Chart Data Compiled From *Billboard's* Pop Album Charts 1955-2001.

ISBN 0-89820-147-0

Record Research Inc.
P.O. Box 200
Menomonee Falls, Wisconsin 53052-0200   U.S.A.

Phone: (262) 251-5408
Fax: (262) 251-9452
E-Mail: books@recordresearch.com
Website: www.recordresearch.com

CONTENTS

An alphabetical listing, by artist, of every album to chart on
Billboard's Popular Albums charts from January 8, 1955 through June 30, 2001.
Each listing includes an alphabetical index of cuts to appear on each album.

Most Charted Albums	Most Consecutive #1 Albums
Most Top 40 Albums	Most Gold & Platinum Albums
Most Top 10 Albums	Top Artists Who Never Hit #1
Most #1 Albums	Artists With Longest Chart Careers
Most Weeks At The #1 Position	One-Hit Wonders

A chronological listing, by peak date, of every #1 album.

Dedicated to my four favorite artists…

…their first releases enthralled me in the '50s and their music still captivates me today…
(in alphabetical order)

Duane Eddy

The Everly Brothers

Ricky Nelson

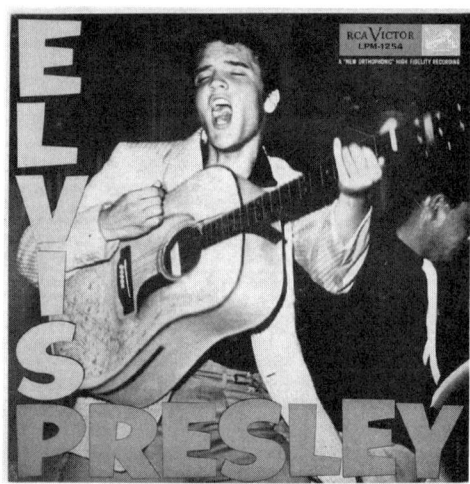

Elvis Presley

Special thanks…

…to my Record Research staff: Bill Hathaway, Kim Bloxdorf, Brent Olynick, Paul Haney, Jeanne Olynick, Kay Wagner, Susette Hustad, Fran Whitburn, and Nestor Vidotto.

…and to Troy Kluess for his research on the Midline/Catalog charts.

The stature of the album configuration has come a long way over the 46 years covered in this book. Back in 1955, finding the 15-position, biweekly Popular Albums chart within *Billboard* magazine required some digging. Key placement of the albums chart in the magazine was not necessary, since singles dominated the music scene.

Today, *"The Billboard 200"* (albums chart) is a highly prominent and top-quoted feature of the magazine, week in and week out. This is evidence of the album's continued growth and eventual surpassing of the single as the most-watched configura-tion in the music industry.

Currently, the music market revolves around the compact disc album. *"The Billboard 200,"* a weekly ranking of the top-selling CDs, is truly the leading barometer of America's musical tastes. The chart encompasses all genres of music: rock, rap, reggae, country, classical, jazz, swing, gospel, pop, and more. This book, the unabridged chronicle of *Billboard's* albums chart, covers its multi-faceted history.

Each new addition of *Top Pop Albums* compels me to include as much as possible about each of the 22,000+ entries that ever appeared on *Billboard's* albums chart, whether they barely scratched its bottom edge or lingered at the top as a multi-platinum seller. This fifth edition features even more about each entry and has valuable updates as well. In addition, I've gone beyond *Billboard's* albums chart to include all of the albums that made *Billboard's* Catalog and Christmas charts! I handpicked the albums and CDs for the book's photographs, spending two weeks in my vault looking at every album and CD that made the charts. Visit our website for a special "albums in color" treat.

For my fellow music lover, I am proud to present you with the results of this research. As always the eye-straining research and the continual fact checking are truly a labor of love for me. I hope that this book increases your appreciation of music past and present.

Joel Whitburn

From an eager record-collecting teenager in the 1950s to a world-renown musicologist in the 21st century, Joel Whitburn's passion for music and the *Billboard* charts is ongoing. Joel turned his chart-watching hobby into a business in 1970 with the publication of his first book. Over the past 31 years, Joel's company, Record Research, has published 86 reference books, which chronicle over a century of American music. These, as well as Joel's books published by Billboard Books, are required reading for virtually anyone with a serious interest in music. He has also collaborated with Rhino Records on a series of 147 CD compilations of America's top charted hits. Joel's own comprehensive charted music collection is the backbone of his research.

Ever the hobbyist, Joel participates in a wide variety of water, winter and motor sports, but the active, six-and-a-half footer ranks basketball and softball as his top sports. The Wisconsinite and his wife, Fran, a native of Honduras, enjoy spending time in southern Florida and central Wisconsin.

VALUABLE VINYL

(see "Most Valuable Albums" on page 1173)

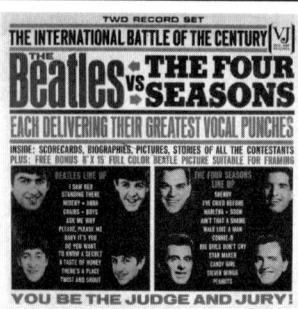

The Beatles vs. The Four Seasons...
The Beatles/The Four Seasons — $800

He's A Rebel...
The Crystals — $600

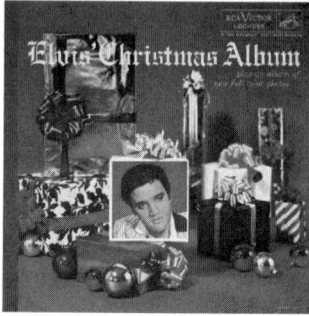

Elvis' Christmas Album...
Elvis Presley — $500

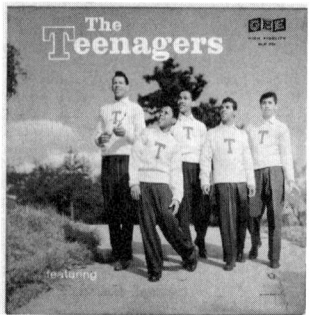

The Teenagers featuring Frankie Lymon...
The Teenagers — $500

...presenting the fabulous Ronettes featuring Veronica...*The Ronettes — $400*

Bluejean Bop!...
Gene Vincent — $400

The Fabulous Miracles...
The Miracles — $300

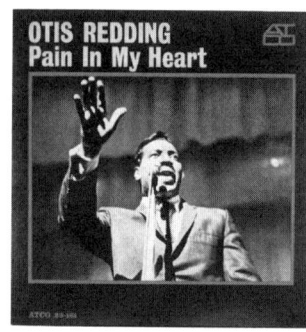

Pain In My Heart...
Otis Redding — $250

Stormsville...
Johnny & The Hurricanes — $200

Llllloco-Motion...
Little Eva — $200

Wild Weekend...
Rockin' Rebels — $200

For Your Love...
The Yardbirds — $200

This fifth edition of *Top Pop Albums* marks the debut of the following new features:

CATALOG CHARTS

We broke new ground by including the research of *Billboard's* "Midline LPs" (1982-88) and "Catalog Albums" (1991-2001) charts. These weekly charts have been home to scores of classic albums, early releases by hot artists and much more. You will find inside all albums that made those charts (even if they did not hit the popular albums chart), and their peak positions and weeks charted on the Midline/Catalog charts.

CHRISTMAS CHARTS

This is the first edition to incorporate all albums that appeared on *Billboard's* seasonal "Christmas Albums" chart into the main section. In some years, the chart listed over 100 titles for a single week. In the previous edition, we showed only the albums that made the Top 10 of the Christmas chart within a special section in the back of the book.

CD AVAILABILITY

See at a glance which albums were released on CD, indicated with a special symbol (©). This includes any vinyl album that made the charts and has since been reissued on CD. This is a helpful feature regarding albums which charted prior to 1990 when vinyl was the album's primary configuration.

EP CHART – 1955

This edition also debuts our research of *Billboard's* "Best Selling Popular Albums – EP's" chart from January 8, 1955, until the chart's end on November 26, 1955. We have included EPs that did not chart on the "Best Selling Popular Albums – LP's" chart and also show EP chart data for albums that hit both charts.

ALBUM COVER PHOTO SECTIONS

Joel Whitburn spent days perusing every album and CD that appears in this book just so he could hand-select over 200 covers for special photograph sections. The covers featured herein span the entire 46-year era of this book and are some of the more obscure, yet most intriguing, of the more than 22,000 that he surveyed. If you're interested in seeing all 216 of these photos in vivid color, visit our website at www.recordresearch.com and click on "Album Photos."

VARIOUS ARTISTS TOGETHER

Because many of the various artist specialty albums could fall under several categories, we decided to combine them into one category, Various Artist Compilations, in alphabetical order by album title so that you can locate them faster rather than looking through the many categories as found in previous editions. Separate categories of albums are still shown for Movie Soundtracks, Movie Soundtrack Compilations, Original Casts, Television Soundtracks, and Christmas (Various Artists).

Billboard magazine began publishing a Top 5 Popular Albums chart in 1945. Today, *Billboard's* Popular Albums chart numbers 200 positions and is known as "*The Billboard 200.*" Throughout its long history, this chart has been home to America's most popular long-play recordings (from vinyl albums to compact discs) representing hundreds of musical genres.

This book's chart research begins with *Billboard's* first Popular Albums chart of 1955 (January 8), since 1955 is widely recognized as the debut year of the rock era. Every album that hit the Popular Albums charts from 1955 through June 30, 2001, appears in this book. The research cutoff date for albums that were on the June 30, 2001 chart is September 29, 2001; weeks charted and peak positions are current through that chart.

This is our first book to feature the 1955 research of *Billboard's* EPs. Under the heading of "Best Selling Popular Albums," *Billboard* published biweekly, two separate, 15-position charts: "LP's" and "EP's." Both of these charts had evolved from *Billboard's* earlier "33 1/3 R.P.M." and "45 R.P.M." charts. (The research of those two charts will appear in an upcoming book featuring all of *Billboard's* early albums charts from 1945-54.) We pick up the research of the EPs chart with the beginning date of this book, January 8, 1955, and end it with the last EPs chart of November 26, 1955. For those EP albums that hit both the LPs and the EPs charts, the peak positions on both charts appear in title trivia; the peak position that appears in the peak column is of the chart on which the EP charted the highest. The chart debut date in the debut column is of the chart on which the EP appeared first. No title trivia is shown for the 15 EPs that only hit the EPs chart in 1955; you will recognize these EPs as they charted in 1955 and have [EP] in the symbol column. (*Billboard* later published a "Best Selling Pop EP's" chart from October 7, 1957, through October 10, 1960. The 131 EPs that made those charts are not included in this book, but are shown and researched in a special "EP Photo Section" in our *Bubbling Under Singles & Albums* book.)

To make this book a complete digest of all of *Billboard's* Popular Albums charts of the rock era, we also consulted two Popular Albums charts not outlined in the *Synopsis Of Billboard's Pop Albums Charts* (page x). The "Most Played by Jockeys" chart, published from July 14, 1956, to December 8, 1958, was a top 15 chart. The "Pop Albums Coming Up Strong" chart, published from July 14, 1956 through August 26, 1957, served the purpose of a "Bubbling Under The Top LPs" chart. We checked the "Most Played by Jockeys" and "Pop Albums Coming Up Strong" charts only for albums which made these charts but did not make the *Billboard* Popular Albums charts. To the 47 albums that only charted on the "Most Played by Jockeys" chart, we added 10 points (or positions) to their peak position. To the 39 albums that only charted on the "Coming Up Strong" charts, we added 15 points (or positions) to their peak position.

From 1959 to 1961, *Billboard* ran concurrent Mono and Stereo charts. For the characteristics and method of researching those charts, see the *Synopsis Of Billboard's Pop Albums Charts*.

Prior to 1963, *Billboard* charted all best-selling Christmas albums on the Popular Albums charts. From 1963 through 1973, *Billboard* did not chart Christmas albums on their Popular Albums charts, but issued special "Christmas Albums" charts for three to four weeks during each holiday season. *Billboard* discontinued the Christmas chart from 1974 through 1982 and returned to charting best-selling Chrismas albums on their regular albums charts. *Billboard* again published "Christmas Albums" charts from 1983-85; however, they also charted the best-selling Christmas albums on their Popular Albums charts. They did not publish a "Christmas Albums" chart in 1986, but have annually since 1987. Albums that only made the "Christmas Albums" chart are indicated with a superscript "X" following their peak position in the peak column. For albums that made the Popular Albums

charts and the "Christmas Albums" charts, their peak positions on the latter chart appears in title trivia.

From 1976 through 1991, *Billboard* did not publish an issue on the final week of the year. The last published chart of the year was considered "frozen" and all chart positions of that final issue remained the same for the unpublished week. This frozen chart data is included in our tabulations. Since 1992, *Billboard* has compiled a Popular Albums chart for the last week of the year, even though an issue is not published. This chart is only available through *Billboard's* computerized information network (BIN) or by mail. Our tabulations include this unpublished chart data.

Also making its debut in this edition is our research of *Billboard's* Midline, later known as Catalog, Albums charts. The bi-weekly "Midline LPs" chart first appeared in *Billboard* on July 24, 1982. The 50-position chart was cut back to 40 positions on October 24, 1982, was renamed "Top Midline Albums," and appeared in *Billboard* every three weeks, until its final chart on October 22, 1988. The Midline chart generally included albums that were $2.00-$3.00 less than the albums on the "Top 200 Albums" chart. On May 25, 1991, *Billboard* introduced the weekly, 50-position "Top Pop Catalog Albums" chart. The Catalog chart was a continuation of the Midline chart as it included several albums that had earlier appeared on the latter chart. According to *Billboard*, "Catalog albums are two-year-old titles that have fallen below #100 on *The Billboard 200*" or reissues of older albums." The Catalog Albums chart still runs today. For albums that hit the Midline/Catalog chart but not the "*The Billboard 200*" chart, we show a superscript "C" following the peak position in the peak column. For all titles that hit the Midline/Catalog charts and "*The Billboard 200*," we show its peak position from the Midline/Catalog charts on the line to the right of the title.

Billboard's compilation of the Popular Albums charts has always been based on album sales. For over 30 years, *Billboard* tallied the Popular Albums charts from rankings of best-selling albums as reported by a representative sampling of stores nationwide. On May 25, 1991, *Billboard* ushered in a new era in sales charts compilation. *Billboard* now bases the Popular Albums chart on actual units sold data as collected by point-of-sale scanning machines which read the album's UPC bar code. The music research firm SoundScan Inc. provides *Billboard* with the actual sales of all albums from a continually revised representative sampling of stores.

MONO VS. STEREO NUMBERS

During the 1960s, *Billboard* frequently showed both mono and stereo numbers for an album on the album charts. The only numbering system that had major differences was the Columbia label. We have shown both the mono and stereo numbers for those albums on Columbia in the main artist listings. For the labels listed below we generally show stereo numbers only in the main artist listings. For your information, here is a list of other mono/stereo variations used on the charts (variations are shown in bold — label numbers are examples only):

RECORD COMPANY	MONO	STEREO
Coral, Decca & Brunswick	57487	**7**57487
Dolton & Sunset	**2**049	**8**049
Epic	2**4**022	2**6**022
Hi	**1**2002	**3**2002
Kapp	**1**368	**3**368
Liberty	**3**522	**7**522
London	**3**338 or 5943	338 or 2**5**943
Mercury	**2**0837	**6**0837
Philips	**200**223	**600**223
United Artists	**3**536	**6**536
Viva	6010	**3**6010

SYNOPSIS OF BILLBOARD'S POP ALBUMS CHARTS

DATE	POSITIONS		CHART TITLE
1/8/55	15	*	**BEST SELLING POPULAR ALBUMS**
			(a biweekly chart featuring a 15-position "LP's" chart and a 15-position "EP's" chart – "EP's" chart discontinued after November 26, 1955)
3/24/56	10-15-20-30		**BEST SELLING POPULAR ALBUMS**
			(published weekly with size varying from a top 10 to a top 30)
6/2/56	15		**BEST SELLING POP ALBUMS**
9/2/57	25		**BEST SELLING POP LPs**
5/25/59	50	*	**BEST SELLING MONOPHONIC LPs**
5/25/59	30	*	**BEST SELLING STEREOPHONIC LPs**
			(separate Stereo and Mono charts published through 8/10/63)
1/4/60	40	*	**MONO ACTION CHARTS** (mono albums charted 39 weeks or less)
1/4/60	30	*	**STEREO ACTION CHARTS** (stereo albums charted 19 weeks or less; changed to 29 weeks or less on 5/30/60)
1/4/60	25	*	**ESSENTIAL INVENTORY – MONO** (mono albums charted 40 weeks or more)
1/4/60	20	*	**ESSENTIAL INVENTORY – STEREO** (stereo albums charted 20 weeks or more; changed to 30 weeks or more on 5/30/60)
1/9/61	25		**ACTION ALBUMS – MONOPHONIC** (mono albums charted nine weeks or less)
1/9/61	15		**ACTION ALBUMS – STEREOPHONIC** (stereo albums charted nine weeks or less)
1/9/61	—		Approximately 200 albums listed by category (no positions) and shown as essential inventory
4/3/61	150		**TOP LP's – MONAURAL**
4/3/61	50		**TOP LP's – STEREO**
8/17/63	150		**TOP LP's** (one chart)
4/1/67	175		**TOP LP's**
5/13/67	200		**TOP LP's**
11/25/67	200		**TOP LP's** (three pages)
2/15/69	200		**TOP LP's** (two pages with A-Z artist listing)
2/19/72	200		**TOP LP's & TAPES**
10/20/84	200		**TOP 200 ALBUMS**
1/5/85	200		**TOP POP ALBUMS**
9/7/91	200		**THE BILLBOARD 200 TOP ALBUMS**
3/14/92	200		**THE BILLBOARD 200**

An album appearing on both the Mono and Stereo charts in the same week is tabulated as one weekly appearance. The album's highest position is determined by the chart (Mono or Stereo) on which the album reached its highest position.

The Essential Inventory charts list albums which have already been charted for months on the Mono and Stereo charts; therefore, we researched the Essential Inventory charts for weeks charted only and did not count peak positions reached on this chart.

Synopsis of *Billboard's* **Midline/Catalog Albums** and **Christmas Albums** charts:

DATE	POSITIONS		CHART TITLE
7/24/82	50	*	**MIDLINE LPs** (a biweekly chart)
10/24/82	40		**TOP MIDLINE ALBUMS** (a triweekly chart –discontinued after October 22, 1988)
5/25/91	50		**TOP POP CATALOG ALBUMS** (a weekly chart)

DATE	POSITIONS		CHART TITLE
1963-73	5-117	*	**CHRISTMAS LP's**
1983-85	10		**CHRISTMAS ALBUMS**
1987-93	30		**TOP CHRISTMAS ALBUMS**
1994-00	40		**TOP HOLIDAY ALBUMS**

* view samples of these charts on the following 5 pages

•Best Selling Popular Albums

Albums are ranked in order of their national sales strength at the retail level according to The Billboard's weekly survey of top dealers in all key markets.

LP'S

1. CRAZY OTTO ....Decca DL 8113
2. STARRING SAMMY DAVIS JR ....Decca DL 8118
3. THE STUDENT PRINCE—Mario Lanza..RCA Victor LM 1837
4. MUSIC, MARTINIS AND MEMORIES—Jackie Gleason ...
...................................Captiol W 509
5. IN THE WEE SMALL HOURS—Frank Sinatra ..Capitol W 581
6. MUSIC FOR LOVERS ONLY—Jackie Gleason..Capitol H 352
7. MUSIC FOR TONIGHT—Steve Allen ......Coral CRL 57004
8. BENNY GOODMAN IN HI-FI ....Capitol W 565
9. BRUBECK TIME—Dave Brubeck.........Columbia CL 622
10. HOLIDAY IN ROME—Michel LeGrand .....Columbia CL 647
11. I LOVE PARIS—Michel LeGrand ....Columbia CL 555
12. I LOVE YOU—Eddie Fisher ....RCA Victor LPM 1097
13. ARTHUR GODFREY PRESENTS CARMEL QUINN ......
.............................Columbia CL 629
14. SOFT AND SWEET—The Three Suns ..RCA Victor LPM 1041
15. MUSIC TO REMEMBER HER—Jackie Gleason ..Capitol W 570

EP'S

1. THE STUDENT PRINCE—Mario Lanza..RCA Victor ERB 1837
2. STARRING SAMMY DAVIS JR ....Decca ED 2214-6
3. MUSIC FOR LOVERS ONLY—Jackie Gleason..Capitol EBF 352
4. CRAZY OTTO, PART 1 ....Decca ED 2201
5. CRAZY OTTO, PART 2 ....Decca ED 2202
6. IN THE WEE SMALL HOURS—Frank Sinatra ....
.............................Capitol EBF 581
7. GLENN MILLER PLAYS SELECTIONS FROM "THE GLENN MILLER STORY" ....RCA Victor EPBT 3057
8. MUSIC, MARTINIS AND MEMORIES—Jackie Gleason ...
.............................Capitol EAP 509
9. I LOVE YOU—Eddie Fisher ....RCA Victor EPB 1097
10. SHAKE, RATTLE AND ROLL—Bill Haley ....Decca ED 2168
11. ARTHUR GODFREY PRESENTS CARMEL QUINN ......
.............................Columbia B 491
12. LES AND MARY—Les Paul & Mary Ford .....Capitol EBF 577
13. PETER PAN—Original Cast .....`.....RCA Victor EOC 1019
14. BENNY GOODMAN IN HI-FI ....Capitol EAP 565
15. LITTLE GIRL BLUE—Joni James ....M-G-M X 272

Billboard TOP LP'S

^{The}

FOR THE WEEK
ENDING JULY 19

BEST SELLING MONOPHONIC LP'S

ONE WEEK AGO	THIS WEEK	TITLE, Artist, Company, Record Number.	WEEKS ON CHART
1	(1)	EXOTICA, VOL. I, Martin Denny, Liberty LRP 3034	12
2	(2)	KINGSTON TRIO AT LARGE, Kingston Trio, Capitol T 1199	5
4	(3)	PETER GUNN, Henry Mancini, RCA Victor LPM 1956	23
3	(4)	FROM THE HUNGRY I, The Kingston Trio, Capitol T 1107	23
5	(5)	GIGI, Sound Track, M-G-M E 3641 ST	55
6	(6)	INSIDE SHELLY BERMAN, Verve MGV 15003	13
7	(7)	HOLD THAT TIGER, Fabian, Chancellor CHL 5003	10
10	(8)	SING ALONG WITH MITCH, Mitch Miller, Columbia CL 1160	54
9	(9)	SOUTH PACIFIC, Sound Track, RCA Victor LOC 1032	69
11	(10)	COME DANCE WITH ME, Frank Sinatra, Capitol W 1069	23
12	(11)	MY FAIR LADY, Original Cast, Columbia OL 5090	172
13	(12)	JOHNNY'S GREATEST HITS, Johnny Mathis, Columbia CL 1133	64
21	(13)	MORE MUSIC FROM PETER GUNN, Henry Mancini, RCA Victor LPM 2040	5
8	(14)	LOOK TO YOUR HEART, Frank Sinatra, Capitol W 1164	8
14	(15)	RODGERS: VICTORY AT SEA, VOL. II, RCA Victor Symphony Orch. (Bennett), RCA Victor LM 2226	19
19	(16)	THE MUSIC MAN, Original Cast, Capitol WAO 990	73
20	(17)	FILM ENCORES, VOL. II, Mantovani, London LL 3117	6
23	(18)	TABOO IN HI-FI, Arthur Lyman, Hi Fi Records R 806	18
24	(19)	KINGSTON TRIO, Capitol T 996	5
15	(20)	BUT NOT FOR ME, Ahmad Jamal Trio, Argo LP 628	29
16	(21)	MORE SING ALONG WITH MITCH, Mitch Miller, Columbia CL 1243	34
22	(22)	FILM ENCORES, VOL. I, Mantovani, London LL 1700	89
26	(23)	PORGY AND BESS, Harry Belafonte & Lena Horne, RCA Victor LOP 1507	5
17	(24)	FLOWER DRUM SONG, Original Cast, Columbia OL 5350	27
31	(25)	SECRET SONGS FOR YOUNG LOVERS, Andre Previn & David Rose, M-G-M E 3716	4
18	(26)	77 SUNSET STRIP, Warren Barker, Warner Bros. WB 1289	14
29	(27)	HAVE TWANGY GUITAR, WILL TRAVEL, Duane Eddy, Jamie JLP 3000	25
27	(28)	OPEN FIRE, TWO GUITARS, Johnny Mathis, Columbia CL 1270	24
32	(29)	HOLLYWOOD IN RHYTHM, Ray Conniff, Columbia CL 1310	4
30	(30)	MORE SONGS OF THE FIFTIES, Roger Williams, Kapp KL 1113	6
35	(31)	THE KING AND I, Sound Track, Capitol W 740	144
25	(32)	LOVE IS A GENTLE THING, Harry Belafonte, RCA Victor LPM 1927	9
36	(33)	OKLAHOMA! Sound Track, Capitol SAO 595	180
41	(34)	TENDERLY, Pat Boone, Dot DLP 3180	2
—	(35)	GYPSY, Original Cast, Columbia OL 5420	1
28	(36)	FOLK SONGS SING ALONG WITH MITCH, Mitch Miller, Columbia CL 1316	8
37	(37)	TCHAIKOVSKY: PIANO CONCERTO NO. 1, Van Cliburn, RCA Victor LM 2252	47
40	(38)	ONLY THE LONELY, Frank Sinatra, Capitol W 1053	34
42	(39)	WARM, Johnny Mathis, Columbia CL 1078	49
45	(40)	GEMS FOREVER, Mantovani, London LL 3032	38
33	(41)	THE BUDDY HOLLY STORY, Coral CRL 57279	13
38	(42)	STILL MORE SING ALONG WITH MITCH, Mitch Miller, Columbia CL 1283	14
43	(43)	SOUTH PACIFIC, Original Cast, Columbia OL 4180	268
46	(44)	RACHMANINOFF: PIANO CONCERTO NO. 3, Van Cliburn, RCA Victor LM 2355	2
34	(45)	CRAZY HE CALLS ME, Dakota Staton, Capitol T 1170	8
39	(46)	IMPROVISATIONS TO MUSIC, Mike Nichols & Elaine May, Mercury MG 20376	7
48	(47)	TO WHOM IT MAY CONCERN, Nat King Cole, Capitol W 1190	5
—	(48)	I WANT TO LIVE! Gerry Mulligan's Jazz Combo, United Artists UAL 4006	5
44	(49)	BLUE HAWAII, Billy Vaughn, Dot DLP 3165	8
49	(50)	'S MARVELOUS, Ray Conniff, Columbia CS 8037	6

BEST SELLING STEREOPHONIC LP'S

ONE WEEK AGO	THIS WEEK	TITLE, Artist, Company, Record Number.	WEEKS ON CHART
2	(1)	SOUTH PACIFIC, Sound Track, RCA Victor LSO 1032	9
1	(2)	FILM ENCORES, VOL. I, Mantovani, London PS 124	9
6	(3)	RODGERS: VICTORY AT SEA, VOL. II, RCA Victor Symphony Orch. (Bennett), RCA Victor LSC 2226	7
3	(4)	GIGI, Sound Track, M-G-M SE 3461 ST	9
4	(5)	PETER GUNN, Henry Mancini, RCA Victor LSP 1956	9
5	(6)	MY FAIR LADY, Original Cast, Columbia OS 2015	9
7	(7)	COME DANCE WITH ME, Frank Sinatra, Capitol SW 1069	9
8	(8)	TABOO IN HI-FI, Arthur Lyman, Hi-Fi Record SR 806	9
10	(9)	THE MUSIC MAN, Original Cast, Capitol SWAO 990	7
15	(10)	KINGSTON TRIO AT LARGE, Kingston Trio, Capitol ST 1199	3
9	(11)	MANTOVANI SHOWCASE, London SS 1	8
13	(12)	GEMS FOREVER, Mantovani, London PS 164	5
16	(13)	TCHAIKOVSKY: 1812 OVERTURE, Minneapolis Symphony Orch. (Dorati), Mercury SR 90054	7
18	(14)	EXOTICA, VOL. I, Martin Denny, Liberty LST 7034	2
11	(15)	ONLY THE LONELY, Frank Sinatra, Capitol SW 1053	9
14	(16)	MORE SONGS OF THE FIFTIES, Roger Williams, Kapp KS 3013	5
17	(17)	FILM ENCORES, VOL. II, Mantovani, London PS 164	5
12	(18)	OKLAHOMA! Sound Track, Capitol SWAO 595	7
19	(19)	PORGY AND BESS, Harry Belafonte and Lena Horne, RCA Victor LSO 1507	2
21	(20)	CONTINENTAL ENCORES, Mantovani, London PS 147	9
20	(21)	MORE MUSIC FROM PETER GUNN, Henry Mancini, RCA Victor LSP 2040	2
22	(22)	SOUL OF SPAIN, 101 Strings, Stereo Fidelity SF 6000	9
25	(23)	RACHMANINOFF: PIANO CONCERTO NO. 3, Van Cliburn, RCA Victor LSC 2355	2
—	(24)	77 SUNSET STRIP, Warren Barker, Warner Bros. WS 1289	6
—	(25)	THE KING AND I, Sound Track, Capitol SW 740	5
23	(26)	PORGY AND BESS, Percy Faith, Columbia CS 8105	9
—	(27)	BILLY VAUGHN PLAYS MILLION SELLERS, Dot DLP 25119	1
26	(28)	THE FLOWER DRUM SONG, Original Cast, Columbia OS 2009	2
28	(29)	TILL, Roger Williams, Kapp KLS 1081	4
24	(30)	'S MARVELOUS, Ray Conniff, Columbia CS 8037	6

Album Cover of the Week

Mozart

MOZART: THE MARRIAGE OF FIGARO, RCA Victor LM 6408. Robert Jones has designed a charming package in the form of a portfolio, complete with a flip top and a lock. Cover sports photos of five gaily costumed principals who star in recording.

Best Selling Low-Priced LP's on the Racks

This chart has been tabulated from the sales made by the nation's leading rack service merchandisers and jobbers. Over a four-week cycle, it covers the main types of packaged records sold from racks. These include: Best-Selling LP's ($3 or more suggested retail price); Best-Selling Low-Priced LP's ($2.99 or less suggested retail price); Best-Selling EP's, and Best-Selling Kiddie Records.

1. **Perry Como Sings Just for You** .....Camden CAL 440
2. **Soul of Spain** 101 Strings .....Somerset P 6600
3. **Good Housekeeping Plan for Reducing Off the Record** .....Harmony HL 7145
4. **Music From Peter Gunn** Aaron Bell Ork .....Lion L 70112
5. **Flower Drum Song** Various Artists .....Design DLP 98
6. **77 Sunset Strip** Aaron Bell Ork .....Lion L 70164
7. **Porgy and Bess** Mundell Lowe .....Camden CAL 490
8. **Grand Canyon Suite** Wilhelm Schnechter .....Somerset C 7900
9. **TV Action Jazz** Video Stars .....Somerset P 880
10. **Eddy Arnold** .....Camden CAL 428

Best Selling Pop EP's

The information given in this chart is based on actual sales to customers in a scientific sample of the nation's retail record outlets during the week ending on the date shown above. Sample design, sample size, and all methods used in this continuing study of retail record sales are under the direct and continuing supervision and control of the School of Retailing of New York University.

1. **Side by Side** Pat & Shirley Boone .....Dot DEP 1076
2. **King Creole, Vol. I** Elvis Presley .....RCA Victor EPA 4319
3. **Peter Gunn** Henry Mancini .....RCA Victor EPA 4333
4. **Songs Our Daddy Taught Us** Everly Brothers .....Cadence CEP 110
5. **Ricky Sings Again** Ricky Nelson .....Imperial BP 159
6. **Nearer the Cross** Tennessee Ernie Ford .....Capitol EAP 1-1005
7. **Spirituals** Tennessee Ernie Ford .....Capitol EAP 1-818
8. **Crazy He Calls Me** Dakota Staton .....Capitol EAP 1-1170
9. **Como's Golden Records** Perry Como .....RCA Victor EPA 5013
10. **Come Dance With Me** Frank Sinatra .....Capitol EAP 1-1069

FOR WEEK ENDING JULY 10 ▶ The Billboard TOP LP'S

BEST SELLING MONOPHONIC LP'S

MONO ACTION ALBUMS --- on the charts 39 weeks or less

This Week	Last Week	Title, Artist, Label and Number	Weeks on Chart
1	1.	SOLD OUT ....11 Kingston Trio ....Capitol T 1352	
2	3.	BUTTON-DOWN MIND OF BOB NEWHART... 8 ....Warner Brothers, W 1379	
3	2.	ELVIS IS BACK ....9 Elvis Presley ....RCA Victor LPM 2231	
4	6.	THEME FROM A SUMMER PLACE ...16 Billy Vaughn ....Dot DLP 3276	
5	4.	THE SOUND OF MUSIC ....29 Original Cast ....Columbia KOL 5450	
6	5.	MR. LUCKY ....15 Henry Mancini ....RCA Victor LPM 2198	
7	8.	LANZA SINGS CARUSO—CARUSO FAVORITES. 7 Mario Lanza/Enrico Caruso ....RCA Victor LM 2393	
8	7.	CAN CAN ....10 Sound Track ....Capitol W 1301	
9	9.	ENCORES OF GOLDEN HITS ....17 Platters ....Mercury MG 20472	
10	12.	ITALIAN FAVORITES ....22 Connie Francis ....M-G-M E 3791	
11	9.	SIXTY YEARS OF MUSIC AMERICA LOVES BEST.32 Assorted Artists ....RCA Victor LM 6074	
12	11.	IT'S EVERLY TIME ....5 Everly Brothers .....Warner Brothers WB 1381	
13	14.	BEN-HUR ....11 Rome Symphony Orch./Savina.......M-G-M 1E1	
14	18.	PERSUASIVE PERCUSSION ....12 Terry Snyder and the All Stars..Command LP 800	
15	15.	BELAFONTE AT CARNEGIE HALL .....35 Harry Belafonte ....RCA Victor LOC 6006	
16	17.	THIS IS DARIN ....18 Bobby Darin ....Atco LP 33-115	
17	13.	BROTHERS FOUR ....12 ....Columbia CL 1402	
18	19.	HE'LL HAVE TO GO ....7 Jim Reeves ....RCA Victor LPM 2223	
19	22.	FAITHFULLY ....25 Johnny Mathis ....Columbia CL 1422	
20	20.	HERE WE GO AGAIN ....35 Kingston Trio ....Capitol T 1258	
21	16.	LATIN A LA LEE ....13 Peggy Lee ....Capitol T 1290	
22	—	REJOICE DEAR HEARTS ....2 Brother Dave Gardner ....RCA Victor LPM 2083	
23	32.	LAUGHING ROOM ....4 Woody Woodbury ....Stereoddities MW 2	
24	21.	OUTSIDE SHELLEY BERMAN ....32 ....Verve MGV 15007	
25	24.	WOODY WOODBURY LOOKS AT LOVE AND LIFE.18 ....Stereoddities MW 1	
26	26.	LISTEN TO DAY ....6 Doris Day ....Columbia DD 1	
27	25.	SATURDAY NIGHT SING ALONG WITH MITCH..14 Mitch Miller ....Columbia CL 1414	
28	27.	GENIUS OF RAY CHARLES ....20 ....Atlantic LP 1321	
29	28.	FIORELLO! ....18 Original Cast ....Capitol WAO 1321	
30	33.	WONDERFUL WORLD OF JONATHAN WINTERS.19 ....Verve MGV 15009	
31	37.	SING A HYMN WITH ME ....8 Tennessee Ernie Ford .....Capitol TAO 1332	
32	29.	GUNFIGHTER BALLADS AND TRAIL SONGS...28 Marty Robbins ....Columbia CL 1349	
33	30.	CONNIE'S GREATEST HITS ....8 Connie Francis ....M-G-M E 3793	
34	36.	SENTIMENTAL SING ALONG WITH MITCH....2 Mitch Miller ....Columbia CL 1457	
35	—	LIKE LOVE ....1 Andre Previn ....Columbia CL 1437	
36	34.	COME FLY WITH ME ....18 Frank Sinatra ....Capitol W 920	
37	40.	SING AGAIN WITH THE CHIPMUNKS ...3 Chipmunks/David Seville .....Liberty LRP 3159	
38	—	PAUL ANKA SINGS HIS BIG 15 ....1 ....ABC Paramount LP 323	
39	—	TCHAIKOVSKY: 1812 OVERTURE/RAVEL: BOLERO ....7 Morton Gould ....RCA Victor LM 2345	
40	—	STUDENT PRINCE ....15 Mario Lanza ....RCA Victor LM 2339	

ESSENTIAL INVENTORY (MONO ALBUMS) on the charts 40 weeks or more

This Week	Last Week	Title, Artist, Label and Number	Weeks on Chart
1	1.	INSIDE SHELLEY BERMAN . . . Verve MGV 15003....63	
2	6.	SOUTH PACIFIC, Sound Track, RCA Victor LOC 1032.......119	
3	2.	OLDIES BUT GOODIES, Assorted Artists, Original Sound S-001 42	
4	3.	MY FAIR LADY, Original Cast, Columbia OL 5090.........222	
5	5.	KINGSTON TRIO . . . Capitol T 996...............55	
6	4.	HEAVENLY, Johnny Mathis, Columbia CL 1351..........42	
7	8.	THE MUSIC MAN, Original Cast, Capitol WAO 990........123	
8	7.	FROM THE HUNGRY I, Kingston Trio, Capitol T 1107......73	
9	10.	GIGI, Sound Track, M-G-M 3641 ST 105	
10	11.	SOUTH PACIFIC, Original Cast, Columbia OL 4180.......318	
11	18.	MORE SING ALONG WITH MITCH, Mitch Miller, Columbia CL 1243 77	
12	16.	HYMNS, Tennessee Ernie Ford, Capitol T 756.........156	
13	—	THAT'S ALL, Bobby Darin, Atco LP 33-104 40	
14	17.	STILL MORE SING ALONG WITH MITCH, Mitch Miller, Columbia CL 1283 57	
15	9.	JOHNNY'S GREATEST HITS, Johnny Mathis, Columbia CL 1133 114	
16	12.	KING AND I, Sound Track, Capitol W 740 192	
17	13.	KINGSTON TRIO AT LARGE . . . Capitol T 1199.......55	
18	23.	BUT NOT FOR ME, Ahmad Jamal, Argo LP 628........77	
19	21.	MORE JOHNNY'S GREATEST HITS, Johnny Mathis, Columbia CL 1344 50	
20	14.	PORGY AND BESS, Sound Track, Columbia CL 5410....51	
21	15.	SING ALONG WITH MITCH, Mitch Miller, Columbia CL 1160.104	
22	20.	ONLY THE LONELY, Frank Sinatra, Capitol W 1053.....77	
23	19.	PETER GUNN, Henry Mancini, RCA Victor LPM 1956......72	
24	25.	GEMS FOREVER, Mantovani, London LL 3032..........70	
25	22.	FLOWER DRUM SONG, Original Cast, Columbia OL 5350...67	

BEST SELLING STEREOPHONIC LP'S

STEREO ACTION ALBUMS --- on the charts 29 weeks or less

This Week	Last Week	Title, Artist, Label and Number	Weeks on Chart
1	1.	PERSUASIVE PERCUSSION ....24 Terry Snyder and the All Stars...Command S 800	
2	2.	PROVOCATIVE PERCUSSION ....24 Enoch Light and the Light Brigade....Command S 806	
3	3.	SOLD OUT ....10 Kingston Trio ....Capitol T 1352	
4	4.	MR. LUCKY ....15 Henry Mancini ....RCA Victor LSP 2198	
5	6.	THEME FROM A SUMMER PLACE ....14 Billy Vaughn ....Dot DLP 25276	
6	7.	LANZA SINGS CARUSO—CARUSO FAVORITES. 8 Mario Lanza-Enrico Caruso ....RCA Victor LSC 2393	
7	5.	SOUND OF MUSIC ....26 Original Cast ....Columbia KOS 2020	
8	8.	BEN-HUR ....7 Rome Symphony Orch./Savina ......M-G-M 1E1	
9	16.	GUNFIGHTER BALLADS AND TRAIL SONGS...21 Marty Robbins ....Columbia CS 8158	
10	10.	NEW ORLEANS ....19 Pete Fountain ....Coral CRL 7-57282	
11	13.	LORD'S PRAYER ....24 Mormon Tabernacle Choir ..Columbia MS 6068	
12	12.	MORE SING ALONG WITH MITCH ....21 Mitch Miller ....Columbia CS 8043	
13	15.	EXOTICA, VOL. I ....24 Martin Denny ....Liberty LST 7034	
14	19.	CONCERT IN RHYTHM, VOL. I ......24 Ray Conniff ....Columbia CS 8022	
15	23.	TCHAIKOVSKY: 1812 OVERTURE/RAVEL: BOLERO ....23 Morton Gould ....RCA Victor LSC 2345	
16	17.	'S AWFUL NICE ....18 Ray Conniff ....Columbia CS 8001	
17	—	THIS IS DARIN ....9 Bobby Darin ....Atco SC 115	
18	—	ONLY THE LONELY ....21 Frank Sinatra ....Capitol-SW 1053	
19	11.	NEARER THE CROSS ....24 Tennessee Ernie Ford .....Capitol ST 1005	
20	14.	CONNIFF MEETS BUTTERFIELD .....24 Ray Conniff ....Columbia CS 8155	
21	26.	AMERICAN SCENE ....15 Mantovani ....London PS 182	
22	27.	BILLY VAUGHN PLAYS MILLION SELLERS....18 Original Cast ....Dot DLP 25119	
23	20.	STILL MORE SING ALONG WITH MITCH....23 Mitch Miller ....Columbia CS 8009	
24	24.	PORGY AND BESS ....23 Sound Track ....Columbia OS 2016	
25	9.	FAITHFULLY ....22 Johnny Mathis ....Columbia CS 8219	
26	18.	LATIN A LA LEE ....2 Peggy Lee ....Capitol ST 1290	
27	22.	FIORELLO! ....24 Original Cast ....Capitol SWAO 1321	
28	—	LET'S ALL SING WITH THE CHIPMUNKS...20 Chipmunks/David Seville .....Liberty LST 7132	
29	18.	BOUQUET ....17 Percy Faith ....Columbia CS 3124	
30	21.	LET'S DANCE AGAIN ....21 David Carroll ....Mercury SR 60152	

ESSENTIAL INVENTORY (STEREO ALBUMS) on the charts 30 weeks or more

This Week	Last Week	Title, Artist, Label and Number	Weeks on Chart
1	2.	SOUTH PACIFIC, Sound Track, RCA Victor LSO 1032.....59	
2	4.	MY FAIR LADY, Original Cast, Columbia OS 2015.........59	
3	1.	BELAFONTE AT CARNEGIE HALL, Harry Belafonte, RCA Victor LSO 6006 33	
4	7.	HERE WE GO AGAIN, Kingston Trio, Capitol ST 1258.....35	
5	3.	HEAVENLY, Johnny Mathis, Columbia CS 8152..........41	
6	6.	GIGI, Sound Track, M-G-M SE 3461 ST.............59	
7	5.	COME DANCE WITH ME, Frank Sinatra, Capitol SW 1069...59	
8	8.	KINGSTON TRIO AT LARGE . . . Capitol ST 1199......44	
9	10.	RODGERS: VICTORY AT SEA, VOL. II, RCA Victor Symphony Orch. (Bennett), RCA Victor LSC 2226.......57	
10	13.	MUSIC MAN, Original Cast, Capitol SWAO 990........48	
11	9.	GEMS FOREVER, Mantovani, London PS 106..........47	
12	15.	PETER GUNN THEME, Henry Mancini, RCA Victor LSP 1956..57	
13	11.	BLUE HAWAII, Billy Vaughn, Dot DLP 25165..........40	
14	12.	FOR THE FIRST TIME, Mario Lanza, RCA Victor LSC 2338...36	
15	14.	STRAUSS WALTZES, Mantovani, London PS 118.........43	
16	17.	QUIET VILLAGE, Martin Denny, Liberty LST 7122.......33	
17	16.	FILM ENCORES, VOL. I, Mantovani, London PS 124.......53	
18	—	MORE JOHNNY'S GREATEST HITS, Johnny Mathis, Columbia CS 8150 34	
19	—	SING ALONG WITH MITCH, Mitch Miller, Columbia CS 8043..30	
20	—	RACHMANINOFF: PIANO CONCERTO NO. 3, Van Cliburn, RCA Victor LSC 2355 31	

Billboard ® Survey For Week Ending 7/24/82

Midline LPs ™

THIS WEEK	LAST REPORT	WEEKS ON CHART	TITLE Artist Label, No. (Dist. Label)	Dist. Co.	Suggested List Prices LP, Cassettes, 8-Track
☆ 1	—	1	**TAPESTRY** Carole King Epic PE 32946 — WEEKS AT #1: 1		
2	—	1	**THE DOORS** The Doors Elektra EKS 74007		5.98
3	—	1	**SOUVENIRS** Dan Fogelberg Epic PE 33132		
4	—	1	**SO FAR** Crosby, Stills and Nash Atlantic SD 19119		5.98
5	—	1	**NETHERLANDS** Dan Fogelberg Epic PE 34185		
6	—	1	**PIANO MAN** Billy Joel Columbia PE 32544		
7	—	1	**THE RISE AND FALL OF ZIGGY STARDUST & THE SPIDERS FROM MARS** David Bowie RCA AY 3843		5.98
8	—	1	**SOFT PARADE** The Doors Elektra EKS 75005		5.98
9	—	1	**FRAGILE** Yes Atlantic SD 19132		5.98
10	—	1	**ON THE BORDER** Eagles Elektra Asylum 7E 1004		5.98
11	—	1	**HOME FREE** Dan Fogelberg Columbia PC 31751		
12	—	1	**WAITING FOR THE SUN** The Doors Elektra EKS 74024		5.98
13	—	1	**BLOW BY BLOW** Jeff Beck Epic PE 33409		
14	—	1	**CAPTURED ANGEL** Dan Fogelberg Epic PE 33499		
15	—	1	**AXIS: BOLD AS LOVE** Jimi Hendrix Warner Bros. Reprise RS6281		5.98
16	—	1	**LOOK SHARP** Joe Jackson A&M 4743		5.98
17	—	1	**ROCK 'N ROLL** John Lennon Capitol SN 16069		5.98
18	—	1	**BEST OF FRIENDS** Loggins & Messina Columbia PC 34388		
19	—	1	**MORE SONGS ABOUT BUILDINGS AND FOOD** Talking Heads Warner Bros. Sire Sir 6058		5.98
20	—	1	**ROCK 'N' ROLL, VOLUME 1** The Beatles Capitol SN 16020		5.98
21	—	1	**ROCK 'N' ROLL, VOLUME 2** The Beatles Capitol SN 16021		5.98
22	—	1	**STRAIGHT SHOOTER** Three Is Bad Company Atlantic Swan Song SS 8502		5.98
23	—	1	**THRESHOLD OF A DREAM** Moody Blues Polygram Deram DES 18025		5.98
24	—	1	**THE PRETENDERS** Pretenders Warner Bros. Sire Sir Mini 3563		5.98
25	—	1	**THE ART OF TEA** Michael Franks Warner Bros. Reprise MS 2230		5.98

THIS WEEK	LAST REPORT	WEEKS ON CHART	TITLE Artist Label, No. (Dist. Label)	Dist. Co.	Suggested List Prices LP, Cassettes, 8-Track
26	—	1	**RUSH** Rush Polygram Mercury SRM-1-1011		5.98
27	—	1	**AND THEN THERE WERE** Genesis Atlantic SD 19173		5.98
28	—	1	**IN SEARCH OF THE LOST CHORD** Moody Blues Polygram Deram DES 18017		5.98
29	—	1	**BLACK SABBATH** Black Sabbath Warner Bros. WS 1871		5.98
30	—	1	**MIND GAMES** John Lennon Capitol SN 16088		5.98
31	—	1	**BEST OF GUESS WHO** Guess Who RCA AYL1-3662		5.98
32	—	1	**A QUESTION OF BALANCE** Moody Blues Polygram Threshold THS 3		5.98
33	—	1	**AGENTS OF FORTUNE** Blue Oyster Cult Columbia PC 34164		
34	—	1	**TRES HOMBRES** ZZ Top Warner Bros. BSK 3270		5.98
35	—	1	**EVE** Alan Parsons Arista AMB 9504		5.98
36	—	1	**YES** Yes Atlantic SD 8243		5.98
37	—	1	**CELEBRATE ME HOME** Kenny Loggins Columbia PC 34655		
38	—	1	**LIVE AT FILLMORE EAST** Allman Bros. Polygram CPN 2 0131		9.98
39	—	1	**MESOPOTAMIA** The B-52's Warner Bros. Mini 3641		5.98
40	—	1	**SABBATH, BLOODY SABBATH** Black Sabbath Warner Bros. BS 2695		5.98
41	—	1	**EAT A PEACH** Allman Bros. Polygram CPN 2 0101		9.98
42	—	1	**THE MONKEES' GREATEST HITS** The Monkees Arista AMB 4089		5.98
43	—	1	**TALKING HEADS '77** Talking Heads Warner Bros. Sire SR 6035		5.98
44	—	1	**TO OUR CHILDRENS . . .** Moody Blues Polygram Threshold THS 1		5.98
45	—	1	**WORST OF JEFFERSON AIRPLANE** Jefferson Airplane RCA AYL1-3661		5.98
46	—	1	**WIND AND WUTHERING** Genesis Atlantic Atco 38-100		5.98
47	—	1	**EXCITABLE BOY** Warren Zevon Elektra Asylum 6E-118		5.98
48	—	1	**MASTER OF REALITY** Black Sabbath Warner Bros. BS 2562		5.98
49	—	1	**RIDING THE STORM** REO Speedwagon Epic PE 32378		
50	—	1	**NEVER MIND THE BOLLOCKS HERE'S THE SEX PISTOLS** Sex Pistols Warner Bros. B515 3147		5.98

Billboard *BEST BETS FOR CHRISTMAS*

BEST SELLING CHRISTMAS LP'S

1. **THE LITTLE DRUMMER BOY**—Harry Simeone Chorale, 20th Century-Fox TFM 3100 (M); TFS 4100 (S)
2. **MERRY CHRISTMAS** — Johnny Mathis, Columbia CL 1195 (M); CS 8021 (S)
3. **MERRY CHRISTMAS** — Andy Williams, Columbia CL 2420 (M); CS 9220 (S)
4. **THE DEAN MARTIN CHRISTMAS ALBUM**—Reprise R 6222 (M); RS 6222 (S)
5. **ELVIS' CHRISTMAS ALBUM**—Elvis Presley, RCA Victor LPM 1951 (M); LSP 1951 (S)
6. **NOEL**—Joan Baez, Vanguard VRS 9230 (M); VSD 79230 (S)
7. **MERRY CHRISTMAS**—Bing Crosby, Decca DL 8128 (M); DL 78128 (S)
8. **THE CHRISTMAS SONG**—Nat King Cole, Capitol W 1967 (M); SW 1967 (S)
9. **NAVIDAD MEANS CHRISTMAS** — Eydie Gorme & Trio Los Panchos, Columbia CL 2557 (M); CS 9357 (S)
10. **SONGS FOR A MERRY CHRISTMAS**—Wayne Newton, Capitol T 2588 (M); ST 2588 (S)
11. **SEASON'S GREETINGS FROM PERRY COMO**—RCA Victor LPM 2066 (M); LSP 2066 (S)
12. **THE SOUND OF CHRISTMAS**—Ramsey Lewis Trio, Cadet CLP 687 (M); CLPS 687 (S)
13. **MERRY CHRISTMAS**—Supremes, Motown 638 (M); ST 638 (S)
14. **MORE SOUNDS OF CHRISTMAS**—Ramsey Lewis Trio, Cadet CLP 745 (M); CLPS 745 (S)
15. **O BAMBINO/THE LITTLE DRUMMER BOY**—Harry Simeone Chorale, Kapp KL 1450 (M); KS 3450 (S)
16. **JAMES BROWN SINGS CHRISTMAS SONGS** — King 1010 (M); 1010 (S)
17. **SONGS FOR CHRISTMAS** — Mahalia Jackson, Columbia CL 1903 (M); CS 8703 (S)
18. **JOHN GARY CHRISTMAS ALBUM**—RCA Victor LPM 2940 (M); LSP 2940 (S)
19. **JACK JONES CHRISTMAS ALBUM** — Kapp KL 1399 (M); KS 3399 (S)
20. **HOLIDAY CHEER** — Dean Martin, Capitol T 2343 (M); ST 2343 (S)
21. **CHRISTMAS WONDERLAND**—Bert Kaempfert & His Ork, Decca DL 4441 (M); DL 7444 (S)
22. **HERE WE COME A-CAROLING**—Ray Conniff & the Singers, Columbia CL 1701 (M); CS 8501 (S)
23. **MERRY CHRISTMAS**—Brenda Lee, Decca DL 4583 (M); DL 74583 (S)
24. **CHRISTMAS TIME** — Roger Williams, Kapp KL 1164 (M); KS 3048 (S)
25. **HOLIDAY SING ALONG WITH MITCH** — Mitch Miller & the Gang, Columbia CL 2406 (M); CS 8501 (S)
26. **A MERRY MANCINI CHRISTMAS** — Henry Mancini Ork & Chorus, RCA Victor LPM 3612 (M); LSP 3612 (S)
27. **CHRISTMAS WITH BUCK OWENS**—Capitol T 2396 (M); ST 2396 (S)
28. **KATE SMITH CHRISTMAS ALBUM**—RCA Victor LBE 3607 (M); LSP 3607 (S)
29. **CHARLES BROWN SINGS CHRISTMAS** — King 775 (M); (No Stereo)
30. **BEACH BOYS' CHRISTMAS ALBUM**—Capitol T 2164 (M); ST 2164 (S)
31. **IN THE CHRISTMAS SPIRIT**—Booker T. & the M.G.'s, Stax 713 (M); SD 713 (S)
32. **THE VENTURES CHRISTMAS ALBUM** — Dolton BLP 2038 (M); CS 8021 (S)
33. **CHRISTMAS WITH CHET ATKINS**—RCA Victor LPM 2423 (M); LSP 2423 (S)
34. **CHRISTMAS CAROLS OF EUROPE**—Prague Madrigal Singers, Crossroads 22160053 (M); 22160054 (S)
35. **CHRISTMAS IS PERCY FAITH** — Columbia CL 2577 (M); CS 9377 (S)
36. **WISHING YOU A MERRY CHRISTMAS**—Andre Kostelanetz/St. Killan Boychoir, Columbia ML 6179 (M); MS 6779 (S)
37. **JIMMY DEAN'S CHRISTMAS CARD** — Columbia CL 2404 (M); CS 9204 (S)
38. **WINTER WONDERLAND**—Earl Grant, Decca DL 4677 (M); DL 74677 (S)
39. **FOR CHRISTMAS THIS YEAR**—Lettermen, Capitol T 2587 (M); ST 2587 (S)
40. **CHRISTMAS WITH THE CHIPMUNKS**—Liberty LRP 3256 (M); LS 7256 (S)
41. **CHRISTMAS HYMNS AND CAROLS**—Robert Shaw Chorale, RCA Victor LPM 2139 (M); LSC 2139 (S)
42. **JOLLY CHRISTMAS FROM FRANK SINATRA**—Capitol W 894 (M); DM 894 (S)
43. **CHRISTMAS GREETINGS FROM THE MANTOVANI ORK**—London LL 3338 (M); PS 3388 (S)
44. **SONGS OF CHRISTMAS**—Norman Luboff, Columbia CL 926 (M); CS 8816 (S)
45. **SOUNDS OF CHRISTMAS** — Johnny Mathis, Mercury MG 20837 (M); SR 69337 (S)
46. **MERRY CHRISTMAS FROM JACKIE WILSON** — Brunswick BL 54112 (M); BL 754112
47. **HAVE YOURSELF A SOULFUL CHRISTMAS**—Kenny Burrell, Cadet LP 779 (M); LPS 779 (S)
48. **HEART OF CHRISTMAS**—Sergio Franchi, RCA Victor LPM 3437 (M); LSP 3437 (S)
49. **TWELVE SONGS OF CHRISTMAS**—Jim Reeves, RCA Victor LPM 2758 (M); LSP 2758 (S)
50. **CHRISTMAS CAROLS AROUND THE WORLD** — Mormon Tabernacle Choir, Columbia ML 5684 (M); MS 6284 (S)

BEST SELLING CHRISTMAS SINGLES

1. **THE LITTLE DRUMMER BOY**—Harry Simeone Chorale, 20th Century-Fox 429
2. **SLEEP IN HEAVENLY PEACE (Silent Night)** — Barbra Streisand, Columbia 43896
3. **IF EVERYDAY WAS LIKE CHRISTMAS**—Elvis Presley, RCA Victor 8950
4. **PLEASE COME HOME FOR CHRISTMAS** — Charles Brown, King 5405
5. **MERRY CHRISTMAS BABY** — Charles Brown, Hollywood 1021
6. **JINGLE BELL ROCK**—Bobby Helms, Decca 30513
7. **LONESOME CHRISTMAS** — Lowell Fulson, Hollywood 1022
8. **THE CHRISTMAS SONG**—Nat King Cole, Capitol 3561
9. **WHITE CHRISTMAS**—Bing Crosby, Decca 23778
10. **SWEET LITTLE BABY BOY** — James Brown & His Famous Flames, King 6065
11. **BAREFOOT SANTA CLAUS**—Sonny James, Capitol 5733
12. **CHRISTMAS SONG** — James Brown & His Famous Flames, King 6064
13. **ALL I WANT FOR CHRISTMAS IS YOU** — Carla Thomas, Stax 206
14. **ROCKIN' AROUND THE CHRISTMAS TREE** — Brenda Lee, Decca 30776
15. **BLUE CHRISTMAS**—Elvis Presley, RCA Victor 0647
16. **LITTLE DRUMMER BOY**—Joan Baez, Vanguard 35046
17. **WHITE CHRISTMAS**—Drifters, Atlantic 1048
18. **SILENT NIGHT**—Bing Crosby, Decca 23777
19. **SILVER BELLS**—Al Martino, Capitol 5311
20. **SILVER BELLS**—Earl Grant, Decca 25703
21. **JINGLE BELLS**—Booker T. & the M.G.'s, Stax 203
22. **SILVER BELLS**—Bing Crosby, Decca 27229
23. **WINTER WONDERLAND**—Ramsey Lewis, Cadet 5337
24. **SOME DAY AT CHRISTMAS**—Stevie Wonder, Tamla 54142
25. **CHRISTMAS TEARS**—Freddy King, Federal 12439
26. **I'LL BE HOME FOR CHRISTMAS**—Brothers Four, Columbia 43919
27. **RUDOLPH THE RED-NOSED REINDEER** — David Seville & the Chipmunks, Liberty 55289

FORMAT

Below each artist's chronological listing of charted albums is an alphabetical title index of all of the cuts from those albums.

The number(s) in parentheses listed to the immediate right of the cut title refers to our sequential album count of the album on which the cut appears. If the artist had only one charted album, no numbers are listed next to the cuts.

A slightly different format appears for Movie Soundtracks through Various Artist Compilations. The cuts for these albums appear below each individual album title.

HOT 100 HITS

All cuts that charted on *Billboard's Hot 100* chart (and *Billboard's* multiple pre-*Hot 100* pop singles charts from 1955-58) are highlighted in bold type with their peak position listed to the right in bold, italics type. If a song hit the charts as a B-side and never achieved its own highest position, then "flip" is listed to the right in bold, italics type.

If the spelling on the *Hot 100* single differs from the spelling listed on the album, we show the title's spelling as it appears on the single (and thus, as it appears in our *Top Pop Singles* book).

If the <u>same</u> version of a song hit the pop singles charts more than once, only the highest position is shown.

If the *Hot 100* version of a song did not appear on any of the artist's charted albums but a different (live, studio or remix) version did, that title is <u>not</u> highlighted and the *Hot 100* position is not shown. (Also see the rules for DIFFERENT VERSIONS below.)

VINYL ALBUMS vs. COMPACT DISCS

Cuts were taken from the vinyl releases of albums that charted prior to 1990. The title trivia note "not released on vinyl" appears only for compact disc albums that charted prior to 1990.

For albums that charted from 1990 through 2001, the listed cuts refer to the album's release on compact disc.

Whenever possible, title trivia notes indicate if bonus cuts were available on compact disc and/or cassette. The CD bonus cuts of albums that charted since 1990 appear in the index; they do not appear in the index for albums that charted prior to 1990.

Non-music cuts are listed if they are separately titled on the album (as are some monologues on comedy albums or speeches on spoken word albums) and are, in most cases, longer than one minute.

WHICH CUTS ARE NOT LISTED

Generally, album content <u>not</u> listed are segments (usually less-than-a-minute long comprised of talking, sound effects, etc.) and untitled cuts not listed on either the album's label or jacket cover.

Not shown within the Artist Section are segments which are <u>titled</u> or <u>feature within their titles</u>: Intro, Introduction, Introductions, Prologue, Opening, Prelude, Narration, Reprise, Overture, Epilogue, Outro, Finale or Ending; however, these do appear within the Movie Soundtrack and Original Cast Sections. All skits, regardless of length, have been eliminated from the listings.

DIFFERENT VERSIONS

In most cases, different versions of a song (live, studio, acoustic, a capella or instrumental, etc.) are grouped together under one title. The album symbols listed across from the album titles, such as [L] for a live album, and notes in the album title trivia are good indications as to which version appears on a particular album. The exception to this rule is if more than one version of a song hit the *Hot 100* chart; then the versions are separated and specified (live, instrumental, remix, etc.) and their peak positions are listed. For example, the two *Hot 100* versions of "Lola" by The Kinks are shown as: **Lola** (11,13,14,25) *9*
Lola [live] (24, 29) *81*

ALPHABETIZATION

If the article A, An, The, or Tha is the first word of a title, it is not shown. However, if the title is made up of only one other word, then it is shown (example: Wanderer, The).

Cuts that begin with Theme From, Love Theme From, Ballad Of, etc. are alphabetized under the subsequent part of the title (example: Romeo & Juliet, Love Theme From).

MEDLEYS

If a medley has a name (example: Bomber Medley) and the songs within the medley do not appear as separate cuts on any of the artist's albums, then the name of the medley appears as the track title. If a medley does not have a specific name and the songs are simply separated by slashes, then each of the songs are listed individually within the cuts index and (medley) appears after each title.

If a song within a medley also appears as an individual track on an album(s), then that title is not shown with a medley designation. For example, Paul McCartney's *Jet* appears as an individual track on four albums and as part of a medley on a live album, so it is listed as follows: **Jet** (5,8,10,18,20) **7**

The songs of a medley are not separated within the cuts title index if the medley is a *Hot 100* hit, such as the 5th Dimension's "Aquarius/Let The Sunshine In," in which the two songs are listed as one title.

DUOS

For duo or trio albums in which each of the participating artists contributed solo cuts to the album, the solo cuts will appear in the <u>performing</u> artist's cuts index. For example, Harry Belafonte and Miriam Makeba's album, *An Evening With Belafonte/Makeba*, is listed under both artists; however, their solo cuts are only listed under the artist who sang them.

In rare instances, cuts are performed on an album by a person or group that does not have a charted solo album. Those cuts are listed in title trivia and do not appear in the cuts index. For example, on the album *The Beatles with Tony Sheridan and Their Guests*, a group named The Titans perform six solo songs; those titles are noted in title trivia and are not shown in the Beatles' cuts index.

RECORD PRICING

This is the third edition of *Top Pop Albums* to feature prices. The dollar amounts listed in the price column are estimates of the dealer-asking prices for *near-mint* commercial vinyl albums prior to 1990 and for new commercial CD albums from 1990 on.

A special symbol (©) is shown for any album reissued on CD. Pricing for albums from 1955 through 1989 is for the vinyl album and <u>not</u> for the CD, even though a very early album is available on CD. This is for the benefit of collectors dealing in rare and collectible vinyl albums.

Pricing for albums from 1990 through 2001 is for the CD. Prices reflect an average for new CDs available from large retail outlets, such as Best Buy, Barnes & Noble, Amazon, etc. Generally, the large retail outlets display their prices on their websites.

From approximately 1958 through 1968, most albums were issued concurrently in both mono and stereo. When format is not specified by the manufacturer's prefix and/or number, the price reflects an average of mono and stereo copies. In most cases, there is little or no difference between the two. Keep in mind that for some late '50s and early '60s albums, the stereo pressing is considerably rarer and thus more valuable than the mono. Conversely, several late '60s albums can be much more valuable in mono than in stereo.

The Artist Section lists by artist name, alphabetically, every album that charted on *Billboard* magazine's Pop Albums charts from January 8, 1955 through June 30, 2001. (See page x for a chart synopsis.) Each artist's charted hits are listed in chronological order and are sequentially numbered. At the bottom of each artist's album listing is a comprehensive index of all musical cuts from their charted albums. (See *Cuts Index* on page xvi for further explanation.)

EXPLANATION OF COLUMNAR HEADINGS

DEBUT: Date album first charted

PEAK: Highest charted position (highlighted in bold type)

WKS: Total weeks charted

RIAA: RIAA-certified gold or platinum album

CD: Album released on compact disc

Catalog: Peak position/Weeks charted on the Catalog chart

Sym: Symbol (see "Letters In Brackets" on next page)

$: Price guide for vinyl albums and compact discs

Label & Number: Original label and number of album when first charted

EXPLANATION OF SYMBOLS AND NUMBERS

★34★   Number next to an artist name denotes an artist's ranking among the Top 500 Album Artists of All Time

'68   Year of an artist's peak popularity

2^1 Superscript number to the right of the #1 or #2 peak position is the total weeks the album held that position

+   Beside debut date indicates that album peaked in the year after it first charted

↑   Beside the peak position and/or weeks charted indicates that the album was still on the charts as of the September 29, 2001 research cutoff date

25^C Superscript C following the peak position in the "PEAK" column indicates album only charted on the Catalog Albums chart and <u>not</u> on the Pop Albums chart. The preceeding peak position is from the Catalog chart.

15^X Superscript X following the peak position in the "PEAK" column indicates album only charted on the Christmas Albums chart and <u>not</u> on the Pop Albums chart. The preceeding peak position is from the Christmas chart.

     For an album that charted on the Christmas <u>and</u> the Popular Albums charts, its Christmas chart's peak position and year of debut appears in title trivia.

C: Indicates that an album which hit the Pop Albums chart <u>also</u> hit the Catalog chart. The "C:" appears on the line to the right of an album title and is followed by its Catalog chart's peak position and weeks charted.

©   Album released on compact disc

●   RIAA-certified gold album (500,000 units sold)

▲ RIAA-certified platinum album (1,000,000 units sold)

The Recording Industry Association of America (RIAA) began certifying gold albums in 1958, platinum albums in 1976 and multi-platinum albums in 1984. Some record labels have never requested RIAA certification for albums which would otherwise have qualified for these awards.

A superscript number to the right of the platinum triangle indicates album was awarded multi-platinum status (ex.: ▲^{3} indicates an album was certified triple platinum).

UNDERLINED & SHADED TITLES

The highest-charting album by an artist with 5 or more charted albums is underlined with a heavy rule. This does not necessarily mean that it is their best-selling album. For example, Pink Floyd's *The Dark Side Of The Moon* spent over 14 years on the charts and has, so far, received 15 platinum designations yet it spent only one week at the top of the charts; whereas, the underlined album *The Wall* was #1 for 15 weeks. Ties are broken based on peak weeks and total weeks charted. All Top 10 albums are shaded with a light gray background.

LETTER(S) IN BRACKETS AFTER TITLES (Sym column)

C - Comedy

E - Earlier Recordings/Releases

EP - 7" Extended Play Album

F - Foreign Language

G - Greatest Hits

I - Instrumental Recording

K - Compilation

L - Live Recording

M - Mini Album (10" or 12" EP, lower-priced CD)

N - Novelty

OC - Original Cast

R - Reissue or re-release **with a new label number** of a previously charted album or Christmas re-release of album with or without the same label number

S - Movie Soundtrack

T - Talk/Spoken Word Recording

TV - Television Program Soundtrack

X - Christmas (If an album also charted on *Billboard's* special Christmas charts, a title note lists the highest position reached and year it made the Christmas albums chart. For example a note may read:

Christmas charts: 5/'67, 10/'68

(indicating that an album peaked at position five on the Christmas chart in 1967 and position 10 in 1968.)

ARTIST & TITLE NOTES

Pertinent biographical information is shown below nearly every artist name. Directly under some album titles are notes indicating guest artists, the location of live recordings, the names of famous producers, etc. Duets and other important name variations are shown in bold capital letters. We highlighted in bold type the names of artists mentioned in the artist and title notes of other charted pop album artists if they have their own album listing elsewhere in this book. All movie, TV and album titles, and other major works, appear in italics.

CUTS INDEX

Below each artist's chronological listing of charted albums is an alphabetical title index of all of the cuts on those albums. The number(s) in parentheses listed to the immediate right of the title refers to the sequential album count of the album on which the cut appears. All cuts that charted on *Billboard's Hot 100* chart (and *Billboard's* multiple pre-*Hot 100* pop singles charts from 1955-58) are highlighted in bold type with their peak position listed to the right in bold, italics type.

See *Cuts Index* on page xvi for further guidelines.

ALBUMS BY ARTIST

Lists, alphabetically by artist name, every album that charted on *Billboard's* Pop Albums chart from January 8, 1955 through June 30, 2001. Each artist listing includes an alphabetical index of all cuts from every one of their albums.

CONTACT US

Artists, group members, producers or label personnel are requested to get in touch with us via email, fax or phone (see page ii) if any of your biographical data is incorrect or needs to be updated. In one day alone, we heard from Andy Kim, Ronnie Dove, and Rosie (Rosie & The Originals) with updated information. Please contact us — we'd love to hear from you and get your comments as to how we're doing.

A

AALIYAH '97
Born Aaliyah Haughton on 1/16/79 in Brooklyn, New York; raised in Detroit. Died in a plane crash on 8/25/2001 (age 22). Female R&B singer/actress. Played "Trish O'Day" in the movie *Romeo Must Die*.

6/11/94	18	37	▲	©	1 Age Ain't Nothing But A Number	$10	Blackground 41533
9/14/96+	18	67	▲²	©	2 One In A Million	$10	Blackground 92715

Age Ain't Nothing But A Number (1) 75	Came To Give Love (2)	4 Page Letter (2)	I Gotcha' Back (2)	Never Givin' Up (2)	Street Thing (1)
At Your Best (You Are Love) (1) 6	Choosey Lover (Old School/New School) (2)	Girl Like You (2)	I'm Down (1)	No One Knows How To Love Me Quite Like You Do (1)	Throw Your Hands Up (1)
Back & Forth (1) 5	Down With The Clique (1)	Giving You More (2)	I'm So Into You (1)	Old School (1)	Young Nation (1)
Beats 4 Da Streets (2)	Everything's Gonna Be Alright (2)	Got To Give It Up (2)	If Your Girl Only Knew (2) 11	One I Gave My Heart To (2) 9	
		Heartbroken (2)	Ladies In Da House (2)	One In A Million (1)	
		Hot Like Fire (2)	Never Comin' Back (2)		

★289★ ABBA '78
Pop group from Stockholm, Sweden: Anni-Frid (**Frida**) Lyngstad and **Agnetha Fältskog** (vocals), Bjorn Ulvaeus (guitar) and Benny Andersson (keyboards). ABBA is an acronym of members' first initials. Benny and Bjorn recorded together in 1966. Bjorn and Agnetha were married from 1971-79. Benny and Frida were married from 1978-81. Disbanded in the early 1980s. Bjorn and Benny cowrote the musical *Chess* with Tim Rice.

1)The Album 2)Super Trouper 3)Voulez-Vous

8/17/74	145	8		©	1 Waterloo	$20	Atlantic 18101
11/15/75	174	3		©	2 Abba	$20	Atlantic 18146
9/18/76	48	61	▲	©	3 Greatest Hits	[G] $15	Atlantic 18189
1/22/77	20	50	●	©	4 Arrival	$15	Atlantic 18207
2/18/78	14	41	▲	©	5 The Album	$15	Atlantic 19164
7/7/79	19	27	●	©	6 Voulez-Vous	$15	Atlantic 16000
					title is French for "Will You"		
12/22/79+	46	14	●	©	7 Greatest Hits, Vol. 2	[G] $15	Atlantic 16009
12/13/80+	17	38	●	©	8 Super Trouper	$15	Atlantic 16023
1/9/82	29	17		©	9 The Visitors	$15	Atlantic 19332
12/18/82+	62	18		©	10 The Singles (The First Ten Years)	[G] $20	Atlantic 80036 [2]
10/9/93	63	104	▲³	©	11 Gold - Greatest Hits	C:#11/122 [G] $10	Polydor 517007

Andante, Andante (8)	Fernando (3,10,11) 13	I Wonder (Departure) (5,7)	Me And I (8)	Rock Me (2,7)	Tropical Loveland (2)
Angeleyes (6,7) 64	Gimme! Gimme! Gimme! (A Man After Midnight) (7,10,11)	I'm A Marionette (5)	Money, Money, Money (4,7,10,11) 56	SOS (2,3,10,11) 15	Two For The Price Of One (9)
Another Town, Another Train (3)	Gonna Sing You My Lovesong (1)	I've Been Waiting For You (2)	Move On (5)	Sitting In The Palmtree (1)	Under Attack (10)
Arrival (4)	Happy New Year (8)	If It Wasn't For The Nights (6)	My Love, My Life (4)	Slipping Through My Fingers (9)	Visitors, The (9) 63
As Good As New (6)	Hasta Manana (1)	Intermezzo No I (2)	My Mama Said (1)	So Long (2,3,10)	Voulez-Vous (6,10,11) 80
Bang-A-Boomerang (2,3)	He Is Your Brother (3)	King Has Lost His Crown (6)	Name Of The Game (5,7,10,11) 12	Soldiers (3)	Watch Out (1)
Chiquitita (6,7,10,11) 29	Head Over Heels (9)	King Kong Song (1)	Nina Pretty Ballerina (3)	Summer Night City (7,10)	Waterloo (1,3,10,11) 6
Dance (While The Music Still Goes On) (1,3)	Hey, Hey Helen (2)	Kisses Of Fire (6)	On And On And On (8) 90	Super Trouper (8,10,11) 45	Way Old Friends Do (8)
Dancing Queen (4,7,10,11) 1	Hole In Your Soul (5)	Knowing Me, Knowing You (4,7,10,11) 14	One Man, One Woman (5)	Suzy-Hang-Around (1)	What About Livingstone (1)
Day Before You Came (10)	Honey, Honey (1,3) 27	Lay All Your Love On Me (8,11)	One Of Us (9,10,11) 3	Take A Chance On Me (5,7,10,11) 3	When All Is Said And Done (9) 27
Does Your Mother Know (6,7,10,11) 19	I Do, I Do, I Do, I Do, I Do (2,3,10) 15	Like An Angel Passing Through My Room (9)	Our Last Summer (8)	Thank You For The Music (5,7,11)	When I Kissed The Teacher (4)
Dum Dum Diddle (4)	I Have A Dream (6,10,11)	Lovers (Live A Little Longer) (6)	People Need Love (3)	That's Me (4)	Why Did It Have To Be Me (4)
Eagle (5,7)	I Let The Music Speak (9)	Mamma Mia (2,3,10,11) 32	Piper, The (8)	Tiger (4)	Winner Takes It All (8,10,11) 8
		Man In The Middle (2)	Ring Ring (1,3,10)		

ABBOTT, Gregory '87
Born on 4/2/54 in New York City. R&B singer/songwriter. Dual citizen of U.S. and Antigua; his father is Antiguan and mother is Venezuelan. Previously taught English at Berkeley.

11/1/86+	22	36	●	©	1 Shake You Down	$10	Columbia 40437
6/4/88	132	9		©	2 I'll Prove It To You	$10	Columbia 44087

Back To Stay (2)	I'll Find A Way (1)	Prisoner Of Love (2)	Shake You Down (1) 1	Unfinished Business (1)
Crazy Over You (2)	I'll Prove It To You (2)	Rhyme And Reason (1)	She's An Entertainer (2)	Wait Until Tomorrow (1)
I Got The Feelin' (It's Over) (1) 56	Let Me Be Your Hero (2)	Runaway (2)	Take Me Back (2)	You're My Angel (1)
	Magic (1)	Say You Will (1)	Two Of A Kind (2)	

ABC '83
Electro-pop group from Sheffield, England: Martin Fry (vocals), Mark White (guitar), Stephen Singleton (sax), Mark Lickley (bass) and David Palmer (drums). After their second album the latter three left, leaving duo of Fry and White.

9/25/82+	24	39	●	©	1 the Lexicon of Love	$10	Mercury 4059
12/17/83+	69	14		©	2 Beauty Stab	$10	Mercury 814661
10/5/85	30	41		©	3 how to be a...Zillionaire!	$10	Mercury 824904
8/22/87	48	25		©	4 Alphabet City	$10	Mercury 832391

A To Z (3)	Between You & Me (3)	(How To Be A) Millionaire (3) 20	Look Of Love (Part Four) (1)	Power Of Persuasion (2)	Think Again (4)
All Of My Heart (1)	Bite The Hand (2)	If I Ever Thought You'd Be Lonely (2)	Love's A Dangerous Language (2)	Rage And Then Regret (4)	Tower Of London (3)
Ark-Angel (4)	By Default By Design (2)	Jealous Lover (4)	Many Happy Returns (3)	S.O.S. (2)	United Kingdom (3)
Avenue A (4)	Date Stamp (1)	King Money (2)	Night You Murdered Love (4)	Show Me (1)	Unzip (2)
Avenue Z (4)	Fear Of The World (3)	King Without A Crown (4)	Ocean Blue (3)	So Hip It Hurts (3)	Valentine's Day (1)
Bad Blood (4)	15 Storey Halo (3)	Look Of Love (Part One) (1) 18	One Day (4)	Tears Are Not Enough (1)	Vanity Kills (3) 91
Be Near Me (3) 9	4 Ever 2 Gether (1)		Poison Arrow (1) 25	That Was Then But This Is Now (2) 89	When Smokey Sings (4) 5
Beauty Stab (2)	Hey Citizen (3)				

ABDUL, Paula '89
Born on 6/19/62 in Los Angeles. Singer/choreographer. While still a teen, was the member and choreographer of the NBA's Los Angeles Lakers cheerleaders. Choreographed **Janet Jackson**'s *Control* videos and **Tracey Ullman**'s TV show. Married to actor Emilio Estevez from 1992-94.

7/23/88+	❶¹⁰	175	▲⁷	©	1 Forever Your Girl	$10	Virgin 90943
5/26/90	7	35	▲	©	2 Shut Up And Dance (The Dance Mixes)	[K] $10	Virgin 91362
6/1/91	❶²	70	▲³	©	3 Spellbound	$10	Captive 91611
7/1/95	18	18	●	©	4 Head Over Heels	$10	Captive 40525

Ain't Never Gonna Give You Up (4)	Blowing Kisses In The Wind (3) 6	Crazy Cool (4) 58	Ho-Down (4)	It's All About Feeling Good (4)	Love Don't Come Easy (4)
Alright Tonight (3)	Choice Is Yours (4)	Cry For Me (4)	I Need You (1)	(It's Just) The Way That You Love Me (1,2) 3	Missing You (4)
	Cold Hearted (1,2) 1	Forever Your Girl (1,2) 1	I Never Knew It (4)	Knocked Out (1,2) 41	My Foolish Heart (3)
		Get Your Groove On (4)	If I Were Your Girl (4)		My Love Is For Real (4) 28

3

ABDUL, Paula — Cont'd

Next To You (1)	**Opposites Attract** (1,2) *1*	**Rush, Rush** (3) *1*	State Of Attraction (1)	U (3)	**Will You Marry Me?** (3) *19*
1990 Medley Mix (2)	**Promise Of A New Day** (3) *1*	Sexy Thoughts (4)	**Straight Up** (1,2) *1*	Under The Influence (4)	
One Or The Other (1,2)	Rock House (3)	Spellbound (3)	To You (3)	**Vibeology** (3) *16*	

ABOVE THE LAW '93

Rap trio from Pamona, California: Don Hutchinson, Kevin Gulley and Anthony Stewart. Hutchinson is the nephew of **Willie Hutch**.

4/14/90	75	16	©	1	Livin' Like Hustlers	$10	Ruthless 46041
8/3/91	120	4	©	2	Vocally Pimpin'	[M] $10	Ruthless 47934
2/20/93	37	7	©	3	Black Mafia Life	$10	Ruthless 24477
7/30/94	113	13	©	4	Uncle Sam's Curse	$10	Ruthless 5524
11/9/96	80	2	©	5	Time Will Reveal	$10	Tommy Boy 1154
3/14/98	142	2	©	6	Legends	$10	Tommy Boy 1233

Adventures Of... (6)	Deep Az The Root (6)	Gangsta Madness (4)	Mee Vs. My Ego (3)	Process Of Elimination	Uncle Sam's Curse (4)
Another Execution (1)	Dose Of The Mega Flex (2)	Gorillapimpin' (5)	Menace To Society (1)	(Untouchakickamurdaqtion)	Untouchable (1)
Apocalypse Now (5)	Encore (5)	G-Rupies Best Friend (3)	Murder Rap (3)	(3)	V.S.O.P. (3)
Ballin' (1)	Endonesia (5)	Harda U R Tha Doppa U Faal	My World (5)	Promise Me (6)	Who Ryde (4)
Be About Yo Bizniz (6)	Everything Will Be Alright (4)	(3)	Never Missin' A Beat (3)	Rain Be For Rain Bo (4)	Why Must I Feel Like Dat (3)
Black Superman (4)	Evil That Men Do (5)	In God We Trust (6)	1996 (5)	Return Of The Real Shit (4)	Wicked (2)
Black Triangle (3)	Flow On (Move Me No	Just Kickin' Lyrics (1)	100 Spokes (3)	Set Free (4)	Worldwide (6)
Call It What U Want (3)	Mountain) (1)	Kalifornia (4)	One Time Two Meny (4)	Set Trippin' (6)	X.O. Wit Me (6)
City Of Angels (3)	4 The Funk Of It (2)	Karma (4)	Outro (3)	Shout 2 The True (5)	
Clinic Niggaz (6)	Freedom Of Speech (1)	Killaz In The Park (5)	Pimp Clinic (3)	Soliciting (6)	
Clinic 2000 (5)	"G" In Me (4)	L.A. Vibe (6)	Pimpology 101 (3)	Soul Searching (6)	
Commin' Up (3)	G's & Macaronies (3)	Last Song (1)	Playaz & Gangstas (5)	Streets, The (6)	
Concreat Jungle (4)	Game Wreck-Oniz-Iz Game (3)	Livin' Like Hustlers (1,2)	Playin' Your Game (2)	Sumner Days (6)	

ABRAMS, Colonel '86

Born Colonel Abrams in Detroit; raised in New York City. R&B singer/songwriter.

4/19/86	75	11			Colonel Abrams	$10	MCA 5682

I'm Not Gonna Let You	Never Change	Picture Me In Love With You	Table For Two	Truth, The
Margaux	Over And Over	Speculation	Trapped	

ACCEPT '84

Hard-rock group from Germany: Udo Dirkschneider (vocals), Wolf Hoffmann and Hermann Frank (guitars), Peter Baltes (bass) and Stefan Kaufmann (drums). Jorg Fischer replaced Frank in 1985. In 1987, Dirkschneider and Fischer left; replaced by Colorado-born David Reece and Jim Stacey.

2/4/84	74	26	● ©	1	Balls To The Wall	$10	Portrait 39241
3/30/85	94	14	©	2	Metal Heart	$10	Portrait 39974
5/17/86	114	9	©	3	Russian Roulette	$10	Portrait 40354
6/24/89	139	9	©	4	Eat The Heat	$10	Epic 44368

Aiming High (3)	Generation Clash (4)	Losers And Winners (1)	Mistreated (4)	Teach Us To Survive (2)	X-T-C
Another Second To Be (3)	Guardian Of The Night (1)	Losing More Than You've Ever	Monsterman (3)	Too High To Get It Right (2)	
Balls To The Wall (1)	Head Over Heels (1)	Had (1)	Prisoner (4)	Turn Me On (1)	
Bound To Fail (2)	Heaven Is Hell (3)	Love Child (1)	Russian Roulette (3)	Turn The Wheel (4)	
Chain Reaction (4)	Hellhammer (4)	Love Sensation (4)	Screaming For A Love-Bite (4)	Up To The Limit (2)	
D-Train (4)	It's Hard To Find A Way (3)	Man Enough To Cry (3)	Stand 4 What U R (4)	Walking In The Shadow (3)	
Dogs On Leads (2)	Living For Tonite (2)	Metal Heart (2)	Stand Tight (3)	Winterdreams (1)	
Fight It Back (1)	London Leatherboys (1)	Midnight Mover (2)	T.V.War (3)	Wrong Is Right (2)	

AC/DC ★67★ '81

Hard-rock group from Sydney, Australia: brothers Angus and Malcolm Young (guitars), Ron Belford "Bon" Scott (vocals), Mark Evans (bass) and Phil Rudd (drums). Cliff Williams replaced Evans in 1977. Bon Scott died on 2/19/80 (age 33) from alcohol abuse and was replaced by Brian Johnson. Simon Wright replaced Rudd in 1985. Wright joined **Dio** in 1989, replaced by Chris Slade of **The Firm**. Rudd returned in 1995. Angus and Malcolm are the younger brothers of George Young of **The Easybeats**.

1)For Those About To Rock We Salute You 2)The Razors Edge 3)Dirty Deeds Done Dirt Cheap

8/13/77	154	11	▲[2] ©	1	Let There Be Rock	C:#9/23	$25	Atco 151
6/24/78	133	17	▲ ©	2	Powerage		$15	Atlantic 19180
12/23/78+	113	14	▲ ©	3	If You Want Blood You've Got It	[L]	$15	Atlantic 19212
8/25/79	17	83	▲[6] ©	4	Highway To Hell	C:#23/20	$10	Atlantic 19244
8/23/80	4	131	▲[19] ©	5	Back In Black	C:❶[1]/472	$10	Atlantic 16018
4/18/81	3	55	▲[6] ©	6	Dirty Deeds Done Dirt Cheap	C:#47/2 [E]	$10	Atlantic 16033
7/18/81+	146	19	▲[2] ©	7	High Voltage	[E]	$10	Atco 142
					above 2 albums recorded in 1976			
12/12/81	❶[3]	30	▲[4] ©	8	For Those About To Rock We Salute You		$10	Atlantic 11111
9/10/83	15	23	▲ ©	9	Flick Of The Switch		$10	Atlantic 80100
11/17/84	76	14	▲ ©	10	'74 Jailbreak	[E-M]	$10	Atlantic 80178
					Australian releases from 1975-76			
7/20/85	32	30	▲ ©	11	Fly On The Wall		$10	Atlantic 81263
6/21/86	33	42	▲[5] ©	12	Who Made Who	C:#14/44 [K-S]	$10	Atlantic 81650
					soundtrack from the movie Maximum Overdrive			
3/5/88	12	24	▲ ©	13	Blow Up Your Video		$10	Atlantic 81828
10/6/90	2[1]	77	▲[4] ©	14	The Razors Edge		$10	Atco 91413
11/14/92	15	48	▲[3] ©	15	Live	C:#13/116 [L]	$10	Atco 92215
					14 tracks from album #16 below			
11/14/92	34	14	▲[2] ©	16	Live (Special Collector's Edition)	[L]	$15	Atco 92212 [2]
10/14/95	4	30	▲[2] ©	17	Ballbreaker		$10	EastWest 61780
12/6/97	90	5	▲ ©	18	Bonfire	[K]	$50	EastWest 62119 [5]
					box set tribute to former lead singer Bon Scott; contains recordings from 1976-80			
3/18/00	7	28	▲ ©	19	Stiff Upper Lip		$10	EastWest 62494

4

AC/DC — Cont'd

Ain't No Fun (Waiting Round To Be A Millionaire) (6)
All Screwed Up (19)
Are You Ready (14,16)
Baby, Please Don't Go (10)
Back In Black (5,15,16,18) 37
Back In Business (11)
Back Seat Confidential (18)
Bad Boy Boogie (1,3,18)
Badlands (9)
Ballbreaker (17)
Beating Around The Bush (4)
Bedlam In Belgium (9)
Big Balls (6)
Bonny (16)
Boogie Man (17)
Brain Shake (9)
Breaking The Rules (8)
Burnin' Alive (11)
C.O.D. (8)
Can I Sit Next To You Girl (7)
Can't Stand Still (19)
Can't Stop Rock 'N' Roll (19)
Caught With Your Pants Down (17)
Chase The Ace (12)
Come And Get It (19)
Cover You In Oil (17)
D.T. (12)

Damned (19)
Danger (11)
Deep In The Hole (9)
Dirty Deeds Done Dirt Cheap (6,15,16)
Dirty Eyes (18)
Dog Eat Dog (1,18)
Down Payment Blues (2)
Evil Walks (8)
Fire Your Guns (14,16)
First Blood (11)
Flick Of The Switch (9)
Fly On The Wall (11)
For Those About To Rock (We Salute You) (8,12,15,16)
Furor, The (17)
Get It Hot (4,18)
Gimme A Bullet (2)
Girls Got Rhythm (4,18)
Give It Up (19)
Given The Dog A Bone (5,18)
Go Down (1)
Go Zone (13)
Gone Shootin' (2)
Goodbye & Good Riddance To Bad Luck (14)
Got You By The Balls (14)
Guns For Hire (9) 84
Hail Caesar (17)

Hard As A Rock (17)
Have A Drink On Me (5,18)
Heatseeker (13,15,16)
Hell Ain't A Bad Place To Be (1,3,18)
Hell Or High Water (11)
Hells Bells (5,12,15,16,18)
High Voltage (3,7,16,18)
Highway To Hell (4,15,16,18) 47
Hold Me Back (19)
Honey Roll (17)
House Of Jazz (19)
If You Dare (11)
If You Want Blood (You've Got It) (1,18)
Inject The Venom (8)
It's A Long Way To The Top (If You Wanna Rock 'N' Roll) (7,18)
Jack, The (3,7,15,16,18)
Jailbreak (10,16)
Kicked In The Teeth (3)
Kissin' Dynamite (13)
Landslide (9)
Let Me Put My Love Into You (5,18)
Let There Be Rock (1,3,16,18)
Let's Get It Up (8) 44
Lets Make It (14)

Little Lover (7)
Live Wire (7,18)
Love At First Feel (6)
Love Bomb (17)
Love Hungry Man (4)
Meanstreak (13)
Meltdown (18)
Mistress For Christmas (14)
Moneytalks (14,15,16) 23
Nervous Shakedown (9)
Nick Of Time (13)
Night Of The Long Knives (8)
Night Prowler (4)
Overdose (1)
Playing With Girls (11)
Problem Child (1,3,6,18)
Put The Finger On You (8)
Razors Edge (14,16)
Ride On (6,12,18)
Riff Raff (2,3)
Rising Power (9)
Rock And Roll Ain't Noise Pollution (5,18)
Rock 'N' Roll Damnation (2,3)
Rock 'N' Roll Singer (7)
Rock Your Heart Out (14)
Rocker (3,6,18)
Ruff Stuff (13)
Safe In New York City (19)

Satellite Blues (19)
School Days (18)
Send For The Man (11)
Shake A Leg (5,18)
Shake Your Foundations (11,12)
She's Got Balls (7,18)
Shoot To Thrill (5,15,16,18)
Shot Down In Flames (4,18)
Shot Of Love (14)
Show Business (10)
Sin City (2,16,18)
Sink The Pink (11,12)
Snowballed (8)
Some Sin For Nuthin' (13)
Soul Stripper (10)
Spellbound (8)
Squealer (6)
Stand Up (11)
Stiff Upper Lip (19)
T.N.T. (7,15,16,18)
That's The Way I Wanna Rock N Roll (13,16)
There's Gonna Be Some Rockin' (18)
This House Is On Fire (9)
This Means War (13)
Thunderstruck (14,15,16)
Touch Too Much (4,18)

Two's Up (13)
Up To My Neck In You (2)
Walk All Over You (4,18)
What Do You Do For Money Honey (5,18)
What's Next To The Moon (2)
W hiskey On The Rocks (17)
Who Made Who (12,15,16)
Whole Lotta Rosie (1,3,15,16,18)
You Ain't Got A Hold On Me (10)
You Shook Me All Night Long (5,12,15,16,18) 35

ACE '75

Pop-rock group from Sheffield, England: Paul Carrack (vocals), Phil Harris and Alan King (guitars), Terry Comer (bass) and Fran Byrne (drums). Harris replaced by Jon Woodhead by 1976. Disbanded in 1977. Carrack joined **Squeeze** in 1981, then **Mike + The Mechanics** in 1985.

3/15/75	11	22			1 **Five-A-Side (an Ace album)**			$15	Anchor 2001
12/27/75+	153	6			2 **Time For Another**			$15	Anchor 2013
2/12/77	170	2			3 **No Strings**			$15	Anchor 2020

Ain't Gonna Stand For This No More (2)
C'est La Vie (3)
Crazy World (3)
Does It Hurt You (2)
Found Out The Hard Way (3)

Gleaming In The Gloom (3)
How Long (1) 3
I Think It's Gonna Last (2)
I'm A Man (2)
I'm Not Takin' It Out On You (3)
Know How It Feels (1)

Let's Hang On (3)
Message To You (2)
Movin' (3)
No Future In Your Eyes (2)
Real Feeling (1)
Rock & Roll Runaway (1) 71

Rock And Roll Singer (2)
Sail On My Brother (3)
Satellite (1)
Sniffin' About (1)
So Sorry Baby (1)
This Is What You Find (2)

Time Ain't Long (1)
Tongue Tied (2)
24 Hours (1)
Why? (1)
Why Did You Leave Me (3)
You Can't Lose (2)

You're All That I Need (3

ACE OF BASE '94

Pop group from Gothenburg, Sweden: vocalists/sisters Jenny and Linn Berggren with keyboardists Jonas "Joker" Berggren (their brother) and Ulf "Buddha" Ekberg.

12/11/93+	**❶**[2]	102	▲[9]	©	1 **The Sign**			$10	Arista 18740
12/2/95+	29	29	▲	©	2 **The Bridge**			$10	Arista 18806
8/1/98	101	10		©	3 **Cruel Summer**			$10	Arista 19021

Adventures In Paradise (3)
All That She Wants (1) 2
Always Have, Always Will (3)
Angel Eyes (3)
Beautiful Life (2) 15
Blooming 18 (2)
Cecilia (3)

Cruel Summer (3) 10
Dancer In A Daydream (1)
Don't Go Away (3)
Don't Turn Around (1) 4
Donnie (3)
Edge Of Heaven (2)
Everytime It Rains (3)

Experience Pearls (2)
Happy Nation (1)
He Decides (3)
Just 'N' Image (2)
Living In Danger (1) 20
Lucky Love (2) 30
My Deja Vu (2)

My Mind (Mindless Mix) (1)
Never Gonna Say I'm Sorry (2)
Perfect World (2)
Que Sera (2)
Ravine (2)
Sign, The (1) 1
Strange Ways (2)

Tokyo Girl (3)
Travel To Romantis (3)
Voulez-Vous Danser (1)
Waiting For Magic (1)
Wave Wet Sand (2)
Wheel Of Fortune (1)

Whenever You're Near Me (3) 76
Whispers In Blindness (2)
Young And Proud (1)

ACE SPECTRUM '75

R&B vocal group from New York City: Ed Zant, Aubrey Johnson, Elliot Isaac and Rudy Gay.

8/23/75	138	7			**Low Rent Rendezvous**			$15	Atlantic 18143

Beautiful Love
Do You Remember Yesterday

I Just Want To Spend The Night With You

Keep Holding On
Laughter In The Rain

Third Rate Romance (Low Rent Rendezvous)

Trust Me
Without You

You Ain't No Match For Me

ACKLES, David '72

Born on 2/20/37 in Rock Island, Illinois. Died of cancer on 3/2/99 (age 62). Pop singer/songwriter. Moved to California as a child and began movie and stage career.

8/12/72	167	10			**American Gothic**			$15	Elektra 75032

American Gothic
Another Friday Night

Ballad Of The Ship Of State
Blues For Billy Whitecloud

Family Band
Love's Enough

Midnight Carousel
Montana Song

Oh, California!
One Night Stand

Waiting For The Moving Van

ACKLIN, Barbara '68

Born on 2/28/42 in Chicago. Died of pneumonia on 11/27/98 (age 56). R&B singer/songwriter. Formerly married to Eugene Record of **The Chi-Lites**.

10/5/68	146	5	©		**Love Makes A Woman**			$25	Brunswick 754137

Be By My Side
Come And See Me Baby

I've Got You Baby
Look Of Love

Love Makes A Woman 15
Old Matchmaker

Please Sunrise, Please
To Sir, With Love

What The World Needs Now Is Love

Yes I See The Love (I Missed)
Your Sweet Loving

ADAM & THE ANTS — see ANT, Adam

ADAMS, Andy — see EGG CREAM

★309★

ADAMS, Bryan '85

Born on 11/5/59 in Kingston, Ontario, Canada. Rock singer/songwriter/guitarist. Lead singer of Sweeney Todd in 1976. Teamed with Jim Vallance in 1977 in songwriting partnership. Cameo appearance in the movie *Pink Cadillac*.

1/30/82	118	13		©	1 **You Want It, You Got It**	C:#39/4		$10	A&M 4864
2/19/83	8	89	▲	©	2 **Cuts Like A Knife**			$10	A&M 4919
11/24/84+	**❶**[2]	83	▲[5]	©	3 **Reckless**	C:#27/10		$10	A&M 5013
4/18/87	7	33	▲	©	4 **Into The Fire**			$10	A&M 3907

ADAMS, Bryan — Cont'd

DEBUT	PEAK	WKS	RIAA	CD	Album Title	Catalog/Sym	$	Label & Number
10/12/91	6	75	▲⁴	© 5	Waking Up The Neighbours		$10	A&M 5367
11/27/93+	6	66	▲⁵	© 6	So Far So Good	C:#38/13 [G]	$10	A&M 540157
6/22/96	31	50	▲	© 7	18 Til I Die		$10	A&M 540551
12/27/97+	88	14		© 8	MTV Unplugged	[L]	$10	A&M 540831

recorded on 9/26/97 at the Hammerstein Ballroom in New York City

| 11/14/98 | 103 | 2 | | © 9 | On A Day Like Today | | $10 | A&M 541014 |

Ain't Gonna Cry (3)
All I Want Is You (5)
Another Day (4)
Back To You (8)
Before The Night Is Over (9)
Best Was Yet To Come (2)
Black Pearl (7)
Can't Stop This Thing We Started (5,6) *2*
Cloud Number Nine (9)
C'mon C'mon C'mon (9)
Coming Home (1)
Cuts Like A Knife (2,6,8) *15*
Depend On Me (5)
Do I Have To Say The Words? (5,6) *11*
Do To You (7)
Don't Drop That Bomb On Me (5)

Don't Leave Me Lonely (2)
Don't Look Now (1)
18 Til I Die (7,8)
(Everything I Do) I Do It For You (5,6) *1*
Fearless (9)
Fits Ya Good (1,8)
Getaway (9)
Have You Ever Really Loved A Woman? (7)
Hearts On Fire (4) *26*
Heat Of The Night (4,6) *6*
Heaven (3,6,8) *1*
Hey Honey - I'm Packin' You In! (5)
Home Again (4)
House Arrest (5)
How Do Ya Feel Tonight (9)
I Don't Wanna Live Forever (9)

I Think About You (7,8)
(I Wanna Be) Your Underwear (7)
I'll Always Be Right There (7,8)
I'm A Liar (9)
I'm Ready (2,8)
If I Had You (9)
If Ya Wanna Be Bad - Ya Gotta Be Good (medley) (8)
If You Wanna Leave Me (Can I Come Too?) (5)
Inside Out (9)
Into The Fire (4)
Is Your Mama Gonna Miss Ya? (5)
It Ain't A Party...If You Can't Come 'Round (7)
It's Only Love (3,6) *15*
Jealousy (1)

Kids Wanna Rock (3,6)
Last Chance (7)
Let Him Know (2)
Let's Make A Night To Remember (7,8) *24*
Little Love (8)
Lonely Nights (1) *84*
Long Gone (3)
Native Son (4)
No One Makes It Right (1)
Not Guilty (5)
On A Day Like Today (9)
One Good Reason (1)
One Night Love Affair (3) *13*
Only One (2)
Only The Strong Survive (4)
Only Thing That Looks Good On Me Is You (7,8) *52*
Please Forgive Me (6) *7*

Rebel (4)
Remembrance Day (4)
Run To You (3,6) *6*
She's Only Happy When She's Dancin' (3)
Somebody (3,6) *11*
Star (7)
Straight From The Heart (2,6) *10*
Summer Of '69 (3,6,8) *5*
Take Me Back (2)
There Will Never Be Another Tonight (5) *31*
This Time (2,6) *24*
Thought I'd Died And Gone To Heaven (5) *13*
Tonight (1)
Touch The Hand (5)
Vanishing (5)

Victim Of Love (4) *32*
We're Gonna Win (7)
What's It Gonna Be (2)
When You Love Someone (8)
When You're Gone (9)
Where Angels Fear To Tread (9)
You Want It, You Got It (1)
You're Still Beautiful To Me (7)

ADAMS, Oleta '91
Born on 5/4/62 in Seattle. Female R&B singer/pianist.

DEBUT	PEAK	WKS		CD	Album Title		$	Label & Number
9/1/90+	20	44	●	© 1	Circle Of One		$10	Fontana 846346
8/21/93	67	13		© 2	Evolution		$10	Fontana 514965
11/25/95	194	1		© 3	Moving On		$10	Fontana 528684

Circle Of One (1)
Come When You Call (2)
Day I Stop Loving You (2)
Don't Let Me Be Lonely Tonight (2)
Don't Look Too Closely (1)
Easier To Say (Goodbye) (2)

Everything Must Change (1)
Evolution (2)
Get Here (1) *5*
Hold Me For A While (2)
I Just Had To Hear Your Voice (2)
I Knew You When (3)

I've Got A Right (1)
I've Got To Sing My Song (1)
If This Love Should Ever End (3)
Life Keeps Moving On (3)
Long Distance Love (3)
Love Begins At Home (3)

Lover's Holiday (2)
My Heart Won't Lie (2)
Never Knew Love (3)
New Star (3)
New York State Of Mind (2)
Once In A Lifetime (3)
Rhythm Of Life (1)

Slow Motion (3)
This Is Real (3)
We Will Meet Again (3)
When Love Comes To The Rescue (2)
Will We Ever Learn (1)
Window Of Hope (2)

You Need To Be Loved (3)
You've Got To Give Me Room (1)

ADAMS, Yolanda '00
Born on 10/21/63 in Houston. Female gospel singer.

DEBUT	PEAK	WKS		CD	Album Title		$	Label & Number
10/9/99+	24	54	▲	© 1	Mountain High...Valley Low		$10	Elektra 62439
12/2/00	86	9		© 2	Christmas With Yolanda Adams	[X]	$10	Elektra 62567

Christmas chart: 4/'00

| 4/7/01 | 63 | 11 | | © 3 | The Experience | [L] | $10 | Elektra 62629 |

Already Alright (1,3)
Angels We Have Heard On High (medley) (2)
Born This Day (2)
Carol Of The Bells (medley) (2)
Christmas Song (2)
Continual Praise (1,3)

First Noel (2)
Fragile Heart (1,3)
Hark The Herald Angels Sing (medley) (2)
Have Yourself A Merry Little Christmas (2)
He'll Arrive (Coming Back) (1)

I Believe I Can Fly (3)
In The Midst Of It All (1,3)
It Came Upon A Midnight Clear (2)
Joy To The World (medley) (2)
Little Drummer Boy (2)
O Holy Night (2)

Ode To Joy (medley) (2)
Open My Heart (1,3) *57*
Silent Night (2)
That Name (1,3)
Things We Do (1)
Time To Change (1)
What About The Children? (3)

What Child Is This (medley) (2)
Wherever You Are (1)
Ye Of Little Faith (3)
Yeah (1,3)

ADC BAND '79
Disco group: Audrey Matthews (vocals), Michael Judkins (vocals, keyboards), Pervis Johnson (guitar), Kublah Khan (congas), Mark Patterson (bass) and Artwell Matthews (drums).

DEBUT	PEAK	WKS		CD	Album Title		$	Label & Number
12/16/78+	139	9			Long Stroke		$12	Cotillion 5210

Baby Love
Cause I Love You

Fire Up
Just Another Song

Long Stroke
More & More Disco

Reggae Disco
That's Life

ADDEO, Leo, & His Orchestra '61
Born on 4/21/14 in Brooklyn, New York. Died in May 1979 (age 65). His orchestra featured guitarists Al Caiola and Billy Mure (of **The Palm Beach Boys**).

DEBUT	PEAK	WKS		CD	Album Title		$	Label & Number
1/9/61	143	13			Hawaii In Hi-Fi	[I]	$20	RCA Camden 510

Aloha Oe
Blue Hawaii

Drifting And Dreaming
Hindustan

Hula Blues
I Get The Blues When It Rains

My Little Grass Shack (In Kealakekua, Hawaii)

On Miami Shore
Sweet Leilani

Yaaka Hula Hickey Dula

ADDERLEY, "Cannonball", Quintet '63
Born Julian Adderley on 9/15/28 in Tampa, Florida. Died of a stroke on 8/8/75 (age 46). Alto saxophonist. His quintet consisted of brother Nat Adderley (coronet), Joe Zawinul (keyboards), Walter Booker (bass) and Roy McCurdy (drums). Zawinul later formed **Weather Report**.
1)Jazz Workshop Revisited 2)Mercy, Mercy, Mercy! 3)Nancy Wilson/Cannonball Adderley

DEBUT	PEAK	WKS		CD	Album Title		$	Label & Number
5/5/62	30	21		© 1	Nancy Wilson/Cannonball Adderley		$30	Capitol 1657
3/30/63	11	25		© 2	Jazz Workshop Revisited	[I-L]	$25	Riverside 444

CANNONBALL ADDERLEY Sextet
recorded in San Francisco

| 2/25/67 | 13 | 27 | | © 3 | Mercy, Mercy, Mercy! | [I-L] | $20 | Capitol 2663 |

recorded at the Club De Lisa in Chicago

6/10/67	148	12		4	Why Am I Treated So Bad!	[I-L]	$20	Capitol 2617
12/9/67	186	2		5	74 Miles Away - Walk Tall	[I-L]	$20	Capitol 2822
3/14/70	136	22		© 6	Country Preacher	[I-L]	$20	Capitol 404

recorded in Chicago; introduction by Rev. Jesse Jackson

9/26/70	194	2		7	Experience In E, Tensity, Dialogues	[I]	$20	Capitol 484
3/6/71	169	2		8	The Price You Got To Pay To Be Free	[L]	$25	Capitol 636 [2]
2/26/72	167	3		9	The Black Messiah	[L]	$25	Capitol 846 [2]
7/1/72	74	20		10	Soul Zodiac		$25	Capitol 11025 [2]

"CANNONBALL" ADDERLEY (above 2)
featuring the Nat Adderley Sextet; narration by Rick Holmes

ADDERLEY, "Cannonball" — Cont'd

9/29/73	179	5		© 11	Inside Straight		[I-L]	$15	Fantasy 9435
9/20/75	121	8		© 12	Phenix		[I-K]	$20	Fantasy 79004 [2]

"CANNONBALL" ADDERLEY

Afro-Spanish Omelet (6)
Alto Sex (9)
Aquarius (10)
Aries (10)
Black Messiah (9)
Bridges (8)
Cancer (10)
Capricorn (10)
Chocolate Nuisance (9)
Circumference (9)
Country Preacher (6,12) *86*
Devastatement (3)
Dialogues For Jazz Quintet And Orchestra (7)
Directions (8)
Do Do Do (What Now Is Next) (5)
Dr. Honouris Cousa (9)

Domination (12)
Down In Black Bottom (8)
End, The (11)
Episode From The Music Came (9)
Experience In E (7)
Exquisition (8)
Eye Of The Cosmos (9)
Five Of A Kind (11)
Fun (3)
Games (3)
Gemini (10)
Get Up Off Your Knees (8)
Hamba Nami (12)
Happy Talk (1)
Heritage (9)
High Fly (12)
Hippodelphia (3)

Hummin' (6)
I Can't Get Started (9)
I Remember Bird (5)
I'm On My Way (4)
Inner Journey (11)
Inquisition (8)
Inside Straight (11)
Introduction (3,10,11)
Jessica's Birthday (2)
Jive Samba (2,12) *66*
Leo (10)
Libra (10)
Lillie (2)
Little Benny Hen (9)
Lonesome Stranger (8)
Marney (2)
Masquerade Is Over (1)
Mellow Buno (2)

Mercy, Mercy, Mercy (3,12) *11*
Mini Mama (4)
Never Say Yes (1)
Never Will I Marry (1)
Oh Babe (5,6)
Old Country (1)
One For Newk (4)
One Man's Dream (1)
1-2-3-Go-o-o-o! (8)
Other Side (4)
Out And In (8)
Painted Desert (8)
Pisces (10)
Pra Dizer Adeus (To Say Goodbye) (8)
Pretty Paul (9)
Price You Got To Pay To Be Free (8)

Primitivo (2)
Rumplestiltskin (8)
Sack O'Woe (3,12)
Sagittarius (8)
Saudade (11)
Save Your Love For Me (1)
Scene, The (4,6,8,9)
Scorpio (10)
Second Son (12)
74 Miles Away (5,12)
Sidewalks Of New York (12)
Sleepin' Bee (1)
Snakin' The Grass (11)
Some Time Ago (8)
Soul Virgo (8)
Stars Fell On Alabama (12)
Steam Drill (4)
Sticks (3)

Taurus (10)
Teaneck (1)
Tensity (7)
This Here (12)
Together (8)
Unit 7 (1)
Untitled (9)
Virgo (10)
Walk Tall (5,6,12)
Why? (Am I Treated So Bad) (4) *73*
Wild-Cat Pee (8)
Work Song (12)
Yvette (4)
Zanek (9)

ADDRISI BROTHERS, The '77

Pop singing/songwriting duo from Winthrop, Massachusetts. Dick was born on 7/4/41. Don was born on 12/14/38; died on 11/13/84 (age 45).

4/8/72	137	3		© 1	We've Got To Get It On Again			$15	Columbia 31296
7/2/77	118	14		2	Addrisi Brothers			$12	Buddah 5694

Baby, Love Is A Two-Way Street (2)
Baguio (2)
Does She Do It Like She Dances (2) *74*

Emergency (2)
I Can Feel You (1)
Love Is On The Line (1)
Monkey See, Monkey Do (2)
Never My Love (1,2) *80*

One Last Time (1)
She's Just Laughing At Me (1)
Slow Dancin' Don't Turn Me On (2) *20*
Spoiled Like A Baby (2)

Twogether (1)
We've Got To Get It On Again (1) *25*
When I Wanted You (2)
Windy Wakefield (1)

Words And Music (1)
You Make It All Worthwhile (1)

ADE, King Sunny, & His African Beats '83

Born Sunday Adeniyi on 9/1/46 in Oshogbo, Nigeria. Best known for his native JuJu Music.

4/9/83	111	29		© 1	JuJu Music		[F]	$10	Mango 9712
8/20/83	91	10		© 2	Synchro System		[F]	$10	Mango 9737

E Saiye Re (2)
E Wele (2)
Eje Nlo Gba Ara Mi (1)

Ja Funmi (2)
Ma Jaiye Oni (1)
Maajo (1)

Mo Beru Agba (1)
Mo Ti Mo (2)
Penkele (2)

Samba/E Falabe Lewe (1)
Sunny Ti De Ariya (1)
Synchro Feelings - Ilako (2)

Synchro System (2)
365 Is My Number/The Message (1)

Tolongo (2)

ADKINS, Trace '97

Born on 1/13/62 in Springhill, Louisiana. Male country singer/songwriter/guitarist.

10/19/96+	53	56	▲ © 1	Dreamin' Out Loud				$10	Capitol 37222
11/8/97	50	21	● © 2	Big Time				$10	Capitol 55856
11/20/99	82	3	© 3	More...				$10	Capitol 96618

All Hat, No Cattle (3)
Bad Way Of Saying Goodbye (1)
Big Time (2)
Can I Want Your Love (3)
Don't Lie (3)
Dreamin' Out Loud (1)
Every Light In The House (1) *78*

Every Other Friday At Five (3)
Everything Takes Me Back (3)
Hold You Now (2)
I Can Dig It (3)
I Can Only Love You Like A Man (1)
I Left Something Turned On At Home (1)

I'm Gonna Love You Anyway (3)
If I Fall (You're Goin' With Me) (1)
It Was You (1)
Lonely Won't Leave Me Alone (2)
More (3) *65*
Night He Can't Remember (3)

Nothin' But Taillights (2)
Out Of My Dreams (2)
Rest Of Mine (2) *70*
See Jane Run (2)
She's Still There (3)
634-5789 (1)
Snowball In El Paso (2)
Someday (3)
There's A Girl In Texas (1)

(This Ain't) No Thinkin' Thing (1)
Took Her To The Moon (3)
Twenty-Four, Seven (2)
Wayfaring Stranger (2)
Working Man's Wage (3)

ADVENTURES, The '88

Pop group from Belfast, Ireland: Terry Sharpe, Eileen Gribben and Spud Murphy (vocals), Pat Gribben (guitar), Tony Ayre (bass) and Paul Crowder (drums).

4/16/88	144	9		©	The Sea Of Love			$10	Elektra 60772

Broken Land *95*
Drowning In The Sea Of Love

Heaven Knows Which Way
Hold Me Now

One Step From Heaven
Sound Of Summer

Trip To Bountiful (When The Rain Comes Down)

When Your Heart Was Young
You Don't Have To Cry Anymor

AEROSMITH ★42★ '93

Rock group from Sunapee, New Hampshire: Steven Tyler (vocals), Joe Perry and Brad Whitford (guitars), Tom Hamilton (bass) and Joey Kramer (drums). Perry left for own **Joe Perry Project** in 1979; replaced by Jimmy Crespo (of **The Flame**). Whitford left in 1981; replaced by Rick Dufay. Original band reunited in April 1984. Tyler is the father of actress/model Liv Tyler. Group appeared in the movies *Sgt. Pepper's Lonely Hearts Club Band* and *Wayne's World 2*. Group inducted into the Rock and Roll Hall of Fame in 2001.

1)Get A Grip 2)Nine Lives 3)Just Push Play 4)Rocks 5)Pump

10/13/73+	21	59	▲² © 1	Aerosmith				$15	Columbia 32005
4/6/74+	74	86	▲³ © 2	Get Your Wings				$15	Columbia 32847
4/26/75	11	128	▲⁶ © 3	Toys In The Attic		C:#9/197		$15	Columbia 33479
5/29/76	3	53	▲⁴ © 4	Rocks				$15	Columbia 34165
12/24/77+	11	20	▲² © 5	Draw The Line				$15	Columbia 34856
11/11/78+	13	22	▲ © 6	Live! Bootleg			[L]	$20	Columbia 35564 [2]
12/1/79+	14	19	▲ © 7	Night In The Ruts				$15	Columbia 36050
11/29/80	53	40	▲¹⁰ © 8	Aerosmith's Greatest Hits		C:❶⁸³/580	[G]	$12	Columbia 36865
9/25/82	32	19	● © 9	Rock In A Hard Place				$12	Columbia 38061
11/30/85	36	28	● © 10	Done With Mirrors				$10	Geffen 24091
4/26/86	84	12	▲ © 11	Classics Live!			[L]	$10	Columbia 40329
9/19/87	11	67	▲⁵ © 12	Permanent Vacation		C:#36/33		$10	Geffen 24162

AEROSMITH — Cont'd

DEBUT	PEAK	WKS	RIAA	CD	ARTIST — Album Title	Catalog	Sym	$	Label & Number
12/10/88+	133	11	●	© 13	**Gems**		[K]	$10	Columbia 44487
9/30/89	5	110	▲7	© 14	**Pump**		C:#37/12	$10	Geffen 24254
12/7/91+	45	9	▲	© 15	**Pandora's Box** .... recordings from 1972-82		[K]	$30	Columbia 46209 [3]
5/8/93	●1	92	▲7	© 16	**Get A Grip**			$10	Geffen 24455
11/19/94	6	48	▲4	© 17	**Big Ones**		C:#9/122 [G]	$10	Geffen 24716
4/5/97	●1	77	▲2	© 18	**Nine Lives**			$10	Columbia 67547
11/7/98	12	20	▲	© 19	**A Little South Of Sanity**		[L]	$15	Geffen 25221 [2]
3/24/01	2¹	27	▲	© 20	**Just Push Play**			$10	Columbia 62088

Adam's Apple (3,13,15)
Ain't That A Bitch (18)
All Your Love (15)
Amazing (16,17,19) *24*
Angel (12,17,19) *3*
Attitude Adjustment (18)
Avant Garden (20)
Back In The Saddle (4,6,8,15,19) *38*
Beyond Beautiful (20)
Big Ten Inch Record (3,15)
Bitch's Brew (9)
Blind Man (17) *48*
Bolivian Ragamuffin (9)
Bone To Bone (Coney Island White Fish Boy) (7,15)
Boogie Man (16)
Bright Light Fright (5)
Cheese Cake (7,15)
Chip Away The Stone (6,13,15) *77*
Chiquita (7)
Combination (4)
Come Together (6,8,15) *23*
Crash (4)
Crazy (16,17,19) *17*
Critical Mass (5,13,15)
Cry Me A River (9)
Cryin' (16,17,19) *12*

Deuces Are Wild (17)
Don't Get Mad, Get Even (14)
Downtown Charlie (15)
Draw The Line (5,8,15) *42*
Drop Dead Gorgeous (20)
Dude (Looks Like A Lady) (12,17,19) *14*
Eat The Rich (16,17,19)
Fallen Angels (18)
Falling In Love (Is Hard On The Knees) (18,19) *35*
Farm, The (18)
Fever (16)
F.I.N.E. (14)
Flesh (16)
Fly Away From Here (20)
Full Circle (18)
Get It (9)
Get Up (5)
Get The Lead Out (4)
Girl Keeps Coming Apart (12)
Gotta Love It (16)
Gypsy Boots (19)
Hand That Feeds (5)
Heart's Done Time (18)
Helter Skelter (15)
Hole In My Soul (18,19) *51*

Home Tonight (4) *71*
Hop, The (10)
I Ain't Got You (6)
I Live In Connecticut (15)
I Wanna Know Why (5,15)
I'm Down (12)
Jaded (20) *7*
Jailbait (9,13,15)
Janie's Got A Gun (14,17,19) *4*
Jig Is Up (9)
Joanie's Butterfly (9)
Just Push Play (20)
Kings And Queens (5,8,11,15) *70*
Kiss Your Past Good-bye (18)
Krawhitham (15)
Last Child (6,8,15,19) *21*
Let It Slide (15)
Let The Music Do The Talking (10)
Lick And A Promise (4,13,15)
Light Inside (20)
Lightning Strikes (9)
Line Up (16)
Livin' On The Edge (16,17,19) *18*
Lord Of The Thighs (2,6,11,13,15)

Love In An Elevator (14,17,19) *5*
Luv Lies (20)
Magic Touch (12)
Major Barbra (11,15)
Make It (1,15)
Mama Kin (1,6,11,13,15,19)
Mia (7)
Milk Cow Blues (5,15)
Monkey On My Back (14,19)
Mother Popcorn (6)
Movie, The (12)
Movin' Out (1,15)
My Fist Your Face (10)
My Girl (14)
Nine Lives (18)
No More No More (3,15)
No Surprize (7,13,15)
Nobody's Fault (4,13,15)
On The Road Again (15)
One Way Street (1,15)
Other Side (14,17,19) *22*
Outta Your Head (20)
Pandora's Box (2,15)
Permanent Vacation (12)
Pink (18) *27*
Prelude To Joanie (9)
Push Comes To Shove (9)
Rag Doll (12,17,19) *17*

Rats In The Cellar (4,13,15)
Rattlesnake Shake (15)
Reason A Dog (10)
Reefer Head Woman (7,11)
Remember (Walking In The Sand) (7,8) *67*
Riff & Roll (15)
Rock In A Hard Place (Cheshire Cat) (9)
Round And Round (3,13,15)
S.O.S. (Too Bad) (2,6)
Same Old Song And Dance (2,8,15,19)
Seasons Of Wither (2,15)
Shame On You (10)
Sharpshooter (15)
She's On Fire (10)
Shela (10)
Shit House Shuffle (15)
Shut Up And Dance (16)
Sick As A Dog (4,6)
Sight For Sore Eyes (5,6)
Simoriah (12)
Somebody (1)
Something's Gotta Give (18)
Soul Saver (15)
South Station Blues (15)
Spaced (2)
St. John (12)

Sunshine (20)
Sweet Emotion (3,6,8,11,15,19) *36*
Taste Of India (18)
Think About It (7)
Three Mile Smile (7,11,15)
Toys In The Attic (3,6,15)
Train Kept A Rollin' (2,6,11,13,15)
Trip Hoppin' (20)
Uncle Salty (3)
Under My Skin (20)
Voodoo Medicine Man (14)
Walk On Down (16,19)
Walk On Water (17)
Walk This Way (3,6,8,15,19) *10*
Walkin' The Dog (1,15)
What It Takes (14,17,19) *9*
When I Needed You (15)
Woman Of The World (20)
Write Me A Letter (1,15)
You See Me Crying (3,15)
Young Lust (14)

AFGHAN WHIGS, The   '96

Rock group from Cincinnati: Greg Dulli (vocals), Rick McCollum (guitar), John Curley (bass) and Paul Buchignani (drums). Michael Horrigan replaced Buchignani in 1997.

DEBUT	PEAK	WKS		CD	ARTIST — Album Title			$	Label & Number
3/30/96	79	2		© 1	**Black Love**			$10	Elektra 61896
11/14/98	176	1		© 2	**1965**			$10	Columbia 69450

Blame, Etc. (1)
Bulletproof (1)
Citi Soleil (2)
Crazy (2)

Crime Scene Part One (1)
Double Day (1)
Faded (1)
Going To Town (1)

Honky's Ladder (1)
John The Baptist (2)
My Enemy (1)
Neglekted (2)

Night By Candlelight (1)
Omerta (2)
66 (2)
Slide Song (2)

Somethin' Hot (2)
Step Into The Light (1)
Summer's Kiss (1)
Sweet Son Of A Bitch (2)

Uptown Again (2)
Vampire Lanois (2)

AFI   '00

Hard-rock group from San Francisco: Davey Havok (vocals), Jade Puget (guitar), Hunter (bass) and Adam Carson (drums). AFI: A Fire Inside.

DEBUT	PEAK	WKS		CD	ARTIST — Album Title			$	Label & Number
10/14/00	174	1		©	**The Art Of Drowning**			$10	Nitro 15835

Catch A Hot One
Days Of The Phoenix
Despair Factor

Ever And A Day
Lost Souls
Morningstar

Nephilim, The
Of Greetings And Goodbyes
Sacrifice Theory

6 To 8
Smile
Story At Three

Wester

AFRIQUE   '73

Instrumental session group featuring **David T. Walker** (guitar) and Chuck Rainey (bass).

DEBUT	PEAK	WKS		CD	ARTIST — Album Title			$	Label & Number
6/16/73	152	8			**Soul Makossa**		[I]	$15	Mainstream 394

Dueling Guitars
Get It

Hot Doggin'
Hot Mud

House Of Rising Funk
Kissing My Love

Let Me Do My Thing
Sleepwalk

Slow Motion
Soul Makossa *47*

AFTER 7   '90

R&B vocal trio from Indianapolis: Keith Mitchell with brothers Melvin and **Kevon Edmonds**. Keith is the cousin of L.A. Reid. Kevon and Melvin are the brothers of **Babyface**. Keith left in 1997.

DEBUT	PEAK	WKS		CD	ARTIST — Album Title			$	Label & Number
10/14/89+	35	72	▲	© 1	**After 7**			$10	Virgin 91061
9/12/92	76	36	●	© 2	**Takin' My Time**			$10	Virgin 86349
8/5/95	40	17	●	© 3	**Reflections**			$10	Virgin 40547
3/29/97	97	8		© 4	**The Very Best Of After 7**		[G]	$10	Virgin 42756

All About Love (2)
Baby I'm For Real (2,4) *55*
Can He Love U Like This (2,4)
Can't Stop (1,4) *6*
Cryin For It (3)
Damn Thing Called Love (3)
Don't Cha' Think (1)

G.S.T. (2)
Givin Up This Good Thing (2)
Gonna Love You Right (4)
He Said, She Said (2)
Heat Of The Moment (1,4) *19*
Honey (Oh How I Need You) (3)
How Could You Leave (3)

How Did He Love You (3)
How Do You Tell The One (3)
I Like It Like That (3)
Kickin' It (2) *45*
Love By Day, Love By Night (2)
Love's Been So Nice (1)
My Only Woman (1)

Nights Like This (4)
No Better Love (2)
Not Enough Hours In The Night (4)
One Night (1,4)
Ready Or Not (1,4) *7*
Sara Smile (4)

Save It Up (3)
Sayonara (1)
Sprung On It (3)
Takin' My Time (2,4)
'Til You Do Me Right (3,4) *31*
Truly Something Special (2)
What U R 2 Me (1)

AFTER THE FIRE   '83

Rock group from England: Andy Piercy (vocals, bass), John Russell (guitar), **Peter Banks** (keyboards) and Pete King (drums). Banks was a member of **Yes** and **Flash**.

DEBUT	PEAK	WKS		CD	ARTIST — Album Title			$	Label & Number
3/12/83	25	20		©	**ATF**			$10	Epic 38282

Carry Me Home
Dancing In The Shadows *85*

Der Kommissar *5*
Frozen Rivers

Laser Love
Love Will Always Make You Cry

1980-F
One Rule For You

Sailing Ship
Sometimes

Starflight

AFU-RA '00
Born Aaron Phillips in New York City. Male rapper.

| 11/11/00 | 183 | 1 | | © | Body Of The Life Force .... | | | $10 | D&D 8210 |

All That
Bigacts Littleacts
Bring It Right

Caliente
D&D Soundclash
Defeat

Equality
Mic Stance
Monotony

Mortal Kombat
Quotations
Self Mastery

Soul Assassination
Warfare
Whirlwind Thru Cities

AGUILERA, Christina '99
Born on 12/18/80 in Staten Island, New York; raised in Wexford, Pennsylvania. Regular on TV's *The Mickey Mouse Club* (1992-93). Won the 1999 Best New Artist Grammy Award.

| 9/11/99 | ❶[1] | 97 | ▲[8] | © | 1 Christina Aguilera | | | $10 | RCA 67690 |
| 9/30/00 | 27 | 18 | ● | © | 2 Mi Reflejo | | [F] | $10 | RCA 69323 |

title is Spanish for "My Reflection"

| 11/11/00 | 28 | 12 | ▲ | © | 3 My Kind Of Christmas | | [X] | $10 | RCA 69343 |

Christmas chart: 1/'00

Angels We Have Heard On High (3)
Blessed (1)
Christmas Song (Chestnuts Roasting On An Open Fire) (3) 18
Christmas Time (3)

Come On Over Baby (All I Want Is You) (1) 1
Contigo En La Distancia (2)
Cuando No Es Contigo (2)
El Beso Del Final (2)
Falsas Esperanzas (2)
Genie In A Bottle (1) 1

Genio Atrapado (2)
Have Yourself A Merry Little Christmas (3)
I Turn To You (1) 3
Love For All Seasons (1)
Love Will Find A Way (1)
Merry Christmas, Baby (3)

Mi Reflejo (2)
Obvious (1)
Oh Holy Night (3)
Pero Me Acuerdo De Tí (2)
Por Siempre Tú (2)
Reflection (1)
Si No Te Hubiera Conocido (2)

So Emotional (1)
Somebody's Somebody (1)
These Are The Special Times (3)
This Christmas (3)
This Year (3)
Una Mujer (2)

Ven Conmigo (Solamente Tú) (2)
What A Girl Wants (1) 1
When You Put Your Hands On Me (1)
Xtina's Xmas (3)

A-HA '85
Pop trio from Oslo, Norway: Morten Harket (vocals), Pal Waaktaar (guitar) and Magne "Mags" Furuholmen (keyboards).

7/20/85	15	47	▲	©	1 Hunting High And Low			$10	Warner 25300
11/1/86	74	20		©	2 Scoundrel Days			$10	Warner 25501
6/4/88	148	6		©	3 Stay On These Roads			$10	Warner 25733

And You Tell Me (1)
Blood That Moves The Body (3)
Blue Sky (1)
Cry Wolf (2) 50
Here I Stand And Face The Rain (1)

Hunting High And Low (1)
Hurry Home (3)
I Dream Myself Alive (1)
I've Been Losing You (2)
Living A Boy's Adventure Tale (1)

Living Daylights (3)
Love Is Reason (1)
Manhattan Skyline (2)
Maybe Maybe (2)
October (2)
Out Of Blue Comes Green (3)

Scoundrel Days (2)
Soft Rains Of April (3)
Stay On These Roads (3)
Sun Always Shines On T.V. (1) 20
Swing Of Things (2)

Take On Me (1) 1
There's Never A Forever Thing (3)
This Alone Is Love (3)
Touchy! (3)
Train Of Thought (1)

We're Looking For The Whales (2)
Weight Of The Wind (2)
You Are The One (3)
You'll End Up Crying (3)

AIR '01
Electronic duo from Versailles, France: Nicolas Godin and Jean-Benoit Dunckel.

| 3/18/00 | 161 | 1 | | © | 1 The Virgin Suicides .... | | [I-S] | $10 | Astralwerks 48848 |
| 6/16/01 | 88 | 3 | | © | 2 10,000Hz Legend .... | | | $10 | Source 10332 |

Afternoon Sister (1)
Bathroom Girl (1)
Caramel Prisoner (2)
Cemetary Party (1)
Clouds Up (1)

Dark Messages (1)
Dead Bodies (1)
Dirty Trip (1)
Don't Be Light (2)
Electronic Performers (2)

Empty House (1)
Ghost Song (1)
Highschool Lover (1)
How Does It Make You Feel? (2)

Lucky And Unhappy (2)
People In The City (2)
Playground Love (1)
Radian (2)
Radio #1 (2)

Sex Born Poison (2)
Suicide Underground (1)
Vagabond, The (2)
Wonder Milky Bitch (2)
Word 'Hurricane' (1)

AIR FORCE — see BAKER, Ginger

AIR SUPPLY '83
Pop vocal duo from Melbourne, Australia: Russell Hitchcock (born on 6/15/49 in Melbourne) and Graham Russell (born on 6/1/50 in Nottingham, England).

5/17/80	22	104	▲[2]	©	1 Lost In Love			$10	Arista 4268
6/13/81	10	60	▲	©	2 The One That You Love			$10	Arista 9551
6/19/82	25	38	▲	©	3 Now And Forever			$10	Arista 9587
8/20/83	7	51	▲[5]	©	4 Greatest Hits		[G]	$10	Arista 8024
6/29/85	26	21	●	©	5 Air Supply			$10	Arista 8283
9/6/86	84	9		©	6 Hearts In Motion			$10	Arista 8426
12/19/87+	10[X]	3		©	7 The Christmas Album		[X]	$10	Arista 8528

Christmas charts: 17/'87, 10/'88

After All (5)
All Out Of Love (1,4) 2
American Hearts (1)
Black And Blue (5)
Chances (1,4)
Christmas Song (Chestnuts Roasting On An Open Fire) (7)
Come What May (3)
Don't Be Afraid (3)
Don't Turn Me Away (2)
Even The Nights Are Better (3,4) 5

Every Woman In The World (1,4) 5
Eyes Of A Child (7)
First Noel (7)
Great Pioneer (5)
Having You Near Me (1)
Heart & Soul (6)
Here I Am (Just When I Thought I Was Over You) (2,4) 5
Hope Springs Eternal (6)
I Can't Get Excited (1)
I Can't Let Go (5)

I Wanna Hold You Tonight (5)
I Want To Give It All (2)
I'd Die For You (6)
I'll Never Get Enough Of You (2)
I've Got Your Love (2)
It's Not Too Late (4)
Just Another Woman (1)
Just As I Am (5)
Keeping The Love Alive (2)
Little Drummer Boy (7)
Lonely Is The Night (6) 76
Lost In Love (1,4) 3

Love Is All (7)
Make It Right (5)
Making Love Out Of Nothing At All (4) 2
My Best Friend (1)
My Heart's With You (6)
Never Fade Away (5)
Now And Forever (3)
O Come All Ye Faithful (7)
Old Habits Die Hard (1)
One More Chance (6)
One Step Closer (3)
One That You Love (2,4) 1

Power Of Love (You Are My Lady) (5) 68
Put Love In Your Life (6)
Sandy (1)
She Never Heard Me Call (3)
Silent Night (7)
Sleigh Ride (7)
Stars In Your Eyes (6)
Sunset (5)
Sweet Dreams (2,4) 5
Taking The Chance (3)
This Heart Belongs To Me (2)
Time For Love (6)

Tonite (2)
Two Less Lonely People In The World (3) 38
What Kind Of Girl (3)
When The Time Is Right (5)
White Christmas (7)
Winter Wonderland (7)
You're Only In Love (6)
Young Love (3) 38

AIRTO — see DEODATO

AKINS, Rhett '96
Born Thomas Rhett Akins on 10/13/69 in Valdosta, Georgia. Country singer/songwriter/guitarist.

| 6/22/96 | 102 | 10 | | © | Somebody New .... | | | $10 | Decca 11424 |

Carolina Line
Don't Get Me Started

Every Cowboy's Dream
I Was Wrong

K-I-S-S-I-N-G
Love You Back

No Match (For That Old Flame)
Somebody Knew

Too Much Texas
Where Angels Live

AKINYELE '96
Born Akinyele Adams in 1970 in Queens, New York. Male rapper.

| 8/31/96 | 127 | 4 | | © | Put It In Your Mouth (a.k.a. fella) .... | | [M] | $10 | Stress 11142 |

F*ck Me For Free
In The World
Put It In Your Mouth
Robbery Song
Thug Sh*t

9

DEBUT	PEAK	WKS	RIAA	CD	ARTIST — Album Title	Catalog	Sym	$	Label & Number

AKKERMAN, Jan '73

Born on 12/24/46 in Amsterdam. Former guitarist with **Focus**.

10/13/73	192	4		©	1 **Profile**		[I]	$20	Sire 7407
3/2/74	195	2			2 **Tabernakel**		[I]	$15	Atco 7032
4/8/78	198	2			3 **Jan Akkerman**		[I]	$12	Atlantic 19159

Andante Sostenuto (1)
Angel Watch (3)
Blue Boy (1)
Britannia By John Dowland (2)
Coranto For Mrs. Murcott By Francis Pilkington (2)
Crackers (3)
Earl Of Derby, His Galliard By John Dowland (2)
Etude (1)
Fantasy By Laurencini Of Rome (2)
Farmers Dance (medley) (1)
Floatin' (3)
Fresh Air (1)
Galliard By Anthonie Holborne (2)
Galliard By John Dowland (2)
Gate To Europe (3)
House Of The King (2)
Javeh (2)
Kemps Jig (1)
Lammy (2)
Maybe Just A Dream (1)
Minstrel (medley) (1)
Pavan By Thomas Morley (2)
Pavane (3)
Skydancer (3)
Stick (1)
Streetwalker (3)

ALABAMA ★73★ '83

Country group from Fort Payne, Alabama: Randy Owen (vocals, guitar), Jeff Cook (keyboards, fiddle), Teddy Gentry (bass, vocals) and Mark Herndon (drums, vocals). Randy, Jeff and Teddy are cousins.

1)The Closer You Get... 2)Mountain Music 3)For The Record 4)Feels So Right 5)Roll On

7/19/80	71	21	▲²	©	1 **My Home's In Alabama**			$15	RCA Victor 3644
3/28/81	16	161	▲⁴	©	2 **Feels So Right**			$10	RCA Victor 3930
3/13/82	14	114	▲⁵	©	3 **Mountain Music**			$10	RCA Victor 4229
3/26/83	10	70	▲⁴	©	4 **The Closer You Get...**			$10	RCA Victor 4663
2/11/84	21	62	▲⁴	©	5 **Roll On**		C:#33/4	$10	RCA Victor 4939
2/23/85	28	40	▲²	©	6 **40 Hour Week**			$10	RCA Victor 5339
11/23/85	75	9	▲²	©	7 **Christmas**		C:#25/12 [X]	$10	RCA Victor 7014
					Christmas charts: 1/'85, 16/'87, 8/'88, 18/'89, 20/'90, 15/'91, 30/'92, 28/'93				
3/1/86	24	38	▲⁵	©	8 **Greatest Hits**		[G]	$10	RCA Victor 7170
10/25/86	42	30	▲	©	9 **The Touch**			$10	RCA Victor 5649
10/17/87	55	28	●	©	10 **Just Us**			$10	RCA Victor 6495
6/25/88	76	19	▲	©	11 **Alabama Live**		[L]	$10	RCA 6825
2/18/89	62	21	▲	©	12 **Southern Star**			$10	RCA 8587
6/16/90	57	41	▲	©	13 **Pass It On Down**			$10	RCA 2108
10/26/91	72	31	▲	©	14 **Greatest Hits II**		[G]	$10	RCA 61040
8/29/92	46	51	▲	©	15 **American Pride**			$10	RCA 66044
10/30/93	76	38	▲	©	16 **Cheap Seats**			$10	RCA 66296
10/15/94+	56	49	▲²	©	17 **Greatest Hits - Vol. III**		[G]	$10	RCA 66410
9/2/95	100	21	▲	©	18 **In Pictures**			$10	RCA 66525
11/30/96	117	6		©	19 **Christmas Volume II**		[X]	$10	RCA 66927
					Christmas chart: 12/'96				
4/26/97	55	26	●	©	20 **Dancin' On The Boulevard**			$10	RCA 67426
9/12/98	13	33	▲⁴	©	21 **For The Record - 41 Number One Hits**		[G]	$15	RCA 67633 [2]
7/3/99	51	10	●	©	22 **Twentieth Century**			$10	RCA 67793
2/3/01	37	8		©	23 **When It All Goes South**			$10	RCA 69337

Alabama Sky (4)
American Pride (15)
Angels Among Us (16,17)
Anytime (I'm Your Man) (20)
As Right Now (6)
Barefootin' (12)
Better Word For Love (16)
Between The Two Of Them (15)
Blessings, The (19)
Borderline, The (12)
Born Country (14,21)
Boy, The (5)
Burn Georgia Burn (2)
Calling All Angels (20)
Can't Forget About You (1)
Can't Keep A Good Man Down (6,11,21)
Can't You See (11)
Candle In The Window (7)
Carolina Mountain Dewe (5)
Changes Comin' On (3)
Cheap Seats (16)
Christmas In Dixie (7)
Christmas In Your Arms (19)
Christmas Is Love (19)
Christmas Memories (7)
Christmas Spirit (7)
Clear Across America Tonight (23)
Clear Water Blues (16)
Close Enough To Perfect (3,21) **65**
Closer You Get (4,14,21) **38**
Country Side Of Life (5)
Cruisin' (3)
Dancin', Shaggin' On The Boulevard (20)
Dixie Boy (4)
Dixieland Delight (4,14,21)
Down Home (13,21)
Down On Longboat Key (6)
Down On The River (12)
Down This Road (23)
End Of The Lyin' (5)
Face To Face (10,17,21)
Fallin' Again (10,14,21)
Fans, The (8)
Fantasy (2)
Fire On Fire (13)
Fireworks (11)
Five O'Clock 500 (21)
Food On The Table (5)
Forever's As Far As I'll Go (13,17,21)
40 Hour Week (For A Livin') (6,8,21)
Get It While It's Hot (1)
Getting Over You (1)
Give Me One More Shot (17,21)
God Must Have Spent A Little More Time On You (22) **29**
Gonna Have A Party (3,11)
Goodbye (Kelly's Song) (13)
Green River (4)
Gulf Of Mexico (13)
Hangin' 'Round The Mistletoe (19)
Hanging Up My Travelin' Shoes (1)
Happy Birthday Jesus (19)
Happy Holidays (7)
Hats Off (14)
Heartbreak Express (18)
Here We Are (13,21)
Hey Baby (20)
High Cotton (12,14,21)
Hollywood (2)
Homecoming Christmas (7)
Homesick Fever (15)
Hometown Honeymoon (15,21)
How Do You Fall In Love (21) **82**
I Ain't Got No Business Doin' Business Today (13)
I Can't Hide My Heart (23)
I Can't Love You Any Less (23)
I Can't Stop (10)
I Just Couldn't Say No (20)
I Love You Enough To Let You Go (22)
I Saw The Time (10)
I Taught Her Everything She Knows (9)
I Wanna Come Over (1)
I Want To Know You Before We Make Love (6)
I Was Young Once Too (19)
(I Wish It Could Always Be) '55 (10)
I Write A Little (23)
I'm A Hurry (And Don't Know Why) (15,17,21)
I'm In That Kind Of Mood (22)
I'm Not That Way Anymore (5)
I'm Stoned (2)
I've Loved A Lot More Than I've Hurt (18)
If I Could Just See You Now (10)
If I Had You (12,21)
If It Ain't Dixie (It Won't Do) (6)
If You're Gonna Play In Texas (You Gotta Have A Fiddle In The Band) (5,17,21)
In Pictures (18,21)
Is The Magic Still There (20)
Is This How Love Begins (9)
It Works (18)
It's All Comin' Back To Me Now (9)
Joseph And Mary's Boy (7)
Jukebox In My Mind (13,17,21)
Katy Brought My Guitar Back Today (16)
Keep On Dreamin' (1)
Keepin' Up (21) **69**
Lady Down On Love (4,11,14,21) **76**
Let's Hear It For The Girl (9)
Life's Too Short To Love This Fast (22)
Little Drummer Boy (19)
Little Things (22)
Louisiana Moon (6)
Love In The First Degree (2,8,11,21) **15**
Love Remains (23)
Lovin' Man (4)
Lovin' You Is Killin' Me (3)
Maker Said Take Her (18)
Mist Of Desire (22)
Moonlight Lounge (13)
Mountain Music (3,8,21)
My Girl (20)
My Home's In Alabama (1)
My Love Belongs To You (18)
Never Be One (3)
New Year's Eve 1999 (19)
Night Before Christmas (19)
Nothing Comes Close (18)
O Little Town Of Bethlehem (19)
Of Course I'm Alright (20)
Old Flame (2,8,21)
Old Man (10)
"Ole" Baugh Road (12)
On This Side Of The Moon (10)
Once Upon A Lifetime (15,21)
One More Time Around (20)
Pass It On Down (13)
Pictures And Memories (15)
Pony Express (9)
Reckless (16,21)
Red River (4,11)
Reinvent The Wheel (23)
Richard Petty Fans (15)
Ride The Train (2)
Right Where I Am (23)
Rockin' Around The Christmas Tree (19)
Roll On (Eighteen Wheeler) (5,14,21)
Sad Lookin' Moon (20,21)
Santa Claus (I Still Believe In You) (7)
Say I (18)
See The Embers, Feel The Flame (2)
She Ain't Your Ordinary Girl (18,21)
She And I (8,21)
She Can (12)
She Put The Sad In All His Songs (4)
(She Won't Have A Thing To Do With) Nobody But Me (6)
She's Got That Look In Her Eyes (20)
Simple As That (23)
Small Stuff (22)
Some Other Place, Some Other Time (1)
Sometimes Out Of Touch (15)
Song Of The South (12,14,21)
Southern Star (18)
Spin The Wheel (18)
Start Living (23)
Starting Tonight (13)
Still Goin' Strong (16)
Sunday Drive (18)
T.L.C. A.S.A.P. (16)
Take A Little Trip (15)
Take Me Down (3,11,14,21) **18**
Tar Top (10)
Tennessee Christmas (7)
Tennessee River (1,8,11,17,21)
That Feeling (16)
Then Again (14,21)
Then We Remember (22)
(There's A) Fire In The Night (5,21)
There's No Way (6,11,17,21)
This Love's On Me (16)
Thistlehair The Christmas Bear (7)
Tonight Is Christmas (7)
Too Much Love (22)
Touch Me When We're Dancing (9,21)
True, True Housewife (9)
Twentieth Century (22)
Until It Happens To You (13)
Vacation (9)
Very Special Love (4)
We Can't Love Like This Anymore (17)
We Made Love (22)
What In The Name Of Love (4)
When It All Goes South (23)
When It Comes To Christmas (19)
When We Make Love (5,11,17,21) **72**
Why Lady Why (1,8,21)
Will You Marry Me (23)
Woman Back Home (2)
Woman He Loves (23)
Wonderful Waste Of Time (23)
Words At Twenty Paces (3)
Write It Down In Blue (22)
You Can't Take The Country Out Of Me (15)
You Only Paint The Picture Once (23)
You Turn Me On (3)
You're My Explanation For Living (10)
"You've Got" The Touch (9,21)

ALARM, The '86
Rock group from Rhyl, Wales: Mike Peters (vocals), Dave Sharp (guitar), Eddie MacDonald (bass) and Nigel Twist (drums).

DEBUT	PEAK	WKS						$	Label & Number
7/30/83+	126	37			1 The Alarm		[M]	$10	I.R.S. 70504
3/10/84	50	22	©		2 Declaration			$10	I.R.S. 70608
11/9/85+	39	36	©		3 Strength			$10	I.R.S. 5666
11/7/87	77	30	©		4 Eye Of The Hurricane			$10	I.R.S. 42061
10/29/88	167	5	©		5 Electric Folklore Live		[L]	$10	I.R.S. 39108
					recorded on 4/26/88 in Boston				
10/14/89	75	23	©		6 Change.			$10	I.R.S. 82018
12/15/90	177	3	©		7 Standards		[G]	$10	I.R.S. 13056
5/18/91	161	1	©		8 Raw			$10	I.R.S. 13087

Absolute Reality (3,7)
Across The Border (1)
Blaze Of Glory (2,5,7)
Change II (6)
Dawn Chorus (3)
Day The Ravens Left The Tower (3)
Deceiver, The (2)
Declaration (2)
Deeside (3)
Devolution Workin' Man Blues (6,7)
Eye Of The Hurricane (4)
Father To Son (3)
For Freedom (Live) (1)
God Save Somebody (8)
Hallowed Ground (4)
Happy Christmas (War Is Over) (7)
Hardland (6)
Hell Or High Water (8)
Howling Wind (2)
Knife Edge (3)
Lead Me Through The Darkness (8)
Let The River Run Its Course (8)
Lie Of The Land (1)
Love Don't Come Easy (6)
Marching On (1,2,7)
Moments In Time (8)
New South Wales (2)
Newtown Jericho (4)
No Frontiers (8)
One Step Closer To Home (4)
Only Love Can Set Me Free (4)
Only The Thunder (3)
Permanence In Change (4,5)
Presence Of Love (4) *77*
Prison Without Prison Bars (6)
Rain In The Summertime (4,5,7) *71*
Raw (8)
Rescue Me (4,5,7)
Rivers To Cross (6)
Road, The (7)
Rock, The (6)
Rockin' In The Free World (8)
Save Your Crying (8)
Scarlet (6)
Shelter (4)
Shout To The Devil (3)
Sixty Eight Guns (2,7)
Sold Me Down The River (6,7) *50*
Spirit Of '76 (3,5,7)
Stand, The (1,7)
Stand (Prophecy) (2)
Strength (3,5,7) *61*
Tell Me (2)
Third Light (2)
Unsafe Building (7)
Walk Forever By My Side (3)
We Are The Light (2)
Where A Town Once Stood (6)
Where Were You Hiding When The Storm Broke? (2,7)
Wind Blows Away My Words (8)
Wonderful World (8)

ALBERT, Morris '75
Born Morris Albert Kaisermann on 9/7/51 in Brazil. Singer/songwriter.

DEBUT	PEAK	WKS						$	Label & Number
9/6/75	37	31	©		1 Feelings			$12	RCA Victor 1018
6/12/76	135	7			2 Morris Albert			$12	RCA Victor 1496

Back To The Rock (2)
Boombamakaoo (medley) (1)
Christine (1)
Come To My Life (1)
Down To Mexico (medley) (2)
Everybody Loves Somebody (2)
Falling Tears (1)
Father (2)
Feelings (1) *6*
Gipsy (1)
Gonna Love You More (1)
Gotta Go Home (1)
La Puerta (medley) (2)
Land Of Love (2)
Memories (2)
Run Away (1)
Same Things (2)
She's My Girl (2)
Summer In Paris (2)
Sweet Loving Man (1) *93*
This World Today Is A Mess (1)
Ways Of Fire (medley) (1)
Where Is The Love Of The World (1)
Woman (1)

ALBRIGHT, Gerald '94
Born in 1957 in Los Angeles. R&B session saxophonist.

DEBUT	PEAK	WKS						$	Label & Number
2/27/88	181	5	©		1 Just Between Us		[I]	$10	Atlantic 81813
3/12/94	151	10	©		2 Smooth		[I]	$10	Atlantic 82552
10/17/98	169	3	©		3 Pleasures Of The Night			$10	Verve Forecast 557613
					WILL DOWNING & GERALD ALBRIGHT				

Anniversary (2)
Back To The Roots (3)
Come Back To Me (1)
Don't Worry About It (2)
G & Lee (2)
Girl Blue (3)
Here's That Rainy Day (3)
I Surrender (2)
Just Between Us (1)
Just 2 B With You (2)
King Boulevard (1)
Like A Lover (3)
Look Of Love (3)
Michelle (3)
Nearness Of You (3)
New Girl On The Block (1)
Passion (2)
Pleasures Of The Night (3)
Say It With Feeling (2)
Sedona (2)
So Amazing (1)
Softly At Sunrise (1)
Stop, Look, Listen To Your Heart (2)
Sweet Baby (2)
This Is For The Lover In You (2)
Trying To Find A Way (1)
We'll Be Together Again (3)
You Don't Even Know (1)
You're My #1 (1)

AL B. SURE! '88
Born Al Brown in 1969 in Boston; raised in Mt. Vernon, New York. R&B singer/songwriter.

DEBUT	PEAK	WKS						$	Label & Number
5/14/88	20	54	▲²		1 In Effect Mode			$10	Warner 25662
11/3/90	20	19	● ©		2 Private Times...And The Whole 9!			$10	Warner 26005
10/10/92	41	11	©		3 Sexy Versus			$10	Warner 26973

Channel J (2)
Die For You (3)
Had Enuf? (2)
Hotel California (2)
I Don't Wanna Cry (3)
I Want To Know (2)
I'll Never Hurt You Again (3)
If I'm Not Your Lover (2)
Just A Taste Of Lovin' (1)
Just For The Moment (2)
Kick In The Head (3)
Killing Me Softly (1) *80*
Misunderstanding (2) *42*
Natalie (3)
Naturally Mine (1)
Nite And Day (1) *7*
No Matter What You Do (2)
Off On Your Own (Girl) (1) *45*
Ooh 4 You Girl (3)
Ooh This Jazz Is So (2)
Oooh This Love Is So (1)
Papes In The End (3)
Playing Games (3)
Private Times (2)
Rescue Me (1)
Right Now (3) *47*
See The Lady (3)
Shades Of Grey (3)
So Special (2)
Sure! Thang (2)
Thanks 4 A Great Time Last Nite (2)
Touch You (2)
Turn You Out (2)
U & I (3)
You Excite Me (2)

ALCATRAZZ '84
Hard-rock group: Graham Bonnet (vocals), Yngwie J. Malmsteen (guitar), Jimmy Waldo (keyboards), Gary Shea (bass) and Jan Uvena (drums). Shea and Waldo were with New England. Bonnet was also with Rainbow, Michael Schenker Group and Impellitteri. By 1985, Steve Vai had replaced Malmsteen. Group named after the notorious maximum-security prison near San Francisco.

DEBUT	PEAK	WKS						$	Label & Number
1/7/84	128	18	©		1 No Parole From Rock 'N' Roll			$25	Rocshire 22016
6/9/84	133	10	©		2 Live Sentence		[L]	$25	Rocshire 22020
					recorded on 1/28/84 in Tokyo				
4/20/85	145	16	©		3 Disturbing The Peace			$20	Capitol 12385

All Night Long (2)
Big Foot (1)
Breaking The Heart Of The City (3)
Coming Bach (2)
Desert Diamond (3)
Evil Eye (2)
General Hospital (1)
God Blessed Video (3)
Hiroshima Mon Amour (1,2)
Incubus (1)
Island In The Sun (1,2)
Jet To Jet (1)
Kree Nakoorie (1,2)
Lighter Shade Of Green (3)
Mercy (3)
Night Games (2)
Painted Lover (3)
Since You've Been Gone (2)
Skyfire (3)
Sons And Lovers (3)
Starcarr Lane (1)
Stripper (3)
Suffer Me (1)
Too Young To Die, Too Drunk To Live (1,2)
Will You Be Home Tonight (3)
Wire And Wood (3)

ALDRICH, Ronnie, And His Two Pianos '62
Born on 2/15/16 in Erith, Kent, England. Died of cancer on 9/30/93 (age 77). Pianist/arranger. Musical director of the *Benny Hill* TV variety series.

DEBUT	PEAK	WKS						$	Label & Number
10/23/61+	20	33			1 Melody And Percussion For Two Pianos		[I]	$20	London Phase 4 44007
10/6/62	36	4			2 Ronnie Aldrich And His Two Pianos		[I]	$20	London Phase 4 44018
5/22/71	169	6			3 Love Story		[I]	$25	London Phase 4 22 [2]

Air On The 'G' String (3)
Amazing Grace (3)
April In Portugal (1)
April Love (1)
Autumn Leaves (1)
Barcarolle (3)
Baubles, Bangles And Beads (2)
Candida (3)
Clair De Lune (2,3)
El Condor Pasa (3)
Full Moon And Empty Arms (2)
Gipsy (3)
Golden Earrings (1)
Goodbye Again, Theme From (2)
(I Never Promised You A) Rose Garden (3)
I Think I Love You (3)
I'm Always Chasing Rainbows (2)
It's Impossible (3)
Liebestraum (2)
Love Story, Theme From (3)
Meditation (3)
Misty (1)
Mr Bojangles (3)
My One And Only Love (1)
My Sweet Lord (3)
Nocturne (3)
None But The Lonely Heart (3)
Reverie (3)
Ruby (1)
Secret Love (1)
Serenade (3)
Story Of A Starry Night (2)
Story Of Three Loves (2)
Stranger In Paradise (2)
Theme From Mozart's Piano Concerto No. 21 (3)
Theme From Rachmaninoff's Piano Concert No. 2 (3)
Till The End Of Time (2)
To Each His Own (1)
Togetherness (3)
Tonight We Love (2)
Unforgettable (1)
Vocalise (3)
What Is Life (3)
Woodstock (3)
Young-At-Heart (1)

ALI, Tatyana '98

Born on 1/24/79 in Long Island, New York. Singer/actress. Played "Ashley Banks" on TV's *The Fresh Prince Of Bel-Air*.

9/12/98 **106** 11 © **Kiss The Sky** .... **$10** MJJ Music 68656
Boy You Knock Me Out
Daydreamin' *6*

| Everytime | If I Ever Love Again | Kiss The Sky | Through Life Alone |
| He Loves Me | If You Only Knew | Love The Way You Love Me | Yesterday |

ALIAS '91

Rock group formed in Los Angeles by former **Sheriff** members Freddy Curci (vocals) and Steve DeMarchi (guitar), with former **Heart** members Roger Fisher (guitar), Steve Fossen (bass) and Mike Derosier (drums).

10/6/90+ **114** 28 © **Alias** .... **$10** EMI 93908
After All The Love Is Gone
Haunted Heart

| Heroes | One More Chance | Say What I Wanna Say | True Emotion | What To Do |
| **More Than Words Can Say** *2* | Power, The | Standing In The Darkness | **Waiting For Love** *13* | |

ALICE DEEJAY '00

Female dance trio from Holland: Judith, Gaby and Jane.

4/15/00 **76** 26 © **Who Needs Guitars Anyway?** .... **$10** Republic 157672
Alice Deejay
Back In My Life
Better Off Alone *27*

Celebrate Our Love	Fairytales	Lonely One	Who Needs Guitars Anyway?
Elements Of Life	Got To Get Away	No More Lies	Will I Ever
Everything Begins With An E	I Can See (See It In Your Eyes)	Waiting For Your Love	

★356★ ALICE IN CHAINS '94

Male hard-rock group formed in Seattle: Layne Staley (vocals), **Jerry Cantrell** (guitar), Mike Starr (bass) and Sean Kinney (drums). Starr replaced by Mike Inez (former bassist for **Ozzy Osbourne**) by 1994. In 1995, Inez recorded with **Slash's Snakepit** and Staley recorded with **Mad Season**. Scott Olson (guitar) joined in 1996.

4/27/91	**42**	59	▲²	©	1 Facelift .... C:#23/65	$10	Columbia 46075
10/17/92	**6**	102	▲⁴	©	2 **Dirt** .... C:#28/29	$10	Columbia 52475
2/12/94	**❶**¹	59	▲²	©	3 **Jar Of Flies** .... [M]	$10	Columbia 57628
4/15/95	**29**ᶜ	7		©	4 Sap .... [M]	$10	Columbia 67059
11/25/95	**❶**¹	46	▲²	©	5 **Alice In Chains**	$10	Columbia 67248
8/17/96	**3**	33	▲	©	6 **MTV Unplugged** .... [L]	$10	Columbia 67703

recorded on 4/10/96 at the Majestic Theater in New York City

7/17/99	**20**	17	●	©	7 **Nothing Safe** .... [K]	$10	Columbia 63649
11/13/99	**123**	1		©	8 **Music Bank** .... [K]	$40	Columbia 69580 [4]
12/23/00	**142**	2		©	9 Live .... [E-L]	$10	Columbia 85274

recorded from 1991-93

Again (5,7,8,9)	Don't Follow (3)	Head Creeps (5,8)	Killing Yourself (8)	Queen Of The Rodeo (8,9)	So Close (5)
Am I Inside (4,8)	Down In A Hole (2,6,7,8)	Heaven Beside You (5,6,8)	Little Bitter (8,9)	Rain When I Die (2,8)	Social Parasite (8)
Angry Chair (2,6,7,8,9)	Fear The Voices (8)	I Can't Have You Blues (8)	Love, Hate, Love (1,8,9)	Real Thing (1)	Sunshine (1)
Bleed The Freak (1,8,9)	Frogs (5,6,8)	I Can't Remember (1,8)	Lying Season (8)	Right Turn (4,8)	Swing On This (3)
Brother (4,6,8)	Get Born Again (7,8)	I Know Somethin (Bout You) (1)	Man In The Box (1,7,8,9)	Rooster (2,6,7,8,9)	Them Bones (2,7,8,9)
Brush Away (5)	God Am (5,8,9)	I Stay Away (3,7,8)	No Excuses (3,6,7,8)	Rotten Apple (3)	We Die Young (1,7,8)
Confusion (1,8)	God Smack (2,8)	Iron Gland (7,8)	Nothin' Song (5)	Sea Of Sorrow (1,8)	Whale & Wasp (3)
Dam That River (2,8,9)	Got Me Wrong (4,6,7,8)	It Ain't Like That (1,8)	Nutshell (3,6,8)	Shame In You (5)	What The Hell Have I (7,8)
Died (8)	Grind (5,7,8)	Junkhead (2,8,9)	Over Now (5,6,8)	Sickman (2,8)	Whatcha Gonna Do (8)
Dirt (2,8,9)	Hate To Feel (2,8)	Killer Is Me (6,8)	Put You Down (1)	Sludge Factory (5,6)	Would? (2,6,7,8,9)

ALIEN ANT FARM '01

Rock group from Los Angeles: Dryden Mitchell (vocals), Terry Corso (guitar), Tye Zamora (bass) and Mike Cosgrove (drums).

3/24/01 **11** 28↑▲ © **ANThology** .... **$10** New Noize 450293
Attitude
Calico
Courage

Death Day	Smooth Criminal	Summer	Wish
Flesh And Bone	Sticks And Stones	Universe	
Movies	Stranded	Whisper	

ALISHA '90

Born in Brooklyn, New York. Female dance singer.

6/23/90 **166** 4 © **Bounce Back** .... **$10** MCA 6378
(Ain't No) Better Love
Bounce Back *54*

| Don't Let Our Love Go | I Need Forever | Love Will Talk | Wrong Number |
| Everything You Do | Kiss Me Quick | Rescue Me | You've Really Gotten To Me |

ALIVE 'N KICKIN' '70

Pop-rock group from New York City: Pepe Cardona (male vocals), Sandy Toder (female vocals), John Parisio (guitar), Bruce Sudano (organ), Thomas Wilson (bass) and Vito Albano (drums). Sudano married **Donna Summer** on 7/16/80 and was a member of **Brooklyn Dreams**.

10/17/70 **129** 3 © **Alive 'N Kickin'** .... **$30** Roulette 42052
Hitter Man
Jordan

produced by **Tommy James**

| Junction Creek | Kentucky Rain | Mother Carey's Chicken | **Tighter, Tighter** *7* |
| **Just Let It Come** *69* | Mississippi Mud | Sunday Morning | |

ALKAHOLIKS, Tha '95

Rap trio from Los Angeles: James Robinson, Rico "**Tash**" Smith and Eric Brooks. Changed name to Tha Liks in 2001.

9/11/93	**124**	6	©	1 21 & Over	$10	Loud 66280
3/18/95	**50**	3	©	2 **Coast II Coast**	$10	Loud 66446
9/13/97	**57**	5	©	3 **Likwidation**	$10	Loud 67435

All Night (3)	Captain Hook (3)	**Hip Hop Drunkies** (3) *66*	Likwidation (3)	Off The Wall (3)	Tore Down (3)
All The Way Live (2)	Contents Unda Pressure (3)	Hit And Run (2)	Likwit (1)	Only When I'm Drunk (1)	Turn Tha Party Out (1)
Aww Sh*t! (3)	DAAAM! (2)	Keep It Pourin' (3)	Likwit Ridas (3)	Pass Out (3)	2014 (2)
Bottoms Up (2)	Feel The Real (3)	Killin' It (3)	Make Room (1)	Read My Lips (2)	21 And Under (2)
Bullshit (1)	Flashback (2)	Last Call (1)	Mary Jane (1)	Rockin' With The Best (3)	WLIX (2)
Can't Tell Me Shit (1)	Funny Style (3)	Let It Out (2)	Next Level (2)	Soda Pop (1)	Who Dem Niggas (1)

ALKALINE TRIO '01

Rock trio from Chicago: Matt Skiba (vocals, guitar), Rob Doran (bass) and Glenn Porter (drums).

4/21/01 **199** 1 © **From Here To Infirmary** .... **$10** Vagrant 353
Another Innocent Girl
Armageddon

| Bloodied Up | I'm Dying Tomorrow | Private Eye | Stupid Kid | Trucks And Trains |
| Crawl | Mr. Chainsaw | Steamer Trunk | Take Lots With Alcohol | You're Dead |

ALLAN, Davie, And The Arrows '67

Born in Los Angeles. Session guitarist. The Arrows consisted of Jared Hendler (keyboards), Drew Bennett (bass) and Larry Brown (drums).

10/15/66+	**17**	71			1 **The Wild Angels**	[S]	$30	Tower 5043

includes "Lonely In The Chapel" and "Midnight Rider" by The Hands Of Time

| 4/22/67 | **94** | 18 | | | 2 **The Wild Angels, Vol. II** .... | [I-S] | $30 | Tower 5056 |
| 8/19/67 | **165** | 2 | | | 3 **Devil's Angels** .... | [I-S] | $30 | Tower 5074 |

Arriba (2)
Blue's Theme (1,2) *37*
Bongo Party (1)
Chase, The (1)
Cody's Theme (3)

Cycle Party (2)
Dark Alley (2)
Devil's Angels (3) *97*
Devil's Rumble (3)
Devils Carnival (3)

Funky (3)
Ghost Story (3)
Hell Rider (3)
Hole In The Wall (3)
Last Ride (2)

Lonely Rider (1)
Losers Burial (2)
Losers Lament (2)
Make-Believe Love (3)
Makin' Love Is Fun (2)

Rockin' Angel (1)
Unknown Rider (1)
Wild Angels, Theme From The (1) *99*
Wild Angels Ballad (Dirge) (1)

Wild Angels Chase (2)
Wild Orgy (2)

ALLAN, Gary '99

Born Gary Herzberg on 12/5/67 in Montebello, California; raised in La Mirada, California. Country singer.

11/9/96+	**136**	16	©	1 **Used Heart For Sale**	$10	Decca 11482
6/6/98	**132**	6	©	2 **It Would Be You**	$10	Decca 70012
11/13/99	**84**	47	● ©	3 **Smoke Rings In The Dark**	$10	MCA 170101

All I Had Going Is Gone (1)
Baby I Will (2)
Bourbon Borderline (3)
Cowboy Blues (3)
Cryin' For Nothin' (3)
Don't Leave Her Lonely Too Long (2)
Don't Tell Mama (3)

Forever And A Day (1)
Forgotten, But Not Gone (2)
From Where I'm Sitting (1)
Greenfields (3)
Her Man (1)
I Ain't Runnin Yet (2)
I'll Take Today (2)
I'm The One (3)

I've Got A Quarter In My Pocket (2)
It Took Us All Night Long To Say Goodbye (2)
It Would Be You (2)
Learning To Live With Me (3)
Living In A House Full Of Love (1)

Lovin' You Against My Will (3)
No Man In His Wrong Heart (2)
Of All The Hearts (1)
Red Lips, Blue Eyes, Little White Lies (2)
Right Where I Need To Be (3) *42*
Runaway (3)

Send Back My Heart (1)
She Loves Me, She Don't Love You (2)
Smoke Rings In The Dark (3) *76*
Sorry (3)
Used Heart For Sale (1)
Wake Up Screaming (1)

Wine Me Up (1)

ALLEN, Dayton '60

Born on 9/24/19 in New York City. Comedian on **Steve Allen**'s TV show. Voice of *Deputy Dawg* TV cartoon and "Phineas T. Bluster" of TV's *Howdy Doody*.

| 12/19/60 | **35** | 1 | | **Why Not!** .... | [C] | $30 | Grand Award 424 |

Botanist
Congressman "Dudley"

Criminologist
General Zugsmith

Hello Sickies
International T.V.

Mailman
Safari

Salvador Dooley
Squaw Valley Olympics

Surgeon

ALLEN, Deborah '84

Born Deborah Lynn Thurmond on 9/30/53 in Memphis. Country singer/songwriter.

| 12/3/83+ | **67** | 20 | | **Cheat The Night** .... | [M] | $10 | RCA Victor 8514 |

Baby I Lied *26*

Cheat The Night

Fool's Paradise

I Hurt For You

I've Been Wrong Before

What's The Matter With Me

ALLEN, Donna '87

Born in Key West, Florida; raised in Tampa. R&B singer. Former cheerleader for the NFL's Tampa Bay Buccaneers.

| 4/4/87 | **133** | 13 | © | **Perfect Timing** .... | $10 | 21 Records 90548 |

Another Affair
Bad Love

Bit By Bit
Daydreams

Perfect Timing
Satisfied

Serious *21*
Sweet Somebody

Wild Nights

ALLEN, Peter '81

Born Peter Allen Woolnough on 2/10/44 in Tenterfield, Australia. Died of AIDS on 6/18/92 (age 48). Cabaret-style performer/songwriter. Married to **Liza Minnelli** from 1967-73. Co-writer of "Arthur's Theme" and "I Honestly Love You."

4/21/79	**171**	3		1 **I Could Have Been A Sailor**	$12	A&M 4739
11/29/80+	**123**	20	©	2 **Bi-Coastal**	$12	A&M 4825
3/12/83	**170**	6	©	3 **Not The Boy Next Door**	$10	Arista 9613

Angels With Dirty Faces (1)
Bi-Coastal (2)
Don't Cry Out Loud (1)
Don't Leave Me Now (1)
Don't Wish Too Hard (1)
Easy On The Weekend (3)
Fade To Black (3)
Fly Away (2) *55*

Hit In The Heart (2)
I Could Have Been A Sailor (1)
I Could Really Show You Around (2)
I Don't Go Shopping (2)
I'd Rather Leave While I'm In Love (1)
If You Were Wondering (1)

Just Another Make Out Song (3)
Not The Boy Next Door (3)
Once Before I Go (3)
One Step Over The Borderline (2)
Paris At 21 (1)
Pass This Time (2)

Simon (2)
Somebody's Angel (2)
Somebody's Got Your Love (3)
Two Boys (1)
We've Come To An Understanding (1)
When This Love Affair Is Over (2)

You And Me (We Wanted It All) (3)
You Haven't Heard The Last Of Me (3)
You'll Always Get Your Way (3)

ALLEN, Steve '55

Born on 12/26/21 in New York City. Died of heart failure on 10/30/2000 (age 78). Comedian/actor/songwriter/author. In 1954, became the first host of TV's *Tonight Show*. Played **Benny Goodman** in the 1956 movie *The Benny Goodman Story*. Hosted own variety and talk shows (1956-80). Married actress Jayne Meadows.

5/14/55	**7**	10		1 Music For Tonight	[I]	$30	Coral 57004
3/16/63	**65**	11		2 **Funny Fone-Calls**	[C]	$25	Dot 3472
4/27/63	**41**	22		3 **Gravy Waltz And 11 Current Hits!**	[I]	$25	Dot 3515

Arthur Goldstein's Mother (2)
Boss Guitar (3)
Call To Eddie, Sr. (2)
Call To Seattle (2)
Calling The Auto Club (2)
Candlelight (1)
Cast Your Fate To The Wind (3)

For Sale: Espresso Machine & Birds Wanted (2)
For The Very First Time (1)
Gravy Waltz (3) *64*
I Fall In Love Too Easily (1)
I'm Glad There Is You (In This World Of Ordinary People) (1)

Imagination (1)
Isn't It Romantic? (1)
It Can't Be Wrong (1)
Lawrence Of Arabia, Theme From (3)
Long Ago (And Far Away) (1)
Love For Sale (3)

Man With A Horn (3)
Preacherman (3)
Rebel-'Rouser (3)
Rinky Dink (3)
Rose And The Butterfly (3)
Share The Ride (2)
Singer Wanted (2)

Stay Just A Little While (1)
Tonight (1)
Wanted: Girl To Share Apartment (2)
Where Are You? (1)
Whistle Bait (3)
Yakety Sax (3)

Your Theme (3)

ALLEN, Woody '64

Born Allen Stewart Konigesberg on 12/1/35 in New York City. Prolific movie director/actor/comedian/writer. Had a child with actress Mia Farrow (never married; highly publicized breakup in 1992).

| 8/15/64 | **63** | 11 | | **Woody Allen** .... | [C] | $30 | Colpix 518 |

no track titles listed on this album

ALL-4-ONE '94

Male vocal group from Los Angeles: Jamie Jones, Delious Kennedy, Alfred Nevarez and Tony Borowiak.

4/30/94	**7**	72	▲⁴ ©	1 All-4-One	$10	Blitzz 82588
6/24/95	**27**	35	▲ ©	2 **And The Music Speaks**	$10	Blitzz 82746
12/2/95	**91**	7	©	3 **An All-4-One Christmas**	[X]	$10	Blitzz 82846

Christmas charts: 13/'95, 30/'96

Better Man (1)
Bomb, The (1)
Breathless (1)

Christmas Song (Chestnuts Roasting On An Open Fire) (3)

Christmas With My Baby (3)
Colors Of Love (2)
Could This Be Magic (2)

Down To The Last Drop (1)
First Noel (3)

Frosty The Snowman (medley) (3)

Giving You My Heart Forever (2)
Here For You (2)

ALL-4-ONE — Cont'd

Here If You're Ready (1)
I Can Love You Like That (2) *5*
I Swear (1) *1*
I'm Sorry (2)
I'm Your Man (2)
Love Is More Than Just Another Four-Letter Word (2)

Mary's Little Boy Child (3)
O Come, All Ye Faithful (3)
Oh Girl (1)
Roll Call (2)
Rudolph The Red Nosed Reindeer (medley) (3)

Santa Claus Is Comin' To Town (3)
(She's Got) Skillz (1) *57*
Silent Night (3)
So Much In Love (1) *5*
Something About You (1)
These Arms (2)

Think You're The One For Me (2)
This Christmas (3)
We Dedicate (2)
We Wish You A Merry Christmas (3)
What Child Is This? (3)

When You Wish Upon A Star (3)
Without You (1)

ALLFRUMTHA I   '98

Male rap duo from Inglewood, California: Ryan Garner and Marcus Moore.

| 5/23/98 | 168 | 1 | | © | **AllFrumTha I** .... | | | $10 | Priority 50588 |

Caps
County Jail

Dopest On Tha Planet
Fill My Cup (To Tha Rim)

Gangsta's Prayer
Get Yo Bang On

Guess Who
Hoo-Ride 'N'

Make You Dance
Rollin Wit Connect

Unthinkable

ALLMAN, Duane   '73

Born Howard Duane Allman on 11/20/46 in Nashville; raised in Daytona Beach, Florida. Died in a motorcycle crash on 10/29/71 (age 24). Lead guitarist of **The Allman Brothers Band**.

| 12/9/72+ | 28 | 26 | ● | © | 1 **An Anthology** .... | [K] | | $30 | Capricorn 0108 [2] |
| 8/31/74 | 49 | 16 | | © | 2 **An Anthology, Vol. II** .... | [K] | | $30 | Capricorn 0139 [2] |

B.B. King Medley (1)
Been Gone Too Long (2)
Born To Be Wild (2)
Come On In My Kitchen (2)
Dimples (2)
Dirty Old Man (2)
Don't Keep Me Wondering (1)

Don't Tell Your Troubles (2)
Done Somebody Wrong (2)
Down Along The Cove (1)
Dreams (1)
Games People Play (1)
Goin' Down Slow (1)
Goin' Up The Country (2)

Goin Upstairs (2)
Happily Married Man (2)
Hey, Jude (1)
It Ain't Fair (2)
Layla (1)
Leave My Blues At Home (2)
Little Martha (1)

Livin' On The Open Road (1)
Loan Me A Dime (1)
Matchbox (2)
Mean Old World (1)
Midnight Rider (1)
No Money Down (2)
Please Be With Me (1)

Push Push (2)
Road Of Love (1)
Rollin' Stone (1)
Shake For Me (1)
Standback (1)
Statesboro Blues (1)
Stuff You Gotta Watch (2)

Waiting For A Train (2)
Walk On Gilded Splinters (2)
Weight, The (1,2)
You Reap What You Sow (2)

ALLMAN, Gregg   '74

Born on 12/8/47 in Nashville; raised in Daytona Beach, Florida. Rock singer/keyboardist. In 1965, Greg and brother **Duane Allman** formed the Allman Joys, which evolved into **The Allman Brothers Band** by 1969. Married to **Cher** from 1975-77. His band included Dan Toler, David Toler, Tim Heding, Chaz Trippy and Bruce Waibel. Acted in the movie *Rush*.

11/24/73+	13	39	●	©	1 **Laid Back**			$15	Capricorn 0116
11/16/74	50	12		©	2 **The Gregg Allman Tour**	[L]		$20	Capricorn 0141 [2]
					recorded at Carnegie Hall and the Capitol Theater in New Jersey				

THE GREGG ALLMAN BAND:

6/11/77	42	12		©	3 **Playin' Up A Storm**			$12	Capricorn 0181
3/7/87	30	28	●	©	4 **I'm No Angel**			$10	Epic 40531
8/6/88	117	11		©	5 **Just Before The Bullets Fly**			$10	Epic 44033

All My Friends (1)
Anything Goes (4)
Are You Lonely For Me Baby (2)
Before The Bullets Fly (5)
Brightest Smile In Town (3)
Bring It On Back (3)
Can't Get Over You (5)
Can't Keep Running (4)

Come And Go Blues (3)
Cryin' Shame (3)
Demons (5)
Don't Mess Up A Good Thing (1,2)
Don't Want You No More (4)
Double Cross (2)
Dreams (2)
Every Hungry Woman (5)

Evidence Of Love (4)
Faces Without Names (4)
Fear Of Falling (5)
Feel So Bad (2)
I'm No Angel (4) *49*
Island (3)
It Ain't No Use (3)
It's Not My Cross To Bear (4)
Lead Me On (4)

Let This Be A Lesson To Ya' (4)
Matthew's Arrival (3)
Midnight Rider (1) *19*
Multi-Colored Lady (4)
Night Games (5)
Ocean Awash The Gunwale (5)
Oncoming Traffic (2)
One More Try (3)
Please Call Home (1)

Queen Of Hearts (1,2)
Slip Away (5)
Stand Back (2)
Sweet Feelin' (3)
These Days (1)
Things That Might Have Been (4)
Thorn And A Wild Rose (5)
Time Will Take Us (2)

Turn On Your Love Light (2)
Where Can You Go? (2)
Will The Circle Be Unbroken (1,2)
Yours For The Asking (4)

ALLMAN BROTHERS BAND, The ★117★   '73

Rock group from Macon, Georgia: brothers **Duane Allman** (lead guitar) and **Gregg Allman** (keyboards), **Dickey Betts** (guitar), Berry Oakley (bass), and the drum duo of Butch Trucks and Jai Johnny Johanson (pronounced: Jay Johnny Johnson). Duane and Gregg known earlier as the **Allman Joys** and Hour Glass. Duane was the top session guitarist at Muscle Shoals studio; killed in a motorcycle crash on 10/29/71 (age 24). Oakley died in a motorcycle crash on 11/11/72 (age 24); replaced by Lamar Williams (d: 1/25/83). Chuck Leavell (keyboards) added in 1972. Group split up in 1976. Gregg formed the Gregg Allman Band. Betts formed Great Southern. Leavell, Williams and Johanson formed the fusion-rock band **Sea Level**. Allman and Betts reunited with a new Allman Brothers lineup in 1978. Disbanded in 1981. Allman, Betts, Trucks and Johanson regrouped with Warren Haynes (guitar), Allen Woody (bass) and Johnny Neel (keyboards) in 1989. Neel left in 1990, replaced by Mark Quinones. Woody died on 8/26/2000 (age 44). Group inducted into the Rock and Roll Hall of Fame in 1995.

1)Brothers And Sisters 2)Eat A Peach 3)Win, Lose Or Draw 4)Enlightened Rogues 5)At Fillmore East

1/24/70	188	5		©	1 **The Allman Brothers Band** ....C:#50/4			$25	Atco 308
					also see #6 below				
10/24/70	38	22		©	2 **Idlewild South**			$25	Atco 342
					also see #6 below				
7/24/71	13	47	▲	©	3 **At Fillmore East** ....C:#23/8	[L]		$30	Capricorn 802 [2]
					recorded on 3/12/71 in New York City				
3/18/72	4	48	▲	©	4 **Eat A Peach** ....C:#21/21	[L]		$30	Capricorn 0102 [2]
5/13/72	129	8			5 **Duane & Gregg Allman**	[E]		$25	Bold 301
					recorded in 1968				
3/10/73	25	55	●	©	6 **Beginnings**	[R]		$30	Atco 805 [2]
					reissue of albums #1 and #2 above				
8/25/73	❶⁵	56	▲	©	7 **Brothers And Sisters**			$15	Capricorn 0111
11/3/73	171	8		©	8 **Early Allman**	[E]		$15	Dial 6005
					ALLMAN JOYS recorded in 1966				
9/13/75	5	14	●	©	9 **Win, Lose Or Draw**			$15	Capricorn 0156
12/13/75+	43	14			10 **The Road Goes On Forever, A Collection Of Their Greatest Recordings**	[G]		$20	Capricorn 0164 [2]
12/4/76	75	10		©	11 **Wipe The Windows-Check The Oil-Dollar Gas**	[L]		$20	Capricorn 0177 [2]
3/17/79	9	24	●	©	12 **Enlightened Rogues**			$12	Capricorn 0218
8/23/80	27	13		©	13 **Reach For The Sky**			$10	Arista 9535
8/22/81	44	12		©	14 **Brothers Of The Road**			$10	Arista 9564
11/21/81	189	3	●	©	15 **The Best Of The Allman Brothers Band**	[G]		$10	Polydor 6339
7/15/89	103	11	●	©	16 **Dreams**	[K]		$60	Polydor 839417 [6]
7/21/90	53	16		©	17 **Seven Turns**			$10	Epic 46144

ALLMAN BROTHERS BAND, The — Cont'd

7/20/91	85	17		© 18	Shades Of Two Worlds			$10	Epic 47877
6/27/92	80	8		© 19	An Evening With The Allman Brothers Band		[L]	$10	Epic 48998
5/21/94	45	21	●	© 20	Where It All Begins			$10	Epic 64232
5/27/95	88	4		© 21	2nd Set - An Evening With The Allman Brothers Band		[L]	$10	Epic 66795

Ain't No Good To Cry (16)
Ain't Wastin' Time No More (4,10,11,16) *77*
All Night Train (20)
Angeline (13,16) *58*
BB King Medley (16)
Back Down Home With You (5)
Back Where It All Begins (20,21)
Bad Rain (18)
Bell Bottom Britches (8)
Black Hearted Woman (1,6,10)
Blind Love (12)
Blue Sky (4,10,15,16,19)
Bougainvillea (16)
Brothers Of The Road (14)
Can You Fool (16)
Can't Lose What You Never Had (9,11,16)
Can't Take It With You (12,16)
Cast Off All My Fears (16)
Change My Way Of Living (20)
Changing Of The Guard (8)
Come And Go Blues (7,11,16)
Come Down And Get Me (5)
Come On In My Kitchen (18)
Crazy Love (12,15,16) *29*

Crossroads (16)
Demons (16)
Desert Blues (18)
Dimples (16)
Doctor Fone Bone (8)
Don't Keep Me Wonderin' (2,6)
Don't Want You No More (1,6,11,16)
Done Somebody Wrong (3)
Down In Texas (16)
Dreams (1,6,10,15,16,19)
Drunken Hearted Boy (16)
Duane's Tune (16)
End Of The Line (18,19)
Every Hungry Woman (1,6)
Everybody's Got A Mountain To Climb (20)
Famous Last Words (13)
Forest For The Trees (8)
From The Madness Of The West (13)
Gambler's Roll (17)
Get On With Your Life (18,19)
God Rest His Soul (5,16)
Goin' Down Slow (16)
Good Clean Fun (17)
Good Time Feeling (16)

Gotta Get Away (8)
Heat Is On (14)
Hell & High Water (13)
High Falls (19)
Hoochie Coochie Man (2,6,10,16)
Hot'Lanta (3,10)
I Beg Of You (14)
I Feel Free (16)
I Got A Right To Be Wrong (13)
I'll Change For You (16)
I'm Gonna Move To The Outskirts Of Town (16)
I'm No Angel (16)
In Memory Of Elizabeth Reed (2,3,11,16,21)
In The Morning When I'm Real (1,6,11,16)
It Ain't Over Yet (17)
It's Not My Cross To Bear (1,6,11,16)
Jelly Jelly (7)
Jessica (7,10,11,15,16,21) *65*
Judgment, The (14)
Just Ain't Easy (12,16)
Just Another Love Song (9)
Keep On Keepin' On (13)

Kind Of Bird (18)
Leave My Blues At Home (2,6)
Leavin' (14)
Les Brers In A Minor (4)
Let Me Ride (17)
Little Martha (4,10,15,16)
Loaded Dice (17)
Long Time Gone (16)
Louisiana Lou And Three Card Monty John (9) *78*
Low Down Dirty Mean (17)
Maybe We Can Go Back To Yesterday (14)
Mean Woman Blues (20)
Melissa (4,5,10,15,16,19) *86*
Midnight Blues (19)
Midnight Man (18)
Midnight Rider (4,6,10,15,16)
Morning Dew (5,16)
Mountain Jam (4)
Mystery Woman (13)
Nancy (16)
Need Your Love So Bad (12)
Never Knew How Much (I Needed You) (14)
Nevertheless (9) *67*
No One To Run With (20,21)

Nobody Knows (18,19)
Nobody Knows You When You're Down And Out (5)
Northern Boundry (8)
Oh John (8)
Old Man River (8)
One More Ride (16)
One Way Out (4,10,16) *86*
Please Call Home (2,6)
Pony Boy (7)
Rain (16)
Ramblin' Man (7,10,11,15,16) *2*
Revival (Love Is Everywhere) (2,6,19) *92*
Sail Away (12)
Sailin' 'Cross The Devil's Sea (20,21)
Same Thing (21)
Seven Turns (17)
Shapes Of Things (16)
She Has Funny Cars (16)
Shine It On (17)
So Long (13)
Soul Serenade (medley) (16)
Soulshine (20,21)
Southbound (7,11,15,16,19)

Spoonful (8,16)
Stalling For Time (8)
Stand Back (4,10,15)
Statesboro Blues (3,10,15,16)
Stormy Monday (3,10)
Straight From The Heart (14) *39*
Street Singer (8)
Sweet Mama (9)
Temptation Is A Gun (20)
Things You Used To Do (14,16)
Trouble No More (1,4,6,16)
Try It One More Time (12)
Two Rights (14)
Wasted Words (7,10,11,16)
Well I Know Too Well (5)
What's Done Is Done (16)
Whipping Post (1,3,6,10,16)
Win, Lose Or Draw (9,15)
You Don't Love Me (3,16,21)
You'll Learn Someday (8)

ALL SAINTS   '98
Female vocal group from London: sisters Natalie and Nicky Appleton, with Shaznay Lewis and Melanie Blatt.

3/28/98	40	49	▲	©	All Saints			$10	London 828997

Alone
Beg
Bootie Call

Heaven
I Know Where It's At *36*

If You Want To Party (I Found Lovin')
Lady Marmalade

Never Ever *4*
Take The Key
Trapped

Under The Bridge
War Of Nerves

ALLURE   '97
Female R&B vocal group from New York City: Alia Davis, Akissa Mendez, Lalisha McLean and Linnie Belcher.

5/24/97	108	27	●	©	Allure			$10	Crave 67848

All Cried Out *4*
Anything You Want
Come Into My House

Give You All I Got
Head Over Heels *35*
I'll Give You Anything

Last Chance
Mama Said
No Question

Story, The
Wanna Get With You
When You Need Someone

You're Gonna Love Me

ALMEIDA, Laurindo, and The Bossa Nova All Stars   '63
Born on 9/2/17 in Sao Paulo, Brazil. Died of cancer on 7/26/95 (age 77). Guitarist/bandleader. Member of **Stan Kenton**'s orchestra until 1950. Helped popularize the bossa nova style. Worked on the scores of many movies.

12/8/62+	9	27			Viva Bossa Nova!		[I]	$25	Capitol 1759

Desafinado
Lazy River

Lollipops And Roses
Maria

Moon River
Mr. Lucky

Naked City Theme
One Note Samba

Petite Fleur
Ramblin' Rose

Route 66 Theme
Teach Me Tonight

ALMOND, Marc   '89
Born Peter Marc Almond on 7/9/57 in Southport, England. Half of the **Soft Cell** duo.

1/28/89	144	11		©	The Stars We Are			$10	Capitol 91042

Bitter Sweet
Only The Moment

Sensualist, The
She Took My Soul In Istanbul

Somethings Gotten Hold Of My Heart

Stars We Are
Tears Run Rings *67*

These My Dreams Are Yours
Very Last Pearl

Your Kisses Burn

ALPERT, Herb, & The Tijuana Brass ★26★   '66
Born on 3/31/35 in Los Angeles. Producer/composer/trumpeter/bandleader. Played trumpet since age eight. Formed A&M Records with Jerry Moss in 1962. Used studio musicians until early 1965, then formed own band. Alpert and Moss formed the Almo Sounds label in 1994.

1)What Now My Love 2)Whipped Cream & Other Delights 3)Going Places 4)The Beat Of The Brass 5)Sounds Like

12/29/62+	10	157	●	© 1	The Lonely Bull		[I]	$20	A&M 101
1/16/65+	6	163	●	© 2	South Of The Border		[I]	$20	A&M 108
5/15/65	❶8	185	●	© 3	Whipped Cream & Other Delights		[I]	$20	A&M 110
10/16/65+	❶6	164	●	© 4	Going Places		[I]	$20	A&M 112
1/15/66	17	56	●	© 5	Herb Alpert's Tijuana Brass, Volume 2		[I]	$20	A&M 103
					released in 1963				
5/14/66	❶9	129	●	© 6	What Now My Love		[I]	$15	A&M 4114
12/10/66	26	85	●	7	S.R.O.		[I]	$15	A&M 4119
6/3/67	❶1	53	●	8	Sounds Like		[I]	$15	A&M 4124
12/23/67+	4	49	●	9	Herb Alpert's Ninth		[I]	$15	A&M 4134
5/11/68	❶2	54	●	© 10	The Beat Of The Brass		[I]	$15	A&M 4146
12/7/68	❶2X	10	●	© 11	Christmas Album		[X-I]	$15	A&M 4166
					Christmas charts: 1/68, 6/'69, 17/'70				
7/5/69	28	26	●	12	Warm		[I]	$15	A&M 4190
11/22/69+	30	20	●	13	The Brass Are Comin'		[I]	$15	A&M 4228
3/21/70	43	32	●	© 14	Greatest Hits		[G-I]	$15	A&M 4245

ALPERT, Herb, & The Tijuana Brass — Cont'd

DEBUT	PEAK	WKS			Album	Sym	$	Label & Number
7/24/71	111	10			15 Summertime	[I]	$15	A&M 4314
6/17/72	135	9	©		16 Solid Brass	[I-K]	$15	A&M 4341
12/8/73	196	4	©		17 Foursider	[I-K]	$20	A&M 3521 [2]
6/1/74	66	11			18 You Smile-The Song Begins	[I]	$12	A&M 3620
4/26/75	88	10			19 Coney Island	[I]	$12	A&M 4521
2/11/78	65	19	©		20 Herb Alpert/Hugh Masekela	[I]	$12	Horizon 728

HERB ALPERT:

DEBUT	PEAK	WKS			Album	Sym	$	Label & Number
10/13/79	6	39	▲ ©		21 Rise	[I]	$12	A&M 4790
7/26/80	28	12			22 Beyond	[I]	$10	A&M 3717
8/22/81	61	10	©		23 Magic Man	[I]	$10	A&M 3728
5/29/82	100	26	©		24 Fandango	[I]	$10	A&M 3731
9/24/83	120	8	©		25 Blow Your Own Horn	[I]	$10	A&M 4949
8/25/84	75	10			26 Bullish	[I]	$10	A&M 5022

HERB ALPERT/TIJUANA BRASS

DEBUT	PEAK	WKS			Album	Sym	$	Label & Number
8/24/85	151	10	©		27 Wild Romance	[I]	$10	A&M 5082
4/25/87	18	31	● ©		28 Keep Your Eye On Me	[I]	$10	A&M 5125

A Banda (Ah Bahn-da) (9,16) 35
Acapulco (16)
Acapulco 1922 (1)
Adios, Mi Corazon (2)
African Flame (27)
African Summer (20)
All My Loving (2)
Alone Again (Naturally) (18)
Always Have A Dream (Pour Le Coeur, A Mon Pere) (26)
A-Me-Ri-Ca (5,14)
And The Angels Sing (4)
Angel (24)
Angelina (21)
Angelito (2)
Anna (13)
Aranjuez (Mon Amour) (21)
Aria (24)
Bean Bag (7)
Beautiful Friend (10)
Behind The Rain (21)
Bell That Couldn't Jingle (11)
Belz Mein Shtetele Belz (My Home Town) (10)
Besame Mucho (23)
Beyond (22) 50
Bittersweet Samba (3)
Blow Your Own Horn (25)
Blue Sunday (7)
Bo-Bo (8)
Brasilia (6)
Brass Are Comin' (The Little Train Of Caipira) (13)
Bud (9)
Bullish (26) 90
Butterball (3)
Cabaret (10,17) 72
California Blues (24)
Cantina Blue (6)
Carmen (9) 51
Carmine (19)
Casino Royale (8,16,17) 27
Cat Man Do (28)
Catch A Falling Star (15)
Catch Me (27)
Catfish (19)
Charmer, The (8)

Christmas Song (Chestnuts Roasting On An Open Fire) (11)
Cinco De Mayo (4)
Coco Loco (La Guajira) (24)
Coney Island (19)
Continental, The (12,22)
Country Lake (13)
Cowboys And Indians (9)
Crave, The (19)
Crawfish (1)
Crea Mi Amor (5)
Dancing In The Light (27)
Darlin' (15)
Desafinado (1)
Dida (18)
Don't Go Breaking My Heart (7)
"8" Ball (27)
El Garbanzo (3)
El Lobo (The Wolf) (1)
El Presidente (2)
Factory, The (22)
Fandango (24)
Fantasy Island (23)
Felicia (4)
Five Minutes More (6)
Flamingo (7,16) 28
Flea Bag (9)
For Carlos (7)
Fox Hunt (18) 84
Freckles (6)
Freight Train Joe (7)
Garden Party (25) 81
Gently (Suavemente) (25)
Girl From Ipanema (2,17)
Girl Talk (12)
Good Morning, Mr. Sunshine (13)
Gotta Lotta Livin' To Do (8)
Great Manolete (La Virgen De La Macarena) (5)
Green Leaves Of Summer (5)
Green Peppers (3)
Happening, The (9) 32
Happy Hanna (20)
Hello, Dolly (2,17)
Hot Shot (28)

Hurt So Bad (15)
I Belong (19)
I Can't Go On Living Baby Without You (18)
I Get It From You (23)
I Have Dreamed (19)
I Might Frighten Her Away (18)
I Will Wait For You (7)
I'll Be Back (13)
I'll Be There For You (20)
I'm An Old Cowhand (From The Rio Grande) (13)
I'm Getting Sentimental Over You (4,14)
I've Grown Accustomed To Her Face (2)
If I Were A Rich Man (6,17)
If You Could Read My Mind (15)
In A Little Spanish Town (8)
Interlude (For Erica) (22)
It Was A Very Good Year (6)
It's All For You (27)
Jerusalem (15,16) 74
Jesu, Joy Of Man's Desiring (11)
Jingle Bell Rock (11)
Jingle Bells (11)
Kamali (22)
Keep It Goin' (22)
Keep Your Eye On Me (28) 46
Lady Godiva (8)
Lady Love (27)
Ladyfingers (3)
Las Mañanitas (11)
Last Tango In Paris (17,18) 77
Latin Lady (25)
Latin Medley (24)
Legend Of The One-Eyed Sailor (18)
Lemon Tree (3)
Let It Be Me (1)
Let It Snow, Let It Snow, Let It Snow (11)
Life Is My Song (26)
Limbo Rock (1)
Lobo (20)
Lollipops And Roses (3)

Lonely Bull (1,14,17) 6
Love Is (21)
Love Nest (9)
Love Potion #9 (3,14)
Love So Fine (9)
Love Without Words (26)
Mae (4)
Magic Trumpet (6)
Make A Wish (26)
Making Love In The Rain (28) 35
Maltese Melody (13,16)
Mame (7,17) 19
Manhattan Melody (23)
Maniac (25)
Marching Thru Madrid (5) 96
Margarita (24)
Marjorine (12)
Martha My Dear (15)
Memories Of Madrid (6)
Mexican Corn (5)
Mexican Road Race (7)
Mexican Shuffle (2,14) 85
Mexico (1)
Mickey (C'Est Ainsi Que Les Choses Arrivent) (19)
Midnight Tango (25)
Milord (5)
Miss Frenchy Brown (8)
Moments (13)
Monday, Monday (10)
Montezuma's Revenge (15)
Moon River (13,17)
Moonza (20)
More (5,17)
More And More Amor (1)
My Favorite Things (11)
My Heart Belongs To Daddy (9)
Never On Sunday (1,14)
Nicest Things Happen (15)
1980 (21)
No Time For Time (27)
Numero Cinco (2)
Ob-La-Di, Ob-La-Da (12)
Oriental Eyes (25)
Our Day Will Come (7)

Our Song (28)
Panama (10)
Paradise Cove (25)
Passion Play (26)
Peanuts (3)
Pillow (28)
Plucky (6)
Pretty World (12)
Promises, Promises (18)
Push And Pull (24)
Quiereme Tal Como Soy (Love Me The Way I Am) (24)
Quiet Tear (Lagrima Quieta) (1)
Ratatouille (Rata Too Ee) (Coisa No. I) (19)
Reach For The Stars (22)
Red Hot (22,25) 77
Ring Bell (20)
Rise (21) 1
Robbers And Cops (13)
Robin, The (10)
Rocket To The Moon (28)
Rotation (21) 30
Route 101 (24) 37
Salud, Amor Y Dinero (2)
Sandbox (12)
Save The Sunlight (18)
Sea Is My Soil (12)
Secret Garden (23)
Senor Mouse (19)
Shades Of Blue (8)
Shadow Of Your Smile (6,17)
She Touched Me (10)
Skokiaan (20)
Sleigh Ride (11)
Slick (10,16)
So What's New? (6,16)
Song For Herb (18)
South Of The Border (2,14)
Spanish Flea (4,14) 27
Spanish Harlem (5)
Stranger On The Shore (28)
Street Life (21)
Strike Up The Band (15)
Struttin' On Five (26)
Struttin' With Maria (1)
Sugarloaf (24)

Summertime (15,16)
Sundown (25)
Sunny (13,17)
Surfin' Senorita (5)
Sweet Georgia Brown (19)
Swinger From Seville (5)
Talk To The Animals (10)
Tangerine (3)
Taste Of Honey (3,14,17) 7
Thanks For The Memory (10)
That's The Way Of The World (22)
3rd Man Theme (4) 47
This Guy's In Love With You (10,16,17) 1
This Masquerade (19)
This One's For Me (23)
Tijuana Sauerkraut (1)
Tijuana Taxi (4,14,17) 38
To Wait For Love (12) 51
Town Without Pity (8)
Traffic Jam (28)
Treasure Of San Miguel (1)
Trolley Song (9)
True Confessions (25)
Up Cherry Street (2,18)
Vento Bravo (19)
Wade In The Water (8,16) 37
Walk, Don't Run (4)
Walk In The Black Forest (4)
Wall Street Rag (7)
Warm (12,17)
What Now My Love (6,16,17) 24
Whipped Cream (3,14,17) 68
Wild Romance (27)
Winds Of Barcelona (1)
Winter Wonderland (11)
With A Little Help From My Friends (9,17)
Without Her (12,16,17) 63
Work Song (7,16) 18
You Are My Life (13)
You Are The One (2)
You Smile-The Song Begins (18,23)
Zazueira (12) 78
Zorba The Greek (4,14,17) 11

ALPHAVILLE '85

Male pop trio from Berlin, Germany: Marian Gold (vocals), Frank Mertens (keyboards) and Bernhard Lloyd (drums). Ricky Echolette replaced Mertens by 1986.

DEBUT	PEAK	WKS			Album	$	Label & Number
12/22/84+	180	15	©		1 Forever Young	$10	Atlantic 80186
8/30/86	174	6	©		2 Afternoons In Utopia	$10	Atlantic 81667

Afternoons In Utopia (2)
Big In Japan (1) 66
Carol Masters (2)
Dance With Me (2)

Fallen Angel (1)
Fantastic Dream (2)
Forever Young (1) 65
IAO (2)

In The Mood (1)
Jerusalem (2)
Jet Set (1)
Lady Bright (2)

Lassie Come Home (2)
Lies (1)
Red Rose (2)
Sensations (2)

Sounds Like A Melody (1)
Summer In Berlin (1)
To Germany With Love (1)
20th Century (2)

Universal Daddy (1)
Victory Of Love (1)
Voyager, The (2)

ALVIN, Dave '87

Born on 11/11/55 in Los Angeles. Songwriter/lead guitarist with **The Blasters**, The Knitters, and **X**. Younger brother of Blasters' lead singer, Phil Alvin.

DEBUT	PEAK	WKS			Album	$	Label & Number
9/26/87	116	13	©		Romeo's Escape	$10	Epic 40921

Border Radio
Brother On The Line

Every Night About This Time
Far Away

Fourth Of July
I Wish It Was Saturday Night

Jubilee Train
Long White Cadillac

New Tattoo
Romeo's Escape

You Got Me

AMAZING RHYTHM ACES, The '77

Country-rock group from Memphis: Russell Smith (vocals, guitar), Barry Burton (guitar, dobro), Billy Earhart (keyboards), Jeff Davis (bass) and Butch McDade (drums). McDade died of cancer on 11/29/98 (age 52).

DEBUT	PEAK	WKS			Album	$	Label & Number
10/18/75	120	8	©		1 Stacked Deck	$20	ABC 913
6/5/76	157	7	©		2 Too Stuffed To Jump	$15	ABC 940
4/16/77	114	11	©		3 Toucan Do It Too	$15	ABC 1005
4/15/78	116	9	©		4 Burning The Ballroom Down	$15	ABC 1063

AMAZING RHYTHM ACES, The — Cont'd

2/17/79	144	7	©	5	The Amazing Rhythm Aces..	$15	ABC 1123
10/4/80	175	3		6	How The Hell Do You Spell Rythum?...	$12	Warner 3476

All That I Had Left (With You) (4)
Amazing Grace (Used To Be Her Favorite Song) (1) 72
Anything You Want (1)
Ashes Of Love (4)
Beautiful Lie (1)
Big Ole Brew (6)
Burning The Ballroom Down (4)
Dancing The Night Away (2)
Della's Long Brown Hair (4)
"Ella B" (1)
Emma-Jean (1)
End Is Not In Sight (The Cowboy Tune) (2) 42

Everybody's Talked Too Much (3)
Farther On Down The Road (6)
Fool For The Woman (2)
Geneva's Lullaby (3)
Give Me Flowers While I'm Living (6)
Hit The Nail On The Head (1)
Homestead In My Heart (5)
I Got The Feeling (6)
I Musta Died And Gone To Texas (4)
I Pity The Mother And The Father (When The Kids Move Away) (4)

I'll Be Gone (2)
I'm Setting You Free (3)
If I Just Knew What To Say (2)
If You Gotta Make A Fool Of Somebody (5)
Jackass Gets His Oats (4)
Just Between You And Me And The Wall, You're A Fool (3)
King Of The Cowboys (1)
Last Letter Home (3)
Life's Railway To Heaven (1)
Lipstick Traces (On A Cigarette) (5)
Little Italy Rag (4)
Living In A World Unknown (3)

Living On Borrowed Time (6)
Lonely One (5)
Love And Happiness (5)
My Tears Still Flow (1)
Never Been Hurt (3)
Never Been To The Islands (Howard & Hugh's Blues) (3)
Object Of My Affection (6)
Out Of Control (4)
Out Of The Snow (2)
Pretty Words (5)
Red To Blue (When Dreams Come True) (4)
Rodrigo, Rita And Elaine (5)
Same Ole' Me (2)

Say You Lied (5)
Spirit Walk (4)
These Dreams Of Losing You (2)
Third Rate Romance (1) 14
Two Can Do It Too (3)
Typical American Boy (2)
What Kind Of Love Is This? (6)
Whispering In The Night (5)
Who Will The Next Fool Be (1)
Who's Crying Now (3)
Why Can't I Be Satisfied (1)
Wild Night (6)
You Left The Water Running (6)

AMBOY DUKES, The   '68

Hard-rock group formed in Chicago: John Drake (vocals), **Ted Nugent** and Steve Farmer (guitars), Rick Lorber (keyboards), Bill White (bass) and Dave Palmer (drums). Several personnel changes with Nugent the only constant until his solo career started in 1975.

2/10/68	183	4	1	The Amboy Dukes..	$50	Mainstream 6104
6/15/68	74	23	2	Journey To The Center Of The Mind................................	$50	Mainstream 6112
3/21/70	191	2	3	Marriage On The Rocks/Rock Bottom..............................	$25	Polydor 4012
3/6/71	129	5	4	Survival Of The Fittest/Live................................... [L]	$25	Polydor 4035

TED NUGENT AND THE AMBOY DUKES
recorded on 7/31/70 at the Eastowne Theater in Detroit

Baby Please Don't Go (1)
Brain Games Of Yesteryear (3)
Breast-Fed 'Gator (Bait) (3)
Children Of The Woods (3)
Colors (1)
Conclusion (2)
Death Is Life (2)
Dr. Slingshot (2)
Down On Philips Escalator (1)

Flight Of The Byrd (2)
Get Yer Guns (3)
Gimme Love (1)
I Feel Fine (1)
I'll Prove I'm Right (2)
Inexhaustible Quest For The Cosmic Cabbage Part 1 & 2 (3)
It's Not True (1)

Ivory Castles (2)
Journey To The Center Of The Mind (2) 16
Let's Go Get Stoned (1)
Lovely Lady (1)
Marriage Parts 1-3 (3)
Missionary Mary (2)
Mississippi Murder (2)
Mr. Jones' Hanging Party (4)

Night Time (1)
Non-Conformist Wilderbeast Man (3)
Papa's Will (4)
Prodigal Man (4)
Psalms Of Aftermath (1)
Rattle My Snake (4)
Saint Philips Friend (2)
Scottish Tea (1)

Slidin' On (4)
Surrender To Your Kings (2)
Survival Of The Fittest (4)
Today's Lesson (Ladies & Gentlemen) (3)
Why Is A Carrot More Orange Than An Orange (2)
Young Love (1)

AMBROSIA   '78

Pop group from Los Angeles: David Pack (vocals, guitar), Joe Puerta (vocals, bass), Christopher North (keyboards) and Burleigh Drummond (drums). North left in 1977. Puerta later joined **Bruce Hornsby & The Range**.

5/3/75	22	33	©	1	Ambrosia..	$12	20th Century 434
9/18/76	79	17	©	2	Somewhere I've Never Travelled	$12	20th Century 510
8/12/78	19	29	©	3	Life Beyond L.A.	$10	Warner 3135
4/19/80	25	33	©	4	One Eighty...	$10	Warner 3368
5/29/82	115	7		5	Road Island..	$10	Warner 3638

And (2)
Angola (3)
Apothecary (3)
Art Beware (3)
Biggest Part Of Me (4) 3
Brunt, The (2)
Can't Let A Woman (2)
Cowboy Star (2)
Cryin' In The Rain (4)

Dancin' By Myself (3)
Danse With Me George (2)
Drink Of Water (4)
Endings (5)
Feelin' Alive Again (5)
Fool Like Me (5)
For Openers (Welcome Home) (5)
Harvey (2)

Heart To Heart (3)
Holdin' On To Yesterday (1) 17
How Can You Love Me (5) 86
How Much I Feel (3) 3
I Wanna Know (2)
Ice Age (5)
If Heaven Could Find Me (3)
Kamikaze (4)

Kid No More (5)
Life Beyond L.A. (3)
Livin' On My Own (4)
Lover Arrive (1)
Make Us All Aware (1)
Mama Frog (1)
Nice, Nice, Very Nice (1) 63
No Big Deal (4)
Not As You Were (3)

Ready (4)
Ready For Camarillo (3)
Rock N' A Hard Place (4)
Runnin' Away (2)
Shape I'm In (4)
Somewhere I've Never Travelled (2)
Still Not Satisfied (5)
Time Waits For No One (1)

We Need You Too (2)
World Leave Me Alone (1)
You're The Only Woman (You & I) (4) 13

AMECHE, Don, & Frances Langford   '62

Ameche was born on 5/31/08 in Kenosha, Wisconsin. Died of cancer on 12/6/93 (age 85). Langford was born on 4/4/13 in Lakeland, Florida. Both began their movie careers in 1935. Their ongoing skit as the quarreling "John & Blanche Bickerson" began as a radio comedy in 1946.

4/7/62	76	12	1	The Bickersons..	[C]	$20	Columbia 1692
11/3/62	109	6	2	The Bickersons Fight Back	[C]	$20	Columbia 1883

Bickersons At Sea (1)

Breakfast With John And Blanche (1)

Later That Same Evening (1)
Round I-IV (2)

Wedding Anniversary (1)

AMERICA   '72
★209★

Soft-rock trio formed in London. Consisted of Americans Dan Peek and Gerry Beckley, with Englishman Dewey Bunnell. All played guitars. Met at U.S. Air Force base. Moved to the U.S. in February 1972. Won the 1972 Best New Artist Grammy Award. Peek left in 1976.

1)America 2)History/America's Greatest Hits 3)Holiday

2/19/72	❶	5	40	▲	©	1	America	$12	Warner 2576
12/2/72+	9		32	▲	©	2	Homecoming	$12	Warner 2655
11/17/73	28		18			3	Hat Trick	$12	Warner 2728
7/13/74	3		53	●		4	Holiday	$12	Warner 2808
4/5/75	4		44	●		5	Hearts	$12	Warner 2852
11/22/75	3		63	▲⁴	©	6	History/America's Greatest Hits [G]	$12	Warner 2894
5/1/76	11		22	●		7	Hideaway	$12	Warner 2932
3/12/77	21		14			8	Harbor	$12	Warner 3017
12/17/77+	129		7			9	America/Live [L]	$12	Warner 3136
							recorded at the Greek Theatre in Los Angeles		
7/7/79	110		6			10	Silent Letter	$10	Capitol 11950
9/6/80	142		6			11	Alibi	$10	Capitol 12098
8/28/82	41		28		©	12	View From The Ground	$10	Capitol 12209
7/2/83	81		14			13	Your Move	$10	Capitol 12277
11/10/84	185		3			14	Perspective	$10	Capitol 12370

All Around (10)
All My Life (10)
All Night (1)

Amber Cascades (7,9) 75
And Forever (10)
Another Try (4,9)

Are You There (8)
Baby It's Up To You (4)
Bell Tree (5)

Border, The (13) 33
California Revisited (2)

(Can't Fall Asleep To A) Lullaby (14)
Can't You See (7)

Cast The Spirit (13)
Catch That Train (11)
Children (1)

AMERICA — Cont'd

Cinderella (14)
Clarice (1)
Coastline (11)
Company (5,9)
Cornwall Blank (2)
Daisy Jane (5,6,9) *20*
Desperate Love (12)
Don't Cross The River (2,6) *35*
Don't Let It Get You Down (7)
Don't Let Me Be Lonely (13)
Don't You Cry (8)
Donkey Jaw (1)
Down To The Water (8)
Even The Score (12)
Fallin' Off The World (14)
5th Avenue (14)
Foolin' (10)
Glad To See You (4)
God Of The Sun (8)
Goodbye (3)
Green Monkey (3)

Half A Man (5)
Hangover (11)
Hat Trick (3)
Head & Heart (2)
Here (1)
Hideaway Part I & II (7)
High In The City (10)
Hollywood (4,9)
Honey (13)
Horse With No Name (1,6,9) *1*
Hurricane (8)
I Do Believe In You (11)
I Don't Believe In Miracles (11)
I Need You (1,6,9) *9*
In The Country (4)
Inspector Mills (12)
It's Life (3)
(It's Like You) Never Left At All (14)
Jet Boy Blue (7)
Jody (12)

Lady With A Bluebird (14)
Letter (7)
Lonely People (4,6) *5*
Love On The Vine (12)
Love's Worn Out Again (13)
Lovely Night (7)
Mad Dog (4)
Midnight (5)
Might Be Your Love (11)
Miniature (4)
Molten Love (3)
Monster (8)
Moon Song (2)
Muskrat Love (3,6,9) *67*
My Dear (13)
My Kinda Woman (13)
Never Be Lonely (12)
Never Found The Time (1)
1960 (10)
No Fortune (10)
Old Man Took (4,9)

Old Virginia (5)
One In A Million (11)
One Morning (10)
Only Game In Town (10)
Only In Your Heart (2,6) *62*
People In The Valley (5)
Pigeon Song (1)
Political Poachers (8)
Rainbow Song (3)
Rainy Day (1)
Right Back To Me (11)
Right Before Your Eyes
 (12) *45*
Riverside (1)
Sandman (1,6)
Sarah (8)
Saturn Nights (2)
Seasons (5)
See How The Love Goes (14)
Sergeant Darkness (8,9)
She's A Liar (7)

She's A Runaway (13)
She's Beside You (7)
She's Gone (8)
She's Gonna Let You Down (3)
Slow Down (8)
Someday Woman (13)
Sometimes Lovers (12)
Special Girl (14)
Stereo (14)
Story Of A Teenager (15)
Submarine Ladies (3)
Survival (14)
Tall Treasures (10)
These Brown Eyes (8)
Three Roses (1)
Till The Sun Comes Up Again
 (2)
Tin Man (4,6,9) *4*
To Each His Own (2,9)
Today's The Day (7) *23*

Sister Golden Hair (5,6,9) *1*

Tomorrow (5)
Tonight Is For Dreamers (13)
Unconditional Love (14)
Valentine (11)
Ventura Highway (2,6,9) *8*
Watership Down (7)
We Got All Night (14)
What Does It Matter (4)
Who Loves You (7)
Willow Tree Lullaby (3)
Wind Wave (3)
Woman Tonight (5,6) *44*
You (4)
You Can Do Magic (12) *8*
You Could've Been The One
 (11)
You Girl (12)
Your Move (13)

AMERICAN ANGEL   '90

Hard-rock group from New Jersey: Rocco Furiero (vocals), Petey D. and Danny Monchek (guitars), Steve Evetts (bass) and Eric Nilla (drums).

DEBUT	PEAK	WKS	RIAA	CD	ARTIST — Album Title	$	Label & Number
3/24/90	164	9		©	American Angel	$10	Grudge 4518

After The Laughter
Back To You

Bring The World Back
Grand Theft Ecstasy

How Can I Miss You
I Wanna Be A Millionaire

It Don't Come Easy
Lessons

Lonely Brown
Teenage Runaway

AMERICAN BREED, The   '68

Pop-rock group from Chicago: Gary Loizzo (vocals, guitar), Al Ciner (guitar), Chuck Colbert (bass) and Lee Graziano (drums). Later members Kevin Murphy (keyboards) and Andre Fischer (drums) went on to form **Rufus**.

DEBUT	PEAK	WKS			ARTIST — Album Title	$	Label & Number
2/24/68	99	10			Bend Me, Shape Me	$30	Acta 38003

Before And After
Bend Me, Shape Me *5*

Bird
Don't It Make You Cry

Don't Make Me Leave You
Green Light *39*

I've Been Tryin'
Mindrocker

No Easy Way Down
Something You've Got

Sometime In The Morning

AMERICAN DREAM, The   '70

Rock group: Nicky Indelicato (vocals), Nick Jameson and Don Lee Van Winkle (guitars), Don Ferris (bass) and Mickey Brook (drums). Jameson went on to produce several albums as a member of **Foghat**.

DEBUT	PEAK	WKS			ARTIST — Album Title	$	Label & Number
2/28/70	194	2			The American Dream	$20	Ampex 10101

produced by **Todd Rundgren**

Big Brother
Cadillac

Credemphels
Frankford El

Future's Folly
Good News

I Ain't Searchin'
I Am You

My Babe
Other Side

Raspberries
Storm

AMERICAN FLYER   '76

Folk-rock group: Craig Fuller (**Pure Prairie League**), Eric Kaz (**Blues Magoos**), Steve Katz (**Blood, Sweat & Tears**) and Doug Yule (**The Velvet Underground**).

DEBUT	PEAK	WKS			ARTIST — Album Title	$	Label & Number
9/4/76	87	10			1 American Flyer	$12	United Artists 650
7/2/77	171	5			2 Spirit Of A Woman	$12	United Artists 720

Back In '57 (1)
Call Me, Tell Me (1)
Dear Carmen (2)
Drive Away (1)

End Of A Love Song (1)
Flyer (2)
Gamblin Man (2)
Good Years (2)

I'm Blowin' Away (2)
Keep On Tryin' (2)
Lady Blue Eyes (1)
Let Me Down Easy (1) *80*

Light Of Your Love (1)
Love Has No Pride (1)
M (1)
My Love Comes Alive (2)

Queen Of All My Days (1)
Spirit Of A Woman (2)
Such A Beautiful Feeling (1)
Victoria (2)

Woman In Your Heart (1)

AMERICAN HI-FI   '01

Male rock group from Boston: Stacy Jones (vocals), Jaime Arentzen (guitar), Drew Parsons (bass) and Brian Nolan (drums). Jones was drummer with **Letters To Cleo**.

DEBUT	PEAK	WKS			ARTIST — Album Title	$	Label & Number
3/17/01	81	25		©	American Hi-Fi	$10	Island 542871

Another Perfect Day
Bigger Mood
Blue Day

Don't Wait For The Sun
Flavor Of The Weak *41*
Hi-Fi Killer

I'm A Fool
My Only Enemy
Safer On The Outside

Scar
Surround
Wall Of Sound

What About Today

★434★ AMES, Ed   '67

Born Ed Urick on 7/9/27 in Malden, Massachusetts. One of **The Ames Brothers**. Actor on Broadway and TV. Played "Mingo" on the *Daniel Boone* TV series.

1)My Cup Runneth Over 2)Who Will Answer? 3)When The Snow Is On The Roses

DEBUT	PEAK	WKS	RIAA	CD	ARTIST — Album Title	$	Label & Number
11/5/66	90	7			1 More I Cannot Wish You	$15	RCA Victor 3636
3/4/67	4	81	●	©	2 My Cup Runneth Over	$15	RCA Victor 3774
7/8/67	77	38			3 Time, Time	$15	RCA Victor 3834
12/9/67	11[X]	8			4 Christmas with Ed Ames [X]	$15	RCA Victor 3838
					Christmas charts: 11/67, 12/68		
12/16/67+	24	25			5 When The Snow Is On The Roses	$15	RCA Victor 3913
2/24/68	13	50	●	©	6 Who Will Answer? And Other Songs Of Our Time	$15	RCA Victor 3961
8/10/68	135	14			7 Apologize	$15	RCA Victor 4028
12/21/68	186	6			8 The Hits Of Broadway And Hollywood	$15	RCA Victor 4079
3/8/69	114	14			9 A Time For Living, A Time For Hope	$15	RCA Victor 4128
7/5/69	157	6			10 The Windmills Of Your Mind	$15	RCA Victor 4172
10/18/69	119	16			11 The Best Of Ed Ames [G]	$15	RCA Victor 4184
1/3/70	172	6			12 Love Of The Common People	$15	RCA Victor 4249
7/11/70	194	2			13 Sing Away The World	$15	RCA Victor 4381
2/20/71	199	1			14 The Songs Of Bacharach And David	$15	RCA Victor 4453

Adios Amor (Goodbye My Love)
 (13)
After All The Loves Of My Life
 (7)
Alfie (14)
Apologize (7,11) *79*
Au Revoir (2)

Away In The Manger (4)
Ballad Of The Christmas
 Donkey (4)
Ballad Of The Sad Young Men
 (1)
Blowin' In The Wind (6)
Bon Soir Dame (2,11)

Born Free (7)
Bound For Glory (El Camino
 Real) (2)
Bridge Over Troubled Water
 (13)
Cabaret (3)
Can't Take My Eyes Off You (6)

Canticle ..see: Scarborough
 Fair
Cast Your Fate To The Wind (1)
Changing, Changing (9,11)
Cherish (6)
Climb Ev'ry Mountain (1)
Color Of Snow (7,11)

Deck The Halls (4)
Deserted Carousel (1)
Do You Hear What I Hear (4)
Do You Know The Way To San
 Jose (14)
Don't Blame Me (2)
Early In The Morning (13)

Edelweiss (2)
Elvira (7)
Feelings (10)
First Noël (4)
Funny Girl (8)
Games People Play (12)
Happy Heart (10)

AMES, Ed — Cont'd

Here With You (3)
Honey (7)
Honey, What's The Matter? (13)
How Are Things In Glocca Morra (8)
How Does A Man Become A Puppet (14)
I Believe (9)
I Can't Give You Anything But Love (8)
I Heard The Bells On Christmas Day (4)
I Just Can't Help Believin' (10)
I Say A Little Prayer (14)
I Still See Elisa (1)
I Wanna Be Free (6)
I Wonder As I Wander (4)
I'll Get By (As Long As I Have You) (5)
I'll Never Fall In Love Again (13)
I'll Stay Lonely (10)
If I Can Dream (9)
If I Can Help Somebody (9)

If I Ever Get To Saginaw Again (10)
If I Had A Hammer (The Hammer Song) (9)
If She Walked Into My Life (1)
Impossible Dream (The Quest) (1,11)
In The Arms Of Love (2)
It's Today (1)
Joy To The World (4)
Just A Drop Of Rain (9)
Kiss Her Now (8,11)
Let It Snow! Let It Snow! Let It Snow! (4)
Let Me So Love (5)
Let's Get Together (12)
Lift Ev'ry Voice And Sing (12)
Little Green Apples (12)
Look Of Love (8,14)
Love Is Blue (7)
Love Of The Common People (12)

Love That Lasts Forever (3)
Make It Easy On Yourself (14)
Mary In The Morning (5)
Massachusetts (6)
Melinda (2)
Michelle (2)
Monday, Monday (6)
More (5)
More I Cannot Wish You (1)
My Cup Runneth Over (2,11) *8*
My Love Is Gone From Me (5)
Nikki (5,14)
O Come, All Ye Faithful (Adeste Fideles) (4)
On A Clear Day (You Can See Forever) (8)
One Little Girl At A Time (3)
Other Man's Grass Is Always Greener (6)
Our Love Is A Living Thing (2)
Pale Venetian Blind (6)
Peaceful Waters (9)
Sweet Little Jesus Boy (4)

Proud Mary (10)
Put A Little Love In Your Heart (12)
Raindrops Keep Fallin' On My Head (13,14)
Rose Of Washington Square (1)
Scarborough Fair/Canticle (7)
Seasons Of Love (5)
Shadow Of Your Smile (8)
Sing Away The World (13)
(Sittin' On) The Dock Of The Bay (10)
Six Words (9)
Somethin' Stupid (3)
Somewhere (9)
Somewhere, My Love (8)
Son Of A Travelin' Man (10) *92*
Sound Of Silence (9)
Strangers (5)
Sunny (7)
Sunrise, Sunset (3)

There's A Kind Of Hush (All Over The World) (6)
There's A Time For Everything (2)
There's No Business Like Show Business (8)
(They Long To Be) Close To You (14)
Thing Called Love (12)
Thirty Days Hath September (7)
This Guy's In Love With You (12)
Three Good Reasons (13)
Time, Time (3,11) *61*
Timeless Love (5)
To Say Goodbye To Anne (10)
Today Is The First Day Of The Rest Of Our Lives (12)
Traces (5)
Travelin' Band (7)
Trolley Song (1)
True Love (2)
Try To Remember (11) *73*

Two Different Worlds (13)
Two For The Road (5)
Until It's Time For You To Go (13)
Walking Happy (8)
Watch What Happens (2)
What A Wonderful World (9)
What Are You Doing The Rest Of Your Life (13)
What The World Needs Now Is Love (3,14)
When The Snow Is On The Roses (5,11) *98*
Who Will Answer? (6,11) *19*
Who Will Buy? (8)
Windmills Of Your Mind (10)
Wish Me A Rainbow (3)
Without A Song (1)
Wives And Lovers (14)
Yesterday (6)

AMES, Nancy   '66
Born Nancy Alfaro in 1937 in Washington DC. Singer/actress. Her grandfather was president of Panama. Cast as the "TW3 Girl" on TV's satirical revue *That Was The Week That Was.*

9/26/64	133	4	1 **This Is The Girl That Is**	[F] $20	Liberty 7369
10/29/66	133	8	2 **Latin Pulse**	[F] $15	Epic 26189

Anna (1)
Ayer (Yesterday) (2)
Besame Mucho (1)
Carcara (2)

Choucoune (1)
Dimelo (Call Me) (2)
El Dia Que Me Quieras (2)
El Gallito Kikiriki (1)

El Tambor De La Alegria (1)
Eso Beso (That Kiss!) (2)
Fay-O (1)
Guantanamera (1)

Guarare (1)
La Sombra De Tu Sonrisa (The Shadow Of Your Smile) (2)
La Ultima Noche (1)

Malaguena Salerosa (1)
Michel (2)
Noche De Ronda (1)
1-2-3 (2)

Perdoname Mi Vida (2)
Un Gusto A Miel (A Taste Of Honey) (2)
Yours (Quiereme Mucho) (1)

AMES BROTHERS, The   '57
Pop vocal group from Malden, Massachusetts: brothers Gene, Joe, Vic and **Ed Ames**. Vic died in a car crash on 1/23/78 (age 51). Also see *Merry Christmas* (Christmas Albums section).

12/2/57	16	4	**There'll Always Be A Christmas**	[X] $30	RCA Victor 1541

C-H-R-I-S-T-M-A-S
Christmas Song (Chestnuts Roasting On An Open Fire)
Deck The Halls

Go Tell It On The Mountain
Good King Wenceslas
Jingle Bells
Night Before Christmas Song

O Holy Night! (Cantique De Noel)
Santa Claus Is Comin' To Town
Silver Bells

There'll Always Be A Christmas
What Child Is This (Greensleeves)

AMG   '92
Born Jason Lewis on 9/29/70 in Brooklyn, New York. Male rapper.

12/21/91+	63	32	● ©	1 **Bitch Betta Have My Money**	$10	Select 21642
6/24/95	100	3	©	2 **Ballin' Outta Control**	$10	Select 21654
					Yo Momma Told Me... (1)

Around The World (2)
Baby Is It Maybe? (2)
Backseat Queenz (2)
Ballin' Outta Control (2)
Be Mai Bitch (2)

Bitch Betta Have My Money (1)
Booty Up (1)
Butt Booty Naked (2)
D. Control (1)
Fly Way (2)

Givva Dogga Bone (1)
I Wanna Be Yo Ho (1)
Jiggable Pie (1)
Leather And Wood (2)
Lick 'Em Low Lover (1)

Mai Sista Izza Bitch (1)
Nu Exasize (1)
Once A Dawg (Janine 2) (1)
Pimp Of The Century (1)
Sucka For Luv (2)

304 Thang (1)
Trunk O' Funk (1)
Vertical Interlude (1)
Vertical Joyride (1)
Word 2 Tha D (1)

AMIL   '00
Born Amil Whitehead in New York City. Female rapper.

10/7/00	45	6	©	**A.M.I.L. (All Money Is Legal)**	$10	Roc-A-Fella 63936

All Money Is Legal (A.M.I.L.)
Anyday
4 Da Fam

Get Down
Girlfriend
Heard It All

I Got That
No 1 Can Compare
Quarrels

Raw
Smile 4 Me
That's Right

Ya'll Dead Wrong

AMMONS, Gene   '63
Born Eugene Ammons on 4/14/25 in Chicago. Died of cancer on 8/6/74 (age 49). Tenor saxophonist. Nicknamed "Jug." Son of boogie-woogie pianist Albert Ammons.

12/22/62+	53	17	©	1 **Bad! Bossa Nova**	[I] $40	Prestige 7257
6/6/70	174	2	©	2 **The Boss Is Back!**	[I] $20	Prestige 7739

Anna (1)
Ca'Purange (1)

Cae' Cae' (1)
Feeling Good (2)

Here's That Rainy Day (2)
I Wonder (2)

Jungle Boss (2)
Madame Queen (2)

Moito Mato Grosso (1)
Pagan Love Song (2)

Tastin' The Jug (2)
Yellow Bird (1)

AMOS, Tori   '96
Born Myra Ellen Amos on 8/22/63 in Newton, North Carolina; raised in Baltimore. Singer/songwriter/pianist.

4/4/92	54	38	▲² ©	1 **Little Earthquakes**	C:#24/22 $10	Atlantic 82358
2/19/94	12	35	▲² ©	2 **Under The Pink**	$10	Atlantic 82567
2/10/96	2¹	29	▲ ©	3 **Boys For Pele**	$10	Atlantic 82862
9/7/96	94	3	©	4 **Hey Jupiter**	[L-M] $10	Atlantic 82955
5/23/98	5	20	▲ ©	5 **From The Choirgirl Hotel**	$10	Atlantic 83095
10/9/99	12	11	▲ ©	6 **To Venus And Back**	[L] $15	Atlantic 83230 [2]

Disc 1: new studio recordings; Disc 2: live recordings

Agent Orange (3)
Baker Baker (2)
Bells For Her (2,6)
Black-Dove (January) (5)
Blood Roses (3)
Bliss (6) *91*
Caught A Lite Sneeze (3) *60*
China (1)
Cloud On My Tongue (2,6)
Concertina (6)
Cooling (6)
Cornflake Girl (2,6)

Crucify (1)
Cruel (5,6)
Datura (6)
Doughnut Song (3)
Father Lucifer (3)
Girl (1,6)
Glory Of The 80's (6)
God (2) *72*
Happy Phantom (1)
Hey Jupiter (3,4)
Honey (4)
Horses (3)

Hotel (5)
Icicle (1)
iieee (5)
In The Springtime Of His Voodoo (3)
Jackie's Strength (5) *54*
Josephine (3)
Juárez (3)
Leather (1)
Liquid Diamonds (5)
Little Amsterdam (3)
Little Earthquakes (1,6)

Lust (6)
Marianne (3)
Me And A Gun (1)
Mother (1)
Mr Zebra (3,6)
Muhammad My Friend (3)
Northern Lad (5)
Not The Red Baron (3)
Pandora's Aquarium (5)
Past The Mission (2)
Playboy Mommy (5)
Precious Things (1,6)

Pretty Good Year (2)
Professional Widow (3,4)
Purple People (6)
Putting The Damage On (3)
Raspberry Swirl (5)
Riot Proof (6)
She's Your Cocaine (5)
Silent All These Years (1) *65*
Somewhere Over The Rainbow (4)
Space Dog (2,6)
Spark (5) *49*

Spring Haze (6)
Suede (6)
Sugar (4,6)
Talula (6)
Tear In Your Hand (1)
1000 Oceans (6)
Twinkle (3)
Waitress, The (2,6)
Way Down (3)
Winter (1)
Wrong Band (2)
Yes, Anastasia (2)

ANA — '90
Born Ana Rodriguez on 2/22/72 in Cuba; raised in Orlando, Florida. Female dance singer.

| 6/23/90 | 191 | 2 | © | **Body Language** .... | | | $10 | Parc 45355 |

Angel Of Love   Everytime We Say Goodbye   **Got To Tell Me Something** 66   Over And Over   Three Steps Closer
Body Language   Friendly   Miracles   So Outrageous   What Could I Do

ANASTACIA — '01
Born Anastacia Newkirk on 9/17/75 in New York City; raised in Chicago. Female singer.

| 4/14/01 | 168 | 4 | © | **Not That Kind**.. | | | $10 | Daylight 69948 |

Black Roses   I Ask Of You   Made For Lovin' You   Same Old Story   Yo Trippin'
Cowboys & Kisses   **I'm Outta Love** 92   Not That Kind   Who's Gonna Stop The Rain
Don'tcha Wanna   Late Last Night   One More Chance   Why'd You Lie To Me

ANDA, Geza — '68
Born in Budapest, Hungary. Classical pianist.

| 6/29/68 | 115 | 17 | | **Mozart: Piano Concertos Nos. 17 & 21** .... | [I] | | $20 | DG 138783 |

Concerto For Piano And   Concerto For Piano And
  Orchestra No. 17 In G Major,   Orchestra No. 21 In C Major,
  K. 453   K. 467

ANDERSEN, Eric — '75
Born on 2/14/43 in Pittsburgh. Folk singer/songwriter.

| 7/15/72 | 169 | 11 | © | 1 | **Blue River** .... | | | $15 | Columbia 31062 |
| 4/19/75 | 113 | 9 | | 2 | **Be True To You**.. | | | $12 | Arista 4033 |

Be True To You (2)   Can't Get You Out Of My Life   Is It Really Love At All (1)   More Often Than Not (1)   Sheila (1)   Wind And Sand (1)
Blue River (1)   (2)   Liza, Light The Candle (2)   Ol '55 (2)   Time Run Like A Freight Train   Woman, She Was Gentle (2)
Blues Keep Fallin' Like The   Faithful (1)   Love Is Just A Game (2)   Pearl's Goodtime Blues (1)   (2)
  Rain (2)   Florentine (1)   Moonchild River Song (2)   Round The Bend (1)   Wildcrow Blues (2)

ANDERSON, Bill — '63
Born James William Anderson III on 11/1/37 in Columbia, South Carolina. Country singer/songwriter/actor. Known as "Whispering Bill."

| 7/6/63 | 36 | 17 | | **Still**.. | | | $25 | Decca 74427 |

Down Came The Rain   Happiness   Little Band Of Gold   Reverend Mr. Black   Take These Chains From My
From A Jack To A King   I Wish It Was Mine   Molly   **Still** 8   Heart
Get A Little Dirt On Your Hands   It's Been So Long Darling   Restless

ANDERSON, Carl — '86
Born on 2/27/45 in Lynchburg, Virginia. R&B singer/actor. Played "Judas" in the original Broadway cast and movie version of the rock opera *Jesus Christ Superstar*.

| 8/23/86 | 87 | 12 | © | **Carl Anderson** .... | | | $10 | Epic 40410 |

Buttercup   Can't Stop This Feeling   **Friends And Lovers** 2   Mr. V.J.   You Are My Shining Star
C'est La Vie   First Time On A Ferris Wheel   Just A Little Love   Woman In Love

ANDERSON, Ernestine — '58
Born on 11/11/28 in Houston. Jazz singer.

| 10/20/58 | 15 | 6 | | **Hot Cargo!** .... | | | $40 | Mercury 20354 |

Autumn In New York   Experiment   Little Girl Blue   My Man   Wrap Your Troubles In Dreams
Day Dream   Ill Wind (You're Blowin' Me No   Love For Sale   Song Is Ended   (And Dream Your Troubles
Did I Remember   Good)   Mad About The Boy   That Old Feeling   Away)

ANDERSON, John — '92
Born on 12/13/54 in Orlando, Florida; raised in Apopka, Florida. Country singer/songwriter/guitarist.

4/9/83	58	12	● ©	1	**Wild & Blue**			$10	Warner 23721
10/29/83	163	5		2	**All The People Are Talkin'**			$10	Warner 23912
2/29/92	35	75	▲² ©	3	**Seminole Wind**			$10	BNA 61029
7/10/93	75	20	● ©	4	**Solid Ground**			$10	BNA 66232
8/16/97	138	4	©	5	**Takin' The Country Back**			$10	Mercury 536004

All The People Are Talkin' (2)   Goin' Down Hill (1)   It's A Long Way Back (5)   Nashville Tears (4)   South Moon Under (5)   Who's Who (5)
All Things To All Things (4)   Haunted House (2)   Jump On It (5)   Occasional Eagle (2)   Steamy Windows (3)   Wild And Blue (1)
Bad Love Gone Good (4)   Hillbilly Hollywood (3)   Last Night I Laid Your Memory   Old Mexico (2)   Straight Tequila Night (3)
Black Sheep (2)   Honky Tonk Hearts (1)   To Rest (3)   Price Of A Thin Silver Dime (1)   Swingin' (1) 43
Blue Lights And Bubbles (2)   Honky Tonk Saturday Night (1)   Let Go Of The Stone (3)   Sara (5)   Takin' The Country Back (5)
Brown Eyed Girl (5)   I Fell In The Water (4)   Let Somebody Else Drive (2)   Seminole Wind (3)   Things Ain't Been The Same
Call On Me (2)   I Used To Love Her (5)   Long Black Veil (1)   She Never Looked That Good   Around The Farm (2)
Can't Get Away From You (4)   I Wish I Could Have Been   Look Away (3)   When She Was Mine (1)   Waltz You Saved For Me (1)
Cold Day In Hell (3)   There (4)   Look What Followed Me Home   Small Town (5)   When It Comes To You (3)
Disappearing Farmer (1)   I've Got It Made (4)   (2)   Solid Ground (4)   Where I Come From (4)
Fall, The (5)   If A Broken Heart Could Kill (1)   Money In The Bank (4)   Somebody Slap Me (5)   Who Got Our Love (3)

ANDERSON, John W. — see KASANDRA

ANDERSON, Jon — '76
Born on 10/25/44 in Lancashire, England. Lead singer of **Yes**. Half of **Jon & Vangelis** duo.

7/24/76	47	13		1	**Olias Of Sunhillow**			$12	Atlantic 18180
12/6/80+	143	11		2	**Song Of Seven**..			$10	Atlantic 16021
7/3/82	176	5		3	**Animation**			$10	Atlantic 19355
12/28/85+	166	5		4	**3 Ships**	[X]		$10	Elektra 60469

All Gods Children (3)   Ding Dong Merrily On High (4)   Heart Of The Matter (2)   Much Better Reason (3)   Solid Space (1)   Unlearning (The Dividing Line)
All In A Matter Of Time (3)   Don't Forget (Nostalgia) (2)   Holly And The Ivy (4)   Ocean Song (1)   Some Are Born (2)   (3)
Animation (3)   Easier Said Than Done (4)   How It Hits You (4)   Oh Holy Night (4)   Song Of Seven (2)   Where Were You? (4)
Boundaries (3)   Everybody Loves You (2)   Jingle Bells (4)   Olympia (3)   Surrender (3)
Dance Of Ranyart Olias (To   Flight Of The Moorglade (1)   Meeting (Garden Of Geda)   Pressure Point (3)   Take Your Time (2)
  Build The Moorglade) (1)   For You For Me (2)   Sound Out The Galleon (1)   Qoquaq En Transic Naon   Three Ships (4)
Day Of Days (4)   Forest Of Fire (4)   Moon Ra Chords Song Of   Transic To (1)   To The Runner (1)
Days (2)   Hear It (2)   Search (1)   Save All Your Love (4)   2,000 Years (4)

ANDERSON, Laurie '84

Born on 6/5/47 in Chicago. Avant-garde performance artist.

DEBUT	PEAK	WKS		CD	#	Album Title	Sym	$	Label & Number
5/29/82	124	12		©	1	**Big Science**		$10	Warner 3674
3/17/84	60	19		©	2	**Mister Heartbreak**		$10	Warner 25077
1/26/85	192	5		©	3	**United States Live**	[L]	$50	Warner 25192 [5]
						recorded in February 1983 at the Brooklyn Academy of Music			
4/26/86	145	12		©	4	**Home Of The Brave**	[S]	$10	Warner 25400
11/18/89	171	12		©	5	**Strange Angels**		$10	Warner 25900
11/12/94	195	1		©	6	**Bright Red**		$10	Warner 45534

Babydoll (5)
Bagpipe Solo (3)
Beautiful Pea Green Boat (6)
Beautiful Red Dress (5)
Beginning French (3)
Big Science (1,3)
Big Top (3)
Blue Lagoon (2,3)
Born, Never Asked (1,3)
Bright Red (6)
Cartoon Song (3)
Cello Solo (3)
City Song (3)
Classified (3)
Closed Circuits (3)
Coolsville (5)
Credit Racket (4)
Curious Phenomenon (3)
Dance Of Electricity (3)
Day The Devil (5)
Democratic Way (3)

Difficult Listening Hour (3)
Dr. Miller (3)
Dog Show (3)
Dream Before (5)
English (3)
Example #22 (1,3)
Excellent Birds (2)
False Documents (3)
Finnish Farmers (3)
Fireworks (3)
For A Large And Changing Room (3)
Four, Three, Two, One (3)
Frames For The Pictures (3)
Freefall (3)
From The Air (1,3)
Going Somewhere? (3)
Gravity's Angel (2)
Healing Horn (3)
Hey Ah (3)
Hiawatha (5)

Hothead (La Langue D'Amour) (3)
I Dreamed I Had To Take A Test (3)
If You Can't Talk About It, Point To It (3)
In Our Sleep (6)
It Tango (1,3)
It Was Up In The Mountains (3)
Kokoku (2)
Language Is A Virus From Outer Space (3,4)
Language Of The Future (3)
Langue D'Amour (2)
Late Show (4)
Let X=X (1,3)
Lighting Out For The Territories (3)
Looking For You (3)
Love Among The Sailors (6)
Mach 20 (3)

Mailman's Nightmare (3)
Monkey's Paw (5)
Muddy River (6)
My Eyes (5)
Neon Duet (3)
New Jersey Turnpike (3)
New York Social Life (3)
Night In Baghdad (6)
O Superman (For Massenet) (1,3)
Odd Objects (3)
Over The River (3)
Pictures Of It (3)
Poison (6)
Private Property (3)
Puppet Motel (6)
Radar (4)
Ramon (5)
Red Map (3)
Reverb (3)
Rising Sun (3)

Running Dogs (3)
Same Time Tomorrow (6)
Sax Duet (3)
Sax Solo (3)
Say Hello (3)
Sharkey's Day (2)
Sharkey's Night (2,4)
Small Voice (3)
Smoke Rings (4)
So Happy Birthday (3)
Song For Two Jims (3)
Speak My Language (6)
Speechless (6)
Steven Weed (3)
Stiff Neck (3)
Strange Angels (5)
Stranger, The (3)
Strike (3)
Sweaters (1,3)
Talk Normal (4)
Talkshow (3)

Telephone Song (3)
Three Songs For Paper, Film And Video (3)
Three Walking Songs (3)
Tightrope (6)
Time And A Half (3)
Violin Solo (3)
Violin Walk (3)
Visitors, The (3)
Voices On Tape (3)
Walk The Dog (3)
Walking And Falling (1,3)
We've Got Four Big Clocks (And They're All Ticking) (3)
White Lily (4)
World Without End (6)
Yankee See (3)

ANDERSON, Lynn '71

Born on 9/26/47 in Grand Forks, North Dakota; raised in Sacramento, California. Country singer. Daughter of country singer Liz Anderson.

1)Rose Garden 2)You're My Man 3)Cry

DEBUT	PEAK	WKS		CD	#	Album Title	Sym	$	Label & Number
4/12/69	197	2			1	**With Love, From Lynn**		$20	Chart 1013
5/3/69	180	3			2	**The Best Of Lynn Anderson**	[G]	$20	Chart 1009
1/9/71	19	33	▲	©	3	**Rose Garden**		$15	Columbia 30411
7/24/71	99	14		©	4	**You're My Man**		$15	Columbia 30793
10/30/71	174	4			5	**The World Of Lynn Anderson**	[K]	$20	Columbia 30902 [2]
12/4/71	132	5			6	**How Can I Unlove You**		$15	Columbia 30925
12/18/71	13[X]	1		©	7	**The Christmas Album**	[X]	$15	Columbia 30957
4/8/72	114	9			8	**Cry**		$15	Columbia 31316
9/9/72	160	7			9	**Listen To A Country Song**		$15	Columbia 31647
11/11/72	129	14	●	©	10	**Lynn Anderson's Greatest Hits**	[G]	$15	Columbia 31641
8/11/73	179	3			11	**Top Of The World**		$15	Columbia 32429

Alabam' (5)
All Day Sucker (5,6)
All You Add Is Love (1)
Another Lonely Night (3)
Ask Any Woman (8)
Auctioneer (1)
Be Quiet Mind (1)
Bedtime Story (8)
Beggars Can't Be Choosers (2)
Big Girls Don't Cry (2)
Cotton Jenny (8)
Country Girl (5)
Cry (8,10) *63*
Cry, Cry Again (4)
Danny's Song (11)
Ding-A-Ling The Christmas Bell (7)
Don't Leave The Leaving Up To Me (5)
Don't Say Things You Don't Mean (6,10)
Don't Wish Me Merry Christmas (7)
Easy Lovin' (6)
Everybody's Reaching Out For Someone (9)
Fancy (5)
Fickle Fortune (11)
Flattery Will Get You Everywhere (1)
Flower Of Love (1)

Flying Machine (4)
Fool Me (9)
For The Good Times (3)
Frosty The Snowman (7)
Good (5)
Heavenly Sunshine (5)
Hello Darlin' (5)
Help Me Make It Through The Night (4)
Here I Go Again (6)
Honey Come Back (5)
How Can I Unlove You (6,10) *63*
Husband Hunting (5)
I Can Spot A Cheater (4)
I Don't Want To Play House (3)
I Live To Love You (2)
I Might As Well Be Here Alone (4)
I Saw Mommy Kissing Santa Claus (7)
I Still Belong to You (3)
I Wish I Was A Little Boy Again (3)
I Won't Mention It Again (8)
I'd Run A Mile To You (5)
I'm Gonna Write A Song (4,10)
I'm Still Loving You (11)
I've Been Everywhere (2)
If I Can't Be Your Woman (9)

If I Kiss You (Will You Go Away) (2)
It Don't Do No Good To Be A Good Girl (9)
It's Only Make Believe (3)
Jingle Bell Rock (7)
Joy To The World (4)
Just Keep It Up (9)
Kids Say The Darndest Things (11)
Killing Me Softly With His Song (11)
Kiss Away (8)
Knock Three Times (4)
Listen To A Country Song (9,10)
Lonely Women Make Good Lovers (11)
Million Shades Of Blue (1)
Mr. Mistletoe (7)
Never Ending Song Of Love (8)
Night The Lights Went Out In Georgia (11)
No Another Time (2)
No Love At All (5,10)
Nobody Wins (1)
Nothing Between Us (3,10)
Only Baby That'll Walk The Line (1)
Our House Is Not A Home (For It's Never Been Loved In) (1)

Promises, Promises (2)
Proud Mary (4)
Put Your Hand In The Hand (4)
Reason To Believe (9)
Ride, Ride, Ride (2)
Rockin' Around The Christmas Tree (7)
Rose Garden (3,10) *3*
Rudolph The Red-Nosed Reindeer (7)
Simple Words (6)
Sing About Love (11)
Sing Me A Sad Song (2)
Snowbird (3)
Someday Soon (5)
Soon It Will Be Christmas Day (7)
Spirit Of Chistmas (7)
Stand By Your Man (1)
Stay There 'Til I Get There (5,10)
Strangers (2)
Sunday Morning Coming Down (3)
Take Me Home, Country Roads (6)
Take Me To Your World (9)
That's What Loving You Has Meant To Me (6,9,10)
There Oughta Be A Law (2)
There's A Party Goin' On (9)

There's Never Been Anyone Like You (6)
Thing Called Love (11)
Time's Just Right (5)
Tomorrow Never Comes (5)
Tonight My Baby's Coming Home (8)
Too Many Dollars, Not Enough Sense (1)
Too Much Of You (2)
Top Of The World (11) *74*
True Love's A Blessing (5)
Wave By Bye To The Man (1)
We Can Make It (8)
We've Got To Get It On Again (8)
What's Made Milwaukee Famous (6)
When You Hurt Me More Than I Love You (5)
When You Say Love (8)
Whistle And A Whisker Away (7)
Wife You Save May Be Your Own (1)
Woman Lives For Love (5)
Words (5)
You're Everything (9)
You're My Man (4,10) *63*
You've Got A Friend (6)
Your Sweet Love Lifted Me (3)

ANDERSON, Michael '88

Born in Grand Rapids, Michigan. Rock singer/songwriter.

DEBUT	PEAK	WKS		CD	Album Title		$	Label & Number
8/13/88	194	2			**Sound Alarm**		$10	A&M 5203

I Know That You Can Stand
I Need You

Little Bit O' Love
Memphis Radio

Sanctuary
Shine A Light

Sound Alarm
Soweto Soul

Time To Go Home
Until You Loved Me

ANDERSON, Sunshine '01

Born in 1975 in Charlotte, North Carolina. Female R&B singer.

DEBUT	PEAK	WKS		CD	Album Title		$	Label & Number
5/5/01	5	17	●	©	**Your Woman**		$10	Soulife 93011

Being Away
Better Off
Crazy Love

He Said, She Said
Heard It All Before *18*
Last Night

Letting Down My Guard
Little Sunshine
Lunch Or Dinner

Saved The Day
Where Have You Been
You Do You

Your Woman

ANDERSON, BRUFORD, WAKEMAN, HOWE — see YES

ANDREWS, Jessica   '01
Born on 12/29/83 in Huntingdon, Tennessee. Country singer.

| 3/17/01 | 22 | 29↑ | © | **Who I Am** | $10 | DreamWorks 450248 |

Every Time — Helplessly, Hopelessly — Karma — Never Had It So Good — Show Me Heaven — **Who I Am** *28*
Good Friend To Me — I Don't Like Anyone — Make Me Love You — Now I Know — These Wings — Wishing Well

ANDREWS, Julie   '62
Born Julia Wells on 10/1/35 in Walton-on-Thames, England. Noted Broadway and movie actress.

| 9/1/62 | 85 | 9 | | 1 **Julie And Carol at Carnegie Hall** | [L] | $25 | Columbia 2240 / 5840 |

JULIE ANDREWS & CAROL BURNETT
recorded on 6/11/62

| 12/2/67 | 9ˣ | 6 | © | 2 **A Christmas Treasure** | [X] | $20 | RCA Victor 3829 |

JULIE ANDREWS WITH ANDRÉ PREVIN
Christmas charts: 9/'67, 52/'68

Angels From The Realm Of Glory (2) — From Switzerland: The Pratt Family (1) — Irish Carol (2) — No Mozart Tonight (1) — You're So London (1)
Away In A Manger (2) — From Texas: Big "D" (1) — It Came Upon The Midnight Clear (2) — Oh Dear What Can The Matter Be (1)
Bells Of Christmas (2) — God Rest You Merry, Gentlemen (2) — Jingle Bells (2) — Oh Little Town Of Bethlehem (2)
Deck The Halls (2) — Greensleeves (2) — Joy To The World (2) — Sunny Bank (2)
From Russia: The Nausiev Ballet (1) — History Of Musical Comedy (1) — Lamb Of God (2) — Meantime (1) — Wexford Carol (2)

ANDREWS SISTERS   '73
Female vocal trio from Minneapolis: sisters Patty, Maxene and LaVerne Andrews. LaVerne died of cancer on 5/8/67 (age 51). Maxene died of a heart attack on 10/21/95 (age 77). The trio had several popular chart hits and appeared in many movies during the 1940s.

10/6/73	126	9		1 **The Best Of The Andrews Sisters**	[G]	$20	MCA 4024 [2]
10/13/73	167	7		2 **Boogie Woogie Bugle Girls**	[K]	$15	Paramount 6075
7/13/74	137	3		3 **Over Here!**	[OC]	$15	Columbia 32961
7/20/74	198	1		4 **In The Mood**	[K]	$20	Paramount 1023 [2]

Beat Begins (Overture) (3) — Dixie (4) — I Can Dream, Can't I? (1,4) — Old Piano Roll Blues (2,4) — There Will Never Be Another You (1)
Beat Me Daddy, Eight To The Bar (1,2,4) — Don't Shoot The Hooey To Me, Louie (3) — I Wanna Be Loved (1,4) — Over Here! (3) — Three Little Fishes (Itty Bitty Poo) (2,4)
Beer Barrel Polka (1,4) — Don't Sit Under The Apple Tree (With Anyone Else But Me) (1,2) — I'll Be With You In Apple Blossom Time (1) — Pennsylvania Polka (1,2,4) — Ti-Pi-Tin (1)
Bei Mir Bist Du Schoen (1,2,4) — In The Mood (2,4) — Pistol Packin' Mama (2,4) — Tico-Tico (1)
Big Beat (3) — Down In The Valley (4) — Joseph! Joseph! (1) — Rhumboogie (1,2,4) — Wait For Me, Marlena (3)
Blue Hawaii (4) — Dream Drummin' (medley) (3) — My Dream For Tomorrow (3) — Rum And Coca-Cola (1,2) — Wartime Wedding (3)
Boogie Woogie Bugle Boy (1,2,4) — Good Time Girl (3) — Near You (4) — Sabre Dance (4) — We Got It! (3)
Buy A Victory Bond (3) — Grass Grows Green (medley) (3) — No Goodbyes (3) — Say "Si Si" (1,4) — Well All Right (3)
Charlie's Place (3) — Hawaiian Wedding Song (4) — Nobody's Darling' But Mine (4) — Since You're Not Around (3) — Where Did The Good Times Go? (3)
Ciribiribin (4) — Hey Yvette (medley) (3) — Oh Johnny, Oh Johnny, Oh! (1,2) — Soft Music (medley) (3) — Yes, My Darling Daughter (1)
Cool Water (4) — Hold Tight (Sea Food) (1,2) — Oh! Ma-Ma! (The Butcher Boy) (1,4) — Sonny Boy (1)
Daddy (2) — South American Way (1) — Strip Polka (1) — Tennessee Waltz (4)

ANGEL   '78
Hard-rock group from Washington DC: Frank DiMino (vocals), Punky Meadows (guitar), Gregg Giuffria (keyboards), Mickey Jones (bass) and Barry Brandt (drums). Felix Robinson replaced Jones by 1978. Giuffria later formed **Giuffria** and **House Of Lords**.

12/20/75+	156	6	©	1 **Angel**		$12	Casablanca 7021
6/19/76	155	10	©	2 **Helluva Band**		$12	Casablanca 7028
3/5/77	76	12	©	3 **On Earth As It Is In Heaven**		$12	Casablanca 7043
2/4/78	55	13	©	4 **White Hot**		$12	Casablanca 7085
3/3/79	159	5	©	5 **Sinful**		$12	Casablanca 7127
2/23/80	149	4	©	6 **Live Without A Net**	[L]	$15	Casablanca 7203 [2]

Ain't Gonna Eat Out My Heart Anymore (4,6) *44* — Cast The First Stone (3) — Fortune, The (2) — Long Time (1) — Rock & Rollers (1) — Waited A Long Time (5)
All The Young Dudes (6) — Chicken Soup (2) — Got Love If You Want It (4,6) — Lovers Live On (5) — She's A Mover (3) — White Lightning (3,6)
Angel (Theme) (1,2) — Dr. Ice (2) — Hold Me, Squeeze Me (4,6) — Mariner (1) — Stick Like Glue (4) — Wild And Hot (5,6)
Anyway You Want It (2,6) — Don't Leave Me Lonely (4,6) — I'll Bring The Whole World To Your Door (5) — Mirrors (2) — Sunday Morning (1) — Winter Song (4)
Bad Time (5) — Don't Take Your Love (5) — I'll Never Fall In Love Again (5) — On & On (1) — Telephone Exchange (3,6) — You Can't Buy Love (5)
Big Boy (Let's Do It Again) (3) — Feelin' Right (2,6) — Just A Dream (3) — On The Rocks (3,6) — **That Magic Touch** (3) *77* — You Could Lose Me (4)
Broken Dreams (1) — Feelings (2) — Just Can't Take It (5) — Over And Over (4,6) — Tower (1,6) — You're Not Fooling Me (3)
Can You Feel It (3,6) — Flying With Broken Wings (Without You) (4) — L.A. Lady (5) — Pressure Point (3) — 20th Century Foxes (6)
Rock & Rollers (6) — Under Suspicion (4)

ANGEL CITY   '80
Hard-rock group from Australia: Doc Neeson (vocals), brothers Rick and John Brewster (guitars), Jim Hilbun (bass) and Brent Eccles (drums).

5/10/80	152	7	©	1 **Face To Face**		$10	Epic 36344
11/8/80	133	6		2 **Darkroom**		$10	Epic 36543
3/20/82	174	5		3 **Night Attack**		$10	Epic 37702

After The Rain (1) — Comin' Down (1) — Living On The Outside (3) — No Exit (1) — Shadow Boxer (1) — Wasted Sleepless Nights (medley) (2)
Am I Ever Gonna See Your Face Again (1) — Darkroom (medley) (2) — Long Night (3) — No Secrets (2) — Storm The Bastille (3)
Back On You (3) — Devil's Gate (2) — Marseilles (1) — Nothin To Win (3) — Straightjacket (2)
Can't Shake It (1) — Face The Day (2) — Moment, The (2) — Out Of The Blue (1) — Take A Long Line (1)
City Out Of Control (3) — Fashion & Fame (3) — Night Attack (3) — Poor Baby (3) — Talk About You (3)
Ivory Stairs (2) — Night Comes Early (2) — Runnin Wild (3) — Waiting For The World (1)

ANGELS, The   '63
Female vocal trio from Orange, New Jersey: sisters Phyllis and Barbara Allbut, with Peggy Santiglia.

| 9/28/63 | 33 | 14 | | **My Boyfriend's Back** | | $75 | Smash 67039 |

Guy With The Black Eye — Hurdy-Gurdy Man — Someday My Prince Will Come — Why Don't The Boy Leave Me
Has Anybody Seen My Boyfriend — Love Me Now — **Thank You And Goodnight** *84* — Alone
He's So Fine — Night Has A Thousand Eyes — **My Boyfriend's Back** *1* — World Without Love
'Til *14*

ANIMAL LOGIC '90
All-star rock trio: Deborah Holland (vocals), **Stanley Clarke** (bass) and **Stewart Copeland** (drums).

12/9/89+	**106**	21		©	Animal Logic			$10	I.R.S. 82020

As Soon As The Sun Goes Down • Firing Up The Sunset Gun • I'm Sorry Baby (I Want You In My Life) • Someday We'll Understand • There's A Spy (In The House Of Love) • Elijah • I Still Feel For You • I'm Through With Love • Someone To Come Home To • Winds Of Santa Ana

★237★ ANIMALS, The '66
Rock group from Newcastle, England: **Eric Burdon** (vocals), Hilton Valentine (guitar), **Alan Price** (keyboards), Bryan "Chas" Chandler (bass) and John Steel (drums). Price left in May 1965, replaced by Dave Rowberry. Chandler pursued a management career and discovered **Jimi Hendrix** in 1966; died in his sleep of an apparent heart attack on 7/17/96 (age 57). Steel left in 1966, replaced by Barry Jenkins. Group disbanded in July 1968. After a period with **War**, Burdon and the other originals reunited in 1976 and again in 1983. Inducted into the Rock and Roll Hall of Fame in 1994.
1)The Best Of The Animals 2)The Animals 3)Animalization

9/5/64	**7**	27		1	The Animals			$30	MGM 4264
3/20/65	**99**	9		2	The Animals On Tour			$30	MGM 4281
9/18/65	**57**	25		3	Animal Tracks			$30	MGM 4305
2/12/66	**6**	113	● ©	4	The Best Of The Animals	[G]		$30	MGM 4324
8/20/66	**20**	30		5	Animalization			$30	MGM 4384
12/3/66+	**33**	22	©	6	Animalism			$30	MGM 4414

ERIC BURDON & THE ANIMALS:

3/25/67	**121**	13	©	7	Eric Is Here			$30	MGM 4433
6/10/67	**71**	24		8	The Best Of Eric Burdon And The Animals, Vol. II	[G]		$30	MGM 4454
9/23/67	**42**	20		9	Winds Of Change			$30	MGM 4484
4/6/68	**79**	29	©	10	The Twain Shall Meet			$30	MGM 4537
8/24/68	**152**	8	©	11	Every One Of Us			$30	MGM 4553
1/11/69	**123**	10	©	12	Love Is			$50	MGM 4591 [2]
3/15/69	**153**	6		13	The Greatest Hits Of Eric Burdon And The Animals	C:#40/6 [G]		$30	MGM 4602

THE ANIMALS:

8/25/73	**188**	2		14	Best Of The Animals	[G]		$20	Abkco 4226
8/27/77	**70**	11	©	15	Before We Were So Rudely Interrupted			$15	United Artists 790
9/10/83	**66**	10	©	16	Ark			$12	I.R.S. 70037
9/15/84	**193**	4	©	17	Rip It To Shreds - The Animals Greatest Hits Live!	[L]		$12	I.R.S. 70043

recorded on 12/31/83 at Wembley Arena in London

Ain't Got You (2) • All Is One (10) • All Night Long (6) • Anything (9,13) 80 • Around And Around (1,14) • As The Crow Flies (15) • As The Years Go Passing By (12) • Baby Let Me Take You Home (1,14) • Being There (16) • Biggest Bundle Of Them All (7) • Black Plague (9) • Blue Feeling (1) • Boom Boom (2,4,14,17) 43 • Bright Lights, Big City (2) • Bring It On Home To Me (3,4,14,17) 32 • Brother Bill (The Last Clean Shirt) (15) • Bury My Body (3,14) • Cheating (9,13) • Closer To The Truth (10) • Club A-GoGo (3) • Colored Rain (12) • Crystal Nights (16) • Dimples (2,14) • **Don't Bring Me Down** (5,8,17) 12 • **Don't Let Me Be Misunderstood** (3,4,17) 15 • Fire On The Sun (15) • Fool, The (15) • For Miss Caulker (3) • Gemini - The Madman (12) • Gin House Blues (5) • Girl Can't Help It (1) • Girl Named Sandoz (8) • Going Down Slow (6) • **Gonna Send You Back To Walker (Gonna Send You Back To Georgia)** (1,4,14) 57 • Good Times (9) • Gotta Get Back To You (14) • Hallelujah, I Love Her So (2) • Hard Times (16) • **Help Me Girl** (7,8) 29 • Hey Gyp (6,8) • Hit The Road, Jack (6) • Hotel Hell (9) • House Of The Rising Sun (1,4,14,17) 1 • How You've Changed (2) • I Believe To My Soul (3) • I Can't Believe It (3) • I Put A Spell On You (5) • I Think It's Gonna Rain Today (7) • I'm An Animal (12) • **I'm Crying** (2,4,14,17) 19 • I'm Dying, Or Am I? (12) • I'm In Love Again (1,4,14) • I'm Mad (1,4) • I've Been Around (1) • Immigrant Lad (1) • In The Night (7) • **Inside-Looking Out** (5,8) 34 • It's All Meat (9) • It's All Over Now, Baby Blue (15) • It's Been A Long Time Comin' (7) • **It's My Life** (4,14,17) 23 • It's Not Easy (7) • It's Too Late (17) • Just A Little Bit (15) • Just Can't Get Enough (16) • Just The Thought (10) • Let The Good Times Roll (2) • Lonely Avenue (15) • Loose Change (16) • Losin' Control (7) • Louisiana Blues (6) • Love Is For All Time (16) • Lucille (6) • Mama Told Me Not To Come (7) • Man - Woman (9) • Many Rivers To Cross (15) • Maudie (5) • Melt Down (16) • Memphis, Tennessee (1) • Mess Around (2) • **Monterey** (10,13) 15 • My Favorite Enemy (16) • New York 1963-America 1968 (11) • **Night, The** (16) 48 • No Self Pity (10) • O Lucky Man! (17) • One Monkey Don't Stop No Show (5) • Orange And Red Beams (10) • Other Side Of This Life (6,8) • Outcast (6) • Paint It Black (9) • Please Send Me Someone To Love (15) • Poem By The Sea (9) • Prisoner Of The Light (16) • Right Time (1) • Ring Of Fire (12) • River Deep, Mountain High (12,13) • Riverside County (15) • Roberta (3,4) • Rock Me Baby (6) • **San Franciscan Nights** (9,13) 9 • **See See Rider** (5,8) 10 • Serenade To A Sweet Lady (11) • Shake (6) • She Said Yeah (2) • She'll Return It (5,8) • **Sky Pilot (Part One)** (10,13) 14 • Smoke Stack Lightning (6) • St. James Infirmary (15) • Story Of Bo Diddley (3,14) • Sweet Little Sixteen (5) • Take It Easy Baby (3) • Talkin' 'Bout You (1,14) • That Ain't Where It's At (7,8) • That's All I Am To You (6) • This Side Of Goodbye (7) • To Love Somebody (12,13) • True Love (Comes Only Once In A Lifetime) (7) • Trying To Get To You (16) • Uppers And Downers (11) • Wait Till Next Year (7) • **We Gotta Get Out Of This Place** (3,4,14,17) 13 • We Love You Lil (10) • What Am I Living For (5) • **When I Was Young** (8) 15 • **White Houses** (11,13) 67 • Winds Of Change (9,13) • Worried Life Blues (2) • Year Of The Guru (11,13) • Yes I Am Experienced (9) • You're On My Mind (5,8)

ANIMOTION '85
Techno-pop group: Astrid Plane (female vocals), Bill Wadhams (male vocals, keyboards), Don Kirkpatrick (guitar), Charles Ottavio (bass) and Frency O'Brien (drums). Plane and Wadhams left by 1988, replaced by Cynthia Rhodes and Paul Engemann. Rhodes was an actress (in movies *Staying Alive* and *Dirty Dancing*). Engemann was formerly with **Device**. Rhodes married **Richard Marx** on 1/8/89. Plane and Ottavio married on 10/13/90.

2/23/85	**28**	30	©	1	Animotion			$10	Mercury 822580
3/15/86	**71**	14	©	2	Strange Behavior			$10	Casablanca 826691
3/25/89	**110**	17	©	3	Animotion			$10	Polydor 837314

Anxiety (2) • Best Mistake (3) • **Calling It Love** (3) 53 • Do Like I Do (3) • Essence, The (2) • Everything's Leading To You (1) • Fun Fun Fun (1) • Ground Zero (3) • Holding You (1) • House Of Love (3) • **I Engineer** (2) 76 • **I Want You** (2) 84 • Let Him Go (1) 39 • Message Of Love (3) • **Obsession** (1) 6 • One Step Ahead (2) • Open Door (1) • Out Of Control (2) • **Room To Move** (3) 9 • Run To Me (1) • Send It Over (3) • Staring Down The Demons (2) • Stealing Time (2) • Stranded (2) • Strange Behavior (2) • Tremble (1) • Turn Around (1) • Way Into Your Heart (3)

★261★ ANKA, Paul '60
Born on 7/30/41 in Ottawa, Ontario, Canada. Singer/songwriter. Wrote "She's A Lady" for **Tom Jones** and the English lyrics to "My Way" for **Frank Sinatra**. Also wrote theme for TV's *Tonight Show*. Own TV variety show in 1973. Cameo appearances in the 1962 movie *The Longest Day* and the 1992 movie *Captain Ron*.
1)Paul Anka Sings His Big 15 2)Anka 3)Times Of Your Life

7/4/60	**4**	140		1	Paul Anka Sings His Big 15	[G]		$50	ABC-Paramount 323
12/5/60+	**23**	27		2	Anka At The Copa	[L]		$50	ABC-Paramount 353

recorded on 7/6/60 at the Copacabana in New York City

9/25/61	**72**	12		3	Paul Anka Sings His Big 15, Vol. 2	[G]		$50	ABC-Paramount 390
4/14/62	**61**	12		4	Young, Alive And In Love!			$30	RCA Victor 2502
9/15/62	**137**	2		5	Let's Sit This One Out			$30	RCA Victor 2575

ANKA, Paul — Cont'd

DEBUT	PEAK	WKS			ARTIST — Album Title	Sym	$	Label & Number
7/6/63	65	33	©	6	Paul Anka's 21 Golden Hits	[G]	$30	RCA Victor 2691
					newly recorded versions of his ABC-Paramount hits			
3/15/69	101	11		7	Goodnight My Love		$25	RCA Victor 4142
12/27/69+	194	2		8	Life Goes On		$25	RCA Victor 4250
1/15/72	188	4		9	Paul Anka		$20	Buddah 5093
6/3/72	192	4		10	Jubilation		$20	Buddah 5114
8/31/74	9	28	●	11	Anka		$15	United Artists 314
12/14/74+	125	9		12	Paul Anka Gold	[G]	$20	Sire 3704 [2]
					original ABC-Paramount recordings			
4/5/75	36	29		13	Feelings		$15	United Artists 367
12/13/75+	22	25	●	14	Times Of Your Life	[K]	$15	United Artists 569
					9 of 10 cuts from previous 2 United Artists albums			
10/23/76+	85	15		15	The Painter		$15	United Artists 653
6/18/77	195	3		16	The Music Man		$15	United Artists 746
11/25/78	179	7		17	Listen To Your Heart		$12	RCA Victor 2892
5/9/81	171	6		18	Both Sides Of Love		$12	RCA Victor 3926
8/13/83	156	8		19	Walk A Fine Line		$10	Columbia 38442

Adam And Eve (1,6,12) 90
Aldous (15)
(All Of A Sudden) My Heart Sings (1,2,12) 15
Anchors Aweigh (2)
Anytime (I'll Be There) (13,14) 33
Aren't You Glad You're You? (4)
Bring The Wine (11,14)
Brought Up In New York (Brought Down In L.A.) (17)
Can't Get You Out Of My Mind (8)
Cinderella (6,12) 70
Closing Doors (15)
Crazy Love (1,6,12) 15
Daddy's Home (7)
Dance On Little Girl (3,6,12) 10
Dannon (16)
Darlin', Darlin' (19)
Diana (1,2,6,12) 1
Do I Love You (9,15) 53
Do What You Gotta Do (8)
Don't Ever Leave Me (1,6,12)
Don't Ever Say Goodbye (17)
Don't Gamble With Love (1,6,12)
Double Life (10)
Down By The Riverside (2)
Eleanor Rigby (8)
Embraceable You (5)
Everybody Ought To Be In Love (16) 75
Everything's Been Changed (9)
Falling In Love With Love (4)
Find My Way (8)
For Once In My Life (7)
Forgive And Forget (7)
Gimme The Word (19)
Girl, You Turn Me On (13)
Golden Boy (19)

Goodnight My Love (7) 27
Happier (15) 60
Happy (8) 86
Hello Young Lovers (2,12) 23
Hold Me 'Til The Mornin' Comes (19) 40
How Can Anything Be Beautiful (After You) (11)
(I Believe) There's Nothing Stronger Than Our Love (13,14) 15
I Can't Give You Anything But Love (2)
I Don't Like To Sleep Alone (13,14) 8
I Gave A Little And Lost A Lot (11)
I Love Life (4)
I Love You (4)
I Love You, Baby (1,6,12) 97
I Love You In The Same Old Way (3,6,12) 40
I Miss You So (1,12) 33
I Only Have Eyes For You (5)
I Wanna Be Loved (5)
I Was There (8)
I'd Even Let You Go (18)
I'd Have To Share (3)
I'll Help You (15)
I'll See You In My Dreams (5)
I'm A Do-It-Yourself Type Song Man (medley) (2)
I'm By Myself Again (17)
I'm Glad There Is You (In This World Of Ordinary People) (5)
I'm Still Waiting Here For You (6)
I've Been Waiting For You All Of My Life (18) 48
I've Gotta Be Me (7)
If I Had My Life To Live Over (16)
In The Still Of The Night (7) 64

It Doesn't Matter Any More (6,11)
It Had To Be You (5)
It's Sad To See The Old Hometown Again (13)
It's Time To Cry (1,2,12) 4
Jealous Lady (16)
Jubilation (10) 65
Just Young (3,12) 80
Kathum (10)
Keeping One Foot In The Door (8)
Kissin' On The Phone (12) 35
Lady Lay Down (18)
Late Last Night (3)
Les Filles De Paris (9)
Let Me Be The One (10)
Let Me Get To Know You (11,14) 80
Let The Bells Keep Ringing (3,12) 16
Let's Fall In Love (5)
Let's Sit This One Out (5)
Let's Start It Over (17)
Life Goes On (8)
Life Is Just A Bowl Of Cherries (4)
Life Song (10)
Listen To Your Heart (17)
Living Isn't Living (15)
Lonely Boy (1,2,6,12) 1
Longest Day (16)
Look What You've Done (18)
Love Is (10)
Love Is A Lonely Song (11)
Love Land (6)
Love Me Lady (17)
Love Your Spell Is Everywhere (4)
Mexican Night (16)
Midnight (1,12) 69
Music Man (16)
My Best Friend's Wife (16) 80

My Home Town (2,3,6,12) 8
My Little Girl's Become A Big Girl Now (16)
My Way (9)
Nearness Of You (5)
Never Gonna Fall In Love Again (Like I Fell In Love With You) (15)
Next Year (7)
No Way Out (19)
One For My Baby (And One More For The Road) (2)
One Man Woman/One Woman Man (11,14) 7
Out Of My Mind In Love (13)
Painter, The (15)
Papa (11,14)
Pickin' Up The Pieces (7)
Prelude (15)
Pretty Good (10)
Puppy Love (1,6,12) 2
Put Your Head On My Shoulder (1,2,6,12) 2
Roses Ain't Red (18)
Second Chance (19)
Second Thoughts (16)
She's A Lady (9)
Silhouettes (17)
Sing Sing Sing (medley) (2)
Slowdown (16)
Some Kind Of Friend (10)
Something About You (11)
Something Good Is Coming (10)
Something Happened (3,12) 41
Something Has Changed Me (3)
Starmaker (17)
Starting All Over Again (17)
Story Of My Love (3,12) 16
Summer's Gone (3,6,12) 11
Swanee (1)

Take Me In Your Arms (19)
Teach Me Tonight (5)
Tell It Like It Is (8)
Tell Me That You Love Me (3)
That's Love (1)
That's What Living's About (9)
There Is Something I'd Like To Say To You (9)
Think I'm In Love Again (18)
Think It Over Baby (7)
This Is Love (17) 35
This Is The First Time (19)
This Life Of Mine (4)
Time To Cry (6)
Times Of Your Life (14) 7
Today I Became A Fool (13)
Tonight (16)
Tonight My Love, Tonight (3,6,12) 5
Waiting For You (12)
Wake Up (13,14)
Walk A Fine Line (19)
Walk Away (13)
Water Runs Deep (13)
We Love Each Other (18)
We Made It Happen (9)
What's Forever For (18)
When I Stop Loving You (That'll Be The Day) (3)
Why Don't We Sleep On It Tonight (18)
Wildflower (15)
Yesterday My Life (9)
You And Me Today (10)
You And The Night And The Music (5)
You Are My Destiny (1,2,6,12) 7
(You Bring Out) The Best In Me (15)
You Go To My Head (5)
You Made Me Love You (2)

You Make Me Feel So Young (4)
You Send Me (7)
You Spoiled Me (17)
(You're) Having My Baby (11,14) 1
You're Just In Love (4)
You're Still A Part Of Me (18)
Young, Alive, And In Love (4)
Young And Foolish (4)
Younger Than Springtime (4)
Your Love (3,12)

ANNETTE   '60
Born Annette Funicello on 10/22/42 in Utica, New York. Became a Mouseketeer in 1955. Acted in several teen movies in the early '60s. Co-starred with **Frankie Avalon** in the 1987 movie *Back To The Beach*. Diagnosed with multiple sclerosis in 1987.

DEBUT	PEAK	WKS			ARTIST — Album Title	Sym	$	Label & Number
3/21/60	21	21		1	Annette Sings Anka		$100	Buena Vista 3302
9/26/60	38	3		2	Hawaiiannette		$75	Buena Vista 3303
10/19/63	39	13		3	Annette's Beach Party	[S]	$75	Buena Vista 3316
					half of the songs are from the movie *Beach Party* starring Annette and **Frankie Avalon**			

Aloha Oe (2)
And So It's Goodbye (1)
Battle Of San Onofre (3)
Beach Party (3)
Blue Hawaii (2)
Blue Muu Muu (2)

California Sun (3)
Don't Stop Now (3)
(Every Night Is) Date Night In Hawaii (2,3)
Hawaiiannette (2)
Hey, Mama (1)

Holiday In Hawaii (2)
Hukilau Song (2)
I Love You (1)
I Love You Baby (1)
It's Really Love (1)
Like A Baby (1)

Lonely Girl (1)
Luau Cha Cha Cha (2)
My Little Grass Shack (In Kealakekua, Hawaii) (2)
Now Is The Hour (2)
Pineapple Princess (2,3) 11

Promise Me Anything (3)
Secret Surfin' Spot (3)
Song Of The Islands (Na Lei O'Hawaii) (2,3)
Surfin' Luau (3)
Swingin' And Surfin' (3)

Talk To Me Baby (1) 92
Teddy (1)
Tell Me That You Love Me (1)
Train Of Love (1) 36
Treat Him Nicely (3)
Waiting For You (1)

ANN-MARGRET — see GARY, John / HIRT, Al

ANOINTED   '99
Gospel trio from Columbus, Ohio: Steve Crawford and his sister Da'dra Crawford, with Denise Walls.

DEBUT	PEAK	WKS			ARTIST — Album Title	Sym	$	Label & Number
5/8/99	159	2	©		Anointed		$10	Myrrh 69616

Anything Is Possible
Godspot

Head Above Water
It's All Good

Love By Grace
Must Have Been Angels

Ooh, Baby
Revive Us

Something Was Missing
Take It Eazy

ANOTHER BAD CREATION   '91
R&B vocal group from Atlanta: Chris Sellers, Dave Shelton, Romell Chapman, with brothers Marliss and Demetrius Pugh. Group appeared in the movie *The Meteor Man*.

DEBUT	PEAK	WKS			ARTIST — Album Title	Sym	$	Label & Number
3/9/91	7	52	▲ ©		Coolin' At The Playground Ya' Know!		$10	Motown 6318

A.B.C.
Iesha 9

Jealous Girl
Little Soldiers

My World
Parents

Playground 10
Spydermann

That's My Girl

ANT, Adam '83

Born Stuart Goddard on 11/3/54 in London. Formed romantic-punk group **Adam And The Ants** in 1976. Three original Ants left to join **Bow Wow Wow** and Ant headed new lineup in 1980. Ant went solo in 1982. Acted in several movies and TV shows.

ADAM AND THE ANTS:

DEBUT	PEAK	WKS	RIAA	CD	ARTIST — Album Title	$	Label & Number
2/28/81	44	35	●	© 1	Kings Of The Wild Frontier	$10	Epic 37033
12/12/81+	94	21		© 2	Prince Charming	$10	Epic 37615

ADAM ANT:

DEBUT	PEAK	WKS	RIAA	CD	ARTIST — Album Title	$	Label & Number
12/11/82+	16	36	●	© 3	Friend Or Foe	$10	Epic 38370
12/10/83	65	26		© 4	Strip	$10	Epic 39108
10/19/85	131	7		© 5	Vive Le Rock	$10	Epic 40159
3/3/90	57	20		© 6	Manners & Physique	$10	MCA 6315
3/25/95	143	9		© 7	Wonderful	$10	Capitol 30335

Alien (7)
Amazon (4)
Angel (7)
Anger Inc. (6)
Ant Rap (2)
Antmusic (1)
Ants Invasion (1)
Apollo 9 (5)
Baby, Let Me Scream At You (4)
Beautiful Dream (7)
Bright Lights Black Leather (6)
Cajun Twisters (3)
Can't Set Rules About Love (6)
Crackpot History And The Right To Lie (3)
Desperate But Not Serious (3) *66*
Dog Eat Dog (1)
Don't Be Square (Be There) (1)
Feed Me To The Lions (3)
5 Guns West (2)
Friend Or Foe (3)
Goody Two Shoes (3) *12*
Gotta Be A Sin (7)
Hell's Eight Acres (3)
Hello, I Love You (3)
Here Comes The Grump (3)
Human Beings (1)
If You Keep On (6)
Image Of Yourself (7)
Jolly Roger (1)
Killer In The Home (1)
Kings Of The Wild Frontier (1)
Libertine (4)
Los Rancheros (1)
Made Of Money (3)
Magnificent Five (1)
Man Called Marco (3)
Manners & Physique (6)
Mile High Club (3)
Miss Thing (5)
Mohair Lockeroom Pin-Up Boys (5)
Montreal (4)
Mowhok (2)
Navel To Neck (4)
1969 Again (7)
No Zap (5)
P.O.E. (5)
Physical (You're So) (1)
Picasso Visita El Planeta De Los Simios (2)
Piccadilly (3)
Place In The Country (3)
Playboy (4)
Press Darlings (1)
Prince Charming (2)
Puss 'N Boots (4)
Razor Keen (5)
Rip Down (5)
Room At The Top (6) *17*
Rough Stuff (6)
Scorpio Rising (5)
Scorpios (2)
S.E.X. (3)
Something Girls (3)
Spanish Games (4)
Stand And Deliver (2)
Strip (4) *42*
That Voodoo (7)
Try This For Sighs (3)
U.S.S.A. (6)
Vampires (7)
Vanity (4)
Very Long Ride (7)
Vive Le Rock (5)
Won't Take That Talk (7)
Wonderful (7) *39*
Yin & Yang (7)
Young Dumb And Full Of It (6)

ANTHONY, Marc '99

Born on 9/16/69 in New York City. Latin singer/actor. Starred in **Paul Simon**'s Broadway musical *The Capeman*.

DEBUT	PEAK	WKS	RIAA	CD	ARTIST — Album Title	Sym	$	Label & Number
11/22/97	74	9	●	© 1	Contra La Corriente	[F]	$10	RMM 82156

title is Spanish for "Against The Current"

DEBUT	PEAK	WKS	RIAA	CD	ARTIST — Album Title	Sym	$	Label & Number
10/16/99	8	83	▲³	© 2	Marc Anthony		$10	Columbia 69726
12/4/99+	151	18		© 3	Desde Un Principio / From The Beginning	[F]	$10	Sony Discos 83580

Am I The Only One (2)
Como Ella Me Quiere A Mí (She's Been Good To Me) (2)
Contra La Corriente (1,3)
Da La Vuelta (2)
Dímelo (I Need To Know) (2)
Don't Let Me Leave (2)
El Ultimo Beso (3)
Hasta Ayer (3)
Hasta Que Te Conoci (3)
How Could I (2)
I Need To Know (2) *3*
La Luna Sobre Nuestro Amor (1)
Love Is All (2)
Me Voy A Regalar (1)
My Baby You (2) *70*
Nadie Como Ella (3)
Necesito Amarte (3)
No Me Ames (3)
No Me Conoces (1,3)
No One (2)
No Sabes Como Duele (1,3)
Preciosa (3)
Remember Me (2)
She's Been Good To Me (3)
Si Te Vas (1)
Si Tu No Te Fueras (3)
Suceden (1)
Te Amare (3)
Te Conozco Bien (3)
That's Okay (2)
Un Mal Sueño (1)
Vivir Lo Nuestro (3)
When I Dream At Night (2)
Y Hubo Alguien (1,3)
You Sang To Me (2) *2*

ANTHONY, Ray '55

Born Raymond Antonini on 1/20/22 in Bentleyville, Pennsylvania; raised in Cleveland. Big band leader/trumpeter. Own TV series in the 1950s. Appeared in the movie *Daddy Long Legs*. Married for a time to actress Mamie Van Doren.

DEBUT	PEAK	WKS	RIAA	CD	ARTIST — Album Title	Sym	$	Label & Number
3/19/55	10	6		1	Golden Horn	[I]	$30	Capitol 563

LP: Capitol T-563 (#10); EP: Capitol ECF-563 (#11)

DEBUT	PEAK	WKS	RIAA	CD	ARTIST — Album Title	Sym	$	Label & Number
6/23/56	15	1		2	Dream Dancing	[I]	$30	Capitol 723
10/28/57	11	21		3	Young Ideas	[I]	$30	Capitol 866
5/19/58	12	10	©	4	The Dream Girl	[I]	$30	Capitol 969
7/21/62	14	19		5	Worried Mind	[I]	$25	Capitol 1752

Amor (1)
Bewitched (4)
Birth Of The Blues (1)
Born To Lose (5)
Brave Bulls (1)
Button Up Your Overcoat (3)
Careless Love (5)
Coquette (1)
Darn That Dream (4)
Dream Dancing (1)
Dream Girl (4)
Embraceable You (2)
Golden Horn (1)
Half As Much (5)
Holiday For Strings (1)
I Can't Stop Loving You (5)
I Didn't Know What Time It Was (4)
I Don't Know Why (I Just Do) (2)
I Fell In Love (4)
I Love You (3)
I Only Have Eyes For You (2)
I'll Never Smile Again (2)
It Ain't Necessarily So (1)
It Makes No Difference Now (5)
It's The Talk Of The Town (4)
Jeepers Creepers (1)
Just One Of Those Things (3)
Laura (2)
Lonely Night In Paris (3)
Moonglow (3)
Moonlight In Vermont (2)
My Foolish Heart (4)
My Private Melody (4)
Nearness Of You (4)
Nice Work If You Can Get It (3)
Out Of Nowhere (4)
Pretend (4)
Release Me (5)
September Song (2)
Skylark (1)
Stars Fell On Alabama (4)
Street Of Dreams (2)
Taking A Chance On Love (1)
Tango La Polma (1)
That Old Feeling (3)
This Love Of Mine (2)
Too Late To Worry - Too Blue To Cry (5)
Trumpet Sorrento (1)
Trumpeter's Lullaby (1)
Walking The Floor Over You (5)
Weary Blues From Waitin' (5)
When I Fall In Love (4)
Why Do I Love You? (3)
Worried Mind (5) *74*
Wrap Your Troubles In Dreams (And Dream Your Troubles Away) (3)
You Nearly Lose Your Mind (5)
You Turned The Tables On Me (3)
You'll Never Know (4)
Young Ideas (3)
Your Cheatin' Heart (5)

★436★ ANTHRAX '93

Hard-rock group from New York City: Joey Belladonna (vocals), Scott Ian and Dan Spitz (guitars), Frank Bello (bass) and Charlie Benante (drums). Belladonna left in early 1992; replaced by John Bush. Spitz left in 1994. Group appeared on TV's *Married...With Children* in 1992.

DEBUT	PEAK	WKS	RIAA	CD	ARTIST — Album Title	Sym	$	Label & Number
12/21/85+	113	18		© 1	Spreading The Disease		$10	Island 90480
4/11/87	62	36	●	© 2	Among The Living		$10	Island 90584
12/19/87+	53	40	▲	© 3	I'm The Man	[L-M]	$10	Island 90685

recorded on 7/11/87 in Dallas

DEBUT	PEAK	WKS	RIAA	CD	ARTIST — Album Title	Sym	$	Label & Number
10/8/88	30	36	●	© 4	State Of Euphoria		$10	Island 91004
9/8/90	24	31	●	© 5	Persistence Of Time		$10	Island 846480
7/13/91	27	25	●	© 6	Attack Of The Killer B's	[K]	$10	Island 848804

unreleased material and B-sides recorded from 1988-91

DEBUT	PEAK	WKS	RIAA	CD	ARTIST — Album Title	$	Label & Number
6/12/93	7	17	●	© 7	Sound Of White Noise	$10	Elektra 61430
11/11/95	47	3		© 8	Stomp 442	$10	Elektra 61856
8/8/98	118	2		© 9	Volume 8 - The Threat Is Real!	$10	Ignition 4034

A.D.I. (medley) (2)
Aftershock (1)
A.I.R. (1)
Alpha Male (9)
American Pompeii (8)
Among The Living (2)
Antisocial (4)
Armed And Dangerous (1)
Bare (4)
Be All, End All (4)
Belly Of The Beast (5,6)
Big Fat (9)
Black Lodge (7)
Blood (5)
Born Again Idiot (9)
Bring The Noise (6)
Burst (9)
C¹¹ H¹⁷ N² O² S Na (7)
Catharsis (8)
Caught In A Mosh (2,3)
Chromatic Death (6)
Crush (9)
Discharge (5)
Drop The Ball (8)
Efilnikufesin (N.F.L.) (2)
Enemy, The (1)
Finale (4)
Fueled (8)
Got The Time (5)
Gridlock (9)
Gung-Ho (4)
Harms Way (9)
H8 Red (5)
Hog Tied (9)
Horror Of It All (medley) (2)
Hy Pro Glo (7)
I Am The Law (2,3)
I'm The Man (6)
I'm The Man '91 (3)
Imitation Of Life (2)
In A Zone (8)
In My World (5)
Indians (2)
Inside Out (9)
Intro To Reality (5)
Invisible (7)
Keep It In The Family (5,6)
Killing Box (7)
King Size (6)
Lone Justice (1)
Madhouse (1)
Make Me Laugh (4)
Medusa (1)
Milk (Ode To Billy) (6)
Misery Loves Company (4)
N.F.B. (Dallabnikufesin) (6)
Nothing (8)
Now It's Dark (4)
One Man Stands (5)
One World (2)
Only (7)
Out Of Sight, Out Of Mind (4)
P & V (9)
Packaged Rebellion (7)
Parasite (6)
Perpetual Motion (8)

ANTHRAX — Cont'd

Pipeline (6)
Potters Field (7)
Protest And Survive (6)
Random Acts Of Senseless
  Violence (8)

Riding Shotgun (8)
Room For One More (7)
S.S.C. (medley) (1)
Sabbath Bloody Sabbath (3)
Schism (4)

Sects (8)
Skeleton In The Closet (2)
Stand Or Fall (medley) (1)
Startin' Up A Posse (6)
Stealing From A Thief (9)

Tester (8)
13 (4)
This Is Not An Exit (7)
1000 Points Of Hate (7)
Time (5)

Toast To The Extras (9)
Who Cares Wins (4)

ANVIL '87
Hard-rock group from Toronto: Steve "Lips" Kudlow (vocals, guitar), Dave Allison (guitar), Ian Dickson (bass) and Robb Reiner (drums).

| 7/18/87 | 191 | 2 | © | **Strength Of Steel** .... | $10 | Enigma 73267 |

Bumble Beast
Concrete Jungle
Cut Loose

I Dreamed It Was The End Of
  The World
Kiss Of Death

Mad Dog
9-2-5
Paper General

Straight Between The Eyes
Strength Of Steel
Wild Eyes

AORTA '69
Rock group from Chicago: Jim Donlinger (vocals, guitar), Jim Nyeholt (keyboards), Bobby Jones (bass) and Billy Herman (drums).

| 4/12/69 | 167 | 8 | | **Aorta** .... | $30 | Columbia 9785 |

Catalyptic
Heart Attack

Magic Bed
Main Vein I-IV
Sleep Tight

Ode To Missy Mztsfpklk
Strange

Sprinkle Road To Cork Street
Thoughts And Feelings
  (medley)

Thousand Thoughts
What's In My Mind's Eye

APACHE '93
Born Anthony Teaks in Jersey City, New Jersey. Male rapper.

| 2/27/93 | 69 | 6 | © | **Apache Ain't Shit** .... | $10 | Tommy Boy 1068 |

Apache Ain't Shit
Beginning, The
Blunted Snap Session

Do Fa Self
Fight, A
Gangsta Bitch *67*

Get Ya Weight Up
Hey Girl
Make Money

Tonto
Wayz Of A Murderahh
Who Freaked Who

Woodchuck

APOLLONIA 6 '84
Female R&B trio formed by **Prince**. Led by Patty "Apollonia" Kotero (co-star of movie *Purple Rain* and cast member of TV's *Falcon Crest*, 1985-86). With former **Vanity 6** members Brenda Bennett and Susan Moonsie.

| 10/27/84 | 62 | 17 | | **Apollonia 6** .... | $10 | Warner 25108 |

Blue Limousine
Happy Birthday, Mr. Christian

In A Spanish Villa
Million Miles (I Love You)

Ooo She She Wa Wa
Sex Shooter *85*

Some Kind Of Lover

APOLLO 100 '72
Studio group from England: Tom Parker, Clem Cattini, Vic Flick, Jim Lawless and Brian Odgers.

| 2/19/72 | 47 | 16 | | **Joy** .... [I] | $15 | Mega 1010 |

Air For The G String
Classical Wind
Evil Midnight (Danse Macabre)

Exercise In A Minor
Jazz Pizzicato
Joy *6*

Libido
Mad Mountain King (Hall Of
  The Mountain King)

**Mendelssohn's 4th (Second
  Movement)** *94*
Reach For The Sky

Tamara

APPALOOSA '69
Folk-rock group from Boston: John Parker Compton (vocals, guitar), Robin Batteau (violin), Gene Rosor (cello) and David Reiser (bass).

| 8/16/69 | 178 | 4 | © | **Appaloosa** .... | $20 | Columbia 9819 |

Bi-Weekly
Feathers

Georgia Street
Glossolalia

Now That I Want You
Pascal's Paradox

Rivers Run To The Sea
Rosalie

Thoughts Of Polly
Tulu Rogers

Yesterday's Roads

APPICE, Carmine — see BECK, Jeff

APPLE, Fiona '99
Born Fiona Apple Maggart on 9/13/77 in New York City. Singer/songwriter/pianist. Daughter of singer Diane McAfee and actor Brandon Maggart.

| 9/28/96+ | 15 | 91 | ▲³ | © | 1 **Tidal** .... | $10 | Clean Slate 67439 |
| 11/27/99 | 13 | 20 | ● | © | 2 **When The Pawn** .... | $10 | Clean Slate 69195 |

entire album title: When The Pawn Hits The Conflicts He Thinks Like A King What He Knows Throws The Blows When He Goes To
The Fight And He'll Win The Whole Thing 'Fore He Enters The Ring There's No Body To Batter When Your Mind Is Your Might So
When You Go Solo, You Hold Your Own Hand And Remember That Depth Is The Greatest Of Heights And If You Know Where You
Stand, Then You Know Where To Land And If You Fall It Won't Matter, Cuz You'll Know That You're Right

Carrion (1)
Child Is Gone (1)
Criminal (1) *21*
Fast As You Can (2)

First Taste (1)
Get Gone (2)
I Know (2)
Limp (2)

Love Ridden (2)
Mistake, A (2)
Never Is A Promise (1)
On The Bound (2)

Pale September (1)
Paper Bag (2)
Shadowboxer (1)
Sleep To Dream (1)

Slow Like Honey (1)
Sullen Girl (1)
To Your Love (2)
Way Things Are (2)

APRIL WINE '81
Rock group from Montreal: Myles Goodwyn (vocals, guitar), Brian Greenway and Gary Moffet (guitars), Steve Lang (bass) and Jerry Mercer (drums). Lang, Moffet and Mercer replaced by Daniel Barbe (keyboards), Jean Pellerin (bass) and Marty Simon (drums) in 1985.

4/21/79	114	11		©	1 **First Glance**	$12	Capitol 11852
11/10/79	64	40	●	©	2 **Harder...Faster**	$12	Capitol 12013
1/31/81	26	34	▲	©	3 **The Nature Of The Beast**	$10	Capitol 12125
7/10/82	37	20		©	4 **Power Play**	$10	Capitol 12218
3/17/84	62	12		©	5 **Animal Grace**	$10	Capitol 12311
10/5/85	174	4		©	6 **Walking Through Fire**	$10	Capitol 12433

Ain't Got Your Love (4)
All It Will Ever Be (6)
All Over Town (3)
Anejo (6)
Anything You Want, You Got It
  (4)
Babes In Arms (2)
Bad Boys (3)
Before The Dawn (2)
Beg For Your Love (6)
Better Do It Well (2)
Big City Girls (3)
Blood Money (4)

Caught In The Crossfire (3)
Comin' Right Down On Top Of
  Me (1)
Crash And Burn (3)
Doin' It Right (4)
Enough Is Enough (4) *50*
Future Tense (3)
Get Ready For Love (1)
Gimme That Thing Called Love
  (5)
Hard Rock Kid (5)
Hold On (6)
Hot On The Wheels Of Love (1)

I Like To Rock (2) *86*
I'm Alive (1)
If You See Kay (4)
Just Between You And Me
  (3) *21*
Ladies Man (2)
Last Time I'll Ever Sing The
  Blues (5)
Let Yourself Go (1)
Love Has Remembered Me (6)
Money Talks (5)
One More Time (3)
Open Soul Surgery (6)

Right Down To It (1)
Rock Myself To Sleep (6)
Rock N' Roll Is A Vicious Game
  (1)
Rock Tonite (5)
Roller (1) *34*
Runners In The Night (4)
Say Hello (2)
Sign Of The Gypsy Queen
  (3) *57*
Silver Dollar (1)
Sons Of The Pioneers (5)
Tell Me Why (4)

Tellin' Me Lies (3)
This Could Be The Right One
  (5) *58*
Tonite (2)
Too Hot To Handle (5)
21st Century Schizoid Man (2)
Wait Any More (6)
Waiting On A Miracle (4)
Wanna Rock (3)
Wanted Dead Or Alive (6)
What If We Fall In Love (4)
Without Your Love (5)

You Don't Have To Act That
  Way (6)

AQUA '97
Pop/dance group from Denmark: Lene Grawford Nystrom, Rene Dif, Claus Norreen and Soren Rasted.

9/27/97	7	50	▲³ ©	1	Aquarium			$10	MCA 11705
4/8/00	82	6	©	2	Aquarius			$10	MCA 157305

Apple A Day (2) | Barbie Girl (1) 7 | Cartoon Heroes (2) | Good Guys (2) | Happy Boys & Girls (1) | Roses Are Red (1)
Aquarius (2) | Be A Man (1) | Cuba Libre (2) | Good Morning Sunshine (1) | Heat Of The Night (1) | Turn Back Time (1)
Around The World (2) | Bumble Bees (2) | Doctor Jones (1) | Goodbye To The Circus (2) | Lollipop (Candyman) (1) 23 | We Belong To The Sea (2)
Back From Mars (2) | Calling You (1) | Freaky Friday (2) | Halloween (2) | My Oh My (1) |

AQUABATS, The '97
Ska-rock group from Huntington Beach, California: Christian Jacobs (vocals), Courtney Pollack (guitar), James Briggs, Adam Diebert and Boyd Terry (horns), Charles Grey (keyboards), Chad Larson (bass) and Travis Barker (drums). Barker joined **Blink 182** in 1998.

11/15/97	172	1	©		The Fury Of The Aquabats!			$10	Goldenvoice 43512

Attacked By Snakes! | Cat With 2 Heads! | Lobster Bucket! | My Skateboard! | Red Sweater! | Theme Song!
Captain Hampton And The | Fight Song! | Magic Chicken! | Phantasma Del Mar! | Story Of Nothing! |
Midget Pirates! | Idiot Box! | Martian Girl! | Powdered Milk Man! | Super Rad! |

AQUARIAN DREAM '76
Disco group: Pat Shannon and Connie Harvey (vocals), Pete Bartee (guitar), Claude Bartee (horns), Winston Daley (keyboards), David Worthy (percussion), Ernie Adams (bass) and Jim Morrison (drums).

10/9/76	154	6	©		Norman Connors presents Aquarian Dream			$12	Buddah 5672

East 6th Street | I'll Always Love You "T" | Look Ahead | Phoenix | Treat Me Like The One You
Guitar Talk | Let Me Be The One | Once Again | | Love

AQUARIANS '69
Instrumental studio group led by pianist Vladimir Vassilieff.

11/1/69	192	2			Jungle Grass		[I]	$20	United Artists 73053

Adela | Bayu-Bayu | Jungle Grass | What Do You Mean, What Do I
Aquarians, The | Excuses, Excuses | Mucho Soul | Mean?
Batakum | Head, The | Saja |

ARABIAN PRINCE '89
Born Michael Lezan in Compton, California. Male rapper. Former member of **Bobby Jimmy & The Critters**.

12/16/89	193	3			Brother Arab			$10	Orpheus 175614

Get On Up | It's A Dope Thang | Let The Good Times Roll | Never Caught Slippin' | She's Got A Big Posse | Sound Check
Gettin' Down | It's Time To Bone | (Nickel Bag) | Now You Have To Understand | Situation Critical

ARBORS, The '67
Pop vocal group formed in Ann Arbor, Michigan, by two pairs of brothers: Edward and Fred Farran, and Scott and Tom Herrick.

2/11/67	144	2			A Symphony For Susan			$20	Date 3003

Day In The Life Of A Fool | Just Let It Happen | My Foolish Heart | **Symphony For Susan 51**
(Manha De Carnaval) | Love Is The Light | Open A New Window | When I Fall In Love
Dreamer Girl | Mas Que Nada (Pow Pow Pow) | So Nice (Summer Samba) | You Are The Girl

ARCADE '93
Hard-rock group formed in Los Angeles: Stephen Pearcy (vocals; **Ratt**), Frank Wilsex (**Sea Hags**) and Donny Syracuse (guitars), Michael Andrews (bass) and Fred Coury (drums; **Cinderella**).

4/24/93	133	2	©		Arcade			$10	Epic 53012

All Shook Up | Cry No More | Livin' Dangerously | Mother Blues | Nothin' To Lose | So Good... So Bad...
Calm Before The Storm | Dancin' With The Angels | Messed Up World | Never Goin' Home | Screamin' S.O.S. | Sons And Daughters

ARCADIA '86
Pop-rock trio from England: **Duran Duran**'s Simon LeBon (vocals), Nick Rhodes (keyboards) and Roger Taylor (drums).

12/21/85+	23	17	▲ ©		So Red The Rose			$10	Capitol 12428

El Diablo | Flame, The | Keep Me In The Dark | Missing | Rose Arcana
Election Day 6 | **Goodbye Is Forever 33** | Lady Ice | Promise, The

ARC ANGELS '92
Rock group formed in Austin, Texas: **Charlie Sexton** (vocals, guitar), Doyle Bramhall II (guitar), Tommy Shannon (bass) and Chris Layton (drums). Shannon, Layton and Bramhall's father were members of **Stevie Ray Vaughan**'s band. ARC: Austin Rehearsal Complex.

5/16/92	127	22	©		Arc Angels			$10	DGC 24465

Always Believed In You | Famous Jane | Living In A Dream | See What Tomorrow Brings | Shape I'm In | Sweet Nadine
Carry Me On | Good Time | Paradise Cafe | Sent By Angels | Spanish Moon | Too Many Ways To Fall

ARCHER, Tasmin '93
Born in 1964 in Bradford, Yorkshire, England. Female singer of Jamaican parentage.

4/24/93	115	10	©		Great Expectations			$10	SBK 80134

Arienne | Hero | In Your Care | Ripped Inside | Somebody's Daughter | When It Comes Down To It
Halfway To Heaven | Higher You Climb | Lords Of The New Church | **Sleeping Satellite 32** | Steeltown

ARCHIES, The '69
Studio group created by Don Kirshner; based on the Saturday morning cartoon television series. Lead vocalist Ron Dante was also the ghost voice of **The Cuff Links** and co-producer of many of **Barry Manilow**'s hits. All tunes written and produced by Jeff Barry, who was half of a prolific hit-writing partnership with his then-wife Ellie Greenwich.

11/2/68+	88	21		1	The Archies			$25	Calendar 101
9/6/69	66	36	©	2	Everything's Archie			$25	Calendar 103
1/3/70	125	10		3	Jingle Jangle			$25	Kirshner 105
9/12/70	137	6		4	Sunshine			$25	Kirshner 107
11/28/70	114	12		5	The Archies Greatest Hits		[G]	$25	Kirshner 109

Archie's Party (3) | Circle Of Blue (2) | Hide And Seek (1) | La Dee Doo Down Down (1) | One Big Family (4) | Suddenly Susan (4)
Archie's Theme (Everything's | Comes The Sun (4) | Hot Dog (2) | Look Before You Leap (3) | Over And Over (4,5) | Sugar And Spice (3,5)
Archie) (1) | Dance (4) | I'm In Love (1) | Love And Rock 'N Roll Music | Ride, Ride, Ride (1) | **Sugar, Sugar** (2,5) 1
Bang-Shang-A-Lang (1,5) 22 | Don't Touch My Guitar (2) | Inside Out - Upside Down (2) | (4) | Rock & Roll Music (2) | Summer Prayer For Peace (4)
Bicycles, Roller Skates And | Everything's Alright (3,5) | It's The Summertime (4) | Love Light (2) | Rock & Roll Music (2) | **Sunshine** (4,5) 57
You (2) | **Feelin' So Good** | **Jingle Jangle** (3,5) 10 | Melody Hill (2) | Senorita Rita (3) | Time For Love (1)
Boys And Girls (1) | (S.k.o.o.b.y-D.o.o.) (2,5) 53 | Justine (2) | Mr. Factory (4) | Seventeen Ain't Young (1,5) | Truck Driver (1)
Catchin' Up On Fun (1) | Get On The Line (3,5) | Kissin' (2) | Nursery Rhyme (3) | She's Putting Me Thru Changes | Waldo P. Emerson Jones (4,5)
| | | | (3) |

ARCHIES, The — Cont'd

Who's Gonna Love Me (4)
Who's Your Baby? (5) *40*
Whoopee Tie Ai A (3)
You Know I Love You (3)
You Little Angel, You (2)
You Make Me Wanna Dance (1)

ARDEN, Jann '96
Born on 3/27/62 in Calgary, Alberta, Canada. Female singer/songwriter.

| 3/30/96 | 76 | 32 | ● | © | **Living Under June** | | | $10 | A&M 540336 |

Could I Be Your Girl
Demolition Love
Gasoline
Good Mother
I Would Die For You
Insensitive *12*
It Looks Like Rain
Living Under June
Looking For It (Finding Heaven)
Unloved
Wonderdrug

AREA CODE 615 '69
Country session group which included **Charlie McCoy** (harmonica) and Norbert Putnam (bass). The 615 area code is in Tennessee.

| 10/18/69 | 191 | 4 | | © | **Area Code 615** | [I] | | $20 | Polydor 4002 |

Classical Gas
Crazy Arms (medley)
Get Back (medley)
Hey Jude
I've Been Loving You Too Long (To Stop Now)
Lil' Maggie
Just Like A Woman
Lady Madonna
Nashville 9 - New York 1
Ruby
Southern Comfort
Why Ask Why?

ARENA, Tina '96
Born Philopina Arena on 11/1/67 in Melbourne, Australia. Female singer.

| 5/18/96 | 101 | 8 | | © | **Don't Ask** | | | $10 | Epic 67533 |

Be A Man
Chains *38*
Greatest Gift
Heaven Help My Heart
Love Is The Answer
Message
Show Me Heaven
Sorrento Moon (I Remember)
Standing Up
That's The Way A Woman Feels
Wasn't It Good

ARENA BRASS '63
Studio group conducted by Robert Mersey.

| 1/5/63 | 130 | 5 | | | **The Lonely Bull** | [I] | | $20 | Epic 26039 |

Amor
Comancheros, The
Desafinado
Eso Beso (That Kiss!)
La Bamba
La Paloma (The Dove)
La Virgen De La Macarena
Lonely Bull
Mexico
Spanish Harlem
Spanish Lace
Tequila

ARGENT '72
Rock group from England: Rod Argent (vocals, keyboards), **Russ Ballard** (guitar), Jim Rodford (bass) and Robert Henrit (drums). Argent was leader of **The Zombies**. Henrit later joined **Charlie**. Rodford and Henrit later joined **The Kinks**.

7/1/72	23	23		©	1 **All Together Now**			$20	Epic 31556
4/7/73	90	11		©	2 **In Deep**			$20	Epic 32195
5/4/74	149	6			3 **Nexus**			$20	Epic 32573
1/11/75	151	4		©	4 **Encore-Live In Concert**	[L]		$30	Epic 33079 [2]
3/29/75	171	3			5 **Circus**			$20	Epic 33422

Be Glad (2)
Be My Lover, Be My Friend (1)
Candles On The River (2)
Christmas For The Free (2)
Circus (5)
Clown (5)
Coming Of Kohoutek (3,4)
God Gave Rock And Roll To You (2,4)
Gonna Meet My Maker (3)
He's A Dynamo (1)
Highwire (5)
Hold Your Head Up (1,4) *5*
I Am The Dance Of Ages (1,4)
I Don't Believe In Miracles (4)
Infinite Wanderer (3)
It's Only Money Part 1 & 2 (2,4)
Jester, The (5)
Keep On Rollin' (1,4)
Keeper Of The Flame (4)
Losing Hold (2)
Love (3)
Man For All Reasons (3)
Music From The Spheres (3,4)
Once Around The Sun (3)
Pure Love Medley (1)
Ring, The (5)
Rosie (2)
Shine On Sunshine (5)
Thunder And Lightning (3,4)
Time Of The Season (4)
Tragedy (1)
Trapeze (5)

ARJONA, Ricardo '00
Born in Antigua, Guatemala. Singer/songwriter/guitarist.

| 9/16/00 | 136 | 2 | | © | **Galeria Caribe** | [F] | | $10 | Sony Discos 84014 |
| | | | | | title is Spanish for "Caribbean Gallery" | | | | |

Carabelas
Cuándo
Lo Poco Que Queda De Mí
Mesías
Mujer De Guanahaní
Pensar En Ti
Porque Hablamos
Receta
Si Usted La Viera (El Confesor)
Sólo Quería Un Café
Te Enamoraste De Ti
Un Caribe En Nueva York

ARMADA ORCHESTRA, The '76
Studio group featuring members of **The London Symphony Orchestra**.

| 1/17/76 | 196 | 2 | | | **The Armada Orchestra** | [I] | | $12 | Scepter 5123 |

Band Of Gold
Cochise
Do Me Right
Drifter, The
Feel The Need In Me
Hustle, The
Same Old Song
Tell Me What You Want
You Want It You Got It

ARMAGEDDON '75
Rock group formed in England: Keith Relf (vocals), Martin Pugh (guitar), Louis Cennamo (bass) and Bobby Caldwell (drums). Relf was a member of **The Yardbirds** and **Renaissance**. Caldwell (not to be confused with the same-named solo artist) was with **Johnny Winter**'s band.

| 6/7/75 | 151 | 6 | | | **Armageddon** | | | $15 | A&M 4513 |

Basking In The White Of The Midnight Sun Medley
Buzzard
Last Stand Before
Paths And Planes And Future Gains
Silver Tightrope

★382★ ARMATRADING, Joan '80
Born on 12/9/50 in St. Kitts, West Indies; raised in Birmingham, England. Singer/songwriter/guitarist.

1)Me Myself I 2)The Key 3)Show Some Emotion

10/9/76+	67	27		©	1 **Joan Armatrading**			$12	A&M 4588
10/22/77	52	21		©	2 **Show Some Emotion**			$12	A&M 4663
11/11/78	125	12		©	3 **To The Limit**			$12	A&M 4732
12/8/79+	136	18			4 **How Cruel**	[M]		$10	A&M 3302
6/7/80	28	23		©	5 **Me Myself I**			$10	A&M 4809
10/17/81+	88	32		©	6 **Walk Under Ladders**			$10	A&M 4876
4/30/83	32	22		©	7 **The Key**			$10	A&M 4912
1/21/84	113	10		©	8 **Track Record**	[G]		$10	A&M 4987
3/30/85	73	19		©	9 **Secret Secrets**			$10	A&M 5040
7/5/86	68	16		©	10 **Sleight Of Hand**			$10	A&M 5130
8/20/88	100	13		©	11 **The Shouting Stage**			$10	A&M 5211
6/30/90	161	10		©	12 **Heart And Flowers**			$10	A&M 5298

All A Woman Needs (11)
All The Way From America (5)
Always (12)
Am I Blue For You (3)
Angel Man (10)
At The Hop (6)
Baby (5)
Bad Habits (7)
Barefoot And Pregnant (3)
Bottom To The Top (3)
Can't Let Go (12)
Dark Truths (11)
Dealer, The (7)
Devil I Know (11)
Did I Make You Up (11)
Don Juan (10)
Down To Zero (1,8)
Drop The Pilot (7,8) *78*
Eating The Bear (6)
Everybody Gotta Know (7)
Feeling In My Heart (For You) (5)
Figure Of Speech (10)
Foolish Pride (7)
Free (12)
Friends (5)
Friends Not Lovers (9)
Frustration (8)
Game Of Love (7)
Get In The Sun (2)

ARMATRADING, Joan — Cont'd

Good Times (12)
He Wants Her (4)
Hearts And Flowers (12)
Heaven (8)
Help Yourself (1)
How Cruel (4)
I Can't Lie To Myself (6)
(I Love It When You) Call Me Names (7,8)
I Love My Baby (7)
I Need You (5)
I Really Must Be Going (4)
I Wanna Hold You (6)
I'm Lucky (6,8)
Is It Tomorrow Yet (5)

Jesse (4)
Join The Boys (1)
Key, The (7)
Killing Time (10)
Kind Words (And A Real Good Heart) (1)
Kissin' And A Huggin' (2)
Laurel And The Rose (10)
Let It Last (3)
Like Fire (1)
Living For You (11)
Love And Affection (1,8)
Love By You (9)
Ma-Me-O-Beach (5)
Mama Mercy (2)

Me Myself I (5,8)
More Than One Kind Of Love (12)
Moves (9)
Never Is Too Late (2)
No Love (6)
One More Chance (10)
One Night (9)
Only One (6)
Opportunity (2)
Peace In Mind (2)
People (1)
Persona Grata (9)
Power Of Dreams (12)
Promise Land (12)

Reach Out (10)
Romancers (6)
Rosie (4,8)
Russian Roulette (10)
Save Me (1)
Secret Secrets (9)
Shouting Stage (11)
Show Some Emotion (2,8)
Simon (4)
Somebody Who Loves You (1)
Someone's In The Background (12)
Something In The Air Tonight (12)
Straight Talk (11)

Strange (9)
Stronger Love (11)
Taking My Baby Up Town (3)
Talking To The Wall (9)
Tall In The Saddle (1)
Tell Tale (7)
Temptation (9)
Thinking Man (9)
Turn Out The Light (5)
Warm Love (2)
Watch Your Step (11)
Water With The Wine (1)
Weakness In Me (6,8)
What Do Boys Dream (7)
What Do You Want (9)

When I Get It Right (6,8)
When You Kisses Me (5)
Willow (2,8)
Wishing (3)
Woncha Come On Home (2)
Words (11)
You Rope You Tie Me (3)
Your Letter (3)

ARMORED SAINT   '86

Hard-rock group from Los Angeles: John Bush (vocals), Dave Prichard and Phil Sandoval (guitars), Joey Vera (bass) and Gonzo (drums). Prichard left after first album.

12/22/84+	138	16		©	1	March Of The Saint		$10	Chrysalis 41476
12/7/85+	108	19		©	2	Delirious Nomad		$10	Chrysalis 41516
9/26/87	114	12		©	3	Raising Fear		$10	Chrysalis 41601

Aftermath (2)
Book Of Blood (3)
Can U Deliver (1)
Chemical Euphoria (3)
Conqueror (2)
Envy (1)

False Alarm (1)
For The Sake (2)
Frozen Will (medley) (3)
Glory Hunter (1)
Human Vulture (3)
In The Hole (2)

Isolation (3)
Laugh, The (2)
Legacy (medley) (3)
Long Before I Die (2)
Mad House (1)
March Of The Saint (1)

Mutiny On The World (1)
Nervous Man (2)
Out On A Limb (3)
Over The Edge (2)
Raising Fear (3)
Released (2)

Saturday Night Special (3)
Seducer (1)
Stricken By Fate (1)
Take A Turn (1)
Terror (1)
Underdogs (3)

You're Never Alone (2)

ARMSTRONG, Louis   '64

Born Daniel Louis Armstrong on 8/4/01 in New Orleans. Died of heart failure on 7/6/71 (age 69). Legendary singer/trumpet player. Nicknamed "Satchmo." Numerous appearances on radio, TV and in movies. Won Grammy's Lifetime Achievement Award in 1972. Inducted into the Rock and Roll Hall of Fame in 1990 as a forefather of rock music.

10/1/55	10	2		©	1	Satch Plays Fats		$50	Columbia 708
						LOUIS ARMSTRONG and His All-Stars			
						a tribute to Fats Waller			
12/15/56	12	2		©	2	Ella And Louis		$50	Verve 4003
						ELLA FITZGERALD and LOUIS ARMSTRONG			
5/16/64	❶⁶	74	●	©	3	Hello, Dolly!		$20	Kapp 3364
11/21/98	21ˣ	7		©	4	It's Christmas Time ....C:#13/5	[X]	$10	LaserLight 15152
						BING CROSBY • FRANK SINATRA • LOUIS ARMSTRONG			
7/15/00	192	1		©	5	The Millennium Collection: The Best Of Louis Armstrong	[G]	$10	MCA 11940
1/27/01	142	5		©	6	Ken Burns Jazz - The Definitive Louis Armstrong	[K-TV]	$10	Legacy 61440
						songs from the Ken Burns PBS-TV special *Jazz*			

Ain't Misbehavin' (1,6)
All That Meat And No Potatoes (1)
April In Paris (2)
Be My Life's Companion (3)
Black And Blue (6)
Blue Again (6)
Blue Turning Grey Over You (1)
Blueberry Hill (3,5,6) *29*
Cabaret (6)
Cake Walkin' Babies (From Home) (6)

Can't We Be Friends (2)
Cheek To Cheek (2)
Chimes Blues (6)
Chinatown, My Chinatown (6)
Christmas In New Orleans (4)
Dream A Little Dream Of Me (4)
Fine Romance (2)
Foggy Day (2)
Gone Fishin' (5)
Heebie Jeebies (6)
Hello, Dolly! (3,5,6) *1*
Hey, Look Me Over (6)

Honeysuckle Rose (1)
I Double Dare You (6)
I Still Get Jealous (3,5) *45*
I'm Crazy 'Bout My Baby And My Baby's Crazy 'Bout Me (1)
I've Got A Feeling I'm Falling (1)
Isn't This A Lovely Day (2)
It's Been A Long, Long Time (1)
Jeepers Creepers (3)
Keepin' Out Of Mischief Now (1)
Kiss To Build A Dream On (3,5)
Lazy River (6)

Lot Of Livin' To Do (3)
Mack The Knife (6) *20*
Mahogany Hall Stomp (6)
Marie (6)
Moon River (3)
Moonlight In Vermont (2)
Nearness Of You (2)
Potato Head Blues (6)
Rockin' Chair (6)
Shadrack (3)
Someday (3)
Squeeze Me (1)

St. Louis Blues (6)
Star Dust (3)
Stars Fell On Alabama (2)
Tenderly (2)
That Lucky Old Sun (5)
They Can't Take That Away From Me (2)
Tight Like This (6)
Under A Blanket Of Blue (2)
West End Blues (6)
What A Wonderful World (5,6) *32*

(What Did I Do To Be So) Black And Blue (1)
When It's Sleepy Time Down South (5,6)
When The Saints Go Marching In (6)
You Are Woman, I Am Man (3)
Zat You Santa Claus (4)

★231★ ARNOLD, Eddy   '66

Born Richard Edward Arnold on 5/15/18 in Henderson, Tennessee. Legendary country singer.
1)My World 2)I Want To Go With You 3)The Best Of Eddy Arnold

10/26/63	131	5		©	1	Cattle Call		$30	RCA Victor 2578
10/16/65+	7	58	●		2	My World		$20	RCA Victor 3466
3/26/66	26	28			3	I Want To Go With You		$20	RCA Victor 3507
7/30/66	46	22			4	The Last Word In Lonesome		$20	RCA Victor 3622
12/24/66+	27ˣ	8		©	5	Christmas with Eddy Arnold	[X]	$20	RCA Victor 2554
						first released in 1962; Christmas charts: 64'/66, 27'/67, 39'/68			
12/24/66+	36	30			6	Somebody Like Me		$20	RCA Victor 3715
3/18/67	57	24			7	Lonely Again		$20	RCA Victor 3753
5/6/67	34	57	●	©	8	The Best Of Eddy Arnold	[G]	$20	RCA Victor 3565
10/7/67	34	36			9	Turn The World Around		$20	RCA Victor 3869
2/24/68	122	21			10	The Everlovin' World Of Eddy Arnold		$20	RCA Victor 3931
6/15/68	56	32			11	The Romantic World Of Eddy Arnold		$20	RCA Victor 4009
11/9/68	70	13			12	Walkin' In Love Land		$20	RCA Victor 4089
3/8/69	77	13			13	Songs Of The Young World		$20	RCA Victor 4110
7/5/69	167	5			14	The Glory Of Love		$20	RCA Victor 4179
11/1/69	116	8			15	The Warmth Of Eddy		$20	RCA Victor 4231
5/2/70	191	3			16	Love & Guitars		$15	RCA Victor 4304
5/30/70	146	2			17	The Best Of Eddy Arnold, Volume II	[G]	$15	RCA Victor 4320
3/13/71	141	4			18	Portrait Of My Woman		$15	RCA Victor 4471

After Losing You (3)
After The Laughter (Comes The Tears) (4)
All I Have To Do Is Dream (12)
All The Time (10,17)
Am I That Easy To Forget (11)
Anything That's Part Of You (18)

Anytime (8)
Apples, Raisins And Roses (12)
As Long As I Love (14)
As Usual (2)
At Sunset (6)
Baby (7)
Baby I Will (18)

Baby That's Living (10)
Band Of Gold (15)
Bear With Me A Little Longer (7)
Boquet Of Roses (8)
But For Love (14)
By The Time I Get To Phoenix (11)

Can't Take My Eyes Off You (11)
Carry Me Back To The Lone Prairie (1)
Castle Made Of Walls (9)
Cattle Call (1,8) *42*
C-H-R-I-S-T-M-A-S (5)

Christmas Can't Be Far Away (5)
Come By Me Nice And Slow (6)
Come Live With Me And Be My Love (3)
Cool Water (1)
Cowboy's Dream (1)
Cowpoke (1)

Cycles (15)
Days Gone By (2)
Dear Heart (10)
Did It Rain (7)
Don't Forget I Still Love You (3)
Don't Keep Me Lonely Too Long (9)
Don't Laugh At My Love (6)

DEBUT	PEAK	WKS	RIAA	CD	ARTIST — Album Title	Catalog	Sym	$	Label & Number

ARNOLD, Eddy — Cont'd

Don't Touch Me (4)
Ev'ry Step Of The Way (6)
Evergreen (11)
Faithfully (14)
Forty Shades Of Green (18)
From This Minute On (11)
Gentle On My Mind (11)
Glory Of Love (14)
Good Woman's Love (3)
Good-bye Sunshine (3)
He's Got You (7)
Heaven Below (14)
Heaven Everyday (18)
Here Comes Heaven (10) *91*
Here Comes My Baby (4)
Honey (11)
How Is She (10)
I Get Baby On My Mind (13)
I Guess I'll Never Understand (9)
I Heard The Bells On Christmas Day (5)
I Just Can't Help Believin' (16)
I Love How You Love Me (13)
I Love You Drops (6)
I Really Don't Want To Know (8,18)
I Really Go For You (11)
I Started A Joke (15)
I Want To Go With You (3,8) *36*
I Was Born To Love You (18)
I'll Always Be In Love With You (3)
I'll Give You Three Guesses (16)

I'll Hold You In My Heart (8)
I'll Love You More (9)
I'll Never Smile Again (12)
I'm In Love With You (13)
I'm Letting You Go (2)
I'm Walking Behind You (2)
If You Were Mine, Mary (2)
In The Misty Moonlight (10)
It Ain't No Big Thing (18)
It Came Upon The Midnight Clear (5)
It Comes And Goes (2)
It's Only Love (6)
It's Over (11,17) *74*
It's Such A Pretty World Today (9,17)
(Jim) I Wore A Tie Today (1)
Jingle Bell Rock (5)
Jolly Old Saint Nicholas (5)
Just A Bend In The Road (14)
Just A Little Lovin' (Will Go A Long Way) (8)
Just Across The Mountain (12)
Just Enough To Start Me Dreamin (16)
Last Word In Lonesome Is Me (4,8) *40*
Lay Some Happiness On Me (6)
Leanin' On The Old Top Rail (1)
Leaving On A Jet Plane (16)
Little Girls And Little Boys (12)
Little Green Apples (13)
Lonely Again (7,17) *87*
Long, Long Friendship (4)
Love Finds A Way (9)

Love Me Like That (3)
Love On My Mind (6)
Make The World Go Away (2,8) *6*
Man's Kind Of Woman (16)
Mary Claire Melvina Rebecca Jane (2)
Mary In The Morning (16)
Mary Who (7)
Meet Me At The Altar (7)
Millions Of Roses (4)
Misty Blue (4,17) *57*
My Dream (12)
My Home Town Sweetheart (4)
My Way (15)
No Matter Whose Baby You Are (11)
Nobody's Darling But Mine (7)
Nothing But Time (10)
O Little Town Of Bethlehem (5)
Oh So Far From Home (7)
Ole Faithful (1)
Olive Tree (12)
One Kiss For Old Times' Sake (3)
Other Side Of Lonely (4)
Pardon Me (3)
Please Don't Go (14)
Portrait Of My Woman (18)
Release Me (And Let Me Love Again) (9,17)
San Francisco Is A Lonely Town (11)
Santa Claus Is Comin' To Town (5)
Secret Love (10)

Shadows Of Her Mind (16)
She's Everywhere (18)
Sierra Sue (1)
Since You've Been Loving Me (13)
Somebody Like Me (6,17) *53*
Somebody Loves You (3)
Song For Shara (10)
Song Of Long Ago (14)
Soul Deep (16)
Streets Of Laredo (1)
Suddenly My Thoughts Are All Of You (13)
Summer Wind (12)
Sunny (4)
Sunshine Belongs To Me (13)
Sweet Bird Of Youth (14)
Sweet Marilyn (13)
Take A Little Time (13)
Taking Chances (4)
Tender Is Her Name (13)
Tennessee Stud (17) *48*
That's A Lie (4)
That's All I Want From You (7)
That's All That's Left Of My Baby (9)
That's How Much I Love You (8)
Then I'll Be Over You (15)
Then She's A Lover (14)
Then You Can Tell Me Goodbye (12,17) *84*
There You Go (10)
There's Always Me (6)
There's This About You (9)
They Don't Make Love Like They Used To (13) *99*

Thing Called Sadness (4)
Tip Of My Fingers (6,17) *43*
To Sleep With You (15)
(Today) I Started Loving You Again (16)
Too Many Rivers (2)
Town And Country (14)
Turn Around, Look At Me (12)
Turn The World Around (9,17) *66*
Until It's Time For You To Go (12)
Up On The Housetop (5)
Wait For Sunday (18)
Walk With Me (9)
Walkin' In Love Land (12)
Wayward Wind (1)
What A Wonderful World (11)
What Have I Done For Her Lately (15)
What Now My Love (11)
What's He Doing In My World (2,8) *60*
Wheel Of Hurt (7)
When The Wind Blows (In Chicago) (16)
When There's A Fire In Your Heart (9)
When Your World Stops Turning (7)
Where The Mountains Meet The Sky (1)
White Christmas (5)
Why (4)
Wichita Lineman (13)

Will Santy Come To Shanty Town (5)
Winter Wonderland (5)
With Pen In Hand (16)
World I Used To Know (10)
Yesterday, When I Was Young (15)
You Don't Know Me (8)
You Don't Need Me Anymore (15)
You Fool (15)
You Gave Me A Mountain (14,17)
You Made Up For Everything (6)
You Still Got A Hold On Me (2)
You'd Better Stop Tellin' Lies (About Me) (3)

ARPEGGIO   '79
Disco studio group assembled by producer Simon Soussan.

| 2/10/79 | 75 | 16 | | | Let The Music Play | | | $12 | Polydor 6180 |

Let The Music Play Medley | Love And Desire (Part I) *70* | Runaway | Spellbound

ARRESTED DEVELOPMENT   '93
Rap group from Atlanta: Todd "Speech" Thomas, **Dionne Farris**, Aerlee Taree, Tim Barnwell, Montsho Eshe, Rasa Don and Baba Oje. Won the 1992 Best New Artist Grammy Award.

| 4/18/92+ | 7 | 76 | ▲4 | © | 1 **3 Years, 5 Months & 2 Days In The Life Of ...** | | | $10 | Chrysalis 21929 |

title refers to the length of time between group's formation and the signing of its recording contract

| 4/10/93 | 60 | 12 | ● | © | 2 **Unplugged** | | [L] | $10 | Chrysalis 21994 |

recorded on 1/6/93

| 7/2/94 | 55 | 8 | | © | 3 **Zingalamaduni** | | | $10 | Chrysalis 29274 |

title is Swahili for "Beehive of Culture"

Ache'n For Acres (3)
Africa's Inside Me (3)
Blues Happy (1)
Children Play With Earth (1)
Dawn Of The Dreads (1)
Drum, The (3)

Ease My Mind (3) *45*
Eve Of Reality (3)
Fishin' 4 Religion (1,2)
Fountain Of Youth (3)
Gettin', The (3)
Give A Man A Fish (1,2)

In The Sunshine (3)
Kneelin' At My Altar (3)
Mama's Always On Stage (1,2)
Man's Final Frontier (1)
Mister Landlord (3)
Mr. Wendal (1,2) *6*

Natural (1,2)
People Everyday (1,2) *8*
Praisin' U (3)
Pride (2)
Raining Revolution (1,2)
Searchin' For One Soul (2)

Shell (3)
Tennessee (1) *6*
Time (2)
U (1,2)
United Front (3)
United Minds (3)

WMFW (We Must Fight & Win) Fm (3)
Warm Sentiments (3)
Washed Away (1)

ARRINGTON, Steve   '83
Born in Dayton, Ohio. R&B singer/drummer. Former member of **Slave**.

| 3/12/83 | 101 | 17 | | © | 1 **Steve Arrington's Hall Of Fame: I** | | | $10 | Atlantic 80049 |
| 2/25/84 | 141 | 9 | | | 2 **Positive Power** | | | $10 | Atlantic 80127 |

STEVE ARRINGTON'S Hall Of Fame (above 2)

| 5/18/85 | 185 | 5 | | | 3 **Dancin' In The Key Of Life** | | | $10 | Atlantic 81245 |

Beddie-Biey (1)
Brown Baby Boy (3)
Dancin' In The Key Of Life (3) *68*
Feel So Real (3)

15 Rounds (2)
Gasoline (3)
Hump To The Bump (2)
Last Nite/Nite Before (1)
Mellow As A Cello (2)

Money On It (3)
Nobody Can Be You (1)
Positive Power (2)
She Just Don't Know (1)
Speak With Your Body (1)

Stand With Me (3)
Strange (Soft & Hard) (1)
Sugar Momma Baby (1)
Turn Up Love (3)
Way Out (1)

Weak At The Knees (1)
What Do You Want From Me (2)
Willie Mae (3)
You Meet My Approval (1)

Young And Ready (2)

ARROWS, The — see ALLAN, Davie

ARTIFACTS   '97
Rap duo from Newark, New Jersey: El Sensei and Tame One.

| 11/12/94 | 137 | 1 | | © | 1 **Between A Rock And A Hard Place** | | | $10 | Big Beat 92397 |
| 5/3/97 | 134 | 1 | | | 2 **That's Them** | | | $10 | Big Beat 92753 |

Art Of Facts (2)
Attack Of New Jeruzalem (1)
Break It Down (2)
Collaboration Of Mics (2)
C'mon Wit Da Git Down (1)

Cummin' Thru Ya F--kin' Block (1)
Drama (Mortal Kombat Fatality) (1)
Dynamite Soul (1)

Flexi Wit Da Tech(nique) (1)
Heavy Ammunition (1)
Ingredients To Time Travel (2)
Interview, The (2)
It's Gettin' Hot (2)

Lower Da Boom (1)
Notty Headed Nigguhz (1)
Return To Da Wrongside (2)
Skwad Training (2)
31 Bumrush (2)

This Is Da Way (2)
To Ya Chest (2)
Ultimate, The (2)
Whassup Now Muthaf--cka? (1)
What Goes On? (1)

Whayback (1)
Where Yo Skillz At? (2)
Who's This? (2)
Wrong Side Of Da Tracks (1)

ART IN AMERICA   '83
Pop-rock trio from Detroit: brothers Chris (vocals, guitar) and Dan (drums) Flynn, with sister Shishonee Flynn (vocals, harp).

| 3/26/83 | 176 | 3 | | © | **Art In America** | | | $10 | Pavillion 38517 |

Art In America
Brett & Hibby
If I Could Fly
Line, The
Loot
Sinatra Serenade
Too Shy To Say
Undercover Lover
Won't It Be Strange

ARTISTS UNITED AGAINST APARTHEID '85

Benefit group of 49 superstar artists formed to protest the South African apartheid government; proceeds went to political prisoners in South Africa. Organized by **Little Steven** and Arthur Baker. Featuring **Pat Benatar**, Bono (**U2**), **Jackson Browne**, **Jimmy Cliff**, **Bob Dylan**, **Peter Gabriel**, **Bonnie Raitt**, **Lou Reed**, **Bruce Springsteen**, and many others.

11/23/85	31	18		©	**Sun City**			$10	Manhattan 53019

Let Me See Your I.D.   No More Apartheid   Revolutionary Situation   Silver And Gold   Struggle Continues   **Sun City** *38*

ART OF NOISE, The '86

Techno-pop trio from England: Anne Dudley (keyboards), J.J. Jeczalik (keyboards, programmer) and Gary Langan (engineer).

7/14/84	85	13		©	1 **(Who's Afraid Of?) The Art Of Noise!**			$10	Island 90179
5/3/86	53	30		©	2 **In Visible Silence**			$10	Chrysalis 41528
10/17/87	134	9		©	3 **In-No-Sense? Nonsense!**			$10	Chrysalis 41570
12/17/88+	83	14		©	4 **The Best Of The Art Of Noise**		[G]	$10	China 837367

Backbeat (2)   Beat Box (Diversion One) (1,4)   Beatback (2)   Camilla (2)   Chameleon's Dish (2)   Close (To The Edit) (1,4)   Counterpoint (3)   Crusoe (3)   Day At The Races (3)   Debut (3)   Dragnet (3)   Dragnet '88 (4)   E.F.L. (3)   Eye Of A Needle (2)   Fin Du Temps (3)   Galleons Of Stone (3)   How Rapid? (3)   How To Kill (1)   Instruments Of Darkness (2)   **Kiss** (4) *31*   Legacy (4)   Legs (2)   Momento (1)   Moments In Love (1,4)   Nothing Was Going To Stop Them Then, Anyway (3)   Ode To Don Jose (3)   One Earth (3)   Opus For Four (3)   Opus 4 (2,4)   **Paranoimia** (2,4) *34*   **Peter Gunn** (2,4) *50*   Ransom On The Sand (3)   Realization (1)   Roller 1 (3)   Roundabout 727 (3)   Slip Of A Tongue (2)   Snapshot (1)   Something Always Happens (4)   Time For Fear (Who's Afraid) (1)   Who's Afraid (Of The Art Of Noise) (1)

A's, The '81

Pop-rock group from Philadelphia: Richard Bush (vocals), Rick DiFonzo (guitar), Rocco Notte (keyboards), Terry Bortman (bass) and Mike Snyder (drums).

7/11/81	146	7			**A Woman's Got The Power**			$10	Arista 9554

Electricity   Heart Of America   How Do You Live   I Pretend She's You   Insomnia   Johnny Silent   Little Mistakes   When The Rebel Comes Home   Woman's Got The Power   Working Man

ASH, Daniel '91

Born on 7/31/57 in Northampton, England. Singer/songwriter/guitarist. Former member of **Bauhaus** and **Love And Rockets**.

3/9/91	109	10		©	**Coming Down**			$10	Beggars Banquet 3014

Blue Angel   Blue Moon   Candy Darling   Closer To You   Coming Down   Coming Down Fast   Day Tripper   Me And My Shadow   Not So Fast   Sweet Little Liar   This Love   Walk This Way

ASHCROFT, Richard '00

Born on 9/11/71 in Lancashire, England. Former lead singer of **The Verve**.

7/15/00	127	1		©	**Alone With Everybody**			$10	Virgin 49494

Brave New World   C'mon People (We're Making It Now)   Crazy World   Everybody   I Get My Beat   Money To Burn   New York   On A Beach   Slow Was My Heart   Song For The Lovers   You On My Mind In My Sleep

★363★ ASHFORD & SIMPSON '78

Husband-and-wife R&B vocal/songwriting duo: Nick Ashford (born on 5/4/43 in Fairfield, South Carolina) and **Valerie Simpson** (born on 8/26/48 in New York City). Joined staff at Motown and wrote and produced for many of the label's top stars. Valerie recorded solo in 1972. They married in 1974. Valerie's brother, Ray Simpson, was the lead singer of **Village People**.

1)Is It Still Good To Ya 2)Stay Free 3)Solid

11/10/73+	156	13			1 **Gimme Something Real**			$15	Warner 2739
7/20/74	195	4			2 **I Wanna Be Selfish**			$15	Warner 2789
5/8/76	189	4			3 **Come As You Are**			$15	Warner 2858
2/5/77	180	3		©	4 **So So Satisfied**			$15	Warner 2992
10/15/77	52	46	●	©	5 **Send It**			$12	Warner 3088
9/9/78	20	28	●	©	6 **Is It Still Good To Ya**			$12	Warner 3219
9/1/79	23	23	●	©	7 **Stay Free**			$12	Warner 3357
8/23/80	38	12		©	8 **A Musical Affair**			$12	Warner 3458
10/17/81	125	6			9 **Performance**		[L]	$15	Warner 3524 [2]
5/29/82	45	20			10 **Street Opera**			$10	Capitol 12207
9/17/83	84	12			11 **High-Rise**			$10	Capitol 12282
11/10/84+	29	36		©	12 **Solid**			$10	Capitol 12366
9/6/86	74	18			13 **Real Love**			$10	Capitol 12469
3/18/89	135	8		©	14 **Love Or Physical**			$10	Capitol 46946

Ain't It A Shame (6)   Ain't No Mountain High Enough (medley) (9)   Ain't Nothin' But A Maybe (2)   Ain't Nothing Like The Real Thing (medley) (9)   Ain't That Good Enough (1)   Ain't That Somethin' (2)   As Long As It Holds You (6)   Babies (12)   Believe In Me (3)   Bend Me (1)   Boss, The (medley) (9)   Bourgie Bourgie (5,9)   By Way Of Love's Express (5)   Can You Make It Brother (1)   Caretaker (3)   Cherish Forever More (12)   Closest To Love (12)   Clouds (medley) (9)   Come On, Pretty Baby (9)   Comes With The Package (14)   Cookies And Cake (14)   Couldn't Get Enough (4)   **Count Your Blessings** (13) *84*   Crazy (7)   Dance Forever (7)   Debt Is Settled (6)   Destiny (7)   **Don't Cost You Nothing** (5,9) *79*   Don't Fight It (2)   Everybody's Got To Give It Up (2)   Experience (Love Had No Face) (11)   Finally Got To Me (7)   Flashback (6)   Follow Your Heart (7)   **Found A Cure** (7,9) *36*   Get Out Your Handkerchief (8)   Get Up And Do Something (6)   Gimme Something Real (1,9)   Happy Endings (8)   Have You Ever Tried It (1)   High-Rise (11)   Honey I Love You (12)   How Does It Fit (13)   I Ain't Asking For Your Love (9)   I Had A Love (2)   I Need Your Light (1,9)   I Waited Too Long (5)   I Wanna Be Selfish (2)   **(I'd Know You) Anywhere** (1) *88*   I'll Be There For You (14)   I'll Take The Whole World On (10)   I'm Determined (1)   I'm Not That Tough (11)   If You're Lying (4)   In Your Arms (14)   Is It Still Good To Ya (6,9)   It Came To Me (3)   It Seems To Hang On (6,9)   It Shows In The Eyes (9)   It'll Come, It'll Come, It'll Come (3)   It's A Rush (11)   It's Much Deeper (11)   It's The Long Run (9)   It's You (4)   Jungle, The (12)   Landlord (medley) (9)   Let Love Use Me (5)   Love Don't Make It Right (8,9)   Love It Away (10)   Love Or Physical (14)   Make It To The Sky (8)   Make It Work Again (10)   Maybe I Can Find It (14)   Mighty Mighty Love (10)   My Kinda Pick Me Up (11)   Nobody Knows (7,9)   Nobody Walks In L.A. (13)   One More Try (3)   Outta The World (12)   Over And Over (4)   Over To Where You Are (2)   Real Love (13)   Relations (11)   Rushing To (8)   Sell The House (3)   Send It (5)   Side Effect (11)   So So Satisfied (4)   Somebody Told A Lie (3)   Something To You (14)   Spoiled (2)   Stay Free (7)   Still Such A Thing (11)   **Street Corner** (10) *56*   Take All The Time You Need (2)   Tell It All (3)   10th Round (13)   Til We Get It Right (14)   Time (1)   Times Will Be Good Again (10)   Timing (14)   Tonight We Escape (We Make Love) (12)   Too Bad (5)   Top Of The Stairs (5)   Tried, Tested And Found True (4)   Way Ahead (13)   We'll Meet Again (8)   What Becomes Of Love (13)   Who Will They Look To (10)   Working Man (13)   You Always Could (6)   You Never Left Me Alone (8)   You're All I Need (medley) (9)

ASHTON, Susan '96
Born Susan Rae Hill on 7/17/67 in Houston. Christian singer/songwriter.

10/26/96	163	1		©	A Distant Call			$10	Sparrow 51458

All Kinds Of People / Body And Soul / Hundreds Of Tears / Lonely River / Send A Message / You Move Me
Blind Side / Crooked Man / I Will Follow / Love Profound / Spinning Like A Wheel

ASHTON, GARDNER & DYKE '71
Pop trio from England: Tony Ashton (vocals, keyboards), Kim Gardner (bass) and Roy Dyke (drums). Ashton died of cancer on 5/28/2001 (age 55).

| 8/7/71 | 185 | 6 | | | Resurrection Shuffle .... | | | $15 | Capitol 563 |

Don't Want No War No More / I'm Your Spiritual Breadman / Mister Freako / Oh Lord / Paper Head, Paper Mind / Resurrection Shuffle 40
Hymn To Everyone / Let It Roll / Momma's Getting Married / Paper Head, Paper Mind / Sweet Patti O'Hara Smith

ASIA '82
Rock supergroup from England: John Wetton (vocals, bass; **King Crimson, Uriah Heep, U.K.**), **Steve Howe** (guitar; **Yes**), Geoff Downes (keyboards; Yes, **The Buggles**) and Carl Palmer (drums; **Emerson, Lake & Palmer, Atomic Rooster**). Howe replaced by Mandy Meyer (**Krokus**) in 1985. Meyer replaced by Pat Thrall (**Automatic Man**) in 1990.

4/3/82	❶9	64	▲4	©	1	Asia		$10	Geffen 2008
8/27/83	6	25	▲	©	2	Alpha		$10	Geffen 4008
12/7/85	67	17		©	3	Astra		$10	Geffen 24072
9/1/90	114	10	●		4	Then & Now .... [G]		$10	Geffen 24298

After The War (3) / Hard On Me (3) / My Own Time (I'll Do What I / **Smile Has Left Your Eyes** / True Colors (2)
Am I In Love? (4) / Heat Goes On (2) / Want) (2) / (2,4) 34 / Voice Of America (3,4)
Countdown To Zero (3) / **Heat Of The Moment** (1,4) 4 / Never In A Million Years (2) / Sole Survivor (1) / Wildest Dreams (1,4)
Cutting It Fine (1) / Here Comes The Feeling (1) / One Step Closer (1) / Summer (Can't Last Too Long) / Wishing (3)
Days Like These (4) 64 / Last To Know (2) / **Only Time Will Tell** (1,4) 17 / (4) / Without You (1)
Don't Cry (2,4) 10 / Love Now Till Eternity (3) / Open Your Eyes (3) / Suspicion (3)
Eye To Eye (2) / Midnight Sun (2) / Prayin' 4 A Miracle (4) / Time Again (1)
Go (3) 46 / Rock And Roll Dream (3) / Too Late (3)

ASLEEP AT THE WHEEL '75
Country group from Paw Paw, West Virginia: Ray Benson (male vocals, guitar), Chris O'Connell (female vocals, guitar), Reuben "Lucky Oceans" Gosfield (steel guitar), Danny Levin (fiddle, mandolin), and Jim "Floyd Domino" Haber (piano). Numerous personnel changes with Benson the only constant.

9/20/75	136	8	©	1	Texas Gold			$12	Capitol 11441
9/18/76	179	3		2	Wheelin' And Dealin'			$12	Capitol 11546
4/16/77	162	4		3	The Wheel			$12	Capitol 11620
9/6/80	191	2		4	Framed			$10	MCA 5131
11/20/93	159	7	©	5	Tribute To The Music Of Bob Wills And The Texas Playboys			$10	Liberty 81470

Across The Alley From The / Corine, Corina (5) / I Wonder (3) / Miles And Miles Of Texas (2) / Route 66 (2) / Trouble With Lovin' Today (2)
Alamo (5) / Deep Water (5) / I Wonder If You Feel The Way I / Misery (5) / Runnin' After Fools (1) / Up, Up, Up (4)
All Night Long (5) / Dollar Short & A Day Late (3) / Do (5) / Musical Talk (4) / Shout Wa Hey (2) / We've Gone As Far As We Can
Am I High? (3) / Don't Get Caught Out In The / Ida Red (5) / My Baby Thinks She's A Train / Slow Dancing (4) / Go (2)
Big Ball's In Cowtown (5) / Rain (4) / If I Can't Love You (2) / (3) / Somebody Stole His Body (3) / Whatever It Takes (4)
Billy Dale (5) / Dusty Skies (5) / Let Me Go Home Whiskey (1) / Nothin' Takes The Place Of You / Still Water Runs The Deepest / Wheel, The (3)
Blues For Dixie (2,5) / Fat Boy Rag (1) / Let's Face Up (3) / (1) / (3) / When Love Goes Wrong (3)
Bring It On Down To My House / Fiddle Funk – Corn Fusion (4) / Letter That Johnny Walker / Old Fashioned Love (5) / They Raided The Joint (2) / Where No One Stands Alone
(5) / Got A Letter From My Kid / Read (1) / Ragtime Annie (3) / Tonight The Bartender Is On / (1)
Bump Bounce Boogie (1) / Today (5) / Lonely Avenue Revisited (4) / Red Stick (3) / The Wrong Side Of The Bar / Yearning (Just For You) (5)
Cajun Stripper (2) / Hubbin' It (5) / Lost Mind (2) / Red Wing (5) / (1) / You Wanna Give Me A Lift (4)
Cool As A Breeze (4) / I Can't Handle It Now (3) / Midnight In Memphis (4) / Roll 'Em Floyd (1) / Trouble In Mind (1)

★381★ ASSOCIATION, The '69
Pop group from Los Angeles: Gary Alexander, Russ Giguere and Jim Yester (guitars), Terry Kirkman (keyboards), Brian Cole (bass) and Ted Bluechel (drums). All shared vocals. Larry Ramos (guitar) joined in 1967. Richard Thompson replaced Giguere in 1970. Cole died of a heroin overdose on 8/2/72 (age 29).

1)Greatest Hits 2)And Then...Along Comes The Association 3)Insight Out

8/20/66	5	59	●	1	And Then...Along Comes The Association			$30	Valiant 5002
1/7/67	34	15		2	Renaissance			$30	Valiant 5004
7/22/67	8	68	●	3	Insight Out			$20	Warner 1696
5/4/68	23	26		4	Birthday			$20	Warner 1733
12/28/68+	4	75	▲2	©	5	Greatest Hits	[G]		$20	Warner 1767
5/10/69	99	18		6	Goodbye, Columbus .... [S]			$20	Warner 1786

includes "Dartmouth? Dartmouth!!," "How Will I Know You?," "Love Has A Way," "A Moment To Share," "Ron's Reverie Medley" and "A Time For Love" by Charles Fox

10/4/69	32	17		7	The Association			$20	Warner 1800
7/18/70	79	12		8	The Association "Live" .... [L]			$25	Warner 1868 [2]
8/14/71	158	4		9	Stop Your Motor			$20	Warner 1927
5/20/72	194	5		10	Waterbeds In Trinidad!			$15	Columbia 31348

All Is Mine (2) / Come On In (4) / I'll Be Your Man (1,8) / Nest, The (7) / Round Again (1) / Travelers Guide (Spanish Flyer)
Along Comes Mary (1,5,8) 7 / Come The Fall (10) / I'm The One (2) / **Never My Love** (3,5,8) 2 / Seven Man Band (8) / (9)
Along The Way (9) / Come To Me (2) / Indian Wells Woman (10) / **No Fair At All** (2,5) 51 / Seven Virgins (9) / Under Branches (7)
Angeline (2) / Darling Be Home Soon (10) / It's Gotta Be Real (6,9) / On A Quiet Night (3) / Silent Song Thru The Land (10) / Wantin' Ain't Gettin' (3)
Another Time, Another Place / Don't Blame It On Me (1) / Just About The Same (8) / One Too Many Mornings (8) / Silver Morning (9) / Wasn't It A Bit Like Now (3,8)
(2) / Dream Girl (Dressing Room) (8) / Kicking The Gong Around (10) / P.F. Sloan (9) / **Six Man Band** (5) 47 / We Love Us (3,5)
Are You Ready (7,8) / Dubuque Blues (7,8) / Last Flower (8) / **Pandora's Golden Heebie** / Snow Queen (10) / What Were The Words (7,8)
Babe, I'm Gonna Leave You (8) / Enter The Young (1,5,8) / Let's Get Together (8) / **Jeebies** (2) 35 / So Kind To Me (Brenda's / When Love Comes To Me (3)
Barefoot Gentleman (4) / **Everything That Touches You** / Like Always (4,5) / Please Don't Go (Round The / Theme) (6) / **Windy** (3,5,8) 1
Birthday Morning (4) / (4,5) 10 / Little Road And A Stone To Roll / Bend) (10) / Sometime (6) / Yes, I Will (7)
Blistered (1,8) / First Sound (9) / (10) / Rainbows Bent (10) / Songs In The Wind (2) / You Hear Me Call Your Name
Boy On The Mountain (7) / Funny Kind Of Song (9) / Look At Me, Look At You (7) / Remember (1,8) / Standing Still (1) / (2)
Bring Yourself Home (9) / **Goodbye Columbus** (6,8) 80 / Looking Glass (2) / Reputation (3) / That's Racin' (9) / You May Think (2)
Broccoli (7) / Goodbye Forever (7,8) / Love Affair (7) / **Requiem For The Masses** / Time For Livin' (4,5) 39 / Your Own Love (1)
Bus Song (9) / Happiness (3) / Memories Of Love (1) / (3,5,8) 100 / Time It Is Today (4,5,8)
Changes (1) / Hear In Here (4) / Message Of Our Love (1) / Rose Petals, Incense And A / Toymaker (4)
Cherish (1,5,8) 1 / I Am Up For Europe (7) / Midnight Wind (10) / Kitten (4)

ASTLEY, Jon — '87

Born in Manchester, England. Noted rock producer (**The Who**, **Eric Clapton** and **Corey Hart**).

8/1/87	135	10		©	Everyone Loves The Pilot (Except The Crew)		$10	Atlantic 81740

Animal, The
Better Never Than Late
Disclaimer
Emperor, The
I Want To Dance
Jane's Getting Serious 77
Jumping In The Deep End
Lipservice
Suffering Fools
Target Practise

ASTLEY, Rick — '88

Born on 2/6/66 in Warrington, England. Pop singer.

1/23/88	10	60	▲²	©	1	Whenever You Need Somebody	$10	RCA 6822
1/28/89	19	23	●	©	2	Hold Me In Your Arms	$10	RCA 8589
3/30/91	31	18		©	3	Free	$10	RCA 3004
10/16/93	185	1		©	4	Body & Soul	$10	RCA 66295

Ain't Too Proud To Beg (2) 89
Be With You (3)
Behind The Smile (3)
Body And Soul (4)
Bottom Line (3)
Cry For Help (3) 7
Dial My Number (2)
Don't Say Goodbye (1)
Dream For Us (4)

Enough Love (4)
Everytime (4)
Giving Up On Love (2) 38
Hold Me In Your Arms (2)
Hopelessly (4) 28
I Don't Want To Be Your Lover (2)
I Don't Want To Lose Her (2)
I'll Never Let You Down (2)

In The Name Of Love (3)
Is This Really Love? (3)
It Would Take A Strong Strong Man (1) 10
Love Has Gone (1)
Move Right Out (3) 81
Natures Gift (3)
Never Gonna Give You Up (1) 1

Never Knew Love (3)
No More Looking For Love (1)
Ones You Love (4)
Really Got A Problem (3)
Remember The Days (4)
She Wants To Dance With Me (2) 6
Slipping Away (1)
Take Me To Your Heart (2)

This Must Be Heaven (3)
Till Then (Time Stands Still) (2)
Together Forever (1) 1
Waiting For The Bell To Ring (4)
When I Fall In Love (1)
When You Love Someone (4)
Whenever You Need Somebody (1)

Wonderful You (3)
You Move Me (1)

ASTRONAUTS, The — '63

Surf-rock group from Boulder, Colorado. Guitarists Bob Demmon, Dennis Lindsey, Rich Fifield and Storm Patterson, with drummer Jim Gallagher. Fifield and Patterson share vocals.

8/3/63	61	14		©	1	Surfin' With The Astronauts	$80	RCA Victor 2760
2/8/64	100	9			2	Everything Is A-OK!	[L] $60	RCA Victor 2782
3/28/64	123	5		©	3	Competition Coupe	$60	RCA Victor 2858

Baby Let's Play House (1)
Baja (1) 94
Banzai Pipeline (1)
Batman (1)
Big Boss Man (2)
Bo Diddley (2)

Chevy Scarfer (3)
Competition Coupe (3)
Devil Driver (3)
Devil Driver's Theme (3)
Dream Lover (3)
El Aguila (The Eagle) (3)

'55 Bird (3)
4:56 Stingray (3)
Happy Ho-Daddy (3)
Hearse, The (3)
I Need You (2)
If I Had A Hammer (2)

It's So Easy (2)
Kuk (1)
Let's Go Trippin' (1)
Little Ford Ragtop (1)
Misirlou (1)
Money (2)

Movin' (1)
Our Car Club (3)
Pipeline (1)
Shortnin' Bread (2)
650 Scrambler (3)
Stormy Monday Blues (3)

Surfer's Stomp (1)
Surfin' U.S.A. (1)
Susie-Q (1)
What'd I Say (2)
Wine, Wine, Wine (2)

ASWAD — '88

Reggae trio from London: Brinsley Forde (vocals, guitar), Tony Robinson (keyboards) and Angus Gaye (drums). Aswad means "black" in Arabic.

8/13/88	173	7		©	Distant Thunder	$10	Mango 9810

Bittersweet
Don't Turn Around
Feelings
Give A Little Love
I Can't Get Over You
International Melody
Justice
Message, The
Set Them Free
Smokey Blues
Tradition

ATC — '01

Pop vocal group: Joe (from New Zealand), Sarah (from Australia), Tracey (from England) and Livio (from Italy). ATC: A Touch of Class.

2/24/01	73	11		©	Planet Pop	$10	Republic 013572

Around The World (La La La La La) 28
Let Me Come & Let Me Go
Lonely

Lonesome Suite
Love Is Blind
Mind Machine
Mistake No. 2

My Heart Beats Like A Drum (Dum Dum Dum)
Notte D'Amore Con Te
So Magical

Thinking Of You
Until
Why Oh Why
With You

Without Your Love

A*TEENS — '01

Teen **Abba** tribute group from Stockholm, Sweden: Dhani Lennevald, Sara Lumholdt, Amit Paul and Marie Serneholt.

6/3/00	71	41	●	©	1	The ABBA Generation	$10	Stockholm 159007
3/17/01	50	28		©	2	Teen Spirit	$10	Stockholm 013666

All My Love (2)
Around The Corner Of Your Eye (2)
Back For More (2)
Bouncing Off The Ceiling (Upside Down) (2) 93

Dancing Queen (1) 95
Don't Even Know Your Name (2)
Firefly (2)
For All That I Am (2)

Gimme! Gimme! Gimme! (A Man After Midnight) (1)
Halfway Around The World (2)
Lay All Your Love On Me (1)
Mamma Mia (1)
Morning Light (2)

Name Of The Game (1)
One Of Us (1)
Our Last Summer (1)
Rockin' (2)
S.O.S. (1)
Slammin' Kinda Love (2)

Sugar Rush (2)
Super Trouper (1)
Take A Chance On Me (1)
That's What (It's All About) (2)
...To The Music (2)
Voulez-Vous (1)

★239★ ATKINS, Chet — '61

Born on 6/20/24 in Luttrell, Tennessee. Died of cancer on 6/30/2001 (age 77). Legendary country guitarist. Moved to Nashville in 1950 and became prolific studio musician/producer. RCA's A&R manager in Nashville from 1960-68; RCA Vice President from 1968-82. Won Grammy's Lifetime Achievement Award in 1993. Recipient of *Billboard's* Century Award in 1997.

1)Chet Atkins' Workshop 2)Teensville 3)Chet Atkins At Home 4)Down Home 5)Caribbean Guitar

6/16/58	21	4			1	Chet Atkins At Home	[I] $50	RCA Victor 1544
2/22/60	16	12			2	Teensville	[I] $40	RCA Victor 2161
2/13/61	7	24		©	3	Chet Atkins' Workshop	[I] $30	RCA Victor 2232
7/10/61	119	10		©	4	The Most Popular Guitar	[I] $30	RCA Victor 2346
3/17/62	31	24		©	5	Down Home	[I] $30	RCA Victor 2450
10/13/62	33	9		©	6	Caribbean Guitar	[I] $30	RCA Victor 2549
3/23/63	135	5			7	Our Man In Nashville	[I] $30	RCA Victor 2616
9/21/63	93	6			8	Teen Scene	[I] $30	RCA Victor 2719
12/14/63+	12ˣ	16		©	9	Christmas with Chet Atkins	[X] $30	RCA Victor 2423
						first released in 1961; Christmas charts: 16/'63, 22/'64, 28/'66, 43/'67, 32/'68, 12/'69		
2/29/64	64	8		©	10	Guitar Country	[I] $30	RCA Victor 2783
4/9/66	112	13		©	11	Chet Atkins Picks On The Beatles	[I] $30	RCA Victor 3531
6/18/66	62	23			12	The "Pops" Goes Country	[I] $30	RCA Victor 2870
						CHET ATKINS/BOSTON POPS/ARTHUR FIEDLER		
12/17/66+	140	4			13	From Nashville With Love	[I] $25	RCA Victor 3647
5/6/67	148	9		©	14	It's A Guitar World	[I] $25	RCA Victor 3728
1/20/68	189	2			15	Class Guitar	[I] $25	RCA Victor 3885
3/30/68	184	3			16	Solo Flights	[I] $25	RCA Victor 3922

DEBUT	PEAK	WKS	RIAA	CD	ARTIST — Album Title	Catalog	Sym	$	Label & Number

ATKINS, Chet — Cont'd

DEBUT	PEAK	WKS			Title		Sym	$	Label & Number
10/11/69	160	4			17 Chet Picks On The Pops		[I]	$25	RCA Victor 3104

CHET ATKINS/BOSTON POPS/ARTHUR FIEDLER

12/13/69+	150	7			18 Solid Gold '69		[I]	$20	RCA Victor 4244
4/25/70	139	5			19 Yestergroovin'		[I]	$20	RCA Victor 4331
5/29/76	172	5	©		20 Chester & Lester		[I]	$12	RCA Victor 1167

CHET ATKINS & LES PAUL

| 4/27/85 | 145 | 13 | © | | 21 Stay Tuned | | [I] | $10 | Columbia 39591 |
| 11/3/90 | 127 | 25 | © | | 22 Neck And Neck | | [I] | $10 | Columbia 45307 |

CHET ATKINS/MARK KNOPFLER

Acutely Cute (15)
Adios Amigo (12)
After The Tears (13)
Al-Di-La (13)
Alabama Jubilee (12)
Alexander's Ragtime Band (7)
Alley Cat (8)
Always On Saturday (7)
And I Love Her (11)
April In Portugal (1)
Aquarius (18)
Autumn Leaves (16)
Avalon (20)
Ave Maria (15)
Ay-Ay-Ay (1)
Back Home Again In Indiana (8)
Banana Boat Song (6)
Bandit, The (6)
Battle Of New Orleans (medley) (17)
Birth Of The Blues (20)
Black Orpheus, Theme From ..see: Manha De Carnaval
Blackbird (17)
Blue Christmas (19)
Blue Steel Blues (5)
Bonita (3)
Boo Boo Stick Beat (2) *49*
Boot And The Stone (21)
Both Sides Now (18)
Bring Me Sunshine (19)
By The Time I Get To Phoenix (17)
Bye Bye Birdie (8)
Can't Buy Me Love (11)
Cancion Triste (Sad Song) (15)
Canticle ..see: Scarborough Fair
Caravan (20)
Cast Your Fate To The Wind (14)
Cheek To Cheek (16)
Cherokee (19)
Chet's Tune (16)
Choro Da Saudade (16)
Cindy, Oh Cindy (16)
Cold, Cold Heart (12)
Come September, Theme From (6)
Come Softly To Me (2)

Come To The Mardi Gras (6)
Copper Kettle (10)
Cosmic Square Dance (21)
Country Champagne (19)
Country Gentleman (12)
Coventry Carol (medley) (9)
Cricket Ballet (21)
Czardas (1)
Deck The Halls (9)
Deed I Do (20)
Delilah (17)
Django's Castle (Manoir De Mes Reves) (2)
Dobro (10)
Down Home (7)
Drina (13)
Drive-In (16)
Drown In My Own Tears (7)
East Of The Sun (West Of The Moon) (4)
El Humahuaqueno (Carnavalito) (15)
Enchanted Sea (6)
English Leather (13)
Et Maintenant (What Now My Love) (14)
Faded Love (12)
First Noël (9)
Folsom Prison Blues (18)
For No One (14)
Freight Train (10)
From Nashville With Love (13)
Galveston (17)
Georgy Girl (16)
Girl Friend Of The Whirling Dervish (5)
Give The World A Smile (5)
God Rest Ye Merry, Gentlemen (medley) (9)
Goin' Home (4)
Gone (10)
Gonna Get Along Without You Now (16)
Goodnight Irene (7)
Goofus (8)
Gotta Travel On (19)
Guitar Country (10)
Hard Day's Night (11)
Hark! The Herald Angels Sing (9)

Hey Jude (18)
Hi-Lili, Hi-Lo (4)
Hot Mocking Bird (3)
Hot Toddy (2)
House In New Orleans (7)
How High The Moon (19)
I Ain't Gonna Work Tomorrow (5)
I Feel Fine (11)
I Feel Pretty (15)
I Got A Woman (8)
I Love How You Love Me (8)
I Love Paris (13)
I Will (8)
I'll Cry Instead (11)
I'll Fly Away (12)
I'll Follow The Sun (11)
I'll Never Fall In Love Again (18)
I'll See You In My Dreams (22)
I'm A Pilgrim (5)
I'm Thinking Tonight Of My Blue Eyes (12)
If I Fell (11)
If I Should Lose You (21)
In A Little Spanish Town ('Twas On A Night Like This) (3)
In The Chapel In The Moonlight (1)
In The Pines (medley) (12)
Inka Dinka Doo (19)
Intermezzo (4)
It Ain't Necessarily So (4)
It Had To Be You (20)
It's Been A Long, Long Time (20)
January In Bombay (14)
Jean (18)
Jingle Bell Rock (9)
Jingle Bells (9)
John Henry (medley) (12)
Jolly Old St. Nicholas (9)
Jungle Dream (6)
Jungle Drums (1)
Just One Time (22)
Kentucky (10)
La Fiesta (13)
Lagrima (medley) (15)
Lambeth Walk (3)
Lara's Theme (14)
Last Waltz (17)

Liberty (19)
Listen To The Mockingbird (medley) (12)
Little Bit Of Blues (10)
Little Bitty Tear (7)
Little Drummer Boy (9)
Little Evil (8)
Little Feet (5)
Little Music Box (La Alborada) (medley) (15)
Lover Come Back To Me (20)
Lullaby Of Birdland (3)
Malaguenas (15)
Manha De Carnaval (15)
Marie (3)
Martha (1)
Mayan Dance (6)
Melissa (7)
Mercy, Mercy, Mercy (16)
Michelle (11)
Monte Carlo Melody (4)
Montego Bay (6)
Moon Over Miami (6)
Moonglow/Picnic (20)
Morenita Do Brazil (15)
Moulin Rouge (Where Is Your Heart), Song From (13)
Mouse In The House (21)
Music To Watch Girls By (16)
My Dear Little Sweetheart (4)
My Prayer (4)
My Way (18)
'Na Voce, 'Na Chitarra E'o Poco 'E Luna (14)
Nagasaki (1)
Never On Sunday (5)
Next Time I'm In Town (22)
Night Train (2)
Nine Pound Hammer (10)
O Come, All Ye Faithful (9)
Ode To Billy Joe (7)
Oh, Lonesome Me (2)
Old Double Shuffle (7)
On Top Of Old Smoky (medley) (12)
One Mint Julep (2) *82*
Orange Blossom Special (12)
Out Of Nowhere (20)
Pickin' Nashville (14)
Picnic ..see: Moonglow

Please Stay Tuned (21)
Poor Boy Blues (22)
Que Sera, Sera ..see: Whatever Will Be, Will Be
Quiet Eyes (21)
Ranjana (14)
Rock-A-Bye Bay (4)
Rocky Top (19)
Romance (13)
Romeo And Juliet, Love Theme From (18)
Rumpus (8)
Salty Dog Rag (5)
Say "Si Si" (1)
Scarborough Fair/Canticle (17)
Scare Crow (7)
Scherzino Mexicano (15)
Sempre (14)
She Loves You (11)
She's A Woman (11)
Silent Night (9)
Silver Bells (9)
Sleep (3)
Sleep Walk (2)
So Soft, Your Goodbye (22)
So What's New (18)
Some Leather And Lace (21)
Someday Sweetheart (20)
Something Tender (13)
Son Of A Preacher Man (18)
Sophisticated Lady (1)
Soul Journey (13)
Spanish Harlem (7,17)
Star-Time (21)
Stay As Sweet As You Are (4)
Steel Guitar Rag (5)
Steeplechase Lane (19)
Stranger On The Shore (13)
Streamlined Cannon Ball (7)
Sugarfoot Rag (10,17)
Summer Place, Theme From A (3)
Sunrise (21)
Susie-Q (8)
Sweet Dreams (22)
Sweetie Baby (8)
Tahitian Skies (22)
Take A Message To Mary (2)
Tammy (3)

Tap Room (21)
Taste Of Honey (14)
Tears (22)
Teen Scene (8)
Teensville (2) *73*
Temptation (6)
Tennessee Pride (14)
Tennessee Waltz (12)
Testament Of Amelia (15)
There'll Be Some Changes Made (22)
Things We Said Today (11)
This Guy's In Love With You (17)
Three Little Words (16)
Till There Was You (2)
To Be In Love (15)
Trambone (5)
Tuxedo Junction (5)
Vanessa (4)
Vaya Con Dios (10)
Vilia (1)
Walk Right In (8)
(What Now My Love) ..see: Et Maintenant
What'd I Say (14)
Whatever Will Be, Will Be (Que Sera, Sera) (3)
When Day Is Done (4)
When You Wish Upon A Star (16)
(Where Is Your Heart) ..see: Moulin Rouge
Whispering (3)
White Christmas (9)
White Silver Sands (2)
Wild Orchids (8)
Wildwood Flower (medley) (12)
Wimoweh (17)
Windy And Warm (5,12)
Winter Walkin' (14)
Winter Wonderland (9)
Yakety Axe (22)
Yankee Doodle Dixie (1)
Yellow Bird (6,15)
Yes Ma'am (10)
Yesterday (11)
Yestergroovin' (19)
You're Just In Love (1)

ATLANTA '84

Country group from Atlanta: Brad Griffis and Bill Davidson (vocals), Tony Ingram (vocals, fiddle), Alan David (guitar), Allen Collay and Bill Packard (keyboards), Jeff Baker (harmonica), Dick Stevens (bass) and John Holder (drums).

| 5/26/84 | 140 | 7 | | | Pictures | | | $10 | MCA 5463 |

Atlanta Burned Again Last Night
Blue Side Of The Grey
Dixie Dreaming
Long Cool Woman In A Black Dress
(Nothing Left Between Us) But Alabama
Pictures
Sweet Country Music
Sweet Was Our Rose
Wishful Drinkin'
You Are The Wine

ATLANTA DISCO BAND, The '76

Disco studio group from Atlanta assembled by producer Dave Crawford. Includes members of MFSB.

| 1/17/76 | 172 | 9 | | | Bad Luck | | [I] | $12 | Ariola America 50004 |

Bad Luck *94*
Buckhead
Do What You Feel
I Am Trying
It's Love
Let It Ride
My Soul Is Satisfied
Ole Goat

★448★ ATLANTA RHYTHM SECTION '78

Rock group formed in Doraville, Georgia: Ronnie Hammond (vocals), Barry Bailey and J.R. Cobb (guitars), Dean Daughtry (keyboards), Paul Goddard (bass) and Robert Nix (drums). Daughtry and Nix were with **Roy Orbison**'s band, **The Candymen**. Cobb, Daughtry and band manager/producer Buddy Buie were with the **Classics IV**. Nix left in late 1978, replaced by Roy Yeager.

1)Champagne Jam 2)A Rock And Roll Alternative 3)Underdog

9/14/74	74	12			1 Third Annual Pipe Dream			$12	Polydor 6027
9/6/75	113	9			2 Dog Days			$12	Polydor 6041
6/5/76	146	15			3 Red Tape			$12	Polydor 6060
1/15/77	11	39	●	©	4 A Rock And Roll Alternative			$12	Polydor 6080
4/9/77	154	4			5 Atlanta Rhythm Section		[E]	$15	MCA 4114 [2]
					recordings from 1972-73				
4/1/78	7	40	▲	©	6 Champagne Jam			$12	Polydor 6134
6/23/79	26	21	●		7 Underdog			$12	Polydor 6200
11/10/79	51	12			8 Are You Ready!		[L]	$15	Polydor 6236 [2]
8/16/80	65	11			9 The Boys From Doraville			$12	Polydor 6285
9/19/81	70	16		©	10 Quinella			$10	Columbia 37550

34

ATLANTA RHYTHM SECTION — Cont'd

Alien (10) *29*
All In Your Mind (5)
All Night Rain (2)
Angel (What In The World's Come Over Us) (1,8) *79*
Another Man's Woman (3,5,8)
Baby No Lie (5)
Back Up Against The Wall (5,8)
Ballad Of Lois Malone (6)
Beautiful Dreamers (3)
Bless My Soul (2)
Blues In Maude's Flat (1)
Boogie Smoogie (2)
Born Ready (7)
Can't Stand It No More (5)
Champagne Jam (6,8) *43*
Close The Door (1)

Cocaine Charlie (9)
Cold Turkey, Tenn. (5)
Conversation (5,8)
Crazy (2)
Cuban Crisis (2)
Do It Or Die (7) *19*
Dog Days (2) *64*
Don't Miss The Message (4)
Doraville (1,8) *35*
Earnestine (5)
Everybody Gotta Go (4)
Evileen (6)
Forty Days And Forty Nights (5)
Free Spirit (3) *85*
Georgia Rhythm (4,8) *68*

Get Your Head Out Of Your Heart (1)
Going To Shangri-La (10)
Great Escape (6)
Help Yourself (1)
Higher (1)
Hitch Hikers' Hero (4)
Homesick (10)
I Ain't Much (9)
I Hate The Blues (medley) (7)
I'm Not Gonna Let It Bother Me Tonight (6,8) *14*
Imaginary Lover (6,8) *7*
Indigo Passion (7)
It Just Ain't Your Moon (2)
It Must Be Love (5)
It's Only Music (7)

Jesus Hearted People (1)
Join The Race (1)
Jukin (3) *82*
Large Time (6,8)
Let's Go Get Stoned (medley) (7)
Livin' Lovin' Wreck (5)
Long Tall Sally (5)
Love Me Just A Little (Sometime) (5)
Make Me Believe It (5)
Mixed Emotions (3)
My Song (7)
Neon Nites (4) *42*
Next Year's Rock & Roll (9)
Normal Love (6)
Oh What A Feeling (3)

One More Problem (5)
Outlaw Music (10)
Outside Woman Blues (4)
Pedestal (2)
Police! Police! (3)
Pretty Girl (10)
Putting My Faith In Love (9)
Quinella (10)
Redneck (5)
Rough At The Edges (9)
Shanghied (8)
Silent Treatment (2)
Silver Eagle (9)
Sky High (4,8)
So In To You (4,8) *7*
Southern Exposure (10)
Spooky (7) *17*

Strictly R & R (9)
Superman (5)
Tara's Theme (8)
Try My Love (9)
War Is Over (1)
What You Gonna Do About It (5)
While Time Is Left (7)
Who You Gonna Run To (1)
Will I Live On (5)
Wrong (5)
You're So Strong (10)
Yours And Mine (5)

★491★ ATLANTIC STARR   '86

R&B group from White Plains, New York: brothers David (guitar), Wayne (keyboards) and Jonathan (trumpet) Lewis, with **Sharon Bryant** (vocals), Cliff Archer (bass) and Porter Carroll (drums). Barbara Weathers replaced Bryant in 1984. Rachel Oliver replaced Weathers in 1991.

DEBUT	PEAK	WKS	RIAA	CD	ARTIST — Album Title	$	Label & Number
8/26/78	67	13			1 **Atlantic Starr**	$12	A&M 4711
6/2/79	142	7			2 **Straight To The Point**	$12	A&M 4764
3/14/81	47	30			3 **Radiant**	$10	A&M 4833
3/27/82	18	29			4 **Brilliance**	$10	A&M 4883
11/19/83+	91	28			5 **Yours Forever**	$10	A&M 4948
5/25/85+	17	68	●	©	6 **As The Band Turns**	$10	A&M 5019
4/25/87	18	31	▲	©	7 **All In The Name Of Love**	$10	Warner 25560
5/20/89	125	6		©	8 **We're Movin' Up**	$10	Warner 25849
2/8/92	134	14			9 **Love Crazy**	$10	Reprise 26545

All In The Name Of Love (7)
Always (7) *1*
Am I Dreaming (3)
Being In Love With You Is So Much Fun (1)
Bring It Back Home Again (8)
Bullseye (2)
Circles (4) *38*
Come Lover (9)
Cool, Calm, Collected (6)
Does It Matter (3)
Don't Abuse My Love (1)
Don't Start The Fire (8)
Don't Take Me For Granted (7)
Fallin' In Love With You (2)

Females (7)
Freak-A-Ristic (6) *90*
Friends (8)
Gimme Your Luvin' (1)
Girl, Your Love's So Fine (9)
Hold On (9)
I Can't Wait (8,9)
I Want Your Love (5)
(I'll Never Miss) The Love I Never Had (1)
I'm In Love With You (8)
If You Knew What's Good For You (9)
If Your Heart Isn't In It (6) *57*
In The Heat Of Passion (6)

Interlude (7)
Island Dream (5)
Keep It Comin' (1)
Kissin' Power (2)
Let The Spirit Move Ya (2)
Let The Sun In (7)
Let's Get Closer (4)
(Let's) Rock 'N' Roll (2)
Let's Start It Over (6)
Lookin' For Love Again (9)
Losin' You (2)
Love Crazy (9) *75*
Love Me Down (4)
Love Moves (4)
Masterpiece (9) *3*

More, More, More (5)
More Time For Me (5)
My First Love (8)
My Mistake (7)
My Special Lover (9)
My Sugar (8)
My Turn Now (3)
Mystery Girl (3)
One Love (6)
One Lover At A Time (7) *58*
Perfect Love (4)
Second To None (6)
Secret Lovers (6) *3*
Send For Me (3)
Sexy Dancer (4)

Silver Shadow (6)
Stand Up (1)
Straight To The Point (2)
Thank You (6)
Thankful (7)
Think About That (3)
Touch A Four Leaf Clover (5) *87*
Tryin' (3)
Unconditional Love (9)
Under Pressure (3)
Under Your Spell (8)
Visions (1)
We Got It Together (9)
We're Movin' Up (8)

What 'Cha Feel Inside (2)
When Love Calls (3)
Where There's Smoke There's Fire (1)
Who Could Love You Better? (5)
With Your Love I Come Alive (1)
You Belong With Me (7)
You Deserve The Best (8)
You Hit The Spot (9)
You're The One (4)
Your Love Finally Ran Out (4)
Yours Forever (5)

ATOMIC ROOSTER   '71

British rock group co-founded by Vincent Crane (keyboards) and Carl Palmer (drums; **Emerson, Lake & Palmer, Asia**), both were with **The Crazy World of Arthur Brown**. Palmer left before first album. Fluctuating lineup included vocalist Chris Farlowe on third album, earlier of **Colosseum**. Crane committed suicide on 2/14/89 (age 44).

DEBUT	PEAK	WKS	RIAA	CD	ARTIST — Album Title	$	Label & Number
7/3/71	90	15			1 **Death Walks Behind You**	$20	Elektra 74094
12/11/71+	167	9			2 **In Hearing Of Atomic Rooster**	$20	Elektra 74109
10/7/72	149	8		©	3 **Made In England**	$20	Elektra 75039

All In Satan's Name (3)
Black Snake (2)
Break The Ice (2)
Breakthrough (2)
Breathless (3)
Close Your Eyes (3)

Death Walks Behind You (1)
Decision/Indecision (2)
Devil's Answer (2)
Don't Know What Went Wrong (3)
Gershatzer (1)

Head In The Sky (2)
I Can't Take No More (1)
Introduction (3)
Little Bit Of Inner Air (3)
Never Too Late (3)
Nobody Else (1)

People You Can't Trust (3)
Price, The (2)
Rock, The (2)
Seven Streets (1)
Sleeping For Years (1)
Space Cowboy (3)

Spoonful Of Bromide Helps The Pulse Rate Go Down (2)
Stand By Me (3)
Time Take My Life (3)
Tomorrow Night (1)
Vug (1)

AT THE DRIVE-IN   '01

Rock group from El Paso, Texas: Cedric Bixler (vocals), Omar Rodriguez and Jim Ward (guitars), Paul Hinojos (bass) and Tony Hajjar (drums).

DEBUT	PEAK	WKS	RIAA	CD	ARTIST — Album Title	$	Label & Number
9/30/00+	116	14		©	**Relationship Of Command**	$10	Grand Royal 49999

Arcarsenal
Cosmonaut

Enfilade
Invalid Litter Dept.

Mannequin Republic
Non-Zero Possibility

One Armed Scissor
Pattern Against.User

Quarantined
Rolodex Propaganda

Sleepwalk Capsules

AUDIENCE   '72

Rock group from London: Howard Werth (vocals, guitar), Patrick Neubergh (sax), Nick Judd (keyboards), Trevor Williams (bass) and Tony Connor (drums).

DEBUT	PEAK	WKS	RIAA	CD	ARTIST — Album Title	$	Label & Number
6/24/72	175	5		©	**Lunch**	$15	Elektra 75026

Ain't The Man You Need
Barracuda Dan

Buy Me An Island
Hula Girl

In Accord
Party Games

Seven Sore Bruises
Stand By The Door

Thunder And Lightning
Trombone Gulch

AUDIO ADRENALINE   '96

Christian pop-rock group from Grayson, Kentucky: Mark Stuart (vocals), Barry Blair (guitar), Bob Herdman (keyboards), Will McGinniss (bass) and Ben Cissel (drums). Tyler Burkham replaced Blair in early 1997.

DEBUT	PEAK	WKS	RIAA	CD	ARTIST — Album Title	Sym	$	Label & Number
3/9/96	77	11	●	©	1 **Bloom**		$10	ForeFront 25144
12/6/97	99	5		©	2 **Some Kind Of Zombie**		$10	ForeFront 25182
10/2/99	76	7		©	3 **Underdog**		$10	ForeFront 25225
4/7/01	186	2			4 **Hit Parade**	[G]	$10	ForeFront 25273

Bag Lady (1)
Big House (4)
Blitz (2,4)
Chevette (2,4)
DC-10 (3,4)
Flicker (4)
Free Ride (1)

Get Down (3,4)
Gloryland (1)
God-Shaped Hole (2)
Good Life (3)
Good People (1)
Hands And Feet (3)
Houseplant Song (3)

I Hear Jesus Calling (1)
I'm Not The King (1,4)
It Is Well With My Soul (3)
It's Over (3)
Jazz Odyssey (1)
Jesus Movement (3)
Let My Love Open The Door (3)

Lighthouse (2)
Man Of God (1,4)
Memoir (1)
Mighty Good Leader (3,4)
Never Gonna Be As Big As Jesus (1,4)
New Body (2)

One Like You (4)
Original Species (2)
People Like Me (2)
Rest Easy (4)
Secret (1)
See Through (1)

Some Kind Of Zombie (2,4)
Superfriend (2)
This Day (3)
Underdog (3,4)
Walk On Water (1,4)
We're A Band (4)
Will Not Fade (4)

AUDIO TWO '88
Rap duo from Brooklyn, New York: brothers Kirk and Gene Robinson.

6/25/88 **185** 4 © **What More Can I Say?** .... $10 First Priority 90907

Giz Starts Buggin'	I Don't Care	Make It Funky	Questions, The	What More Can I Say?
Hickeys Around My Neck	I Like Cherries	Put It 2 Music	Top Billin'	When The 2 Is On The Mic

AUER, Barbara Ann '81
Born in Los Angeles. Aerobic dance instructor.

6/20/81 **145** 15 **Aerobic Dancing** .... $12 Gateway 7610

Beyond Orion [Disco From Another Galaxy]	Love Letters [Salsoul Orchestra]	Magic Bird Of Fire [Salsoul Orchestra]	Queens Red [Michael Colombier]
From A Dream [Neil Larsen]		Promenade [Neil Larsen]	

AUGER, Brian '74
Born on 7/18/39 in Bihar, India; raised in London. Jazz-rock keyboardist. The Trinity consisted of Julie Driscoll (vocals), Gary Boyle (guitar), Dave Ambrose (bass) and Clive Thacker (drums). Disbanded in mid-1970. Everchanging personnel of Oblivion Express included future **AWB** members Robbie McIntosh and Steve Ferrone, and Alex Ligertwood, later of **Santana**.
1)Streetnoise 2)Straight Ahead 3)Live Oblivion, Vol. 1

JULIE DRISCOLL/BRIAN AUGER & THE TRINITY:

5/10/69 **194** 2 © 1 **Jools & Brian** .... $20 Capitol 136
6/14/69 **41** 16 © 2 **Streetnoise** .... $25 Atco 701 [2]

BRIAN AUGER & THE TRINITY:

8/1/70 **184** 3 © 3 **Befour** .... $15 RCA Victor 4372

BRIAN AUGER'S OBLIVION EXPRESS:

6/3/72 **170** 7 © 4 **Second Wind** .... $15 RCA Victor 4703
8/4/73 **64** 31 © 5 **Closer To It!** .... $15 RCA Victor 0140
4/6/74 **45** 20 © 6 **Straight Ahead** .... $15 RCA Victor 0454
12/7/74+ **51** 13 © 7 **Live Oblivion, Vol. 1** .... [L] $15 RCA Victor 0645
recorded at the Whiskey-A-Go-Go in Hollywood
10/11/75 **115** 8 © 8 **Reinforcements** .... $12 RCA Victor 1210
3/13/76 **169** 4 © 9 **Live Oblivion, Vol. 2** .... [L] $15 RCA Victor 1230 [2]
recorded at the Whiskey-A-Go-Go in Hollywood
2/19/77 **127** 5 10 **Happiness Heartaches** .... $12 Warner 2981
4/23/77 **151** 3 © 11 **The Best Of Brian Auger** .... [G] $12 RCA Victor 2249

Adagio Per Archi E Organo (3)	Ellis Island (2)	Happiness Is Just Around The Bend (5,9,11)	Inner City Blues (5,9,11)	Oh, Baby Won't You Come Back Home To Croydon,	Straight Ahead (6,9,11)
All Blues (2)	Finally Found You Out (2)	I Didn't Want To Have To Do It	Just You Just Me (3,4)	Where Everybody Beedle An'	Take Me To The Water (2)
Back Street Bible Class (10)	Flesh Failures (Let The	(1)	Kiko (1)	Bo's (1)	Thoughts From Afar (8)
Beginning Again (6,7)	Sunshine In) (2)	I Got Life (2)	Let's Do It Tonight (1)	Paging Mr. McCoy (10)	Tiger (1)
Big Yin (8)	Fool Killer (1)	I Know You (1)	Light My Fire (2)	Pavane (2)	Tropic Of Capricorn (2)
Brain Damage (8)	Foolish Girl (8,11)	I Know You Love Me Not (1)	Light On The Path (5)	Plum (8)	Truth (4,7)
Bumpin' On Sunset (6,7)	Freedom Jazz Dance (4,9,11)	I Wanna Take You Higher (3)	Listen Here (3,11) *100*	Save The Country (2)	Vauxhall To Lambeth Bridge (2)
Change (6)	Future Pilot (8)	If You Should Ever Leave Me	Looking In The Eye Of The	Second Wind (4,9)	Voices Of Other Times (5)
Compared To What (5,9)	Gimme A Funky Break (10)	(1)	World (2)	Somebody Help Us (4)	When I Was A Young Girl (2)
Czechoslovakia (2)	Got To Be Born Again (10)	In Search Of The Sun (2)	Maiden Voyage (3,9)	Something Out Of Nothing (8)	Whenever You're Ready (5,9)
Don't Do It No More (1)	Green Onions (1)	Indian Rope Man (2)	Never Gonna Come Down (10)	Spice Island (10)	Word About Color (2)
Don't Look Away (4,7)	Happiness Heartaches (10)		No Time To Live (3)		You'll Stay In My Heart (6)

AURRA '82
Funk group from Dayton, Ohio: Starleana Young and Curt Jones (vocals), Steve Washington and Tom Lockett (horns) and Philip Fields (keyboards). All but Fields were members of **Slave**. Young and Jones later formed **Déja**.

6/13/81 **103** 13 © 1 **Send Your Love** .... $10 Salsoul 8538
2/27/82 **38** 15 2 **A Little Love** .... $10 Salsoul 8551

Are You Single (1)	In My Arms (2)	Kingston Lady (1)	Make Up Your Mind (2) *71*	Patience (2)	Thinking Of You (2)
Checking You Out (2)	It's You (2)	Little Love (2)	Nasty Disposition (1)	Send Your Love (1)	
Forever (1)	Keep Doin' It (1)	Living Too Fast (1)	Party Time (1)	Still Free (2)	

AUSTIN, Patti '83
Born on 8/10/48 in New York City. R&B singer.

12/3/77+ **116** 13 © 1 **Havana Candy** .... $12 CTI 5006
10/3/81+ **36** 44 © 2 **Every Home Should Have One** .... $10 Qwest 3591
3/31/84 **87** 18 © 3 **Patti Austin** .... $10 Qwest 23974
11/9/85 **182** 4 4 **Gettin' Away With Murder** .... $10 Qwest 25276
4/14/90 **93** 17 © 5 **Love Is Gonna Getcha** .... $10 GRP 9603

All Behind Us Now (3)	Fine Fine Fella (Got To Have	Honey For The Bees (4)	It's Gonna Be Special (3) *82*	Starstruck (3)	Way I Feel (2)
Any Way You Can (3)	You) (3)	Hot! In The Flames Of Love (3)	Little Baby (1)	Stop, Look, Listen (2)	We're In Love (1)
Anything Can Happen Here (4)	First Time Love (5)	I Just Want To Know (1)	Lost In The Stars (1)	Summer Is The Coldest Time	
Baby, Come To Me (2) *1*	Genie, The (2)	I Need Somebody (1)	Love Is Gonna Getcha (5)	Of Year (4)	
Believe The Children (5)	Gettin' Away With Murder (4)	I've Got My Heart Set On You	Love Me To Death (1)	Symphony Of Love (2)	
Big Bad World (4)	Girl Who Used To Be Me (5)	(3)	Oh No, Margarita (2)	Talkin' 'Bout My Baby (4)	
Change Your Attitude (3)	Golden Oldies (1)	If I Believed (4)	Only A Breath Away (4)	That's Enough For Me (1)	
Do You Love Me? (2)	Good In Love (5)	In My Dream (5)	Ooh-Whee (The Carnival) (5)	Through The Test Of Time (5)	
Every Home Should Have	Havana Candy (1)	In My Life (5)	Rhythm Of The Street (3)	Too Soon To Know (5)	
One (2) *62*	Heat Of Heat (4) *55*	Island, The (2)	Shoot The Moon (3)	Wait For Me (5)	

AUSTIN, Sherrié '99
Born on 8/28/70 in Sydney, Australia; raised in Townsville, Australia. Country singer/actress. Played "Pippa McKenna" on TV's *The Facts of Life* (1987-88).

8/28/99 **150** 3 © **Love In The Real World** .... $10 Arista 18881

All That Matters	Good Love Comin' On	Little Bird	Sarah	Wish
All The Love A Heart Can Hold	Heart Hold On	Love In The Real World	That's No Way To Break A	
Dreaming Out Loud	Heart To Heart	Never Been Kissed *89*	Heart	

AUTOGRAPH '85

Rock group from Los Angeles: Steve Plunkett (vocals, guitar), Steve Lynch (guitar), Steven Isham (keyboards), Randy Rand (bass) and Keni Richards (drums).

DEBUT	PEAK	WKS	RIAA	CD	ARTIST — Album Title	$	Label & Number
1/5/85	29	29	●	©	1 Sign In Please	$10	RCA Victor 8040
11/16/85	92	15		©	2 That's The Stuff	$10	RCA Victor 7009
4/11/87	108	15		©	3 Loud And Clear	$10	RCA Victor 5796

All I'm Gonna Take (1)
Bad Boy (3)
Blondes In Black Cars (2)
Built For Speed (2)
Changing Hands (2)
Cloud 10 (1)
Crazy World (2)
Dance All Night (3)
Deep End (1)
Down 'N Dirty (3)
Everytime I Dream (3)
Friday (1)
Hammerhead (1)
In The Night (1)
Just Got Back From Heaven (3)
Loud And Clear (3)
More Than A Million Times (3)
My Girlfriend's Boyfriend Isn't Me (1)
Night Teen & Non Stop (1)
Paint This Town (2)
Send Her To Me (1)
She Never Looked That Good For Me (1)
She's A Tease (3)
Six String Fever (2)
Take No Prisoners (2)
That's The Stuff (2)
Thrill Of Love (1)
Turn Up The Radio (1) 29
When The Sun Goes Down (3)
You'll Get Over It (2)

AUTOMATIC MAN '77

Rock group from San Francisco: Bayete (vocals, keyboards), Pat Thrall (guitar; **Asia**), Donni Harvey (bass) and **Michael Shrieve** (drums; **Santana**). After first album, Shrieve and Harvey left; replaced by Glenna Symmonds and Jerome Rinson.

DEBUT	PEAK	WKS	RIAA	CD	ARTIST — Album Title	$	Label & Number
10/2/76	120	7			1 Automatic Man	$12	Island 9397
10/8/77	109	8			2 Visitors	$12	Island 9429

Atlantis Rising Fanfare (1)
Atlantis Rising Theme (Turning Of The Axis) (1)
Automatic Man (1)
Comin' Through (1)
Daughter Of Neptune (2)
Geni-Geni (1)
Give It To Me (2)
Here I Am Now (2)
I.T.D. Interstellar Tracking Devices (1)
Live Wire (2)
My Pearl (1) 97
Newspapers (1)
One And One (1)
Right Back Down (1)
So You Wanna Be (2)
There's A Way (1)
Visitors (2)
What's Done (1)
Y - 2 - Me (2)

AVALON '01

Christian vocal group: Jody McBrayer and Michael Passons (male vocals), Nikki Hassman and Janna Potter (female vocals). Cherie Paliotta replaced Hassman after first album.

DEBUT	PEAK	WKS	RIAA	CD	ARTIST — Album Title	Sym	$	Label & Number
2/20/99	153	1	●	©	1 A Maze Of Grace		$10	Sparrow 51639
4/10/99	81	13	●	©	2 In A Different Light		$10	Sparrow 51687
11/18/00	115	8		©	3 Joy: A Christmas Collection	[X]	$10	Sparrow 51733
6/9/01	37	11		©	4 Oxygen		$10	Sparrow 51796

Adonai (1)
Always Have, Always Will (2)
Angels Medley (3)
Best Thing (4)
By Heart, By Soul (4)
Can't Live A Day (2)
Christmas Song (3)
Come And Fill My Heart (4)
Don't Save It All For Christmas Day (3)
Dreams I Dream For You (1)
First Love (4)
Forgive + Forget (1)
Glory, The (4)
Good News (3)
Hide My Soul (2)
I Don't Want To Go (4)
I'm Speechless (2)
If My People Pray (2)
In A Different Light (2)
In Not Of (2)
Jesus Born On This Day (3)
Joy (To The World) (3)
Knockin' On Heaven's Door (1)
Let Your Love (2)
Light A Candle (3)
Love Remains (4)
Make It Last Forever (4)
Manger Medley (3)
Maze Of Grace (1)
Move, The (1)
Never Givin' Up (4)
Only For The Weak (2)
Oxygen (4)
Reason Enough (1)
Speed Of Light (1)
Take You At Your Word (2)
Testify To Love (1)
Undeniably You (4)
We Are The Reason (3)
Winter Wonderland (3)
Wonder Why (4)
World Away (1)

AVALON, Frankie '60

Born Francis Avallone on 9/18/39 in Philadelphia. Singer/actor. Co-starred in many movies with **Annette**.

DEBUT	PEAK	WKS	RIAA	CD	ARTIST — Album Title	Sym	$	Label & Number
12/28/59+	9	14			1 Swingin' On A Rainbow		$75	Chancellor 5004
10/23/61+	59	20			2 A Whole Lotta Frankie	[G]	$75	Chancellor 5018

All Of Everything (2) 70
Birds Of A Feather (1)
Bobby Sox To Stockings (2) 8
Call Me Anytime (2)
Dede Dinah (2) 7
Don't Let Love Pass Me By (2) 85
Don't Throw Away All Those Teardrops (2) 22
Ginger Bread (2) 9
I Do Adore Her (1)
I'll Wait For You (2) 15
Just Ask Your Heart (2) 7
Perfect Love (2) 47
Sandy (1)
Secret Love (1)
She's Funny That Way (1)
Step In The Right Direction (1)
Swingin' On A Rainbow (1) 39
Talk, Talk, Talk (1,2)
Them There Eyes (1)
Togetherness (2) 26
Trouble With Me Is You (1)
Try A Little Tenderness (1)
Tuxedo Junction (2) 82
Two Fools (2) 54
Venus (2) 1
What's The Reason (I'm Not Pleasin' You) (1)
Where Are You (2) 32
Why (2) 1
You're Just Too Much (1)

AVANT '00

Born Myron Avant in 1978 in Cleveland. Male R&B singer.

DEBUT	PEAK	WKS	RIAA	CD	ARTIST — Album Title	$	Label & Number
5/27/00	45	44	●	©	My Thoughts	$10	Magic Johnson 112069

Destiny
Get Away
Happy
I Wanna Know
Let's Make A Deal
My First Love 26
Ooh Aah
Reaction
Separated 23
Serious
This Time
Why

★369★ AWB (AVERAGE WHITE BAND) '75

White funk group from Scotland: Alan Gorrie (vocals, bass), Onnie McIntyre (guitar, vocals), Hamish Stuart (guitar, vocals), Malcolm Duncan (sax), Roger Ball (sax, keyboards) and Robbie McIntosh (drums). Gorrie and McIntyre were members of **Forever More**. McIntosh died of a drug overdose on 9/23/74 (age 24), replaced by Steve Ferrone. McIntosh and Ferrone were members of **Brian Auger's Oblivion Express**. Stuart later joined **Paul McCartney**'s touring band.

1)AWB 2)Cut The Cake 3)Soul Searching

DEBUT	PEAK	WKS	RIAA	CD	ARTIST — Album Title	Sym	$	Label & Number
9/21/74+	❶[1]	43	●	©	1 AWB		$12	Atlantic 7308
4/5/75	39	13			2 Put It Where You Want It	[E]	$12	MCA 475
					released in 1973 as Show Your Hand on MCA 345 ($20)			
6/28/75	4	24	●	©	3 Cut The Cake		$12	Atlantic 18140
7/17/76	9	32	▲	©	4 Soul Searching		$12	Atlantic 18179
1/22/77	28	18	●	©	5 Person To Person	[L]	$15	Atlantic 1002 [2]
7/23/77	33	21			6 Benny And Us		$12	Atlantic 19105
					AVERAGE WHITE BAND & BEN E. KING			
4/1/78	28	17	●	©	7 Warmer Communications		$12	Atlantic 19162
4/7/79	32	15		©	8 Feel No Fret		$12	Atlantic 19207
5/31/80	116	12			9 Shine		$10	Arista 9523
9/20/80	182	2		©	10 Volume VIII	[G]	$10	Atlantic 19266

Ace Of Hearts (8)
Atlantic Avenue (8)
Back In '67 (2)
Big City Lights (7)
Catch Me (Before I Have To Testify) (9)
Cloudy (3,5)
Cut The Cake (3,5,10) 10
Daddy's All Gone (7)
Digging Deeper (4)
Everybody's Darling (4)
Feel No Fret (8)
Fire Burning (8)
Fool For You Anyway (6)
For You, For Love (9)
Get It Up For Love (6)
Goin' Home (4)
Got The Love (1)
Groovin' The Night Away (3)
Growing Pains (10)
Help Is On The Way (9)
High Flyin' Woman (3)
How Can You Go Home (2)
How Sweet Can You Get (3)
I Heard It Through The Grapevine (5)
I Just Can't Give You Up (1)
I'm The One (4,5)
If I Ever Lose This Heaven (3,5) 39
If Love Only Lasts For One Night (3)
Imagine (6)
Into The Night (9)
It's A Mystery (3)
Just Wanna Love You Tonight (1)
Keepin' It To Myself (1,6)
Kiss Me (10)
Let's Go 'Round Again (9) 53
Love Gives, Love Takes Away (10)
Love Of Your Own (4,10)
Love Won't Get In The Way (10)
Love Your Life (4,5)
Message, The (6)
Nothing You Can Do (1)
One Look Over My Shoulder (Is This Really Goodbye?) (7)
Our Time Has Come (9)
Overture (4)
Person To Person (1,5,10)
Pick Up The Pieces (1,5,10) 1
Please Don't Fall In Love (8)
Price Of The Dream (7)
Put It Where You Want It (2)
Queen Of My Soul (4,10) 40
Reach Out (2)
Same Feeling, Different Song (7)
School Boy Crush (3,5) 33
She's A Dream (7)
Shine (9)
Show Your Hand (2)
Someday We'll All Be Free (6)
Soul Searching (4)
Star In The Ghetto (8)
Stop The Rain (8)
Sunny Days (Make Me Think Of You) (4)

DEBUT	PEAK	WKS	RIAA	CD	ARTIST — Album Title	Catalog	Sym	$	Label & Number

AWB (AVERAGE WHITE BAND) — Cont'd

Sweet & Sour (7)
T.L.C. (2,5)
There's Always Someone Waiting (1)
This World Has Music (2)
Too Late To Cry (8)
Twilight Zone (2)
Walk On By (8) *92*
Warmer Communications (7)
What Is Soul (6)
Whatcha' Gonna Do For Me (9)
When They Bring Down The Curtain (3)
When Will You Be Mine (8)
Why (3)
Work To Do (1)
Would You Stay (4)
You Got It (1)
Your Love Is A Miracle (7)

AXE '82

Rock group from Gainesville, Florida: Bobby Barth (vocals, guitar), Michael Osborne (guitar), Edgar Riley (keyboards), Wayne Haner (bass) and Ted Mueller (drums). Disbanded in 1984. Group made the Adult Contemporary chart in 1976 as Babyface. Osborne died in a car crash on 7/21/84 (age 34).

| 6/26/82 | 81 | 20 | | | 1 **Offering** | | | $10 | Atco 148 |
| 9/10/83 | 156 | 6 | | | 2 **Nemesis** | | | $10 | Atco 90099 |

All Through The Night (2)
Burn The City Down (1)
Eagle Flies Alone (2)
Foolin' Your Mama Again (2)
Girls, Girls, Girls (2)
Heat In The Street (2)
Holdin' On (1)
I Got The Fire (1)
I Think You'll Remember Tonight (2) *94*
Jennifer (1)
Keep Playing That Rock 'N' Roll (2)
Let The Music Come Back (2)
Masquerade (2)
Now Or Never (1) *64*
Rock 'N' Roll Party In The Streets (2)
She's Had The Power (2)
Silent Soldiers (1)
Steal Another Fantasy (1)
Video Inspiration (1)
Young Hearts (2)

AXTON, Hoyt '76

Born on 3/25/38 in Duncan, Oklahoma. Died of a heart attack on 10/26/99 (age 61). Country singer/songwriter/actor. Son of songwriter Mae Axton ("Heartbreak Hotel"). Acted in the movies *The Black Stallion* and *Gremlins*.

| 4/12/75 | 188 | 2 | | | 1 **Southbound** | | | $12 | A&M 4510 |
| 4/10/76 | 171 | 4 | | | 2 **Fearless** | | | $12 | A&M 4571 |

Beyond These Walls (2)
Blind Fiddler (1)
Devil, The (2)
Evangelina (2)
Flash Of Fire (2)
Greensleeves (1)
Gypsy Moth (2)
I Love To Sing (1)
Idol Of The Band (2)
In A Young Girls Mind (1)
Jealous Man (2)
Lay, Lady, Lay (2)
Lion In The Winter (1)
Nashville (1)
No No Song (1)
Old Greyhound (2)
Paid In Advance (2)
Penny Whistle Song (2)
Pride Of Man (1)
Roll Your Own (1)
Sometimes It's Easy (1)
Southbound (1)
Speed Trap (Out Of State Cars) (1)
Stone And A Feather (2)
Whiskey (1)

★457★ AYERS, Roy '78

Born on 9/10/40 in Los Angeles. R&B-jazz vibraphone player/keyboardist/vocalist. With **Herbie Mann** from 1966-70. In 1970, formed **Ubiquity** whose guest players included drummer **Billy Cobham**, guitarist **George Benson**, trombonist Wayne Henderson (**The Crusaders**) and vocalist **Dee Dee Bridgewater**.

1)Let's Do It 2)You Send Me 3)Everybody Loves The Sunshine

ROY AYERS UBIQUITY:

10/5/74	156	4			1 **Change Up The Groove**			$50	Polydor 6032
2/21/76	90	18		©	2 **Mystic Voyage**			$50	Polydor 6057
8/14/76	51	17		©	3 **Everybody Loves The Sunshine**			$50	Polydor 6070
1/15/77	74	12			4 **Vibrations**			$50	Polydor 6091
7/2/77	72	25			5 **Lifeline**			$50	Polydor 6108

ROY AYERS:

3/11/78	33	13			6 **Let's Do It**			$20	Polydor 6126
8/19/78	48	15			7 **You Send Me**			$20	Polydor 6159
5/26/79	67	15			8 **Fever**			$20	Polydor 6204
12/15/79+	82	18			9 **No Stranger To Love**			$20	Polydor 6246
11/1/80	157	3			10 **Love Fantasy**			$20	Polydor 6301
8/15/81	197	2			11 **Africa, Center Of The World**			$20	Polydor 6327
3/20/82	160	7			12 **Feeling Good**			$20	Polydor 6348

Africa, Center Of The World (11)
And Don't You Say No (7)
Baby Bubba (10)
Baby I Need Your Love (4)
Baby You Give Me A Feeling (4)
Believe In Yourself (10)
Betcha Gonna (10)
Better Days (4)
Black Five (2)
Boogie Back (1)
Brother Green (The Disco King) (2)
Can't You See Me? (7)
Change Up The Groove (1)
Cincinnati Growl (5)
Come Out And Play (4)
Destination Motherland (11)
Domelo (Give It To Me) (4)
Don't Hide Your Love (9)
Don't Let Our Love Slip Away (9)
Don't Stop The Feeling (9)
Don't You Worry 'Bout A Thing (1)
Everybody Loves The Sunshine (3)
Everytime I See You (7)
Evolution (2)
Feel Like Makin' Love (1)
Feeling Good (12)
Fever (8)
Fikisha (1)
Fire Up The Funk (12)
Freaky Deaky (6)
Fruit (5)
Funky Motion (2)
Get On Up, Get On Down (7)
Golden Rod (3)
Gotta Find A Lover (5)
Hey Uh-What You Say Come On (3)
Higher (4)
I Still Love You (5)
I Wanna Feel It (I Wanna Dance) (3)
I Wanna Touch You Baby (7)
I'll Just Keep Trying (11)
If You Love Me (8)
Is It Too Late To Try? (8)
It Ain't Your Sign It's Your Mind (3,7)
Keep On Walking (3)
Kiss (6)
Knock, Knock (12)
Land Of Fruit & Honey (11)
Leo (8)
Let's Do It (6)
Let's Stay Together (12)
Life Is Just A Moment (2)
Lifeline (5)
Lonesome Cowboy (3)
Love Fantasy (10)
Love Will Bring Us Back Together (8)
Mash, Theme From (1)
Melody Maker (6)
Memory, The (4)
Mo Mise Si E (I Love You) (11)
Moving, Grooving (4)
Mystic Voyage (2)
No Stranger To Love (medley) (9)
One Sweet Love To Remember (4)
Ooh (12)
Our Time Is Coming (12)
People And The World (3)
Rhythm (7)
River Niger (11)
Rock Your Roll (10)
Running Away (5)
Sanctified Feeling (5)
Searching (4)
Sensitize (1)
Shack Up, Pack Up, It's Up (When I'm Gone) (9)
"Sigh" (Feel The Vibration) (10)
Simple And Sweet (8)
Slyde (9)
Spirit Of Doo Do (2)
Stairway To The Stars (12)
Stranded In The Jungle (5)
Sweet Tears (6)
Take All The Time You Need (2)
Take Me Out To The Ball Game (8)
There's A Master Plan (11)
Third Eye (3,11)
This Side Of Sunshine (5)
Together (5)
Tongue Power (3)
Turn Me Loose (12)
Vibrations (4)
Want You (medley) (9)
Wee Bit (2)
What You Won't Do For Love (9)
When Is Real, Real? (1,6)
You And Me My Love (3)
You Came Into My Life (6)
You Send Me (7)

AZ '95

Born Anthony Cruz in Brooklyn, New York. Male rapper. Member of **The Firm**.

10/28/95	15	6		©	1 **Doe Or Die**			$10	EMI 32631
4/25/98	22	6		©	2 **Pieces Of A Man**			$10	Noo Trybe 56715
6/30/01	23	7		©	3 **9 Lives**			$10	Motown 013786

AZ's Back (3)
At Night (3)
Betcha Don't Know (2)
Born Alone, Die Alone (1)
Doe Or Die (1)
Everything's Everything (3)
Gimme Your's (1)
Ho Happy Jackie (1)
How Many Wanna (3)
How Ya Livin' (2)
I Don't Give A F**k (3)
I Feel For You (1)
I'm Known (2)
It's A Boy Thing (2)
Just Because (2)
Last Dayz (2)
Let's Toast (3)
Love Is Love (2)
Love Me (3)
Mo Money, Mo Murder (Homicide) (1)
New Life (2)
Pay Back (2)
Pieces Of A (Black) Man (2)
Problems (3)
Quiet Money TBS (3)
Rather Unique (1)
Sosa (2)
Sugar Hill (1) *25*
That's Real (3)
Trading Places (2)
Trial Of The Century (2)
Uncut Raw (1)
We Can't Win (1)
What Cha Day About (3)
What Ya'll N****s Want (3)
What's The Deal (2)
Whatever Happened (The Birth) (2)
Your World Don't Stop (1)

AZTECA '73

Latin jazz-rock ensemble led by brothers Pete (vocals) and Coke Escovedo (percussion). Pete is the father of **Sheila E**. Coke died on 7/13/86 (age 45).

| 1/13/73 | 151 | 9 | | © | **Azteca** | | | $15 | Columbia 31776 |

Ah! Ah!
Ain't Got No Special Woman
Azteca
Can't Take The Funk Out Of Me
Empty Prophet
La Piedra Del Sol
Love Not Then
Mamita Linda
Non Pacem
Peace Everybody

AZTEC CAMERA   '83

Pop-rock group formed by singer/songwriter Roddy Frame (born on 1/29/64 in East Kilbride, Scotland). Numerous personnel changes with Frame the only constant.

9/10/83	**129**	10		©	1 **High Land, Hard Rain**			$10	Sire 23899
10/13/84	**175**	6			2 **Knife**			$10	Sire 25183
					produced by **Mark Knopfler**				
4/13/85	**181**	3			3 **Aztec Camera**		[L-M]	$10	Sire 25285
					recorded on 10/16/84 at the Dominion Theatre in London				
12/19/87	**193**	3		©	4 **Love**			$10	Sire 25646

All I Need Is Everything (2) — Boy Wonders (1) — Head Is Happy (Heart's Insane) (2) — Killermont Street (4) — Oblivious (1) — One And One (4) — Somewhere In My Heart (4) — Still On Fire (2)
Back Door To Heaven (2) — Bugle Sounds Again (1,3) — How Men Are (4) — Knife (2) — Paradise (4) — Walk Out To Winter (1)
Back On Board (1) — Deep & Wide & Tall (4) — Jump (1) — Lost Outside The Tunnel (1) — Pillar To Post (1) — We Could Send Letters (1)
Backwards And Forwards (2,3) — Down The Dip (1) — Just Like The USA (2) — Mattress Of Wire (3) — Release (1) — Working In A Goldmine (4)
Birth Of The True (2,3) — Everybody Is A Number One (4) — More Than A Law (4)

AZTEC TWO-STEP   '77

Pop-rock duo from Boston: guitarists/vocalists Rex Fowler and Neal Shulman.

12/25/76+	**181**	4			**Two's Company**			$12	RCA Victor 1497

Conversation In A Car — Give It Away — Loving Game — Penthouse — Where'd Our Loving Go — You've Got A Way
Finding Somebody New — Isn't It Sweet To Think So — Pajama Party — So We Danced — Whiskey Man

AZ YET   '96

R&B vocal group from Philadelphia: Dion Allen, Darryl Anthony, Marc Nelson, Shawn Rivera and Kenny Terry.

11/16/96	**60**	41	●	©	**Az Yet**			$10	LaFace 26034

Care For Me — **Hard To Say I'm Sorry** 8 — Inseparable Lovers — Sadder Than Blue — Secrets — Through My Heart (The Arrow)
Every Little Bit Of My Heart — I Don't Want To Be Lonely — **Last Night** 9 — Saved For Someone Else — That's All I Want — Time To End The Story

B

BABE RUTH   '75

Rock group from Hatfield, Hertfordshire, England: Janita "Jenny" Haan (vocals), Alan Shacklock (guitar), Dave Punshon (piano), Dave Hewitt (bass) and Dick Powell (drums). In 1974, Steve Gurl replaced Punshon and Ed Spevock replaced Powell. In mid-1975, Bernie Marsden replaced Shacklock. Group named after the baseball great.

8/11/73	**178**	6		©	1 **First Base**			$15	Harvest 11151
2/22/75	**75**	7		©	2 **Babe Ruth**			$12	Harvest 11367
10/25/75	**169**	6		©	3 **Stealin' Home**			$12	Harvest 11451

Black Dog (1) — Elusive (3) — Joker (1) — Sad But Rich (2) — Turquoise (3) — Winner Takes All (3)
Can You Feel It (3) — Fascination (3) — King Kong (1) — Say No More (3) — 2000 Sunsets (3)
Caught At The Plate (3) — Fistful Of Dollars (2) — Mexican, The (1) — Somebody's Nobody (2) — We People Who Are Darker
Dancer (2) — It'll Happen In Time (3) — Private Number (2) — Tomorrow (Joining Of The Day) — Than Blue (2)
Duchess Of Orleans (2) — Jack O'Lantern (2) — Runaways, The (1) — (3) — Wells Fargo (2)

BABYFACE   '96

Born Kenneth Edmonds on 4/10/59 in Indianapolis. R&B singer/songwriter/multi-instrumentalist. Formerly with **Manchild** and **The Deele**. Brother of Melvin and **Kevon Edmonds** of **After 7**. Formed prolific songwriting partnership with Antonio "L.A." Reid; they co-founded LaFace Records in 1989. Babyface's wife, Tracey, is president of Yab Yum Records.

8/5/89+	**14**	61	▲³	©	1 **Tender Lover**			$10	Solar 45288
9/4/93	**16**	83	▲³	©	2 **For The Cool In You**			$10	Epic 53558
11/16/96	**6**	46	▲²	©	3 **The Day**			$10	Epic 67293
12/13/97	**106**	13	●	©	4 **MTV Unplugged NYC 1997**		[L]	$10	Epic 68779
12/12/98	**101**	5		©	5 **Christmas With Babyface**	C:#43/1	[X]	$10	Epic 69617
					Christmas charts: 11/'98, 33/'99				
12/2/00	**75**	7		©	6 **A Collection Of His Greatest Hits**		[G]	$10	Epic 85132

All Day Thinkin' (3) — First Noel (medley) (5) — It Came Upon A Midnight Clear — Saturday (2) — When Men Grow Old (6)
And Our Feelings (2) 21 — **For The Cool In You** (2,6) 81 — (medley) (5) — Seven Seas (3) — When Your Body Gets Weak
Bit Old-Fashioned (2) — Given A Chance (1) — **It's No Crime** (1,6) 7 — Silent Night (5) — (3)
Breathe Again (2) — Gone Too Soon (4) — Lady, Lady (2) — Simple Days (3) — Where Will You Go (1,6)
Can't Stop My Heart (1) — How Come, How Long (3,4,6) — Let's Be Romantic (1) — Sleigh Ride (5) — White Christmas (5)
Change The World (4,6) — I Care About You (4) — Little Drummer Boy (5) — Soon As I Get Home (1,6) — **Whip Appeal** (1,4,6) 6
Christmas Song (5) — I Love You Babe (6) — **My Kinda Girl** (1) 30 — Sunshine (1) — Winter Wonderland (5)
Day (That You Gave Me A Son) — I Said I Love You (3) — **Never Keeping Secrets** — Talk To Me (3,4) — You Are So Beautiful (2)
(3,4) — I'll Always Love You (2) — (2,6) 15 — **Tender Lover** (1) 14 — You Were There (5)
End Of The Road (medley) (4) — I'll Be Home For Christmas (5) — Reason For Breathing (6) — This Is For The Lover In You
Every Time I Close My Eyes — I'll Make Love To You (medley) — Rock Bottom (2) — (3,6) 6
(3,6) 6 — (4) — Rudolph The Red Nosed — Well Alright (2)
Exhale (Shoop Shoop) (4) — Illusions (2) — Reindeer (5) — **When Can I See You** (2,6) 4

BABYLON A.D.   '90

Hard-rock group from San Francisco: Derek Davis (vocals), Danny De La Rosa and Ron Freschi (guitars), Robb Reid (bass) and James Pacheco (drums).

12/2/89+	**88**	28		©	**Babylon A.D.**			$10	Arista 8580

Back In Babylon — Caught Up In The Crossfire — Hammer Swings Down — Maryanne — Shot O' Love
Bang Go The Bells — Desperate — Kid Goes Wild — Sally Danced — Sweet Temptation

BABYS, The   '79

Rock group from England: John Waite (vocals), Walt Stocker (guitar), Mike Corby (keyboards) and Tony Brock (drums). In 1978, Jonathan Cain replaced Corby and Ricky Phillips (bass) joined. Cain later joined **Journey**. Waite later formed **Bad English** with Phillips and Cain.

3/5/77	**133**	13		©	1 **The Babys**			$15	Chrysalis 1129
10/8/77	**34**	26		©	2 **Broken Heart**			$12	Chrysalis 1150
1/27/79	**22**	25		©	3 **Head First**			$12	Chrysalis 1195
1/19/80	**42**	22		©	4 **Union Jacks**			$12	Chrysalis 1267
11/15/80	**71**	15		©	5 **On The Edge**			$12	Chrysalis 1305
11/7/81	**138**	7		©	6 **Anthology**		[G]	$12	Chrysalis 1351

BABYS, The — Cont'd

And If You Could See Me Fly (2)
Anytime (4)
Back On My Feet Again (4,6) *33*
Broken Heart (2)
California (3)
Darker Side Of Town (5)
Downtown (5)
Dying Man (1)

Every Time I Think Of You (3,6) *13*
Give Me Your Love (2,6)
Golden Mile (2)
Gonna Be Somebody (5)
Head First (3,6) *77*
I Believe In Love (1)
I Love How You Love Me (1)
I Was One (3)
I'm Falling (2)

If You've Got The Time (1,6) *88*
In Your Eyes (4)
Isn't It Time (2,6) *13*
Jesus, Are You There? (4)
Laura (1)
Looking For Love (1)
Love Don't Prove I'm Right (3)
Love Is Just A Mystery (4)
Love Won't Wait (5)

Midnight Rendezvous (4,6) *72*
Money (6)
Over And Over (1)
Piece Of The Action (2)
Please Don't Leave Me Here (3)
Postcard (5)
Read My Stars (1)
Rescue Me (2)
Rock 'N' Roll Is (Alive And Well) (5)

Rodeo (1)
Run To Mexico (3)
She's My Girl (5)
Silver Dreams (2) *53*
Sweet 17 (5,6)
Too Far Gone (5)
True Love True Confession (4)
Turn And Walk Away (5,6) *42*
Turn Around In Tokyo (4)
Union Jack (4)

White Lightning (3)
Wild Man (1)
Wrong Or Right (2)
You (Got It) (3)

BACHARACH, Burt   '71

Born on 5/12/28 in Kansas City. Conductor/arranger/composer. Formed prolific songwriting team with lyricist Hal David. Married to actress Angie Dickinson from 1965-80. Married to songwriter **Carole Bayer Sager** from 1982-91.

DEBUT	PEAK	WKS	RIAA	CD		ARTIST — Album Title	Catalog	Sym	$	Label & Number
10/28/67+	96	65	●	©	1	Reach Out			$15	A&M 4131
6/28/69	51	87	●	©	2	Make It Easy On Yourself			$15	A&M 4188
6/19/71	18	24	●		3	Burt Bacharach			$15	A&M 3501
1/5/74	181	6			4	Living Together			$12	A&M 3527
12/14/74	173	5		©	5	Burt Bacharach's Greatest Hits	[G]		$12	A&M 3661
10/17/98	78	6		©	6	Painted From Memory			$10	Mercury 538002

ELVIS COSTELLO WITH BURT BACHARACH

Alfie (1,5)
All Kinds Of People (3)
And The People Were With Her (3)
Any Day Now (2)
April Fools (3)
Are You There (With Another Girl) (1)
Balance Of Nature (4)
Bond Street (1)
Do You Know The Way To San Jose (2)
Freefall (3)
God Give Me Strength (6)

Hasbrook Heights (3)
House Is Not A Home (1)
I Come To You (4)
I Might Frighten Her Away (4)
I Say A Little Prayer (1,5)
I Still Have That Other Girl (6)
I'll Never Fall In Love Again (2,5) *93*
In The Darkest Place (6)
Knowing When To Leave (2)
Lisa (1)
Living Together, Growing Together (4,5)
Long Ago Tomorrow (4)

Long Division (6)
Look Of Love (1,5)
Lost Horizon (4)
Make It Easy On Yourself (2,5)
Message To Michael (1)
Mexican Divorce (4)
Monterey Peninsula (4)
My Thief (6)
Nikki (3)
One Less Bell To Answer (3)
Pacific Coast Highway (2)
Painted From Memory (6)
Promises, Promises (3)

Raindrops Keep Fallin' On My Head (5)
Reach Out For Me (1,5)
Reflections (4)
She's Gone Away (2)
Something Big (4)
Such Unlikely Lovers (6)
Sweetest Punch (6)
Tears At The Birthday Party (6)
(They Long To Be) Close To You (3,5)
This Guy's In Love With You (2,5)
This House Is Empty Now (6)

Toledo (6)
Walk The Way You Talk (4)
Wanting Things (2)
What The World Needs Now Is Love (1,5)
What's Her Name Today? (6)
Whoever You Are I Love You (2)
Windows Of The World (1)
Wives & Lovers (3,5)

BACHELORS, The   '64

Pop vocal trio from Dublin, Ireland: brothers Declan and Con Cluskey, with John Stokes.

DEBUT	PEAK	WKS				ARTIST — Album Title	Catalog	Sym	$	Label & Number
6/20/64	70	16			1	Presenting: The Bachelors			$20	London 353
11/7/64	142	3			2	Back Again			$20	London 393
4/3/65	136	4			3	No Arms Can Ever Hold You			$20	London 418
9/4/65	89	6			4	Marie			$20	London 435

Always (4)
Charmaine (1)
Danny Boy (4)
Diane (1) *10*
Down Among The Sheltering Palms (4)
Dream (1)
Far Away Places (4)
Far Far Away (1)
He's Got The Whole World In His Hands (2)

I Believe (1,4) *33*
I Do Adore Her (3)
I Wouldn't Trade You For The World (2) *69*
I'll Be With You In Apple Blossom Time (4)
I'm Getting Sentimental Over You (3)
I'm Yours (3)
If (1)
If I Should Fall In Love Again (3)

Light A Candle In The Chapel (4)
Little White Cloud That Cried (2)
Love To Last A Lifetime (4)
Maybe (2,4)
Melody Of Love (2)
Mistakes (3)
Moments To Remember (1)
Moonlight And Roses (2)

No Arms Can Ever Hold You (3) *27*
Old Bill (1)
Only You (1)
Pagan Love Song (2)
Pennies From Heaven (3)
Put Your Arms Around Me, Honey (2)
Ramona (2)
Saints, The (3)
Sittin' In The Sun (4)

Skip To My Lou (3)
Ten Pretty Girls (2)
Till Then My Love (4)
Whispering (1)
Whispering Grass (1)
Whistle Down The Wind (3)
With All My Heart (3)
With These Hands (1,2)
You'll Never Walk Alone (1)
You're Next (4)

BACHMAN, Tal   '99

Born on 8/13/69 in Vancouver. Male rock singer/songwriter/guitarist. Son of Randy Bachman (of **Bachman-Turner Overdrive**).

DEBUT	PEAK	WKS				ARTIST — Album Title	Catalog	Sym	$	Label & Number
8/7/99	124	10		©		Tal Bachman			$10	Columbia 67956

Beside You
Darker Side Of Blue
I Am Free

I Wonder
If You Sleep
Looks Like Rain

Romanticide
She's So High *14*
Strong Enough

You Don't Know What It's Like (You Love) Like Nobody Loves Me

You're My Everything

★378★   BACHMAN-TURNER OVERDRIVE   '74

Hard-rock group from Vancouver: brothers Randy (vocals, guitar) and Robbie (drums) Bachman, with C. Fred Turner (vocals, bass) and Blair Thornton (guitar). Originally known as Brave Belt. Randy was a member of **The Guess Who**. Randy left in 1977 to form **Ironhorse**. Randy and Tim regrouped with C.F. Turner in 1984. Randy is the father of **Tal Bachman**.

1)Not Fragile 2)Bachman-Turner Overdrive II 3)Four Wheel Drive

DEBUT	PEAK	WKS	RIAA	CD		ARTIST — Album Title	Catalog	Sym	$	Label & Number
8/18/73+	70	68	●	©	1	Bachman-Turner Overdrive			$12	Mercury 673
1/19/74	4	75	●	©	2	Bachman-Turner Overdrive II			$12	Mercury 696
8/31/74	❶¹	50	●	©	3	Not Fragile			$12	Mercury 1004
3/8/75	180	3			4	Bachman-Turner-Bachman As Brave Belt	[E]		$12	Reprise 2210
						first released in 1972 as *Brave Belt II* on Reprise 2057 ($15)				
5/31/75	5	22	●	©	5	Four Wheel Drive			$12	Mercury 1027
1/3/76	23	21	●	©	6	Head On			$12	Mercury 1067
8/14/76	19	15	▲		7	Best Of B.T.O. (So Far)	C:#29/8	[G]	$12	Mercury 1101
3/19/77	70	9		©	8	Freeways			$12	Mercury 3700
3/18/78	130	4		©	9	Street Action			$12	Mercury 3713
4/7/79	165	4		©	10	Rock N' Roll Nights			$12	Mercury 3748
						BTO (above 2)				
9/29/84	191	2		©	11	Bachman Turner Overdrive			$10	Compleat 1010

Amelia Earhart (10)
Another Fool (11)
Another Way Out (4)
Average Man (6)
Away From Home (6)
Be A Good Man (4)
Blown (2)
Blue Collar (1,7) *68*

Blue Moanin' (3)
Can We All Come Together (8)
Can You Feel It (4)
City's Still Growin' (11)
Don't Get Yourself In Trouble (1)
Don't Let The Blues Get You Down (5)
Down And Out Man (1)

Down, Down (8)
Down The Road (9)
Dunrobin's Gone (4)
Easy Groove (8)
End Of The Line (10)
Find Out About Love (6)
Flat Broke Love (9)
For Love (9)

For The Weekend (11)
Four Wheel Drive (5)
Free Wheelin' (3) *flip*
Freeways (8)
Gimme Your Money Please (1,7) *70*
Give It Time (2)
Givin' It All Away (3)
Goodbye, Soul Shy (4)

Heartaches (10) *60*
Heaven Tonight (10)
Here She Comes Again (10)
Hey (5,7) *21*
Hold Back The Water (1)
I Don't Have To Hide (5)
I'm In Love (9)
It's Over (6)

Jamaica (3)
Just For You (8)
Just Look At Me Now (11)
Let It Ride (2,7) *23*
Life Still Goes On (I'm Lonely) (8)
Little Gandy Dancer (1)
Long Time For A Little While (9)
Long Way 'Round (4)

BACHMAN-TURNER OVERDRIVE

Lookin' Out For #1 (6,7) 65
Lost In A Fantasy (11)
Lowland Fling (5)
Madison Avenue (9)
My Sugaree (11)
My Wheels Won't Turn (8)
Never Comin' Home (4)
Not Fragile (3)
Put It In A Song (4)

Quick Change Artist (5)
Rock And Roll Hell (11)
Rock And Roll Nights (10)
Rock Is My Life, And This Is My Song (3)
Roll On Down The Highway (3,7) **14**
Second Hand (3)
Service With A Smile (11)

She's A Devil (5)
She's Keepin' Time (5)
Shotgun Rider (8)
Sledgehammer (3)
Stay Alive (6)
Stayed Awake All Night (1)
Stonegates (2)
Street Action (9)
Summer Soldier (5)

Take It Like A Man (6,7) **33**
Takes A Lot Of People (9)
Takin' Care Of Business (2,7) **12**
Thank You For The Feelin' (1)
Toledo (11)
Too Far Away (4)
Tramp (2)
Wastin' Time (10)

Waterloo Country (4)
Welcome Home (2)
Wild Spirit (6)
Woncha Take Me For A While (6)
World Is Waiting For A Love Song (9)
You Ain't Seen Nothing Yet (3,7) **1**

You're Gonna Miss Me (9)

BACKSTREET BOYS '99

Pop vocal group from Orlando, Florida: Nick Carter, Howie Dorough, Brian Littrell, A.J. McLean and Kevin Richardson. Carter is the older brother **Aaron Carter**.

DEBUT	PEAK	WKS	RIAA	CD		Album	Catalog	Sym	$	Label & Number
8/30/97+	**4**	133	▲14	©	1	Backstreet Boys	C:#2⁴/41		$10	Jive 41589
6/5/99	❶10	93	▲13	©	2	Millennium	C:#23/7		$10	Jive 41672
12/9/00	❶²	42	▲8	©	3	Black & Blue			$10	Jive 41743

All I Have To Give (1) 5
Answer To Our Life (3)
Anywhere For You (1)
As Long As You Love Me (1)
Back To Your Heart (2)
Call, The (3) **52**
Darlin' (1)
Don't Wanna Lose You Now (2)
Don't Want You Back (2)

Everybody (Backstreet's Back) (1) 4
Everyone (3)
Get Another Boyfriend (3)
Get Down (You're The One For Me) (1)
Hey, Mr. DJ (Keep Playin' This Song) (1)
How Did I Fall In Love With You (3)

I Need You Tonight (2)
I Promise You (With Everything I Am) (1)
I Want It That Way (2) **6**
I'll Never Break Your Heart (1) 35
If You Want It To Be Good Girl (Get Yourself A Bad Boy) (1)
It's Gotta Be You (2)
It's True (3)

Larger Than Life (2) **25**
More Than That (3) **27**
No One Else Comes Close (2)
Not For Me (3)
One, The (2) **30**
Perfect Fan (2)
Quit Playing Games (With My Heart) (1) **2**
Set Adrift On Memory Bliss (1)

Shape Of My Heart (3) 9
Shining Star (3)
Show Me The Meaning Of Being Lonely (2) **6**
Spanish Eyes (2)
Time (3)
We've Got It Goin' On (1)
Yes I Will (3)

BACK STREET CRAWLER '77

Rock group from England: Terry Wilson-Slesser (vocals), **Paul Kossoff** (guitar; **Free**), Mike Montgomery (keyboards), Terry Wilson (bass) and Tony Brunagel (drums). After first album, John Bundrick replaced Montgomery. Kossoff died of heart failure on 3/19/76 (age 25; after completion of second album). Geoff Whitehorn replaced Kossoff and group shortened name to **Crawler**.

DEBUT	PEAK	WKS	RIAA	CD		Album			$	Label & Number
11/15/75	**111**	10			1	The Band Plays On			$15	Atco 125
8/14/76	**140**	5			2	2nd Street			$15	Atco 138
9/10/77	**85**	13			3	Crawler			$12	Epic 34900

All The Girls Are Crazy (1)
Band Plays On (1)
Blue Soul (2)
Hoo Doo Woman (1)
It's A Long Way Down To The Top (1)

Jason Blue (1)
Just For You (2)
Leaves In The Wind (2)
Never Loved A Woman (2)
New York, New York (1)
On Your Life (2)

One Too Many Lovers (3)
Pastime Dreamer (3)
Raging River (2)
Rock & Roll Junkie (1)
Selfish Lover (2)
Sold On Down The Line (3)

Some Kind Of Happy (2)
Stealing My Way (1)
Stone Cold Sober (3)
Stop Doing What You're Doing (2)
Survivor (1)

Sweet, Sweet Beauty (2)
Train Song (1)
Without You Babe (3)
You And Me (3)
You Are My Saviour (3)
You Got Money (3)

BAD AZZ '98

Born in 1975 in Los Angeles. Male rapper.

DEBUT	PEAK	WKS	RIAA	CD		Album			$	Label & Number
10/17/98	**182**	1		©		Word On Tha Streets			$10	Priority 50741

Addicted To Crime
Continued Dedication
Cookin' Cookies

Everythang Happens Fo' A Reason
Ghetto Star

Hold On Hip Hop
I Ain't Concerned
Last Time

Livin It Up
Money, Houses And Cars
My People

Sh*t (Why U F**k Wit Me?)
Stand, Tha
This Life Of Mine

We Be Puttin It Down!

★233★ BAD COMPANY '74

Rock group from England: **Paul Rodgers** (vocals), Mick Ralphs (guitar), Raymond "Boz" Burrell (bass) and Simon Kirke (drums). Rodgers and Kirke from **Free**; Ralphs from **Mott The Hoople**; and Burrell from **King Crimson**. Rodgers, who left group in late 1982, was a member of **The Firm** (1984-86) and **The Law** (in 1991). Vocalist Brian Howe joined in 1986. Burrell left in 1987. Dave "Bucket" Colwell (guitar) and Rick Wills (of **Foreigner**; bass) joined in late 1992. Howe left in early 1995; replaced by Robert Hart. Band named after a 1972 Jeff Bridges movie.

1)Bad Company 2)Desolation Angels 3)Straight Shooter

DEBUT	PEAK	WKS	RIAA	CD		Album	Catalog	Sym	$	Label & Number
7/27/74	❶¹	64	▲5	©	1	Bad Company			$12	Swan Song 8410
4/19/75	**3**	33	▲3	©	2	Straight Shooter	C:#12/23		$12	Swan Song 8413
2/14/76	**5**	28	▲	©	3	Run With The Pack			$12	Swan Song 8415
3/26/77	**15**	24	●	©	4	Burnin' Sky			$12	Swan Song 8500
3/31/79	**3**	37	▲²	©	5	Desolation Angels			$12	Swan Song 8506
9/4/82	**26**	18		©	6	Rough Diamonds			$12	Swan Song 90001
1/18/86	**137**	14	▲²	©	7	10 From 6	C:#11/71	[G]	$10	Atlantic 81625
10/25/86	**106**	9		©	8	Fame And Fortune			$10	Atlantic 81684
9/17/88	**58**	40	●	©	9	Dangerous Age			$10	Atlantic 81884
6/30/90	**35**	75	▲	©	10	Holy Water			$10	Atco 91371
10/10/92	**40**	20	●	©	11	Here Comes Trouble			$10	Atco 91759
6/24/95	**159**	3		©	12	Company Of Strangers			$10	EastWest 61808
4/10/99	**189**	1		©	13	The 'Original' Bad Co. Anthology		[K]	$15	Elektra 62349 [2]

Abandoned And Alone (12)
Ain't It Good (13)
Anna (2)
Bad Company (1,7,13)
Bad Man (8)
Ballad Of The Band (6)
Both Feet In The Water (11)
Boys Cry Tough (10)
Brokenhearted (11)
Burnin' Sky (4,13) **78**
Burning Up (8)
Call On Me (9)
Can't Get Enough (1,7,13) **5**
Clearwater Highway (12)
Company Of Strangers (12)
Crazy Circles (5)
Cross Country Boy (9)
Dance With The Devil (12)
Dangerous Age (9)
Dead Of The Night (10)

Deal With The Preacher (2,13)
Dirty Boy (9)
Do Right By Your Woman (3,13)
Don't Let Me Down (1)
Down And Dirty (12)
Down Down Down (12)
Downhill Ryder (6,13)
Early In The Morning (5)
Easy On My Soul (13)
Electricland (6,7) **74**
Everything I Need (4)
Evil Wind (5,13)
Fade Away (3)
Fame And Fortune (8)
Fearless (10)
Feel Like Makin' Love (2,7,13) **10**
Gimme Gimme (12)
Gone, Gone, Gone (5) **56**

Good Lovin' Gone Bad (2,13) **36**
Hammer Of Love (13)
Heartbeat (4,13)
Here Comes Trouble (11)
Hey, Hey (13)
Hold On My Heart (8)
Hold On To My Heart (11)
Holy Water (10) **89**
Honey Child (3,13) **59**
How About That (11) **38**
I Can't Live Without You (10)
I Don't Care (10)
If I'm Sleeping (8)
If You Needed Somebody (10) **16**
Judas My Brother (12)
Kickdown (6)
Lay Your Love On Me (13)
Leaving You (4)

Like Water (4)
Little Angel (11)
Little Martha (12)
Little Miss Fortune (13)
Live For The Music (3,7)
Lonely For Your Love (5)
Long Walk (8)
Love Attack (9)
Love Me Somebody (3)
Loving You Out Loud (13)
Man Needs Woman (4)
Master Of Ceremony (4)
Morning Sun (4)
Movin' On (1,7,13) **19**
My Only One (11)
Never Too Late (10)
No Smoke Without A Fire (9)
Nuthin' On The TV (6)
Oh, Atlanta (5,13)
Old Mexico (6)

100 Miles (10)
One Night (9)
Painted Face (6)
Passing Time (4)
Peace Of Mind (4)
Pretty Woman (12)
Racetrack (6)
Ready For Love (1,7,13)
Rhythm Machine (5,13)
Rock 'N' Roll Fantasy (5,7,13) **13**
Rock Of America (9)
Rock Steady (1,13)
Run With The Pack (3,7,13)
Seagull (1,13)
Shake It Up (9) **82**
She Brings Me Love (8)
Shooting Star (2,7,13)
Silver, Blue & Gold (3,13)
Simple Man (3)

Smokin' 45 (13)
Something About You (9)
Stranger Stranger (10)
Stranger Than Fiction (11)
Superstar Woman (13)
Sweet Lil' Sister (3)
Take The Time (5)
Take This Town (11)
Tell It Like It Is (8)
That Girl (8)
This Could Be The One (11) **87**
This Love (8) **85**
Too Bad (4,13)
Tracking Down A Runaway (13)
Untie The Knot (6,13)

BAD COMPANY — Cont'd

Valerie (8)	Way That It Goes (9)	When We Made Love (8)	Wild Fire Woman (2,13)	**Young Blood** (3) *20*
Walk Through Fire (10) *28*	Weep No More (2)	Where I Belong (12)	With You In A Heartbeat (10)	
Way I Choose (1)	What About You (11)	Whiskey Bottle (13)	You're The Only Reason (12)	

BAD ENGLISH '89

Rock supergroup: **John Waite** (vocals), **Neal Schon** (guitar), **Jonathan Cain** (keyboards), Ricky Phillips (bass) and Deen Castronovo (drums). Waite, Phillips and Cain were members of **The Babys**. Cain and Schon were members of **Journey**.

DEBUT	PEAK	WKS	RIAA	CD		$	Label & Number
7/15/89	21	52	▲	© 1	Bad English	$10	Epic 45083
9/14/91	72	8		© 2	Backlash	$10	Epic 46935

Best Of What I Got (1)	Ghost In Your Heart (1)	Make Love Last (1)	Rebel Say A Prayer (2)	**Straight To Your Heart** (2) *42*
Dancing Off The Edge Of The World (2)	**Heaven Is A 4 Letter Word** (1) *66*	Possession (1) *21*	Restless Ones (1)	Time Alone With You (2)
Don't Walk Away (1)	Lay Down (1)	Pray For Rain (2)	Rockin' Horse (1)	Time Stood Still (2)
Forget Me Not (1) *45*	Life At The Top (2)	Price Of Love (1) *5*	Savage Blue (2)	Tough Times Don't Last (1)
		Ready When You Are (1)	So This Is Eden (2)	**When I See You Smile** (1) *1*

BADFINGER '70

Rock group from Swansea, Wales: Pete Ham (guitar) and Joey Molland (guitars), Tom Evans (bass) and Mike Gibbins (drums). All but Gibbins shared vocals. After Ham committed suicide on 4/23/75 (age 27), group disbanded. Molland and Evans reunited in 1979 with new lineup. Evans committed suicide on 11/23/83 (age 36).

DEBUT	PEAK	WKS	CD			$	Label & Number
3/28/70	55	17	© 1	Magic Christian Music		$40	Apple 3364
11/28/70	28	15	© 2	No Dice		$40	Apple 3367
12/25/71+	31	32	© 3	Straight Up	C:#23/1	$60	Apple 3387
				produced by **Todd Rundgren** and **George Harrison**			
12/15/73+	122	8	4	Ass		$30	Apple 3411
3/9/74	161	5	5	Badfinger		$25	Warner 2762
11/9/74	148	6	© 6	Wish You Were Here		$25	Warner 2827
3/24/79	125	8	© 7	Airwaves		$20	Elektra 175
3/28/81	155	6	© 8	Say No More		$15	Radio 16030

Airwaves (7)	Cowboy (4)	I Don't Mind (2)	Look Out California (7)	Name Of The Game (3)	Sympathy (7)
Andy Norris (5)	Crimson Ship (1)	I Got You (8)	Lost Inside Your Love (7)	**No Matter What** (2) *8*	Take It All (3)
Apple Of My Eye (4)	Crocadillo (8)	I Miss You (5)	Love Is Easy (5)	No More (8)	Three Time Loser (8)
Baby Blue (3) *14*	Day After Day (3) *4*	I'd Die Babe (3)	**Love Is Gonna Come At Last** (7) *69*	Passin' Time (8)	Timeless (4)
Beautiful And Blue (1)	Dear Angie (3)	I'm In Love (1)		Perfection (3)	Too Hung Up On You (8)
Because I Love You (8)	Dennis (6)	Icicles (4)	Love Me Do (2)	Rock N' Roll Contract (8)	Walk In The Rain (1)
Believe Me (1)	Dreamer, The (7)	In The Meantime (medley) (6)	Love Time (6)	Rock Of All Ages (1)	Watford John (2)
Better Days (2)	Fisherman (1)	Island (5)	Matted Spam (5)	Sail Away (7)	We're For The Dark (2)
Blind Owl (4)	Flying (3)	It Had To Be (2)	**Maybe Tomorrow** (1) *67*	Shine On (5)	When I Say (4)
Blodwyn (2)	Get Away (4)	It's Over (3)	Meanwhile Back At The Ranch (medley) (6)	Should I Smoke (medley) (6)	Where Do We Go From Here? (5)
Carry On Till Tomorrow (1)	Give It Up (5)	Just A Chance (6)		Some Other Time (medley) (6)	
Come And Get It (1) *7*	Got To Get Out Of Here (6)	King Of The Load (T) (6)	Midnight Caller (2)	Sometimes (3)	Why Don't We Talk? (5)
Come Down Hard (7)	**Hold On** (8) *56*	Knocking Down Our Home (1)	Midnight Sun (1)	Song For A Lost Friend (5)	Winner, The (4,7)
Come One (8)	I Can Love You (4)	Know One Knows (6)	Money (3)	Suitcase (3)	Without You (2)
Constitution (4)	I Can't Take It (2)	Lonely You (5)	My Heart Goes Out (5)	Sweet Tuesday Morning (3)	Your So Fine (6)

BADGER '73

Rock group from England: Tony Kaye (keyboards; **Yes**, **Badfinger**), Brian Parrish (guitar), Dave Foster (bass) and Roy Dyke (drums).

DEBUT	PEAK	WKS			$	Label & Number
8/11/73	167	8		One Live Badger	[L] $15	Atco 7022
				recorded on 12/15/72 at the Rainbow Theatre		

Fountain	On The Way Home	Preacher, The	River	Wheel Of Fortune	Wind Of Change

BADLANDS '89

Hard-rock group from England: Ray Gillen (vocals), Jake E. Lee (former guitarist with **Ozzy Osbourne**), Greg Chaisson (bass) and Eric Singer (drums; **Black Sabbath**). Singer replaced by Jeff Martin in 1990. Gillen died of cancer on 12/1/93 (age 33).

DEBUT	PEAK	WKS	CD			$	Label & Number
6/10/89	57	26	© 1	Badlands		$10	Atlantic 81966
6/29/91	140	3	© 2	Voodoo Highway		$10	Atlantic 82251

Dancing On The Edge (1)	Hard Driver (1)	Jade's Song (1)	Rumblin' Train (1)	Silver Horses (1)	Voodoo Highway (2)
Devil's Stomp (1)	Heaven's Train (2)	Joe's Blues (1)	Seasons (1)	Soul Stealer (2)	Whiskey Dust (1)
Dreams In The Dark (1)	High Wire (1)	Last Time (2)	Shine On (2)	Streets Cry Freedom (1)	Winter's Call (1)
Fire And Rain (2)	In A Dream (2)	Love Don't Mean A Thing (2)	Show Me The Way (2)	3 Day Funk (2)	

BAD RELIGION '96

Punk-rock group from Woodland Hills, California: Greg Graffin (vocals), Brett Gurewitz and Greg Hetson (guitars), Jay Bentley (bass) and Bobby Schayer (drums). Brian Baker replaced Gurewitz in 1995. Gurewitz owns the Epitaph record label.

DEBUT	PEAK	WKS	RIAA	CD			$	Label & Number
9/24/94	87	7	●	© 1	Stranger Than Fiction		$10	Atlantic 82658
3/16/96	56	5		© 2	The Gray Race		$10	Atlantic 82870
					co-produced by **Ric Ocasek**			
5/23/98	78	2		© 3	No Substance		$10	Atlantic 83094
5/27/00	88	2		© 4	The New America		$10	Atlantic 83303

All Fantastic Images (3)	Gray Race (2)	Inner Logic (1)	Pity The Dead (2)	Strange Denial (3)	Victims Of The Revolution (3)
At The Mercy Of Imbeciles (3)	Handshake, The (1)	It's A Long Way To The Promise Land (4)	Punk Rock Song (2)	Stranger Than Fiction (1)	Victory (2)
Believe It (4)	Hear It (3)		Raise Your Voice! (3)	Streetkid Named Desire (4)	Voracious March Of Godliness (3)
Better Off Dead (1)	Hippy Killers (3)	Leave Mine To Me (1)	Same Person (3)	Streets Of America (2)	
Biggest Killer In American History (3)	Hooray For Me... (1)	Let It Burn (4)	Shades Of Truth (3)	Television (1)	Walk, A (2)
	Hopeless Housewife (4)	Marked (1)	Slumber (1)	Ten In 2010 (3)	What It Is (1)
Cease (2)	I Love My Computer (4)	Mediocre Minds (3)	Sowing The Seeds Of Utopia (3)	Them And Us (2)	Whisper In Time (4)
Come Join Us (2)	In So Many Ways (3)	New America (4)		There Will Be A Way (4)	World Without Melody (4)
Don't Sell Me Short (4)	Incomplete (1)	No Substance (3)	Spirit Shine (2)	1000 Memories (4)	You've Got A Chance (4)
Drunk Sincerity (1)	Individual (1)	Nobody Listens (4)	State Of The End Of The Millenium Address (3)	Tiny Voices (1)	
Empty Causes (2)	Infected (1)	Parallel (2)		21st Century (Digital Boy) (1)	

BADU, Erykah '97

Born Erica Wright on 2/26/71 in Dallas. R&B singer/actress. Played "Rose Rose" in the movie *The Cider House Rules*.

DEBUT	PEAK	WKS	RIAA	CD			$	Label & Number
3/1/97	2[1]	58	▲[3]	© 1	Baduizm		$10	Kedar 53027
12/6/97	4	30	▲[2]	© 2	Live		[L] $10	Kedar 53109
					recorded on 10/1/97 at Sony Studios in New York City			
12/9/00	11	25	▲	© 3	Mama's Gun		$10	Motown 153259

A.D. 2000 (3)	All Night (medley) (2)	Appletree (1,2)	Boogie Nights (medley) (2)	Certainly (1,2)	Didn't Cha Know (3)
Afro (1)	...& On (3)	**Bag Lady** (3) *6*	Booty (3)	Cleva (3)	Drama (1)

DEBUT	PEAK	WKS	RIAA	CD	ARTIST — Album Title	Catalog	Sym	$	Label & Number

BADU, Erykah — Cont'd

4 Leaf Clover (1)
Green Eyes (3)
Hey Sugah (3)

In Love With You (3)
Kiss Me On My Neck (Hesi) (3)
My Life (3)

Next Lifetime (1,2)
No Love (1)
On&On (1,2) *12*

Orange Moon (3)
Otherside Of The Game (1,2)
Penitentiary Philosophy (3)

Searching (2)
Sometimes... (1)
Stay (2)

Time's A Wastin' (3)
Tyrone (2)
Ye Yo (2)

BAERWALD, David   '90
Born in 1960 in Oxford, Ohio. Half of the **David & David** duo.

| 7/7/90 | 149 | 19 | | © | **Bedtime Stories** .... | | | $10 | A&M 5289 |

All For You
Best Inside You

Colette
Dance

Good Times
Hello Mary

In The Morning
Liberty Lies

Sirens In The City
Stranger

Walk Through Fire
Young Anymore

BAEZ, Joan ★77★   '62
Born on 1/9/41 in Staten Island, New York. Legendary folk singer/political activist. Influential in fostering career of **Bob Dylan**. Married to Stanford University student leader David Harris from 1968-71. Appeared in Bob Dylan's Rolling Thunder Revue in 1975 and his 1978 movie *Renaldo And Clara*. Joan's sister Mimi Farina was in a folk songwriting/singing duo with her husband, the late Richard Farina.

1)*Joan Baez In Concert, Part 2* 2)*Joan Baez In Concert* 3)*Farewell, Angelina* 4)*Blessed Are*
5)*Diamonds & Rust*

11/27/61+	13	125	●	©	1 **Joan Baez, Vol. 2**			$40	Vanguard 2097
3/3/62	15	140	●	©	2 **Joan Baez**			$40	Vanguard 2077
					first released in 1960				
10/27/62	10	114	●	©	3 **Joan Baez In Concert**	[L]		$40	Vanguard 2122
11/23/63	45	18			4 **The Best Of Joan Baez**	[E]		$40	Squire 33001
					first recordings from 1959 with Bill Wood and Ted Alevizos				
12/7/63+	7	36		©	5 **Joan Baez In Concert, Part 2**	[L]		$40	Vanguard 2123
11/21/64	12	66		©	6 **Joan Baez/5**			$25	Vanguard 79160
10/23/65	10	27		©	7 **Farewell, Angelina**			$25	Vanguard 79200
12/3/66	6^X	13		©	8 **Noël**	[X]		$25	Vanguard 79230
					Christmas charts: 6/'66, 10/'67, 11/'71, 14/'72, 12/'73				
9/2/67	38	20		©	9 **Joan**			$25	Vanguard 79240
8/10/68	84	25		©	10 **Baptism**			$25	Vanguard 79275
1/25/69	30	20	●	©	11 **Any Day Now**			$30	Vanguard 79306 [2]
					songs of Bob Dylan				
6/7/69	36	14		©	12 **David's Album**			$20	Vanguard 79308
					dedicated to her husband, David Harris, imprisoned for draft resistance				
3/21/70	80	14		©	13 **One Day At A Time**			$20	Vanguard 79310
11/21/70	73	11		©	14 **The First 10 Years**	[K]		$25	Vanguard 6560 [2]
9/18/71	11	23	●	©	15 **Blessed Are**	[K]		$25	Vanguard 6570 [2]
1/1/72	164	5		©	16 **Carry It On**	[S]		$20	Vanguard 79313
5/27/72	48	24		©	17 **Come From The Shadows**			$15	A&M 4339
12/16/72+	188	7			18 **The Joan Baez Ballad Book**	[K]		$20	Vanguard 41/42 [2]
5/19/73	138	9			19 **Where Are You Now, My Son?**			$15	A&M 4390
7/7/73	163	8		©	20 **Hits/Greatest & Others**	[G]		$15	Vanguard 79332
5/17/75	11	46	●	©	21 **Diamonds & Rust**			$12	A&M 4527
2/7/76	34	17		©	22 **From Every Stage**	[L]		$15	A&M 3704 [2]
11/6/76	62	17			23 **Gulf Winds**			$12	A&M 4603
6/25/77	54	14		©	24 **Blowin' Away**			$12	Portrait 34697
12/17/77+	121	8		©	25 **The Best Of Joan C. Baez**	[G]		$12	A&M 4668
8/4/79	113	7		©	26 **Honest Lullaby**			$12	Portrait 35766

Adeste Fidelis (medley) (8)
(Ain't Gonna Let Nobody) Turn Me Around (22)
All In Green Went My Love Riding (10)
All My Trials (2,18)
Alter Boy And The Thief (24)
Amazing Grace (22)
Angeline (15)
Angels We Have Heard On High (8)
Annabel Lee (9)
Astrapsen (The Sun Is Risen) (4)
Ate Amanha (3)
Ave Maria (8)
Away In A Manger (medley) (8)
Babe, I'm Gonna Leave You (3)
Bachianas Brasileiras No. 5 - Aria (9)
Ballad Of Sacco & Vanzetti (22)
Banks Of The Ohio (1,4)
Barbara Allen (1,18)
Battle Hymn Of The Republic (5)
Be Not Too Hard (9)
Before The Deluge (26)
Best Of Friends (19)
Birmingham Sunday (5)
Black Is The Color Of My True Love's Hair (3,4,18)
Blessed Are... (15,20,22)
Blowin' In The Wind (22)

Blue Sky (21) *57*
Boots Of Spanish Leather (11)
Boulder To Birmingham (22)
Brand New Tennessee Waltz (15,20)
Bring A Torch, Jeannette, Isabella (medley) (8)
Cantique De Noël (8)
Careless Love (4)
Carol Of The Birds (8)
Carry It On (13,14,16)
Caruso (3)
Casida Of The Lament (10)
Cherry Tree Carol (1)
Childhood III (10)
Children And All That Jazz (21,25)
Children Of Darkness (9)
Colours (7,10)
Copper Kettle (4)
Coventry Carol (medley) (8)
Cry Me A River (24)
Daddy, You Been On My Mind (7)
Danger Waters (3)
Dangling Conversation (9,20)
Danny Boy (medley) (21)
David's Song (13)
Dear Landlord (11)
Death Of Queen Jane (6)
Deck The Halls (medley) (8)
Diamonds And Rust (21,22,25) *35*
Dida (21)

Do Right Woman, Do Right Man (16)
Don't Think Twice, It's All Right (5,14)
Don't Weep After Me (4)
Donna Donna (2)
Down In Yon Forest (8)
Drifter's Escape (11)
East Virginia (2,18)
El Preso Numero Nueve (The Ninth Prisoner) (2)
Eleanor Rigby (9,20)
Engine 143 (1)
Epitaph For A Poet (10)
Evil (10)
Fare Thee Well ..see: Ten Thousand Miles
Farewell Angelina (7,14)
Fennario (5,18)
Fifteen Months (15)
For All We Know (26)
For Sasha (26)
Forever Young (22,25)
Fountain Of Sorrow (21)
Free At Last (26)
From Portrait Of The Artist As A Young Man (10)
Gabriel And Me (18)
Gacela Of The Dark Death (10)
Geordie (3,14)
Ghetto (13,14)
Glad Bluebird Of Happiness (12)

Go 'Way From My Window (6,18)
Good King Wenceslas (medley) (8)
Gospel Ship (3)
Gracias A La Vida (Here's To Life) (25)
Green, Green Grass Of Home (12,14)
Greenwood Side (9)
Gulf Winds (23)
Hard Rain's A-Gonna Fall (7,14)
Heartfelt Line Or Two (24)
Heaven Help Us All (15,20)
Hello In There (21)
Help Me Make It Through The Night (15,20)
Henry Martin (2,18)
Hickory Wind (12,16)
Hitchhikers' Song (15)
Honest Lullaby (26)
House Carpenter (3,18)
House Of The Rising Sun (2,18)
Hush Little Baby (5)
I Dream Of Jeannie (medley) (21)
I Dreamed I Saw St. Augustine (11)
I Pity The Poor Immigrant (11,20)
I Saw The Vision Of Armies (10)
I Shall Be Released (11,16,22)
I Still Miss Someone (6)

I Wonder As I Wander (medley) (8)
I'm Blowin' Away (24)
Idols And Heroes (16)
If I Knew (12,14)
If I Were A Carpenter (9,14)
Imagine (17,25)
In Forty Days (16)
In Guernica (10)
In The Quiet Morning (17) *69*
It Ain't Me, Babe (6)
It's All Over Now, Baby Blue (7)
Jackaroe (5,18)
Jesse (21)
Joe Hill (13,16,22)
John Henry (4)
John Riley (2,14,18)
Jolie Blonde (13)
Just A Closer Walk With Thee (12)
Kingdom Of Childhood (23)
Kitty (4)
Kumbaya (3)
La Colombe - The Dove (3)
Lady Came From Baltimore (9)
Lady Mary (3)
Last, Lonely And Wretched (15)
Last Thing On My Mind (16)
Less Than The Song (19)
Let It Be (15,20) *49*
Let Your Love Flow (26)
Life Is Sacred (16)
Light A Light (26)
Lily Of The West (1,18)

Lily, Rosemary And The Jack Of Hearts (22)
Lincoln Freed Me (The Slave) (15)
Little Drummer Boy (8)
Little Moses (2)
London (10,14)
Lonesome Road (1)
Long Black Veil (5,13)
Love Is Just A Four-Letter Word (11,14,16,20,22) *86*
Love Minus Zero/No Limit (11)
Love Song To A Stranger (17,22,25)
Lowlands (4)
Luba The Baroness (24)
Magic Wood (10)
Manha De Carnaval (5,14)
Many A Mile To Freedom (24)
Marie Flore (medley) (15)
Mary Call (19)
Mary Hamilton (2,14,18)
Mary's Wandering (medley) (8)
Matty Groves (3,18)
Michael (26)
Milanese Waltz (medley) (8)
Minister Of War (10)
Miracles (24)
My Home's Across The Blue Ridge Mountains (12)
Myths (17)
Natalia (22)
Never Dreamed You'd Leave In Summer (21,25)

BAEZ, Joan — Cont'd

Night They Drove Old Dixie Down (15,20,22,25) *3*
No Expectations (13,14)
No Man Is An Iland (10)
No Woman, No Cry (26)
North (9)
North Country Blues (11)
'Nu Bello Cardillo (5)
O Brother! (23)
O Come, O Come, Emmanuel (8)
O'Cangaceiro (6)
Of The Dark Past (10)
Oh, Happy Day (16,22)
Oh, Little Child (10)
Oh! What A Beautiful City (4)
Old Blue (1,18)
Old Welsh Song (10,14)
Once I Had A Sweetheart (5,18)
Once I Knew A Pretty Girl (1)
One Day At A Time (13)
One Too Many Mornings (11)

Only Heaven Knows (Ah, The Sad Wind Blows) (19)
Outside The Nashville City Limits (15)
Pal Of Mine (1)
Parable Of The Old Man And The Young (10)
Partisan, The (17)
Pauvre Ruteboeuf (7)
Plaisir D'Amour (1)
Please Come To Boston (22,25)
Poems From The Japanese (10)
Poor Wayfaring Stranger (12)
Portland Town (5)
Pretty Boy Floyd (3)
Prison Trilogy (Billy Rose) (17,25)
Put Your Hand In The Hand (15)
Queen Of Hearts (5,18)
Railroad Boy (1,18)

Rainbow Road (17)
Rake And Rambling Boy (2)
Ranger's Command (7)
Restless Farewell (11)
Rider, Pass By (19)
River In The Pines (7)
Rock Salt And Nails (12)
Sad-Eyed Lady Of The Lowlands (11)
Sagt Mir Wo Die Blumen Sind (7)
Saigon Bride (9)
Sail Away Ladies (4)
Sailing (24)
Salt Of The Earth (15)
San Francisco Mabel Joy (15)
Satisfied Mind (7)
Seabirds (23)
Seven Bridges Road (13)
Silent Night (8)
Silkie (1,18)
Silver Dagger (2,14,18)
Simple Twist Of Fate (21,25)
33rd Of August (15)

So Soon In The Morning (4)
So We'll Go No More A Roving (6)
Song At The End Of The Movie (26)
Song In The Blood (10)
Song Of Bangladesh (17)
Stephanie's Room (23)
Stewball (6,22)
Still Waters At Night (23)
Stranger In My Place (17)
Suzanne (16,22)
Sweet Sir Galahad (13,14)
Sweeter For Me (23,25)
Swing Low, Sweet Chariot (22)
Take Me Back To The Sweet Sunny South (13)
Te Ador (5,14)
Tears Of Rage (11)
Ten Thousand Miles (2,18)
There But For Fortune (6,14,20) *50*

Three Fishers (5)
Three Horses (15)
Time Is Passing Us By (23)
Time Rag (24)
To Bobby (17)
Tramp On The Street (12)
Travellin' Shoes (4)
Trees They Do Grow High (1,18)
Tumbleweed (17)
Turquoise (9,14)
Unquiet Grave (6)
Wagoner's Lad (1,18)
Walie Walie (4)
Walkin' Down The Line (11)
Walls Of Redwing (11)
We Shall Overcome (5,16) *90*
Weary Mothers (People's Union 1) (17)
What Child Is This (8)
What Have They Done To The Rain (3)

What You Gonna Call Your Pretty Little Baby (4)
When Time Is Stolen (15)
When You Hear Them Cuckoos Hollerin' (6)
Where Are You Now, My Son? (19)
Who Murdered The Minutes (10)
Wild Mountain Thyme (7)
Wildwood Flower (2)
Will The Circle Be Unbroken (12,14)
Windrose (19)
Winds Of The Old Days (21)
With God On Our Side (5,14)
Yellow Coat (24)
You Ain't Goin' Nowhere (11,14)
Young Gypsy (19)

BAHAMADIA   '96

Born Antonia Reed in Philadelphia. Female rapper.

4/20/96	126	5		©	**Kollage**				$10	Chrysalis 35484

Biggest Part Of Me
Da Jawn

I Confess
Innovation

Rugged Ruff
Spontaneity

3 Tha Hard Way
Total Wreck

True Honey Buns (Dat Freak Sh*t)

UKNOWHOWWEDU
WordPlay

BAHA MEN   '00

R&B group from the Bahamas: Rick Carey and Omerit Hield (vocals), Marvin Prosper (rapper), Herschel Small and Patrick Carey (guitars), Tony Flowers (percussion), Jeff Cher (keyboards), Isaiah Taylor (bass) and Colyn Grant (drums).

8/26/00	5	46	▲³	©	**Who Let The Dogs Out**				$10	S-Curve 751052

Get Ya Party On
Getting Hotter

It's All In The Mind
Shake It Mamma

Summer Of Love
What's Up, Come On

Where Did I Go Wrong
Who Let The Dogs Out *40*

You All Dat *94*
You Can Get It

You're Mine

BAILEY, Philip   '85

Born on 5/8/51 in Denver. Co-lead singer of **Earth, Wind & Fire**.

9/10/83	71	14			1 **Continuation**				$10	Columbia 38725
11/10/84+	22	35	©		2 **Chinese Wall**				$10	Columbia 39542
5/24/86	84	11	©		3 **Inside Out**				$10	Columbia 40209

Back It Up (3)
Because Of You (3)
Children Of The Ghetto (2)
Day Will Come (3)
Desire (1)
Don't Leave Me Baby (3)
Easy Lover (2) *2*

Echo My Heart (3)
For Every Heart That's Been Broken (2)
Go (2)
Good Guy's Supposed To Get The Girls (1)
I Go Crazy (3)

I Know (1)
I'm Waitin' For Your Love (1)
It's Our Time (1)
Long Distance Love (3)
Photogenic Memory (2)
Show You The Way To Love (2)
Special Effect (3)

State Of The Heart (3)
Take This With You (3)
Time Is A Woman (2)
Trapped (1)
Vaya (Go With Love) (1)
Walking On The Chinese Wall (2) *46*

Welcome To The Club (3)
Woman (2)
Your Boyfriend's Back (1)

BAILEY, Razzy   '82

Born Rasie Michael Bailey on 2/14/39 in Five Points, Alabama. Country singer/songwriter.

6/20/81	183	2			1 **Makin' Friends**				$10	RCA Victor 4026
2/27/82	176	4			2 **Feelin' Right**				$10	RCA Victor 4228

Anywhere There's A Jukebox (1)
Bad News Look (2)
Best Kept Secret In Town (1)
Blaze Of Glory (2)

Blind Faith And The Naked Truth (1)
Everytime You Cross My Mind (You Break My Heart) (2)
Friends (1)

I Loved 'Em All (2)
I've Had My Limit (Of Two-Timing Women) (2)
Late Night Honky Tonk Country Song (1)

Midnight Hauler (1)
Night Life (2)
Old No Homer (1)
Scratch My Back (And Whisper In My Ear) (1)

She Left Love All Over Me (2)
Sittin' Here Wishing (I Was Someplace Else) (2)
Spending My Nights With You (1)

Too Far Gone And Much Too Close To You (1)
Travelin' Time (2)
Your Momma And Daddy Sure Did Something Right (2)

BAINBRIDGE, Merril   '96

Born on 6/2/68 in Melbourne, Australia. Female singer/songwriter.

10/26/96	101	20		©	**The Garden**				$10	Universal 53019

Being Boring
Garden In My Room

Julie
Miss You

Mouth *4*
Power Of One

Reasons Why
Sleeping Dogs

Song For Neen
Spinning

State Of Mind
Under The Water *91*

BAIO, Scott   '82

Born on 9/22/60 in New York City. Singer/actor. Played "Chaci Arcola" on TV's *Happy Days*.

9/4/82	181	4			**Scott Baio**				$10	RCA Victor 8025

Half The World
How Do You Talk To Girls

Looking For The Right Girl
Midnight Confessions

Runnin' Out Of Reasons To Go
Wanted For Love

What Am I Supposed To Do
What Was In That Kiss

When You Find Someone Who Loves You

Woman, I Love Only You

BAJA MARIMBA BAND   '67

Group led by marimbist Julius Wechter (born on 5/10/35 in Chicago; died of cancer on 2/1/99, age 63). Group featured various studio musicians with Wechter the only constant. Wechter also played with **Herb Alpert** and **Martin Denny**.
1)*Watch Out!* 2)*Heads Up!* 3)*Baja Marimba Band*

4/25/64	88	12			1 **Baja Marimba Band**		[I]	$15	A&M 104
4/24/65	123	3			2 **Baja Marimba Band Rides Again**		[I]	$15	A&M 109
1/8/66	102	16			3 **For Animals Only**		[I]	$15	A&M 113
11/19/66+	54	43			4 **Watch Out!**		[I]	$15	A&M 4118
5/27/67	77	44			5 **Heads Up!**		[I]	$15	A&M 4123

JULIUS WECHTER AND THE BAJA MARIMBA BAND:

1/20/68	168	9			6 **Fowl Play**		[I]	$15	A&M 4136
8/31/68	171	8			7 **Do You Know The Way To San Jose?**		[I]	$15	A&M 4150
3/8/69	117	10			8 **Those Were The Days**		[I]	$15	A&M 4167
10/18/69	176	3			9 **Fresh Air**		[I]	$15	A&M 4200

BAJA MARIMBA BAND — Cont'd

| 4/4/70 | 180 | 6 | | | 10 Greatest Hits .... [G-I] | | | $15 | A&M 4248 |

Acapulco 1922 (1,10)
Along Comes Mary (6,10) *96*
Back To Cuernavaca (1)
Baja Humbug (6)
Baja Nights (1)
Baja Nova (5)
Ballad Of Bonnie And Clyde (7)
Big Red (9)
Born Free (5)
Brasilia (2,10)
By The Time I Get To Phoenix (7)
Cabeza Arriba! (Heads Up!) (5)
Cast Your Fate To The Wind (4)
Charade (1)
Cielito Lindo (9)
Comin' In The Back Door (1,10) *41*

Cry Of The Wild Goose (5)
Dear Heart (2)
December's Child (1)
Do You Know The Way To San Jose (7)
Domingo (5)
Dream A Little Dream Of Me (8)
El Gazelle (3)
Eleanor Rigby (9)
Elenore (8)
Elephant Soul (3)
Fiddler On The Roof (6)
Flyin' High (8)
For Animals Only (3)
For Bud (7)
Fowl Play (6,10)
Fresh Air (9)
Gay Ranchero (4)
Georgy Girl (5,10) *98*

Ghost Riders In The Sky (4,10) *52*
Gnu Bossa Nova (3)
Goin' Out The Side Door (2)
Guacamole (2)
Happening To Me (8)
Hecho En Mexico (2)
Here (9)
Here, Th
ere And Everywhere (8)
How Much Is That Doggie In The Window (8)
I Don't Want To Walk Without You (9)
I Say A Little Prayer (7)
I'll Marimba You (9)
In A Vera Cruz Vein (5)
Juarez (2)
Knowing When To Leave (8)

La Cucaracha (3)
Las Mananitas (3)
Last Of The Red Hot Llamas (9)
Les Bicyclettes De Belsize (8)
Look Of Love (6,10)
Madagascar (9)
Majorca (2)
Maria Elena (1,10)
Maria's First Rose (1)
Moonglow/Picnic Theme (1)
More (2)
More I See You (4)
Odd One (5)
Partridge In A Pear Tree (Twelve Days Of Christmas) (3)
Pedro's Porch, Part II (1)
Peru '68 (8)
Portuguese Washerwoman (4)

Puff (The Magic Dragon) (3)
Red Roses For A Blue Lady (2)
Rhode Island Red (6)
Sabor A Mi (Be True To Me) (4)
Samba De Orfeu (1)
Samba Nuevo (9)
San Fernando (7)
She's Leaving Home (6)
Somewhere My Love (4,10)
Sounds Of Silence (6)
Spanish Eyes (5,10)
Spanish Moss (4)
Spanish Rose (2)
Summer Samba (4)
Sunday Mornin' (7)
Sunrise, Sunset (5)
Swan Waltz (3)
Telephone Song (4)
Temptation (5)

(There's) Always Something There To Remind Me (8)
There's Gotta Be Something Better Than This (7)
They Call The Wind Maria (5)
Those Were The Days (8)
Tomorrow Will Be Better (4)
Up Cherry Street (1)
Walk On By (2)
Wave (9)
Winchester Cathedral (5)
Windmills Of Your Mind (9)
Windy (6)
Woody Woodpecker Song (5)
Yellow Bird (3)
Yellow Days (6)
Yes Sir, That's My Baby (7)
Yours (4,10)

BAKER, Anita   '88

Born on 12/20/57 in Toledo, Ohio; raised in Detroit. R&B/jazz-styled singer.

10/29/83	139	11		©	1 The Songstress			$12	Beverly Glen 10002
4/19/86+	11	157	▲⁵	©	2 Rapture			$10	Elektra 60444
11/5/88	❶⁴	42	▲³	©	3 Giving You The Best That I Got			$10	Elektra 60827
7/21/90	5	40	▲	©	4 Compositions			$10	Elektra 60922
10/1/94	3	38	▲²	©	5 Rhythm Of Love			$10	Elektra 61555

Angel (1)
Baby (5)
Been So Long (2)
Body And Soul (5) *36*
Caught Up In The Rapture (2) *37*
Do You Believe Me (1)
Fairy Tales (4)

Feel The Need (1)
Giving You The Best That I Got (3) *3*
Good Enough (3)
Good Love (3)
I Apologize (5) *74*
It's Been You (5)
Just Because (3) *14*

Lead Me Into Love (3)
Lonely (4)
Look Of Love (5)
Love You To The Letter (4)
More Than You Know (4)
My Funny Valentine (5)
Mystery (2)
No More Tears (1)

No One In The World (2) *44*
No One To Blame (4)
Only For A While (5)
Perfect Love Affair (4)
Plenty Of Room (5)
Priceless (3)
Rhythm Of Love (5)
Rules (3)

Same Ole Love (365 Days A Year) (2) *44*
Sometimes (1)
Sometimes I Wonder Why (5)
Soul Inspiration (4) *72*
Squeeze Me (1)
Sweet Love (2) *8*
Talk To Me (4) *44*

Watch Your Step (2)
Whatever It Takes (4)
Will You Be Mine (1)
Wrong Man (5)
You Belong To Me (3,5)
You Bring Me Joy (2)
You're The Best Thing Yet (1)

BAKER, George, Selection   '70

Born Johannes Bouwens on 12/9/44 in Holland. His Selection consisted of Jan Hop, Jacobus Greuter, George The and Jan Visser. Female singer Nelleke Brzoskowsky joined in 1975.

| 7/4/70 | 107 | 6 | | © | 1 Little Green Bag .... | | | $20 | Colossus 1002 |
| 1/31/76 | 153 | 7 | | | 2 Paloma Blanca .... | | | $15 | Warner 2905 |

African Dream (2)
As Long As The Sun Will Shine (2)
Dear Ann (1) *93*

Fisherman, The (2)
Fly (1)
Funny Girl (1)
Goodbye (1)
Have Another Drink (1)

I Wanna Love You (1)
I'll Be Your Baby Tonight (1)
Impressions (1)
Israel (1)
Little Green Bag (1) *21*

Morning Sky (2)
Paloma Blanca (2) *26*
Prisoner, The (1)
Road Of Peace (1)
Seagull (2)

Send Me The Pillow You Dream On (2)
Song For You (2)
Superstar (1)
Take Me Home (2)

Winter Time (1)

BAKER('S), Ginger, Air Force   '70

Born Peter Baker on 8/19/39 in Lewisham, London, England. Drummer for **Cream** and **Blind Faith**. Got start as replacement for Charlie Watts (who left to join **The Rolling Stones**) in Alexis Korner's Blues Inc. (**C.C.S.**) in 1962. Then with the Graham Bond Organization. Ten-member Air Force featured **Steve Winwood** (vocals), Denny Laine (guitar; **Moody Blues**, **Wings**) and Rick Grech (bass; **Family**, **Traffic**, Blind Faith). Also see **Baker Gurvitz Army**.

| 5/23/70 | 33 | 15 | | © | Ginger Baker's Air Force .... [L] | | | $20 | Atco 703 [2] |

recorded at the Royal Albert Hall in London

Aiko Biaye
Da Da Man

Do What You Like
Doin' It

Don't Care
Early In The Morning

Man Of Constant Sorrow *85*
Toad

BAKER GURVITZ ARMY   '75

Rock trio from England: drummer **Ginger Baker** with brothers Paul (bass) and Adrian (guitar) Gurvitz. All shared vocals.

| 2/15/75 | 140 | 7 | | © | 1 The Baker Gurvitz Army .... | | | $20 | Janus 7015 |
| 11/15/75 | 165 | 5 | | | 2 Elysian Encounter .... | | | $15 | Atco 123 |

Artist, The (2)
Dreamer, The (2)
4 Phil (1)

Gambler, The (2)
Help Me (1)
Hustler, The (2)

I Wanna Live Again (1)
Inside Of Me (1)
Key, The (2)

Love Is (1)
Mad Jack (1)
Memory Lane (1)

People (2)
Remember (2)
Since Beginning (1)

Time (2)

BALAAM & THE ANGEL   '88

Rock trio from Motherwell, Scotland: brothers Mark (vocals), Jim (guitar) and Des (drums) Morris. Discovered by Ian Astbury of **The Cult**. Ian McKean (guitar) joined in 1989.

| 4/30/88 | 174 | 3 | | © | Live Free Or Die .... | | | $10 | Virgin 90869 |

Big City Fun Time Girl
I Love The Things You Do To Me

I Won't Be Afraid
I'll Show You Something
Special

It Goes On
Live Free Or Die
Long Time Loving You

On The Run
Running Out Of Time
Would I Die For You

BALANCE   '81

Pop-rock trio from New York City: Peppy Castro (vocals; **Blues Magoos**), Bob Kulick (guitar; brother of Bruce Kulick of **Kiss**) and Doug Katsaros (keyboards).

| 8/29/81 | 133 | 12 | | © | Balance .... | | | $10 | Portrait 37357 |

American Dream
Breaking Away *22*

Falling In Love *58*
Fly Through The Night

Haunting
Hot Summer Nights

I'm Through Loving You
It's So Strange

(Looking For The) Magic
No Getting Around My Love

BALDRY, Long John   '71

Born on 1/12/41 in London. Influential blues rocker. Formed Steampacket with **Rod Stewart**, and Bluesology with **Elton John**.

| 7/3/71 | 83 | 18 | | | 1 It Ain't Easy .... | | | $15 | Warner 1921 |
| 5/6/72 | 180 | 6 | | | 2 Everything Stops For Tea .... | | | $15 | Warner 2614 |

above 2 produced by **Rod Stewart** and **Elton John**

Armit's Trousers (2)
Black Girl (1)
Come Back Again (2)

Don't Try To Lay No Boogie-Woogie On The (1) *73*

King Of Rock And Roll (1) *73*
Everything Stops For Tea (2)

Flying (1)
Hambone (2)
I'm Ready (1)

Iko Iko (2)
It Ain't Easy (1)
Jubilee Cloud (2)

Let's Burn Down The Cornfield (1)
Lord Remember Me (2)

BALDRY, Long John — Cont'd

Morning, Morning (1)	Mr. Rubin (1)	Seventh Son (2)	You Can't Judge A Book By
Mother Ain't Dead (2)	Rock Me When He's Gone (1)	Wild Mountain Thyme (2)	The Cover (2)

BALIN, Marty '81

Born Martyn Buchwald on 1/30/43 in Cincinnati. Lead singer of **Jefferson Airplane/Starship** and **KBC Band**.

| 6/6/81 | 35 | 23 | | | 1 Balin .... | | | $10 | EMI America 17054 |
| 3/12/83 | 156 | 6 | | | 2 Lucky .... | | | $10 | EMI America 17088 |

All We Really Need (2)	Do It For Love (2)	I Do Believe In You (1)	Palm Of Your Hand (2)	**What Love Is** (2) *63*
Atlanta Lady (Something	Elvis And Marilyn (1)	Just Like That (2)	Spotlight (1)	When Love Comes (2)
About Your Love) (1) *27*	Heart Of Stone (2)	Lydia! (1)	Tell Me More (1)	Will You Forever (2)
Born To Be A Winner (2)	**Hearts** (1) *8*	Music Is The Light (1)	What Do People Like (2)	You Left Your Mark On Me (1)

BALL, David '94

Born on 7/9/53 in Rock Hill, South Carolina. Country singer/songwriter/guitarist.

| 7/2/94 | 53 | 55 | ▲ | © | Thinkin' Problem .... | | | $10 | Warner 45562 |

Blowin' Smoke	Down At The Bottom Of A	Look What Followed Me Home	Walk On The Wild Side Of Life	When The Thought Of You
Don't Think Twice	Broken Heart	**Thinkin' Problem** *40*	What Do You Want With His	Catches Up With Me
	Honky Tonk Healin'	12-12-84	Love	

BALL, Kenny, and His Jazzmen '62

Born on 5/22/30 in Ilford, Essex, England. Trumpet player. His Jazzmen consisted of Diz Disley (banjo), Johnny Bennett (trombone), Dave Jones (clarinet), Colin Bates (piano), Vic Pitts (bass) and Ron Bowden (drums).

| 3/17/62 | 13 | 32 | | | Midnight In Moscow .... | | [I] | $25 | Kapp 1276 |

American Patrol	Dark Eyes	My Mother's Eyes	Tin Roof Blues	You Must Have Been A
Big Noise From Winnetka	High Society	Puttin' On The Ritz	Yes She Do, No She Don't (I'm	Beautiful Baby
	Midnight In Moscow *2*	Savoy Blues	Satisfied With My Girl)	

BALLARD, Russ '84

Born on 10/31/45 in Waltham Cross, Hertfordshire, England. Pop-rock singer/songwriter/producer. Guitarist of **Argent** from 1969-74.

8/16/80	187	2		©	1 Barnet Dogs			$12	Epic 36186
6/9/84	147	13		©	2 Russ Ballard			$10	EMI America 17108
8/3/85	166	4		©	3 The Fire Still Burns			$10	EMI America 17162

Ain't No Turning Back (1)	Feels Like The Real Thing (1)	It's Too Late (1)	Playing With Fire (2)	Time (3)
Bad Boy (1)	Fire Still Burns (3)	Last Time (2)	Rene Didn't Do It (1)	Two Silhouettes (2)
Beware (1)	Hey Bernadette (3)	Omen, The (3)	Riding With The Angels (1)	Voices (2)
Day To Day (2)	I Can't Hear You No More (2)	**On The Rebound** (1) *58*	Searching (3)	Woman Like You (2)
Dream On (3)	In The Night (2)	Once A Rebel (3)	She Said "Yeah" (1)	Your Time Is Gonna Come (3)

BALLINGER, Lon '01

Born in Toronto. Male DJ/dance producer.

| 5/12/01 | 167 | 2 | | © | Webster Hall Tranzworld 4 .... | | [I] | $10 | Webster Hall NYC 22 |
| | | | | | | | | | Trance Airport 2000 |

Africa	Colours	Into The Inner Space	La Galera	Nostradamus
Capricorn	Dying	Journey Into Trance	Memories Like Radium	Phantom Anthem

BALLIN' JACK '71

Interracial jazz-rock group from San Francisco: Jim Walters (vocals, trumpet), Glenn Thomas (guitar), Jim Coile (sax), Tim McFarland (trombone), Luther Rabb (bass) and Ronnie Hammond (drums). Rabb and Hammond joined **War** in 1979.

| 1/2/71 | 180 | 8 | | | Ballin' Jack .... | | | $15 | Columbia 30344 |

Ballin' The Jack	Festival	Hold On	Only A Tear	**Super Highway** *93*
Carnival	Found A Child	Never Let 'Em Say	Street People	Telephone

BALTIMORA '86

Born Jimmy McShane on 5/23/57 in Londonderry, Northern Ireland. Died of AIDS on 3/28/95 (age 37). Pop singer.

| 1/18/86 | 49 | 17 | | | Living In The Background .... | | | $10 | Manhattan 53026 |

Chinese Restaurant	**Living In The Background** *87*	Running For Your Love	Up With Baltimora	
Jukebox Boy	Pull The Wires	**Tarzan Boy** *13*	Woody Boogie	

BALTIMORE AND OHIO MARCHING BAND, The '68

Studio group assembled by producers Joey Day and Alan Dischel.

| 1/20/68 | 177 | 3 | | | Lapland .... | | [I] | $15 | Jubilee 8008 |

B&O Marching Band Song	Col. Bogey March	Happy Wanderer	Seventy-Six Trombones	Whistle While You Work
Bach Minuet	Do Re Mi	Kazoo Special	St. Louie Street March	(medley)
Children's Marching Song	Girl Watchers Theme	**Lapland** *94*		Yellow Rose Of Texas (medley)

BANANARAMA '86

Female vocal trio from London: Sarah Dallin, Keren Woodward and Siobhan Fahey. Group name is a combination of the children's TV show *The Banana Splits* and the **Roxy Music** song "Pyjamarama." Fahey married David A. Stewart (of **Eurythmics**) on 8/1/87; later formed duo **Shakespear's Sister**.

4/16/83	63	19		©	1 Deep Sea Skiving			$10	London 810102
6/2/84	30	36		©	2 Bananarama			$10	London 820036
8/16/86	15	28	●	©	3 True Confessions			$10	London 828013
9/26/87	44	26		©	4 Wow!			$10	London 828061
12/3/88	151	9		©	5 Greatest Hits Collection		[G]	$10	London 828127

Bad For Me (4)	Dream Baby (2)	King Of The Jungle (2)	Perfect World (3)	State I'm In (2)	Young At Heart (1)
Boy Trouble (1)	He Was Really Sayin'	**Love In The First Degree**	Promised Land (3)	Strike It Rich (4)	
Cheers Then (1)	Somethin' (1,5)	(4,5) *48*	Ready Or Not (3)	Through A Childs Eyes (4)	
Come Back With My Heart (4)	Hey Young London (1)	**Love, Truth & Honesty** (5) *89*	**Robert DeNiro's Waiting**	**Trick Of The Night** (3) *76*	
Cruel Summer (2,5) *9*	Hooked On Love (3)	**More Than Physical** (3) *73*	(2,5) *95*	True Confessions (3)	
Cut Above The Rest (3)	Hot Line To Heaven (2)	Na Na Hey Hey Kiss Him	Rough Justice (2)	**Venus** (3,5) *1*	
Dance With A Stranger (3)	**I Can't Help It** (4,5) *47*	Goodbye (1,5)	**Shy Boy (Don't It Make You**	What A Shambles (1)	
Do Not Disturb (3)	**I Heard A Rumour** (4,5) *4*	Nathan Jones (4,5)	**Feel Good)** (1,5) *83*	**Wild Life** (2) *70*	
Doctor Love (1)	I Want You Back (4,5)	Once In A Lifetime (4)	Some Girls (4)	Wish You Were Here (1)	

BAND, The ★191★ '74

Rock group formed in Woodstock, New York: **Robbie Robertson** (guitar, vocals), Richard Manuel (piano), Garth Hudson (organ), **Rick Danko** (bass) and **Levon Helm** (drums, vocals). All hailed from Canada (except Helm from Arkansas). Group's "farewell concert" on Thanksgiving Day in 1976 was documented in the Martin Scorcese movie *The Last Waltz*. Manuel committed suicide on 3/4/86 (age 42). Helm, Danko and Hudson reunited in 1993 with Jim Weider (guitar), Richard Bell (piano) and Randy Ciarlante (drums). Danko died on 12/10/99 (age 56). Group inducted into the Rock and Roll Hall of Fame in 1994.

1)Planet Waves 2)Before The Flood 3)Stage Fright

8/10/68	30	40	●	©	1	Music From Big Pink			$20	Capitol 2955
10/18/69+	9	49	▲	©	2	The Band			$15	Capitol 132
9/5/70	5	22	●	©	3	Stage Fright			$15	Capitol 425
10/16/71	21	14		©	4	Cahoots			$15	Capitol 651
9/9/72	6	28	●	©	5	Rock Of Ages		[L]	$20	Capitol 11045 [2]

recorded on 12/31/71 at the Academy of Music in New York City

| 11/17/73+ | 28 | 20 | | © | 6 | Moondog Matinee | | | $15 | Capitol 11214 |
| 2/9/74 | ❶⁴ | 21 | ● | © | 7 | Planet Waves | | | $15 | Asylum 1003 |

BOB DYLAN With The Band

| 7/13/74 | 3 | 19 | ▲ | © | 8 | Before The Flood | | [L] | $20 | Asylum 201 [2] |

BOB DYLAN/THE BAND

| 7/26/75 | 7 | 14 | ● | © | 9 | The Basement Tapes | | [E] | $20 | Columbia 33682 [2] |

BOB DYLAN AND THE BAND

12/13/75+	26	19		©	10	Northern Lights-Southern Cross			$12	Capitol 11440
9/4/76	51	14	●	©	11	The Best Of The Band		[G]	$12	Capitol 11553
3/26/77	64	10		©	12	Islands			$12	Capitol 11602
4/29/78	16	20		©	13	The Last Waltz		[L-S]	$20	Warner 3146 [3]

recorded on 11/25/76 at Winterland in San Francisco

| 11/20/93 | 166 | 1 | | © | 14 | Jericho | | | $10 | Pyramid 71564 |

Acadian Driftwood (10)
Across The Great Divide (2,5)
Ain't Got No Home (6) *73*
Ain't No More Cane (9)
Ain't That A Lot Of Love (11)
All Along The Watchtower (8)
All La Glory (3)
Amazon (River Of Dreams) (14)
Apple Suckling Tree (9)
Atlantic City (14)
Baby Let Me Follow You Down (13)
Ballad Of A Thin Man (8)
Bessie Smith (9)
Blind Willie McTell (14)
Blowin' In The Wind (8)
Blues Stay Away From Me (14)
Caledonia Mission (1,5)
Caravan (13)
Caves Of Jericho (14)
Change Is Gonna Come (6)
Chest Fever (1,5)
Christmas Must Be Tonight (12)
Clothes Line Saga (9)
Country Boy (14)
Coyote (13)
Crash On The Levee (Down In The Flood) (9)
Daniel And The Sacred Harp (3)

Dirge (7)
Don't Do It (5,11) *34*
Don't Think Twice, It's All Right (8)
Don't Ya Tell Henry (9)
Down South In New Orleans (13)
Dry Your Eyes (3)
Endless Highway (8)
Evangeline (13)
Forbidden Fruit (10)
Forever Young (7,13)
4% Pantomime (4)
Further On Up The Road (13)
Genetic Method (5)
Georgia On My Mind (12)
Get Up Jake (5)
Goin' To Acapulco (9)
Going Going Gone (7)
Great Pretender (6)
Hazel (7)
Helpless (13)
Highway 61 Revisited (8)
Hobo Jungle (10)
Holy Cow (6)
I Don't Believe You (She Acts Like We Never Have Met) (13)
(I Don't Want To) Hang Up My Rock And Roll Shoes (5)
I Shall Be Released (1,8,13)

I'm Ready (6)
In A Station (11)
Islands (12)
It Ain't Me Babe (8)
It Makes No Difference (10,11,13)
It's Alright, Ma (I'm Only Bleeding) (8)
Jawbone (2)
Jemima Surrender (2)
Jupiter Hollow (10)
Just Another Whistle Stop (3)
Just Like A Woman (8)
Katie's Been Gone (9)
King Harvest (Has Surely Come) (2,5)
Knockin' Lost John (12)
Knockin' On Heaven's Door (8)
Last Of The Blacksmiths (4)
Last Waltz, Theme From (13)
Last Waltz Refrain (13)
Lay Lady Lay (8)
Let The Night Fall (12)
Life Is A Carnival (4,5,11,13) *72*
Like A Rolling Stone (8)
Livin' In A Dream (12)
Lo And Behold! (9)
Lonesome Suzie (1)
Long Black Veil (1)

Long Distance Operator (9)
Look Out Cleveland (2)
Mannish Boy (13)
Million Dollar Bash (9)
Moon Struck One (4)
Most Likely You Go Your Way (And I'll Go Mine) (8) *66*
Move To Japan (14)
Mystery Train (6,13)
Never Say Goodbye (7)
Night They Drove Old Dixie Down (2,5,8,11,13)
Nothing Was Delivered (9)
Odds And Ends (9)
On A Night Like This (7) *44*
Open The Door, Homer (9)
Ophelia (10,11,13) *62*
Orange Juice Blues (Blues For Breakfast) (9)
Out Of The Blue (13)
Please, Mrs. Henry (9)
Promised Land (6)
Rag Mama Rag (2,5) *57*
Rags And Bones (10)
Rainy Day Women #12 & 35 (8)
Remedy (14)
Right As Rain (12)
Ring Your Bell (10)
River Hymn (4)
Rockin' Chair (2)

Ruben Remus (9)
Rumor, The (13)
Saga Of Pepote Rouge (12)
Same Thing (14)
Saved (6)
Shape I'm In (3,5,8,11,13)
Share Your Love (6)
Shine A Light (14)
Shoot Out In Chinatown (4)
Sleeping (13)
Smoke Signal (4)
Something There Is About You (7)
Stage Fright (3,5,8,11,13)
Strawberry Wine (3)
Street Walker (12)
Stuff You Gotta Watch (14)
Such A Night (13)
Tears Of Rage (1,9,11)
Thinkin' Out Loud (4)
Third Man Theme (6)
This Wheel's On Fire (1,5,9)
Time To Kill (3) *77*
Tiny Montgomery (9)
To Kingdom Come (13)
Too Much Of Nothing (9)
Too Soon Gone (14)
Tough Mama (7)
Tura Lura Lural (That's An Irish Lullaby) (13)

Twilight (11)
Unfaithful Servant (2,5)
Up On Cripple Creek (2,8,11,13) *25*
Volcano (4)
W.S. Walcott Medicine Show (3,5)
We Can Talk (1)
Wedding Song (7)
Weight, The (1,5,8,11,13) *63*
Well, The (13)
When I Paint My Masterpiece (4)
When You Awake (2,8)
Where Do We Go From Here? (4)
Whispering Pines (2)
Who Do You Love (13)
Yazoo Street Scandal (9)
Yea! Heavy And A Bottle Of Bread (9)
You Ain't Goin' Nowhere (9)
You Angel You (7)

BANDA EL RECODO '01

Group of various Mexican musicians assembled by producer Don Cruz.

| 4/7/01 | 188 | 2 | | © | | Contigo Por Siempre... | | [F] | $10 | Fonovisa 6102 |

title is Spanish for "With You Always"

Cada Vez Te Extraño Mas
Como Pudiste
Contigo Por Siempre

Interactivo
La Chiquilla
La Crazy Loca

Pero No Me Quieres
Pero Vas A Pagar
Quisiera Ser

Te Equivocaste
Tu No Eres Facil De Querer
Vuelve Amor

Y Llegaste Tu

BAND OF THE BLACK WATCH, The '76

Scottish military unit.

| 3/20/76 | 164 | 4 | | | | Scotch On The Rocks | | [I] | $12 | Private Stock 2007 |

Birmingham Brass Band
Bump, The

Caribbean Honeymoon
Highland Safari

Hoots Mon!
Lass Of Fyve

Let's Go To Jersey
Pipers Waltz

Purple Heather
Scotch On The Rocks *75*

Sons Of The Thistle
Y Viva Espana

BANDY, Moe, & Joe Stampley '81

Country duo. Bandy was born on 2/12/44 in Meridian, Mississippi. Stampley was born on 6/6/43 in Springhill, Louisiana.

| 4/11/81 | 170 | 4 | | | | Hey Joe!/Hey Moe! | | | $10 | Columbia 37003 |

Country Boys
Drinkin', Dancin'

Drunk Front
Get Off My Case

Girl Don't Ever Get Lonely
Hey Joe (Hey Moe)

Honky Tonk Queen
I'd Rather Be A-Pickin'

Let's Hear It For The Workin' Man

Two Beers Away

BANG '72

Rock trio from Florida: Frank Ferrara (vocals, bass), Frank Gilcken (guitar) and Tony D'Lorio (drums).

| 4/8/72 | 164 | 10 | | | | Bang | | | $15 | Capitol 11015 |

Come With Me
Future Shock

Last Will & Testament
Lions, Christians

Our Home
Queen, The

Questions *90*
Redman

B ANGIE B '91
Born Angela Boyd in Morton, Mississippi. R&B singer.

5/4/91	133	6		©	B Angie B			$10	Bust It 95236

I Am Angie B
I Don't Want To Lose Your Love *54*

I'm So Sorry
Men Get Lonely
My Prayer To You

Pump It Up
So Much Love
Sweet Thang

This Is A Jam For You
Woman's Perspective

BANGLES '86
Female pop-rock group from Los Angeles: sisters Vicki (lead guitar) and Debbi (drums) Peterson, Michael Steele (bass) and **Susanna Hoffs** (guitar). Originally named The Bangs. Steele was previously in **The Runaways**.

8/4/84	80	30		©	1 All Over The Place			$10	Columbia 39220
2/1/86+	2²	82	▲³ ©		2 Different Light			$10	Columbia 40039
11/5/88+	15	42	▲	©	3 Everything			$10	Columbia 44056
5/26/90	97	9	▲	©	4 Greatest Hits		[G]	$10	Columbia 46125

All About You (1)
Angels Don't Fall In Love (2)
Be With You (3,4) *30*
Bell Jar (3)
Complicated Girl (3)
Crash And Burn (3)
Dover Beach (1)

Eternal Flame (3,4) *1*
Everything I Wanted (4)
Following (2,4)
Glitter Years (3)
Going Down To Liverpool (1,4)
Hazy Shade Of Winter (4) *2*
He's Got A Secret (1)

Hero Takes A Fall (1,4)
I'll Set You Free (3,4)
If She Knew What She Wants (2,4) *29*
In A Different Light (2)
In Your Room (3,4) *5*
James (1)

Let It Go (2)
Live (1)
Make A Play For Her Now (3)
Manic Monday (2,4) *2*
More Than Meets The Eye (1)
Not Like You (2)
Restless (1)

Return Post (2)
September Gurls (2)
Silent Treatment (1)
Some Dreams Come True (3)
Something To Believe In (3)
Standing In The Hallway (2)
Tell Me (1)

Waiting For You (3)
Walk Like An Egyptian (2,4) *1*
Walking Down Your Street (2,4) *11*
Watching The Sky (3)
Where Were You When I Needed You (4)

BANGOR FLYING CIRCUS '69
Pop trio from Chicago: David Wolinski (vocals, guitar), Alan DeCarlo (keyboards, bass) and Michael Tegza (drums). Wolinski and DeCarlo went on to form **Madura**. Wolinski later joined **Rufus**.

12/27/69	190	2		©	Bangor Flying Circus			$15	Dunhill/ABC 50069

Change In Our Lives
Come On People
Concerto For Clouds

In The Woods

Mama Don't You Know (That Your Daughter's Acting Mighty Strange)

Norwegian Wood (This Bird Has Flown)
Ode To Sadness

Someday I'll Find
Violent Man

BANG TANGO '89
Hard-rock group from Los Angeles: Joe LeSte (vocals), Mark Knight and Kyle Stevens (guitars), Kyle Kyle (bass) and Tigg Ketler (drums).

7/1/89	58	39		©	1 Psycho Cafe			$10	Mechanic 6300
6/15/91	113	3		©	2 Dancin' On Coals			$10	Mechanic 10196

Attack Of Life (1)
Big Line (2)
Breaking Up A Heart Of Stone (1)

Cactus Juice (2)
Dancin' On Coals (2)
Do What You're Told (1)
Don't Stop Now (1)

Dressed Up Vamp (2)
Emotions In Gear (2)
I'm In Love (2)
Just For You (1)

Last Kiss (2)
Love Injection (1)
Midnight Struck (2)
My Saltine (2)

Shotgun Man (1)
Someone Like You (1)
Soul To Soul (2)
Sweet Little Razor (1)

Untied And True (2)
Wrap My Wings (1)

BANKS, Ant '97
Born Anthony Banks in Oakland. Male rapper/producer. Also see **T.W.D.Y.**

4/10/93	123	7		©	1 Sittin' On Somethin' Phat			$10	Jive 41496
7/2/94	80	5		©	2 The Big Badass			$10	Jive 41534
7/26/97	20	10		©	3 Big Thangs			$10	Priority 50698

Big Badass (2)
Big Thangs (3)
Can't Stop (3)
Clownin' Wit Da Crew (2)
Cutaluff (3)
Drunken Fool (2)

End, The (1)
Fien (3)
4 Tha Hustlas (3)
****** Wit Banks (2)
Hard As Hell (2)
Hard Knox (3)

Hit It (1)
Hoo-Ride Ant Banks (3)
Late Nite (1)
Livin' The Life (1)
Loot, The (2)
Lyin' On Yo (1)

Make Money (3)
Only Out To (1)
Packin' A Gat (2)
Parlayin' (2)
Pimp Style Gangstas (2)
Playa Paraphernalia (3)

Roll 'Em Phat (1)
Sittin' On Somethin' Phat (1)
Spice 1 Wit Da Banksta (1)
Straight Hustlin' (2)
Streets Of Oakland (2)
Time Is Tickin' (3)

2 Kill A G (2)
2 The Head (1)
U Just A Punk (1)
West Riden' (3)
You Want Me Back (3)

BANKS, Peter '73
Born on 4/8/47 in England. Former member of **Yes** and **Flash**. Later joned **After The Fire**.

9/8/73	152	8		©	Two Sides Of Peter Banks			$15	Sovereign 11217

Battles
Beyond The Loneliest Sea

Get Out Of My Fridge
Knights Medley

Last Eclipse
Stop That!

Vision Of The King
White Horse Vale Medley

BANKS, Tony '80
Born on 3/27/51 in East Heathly, Sussex, England. Keyboardist with **Genesis**.

12/15/79+	171	5		©	A Curious Feeling			$12	Charisma 2207

After The Lie
Curious Feeling

For A While
Forever Morning

From The Undertow
In The Dark

Lie, The
Lucky Me

Somebody Else's Dream
Waters Of Lethe

You

BANTON, Buju '95
Born Mark Myrie 1973 in Kingston, Jamaica. Male reggae singer.

8/21/93	159	7		©	1 Voice Of Jamaica			$10	Mercury 518013
8/5/95	148	2		©	2 'Til Shiloh			$10	Loose Cannon 524119
9/9/00	128	2		©	3 Unchained Spirit			$10	Anti 86580

Better Must Come (3)
Champion (2)
Chuck It So (2)
Commitment (1)
Complaint (2)
Deportees (Things Change) (1)
Gone A Lead (1)
Good Body (1)

Guns And Bombs (3)
Him Take Off (1)
How Could You (2)
Hush Baby Hush (2)
If Loving Was A Crime (1)
It's All Over (2)
Law And Order (3)
Life Is A Journey (3)

Little More Time (1)
Make My Day (1)
Mighty Dread (3)
Murderer (2)
No More Misty Days (3)
No Respect (1)
Not An Easy Road (2)
Only Man (2)

Operation Ardent (1)
Poor Old Man (3)
Pull It Up (3)
Red Rose (1)
Reunion (3)
Searching (1)
Shiloh (2)
Sudan (3)

'Til I'm Laid To Rest (2)
Tribal War (1)
23rd Psalm (3)
Untold Stories (2)
Voice Of Jah (3)
Wanna Be Loved (3)
We'll Be Alright (1)
What Ya Gonna Do (2)

Wicked Act (1)
Willy (Don't Be Silly) (1)
Woman Dem Phat (3)

BARBER, Frank, Orch. '82
Big band led by British arranger/conductor Frank Barber.

6/5/82	94	16			Hooked On Big Bands		[I]	$10	Victory 702

Artie Shaw Medley

Benny Goodman Medley

Dorsey Brothers Medley

Duke Ellington Medley

Glenn Miller Medley *61*
Louis Armstrong Medley

BARBIERI, Gato '77
Born Leandro Barbieri on 11/28/33 in Rosario, Argentina. Tenor saxophonist.

5/5/73	166	7		©	1 Last Tango In Paris		[I-S]	$15	United Artists 045
10/26/74	160	3		©	2 Chapter Three - Viva Emiliano Zapata ...		[I]	$15	Impulse! 9279

BARBIERI, Gato — Cont'd

DEBUT	PEAK	WKS	RIAA	CD	Album Title	Sym	$	Label & Number
10/2/76+	75	32	● ©	3	Caliente! .... title is Spanish for "Hot!"	[I]	$12	A&M 4597
10/29/77	66	20	©	4	Ruby, Ruby	[I]	$12	A&M 4655
7/29/78	96	7	©	5	Tropico	[I]	$12	A&M 4710
8/11/79	116	9		6	Euphoria	[I]	$12	A&M 4774

Adios (3,4)
Behind The Rain (3)
Blue Angel (4)
Bolero (5)
Carnavalito (6)
Cuando Vuelva A Tu Lado (What A Difference A Day Makes) (2)

Don't Cry Rochelle (3)
El Sublime (2)
Europa (Earth's Cry Heaven's Smile) (2)
Evil Eyes (5)
Fake Ophelia (1)
Fiesta (3)
Fireflies (3)
Firepower, Theme From (6)

Girl In Black (Para Mi Negra) (1)
Gods And Astronauts (3)
Goodbye (Un Largo Adios) (1)
I Want You (3)
It's Over (1)
Jeanne (1)
La Podrida (2)
Last Tango In Paris (1)

Latin Lady (5)
Latin Reaction (4)
Lions Also Cry (6)
Lluvia Azul (2)
Los Desperados (3)
Midnight Tango (4)
Milonga Triste (2)
Ngiculela - Es Una Historia - I Am Singing (4)

Nostalgia (4)
Odara (5)
Picture In The Rain (1)
Poinciana (Song Of The Tree) (5)
Return (La Vuelta) (1)
Ruby (4)
Secret Fiesta (6)
She Is Michelle (5)

Sophia (6)
Speak Low (6)
Sunride (4)
Viva Emiliano Zapata (2)
Where Is The Love (5)
Why Did She Choose You (1)

BARBOUR, Keith '69
Born on 1/21/41 in New York City. Pop singer/songwriter. Formerly with **The New Christy Minstrels**. Married to TV actress Deidre Hall (*Our House* and *Days of Our Lives*) from 1971-78.

DEBUT	PEAK	WKS	CD	Album Title	$	Label & Number
11/1/69	163	4	©	Echo Park	$20	Epic 26485

All Of Your Loving
Baby Lit A Candle

Echo Park *40*
Here I Am Losing You

Here I Find
Home

If Only I Could Touch You
Reaching High

Today
Wind Is The Color Of Lace

You Try Not To Show

BARCLAY JAMES HARVEST '77
Art-rock group from Oldham, England: John Lees (vocals, guitar), Stewart Wolstenholme (keyboards), Les Holroyd (bass) and Mel Pritchard (drums).

DEBUT	PEAK	WKS	Album Title	$	Label & Number
2/19/77	174	3	Octoberon	$12	MCA 2234

Believe In Me
May Day

Polk Street Rag
Ra

Rock 'N' Roll Star
Suicide?

World Goes On

BARDENS, Pete '87
Born on 6/19/45 in London. Rock keyboardist. Former member of **Them** and **Camel**.

DEBUT	PEAK	WKS	CD	Album Title	Sym	$	Label & Number
10/17/87	148	5	©	Seen One Earth	[I]	$10	Cinema 12555

Home Thoughts
In Dreams

Man Alive
Many Happy Returns

Prelude
Seascape

Seen One Earth
Stargate, The

BARDEUX '88
Female dance duo from Los Angeles: Stacy Smith and Jaz. Melanie Taylor replaced Jaz in 1989.

DEBUT	PEAK	WKS	CD	Album Title	$	Label & Number
4/30/88	104	12	©	1 Bold As Love	$10	Enigma 73312
10/14/89	133	7	©	2 Shangri-La	$10	Enigma 73522

Bleeding Heart (1)
Caution (1)
Dancing In The Wind (1)
Hardline (2)

Hold Me, Hold Me (1)
I Love To Bass (2) *68*
Just Say The Word (2)
Magic Carpet Ride (1) *81*

Nervous (2)
Now I've Got Your Number (2)
Now Or Never (2)
One Last Kiss (2)

Sex Machine (1)
Shangri-La (2)
Three Time Lover (1)
Thumbs Up (2)

When We Kiss (1) *36*
You Can Rock My Body (2)
You're My Only Kind Of Lover (1)

BARE, Bobby '63
Born on 4/7/35 in Ironton, Ohio. Country singer/songwriter/guitarist. Acted in the movie *A Distant Trumpet* in 1964. Own TV series in the mid-1980s.

DEBUT	PEAK	WKS	Album Title	$	Label & Number
10/26/63	119	3	1 "Detroit City" And Other Hits	$25	RCA Victor 2776
2/1/64	133	5	2 500 Miles Away From Home	$25	RCA Victor 2835

Abilene (2)
All American Boy (1) *2*
Book Of Love (1)
Brooklyn Bridge (1)
Dear Wastebasket (1)

Detroit City (1) *16*
500 Miles Away From Home (2) *10*
God's Were Angry With Me (1)
Gotta Travel On (2)

Homestead On The Farm (2)
I Don't Believe I'll Fall In Love Today (1)
I Wonder Where You Are Tonight (2)

I'd Fight The World (1)
Is It Wrong (For Loving You) (1)
Jeannie's Last Kiss (2)
Let Me Tell You About Mary (2)
Lorena (1)

Lynchin' Party (2)
Noah's Ark (2)
Sailor Man (2)
Shame On Me (1) *23*
She Called Me Baby (1)

What Kind Of Bird Is That (2)
Worried Man Blues (2)

BARENAKED LADIES '98
Pop-rock group from Toronto: Steven Page (vocals), Ed Robertson (vocals, guitar), brothers Andrew (keyboards) and Jim (bass) Creeggan and Tyler Stewart (drums). Kevin Hearn replaced Andrew Creeggan in 1996.

DEBUT	PEAK	WKS	RIAA	CD	Album Title	Catalog	Sym	$	Label & Number
9/3/94	175	1		©	1 Maybe You Should Drive			$10	Reprise 45709
4/6/96	111	2	●	©	2 Born On A Pirate Ship			$10	Reprise 46128
7/5/97+	86	56	▲	©	3 Rock Spectacle	C:#16/19	[L]	$10	Reprise 46393
7/25/98	3	63	▲⁴	©	4 Stunt			$10	Reprise 46963
7/25/98	36ᶜ	13	●	©	5 Gordon .... released in 1992		[E]	$10	Reprise 26956
9/30/00	5	27	▲		6 Maroon			$10	Reprise 47814

A (1)
Alcohol (4)
Alternative Girlfriend (1)
Am I The Only One? (1)
Baby Seat (6)
Be My Yoko Ono (5)
Blame It On Me (5)
Box Set (1)
Break Your Heart (2,3)
Brian Wilson (3,5) *68*
Call And Answer (4)
Call Me Calmly (2)

Conventioneers (6)
Crazy (5)
Enid (5)
Everything Old Is New Again (1)
Falling For The First Time (6)
Flag, The (5)
Go Home (6)
Grade 9 (5)
Great Provider (1)
Helicopters (6)
Hello City (3,5)
Humour Of The Situation (6)

I Know (2)
I Live With It Every Day (2)
I Love You (5)
I'll Be That Girl (4)
If I Had $1000000 (3,5)
In The Car (4)
In The Drink (2)
Intermittently (1)
It's All Been Done (4) *44*
Jane (1,3)
Just A Toy (2)
King Of Bedside Manor (5)

Leave (4)
Life, In A Nutshell (1,3)
Light Up My Room (4)
Little Tiny Song (1)
Never Do Anything (6)
Never Is Enough (4)
New Kid (On The Block) (5)
Off The Hook (6)
Old Apartment (2,3) *88*
One Week (4) *1*
Pinch Me (6) *15*
Same Thing (2)

Sell Sell Sell (6)
Shoe Box (2)
Some Fantastic (4)
Spider In My Room (2)
Stomach Vs. Heart (2)
Straw Hat And Old Dirty Hank (2,3)
These Apples (1,3)
This Is Where It Ends (2)
Told You So (4)
Tonight Is The Night I Fell Asleep At The Wheel (6)

Too Little Too Late (6) *86*
What A Good Boy (3,5)
When I Fall (2,3)
When You Dream (4)
Who Needs Sleep? (4)
Wrap Your Arms Around Me (5)
Wrong Man Was Convicted (1)
You Will Be Waiting (1)

★329★ **BAR-KAYS** '79
Funk group from Memphis: Jimmy King (guitar), Ronnie Caldwell (organ), Phalon Jones (sax), Ben Cauley (trumpet), James Alexander (bass) and Carl Cunningham (drums). The plane crash that killed **Otis Redding** (on 12/10/67 in Madison, Wisconsin) also claimed the lives of all the Bar-Kays except Alexander (not on the plane) and Cauley (survived the crash). Alexander re-formed the group with Larry Dodson (vocals), Barry Wilkins (guitar), Harvey Henderson (sax), Winston Stewart (organ) and Willie Hall (drums).
1)Injoy 2)Flying High On Your Love 3)Propositions

DEBUT	PEAK	WKS	CD	Album Title	$	Label & Number
2/27/71	90	12	©	1 Black Rock	$25	Volt 6011
11/13/76+	69	22		2 Too Hot To Stop	$12	Mercury 1099
12/10/77+	47	23	●	3 Flying High On Your Love	$12	Mercury 1181

Angel Eyes (5)
Anticipation (9)
Are You Being Real (5)
As One (7)
Attitudes (3)
Baby I Love You (1)
Backseat Driver (8)
Bang, Bang (Stick 'Em Up) (2)
Banging The Walls (11)
Bodyfever (9)
Boogie Body Land (7)
(Busted) (9)
Can't Keep My Hands Off You (3)
Certified True (12)
Contagious (12)
Cozy (2)
Dance, Party, Etc. (10)

Dance To The Music (1)
Dance Your Body, Desara (11)
Dangerous (10)
Deliver Us (7)
Dirty Dancer (10)
Do It (Let Me See You Shake) (9)
Don't Hang Up (12)
Feelin' Alright (4)
Feels Like I'm Falling In Love (8)
Flying High On Your Love (3)
Freak City U.S.A. (12)
Freakshow On The Dance Floor (1) 73
Freaky Behavior (8)
Get Up 'N Do It (5)
Gina (11)
Girl I'm On Your Side (6)

Give It Up (5)
Hit And Run (8)
Holy Ghost (4)
How Sweet It Would Be (1)
I Can't Believe You're Leaving Me (9)
I Lean On You/You Lean On Me (1)
I'll Dance (5)
I've Been Trying (1)
Let's Have Some Fun (3)
Loose Talk (10)
Love Don't Wait (11)
Love's What It's All About (5)
Lovers Should Never Fall In Love (10)
Loving You Is My Occupation (6)
Make Believe Lover (10)

Many Mistakes (12)
Mean Mistreater (4)
Missiles On Target (11)
Money Talks (4)
Monster (4)
Montego Bay (1)
More And More (6)
Move Your Boogie Body (6) 57
Nightcruising (8)
Open Your Heart (7)
Paper Doll (11)
Piece Of Your Peace (1)
Propositions (9)
Running In And Out Of My Life (6)
Say It Through Love (7)
Sex Driver (11)
Sexomatic (10)

Shake Your Rump To The Funk (2) 23
She Talks To Me With Her Body (9)
Shine (5)
Shut The Funk Up (3)
Six O'Clock News Report (1)
Something In The Air (12)
Spellbound (2)
Standing On The Outside (3)
Summer Of Our Love (2)
Take The Time To Love Somebody (7)
This Could Be The Night (12)
Time Out (12)
Today Is The Day (6) 60
Too Hot To Stop (Pt. 1) (2) 74
Touch (12)
Touch Tone (8)

Traffic Jammer (8)
Tripping Out (9)
Unforgettable Dream (8)
Up In Here (6)
We're The Happiest People In The World (5)
Whatever It Is (3)
Whitehouseorgy (2)
Woman Of The Night (3)
Work It Out (7)
You Can't Run Away (3)
You Don't Know Like I Know (3)
You Made A Change In My Life (9)
You're So Sexy (2)
You've Been (1)
Your Place Or Mine (11)

BARNES, Jimmy '88
Born on 4/28/56 in Glasgow, Scotland; raised in Australia. Lead singer of **Cold Chisel**.

American Heartbeat (1)
Boys Cry Out For War (1)
Daylight (1)
Do Or Die (2)
Driving Wheels (1)

I Wanna Get Started With You (2)
I'd Die To Be With You Tonight (1)
I'm Still On Your Side (2)

Last Frontier (2)
Lessons In Love (2)
No Second Prize (1)
Paradise (1)
Promise Me You'll Call (1)

Ride The Night Away (1)
Seven Days (2)
Thick Skinned (1)
Too Much Ain't Enough Love (2) 91

Waitin' For The Heartache (2)
Walk On (2)
Without Your Love (1)
Working Class Man (1) 74

BARRABAS '75
Disco group: Jo Tejada (vocals), Ricky Morales (guitar), Juan Vidal (keyboards), Ernesto Duarte Duarte (percussion), Miguel Morales (bass) and Daniel Louis (drums).

Along The Shore
Checkmate

Family Size
Four Season Woman

Make It Easy
Mellow Blow

Take A Wild Ride
Thank You Love

BARRETT, Syd '74
Born Roger David Barrett on 1/6/46 in Cambridge, England. Original lead guitarist of **Pink Floyd**.

Baby Lemonade
Dark Globe
Dominoes
Effervescing Elephant (medley)
Feel

Gigolo Aunt
Golden Hair
Here I Go
I Never Lied To You (medley)
If It's In You

It Is Obvious
Late Night
Long Gone
Love Song
Love You

Maisie
No Good Trying
No Man's Land
Octopus
Rats

She Took A Long Cold Look
Terrapin
Waving My Arms In The Air (medley)
Wined And Dined

Wolfpack (medley)

BARRY, Claudja '79
Born in Jamaica; raised in Toronto. Disco singer/actress.

Boogie Tonight (2)
Boogie Woogie Dancin' Shoes (2) 56
Cold Fire (2)

Dancin' Fever (1) 72
Every Beat Of My Heart (1)
Forget About You (2)
Give It Up (1)

Heavy Makes You Happy (2)
Johnny, Johnny Please Come Home (1)
Love Machine (1)

Nobody But You (2)
Open The Door (1)
Sexy Talkin' Lover (1)
Take It Easy (1)

Take Me In Your Arms (1)
Way You Are Dancing (2)
When Life Was Just A Game (1)

BARRY, Len '65
Born Leonard Borisoff on 6/12/42 in Philadelphia. Lead singer of **The Dovells** from 1957-63.

At The Hop '65
Bullseye
Don't Throw Your Love Away

Happiness (Is A Girl Like Mine)
I.O.U.
Like A Baby 27

Lip Sync (To The Tongue Twisters) 84

1-2-3 2
Treat Her Right
Will You Love Me Tomorrow

Would I Love You?
You Baby

BARTON, Lou Ann '82
Born on 2/17/54 in Fort Worth, Texas. Female blues singer.

produced by Glenn Frey

Brand New Lover
Doodle Song

Every Night Of The Week
Finger Poppin' Time

I'm Old Enough
It Ain't Right

It's Raining
Maybe

Stop These Teardrops
Sudden Stop

BASIA '90
Born Basia Trzetrzelewska on 9/30/59 in Jaworzno, Poland. Female pop singer.

Astrud (1)
Baby You're Mine (2)
Best Friends (2)
Brave New Hope (2)
Copernicus (2)
Cruising For Bruising (2) 29

Drunk On Love (3)
Freeze Thaw (1)
From Now On (1)
How Dare You (1)
Miles Away (1)
More Fire Than Flame (3)

My Cruel Ways (3)
New Day For You (1) 53
Not An Angel (3)
Olive Tree (3)
Ordinary People (3)
Perfect Mother (3)

Prayer Of A Happy Housewife (3)
Prime Time TV (1)
Promises (1)
Reward (3)
Run For Cover (1)

She Deserves It/Rachel's Wedding (3)
Simple Pleasures (3)
Sweetest Illusion (3)
Take Him Back, Rachel (3)
Third Time Lucky (3)

Time And Tide (1) 26
Until You Come Back To Me (2)
Yearning (3)

BASIC BLACK   '90
R&B group from Los Angeles: Darryl Adams (vocals), Walter Scott and Lloyd Turner (keyboards) and Kelvin Bradshaw (drums).

| 11/17/90 | **178** | 1 | | © | **Basic Black** | | | $10 | Motown 6307 |

Baby Can We Talk   Give Your Love To Me   Nothing But A Party   She's Mine   Stupid
Don't Make Me Fall In Love   It's A Man's Thang   Now Or Never   Special Kind Of Fool   What Ever It Takes

★494★   BASIE, Count   '63
Born William Basie on 8/21/04 in Red Bank, New Jersey. Died of cancer on 4/26/84 (age 79). Legendary jazz, big-band leader/pianist/organist. Appeared in many movies. Won the Grammy Trustees Award in 1981.
1)Sinatra-Basie 2)It Might As Well Be Swing 3)This Time By Basie! Hits of the 50's And 60's

2/2/63	**5**	42		©	1 Sinatra-Basie			$25	Reprise 1008
					FRANK SINATRA/COUNT BASIE				
7/20/63	**19**	27		©	2 This Time By Basie! Hits Of The 50's And 60's		[I]	$20	Reprise 6070
9/7/63	**123**	5		©	3 Li'l Ol' Groovemaker...Basie!		[I]	$20	Verve 8549
10/19/63	**69**	20		©	4 Ella And Basie!			$30	Verve 4061
					ELLA FITZGERALD/COUNT BASIE				
2/22/64	**150**	1			5 More Hits Of The 50's And 60's		[I]	$20	Verve 8563
8/22/64	**13**	31		©	6 It Might As Well Be Swing			$20	Reprise 1012
					FRANK SINATRA/COUNT BASIE				
3/27/65	**141**	4		©	7 Our Shining Hour			$20	Verve 8605
					SAMMY DAVIS • COUNT BASIE				
3/26/66	**107**	13			8 Arthur Prysock/Count Basie			$20	Verve 8646
12/10/66	**143**	2			9 Broadway Basie's...Way		[I]	$15	Command 905
4/6/68	**145**	6			10 The Board Of Directors			$15	Dot 25838
					COUNT BASIE & THE MILLS BROTHERS				
6/1/68	**195**	3		©	11 Manufacturers Of Soul			$20	Brunswick 754134
					JACKIE WILSON/COUNT BASIE				

Ain't Misbehavin' (4)
Ain't No Use (8)
All Of Me (5)
Apartment, Theme From The (2)
April In Paris (7,10)
Baubles, Bangles And Beads (9)
Belly Roll (3)
Best Is Yet To Come (6)
Bill Basie Won't You Please Come Home (7)
Blues For Mr. Charlie (7)
Boody Rumble (3)
Chain Gang (11) *84*
Come Fly With Me (5)
Come Home (8)
Come Rain Or Come Shine (8)
Count 'Em (3)
December (10)
'Deed I Do (4)
Don't Go To Strangers (8)
Down - Down - Down (10)
Dream A Little Dream Of Me (4)
Dum Dum (3)
Even When You Cry (11)

Everything's Coming Up Roses (9)
Fly Me To The Moon (2,6)
For Your Precious Love (11) *49*
From This Moment On (9)
Funky Broadway (11)
Girl From Ipanema (7)
Gone Again (8)
Good Life (6)
Hello, Dolly! (6)
Hello Young Lovers (9)
Here's That Rainy Day (9)
Hey, Jealous Lover (5)
Honeysuckle Rose (4)
I Believe In You (6)
I Can't Stop Loving You (2,6) *77*
I Could Have Told You (8)
I Could Write A Book (8)
I Dig Rock And Roll Music (10)
I Left My Heart In San Francisco (2)
I May Be Wrong But I Think You're Wonderful (10)

I Never Loved A Woman (The Way I Love You) (11)
I Only Have Eyes For You (1)
I Thought About You (5)
I Wanna Be Around (6)
I Want To Be Happy (10)
I Was Made To Love Her (11)
I Wish You Love (6)
I Won't Dance (1)
I Worry 'Bout You (8)
I'll Never Smile Again (5)
I'm Beginning To See The Light (4)
I'm Gonna Sit Right Down And Write Myself A Letter (1,8)
I'm Lost (8)
In The Midnight Hour (11)
In The Wee Small Hours Of The Morning (5)
Into Each Life Some Rain Must Fall (4)
It's All Right With Me (9)
Just In Time (9)
Kansas City Wrinkles (3)
Keepin' Out Of Mischief Now (7)
Lazy River (10)

Learnin' The Blues (1) *1*
Let Me Dream (10)
Li'l Ol' Groovemaker...Basie (3)
Looking At The World Thru Rose Colored Glasses (1)
Lot Of Livin' To Do (9)
(Love Is) The Tender Trap (1) *7*
Lullabye For Jolie (3)
Mame (9)
Moon River (2)
More (9)
My Girl (11)
My Kind Of Girl (1)
My Last Affair (4)
My Shining Hour (7)
Nasty Magnus (3)
New York City Blues (7)
Nice 'N' Easy (2)
Nice Work If You Can Get It (1)
Ode To Billy Joe (11)
On A Clear Day (You Can See Forever) (9)
On The Road To Mandalay (5)
On The Street Where You Live (9)

On The Sunny Side Of The Street (4)
One Mint Julep (2)
Only The Lonely (5)
Pennies From Heaven (3)
People (9)
Please Be Kind (1)
Pleasingly Plump (3)
Release Me (10)
Respect (11)
Satin Doll (4)
Saturday Night (Is The Loneliest Night Of The Week) (5)
Second Time Around (4)
She's A Woman (7)
Shiny Stockings (4)
South Of The Border (Down Mexico Way) (5)
Swingin' Shepherd Blues (2)
Tea For Two (4)
Teach Me Tonight (7)
Them There Eyes (4)
This Could Be The Start Of Something Big (2)
This Love Of Mine (5)

Tiny Bubbles (10)
Uptight (Everything's Alright) (11)
Walk, Don't Run (2)
What Kind Of Fool Am I? (2)
What Will I Tell My Heart (8)
Whiffenpoof Song (10)
Why Try To Change Me Now (7)
Wives And Lovers (6)
Work Song (7)
You're Nobody Till Somebody Loves You (7)

BASIL, Toni   '82
Born Antonia Basilotta in 1950 in Philadelphia. Choreographer/actress. Worked on TV shows *Shindig* and *Hullabaloo*. Choreographed the movie *American Graffiti*. Appeared in the movie *Easy Rider*.

| 10/23/82 | **22** | 30 | ● | | Word Of Mouth | | | $10 | Chrysalis 1410 |

Be Stiff   **Mickey** *1*   Rock On   Space Girls   Time After Time
Little Red Book   Nobody   **Shoppin' From A To Z** *77*   Thief On The Loose   You Gotta Problem

BASS, Fontella   '66
Born on 7/3/40 in St. Louis. R&B singer/pianist.

| 2/26/66 | **93** | 8 | | © | The New Look | | | $50 | Checker 2997 |

Come And Get These Memories   How Glad I Am   Impossible   **Rescue Me** *4*   You've Lost That Lovin' Feelin'
Gee Whiz   I Know   Oh No, Not My Baby   Since I Fell For You
    I'm A Woman   Our Day Will Come   Soul Of The Man

BASS BOY   '92
Born James McCauley in Sarasota, Florida. Mixer/scratcher of bass-heavy samples. Also see **Bass Outlaws**.

| 6/6/92 | **160** | 12 | | © | I Got The Bass | | | $10 | Newtown 2209 |

Bass Boy Crazy   Bass Wave   Blinded By The Bass   I Got The Bass   Non-Stop Bass
Bass Me Up   Big 10"   Funkin' Bass   Mo' Better Bass   Rebel Bass

BASSEY, Shirley   '73
Born on 1/8/37 in Tiger Bay, Cardiff, Wales. R&B singer.
1)Never, Never, Never 2)Shirley Bassey Belts The Best! 3)I Capricorn

4/24/65	**85**	9			1 Shirley Bassey Belts The Best!			$20	United Artists 6419
10/17/70	**105**	13			2 Shirley Bassey Is Really "Something"			$15	United Artists 6765
6/12/71	**123**	24			3 Something Else			$15	United Artists 6797
3/18/72	**94**	13			4 I Capricorn			$15	United Artists 5565
11/25/72	**171**	8			5 And I Love You So			$15	United Artists 5643
5/26/73	**60**	19			6 Never, Never, Never			$15	United Artists 055
9/22/73	**136**	8			7 Live At Carnegie Hall		[L]	$20	United Artists 111 [2]
					recorded on 5/11/73				
9/21/74	**142**	6			8 Nobody Does It Like Me			$12	United Artists 214
11/29/75	**186**	3			9 Good, Bad But Beautiful			$12	United Artists 542

BASSEY, Shirley — Cont'd

10/9/76 149 8 10 Love, Life And Feelings .... **$12** United Artists 605

All In Love Is Fair (9)
All That Love Went To Waste (8)
Alone Again (Naturally) (10)
And I Love You So (5,7)
Baby I'm-A Want You (6)
Ballad Of The Sad Young Men (5)
Big Spender (7)
Bless The Beasts And Children (5)
Born To Lose (10)
Breakfast In Bed (3)
Bridge Over Troubled Water (3)
Davy (8)
Day By Day (5,7)
Diamonds Are Forever (7) **57**
Easy To Be Hard (2)
Emotion (9)
Everything That Touches You (10)
Everything's Coming Up Roses (1)
Excuse Me (3)

Feel Like Makin' Love (9)
Feelings (10)
First Time Ever I Saw Your Face (5)
For All We Know (4,7)
Going, Going, Gone (6)
Goldfinger (1,7) **8**
Good, Bad But Beautiful (9)
Greatest Performance Of My Life (9)
He Loves Me (1)
Hungry Years (10)
I Believe In You (1)
I, Capricorn (4,7)
I Could Have Danced All Night (1)
I Don't Know How To Love Him (5)
I Who Have Nothing (7)
I Won't Last A Day Without You (6)
I'd Do It All Again (5)
I'd Like To Hate Myself In The Morning (And Raise A Little Hell Tonight) (3,7)

I'll Be Your Audience (9)
I'm Not Anyone (8)
I'm Nothing Without You (8)
I've Never Been A Woman Before (4)
If Ever I Would Leave You (1)
If I Never Sing Another Song (10)
If We Only Have Love (5)
Isn't It A Shame (10)
It's Impossible (Somos Novios) (3)
Jesse (9)
Jezahel (8)
Johnny One Note (7)
Killing Me Softly With His Song (6)
Leave A Little Room (8)
Let Me Sing And I'm Happy (7)
Life Goes On (2)
Light My Fire (2)
Living (9)
Look Of Love (4)
Losing My Mind (4)
Lost And Lonely (4)

Lot Of Livin' To Do (1)
Love (4)
Love Story, Theme From (3)
Lovely Way To Spend An Evening (7)
Make The World A Little Younger (6)
Midnight Blue (10)
Morning In Your Eyes (8)
My Way (2)
Natali (10)
Never, Never, Never (6,7) **48**
No Regrets (6)
Nobody Does It Like Me (8)
Old-Fashioned Way (6)
Once In A Lifetime (1)
One Less Bell To Answer (4)
Other Side Of Me (9)
Party's Over (7)
People (1)
Pieces Of Dreams (9)
Run On And On And On (9)
Sea And Sand (2)
Send In The Clowns (9)

Sing (2)
Someday (5)
Somehow (6)
Someone Who Cares (6)
Something (2,7) **55**
Something Wonderful (1)
Somewhere (1)
Spinning Wheel (2)
Sweetest Sounds (1)
There's No Such Thing As Love (6)
This Is My Life (La Vita) (7)
Till Love Touches Your Life (3)
Together (6)
Trouble With Hello Is Goodbye (8)
Until It's Time For You To Go (3)
Way A Woman Loves (4)
Way I Want To Touch You (10)
Way Of Love (5)
Way We Were (9)
What About Today? (2)
What Are You Doing The Rest Of Your Life? (2)

What I Did For Love (10)
What's Done Is Done (3)
When You Smile (8)
Where Am I Going (4,7)
(Where Do I Begin) ..see: Love Story
Where Is Love (4)
Without You (5)
Yesterday I Heard The Rain (2)
Yesterday When I Was Young (Hier Encore) (2)
You And I (2,7)
You Are The Sunshine Of My Life (8)
You've Made Me So Very Happy (10)

BASS OUTLAWS   '93

Hardcore bass duo: **Bass Boy** and **Techmaster P.E.B.**

1/30/93 165 8 © Illegal Bass .... [I] **$10** Newtown 2210

Bass My Beat
Bass On It
Beau's Bass

Boomin' Bass
I Want Some Bass
Illegal Bass

In Your Bass
It's Bass
Slo Mello Bass

Slow Down The Bass
Stereo Bass (Extreme Woofer Test)

3 Kinds Of Bass

BATDORF & RODNEY   '75

Pop duo: John Batdorf and Mark Rodney. Batdorf formed the group **Silver** in 1976.

10/28/72 185 7 1 Batdorf & Rodney .... **$15** Asylum 5056
7/12/75 140 10 2 Life Is You .... **$12** Arista 4041

Ain't It Like Home (2)
All I Need (1)
Another Part Of Me (2)
Between The Ages (1)

By Today (1)
Caught In The Rain (2)
Grab At A Straw (2)
Happy Town (1)

Home Again (1)
Is It Love (2)
Let Me Live The Life (1)
Life Is You (2)

Long Way From Heaven (2)
Oh, Can You Tell Me (1)
Poor Man's Dream (1)
She Made Me Smile (2)

To A Gentler Time (2)
Under Five (1)
You Are A Song (2) **87**

BATON ROUGE   '90

Hard-rock group from New Orleans: Kelly Keeling (vocals, guitar), Lance Bulen (guitar), David Cremin (keyboards), Scott Bender (bass) and Corky McClellan (drums).

6/2/90 160 12 © Shake Your Soul .... **$10** Atlantic 82073

Baby's So Cool
Bad Time Comin' Down

Big Trouble
Doctor

Hot Blood Movin'
It's About Time

Melenie
Midge, The

Spread Like Fire
There Was A Time (The Storm)

Walks Like A Woman
Young Hearts

BATTLE, Kathleen, & Jessye Norman   '91

Duo of opera stars. Battle was born on 8/13/48 in Portsmouth, Ohio. Norman was born on 9/15/45 in Augusta, Georgia.

5/4/91 186 2 © Spirituals In Concert .... [L] **$10** Deutsche G. 429790
recorded on 3/18/90 at Carnegie Hall

Calvary (medley)
Gospel Train
Great Day
He's Got The Whole World In His Hand

I Believe I'll Go Back Home (medley)
In That Great Getting Up Morning
Lil' David (medley)

Lord, How Come Me Here
Lordy, Won't You Help Me (medley)
My God Is So High
Oh, Glory

Oh, What A Beautiful City
Over My Head (medley)
Ride On, King Jesus
Ride Up In The Chariot (medley)

Scandalize My Name
Sinner, Please Don't Let This Harvest Pass
Swing Low, Sweet Chariot (medley)

Talk About A Child
There Is A Balm In Gilead
They Crucified My Lord (medley)
You Can Tell The World

BAUHAUS   '89

Rock group from Northamptonshire, England: **Peter Murphy** (vocals, keyboards), **Daniel Ash** (guitar), David Jay (bass) and Kevin Haskins (drums). Disbanded in 1983. Murphy went solo. The latter three formed **Love & Rockets**.

8/12/89 169 6 © Swing The Heartache - The BBC Sessions .... [E] **$10** Beggars Ban. 9804 [2]
recorded from 1980-83

Departure
Double Dare
God In An Alcove

In Fear Of Fear
In The Flat Field
Night Time

Party Of The First Part
Poison Pen
She's In Parties

Silent Hedges
Spy In The Cab
St. Vitus Dance

Swing The Heartache
Telegram Sam
Terror Couple Kill Colonel

Third Uncle
Three Shadows (Part 2)
Ziggy Stardust

BAXTER, Les, & His Orchestra   '56

Born on 3/14/22 in Mexia, Texas. Died of a heart attack on 1/15/96 (age 73). Orchestra leader/arranger.

6/11/55 14 10 1 Blue Mirage .... [EP] **$25** Capitol 599
1/28/56 6 2 © 2 Tamboo! .... [I] **$40** Capitol 655
3/16/57 21 2 © 3 Skins! .... [I] **$40** Capitol 774

Afro-Deesia (3)
Batumba (2)
Blue Mirage (Don't Go) (1)
Brazilian Bash (3)
Bustin' The Bongos (3)

Conversation (3)
Cuchibamba (2)
Gringo (3)
Havana (2)
If You've Forgotten Me (1)

Lonely Wine (1)
Maracaibo (2)
Mood Tattooed (3)
Mozambique (2)
Oasis Of Dakhla (2)

Pantan (2)
Poppin' Panderos (3)
Reverberasia (3)
Rio (2)
Shoutin' Drums (3)

Simba (2)
Talkin' Drums (3)
Tehran (2)
Unchained Melody (1) **1**
Wotuka (2)

Zambezi (2)

BAY CITY ROLLERS   '76

Pop-rock group from Edinburgh, Scotland: Les McKeown (vocals), brothers Alan (guitar) and Derek (drums) Longmuir, Eric Faulkner (guitar) and Stuart "Woody" Wood (bass). Alan Longmuir left in mid-1976; returned in 1978. Ian Mitchell (guitar) joined briefly in 1976.

9/27/75+ 20 35 ● 1 Bay City Rollers .... **$12** Arista 4049
3/20/76 31 16 ● 2 Rock N' Roll Love Letter .... **$12** Arista 4071
9/18/76 26 25 ● 3 Dedication .... **$12** Arista 4093
7/23/77 23 11 ● 4 It's A Game .... **$12** Arista 7004
12/3/77+ 77 11 © 5 Greatest Hits .... [G] **$12** Arista 4158

BAY CITY ROLLERS — Cont'd

| 10/14/78 | 129 | 4 | | | 6 Strangers In The Wind | | | $12 | Arista 4194 |

All Of The World Is Falling In Love (6)
Another Rainy Day In New York City (6)
Are You Cuckoo (3)
Back On The Street (6)
Be My Baby (1)
Bye Bye Baby (1)
Dance Dance Dance (4)
Dedication (3,5) *60*
Disco Kid (2)

Don't Let The Music Die (4)
Don't Stop The Music (2,5)
Don't Worry Baby (3)
Eagles Fly (2)
Every Tear I Cry (6)
Give A Little Love (1)
I Only Wanna Dance With You (2)
I Only Want To Be With You (3,5) *12*
If You Were My Woman (6)

Inside A Broken Dream (4)
It's A Game (4)
Keep On Dancing (1)
La Belle Jeane (2)
Let's Go (A Huggin' And A Kissin' In The Moonlight) (1)
Let's Pretend (3)
Love Brought Me Such A Magical Thing (6)
Love Fever (4)
Love Power (4)

Marlina (1)
Maybe I'm A Fool To Love You (2,5)
Money Honey (2,5) *9*
My Lisa (3)
My Teenage Heart (1)
Rebel Rebel (4)
Remember (Sha La La La) (1)
Rock And Roll Love Letter (2,5) *28*
Rock N' Roller (3)

Saturday Night (1,5) *1*
Shang-A-Lang (1)
Shanghai'd In Love (2)
Shoorah Shoorah For Hollywood (5)
Strangers In The Wind (6)
Summer Love Sensation (1)
Sweet Virginia (4)
Too Young To Rock & Roll (2)
Way I Feel Tonight (4,5) *24*

When I Say I Love You (The Pie) (6)
Where Will I Be Now (6)
Wouldn't You Like It (2)
Write A Letter (3)
Yesterday's Hero (3,5) *54*
You Made Me Believe In Magic (4,5) *10*
You're A Woman (3)

B.B.&Q. BAND — see BROOKLYN, BRONX & QUEENS BAND

BBMAK   '00

Male vocal trio from Liverpool, England: Mark Barry, Christian Burns and Steve McNally.

| 6/3/00 | 38 | 44 | ● | | Sooner Or Later | | | $10 | Hollywood 62260 |

Again
Always

Back Here *13*
Can't Say

Ghost Of You And Me
I Can Tell

I'm Not In Love
Love Is Leaving

Love On The Outside
Next Time

Still On Your Side *54*
Unpredictable

BEACH BOYS, The ★13★   '64

Pop-rock group from Hawthorne, California: brothers **Brian Wilson** (keyboards, bass), **Carl Wilson** (guitar) and **Dennis Wilson** (drums); their cousin Mike Love (lead vocals, saxophone) and Al Jardine (guitar). Jardine replaced by David Marks from March 1962 to March 1963. Brian quit touring with group in December 1964; replaced briefly by **Glen Campbell** until Bruce Johnston (of Bruce & Terry) joined permanently in April 1965. Johnston and Campbell also recorded in the studio band Sagittarius in 1967. Brian continued to write for and produce group, returned to stage in 1983. Daryl Dragon (**Captain & Tennille**) was a keyboardist in their stage band. Dennis Wilson drowned on 12/28/83 (age 39). Carl Wilson died of cancer on 2/6/98 (age 51). **Carnie and Wendy Wilson**, daughters of Brian Wilson, were members of **Wilson Phillips**. Group inducted into the Rock and Roll Hall of Fame in 1988.

1)Beach Boys Concert 2)Endless Summer 3)Surfin' U.S.A. 4)Summer Days (And Summer Nights!!)
5)The Beach Boys Today!

11/24/62+	32	37		©	1 Surfin' Safari			$50	Capitol 1808
5/4/63	2²	78	●	©	2 Surfin' U.S.A.			$50	Capitol 1890
					also see #20 below				
10/12/63	7	56	●	©	3 Surfer Girl			$50	Capitol 1981
11/9/63+	4	46	▲	©	4 Little Deuce Coupe			$50	Capitol 1998
4/11/64	13	38	●	©	5 Shut Down, Volume 2			$50	Capitol 2027
8/1/64	4	49	●	©	6 All Summer Long			$50	Capitol 2110
					also see #20 below				
11/7/64	❶⁴	62	●	©	7 Beach Boys Concert		[L]	$50	Capitol 2198
					recorded on 8/1/64 at the Civic Auditorium in Sacramento, California				
12/5/64	6ˣ	13	●	©	8 The Beach Boys' Christmas Album		[X]	$50	Capitol 2164
					Christmas charts: 6/'64, 7/'65, 26/'66, 72/'67, 14/'68; also see #48 below				
3/27/65	4	50	●	©	9 The Beach Boys Today!			$40	Capitol 2269
7/24/65	2¹	33	●	©	10 Summer Days (And Summer Nights!!)			$40	Capitol 2354
11/27/65+	6	24		©	11 Beach Boys' Party!			$40	Capitol 2398
5/28/66	10	39	▲	©	12 Pet Sounds			$40	Capitol 2458
					also see #23 and #42 below				
7/23/66	8	78	▲²	©	13 Best Of The Beach Boys		[G]	$30	Capitol 2545
8/12/67	50	22	▲²	©	14 Best Of The Beach Boys, Vol. 2		[G]	$30	Capitol 2706
9/30/67	41	21		©	15 Smiley Smile			$30	Brother 9001
					also see #28 below				
12/30/67+	24	15		©	16 Wild Honey			$30	Capitol 2859
					also see #27 below				
7/6/68	126	10		©	17 Friends			$30	Capitol 2895
					also see #28 below				
9/7/68	153	6			18 Best Of The Beach Boys, Vol. 3		[G]	$30	Capitol 2945
3/1/69	68	11		©	19 20/20			$30	Capitol 133
8/16/69	136	6			20 Close-Up		[R]	$40	Capitol 253 [2]
					reissue of albums #2 and #6 above				
9/26/70	151	4		©	21 Sunflower			$30	Brother 6382
9/11/71	29	17		©	22 Surf's Up			$20	Brother 6453
6/3/72	50	20		©	23 Pet Sounds/Carl And The Passions - So Tough		[R]	$25	Brother 2083 [2]
					record 1 is a reissue of #12 above				
1/27/73	36	30		©	24 Holland			$20	Brother 2118
12/8/73+	25	24	●	©	25 The Beach Boys In Concert		[L]	$25	Brother 6484 [2]
7/20/74	❶¹	156	●	©	26 Endless Summer		[K]	$20	Capitol 11307 [2]
8/3/74	50	11			27 Wild Honey & 20/20		[R]	$20	Brother 2166 [2]
					reissue of #16 and #19 above				
11/9/74	125	6			28 Friends & Smiley Smile		[R]	$20	Brother 2167 [2]
					reissue of #15 and #17 above				
5/3/75	8	43	●	©	29 Spirit Of America		[K]	$20	Capitol 11384 [2]
7/19/75	25	23			30 Good Vibrations-Best Of The Beach Boys		[G]	$15	Brother 2223
7/17/76	8	27	●	©	31 15 Big Ones			$15	Brother 2251
12/11/76+	75	10		©	32 Beach Boys '69 (The Beach Boys Live In London)		[L]	$15	Capitol 11584
4/30/77	53	7		©	33 Love You			$15	Brother 2258
10/21/78	151	4		©	34 M.I.U. Album			$15	Brother 2268
					MIU: Maharishi International University				

DEBUT	PEAK	WKS	RIAA	CD	ARTIST — Album Title	Catalog	Sym	$	Label & Number

BEACH BOYS, The — Cont'd

DEBUT	PEAK	WKS	CD		ARTIST — Album Title	$	Label & Number
4/7/79	100	13	©	35	L.A. (Light Album)	$10	Caribou 35752
4/12/80	75	6	©	36	Keepin' The Summer Alive	$10	Caribou 36283
12/26/81+	156	8	©	37	Ten Years Of Harmony (1970-1980) .... [K]	$15	Caribou 37445 [2]
7/3/82	180	6		38	Sunshine Dream .... [K]	$15	Capitol 12220 [2]
6/29/85	52	14	©	39	The Beach Boys	$10	Caribou 39946
7/26/86	96	12	●	40	Made In U.S.A. .... [G]	$15	Capitol 12396 [2]
9/16/89	46	22	● ©	41	Still Cruisin' .... [K]	$10	Capitol 92639
6/16/90	162	5	©	42	Pet Sounds .... [R]	$10	Capitol 48421
4/20/96	198	1	▲² ©	43	20 Good Vibrations - The Greatest Hits ....C:#22/18 [G]	$10	Capitol 29418
					also see #46 below		
9/7/96	101	8	©	44	Stars And Stripes Vol. 1	$10	River North 1205
3/18/00	26ᶜ	1	©	45	The Best Of The Beach Boys	$10	EMI-Capitol 19707
3/18/00	95	11	©	46	The Greatest Hits - Volume 1: 20 Good Vibrations ....C:#7/15 [G-R]	$10	Capitol 21860
					reissue of #43 above		
3/18/00	192	1	©	47	The Greatest Hits - Volume 2: 20 More Good Vibrations .... [G]	$10	Capitol 20238
11/25/00+	20ˣ	3	©	48	Ultimate Christmas ....C:#26/2 [X]	$20	Capitol 95734
					includes all 12 tracks from #8 above plus 14 additional tracks		

Add Some Music To Your Day (21,30,37) **64**
Airplane (33)
All I Wanna Do (21)
All I Want To Do (19,27,38)
All Summer Long (6,20,26,47)
All This Is That (23)
Alley Oop (3)
Amusement Parks U.S.A. (18)
And Your Dream Comes True (10)
Angel Come Home (35)
Anna Lee, The Healer (17,28)
Aren't You Glad (16,27,32,38)
At My Window (21)
Auld Lang Syne (8,48)
Baby Blue (35)
Back Home (31)
Ballad Of Ole' Betsy (4)
Barbara Ann (11,14,29,32,40,43,45,46) **2**
Be Here In The Mornin' (17,28,38)
Be Still (17,28)
Be True To Your School (4,26,40,43,44,45,46) **6**
Be With Me (19,27)
Beach Boys Medley (38) **12**
Beaks Of Eagles (medley) (24)
Belles Of Paris (34)
Bells Of Christmas (48)
Big Sur (medley) (24)
Blue Christmas (8,48)
Blueberry Hill (35)
Bluebirds Over The Mountain (19,27,32,38,47) **61**
Boogie Woogie (33)
Break Away (29,47) **63**
Busy Doin' Nothin' (17,28)
Cabinessence (19,27)
California (medley) (24,37)
California Calling (39)
California Dreamin' (40) **57**
California Girls (10,14,25,26, 32,40,41,43,45,46) **3**
California Saga (On My Way To Sunny Californ-i-a) (medley) (24,37) **84**
Car Crazy Cutie (4)
Carl's Big Chance (6)
Caroline, No (12,23,25,30,38, 40,42,44,47) **32**
"Cassius" Love Vs "Sonny" Wilson (5)
Casual Look (31)
Catch A Wave (3,13,26,43,46)
Chapel Of Love (31)
Cherry, Cherry Coupe (4)
Child Of Winter (Christmas Song) (48)
Christmas Day (8,48)
Christmas Time Is Here Again (48)
Chug-A-Lug (1)
Come On With Me (34,37,40) **18**
Cool, Cool Water (21,37)
Cotton Fields (19,27,38,47)

Country Air (16,27)
County Fair (1)
Crack At Your Love (39)
Cuckoo Clock (1)
Cuddle Up (23)
Custom Machine (4,29)
Dance, Dance, Dance (9,18,29,40,43,46) **8**
Darlin' (16,18,25,27,30,32,37,38,47) **19**
Day In The Life Of A Tree (22)
Deirdre (21,37)
Denny's Drums (5)
Devoted To You (11)
Diamond Head (17,28)
Ding Dang (33)
Disney Girls (1957) (22,37)
Do It Again (19,27,30,32,38,40,47) **20**
Do You Remember? (6,20,29)
Do You Wanna Dance? (9,29,43,46) **12**
Don't Back Down (6,20,29)
Don't Go Near The Water (22,37)
Don't Hurt My Little Sister (9)
Don't Talk (Put Your Head On My Shoulder) (12,23,42)
Don't Worry Baby (5,14,25,26,40,44,47) **24**
Drive-In (6,20,29)
Endless Harmony (36)
Everyone's In Love With You (11)
Fall Breaks And Back To Winter (15,28)
Farmer's Daughter (2,20)
Feel Flows (22,37)
Finders Keepers (2,20)
Forever (21)
409 (1,4,14,18,29,40,43,44,46) **76**
Friends (17,28,30,38,47) **47**
Full Sail (35)
Fun, Fun, Fun (5,7,13,25,26,40,43,44,45,46) **5**
Funky Pretty (24,25)
Getcha Back (39,40) **26**
Gettin' Hungry (15,28)
Girl Don't Tell Me (10,18,26)
Girl From New York City (10)
Girls On The Beach (6,20,26)
God Only Knows (12,18,23,30,32,38,40,42,43,46) **39**
Goin' On (36,37) **83**
Goin' South (35)
Good Time (33)
Good Timin' (35,37) **40**
Good To My Baby (9,29)
Good Vibrations (15,18,25,28,30,32,38,40,43,45,46) **1**
Got To Know The Woman (21)
Graduation Day (7,29)
Had To Phone Ya (31)
Hang On To Your Ego (42)

Hawaii (3,7,29)
He Come Down (23)
Heads You Win - Tails I Lose (1)
Help Me, Rhonda (9,10,14,25,26,40,43,44,45,46) **1**
Here Comes The Night (16,27,35) **44**
Here She Comes (23)
Here Today (12,23,38,42)
Heroes And Villains (15,18,25,28,30,38,40,47) **12**
Hey Little Tomboy (34)
Hold On Dear Brother (23)
Honkin' Down The Highway (33)
Honky Tonk (2,20)
How She Boogalooed It (16,27,38)
Hully Gully (11)
Hushabye (6,29)
I Can Hear Music (19,27,38,44,47) **24**
I Do Love You (39)
I Get Around (6,7,11,14,20,26,40,41,43,44, 45,46) **1**
I Just Wasn't Made For These Times (12,23,42)
I Know There's An Answer (12,23,42)
(I Saw Santa) Rockin' Around The Christmas Tree (48)
I Should Have Known Better (11)
I Wanna Pick You Up (33)
I Was Made To Love Her (16,27)
I Went To Sleep (19,27)
I'd Love Just Once To See You (16,27)
I'll Be Home For Christmas (8,48)
I'll Bet He's Nice (33)
I'm Bugged At My Ol' Man (10)
I'm So Lonely (9)
I'm So Young (9)
I'm Waiting For The Day (12,23,38,42)
In My Car (41)
In My Room (3,7,13,26,47) **23**
In The Back Of My Mind (9)
In The Parkin' Lot (5)
In The Still Of The Night (31)
Island Girl (41)
It's A Beautiful Day (37)
It's About Time (21)
It's Gettin' Late (39) **82**
It's Just A Matter Of Time (39)
It's O.K. (31,37) **29**
Johnny B. Goode (7)
Johnny Carson (33)
Just Once In My Life (31)
Keep An Eye On Summer (5,38)
Keepin' The Summer Alive (36)
Kiss Me, Baby (9,13)
Kokomo (41,43,46) **1**

Kona Coast (34)
Lady Lynda (35,37)
Lana (2,20)
Leaving This Town (24,25)
Let Him Run Wild (10,14,26)
Let The Wind Blow (16,25,27)
Let Us Go On This Way (33)
Let's Go Away For Awhile (12,23,42)
Let's Go Trippin' (2,7)
Let's Put Our Hearts Together (33)
Little Bird (17,28)
Little Deuce Coupe (3,4,7,11,13,26,43,44,46) **15**
Little Girl I Once Knew (18,29,47) **20**
Little Girl (You're My Miss America) (1)
Little Honda (6,13,20,29,47) **65**
Little Old Lady From Pasadena (7)
Little Pad (15,28)
Little Saint Nick (8,14,48)
Livin' With A Heartache (36)
Lonely Sea (2,20)
Long Promised Road (22,37) **89**
Long, Tall Texan (7,14,44)
Lookin' At Tomorrow (A Welfare Song) (22)
Louie, Louie (5,13)
Love Is A Woman (33)
Love Surrounds Me (35)
Make It Big (41)
Make It Good (23)
Mama Says (16,27)
Man With All The Toys (8,48)
Marcella (23,25,37)
Match Point Of Our Love (34)
Maybe I Don't Know (39)
Meant For You (17,28)
Melekalikimaka (8,48)
Merry Christmas, Baby (8,48)
Misirlou (2)
Mona (33)
Monster Mash (7)
Moon Dawg (1)
Morning Christmas (48)
Mountain Of Love (11)
My Diane (34)
Nearest Faraway Place (19,27)
Never Learn Not To Love (19,27)
Night Was So Young (33)
No-Go Showboat (4)
Noble Surfer (2,20)
Oh Darlin' (36)
Only With You (24)
Our Car Club (3,4)
Our Prayer (17,28)
Our Sweet Love (21)
Palisades Park (31)
Papa-Oom-Mow-Mow (7,11)
Passing By (17,28)
Passing Friend (39)
Peggy Sue (34) **59**
Pet Sounds (12,23,42)

Pitter Patter (34)
Please Let Me Wonder (9,14,29,47) **52**
Pom, Pom Play Girl (5)
River Song (37)
Rock And Roll Music (31,37,40) **5**
Rock 'N' Roll To The Rescue (40) **68**
Rocking Surfer (3)
Roller Skating Child (33,37)
Sail On Sailor (24,25,30,37) **49**
Salt Lake City (10,29)
San Miguel (37)
Santa Ana Winds (36)
Santa Claus Is Comin' To Town (8,48)
Santa's Beard (8,48)
Santa's Got An Airplane (48)
School Day (Ring! Ring! Goes The Bell) (36,37)
Sea Cruise (37)
She Believes In Love Again (39)
She Knows Me Too Well (9,18)
She's Goin' Bald (15,28)
She's Got Rhythm (34,37)
Shift, The (1)
Shortenin' Bread (35)
Shut Down (2,4,5,20,26,43,46) **23**
Slip On Through (21)
Sloop John B (12,23,25,30,32, 38,40,42,43,46) **3**
Solar System (33)
Some Of Your Love (36)
Somewhere Near Japan (41)
South Bay Surfer (3)
Spirit Of America (4,29)
Steamboat (24)
Still Cruisin' (41) **93**
Stoked (2,20)
Student Demonstration Time (22)
Sumahama (35)
Summer Means New Love (10)
Summertime Blues (1)
Sunshine (36)
Surf Jam (2,20)
Surf's Up (22,30,37)
Surfer Girl (3,13,25,26,40,43,45,46) **7**
Surfer Moon (3)
Surfer's Rule (3)
Surfin (1,18) **75**
Surfin' Safari (1,14,26,40,43,46) **14**
Surfin' U.S.A. (2,13,20,25,26,40,43,45,46) **3**
Susie Cincinnati (31)
Sweet Sunday Kinda Love (34)
T M Song (31)
Take A Load Off Your Feet (22)
Talk To Me (31)
Tears In The Morning (21)
Tell Me Why (11,29)
Ten Little Indians (1) **49**
That Same Song (31)

That's Not Me (12,23,42)
Their Hearts Were Full Of Spring (32)
Then I Kissed Her (10,38)
There's No Other (Like My Baby) (11,38)
Thing Or Two (16,27)
This Car Of Mine (5,29)
This Whole World (21,37)
'Til I Die (22,37)
Time To Get Alone (19,27)
Times They Are A-Changin' (17,28)
Trader, The (24,25,37)
Transcendental Meditation (17,28)
Trombone Dixie (42)
Vegetables (15,28,38)
Wake The World (17,28,32)
Wanderer, The (7)
Warmth Of The Sun (5,13,26,44,47)
We Got Love (25)
We Three Kings Of Orient Are (8,48)
We'll Run Away (6,20)
Wendy (6,13,20,26,47) **44**
When A Man Needs A Woman (17,28)
When Girls Get Together (36)
When I Grow Up (To Be A Man) (9,14,29,40,47) **9**
Where I Belong (39)
Whistle In (15,28)
White Christmas (8,48)
Why Do Fools Fall In Love (5,29)
Wild Honey (16,27,38,47) **31**
Wind Chimes (15,28)
Winds Of Change (34)
Winter Symphony (48)
Wipeout (41) **12**
With Me Tonight (15,28)
Wonderful (15,28)
Wontcha Come Out Tonight (34,37)
Wouldn't It Be Nice (12,23,25, 30,32,38,40,41,42,43,45,46) **8**
You Need A Mess Of Help To Stand Alone (23)
You Still Believe In Me (12,23,42)
You're So Good To Me (10,13,26,47)
You've Got To Hide Your Love Away (11)
Young Man Is Gone (4,29)
Your Summer Dream (3)

BEACON STREET UNION   '68

Rock group from Boston: John Lincoln Wright (vocals), Paul Tartachny (guitar), Robert Rhodes (keyboards), Wayne Ulaky (bass) and Richard Weisberg (drums).

DEBUT	PEAK	WKS	CD		ARTIST — Album Title	$	Label & Number
3/9/68	75	16	©	1	The Eyes Of The Beacon Street Union	$30	MGM 4517
9/14/68	173	10	©	2	The Clown Died In Marvin Gardens	$30	MGM 4568

DEBUT	PEAK	WKS	RIAA	CD	ARTIST — Album Title	Catalog	Sym	$	Label & Number

BEACON STREET UNION — Cont'd

Angus Of Aberdeen (2)	Blue Suede Shoes (2)	Four Hundred And Five (1)	My Love Is (1)	Prophet, The (1)	Speed Kills (1)
Baby Please Don't Go (2)	Clown Died In Marvin Gardens (2)	Green Destroys The Gold (1)	Mystic Mourning (2)	Sadie Said No (1)	Sportin' Life (1)
Beautiful Delilah (1)	Clown's Overture (2)	King Of The Jungle (2)	Not Very August Afternoon (2)	South End Incident (I'm Afraid) (1)	
Blue Avenue (1)		May I Light Your Cigarette (2)	Now I Taste The Tears (2)		

BEAR, Edward — see EDWARD

BEARS, The   '88
Pop-rock group: **Adrian Belew** (vocals), Rob Fetters (guitar), Bob Nyswonger (bass) and Chris Arduser (drums).

| 4/30/88 | 159 | 5 | © | Rise And Shine .... | $10 | I.R.S. 42139 |

Aches And Pains	Girl With Clouds	Little Blue River	Old Fat Cadillac	Save Me
Best Laid Plans	Highway 2	Nobody's Fool	Rabbit Manor	You Can Buy Friends
Complicated Potatoes	Holy Mack	Not Worlds Apart	Robobo's Beef	

BEAST   '69
Rock group from Denver: David Raines (vocals), Robert Yeazel (guitar), Gerry Fike (organ), Michael Kerns (flute), Dominick Todero (trumpet), Ken Passarelli (bass) and Larry Ferris (drums).

| 9/13/69 | 195 | 2 | | Beast .... | $20 | Cotillion 9012 |

Alley Sam (I Feel A Change)	Ev'ry Man Hears Different	Goin' Downtown	On My Way	(Strange Places Like) Santo	When We Rise
Cannabis Sativa L	Music	Listen	Prelude For Today	Domingo	Wow Wow
Dear Ruth	Floating (Down By The River)	Love Like	Spaceman	Treat Her Right	

★206★ BEASTIE BOYS   '87
White rap-punk trio from New York City: Adam Horovitz, Adam Yauch and Mike Diamond. Horovitz starred in the movie *Lost Angels*; married actress Ione Skye (daughter of **Donovan**). Group started own Grand Royal record label.

11/29/86+	❶[7]	68	▲[9]	©	1 **Licensed To Ill**	C:❶[26]/378	$10	Def Jam 40238
8/12/89	14	15	▲[2]	©	2 **Paul's Boutique**	C:#6/28	$10	Capitol 91743
5/9/92	10	35	▲[2]	©	3 **Check Your Head**	C:#11/16	$10	Capitol 98938
2/26/94	46	7		©	4 **Some Old Bullshit**	[K]	$10	Grand Royal 89843
6/18/94	❶[1]	62	▲[3]	©	5 **Ill Communication**	C:#21/11	$10	Grand Royal 28599
6/10/95	50	8		©	6 **Root Down**	[L-M]	$10	Grand Royal 33603
4/20/96	45	7		©	7 **The In Sound From Way Out!**	[I]	$10	Grand Royal 33590
8/1/98	❶[3]	48	▲[3]	©	8 **Hello Nasty**		$10	Grand Royal 37716
12/11/99	19	17		©	9 **Beastie Boys Anthology: The Sounds Of Science**	[K]	$15	Grand Royal 22940 [2]

Alive (9)	Dedication (8)	Groove Holmes (3,7)	Mark On The Bus (3)	Ricky's Theme (5,7)	Sounds Of Science (2)
Alright Hear This (5)	Do It (5)	Heart Attack Man (5,6)	Michelle's Farm (4)	Root Down (5,6,9)	Stand Together (3)
And Me (8)	Dr. Lee, PhD (8)	**Hey Ladies** (2,9) *36*	Move, The (8)	Sabotage (5,9)	Super Disco Breakin' (8)
Ask For Janice (2)	Drinkin' Wine (7)	High Plains Drifter (2)	Namaste (3,7)	Sabrosa (5,6,7,9)	Sure Shot (5)
B-Boy Bouillabaisse Medley (2)	Dub The Mic (9)	Hold It Now, Hit It (1)	Negotiation Limerick File (8,9)	Scoop, The (5)	Three MC's And One DJ (8,9)
B-Boys Makin' With The Freak Freak (5)	Egg Man (2)	Holy Snappers (4)	Netty's Girl (9)	Shadrach (2,9)	3-Minute Rule (2)
	Egg Raid On Mojo (4,9)	I Don't Know (8)	New Style (1)	Shake Your Rump (2,9)	Time For Livin' (3,6,9)
Beastie Boys (9)	Electrify (8)	I Want Some (9)	No Sleep Till Brooklyn (1)	Shambala (5,7)	Time To Get Ill (1,6)
Beastie Revolution (4)	Eugene's Lament (5,7)	In 3's (3,7)	Ode To... (4)	She's Crafty (1)	To All The Girls (2)
Believe Me (9)	Fight For Your Right (9)	Instant Death (8)	POW (3)	She's On It (9)	Transit Cop (4)
Benny And The Jets (9)	Finger Lickin' Good (3)	**Intergalactic** (8,9) *28*	Pass The Mic (3,9)	Skills To Pay The Bills (9)	Transitions (5,7)
Biz Vs. The Nuge (9)	5-Piece Chicken Dinner (2)	Jimi (4)	Paul Revere (1)	Slow And Low (1,9)	Twenty Questions (9)
Bobo On The Corner (5,7)	Flowin' Prose (8)	Jimmy James (3,9)	Picture This (8)	Slow Ride (1)	Unite (8)
Bodhisattva Vow (5,9)	Flute Loop (5,6)	Johnny Ryall (2)	Posse In Effect (1)	Sneakin' Out The Hospital (8)	What Comes Around (2)
Body Movin' (8,9)	Funky Boss (3)	Just A Test (8)	Pow (7)	So What'cha Want (3,9) *93*	**(You Gotta) Fight For Your**
Bonus Batter (4)	Futterman's Rule (5,9)	Lighten Up (3)	Professor Booty (3)	Soba Violence (9)	**Right (To Party!)** (1) *7*
Boomin' Granny (9)	Get It Together (5,9)	Live At P.J.'s (3)	Putting Shame In Your Game (8)	Something's Got To Give (3,6,9)	
Brass Monkey (1,9) *48*	Girls (1)	Live Wire (9)	Railroad Blues (9)	Son of Neckbone (7,9)	
Car Thief (2)	Grasshopper Unit (Keep Movin') (8)	Looking Down The Barrel Of A Gun (2)	Remote Control (8,9)	Song For Junior (8)	
Cooky Puss (4)	Gratitude (3,9)	Maestro, The (3,6)	Rhymin & Stealin (1)	Song For The Man (8,9)	
Country Mike's Theme (9)					

BEAT FARMERS, The   '87
Rock group from Los Angeles: Joey Harris (vocals, guitar), Jerry Raney (guitar), Rollie Love (bass) and Country Dick Montana (drums). Montana died of a heart attack on 11/8/95 (age 40).

6/8/85	186	3	©	1 **Tales Of The New West**	$10	Rhino 853
7/12/86	135	9	©	2 **Van Go**	$10	MCA/Curb 5759
9/5/87	131	8	©	3 **The Pursuit Of Happiness**	$10	MCA/Curb 5993

Big Big Man (3)	Buy Me A Car (2)	Goldmine (1)	Lonesome Hound (1)	Ridin' (3)	Showbiz (1)
Big River (3)	California Kid (1)	Gun Sale At The Church (2)	Lost Weekend (1)	Riverside (2)	Texas (3)
Big Ugly Wheels (2)	Dark Light (3)	Happy Boy (1)	Make It Last (3)	Road To Ruin (2)	There She Goes Again (1)
Bigger Fool Than Me (2)	Deceiver (2)	Hollywood Hills (3)	Never Going Back (1)	Rosie (3)	Where Do They Go (1)
Bigger Stones (1)	Elephant Day Parade (3)	I Want You, Too (2)	Powderfinger (2)	Selfish Heart (1)	
Blue Chevrolet (2)	God Is Here Tonight (3)	Key To The World (3)	Reason To Believe (1)	Seven Year Blues (2)	

55

BEATLES, The ★3★   '64

The world's #1 rock group was formed in Liverpool, England, in the late 1950s. Known in early forms as The Quarrymen, Johnny & the Moondogs, The Rainbows, and the Silver Beatles. Named The Beatles in 1960. Originally consisted of **John Lennon**, **Paul McCartney**, **George Harrison** (guitars), Stu Sutcliffe (bass) and Pete Best (drums). Sutcliffe left in April 1961 (died of a brain hemorrhage on 4/10/62, age 21); McCartney moved to bass. Best replaced by **Ringo Starr** in August 1962. Group managed by Brian Epstein (died of a sleeping-pill overdose on 8/27/67, age 32) and produced by **George Martin**. First U.S. tour in February 1964. Won the 1964 Best New Artist Grammy Award. Group starred in the movies *A Hard Day's Night* (1964), *Help* (1965), *Magical Mystery Tour* (1967) and *Let It Be* (1970); contributed soundtrack to the animated movie *Yellow Submarine* (1968). Own Apple label in 1968. McCartney publicly announced group's dissolution on 4/10/70. Won the Grammy's Trustees Award in 1972. Lennon was shot to death on 12/8/80 (age 40). Group inducted into the Rock and Roll Hall of Fame in 1988.

1)Sgt. Pepper's Lonely Hearts Club Band 2)A Hard Day's Night 3)Abbey Road 4)Meet The Beatles!
5)The Beatles [White Album]

DEBUT	PEAK	WKS	RIAA	CD	#	Album Title	Catalog/Sym	$	Label & Number
2/1/64	❶[11]	71	▲[5]		1	**Meet The Beatles!**		$150	Capitol 2047
2/8/64	2[9]	49			2	**Introducing...The Beatles**		$800	Vee-Jay 1062
						releazed in July 1963; also see #9 and #10 below			
2/15/64	68	14			3	**The Beatles with Tony Sheridan and Their Guests**	[E]	$200	MGM 4215
						includes "Darktown Strutters' Ball," "Flying Beat," "Happy New Year Beat," "Johnson Rag," "Rye Beat" and "Summertime Beat" by The Titans			
4/4/64	104	6			4	**Jolly What! The Beatles & Frank Ifield**	[K]	$500	Vee-Jay 1085
						includes "Anytime," "I Listen To My Heart," "I Remember You," "I'm Smiling Now," "Lovesick Blues," "Nobody's Darling," "Unchained Melody" and "The Wayward Wind" by **Frank Ifield**; a repackaged version showing a portrait of The Beatles on cover was released briefly in late 1964 and is valued at $3000-$6000 for a stereo copy			
4/25/64	❶[5]	55	▲[2]		5	**The Beatles' Second Album**		$100	Capitol 2080
6/6/64	20	13			6	**The American Tour With Ed Rudy**	[T]	$100	RadioPulsebeat 2
						interviews with The Beatles			
7/18/64	❶[14]	51	▲[4]	©	7	**A Hard Day's Night**	C:#20/2 [S]	$100	United Artists 6366
						includes "And I Love Her," "Hard Day's Night," "I Should Have Known Better" and "Ringo's Theme (This Boy)" by **George Martin**			
8/8/64	2[9]	41	▲[2]		8	**Something New**		$100	Capitol 2108
10/10/64	142	3			9	**The Beatles vs. The Four Seasons**	[R]	$800	Vee-Jay 30 [2]
						reissue of #2 above and *Golden Hits of The 4 Seasons*			
10/31/64	63	11			10	**Songs, Pictures And Stories Of The Fabulous Beatles**	[R]	$500	Vee-Jay 1092
						2nd reissue of #2 above			
12/12/64+	7	17	●		11	**The Beatles' Story**	[T]	$100	Capitol 2222 [2]
						narrative featuring bits of their hits			
1/2/65	❶[9]	71	▲[3]		12	**Beatles '65**		$100	Capitol 2228
4/24/65	43	35	▲		13	**The Early Beatles**	[E]	$100	Capitol 2309
						reissue by Capitol of Vee-Jay recordings			
6/26/65	❶[6]	41	▲		14	**Beatles VI**		$100	Capitol 2358
8/28/65	❶[9]	44	▲[3]	©	15	**Help!**	C:#29/8 [S]	$100	Capitol 2386
						includes "The Bitter End," "Another Hard Day's Night," "The Chase," "From Me To You Fantasy" and "In The Tyrol" by Ken Thorne			
12/25/65+	❶[6]	59	▲[6]	©	16	**Rubber Soul**	C:#6/33	$100	Capitol 2442
7/9/66	❶[5]	31	▲[2]		17	**"Yesterday"...And Today**	[G]	$100	Capitol 2553
						originally featured the "butcher cover" (proper name of photo on cover is "Somnambulant Adventure") which is valued at $3000-$5000 for a mono copy and $5000-$10,000 for stereo; album quickly withdrawn after its release and a new photo was pasted over the controversial original cover			
9/3/66	❶[6]	77	▲[5]	©	18	**Revolver**	C:#13/25	$100	Capitol 2576
6/24/67	❶[15]	175	▲[11]	©	19	**Sgt. Pepper's Lonely Hearts Club Band**	C:❶[1]/175	$100	Capitol 2653
						1967 Grammy winner: Album of the Year			
12/23/67+	❶[8]	91	▲[6]	©	20	**Magical Mystery Tour**	C:#13/20 [G-S]	$100	Capitol 2835
12/14/68	❶[9]	155	▲[19]	©	21	**The Beatles [White Album]**	C:#2[1]/90	$200	Apple 101 [2]
						simply titled *The Beatles*, however, because of stark cover, commonly referred to as *The White Album*			
2/8/69	2[2]	25	▲	©	22	**Yellow Submarine**	[S]	$50	Apple 153
						includes "March Of The Meanies," "Pepperland," "Pepperland Laid Waste," "Sea Of Time/Sea Of Holes," "Sea Of Monsters" and "Yellow Submarine In Pepperland" by **George Martin**; also see #45 below			
10/18/69	❶[11]	129	▲[12]	©	23	**Abbey Road**	C:#2[1]/157	$50	Apple 383
3/21/70	2[4]	33	▲[3]		24	**Hey Jude**	[G]	$50	Apple 385
5/16/70	117	7			25	**The Beatles Featuring Tony Sheridan - In The Beginning (Circa 1960)**	[E]	$50	Polydor 4504
5/30/70	❶[4]	59	▲[4]	©	26	**Let It Be**	C:#32/3 [S]	$50	Apple 34001
4/14/73	3	164	▲[15]	©	27	**The Beatles/1962-1966**	C:#2[2]/63	[G] $40	Apple 3403 [2]
4/14/73	❶[1]	169	▲[16]	©	28	**The Beatles/1967-1970**	C:❶[3]/88	[G] $40	Apple 3404 [2]
6/26/76	2[2]	30	▲		29	**Rock 'N' Roll Music**	[K]	$20	Capitol 11537 [2]
						also see #35 and #36 below			
5/21/77	2[2]	17	▲		30	**The Beatles At The Hollywood Bowl**	[E-L]	$15	Capitol 11638
						recorded on 8/23/64 and 8/30/65			
7/2/77	111	7		©	31	**The Beatles Live! at the Star-Club in Hamburg, Germany; 1962**	[E-L]	$20	Lingasong 7001 [2]
11/12/77	24	31	▲[3]		32	**Love Songs**	[K]	$20	Capitol 11711 [2]
4/12/80	21	15	●		33	**Rarities**	[K]	$12	Capitol 12060
4/10/82	19	12	●		34	**Reel Music**	[K]	$12	Capitol 12199
7/24/82	11[C]	71	▲		35	**Rock 'N' Roll Music, Volume 1**	[R]	$12	Capitol 16020
7/24/82	7[C]	95	▲		36	**Rock 'N' Roll Music, Volume 2**	[R]	$12	Capitol 16021
						above 2 are single album reissues of #29 above			
11/13/82+	50	28	▲[2]		37	**20 Greatest Hits**	[G]	$12	Capitol 12245
4/2/88	149	6	▲	©	38	**Past Masters - Volume One**	C:#39/1 [K]	$12	Capitol 90043
4/2/88	121	7	▲	©	39	**Past Masters - Volume Two**	C:#30/2 [K]	$12	Capitol 90044
11/14/92	38[C]	1	▲	©	40	**Please Please Me**	[E]	$10	Capitol 46435
						first released in England in 1963			
12/24/94	3	24	▲[4]	©	41	**Live At The BBC**	[E-L]	$20	Apple 31796 [2]

BEATLES, The — Cont'd

DEBUT	PEAK	WKS	RIAA	CD	ARTIST — Album Title	Sym	$	Label & Number
12/9/95	❶³	29	▲⁸	© 42	**Anthology 1**	[K]	$20	Apple 34445 [2]
4/6/96	❶¹	37	▲⁴	© 43	**Anthology 2**	[K]	$20	Apple 34448 [2]
11/16/96	❶¹	16	▲³	© 44	**Anthology 3**	[K]	$20	Apple 46332 [2]
10/2/99	15	15	●	© 45	**Yellow Submarine Songtrack**	[S-R]	$10	Apple 21481

includes 9 songs not on the original release in 1969

| 12/2/00 | ❶⁸ | 44↑ | ▲⁷ | © 46 | **1** | [G] | $10 | Apple 29325 |

Across The Universe (26,28,33,39,43)
Act Naturally (17) 47
Ain't Nothing Shakin' (Like The Leaves On A Tree) (31)
Ain't She Sweet (25,42,44) 19
All I've Got To Do (1)
All My Loving (1,27,30,41,42) 45
All Things Must Pass (44)
All Together Now (22,45)
All You Need Is Love (20,22,28,34,37,45,46) 1
And I Love Her (7,8,27,32,33,34,42) 12
And Your Bird Can Sing (17,43)
Anna (2,9,10,13,40)
Another Girl (15)
Any Time At All (8,29,36)
Ask Me Why (2,4,9,10,13,40)
Baby It's You (2,9,10,13,40,41) 67
Baby You're A Rich Man (20,45) 34
Baby's In Black (12)
Back In The U.S.S.R. (21,28,29,36)
Bad Boy (14,29,35,38)
Ballad Of John And Yoko (24,28,39,46) 8
Be-Bop-A-Lula (31)
Because (23,44)
Beginning, A (44)
Being For The Benefit Of Mr. Kite (19,43)
Besame Mucho (31,42)
Birthday (21,29,36)
Blackbird (21,44)
Blue Jay Way (20)
Blue Suede Shoes (medley) (44)
Boys (2,9,10,13,29,30,35,40,42)
Can't Buy Me Love (7,24,27,30,34,37,41,42,46) 1
Carol (41)
Carry That Weight (23)
Cayenne (42)
Chains (2,9,10,13,40)
Clarabella (41)
Come And Get It (44)
Come Together (23,28,37,44,46) 1
Continuing Story of Bungalow Bill (21)
Cry Baby Cry (21,44)
Cry For A Shadow (3,25,42)
Crying, Waiting, Hoping (41)
Day In The Life (19,28,43)
Day Tripper (17,27,39,46) 5
Dear Prudence (21)
Devil In Her Heart (5)
Dig A Pony (44)
Dig It (26)
Dizzy Miss Lizzie (14,29,30,36,41)
Do You Want To Know A Secret (2,9,10,13,40) 2
Dr. Robert (17)
Don't Bother Me (1)
Don't Ever Change (41)
Don't Let Me Down (24,28,39) 35
Don't Pass Me By (21,33,44)
Drive My Car (17,27,29,36)

Eight Days A Week (14,27,37,42,46) 1
Eleanor Rigby (18,27,43,45,46) 11
End, The (23,44)
Every Little Thing (14,32)
Everybody's Got Something To Hide Except Me And My Monkey (21)
Everybody's Trying To Be My Baby (12,29,31,36,41,43) 68
hit "Hot 100" as part of "4-By The Beatles"
Falling In Love Again (31)
Fixing A Hole (19)
Flying (20)
Fool On The Hill (20,28,43)
For No One (18,32)
For You Blue (26,44) flip
Free As A Bird (42) 6
From Me To You (4,27,38,42,46) 41
From Us To You (41)
Get Back (26,28,29,34,36,37,39,44,46) 1
Getting Better (19)
Girl (16,27,32)
Glad All Over (41)
Glass Onion (21,44)
Golden Slumbers (23)
Good Day Sunshine (18)
Good Morning Good Morning (19,43)
Good Night (21,44)
Got To Get You Into My Life (18,29,36,43) 7
Hallelujah I Love Her So (31,42)
Happiness Is A Warm Gun (21,44)
Hard Day's Night (7,27,30,34,37,41,42,46) 1
Hello Goodbye (20,28,37,43,46) 1
Hello Little Girl (42)
Help! (15,27,30,33,34,37,43,46) 1
Helter Skelter (21,29,33,36,44)
Her Majesty (23)
Here Comes The Sun (23,28)
Here, There And Everywhere (18,32)
Hey Bulldog (22,29,36,45)
Hey, Hey, Hey, Hey (medley) (14,29,31,35,41,42)
Hey Jude (24,28,37,39,44,46) 1
Hippy Hippy Shake (31,41)
Hold Me Tight (1)
Honey Don't (12,41) 68
hit "Hot 100" as part of "4-By The Beatles"
Honey Pie (21,44)
Honeymoon Song (41)
How Do You Do It (42)
I Am The Walrus (20,28,33,34,43) 56
I Call Your Name (5,29,35,38)
I Dig A Pony (26)
I Don't Want To Spoil The Party (14) 39
I Feel Fine (12,27,37,38,41,43,46) 1
I Forgot To Remember To Forget (41)
I Got A Woman (41)

I Got To Find My Baby (41)
I Just Don't Understand (41)
I Me Mine (26,44)
I Need You (15,32)
I Remember You (31)
I Saw Her Standing There (1,2,9,10,29,35,40,41,42) 14
I Should Have Known Better (7,24,34) 53
I Wanna Be Your Man (1,29,35,41)
I Want To Hold Your Hand (1,27,37,38,42,46) 1
I Want To Tell You (18)
I Want You (She's So Heavy) (23)
I Will (21,32,44)
I'll Be Back (12,32,42)
I'll Be On My Way (41)
I'll Cry Instead (7,8) 25
I'll Follow The Sun (12,32)
I'll Get You (5,38,42)
I'm A Loser (12,41) 68
hit "Hot 100" as part of "4-By The Beatles"
I'm Down (29,36,38,43)
I'm Gonna Sit Right Down And Cry Over You (31,41)
I'm Happy Just To Dance With You (7,8) 95
I'm Looking Through You (16,43)
I'm Only Sleeping (17,33,43)
I'm So Tired (21,44)
I've Got A Feeling (26,44)
I've Just Seen A Face (16)
If I Fell (7,8,32) 53
If I Needed Someone (17)
If You've Got Trouble (43)
In My Life (16,27,32)
In Spite Of All The Danger (41)
Inner Light (33,39) 96
It Won't Be Long (1)
It's All Too Much (22,45)
It's Only Love (16,32,43)
Johnny B Goode (41)
Julia (21,44)
Junk (44)
Kansas City (medley) (14,29,31,35,41,42)
Keep Your Hands Off My Baby (41)
Komm, Gib Mir Deine Hand (I Want To Hold Your Hand) (8,38)
Lady Madonna (24,28,39,43,46) 4
Leave My Kitten Alone (41)
Lend Me Your Comb (31,42)
Let It Be (26,28,34,37,39,44,46) 1
Let's Dance (25)
Like Dreamers Do (42)
Little Child (1)
Little Queenie (31)
Lonesome Tears In My Eyes (41)
Long And Winding Road (26,28,32,34,37,44,46) 1
Long, Long, Long (21)
Long Tall Sally (5,29,30,31,35,38,41,42)
Los Paranoias (medley) (44)
Love Me Do (2,13,27,33,37,38,40,41,42,46) 1
Love You To (18,45)

Lovely Rita (19)
Lucille (41)
Lucy In The Sky With Diamonds (19,28,43,45)
Maggie Mae (26)
Magical Mystery Tour (20,28,34)
hit #12 on "Hot 100" as part of "Beatles' Movie Medley"
Mailman, Bring Me No More Blues (44)
Martha My Dear (21)
Matchbox (8,29,31,35,38,41) 17
Maxwell's Silver Hammer (23,44)
Mean Mr. Mustard (23,44)
Memphis, Tennessee (41)
Michelle (16,27,32)
Misery (2,9,10,33,40)
Money (That's What I Want) (5,29,35,42)
Moonlight Bay (42)
Mother Nature's Son (21,44)
hit "Hot 100" as part of "4-By The Beatles"
Mr. Moonlight (12,31,42) 68
My Bonnie My Bonnie Lies Over The Ocean (3,25,42) 26
Night Before (15,29,36)
No Reply (12,42)
Nobody's Child (3)
Norwegian Wood (This Bird Has Flown) (16,27,32,43)
Not A Second Time (1)
Not Guilty (44)
Nothin' Shakin' (41)
Nowhere Man (17,27,45) 3
Ob-La-Di, Ob-La-Da (21,28,44) 49
Octopus's Garden (23,28,44)
Oh! Darling (23,44)
Old Brown Shoe (24,28,39,44)
One After 909 (26,42)
Only A Northern Song (22,43,45)
Ooh! My Soul (41)
P.S. I Love You (2,13,32,40) 10
Paperback Writer (24,27,37,39,46) 1
Penny Lane (20,28,33,37,43,46) 1
Piggies (21,44)
Please Mister Postman (5) 92
hit "Hot 100" as part of "Four By The Beatles"
Please Please Me (2,4,9,10,13,27,40,42) 3
Polythene Pam (23,44)
Rain (24,39) 23
Real Love (43) 11
Red Sails In The Sunset (31)
Revolution (21,24,28,29,36,39) 12
Revolution 9 (21)
Ringo's Theme ..see: This Boy
Rip It Up (medley) (44)
Rock And Roll Music (12,29,35,41,43)
Rocky Raccoon (21,44)
Roll Over Beethoven (5,29,30,31,35,41,42) 68
Ruby Baby (25)
Run For Your Life (16)

Saints (When The Saints Go Marching In) (3,25)
Savoy Truffle (21)
Searchin' (42)
Sexy Sadie (21,44)
Sgt. Pepper's Lonely Hearts Club Band (19,28,43,45) 71
hit "Hot 100" as a medley with "With A Little Help From My Friends"
Shake, Rattle And Roll (medley) (44)
She Came In Through The Bathroom Window (23,44)
She Loves You (5,27,30,37,38,42,46) 1
She Said She Said (18)
She's A Woman (12,30,38,41,43) 4
She's Leaving Home (19,32)
Sheik Of Araby (42)
Sheila (31)
Shimmy Shake (31)
Shot Of Rhythm And Blues (41)
Shout (42)
Sie Liebt Dich (She Loves You) (33,38) 97
Slow Down (8,29,35,38,41) 25
So How Come (No One Loves Me) (41)
Soldier Of Love (41)
Some Other Guy (41)
Something (23,28,32,44,46) 3
Step Inside Love (medley) (44)
Strawberry Fields Forever (20,28,43) 8
Sun King (23)
Sure To Fall (In Love With You) (41)
Swanee River (23)
Sweet Georgia Brown (25)
Sweet Little Sixteen (31,41)
Take Out Some Insurance On Me, Baby (25)
Talkin' 'Bout You (31)
Taste Of Honey (2,9,10,13,31,40,41)
Taxman (18,29,36,43)
Teddy Boy (44)
Tell Me What You See (14,32)
Tell Me Why (7,8)
Thank You Girl (4,5,38,41) 35
That Means A Lot (43)
That'll Be The Day (42)
That's All Right (Mama) (41)
There's A Place (2,9,10,33,40) 74
Things We Said Today (8,30,41)
Think For Yourself (16)
This Boy (1,32,38,42) 92
hit "Hot 100" as part of "Four By The Beatles"
Three Cool Cats (42)
Ticket To Ride (15,27,30,34,37,41,43,46) 1
Till There Was You (1,31,41,42)
To Know Her Is To Love Her (31,41)
Tomorrow Never Knows (18,43)
Too Much Monkey Business (41)
12-Bar Original (43)
Twist And Shout (2,9,10,13,29,30,35,40,42) 2
Two Of Us (26,44)

Wait (16)
Wanna Be Your Man (42)
We Can Work It Out (17,27,37,39,46) 1
What You're Doing (14)
What'd I Say (25)
What's The New Mary Jane (44)
When I Get Home (8)
When I'm Sixty-Four (19,45)
Where Have You Been All My Life (31)
While My Guitar Gently Weeps (21,28,44)
Why (3,25) 88
Why Don't We Do It In The Road? (21,44)
Wild Honey Pie (21)
With A Little Help From My Friends (19,28,45) 71
hit "Hot 100" as a medley with "Sgt. Pepper's Lonely Hearts Club Band"
Within You Without You (19,43)
Word, The (16)
Words Of Love (14,32)
Ya Ya (25)
Yellow Submarine (18,22,27,34,45,46) 2
Yer Blues (21)
Yes It Is (14,32,38,43) 46
Yesterday (17,27,32,37,43,46) 1
You Are My Sunshine (31)
You Can't Do That (5,29,35,42) 48
You Know My Name (Look Up My Number) (33,39,43)
You Know What to Do (42)
You Like Me Too Much (14)
You Never Give Me Your Money (41)
You Really Got A Hold On Me (5,41,42)
You Won't See Me (16)
You'll Be Mine (42)
You're Going To Lose That Girl (15,32)
You've Got To Hide Your Love Away (15,27,32,34,43)
hit #12 on "Hot 100" as part of "Beatles' Movie Medley"
Young Blood (42)
Your Feets Too Big (31)
Your Mother Should Know (20,43)

BEATNUTS, The

Rap trio from New York City: Les Fernandez, Jerry Tineo and Bert Smalls (left after first album).

'99

DEBUT	PEAK	WKS	RIAA	CD	ARTIST — Album Title	$	Label & Number
7/9/94	182	2		© 1	**The Beatnuts**	$10	Relativity 1179
7/12/97	154	1		© 2	**Stone Crazy**	$10	Relativity 1508
9/18/99	35	8		© 3	**A Musical Massacre**	$10	Violator 1722
4/7/01	51	7		© 4	**Take It Or Squeeze It**	$10	Loud 1906

Are You Ready (1)
Beatnuts Forever (3)
Bless The M.I.C. (2)
Buddah In The Air (3)
Contact (4)
Do You Believe? (2)

Find That (2)
Fried Chicken (1)
Get Funky (2)
Give Me Tha Ass (2)
Hammer Time (4)
Hellraiser (1)

Here's A Drink (2)
Hit Me With That (1)
Hood Thang (4)
I Love It (3)
If It Ain't Gangsta (4)
It's Da Nuts (4)

Let Off A Couple (1)
Let's Git Doe (4)
Lick The Pussy (1)
Look Around (3)
Mayonnaise (4)
Monster For Music (3)

Muchachacha (3)
Niggaz Know (2)
No Escapin' This (4)
Off The Books (2) 86
Prendelo (Light It Up) (4)
Props Over Here (1)

Psycho Dwarf (1)
Puffin' On A Cloud (3)
Rik's Joint (1)
Sandwiches (1)
Se Acabo (It's Over) (3,4)
Slam Pit (3)

BEATNUTS, The — Cont'd

Spelling Beatnuts With Lil' Donny (3)
Stone Crazy (2)
Story 2000 (3)
Straight Jacket (1)
Strokes (2)
Supa Supreme (2)
Superbad (1)
Thinkin 'Bout Cash (2)
Turn It Out (3)
2-3 Break (1)
U Don't Want It (4)
Uncivilized (2)
Watch Out Now (3) *84*
Who You're Fuckin' Wit (3)
Who's Comin Wit Da Shit Na (4)
Wild, Wild, What! (3)
World Famous (2)
Ya Don't Stop (1)
Yeah You Get Props (1)
Yo Yo Yo (4)
You're A Clown (3)

BEATS INTERNATIONAL   '90

Dance group from England: Lester Noel and Lindy Layton (vocals), Andy Boucher (keyboards), Norman Cook (bass) and Luke Creswell (drums). Cook was a member of **The Housemartins** and later recorded as **Fatboy Slim**.

5/19/90	162	6		©	Let Them Eat Bingo			$10	Elektra 60921

Babies Makin' Babies
Before I Grow Too Old
Blame It On The Bassline
Burundi Blues
Dance To The Drummer's Beat
Dub Be Good To Me *76*
For Spacious Lies
Ragged Trousered Percussionists
Tribute To King Tubby
Whole World's Down On Me
Won't Talk About It *76*

BEAU BRUMMELS, The   '65

Rock group from San Francisco: Sal Valentino (vocals), Ron Elliott (guitar), Ron Meagher (bass) and John Petersen (drums). Petersen later joined **Harpers Bizzare**.

5/8/65	24	21		©	1	Introducing The Beau Brummels		$50	Autumn 103
						produced by **Sly Stone**			
9/30/67	197	2			2	Triangle		$25	Warner 1692
7/5/75	180	3			3	The Beau Brummels		$20	Warner 2842

Ain't That Loving You Baby (1)
And I've Seen Her (2)
Are You Happy? (2)
Down To The Bottom (3)
First In Line (3)
Gate Of Hearts (3)
Goldrush (3)
I Want More Loving (1)
I Would Be Happy (1)
It Won't Get Better (2)
Just A Little (1) *8*
Just Wait And See (1)
Keeper Of Time (2)
Laugh, Laugh (1) *15*
Lonely Side (3)
Magic Hollow (2)
Nine Pound Hammer (2)
Not Too Long Ago (1)
Oh Lonesome Me (1)
Old Kentucky Home (2)
Only Dreaming Now (2)
Painter Of Women (2)
Singing Cowboy (3)
Stick Like Glue (1)
Still In Love With You Baby (1)
Tennessee Walker (3)
That's, If You Want Me To (1)
They'll Make You Cry (1)
Today By Day (3)
Triangle (2)
Wolf (3)
Wolf Of Velvet Fortune (2)
You Tell Me Why (3) *38*

BEAUVOIR, Jean   '86

Born in Chicago of Haitian parentage; raised in New York City. Male singer/bassist. Member of the **Plasmatics** and **Little Steven and the Disciples Of Soul**.

6/28/86	93	15		©	Drums Along The Mohawk			$10	Columbia 40403

Drive You Home
Feel The Heat *73*
If I Was Me
Missing The Young Days
Never Went Down
Nina
Rockin In The Street
Same Song Plays On And On
Sorry I Missed Your Wedding
Day
This Is Our House

BEAVIS & BUTT-HEAD — see TELEVISION SOUNDTRACKS

BE-BOP DELUXE   '77

Rock group from England: Bill Nelson (vocals), Andy Clark (keyboards), Charles Tumahai (bass) and Simon Fox (drums). Tumahai died of a heart attack on 12/21/95.

2/7/76	96	17			1	Sunburst Finish		$12	Harvest 11478
10/16/76	88	8			2	Modern Music		$12	Harvest 11575
8/20/77	65	15		©	3	Live! In The Air Age .... [L]	$15	Harvest 11666 [2]
3/11/78	95	9			4	Drastic Plastic		$12	Harvest 11750

Adventures In A Yorkshire Landscape (3)
Beauty Secrets (1)
Bird Charmer's Destiny (2)
Blazing Apostles (1,3)
Bring Back The Spark (2)
Crying To The Sky (1)
Crystal Gazing (1)
Dance Of The Uncle Sam Humanoids (2)
Dancing In The Moonlight (All Alone) (2)
Dangerous Stranger (4)
Down On Terminal Street (2)
Electrical Language (4)
Fair Exchange (1,3)
Forbidden Lovers (2)
Gold At The End Of My Rainbow (2)
Heavenly Homes (1)
Honeymoon On Mars (2)
Islands Of The Dead (3)
Japan (4)
Kiss Of Light (2)
Life In The Air Age (1,3)
Like An Old Blues (1)
Lost In The Neon World (2)
Love In Flames (4)
Maid In Heaven (1)
Make The Music Magic (2)
Mill Street Junction (3)
Modern Music (2)
New Mysteries (4)
New Precision (4)
Orphans Of Babylon (2)
Panic In The World (4)
Piece Of Mine (3)
Possession (4)
Shine (3)
Ships In The Night (1,3)
Sister Seagull (1)
Sleep That Burns (1)
Superenigmatix (Lethal Appliances For The Home With Everything) (4)
Surreal Estate (4)
Twilight Capers (4)

BECK   '94

Born Beck David Campbell on 7/8/70 near Kansas City; raised in Los Angeles. Male rock singer/songwriter/guitarist.

3/19/94	13	24	▲	©	1	Mellow Gold		$10	DGC 24634
7/6/96	16	88	▲²	©	2	Odelay		$10	DGC 24823
11/21/98	13	14	●	©	3	Mutations		$10	DGC 25309
12/11/99	34	18	●	©	4	Midnite Vultures		$10	DGC 490485

Beautiful Way (4)
Beercan (1)
Blackhole (1)
Bottle Of Blues (3)
Broken Train (4)
Canceled Check (3)
Cold Brains (3)
Dead Melodies (3)
Debra (4)
Derelict (2)
Devils Haircut (2) *94*
Fuckin With My Head (Mountain Dew Rock) (1)
Get Real Paid (4)
High 5 (Rock The Catskills) (2)
Hollywood Freaks (4)
Hotwax (2)
Jack-Ass (2) *73*
Lazy Flies (3)
Lord Only Knows (2)
Loser (1) *10*
Milk & Honey (4)
Minus (2)
Mixed Bizness (4)
Mutherfuker (1)
New Pollution (2) *78*
Nicotine & Gravy (4)
Nitemare Hippy Girl (1)
Nobody's Fault But My Own (3)
Novacane (4)
O Maria (3)
Pay No Mind (Snoozer) (1)
Peaches & Cream (4)
Pressure Zone (4)
Ramshackle (2)
Readymade (2)
Sexx Laws (4)
Sing It Again (3)
Sissyneck (2)
Soul Suckin Jerk (1)
Static (2)
Steal My Body Home (1)
Sweet Sunshine (1)
Tropicalia (3)
Truckdrivin Neighbors Downstairs (Yellow Sweat) (1)
We Live Again (3)
Where It's At (2) *61*
Whiskeyclone, Hotel City 1997 (1)

BECK, Jeff   ★187★   '75

Born on 6/24/44 in Wallington, Surrey, England. Prolific rock guitarist. With **The Yardbirds** from 1965-66. Lineup of **Jeff Beck Group** from 1968-69: Beck, **Rod Stewart** (vocals), **Ronnie Wood** (bass), **Nicky Hopkins** (keyboards) and Tony Newman (drums); group's lineup from 1970-72: Beck, Bob Tench (vocals), Clive Chaman (bass), Max Middleton (piano) and Cozy Powell (drums; **Emerson, Lake & Powell**; **Black Sabbath**). Member of **The Honeydrippers**.

1)Blow By Blow   2)Jeff Beck, Tim Bogert, Carmine Appice   3)Truth

8/24/68	15	33	●	©	1	Truth		$20	Epic 26413
7/12/69	15	21	●	©	2	Beck-Ola		$20	Epic 26478
11/6/71	46	16		©	3	Rough And Ready		$15	Epic 30973
5/13/72	19	26	●	©	4	Jeff Beck Group		$15	Epic 31331
						JEFF BECK GROUP (above 3)			
4/7/73	12	27	●	©	5	Jeff Beck, Tim Bogert, Carmine Appice		$15	Epic 32140
4/12/75	4	25	▲	©	6	Blow By Blow	C:#12/209 [I]	$12	Epic 33409
6/26/76	16	25	▲	©	7	Wired	C:#21/96 [I]	$12	Epic 33849

58

BECK, Jeff — Cont'd

DEBUT	PEAK	WKS	RIAA	CD	ARTIST — Album Title	Catalog	Sym	$	Label & Number
4/2/77	23	15	●	© 8	Jeff Beck with The Jan Hammer Group Live	[I-L]		$12	Epic 34433
					recorded at Scorpio Sound Studios in London				
7/12/80	21	20		© 9	There And Back	[I]		$12	Epic 35684
7/20/85	39	18		© 10	Flash			$10	Epic 39483
10/21/89	49	18		© 11	Jeff Beck's Guitar Shop	[I]		$10	Epic 44313
					JEFF BECK WITH TERRY BOZZIO & TONY HYMAS				
7/17/93	171	1		© 12	Crazy Legs			$10	Epic 53562
					JEFF BECK and The Big Town Playboys				
					tribute to Gene Vincent				
4/3/99	99	5		© 13	Who Else!	[I]		$10	Epic 67987
2/24/01	110	2		© 14	You Had It Coming	[I]		$10	Epic 61625

Air Blower (6)
All Shook Up (2)
Ambitious (10)
Angel (Footsteps) (13)
Another Place (13)
B-I-Bickey-Bi-Bo-Bo-Go (12)
Baby Blue (12)
Beck's Bolero (1)
Behind The Veil (11)
Big Block (11)
Black Cat Moan (5)
Blackbird (14)
Blast From The East (13)
Blue Wind (7,8)
Blues De Luxe (1)
Blues Stay Away From Me (12)
Brush With The Blues (13)
Catman (12)
Cause We've Ended As Lovers (6)
Come Dancing (7)
Constipated Duck (6)
Crazy Legs (12)

Cruisin' (12)
Darkness (medley) (8)
Day In The House (11)
Declan (13)
Definitely Maybe (4)
Diamond Dust (6)
Dirty Mind (14)
Double Talkin' Baby (12)
Earth In Search Of A Sun (medley) (8)
Earth (Still Our Only Home) (8)
Earthquake (14)
Ecstasy (10)
El Becko (9)
Escape (10)
Even Odds (13)
Final Peace (9)
Five Feet Of Lovin' (12)
Freeway Jam (6,8)
Full Moon Boogie (8)
Get Workin' (10)
Gets Us All In The End (10)
Girl From Mill Valley (2)

Glad All Over (4)
Going Down (4)
Golden Road (9)
Goodbye Pork Pie Hat (7)
Got The Feeling (3)
Greensleeves (1)
Guitar Shop (11)
Hangman's Knee (2)
Head For Backstage Pass (7)
Highways (4)
Hip-Notica (13)
Hold Me, Hug Me, Rock Me (12)
I Ain't Superstitious (1)
I Can't Give Back The Love I Feel For You (4)
I Got To Have A Song (4)
I'm So Proud (5)
I've Been Used (3)
Ice Cream Cakes (1)
Jailhouse Rock (2)
Jody (3)
Lady (5)

Led Boots (7)
Left Hook (14)
Let Me Love You (1)
Livin' Alone (5)
Loose Cannon (14)
Lose Myself With You (5)
Lotta Lovin' (12)
Love Is Green (7)
Max's Tune (3)
Morning Dew (1)
Nadia (14)
New Ways (medley) (3)
Night After Night (10)
Oh To Love You (5)
Ol' Man River (1)
People Get Ready (10) *48*
Pink Thunderbird (12)
Play With Me (7)
Plynth (Water Down The Drain) (2)
Pretty Pretty Baby (12)
Psycho Sam (13)
Pump, The (9)

Race With The Devil (12)
Red Blue Jeans And A Pony Tail (12)
Rice Pudding (2)
Rock My Plimsoul (1)
Rollin' And Tumblin' (14)
Rosebud (14)
Roy's Toy (14)
Savoy (11)
Say Mama (12)
Scatterbrain (6,8)
Shapes Of Things (1)
She's A Woman (6,8)
Short Business (3)
Situation (3)
Sling Shot (11)
Sophie (7)
Space Boogie (9)
Space For The Papa (13)
Spanish Boots (2)
Stand On It (11)
Star Cycle (9)
Stop, Look And Listen (10)

Sugar Cane (4)
Superstition (5)
Suspension (14)
Sweet Sweet Surrender (5)
THX138 (13)
Thelonius (6)
Tonight I'll Be Staying Here With You (4)
Too Much To Lose (9)
Train Train (medley) (3)
Two Rivers (11)
What Mama Said (13)
Where Were You (11)
Who Slapped John? (12)
Why Should I Care (5)
Woman Love (12)
You Better Believe (12)
You Know, We Know (10)
You Know What I Mean (6)
You Never Know (9)
You Shook Me (1)

BECK, Joe   '75
Born on 7/29/45 in Philadelphia. Jazz-funk guitarist.

DEBUT	PEAK	WKS	RIAA	CD	ARTIST — Album Title	Catalog	Sym	$	Label & Number
6/28/75	140	5			Beck	[I]		$12	Kudu 21

Brothers And Others   Cactus   Cafe Black Rose   Red Eye   Star Fire   Texas Ann

BEE GEES ★29★   '78
Trio of brothers from Manchester, England: **Barry Gibb** (b: 9/1/47) and twins Maurice and Robin Gibb (b: 12/22/49). Moved to Australia in 1958, performed as the Gibbs, later as BG's, finally the Bee Gees. Returned to England in February 1967, with guitarist Vince Melouney and drummer Colin Peterson. Melouney left in December 1968; Robin left for solo career in 1969. When Peterson left in August 1969, Barry and Maurice went solo. After eight months, the brothers reunited. Composed soundtracks for *Saturday Night Fever* and *Staying Alive*. Acted in the movie *Sgt. Pepper's Lonely Hearts Club Band*. Youngest brother, **Andy Gibb**, was a successful solo singer (d: 3/10/88). Trio inducted into the Rock and Roll Hall of Fame in 1997.

1)Saturday Night Fever 2)Spirits Having Flown 3)Bee Gees Greatest 4)Staying Alive 5)Bee Gees' 1st

DEBUT	PEAK	WKS	RIAA	CD	ARTIST — Album Title	Catalog	Sym	$	Label & Number
8/26/67	7	52		© 1	Bee Gees' 1st			$30	Atco 223
2/10/68	12	22		© 2	Horizontal			$30	Atco 233
8/31/68	17	27		© 3	Idea			$30	Atco 253
12/7/68+	99	12		4	Rare Precious & Beautiful	[E]		$30	Atco 264
					early Australian recordings (1963-1966)				
2/22/69	20	25		© 5	Odessa			$40	Atco 702 [2]
7/26/69	9	49	●	© 6	Best Of Bee Gees	C:#37/1	[G]	$30	Atco 292
3/28/70	100	8		7	Rare Precious & Beautiful, Volume 2	[E]		$30	Atco 321
					more Australian recordings (1963-1966)				
5/9/70	94	8		© 8	Cucumber Castle			$20	Atco 327
1/30/71	32	14		© 9	2 Years On			$20	Atco 353
9/25/71	34	14		© 10	Trafalgar			$20	Atco 7003
11/11/72	35	14		© 11	To Whom It May Concern			$20	Atco 7012
2/3/73	69	13		© 12	Life In A Tin Can			$15	RSO 870
8/4/73	98	16		© 13	Best Of Bee Gees, Vol. 2		[G]	$15	RSO 875
6/15/74	178	5		© 14	Mr. Natural			$12	RSO 4800
6/21/75+	14	75	●	© 15	Main Course			$12	RSO 4807
10/2/76	8	63	▲	© 16	Children Of The World			$12	RSO 3003
11/13/76+	50	33	●	17	Bee Gees Gold, Volume One		[G]	$12	RSO 3006
6/4/77	8	90	▲	© 18	Here At Last...Bee Gees...Live	[L]		$20	RSO 3901 [2]
11/26/77+	❶24	120	▲15	© 19	Saturday Night Fever	C:#6/27	[S]	$20	RSO 4001 [2]
					1978 Grammy winner: Album of the Year; includes "Boogie Shoes" by KC & The Sunshine Band, "Calypso Breakdown" by Ralph MacDonald, "Disco Inferno" by The Trammps, "A Fifth Of Beethoven" by Walter Murphy, "If I Can't Have You" by Yvonne Elliman, "K-Jee" by MFSB, "Open Sesame" by Kool & The Gang, "More Than A Woman" by Tavares and "Manhattan Skyline," "Night On Disco Mountain" and "Salsation" by David Shire				
2/17/79	❶6	55	▲	© 20	Spirits Having Flown			$12	RSO 3041
11/17/79+	❶1	32	▲2	© 21	Bee Gees Greatest	C:#3/56	[G]	$20	RSO 4200 [2]
11/21/81	41	12		© 22	Living Eyes			$12	RSO 3098
7/16/83	6	27	▲	© 23	Staying Alive		[S]	$20	RSO 813269
					includes "Far From Over" and "Moody Girl" by Frank Stallone, "Finding Out The Hard Way" by Cynthia Rhodes, "I'm Never Gonna Give You Up" by Frank Stallone & Cynthia Rhodes and "Look Out For Number One" and "(We Dance) So Close To The Fire" by Tommy Faragher				

DEBUT	PEAK	WKS	RIAA	CD	ARTIST — Album Title	Catalog	Sym	$	Label & Number

BEE GEES — Cont'd

DEBUT	PEAK	WKS						$	Label & Number
10/17/87	96	9		© 24	E-S-P..			$10	Warner 25541
8/19/89	68	13		© 25	One...			$10	Warner 25887
11/20/93	153	3		© 26	Size Isn't Everything......................................			$10	Polydor 521055
5/24/97	11	21	▲	© 27	Still Waters..			$10	Polydor 537302
11/21/98+	72	42	▲	© 28	One Night Only..	C:#2¹/18	[L]	$10	Polydor 559220
					recorded on 11/14/97 at the MGM Grand in Las Vegas				
5/12/01	16	8		© 29	This Is Where I Came In..................................			$10	Universal 549626

Above And Beyond (26)
Alive (11,13) *34*
All Of My Life (7)
All This Making Love (15)
Alone (27,28) *28*
Alone Again (9)
And The Sun Will Shine (2,13,28)
Angela (24)
Anything For You (26)
Baby As You Turn Away (15)
Back Home (9)
Backtafunk (24)
Bad Bad Dreams (11)
Be Who You Are (22)
Big Chance (4)
Birdie Told Me (2)
Black Diamond (5)
Blue Island (26)
Bodyguard (25)
Boogie Child (16,18) *12*
Born A Man (4)
Breakout (23)
British Opera (5)
Bury Me Down By The River (8)
Can't Keep A Good Man Down (16,18)
Chance Of Love (8)
Change Is Made (2)
Charade (14)
Cherry Red (7)
Children Of The World (16,21)
Claustrophobia (7)
Close Another Door (1)
Closer Than Close (27,28)
Come Home Johnny Bride (12)
Come On Over (15,18)
Could It Be (7)
Country Lanes (15)
Craise Finton Kirk Royal Academy Of Arts (1)
Crazy For Your Love (24)
Cryin' Every Day (22)
Cucumber Castle (1)
Day Time Girl (2)
Dearest (10)
Déjà Vu (29)
Dogs (14)
Don't Fall In Love With Me (2)
Don't Forget To Remember (8,13) *73*
Don't Say Goodbye (7)

Don't Wanna Live Inside Myself (10,13) *53*
Down The Road (14,18)
Down To Earth (3)
E-S-P (24)
Earnest Of Being George (2)
Edge Of The Universe (15,18) *26*
Edison (5)
Embrace (29)
Every Christian Lion Hearted Man Will Show You (1,6)
Every Second, Every Minute (9)
Everyday I Have To Cry (7)
Extra Mile (29)
Fallen Angel (26)
Fanny (Be Tender With My Love) (15,21) *12*
1st Mistake I Made (9)
First Of May (5,6) *37*
Flesh And Blood (25)
Follow The Wind (7)
For Whom The Bell Tolls (26)
Give Your Best (5)
Give A Hand, Take A Hand (14)
Giving Up The Ghost (5)
Glass House (4)
Grease (28)
Greatest Man In The World (10)
Guilty (28)
Had A Lot Of Love Last Night (14)
Harry Braff (2)
Haunted House (26)
He's A Liar (22) *30*
Heart Like Mine (26)
Heartbreaker (28)
Heavy Breathing (14)
Holiday (1,6,17,18) *16*
Horizontal (2)
House Of Shame (25)
How Can You Mend A Broken Heart (10,13,17,18,28) *1*
How Deep Is Your Love (19,21,28) *1*
How Many Birds (4)
How To Fall In Love, Pt. I (26)
I.O.I.O. (8,13) *94*
I Can Bring Love (11)
I Can't Let You Go (14)
I Can't See Nobody (1,6,17,18,28)

I Close My Eyes (1)
I Could Not Love You More (27)
I Do Adore Her (1)
I Don't Know Why I Bother Myself (4)
I Don't Wanna Be The One (12)
I Have Decided To Join The Air Force (3)
I Held A Party (11)
I Laugh In Your Face (5)
I Lay Down And Die (8)
I Love You Too Much (23)
I Started A Joke (3,6,17,18,28) *6*
I Still Love You (22)
I Surrender (27)
I Was A Lover, A Leader Of Men (7)
I Was The Child (8)
I Will (27)
I'm Satisfied (20)
I'm Weeping (9)
I've Gotta Get A Message To You (3,6,17,18) *8*
Idea (3)
If I Can't Have You (21)
If Only I Had My Mind On Something Else (8) *91*
Immortality (28)
In My Own Time (1)
In The Summer Of His Years (3)
Indian Gin And Whisky Dry (3)
Irresistible Force (27)
Islands In The Stream (28)
Israel (10)
It's Just The Way (10)
It's My Neighborhood (25)
Jingle Jangle (4)
Jive Talkin' (15,18,19,21,28) *1*
Kilburn Towers (3)
Kiss Of Life (26)
Kitty Can (3)
Lamplight (5)
Lay It On Me (9)
Lemons Never Forget (2)
Let There Be Love (3,13)
Life Goes On (23)
(Lights Went Out In) Massachusetts (2,6,17,18,28) *11*
Lion In Winter (10)

Live Or Die (Hold Me Like A Child) (24)
Living Eyes (22) *45*
Living In Chicago (12)
Living Together (20)
Lonely Days (9,13,17,18,28) *3*
Longest Night (24)
Loose Talk Costs Lives (29)
Lord, The (8)
Lost In Your Love (14)
Love Me (16,21)
Love So Right (16,18,21) *3*
Love You Inside Out (20,21) *1*
Lovers (16)
Man For All Seasons (9,13)
Man In The Middle (29)
Marley Purt Drive (5)
Melody Fair (5,13)
Method To My Madness (12)
Miracles Happen (27)
Monday's Rain (4)
More Than A Woman (19,21,28)
Morning Of My Life (In The Morning) (13)
Mr. Natural (14) *93*
My Life Has Been A Song (12)
My Lover's Prayer (27)
My Thing (8)
My World (13,17) *16*
Never Been Alone (11)
Never Say Never Again (5)
New York Mining Disaster 1941 (Have You Seen My Wife, Mr. Jones) (1,6,17,18,28) *14*
Night Fever (19,21,28) *1*
Nights On Broadway (15,18,21,28) *7*
Nothing Could Be Good (22)
Obsessions (27)
Odessa (City On The Black Sea) (5)
Omega Man (26)
One (25) *7*
One Minute Woman (1)
Ordinary Lives (25)
(Our Love) Don't Throw It All Away (21,28)
Overnight (24)
Paper Mache, Cabbages & Kings (11)

Paradise (22)
Paying The Price Of Love (26) *74*
Playdown (4)
Please Don't Turn Out The Lights (11)
Please Read Me (1)
Portrait Of Louise (9)
Reaching Out (20)
Really And Sincerely (2)
Red Chair, Fade Away (1)
Remembering (9)
Rest Your Love On Me (21)
Road To Alaska (11)
Run To Me (11,13,17,18) *16*
Sacred Trust (29)
Saved By The Bell (13)
Saw A New Morning (12) *94*
Sea Of Smiling Faces (11)
Search, Find (20)
Second Hand People (4)
Seven Seas Symphony (5)
She Keeps On Coming (29)
Sincere Relation (9)
Smoke And Mirrors (27)
Soldiers (22)
Somebody Stop The Music (10)
Someone Belonging To Someone (23) *49*
Songbird (15)
Sound Of Love (5)
South Dakota Morning (12)
Spicks And Specks (4,6)
Spirits (Having Flown) (20,21)
Stayin' Alive (19,21,23,28) *1*
Still Waters Run Deep (27) *57*
Stop (Think Again) (20)
Subway (16)
Suddenly (4)
Swan Song (3)
Sweet Song Of Summer (11)
Sweetheart (8)
Take Hold Of That Star (7)
Tears (27)
Technicolor Dreams (29)
Tell Me Why (9)
Then You Left Me (8)
This Is Where I Came In (29)
This Is Your Life (2)
Three Kisses Of Love (7)
Throw A Penny (8)

Tint Of Blue (4)
To Be Or Not To Be (7)
To Love Somebody (1,6,17,18,28) *17*
Tokyo Nights (25)
Too Much Heaven (20,21) *1*
Trafalgar (10)
Tragedy (20,21,28) *1*
Travels Of Jamie McPheeters, Theme From The (7)
Turn Of The Century (1)
Turning Tide (8)
2 Years On (9)
Until (20)
Voice in The Wilderness (29)
Voices (14)
Walking Back To Waterloo (10)
Walking On Air (29)
Way It Was (16)
We Lost The Road (11)
Wedding Day (29)
When Do I (10)
When The Swallows Fly (3)
Where Are You (4)
While I Play (12)
Whisper Whisper (5)
Will You Ever Let Me (25)
Wind Of Change (15,18,21)
Wish You Were Here (25)
With All Nations (International Anthem) (5)
With My Eyes Closed (27)
With The Sun In My Eyes (2)
Woman In You (23) *24*
Words (6,17,18,28) *15*
World (2,6,18)
Wouldn't I Be Someone (13)
You Know It's For You (11)
You Should Be Dancing (16,18,19,21,28) *1*
You Stepped Into My Life (16,21)
You Win Again (24) *75*
You'll Never See My Face Again (5)

BEELOW
Born Bruce Moore in Baton Rouge, Louisiana. Male rapper.   **'00**

DEBUT	PEAK	WKS						$	Label & Number
3/18/00	146	2		©	Ballaholic..			$10	Ballin 417105

Actin Badd II
All I Hear (Murderer)
Ballaholic
Big Body Remix

Big Mouth
Da Heist
From Baton Rouge To New Orleans
I'm A Baller

Hoodlum & Ballers
How Many Dollars
I Wish U Would

My Niggaz
On Da Grind (Like A Man Bra)
Slow Yo Roll
10 Niggaz

Too Late
Watch Dem Haters
Watch Yo Ass
Wooday

BEENIE MAN
Born Anthony Davis on 8/22/73 in Kingston, Jamaica. Reggae singer/rapper.   **'00**

DEBUT	PEAK	WKS						$	Label & Number
3/21/98	151	12		© 1	Many Moods Of Moses......................................			$10	VP 1513
7/29/00	68	20		© 2	Art And Life..			$10	Shocking Vibes 49093

Ain't Gonna Figure It Yet (1)
Analyze This (2)
Art And Life (2)
Bad Man (1)
Bad Mind Is Active (My Prerogative) (1)

Best That I Got (2)
Crazy Notion (2)
Foundation (1)
Girls Dem Sugar (2) *54*
Got To Be There (1)
Haters And Fools (2)

Have You Ever (1)
Heaven On Earth (1)
Heights Of Great Men (2)
I've Got A Date (2)
Jamaica Way (1)
Long Road (1)

Love Me Now (2)
Miss You (1)
Monster Look (1)
9 To 5 (2)
Ola (2)
Original Tune (2)

Oysters & Conch (1)
Sincerely (1)
So Hot (1)
Some Tonight (2)
Steve Biko (1)
Trus Me (2)

Tumble (La Caida) (2)
Who Am I (1) *40*
Woman A Sample (1)

BEGA, Lou
Born David Lubega in 1975 in Munich, Germany (Sicilian mother/Ugandan father).   **'99**

DEBUT	PEAK	WKS						$	Label & Number
9/11/99	3	47	▲³	©	A Little Bit Of Mambo			$10	RCA 67887

Baby Keep Smiling
Beauty On The TV-Screen
Behind Stage
Can I Tico Tico You

I Got A Girl
Icecream
Lou's Café
Mambo Mambo

Mambo No. 5 (A Little Bit Of...) *3*
Most Expensive Girl In The World

1+1=2
Tricky, Tricky *74*
Trumpet Part II

BELAFONTE, Harry ★51★   '56

Born on 3/1/27 in Harlem, New York. Calypso singer/actor. Rode the crest of the calypso craze to worldwide stardom. Starred in several movies. Became UNICEF goodwill ambassador in 1987. Father of actress Shari Belafonte.

1)Calypso 2)Belafonte 3)An Evening With Belafonte 4)Belafonte Sings Of The Caribbean
5)"Mark Twain" And Other Folk Favorites

1/28/56	3	6			1 "Mark Twain" And Other Folk Favorites	$50	RCA Victor 1022
2/25/56	❶6	62	●		2 Belafonte	$50	RCA Victor 1150
6/16/56	❶31	99	●	©	3 Calypso	$30	RCA Victor 1248
3/30/57	2²	20	●		4 An Evening With Belafonte	$30	RCA Victor 1402
9/16/57	3	16			5 Belafonte Sings Of The Caribbean	$30	RCA Victor 1505
10/20/58	16	15			6 Belafonte Sings The Blues	$30	RCA Victor 1006
5/25/59	18	11			7 Love Is A Gentle Thing	$30	RCA Victor 1927
6/22/59	13	22			8 Porgy & Bess	$30	RCA Victor 1507
					LENA HORNE/HARRY BELAFONTE		
11/9/59+	3	168	●	©	9 Belafonte At Carnegie Hall [L]	$50	RCA Victor 6006 [2]
					recorded on 4/20/59		
3/21/60	34	1			10 My Lord What A Mornin'	$30	RCA Victor 2022
12/26/60+	3	39	●	©	11 Belafonte Returns To Carnegie Hall [L]	$40	RCA Victor 6007 [2]
					recorded on 5/2/60; includes "I've Been Driving On Bald Mountain/Water Boy" by **Odetta**, "The Click Song" by **Miriam Makeba** and "Ballad Of Sigmund Freud," "I Do Adore Her" and "Vaichazkem (Vayiven Uziaho)" by the **Chad Mitchell Trio**		
8/28/61	3	67	●	©	12 Jump Up Calypso	$30	RCA Victor 2388
5/12/62	8	24			13 The Midnight Special	$40	RCA Victor 2449
					Bob Dylan (harmonica on title track - his first appearance on record)		
10/20/62	25	22			14 The Many Moods Of Belafonte	$20	RCA Victor 2574
12/22/62	125	2		©	15 To Wish You A Merry Christmas [X]	$20	RCA Victor 2626
					first released in 1958 on RCA 1887; Christmas charts: 34/'64, 58/'66, 47/'67		
6/22/63	30	26			16 Streets I Have Walked	$20	RCA Victor 2695
4/18/64	17	20			17 Belafonte At The Greek Theatre [L]	$30	RCA Victor 6009 [2]
					recorded on 8/23/63		
10/17/64	103	7			18 Ballads, Blues And Boasters	$20	RCA Victor 2953
7/10/65	85	11			19 An Evening With Belafonte/Makeba	$20	RCA Victor 3420
					HARRY BELAFONTE/MIRIAM MAKEBA		
4/9/66	124	8			20 An Evening With Belafonte/Mouskouri	$20	RCA Victor 3415
					HARRY BELAFONTE/NANA MOUSKOURI		
7/16/66	82	10			21 In My Quiet Room	$20	RCA Victor 3571
4/29/67	172	2			22 Calypso In Brass	$20	RCA Victor 3658
7/29/67	199	3			23 Belafonte On Campus	$20	RCA Victor 3779
1/10/70	192	3			24 Homeward Bound	$20	RCA Victor 4255

All My Trials (7,9)
Amen (16)
Ananias (18)
Angelina (12)
Angelique-O (5)
Baby Boy (12)
Back Of The Bus (18)
Bally Mena (12)
Bamotsweri (14)
Banana Boat (Day-O) (3,9) *5*
Be My Woman, Gal (medley) (17)
Bella Rosa (7)
Bess, Oh Where's My Bess (8)
Bess, You Is My Woman (8)
Betty An' Dupree (14)
Big Boat Up The River (18)
Black Betty (18)
Blue Willow Moan (18)
Boot Dance (17)
Borning Day (16)
Boy (18)
Brown Skin Girl (3)
Buked And Scorned (10)
Chickens (11)
Christmas Is Coming (15)
Cocoanut Woman (5,22) *25*
Come Away Melinda (16)
Come Back Liza (3,9)
Come O My Love (4)
Contemporary Dance (17)
Cordelia Brown (5)
Cotton Fields (6,9)
Crawdad Song (13)
Cruel War (7)
Cu Cu Ru Cu Cu Paloma (4,9)
Danny Boy (4,9)
Dark As A Dungeon (14)
Darlin' Cora (9)
Day-O ..see: Banana Boat
Deck The Halls (medley) (15)
Delia (1,23)
Delia's Gone (7)

Did You Hear About Jerry (13)
Didn't It Rain *[Belafonte Folk Singers]* (11)
Dog Named (Your Dog) (23)
Dolly Dawn (5)
Dolphin, The (24)
Don't Ever Love Me (5) *90*
Don't Talk Now (24)
Drummer And The Cook (1,4)
Eden Was Like This (4)
Erev Shel Shoshanim (Night Of Roses) (16)
Ezekiel (10)
Far Side Of The Hill (23)
Fare Thee Well (6)
Fifteen (7)
First Noël (medley) (15)
First Time Ever I Saw Your Face (23)
Fool For You (6)
Four Strong Winds (18)
Fox, The (1)
Gifts They Gave (15)
Girls In Their Summer Dresses (21)
Give Us Our Land (19)
Gloria (12)
Glory Manger (17)
Go Down Emanuel Road (12)
Go 'Way From My Window (7)
God Bless' The Child (6)
God Rest Ye Merry, Gentlemen (medley) (15)
Goin' Down Jordan (2)
Gone Are My Children (19)
Gotta Travel On (13)
Green Grow The Lilacs (7)
Haiti Cherie (5)
Hallelujah I Love Her So (6)
Hands I Love (23)
Hava Nageela (16)
Hayoshevet Baganim (17)
Hene Ma Tov (11)
Hoedown Blues (17)

Hold On To Me Babe (23)
Hole In The Bucket (11)
Homeward Bound (24)
Honey Wind Blows (21)
Hosanna (3)
Hush, Hush (19)
I Do Adore Her (3,12)
I Heard The Bells On Christmas Day (15)
I Know Where I'm Going (11)
I Never Will Marry (7)
I Wants To Stay Here (8)
I'm Goin' Away (7)
I'm Just A Country Boy (21)
I'm On My Way To Saturday (14)
If I Were A Carpenter (24)
If You Are Thirsty (20)
In My Father's House (17)
In That Great Gettin' Up Mornin' (2)
In The Evenin' Mama (6)
In The Small Boat (20)
Irene (20)
It Ain't Necessarily So (8)
Jack-Ass Song (3)
Jamaica Farewell (3,9) *14*
Jehovah The Lord Will Provide (15)
John Henry (1,9)
John The Revelator (18)
Joy To The World (medley) (15)
Joys Of Christmas (medley) (15)
Judy Drownded (5,22)
Jump And Bray Medley (22)
Jump Down, Spin Around (2,11)
Jump In The Line (12,22)
Kalenda Rock (1)
Kingston Market (12)
La Bamba (11)
Land Of The Sea And Sun (12)
Last Thing On My Mind (23)

Last Time I Saw Her (24)
Lead Man Holler (5)
Little Bird (24)
Little Lyric Of Great Importance (11)
'Long About Now (14,21)
Look Over Yonder (medley) (17)
Lord Randall (1)
Losing Hand (6)
Love, Love Alone (5)
Lucy's Door (5)
Lullaby (19)
Lyla, Lyla (13)
Makes A Long Time Man Feel Bad (13)
Mama Look At Bubu (9,22) *11*
Man Piaba (1,9)
Man Smart (Woman Smarter) (3,9,22)
Mangwene Mpulele (16)
March Down To Jordan (10)
Marching Saints ..see: When The Saints Go Marching In
Mark Twain (1)
Mary Ann (6)
Mary, Mary (15)
Mary's Boy Child (4,15) *12*
Matilda (2,9)
Memphis Tennessee (13)
Merci Bon Dieu (4,9)
Merry Minuet (17)
Michael Row The Boat Ashore (13)
Midnight Special (13)
Mo Mary (1)
Monkey (12)
Muleskinner (13)
My Angel (19)
My Lord What A Mornin' (10)
My Love Is A Dewdrop (18)
My Man's Gone Now (8)
My Moon (20)
My Old Paint (16)

Naughty Little Flea (22)
Next Big River (1)
Noah (2)
O Come, All Ye Faithful (medley) (15)
O Little Town Of Bethlehem (medley) (15)
Oh Freedom (10)
Oh, I Got Plenty Of Nothin' (8)
Oh Let Me Fly (10)
Old King Cole (1)
On Top Of Old Smokey (13)
Once Was (4)
One For My Baby (6)
One More Dance (11)
Our Time For Loving (21)
Ox Drivers *[Belafonte Folk Singers]* (11)
Pastures Of Plenty (18)
Pig (17)
Portrait Of A Sunday Afternoon (21)
Quiet Room (21)
Raindrops (21)
Red Rosy Bush *[Belafonte Folk Singers]* (11)
Reincarnation (22)
Roll On, Buddy (13)
Sad Heart (24)
Sail Away Ladies (23)
Sailor Man (16)
Sakura (16)
Scarlet Ribbons (For Her Hair) (2)
Scratch, Scratch (5)
Shake That Little Foot (17)
Shenandoah (4,9)
Show Me The Way, My Brother (19)
Silent Night (15)
Sinner's Prayer (6)
Sit Down (16)
Small One (7)
Softly (24)

Soldier, Soldier (1)
Son Of Mary (15)
Star In The East (15)
Star O (3)
Stars Shinin' (By 'N By) (10)
Steal Away (10)
Street Calls Medley (8)
Summertime (8)
Summertime Love (14,21)
Suzanne (24)
Suzanne (Every Night When The Sun Goes Down) (2,11)
Sweetheart From Venezuela (12,22)
Swing Low (10)
Sylvie (2,9)
Take My Mother Home (2,9)
There's A Boat That's Leavin' Soon For New York (8)
These Are The Times (12)
This Land Is Your Land (16)
This Wicked Race (16)
Those Three Are On My Mind (23)
Times Are Gettin' Hard (7)
Tol' My Captain (1)
Tomorrow Is A Long Time (24)
Tone The Bell Easy (18)
Tongue Tie Baby (14,22)
Train Song (16)
Troubles (2)
Try To Remember (14,17,21)
Tunga (16)
Turn Around (7)
Twelve Days Of Christmas (15)
Unchained Melody (2)
Wake Up Jacob (10)
Walkin' On The Green Grass (7)
Walking On The Moon (20)
Waltzing Matilda (16)
Waly, Waly (23)
Waterboy (2)
Way That I Feel (6)

61

BELAFONTE, Harry — Cont'd

We Wish You A Merry Christmas (medley) (15)
Were You There When They Cruolfied My Lord (10)
When The Saints Go Marching In (4,9)
Where The Little Jesus Sleeps (15)
Who's Gonna Be Your Man (14)
Why 'N' Why (17)
Wide Sea (20)
Will His Love Be Like His Rum (3)
Windin' Road (17)
Woman Is A Sometime Thing (8)
Zombie Jamboree (14,17,22)

BELEW, Adrian '82

Born Robert Steven Belew on 12/23/49 in Covington, Kentucky. Prolific rock guitarist. Member of **King Crimson** from 1981-84 and **The Bears** from 1985-88.

7/24/82	82	9		1 **Lone Rhino**	$10 Island 9751
10/1/83	146	7		2 **Twang Bar King**	$10 Island 90108
7/22/89	114	11	©	3 **Mr. Music Head**	$10 Atlantic 81959
6/2/90	118	11	©	4 **Young Lions**	$10 Atlantic 82099

Adidas In Heat (1)
Animal Grace (1)
Another Time (2)
Bad Days (3)
Ballet For A Blue Whale (2)
Big Electric Cat (1)
Bird In A Box (3)
Bumpity Bump (3)
Coconuts (3)
Final Rhino (1)
Fish Head (2)
Gunman (4)
Heartbeat (4)
Hot Sun (1)
Hot Zoo (3)
House Of Cards (3)
I Am What I Am (4)
I Wonder (2)
I'm Down (2)
Ideal Woman (2)
Life Without A Cage (2)
Lone Rhinoceros (1)
Looking For A U.F.O. (3)
Man In The Moon (1)
Men In Helicopters (4)
Momur, The (1)
Motor Bungalow (3)
Naive Guitar (1)
1967 (3)
Not Alone Anymore (4)
Oh Daddy (3) *58*
One Of Those Days (3)
Paint The Road (2)
Peaceable Kingdom (3)
Phone Call From The Moon (4)
Pretty Pink Rose (4)
Rail Song (3)
Sexy Rhino (2)
She Is Not Dead (2)
Small World (4)
Stop It (1)
Swingline (1)
Twang Bar King (2)
Young Lions (4)

BELL, Archie, & The Drells '76

Born on 9/1/44 in Henderson, Texas. R&B singer. The Drells consisted of James Wise, Lee Bell and Willie Parnell.

5/25/68	142	8	1 **Tighten Up**	$50 Atlantic 8181
8/16/69	163	3	2 **There's Gonna Be A Showdown**	$30 Atlantic 8226
1/10/76	95	20	3 **Dance Your Troubles Away**	$15 TSOP 33844

Dance Your Troubles Away (3)
Do The Hand Jive (2)
Girl You're Too Young (2) *59*
Give Me Time (1)
Giving Up Dancing (2)
Go For What You Know (2)
Green Power (2)
Here I Go Again (2)
Houston Texas (2)
I Could Dance All Night (3)
I Don't Wanna Be A Playboy (1)
I Love My Baby (2) *94*
I Love You (But You Don't Even Know It) (3)
I Won't Leave You Honey, Never (3)
In The Midnight Hour (1)
Just A Little Closer (2)
Knock On Wood (1)
Let's Go Disco (3)
Let's Groove (3)
Mama Didn't Teach Me That Way (2)
My Balloon's Going Up (2) *87*
Soldier's Prayer, 1967 (1)
Soul City Walk (3)
There's Gonna Be A Showdown (2) *21*
Thousand Wonders (1)
Tighten Up (1) *1*
Tighten Up (Part 2) (1)
When You Left Heartache Began (1)
You're Mine (1)

BELL, Maggie '74

Born on 1/12/45 in Glasgow, Scotland. Lead singer of Stone The Crows.

4/20/74	122	13	1 **Queen Of The Night**	$12 Atlantic 7293
4/5/75	130	8	2 **Suicide Sal**	$12 Swan Song 8412

After Midnight (1) *97*
As The Years Go Passing By (1)
Caddo Queen (1)
Comin' On Strong (2)
Hold On (2)
I Saw Him Standing There (2)
I Was In Chains (2)
If You Don't Know (2)
In My Life (2)
It's Been So Long (2)
Oh My My (1)
Other Side (1)
Queen Of The Night (1)
Souvenirs (1)
Suicide Sal (2)
Trade Winds (1)
We Had It All (1)
What You Got (2)
Wishing Well (2)
Woman Left Lonely (1)
Yesterday's Music (1)

BELL, Vincent '70

Born Vincent Gambella on 7/28/35 in Brooklyn, New York. Prolific studio guitarist.

6/20/70	75	8	**Airport Love Theme**	[I] $15 Decca 75212

Airport Love Theme (Gwen And Vern) *31*
Damned, Theme From The
Darling Lili
Everybody's Talkin'
Farewell, Farewell
Loss Of Love
Marilyn's Theme
Nikki
Romeo & Juliet, Love Theme From ..see: Time For Us
Shadow Of Your Smile
Time For Us

BELL, William '77

Born William Yarborough on 7/16/39 in Memphis. R&B singer.

4/2/77	63	12	© **Coming Back For More**	$12 Mercury 1146

Coming Back For More
I Absotivly, Posolutely Love You
I Wake Up Cryin'
If Sex Was All We Had
Just Another Way To Feel
Malnutrition
Relax
Tryin' To Love Two *10*
You Don't Miss Your Water
You've Really Got A Hold On Me

BELLAMY BROTHERS '76

Country duo from Darby, Florida: brothers Howard (born on 2/2/46) and David (born on 9/16/50) Bellamy.

5/15/76	69	12	● **Bellamy Brothers**	$12 Warner/Curb 2941

Hell Cat *70*
Highway 2-18 (Hang On To Your Dreams)
I'm The Only Sane Man Left Alive
Inside Of My Guitar
Let Fantasy Live
Let Your Love Flow *1*
Livin' In The West
Nothin' Heavy
Rainy, Windy, Sunshine (Roadeo Road)
Satin Sheets *73*

BELL & JAMES '79

R&B duo of Leroy Bell and Casey James. Began as songwriting team for Bell's uncle, producer Thom Bell.

2/3/79	31	19	1 **Bell & James**	$12 A&M 4728
11/3/79	125	4	2 **Only Make Believe**	$12 A&M 4784

Ask Billie (They Tell Me) (1)
(Babe) You Don't Love Me Like You Should (2)
Don't Let The Man Get You (1)
Fare Thee Well (1)
I Love The Music (1)
I Need You (Beside Me) (1)
Just Can't Get Enough (Of Your Love) (1)
Laughing In The Face Of Love (2)
Only Make Believe (2)
Livin' It Up (Friday Night) (1) *15*
Nobody Knows It (2)
Say It's Gonna Last Forever (2)
Shakedown (2)
Stay (2)
Three Way Love Affair (1)
You Never Know What You've Got (1)

BELL BIV DeVOE '90

R&B trio of **New Edition** members: Ricky Bell, Michael Bivins and Ronnie DeVoe.

4/7/90	5	77	▲4 ©	1 **Poison**	$10 MCA 6387
9/14/91	18	27	● ©	2 **WBBD - Bootcity! The Remix Album** ..... [K]	$10 MCA 10345
7/10/93	19	18	●	3 **Hootie Mack**	$10 MCA 10682

Above The Rim (3)
Ain't Nut'in' Changed! (1,2)
B.B.D. (I Thought It Was Me)? (1,2) *26*
Do Me! (1,2) *3*
Dope! (3)
From The Back (3)
Ghetto Booty (3)
Hootie Mack (3)
I Do Need You (1,2)
Let Me Know Something?! (1,2)
Lost In The Moment (3)
Lovely (3)
Nickel (3)
Please Come Back (3)
Poison (1,2) *3*
Ronnie, Bobby, Ricky, Mike, Ralph And Johnny (Word To The Mutha)! (1,2)
She's Dope! (2)
Show Me The Way (3)
Situation, The (3)
Something In Your Eyes (3) *38*
When Will I See You Smile Again? (1,2) *63*

BELLE, Regina '89
Born on 7/15/63 in Englewood, New Jersey. R&B singer.

DEBUT	PEAK	WKS		CD	Title			$	Label & Number
7/11/87	85	15		© 1	All By Myself			$10	Columbia 40537
9/16/89	63	44	●	© 2	Stay With Me			$10	Columbia 44367
3/6/93	63	23	●	© 3	Passion			$10	Columbia 48826
9/23/95	115	9		© 4	Reachin' Back			$10	Columbia 66813

After The Love Has Lost Its Shine (1) · Baby Come To Me (2) 60 · Could It Be I'm Falling In Love (4) · Deeper I Love (3) · Didn't I (Blow Your Mind This Time) (4) · Do You Wanna Get Serious (3) · Dream In Color (3) · Dream Lover (2) · Good Lovin' (2) · Gotta Give It Up (1) · Heaven's Just A Whisper Away (3) · How Could You Do It To Me (3) · Hurry Up This Way Again (4) · I'll Be Around (3) · If I Could (3) 52 · Intimate Relations (1) · It Doesn't Hurt Anymore (2) · (It's Gonna Take) All Our Love (2) · Just Don't Want To Be Lonely (4) · Let Me Make Love To You (4) · Love (3) · Love T.K.O. (4) · Make It Like It Was (2) 43 · My Man (3) · One Love (3) · Passion (3) · Please Be Mine (3) · Quiet Time (3) · Save The Children (medley) (2) · Show Me The Way (1) 68 · So Many Tears (1) · Someday We'll Be All Free (medley) (2) · Take Your Love Away (1) · Tango In Paris (3) · This Is Love (2) · What Goes Around (2) · When Will You Be Mine (2) · Whole New World (Aladdin's Theme) (3) 1 · Whole Town's Laughing At Me (4) · You Are Everything (4) · You Got The Love (1) · You Make Me Feel Brand New (4)

BELLE AND SEBASTIAN '00
Rock group from Scotland: Stuart Murdoch and Isobel Campbell (vocals), Stevie Jackson (guitar), Chris Geddes (keyboards), Stuart David (bass) and Richard Colburn (drums).

DEBUT	PEAK	WKS		CD	Title			$	Label & Number
7/31/99	39 C	1		© 1	Tigermilk			$10	Jeepster 361
6/24/00	80	3		© 2	Fold Your Hands Child, You Walk Like A Peasant			$10	Jeepster 429

Beyond The Sunrise (2) · Chalet Lines (2) · Don't Leave The Light On Baby (2) · Electronic Renaissance (1) · Expectations (1) · Family Tree (2) · I Could Be Dreaming (1) · I Don't Love Anyone (1) · I Fought In A War (2) · Mary Jo (1) · Model, The (2) · My Wandering Days Are Over (1) · Nice Day For A Sulk (2) · She's Losing It (1) · State I Am In (1) · There's Too Much Love (2) · Waiting For The Moon To Rise (2) · We Rule The School (1) · Women's Realm (2) · Wrong Girl (1) · You're Just A Baby (1)

BELLE STARS, The '83
Female group from England: Jennie McKeown (vocals), Sarah-Jane Owen and Stella Barker (guitars), Miranda Joyce and Clare Hirst (saxaphones), Lesley Shone (bass) and Judy Parsons (drums).

DEBUT	PEAK	WKS			Title			$	Label & Number
5/28/83	191	2			The Belle Stars			$10	Warner 23866

Baby I'm Yours · Burning · Ci Ya Ya · Clapping Song · Harlem Shuffle · Iko Iko · *new version charted at #14 on "Hot 100" in 1989* · Indian Summer · Mockingbird · Needle In A Haystack · Reason, The · Sign Of The Times 75 · Snake, The

BELLS, The '71
Pop group from Canada: Jacki Ralph and Cliff Edwards (vocals), Charles Clarke (guitar), Dennis Will (keyboards), Michael Waye (bass) and Douglas Gravelle (drums).

DEBUT	PEAK	WKS			Title			$	Label & Number
5/1/71	90	14			Fly, Little White Dove, Fly			$15	Polydor 4510

Fly Little White Dove Fly 95 · I Can Make It With You · I'm Gonna Get Out · Maxwell's Silver Hammer · Moody Manitoba Morning · Proud Mary · Rain · Sing A Song Of Freedom · Stay Awhile 7 · Yesterday Will Never Come Again

BELLY '93
Pop-rock group from Newport, Rhode Island: Tanya Donelly (vocals, guitar) with brothers Thomas (guitar) and Chris (drums) Gorman. Gail Greenwood (bass) joined by mid-1993. Donelly was a member of Throwing Muses and **The Breeders**.

DEBUT	PEAK	WKS		CD	Title			$	Label & Number
2/20/93	59	28	●	© 1	Star			$10	Sire 45187
3/4/95	57	6		© 2	King			$10	Sire 45833

Angel (1) · Bees, The (2) · Dusted (1) · Every Word (1) · Feed The Tree (1) 95 · Full Moon, Empty Heart (1) · Gepetto (1) · Judas My Heart (2) · King (2) · L'il Ennio (2) · Low Red Moon (1) · Now They'll Sleep (2) · Puberty (2) · Red (2) · Sad Dress (1) · Seal My Fate (2) · Silverfish (2) · Slow Dog (1) · Someone To Die For (1) · Star (1) · Stay (1) · Super-Connected (2) · Untitled And Unsung (1) · Untogether (1) · White Belly (1) · Witch (1)

BELMONTS, The '62
Vocal trio from the Bronx, New York: Angelo D'Aleo, Fred Milano and Carlo Mastrangelo. Sang with **Dion** from 1957-60. Frank Lyndon replaced Mastrangelo in May 1962.

DEBUT	PEAK	WKS			Title			$	Label & Number
10/27/62	113	7			The Belmonts' Carnival Of Hits		[G]	$150	Sabina 5001

Come On Little Angel 28 · Don't Get Around Much Anymore 57 · Have You Heard · Hombre · How About Me · I Confess · I Don't Know How To Cry · I Need Some One 75 · Searching For A New Love · Tell Me Why 18 · That American Dance · This Love Of Mine

BELOVED, The '90
Pop-rock duo from England: Jon Marsh (vocals, keyboards) and Steve Waddington (guitars).

DEBUT	PEAK	WKS		CD	Title			$	Label & Number
4/14/90	154	9		©	Happiness			$10	Atlantic 82047

Don't You Worry · Found · Hello · I Love You More · Scarlet Beautiful · Sun Rising · Time After Time · Up, Up And Away · Wake Up Soon · Your Love Takes Me Higher

BELTRAN, Graciela — see SELENA

BENATAR, Pat ★215★ '81
Born Patricia Andrzejewski on 1/10/53 in Lindenhurst, Long Island, New York. Rock singer. Married her producer/guitarist Neil Giraldo on 2/20/82. Acted in the movie *Union City*.

1)Precious Time 2)Crimes Of Passion 3)Get Nervous

DEBUT	PEAK	WKS	RIAA	CD	Title			$	Label & Number
10/20/79+	12	122	▲	© 1	In The Heat Of The Night			$10	Chrysalis 1236
8/23/80+	2⁵	93	▲⁴	© 2	Crimes Of Passion			$10	Chrysalis 1275
7/25/81	❶¹	54	▲²	© 3	Precious Time			$10	Chrysalis 1346
11/20/82+	4	46	▲	© 4	Get Nervous			$10	Chrysalis 1396
10/15/83	13	34	▲	© 5	Live From Earth		[L]	$10	Chrysalis 41444
11/24/84	14	22	▲	© 6	Tropico			$10	Chrysalis 41471
12/14/85	26	20	●	© 7	Seven The Hard Way			$10	Chrysalis 41507
7/23/88	28	29	●	© 8	Wide Awake In Dreamland			$10	Chrysalis 41628
11/25/89	67	20	▲	© 9	Best Shots		[G]	$10	Chrysalis 21715
4/27/91	37	22		© 10	True Love			$10	Chrysalis 21805
6/19/93	85	9		© 11	Gravity's Rainbow			$10	Chrysalis 21982
6/21/97	171	1		© 12	Innamorata			$10	CMC Int'l. 86216

All Fired Up (8,9) 19 · Angry (12) · Anxiety (Get Nervous) (4) · Art Of Letting Go (7) · At This Time (12) · Big Life (7) · Bloodshot Eyes (10) · Cerebral Man (8) · Cool Zero (8) · Crazy (11) · Crazy World Like This (6) · Diamond Field (6)

BENATAR, Pat — Cont'd

Dirty Little Secrets (12)
Disconnected (11)
Don't Happen No More (10)
Don't Let It Show (1)
Don't Walk Away (8)
Evening (10)
Every Time I Fall Back (11)
Everybody Lay Down (11)
Evil Genius (3)
Fight It Out (4)
Fire And Ice (3,5,9) *17*
Gina's Song (12)
Good Life (10)
Hard To Believe (3)
Heartbreaker (1,5,9) *23*
Hell Is For Children (2,5,9)
Helter Skelter (3)

Hit Me With Your Best Shot (2,5,9) *9*
I Don't Want To Be Your Friend (12)
I Feel Lucky (10)
I Get Evil (10)
I Need A Lover (1)
I Want Out (4,5)
I'll Do It (4)
I'm Gonna Follow You (2)
I've Got Papers On You (10)
If You Think You Know How To Love Me (1)
In The Heat Of The Night (1)
In These Times (12)
Innamorata (12)
Invincible (7,9) *10*

It's A Tuff Life (3)
Just Like Me (3)
Kingdom Key (11)
Le Bel Age (7) *54*
Let's Stay Together (8)
Lift 'Em On Up (8)
Lipstick Lies (5)
Little Paradise (2)
Little Too Late (4) *20*
Looking For A Stranger (4,5) *39*
Love In The Ice Age (6)
Love Is A Battlefield (5,9) *5*
My Clone Sleeps Alone (1)
Never Wanna Leave You (2)
No You Don't (1)
One Love (8,9)

Only You (12)
Ooh Ooh Song (6) *36*
Out-A-Touch (2)
Outlaw Blues (6)
Painted Desert (6)
Papa's Roses (12)
Payin' The Cost To Be The Boss (11)
Please Come Home For Christmas (10)
Precious Time (3)
Prisoner Of Love (2)
Promises In The Dark (3,5,9) *38*
Purgatory (12)
Rated X (1)
Red Vision (7)

Rise (Part 2) (11)
River Of Love (12)
Run Between The Raindrops (7)
Sanctuary (11)
7 Rooms Of Gloom (7)
Sex As A Weapon (7) *28*
Shadows Of The Night (4,9) *13*
Silent Partner (4)
So Long (10)
So Sincere (1)
Somebody's Baby (11)
Strawberry Wine (12)
Suburban King (10)
Suffer The Little Children (8)
Take It Anyway You Want It (3)

Takin' It Back (6)
Tell It To Her (4)
Temporary Heroes (6)
Ties That Bind (1)
Too Long A Soldier (8)
Tradin' Down (11)
Treat Me Right (2) *18*
True Love (10)
Victim, The (4)
Walking In The Underground (7)
We Belong (6,9) *5*
We Live For Love (1,5,9) *27*
Wide Awake In Dreamland (8)
Wuthering Heights (2)
You & I (11)
You Better Run (2) *42*

BENEDICTINE MONKS OF SANTO DOMINGO DE SILOS '94

Group of 36 monks who live in an eighth-century monastery in north-central Spain. They sing 1,000-year-old Gregorian chants in Latin.

DEBUT	PEAK	WKS		CD	ARTIST — Album Title	Catalog	Sym	$	Label & Number
4/2/94	3	53	▲²	© 1	**Chant**		[F]	$10	Angel 55138
11/26/94	78	7		© 2	**Chant Noel**		[X-F]	$10	Angel 55206
					Christmas chart: 9/'94				
12/23/95+	172	3		© 3	**Chant II**		[E-F-L]	$10	Angel 55504
					recorded on 11/21/72 at Teatro Real in Madrid, Spain				

Agnus Dei, Qui Tollis Peccata Mundi (3)
Alleluia, Beatus Vir Qui Suffert (1)
Alleluia. Domine In Virtute Tua (2)
Alleluia. Oportebat (2)
Alleluia. Veni Sancte Spiritus (3)
Alleluia. Vir Dei Benedictus (3)
Ave Mundi Spes Maria (1,3)

Christus Factus Est Pro Nobis (1)
Cibavit Eos Ex Adipe Frumenti (3)
Da Pacem, Domine (3)
De Ore Leonis (2)
Genuit Puerpera Regem (1)
Gloria In Excelsis Deo (2,3)
Gloria, Laus Et Honor (2)
Haec Dies Quam Fecit Dominus (3)
Hodie Christus Natus Est (2)

Hodie Nobis Caelorum Rex (2)
Hodie Nobis De Caelo (2)
Hosanna Filio David (1)
Improperium (1)
In Principio (2)
Jacta Cogitatum Tuum (1)
Jucundare Filia Sion (2)
Kyrie XI, A (1)
Kyrie Fons Bonitatis (1,3)
Kyrie "Lux Et Origo" (3)
Laetatus Sum (1)
Mandatum Novum Do Vobis (1)

Media Vita In Morte Sumus (1,3)
Occuli Omnium (1)
Oculi Omnium In Te Sperant (3)
Os Iusti (2)
Os Justi Meditabitur Sapientiam (3)
Puer Natus Est Nobis (1)
Puer Natus In Bethlehem (1)
Pueri Hebraeorum (1)
Quam Magnificata Sunt Opera Tua Domine (3)

Qui Manducat (2)
Respice, Domine (2)
Rorate Caeli Desuper (2)
Salve, Regina, Mater Misericordiae (2)
Sanctus Dominus Deus Sabaoth (3)
Spiritus Domini (1)
Spiritus Domini Replevit Orbem Terrarum (2)
Super Flumina Babylonis (2)
Tui Sunt Caeli (2)

Ubi Caritas (2)
Ut Queant Laxis Resonare Fibris (3)
Veni Sancte Spiritus (1)
Verbum Caro Factum Est (1,2)
Victimae Paschali Laudes (3)
Viderunt Omnes (2)
Zelus Domus Tuae (2)

BENÉT, Eric   '99

Born Eric Benét Jordan on 10/5/69 in Milwaukee. R&B singer/songwriter. Married actress Halle Berry on 1/19/2001.

DEBUT	PEAK	WKS		CD	ARTIST — Album Title	Catalog	Sym	$	Label & Number
4/26/97	174	5		© 1	**True To Myself**			$10	Warner 46270
5/15/99	25	49	●	© 2	**A Day In The Life**			$10	Warner 47072

All In The Game (1)
Chains (1)
Come As You Are (2)
Dust In The Wind (2)
Femininity (1)

Georgy Porgy (2) *55*
Ghetto Girl (1)
I'll Be There (1)
If You Want Me To Stay (1)
Just Friends (1)

Lamentation (2)
Let's Stay Together (2)
Love Of My Own (1)
Love The Hurt Away (2)
Loving Your Best Friend (2)

More Than Just A Girlfriend (1)
Something Real (2)
Spend My Life With You (2) *21*
Spiritual Thang (1)

That's Just My Way (2)
True To Myself (1)
What If We Was Cool (1)
When You Think Of Me (2)
While You Were Here (1)

Why You Follow Me (2)

BENITEZ, Jellybean — see JELLYBEAN

BENNETT, Tony ★93★   '62

Born Anthony Benedetto on 8/3/26 in Queens, New York. Legendary pop/jazz-styled singer. Appeared in the movie *The Oscar*. Breakthrough with **Bob Hope** in 1949 who suggested that he change his then-stage name, Joe Bari, to Tony Bennett.

1)*I Left My Heart In San Francisco* 2)*I Wanna Be Around* 3)*Tony* 4)*The Movie Song Album* 5)*The Many Moods Of Tony*

DEBUT	PEAK	WKS		CD	ARTIST — Album Title	Catalog	Sym	$	Label & Number
2/23/57	14	9		1	**Tony**			$30	Columbia 938
7/7/62	5	149	●	© 2	**I Left My Heart In San Francisco**			$20	Columbia 1869 / 8669
10/13/62	37	19		© 3	**Tony Bennett At Carnegie Hall**		[L]	$25	Columbia 23 [2]
					recorded on 6/9/62				
4/6/63+	5	44		© 4	**I Wanna Be Around**			$20	Columbia 2000 / 8800
8/24/63	24	30		5	**This Is All I Ask**			$20	Columbia 2056 / 8856
2/22/64	20	24		6	**The Many Moods Of Tony**			$20	Columbia 2141 / 8941
5/23/64	79	12		7	**When Lights Are Low**			$20	Columbia 2175 / 8975
12/19/64+	42	19		© 8	**Who Can I Turn To**			$20	Columbia 2285 / 9085
5/22/65	47	22		© 9	**If I Ruled The World - Songs For The Jet Set**			$20	Columbia 2343 / 9143
8/21/65	20	42	●	10	**Tony's Greatest Hits, Volume III**		[G]	$20	Columbia 2373 / 9173
3/12/66	18	29		© 11	**The Movie Song Album**			$20	Columbia 2472 / 9272
10/8/66+	68	18		12	**A Time For Love**			$20	Columbia 2560 / 9360
5/13/67	178	6		13	**Tony Makes It Happen!**			$20	Columbia 2653 / 9453
1/13/68	164	7		14	**For Once In My Life**			$20	Columbia 9573
12/14/68	10ˣ	14		© 15	**Snowfall/The Tony Bennett Christmas Album**	C:#17/13	[X]	$20	Columbia 9739
					Christmas charts: 10/'68, 22/'94, 31/'95				
5/10/69	174	8		16	**Tony Bennett's Greatest Hits, Volume IV**		[G]	$20	Columbia 9814
9/6/69	137	5		17	**I've Gotta Be Me**			$20	Columbia 9882
2/28/70	144	11		18	**Tony Sings The Great Hits Of Today!**			$20	Columbia 9980
11/14/70	193	2		© 19	**Tony Bennett's "Something"**			$15	Columbia 30280
3/6/71	67	13		20	**Love Story**			$15	Columbia 30558
11/20/71	195	2		21	**Get Happy with the London Philharmonic Orchestra**		[L]	$15	Columbia 30953
					recorded on 1/31/71				
2/19/72	182	4		22	**Summer Of '42**			$15	Columbia 31219

BENNETT, Tony — Cont'd

DEBUT	PEAK	WKS	RIAA	CD	ARTIST — Album Title	$	Label & Number
7/1/72	167	14			23 **With Love**	$15	Columbia 31460
10/21/72	175	7	●	©	24 **Tony Bennett's All-Time Greatest Hits** .... [G]	$20	Columbia 31494 [2]
12/9/72	196	6			25 **The Good Things In Life**	$15	MGM/Verve 5088
6/21/86	160	8		©	26 **The Art Of Excellence**	$10	Columbia 40344
10/3/92	102	26	●	©	27 **Perfectly Frank**	$10	Columbia 52965
					tribute to Frank Sinatra		
10/23/93+	128	16	●	©	28 **Steppin' Out**	$10	Columbia 57424
7/16/94+	48	27	▲	©	29 **MTV Unplugged** .... [L]	$10	Columbia 66214
					recorded on 4/12/94; 1994 Grammy winner: Album of the Year		
11/11/95	96	9		©	30 **Here's To The Ladies**	$10	Columbia 67349
2/22/97	101	5		©	31 **On Holiday - A Tribute To Billie Holiday**	$10	Columbia 67774
10/16/99	161	3		©	32 **Bennett Sings Ellington Hot & Cool**	$10	RPM/Columbia 63668

Ain't Misbehavin' (7)
Alfie (17)
All My Tomorrows (9)
All Of Me (31)
All Of You (28,29)
All The Things You Are (3)
Always (1,3)
Angel Eyes (27)
Anything Goes (3)
April In Paris (3)
Autumn In Rome (5)
Autumn Leaves (8,29)
Azure (32)
Baby Don't You Quit Now (17)
Baby, Dream Your Dream (14)
Beautiful Friendship (13)
Because Of You (3,24)
Best Is Yet To Come (2,10)
Best Thing To Be Is A Person (8)
Between The Devil And The Deep Blue Sea (8)
Blue Velvet (3)
Blues For Breakfast (25)
Body And Soul (29)
Boulevard Of Broken Dreams (1,24)
Brightest Smile In Town (8)
Broadway (medley) (14)
By Myself (28)
Call Me Irresponsible (27)
Can't Get Out Of This Mood (13)
Candy Kisses (2)
Caravan (6,32)
Change Partners (medley) (28)
Cheek To Cheek (medley) (28)
Chelsea Bridge (32)
Christmas Song (Chestnuts Roasting On An Open Fire) (15)
Christmasland (15)
City Of The Angels (26)
Climb Ev'ry Mountain (3) *74*
Cloudy Morning (30)
Coco (19)
Coffee Break (22)
Come Saturday Morning (19)
Country Girl (13,20,21)
Crazy Rhythm (medley) (14)
Crazy She Calls Me (31)
Cute (25)
Dancing In The Dark (28)
Day Dream (32)
Day In, Day Out (27)
Day You Leave Me (26)
Daybreak (30)
Days Of Love (14)
Days Of Wine And Roses (11)
De Glory Road (3)
Do Nothin' Till You Hear From Me (32)
Don't Get Around Much Anymore (13,32)
Don't Wait Too Long (6) *54*
Don't Worry 'Bout Me (27)
Down In The Depths (30)
Dream (23)
East Of The Sun (West Of The Moon) (27)
Easy Come, Easy Go (23)
Eleanor Rigby (19)
Emily (11)
End Of A Love Affair (25)
Everybody Has The Blues (26)
Everybody's Talkin' (19)

Firefly (3,24) *20*
Fly Me To The Moon (In Other Words) (9,16,29) *84*
Foggy Day (27,29)
For Once In My Life (14,16,21,24) *91*
Forget The Woman (24)
Gentle Rain (11,16,20)
Georgia Rose (12,16) *89*
Get Happy (21)
Girl I Love (a/k/a The Man I Love) (29)
Girl Talk (11)
God Bless The Child (30,31)
Good Life (4,10,29) *18*
Good Morning, Heartache (31)
Good Things In Life (25)
Got Her Off My Hands (But Can't Get Her Off My Mind) (5)
Got The Gate On The Golden Gate (8)
Harlem Butterfly (23)
Have I Told You Lately? (2)
Have Yourself A Merry Little Christmas (15)
He Loves And She Loves (28)
Here (18)
Here, There And Everywhere (18)
Here's That Rainy Day (23,27)
Honeysuckle Rose (30)
How About You (3)
How Do You Keep The Music Playing? (26)
How Do You Say Auf Wiedersehen (14)
How Insensitive (9,16)
I Can't Give You Anything But Love (1)
I Concentrate On You (28)
I Do Not Know A Day I Did Not Love You (20)
I Don't Know Why (I Just Do) (13)
I Fall In Love Too Easily (27)
(I Got A Woman Crazy For Me) She's Funny That Way (13)
I Got Lost In Her Arms (24)
I Got Rhythm (30)
I Guess I'll Have To Change My Plan (28)
I Left My Heart In San Francisco (2,3,10,21,24,29) *19*
I Let A Song Go Out Of My Heart (13)
I Love A Piano (29)
I Love The Winter Weather (medley) (15)
I See Your Face Before Me (27)
I Thought About You (27)
I Walk A Little Faster (8)
I Wanna Be Around (4,10,21,24,29) *14*
I Wanna Be In Love Again (27)
I Want To Be Happy (20,21)
I Will Live My Life For You (4) *85*
I Wished On The Moon (27,31)
I'll Be Around (8)
I'll Be Seeing You (1,27)
I'll Begin Again (20,21)
I'll Only Miss Her When I Think Of Her (12)
I'm Always Chasing Rainbows (2)

I'm Glad There Is You (27)
I'm In Love Again (30)
I'm Just A Lucky So And So (1,3,32)
I'm Losing My Mind (22)
I've Got Just About Everything (7)
I've Got My Love To Keep Me Warm (medley) (15)
I've Got The World On A String (27)
I've Got Your Number (4)
I've Gotta Be Me (17)
I've Never Seen (8)
If I Could Be With You (One Hour Tonight) (31)
I Love Again (4)
If I Ruled The World (9,10,21) *34*
If You Were Mine (4)
Ill Wind (You're Blowin' Me No Good) (31)
In A Mellow Tone (32)
In A Sentimental Mood (32)
In The Wee Small Hours (12)
Indian Summer (27,29)
Individual Thing (20)
Invitation (25)
Irena (22)
Is That All There Is? (18)
It Amazes Me (3,29)
It Could Happen To You (7)
It Don't Mean A Thing If It Ain't Got That Swing (29,32)
It Had To Be You (1,7,29)
It Only Happens When I Dance With You (28)
It Was Me (4,22)
It Was You (25)
It's A Sin To Tell A Lie (7) *99*
Jingle Bells (medley) (15)
Judy (7)
Just In Time (3,24) *46*
Keep Smiling At Trouble (Trouble's A Bubble) (5,14)
Kid's A Dreamer (The Kid From Fool's Paradise) (6)
Lady Is A Tramp (27)
Lady's In Love With You (13)
Last Night When We Were Young (27)
Laughing At Life (31)
Lazy Afternoon (3)
Lazy Day (23)
Let There Be Love (21)
Let's Face The Music And Dance (4)
Limehouse Blues (6)
Listen, Little Girl (8)
Little Boy (5) *52*
Little Green Apples (18)
Live For Life (18)
London By Night (25)
Lonely Place (17)
Long About Now (5)
Long And Winding Road (19)
Look Of Love (18)
Lost In The Stars (1,3)
Love (23)
Love For Sale (2)
Love Is Here To Stay (3)
Love Look Away (3,24)
Love Scene (9)
Love Story, Love Theme From ..see: (Where Do I Begin)
Lullaby Of Broadway (3,14)

MacArthur Park (18)
Make It Easy On Yourself (19)
Marry Young (2)
(Maybe September) ..see: Oscar
Maybe This Time (23,24,30)
Me, Myself And I (Are All In Love With You) (31)
Midnight Sun (25)
Mimi (25)
Moment Of Truth (5,10)
Moments Like This (26)
Mood Indigo (32)
Moonglow (29)
Moonlight In Vermont (30)
More And More (22)
My Cherie Amour (18)
My Favorite Things (15,16)
My Funny Valentine (12)
My Heart Tells Me (3)
My Ideal (30)
My Inamorata (22)
My Love Went To London (30)
My Old Flame (31)
Nancy (27)
Never Too Late (11)
Nice Work If You Can Get It (28)
Night And Day (27)
Nightingale Sang In Berkeley Square (27)
Nobody Else But Me (7)
O Come, All Ye Faithful (medley) (15)
O Sole Mio (3)
Oh Lady Be Good (25)
Oh! You Crazy Moon (7)
Ol' Man River (3)
Old Devil Moon (13,21,29)
On A Clear Day (You Can See Forever) (19)
On Green Dolphin Street (3)
On The Other Side Of The Tracks (5)
On The Sunny Side Of The Street (13,21)
Once Upon A Summertime (4)
Once Upon A Time (2,10)
One For My Baby (And One More For The Road) (3,27) *47*
Oscar, Song From The (11)
Out Of This World (14)
Over The Sun (17)
Passing Strangers (24)
Pawnbroker, The (11)
People (16,30)
Play It Again, Sam (17)
Poor Butterfly (30)
Prelude To A Kiss (32)
Put On A Happy Face (24)
Quiet Nights Of Quiet Stars (Corcovado) (4,10)
Rags To Riches (3,24,29)
Remind Me (2)
Right To Love (9)
Riviera, The (3)
Rules Of The Road (2,7)
Samba De Orfeu (11)
Sandpiper (The Shadow Of Your Smile), Love Theme From The (11,16,24) *95*
Sandy's Smile (5)
Santa Claus Is Comin' To Town (15)
Second Time Around (11)
Sentimental Journey (30)

(Shadow Of Your Smile) ..see: Sandpiper
Shall We Dance (28)
She's Funny That Way (I Got A Woman, Crazy For Me) (31)
She's Got It Bad (And That Ain't Good) (32)
Shine On Your Shoes (28)
Shining Sea (12,22)
Silent Night, Holy Night (medley) (15)
Sing You Sinners (3,24)
Sleepy Time Gal (12)
Smile (2,11,24) *73*
Snowfall (15)
So Long, Big Time! (6)
Solitude (3,31)
Some Other Spring (31)
Someone To Light Up My Life (Se Todos Fossem Iguals A Voce) (25)
Someone To Love (4)
Something (18,19,24)
Something In Your Smile (14)
Sometimes I'm Happy (3,14)
Somewhere Along The Line (22)
Somewhere Over The Rainbow (30)
Song Of The Jet (Samba Do Aviao) (9)
Soon It's Gonna Rain (6,20)
Sophisticated Lady (32)
Speak Low (7,29)
Spring In Manhattan (6) *92*
Steppin' Out With My Baby (28,29)
Stranger In Paradise (3,24)
Street Of Dreams (23)
Summer Of '42 (The Summer Knows), Theme From (22)
Sunrise, Sunset (18)
Sweet Lorraine (9)
Take The Moment (9)
Taking A Chance On Love (1,2)
Tangerine (28)
Taste Of Honey (6,10,20) *94*
Tea For Two (20,21)
Tender Is The Night (2)
Tenderly (30)
That Night (17)
That Ole Devil Called Love (31)
That's Entertainment (28)
Then Was Then And Now Is Now (9)
There Will Never Be Another You (21)
There's A Lull In My Life (8)
These Foolish Things (Remind Me Of You) (1,31)
They All Laughed (17,28)
They Can't Take That Away From Me (14,20,28,29)
This Is All I Ask (5,10,24) *70*
Till (22)
Time After Time (27)
Time For Love (12,16,24)
Top Hat, White Tie And Tails (28)
Touch The Earth (12)
Trapped In The Web Of Love (12)
Trav'lin' Light (31)
Tricks (5)
Trolley Song (11,21)
True Blue Lou (5) *99*
Twilight World (23)

Two By Two (9)
Until I Met You (4)
Valley Of The Dolls, Theme From (17)
Very Thought Of You (12)
Walkabout (22)
Waltz For Debby (4)
Watch What Happens (9,16)
Wave (19,21)
Way That I Feel (5)
We Wish You A Merry Christmas (medley) (15)
What A Little Moonlight Can Do (31)
What A Wonderful World (19)
What Are You Afraid Of? (26)
What Good Does It Do (3)
What Makes It Happen (13)
What The World Needs Now Is Love (17,21)
When A Woman Loves A Man (31)
When I Look In Your Eyes (19)
When Joanna Loved Me (6,10,20,29) *94*
When Lights Are Low (7)
When Love Was All We Had (26)
(When We're Together Again) Think How It's Gonna Be (19)
(Where Do I Begin) Love Story (20,21,24)
Where Is Love (medley) (15)
White Christmas (15)
Who Can I Turn To (When Nobody Needs Me) (8,10,24) *33*
Who Cares? (28)
Whoever You Are, I Love You (17)
Why Do People Fall In Love (26)
Willow Weep For Me (31)
Winter Wonderland (15)
Without A Song (1)
Wrap Your Troubles In Dreams (And Dream Your Troubles Away) (8)
Yellow Days (19)
Yesterday I Heard The Rain (Esta Tarde Vi Llover) (16)
Yesterdays (17)
You Can Depend On Me (1)
You Go To My Head (27)
You Showed Me The Way (30)
You're All The World To Me (28,29)
You're Easy To Dance With (medley) (28)
You've Changed (6)
Young And Foolish (5)

BENNO, Marc '72

Born on 7/1/47 in Dallas. Rock guitarist/songwriter/singer. Formed partnership, **Asylum Choir**, with **Leon Russell** in 1968. Songwriter for **Rita Coolidge** and session work for **The Doors**.

12/4/71+	70	20	©	1	Asylum Choir II	[E]	$15	Shelter 8910

LEON RUSSELL & MARC BENNO
recorded in 1969

9/23/72	171	8		2	Ambush		$15	A&M 4364

Ballad For A Soldier (1) Hall Street Jive (2) Lady In Waiting (1) Share (2) Sweet Home Chicago (1)
Donut Man (2) Hello, Little Friend (1) Learn How To Boogie (1) Southern Woman (2) Tryin' To Stay 'Live (1)
Down On The Base (1) Here To Stay Blues (2) Poor Boy (2) Straight Brother (1) When You Wish Upon A Fag
Either Way It Happens (2) Jive Fade Jive (2) Salty Candy (1) Sunshine Feelin (2) (1)

BENOIT, David '89

Born in Hermosa Beach, California. Jazz keyboardist.

6/4/88	129	14	©	1	Every Step Of The Way	[I]	$10	GRP 1047
5/13/89	101	14	©	2	Urban Daydreams	[I]	$10	GRP 9587
11/11/89	187	3	©	3	Waiting For Spring	[I]	$10	GRP 9595
10/27/90	161	4	©	4	Inner Motion	[I]	$10	GRP 9621
3/12/94	118	7	©	5	The Benoit/Freeman Project	[I]	$10	GRP 9739

DAVID BENOIT/RUSS FREEMAN

After The Love Has Gone (5) End Of Our Season (5) Last Request (4) ReBach (1) Smartypants (5) When The Winter's Gone (Song
After The Snow Falls (3) Every Corner Of The World (4) Looking Back (2) Remembering What You Said Snow Dancing (2) For A Stranger) (2)
Along Love's Highway (4) Every Step Of The Way (1) M.W.A. (Musicians With (1) Some Other Sunset (3) Wild Kids (2)
Cabin Fever (3) Funkallero (3) Attitude) (4) Reunion (5) South East Quarter (4)
Cast Your Fate To The Wind (3) Houston (4) Mediterranean Nights (5) Safari (2) Swept Away (5)
Cat On A Windowsill (3) I Just Can't Stop Loving You (1) Mirage (5) Sailing Through The City (2) That's All I Could Say (5)
Cloud Break (2) I Remember Bill Evans (3) My Romance (3) Sao Paulo (4) Turn Out The Stars (3)
Coconut Roads (4) It's The Thought That Counts No Worries (1) Seattle Morning (2) Urban Daydreams (2)
Deep Light (4) (5) Once Running Free (1) Shibuya Station (1) Waiting For Spring (3)
El Camino Real (4) Key To You (1) Painted Desert (1) 6-String Poet (4) When She Believed In Me (5)

BENSON, George ★132★ '76

Born on 3/22/43 in Pittsburgh. R&B/jazz-styled singer/guitarist. Played guitar from age eight. Played in **Brother Jack McDuff**'s trio in 1963. House musician at CTI Records to early 1970s. Member of **Fuse One**.

1)Breezin' 2)Give Me The Night 3)Weekend In L.A. 4)Livin' Inside Your Love 5)In Flight

8/23/69	145	3		©	1	Tell It Like It Is	[I]	$20	A&M 3020
12/28/74+	78	19		©	2	Bad Benson	[I]	$12	CTI 6045
4/17/76	❶2	78	▲3	©	3	Breezin'		$12	Warner 2919
6/26/76	51	16		©	4	Good King Bad	[I]	$12	CTI 6062
7/24/76	125	8		©	5	The Other Side Of Abbey Road	[E]	$12	A&M 3028

recorded in 1969

10/30/76	100	8		©	6	Benson & Farrell	[I]	$12	CTI 6069

GEORGE BENSON & JOE FARRELL

1/29/77	122	8		©	7	George Benson In Concert-Carnegie Hall	[I-L]	$12	CTI 6072

recorded on 1/11/75

2/12/77	9	35	▲	©	8	In Flight		$12	Warner 2983
2/11/78	5	38	▲	©	9	Weekend In L.A.	[L]	$15	Warner 3139 [2]

recorded on 10/1/77 at the Roxy

3/17/79	7	26	●	©	10	Livin' Inside Your Love		$15	Warner 3277 [2]
8/9/80	3	38	▲	©	11	Give Me The Night		$10	Warner 3453
11/21/81+	14	26	●	©	12	The George Benson Collection	[G]	$15	Warner 3577 [2]
6/18/83	27	35	●	©	13	In Your Eyes		$10	Warner 23744
1/26/85	45	32	●	©	14	20/20		$10	Warner 25178
9/20/86	77	24		©	15	While The City Sleeps...		$10	Warner 25475
7/11/87	59	31	●	©	16	Collaboration	[I]	$10	Warner 25580

GEORGE BENSON/EARL KLUGH

9/24/88	76	10		©	17	Twice The Love		$10	Warner 25705
8/5/89	140	6		©	18	Tenderly		$10	Warner 25907
8/17/96	150	10		©	19	That's Right	[I]	$10	GRP 9823
6/10/00	125	3		©	20	Absolute Benson	[I]	$10	GRP 543586

Affirmation (3) Deeper Than You Think (20) Gone (7) Inside Love (So Personal) Living On Borrowed Love (17) Nature Boy (8,12)
Are You Happy? (1) Did You Hear Thunder (15) Gonna Love You More (8) 71 (13) 43 Love All The Hurt Away Never Give Up On A Good
At The Mambo Inn (18) Dinorah, Dinorah (11) Good Habit (17) It's All In The Game (9) (12) 46 Thing (12) 52
Because (medley) (5) Dontcha Hear Me Callin' To Ya Greatest Love Of All (9,12) 24 Jackie, All (1) Love Ballad (10,12) 18 Never Too Far To Fall (13)
Before You Go (10) (1) Here Comes The Sun (5,12) Jama Joe (1) Love Dance (11) New Day (11)
Being With You (13) Down Here On The Ground (9) Here, There And Everywhere Jamaica (16) Love Is A Hurtin' Thing (10) No One Emotion (14)
Beyond The Ozone (6) Dreamin' (16) (18) Jazzenco (20) Love Is Here Tonight (15) No Sooner Said Than Done (2)
Beyond The Sea (La Mer) (14) El Barrio (20) Hey Girl (10) Johnnie Lee (19) Love X Love (11) 61 Nothing's Gonna Change My
Brazilian Stomp (16) Em (4) Hipping The Hop (20) Kisses In The Moonlight (15) Love Will Come Again (13) Love For You (14)
Breezin' (3,12) 63 End, The (5) Hold Me (5) Lady (3) Marvin Gaye (19) Octane (7)
California P.M. (9) Everybody Does It (17) Holdin' On (19) Lady Blue (9) Medicine Man (20) Octopus's Garden (medley) (5)
Camel Hump (6) Everything Must Change (8) I Could Write A Book (20) **Lady Love Me (One More** Midnight Love Affair (11) Ode To A Kudu (9)
Cast Your Fate To The Wind Feel Like Making Love (13) I Just Wanna Hang Around You **Time)** (13) 30 Mimosa (16) Off Broadway (11)
(4,12) Flute Song (6) (14) Land Of 1000 Dances (11) Moody's Mood (11,12) Oh! Darling (5)
Change Is Gonna Come (10) Footprints In The Sand (19) I Want You (She's So Heavy) Last Train To Clarksville (12) Mt. Airy Road (16) Old Devil Moon (6)
Changing World (2) Full Compass (2) (5) Late At Night (13) My Cherie Amour (1) **On Broadway** (9,12) 7
Collaboration (16) Ghetto, The (20) In Search Of A Dream (13) Lately (20) My Latin Brother (2) One On One (20)
Come Back Baby (20) **Give Me The Night** (11,12) 4 In Your Eyes (13) Let's Do It Again (17) My Woman's Good To Me (1) One Rock Don't Make No
Come Together (medley) (5) Golden Slumbers (5) Livin' Inside Your Love (10,12) Nassau Day (10) Boulder (4)

DEBUT	PEAK	WKS	RIAA	CD	ARTIST — Album Title	Catalog	Sym	$	Label & Number

BENSON, George — Cont'd

Out In The Cold Again (1)
P Park (19)
Please Don't Walk Away (14)
Prelude To Fall (10)
Rolling Home (6)
Secrets In The Night (15)
Shell Of A Man (4)
Shiver (15)
Siberian Workout (4)
Since You're Gone (16)
Six To Four (3)

So This Is Love? (3)
Something (medley) (5)
Song For My Brother (19)
Soul Limbo (1)
Soulful Strut (10)
Stand Up (14)
Star Of A Story (X) (11)
Stardust (18)
Starting All Over (17)
Stella By Starlight (18)
Stephanie (17)
Summer Love (19)

Summer Wishes, Winter Dreams (2)
Summertime (2)
Take Five (2,7)
Teaser (15)
Tell It Like It Is (1)
Tender Love (17)
Tenderly (18)
That's Right (19)
Theme From Good King Bad (4)
Thinker, The (19)

This Is All I Ask (18)
This Masquerade (3,12) 10
Too Many Times (15)
True Blue (19)
Turn Out The Lamplight (11)
Turn Your Love Around (12) 5
20/20 (14) 48
Twice The Love (17)
Unchained Melody (10)
Until You Believe (17)
Use Me (13)
Valdez In The Country (8)

Water Brother (1)
We All Remember Wes (9)
We As Love (9)
We Got The Love (12)
Weekend In L.A. (9)
Welcome Into My World (10)
What's On Your Mind (11)
While The City Sleeps (15)
White Rabbit (12)
Wind And I (8)
Windsong (9)
World Is A Ghetto (8)

You Are The Love Of My Life (14)
You Don't Know What Love Is (18)
You Never Give Me Your Money (5)
You're Never Too Far From Me (10)
You're Still My Baby (17)

BENTON, Brook   '70
Born Benjamin Franklin Peay on 9/19/31 in Camden, South Carolina. Died of spinal meningitis on 4/9/88 (age 56). R&B singer/songwriter.

DEBUT	PEAK	WKS			ARTIST — Album Title		Sym	$	Label & Number
6/5/61	82	20			1 Golden Hits		[G]	$30	Mercury 60607
9/25/61	70	13			2 The Boll Weevil Song And 11 Other Great Hits			$30	Mercury 60641
2/17/62	77	7			3 If You Believe			$30	Mercury 60619
10/27/62	40	15			4 Singing The Blues - Lie To Me			$30	Mercury 60740
4/13/63	82	6			5 Golden Hits, Volume 2		[G]	$30	Mercury 60774
10/28/67	156	4			6 Laura (What's He Got That I Ain't Got)			$20	Reprise 6268
7/19/69	189	2			7 Do Your Own Thing			$15	Cotillion 9002
2/21/70	27	23			8 Brook Benton Today			$15	Cotillion 9018
8/22/70	199	2			9 Home Style			$15	Cotillion 9028

Are You Sincere (9)
Aspen Colorado (9)
Baby (8)
Boll Weevil Song (2,5) 2
Born Under A Bad Sign (9)
Break Out (7)
Can't Take My Eyes Off You (8)
Careless Love (2)
Chains Of Love (4)
Child Of The Engineer (2)
Deep River (3)
Desertion (8)
Destination Heartbreak (7)
Do Your Own Thing (7) 99
Don't It Make You Want To Go Home (9) 45
Don't Think Twice It's All Right (9)
Endlessly (1) 12
Fools Rush In (Where Angels Fear To Tread) (5) 24

For Lee Ann (9)
Four Thousand Years Ago (2)
Frankie And Johnny (2,5) 20
Glory Of Love (6)
Go Tell It On The Mountain (3)
Going Home (3)
Got You On My Mind (4)
He'll Understand And Say Well Done (3)
Here We Go Again (6)
Hiding Behind The Shadow Of A Dream (7)
Hit Record (5) 45
Hither And Thither And Yon (1) 58
Honey Babe (2)
Hotel Happiness (5) 3
How Many Times (1)
Hurtin' Inside (1) 78
I Got What I Wanted (4) 28
I Just Don't Know What To Do With Myself (1)

I Left My Heart In San Francisco (medley) (6)
I've Gotta Be Me (8)
Intoxicated Rat (2)
It's All In The Game (9)
It's Just A House Without You (5) 45
It's Just A Matter Of Time (1) 3
It's My Lazy Day (2)
Johnny-O (3)
Just A Closer Walk With Thee (3)
Key To The Highway (2)
Kiddio (1) 7
Laura (Tell Me What He's Got That I Ain't Got) (6) 78
Let Me Fix It (7)
Lie To Me (4,5) 13
Life Has Its Little Ups And Downs (8)
Lingering On (6)

Little Bit Of Soap (8)
Looking Back (4)
Lost Penny (3) 77
Man Without Love (7)
My Last Dollar (2)
My True Confession (4) 22
My Way (8) 72
Nothing Can Take The Place Of You (7) 74
Ode To Billie Joe (6)
Oh Lord, Why Lord (7)
Only Believe (3)
Pledging My Love (4)
Rainy Night In Georgia (8) 4
Remember Me (3)
Revenge (9) 15
Same One (1) 16
San Francisco (Be Sure To Wear Some Flowers In Your Hair) (medley) (6)
Send For Me (4)
Set Me Free (7)

Shadrack (3,5) 19
She Knows What To Do For Me (7)
So Close (1) 38
So Many Ways (1) 6
Steal Away (3)
Stick-To-It-Ivity (6)
Still Waters Run Deep (5) 89
Take Good Care Of Her (4)
Thank You Pretty Baby (1) 16
(There Was A) Tall Oak Tree (6)
Think Twice (5) 11
Ties That Bind (1) 37
Tomorrow Night (4)
Touch 'Em With Love (7)
Valley Of Tears (4)
Walk On The Wild Side (5) 43
We're Gonna Make It (8)
Where Do I Go From Here? (8)

Whoever Finds This I Love You (9)
Will You Love Me Tomorrow (4)
Willie And Laura Mae Jones (9)
With All Of My Heart (1) 82
With Pen In Hand (7)
Worried Man (2)
You're The Reason I'm Living (6)

BERG, Gertrude   '65
Born Gertrude Edelstein on 10/3/1899 in New York City. Died of heart failure on 9/14/66 (age 66). Actress. Played "Molly Goldberg" on radio and TV.

| 7/17/65 | 131 | 12 | | | How To Be A Jewish Mother | | [C] | $25 | Amy 8007 |

Basic Techniques Of Jewish Motherhood
Glossary Of Terms: Final Word

How To Be A Jewish Grandmother
Jewish Mother's Guide To Education

Jewish Mother's Guide To Entertaining
Jewish Mother's Guide To Food Distribution

Jewish Mother's Guide To Relaxation
Jewish Mother's Guide To Sex And Marriage

Jewish Mother's Guide To Thrift

BERGEN, Edgar, & Charlie McCarthy — see FIELDS, W.C.

BERGEN, Polly   '57
Born Nellie Burgin on 7/4/30 in Knoxville, Tennessee. Singer/actress. Appeared in several movies and TV shows.

| 6/10/57 | 10 | 5 | | © | 1 Bergen Sings Morgan | | | $30 | Columbia 994 |

tribute to Helen Morgan

| 11/4/57 | 20 | 1 | | © | 2 The Party's Over | | | $30 | Columbia 1031 |

Bill (medley) (1)
Body And Soul (2)
But Not For Me (2)
Can't Help Lovin' That Man (1)
Don't Ever Leave Me! (1)

Ev'ry Time We Say Goodbye (2)
(Here Am I) Broken Hearted (1)
I Guess I'll Have To Change My Plan (2)

I'm Thru With Love (2)
(I've Got) Sand In My Shoes (1)
It Never Entered My Mind (2)
Little Things You Used To Do (1)
Make The Man Love Me (2)

Mean To Me (1)
More Than You Know (1)
My Melancholy Baby (1)
Party's Over (2)
Something To Remember You By (1)

What Wouldn't I Do For That Man! (1)
(When Your Heart's On Fire) Smoke Gets In Your Eyes (2)
Where's The Boy I Saved For A Rainy Day? (2)

Why Was I Born? (medley) (1)
You Don't Know What Love Is (2)
You'll Never Know (2)

BERLIN   '84
Electro-pop group from Los Angeles: Terri Nunn (vocals), Rick Olsen (guitar), Matt Reid and David Diamond (keyboards), John Crawford (bass) and Rob Brill (drums). Pared down to a trio in 1985 with Nunn, Crawford and Brill.

2/19/83	30	34	▲	©	1 Pleasure Victim			$10	Geffen 2036
3/31/84	28	30	●	©	2 Love Life			$10	Geffen 4025
11/8/86	61	20		©	3 Count Three And Pray			$10	Geffen 24121

Beg, Steal Or Borrow (2)
Dancing In Berlin (2)
Fall (2)
For All Tomorrow's Lies (2)
Heartstrings (3)

Hideaway (3)
In My Dreams (2)
Like Flames (3) 82
Masquerade (1) 82
Metro, The (1) 58

No More Words (2) 23
Now It's My Turn (2) 74
Pictures Of You (2)
Pink And Velvet (3)
Pleasure Victim (1)

Sex (I'm A...) (1) 62
Sex Me, Talk Me (3)
Take My Breath Away (3) 1
Tell Me Why (4)
Torture (1)

Touch (2)
Trash (3)
When Love Goes To War (3)
When We Make Love (3)
Will I Ever Understand You (3)

World Of Smiles (1)
You Don't Know (3)

BERLIN SYMPHONY — see CHRISTMAS (Various Artists)

BERMAN, Shelley   '59
Born on 2/3/26 in Chicago. Male comedian/actor. Appeared in many TV shows and movies.

4/27/59	2⁵	134			1 Inside Shelley Berman		[C]	$25	Verve 15003
11/30/59	6	77			2 Outside Shelley Berman		[C]	$25	Verve 15007
7/25/60	4	52			3 The Edge Of Shelley Berman		[C]	$25	Verve 15013

DEBUT	PEAK	WKS	RIAA	CD	ARTIST — Album Title	Catalog	Sym	$	Label & Number

BERMAN, Shelley — Cont'd

DEBUT	PEAK	WKS			Album Title	Catalog		$	Label & Number
11/6/61+	25	19			4 **A Personal Appearance**	[C]		$25	Verve 15027

no track titles listed for above 4 albums

| 9/26/64 | 88 | 8 | | | 5 **The Sex Life Of The Primate (and other Bits of Gossip)** | [C] | | $25 | Verve 15043 |

with Jerry Stiller, Anne Meara and Lovelady Powell

Associated Wives Of America (5) • Beginning Is A Clean, The End Is A Dirty (5) • Cleans And Dirtys (5) • Cleans And Dirtys Rise Again (5) • Divorce New York Style (5) • Drugstore Problem (5) • Expurgated...., An (5) • "It Was The Lark" Or Goodnight Already (5) • More Cleans And Dirtys (5) • My Friends The Gorillas (5) • Ooby Dooby Ooby Doo (5) • Sex Is Un-American (5) • Spermatozoa Plus The Roe Make The Little Fishes Grow (5)

BERNARDI, Herschel '67

Born on 10/20/23 in New York City. Died on 5/9/86 (age 62). Actor. Played "Tevye" in Broadway's *Fiddler On The Roof*.

| 11/12/66+ | 138 | 5 | | | **Fiddler On The Roof** | | | $20 | Columbia 6610 |

Anatevka • Fiddler On The Roof • If I Were A Rich Man • Matchmaker, Matchmaker • Miracle Of Miracles • Sabbath Prayer • Sunrise, Sunset • To Life • Tradition • When Messiah Comes

BERNSTEIN, Leonard '61

Born on 8/25/18 in Lawrence, Massachusetts. Died of a heart attack on 10/14/90 (age 72). Conductor/pianist/composer. Conductor of numerous major orchestras worldwide, including the New York Philharmonic and the Vienna Philharmonic. Composed music for several movies and Broadway shows. Won Grammy's Lifetime Achievement Award in 1985.

| 12/12/60+ | 13 | 15 | | | 1 **Bernstein Plays Brubeck Plays Bernstein** | [I] | | $25 | Columbia 1466 / 8257 |

side 1: **New York Philharmonic** with the **Dave Brubeck Quartet** conducted by Leonard Bernstein; side 2: **Dave Brubeck Quartet**

| 12/21/63+ | 8[X] | 12 | ● | | 2 **The Joy of Christmas** | [X] | | $25 | Columbia 5899 / 6499 |

LEONARD BERNSTEIN/NEW YORK PHILHARMONIC/THE MORMON TABERNACLE CHOIR
Christmas charts: 12/63, 32/64, 8/65, 62/66, 106/67, 28/68, 20/70

| 12/25/71+ | 53 | 20 | | | 3 **Mass (from the Liturgy of the Roman Mass)** | | | $20 | Columbia 31008 [2] |

created for the opening of the **John F. Kennedy** Center for the Performing Arts

| 5/25/85 | 70 | 20 | | | 4 **West Side Story** | | | $20 | DG 415253 [2] |

studio production featuring opera stars **Kiri Te Kanawa**, **José Carreras**, Tatiana Troyanos, Kurt Ollmann and Marilyn Horne

Agnus Dei (3) • America (3) • Animal Carol (2) • Away In A Manger (2) • Balcony Scene (4) • Ballet Sequence (4) • Boy Like That (medley) (4) • Bye Bye Johnny (4) • Carol Of The Bells (2) • Confession (3) • Cool (4) • Credo (3) • Dance At The Gym (4) • Deck The Hall With Boughs Of Holly (2) • Devotions Before Mass (3) • Dialogues For Jazz Combo And Orchestra (Movements 1-4) (1) • Epistle: The Word Of The Lord (3) • Finale (4) • First Introit (Rondo) (3) • Fraction: "Things Get Broken" (3) • Gee, Officer Krupke (4) • Gloria (3) • God Rest Ye Merry, Gentlemen (2) • Gospel-Sermon: "God Said" (3) • I Feel Pretty (4) • I Have A Love (medley) (4) • Jet Song (4) • Joseph Dearest, Joseph Mine (2) • Joy To The World (2) • La Virgen Lava Panales (2) • Lord's Prayer (3) • Lullay My Liking (2) • Maria (4) • Meditation #1, 2 & 3 (3) • O Come, All Ye Faithful (2) • O Little Town Of Bethlehem (2) • Offertory (3) • Once In Royal David's City (2) • One Hand, One Heart (4) • Patapan (2) • Pax: Communion (3) • Prologue (4) • Rumble, The (4) • Sanctus (3) • Second Introit (3) • Silent Night, Holy Night (2) • Something's Coming (4) • Taunting Scene (4) • Tonight (4) • Twelfth Night Song (2) • Twelve Days Of Christmas (2)

BERRY, Chuck '72

Born on 10/18/26 in St. Louis. Highly influential singer/songwriter/guitarist. Appeared in several movies. Won Grammy's Lifetime Achievement Award in 1984. Inducted into the Rock and Roll Hall of Fame in 1986. Movie documentary/concert tribute to Berry, *Hail! Hail! Rock 'N' Roll*, released in 1987.

| 8/24/63 | 29 | 17 | | | 1 **Chuck Berry On Stage** | | | $60 | Chess 1480 |

not a live album; audience dubbed in; although "Surfin' USA" is listed on the cover, it does not appear on the album

6/6/64	34	21			2 **Chuck Berry's Greatest Hits**	[G]		$50	Chess 1485
12/12/64+	124	7		©	3 **St. Louis To Liverpool**			$50	Chess 1488
5/20/67+	72	20			4 **Chuck Berry's Golden Decade**	[G]		$30	Chess 1514 [2]
6/10/72	8	47	●	©	5 **The London Chuck Berry Sessions**	[L]		$20	Chess 60020

side 1: studio; side 2: recorded live at the Lanchester Arts Festival in Coventry, England (with **Average White Band** backing)

| 11/4/72 | 185 | 7 | | | 6 **St. Louie To Frisco To Memphis** | [L] | | $25 | Mercury 6501 [2] |

record 1: live at the Fillmore with the **Steve Miller Band**

| 2/24/73 | 110 | 8 | | | 7 **Chuck Berry's Golden Decade, Vol. 2** | [G] | | $25 | Chess 60023 [2] |
| 9/8/73 | 175 | 6 | | | 8 **Chuck Berry/Bio** | | | $20 | Chess 50043 |

All Aboard (1) • **Almost Grown** (4) *32* • **Anthony Boy** (4) *60* • **Back In The U.S.A.** (4) *37* • Back To Memphis (6) • Betty Jean (7) • Bio (4) • Brenda Lee (3) • Brown Eyed Handsome Man (1,2,4) • Bye Bye Johnny (4) • **Carol** (7) *18* • Check Me Out (6) • Come On (7) • Deep Feeling (4) • Don't You Lie To Me (7) • Down The Road Apiece (7) • Driftin' Aimlessly (8) • Driftin' Blues (6,7) • Everyday I Have The Blues (medley) (6) • Feelin' It (6) • Fillmore Blues (6) • Flying Home (6) • Go Bobby Soxer (3) • Go Go Go (1,7) • Got It And Gone (8) • Guitar Boogie (7) • Havana Moon (6) • Hello Little Girl, Goodbye (8) • I Can't Believe (6) • I Do Really Love You (6) • I Just Want To Make Love To You (1) • I Love You (5) • I Will Not Let You Go (5) • I'm Talking About You (7) • I'm Your Hoochie Cooche Man (6) • It Don't Take But A Few Minutes (7) • It Hurts Me Too (6) • It's Too Dark In There (6) • Jaguar & The Thunderbird (4) • **Joe Joe Gun** (7) *83* • **Johnny B. Goode** (2,4,5,6) *8* • La Juanda (Espanola) (7) • **Let It Rock** (7) *64* • Let's Boogie (5) • Little Fox (6) • **Little Marie** (3) *54* • **Little Queenie** (7) *80* • Liverpool Drive (6) • London Berry Blues (5) • Louis To Frisco (6) • Ma Dear, Ma Dear (6) • Mad Lad (7) • Man And The Donkey (1) • Mean Old World (5) • Memphis (1,2,4) • **Merry Christmas Baby** (3,7) *71* • Misery (6) • **My Ding-A-Ling** (5) *1* • My Heart Will Always Belong To You (6) • My Tambourine (6) • **Nadine (Is It You?)** (2,4) *23* • Night Beat (3) • No Money Down (7) • **No Particular Place To Go** (3,4) *10* • **Oh Baby Doll** (2,4) *57* • Our Little Rendezvous (3) • **Promised Land** (3,7) *41* • Rain Eyes (8) • **Reelin' & Rockin'** (4,5) *27* • **Rock & Roll Music** (2,4) *8* • Rockin' At The Fillmore (medley) (6) • Rockin' At The Philharmonic (7) • Rocking On The Railroad (1) • **Roll Over Beethoven** (2,4) *29* • 'Round And 'Round (4) • **Run Rudolph Run** (7) *69* • **School Day** (2,4) *3* • So Long (6) • Soul Rockin' (6) • Still Got The Blues (1) • Surfing Steel (1) • **Sweet Little Rock And Roll** (7) *47* • **Sweet Little Sixteen** (2,4) *2* • Talkin' About My Buddy (8) • Things I Used To Do (3) • Thirty Days (2,4) • Together We Will Always Be (7) • Too Much Monkey Business (2,4) • **Too Pooped To Pop ("Casey")** (4) *42* • Trick Or Treat (1) • Wee Baby Blues (6) • Wee Wee Hours (4) • Woodpecker (8) • You Can't Catch Me (4) • **You Never Can Tell** (3,7) *14* • You Two (3)

BERRY, John '95

Born on 9/14/59 in Aiken, South Carolina; raised in Atlanta. Country singer/songwriter.

4/16/94	85	43	▲	©	1 **John Berry**			$10	Liberty 80472
3/15/95	69	39	●	©	2 **Standing On The Edge**			$10	Patriot 28495
12/2/95	110	6		©	3 **O Holy Night**			$10	Capitol 32663

Christmas chart: 18/'95

| | | | | | | C:#36/3 | [X] | | |
| 10/5/96 | 83 | 13 | ● | © | 4 **Faces** | | | $10 | Capitol 35464 |

Away In A Manger (3) • Change My Mind (4) • Christmas Song (3) • Desperate Measures (2) • Destiny (1) • Every Time My Heart Calls Your Name (2) • Faithfully (4) • Forty Again (4) • God Rest Ye Merry Gentlemen (3) • He Doesn't Even Know Her (4) • I Give My Heart (4) • I Never Lost You (1) • I Think About It All The Time (2) • I Will, If You Will (4) • I'll Be Home For Christmas (3) • If I Had Any Pride Left At All (2) • Joy To The World (3) • Kiss Me In The Car (1) • Little Drummer Boy (3) • Livin' On Love (4) • Love Is Everything (4) • Mind Of Her Own (1) • More Sorry Than You'll Ever Know (1) • More Than Just A Little (1) • Ninety Miles An Hour (2) • O Come All Ye Faithful (3) • O Come Emmanuel (3) • O Holy Night (3) • Prove Me Wrong (2) • She's Taken A Shine (4) • Silent Night (3) • Somebody (1) • Standing On The Edge Of Goodbye (2) • There's No Cross That Love Won't Bear (2) • Time To Be A Man (4) • What Are We Fighting For (2) • What's In It For Me (1) • When Love Dies (1) • You And Only You (1,2) • Your Love Amazes Me (1)

BETH, Karen '69
Born in 1948 in New York City. Folk-rock singer/songwriter/keyboardist.

9/6/69	171	6			**The Joys Of Life**			$15	Decca 75148

April Rain	I Know That You Know	It's All Over Now	Nothing Lasts	Song To A Shepherd	White Dakota Hill
Come December	In The Morning	Joys Of Life	Something To Believe In	Tomorrow's A New Day	

BETTER THAN EZRA '95
Rock trio from New Orleans: Kevin Griffin (vocals, guitar), Tom Drummond (bass) and Cary Bonnecaze (drums). Travis McNabb replaced Bonnecaze by 1996.

4/22/95	35	42	▲	© 1	**Deluxe**			$10	Elektra 61784
8/31/96	64	19		© 2	**Friction, Baby**			$10	Elektra 61944
9/12/98	129	1		© 3	**How Does Your Garden Grow?**			$10	Elektra 62247

Allison Foley (3)	Everything In 2's (3)	Je Ne M'en Souviens Pas (3)	Normal Town (2)	Rewind (2)	Teenager (3)
At Ch. DeGaulle, Etc. (2)	**Good** (1) *30*	Killer Inside (3)	One More Murder (3)	**Rosealia** (1) *71*	This Time of Year (1)
At The Stars (3) *78*	Happy Day MāMā (3)	King Of New Orleans (2)	Particle (2)	Scared Are You? (2)	Under You (3)
Beautiful Mistake (3)	Happy Endings (2)	Like It Like That (3)	Porcelain (1)	Southern Girl (1)	WWOZ (2)
Coyote (3)	Heaven (1)	Live Again (3)	Pull (3)	Speeding Up To Slow Down (2)	Waxing Or Waning? (3)
Cry in the Sun (1)	Hung The Moon (2)	Long Lost (2)	Return Of The Post Moderns	Still Life With Cooley (3)	
Desperately Wanting (2) *48*	In The Blood (1)	New Kind Of Low (3)	(2)	Summer House (1)	

BETTS, Dickey '74
Born on 12/12/43 in Sarasota, Florida. Singer/guitarist of **The Allman Brothers Band**. In the late 1970s, formed Great Southern: Dan Toler (guitar), Ken Tibbets (bass), Tom Broome (keyboards) and Jerry Thompson and Doni Sharbono (drums). By 1978, Tibbets, Broome and Thompson left; Dave Goldflies (bass), Michael Workman (keyboards) and David Toler (drums; brother of Dan) joined. The Toler brothers later joined **The Gregg Allman Band**. **The Dickey Betts Band** included: Warren Haynes (guitar), Johnny Neel (piano), Marty Privette (bass) and Matt Abts (drums). Haynes and Neel were also with The Allman Brothers Band. Betts was fired from the Allman Brothers Band in 2000.

8/31/74	19	16		© 1	**Highway Call**			$15	Capricorn 0123
					RICHARD BETTS				
4/30/77	31	12		© 2	**Dickey Betts & Great Southern**			$12	Arista 4123
4/29/78	157	5		© 3	**Atlanta's Burning Down**			$12	Arista 4168
11/12/88	187	4		© 4	**Pattern Disruptive**			$10	Epic 44289
					THE DICKEY BETTS BAND				

Atlanta's Burning Down (3)	Dealin' With The Devil (3)	Highway Call (1)	Mr. Blues Man (3)	Shady Streets (3)	You Can Have Her (I Don't
Back On The Road Again (3)	Duane's Tune (4)	Kissimmee Kid (1)	Nothing You Can Do (2)	Stone Cold Heart (4)	Want Her) (3)
Blues Ain't Nothin' (4)	Far Cry (4)	Leavin' Me Again (3)	Out To Get Me (2)	Sweet Virginia (2)	
Bougainvillea (2)	Good Time Feeling (3)	Let Nature Sing (1)	Rain (1)	Time To Roll (4)	
C'est La Vie (4)	Hand Picked (1)	Long Time Gone (1)	Rock Bottom (4)	Under The Guns Of Love (4)	
California Blues (2)	Heartbreak Line (4)	Loverman (4)	Run Gypsy Run (2)	Way Love Goes (2)	

B-52's, The ★375★ '90
Pop-rock group from Athens, Georgia: Fred Schneider (vocals, keyboards), Kate Pierson (vocals, organ), Cindy Wilson (guitar, vocals) and her brother Ricky Wilson (guitar) and Keith Strickland (drums). Ricky Wilson died of AIDS on 10/12/85 (age 32). Strickland then moved to guitar. Cindy Wilson left in 1991, replaced on tour by **Julee Cruise**. Appeared as The B.C. 52's in the movie *The Flintstones*. B-52 is slang for the bouffant hairstyle worn by Kate and Cindy.

1)*Cosmic Thing* 2)*Good Stuff* 3)*Wild Planet*

8/11/79+	59	74	▲	© 1	**The B-52's**			$10	Warner 3355
9/20/80	18	27	●	© 2	**Wild Planet**			$10	Warner 3471
8/8/81	55	11			3 **Party Mix!**	[K-M]		$10	Warner 3596
					6-cut party remix of *Wild Planet* album				
2/20/82	35	18			4 **Mesopotamia**	C:#31/8	[M]	$10	Warner 3641
5/21/83	29	26	●	© 5	**Whammy!**			$10	Warner 23819
10/4/86	85	15		© 6	**Bouncing Off The Satellites**			$10	Warner 25504
7/22/89+	4	65	▲⁴	© 7	Cosmic Thing			$10	Reprise 25854
2/23/91	184	3		© 8	**Party Mix!/Mesopotamia**	[R]		$10	Reprise 26401
					albums #3 and 4 above released together on 1 CD; *Mesopotamia* remixed in summer of 1990				
7/11/92	16	15	●	© 9	**Good Stuff**			$10	Reprise 26943
6/13/98	93	11		© 10	**Time Capsule - Songs For A Future Generation**	[G]		$10	Reprise 46920

Ain't It A Shame (6)	**Deadbeat Club** (7,10) *30*	Follow Your Bliss (7)	Lava (1,3,8)	Revolution Earth (9)	There's A Moon In The Sky
Bad Influence (9)	Debbie (10)	Girl From Ipanema Goes To	**Legal Tender** (5) *81*	Roam (7,10) *3*	(Called The Moon) (1)
Big Bird (1)	Deep Sleep (4,8)	Greenland (6)	Love Shack (7,10) *3*	**Rock Lobster** (1,10) *56*	Throw That Beat In The
Breezin' (9)	Detour Thru Your Mind (6)	Give Me Back My Man (2,3,8)	Loveland (4,8)	Runnin' Around (2)	Garbage Can (4,8)
Bushfire (7)	Devil In My Car (2)	**Good Stuff** (9,10) *28*	Mesopotamia (4,8,10)	She Brakes For Rainbows (6)	Topaz (7)
Butterbean (5)	Dirty Back Road (2)	Hallucinating Pluto (10)	Nip It In The Bud (4,8)	6060-842 (1)	Trism (5)
Cake (4,8)	Don't Worry (5)	Hero Worship (1)	Nude Beach, Theme For A (4)	Song For A Future Generation	Vision Of A Kiss (9)
Channel Z (7,10)	Downtown (1)	Hot Pants Explosion (9)	Party Out Of Bounds (2,3,8,10)	(5,10)	Whammy Kiss (5)
Communicate (6)	Dreamland (9)	Housework (5)	Planet Claire (1,10)	Strobe Light (2,10)	Wig (6)
Cosmic Thing (7)	Dry County (7)	Is That You Mo-Dean? (9,10)	**Private Idaho** (2,3,8,10) *74*	Summer Of Love (6,10)	Work That Skirt (5)
Dance This Mess Around	53 Miles West Of Venus (2)	Juicy Jungle (6)	Queen Of Las Vegas (5)	Tell It Like It T-I-Is (9)	World's Green Laughter (9)
(1,3,8)	52 Girls (1,3,8,10)	Junebug (7)	Quiche Lorraine (2,10)		

B.G. '99
Born Christopher Dorsey in 1980 in New Orleans. Male rapper. B.G.: Baby Gangsta. Member of **Cash Money Millionaires** and **Hot Boy$**.

11/15/97	184	1		© 1	**It's All On U Vol. 2**			$10	Cash Money 9616
5/8/99	9	42	●	© 2	Chopper City In The Ghetto			$10	Cash Money 53265
12/9/00	21	15		© 3	**Checkmate**			$10	Cash Money 860909

Ah Ha ... (3)	Clean Up Man (1)	Hot Boyz 226 (1)	Play'n It Raw (2)	Thug'n (2)
Big Tymers (3)	Dog Ass (2)	I Know (3)	Press One (3)	To My People (3)
Bling Bling (2) *36*	Don't Hate Me (1)	I'm Try'n (1)	Problems (3)	Trigga Play (3)
Bounce With Me (3)	Get In Line (3)	Jungle (3)	Real Niggaz (2)	"U" All "N" (1)
'Bout My Paper (2)	Get Your Shine On (1)	Knock Out (2)	Ride Or Die (1)	U Know How We Do (3)
Cash Money Is An Army (2)	Gun Slinger (3)	Livin Legend (1)	Run With My Chopper (3)	Uptown My Home (2)
Cash Money Roll (2)	Hard Times (2)	Made Man (2)	6 Figure (1)	What U Want Do (1)
Change The World [Hot Boys	He Used 2 Be A Man (3)	Niggaz In Trouble (2)	Stay "N" Line Hoe (1)	What's That Smell (1)
Feat. Big Tymers] (3)	Hennessey & XTC (3)	Plan Went Sour (1)	This N___ Die (3)	With Tha B.G. (2)

B.G. KNOCC OUT & DRESTA — '95

Male rap duo from Los Angeles.

| 9/2/95 | 128 | 5 | © | **Real Brothas** | $10 | OutBurst 527899 |

B.G. Knocc Out
Compton & Watts
Compton Hoe
Compton Swangin'
D.P.G./K
Do Or Die
Down Goes Anotha Nigga
Everyday Allday
50/50 Luv
Jealousy
Life's A Puzzle
Micc Checc
Real Brothas
Take A Ride
Whose The "G"

BICKERSONS, The — see AMECHE, Don

BIDDU ORCHESTRA — '76

Biddu was born in Bangalore, India. Male songwriter/producer/arranger.

| 2/21/76 | 170 | 3 | | **Biddu Orchestra** | [I] $12 | Epic 33903 |

Aranjuez Mon Amour
Black Magic Man
Blue Eyed Soul
Couldn't We Be Friends
Exodus (Main Theme)
Hot Ice
I Could Have Danced All Night *72*
Jump For Joy *flip*
Northern Dancer
Summer Of '42 *57*
You Don't Stand A Chance (If
You Don't Dance)

BIG AUDIO DYNAMITE — '91

Rock group from England. Formed by singer/guitarist Mick Jones (co-founder of **The Clash**; not to be confused with Mick Jones of Foreigner). Included Don Letts (keyboards), Greg Roberts (drums), Dan Donovan (keyboards; married to Eighth Wonder's Patsy Kensit, 1989-91) and Leo Williams (bass). Disbanded in 1989. Jones formed **Big Audio Dynamite II** in 1990 with Nick Hawkins (guitar; **Sigue Sigue Sputnik**), Gary Stonadge (bass) and Chris Kavanagh (drums). By 1994, group simply known as Big Audio.

11/23/85+	103	35		©	1	**This Is Big Audio Dynamite**	$10	Columbia 40220
11/1/86	119	23		©	2	**No. 10, Upping St.**	$10	Columbia 40445
8/13/88	102	12		©	3	**Tighten Up Vol. '88**	$10	Columbia 44074
9/23/89	85	13		©	4	**Megatop Phoenix**	$10	Columbia 45212
8/24/91	76	37	●	©	5	**The Globe**	$10	Columbia 46147

BIG AUDIO DYNAMITE II

All Mink & No Manners (4)
Applecart (3)
Around The Girl In 80 Ways (4)
Baby, Don't Apologise (4)
Bad (1)
Battle Of All Saints Road (3)
Beyond The Pale (2)
Bottom Line (1)
Can't Wait (5)
Champagne (3)
C'mon Every Beatbox (2)
Contact (4)
Dial A Hitman (2)
Dragon Town (4)
E=MC (1)
End (4)
Esquerita (3)
Everybody Needs A Holiday (4)
Funny Names (3)
Globe, The (5) *72*
Green Grass (5)
Green Lady (4)
Hip, Neck & Thigh (3)
Hollywood Boulevard (4)
House Arrest (4)
I Don't Know (5)
In My Dreams (5)
Innocent Child (4)
Is Yours Working Yet? (4)
James Brown (4)
Just Play Music! (3)
Kool-Aid (5)
Limbo The Law (2)
London Bridge (4)
Medicine Show (1)
Mick's A Hippie Burning (4)
Mr. Walker Said (3)
Other 99 (3)
Party, A (1)
Rewind (4)
Rock Non Stop (All Night Long)
  (3)
Rush (5) *32*
Sambadrome (2)
Sightsee M.C! (2)
Sony (1)
Stalag 123 (4)
Start (4)
Stone Thames (1)
Sudden Impact! (1)
Tea Party (5)
Ticket (2)
Tighten Up Vol. '88 (3)
2000 Shoes (3)
Union, Jack (4)
V. Thirteen (2)
When The Time Comes (5)

BIG BAD VOODOO DADDY — '98

Eclectic-jazz group from Ventura, California: Scotty Morris (vocals, guitar), Joshua Levy (piano), Jeff Harvis, Karl Hunter, Glen Marhevka and Andy Rowley (horns), Dirk Shumaker (bass) and Kurt Sodergen (drums). Harvis left after first album. Group appeared as the band in the movie *Swingers*.

| 3/14/98 | 47 | 56 | ▲ | © | 1 | **Big Bad Voodoo Daddy** | $10 | Coolsville 93338 |
| 11/6/99 | 93 | 3 | | © | 2 | **This Beautiful Life** | $10 | Coolsville 90387 |

Big And Bad (2)
Big Time Operator (2)
Boogie Bumper (1)
Go Daddy-O (1)
I Wanna Be Like You (4)
I'm Not Sleepin' (2)
Jump With My Baby (1)
Jumpin' Jack (1)
King Of Swing (1)
Maddest Kind Of Love (1)
Mambo Swing (1)
Minnie The Moocher (1)
Mr. Pinstripe Suit (1)
Please Baby (1)
Sleep Tight (2)
So Long-Farewell-Goodbye (1)
Some Things (2)
Still In Love With You (1)
2000 Volts (2)
What's Next? (2)
When It Comes To Love (2)
Who's That Creepin'? (2)
You & Me & The Bottle Makes 3
  Tonight (Baby) (1)

BIG BROTHER & THE HOLDING COMPANY — '68

Rock group from San Francisco: **Janis Joplin** (vocals), Sam Andrew and James Gurley (guitars), Peter Albin (bass) and David Getz (drums). Joplin died of a heroin overdose on 10/4/70 (age 27).

9/2/67	60	30			1	**Big Brother & The Holding Company**	$50	Mainstream 6099
8/31/68	❶[8]	66	▲[2]	©	2	**Cheap Thrills**	$25	Columbia 9700
11/28/70	134	6			3	**Be A Brother**	$25	Columbia 30222
5/15/71	185	4		©	4	**Big Brother & The Holding Company**	[R] $25	Columbia 30631
9/4/71	157	3			5	**How Hard It Is**	$25	Columbia 30738

All Is Loneliness (1,4)
Ball And Chain (2)
Be A Brother (3)
Black Widow Spider (5)
Blindman (1,4)
Buried Alive In The Blues (5)
Bye, Bye Baby (1,4)
Call On Me (1,4)
Caterpillar (1,4)
Combination Of The Two (2)
Coo Coo (1,4) *84*
Down On Me (1,4) *43*
Easy Rider (1,4)
Funkie Jim (3)
Heartache People (3)
Home On the Strange (3)
House On Fire (4)
How Hard It Is (5)
I Need A Man To Love (2)
I'll Change Your Flat Tire, Merle
  (1,4)
Intruder (1,4)
Joseph's Coat (3)
Keep On (3)
Last Band On Side One (5)
Last Time (1,4)
Light Is Faster Than Sound
  (1,4)
Maui (5)
Mr. Natural (3)
Nu Boogaloo Jam (5)
Oh, Sweet Mary (2)
Piece Of My Heart (2) *12*
Promise Her Anything But Give
  Her Arpeggio (5)
Shine On (5)
Someday (3)
Summertime (2)
Sunshine Baby (3)
Turtle Blues (2)
Women Is Losers (1,4)
You've Been Talkin' 'Bout Me,
  Baby (5)

BIG BUB — '97

Born Frederick Lee Drakeford in Engelwood, New Jersey. Male singer/rapper. Former member of **Today**.

| 11/8/97 | 104 | 3 | | © | **Timeless** | $10 | Kedar 53074 |

Bring It On
Call Me
Everybody
My Way
Need Your Love *70*
No One
Settle Down
Strung
Take It Off
Zoom

BIG COUNTRY — '83

Pop-rock group from Dunfermline, Scotland: Stuart Adamson (vocals, guitar), Bruce Watson (guitar), Tony Butler (bass) and Mark Brzezicki (drums).

9/24/83	18	42	●	©	1	**The Crossing**	$10	Mercury 812870
5/5/84	65	12			2	**Wonderland**	[M] $10	Mercury 818835
11/24/84	70	17		©	3	**Steeltown**	$10	Mercury 822831
7/19/86	59	17		©	4	**The Seer**	$10	Mercury 826844
10/29/88	160	6		©	5	**Peace In Our Time**	$10	Reprise 25787

All Fall Together (2)
Angle Park (2)
Broken Heart (Thirteen Valleys)
  (5)
Chance (1)
Close Action (1)
Come Back To Me (3)
Crossing, The (2)
East Of Eden (3)
Eiledon (4)
Everything I Need (5)
Fields Of Fire (1) *52*
Flame Of The West (3)
From Here To Eternity (5)
Girl With Grey Eyes (4)
Great Divide (3)
Harvest Home (4)
Hold The Heart (4)
I Could Be Happy Here (5)
I Walk The Hill (4)
In A Big Country (1) *17*
In This Place (5)
Inwards (1)
Just A Shadow (3)
King Of Emotion (5)
Look Away (4)
Lost Patrol (1)
One Great Thing (4)
One Great Thing (4)
1000 Stars (1)
Peace In Our Time (5)
Porrohman (2)
Rain Dance (3)
Red Fox (4)
Remembrance Day (4)
River Of Hope (5)
Sailor, The (4)
Seer, The (4)
Steeltown (3)
Storm, The (1)
Tall Ships Go (3)
Teacher, The (4)
Thousand Yard Stare (5)
Time For Leaving (5)
Where The Rose Is Sown (4)
Wonderland (2) *86*

BIGDUMBFACE '01
Rock group formed in Jacksonville, Florida: Wes Borland (vocals, guitar), Kyle Weeks (guitar), Chris Gibbs (bass) and Greg Isabel (drums). Borland is also a member of **Limp Bizkit**.

3/24/01	194	1		©	**Duke Lion Fights The Terror!!**.........................			$10	Flip 490893

Blood Red Head On Fire | Duke Lion | It's Right In Here | Mighty Penis Laser | Rebel | Space Adventure
Burgalveist | Fightin' Stance | Kali Is The Sweethog | Organ Splitter | Robot | Voices In The Wall

BIG ED '98
Born Edward Knight in Richmond, California. Male rapper.

9/19/98	16	6		©	**The Assassin**......................................			$10	No Limit 50729

Assassin | Come Home w/Me | I'm Yo Soldier | Make Some Room | Scriptures | We Represent
Buck 'Em | Go 2 War | Just Me & U | My Entourage | Shake'm Up | We Some
Come Get Me | I Miss 'Em | Life | Rodeo | Uh Oh |

BIG HEAD TODD & THE MONSTERS '94
Rock trio from Boulder, Colorado: Todd Park Mohr (guitar, keyboards), Rob Squires (bass) and Brian Nevin (drums). All share vocals.

3/13/93+	117	64	▲	© 1	**Sister Sweetly**.....................................			$10	Giant 24486
10/15/94	30	8		© 2	**Strategem**..			$10	Giant 24580
3/1/97	54	10		© 3	**Beautiful World**...................................			$10	Revolution 24661

Angel Leads Me On (2) | Candle 99 (2) | Groove Thing (1) | Kensington Line (2) | Shadowlands (2) | Tower (3)
Beautiful World (3) | Caroline (1) | Heart Of Wilderness (3) | Magdelina (2) | Sister Sweetly (1) | True Lady (3)
Bittersweet (1) | Circle (1) | Helpless (3) | Neckbreaker (2) | Soul For Every Cowboy (2) | Turn The Light Out (1)
Boom Boom (3) | Crazy Mary (3) | If You Can't Slow Down (3) | Please Don't Tell Her (1) | Strategem (2) | Wearing Only Flowers (2)
Broken Hearted Savior (1) | Ellis Island (1) | In The Morning (2) | Poor Miss (1) | These Days Without You (3) |
Brother John (1) | Greyhound (2) | It's Alright (1) | Resignation Superman (3) | Tomorrow Never Comes (1) |

BIG L '00
Born Lamont Coleman on 5/30/74 in Harlem, New York. Shot to death in New York City on 2/15/99 (age 24). Male rapper.

4/15/95	149	2		© 1	**Lifestylez Ov Da Poor & Dangerous**................			$10	Columbia 53795
8/19/00	13	9	●	© 2	**The Big Picture**...................................			$10	Rawkus 26136

All Black (1) | Ebonics (2) | Flamboyant (2) | I Don't Understand It (1) | '98 Freestyle (2) | Street Struck (1)
Casualties Of A Dice Game (2) | 8 Iz Enuff (1) | Games (2) | Let 'Em Have It *L* (1) | No Endz, No Skinz (1) | Triboro, The (2)
Da Graveyard (1) | Enemy, The (2) | Heist, The (2) | Lifestylez Ov Da Poor & | Platinum Plus (2) | Who You Slidin' Wit (2)
Danger Zone (1) | Fall Back (2) | Heist Revisited (2) | Dangerous (1) | Put It On (1) |
Deadly Combination (1) | Fed Up Wit The Bullshit (2) | Holdin' It Down (2) | MVP (1) | Size 'Em Up (2) |

BIG MIKE '97
Born Michael Barnett on 9/27/71 in New Orleans. Male rapper. Member of **The Geto Boys**.

7/16/94	40	20	●	© 1	**Somethin' Serious**.................................			$10	Rap-A-Lot 53907
4/26/97	16	11		© 2	**Still Serious**......................................			$10	Rap-A-Lot 44099
					includes "Grey Skies" by Ill				
6/12/99	63	3		© 3	**Hard To Hit**.......................................			$10	Rap-A-Lot 50104

All A Dream (2) | Creepin - Rollin (1) | Hard To Hit (3) | On Da 1 (1) | Smoke Em & Choke Em (1) | Sunday Morning (3)
All My Love (3) | Daddy's Gone (With Mr. | Havin Thangs (1) | On Da Real (1) | Somethin Serious (1) | This Goes Out (3)
Better Now (3) | Scarface) (1) | Heads Like Us (3) | 1000 Guns (3) | Southern Comfort (On & On) (2) | 12 O'Clock (3)
Black Lacquer (2) | Everybody Wants A Name (1) | How You Want It (3) | One Time (3) | Southern Dialect (2) | Twirk It (3)
'Burban & Impalas (2) | Fire (1) | Hustlers (3) | Playa Playa (3) | Southern Supreme (3) | Uhh! Uhh! (3)
Candy's 4 Babies (2) | Get Over That (1) | It's Alright (2) | Playas To Governors (2) | Southern Thang (1) | World Of Mind (1)
Claimin' Real (3) | Ghetto Love (1) | Made Men (3) | Return Of The Gangsta (3) | Still Serious (3) |
Comin From The Swamp (1) | Giddy Up (3) | None (3) | Seal It W/A Kiss (2) | Suckers 2 Me (3) |

BIG MOE '00
Born in Houston. Male rapper.

8/5/00	176	2		©	**City Of Syrup**.....................................			$10	Wreckshop 4441

Barre Baby | Freestyle (June27) | I'll Do It | Payin' Dues | We Da' Sh*t!
Choppaz | Get Back | Leanin' | Po' It Up | Whatcha Want?
City Of Syrup | I Wonder | Maan!! | Ridin' Candy | X(time) 4 Change

BIG MOUNTAIN '94
Reggae group from San Diego: Quino (vocals, guitar), Jerome Cruz (guitar), Manfred Reinke (keyboards), Gregory Blakney (percussion), Lynn Copeland (bass) and Lance Rhodes (drums).

8/6/94	174	5		©	**Unity**...			$10	Giant 24563

Baby, I Love Your Way *6* | Border Town | I Would Find A Way | **Sweet Sensual Love** *80* | Time Has Come | Young Revolutionaries
Big Mountain | Fruitful Days | Revolution | Tengo Ganas | Upful & Right

BIG PIG '88
Rock group from Australia: male singers Nick Disbray, Tony Antoniades, Tim Rosewarne and Oleh Witer, with female singer Sherine, and drummers Adrian Scaglione and Neil Baker.

3/26/88	93	17		©	**Bonk**...			$10	A&M 5185

Big Hotel | Charlie | Hungry Town | Iron Lung | Tin Drum
Boy Wonder | Devil's Song | I Can't Break Away ..see: | Money God |
Breakaway *60* | Fine Thing | Breakaway | Nation |

BIG PUN '00
Born Christopher Rios on 11/9/71 in New York City. Died of a heart attack on 2/7/2000 (age 28). Male rapper. Member of **Terror Squad**.

5/16/98	5	28	▲	© 1	**Capital Punishment**			$10	Loud 67512
					BIG PUNISHER				
4/22/00	3	23	●	© 2	**Yeeeah Baby**			$10	Loud 63843
4/21/01	7	9		© 3	**Endangered Species**			$10	Loud 1963

Banned From T.V. (3) | Dream Shatterer (1,3) | John Blaze (3) | New York Giants (2) | Super Lyrical (1) | Wishful Thinking (3)
Beware (1) | Fast Money (1) | Laughing At You (2) | Nigga Shit (2) | Top Of The World (3) | Wrong Ones (2)
Boomerang (1) | Fire Water (3) | Leather Face (2) | Off The Books (3) *86* | Tres Leches (Triboro Trilogy) | You Ain't A Killer (1,3)
Brave In The Heart (3) | Freestyle With Remy Martin (3) | Livin' La Vida Loca (3) | Off Wit His Head (2) | (1) | You Came Up (1)
Capital Punishment (1) | Glamour Life (3) | Mamma (2) | 100% (2) | Twinz (Deep Cover 98) (1,3) | You Was Wrong (2)
Caribbean Connection (1) | How We Roll (3) | Ms. Martin (2) | Parental Discretion (1) | Uncensored (2) |
Charlie Rock Shout (skit) (1) | How We Roll '98 (3) | My Dick (2) | Pina Colada (3) | Watch Those (2) |
Classic Verses (Drop It Heavy | **I'm Not A Player** (1) *57* | My Turn (2) | Punish Me (1) | We Don't Care (2) |
and Fantastic 4) (3) | **It's So Hard** (2) *75* | My World (3) | **Still Not A Player** (1,3) *24* | Whatcha Gon Do (3) |

BIG TYMERS '00

Rap duo from New Orleans: Mannie Fresh and Brian Williams. Members of **Cash Money Millionaires**.

DEBUT	PEAK	WKS		CD	#	Title		$	Label & Number
3/14/98	168	1		©	1	How You Luv That?		$10	Cash Money 9617
10/10/98	105	2		©	2	How You Luv That? Vol. 2		$10	Cash Money 53170
6/3/00	3	29	▲		3	I Got That Work		$10	Cash Money 157673

Ballin' (1,2) • Drivin' Em (1) • Money & Power (2) • Pimp On (3) • Suga & Pac, Puff & Big (6 Fig) • Try'n 2 Make A Million (1)
Beautiful (1,2) • Drop It Like It's Hot (2) • My Life (3) • Playboy (Don't Hate Me) (1,2) • (1,2) • We Ain't Stoppin' (3)
Big Ballin' (2) • Get Your Roll On (3) • Nigga Couldn't Know (3) • Preppy Pimp (1) • Sunday Night (3) • We Hustle (3)
Big Tymers (3) • Hard Life (3) • No, No (3) • Rocky (3) • Tear It Up (1,2)
Broads (1) • How Should I Ride (2) • #1 Stunna (3) • Snake (3) • Tell Me (2)
Cutlass, Monte Carlo's, & • How U Luv That (1,2) • On Top Of The World (2) • Stun'n (1,2) • 10 Wayz (3)
Regals (1,2) • Millionaire Dream (1,2) • Phone Call (1,2) • Stuntastic (3) • Top Of Tha Line Nigga (1,2)

BILK, Mr. Acker '62

Born Bernard Stanley Bilk on 1/28/29 in Somerset, England. Clarinet player.

DEBUT	PEAK	WKS		CD	#	Title	Sym	$	Label & Number
5/5/62	3	29	●		1	Stranger On The Shore	[I]	$25	Atco 129
9/1/62	48	9			2	Above The Stars & Other Romantic Fancies	[I]	$25	Atco 144

Above The Stars (2) 59 • Brahms' Lullaby (1) • Della (2) • Limelight (2) 92 • Moonlight Becomes You (2) • Soft Sands (2)
Acker's Lacquer (2) • Carolina Moon (1) • Greensleeves (1) • Londonderry Air (2) • Nobody Knows The Trouble (1) • Stranger On The Shore (1) 1
And The Angels Sing (2) • Cielito Lindo (1) • I Can't Get Started (1) • Lonely (2) • Sentimental Journey (1) • Take My Lips (1)
Babette (2) • Deep Purple (1) • Is This The Blues? (1) • Mean To Me (1) • Skye Boat Song (1) • When You Smile (2)

BILLION DOLLAR BABIES '77

Backing group for **Alice Cooper**: Michael Bruce (vocals), Mike Marconi (guitar), Bob Dolin (keyboards), Dennis Dunaway (bass) and Neal Smith (drums). Group named after Cooper's 1973 album.

DEBUT	PEAK	WKS		CD		Title		$	Label & Number
6/11/77	198	2				Battle Axe		$15	Polydor 6100

Battle Axe (medley) • Ego Mania • Love Is Rather Blind • Rock N' Roll Radio • Sudden Death (medley) • Wasn't I The One
Dance With Me • I Miss You • Rock Me Slowly • Shine Your Love • Too Young • Winner

BILLY & THE BEATERS — see VERA, Billy

BILLY SATELLITE '84

Rock group from Oakland: Monty Byrom (vocals), Danny Chauncey (guitar), Ira Walker (bass) and Tom Falletti (drums).

DEBUT	PEAK	WKS		CD		Title		$	Label & Number
9/1/84	139	6				Billy Satellite		$10	Capitol 12340

Bye Bye Baby • I Wanna Go Back 78 • Lonely One • Satisfy Me 64 • Trouble
Do Ya • Last Call • Rockin' Down The Highway • Standin' With The Kings • Turning Point

BIOHAZARD '94

Hard-rock group from Brooklyn, New York: Bobby Hambel (vocals), Billy Graziadei (guitar), Evan Seinfeld (bass) and Danny Schuler (drums). Hambel left in 1995, Graziadei and Seinfeld took over vocals. Rob Echeverria (guitar) joined in 1998.

DEBUT	PEAK	WKS		CD	#	Title		$	Label & Number
6/11/94	48	8		©	1	State Of The World Address		$10	Warner 45595
7/13/96	170	1		©	2	Mata Leão		$10	Warner 46208
6/26/99	187	1		©	3	New World Disorder		$10	King 546032

Abandon In Place (3) • Control (2) • Failed Territory (1) • Lot To Learn (2) • Skin (3) • Waiting To Die (2)
All For None (3) • Cornered (1) • Five Blocks To The Subway (1) • Love Denied (1) • State Of The World Address (1) • Way, A (2)
Authority (3) • Cycle Of Abuse (3) • Gravity (3) • Modern Democracy (2) • Stigmatized (2) • What Makes Us Tick (1)
Better Days (2) • Decline (3) • How It Is (1) • New World Disorder (3) • Switchback (3)
Breakdown (3) • Dogs Of War (3) • Human Animal (1) • Pride (1) • Tales From The Hard Side (1)
Camouflage (3) • Down For Life (3) • In Vain (1) • Remember (1) • These Eyes (Have Seen) (2)
Cleansing (2) • Each Day (1) • Inner Fear On (3) • Resist (3) • Thorn (2)
Competition (2) • End Of My Rope (3) • Lack There Of (1) • Salvation (3) • True Strengths (3)

BIONIC BOOGIE '78

Disco studio group assembled by producer Gregg Diamond.

DEBUT	PEAK	WKS		CD		Title		$	Label & Number
1/28/78	88	16				Bionic Boogie		$12	Polydor 6123

Big West • Dance Little Dreamer • Don't Lose That Number • Feel Like Dancing • Stop The Music
Boogie Boo • • (Mumbo Jumbo) • Risky Changes • We Must Believe In Magic

BIRKIN, Jane, & Serge Gainsbourg '70

Actress Birkin was born on 12/14/46 in London. Singer/songwriter Lucien "Serge" Gainsbourg was born on 4/2/28 in Paris. Died of heart failure on 3/2/91 (age 62). Couple were married from 1968-80.

DEBUT	PEAK	WKS		CD		Title	Sym	$	Label & Number
3/7/70	196	2				Je T'Aime (Beautiful Love)	[F]	$20	Fontana 67610

18-39 • L'Amanour (The Lover) • Les Sucettes (The Little • 69 Annee Erotique (69 The
Elisa • Le Canari Est Sur Le Balcon • Sweets) • Erotic Year)
Jane B • (The Canary Is On The • Manon • Sous Le Soleil Exactement
Je T'Aime...Moi Non Plus 58 • Balcony) • Orang Outan (Orangutan) • (Underneath The Sun Exactly)

BISHOP, Elvin '76

Born on 10/21/42 in Tulsa, Oklahoma. Lead guitarist with The **Paul Butterfield** Blues Band (1965-68).

DEBUT	PEAK	WKS		CD	#	Title	Sym	$	Label & Number
7/27/74	100	17		©	1	Let It Flow		$15	Capricorn 0134
5/10/75	46	17		©	2	Juke Joint Jump		$15	Capricorn 0151
1/24/76	18	34		©	3	Struttin' My Stuff		$15	Capricorn 0165
11/20/76	70	12		©	4	Hometown Boy Makes Good!		$15	Capricorn 0176
8/27/77	38	12		©	5	Live! Raisin' Hell	[L]	$20	Capricorn 0185 [2]

Arkansas Line (2) • D.C. Strut (4) • Have A Good Time (2,5) • Juke Joint Jump (2,5) • Rock My Soul (5) • Sure Feels Good (2,5) 83
Bourbon Street (1) • Do Nobody Wrong (2) • Hey, Good Lookin' (1) • Keep It Cool (4) • Rollin' Home (2) • Travelin' Shoes (1,5) 61
Bring It On Home To Me • Fishin' (1) • Hey, Hey, Hey, Hey (3,5) • Let It Flow (1) • Sidelines (4) • Twist & Shout (4)
(medley) (5) • Fooled Around And Fell In • Hold On (2) • Let The Good Times Roll • Slick Titty Boom (3) • Wide River (2)
Calling All Cows (2,5) • Love (3,5) 3 • Holler And Shout (3) • (medley) (5) • Spend Some Time (4) 93 • Yes Sir (4,5
Can't Go Back (1) • Give It Up (4,5) • Honey Babe (1) • Little Brown Bird (5) • Stealin' Watermelons (1,5) • '
Change Is Gonna Come • Grab All The Love (3) • I Can't Hold Myself In Line (1) • My Girl (3) • Struttin' My Stuff (3,5) 68
(medley) (5) • Graveyard Blues (4) • I Love The Life I Lead (3) • Once In A Lifetime (4) • Sugar Dumplin' (2)
Crawlin' Kingsnake (2) • Ground Hog (1) • Joy (3,5) • Raisin' Hell (5) • Sunshine Special (1)

BISHOP, Stephen '77

Born on 11/14/51 in San Diego. Pop-rock singer/songwriter. Wrote several movie themes. Cameo role as the "Charming Guy With Guitar" in *National Lampoon's Animal House*.

| 1/8/77 | 34 | 32 | | © | 1 **Careless** | | | $12 | ABC 954 |
| 9/16/78 | 35 | 19 | ● | | 2 **Bish** | | | $12 | ABC 1082 |

Bish's Hideaway (2)
Careless (1)
Every Minute (1)
Everybody Needs Love (2) *32*
Fool At Heart (2)

I've Never Known A Nite Like This (2)
If I Only Had A Brain (2)
Little Italy (1)
Looking For The Right One (2)

Losing Myself In You (2)
Madge (1)
Never Letting Go (1)
On And On (1) *11*
One More Night (1)

Only The Heart Within You (2)
Recognized (2)
Rock And Roll Slave (1)
Same Old Tears On A New Background (1)

Save It For A Rainy Day (1) *22*
Sinking In An Ocean Of Tears (1)
Vagabond From Heaven (2)
What Love Can Do (2)

When I Was In Love (2)

BIZ MARKIE '89

Born Marcel Hall on 4/8/64 in Harlem. Rapper/actor. Appeared in the movie *The Meteor Man*.

3/19/88	90	18		©	1 **Goin' Off**			$10	Cold Chillin' 25675
10/28/89	66	30	●	©	2 **The Biz Never Sleeps**			$10	Cold Chillin' 26003
					THE DIABOLICAL BIZ MARKIE				
9/14/91	113	2		©	3 **I Need A Haircut**			$10	Cold Chillin' 26648

Albee Square Mall (1)
Alone Again (3)
Biz Dance (Part One) (1)
Biz In Harmony (2)
Biz Is Goin' Off (1)
Buck Wild (3)
Busy Doing Nuthin' (3)

Check It Out (2)
Cool V's Tribute To Scratching (1)
Dedication (2)
Dragon, The (2)
I Hear Music (2)
I Told You (3)

Just A Friend (2) *9*
Kung Fu (3)
Let Go My Eggo (3)
Make The Music With Your Mouth Biz (1)
Me Versus Me (2)
Mudd Foot (2)

My Man Rich (2)
Nobody Beats The Biz (1)
On And On (3)
Pickin' Boogers (1)
Return Of The Biz Dance (1)
Road Block (2)
Romeo And Juliet (3)

She's Not Just Another Woman (Monique) (2)
Spring Again (2)
T.S.R. (Toilet Stool Rap) (3)
Take It From The Top (3)
Thing Named Kim (2)
Things Get A Little Easier (2)

This Is Something For The Radio (1)
To My Boys (3)
Vapors (1)
What Comes Around Goes Around (3)

BIZZY BONE '98

Born Charles Scruggs in Cleveland. Male rapper. Member of **Bone Thugs-N-Harmony**.

| 10/24/98 | 3 | 19 | ● | © | 1 **Heaven'z Movie** | | | $10 | Mo Thugs 1670 |
| 4/7/01 | 44 | 7 | | © | 2 **The Gift** | | | $10 | AMC 71150 |

Be Careful (2)
Before I Go (2)
Brain On Drugs (1)
Demons Surround Me (1)
Don't Be Dumb (2)

Don't Doubt Me (2)
Father (2)
Fried Day (2)
Jesus (2)
Marchin' On Washington (1)

Menensky Mobbin' (1)
Mr. Majesty II (1)
Murderah (2)
Never Grow (2)
Nobody Can Stop Me (1)

On The Freeway (2)
Roll Call (1)
(Roof Is) On Fire (1)
Schizophrenic (2)
Social Studies (1)

Still Thuggish Ruggish (2)
Thugz Cry (1)
Time Passing Us By (2)
Voices In The Head (2)
Waitin' For Warfare (1)

Whole Wide World (2)
Yes Yes Y'all (1)

BJOERLING, Jussi '61

Born on 2/5/11 in Stora Tuna, Sweden. Died on 9/9/60 (age 49). Male opera tenor.

| 4/17/61 | 142 | 1 | | | **The Beloved Bjoerling, Volume One** | | [E] | $30 | Capitol 7239 |
| | | | | | recordings from 1936-48 | | | | |

Che Gelida Manina
Cielo E Mar
Donna Non Vidi Mai!

E La Solita Storia
Instant Charmant...(Act 1 & 2)

La Fleur Que Tu M'Avais Jetee (Flower Song)
Mi Batte Il Cor...O Paradiso

Nessun Dorma
O Lola, Bianca Come Fior (Siciliana)

Questa O Quella
Una Furtiva Lagrima
Vesti La Giubba

BJÖRK '95

Born Björk Gudmundsdottir on 11/12/65 in Reykjavik, Iceland. Female singer/actress. Lead singer of **The Sugarcubes**.

7/31/93	61	31	▲	©	1 **Debut**			$10	Elektra 61468
7/1/95	32	20	▲	©	2 **Post**			$10	Elektra 61740
2/1/97	66	5		©	3 **Telegram**		[K]	$10	Elektra 61897
					contains remixes of songs from #2 above				
10/11/97	28	9	●	©	4 **Homogenic**			$10	Elektra 62061
10/7/00	41	7		©	5 **Selmasongs**			$10	Elektra 62533

Aeroplane (1)
Alarm Call (4)
All Is Full Of Love (4)
All Neon Like (4)
Anchor Song (1)
Army Of Me (2,3)
Bachelorette (4)

Big Time Sensuality (1) *88*
Come To Me (3)
Cover Me (2,3)
Crying (1)
Cvalda (5)
Enjoy (2,3)
5 Years (4)

Headphones (2,3)
Human Behaviour (1)
Hunter (4)
Hyper-ballad (2,3)
I Miss You (2,3)
I've Seen It All (5)
Immature (4)

In The Musicals (5)
Isobel (2,3)
It's Oh So Quiet (2)
Joga (4)
Like Someone In Love (1)
Modern Things (2)
My Spine (3)

New World (5)
One Day (1)
107 Steps (5)
Pluto (4)
Possibly Maybe (2,3)
Scatterheart (5)

There's More To Life Than This (1)
Unravel (4)
Venus As A Boy (1)
Violently Happy (1)
You've Been Flirting Again (2,3)

BLACK('S), Bill, Combo '60

Born on 9/17/26 in Memphis. Died of a brain tumor on 10/21/65 (age 39). Bass guitarist. Session work in Memphis; backed **Elvis Presley** (with Scotty Moore, guitar; D.J. Fontana, drums) on most of his early records. Formed own band in 1959. Labeled as "The Untouchable Sound." Larry Rogers and Bob Tucker led group after Black's death; recorded well into the 1970's.

11/14/60	23	28		©	1 **Solid And Raunchy**		[I]	$40	Hi 12003
1/20/62	35	19		©	2 **Let's Twist Her**		[I]	$30	Hi 12006
					originally released in 1961 as *Bill Black's Record Hop*				
7/11/64	143	4		©	3 **Plays Tunes By Chuck Berry**		[I]	$30	Hi 32017
11/28/64	139	3		©	4 **Bill Black's Combo Goes Big Band**		[I]	$30	Hi 32020
8/19/67	195	2		©	5 **Bill Black's Greatest Hits**		[G-I]	$25	Hi 32012
9/13/69	168	4		©	6 **Solid And Raunchy The 3rd**		[I]	$25	Hi 32052

Blue Tango (5) *16*
Blueberry Hill (5)
Bo Diddley (1)
Brown Eyed Handsome Man (3)
Cab Driver (3)
Canadian Sunset (4)
Carol (3)
Cherry Pink (1)
Coco Brown (6)
Come See About Me (6)
Corrina, Corrina (2)
Creepin' Around (6)

Do It -- Rat Now (5) *51*
Don't Be Cruel (1,5) *11*
Groovin' Easy (6)
Hearts Of Stone (5) *20*
Hold It Down (4)
Honky Tonk (1)
Huckle-Buck (Twist) (4)
I Almost Lost My Mind (1)
If I Had A Hammer (6)
In The Mood (5)
Java (4)
Johnny B. Goode (2,3)

Josephine (5) *18*
Leap Frog (4)
Leavin' Town (6)
Little Queenie (3) *73*
Love Is Here And Now You're Gone (6)
Mabellene (3)
Mack The Knife (1)
Memphis Tennessee (3)
Mona Lisa (1)
My Girl Josephine (2)
Nadine (3)

Near You (4)
Night Train (2)
O (Oh!) (4)
Ole Buttermilk Sky (5) *25*
Raunchy (1)
Reelin' And Rockin' (3)
Roll Over Beethoven (3)
Rollin' (5)
Royal Blue (5)
Royal Twist (2)
School Days (3)
Sentimental Journey (4)

Singin' The Blues (4)
Slippin' & Slidin' (Twist) (2)
Smokie -- Part 2 (5) *17*
Smokie Part II (Twist) (2)
So Rare (4)
Son Of Hickory Holler's Tramp (6)
Stranger On The Shore (4)
Sweet Little Sixteen (3)
T.D.'s Boogie Woogie (4)
Tequila (1) *91*
Thirty Days (3)

Tuxedo Junction (4)
Twist-Her (2) *26*
Twist With Me Baby (2)
Twisteroo (2)
Two O'Clock Jump (4)
Watch Your Step (6)
White Silver Sands (5) *9*
Willie (5)
Yogi (5)
Yogi (Twist) (2)
You Win Again (1)

★332★ BLACK, Clint '90

Born on 2/4/62 in Long Branch, New Jersey; raised in Houston. Country singer/guitarist. Married actress Lisa Hartman on 10/20/91.

DEBUT	PEAK	WKS	RIAA	CD	#	Album Title	Sym	$	Label & Number
6/10/89+	31	143	▲³	©	1	Killin' Time		$10	RCA 9668
11/24/90	18	80	▲³	©	2	Put Yourself In My Shoes		$10	RCA 2372
8/1/92	8	41	▲	©	3	The Hard Way		$10	RCA 66003
7/31/93	14	52	▲	©	4	No Time To Kill		$10	RCA 66239
10/22/94	37	33	▲	©	5	One Emotion		$10	RCA 66419
11/11/95	138	7		©	6	Looking For Christmas	[X]	$10	RCA 66593
						Christmas chart: 20/'95			
10/12/96	12	40	▲	©	7	The Greatest Hits	[G]	$10	RCA 66671
8/16/97	43	43	●	©	8	Nothin' But The Taillights		$10	RCA 67515
10/16/99	75	23	●	©	9	D'lectrified		$10	RCA 67823

Are You Sure Waylon Done It This Way (9)
Back To Back (4)
Bad Goodbye (4,7) *43*
Better Man (1,7)
Birth Of The King (6)
Bitter Side Of Sweet (8)
Bob Away My Blues (9)
Burn One Down (3,7,9)
Buying Time (3)
Cadillac Jack Favor (7)
Change In The Air (5)
Christmas For Every Boy And Girl (6)
Coolest Pair (6)
Desperado (7)
Dixie Lullaby (9)
Finest Gift (6)
Galaxy Song (9)
Good Old Days (9)
Good Run Of Bad Luck (4,7)
Goodnight-Loving (2)
Gulf Of Mexico (3)
Half The Man (4)
Half Way Up (7)
Hand In The Fire (9)
Happiness Alone (4)
Hard Way (8)
Harmony (9)
Heart Like Mine (2)
Hey Hot Rod (5)
I Can Get By (5)
I'll Take Texas (4)
Kid, The (6)
Killin' Time (1)
Life Gets Away (5,7)
Like The Rain (7)
Live And Learn (1)
Looking For Christmas (6)
Loosen Up My Strings (8)
Love She Can't Live Without (9)
Loving Blind (2)
Muddy Water (2)
No Time To Kill (4,7,9)
Nobody's Home (1)
Nothin' But The Taillights (8)
Nothing's News (1)
Ode To Chet (8)
Old Man (2)
One Emotion (5)
One More Payment (2)
Our Kind Of Love (8)
Put Yourself In My Shoes (2,7)
Shoes You're Wearing (8)
Slow As Christmas (6)
Something That We Do (8) *76*
Something To Cry About (3)
State Of Mind (4,7)
Still Holding On (8)
Straight From The Factory (1)
Summer's Comin' (5,7)
That Something In My Life (8)
There Never Was A Train (3)
Thinkin' Again (4)
This Nightlife (2)
Til' Santa's Gone (Milk And Cookies) (6)
Tuckered Out (4)
Under The Mistletoe (6)
Untanglin' My Mind (5)
Wake Up Yesterday (3)
Walkin' Away (1)
We Tell Ourselves (3,7)
What I Feel Inside (8)
When I Said I Do (9) *31*
When My Ship Comes In (3)
Where Are You Now (2)
Where Your Love Won't Go (9)
Wherever You Go (5,7)
Who I Use To Be (9)
Winding Down (1)
Woman Has Her Way (3)
You Don't Need Me Now (8)
You Know It All (8)
You Made Me Feel (5)
You Walked By (5)
You're Gonna Leave Me Again (1)

BLACK, Frank '93

Born Charles Thompson in 1965 in Long Beach, California. Rock singer/guitarist. Former leader of the **Pixies**.

DEBUT	PEAK	WKS	CD	#	Album Title	$	Label & Number
3/27/93	117	5	©	1	Frank Black	$10	4 A D 61467
6/11/94	131	2	©	2	Teenager Of The Year	$10	4 A D 61618
2/17/96	127	1	©	3	The Cult Of Ray	$10	American 43070

Adda Lee (1)
Adventure And The Resolution (3)
Big Red (2)
Big, Wicked World (2)
Brackish Boy (1)
Calistan (2)
Creature Crawling (3)
Cult Of Ray (3)
Czar (1)
Dance War (3)
Don't Ya Rile 'Em (1)
Every Time I Go Around Here (1)
Fazer Eyes (2)
Fiddle Riddle (2)
Freedom Rock (2)
Fu Manchu (1)
Hang on to Your Ego (1)
Headache (2)
Hostess with the Mostest (2)
I Could Stay Here Forever (2)
I Don't Want To Hurt You (Every Single Time) (3)
I Heard Ramona Sing (1)
(I Want to Live on an) Abstract Plain (2)
Jesus Was Right (3)
Kicked In The Taco (3)
Last Stand Of Shazeb Andleeb (3)
Los Angeles (1)
Marsist, The (3)
Men In Black (3)
Mosh, Don't Pass The Guy (3)
Old Black Dawning (1)
Ole Mulholland (2)
Parry the Wind High, Low (1)
Pie in the Sky (2)
Places Named After Numbers (1)
Punk Rock City (3)
Pure Denizen Of The Citizens Band (2)
Sir Rockaby (2)
Space is Gonna do me Good (2)
Speedy Marie (2)
Superabound (2)
Ten Percenter (1)
Thalassocracy (2)
Tossed (1)
Two Reelers (2)
Two Spaces (1)
Vanishing Spies (2)
Whatever Happened to Pong? (2)
White Noise Maker (2)
You Ain't Me (3)

BLACK, Stanley, and His Orchestra '62

Born on 6/14/13 in London. Pianist/arranger/composer. Wrote many movie scores.

DEBUT	PEAK	WKS	#	Album Title	Sym	$	Label & Number
2/10/62	30	8	1	Exotic Percussion	[I]	$20	London Phase 4 44004
8/18/62	33	10	2	Spain	[I]	$20	London Phase 4 44016
8/10/63	50	4	3	Film Spectacular	[I]	$20	London Phase 4 44025
6/12/65	148	3	4	Music Of A People	[I]	$20	London Phase 4 44060

Adieu Tristesse (1)
And The Angels Sing (4)
Around The World (3)
Ay-Ay-Ay (2)
Babalu (1)
Baia (1)
Big Country (1)
Breakfast At Tiffany's (3)
Bulerias (2)
By The Waters Of Minnetonka (1)
Caravan (1)
Carmen Fantasy (2)
Eili Eili (2)
Estrellita (2)
Exodus (3)
Flamingo (1)
Granada (2)
Hatikvah (4)
Hava Nagila (medley) (4)
Hebrew Melody (4)
Henry V (3)
Hymn To The Sun (1)
Joseph! Joseph! (4)
Jungle Drums (1)
Letter To My Mother (4)
Longest Day (3)
Macarenas (2)
Malaguena (2)
Misirlou (1)
Moon Of Manakoora (1)
Old Devil Moon (1)
Raisins And Almonds (4)
Ritual Fire Dance (2)
Samson And Delilah (2)
Sevillanas (2)
Shema (medley) (4)
Temptation (1)
Tzena Tzena Tzena (4)
Valencia (2)
West Side Story (3)
Yes, My Darling Daughter (4)

BLACK BOX '90

Male Italian dance trio of producer Daniele Davoli and musicians Mirko Limoni and Valerio Semplici. **Martha Wash** is the uncredited lead vocalist.

DEBUT	PEAK	WKS	RIAA	CD	#	Album Title	$	Label & Number
8/11/90	56	61	●	©		Dreamland	$10	RCA 2221

Dreamland
Everybody Everybody *8*
Fantasy
Ghost Box
Hold On
I Don't Know Anybody Else *23*
Open Your Eyes
Ride On Time
Strike It Up *8*

BLACKBYRDS, The '76

R&B group from Washington DC. Core members: **Donald Byrd** (trumpet), Joe Hall (vocals, bass), Kevin Toney (vocals, keyboards) and Keith Killgo (vocals, drums).

DEBUT	PEAK	WKS	RIAA	CD	#	Album Title	Sym	$	Label & Number
6/22/74	96	23		©	1	The Blackbyrds		$15	Fantasy 9444
12/7/74+	30	39		©	2	Flying Start		$15	Fantasy 9472
7/5/75	150	6			3	Cornbread, Earl And Me	[S]	$15	Fantasy 9483
11/22/75+	16	40	●	©	4	City Life		$15	Fantasy 9490
11/27/76+	34	24	●	©	5	Unfinished Business		$15	Fantasy 9518
10/8/77	43	30	●	©	6	Action		$15	Fantasy 9535
1/6/79	159	7			7	Night Grooves	[G]	$15	Fantasy 9570
1/17/81	133	11		©	8	Better Days		$15	Fantasy 9602

All I Ask (4)
April Showers (2)
At The Carnival (3)
Baby, The (2)
Better Days (8)
Blackbyrds' Theme (2)
Candy Store Dilemma (3)
City Life (4)
Cornbread (3)
Courtroom Emotions (3)
Dancin' Dancin' (8)
Do It, Fluid (1,7) *69*
Do It Girl (8)
Do You Wanna Dance? (8)
Don't Know What To Say (8)
Dreaming About You (6)
Enter In (5)
Flyin' High (4) *70*
Funky Junkie (1)
Future Children, Future Hopes (2)
Gut Level (1,7)
Gym Fight (3)
Happy Music (4,7) *19*
Hash And Eggs (4)
Heavy Town (3)
Hot Day Today (1)
I Need You (2)
In Life (5)
Lady (3)
Life Styles (1)
Lonelies For Your Love (8)
Lookin' Ahead (6)
Love Don't Strike Twice (8)
Love Is Love (2)
Love So Fine (4)
Mother/Son Bedroom Talk (3)
Mother/Son Talk (3)
Mother/Son Theme (3)
Mysterious Vibes (6)
One-Eye Two-Step (3)
One-Gun Salute (3)
Party Land (5)
Reggins (1)
Riot (3)
Rock Creek Park (4,7) *93*
Runaway, The (1)
Soft And Easy (6,7)
Something Special (6)
Soulful Source (6)
Spaced Out (2)
Street Games (6)
Summer Love (1)
Supernatural Feeling (6,7)

BLACKBYRDS, The

Thankful 'Bout Yourself (4)	Unfinished Business (5)	What We Have Is Right (8)	Wilford's Gone (3)	You've Got That Something (5)
Time Is Movin' (5) **95**	**Walking In Rhythm** (2,7) **6**	What's On Your Mind (8)	Without Your Love (8)	

★397★   BLACK CROWES, The   '92

Rock group from Atlanta: brothers Chris (vocals) and Rich (guitar) Robinson, Jeff Cease (guitar), Johnny Colt (bass) and Steve Gorman (drums). Marc Ford replaced Cease in late 1991. Eddie Harsch (keyboards) joined in late 1992. Ford left in August 1997. Audley Freed replaced Colt in 1998. Chris Robinson married actress Kate Hudson (daughter of Goldie Hawn) on 12/31/2000.

3/24/90+	4	165	▲5	©	1 Shake Your Money Maker	C:#32/15	$10	Def American 24278
5/30/92	❶1	51	▲2	©	2 The Southern Harmony And Musical Companion		$10	Def American 26916
11/19/94	11	18	●	©	3 Amorica		$10	American 43000
8/10/96	15	14		©	4 Three Snakes And One Charm		$10	American 43082
1/30/99	26	10		©	5 By Your Side		$10	American 69361
7/8/00	143	4		©	6 A Tribute To A Work In Progress...Greatest Hits 1990-1999	[G]	$10	American 63666
7/22/00	64	9	●	©	7 Live At The Greek	[L]	$15	TVT 2140 [2]

JIMMY PAGE & THE BLACK CROWES

5/26/01	20	6		©	8 Lions		$10	V2 27091

Bad Luck Blue Eyes Goodbye (2,6)	Cypress Tree (8)	HorseHead (8)	Nebakanezer (4)	Shapes Of Things To Come (7)	Twice As Hard (1,6)
Ballad In Urgency (3)	Descending (3)	Hotel Illness (2)	No Speak No Slave (2)	She Gave Good Sunflower (3)	Under A Mountain (4)
Better When You're Not Alone (4)	Diamond Ring (5)	How Much For Your Wings? (4)	No Use Lying (8)	**She Talks To Angels** (1,6) **30**	Virtue And Vice (5)
Black Moon Creeping (2)	Downtown Money Waster (3)	In My Time Of Dying (7)	Nobody's Fault But Mine (7)	Sick Again (7)	Welcome To The Goodtimes (5)
Blackberry (4,6)	Evil Eye (4)	**Jealous Again** (1,6) **75**	Nonfiction (3)	Sister Luck (1)	What Is And What Should Never Be (7)
Bring On, Bring On (4)	Girl From A Pawnshop (4)	Kickin' My Heart Around (5,6)	Oh Well (7)	Sloppy Drunk (7)	Whole Lotta Love (7)
By Your Side (5,6)	Go Faster (5,6)	Lay It All On Me (8)	One Mirror Too Many (4)	Sometimes Salvation (2)	Wiser Time (3,6)
Celebration Day (7)	Go Tell The Congregation (5)	Lemon Song (7)	Only A Fool (5,6)	Soul Singing (8)	Woke Up This Morning (7)
Come On (8)	Gone (3)	Let Me Share The Ride (4)	(Only) Halfway To Everywhere (4)	Stare It Cold (1)	You Shook Me (7)
Conspiracy, A (3,6)	Good Friday (4,6)	Lickin' (8)	Out On The Tiles (7)	Sting Me (2,6)	Young Man, Old Man (8)
Cosmic Friend (8)	Greasy Grass River (8)	Losing My Mind (8)	Ozone Mama (8)	Struttin' Blues (1)	Your Time Is Gonna Come (7)
Could I've Been So Blind (1)	**Hard To Handle** (1,6) **26**	Mellow Down Easy (7)	P. 25 London (3)	Ten Years Gone (7)	
Cursed Diamond (3)	Heartbreaker (7)	Midnight From The Inside Out (8)	**Remedy** (2,6) **48**	Then She Said My Name (5)	
Custard Pie (7)	Heavy (5)	Miracle To Me (8)	Seeing Things (1)	Thick N' Thin (1)	
	Hey Hey What Can I Do (7)	My Morning Song (2)	Shake Your Money Maker (7)	**Thorn In My Pride** (2,6) **80**	
	High Head Blues (3)			Time Will Tell (2)	

BLACK EYED PEAS   '00

Rap trio from Los Angeles: Will.I.Am, Alp.De.Ap and Taboo.

7/18/98	129	9		©	1 Behind The Front		$10	Interscope 90152
10/14/00	67	5		©	2 Bridging The Gap		$10	Interscope 490661

A8 (1)	Cali To New York (2)	Get Original (2)	Karma (1)	Positivity (1)	Say Goodbye (1)
Be Free (1)	Clap Your Hands (1)	Go Go (2)	Lil' Lil' (2)	¿Que Dices? (1)	Tell Your Mama Come (2)
Bep Empire (2)	Communication (1)	Head Bobs (1)	Love Won't Wait (1)	Rap Song (2)	Way U Make Me Feel (1)
Bridging The Gaps (2)	Duet (1)	Hot (2)	Movement (1)	Release (2)	Weekends (2)
Bringing It Back (2)	Fallin' Up (1)	Joints & Jam (1)	On My Own (2)	**Request Line** (2) **63**	What It Is (1)

BLACKFOOT   '79

Rock group from Jacksonville, Florida: Rickey Medlocke (vocals), Charlie Hargrett (guitar), Greg Walker (bass) and Jakson Spires (drums). Medlocke and Walker were original members of **Lynyrd Skynyrd** (Medlocke rejoined group in 1995). Hargrett left in 1983. **Ken Hensley** (keyboards; **Uriah Heep**) joined in early 1984.

5/12/79	42	41	▲	©	1 Strikes		$12	Atco 112
6/21/80	50	20		©	2 Tomcattin'		$12	Atco 101
7/25/81	48	12		©	3 Marauder		$12	Atco 107
6/11/83	82	13			4 Siogo		$10	Atco 90080
10/27/84	176	5			5 Vertical Smiles		$10	Atco 90218

Baby Blue (1)	Fire Of The Dragon (3)	Heartbeat And Heels (3)	Morning Dew (5)	Run And Hide (1)	Teenage Idol (4)
Crossfire (4)	**Fly Away** (3) **42**	**Highway Song** (1) **26**	On The Run (2)	Run For Cover (4)	Too Hard To Handle (4)
Diary Of A Workingman (3)	Fox Chase (2)	I Got A Line On You (1)	Pay My Dues (1)	Sail Away (4)	**Train, Train** (1) **38**
Dream On (2)	Get It On (5)	In For The Kill (5)	Payin' For It (3)	Searchin' (3)	Warped (4)
Drivin' Fool (4)	Gimme, Gimme, Gimme (2)	In The Night (2)	Rattlesnake Rock 'N' Roller (3)	Send Me An Angel (4)	We're Goin' Down (4)
Dry County (3)	Goin' In Circles (4)	Left Turn On A Red Light (1)	Reckless Abandoner (2)	Spendin' Cabbage (2)	White Man's Land (4)
Every Man Should Know (Queenie) (2)	Good Morning (3)	Legend Never Dies (5)	Ride With You (5)	Street Fighter (4)	Wishing Well (1)
	Heart's Grown Cold (4)	Livin' In Limelight (5)	Road Fever (1)	Summer Days (5)	Young Girl (5)

BLACK 47   '93

Rock group from Ireland: Larry Kirwan (vocals, guitar), Geoffrey Blythe (saxophone; **Dexys Midnight Runners**), Chris Byrne (pipes), Fred Parcells (trombone), David Conrad (bass) and Thomas Hamlin (drums). Group name stands for the blackest year in the Irish potato famine, 1847.

4/10/93	176	1		©	Fire Of Freedom		$10	SBK 80686

co-produced by **Ric Ocasek**

Banks Of The Hudson	Fanatic Heart	40 Shades Of Blue (3)	James Connolly	Maria's Wedding	Rockin' The Bronx
Black 47	Fire Of Freedom	Funky Ceili (Bridie's Song)	Livin' In America	New York, NY 10009	Sleep Tight In New York City/Her Dear Old Donegal

BLACKHAWK   '95

Country vocal trio: **Henry Paul**, **Van Stephenson** and Dave Robbins. Stephenson died of cancer on 4/8/2001 (age 47).

2/19/94	98	83	▲2	©	1 BlackHawk		$10	Arista 18708
9/30/95	22	32	●	©	2 Strong Enough		$10	Arista 18792
8/16/97	79	9		©	3 Love & Gravity		$10	Arista 18837
10/17/98	192	2		©	4 The Sky's The Limit		$10	Arista 18872
6/3/00	152	3		©	5 Greatest Hits	[G]	$10	Arista 18907

Almost A Memory Now (2,5)	Every Once In A While (1,5)	I'm Not Strong Enough To Say No (2,5)	Last Time (4)	Nobody's Fool (3)	**There You Have It** (4,5) **41**
Always Have, Always Will (4,5)	Goin' Down Fightin' (4)	If That Was A Lie (3)	Let 'Em Whirl (1)	One More Heartache (1)	Think Again (4)
Any Man With A Heartbeat (2)	Goodbye Says It All (1,5)	In My Heart Of Hearts (4)	Like There Ain't No Yesterday (2,5)	Postmarked Birmingham (3,5)	Walkin' On Water (4)
Bad Love Gone Good (2)	Hold Me Harmless (3)	It Ain't About Love Anymore (3)	Lonely Boy (3)	She Dances With Her Shadow (3)	When I Find It, I'll Know It (4)
Between Ragged And Wrong (1)	Hole In My Heart (3)	It Takes A Woman (5)	Love And Gravity (3)	Ships Of Heaven (5)	Who Am I Now (4)
Big Guitar (2,5)	Hook, Line And Sinker (2)	King Of The World (2)	Love Like This (1)	Stepping Stones (4)	Will You Be There (In The Morning) (3)
Cast Iron Heart (2)	I Need You All The Time (5)	Kiss Is Worth A Thousand Words (2)	Nobody Knows What To Say (4)	Stone By Stone (1)	Your Own Little Corner Of My Heart (4)
Down In Flames (1,5)	I Sure Can Smell The Rain (1,5)			That's Just About Right (1,5)	

BLACK IVORY   '72

R&B vocal trio from New York City: Leroy Burgess, Stuart Bascombe and Russell Patterson.

4/22/72	**158**	9	©	**1 Don't Turn Around** .... $15 Today 1005
1/20/73	**188**	9		**2 Baby, Won't You Change Your Mind** .... $15 Today 1008

Baby, Won't You Change Your Mind (2)
Don't Turn Around (1)
Find The One Who Loves You (1)

Got To Be There (1)
I Keep Asking You Questions (1)
I'll Find A Way (1)
If I Could Be A Mirror (1)

Just Leave Me Some (2)
No If's Ands Or Buts (2)
One Way Ticket To Loveland (2)
Our Future (1)

Push Come To Shove (1)
She Said That She's Leaving (1)
Spinning Around (2)
Surrender (1)

Time Is Love (2)
Time To Say Goodbye (2)
Wishful Thinking (2)
You And I (1)

BLACKJACK   '79

Rock group from New York City: Michael Bolotin (vocals), Bruce Kulick (guitar), Jimmy Haslip (bass) and Sandy Gennaro (drums). Haslip joined the **Yellowjackets**. Bolotin began solo career in 1983 as **Michael Bolton**. Kulick joined **Kiss** in 1985.

7/21/79	**127**	7		**Blackjack** .... $12 Polydor 6215

Countin' On You
Fallin'

For You
Heart Of Mine

Heart Of Stone
I'm Aware Of Your Love

Love Me Tonight *62*
Night Has Me Calling For You

Southern Ballad (If This Means) Without Your Love
Losing You)

BLACK MOON   '99

Rap trio from Brooklyn, New York: Kenyatta Blake, 5 Ft. Excellerator and Edward Pewgarde.

4/3/99	**35**	5	©	**War Zone** .... $10 Duck Down 50039

Annihilation
Come Get Some
Duress

Evil Dee Is On The Mix
For All Ya'll
Frame

Freestyle
One-Two
Onslaught, The

Showdown
This Is What It Sounds Like (Worldwind)
War Zone

Throw Your Hands In The Air
Two Turntables & A Mic

Weight Of The World

BLACKMORE, Ritchie — see RAINBOW

BLACK 'N BLUE   '86

Hard-rock group from Portland, Oregon: Jaime St. James (vocals), Tom Thayer and Jeff Warner (guitars), Patrick Young (bass) and Pete Holmes (drums).

9/15/84	**116**	11		**1 Black 'N Blue** .... $10 Geffen 24041
10/25/86	**110**	20		**2 Nasty Nasty** .... $10 Geffen 24111
4/23/88	**133**	9	©	**3 In Heat** .... $10 Geffen 24180

Action (1)
Autoblast (1)
Best In The West (1)
Chains Around Heaven (1)
Do What You Wanna Do (2)

Does She Or Doesn't She (2)
Get Wise To The Rise (3)
Gimme Your Love (3)
Great Guns Of Fire (3)
Heat It Up! Burn It Out! (3)

Hold On To 18 (1)
I Want It All (I Want It Now) (2)
I'll Be There For You (2)
I'm The King (1)
Kiss Of Death (2)

Live It Up (3)
Nasty Nasty (2)
One For The Money (1)
Rock On (3)
Rules (2)

School Of Hard Knocks (1)
Show Me The Night (1)
Sight For Sore Eyes (3)
Snake, The (3)
Stranger (3)

Strong Will Rock (1)
Suspicious (3)
12 O'Clock High (2)
Wicked Bitch (1)

BLACK OAK ARKANSAS   '74

Rock group from Black Oak, Arkansas: Jim "Dandy" Mangrum (vocals), Ricky Reynolds, Jimmy Henderson and Stan Knight (guitars), Pat Daugherty (bass) and Wayne Evans (drums).

1)High On The Hog 2)Street Party 3)Raunch 'N' Roll/Live

8/28/71	**127**	12	● ©	**1 Black Oak Arkansas** .... $15 Atco 354
2/12/72	**103**	10	©	**2 Keep The Faith** .... $15 Atco 381
7/8/72	**93**	19	©	**3 If An Angel Came To See You, Would You Make Her Feel At Home?** .... $15 Atco 7008
3/17/73	**90**	16	● ©	**4 Raunch 'N' Roll/Live** .... [L] $15 Atco 7019
11/24/73+	**52**	22	● ©	**5 High On The Hog** .... $15 Atco 7035
7/27/74	**56**	12	©	**6 Street Party** .... $15 Atco 101
5/31/75	**145**	8	©	**7 Ain't Life Grand** .... $15 Atco 111
10/18/75+	**99**	17		**8 X-Rated** .... $15 MCA 2155
2/28/76	**194**	2	©	**9 Live! Mutha** .... [L] $15 Atco 128

recorded on 5/11/75 at the Long Beach Auditorium in California

6/12/76	**173**	7		**10 Balls Of Fire** .... $15 MCA 2199

Ace In The Hole (8)
All My Troubles (10)
Back Door Man (7)
Back To The Land (9)
Big One's Still Coming (6)
Brink Of Creation (6)
Bump 'N' Grind (8)
Cryin' Shame (7,9)
Dancing In The Streets (6)
Diggin' For Gold (7)
Dixie (6)
Don't Confuse What You Don't Know (2)
Everybody Wants To See Heaven "Nobody Wants To Die" (6)
Fancy Nancy (7,9)

Feet On Earth, Head In Sky (2)
Fertile Woman (3)
Fever In My Mind (2,9)
Fightin' Cock (3)
Fistful Of Love (10)
Flesh Needs Flesh (8)
Full Moon Ride (3)
Gettin' Kinda Cocky (4)
Gigolo (4)
Goin' Home (6)
Good Good Woman (6)
Good Stuff (7)
Gravel Roads (3)
Great Balls Of Fire (10)
Happy Hooker (5)
Hey Ya'll (6,9)
High Flyer (8)

High 'N' Dry (5)
Highway Pirate (8)
Hills Of Arkansas (1)
Hot And Nasty (1,4,9)
Hot Rod (4)
I Can Feel Forever (10)
I Could Love You (1)
I'm A Man (6)
Jail Bait (6)
Jim Dandy (5,9) *25*
Just To Fall In Love (10)
Keep On (7)
Keep The Faith (2)
Leather Angel (10)
Let Life Be Good To You (7)
Lord Have Mercy On My Soul (1,9)

Love Can Be Found (7)
Mad Man (5)
Make That Scene (10)
Memories At The Window (1)
Moonshine Sonata (5)
Movin' (5)
Mutants Of The Monster (3,4)
Our Eyes Ere On You (3)
Our Minds Eye (3)
Ramblin' Gamblin' Man (10)
Rebel (3)
Red Hot Lovin' (5)
Revolutionary All American Boys (2)
Rock 'N' Roll (10)
Short Life Line (2)
Singing The Blues (7)

Son Of A Gun (6)
Spring Vacation (3)
Sting Me (6)
Storm Of Passion (10)
Strong Enough To Be Gentle (8) *89*
Sure Been Workin' Hard (6)
Swimmin' In Quicksand (5)
Taxman (7,9)
To Make Us What We Are (3)
Too Hot To Stop (8)
Uncle Lijiah (1)
Up (4)
We Help Each Other (3)
We Live On Day To Day (2)
When Electricity Came To Arkansas (1,4)

White-Headed Woman (2)
Why Shouldn't I Smile (5)
Wild Men From The Mountains (8)

BLACK PEARL   '69

Rock group formed in San Francisco: Bernie "B.B." Fieldings, Bruce Benson, Jeff Morris, Tom Molcahy and Jerry Causi. Benson, Morris and Causi were members of The Barbarians.

5/3/69	**130**	5		**1 Black Pearl** .... $25 Atlantic 8220
10/17/70	**189**	2		**2 Black Pearl-Live!** .... [L] $25 Prophesy 1001

recorded in October 1968 at the Fillmore West

Bent Over (1)
Climbing Up The Walls (1)
Cold Sweat (2)

Crazy Chicken (1)
Endless Journey (1)
Forget It (1)

Hermit Freak Show (2)
I Get The Blues Most Every Night (2)

Mr. Soul Satisfaction (1)
People Get Ready (2)
Reach Up (1)

Thinkin' 'Bout The Good Times (1)
Uptown (2)

White Devil (1)

BLACK ROB   '00

Born Robert Ross in 1970 in New York City. Male rapper.

3/25/00	**3**	19	▲ ©	**Life Story** .... $10 Bad Boy 73026

B.R.
Can I Live
Down The Line Joint

Espacio
I Dare You
I Love You Baby

Jasmine
Life Story
Lookin' At Us

Muscle Game
Po World Tour
Spanish Fly

Thug Story
Whoa! *43*
You Don't Know Me

BLACK SABBATH ★129★   '71

Hard-rock group from Birmingham, England: **Ozzy Osbourne** (vocals), **Tony Iommi**(guitar), Terry Butler (bass) and William Ward (drums). Osbourne left in 1979, replaced by Ronnie James **Dio** (**Rainbow**). Ward left for a year in 1981, replaced by Vinnie Appice (younger brother of Carmine Appice). In 1983, Ian **Gillan** (**Deep Purple**) replaced Dio who, with Appice, formed Dio. Fluctuating lineup since 1986. Iommi was the only original member in lineups that included vocalists Glenn Hughes (1986; ex-bassist of Deep Purple) and Tony Martin (since 1987); bassists Dave Spitz (1986-87), Bob Daisley (1987), Laurence Cottle (1989) and Neil Murray (since 1990); drummers Eric Singer (1986-87), Bev Bevan (1987; **Move, ELO**) and Cozy Powell (since 1989; **Jeff Beck Group**, **Emerson, Lake & Powell**), and keyboardist Geoff Nicholls (1983-89). Singer later joined **Kiss**. In 1991, reunion of Iommi, Butler, Appice and Dio. Lineup in 1994: Iommi, Butler, Martin, Nichols and Bobby Rondinelli (drums). Powell died in a car crash on 4/5/98 (age 50). Original lineup reunited in 1997.

1)Master Of Reality 2)Sabbath Bloody Sabbath 3)Reunion

8/29/70	23	65	▲	©	1 **Black Sabbath** .... C:#29/29			$20	Warner 1871
2/20/71	12	70	▲⁴	©	2 **Paranoid**			$20	Warner 1887
9/4/71	8	43	▲²	©	3 **Master Of Reality**	C:#6/19		$15	Warner 2562
10/21/72	13	31	▲	©	4 **Black Sabbath, Vol. 4** .... C:#42/2			$15	Warner 2602
1/26/74	11	32	▲	©	5 **Sabbath Bloody Sabbath** .... C:#34/19			$15	Warner 2695
8/23/75	28	14	●	©	6 **Sabotage**			$15	Warner 2822
2/28/76	48	10	▲²	©	7 **We Sold Our Soul For Rock 'N' Roll**		[K]	$20	Warner 2923 [2]
10/30/76	51	12	●	©	8 **Technical Ecstasy**			$15	Warner 2969
10/28/78	69	14	●	©	9 **Never Say Die!**			$12	Warner 3186
6/14/80	28	24	▲	©	10 **Heaven And Hell**			$12	Warner 3372
11/28/81	29	18	●	©	11 **Mob Rules**			$12	Warner 3605
2/5/83	37	12		©	12 **Live Evil**		[L]	$15	Warner 23742 [2]
10/22/83	39	16			13 **Born Again**			$10	Warner 23978
2/15/86	78	11			14 **Seventh Star**			$10	Warner 25337

BLACK SABBATH Featuring Tony Iommi

12/26/87+	168	6		©	15 **The Eternal Idol**			$10	Warner 25548
5/13/89	115	8			16 **Headless Cross**			$10	I.R.S. 82002
7/18/92	44	8			17 **Dehumanizer**			$10	Reprise 26965
2/26/94	122	2		©	18 **Cross Purposes**			$10	I.R.S. 13222
11/7/98	11	18	▲	©	19 **Reunion**		[L]	$15	Epic 69115 [2]

recorded 12/5/97 in Birmingham, England

After All (The Dead) (17)
After Forever (3)
Air Dance (9)
All Moving Parts (Stand Still) (8)
Am I Going Insane (Radio) (6,7)
Ancient Warrior (15)
Angry Heart (14)
Back Street Kids (8)
Back To Eden (18)
Bassically (1)
Behind The Wall Of Sleep (1,19)
Bit Of Finger (1)
Black Moon (16)
Black Sabbath (1,7,12,19)
Born Again (13)
Born To Lose (15)
Breakout (9)
Buried Alive (17)
Call Of The Wild (16)
Cardinal Sin (18)
Changes (4,7)
Children Of The Grave (3,7,12,19)
Children Of The Sea (10,12)

Computer God (17)
Cornucopia (17)
Country Girl (11)
Cross Of Thorns (18)
Danger Zone (14)
Dark, The (13)
Devil And Daughter (16)
Die Young (10)
Digital Bitch (13)
Dirty Women (8,19)
Disturbing The Priest (13)
Don't Start (Too Late) (6)
Dying For Love (18)
E5I50 (11,12)
Electric Funeral (2)
Embryo (3)
Eternal Idol (15)
Every Day Comes And Goes (medley) (4)
Evil Eye (18)
FX (4)
Fairies Wear Boots (2,7,19)
Falling Off The Edge Of The World (11)
Fluff (5,12)
Gates Of Hell (16)

Glory Ride (15)
Gypsy (8)
Hand Of Doom (2)
Hand That Rocks The Cradle (18)
Hard Life To Love (15)
Hard Road (9)
Headless Cross (16)
Heart Like A Wheel (14)
Heaven And Hell (10,19)
Hole In The Sky (6)
Hot Line (13)
I (17)
I Witness (18)
Immaculate Deception (18)
In For The Kill (14)
In Memory... (14)
Into The Void (3,19)
Iron Man (2,7,12,19) *52*
It's Alright (8)
Jack The Stripper (medley) (2)
Johnny Blade (9)
Junior's Eyes (9)
Keep It Warm (13)
Kill In The Spirit World (16)
Killing Yourself To Live (5)

Lady Evil (10)
Laguna Sunrise (4,7)
Letters From Earth (17)
Lonely Is The Word (10)
Looking For Today (5)
Lord Of This World (3,19)
Lost Forever (15)
Luke's Wall (medley) (2)
Master Of Insanity (17)
Megalomania (6)
Mob Rules (11,12)
N.I.B. (1,7,12,19)
National Acrobat (5)
Neon Knights (10,12)
Never Say Die (9)
Nightmare (15)
Nightwing (16)
No Stranger To Love (14)
Orchid (3,19)
Over And Over (11)
Over To You (9)
Paranoid (2,7,12,19) *61*
Planet Caravan (2)
Psycho Man (19)
Psychophobia (18)
Rat Salad (2)

Rock 'N' Roll Doctor (8)
Sabbath, Bloody Sabbath (5,7,19)
Sabbra Cadabra (5)
Scarlet Pimpernel (15)
Selling My Soul (19)
Seventh Star (14)
She's Gone (8)
Shining, The (15)
Shock Wave (9)
Sign Of The Southern Cross (11,12)
Sins Of The Father (17)
Sleeping Village (1)
Slipping Away (11)
Snowblind (4,7,19)
Solitude (3)
Sphinx (The Guardian) (14)
Spiral Architect (5,19)
St. Vitus' Dance (4)
Stonehenge (13)
Supernaut (4)
Supertzar (8)
Sweet Leaf (3,7,19)
Swinging The Chain (9)
Symptom Of The Universe (6)

TV Crimes (17)
Thrill Of It All (16)
Time Machine (17)
Tomorrow's Dream (4,7)
Too Late (17)
Trashed (13)
Turn To Stone (14)
Turn Up The Night (11)
Under The Sun (medley) (4)
Virtual Death (18)
Voodoo (11,12)
Walk Away (10)
War Pigs (2,7,12,19)
Warning (1,7)
Wasp (1)
Wheels Of Confusion (4)
When Death Calls (16)
Who Are You? (5)
Wicked World (1)
Wishing Well (10)
Wizard, The (1,7)
Writ, The (6)
You Won't Change Me (8)
Zero The Hero (13)

BLACK SHEEP   '92

Rap duo from the Bronx, New York: Andre Titus and William McLean.

| 11/9/91+ | 30 | 41 | ● | © | 1 **A Wolf In Sheep's Clothing** .... | | | $10 | Mercury 848368 |
| 12/24/94 | 107 | 3 | | © | 2 **Non-Fiction** | | | $10 | Mercury 522685 |

Are You Mad? (1)
Autobiographical (2)
B.B.S. (1)
Black With N.V. (No Vision) (1)
Blunted 10 (1)
Butt In The Meantime (1)

Choice Is Yours (1) *57*
City Lights (2)
Do Your Thing (2)
E.F.F.E.C.T. (2)
Flavor Of The Month (1)
For Doz That Slept (1)

Freak Y'All (2)
Gimme The Finga (1)
Go To Hail (1)
Gotta Get Up (2)
Have U.N.E. Pull (1)
Hoes We Knows (1)

L.A.S.M. (1)
La Menage (1)
Let's Get Cozy (2)
Me & My Brother (2)
North South East West (2)
Pass The 40 (1)

Peace To The Niggas (2)
Similak Child (1)
Strobelite Honey (1) *80*
Summa Tha Time (2)
To Whom It May Concern (1)
Try Counting Sheep (1)

U Mean I'm Not (1)
We Boys (2)
Who's Next? (2)
Without A Doubt (2)
Yes (1)

BLACK STAR   '98

Rap duo from New York City: **Mos Def** and **Talib Kweli**.

| 10/17/98 | 53 | 5 | | © | **Black Star** .... | | | $10 | Rawkus 1158 |

MOS DEF & TALIB KWELI ARE BLACK STAR

Astronomy (8th Light)
B Boys Will Be Boys

Brown Skin Lady
Children's Story

Definition *60*
Hater Players

K.O.S. (Determination)
RE: DEFinition

Respiration
Thieves In The Night

Twice Inna Lifetime
Yo Yeah

BLACKSTREET   '96

R&B vocal group: Teddy Riley, Chauncey Hannibal, Levi Little and **Dave Hollister**. Riley was a member of **Guy**. Hollister and Little left in late 1995, replaced by Eric Williams and Mark Middleton.

7/9/94	52	51	▲	©	1 **Blackstreet**			$10	Interscope 92351
9/28/96	3	60	▲⁴	©	2 **Another Level**			$10	Interscope 90071
4/10/99	9	12	●	©	3 **Finally**			$10	Lil' Man 90274

Baby Be Mine (1)
Before I Let You Go (1) *7*
Black & White (3)
BLACKstreet (On The Radio) (2)

Booti Call (1) *34*
Can You Feel Me (3)
Don't Leave Me (2)
Drama (3)
Falling In Love Again (1)

Finally (3)
Fix (2) *58*
Girlfriend/Boyfriend (3) *47*
Givin' You All My Lovin' (1)
Good Life (1)

Good Lovin' (2)
Happy Home (1)
Happy Song (Tonite) (2)
Hustler's Prayer (3)

I Can't Get You (Out Of My Mind) (1)
I Got What You On (3)
I Like The Way You Work (1)
I Wanna Be Your Man (2)

I'll Give It To You (3)
I'm Sorry (3)
In A Rush (3)
Joy (1) *43*
Let's Stay In Love (2)

BLACKSTREET — Cont'd

Lord Is Real (Time Will Reveal) (2)
Love's In Need (1)
Make U Wet (1)
(Money Can't) Buy Me Love (2)
Motherlude (2)
My Paradise (2)
Never Gonna Let Me Go (2)
No Diggity (2) *1*
On The Floor (3)
Physical Thing (1)
Take Me There (3) *14*
Think About You (3)
This Is How We Roll (2)
Tonight's The Night (1) *80*
U Blow My Mind (1)
Wanna Make Love (1)
Yo Love (3)

BLACK UHURU '90

Reggae vocal trio from Jamaica: Don Carlos, Duckie Simpson and Garth Dennis. Carlos and Dennis left in 1977, Michael Rose and female vocalist Puma Jones joined. Rose and Jones left in 1985, Delroy Reid and Janet Reid were added. Carlos, Simpson and Dennis reunited in 1987. Uhuru means freedom in Swahili.

7/24/82	146	7	©	1	Chill Out			$10	Island 9752
3/10/90	121	11	©	2	Now			$10	Mesa 79021

Army Band (2)
Chill Out (1)
Darkness (1)
Emotional Slaughter (1)
Eye Market (1)
Fleety Foot (1)
Freedom Fighter (2)
Heathen (2)
Hey Joe (1)
Imposter (2)
Mondays (1)
Moya (Queen Of I Jungle) (1)
Peace And Love (2)
Reggae Rock (2)
Right Stuff (1)
Take Heed (2)
Thinking About You (2)
Wicked Act (1)
Word Sound (1)

BLADES, Ruben '88

Born on 7/16/48 in Panama City, Panama. Latin singer/actor. Appeared in several movies.

5/7/88	156	6	©		Nothing But The Truth			$10	Elektra 60754

Calm Before The Storm
Chameleons
Hit, The
Hopes On Hold
I Can't Say
In Salvador
Letter, The
Letters To The Vatican
Miranda Syndrome
Ollie's Doo-Wop
Shamed Into Love

BLANCHARD, Jack, & Misty Morgan '70

Husband-and-wife country duo. Both born in Buffalo. Jack (b: 5/8/42) plays saxophone and keyboards. Misty (b: 5/23/45) plays keyboards. Met and married while working in Florida.

7/4/70	185	5			Birds Of A Feather			$15	Wayside 001

Bethlehem Steel
Big Black Bird (Spirit Of My Love)
Changin' Times
Chapel Hill
Clock Of St. James
Dum Song
Humphrey The Camel *78*
Poor Jody
Tennessee Bird Walk *23*
With Pen In Hand
Yellow Bellied Sapsucker
You've Got Your Troubles (I've Got Mine)

BLAND, Bobby '63

Born on 1/27/30 in Rosemark, Tennessee. Blues singer/guitarist. Nicknamed "Blue." Inducted into the Rock and Roll Hall of Fame in 1992.

1)Call On Me/That's The Way Love Is 2)Together For The First Time...Live 3)Here's The Man!!!

9/1/62	53	7		1	Here's The Man!!!			$100	Duke 75
7/13/63	11	26		2	Call On Me/That's The Way Love Is			$100	Duke 77
8/1/64	119	8		3	Ain't Nothing You Can Do			$100	Duke 78
11/3/74+	136	19	©	4	His California Album			$15	Dunhill/ABC 50163
					BOBBY BLUE BLAND				
8/3/74	172	7	©	5	Dreamer			$15	Dunhill/ABC 50169
10/26/74+	43	20	● ©	6	Together For The First Time...Live		[L]	$20	Dunhill/ABC 50190 [2]
					B.B. KING & BOBBY BLAND				
9/13/75	154	5	©	7	Get On Down With Bobby Bland			$12	ABC 895
7/17/76	73	14	©	8	Together Again...Live		[L]	$12	ABC/Impulse 9317
					BOBBY BLAND & B.B. KING				
5/14/77	185	4	©	9	Reflections In Blue			$12	ABC 1018
7/1/78	185	3		10	Come Fly With Me			$12	ABC 1075
10/27/79	187	2		11	I Feel Good, I Feel Fine			$12	MCA 3157

After It's Too Late (3)
Ain't God Something (10)
Ain't It A Good Thing (2)
Ain't No Love In The Heart Of The City (5) *91*
Ain't Nothing You Can Do (3) *20*
Ain't That Loving You (1) *86*
Black Night (3,6) *99*
Blind Man (3) *78*
Blues In The Night (1)
Bobby's Blues (2)
Call On Me (2) *22*
Care For Me (2)
Chains Of Love (medley) (6)
Cherry Red (medley) (6)
Cold Day In Hell (6)
Come Fly With Me (10)
Cry, Lover, Cry (2)
Don't Answer The Door (6)
Don't Cry No More (6)
Dreamer (5)
Driftin' Blues (6)
Driving Wheel (medley) (6)
End Of The Road (5)
Everyday (I Have The Blues) (8)
Feel So Bad (8)
Feeling Is Gone (2) *91*
Five Long Years (8)
Friday The 13th Child (4)
Goin' Down Slow (4,6) *69*
Gonna Get Me An Old Woman (medley) (6)
Good To Be Back Home (medley) (6)
Help Me Through The Day (4)
Honky Tonk (2)
I Ain't Gonna Be The First To Cry (5,8)
I Can't Take No Mo' (11)
I Feel Good, I Feel Fine (11)
I Got The Same Old Blues (9)
I Hate You (7)
I Intend To Take Your Place (9)
I Like To Live The Love (6)
I Take It On Home (7)
I Wouldn't Treat A Dog (The Way You Treated Me) (5) *88*
I'll Be Your Fool Once More (9)
I'll Take Care Of You (6)
I'm Gonna Cry (3)
I'm Just Your Man (10)
I'm Sorry (6)
I've Got To Use My Imagination (4)
If Fingerprints Showed Up On Skin (7)
If I Hadn't Called You Back (3)
If I Weren't A Gambler (9)
(If Loving You Is Wrong) I Don't Want To Be Right (4)
If You Could Read My Mind (3)
In His Eyes (11)
It Ain't The Real Thing (9)
It's All Over (9)
It's My Own Fault (6)
It's Not The Spotlight (4)
Jelly Jelly (11)
Lady Lonely (10)
Let The Good Times Roll (8)
Little Mama (11)
Loneliness Hurts (3)
Love To See You Smile (10)
Lovin' On Borrowed Time (5)
Mean Old World (8)
Mother-In-Law Blues (medley) (8)
Night Games (10)
No Sweeter Girl (2)
Presenting Dynamic Bobby Bland 36-22-36 (1)
Queen For A Day (2)
Reconsider (3)
Red Sails In The Sunset (11)
Right Place At The Right Time (4)
Rock Me Baby (medley) (6)
Share Your Love With Me (2) *42*
Sittin' On A Poor Man's Throne (9)
Someone To Belong To (11)
Someone To Give My Love To (7)
Soon As The Weather Breaks (11)
Soul Of A Man (9)
Steal Away (3)
Stormy Monday Blues (1,8) *43*
Strange Things Happen (medley) (8)
That's The Way Love Is (2,6) *33*
This Bitter Earth (10)
This Time I'm Gone For Good (4) *42*
3 O'Clock Blues (6)
Thrill Is Gone (medley) (8)
Tit For Tat (11)
To Be Friends (10)
Today (3)
Today I Started Loving You Again (7)
Too Far Gone (7)
Turn On Your Love Light (1) *28*
Twenty-Four Hour Blues (5)
Twistin' Up The Road (1)
Up And Down World (4)
When You Put Me Down (3)
Where Baby Went (4)
Who Will The Next Fool Be (1) *76*
Who's Foolin' Who (5)
Why I Sing The Blues (6)
Wishing Well (2)
Worried Life Blues (medley) (6)
Yolanda (5)
You Can Count On Me (10)
You're Gonna Love Yourself (In The Morning) (7)
You're The One (That I Adore) (1)
You're Worth It All (1)
You've Always Got The Blues (7)
You've Never Been This Far Before (7)
Your Friends (1)

BLAQUE '00

Female R&B vocal trio from Atlanta: Shamari Fears, Natina Reed and Brandi Williams.

6/19/99+	53	54	▲ ©		Blaque			$10	Track Masters 68987

Bring It All To Me *5*
Don't Go Looking For Love
808 *8*
I Do
Leny
Mind Of A King
Rainbow Drive
Release Me
Right Next To Me
Roll With Me
Stay By Your Side
Time After Time
When The Last Teardrop Falls

BLASTERS, The '82

Rock group from Los Angeles: brothers Phil (vocals, guitar) and **Dave Alvin** (guitar), Gene Taylor (piano), John Bazz (bass), and Bill Bateman (drums).

1/9/82	36	30	©	1	The Blasters			$10	Slash 3680
10/30/82	117	8		2	Over There-Live At The Venue, London		[L-M]	$10	Slash 23735
					recorded on 5/22/82				
5/14/83	95	8		3	Non Fiction			$10	Slash 23818
3/23/85	86	19		4	Hard Line			$10	Slash 25093

BLASTERS, The — Cont'd

American Music (1)	Dark Night (4)	Hollywood Bed (1)	Keep A Knockin' (2)	One More Dance (3)	Stop The Clock (1)
Barefoot Rock (3)	Fool's Paradise (3)	I Don't Want To (2)	Leaving (3)	Red Rose (3)	Tag Along (3)
Boomtown (3)	Go, Go, Go (2)	I Love You So (1)	Little Honey (4)	Rock And Roll Will Stand (4)	This Is It (1)
Border Radio (1)	Help You Dream (4)	I'm Shakin' (1)	Long White Cadillac (3)	Rock Boppin' Baby (2)	Trouble Bound (4)
Bus Station (3)	Hey, Girl (4)	It Must Be Love (3)	Marie Marie (1)	Roll 'Em Pete (2)	
Colored Lights (4)	High School Confidential (2)	Jubilee Train (3)	Never No More Blues (1)	Samson And Delilah (4)	
Common Man (4)	Highway 61 (1)	Just Another Sunday (4)	No Other Girl (1)	So Long Baby Goodbye (1)	

B-LEGIT '96

Born Brandt Jones in San Francisco. Male rapper. Member of **The Click**. Cousin of **E-40**.

12/14/96	55	10	©	1	The Hemp Museum			$10	Sick Wid' It 41593
9/30/00	64	6	©	2	Hempin' Ain't Easy			$10	Koch 8167

Blaze It (2)	Destiny (2)	Gotta Buy Your Dope From Us	I'm Dyin' With Mine (2)	Rap Star (2)	Where The Gangstas At (2)
Can My Nine Get Ate (1)	For So Long (1)	(1)	It's In The Game (2)	Rollin' Wit Hustlers (1)	World Is A Mutha (2)
Check It Out (1)	Game Is Cold (2)	Grape Vine (2)	Keep It P.I. (2)	Scared Man (2)	
City 2 City (1)	Get's Down Like That (1)	Hard Head Nigga (2)	My Flow Of Cash (1)	To All My Playaz (2)	
D-Boy Blues (1	Ghetto Smile (1)	Hemp Museum (1)	Neva Bite (2)	Touch You There (2)	
)	Gold Ones (2)	Hood Ratz & Knuckle Heads (2)	Niggaz Get They Wig Split (1)	What They Talkin' 'Bout (2)	

BLESSID UNION OF SOULS '95

Pop group from Cincinnati: Eliot Sloan (vocals), Jeff Pence (guitar), Charly Roth (keyboards), Tony Clark (bass) and Eddie Hedges (drums).

4/22/95	78	29	●	©	1	Home			$10	EMI 31836
6/7/97	127	10		©	2	Blessid Union Of Souls			$10	EMI 56716
6/5/99	143	15		©	3	Walking Off The Buzz			$10	Push 27047
3/17/01	178	1		©	4	The Singles	[G]	$10	V2 27086

All Along (1,4) 70	Hey Leonardo (she likes me	It's Your Day (Bronson's Song)	Nora (1)	South Hampton Avenue (3)	What Have I Got To Lose (3)
...And Then She Hit Me (4)	for me) (3,4) 33	(2)	Oh Virginia (1,4)	Standing At The Edge Of The	When She Comes (2)
Brother My Brother (4)	Hold Her Closer (2)	Jelly (2)	Peace And Love (2)	Earth (3,4)	Where We Were Before (2)
End Of The World (2)	Home (1)	Last Day (3)	Real Good Friends (3)	Stone Glass Window (3)	Would You Be There (1)
Forever For Tonight (1)	Humble Star (2)	Let Me Be The One (1,4) 29	Rest Of My Life (4)	Storybook Life (4)	
Heaven (1)	I Believe (1,4) 8	Light In Your Eyes (2,4) 48	Rev It Up (NASCAR Rocks) (4)	That's The Girl I've Been Telling	
	I Wanna Be There (2,4) 39	Lucky To Be Here (1)	Scenes From A Coffee House	You About (3,4)	
	If She Couldn't Sleep (3)	My Friend (2)	(You'll Always Be Mine) (2)	Walking Off The Buzz (3)	

BLESSING, Adam — see DAMNATION OF

BLIGE, Mary J. '97

Born Mary Jane Blige on 1/11/71 in Atlanta; raised in Yonkers, New York. R&B singer.

8/15/92	6	58	▲³	©	1	What's The 411?			$10	Uptown 10681
12/25/93+	118	14	●	©	2	What's The 411? Remix	[K]	$10	Uptown 10942
12/17/94+	7	46	▲³	©	3	My Life			$10	Uptown 11156
5/10/97	❶¹	57	▲³	©	4	Share My World			$10	MCA 11606
8/15/98	21	12	●	©	5	The Tour	[L]	$10	MCA 11848
9/4/99	2¹	57	▲²	©	6	Mary			$10	MCA 11929

All That I Can Say (6) 44	Everything (4,5) 24	I'm The Only Woman (3,5)	Memories (6)	Reminisce (1,2,5) 57	What's The 411? (1,2)
Be Happy (3) 29	Get To Know You Better (4)	It's On (4)	Missing You (4,5)	Round And Round (4)	You Bring Me Joy (3) 57
Be With You (3)	Give Me You (6) 68	Keep Your Head (4,5)	Misty Blue (5)	Searching (4)	You Don't Have To Worry
Beautiful Ones (6)	I Can Love You (4,5) 28	Leave A Message (1,2)	My Life (3,5)	Seven Days (4,5)	(2) 63
Can't Get You Off My Mind (4)	I Don't Want To Do Anything	Let No Man Put Asunder (6)	My Love (1,2)	Sexy (6)	You Gotta Believe (3,5)
Changes I've Been Going	(1,2)	Love I Never Had (4)	No Happy Holidays (6)	Share My World (4,5)	You Remind Me (1,2,5) 29
Through (1,2)	I Love You (3) 65	Love Is All We Need (4)	No One Else (4)	Slow Down (1,5)	Your Child (6)
Day Dreaming (5)	I Never Wanna Live Without	Love No Limit (1,2,5) 44	Not Gon' Cry (4,5) 2	Summer Madness (5)	
Deep Inside (6) 63	You (3)	Mary & Andre (2)	Not Lookin' (6)	Sweet Thing (1,2,5) 28	
Don't Go (3)	I'm Goin' Down (3,5) 22	Mary Jane (All Night Long) (3,5)	Our Love (4)	Thank You Lord (5)	
Don't Waste Your Time (6)	I'm In Love (6)	Mary's Joint (3,5)	Real Love (1,2,5) 7	Time (6)	

BLIND FAITH '69

Rock supergroup from England: **Eric Clapton** (**The Yardbirds**, **Cream**), **Steve Winwood** (**Spencer Davis Group**, **Traffic**), **Ginger Baker** (**Cream**) and **Rick Grech** (**Family**, **Traffic**). Formed and disbanded in 1969.

8/16/69	❶²	37	▲	©	1	Blind Faith			$25	Atco 304
						original cover depicted a prepubescent nude girl; quickly withdrawn and replaced by a photo of the band
2/26/77	126	8		©	2	Blind Faith	[R]	$15	RSO 3016
						re-issued with the original, controversial cover

Can't Find My Way Home (1,2)	Do What You Like (1,2)	Had To Cry Today (1,2)	Presence Of The Lord (1,2)	Sea Of Joy (1,2)	Well All Right (1,2)

BLIND MELON '93

Male rock group formed in Los Angeles: Shannon Hoon (vocals), Rogers Stevens and Christopher Thorn (guitars), Brad Smith (bass) and Glen Graham (drums). Stevens, Smith and Graham are from West Point, Mississippi. Hoon died of a drug overdose on 10/21/95 (age 28).

7/24/93	3	44	▲⁴	©	1	Blind Melon			$10	Capitol 96585
9/2/95	28	9		©	2	Soup			$10	Capitol 28732
11/30/96	161	1		©	3	Nico	[K]	$10	Capitol 37451
						recordings from 1991-95

All That I Need (3)	Dumptruck (2)	Lemonade (2)	Pull (3)	Soup (3)	Vernie (2)
Car Seat (God's Presents) (2)	Galaxie (2)	Letters From A Porcupine (3)	Pusher, The (3)	St. Andrew's Fall (2,3)	Walk (2)
Change (1)	Glitch (3)	Life Ain't So Shitty (3)	Seed to a Tree (1)	Swallowed (3)	Wilt (2)
Dear Ol' Dad (1)	Hell (3)	Mouthful Of Cavities (3)	Skinned (2)	Time (1)	
Deserted (1)	Holyman (1)	New Life (2)	Sleephouse (1)	Toes Across The Floor (2)	
Drive (1)	I Wonder (1)	No Rain (1,3) 20	Soak The Sin (1)	Tones Of Home (1)	
Duke, The (2)	John Sinclair (3)	Paper Scratcher (1)	Soul One (3)	2 X 4 (2)	

BLINK 182 '01

Rock trio from San Diego: Mark Hoppus (vocals, bass), Tom Delonge (guitar) and Scott Raynor (drums). Travis Barker (formerly of **The Aquabats**) replaced Raynor in late 1998.

7/5/97+	67	48	▲	©	1	Dude Ranch	C:#27/7	$10	MCA 11624
6/19/99	9	86	▲⁵	©	2	Enema Of The State	C:#6/16	$10	MCA 11950
11/25/00	8	17	●	©	3	The Mark, Tom, And Travis Show (The Enema Strikes Back!)	[L]	$10	MCA 112379
6/30/01	❶¹	14↑	▲	©	4	Take Off Your Pants And Jacket			$10	MCA 112627

BLINK 182 — Cont'd

Adam's Song (2,3)
Aliens Exist (2,3)
All The Small Things (2,3) *6*
Anthem (2,4)
Apple Shampoo (1)
Blew Job (3)
Boring (1)
Carousel (3)

Country Song (3)
Dammit (1,3)
Degenerate (1)
Dick Lips (1)
Don't Leave Me (2,3)
Dumpweed (2,3)
Dysentery Gary (2)
Emo (1)

Enthused (1)
Everytime I Look For You (4)
Family Reunion (3)
First Date (4)
Give Me One Good Reason (4)
Going Away To College (2,3)
Happy Holidays, You Bastard (4)

I'm Sorry (1)
Josie (1)
Lemmings (1)
Man Overboard (3)
Mutt (2,3)
New Hope (1)
Online Songs (4)
Party Song (2)

Pathetic (1,3)
Peggy Sue (3)
Please Take Me Home (4)
Reckless Abandon (4)
Rich Lips (3)
Rock Show (4)
Roller Coaster (4)
Shut Up (4)

Stay Together For The Kids (4)
Story Of A Lonely Guy (4)
Untitled (1,3)
Voyeur (1,3)
Waggy (1)
Wendy Clear (2,3)
What's My Age Again?
(2,3) *58*

BLODWYN PIG '70

Rock group from England: Mick Abrahams (vocals, guitar; **Jethro Tull**), Jack Lancaster (sax), Andy Pyle (bass) and Ron Berg (drums).

12/13/69+	149	5		© 1	Ahead Rings Out			$15	A&M 4210
6/27/70	96	5		© 2	Getting To This			$15	A&M 4243

Ain't Ya Coming Home? (1)
Backwash (1)
Change Song (1)
Dear Jill (1)

Drive Me (2)
It's Only Love (1)
Long Bomb Blues (2)
Meanie Mornay (2)

Modern Alchemist (1)
San Francisco Sketches Medley (2)
See My Way (1)

Send Your Son To Die (2)
Squirreling Must Go On (2)
Summer Day (1)
Toys (2)

Variations On Nainos (2)
Walk On The Water (1)
Worry (2)

★465★ BLONDIE '79

Pop-rock group formed in New York City: **Debbie Harry** (vocals), Chris Stein and Frank Infante (guitars), Jimmy Destri (keyboards), Nigel Harrison (bass) and Clem Burke (drums). Harry had been in the folk-rock group **The Wind In The Willows**. Group disbanded in 1982; reunited in 1999.

2/25/78	72	17		© 1	Plastic Letters			$12	Chrysalis 1166
9/23/78+	6	103	▲	© 2	Parallel Lines			$12	Chrysalis 1192
10/20/79	17	51	▲	© 3	Eat To The Beat			$12	Chrysalis 1225
12/13/80+	7	34	▲	© 4	Autoamerican			$12	Chrysalis 1290
10/31/81	30	23	▲	© 5	The Best Of Blondie ....C:#13/25		[G]	$12	Chrysalis 1337
6/19/82	33	12		© 6	The Hunter			$12	Chrysalis 1384
3/13/99	18	15		© 7	No Exit			$10	Beyond 78003

Accidents Never Happen (3)
Angels On The Balcony (4)
Atomic (3,5) *39*
Beast, The (6)
Bermuda Triangle Blues (Flight 45) (1)
Boom Boom In The Zoom Zoom Room (7)
Call Me (5) *1*
(Can I) Find The Right Words (To Say) (6)
Cautious Lip (1)
Contact In Red Square (1)
Danceway (1)
Denis (1)

Detroit 442 (1)
Die Young Stay Pretty (3)
Dig Up The Conjo (7)
Divine (1)
Do The Dark (4)
Double Take (7)
Dragonfly (6)
Dream's Lost On Me (7)
Eat To The Beat (3)
11:59 (2)
English Boys (6)
Europa (4)
Faces (4)
Fade Away And Radiate (2)

Fan Mail (1)
Follow Me (4)
For Your Eyes Only (6)
Forgive And Forget (7)
Go Through It (4)
Hanging On The Telephone (2,5)
Happy Dog (7)
Hardest Part (3) *84*
Heart Of Glass (2,5) *1*
Here's Looking At You (4)
Hunter Gets Captured By The Game (6)
I Didn't Have The Nerve To Say No (1)

I Know But I Don't Know (2)
(I'm Always Touched By Your) Presence, Dear (1,5)
I'm Gonna Love You Too (2)
I'm On E (1)
In The Flesh (5)
Island Of Lost Souls (6) *37*
Just Go Away (2)
Kidnapper (1)
Little Caesar (6)
Live It Up (4)
Living In The Real World (3)
Love At The Pier (1)
Maria (7) *82*
Night Wind Sent (7)

No Exit (7)
No Imagination (1)
Nothing Is Real But The Girl (7)
One Way Or Another (2,5) *24*
Orchid Club (6)
Out In The Streets (7)
Picture This (1)
Pretty Baby (2)
Rapture (4,5) *1*
Rip Her To Shreds (5)
Screaming Skin (7)
Shayla (3)
Slow Motion (3)
Sound-A-Sleep (3)
Sunday Girl (2,5)

T-Birds (4)
Tide Is High (4,5) *1*
Under The Gun (7)
Union City Blue (3)
Victor (3)
Walk Like Me (4)
War Child (6)
Will Anything Happen? (2)
Youth Nabbed As Sniper (1)

BLOODHOUND GANG '00

Rock group from Philadelphia: Jimmy Pop Ali (vocals), Lupus (guitar), Q-Ball (DJ), Evil Jared (bass) and Spanky G (drums).

1/18/97	57	26	●	© 1	One Fierce Beer Coaster			$10	Geffen 25124
3/18/00	14	29	▲	© 2	Hooray For Boobies			$10	Republic 490455

Along Comes Mary (2)
Asleep At The Wheel (1)
Bad Touch (2) *52*
Ballad Of Chasey Lain (2)
Boom (1)
Fire Water Burn (1)
Going Nowhere Slow (1)

Hell Yeah (2)
I Hope You Die (2)
I Wish I Was Queer So I Could Get Chicks (1)
Inevitable Return Of The Great White Dope (2)
It's Tricky (1)

Kiss Me Where It Smells Funny (1)
Lap Dance Is So Much Better When The Stripper Is Crying (2)
Lift Your Head Up High (And Blow Your Brains Out) (1)

Magna Cum Nada (2)
Mama's Boy (2)
Mope (2)
R.S.V.P. (2)
Right Turn Clyde (2)
Shut Up (1)
Take The Long Way Home (2)

Ten Coolest Things About New Jersey (2)
That Cough Came With A Prize (2)
This Is Stupid (2)
Three Point One Four (2)

Why's Everybody Always Pickin' On Me? (1)
Your Only Friends Are Make Believe (1)
Yummy Down On This (2)

BLOODROCK '71

Rock group from Fort Worth, Texas: Jim Rutledge (vocals), Lee Pickens and Nick Taylor (guitars), Stevie Hill (keyboards), Eddie Grundy (bass) and Rick Cobb (drums). Rutledge left in 1972, replaced by Warren Ham. Rutledge headed own production company in the 1970s; produced Meri Wilson's 1977 Hot 100 hit "Telephone Man."

4/25/70	160	5		© 1	Bloodrock			$20	Capitol 435
11/7/70+	21	37	●	© 2	Bloodrock 2			$20	Capitol 491
4/10/71	27	23		3	Bloodrock 3			$20	Capitol 765
11/6/71	88	7		4	Bloodrock U.S.A.			$20	Capitol 645
6/3/72	67	22		5	Bloodrock Live		[L]	$25	Capitol 11038 [2]
					recorded at the Chicago Ampitheater				
9/30/72	104	14		6	Bloodrock Passage			$20	Capitol 11109

Abracadaver (4)
America, America (3)
American Burn (4)
Breach Of Lease (3,5)
Castle Of Thoughts (1,5)
Certain Kind (3)
Cheater (2,5)
Children's Heritage (2)

Crazy 'Bout You Babe (4)
D.O.A. (2,5) *36*
Days And Nights (6)
Dier Not A Lover (2)
Don't Eat The Children (4)
Double Cross (1)
Fallin' (2)
Fancy Space Odyssey (2)

Fantastic Piece Of Architecture (1)
Fantasy (6)
Fatback (1)
Gimme Your Head (1)
Gotta Find A Way (1,5)
Hangman's Dance (4)
Help Is On The Way (6)

It's A Sad World (4)
Jessica (3,5)
Juice (6)
Kool-Aid-Kids (3,5)
Life Blood (6)
Lost Fame (6)
Lucky In The Morning (2,5)
Magic Man (4)

Melvin Laid An Egg (1)
Power, The (6)
Promises (4)
Rock & Roll Candy Man (4)
Sable And Pearl (2)
Scottsman (6)
Song For A Brother (3)
Thank You Daniel Ellsberg (6)

Timepiece (1)
Whiskey Vengeance (3)
Wicked Truth (1)
You Gotta Roll (3,5)

BLOODS & CRIPS '93

Rap group from Los Angeles made up of members of two rival street gangs. Features a revolving lineup of rappers.

3/27/93	86	19		© 1	Bangin On Wax			$10	Dangerous 19138
10/8/94	139	4		© 2	Bangin On Wax 2...the saga continues			$10	Dangerous 6715

Another Slob Bites The Dust (1)
Bangin' On Wax (1)
Brothers To Brothers (2)
C-K Ride (1)
C-Sick (1)

Can't Stop, Won't Stop (2)
Crip, Crip, Crip (1)
Crip 4 Life (2)
Crippin' Aint Easy (1)
East Side Rip Rider (2)

Every Dog Has His Day (2)
Gangsta Shit (2)
Gangsta Talk (1)
Gs & LOC's (2)
I Killed Ya Dead Homies (1)

K's Up (1)
Mackin' To Slob Bitches (1)
Mafia Lane (2)
No Way Out (1)
Piru Love (1)

Puttin' In Work (1)
Rip A Crab In Half (1)
Send That Crab Off To Die (2)
Set Trippin' (2)
Shuda Beena B-Dog (1)

Slobs Keep On Slippin' (2)
Steady Dippin' (1)
Time Is Gone Nigga (2)
Wish You Were Here (2)

BLOODSTONE   '73

R&B group from Kansas City, Missouri: Charles Love (vocals, guitar), Willis Draffen (guitar), Harry Williams and Roger Durham (percussion), Charles McCormick (bass) and Melvin Webb (drums). Durham died after falling off a horse in 1973. Webb died of diabetes in 1973; replaced by Eddie Summers. Group acted in the 1975 movie *Train Ride To Hollywood*.

DEBUT	PEAK	WKS		CD	# Title			$	Label & Number
4/14/73	30	36		©	1 Natural High			$12	London 620
1/5/74	110	22		©	2 Unreal			$12	London 634
8/10/74	141	8			3 I Need Time			$12	London 647
2/22/75	147	6			4 Riddle Of The Sphinx			$12	London 645
7/17/82	95	11		©	5 We Go A Long Way Back			$10	T-Neck 38115

Closer Together (3)
Damn That Rock 'N' Roll Medley (1)
Everybody Needs Love (2)
For The First Time Medley (4)
Funkin' Around (5)
Funky Park (3)
Get Up (Or Get Out) (3)
Go On And Cry (4)

How Does It Feel (5)
I Believe You Now (3)
I Just Learned To Walk (4)
I Need Time (3)
I Need Your Love (1)
Keep Our Own Thing Together (2)
Let Me Ride (2)
Little Linda (3)

Loving You Is Just A Pastime (3)
Moulded Oldies Medley (2)
My Kind Of Woman (5)
My Little Lady (4) **57**
My Love Grows Stronger (5)
Natural High (1) **10**
Never Let You Go (1) **43**
Nite Time Fun (5)

Nobody But You (4)
Out Of My Life (3)
Outside Woman (2) **34**
Peter's Jones (1)
Ran It In The Ground (1)
Save Me Medley (4)
Sign For Me Dad (4)
Something (2)
Something's Missing (4)

Tell It To My Face (1)
That's Not How It Goes (3) **82**
That's The Way We Make Our Music (1)
This World Is Funky (4)
Time For Reflection (4)
Traffic Cop (Dance) (2)
Unreal (2)
Wasted Time (4)

We Did It (3)
We Go A Long Way Back (5)
What Did You Do To Me? Part 1 & 2 (2)
Who Has The Last Laugh Now (1)
You Know We've Learned (1)
Young Times Old Times (4)

★303★   BLOOD, SWEAT & TEARS   '69

Pop-jazz group formed by **Al Kooper** (Royal Teens, **Blues Project**) in New York City. Nucleus consisted of Kooper (keyboards), Steve Katz (guitar; Blues Project), Bobby Colombo (drums) and Jim Fielder (bass). Kooper replaced by lead singer **David Clayton-Thomas** by 1969. Clayton-Thomas replaced by Jerry Fisher in 1972. Katz left in 1973. Clayton-Thomas rejoined in 1974.

1)*Blood, Sweat & Tears* 2)*Blood, Sweat & Tears 3* 3)*B, S & T; 4*

DEBUT	PEAK	WKS		CD	# Title			$	Label & Number
4/13/68	47	55	●	©	1 Child Is Father To The Man			$25	Columbia 9619
2/1/69	❶[7]	109	▲[4]	©	2 Blood, Sweat & Tears			$15	Columbia 9720
					1969 Grammy winner: Album of the Year				
7/18/70	❶[2]	41	●	©	3 Blood, Sweat & Tears 3			$15	Columbia 30090
7/10/71	10	23	●	©	4 B, S & T; 4			$15	Columbia 30590
3/11/72	19	27	▲[2]	©	5 Blood, Sweat & Tears Greatest Hits		[G]	$15	Columbia 31170
11/4/72	32	17			6 New Blood			$12	Columbia 31780
8/25/73	72	12			7 No Sweat			$12	Columbia 32180
9/7/74	149	6			8 Mirror Image			$12	Columbia 32929
5/31/75	47	13			9 New City			$12	Columbia 33484
7/31/76	165	3			10 More Than Ever			$12	Columbia 34233

Almost Sorry (7)
Alone (6)
And When I Die (2,5) **2**
Applause (9)
Are You Satisfied (8)
Back Up Against The Wall (1)
Battle, The (3)
Blues - Part II (2)
Cowboys And Indians (4)
Django (An Excerpt) (7)
Down In The Flood (6)
Empty Pages (7)
Fire And Rain (3)
For My Lady (4)
40,000 Headman (3)
Go Down Gamblin' (4,5) **32**
God Bless The Child (2,3,5)

Got To Get You Into My Life (9) **62**
He's A Runner (3)
Heavy Blue (10)
Hi-De-Ho (3,5) **14**
High On A Mountain (4)
Hip Pickles (7)
Hold On To Me (8)
Hollywood (10)
House In The Country (1)
I Can't Move No Mountains (3)
I Can't Quit Her (1,5)
I Love You More Than Ever (10)
I Love You More Than You'll Ever Know (1,5)
I Was A Witness To A War (9)

Inner Crisis (7)
John The Baptist (Holy John) (4)
Just One Smile (1)
Katy Bell (10)
Life (9)
Lisa, Listen To Me (4,5) **73**
Lonesome Suzie (1)
Look To My Heart (4)
Look Up To The Sky (8)
Love Looks Good On You (You're Candy Sweet) (8)
Lucretia Mac Evil (3,5) **29**
Lucretia's Reprise (3)
Maiden Voyage (6)
Mama Gets High (4)
Mary Miles (7)
Meagan's Gypsy Eyes (1)

Mirror Image (8)
Modern Adventures of Plato, Diogenes And Freud (1)
More And More (2)
Morning Glory (1)
My Days Are Numbered (1)
My Old Lady (7)
Naked Man (9)
No Show (9)
One Room Country Shack (9)
Over The Hill (6)
Overture (1)
Redemption (4)
Ride Captain Ride (9)
Roller Coaster (7)
Rosemary (7)
Save Our Ship (7)

Saved By The Grace Of Your Love (10)
She's Coming Home (8)
Smiling Phases (2)
Snow Queen (6)
So Long Dixie (6) **44**
So Much Love (1)
Somethin' Comin' On (3)
Somethin' Goin' On (1)
Sometimes In Winter (2,5)
Song For John (7)
Spinning Wheel (2,5) **2**
Sweet Sadie The Savior (10)
Sympathy For The Devil (medley) (3)
Symphony For The Devil (medley) (3)

Take Me In Your Arms (Rock Me A Little While) (4)
Takin' It Home (9)
Tell Me That I'm Wrong (8) **83**
They (10)
Thinking Of You (8)
Touch Me (6)
Valentine's Day (4)
Variations On A Theme By Erik Satie (1st And 2nd Movements) (2)
Velvet (6)
Without Her (1)
Yesterday's Music (9)
You're The One (10)
You've Made Me So Very Happy (2,5) **2**

BLOOM, Bobby   '70

Born in 1945 in New York City. Died from an accidental shooting on 2/28/74 (age 28). Pop singer/songwriter. Much session work in the 1960s.

DEBUT	PEAK	WKS			# Title			$	Label & Number
11/28/70	126	3			The Bobby Bloom Album			$15	L&R 1035

Brighten Your Flame
Careful Not To Break The Spell

Fanta
Give 'Em A Hand

Heavy Makes You Happy
Heidi

Little On The Heavy Side
Montego Bay 8

Oh I Wish You Knew
This Thing I've Gotten Into

Try A Little Harder

BLOOMFIELD, Mike   '68

Born on 7/28/44 in Chicago. Died of a drug overdose on 2/15/81 (age 36). Blues guitarist. With The **Paul Butterfield** Blues Band and **Electric Flag**. Later joined KGB.

DEBUT	PEAK	WKS		CD	# Title			$	Label & Number
8/31/68	12	37	●	©	1 Super Session			$20	Columbia 9701
					MIKE BLOOMFIELD/AL KOOPER/STEVE STILLS				
2/8/69	18	20		©	2 The Live Adventures Of Mike Bloomfield And Al Kooper		[L]	$25	Columbia 6 [2]
					MIKE BLOOMFIELD & AL KOOPER				
					recorded on 9/27/68 at the Fillmore in San Francisco				
10/11/69	127	5			3 It's Not Killing Me			$20	Columbia 9883
					MICHAEL BLOOMFIELD				
6/16/73	105	12		©	4 Triumvirate			$15	Columbia 32172
					MIKE BLOOMFIELD/JOHN PAUL HAMMOND/DR. JOHN				

Albert's Shuffle (1)
Baby Let Me Kiss You (4)
Cha-Dooky-Doo (4)
Dear Mr. Fantasy (2)
Don't Think About It, Baby (3)
Don't Throw Your Love On Me So Strong (2)
Far Too Many Nights (3)

59th Street Bridge Song (Feelin' Groovy) (2)
For Anyone You Meet (3)
Good Old Guy (4)
Goofers (3)
Green Onions (2)
Ground Hog Blues (4)
Harvey's Tune (3)

Her Holy Modal Highness (2)
His Holy Modal Majesty (1)
I Wonder Who (2)
I Yi Yi (4)
If You See My Baby (3)
It Hurts Me Too (4)
It Takes A Lot To Laugh, It Takes A Train To Cry (1)

It's Not Killing Me (3)
Just To Be With You (4)
Last Night (4)
Man's Temptation (1)
Mary Ann (2)
Michael's Lament (3)
Next Time You See Me (3)
No More Lonely Nights (2)

Ones I Loved Are Gone (3)
Pretty Thing (4)
Really (1)
Refugee (2)
Rock Me Baby (4)
Season Of The Witch (1)
Sho Bout To Drive Me Wild (4)
Sonny Boy Williamson (2)

Stop (1)
That's All Right (2)
Together 'Til The End Of Time (2)
Weight, The (2)
Why Must My Baby (3)
You Don't Love Me (1)

BLOW, Kurtis   '80

Born Kurtis Walker on 8/9/59 in New York City. Male rapper. Appeared in the movie *Krush Groove*.

DEBUT	PEAK	WKS		CD	# Title			$	Label & Number
10/18/80	71	10		©	1 Kurtis Blow			$10	Mercury 3854
7/18/81	137	5			2 Deuce			$10	Mercury 4020
10/9/82	167	5			3 Tough		[M]	$10	Mercury 505

BLOW, Kurtis — Cont'd

10/13/84+	83	37		4 **Ego Trip**	$10 Mercury 822420
11/2/85	153	15		5 **America**	$10 Mercury 826141
12/13/86	196	2	©	6 **Kingdom Blow**	$10 Mercury 830215

AJ Is Cool (5)
AJ Meets Davy DMX (5)
AJ Scratch (4)
All I Want In This World (Is To Find That Girl) (1)
America (3)
Baby, You've Got To Go (3)
Basketball (4) 71

Boogie Blues (3)
Breaks, The (Part 1) (1) 87
Bronx, The (6)
Daydreamin' (3)
Deuce, The (2)
Do The Do (3)
Don't Cha Feel Like Making Love (5)

Ego Trip (4)
8 Million Stories (4)
Fallin' Back In Love Again (4)
Getaway (2)
Hard Times (1)
Hello Baby (5)
I Can't Take It No More (4)
I'm Chillin' (6)

If I Ruled The World (5)
It's Gettin' Hot (2)
Juice (3)
Kingdom Blow (6)
MC Lullaby (5)
Magilla Gorilla (5)
Rappin' Blow (Part 2) (1)
Reasons For Wanting You (6)

Respect To The King (5)
Rockin' (2)
Starlife (2)
Street Rock (6)
Summertime Groove (5)
Sunshine (6)
Super Sperm (5)
Take It To The Bridge (2)

Takin' Care Of Business (1)
Throughout Your Years (1)
Tough (3)
Under Fire (4)
Unity Party Jam (6)
Way Out West (1)

BLOWFLY '80

Born Clarence Reid on 2/14/45 in Cochran, Georgia. X-rated singer/songwriter/producer.

5/24/80	82	20		**Blowfly's Party [X-Rated]**	$12 Weird World 2034

Blowfly's Rapp
Can I Come In Your Mouth

Nobody's Butt Yours, Babe
Panty Lines

Prick Ryder
Rapp Dirty

Show Me A Man Who Don't Like To Fuck

Who Did I Eat Last Night?

BLOW MONKEYS, The '86

Pop-rock group from England: "Dr. Robert" Howard (vocals, guitar), Neville Henry (sax), Mick Anker (bass) and Tony Kiley (drums).

6/21/86	35	18		1 **Animal Magic**	$10 RCA Victor 8065
4/25/87	134	8	©	2 **She Was Only A Grocer's Daughter**	$10 RCA Victor 6246

Aeroplane City Lovesong (1)
Animal Magic (1)
Beautiful Child (2)
Burn The Rich (1)
Cash (2)
Checking Out (2)

Day After You (2)
Digging Your Scene (1) 14
Don't Be Scared Of Me (1)
Don't Give It Up (2)
Forbidden Fruit (1)

Heaven Is A Place I'm Moving To (1)
How Long Can A Bad Thing Last (2)
I Backed A Winner (In You) (1)
I Nearly Died Laughing (1)

It Doesn't Have To Be This Way (2)
Man At The End Of His Tether (2)
Out With Her (2)
Rise Above (2)

Some Kind Of Wonderful (2)
Sweet Murder (1)
Wicked Ways (1)

BLUE CHEER '68

Hard-rock trio from San Francisco: Dickie Peterson (vocals, bass), Leigh Stephens (guitar) and Paul Whaley (drums). Considered to be the first "heavy metal" band.

3/9/68	11	27	©	1 **Vincebus Eruptum**	$40 Philips 264
9/28/68	90	16	©	2 **Outsideinside**	$40 Philips 278
5/3/69	84	14	©	3 **New! Improved! Blue Cheer**	$40 Philips 305
11/7/70	188	5	©	4 **The Original Human Being**	$40 Philips 347

Aces 'N' Eights (3)
As Long As I Live (3)
Babaji (Twilight Raga) (4)
Babylon (2)
Black Sun (4)
Come And Get It (2)
Doctor Please (1)
Feathers From Your Tree (2)

Fruit & Iceburgs (3)
Good Times Are So Hard To Find (4)
Gypsy Ball (2)
Honey Butter Lover (3)
Hunter, The (2)
(I Can't Get No) Satisfaction (2)
I Want My Baby Back (3)

It Takes A Lot To Laugh, It Takes A Train To Cry (3)
Just A Little Bit (2) 92
Love Of A Woman (4)
Magnolia Caboose Babyfinger (2)
Make Me Laugh (4)
Man On The Run (4)

Out Of Focus (1)
Parchment Farm (1)
Peace Of Mind (3)
Pilot (4)
Preacher (4)
Rest At Ease (4)
Rock Me Baby (1)
Sandwich (4)

Second Time Around (1)
Summertime Blues (1) 14
Sun Cycle (4)
Tears By My Bed (4)
West Coast Child Of Sunshine (3)
When It All Gets Old (3)

BLUE MAGIC '74

R&B vocal group from Philadelphia: Theodore Mills, Vernon Sawyer, Wendell Sawyer, Keith Beaton and Richard Pratt.

3/16/74	45	34		1 **Blue Magic**	$12 Atco 7038
12/28/74+	71	13		2 **The Magic Of The Blue**	$12 Atco 103
10/4/75	50	12		3 **Thirteen Blue Magic Lane**	$12 Atco 120
9/25/76	170	5		4 **Mystic Dragons**	$12 Atco 140

Answer To My Prayer (1)
Born On Halloween (3)
Chasing Rainbows (3)
Freak-N-Stein (4)
Haunted (By Your Love) (3)
I Like You (3)
It's Something About Love (4)
Just Don't Want To Be Lonely (1)

Let Me Be The One (2)
Loneliest House On The Block (3)
Look Me Up (1)
Looking For A Friend (2)
Love Has Found Its Way To Me (2)
Magic Of The Blue (3)
Making Love To A Memory (4)

Maybe Just Maybe (We Can Fall In Love Again) (3)
Mother Funk (4)
Never Get Over You (2)
Rock N Roll Revival (4)
See The Bedroom (4)
Sideshow (1) 8
Spark Of Love (4)
Spell (1)

Stop And Get A Hold Of Yourself (3)
Stop To Start (1) 74
Stringin' Me Along (2)
Summer Snow (4)
Talking To Myself (2)
Tear It Down (1)
Three Ring Circus (2) 36

To Get Love (You Must Give Love) (4)
We're On The Right Track (3)
Welcome To The Club (1)
What's Come Over Me (1,3)
When Ya Coming Home (2)
You Won't Have To Tell Me Goodbye (2)

BLUE MAN GROUP '01

Experimental musical theatre trio: Matt Goldman, Phil Stanton and Chris Wink. Perform with various inventive percussion instruments while dressed in blue-painted skin, skullcaps and black clothing.

5/19/01	175	1	©	**Audio**	[I] $10 Blue Man Group 48613

Cat Video
Club Nowhere
Drumbone

Endless Column
Klein Mandelbrot
Mandelgroove

Opening Mandelbrot
PVC IV
Rods And Cones

Shadows
Synaesthetic
TV Song

Tension 2
Utne Wire Man

BLUE MERCEDES '88

Pop duo from London: David Titlow (vocals) and Duncan Millar (keyboards).

5/14/88	165	5	©	**Rich And Famous**	$10 MCA 42143

Crunchy Love Affaire
Heaven On Earth
I Hate New York

I Want To Be Your Property 66
Love Is The Gun

Run For Your Love
See Want Must Have
Treehouse

Welcome To Lovesville
Your Secret Is Safe With Me

BLUE MURDER '89

Rock trio: John Sykes (guitar, vocals; **Thin Lizzy**, **Whitesnake**), Tony Franklin (bass; **The Firm**) and Carmine Appice (drums; **Vanilla Fudge**, **Cactus**, and **KGB**).

5/13/89	69	21	©	**Blue Murder**	$10 Geffen 24212

Billy
Black-Hearted Woman

Blue Murder
Jelly Roll

Out Of Love
Ptolemy

Riot
Sex Child

Valley Of The Kings

BLUE NILE, The '90

Melodic-pop trio from Glasgow, Scotland: Paul Buchanan (vocals, guitar), Robert Bell (bass) and Paul Moore (keyboards).

2/24/90	108	14	©	**Hats**	$10 A&M 5284

Downtown Lights
From A Late Night Train

Headlights On The Parade
Let's Go Out Tonight

Over The Hillside
Saturday Night

Seven A.M.

★274★ BLUE ÖYSTER CULT '76

Hard-rock group from Long Island, New York: Eric Bloom (vocals), Donald "Buck Dharma" Roeser (guitar), Allen Lanier (keyboards), and brothers Joe (bass) and Albert (drums) Bouchard. Rick Downey replaced Albert Bouchard in 1982. Downey left in 1984. Tommy Zvoncheck (keyboards) and Jimmy Wilcox (drums) joined in 1985. Original lineup reunited in 1988. Bloom is a cousin of DJ Howard Stern.

1)On Your Feet Or On Your Knees 2)Fire Of Unknown Origin 3)Extraterrestrial Live

DEBUT	PEAK	WKS	RIAA	CD	#	ARTIST — Album Title	Catalog	Sym	$	Label & Number
5/20/72	172	8		©	1	Blue Öyster Cult			$15	Columbia 31063
3/17/73	122	13		©	2	Tyranny And Mutation			$15	Columbia 32017
4/27/74	53	14	●	©	3	Secret Treaties			$15	Columbia 32858
3/15/75	22	13	●	©	4	On Your Feet Or On Your Knees		[L]	$20	Columbia 33371 [2]
						recorded at the Academy of Music in New York City				
6/19/76	29	35	▲	©	5	Agents Of Fortune	C:#17/12		$12	Columbia 34164
11/12/77	43	14	●	©	6	Spectres			$12	Columbia 35019
9/30/78	44	12	▲	©	7	Some Enchanted Evening	C:#27/35	[L]	$12	Columbia 35563
7/7/79	44	17		©	8	Mirrors			$12	Columbia 36009
7/12/80	34	16		©	9	Cultosaurus Erectus			$12	Columbia 36550
7/11/81	24	31	●	©	10	Fire Of Unknown Origin			$12	Columbia 37389
5/15/82	29	19		©	11	Extraterrestrial Live		[L]	$15	Columbia 37946 [2]
11/26/83+	93	16		©	12	The Revolution By Night			$10	Columbia 38947
2/22/86	63	14		©	13	Club Ninja			$10	Columbia 39979
8/20/88	122	8		©	14	Imaginos			$10	Columbia 40618

After Dark (10)
Astronomy (3,7,14)
Baby Ice Dog (2)
Beat 'Em Up (13)
Before The Kiss, A Redcap (1,4)
Black Blade (9,11)
Blue Oyster Cult (14)
Born To Be Wild (4)
Buck's Boogie (4)
Burnin' For You (10,11) *40*
Cagey Cretins (3)
Career Of Evil (3)
Celestial The Queen (6)
Cities On Flame With Rock And Roll (1,4,11)
Dancin' In The Ruins (13)
Deadline (9)
Death Valley Nights (6)
Debbie Denise (5)
Del Rio's Song (14)

Divine Wind (9)
Dr. Music (8,11)
Dominance And Submission (3,11)
(Don't Fear) The Reaper (5,7,11) *12*
Don't Turn Your Back (10)
Dragon Lady (12)
E.T.I. (Extra Terrestrial Intelligence) (5,7,11)
Eyes On Fire (9)
Fallen Angel (9)
Feel The Thunder (12)
Fire Of Unknown Origin (10)
Fireworks (3)
Flaming Telepaths (3)
Godzilla (6,7,11)
Goin' Through The Motions (6)
Golden Age Of Leather (6)
Great Sun Jester (8)
Harvester Of Eyes (3,4)

Heavy Metal: The Black And Silver (10)
Hot Rails To Hell (2,4,11)
Hungry Boys (9)
I Ain't Got You (4)
I Am The One You Warned Me Of (14)
I Am The Storm (8)
I Love The Night (6)
I'm On The Lamb But I Ain't No Sheep (1)
Imaginos (14)
In The Presence Of Another World (14)
In Thee (8) *74*
Joan Crawford (10,11)
Kick Out The Jams (7)
Les Invisibles (14)
Let Go (12)
Light Years Of Love (12)
Lips In The Hills (9)

Lonely Teardrops (8)
ME 262 (3,4)
Madness To The Method (13)
Magna Of Illusion (14)
Make Rock Not War (13)
Marshall Plan (9)
Mirrors (8)
Mistress Of The Salmon Salt (Quicklime Girl) (2)
Monsters (9)
Moon Crazy (8)
Morning Final (5)
Nosferatu (6)
O.D.'d On Life Itself (2)
Perfect Water (13)
R. U. Ready 2 Rock (6,7)
Red & The Black (2,4,11)
Redeemed (3)
Revenge Of Vera Gemini (5)
Roadhouse Blues (11)
Screams (3)

Searchin' For Celine (6)
7 Screaming Diz-Busters (2,4)
Shadow Of California (12)
Shadow Warrior (13)
She's As Beautiful As A Foot (1)
Shooting Shark (12) *83*
Siege And Investiture Of Baron Von Frankenstein's Castle At Weisseria (14)
Sinful Love (5)
Sole Survivor (10)
Spy In The House Of The Night (13)
Stairway To The Stars (1)
Subhuman (3,4)
Take Me Away (12)
Tattoo Vampire (5)
Teen Archer (4)
Tenderloin (5)
Then Came The Last Days Of May (1,4)

This Ain't The Summer Of Love (5)
Transmaniacon (1)
True Confessions (5)
Unknown Tongue (9)
Veins (12)
Vengeance (The Pact) (10)
Veteran Of The Psychic Wars (10,11)
Vigil, The (8)
We Gotta Get Out Of This Place (7)
When The War Comes (13)
White Flags (13)
Wings Wetted Down (2)
Workshop Of The Telescopes (1)
You're Not The One (I Was Looking For) (8)

BLUE RIDGE RANGERS — see FOGERTY, John

BLUES BROTHERS '79

Duo of comedians John Belushi (as "Jake Blues") and Dan Aykroyd (as "Elwood Blues"). Originally created for TV's *Saturday Night Live*. Starred in their own movie. Belushi was born on 1/24/49 in Wheaton, Illinois. Died of a drug overdose on 3/5/82 (age 33). Aykroyd was born on 7/1/52 in Ottawa, Ontario, Canada. Backing band included Paul Shaffer, **Steve Cropper** and Donald "Duck" Dunn. Actor John Goodman replaced Belushi for the *Blues Brothers 2000* movie.

DEBUT	PEAK	WKS	RIAA	CD	#	ARTIST — Album Title	Sym	$	Label & Number
12/23/78+	❶¹	29	▲²	©	1	Briefcase Full Of Blues	[L]	$15	Atlantic 19217
						recorded at the Universal Ampitheater in Los Angeles			
6/28/80	13	19	▲	©	2	The Blues Brothers	[S]	$12	Atlantic 16017
						includes "Think" by Aretha Franklin, "Minnie The Moocher" by Cab Calloway, and "The Old Landmark" by James Brown			
12/27/80+	49	12		©	3	Made In America	[L]	$12	Atlantic 16025
						recorded at the Universal Ampitheater in Los Angeles			
1/9/82	143	3		©	4	Best Of The Blues Brothers	[G]	$12	Atlantic 19331
2/21/98	12	10	●	©	5	Blues Brothers 2000	[S]	$10	Universal 53116
						includes "Born In Chicago" by Paul Butterfield Blues Band, "Harmonica Musings" by John Popper, "Maybe I'm Wrong" by Blues Traveler, "Let There Be Drums" by Carl LaFong Trio, and "How Blue Can You Get" by Louisiana Gator Boys			

"B" Movie Box Car Blues (1,4)
Blues Don't Bother Me (5)
Born In Chicago (5)
Can't Turn You Loose (5)
Cheaper To Keep Her (5)
Do You Love Me (medley) (3)
Everybody Needs Somebody To Love (2,4)
Expressway To Your Heart (4)

Flip, Flop And Fly (1,4)
From The Bottom (3)
Funky Broadway (medley) (3)
Funky Nassau (5)
Gimme Some Lovin' (2,4) *18*
Going Back To Miami (3,4)
Green Onions (3)
Groove Me (1)
Guilty (3)

Hey Bartender (1)
I Ain't Got You (3)
I Can't Turn You Loose (1)
I Don't Know (1)
(I Got Every Thing I Need) Almost (1)
Jailhouse Rock (2)
John The Revelator (5)
Looking For A Fox (5)

Messin' With The Kid (1)
Mother Popcorn (You Got To Have A Mother For Me) (medley) (3)
New Orleans (5)
Perry Mason Theme (3,5)
Peter Gunn Theme (1)
Rawhide, Theme From (2)
R-E-S-P-E-C-T (5)

Riders In The Sky (A Cowboy Legend) (5)
Riot In Cell Block Number Nine (3)
Rubber Biscuit (1,4) *37*
Season Of The Witch (5)
Shake Your Tailfeather (2)
She Caught The Katy (2,4)
Shot Gun Blues (1)

634-5789 (5)
Soul Finger (medley) (3)
Soul Man (1,4) *14*
Sweet Home Chicago (2)
Turn On Your Love Light (5)
Who's Making Love (3) *39*

BLUES IMAGE '69

Rock group from Tampa, Florida: Mike Pinera (vocals, guitar; **Iron Butterfly**), Frank Konte (keyboards), Joe Lala (percussion), Malcolm Jones (bass) and Manuel Bertematti (drums).

DEBUT	PEAK	WKS	#	ARTIST — Album Title	$	Label & Number
8/16/69	112	9	1	Blues Image	$25	Atco 300
4/25/70	147	13	2	Open	$20	Atco 317

Clean Love (2)
Consuelate (2)
(Do You Have) Somethin' To Say (1)
Fugue U (2)

In Front Behind You (1)
La Bamba (2)
Lay Your Sweet Love On Me (1)
Lazy Day Blues (1)

Leaving My Troubles Behind (1)
Love Is The Answer (2)
Outside Was Night (1)
Parchman Farm (2)
Pay My Dues (2)

Reality Does Not Inspire (1)
Ride Captain Ride (2) *4*
Running The Water (2)
Take Me (2)
Take Me To The Sunrise (1)

Wrath Of Daisey (2)
Yesterday Could Be Today (1)

BLUES MAGOOS '67

Psychedelic-rock group from the Bronx, New York: Emil "Peppy Castro" Thielhelm (vocals, guitar), Mike Esposito (guitar), Ralph Scala (keyboards), Ronnie Gilbert (bass) and Geoff Daking (drums). Castro later became lead singer of **Balance**.

DEBUT	PEAK	WKS	CD	#	ARTIST — Album Title	$	Label & Number
12/3/66+	21	32	©	1	Psychedelic Lollipop	$50	Mercury 61096
4/22/67	74	16	©	2	Electric Comic Book	$40	Mercury 61104

Albert Common Is Dead (2)
Baby, I Want You (2)
Gloria (1)
Gotta Get Away (1)

I'll Go Crazy (1)
Let's Get Together (2)
Life Is Just A Cher O'Bowlies (2)

Love Seems Doomed (1)
One By One (1) *71*
Pipe Dream (2) *60*
Queen Of My Nights (1)

Rush Hour (2)
She's Coming Home (1)
Sometimes I Think About (1)
Summer Is The Man (2)

Take My Love (2)
That's All Folks (2)
There's A Chance We Can Make It (2) *81*

Tobacco Road (1)
(We Ain't Got) Nothin' Yet (1) *5*
Worried Life Blues (1)

BLUES PROJECT, The '67

Blues group formed in New York City by Danny Kalb (guitar) and Roy Blumenfeld (drums). Vocalist Tommy Flanders left group after first album. Guitarist Steve Katz and organist **Al Kooper** took over vocals. Katz and Kooper left to form **Blood, Sweat & Tears** in 1968.

DEBUT	PEAK	WKS		#	Title		Sym	$	Label & Number
5/21/66	77	21		1	Live At The Cafe Au Go Go		[L]	$25	Verve Folkways 3000
					recorded on 11/25/65 in New York City				
12/17/66+	52	36		2	Projections			$25	Verve Folkways 3008
10/7/67	71	11	©	3	The Blues Project Live At Town Hall		[L]	$20	Verve Forecast 3025
8/9/69	199	2	©	4	Best Of The Blues Project		[G]	$20	Verve Forecast 3077

Alberta (1)
Back Door Man (1)
Caress Me Baby (2)
Catch The Wind (1)
Cheryl's Going Home (2,4)
Flute Thing (2,3,4)

Fly Away (2)
Goin' Down Louisiana (1)
I Can't Keep From Crying (2,3,4)
I Want To Be Your Driver (1,4)
Jelly Jelly Blues (1)

Love Will Endure (3)
Mean Old Southern (3)
No Time Like The Right Time (3,4) *96*
Spoonful (1)
Steve's Song (2,4)

Two Trains Running (2)
Violets Of Dawn (1,4)
Wake Me, Shake Me (2,3,4)
Way My Baby Walks (1)
Where There's Smoke, There's Fire (3)

Who Do You Love (1)
You Can't Catch Me (2)
You Go, And I'll Go With You (1)

BLUES TRAVELER '95

Blues-rock group from New York City: **John Popper** (vocals, harmonica), Chan Kinchla (guitar), Bobby Sheehan (bass) and Brendan Hill (drums). Sheehan died of a drug overdose on 8/20/99 (age 31); replaced by Chan's brother, Tad Kinchla. Ben Wilson (keyboards) joined in 2000.

DEBUT	PEAK	WKS	RIAA	CD	#	Title		Sym	$	Label & Number
3/2/91	136	12	●	©	1	Blues Traveler	C:#41/3		$10	A&M 5308
9/21/91	125	5	●	©	2	Travelers & Thieves			$10	A&M 5373
4/24/93	72	13	●	©	3	Save His Soul			$10	A&M 540080
10/1/94+	8	96	▲⁶	©	4	four			$10	A&M 540265
7/20/96	46	11	▲	©	5	Live From The Fall		[L]	$15	A&M 540515 [2]
7/19/97	11	24	▲	©	6	Straight On Till Morning			$10	A&M 540750
5/26/01	91	6		©	7	Bridge			$10	A&M 490895

All Hands (7)
All In The Groove (2)
Alone (1,5)
Back In The Day (7)
Bagheera (7)
Battle Of Someone (6)
Believe Me (3)
Best Part (2)
Breakfast (5)
Brother John (4)
Bullshitter's Lament (3)
Business As Usual (6)
But Anyway (1,5)
Canadian Rose (6)

Carolina Blues (6)
Closing Down The Park (5)
Conquer Me (3)
Crash Burn (4,5)
Crystal Flame (1)
Decision Of The Skies (7)
Defense & Desire (3)
Dropping Some NYC (1)
Fallible (6)
Felicia (6)
Fledgling (3)
Freedom (4,5)
Gina (1,5)
Girl Inside My Head (7)

Go (5)
Go Outside & Drive (3)
Good, The Bad, And The Ugly (4)
Gotta Get Mean (1)
Great Big World (6)
Gunfighter, The (6)
Hippie (medley) (5)
Hook (4) *23*
I Have My Moments (2)
Imagine (medley) (5)
Ivory Tusk (2)
Just For Me (7)
Just Wait (4)

Justify The Thrill (6)
Last Night I Dreamed (6)
Letter From A Friend (3)
Look Around (4)
Love & Greed (3,5)
Love Of My Life (3)
Low (medley) (5)
Make My Way (6)
Manhattan Bridge (3)
Most Precarious (6)
Mountain Cry (2,5)
Mountains Win (5)
Mountains Win Again (4)
Mulling It Over (1,5)

NY Prophesie (3,5)
100 Years (1,5)
Onslaught (4)
Optimistic Thought (2)
Pretty Angry (7)
Price To Pay (4)
Psycho Joe (6)
Rage (7)
Regarding Steven (5)
Run-Around (4,5) *8*
Sadly A Fiction (7)
Save His Soul (3)
Slow Change (1)
Stand (4)

Support Your Local Emperor (2)
Sweet Pain (2)
Sweet Talking Hippie (1)
Tiding, The (2)
Trina Magna (3)
Warmer Days (1)
Way, The (7)
What's For Breakfast (2)
Whoops (3)
You Lost Me There (7)
You Reach Me (7)
You're Burning Me (7)
Yours (6)

BLUE SWEDE '74

Pop group from Sweden: Bjorn Skifs (vocals), Michael Areklew (guitar), Anders Berglund (keyboards), Hinke Ekestubbe (sax), Thomas Berglund (trumpet), Bosse Liljedahl (bass) and Jan Guldback (drums).

DEBUT	PEAK	WKS			Title			$	Label & Number
4/6/74	80	17			Hooked On A Feeling			$12	EMI 11286

Destiny
Gotta Have Your Love

Hooked On A Feeling *1*
Lonely Sunday Afternoon

Never My Love *7*
Pinewood Rally

Silly Milly *71*
Something's Burning

(There's) Always Something There To Remind Me

Working In The Coal Mine

BLUR '95

Techno-rock group from London: Damon Albarn (vocals), Graham Coxon (guitar), Alex James (bass) and Dave Rowntree (drums).

DEBUT	PEAK	WKS		CD	#	Title		Sym	$	Label & Number
10/14/95	150	1		©	1	The Great Escape			$10	Food 40855
3/29/97	61	37	●	©	2	Blur			$10	Food 42876
4/10/99	80	5		©	3	13			$10	Food 99129
12/9/00	186	1		©	4	Blur: The Best Of		[G]	$15	Food 50457 [2]

disc 2: recorded on 12/12/99 at Wembley Arena

B.L.U.R.E.M.I. (3)
Battle (3)
Beetlebum (2,4)
Best Days (1)
Bugman (3)
Caramel (3)
Charmless Man (1,4)
Chinese Bombs (2)
Coffee & TV (3,4)

Country House (1,4)
Country Sad Ballad Man (2)
Dan Abnormal (1)
Death Of A Party (2)
End Of A Century (4)
Entertain Me (1)
Ernold Same (1)
Essex Dogs (1)
Fade Away (1)

For Tomorrow (4)
Girls And Boys (4)
Globe Alone (1)
He Thought Of Cars (1)
I'm Just A Killer For Your Love (2)
It Could Be You (1)
Look Inside America (2)
M.O.R. (2,4)

Mellow Song (3)
Movin' On (2)
Mr. Robinson's Quango (1)
Music Is My Radar (4)
1992 (3)
No Distance Left To Run (3,4)
On Your Own (2,4)
Optigan 1 (3)
Parklife (4)

She's So High (4)
Song 2 (2,4)
Stereotypes (1,4)
Strange News From Another Star (2)
Swamp Song (3)
Tender (3,4)
Theme From Retro (2)
There's No Other Way (4)

This Is A Low (4)
To The End (4)
Top Man (1)
Trailerpark (3)
Trimm Trabb (3)
Universal, The (1,4)
You're So Great (2)
Yuko & Hiro (1)

BOB & TOM '97

DJ morning team of Bob Kevoian and Tom Griswold of radio station WFBQ-Indianapolis.

DEBUT	PEAK	WKS		CD		Title		Sym	$	Label & Number
9/27/97	164	2		©		Fun House		[C]	$10	Big Mouth 97

Cathy & Pappy
Ch-Ch-Ch-Chick
Crime & Punishment
Douche Commercial
Feminine Hygiene
Fred

Girl Like You
Guiding Shiite
Harrassaway
Harry & Miss Universe
He Said, She Heard
Hockers

Hot Coffee
Hurt Me Elmo
I Kill You
Ian & The Dinosaur
Marge & Martha
Marge & Paula

Men & Women
Mom
Nail, The
Pallbearer, The
Phone Message To Dad
Pictionary, Etc.

Pull My Finger Charlie
Sexy Trekkie
Skeleton, The
Spit Take Theater
Tim's Blues
Time To Go

Working
Yiddish For Rednecks
You Can Be Mean To Me

BOBBY & THE MIDNITES '81

Rock group led by **Grateful Dead** guitarist **Bob Weir**. Group also included Grateful Dead member Brent Mydland (keyboards), Bobby Cochran (guitar), Matthew Kelly (harmonica), Alphonso Johnson (bass) and **Billy Cobham** (drums).

DEBUT	PEAK	WKS		CD	#	Title			$	Label & Number
11/21/81	158	7		©	1	Bobby & The Midnites			$12	Arista 9568
8/25/84	166	4		©	2	Where the Beat Meets the Street			$10	Columbia 39276

Ain't That Pecuiliar (2)
Book Of Rules (1)
Carry Me (1)
Falling (2)
Far Away (1)

Festival (1)
Gloria Monday (1)
Haze (1)
(I Want To) Fly Away (1)
(I Want To Live In) America (2)

Josephine (1)
Lifeguard (2)
Lifeline (2)
Me, Without You (1)
Rock In The 80's (1)

She's Gonna Win Your Heart (2)
Thunder & Lightning (2)
Too Many Losers (1)

Where The Beat Meets The Street (2)

BOBBY JIMMY & THE CRITTERS '86

Comedic rap group from Los Angeles: Russ Parr ("Bobby Jimmy"), **Arabian Prince**, Buckwheat and Bo.

11/29/86	200	1			Roaches: The Beginning .... [N]			$10	Macola 0933

Bag Bobby Jimmy Jam · Bring It On Home · New York Rapper · Rush It
Big Butt · Gotta Party · Roaches · We Like Ugly Women

BOBO, Willie '66

Born William Correa on 2/28/34 in New York City. Died on 9/15/83 (age 49). Latin-jazz percussionist. Joined the bands of Tito Puente (1954-57), **Cal Tjader** (1958-61) and **Mongo Santamaria** (1961-62).

2/26/66	137	8			Spanish Grease .... [I]			$20	Verve 8631

Blind, Man, Blind Man (medley) · Elation · Hurt So Bad · Nessa · Shot Gun (medley)
Blues In The Closet · Haitian Lady · It's Not Unusual · Our Day Will Come · Spanish Grease

BOCELLI, Andrea '99

Born on 9/22/58 in Lajatico, Italy. Male operatic tenor. Blind since age 12.

12/20/97+	35	91	▲²	© 1	Romanza C:❶²/92	[F]		$10	Philips 539207
3/28/98	153	21	●	© 2	Viaggio Italiano .... C:#19/1	[F]		$10	Philips 533123
					title is Italian for "Italian Travel"				
4/25/98	59	69	▲	© 3	Aria: The Opera Album .... C:#29/4	[F]		$10	Philips 462033
4/17/99	4	72	▲²	© 4	Sogno	[F]		$10	Polydor 547222
5/8/99	163	2		© 5	Sueño	[F]		$10	Polydor 547224
11/27/99+	22	30	▲	© 6	Sacred Arias	[F]		$10	Philips 462600
9/30/00	23	23	●	© 7	Verdi...	[F]		$10	Philips 464600

A Mio Padre (4,5) · Come Un Bel Di Di Maggio (3) · Ella Mi Fu Rapita! (7) · Lamento di Federico (2) · Oh Mio Rimorso! (7) · Silent Night (6)
A Volte Il Cuore (4,5) · Come Un Fiume Tu (4,5) · Frondi Tenere...Ombra Mai Fu (6) · Le Fleur Que Tu M'Avais Jetée (3) · Panis Angelicus (2,6) · Sogno (Dream) (4)
Addio, Fiorito Asil (3) · Con Te Partirò ...see: Time To Say Goodbye · Gloria A Te, Cristo Gesù (6) · Le Tue Parole (1) · Per Amore (1) · Sueño (5)
Adeste Fideles (2,6) · Con Te Partirò (1) · I Love Rossini (4,5) · Ma Se M'è Forza Perderti (7) · Pietà, Signore (6) · Te, O Cara (3)
Ah, La Paterna Mano (2) · Core N'Grato (2) · I' Te Vurria Vasà (2) · Macchine Da Guerra (1) · Piscatore 'E Pusilleco (2) · Time To Say Goodbye (Con Te Partirò) (1)
Ah Si, Ben Mio (7) · Cujus Animam (6) · Il Mare Calmo Della Sera (1) · Mai Piu' Così' Lontano (4,5) · Possente Amor Mi Chiama (7) · Tombe Degli Avi Miei - Fra Poco A Me Ricovero (3)
Amor Ti Vieta (3) · De' Miei Bollenti Spiriti (7) · Immenso (3) · Marinarello (2) · Pour Mon Âme (3) · Tremo E T' Amo (4,5)
Ave Maria (4) · Der Engel (6) · Ingemisco (6) · Mercé, Diletti Amici (7) · Pourquoi Me Réveiller (3) · Tu, 'Ca Nun Chiagne! (2)
Ave Verum Corpus (6) · Di Quella Pira (7) · Io La Vidi E Il Suo Sorriso (7) · Mille Cherubini In Coro (6) · Prayer, The (4,5) · Un Canto (4,5)
Cantico (4,5) · Di Rigori Armato Il Seno (3) · La Dolcissima Effigie (3) · Miserere (1) · Quando Le Sere Al Placido (7) · Una Furtiva Lagrima (2)
Canto De La Tierra (4,5) · Di' Tu Se Fedele (7) · La Donna È Mobile (2,7) · Musetta! - Testa Adorata (3) · Questa O Quella (3) · Vivere (1)
Caruso (1) · Domine Deus (6) · La Luna Che Non C'è (1) · Nel Cuore Lei (4,5) · Rapsodia (1) · Vivo Per Lei (1)
Celeste Aida (7) · E Chiove (1) · La Mia Letizia Infondere Vorrei (7) · Nessun Dorma (2) · Recondita Armonia (3) · Voglio Restare Così (1)
Che Gelida Manina (3) · E Lucevan Le Stelle (3) · La Vita È Inferno All'Infelice (7) · 'O Mare E Tu (1) · Romanza (1)
Ch'ella Mi Creda (3) · El Mar Y Tu (5) · O Sole Mio (2) · Sancta Maria (6)
Cielo E Mar! (3) · Santa Lucia Luntana (2)

BoDEANS '87

Folk-rock group from Waukesha, Wisconsin: Kurt Neumann and Sam Llanas (guitar, vocals), Bob Griffin (bass) and Guy Hoffman (drums). In 1989, Hoffman left; Michael Ramos (keyboards) and Danny Gayol (drums) joined. In 1995, Gayol was replaced by Nick Kitsos.

6/7/86	115	19		© 1	Love & Hope & Sex & Dreams			$10	Slash 25403
10/10/87	86	20		© 2	Outside Looking In			$10	Slash 25629
7/22/89	94	13		© 3	home...			$10	Slash 25876
4/20/91	105	5		© 4	Black And White			$10	Slash 26487
10/30/93	127	3		© 5	Go Slow Down			$10	Slash 45455
8/26/95	161	1		© 6	Joe Dirt Car .... [L]			$15	Slash 45945 [2]
11/23/96	132	2		© 7	Blend			$10	Slash 46216

All I Ever Wanted (7) · Cold Winter's Day (5) · Forever Young (The Wild Ones) (2) · Idaho (5,6) · Red River (3) · Texas Ride Song (5,6)
Angels (1) · Count On Me (7) · Freedom (3) · Long Hard Day (4) · Red Roses (7) · That's All (1)
Any Given Day (4) · Do I Do (4) · Go Slow Down (5,6) · Lookin' For Me Somewhere (1,6) · Rickshaw Riding (1) · True Devotion (4,6)
Bad For You (4) · Do What You Want (7) · Going Home (4,6) · Lullabye (7) · Save A Little (5) · Ultimately Fine (1)
Ballad Of Jenny Rae (2,6) · Don't Be Lonely (2) · Good Things (4,6) · Misery (1,6) · Say About Love (2,6) · Understanding, The (7)
Beaujolais (3) · Dreams (2) · Good Work (3,6) · Naked (4,6) · Say You Will (1) · Walking After Midnight (6)
Beautiful Rain (3) · Fadeaway (1,6) · Hand In Hand (3) · No One (3) · She's A Runaway (1,6) · What It Feels Like (3)
Black, White And Blood Red (4,6) · Far Far Away From My Heart (3,6) · Heart Of A Miracle (7) · Only Love (2) · Someday (7) · When The Love Is Good (3)
Brand New (3) · Feed The Fire (5,6) · Hell Of A Chance (4) · Ooh (She's My Baby) (6) · Something's Telling Me (5) · Worlds Away (3)
Can't Stop Thinking (7) · Fire In The Hole (5) · Hey Pretty Girl (7) · Other Side (1) · Stay On (5) · You Don't Get Much (3,6)
Closer To Free (5,6) *16* · Forever On My Mind (4) · Hurt By Love (7) · Paradise (4,6) · Still The Night (1,6)
· I'm In Trouble Again (6) · Pick Up The Pieces (2) · Strangest Kind (1)
· Take It Tomorrow (2)

BODY COUNT '92

Speed-metal group formed by rapper **Ice-T** (vocals) and Ernie-C (guitar), with D-Roc (guitar), Mooseman (bass) and Beatmaster V (drums). All are alumni of Crenshaw High School in South Central Los Angeles. Beatmaster V (real name: Victor Wilson) died of leukemia on 4/30/96 (age 37).

4/18/92	26	20	●	© 1	Body Count...			$10	Sire 26878
9/24/94	74	3		© 2	Born Dead			$10	Virgin 39802

Body Count (1) · Bowels Of The Devil (1) · Freedom Of Speech (1) · Masters Of Revenge (2) · Surviving The Game (2) · Winner Loses (1)
Body Count Anthem (1) · C Note (1) · Hey Joe (2) · Momma's Gotta Die Tonight (1) · There Goes The Neighborhood (1)
Body Count's In The House (1) · Cop Killer (1) · KKK Bitch (1) · Necessary Evil (2)
Body M/F Count (2) · Drive By (2) · Killin' Floor (1) · Shallow Graves (2) · Voodoo (1)
Born Dead (2) · Evil Dick (2) · Last Breath (2) · Street Lobotomy (2) · Who Are You (2)

BOFILL, Angela '80

Born in 1954 in New York City. R&B/jazz-styled singer/songwriter.

2/17/79	47	26		© 1	Angie			$12	GRP 5000
11/3/79+	34	33		© 2	Angel of the Night			$12	GRP 5501
11/21/81	61	22		3	Something About You			$10	Arista 9576
2/12/83	40	32		4	Too Tough...			$10	Arista 9616
11/26/83+	81	21		© 5	Teaser..			$10	Arista 8198

Accept Me (I'm Not A Girl Anymore) (4) · Baby, I Need Your Love (1) · Crazy For Him (5) · I Do Love You (3) · Love You Too Much (4) · Only Thing I Would Wish For (1)
Ain't Nothing Like The Real Thing (4) · Break It To Me Gently (3) · Feelin's Love (2) · I Try (2) · Nothin' But A Teaser (5) · Penetration (5)
Angel Of The Night (2) · Call Of The Wild (5) · Gotta Make It Up To You (5) · I'm On Your Side (5) · On And On (3) · People Make The World Go 'Round (2)
· Children Of The World United (1) · Holdin' Out For Love (3) · Is This A Dream (4) · Only Love (3)
· I Can See It In Your Eyes (4) · Love To Last (2)

BOFILL, Angela — Cont'd

Rainbow Child (Little Pas) (2)	Song For A Rainy Day (4)	This Time I'll Be Sweeter (1)	Tropical Love (3)
Rainbow Inside My Heart (4)	Special Delivery (5)	Three Blind Mice (3)	Under The Moon And Over The
Rough Times (1)	Still A Thrill (2)	Time To Say Goodbye (3)	Sky (1)
Share Your Love (1)	Stop Look Listen (3)	Tonight I Give In (4)	Voyage, The (2)
Something About You (3)	Summer Days (1)	Too Tough (4)	

What I Wouldn't Do (For The Love Of You) (2)
You Could Come Take Me Home (4)
You Should Know By Now (3)
You're A Special Part Of Me (5)

BOGERT, Tim — see BECK, Jeff

BOGGUSS, Suzy   '92
Born on 12/30/56 in Aledo, Illinois. Country singer/songwriter/guitarist.

2/1/92	83	53	▲	©	1 **Aces**..		$10	Capitol 95847
10/31/92	116	23	●	©	2 **Voices In The Wind**		$10	Liberty 98585
10/9/93	121	18	●	©	3 **Something Up My Sleeve**		$10	Liberty 89261
4/2/94	190	1	●	©	4 **Greatest Hits**	[G]	$10	Liberty 28457

Aces (1,4)	Heartache (2,4)	In The Day (2)	No Green Eyes (3)
Cold Day In July (2)	Hey Cinderella (3)	Just Like The Weather (3)	Other Side Of The Hill (2)
Cross My Broken Heart (4)	Hopelessly Yours (4)	Let Goodbye Hurt (1)	Outbound Plane (1,4)
Diamonds And Tears (3)	How Come You Go To Her (4)	Letting Go (1,2,4)	Part Of Me (1)
Don't Wanna (3)	I Keep Comin' Back To You (3)	Love Goes Without Saying (2)	Save Yourself (1)
Drive South (2,4)	I Want To Be A Cowboy's	Lovin' A Hurricane (2)	Someday Soon (1,4)
Eat At Joe's (2)	Sweetheart (4)	Music On The Wind (1)	Something Up My Sleeve (3)

Somewhere Between (4)
Souvenirs (3)
Still Hold On (1)
Yellow River Road (1)
You Never Will (3)
You Wouldn't Say That To A Stranger (3)
You'd Be The One (3)

BOHANNON, Hamilton   '78
Born on 3/7/42 in Newnan, Georgia. Session drummer. Worked for **Stevie Wonder** from 1965-67.

| 8/12/78 | 58 | 19 | | | **Summertime Groove**............................ | | $12 | Mercury 3728 |

I Wonder Why	Let's Start The Dance	Listen To The Children Play	Me And The Gang

Street Dance
Summertime Groove

BOHN, Rudi, and His Band   '61
Born in Germany. Polka bandleader.

| 10/16/61 | 38 | 9 | | | **Percussive Oompah**............................ | [I] | $20 | London Phase 4 44009 |

Accordion Joe	Good-Bye	In Munchen Steht Ein	Mack The Knife-March
Auf Wiederseh'n Sweetheart	Happy Wanderer	Hofbrauhaus	O Du Lieber Augustin
Beer Barrel Polka		Liechtensteiner Polka	Pennsylvania Polka

Too Fat Polka
Trink, Trink, Bruderlein, Trink

BOLIN, Tommy   '76
Born on 8/1/51 in Sioux City, Iowa. Died of a drug overdose on 12/4/76 (age 25). Guitarist with **The James Gang**, **Deep Purple** and **Zephyr**.

| 12/20/75+ | 96 | 14 | | © | 1 **Teaser**.. | | $15 | Nemperor 436 |
| 10/2/76 | 98 | 8 | ● | © | 2 **Private Eyes**.................................... | | $12 | Columbia 34329 |

Bustin' Out For Rosey (2)	Hello, Again (2)	People, People (1)	Someday Will Bring Our Love
Dreamer (1)	Homeward Strut (1)	Post Toastee (2)	Home (2)
Grind, The (1)	Lotus (1)	Savannah Woman (1)	Sweet Burgundy (2)
Gypsy Soul (2)	Marching Powder (1)	Shake The Devil (2)	Teaser (1)

Wild Dogs (1)
You Told Me That You Loved Me (2)

★219★ BOLTON, Michael   '91
Born Michael Bolotin on 2/26/53 in New Haven, Connecticut. First recorded for Epic in 1968. Lead singer of **Blackjack** in the late 1970s. Began recording as Michael Bolton in 1983.
1)Time, Love & Tenderness 2)Timeless (The Classics) 3)Soul Provider

5/7/83	89	13	●	©	1 **Michael Bolton**		$10	Columbia 38537
10/10/87+	46	41	▲²	©	2 **The Hunger** ....C:#8/37		$10	Columbia 40473
7/22/89+	3	202	▲⁶	©	3 **Soul Provider** ....C:#32/14		$10	Columbia 45012
5/11/91	❶¹	149	▲⁸	©	4 **Time, Love & Tenderness**		$10	Columbia 46771
10/17/92	❶¹	47	▲⁴	©	5 **Timeless (The Classics)**		$10	Columbia 52783
12/4/93	3	45	▲³	©	6 **The One Thing**		$10	Columbia 53567
10/7/95	5	42	▲³	©	7 **Greatest Hits 1985-1995**	[G]	$10	Columbia 67300
10/19/96	11	15	▲	©	8 **This Is The Time - The Christmas Album** ....C:#6/9	[X]	$10	Columbia 67621
					Christmas charts: 2/'96, 7/'97, 26/'98			
11/22/97	39	17	●	©	9 **All That Matters**		$10	Columbia 68510
12/20/97	192	2		©	10 **Merry Christmas From Vienna**	[X-L]	$10	Sony Classical 62970
					PLÁCIDO DOMINGO/YING HUANG/MICHAEL BOLTON			
					recorded on 12/16/96 at the Austria Center in Vienna			
2/14/98	112	8		©	11 **My Secret Passion - The Arias**	[F]	$10	Sony Classical 63077

Ain't Got Nothing If You Ain't	E Lucevan Le Stelle (11)	**How Can We Be Lovers**	Missing You Now (4,7) *12*
Got Love (1)	Fallin' (6)	(3,7) *3*	Nessun Dorma! (11)
Aleluya (medley) (10)	Fanfare (10)	Hunger, The (2)	Never Get Enough Of Your
Ave Maria (8,10)	Fighting For My Life (1)	I Almost Believed You (1)	Love (6)
Back In My Arms Again (1)	First Nowell (10)	I Found Someone (7)	New Love (4)
Best Of Love (9)	**Fools Game** (1) *82*	I Promise You (7)	Noche De Paz ..see: Silent
Bring It On Home To Me (5)	Forever Isn't Long Enough (4)	I'm Not Made Of Steel (6)	Night
Can I Touch You...There?	Forever's Just A Matter Of Time	In The Arms Of Love (6)	Now That I Found You (4)
(7) *27*	(9)	It's Only My Heart (3)	Nu År Det Jul Igen (medley)
Can't Get Close Enough To You	From Now On (3)	Jingle Bells (medley) (10)	(10)
(9)	Fum, Fum, Fum (medley) (10)	Joy To The World (8,10)	O Holy Night (8)
Can't Hold On, Can't Let Go (1)	**Georgia On My Mind** (3,7) *36*	Kling Glöckchen (medley) (10)	O Soave Fanciulla (11)
Carrie (1)	Gina (2)	Knock On Wood (5)	One Thing (6)
Celeste Aïda (11)	**Go The Distance** (9) *24*	Lean On Me (5)	Paradise (1)
Che Gelida Manina (11)	Have Yourself A Merry Little	Let There Be Love (9)	Pleasure Or Pain (9)
Children Of Christmas (10)	Christmas (8)	Let's Make A Long Story Longer	Pourquoi Me Réveiller? (11)
Christmas Song (8)	Heart Can Only Be So Strong	(9)	Pujdem Spolu Do Betlema
Completely (6) *32*	(9)	Love Cuts Deep (3)	(medley) (10)
Corramos, Corramos (medley)	Hold On, I'm Coming (5)	**Love Is A Wonderful Thing**	Reach Out I'll Be There (5)
(10)	Hometown Hero (1)	(4) *4*	Recondita Armonia (11)
Dormi, Dormi (medley) (10)	Hot Love (2)	Love Is The Power (8)	Safe Place From The Storm (9)
Drift Away (5)	**How Am I Supposed To Live**	Love So Beautiful (7)	**Said I Loved You...But I Lied**
È La Solita Storia (11)	**Without You** (3,7) *1*	M'appari (11)	(6,7) *6*

Santa Claus Is Coming To Town (8)
Save Me (4)
She Did The Same Thing (1)
Show Her The Way (9)
Silent Night (8,10)
Since I Fell For You (5)
(Sittin' On) The Dock Of The Bay (2,7) *11*
Soul Of My Soul (6)
Soul Provider (3,7) *17*
Stand Up For Love (3)
Steel Bars (4,7)
Take A Look At My Face (2)
That's What Love Is All About (2,7) *19*
This Is The Time (8)
This River (2)
Time For Letting Go (6)
Time, Love And Tenderness (4,7) *7*
To Love Somebody (5) *11*
Una Furtiva Lagrima (11)

Vesti La Giubba (11)
Wait On Love (2) *79*
Walk Away (2)
We're Not Makin' Love Anymore (4)
When A Man Loves A Woman (4,7) *1*
When I'm Back On My Feet Again (3,7) *7*
Whenever I Remember Loving You (9)
White Christmas (5,8,10)
Why Me (9)
Yesterday (5)
You Send Me (5)
You Wouldn't Know Love (3)
You're All That I Need (2)

BOLTZ, Ray '95
Born in Muncie, Indiana. Gospel singer.

9/9/95	194	1	●	© 1	The Concert Of A Lifetime		[L]	$10	Word 641601
10/26/96	173	1		© 2	No Greater Sacrifice			$10	Word 67867
11/29/97	169	5		© 3	A Christmas Album		[X]	$10	Word 68512

Christmas chart: 15/'97

Altar, The (1)
Anchor Holds (1)
At The Foot Of The Cross (2)
Behold (1)
Bethlehem Star (1)
Brave New World (2)
Children Of The World (medley) (2)
Everyone Wins (2)
Feel The Nails (1)
Gift, The (3)
Glad Tidings (3)
Go Tell It On The Mountain (3)
God Gave Me Back Tomorrow (2)
Hammer, The (1)
Heaven Is Counting On You (1)
I Believe In Bethlehem (3)
I Go To The River (1)
I Pledge Allegiance To The Lamb (1)
I Will Praise The Lord (1)
I've Come To Serve (1)
Is There A Heaven For Me? (medley) (2)
Oh, What A Beautiful Name (3)
One Drop Of Blood (2)
One Single Flame (2)
Perfect Tree (3)
Sent By The Father (3)
Still Her Little Child (3)
Stones, The (1)
Storm, The (1)
Thank You (1)
There Stood A Lamb (2)
Touching Him (1)
Until All Have Been Served (2)
Watch The Lamb (1)
What If I Give All (2)
When Her Eyes Are On The Child (3)

BONAMY, James '96
Born on 4/29/72 in Winter Park, Florida; raised in Daytona Beach, Florida. Country singer.

8/3/96	112	13		©	What I Live To Do			$10	Epic 67069

All I Do Is Love Her
Amy Jane
Brain In A Jar
Couple, The
Devil Goes Fishin'
Dog On A Toolbox
Heartbreak School
I Don't Think I Will
Jimmy And Jesus
She's Got A Mind Of Her Own

BOND '01
Female classical-folk group from England: Eos and Haylie Ecker (violins), Tania Davis (viola) and Gay-Yee Westerhoff (cello).

4/21/01	108	8		©	Born		[I]	$10	MBO 467091

Alexander The Great
Bella Donna
Dalalai
Duel
1812, The
Hymn
Kismet
Korobushka
Oceanic
Quixote
Victory
Winter

BOND, Angelo '75
Born in Detroit. R&B singer/songwriter.

8/2/75	179	2			Bondage			$12	ABC 889

Eve
Goodbye My Love
He Gained The World (But Lost His Soul)
I Love You For What You Are
I Never Sang For My Baby
Man Can't Serve Two Masters
Reach For The Moon (Poor People)
What's Bad About Feeling Good

BOND, Johnny '65
Born Cyrus Whitfield Bond on 6/1/15 in Enville, Oklahoma. Died of a heart attack on 6/12/78 (age 63). Country singer/songwriter/actor. Appeared in several movies.

5/29/65	142	3			Ten Little Bottles		[N]	$40	Starday 333

Barrel House Bessie
Dang Hangover (Tall Tale)
Judge Roy Bean's Court (Tall Tale)
New Year's Day (Tall Tale)
Sadie Was A Lady
Sick, Sober, And Sorry
10 Little Bottles 43
Three Sheets In The Wind
Winter Blizzard (Tall Tale)

BONDS, Gary (U.S.) '61
Born Gary Anderson on 6/6/39 in Jacksonville, Florida. R&B singer.

8/7/61	6	28		© 1	Dance 'til Quarter To Three			$100	Legrand 3001
					U.S. BONDS				
5/2/81	27	20		© 2	Dedication			$10	EMI America 17051
6/26/82	52	17		© 3	On The Line			$10	EMI America 17068

above 2 produced by **Bruce Springsteen** and "**Little Steven**" Van Zant.

All I Need (3)
Angelyne (3)
Bring Her Back (3)
Cecilia (1)
Club Soul City (3)
Daddy's Come Home (2)
Dedication (2)
Don't Go To Strangers (1)
From A Buick 6 (2)
Hold On (To What You Got) (3)
I Know Why Dreamers Cry (1)
It's Only Love (2)
Jole Blon (2) 65
Just Like A Child (2)
Last Time (3)
Love's On The Line (3)
Minnie The Moocher (1)
New Orleans (1) 6
Not Me (1)
One Million Tears (1)
Out Of Work (3) 21
Please Forgive Me (1)
Pretender, The (2)
Quarter To Three (1) 1
Rendezvous (3)
School Is Out (1) 5
Soul Deep (3)
That's All Right (1)
This Little Girl (2) 11
Trip To The Moon (1)
Turn The Music Down (1)
Way Back When (2)
Your Love (2)

★432★ BONE THUGS-N-HARMONY '95
Male rap group from Cleveland: Anthony Henderson ("**Krayzie Bone**"), Steven Howse ("**L-Burna a.k.a. Layzie Bone**"), Charles Scruggs ("**Bizzy Bone**"), Byron McCane ("**Wish Bone**") and Stanley Howse ("**Flesh-N-Bone**"; left in 1996). Previously known as **Bone Enterprise**.

7/30/94	12	96	▲²	© 1	Creepin On Ah Come Up		[M]	$10	Ruthless 5526
7/22/95	188	2		© 2	Faces Of Death		[E]	$10	Stoney Burke 70020
					BONE ENTERPRISE				
					recordings from 1993				
8/12/95	❶²	104	▲⁴	© 3	E. 1999 Eternal	C:#12/19		$10	Ruthless 5539
8/16/97	❶¹	32	▲⁴	© 4	The Art Of War			$15	Ruthless 6340 [2]
12/12/98	32	28	▲	© 5	The Collection Volume One		[G]	$10	Ruthless 69715
3/18/00	2¹	28	▲	© 6	BTNHRESURRECTION			$10	Ruthless 63581
12/2/00	41	11		© 7	The Collection Volume Two		[K]	$10	Ruthless 85172

Ain't Nothin Changed (Everyday Thang part 2) (4)
All Good (7)
All Original (4)
BNK (4)
Battlezone (6)
Bless Da 40 oz. (2)
Body Rott (4,5)
Breakdown (5)
Buddah Lovaz (3)
Budsmokers Only (3)
C Land I.A. (7)
Can't Give It Up (6,7)
Change The World (6,7)
Clog Up Yo Mind (4)
Creepin On Ah Come Up (1)
Crept And We Came (3)
Crossroads, Tha (3,5) 1
Days Of Our Livez (5)
Def Dick (3)
Die Die Die (3)
Don't Hate On Me (7)
Don't Worry (6)
Down Foe My Thang (1)
Down '71 (The Getaway) (3)
East 1999 (3) 62
Ecstasy (6)
Eternal (3)
Everyday Thang (2)
Evil Paradise (4)
Family Tree (4)
1st Of Tha Month (3,5) 14
Flow Motion (2)
Foe Tha Love Of $ (1,5) 41
Friends (How Many Of Us Have Them) (4)
Frontline Warrior (7)
F--- Tha Police (5)
Ganksta Attitude (2)
Gett Cha Thug on (Wish Bone) (4)
Ghetto Cowboy (7) 15
Handle The Vibe (4)
Hatin Nation (4)
Hell Sent (2)
Hook It Up (7)
If I Could Teach The World (4) 27
It's All Mo' Thug (4)
It's All Real (4)
Land Of Tha Heartless (3)
Let The Law End (4)
Look Into My Eyes (4,7) 4
Me Killa (3)
Mind Of A Souljah (4)
Mind On Our Money (6)
Mo' Murda (3)
Mo' Thug · Family Tree (4)
Moe Cheese (1)
Mr. Bill Collector (3)
Mr. Ouija (1)
Mr. Ouija 2 (3)
Murder One (6)
No Shorts, No Losses (3)
No Surrender (1)
No Way Out (6)
Notorious Thugs (5)
#1 Assassin (2)
One Night Stand (6)
P.O.D. (5)
Ready 4 War (4)
Resurrection (Paper, Paper) (6)
Righteous Ones (6)
Servin' Tha Fiends (6)
7 Sign (4)
Shoot 'Em Up (3)
Shotz To Tha Double Glock (3)
Show 'Em (6)
Sleepwalkers (7)
Sons of Assassins (2)
Souljahs Marching (6)
Thug Luv (4,7)
Thuggish Ruggish Bone (1,5) 22
2 Glocks (6,7)
U Ain't Bone (4)
War (5)
Wasteland Warriors (4)
We Be Fiendin' (2)
Weed Song (4)
Weedman (7)
Whom Die They Lie (4)

BONEY JAMES '00

Born James Oppenheim in Massachusetts; raised in New York City and Los Angeles. Male saxophonist.

6/14/97	112	11	●	©	1 Sweet Thing		[I]	$10	Warner 46548
3/13/99	91	18	●	©	2 Body Language		[I]	$10	Warner 47283
6/17/00	78	15		©	3 Shake It Up...		[I]	$10	Warner 47557

BONEY JAMES/RICK BRAUN

After The Rain (1)	Boneyizm (3)	I Get Lonely (2)	It's All Good (1)	Nothin' But Love (1)	Sweet Thing (1)
All Night Long (2)	Central Ave. (3)	I Still Dream (1)	Ivory Coast (1)	R.S.V.P. (3)	Words (Unspoken) (1)
Are You Ready? (2)	Chain Reaction (3)	I'll Always Love You (2)	Love's Like That (3)	Shake It Up (3)	
Bedtime Story (2)	East Bay (1)	Innocence (1)	Lovefest (2)	Song For My Father (3)	
Body Language (2)	Grazin' In The Grass (3)	Into The Blue (2)	More Than You Know (3)	Stars Above (3)	

BONEY M '78

Vocal group created in Germany by producer/composer Frank Farian. Consisted of Marcia Barrett, Maizie Williams, Liz Mitchell and Bobby Farrell. All were from the West Indies. Farian created the Far Corporation in 1986 and **Milli Vanilli** in 1988.

| 9/2/78 | 134 | 10 | | | Nightflight To Venus .... | | | $12 | Sire 6062 |

| Brown Girl In The Ring | Heart Of Gold | Never Change Lovers In The | Nightflight To Venus | Rasputin | Voodoo Night |
| He Was A Steppenwolf | King Of The Road | Middle Of The Night | Painter Man | **Rivers Of Babylon 30** | |

BONFIGLIO '95

Born Robert Bonfiglio in Iowa; raised in New York. Classical harmonica player.

| 10/21/95 | 21^C | 1 | | © | Through The Raindrops .... | | [I] | $10 | High Harmony 1000 |

| Chelsea Day | Fleur D'Ennui | Quiet Jungle | Sleepwalk | Through The Raindrops |
| Deborah's Theme | In The Rain | Riverside | Street Song | Troubland Bolero |

BONHAM '89

Hard-rock group from England. Led by drummer Jason Bonham, the son of **Led Zeppelin**'s drummer, the late John Bonham. Includes Daniel MacMaster (vocals), Ian Hatton (guitar) and John Smithson (keyboards, bass).

| 10/7/89 | 38 | 29 | ● | © | The Disregard Of Timekeeping .... | | | $10 | WTG 45009 |

| Bringing Me Down | Disregard Of Timekeeping | Dreams | Holding On Forever | Playing To Win | **Wait For You 55** |
| Cross Me And See | Don't Walk Away | Guilty | Just Another Day | Room For Us All | |

BONHAM, Tracy '96

Born in 1969 in Eugene, Oregon. Female singer/songwriter/guitarist.

| 4/27/96 | 54 | 25 | ● | © | The Burdens Of Being Upright .... | | | $10 | Island 524187 |

| Brain Crack | Every Breath | Mother Mother | One, The | Real, The | Tell It To The Sky |
| Bulldog | Kisses | Navy Bean | One Hit Wonder | Sharks Can't Sleep | 30 Seconds |

BON JOVI ★156★ '86

Rock group from Sayreville, New Jersey: **Jon Bon Jovi** (vocals, born on 3/2/62), **Richie Sambora** (guitar), Dave Bryan (keyboards), Alec John Such (bass) and Tico Torres (drums). Hugh McDonald replaced Such in 2000. Jon acted in the movies *Moonlight and Valentino*, *The Leading Man*, *No Looking Back*, *U-571* and *Pay It Forward*.

1)Slippery When Wet 2)New Jersey 3)Blaze Of Glory/Young Guns II

2/25/84	43	86	▲^{2}	©	1 Bon Jovi..			$10	Mercury 814982
5/18/85	37	104	▲	©	2 7800° Fahrenheit			$10	Mercury 824509
9/13/86	❶^8	94	▲^{12}	©	3 Slippery When Wet	C:#19/65		$10	Mercury 830264
10/8/88	❶^4	76	▲^{7}	©	4 New Jersey			$10	Mercury 836345
8/25/90	3	41	▲^{2}	©	5 Blaze Of Glory/Young Guns II		[S]	$10	Mercury 846473

JON BON JOVI

songs from and songs inspired by the movie *Young Guns II* starring Emilio Estevez and Kiefer Sutherland

11/21/92	5	46	▲^{2}	©	6 Keep The Faith			$10	Jambco 514045
11/5/94	8	50	▲^{4}	©	7 Cross Road	C:#5/61	[G]	$10	Mercury 526013
7/15/95	9	20	▲	©	8 These Days			$10	Mercury 528181
7/5/97	31	9		©	9 Destination Anywhere			$10	Mercury 534903

JON BON JOVI

| 7/1/00 | 9 | 51 | ▲^{2} | © | 10 Crush .... | | | $10 | Island 542474 |
| 6/9/01 | 20 | 14 | | © | 11 One Wild Night: Live 1985 - 2001 .... | | [L] | $10 | Island 548684 |

Always (7) **4**	Diamond Ring (8)	If I Was Your Mother (6)	**Living In Sin** (4) **9**	Rockin' In The Free World (11)	**Thank You For Loving Me**
Always Run To You (2)	Dry County (6)	If That's What It Takes (8)	Love For Sale (4)	Roulette (1)	(10) **57**
August 7, 4:15 (9)	Dyin' Ain't Much Of A Livin' (5)	**In And Out Of Love** (2,7,11) **69**	Love Lies (2)	**Runaway** (1,7,11) **39**	These Days (8)
Bad Medicine (4,7,11) **1**	Every Word Was A Piece Of My	In These Arms (6) **27**	Midnight In Chelsea (9)	Santa Fe (5)	**This Ain't A Love Song** (8) **14**
Bang A Drum (5)	Heart (6)	(It's Hard) Letting You Go (8)	**Miracle** (5) **12**	Save The World (10)	To The Fire (2)
Bed Of Roses (6,7) **10**	Fear (6)	It's Just Me (9)	My Guitar Lies Bleeding In My	Say It Isn't So (10)	Tokyo Road (2)
Billy Get Your Guns (5)	Get Ready (1)	**It's My Life** (10,11) **33**	Arms (8)	Secret Dreams (2)	Two Story Town (10)
Blame It On The Love Of Rock	Guano City (5)	Janie, Don't Take Your Love To	Mystery Train (10)	**She Don't Know Me** (1) **48**	Ugly (9)
& Roll (6)	Hardest Part Is The Night (2)	Town (9)	Naked (9)	She's A Mystery (10)	**Wanted Dead Or Alive**
Blaze Of Glory (5,7) **5**	Hearts Breaking Even (8)	Just Older (10,11)	Never Say Die (5)	Shot Through The Heart (1)	(3,7,11) **7**
Blood Money (5)	Hey God (8)	Justice In The Barrel (5)	Never Say Goodbye (3)	Silent Night (2)	Wild In The Streets (3)
Blood On Blood (4)	Homebound Train (4)	**Keep The Faith** (6,7,11) **29**	99 In The Shade (4)	Social Disease (4)	Wild Is The Wind (4)
Born To Be My Baby (4) **3**	I Believe (6)	King Of The Mountain (2)	One Wild Night (10,11)	Someday I'll Be Saturday Night	Without Love (3)
Breakout (1)	I Don't Like Mondays (11)	**Lay Your Hands On Me** (4,7) **7**	**Only Lonely** (2) **54**	(7,11)	Woman In Love (6)
Burning For Love (1)	I Got The Girl (10)	Learning How To Fall (9)	Prayer '94 (7)	**Something For The Pain**	**You Give Love A Bad Name**
Captain Crash & The Beauty	I Want You (6)	Let It Rock (3)	Price Of Love (3)	(8,11) **76**	(3,7,11) **1**
Queen From Mars (10)	I'd Die For You (3)	**Lie To Me** (8) **88**	Queen Of New Orleans (9)	Something To Believe In (8,11)	You Really Got Me Now (5)
Come Back (1)	**I'll Be There For You** (4,7) **1**	Little Bit Of Soul (6)	Raise Your Hands (3)	Staring At Your Window With A	
Damned (8)	**I'll Sleep When I'm Dead**	Little City (9)	Ride Cowboy Ride (4)	Suitcase In My Hand (9)	
Destination Anywhere (9)	(6) **97**	**Livin' On A Prayer** (3,7,11) **1**		Stick To Your Guns (4)	

BONOFF, Karla '79
Born on 12/27/51 in Los Angeles. Pop singer/songwriter/pianist.

10/1/77	52	40	●	© 1	**Karla Bonoff**	$12	Columbia 34672
9/29/79	31	26		© 2	**Restless Nights**	$12	Columbia 35799
4/3/82	49	35		© 3	**Wild Heart Of The Young**	$10	Columbia 37444

Baby Don't Go (2) *69*
Dream (3)
Even If (3)
Faces In The Wind (1)
Falling Star (1)

Flying High (1)
Gonna Be Mine (3)
Home (1)
I Can't Hold On (1) *76*
I Don't Want To Miss You (3)

If He's Ever Near (1)
Isn't It Always Love (1)
It Just Takes One (3)
Just Walk Away (3)
Letter, The (2)

Lose Again (1)
Loving You (2)
Never Stop Her Heart (2)
Only A Fool (2)
Personally (3) *19*

Please Be The One (3) *63*
Restless Nights (2)
Rose In The Garden (1)
Someone To Lay Down Beside Me (1)

Trouble Again (2)
Water Is Wide (2)
When You Walk In The Room (2)
Wild Heart Of The Young (3)

BONZO DOG BAND '72
Satirical rock group from England. Member Neil Innes was later with **The Rutles**. Group appeared in the 1967 **Beatles** movie *Magical Mystery Tour*. Member Vivian Stanshall died in a fire on 3/5/95 (age 51).

6/10/72	199	2		©	**Let's Make Up And Be Friendly**	$15	United Artists 5584

Bad Blood
Don't Get Me Wrong

Fresh Wound
King Of Scurf

Rawlinson End
Rusty (Champion Thrust)

Slush
Straight From My Heart

Strain, The
Turkeys

Waiting For The Wardrobe

BOOGIE BOYS, The '85
Rap trio from Harlem, New York: William Stroman, Joe Malloy and Rudy Sheriff.

8/31/85	53	17		1	**City Life**	$10	Capitol 12409
8/9/86	124	9		2	**Survival Of The Freshest**	$10	Capitol 12488
3/19/88	117	11		© 3	**Romeo Knight**	$10	Capitol 46917

Always On My Mind (3)
Body (3)
Break Dancer (1)
City Life (1)
Colorblind World (2)

Dealin' With Life (2)
Do Or Die (1)
Fly Girl (1)
Friend Or Foe (2)
Girl Talk (2)

Home Girl (3)
I'm A Lover (3)
I'm Comin' (3)
Kick It (3)
Love List (2)

Party Asteroid (1)
Peep It (3)
Pit Bull (3)
Pussi Cat (3)
Rise Up (3)

Romeo Knight (3)
Run It (2)
Runnin' From Your Love (1)
Shake And Break (1)
Share My World (2)

Starvin' Marvin (2)
This Is Us (3)
You Ain't Fresh (1)

BOOGIE DOWN PRODUCTIONS '90
Rap group from the Bronx, New York. Founded by Lawrence Parker ("**KRS-ONE**") and Scott Sterling (shot to death on 8/25/87, age 24). Group includes a revolving lineup of rappers.

4/30/88	75	23	●	© 1	**By All Means Necessary**	$10	Jive 1097
7/22/89	36	17	●	© 2	**Ghetto Music: The Blueprint Of Hip Hop**	$10	Jive 1187
8/25/90	32	16	●	© 3	**Edutainment**	$10	Jive 1358
4/6/91	115	7		© 4	**Live Hardcore Worldwide**	[L] $10	Jive 1425
3/14/92	42	9		© 5	**Sex And Violence**	$10	Jive 41470

Beef (3)
Blackman In Effect (3)
Blueprint, The (2)
Bo! Bo! Bo! (2,4)
Breath Control (2,4)
Breath Control II (3)
Bridge Is Over (4)
Build And Destroy (5)
Come To The Teacher (4)
Criminal Minded (4)
Drug Dealer (5)

Duck Down (5)
Edutainment (3)
Eye Opener (4)
Ghetto Music (2)
Gimme Dat, (Woy) (2)
Hip Hop Rules (2)
Homeless, The (3)
House Nigga's (3,4)
How Not To Get Jerked (5)
I'm Still #1 (1,4)
Illegal Business (1)

Jack Of Spades (2,4)
Jah Rulez (2)
Jimmy (1,4)
Kenny Parker Show (3)
Lick A Shot (4)
Like A Throttle (5)
Love's Gonna Get'cha (Material Love) (3)
My Philosophy (1,4)
Necessary (1)
Nervous (1)

100 Guns (3)
Original Lyrics (3)
Original Way (5)
Part Time Suckers (1)
Poetry (4)
Poisonous Products (5)
Questions And Answers (3)
Racist, The (3)
Real Holy Place (5)
Reggae Medley (4)
Ruff Ruff (5)

Say Gal (5)
Self Destruction (4)
7 Dee Jays (3)
Sex And Violence (4)
South Bronx (4)
Stop The Violence (1,4)
Style You Haven't Done Yet (2)
Super Hoe (4)
T'cha - T'cha (1)
13 And Good (5)
30 Cops Or More (3)

Up To Date (4)
We In There (5)
Who Are The Pimps? (5)
Who Protects Us From You? (2)
Why Is That? (2,4)
World Peace (2)
Ya Know The Rules (3,4)
Ya Slippin' (1)
Ya Strugglin' (3)
You Must Learn (2)

BOOKER, Chuckii '89
Born in 1966 in Los Angeles. Singer/songwriter/multi-instrumentalist.

7/22/89	116	10		©	**Chuckii**	$10	Atlantic 81947

(Don't U Know) I Love U
Heavenly Father

Hotel Happiness
Let Me Love U

Oh Lover
Res Q Me

That's My Honey
Touch

Turned Away *42*

★402★ ## BOOKER T. & THE MG'S '63
Instrumental group from Memphis: Booker T. Jones (keyboards; born on 11/12/44), **Steve Cropper** (guitar), Donald "Duck" Dunn (bass) and Al Jackson, Jr. (drums). MG stands for Memphis Group. Jackson was murdered on 10/1/75 (age 39). Cropper and Dunn had been in the **Mar-Keys** before. Cropper and Dunn later joined the **Blues Brothers** band. Jones married and recorded with Priscilla Coolidge (sister of **Rita Coolidge**). Group inducted into the Rock and Roll Hall of Fame in 1992.
1)Green Onions 2)Hip Hug-Her 3)Melting Pot

11/10/62+	33	17		© 1	**Green Onions**	[I] $100	Stax 701
12/17/66+	13^X	10		© 2	**Booker T. & The MG's in the Christmas Spirit**	[X-I] $200	Stax 713

originally issued in 1966 with a "hands and piano keys" cover ($400); issued with a "Santa Claus ornament" cover from 1967-on; Christmas charts: 31/'66, 13/'67, 54/'68, 14/'69

6/24/67	35	29		© 3	**Hip Hug-Her**	[I] $50	Stax 717
8/26/67	98	4		© 4	**Back To Back**	[I-L] $50	Stax 720

THE MAR-KEYS/BOOKER T. & THE MG's
includes "Grab This Thing", "Last Night" and "Philly Dog" by **The Mar-Keys**

5/18/68	176	4		© 5	**Doin' Our Thing**	[I] $50	Stax 724
10/19/68	127	9		© 6	**Soul Limbo**	[I] $30	Stax 2001
11/23/68	167	11		© 7	**The Best Of Booker T. & The MG's**	[G-I] $30	Atlantic 8202
2/8/69	98	27		© 8	**Uptight**	[S] $30	Stax 2006
6/14/69	53	18		© 9	**The Booker T. Set**	[I] $30	Stax 2009
5/2/70	107	15		© 10	**McLemore Avenue**	[I] $30	Stax 2027
11/14/70	132	8		© 11	**Booker T. & The M.G.'s Greatest Hits**	[G-I] $25	Stax 2033
2/13/71	43	38		© 12	**Melting Pot**	[I] $25	Stax 2035

BOOKER T. & PRISCILLA:

8/14/71	106	6			13	**Booker T. & Priscilla**	$20	A&M 3504 [2]
7/22/72	190	4			14	**Home Grown**	$15	A&M 4351

Back Home (12)
Be Young, Be Foolish, Be Happy (6)
Beat Goes On (5)
Because (medley) (10)

Behave Yourself (1)
Blue Christmas (2)
Blue On Green (5)
Blues In The Gutter (8)
Booker Loo (4)

Booker's Notion (3)
Boot-Leg (7) *58*
Born Under A Bad Sign (6,14)
California Girl (13)
Can't Be Still (7)

Carnaby St. (3)
Carry That Weight (medley) (10)
Chicken Pox (12)
Children Don't Weary (8)

Christmas Song (2)
Cleveland Now (8)
Color Your Mama (14)
Come Together (medley) (10)
Comin' Home Baby (1)

Cool Black Dream (13)
Deadwood Dick (8)
Delta Song (13)
Doin' Our Thing (5)

BOOKER T. & THE MG'S — Cont'd

Don't Think Twice, It's All Right (14)
Double Or Nothing (3)
Down At Ralph's Joint (8)
Earth Children (13)
Eleanor Rigby (6,11)
End, The (medley) (10)
Exodus Song (5)
Expressway (To Your Heart) (5)
For Priscilla (13)
Foxy Lady (6)
Funny Honey (13)
Fuquawi (12)
Get Ready (3)
Gimme Some Lovin' (4)
Golden Slumbers (medley) (10)
Green Onions (1,4,7) *3*
Groovin' (3,7) *21*
Hang 'Em High (6,11) *9*
He (13)
Heads Or Tails (6,11)

Here Comes The Sun (medley) (10)
Hi Ride (12)
Hip Hug-Her (3,4,7,11) *37*
Horse, The (9)
I Can Dig It (5)
I Can't Sit Down (1)
I Got A Woman (1)
I Want You (medley) (10)
I've Never Found A Girl (9)
Indian Song (13)
It's Your Thing (9)
Jellybread (7) *82*
Jingle Bells (2)
Johnny, I Love You (8,11)
Kinda Easy Like (12)
L.A. Jazz Song (12)
La La Means I Love You (6)
Lady Madonna (9)
Let's Go Get Stoned (5)
Light My Fire (9)

Lonely Avenue (1)
Love Child (9)
Maggie's Farm (14)
Mean Mr. Mustard (medley) (10)
Meditation (11)
Medley From The Jones Ranch (13)
Melting Pot (12) *45*
Merry Christmas Baby (2)
Michelle (9)
Mississippi Voodoo (13)
Mo-Onions (1,7) *97*
More (3)
Mrs. Robinson (9,11) *37*
Muddy Road (14)
Never My Love (5)
Ode To Billie Joe (5)
Ole Man Trouble (13)
One Who Really Loves You (1)
Outrage (4)

Over Easy (6,11)
Pigmy (3)
Polythene Pam (medley) (10)
Red Beans And Rice (4,7)
Rinky-Dink (1)
Run Tank Run (8)
Santa Claus Is Coming To Town (2)
Save Us From Ourselves (14)
Sea Gull (13)
Sequence, The (14)
She (13)
She Came In Through The Bathroom Window (medley)
She's So Heavy (medley) (10)
Silent Night (2)
Silver Bells (2)
Sing A Simple Song (9)
Sister Babe (13)
Slim Jenkin's Place (3,7) *70*

Something (10,11) *76*
Soul Dressing (7) *95*
Soul-Limbo (6,11) *17*
Soul Sanction (3)
Stranger On The Shore (1)
Summertime (7)
Sun Don't Shine (13)
Sun King (medley) (10)
Sunny (3)
Sunny Monday (12)
Sweet Child You're Not Alone (13)
Sweet Little Jesus Boy (2)
(Sweet, Sweet, Baby) Since You've Been Gone (6)
Tank's Lament (8)
This Guy's In Love With You (9)
Tic-Tac-Toe (4,7)
Time Is Tight (8,11) *6*
Twist And Shout (3)
Water Brothers (13)

We Three Kings (2)
We Wish You A Merry Christmas (2)
We've Got Johnny Wells (8)
Wedding Song (13)
White Christmas (2)
Who Killed Cock Robin? (14)
Why (13)
Willow Weep For Me (6)
Winter Wonderland (2)
You Don't Love Me (5)
You Keep Me Hanging On (5)
Woman, A Lover, A Friend (1)
You Never Give Me Your Money (medley) (10)
You're All I Need To Get By (9)

BOOK OF LOVE   '88

Dance-pop group from New York City: Susan Ottaviano (lead vocals), Ted Ottaviano and Lauren Roselli (keyboards), and Jade Lee (percussion). The Ottavianos are not related.

7/23/88	156	10	©	1 Lullaby..	$10 Sire 25700
2/23/91	174	4	©	2 Candy Carol......................................	$10 Sire 26389

Alice Everyday (2)
Butterfly (2)
Candy Carol (2)
Champagne Wishes (1)
Counting The Rosaries (2)

Flower Parade (2)
Lullaby (1)
Melt My Heart (1)
Miss Melancholy (2)
Orange Flip (2)

Oranges And Lemons (1)
Pretty Boys And Pretty Girls (1) *90*
Quiver (2)
Sea Of Tranquility (1)

Sunny Day (2)
Tubular Bells (1)
Turn The World (2)
Wall Song (2)
Witchcraft (1)

With A Little Love (1)
You Look Through Me (1)

BOOM, Taka   '79

Born Yvonne Stevens in 1954 in Chicago. R&B singer. Sister of **Chaka Khan**.

6/9/79	171	4	Taka Boom...	$12 Ariola 50041

Anything You Want
Cloud Dancer

Dance Baby Dance
Dance Like You Do At Home

Night Dancin' *74*
Red Hot

Troubled Waters
You're My Everything

BOOMTOWN RATS, The   '80

Rock group from Dun Laoghaire, Ireland: **Bob Geldof** (vocals), Gerry Cott and Garry Roberts (guitars), Johnnie Fingers (keyboards), Pete Briquette (bass) and Simon Crowe (drums). Cott left in 1980. Geldof organized Band Aid.

3/3/79	112	13	©	1 A Tonic For The Troops.......................	$12 Columbia 35750
12/1/79+	103	16	©	2 The Fine Art Of Surfacing..................	$12 Columbia 36248
2/21/81	116	8	©	3 Mondo Bongo..................................	$10 Columbia 37062
5/25/85	188	4		4 In The Long Grass...........................	$10 Columbia 39335

Another Piece Of Red (3)
Another Sad Story (4)
Banana Republic (3)
Blind Date (1)
Diamond Smiles (2)
Don't Believe What You Read (1)
Don't Talk To Me (3)

Drag Me Down (4)
Elephants Graveyard (3)
Go Man Go (3)
Hard Times (4)
Having My Picture Taken (2)
Hold Of Me (4)
Hurt Hurts (3)
I Don't Like Mondays (2) *73*

(I Never Loved) Eva Braun (1)
Icicle In The Sun (4)
Joey's On The Street Again (1)
Keep It Up (2)
Like Clockwork (1)
Living In An Island (1)
Lucky (4)
Mary Of The 4th Form (1)

Me And Howard Hughes (1)
Mood Mambo (3)
Nice 'N' Neat (2)
Nothing Happened Today (2)
Over Again (4)
Please Don't Go (3)
Rain (4)
Rat Trap (1)

She's So Modern (1)
Sleep (Fingers' Lullaby) (2)
Someone's Looking At You (2)
Straight Up (3)
This Is My Room (3)
Tonight (4)
Under Their Thumb...Is Under My Thumb (3)

Up All Night (3)
Up Or Down (4)
When The Night Comes (2)
Wind Chill Factor (Minus Zero) (2)

BOONE, Daniel   '72

Born Peter Lee Stirling on 7/31/42 in Birmingham, England. Singer/songwriter.

10/7/72	142	9	Beautiful Sunday...	$15 Mercury 649

Annabelle *86*
Beautiful Sunday *15*

Crying
Darling Honey

Funny Little Things
Home Again

In Love Again
In Ohio

Sleepy Head
Sunshine Lover

Sweet Joanna
Taste The Wine

BOONE, Debby   '77

Born on 9/22/56 in Leonia, New Jersey. Daughter of **Pat Boone**. Won the 1977 Best New Artist Grammy Award. Married Gabriel Ferrer (son of **Rosemary Clooney** and actor Jose Ferrer) on 9/1/79.

10/29/77	6	37	▲	1 You Light Up My Life	$12 Warner/Curb 3118
8/12/78	147	5		2 Midstream	$12 Warner/Curb 3130

Another Goodbye (2)
Baby, I'm Yours (1) *flip*
California (2) *50*
Come Share My Love (2)
Don't You Want Me Anymore (2)

End Of The World (1)
From Me To You (1)
God Knows (2) *74*
Hasta Manana (1)
Hey Everybody (1)

I'd Rather Leave While I'm In Love (2)
If Ever I See You Again (2)
It Was Such A Good Day (2)
It's Just A Matter Of Time (1)
Micol's Theme (1)

Oh, No, Not My Baby (2)
Rock And Roll Song (1)
What Becomes Of My World (2)
When I Look At You (My Love) (1)
When It's Over (2)

When The Lovelight Starts Shining Through His Eyes (1)
When You're Loved (2)
You Light Up My Life (1) *1*
Your Love Broke Through (1)

BOONE, Pat ★174★ '58

Born Charles Eugene Boone on 6/1/34 in Jacksonville, Florida: raised in Nashville. Direct descendant of Daniel Boone. Married country singer Red Foley's daughter, Shirley, on 11/7/53. Father of **Debby Boone**. Hosted own TV show, *The Pat Boone-Chevy Showroom*, 1957-60. Appeared in several movies. Wrote several books. Recording artist Nick Todd is his younger brother.

1)Star Dust 2)Pat's Great Hits 3)Four By Pat

DEBUT	PEAK	WKS	CD		ARTIST — Album Title	Sym	$	Label & Number
10/27/56	14	4		1	Howdy!		$50	Dot 3030
6/24/57	13	7		2	A Closer Walk With Thee	[EP]	$25	Dot 1056
7/8/57	19	3		3	"Pat"		$50	Dot 3050
9/2/57	5	5		4	Four By Pat	[EP]	$25	Dot 1057
10/7/57	20	2		5	Pat Boone	[E]	$50	Dot 3012
					released in 1956			
10/21/57	3	36	●	6	Pat's Great Hits	[G]	$50	Dot 3071
12/23/57+	12	13		7	April Love	[S]	$50	Dot 9000
					includes "Main Title," "First Meeting," "Tugfire," "Tugfire's Escape," "Sulky Race," "Lovers' Quarrel," "Tugfire's Illness" and "Finale" by Lionel Newman			
12/23/57	21	4		8	Hymns We Love		$30	Dot 3068
7/28/58	2[1]	32		9	Star Dust		$30	Dot 3118
11/24/58	13	2		10	Yes Indeed!		$30	Dot 3121
7/13/59	17	11		11	Tenderly		$30	Dot 3180
5/23/60	26	3		12	Moonglow		$30	Dot 3270
7/17/61	29	30		13	Moody River		$25	Dot 3384
1/6/62	39	2		14	White Christmas	[X-E]	$25	Dot 3222
					released in 1959; Christmas chart: 50/'66			
9/15/62	66	13		15	Pat Boone's Golden Hits	[G]	$25	Dot 3455
12/29/62	116	1		16	White Christmas	[X-E-R]	$25	Dot 3222
2/15/97	125	2	©	17	In A Metal Mood: No More Mr. Nice Guy		$10	Hip-O 40025

Adeste Fideles (14,16)
Again (12)
Ain't Nobody Here But Us Chickens (3)
Ain't That A Shame (5) *1*
Alabam (15) *47*
All I Do Is Dream Of You (1)
American Beauty Rose (10)
Anastasia (6) *37*
Angel On My Shoulder (13)
Anniversary Song (9)
April Love (7) *1*
At My Front Door (Crazy Little Mama) (5) *7*
Autumn Leaves (9)
Because Of You (11)
Beg Your Pardon (1)
Begin The Beguine (1)
Bentonville Fair (7)
Bernardine (6) *14*
Beyond The Sunset (8) *71*
Big Cold Wind (15) *19*
Blue Moon (13)
Blueberry Hill (9)
Carnival ..see: Love Makes The World Go 'Round
Cathedral In The Pines (4)
Chains Of Love (6) *10*
Chattanooga Shoe Shine Boy (1)
Clover In The Meadow (7)
Cold, Cold Heart (9)
Corinna, Corinna (13)
Crazy Train (17)
Dear John (15) *44*
Deep Purple (9)
Do It Yourself (1)

Don't Forbid Me (6) *1*
Don't Worry 'Bout Me (10)
Ebb Tide (9)
Enter Sandman (17)
Ev'ry Little Thing (1)
Fascination (11)
First Noel (14,16)
Five, Ten, Fifteen Hours (3)
Flip, Flop And Fly (3)
For A Penny (15) *23*
Forgive Me (1)
Friendly Persuasion (Thee I Love) (6) *5*
Gee Whittakers! (5) *19*
Georgia On My Mind (13)
Girl Of My Dreams (12)
Give Me A Gentle Girl (7)
God Rest Ye Merry, Gentlemen (14,16)
Gone Fishin' (10)
Great Pretender (13)
Hands Across The Table (12)
Harbor Lights (1)
Hark! The Herald Angels Sing (14,16)
Have Thine Own Way, Lord (3)
He'll Understand (And Say "Well Done") (2)
Heartaches (9)
Here Comes Santa Claus (14,16)
Holy Diver (17)
Honey Hush (3)
How Soon (11)
Hummin' The Blues (1)
I Almost Lost My Mind (6) *1*
I'll Be Home (5) *4*

I'll Be Home For Christmas (14,16)
I'll Build A Stairway To Paradise (10)
I'll Walk Alone (9)
I'm In Love Again (1)
I'm In Love With You (6) *57*
I'm In The Mood For Love (11)
I'm Waiting Just For You (6) *27*
I've Heard That Song Before (14,16)
I've Told Ev'ry Little Star (13)
Imagination (12)
In The Garden (8)
It Came Upon A Midnight Clear (14,16)
It Is No Secret (8)
It's A Long Way To The Top (If You Wanna Rock 'N Roll) (17)
It's A Pity To Say Goodnight (10)
It's A Sin To Tell A Lie (12)
Jingle Bells (14,16)
Johnny Will (15) *35*
Joy To The World (14,16)
Just A Closer Walk With Thee (2)
Lazy River (10)
Little White Lies (9)
Lonesome Road (10)
Louella (4)
Love Hurts (17)
Love Letters In The Sand (6) *1*
Love Makes The World Go 'Round (13)
Maybe You'll Be There (11)

Money Honey (3)
Moody River (13) *1*
Moonglow (12)
More Than You Know (11)
My Baby Just Cares For Me (10)
My God Is Real (Yes, God Is Real) (8)
Nearness Of You (11)
No More Mr. Nice Guy (17)
No Other Arms (No Arms Can Ever Hold You) (5) *26*
Now I Know (5)
Now The Day Is Over (8)
O Come, All Ye Faithful ..see: Adeste Fideles
O Come, All Ye Faithful ..see: Adeste Fideles
O Holy Night (14,16)
O Little Town Of Bethlehem (14,16)
Old Rugged Cross (8)
Panama (17)
Paradise City (17)
Peace In The Valley (2)
Please Send Me Someone To Love (3)
Pledging My Love (3)
Remember You're Mine (6) *6*
Rich In Love (5)
Robins And Roses (10)
Rock Around The Clock (3)
San Antonio Rose (12)
Santa Claus Is Comin' To Town (14,16)
Secret Love (11)
September Song (9)

Shake A Hand (3)
Shot Gun Boogie (3)
Silent Night (14,16)
Silver Bells (14,16)
Sleep (13)
Smoke On The Water (17)
Softly And Tenderly (8)
Solitude (9)
Speedy Gonzales (15) *6*
St. Louis Blues (9)
Stairway To Heaven (17)
Star Dust (9)
Steal Away (2)
Sunday (1)
Sweet Georgia Brown (10)
Sweet Hour Of Prayer (8)
Sweet Sue (11)
Take The Time (5)
Technique (4)
Tenderly (11)
Tennessee Saturday Night (5)
That Lucky Old Sun (1)
There's A Gold Mine In The Sky (6) *14*
There's A Moon Out Tonight (13)
They Can't Take That Away From Me (11)
Thousand Years (13)
To Each His Own (9)
Tomorrow Night (3)
Tra-La-La (5)
True Love (11)
Tutti' Frutti (5) *12*
Twixt Twelve And Twenty (15) *17*
Two Hearts (5) *16*

Unchained Melody (12)
Very Thought Of You (12)
Walking The Floor Over You (15) *44*
Wang Dang Taffy-Apple Tango (15) *62*
We Love But Once (12)
(Welcome) New Lovers (15) *18*
Whispering Hope (8)
White Christmas (14,16)
Who's Sorry Now (12)
Why Baby Why (6) *5*
Why Don't You Believe Me (11)
Will The Circle Be Unbroken (8)
Will You Love Me Tomorrow (13)
Wind Cries Mary (17)
With The Wind And The Rain In Your Hair (15) *21*
With You (1)
Without My Love (4)
Words (15) *94*
Would You Like To Take A Walk (1)
Yes Indeed (10)
Yield Not To Temptation (8)
You Always Hurt The One You Love (12)
You Belong To Me (11)
You've Got Another Thing Comin' (17)

BOOT CAMP CLIK '97

Collective of rap acts: BDI, **Cocoa Brovaz**, **Heltah Skeltah**, **Originoo Gunn Clappaz**, The Reps, B.T.J's, Swan & Boogie Brown, F.L.O.W. and Illa Noyz.

DEBUT	PEAK	WKS	CD		ARTIST — Album Title	$	Label & Number
6/7/97	15	9	©		For The People	$10	Priority 50646

Blackout
Down By Law
Dugout, The

Go For Yours
Headz Are Reddee Pt. II
Illa Noyz

Last Time
Likkle Youth Man Dem
Night Riders

Ohkeedoke
1-900 Get Da Boot
Rag Time

Rugged Terrain
Watch Your Step

BOOTLEG '99

Born Ira Dorsey in Flint, Michigan. Male rapper. Member of group **The Dayton Family**.

DEBUT	PEAK	WKS	CD		ARTIST — Album Title	$	Label & Number
4/17/99	91	5	©		Death Before Dishonesty	$10	Relativity 1726

Bad Guy
Celebrate
Death Before Dishonesty

Fantasies
Fly Away
If I Die

MaMa
No Future
Run For Cover

Set Up
Sideways
Sophisticated Thugs

We Gone Ride

BOOTSY'S RUBBER BAND '78

Born William Collins on 10/26/51 in Cincinnati. Member of **James Brown**'s **JB's** from 1969-71. Became bassist of **Funkadelic/Parliament** in 1972. Later formed own group, Bootsy's Rubber Band.

DEBUT	PEAK	WKS		CD				$	Label
5/1/76	59	27		© 1	Stretchin' Out In Bootsy's Rubber Band			$15	Warner 2920
2/5/77	16	23	●	© 2	Ahh...The Name Is Bootsy, Baby!			$15	Warner 2972
2/25/78	16	24	●	© 3	Bootsy? Player Of The Year			$15	Warner 3093
7/21/79	52	9		4	This Boot Is Made For Fonk-n			$15	Warner 3295
12/6/80	70	9		© 5	Ultra Wave			$15	Warner 3433

BOOTSY

| 5/29/82 | 120 | 8 | | © 6 | The One Giveth, The Count Taketh Away | | | $15 | Warner 3667 |

WILLIAM "BOOTSY" COLLINS

Ahh...The Name Is Bootsy, Baby (2) • Another Point Of View (1) • As In (I Love You) (3) • Bootsy Get Live (4) • Bootsy? (What's The Name Of This Town) (3) • Bootzilla (3) • Can't Stay Away (2) • Chug-A-Lug (The Bunn Patrol) (4)
Countracula (This One's For You) (6) • Excon (Of Love) (6) • F-Encounter (5) • Fat Cat (5) • Funky Funktioneer (6) • Hollywood Squares (3) • I'd Rather Be With You (1) • Is That My Song? (5) • It's A Musical (5) • Jam Fan (Hot) (4)
Landshark (Just When You Thought It Was Safe) (6) • Love Vibes (1) • May The Force Be With You (3) • Mug Push (5) • Munchies For Your Love (2) • Music To Smile By (6) • #1 Funkateer (6) • Oh Boy Gorl (4) • Physical Love (1) • Pinocchio Theory (2) • Play On Playboy (6)
Preview Side Too (2) • Psychoticbumpschool (1) • Roto-Rooter (3) • Rubber Duckie (2) • Sacred Flower (5) • Shejam (Almost Bootsy Show) (4) • Shine-O-Myte (Rag Popping) (6) • So Nice You Name Him Twice (6) • Sound Crack (5)
Stretchin' Out (In A Rubber Band) (1) • Take A Lickin' And Keep On Kickin' (6) • Under The Influence Of A Groove (4) • Vanish In Our Sleep (1) • Very Yes (3) • We Want Bootsy (2) • What's A Telephone Bill? (2) • What's W-R-O-N-G Radio (6)

BOO-YAA T.R.I.B.E. '90

Rap group from Los Angeles: Samoan brothers Ted, Donald, David, Danny, Paul and Roscoe Devoux.

| 4/28/90 | 117 | 15 | | © | New Funky Nation | | | $10 | 4th & B'way 4017 |

Don't Mess • New Funky Nation
Once Upon A Drive By • Pickin' Up Metal
Psyko Funk • R.A.I.D.
Rated R • Riot Pump
Six Bad Brothas • T.R.I.B.E.
Walk The Line

BORDEN, Lizzy — see LIZZY

BORN JAMERICANS '94

Dancehall reggae duo: Horace Payne and Norman Howell.

| 6/25/94 | 188 | 1 | | © | Kids From Foreign | | | $10 | Delicious Vinyl 92349 |

Ain't No Stoppin' • Boom Shak-A-Tack
Cease & Seckle • Informa Fe Dead
Nobody Knows • Oh Gosh
So Ladies • Sweet Honey
Warning Sign • Why Do Girls

BOSS '93

Born Lichelle Laws in 1973 in Southfield, Michigan. Female rapper.

| 6/12/93 | 22 | 18 | | © | Born Gangstaz | | | $10 | DJ West 52903 |

Born Gangsta • Catch A Bad One • Comin' To Getcha
Deeper *65* • Diary Of A Mad Bitch • Drive By
I Don't Give A Fuck • Livin' Loc'd • Mai Sista Izza Bitch
1-800-Body-Bags • Progress Of Elimination • Recipe Of A Hoe
2 To Da Head

★490★ BOSTON '86

Rock group from Boston: Brad Delp (vocals), Tom Scholz (guitar, keyboards), Barry Goudreau (guitar), Fran Sheehan (bass) and Sib Hashian (drums). Goudreau formed **Orion The Hunter** in 1982. By 1986, reduced to a duo of Scholz and Delp. Delp and Goudreau formed **RTZ**. Scholz's 1994 Boston lineup: Fran Cosmo and Tommy Funderburk (vocals), Gary Pihl (guitar), David Sikes (bass) and Doug Huffman (drums). Scholz is an avid inventor with several patented inventions.

9/25/76	3	132	▲16 ©	1	Boston	C:#37/28		$12	Epic 34188
9/2/78	❶2	45	▲7 ©	2	Don't Look Back	C:#20/21		$12	Epic 35050
10/18/86	❶4	50	▲4 ©	3	Third Stage			$10	MCA 6188
6/25/94	7	16	▲ ©	4	Walk On			$10	MCA 10973
6/21/97	47	16	▲ ©	5	Greatest Hits	[G]		$10	Epic 67622

Amanda (3,5) *1* • Can'tcha Say (You Believe In Me)/Still In Love (3) *20* • Cool The Engines (3,5) • Don't Be Afraid (2) • Don't Look Back (2,5) *4* • Feelin' Satisfied (2,5) *46*
4th Of July Reprise (medley) (5) • Higher Power (5) • Hitch A Ride (1) • Hollyann (3) • I Need Your Love (4) *51* • I Think I Like It (3) • It's Easy (2)
Journey, The (3) • Launch Medley (3) • Let Me Take You Home Tonight (1) • Livin' For You (4,5) • Long Time (1,5) *22* • Magdalene (3)
Man I'll Never Be (2,5) *31* • More Than A Feeling (1,5) *5* • My Destination (3) • New World (3) • Party (2,5) • Peace Of Mind (1,5) *38* • Rock & Roll Band (1,5)
Smokin' (1,5) • Something About You (1) • Star Spangled Banner (medley) (5) • Surrender To Me (4) • Tell Me (5) • To Be A Man (3)
Used To Bad News (2) • Walk On Medley (4) • We Can Make It (4) • We're Ready (3) *9* • What's Your Name (4)

★243★ BOSTON POPS ORCHESTRA '63

Founded in 1885 by Henry Lee Higginson, conductor of the Boston Symphony Orchestra. Arthur Fiedler (b: 12/17/1894 in Boston; d: 7/10/79, age 84) joined the orchestra in 1915 as a violist; began his reign as its conductor in 1930 and remained until his death. National public TV program *Evening at Pops* began in 1969. **John Williams** succeeded Fiedler in 1980. Keith Lockhart (former Cincinnati Pops conductor) succeeded Williams in 1995.

1)"Jalousie" And Other Favorites In The Latin Flavor 2)Offenbach: Gaite Parisienne 3)"Pops" Goes The Trumpet 4)Star Dust 5)Pops Roundup

BOSTON POPS/ARTHUR FIEDLER:

2/2/59	9	16	©	1	Offenbach: Gaite Parisienne; Khachaturian: Gayne Ballet Suite	[I]		$25	RCA Victor 2267
7/14/62	29	14	©	2	Pops Roundup	[I]		$25	RCA Victor 2595
3/9/63	36	6		3	Our Man In Boston	[I]		$25	RCA Victor 2599
4/6/63	5	23		4	"Jalousie" And Other Favorites In The Latin Flavor	[I]		$25	RCA Victor 2661
6/22/63	29	14		5	Star Dust	[I]		$25	RCA Victor 2670
10/19/63	116	4		6	Concert In The Park	[I]		$25	RCA Victor 2677
9/26/64	18	31		7	"Pops" Goes The Trumpet	[I]		$25	RCA Victor 2729

AL HIRT/BOSTON POPS/ARTHUR FIEDLER

| 11/21/64+ | 53 | 14 | | 8 | Peter And The Commissar | [C] | | $25 | RCA Victor 2773 |

ALLAN SHERMAN/BOSTON POPS/ARTHUR FIEDLER

| 10/23/65 | 86 | 16 | | 9 | Nero Goes "Pops" | [I] | | $25 | RCA Victor 2821 |

PETER NERO/ARTHUR FIEDLER/BOSTON POPS

| 12/25/65 | 58ˣ | 1 | © | 10 | Pops Christmas Party | [X-I] | | $25 | RCA Victor 2329 |
| | | | | | first released in 1959 | | | | |

DEBUT	PEAK	WKS	RIAA	CD	ARTIST — Album Title	Catalog	Sym	$	Label & Number
					BOSTON POPS ORCHESTRA — Cont'd				
5/14/66	145	3			11 The Duke At Tanglewood	[I-L]		$25	RCA Victor 2857
					DUKE ELLINGTON/BOSTON POPS/ARTHUR FIEDLER				
6/18/66	62	23			12 The "Pops" Goes Country	[I]		$30	RCA Victor 2870
					CHET ATKINS/BOSTON POPS/ARTHUR FIEDLER				
10/26/68	157	7			13 Up Up And Away	[I]		$25	RCA Victor 3041
4/5/69	192	2			14 Glenn Miller's Biggest Hits	[I]		$25	RCA Victor 3064
10/11/69	160	4			15 Chet Picks On The Pops	[I]		$25	RCA Victor 3104
					CHET ATKINS/BOSTON POPS/ARTHUR FIEDLER				
12/19/70	9[X]	2		©	16 A Christmas Festival	[X-I]		$15	Polydor 5004
1/9/71	190	2			17 Fabulous Broadway	[I]		$15	Polydor 5003
12/4/71	174	5			18 Arthur Fiedler "Superstar"	[I]		$15	Polydor 5008
2/26/72	196	3			19 The Music Of Paul Simon	[I]		$15	Polydor 5018
9/8/79	147	6			20 Saturday Night Fiedler	[I]		$12	Midsong Int. 011
					BOSTON POPS/JOHN WILLIAMS:				
12/20/80+	181	6		©	21 Pops In Space	[I]		$10	Philips 9500 921
5/17/86	155	8		©	22 Swing, Swing, Swing	[I]		$10	Philips 412626
7/20/96	62	7		©	23 Summon The Heroes	[I]		$10	Sony Classical 62592
					BOSTON POPS				
					official centennial Olympic theme for the 1996 Summer Olympics in Atlanta				

Adios Amigo (12)
Alabama Jubilee (12)
American Patrol (14)
"And Now A Word From Our Sponsor" Medley (3)
Apartment, Theme From The (3)
Austrian Peasant Dances, Op. 14 (6)
Bachmania (20)
Battle Of New Orleans (medley) (15)
Begin The Beguine (22)
Bidin' My Time (9)
Blue Moon (5)
Brazilian Dance (4)
Bridge Over Troubled Water (18,19)
Bugler's Dream (medley) (23)
Bugler's Holiday (3,7)
By The Time I Get To Phoenix (15)
Cabaret (13)
Canticle ..see: Scarborough Fair
Caravan (21)
Carnival Of Venice (7)
Cecilia (13)
Chariots Of Fire (Theme) (23)
Chattanooga Choo Choo (14)
Chester (6)
Christmas Festival (10)
Clair De Lune (Moonlight) (5)
Close Encounters Of The Third Kind Suite (21)
Cold, Cold Heart (12)
Company Medley (17)
Conquest Of Paradise (Theme) (23)
Cool Water (2)
Country Gentleman (12)
Dance Of The Sugar Plum Fairy (10)

Dangling Conversation (19)
Danze Piemontesi Op. 31, No. 1 (4)
Deck The Halls (medley) (16)
Deep Purple (5)
Delilah (15)
Do Nothin' 'Til You Hear From Me (11)
Dream Pantomime (10)
El Condor Pasa (19)
Eili, Eili (7)
Embraceable You (9)
Empire Strikes Back Medley (21)
End Of A Symphony (8)
Espana Cani (4)
Exodus, Theme From (3)
Faded Love (12)
Festive Overture, Op. 96 (23)
Fiddler On The Roof Medley (17)
59th Street Bridge Song (Feelin' Groovy) (19)
First Noel (medley) (16)
Funeral March Of A Marionette (6)
Gaite Parisienne (1)
Galveston (15)
Gayne Ballet Suite - Medley (1)
Gentle On My Mind (18)
Georgy Girl (13)
Glow Worm (5)
God Rest Ye Merry, Gentlemen (medley) (16)
Good King Wenceslas (medley) (16)
Grand Galop Chromatique, Op. 12 (6)
Guys And Dolls Medley (3)
Hair Medley (17)
Hallelujah Chorus (16)
Hark! The Herald Angels Sing (medley) (16)

Hazy Shade Of Winter (19)
Hey, Look Me Over (3)
Home On The Range (2)
Homeward Bound (19)
I Got It Bad And That Ain't Good (11)
I Got Rhythm (9)
I Let A Song Go Out Of My Heart (11)
I Think I Love You (18)
I'll Fly Away (12)
I'm Beginning To See The Light (11)
I'm Thinking Tonight Of My Blue Eyes (12)
Il Guarany-Overture (4)
In The Mood (14,22)
In The Pines (medley) (12)
Jalousie (4)
Jamaican Rhumba (4)
Java (4)
Javelin (23)
Jesus Christ Superstar (18)
Jingle Bells (medley) (16)
John Henry (medley) (12)
Joy To The World (medley) (16)
La Sorella-March (4)
La Virgen De La Macarena (4)
Lara's Theme (13)
Last Roundup (2)
Last Waltz (15)
Le Cid (4)
Let It Be (18)
Listen To The Mockingbird (medley) (12)
Little Brown Jug (14)
Lost Chord (7)
Love Is Blue (13)
Love Is Here To Stay (9)
Love Me Tonight (18)
Love Scene (11)
Love Story, Theme From (18)

Lover's Concerto (13)
Mack The Knife (3)
Mah-Na Mah-Na (18)
Man And A Woman (13)
Man I Love (9)
Man Of La Mancha Medley (17)
March Of The Charioteers (3)
Michelle (13)
Mooch, The (11)
Mood Indigo (11)
Moonlight Cocktail (14)
Moonlight Serenade (14,22)
Mosquito Dance (4)
Mrs. Robinson (19)
Never On Sunday (5)
Night Was Made For Love (5)
O Bury Me Not On The Lone Prairie (2)
O Come All Ye Faithful (medley) (16)
O Fortuna (23)
Ode To Billy Joe (15)
Ode To Zeus (23)
Old Friends (19)
Olympic Fanfare and Theme (medley) (23)
Olympic Hymn (23)
Olympic Spirit (23)
On Top Of Old Smoky (medley) (12)
Opus One (22)
Orange Blossom Special (12)
Parade Of Charioteers (23)
Parade Of The Wooden Soldiers (10)
Pavanne (7)
Peter And The Commissar (8)
Piano Concerto No. 21: Andante (13)
Pops Hoe-Down (2)
Pops Roundup (2)
Prayer Of Thanksgiving (6)

Proud Mary (18)
Red River Valley (2)
Reverie (5)
Rhapsody In Blue (9)
Riders In The Sky (2)
Rudolph The Red-Nosed Reindeer (10,16)
Santa Claus Is Comin' To Town (10,16)
Satin Doll (11,22)
Saturday Night Fever Medley (20)
Scarborough Fair/Canticle (15,19)
Shepherds' Pastorale (16)
Silent Night (medley) (16)
Sing, Sing, Sing (22)
Sleepy Lagoon (14,22)
Sleigh Ride (10,16)
Smoke Gets In Your Eyes (3)
Snowfall (22)
Solitude (11)
Song Fest Medley (6)
Song Of India (2)
Song Of The Volga Boatmen (14)
Sophisticated Lady (11)
Sound Of Silence (19)
Spanish Harlem (15)
St. Louis Blues March (14)
Stairway To The Stars (5)
Star Dust (5)
Star Wars Medley (21)
Stompin' At The Savoy (22)
String Of Pearls (14,22)
Sugarfoot Rag (medley) (15)
Summon The Heroes (23)
Sunrise Serenade (14,22)
Superman Medley (21)
Swing, Swing, Swing (22)
Tennessee Waltz (12)

They Can't Take That Away From Me (9)
This Guy's In Love With You (15)
Timon Of Athens March (11)
Tonight (5)
Toward A New Life (23)
Toy Trumpet (7)
Trumpet Concerto (7)
Trumpeter's Lullaby (7)
Tumbling Tumbleweeds (2)
Tuxedo Junction (14,22)
Up, Up And Away (13)
Valley Of The Dolls, Theme From (13)
Variations On "How Dry I Am" (8)
Victor Herbert Favorites Medley (6)
Wagon Wheels (2)
Waltz Of The Flowers (16)
Wedding Dance (Freilachs) (6)
What Have They Done To My Song, Ma (18)
When You Wish Upon A Star (5)
White Christmas (10,16)
Whoopie-Ti-Yi-Yo (Git Along Little Dogies) (2)
Wildwood Flower (medley) (12)
Wimoweh (15)
Windy And Warm (12)
Winter Wonderland (10)
Wunderbar (5)
Yellow Rose Of Texas (2)
Yesterday (13)
You And The Night And The Music (5)
Zacatecas-March (4)

BOSTON SYMPHONY ORCHESTRA   '63

Orchestra founded in 1880. Conductors have included **Charles Munch**, **Erich Leinsdorf** and Seiji Ozawa.

DEBUT	PEAK	WKS			ARTIST — Album Title	Catalog		$	Label & Number
5/11/63	17	8			1 Ravel: Bolero/Pavan For A Dead Princess/La Valse	[I]		$20	RCA Victor 2664
					Charles Munch, conductor				
5/18/63	41	4			2 Mahler: Symphony No. 1	[I]		$20	RCA Victor 2642
					Erich Leinsdorf, conductor				
3/28/64	82	12			3 Mozart: Requiem Mass			$25	RCA Victor 7030 [2]
					a Requiem Mass conducted by **Erich Leinsdorf** in memory of President **John F. Kennedy** - celebrated by Richard Cardinal Cushing, the Archbishop of Boston, on 1/19/64 at Boston's Cathedral of the Holy Cross				

Bolero (1)   La Valse (1)   Pavan For A Dead Princess (1)   Requiem Mass (3)   Symphony No. 1 In D (2)

BOUNTY KILLER   '96

Born Rodney Pryce on 6/26/72 in Riverton City, Jamaica. Reggae singer.

DEBUT	PEAK	WKS			ARTIST — Album Title	Catalog		$	Label & Number
10/5/96	145	4		©	My Xperience			$10	TVT 1461

Benz & The Bimma
Change Like The Weather
Fedup
Gun Down

Guns & Roses
Hip-Hopera 81
Living Dangerously
Lord Is My Light & Salvation

Mama
Maniac
Marathon ("To Chicago")
Mi Nature

My Experience
Revolution III
Seek God
Suicide Or Murder

Virgin Island
War Beyond The Stars
War Face
Who Send Dem

BOURGEOIS TAGG   '87

Rock group from Los Angeles: Brent Bourgeois (vocals, keyboards), Larry Tagg (vocals, bass), Lyle Workman (guitar), Scott Moon (keyboards) and Michael Urbano (drums).

| 5/31/86 | 139 | 7 | © | 1 | Bourgeois Tagg | | | $10 | Island 90496 |
| 10/24/87 | 84 | 21 | © | 2 | YoYo | | | $10 | Island 90638 |

Best Of All Possible Worlds (2)
Body Count (1)
Changed (1)
Coma (2)

Cry Like A Baby (2)
Dying To Be Free (1)
Electric Train (1)
15 Minutes In The Sun (2)

Heart Of Darkness (1)
I Don't Mind At All (2) *38*
Let The War Begin (1)
Move Up (1)

Mutual Surrender (What A Wonderful World) (1) *62*
Out Of My Mind (2)
Pencil & Paper (2)

Perfect Life (1)
Stress (2)
Waiting For The Worm To Turn (2)

What's Wrong With This Picture (2)

BOWIE, David   ★28★   '73

Born David Jones on 1/8/47 in London. Pop-rock singer/actor. Joined Lindsay Kemp Mime Troupe in 1967. Adopted new personas (Ziggy Stardust, Alladin Sane, Thin White Duke) to accompany several of his musical phases. Married to Angie Barnett, the subject of **The Rolling Stones'** song "Angie," from 1970-80. Acted in several movies. Starred in *The Elephant Man* on Broadway. Formed **Tin Machine** in 1988. Married Somalian actress/supermodel Iman on 4/24/92. Inducted into the Rock and Roll Hall of Fame in 1996. Also see **Spiders From Mars**.

1)Station To Station 2)Let's Dance 3)Diamond Dogs 4)David Live 5)Young Americans

4/15/72+	93	16		©	1	Hunky Dory	C:#39/16		$20	RCA Victor 4623
6/17/72+	75	72	●	©	2	The Rise And Fall Of Ziggy Stardust And The Spiders From Mars	C:❶⁴⁶/277		$20	RCA Victor 4702
						also see #30 below				
11/18/72+	16	36		©	3	Space Oddity	[E]		$20	RCA Victor 4813
						first released in 1968 as Man Of Words, Man Of Music on Mercury 61246 ($150)				
11/18/72+	105	23		©	4	The Man Who Sold The World	[E]		$20	RCA Victor 4816
						first released in 1970 on Mercury 61325 ($40)				
3/17/73	144	9			5	Images 1966-1967	[E]		$50	London 628/9 [2]
						first recordings in London on Pye and Decca labels				
5/12/73	17	22	●	©	6	Aladdin Sane	C:#41/20		$20	RCA Victor 4852
11/10/73	23	21		©	7	Bowie Pin Ups	C:#32/16		$20	RCA Victor 0291
6/15/74	5	25	●	©	8	Diamond Dogs	C:#9/48		$20	RCA Victor 0576
						BOWIE				
						original cover, which is worth $4000, features Bowie as a dog with his genitals visible -- controversial and quickly withdrawn				
10/26/74	8	21	●	©	9	David Live	[L]		$25	RCA Victor 0771 [2]
						recorded on 7/12/74 at the Tower Theatre in Philadelphia				
3/22/75	9	51	●	©	10	Young Americans			$15	RCA Victor 0998
2/7/76	3	32	●	©	11	Station To Station			$15	RCA Victor 1327
6/19/76	10	39	▲	©	12	Changesonebowie	[G]		$15	RCA Victor 1732
1/29/77	11	19		©	13	Low			$15	RCA Victor 2030
11/12/77	35	19		©	14	"Heroes"	C:#18/60		$15	RCA Victor 2522
5/6/78	136	8		©	15	David Bowie narrates Prokofiev's "Peter and The Wolf"			$15	RCA Victor 2743
						DAVID BOWIE/EUGENE ORMANDY & THE PHILADELPHIA ORCHESTRA				
						side 1: above title; side 2: Britten: Young Person's Guide to the Orchestra - both sides feature The Philadelphia Orch.				
10/21/78	44	13		©	16	Stage	[L]		$20	RCA Victor 2913 [2]
						recorded on 4/28/78 at the Spectrum in Philadelphia				
6/16/79	20	15		©	17	Lodger			$12	RCA Victor 3254
10/4/80	12	27		©	18	Scary Monsters			$12	RCA Victor 3647
12/12/81+	68	18		©	19	Changestwobowie	[G]		$12	RCA Victor 4202
4/3/82	135	7			20	Christiane F.	[S]		$12	RCA Victor 4239
4/30/83	4	68	▲	©	21	Let's Dance			$10	EMI America 17093
8/27/83	99	9		©	22	Golden Years	[K]		$10	RCA Victor 4792
11/12/83	89	15		©	23	Ziggy Stardust/The Motion Picture	[L-S]		$15	RCA Victor 4862 [2]
						recorded on 7/3/73 at the Hammersmith Odeon in London				
4/21/84	147	6		©	24	Fame and Fashion (David Bowie's All Time Greatest Hits)	[G]		$10	RCA Victor 4919
10/20/84	11	24	▲	©	25	Tonight			$10	EMI America 17138
7/19/86	68	8		©	26	Labyrinth	[S]		$10	EMI America 17206
						includes "Into The Labyrinth," "Sarah," "Hallucination," "The Goblin Battle," "Thirteen O'Clock" and "Home At Last" by Trevor Jones				
5/23/87	34	26	●	©	27	Never Let Me Down			$10	EMI America 17267
10/14/89	97	16	●	©	28	Sound + Vision	[K]		$60	Rykodisc 0120 [6]
						recordings from 1969-80				
4/7/90	39	27	▲	©	29	Changesbowie	[G]		$10	Rykodisc 20171
7/7/90	93	9		©	30	The Rise And Fall Of Ziggy Stardust And The Spiders From Mars	[R]		$10	Rykodisc 10134
4/24/93	39	8		©	31	Black Tie White Noise			$10	Savage 50212
10/14/95	21	6		©	32	Outside - The Nathan Adler Diaries: A Hyper Cycle			$10	Virgin 40711
3/1/97	39	6		©	33	Earthling			$10	Virgin 42627
10/23/99	47	4		©	34	'Hours...			$10	Virgin 48157
10/14/00	181	1		©	35	Bowie At The Beeb	[E-L]		$25	Virgin 28958 [3]
						recorded from 1968-72 for the BBC				

Absolute Beginners (35)
Across The Universe (10)
African Night Flight (17)
After All (4)
After Today (28)
Aladdin Sane (1913-1938-197?) (6,9,19)
All The Madmen (4)
All The Young Dudes (9,23)
Almost Grown (35)
Always Crashing In The Same Car (13,35)

Amsterdam (35)
Andy Warhol (1,35)
Anyway, Anyhow, Anywhere (7,28)
Art Decade (13,16)
Ashes To Ashes (18,19,22,24,28,29,35)
Bang Bang (27)
Battle For Britain (The Letter) (33)
Be My Wife (13,28)

Beat Of Your Drum (27)
Beauty And The Beast (14,16)
Because You're Young (18)
Bewlay Brothers (1,28)
Big Brother (8,9,28)
Black Country Rock (4,28)
Black Tie White Noise (31)
Blackout (14,16)
Blue Jean (25,29) *8*
Bombers (35)
Boys Keep Swinging (17,20,28)

Breaking Glass (13,16,28)
Brilliant Adventure (34)
Can You Hear Me (10)
Candidate (8)
Cat People (Putting Out Fire) (21) *67*
Changes (1,9,13,23,24,28,29,35)
Chant Of The Ever Circling Skeletal Family (8)
Chilly Down (26)
China Girl (21,29) *10*

Come And Buy My Toys (5)
Cracked Actor (6,9,23,28,35)
Criminal World (21)
Cygnet Committee (3,35)
D. J. (17,19,24)
Dancing With The Big Boys (25)
Day-In Day-Out (27) *21*
Dead Man Walking (33)
Diamond Dogs (8,9,12,29)
Did You Ever Have A Dream (5)
Dodo (medley) (28)

Don't Bring Me Down (7,28)
Don't Let Me Down & Down (31)
Don't Look Down (25)
Dreamers, The (34)
Drive-In Saturday (6,28)
Eight Line Poem (1,35)
'87 And Cry (27)
Everything's All Right (7)
Fame (10,12,16,24,35) *1*
Fame '90 (29)

BOWIE, David — Cont'd

Fantastic Voyage (17)
Fascination (10,28)
Fashion (18,19,22,24,29) **70**
Fill Your Heart (medley) (1)
Five Years (2,16,30,35)
Friday On My Mind (7)
Future Legend (8)
Glass Spider (27)
God Knows I'm Good (3,35)
God Only Knows (25)
Golden Years
   (11,12,22,24,29) **10**
Gospel According To Tony Day
   (5)
Hallo Spaceboy (32,35)
Hang On To Yourself
   (2,16,23,30,35)
Hearts Filthy Lesson (32) **92**
Helden (20,28)
Here Comes The Night (7)
Heroes (14,16,20,24,29)
I Am With Name (32)
I Can't Explain (7,22)
I Feel Free (31)
I Have Not Been To Oxford
   Town (32)
I Keep Forgetting (25)
I Know It's Gonna Happen
   Someday (31)
I Wish You Would (7)
I'm Afraid Of Americans
   (33,35) **66**
I'm Deranged (32)
If I'm Dreaming My Life (34)
In The Heat Of The Morning
   (5,35)
It Ain't Easy (2,30,35)
It's Hard To Be A Saint In The
   City (28)

It's No Game (Part 1 & 2) (18)
Janine (3,35)
Jean Genie (6,9,12,29) **71**
Joe The Lion (14,22,28)
John, I'm Only Dancing
   (12,28,29,30)
John I'm Only Dancing (Again)
   1975 (19)
Join The Gang (5)
Jump They Say (31)
Karma Man (5,35)
Kingdom Come (18,28)
Knock On Wood (9)
Kooks (1,35)
Lady Grinning Soul (6)
Lady Stardust (2,30,35)
Last Thing You Should Do (33)
Laughing Gnome (5)
Law (Earthlings On Fire) (33)
Leon Takes Us Outside (32)
Let Me Sleep Beside You (5,35)
Let's Dance (21,29,35) **1**
Let's Spend The Night Together
   (6,23)
Letter To Hermione (3)
Life On Mars? (1)
Little Bombadier (5)
Little Wonder (33,35)
London Boys (5)
London Bye Ta-Ta (28,35)
Look Back In Anger
   (17,20,22,28)
Looking For A Friend (35)
Looking For Lester (31)
Looking For Satellites (33)
Love You Till Tuesday (5)
Loving The Alien (25)
Lucy Can't Dance (31)
Magic Dance (26)

Maid Of Bond Street (5)
Man Who Sold The World
   (4,28,35)
Memory Of A Free Festival
   (3,35)
Miracle Goodnight (31)
Modern Love (21,29) **14**
Moonage Daydream
   (2,9,23,28,30,35)
Moss Garden (14)
Motel, The (32)
Move On (17)
My Death (23)
Neighborhood Threat (25)
Neuköln (14)
Never Let Me Down (27) **27**
New Angels Of Promise (34)
New Career In A New Town
   (13)
New York's In Love (27)
1984 (8,9,19,24,28)
Nite Flights (31)
No Control (32)
Occasional Dream (3)
Oh! You Pretty Things
   (1,19,23,35)
On Broadway (medley) (19)
Outside (32)
Pallas Athena (31)
Panic In Detroit (6,28)
Peter And The Wolf, Op. 67
   (15)
Please Mr. Gravedigger (5)
Prettiest Star (6,28)
Pretty Things Are Going To Hell
   (34)
Queen Bitch (1,35)
Quicksand (1)
Rebel Rebel (8,9,12,28,29) **64**

Red Money (17)
Red Sails (17,22,28)
Repetition (17)
Ricochet (21)
Right (10)
Rock 'N' Roll Suicide
   (2,9,23,28,30,35)
Rock 'N' Roll With Me (8,9)
Rosalyn (7)
Round And Round (28)
Rubber Band (5)
Running Gun Blues (4)
Saviour Machine (4)
Scary Monsters (And Super
   Creeps) (18,22)
Scream Like A Baby (18)
Secret Life Of Arabia (14)
See Emily Play (7)
Sell Me A Coat (5)
Sense Of Doubt (14,16,20)
Seven (34,35)
Seven Years In Tibet (33)
Shake It (21)
Shapes Of Things (7)
She Shook Me Cold (4)
She's Got My Medals (5)
Shining Star (Makin' My Love)
   (27)
Silly Boy Blue (5,35)
Small Plot Of Land (32)
Somebody Up There Likes Me
   (10)
Something In The Air (34)
Song For Bob Dylan (1)
Sons Of The Silent Age (14,28)
Sorrow (7,28)
Soul Love (2,16,30)
Sound And Vision
   (13,19,28) **69**

Space Oddity
   (3,12,23,24,28,29,35) **15**
Speed Of Life (13,16,28)
Star (2,16,30)
Starman (2,19,24,30,35) **65**
Station To Station (11,16,20,28)
Stay (11,20,35)
Strangers When We Meet (32)
Subterraneans (13)
Suffragette City
   (2,9,12,23,28,29,30,35)
Supermen, The (4,35)
Survive (34,35)
Sweet Head (30)
Sweet Thing (8,9)
TVC 15 (11,16,20,24,28) **64**
Teenage Wildlife (18)
Telling Lies (33)
There Is A Happy Land (5)
This Is Not America (35)
Thru' These Architects Eyes
   (32)
Thursday's Child (34)
Time (6,23)
Time Will Crawl (27)
Tonight (25) **53**
Too Dizzy (27)
Tumble And Twirl (25)
Uncle Arthur (5)
Underground (26)
Unwashed And Somewhat
   Slightly Dazed (3,35)
Up The Hill Backwards (18,28)
V-2 Schneider (14,20)
Velvet Goldmine (30)
Voyeur Of Utter Destruction (As
   Beauty) (32)
Waiting For The Man (35)
Warszawa (13,16,20,28)

Watch That Man (6,9,23,28)
We Are Hungry Men (5)
We Are The Dead (8)
We Prick You (32)
Wedding, The (31)
Wedding Song (31)
Weeping Wall (13)
What In The World (13,16)
What's Really Happening? (34)
When I Live My Dream (5)
Where Have All The Good
   Times Gone! (7)
White Light/White Heat
   (23,28,35)
Width Of A Circle (4,9,23,35)
Wild Eyed Boy From Freecloud
   (3,23,28,35)
Wild Is The Wind
   (11,19,22,28,35)
Win (10)
Wishful Beginnings (32)
Within You (26)
Without You (21) **73**
Word On A Wing (11)
Yassassin (17)
You've Been Around (31)
Young Americans
   (10,12,24,28,29) **28**
Young Person's Guide To The
   Orchestra, Op. 34 (15)
Zeroes (27)
Ziggy Stardust
   (2,12,16,23,28,29,30,35)

BOW WOW WOW '82

New-wave group assembled in London by Malcolm McLaren (former **Sex Pistols** manager). Consisted of Annabella Lwin (vocals; born Myant Myant Aye in Burma), Matthew Ashman (guitar), Leroy Gorman (bass) and Dave Barbarossa (drums). The latter three were members of **Adam And The Ants** until 1980. Ashman died of diabetes on 11/21/95 (age 36).

11/21/81	192	2		©	1 **See Jungle! See Jungle! Go Join Your Gang Yeah! City All Over, Go Ape Crazy**			$10	RCA Victor 4147
5/15/82	67	22			2 **The Last Of The Mohicans**		[M]	$10	RCA Victor 4314
9/18/82	123	9		©	3 **I Want Candy**			$10	RCA Victor 4375
3/26/83	82	13		©	4 **When The Going Gets Tough, The Tough Get Going**			$10	RCA Victor 4570

Aphrodisiac (4)
Baby, Oh No (3)
Chihuahua (1)
Cowboy (2,3)
Do You Wanna Hold Me?
   (4) **77**

El Boss Dicho (3)
Elimination Dancing (1)
Go Wild In The Country (1,3)
Golly! Golly! Go Buddy! (1)
Hello, Hello Daddy (I'll Sacrifice
   You) (1)

I Want Candy (2,3) **62**
(I'm A) T.V. Savage (1,3)
I'm Not A Know It All (1)
Jungle Boy (1,3)
King Kong (1,3)
Lonesome Tonight (4)

Louis Quatorze (2,3)
Love Me (4)
Love, Peace And Harmony (4)
Man Mountain (4)
Mario (Your Own Way To
   Paradise) (4)

Mickey, Put It Down (1)
Mile High Club (2,3)
Orang-outang (1)
Quiver (Arrows In My) (4)
Rikki Dee (4)
Roustabout (4)

Sinner! Sinner! Sinner! (Prince
   Of Darkness) (4)
Tommy Tucker (4)
What's The Time (Hey Buddy)
   (4)
Why Are Babies So Wise? (1)

BOX OF FROGS '84

Rock group from England: John Fiddler (vocals), Chris Dreja (guitar), Paul Samwell-Smith (bass) and Jim McCarty (drums). The latter three were members of **The Yardbirds**. McCarty also with **Renaissance** and **Illusion**.

7/7/84	45	20		©	1 **Box Of Frogs**			$10	Epic 39327
6/14/86	177	3		©	2 **Strange Land**			$10	Epic 39923

Another Wasted Day (1)
Asylum (2)
Average (2)
Back Where I Started (1)

Edge, The (1)
Get It While You Can (2)
Hanging From The Wreckage
   (2)

Harder (1)
Heart Full Of Soul (2)
House On Fire (2)
Into The Dark (1)

Just A Boy Again (1)
Love Inside You (1)
Poor Boy (1)
Strange Land (2)

Trouble (2)
Two Steps Ahead (1)
You Mix Me Up (2)

BOX TOPS, The '68

Pop-rock group from Memphis: Alex Chilton (vocals), Gary Talley (guitar), John Evans (organ), Bill Cunningham (bass) and Danny Smythe (drums). Evans and Smythe left in late 1967; replaced by Rick Allen and Tom Boggs. Disbanded in 1970. Chilton later formed the power-pop band Big Star. Cunningham is the brother of B.B. Cunningham of **The Hombres**.

11/18/67+	87	15		©	1 **The Letter/Neon Rainbow**			$25	Bell 6011
4/27/68	59	19		©	2 **Cry Like A Baby**			$20	Bell 6017
12/7/68+	45	26			3 **The Box Tops Super Hits**		[G]	$20	Bell 6025
9/6/69	77	11		©	4 **Dimensions**			$20	Bell 6032

Ain't No Way (4)
Break My Mind (1,3)
Choo Choo Train (3) **26**
Cry Like A Baby (2,3) **2**
Deep In Kentucky (2)
Every Time (2)
Everything I Am (1)

Fields Of Clover (2)
Gonna Find Somebody (1)
Good Morning Dear (2)
Happy Song (4)
Happy Times (1)
I Met Her In Church (3) **37**
I Must Be The Devil (4)

I Pray For Rain (4)
I Shall Be Released (4) **67**
I'll Hold Out My Hand (4)
I'm The One For You (4)
I'm Your Puppet (1,3)
Letter, The (1,3) **1**
Lost (2)

Midnight Angel (4)
Neon Rainbow (1,3) **24**
People Make The World (1)
Rock Me Baby (4)
727 (2)
She Knows How (1)
She Shot A Hole In My Soul (3)

Soul Deep (4) **18**
**Sweet Cream Ladies, Forward
   March** (4) **28**
Together (4)
Trains & Boats & Planes (1,3)
Trouble With Sam (2)
Weeping Analeah (2)

Whiter Shade Of Pale (1,3)
You Keep Me Hanging On (2,3)

BOYCE, Tommy, & Bobby Hart '68

Songwriting/singing/production duo. Boyce was born on 9/29/44 in Charlottesville, Virginia. Died of a self-inflicted gunshot wound on 11/23/94 (age 50). Hart was born in 1944 in Phoenix.

9/9/67	200	1			1 **Test Patterns**			$30	A&M 4126
4/20/68	109	5			2 **I Wonder What She's Doing Tonite?**			$30	A&M 4143

Abe's Tune (2)
Countess, The (2)
For Baby (1)
Girl, I'm Out To Get You (1)

**Goodbye Baby (I Don't Want
   To See You Cry)** (2) **53**
I Should Be Going Home (1)
I Wanna Be Free (2)

**I Wonder What She's Doing
   Tonite** (2) **8**
I'm Digging You, Digging Me (2)
In The Night (1)

Leaving Again (2)
Life Medley (1)
Love Every Day (2)
My Little Chickadee (1)

Out & About (1) **39**
Population (1)
Pretty Flower (2)
Shadows (1)

Sometimes She's A Little Girl
   (1)
Teardrop City (2)
Two For The Price Of One (2)

BOYER, Charles '66
Born on 8/28/1897 in Figeac, France. Committed suicide on 8/26/78 (age 80). Prolific actor.

| 1/8/66 | 148 | 2 | | | **Where Does Love Go**.. [T] | $25 | Valiant 5001 |

All The Things You Are
Autumn Leaves
Gigi
Hello, Young Lovers
I Believe
La Vie En Rose
Once Upon A Time
Softly, As I Leave You
Venice Blue
What Now My Love
When The World Was Young
Where Does Love Go

BOY GEORGE '89
Born George O'Dowd on 6/14/61 in Bexleyheath, England. Former lead singer of **Culture Club**. Brief stint as Lieutenant Lush, a backing singer with **Bow Wow Wow**.

8/1/87	145	5		© 1	**Sold**			$10	Virgin 90617
3/25/89	126	11		© 2	**High Hat**			$10	Virgin 91022
11/20/93	169	3		© 3	**At Worst...The Best Of Boy George And Culture Club** .... [G]			$10	SBK 39014

After The Love (3)
Bow Down Mister (3)
Church Of The Poison Mind
   (3) *10*
Crying Game (3) *15*
**Do You Really Want To Hurt
   Me** (3) *2*
Don't Cry (2,3)\
Don't Take My Mind On A Trip
   (2)
Everything I Own (1,3)
Freedom (1)
Generations Of Love (3)
Girl With Combination Skin (2)
I Asked For Love (1)
I'll Tumble 4 Ya (3) *9*
I'm Not Sleeping Anymore (2)
It's A Miracle (3) *13*
Just Ain't Enough (1)
Karma Chameleon (3) *1*
Keep Me In Mind (1)
Kipsy (2)
Little Ghost (1)
Love Hurts (3)
Love Is Love (3)
Miss Me Blind (3) *5*
More Than Likely (3)
Move Away (3) *12*
Next Time (1)
Sold (1)
Something Strange Called Love
   (2)
Sweet Toxic Love (3)
Time (Clock Of The Heart)
   (3) *2*
To Be Reborn (1)
Victims (3)
We've Got The Right (1)
Where Are You Now? (1)
Whether They Like It Or Not (2)
Whisper (2)
You Are My Heroin (2)
You Found Another Guy (2)

BOY HOWDY '94
Country group from Los Angeles: brothers Cary and Larry Parks (guitars), Jeffrey Steele (vocals, bass) and Hugh Wright (drums).

| 1/29/94 | 103 | 14 | | © | **She'd Give Anything** .... [M] | $10 | Curb 77656 |

Come On, Come On
Cowboy's Born With A Broken
   Heart
Homegrown Love
One That Got Away
She'd Give Anything
They Don't Make Them Like
   That Anymore

BOYLAN, Terence '77
Born in 1948 in Buffalo, New York. Brother of record producer John Boylan.

| 11/5/77 | 181 | 3 | | | **Terence Boylan** .... | $12 | Asylum 1091 |

Don't Hang Up Those Dancing
   Shoes
Hey Papa
Rain King
Shake It
Shame
Sundown Of Fools
Trains
War Was Over
Where Are You Hiding?

BOY MEETS GIRL '89
Songwriting/recording duo from Seattle: Shannon Rubicam and George Merrill. Married in 1988.

| 5/4/85 | 76 | 11 | | © 1 | **Boy Meets Girl** | | | $10 | A&M 5046 |
| 10/22/88+ | 50 | 26 | | © 2 | **Reel Life** | | | $10 | RCA 8414 |

Be My Baby (1)
Bring Down The Moon (2) *49*
Don't Tell Me We Have Nothing
   (1)
From Now On (1)
I Wish You Were Here (1)
If You Run (2)
In Your Eyes (1)
Is Anybody Out There In Love
   (2)
Kissing, Falling, Flying (1)
No Apologies (2)
Oh Girl (1) *39*
One Sweet Dream (2)
Pieces (1)
Premonitions (1)
Restless Dreamer (2)
Someone's Got To Send Out
   Love (2)
Stay Forever (2)
Stormy Love (2)
Touch, The (1)
Waiting For A Star To Fall
   (2) *5*

BOYS, The '89
R&B vocal group from Northridge, California: Khiry, Hakeem, Tajh and Bilal Samad.

11/26/88+	33	36	▲	© 1	**Messages From The Boys**			$10	Motown 6260
10/27/90	108	7	●	© 2	**The Boys**			$10	Motown 6302
5/30/92	191	1		© 3	**The Saga Continues...**			$10	Motown 6336

Applejuice (3)
Be My Girl (1)
Be Yo Man (3)
Bush, The (2)
Crazy (2) *29*
Dial My Heart (1) *13*
Doin' It With The B (3)
Freak Of The Week (3)
Funny (2)
Funny '92 (3)
Got To Be There (2)
Hak's House Of Pleasure (3)
Happiness (3)
Happy (1)
I Had A Dream (2)
I'm Yours (3)
Just For The Fun Of It (1)
Let's Dance (1)
Little Romance (1)
Love Gram (1)
Lucky Charm (1)
My Love (2)
Personality (1)
Saga Continues... (3)
Smpte (2)
Strings 'N Things (2)
Sunshine (1)
Thanx 4 The Funk (2)
Thing Called Love (2)
Thought You Knew (3)
Tonite (3)
You Got Me Cryin' (3)

BOYS CLUB '89
Vocal duo from Minneapolis: Gene Hunt and Joe Pasquale. Hunt (real name: Eugene Wolfgramm) was a member of **The Jets**.

| 11/26/88+ | 93 | 16 | | © | **Boys Club** | | | $10 | MCA 42242 |

At It Again
Danglin' On A String
I Remember Holding You *8*
Loneliest Heart
Naked Truth
Step By Step
Tell Me
Time Starts Now
Victim Of The Heart
When You're Letting Go

BOYS DON'T CRY '86
British pop-rock quintet: Nick Richards (vocals), Nico Ramsden (guitar), Brian Chatton (keyboards), Mark Smith (bass) and Jeff Seopardi (drums).

| 6/21/86 | 55 | 19 | | © | **Boys Don't Cry** .... | $10 | Profile 1219 |

Cities On Fire
Hearts Bin Broken
I Wanna Be A Cowboy *12*
Josephine
Lipstick
Ships In The Night
Take My Love And Run
Turn Over (I Like It Better That
   Way)
22nd Century Boy

BOYZONE '99
Male vocal group from Dublin, Ireland: Mikey Graham, Keith Duffy, Shane Lynch, Ronan Keating and Stephen Gately.

| 9/18/99 | 167 | 4 | | © | **Where We Belong** .... | $10 | Ravenous 559171 |

All That I Need
All The Time In The World
And I
Baby Can I Hold You
I Love The Way You Love Me
I'll Never Not Need You
Must Have Been High
No Matter What
One Kiss At A Time
Picture Of You
That's How Love Goes
Walk On (So They Told Me)
Where Did You Go?
Will Be Yours
You Flew Away

★348★ BOYZ II MEN '94
R&B vocal group from Philadelphia: Wanya Morris, Michael McCary, Shawn Stockman and Nathan Morris.

6/1/91	3	133	▲⁹	© 1	**Cooleyhighharmony** C:❶⁷/75	$10	Motown 6320
10/23/93	19	15	▲²	© 2	**Christmas Interpretations** .... C:#3/30 [X]	$10	Motown 6365
					Christmas charts: 2/'93, 5/'94, 6/'95, 13/'96, 21/'97		
1/8/94	154	6		© 3	**Cooleyhighharmony** .... C:#27/2 [R]	$10	Motown 0231
					expanded edition of their first album, includes 7 extra tracks		
9/17/94	❶⁵	99	▲¹²	© 4	**II** .... C:#46/2	$10	Motown 0323
11/25/95	17	19	▲	© 5	**The Remix Collection** .... [K]	$10	Motown 0584
10/11/97	❶¹	50	▲²	© 6	**Evolution**		$10	Motown 0819

BOYZ II MEN — Cont'd

| 9/30/00 | 4 | 23 | ● | © 7 | Nathan/Michael/Shawn/Wanya | | | $10 | Universal 159281 |

Al Final Del Camino (End Of The Road - Spanish Version) (3)
All Around The World (4)
All Night Long (6)
Baby C'mon (6)
Beautiful Women (7)
Bounce, Shake, Move, Swing (7)
Brokenhearted (5)
Can You Stand The Rain (6)
Can't Let Her Go (6)
Cold December Nights (2)
Come On (6)
Dear God (6)
Do They Know (2)
Do You Remember (7)
Doin' Just Fine (6)
Dreams (7)
End of the Road (3) 1
50 Candles (4)
4 Seasons Of Loneliness (6) 1
Girl In The Life Magazine (6)
Good Guy (7)
Hey Lover (4)
Human II (Don't Turn Your Back On Me) (6)
I Do (7)
I Finally Know (7)
I Remember (5) 46
I Sit Away (4)
I'll Make Love To You (4,5) 1
In The Still Of The Nite (I'll Remember) (3) 3
It's So Hard To Say Goodbye To Yesterday (1,3) 2
Jezzebel (4)
Joyous Song (2)
Know What You Want (7)
Let It Snow (2) 32
Little Things (1,3)
Lonely Heart (1,3)
Lovely (7)
Motownphilly (1,3,5) 3
Never (6)
Never Go Away (7)
On Bended Knee (4,5) 1
Pass You By (7)
Please Don't Go (1,3) 49
Share Love (7)
Silent Night (2)
Song For Mama (6) 7
Step On Up (7)
Sympin (1,3)
Thank You (4) 21
Thank You In Advance (7) 80
This Is My Heart (1,3)
To The Limit (6)
Trying Times (4)
U Know (4,5)
Uhh Ahh (1,3,5) 16
Under Pressure (1,3,5)
Vibin' (4,5) 56
Water Runs Dry (4,5) 2
What The Deal (7)
Who Would Have Thought (2)
Why Christmas (2)
Yesterday (4)
You're Not Alone (2)
Your Love (1,3)

BRADY BUNCH, The   '72

Vocal group consisting of the child actors of TV's *The Brady Bunch*. Barry Williams (Greg), Chris Knight (Peter), Mike Lookinland (Bobby), Maureen McCormick (Marsha), Eve Plumb (Jan) and Susan Olsen (Cindy).

| 12/25/71 | 6 [X] | 1 | © 1 | Merry Christmas from The Brady Bunch | [X] | $75 | Paramount 5026 |
| 5/13/72 | 108 | 19 | © 2 | Meet The Brady Bunch | | $50 | Paramount 6032 |

Ain't It Crazy (2)
American Pie (2)
Away In A Manger (1)
Baby, I'm-A Want You (2)
Come Run With Me (2)
Day After Day (2)
First Noel (1)
Frosty The Snowman (1)
I Believe In You (2)
I Just Want To Be Your Friend (2)
Jingle Bells (1)
Little Drummer Boy (1)
Love My Life Away (2)
Me And You And A Dog Named Boo (2)
O Come All Ye Faithful (1)
O Holy Night (1)
Rudolph The Red-Nosed Reindeer (1)
Santa Claus Is Coming To Town (1)
Silent Night (1)
Silver Bells (1)
Time To Change (2)
We Can Make The World A Whole Lot Brighter (2)
We Wish You A Merry Christmas (1)
We'll Always Be Friends (2)

BRAGG, Billy, & Wilco   '00

Born Steven William Bragg on 12/20/57 in Barking, Essex, England. Rock singer/songwriter.

| 11/5/88 | 198 | 1 | © 1 | Workers Playtime | | $10 | Elektra 60824 |

BILLY BRAGG

| 7/11/98 | 90 | 7 | © 2 | Mermaid Avenue | | $10 | Elektra 62204 |
| 6/17/00 | 88 | 4 | © 3 | Mermaid Avenue Vol. II | | $10 | Elektra 62522 |

Aginst Th' Law (3)
Airline To Heaven (3)
All You Fascists (3)
Another Man's Done Gone (2)
At My Window Sad And Lonely (2)
Birds And Ships (2)
Black Wind Blowing (3)
Blood Of The Lamb (3)
California Stars (2)
Christ For President (2)
Eisler On The Go (2)
Feed Of Man (3)
Hesitating Beauty (2)
Hoodoo Voodoo (2)
Hot Rod Hotel (3)
I Guess I Planted (2)
I Was Born (3)
Ingrid Bergman (2)
Joe Dimaggio Done It Again (3)
Life With The Lions (1)
Little Time Bomb (2)
Meanest Man (3)
Must I Paint You A Picture (1)
My Flying Saucer (3)
One By One (2)
Only One (1)
Price I Pay (1)
Remember The Mountain Bed (3)
Rotting On Remand (1)
Secret Of The Sea (3)
She Came Along To Me (2)
She's Got A New Spell (1)
Short Answer (1)
Someday Some Morning Sometime (2)
Stetson Kennedy (2)
Tender Comrade (1)
Unwelcome Guest (2)
Valentine's Day Is Over (1)
Waiting For The Great Leap Forwards (1)
Walt Whitman's Niece (2)
Way Over Yonder In The Minor Key (2)

BRAINSTORM   '77

Disco group from Detroit: Belita Woods, Charles Overton, Jeryl Bright, Larry Sims, Gerald Kent, Trenita Womack, Lamont Johnson, Willie Wooten and Renell Gonsalves.

| 3/26/77 | 145 | 16 | | | Stormin' | | | $12 | Tabu 2048 |

Easy Thangs
Hangin' On
Lovin' Is Really My Game
Prelude
Stormin'
This Must Be Heaven
Waiting For Someone
Wake Up And Be Somebody 86
We Know A Place

BRAMLETT, Bonnie   '75

Born Bonnie O'Farrell on 11/8/44 in Acton, Illinois. Singer/actress. Half of **Delaney & Bonnie**. Married to Delaney Bramlett from 1967-72. Their daughter Bekka briefly joined **Fleetwood Mac**. Played "Bonnie Watkins" on TV's *Roseanne*.

| 2/22/75 | 168 | 5 | | | It's Time | | | $15 | Capricorn 0148 |

Atlanta, Georgia
Cover Me
Cowboys And Indians
Higher & Higher
It's Time
Oncoming Traffic
Since I Met You Baby
Where You Come From
Your Kind Of Kindness
(Your Love Has Brought Me From A) Mighty Long Way

BRAM TCHAIKOVSKY   '79

Rock trio from Lincolnshire, England: Peter Bramall (vocals, guitar), Micky Broadbent (bass) and Keith Boyce (drums).

6/30/79	36	18		1	Strange Man, Changed Man			$12	Polydor 6211
5/17/80	108	10		2	Pressure			$12	Polydor 6273
5/23/81	158	8		3	Funland			$10	Arista 4292

Bloodline (1)
Breaking Down The Walls Of Heartache (3)
Can't Give You Reasons (2)
Egyptian Mummies (3)
Girl Of My Dreams (1) 37
Heart Of Stone (3)
Heartache (2)
Hollywood Nightmare (2)
I'm A Believer (1)
I'm The One That's Leaving (1)
Jeux Sans Frontieres (Game With No Rules) (2)
Lady From The U.S.A. (1)
Let's Dance (2)
Letter From The USA (2)
Lonely Dancer (1)
Miracle Cure (1)
Missfortune (2)
Mister President (2)
Model Girl (3)
New York Paranoia (2)
Nobody Knows (1)
Pressure (2)
Robber (1)
Russians Are Coming (2)
Sarah Smiles (1)
Shall We Dance? (3)
Soul Surrender (3)
Stand And Deliver (3)
Strange Man, Changed Man (1)
Together My Love (3)
Turn On The Light (1)
Used To Be My Used To Be (3)
Why Does My Mother 'Phone Me? (3)

BRAND NEW HEAVIES, The   '94

Funk group from London: N'Dea Davenport (vocals), Simon Bartholomew (guitar), Andrew Levy (bass) and Jan Kincaid (drums). Davenport left in 1996; replaced by Siedah Garrett.

8/22/92	139	3	©	1	Heavy Rhyme Experience: Vol. 1			$10	Delicious Vinyl 92178
4/9/94	95	9	©	2	Brother Sister			$10	Delicious Vinyl 92319
5/31/97	118	5	©	3	Shelter			$10	Delicious Vinyl 5019

After Forever (3)
Back To Love (2)
Bonafied Funk (1)
Brother Sister (2)
Crying Water (3)
Day Break (2)
Day By Day (3)
Death Threat (1)
Do Whatta I Gotta Do (1)
Dream On Dreamer (2) 51
Fake (2)
Feels Like Right (3)
Forever (2)
Have A Good Time (2)
Highest High (3)
I Like It (3)
It's Gettin Hectic (1)
Jump N' Move (1)
Keep Together (2)
Last To Know (3)
Mind Trips (2)
Once Is Twice Enough (3)
People Giving Love (2)
Shelter (3)
Snake Hips (2)
Sometimes (3) 88
Soul Flower (1)
Spend Some Time (2)
State Of Yo (1)
Stay Gone (3)
Ten Ton Take (2)
Wake Me When I'm Dead (1)
Whatgabouthat (1)
Who Makes The Loot? (1)
You Are The Universe (3)
You Can Do It (3)

BRAND NUBIAN   '93

Rap trio from New Rochelle, New York: Maxwell Dixon ("Grand Puba"), Derek Murphy ("Sadat X") and Lorenzo DeChalus ("Lord Jamar"). Dixon left in 1992, replaced by Terence Perry ("Sincere Allah"). Dixon returned in 1998.

| 2/23/91 | 130 | 28 | © | 1 | One For All | | | $10 | Elektra 60946 |
| 2/20/93 | 12 | 10 | © | 2 | In God We Trust | | | $10 | Elektra 61381 |

BRAND NUBIAN — Cont'd

| 11/19/94 | 54 | 3 | © 3 Everything Is Everything .... | $10 | Elektra 61682 |
| 10/17/98 | 59 | 5 | © 4 Foundation... | $10 | Arista 19024 |

Ain't No Mystery (2)
All For One (1)
Alladat (3)
Allah And Justice (1)
Allah U Akbar (2)
Another Day In The Beast (Thoughts From A Criminal) (3)
Back Up Off The Wall (4)
Beat Change (4)
Black And Blue (2)

Black Star Line (2)
Brand Nubian (1,4)
Brand Nubian Rock The Set (2)
Claimin' I'm A Criminal (3)
Concerto In X Minor (1)
Dance To My Ministry (1)
Dedication (1)
Don't Let It Go To Your Head (4) *54*
Down For The Real (3)
Drop The Bomb (1)

Feels So Good (1)
Foundation (4)
Gang Bang (3)
Godz..., The (2)
Grand Puba, Positive And L.G. (1)
Here We Go (4)
Hold On (5)
I'm Black And I'm Proud (4)
Let's Dance (4)
Lick Dem Muthaphuckas (3)

Love Me Or Leave Me Alone (2) *92*
Love Vs. Hate (4)
Maybe One Day (4)
Meaning Of The 5% (2)
Nubian Jam (3)
Pass The Gat (2)
Probable Cause (4)
Punks Jump Up To Get Beat Down (2) *77*
Ragtime (1)

Return, The (4)
Return Of The Dread (3)
Shinin' Star (4)
Sincerely (4)
Slow Down (1)
Steady Bootleggin' (2)
Steal Ya 'Ho (2)
Step Into Da Cipher (3)
Step To The Rear (1)
Straight Off Da Head (3)
Straight Outta Now Rule (4)

Sweatin Bullets (3)
To The Right (1)
Too Late (4)
Travel Jam (2)
Try To Do Me (1)
U For Me (4)
Wake Up (1)
What The Fuck... (3)
Who Can Get Busy Like This Man... (1)
Word Is Bond (3) *94*

BRANDOS, The   '87
Rock group from New York City: Dave Kincaid (vocals), Ed Rupprecht (guitar), Ernie Mendillo (bass) and Larry Mason (drums).

| 9/26/87 | 108 | 19 | © Honor Among Thieves.. | $10 | Relativity 8192 |

Come Home
Gettysburg

Hard Luck Runner
Honor Among Thieves

In My Dreams
Matter Of Survival

Nothing To Fear
Strychnine

Walking On The Water

BRANDT, Paul   '96
Born on 7/21/72 in Calgary, Alberta, Canada. Country singer/songwriter.

| 6/29/96 | 102 | 30 | ● © Calm Before The Storm....................................... | $10 | Reprise 46180 |

All Over Me
Calm Before The Storm
I Do

I Meant To Do That
My Heart Has A History
On The Inside

One And Only One
Pass Me By (If You're Only Passing Through)

Take It From Me
12 Step Recovery

BRAND X   '77
Jazz-fusion group from England: **Phil Collins** (drums; **Genesis**), John Goodsall (guitar), Robin Lumley (keyboards), Percy Jones (bass) and Morris Pert (percussion).

11/13/76	191	3	© 1 Unorthodox Behaviour	[I]	$12	Passport 98019
5/21/77	125	8	© 2 Moroccan Roll	[I]	$12	Passport 98022
11/3/79	165	6	© 3 Product..	[I]	$12	Passport 9840

Algon (Where An Ordinary Cup Of Drinking Chocolate Costs £8,000,000,000) (3)
...And So To F... (3)
April (3)
Born Ugly (1)

Collapsar (2)
Dance Of The Illegal Aliens (3)
Disco Suicide (2)
Don't Make Waves (3)
Euthanasia Waltz (1)
Hate Zone (2)

Macrocosm (2)
Malaga Virgen (2)
...Maybe I'll Lend You Mine After All (2)
Not Good Enough-See Me! (1)
Nuclear Burn (1)

Orbits (2)
Rhesus Perplexus (3)
Running On Three (1)
Smacks Of Euphoric Hysteria (1)
Soho (3)

Sun In The Night (2)
Touch Wood (1)
Unorthodox Behaviour (1)
Wal To Wal (3)

Why Should I Lend You Mine (When You've Broken Yours Off Already) (2)

BRANDY   '95
Born Brandy Norwood on 2/11/79 in McComb, Mississippi; raised in California. Singer/actress. Star of the TV series *Moesha*.

| 10/15/94+ | 20 | 89 | ▲⁴ © 1 Brandy .... | $10 | Atlantic 82610 |
| 6/27/98 | 2¹ | 72 | ▲⁴ © 2 Never S-a-y Never | $10 | Atlantic 83039 |

Almost Doesn't Count (2) *16*
Always On My Mind (1)
Angel In Disguise (2) *72*
As Long As You're Here (1)
Baby (1) *4*

Best Friend (1) *34*
Boy Is Mine (2) *1*
Brokenhearted (1) *9*
(Everything I Do) I Do It For You (2)

Give Me You (1)
Happy (1)
Have You Ever? (2) *1*
I Dedicate (Parts I-III) (1)
I Wanna Be Down (1) *6*

I'm Yours (1)
Learn The Hard Way (2)
Love Is On My Side (1)
Movin' On (1)
Never Say Never (2)

One Voice (2)
Put That On Everything (2)
Sunny Day (1)
Tomorrow (2)
Top Of The World (2)

Truthfully (2)
U Don't Know Me (Like U Used To) (2) *79*

BRANIGAN, Laura   '84
Born on 7/3/57 in Brewster, New York. Singer/actress. Played "Monica" in the 1984 movie *Delta Pi*.

9/25/82	34	36	● © 1 Branigan..	$10	Atlantic 19289
4/9/83	29	37	● © 2 Branigan 2...	$10	Atlantic 80052
4/28/84	23	45	▲ © 3 Self Control	$10	Atlantic 80147
8/10/85	71	15	© 4 Hold Me	$10	Atlantic 81265
8/1/87	87	28	© 5 Touch	$10	Atlantic 81747
4/28/90	133	6	© 6 Laura Branigan..	$10	Atlantic 82086

All Night With Me (1) *69*
Angels Calling (5)
Bad Attitude (6)
Best Was Yet To Come (6)
Breaking Out (3)
Close Enough (2)
Cry Wolf (5)
Deep In The Dark (2)
Don't Show Your Love (2)
Down Like A Rock (1)
Find Me (2)

Foolish Lullaby (4)
Forever Young (4)
Gloria (1) *2*
Heart (3)
Hold Me (4) *82*
How Am I Supposed To Live Without You (2) *12*
I Found Someone (4) *90*
I Wish We Could Be Alone (1)
I'm Not The Only One (2)
If You Loved Me (1)

Let Me In (6)
Living A Lie (1)
Lovin' You Baby (1)
Lucky (2)
Lucky One (3) *20*
Mama (2)
Maybe I Love You (1)
Maybe Tonight (1)
Meaning Of The Word (5)
Moonlight On Water (6) *59*
Name Game (5)

Never In A Million Years (6)
No Promise, No Guarantee (6)
Over Love (5)
Please Stay, Go Away (1)
Power Of Love (5) *26*
Reverse Psychology (6)
Sanctuary (4)
Satisfaction (3)
Self Control (3) *4*
Shadow Of Love (5)
Shattered Glass (5) *48*

Silent Partners (3)
Smoke Screen (6)
Solitaire (2) *7*
Spanish Eddie (4) *40*
Spirit Of Love (5)
Squeeze Box (2)
Take Me (3)
Tenderness (4)
Ti Amo (3) *55*
Touch (5)
Turn The Beat Around (6)

Unison (6)
Whatever I Do (5)
When I'm With You (4)
When The Heat Hits The Streets (4)
Will You Still Love Me Tomorrow (3)
With Every Beat Of My Heart (3)

BRANNEN, John   '88
Born in Savannah, Georgia; raised in Charleston, South Carolina. Country-rock singer.

| 3/12/88 | 156 | 14 | © Mystery Street... | $10 | Apache 71650 |

Desolation Angel
Dreaming Girl

Drifter, The
Mystery Street

Paradise Highway
Primitive Emotion

Running With The Storm
Searching For Satisfaction

Shadows In The Night
Twilight Is Over

Wild One

BRASS CONSTRUCTION   '76
Disco group from New York City: Randy Muller (vocals, keyboards), Joe Wong (guitar), Wayne Parris, Morris Price, Jesse Ward and Mickey Grudge (horn section), Sandy Billups (congas), Wade Williamston (bass) and Larry Payton (drums). Muller later formed **Skyy**.

2/7/76	10	35	▲ 1 Brass Construction	$12	United Artists 545
11/20/76	26	22	● 2 Brass Construction II..	$12	United Artists 677
11/19/77	66	14	● 3 Brass Construction III...	$12	United Artists 775
11/18/78	174	4	4 Brass Construction IV	$12	United Artists 916
12/15/79+	89	20	5 Brass Construction 5...	$12	United Artists 977
9/20/80	121	5	6 Brass Construction 6...	$12	United Artists 1060
5/22/82	114	8	7 Attitudes...	$10	Liberty 51121

BRASS CONSTRUCTION — Cont'd

| 6/11/83 | 176 | 6 | | | 8 **Conversations** .... | | | $10 | Capitol 12268 |

Attitude (7)
Blame It On Me (Introspection) (2)
Breakdown (8)
Can You See The Light (7)
Celebrate (3)
Changin' (1)
Dance (1)
Do That Thang (7)
Do Ya (6)
Don't Try To Change Me (6)
E.T.C. (7)
Easy (8)

Forever Love (7)
Funtimes (7)
Get It Together (3)
Get To The Point (Summation) (2)
Get Up (4)
Get Up To Get Down (5)
Ha Cha Cha (Funktion) (2) 51
Happy People (3)
Help Yourself (4)
Hotdog (7)
How Do You Do (What You Do To Me) (8)

I Do Love You (8)
I Want Some Action (5)
I'm Not Gonna Stop (6)
It's A Shame (8)
It's Alright (5)
Love (1)
L-O-V-E-U (3)
Message (Inspiration) (2)
Movin' (1) 14
Music Makes You Feel Like Dancing (5)
Night Chaser (4)
No Communication (8)

Now Is Tomorrow (Anticipation) (2)
One To One (4)
Peekin' (1)
Perceptions (What's The Right Direction) (4)
Physical Attraction (8)
Pick Yourself Up (4)
Right Place (5)
Sambo (Progression) (2)
Screwed (Conditions) (2,5,6)
Shakit (5)
Starting Tomorrow (4)

Sweet As Sugar (4)
Talkin' (1)
Top Of The World (3)
Wake Up (3)
Walkin' The Line (8)
Watch Out (5)
We (3)
We Are Brass (6)
We Can Do It (6)
We Can Work It Out (8)
What's On Your Mind (Expression) (2)
Working Harder Every Day (6)

Yesterday (3)

BRASS RING, The　　'66

Studio group assembled by producer/arranger/saxophonist Phil Bodner.

6/25/66	109	8			1 **Love Theme From The Flight Of The Phoenix**		[I]	$15	Dunhill 50008
4/15/67	157	3			2 **Sunday Night At The Movies**		[I]	$15	Dunhill 50015
6/24/67	193	2			3 **The Dis-Advantages Of You**		[I]	$15	Dunhill 50017

Al Di La (2)
Amen (2)
Baby The Rain Must Fall (2)
Born Free (2)
California Dreamin' (3)
Colonel Bogey March (2)
Dating Game (3)
Day In The Life Of A Fool (2)

Dis-Advantages Of You (3) 36
Hud, Theme From (2)
I Will Wait For You (3)
Lara's Theme (1)
Laura (1)
Lightening Bug (3)
Long Ships (2)
Look For A Star (2)

Love Is A Many Splendored Thing (1)
Man & A Woman (3)
Moment To Moment (1)
Moon River (1)
Moonglow & Theme From Picnic (3)
Music To Watch Girls By (3)

My Foolish Heart (1)
Pakistan (3)
Phoenix Love Theme (1) 32
Sambe De Orfeo (2)
Sand Pebbles (And We Were Lovers), Theme From The (3)
Secret Love (1)
Shadow Of Your Smile (1)

Somewhere, My Love ..see: Lara's Theme
Summer Place, Theme From A (1)
Tara's Theme (1)
True Love (2)
Unchained Melody (1)
Very Precious Love (2)

Wait For Me (3)

BRAUN, Bob　　'62

Born Robert Brown on 4/20/29 in Ludlow, Kentucky. Died of Parkinson's disease on 1/15/2001 (age 71). Hosted own TV show in Cincinnati.

| 10/27/62 | 99 | 6 | | | **Till Death Do Us Part** .... | | | $20 | Decca 74339 |

Because Of You
How Deep Is The Ocean (How High Is The Sky)

Is It Right Or Wrong?
Just In Time
Nearness Of You

Our Anniversary Of Love
That Certain Something (We Call Love)

Till Death Do Us Part 26
Wasn't The Summer Short
When I Fall In Love

Why I Love You
You'll Never Know

BRAUN, Rick　　'00

Born in Allentown, Pennsylvania. Jazz saxophonist.

| 6/17/00 | 78 | 15 | | © | 1 **Shake It Up** .... | | [I] | $10 | Warner 47557 |

BONEY JAMES/RICK BRUAN

| 3/17/01 | 182 | 1 | | © | 2 **Kisses In The Rain** .... | | [I] | $10 | Warner 47994 |

Car Wash 2000 (2)
Central Ave. (1)
Chain Reaction (1)
Emma's Song (2)

Grazin' In The Grass (1)
Grover's Groove (2)
Kisses In The Rain (2)
Love's Like That (1)

Middle Of The Night (2)
More Than You Know (1)
One For The Girls (2)
R.S.V.P. (1)

Shake It Up (1)
Simplicity (2)
Song For My Father (1)
Song For You (2)

Stars Above (1)
Use Me (2)
Your World (2)

BRAVE BELT — see BACHMAN-TURNER OVERDRIVE

BRAXTON, Toni　　'94

Born on 10/7/68 in Severn, Maryland. Female R&B singer. Former member of **The Braxtons**. Sister of **Tamar**. Married Keri Lewis (of **Mint Condition**) on 4/21/2001. Won the 1993 Best New Artist Grammy Award.

7/31/93+	❶²	96	▲⁸	©	1 Toni Braxton		C:#46/1	$10	LaFace 26007
7/6/96	2¹	92	▲⁸	©	2 Secrets			$10	LaFace 26020
5/13/00	2¹	47	▲²	©	3 The Heat			$10	LaFace 26069

Another Sad Love Song (1) 7
Art Of Love (3)
Best Friend (1)
Breathe Again (1) 3
Candlelight (1)
Come On Over Here (2)
Fairy Tale (3)

Find Me A Man (2)
Gimme Some (3)
He Wasn't Man Enough (3) 2
Heat, The (3)
How Could An Angel Break My Heart (2)
How Many Ways (1) 35

I Belong To You (1) 28
I Don't Want To (2) 19
I Love Me Some Him (2) flip
I'm Still Breathing (3)
In The Late Of Night (2)
Just Be A Man About It (3) 32
Let It Flow (2) flip

Love Affair (1)
Love Shoulda Brought You Home (1) 33
Maybe (3)
Never Just For A Ring (3)
Seven Whole Days (1)
Spanish Guitar (3) 98

Speaking In Tongues (3)
Spending My Time With You (1)
Talking In His Sleep (3)
There's No Me Without You (2)
Un-Break My Heart (2) 1
Why Should I Care (2)

You Mean The World To Me (1) 7
You're Makin Me High (2) 1
You've Been Wrong (1)

BRAXTONS, The　　'96

Vocal trio of sisters from Severn, Maryland: **Tamar**, Trina and Towanda Braxton. Began as a quintet, with Traci and **Toni Braxton**. Toni went solo in 1992; Traci went solo in 1995.

| 8/31/96 | 113 | 6 | | © | **So Many Ways** .... | | | $10 | Atlantic 82875 |

Boss, The
Girl On the Side

I'd Still Say Yes
In A Special Way

L.A.D.I.
Never Say Goodbye

Only Love
Slow Flow

So Many Ways 83
Take Home To Momma

What Does It Take
Where's The Good In Goodbye

★389★　　BREAD　　'73

Soft-rock group formed in Los Angeles: **David Gates** (vocals, guitar, keyboards), James Griffin (guitar), Robb Royer (guitar) and Jim Gordon (drums). Mike Botts replaced Gordon after first album. Larry Knechtel replaced Royer in 1971. Disbanded in 1973, reunited briefly in 1976.

10/18/69	127	9		©	1 **Bread**			$15	Elektra 74044
8/8/70	12	32	●	©	2 **On The Waters**			$15	Elektra 74076
3/27/71	21	25	●	©	3 **Manna**			$15	Elektra 74086
2/5/72	3	56	●	©	4 **Baby I'm-A Want You**			$15	Elektra 75015
11/18/72	18	29	●	©	5 **Guitar Man**			$15	Elektra 75047
3/31/73	2¹	119	▲⁵	©	6 **The Best Of Bread**		[G]	$15	Elektra 75056
6/1/74	32	18	●		7 **The Best Of Bread, Volume Two**		[G]	$12	Elektra 1005
1/15/77	26	16	●	©	8 **Lost Without Your Love**			$12	Elektra 1094

Any Way You Want Me (1)
Aubrey (5,7) 15
Baby I'm-A Want You (4,6) 3
Be Kind To Me (3)
Been Too Long On The Road (2,7)
Belonging (8)

Blue Satin Pillow (2)
Call On Me (2)
Change Of Heart (8)
Chosen One (8)
Come Again (3)
Coming Apart (1)
Could I (1)

Daughter (4,7)
Diary (4,6) 15
Didn't Even Know Her Name (5)
Dismal Day (1)
Don't Shut Me Out (1)
Don't Tell Me No (5)
Down On My Knees (4,6)

Dream Lady (4,7)
Easy Love (2)
Everything I Own (4,6) 5
Family Doctor (1)
Fancy Dancer (5,7)
Fly Away (8)
Friends And Lovers (1,7)

Games Of Magic (4)
Guitar Man (5,7) 11
He's A Good Lad (3,7)
Hold Tight (8)
Hooked On You (8) 60
I Am That I Am (2)
I Don't Love You (4)

I Say Again (3)
I Want You With Me (2)
If (3,6) 4
In The Afterglow (2)
It Don't Matter To Me (1,6) 10
Just Like Yesterday (4,7)
Last Time (1)

BREAD — Cont'd

Lay Your Money Down (8)
Let Me Go (5)
Let Your Love Go (3,6) *28*
Live In Your Love (3)
London Bridge (1,7)
Look At Me (1)

Look What You've Done (2,6)
Lost Without Your Love (8) *9*
Make It By Yourself (5)
Make It With You (2,6) *1*
Mother Freedom (4,6) *37*
Move Over (1)

Nobody Like You (4)
Other Side Of Life (2)
Our Lady Of Sorrow (8)
Picture In Your Mind (5)
She Was My Lady (3)
She's The Only One (8)

Sweet Surrender (5,7) *15*
Take Comfort (3)
Tecolote (5)
This Isn't What The
  Governmeant (4)
Today's The First Day (8)

Too Much Love (3,6)
Truckin' (3,6)
Welcome To The Music (5)
What A Change (3)
Why Do You Keep Me Waiting
  (2)

You Can't Measure The Cost
  (1)
Yours For Life (5,7)

BREAKFAST CLUB   '87

Pop-dance group from New York City: brothers Dan (vocals) and Eddie (guitar) Gilroy, Gary Burke (bass) and Stephen Bray (drums). **Madonna** was the group's drummer for a short time in 1979.

| 3/28/87 | **43** | 30 | © | Breakfast Club.. | | | $10 | MCA 5821 |

Always Be Like This
Expressway To Your Heart

Kiss And Tell *48*
Never Be The Same

Rico Mambo
Right On Track *7*

Specialty
Standout

Tongue Tied

BREAKWATER   '80

Disco group from Philadelphia: Gene Robinson (vocals), Lincoln Gilmore (guitar), Kae Williams (keyboards), John Braddock (percussion), Vince Garnell and Greg Scott (horns), Steve Green (bass) and James Jones (drums).

| 4/21/79 | **173** | 5 | | 1 Breakwater.. | | | $12 | Arista 4208 |
| 6/7/80 | **141** | 5 | | 2 Splashdown.. | | | $12 | Arista 4264 |

Do It Till The Fluid Gets Hot (1)
Feel Your Way (1)
Free Yourself (1)

Let Love In (2)
Love Of My Life (2)
No Limit (2)

One In My Dreams (2)
Release The Beast (2)
Say You Love Me Girl (2)

Splashdown Time (2)
That's Not What We Came
  Here For (1)
Work It Out (1)

Time (2)
Unnecessary Business (1)

You (2)
You Know I Love You (1)

BREATHE   '88

Pop group from London: David Glasper (vocals), Marcus Lillington (guitar), Michael Delahunty (bass) and Ian Spice (drums). Delahunty left in 1988.

| 6/4/88 | **34** | 51 | ● © | 1 All That Jazz.. | | | $10 | A&M 5163 |
| 9/22/90 | **116** | 20 | © | 2 Peace Of Mind.. | | | $10 | A&M 5320 |

All That Jazz (1)
All This I Should Have Known
  (1)
Any Trick (1)

Does She Love That Man?
  (2) *34*
Don't Tell Me Lies (1) *10*
Got To Get By (2)
Hands To Heaven (1) *2*

How Can I Fall? (1) *3*
I Hear You're Doing Fine (2)
Jonah (1)
Liberties Union (1)
Mississippi Water (1)

Monday Morning Blues (1)
Perfect Love (2)
Say A Prayer (2) *21*
Say Hello (2)
Where Angels Fear (2)

Will The Circle Be Unbroken?
  (2)
Without Your Love (2)
Woman (2)
Won't You Come Back? (1)

BRECKER BROTHERS, The   '76

Duo of Philadelphia-born brothers Randy (b: 11/27/45; trumpet) and Michael (b: 3/29/49; reeds) Brecker. The brothers began recording together in their group **Dreams**; also with **Spyro Gyra**.

6/7/75	**102**	13	©	1 The Brecker Brothers................................	[I]	$12	Arista 4037
2/28/76	**82**	16	©	2 Back To Back..	[I]	$12	Arista 4061
5/7/77	**135**	6	©	3 Don't Stop The Music................................	[I]	$12	Arista 4122
6/20/81	**176**	3	©	4 Straphangin'..	[I]	$12	Arista 9550

As Long As I've Got Your Love
  (3)
Bathsheba (4)
Creature Of Many Faces (1)
D.B.B. (1)
Dig A Little Deeper (2)
Don't Stop The Music (3)

Finger Lickin' Good (3)
Funky Sea, Funky Dew (3)
Grease Piece (2)
I Love Wastin' Time With You
  (2,3)
If You Wanna Boogie...Forget It
  (2)

Jacknife (2)
Keep It Steady (Brecker Bump)
  (2)
Levitate (1)
Lovely Lady (2)
Night Flight (2)
Not Ethiopia (4)

Oh My Stars (1)
Petals (3)
Rocks (1)
Slick Stuff (2)
Sneakin' Up Behind You
  (1) *58*
Some Skunk Funk (1)

Sponge (1)
Spreadeagle (4)
Squids (1)
Straphangin' (4)
Tabula Rasa (3)
Threesome (4)
Twilight (1)

What Can A Miracle Do (2,3)
Why Can't I Be There (4)

BREEDERS, The   '94

Rock group from Dayton, Ohio: twin sisters/guitarists/vocalists Kim and Kelley Deal, bassist Josephine Wiggs (native of Bedfordshire, England) and drummer Jim MacPherson. Kim was a member of the **Pixies**. Tanya Donelly (Throwing Muses), **Belly**) was an early member.

| 9/18/93+ | **33** | 36 | ▲ © | Last Splash.. | | | $10 | 4 A D 61508 |

Cannonball *44*
Divine Hammer
Do You Love Me Now?

Drivin' On 9
Flipside
Hag

I Just Wanna Get Along
Invisible Man
Mad Lucas

New Year
No Aloha
Roi

S.O.S.
Saints

BREMERS, Beverly   '72

Born on 3/10/50 in Chicago. Singer/actress.

| 9/16/72 | **124** | 8 | | I'll Make You Music................................ | | | $15 | Scepter 5102 |

All That's Left Is The Music
At My Place
Baby I Don't Know You
Colors Of Love

Don't Say You Don't
  Remember *15*
Get Smart Girl
Guy Like You

I Made A Man Out Of You
  Jimmy
I'll Make You Music *63*

May The Road Rise To Meet
  You
Poor Side Of Town
We're Free *40*

BRENDA & THE TABULATIONS   '67

R&B vocal group from Philadelphia: Brenda Payton, Jerry Jones, Eddie Jackson and Maurice Coates. Payton died on 6/14/92.

| 7/1/67 | **191** | 4 | © | Dry Your Eyes.. | | | $50 | Dionn 2000 |

Dry Your Eyes *20*
Forever
God Only Knows
Hey Boy

Just Once In A Lifetime *97*
Oh Lord What Are You Doing
  To Me

Stay Together Young
  Lovers *66*
Summertime
Walk On By

Wash, The
Where Did Our Love Go
Who's Lovin' You *66*

BRENNAN, Walter   '62

Born on 7/25/1894 in Swampscott, Massachusetts. Died of emphysema on 9/21/74 (age 80). Famous character actor. Appeared in several movies and TV shows.

| 6/23/62 | **54** | 10 | © | Old Rivers.. | | | $25 | Liberty 3233 |

Boll Weevil
Conversation With A Mule

Farmer And The Lord
Happy Birthday Old Folk

It Takes A Heap Of Living (To
  Make A House A Home)

Old Kelly Place
Old Rivers *5*

Old Rivers' Trunk
Pickin' Time

Steal Away

BREWER, Teresa   '55

Born Theresa Breuer on 5/7/31 in Toledo, Ohio. Pop singer.

| 3/19/55 | **10** | 6 | | Especially For You... | [EP] | $25 | Coral 81115 |

How Important Can It Be? *flip*   Pledging My Love *17*   Rock Love   Tweedle Dee

BREWER & SHIPLEY '71
Folk-rock duo formed in Los Angeles: Mike Brewer (b: 1944 in Oklahoma City) and Tom Shipley (b: 1942 in Mineral Ridge, Ohio).

3/6/71	34	26		©	1 Tarkio			$15	Kama Sutra 2024
12/25/71+	164	8			2 Shake Off The Demon			$15	Kama Sutra 2039
1/27/73	174	7			3 Rural Space			$15	Kama Sutra 2058
5/11/74	185	5			4 ST-11261			$12	Capitol 11261

album title refers to the label prefix and number

Back To The Farm (2)
Ballad Of A Country Dog (4)
Black Sky (3)
Blue Highway (3)
Bound To Fall (4)
Can't Go Home (1)
Crested Butte (3)
Don't Want To Die In Georgia (1)
Eco-Catastrophe Blues (4)
Fair Play (4)
Fifty States Of Freedom (1)
Fly, Fly, Fly (This Seat Is Occupado) (3)
Got To Get Off The Island (3)
Have A Good Life (3)
How Are You (4)
It Did Me In (4)
Keeper Of The Keys (4)
Light, The (1)
Look Up, Look Out (4)
Merciful Love (2)
Message From The Mission (Hold On) (2)
Natural Child (2)
Oh Mommy (1)
Oh So Long (4)
One By One (2)
One Toke Over The Line (1) **10**
Platte River, Song From (1)
Rock Me On The Water (2)
Ruby On The Morning (1)
Seems Like A Long Time (1)
Shake Off The Demon (2) **98**
Shine So Strong (4)
Sleeping On The Way (3)
Sweet Love (2)
Tarkio Road (1) **55**
When Everybody Comes Home (2)
When The Truth Finally Comes (3)
Where Do We Go From Here (3)
Working On The Well (2)
Yankee Lady (3)

BRICK '77
Disco group from Atlanta: Jimmy Brown (sax), Reggie Hargis (guitar), Don Nevins (keyboards), Ray Ransom (bass) and Eddie Irons (drums). All share vocals.

11/13/76+	19	24			1 Good High			$12	Bang 408
9/10/77	15	32			2 Brick			$12	Bang 409
5/19/79	100	8			3 Stoneheart			$12	Bang 35969
7/12/80	179	5			4 Waiting On You			$12	Bang 36262
9/5/81	89	10			5 Summer Heat			$12	Bang 37471

Ain't Gonna' Hurt Nobody (2) **92**
All The Way (4)
Babe (4)
Brick City (1)
By The Moonlight (3)
Can't Wait (1)
Dancin' Man (3)
Dazz (1) **3**
Don't Ever Lose Your Love (4)
Dusic (2) **18**
Free (4)
Fun (2)
Get Fired Up (4)
Get Started (4)
Good High (1)
Good Morning Sunshine (2)
Happening, The (5)
Happy (2)
Hello (2)
Here We Come (1)
Honey Chile (2)
I Want You To Know (That I'm In Love With You) (5)
Let Me Make You Happy (4)
Life Is What You Make It (2)
Living From The Mind (2)
Magic Woman (2)
Music Matic (1)
Push, Push (4)
Raise Your Hands (3)
Right Back (Where I Started From) (5)
Sea Side Vibes (5)
Sister Twister (1)
Southern Sunset (1)
Spread Love (4)
Stoneheart (3)
Summer Heat (5)
Sure Feels Good (5)
Sweat (Till You Get Wet) (5)
Sweet Lips (4)
That's What It's All About (1)
To Me (3)
Waiting On You (4)
We Don't Wanna' Sit Down (We Wanna' Git Down) (2)
We'll Love (3)
Wide Open (5)

BRICKELL, Edie, & New Bohemians '89
Born on 3/10/66 in Oak Cliff, Texas. Female singer/songwriter. New Bohemians consisted of Kenny Withrow (guitar), Brad Houser (bass) and John Bush (drums). Joining the band by 1990 were Wes Burt-Martin (guitar) and Matt Chamberlain (drums). Brickell married **Paul Simon** on 5/30/92.

9/24/88+	4	54	▲²	©	1 Shooting Rubberbands At The Stars			$10	Geffen 24192
11/17/90	32	18		©	2 Ghost Of A Dog			$10	Geffen 24304
9/3/94	68	10		©	3 Picture Perfect Morning			$10	Geffen 24715

EDIE BRICKELL

Air Of December (1)
Another Woman's Dream (3)
Beat The Time (1)
Black & Blue (2)
Carmelito (2)
Circle (1) **48**
Forgiven (1)
Ghost Of A Dog (2)
Good Times (3) **60**
Green (3)
Hard Times (3)
He Said (2)
In The Bath (2)
Keep Coming Back (1)
Little Miss S. (1)
Lost In The Moment (3)
Love Like We Do (1)
Mama Help Me (2)
Me By The Sea (2)
Nothing (1)
Now (1)
Oak Cliff Bra (2)
Olivia (3)
Picture Perfect Morning (3)
She (1)
Stay Awhile (3)
Strings Of Love (2)
Stwisted (2)
10,000 Angels (2)
This Eye (2)
Times Like This (2)
Tomorrow Comes (3)
What I Am (1) **7**
Wheel, The (1)
When The Lights Go Down (3)
Woyaho (2)

BRICKMAN, Jim '96
Born on 11/20/61 in Cleveland. New Age pianist.

2/17/96	187	4	●	©	1 By Heart: Piano Solos		[I]	$10	Windham Hill 11164
2/15/97	30	29	●	©	2 Picture This		[I]	$10	Windham Hill 11211
11/1/97	48	11	●	©	3 The Gift	C:#16/8	[X-I]	$10	Windham Hill 11242

Christmas charts: 3/'97, 17/'98, 26/'99

2/13/99	42	16	●	©	4 Destiny		[I]	$10	Windham Hill 11396
9/9/00	75	12		©	5 My Romance...An Evening With Jim Brickman		[I-L]	$10	Windham Hill 11557

recorded on 3/27/00 at the Capitol Theatre in Salt Lake City

All I Ever Wanted (1)
Angel Eyes (1)
Angels (3)
Bittersweet (4)
By Chance (4)
By Heart (1,5)
Change Of Heart (5)
Circles (5)
Coming Home (2)
Crooked River (4)
Crossroads (4)
Destiny (4)
Dream Come True (2)
Dreams Come True (3)
Edgewater (2,5)
Fireside (3)
First Noel (3)
First Steps (2)
Freedom (4,5)
Frere Jacques (2)
Gift, The (3)
Glory (5)
Hero's Dream (2)
Hope Is Born Again (3)
Hush Li'l Baby (4)
If You Believe (1)
In A Lover's Eyes (1)
It Came Upon A Midnight Clear (3)
Joy To The World (3)
Lake Erie Rainfall (1,5)
Little Star (1)
Little Town Of Bethlehem (3)
Looking Back (1)
Love I Found In You (5)
Love Of My Life (4,5)
Meant To Be (4)
Nothing Left To Say (1)
Oh Christmas Tree (3)
On The Edge (1)
Part Of My Heart (4)
Partners In Crime (5)
Picture This (2,5)
Rainbow Connection (4)
Remembrance (4)
Rendezvous (4)
Rocket To The Moon (5)
Secret Love (2)
Sound Of Your Voice (4)
Starbright (3)
Starbright (The Lullaby Medley) (3)
Sudden Inspiration (1)
Sun, Moon & Stars (2)
Sweet Dreams (4)
Valentine (2,5)
What Child Is This? (3)
Where Are You Now? (1)
Winter Peace (3)
You Never Know (4)
Your Love (4)

BRIDES OF FUNKENSTEIN, The '78
Female singers from **George Clinton's Parliament/Funkadelic** corporation. Duo in 1978 of Dawn Silva and Lynn Mabry. Trio in 1979 of Silva, Sheila Horn (later known as Sheila Washington) and Jeanette McGruder.

11/4/78	70	13			1 Funk Or Walk			$15	Atlantic 19201
2/16/80	93	7			2 Never Buy Texas From A Cowboy			$15	Atlantic 19261

Amorous (1)
Birdie (1)
Didn't Mean To Fall In Love (2)
Disco To Go (1)
I'm Holding You Responsible (2)
Just Like You (1)
Mother May I? (2)
Nappy (2)
Never Buy Texas From A Cowboy (2)
Party Up In Here (2)
Smoke Signals (2)
War Ship Touchante (1)
When You're Gone (1)

BRIDGES, Alicia '79
Born on 7/15/53 in Lawndale, North Carolina. Disco singer/songwriter.

9/30/78+	33	32			Alicia Bridges			$12	Polydor 6158

Body Heat *86*
Break Away
Broken Woman
City Rhythm
Diamond In The Rough
High Altitudes
I Love The Nightlife (Disco 'Round) *5*
In The Name Of Love
Self Applause
We Are One

BRIDGEWATER, Dee Dee '78
Born on 5/27/50 in Memphis; raised in Flint, Michigan. Jazz singer/actress.

| 5/6/78 | 170 | 7 | | | 1 **Just Family** .... | | | $12 | Elektra 119 |
| 5/26/79 | 182 | 4 | | | 2 **Bad For Me** .... | | | $12 | Elektra 188 |

Back Of Your Mind (2)
Bad For Me (2)
Children Are The Spirit (Of The World) (1)

Don't Say It (If You Don't Mean It) (2)
For The Girls (2)
Is This What Feeling Gets? (2)
It's The Fallin In Love (2)

Just Family (1)
Love Won't Let Me Go (2)
Maybe Today (1)
Melody Maker (1)
Night Moves (1)

Open Up Your Eyes (1)
Sorry Seems To Be The Hardest Word (1)
Streetsinger (2)
Sweet Rain (1)

Tequila Mockingbird (2)
Thank The Day (1)

BRIGHTMAN, Sarah '00
Born on 8/14/61 in England. Singer/actress. Starred on Broadway's *The Phantom Of The Opera*. Formerly married to **Andrew Lloyd Webber**.

2/28/98	71	27	▲	©	1 **Time To Say Goodbye** .... C:#35/6			$10	Angel 56511
5/8/99	65	24		©	2 **Eden**			$10	Angel 56769
6/26/99	110	17	●	©	3 **The Andrew Lloyd Webber Collection** .... [K]			$10	Really Useful 539330
9/16/00	17	31	●	©	4 **La Luna**			$10	Angel 56968

All I Ask Of You (3)
Alleluja (1)
Amigos Para Siempre (Friends For Life) (3)
Another Suitcase In Another Hall (3)
Anything But Lonely (3)
Anytime, Anywhere (2)
Bailero (2)
Bilitis-Gènèrique (1)
Chanson D'enfance (3)

Deliver Me (2)
Don't Cry For Me Argentina (3)
Dust In The Wind (3)
Eden (2)
En Aranjuez Con Tu Amor (1)
Figlio Perduto (4)
Gloomy Sunday (4)
Gus: The Theatre Cat (3)
He Doesn't See Me (4)
Here With Me (4)
Hijo de la Luna (4)

How Fair This Place (4)
Il Mio Cuore (2)
In Pace (1)
In Paradisum (2)
In Trutina (1)
Just Show Me How To Love You (1)
La Califfa (4)
La Luna (4)
La Lune (4)
La Wally (1)

Lascia Ch'io Pianga (2)
Last Words You Said (2)
Love Changes Everything (3)
Macavity: The Mystery Cat (3)
Memory (3)
Music Of The Night (3)
Naturaleza Muerta (1)
Nella Fantasia (2)
Nessun Dorma (2)
No One Like You (1)
O Mio Babbino Caro (1)

Only An Ocean Away (2)
Phantom Of The Opera (4)
Pie Jesu (4)
Scarborough Fair (4)
Scéne D'Amour (2)
Serenade (4)
So Many Things (2)
Solo Con Te (4)
Tell Me On A Sunday (3)
There For Me (1)
This Love (4)

Time To Say Goodbye (1)
Tu (2)
Tu Quieres Volver (1)
Un Jour Il Viendra (2)
Unexpected Song (3)
Whiter Shade Of Pale (4)
Who Wants To Live Forever (1)
Winter In July (4)
Wishing You Were Somehow Here Again (3)

BRILEY, Martin '83
Born in England. Rock singer/songwriter/guitarist.

| 5/7/83 | 55 | 22 | | | 1 **One Night With A Stranger** .... | | | $10 | Mercury 810332 |
| 2/9/85 | 85 | 10 | | © | 2 **Dangerous Moments** .... | | | $10 | Mercury 822423 |

Alone At Last (2)
Before The Party Ends (2)
Dangerous Moments (2)
Dirty Windows (2)

Dumb Love (1)
Ghosts (2)
I Wonder What She Thinks Of Me (1)

If This Is What It Means (2)
It Shouldn't Have To Hurt That Much (2)
Just A Mile Away (1)

Maybe I've Waited Too Long (1)
One Night With A Stranger (1)
Put Your Hands On The Screen (1)

Rainy Day In New York City (1)
Salt In My Tears (1) *36*
School For Dogs (1)
She's So Flexible (1)

Think Of Me (2)
Underwater (2)

BRINKLEY, David — HUNTLEY, Chet

BRISTOL, Johnny '74
Born on 2/3/39 in Morganton, North Carolina. R&B singer/songwriter/producer.

| 8/31/74 | 82 | 17 | | | 1 **Hang On In There Baby** .... | | | $15 | MGM 4959 |
| 12/11/76+ | 154 | 11 | | | 2 **Bristol's Creme** .... | | | $12 | Atlantic 18197 |

Baby's So Much Fun To Dream About (2)
Do It To My Mind (2) *43*
Hang On In There Baby (1) *8*

Have Yourself A Good Time (2)
Thinkin' 'Bout The Good Times... (2)
I Got Cha Number (1)

I Love Talkin' 'Bout Baby (2)
I Sho Like Groovin' With Ya (2)
It Don't Hurt No More (1)
Love Me For A Reason (1)

Love To Have A Chance To Taste The Wine (2)
Memories Don't Leave Like People Do (1)

Reachin' Out For Your Love (1)
She Came Into My Life (2)
Take Care Of You For Me (1)
Woman, Woman (1)

You And I (1) *48*
You Turned Me On To Love (2)

BRITISH LIONS '78
Rock group from Birmingham, England: John Fiddler (vocals), Ray Major (guitar), Morgan Fisher (keyboards), Pete "Overend" Watts (bass) and Dale "Buffin" Griffin (drums). Fisher, Watts and Griffin were members of **Mott The Hoople**.

| 4/29/78 | 83 | 15 | | © | **British Lions** .... | | | $12 | RSO 3032 |

Big Drift Away
Booster

Break This Fool
Eat The Rich

Fork Talking Man
International Heroes

My Life's In Your Hands
One More Chance To Run

Wild In The Streets *87*

BRITNY FOX '88
Hard-rock group from Philadelphia: "Dizzy" Dean Davidson (vocals), Michael Kelly Smith (guitar), Billy Childs (bass) and Johnny Dee (drums).

| 7/23/88 | 39 | 37 | ● | © | 1 **Britny Fox** .... | | | $10 | Columbia 44140 |
| 11/25/89 | 79 | 23 | | © | 2 **Boys In Heat** .... | | | $10 | Columbia 45300 |

Angel In My Heart (2)
Don't Hide (1)
Dream On (2)
Fun In Texas (1)

Girlschool (1)
Gudbuy T' Jane (1)
Hair Of The Dog (2)
Hold On (1)

In America (1)
In Motion (2)
Kick 'N' Fight (1)
Left Me Stray (2)

Livin' On A Dream (2)
Long Way From Home (2)
Long Way To Love (1) *100*
Longroad (2)

Plenty Of Love (2)
Rock Revolution (1)
Save The Weak (1)
She's So Lonely (2)

Shine On (2)
Standing In The Shadows (2)
Stevie (2)

BRITTEN, Benjamin '63
Born on 11/22/13 in Lowestoft, Norfolk, England. Died on 12/4/76 (age 63). Composer/conductor.

| 9/7/63 | 68 | 8 | | | **Britten: War Requiem** .... | | | $25 | London 4255 [2] |

War Requiem, Op. 66 (Dies Trae (Conclusion)/Offertorium)

War Requiem, Op. 66 (Libera Me)

War Requiem, Op. 66 (Requiem Aeternam/Dies Irae)

War Requiem, Op. 66 (Sanctus/Agnus Dei)

BROCK, Chad '00
Born on 7/31/63 in Ocala, Florida. Country singer/songwriter/guitarist.

| 5/20/00 | 125 | 2 | | © | **Yes!** .... | | | $10 | Warner 47659 |

Country Boy Can Survive *75*
Hey Mister
If I Were You

Love Lives (Events Of The Heart)
She Does

This
Visit, The
Yes! *22*

You Had To Be There
Young Enough To Know It All

BRODSKY QUARTET, The — see COSTELLO, Elvis

BROMBERG, David '76
Born on 9/19/45 in Philadelphia. Folk singer/songwriter/guitarist.

3/25/72	194	2			1 **David Bromberg**			$15	Columbia 31104
2/23/74	167	5		©	2 **Wanted Dead Or Alive**			$15	Columbia 32717
7/12/75	173	3		©	3 **Midnight On The Water**			$15	Columbia 33397

BROMBERG, David — Cont'd

DEBUT	PEAK	WKS						$	Label & Number
10/9/76	104	11	©	4	How Late'll Ya Play 'Til?		[L]	$20	Fantasy 79007 [2]

record 1: studio; record 2: recorded on 6/18/76 at the Great American Music Hall in San Francisco

11/19/77	132	9	©	5	Reckless Abandon			$12	Fantasy 9540
6/17/78	130	9	©	6	Bandit In A Bathing Suit			$12	Fantasy 9555
2/24/79	152	4	©	7	My Own House			$12	Fantasy 9572

Baby Breeze (5)
Bandit In A Bathing Suit (6)
Battle Of Bull Run Medley (5)
Beware Brother Beware (5)
Black And Tan (7)
Blackberry Blossom (medley) (6)
Bluebird (4)
Boggy Road To Milledgeville (Arkansas Traveler) (1)
Bullfrog Blues (4)
Child's Song (5)
Chubby Thighs (4)
Chump Man Blues (7)
Church Bell Blues (medley) (2)
Cocaine Blues (7)
Come On In My Kitchen (4)

Dallas Rag (medley) (4)
Danger Man (2)
Danger Man II (4)
Dark Hollow (3)
Dehlia (3)
Dixie Hoedown (medley) (6)
Don't Let Your Deal Go Down Medley (7)
Don't Put That Thing On Me (3)
Dyin' Crapshooter's Blues (7)
Early This Morning (7)
Fiddle Tunes (medley) (4)
Georgia On My Mind (7)
Get Up And Go (medley) (4)
Holdup, The (1,2)
I Like To Sleep Late In The Morning (3)

I Want To Go Home (5)
Idol With A Golden Head (4)
If I Get Lucky (3)
If You Don't Want Me Baby (6)
Joke's On Me (3)
June Apple (medley) (6)
Kaatskill Serenade (4)
Kansas City (2)
Kitchen Girl (7)
Last Song For Shelby Jean (1)
Lonesome Dave's Lovesick Blues #3 (1)
Love Please Come Home (medley) (6)
Lower Left Hand Corner Of The Night (7)
Main Street Moan (2)

Maple Leaf Rag (medley) (4)
Midnight On The Water Medley (3)
Mississippi Blues (1)
Mr. Blue (3)
Mrs. Delion's Lament (5)
My Own House Medley (7)
New Lee Highway Blues (2)
Nobody's (3)
Nobody's Fault But Mine (5)
Northeast Texas Women (6)
Peanut Man (5)
Pine Tree Woman (1)
Queen Ellen (6)
Sally Goodin' Medley (5)
Sammy's Song (1)

Send Me To The 'Lectric Chair (2)
Sheebeg And Sheemore (7)
Sloppy Drunk (4)
Someone Else's Blues (2)
Spanish Johnny (7)
Statesboro Blues (medley) (2)
Stealin' (5)
Such A Night (4)
Suffer To Sing The Blues (1)
Summer Wages (4)
Sweet Home Chicago (4)
Sweet Sweet Sadness (6)
To Know Her Is To Love Her (7)
Travelling Man (6)
Ugly Hour (6)

Wallflower (2)
What A Town (5)
(What A) Wonderful World (3)
Whoopee Ti Yi Yo (4)
Will Not Be Your Fool (4)
Yankee's Revenge Medley (3)
Young Westley (4)

BRONSKI BEAT '85

Techno-pop trio from England: **Jimmy Somerville** (vocals), Steve Bronski and Larry Steinbachek (synthesizers). Somerville formed the **Communards**.

| 1/19/85 | 36 | 25 | © | 1 | The Age Of Consent | | | $10 | MCA 5538 |
| 8/2/86 | 147 | 6 | © | 2 | Truthdare Doubledare | | | $10 | MCA 5751 |

C'Mon! C'Mon! (2)
Do It (2)
Dr. John (2)
Heatwave (1)

Hit That Perfect Beat (2)
I Feel Love (medley) (1)
In My Dreams (2)
It Ain't Necessarily So (1)

Johnny Remember Me (medley) (1)
Junk (1)
Love And Money (1)

Need A Man Blues (1)
No More War (1)
Punishment For Love (1)
Screaming (1)

Smalltown Boy (1) **48**
This Heart (2)
Truthdare Doubledare (2)
We Know How It Feels (2)

Why? (1)

BROOD, Herman '79

Born on 11/5/46 in Zwolle, Holland. Committed suicide on 7/11/2001 (age 54). Leader of Dutch rock band Wild Romance.

| 5/26/79 | 122 | 19 | | | Herman Brood & His Wild Romance | | | $12 | Ariola 50059 |

Back (In Y'r Love)
Champagne (& Wine)
Doin' It

Dope Sucks
Doreen
Get Lost

Hit
Hot Talk
Never Enough

Pain
Prisoners
R & Roll Junkie

Saturdaynight 35
Skid Row

BROOKE, Jonatha '01

Born in Boston. Female folk-pop singer/songwriter.

| 3/3/01 | 192 | 1 | © | | Steady Pull | | | $10 | Bad Dog 60801 |

Digging
How Deep Is Your Love?

I'll Take It From Here
Linger

Lullaby
New Dress

Out Of Your Mind
Red Dress

Room In My Heart
Steady Pull

Walking
Your House

BROOKLYN BRIDGE '69

Pop group from Long Island, New York: Johnny Maestro (lead vocals), Fred Ferrara, Les Cauchi and Mike Gregorie (backing vocals), Richie Macioce (guitar), Tom Sullivan and Joe Ruvio (saxophones), Shelly Davis (trumpet), Carolyn Wood (organ), Jimmy Rosica (bass) and Artie Catanzarita (drums). Maestro was lead singer of The Crests.

3/29/69	54	30		1	Brooklyn Bridge			$25	Buddah 5034
10/11/69	145	8		2	The Second Brooklyn Bridge			$25	Buddah 5042
10/18/69	169	4		3	Live At Yankee Stadium		[L]	$30	T-Neck 3004 [2]

side A: **Isley Brothers**; side B: **Edwin Hawkins Singers**; side C: Brooklyn Bridge; side D: "Don't Change Your Love" by **The Five Stairsteps**, "Somebody's Been Messin'" by Judy White and "Love Is What You Make It" by Sweet Cherries; recorded on 6/21/69

Also Sprach Zarathustra ..see: Space Odessey
Amen (medley) (3)
Blessed Is The Rain (1) **45**
Caroline (2)
Echo Park (2)
Free As The Wind (1)
Glad She's A Woman (1)

I'm So Proud (medley) (3)
I've Been Lonely Too Long (1)
In The End (2)
Inside Out (Upside Down) (2)
It's All Right (medley) (3)
Keep On Pushin' (medley) (3)
Look At Me (2)
Minstral Sunday (2)

People Get Ready (medley) (3)
Piece Of My Heart (1)
Requiem (1)
Space Odessey-2001 (Thus Spake Zarathustra) (1)
Talkin' About My Baby (medley) (3)
12:29 Is Taking My Baby Away (2)

Welcome Me Love (1) **48**
Which Way To Nowhere (1)
Without Her (Father Paul) (2)
Worst That Could Happen (1) **3**
You Must Believe Me (medley) (3)
You'll Never Walk Alone (2) **51**

Your Husband - My Wife (2) **46**
Your Kite, My Kite (1)

BROOKLYN, BRONX & QUEENS BAND, The '81

R&B group from New York City: Lucious Floyd (vocals), Abdul Walli Mohammed (guitar), Kevin Nance (keyboards), PeeWee Ford (bass) and Dwayne Perdue (drums).

| 8/29/81 | 109 | 9 | | | The Brooklyn, Bronx & Queens Band | | | $10 | Capitol 12155 |

Don't Say Goodbye
I'll Cut You Loose

Lovin's What We Should Do
Mistakes

On The Beat
Starlette

Time For Love

BROOKLYN DREAMS '79

Disco trio from New York City: Joe "Bean" Esposito (vocals, guitar), Bruce Sudano (keyboards, **Alive And Kicking**) and Eddie Hokenson (drums). Sudano married **Donna Summer** on 7/16/80.

| 3/24/79 | 151 | 7 | | | Sleepless Nights | | | $12 | Casablanca 7135 |

Coming Up The Hard Way
Fashion For Me
First Love

Heaven Knows 4
Long Distance
Make It Last 69

Send Me A Dream (medley)
Sleepless Nights (medley)
Street Man

That's Not The Way That Your Mama Taught You To Be
Touching In The Dark

BROOKLYN TABERNACLE CHOIR '00

Choir founded in 1972 by Jim Cymbala in Brooklyn, New York. Comprised of 240 members.

| 5/6/00 | 59 | 3 | © | | God Is Working - Live | | [L] | $10 | Word 63805 |

All The Way To Calvary
Church Medley

For Every Mountain
God Is Working

Holy Like You
I Found The Answer

It's Amazing
Keep Me True

Lift Your Voice
More Than Enough

Nothing Is Impossible

BROOKS, Garth ★52★   '91

Born Troyal Garth Brooks on 2/7/62 in Luba, Oklahoma; raised in Yukon, Oklahoma. Best-selling country artist of all-time. Also recorded as alter-ego pop singer "Chris Gaines."

1)Ropin' The Wind 2)The Hits 3)The Chase

DEBUT	PEAK	WKS	RIAA	CD	#	Album Title	Catalog	$	Label & Number
5/12/90+	13	224	▲⁹	©	1	Garth Brooks	C:#48/1	$10	Capitol 90897
9/22/90+	3	224	▲¹⁶	©	2	No Fences	C:#17/15	$10	Capitol 93866
9/28/91	❶¹⁸	132	▲¹⁴	©	3	Ropin' The Wind		$10	Capitol 96330
9/12/92	2¹	24	▲³	©	4	Beyond The Season	C:#3/42 [X]	$10	Liberty 98742
						Christmas charts: 1/'92, 11/'93, 16/'94, 17/'95, 25/'96, 37/'97, 10/'98			
10/10/92	❶⁷	64	▲⁸	©	5	The Chase		$10	Liberty 98743
9/18/93	❶⁵	76	▲⁸	©	6	In Pieces		$10	Liberty 80857
12/31/94+	❶⁸	110	▲¹⁰	©	7	The Hits	C:❶¹²/102 [G]	$10	Liberty 29689
12/9/95	2²	66	▲⁶	©	8	Fresh Horses		$10	Capitol 32080
12/13/97	❶⁵	58	▲⁷	©	9	Sevens		$10	Capitol 56599
5/23/98	❶²	34		©	10	The Limited Series	[K-R]	$50	Capitol 94572 [6]
						package of his albums *Garth Brooks*, *No Fences*, *Ropin' The Wind*, *The Chase*, *In Pieces* and *Fresh Horses*, with one additional track on each; includes a 61-page booklet			
12/5/98	❶⁵	56	▲¹⁴	©	11	Double Live	[L]	$15	Capitol 97424 [2]
10/16/99	2¹	18	▲²	©	12	Garth Brooks In...The Life Of Chris Gaines		$10	Capitol 20051
12/11/99	7	7	▲	©	13	Garth Brooks & The Magic Of Christmas	C:#6/8 [X]	$10	Capitol 23550
						Christmas charts: 1/'99, 10/'00			

Against The Grain (3,10)
Ain't Going Down (Til The Sun Comes Up) (6,7,10,11)
Alabama Clay (1,10)
American Honky-Tonk Bar Association (6,7,10,11)
Anonymous (10)
Baby Jesus Is Born (13)
Beaches Of Cheyenne (8,10,11)
Belleau Wood (9)
Burning Bridges (3,10)
Callin' Baton Rouge (6,7,10,11)
Change, The (8,10)
Christmas Song (13)
Cold Shoulder (3,10)
Cowboy Bill (1,10)
Cowboy Cadillac (9)
Cowboy Song (6,10)
Cowboys And Angels (8,10)
Dance, The (1,7,10,11)
Digging For Gold (12)
Dixie Chicken (5,10)
Do What You Gotta Do (9) *69*

Driftin' Away (12)
Every Now And Then (5,10)
Everytime That It Rains (1,10)
Face To Face (5,10)
Fever, The (8,10,11)
Fit For A King (9)
Friend To Me (9)
Friendly Beasts (4)
Friends In Low Places (2,7,10,11)
Gift, The (4)
Go Tell It On The Mountain (4,13)
God Rest Ye Merry Gentlemen (4,13)
Have Yourself A Merry Little Christmas (13)
How You Ever Gonna Know (9)
I Don't Have To Wonder (9)
I Know One (1,10)
I've Got A Good Thing Going (1,10)
If Tomorrow Never Comes (1,7,10,11)

In Another's Eyes (9)
In Lonesome Dove (3,10)
Ireland (8,10)
It Don't Matter To The Sun (12)
It's Midnight Cinderella (8,10)
It's The Most Wonderful Time Of The Year (13)
It's Your Song (11) *62*
Kickin' And Screamin' (6,10)
Learning To Live Again (5,10)
Let It Snow (13)
Longneck Bottle (9,11)
Lost In You (12) *5*
Main Street (12)
Mary's Dream (4)
Maybe (12)
Mr. Blue (2,10)
Mr. Right (5,10)
Much Too Young (To Feel This Damn Old) (1,7,10)
My Love Tells Me So (12)
New Way To Fly (2,10)
Night I Called The Old Man Out (6,10)

Night Rider's Lament (5,10)
Night Will Only Know (6,10)
Nobody Gets Off In This Town (1,10)
Not Counting You (1,10)
O Little Town Of Bethlehem (13)
Old Man's Back In Town (4)
Old Stuff (8,10)
One Night A Day (6,10)
Papa Loved Mama (3,7,10,11)
Red Strokes (6,10)
Right Now (12)
River, The (3,7,10,11)
Rodeo (3,7,10,11)
Rollin' (8,10)
Same Old Story (2,10)
Santa Looked A Lot Like Daddy (4)
Shameless (3,7,10,11)
She's Every Woman (8,10)
She's Gonna Make It (9)
Silent Night (4)
Silver Bells (13)

Sleigh Ride (13)
Snow In July (12)
Something With A Ring To It (10)
Somewhere Other Than The Night (5,10)
Standing Outside The Fire (6,7,10,11)
Take The Keys To My Heart (9)
Tearin' It Up (And Burnin' It Down) (11)
That Ol' Wind (8,10)
That Summer (5,7,10,11)
That's The Way I Remember It (12)
(There's No Place Like) Home For The Holidays (13)
This Ain't Tennessee (10)
Thunder Rolls (2,7,10,11)
To Make You Feel My Love (10,11)
Two Of A Kind, Workin' On A Full House (2,7,10,11)
Two Piña Coladas (9,11)

Unanswered Prayers (2,7,10,11)
Unsigned Letter (12)
Unto You This Night (4)
Uptown Downhome Good Ol' Boy (10)
Victim Of The Game (2,10)
Walking After Midnight (5,10)
Way Of The Girl (12)
We Bury The Hatchet (3,10)
We Shall Be Free (5,7,10,11)
What Child Is This (4)
What She's Doing Now (3,7,10)
When There's No One Around (9)
Which One Of Them (10)
White Christmas (4,13)
White Flag (12)
Wild As The Wind (11)
Wild Horses (2,10) *50*
Winter Wonderland (13)
Wise Men's Journey (13)
Wolves (5,10)
You Move Me (9)

BROOKS, Mel — see REINER, Carl

BROOKS, Meredith   '97

Born on 6/12/66 in Oregon City, Oregon. Female rock singer/guitarist. Former member of **The Graces**.

5/24/97	22	47	▲	©	Blurring The Edges	$10	Capitol 36919

Birthday
Bitch *2*
I Need
It Don't Get Better
My Little Town
Pollyanne
Shatter
Somedays
Stop
Wash My Hands
Watched You Fall
What Would Happen *46*

★286★   BROOKS & DUNN   '97

Country vocal duo: Kix Brooks (b: 5/12/55 in Shreveport, Louisiana) and Ronnie Dunn (b: 6/1/53 in Coleman, Texas).

DEBUT	PEAK	WKS	RIAA	CD	#	Album Title	Catalog	$	Label & Number
9/7/91+	10	153	▲⁵	©	1	Brand New Man		$10	Arista 18658
3/13/93	9	99	▲⁴	©	2	Hard Workin' Man		$10	Arista 18716
10/15/94	15	59	▲³	©	3	Waitin' On Sundown		$10	Arista 18765
5/4/96	5	70	▲²	©	4	Borderline		$10	Arista 18810
10/4/97	4	86	▲³	©	5	The Greatest Hits Collection	C:#21/81 [G]	$10	Arista 18852
6/20/98	11	40	▲²	©	6	If You See Her		$10	Arista 18865
10/9/99	31	14	●	©	7	Tight Rope		$10	Arista 18895
5/5/01	4	22↑	●	©	8	Steers & Stripes		$10	Arista 67003

Ain't Nothing 'Bout You (8) *25*
All Out Of Love (7,10)
Beer Thirty (7)
Boot Scootin' Boogie (1,5) *50*
Born And Raised In Black And White (7)
Brand New Man (1,5)
Brand New Whiskey (6)
Can't Stop My Heart (7)
Cheating On The Blues (1)
Cool Drink Of Water (1)
Days Of Thunder (5)
Deny, Deny, Deny (8)
Don't Look Back Now (7)

Every River (8)
Few Good Rides Away (3)
Go West (8)
Goin' Under Gettin' Over You (7)
Good Girls Go To Heaven (8)
Hard Workin' Man (2,5)
He's Got You (5)
Heartbroke Out Of My Mind (2)
Honky Tonk Truth (5)
How Long Gone (6)
Hurt Train (7)
Husbands And Wives (6) *36*
I Am That Man (4)

I Can't Get Over You (6) *51*
I Can't Put Out This Fire (2)
I Fall (8)
I Love You More (7)
I'll Never Forgive My Heart (3)
I'm No Good (1)
I've Got A Lot To Learn (1)
If That's The Way You Want It (3)
If You See Him/If You See Her (6)
Last Thing I Do (8)
Little Miss Honky Tonk (3,5)
Long Goodbye (8)

Lost And Found (1,5)
Lucky Me, Lonely You (8)
Mama Don't Get Dressed Up For Nothing (4,5)
Man This Lonely (4)
Mexican Minutes (2)
Missing You (7) *75*
More Than A Margarita (4)
My Heart Is Lost To You (8)
My Kind Of Crazy (3)
My Love Will Follow You (4)
My Maria (4,5) *79*
My Next Broken Heart (1,5)
Neon Moon (1,5)

One Heartache At A Time (4)
Only In America (8)
Our Time Is Coming (2)
Redneck Rhythms & Blues (4)
Rock My World (Little Country Girl) (2,5) *97*
See Jane Dance (8)
She Used To Be Mine (2,5)
She's Not The Cheatin' Kind (3,5)
She's The Kind Of Trouble (3)
Silver And Gold (3)
South Of Santa Fe (8)
Still In Love With You (1)

Temptation #9 (7)
Tequila Town (4)
Texas And Norma Jean (7)
Texas Women (Don't Stay Lonely Long) (2)
That Ain't No Way To Go (2,5)
Too Far This Time (7)
Trouble With Angels (7)
Unloved (8)
Way Gone (6)
We'll Burn That Bridge (2,5)
When Love Dies (6)
When She's Gone, She's Gone (8)

BROOKS & DUNN — Cont'd

Whiskey Under The Bridge (3,5)
White Line Casanova (4)

Why Would I Say Goodbye (4)
You'll Always Be Loved By Me (7) *55*

You're Gonna Miss Me When I'm Gone (3,5)
You're My Angel (6)

Your Love Don't Take A Backseat To Nothing (6)

BROS '88
Pop trio from London: twin brothers Matt (vocals) and Luke (drums) Goss, with Craig Logan (bass). Group's name rhymes with "cross."

| 7/23/88 | 171 | 5 | © | **Push** .... | | | **$10** | Epic 44285 |

Cat Among The Pigeons
Drop The Boy

I Owe You Nothing
I Quit

It's A Jungle Out There
Liar

Love To Hate You
Shocked

Ten Out Of Ten
When Will I Be Famous? *83*

BROTHA LYNCH HUNG '97
Born Kevin Mann on 2/29/72 in Sacramento, California. Male rapper.

3/18/95	162	2	©	1	**Season Of Da Siccness - The Resurrection**			**$10**	Black Market 53967
10/18/97	28	5	©	2	**Loaded**			**$10**	Black Market 50648
7/15/00	86	6	©	3	**EBK4**			**$10**	Black Market 4321

Blood On Da Rug (3)
Bonus Trackz (2)
Can't Have It (3)
Catch You (3)
Datz Real Gangsta [Gangsta Shit] (1)
De One Below (3)

Dead Man Walking (1)
Deep Down (1)
Did It And Did It (2)
Die; 1 By 1 (2)
Dogg Market (3)
Dramatic (3)
Every Single Bitch (3)
Feel My Nature Rize (3)

Heataz (2)
Holding On (3)
Hunta Killa (3)
Inhale With Da Devil (3)
Liquor Sicc (1)
Locc 2 Da Brain (1)
My Love (3)
My Soul To Keep (2)

Naked Cheese (3)
On My Brief Case (2)
One A Da Las Sicc Niggaz (2)
One Mo Pound (2)
One Time (3)
Raw Meat (3)
Real Loccs (1)
Rest In Piss (1)

Return Of Da Baby (1)
Season Of Da Siccness (1)
Secondz A Way (2)
Siccmade (1)
Siccmade House (2)
Situation (3)
Split Yo Face (3)
Thatz What I Said (2)

Welcome 2 Your Own Death (1)
Went Way (2)
Xcaliber (3)

BROTHER CANE '95
Rock group from Birmingham, Alabama: Damon Johnson (vocals, guitar), Roman Glick (guitar), Glenn Maxey (bass) and Scott Collier (drums). Maxey replaced by David Anderson by 1995.

| 8/12/95 | 184 | 7 | © | | **Seeds**.. | | | **$10** | Virgin 40564 |

And Fools Shine On
Bad Seeds

Breadmaker
High Speed Freezin'

Horses & Needles
Hung On A Rope

Intempted
Kerosene

Rise On Water
Stain

20/20 Faith
Voice Of Eujena

BROTHERHOOD OF MAN, The '70
Studio group from England featuring Tony Burrows (lead singer of Edison Lighthouse, First Class, **The Pipkins** and **White Plains**).

| 8/8/70 | 168 | 8 | | | **United We Stand**.. | | | **$15** | Deram 18046 |

For Old Times Sake
For The Rest Of Our Lives

Little Bit Of Heaven
Living In The Land Of Love

Love Is A Good Foundation
Love One Another

Say A Prayer
Sing In The Sunshine

Too Many Heartaches
United We Stand *13*

Where Are You Going To My Love *61*

★455★ BROTHERS FOUR, The '61
Folk-pop group formed at the University of Washington: Dick Foley, Bob Flick, John Paine and Mike Kirkland.
1)B.M.O.C. (Best Music On/Off Campus) 2)The Brothers Four 3)The Big Folk Hits

4/18/60	11	19	©	1	**The Brothers Four**			**$20**	Columbia 1402 / 8197
2/13/61	4	35	©	2	**B.M.O.C. (Best Music On/Off Campus)**			**$20**	Columbia 1578 / 8378
12/18/61	71	14	©	3	**The Brothers Four Song Book**			**$20**	Columbia 1697 / 8497
10/6/62	102	4	©	4	**The Brothers Four: In Person**	[L]		**$20**	Columbia 1828 / 8628
5/4/63	81	12	©	5	**Cross-Country Concert**	[L]		**$20**	Columbia 1946 / 8746
10/12/63	56	20	©	6	**The Big Folk Hits**			**$20**	Columbia 2033 / 8833
10/31/64	134	4		7	**More Big Folk Hits**			**$20**	Columbia 2213 / 9013
5/1/65	118	5		8	**The Honey Wind Blows**			**$20**	Columbia 2305 / 9105
11/13/65+	76	15		9	**Try To Remember**			**$20**	Columbia 2379 / 9179
7/30/66	97	7		10	**A Beatles' Songbook (The Brothers Four sing Lennon/McCartney)**............			**$20**	Columbia 2502 / 9302

Across The Sea (4)
All My Loving (10)
And I Love Her (10)
Angelique(10)
Banana Boat Song (7)
Banua (1)
Battle Of New Orleans (7)
Beast (Song Of The Punch Press Operator) (5)
Beautiful Brown Eyes (2)
Boa Constrictor (5)
Born Free (9)
Brady, Brady, Brady (5)
Brandy Wine Blues (5)
Brother Where Are You (7)
Cleano (3)
Come For To Carry Me Home (3)
Come Kiss Me Love (9)
Come To My Bedside, My Darlin' (7)
Damsel's Lament (I Never Will Marry) (1)
Darlin' Sportin' Jenny (4)

Darlin', Won't You Wait (1)
Darling Corey (6)
Don't Let The Rain Come Down (Crooked Little Man) (7)
Don't Think Twice, It's All Right (7)
Drillers' Song (3)
East Virginia (1)
Eddystone Light (1)
El Paso (6)
Feed The Birds (8)
First Battalion (4)
500 Miles (6)
Frogg (3) *32*
Gimme That Wine (9)
Girl (10)
Goodnight, Irene (3)
Green Leaves Of Summer (2) *65*
Greenfields (1,4) *2*
Hard Travelin' (1)
Help! (10)
Honey Wind Blows (8)
House Of The Rising Sun (8)

I Am A Roving Gambler (2,4)
I Remember When I Loved Her (9)
I Fell (10)
I'll Follow The Sun (10)
I'm Just A Country Boy (7)
If I Fell (10)
If I Had A Hammer (6)
Island In The Sun (5)
Jamaica Farewell (6)
John B. Sails (6)
Just A Little Rain (Low Down You Big Thunderhead) (5)
Lady Greensleeves (3)
Lazy Harry's (8)
Little Play Soldiers (8)
Malaika (3)
Michael Row The Boat Ashore (6)
Michelle (10)
Midnight Special (4)
Moulin Rouge (Where Is Your Heart), Song From (9)
Mr. Tambourine Man (8)
Muleskinner (7)

My Little John Henry (Got A Mighty Know) (2)
Nancy O. (8)
New "Frankie And Johnnie" Song (5)
Nobody Knows (3)
Norwegian Wood (This Bird Has Flown) (10)
Nowhere Man (10)
Old Settler's Song (2)
Ole Smokey (3)
Poverty Hill (8)
Pretty Girl Is Like A Little Bird (2)
Puff (The Magic Dragon) (7)
Riders In The Sky (5)
Rock Island Line (3,4)
Run, Come, See Jerusalem (3)
Sakura (9)
Sama Kama Wacky Brown (1)
San Francisco Bay Blues (7)
Scarlet Ribbons (For Her Hair) (6)
Silver Threads And Golden Needles (6)

Since My Canary Died (5)
Sloth (9)
Somewhere (8)
Song Of The Ox Driver (3)
St. James Infirmary (2)
Summer Days Alone (3)
Summertime (4)
Superman (1)
Sweet Rosyanne (2)
Symphonic Variation (The Violins Play Along) (5)
Tarrytown (8)
Tavern Song (3)
Thinking Man, John Henry (4)
Tie Me Kangaroo Down, Sport (6)
Try To Remember (9) *91*
Turn Around (3)
25 Minutes To Go (5)
Variation On An Old English Theme (4)
Viva La Compagnie (3)
Walk Right In (6)
Waves Roll Out (8)
We Can Work It Out (10)

We Shall Overcome (7)
Well, Well, Well (2)
What Now My Love (9)
When Everything Was Green (9)
When The Sun Goes Down (2)
Where Have All The Flowers Gone (7)
Whoa, Back, Buck! (4)
Wild Colonial Boy (9)
Winken, Blinken And Nod (5)
Wish I Was In Bowling Green (5)
With You Fair Maid (2)
Wolverton Mountain (6)
Yellow Bird (7)
Yesterday (10)
Zulu Warrior (1)

BROTHERS JOHNSON, The '80
R&B duo of brothers from Los Angeles: George (guitar; b: 5/17/53) and Louis (bass; b: 4/13/55) Johnson. With **Billy Preston**'s band from 1973-75. Also see **Quincy Jones**.

3/6/76	9	49	▲	©	1	**Look Out For #1**			**$12**	A&M 4567
5/21/77	13	31	▲	©	2	**Right On Time**			**$12**	A&M 4644
8/12/78	7	24	▲	©	3	**Blam!!**			**$12**	A&M 4714
3/8/80	5	30	▲	©	4	**Light Up The Night**			**$10**	A&M 3716
7/18/81	48	13			5	**Winners**			**$10**	A&M 3724
1/22/83	138	5			6	**Blast! (The Latest And The Greatest)**	[G]		**$10**	A&M 4927

BROTHERS JOHNSON, The — Cont'd

8/4/84	**91**	11			7 Out Of Control .... $10 A&M 4965

Ain't We Funkin' Now (3,6)
All About The Heaven (4)
Blam!! (3)
Brother Man (2)
Caught Up (5)
Celebrations (4)
Closer To The One That You Love (4)
Come Together (1)
Dancin' And Prancin' (1)
Dancin' Free (5)

Daydreamer Dream (5)
Dazed (7)
Devil, The (1)
Do It For Love (5)
Do You (7)
Free And Single (1)
Free Yourself, Be Yourself (7)
Funk It (Funkadelala) (6)
Get The Funk Out Ma Face (1,6) **30**
Great Awaking (6)

Hot Mama (5)
I Came Here To Party (7)
I Want You (5)
I'll Be Good To You (1,6) **3**
I'm Giving You All Of My Love (6)
In The Way (5)
It's All Over Now (7)
It's You Girl (3)
Land Of Ladies (4)
Let's Try Love Again (7)

Light Up The Night (4)
Love Is (2)
Lovers Forever (7)
Mista' Cool (3)
Never Leave You Lonely (2)
Out Of Control (7)
"Q" (2)
Real Thing (5,6) **67**
Ride-O-Rocket (3)
Right On Time (2)
Runnin' For Your Lovin' (2)

Save Me (7)
Smilin' On Ya (4)
So Won't You Stay (3)
Stomp! (4,6) **7**
Strawberry Letter 23 (2,6) **5**
Streetwave (3)
Sunlight (5)
Teaser (5)
This Had To Be (4)
Thunder Thumbs And Lightnin' Licks (1)

Tokyo (7)
Tomorrow (1)
Treasure (4) **73**
Welcome To The Club (6)
You Keep Me Coming Back (7)
You Make Me Wanna Wiggle (4)

BROWN, Arthur, The Crazy World Of   '68

Born Arthur Wilton on 6/24/42 in Whitby, Yorkshire, England. Theatrical rock singer. His band consisted of Sean Nicholas (guitar), Vince Crane (organ; **Atomic Rooster**) and Carl Palmer (drums; Atomic Rooster, **Emerson, Lake & Palmer**, **Asia**). Crane committed suicide on 2/14/89 (age 44).

9/7/68	**7**	24		©	The Crazy World Of Arthur Brown .... $25 Track 8198

Child Of My Kingdom
Come And Buy

Confusion (medley)
Fire 2

Fire Poem
I Put A Spell On You

I've Got Money
Nightmare

Rest Cure
Spontaneous Apple Creation

Time (medley)

BROWN, Bobby   '89

Born on 2/5/69 in Roxbury, Massachusetts. R&B singer. Former member of **New Edition**. Appeared in the movies *Ghostbusters II*, *Panther* and *A Thin Line Between Love & Hate*. Married **Whitney Houston** on 7/18/92.

12/13/86+	**88**	17		©	1	King Of Stage	$10 MCA 5827
7/23/88+	**❶**6	97	▲7	©	2	Don't Be Cruel	$10 MCA 42185
12/2/89+	**9**	33	▲	©	3	Dance!...Ya Know It!	[K] $10 MCA 6342
9/12/92	**2**1	43	▲2	©	4	Bobby	$10 MCA 10417
11/22/97	**61**	3		©	5	Forever	$10 MCA 11691

All Day All Night (2)
Baby, I Wanna Tell You Something (1,3)
Been Around The World (5)
College Girl (4)
Don't Be Cruel (2,3) **8**
Every Little Step (2,3) **3**
Feelin' Inside (5)

Forever (5)
Get Away (4) **14**
Girl Next Door (1,3)
Girlfriend (1) **57**
Give It Up (5)
Good Enough (4) **7**
Happy Days (5)
Heart And Soul (5)

Humpin' Around (4) **3**
I Really Love You Girl (2)
I'll Be Good To You (2)
I'm Your Friend (4)
It's Still My Thang (5)
King Of Stage (1)
Love Obsession (1)
Lovin' You Down (4)

My Place (5)
My Prerogative (2,3) **1**
On Our Own (3)
One More Night (4)
Pretty Little Girl (4)
Rock Wit'cha (2,3) **7**
Roni (2,3) **3**
Seventeen (1,3)

She's All I Need (5)
Something In Common (4)
Spending Time (1)
Storm Away (4)
Sunday Afternoon (5)
Take It Slow (2)
That's The Way Love Is (4) **57**
Til The End Of Time (4)

Two Can Play That Game (4)
You Ain't Been Loved Right (1)
Your Tender Romance (1)

BROWN, Charles   '70

Born on 9/13/22 in Texas City, Texas. Died of heart failure on 1/21/99 (age 76). R&B singer/pianist.

12/12/64+	**17**X	10		©	Charles Brown sings Christmas Songs .... [X] $200 King 775

first released in 1961; Christmas charts: 22/'64, 29/'66, 19/'67, 36/'68, 17/'70

Bringing In A Brand New Year
Christmas Blues
Christmas Comes But Once A Year

Christmas In Heaven
Christmas Questions
Christmas With No One To Love

It's Christmas All Year 'Round
It's Christmas Time
Let's Make Every Day A Christmas Day

Merry Christmas Baby
Please Come Home For Christmas

Wrap Yourself In A Christmas Package

BROWN, Chuck, & The Soul Searchers   '79

Funk group from Washington DC: Chuck Brown (vocals), John Buchanan and Curtis Johnson (keyboards), Don Tillery (trumpet), Leroy Fleming (sax), Gregory Gerran (congas), Jerry Wilder (bass) and Ricky Wellman (drums).

2/17/79	**31**	14	●	©	1	Bustin' Loose	$12 Source 3076
6/2/01	**193**	1		©	2	Your Game... Live At The 9:30 Club, Washington, D.C.	[L] $10 Raw Venture 9

CHUCK BROWN

Berro E Sombaro (1)
Bustin' Loose Part 1 (1) **34**
Chameleon (2)
Could It Be Love (1)
Do You Know What Time It Is (2)
Feel Like Movin' That Body (2)

Game Seven (1)
Get Your Hands Up (medley) (2)
Go Go Swing Outro (2)
Hah Man (Sinbad, Main Title) (2)
Hey Go Go Mickey (2)

Hoochie Coochie Man (medley) (2)
I Gotcha Now (1)
If It Ain't Funky (1)
It's Love (2)
Never Gonna Give You Up (1)
No Diggity (2)

One On One (2)
People Make The World Go Round (2)
Playing Your Game Baby (medley) (2)
2001 (That'll Work) (2)

Wind Me Up Chuck (medley)
Wind Us Up Funk & Benny (2)

BROWN, Danny Joe   '81

Born in 1951 in Jacksonville, Florida. Lead singer of **Molly Hatchet**. Brown's band included: Bobby Ingram, Steve Wheeler and Kenny McVay (guitars), John Galvin (keyboards), Buzzy Meekins (bass) and Jimmy Glenn (drums).

7/4/81	**120**	7			Danny Joe Brown And The Danny Joe Brown Band .... $10 Epic 37385

Alamo, The
Beggar Man

Edge Of Sundown
Gambler's Dream

Hear My Song
Hit The Road

Nobody Walks On Me
Run For Your Life

Sundance
Two Days Home

BROWN, Foxy   '99

Born Inga Marchand on 9/6/79 in Brooklyn, New York. Female rapper. Took her name from the action movie character played by actress Pam Grier. Member of **The Firm**.

12/7/96	**7**	43	▲	©	1	Ill Na Na	$10 Violator 533684
2/13/99	**❶**1	20	▲	©	2	Chyna Doll	$10 Violator 558933

BWA (2)
Baby Mother (2)
Baller Bitch (2)
Birth Of Foxy Brown (2)
Bomb Ass (2)
Bonnie & Clyde Part II (2)

Can U Feel Me Baby (2)
Chase, The (1)
Chyna Whyte (2)
Dog & A Fox (2)
4-5-6 (2)
Fox Boogie (1)

Foxy's Bells (1)
Get Me Home (1)
(Holy Matrimony) Letter To The Firm (1)
Hot Spot (2) **91**
I Can't (2)

I'll Be (1) **7**
If I... (1)
Ill Na Na (1)
It's Hard Being Wifee (2)
JOB (2)
My Life (2)

No One's (1)
Promise, The (1)
Ride (Down South) (2)
Tramp (2)

BROWN, Horace   '96

Born in Charlotte, North Carolina. R&B singer.

7/6/96	**145**	2		©	Horace Brown .... $10 Motown 530625

Gotta Find A Way
How Can We Stop

I Like
I Want You Baby

Just Let Me Know
One For The Money **62**

Taste Your Love
Things We Do For Love **95**

Trippin'
Why Why Why

You Need A Man

DEBUT	PEAK	WKS	RIAA	CD		ARTIST — Album Title	Catalog Sym	$	Label & Number

BROWN, James ★15★   '63

Born on 5/3/33 in Barnwell, South Carolina; raised in Augusta, Georgia. Acclaimed as one of the most influential "soul" artists of all-time. Various nicknames include "The Godfather of Soul" and "The Hardest Working Man In Show Business." Inducted into the Rock and Roll Hall of Fame in 1986. On 12/15/88, received a six-year prison sentence after leading police on an interstate car chase; released from prison on 2/27/91. Won Grammy's Lifetime Achievement Award in 1992.

1)Live At The Apollo 2)Pure Dynamite! Live At The Royal 3)I Can't Stand Myself 4)Hot Pants 5)Papa's Got A Brand New Bag

DEBUT	PEAK	WKS	CD	#	Album Title	Sym	$	Label & Number
6/29/63	2²	66	©	1	**Live At The Apollo**	[L]	$200	King 826
					recorded on 10/24/62 at the Apollo Theater in New York City; also see #49 below			
9/28/63	73	17		2	Prisoner Of Love		$200	King 851
2/29/64	10	22		3	**Pure Dynamite! Live At The Royal**	[L]	$200	King 883
					recorded at The Royal Theater in Baltimore			
5/9/64	61	18		4	Showtime		$50	Smash 67054
					not a live album; audience effects are dubbed in			
4/10/65	124	10		5	Grits & Soul	[I]	$50	Smash 67057
9/11/65+	26	27		6	Papa's Got A Brand New Bag		$100	King 938
11/20/65+	42	19		7	James Brown Plays James Brown - Today & Yesterday	[I]	$50	Smash 67072
1/22/66	36	17		8	I Got You (I Feel Good)		$100	King 946
4/16/66	101	11		9	James Brown Plays New Breed	[I]	$50	Smash 67080
9/10/66	90	9		10	It's A Man's Man's Man's World		$100	King 985
12/3/66+	13ˣ	11		11	James Brown sings Christmas Songs	[X]	$100	King 1010
					album cover issued in 1966 with a Christmas wreath on a gray wall; issued with a different wreath on a white wall from 1967-on; Christmas charts: 15/'66, 13/'67, 15/'68			
12/3/66	135	3		12	Handful Of Soul	[I]	$50	Smash 67084
4/8/67	88	14	©	13	Raw Soul		$50	King 1016
6/10/67	41	17		14	Live At The Garden	[L]	$50	King 1018
7/15/67	164	5		15	James Brown Plays The Real Thing	[I]	$50	Smash 67093
9/16/67	35	17	©	16	Cold Sweat		$50	King 1020
3/23/68	17	14		17	I Can't Stand Myself (When You Touch Me)		$50	King 1030
5/18/68	135	14		18	I Got The Feelin'		$50	King 1031
8/24/68	150	5		19	James Brown Plays Nothing But Soul	[I]	$50	King 1034
9/7/68	32	39	©	20	Live At The Apollo, Volume II	[L]	$75	King 1022 [2]
					recorded at the Apollo Theater in New York City			
4/12/69	53	22	©	21	Say It Loud-I'm Black And I'm Proud		$50	King 1047
5/31/69	99	14		22	Gettin' Down To It		$50	King 1051
8/23/69	40	22		23	James Brown plays & directs The Popcorn	[I]	$40	King 1055
9/6/69	26	24		24	It's A Mother		$40	King 1063
12/13/69	10ˣ	3		25	**A Soulful Christmas**	[X]	$40	King 1040
					first released in 1968			
2/14/70	43	12		26	Ain't It Funky	[I]	$40	King 1092
5/16/70	125	10		27	Soul On Top		$40	King 1100
					with the Louie Bellson Orchestra			
7/4/70	121	6		28	It's A New Day So Let A Man Come In		$40	King 1095
9/12/70	29	31	©	29	Sex Machine		$60	King 1115 [2]
					not a live album; audience effects are dubbed in			
1/30/71	61	15		30	Super Bad		$40	King 1127
					not a live album; audience effects are dubbed in			
5/1/71	137	4		31	Sho Is Funky Down Here	[I]	$40	King 1110
9/4/71	22	18	©	32	Hot Pants		$40	Polydor 4054
12/25/71+	39	21	©	33	Revolution Of The Mind - Live At The Apollo, Volume III	[L]	$60	Polydor 3003 [2]
					recorded at the Apollo Theater in New York City			
6/17/72	83	16		34	James Brown Soul Classics	[G]	$25	Polydor 5401
7/8/72	60	21	©	35	There It Is		$40	Polydor 5028
12/9/72+	68	17	©	36	Get On The Good Foot		$60	Polydor 3004 [2]
3/3/73	31	21	©	37	Black Caesar	[S]	$50	Polydor 6014
7/28/73	92	11	©	38	Slaughter's Big Rip-Off	[S]	$50	Polydor 6015
1/5/74	34	36	● ©	39	The Payback		$50	Polydor 3007 [2]
7/27/74	35	19	©	40	Hell		$80	Polydor 9001 [2]
1/25/75	56	10	©	41	Reality		$40	Polydor 6039
5/24/75	103	8		42	Sex Machine Today		$40	Polydor 6042
10/4/75	193	2		43	Everybody's Doin' The Hustle & Dead On The Double Bump		$40	Polydor 6054
8/14/76	147	8		44	Get Up Offa That Thing		$40	Polydor 6071
1/15/77	126	10		45	Bodyheat		$40	Polydor 6093
5/6/78	121	22		46	Jam/1980's		$40	Polydor 6140
8/11/79	152	6		47	The Original Disco Man		$30	Polydor 6212
8/16/80	170	5		48	James Brown...Live/Hot On The One	[L]	$50	Polydor 6290 [2]
					recorded in Tokyo			
11/22/80	163	3		49	Live And Lowdown At The Apollo, Vol. 1	[L-R]	$15	Solid Smoke 8006
					reissue of album #1 above			
10/18/86	156	6	©	50	Gravity		$10	Scotti Brothers 40380
6/18/88	96	14	©	51	I'm Real		$10	Scotti Brothers 44241

After You Done It (26)
After You're Through (5)
Again (2)
Ain't It A Groove (36)

Ain't It Funky Now (Parts 1 and 2) (26) *24*
Ain't Nobody Here But Us Chickens (4)
Ain't That A Groove (10,14) *42*

All About My Girl (9)
All For One (41)
All The Way (22)
And I Do Just What I Want (6)

Any Day Now (24)
Baby, Baby, Baby, Baby (17)
Baby, You're Right (6) *49*
Back Stabbin' (16)

Believers Shall Enjoy (Non Believers Shall Suffer) (25)
Bells, The (10) *68*
Bernadette (15)

Bewildered
(1,2,10,29,33,49) *40*
Big Strong (38)
Blind Man Can See It (37)
Blues & Pants (32)

DEBUT	PEAK	WKS	RIAA	CD	ARTIST — Album Title	Catalog	Sym	$	Label & Number

BROWN, James — Cont'd

Blues For My Baby (4)
Bob Scoward (31)
Bodyheat (45,48) *88*
Boss, The (37)
Bring It Up (13,14,20) *29*
Brother Rap (29,38)
Buddy-E (19)
By The Time I Get To Phoenix (30)
Caledonia (4) *95*
Calm & Cool (43)
Can Mind (31)
(Can You) Feel It (Part 1) (2)
Can't Git Enough (2)
Can't Stand It (32)
  (also see: I Can't Stand It)
Can't Take It With You (44)
Chase, The (23,37)
Check Your Body (41)
Chicago (22)
Chicken, The (23)
Christmas In Heaven (11)
Christmas Is Coming (25)
Christmas Song (Version 1 & 2) (11)
Cold Sweat (16,20,22,26,34,36) *7*
Coldblooded (40) *flip*
Come Over Here (19)
Come Rain Or Come Shine (16)
Cross Firing (6)
"D" Thing (15)
Dancin' Little Thing (8)
Dead On It (42)
Deep In It (42)
Devil's Hideaway (5)
Dirty Harri (36,37)
Doin' The Limbo (6)
Doing The Best I Can (39)
Don't Be A Drop Out (13) *50*
Don't Cry Baby (4)
Don't Fence Me In (41)
Don't Mind (31)
Don't Tell A Lie About Me And I Won't Tell The Truth On You (40)
Don't Tell It (45)
Down And Out In New York City (37) *50*
Escape-ism (32,33) *35*
Every Beat Of My Heart (7) *99*
Every Day I Have The Blues (27)
Evil (4)
Eyesight (46)
Fat Soul (19)
Fat Wood (Parts 1 And 2) (26)
Fever (16)
For Once In My Life (27)
For You My Love (4)
Forever Suffering (39)
Funky Broadway (15)
Funky President (People It's Bad) (41) *44*
Funky Side Of Town (36)
Funky Soul #1 (17)
Further On Up The Road (41)
Georgia On My Mind (28)
Get It Together (17) *40*
Get Loose (12)
Get On The Good Foot (36,48) *18*
Get Up, Get Into It, Get Involved (39)
Get Up I Feel Like Being Like A Sex Machine (29,33,34) *15*
  (also see: Sex Machine)

Get Up Off Of Me (42)
Get Up Offa That Thing (44,48) *45*
Gittin' A Little Hipper (19)
Give It Up Or Turnit A Loose (26,28,29,33,34) *15*
Giving Out Of Juice (30)
Go On Now (19)
Godfather Runnin' The Joint (51)
Goliath (50)
Gonna Have A Funky Good Time (48)
Good, Good Loving (3,8)
Good Rockin' Tonight (16)
Goodbye My Love (21) *31*
Gravity (50) *93*
Grits (5)
Happy For The Poor (38)
Have Mercy Baby (6) *92*
Headache (5)
Hell (40)
Here I Go (18)
Hip Bag '67 (14)
Hold It (7)
Hold On, I'm Comin' (12)
Home Again (44)
Hooks (9)
Hot Mix (12)
Hot Pants (She Got To Use What She Got To Get What She Wants) (32,33) *15*
How Do You Stop (50)
How Long Can I Keep It Up (38)
How Long Darling (2)
Hustle!!! (Dead On It) (43)
I Can't Help It (I Just Do-Do-Do) (8)
I Can't Stand It (33)
I Can't Stand It "76" (40)
  (also see: Can't Stand It)
I Can't Stand Myself (When You Touch Me) (17,29) *28*
I Don't Mind (1,10,49) *47*
I Don't Want Nobody To Give Me Nothing (29)
I Feel Good (42)
I Found Someone (1,49)
I Got A Bag Of My Own (36) *44*
I Got The Feelin' (18,29,33,48) *6*
I Got You (I Feel Good) (8,14,20,34) *3*
I Guess I'll Have To Cry, Cry, Cry (21) *55*
I Love You (21)
I Love You) For Sentimental Reasons (22)
I Love You, Yes I Do (1,10,49)
I Loves You Porgy (16)
I Need Help (I Can't Do It Alone) (35)
I Need Your Key (To Turn Me On) (27)
I Never Loved A Man The Way I Love You (15)
I Never, Never, Never Will Forget (46)
I Refuse To Lose (44)
I Stay In The Chapel Every Night (Just Won't Do Right) (6)
I Want To Be Around (16,20)
I Want You So Bad (1,49)
I'll Go Crazy (1,49)
I'll Lose My Mind (21)
I'll Never Let You Go (3)

I'm A Greedy Man (Part 1 And 2) (35) *35*
I'm Broken Hearted (41)
I'm Not Demanding (Part 1) (28)
I'm Real (51)
I'm Satisfied (45)
I'm Shook (24)
I've Got Money (8)
If I Ruled The World (18,24,28,29)
In The Middle (23,25)
In The Wee Wee Hours (Of The Nite) (10)
Infatuation (5)
Is It Yes Or Is It No? (10)
It Had To Be You (22)
It May Be The Last Time (14,20)
It Won't Be Me (18)
It's A Man's Man's Man's World (10,20,27,28,29,34,48) *8*
It's A New Day (Part 1 And 2) (28) *57*
It's A New Day So Let A Man Come In And Do The Popcorn (33)
It's Magic (2)
It's Too Funky In Here (47,48)
It's Your Money$ (51)
Jabo (9)
Jam (46)
Jam 1980 (48)
James Brown's Boo-Ga-Loo (9)
Jimmy Mack (15)
Just Enough Room For Storage (31)
Just Plain Funk (18)
Just You Me, Darling (10)
Kansas City (16,20,43) *55*
Keep Keepin' (51)
King, The (12)
King Heroin (35) *40*
King Slaughter (38)
Kiss In 77 (45)
Let A Man Come In And Do The Popcorn (Part 1) (28) *21*
Let A Man Come In And Do The Popcorn (Part 2) (28) *40*
Let It Be Me (30)
Let The Boogie Do The Rest (47)
Let Them Talk (21)
Let Yourself Go (13,14,20) *46*
Let's Get Personal (50)
Let's Go Get Stoned (12)
Let's Make Christmas Mean Something This Year (11)
Let's Unite The Whole World At Christmas (25)
Licking Stick - Licking Stick (21,29) *14*
Like A Baby (3)
Like It Is, Like It Was (37)
Little Fellow (19)
Little Groove Maker Me (20,24)
Living In America (50) *4*
Lost In The Mood Of Changes (9)
Lost Someone (1,2,8,20,36,40,49) *48*
Love Don't Love Nobody (6,8)
Low Down Popcorn (29)
Make It Funky (33,34) *22*
Make It Funky (My Part) (34,36) *68*
Make It Good To Yourself (37)
Mama Feelgood (37)

Mama's Dead (37)
Man Has To Go Back To The Crossroads (30,40)
Man In The Glass (27,28)
Mashed Potato Popcorn (24)
Mashed Potatoes U.S.A. (6) *82*
Maybe Good-Maybe Bad (18)
Maybe I'll Understand (18,21)
Maybe The Last Time (7)
Mercy, Mercy, Mercy (15)
Merry Christmas Baby (11)
Merry Christmas, I Love You (11)
Message To Michael (12)
Mind Power (39)
Mister Hip (5)
Mona Lisa (16)
Money Won't Change You (13) *53*
Mother Popcorn (You Got To Have A Mother For Me) (24,29,33) *11*
My Thang (40) *29*
Nature (46)
Nature Boy (16)
Nearness Of You (13)
Need Your Love So Bad (17)
Never Can Say Goodbye (35)
New Breed (9)
New Shift (23)
Night Train (1,8,49) *35*
Nobody Knows (13)
Nose Job (26)
Nothing Beats A Try But A Fail (36)
Oh Baby Don't You Weep (3,7) *23*
Oh! Henry (12)
Only You (13)
Original Disco Man (47)
Our Day Will Come (12)
Out Of Sight (7,14,20)
Out Of The Blue (4)
Papa Don't Take No Mess (40) *31*
Papa's Got A Brand New Bag (6,7,27,34,43,48) *8*
Payback, The (39) *26*
Peewee's Groove In "D" (15)
People Get Up And Drive Your Funky Soul (38)
Please Come Home For Christmas (11)
Please Don't Go (1,49)
Please, Please (36)
Please, Please, Please (1,3,14,20,29,40,48,49) *95*
Popcorn, The (23) *30*
Popcorn With A Feeling (24)
Prisoner Of Love (2,14,20) *18*
Problems (29)
Public Enemy #1 (Part 1 And 2) (35)
Reality (41) *80*
Really, Really, Really (38)
Release The Pressure (medley) (44)
Repeat The Beat (Faith) (50)
Return To Me (50)
Santa Claus Gave Me A Brand New Start (24)
Santa Claus Go Straight To The Ghetto (25)
Santa Claus, Santa Claus (25)
Say It Loud - I'm Black And I'm Proud (21,25) *10*
Sayin' It And Doin' It (40)

Scratch, The (10)
September Song (27)
Sex Machine Part I And Part II (42,48) *61*
  (also see: Get Up I Feel Like Being Like A Sex Machine)
Sexy, Sexy, Sexy (38) *50*
Shades Of Brown (21)
She Looks All Types A'Good (51)
Shhhhhhh (For A Little While) (18)
Sho Is Funky Down Here (31)
Shoot Your Shot (39)
Shout And Shimmy (12)
Sidewinder (7)
Signed, Sealed, And Delivered (2,3) *77*
Signs Of Christmas (11)
634-5789 (12)
Slaughter Theme (38)
Slow Walk (9)
So Long (2)
Somebody Changed The Lock On My Door (4)
Sometime (30,40)
Song For My Father (7)
Soul Of J.B. (17)
Soul Power (33,34) *29*
Soul Pride (Part 1 & 2) (23)
Soul With Different Notes (19)
Soulful Christmas (25)
Spank, The (46)
Spinning Wheel (29) *90*
Sportin' Life (37)
Stagger Lee (16)
Star Generation (47)
Static (Part 1 And 2) (51)
Still (47)
Stone Fox (13,18)
Stoned To The Bone (39) *58*
Stormy Monday (40)
Straight Ahead (38)
Strangers In The Night (22)
Suds (8)
Sudsy (23)
Sumpin' Else (9)
Sunny (22)
Super Bad (30,33,34) *13*
Superbad, Superslick (43)
Sweet Little Baby Boy (Part 1 & 2) (11)
Sweet Lorraine (4)
Take Some-Leave Some (39)
Talking Loud And Saying Nothing (35) *27*
Tell Me That You Love Me (13)
Tempted (5)
That's Life (20,22)
That's My Desire (27)
Then You Can Tell Me Goodbye (21)
There (5)
There It Is (Part 1 And 2) (35) *43*
There Was A Time (17,20,22,29) *36*
These Foolish Things (3,40)
Thing In "G" (2)
Things That I Used To Do (4) *99*
Think (1,8,20,49) *33*
This Feeling (44)
This Is My Lonely Christmas (Part 1 & 2) (11)
This Old Heart (6) *79*

Three Hearts In A Tangle (8) *93*
Till Then (13)
Time After Time (17,22)
Time Is Running Out Fast (39)
Time To Get Busy (51)
Tit For Tat (Ain't No Taking Back) (25) *86*
To My Brother (38)
Top Of The Stack (24)
Transmograpfication (38)
Tribute (51)
Try Me (1,2,14,20,33,48,49) *48*
Try Me [instrumental] (7) *63*
Tryin' To Get Over (38)
Turn Me Loose, I'm Dr. Feelgood (50)
Turn On The Heat And Build Some Fire (43)
Twist, The (41)
Uncle (22)
Use Your Mother (26)
Vonshelia (9)
Waiting In Vain (2)
Wake Up And Give Yourself A Chance To Live (45)
Wee Wee (9)
What Do You Like (15)
What Kind Of Fool Am I (27)
What The World Needs Now Is Love (45)
When A Man Loves A Woman (12)
When The Saints Go Marching In (40)
White Lightning (I Mean Moonshine) (37)
Who Am I (35)
Who Can I Turn To (41)
Who's Afraid Of Virginia Woolf? (5)
Whole World Needs Liberation (36)
Why Am I Treated So Bad (23)
Why Did You Take Your Love Away From Me (17)
Why Do You Do Me (1,49)
Why Does Everything Happen To Me (1,49)
Willow Weep For Me (22)
Woman (45)
Women Are Something Else (39)
World (Part 1 And Part 2) (28) *37*
You And Me (51)
You Don't Have To Go (6)
You Know It (25)
You Mother (31)
You Took My Heart (44)
You're Nobody Till Somebody Loves You (4)
You're Still Out Of Sight (24)
You've Got The Power (1,8,18,49) *86*
You've Got To Change Your Mind (17)
Your Cheating Heart (27)
Your Love (43)
Your Love Was Good For Me (36)
Yours And Mine (13)

BROWN, Jim Ed   '71

Born on 4/1/34 in Sparkman, Arkansas. Country singer. Leader of The Browns.

| 2/6/71 | 81 | 9 | | | **Morning** | | | $15 | RCA Victor 4461 |

Ain't Life Sweet / Dime At A Time / Every Mile Of The Way / Good Brother John / How To Lose A Good Woman / Laying Here Lying In Bed / **Morning** *47* / Rainy Jane / Sunday Morning We'll Be Singing / Wake Me Up In Oklahoma

BROWN, Julie   '85

Born in 1958 in Van Nuys, California. Comedic singer/actress. Appeared in several movies and TV shows. Not to be confused with former MTV VJ "Downtown" Julie Brown.

| 2/2/85 | 168 | 7 | | | **Goddess In Progress** | | [M-N] | $10 | Rhino 610 |

'Cause I'm A Blonde / Earth Girls Are Easy / Homecoming Queen's Got A Gun / I Like 'Em Big And Stupid / Will I Make It Through The Eighties?

BROWN, Les, And His Orchestra   '55
Born on 3/14/12 in Reinerton, Pennsylvania. Died of cancer on 1/4/2001 (age 88). Big band leader/clarinetist.

| 2/19/55 | **15** | 2 | | | **Concert At The Palladium** .... [I-L] | $30 | Coral CX-1 [2] |

recorded in September 1953 at the Hollywood Palladium

Baby, I Need You
Back In Your Own Backyard
Begin The Beguine
Brown's Little Jug
Caravan

Cherokee (Indian Love Song)
Crazy Legs
Flying Home
From This Moment On
Happy Holligan

I Let A Song Go Out Of My Heart
I Would Do Anything For You
Invitation
Jersey Bounce

Laura
Midnight Sun
Montoona Clipper
One O'Clock Jump
Rain

Sentimental Journey
Speak Low (When You Speak, Love)
Strange
Street Of Dreams

You're The Cream In My Coffee

BROWN, Maxine   '69
Born on 4/27/32 in Kingstree, South Carolina. R&B singer.

| 11/29/69 | **195** | 2 | | | **We'll Cry Together** .... | $20 | Commonwealth U. 6001 |

Darling, Be Home Soon
Didn't You Know (You'd Have To Cry Sometime)

I Can't Get Along Without You
Johnny's Coming Home
Piece Of My Heart

Reason To Believe
See And Don't See
We'll Cry Together *73*

You're The Reason I'm Living

BROWN, Norman   '94
Born in Los Angeles. Jazz guitarist.

| 6/4/94 | **140** | 13 | | © | 1 **After The Storm** .... [I] | $10 | MoJazz 0301 |
| 7/6/96 | **162** | 3 | | © | 2 **Better Days Ahead** .... [I] | $10 | MoJazz 530545 |

Acoustic Time (1)
After The Love Is Gone (2)
After The Storm (1)
Any Love (1)

Better Days Ahead (2)
Come Closer To Me (2)
El Dulce Sol (1)
Facts Of Love (2)

Family (1)
For The Love Of You (1)
It Costs To Love (1)
Let's Come Together (1)

Lydian (1)
N-Control (2)
Places In The Heart (2)
Serenade (2)

Take Me There (1)
That's The Way Love Goes (1)
Third World (2)
This Time Around (2)

Trashman (1)
Your Body's Callin' (2)

BROWN, Odell, & The Organ-Izers   '67
Born in 1938 in Louisville, Kentucky. Jazz organist.

| 9/9/67 | **173** | 4 | | | **Mellow Yellow** .... [I] | $20 | Cadet 788 |

Ain't That A Groove
Baby, You Just Don't Know

Mas Que Nada
Mellow Yellow

Que Son Uno
Quiet Village

Tommy's Thing

BROWN, Peter   '78
Born on 7/11/53 in Blue Island, Illinois. Disco singer/keyboardist.

| 1/14/78 | **11** | 44 | | © | **A Fantasy Love Affair** .... | $12 | Drive 104 |

Dance With Me *8*
Do Ya Wanna Get Funky With Me *18*

Fantasy Love Affair
For Your Love

It's True What They Say About Love
Singer's Become A Dancer

Without Love
You Should Do It *54*

BROWN, Shirley   '75
Born on 1/6/47 in West Memphis, Arkansas; raised in St. Louis. R&B singer.

| 1/25/75 | **98** | 11 | | © | **Woman To Woman** .... | $12 | Truth 4206 |

Between You And Me
I Can't Give You Up

I Need You Tonight
I've Got To Go On Without You

It Ain't No Fun *94*
Long As You Love Me

Passion
So Glad To Have You

Stay With Me Baby
Woman To Woman *22*

BROWNE, Duncan   '79
Born on 3/25/47 in England. Died of cancer on 5/28/93 (age 46). Rock singer/songwriter.

| 5/19/79 | **174** | 5 | | | **The Wild Places** .... | $12 | Sire 6065 |

Camino Real (Part 1, 2 & 3)
Crash, The

Kisarazu
Planet Earth

Roman Vecu
Samurai

Wild Places

BROWNE, Jackson   '80
| | ★226★ | | | | | | |

Born on 10/9/48 on a U.S. Army base in Heidelberg, Germany; raised in Los Angeles. Pop-rock singer/songwriter/guitarist/pianist. Worked with the **Eagles** and **Warren Zevon**. Wife, Phyllis, committed suicide on 3/25/76. A prominent activist against nuclear power.

1)Hold Out 2)Running On Empty 3)The Pretender

| 3/18/72 | **53** | 23 | ▲ | © | 1 **Jackson Browne** .... | $20 | Asylum 5051 |

album also known as *Saturate Before Using*

11/10/73	**43**	38	▲	©	2 **For Everyman**	$15	Asylum 5067
10/12/74	**14**	29	▲	©	3 **Late For The Sky**	$12	Asylum 1017
11/20/76	**5**	35	▲²	©	4 **The Pretender**	$12	Asylum 1079
1/7/78	**3**	65	▲⁷	©	5 **Running On Empty**	$12	Asylum 113
7/19/80	**❶¹**	38	▲²	©	6 **Hold Out**	$12	Asylum 511
8/20/83	**8**	33	▲	©	7 **Lawyers In Love**	$10	Asylum 60268
3/22/86	**23**	31	●	©	8 **Lives In The Balance**	$10	Asylum 60457
6/24/89	**45**	16		©	9 **World In Motion**	$10	Elektra 60830
11/13/93	**40**	21	●	©	10 **I'm Alive**	$10	Elektra 61524
3/2/96	**36**	9		©	11 **Looking East**	$10	Elektra 61867
10/11/97	**47**	13		©	12 **The Next Voice You Hear - The Best Of Jackson Browne** .... [G]	$10	Elektra 62111

Alive In The World (11)
All Good Things (10)
Anything Can Happen (9)
Baby How Long (11)
Barricades Of Heaven (11,12)
Before The Deluge (3)
Black And White (8)
Boulevard (6) *19*
Call It A Loan (6,12)
Candy (8)
Chasing You Into The Light (9)
Child In These Hills (1)
Cocaine (5)
Colors Of The Sun (2)
Culver Moon (11)
Cut It Away (9)
Daddy's Tune (4)
Disco Apocalypse (6)

Doctor My Eyes (1,12) *8*
Downtown (7)
Enough Of The Night (9)
Everywhere I Go (10)
Farther On (3)
For A Dancer (3)
For A Rocker (7) *45*
For America (8) *30*
For Everyman (2)
Fountain Of Sorrow (3,12)
From Silver Lake (1)
Fuse, The (4)
Here Come Those Tears Again (4) *23*
Hold On Hold Out (6)
Hold Out (6)
How Long (9)
I Am A Patriot (9)

I Thought I Was A Child (2)
I'll Do Anything (11)
I'm Alive (10)
I'm The Cat (11)
In The Shape Of A Heart (8,12) *70*
Information Wars (11)
It Is One (11)
Jamaica Say You Will (1)
Knock On Any Door (7)
Late For The Sky (3,12)
Late Show (3)
Lawless Avenues (9)
Lawyers In Love (7) *13*
Lights And Virtues (9)
Linda Paloma (4)
Lives In The Balance (8,12)
Load-Out, The (5) *flip*

Looking East (11)
Looking Into You (1)
Love Needs A Heart (5)
Miles Away (10)
My Opening Farewell (1)
My Personal Revenge (9)
My Problem Is You (10)
Next Voice You Hear (12)
Nino (11)
Nothing But Time (5)
Of Missing Persons (6)
On The Day (7)
Only Child (4)
Our Lady Of The Well (2)
Pretender, The (4,12) *58*
Ready Or Not (2)
Rebel Jesus (12)
Redneck Friend (2) *85*

Road, The (5)
Road And The Sky (3)
Rock Me On The Water (1) *48*
Rosie (2)
Running On Empty (5,12) *11*
Say It Isn't True (7)
Shaky Town (5)
Sing My Songs To Me (3)
Sky Blue And Black (10,12)
Sleep's Dark And Silent Gate (4)
Soldier Of Plenty (8)
Some Bridges (11)
Somebody's Baby (12)
Something Fine (1)
Song For Adam (1)
Stay (5) *20*
Take Easy (2)

Take This Rain (10)
Tender Is The Night (7,12) *25*
That Girl Could Sing (6) *22*
These Days (2,12)
Till I Go Down (8)
Times You've Come (2)
Too Many Angels (10)
Two Of Me, Two Of You (10)
Under The Falling Sky (1)
Walking Slow (3)
When The Stone Begins To Turn (9)
Word Justice (9)
World In Motion (9)
You Love The Thunder (5)
Your Bright Baby Blues (4)

BROWNE, Tom '80

Born in 1959 in New York City. Jazz-funk trumpeter. Member of **Fuse One**.

DEBUT	PEAK	WKS	RIAA	CD	#	Title	Sym	$	Label & Number
8/11/79	147	6		©	1	Browne Sugar	[I]	$12	GRP 5003
7/26/80	18	26	●		2	Love Approach	[I]	$12	GRP 5008
2/21/81	37	19			3	Magic		$12	GRP 5503
12/12/81+	97	14			4	Yours Truly		$12	GRP 5507
12/3/83+	147	12			5	Rockin' Radio	[I]	$10	Arista 8107

Angeline (5)
Antoinette Like (1)
Bebopafunkadiscolypso (medley) (4)
Brighter Tomorrow (5)
Brother, Brother (1)
Bye Gones (4)
Can't Give It Away (4)
Charisma (4)
Closer I Get To You (1)
Come For The Ride (4)
Crusin' (5)
Dreams Of Lovin' You (2)
Feel Like Making Love (5)
Forever More (2)
Fungi Mama (medley) (4)
Funkin' For Jamaica (N.Y.) (2)
God Bless The Child (3)
Her Silent Smile (2)
Herbal Scent (1)
I Know (3)
I Never Was A Cowboy (1)
Lazy Bird (3)
Let's Dance (3)
Magic (3)
Making Plans (3)
Martha (2)
Message (Pride And Pity) (4)
Midnight Interlude (3)
Moon Rise (2)
Mr. Business (5)
My Latin Sky (4)
Naima (4)
Never My Love (5)
Night Wind (3)
Nocturne (2)
Promises For Spring (1)
Rockin' Radio (5)
Thigh's High (Grip Your Hips And Move) (3)
Throw Down (1)
Turn It Up (Come On Y'all) (5)
Weak In The Knees (2)
What's Going On (1)

BROWNSTONE '95

Female R&B vocal trio form Los Angeles: Monica Doby, Nichole Gilbert and Charmayne Maxwell. Doby left group for health reasons in June 1995; replaced by Kina Cosper.

DEBUT	PEAK	WKS	RIAA	CD	#	Title	Sym	$	Label & Number
1/28/95	29	37	▲	©	1	From The Bottom Up		$10	MJJ Music 57827
7/12/97	51	11		©	2	Still Climbing		$10	MJJ Music 67524

All I Do (2)
Around You (2)
Baby Love (2)
Deeper Feelings (Ooh La La) (1)
Don't Cry For Me (1)
5 Miles To Empty (2) *39*
Foolish Pride (2)
Fruit Of Life (1)
Grapevine (1) *49*
Half Of You (1)
I Can't Tell You Why (1) *54*
If You Love Me (1) *8*
If You Play Your Cards Right (2)
In The Game Of Love (2)
Kiss And Tell (2)
Let's Get It Started (2)
Love Me Like You Do (2)
Party Wit Me (1)
Pass The Lovin' (1)
Revenge (2)
Sometimes Dancin' (1)
True To Me (1)
Wipe It Up (1)
You Give Good Love (2)

BROWNSVILLE STATION '74

Rock trio from Ann Arbor, Michigan: Michael Lutz (vocals, bass), Michael "Cub" Koda (guitar), and Henry Weck (drums). Koda died of kidney failure on 7/1/2000 (age 51).

DEBUT	PEAK	WKS	RIAA	CD	#	Title	Sym	$	Label & Number
10/7/72	191	5			1	A Night On The Town		$15	Big Tree 2010
9/15/73+	98	19			2	Yeah!		$15	Big Tree 2102
6/15/74	170	8			3	School Punks		$15	Big Tree 89500

All Night Long (2)
Barefootin' (2)
Country Flavor (1)
Fast Phyllis (3)
Go Out And Get Her (2)
Hey Little Girl (3)
I Get So Excited (3)
I Got It Bad For You (3)
I Got Time (1)
I'm A King Bee (medley) (3)
I'm The Leader Of The Gang (3) *48*
I've Got Love If You Want It (medley) (3)
Jonah's Here To Stay (1)
Kings Of The Party (3) *31*
Leavin' Here (1)
Let Your Yeah Be Yeah (2) *57*
Lightnin' Bar Blues (2)
Love, Love, Love (2)
Lovin' Lady Lee (1)
Mad For Me (1)
Mama Don't Allow No Parkin' (3)
Man Who Wanted More (Saints Rock & Roll) (1)
Meet Me On The Fourth Floor (3)
Mister Robert (1)
Ostrich (3)
Question Of Temperature (2)
Rock With The Music (1)
Smokin' In The Boy's Room (2) *3*
Sweet Jane (2)
Take It Or Leave It (2)
Wanted (Dead Or Alive) (1)

BRUBECK, Dave, Quartet ★168★ '61

Born David Warren on 12/6/20 in Concord, California. Leader of jazz quartet consisting of Brubeck (piano), **Paul Desmond** (alto sax), Eugene Wright (bass) and Joe Morello (drums). One of America's all-time most popular jazz groups on college campuses. Desmond died on 5/30/77 (age 52). Brubeck won Grammy's Lifetime Achievement Award in 1996.

1)Time Out Featuring "Take Five" 2)Brubeck Time 3)Jazz: Red Hot And Cool

DEBUT	PEAK	WKS	RIAA	CD	#	Title	Sym	$	Label & Number
2/5/55	8	6			1	Dave Brubeck At Storyville: 1954	[I-L]	$80	Columbia 590
						recorded at the Storyville nightclub in Boston			
3/19/55	5	22		©	2	Brubeck Time	[I]	$60	Columbia 622
						LP: Columbia CL-622 (#5); EP: Columbia B-473 (#10)			
11/12/55	7	3		©	3	Jazz: Red Hot And Cool	[I-L]	$60	Columbia 699
						recorded at the Basin Street nightclub in New York City; LP: Columbia CL-699 (#7); EP: Columbia B-699 (#8)			
7/8/57	18	1			4	Jazz Impressions of the U.S.A.	[I]	$50	Columbia 984
9/30/57	24	1			5	Jazz Goes To Junior College	[I-L]	$40	Columbia 1034
						sequel to Brubeck's 1954 album *Jazz Goes To College* (#8)			
11/28/60+	2[1]	164	▲	©	6	Time Out Featuring "Take Five"	C:#42/2 [I]	$25	Columbia 1397 / 8192
12/12/60+	13	15			7	Bernstein Plays Brubeck Plays Bernstein	[I]	$25	Columbia 1466 / 8257
						side 1: **New York Philharmonic** with the Dave Brubeck Quartet conducted by **Leonard Bernstein**; side 2: Dave Brubeck Quartet			
12/25/61+	8	46		©	8	Time Further Out	[I]	$25	Columbia 1690 / 8490
6/16/62	24	21			9	Countdown - Time In Outer Space	[I]	$25	Columbia 1775 / 8575
3/16/63	14	15			10	Bossa Nova U.S.A.	[I]	$25	Columbia 8798
7/27/63	37	4		©	11	The Dave Brubeck Quartet At Carnegie Hall	[I-L]	$30	Columbia 826 [2]
12/21/63	137	3		©	12	Brandenburg Gate: Revisited	[I]	$25	Columbia 1963 / 8763
4/18/64	81	9			13	Time Changes	[I]	$25	Columbia 2127 / 8927
2/27/65	142	4		©	14	Jazz Impressions Of New York	[I]	$25	Columbia 2275 / 9075
10/9/65	122	3			15	Angel Eyes	[I]	$25	Columbia 2348 / 9148
3/26/66	133	5			16	My Favorite Things	[I]	$20	Columbia 2437 / 9237
7/30/66	104	4	●	©	17	Dave Brubeck's Greatest Hits	[G-I]	$20	Columbia 2484 / 9284
1/10/76	167	5		©	18	1975: The Duets	[I]	$15	Horizon 703

DAVE BRUBECK & PAUL DESMOND

Alice In Wonderland (18)
Angel Eyes (15)
Audrey (2)
Autumn In Washington Square (14)
Back Bay Blues (1)
Back To Earth (9)
Balcony Rock (18)
Blue Dove (18)
Blue Rondo A La Turk (6,11,17)
Blue Shadows In The Street (8)
Bluette (8)
Bossa Nova U.S.A. (10,11,17) *69*
Brandenburg Gate Medley (12)
Broadway Bossa Nova (14)
Broadway Romance (14)
Brother, Can You Spare A Dime (2)
Bru's Blues (5)
Bru's Boogie Woogie (8)
Cable Car (8)
Camptown Races (17)
Cantiga Nova Swing (10)
Castilian Blues (9)
Castilian Drums (9,11)
Charles Matthew Hallelujah (8)
Circus On Parade (16)
Coracao Sensivel (Tender Heart) (10)
Countdown (9)
Curtain Time (4)
Danse Duet (9)
Dialogues For Jazz Combo And Orchestra (Movements 1-4) (7)
Don't Worry 'Bout Me (1)
Duke, The (3,17)
Elementals (13)
Eleven Four (9,11)
Everybody's Jumpin' (6)
Everything Happens To Me (15)
Far More Blue (8)
Far More Drums (8)
Fare Thee Well, Annabelle (3)
Fast Life (9)
Fine Romance (2)
For All We Know (11)
G Flat Theme (12)
Gone With The Wind (1)
Here Lies Love (1)

BRUBECK, Dave, Quartet — Cont'd

History Of A Boy Scout (4)
Home At Last (4)
I Feel Pretty (7)
I'm Afraid The Masquerade Is Over (5)
I'm In A Dancing Mood (17)
Iberia (13)
In Your Own Sweet Way (12,17)
Indiana (3)
Irmao Amigo (Brother Friend) (10)
It's A Raggy Waltz (8,11,17)
Jeepers Creepers (2)
June, Theme For (10)

Kathy's Waltz (6,12)
Keepin' Out Of Mischief Now (2)
King For A Day (11)
Koto Song (18)
Lamento (10)
Let's Get Away From It All (15)
Little Girl Blue (3,16)
Little Man With A Candy Cigar (15)
Lonely Mr. Broadway (14)
Love Walked In (3)
Lover (3)
Maori Blues (8)
Maria (7)

Most Beautiful Girl In The World (16)
Mr. Broadway, Theme From (14,17)
My Favorite Things (16)
My Romance (14)
Night We Called It A Day (15)
Ode To A Cowboy (4)
On The Alamo (1)
One Moment Worth Years (5)
Over And Over Again (16)
Pennies From Heaven (2,11)
Pick Up Sticks (6)
Plain Song (4)
Quiet Girl (7)

Shim Wha (13)
Sixth Sense (14)
Someday My Prince Will Come (9)
Something To Sing About (14)
Sometimes I'm Happy (3)
Somewhere (7)
Sounds Of The Loop (4)
Southern Scene (Briar Bush) (11)
Spring In Central Park (14)
St. Louis Blues (5,11)
Stardust (18)
Stompin' For Mili (2)
Strange Meadow Lark (6)

Summer On The Sound (14)
Summer Song (4,12,18)
Take Five (6,11,17) 25
There'll Be No Tomorrow (10)
These Foolish Things (5,18)
This Can't Be Love (10,16)
Three To Get Ready (6,11)
Three's A Crowd (9)
Tonight (7)
Trolley Song (10,17)
Unisphere (13)
Unsquare Dance (8,17) 74
Upstage Rumba (14)
Vento Fresco (Cool Wind) (10)
Violets For Your Furs (15)

Waltz Limp (9)
When You're Smiling (The Whole World Smiles With You) (1)
Why Can't I? (16)
Why Do I Love You (2)
Why Phillis (9)
Will You Still Be Mine? (15)
Winter Ballad (14)
World's Fair (13)
Yonder For Two (4)
You Go To My Head (18)

BRUCE, Jack '81

Born John Asher on 5/14/43 in Glasgow, Scotland. Bass player of **Cream**. Started career with Alexis Korner's Blues Inc. (**C.C.S.**). Prior to Cream was with the Graham Bond Organization, **John Mayall**'s Bluesbreakers and **Manfred Mann**. Also see **West, Bruce & Laing**.

DEBUT	PEAK	WKS	RIAA	CD	#	Album Title	Catalog	Sym	$	Label & Number
10/25/69	55	11		©	1	Songs For A Tailor			$15	Atco 306
12/7/74	160	3		©	2	Out Of The Storm			$12	RSO 4805
5/7/77	153	5		©	3	How's Tricks			$12	RSO 3021

JACK BRUCE BAND

DEBUT	PEAK	WKS	RIAA	CD	#	Album Title	Catalog	Sym	$	Label & Number
12/13/80	182	2			4	I've Always Wanted To Do This			$10	Epic 36827

JACK BRUCE & FRIENDS

DEBUT	PEAK	WKS	RIAA	CD	#	Album Title	Catalog	Sym	$	Label & Number
3/21/81	37	16		©	5	B.L.T.			$10	Chrysalis 1324

JACK BRUCE/BILL LORDAN/ROBIN TROWER

DEBUT	PEAK	WKS	RIAA	CD	#	Album Title	Catalog	Sym	$	Label & Number
1/30/82	109	6		©	6	Truce			$10	Chrysalis 1352

JACK BRUCE/ROBIN TROWER

Baby Jane (3)
Bird Alone (4)
Boston Ball Game, 1967 (1)
Carmen (5)
Clearout, The (1)
Dancing On Air (4)
End Game (3)
Facelift 318 (4)
Fall In Love (6)
Fat Gut (6)
Feel The Heat (5)
Golden Days (2)

Gone Too Far (6)
Gonna Shut You Down (6)
He The Richmond (1)
Hit And Run (4)
How's Tricks? (3)
Imaginary Western, Theme For An (1)
In This Way (4)
Into Money (5)
Into The Storm (2)
It's Too Late (3)
Johnny B '77 (3)

Keep It Down (2)
Keep On Wondering (2)
Last Train To The Stars (6)
Life On Earth (5)
Little Boy Lost (6)
Livin' Without Ja (4)
Lost Inside A Song (3)
Madhouse (3)
Mickey The Fiddler (4)
Ministry Of Bag (1)
Never Tell Your Mother She's Out Of Tune (1)

No Island Lost (5)
Once The Bird Has Flown (5)
One (2)
Out To Lunch (4)
Outsiders (3)
Pieces Of Mind (2)
Rope Ladder To The Moon (1)
Running Back (4)
Running Through Our Hands (2)
Shadows Touching (6)
Something To Live For (3)

Take Good Care Of Yourself (6)
Thin Ice (6)
Tickets To Water Falls (1)
Times (3)
Timeslip (2)
To Isengard (1)
Waiting For The Call (3)
Weird Of Hermiston (1)
What It Is (3)
Wind And The Sea (4)
Without A Word (3)
Won't Let You Down (5)

BRUCE, Lenny '75

Born Leonard Schneider on 10/13/25 in Long Island, New York. Died of a heroin overdose on 8/3/66 (age 40). Satirical comedian. Dustin Hoffman portrayed Bruce in the 1974 autobiographical movie. Also see **Movie Soundtracks**: *Lenny*.

DEBUT	PEAK	WKS	RIAA	CD	#	Album Title	Catalog	Sym	$	Label & Number
3/15/75	178	2		©	1	Lenny Bruce/Carnegie Hall		[C]	$30	United Artists 9800 [3]
						recorded on 2/4/61				
4/5/75	191	2			2	The Real Lenny Bruce		[C-E]	$20	Fantasy 79003 [2]
						recorded 1958-1959				

Airlines, The (1)
Burlesque House (1)
Christ And Moses (1)
Clap, The (1)
Comic At The Palladium (2)
Dear Abby (1)
Djinni In The Candy Store (2)
Dykes And Faggots (1)

Enchanting Transylvania (2)
End, The (1)
Equality (1)
Fat Boy (2)
Father Flotski's Triumph (Unexpurgated) (2)
Flag And Communism (1)
Girl Singing (1)

Homosexuality (1)
How To Relax Your Colored Friends At Parties (2)
Internal Revenue (1)
Joke, The (1)
Judge Saperstein Decision (1)
Kennedy Acceptance Speech (1)

Kidnap, The (1)
Ku Klux Klan (1)
Las Vegas Tits And Ass (1)
Lima, Ohio (1)
Miracle On 57th Street (1)
My Werewolf Mama (2)
Nightclubs (1)
Non Skeddo Flies Again (2)

On Contemporaries (1)
On Humor (1)
Operation, The (1)
Pills (1)
Point Of View (1)
Religions, Inc. (2)
Shelley Berman (1)
Sound, The (1,2)

Tarzan (2)
Thank You Masked Man (2)
What's It Mean (1)
White Collar Drunk (2)

BRUFORD, Bill '79

Born on 5/17/49 in Sevenoaks, Kent, England. Drummer with **Yes**, **King Crimson**, **Genesis** and **Anderson, Bruford, Wakeman, Howe**.

DEBUT	PEAK	WKS	RIAA	CD	#	Album Title	Catalog	Sym	$	Label & Number
7/7/79	123	5		©	1	One Of A Kind		[I]	$12	Polydor 6205
3/29/80	191	2		©	2	Gradually Going Tornado		[I]	$12	Polydor 6261

Abingdon Chasp (1)
Age Of Information (1)
Fainting In Coils (1)
Five G (1)

Forever Until Sunday (1)
Gothic 17 (2)
Hell's Bells (1)
Joe Frazier (1)

Land's End (2)
One Of A Kind - Part One & Two (1)
Palewell Park (2)

Plans For J.D. (2)
Q. E. D. (2)
Sahara Of Snow - Part One & Two (1)

Sliding Floor (2)
Travels With Myself-And Someone Else (1)

BRYANT, Anita '62

Born on 3/25/40 in Barnsdale, Oklahoma. Pop singer.

DEBUT	PEAK	WKS	RIAA	CD	#	Album Title	Catalog	Sym	$	Label & Number
9/15/62	145	2			1	In A Velvet Mood			$20	Columbia 1885 / 8685
1/21/67	146	4			2	Mine Eyes Have Seen The Glory			$15	Columbia 2573 / 9373
12/2/67	25[X]	5			3	Christmas With Anita Bryant/Do You Hear What I Hear?		[X]	$15	Columbia 2720 / 9520

All The Way (1)
America (2)
America The Beautiful (2)
Away In A Manger (3)
Battle Hymn Of The Republic (2)
Cry Me A River (1)

Do You Hear What I Hear? (3)
First Noel (3)
God Bless America (2)
House I Live In (That's America To Me) (2)
In A Humble Place (3)
In God We Trust (2)

It Came Upon The Midnight Clear (3)
Love Is A Many-Splendored Thing (1)
Love Letters In The Sand (1)
Mary's Lullaby (Sleep Baby, Sleep) (3)

Misty (1)
Moon River (1)
Moulin Rouge (Where Is Your Heart), Song From (1)
My Prayer (1)
Never On Sunday (1)
O Come, All Ye Faithful (3)

O Holy Night (3)
Oh Little Town Of Bethlehem (3)
Onward, Christian Soldiers (2)
Power And The Glory (2)
Silent Night, Holy Night (3)
Star-Spangled Banner (2)

Story Of Christmas (3)
Tammy (1)
This Is My Country (2)
This Is Worth Fighting For (2)
Tonight (1)
Volare (Nel Blu Dipinto Di Blu) (1)

BRYANT, Ray '66

Born Raphael Bryant on 12/24/31 in Philadelphia. Jazz pianist.

DEBUT	PEAK	WKS	RIAA	CD	#	Album Title	Catalog	Sym	$	Label & Number
6/25/66	111	12			1	Gotta Travel On		[I]	$20	Cadet 767
5/13/67	193	3			2	Slow Freight		[I]	$20	Cadet 781

Ah, The Apple Tree (When The World Was Young) (2)
All Things Are Possible (1)

Amen (2)
Bag's Groove (1)
Erewhon (1)

Fox Stalker (2)
Gotta Travel On (1)
If You Go Away (2)

It Was A Very Good Year (1)
Little Soul Sister (1)
Midnight Stalkin' (1)

Monkey Business (1)
Return Of The Prodigal Son (2)
Satin Doll (2)

Slow Freight (2)
Smack Dab In The Middle (1)

BRYANT, Sharon '89

Born on 8/14/56 in Westchester County, New York. Lead singer of **Atlantic Starr** from 1976-84.

| 9/9/89 | 139 | 13 | | © | Here I Am .... | | | $10 | Wing 837313 |

Body Talk Foolish Heart *90* In The Nite Time No More Lonely Nights
Falling Here I Am Let Go *34* Old Friend

★284★ BRYSON, Peabo '83

Born Robert Peabo Bryson on 4/13/51 in Greenville, South Carolina. R&B singer/producer.
1)Born To Love 2)Crosswinds 3)I Am Love

3/11/78	49	29	●	©	1 Reaching For The Sky			$12	Capitol 11729
12/9/78+	35	26	●		2 Crosswinds			$12	Capitol 11875
12/15/79+	44	19		©	3 We're The Best Of Friends			$12	Capitol 12019

NATALIE COLE/PEABO BRYSON

| 5/3/80 | 79 | 16 | | | 4 Paradise .... | | | $12 | Capitol 12063 |
| 12/20/80+ | 52 | 19 | | © | 5 Live & More .... | | [L] | $15 | Atlantic 7004 [2] |

ROBERTA FLACK & PEABO BRYSON
recorded at the Holiday Star Theater in Merrillville, Indiana

2/28/81	82	11			6 Turn The Hands Of Time			$10	Capitol 12138
11/28/81+	40	24			7 I Am Love			$10	Capitol 12179
12/4/82+	55	21			8 Don't Play With Fire			$10	Capitol 12241
8/13/83	25	42	●	©	9 Born To Love			$10	Capitol 12284

PEABO BRYSON/ROBERTA FLACK

6/16/84	44	26		©	10 Straight From The Heart			$10	Elektra 60362
7/14/84	168	10		©	11 The Peabo Bryson Collection		[G]	$10	Capitol 12348
7/6/85	102	13		©	12 Take No Prisoners			$10	Elektra 60427
2/13/88	157	6		©	13 Positive			$10	Elektra 60753
7/13/91	88	19	●	©	14 Can You Stop The Rain			$10	Columbia 46823

Another Love Song (6) Gimme Some Time (3) I've Been Down (6) Love Is A Waiting Game (5) She's A Woman (2) We Don't Have To Talk (About
Back Together Again (5) Give Me Your Love (8) **If Ever You're In My Arms** Love Is On The Rise (7) She's Over Me (12) Love) (8,11)
Blame It On Me (9) Go For It (8) **Again** (10) *10* Love Is Watching You (2) Shower You With Love (14) We're The Best Of Friends (3)
Born To Love (9) God Don't Like Ugly (5) If It's Really Love (14) Love Means Forever (10) **Slow Dancin'** (10) *82* What You Won't Do For Love
Can We Find Love Again (9) Have A Good Time (1) If Only For One Night (5) Love Walked Out On Me (1) Smile (2) (3,11)
Can You Stop The Rain Heaven Above Me (9,11) Impossible (7) Love Will Find You (3) Soul Provider (14) When We Need It Bad (13)
(14) *52* Hold On To The World (1) Irresistible (Never Run Away Make The World Stand Still (5) Split Decision (7) When Will I Learn (4,5)
Closer Than Close (14) Hurt (13) From Love) (12) Man On A String (6) Spread Your Wings (2) When You Talk To Me (12)
Come On Over Tonight (13) I Am Love (7) Killing Me Softly With His Song Maybe (9) Still Water (13) Why Don't You Make Up Your
Comin' Alive (9) I Believe In You (4,5) (5) Minute By Minute (4) Straight From The Heart (10) Mind (6)
Crosswinds (2) I Can't Imagine (14) Learning The Ways Of Love More Than Everything (5) **Take No Prisoners (In The** **Without You** (13) *89*
Don't Make Me Wait Too Long I Get Nervous (10) (10) Move Your Body (2) **Game Of Love)** (12) *78* Words (8)
(5) I Just Came Here To Dance Let Me Be The One You Need My Life (6) There's No Getting Over You You (7)
Don't Play With Fire (8) (9,11) (8) Only Heaven Can Wait (For (La Theme De Sharon) (10) You Are My Heaven (medley)
Don't Touch Me (2) I Just Had To Fall (14) **Let The Feeling Flow** (7,11) *42* Love) (medley) (5) There's No Guarantee (7) (5)
Dwellers Of The City (6) I Love The Way You Love (4) Let's Apologize (13) Paradise (4) There's Nothin' Out There (12) You Don't Have To Beg (14)
Falling For You (12) I Wanna Be With You (14) Let's Fall In Love (medley) (3) Piece Of My Heart (6) This Love Affair (3) You Haven't Learned About
Feel Like Makin' Love (5) I Want To Be Where You Are Life Is A Child (4) Point Of View (2) This Time Around (13) Love (1)
Feel The Fire (1,5,11) (3) Lost In The Night (14) Positive (13) Tonight (13) You Send Me (medley) (3)
Fool Already Knows (1) I Want To Know (13) Love Always Finds A Way (12) Reaching For The Sky (1,5,11) **Tonight, I Celebrate My Love** **You're Looking Like Love To**
Fool Such As I (6) I Wish You Love (14) Love From Your Heart (1) Real Deal (10) (9,11) *58* **Me** (9,11) *58*
Friction (5) I'm In Love (12) Love Has No Shame (4) Remember When (So Much In Turn It On (8) Your Lonely Heart (3)
Get Ready To Cry (7) I'm So Into You (2,11) Love In Every Season (4,5) Love) (8) Turn The Hands Of Time (6)

BT '00

Born Brian Transeau in 1973 in Washington DC. Electronic keyboardist/producer.

| 8/26/00 | 166 | 2 | | © | Movement In Still Life .... | | | $10 | Nettwerk 30154 |

Dreaming Love On Haight Street Mercury And Solace Never Gonna Come Back Down Satellite
Godspeed MadSkillz-Mic Chekka Movement In Still Life Running Down The Way Up Shame Smartbomb

B.T. EXPRESS '75

Disco group from Brooklyn, New York. Core members: Barbara Joyce (female vocals), brothers Louis (vocals, bass) and Bill (sax) Risbrook, Richard Thompson (guitar), Carlos Ward (flute) and Dennis Rowe (congas). Keyboardist Michael Jones, who was with the group from 1976-79, later recorded solo as techno-funk musician **Kashif**.

11/23/74+	5	31	●	©	1 Do It ('Til You're Satisfied)			$15	Roadshow 5117
8/2/75	19	19		©	2 Non-Stop			$12	Roadshow 41001
5/29/76	43	12			3 Energy To Burn			$12	Columbia 34178
5/28/77	111	5			4 Function At The Junction			$12	Columbia 34702
2/25/78	67	11			5 Shout!			$12	Columbia 35078
5/31/80	164	4			6 B.T. Express 1980			$12	Columbia 36333

Better Late Than Never (6) Does It Feel Good (6) Give Up The Funk (Let's Make Your Body Move (3) Sunshine (4)
Can't Stop Groovin' Now, Door To My Mind (4) Dance) (6) Mental Telepathy (1) Takin' Off (6)
Wanna Do It Some More Energy Level (3) Happiness (2) Now That We Found Love (3) That's What I Want For You
(3) *52* Energy To Burn (3) Have Some Fun (6) Once You Get It (1) Baby (1)
Close To You (2) *82* Everything Good To You (Ain't Heart Of Fire (6) **Peace Pipe** (2) *31* This House Is Smokin' (1)
Closer (6) Always Good For You) (1) Herbs (3) Put It In (In The Pocket) (5) Time Tunnel (3)
Depend On Yourself (3) Expose Yourself (4) How Big Can You Dream (4) Ride On B. T. (5) We Got It Together (4)
Devil's Workshop (2) **Express** (1) *4* I Want You With Me (5) Scratch My Itch (4) What You Do In The Dark (5)
Discotizer (2) Eyes (4) If It Don't Turn You On (You Shake It Off (5) Whatcha Think About That? (2)
Do It ('Til You're Satisfied) Funk Theory (6) Oughta' Leave It Alone) (1) Shout It Out (5) You Got It-I Want It (2)
(1) *2* Funky Music (4) It's In Your Blood (5) Star Gazer (4) You Got Something (5)
Do You Like It (1) **Give It What You Got** (2) *40* Look At The People (5) Still Good-Still Like It (2)

BUBBLE PUPPY '69

Psychedelic-rock group from Houston: Rod Price (vocals), Todd Potter (guitar), Roy Cox (bass) and David Fore (drums).

| 5/17/69 | 176 | 6 | | © | A Gathering Of Promises .... | | | $100 | Int'l. Artists 10 |

Beginning Gathering Of Promises Hurry Sundown It's Safe To Say Road To St. Stephens
Elizabeth **Hot Smoke & Sasafrass** *14* I've Got To Reach You Lonely Todd's Tune

BUCHANAN, Roy　　　'73

Born on 9/23/39 in Ozark, Arkansas; raised in Pixley, California. Committed suicide on 8/14/88 (age 48). Prolific rock/blues guitarist.
1)Second Album 2)Loading Zone 3)Roy Buchanan

DEBUT	PEAK	WKS	CD	# Album Title	Sym	$	Label & Number
9/9/72	107	12	©	1 Roy Buchanan		$15	Polydor 5033
3/10/73	86	13	©	2 Second Album	[I]	$15	Polydor 5046
2/23/74	152	10	©	3 That's What I Am Here For		$15	Polydor 6020
12/28/74+	160	6	©	4 In The Beginning		$15	Polydor 6035
5/15/76	148	7		5 A Street Called Straight		$12	Atlantic 18170
6/18/77	105	8		6 Loading Zone	[I]	$12	Atlantic 18219
5/20/78	119	7		7 You're Not Alone	[I]	$12	Atlantic 19170
1/24/81	193	2	©	8 My Babe		$10	Waterhouse 12
8/3/85	161	13	©	9 When A Guitar Plays The Blues		$10	Alligator 4741
6/28/86	153	8	©	10 Dancing On The Edge		$10	Alligator 4747

Adventures Of Brer Rabbit And Tar Baby (6)
After Hours (2)
Baby, Baby, Baby (10)
Beer Drinking Woman (10)
Blues For Gary (8)
CC Ryder (4)
Cajun (1)
Caruso (5)
Chicago Smokeshop (9)
Chokin' Kind (10)
Circle, The (6)
Country Boy (9)
Country Preacher (4)
Cream Of The Crop (10)
Dizzy Miss Lizzy (8)
Dr. Rock & Roll (8)
Done Your Daddy Dirty (6)
Down By The River (7)
Drowning On Dry Land (10)
1841 Shuffle (7)
Filthy Teddy (2)
Five String Blues (2)
Fly...Night Bird (7)
Good God Have Mercy (5)
Green Onions (4)
Guitar Cadenza (5)
Haunted House (1)
Hawaiian Punch (9)
Heat Of The Battle (6)
Hey, Good Lookin' (1)
Hey Joe (3)
Hidden (6)
Home Is Where I Lost Her (3)
I Am A Lonesome Fugitive (1)
I Still Think About Ida Mae (5)
I Won't Tell You No Lies (2)
I'm A Ram (4)
If Six Was Nine (5)
In The Beginning (4)
It Should've Been Me (8)
John's Blues (1)
Judy (6)
Jungle Gym (10)
Keep What You Got (5)
Lack Of Talent (8)
Man On The Floor (5)
Matthew (10)
Messiah Will Come Again (1,5)
Mrs. Pressure (9)
My Babe (8)
My Baby Says She's Gonna Leave Me (8)
My Friend Jeff (5)
My Sonata (8)
Nephesh (3)
Nickel And A Nail (9)
Okay (5)
Opening...Miles From Earth (7)
Petal To The Metal (10)
Pete's Blue (1)
Peter Gunn (10)
Please Don't Turn Me Away (3)
Ramon's Blues (6)
Rescue Me (4)
Rodney's Song (3)
Roy's Bluz (3)
Running Out (5)
Secret Love (8)
She Can't Say No (4)
She Once Lived Here (2)
Short Fuse (9)
Sneaking Godzilla Through The Alley (9)
Supernova (7)
Sweet Dreams (1)
Thank You Lord (9)
That's What I Am Here For (3)
Treat Her Right (2)
Tribute To Elmore James (2)
Turn To Stone (7)
Voices (3)
Wayfairing Pilgrim (4)
When A Guitar Plays The Blues (9)
Whiplash (10)
Why Don't You Want Me? (9)
You Can't Judge A Book By The Cover (10)
You Gotta Let Me Know (8)
You're Killing My Love (4)
You're Not Alone (7)
Your Love (6)

BUCKCHERRY　　　'01

Rock group from Los Angeles: Joshua Todd (vocals), Keith Nelson and Yogi (guitars), Jon Brightman (bass) and Devon Glenn (drums).

DEBUT	PEAK	WKS	RIAA	CD	# Album Title	$	Label & Number
4/24/99	74	30	●	©	1 Buckcherry	$10	DreamWorks 50044
4/14/01	64	5		©	2 Time Bomb	$10	DreamWorks 450287

Baby (1)
Borderline (1)
Check Your Head (1)
Crushed (1)
Dead Again (1)
Dirty Mind (1)
Drink The Water (1)
Fall (2)
For The Movies (1)
Frontside (2)
Get Back (1)
Lawless And Lulu (2)
Lit Up (1)
Place In The Sun (2)
Porno Star (2)
Related (1)
Ridin' (2)
(Segue) Helpless (2)
Slamin' (2)
Slit My Wrists (2)
Time Bomb (2)
Underneath (2)
Whiskey In The Morning (2)
You (2)

BUCKINGHAM, Lindsey　　　'81

Born on 10/3/47 in Palo Alto, California. Rock singer/songwriter/guitarist. Formed **Buckingham-Nicks** duo with then-girlfriend, Stevie Nicks. Both joined **Fleetwood Mac** in 1975.

DEBUT	PEAK	WKS	CD	# Album Title	$	Label & Number
11/7/81	32	24	©	1 Law And Order	$10	Asylum 561
1/29/83+	28 C	22	©	2 Buckingham Nicks	$10	Polydor 5058
				first released in 1973		
9/1/84	45	16	©	3 Go Insane	$10	Elektra 60363
7/4/92	128	9	©	4 Out Of The Cradle	$10	Reprise 26182

All My Sorrows (4)
Bang The Drum (3)
Bwana (1)
Countdown (4)
Crying In The Night (2)
Crystal (2)
D.W. Suite (3)
Django (2)
Doing What I Can (4)
Don't Let Me Down Again (2)
Don't Look Down (4)
Frozen Love (2)
Go Insane (3) *23*
I Must Go (3)
I Want You (3)
I'll Tell You Now (1)
It Was I (1)
Johnny Stew (1)
Lola (My Love) (2)
Long Distance Winner (2)
Love From Here, Love From There (1)
Loving Cup (3)
Mary Lee Jones (1)
Play In The Rain (3)
Races Are Run (2)
Satisfied Mind (4)
Say We'll Meet Again (4)
September Song (1)
Shadow Of The West (1)
Slow Dancing (3)
Soul Drifter (4)
Stephanie (2)
Street Of Dreams (4)
Surrender The Rain (4)
That's How We Do It In L.A. (1)
This Is The Time (4)
This Nearly Was Mine (4)
Trouble (1) *9*
Turn It On (4)
Without A Leg To Stand On (2)
Wrong (4)
You Do Or You Don't (4)

BUCKINGHAMS, The　　　'68

Pop-rock group from Chicago: Dennis Tufano (vocals), Carl Giammarese (guitar), Martin Grebb (keyboards), Nick Fortune (bass) and Jon Paulos (drums). Paulos died of a drug overdose on 3/26/80 (age 32). Grebb formed **The Fabulous Rhinestones**.

DEBUT	PEAK	WKS	CD	# Album Title	Sym	$	Label & Number
3/25/67	109	8	©	1 Kind Of A Drag		$50	U.S.A. 107
6/10/67	58	23	©	2 Time & Charges		$25	Columbia 9469
2/10/68	53	16	©	3 Portraits		$25	Columbia 9598
9/21/68	161	5	©	4 In One Ear And Gone Tomorrow		$25	Columbia 9703
5/24/69	73	12	©	5 The Buckinghams' Greatest Hits	[G]	$25	Columbia 9812

And Our Love (2,5)
Any Place In Here (3)
Are You There (With Another Girl) (4)
Back In Love Again (4,5) *57*
Beginners Love (1)
Big Business Advisor (3)
Can I Get A Witness (4)
Can't Find The Words (4)
C'mon Home (3)
Don't Want To Cry (1)
Don't You Care (2,5) *6*
Foreign Policy (2,5)
Have You Noticed You're Alive (3)
Hey Baby (They're Playing Our Song) (3,5) *12*
I Call Your Name (1)
I Know I Think (4)
I Love All Of The Girls (3)
I'll Be Back (2)
I'll Go Crazy (1,5)
I've Been Wrong (1)
Inside Looking Out (3)
Just Because I've Fallen Down (3)
Kind Of A Drag (1,5) *1*
Laudy Miss Claudy (5) *41*
Love Ain't Enough (1)
Mail, The (3)
Makin' Up & Breakin' Up (1)
Married Life (2)
Mercy, Mercy, Mercy (2,5) *5*
Our Wrong To Be Right (4)
Pitied Be The Dragon Hunter (2)
Remember (2)
Simplicity (4)
Song Of The Breeze (4)
Summertime (1)
Susan (3,5) *11*
Sweets For My Sweet (1)
Till The Sun Doesn't Shine (4)
Time Of My Life (4)
Virginia Wolf (1)
We Just Know (3)
What Is Love (4)
Why Don't You Love Me (2,5)
You Are Gone (2)
You Make Me Feel So Good (1)

BUCKLEY, Jeff　　　'98

Born on 11/17/66 in Los Angeles. Drowned in Memphis on 5/29/97 (age 30). Singer/songwriter/guitarist. Son of **Tim Buckley**.

DEBUT	PEAK	WKS	CD	# Album Title	Sym	$	Label & Number
5/20/95	149	7	©	1 Grace		$10	Columbia 57528
6/13/98	64	3	©	2 Sketches For My Sweetheart The Drunk		$15	Columbia 67228 [2]
5/27/00	133	1	©	3 Mystery White Boy - Live '95-'96	[L]	$10	Columbia 69592

Back In N.Y.C. (2)
Corpus Christi Carol (1)
Demon John (2)
Dream Brother (1,3)
Eternal Life (1,3)
Everybody Here Wants You (2)
Grace (1,3)
Hallelujah (1,3)
Haven't You Heard (2)
I Know It's Over (medley) (2)
I Know We Could Be So Happy Baby (If We Wanted To Be) (2)
I Woke Up In A Strange Place (2)
Jewel Box (2)
Kanga Roo (3)
Last Goodbye (1,3)
Lilac Wine (1,3)
Lover, You Should've Come Over (1)
Man That Got Away (3)
Mojo Pin (1,3)
Moodswing Whiskey (3)
Morning Theft (2)
Murder Suicide Meteor Slave (2)
New Year's Prayer (2)
Nightmares By The Sea (2)
Opened Once (2)
Satisfied Mind (2)
Sky Is A Landfill (2)
So Real (1)
Vancouver (2)
What Will You Say (3)
Witches' Rave (2)
Yard Of Blonde Girls (2)
You & I (2)
Your Flesh Is So Nice (2)

BUCKLEY, Tim '69
Born on 2/14/47 in Washington DC. Died of a drug overdose on 6/29/75 (age 28). Folk singer/songwriter. Father of **Jeff Buckley**.

11/4/67	171	5		© 1	Goodbye And Hello			$25	Elektra 74018
4/19/69	81	12		© 2	Happy Sad			$25	Elektra 74045
2/7/70	192	2		© 3	Blue Afternoon			$30	Straight 1060

Blue Melody (3)
Buzzin' Fly (2)
Cafe (3)
Carnival Song (1)
Chase The Blues Away (3)
Dream Letter (2)

Goodbye And Hello (1)
Gypsy Woman (1)
Hallucinations (1)
Happy Time (1)
I Must Have Been Blind (3)

I Never Asked To Be Your Mountain (1)
Knight-Errant (1)
Love From Room 109 At The Islander (On Pacific Coast Highway) (2)

Morning Glory (1)
No Man Can Find The War (1)
Once I Was (1)
Phantasmagoria In Two (1)
Pleasant Street (1)
River, The (3)

Sing A Song For You (2)
So Lonely (3)
Strange Feelin' (2)
Train, The (3)

BUCKNER & GARCIA '82
Novelty duo from Atlanta: Jerry Buckner (keyboards) and Gary Garcia (vocals).

| 3/13/82 | 24 | 16 | ● | | Pac-Man Fever | | [N] | $10 | Columbia 37941 |

Defender, The
Do The Donkey Kong

Froggy's Lament
Goin' Berzerk

Hyperspace
Mousetrap

Ode To A Centipede
Pac-Man Fever 9

BUCK-O-NINE '97
Ska-rock group from San Diego: Jon Pebsworth (vocals), Jonas Kleiner (guitar), Anthony Curry (trumpet), Dan Albert (trombone), Craig Yarnold (sax), Scott Kennerly (bass) and Steve Bauer (drums).

| 9/6/97 | 190 | 1 | © | | Twenty-Eight Teeth | | | $10 | TVT 5760 |

Albequerque
I'm The Man
Jennifer's Cold

Little Pain Inside
My Town
Nineteen

Peach Fish
Record Store
Round Kid

Steve Was Dead
Tear Jerky
Twenty-Eight Teeth

What Happened To My Radio?
You Go You're Gone

BUCKWHEAT '72
Pop group from Los Angeles: Debbie Campbell (vocals), Michael Smotherman (vocals, keyboards), Randy James (guitar), Mark Durham (bass) and Timmy Harrison (drums).

| 4/1/72 | 179 | 6 | | | Movin' On | | | $15 | London 609 |

Crazy Songs And Looney Tunes

Does Anybody Care
Good Book

Gunfighter, The
I'm Goin' Home

Indian Song
Movin' On (Part I & II)

Simple Song Of Freedom 84
Song For Billy

BUCKWHEAT ZYDECO '88
Born Stanley Dural on 11/14/47 in Lafayette, Louisiana. Singer/songwriter/accordianist.

11/14/87	172	5	© 1		On A Night Like This			$10	Island 90622
9/17/88	104	7	© 2		Taking It Home			$10	Island 90968
7/7/90	140	11	© 3		Where There's Smoke There's Fire			$10	Island 842925

Be Good Or Be Gone (3)
Beast Of Burden (3)
Buck's Hot Rod (3)
Buckwheat's Special (1)
Creole Country Part 1 & 2 (2)
Down Dallas Alley (2)

Drivin' Old Grey (2)
Hey, Good Lookin' (3)
Hot Tamale Baby (2)
In And Out Of My Life (2)
It's Getting Late (3)
Ma 'Tit Fille (1)

Make A Change (2)
Marie Marie (1)
Maybe I Will (3)
On A Night Like This (1)
Ooh Wow (2)
People's Choice (1)

Pour Tout Quelque'un (3)
Route 66 (3)
Space Zydeco (1)
Taking It Home (2)
These Things You Do (2)
Time Is Tight (1)

We're Having A Party (3)
What You Gonna Do? (3)
Where There's Smoke There's Fire (3)
Why Does Love Got To Be So Sad (2)

Zydeco Honky Tonk (1)

BUD AND TRAVIS '63
Folk duo from San Francisco: Bud Dashiel and Travis Edmonson. Dashiel died on 6/2/89.

11/9/63	126	4		1	Bud & Travis...In Concert		[L]	$30	Liberty 11001 [2]
					recorded on 3/24/60 at the Civic Auditorium in Santa Monica				
3/28/64	129	6		2	Perspective On Bud & Travis			$25	Liberty 7341

Abilene (2)
Ay! Jalisco (2)
Ay, Maria (2)
Bonsoir Dame (1)
Carmen Carmella (1)
Cloudy Summer Afternoon (1)

Come To The Dance (Vamos Al Baile) (1)
Delia's Gone (1)
Everybody Loves Saturday Night (1)
Fiesta In Guadalajara (2)

Goin' To California (3)
Guess I'll Go Home (1)
I Never Will Marry (2)
Johnny, I Hardly Knew Ye' (1)
La Vaquila Colorada (1)
Long Time Back (2)

Malaguena Salerosa (1)
Maria Cristina (2)
Merry Minuet (Rioting In Africa) (1)
Mexican Wedding Dance (La Bamba) (1)

Myra (1)
Raspberries, Strawberries (1)
Sabras Que Te Quiero (2)
Sloop John B (1)
So Long, Stay Well (2)
Take Off Your Old Coat (2)

They Call The Wind Maria (1)
Tomorrow Is A Long Time (2)
Two Brothers (2)

BUENA VISTA SOCIAL CLUB '99
Group of Cuban musicians assembled by American guitarist **Ry Cooder**: Company Segundo and **Ibrahim Ferrer** (vocals), Eliades Ochoa (guitar) and Ruben Gonzalez (piano).

| 3/14/98+ | 80 | 19 | ▲ © | | Buena Vista Social Club | C:❶3/57 | [F] | $10 | World Circuit 79478 |

Amor de Loca Juventud
Buena Vista Social Club
Candela

Chan Chan
De Camino a La Vereda
Dos Gardenias

El Carretero
El Cuarto de Tula
La Bayamesa

Murmullo
Orgullecida
Pueblo Nuevo

Veinte Años
¿Y Tú Qué Has Hecho?

BUFFALO SPRINGFIELD, The '69
Superstar group formed in Los Angeles: **Stephen Stills** (vocals, guitar), **Neil Young** and **Richie Furay** (guitars), Bruce Palmer (bass) and Dewey Martin (drums). **Jim Messina** replaced Palmer after second album. Disbanded in 1968. Stills and Young formed **Crosby, Stills, Nash & Young**. Furay and Messina formed **Poco**. Group inducted into the Rock and Roll Hall of Fame in 1997.

3/25/67	80	16	© 1		Buffalo Springfield			$25	Atco 200
11/18/67+	44	14	© 2		Buffalo Springfield Again			$25	Atco 226
8/17/68	42	19	© 3		Last Time Around			$25	Atco 256
3/1/69	42	24	▲ © 4		Retrospective/The Best Of Buffalo Springfield	C:#33/6	[G]	$25	Atco 283
12/8/73	104	13	© 5		Buffalo Springfield		[K]	$20	Atco 806 [2]

Bluebird (2,4,5) *58*
Broken Arrow (2,4,5)
Burned (1,5)
Carefree Country Day (3)
Child's Claim To Fame (2,5)
Do I Have To Come Right Out And Say It (1)
Everybody's Wrong (1)

Everydays (2)
Expecting To Fly (2,4,5) *98*
Flying On The Ground Is Wrong (1)
For What It's Worth (Stop, Hey What's That Sound) (1,4,5) *7*
Four Days Gone (3,5)

Go And Say Goodbye (1,4,5)
Good Time Boy (3)
Hot Dusty Roads (1)
Hour Of Not Quite Rain (3,5)
Hung Upside Down (2,5)
I Am A Child (3,4,5)
It's So Hard To Wait (3)
Kind Woman (3,4,5)

Leave (1,5)
Merry-Go-Round (3)
Mr. Soul (2,4,5)
Nowadays Clancy Can't Even Sing (1,4,5)
On The Way Home (3,4,5) *82*
Out Of My Mind (1,5)
Pay The Price (1,5)

Pretty Girl Why (3,5)
Questions (3,5)
Rock 'N' Roll Woman (2,4,5) *44*
Sad Memory (4)
Sit Down I Think I Love You (1,4,5)
Special Care (3,5)

Uno Mundo (3,5)

BUFFALO TOM '95
Rock trio from Boston: Bill Janovitz (vocals, guitar), Chris Colbourn (bass) and Tom Maginnis (drums).

| 10/9/93 | 185 | 1 | © 1 | | [big red letter day] | | | $10 | Beggars Banquet 92292 |
| 7/29/95 | 160 | 1 | © 2 | | Sleepy Eyed | | | $10 | EastWest 61782 |

Anything That Way (1)
Clobbered (2)
Crueler (2)

Dry Land (1)
I'm Allowed (2)
It's You (2)

Kitchen Door (2)
Late At Night (1)
Latest Monkey (1)

My Responsibility (1)
Rules (2)
Sodajerk (1)

Souvenir (2)
Sparklers (2)
Summer (2)

Sunday Night (2)
Sundress (2)
Suppose (1)

BUFFALO TOM — Cont'd

Tangerine (2)
Torch Singer (1)

Tree House (1)
Twenty-Points (2)

When You Discover (2)
Would Not Be Denied (1)

Your Stripes (2)

BUFFETT, Jimmy ★46★   '96

Born on 12/25/46 in Pascagoula, Mississippi; raised in Mobile, Alabama. Singer/songwriter/guitarist. Settled in Key West, Florida, in 1971. Author of several books. Appeared in the movie *FM*. Faithful fans known as "Parrotheads."

1)Banana Wind 2)Fruitcakes 3)Barometer Soup 4)Beach House On The Moon 5)Son Of A Son Of A Sailor

DEBUT	PEAK	WKS	RIAA	CD	#	Album Title	Chart	$	Label & Number
3/2/74	176	13		©	1	Living and Dying in 3/4 Time	C:#21/56	$15	Dunhill/ABC 50132
2/8/75	25	27		©	2	A1A		$15	Dunhill/ABC 50183
2/14/76	65	14		©	3	Havana Daydreamin'		$12	ABC 914
2/12/77	12	42	▲	©	4	Changes In Latitudes, Changes In Attitudes	C:#10/218	$12	ABC 990
4/8/78	10	29	▲	©	5	Son Of A Son Of A Sailor	C:#30/48	$12	ABC 1046
11/11/78	72	18	●	©	6	You Had To Be There	[L]	$15	ABC 1008 [2]
9/15/79	14	28	●	©	7	Volcano		$10	MCA 5102
2/21/81	30	18		©	8	Coconut Telegraph		$10	MCA 5169
1/23/82	31	15		©	9	Somewhere Over China		$10	MCA 5285
10/8/83	59	24		©	10	One Particular Harbour		$10	MCA 5447
9/29/84	87	14		©	11	Riddles In The Sand		$10	MCA 5512
7/6/85	53	20		©	12	Last Mango In Paris		$10	MCA 5600
11/16/85	100	24	▲6	©	13	Songs You Know By Heart - Jimmy Buffett's Greatest Hit(s)	C:❶5/478 [G]	$10	MCA 5633
6/28/86	66	16		©	14	Floridays		$10	MCA 5730
7/9/88	46	14		©	15	Hot Water		$10	MCA 42093
7/15/89	57	13		©	16	Off To See The Lizard		$10	MCA 6314
11/17/90	68	15	●	©	17	Feeding Frenzy	C:#32/4 [L]	$10	MCA 10022
6/6/92	68	19	▲4	©	18	Boats Beaches Bars & Ballads	[K]	$40	Margaritaville 10613 [4]
6/12/93	169	2		©	19	Before The Beach	[E]	$10	Margaritaville 10823
6/11/94	5	19	▲	©	20	Fruitcakes		$10	Margaritaville 11043
8/19/95	6	17	●	©	21	Barometer Soup		$10	Margaritaville 11247
6/22/96	4	18	▲	©	22	Banana Wind		$10	Margaritaville 11451
10/26/96	27	14	▲	©	23	Christmas Island	C:#12/14 [X]	$10	Margaritaville 11489
						Christmas charts: 4/96, 17/97, 25/99			
5/16/98	15	11	●	©	24	Don't Stop The Carnival		$10	Margaritaville 524485
6/5/99	8	17	●	©	25	Beach House On The Moon		$10	Margaritaville 524660
11/27/99	37	11	●	©	26	Buffett Live: Tuesdays, Thursdays, Saturdays	[L]	$10	Mailboat 2000

Ace (19)
African Friend (5,18)
Apocalypso (20)
Baby's Gone Shoppin' (15)
Ballad Of Skip Wiley (21)
Ballad Of Spider John (1,18)
Banana Republics (4)
Banana Wind (22)
Bank Of Bad Habits (21)
Barefoot Children (21)
Barometer Soup (21)
Beach House On The Moon (25)
Bend A Little (19)
Beyond The End (12)
Big Rig (3)
Bigger Than The Both Of Us (11)
Biloxi (4,18)
Blue Heaven Rendezvous (21)
Boat Drinks (7,13,18)
Bob Robert's Society Band (22)
Boomerang Love (16)
Brahma Fear (1)
Brand New Country Star (1)
Bring Back The Magic (15)
Brown Eyed Girl (10,18,26)
Burn That Bridge (11)
Calaloo (24)
California Promises (10,18)
Captain America (19)
Captain And The Kid (3,6,18,19)
Carnival World (16)
Champagne Sí, Agua No (24)
Changes In Latitudes, Changes In Attitudes (4,6,13,18) 37
Changing Channels (16,18)
Chanson Pour Les Petits Enfants (7)
Cheeseburger In Paradise (5,13,17,18,26) 32
Christmas In The Caribbean (18)
Christmas Island (23)

City, The (17)
Cliches (3)
Coast Of Marseilles (5,18)
Coconut Telegraph (8,18,26)
Come Monday (1,6,13,17,18,26) 30
Come To The Moon (11)
Comin' Down Slow (medley) (19)
Cowboy In The Jungle (5)
Creola (14)
Cuban Crime Of Passion (18)
Cultural Infidel (22)
Cumberland High Dilemma (19)
Dallas (2)
Death Valley Lives (19)
Defying Gravity (3,18)
Delaney Talks To Statues (20)
Desdemona's Building A Rocket Ship (22)
Desperation Samba (Halloween In Tijuana) (12,18)
Diamond As Big As The Ritz (21)
Distantly In Love (10,18)
Dixie Diner (4)
Domicile (24)
Domino College (18)
Don't Chu-Know (21)
Door Number Three (2)
Dreamsicle (7)
Ellis Dee (19)
Elvis Imitators (18)
England (19)
Everlasting Moon (11)
Everybody's Got A Cousin In Miami (20)
Everybody's On The Run (19)
False Echoes (22)
Fat Person Man (24)
Fins (7,13,17,18,26) 35
First Look (14,18)
Flesh And Bone (25)
Floridays (14)
Fool Button (19)
Frank And Lola (12,18)

Frenchman For The Night (20)
Fruitcakes (20,26)
Funeral Dance (24)
God Don't Own A Car (19)
God's Own Drunk (1,6)
Good Fight (8)
Grapefruit-Juicy Fruit (6,13,18)
Gravity Storm (16)
Great Filling Station Holdup (18)
Great Heart (15)
Growing Older But Not Up (8)
Gypsies In The Palace (12,17)
Hang-Out Gang (19)
Happily Ever After (Now And Then) (22)
Happy Hours (War Is Over) (23)
Havana Daydreamin' (3,6,18)
He Went To Paris (6,13,18)
Henny's Song: The Key To My Man (24)
High Cumberland Jubilee (medley) (19)
Hippolyte's Habitat (Qui Moun' Qui) (24)
Ho Ho Ho And A Bottle Of Rhum (23)
Holiday (22)
Homemade Music (15)
Honey Do (10,17)
I Can't Be Your Hero Today (19)
I Don't Know And I Don't Care (25)
I Have Found Me A Home (18)
I Heard I Was In Town (9,18)
I Love The Now (14)
I Used To Have Money One Time (10)
I Will Play For Gumbo (25)
I Wish Lunch Would Last Forever (16)
I'll Be Home For Christmas (23)

If I Could Just Get It On Paper (9)
If It All Falls Down (14)
If The Phone Doesn't Ring, It's Me (12,18)
In The Shelter (4,19)
Incommunicado (8,18)
Island (8,18)
Island Fever (24)
It's All About The Water (24)
It's Midnight And I'm Not Famous Yet (9)
It's My Job (8) 57
Jamaica Farewell (17)
Jamaica Mistaica (22)
Jimmy Dreams (21)
Jingle Bells (23)
Jolly Mon Sing (12,17,18)
Just An Old Truth Teller (24)
Kick It In Second Wind (3,18)
King Of Somewhere Hot (15)
Kinja (medley) (24)
Kinja Rules (24)
Knees Of My Heart (11,18)
L'Air De La Louisiane (15)
La Vie Dansante (11)
Lady I Can't Explain (7)
Lage Nom Ai (21)
Landfall (4,6)
Last Line (5)
Last Mango In Paris (12,17)
Legend Of Norman Paperman (medley) (24)
Life Is Just A Tire Swing (2)
Lip Service (9)
Little Miss Magic (8,18)
Livin' It Up (10)
Livingston Saturday Night (5,18) 52
Livingston's Gone To Texas (1,19)
Lone Palm (21)
Love And Luck (18,26)
Love In Decline (11)
Love In The Library (20)

Love Song (From A Different Point Of View) (17)
Lovely Cruise (4,18)
Lucky Stars (25)
Makin' Music For Money (2)
Mañana (5,18) 84
Margaritaville (4,6,13,17,18,26) 8
Math Suks (25)
Meet Me In Memphis (14)
Mele Kalikimaka (23)
Mental Floss (22)
Mermaid In The Night (16)
Merry Christmas, Alabama (Never Far From Home) (23)
Mexico (21)
Middle Of The Night (18)
Migration (2)
Mile High In Denver (19)
Miss You So Badly (4,6)
Missionary, The (19)
Money Back Guarantee (18)
Morris' Nightmare (6)
My Barracuda (15)
My Head Hurts, My Feet Stink And I Don't Love Jesus (3)
Nautical Wheelers (2,18)
Night I Painted The Sky (21)
No Plane On Sunday (14)
Nobody Speaks To The Captain No More (14)
Off To See The Lizard (16)
On A Slow Boat To China (9,18)
One Particular Harbour (10,17,18,26)
Only Time Will Tell (22)
Overkill (22)
Oysters And Pearls (25)
Pacing The Cage (25)
Pascagoula Run (16,18)
Pencil Thin Mustache (1,6,13,18,26)
Perfect Partner (11)
Permanent Reminder Of A Temporary Feeling (25)

Perrier Blues (6)
Pirate Looks At Forty (2,6,13,17,18)
Please Bypass This Heart (12)
Pre-You (15,18)
Presents To Send You (2)
Prince Of Tides (15)
Public Relations (24)
Quietly Making Noise (20)
Ragtop Day (11,18)
Remittance Man (21)
Ringling, Ringling (11)
Rockefeller Square (19)
Run Rudolph Run (23)
Sailor's Christmas (23)
Saxophones (1)
School Boy Heart (22)
Semi-True Story (25)
Sendin' The Old Man Home (7,18)
She's Going Out Of My Mind (11)
She's Got You (20)
Sheila Says (24)
Six String Music (20)
Smart Woman (In A Real Short Skirt) (15)
Something So Feminine About A Mandolin (3)
Somewhere Over China (9)
Son Of A Son Of A Sailor (5,6,13,18,26)
Southern Cross (26)
Spending Money (25)
Stars Fell On Alabama (8,18)
Stars On The Water (10,18)
Steamer (9,18)
Stories We Could Tell (7)
Stranded On A Sandbar (7)
Strange Bird (16)
Sunny Afternoon (20)
Survive (7,18) 77
Take Another Road (16)
Take It Back (18)
Tampico Trauma (4,6,18)

BUFFETT, Jimmy — Cont'd

That's My Story And I'm Stickin' To It (16)
That's What Living Is To Me (15)
There's Nothin' Soft About Hard Times (19)
They Don't Dance Like Carmen No More (18)
This Hotel Room (3)
Thousand Steps To Nowhere (24)

Time To Go Home (24)
Tin Cup Chalice (2,18,26)
Today's Message (17)
Travelin' Clean (19)
Treat Her Like A Lady (7,18)
Truckstop Salvation (19)
Trying To Reason With Hurricane Season (2,18,26)
Turnabout (19)
Twelve Volt Man (10,18)

Uncle John's Band (20)
Up On The Hill (24)
Up On The House Top (23)
Vampires, Mummies And The Holy Ghost (20)
Volcano (7,13,17,18,26) 66
Waiting For The Next Explosion (25)
We Are The People Our Parents Warned Us About (10)

Weather Is Here, Wish You Were Beautiful (8,18)
West Nashville Grand Ballroom Gown (1)
When Salome Plays The Drum (9,18)
When The Coast Is Clear (14,18)
When The Wild Life Betrays Me (11)
Where's The Party (9)

Who Are We Trying To Fool? (24)
Who's The Blonde Stranger? (11,18)
Why Don't We Get Drunk And Screw (6,13,18)
Why The Things We Do (16)
Why You Wanna Hurt My Heart (10)
Wino And I Know (1,18)

Woman Goin' Crazy On Caroline Street (3)
Wonder Why We Ever Go Home (4,6)
You Call It Jogging (25)
You'll Never Work In Dis Bidness Again (14,17)

BUGGLES, The   '82

New-wave duo from England: Geoff Downes and Trevor Horn. Both joined the group **Yes** in 1980. Downes joined **Asia** in 1981. Horn became a prolific producer.

DEBUT	PEAK	WKS	RIAA	CD	ARTIST — Album Title	Sym	$	Label & Number
3/27/82	161	5			Adventures In Modern Recording		$10	Carrere 37926

Adventures In Modern Recording
Beatnik
I Am A Camera
Inner City
Lenny
On T.V.
Rainbow Warrior
Vermillion Sands

BUGNON, Alex   '89

Born in 1962 in Montreux, Switzerland. Keyboardist. Nephew of jazz trumpeter **Donald Byrd**.

| 4/1/89 | 127 | 11 | | © 1 | Love Season | | $10 | Orpheus 75602 |
| 5/26/90 | 131 | 7 | | © 2 | Head Over Heels | [I] | $10 | Orpheus 75615 |

Any Love (2)
Around 12:15 AM (1)
Can't Get Over You (2)

Dance Of The Ghosts (2)
Elis (2)
Falling For You (1)

Going Out (1)
Head Over Heels (2)
Human Epilogue (2)

Love Season (1)
Magie Noire (1)
Missing You (2)

No Other Love (2)
Piano In The Dark (1)
Time Is Running Out (1)

Winnie (2)
Yearning For Your Love (1)

BUILT TO SPILL   '99

Rock trio from Boise, Idaho: Doug Martsch (vocals, guitar), Brett Nelson (bass) and Andy Capps (drums).

| 3/13/99 | 120 | 1 | | © | Keep It Like A Secret | | $10 | Warner 46952 |

Bad Light
Broken Chairs
Carry The Zero
Center Of The Universe
Else
Plan, The
Sidewalk
Temporarily Blind
Time Trap
You Were Right

BULGARIAN STATE FEMALE VOCAL CHOIR   '89

Twenty-six-member female choir, conducted by Dora Hriztova. Established in 1951 in Bulgaria by Philip Koutev, choir's vocal sound is a combination of Bulgarian folk and Western classical music.

| 12/17/88+ | 165 | 10 | | © | Le Mystere des Voix Bulgares | [F-K] | $10 | Nonesuch 79165 |

translation of Bulgarian title: The Mystery of Bulgarian Voices; compiled over a 20-year period, tracks feature various conductors and choir members

Brei Yvane (Dancing Song)
Erghen Diado (Song Of Schopsko)
Kalimankou Denkou (The Evening Gathering)

Messetschinko Lio Greilivko (Love Song From The Mountains)
Mir Stanke Le (Harvest Song from Thrace)

Pilentze Pee (Pilentze Sings)
Polegnala E Pschenitza (Harvest Song from Thrace)
Polegnala E Todora (Love Song)

Pritouritze Planinata (Song From The Thracian Plain)
Sableyalo Mi Agontze (The Bleating Lamb)

Schopska Pesen (Diaphonic Chant)
Strati Na Angelaki Doumasche (Haiduk Song)
Svatba (The Wedding)

BULLDOG   '73

Rock group from New York City: Billy Hocher (vocals, bass), Eric Thorngren and Gene Cornish (guitars), John Turi (keyboards) and Dino Danelli (drums). Cornish and Danelli were members of **The Rascals**. Thorngren later became a prolific record mixer. Also see **Fotomaker**.

| 11/18/72+ | 176 | 11 | | | Bulldog | | $20 | Decca 75370 |

Don't Blame It On Me
Good Times Are Comin'

Have A Nice Day
I'm A Madman

Juicin' With Lucy
No 44

Parting People Should Be Good
Friends

Rockin' Robin
Too Much Monkey Business

You Underlined My Life

BULLETBOYS   '89

Hard-rock group from Los Angeles: Marq Torien (vocals), Mick Sweda (guitar), Lonnie Vincent (bass) and Jimmy D'Anda (drums).

| 10/29/88+ | 34 | 47 | ● | © 1 | BulletBoys | | $10 | Warner 25782 |
| 3/30/91 | 69 | 8 | | © 2 | Freakshow | | $10 | Warner 26168 |

Badlands (1)
Crank Me Up (2)
Do Me Raw (2)
F#9 (1)

For The Love Of Money (1) 78
Freakshow (2)
Goodgirl (2)
Hang On St. Christopher (2)

Hard As A Rock (1)
Hell On My Heels (1)
Hell Yeah! (2)
Huge (2)

Kissin' Kitty (1)
O Me O My (2)
Owed To Joe (1)
Ripping Me (2)

Say Your Prayers (2)
Shoot The Preacher Down (1)
Smooth Up (1) 71
THC Groove (2)

Talk To Your Daughter (2)
Thrill That Kills (2)

BUONO, Victor   '71

Born on 2/3/38 in San Diego. Died of a heart attack on 1/1/82 (age 43). Prolific character actor.

| 9/18/71 | 66 | 17 | | | Heavy! | [C] | $15 | Dore 325 |

Bless Me Doctor
Fat Man's Prayer

I Am
I'm Fat

Lard Lib
New Gig

Skinny Poems For Fat Lovers
Someday When I'm Skinny

We're The Most
Word To The Wide

You Don't Have To Be Fat To Hate Rome

BURDON, Eric, And War   '70

Born on 5/11/41 in Walker, Newcastle, England. After leaving **The Animals**, Burdon teamed up with the funk band **War** for two albums. Starred in the 1982 movie *Comeback* and made a cameo appearance in *The Doors*.

| 5/16/70 | 18 | 27 | | © 1 | Eric Burdon Declares "War" | | $20 | MGM 4663 |
| 12/26/70+ | 82 | 9 | | © 2 | The Black-Man's Burdon | | $25 | MGM 4710 [2] |

THE ERIC BURDON BAND:

| 12/21/74+ | 51 | 16 | | 3 | Sun Secrets | | $15 | Capitol 11359 |
| 8/9/75 | 171 | 5 | | 4 | Stop | | $15 | Capitol 11426 |

WAR FEATURING ERIC BURDON:

| 12/25/76+ | 140 | 5 | | © 5 | Love Is All Around | [E] | $12 | ABC 988 |

recorded 1969-70

All I Do (4)
Bare Back Ride (2)
Be Mine (4)
Beautiful New Born Child (2)
Bird & The Squirrel (2)
Birth (1)
Black Bird (2)
Black On Black In Black (2)
City Boy (4)
Danish Pastry (1)

Day In The Life (5)
Dedication (1)
Don't Let Me Be Misunderstood (medley) (3)
Funky Fever (4)
Gotta Get It On (4)
Gun (2)
Home Cookin' (2)
Home Dream (5)
I Have A Dream (1)

I'm Lookin' Up (4)
It's My Life (3)
Jimbo (2)
Laurel & Hardy (2)
Letter From The County Farm (3)
Love Is All Around (5)
Magic Mountain (5)
Man, The (4)
Mother Earth (1)

Mr. Charlie (1)
Nights In White Satin I & II (2)
Nina's School (medley) (3)
Nuts, Seeds & Life (2)
Out Of Nowhere (2)
P.C. 3 (2)
Paint It Black (2,5)
Pintelo Negro II (2)
Pretty Colors (4)
Rainbow (4)

Real Me (3)
Ring Of Fire (3)
Roll On Kirk (1)
Spill The Wine (1) 3
Spirit (2)
Stop (4)
Sun/Moon (2)
Sun Secrets (3)
They Can't Take Away Our Music (2) 50

Tobacco Road (1,5)
War Child (medley) (3)
Way It Should Be (4)
When I Was Young (medley) (3)
You're No Stranger (1)

BURKE, Solomon '69
Born in 1936 in Philadelphia. R&B singer. Inducted into the Rock and Roll Hall of Fame in 2001.

| 7/31/65 | 141 | 3 | © | 1 The Best Of Solomon Burke | [G] | $30 | Atlantic 8109 |
| 7/5/69 | 140 | 4 | © | 2 Proud Mary | | $20 | Bell 6033 |

Cry To Me (1) *44*
Don't Wait Too Long (2)
Down In The Valley (1) *71*
Everybody Needs Somebody To Love (1) *58*

Got To Get You Off My Mind (1)
Home In Your Heart (1)
How Big A Fool (Can A Fool Be) (2)
I Can't Stop (2)

I Really Don't Want To Know (1) *93*
I'll Be Doggone (2)
I'm Hanging Up My Heart For You (1) *85*
If You Need Me (1) *37*

Just Out Of Reach (Of My Two Open Arms) (1) *24*
Please Send Me Someone To Love (2)
Price, The (1) *57*
Proud Mary (2) *45*

That Lucky Old Sun (2)
These Arms Of Mine (2)
Tonight's The Night (1) *28*
Uptight Good Woman (2)
What Am I Living For (2)
Words (1)

BURNETT, Carol '62
Born on 4/26/33 in San Antonio. Comedic actress. Star of own variety TV show from 1967-78.

| 9/1/62 | 85 | 9 | | 1 Julie And Carol at Carnegie Hall | [L] | $25 | Columbia 2240 / 5840 |
JULIE ANDREWS & CAROL BURNETT
recorded on June 11, 1962

| 1/29/72 | 199 | 2 | | 2 Carol Burnett featuring If I Could Write A Song | | $15 | Columbia 31048 |

For All We Know (2)
From Russia: The Nausiev Ballet (1)
From Switzerland: The Pratt Family (1)

From Texas: Big "D" (1)
Guess Who (medley) (2)
History Of Musical Comedy (1)
If I Could Write A Song (2)
It's Too Late (2)

Meantime (1)
No Mozart Tonight (1)
Oh Dear What Can The Matter Be (1)
Rainy Days And Monday (2)

Rose Garden (2)
Saturday Morning Confusion (2)
Sunrise, Sunset (2)
Those Were The Days (2)
Try To Remember (2)

Turn Around, Look At Me (medley) (2)
Who's Sorry Now (2)
You're So London (1)

BURNETT, T-Bone '83
Born John Henry Burnett on 1/14/48 in St. Louis; raised in Fort Worth, Texas. Rock singer/songwriter/guitarist. Married **Sam Phillips** in 1989.

| 10/1/83 | 188 | 5 | | Proof Through The Night | | $10 | Warner 23921 |

After All These Years
Baby Fall Down

Fatally Beautiful
Hefner And Disney

Hula Hoop
Murder Weapon

Pressure
Shut It Tight

Sixties, The
Stunned

When The Night Falls

BURNETTE, Rocky '80
Born on 6/12/53 in Memphis. Son of Johnny Burnette, nephew of Dorsey Burnette and cousin of Billy Burnette (of **Fleetwood Mac**).

| 6/21/80 | 53 | 14 | | The Son Of Rock And Roll | | $10 | EMI America 17033 |

Angel In Chambray
Anywhere Your Body Goes

Baby Tonight
Boogie Man

Clowns From Outer Space
Fallin' In Love (Bein' Friends)

Roll Like A Wheel
Tired Of Toein' The Line *8*

Woman In Love
You're So Easy To Love

BURNING SENSATIONS '83
Rock group from Los Angeles: Tim McGovern (vocals, guitar; **Motels**), Morley Bartnof (keyboards), Jeff Hollie (sax), Michael Temple (percussion), Rob Hasick (bass) and Barry Wisdom (drums).

| 7/30/83 | 175 | 4 | | Burning Sensations | [M] | $10 | Capitol 15009 |

Belly Of The Whale

Carnivals Of Souls

Check Your Mail

Jokenge

BURNS, George '80
Born Nathan Birnbaum on 1/20/1896 in New York City. Died on 3/9/96 (age 100). Popular radio, movie and TV comedian. Starred in several movies including *The Sunshine Boys* and *Oh God*.

| 2/9/80 | 93 | 10 | | I Wish I Was Eighteen Again | | $10 | Mercury 5025 |

Arizona Whiz
Baby Song
Forgive Her A Little (And Love Her A Lot)

I Wish I Was Eighteen Again *49*
Nickels And Dimes
Old Bones

Old Dogs, Children And Watermelon Wine
One Of The Mysteries Of Life
Only Way To Go

Real Good Cigar

BURRELL, Kenny '63
Born on 7/31/31 in Detroit. Jazz guitarist.

| 11/30/63 | 108 | 4 | © | 1 Blue Bash! | [I] | $25 | Verve 8553 |
KENNY BURRELL/JIMMY SMITH
| 12/17/66+ | 15[X] | 8 | © | 2 Have Yourself A Soulful Little Christmas | [X-I] | $25 | Cadet 779 |
Christmas charts: 43/'66, 21/'67, 15/'68
| 12/17/66 | 146 | 2 | | 3 The Tender Gender | [I] | $25 | Cadet 772 |
| 8/31/68 | 191 | 2 | | 4 Blues-The Common Ground | [I] | $25 | Verve 8746 |

Angel Eyes (4)
Away In A Manger (2)
Blue Bash (1)
Blues For Del (1)
Burning Spear (4)
Christmas Song (2)
Common Ground (4)
Easy Living (1)

Every Day (I Have The Blues) (4)
Everydays (4)
Fever (1)
Girl Talk (3)
Go Where I Send Thee (2)
God Rest Ye Merry Gentlemen (2)

Have Yourself A Merry Little Christmas (2)
Hot Bossa (3)
I'm Confessin' (3)
If Someone Had Told Me (3)
Isabella (3)
Kenny's Sound (1)
La Petite Mambo (3)
Little Drummer Boy (2)

Mary's Little Boy Chile (2)
Merry Christmas Baby (2)
Mother-In-Law (3)
My Favorite Things (2)
People (3)
Preacher, The (4)
Sausalito Nights (4)
See See Rider (4)
Silent Night (2)

Soft Winds (1)
Soulful Brothers (4)
Suzy (3)
Tender Gender (3)
Travelin' (1)
Twelve Days Of Christmas (2)
Were You There (4)
White Christmas (2)
Wonder Why (4)

BURRELL, Kim '01
Born on 8/26/72 in Houston. Gospel singer.

| 3/24/01 | 138 | 3 | © | Live In Concert | [L] | $10 | Tommy Boy 1450 |

Anything
Calvary

Everywhere You Go
Holy Ghost

How Will You Know?
I'll Keep Holding On

Since Jesus
Try Me Again

Victory

BURTNICK, Glen '87
Born in New Jersey. Pop singer/guitarist. Joined **Styx** in 1990.

| 10/24/87 | 147 | 6 | | Heroes & Zeros | | $10 | A&M 5166 |

Abalene
Day Your Ship Gets Thru

Follow You *65*
Heard It On The Radio

Here Comes Sally
Love Goes On

Scattered
Spinning My Wheels

Stupid Boys (Suckers For Love)
Walls Came Down

BURTON, Jenny '84
Born on 11/18/57 in New York City. R&B singer.

| 3/24/84 | 181 | 4 | | In Black And White | | $10 | Atlantic 80122 |

All The Time (medley)
Players

Remember What You Like *81*
Rock Steady

Small Rewards
Time (medley)

Vena Cava
You'll Never Come Again

DEBUT	PEAK	WKS	RIAA	CD	ARTIST — Album Title	Catalog	Sym	$	Label & Number

BUS BOYS, The   '81

R&B group from Los Angeles: Gus Lounderman (vocals), brothers Brian (keyboards) and Kevin (bass) O'Neal, Victor Johnson (guitar), Michael Jones (keyboards) and Steve Felix (drums). Group appeared in the movie *48 HRS*.

11/29/80+	85	15			1 **Minimum Wage Rock & Roll**			$10	Arista 4280
8/21/82	139	7			2 **American Worker**			$10	Arista 9569

American Workers (2)	Dr. Doctor (1)	I Get Lost (2)	Minimum Wage (1)	Soul Surfing U.S.A. (2)	We Stand United (1)
Anggie (1)	Falling In Love (2)	Johnny Soul'd Out (1)	New Shoes (2)	Tell The Coach (1)	Yellow Lights (2)
D-Day (1)	Heart And Soul (2)	KKK (1)	Opportunity (2)	There Goes The Neighborhood	
Did You See Me? (1)	I Believe (2)	Last Forever (2)	Respect (1)	(1)	

BUSH   '96

Rock group from London: Gavin Rossdale (vocals, guitar), Nigel Pulsford (guitar), Dave Parsons (bass) and Robin Goodridge (drums).

1/28/95+	4	109	▲6	©	1 **Sixteen Stone**	C:#3/42		$10	Trauma 92531
12/7/96	❶2	45	▲3	©	2 **Razorblade Suitcase**			$10	Trauma 90091
11/29/97	36	15	●	©	3 **Deconstructed**		[K]	$10	Trauma 90161
					contains remixes of previous recordings				
11/13/99	11	30	▲	©	4 **The Science Of Things**			$10	Trauma 490483

Alien (1)	Comedown (1,3) *30*	Everything Zen (1,3)	Jesus Online (4)	Personal Holloway (2,3)	Tendency To Start Fires (2)
Altered States (4)	Communicator (4)	40 Miles From The Sun (4)	Letting The Cables Sleep (4)	Prizefighter (4)	Testosterone (1)
Body (1)	Dead Meat (4)	Glycerine (1) *28*	Little Things (1)	Spacetravel (4)	Warm Machine (4)
Bomb (1)	Disease Of The Dancing Cats	Greedy Fly (2)	Machinehead (1) *43*	Straight No Chaser (2)	X-Girlfriend (1)
Bonedriven (2,3)	(4)	History (2,3)	Mindchanger (4)	Swallowed (2,3)	
Chemicals Between Us (4) *67*	Distant Voices (2)	In A Lonely Place (4)	Monkey (1)	Swim (1)	
Cold Contagious (2)	English Fire (4)	Insect Kin (2,3)	Mouth (2,3)	Synapse (2,3)	

BUSH, Kate   '93

Born on 7/30/58 in Bexleyheath, Kent, England. Singer/songwriter.

11/13/82	157	11		©	1 **The Dreaming**			$10	EMI America 17084
7/9/83	148	6			2 **Kate Bush**		[M]	$10	EMI America 19004
10/26/85	30	27		©	3 **Hounds Of Love**			$10	EMI America 17171
12/20/86+	76	27		©	4 **The Whole Story**		[G]	$10	EMI America 17242
11/4/89	43	26	●	©	5 **The Sensual World**			$10	Columbia 44164
11/20/93	28	14		©	6 **The Red Shoes**			$10	Columbia 53737

All The Love (1)	Cloudbusting (3,4)	Houdini (1)	Morning Fog (3)	Sat In Your Lap (1,2,4)	Waking The Witch (3)
And Dream Of Sheep (3)	Constellation of the Heart (6)	Hounds Of Love (3,4)	Mother Stands For Comfort (3)	Sensual World (5)	Watching You Without Me (3)
And So is Love (6)	Deeper Understanding (5)	James And The Cold Gun (2)	Never Be Mine (5)	Song of Solomon (6)	Why Should I Love You? (6)
Army Dreamers (4)	Dreaming, The (1,4)	Jig Of Life (3)	Night Of The Swallow (1)	Suspended In Gaffa (1,2)	Wow (4)
Babooshka (4)	Eat the Music (6)	Leave It Open (1)	Pull Out The Pin (1)	There Goes A Tenner (1)	Wuthering Heights (4)
Between A Man And A Woman	Experiment IV (4)	Lily (6)	Reaching Out (5)	This Woman's Work (5)	You're the One (6)
(5)	Fog, The (5)	Love And Anger (5)	Red Shoes (6)	Top of the City (6)	
Big Sky (3)	Get Out Of My House (1)	**Man With The Child In His**	Rocket's Tail (5)	Un Baisser D'Enfant (The Infant	
Big Stripey Lie (6)	Heads We're Dancing (5)	**Eyes** (4) *85*	**Rubberband Girl** (6) *88*	Kiss) (2)	
Breathing (4)	Hello Earth (5)	Moments of Pleasure (6)	**Running Up That Hill** (3,4) *30*	Under Ice (3)	

BUSHKIN, Joe   '56

Born on 11/7/16 in New York City. Pianist/composer.

5/26/56	14	1			**Midnight Rhapsody**		[I]	$25	Capitol 711

Above All, You	Come Rain Or Come Shine	I Can't Get Started	It's The Talk Of The Town	Manhattan	Song Is You
As Time Goes By	Embraceable You	I Cover The Waterfront	Laura	September Song	Stormy Weather

BUSHWICK BILL   '92

Born Richard Shaw on 12/8/66 in Kingston, Jamaica. Member of **The Geto Boys**. Lost his right eye in a shooting on 5/10/91.

10/17/92	32	9		©	1 **Little Big Man**			$10	Rap-A-Lot 57189
7/29/95	43	7		©	2 **Phantom Of The Rapra**			$10	Rap-A-Lot 40512

Already Dead (2)	Copper To Cash (1)	Ex-Girlfriend (2)	Little Big Man (1)	Stop Lying (1)	Wha Cha Gonna Do? (2)
Bushwicken, The (2)	Dollars And Sense (1)	Inhale Exhale (2)	Mr. President (2)	Subliminal Criminal (2)	Who's The Biggest (2)
Call Me Crazy (1)	Don't Come To Big (1)	Intro (1)	Only God Knows (2)	Take Em' Off (1)	
Chuckwick (1)	Ever So Clear (1)	Letter From KKK (1)	Skitso (1)	Times Is Hard (2)	

BUSTA RHYMES   '97

Born Trevor Smith on 5/20/72 in Brooklyn, New York. Male rapper. Member of **Leaders Of The New School**.

4/13/96	6	21	▲	©	1 **The Coming**			$10	Elektra 61742
10/4/97	3	44	▲	©	2 **When Disaster Strikes...**			$10	Elektra 62064
1/2/99	12	32	▲	©	3 **E.L.E.: Extinction Level Event * The Final World Front**			$10	Flipmode 62211
7/8/00	4	14	▲	©	4 **Anarchy**			$10	Flipmode 62517

Abandon Ship (1)	End Of The World (1)	Get Out!! (4)	Keepin' It Tight (3)	Street Shit (4)	We Could Take It Outside (2)
Against All Odds (3)	Enjoy Da Ride (4)	Gimme Some More (3)	Live It Up (4)	Survival Hungry (2)	We Put It Down For Y'all (4)
All Night (4)	Everybody Rise (3)	Heist, The (4)	Make Noise (4)	Take It Off (3)	What The Fuck You Want!! (3)
Anarchy (4)	**Everything Remains Raw**	Here We Go Again (4)	One (2)	Tear Da Roof Off (3)	**What's It Gonna Be** (3) *3*
Bladow!! (4)	(1) *flip*	Hot Fudge (1)	Party Is Goin' On Over Here (3)	There's Not A Problem My	When Disaster Strikes (2)
Body Rock (2)	Extinction Level Event [The	Hot Shit Makin' Ya Bounce (3)	Put Your Hands Where My	Squad Can't Fix (2)	Where We Are About To Take It
C'mon All My Niggaz, C'mon All	Song Of Salvation] (3)	How Much We Grew (4)	Eyes Could See (2)	Things We Be Doin' For Money	(3)
My Bitches (4)	Finish Line (1)	I'll Vibe (1)	Ready For War (4)	Part 1 & 2 (2)	Whole World Lookin' At Me (2)
Coming, The (1)	Fire (4)	**It's A Party** (1) *52*	Rhymes Galore (2)	This Means War!! (3)	Why We Die (4)
Dangerous (2) *9*	Flipmode Squad Meets Def	Iz They Wildin Wit Us & Gettin'	Salute Da Gods!! (4)	Trip Out Of Town (4)	**Woo Hah!! Got You All In**
Do It To Death (3)	Squad (1)	Rowdy With Us (3)	Show Me What You Got (4)	**Turn It Up [Remix]/Fire It Up**	**Check** (1) *8*
Do My Thing (1)	Get High Tonight (2)	Just Give It To Me Raw (4)	So Hardcore (2)	(2) *10*	
Do The Bus A Bus (3)	Get Off My Block (2)	Keep It Movin' (1)	Still Shining (1)	We Comin' Through (4)	

BUTCHER, Jon, Axis   '85

Born in Boston. Black rock singer/guitarist. The Axis included Chris Martin (bass) and Derek Blevins (drums). Martin left in early 1985. Thom Gimbel (keyboards) and Jimmy Johnson (bass) joined in 1985. Butcher went solo in early 1987.

3/26/83	91	13			1 **Jon Butcher Axis**			$10	Polydor 810059
3/31/84	160	6			2 **Stare At The Sun**			$10	Polydor 817493
10/12/85	66	17			3 **Along The Axis**			$10	Capitol 12425
					JON BUTCHER:				
4/4/87	77	27		©	4 **Wishes**			$10	Capitol 12542

BUTCHER, Jon, Axis — Cont'd

| 2/18/89 | 121 | 8 | © | 5 | Pictures From The Front | $10 | Capitol 90238 |

Along The Axis (3)
Angel Dressed In Blue (4)
Beating Drum (5)
Between The Lines (3)
Breakout (2)
Call To Arms (2)
Can't Be The Only Fool (1)
Can't Tell The Dancer From The Dance (2)
Carrie (3)

Churinga (4)
Come And Get It (5)
Division Street (5)
Don't Say Goodnight (2)
Dreams Fade Away (2)
Electricity (3)
Eros Arriving (2)
Fairlight (1)
Goodbye Saving Grace (4)
Holy War (4)

I'm Only Dreaming (5)
I've Got Money (3)
It's Only Words (1)
Life Takes A Life (1)
Little Bit Of Magic (4)
Live Or Die (1)
Living For Tomorrow (4)
Long Way Home (4)
Might As Well Be Free (5)
Mission, The (5)

New Man (1)
99 (May Be All You Need) (5)
Ocean In Motion (1)
Only The Fox (3)
Partners In Crime (4)
Prisoners Of The Silver Chain (4)
Ritual, The (3)
Send Me Somebody (5)
Send One, Care Of (1)

Sentinel (1)
Show Me Some Emotion (4)
Sounds Of Your Voice (3) 94
Stay Low (2)
Stop (3)
That's How Strong My Love Is (3)
2 Hearts Running (3)
Victims (2)
Waiting For A Miracle (5)

Walk Like This (1)
Walk On The Moon (2)
We Will Be As One (1)
Wind It Up (2)
Wishes (4)

BUTLER, Carl '63
Born on 6/2/27 in Knoxville, Tennessee. Died on 9/4/92 (age 65). Country singer.

| 4/27/63 | 104 | 9 | © | | Don't Let Me Cross Over | $25 | Columbia 2002 |

Don't Let Me Cross Over 88
For The First Time
Grief In My Heart

Honky Tonkitis
I Know What It Means To Be Lonesome

I Know Why I Cry
I Know You Don't Love Me
I Like To Pretend

I'll Cry Again Tomorrow
I'm A Prisoner Of Love
River Of Tears

Wonder Drug

★496★ BUTLER, Jerry '69
Born on 12/8/39 in Sunflower, Mississippi; raised in Chicago. R&B singer. Member of **The Impressions** from 1957-58. Nicknamed "The Ice Man."
1)The Ice Man Cometh 2)Ice On Ice 3)Thelma & Jerry

| 10/3/64 | 102 | 11 | © | 1 | Delicious Together | $50 | Vee-Jay 1099 |

BETTY EVERETT & JERRY BUTLER

| 1/20/68 | 154 | 7 | | 2 | Mr. Dream Merchant | $20 | Mercury 61146 |
| 3/16/68 | 178 | 2 | | 3 | Jerry Butler's Golden Hits Live | [L] | $20 | Mercury 61151 |

recorded in September 1967 at Morgan State College in Baltimore

7/27/68	195	2		4	The Soul Goes On	$20	Mercury 61171
1/4/69	29	47		5	The Ice Man Cometh	$20	Mercury 61198
10/4/69	41	23		6	Ice On Ice	$20	Mercury 61234
6/27/70	167	5		7	The Best Of Jerry Butler	[G]	$15	Mercury 61281
7/11/70	172	4		8	You & Me	$15	Mercury 61269
2/6/71	186	4		9	Jerry Butler Sings Assorted Sounds	$15	Mercury 61320
3/27/71	143	5		10	Gene & Jerry - One & One	$20	Mercury 61330

GENE CHANDLER & JERRY BUTLER

10/2/71+	123	22		11	The Sagittarius Movement	$15	Mercury 61347
6/17/72	92	24		12	The Spice Of Life	$20	Mercury 7502 [2]
2/5/77	199	2		13	The Vintage Years	[G]	$20	Sire 3717 [2]

featuring 13 hits by Jerry Butler, 13 by **The Impressions** (see for cuts), and 2 by Curtis Mayfield: "Freddie's Dead" and "Superfly"

| 3/12/77 | 146 | 11 | © | 14 | Suite For The Single Girl | $12 | Motown 878 |
| 6/18/77 | 53 | 12 | © | 15 | Thelma & Jerry | $15 | Motown 887 |

THELMA HOUSTON & JERRY BUTLER

| 1/13/79 | 160 | 4 | | 16 | Nothing Says I Love You Like I Love You | $12 | Philadelphia Int'l. 35510 |

Ain't That Good News (4)
Ain't That Loving You Baby (1)
Ain't Understanding Mellow (11) 21
Alfie (2)
All Kinds Of People (12)
Amen (5) 39
And You've Got Me (15)
Are You Lonely Tonight (16)
Baby I'm A Want You (12)
Be Yourself (10)
Been A Long Time (6)
Beside You (2)
Brand New Me (6,7)
Built My World Around You (9)
Can't Forget About You, Baby (5)
Cause I Love You So (3)
Chain Gang (4)
Chalk It Up (14)
Change Is Gonna Come (4)
Close To You Love (9)
Do You Finally Need A Friend (9)
Don't Let Love Hang You Up (6) 44
Don't Rip Me Off (12)
Dream Music (medley) (14)
Dream World (16)
Everybody Is Waiting (10)
Fever (1)
Find Another Girl (13) 27

For Your Precious Love (3,7,13) 11
Get On The Case (12)
Girl In His Mind (11)
Give Up A Taste (12)
Giving Up On Love (13) 56
Go Away-Find Yourself (5)
Going Back To My Baby's Love (9)
Goodnight My Love (4)
Got To See If I Can't Get Mommy (To Come Back Home) (6,7) 62
Guess Who (4)
He Will Break Your Heart (3,13) 1
Hey, Western Union Man (5,7,13) 16
How Can I Get In Touch With You (5)
How Did We Lose It Baby (9) 85
How Does It Feel (9)
I Can't Stand It (1)
I Come To You (2)
I Could Write A Book (8) 46
I Dig You Baby (3,7) 60
I Forgot To Remember (6)
I Found That I Was Wrong (10)
I Love You Through Windows (15)
I Need You (12)
I Only Have Eyes For You (12) 85

I Stand Accused (3)
I Stop By Heaven (5)
I Wanna Do It To You (14) 51
I'm A Telling You (13) 25
I'm Glad To Be Back (16)
(I'm Just Thinking About) Cooling Off (13)
I've Been Loving You Too Long (4)
If I Could Remember (Not Ever Having You) (12)
If It's Real What I Feel (9) 69
If You Leave Me Now (medley) (15)
Introduction (3)
It's A Lifetime Thing (15)
It's All Right (1)
Joy Inside My Tears (15)
Just Be True (1)
Just Because I Really Love You (5)
Let It Be Me (1,3) 5
Let Me Be (1)
Let The Good Times Roll (1)
Let's Get Together (15)
Let's Go Get Out Of Town (14)
Let's Make Love (16)
Let's Pretend ..see: (Play The Game Of)
Life's Unfortunate Sons (16)
Loneliness (8)
Lost (2,5,7) 62
Love Is Strange (1)

Love So Right (medley) (15)
Mail Call Time (10)
Make It Easy On Yourself (3,13) 20
Masquerade Is Over (medley) (12)
Mighty Good People (16)
Moody Woman (6,7,13) 11
Moon River (3,13) 11
Mr. Dee Jay (I Got A Heartache) (2)
Mr. Dream Merchant (2,7,13) 38
Ms. Fine (14)
Music In Her Dreams (medley) (14)
Need To Belong (13) 31
Never Give You Up (4,5,7,13) 20
No Money Down (8)
(Nobody Ever Loved Anybody) The Way I Love You (2)
Nothing Says I Love You Like I Love You (16)
One Hand Washes The Other (10)
100 Lbs. Of Clay (2)
One Night Affair (12) 52
One Woman Man (8)
Only Pretty Girls (14)
Only The Beginning (15)
Only The Strong Survive (5,7,13) 4
Ordinary Joe (8)

Our Day Will Come (1)
(Play The Game Of) Let's Pretend (15)
Prayer, A (12)
Real Good Man (8)
Respect (4)
Sad Eyes (16)
Said A Mother Said A Father (11)
Sail Away (11)
Sho' Is Groovin' (10)
Simple Country Girl (11)
Since I Don't Have You (1)
Since I Fell For You (medley) (12)
Since I Lost You Lady (6)
Sittin' On The Dock Of The Bay (4)
So Far Away (12)
Something (8)
Special Memory (9)
Stop Steppin' On My Dreams (12)
(Strange) I Still Love You (5)
Strong Enough To Take It (9)
Suite For The Single Girl (14)
Sweet Love I've Found (15)
Tammy Jones (8)
Ten And Two (Take This Woman Off The Corner) (10)
That's The Way It Was (That's The Way It Is) (12)
These Arms Of Mine (4)

Our Day Will Come (1)
(They Long To Be) Close To You (12) 91
To Make A Big Man Cry (2)
True Love Don't Come Easy (11)
Walk Easy My Son (11) 93
Walking Around In Teardrops (6)
Way You Do The Things You Do (1)
What A Pleasant Surprise (14)
What Is It (1)
What's So Good About It (You're My Baby) (12)
What's The Use Of Breaking Up (6,7,13) 20
When A Woman Loves A Man (When A Man Loves A Woman) (2)
When You're Alone (6)
Why Are You Leaving Me (9)
Windy City Soul (11)
Winter Of A Loving Heart (8)
World Keeps Changing (10)
Yes, My Goodness, Yes (4)
Yesterday (2)
You And Me (8)
You Can't Always Tell (12)
You Gotta Believe In Me (14)
You Just Can't Win (You're Making The Same Mistake) (10) 94
You Send Me (4)

BUTLER, Jonathan '87
Born in Capetown, South Africa. R&B singer/songwriter/guitarist.

5/24/86	101	16	©	1	Introducing Jonathan Butler	$10	Jive 8408
5/30/87	50	33	● ©	2	Jonathan Butler	$15	Jive 1032 [2]
11/5/88	113	22	©	3	More Than Friends	$10	Jive 1136

Afrika (1)
All Over You (2)
Baby Please Don't Take It (I Need Your Love) (1)
Barenese (2)

Breaking Away (3)
Calm Before The Storm (1)
Crossroads Revisited (1)
Gentle Love (1)
Give A Little More Lovin' (2)

Going Home (3)
Haunted By Your Love (1)
High Tide (2)
Holding On (2)
I Miss Your Love Tonight (2)

It's So Hard To Let You Go (3)
Lies (2) 27
Love Songs, Candlelight And You (2)
Loving You (2)

More Than Friends (3)
One More Dance (2)
Overflowing (2)
Reunion (2)
Rumours (1)

Sarah Sarah (3)
Say We'll Be Together (2)
Sekona (3)
7th Avenue South (1)
She's A Teaser (3)

DEBUT	PEAK	WKS	RIAA	CD	ARTIST — Album Title	Catalog	Sym	$	Label & Number

BUTLER, Jonathan — Cont'd

She's Hot (Burning Up) (3)	Sunset (2)	Take Me Home (3)	There's One Born Every Minute	Thinking Of You (1)
Song For Jon (1)	Take Good Care Of Me (2)		(I'm A Sucker For You) (3)	True Love Never Fails (3)

BUTTERFIELD, Billy — see CONNIFF, Ray

BUTTERFIELD, Paul   '68

Born on 12/17/42 in Chicago. Died on 5/4/87 (age 44). White blues singer/harmonica player. Formed interracial blues band in Chicago in 1965. His University of Chicago classmate **Elvin Bishop** was guitarist with group through 1968. **Mike Bloomfield** was the slide guitarist from 1965-66. Various members including saxophonist **David Sanborn** worked on and off with Butterfield from 1967-72.

1)The Resurrection Of Pigboy Crabshaw 2)East-West 3)The Butterfield Blues Band/Live

12/4/65+	123	9	©	1	The Paul Butterfield Blues Band			$25	Elektra 7294

THE BUTTERFIELD BLUES BAND:

| 10/8/66+ | 65 | 29 | © | 2 | East-West .... | | | $25 | Elektra 7315 |
| 1/13/68 | 52 | 16 | © | 3 | The Resurrection Of Pigboy Crabshaw | | | $20 | Elektra 74015 |

Pigboy Crabshaw is **Elvin Bishop**'s nickname

8/24/68	79	17		4	In My Own Dream			$20	Elektra 74025
11/1/69	102	10		5	Keep On Moving			$20	Elektra 74053
1/16/71	72	12		6	The Butterfield Blues Band/Live		[L]	$25	Elektra 2001 [2]

recorded at The Troubador in Los Angeles

| 9/4/71 | 124 | 6 | | 7 | Sometimes I Just Feel Like Smilin' .... | | | $20 | Elektra 75013 |
| 5/20/72 | 136 | 6 | | 8 | Golden Butter/The Best Of The Paul Butterfield Blues Band .... | | [G] | $25 | Elektra 2005 [2] |

PAUL BUTTERFIELD'S BETTER DAYS:

| 2/3/73 | 145 | 13 | © | 9 | Better Days .... | | | $15 | Bearsville 2119 |
| 11/3/73 | 156 | 8 | © | 10 | It All Comes Back .... | | | $15 | Bearsville 2170 |

All In A Day (5)	Drivin' Wheel (3)	I Got My Mojo Working (1)	Love Disease (5,6)	One More Mile (8)	Song For Lee (7)
All These Blues (2)	Droppin' Out (3)	I Want To Be With You (6)	Love March (5,8)	1000 Ways (7)	Spoonful (8)
Baby Please Don't Go (9)	Drowned In My Own Tears (7)	If You Live (10)	Mary, Mary (2,8)	Our Love Is Drifting (1,8)	Take Your Pleasure Where You
Blind Leading The Blind (7,8)	Drunk Again (4)	In My Own Dream (4,8)	Mellow Down Easy (1,8)	Pity The Fool (3)	Find It (10)
Blues With A Feeling (1)	East West (2,8)	It All Comes Back (10)	Mine To Love (4)	Play On (7)	Thank You Mr. Poobah (1)
Born In Chicago (1,8)	Everything Going To Be Alright	It's Getting Harder To Survive	Morning Blues (4)	Please Send Me Someone To	Tollin' Bells (3)
Born Under A Bad Sign (3,6)	(6)	(10)	Morning Sunrise (5)	Love (9)	Too Many Drivers (10)
Boxer, The (6)	Except You (5)	Just To Be With You (4)	Mystery Train (1,8)	Poor Boy (10)	Trainman (7)
Broke My Baby's Heart (9)	Get Out Of My Life, Woman	Keep On Moving (5)	Never Say No (2)	Pretty Woman (7)	Two Trains Running (2)
Buddy's Advice (5)	(2,8)	Last Hope's Gone (4,8)	New Walkin Blues (9)	Rule The Road (9)	Walkin' Blues (2,8)
Buried Alive In The Blues (9)	Get Together Again (6)	Last Night (1)	Night Child (7)	Run Out Of Time (3)	Walking By Myself (5)
Done A Lot Of Wrong Things	Get Yourself Together (4)	Little Piece Of Dying (7)	No Amount Of Loving (5,6)	Screamin' (1)	Where Did My Baby Go (5)
(9)	Highway 28 (9)	Look Over Yonders Wall (1,8)	Nobody's Fault But Mine (9)	Shake Your Money-Maker (1,8)	Win Or Lose (10)
Double Trouble (3)	I Got A Mind To Give Up Living	Losing Hand (5)	Number Nine (6)	Small Town Talk (10)	Work Song (2)
Driftin' And Driftin' (3,6,8)	(2)	Louisiana Flood (10)	One More Heartache (3,8)	So Far So Good (5,6)	

BUTTHOLE SURFERS   '96

Rock group from San Antonio, Texas: Gibby Haynes (vocals), Paul Leary (guitar), Jeff Pinkus (bass) and King Coffey (drums).

| 4/10/93 | 154 | 12 | © | 1 | Independent Worm Saloon .... | | | $10 | Capitol 98798 |
| 6/1/96 | 31 | 24 | ● © | 2 | Electriclarryland .... | | | $10 | Capitol 29842 |

Ah Ha (2)	Cough Syrup (2)	Jingle Of A Dog's Collar (2)	Pepper (2)	Thermador (2)	You Don't Know Me (1)
Alcohol (1)	Dancing Fool (1)	L.A. (2)	Some Dispute Over T-Shirt	Tongue (1)	
Annoying Song (1)	Dog Inside Your Body (1)	Leave Me Alone (1)	Sales (1)	Ulcer Breakout (2)	
Ballad Of Naked Man (1)	Dust Devil (1)	Let's Talk About Cars (2)	Space (2)	Who Was In My Room Last	
Birds (2)	Edgar (1)	Lord Is A Monkey (2)	Strawberry (1)	Night? (1)	
Clean It Up (1)	Goofy's Concern (1)	My Brother's Wife (2)	TV Star (2)	Wooden Song (1)	

BUZZCOCKS   '80

Pop-punk group from Manchester, England: **Pete Shelley** (vocals, guitar), Steve Diggle (guitar), Steve Garvey (bass) and John Maher (drums).

| 2/23/80 | 163 | 6 | © | | A Different Kind Of Tension .... | | | $12 | I.R.S. 009 |

Different Kind Of Tension	I Don't Know What To Do With	Money	Raison D'être	You Say You Don't Love Me
Hollow Inside	My Life	Paradise	Sitting Round At Home	
I Believe	Mad Mad Judy	Radio Nine	You Know You Can't Help It	

B*WITCHED   '99

Female vocal group from Dublin, Ireland: twin sisters Edele and Keavy Lynch, with Sinead O'Carroll and Lindsay Armaou.

| 4/3/99 | 12 | 29 | ▲ © | 1 | B*Witched .... | | | $10 | Epic 69751 |
| 11/13/99 | 91 | 10 | ● © | 2 | Awake And Breathe .... | | | $10 | Epic 63985 |

Are You A Ghost? (2)	Freak Out (1)	Jesse Hold On (2)	Like The Rose (1)	Rev It Up (1)	We Four Girls (1)
Blame It On The Weatherman	I Shall Be There (2)	Jump Down (2)	My Superman (2)	Rollercoaster (1) 67	
(1,2)	If It Don't Fit (2)	Leaves (2)	Never Giving Up (1)	Shy One (2)	
C'est La Vie (1) 9	In Fields Where We Lay (2)	Let's Go (The B*Witched Jig)	Oh Mr. Postman (1)	Someday (2)	
Castles In The Air (1)	It Was Our Day (2)	(1)	Red Indian Girl (2)	To You I Belong (1)	

BY ALL MEANS   '90

R&B trio from Los Angeles: Lynn Roderick (female vocals), James Varner (male vocals, piano) and Billy Sheppard (guitar).

| 1/20/90 | 160 | 11 | © | | Beyond A Dream .... | | | $10 | Island 91319 |

Do You Remember	I Know You Well	I'd Rather Be Lonely	More You Give, The More You	Point Of View	Tender Love
Early Fall	I Think I Fell In Love	Let's Get It On	Get	Stay With Me Tonight	

BYRD, Charlie   '63

Born on 9/16/25 in Chuckatuch, Virginia. Jazz and classical guitar virtuoso.

| 9/15/62+ | ❶¹ | 70 | © | 1 | Jazz Samba .... | [I] | | $25 | Verve 8432 |

STAN GETZ/CHARLIE BYRD

| 3/23/63 | 128 | 5 | © | 2 | Bossa Nova Pelos Passaros .... | [I] | | $25 | Riverside 9436 |

translation of Pelos Passaros: By The Birds

12/9/67	40ˣ	4		3	Christmas Carols For Solo Guitar	[X-I]		$25	Columbia 2555 / 9355
6/28/69	197	4		4	Aquarius	[I]		$20	Columbia 9841
9/6/69	129	4		5	Let Go	[I-L]		$20	Columbia 9869

THE CHARLIE BYRD QUARTET

recorded on 2/28/69 at the Century Plaza Hotel in Los Angeles

BYRD, Charlie — Cont'd

Aquarius (medley) (4)
Baia (1)
Bells Of Bethlehem (3)
Bim Bom (2)
Bird Of Paradise (5)
Blues 13 (5)
Coisa Mais Linda (A Most Beautiful Thing) (2)
Coventry Carol (3)
Desafinado (1,2) *15*
Do You Hear What I Hear? (3)
E Luxo So (1)

Ela Me Deixou (She Has Gone) (2)
Esperando O Sol (5)
First Noël (3)
Galveston (4)
God Rest Ye Merry, Gentlemen (3)
Good King Wenceslas (3)
Happy Heart (4)
Hark! The Herald Angels Sing (3)
Here's That Rainy Day (5)

Ho-Ba-La-La (2)
How Long Has This Been Going On (5)
It Came Upon The Midnight Clear (3)
Joy To The World (3)
Julia (4)
Let Go (Canto de Ossanha) (5)
Let The Sunshine In (medley) (4)
Lonely Princess (5)
Meditation (Meditacao) (2) *66*

Mood Indigo (medley) (5)
My Way (4)
O Barquinho (Little Boat) (2)
O Holy Night (3)
O Passaro (The Bird) (2)
O Pato (1)
Oh Little Town Of Bethlehem (3)
Promises, Promises (5)
Samba De Uma Nota So (One Note Samba) (1)
Samba Dees Days (1)

Samba Triste (1,2)
Satin Doll (medley) (5)
Silent Night, Holy Night (3)
This Guy's In Love With You (5)
Time Of The Season (4)
Traces (4)
Un Abraco Do Bonfa (A Salute To Bonfa) (2)
Voce E Eu (You And I) (2)
Way It Used To Be (4)
We Three Kings (3)

What Child Is This? (Greensleeves) (3)
Where's The Playground Susie? (4)
While My Guitar Gently Weeps (4)
You've Made Me So Very Happy (4)
Yvone (2)

BYRD, Donald   '74

Born on 12/9/32 in Detroit. R&B-jazz trumpeter/flugelhorn player. Founded **The Blackbyrds** in 1973 while teaching jazz at Howard University in Washington DC.

DEBUT	PEAK	WKS	CD	#	Album Title	Sym	$	Label & Number
7/11/64	110	8	©	1	A New Perspective	[I]	$20	Blue Note 84124
4/28/73	36	34	©	2	Black Byrd		$15	Blue Note 047
3/30/74	33	28	©	3	Street Lady	[I]	$15	Blue Note 140
3/29/75	42	19	©	4	Stepping Into Tomorrow	[I]	$15	Blue Note 368
11/15/75+	49	29	©	5	Places And Spaces		$15	Blue Note 549
12/18/76+	167	4		6	Donald Byrd's Best	[G]	$15	Blue Note 700
2/12/77	60	14		7	Caricatures		$15	Blue Note 633
11/18/78	191	4		8	Thank You...For F.U.M.L. (Funking Up My Life)		$12	Elektra 144
10/3/81	93	10		9	Love Byrd		$10	Elektra 531

Beast Of Burden (1)
Black Byrd (2,6) *88*
Black Disciple (1)
Butterfly (9)
Caricatures (7)
Change (Makes You Want To Hustle) (5,6)
Chant (1)
Close Your Eyes And Look Within (8)
Cristo Redentor (1,8)

Dance Band (7)
Dancing In The Street (7)
Design A Nation (4)
Dominoes (5)
Elijah (1)
Falling (9)
Flight Time (2,6)
Have You Heard The News? (8)
I Feel Like Loving You Today (9)
I Love The Girl (4)

I Love Your Love (9)
I'll Always Love You (9)
In Love With Love (8)
Just My Imagination (5)
Lansana's Priestess (3,6)
Love For Sale (9)
Love Has Come Around (9)
Love's So Far Away (2)
Loving You (8)
Makin' It (4)
Miss Kane (3)

Mr. Thomas (2)
Night Whistler (5)
Onward 'Til Morning (7)
Places And Spaces (6)
Return Of The King (7)
Rock And Roll Again (4,6)
Science Funktion (7)
Sister Love (3)
Sky High (2,6)
Slop Jar Blues (2)
Stepping Into Tomorrow (4,6)

Street Lady (3,6)
Sunning In Your Loveshine (8)
Tell Me (7)
Thank You For Funking Up My Life (8)
Think Twice (4)
We're Together (4)
Where Are We Going? (2)
Wild Life (7)
Wind Parade (5)
Witch Hunt (3)

Woman Of The World (3)
You And Music (5)
You Are The World (4)
Your Love Is My Ecstasy (5)

BYRD, Tracy   '95

Born on 12/18/66 in Beaumont, Texas; raised in Vidor, Texas. Male country singer.

DEBUT	PEAK	WKS		CD	#	Album Title	Sym	$	Label & Number
5/15/93	115	6	●	©	1	Tracy Byrd		$10	MCA 10649
6/25/94+	30	78	▲²	©	2	No Ordinary Man		$10	MCA 10991
8/5/95	44	31	●	©	3	Love Lessons		$10	MCA 11242
11/9/96+	106	22	●	©	4	Big Love		$10	MCA 11485
5/30/98	58	8		©	5	I'm From The Country		$10	MCA 70016
3/13/99	70	10	●	©	6	Keepers / Greatest Hits	[G]	$10	MCA 70048
11/20/99	174	1		©	7	It's About Time		$10	RCA 67881

Ain't It Just Like A Woman (7)
Anybody Else's Heart But Mine (2)
Back In The Swing Of Things (1)
Back To Texas (5)
Big Love (4,6)
Can't Have One Without The Other (7)
Cowgirl (4)
Don't Love Make A Diamond Shine (4)
Don't Need That Heartache (3)
Don't Take Her She's All I Got (4,6)

Down On The Bottom (3)
Driving Me Out Of Your Mind (4)
Edge Of A Memory (1)
Every Time I Do (7)
First Step (4)
For Me It's You (5)
Gettin' Me Over Mountains (5)
Good Ol' Fashioned Love (4)
Hat Trick (1)
Have A Good One (3)
Heaven In My Woman's Eyes (3,6)
Holdin' Heaven (1,6)

Honky-Tonk Dancing Machine (3)
I Don't Believe That's How You Feel (4)
I Love You, That's All (4)
I Still Love The Night Life (5)
I Wanna Feel That Way Again (5)
I'm From The Country (5,6) *63*
I've Got What It Takes (5)
If I Stay (4)
It's About Time (7)
Keeper Of The Stars (2,6) *68*
Lifestyles Of The Not So Rich And Famous (2,6)

Little Love (7)
Love Lessons (3,6)
Love, You Ain't Seen The Last Of Me (7)
No Ordinary Man (2)
Old One Better (5)
On Again, Off Again (5)
Out Of Control Raging Fire (1)
Pink Flamingos (2)
Proud Of Me (7)
Put Your Hand In Mine (7) *76*
Redneck Roses (2)
Right About Now (2)
Someone To Give My Love To (1,6)

Something To Brag About (7)
Take Me With You When You Go (7)
Talk To Me Texas (1)
That's The Thing About A Memory (1)
Tucson Too Soon (4)
Undo The Right (7)
Walkin' In (3)
Walkin' The Line (5)
Walking To Jerusalem (3) *92*
Watermelon Crawl (2,6) *81*
When Mama Ain't Happy (6)
Why (1)

Why Don't That Telephone Ring (1)
You Lied To Me (3)
You Never Know Just How Good You've Got It (2)

★211★ BYRDS, The   '65

Folk-rock group formed in Los Angeles: **Roger McGuinn** and **David Crosby** (guitars), **Gene Clark** (tambourine, guitar), **Chris Hillman** (bass) and Mike Clarke (drums). All shared vocals. McGuinn had been with the **Chad Mitchell Trio**. Gene Clark had been with the **New Christy Minstrels**; left in 1966. Crosby left in late 1967 to form **Crosby, Stills & Nash**. Re-formed in 1968 with McGuinn, Hillman, Kevin Kelly (drums) and **Gram Parsons** (guitar). Hillman and Parsons left that same year to form the **Flying Burrito Brothers**. McGuinn again re-formed with Clarence White (guitar), John York (bass) and Gene Parsons (drums). Reunions with original members in 1973 and 1979. Gram Parsons died of a heroin overdose on 9/19/73 (age 26). **McGuinn, Clark & Hillman** later recorded as a trio. In 1986, Hillman formed popular country group **The Desert Rose Band**. McGuinn, Crosby and Hillman reunited on stage on 2/24/90 for a **Roy Orbison** tribute. Gene Clark died on 5/24/91 (age 46). Mike Clarke, also with the Flying Burrito Brothers and **Firefall**, died of liver failure on 12/19/93 (age 49). Group inducted into the Rock and Roll Hall of Fame in 1991.

1)Mr. Tambourine Man 2)The Byrds' Greatest Hits 3)Turn! Turn! Turn!

DEBUT	PEAK	WKS	CD	#	Album Title	Sym	$	Label & Number
6/26/65	6	38	©	1	Mr. Tambourine Man		$40	Columbia 2372 / 9172
1/1/66	17	40	©	2	Turn! Turn! Turn!		$25	Columbia 2454 / 9254
8/27/66	24	28	©	3	Fifth Dimension		$25	Columbia 2549 / 9349
3/18/67	24	24	©	4	Younger Than Yesterday		$25	Columbia 2642 / 9442
9/2/67	6	29	▲ ©	5	The Byrds' Greatest Hits	[G]	$20	Columbia 2716 / 9516
2/3/68	47	19	©	6	The Notorious Byrd Brothers		$20	Columbia 2775 / 9575
8/31/68	77	10	©	7	Sweetheart Of The Rodeo		$20	Columbia 9670
3/15/69	153	7	©	8	Dr. Byrds & Mr. Hyde		$20	Columbia 9755
9/6/69	84	12		9	Preflyte	[E]	$20	Together 1001
					recorded in 1964; also see #16 below			
12/13/69+	36	17	©	10	Ballad Of Easy Rider		$20	Columbia 9942
10/17/70	40	21	©	11	The Byrds (Untitled)	[L]	$25	Columbia 30127 [2]
					record 1: live; record 2: studio			

BYRDS, The — Cont'd

DEBUT	PEAK	WKS			Title		Sym	$	Label & Number
7/24/71	46	10	©	12	Byrdmaniax			$20	Columbia 30640
12/25/71+	152	7	©	13	Farther Along			$20	Columbia 31050
12/16/72+	114	13	©	14	The Best Of The Byrds (Greatest Hits, Volume II)		[G]	$20	Columbia 31795
3/24/73	20	17		15	Byrds			$15	Asylum 5058
					reunion of original 5 Byrds				
9/8/73	183	3		16	Preflyte		[E-R]	$15	Columbia 32183
					new cover features a futuristic drawing of the band				
11/10/90	151	4	©	17	The Byrds		[K]	$40	Columbia 46773 [4]

Absolute Happiness (12)
Airport Song (9,16)
All I Really Want To Do (1,5,17) **40**
All The Things (11)
America's Great National Pastime (13,14)
Antique Sandy (13)
Armstrong, Aldrin And Collins (10)
Artificial Energy (6)
B.B. Class Road (13)
B. J. Blues (medley) (8)
Baby, What Do You Want Me To Do (medley) (8)
Bad Night At The Whiskey (8,17)
Ballad Of Easy Rider (10,14,17) **65**
Bells Of Rhymney (1,5,17)
Black Mountain Rag (Soldier's Joy) (17)
Blue Canadian Rockies (7)
Born To Rock 'N Roll (15)
Borrowing Time (15)
Boston (9,16)
Bristol Steam Convention Blues (13)
Bugler (13,17)
C.T.A. - 102 (4)
Candy (8)
Captain Soul (3)
Change Is Now (6)

Changing Heart (15)
Chestnut Mare (11,14,17)
Child Of The Universe (8)
Chimes Of Freedom (1,5,17)
Christian Life (7,17)
Citizen Kane (12,14)
Cowgirl In The Sand (14)
Day Walk (Never Before) (17)
Deportee (Plane Wreck At Los Gatos) (10,17)
Dolphins' Smile (6,17)
Don't Doubt Yourself, Babe (1)
Draft Morning (6,17)
Drug Store Truck Drivin' Man (8,14,17)
Eight Miles High (3,5,11,17) **14**
Everybody's Been Burned (4,17)
Farther Along (13,17)
Fido (10)
5 D (Fifth Dimension) (3,5,17) **44**
For Free (15)
For Me Again (9,16)
From A Distance (17)
Full Circle (15)
Get Down Your Line (13)
Get To You (6)
Girl With No Name (4,17)
Glory, Glory (12,17)
Goin' Back (6,17) **89**
Green Apple Quick Step (12,17)

Gunga Din (10)
Have You Seen Her Face (4,17) **74**
He Was A Friend Of Mine (2,14,17)
Here Without You (1,9,16)
Hey Joe (Where You Gonna Go) (3,17)
Hickory Wind (7,17)
Hungry Planet (11)
I Am A Pilgrim (7,17)
I Come And Stand At Every Door (3)
I Knew I'd Want You (1,9,16)
I Know My Rider (17)
I See You (17)
I Trust (12,17)
I Wanna Grow Up To Be A Politician (12,14,17)
I'll Feel A Whole Lot Better (1,5,17)
If You're Gone (2)
It Happens Each Day (17)
It Won't Be Wrong (2,17) **63**
It's All Over Now, Baby Blue (10,17)
It's No Use (1)
Jack Tarr The Sailor (10)
Jamaica Say You Will (12)
Jesus Is Just Alright (10,14,17) **97**
John Riley (3,17)
Just A Season (11,17)

Just Like A Woman (17)
Kathleen's Song (12,17)
King Apathy III (8)
Lady Friend (17) **82**
Laughing (15)
Lay Down Your Weary Tune (2,17)
Lay Lady Lay (17)
Lazy Days (17)
Lazy Waters (13,17)
Life In Prison (7)
Long Live The King (15)
Love That Never Dies (17)
Lover Of The Bayou (11,17)
Mae Jean Goes to Hollywood (17)
Mind Gardens (4)
Mr. Spaceman (3,5,11,17) **36**
Mr. Tambourine Man (1,5,9,11,16,17) **1**
My Back Pages (4,5,8,17) **30**
My Destiny (12)
Nashville West (8,11,17)
Natural Harmony (6)
Nothing Was Delivered (7,17)
Oh! Susannah! (5)
Oil In My Lamp (10,17)
Old Blue (8,17)
Old John Robertson (6,17)
One Hundred Years From Now (7,17)
Pale Blue (12)
Paths Of Victory (17)

Positively 4th Street (11,17)
Precious Kate (13)
Pretty Boy Floyd (7,17)
Pretty Polly (17)
Psychodrama City (17)
Reason Why (9,16)
Renaissance Fair (4,17)
Reputation (17)
Roll Over Beethoven (17)
Satisfied Mind (7)
(See The Sky) About To Rain (15)
Set You Free This Time (2) **79**
She Don't Care About Time (17)
She Has A Way (9,16,17)
So Fine (13)
So You Want To Be A Rock 'N' Roll Star (4,5,11,17) **29**
Space Odyssey (6)
Spanish Harlem Incident (1,17)
Stanley's Song (17)
Sweet Mary (15)
Take A Whiff (On Me) (11)
There Must Be Someone (10)
Things Will Be Better (15)
This Wheel's On Fire (8,17)
Thoughts And Words (4)
Tiffany Queen (13,14,17)
Time Between (4,17)
Times They Are A-Changin' (2,17)
Triad (17)
Tribal Gathering (6)

Truck Stop Girl (11,17)
Tulsa County (10,17)
Tunnel Of Love (12)
Turn! Turn! Turn! (To Everything There Is A Season) (2,5,17) **1**
2-4-2 Fox Trot (The Lear Jet Song) (3)
Wait And See (2)
Wasn't Born To Follow (6,14,17)
Way Beyond The Sun (17)
We'll Meet Again (1)
Well Come Back Home (11)
What's Happening?!?! (3)
White's Lightning (17)
Why (4,17)
Wild Mountain Thyme (3)
Willin' (17)
World Turns All Around Her (2,17)
Yesterday's Train (11)
You Ain't Going Nowhere (7,14,17) **74**
You All Look Alike (17)
You Don't Miss Your Water (7,17)
You Movin' (9,16)
You Showed Me (9,16)
You Won't Have To Cry (1,9,16)
You're Still On My Mind (7)
Your Gentle Way Of Loving Me (8)

BYRNE, David   '81

Born on 5/14/52 in Dumbarton, Scotland; raised in Baltimore. Lead singer of the **Talking Heads**. Composed scores for several movies and plays. Formed own Luaka Bop record label.

DEBUT	PEAK	WKS			Title		Sym	$	Label & Number
3/21/81	44	13	©	1	My Life In The Bush Of Ghosts		[I]	$10	Sire 6093
					BRIAN ENO-DAVID BYRNE				
12/19/81+	104	12	©	2	The Catherine Wheel		[OC]	$10	Sire 3645
6/1/85	141	6		3	Music for The Knee Plays			$10	ECM 25022
10/21/89	71	18	©	4	Rei Momo			$10	Luaka Bop 25990
3/21/92	125	6	©	5	Uh-Oh			$10	Luaka Bop 26799
6/11/94	139	6	©	6	David Byrne			$10	Luaka Bop 45558
7/5/97	155	1	©	7	Feelings			$10	Luaka Bop 46605
5/26/01	120	4	©	8	Look Into The Eyeball			$10	Luaka Bop 50924

Accident, The (8)
Admiral Perry (3)
America Is Waiting (1)
Amnesia (7)
Angels (6)
Back In The Box (8)
Big Blue Plymouth (Eyes Wide Open) (2)
Big Business (2)
Broken Things (8)
Buck Naked (6)
Burnt By The Sun (7)
Call Of The Wild (4)
Carnival Eyes (4)
Carrier, The (1)
Civil Wars (7)
Cloud Chamber (2)
Come With Us (1)

Cowboy Mambo (Hey Lookit Me Now) (5)
Crash (6)
Daddy Go Down (7)
Dance On Vaseline (5)
Desconocido Soy (8)
Dirty Old Town (4)
Don't Want To Be Part Of Your World (4)
Dream Police (4)
Eggs In A Briar Patch (2)
Everyone's In Love With You (8)
Finite=Alright (7)
Fuzzy Freaky (7)
Gates Of Paradise (7)
(Gift Of Sound) Where The Sun Never Goes Down (4)

Girls On My Mind (5)
Great Intoxication (8)
Hanging Upside Down (5)
Help Me Somebody (1)
His Wife Refused (2)
I Bid You Goodnight (3)
I Know Sometimes A Man Is Wrong (4)
I've Tried (3)
In The Future (3)
In The Upper Room (3)
Independence Day (4)
Jezebel Spirit (1)
Jungle Book (3)
Lie To Me (4)
Light Bath (2)
Like Humans Do (8)
Lilies Of The Valley (5)

Long Time Ago (6)
Make Believe Mambo (4)
Marching Through The Wilderness (4)
Mea Culpa (1)
Million Miles Away (5)
Miss America (7)
Moment Of Conception (8)
Monkey Man (5)
Moonlight In Glory (1)
Mountain Of Needles (1)
My Big Hands (Fall Through The Cracks) (2)
My Love Is You (6)
Neighborhood (8)
Nothing At All (6)
Now I'm Your Mom (5)
Poison (2)

Qu'Ran (1)
Red House (2)
Regiment (1)
Revolution, The (8)
Rose Tattoo (8)
Sad Song (6)
Secret Life (4)
Self-Made Man (6)
She's Mad (7)
Smile (6)
Social Studies (3)
Soft Seduction (7)
Somebody (5)
Something Ain't Right (5)
Sound Of Business (3)
Strange Ritual (6)
Theadora Is Dozing (3)

They Are In Love (7)
Tiny Town (5)
Tree (Today Is An Important Occasion) (3)
Twistin' In The Wind (5)
Two Soldiers (2)
U.B. Jesus (8)
Walk In The Dark (5)
Walk On Water (8)
What A Day That Was (2)
Wicked Little Doll (7)
Winter (7)
Women Vs. Men (4)
You & Eye (6)
You Don't Know Me (7)

BYRON, D.L.   '80

Born David Byron in New York City. Singer/songwriter/guitarist.

DEBUT	PEAK	WKS			Title		Sym	$	Label & Number
2/16/80	133	10			This Day And Age			$12	Arista 4258

Am I Falling In Love Again
Backstage Girl
Big Boys

Get With It
Listen To The Heartbeat
Lorryanne

Love In Motion
No Romance, No Weekend, No Love

Today
21st Century Man

C

CACTUS — '70

Rock group formed in New York City: Rusty Day (vocals), Jim McCarty (guitar), Tim Bogert (bass) and Carmine Appice (drums). McCarty was with **Mitch Ryder & The Detroit Wheels**. Bogert and Appice were with **Vanilla Fudge**. Day and McCarty left in 1972, replaced by Peter French (vocals), Werner Fritzschings (guitar) and Duane Hitchings (keyboards). Hitchings formed New Cactus Band in 1972 with Mike Pinera (vocals, guitar; **Iron Butterfly**, **Blues Image**, **Ramatam**), Roland Robinson (bass) and Jerry Norris (drums). Day died on 6/3/82. Hitchings and Appice later joined **Rod Stewart**'s band.

7/25/70	54	18			1 Cactus			$20	Atco 340
3/20/71	88	13		©	2 One Way...Or Another			$20	Atco 356
11/27/71	155	10			3 Restrictions			$20	Atco 377
10/28/72	162	5			4 'Ot 'N' Sweaty		[L]	$20	Atco 7011
5/12/73	183	6			5 Son Of Cactus			$20	Atco 7017

NEW CACTUS BAND

Alaska (3)
Bad Mother Boogie (4)
Bad Stuff (4)
Bag Drag (3)
Bedroom Mazurka (4)
Big Mama Boogie - Parts I & II (2)
Blue Gypsy Woman (5)
Bringing Me Down (4)
Bro. Bill (1)
Daddy Ain't Gone (5)
Evil (3)
Feel So Bad (2)
Feel So Good (1)
Guiltless Glider (3)
Hold On To My Love (5)
Hometown Bust (2)
Hook Line And Sinker (5)
I Can't Wait (5)
It's Getting Better (5)
It's Just A Feelin' (5)
Lady (Spend My Life With You) (5)
Let Me Swim (1)
Long Tall Sally (2)
Man Is A Boy (5)
Mean Night In Cleveland (3)
My Lady From South Of Detroit (1)
No Need To Worry (1)
Oleo (1)
One Way...Or Another (2)
Our Lil Rock-N-Roll Thing (4)
Parchman Farm (1)
Ragtime Suzy (5)
Restrictions (3)
Rock N' Roll Children (2)
Rockout, Whatever You Feel Like (2)
Senseless Rebel (5)
Song For Aries (2)
Sweet Sixteen (3)
Swim (4)
Telling You (4)
Token Chokin' (3)
Underneath The Arches (4)
You Can't Judge A Book By The Cover (1)

CACTUS WORLD NEWS — '86

Rock group from Ireland: Eoin McEvoy (vocals), Frank Kearns (guitar), Fergal MacAindris (bass) and Wayne Sheehy (drums).

8/9/86	179	5			Urban Beaches			$10	MCA 5747

Bridge, The
Church Of The Cold
In A Whirlpool
Jigsaw Street
Maybe This Time
Pilots Of Beka
Promise, The
State Of Emergency
Worlds Apart
Years Later

CAEDMON'S CALL — '00

Christian pop-rock group from Houston: Danielle Glenn (vocals), Cliff Young and Derek Webb (vocals, guitars), Garett Buell (percussion), Aric Nitzberg (bass) and Todd Bragg(drums). Randy Holsapple (keyboards) joined in 1998. Josh Moore replaced Holsapple and Jeff Miller replaced Nitzberg in early 2000. Band named after a seventh-century folk tale about a herdsman's God-given singing voice.

4/12/97	110	2		©	1 Caedmon's Call			$10	Warner Alliance 46463
5/1/99	61	9		©	2 40 Acres			$10	Essential 10486
10/28/00	58	2		©	3 Long Line Of Leavers			$10	Essential 10559

Ballad Of San Francisco (3)
Bus Driver (1)
Can't Lose You (3)
Center Aisle (1)
Climb On (A Back That's Strong) (2)
Close Of Autumn (1)
Coming Home (1)
Dance (3)
Daring Daylight Escape (2)
Faith My Eyes (2)
40 Acres (2)
Hope To Carry On (1)
I Just Don't Want Coffee (1)
Lead Of Love (1)
Love Alone (1)
Love Is Different (3)
Masquerade (3)
Mistake Of My Life (3)
Not Enough (1)
Not The Land (1)
Only One (3)
Petrified Heart (2)
Piece Of Glass (3)
Prepare Ye The Way (3)
Prove Me Wrong (3)
Shifting Sand (2)
Somewhere North (2)
Standing Up For Nothing (1)
Stupid Kid (1)
Table For Two (2)
Thankful (2)
There You Go (2)
This World (1)
Valleys Fill First (3)
What You Want (3)
Where I Began (2)

CAFFERTY, John, And The Beaver Brown Band — '84

Rock group from Narragansett, Rhode Island: John Cafferty (vocals, guitar), Gary Gramolini (guitar), Robert Cotoia (keyboards), Michael Antunes (sax), Pat Lupo (bass) and Ken Silva (drums). Wrote and recorded the music for the soundtrack Eddie And The Cruisers.

10/15/83+	9	62	▲³	©	1 Eddie And The Cruisers		[S]	$10	Scotti Brothers 38929
6/8/85	40	32		©	2 Tough All Over			$10	Scotti Brothers 39405
8/26/89	121	6		©	3 Eddie And The Cruisers II		[S]	$10	Scotti Brothers 45297

Betty Lou's Got A New Pair Of Shoes (1)
Boardwalk Angel (1)
C-I-T-Y (2) *18*
Dixieland (2)
Down On My Knees (1)
Emotional Storm (3)
Garden Of Eden (3)
Hang Up My Rock And Roll Shoes (1)
Just A Matter Of Time (3)
(Keep My Love) Alive (3)
Maryia (3)
More Than Just One Of The Boys (2)
NYC Song (3)
On The Dark Side (1) *7*
Open Road (3)
Pride & Passion (3) *66*
Runaround Sue (1)
Runnin' Thru The Fire (3)
Season In Hell (Fire Suite) (3)
Small Town Girl (2) *64*
Some Like It Hot (3)
Strangers In Paradise (2)
Tender Years (1) *31*
Tex-Mex (Crystal Blue) (2)
Those Oldies But Goodies (Remind Me Of You) (1)
Tough All Over (2) *22*
Voice Of America's Sons (2) *62*
Where The Action Is (2)
Wild Summer Nights (1)

CAIN, Tané — '82

Born in 1958 in Hawaii. Former wife of Jonathan Cain (**The Babys**, **Journey**, **Bad English**). Daughter of actor Doug McClure.

9/11/82	121	10			Tané Cain			$10	RCA Victor 4381

Almost Any Night
Crazy Eyes
Danger Zone
Holdin' On *37*
Hurtin' Kind
My Time To Fly
Suspicious Eyes
Temptation
Vertigo

CAKE — '98

Rock group from Sacramento, California: John McCrea (vocals, guitar), Greg Brown (guitar), Vince DiFiore (trumpet), Victor Damiani (bass) and Todd Roper (drums). Brown left in 1997. Gabriel Nelson replaced Damiani in early 1998.

10/5/96+	36	51	▲	©	1 Fashion Nugget		C:#48/1	$10	Capricorn 532867
10/24/98	33	36	▲	©	2 Prolonging The Magic			$10	Capricorn 538092

Alpha Beta Parking Lot (2)
Cool Blue Reason (2)
Daria (1)
Distance, The (1)
Frank Sinatra (1)
Friend Is A Four Letter Word (1)
Guitar (2)
Hem Of Your Garment (2)
I Will Survive (1)
It's Coming Down (1)
Italian Leather Sofa (1)
Let Me Go (2)
Mexico (2)
Never There (2) *78*
Nugget (1)
Open Book (1)
Perhaps, Perhaps, Perhaps (2)
Race Car Ya-Yas (1)
Sad Songs And Waltzes (2)
Satan Is My Motor (2)
She'll Come Back To Me (1)
Sheep Go To Heaven (2)
Stickshifts And Safetybelts (1)
Walk On By (2)
When You Sleep (2)
Where Would I Be? (2)
You Turn The Screws (2)

CALDERA — '77

Jazz instrumental group: Jorge Strunz (guitar), Eduardo Del Barrio (piano), Steve Tavaglione (flute), Mike Azevedo (congas), Hector Andrade (percussion), Dean Cortez (bass) and Carlos Vega (drums). Also see **Strunz & Farah**.

10/1/77	159	4			Sky Islands		[I]	$12	Capitol 11658

Ancient Source
Carnavalito
Indigo Fire
It Used To Be
Pegasus
Pescador (Fisherman)
Seraphim (Angels)
Sky Islands
Triste

CALDWELL, Bobby — '79

Born on 8/15/51 in New York City; raised in Miami. Multi-instrumentalist/songwriter.

11/18/78+	21	31		©	1 Bobby Caldwell			$12	Clouds 8804
3/29/80	113	15		©	2 Cat In The Hat			$12	Clouds 8810
4/17/82	133	13		©	3 Carry On			$10	Polydor 6347

All Of My Love (3) *77*
Can't Say Goodbye (1)
Carry On (3)
Catwalk (3)
Come To Me (1)
Coming Down From Love (2) *42*
Down For The Third Time (1)
I Don't Want To Lose Your Love (2)

CALDWELL, Bobby — Cont'd

It's Over (2)	Love Won't Wait (1)	My Flame (1)	Sunny Hills (3)	What You Won't Do For Love	Wrong Or Right (2)
Jamaica (3)	Loving You (3)	Open Your Eyes (2)	Take Me Back To Then (1)	(1) *9*	You Belong To Me (3)
Kalimba Song (1)	Mother Of Creation (2)	Special To Me (1)	To Know What You've Got (2)	Words (3)	You Promised Me (2)

CALE, J.J.   '72
Born Jean Jacques Cale on 12/5/38 in Oklahoma City. Rock singer/songwriter/guitarist.

1/22/72	51	32	©	1	**Naturally**		$15	Shelter 8098
12/30/72+	92	11	©	2	**Really**		$15	Shelter 8912
6/15/74	128	11	©	3	**Okie**		$15	Shelter 2107
9/25/76	84	18	©	4	**Troubadour**		$15	Shelter 52002
9/8/79	136	9	©	5	**5**		$15	Shelter 3163
2/28/81	110	7	©	6	**Shades**		$12	MCA 5158
4/3/82	149	8	©	7	**Grasshopper**		$12	Mercury 4038
3/17/90	131	10	©	8	**Travel-Log**		$10	Silvertone 1306

After Midnight (1) *42*	Deep Dark Dungeon (6)	Hold On (4)	Lou-Easy-Ann (5)	Ride Me High (4)	Who's Talking (8)
Anyway The Wind Blows (3)	Devil In Disguise (8)	Hold On Baby (8)	Louisiana Women (2)	Ridin' Home (2)	Wish I Had Not Said That (6)
Boilin' Pot (5)	Disadvantage (8)	Humdinger (3)	Love Has Been Gone (6)	Right Down Here (2)	Woman I Love (1)
Bringing It Back (1)	Dr. Jive (7)	I Got The Same Old Blues (3)	Magnolia (1)	River Boat Song (8)	Woman That Got Away (4)
Cajun Moon (3)	Does Your Mama Like To	I'd Like To Love You Baby (3)	Mama Don't (6)	River Runs Deep (1)	You Got Me On So Bad (4)
Call Me The Breeze (1)	Reggae (7)	I'll Be There (If You Ever Want	Mississippi River (7)	Rock And Roll Records (3)	You Got Something (4)
Call The Doctor (1)	Don't Cry Sister (5)	Me) (3)	Mo Jo (2)	Runaround (6)	You Keep Me Hangin' On (7)
Can't Live Here (7)	Don't Go To Strangers (1)	I'll Kiss The World Goodbye (3)	Mona (3)	Sensitive Kind (5)	
Carry On (6)	Don't Wait (7)	I'll Make Love To You Anytime	New Orleans (8)	Shanghaid (8)	
Change Your Mind (8)	Downtown L.A. (7)	(5)	No Time (8)	Soulin' (2)	
Changes (2)	Drifters Wife (7)	I'm A Gypsy Man (4)	Nobody But You (7)	Starbound (3)	
Cherry (4)	End Of The Line (8)	If You Leave Her (6)	Nowhere To Run (1)	Super Blue (4)	
City Girls (7)	Everlovin' Woman (3)	If You're Ever In Oklahoma (2)	Okie (3)	That Kind Of Thing (8)	
Cloudy Day (6)	Everything Will Be Alright (2)	Katy Kool Lady (5)	Old Man And Me (3)	Thing Going On (7)	
Clyde (7)	Fate Of A Fool (5)	Lady Luck (8)	One Step Ahead Of The Blues	Thirteen Days (5)	
Cocaine (4)	Friday (5)	Lean On Me (8)	(7)	Tijuana (8)	
Crazy Mama (1) *22*	Going Down (2)	Let Me Do It To You (4)	Pack My Jack (6)	Too Much For Me (5)	
Crying (3)	Grasshopper (7)	Let's Go To Tahiti (5)	Playing In The Street (2)	Travelin' Light (4)	
Crying Eyes (1)	**Hey Baby** (4) *96*	**Lies** (2) *42*	Precious Memories (3)	What Do You Expect (6)	

CALE, John   '90
Born on 3/9/40 in Crynant, West Glamorgan, Wales. Singer/songwriter/producer. Member of the **Velvet Underground**.

4/11/81	154	5		1	**Honi Soit (o nee swa)**		$10	A&M 4849
5/12/90	103	8	©	2	**Songs For Drella**		$10	Sire 26140

LOU REED/JOHN CALE
fictitious account of the life of Andy Warhol

Dead Or Alive (1)	Honi Soit (La Premiere Lecon	Nobody But You (2)	Starlight (2)	Wilson Joliet (1)
Dream, A (2)	De Francais) (1)	Open House (2)	Strange Times In Casablanca	Work (2)
Faces And Names (2)	I Believe (2)	Riverbank (1)	(1)	
Fighter Pilot (1)	Images (2)	Russian Roulette (2)	Streets Of Laredo (1)	
Forever Changed (2)	It Wasn't Me (2)	Slip Away (A Warning) (2)	Style It Takes (2)	
Hello It's Me (2)	Magic & Lies (1)	Smalltown (2)	Trouble With Classicists (2)	

CALHOUN, Slimm   '01
Born in College Park, Georgia. Male rapper.

4/28/01	78	5	©		**The Skinny**		$10	Aquemini 62520

All Da Hustlers	Dirt Work	It's OK	On Tha Grind	Skinny, The	Well
Characters	How Much Can I	Lil' Buddy (Til Death Do Us	Piece Of Tha Pie	This Young G	Worldly Ways
Cut Song	It Ain't Easy	Part)	Red Clay	Timelock	

CALIFORNIA RAISINS, The   '88
Studio group assembled by producer Ross Vannelli (brother of **Gino Vannelli**). Features R&B singer/drummer **Buddy Miles** and singer Alfie Silas. Based on the Claymation characters of a California Raisin Growers TV commercial.

12/5/87+	60	36	▲	©	1	**The California Raisins Sing The Hit Songs**		$10	Priority 9706
10/8/88	140	15		©	2	**Sweet, Delicious, & Marvelous**		$10	Priority 9755
12/24/88	27[X]	3		©	3	**Christmas With The California Raisins**	[X]	$10	Priority 7923

Dancing In The Street (2)	Jingle Bell Rock (3)	Rudolph The Red Nosed	Stand By Me (1)	When A Man Loves A Woman
Frosty The Snowman (3)	La Bamba (1)	Reindeer (3)	Stop! In The Name Of Love (2)	(1)
Happy Christmas (3)	Lean On Me (1)	Santa Claus Is Coming To	Sweet, Delicious & Marvelous	White Christmas (3)
Heartbreak Hotel (1)	Mony, Mony (1)	Town (3)	(California Raisins Theme	Winter Wonderland (3)
I Got You (I Feel Good) (2)	My Girl (2)	Silent Night (3)	Song) (1)	You Can't Hurry Love (1)
I Heard It Through The	Never Can Say Goodbye (2)	(Sittin' On) The Dock Of The	Tracks Of My Tears (2)	You Don't Have To Wait (2)
Grapevine (1,2) *84*	Respect (1)	Bay (2)	What Does It Take (To Win	
It's Christmas Again (3)		Sleigh Ride (3)	Your Love) (2)	

CALL, The   '89
Rock group from California: Michael Been (vocals, guitar), Tom Ferrier (guitar), Greg Freeman (bass) and Scott Musick (drums). Jim Goodwin (keyboards) replaced Freeman in 1984.

3/26/83	84	15		1	**Modern Romans**		$10	Mercury 810307
3/8/86	82	30	©	2	**Reconciled**		$10	Elektra 60440
7/4/87	123	13	©	3	**Into The Woods**		$10	Elektra 60739
7/1/89	64	22	©	4	**Let The Day Begin**		$10	MCA 6303

All About You (1)	Everywhere I Go (2)	It Could Have Been Me (3)	Same Ol' Story (4)	Uncovered (4)	Woods, The (3)
Back From The Front (1)	Expecting (3)	Jealousy (4)	Sanctuary (3)	Violent Times (1)	You Run (4)
Blood Red (America) (2)	Face To Face (1)	**Let The Day Begin** (4) *51*	Surrender (4)	Walk Walk (3)	
Closer (4)	For Love (4)	Memory (3)	Time Of Your Life (4)	**Walls Came Down** (1) *74*	
Day Or Night (3)	I Don't Wanna (3)	Modern Romans (1)	Too Many Tears (3)	Watch (4)	
Destination (1)	I Still Believe (Great Design) (2)	Morning, The (2)	Tore The Old Place Down (2)	When (4)	
Even Now (2)	In The River (3)	Oklahoma (2)	Turn A Blind Eye (1)	With Or Without Reason (2)	

CALLAS, Maria   '65
Born on 12/4/23 in New York City. Died of heart failure on 9/16/77 (age 53). Renowned operatic soprano.

2/27/65	87	8			**Bizet: Carmen**		$30	Angel 3650 [3]

DEBUT	PEAK	WKS	RIAA	CD	ARTIST — Album Title	Catalog	Sym	$	Label & Number

CALLOWAY '90
R&B duo from Cincinnati: brothers Reggie and Vincent Calloway. Both were members of **Midnight Star**.

| 3/31/90 | 80 | 14 | | © | **All The Way** .... | | | $10 | Solar 75310 |

All The Way 63 | Holiday | I Want You | Sir Lancelot | You Are My Everything
Freaks Compete | **I Wanna Be Rich** 2 | Love Circles | Sugar Free | You Can Count On Me

CAMBRIDGE, Godfrey '64
Born on 2/26/33 in New York City. Died of a heart attack on 11/29/76 (age 43). Actor/comedian. Starred in the movie *Watermelon Man*.

| 7/11/64 | 42 | 13 | | | 1 **Ready Or Not...Here's Godfrey Cambridge** .... | | [C] | $25 | Epic 13101 |
| 4/3/65 | 142 | 9 | | | 2 **Them Cotton Pickin' Days Is Over** .... | | [C] | $25 | Epic 13102 |

Airplanes - Next Time Take The Train (2) | I'm A Bad Luck Drunk (2) | Is That The Way He Really Looks? (2) | Method Acting (1) | New Hobbies - Sky Diving (2)
Arthur Uncle (1) | Irresistible Me (Women Around The World) (1) | Las Vegas And Other Goodies (2) | Middle Income Frustrations (1) | Rent-A-Negro Plan (1)
Block Busting (1) | Is Black Muslim Really A Textile? (2) | Manual Of Arms And Other Put-Ons (2) | Misinterpretation - Cary Grant Is The White Godfrey Cambridge (1) | Theater In The Sky (2)
Gadfly Overseas (2) | | | Movies (1) |
I Love Barry (1) |

CAMEL '76
Rock group from Surrey, England: **Pete Bardens** (keyboards; Them), Andy Latimer (guitar), Doug Ferguson (bass) and Andy Ward (drums).

11/30/74	149	13			1 **Mirage**			$15	Janus 7009
7/19/75	162	5			2 **The Snow Goose**		[I]	$15	Janus 7016
5/22/76	118	13			3 **Moonmadness**			$15	Janus 7024
11/12/77	136	5			4 **Rain Dances**			$15	Janus 7035
2/10/79	134	10		©	5 **Breathless**			$12	Arista 4206

Air Born (3) | Echoes (5) | Fritha Alone (medley) (2) | One Of These Days I'll Get An Early Night (4) | Sanctuary (medley) (2) | Supertwister (1)
Another Night (3) | Elke (4) | Great Marsh (2) | Preparation (2) | Skylines (4) | Tell Me (4)
Aristillus (3) | Encounter (medley) (1) | Highways Of The Sun (4) | Procession, The (medley) (1) | Sleeper, The (5) | Unevensong (4)
Breathless (5) | Epitaph (medley) (2) | La Princesse Perdue (2) | Rain Dances (4) | Smiles For You (medley) (1) | White Rider (medley) (1)
Chord Changes (3) | First Light (4) | Lady Fantasy (medley) (1) | Rainbow's End (5) | Snow Goose (2) | Wing And A Prayer (5)
Down On The Farm (5) | Flight Of The Snow Goose (2) | Lunar Sea (3) | Rhavader (2) | Song Within A Song (3) | You Make Me Smile (5)
Dunkirk (2) | Freefall (1) | Metrognome (4) | Rhavader Alone (medley) (2) | Spirit Of The Water (4) |
Earthrise (1) | Friendship (medley) (2) | Migration (medley) (1) | Rhavader Goes To Town (2) | Starlight Ride (5) |
| | Fritha (medley) (1) | Nimrodel (medley) (1) | | Summer Lightning (5) |

★235★ CAMEO '86
R&B-funk group founded in 1974 by Larry Blackmon (producer, vocals, drums) as The New York City Players. Varying members also included Gregory Johnson, Tomi Jenkins, brothers Nathan and Arnett Leftenant, Wayne Cooper, Gary Dow, Eric Durham, Anthony Lockett, Charlie Singleton, Jeryl Bright, Thomas Campbell, Stephen Moore, Aaron Mills and Kevin Kendricks. In mid-'80s, Blackmon relocated group to Atlanta and formed own label, Atlanta Artists. By 1986, group pared to trio of Blackmon, Jenkins and Nathan Leftenant (left by 1992 and Singleton returned).

1)Word Up! 2)Alligator Woman 3)Cameosis

8/20/77	116	15		©	1 **Cardiac Arrest**			$12	Chocolate City 2003
2/18/78	58	23		©	2 **We All Know Who We Are**			$12	Chocolate City 2004
11/4/78	83	15			3 **Ugly Ego**			$12	Chocolate City 2006
7/28/79	46	21	●	©	4 **Secret Omen**			$12	Chocolate City 2008
5/24/80	25	26	●	©	5 **Cameosis**			$12	Chocolate City 2011
12/6/80+	44	17	●	©	6 **Feel Me**			$12	Chocolate City 2016
6/20/81	44	13	●	©	7 **Knights Of The Sound Table**			$12	Chocolate City 2019
4/10/82	23	24	●		8 **Alligator Woman**			$12	Chocolate City 2021
5/7/83	53	12			9 **Style**			$10	Atlanta Artists 811072
3/17/84	27	24	●	©	10 **She's Strange**			$10	Atlanta Artists 814984
7/13/85	58	27	●		11 **Single Life**			$10	Atlanta Artists 824546
9/27/86	8	54	▲	©	12 **Word Up!**			$10	Atlanta Artists 830265
11/12/88	56	19		©	13 **Machismo**			$10	Atlanta Artists 836002
7/14/90	84	8			14 **Real Men...Wear Black**			$10	Atlanta Artists 846297

Alligator Woman (8) | Energy (4) | I Care For You (14) | Just A Broken Heart (14) | Rock, The (4) | Talkin' Out The Side Of Your Neck (10)
Am I Bad Enough (14) | Enjoy Your Life (8) | I Just Want To Be (4) | Keep It Hot (6) | Roller Skates (6) | This Life Is Not For Me (9)
Anything You Wanna Do (3) | Fast, Fierce & Funny (12) | I Like It (7) | Knights By Nights (7) | Secrets Of Time (8) | Throw It Down (6)
Aphrodisiac (9) | Feel Me (6) | I Like The World (13) | Let's Not Talk Slot (9) | Shake Your Pants (5) | Time, Fire & Space (14)
Attack Me With Your Love (11) | Find My Way (1,4) | I Never Knew (7) | Leve Toi! (10) | She's Mine (12) | Tribute To Bob Marley (10)
Attitude (14) | Flirt (8) | I Owe It All To You (8) | Little Boys - Dangerous Toys (11) | Single Life (11) | Two Of Us (3)
Back And Forth (12) *50* | For You (8) | I Want It Now (14) | Love You Anyway (10) | Skin I'm In (13) | Ugly Ego (3)
Be Yourself (8) | Freaky Dancin' (7) | I Want You (3) | Macho (4) | Slow Movin' (9) | Urban Warrior (11)
Better Days (6) | Friend To Me (3) | I'll Always Stay (7) | Me (14) | Smile (1) | Use It Or Lose It (7)
C On The Funk (2) | Funk Funk (1) | I'll Be With You (3) | Nan-Yea (14) | Soul Army (8) | We All Know Who We Are (2)
Cameo's Dance (9) | Get Paid (14) | I'll Never Look For Love (11) | New York (4) | Soul Tightened (13) | We're Goin' Out Tonight (5)
Cameosis (6) | Give Love A Chance (3) | I've Got Your Image (11) | On The One (5) | Sound Table (7) | Why Have I Lost You (2,5)
Can't Help Falling In Love (9) | Good-Bye, A (11) | In The Night (13) | Please You (5) | Sparkle (4) | **Word Up** (12) *6*
Candy (12) *21* | Good Times (1) | Inflation (2) | Post Mortem (1) | Stand Up (4) | **You Make Me Work** (13) *85*
Close Quarters (14) | Groove With You (10) | Insane (3) | Pretty Girls (13) | Stay By My Side (1) | You're A Winner (9)
DKWIG (13) | Hangin' Downtown (10) | Is This The Way (6) | Promiscuous (13) | Still Feels Good (1) | Your Love Takes Me Out (6)
Don't Be Lonely (12) | Heaven Only Knows (9) | It's Over (2) | Rigor Mortis (1) | Style (9) |
Don't Be So Cool (7) | Honey (1) | It's Serious (2) | | |

CAMERON, Rafael '80
Born in 1951 in Georgetown, Guyana. Disco singer.

| 8/2/80 | 67 | 18 | | | 1 **Cameron** .... | | | $12 | Salsoul 8535 |
| 7/18/81 | 101 | 12 | | © | 2 **Cameron's In Love** .... | | | $12 | Salsoul 8542 |

All That's Good To Me (2) | Daisy (2) | Funtown U.S.A. (2) | In Love (2) | Number One (2)
Boogie's Gonna Get Ya' (2) | Feelin' (1) | Get It Off (1) | Let's Get Married (2) | Together (1)
Can't Live Without Ya' (1) | Funkdown (1) | I'd Go Crazy (1) | Magic Of You (1) |

CAMOUFLAGE '89
Dance trio from Germany: Marcus Meyn (vocals), Heiko Maile (keyboards) and Oliver Kreyssig (backing vocals; left in 1990).

| 1/14/89 | 100 | 14 | | © | **Voices & Images** .... | | | $10 | Atlantic 81886 |

From Ay To Bee | Helpless Helpless | Music For Ballerinas | Strangers Thoughts | Where Has The Childhood Gone | Winner Takes Nothing
Great Commandment 59 | I Once Had A Dream | Neighbours | That Smiling Face | |

Aaliyah
Age Ain't Nothing But A Number ('94)

Accept
Russian Roulette ('86)

Dayton Allen
Why Not! ('60)

Animal Logic
Animal Logic ('89)

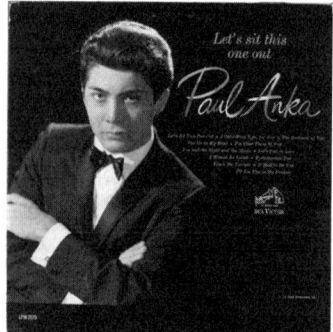

Paul Anka
Let's Sit This One Out ('62)

The Aquabats
The Fury of The Aquabats! ('97)

The Astronauts
Everything Is A-OK! ('64)

Chet Atkins
Christmas With Chet Atkins ('63)

Audio Adrenaline
Underdog ('99)

Joan Baez
Joan Baez In Concert, Part 2 ('63)

Jeff Beck and The Big Town Playboys
Crazy Legs ('93)

Harry Belafonte/Nana Mouskouri
An Evening With Belafonte/Mouskouri ('66)

The Belmonts
The Belmonts Carnival Of Hits ('62)

Tony Bennett
Steppin' Out ('93)

Bjork
Homogenic ('97)

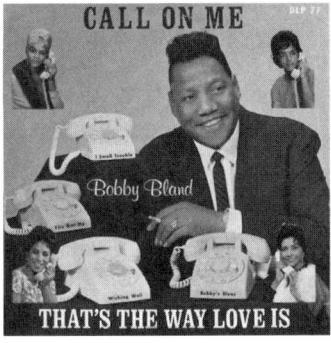

Bobby Bland
Call On Me/That's The Way Love Is ('63)

Kurtis Blow
Kingdom Blow ('86)

David Bowie
Earthling ('97)

The Brass Ring
The Dis-Advantages Of You ('67)

David Bromberg
How Late'll Ya Play 'Til? ('76)

Bubble Puppy
A Gathering Of Promises ('69)

Jimmy Buffett
Christmas Island ('96)

Charlie Byrd
Bossa Nova Pelos Passaros ('63)

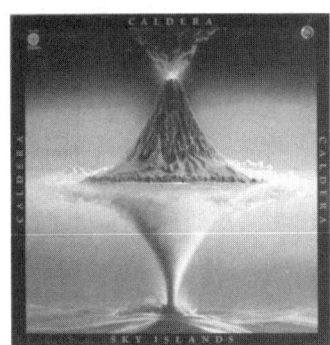

Caldera
Sky Islands ('77)

CAMPBELL, Glen ★85★   '68

Born on 4/22/36 in Delight, Arkansas. Country singer/songwriter/producer. Became prolific studio musician; with The Champs in 1960, **The Hondells** in 1964, **The Beach Boys** in 1965 and Sagittarius in 1967. Own TV show *The Glen Campbell Goodtime Hour*, 1968-72. Acted in the movies *True Grit*, *Norwood* and *Strange Homecoming*; voice in the animated movie *Rock-A-Doodle*. Also see **The Folkswingers**.

1)Wichita Lineman 2)Galveston 3)Gentle On My Mind 4)Bobbie Gentry & Glen Campbell
5)Try A Little Kindness

DEBUT	PEAK	WKS	RIAA	CD		ARTIST — Album Title	Sym	$	Label & Number
12/2/67+	5	75	▲	©	1	Gentle On My Mind		$20	Capitol 2809
12/30/67+	15	80	▲	©	2	By The Time I Get To Phoenix		$20	Capitol 2851
						1968 Grammy winner: Album of the Year			
4/6/68	26	51	●		3	Hey, Little One		$20	Capitol 2878
6/22/68	24	33			4	A New Place In The Sun		$20	Capitol 2907
10/12/68	11	47	●		5	Bobbie Gentry & Glen Campbell		$20	Capitol 2928
11/16/68	❶⁵	46	▲²	©	6	Wichita Lineman		$20	Capitol 103
12/7/68	❶²ˣ	10	●		7	That Christmas Feeling	[X]	$20	Capitol 2978
						Christmas charts: 1/'68, 4/'69, 23/'70, 14/'71			
4/12/69	2¹	42	▲		8	Galveston		$20	Capitol 210
9/20/69	13	29	●		9	Glen Campbell - "Live"	[L]	$25	Capitol 268 [2]
						recorded at the Garden States Art Center in Holmdel, New Jersey			
2/7/70	12	28	●		10	Try A Little Kindness		$15	Capitol 389
5/23/70	38	19			11	Oh Happy Day		$15	Capitol 443
6/27/70	90	13			12	Norwood	[S]	$15	Capitol 475
						includes "Country Girl", "Brass Ensemble Of Ralph, Texas," "Hot Wheels," "Fring Thing," "Chicken Out (Joann's Theme)" and "Different Kind Of Rock" by Al DeLory			
10/3/70	27	21			13	The Glen Campbell Goodtime Album		$15	Capitol 493
4/17/71	39	27	▲	©	14	Glen Campbell's Greatest Hits	[G]	$15	Capitol 752
8/7/71	87	9			15	The Last Time I Saw Her		$15	Capitol 733
12/11/71+	128	8		©	16	Anne Murray/Glen Campbell		$15	Capitol 869
11/25/72+	148	13			17	Glen Travis Campbell		$12	Capitol 11117
6/9/73	154	6			18	I Knew Jesus (Before He Was a Star)		$12	Capitol 11185
11/16/74	166	5			19	Reunion (the songs of Jimmy Webb)		$12	Capitol 11336
8/9/75	17	30	●		20	Rhinestone Cowboy		$12	Capitol 11430
5/1/76	63	9			21	Bloodline		$12	Capitol 11516
11/27/76	116	6	©		22	The Best Of Glen Campbell	[G]	$12	Capitol 11577
3/19/77	22	22	●		23	Southern Nights		$12	Capitol 11601
1/7/78	171	5			24	Live At The Royal Festival Hall	[L]	$15	Capitol 11707 [2]
12/16/78	164	5			25	Basic		$12	Capitol 11722
2/28/81	178	3			26	It's The World Gone Crazy		$12	Capitol 12124

About The Ocean (19)
Adoration (19)
All My Tomorrows (17)
All The Way (10)
Amazing Grace (18,24)
And The World Keeps Spinning (10)
Angels In The Sky (11)
Ann (6)
Any Which Way You Can (26)
As Far As I'm Concerned (13)
Baby Don't Be Givin' Me Up (21)
Back In The Race (2)
Bad Seed (2)
Bloodline (21)
Blue Christmas (7)
Both Sides, Now (10)
Bottom Line (21)
Bowling Green (1)
Break My Mind (3)
Bridge Over Troubled Water (13)
Bring Back The Love (16)
Burning Bridges (14)
By The Time I Get To Phoenix (2,9,14,22,24) 26
(also see: I Say A Little Prayer)
California (25)
Can You Fool (25) 38
Canadian Sunset (16)
Canticle ..see: Scarborough Fair
Catch The Wind (1)
Christiaan No (21)
Christmas Day (7)
Christmas Is For Children (7)
Christmas Song (Merry Christmas To You) (7)
Classical Gas (24)
Cold December (In Your Heart) (2)
Comeback (20)
Count On Me (20)
Country Boy (You Got Your Feet In L.A.) (20,22) 11

Country Girl (10)
Cryin' (1)
Daddy Sang Dass (11)
Daisy A Day (26)
Didn't We (9)
Don't Pull Your Love/Then You Can Tell Me Goodbye (21,22) 27
Down Home (12)
Dream Baby (How Long Must I Dream) (15) 31
Dream Sweet Dreams About Me (13)
Dreams Of The Everyday Housewife (6,9,14,22) 32
Early Morning Song (23)
Ease Your Pain (16)
Elusive Butterfly (3)
Every Time I Itch I Wind Up Scratchin' You (8)
Everything A Man Could Ever Need (21)
Everytime I Sing A Love Song (21)
Fate Of Man (6)
For Cryin' Out Loud (23)
For My Woman's Love (10)
For Once In My Life (9)
Freeborn Man (4)
Friends (8)
Funny Kind Of Monday (13)
Galveston (8,14,22,24) 4
Gentle On My Mind (1,5,9,14,22) 39
Give Me Back That Old Familiar Feeling (18)
God Only Knows (23,24)
Good Ole Mountain Dew (9)
Good Vibrations (medley) (24)
Gotta Have Tenderness (8)
Gotta Travel On (9)
Grafraidh Me Thu (25)
Guide Me (23)
Have I Stayed Away Too Long? (4)

Have Yourself A Merry Little Christmas (7)
He (11)
He Ain't Heavy, He's My Brother (15)
He's Got The Whole World In His Hands (11)
Heart To Heart Talk (9)
Help Make It Through The Night (15)
Help Me, Rhonda (medley) (24)
Here We Go Again (15)
Hey Little One (2,3) 54
Home Again (10)
Homeward Bound (2)
Honey Come Back (10,14) 19
Houston (I'm Comin' To See You) (22) 68
How High Did We Go (23)
I Believe (11)
I Don't Believe You (She Acts Like We Never Have Met) (3)
I Don't Want To Know Your Name (26) 65
I Got Love For You Ruby (21)
I Have No One To Love Me Anymore (4)
I Keep It Hid (19)
I Knew Jesus (Before He Was A Star) (18,22) 45
I Miss You Tonight (20)
I Say A Little Prayer/By The Time I Get To Phoenix (16) 81
I See Love (25)
I Take It On Home (18)
I Wanna Live (3,14) 36
I Want To Be With You Always (18)
I Will Never Pass This Way Again (17) 61
I'd Build A Bridge (20)
I'll Be Home For Christmas (If Only In My Dreams) (7)
I'll Be Lucky Someday (2)
I'll Paint You A Song (1)

(I'm Getting) Used To The Crying (23)
I'm Gonna Love You (25)
If Not For You (18)
If This Is Love (8)
If You Could Read My Mind (15)
If You Go Away (6,9,24)
Impossible Dream (The Quest) (3,9)
In Cars (26)
It Must Be Getting Close To Christmas (7)
It's A Sin (19)
It's Only Make Believe (13,22) 10
(It's Only Your) Imagination (5)
It's Over (1,3,9)
It's The World's Gone Crazy (Cotillion) (26)
It's Your World (26)
Just Another Man (1)
Just Another Piece Of Paper (13)
Just For What I Am (17)
Just This One Time (19)
Last Letter (4)
Last Thing On My Mind (17)
Last Time I Saw Her (15,22) 61
Lay Me Down (Roll Me Out To Sea) (21)
Legend Of Bonnie And Clyde (4)
Less Of Me (5)
Let Go (23)
Let It Be Me (5) 36
Let Me Be The One (16)
(Let Me Be Your) Teddy Bear (medley) (24)
Let's All Sing A Song About It (25)
Little Altar Boy (7)
Little Green Apples (5)
Lord's Prayer (7)
Love Is A Lonesome River (2)
Love Is Not A Game (10)

Love Me As Though There Were No Tomorrow (1)
Love Story (You & Me) (16)
Love Takes You Higher (25)
Loving You (medley) (24)
Mac Arthur Park (13,24)
Marie (12,20)
Mary In The Morning (1)
Moon's A Harsh Mistress (19,22)
More (medley) (9)
Mornin' Glory (5) 74
My Baby's Gone (2)
My Cricket (17)
My Ecstasy (16)
My Elusive Dreams (5)
My Girl (20)
My Way (13)
Never Tell You No Lies (25)
Norwood (Me And My Guitar) (12)
Nothing Quite Like Love (26)
Ocean In His Eyes (19)
Oh Happy Day (11) 40
Oh What A Woman (8)
Ol' Norwood's Comin' Home (12)
Old Toy Trains (7)
On This Road (18)
Once More With Feeling (10)
One Last Time (17) 78
One Pair Of Hands (11)
Pave Your Way Into Tomorrow (13)
Pencils For Sale (20)
People Get Ready (11)
Place In The Sun (4)
Pretty Paper (7)
Reason To Believe (6)
Repo Man (12)
Rhinestone Cowboy (20,22,24) 1
Roll Me Easy (19)
Rollin' (26)
Rose Garden (15)
Running Scared (17)

San Francisco Is A Lonely Town (21)
Scarborough Fair/Canticle (5)
See You On Sunday (21)
She Called Me Baby (4)
She Thinks I Still Care (7)
She Understands Me (15)
Shoulder To Shoulder (26)
(Sittin' On) The Dock Of The Bay (6,9)
Sold American (18)
Soliloquy (24)
Someday Soon (18)
Someone Above (11)
Someone To Give My Love To (17)
Somewhere (medley) (9)
Southern Nights (23,24) 1
Stars (medley) (24)
Straight Life (8)
Stranger In The Mirror (25)
Streets Of London (24)
Sunday Mornin' (5)
Sunflower (23,24) 39
Sunny Day Girl (4)
Surfer Girl (medley) (24)
Surfin' U.S.A. (medley) (24)
Sweet Fantasy (17)
Take Me Back (3)
Take My Hand For A While (8)
Terrible Tangled Web (5)
That's All That Matters (3)
That's Not Home (6)
That's When The Music Takes Me (24)
There's No Place Like Home (7)
This Is Sarah's Song (23,24)
Time (8)
Today (8)
Today Is Mine (15)
Tomorrow Never Comes (2)
Try A Little Kindness (10,14,22,24) 23
Turn Around And Look At Me (3)
Turn It Around In Your Mind (13)

CAMPBELL, Glen — Cont'd

Twelfth Of Never (4)
United We Stand (16)
Until It's Time For You To Go (8)
Visions Of Sugarplums (4)
Walk Right In (9)
We All Pull The Load (16)

We're Over (20)
(When I Feel Like) I Got No Love In Me (25)
Where Do I Begin (15)
Where Do You Go (10)
Where's The Playground Susie (8,9,14) **26**

White Lightning (9)
Why Don't We Just Sleep On It Tonight (26)
Wichita Lineman (6,14,22,24) **3**
William Tell Overture (24)
Wishing Now (19)

Within My Memory (4)
Without Her (1)
Woman, Woman (3)
Words (6)
World I Used To Know (1)
Yakety Sax (9)
You All Come (Y'All Come) (9)

You Better Sit Down Kids (6)
You Might As Well Smile (19)
You'll Never Walk Alone (11)
You're Easy To Love (16)
You're My World (1)
You're The One (18)

You're Young And You'll Forget (2)
(You've Got To) Sing It Nice And Loud For Me Sonny (25)

CAMPBELL, Tevin   '93

Born on 11/12/78 in Waxahachie, Texas. R&B singer. Appeared in the movie *Graffiti Bridge*.

12/7/91+	38	44	▲	©	1 T.E.V.I.N.			$10	Qwest 26291
11/13/93	18	49	▲²	©	2 I'm Ready			$10	Qwest 45388
7/13/96	46	8		©	3 Back To The World			$10	Qwest 46003
3/13/99	88	4		©	4 Tevin Campbell			$10	Qwest 47008

Alone With You (1) *72*
Always In My Heart (2) *20*
Another Way (4) *100*
Back To The World (3) *47*
Beautiful Thing (3)
Break Of Dawn (3)
Brown Eyed Girl (2)
Can We Talk (2) *9*
Confused (1)

Could It Be (3)
Could You Learn To Love (3)
Dandelion (4)
Don't Say Goodbye Girl (2) *71*
Don't Throw Your Life Away (4)
Dry Your Eyes (3)
Everything You Are (4)
For Your Love (4)
Goodbye (1) *85*

Halls Of Desire (1)
I Got It Bad (3)
I Need You (3)
I'll Be There (3)
I'm Ready (2) *9*
Infant Child (2)
Just Ask Me To (1) *88*
Just Begun To Grow (4)
Lil' Brother (1)

Look What We'd Have (If You Were Mine) (1)
Losing All Control (4)
My Love Ain't Blind (4)
Never Again (4)
One Song (1)
Only One For Me (4)
Paris 1798430 (2)
Perfect World (1)

Round And Round (1) *12*
She's All That (1)
Shhh (2)
Siempre Estaras En Mi (Dandelion) (4)
Since I Lost You (4)
Strawberry Letter 23 (1) *53*
Tell Me What You Want Me To Do (1) *6*

Tell Me Where (3)
Uncle Sam (2)
We Can Work It Out (3)
What Do I Say (3)
You Don't Have To Worry (3)

CAMPER VAN BEETHOVEN   '88

Rock group from Santa Cruz, California: David Lowery (vocals, guitar), Greg Lisher (guitar), Morgan Fichter (violin), Victor Krummenacher (bass) and Chris Pedersen (drums). Lowery later formed **Cracker**.

6/18/88	124	17		©	1 Our Beloved Revolutionary Sweetheart			$10	Virgin 90918
10/7/89	141	13		©	2 Key Lime Pie			$10	Virgin 91289

All Her Favorite Fruit (2)
Borderline (2)
Change Your Mind (1)
Come On Darkness (2)
Devil Song (1)
Eye Of Fatima (Pt. 1 & 2) (1)

Flowers (2)
Fool, The (1)
Humid Press Of Days (2)
(I Was Born In A) Laundromat (2)
Jack Ruby (2)

June (2)
Life Is Grand (1)
Light From A Cake (2)
My Path Belated (1)
Never Go Back (1)
O Death (1)

One Of These Days (1)
Pictures Of Matchstick Men (2)
She Divines Water (1)
Sweethearts (1)
Tania (1)
Turquoise Jewelry (1)

Waka (1)
When I Win The Lottery (2)

CAMP LO   '97

Male rap duo from the Bronx, New York: Salahadeen Wallace and Saladine Wilds.

3/1/97	27	9		©	Uptown Saturday Night			$10	Profile 1470

B-Side To Hollywood
Black Connection
Black Nostaljack

Coolie High
Killin' Em Softly
Krystal Karrington

Luchini aka (this is it) *50*
Negro League
Nicky Barnes

Park Joint
Rockin' It
Say Word

Sparkle
Swing

CAM'RON   '98

Born Cameron Giles in 1978 in New York City. Male rapper.

8/8/98	6	10	●	©	1 Confessions Of Fire			$10	Untertainment 68976
10/7/00	14	9		©	2 S.D.E.			$10	Untertainment 69873

All The Chickens (2)
Come Kill Me (2)
Confessions (1)
D Rugs (1)
Death (1)
Do It Again (2)
Double Up (2)

Feels Good (1)
Freak (2)
Fuck You (1,2)
Fuck You At (2)
Glory (1)
Horse & Carriage (1) *41*
Let Me Know (2) *99*

Losin' Weight (2)
Me & My Boo (2)
Me, My Moms & Jimmy (1)
My Hood (2)
Pimp's A Pimp (1)
Prophecy (1)
Rockin' And Rollin' (1)

Shanghai (1)
Sports, Drugs & Entertainment (2)
That's Me (2)
357 (1)
Violence (2)
We Got It (1)

What I Gotta Live For (2)
What Means The World To You (2) *83*
Whatever (2)
Where I'm From (2)
Who's Nice (1)
Why No (2)

Wrong Ones (1)

C & C MUSIC FACTORY   '91

Dance group led by producers/songwriters Robert Clivilles (percussion) and David Cole (keyboards). Featured vocalists include Freedom Williams, Deborah Cooper and Martha Wash. Cole died of spinal meningitis on 1/24/95 (age 32).

1/12/91	2⁷	85	▲⁵	©	1 Gonna Make You Sweat			$10	Columbia 47093
2/29/92	87	9		©	2 Greatest Remixes Vol. I	[K]		$10	Columbia 48840
					CLIVILLES + COLE				
8/27/94	106	9		©	3 Anything Goes!			$10	Columbia 66160

All Damn Night (3)
Bang That Beat (1)
Because Of You (2)
Bounce To The Beat (Can You Dig It) (3)
Clouds (2)
Deeper Love (2) *44*
Do It Properly (2)

Do You Wanna Get Funky (3) *40*
Don't Take Your Love Away (2)
Givin' It To You (1)
Gonna Love U Over (3)
Gonna Make You Sweat (Everybody Dance Now) (1,2) *1*

Groove Of Love (What's This Word Called Love?) (1)
Here We Go (1,2) *3*
Hip Hop Express (3)
I Found Love (3)
Just A Touch Of Love (1) *50*
Just Wanna Chill (2)
Let The Beat Hit 'Em (2)

Let's Get Funkee (1)
Live Happy (1)
Mind Your Business (2)
Notice Me (2)
Oooh Baby (1)
Papermaker (3)
Pride (In The Name Of Love) (2) *54*

Robi-Rob's Boriqua Anthem (3)
Share That Beat Of Love (3)
Take A Toke (3)
Takin' Over (3)
Things That Make You Go Hmmmm... (1,2) *4*
True Love (2)
Two To Make It Right (2)

You Take My Breath Away (2)

CANDLEBOX   '94

Rock group from Seattle: Kevin Martin (vocals), Peter Klett (guitar), Bardi Martin (bass) and Scott Mercado (drums). Dave Krusen replaced Mercado in 1997.

10/9/93+	7	104	▲³	©	1 Candlebox			$10	Maverick 45313
10/21/95	11	17	●	©	2 Lucy			$10	Maverick 45962
8/8/98	65	9		©	3 Happy Pills			$10	Maverick 46975

Arrow (1)
Become (To Tell) (2)
Belmore Place (3)
Best Friend (2)
Blinders (3)
Blossom (1)

Bothered (2)
Breakaway (3)
Butterfly (2)
Change (1)
Cover Me (1)
Crooked Halo (2)

Don't You (1)
Drowned (2)
Far Behind (1) *18*
Happy Pills (3)
He Calls Home (1)
It's Alright (3)

It's Amazing (2)
Look What You've Done (3)
Lucy (2)
Mothers Dream (1)
No Sense (1)
Offerings (3)

Rain (1)
Simple Lessons (2)
So Real (3)
Sometimes (3)
Step Back (3)
Stone's Throw Away (3)

10,000 Horses (3)
Understanding (2)
Vulgar Before Me (2)
You (1) *78*

CANDLEMASS   '89

Hard-rock group from Sweden: Messiah Marcolin (vocals), Lars Johansson and Mats Bjorkman (guitars), Leif Edling (bass) and Jan Lindh (drums).

1/21/89	174	6		©	Ancient Dreams			$10	Metal Blade 73340

Ancient Dreams
Bearer Of Pain

Bell Of Acheron
Cry From The Crypt

Darkness In Paradise
Epistle No. 81

Incarnation Of Evil
Mirror Mirror

CANDYMAN '91

Born on 6/25/68 in Los Angeles. Male rapper.

10/27/90+	**40**	36	● ©	**Ain't No Shame In My Game**	$10 Epic 46947

Ain't No Shame In My Game(show)
Candyman

Don't Leave Home Without It
5 Verses Of Def
Keep On Watcha Doin'

Knockin' Boots 9
Mack Is Back
Melt In Your Mouth 69

Nightgown 91
Playin' On Me
Today's Topic

Who Shakes The Best

CANDYMEN, The '67

Former backing band for **Roy Orbison**: Rodney Justo (vocals), John Adkins (guitar), Dean Daughtry (piano), Billy Gilmore (bass) and Bob Nix (drums). Daughter joined the **Classics IV**. Justo, Daughtry and Nix later joined the **Atlanta Rhythm Section**. Adkins died in June 1989 (age 47).

11/11/67	**195**	4		**The Candymen**	$25 ABC 616

Deep In The Night
Even The Grass Has Died
Georgia Pines *81*

Happier Than Them
Hope
Lonely Eyes

Movies In My Mind
Roses Won't Grow In My Garden

See Saw
Stone Blues Man
Stormy Monday Blues

CANIBUS '98

Born Germaine Williams in New Jersey. Male rapper.

9/26/98	**2**[1]	7	● ©	1 **Can-I-Bus**	$10 Universal 53136
8/5/00	**23**	7	©	2 **2000 B.C. (Before Can-I-Bus)**	$10 Universal 159054

Buckingham Palace (1)
C-Quel, Zero (1)
Channel Zero (1)
Chaos (2)
Die Slow (2)

Doomsday News (2)
Get Retarded (1)
Horsemen (2)
Horsementality (2)
How We Roll (1)

Hype-nitis (1)
I Honor U (1)
I'll Buss 'Em U Punish 'Em (2)
Let's Ride (1)
Life Liquid (2)

Lost @ "C" (2)
Mic-Nificent (2)
Niggonometry (1)
100 Bars (2)
Patriots (1)

Rip Rock (1)
Second Round K.O. (1) *28*
Shock Therapy (2)
2000 B.C. (Before Can-I-Bus) (2)

Watch Who U Beef Wit (2)
What's Going On (1)

★445★ CANNED HEAT '69

Blues-rock group from Los Angeles: Bob "The Bear" Hite (vocals, harmonica), Alan "Blind Owl" Wilson (guitar, harmonica, vocals), Henry Vestine (guitar), Larry Taylor (bass) and Frank Cook (drums). Cook replaced by Fito DeLa Parra in 1968. Vestine replaced by **Harvey Mandel** in 1969. Wilson died of a drug overdose on 9/3/70 (age 27). Hite died of a drug-related heart attack on 4/6/81 (age 36). Vestine died of heart failure on 10/20/97 (age 52).

1)Boogie With Canned Heat 2)Living The Blues 3)Hallelujah

8/12/67	**76**	23		1 **Canned Heat**	$25 Liberty 7526
2/24/68	**16**	52		2 **Boogie With Canned Heat**	$20 Liberty 7541
12/7/68+	**18**	17	©	3 **Living The Blues** .... [L]	$25 Liberty 27200 [2]

record 2: recorded live at the Kaleidoscope in Hollywood; also see #10 below

8/9/69	**37**	15		4 **Hallelujah**	$20 Liberty 7618
12/6/69+	**86**	19		5 **Canned Heat Cook Book (The Best Of Canned Heat)** .... [G]	$20 Liberty 11000
1/17/70	**173**	5		6 **Vintage-Canned Heat** .... [E]	$15 Janus 3009
9/12/70	**59**	19		7 **Future Blues**	$15 Liberty 11002
2/27/71	**73**	16	©	8 **Hooker 'N Heat**	$20 Liberty 35002 [2]

CANNED HEAT & JOHN LEE HOOKER

7/17/71	**133**	9		9 **Canned Heat Concert (Recorded Live In Europe)** .... [L]	$15 United Artists 5509
10/30/71	**182**	2		10 **Living The Blues** .... [L-R]	$20 United Artists 9955 [2]

new cover features a drawing of an open mouth

3/4/72	**87**	12		11 **Historical Figures And Ancient Heads**	$15 United Artists 5557

Alimonia Blues (8)
Amphetamine Annie (2,5)
Back Out On The Road (medley) (9)
Big Fat (4)
Big Road Blues (1,6)
Boogie Chillen No. 2 (8)
Boogie Music (3,5,10)
Bottle Up And Go (8)
Bring It On Home (9)
Bullfrog Blues (1,5)
Burning Hell (8)
Can't Hold On Much Longer (6)
Canned Heat (4)
Catfish Blues (1)
Change My Ways (4)

Cherokee Dance (11)
Dimples (6)
Do Not Enter (4)
Down In The Gutter, But Free (4)
Drifter (8)
Dust My Broom (1)
Evil Is Going On (1)
Evil Woman (2)
Feelin' Is Gone (8)
Fried Hockey Boogie (2,5)
Future Blues (7)
Get Off My Back (4)
Goin' Down Slow (1)
Going Up The Country (3,5,10) *11*

Goodbye For Now (9)
Got My Mojo Working (6)
Help Me (1)
Hill's Stomp (11)
Huautla (4)
I Don't Care What You Tell Me (11)
I Got My Eyes On You (8)
I'm Her Man (4)
Just You And Me (8)
Let's Make It (8)
Let's Work Together (7,9) *26*
London Blues (7,9)
Long Way From L.A. (11)
Louise (6)
Marie Laveau (2)

Meet Me In The Bottom (8)
Messin' With The Hook (8)
My Crime (2)
My Mistake (3,10)
My Time Ain't Long (7)
On The Road Again (2,5,9) *16*
One Kind Favor (3,10)
Owl Song (2)
Parthenogenesis Medley (3,10)
Peavine (8)
Pony Blues (3,10)
Pretty Thing (6)
Pulling Hair Blues (9)
Refried Boogie (Part I & II) (3,10)
Rich Woman (1)

Road Song (1)
Rockin' With The King (11) *88*
Rollin' And Tumblin' (1,5,6)
Same All Over (4,5)
Sandy's Blues (3,10)
Scat (7)
Send Me Your Pillow (8)
Shake It And Break It (7)
Sic 'Em Pigs (4,5)
Sittin' Here Thinkin' (8)
Sneakin' Around (11)
So Sad (The World's In A Tangle) (7)
Spoonful (6)
Story Of My Life (11)
Straight Ahead (6)

Sugar Bee (7)
That's All Right (11)
That's All Right Mama (7,9)
Time Was (4,5) *67*
Turpentine Moan (2)
Utah (11)
Walking By Myself (3,10)
Whiskey And Wimmen' (8)
Whiskey Headed Woman No. 2 (2)
World In A Jug (2)
World Today (8)
You Talk Too Much (8)

CANNIBAL AND THE HEADHUNTERS '65

Vocal group from Los Angeles: Frankie "Cannibal" Garcia, brothers Robert and Joe Jaramillo, and Richard Lopez. Garcia died on 1/21/96 (age 49). Joe Jaramillo died on 5/24/2000 (age 51).

5/8/65	**141**	4		**Land Of 1000 Dances**	$50 Rampart 3302

Boy From New York City
Devil In Disguise

Don't Let Her Go
Fat Man

Get Your Baby
Here Comes Love

Land Of 1000 Dances *30*
My Girl

Out Of Sight
Searchin'

Shotgun
Strange World

CANNIBAL CORPSE '96

Death-metal group from Buffalo: George Fisher (vocals), Jack Owen and Rob Barrett (guitars), Alex Webster (bass) and Paul Mazurkiewicz (drums).

6/8/96	**151**	1	©	**Vile**	$10 Metal Blade 14204

Absolute Hatred
Bloodlands

Devoured By Vermin
Disfigured

Eaten From Inside
Monolith

Mummified In Barbed Wire
Orgasm Through Torture

Perverse Suffering
Puncture Wound Massacre

Relentless Beating

CANNON, Ace '62

Born Hubert Cannon on 5/4/34 in Grenada, Mississippi. Male saxophonist.

5/19/62	**44**	17	©	1 **"Tuff"-Sax** .... [I]	$25 Hi 32007
12/18/65	**23**[X]	5		2 **Christmas Cheers From Ace Cannon** .... [X]	$25 Hi 32022

Christmas charts: 23/'65, 64/'67

Basin Street Blues (1)
Blue Christmas (2)
Blues In My Heart (1)
Blues (Stay Away From Me) (1) *36*
Cannonball (1)

Careless Love (1)
Frosty The Snowman (2)
Here Comes Santa Claus (2)
I Saw Mommy Kissing Santa Claus (2)
I've Got A Woman (1)

Jingle Bell Rock (2)
Jingle Bells (2)
Kansas City (1)
Let It Snow, Let It Snow, Let It Snow (2)
Lonesome Road (1)

Rock Around The Christmas Tree (2)
Rudolph The Red Nosed Reindeer (2)
Santa Claus Is Coming To Town (2)

St. Louis Blues (1)
Trouble In Mind (1)
Tuff (1) *17*
Wabash Blues (1)
White Christmas (2)
Winter Wonderland (2)

CANNON, Freddy '62
Born Frederick Picariello on 12/4/39 in Lynn, Massachusetts. Pop singer. Nickname "Boom Boom" came from big bass drum-sound on his records.

| 9/1/62 | 101 | 5 | | | Freddy Cannon At Palisades Park | | | $150 | Swan 507 |

Buzz Buzz A-Diddle-It *51*   Itsy Bitsy Teenie Weenie Yellow   Meet Me In St. Louis   Splish Splash   Transistor Sister *35*
For Me And My Gal *71*   Polkadot Bikini   Merry-Go-Round Broke Down   Summer's Comin'
Forever True   June, July, August   **Palisades Park 3**   Teen Queen Of The Week *92*

CANO, Eddie '62
Born on 6/6/27 in Los Angeles. Died on 1/30/88 (age 60). Latin-jazz pianist/bandleader.

| 9/1/62 | 31 | 12 | | | Eddie Cano At P.J.'s | | [I] | $20 | Reprise 6030 |

Cal's Pals   First One   Laura   Oye Corazon   Panchita   Trolley Song
Cotton Candy   Hello Young Lovers   Maha   P.J.'s   Taste Of Honey   Watusi Walk

CANTRELL, Jerry '98
Born on 3/18/66 in Tacoma, Washington. Lead guitarist of **Alice In Chains**.

| 4/25/98 | 28 | 14 | © | | Boggy Depot | | | $10 | Columbia 68147 |

Between   Cold Piece   Devil By His Side   Hurt A Long Time   Keep The Light On   Satisfy
Breaks My Back   Cut You In   Dickeye   Jesus Hands   My Song   Settling Down

CANTRELL, Lana '68
Born on 8/7/43 in Sydney, Australia. Female singer/actress.

| 11/16/68 | 166 | 2 | | | Lana! | | | $15 | RCA Victor 4026 |

Baby, Now That I've Found You   Fool On The Hill   Gentle On My Mind   How Can I Be Sure   Music Played (Was Ich Dir   Sound Of Silence
Can't Take My Eyes Off Of You   For Me (Arrastao)   Honey   Mine (Is A Quiet Love)   Sagen Will)   Workin' On A Groovy Thing

CAPALDI, Jim '72
Born on 8/24/44 in Evesham, England. Singer/drummer. Member of **Traffic**.

3/4/72	82	11	©	1	Oh How We Danced			$15	Island 9314
9/7/74	191	3	©	2	Whale Meat Again			$15	Island 9254
2/14/76	193	4	©	3	Short Cut Draw Blood			$15	Island 9336
5/21/83	91	12		4	Fierce Heart			$12	Atlantic 80059
12/17/88+	183	8	©	5	Some Come Running			$10	Island 91024

Anniversary Song (1)   Eve (1) *91*   It's All Up To You (3)   Love Used To Be A Friend Of   Short Cut Draw Blood (3)   Whale Meat Again (2)
Back At My Place (4)   Gifts Of Unknown Things (4)   Johnny Too Bad (3)   Mine (5)   Some Come Running (5)   Yellow Sun (2)
Bad Breaks (4)   Goodbye Love (3)   Keep On Trying (3)   Low Rider (2)   Something So Strong (5)   You Are The One (5)
Big Thirst (1)   How Much Can A Man Really   Last Day Of Dawn (1)   My Brother (2)   Summer Is Fading (2)
Boy With A Problem (3)   Take (1)   Living On A Marble (3)   Oh Lord, Why Lord (5)   Take Me Home (5)
Dancing On The Highway (5)   I'll Always Be Your Fool (4)   **Living On The Edge** (4) *75*   Open Your Heart (1)   **That's Love** (4) *28*
Don't Be A Hero (1)   I've Got So Much Lovin' (1)   **Love Hurts** (1) *97*   Runaway (4)   Tonight You're Mine (4)
Don't Let Them Control You (4)   **It's All Right** (2) *55*   Love Is All You Can Try (1)   Seagull (3)   Voices In The Night (5)

CAPITOLS, The '66
R&B trio from Detroit: Sam George (vocals, drums), Donald Storball (guitar) and Richard McDougall (keyboards). George was fatally stabbed on 3/17/82 (age 39).

| 7/23/66 | 95 | 12 | | | Dance The Cool Jerk | | | $50 | Atco 190 |

Cool Jerk 7   Hello Stranger   Kick, The   My Girl   Zig Zaggin'
Dog & Cat   I Got My Mojo Working   Love Makes The World Go   Please Please Please
Good Lovin'   In The Midnight Hour   Round   Tired Running From You

CAPONE-N-NOREAGA '97
Rap duo from New York City: Kiam "Capone" Holley and Victor "**Noreaga**" Santiago. Capone is a member of **QB Finest**.

| 7/5/97 | 21 | 10 | © | 1 | The War Report | | | $10 | Penalty 3041 |
| 12/9/00 | 31 | 14 | © | 2 | The Reunion | | | $10 | Tommy Boy 3110 |

All We Got Is Us (2)   Brothers (2)   Don't Know Nobody (2)   Illegal Life (1)   Neva Die Alone (1)   Stick You (1)
B EZ (2)   Capone Bone (1)   Driver's Seat (1)   Invincible (2)   Parole Violators (1)   Straight Like That (2)
Bang Bang (2)   Change Is Gonna Come (2)   Full Steezy (2)   Iraq (See The World) (1)   Phonetime (2)   T.O.N.Y. (Top Of New York) (1)
Black Gangstas (1)   Channel 10 (1)   Gunz In Da Air (2)   L.A., L.A. (1)   Queens (2)   Y'All Don't Wanna (2)
Bloody Money (1)   Closer (1)   Halfway Thugs (1)   Live On Live Long (1)   Queens Finest (2)   You Can't Kill Me (2)

CAPPADONNA '98
Born Darryl Hill in New York City. Male rapper.

| 4/11/98 | 3 | 10 | ● © | 1 | The Pillage | | | $10 | Razor Sharp 67947 |
| 4/21/01 | 51 | 4 | © | 2 | The Yin And The Yang | | | $10 | Wu-Tang 69821 |

Big Business (2)   Dart Throwing (1)   Milk The Cow (1)   Revenge (2)   Splish Splash (1)   Young Hearts (1)
Black Boy (1)   Everything Is Everything (1)   Oh-Donna (1)   Run (1)   Supa Ninjaz (1)
Blood On Blood War (1)   Grits, The (2)   One Way 2 Zion (2)   Shake Dat (2)   Super Model (2)
Bread Of Life (2)   Love Is The Message (2)   Pillage (1)   Slang Editorial (1)   War Rats (2)
Check For A Nigga (1)   MCF (1)   Pump Your Fist (1)   South Of The Border (1)   We Know (2)

CAPTAIN & TENNILLE '75
Pop duo: Daryl "The Captain" Dragon (born on 8/27/42 in Los Angeles) and his wife, Toni Tennille (born on 5/8/43 in Montgomery, Alabama). Dragon is the son of noted conductor **Carmen Dragon**. Keyboardist with **The Beach Boys**, nicknamed "The Captain" by Mike Love. Duo had own TV show on ABC from 1976-77.

6/14/75	2[1]	104	● ©	1	Love Will Keep Us Together			$12	A&M 3405
3/20/76	9	61	▲	2	Song Of Joy			$12	A&M 4570
4/23/77	18	15	●	3	Come In From The Rain			$12	A&M 4700
12/10/77+	55	12	● ©	4	Captain & Tennille's Greatest Hits		[G]	$12	A&M 4667
7/22/78	131	30	●	5	Dream			$12	A&M 4707
11/17/79+	23	24	●	6	Make Your Move			$10	Casablanca 7188

Baby You Still Got It (6)   **Come In From The Rain**   Dixie Hummingbird (5)   Feel Like A Man (1)   Happier Than The Morning Sun
Back To The Island (5)   (3,4) *61*   **Do That To Me One More**   Gentle Stranger (1)   (3)
Broddy Bounce (1)   Cuddle Up (1)   **Time** (6) *1*   God Only Knows (1)   **Happy Together (A Fantasy)**
Butterscotch Castle (2)   "D" Keyboard Blues (1)   Don't Be Scared (3)   Going Bananas (2)   (6) *53*
Can't Stop Dancin' (3,4) *13*   Deep In The Dark (6)   Dream (5)   Good Enough (5)   Honey Come Love Me (1)
Circles (3,4)   Disney Girls (1,4)   Easy Evil (3)   Good Songs (1)   How Can You Be So Cold (6)

CAPTAIN & TENNILLE — Cont'd

I Write The Songs (1,4)
I'm On My Way (5) *74*
If There Were Time (5)
Ka-Ding-Dong (3)
Ladybug (3)
Let Mama Know (3)
Lonely Night (Angel Face) (2,4) *3*

Love Is Spreading Over The World (5)
Love Me Like A Baby (5)
Love On A Shoestring (6) *55*
Love Will Keep Us Together (1,4) *1*
Mind Your Love (2)
Muskrat Love (2,4) *4*

Never Make A Move Too Soon (6)
1954 Boogie Blues (2)
No Love In The Morning (6)
Sad Eyes (3)
Shop Around (2,4) *4*
Smile For Me One More Time (2)
Song Of Joy (2)

Thank You, Baby (2)
Way I Want To Touch You (1,4) *4*
We Never Really Say Goodbye (3,4)
Wedding Song (There Is Love) (2,4)
You Need A Woman Tonight (5) *40*

You Never Done It Like That (5) *10*

CAPTAIN BEEFHEART   '75

Born Don Van Vliet on 1/15/41 in Glendale, California. Multi-octave rock singer. Collaborations with high school friend **Frank Zappa**. Backed by various personnel. Beefheart retired from music in 1986 to become a professional painter.

| 2/19/72 | 131 | 9 | © | 1 | The Spotlight Kid | $20 | Reprise 2050 |

CAPTAIN BEEFHEART & THE MAGIC BAND:

12/23/72+	191	7	©	2	Clear Spot	$20	Reprise 2115
4/27/74	192	4	©	3	Unconditionally Guaranteed	$20	Mercury 709
11/1/75	66	8	©	4	Bongo Fury	[L] $20	DiscReet 2234

FRANK ZAPPA/CAPTAIN BEEFHEART/THE MOTHERS
recorded on 5/20/75 in Austin, Texas

Advance Romance (4)
Alice In Blunderland (1)
Big Eyed Beans From Venus (2)
Blabber 'N Smoke (1)
Carolina Hard-Core Ecstasy (4)
Circumstances (2)
Clear Spot (2)
Click Clack (1)
Crazy Little Thing (2)

Cucamonga (4)
Debra Kadabra (4)
Full Moon, Hot Sun (3)
Glider (1)
Golden Birdies (2)
Grow Fins (1)
Happy Love Song (3)
Her Eyes Are A Blue Million Miles (2)
I Got Love On My Mind (3)

I'm Gonna Booglarize You Baby (1)
Lazy Music (3)
Long Neck Bottles (2)
Low Yo Yo Stuff (2)
Magic Be (3)
Man With The Woman Head (4)
Muffin Man (4)
My Head Is My Only House Unless It Rains (2)

New Electric Ride (3)
Nowadays A Woman's Gotta Hit A Man (2)
Peaches (3)
Poofter's Froth Wyoming Plans Ahead (4)
Sam With The Showing Scalp Flat Top (4)
Spotlight Kid (1)
Sugar Bowl (2)

Sun Zoom Spark (2)
There Ain't No Santa Claus On The Evenin' Stage (1)
This Is The Day (3)
Too Much Time (2)
200 Years Old (4)
Upon The My-O-My (3)
When It Blows Its Stacks (1)
White Jam (1)

CAPTAIN BEYOND   '73

Rock group: Rod Evans (vocals; **Deep Purple**), Larry Rheinhart (guitar), Lee Dorman (bass; **Iron Butterfly**) and Bobby Caldwell (drums; **Armageddon**). Various personnel after first album. Evans left after second album; replaced by Willy Daffern.

8/19/72	134	12	©	1	Captain Beyond	$30	Capricorn 0105
9/1/73	90	10	©	2	Sufficiently Breathless	$30	Capricorn 0115
6/11/77	181	2	©	3	Dawn Explosion	$15	Warner 3047

Armworth (1)
As The Moon Speaks (To The Waves Of The Sea) (1)
Astral Lady (1)
Breath Of Fire - Part 1 & 2 (3)
Bright Blue Tango (2)

Dancing Madly Backwards (On A Sea Of Air) (1)
Distant Sun (2)
Do Or Die (3)
Drifting In Space (2)
Everything's A Circle (2)

Evil Men (2)
Fantasy (1)
Frozen Over (1)
I Can't Feel Nothin' (Part I & II) (1)
Icarus (3)

If You Please (3)
Mesmerization Eclipse (1)
Midnight Memories (3)
Myopic Void (1)
Oblivion (medley) (3)
Raging River Of Fear (1)

Space (medley) (3)
Starglow Energy (2)
Sufficiently Breathless (2)
Sweet Dreams (3)

Thousand Days Of Yesterdays (Time Since Come And Gone) (1)
Voyages Of Past Travellers (2)

CAPTAIN SKY   '79

Born Daryl Cameron on 7/10/57 in Chicago. R&B singer/songwriter/producer.

| 1/27/79 | 157 | 12 | | | The Adventures Of Captain Sky | $12 | AVI 6042 |

Can't Stop Now

Now That I Have You

Saturday Night Move-Ease

Super Sporm

Wonder Worm

CAPUANO, Carla   '82

Born in Westfield, New Jersey. Aerobic dance instructor.

| 3/13/82 | 152 | 8 | | | Aerobic Dance Hits, Volume One | $10 | Casablanca 7263 |

Celebration *[Kool & The Gang]*
Hollywood Swinging *[Kool & The Gang]*

I Can't Go For That
Jungle Boogie *[Kool & The Gang]*

Let's Groove
New Empire
Paradise

Physical
Waiting For A Girl Like You
Yesterday's Songs

CARA, Irene   '84

Born on 3/18/59 in New York City. Singer/pianist/actress. Appeared in several movies and TV shows.

| 1/30/82 | 76 | 17 | | 1 | Anyone Can See | $10 | Network 60003 |
| 12/10/83+ | 77 | 37 | © | 2 | What A Feelin' | $10 | Geffen 4021 |

Anyone Can See (1) *42*
Breakdance (2) *8*
Cue Me Up (2)
Don't Throw Your Love Away (1)

Dream (Hold On To Your Dream) (2) *37*
Flashdance...What A Feeling (2) *1*
Keep On (2)

My Baby (He's Something Else) (1)
Reach Out I'll Be There (1)
Receiving (2)
Romance '83 (2)

Slow Down (1)
Thunder In My Heart (1)
True Love (1)
Whad'Ya Want (1)
Why (1)

Why Me? (2) *13*
You Hurt Me Once (1)
You Took My Life Away (2)
You Were Made For Me (2) *78*

CARAVAN   '75

Rock group from Canterbury, England: Pye Hastings (vocals, guitar), Dave Sinclair (piano), Geoff Richardson (viola), Mike Wedgwood (bass) and Richard Coughlan (drums).

| 8/23/75 | 124 | 10 | © | | Cunning Stunts | $15 | BTM 5000 |

Dabsong Conshirtoe Medley

Fear And Loathing In Tollington Park Rag

Lover
No Back Stage Pass

Show Of Our Lives
Stuck In A Hole

Welcome The Day

CARAVELLES, The   '64

Female vocal duo from England: Andrea Simpson and Lois Wilkinson.

| 2/15/64 | 127 | 4 | | | You Don't Have To Be A Baby To Cry | $60 | Smash 67044 |

Don't Blow Your Cool
Don't Sing Love Songs
Forever

Gonna Get Along Without You Now
Half As Much

Have You Ever Been Lonely (Have You Ever Been Blue) *94*

I Really Don't Want To Know
I Was Wrong
Last One To Know

My How The Time Goes By
Tonight You Belong To Me

You Don't Have To Be A Baby To Cry *3*

CARDIGANS, The   '97

Pop-rock group from Sweden: Nina Persson (vocals), Peter Svensson (guitar), Lars-Olof Johansson (keyboards), Magnus Sveningsson (bass) and Bengt Lagersburg (drums).

| 1/4/97 | 35 | 27 | ▲ | © | 1 | First Band On The Moon | $10 | Stockholm 533117 |
| 11/21/98 | 151 | 1 | | © | 2 | Gran Turismo | $10 | Stockholm 559081 |

Been It (1)
Choke (1)
Do You Believe (2)
Erase/Rewind (2)

Explode (2)
Great Divide (1)
Hanging Around (2)
Happy Meal II (1)

Heartbreaker (1)
Higher (2)
Iron Man (1)
Junk Of The Hearts (2)

Losers (1)
Lovefool (1)
Marvel Hill (2)
My Favourite Game (2)

Never Recover (1)
Nil (2)
Paralyzed (2)
Starter (2)

Step On Me (1)
Your New Cuckoo (1)

CAREY, Mariah ★142★   '91

Born on 3/27/70 in Greenlawn, Long Island, New York. Singer/songwriter/producer. Daughter of former opera singer Patricia Carey. Mariah sang backup for **Brenda K. Starr**. Won the 1990 Best New Artist Grammy Award. Married to Tommy Mottola, president of Sony Music Entertainment, from 1993-98. Acted in the movies *The Bachelor* and *Glitter*.

DEBUT	PEAK	WKS	RIAA	CD	ARTIST — Album Title	Catalog	Sym	$	Label & Number
6/30/90+	❶^{11}	113	▲^{9}	©	1 Mariah Carey	C:#30/26		$10	Columbia 45202
10/5/91	4	54	▲^{4}	©	2 Emotions			$10	Columbia 47980
6/20/92	3	57	▲^{3}	©	3 MTV Unplugged EP		[L-M]	$10	Columbia 52758
					recorded on 3/16/92				
9/18/93	❶^8	128	▲^{10}	©	4 Music Box			$10	Columbia 53205
11/19/94	3	13	▲^{4}	©	5 Merry Christmas	C:❶^2/49	[X]	$10	Columbia 64222
					Christmas charts: 1/'94, 3/'95, 3/'96, 7/'97, 7/'98, 14/'99, 19/'00				
10/21/95	❶^6	81	▲^{9}	©	6 Daydream	C:#45/1		$10	Columbia 66700
10/4/97	❶^1	55	▲^{5}	©	7 Butterfly			$10	Columbia 67835
12/5/98	4	62	▲^{4}	©	8 #1's		[G]	$10	Columbia 69670
11/20/99	2^2	35	▲^{3}	©	9 Rainbow			$10	Columbia 63800

After Tonight (9)
Against All Odds (Take A Look At Me Now) (9)
All I Want For Christmas Is You (5) *83*
All I've Ever Wanted (4)
All In Your Mind (1)
Alone In Love (1)
Always Be My Baby (6,8) *1*
And You Don't Remember (2)
Anytime You Need A Friend (4) *12*
Babydoll (7)
Beautiful Ones (7)
Bliss (9)
Breakdown (7)
Butterfly (7)
Can't Let Go (2,3) *2*
Can't Take That Away (Mariah's Theme) (9)
Christmas (Baby Please Come Home) (5)
Close My Eyes (7)
Crybaby (9) *28*
Did I Do That? (9)
Dreamlover (4,8) *1*
Emotions (2,3,8) *1*
Fantasy (6,8) *1*
Forever (6)
Fourth Of July (7)
Gloria (In Excelsis Deo) (medley) (5)
Hark! The Herald Angels Sing (medley) (5)
Heartbreaker (9) *1*
Hero (4,8) *1*
Honey (7,8) *1*
How Much (9)
I Am Free (6)
I Don't Wanna Cry (1,8) *1*
I Still Believe (8) *4*
I'll Be There (5) *1*
I've Been Thinking About You
If It's Over (2,3)
Jesus Born On This Day (5)
Jesus Oh What A Wonderful Child (5)
Joy To The World (5)
Just To Hold You Once Again (4)
Long Ago (6)
Looking In (6)
Love Takes Time (1,8) *1*
Make It Happen (2,3) *5*
Melt Away (6)
Miss You Most (At Christmas Time) (5)
Music Box (4)
My All (7,8) *1*
Never Forget You (4)
Now That I Know (4)
O Holy Night (5)
One Sweet Day (6,8) *1*
Open Arms (6)
Outside (7)
Petals (9)
Prisoner (1)
Roof, The (7)
Santa Claus Is Comin' To Town (5)
Sent From Up Above (1)
Silent Night (5)
So Blessed (2)
Someday (1,3,8) *1*
Sweetheart (8)
Thank God I Found You (9) *1*
There's Got To Be A Way (1)
Till The End Of Time (1)
To Be Around You (2)
Underneath The Stars (6)
Vanishing (1)
Vision Of Love (1,3,8) *1*
When I Saw You (6)
When You Believe (8) *15*
Whenever You Call (7,8)
Wind, The (2)
Without You (4) *3*
X-Girlfriend (9)
You Need Me (1)
You're So Cold (2)

CAREY, Tony   '84

Born on 10/16/52 in Watsonville, California. Rock singer/songwriter/keyboardist. Former member of **Rainbow** and **Planet P**.

DEBUT	PEAK	WKS			ARTIST — Album Title			$	Label & Number
4/2/83	167	9			1 Tony Carey [I Won't Be Home Tonight]			$15	Rocshire 0001
3/31/84	60	24			2 Some Tough City			$10	MCA 5464

Carry My Love (1)
Eddie Goes Underground (2)
Fine Fine Day (2) *22*
First Day Of Summer (2) *33*
Hungry (2)
I Can Stop The World (2)
I Don't Care (1)
I Won't Be Home Tonight (1) *79*
I'll Tell The World About Her (1)
Lonely Life (2)
Natalia (1)
Reach Out (1)
Running Away From The Thought Of You (1)
She Can Bring Me Love (2)
Sing Along (1)
Some Tough City (2)
Something For Nothing (1)
Tinseltown (2)
Vigilante (1)
West Coast Summer Nights (1) *64*

CARGILL, Henson   '68

Born on 2/5/41 in Oklahoma City. Country singer.

DEBUT	PEAK	WKS			ARTIST — Album Title			$	Label & Number
3/23/68	179	2			Skip A Rope			$20	Monument 18094

Black Jack County Chain
By The Time I Get To Phoenix
Distant Drums
Four Long Seasons
Green Green Grass Of Home
It's Over
Just As Much As Ever
Little Girls And Little Boys
Saginaw, Michigan
Skip A Rope *25*
Very Well Traveled Man

CARLIN, George   '72

Born on 5/12/37 in the Bronx, New York. Comedian/actor. Appeared in several movies. Starred in own TV series.

DEBUT	PEAK	WKS		CD	ARTIST — Album Title		Sym	$	Label & Number
2/19/72	13	35	●	©	1 FM & AM		[C]	$15	Little David 7214
10/14/72	22	35	●	©	2 Class Clown		[C]	$15	Little David 1004
11/10/73	35	21	●	©	3 Occupation: Foole		[C]	$15	Little David 1005
12/7/74+	19	17	●	©	4 Toledo Window Box		[C]	$15	Little David 3003
11/8/75+	34	15		©	5 An Evening With Wally Londo Featuring Bill Slaszo		[C]	$15	Little David 1008
5/21/77	90	9		©	6 On The Road		[C]	$15	Little David 1075
1/6/79	112	8			7 Indecent Exposure (some of the best of George Carlin)		[C-K]	$15	Little David 1076
12/19/81+	145	13			8 A Place For My Stuff!		[C]	$10	Atlantic 19326
8/4/84	136	11		©	9 Carlin On Campus		[C]	$10	Eardrum 1001

Abortion (8)
Asshole, Jackoff, Scumbag (8)
Baseball - Football (5,9)
Birth Control (1)
Black Consciousness (3)
Bodily Functions (5,7)
Breakfast Wine And Who's Boss (7)
Cars And Driving (9)
Childhood Cliches (3)
Class Clown (2)
Confessional, The (2,7)
Cute Little Farts (3,7)
Death And Dying (4)
Divorce Game (1)
Drugs (1)
Ed Sullivan Self Taught (1)
11 O'Clock News (1)
Few More Farts (4)
Filthy Words (3,7)
First Leftfielders (9)
Flesh Colored Band-Aids (5)
For Names' Sake (9)
Fourth Leftfielders (9)
Fussy Eater (Part 1 & 2) (8)
Gay Lib (4)
God (4)
Good Sports (5)
Goofy Shit (4)
Grass Swept The Neighborhood (3)
Hair Piece (1)
Hallway Groups (3)
Have A Nice Day (medley) (8)
Head Lines (6)
Heavy Mysteries (2)
High On The Plane (5)
How's Your Dog? (6)
I Used To Be Irish Catholic (2)
Ice Box Man (8)
Incomplete List Of Impolite Words (2)
Interview With Jesus (8)
Join The Book Club (8)
Kids Are Too Small (9)
Let's Make A Deal (1)
Mental Hot Foots (5)
Metric System (4)
Moment Of Silence (9)
Muhammad Ali - America The Beautiful (2)
New News (5)
New York Voices (3)
Nursery Rhymes (4)
Occupation: Foole (3)
On The Road (6)
Parents' Cliches And Children's Secret Answers (6)
Place For My Stuff (8)
Prayer, The (9)
Radio Dial (1)
Raisin Rhetoric (3)
Religious Lift (5)
Rice Krispies (medley) (8)
Rules, Rules, Rules! (6)
Second Leftfielders (9)
Seven Words You Can Never Say On Television (2,7)
Sex In Commercials (1,7)
Shoot (1)
Snot, The Original Rubber Cement (4)
Some Werds (4)
Son Of Wino (1)
Special Dispensation - Heaven, Hell, Purgatory And Limbo (2)
Supermarkets (6)
Teenage Masturbation (5,7)
Third Leftfielders (9)
Toledo Window Box (4)
Unrelated Things (5)
Urinals Are 50 Percent Universal (4,7)
Values (How Much Is That Dog Crap In The Window) (2)
Wasted Time - Sharing A Swallow (2)
Water Sez (4)
Welcome To My Job (3)
White Harlem (3)
Words We Leave Behind (6)
Wurds (5)
Y'Ever (5)

CARLISLE, Belinda '88

Born on 8/17/58 in Hollywood. Lead singer of the **Go-Go's**. Married Morgan Mason (son of actor James Mason) in 1986.

6/7/86	13	34	●	©	1 Belinda			$10	I.R.S. 5741
10/24/87+	13	51	▲	©	2 Heaven On Earth			$10	MCA 42080
10/21/89	37	25	●	©	3 Runaway Horses			$10	MCA 6339

Band Of Gold (1)
Circle In The Sand (2) 7
Deep Deep Ocean (3)
Fool For Love (2)
From The Heart (1)
Gotta Get To You (1)

Heaven Is A Place On Earth (2) 1
I Feel Free (2) 88
I Feel The Magic (1) 82
I Get Weak (2) 2
I Need A Disguise (1)

I Never Wanted A Rich Man (1)
La Luna (3)
Leave A Light On (3) 11
Love Never Dies... (2)
Mad About You (1) 3
Nobody Owns Me (2)

Runaway Horses (3)
Shades Of Michaelangelo (3)
Shot In The Dark (1)
Should I Let You In? (2)
Since You've Gone (1)
Stuff And Nonsense (1)

Summer Rain (3) 30
Valentine (3)
Vision Of You (3)
We Can Change (2)
(We Want) The Same Thing (3)
Whatever It Takes (3)

World Without You (2)

CARLISLE, Bob '97

Born on 9/29/56 in Santa Anna, California. Singer/songwriter/guitarist.

| 5/10/97 | ❶² | 39 | ▲² | © | 1 Butterfly Kisses (Shades Of Grace) | C:#14/1 | | $10 | Jive 41613 |
| 10/17/98 | 191 | 2 | | © | 2 Stories From The Heart | | | $10 | Benson 2312 |

All Of Me (2)
Butterfly Kisses (1)
Father's Love (2)
I Will Shelter You (2)

I'm Gonna Be Ready (1)
In The Hands Of Jesus (2)
International (1)
It Is Well With My Soul (1)

Lately (Dreamin' About Babies)
(2)
Living Water (1)
Man Of His Word (1)

Mighty Love (1)
My Desire (2)
On My Knees (1)
On My Way To Paradise (2)

One Man Revival (1)
Power Of Love (2)
Somewhere (2)
True Believer (2)

We Fall Down (2)
You Must Have Been An Angel
(1)

CARLOS, Walter '69

Born on 11/14/39 in Pawtucket, Rhode Island. Classical musician who performs on the Moog Synthesizer. Had a sex change and known as Wendy Carlos by 1982.

1/18/69	10	56	●		1 Switched-On Bach		[I]	$15	Columbia 7194
1/3/70	199	2		©	2 The Well-Tempered Synthesizer		[I]	$15	Columbia 7286
7/8/72	146	9		©	3 Walter Carlos' Clockwork Orange		[I]	$15	Columbia 31480
7/8/72	168	7		©	4 Sonic Seasonings		[I]	$20	Columbia 31234 [2]

Air For The G String (1)
Brandenburg Concerto No. 3 In
G Major (1)
Brandenburg Concerto No. 4 In
G Major, BWV 1049 (2)
Chorale Prelude "Wachet Auf"
(1)
Clockwork Orange, March From
A (3)

Clockwork Orange, Theme
From A (3)
Clockwork Orange, Title Music
From A (3)
Country Lane (3)
Domine Ad Adjuvandum (2)
Fall (4)
Jesu, Joy Of Man's Desiring (1)

La Gazza Ladra (The Thieving
Magpie), Abridged (3)
Ninth Symphony: Second
Movement (Scherzo) (3)
Orfeo Suite (2)
Prelude And Fugue No. 7 In
E-Flat Major (1)
Prelude And Fugue No. 2 In C
Minor (1)

Sinfonia To Cantata No. 29 (1)
Sonata In D Major, L. 164 (2)
Sonata In D Major, L. 465 (2)
Sonata In E Major, L. 430 (2)
Sonata In G Major, L. 209 (2)
Spring (4)
Summer (4)
Timesteps (3)

Two-Part Invention In B-Flat
Major (1)
Two-Part Invention In D Minor
(1)
Two-Part Invention In F Major
(1)
Water Music (2)
William Tell Overture, Abridged
(3)

Winter (4)

CARLTON, Carl '81

Born in 1952 in Detroit. R&B singer/songwriter.

1/18/75	132	7			1 Everlasting Love			$15	ABC 857
8/8/81	34	19			2 Carl Carlton			$12	20th Century 628
10/23/82	133	7			3 The Bad C.C.			$10	RCA Victor 4425

Baby, I Need Your Loving (3)
Dance With You (3)
Don't You Wanna Make Love
(2)
Everlasting Love (1) 6
Everyone Can Be A Star (3)

Fighting In The Name Of Love
(2)
Fooled Myself Again (3)
Groovin' (3)
Hurt So Bad (1)

I Think It's Gonna Be Alright (2)
I Wanna Be Your Main
Squeeze (1)
I've Got That Boogie Fever (3)
Just One Kiss (3)
La La Song (1)

Let Me Love You 'Til The
Morning Comes (2)
Lonely Teardrops (1)
Morning, Noon And Nightime
(1)
Our Day Will Come (1)

Sexy Lady (2)
She's A Bad Mama Jama
(She's Built, She's Stacked)
(2) 22
Signed, Sealed And Delivered
(1)

Smokin' Room (1) 91
Swing That Sexy Thang (3)
This Feeling's Rated X-Tra (2)
Under The Boardwalk (3)

CARLTON, Larry '82

Born on 3/2/48 in Torrance, California. Top session guitarist. Joined **Fourplay** in 1997.

8/26/78	174	10		©	1 Larry Carlton		[I]	$12	Warner 3221
9/6/80	138	8		©	2 Strikes Twice		[I]	$12	Warner 3380
1/30/82	99	16		©	3 Sleepwalk		[I]	$12	Warner 3635
6/18/83	126	11		©	4 Friends		[I]	$12	Warner 23834
6/28/86	141	11		©	5 Alone/But Never Alone		[I]	$10	MCA 5689
8/1/87	180	6		©	6 Discovery		[I]	$10	MCA 42003
6/10/89	126	8		©	7 On Solid Ground		[I]	$10	MCA 6237
6/30/90	156	5		©	8 Collection		[I-K]	$10	GRP 9611

Ain't Nothin' For A Heartache
(2)
All In Good Time (7)
Alone/But Never Alone (5)
Blues Bird (3)
Blues For T.J. (4,8)
Breaking Ground (4)
Bubble Shuffle (7,8)
Carrying You (5)
Chapter II (7)
Cruisin' (4)

Discovery (6)
Don't Give It Up (1)
For Heaven's Sake (8)
For Love Alone (2)
Frenchman's Flat (3)
Friends (4)
Hello Tomorrow (6,8)
Her Favorite Song (6)
High Steppin' (5,8)
Honey Samba (7)
I Apologize (1)

In My Blood (2)
(It Was) Only Yesterday (1)
Josie (7)
Knock On Wood (6)
L.A., N.Y. (4)
Last Nite (3)
Layla (7)
Lord's Prayer (5)
Magician, The (2)
March Of The Jazz Angels (6)
Midnight Parade (2)

Minute By Minute (6,8)
Mulberry Street (2)
My Home Away From Home (6)
Nite Crawler (1,8)
On Solid Ground (7)
Perfect Peace (5)
Philosopher, The (7)
Place For Skipper (6)
Point It Up (1)
Pure Delight (5)
Rio Samba (1)

Room 335 (1)
Sea Space (7)
Sleepwalk (3,8) 74
Small Town Girl (8)
Smiles And Smiles To Go (5,8)
Song For Katie (3)
Song In The 5th Grade (4)
South Town (4)
Springville (2)
Strikes Twice (2)
10:00 P.M. (3,8)

Tequila (4,8)
Those Eyes (6)
Upper Kern (3)
Waffer, The (7)
Whatever Happens (5)
Where Did You Come From (1)
You Gotta Get It While You Can
(3)

CARMAN '95

Born Carman Licciardello on 1/19/56 in Trenton, New Jersey. Male Christian singer.

11/18/95	45	8	●	©	1 R.I.O.T. (Righteous Invasion Of Truth)			$10	Sparrow 1422
4/19/97	102	12	●	©	2 I Surrender All - 30 Classic Hymns			$10	Sparrow 51565
2/14/98	94	8		©	3 Mission 3:16			$10	Sparrow 51640
4/10/99	179	4		©	4 Passion For Praise Volume One			$10	Sparrow 51704
11/11/00	53	7		©	5 Heart Of A Champion: A Collection Of 30 Hits		[K]	$15	Sparrow 51766 [2]

Addicted To Jesus (5)
All In Life (3)
Alleluia (4)
Amazing Grace (medley) (2)
Amen (1)
America Again (5)
Are You Washed In The Blood
(medley) (2)
Awesome God (4)

Bless The Name Of Jesus (4)
Champion, The (5)
Courtroom, The (3)
Do I (5)
Faith Enough (5)
Give Thanks (4)
God Is Exalted (1)
Grace Greater Than Our Sin
(medley) (2)

Great God (5)
He Keeps Me Singing (medley)
(2)
He Took My Sins Away
(medley) (2)
Heart Of A Champion (5)
His Name Is Wonderful (4)
Holdin' On (5)
Hosanna (medley) (2)

Hunger For Holiness (5)
I Feel Jesus (4,5)
I Love Jesus (medley) (4)
I Love To Tell The Story
(medley) (2)
I Promise (5)
I Surrender All (medley) (2)
I'm So Glad Jesus Lifted Me
(medley) (2)

I've Been Delivered (5)
I've Been Redeemed (medley)
(4)
Isn't He Wonderful (medley) (2)
Jericho: The Shout Of Victory
(5)
Jesus Is The Lamb (3)
Jesus Is The Light (4)

Jesus Is The Sweetest Name I
Know (medley) (2)
Jesus, Keep Me Near The
Cross (2)
Jesus Paid It All (2)
Jesus Period (5)
Just Like He Said (5)
Kingdom Suite (3)

CARMAN — Cont'd

Leaning On The Everlasting Arms (2)
Legendary Mission (3,5)
Let The Fire Fall (4,5)
Lord, I Lift Your Name On High (4)
Mission 3:16 (3,5)
Missione D'Italiano (3)
My Jesus, I Love Thee (medley) (2)

My Story (1,5)
Never Be (3)
New Name In Glory (medley) (2)
No Monsters (1,5)
Not 4 Sale (1)
Nothing But The Blood (medley) (2)
Now's The Time (4,5)
Oh, How I Love Jesus (medley) (2)

Oh, The Blood Of Jesus (medley) (2)
Old Rugged Cross (medley) (2)
Peace Like A River (medley) (2)
People Of God (3)
Praise Him (When The Sun Goes Down) (2)
Prayer (5)
Prayer Anthem (3,4,5)
R.I.O.T. (Righteous Invasion Of Truth) (1,5)

River, The (5)
Satan, Bite The Dust! (5)
Search Me, Oh God (medley) (2)
7 Ways 2 Praise (1)
Shout To The Lord (4)
Since Jesus Came Into My Heart (medley) (2)
Slam (3)
Step Of Faith (1,5)
Sunday School Rock (5)

Surf Mission (3)
Tell Me The Story Of Jesus (medley) (2)
There Is A God (1,5)
'Tis So Sweet To Trust In Jesus (2)
We Are Not Ashamed (3)
What A Friend We Have In Jesus (medley) (2)
When The Roll Is Called Up Yonder (medley) (2)

When The Saints Go Marching In (medley) (2)
When We All Get To Heaven (medley) (2)
Whiter Than Snow (1)
Who's In The House (3)
Witch's Invitation (5)

CARMEN, Eric   '76
Born on 8/11/49 in Cleveland. Singer/songwriter/pianist. Lead singer of the **Raspberries** from 1970-74.

DEBUT	PEAK	WKS	RIAA	CD		ARTIST — Album Title	$	Label & Number
11/15/75+	21	51	●	©	1	Eric Carmen	$12	Arista 4057
9/10/77	45	13			2	Boats Against The Current	$12	Arista 4124
10/28/78	137	12			3	Change Of Heart	$12	Arista 4184
6/28/80	160	5			4	Tonight You're Mine	$12	Arista 9513
2/9/85	128	10		©	5	Eric Carmen	$10	Geffen 24042
6/11/88	59	20		©	6	The Best Of Eric Carmen	[G] $10	Arista 8547

All By Myself (1,6) 2
All For Love (4)
American As Apple Pie (5)
Baby, I Need Your Lovin' (3) 62
Boats Against The Current (2,6) 88
Change Of Heart (3,6) 19
Come Back To My Love (5)

Desperate Fools (3)
End Of The World (3)
Everything (1)
Foolin' Myself (4)
Great Expectations (1)
Haven't We Come A Long Way (3)
Heaven Can Wait (3)
Hey Deanie (3,6)

Hungry Eyes (6) 4
I Think I Found Myself (2)
I Wanna Hear It From Your Lips (5) 35
I'm Through With Love (5) 87
Inside Story (4)
It Hurts Too Much (4,6) 75
Last Night (1)
Living Without Your Love (5)

Lost In The Shuffle (4)
Love Is All That Matters (2)
Marathon Man (2)
Maybe My Baby (5)
My Girl (1)
Never Gonna Fall In Love Again (1,6) 11
No Hard Feelings (1,6)
Nowhere To Hide (2)

On Broadway (1)
Runaway (2)
She Did It (2,6) 23
She Remembered (4)
Sleep With Me (4)
Someday (3)
Spotlight (5)
Sunrise (1) 34
Take It Or Leave It (2)

That's Rock & Roll (1,6)
Tonight You're Mine (4)
Way We Used To Be (5)
You Need Some Lovin' (4)
You Took Me All The Way (5)

CARN, Jean   '77
Born Sarah Jean Perkins in Columbus, Georgia. R&B singer.

DEBUT	PEAK	WKS			ARTIST — Album Title	$	Label & Number
2/19/77	122	10		1	Jean Carn	$12	Philadelphia Int'l. 34394
8/15/81	176	3		2	Sweet And Wonderful	$12	TSOP 36775
9/6/86	162	6		3	Closer Than Close	$10	Omni 90492

JEAN CARNE

Anything For Money (3)
Bet Your Lucky Star (2)
Break Up To Make Up (3)
Candy Love (3)
Closer Than Close (3)
Don't Say No (To Love) (2)

Don't You Know Love When You See It (1)
Everything Must Change (3)
Flame Of Love (3)
Free Love (3)
I Just Thought Of A Way (2)

I'm In Love Once Again (1)
If You Wanna Go Back (1)
It Must Be Love (3)
Love Don't Love Nobody (2)
Love (Makes Me Do Foolish Things) (2)

Lucky Charm (3)
Mystic Stranger (2)
No Laughing Matter (1)
Sexy Eyes (3)
Sweet And Wonderful (2)
Time Waits For No One (1)

We Got Some Catchin' Up To Do (2)
Where Did You Ever Go (1)
You Are All I Need (1)
You Got A Problem (1)

CARNES, Kim   '81
Born on 7/20/45 in Los Angeles. Singer/songwriter/pianist. Member of **The New Christy Minstrels** with husband/co-writer Dave Ellingson.

DEBUT	PEAK	WKS	RIAA	CD		ARTIST — Album Title	$	Label & Number
7/5/80	57	17			1	Romance Dance	$10	EMI America 17030
5/2/81	❶⁴	52	▲	©	2	Mistaken Identity	$10	EMI America 17052
9/25/82	49	22		©	3	Voyeur	$10	EMI America 17078
11/19/83	97	16		©	4	Cafe Racers	$10	EMI America 17106
6/29/85	48	14			5	Barking At Airplanes	$10	EMI America 17159
6/14/86	116	7			6	Light House	$10	EMI America 17198

Abadabadango (5) 67
Along With The Radio (6)
And Still Be Loving You (1)
Arrangement, The (3)
Begging For Favors (Learning How Things Work) (5)
Bette Davis Eyes (2) 1
Black And White (6)
Bon Voyage (6)
Break The Rules Tonight (Out Of School) (2)
Breakin' Away From Sanity (3)
Changin' (1)

Crazy In The Night (Barking At Airplanes) (5) 15
Cry Like A Baby (1) 44
Dancin' At The Lighthouse (6)
Divided Hearts (6) 79
Does It Make You Remember (3) 36
Don't Call It Love (2)
Don't Pick Up The Phone (Pick Up The Phone) (5)
Draw Of The Cards (2) 28

Hangin' On By A Thread (A Sad Affair Of The Heart) (4)
He Makes The Sun Rise (Orpheus) (5)
Hit And Run (2)
Hurricane (4)
I Pretend (4) 74
I'd Lie To You For Your Love (6)
I'll Be Here Where The Heart Is (4)
In The Chill Of The Night (1)
Invisible Hands (4) 40

Kick In The Heart (4)
Looker (3)
Love Me Like You Never Did Before (4)
Merc Man (3)
Met You At The Wrong Time Of My Life (4)
Miss You Tonite (2)
Mistaken Identity (2) 60
More Love (1) 10
My Old Pals (2)
Oliver (Voice On The Radio) (5)

One Kiss (4)
Only Lonely Love (6)
Piece Of The Sky (6)
Rough Edges (6)
Say You Don't Know Me (3)
Still Hold On (2)
Swept Me Off My Feet (The Part Of The Fool) (1)
Take It On The Chin (3)
Tear Me Apart (1)
That's Where The Trouble Lies (6)
Thrill Of The Grill (1)

Touch And Go (5)
Undertow (3)
Universal Song (4)
Voyeur (3) 29
When I'm Away From You (2)
Where Is Your Heart (1)
Will You Remember Me (1)
You Make My Heart Beat Faster (And That's All That Matters) (4) 54
You Say You Love Me (But I Know You Don't) (6)
Young Love (4)

CARNIVAL, The   '69
Pop vocal group from Los Angeles.

DEBUT	PEAK	WKS			ARTIST — Album Title	$	Label & Number
12/6/69	191	2			The Carnival	$15	World Pacific 21894

Canto De Carnival
Famous Myth
Hope

Laia Ladaia
Love So Fine
Reach Out For Me

Son Of A Preacher Man
Sweets For My Sweet
Take Me For A Little While

Turn, Turn, Turn (To Everything There Is A Season)
Walk On By

Word, The

CARPENTER, Mary-Chapin   '94
Born on 2/21/58 in Princeton, New Jersey. Country singer/songwriter/guitarist.

DEBUT	PEAK	WKS	RIAA	CD		ARTIST — Album Title	$	Label & Number
12/9/89+	183	10	●	©	1	State Of The Heart	$10	Columbia 44228
11/3/90+	70	52	▲	©	2	Shooting Straight In The Dark	$10	Columbia 46077
7/18/92	31	134	▲³	©	3	Come On Come On	$10	Columbia 48881
10/22/94	10	40	▲²	©	4	Stones In The Road	$10	Columbia 64327
11/9/96	20	19	●	©	5	A Place In The World	$10	Columbia 67501
6/12/99	43	17	●	©	6	Party Doll And Other Favorites	[K] $10	Columbia 68751
6/16/01	52	10		©	7	Time*Sex*Love*	$10	Columbia 85176

Almost Home (6) 85
Alone But Not Lonely (7)
Better To Dream Of You (5)
Bug, The (3)
Can't Take Love For Granted (2,6)

Come On Come On (3)
Down At The Twist And Shout (2,6)
Down In Mary's Land (1)
Dreaming Road (7)
Dreamland (6)

End Of My Pirate Days (4)
Going Out Tonight (2)
Goodbye Again (1)
Grow Old With Me (2)
Halley Came To Jackson (3)
Hard Way (3,6)

e Thinks He'll Keep Her (3,6)
Hero In Your Own Hometown (5)
House Of Cards (4)
How Do (1)
I Am A Town (3)

I Can See It Now (5)
I Feel Lucky (3,6)
I Take My Chances (3,6)
I Want To Be Your Girlfriend (5)
Ideas Are Like Stars (5)

CARPENTER, Mary-Chapin — Cont'd

In The Name Of Love (7)
It Don't Bring You (1)
John Doe No. 24 (4)
Jubilee (4)
Keeper For Every Flame (4)
Keeping The Faith (5)
King Of Love (4)
Last Word (4)
Late For Your Life (7)

Let Me Into Your Heart (5)
Long Way Home (7)
Maybe World (7)
Middle Ground (2)
Moon And St. Christopher (2)
More Things Change (2)
Naked To The Eye (5)
Never Had It So Good (1)
Not Too Much To Ask (3)

Only A Dream (3)
Outside Looking In (4)
Party Doll (6)
Place In The World (5)
Quittin' Time (1,6)
Read My Lips (1)
Rhythm Of The Blues (3)
Right Now (2)

Shut Up And Kiss Me (4,6) *90*
Simple Life (7)
Slave To The Beauty (7)
Slow Country Dance (1)
Someone Else's Prayer (7)
Something Of A Dreamer (1)
Stones In The Road (4,6)
Sudden Gift Of Fate (5)
Swept Away (7)

10,000 Miles (6)
Tender When I Want To Be (4)
That's Real (5)
This Is Love (4)
This Is Me Leaving You (7)
This Shirt (1,6)
Too Tired (1)
Walking Through Fire (3)
What If We Went To Italy (5)

What Was It Like (7)
What You Didn't Say (2)
When She's Gone (2)
Whenever You're Ready (7)
Where Time Stands Still (4)
Wherever You Are (6)
Why Walk When You Can Fly (4)
You Win Again (2)

CARPENTERS ★188★   '71

Brother-sister duo originally from New Haven, Connecticut: Richard (b: 10/15/46) and Karen Carpenter (b: 3/2/50; d: 2/4/83 of heart failure due to anorexia nervosa, age 32). To Downey, California, in 1963. Richard played piano from age nine. Karen played drums in group with Richard and bass player Wes Jacobs in 1965. The trio recorded for RCA in 1966. After a period with the band Spectrum, the Carpenters recorded as a duo for A&M in 1969. Won the 1970 Best New Artist Grammy Award.

1)The Singles 1969-1973 2)Carpenters 3)Close To You

DEBUT	PEAK	WKS	RIAA	CD		ARTIST — Album Title		Sym	$	Label & Number
9/19/70	2¹	87	▲²	©	1	**Close To You**			$15	A&M 4271
3/6/71	150	16		©	2	**Ticket To Ride**............................			$15	A&M 4205
						first released in 1969 as Offering ($80)				
6/5/71	2²	59	▲⁴	©	3	**Carpenters**			$15	A&M 3502
7/8/72	4	41	▲³	©	4	**A Song For You**			$15	A&M 3511
6/2/73	2¹	41	▲²	©	5	**Now & Then**			$15	A&M 3519
12/1/73+	❶¹	49	▲⁷	©	6	**The Singles 1969-1973**	C:#48/1 [G]		$15	A&M 3601
6/28/75	13	18	▲	©	7	**Horizon**			$12	A&M 4530
7/10/76	33	16	●	©	8	**A Kind Of Hush**..........................			$12	A&M 4581
10/22/77	49	18		©	9	**Passage**			$12	A&M 4703
12/9/78+	145	7	●	©	10	**Christmas Portrait**	[X]		$12	A&M 4726
						also released on A&M 3210; Christmas charts: 5/'83, 2/'84, 7/'85, 7/'87, 7/'88, 8/'89				
7/4/81	52	15		©	11	**Made In America**			$12	A&M 3723
11/19/83+	46	19	●	©	12	**Voice Of The Heart**			$12	A&M 4954
1/5/85	190	1	●	©	13	**An Old-Fashioned Christmas**........	C:#46/1 [X]		$12	A&M 3270
						Christmas charts: 29/'87, 29/'88, 25/'90				
5/25/85	144	8	▲²		14	**Yesterday Once More**	[G]		$15	A&M 6601 [2]
12/22/90+	159	3		©	15	**Christmas Portrait - The Special Edition**.................	C:#5/50 [X-R]		$10	A&M 5173
						expanded edition of #10 above with new sequencing plus some substituted songs; Christmas charts: 8/'90, 5/'91, 10/'92, 18/'93, 20/'94, 21/'95, 24/'96, 19/'97, 40/'98, 36/'00				
4/18/98	106	25	●	©	16	**Love Songs**.............................	[G]		$10	A&M 540838

All I Can Do (2)
All Of My Life (2)
All You Get From Love Is A Love Song (9,14,16) *35*
Angels We Have Heard On High (medley) (13,15)
Another Song (1)
At The End Of A Song (12)
Aurora (7)
Ave Maria (10,15)
Away In A Manger (medley) (10)
B'wana She No Home (9)
Baby It's You (1)
Because We Are In Love (The Wedding Song) (11,14)
Beechwood 4-5789 (11) *74*
Bless The Beasts And Children (4,14) *67*
Boat To Sail (8)
Breaking Up Is Hard To Do (8)
Calling Occupants Of Interplanetary Craft (9,14) *32*
Can't Smile Without You (8)
Carol Of The Bells (10,15)
Christ Is Born (10,15)
Christmas Song (Chestnuts Roasting On An Open Fire) (10,15)
Christmas Waltz (10,15)
Crescent Noon (1)
Crystal Lullaby (4)
Da Doo Ron Ron (When He Walked Me Home) (medley) (5)
Deadman's Curve (medley) (5)
Deck The Hall (medley) (10)
Desperado (7)
Do You Hear What I Hear? (13)

Do You Know The Way To San Jose (medley) (3)
Don't Be Afraid (2)
Don't Cry For Me Argentina (medley) (9)
Druscilla Penny (3)
End Of The World (medley) (5)
Eve (2)
Eventide (7)
First Noel (medley) (13,15)
First Snowfall (medley) (10)
Flat Baroque (4)
For All We Know (3,6,14,16) *3*
Frosty The Snowman (medley) (13,15)
Fun, Fun, Fun (medley) (5)
Gesu Bambino (13,15)
Get Together (2)
God Rest Ye Merry Gentlemen (medley) (10)
Good King Wenceslas (medley) (13,15)
Goodbye To Love (4,6,14,16) *7*
Goofus (8) *56*
Happy (7)
Happy Holiday (medley) (13,15)
Have Yourself A Merry Little Christmas (10,15)
He Came Here For Me (13)
Heather (2)
Help (1)
Here Comes Santa Claus (medley) (13,15)
Home For The Holidays (13,15)
Hurting Each Other (4,6,14,16) *2*
I Believe You (11) *68*
I Can Dream Can't I (7)

I Can't Make Music (5)
I Have You (8)
I Heard The Bells On Christmas Day (13)
I Just Fall In Love Again (9,16)
I Kept On Loving You (1)
I Saw Mommy Kissing Santa Claus (medley) (13,15)
I Saw Three Ships (medley) (10)
I Won't Last A Day Without You (4,14,16) *11*
I'll Be Home For Christmas (10,15)
I'll Never Fall In Love Again (1,3)
(I'm Caught Between) Goodbye And I Love You (7)
In Dulce Jubilo (medley) (13,15)
It Came Upon A Midnight Clear (13,15)
It's Christmas Time (10,15)
It's Going To Take Some Time (4,6,14) *12*
Jambalaya (On The Bayou) (5)
Jingle Bells (10)
Johnny Angel (medley) (5)
Knowing When To Leave (medley) (3)
Let It Snow (medley) (10)
Let Me Be The One (3)
Little Altar Boy (13,15)
Little Jesus (medley) (13,15)
Look To Your Dreams (12)
Love Is Surrender (1)
Love Me For What I Am (7)
Make Believe It's Your First Time (12,14,16)

Make It Easy On Yourself (medley) (3)
Man Smart, Woman Smarter (9)
March Of The Toys (medley) (13,15)
Maybe It's You (1)
Merry Christmas Darling (10,15)
Mr. Guder (3)
My Favorite Things (13)
Night Has A Thousand Eyes (medley) (5)
Now (12)
Nowadays Clancy Can't Even Sing (2)
"Nutcracker" Medley (13,15)
O Come All Ye Faithful (Adeste Fideles) (medley) (10)
O Come, O Come Immanuel (10)
O Holy Night (13,15)
O Little Town Of Bethlehem (medley) (13,15)
Old-Fashioned Christmas (13,15)
On The Balcony Of The Casa Rosada (medley) (9)
One Fine Day (medley) (5)
One Love (3)
One More Time (8)
Only Yesterday (7,14,16) *4*
Ordinary Fool (12)
Our Day Will Come (medley) (5)
Piano Picker (4)
(Place To) Hideaway (3)
Please Mr. Postman (7,14) *1*
Prime Time Love (7)
Rainy Days And Mondays (3,6,14,16) *2*
Reason To Believe (1)

Road Ode (4)
Rudolph The Red-Nosed Reindeer (medley) (13,15)
Sailing On The Tide (12)
Sandy (8)
Santa Claus Is Comin' To Town (10,13,15)
Saturday (3)
Silent Night (10,15)
Silver Bells (medley) (10,15)
Sing (5,6,14) *3*
Sleep Well, Little Children (medley) (10)
Sleigh Ride (10,15)
Solitaire (7,16) *17*
Somebody's Been Lyin' (11)
Someday (7)
Sometimes (3)
Song For You (4,16)
Strength Of A Woman (11)
Superstar (3,6,14,16) *2*
Sweet, Sweet Smile (9,14) *44*
There's A Kind Of Hush (All Over The World) (8,14) *12*
(There's) Always Something There To Remind Me (medley) (3)
(They Long To Be) Close To You (1,6,14,16) *1*
This Masquerade (5,14,16)
Those Good Old Dreams (11,14) *63*
Ticket To Ride (2,6,14) *54*
Top Of The World (4,6,14,16) *1*
Touch Me When We're Dancing (11,14) *16*
Turn Away (2)
Two Lives (12)

Two Sides (9)
Walk On By (medley) (3)
(Want You) Back In My Life Again (11,14) *72*
We've Only Just Begun (1,6,14,16) *2*
What Are You Doing New Year's Eve? (13)
What Child Is This (medley) (10)
What's The Use (2)
When I Fall In Love (16)
When It's Gone (It's Just Gone) (11)
When You've Got What It Takes (11)
Where Do I Go From Here? (16)
White Christmas (medley) (10,15)
Winter Wonderland (medley) (10,15)
Yesterday Once More (5,6,14) *2*
You (8)
You're Enough (12)
You're The One (16)
Your Baby Doesn't Love You Anymore (12)
Your Wonderful Parade (2)

★460★ CARR, Vikki '68

Born Florencia Martinez Cardona on 7/19/41 in El Paso, Texas. Regular on TV's **Ray Anthony** Show.

1)It Must Be Him 2)For Once In My Life 3)Vikki Carr's Love Story

DEBUT	PEAK	WKS	CD	#	Album	Sym	$	Label & Number
7/18/64	114	4		1	Discovery!...		$20	Liberty 7354
10/21/67+	12	47	©	2	It Must Be Him		$15	Liberty 7533
3/23/68	63	16		3	Vikki!...		$15	Liberty 7548
3/29/69	29	34		4	For Once In My Life..............................	[L]	$15	Liberty 7604
					recorded at the Persian Room in New York City			
5/9/70	111	8		5	Nashville by Carr.................................		$15	Liberty 11001
7/10/71	60	14		6	Vikki Carr's Love Story		$12	Columbia 30662
1/8/72	118	4		7	Superstar		$12	Columbia 31040
6/24/72	146	12		8	The First Time Ever (I Saw Your Face)		$12	Columbia 31453
9/9/72	106	25		9	En Espanol	[F]	$12	Columbia 31470
6/23/73	142	7		10	Ms. America		$12	Columbia 32251
11/24/73	172	7		11	Live At The Greek Theatre......................	[L]	$15	Columbia 32656 [2]
9/28/74	155	5		12	One Hell Of A Woman		$12	Columbia 32860

Adoro (9)
After Today (medley) (4)
After You've Gone (medley) (4)
Afternoon Of A Faun (11)
Ahora Que Soy Libre (9)
Ain't No Mountain High Enough (6)
Ain't No Way To Treat A Lady (12)
Alfie (2)
Amanece (9)
Baby Don't Walk Out On Me (10)
Bit Of Love (2)
Bluesette (1)
Brian's Song (The Hands Of Time) (8)
By The Time I Get To Phoenix (3)
Cabaret (8)
Can't Take My Eyes Off You (2,4,11)
Carnival (Manha De Carnaval) (4)
Come Rain Or Come Shine (medley) (4)
Crazy Love (7)
Crying Time (medley) (5)
Daddy's Dream (11)
Danny's Song (10)
Days (4)
Don't Talk To Me (1)
El Triste (9)
Everybody's Talkin' (5)

Everything I Touch Turns To Tears (3)
First Time Ever (I Saw Your Face) (8)
For All We Know (6)
For Once In My Life (3,4)
Forget You (2)
Garland Medley (11)
Go (Vois) (3)
Godfather (Speak Softly Love), Love Theme From The (8)
Grande, Grande, Grande (9)
Gypsies, Tramps And Thieves (8)
Happy Together (4)
Have You Heard The News (11)
Haven't Got Time For The Pain (12)
Help Me Make It Through The Night (8)
Her Little Heart Went To Loveland (2)
Historia De Amor (Love Story) (9)
Hold My Hand (12)
How Can You Mend A Broken Heart? (7)
How Insensitive (Insensatez) (1)
Hurt (6)
I Believe In The Sunshine (11)
I Can't Give Back The Love I Feel For You (7)
I Can't Stop Loving You (11)

I Cry Alone (1)
I Keep It Hid (6)
I Wonder Who's Kissing Her Now (11)
I Would Be Your Friend (10)
I'd Do It All Again (7)
I'll Be Home (6) *96*
I'll Have To Say I Love You In A Song (12)
I'm Gonna Love You (7)
I've Never Been A Woman Before (6)
If I Were Your Woman (6)
If You Could Read My Mind (4)
It Must Be Him (2,4,11) *3*
Killing Me Softly With His Song (10)
La Nave Del Olvido (9)
(Last Night) I Didn't Get To Sleep At All (8)
Last Song (10)
Lazy Day (10)
Lean On Me (11)
Leave A Little Room (11)
Lesson, The (3) *34*
Let Me Be The One (12)
Living On A Prayer, A Hope And A Hand-Me-Down (5)
Look Again (Theme From Irma La Douce) (2)
Love Song (11)
Loving Him Was Easier (Than Anything I'll Ever Do Again) (7)

Make It Rain (5)
Million Years Or So (2)
Ms. America (10)
Need To Be (12)
Neither One Of Us (Wants To Be The First To Say Goodbye) (10)
Never My Love (9)
Never Will I Marry (1)
Night They Drove Old Dixie Down (7)
No Sun Today (3)
One Hell Of A Woman (12)
One Less Bell To Answer (6)
One More Mountain (2)
Other Man's Grass Is Always Greener (4)
Overcrowded Dreams (11)
Pero Te Extrano (9)
Poor Butterfly (medley) (1)
Portrait (7)
Put Your Arms Around Me (3)
Raindrops Keep Fallin' On My Head (5)
Real Me (3)
Rescue Me (10)
Se Acabo (9)
Should I Follow (1)
Singing My Song (5)
Six Weeks Every Summer (Christmas Every Other Year) (6)
Sleeping Between Two People (12)

So Far Away (7)
So In Love (1)
So Much In Love With You (2)
Soap Opera (11)
Some Of These Days (medley) (4)
Somebody Loves You (10)
Somos Novios (It's Impossible) (9)
Song For You (11)
Song Sung Blue (8)
Spanish Harlem (7)
Spanish Medley (11)
Stay (medley) (1)
Summer Of '42 (The Summer Knows), Theme From (8)
Sunday Mornin' Comin' Down (5)
Sunshine On My Shoulders (12)
Superstar (7)
Surrey With The Fringe On Top (1)
That's The Way We Fall In Love (12)
There I Go (Se Pe Te C' E' Soltanto Qull' Uomo) (3)
This Girl Is Gonna Cry (10)
This Girl's In Love With You (medley) (4)
This Is The House That Jack Built (3)
Tip Of My Fingers (5)
Today I Started Loving You Again (medley) (5)

Tomorrow Is My Friend (5)
Tunesmith (2)
Until It's Time For You To Go (5)
Watch What Happens (3)
Way Of Love (8)
We Didn't Know The Time Of Day (10)
What Are You Afraid Of? (1)
Where Are You (1)
(Where Do I Begin) Love Story (6)
Wind Me Up (12)
With Pen In Hand (4,11) *35*
Without You (8)
Y Volvere (9)
Yesterday I Heard The Rain (Esta Tarde Vi Llover) (4)
Yesterday, When I Was Young (Heir Encore) (5)
You Are (5)
You Are The Sunshine Of My Life (11)

CARRACK, Paul '88

Born on 4/22/51 in Sheffield, England. Lead singer of **Ace**, **Squeeze** and **Mike + The Mechanics**.

DEBUT	PEAK	WKS	CD	#	Album	$	Label & Number
9/11/82	78	14	©	1	Suburban Voodoo	$12	Epic 38161
11/21/87+	67	31	©	2	One Good Reason	$10	Chrysalis 41578
11/11/89	120	18	©	3	Groove Approved...	$10	Chrysalis 21709

After The Love Is Gone (3)
Always Better With You (1)
Bad News (At The Best Of Times) (3)
Battlefield (3)
Button Off My Shirt (2) *91*

Call Me Tonight (1)
Collrane (2)
Dedicated (3)
(Do I Figure) In Your Life (2)
Don't Give My Heart A Break (1)

Don't Shed A Tear (2) *9*
Double It Up (2)
Fire With Fire (2)
From Now On (1)
Give Me A Chance (2)
Here I Am (2)

I Found Love (1)
I Live By The Groove (3) *31*
I Need You (1) *37*
I'm In Love (1)
I'm On Your Tail (3)
Lesson In Love (1)

Little Unkind (1)
Love Can Break Your Heart (3)
Loveless (3)
One Good Reason (2) *28*
Only My Heart Can Tell (3)
Out Of Touch (1)

So Right, So Wrong (1)
Tip Of My Tongue (3)
What A Way To Go (1)
When You Walk In The Room (2) *90*

CARRADINE, Keith '76

Born on 8/8/49 in San Mateo, California. Singer/guitarist/actor. Son of actor John Carradine. Half-brother of actor David Carradine. Acted in several movies.

DEBUT	PEAK	WKS	#	Album	$	Label & Number
6/26/76	61	17	1	I'm Easy	$12	Asylum 1066
						Spellbound

Been Gone So Long
High Sierra

Honey Won't You Let Me Be Your Friend

I Will Never Forget Your Face
I'll Be There

I'm Easy *17*
It's Been So Long

Raining In The City
Soul Is Strong

CARRERAS, José '94

Born on 12/5/46 in Barcelona, Spain. Operatic tenor. Member of **The Three Tenors**.

DEBUT	PEAK	WKS	CD	#	Album	Sym	$	Label & Number
12/18/93	154	3	©	1	Christmas In Vienna	[X-L]	$10	Sony Classical 53358
					PLACIDO DOMINGO-DIANA ROSS-JOSÉ CARRERAS			
					recorded on 12/23/92 at the Rathaus in Vienna			
12/21/96	196	2	©	2	A Celebration Of Christmas....................................	[X-L]	$10	Elektra 62000
					JOSÉ CARRERAS-NATALIE COLE-PLÁCIDO DOMINGO			
					recorded on 12/23/95 at the Austria Center in Vienna			

Adeste Fideles (1)
Amazing Grace (2)
Ave Maria (1)
¡Ay! Para Navidad (2)
Cantique De Noël (2)
Carol Of The Drum (1)
Holly And The Ivy (2)

I Walked Today Where Jesus Walked (2)
I'll Be Home For Christmas (2)
Jingle Bells (1)
Joy To The World (medley) (1)
La Virgen Lava Panales (medley) (1)

Lord's Prayer (2)
May Each Day (2)
Mille Cherubini In Coro (1)
Minuit, Chretien (medley) (1)
Navidad (1,2)
O Little Town Of Bethlehem (medley) (1)

O Tannenbaum (medley) (1)
Oh, Du Fröhliche (2)
Panis Angelicus (2)
Pero Mira Como Beben Los Peces En El Río (2)
Silent Night ..see: Stille Nacht
Sleigh Ride (2)

Stille Nacht (1,2)
Tu Scendi Dalle Stelle (medley) (1)
What A Wonderful World (2)
What Child Is This? (2)
White Christmas (2)

DEBUT	PEAK	WKS	RIAA	CD	ARTIST — Album Title	Catalog	Sym	$	Label & Number

CARRINGTON, Rodney　'00
Born in Longview, Texas. Country comedian.

| 9/2/00 | 153 | 3 | | © | Morning Wood ...... | | [C] | $10 | Capitol 24827 |

All About Sex / Fat Girls, Nebraska Farmers, / Great To Be A Man / Morning Wood / Play Your Cards Wrong / T**ties & Beer
Carlos / Japanese Restaurants / In Her Day / Older Women / Rodney's Wife & Kids,
Dozen Roses / Gay Factory Worker / More Of A Man / Pickup Truck / Marriage, Vacations

CARRINGTON, Terri Lyne　'89
Born in 1962 in Medford, Massachusetts. Female jazz drummer. Member of the house band on TV's *The Arsenio Hall Show* until June 1989.

| 4/29/89 | 169 | 7 | | © | Real Life Story ...... | | [I] | $10 | Forecast 837697 |

Blackbird / Message True / Obstacle Illusion / Real Life Story / Skeptic Alert
Human Revolution / More Than Woman / Pleasant Dreams / Shh

CARROLL, David, And His Orchestra　'60
Born Nook Schrier on 10/15/13 in Chicago. Arranger/conductor.

| 6/1/59 | 21 | 6 | | 1 | Let's Dance ...... | | | $20 | Mercury 60001 |
| 1/11/60 | 6 | 30 | | 2 | Let's Dance Again ...... | | | $20 | Mercury 60152 |

Adios (2) / Dancing Tambourine (1) / Glow-Worm, The (1) / My Sin (1) / Soft Shoe Song (The Dance My / Would You Like To Take A
Armen's Theme (1) / Dixie Dawn Patrol (1) / Hey Chick! (2) / Play A Simple Melody (2) / Darling Used To Do) (2) / Walk (2)
Bouncing Ball (2) / Doodlin' Drummer (2) / Irene (2) / Pretty Baby (2) / Swamp Fire (2) / Yearning (1)
Cha-Cha-Panecas (2) / Euphrates (1) / Let's Dance (1) / Puerto Rican Pedlar (1) / Trouble With Harry (1)
Cuddle Up A Little Closer (1) / Gliss To Remember (1) / Let's Dance Again (2) / Side Saddle (2)

CARROLL, Jim, Band　'81
Born on 8/1/50 in New York City. Poet/rock singer. His band included Brian Linsley and Terrell Winn (guitars), Steve Linsley (bass) and Wayne Woods (drums). The 1995 movie *The Basketball Diaries* was based on Carroll's autobiographical book.

| 11/15/80+ | 73 | 23 | © | 1 | Catholic Boy ...... | | | $12 | Atco 132 |
| 5/22/82 | 156 | 7 | | 2 | Dry Dreams ...... | | | $12 | Atco 145 |

Barricades (2) / Day And Night (1) / It's Too Late (1) / Nothing Is True (1) / Them (2)
Catholic Boy (1) / Dry Dreams (2) / Jealous Twin (2) / People Who Died (1) / Three Sisters (1)
City Drops Into The Night (1) / Evangeline (2) / Jody (2) / Rooms (2) / Wicked Gravity (1)
Crow (1) / I Want The Angel (1) / Lorraine (2) / Still Life (2) / Work Not Play (2)

★360★　CARS, The　'79
Pop-rock group from Boston: **Ric Ocasek** (vocals, guitar), **Benjamin Orr** (bass, vocals), **Elliot Easton** (guitar), Greg Hawkes (keyboards) and David Robinson (drums). Orr died of cancer on 10/3/2000 (age 53).

7/1/78+	18	139	▲6 ©	1	The Cars	C:#24/25		$12	Elektra 135
6/30/79	3	62	▲3 ©	2	Candy-O			$12	Elektra 507
9/6/80	5	28	▲	3	Panorama			$12	Elektra 514
11/28/81	9	41	▲ ©	4	Shake It Up			$12	Elektra 567
4/7/84	3	69	▲3	5	Heartbeat City			$10	Elektra 60296
11/23/85	12	39	▲3 ©	6	The Cars Greatest Hits		[G]	$10	Elektra 60464
9/12/87	26	23	● ©	7	Door To Door			$10	Elektra 60747

All Mixed Up (1) / Down Boys (3) / **Hello Again** (5) 20 / Lust For Kicks (2) / Since I Held You (2) / **Why Can't I Have You** (5) 33
Bye Bye Love (1) / Dream Away (4) / I Refuse (5) / **Magic** (5,6) 12 / **Since You're Gone** (4,6) 41 / Wound Up On You (7)
Candy-O (2) / **Drive** (5,6) 3 / I'm In Touch With Your World / Maybe Baby (4) / Stranger (5) / **You Are The Girl** (7) 17
Coming Up You (7) 74 / Everything You Say (7) / (1) / Misfit Kid (3) / **Strap Me In** (7) 85 / You Can't Hold On Too Long
Cruiser (4) / Fine Line (7) / **I'm Not The One** (4,6) 32 / Moving In Stereo (1) / Ta Ta Wayo Wayo (7) / (2)
Dangerous Type (2) / Getting Through (3) / **It's All I Can Do** (2) 41 / **My Best Friend's Girl** (1,6) 35 / Think It Over (4) / **You Might Think** (5,6) 7
Don't Cha Stop (1) / Gimme Some Slack (3) / It's Not The Night (5) / Nightspots (2) / This Could Be Love (4) / You Wear Those Eyes (3)
Don't Tell Me No (3) / Go Away (3) / **Just What I Needed** (1,6) 27 / Panorama (3) / **Tonight She Comes** (6) 7 / You're All I've Got Tonight (1)
Door To Door (7) / **Good Times Roll** (1,6) 41 / Leave Or Stay (7) / Running To You (3) / **Touch And Go** (3,6) 37
Double Life (2) / Got A Lot On My Head (2) / **Let's Go** (2,6) 14 / **Shake It Up** (4,6) 4 / Up And Down (3)
Double Trouble (1) / Heartbeat City (5) / Looking For Love (5) / Shoo Be Doo (2) / Victim Of Love (4)

CARSON, Jeff　'95
Born Jeff Herndon on 12/16/64 in Tulsa, Oklahoma; raised in Gravette, Arkansas. Country singer/songwriter/guitarist.

| 8/12/95 | 152 | 7 | | © | Jeff Carson ...... | | | $10 | MCG/Curb 77744 |

Betty's Takin' Judo / Definite Possibilities / Holdin' Onto Something / Me Too / Preachin' To The Choir / Yeah Buddy
Car, The / Get A Guitar / If I Ain't Got You / **Not On Your Love** 97 / That Last Mile

CARTER, Aaron　'01
Born on 12/7/87 in Tampa, Florida. Pop singer. Younger brother of Nick Carter of the **Backstreet Boys**.

| 10/14/00+ | 4 | 51↑ | ▲2 © | | Aaron's Party (Come Get It) ...... | | | $10 | Jive 41708 |

Aaron's Party (Come Get It) 35 / Bounce / Girl You Shine / Iko Iko / Real Good Time / **That's How I Beat Shaq** 96
Clapping Song / I Want Candy / My Internet Girl / Tell Me What You Want

CARTER, Betty — see CHARLES, Ray

CARTER, Carlene　'80
Born Rebecca Carlene Smith on 9/26/55 in Madison, Tennessee. Country singer/songwriter/guitarist. Daughter of country singers **June Carter** and Carl Smith. Married to **Nick Lowe** from 1979-90. Later married Howie Epstein of **Tom Petty & The Heartbreakers**.

| 10/4/80 | 139 | 6 | | © | 1 | Musical Shapes ...... | | | $12 | Warner 3465 |
| 8/28/93 | 196 | 1 | | © | 2 | Little Love Letters ...... | | | $10 | Giant 24499 |

Appalachian Eyes (1) / First Kiss (2) / I'm So Cool (1) / Rain, The (2) / Too Bad About Sandy (1)
Baby Ride Easy (1) / Foggy Mountain Top (1) / Little Love Letter #1 & 2 (2) / Ring Of Fire (1) / Too Proud (1)
Bandit Of Love (1) / Hallelujah In My Heart (2) / Long Hard Fall (2) / Sweet Meant To Be (2) / Unbreakable Heart (2)
Cry (1) / Heart Is Right (2) / Madness (2) / That Very First Kiss (2) / Wastin' Time With You (2)
Every Little Thing (2) / I Love You 'Cause I Want To (2) / Nowhere Train (2) / To Drunk (Too Remember) (1) / World Of Miracles (2)

CARTER, Clarence　'70
Born on 1/14/36 in Montgomery, Alabama. R&B singer/guitarist. Blind since age one. Married for a time to **Candi Staton**.

12/7/68	200	2		©	1	This Is Clarence Carter			$30	Atlantic 8192
4/5/69	169	4		©	2	The Dynamic Clarence Carter			$30	Atlantic 8199
8/16/69	138	3		©	3	Testifyin'			$30	Atlantic 8238

CARTER, Clarence — Cont'd

9/26/70	44	12	©	4	**Patches**			$25	Atlantic 8267
5/22/71	103	10		5	**The Best Of Clarence Carter**		[G]	$25	Atlantic 8282
2/28/81	189	3		6	**Let's Burn**			$15	Venture 1005

Another Night (6)
Back Door Santa (3)
Bad News (3)
C.C. Blues (4)
Changes (4)
Do What You Gotta Do (1)
Doin' Our Thing (3,5) *46*
Feeling Is Right (3,5) *65*
Funky Fever (1,5) *88*
Getting The Bills (But No Merchandise) (4)

Harper Valley P.T.A. (2)
I Can't Do Without You (3)
I Can't Leave Your Love Alone (4,5) *42*
I Can't See Myself (1)
I Smell A Rat (3,5)
I'd Rather Go Blind (2)
I'm Just A Prisoner (Of Your Good Lovin') (4)
I'm Qualified (2)
I'm So Tired (6)

If I Stay (6)
Instant Reaction (3)
It's All In Your Mind (4) *51*
Jimmy's Disco (6)
Just Searching (6)
Let It Be (4)
Let Me Comfort You (2)
Let's Burn (6)
Light My Fire (2)
Look What I Got (2)
Looking For A Fox (1) *62*

Love Building (6)
Making Love (At The Dark End Of The Street) (3,5)
Part Time Love (1)
Patches (4,5) *4*
Road Of Love (2)
Say Man (4)
Scratch My Back (6)
Set Me Free (1)
She Ain't Gonna Do Right (1)
She's Out To Get Me (6)

Slip Away (1,5) *6*
Slippin' Around (1)
Snatching It Back (3,5) *31*
Soul Deep (3)
Steal Away (2)
Take It Off Him And Put It On Me (5) *94*
That Old Time Feeling (2)
Think About It (2)
Thread The Needle (1) *98*
Till I Can't Take It Anymore (4)

Too Weak To Fight (2,5) *13*
Weekend Love (2)
Willie And Laura Mae Jones (4)
Wind It Up (1)
You Can't Miss What You Can't Measure (3,5)
You've Been A Long Time Comin' (2)
Your Love Lifted Me (4)

CARTER, Deana   '97
Born on 1/4/66 in Nashville. Country singer/songwriter.

9/28/96+	10	86	▲5 ©	1	**Did I Shave My Legs For This?**			$10	Capitol 37514
11/7/98	57	12	● ©	2	**Everything's Gonna Be Alright**			$10	Capitol 21142

Absence Of The Heart (2) *83*
Angels Working Overtime (2)
Before We Ever Heard Goodbye (1)
Brand New Key (2)

Colour Everywhere (2)
Count Me In (1)
Dickson County (2)
Did I Shave My Legs For This? (1) *85*

Everything's Gonna Be Alright (2)
How Do I Get There (1)
I've Loved Enough To Know (1)
If This Is Love (1)

Love Ain't Worth Making (1)
Make Up Your Mind (2)
Michelangelo Sky (2)
Never Comin' Down (2)
People Miss Planes (2)

Ruby Brown (2)
Strawberry Wine (1) *65*
That's How You Know It's Love (1)
To The Other Side (1)

Train Song (2)
We Danced Anyway (1) *72*
You Still Shake Me (2)

CARTER, June — see CASH, Johnny

CARTER, Mel   '65
Born on 4/22/39 in Cincinnati. R&B singer/actor. Acted on several TV shows in the 1970s.

9/18/65	62	12		1	**Hold Me, Thrill Me, Kiss Me**			$20	Imperial 12289
10/1/66	81	11		2	**Easy Listening**			$20	Imperial 12319

Alfie (2)
Can I Trust You? (2)
Detour (1)
Funny World (1)
High Noon (1)

Hold Me, Thrill Me, Kiss Me (1) *8*
I Am (1)
I Just Can't Imagine (1)
I Need You Now (1)

I'll Never Be Free (1)
Impossible Dream (The Quest) (2)
Love Letters (2)
More I See You (2)

Richest Man Alive (1)
Somewhere, My Love (2)
Strangers In The Night (2)
Sweet Little Girl (1)
Take Good Care Of Her (2) *78*

Tar And Cement (2)
Wanted (1)
What's On Your Mind (1)
You Don't Have To Say You Love Me (2)

You You You (2) *49*
You're Gonna Hear From Me (2)

CARTER, Ron   '78
Born on 5/4/37 in Ferndale, Michigan. Jazz bassist. Also see **V.S.O.P.**

3/12/77	193	1	©	1	**Pastels**		[I]	$12	Milestone 9073
10/21/78	178	3		2	**A Song For You**		[I]	$12	Milestone 9086

Ballad (1)
El Ojo De Dios (2)
Good Time (2)

N.O. Blues (2)
One Bass Rag (1)
Pastels (1)

Quiet Place (2)
Someday My Prince Will Come (2)

Song For You (2)
12 + 12 (1)
Woolaphant (1)

CARTER, Valerie   '77
Born in 1954 in New York City. Session singer. Sang backup for **Eddie Money**, **Randy Newman** and **James Taylor**.

4/2/77	182	5	©		**Just A Stone's Throw Away**			$12	Columbia 34155

Back To Blue Some More
City Lights

Cowboy Angel
Face Of Appalachia

Heartache
Ooh Child

Ringing Doorbells In The Rain
So, So Happy

Stone's Throw Away

CARTWRIGHT, Lionel   '91
Born on 2/10/60 in Gallipolis, Ohio; raised in West Virginia. Country singer/actor.

10/5/91	170	2	©		**Chasin' The Sun**			$10	MCA 10307

Family Tree
Great Expectations

I'm Your Man
Leap Of Faith

Smack Dab In The Middle Of Love

Susannah
30 Nothin'

Waitin' For The Sun To Shine
What Kind Of Fool

When You Cross That Line

CASCADES, The   '63
Pop group from San Diego: John Gummoe (vocals, guitar), Eddie Snyder (piano), David Wilson (sax), David Stevens (bass) and David Zabo (drums). Wilson died of cancer on 11/14/2000 (age 63).

4/20/63	111	10			**Rhythm Of The Rain**			$150	Valiant 405

Angel On My Shoulder
Dreamin'

I Wanna Be Your Lover
Last Leaf *60*

Let Me Be
Lucky Guy

My First Day Alone
Punch And Judy

Rhythm Of The Rain *3*
Shy Girl *91*

There's A Reason
Was I Dreamin'?

CASE   '01
Born Case Woodard in New York City. Male R&B singer/songwriter.

8/31/96	42	6	©	1	**Case**			$10	Def Jam 533134
5/8/99	33	28	● ©	2	**Personal Conversation**			$10	Def Jam 538871
5/12/01	5	17	● ©	3	**Open Letter**			$10	Def Soul 548626

Already Have (3)
Another Minute (2)
Caught You (2)
Conversate (3)
Crazy (1)
Crooked Letter (3)

Cryin' Over Time (1)
Day That I Die (1)
Don't Be Afraid (1)
Driving (3)
Even Though (3)
Faded Pictures (2) *10*

Fallin' (1)
Happily Ever After (2) *15*
Having My Baby (2)
He Don't Love You (3)
I Gotcha (1)
If (2)

Love Of My Life (3)
Missing You (3) *4*
More To Love (1)
No Regrets (3)
Not Your Friend (3)
Rain (1)

Scandalous (2)
Sex Games (3)
Shine (3)
Song For Skye (3)
Tell Me (2)
Think Of You (2)

Touch Me Tease Me (1) *14*
What's Wrong? (1)
Where Did Our Love Go (2)
Wishful Thinking (3)

CASH, Johnny ★64★   '69

Born on 2/26/32 in Kingsland, Arkansas. Country singer/songwriter/guitarist. Formed trio with Luther Perkins (guitar) and Marshall Grant (bass) in 1955. Hosted own TV show for ABC from 1969-71. Worked with **June Carter** from 1961, married her in March 1968. Father of **Rosanne Cash**. Elected to the Country Music Hall of Fame in 1980. Won Grammy's Living Legends Award in 1990. Inducted into the Rock and Roll Hall of Fame in 1992.

1)Johnny Cash At San Quentin 2)Hello, I'm Johnny Cash 3)Johnny Cash At Folsom Prison
4)The Fabulous Johnny Cash 5)Ring Of Fire (The Best Of Johnny Cash)

12/8/58	19	11		©	1	The Fabulous Johnny Cash			$50	Columbia 1253 / 8122
3/16/63	80	15		©	2	Blood, Sweat & Tears			$40	Columbia 1930 / 8730
7/27/63	26	68	●	©	3	**Ring Of Fire (The Best Of Johnny Cash)**	[K]		$40	Columbia 2053 / 8853
7/25/64	53	17	●	©	4	I Walk The Line			$30	Columbia 2190 / 8990
11/7/64	47	13		©	5	Bitter Tears (Ballads of The American Indian)			$30	Columbia 2248 / 9048
3/20/65	49	13			6	Orange Blossom Special			$30	Columbia 2309 / 9109
7/9/66	88	9			7	Everybody Loves A Nut	[N]		$30	Columbia 2492 / 9292
7/22/67+	82	71	▲²	©	8	Johnny Cash's Greatest Hits, Volume 1	[G]		$30	Columbia 2678 / 9478
10/7/67	194	3			9	Carryin' On With Johnny Cash & June Carter			$30	Columbia 2728 / 9528
						JOHNNY CASH & JUNE CARTER				
6/15/68	13	122	▲²	©	10	Johnny Cash At Folsom Prison	[L]		$30	Columbia 9639
2/15/69	54	20		©	11	The Holy Land			$30	Columbia 9726
7/5/69	❶⁴	70	▲²	©	12	Johnny Cash At San Quentin	[L]		$30	Columbia 9827
9/27/69	95	13		©	13	Original Golden Hits, Volume I	[G]		$20	Sun 100
9/27/69	98	8		©	14	Original Golden Hits, Volume II	[G]		$20	Sun 101
10/11/69	186	2			15	Johnny Cash	[K]		$20	Harmony 11342
11/29/69	164	6			16	Get Rhythm	[K]		$20	Sun 105
12/13/69	7ˣ	5			17	The Christmas Spirit	[X]		$25	Columbia 2117 / 8917
						first released in 1963; Christmas charts: 7/'69, 14/'70				
12/27/69+	181	4		©	18	Showtime	[K]		$20	Sun 106
12/27/69	197	2		©	19	Story Songs Of The Trains And Rivers	[K]		$20	Sun 104
2/14/70	6	30	●	©	20	Hello, I'm Johnny Cash			$20	Columbia 9943
5/16/70	186	3		©	21	The Singing Story Teller	[K]		$20	Sun 115
						all Sun albums were recorded from 1955-58				
6/6/70	54	34	●	©	22	The World Of Johnny Cash	[K]		$25	Columbia 29 [2]
11/14/70	44	18	●		23	The Johnny Cash Show	[L]		$20	Columbia 30100
						recorded at the *Grand Ole Opry*				
12/12/70	176	6			24	I Walk The Line	[S]		$20	Columbia 30397
6/26/71	56	12			25	Man In Black			$20	Columbia 30550
10/23/71	94	8	▲		26	The Johnny Cash Collection (His Greatest Hits, Volume II)	[G]		$20	Columbia 30887
4/29/72	112	9			27	A Thing Called Love			$20	Columbia 31332
9/16/72	176	7			28	Johnny Cash: America (A 200-Year Salute In Story And Song)			$20	Columbia 31645
2/24/73	188	4			29	Any Old Wind That Blows			$20	Columbia 32091
7/17/76	185	2			30	One Piece At A Time			$15	Columbia 34193
6/1/85	92	35	▲	©	31	Highwayman			$10	Columbia 40056
						WILLIE NELSON/JOHNNY CASH/WAYLON JENNINGS/KRIS KRISTOFFERSON				
6/21/86	87	12		©	32	Class Of '55 (Memphis Rock & Roll Homecoming)	C:#13/2		$10	America Smash 830002
						CARL PERKINS/JERRY LEE LEWIS/ROY ORBISON/JOHNNY CASH				
3/17/90	79	13		©	33	Highwayman 2			$10	Columbia 45240
						WILLIE NELSON/JOHNNY CASH/WAYLON JENNINGS/KRIS KRISTOFFERSON				
5/14/94	110	9		©	34	American Recordings			$10	American 45520
11/23/96	170	2		©	35	Unchained			$10	American 43097
6/27/98	150	2		©	36	VH1 Storytellers	[L]		$10	American 69416
						JOHNNY CASH/WILLIE NELSON				
5/8/99	185	1		©	37	16 Biggest Hits	C:#37/2 [G]		$10	Columbia 69739
11/4/00	88	4		©	38	American III: Solitary Man			$10	American 69691

CASH, Johnny — Cont'd

I Still Miss Someone (1,3,4,10,15,22,36,37)
I Talk To Jesus Every Day (25)
I Walk The Line (4,8,12,13,18,24,37) *17*
I Want To Go Home (22)
I Will Rock And Roll With You (32)
I Won't Back Down (38)
I'd Rather Die Young (1)
I'd Still Be There (1)
I'm Gonna Try To Be That Way (23)
I'm Leavin' Now (38)
I'm So Lonesome I Could Cry (22)
I've Been Everywhere (35)
I've Got A Thing About Trains (20)
If I Had A Hammer (29)
If I Were A Carpenter (20,26) *36*
If Not For Love (25)
In A Young Girl's Mind (10)
In Bethlehem (11)
In Garden Of Gethsemane (11)
In The Jailhouse Now (22,37)
In Them Old Cottonfields Back Home (22)
It Ain't Me, Babe (6,8,9) *58*
Jackson (8,9,10)
Jesus Was A Carpenter (20)
Jim, I Wore A Tie Today (31)
Joe Bean (7)
Just About Time (14)
Kate (27) *75*
Keep My Motor Running (32)
Kentucky Straight (29)
Kneeling Drunkard's Plea (35)
Land Of Israel (11)
Last Cowboy Song (31)
Legend Of John Henry's Hammer (2,22,37)

Let The Train Blow The Whistle (34)
Let There Be Country (30)
Life Goes On (19)
Like A Soldier (34)
Like A Young Colt (28)
Little Drummer Boy (17) *63*
Living Legend (33)
Long Black Veil (6,10,15)
Long-Legged Guitar Pickin' Man (9,26)
Look For Me (25)
Lorena (15,28)
Love Has Lost Again (30)
Loving Gift (27)
Luther's Boogie (14,16)
Mama, You Been On My Mind (6)
Man In Black (25,37) *84*
Man Who Couldn't Cry (34)
Mary Of The Wild Moor (38)
Me And Paul (35)
Mean Eyed Cat (16,35)
Meet Me In Heaven (35)
Melva's Wine (27)
Memories Are Made Of This (35)
Mercy Seat (38)
Michigan City Howdy Do (30)
Miracle Man (27)
Mississippi Sand (27)
Mister Garfield (28)
Mother's Love (11)
Mountain Lady (30)
My Shoes Keep Walking Back To You (22)
My Wife June At Sea Of Galilee (11)
Nazarene (11)
Ned Kelly (25)
New Mexico (16)
Next In Line (13,21) *99*
Night Life (36)

Nine Pound Hammer (2,15)
No, No, No (9)
Nobody (38)
Oh Bury Me Not (34)
Oh Lonesome Me (16) *93*
Oh, What A Good Thing We Had (9)
On The Road Again (36)
On The Via Dolorosa (11)
On Wheels And Wings (28)
One (38)
One More Ride (1,22)
One On The Right Is On The Left (7,8) *46*
One Piece At A Time (30,37) *29*
One Rose (35)
Oney (29)
Opening The West (28)
Orange Blossom Special (6,8,10) *80*
Orphan Of The Road (25)
Our Guide Jacob At Mount Tabor (11)
Pack Up Your Sorrows (9)
Papa Was A Good Man (27)
Paul Revere (28)
Peace In The Valley ..see: (There'll Be)
Pickin' Time (1,22)
Please Don't Play Red River Valley (7)
Port Of Lonely Hearts (19)
Preacher Said, "Jesus Said" (25)
Prologue (11)
Proud Land (28)
Reaching For The Stars (28)
Rebel - Johnny Yuma (3,8)
Redemption (34)
Remember The Alamo (3,28)
Ring Of Fire (3,8,37) *17*
Ringing The Bells For Jim (17)

Road To Kaintuck (28)
Rock And Roll (Fais-Do-Do) (32)
Rock Island Line (18,19) *93*
Roughneck (2)
Route #1, Box 144 (20)
Rowboat (35)
Run Softly, Blue River (1)
Rusty Cage (35)
San Quentin (12)
Sea Of Heartbreak (35)
See Ruby Fall (20) *75*
Send A Picture Of Mother (10)
Shantytown (9)
Shepherd Of My Heart (1)
Silent Night (17)
Silver Stallion (33)
Sing A Traveling Song (20)
Sing It Pretty, Sue (22)
Singin' In Viet Nam Talkin' Blues (25)
Singing Star's Queen (7)
Sixteen Candles (32)
So Doggone Lonesome (13)
Sold Out Of Flagpoles (30)
Solitary Man (38)
Songs That Make A Difference (33)
Southern Accents (35)
Southwestward (28)
Southwind (20)
Spiritual (35)
Standing On The Promises (medley) (24)
Starkville City Jail (12)
Still In Town (4)
Streets Of Laredo (15)
Sugartime (16)
Sunday Morning Coming Down (23,26,37) *46*
Supper-Time (1,22)
Take Me Home (7)
Talking Leaves (5)

Tear Stained Letter (27)
Tell Him I'm Gone (2)
Ten Commandments (11)
Tennessee Flat-Top Box (3) *84*
Tennessee Stud (34)
Texas (33)
Thanks A Lot (14)
That Lucky Old Sun (Just Rolls Around Heaven All Day) (38)
That's All Over (1)
That's Enough (1)
There You Go (13,18)
(There'll Be) Peace In The Valley (For Me) (3,12)
These Are My People (28)
These Hands (23)
Thing Called Love (27)
Thirteen (34)
This Is Nazareth (11)
This Side Of The Law (24)
This Town (24)
To Beat The Devil (20)
To The Shining Mountains (28)
Too Little, Too Late (29)
Town Of Cana (11)
Train Of Love (13,19)
Troubadour, The (1)
Troublesome Waters (4)
Twentieth Century Is Almost Over (31)
25 Minutes To Go (10)
Two Stories Wide (33)
Two Timin' Woman (16)
Unchained (35,36)
Understand Your Man (4,8,37) *35*
Vanishing Race (4)
Waiting For A Train (2,22)
Wall, The (6,10)
Wanted Man (12)
Wayfaring Stranger (38)
Waymore's Blues (37)

Ways Of A Woman In Love (14,21) *24*
We Are The Shepherds (17)
We Remember The King (32)
We're All In Your Corner (33)
Welcome Back Jesus (29)
Welfare Line (31)
Were You There (When They Crucified My Lord) (3)
West, The (28)
What Do I Care (3) *52*
What'd I Say (9)
When It's Springtime In Alaska (It's Forty Below) (6)
When Papa Played The Dobro (15,22)
White Girl (5)
Who Kept The Sheep (17)
Why Me Lord (34)
Wide Open Road (19)
Wildwood Flower (6)
World's Gonna Fall On You (24)
Worried Man (36)
Would You Lay With Me (In A Field Of Stone) (38)
Wreck Of The Old 97 (4,12,18,19)
Wrinkled, Crinkled, Wadded Dollar Bill (1)
You Wild Colorado (6)
You Win Again (16)
You'll Be All Right (9)
You're The Nearest Thing To Heaven (14,21) *flip*
You've Got A New Light Shining In Your Eyes (25)

CASH, Rosanne   '81

Born on 5/24/56 in Memphis. Daughter of **Johnny Cash**. Married to **Rodney Crowell** from 1979-92. Married producer John Leventhal in 1995. Released short-story collection *Bodies of Water* in 1996.

DEBUT	PEAK	WKS		CD				$	
3/28/81	26	32	●	©	1 Seven Year Ache			$10	Columbia 36965
7/10/82	76	12		©	2 Somewhere In The Stars			$10	Columbia 37570
6/22/85	101	21		©	3 Rhythm & Romance			$10	Columbia 39463
8/15/87+	138	20	●	©	4 King's Record Shop			$10	Columbia 40777
4/1/89	152	7	●	©	5 Hits 1979-1989		[G]	$10	Columbia 45054
11/17/90	175	4		©	6 Interiors			$10	Columbia 46079
3/27/93	160	2		©	7 The Wheel			$10	Columbia 52729

Ain't No Money (2)
Black And White (5)
Blue Moon With Heartache (1,5)
Change Partners (7)
Closing Time (3)
Dance With The Tiger (6)
Down On Love (2)
Fire Of The Newly Alive (7)
From The Ashes (7)
Green, Yellow And Red (4)
Halfway House (3)
Hold On (3,5)
Hometown Blues (1)
I Can't Resist (1)

I Don't Have To Crawl (4)
I Don't Know Why You Don't Want Me (3,5)
I Don't Want To Spoil The Party (5)
I Look For Love (2)
I Want A Cure (6)
I Wonder (2,5)
If There's A God On My Side (7)
If You Change Your Mind (4)
It Hasn't Happened Yet (2)
Land Of Nightmares (6)
Looking For A Corner (2)
Mirror Image (6)

My Baby Thinks He's A Train (1,5)
My Old Man (3)
Never Alone (3)
Never Be You (3,5)
Never Gonna Hurt (3)
No Memories Hangin' Around (5)
Oh Yes I Can (2)
On The Inside (6)
On The Surface (6)
Only Human (1)
Paralyzed (6)
Pink Bedroom (3)
Rainin' (1)

Real Me (4)
Real Woman (6)
Roses In The Fire (7)
Rosie Strike Back (4)
Runaway Train (4)
Second To No One (3)
Seven Year Ache (1,5) *22*
Seventh Avenue (7)
Sleeping In Paris (7)
Somewhere In The Stars (2)
Somewhere Sometime (4)
Tears Falling Down (7)
Tennessee Flat Top Box (4,5)
That's How I Got To Memphis (2)

Third Rate Romance (2)
This World (6)
Truth About You (7)
Way We Make A Broken Heart (4,5)
What Kinda Girl? (1)
What We Really Want (6)
Wheel, The (7)
Where Will The Words Come From? (1)
Why Don't You Quit Leaving Me Alone (4)
You Don't Have Very Far To Go (1)
You Won't Let Me In (7)

CA$HFLOW   '86

Funk-rap group from Atlanta: Kary Hubbert (vocals), James Duffie and Regis Ferguson (keyboards) and Gaylord Parsons (drums).

								$	
5/3/86	144	11			Ca$hflow			$10	Atlanta Artists 826028

Can't Let Love Pass Us By
I Need Your Love

It's Just A Dream
Mine All Mine

Party Freak
Reach Out

Spending Money

CASHMAN & WEST   '72

Duo of pop record producers/songwriters/singers Dennis "Terry Cashman" Minogue (born on 7/5/41) and Thomas "Tommy West" Picardo, Jr. (born on 8/17/42). Produced all of **Jim Croce**'s recordings.

								$	
10/14/72	168	8			1 A Song Or Two			$15	Dunhill/ABC 50126
8/11/73	192	2			2 Moondog Serenade			$15	Dunhill/ABC 50141

AM-FM Blues (2)
American City Suite (1) *27*
Because You're Free (1)
Follow The Man With The Music (2)

Girls Next Door (2)
I Belong To You (1)
If You Were A Rainbow (1)
Is It Raining In New York City (2)

It Ain't Easy (1)
King Of Rock 'N Roll (2)
Let Your Feelings Go (2)
Mixed Emotions (2)
Only A Woman Like You (1)

Six-Man Song Band (1)
Somebody Stole The Sun (2)
Songman (1) *59*
Time-Traveler (2)
We Let Love Slip Away (1)

Will You Be My Lady (2)

CASH MONEY MILLIONAIRES   '00

Rap collective of Cash Money artists: **B.G.**, **Big Tymers**, **Juvenile**, **Lil' Wayne** and **Turk**.

								$	
9/30/00	13	24	●	©	Baller Blockin			$10	Cash Money 153291

Baller Blockin
Ballin' Gs
Calling Me Killer

Don't Cry
Family Affair
I Don't Know

I Got To Go
Let Us Stunt
Milk & Honey

Project B!#$h
Rover Truck
Thugged Out

Uptown
What You Gonna Do
Whatever

Win Or Loose

CASINOS, The '67

Pop vocal group from Cincinnati: Gene Hughes, Pete Bolton, Bob Armstrong, Tom Mathews, Ray White, Mickey Denton, Glen Hughes, Joe Patterson and Bill Hawkins.

| 5/13/67 | 187 | 4 | | | Then You Can Tell Me Goodbye .... | | | $50 | Fraternity 1019 |

Certain Girl
Gee Whiz
Gina

Hold On I'm Coming
I Still Love You
Magic Circle

Maybe
Rag Doll
Talk To Me

Then You Can Tell Me Goodbye 6
To Be Loved

What Kind Of Fool Am I

CASSIDY, David '72

Born on 4/12/50 in New York City. Son of actor Jack Cassidy and actress Evelyn Ward. Played "Keith Partridge", the lead singer of TV's **The Partridge Family**. Married to actress Kay Lenz from 1977-81. Co-starred with his half-brother **Shaun Cassidy** on Broadway's *Blood Brothers* in 1993.

2/12/72	15	23	●	© 1	Cherish			$15	Bell 6070
11/11/72	41	17		© 2	Rock Me Baby			$15	Bell 1109
11/3/90	136	11		© 3	David Cassidy			$10	Enigma 73554

All Because Of You (3)
Being Together (1)
Blind Hope (1)
Boulevard Of Broken Dreams (3)
Cherish (1) *9*
Could It Be Forever (1) *37*

Go Now (2)
Hi-Heel Sneakers (3)
How Can I Be Sure (2) *25*
I Am A Clown (1)
I Just Wanna Make You Happy (1)
I Lost My Chance (1)

Labor Of Love (3)
Livin' Without You (3)
Lonely Too Long (2)
Lyin' To Myself (3) *27*
Message To The World (3)
My First Night Alone Without You (1)

(Oh No) No Way (2)
Prisoner (2)
Ricky's Tune (1)
Rock Me Baby (2) *38*
Soft As A Summer Shower (2)
Some Kind Of A Summer (2)
Song For A Rainy Day (2)

Song Of Love (2)
Stranger In Your Heart (3)
Two Time Loser (2)
Warm My Soul (2)
We Could Never Be Friends ('Cause We've Been Lovers Too Long) (1)

Where Is The Morning (1)
You Remember Me (3)

CASSIDY, Eva '01

Born on 2/2/63 in Oxon Hill, Maryland. Died of cancer on 11/2/96 (age 33). Singer/songwriter/guitarist.

| 4/7/01 | ❶⁹ᶜ | 26 | | © 1 | Songbird .... | | | $10 | Blix Street 10045 |
| 6/9/01 | 2¹ᶜ | 6 | | © 2 | Live At Blues Alley .... | | [L] | $10 | Blix Street 10046 |

Autumn Leaves (1,2)
Blue Skies (2)
Bridge Over Troubled Water (2)
Cheek To Cheek (2)

Fields Of Gold (1,2)
Fine And Mellow (2)
Honeysuckle Rose (2)
I Know You By Heart (1)

Oh, Had I A Golden Thread (1,2)
Over The Rainbow (1)
People Get Ready (1,2)

Songbird (1)
Stormy Monday (2)
Take Me To The River (2)
Tall Trees In Georgia (2)

Time Is A Healer (1)
Wade In The Water (1)
Wayfaring Stranger (1)
What A Wonderful World (2)

CASSIDY, Shaun '77

Born on 9/27/59 in Los Angeles. Son of actor Jack Cassidy and actress Shirley Jones of TV's **The Partridge Family**. Played "Joe Hardy" on TV's *The Hardy Boys*. Co-starred with his half-brother David Cassidy on Broadway's *Blood Brothers* in 1993. Cast member of the TV soap *General Hospital* in 1987. Married to model Ann Pennington from 1979-91.

6/25/77	3	57	▲	1	Shaun Cassidy			$12	Warner/Curb 3067
11/26/77+	6	37	▲	2	Born Late			$12	Warner/Curb 3126
8/19/78	33	13	▲	3	Under Wraps			$12	Warner/Curb 3222

Amblin' (1)
Audrey (2)
Baby, Baby, Baby (2)
Be My Baby (1)
Carolina's Comin' Home (2)
Da Doo Ron Ron (1) *1*

Do You Believe In Magic (2) *31*
Girl Like You (2)
Hard Love (3)
Hey Deanie (2) *7*
Hey There Lonely Girl (1)

Holiday (1)
I Wanna Be With You (1)
It's Like Heaven (3)
It's Too Late (1)
It's Up To You (3)
Lie To Me (3)

Midnight Sun (3)
Morning Girl (1)
One More Night Of Your Love (3)
Our Night (3) *80*
Right Before Your Skies (3)

She's Right (3)
Strange Sensation (2)
Take Good Care Of My Baby (1)
Taxi Dancer (3)
Teen Dream (2)

That's Rock 'N' Roll (1) *3*
Walk Away (2)

CASTOR, Jimmy, Bunch '72

Born on 6/2/43 in New York City. R&B singer/saxophonist/composer/arranger. Formed the Jimmy Castor Bunch in 1972, with Gerry Thomas (keyboards), Doug Gibson (bass), Harry Jensen (guitar), Lenny Fridie, Jr. (congas) and Bobby Manigault (drums).

4/22/72	27	23		1	It's Just Begun			$15	RCA Victor 4640
9/23/72	192	4		2	Phase Two			$15	RCA Victor 4783
3/1/75	74	17		3	Butt Of Course			$12	Atlantic 18124
9/25/76	132	9		4	E-Man Groovin'			$12	Atlantic 18186

Bad (1)
Bertha Butt Boogie-Part 1 (3) *16*
Creation (1)
Daniel (3)
Dracula Pt. I & II (4)
E-Man Boogie (3)
E-Man Groovin' (4)

Everything Is Beautiful To Me (4)
Fanfare (2)
First Time Ever I Saw Your Face (2)
Hallucinations (3)
I Don't Want To Lose You (4)
I Love A Mellow Groove (4)

I Promise To Remember (1)
It's Just Begun (1)
L.T.D. (Life, Truth & Death) (1)
Let's Party Now (3)
Luther The Anthropoid (Ape Man) (2)
My Brightest Day (1)
One Precious Word (3)

Paradise (2)
Party Life (2)
Potential (3)
Psyche (1)
Say Leroy (The Creature From The Black Lagoon Is Your Father) (2)
Space Age (4)

Super Love (4)
Tribute To Jimi Medley (2)
Troglodyte (Cave Man) (1) *6*
When? (2)
You Better Be Good (Or The Devil Gon' Getcha) (1)
You Make Me Feel Brand New (3)

CASUAL '94

Born Jonathan Owens. Male rapper.

| 2/19/94 | 108 | 2 | | © | Fear Itself .... | | | $10 | Jive 41520 |

Be Thousand
Chained Minds
Follow The Funk

Get Off It
I Didn't Mean To
Little Something

Lose In The End
Me-O-Mi-O
That Bullshit

That's How It Is
This Is How We Rip Shit
Thoughts Of The Thoughtful

We Got It Like That
Who's It On
You Flunked

CATE BROS. '76

Pop duo of twins Ernie (vocals, piano) and Earl (guitar) Cate. Born on 12/26/42 in Fayetteville, Arkansas.

| 2/7/76 | 158 | 9 | | 1 | Cate Bros. .... | | | $12 | Asylum 1050 |
| 10/30/76 | 182 | 2 | | 2 | In One Eye And Out The Other .... | | | $12 | Asylum 1080 |

Always Waiting (1)
Can't Change My Heart (1) *91*
Can't Stop (2)
Easy Way Out (1)

Give It All To You (2)
I Don't Want Nobody (Standing Over Me) (2)
I Just Wanna Sing (1)

In One Eye And Out The Other (2)
Lady Luck (1)
Let's Just Let It Be (2)

Livin' On Dreams (1)
Music Making Machine (2)
Standin' On A Mountain Top (1)
Start All Over Again (2)

Stuck In Chicago (2)
Time For Us (1)
Travelin' Man (2)
Union Man (1) *24*

When Love Comes (1)
Where Can We Go (2)

CATHEDRALS, The '99

Gospel group formed in 1964 in Akron, Ohio: Glen Payne, George Younce, Scott Fowler and Ernie Haase. Payne died of cancer on 10/15/99 (age 72).

| 12/11/99 | 93 | 4 | | © | A Farewell Celebration .... | | [L] | $10 | Spring House 42223 |

Champion Of Love
Climbing Higher And Higher
Farther Along
Going Home

Haven Of Rest
I Will Serve Thee (medley)
In The Name Of The Lord
Life Will Be Sweeter Some Day

Life's Railway To Heaven
Noah Found Grace In The Eyes Of The Lord
O What A Savior

Sinner Saved By Grace
Suppertime
Thanks To Calvary
That Day At Calvary

There's Something About That Name (medley)
This Old House (medley)
Trying To Get A Glimpse

We Shall See Jesus
When The Saints Go Marching In (medley)
Wonderful Grace Of Jesus

CATHERINE WHEEL '95
Rock group from England: Rob Dickinson (vocals), Brian Futter (guitar), Dave Hawes (bass) and Neil Sims (drums). Dickinson is the cousin of **Bruce Dickinson (Iron Maiden)**.

| 6/24/95 | 163 | 1 | © | 1 | **Happy Days** | $10 | Mercury 526850 |
| 9/13/97 | 178 | 1 | © | 2 | **Adam And Eve** | $10 | Mercury 534864 |

Broken Nose (2)
Delicious (2)
Eat My Dust You Insensitive Fuck (1)
Empty Head (1)

Fizzy Love (1)
For Dreaming (2)
Future Boy (2)
God Inside My Head (1)
Goodbye (2)

Heal (1)
Here Comes The Fat Controller (2)
Hole (1)
Judy Staring At The Sun (1)

Kill My Soul (1)
Little Muscle (1)
Love Tips Up (1)
Ma Solituda (2)
My Exhibition (1)

Phantom Of The American Mother (1)
Receive (1)
Satellite (2)
Shocking (1)

Thunderbird (2)
Waydown (1)

CAT MOTHER and The All Night News Boys '69
Rock group from New York City: Larry Packer (guitar), Bob Smith (piano), Charley Chin (banjo), Roy Michaels (bass) and Michael Equine (drums). All share vocals.

| 7/5/69 | 55 | 15 | © | | **The Street Giveth...And The Street Taketh Away** | $25 | Polydor 4001 |

produced by **Jimi Hendrix**

Bad News
Boston Burglar

Bramble Bush
Can You Dance To It?

Charlie's Waltz
Favors

Good Old Rock 'N Roll *21*
How I Spent My Summer

Marie
Probably Won't

Track In "A" (Nebraska Nights)

CAUSE & EFFECT '92
Pop duo formed in California: Sean Rowley (keyboards) and Robert Rowe (vocals, guitar). Rowley died of asthma-related cardiac arrest on 11/12/92 (age 23).

| 4/4/92 | 141 | 11 | © | | **Another Minute** | $10 | SRC 11019 |

Another Minute *75*
Beginning Of The End

Echoing Green
Farewell To Arms

New World
Nothing Comes To Mind

Something New
What Do You See

You Think You Know Her *38*

CAVE, Nick, & The Bad Seeds '97
Born on 9/22/57 in Warracknabeal, Australia. Rock singer/pianist. The Bad Seeds: Mick Harvey and Blixa Bargeld (guitars), Conway Savage (organ), Warren Ellis (violin), Martyn Casey (bass) and Thomas Wylder (drums).

| 3/22/97 | 155 | 1 | © | 1 | **The Boatman's Call** | $10 | Reprise 46530 |
| 4/28/01 | 180 | 1 | © | 2 | **No More Shall We Part** | $10 | Mute 48039 |

And No More Shall We Part (2)
(Are You) The One That I've Been Waiting For? (1)
As I Sat Sadly By Her Side (2)
Black Hair (1)

Brompton Oratory (1)
Darker With The Day (2)
Far From Me (1)
Fifteen Feet Of Pure White Snow (2)

Gates To The Garden (2)
God Is In The House (2)
Green Eyes (2)
Hallelujah (2)
Idiot Prayer (1)

Into My Arms (1)
Lime-Tree Arbour (1)
Love Letter (2)
Oh My Lord (2)
People Ain't No Good (1)

Sorrowful Wife (2)
Sweetheart Come (2)
There Is A Kingdom (1)
We Came Along This Road (2)
West Country Girl (1)

Where Do We Go Now But Nowhere? (1)

C-BO '98
Born Shawn Thomas in Oakland. Male rapper.

6/24/95	99	9	©	1	**Tales From The Crypt**	$10	AWOL 7197
3/1/97	65	6	©	2	**One Life 2 Live**	$10	AWOL 7201
3/14/98	41	6	©	3	**Til My Casket Drops**	$10	AWOL 45496
3/27/99	81	2	©	4	**The Final Chapter**	$10	AWOL 47206
8/12/00	91	6	©	5	**Enemy Of The State**	$10	West Coast Mafia 2829

Ain't No Sushine (1)
All I Ever Wanted (3)
As The World Turns (4)
Best Recognize (4)
Big Boss (4)
Big Figgas (4)
Big Gangsta (3)
Birds In The Kitchen (1)
Boo Yow! (3)
Born Killaz (3)
Break'um Off (2)
C And The Mac (5)

Can We All Ball (3)
Club Hoppin (2)
Crippin' (5)
Deadly Game (3)
Death Rider'z (5)
Desparado Outlaws (1)
Enemy Of The State (5)
Forever Thugin' (5)
40 & C-BO (5)
Free Style (1)
Get The Chips (4)
Get The Money (5)

Groovin' On A Sunday (1)
Hard Core (1)
Hard Labor (3)
Here We Come, Boy! (5)
How Many (4)
I Can't See Tha Light (2)
I'm A Fool (3)
I'm Gonna Get Mine (2)
It's War (5)
Kill'em Up (2)
Livin Like A Hustler Part 2 (1)
Major Pain & Mr. Bossalini (3)

Menace (2)
Mobb Deep (3)
Money By The Ton (3)
Murder That He Ritt (1)
My True Soldiers (4)
9.6 (5)
No Pain No Gain (3)
No Surrender No Retreat (5)
Nothin' Over My G'z (5)
187 Dance (1)
1 Life 2 Live (2)
Paper Made (5)

Picture Me Ballin' (5)
Pimpin' And Jackin' (5)
Player To Player (4)
Professional Ballers (3)
Raised In Hell (3)
Real Niggas (3)
Ride Til' We Die (3)
Ride Till We Die (5)
Ridin On My Bumper (2)
Spray Yourself (5)
Still Mashin (4)
Stompin' In My Steel Toes (1)

Survival 1st (2)
Take It How You Want Too (1)
357 (3)
3 Gangstas (2)
Till My Casket Drops (3)
Tru 2 Da Game (4)
Tycoon (5)
Want To Be A "G" (1)
Who Ride (1)

C.C.S. '71
British jazz-rock collective. Put together by core trio of vocalists Alexis Korner and Peter Thorup, with arranger John Cameron. Name stands for Collective Consciousness Society. Korner's Blues Inc., a pioneer blues-rock band of the early 1960s, featured future **Rolling Stones** members, **Ginger Baker**, **Jack Bruce** and other rock notables. Korner died of lung cancer on 1/1/84 (age 55).

| 4/3/71 | 197 | 2 | | | **Whole Lotta Love** | $20 | RAK 30559 |

Boom Boom
Dos Cantos

(I Can't Get No) Satisfaction
Living In The Past

Lookin' For Fun
Sunrise

Wade In The Water
Waiting Song

Walking
Whole Lotta Love *58*

CEDARMONT KIDS SINGERS '00
Cedarmont Kids Classics series of recordings for children, featuring a chorus of 14 little girls.

11/25/95	33ˣ	3	©	1	**Christmas Carols**	C:#48/1	[X]	$10	Benson 84054
12/2/95	29ˣ	1	©	2	**Christmas Favorites**	C:#42/1	[X]	$10	Benson 84058
4/15/00	25ᶜ	14	©	3	**Toddler Tunes: 25 Classic Songs For Toddlers**			$10	Benson 84056

Alphabet Song (3)
Angels We Have Heard On High (1)
Are You Sleeping? (3)
Away In A Manger (1)
Baa, Baa, Black Sheep (3)
Be Kind To Your Web-Footed Friends (3)
Children, Go Where I Send Thee (2)
Deck The Hall (2)
Deep And Wide (3)
Eensy, Weensy Spider (3)

Father, We Thank Thee (3)
First Noel (1)
Friendly Beasts (2)
Fum, Fum, Fum (1)
Get On Board (3)
God Made Me (3)
God Rest Ye Merry, Gentlemen (1)
Good Christian Men, Rejoice (1)
Hark! The Herald Angels Sing (1)
Here We Come A-Caroling (3)

Holly And The Ivy (2)
How Great Our Joy! (1)
I Heard The Bells On Christmas Day (1)
I Saw Three Ships (2)
It Came Upon The Midnight Clear (1)
Jack And Jill (3)
Jingle Bells (2)
Joy To The World! (1)
London Bridge (3)
Mary Had A Little Lamb (3)
More We Get Together (3)

Muffin Man (3)
Mulberry Bush (3)
O Christmas Tree (2)
O Come All Ye Faithful (1)
O Come, Little Children (1)
O Little Town Of Bethlehem (1)
Oh Dear! What Can The Matter Be? (2)
Oh, Where, Oh, Where Has My Little Dog Gone? (2)
Old MacDonald (3)
Over The River And Through The Wood (2)

Pat-A-Pan (Willie, Take Your Drum) (2)
Polly, Put The Kettle On (3)
Pop! Goes The Weasel! (3)
Roll Over (3)
Row, Row, Row Your Boat (3)
Silent Night! Holy Night! (1)
There's A Song In The Air (2)
This Old Man (3)
Twelve Days Of Christmas (2)
Virgin Mary Had A Baby Boy (2)
We Three Kings (1)

We Wish You A Merry Christmas (2)
What Child Is This? (2)
Wheels On The Bus (3)

CELI BEE & THE BUZZY BUNCH '77
Puerto Rican disco band led by female vocalist Celinas Soto.

| 7/23/77 | 169 | 5 | | | **Celi Bee & The Buzzy Bunch** | $12 | APA 77001 |

Closer, Closer

Hurt Me, Hurt Me

It's Sad

One Love

Smile

Superman *41*

CELLA DWELLAS '96
Rap duo from Brooklyn, New York: Ug and Phantasm.

| 4/13/96 | 160 | 1 | | © | **Realms 'N Reality** .... | | | $10 | Loud 66521 |

Advance To Boardwalk | Hold U Down | Medina Style | Realm 3 | Worries
Cella Dwellas | Land Of The Lost | Mystic Freestyle | Recognize N Realize | Wussdaplan
Good Dwellas | Line 4 Line | Perfect Match | We Got It Hemmed

CELLY CELL '96
Born Michael McCarver in Vallejo, California. Male rapper.

| 5/18/96 | 26 | 17 | | © 1 | **Killa Kali** .... | | | $10 | Sick Wid' It 41577 |
| 8/15/98 | 53 | 6 | | © 2 | **The G Filez** .... | | | $10 | Sick Wid' It 41622 |

All I Know (2) | Don't Wanna See Us (2) | Function, The (2) | In The Traffic (2) | Red Rum (2) | Sick Wid It Party (2)
Bay, The (2) | Eternal Life (2) | Funk Season (1) | It's Goin' Down (1,2) | Remember Where You Came | Skanlezz Azz Butchez (1)
Bullet, Tha (1) | Every Day Is Tha Weekend (2) | G Filez (2) | Killa Kali (1) | From (1) | What U Niggaz Thought (1)
Can I Kick It? (2) | 4 Tha Scrilla (1) | Get A Real Job (2) | Playerizm (1) | Ride (2) | Why Must I Be Like That? (2)
Can't Tell Me Shit (1) | Fuck Tha World (2) | Get It Crackin' (2) | Pop The Trunk (2) | Round 2 (1) | You Neva Know (2)

CENTRAL LINE '82
R&B group from London: Linton Beckles (vocals, drums), Henry Defoe (guitar), Lipson Francis (keyboards) and Camelle Hinds (bass).

| 1/9/82 | 145 | 9 | | | **Central Line** .... | | | $10 | Mercury 4033 |

Breaking Point | Goodbye | Shake It Up | That's No Way To Treat My | **Walking Into Sunshine** 84
Don't Tell Me | I Need Your Love | | Love

CERRONE '79
Born Jean-Marc Cerrone in 1952 in St. Michel, France. Composer/producer/drummer. A pioneer of the Euro-disco sound. Also see **Kongas**.

2/26/77	153	10		1	**Love In C Minor**			$12	Cotillion 9913
8/6/77	162	5		© 2	**Cerrone's Paradise**			$12	Cotillion 9917
1/21/78	129	8		© 3	**Cerrone 3 - Supernature**			$12	Cotillion 5202
11/18/78+	118	13		4	**Cerrone IV - The Golden Touch**			$12	Cotillion 5208

Black Is Black (1) | In The Smoke (3) | **Love In 'C' Minor - Pt. I** (1) 36 | Midnite Lady (1) | **Supernature** (3) 70 | Time For Love (2)
Cerrone's Paradise (2) | Je Suis Music (4) | Love Is Here (3) | Music Of Life (4) | Sweet Drums (3)
Give Me Love (3) | Look For Love (4) | Love Is The Answer (3) | Rocket In The Pocket (4) | Take Me (2)

CETERA, Peter '86
Born on 9/13/44 in Chicago. Lead singer/bass guitarist of **Chicago** from 1967-85.

1/23/82	143	10		© 1	**Peter Cetera**			$10	Full Moon 3624
7/12/86	23	43	▲	© 2	**Solitude/Solitaire**			$10	Full Moon 25474
8/20/88	58	17		© 3	**One More Story**			$10	Full Moon 25704
8/8/92	163	9		© 4	**World Falling Down**			$10	Warner 26894
6/7/97	134	13		© 5	**You're The Inspiration - A Collection**		[G]	$10	River North 61250

After All (5) 6 | Evil Eye (1) | I Can Feel It (1) | Mona Mona (1) | Queen Of The Masquerade Ball | They Don't Make 'Em Like They
Baby What A Big Surprise (5) | **Feels Like Heaven** (4,5) 71 | **(I Wanna Take) Forever** | Next Time I Fall (2,5) 1 | (2) | Used To (2)
Best Of Times (3) 59 | **Glory Of Love** (2) 1 | **Tonight** (5) 86 | Not Afraid To Cry (1) | **Restless Heart** (4) 35 | Wake Up To Love (2)
Big Mistake (2) 61 | Have You Ever Been In Love | **I Wasn't The One (Who Said** | On The Line (1) | S.O.S. (5) | Where There's No Tomorrow
Body Language (There In The | (4) | **Goodbye)** (5) 93 | One Good Woman (3) 4 | Save Me (3) | (4)
Dark) (1) | Heaven Help This Lonely Man | If You Leave Me Now (5) | One More Story (3) | Scheherazade (3) | Wild Ways (4)
Daddy's Girl (2) | (3) | Ivy Covered Walls (1) | Only Love Knows Why (1) | She Doesn't Need Me Anymore | World Falling Down (4)
Dip Your Wings (4) | Holding Out (3) | Last Place God Made (4) | Peace Of Mind (3) | (5) | You Never Listen To Me (3)
Do You Love Me That Much (5) | Holy Moly (1) | Livin' In The Limelight (1) | Practical Man (1) | Solitude/Solitaire (2) | **You're The Inspiration** (5) 77
Even A Fool Can See (4) 68 | How Many Times (1) | Man In Me (4)

CHACKSFIELD, Frank, And His Orchestra '61
Born on 5/9/14 in Battle, Sussex, England. Died on 6/9/95 (age 81). Pianist/bandleader.

| 1/9/61 | 36 | 14 | | 1 | **Ebb Tide** .... | | | $20 | Richmond 30078 |
| 11/28/64 | 120 | 9 | | 2 | **The New Ebb Tide** .... | | | $10 | London Phase 4 44053 |

Among My Souvenirs (1) | Deep Purple (1) | I Only Have Eyes For You (1) | Moonlight On The Ganges (2) | Shenandoah (2) | Victory At Sea (2)
Autumn Leaves (1) | Deep River (2) | Limelight (1) | Red Sails In The Sunset (1) | Sleepy Lagoon (2)
Boulevard Of Broken Dreams | Ebb Tide (1,2) | Love By Starlight (1) | Sea, The (1) | Smoke Gets In Your Eyes (1)
(1) | How Deep Is The Ocean (2) | Moon River (2) | Sea Mist (2) | Stranger On The Shore (2)

CHAD & JEREMY '65
Folk-pop duo from London: Chad Stuart (born on 12/10/43) and Jeremy Clyde (born on 3/22/44).

9/26/64+	22	39		1	**Yesterday's Gone**			$30	World Artists 2002
3/27/65	69	14		2	**Chad & Jeremy Sing For You**			$30	World Artists 2005
6/26/65	37	18		3	**Before And After**			$25	Columbia 9174
11/6/65	77	11		4	**I Don't Want To Lose You Baby**			$25	Columbia 9198
4/23/66	49	23		© 5	**The Best Of Chad & Jeremy**		[G]	$25	Capitol 2470
8/20/66	144	4		6	**More Chad & Jeremy**		[K]	$25	Capitol 2546
9/24/66	61	14		© 7	**Distant Shores**			$25	Columbia 9364
11/11/67	186	5		© 8	**Of Cabbages And Kings**			$25	Columbia 9471

Ain't It Nice (7) | Early Mornin' Rain (3) | Girl Who Sang The Blues (4) | Lemon Tree (6) | Progress Suite - Movements 1 | Truth Often Hurts The Heart
Baby Don't Go (4) | Everyone's Gone To The Moon | Homeward Bound (7) | Like I Love You Today (1,5) | Thru 5 (8) | (1,6)
Before And After (3) 17 | (7) | **I Don't Wanna Lose You Baby** | Little Does She Know (3) | Rest In Peace (8) | Way You Look Tonight (7)
Busman's Holiday (8) | Evil-Hearted Me (3) | (4) 35 | Morning (7) | Say It Isn't True (3) | **What Do You Want With Me**
Can I See You (8) | Family Way (8) | **I Have Dreamed** (4) 91 | Mr. Tambourine Man (4) | September In The Rain (1,6) | (2,3,5) 51
Can't Get Used To Losing You | Fare Thee Well (I Must Be | I Won't Cry (3) | My Coloring Book (2,6) | Should I (4) | When Your Love Has Gone (7)
(3) | Gone) (3) | I'll Get Around To It When And | My How The Time Goes By | Sleep Little Boy (2) | Why Should I Care (3)
Dirty Old Town (1,6) | For Lovin' Me (3) | If I Can (8) | (2,5) | **Summer Song** (1,5) 7 | **Willow Weep For Me** (1,5) 15
Distant Shores (7) 30 | Four Strong Winds (2,6) | I'm In Love Again (3) | No Other Baby (2) | Tell Me Baby (3) | Woman In You (4)
Don't Make Me Do It (7) | **From A Window** (2,5) 97 | **If I Loved You** (5) 23 | No Tears For Johnnie (1,6) | There But For Fortune (4) | **Yesterday's Gone** (1,5) 21
Don't Think Twice, It's All Right | Funny How Love Can Be (4) | If She Was Mine (1) | Now And Forever (1,6) | These Things You Don't Forget | **You Are She** (7) 87
(4) | Gentle Cold Of Dawn (8) | If You've Got A Heart (2,5) | Only For The Young (1) | (4) | You Know What (2)
Donna, Donna (2,6) | Girl From Ipanema (2,6) | It Was A Very Good Year (6) | Only Those In Love (2,5) | Too Soon My Love (1,5)

CHAIRMEN OF THE BOARD '71
R&B vocal group from Detroit: General Norman Johnson, Danny Woods, Harrison Kennedy and Eddie Curtis.

5/2/70	**133**	10		1 **Give Me Just A Little More Time**	$40	Invictus 7300
11/28/70+	**117**	16		2 **In Session**	$40	Invictus 7304
5/6/72	**178**	3		3 **Bittersweet**	$40	Invictus 9801

All We Need Is Understanding (2) — Come Together (1) — I Can't Find Myself (2) — My Way (1) — Twelfth Of Never (2)
Bittersweet (3) — Didn't We (1) — I'll Come Crawling (1) — Patches (1,2) — Weary Traveler (3)
Bless You (1) — Elmo James (3) — I'm A Sign Of Changing Times (3) — **Pay To The Piper** (2) *13* — When Will She Tell Me She Needs Me (2)
Bravo, Horray (1) — Everything's Tuesday (2) *38* — I'm On My Way To A Better Place (3) — Saginaw County Line (3) — Working On A Building Of Love (3)
Bridge Over Troubled Water (2) — Feelin' Alright? (1) — It Was Almost Something (2) — Since The Days Of Pigtails (And Fairy Tales) (3) — **(You've Got Me) Dangling On A String** (1) *38*
Chairman Of The Board (2) *42* — **Give Me Just A Little More Time** (1) *3* — Men Are Getting Scarce (3) — So Glad You're Mine (3)
Children Of Today (2) — Hanging On To A Memory (2) — Tricked & Trapped (1)

CHAKACHAS, The '72
Studio group from Belgium. Featuring saxophonist Victor Ingeveld.

4/8/72	**117**	11			**Jungle Fever**	[F]	$15	Polydor 5504

Ay Mulata — Chica Chica Bau Bau — El Rico Son — Harlem Nocturne — Latin Can Can — Yo Soy Cubano
Cha Ka Cha — El Canyon Rojo — Eso Es El Amor — **Jungle Fever** *8* — Un Rayo Del Sol

CHAKIRIS, George '62
Born on 9/16/34 in Norwood, Ohio. Actor/singer. Best-known for playing "Bernardo" in the movie *West Side Story*.

9/1/62	**28**	16		1 **George Chakiris**	$20	Capitol 1750
2/2/63	**45**	17		2 **Memories Are Made Of These**	$20	Capitol 1813

All I Need Is The Girl (1) — I Left My Heart In San Francisco (2) — Maria (1) — One Girl (1) — Witchcraft (2)
Autumn Leaves (2) — I'm Falling In Love With Someone (1) — Memories Are Made Of This (2) — Second Time Around (2) — You Stepped Out Of A Dream (1)
By Myself (1) — Moon River (2) — Taste Of Honey (2)
Fever (2) — Ill Wind (1) — Mr. Lucky (1) — Tonight (1)
Hallelujah, I Love Her So (1) — Lollipops And Roses (2) — Naked City Theme (Somewhere In The Night) (2) — Two For The Seesaw (A Second Chance), Song From (2)
I Believe In You (1) — Lot Of Livin' To Do (1) — Once Upon A Time (1)

CHAMBERLAIN, Richard '63
Born George Richard Chamberlain on 3/31/35 in Beverly Hills, California. Leading movie, theater and TV actor. Played lead role in TV's *Dr. Kildare* from 1961-66.

2/2/63	**5**	36		**Richard Chamberlain Sings**	$20	MGM 4088

All I Do Is Dream Of You — Dr. Kildare (Three Stars Will Shine Tonight), Theme From (1) — Hi-Lili, Hi-Lo *64* — I'll Be Around — Love Me Tender *21*
All I Have To Do Is Dream *14* — I Hadn't Anyone Till You — It's A Lonesome Old Town (When You're Not Around) — Quiet Kind Of Love
I Will Love You *65* — **True Love** *98*

CHAMBERS BROTHERS, The '68
Group of brothers from Lee County, Mississippi: Willie (guitar), Joe (guitar), Lester (harmonica) and George (bass) Chambers, with Brian Keenan (drums).

2/17/68	**4**	58	●	©	1 **The Time Has Come**	$20	Columbia 9522
10/12/68	**16**	21		©	2 **A New Time-A New Day**	$20	Columbia 9671
12/27/69+	**58**	33			3 **Love, Peace And Happiness**	[L] $25	Columbia 20 [2]
					record 2: live at Bill Graham's Fillmore East		
12/5/70	**193**	2			4 **The Chambers Brothers Greatest Hits**	[E] $25	Vault 135 [2]
					reissue of 1965-1966 recordings		
2/27/71	**145**	7			5 **New Generation**	$15	Columbia 30032
12/4/71+	**166**	7		©	6 **The Chambers Brothers' Greatest Hits**	[G] $15	Columbia 30871

All Strung Out Over You (1,6) — Going To The Mill (5) — In The Midnight Hour (1,6) — New Time - A New Day (2) — Seventeen (4) — **Wake Up** (3) *92*
Are You Ready (5,6) — Guess Who (2) — It Rained The Day You Left (4) — No, No, No, Don't Say Good-By (2) — So Fine (4) — What The World Needs Now Is Love (1)
Baby Please Don't Go (4) — Have A Little Faith (3) — It's Groovin' Time (4) — People Get Ready (1,3,4,6) — So Tired (1) — When The Evening Comes (5)
Bang Bang (3) — High Heel Sneakers (4) — Johnny B. Goode (4) — Please Don't Leave Me (1) — There She Goes (4) — Where Have All The Flowers Gone (2)
Blues, Get Off My Shoulder (4) — Hooka Tooka (4) — Just A Closer Walk With Thee (4) — Pollution (5) — **Time Has Come Today** (1,6) *11* — You Got The Power - To Turn Me On (2)
Call Me (4) — House Of The Rising Sun (4) — Let's Do It (Do It Together) (3,6) — Practice What You Preach (5) — To Love Somebody (3) — You're So Fine (3)
Do Your Thing (2) — I Can't Stand It (1) — Love Is All I Have (2) — Pretty Girls Everywhere (4) — Travel On My Way (4) — You've Got Me Running (4)
Don't Lose Your Cool (4) — **I Can't Turn You Loose** (2,3,6) *37* — Love! Love! Love! (medley) (3) — Reflections (5) — Undecided (3,4) — Young Girl (5)
Everybody Needs Somebody (3) — I Got It (medley) (4) — **Love, Peace And Happiness** (3,6) *96* — Rock Me Mama (2) — Uptown (1)
Funky (5,6) — I Wish It Would Rain (2) — New Generation (5) — Romeo And Juliet (1) — Wade In The Water (3)
Girls, We Love You (4) — If You Want Me To (3) — Satisfy You (2)

CHAMPAIGN '81
R&B group from Champaign, Illinois: Pauli Carman and Rena Jones (vocals), Leon Reeder (guitar), Michael Day and Dana Walden (keyboards), Michael Reed (bass) and Rocky Maffit (drums).

3/21/81	**53**	20	©	1 **How 'Bout Us**	$10	Columbia 37008
4/2/83	**64**	24		2 **Modern Heart**	$10	Columbia 38284
11/10/84	**184**	3		3 **Woman In Flames**	$10	Columbia 39365

Be Mine Tonight (3) — Get It Again (2) — Intimate Strangers (3) — Mardi Gras (3) — Spinnin' (1) — Woman In Flames (3)
Can You Find The Time? (1) — **How 'Bout Us** (1) *12* — Keep It Up (2) — Off And On Love (3) — This Time (3)
Capture The Moon (3) — I'm On Fire (1) — Let Your Body Rock (2) — Party Line (2) — **Try Again** (2) *23*
Cool Running (2) — If One More Morning (1) — Lighten Up (1) — Party People (1) — Walkin' (2)
Dancin' Together Again (1) — International Feel (1) — Love Games (2) — Prisoner (3) — Whiplash (2)

CHAMPLIN, Bill '82
Born on 5/21/47 in Oakland. Singer/songwriter/guitarist. Founder of **Sons Of Champlin**. Joined **Chicago** in 1982.

2/6/82	**178**	4			**Runaway**	$10	Elektra 563

Fool Is All Alone — One Way Ticket — **Sara** *61* — Stop Knockin' On My Door — **Tonight Tonight** *55*
Gotta Get Back To Love — Runaway — Satisfaction — Take It Uptown — Without You

CHANDLER, Gene '79
Born Eugene Dixon on 7/6/37 in Chicago. R&B singer/producer. Joined The Dukays vocal group in 1957. Own label, Mr. Chand, 1969-73.

3/31/62	**69**	8	©	1 **The Duke Of Earl**	$150	Vee-Jay 1040
1/8/66	**124**	3		2 **Gene Chandler - Live On Stage In '65**	[L] $50	Constellation 1425
				recorded at the Regal Theater in Chicago		
10/31/70	**178**	9		3 **The Gene Chandler Situation**	$20	Mercury 61304

CHANDLER, Gene — Cont'd

DEBUT	PEAK	WKS		ARTIST — Album Title	$	Label & Number
3/27/71	143	5	4	Gene & Jerry - One & One	$20	Mercury 61330
				GENE CHANDLER & JERRY BUTLER		
11/25/78+	47	20	5	Get Down	$15	Chi-Sound 578
8/25/79	153	3	6	When You're #1	$12	20th Century 598
6/7/80	87	18	7	Gene Chandler '80	$12	20th Century 605

Ain't No Use (2)
All About The Paper (7)
Am I Blue (3)
Be Yourself (4)
Big Lie (1)
Bless Our Love (2)
Bright Lights And You, Girl (3)
Daddy's Home (1)
Dance Fever (6)
Do It Baby (7)
Do What Comes So Natural (6)
Does She Have A Friend? (7)

Duke Of Earl (1) *1*
Everybody Is Waiting (4)
Festival Of Love (1)
Get Down (5) *53*
Give Me A Chance (4)
Give Me The Cue (5)
Give Up A Taste (4)
Greatest Love Ever Known (5)
Groovy Situation (3) *12*
Hallelujah, I Love Her So (3)
Hey, Little Angel (3)
I Found That I Was Wrong (4)

I Wake Up Crying (1)
I'll Be There (7)
I'll Follow You (1)
I'll Remember You (6)
I'm The Traveling Kind (5)
If You Can't Be True (2)
It's Your Love I'm After (3)
Just Be True (2)
Kissin' In The Kitchen (1)
Lay Me Gently (7)
Let Me Make Love To You (7)
Lonely Island (1)

Lovequake (5)
Mail Call Time (4)
Monkey Time (2)
Nite Owl (1)
Not The Marrying Kind (3)
One Hand Washes The Other (4)
Please Sunrise (5)
Rainbow '65 (Part I) *69*
Rainbow '80 (7)
Sho' Is Groovin' (4)
Simply Call It Love (3) *75*

So Many Ways (1)
Song Called Soul (2)
Soul Hootenanny (2)
Stand By Me (1)
Stay Here In My Heart (4)
Ten And Two (Take This Woman Off The Corner) (4)
That Funky Disco Rhythm (6)
Tomorrow I May Not Feel The Same (5)
Turn On Your Love Light (1)
Unforgettable (3)

What Now (2,5)
When You're #1 (6) *99*
World Keeps Changing (4)
You Just Can't Win (By Making The Same Mistake) (4) *94*
You've Been So Sweet To Me (7)

CHANGE '80

European-American studio group formed in Italy by producers Jacques Fred Petrus and Mauro Malavasi. Led by Paolo Gianolio (guitar) and David Romani (bass). **Luther Vandross** sang lead on several songs for group's first charted album. Later group, based in New York, included lead vocals by James Robinson and Deborah Cooper (later with **C & C Music Factory**). One-time band member Rick Gallwey married **Sharon Bryant**, former lead singer of **Atlantic Starr**.

DEBUT	PEAK	WKS		CD	ARTIST — Album Title	$	Label & Number
5/10/80	29	25	●	©	1 The Glow Of Love	$12	RFC 3438
4/18/81	46	22			2 Miracles	$10	Atlantic 19301
5/15/82	66	9			3 Sharing Your Love	$10	Atlantic 19342
4/2/83	161	7			4 This Is Your Time	$10	Atlantic 80053
4/28/84	102	15			5 Change of Heart	$10	Atlantic 80151

Angel (4)
Angel In My Pocket (1)
Change Of Heart (5)
Don't Wait Another Night (4)
End, The (1)
Everything And More (3)
Glow Of Love (1)

Got My Eyes On You (5)
Got To Get Up (4)
Hard Times (It's Gonna Be Alright) (3)
Heaven Of My Life (2)
Hold Tight (4) *89*
It Burns Me Up (5)

It's A Girl's Affair (1)
Keep It On (3)
Lovely Lady (5)
Lover's Holiday (1) *40*
Magical Night (4)
Miracles (2)
Oh What A Night (3)

On Top (2)
Paradise (2) *80*
Promise Your Love (3)
Say You Love Me Again (5)
Searching (1)
Sharing Your Love (3)
Stay 'N Fit (4)

Stop For Love (2)
Take You To Heaven (3)
Tell Me Why (4)
This Is Your Time (4)
True Love (5)
Very Best In You (3) *84*
Warm (5)

You Are My Melody (5)
You'll Never Realize (4)
You're My Girl (3)
You're My Number 1 (3)
Your Move (2)

CHANGING FACES '97

Female R&B vocal duo from New York City: Charisse Rose and Cassandra Lucas.

DEBUT	PEAK	WKS		CD	ARTIST — Album Title	$	Label & Number
9/10/94	25	25	●	©	1 Changing Faces	$10	Big Beat 92369
6/28/97	21	15	●	©	2 All Day, All Night	$10	Big Beat 92720
10/28/00	46	6		©	3 Visit Me	$10	Atlantic 83401

All Day, All Night (2)
All Is Not Gone (1)
All Of My Own (2)
All That (2)
Am I Wasting My Time (1)
Baby Tonight (2)
Baby U Ain't Got Me (3)

Baby Your Love (1)
Be A Man (3)
B***h (3)
Come Closer (1)
Come Over (3)
Doin To Me (3)
Don't Cry For Me (3)

Feeling All This Love (1)
Foolin' Around (1) *38*
G.H.E.T.T.O.U.T. (2) *8*
G.H.E.T.T.O.U.T. Part II (2)
Goin' Nowhere (2)
Good Thing (2)
I Apologize (2)

I Got Somebody Else (2)
I Told You (3)
Keep It Right There (1)
Ladies Man (3)
Last Night (3)
Lovin' Ya Boy (1)
More Than A Friend (3)

Movin' On (1)
My Heart Can't Take Much More (2)
My Lovely (2)
No Stoppin' This Groove (2)
One Of Those Things (1)
Out Of Sight (3)

Stroke You Up (1) *3*
That Ain't Me (3)
That Other Woman (3) *64*
Thinkin' About You (2)
Thoughts Of You (1)
Time After Time (2)
Visit Me (3)

CHANNEL, Bruce '62

Born on 11/28/40 in Jacksonville, Texas. Pop singer.

DEBUT	PEAK	WKS		ARTIST — Album Title	$	Label & Number
5/19/62	114	5		Hey! Baby (and 11 Other Songs About Your Baby)	$100	Smash 67008

Ain't Got No Home
Baby, It's You

Baby, You've Got What It Takes
Breakin' Up Is Hard To Do

Chantilly Lace
Dream Baby

Dream Girl
Hey! Baby *1*

If Only I Had Known
Love Me

Since I Met You Baby
Sorry Baby

CHANNEL LIVE '95

Rap duo from New Jersey: Tuffy and Hakeem.

DEBUT	PEAK	WKS		CD	ARTIST — Album Title	$	Label & Number
4/8/95	58	5		©	Station Identification	$10	Capitol 28968

Alpha & Omega
Build & Destroy

Down Goes The Devil
Homicide Ride

Lock It Up
Mad Izm *54*

Reprogram
Sex For The Sport

Station Identification
What! (Cause And Effect)

Who U Represent

CHANSON '79

Disco studio group. Lead vocals by James Jamerson, Jr. and David Williams. Jamerson's father was a prominent Motown bassist. Group name is French for song.

DEBUT	PEAK	WKS		ARTIST — Album Title	$	Label & Number
10/14/78+	41	21		Chanson	$12	Ariola 50039

All The Time You Need

Did You Ever

Don't Hold Back *21*

I Can Tell

I Love You More

Why

CHANTAY'S '63

Teenage surf-rock group from Santa Ana, California: Bob Spickard (lead guitar), Brian Carman (rhythm guitar), Rob Marshall (piano), Warren Waters (bass) and Bob Welsh (drums).

DEBUT	PEAK	WKS		CD	ARTIST — Album Title	Sym	$	Label & Number
5/18/63	26	18		©	Pipeline	[I]	$75	Dot 25516

Banzai
Blunderbus

El Conquistador
Last Night

Lonesome Road
Night Theme

Pipeline *4*
Riders In The Sky

Runaway
Sleep Walk

Tragic Wind
Wayward Nile

★427★ CHAPIN, Harry '74

Born on 12/7/42 in New York City. Died in a car crash on 7/16/81 (age 38). Folk-rock singer/songwriter.

1)*Verities & Balderdash* 2)*Greatest Stories-Live* 3)*Portrait Gallery*

DEBUT	PEAK	WKS		CD	ARTIST — Album Title	Sym	$	Label & Number
3/18/72	60	27	●	©	1 Heads & Tales		$15	Elektra 75023
10/28/72	160	8			2 Sniper and Other Love Songs		$15	Elektra 75042
12/29/73+	61	23			3 Short Stories		$15	Elektra 75065
9/7/74	4	33	●	©	4 Verities & Balderdash		$15	Elektra 1012
10/4/75	53	8		©	5 Portrait Gallery		$15	Elektra 1041
5/1/76	48	19	▲²		6 Greatest Stories-Live	[L]	$20	Elektra 2009 [2]
10/30/76	87	6		©	7 On The Road To Kingdom Come		$12	Elektra 1082

CHAPIN, Harry — Cont'd

DEBUT	PEAK	WKS	CD		Album Title	$	Label & Number
9/17/77	58	10	© 8	Dance Band On The Titanic		$15	Elektra 301 [2]
7/1/78	133	8	© 9	Living Room Suite		$12	Elektra 142
10/27/79	163	3	© 10	Legends Of The Lost And Found - New Greatest Stories Live	[L]	$15	Elektra 703 [2]
11/1/80	58	15	11	Sequel		$12	Boardwalk 36872

And The Baby Never Cries (2) / Any Old Kind Of Day (1) / Babysitter (5) / Barefoot Boy (2) / **Better Place To Be (Parts 1 & 2)** (2,6) *86* / Bluesman (8) / Bummer (5) / Burning Herself (2) / Caroline (7) / **Cat's In The Cradle** (4,6) *1* / Changes (3) / Circle (2,6) / Copper (10) / Corey's Coming (7,10) / Could You Put Your Light On, Please (1) / Country Dreams (8) / Dance Band On The Titanic (8) / Dancin' Boy (9) / Day They Closed The Factory Down (10) / Dirt Gets Under The Fingernails (5)

Dogtown (1) / Dreams Go By (5,6) / Empty (1) / Everybody's Lonely (1) / Fall In Love With Him (7) / Flowers Are Red (9,10) / Get On With It (10) / God Babe, You've Been Good For Me (11) / Greyhound (1) / Halfway To Heaven (4) / I Do It For You, Jane (3) / I Finally Found It Sandy (11) / I Miss America (11) / **I Wanna Learn A Love Song** (4,6) *44* / I Wonder What Happened To Him (8) / I Wonder What Would Happen To This World (9) / If My Mary Were Here (7,10) / If You Want To Feel (9) / It Seems You Only Love Me When It Rains (9)

Jenny (9) / Laugh Man (7) / Legends Of The Lost And Found (10) / Let Time Go Lightly (6) / Love Is Just Another Word (6) / Mail Order Annie (3,10) / Manhood (7) / Mayor Of Candor Lied (7) / Mercenaries (8) / Mismatch (9) / Mr. Tanner (3,6) / My Old Lady (8) / Northwest 222 (11) / Odd Job Man (10) / Old College Avenue (3) / Old Folkie (10) / On The Road To Kingdom Come (7) / One Light In A Dark Valley (An Imitation Spiritual) (8) / Paint A Picture Of Yourself (Michael) (8) / Parade's Still Passing By (7)

Poor Damned Fool (9,10) / Pretzel Man (10) / Remember When The Music (11) / Rock, The (5) / Roll Down The River (7) / Salt And Pepper (11) / Same Sad Singer (1) / Sandy (5) / Saturday Morning (6) / **Sequel** (11) *23* / She Is Always Seventeen (6) / She Sings Songs Without Words (4) / Shooting Star (4) / Short Stories (3) / Shortest Story (6) / Six String Orchestra (4) / Sniper (2) / Somebody Said (9) / Someone Keeps Calling My Name (5) / Sometime, Somewhere Wife (1) / Song For Myself (3)

Song Man (7) / Star Tripper (5) / Stop Singing These Sad Songs (5) / Story Of A Life (11) / Stranger With The Melodies (10) / **Sunday Morning Sunshine** (2) *75* / Tangled Up Puppet (5,10) / **Taxi** (1,6) *24* / There Only Was One Choice (8) / There's A Lot Of Lonely People Tonight (3) / They Call Her Easy (3) / 30,000 Pounds Of Bananas (4,6) / Up On The Shelf (11) / Vacancy (4) / **WOLD** (3,6) *36* / We Grew Up A Little Bit (8) / We Were Three (10)

What Made America Famous? (4) / Why Do Little Girls (2) / Why Should People Stay The Same (8) / Winter Song (2) / Woman Child (2) / You Are The Only Song (10)

CHAPMAN, Gary
'96

Born on 8/19/57 in Waurika, Oklahoma; raised in DeLeon, Texas. Contemporary Christian singer/songwriter. Married to Amy Grant from 1982-99. Hosted TNN's *Prime Time Country* from 1996-99.

DEBUT	PEAK	WKS	CD		Album Title	$	Label & Number
3/16/96	192	1	©	Shelter		$10	Reunion 16200

Anything's Possible / Back Where I Started

Chains Of Clay / Don't Be A Stranger

Gospel Ship / Great Is Thy Faithfulness

If You Ever Need Me / Man After Your Own Heart

Nothing Wrong With You / One Of Two

Soldiers Of The Soul / Written In The Scars

CHAPMAN, Steven Curtis
'96

Born on 11/21/62 in Paducah, Kentucky. Contemporary Christian singer/songwriter.

DEBUT	PEAK	WKS	CD		Album Title		$	Label & Number
11/18/95	61	9	● © 1	The Music Of Christmas	C:#39/3 [X]	$10	Sparrow 51489
				Christmas charts: 7/'95, 39/'96, 39/'98			
12/9/95	195	1	▲ © 2	Heaven In The Real World		$10	Sparrow 51408
				released in July 1994			
9/21/96	20	36	● © 3	Signs Of Life		$10	Sparrow 51554
11/8/97	85	16	● © 4	Greatest Hits	[G]	$10	Sparrow 51630
7/3/99	31	34	▲ © 5	(Speechless)		$10	Sparrow 51695

Angels We Have Heard On High (1) / Away In A Manger (medley) (1) / Be Still And Know (5) / Burn The Ships (2) / Carol Of The Bells (1) / Celebrate You (3) / Change, The (5) / Children Of The Burning Heart (3) / Christmas Is All In The Heart (1) / Dancing With The Dinosaur (2) / Dive (5) / Facts Are Facts (2) / Fingerprints Of God (5)

For The Sake Of The Call (4) / Free (3) / Going Home For Christmas (1) / Great Adventure (4) / Great Expectations (5) / Hark! The Herald Angels Sing (medley) (1) / Heartbeat Of Heaven (2) / Heaven In The Real World (2,4) / Hiding Place (4) / His Eyes (4) / His Strength Is Perfect (4) / Hold On To Jesus (5) / I Am Found In You (4) / I Do Believe (5)

I Will Be Here (4) / Invitation, The (5) / Journey, The (5) / King Of The Jungle (2) / Land Of Opportunity (3) / Let Us Pray (3) / Lord Of The Dance (3,4) / Love And Learn (2) / Miracle Of Mercy (2) / More To This Life (4) / Mountain, The (2) / Music Of Christmas (medley) (1) / Next 5 Minutes (5) / No Better Place (4)

Not Home Yet (4) / O Come All Ye Faithful (1) / O Come, O Come, Emmanuel (1) / O Holy Night (medley) (1) / Only Natural (3) / Our God Is With Us (1) / Precious Promise (1) / Remember Your Chains (2) / Rubber Meets The Road (3) / Signs Of Life (4) / Silent Night (medley) (1) / Speechless (5) / Still Listening (2) / That's Paradise (5)

This Baby (1) / Treasure Of You (2) / Walk, The (3,4) / What I Really Want To Say (5) / What I Would Say (3) / Whatever (5) / With Hope (5)

CHAPMAN, Tracy
'88

Born on 3/20/64 in Cleveland. Folk-R&B singer/songwriter. Won the 1988 Best New Artist Grammy Award.

DEBUT	PEAK	WKS	RIAA	CD		Album Title		$	Label & Number
4/30/88	❶¹	61	▲⁴	© 1	Tracy Chapman	C:#5/65	$10	Elektra 60774
10/21/89	9	26	▲	© 2	Crossroads		$10	Elektra 60888
5/16/92	53	11		© 3	Matters Of The Heart		$10	Elektra 61215
12/2/95+	4	95	▲³	© 4	New Beginning		$10	Elektra 61850
3/4/00	33	22	●	© 5	Telling Stories		$10	Elektra 62478

Across The Lines (1) / All That You Have Is Your Soul (2) / At This Point In My Life (4) / **Baby Can I Hold You** (1) *48* / Bang Bang Bang (3) / Be Careful Of My Heart (2) / Behind The Wall (1) / Born To Fight (1) / Bridges (2)

Cold Feet (4) / **Crossroads** (2) *90* / Devotion (5) / Dreaming On A World (3) / **Fast Car** (1) *6* / First Try (5) / For My Lover (1) / For You (1) / Freedom Now (2) / **Give Me One Reason** (4) *3*

Heaven's Here On Earth (4) / Hundred Years (2) / I Used To Be A Sailor (3) / I'm Ready (4) / If Not Now... (1) / If These Are The Things (3) / It's OK (5) / Less Than Strangers (5) / Love That You Had (3) / Material World (2)

Matters Of The Heart (3) / Mountains O' Things (1) / New Beginning (4) / Nothing Yet (5) / Only One (5) / Open Arms (4) / Paper And Ink (5) / Promise, The (4) / Rape Of The World (4) / Remember The Tinman (4)

She's Got Her Ticket (1) / Short Supply (3) / Smoke And Ashes (4) / So (3) / Speak The Word (5) / Subcity (2) / **Talkin' Bout A Revolution** (1) *75* / Tell It Like It Is (4) / Telling Stories (5)

This Time (2) / Unsung Psalm (5) / Wedding Song (5) / Why? (1) / Woman's Work (3)

CHARLATANS UK, The
'91

Rock group from Northwich, England: Tim Burgess (vocals), Jon Baker (guitar), Rob Collins (organ), Martin Blunt (bass) and Jon Brookes (drums). Mark Collins (guitar) replaced Baker in 1993. Simply known as The Charlatans by 1994. Rob Collins died in a car crash on 7/23/96 (age 32).

DEBUT	PEAK	WKS	CD		Album Title	$	Label & Number
11/10/90+	73	27	© 1	Some Friendly		$10	Beggars Banquet 2411
5/2/92	173	2	© 2	Between 10th & 11th		$10	Beggars Banquet 61108

Believe You Me (1) / Can't Even Be Bothered (2) / Chewing Gum Weekend (2) / End Of Everything (2)

Flower (1) / I Don't Want To See The Sights (2) / Ignition (2)

(No One) Not Even The Rain (2) / Page One (2) / 109 pt2 (1) / Only One I Know (1)

Opportunity (1) / Page One (2) / Polar Bear (1) / Sonic (1)

Sproston Green (1) / Subtitle (2) / Then (1) / Tremelo Song (2)

Weirdo (2) / White Shirt (1) / You're Not Very Well (1)

CHARLENE　'82

Born Charlene Duncan on 6/1/50 in Hollywood, California. Pop-R&B singer.

DEBUT	PEAK	WKS						$	Label & Number
4/10/82	36	20			1 **I've Never Been To Me**			$10	Motown 6009
11/27/82	162	7			2 **Used To Be**			$10	Motown 6027

After The Ball (1)
Can't We Try (1)
Heaven Help Us All (2)
Hey Mama (1)
Hungry (1)

I Need A Man (1)
I Want To Go Back There Again (2)
I Won't Remember Ever Loving You (1)
I've Never Been To Me (1) *3*

If I Could See Myself (1)
If You Take Away The Pain (1)
Until The Morning (2)
It Ain't Easy Comin' Down (1) *97*

Johnny Doesn't Love Here Anymore (1)
Last Song (2)
Rainbows (2)
Richie's Song (For Richard Oliver) (2)

Some Things Never Change (2)
Used To Be (2) *46*
You're Home (2)

CHARLES, Ray ★22★　'62

Born Ray Charles Robinson on 9/23/30 in Albany, Georgia; raised in Greenville, Florida. Legendary R&B singer/pianist. Partially blind at age five, completely blind at seven (glaucoma). Studied classical piano and clarinet at State School for Deaf and Blind Children, St. Augustine, Florida, 1937-45. Formed the McSon Trio (also known as the Maxim Trio and the Maxine Trio) with Gossady McGhee (guitar) and Milton Garred (bass). First recordings were very much in the King Cole Trio style. Formed own band in 1954. The 1950s female vocal group, The Cookies, became his backing group, The Raeletts. Inducted into the Rock and Roll Hall of Fame in 1986. Won Grammy's Lifetime Achievement Award in 1987. Popular performer, with many TV and movie appearances.

1)*Modern Sounds In Country And Western Music*　2)*Modern Sounds In Country And Western*
5)*Ray Charles' Greatest Hits*

DEBUT	PEAK	WKS					Sym	$	Label & Number
2/15/60	17	82	©	1	The Genius Of Ray Charles			$50	Atlantic 1312
7/18/60	13	37		2	Ray Charles In Person		[L]	$40	Atlantic 8039
					recorded on 5/28/59 at Herndon Stadium in Atlanta; also see #33 below				
10/10/60	9	50	©	3	The Genius Hits The Road			$40	ABC-Paramount 335
3/6/61	11	31	©	4	Dedicated To You			$40	ABC-Paramount 355
3/27/61	4	48	©	5	Genius + Soul = Jazz			$40	Impulse! 2
8/28/61+	20	73		6	What'd I Say		[K]	$40	Atlantic 8029
8/28/61	49	17	©	7	The Genius After Hours		[I-K]	$40	Atlantic 1369
9/4/61	52	15	©	8	Ray Charles & Betty Carter			$40	ABC-Paramount 385
11/13/61+	73	12		9	The Genius Sings The Blues		[K]	$30	Atlantic 8052
12/18/61+	11	52		10	Do The Twist!		[K]	$30	Atlantic 8054
4/21/62	❶14	101	● ©	11	Modern Sounds In Country And Western Music			$25	ABC-Paramount 410
8/11/62	14	38		12	The Ray Charles Story		[K]	$40	Atlantic 900 [2]
					all of above Atlantic albums recorded 1952-59				
8/18/62	5	47	●	13	Ray Charles' Greatest Hits		[G]	$25	ABC-Paramount 415
11/3/62	2²	67	● ©	14	Modern Sounds In Country And Western Music (Volume Two)			$25	ABC-Paramount 435
8/31/63	2²	36		15	Ingredients In A Recipe For Soul			$25	ABC-Paramount 465
3/21/64	9	23	©	16	Sweet & Sour Tears			$25	ABC-Paramount 480
8/29/64	36	16	©	17	Have A Smile With Me			$25	ABC-Paramount 495
2/20/65	80	18		18	Ray Charles Live In Concert		[L]	$25	ABC-Paramount 500
					recorded at the Shrine Auditorium in Los Angeles				
9/11/65	116	7		19	Country & Western Meets Rhythm & Blues			$25	ABC-Paramount 520
3/12/66	15	36		20	Crying Time			$25	ABC-Paramount 544
9/17/66	52	17		21	Ray's Moods			$20	ABC 550
3/25/67	77	62	●	22	A Man And His Soul		[G]	$25	ABC 590 [2]
7/8/67	76	34		23	Ray Charles invites you to Listen			$20	ABC/TRC 595
4/13/68	51	24		24	A Portrait Of Ray			$20	ABC/TRC 625
4/5/69	167	11		25	I'm All Yours-Baby!			$20	ABC/TRC 675
7/26/69	172	3		26	Doing His Thing			$20	ABC/TRC 695
7/11/70	155	2		27	My Kind Of Jazz		[I]	$20	Tangerine 1512
8/22/70	192	4		28	Love Country Style			$20	ABC/TRC 707
5/29/71	52	16		29	Volcanic Action Of My Soul			$20	ABC/TRC 726
11/20/71	152	10		30	A 25th Anniversary in Show Business Salute to Ray Charles		[G]	$20	ABC 731 [2]
					record 1: Atlantic hits; record 2: ABC hits				
4/29/72	52	22		31	A Message From The People			$15	ABC/TRC 755
11/25/72+	186	8		32	Through The Eyes Of Love			$15	ABC/TRC 765
5/19/73	182	5	©	33	Ray Charles Live		[L-R]	$20	Atlantic 503 [2]
					record 1: recorded on 7/5/74 at the Newport Jazz Festival; record 2: reissue of album #2 above				
6/28/75	175	3		34	Renaissance			$15	Crossover 9005
12/4/76	138	11	©	35	Porgy & Bess			$20	RCA Victor 1831 [2]
					RAY CHARLES/CLEO LAINE				
					includes "Summertime," "I Got Plenty O'Nuttin'," "Strawberry Woman," "It Ain't Necessarily So," "There's A Boat Dat's Leavin' Soon For New York," "I Loves You, Porgy" and "Oh, Bess, O Where's My Bess" by **Frank DeVol**				
11/12/77	78	20		36	True To Life			$12	Atlantic 19142
2/23/85	75	20	©	37	Friendship			$10	Columbia 39415
5/15/93	145	8	©	38	My World			$10	Warner 26735

Abraham, Martin, And John (31)
After My Laughter Came Tears (16)
Ain't Misbehavin' (7)
Ain't That Love (12,30)
Alabamy Bound (3)
Alexander's Ragtime Band (1)
All For You (23)
All I Ever Need Is You (29)
All Night Long (19)
Alone Together (8)
Am I Blue (1,24)
America The Beautiful (31)
Angel City (27)

Anonymous Love (36)
Baby, Don't You Cry (16,18) *39*
Baby It's Cold Outside (8,22) *91*
Baby Please (26)
Basin Street Blues (3)
Be My Love (36)
Bess, You Is My Woman (35)
Birth Of The Blues (5)
Blue Hawaii (3)
Blue Moon Of Kentucky (Swingova) (19)
Blues Waltz (33)
Bluesette (27)

Booty Butt (27,30) *36*
Born Loser (21)
Born To Be Blue (15)
Born To Lose (11,22,30) *41*
Bright Lights & You Girl (24)
Busted (15,22,30) *4*
But On The Other Hand Baby (13) *72*
Buzzard Song (35)
By The Light Of The Silvery Moon (21)
Bye, Bye, Love (11)
California, Here I Come (3)
Candy (4)

Careless Love (11) *60*
Carry Me Back To Old Virginny (3)
Charlesville (7)
Chattanooga Choo-Choo (3)
Cherry (4)
Chitlins With Candied Yams (21,22)
Cocktails For Two (8)
Come And Get It (26)
Come Back Baby (12)
Come Rain Or Come Shine (1,12) *83*

Cry (16,22) *58*
Cry Me A River (16)
Crying Time (20,22,30) *6*
Danger Zone (13)
Dawn Ray (7)
Deed I Do (1)
Deep In The Heart Of Texas (3)
Diane (4)
Don't Change On Me (28,30) *36*
Don't Cry Baby (12)
Don't Let Her Know (19)
Don't Let The Sun Catch You Cryin' (1,30) *95*

Don't Set Me Free (18)
Don't Tell Me Your Troubles (14)
Don't You Know (12,30)
Don't You Think I Ought To Know (20)
Doodlin' (12)
Down In The Valley (29)
Drifting Blues (21)
Drown In My Own Tears (2,12,30,33)
Early In The Mornin' (9)
Eleanor Rigby (24,30) *35*

CHARLES, Ray — Cont'd

Ev'ry Time We Say Goodbye (8)
Every Saturday Night (31)
Feel So Bad (29,30) 68
Feelin' Sad (9)
Feudin' And Fightin' (17)
Finders Keepers, Losers Weepers (26)
Fool For You (12,30,33)
For All We Know (8)
For Mama (La Mamma) (34)
Frensei (2,33)
Friendship (37)
From The Heart (5,22)
Game Number Nine (36)
Gee, Baby Ain't Good To You (23)
Genius After Hours (7)
Georgia On My Mind (3,13,22,30) 1
Girl I Used To Know (21)
Gloomy Sunday (29)
Going Down Slow (20)
Golden Boy (27)
Good Morning Dear (28)
Goodbye (medley) (8)
Granny Wasn't Grinning That Day (21)
Guess I'll Hang My Tears Out To Dry (16)
Half As Much (11)
Hallelujah I Love Her So (12,18,30)
Hang Your Head In Shame (14)
Hard Times (No One Knows Better Than I) (9)
Hardhearted Hannah (4) 55
Heartbreaker (10)
Heaven Help Us All (31)
Heavenly Music (36)
Here We Go Again (23) 15
Hey Mister (31)
Hide Nor Hair (18)
Hit The Road Jack (13,22,30) 1
Hornful Soul (7)
Hot Rod (33)
How Deep Is The Ocean (How High Is The Sky) (23)
How Long Has This Been Going On (36)
I Believe To My Soul (9,30)
I Can Make It Thru The Days (But Oh Those Lonely Nights) (32) 81
I Can See Clearly Now (36)
I Can't Stop Loving You (11,22,30) 1
I Chose To Sing The Blues (22) 32

I Cried For You (16)
I Didn't Know What Time It Was (25)
I Don't Care (19)
I Don't Need No Doctor (22) 72
I Dream Of You (More Than You Dream I Do) (25)
I Got Plenty O'Nuttin' (35)
I Gotta Woman (Part One) (10,12,18,30,33) 79
I Had The Craziest Dream (25)
I Keep It Hid (28)
I Like To Hear It Sometime (19)
I Love You So Much It Hurts (11)
I May Be Wrong (But I Think You're Wonderful) (29)
I Never See Maggie Alone (17)
I Told You So (26)
I Won't Leave (24)
I Wonder (13)
I Wonder Who (9)
I'll Be Seeing You (23)
I'll Be There (38)
I'll Never Stand In Your Way (14)
I'm Gonna Move To The Outskirts Of Town (5,13) 84
I'm Movin' On (9,10,12) 40
I'm Ready (26)
I've Got A Tiger By The Tail (Swingova) (19)
I've Got News For You (5,13) 66
If I Could (38)
If It Wasn't For Bad Luck (26) 77
If You Were Mine (28,30) 41
If You Wouldn't Be My Lady (32)
In A Little Spanish Town (33)
In The Evening (When The Sun Goes Down) (15)
Indian Love Call (25)
It Ain't Easy Being Green (34)
It Ain't Gonna Worry My Mind (37)
It Ain't Necessarily So (35)
It Had To Be You (1)
It Makes No Difference Now (11)
It Should've Been Me (12,30)
It's A Man's World (21)
Jealous Kind (36)
Josephine (4)
Joy Ride (7)
Jumpin' In The Mornin' (6)
Just A Little Lovin' (11)
Just For A Thrill (1,12,30)
Just You, Just Me (8)

Leave My Woman Alone (10)
Let It Be (36)
Let Me Take Over (38)
Let The Good Times Roll (1,12) 78
Let's Go (5)
Let's Go Get Stoned (20,22,30) 31
Lift Every Voice And Sing (31)
Light Out Of Darkness (19)
Little Hotel Room (37)
Living For The City (34) 91
Lonely Avenue (12,30)
Long And Winding Road (29)
Losing Hand (12)
Love Has A Mind Of Its Own (38)
Love Is Here To Stay (25)
Love Walked In (23)
Ma (She's Making Eyes At Me) (17)
Makin' Whoopee (18,22) 46
Making Believe (14)
Man I Love (7)
Man With The Weird Beard (11)
Margie (4,18)
Marie (4)
Mary Ann (12,30)
Maybe It's Because Of Love (21)
Maybe It's Nothing At All (19)
Memories Of You (25)
Mess Around (12,30)
Midnight (14)
Midnight Hour (9)
Mississippi Mud (5)
Mister C (5)
Moanin' (5)
Moon Over Miami (3)
Moonlight In Vermont (3)
Move It On Over (17)
Mr. Charles Blues (9)
Music, Music, Music (7)
My Bonnie (6,12)
My First Night Alone Without You (32)
My God And I (34)
My World (38)
Nancy (4)
Naughty Lady Of Shady Lane (17)
Never Ending Song Of Love (32)
Never Say Naw (24)
New York's My Home (3)
Next Door To The Blues (19)
(Night Time Is) The Right Time (30) 95
No Letter Today (14)
No One To Cry To (16) 55
No Use Crying (20,22)

Nobody Cares (9)
None Of Us Are Free (38)
Oh, Bess, Oh Where's My Bess (35)
Oh Lawd, I'm On My Way (35)
Oh, Lonesome Me (14)
Oh, What A Beautiful Mornin' (36)
Ol' Man River (15,22)
Ol' Man Time (15)
One Drop Of Love (38)
One Mint Julep (5,13,22,30) 8
Over The Rainbow (15)
Pas-Se-O-Ne Blues (27)
Peace Of Mind (20)
People (23)
People Will Say We're In Love (8)
Perfect Love (32)
Please Forgive And Forget (19)
Please Say You're Fooling (21) 64
Rainy Night In Georgia (32)
Ray's Blues (9)
Right Time (2,9,12,33)
Ring Of Fire (28)
Rock And Roll Shoes (37)
Rockhouse (Part 2) (6,12,30) 79
Roll With My Baby (6)
Rosetta (4)
Ruby (4,13,22,30) 28
Sail Away (34)
Same Thing That Can Make You Laugh (Can Make You Cry) (26)
See You Then (29)
Seems Like I Gotta Do Wrong (31)
Senor Blues (27)
Sentimental Journey (21)
Seven Spanish Angels (37)
She's Funny That Way (I Got A Woman Crazy For Me) (23)
She's Lonesome Again (21)
Sherry (33)
Show Me The Sunshine (28)
Side By Side (8)
Sidewinder (27)
Smack Dab In The Middle (17) 52
So Help Me God (38)
Some Day Baby (9)
Someday (7)
Someday (You'll Want Me To Want You) (14)
Someone To Watch Over Me (32)
Something (29)
Song For You (38)
Spirit-Feel, The (2,33)

Stella By Starlight (4)
Sticks And Stones (13) 40
Still Crazy After All These Years (38)
Stompin' Room Only (5)
Stranger In Town (15)
Strike Up The Band (5)
Summertime (35)
Sun Died (24)
Sun's Gonna Shine Again (12)
Sunshine (34)
Swanee River Rock (Talkin' 'Bout That River) (12,30) 34
Sweet Georgia Brown (4)
Sweet Memories (28)
Sweet Sixteen Bars (12)
Sweet Young Thing Like You (24) 83
Swing A Little Taste (18)
Take Me Home, Country Roads (31)
Take These Chains From My Heart (14) 8
Takes Two To Tango (8,22)
Talkin' 'Bout You (10,12,33)
Tear Fell (16) 50
Teardrops From My Eyes (16,22)
Teardrops In My Heart (14)
Tears (20)
Tell All The World About You (6,12)
Tell Me How Do You Feel (6,10)
Tell Me You'll Wait For Me (1)
Tell The Truth (2,10,33)
That Lucky Old Sun (15) 89
That Thing Called Love (26)
That's Enough (6)
Them That Got (13) 58
Then We'll Be Home (34)
There'll Be No Peace Without All Men As One (31)
There's A Boat Dat's Leavin' Soon For New York (35)
Thing, The (17)
This Here (27)
This Little Girl Of Mine (12)
This Old Heart (Is Gonna Rise Again) (37)
Three Bells (29)
Till I Can't Take It Anymore (28)
Till The End Of Time (25)
Together (32)
Together Again (19) 19
Two Old Cats Like Us (37)
Two Ton Tessie (17)
Two Years Of Torture (11)
Unchain My Heart (13,22,30) 9
Understanding (24,30) 46
Watch It Baby (19)

We Can Make It (26)
We Didn't See A Thing (37)
We Don't See Eye To Eye (20)
We'll Be Together Again (medley) (8)
We're Gonna Make It (34)
What Am I Living For (29) 54
What-Cha Doing In There (I Wanna Know) (21)
What Have They Done To My Song, Ma (31)
What Kind Of Man Are You (6,12)
What'd I Say (Part I) (2,6,10,12,18,22,30,33) 6
When I Stop Dreamin' (24)
When Your Lover Has Gone (1)
Where Can I Go? (15)
Who Cares (37)
Who Cares (For Me) (17)
Wichita Lineman (29)
Willow Weep For Me (16)
Woman Is A Sometime Thing (35)
Worried Mind (11,22)
Yes Indeed! (2,12,30,33)
Yesterday (23,30) 25
Yesterdays (24)
You And I (8)
You Are My Sunshine (14,22,30) 7
You Be My Baby (6,10)
You Don't Know Me (11,18) 2
You Don't Understand (21)
You Leave Me Breathless (32)
You Made Me Love You (I Didn't Wanna Do It) (23)
You Ought To Change Your Ways (26)
You Win Again (11)
You Won't Let Me Go (1)
You'll Never Walk Alone (15)
You're In For A Big Surprise (20)
You're Just About To Lose Your Clown (20) 91
You've Got A Problem (20)
You've Got Me Crying Again (16)
You've Still Got A Place In My Heart (28)
Your Cheating Heart (14) 29
Your Love Is So Doggone Good (28)
Yours (25)
Zig Zag (27)

CHARLES, Ray, Singers   '64

Born Charles Raymond Offenberg on 9/13/18 in Chicago. Arranger/conductor for many TV shows.

4/4/64	11	33	1 Something Special For Young Lovers	$15	Command 866
9/5/64	45	22	2 Al-Di-La and other Extra-Special songs for Young Lovers	$15	Command 870
12/5/64+	88	20	3 Songs For Lonesome Lovers	$15	Command 874
8/21/65	125	6	4 Songs For Latin Lovers	$15	Command 886

Adios (4)
Al-Di-La (2) 29
Amo, Amas, Amamus (4)
Bluesette (2)
By Myself (3)
Call Me Irresponsible (2)
Carnival (Manha De Carnaval) (4)
Charade (1)
Dear Heart (3)
Desafinado (Slightly Out Of Tune) (4)

Do You Want To Know A Secret (2)
Dominique (1)
Friendliest Thing (2)
Girl From Ipanema (2)
Hello, Dolly! (1)
I Ain't Gonna Cry No More (3)
I Left My Heart In San Francisco (1)
I Wish You Love (3)
I'll Never Smile Again (3)
Johann Sebastian Bach (2)

Love Me With All Your Heart (Cuando Calienta El Sol) (1) 3
Maria Elena (4)
More (1)
My Guitar And My Song (Ti Regalo La Luna) (4)
My Love, Forgive Me (Amore, Scusami) (4)
No More Blues (Chega De Saudade) (1)
One More Time (3) 32

Over The Rainbow (3)
People (3)
Quiet Night (Corcovado) (1)
Real Live Girl (2)
Satin Doll (3)
Smile (3)
Something Extra Special (2)
Song Of The Jet (Samba Do Aviao) (4)
Sweet Little Mountain Bird (1)
There I've Said It Again (1)

This Could Be The Start Of Something (1)
This Is All I Ask (1)
This Is My Prayer (3) 72
Till The End Of Time (2) 83
To You (E Lei) (4)
Toy For A Boy (3)
Vaya Con Dios (4)
What Kind Of Fool Am I? (1)
Willow Weep For Me (3)
Yo No Que Te Quiero (1)

You Are Never Far Away From Me (2)
You're Mine (4)

CHARLES, Sonny   '83

Born Charles Hemphill on 9/4/40 in Fort Wayne, Indiana. R&B singer. Leader of **The Checkmates, Ltd.**

| 12/25/82+ | 136 | 7 | The Sun Still Shines | $10 | Highrise 102 |

Always On My Mind
Can't Get Enough

One Eyed Jacks
Per-so-nal-ly

Put It In A Magazine 40
Treasure Of Your Pleasure

Week-end Father Song
Whet Your Whistle

CHARLES & EDDIE   '92

R&B vocal duo: Charles Pettigrew (from Philadelphia) and Eddie Chacon (from Oakland). Pettigrew died of cancer on 4/6/2001 (age 37).

| 10/31/92 | 153 | 5 | © Duophonic | $10 | Capitol 97150 |

Be A Little Easy On Me
December 2
Father To Son

House Is Not A Home
Hurt No More
I Understand

Love Is A Beautiful Thing
N.Y.C.
Shine

Unconditional
Vowel Song
Where Do We Go From Here?

Would I Lie To You? 13

CHARLESTON CITY ALL-STARS '57

Group of studio musicians conducted by **Enoch Light**.

DEBUT	PEAK	WKS			Album		Sym	$	Label & Number
7/8/57+	16	14			1 **The Roaring 20's, Volume 2**		[I]	$20	Grand Award 340
9/2/57	17	2			2 **The Roaring 20's, Volume 3**		[I]	$20	Grand Award 353

Ain't She Sweet (1)
April Showers (2)
Baby Face (2)
Bye, Bye Blackbird (2)
Collegiate (1)
Five Foot Two (1)
I Can't Give You Anything But Love (1)
I Love My Baby, My Baby Loves Me (2)
I'm Just Wild About Harry (2)
I'm Sitting On Top Of The World (2)
Ma, He's Making Eyes At Me (2)
Margie (2)
Paddlin' Madelin' Home (1)
Runnin' Wild (1)
Sheik Of Araby (2)
Show Me The Way To Go Home (1)
Singin' In The Rain (1)
Sleepy Time Gal (2)
Sugar Blues (1)
Swinging Down The Lane (1)
That Certain Party (1)
Varsity Drag (1)
When My Baby Smiles At Me (1)
When The Red, Red Robin Comes Bob, Bob Bobbin' Along (2)

CHARLIE '79

Rock group from England: Terry Thomas (guitar), Julian Colbeck (guitar), John Anderson (bass) and Steve Gadd (drums). Varying membership also included Bob Henrit (drums; **Argent**; joined by 1983) and Terry Slesser (vocals; joined in 1980). Henrit joined **The Kinks** in 1984.

DEBUT	PEAK	WKS			Album	$	Label & Number
6/4/77	111	15			1 **No Second Chance**	$12	Janus 7032
4/15/78	75	14			2 **Lines**	$12	Janus 7036
9/1/79	60	10			3 **Fight Dirty**	$12	Arista 4239
10/10/81	99	11			4 **Fifth Flight**	$12	Vertigo 2003
7/23/83	145	9			5 **Charlie**	$10	Mirage 90098

California (3)
Can't Wait 'Til Tomorrow (5)
Don't Count Me Out (3)
Don't Look Back (1)
End Of It All (3)
Fight Dirty (3)
Guitar Hero (1)
Heartaches Begin (5)
Heartless (3)
I Like To Rock And Roll (2)
It's Inevitable (5) *38*
Johnny Hold Back (1)
Just One More Smiling Face (3)
Keep In Mind (2)
Killer Cut (3) *60*
L.A. Dreamer (2)
Life So Cruel (2)
Love Is Alright (1)
Lovers (1)
Never Too Late (5)
No More Heartache (2)
No Second Chance (1)
No Strangers In Paradise (2)
Out Of Control (2)
Playing To Win (5)
Pressure Point (1)
Runaway (3)
She Loves To Be In Love (2) *54*
So Alone (3)
Spend My Life With You (5)
Tempted (5)
Thirteen (1)
This Time (5)
Too Late (3)
Turning To You (1) *96*
Watching T.V. (2)
You're Everything I Need (5)

CHARO & The Salsoul Orchestra '78

Born Maria Rosario Pilar Martinez on 1/15/42 in Murcia, Spain. Singer/actress. Known as the "Cuchi-Cuchi" girl. Married to bandleader Xavier Cugat from 1963-78.

DEBUT	PEAK	WKS			Album	$	Label & Number
11/26/77+	100	15			**Cuchi-Cuchi**	$12	Salsoul 5519

Borriquito
Cookie Jar
Cuchi-Cuchi
Dance A Little Bit Closer
El Reloj (The Clock)
More Of You
Let's Spend The Night Together
Only You (Can Make My Empty Life Worthwhile)
Speedy Gonzalez
You're Just The Right Size

CHASE '71

Jazz-rock band organized by trumpeter Bill Chase (born in 1935 in Chicago; formerly with **Woody Herman** and **Stan Kenton**). Varying lineup. Chase along with bandmates John Emma, Wallace Yohn and Walter Clark were killed in a plane crash on 8/9/74 near Jackson, Minnesota.

DEBUT	PEAK	WKS		CD	Album	$	Label & Number
5/8/71	22	26		©	1 **Chase**	$15	Epic 30472
4/8/72	71	12		©	2 **Ennea**	$15	Epic 31097
4/27/74	155	10		©	3 **Pure Music**	$15	Epic 32572

Aphrodite Part I & II (Venus) (2)
Bochawa (3)
Boys And Girls Together (1)
Close Up Tight (3)
Cronus (Saturn) (2)
Get It On (1) *24*
Hades (Pluto) (2)
Handbags And Gladrags (1) *84*
Hello Groceries (1)
I Can Feel It (2)
Invitation To A River Medley (1)
It Won't Be Long (2)
Livin' In Heat (1)
Love Is On The Way (3)
Night (2)
Open Up Wide (1)
Poseidon (Neptune) (2)
Run Back To Mama (3)
So Many People (2) *81*
Swanee River (2)
Twinkles (3)
Weird Song #1 (3)
Woman Of The Dark (2)
Zeus (Jupiter) (2)

★221★ CHEAP TRICK '79

Rock group from Rockford, Illinois: Robin Zander (vocals), Rick Nielsen (guitar), Tom Petersson (bass) and Brad "Bun E. Carlos" Carlson (drums). Petersson replaced by Jon Brant in 1980; returned in 1988, replacing Brant.

1)Cheap Trick At Budokan 2)Dream Police 3)Lap Of Luxury

DEBUT	PEAK	WKS	RIAA	CD	Album	Catalog	Sym	$	Label & Number
9/24/77	73	12	●	©	1 **In Color**			$12	Epic 34884
6/10/78	48	22	▲	©	2 **Heaven Tonight**			$12	Epic 35312
2/24/79	4	53	▲³	©	3 **Cheap Trick At Budokan**	C:#34/56	[L]	$12	Epic 35795
					recorded on 4/28/78 in Japan				
10/6/79	6	25	▲	©	4 **Dream Police**			$12	Epic 35773
7/5/80	39	12			5 **Found All The Parts**		[M]	$12	Epic 36453
11/15/80	24	15	●	©	6 **All Shook Up**			$12	Epic 36498
5/29/82	39	27	●		7 **One On One**			$10	Epic 38021
9/10/83	61	11		©	8 **Next Position Please**			$10	Epic 38794
8/17/85	35	18		©	9 **Standing On The Edge**			$10	Epic 39592
10/18/86	115	9		©	10 **The Doctor**			$10	Epic 40405
5/7/88	16	47	▲	©	11 **Lap Of Luxury**			$10	Epic 40922
8/4/90	48	17		©	12 **Busted**			$10	Epic 46013
10/19/91	174	3	▲	©	13 **The Greatest Hits**		[G]	$10	Epic 48681
4/9/94	123	2			14 **Woke Up With A Monster**			$10	Warner 45425
5/17/97	99	2		©	15 **Cheap Trick**			$10	Red Ant 002

Ain't That A Shame (3,13) *35*
All We Need Is A Dream (11)
All Wound Up (11)
Anytime (15)
Are You Lonely Tonight (10)
Auf Wiedersehen (2)
Baby Loves To Rock (6)
Baby No More (15)
Back 'N Blue (12)
Big Eyes (1,3)
Borderline (8)
Busted (12)
California Man (2)
Can't Hold On (5)
Can't Stop Fallin' Into Love (12,13) *12*
Can't Stop But I'm Gonna Try (6)
Carnival Game (15)
Clock Strikes Ten (1,3)
Come On, Come On (1,3)
Cover Girl (9)
Cry Baby (14)
Dancing The Night Away (8)
Day Tripper (5)
Didn't Know I Had It (14)
Doctor, The (10)
Downed (1)
Dream Police (4,13) *26*
Eight Miles Low (15)
Flame, The (11,13) *1*
Four Letter Word (7)
Ghost Town (11) *33*
Girlfriends (14)
Go For The Throat (Use Your Own Imagination) (6)
Gonna Raise Hell (3)
Good Girls Go To Heaven (Bad Girls Go Everywhere) (10)
Goodnight (3)
Had To Make You Mine (12)
Hard To Tell (15)
Heaven Tonight (2)
Hello There (1,3)
Heaven's Falling (8)
High Priest Of Rhythmic Noise (6)
High Roller (2)
House Is Rockin' (With Domestic Problems) (4)
How About You (9)
How Are You (2)
I Can't Take It (8,13)
I Can't Understand It (12)
I Don't Love Here Anymore (8)
I Know What I Want (4)
I Love You Honey But I Hate Your Friends (6)
I Want Be Man (7)
I Want You (7)
I Want You To Want Me (1,3,13) *7*
I'll Be With You Tonight (4)
If You Need Me (12)
If You Want My Love (7,13) *45*
Invaders Of The Heart (8)
It All Comes Back To You (15)
It's Only Love (10)
It's Up To You (10)
Just Got Back (6)
Kiss Me Red (10)
Let Go (11)
Let Her Go (14)
Little Sister (9)
Lookin' Out For Number One (7)
Lookout (3)
Love Comes (9)
Love Comes A-Tumblin' Down (6)
Love Me For A Minute (14)
Love's Got A Hold On Me (7)
Magical Mystery Tour (13)
Man-U-Lip-U-Lator (10)
My Gang (14)
Name Of The Game (10)
Need Your Love (3,4)
Never Had A Lot To Lose (11) *75*
Never Run Out Of Love (14)
Next Position Please (8)
No Mercy (11)
Oh Caroline (1)
On The Radio (4)
On Top Of The World (2)
One On One (7)
Oo La La La (7)
Rearview Mirror Romance (10)
Ride The Pony (14)
Rock All Night (9)
Rock 'N' Roll Tonight (12)
Saturday At Midnight (7)
Say Goodbye (15)
She's Got Motion (9)
She's Tight (7,13) *65*
Shelter (15)
So Good To See You (1)

CHEAP TRICK — Cont'd

Southern Girls (1)
Space (11)
Standing On The Edge (9)
Stiff Competition (2)
Stop This Game (6) *48*
Such A Good Girl (5)
Surrender (2,3,13) *62*

Take Me I'm Yours (5)
Take Me To The Top (10)
Takin' Me Back (2)
Tell Me Everything (14)
This Time Around (9)
3-D (8)
Time Is Runnin' (7)

Tonight It's You (9,13) *44*
Voices (4,13) *32*
Walk Away (12)
Way Of The World (4)
When You Need Someone (12)
Wherever Would I Be (12) *50*
Who D' King (6)

Wild Wild Women (9)
Woke Up With A Monster (14)
Won't Take No For An Answer (8)
World's Greatest Lover (6)
Writing On The Wall (9)
Wrong All Along (15)

Wrong Side Of Love (11)
Y.O.Y.O.Y. (8)
Yeah Yeah (15)
You Drive, I'll Steer (12)
You Let A Lotta People Down (15)
You Say Jump (8)

You're All I Wanna Do (14)
You're All Talk (1)
Younger Girls (8)

CHECKER, Chubby ★145★   '62

Born Ernest Evans on 10/3/41 in Andrews, South Carolina; raised in Philadelphia. Did impersonations of famous singers. First recorded for Parkway in 1959. Dick Clark's then-wife Bobbie suggested that Evans change his name to Chubby Checker due to his resemblance to a teenage **Fats Domino**. Cover version of Hank Ballard's "The Twist" started worldwide dance craze. On 4/12/64, married Miss World 1962, Dutch-born Catharina Lodders ("Loddy Lo" written for her). In the movies *Don't Knock The Twist* and *Twist Around The Clock*.

1)*Your Twist Party* 2)*Twist With Chubby Checker* 3)*Bobby Rydell/Chubby*

DEBUT	PEAK	WKS			ARTIST — Album Title		Sym	$	Label & Number
10/31/60+	**3**	86		1	Twist With Chubby Checker			$60	Parkway 7001
5/29/61	**110**	16		2	It's Pony Time			$60	Parkway 7003
9/25/61+	**11**	47		3	Let's Twist Again			$60	Parkway 7004
12/4/61+	**8**	38		4	For Twisters Only			$60	Parkway 7002
12/11/61+	**2**[6]	67		5	Your Twist Party		[K]	$60	Parkway 7007
12/18/61+	**7**	30		6	Bobby Rydell/Chubby Checker			$60	Cameo 1013
3/31/62	**17**	27		7	For Teen Twisters Only			$60	Parkway 7009
4/28/62	**54**	11		8	Twistin' Round The World			$60	Parkway 7008
6/9/62	**29**	20		9	Don't Knock The Twist		[S]	$60	Parkway 7011
					includes "Bristol Stomp" and "Do The Continental" by **The Dovells**, "Bo Diddley" by Carroll Brothers; "Mashed Potato Time" by **Dee Dee Sharp**, "Smashed Potatoes" (instrumental) and "Salome Twist" by Various Artists				
10/27/62	**23**	24		10	All The Hits (For Your Dancin' Party)			$60	Parkway 7014
11/17/62	**117**	4		11	Down To Earth			$60	Cameo 1029
					CHUBBY CHECKER/DEE DEE SHARP				
12/15/62+	**11**	24		12	Limbo Party			$60	Parkway 7020
12/29/62+	**27**	23		13	Chubby Checker's Biggest Hits		[G]	$60	Parkway 7022
3/30/63	**87**	17		14	Let's Limbo Some More			$60	Parkway 7027
8/10/63	**90**	4		15	Beach Party			$60	Parkway 7030
10/12/63	**104**	4		16	Chubby Checker In Person		[L]	$60	Parkway 7026
					labeled as *Twist It Up*; recorded at the Under 21 Club in Somers Point, New Jersey				
12/23/72+	**152**	10		17	Chubby Checker's Greatest Hits		[G]	$25	Abkco 4219 [2]
3/6/82	**186**	2		18	The Change Has Come			$10	MCA 5291

Alouette (All You Twisters) (8)
At The Hop (4,17)
Baby, Come Back (12)
Ballin' The Jack (3,5)
Banana Boat Limbo Song (12)
Birdland (15,17) *12*
Blueberry Hill (4,5)
Bossa Nova (12)
Burn Up The Night (18)
But Girls! (4)
C.C. Rider Stroll (1)
Charleston, The (17)
Chicken, The (1)
Cindy, Oh Cindy (14)
Class, The (17) *38*
Continental Walk (3)
Dance-A-Long (3)
Dance The Mess Around (13) *24*
Dance With Me, Henry (4)
Dancin' Party (10,13,17) *12*
Dear Lady Twist (7)
Desafinado (Slightly Out Of Tune) (12)
Do The Freddy (17)
Do You Love Me (11)
(Don't Be Afraid,) It's Only Rock And Roll (18)
Don't Knock The Twist (9)
Don't Let Go (16)
Don't You Just Know It (16)
Down To Earth (11)
Fishin' (3)
Fly, The (7,9,13,17) *7*
Girl With The Swingin' Derriere (14)

Good, Good Lovin' (13) *43*
Gravy (For My Mashed Potatoes) (10)
Harder Than Diamond (18)
Hava Nagela (8)
Having A Party (10)
Hey, Bobba Needle (17) *23*
Hi-Ho Silver (2,16)
Hold Tight (4)
Hooka Tooka (17) *17*
Hound Dog (4,5)
How Can You Go? (14)
Hucklebuck, The (1,5,13,17) *14*
Hully Gully (2)
Hully Gully Baby (10)
I Almost Lost My Mind (3)
I Could Have Danced All Night (3,5)
I Love To Twist (9)
I Need Your Loving (10)
I Really Don't Want To Know (11)
I'm Walkin' (16)
I've Got Love (That's Hard To Find) (18)
Jamaica Farewell (12)
Jet, The (3)
Jingle Bell Rock (6) *21*
Jingle Bells Imitations (6)
Johnny B. Goode (16)
Kansas City (16)
Killer, The (15)
La Bamba (12)
La La Limbo (12)
La Paloma Twist (9) *72*

Lazy Elsie Molly (17) *40*
Let The Good Times Roll (11)
Let's Dance, Let's Dance, Let's Dance (2)
Let's Limbo Some More (14,17) *20*
Let's Surf Again (15)
Let's Twist (A La Paloma) (8)
Let's Twist Again (3,5,13,16,17) *8*
Let's Twist Again (Der Twist Beginnt) (8)
Limbo Rock (10,12,13,17) *2*
Limbo Side By Side (15)
Loddy Lo (17) *12*
Lose Your Inhibitions Twist (7)
Lotta Limbo (14)
Love Is Like A Twist (7)
Love Is Strange (1,11)
Loving You (11)
Madison, The (1)
Make Love To Me (11)
Mama Look A Boo Boo (14)
Man Smart, Woman Smarter (12)
Manana (Is Soon Enough For Me) (14)
Mary Ann Limbo (12)
Mashed Potato Love (15)
Mashed Potato Time (10)
Mashed Potatoes (2)
Maybelline (16)
Mess Around (2)
Mexican Hat Twist (1,5)
Miserlou (8)
Mister Twister (4,5)
Mother Goose Limbo (14)

My Baby Just Cares For Me (6)
Never On Sunday (8)
Nothin' But The Twist (15)
O Sole Mio (8)
One More Time (11)
Oo-Kook-A-Boo (15)
Ooh Poo Pah Doo Shimmy (1)
Peanut Butter (3)
Peanut Vendor (14)
Peppermint Twist (7)
Play It Fair (11)
Pledging My Love (11)
Pony, The (17)
Pony Express (2)
Pony Time (2,13,17) *1*
Popeye The Hitchhiker (10,13) *10*
Quarter To Three (3)
Ray Charles-ton (3)
Rip It Up (16)
Rock Around The Clock (4,5)
Rock It To Me Rudy (13)
Rockin' Good Way (To Mess Around And Fall In Love) (medley) (11)
Rum And Coca Cola (14)
Run Around Sue (7)
Run, Chico, Run (14)
Run To Me (18)
Running (18) *91*
Shake Rattle And Roll (4,17)
She Said (15)
She's A Hippy (15)
Shimmy, The (7)
Shout (7)
Side By Side (6)
Slop, The (1)

Slow Twistin' (7,9,13,16,17) *3*
Somebody Bad Stole De Wedding Bell (12)
Strand, The (1)
Stroll, The (2)
Surf Party (15) *55*
Swingin' Together (6)
T-82 (18)
Takes Two To Tango (3)
Tea For Two (8)
Teach Me To Twist (6)
Twenty Miles (14) *15*
Twist, The (1,5,13,16,17) *1*
Twist-A-Long (7)
Twist And Shout (15)
Twist It Up (15,16,17) *25*
Twist Marie (8)
Twist Mit Mir (Mus I Denn) (8)
Twist Train (4)
Twistin' (9)
Twistin' Bones (7)
Twistin' Matilda (8)
Twistin' Round The World (8)
Twistin' The Blues (7)
Twistin' U.S.A. (1,5) *68*
Under My Thumb (18)
Voodoo (You Remind Me Of The Guy) (8)
Wah-Watusi, The (2,10)
Walkin' My Baby Back Home (6)
We Like Birdland (2,10)
(We're Gone) Surfin' (15)
What Are You Doing New Year's Eve (6)
When The Saints Go Limbo In (12)

Whole Lotta Shakin' Goin' On (4,5,13) *42*
You Came A Long Way From St. Louis (11)
Your Feet's Too Big (4)
Your Hits And Mine Medley (6)
Your Lips And Mine (7)
Your Love (18)

CHECKMATES, LTD., The   '69

R&B group from Fort Wayne, Indiana: **Sonny Charles** and Bobby Stevens (vocals), Harvey Trees (guitar), Bill Van Buskirk (bass) and Marvin Smith (drums).

DEBUT	PEAK	WKS			ARTIST — Album Title			$	Label & Number
10/18/69	**178**	4			Love Is All We Have To Give			$25	A&M 4183

Black Pearl *13*   Hair Anthology Suite Medley   I Keep Forgettin'   Love Is All I Have To Give *65*   Proud Mary *69*   Spanish Harlem

DEBUT	PEAK	WKS	RIAA	CD		ARTIST — Album Title	Catalog	Sym	$	Label & Number

★450★ CHEECH & CHONG '72

Duo of comedians Richard "Cheech" Marin (born on 7/13/46 in Watts, California) and Thomas Chong (born on 5/24/38, Edmonton, Alberta, Canada). Starred in several movies. Chong, the father of actress Rae Dawn Chong, was the guitarist of **Bobby Taylor & The Vancouvers**. Cheech was a cast member of TV's *Golden Palace* and *Nash Bridges*.

DEBUT	PEAK	WKS		CD	#	Album Title	Sym	$	Label & Number
9/25/71+	28	64	●	©	1	Cheech And Chong	[C]	$15	Ode 77010
7/1/72	2¹	111	●	©	2	Big Bambu	[C]	$15	Ode 77014
9/8/73	2¹	69	●	©	3	Los Cochinos	[C]	$15	Ode 77019
						title is Spanish for "The Pigs"			
10/19/74	5	25	●	©	4	Cheech & Chong's Wedding Album	[C]	$15	Ode 77025
6/26/76	25	13		©	5	Sleeping Beauty	[C]	$15	Ode 77040
12/2/78+	162	7		©	6	Up In Smoke	[C-S]	$12	Warner 3249
						includes "Low Rider" by **War** and "Here Come The Mounties To The Rescue," "Lost Due To Incompetence (Theme For A Big Green Van)" and "Strawberry's" by Yesca			
7/19/80	173	3			7	Let's Make A New Dope Deal	[C]	$12	Warner 3391
10/12/85	71	11			8	Get Out Of My Room	[C]	$10	MCA 5640

Acapulco Gold Filters (1)
Acupuncture (7)
Adventures Of Red & Roy (The Last Round-Up) (5)
Ajax Lady (6)
Baby Sitters Featuring Pedro & Man (4)
Basketball Jones Featuring Tyrone Shoelaces (3) *15*
Big Sniff (Starring Ralph & Herbie) (5)
Black Lassie Featuring Johnny Stash (4) *55*
Blind Melon Chitlin' (1)
Bloat On Featuring The Bloaters (7) *41*
Born In East L.A. (8) *48*

Bust, The (2)
Championship Wrestling (4)
Cheborneck (3)
China Town (7)
Coming Attractions (4)
Continuing Adventures Of Pedro De Pacas And Man (2)
Cruisin' With Pedro De Pacas (1)
Dave (1)
Disco Disco (7)
Don't Bug Me (3)
Dork Radio (7)
Dorm Radio I, II, & III (8)
Earache My Eye Featuring Alice Bowie (4,6) *9*
Emergency Ward (1)

Evelyn Woodhead Speed Reading Course (3)
Finkelstein Shit Kid (6)
1st Gear, 2nd Gear (6)
Framed (5,6) *41*
Get Out Of My Room (8)
Hey Margaret (4)
I Didn't Know Your Name Was Alex (6)
I'm A (Modern) Man (8)
I'm Not Home Right Now (8)
Jimmy (5)
Juan Coyote (8)
Lard Ass (6)
Les Morpions (3)
Let's Make A New Dope Deal (7)

Love Is Strange (8)
Moe Money (Rudolph The Red Nosed Reindeer) (7)
Music Lesson (8)
Other Tapes (4)
Pedro And Man At The Drive-Inn (3)
Pedro's Request (5)
Peter Rooter (3)
Pope: Live At The Vatican (1)
Queer Wars (7)
Radio News (4)
Rainbow Bar & Grill (7)
Ralph And Herbie (2)
Rebuttal: Speaker Ashley Roachclip (2)
Rock Fight (6)

Sargent Stadanko (3)
Searchin' (6)
17th American Tour (7)
Sister Mary Elephant (Shudd-Up!) (2) *24*
Sleeping Beauty (5)
Sometimes When You Gotta Go, You Can't (6)
Strawberry Revival Festival (3)
Streets Of New York Or Los Angeles Or San Francisco Or... (2)
Stupid Early Show (8)
Sushi Bar (8)
T.W.A.T. (Tactical Women's Alert Team) (5)
Television Medley (2)

Testimonial By R. Zimmerman (4)
Three Little Pigs (4)
Trippin' In Court (1)
Uncle Pervy (5)
Up His Nose (3)
Up In Smoke (6)
Vietnam (1)
Waiting For Dave (1)
Wake Up America (4)
Warren Beatty (8)
Welcome To Mexico (1)
White World Of Sports (3)
Wink Dinkerson (1)

CHEMICAL BROTHERS, The '97

Techno-dance DJ duo from England: Tom Rowlands and Ed Simons.

DEBUT	PEAK	WKS		CD	#	Album Title	Sym	$	Label & Number
4/26/97	14	25	●	©	1	Dig Your Own Hole	[I]	$10	Astralwerks 6180
10/10/98	95	4		©	2	Brother's Gonna Work It Out	[I]	$10	Astralwerks 6243
7/10/99	32	14		©	3	Surrender	[I]	$10	Freestyle Dust 47610

Asleep From Day (3)
Block Rockin' Beats (1,2)
Brother's Gonna Work It Out (medley) (2)
Dig Your Own Hole (2)
Doin' It After Dark (medley) (2)
Don't Stop The Rock (1,2)
Dream On (3)
Elektrobank (1)

Everything Must Go (medley) (2)
Get Up On It Like This (1)
Gimme Some Love (medley) (2)
Got Glint? (3)
Hey Boy Hey Girl (3)
Hot Wheels - The Chase (medley) (2)
I Think I'm In Love (medley) (2)

It Doesn't Matter (1)
It's Just Begun (medley) (2)
Jazz, The (medley) (2)
Let Forever Be (3)
Losing Control (medley) (2)
Lost In The K-Hole (1)
Makin' A Living (medley) (2)
Mars Needs Women (medley) (2)

Morning Lemon (medley) (2)
Mother Earth (medley) (2)
Music: Response (3)
Not Another Drugstore (medley) (2)
Orange Wedge (3)
Out Of Control (3)
Piku (1)
Private Psychedelic Reel (1)

Riot, The (medley) (2)
Setting Sun (1) *80*
Sidewinder (medley) (2)
Sunshine Underground (3)
Surrender (3)
Theme, The (medley) (2)
This Ain't Chicago (medley) (2)
Thunder (medley) (2)

To A Nation Rockin' (medley) (2)
Trip Harder (medley) (2)
Under The Influence (3)
Where Do I Begin (1)

CHEQUERED PAST '84

Hard-rock group: Michael Des Barres (vocals; **Detective**), Tony Sales (guitar), Nigel Harrison (bass), and Steve Jones and Clem Burke (drums). Sales was a member of **Utopia** and later **Tin Machine**. Jones was a founding member of the **Sex Pistols**. Harrison and Burke were members of **Blondie**. Des Barres was touring vocalist for **The Power Station**.

DEBUT	PEAK	WKS				Album Title		$	Label & Number
9/15/84	151	6				Chequered Past		$10	EMI America 17123

Are You Sure Hank Done It This Way
How Much Is Too Much?
Let Me Rock

Never In A Million Years
No Knife

Only The Strong (Will Survive)
Tonight And Every Night

Underworld
World Gone Wild

CHER ★120★ '99

Born Cherilyn Sarkisian on 5/20/46 in El Centro, California. Adopted by stepfather at age 15 and last name changed to La Piere. Worked as backup singer for Phil Spector. Recorded as "Bonnie Jo Mason" and "Cherilyn" in 1964. Recorded with Sonny Bono as "Caesar & Cleo" in 1963, then as **Sonny & Cher** from 1965-73. Married to Bono from 1969-75. Married to **Gregg Allman** from 1975-79. Own TV series with Bono from 1971-74, 1976-77. Member of the group Black Rose in 1980. Acclaimed movie actress (won the 1987 Best Actress Oscar for *Moonstruck*).

1)Believe 2)Heart Of Stone 3)All I Really Want To Do 4)Gypsys, Tramps & Thieves 5)Take Me Home

DEBUT	PEAK	WKS		CD	#	Album Title	Sym	$	Label & Number
9/18/65	16	24		©	1	All I Really Want To Do		$25	Imperial 12292
4/23/66	26	19		©	2	The Sonny Side Of Cher		$25	Imperial 12301
10/1/66	59	16			3	Cher		$25	Imperial 12320
11/18/67+	47	14			4	With Love - Cher		$25	Imperial 12358
11/30/68	195	3			5	Cher's Golden Greats	[G]	$25	Imperial 12406
8/16/69	160	3			6	3614 Jackson Highway		$20	Atco 298
						address of the Muscle Shoals Sound Studio			
9/25/71	16	45	●	©	7	Gypsys, Tramps & Thieves		$15	Kapp 3649
						original pressing simply titled *Cher*			
1/8/72	92	10			8	Cher Superpak	[K]	$20	United Artists 88 [2]
7/29/72	43	22			9	Foxy Lady		$15	Kapp 5514
10/7/72	95	9			10	Cher Superpak, Vol. II	[K]	$20	United Artists 94 [2]
						Superpaks: Imperial recordings			
4/14/73	140	8			11	Bittersweet White Light		$15	MCA 2101
9/22/73	28	25	●		12	Half-Breed		$15	MCA 2104
6/1/74	69	14			13	Dark Lady		$15	MCA 2113
11/16/74	152	7		©	14	Greatest Hits	[G]	$15	MCA 2127
5/10/75	153	7			15	Stars		$12	Warner 2850
2/24/79	25	21	●	©	16	Take Me Home		$12	Casablanca 7133

CHER — Cont'd

DEBUT	PEAK	WKS	RIAA	CD	Album	$	Label & Number
12/5/87+	32	41	▲	© 17	Cher	$10	Geffen 24164
7/22/89	10	53	▲³	© 18	Heart Of Stone	$10	Geffen 24239
7/6/91	48	34	●	© 19	Love Hurts	$10	Geffen 24369
7/13/96	64	10		© 20	It's A Man's World	$10	Reprise 46179
11/28/98+	4	76	▲³	© 21	Believe	$10	Warner 47121
3/27/99	57	23	●	© 22	If I Could Turn Back Time - Cher's Greatest Hits [G]	$10	Geffen 24509

After All (18,22) 6
Alfie (3,5,8) 32
All Because Of You (18)
All I Really Want To Do (1,5,8) 15
All Or Nothing (21)
Am I Blue (11)
Angels Running (20)
Apples Don't Fall Far From The Tree (13)
Bang Bang (My Baby Shot Me Down) (2,5,8,17,22) 2
Behind The Door (4) 97
Believe (21) 1
Bell Bottom Blues (15)
Bells Of Rhymney (1,8)
Bigger They Come The Harder They Fall (15)
Blowin' In The Wind (1,8)
But I Can't Love You More (4)
By Myself (11)
Carnival (10)
Carousel Man (12,14)
Catch The Wind (3,8)
Chastity Sun (12)
Click Song (8)
Come And Stay With Me (1,5,8)
Come To Your Window (19)
Could've Been You (19)
Cruel War (3,10)
Cry Like A Baby (6)
Cry Myself To Sleep (1,10)
Dangerous Times (17)
Dark Lady (13,14,22) 1
David's Song (12)
Dixie Girl (13)
Do Right Woman, Do Right Man (4)
Do You Believe In Magic (8)
Does Anybody Really Fall In Love Anymore? (18)
Don't Come Cryin' To Me (22)
Don't Ever Try To Close A Rose (9)
Don't Hide Your Love (9,14) 46

Don't Think Twice, It's All Right (1,10)
Dov'è L'Amore (21)
Down, Down, Down (9)
Dream Baby (1,5)
Elusive Butterfly (2,5,8)
Emotional Fire (18)
Fire & Rain (7)
Fires Of Eden (19)
First Time (9)
For What It's Worth (6)
Geronimo's Cadillac (15)
Girl Don't Come (1,8)
Girl From Ipanema (2,10)
Git Down (Guitar Groupie) (16)
Give Our Love A Fightin' Chance (17)
Go Now (10)
Greatest Song I Ever Heard (12)
Gunman, The (20)
Gypsys, Tramps & Thieves (7,14,22) 1
Half-Breed (12,14,22) 1
Happy Was The Day We Met (16)
Hard Enough Getting Over You (17)
He Ain't Heavy, He's My Brother (7)
He'll Never Know (7)
Heart Of Stone (18,22) 20
Hey Joe (4,5,10) 94
Homeward Bound (3,8)
House Is Not A Home (8)
How Can You Mend A Broken Heart (12)
How Long Has This Been Going On (11)
I Found Someone (17,22) 10
I Go To Sleep (1)
I Got It Bad And That Ain't Good (11)
I Got You Babe [Sonny & Cher] (22) 1
I Hate To Sleep Alone (7)

I Saw A Man And He Danced With His Wife (13,14) 42
I Threw It All Away (6)
I Walk On Guilded Splinters (6)
I Want You (3,10)
I Wasn't Ready (10)
I Will Wait For You (4,10)
I'll Never Stop Loving You (19)
I'm Blowin' Away (20)
I'm In The Middle (7)
If I Could Turn Back Time (18,22) 3
If I Knew Then (9)
Impossible Dream (The Quest) (10)
It Might As Well Stay Monday (From Now On) (9)
It's A Man's Man's Man's World (16)
It's Not Unusual (2,10)
It's Too Late To Love Me Now (16)
Jolson Medley (11)
Just Enough To Keep Me Hangin' On (6)
Just Like Jesse James (18,22) 8
Just This One Time (15)
Just What I've Been Lookin' For (13)
Kiss To Kiss (18)
Lay Baby Lay (6)
Let Me Down Easy (9)
Let This Be A Lesson To You (16)
Like A Rolling Stone (2,10)
Living In A House Divided (9,14) 22
Long And Winding Road (12)
Look At Me (4)
Love And Understanding (19,22) 17
Love Enough (15)
Love Hurts (15,19)
Love Is The Groove (21)
Love On A Rooftop (18)

Magic In The Air (3)
Main Man (17)
Make The Man Love Me (13)
Mama (When My Dollies Have Babies) (4,8)
Man I Love (11)
Man That Got Away (11)
Melody (12,14)
Milord (2,10)
Miss Subway Of 1952 (13)
More Than You Know (11)
Mr. Soul (15)
My Love (12)
My Song (Too Far Gone) (16)
Needles And Pins (1,5,8)
Never Been To Spain (9)
Not Enough Love In The World (20)
Ol' Man River (2,10)
One By One (20) 52
One Honest Man (7)
One Small Step (19)
Our Day Will Come (2,10)
Pain In My Heart (16)
Paradise Is Here (20)
Perfection (17)
Pied Piper (3)
Please Don't Tell Me (6)
Power, The (21)
Reason To Believe (8)
Rescue Me (13)
Rock And Roll Doctor (15)
Runaway (21)
Same Mistake (20)
Save The Children (6)
Save Up All Your Tears (19,22) 37
Say The Word (16)
See See Rider (14)
She Thinks I Still Care (1,10)
Shoop Shoop Song (It's In His Kiss) (22)
Sing For Your Supper (4,10)
(Sittin' On) The Dock Of The Bay (6)

Skin Deep (17) 79
Song Called Children (10)
Song For You (9)
Stars (15)
Starting Over (18)
Still In Love With You (18)
Strong Enough (21) 57
Sun Ain't Gonna Shine Anymore (20)
Sunny (3,5,8)
Take Me For A Little While (5,10)
Take Me Home (16,22) 8
Takin' Back My Heart (21)
Taxi Taxi (21)
There But For Fortune (4,8)
These Days (11)
This God-Forsaken Day (12)
Time (2,8)
Times They Are A-Changin' (4,10)
Tonight I'll Be Staying Here With You (6)
Touch And Go (7)
Train Of Thought (13,14) 27
Twelfth Of Never (3,10)
Two People Clinging To A Thread (12)
Until It's Time For You To Go (3,8)
Walking In Memphis (20)
Wasn't It Good (16) 49
Way Of Love (7,14,22) 7
We All Sleep Alone (17,21,22) 14
What About The Moonlight (20)
What'll I Do (3)
When Love Calls Your Name (19)
When Lovers Become Strangers (19)
When You Find Out Where You're Goin' Let Me Know (7)
Where Do We Go (2,5,8) 25
Who You Gonna Believe (19)
Why Was I Born (11)

Will You Love Me Tomorrow (3,8)
Working Girl (17)
World Without Heroes (19)
You Better Sit Down Kids (4,5,8) 9
You Don't Have To Say You Love Me (3,8)
You Wouldn't Know Love (18)
Young Girl (2,10)

CHERRELLE
'86

Born Cheryl Norton in 1958 in Los Angeles. R&B singer/drummer. Cousin of singer **Pebbles**.

DEBUT	PEAK	WKS	CD	Album	$	Label & Number
9/8/84	144	8	© 1	Fragile	$10	Tabu 39144
2/1/86	36	30	© 2	High Priority	$10	Tabu 40094
11/19/88	106	15	© 3	Affair	$10	Tabu 44148

Affair (3)
Artificial Heart (2)
Crazy (For Loving You) (3)
Discreet (3)
Everything I Miss At Home (3)
Fragile...Handle With Care (1)
Happy That You're With Me (3)

High Priority (2)
Home (3)
I Didn't Mean To Turn You On (1) 79
I Need You Now (1)
I Will Wait For You (1)
Keep It Inside (3)

Like I Will (1)
Looks Aren't Everything (3)
Lucky (3)
My Friend (3)
New Love (2)
Oh No It's U Again (2)
Pick Me Up (3)

Saturday Love (2) 26
Stay With Me (1)
What More Can I Do For You (3)
When You Look In My Eyes (1)
Where Do I Run To (2)
Who's It Gonna Be (1)

Will You Satisfy? (2)
You Look Good To Me (2)

CHERRY, Don
'56

Born on 1/11/24 in Wichita Falls, Texas. Pop singer. Not to be confused with the jazz trumpeter/father of Eagle-Eye and Neneh Cherry.

DEBUT	PEAK	WKS	Album	$	Label & Number
9/22/56	15	7	Swingin' For Two	$25	Columbia 893

For You
I Didn't Know About You

I Don't Care If The Sun Don't Shine
I'll String Along With You

I'm Gonna Sit Right Down And Write Myself A Letter
I'm Yours

Love Is Just Around The Corner
My Future Just Passed
Please Be Kind

Sleepy Time Gal
So Rare
When The Sun Comes Out

CHERRY, Eagle-Eye
'98

Born in 1970 in Skane, Sweden. Son of trumpeter Don Cherry. Half-brother of **Neneh Cherry**.

DEBUT	PEAK	WKS	RIAA	CD	Album	$	Label & Number
8/22/98	45	39	▲	©	Desireless	$10	Work 69434

Comatose (In The Arms Of Slumber)
Conversation

Death Defied By Will
Desireless
Falling In Love Again

Indecision
Permanent Tears
Rainbow Wings

Save Tonight 5
Shooting Up In Vain
When Mermaids Cry

Worried Eyes

CHERRY, Neneh
'89

Born on 8/10/64 in Stockholm, Sweden; raised in New York City. Female R&B singer. Stepdaughter of jazz trumpeter Don Cherry. Half-sister of **Eagle-Eye Cherry**.

DEBUT	PEAK	WKS	CD	Album	$	Label & Number
6/24/89	40	35	©	Raw Like Sushi	$10	Virgin 91252

Buffalo Stance 3
Heart 73

Inna City Mamma
Kisses On The Wind 8

Love Ghetto
Manchild

Next Generation
Outre Risque Locomotive

Phoney Ladies
So Here I Come

CHERRY POPPIN' DADDIES '98

Eclectic-jazz group from Eugene, Oregon: Steve Perry (vocals, guitar), Jason Moss (guitar), Dana Heitman, Sean Flannery and Ian Early (horns), Darren Cassidy (bass) and Tim Donahue (drums).

2/28/98	17	53	▲² ©	Zoot Suit Riot............................			$10	Mojo 53081

Brown Derby Jump
Cherry Poppin' Daddy Strut
Come Back To Me
Ding-Dong Daddy Of The D-Car Line
Dr. Bones
Drunk Daddy
Here Comes The Snake
Master And Slave
Mister White Keys
No Mercy For Swine
Pink Elephant
Shake Your Lovemaker
When I Change Your Mind
Zoot Suit Riot

CHESNEY, Kenny '00

Born on 3/26/68 in Knoxville; raised in Luttrell, Tennessee. Country singer.

9/28/96+	78	30	● ©	1	Me And You..........................		$10	BNA 66908
8/2/97	95	34	▲ ©	2	I Will Stand........................		$10	BNA 67498
3/20/99	51	82	▲² ©	3	Everywhere We Go..............		$10	BNA 67655
10/14/00	13	51↑▲	©	4	Greatest Hits......................	[G]	$10	BNA 67976

Ain't That Love (1)
All I Need To Know (4)
Another Friday Night (1)
Back In My Arms Again (1)
Back Where I Come From (1,4)
Baptism (3,4)
Because Of Your Love (4)
California (3)
Chance, A (2)
Don't Happen Twice (4) 26
Everywhere We Go (3)
Fall In Love (4)
For The First Time (4)
From Hillbilly Heaven To Honky Tonk Hell (2)
How Forever Feels (3,4) 27
I Lost It (4) 34
I Might Get Over You (3)
I Will Stand (2)
It's Never Easy To Say Goodbye (1)
Kiss Me, Kiss Me, Kiss Me (3)
Life Is Good (3)
Lonely, Needin' Lovin' (2)
Love Me Tonight ..see: [Turn Out The Light And]
Me And You (1,4)
My Poor Old Heart (1)
No Small Miracle (1)
She Always Says It First (2)
She Gets That Way (2)
She Thinks My Tractor's Sexy (3,4) 74
She's Got It All (2,4)
Steamy Windows (2)
That's Why I'm Here (2,4) 79
Tin Man (4)
Turn For The Worse (1)
[Turn Out The Light And] Love Me Tonight (1)
What I Need To Do (3,4) 56
When I Close My Eyes (1,2,4)
Woman Knows (3)
You Had Me From Hello (3,4) 34
You Win, I Win, We Lose (2)

CHESNUTT, Mark '93

Born on 9/6/63 in Beaumont, Texas. Country singer/guitarist.

10/27/90	132	38	▲ ©	1	Too Cold At Home................		$10	MCA 10032
4/18/92	68	57	▲ ©	2	Longnecks & Short Stories....		$10	MCA 10530
7/10/93	43	48	▲ ©	3	Almost Goodbye..................		$10	MCA 10851
10/1/94	98	17	● ©	4	What A Way To Live..............		$10	Decca 11094
10/21/95	116	4	©	5	Wings................................		$10	Decca 11261
12/7/96+	130	14	▲ ©	6	Greatest Hits......................	[G]	$10	Decca 11529
10/11/97	165	4	©	7	Thank God For Believers......		$10	Decca 70006
2/27/99	65	7	©	8	I Don't Want To Miss A Thing..		$10	Decca 70035

Almost Goodbye (3,6)
Any Ole Reason (7)
April's Fool (7)
As The Honky Tonk Turns (5)
Blame It On Texas (1,6)
Broken Promise Land (1)
Brother Jukebox (1,6)
Bubba Shot The Jukebox (2,6)
Danger At My Door (1)
Down In Tennessee (4)
Friends In Low Places (1)
Goin' Through The Big D (4,6)
Gonna Get A Life (4,6)
Goodbye Heartache (7)
Half Of Everything (And All Of My Heart) (4)
Hello Honky Tonk (7)
Hey You There In The Mirror (1)
I Don't Want To Miss A Thing (8) 17
I Just Wanted You To Know (3)
I May Be A Fool (5)
I Might Even Quit Lovin' You (7)
(I Think) I've Finally Broken Mine (1)
I'll Get You Back (8)
I'll Think Of Something (2,6)
I'm Not Getting Any Better At Goodbyes (2)
It Sure Is Monday (3,6)
It Wouldn't Hurt To Have Wings (5)
It's A Little Too Late (6)
It's Almost Like You're Here (4)
It's Not Over (If I'm Not Over You) (2,7)
Jolie (8)
King Of Broken Hearts (3)
Let It Rain (6)
Let's Talk About Our Love (8)
Live A Little (4)
Lucky Man (1)
(Misery's All The Same) ..see: Uptown Downtown
My Heart's Too Broke (To Pay Attention) (3)
My Way Back Home (8)
Numbers On The Jukebox (7)
Old Country (2,6)
Old Flames Have New Names (2)
Postpone The Pain (2)
Pride's Not Hard To Swallow (5)
Rainy Day Woman (4)
Settlin' For What They Get (5)
She Dreams (5)
Strangers (5)
Talking To Hank (2)
Texas Is Bigger Than It Used To Be (3)
Thank God For Believers (7)
That Side Of You (7)
That's The Way You Make An Ex (8)
This Heartache Never Sleeps (8)
This Side Of The Door (4)
Till A Better Memory Comes Along (3)
Tonight I'll Let My Memory Take Me Home (8)
Too Cold At Home (1,6)
Too Good A Memory (1)
Trouble (5)
Uptown Downtown (Misery's All The Same) (2)
Useless (7)
Vickie Vance Gotta Dance (3)
What A Way To Live (4)
What Was You Thinking (8)
Wherever You Are (7)
Who Will The Next Fool Be (2)
Will, The (3)
Woman, Sensuous Woman (3)
Wrong Place, Wrong Time (5)
Your Love Is A Miracle (1)

CHI-ALI '92

Born Chi-Ali Griffith in 1977 in New York City. Male rapper. Acted in the HBO-TV movie *Strapped*. Wanted in the murder of his girlfriend's brother in New York City.

4/18/92	189	2	©		The Fabulous Chi-Ali............		$10	Violator 1082

Age Ain't Nothin' But A #
Check My Record
Chi-Ali Vs. Vanilla Shake
Fabulous Chi
Funky Lemonade
In My Room
Jump To The Rhythm
Let The Horns Blow
Looped It
Maniac Psycho
Murder Chi Wrote
Roadrunner
Shorty Said Nah
Step Up

CHIC '78

R&B-disco group formed in New York City by prolific producers Bernard Edwards (bass) and Nile Rodgers (guitar). Featured drummer Tony Thompson and singers Luci Martin and Norma Jean Wright. Wright began solo career in 1978 as **Norma Jean**; replaced by Alfa Anderson. Rodgers joined **The Honeydrippers** in 1984. Thompson joined **The Power Station** in 1985 and Edwards became their producer. Wright along with supporting Chic member Raymond Jones formed State Of Art in 1991. Rodgers and Edwards regrouped as Chic in 1992 with female lead vocalists/South Carolina natives Sylvester Logan Sharp and Jenn Thomas. Edwards died of pneumonia on 4/18/96 (age 43).

12/17/77+	27	40	● ©	1	Chic....................................		$12	Atlantic 19153
12/2/78	4	48	▲ ©	2	C'est Chic...........................		$12	Atlantic 19209
8/25/79	5	17	▲ ©	3	Risque...............................		$12	Atlantic 16003
12/22/79+	88	9		4	Les Plus Grands Succes De Chic - Chic's Greatest Hits........	[G]	$12	Atlantic 16011
7/26/80	30	15	©	5	Real People........................		$12	Atlantic 16016
12/19/81+	124	9	©	6	Take It Off..........................		$12	Atlantic 19323
12/4/82	173	6		7	Tongue In Chic...................		$10	Atlantic 80031

At Last I Am Free (2)
Baby Doll (6)
Burn Hard (6)
Can't Stand To Love You (3)
Chic Cheer (2,4)
Chic (Everybody Say) (7)
Chip Off The Old Block (5) *flip*
City Lights (7)
Dance, Dance, Dance (Yowsah, Yowsah, Yowsah) (1,4) 6
Everybody Dance (1,4) 38
Falling In Love With You (1)
Flash Back (6)
(Funny) Bone (2)
Good Times (3,4) 1
Hangin' (7)
Happy Man (2)
Hey Fool (7)
I Feel Your Love Comin' On (7)
I Got Protection (5)
I Loved You More (5)
I Want Your Love (2,4) 7
Just Out Of Reach (6)
Le Freak (2,4) 1
My Feet Keep Dancing (3,4)
My Forbidden Lover (3) 43
Open Up (5)
Real People (5) 79
Rebels Are We (5) 61
Sao Paulo (1)
Savoir Faire (7)
Sharing Love (7)
So Fine (6)
Sometimes You Win (2)
Stage Fright (6)
Strike Up The Band (1)
Take It Off (6)
Telling Lies (6)
26 (5)
Warm Summer Night (3)
What About Me (3)
When You Love Someone (7)
Will You Cry (When You Hear This Song) (3)
Would You Be My Baby (6)
You Can Get By (1)
You Can't Do It Alone (5)
Your Love Is Cancelled (6)

CHICAGO ★30★   '72

Jazz-oriented rock group from Chicago: **Peter Cetera** (vocals, bass), Robert Lamm (vocals, keyboards), Terry Kath (vocals, guitar), James Pankow (trombone), Lee Loughnane (trumpet), Walt Parazaider (reeds) and Danny Seraphine (drums). Originally called The Big Thing, later Chicago Transit Authority. To Los Angeles in 1968. Kath died of an accidental self-inflicted gunshot on 1/23/78 (age 31). Guitarist Donnie Dacus joined in 1978, replaced by Chris Pinnick in 1979 (left in 1981). **Bill Champlin** (vocals, keyboards) joined in 1982. Cetera left in 1985, replaced by Jason Scheff. Seraphine left in 1989, guitarist DaWayne Bailey added.

1)Chicago V 2)Chicago VI 3)Chicago IX - Chicago's Greatest Hits 4)Chicago VIII 5)Chicago VII

DEBUT	PEAK	WKS	RIAA	CD	#	Album Title	Sym	$	Label & Number
5/17/69	17	171	▲²	©	1	Chicago Transit Authority		$25	Columbia 8 [2]
2/14/70	4	134	●	©	2	Chicago II		$25	Columbia 24 [2]
1/30/71	2²	63	▲	©	3	Chicago III		$25	Columbia 30110 [2]
11/13/71+	3	46	▲	©	4	Chicago At Carnegie Hall	[L]	$30	Columbia 30865 [4]
						recorded in April 1971			
7/29/72	❶⁹	51	▲²	©	5	Chicago V		$20	Columbia 31102
7/14/73	❶⁵	73	▲²	©	6	Chicago VI		$15	Columbia 32400
3/30/74	❶¹	69	▲	©	7	Chicago VII		$20	Columbia 32810 [2]
4/12/75	❶²	29	▲	©	8	Chicago VIII		$15	Columbia 33100
11/29/75	❶⁵	72	▲⁵	©	9	Chicago IX - Chicago's Greatest Hits	C:#9/99 [G]	$15	Columbia 33900
7/4/76	3	44	▲²	©	10	Chicago X		$15	Columbia 34200
10/1/77	6	20	▲	©	11	Chicago XI		$15	Columbia 34860
10/21/78	12	29	©		12	Hot Streets		$15	Columbia 35512
9/1/79	21	10	●	©	13	Chicago 13		$15	Columbia 36105
8/9/80	71	9		©	14	Chicago XIV		$15	Columbia 36517
12/12/81	171	5		©	15	Chicago - Greatest Hits, Volume II	[G]	$15	Columbia 37682
6/26/82	9	38	▲	©	16	Chicago 16		$12	Full Moon 23689
6/2/84+	4	72	▲⁶	©	17	Chicago 17		$10	Warner 25060
10/18/86+	35	45	●	©	18	Chicago 18		$10	Warner 25509
7/9/88+	37	42	▲	©	19	19		$10	Reprise 25714
12/9/89+	37	25	▲⁵	©	20	Greatest Hits 1982-1989	C:#20/203 [G]	$10	Reprise 26080
2/16/91	66	11		©	21	Twenty 1		$10	Reprise 26391
6/10/95	90	7		©	22	Night & Day		$10	Giant 24615
5/10/97	55	27	●	©	23	The Heart Of Chicago 1967-1997	[G]	$10	Reprise 46554
5/30/98	154	2		©	24	The Heart Of Chicago 1967-1998 Volume II	[G]	$10	Reprise 46911
11/28/98	47	7	●	©	25	Chicago 25 - The Christmas Album	C:#9/7 [X]	$10	Chicago 3035

Christmas charts: 4/98, 18/'99

A.M. Mourning (2)
Ain't It Blue? (8)
Ain't It Time (17)
Aire (7)
Alive Again (12,15) *14*
All Is Well (5)
All Roads Lead To You (24)
Alma Mater (5)
Aloha Mama (13)
Along Comes A Woman (17,20) *14*
American Dream (14)
Another Rainy Day In New York City (10) *32*
Anxiety's Moment (2,4)
Anyway You Want (8)
Approaching Storm (3)
At The Sunrise (3)
Baby, What A Big Surprise (11,15,24) *4*
Bad Advice (16)
(Ballet For A Girl In Buchannon) ...see: Wake Up Sunshine
Beginnings (1,4,9,23) *7*
Birthday Boy (14)
Blues In The Night (22)
Brand New Love Affair (Part I & II) (8) *61*
Byblos (7)
Call On Me (7,9,24) *6*
Canon (3)
Caravan (22)
Chains (16)
Chasin' The Wind (21) *39*
Chicago (22)
Child's Prayer (25)
Christmas Song (25)
Christmas Time Is Here (25)
Colour My World (2,4,9,23) *flip*
Come In From The Night (19)
Critic's Choice (6)
Darlin' Dear (6)
Devil's Sweet (7)
Dialogue (Part I & II) (5,15,24) *24*
Does Anybody Really Know What Time It Is? (1,4,9,23) *7*

Don't Get Around Much Anymore (22)
I Don't Wanna Live Without Your Love (19,20,24) *3*
Dream A Little Dream Of Me (22)
Dreamin' Home (3)
Explain It To My Heart (21)
Fallin' Out (3)
Fancy Colours (2,4)
Feelin' Stronger Every Day (6,9,24) *10*
Feliz Navidad (25)
Flight 602 (3,4)
Follow Me (16)
Forever (18)
Free (3,4) *20*
Free Country (3)
Free Form Guitar (1)
Gently I'll Wake You (10)
Get Away (medley) (16,20,23)
God Rest Ye Merry, Gentlemen (25)
Gone Long Gone (12,15) *73*
Goodbye (5)
Goody Goody (22)
Greatest Love On Earth (12)
Halian From New York (7)
Hanky Panky (7)
Happy 'Cause I'm Going Home (3,4)
Happy Man (7,15)
Hard Habit To Break (17,20,23) *3*
Hard Risin' Morning Without Breakfast (3)
Hard To Say I'm Sorry (medley) (16,20,23) *1*
Harry Truman (8) *13*
Have Yourself A Merry Little Christmas (25)
Heart In Pieces (19)
Here In My Heart (23)
Hideaway (8)
Hit By Varese (5)
Hold On (14)
Holdin' On (21)
Hollywood (6)
Hope For Love (10)
Hot Streets (12)

I Believe (18)
I Don't Wanna Live Without Your Love (19,20,24) *3*
I Don't Want Your Money (3,4)
I Stand Up (19)
I'm A Man (1,4,24) *49*
(I've Been) Searchin' So Long (7,9,24) *9*
If It Were You (21)
If She Would Have Been Faithful... (18,20) *17*
If You Leave Me Now (10,15,23) *1*
In Terms Of Two (6)
In The Country (2,4)
In The Mood (22)
Inner Struggles Of A Man (11)
Introduction (4)
It Better End Soon (Movements 1-5) (2,4)
It's Alright (18)
Jenny (6)
Just You 'N' Me (6,9,23) *4*
Let It Snow! Let It Snow! Let It Snow! (25)
Liberation (1)
Life Is What It Is (13)
Life Saver (7)
Listen (1)
Little Drummer Boy (25)
Little Miss Lovin' (12)
Little One (11) *44*
Loneliness Is Just A Word (3)
Long Time No See (8)
Look Away (19,20,23) *1*
Loser With A Broken Heart (13)
Love Me Tomorrow (16,20,24) *22*
Love Was New (12)
Lowdown (3,4) *35*
Make Me Smile (2,4,9,23) *9*
Mama Mama (10)
Mama Take (13)
Man To Woman (21)
Man Vs. Man: The End (3)
Manipulation (14)
Memories Of Love (2)

Mississippi Delta City Blues (11)
Mongonucleosis (7)
Moonlight Serenade (22)
Morning Blues Again (3)
Mother (3,4)
Motorboat To Mars (3,4)
Movin' In (2)
Must Have Been Crazy (13) *83*
Never Been In Love Before (8)
Niagara Falls (18) *91*
Night & Day (22)
No Tell Lover (12,15,24) *14*
Nothin's Gonna Stop Us Now (18)
Now More Than Ever (2,4)
Now That You've Gone (5)
O Come All Ye Faithful (25)
Off To Work (3)
Oh, Thank You Great Spirit (8)
Old Days (8,15,24) *5*
Once In A Lifetime (17)
Once Or Twice (10)
Once Upon A Time... (3)
One From The Heart (21)
One Little Candle (25)
One More Day (18)
Only One (23)
Only Time Can Heal The Wounded (21)
Only You (17)
Over And Over (18)
Overnight Cafe (14)
P.M. Mourning (3)
Paradise Alley (13)
Please Hold On (17)
Poem 58 (1)
Poem For The People (2)
Policeman (11)
Prelude (2)
Prima Donna (17)
Progress? (3)
Questions 67 And 68 (1,4,15) *24*
Rediscovery (6)
Remember The Feeling (17)
Reruns (13)
Rescue You (16)
Road, The (2)

Run Away (13)
Runaround (19)
Santa Claus Is Coming To Town (25)
Saturday In The Park (5,9,23) *3*
Scrapbook (10)
Show Me A Sign (24)
Show Me The Way (12)
Silent Night (25)
Sing A Mean Tune Kid (3,4)
Sing, Sing, Sing (22)
Skin Tight (10)
Skinny Boy (7)
So Much To Say, So Much To Give (2,4)
Somebody, Somewhere (21)
Someday (1)
Something In This City Changes People (6)
Song For Richard And His Friends (4)
Song For You (14)
Song Of The Evergreens (7)
Sonny Think Twice (16)
Sophisticated Lady (22)
South California Purples (1,4)
State Of The Union (5)
Stay The Night (17,20,24) *16*
Street Player (13)
Take A Chance (12)
Take Me Back To Chicago (11,15) *63*
Take The "A" Train (22)
Takin' It On Uptown (11)
This Time (11)
Thunder And Lightning (14) *56*
Till The End Of Time (11)
Till We Meet Again (8)
To Be Free (2,4)
Together Again (10)
25 Or 6 To 4 (2,4,9,24) *4*
25 Or 6 To 4 (18) *48*
Upon Arrival (14)
Victorious (9)
Vote For Me (11)
Waiting For You To Decide (16)

Wake Up Sunshine (Ballet For A Girl In Buchannon) (2,4)
We Can Last Forever (19,20) *55*
We Can Stop The Hurtin' (17)
West Virginia Fantasies (2,4)
What Can I Say (16)
What Child Is This (25)
What Does It Take (21)
What Else Can I Say (3)
What Kind Of Man Would I Be? (19,20,24) *5*
What You're Missing (16) *81*
What's This World Comin' To (6)
When All The Laughter Dies In Sorrow (3)
Where Did The Lovin' Go (14)
Where Do We Go From Here (2,4)
While The City Sleeps (5)
White Christmas (25)
Who Do You Love (21)
Will You Still Love Me? (18,20,23) *3*
Window Dreamin' (13)
Wishing You Were Here (7,9,23) *11*
Women Don't Want To Love Me (7)
You Are On My Mind (10) *49*
You Come To My Senses (21)
You Get It Up (10)
You're Not Alone (19,24) *10*
You're The Inspiration (17,20,23) *3*

CHIEFTAINS '95

Folk group from Ireland: Kevin Conneff (vocals), Paddy Moloney (pipes, whistles), Martin Fay and Sean Keane (fiddles), Derek Bell (keyboards) and Matt Molloy (flute).

DEBUT	PEAK	WKS	CD	#	Album Title	Catalog	Sym	$	Label & Number
2/28/76	187	4	©	1	The Chieftains 5		[I]	$15	Island 9334
7/23/88	102	13	©	2	Irish Heartbeat			$10	Mercury 834496

VAN MORRISON & THE CHIEFTAINS

| 12/14/91+ | 107 | 5 | ● © | 3 | The Bells Of Dublin | C:#49/2 | [X] | $10 | RCA Victor 60824 |

Christmas charts: 14/'91, 25/'92

| 3/14/92 | 120 | 4 | © | 4 | An Irish Evening-Live At The Grand Opera House, Belfast | | [L] | $10 | RCA Victor 60916 |

recorded on 7/31/91

2/11/95	22	19	● ©	5	The Long Black Veil			$10	RCA Victor 62702
3/30/96	193	1	©	6	Film Cuts		[I]	$10	RCA Victor 68438
3/13/99	56	13	©	7	Tears Of Stone			$10	RCA Victor 68968
3/18/00	96	4	©	8	Water From The Well			$10	RCA Victor 63637

Any Old Iron (medley) (4)
Arrival Of The Wren Boys (3)
Ballyfin Polkas (8)
Barry Lyndon: Love Theme (6)
Bean An Fhir Rua (8)
Behind Blue Eyes (4)
Bells Of Dublin (medley) (3)
Boar's Head (3)
Brafferton Village (medley) (3)
Breton Carol (3)
Buinneán Buí (medley) (8)
Ca Berger (medley) (3)
Carrickfergus (2)
Casadh An Tsúgáin (8)
Celtic Ray (2)
Ceol Bhriotanach (Breton Music) (1)
Changing Your Demeanour (5)
Chieftains Knock On The Door (1)
Christmas Eve (medley) (3)
Circle Of Friends: Air-You're The One (4)
Circle Of Friends: Dublin (6)
Coast Of Malabar (3)
County Tyrone (medley) (8)
Damhsa (4)

Dance Duet-Reels (3)
Danny Boy (3)
Deserted Soldier (7)
Ding Dong Merrily On High (3)
Dingle Set-Dance (3,8)
Dochas (medley) (4)
Don Oiche Ud I mBeithil (3)
Donegal Set (8)
Dunmore Lassies (5)
Dusty Miller (8)
Factory Girl (7)
Far And Away: Fighting for Dough (6)
Farewell, The (3)
Ferny Hill (5)
Fiddling Ladies (4)
Foggy Dew (5)
Ford Econoline (medley) (4)
Gaoth Aneas (8)
Ghe Agus An Gra Geal (The Goose And Bright Love) (1)
God Rest Ye Merry Gentlemen (3)
Grey Fox: Main Theme (6)
Have I Told You Lately That I Love You? (5)
He Moved Through The Fair (5)

Humours Of Carolan (1)
I Know My Love (7)
I Saw Three Ships A Sailing (3)
I'll Tell Me Ma (2)
Il Est Ne (medley) (3)
Ireland Moving: Train Sequence (6)
Irish Heartbeat (2)
Jack Of All Trades (8)
Jimmy Mó Mhile Stór (7)
Kerry Slides (1)
King Of Laois (medley) (4)
Kilfenora Set (8)
Lilly Bolero (medley) (4)
Lily Of The West (5)
Little Love Affairs (4)
Live From Matt Molloy's Pub (8)
Long Black Veil (5)
Lots Of Drops Of Brandy (8)
Love Is Teasin' (5)
Lovely Sweet Banks Of The Moy (8)
Lowlands Of Holland (7)
Magdalene Laundries (7)
Marie's Wedding (2)
Mason's Apron (4)
May Morning Dew (8)

Miscellany Medley (4)
Mo Ghile Mear-"Our Hero" (5)
My Lagan Love (2)
Never Give All The Heart (7)
Newry Hornpipe (medley) (8)
North Americay (4)
O Come All Ye Faithful (3)
O Holy Night (3)
O Murchu's Hornpipe (medley) (4)
O The Holly She Bears A Berry (3)
O'Keefes/Chattering Magpie-Reels (medley) (4)
Old Blackthorn (medley) (8)
Once In Royal David's City (3)
Paddy's Jig (medley) (4)
Past Three O'Clock (3)
Planxty George Brabazon (4)
Poc Ar Buile (8)
Rachamid a Bhean Bheag (medley) (4)
Raglan Road (2,4,7)
Rebel Jesus (3)
Red Is The Rose (4)
Rob Roy: O'Sullivan's March (6)
Robbers' Glen (1)

Rocky Road To Dublin (5)
Sake In The Jar (7)
Samhradh, Samhradh (Summertime, Summertime) (1)
She Moved Through The Fair (2)
Skyline Jig (3)
Sliabh Geal gCua na Feile (medley) (4)
St. Stephen's Day Murders (3)
Star Of The County Down (2)
Stone, The (4)
Stór Mo Chroí (7)
Síuil A Rún (7)
Ta Mo Chleamhnas Deanta (3)
Tabhair Dom Do Lamh (Give Me Your Hand) (1)
Tennessee Mazurka (medley) (5)
Tennessee Waltz (medley) (5)
Three Kerry Polkas (1)
Timpan Reel (1)
Treasure Island: Blind Pew (6)
Treasure Island: French Leave (6)
Treasure Island: Island Theme (6)

Treasure Island: Loyals March (6)
Treasure Island: Opening Theme (6)
Treasure Island: Setting Sail (6)
Treasure Island: Silver and Loyals March (medley) (6)
Treasure Island: The Hispanola (medley) (6)
Treasure Island: Treasure Cave (6)
Tristan And Isolde: Love Theme (6)
Tristan And Isolde: The Departure (6)
Tristan And Isolde: The Falcon (6)
Walsh's Hornpipe (medley) (3)
Wandering Minstrel (medley) (4)
Wexford Carol (3)
White Cockade (medley) (4)
Within A Mile Of Dublin (medley) (8)
Wren In The Furze (3)
Ye Rambling Boys Of Pleasure (7)

CHIFFONS, The '63

Female R&B vocal group from the Bronx, New York: Judy Craig, Barbara Lee Jones, Patricia Bennett and Sylvia Peterson. Jones died of a heart attack on 5/15/92 (age 48).

DEBUT	PEAK	WKS	#	Album Title			$	Label & Number
5/18/63	97	11	1	He's So Fine			$120	Laurie 2018
8/20/66	149	3	2	Sweet Talkin' Guy			$100	Laurie 2036

ABC - 123 (1)
Down, Down, Down (2)
He's So Fine (1) 1
Just A Boy (2)
Keep The Boy Happy (2)

Lucky Me (1)
March (2)
My Block (1) 67
My Boyfriends' Back (2)

Mystic Voice (1)
Nobody Knows What's Goin' On (In My Mind But Me) (2) 49
Oh My Lover (1)

Open Your Eyes (I Will Be There) (2)
Out Of This World (2) 67
See You In September (1,2)
Sweet Talkin' Guy (2) 10

Thumbs Down (2)
Up On The Bridge (2)
When I Go To Sleep At Night (1)
Why Am I So Shy (1)

Why Do Fools Fall In Love (1)
Will You Still Love Me Tomorrow (1)
Wishing (1)

CHILD, Desmond, And Rouge '79

Born John Charles Barrett on 10/28/53 in Miami. Prolific producer/songwriter. Formed vocal group Rouge with Diane Grasselli, Myriam Valle and Maria Vidal.

DEBUT	PEAK	WKS		Album Title			$	Label & Number
3/24/79	157	6		Desmond Child And Rouge			$12	Capitol 11908

City In Heat
Fight, The

Givin' It To My Love
Lazy Love

Lovin' Your Love
Main Man

Otti
Our Love Is Insane 51

Westside Pow Wow

CHILD, Jane '90

Born in Toronto. Female singer/songwriter/keyboardist.

DEBUT	PEAK	WKS	CD		Album Title			$	Label & Number
3/3/90	49	22	©		Jane Child			$10	Warner 25858

Biology
DS 21

Don't Let It Get To You
Don't Wanna Fall In Love 2

Hey Mr. Jones
I Got News For You

Welcome To The Real World 49

World Lullabye
You're My Religion Now

CHILDS, Toni '88

Born in 1958 in Orange, California. Female singer.

DEBUT	PEAK	WKS	RIAA	CD	#	Album Title			$	Label & Number
6/25/88	63	45	●	©	1	Union			$10	A&M 5175
7/13/91	115	13		©	2	House Of Hope			$10	A&M 5358

Daddy's Song (2)
Dead Are Dancing (2)
Don't Walk Away (1) 72
Dreamer (1)

Heaven's Gate (2)
House Of Hope (2)
Hush (1)
I Want To Walk With You (2)

I've Got To Go Now (2)
Let The Rain Come Down (1)
Next To You (2)
Put This Fire Out (2)

Stop Your Fussin' (1)
Three Days (2)
Tin Drum (1)
Walk And Talk Like Angels (1)

Where's The Light (2)
Where's The Ocean (1)
Zimbabwae (1)

CHI-LITES, The '72

R&B vocal group from Chicago: Eugene Record, Robert Lester, Marshall Thompson and Creadel Jones. Record was married to **Barbara Acklin**.

1)A Lonely Man 2)(For God's Sake) Give More Power To The People 3)A Letter To Myself

DEBUT	PEAK	WKS	CD	#	Album Title			$	Label & Number
9/13/69	180	3		1	Give It Away			$25	Brunswick 754152
8/21/71	12	32	©	2	(For God's Sake) Give More Power To The People			$25	Brunswick 754170
4/29/72	5	36	©	3	A Lonely Man			$25	Brunswick 754179
10/21/72	55	24	©	4	The Chi-Lites Greatest Hits		[G]	$25	Brunswick 754184
3/24/73	50	13	©	5	A Letter To Myself			$25	Brunswick 754188
9/15/73	89	14		6	Chi-Lites			$25	Brunswick 754197
7/13/74	181	5	©	7	Toby			$25	Brunswick 754200
11/29/80	179	6		8	Heavenly Body			$12	Chi-Sound 619

CHI-LITES, The — Cont'd

| 4/10/82 | 162 | 7 | | | 9 **Me And You** | | | $12 | Chi-Sound 635 |
| 6/4/83 | 98 | 12 | | | 10 **Bottom's Up** | | | $12 | Larc 8103 |

Ain't Too Much Of Nothin' (3)
All I Wanna Do Is Make Love To You (8)
Are You My Woman? (Tell Me So) (4) *72*
Bad Motor Scooter (10)
Being In Love (3)
Bet You'll Never Be Sorry (6)
Bottom's Up (10)
Changing For You (10)
Coldest Days Of My Life (Part 1) (3,4) *47*
First Time (Ever I Saw Your Face) (7)
(For God's Sake) Give More Power To The People (2,4) *26*
Get Down With Me (9)
Gettin' On Outta Town (7)
Give It Away (1,4) *88*

Give Me A Dream (8)
Go Away Dream (6)
Happiness Is Your Middle Name (7)
Have You Seen Her (2,4,8) *3*
Heavenly Body (8)
Homely Girl (6) *54*
Hot On A Thing (Called Love) (9)
I Forgot To Say I Love You Till I'm Gone (6)
I Found Sunshine (6) *47*
I Heard It Through The Grapevine (7)
I Just Wanna Hold You (10)
I Lied (7)
I Like To Live The Love (That I Sing About) (7)
I Like Your Lovin' (Do You Like Mine) (4) *72*

I Love (10)
I Never Had It So Good (And Felt So Bad) (6)
I Want To Pay You Back (For Loving Me) (2,4) *95*
I'm Gonna Make You Love Me (1)
I'm Ready If I Don't Get To Go (4)
Inner City Blues (Make Me Wanna Holler) (7)
Just Two Teenage Kids (Still In Love) (5)
Let Me Be The Man My Daddy Was (1,4) *94*
Letter To Myself (5) *33*
Living In The Footsteps Of Another Man (3,4)
Lonely Man (3,4) *57*
Love Comes In All Sizes (5)

Love Is (3)
Love Shock (8)
Love Uprising (2,4)
Making Love (10)
Man & The Woman (The Boy & The Girl) (3) *flip*
Marriage License (4)
Me And You (9)
My Heart Just Keeps On Breakin' (5) *92*
My Whole World Ended (9)
Never Speak To A Stranger (9)
Oh Girl (3,4,9) *1*
One Man Band (6)
Round & Round (8)
Sally (5)
Someone Else's Arms (5)
Sound Of Lonely (7)
Stoned Out Of My Mind (6) *30*
Strung Out (8)

Super Mad (About You Baby) (8)
Tell Me Where It Hurts (9)
That's How Long (7) *flip*
That's My Baby For You (1)
There Will Never Be Any Peace (Until God Is Seated At The Conference Table) (7) *63*
To Change My Love (1)
Toby (7) *78*
Too Good To Be Forgotten (6)
Too Late To Turn Back Now (5)
Touch Me (10)
Troubles A'Comin' (2)
Try My Side (Of Love) (9)
Twelfth Of Never (1)
24 Hours Of Sadness (1,4)
We Are Neighbors (2,4) *70*
We Need Order (5) *61*

What Do I Wish For (1,2)
Whole Lot Of Good Good Lovin' (9)
Yes I'm Ready (If I Don't Get To Go) (2)
You Got Me Walkin' (2)
You Got To Be The One (7) *83*
You Smiled The Same Old Way (5)
You Take The Cake (10)
You're No Longer Part Of My Heart (1)

CHILLDRIN OF DA GHETTO   '99
Male rap trio from Chicago: Goldiiz, Bad Seed and P-Child.

| 11/6/99 | 158 | 1 | | © | **Chilldrin Of Da Ghetto** | | | $10 | Hoo Bangin' 50020 |

Across The Street
Better Days

Choke On
Drug Lord

Hoo Bangin' C.O.G. Style
Intention To Kill

It's Time To Roll
Lonely

Luv At First Sight
Mistake

Party
Wild Side

CHILLIWACK   '81
Rock group from Vancouver: Bill Henderson (vocals, guitar), Brian MacLeod (guitar), Ab Bryant (bass) and Rick Taylor (drums). Bryant and MacLeod later joined **Headpins**. Bryant was also with **Prism**. MacLeod died of cancer on 4/25/92.

3/26/77	142	13			1 **Dreams, Dreams, Dreams**			$15	Mushroom 5006
8/12/78	191	4			2 **Lights From The Valley**			$15	Mushroom 5011
10/3/81	78	30			3 **Wanna Be A Star**			$12	Millennium 7759
11/27/82	112	10			4 **Opus X**			$12	Millennium 7766

Arms Of Mary (2) *67*
Baby Blue (1)
California Girl (1)
Don't It Make You Feel Good (4)
(Don't Wanna) Live For A Living (3)

Fly At Night (1) *75*
How Can You Hide Your Love? (2)
I Believe (3) *33*
I Wanna Be The One (2)
In Love With A Look (3)
Lean On Me (4)

Living In Stereo (3)
Lookin' For A Place (2)
Midnight (4)
Mr. Rock (3)
My Girl (Gone, Gone, Gone) (3) *22*
Never Be The Same (2)

Night Time (4)
No Love At All (2)
Rain-O (1)
Really Don't Mind (4)
Rockin' Girl (1)
Roll On (1)
Secret Information (4)

She Don't Know (4)
She Keeps On Cryin' (2)
Sign Here (3)
So You Wanna Be A Star (3)
Something Better (1)
Tell It To The Telephone (3)
Tonight (2)

Too Many Enemies (3)
Walk On (3)
(We Don't Have To) Fall In Love (2)
Whatcha Gonna Do (4) *41*
You're Gonna Last (4)

CHIMES, The   '90
Trio from Scotland: Pauline Henry (vocals), Mike Peden (bass) and James Locke (drums).

| 6/2/90 | 162 | 6 | | © | **The Chimes** | | | $10 | Columbia 46008 |

Don't Make Me Wait
Heaven

I Still Haven't Found What I'm Looking For

Love Comes To Mind
Love So Tender

1-2-3 *86*
Stay

Stronger Together
True Love

Underestimate

CHINA CRISIS   '87
Rock group from Liverpool, England: Garry Daly (vocals, keyboards), Eddie Lundon (guitar), Gary Johnson (bass) and Kevin Wilkinson (drums).

| 6/1/85 | 171 | 4 | | | 1 **Flaunt The Imperfection** | | | $10 | Warner 25296 |
| 3/7/87 | 114 | 12 | | © | 2 **What Price Paradise** | | | $10 | A&M 5148 |

Arizona Sky (2)
Best Kept Secret (2)
Bigger The Punch I'm Feeling (1)

Black Man Ray (1)
Blue Sea (1)
Day's Work For The Dayo's Done (2)

Gift Of Freedom (1)
Hampton Beach (2)
Highest High (1)
It's Everything (2)

June Bride (2)
King In A Catholic Style (1)
Safe As Houses (2)
Strength Of Character (1)

Understudy, The (2)
Wall Of God (1)
We Do The Same (2)
World Spins, I'm Part Of It (1)

Worlds Apart (2)
You Did Cut Me (1)

★384★ CHIPMUNKS, The   '60
Characters created by Ross Bagdasarian ("David Seville") who named Alvin, Simon and Theodore after Liberty executives Alvin Bennett, Simon Waronker and Theodore Keep. The Chipmunks starred in own prime-time animated TV show in the early 1960s and a Saturday morning cartoon series in the mid-1980s. Bagdasarian died on 1/16/72 (age 52). His son, Ross Jr., resurrected the act in 1980.

1)Let's All Sing With The Chipmunks 2)The Chipmunks Sing The Beatles Hits 3)Chipmunks In Low Places

DAVID SEVILLE AND THE CHIPMUNKS:

| 11/30/59+ | 4 | 41 | | | 1 Let's All Sing With The Chipmunks | | [N] | $60 | Liberty 3132 |
| 6/20/60 | 31 | 5 | | © | 2 **Sing Again With The Chipmunks** | | [N] | $50 | Liberty 3159 |

THE CHIPMUNKS WITH DAVID SEVILLE:

12/22/62	84	2		©	3 **Christmas With The Chipmunks**	C:#44/4	[X-N]	$40	Liberty 3256
					Christmas charts: 33/'65, 36/'66, 33/'67, 23/'87, 21/'88				
12/7/63	9^X	13		©	4 Christmas with the Chipmunks, Vol. 2		[X-N]	$30	Liberty 7334
					Christmas charts: 9/'63, 18/'64, 18/'67, 31/'68				
9/5/64	14	23		©	5 **The Chipmunks Sing The Beatles Hits**		[N]	$30	Liberty 7388

THE CHIPMUNKS:

8/9/80	34	26	●		6 **Chipmunk Punk**		[N]	$12	Excelsior 6008
6/6/81	56	35	●	©	7 **Urban Chipmunk**	C:#25/4	[N]	$10	RCA Victor 4027
11/21/81+	72	9	●	©	8 **A Chipmunk Christmas**		[X-N]	$10	RCA Victor 4041
					Christmas charts: 10/'83, 8/'84				
6/5/82	109	6			9 **Chipmunk Rock**		[N]	$10	RCA Victor 4304

ALVIN & THE CHIPMUNKS:

10/24/92+	21	28	▲	©	10 **Chipmunks In Low Places**		[N]	$10	Epic 53006
12/17/94	147	3		©	11 **A Very Merry Chipmunk**		[X-N]	$10	Epic 64434
					Christmas chart: 33/'94				

CHIPMUNKS, The — Cont'd

A Comes Before B (11)
Achy Breaky Heart (10)
(All I Want For Christmas Is) My Two Front Teeth (4)
All My Loving (5)
Alvin's Harmonica (1) *3*
Alvin's Orchestra (2) *33*
Another Somebody Done Somebody Wrong Song (7)
Bette Davis Eyes (9)
Brothers & Old Boots (10)
Call Me (6)
Can't Buy Me Love (5)
Chipmunk Fun (1)
Chipmunk Song (1,3,8,11) *1*
Christmas Time (Greensleeves) (4)
Christmas Time Uptown (11)
Coming 'Round The Mountain (2)
Country Pride (10)
Coward Of The County (7)
Crashcup's Christmas (8)

Crazy Little Thing Called Love (6)
Deck The Halls (4,8)
Do You Want To Know A Secret (5)
Don't Rock The Jukebox (10)
Down At The Twist And Shout (10)
From Me To You (5)
Frosty The Snowman (3)
Frustrated (8)
Gambler, The (7)
Good Girls Don't (6)
Good Morning Song (1)
Gotta Believe In Pumpkins (10)
Hang Up Your Stockin' (4)
Hard Day's Night (5)
Have Yourself A Merry Little Christmas (4,8)
Heartbreaker (9)
Here Comes Christmas (11)
Here Comes Santa Claus (Right Down Santa Claus Lane) (3,8)

Here We Come A-Caroling (4)
Hit Me With Your Best Shot (9)
Hold On Tight (9)
Home On The Range (2)
How Do I Make You (6)
I Ain't No Dang Cartoon (10)
I Don't Want To Be Alone For Christmas (Unless I'm Alone With You) (1)
I Feel Lucky (10)
I Love A Rainy Night (7)
I Saw Her Standing There (5)
I Want To Hold Your Hand (5)
I Wish I Had A Horse (2)
If You Love Me (Alouette) (1)
It's Beginning To Look Like Christmas (3,8)
Jessie's Girl (9)
Jingle-Bell Rock (4)
Jingle Bells (3,8)
Jolly Old Saint Nicholas (4)
Leader Of The Pack (9)
Let's Go (6)
Little Dog (1)

Little Drummer Boy (11)
Losing You (I Really Wanna Lose You) (9)
Love Me Do (5)
Luckenbach, Texas (Back To The Basics Of Love) (7)
Lunchbox (7)
Made For Each Other (7)
Mammas Don't Let Your Babies Grow Up To Be Cowboys Chipmunks (7)
My Sharona (6)
Night Before Christmas (4)
O Christmas Tree (O Tannenbaum) (4)
Old MacDonald Cha Cha Cha (1)
On The Road Again (7)
Outlaws (10)
Over The River And Through The Woods (3,11)
P.S. I Love You (5)
Petit Papa Noel (11)
Please, Please Me (5)

Pop Goes The Weasel (1)
Queen Of Hearts (9)
Ragtime Cowboy Joe (1) *16*
Refugee (6)
Rockin' Around The Christmas Tree (11)
Row Your Boat (2)
Rudolph The Red Nosed Reindeer (3,11) *21*
Santa Claus Is Comin' To Town (3)
Santa's Gonna Come In A Pickup Truck (11)
She Loves You (5)
Silent Night (8)
Silver Bells (3)
Sing A Goofy Song (2)
Sing Again With The Chipmunks (2)
Sleigh Ride (8)
Spirit Of Christmas (8)
Stand By Your Man (10)
Swanee River (2)
Swing Low Sweet Chariot (2)

Take A Chance On Me (9)
Thank God I'm A Country Boy (7)
There Ain't Nothin' Wrong With The Radio (10)
Three Blind-(Folded) Mice (1)
Twelve Days Of Christmas (4)
Twist And Shout (5)
Up On The House-Top (3)
We Wish You A Merry Christmas (3,8)
When Johnny Comes Marching Home (2)
Whip It (9)
Whistle While You Work (1)
White Christmas (3)
Witch Doctor (2)
Wonderful Day (4)
Working On The Railroad (2)
Yankee Doodle (1)
You May Be Right (6)

CHOCOLATE MILK
R&B group from New Orleans: Frank Richard (vocals), Amadee Castanell (saxophone), Joe Foxx (trumpet), Robert Dabon (keyboards), Mario Tio (guitar) and Dwight Richards (drums). **'79**

10/25/75	191	3	©	1	**Action Speaks Louder Than Words**		$12	RCA Victor 1188
6/24/78	171	5		2	We're All In This Together		$12	RCA Victor 2331
4/14/79	161	6		3	Milky Way		$12	RCA Victor 3081
12/12/81+	162	10		4	Blue Jeans		$12	RCA Victor 3896

Action Speaks Louder Than Words (1) *69*
Ain't Nothin' But A Thing (1)
America (2)
Blue Jeans (4)
Chocolate Pleasure (1)

Confusion (1)
Doc (3)
Fertility (2)
Girl Callin' (2)
Grand Theft (2)
Groove City (3)

Help Me Find The Road (2)
Honey Bun (4)
Hurry Down Sunset (3)
I've Been Loving You Too Long (4)
Let's Go All The Way (4)

Like My Lady's Love (4)
Milky Way (3)
My Mind Is Hazy (1)
Out Among The Stars (1)
Over The Rainbow (2)
Paradise (3)

People (1)
Pretty Pimpin' Willie (1)
Running On Empty (4)
Save The Last Dance (3)
Say Won'tcha (3)
That's The Way She Loves (2)

Thinking Of You (2)
Time Machine (1)
Tin Man (1)
Video Queen (4)
We're All In This Together (2)
You're The One (3)

CHOIR OF THE VIENNA HOFBURGKAPELLE
Austrian choir. Conducted by Josef Schabasser. **'94**

7/30/94	185	1	©	**Mystical Chants**	[F]	$10	Special Music 5118

Alleluia For The Third Christmas Mass
Communion For The Feast Of St. Stephen
Communion For The Second Sunday After Epiphany

Communion For The Second Sunday In Lent
Communion For The Third Sunday In Advent
Gradual For Maundy Thursday
Gradual For The Feast Of The Holy Confessor

Hymn For The Christmas Vespers
Introit For Sexagesima Sunday
Introit For The First Sunday In Advent
Introit For The Fourth Sunday In Advent

Introit For The Third Christmas Mass
Introit For The Third Sunday In Advent
Offertory For Maundy Thursday
Offertory For Palm Sunday

Offertory For The Fourth Sunday In Advent
Offertory For The Second Sunday After Epiphany
Tract Of Sexagesima Sunday

CHRISTIANS, The
Rock trio from Liverpool, England: brothers Garry (vocals) and Russell (saxophone) Christian, with multi-instrumentalist Henry Priestman. **'88**

3/12/88	158	8	©	**The Christians**		$10	Island 90852

...And That's Why
Born Again

Forgotten Town
Hooverville

Ideal World
One In A Million
Save A Soul In Every Town

Sad Songs

When The Fingers Point

CHRISTIE
Pop-rock trio from England: Jeff Christie (vocals, bass), Vic Elmes (guitar) and Mike Blakely (drums). Blakely's brother, Alan, was a member of **The Tremeloes**. **'71**

12/12/70+	115	10	©	**Yellow River**		$15	Epic 30403

Coming Home Tonight
Country Boy

Down The Mississippi Line
Gotta Be Free

I've Got A Feeling
Inside Looking Out

Johnny One Time
New York City

Put Your Money Down
San Bernadino *100*

Yellow River *23*

CHRISTIE, Lou
Born Lugee Sacco on 2/19/43 in Glen Willard, Pennsylvania. Pop singer/songwriter. **'66**

8/24/63	124	6	©	1	**Lou Christie**		$100	Roulette 25208
3/5/66	103	14		2	Lightnin' Strikes		$25	MGM 4360

All That Glitters Isn't Gold (1)
Baby We Got To Run Away (2)
Cryin' In The Streets (2)
Diary (2)
Goin' Out Of My Head (2)

Gypsy Cried (1) *24*
Have I Sinned (1)
How Many Teardrops (1) *46*
If I Fell (2)
Jungle (2)

Lightnin' Strikes (2) *1*
Love Is Like A Heat Wave (2)
Mr. Tenor Man (1)
Since I Fell For You (2)
Stay (1)

Tears On My Pillow (1)
(There's) Always Something There To Remind Me (2)
To Be Loved (1)
Tonight (I Fell In Love) (1)

Trapeze (2)
Two Faces Have I (1) *6*
When You Dance (1)
You And I (Have A Right To Cry) (1)

You've Got Your Troubles (2)

CHRISTIÓN
R&B vocal duo from Oakland: Kenny Ski and Allen Anthony. **'97**

11/22/97	146	2	©	**Ghetto Cyrano**		$10	Roc-A-Fella 536281

Aftermath
Anything Goes
Bring Back Your Love

Come To Me
Face Like Yours
Full Of Smoke *53*

Ghetto (Do What Ya Gotta Do)
I Wanna Get Next To You *86*
Midnight X-ta-C

Pull It
Soon
Tonight

Where I'm From

CHRISTOPHER, Gavin
Born in Chicago. Male R&B singer/songwriter/producer. **'86**

7/5/86	74	15		**One Step Closer**		$10	Manhattan 53024

Are We Running From Love
Back In Your Arms

Could This Be The Night
In The Heat Of Passion

Love Is Knocking At Your Door
Once You Get Started

One Step Closer To You *22*
Sparks Turn Into Fire

That's The Kind Of Guy I Am

158

CHRISTY, June '57

Born Shirley Luster on 11/20/25 in Springfield, Illinois. Died of kidney failure on 6/21/90 (age 64). Jazz singer. Achieved national fame with the **Stan Kenton** band. Orchestra conducted by Pete Rugolo.

9/29/56	14	4	© 1	The Misty Miss Christy	$40	Capitol 725
7/22/57	16	4	2	June - Fair and Warmer!	$40	Capitol 833

Best Thing For You (2)	For All We Know (1)	I've Never Been In Love Before (2)	Let There Be Love (2)	'Round Midnight (1)	When Sunny Gets Blue (2)
Better Luck Next Time (2)	I Didn't Know About You (1)	Imagination (2)	Lovely Way To Spend An Evening (1)	Sing Something Simple (1)	Wind, The (1)
Beware My Heart (2)	I Know Why (And So Do You) (2)	Irresistible You (2)	Maybe You'll Be There (1)	That's All (1)	
Day-Dream (1)	I Want To Be Happy (2)	It's Always You (2)	No More (2)	There's No You (1)	
Dearly Beloved (1)				This Year's Kisses (1)	

CHUBB ROCK '91

Born Richard Simpson on 5/28/68 in Jamaica; raised in Brooklyn, New York. Male rapper.

3/23/91	73	10	© 1	Treat 'Em Right	$10	Select 9063
6/8/91	71	21	© 2	The One	$10	Select 21640
9/19/92	127	3	© 3	I Gotta Get Mine Yo! - Book Of Rhymes	$10	Select 61299

Another Statistic (2)	Cat (2)	Hatred, The (2)	Keep It Street (1,2)	Pop 'Nuff Shit (3)	Which Way Is Up (3)
Arrival, The (3)	Chubbster, The (2)	I Don't Want To Be Lonely (3)	Lost In The Storm (3)	Regiments Of Steel (1,2)	Yabadabadoo (3)
Bad Boyz (3)	Don't Drink The Milk (3)	I Gotta Get Mine Yo (3)	Message To The B.A.N. (3)	So Much Things To Say (3)	
Big Man (2)	Enjoy Ya Self (3)	I Need Some Blow (3)	My Brother (3)	Some-O-Next Shit (3)	
Black Trek IV The Voyage Home (3)	Enter The Dragon (3)	I'm The Man (3)	Night Scene (3)	3 Men At Chung King (3)	
Bring 'Em Home Safely (2)	Five Deadly Venoms (2)	I'm Too Much (3)	One, The (2)	Treat 'Em Right (1,2) 95	
	Funky, The (3)	Just The Two Of Us (2)	Organizer, The (1,2)	What's The Word (1,2)	

CHUCK D '96

Born Carlton Ridenhour on 8/1/60 in New York City. Leader of **Public Enemy**.

11/9/96	190	1	©	Autobiography Of Mistachuck	$10	Mercury 532944

But Can You Kill The Nigger In You?	Free Big Willie	Mistachuck	No	Talk Show Created The Fool
Endonesia	Generation Wrekkked	Niggativity...Do I Dare Disturb The Universe?	Paid	Underdog
	Horizontal Heroin		Pride, The	

CHUMBAWAMBA '98

Post-punk group from Leeds, England: Alice Nutter, Lou Watts, Danbert Nubacon, Paul Greco, Jude Abbott, Dunstan Bruce, Neil Ferguson and Harry Hamer.

10/11/97+	3	43	▲³ ©	Tubthumper	$10	Republic 53099

					Smalltown
Amnesia	Creepy Crawling	Good Ship Lifestyle	Mary, Mary	Outsider	
Big Issue	Drip, Drip, Drip	I Want More	One By One	Scapegoat	Tubthumping 6

CHUNKY A '90

Chunkston Arthur Hall is actually comedian Arsenio Hall. Born on 2/12/57 in Cleveland. Hosted own late night talk show (1989-1994) and starred in own sitcom (1997). Acted in several movies.

12/16/89+	71	13	©	Large And In Charge	[N] $10	MCA 6354

Dipstick	Ho Is Lazy	Large And In Charge	Sorry	Very High Key
Dope, The Big Lie	I Command You To Dance	Owwww! 77	Stank Breath	

CHURCH, The '88

Folk-rock group from Canberra, Australia: Steve Kilbey (vocals, bass), Peter Koppes and Marty Willson-Piper (guitars), and Richard Ploog (drums). Ploog left in 1991, replaced by Jay Dee Daugherty.

6/21/86	146	11	© 1	Heyday	$10	Warner 25370
3/12/88	41	36	● © 2	Starfish	$10	Arista 8521
3/31/90	66	20	© 3	Gold Afternoon Fix	$10	Arista 8579
3/28/92	176	2	© 4	Priest = Aura	$10	Arista 18683

Already Yesterday (1)	Disappointment (3)	Grind (3)	Mistress (4)	Paradox (4)	Tantalized (1)
Antenna (2)	Disenchanted (1)	Happy Hunting Ground (1)	Monday Morning (3)	Pharoah (3)	Terra Nova Cain (3)
Aura (4)	Disillusionist, The (4)	Hotel Womb (2)	Myrrh (1)	Reptile (2)	Transient (3)
Blood Money (2)	Dome (4)	Kings (4)	New Season (2)	Ripple (4)	Tristesse (1)
Chaos (4)	Essence (3)	Laughing (3)	Night Of Light (3)	Roman (1)	Under The Milky Way (2) 24
City (3)	Fading Away (3)	Lost (2)	North, South, East And West (2)	Russian Autumn Heart (3)	Witch Hunt (4)
Columbus (1)	Feel (4)	Lustre (4)	Old Flame (4)	Spark (2)	You're Still Beautiful (3)
Destination (2)	Film (4)	Metropolis (3)		Swan Lake (4)	Youth Worshipper (1)

CHURCH, Charlotte '00

Born on 2/21/86 in Cardiff, Wales. Female opera singer.

4/3/99	28	77	▲² © 1	Voice Of An Angel	C:#38/2 $10	Sony Classical 60957
12/4/99+	40	28	▲ © 2	Charlotte Church	$10	Sony Classical 64356
11/4/00	7	12	▲ © 3	Dream A Dream	[X] $10	Sony Classical 89463

Christmas chart: 1/'00

Amazing Grace (1)	Dream A Dream (Elysium) (3)	Lo! How A Rose E'er Blooming (3)	O Mio Babbino Caro (2)	Suo-Gân (1)
Ave Maria (1,3)	Far Over Bethlehem (medley) (3)	If Thou Art Near (2)	Panis Angelicus (1)	Tylluanod (Owls) (1)
Barcarolle (Night Of Stars) (3)	Gabriel's Message (3)	In Trutina (3)	Pie Jesu (1)	Voi Che Sapete (Tell Me What Love Is) (2)
Christmas Song (Chestnuts Roasting On An Open Fire) (3)	God Rest Ye Merry, Gentlemen (3)	Jerusalem (1)	Plaisir D'Amour (2)	What Child Is This? (3)
Coventry Carol (Lully Lullay) (3)	Guide Me, Oh Thou Great Redeemer (2)	Jewel Song (2)	Psalm 23 (1)	When A Child Is Born (3)
Danny Boy (1)	Hark! The Herald Angels Sing (3)	Joy To The World (3)	Mae Hiraeth Yn Y Môr (There's A Longing In The Sea) (3)	She Moved Through The Fair (2)	When At Night I Go To Sleep (1)
Ding Dong! Merrily On High (3)	Holy City (2)	Just Wave Hello (2)	Mary's Boy Child (3)	Silent Night (3)	Winter Wonderland (3)
Draw Tua Bethlehem (medley) (3)		La Pastorella (2)	Men Of Harlech (3)	Songs My Mother Taught Me (2)	Y Gylfinir (The Curlew) (1)
		Lascia Ch'io Pianga (2)	My Lagan Love (1)	Summertime (2)	
		Last Rose Of Summer (2)	O Come, All Ye Faithful (3)		
		Little Drummer Boy (3)	O Holy Night (3)		

CIBO MATTO '99

Rock group from New York City: **Sean Lennon** (son of **John Lennon**; bass), Miho Hatori (vocals, guitar), Yuka Honda (keyboards) and Timo Ellis (drums).

6/26/99	171	1	©	Stereo * Type A	$10	Warner 47345

Blue Train	King Of Silence	Mortming	Spoon	Working For Vacation
Clouds	Lint Of Love	Sci-Fi Wasabi	Stone	
Flowers	Moonchild	Speechless	Sunday Parts I & II	

CINDERELLA '87
Hard-rock group from Philadelphia: Tom Keifer (vocals, guitar), Jeff LaBar (guitar), Eric Brittingham (bass) and Fred Coury (drums; left in 1992 and formed **Arcade**).

DEBUT	PEAK	WKS	RIAA	CD	Album	$	Label & Number
7/19/86+	3	70	▲³	© 1	Night Songs	$10	Mercury 830076
7/23/88	10	66	▲³	© 2	Long Cold Winter	$10	Mercury 834612
12/8/90	19	32	▲	© 3	Heartbreak Station	$10	Mercury 848018
11/26/94	178	1		© 4	Still Climbing	$10	Mercury 522947

All Comes Down (4)
Back Home Again (1)
Bad Attitude Shuffle (4)
Bad Seamstress Blues (medley) (2)
Blood From A Stone (4)
Coming Home (2) *20*
Dead Man's Road (3)

Don't Know What You Got (Till It's Gone) (2) *12*
Easy Come Easy Go (4)
Electric Love (3)
Fallin' Apart At The Seams (medley) (2)
Fire And Ice (2)
Freewheelin (4)

Gypsy Road (2) *51*
Hard To Find The Words (4)
Heartbreak Station (3) *44*
Hell On Wheels (1)
Hot & Bothered (4)
If You Don't Like It (2)
In From The Outside (1)
Last Mile (2) *36*

Long Cold Winter (2)
Love Gone Bad (3)
Love's Got Me Doin' Time (3)
Make Your Own Way (3)
More Things Change (3)
Night Songs (1)
Nobody's Fool (1) *13*
Nothin' For Nothin' (1)

Once Around The Ride (1)
One For Rock And Roll (3)
Push, Push (1)
Road's Still Long (4)
Second Wind (2)
Shake Me (1)
Shelter Me (3) *36*
Sick For The Cure (3)

Somebody Save Me (1) *66*
Still Climbing (4)
Take Me Back (2)
Talk Is Cheap (4)
Through The Rain (4)
Winds Of Change (3)

CIRCUS OF POWER '88
Hard-rock group: Toronto native Alex Mitchell (vocals) with New Yorkers Ricky Beck Mahler (guitar), Gary Sunshine (bass) and Ryan Maher (drums).

DEBUT	PEAK	WKS	RIAA	CD	Album	$	Label & Number
11/12/88	185	2		©	Circus Of Power	$10	RCA 8464

Backseat Mama
Call Of The Wild

Crazy
Heart Attack

In The Wind
Letters Home

Machine
Motor

Needles
White Trash Queen

CITY BOY '78
Pop-rock group from Birmingham, England: Lol Mason (vocals), Mike Slamer (guitar), Max Thomas (keyboards), Steve Broughton (percussion), Chris Dunn (bass) and Roger Kent (drums). In 1978, Roy Ward replaced Kent.

DEBUT	PEAK	WKS	RIAA	CD	Album	$	Label & Number
8/28/76	177	3		© 1	City Boy	$12	Mercury 1098
2/12/77	170	4		© 2	Dinner At The Ritz	$12	Mercury 1121
9/16/78	115	9		© 3	Book Early	$12	Mercury 3737

Beth (3)
Cigarettes (3)
Dangerous Ground (3)
Deadly Delicious (1)
Dinner At The Ritz (2)
Do What You Do, Do Well (3)

Don't Know Can't Tell (medley) (1)
5.7.0.S. (3) *27*
5000 Years (medley) (1)
Goodbye Blue Monday (2)
Goodbye Laurelie (3)
Greatest Story Ever Told (1)

Hap-ki-do Kid (1)
Haymaking Time (1)
Momma's Boy (2)
(Moonlight) Shake My Head And Leave (1)
Moving In Circles (3)
Narcissus (2)

Oddball Dance (1)
Raise Your Glass (To Foolish Me) (3)
State Secrets - A Thriller Medley (3)
Summer In The School Yard (3)
Sunset Boulevard (1)

Surgery Hours (Doctor Doctor) (1)
Violin, The (2)
Walk On The Water (2)
What A Night (3)
World Loves A Dancer (3)

CITY HIGH '01
Hip-hop trio from Willingboro, New Jersey: Claudette Ortiz, Robby Pardio and Ryan Toby.

DEBUT	PEAK	WKS	RIAA	CD	Album	$	Label & Number
6/9/01	34	17↑	●	©	City High	$10	Booga Base. 490890

Best Friends
Caramel
Cat And Dogs

City High Anthem
Didn't Ya
15 Will Get You 20

Only One I Trust
Sista
So Many Things

Song For You
Three Way
What Would You Do *8*

Why
You Don't Know Me

C.J. & CO. '77
Disco group from Detroit: Cornelius Brown, Curtis Durden, Joni Tolbert, Connie Durden and Charles Clark.

DEBUT	PEAK	WKS	RIAA	CD	Album	$	Label & Number
7/9/77	60	23			Devil's Gun	$12	Westbound 6100

Devil's Gun *36*

Free To Be Me

Get A Groove In Order To Move

Sure Can't Go To The Moon

We Got Our Own Thing

CLANCY BROTHERS & TOMMY MAKEM '63
Folk group from Ireland: brothers Tom, Liam and Pat Clancy with Tommy Makem. The brothers first began recording in the 1950s for Tradition Records. Tom acted off-Broadway and in TV through the 1980s; died of cancer on 11/7/90 (age 67). Pat died of cancer on 11/11/98 (age 76).

DEBUT	PEAK	WKS	RIAA	CD	Album	$	Label & Number
11/16/63	60	12		© 1	In Person At Carnegie Hall	[L] $20	Columbia 1950
					recorded on 11/3/62		
5/2/64	91	6		2	The First Hurrah!	$20	Columbia 2165

Au Poc Als Buille (The Mad Goat) (2)
Bonny Charlie (2)
Carrickfergus (2)
Children's Medley (1)

Gallant Forty TWA (2)
Galway Bay (1)
Johnny Todd (2)
Johnson's Motor Car (1)
Jug Of Punch (1)

Juice Of The Barley (1)
Kelly (2)
Leaving Of Liverpool (2)
Legion Of The Rearguard (1)
Mermaid, The (2)

O'Driscoll (The Host Of The Air) (1)
Oro Se Do Bheatha Bhaile (1)
Parting Glass (1)
Patriot Game (1)

Reilly's Daughter (1)
Rocky Road To Dublin (2)
Rosin The Bow (2)
Row, Bullies, Row (2)
West's Awake (1)

CLANNAD '93
Pop group from Ireland: Maire Brennan (vocals) with brothers Pol & Ciaran Brennan, and twin uncles Noel & Padraig Duggan. Pol left by 1993. Group name is Gaelic for family. Singer **Enya**, the sister of the Brennans, was a member from 1980-82.

DEBUT	PEAK	WKS	RIAA	CD	Album	$	Label & Number
3/22/86	131	12		© 1	Macalla	$10	RCA Victor 8063
3/5/88	183	5		© 2	Sirius	$10	RCA 6846
3/20/93	46	24	●	© 3	Anam	$10	Atlantic 82409
7/3/93	110	11	●	© 4	Banba	$10	Atlantic 82503
3/23/96	195	1		© 5	Lore	$10	Atlantic 82753

Alasdair MacColla (5)
Almost Seems (Too Late To Turn) (1)
Anam (4)
Banba Oir (4)
Blackstairs (1)
Bridge (That Carries Us Over) (5)
Broken Pieces (5)
Buachaill On Eirne (1)

Caide Sin Do'n Te Sin (4)
Caislean Oir (1)
Closer To Your Heart (1)
Croi Croga (5)
Dealramh Go Deo (5)
Dobhar (3)
Farewell Love (5)
Fonn Mharta (5)
From Your Heart (5)

Gentle Place (4)
Harry's Game (3)
I Will Find You (4)
In A Lifetime (1,3)
In Fortune's Hand (3)
In Search Of A Heart (2)
Indoor (1)
Journey's End (1)
Live And Learn (2)

Love And Affection (3)
Many Roads (2)
Mystery Game (4)
Na Laethe Bhi (4)
Northern Skyline (1)
Other Side (4)
Poison Glen (5)
Ri Na Cruinne (3)
Seanchas (5)

Second Nature (2)
Sirius (2)
Skellig (2)
Something To Believe In (2)
Soul Searcher (4)
Stepping Stone (2)
Struggle (4)
Sunset Dreams (4)
There For You (4)

Trail Of Tears (5)
Trathnona Beag Areir (5)
Turning Tide (2)
Uirchill An Chreagain (3)
White Fool (2)
Why Worry? (3)
Wild Cry (1)
Wilderness (3)
You're The One (3)

CLAPTON, Eric ★14★   '74

Born Eric Patrick Clapp on 3/30/45 in Ripley, England. Prolific rock-blues guitarist/vocalist. With The Roosters in 1963, **The Yardbirds**, 1963-65, and **John Mayall**'s Bluesbreakers, 1965-66. Formed **Cream** with **Jack Bruce** and **Ginger Baker** in 1966. Formed **Blind Faith** in 1968; worked with **John Lennon**'s Plastic Ono Band, and **Delaney & Bonnie**. Formed **Derek and The Dominos** in 1970. After two years of reclusion (1971-72), Clapton performed his comeback concert at London's Rainbow Theatre in January 1973. Began actively recording and touring again in 1974. Clapton's four-year-old son, Conor, died on 3/20/91 in a 53-floor fall in New York City. Nicknamed "Slowhand" in 1964 while with The Yardbirds. Inducted into the Rock and Roll Hall of Fame in 2000.

1)461 Ocean Boulevard 2)Unplugged 3)From The Cradle 4)Just One Night 5)Slowhand

DEBUT	PEAK	WKS	RIAA	CD	ARTIST — Album Title	Sym	$	Label & Number
7/25/70	13	30		© 1	Eric Clapton		$40	Atco 329
					also see #14 below			
11/21/70	16	65	●	© 2	Layla		$30	Atco 704 [2]
					DEREK AND THE DOMINOS also see #9, #13 and #25 below			
4/15/72	6	42	●		3 History Of Eric Clapton	[K]	$30	Atco 803 [2]
10/14/72	87	17			4 Eric Clapton At His Best	[K]	$30	Polydor 3503 [2]
1/27/73	20	21	● ©		5 Derek & The Dominos In Concert	[L]	$30	RSO 8800 [2]
					DEREK & THE DOMINOS recorded at the Fillmore East in New York City			
2/17/73	67	11			6 Clapton	[K]	$20	Polydor 5526
9/22/73	18	14	©		7 Eric Clapton's Rainbow Concert	[L]	$20	RSO 877
					recorded at the Rainbow Theatre in London			
7/20/74	❶⁴	25	● ©		8 461 Ocean Boulevard		$15	RSO 4801
					address where recorded in Miami, Florida			
8/10/74	107	10			9 Layla	[R]	$20	Polydor 3501 [2]
					DEREK AND THE DOMINOS reissue of #2 above			
4/12/75	21	14	©		10 There's One In Every Crowd		$15	RSO 4806
9/6/75	20	13	©		11 E.C. Was Here	[L]	$15	RSO 4809
10/16/76	15	21	©		12 No Reason To Cry		$15	RSO 3004
2/19/77	183	2			13 Layla	[R]	$20	RSO 3801 [2]
					DEREK AND THE DOMINOS reissue of #2 above			
3/5/77	194	2			14 Eric Clapton	[R]	$15	RSO 3008
					reissue of #1 above			
11/26/77+	2⁵	74	▲³	©	15 Slowhand	C:#48/1	$15	RSO 3030
12/2/78+	8	37	▲	©	16 Backless		$15	RSO 3039
5/3/80	2⁶	31	●	©	17 Just One Night	[L]	$20	RSO 4202 [2]
					recorded December 1979 at the Budokan concert hall in Japan			
3/21/81	7	21	●	©	18 Another Ticket		$12	RSO 3095
5/22/82	101	14	▲⁷	©	19 Time Pieces/The Best Of Eric Clapton	C:❶³⁷/322 [G]	$12	RSO 3099
2/19/83	16	19		©	20 Money And Cigarettes		$12	Duck 23773
4/6/85	34	28	▲	©	21 Behind The Sun		$12	Duck 25166
12/27/86+	37	34	●	©	22 August		$12	Duck 25476
5/7/88	34	26	▲²	©	23 Crossroads	[K]	$50	Polydor 835261 [6]
11/25/89+	16	51	▲²	©	24 Journeyman		$10	Duck 26074
10/6/90	157	5		©	25 The Layla Sessions - 20th Anniversary Edition	[K]	$25	Polydor 847083 [3]
					DEREK AND THE DOMINOS remix of album #2 above plus rare and unreleased cuts from the original *Layla* session tapes			
10/26/91	38	19	●	©	26 24 Nights	[L]	$20	Duck 26420 [2]
					recorded at the Royal Albert Hall in London			
2/1/92	24	31	●	©	27 Rush	[I-S]	$10	Reprise 26794
9/12/92+	❶³	137	▲¹⁰	©	28 Unplugged	C:#25/28 [L]	$10	Duck 45024
					recorded on 3/12/92; 1992 Grammy winner: Album of the Year			
10/1/94	❶¹	41	▲³	©	29 From The Cradle	[L]	$10	Duck 45735
3/25/95	80	30	▲	©	30 The Cream Of Clapton	C:#23/58 [G]	$10	Chronicles 527116
4/20/96	137	1		©	31 Crossroads 2 (Live In The Seventies)	[L]	$40	Chronicles 529305 [4]
3/28/98	4	29	▲	©	32 Pilgrim		$10	Duck 46577
8/14/99	52	9	●	©	33 Blues	[K]	$15	Polydor 547178 [2]
10/30/99	20	28	▲	©	34 Clapton Chronicles - The Best Of Eric Clapton	[G]	$10	Duck 47553
7/1/00	3	43	▲²	©	35 Riding With The King		$10	Reprise 47612
					B.B. KING & ERIC CLAPTON			
3/31/01	5	16	●	©	36 Reptile		$10	Duck 47966

After Midnight (1,4,7,14,17,19,23,30) *18*
Ain't Going Down (20)
Ain't That Lovin' You (23,33)
Alberta (28,33)
All Our Pastimes (12,17)
All Your Love (23)
Another Ticket (18) *78*
Anyday (2,4,9,13,25)
Anyone For Tennis (23) *64*
Anything For Your Love (24)
Baby What's Wrong (23)
Bad Boy (1,6,14)
Bad Influence (22)
Bad Love (24,26,34) *88*
Badge (3,7,23,26,30,31) *60*
Beautiful Thing (12)

Before You Accuse Me (24,28,33,34)
Behind The Mask (22)
Behind The Sun (21)
Believe In Life (36)
Bell Bottom Blues (2,4,6,9,13,25,26,30) *78*
Bernard Jenkins (23)
Better Make It Through Today (10,23)
Black Rose (18)
Black Summer Rain (12)
Blow Wind Blow (18,33)
Blue Eyes Blue (34)
Blues Before Sunrise (29)
Blues Leave Me Alone (29)
Blues Power (1,3,4,5,14,17,23,30) *76*

Boom Boom (23)
Born In Time (32)
Bottle Of Red Wine (1,4,5,14)
Breaking Point (24)
Broken Down (36)
Broken Hearted (32)
Can't Find My Way Home (11,23,31)
Carnival (12)
Catch Me If You Can (18)
Certain Girl (23)
Change The World (34) *5*
Circus (32)
Cocaine (15,17,19,23,30,31) *flip*
Cold Turkey (27)
Come Back Baby (36)

Come Rain Or Come Shine (35)
Comin' Home (23) *84*
Core, The (15,31)
County Jail Blues (12,33)
Crazy Country Hop (20)
Crosscut Saw (20)
Crossroads (3,23,30,31,33) *28*
Cryin' (31,33)
Days Of Old (35)
Don't Blame Me (10)
Don't Know Which Way To Go (27)
Don't Know Why (1,6,14)
Don't Let Me Be Lonely Tonight (36)
Double Trouble (12,17,23,31,33)
Driftin' Blues (31,33)

Drifting Blues (11,29)
Early In The Morning (16,17,31,33)
Easy Now (1,4,14)
Edge Of Darkness (26)
Everybody Oughta Make A Change (20)
Evil (23)
Eyesight To The Blind (medley) (31)
Fall Like Rain (32)
Farther On Up The Road (11,17,23,31,33)
Find Myself (36)
Five Long Years (29)
Floating Bridge (18,33)
For Your Love (23) *6*
Forever Man (21,34) *26*

Get Ready (8,31)
Give Me Strength (8,33)
Goin' Away Baby (29)
Goin' Down Slow (31,32)
Golden Ring (16)
Good Morning Little Schoolgirls (23)
Got To Get Better In A Little While (5,23)
Got To Hurry (23)
Got You On My Mind (36)
Groaning The Blues (29)
Hard Times (24,26)
Have You Ever Loved A Woman (2,5,6,9,11,13,23,25,26,31,33)
Heaven Is One Step Away (23)
Hello Old Friend (12,23,30) *24*

CLAPTON, Eric — Cont'd

Help Me Up (27)
Help The Poor (35)
Hey Hey (28)
Hideaway (3,23)
High (10)
Hold Me Lord (18)
Hold On (22)
Hold On I'm Coming (35)
Holy Mother (22)
Honey In Your Hips (23)
Hoochie Coochie Man (29)
Hoodoo Man (26)
Hound Dog (24)
How Long Blues (29)
Hung Up On Your Love (22)
Hungry (12)
I Ain't Gonna Stand For It (36)
I Ain't Got You (3,23)
I Am Yours (2,9,13,25)
I Can't Hold Out (8)
I Can't Stand It (18,23,30) **10**
I Don't Want To Discuss It (3)
I Feel Free (23,30)
I Found A Love (23)
(I) Get Lost (34)
I Looked Away (2,4,9,13,25)
I Shot The Sheriff (8,19,23,30,31) **1**
I Wanna Be (35)
I Want A Little Girl (36)
I Want To Know (3)
I Wish You Would (23)
I'll Make Love To You Anytime (16)
I'm Tore Down (29)
I've Got A Rock N' Roll Heart (20) **18**

I've Told You For The Last Time (14)
If I Don't Be There By Morning (16,17,23)
Innocent Times (12)
Inside Of Me (32)
It All Depends (21)
It Hurts Me Too (29)
It's In The Way That You Use It (22,34)
It's Too Late (2,9,13,25)
Jam I-V (25)
Just Like A Prisoner (21)
Keep On Growing (2,4,9,13,25)
Key To The Highway (2,4,9,13,23,25,35)
Knock On Wood (21)
Knockin' On Heaven's Door (19,23,30,31)
Kristen And Jim (27)
Lawdy Mama (23)
Lay Down Sally (15,17,19,23,31) **3**
Layla (2,3,4,9,13,19,23,25,30,31) **10**
Layla [live] (28,34) **12**
Lead Me On (24)
Let It Grow (8,23,30)
Let It Rain (1,4,5,14,23,30) **48**
Little Rachel (32)
Little Wing (2,4,7,9,13,25,31)
Lonely Stranger (28)
Lonely Years (23)
Lonesome And A Long Way From Home (1,4,14)

Lovin' You Lovin' Me (1,6,14)
Loving You Is Sweeter Than Ever (31)
Mainline Florida (8)
Malted Milk (28)
Man In Love (20)
Man Overboard (20)
Marry You (35)
May You Never (15)
Mean Old Frisco (15,23,31)
Mean Old World (23,25,33)
Meet Me (Down At The Bottom) (33)
Miss You (22,23)
Modern Girl (34)
Motherless Child (29)
Motherless Children (8,23)
My Father's Eyes (32,34)
Needs His Woman (32)
Never Make You Cry (21)
Next Time You See Her (15)
No Alibis (24)
Nobody Knows You When You're Down And Out (2,6,9,13,25,28)
Old Love (24,26,28)
One Chance (32)
One More Chance (23)
Only You Know And I Know (3) **20**
Opposites (10)
Peaches And Diesel (15)
Pearly Queen (7)
Pilgrim (32)
Please Be With Me (8)
Preludin Fugue (27)

Presence Of The Lord (4,5,7,11,23,30,31)
Pretending (24,26,34) **55**
Pretty Blue Eyes (10)
Pretty Girl (20)
Promises (16,19,23,30) **9**
Ramblin' On My Mind (11,17,23,31)
Realization (27)
Reconsider Baby (29)
Reptile (36)
Riding With The King (35)
Rita Mae (18)
River Of Tears (32,34)
Roll It (16)
Roll It Over (5,7,23)
Rollin' & Tumblin' (28)
Run (22)
Run So Far (24)
Running On Faith (24,26,28,34)
Same Old Blues (21)
San Francisco Bay Blues (28)
Sea Of Joy (3,4)
Second Nature (36)
See What Love Can Do (21) **89**
Setting Me Up (17)
Shape You're In (20,23)
She's Gone (32)
She's Something Special (18)
She's Waiting (21,23,34)
Sick And Tired (32)
Sign Language (12,23)
Signe (28)
Singin' The Blues (10)
Sinner's Prayer (29)
Sky Is Crying (10,23,31,33)

Sleeping In The Ground (23)
Slow Down Linda (20)
Slunky (1,4,14)
Snake Lake Blues (23)
Someday After A While (29)
Someone Like You (23)
Something's Happening (21)
Son & Sylvia (36)
Spoonful (3,23)
Standin' Round Crying (29)
Steady Rollin' Man (8)
Steppin' Out (23)
Stormy Monday (31,33)
Strange Brew (23)
Sunshine Of Your Love (3,23,26,30) **5**
Superman Inside (36)
Swing Low Sweet Chariot (10,19)
Take A Chance (22)
Tales Of Brave Ulysses (23)
Tangled In Love (21)
Tearing Us Apart (22)
Tears In Heaven (27,28,34) **2**
Teasin' (23)
Tell Me That You Love Me (16)
Tell The Truth (2,3,5,6,9,13,23,25,31)
Ten Long Years (35)
Tender Love (25)
Third Degree (29)
Thorn Tree In The Garden (2,9,13,25)
Three O'Clock Blues (35)
To Make Somebody Happy (31,33)

Told You For The Last Time (1,6)
Too Bad (23)
Tracks And Lines (27)
Travelin' Light (36)
Tribute To Elmore (3)
Tulsa Time (16,17,31) **30**
Walk Away (22)
Walk Out In The Rain (16)
Walkin' Blues (28)
Walkin' Down The Road (31)
Wanna Make Love To You (23)
Watch Out For Lucy (16) **40**
Watch Yourself (26)
Water On The Ground (31)
We're All The Way (15,31)
We've Been Told (Jesus Coming Soon) (10)
Whatcha Gonna Do (23)
When My Heart Beats Like A Hammer (35)
(When Things Go Wrong) It Hurts Me Too (23,25)
White Room (23,26,30) **6**
Why Does Love Got To Be So Sad? (2,4,5,9,13,25,31)
Will Gaines (27)
Willie And The Hand Jive (8,19,31) **26**
Wonderful Tonight (15,17,19,23,26,30,31,33) **16**
Worried Life Blues (17,26,31,33,35)
Wrapping Paper (23)
You Were There (32

★258★ CLARK, Dave, Five '64

Born on 12/15/42 in London. Pop-rock drummer. His group consisted of Mike Smith (vocals, keyboards), Lenny Davidson (guitar), Denny Payton (sax) and Rick Huxley (bass). Group starred in the 1965 movie *Having A Wild Weekend*. Clark co-wrote and produced the 1986 London stage musical *Time*.

1)Glad All Over 2)The Dave Clark Five Return! 3)Coast To Coast

DEBUT	PEAK	WKS	RIAA	CD	ARTIST — Album Title		$	Label & Number
4/11/64	3	32	●		1 Glad All Over		$40	Epic 26093
6/20/64	5	22			2 The Dave Clark Five Return!		$40	Epic 26104
8/29/64	11	28		©	3 American Tour		$40	Epic 26117
1/2/65	6	21		©	4 Coast To Coast		$40	Epic 26128
4/3/65	24	23		©	5 Weekend In London		$40	Epic 26139
8/14/65	15	21			6 Having A Wild Weekend	[S]	$40	Epic 26162
12/11/65+	32	16			7 I Like It Like That		$40	Epic 26178
2/26/66	9	62	●		8 The Dave Clark Five's Greatest Hits	[G]	$40	Epic 26185
6/25/66	77	11			9 Try Too Hard		$40	Epic 26198
10/1/66	127	6			10 Satisfied With You		$40	Epic 26212
12/10/66+	103	7			11 The Dave Clark Five/More Greatest Hits	[G]	$40	Epic 26221
3/25/67	119	7			12 5 By 5		$40	Epic 26236
8/12/67	149	3			13 You Got What It Takes		$40	Epic 26312
8/21/93	127	1		©	14 The History Of The Dave Clark Five	[K]	$20	Hollywood 61482 [2]

All Night Long (11,14)
All Of The Time (1)
Any Time You Want Love (3,14)
Any Way You Want It (4,8,14) **14**
At The Place (14)
At The Scene (11,14) **18**
Because (3,8,14) **3**
Bernadette (12)
Best Day's Work (14)
Bits And Pieces (1,8,14) **4**
Blue Monday (7)
Blue Suede Shoes (5)
Can I Trust You (2)
Can't You See That She's Mine (2,8,14) **4**
Catch Us If You Can (6,8,14) **4**
Chaquita (1)
Come Home (5,11,14) **14**
Come On Over (3)
Concentration Baby (14)
Crying Over You (4,14)
Do You Love Me (1,8,14) **11**
Do You Still Love Me? (10,14)
Doctor Rhythm (13,14)

Don't Be Taken In (6,14)
Don't Let Me Down (11,14)
Don't You Know (4)
Don't You Realize (6)
Doo Dah (1)
Dum-Dee-Dee-Dum (6)
Ever Since You've Been Away (9)
Everybody Get Together (14)
Everybody Knows (14)
Everybody Knows (I Still Love You) (8,14) **15**
Forever And A Day (2)
Funny (2)
Glad All Over (1,8,14) **6**
Go On (10)
Good Lovin' (10)
Goodbye My Friends (7)
Having A Wild Weekend (6,14)
Here Comes Summer (14)
How Can I Tell You (12)
Hurting Inside (5,14)
I Am On My Own (7,14)
I Can't Stand It (4)
I Can't Stop Loving You (14)
I Cried Over You (3)

I Know (9)
I Know You (1)
I Like It Like That (7,8,14) **7**
I Love You No More (2)
I Meant You (10)
I Miss You (14)
I Need Love (7,14)
I Need You, I Love You (2)
I Never Will (9)
I Really Love You (9)
I Said I Was Sorry (6)
I Still Need You (10)
I Want You Still (3)
I'll Be Yours My Love (7,14)
I'll Never Know (5)
I'm Thinking (5,11)
I've Got To Have A Reason (13,14) **44**
If You Come Back (6)
Inside And Out (14)
It Don't Feel Good (9)
It'll Only Hurt For A Little While (10)
It's Not True (4)
Let Me Be (13)
Little Bit Of Love (7)

Little Bit Strong (12)
Little Bitty Pretty One (5,14)
Live In The Sky (14)
Long Ago (3)
Look Before You Leap (10,11,14)
Looking In (9)
Lovin' So Good (13)
Maybe It's You (7)
Maze Of Love (14)
Mighty Good Loving (5,14)
Move On (3)
New Kind Of Love (6)
Nineteen Days (12,14) **48**
No Stopping (6)
No Time To Lose (1)
Ol' Sol (3)
On Broadway (2)
On The Move (6)
Over And Over (8,14) **1**
Pick Up Your Phone (12)
Picture Of You (12)
Play With Me (13)
Please Love Me (9)
Please Tell Me Why (10,11,14) **28**

Pumping (7)
Reelin' And Rockin' (11,14) **23**
Remember, It's Me (5)
Rumble (2)
Satisfied With You (10,11,14) **50**
Say You Want Me (4)
Scared Of Falling In Love (9)
She's A Loving Girl (7)
She's All Mine (1)
Sitting Here Baby (12)
Small Talk (12,14)
Somebody Find A New Love (9,14)
Something I've Always Wanted (12)
Sometimes (3)
Stay (1)
Sweet Memories (4)
Tabatha Twitchit (13)
That's How Long Our Love Will Last (7)
Theme Without A Name (2)
Thinking Of You Baby (13,14)
'Til The Right One Comes Along (5,14)
Time (1)

To Me (4)
Today (9)
Try Too Hard (9,11,14) **12**
We'll Be Running (5)
What Is There To Say (4)
When (4,14)
When I'm Alone (6)
Whenever You're Around (3,14)
Who Does He Think He Is (3)
You Don't Play Me Around (13)
You Don't Want My Loving (12)
You Got What It Takes (13,14) **7**
You Know You're Lying (7)
You Never Listen (10)
Your Turn To Cry (5)
Zip-A-Dee-Doo-Dah (2)

CLARK, Gene '74

Born Harold Eugene Clark on 11/17/41 in Tipton, Missouri. Died on 5/24/91 (age 49). Guitarist of **The Byrds**. Also see **McGuinn, Clark & Hillman**.

DEBUT	PEAK	WKS	RIAA	CD	ARTIST — Album Title		$	Label & Number
11/2/74	144	5		©	No Other		$15	Asylum 1016

From A Silver Phial
Lady Of The North

Life's Greatest Fool
No Other

Silver Raven
Some Misunderstanding

Strength Of Strings
True One

162

★321★   CLARK, Petula   '65

Born on 11/15/32 in Epsom, Surrey, England. Pop singer/actress. Hosted own radio and TV shows in England. Starred in several movies including *Finian's Rainbow* and *Goodbye Mr. Chips*.

1)Downtown 2)These Are My Songs 3)Portrait Of Petula

DEBUT	PEAK	WKS	CD	#	ARTIST — Album Title	Sym	$	Label & Number
2/13/65	21	36		1	**Downtown**		$25	Warner 1590
5/29/65	42	17		2	**I Know A Place**		$25	Warner 1598
10/23/65	129	9		3	**The World's Greatest International Hits!**		$25	Warner 1608
4/9/66	68	12		4	**My Love**		$25	Warner 1630
9/3/66	43	16		5	**I Couldn't Live Without Your Love**		$25	Warner 1645
2/18/67	49	27		6	**Color My World/Who Am I**		$25	Warner 1673
9/2/67	27	27		7	**These Are My Songs**		$25	Warner 1698
2/17/68	93	23		8	**The Other Man's Grass Is Always Greener**		$25	Warner 1719
9/7/68	51	21		9	**Petula**		$25	Warner 1743
12/28/68+	57	17		10	**Petula Clark's Greatest Hits, Vol. 1**	[G]	$25	Warner 1765
5/17/69	37	11		11	**Portrait Of Petula**		$20	Warner 1789
12/27/69+	176	7	©	12	**Just Pet**		$20	Warner 1823
8/8/70	198	2	©	13	**Memphis**		$20	Warner 1862
4/10/71	178	3		14	**Warm And Tender**		$20	Warner 1885

Ad, The (11)
Answer Me My Love (8)
At The Crossroads (8)
Baby It's Me (1)
Ballad Of A Sad Young Man (8)
Bang Bang (5)
Be Good To Me (1)
Beautiful (14)
Beautiful In The Rain (9)
Black Coffee (8)
Boy From Ipanema (3)
Butterfly (5)
Call Me (2,10)
Cat In The Window (The Bird In The Sky) (8) *26*
Cherish (8)
Color My World (6,10) *16*
Come Rain Or Come Shine (5)
Couldn't Sleep (14)
Cry Like A Baby (14)
Crying Through A Sleepless Night (1)
Cuando Calienta El Sol (Love Me With All Of Your Heart) (3)
Dance With Me (4)
Dancing In The Street (2)
Days (9)
Don't Give Up (9) *37*
Don't Say I Didn't Tell You So (14)
Don't Sleep In The Subway (7) *5*

Downtown (1,10) *1*
Elusive Butterfly (5)
England Swings (6)
Eternally (7)
Every Little Bit Hurts (2)
Everything In The Garden (2)
Fill The World With Love (12)
Foggy Day (2)
Fool On The Hill (12)
For Free (14)
For Love (8)
For Those In Love (12)
Goin' Out Of My Head (12)
Good Life (9)
Goodnight Sweet Dreams (13)
Gotta Tell The World (2)
Groovin' (12)
Groovy Kind Of Love (5)
Happy Heart (11) *62*
Happy Together (12)
Have Another Dream On Me (9)
Have I The Right (3)
Heart (2)
Hello, Dolly! (3)
Here, There & Everywhere (6)
Hey, Jude (12)
Hold On To What You've Got (4)
Homeward Bound (5)
Houses (12)

How Insensitive (7)
How We Gonna Live To Be A Hundred Years Old Together (13)
I Can't Remember Ever Loving You (4)
I Could Have Danced All Night (8)
I Couldn't Live Without Your Love (5,10) *9*
I Just Can't Wait To Hold You (14)
I Know A Place (2,10) *3*
I Wanna See Morning With Him (13)
I Want To Hold Your Hand (3)
I (Who Have Nothing) (3)
I Will Wait For You (7)
I've Got My Eyes On You (14)
If Ever You're Lonely (11)
If I Only Had Time (12)
If I Were A Bell (4)
Imagine (7)
"In" Crowd (3)
In Love (1)
It Don't Matter To Me (14)
Just Say Goodbye (4)
Kiss Me Goodbye (9) *15*
L'ile De France (8)
Las Vegas (8)
Last Waltz (8)
Let It Be Me (11)

Let Me Be The One (14)
Let Me Tell You Baby (1)
Life And Soul Of The Party (4)
Lights Of Night (12)
Loss Of Love (14)
Love Is Here (7)
Love Is The Only Thing (11)
Lover Man (7)
Lovin' Things (11)
Maybe I'm Amazed (14)
Monday, Monday (5)
Morgen (One More Sunrise) (3)
Music (1)
My Funny Valentine (11)
My Love (4,10) *1*
Neon Rainbow (13)
Never On Sunday (3)
No One Better Than You (12) *93*
Nothing's As Good As It Used To Be (13)
Now That You've Gone (1)
On The Path Of Glory (7)
One In A Million (9)
Other Man's Grass Is Always Greener (8) *31*
People Get Ready (13)
Please Don't Go (6)
Rain (5)
Reach Out, I'll Be There (6)
Resist (7)

Right On (13)
Round Every Corner (10) *21*
San Francisco (Be Sure To Wear Some Flowers In Your Hair) (7)
Sign Of The Times (4,10) *11*
Smile (8)
Some (11)
Song Of My Life (14)
Special People (8)
Strangers And Lovers (2)
Strangers In The Night (5)
Sun Shines Out Of Your Shoes (9)
Tell Me (That It's Love) (1)
That Old Time Feeling (13)
That's What Life Is All About (13)
There Goes My Love, There Goes My Life (3)
Things Bright & Beautiful (12)
Thirty-First Of June (4)
This Girl's In Love With You (9)
This Is Goodbye (1)
This Is My Song (7) *3*
Time And Love (14)
Time For Love (8)
Today, Tomorrow (8)
True Love Never Runs Smooth (1)
Two Rivers (5,10)

Volare (Nel Blu, Dipinto Di Blu) (3)
Wasn't It You (5)
We Can Work It Out (4)
We're Falling In Love Again (9)
What Now My Love (3)
What Would I Be (6)
When I Give My Heart (11)
When I Was A Child (11)
When The World Was Round (13)
Where Did We Go Wrong (4)
While The Children Play (6)
Who Am I (6,10) *21*
Why Can't I Cry? (9)
Why Don't They Understand (3)
Winchester Cathedral (6)
Windmills Of Your Mind (11)
You Belong To Me (1)
You Can't Keep Me From Loving You (3)
You'd Better Come Home (10) *22*
You're The One (2,10)
Your Love Is Everywhere (9)

CLARK, Roy   '69

Born on 4/15/33 in Meherrin, Virginia. Country singer/guitarist. Co-hosted TV's *Hee-Haw*.

DEBUT	PEAK	WKS	#	ARTIST — Album Title	Sym	$	Label & Number
7/5/69	50	20	1	**Yesterday, When I Was Young**		$15	Dot 25953
1/3/70	129	9	2	**The Everlovin' Soul Of Roy Clark**		$15	Dot 25972
8/29/70	176	6	3	**I Never Picked Cotton**		$15	Dot 25980
4/3/71	178	8	4	**The Best Of Roy Clark**	[G]	$15	Dot 25986
8/14/71	197	2	5	**The Incredible Roy Clark**		$15	Dot 25990
7/29/72	112	12	6	**Roy Clark Country!**		$15	Dot 25997
5/5/73	172	6	7	**Roy Clark/Superpicker**	[I]	$15	Dot 26008
4/13/74	186	3	8	**Roy Clark/The Entertainer**		$15	Dot 2001

All The Way (2)
April's Fool (1)
As Far As I'm Concerned (5)
Aura Lee (7)
Back In The Race (5)
Carolyn (6)
Chomp 'N' (8)
Darby's Castle (6)
Days Of Sand And Shovels (1)
Do You Believe This Town (4)
Don't Touch Me (5)
Dozen Pairs Of Boots (6)
Drink To Me Only With Thine Eyes (8)
Duelin' Banjos (8)
Family Man (6)
For Once In My Life (2)
For The Good Times (5)

For The Life Of Me (1)
Hangin' On (5)
He'll Have To Go (6)
Honeymoon Feelin' (8)
I Need To Be Needed (2)
I Never Picked Cotton (3,4)
I Really Don't Want To Know (8)
I Remember Loving Someone (5)
I'll Take The Time (6)
Is Anybody Goin' To San Antone (3)
It's All Over (All Over Again) (8)
January, April And Me (3)
Just Another Man (1)
Kiss An Angel Good Mornin' (6)
Last Letter (2)

Let Me Be There (8)
Lonesome Too Long (3)
Lord, Let It Rain (6)
Love Is Just A State Of Mind (1,4)
Love Story, Theme From (7)
Love's All Around You (8)
Malaguena (7)
Mary Ann Regrets (5)
Me And Bobby McGee (2)
Middle Of The Road (5)
Midnight Cowboy Rides Again (7)
Morningside Of The Mountain (2)
Most Beautiful Girl (8)
My Goal For Today (5)
Never On Sunday (7)

Odds And Ends (Bits And Pieces) (1)
Ode To A Critter (6)
Raggedy Ann (1)
Riders In The Sky (7)
Right Or Left At Oak Street (2,4)
Rocky Top (5)
Roy's Guitar Boogie (7)
Say Amen (2)
September Song (1,4)
She Cried (5)
She Cries For Me (3)
She Makes The Living Worthwhile (8)
She's All I Got (6)
Simple Thing As Love (1,4)
Since December (3)

Snowbird (7)
Somewhere, My Love (7)
Strangers (3)
Sunday Mornin' Comin' Down (3)
Sunday Sunrise (4)
Tara Theme (7)
Thank God And Greyhound (3,4) *90*
That's All That Matters (5)
Then She's A Lover (2,4) *94*
Tips Of My Fingers (1,4)
Today (2)
Today I Started Loving You Again (7)
True Love (7)
Unchained Melody (2)

When A Man Becomes A Man (1)
When The Wind Blows (In Chicago) (6)
Yesterday, When I Was Young (1,4) *19*
You Don't Have Very Far To Go (2)
You Gotta Love People (3)

CLARK, Terri   '96

Born on 8/5/68 in Montreal; raised in Medicine Hat, Alberta, Canada. Female country singer.

DEBUT	PEAK	WKS	RIAA	CD	#	ARTIST — Album Title	$	Label & Number
9/23/95+	79	47	▲	©	1	**Terri Clark**	$10	Mercury 526991
11/23/96	58	25	▲	©	2	**Just The Same**	$10	Mercury 532879
6/6/98	70	16	●	©	3	**How I Feel**	$10	Mercury 558211
10/7/00	85	3		©	4	**Fearless**	$10	Mercury 170157

Any Woman (2)
Better Things To Do (1)
Catch 22 (1)

Cure For The Common Heartache (3)
Easy From Now On (4)

Emotional Girl (2)
Empty (4)
Everytime I Cry (3) *69*

Flowers After The Fact (1)
Getting Even With The Blues (3)

Getting There (4)
Good Mother (4)
Hold Your Horses (2)

I'm Alright (3)
If I Were You (1)
Inside Story (1)

CLARK, Terri — cont'd

Is Fort Worth Worth It (1)	Neon Flame (2)	Real Thing (4)	Take My Time (4)	Twang Thang (2)	When Boy Meets Girl (1)

Is Fort Worth Worth It (1)
Just The Same (2)
Keeper Of The Flame (2)
Last Thing I Wanted (4)
Little Gasoline (4) *75*
Midnight's Gone (4)

Neon Flame (2)
No Fear (4)
Not Getting Over You (3)
Not What I Wanted To Hear (2)
Now That I Found You (3) *72*
Poor, Poor Pitiful Me (2)

Real Thing (4)
Something In The Water (2)
Something You Should've Said (1)
Sometimes Goodbye (4)
Suddenly Single (1)

Take My Time (4)
That's How I Feel (3)
That's Me Not Loving You (3)
This Ole Heart (3)
Till I Get There (3)
To Tell You Everything (4)

Twang Thang (2)
Tyin' A Heart To A Tumbleweed (1)
Unsung Hero (3)
Was There A Girl On Your Boys' Night Out (1)

When Boy Meets Girl (1)
When We Had It Bad (1)
You Do Or You Don't (2)
You're Easy On The Eyes (3) *40*

★478★   ## CLARKE, Stanley   '75

Born on 6/30/51 in Philadelphia. R&B-jazz bassist/violinist/cellist. With **Chick Corea** in **Return To Forever** in 1973. Much session work, solo debut in 1974. Member of **Fuse One** in 1982 and **Animal Logic** in 1989.

1)The Clarke/Duke Project 2)Journey To Love 3)School Days

DEBUT	PEAK	WKS	CD	#	Album Title	Sym	$	Label & Number
1/18/75	59	16	©	1	Stanley Clarke	[I]	$12	Nemperor 431
11/1/75	34	19	©	2	Journey To Love	[I]	$12	Nemperor 433
9/25/76	34	22	©	3	School Days	[I]	$12	Nemperor 439
4/29/78	57	19	©	4	Modern Man	[I]	$12	Nemperor 35303
7/21/79	62	14	©	5	I Wanna Play For You	[I-L]	$15	Nemperor 35680 [2]
6/28/80	95	11	©	6	Rocks, Pebbles And Sand		$10	Epic 36506
5/9/81	33	23	©	7	The Clarke/Duke Project		$10	Epic 36918
					STANLEY CLARKE/GEORGE DUKE			
8/21/82	114	8		8	Let Me Know You		$10	Epic 38086
11/26/83+	146	10	©	9	The Clarke/Duke Project II		$10	Epic 38934
					STANLEY CLARKE/GEORGE DUKE			
4/28/84	149	13	©	10	Time Exposure		$10	Epic 38688

All About (5)
All Hell Broke Loose (6)
Are You Ready (For The Future) (10)
Atlanta (9)
Blues For Mingus (5)
Christopher Ivanhoe (5)
Concerto For Jazz (medley) (2)
Dancer, The (3)
Danger Street (6)
Dayride (4)
Desert Song (3)
Every Reason To Smile (9)
Finding My Way (7)
Force Of Love (8)

Future (10)
Future Shock (10)
Good Times (9)
Got To Find My Own Place (4)
Great Danes (9)
He Lives On (Story About The Last Journey Of A Warrior) (4)
Heaven Sent You (10)
Hello Jeff (2)
Heroes (9)
Hot Fun (3,5)
I Just Want To Be Your Brother (8)
I Just Want To Love You (7)
I Know Just How You Feel (10)

I Wanna Play For You (5)
It's What She Didn't Say (4)
Jamaican Boy (5)
Journey To Love (2)
Just A Feeling (5)
Let Me Know You (8)
Let's Get Started (7)
Life Is Just A Game (3)
Life Suite (Part I, II, III, IV) (1)
Lopsy Lu (1)
Louie Louie (7)
Modern Man (4)
More Hot Fun (4)
My Greatest Hits (5)

Never Judge A Cover By It's Book (7)
New York City (8)
Off The Planet (5)
Play The Bass (8,10)
Power (1)
Put It On The Line (9)
Quiet Afternoon (3,5)
Relaxed Occasion (4)
Rock 'N' Roll Jelly (4,5)
Rock Orchestra (medley) (2)
Rocks, Pebbles And Sand (6)
School Days (3,5)
Secret To My Heart (8)
Serious Occasion (4)

Silly Putty (2)
Slow Dance (4)
Song To John (2)
Spacerunner (10)
Spanish Phases For Strings & Bass (1)
Speedball (10)
Story Of A Man And A Woman Medley (6)
Straight To The Top (8)
Strange Weather (5)
Streets Of Philadelphia (5)
Sweet Baby (7) *19*
Time Exposure (10)
Together Again (5)

Touch And Go (7)
Trip You In Love (9)
Try Me Baby (9)
Underestimation (6)
Vulcan Princess (1)
We Supply (6)
Wild Dog (7)
Winners (7)
Yesterday Princess (1)
You Are The One For Me (4)
You/Me Together (6)
You're Gonna Love It (9)

CLASH, The   '83

Eclectic new wave rock group from London: John "Joe Strummer" Mellor (vocals), Mick Jones (guitar), Paul Simonon (bass) and Nicky "Topper" Headon (drums). Political activists, who wrote songs protesting racism and oppression. Headon left in May 1983; replaced by Peter Howard. Jones (not to be confused with Mick Jones of Foreigner) left band in 1984 to form **Big Audio Dynamite**. Strummer disbanded The Clash in early 1986, and appeared in the 1987 movie *Straight To Hell*. Simonon formed **Havana 3 A.M.** in 1990.

DEBUT	PEAK	WKS	RIAA	CD	#	Album Title	Sym	$	Label & Number
2/24/79	128	10		©	1	Give 'Em Enough Rope		$15	Epic 35543
9/8/79	126	6	●	©	2	The Clash		$15	Epic 36060
2/9/80	27	33	▲	©	3	London Calling		$20	Epic 36328 [2]
11/22/80	74	16			4	Black Market Clash		$15	Epic 36846
2/7/81	24	20	●	©	5	Sandinista!		$25	Epic 37037 [3]
6/12/82+	7	61	▲²	©	6	Combat Rock		$10	Epic 37689
12/7/85+	88	12		©	7	Cut The Crap		$10	Epic 40017
5/28/88	142	8	▲	©	8	The Story Of The Clash, Volume I	[G]	$15	Epic 44035 [2]
11/13/99	193	1		©	9	From Here To Eternity Live	[L]	$10	Epic 65747

recorded from 1978-82

All The Young Punks (New Boots And Contracts) (1)
Are You Red..Y (7)
Armagideon Time (4,8,9)
Atom Tan (6)
Bankrobber (4,8)
Brand New Cadillac (3)
Broadway (5)
Call Up (5)
Capital Radio One (4,8,9)
Car Jamming (6)
Card Cheat (3)
Career Opportunities (2,5,8,9)
Charlie Don't Surf (5)
Cheapskate (1)
Cheat (4)
City Of The Dead (4,9)
Clampdown (3,8)
Clash City Rockers (2,8,9)
Complete Control (2,8,9)
Cool Under Heat (7)
Corner Soul (5)

Crooked Beat (5)
Death Is A Star (6)
Death Or Glory (3)
Dictator (7)
Dirty Punk (7)
Drug-Stabbing Time (1)
English Civil War (1,8)
Equaliser, The (5)
Fingerpoppin' (7)
Four Horsemen (3)
Garageland (2)
Ghetto Defendant (6)
Guns Of Brixton (3,8)
Guns On The Roof (1)
Hate And War (2)
Hateful (3)
Hitsville U.K. (5)
I Fought The Law (2,8,9)
I'm Not Down (3)
I'm So Bored With The U.S.A. (2)
If Music Could Talk (5)

Inoculated City (6)
Ivan Meets G.I. Joe (5)
Jail Guitar Doors (2)
Janie Jones (2,8)
Jimmy Jazz (3)
Julie's In The Drug Squad (1)
Junco Partner (5)
Junkie Slip (5)
Justice Tonight (medley) (4)
Kick It Over (medley) (4)
Kingston Advice (5)
Know Your Rights (6,9)
Koka Kola (3)
Last Gang In Town (1)
Leader, The (5)
Let's Go Crazy (5)
Life Is Wild (7)
Lightning Strikes (Not Once But Twice) (5)
Living In Fame (5)
London Calling (3,8,9)
London's Burning (2,8,9)

Look Here (5)
Lose This Skin (5)
Lost In The Supermarket (3,8)
Lover's Rock (5)
Magnificent Seven (5,8,9)
Mensforth Hill (5)
Midnight Log (5)
Movers And Shakers (7)
North And South (7)
One More Dub (5)
One More Time (5)
Overpowered By Funk (6)
Play To Win (7)
Police And Thieves (2,8)
Police On My Back (5)
Pressure Drop (4)
Prisoner, The (4)
Rebel Waltz (5)
Red Angel Dragnet (6)
Remote Control (2)
Revolution Rock (3)
Right Profile (3)

Rock The Casbah (6,8) *8*
Rudie Can't Fail (3)
Safe European Home (1,8)
Sean Flynn (6)
Shepherds Delight (5)
Should I Stay Or Should I Go? (6,8,9) *45*
Silicone On Sapphire (5)
Somebody Got Murdered (5,8)
Something About England (5)
Sound Of The Sinners (3,8)
Spanish Bombs (3,8)
Stay Free (1,8)
Straight To Hell (6,8,9)
Street Parade (5)
This Is England (7)
This Is Radio Clash (8)
Three Card Trick (7)
Time Is Tight (4)
Tommy Gun (1,8)
Train In Vain (Stand By Me) (3,8,9) *23*

Up In Heaven (Not Only Here) (5)
Version City (5)
Version Pardner (5)
Washington Bullets (5)
We Are The Clash (7)
What's My Name (2,9)
White Man In Hammersmith Palais (2,8,9)
White Riot (2,8)
Wrong 'Em Boyo (3)

CLASSICS IV   '69

Soft-rock group from Jacksonville, Florida: Dennis Yost (vocals), J.R. Cobb and Wally Eaton (guitars), Joe Wilson (bass; replaced by Dean Daughtry) and Kim Venable (drums). Cobb, Daughtry and producer Buddy Buie joined the **Atlanta Rhythm Section** in 1974.

DEBUT	PEAK	WKS	#	Album Title	Sym	$	Label & Number
3/9/68	140	7	1	Spooky		$20	Imperial 12371
2/1/69	196	3	2	Mamas And Papas/Soul Train		$20	Imperial 12407
4/26/69	45	20	3	Traces		$20	Imperial 12429
12/6/69+	50	20	4	Dennis Yost & The Classics IV/Golden Greats-Volume I	[G]	$20	Imperial 16000

Bed Of Roses (1)
Book A Trip (1)
Bus Stop (1)

By The Time I Get To Phoenix (1)
Change Of Heart (4) *49*

Daydream Believer (1)
Everyday With You Girl (3,4) *19*

Free (3)
Girl From Ipanema (Garota De Ipanema) (2)

Goin' Out Of My Head (1)
It Ain't Necessarily So (2)
Just Between You And Me (1)

Ladies Man (2)
Letter, The (1)
Mama's And Papa's (1)

DEBUT	PEAK	WKS	RIAA	CD	ARTIST — Album Title	Catalog	Sym	$	Label & Number

CLASSICS IV — Cont'd

Mary, Mary Row Your Boat (1,4)
Mr. Blue (3)
Nobody Loves You But Me (3)

Our Day Will Come (3)
Pity The Fool (2)
Poor People (1)
Rainy Day (3)

Sentimental Lady (3)
Something I'll Remember (3,4)
Soul Train (2,4) **90**
Spooky (1,4) **3**

Stormy (2,4) **5**
Strange Changes (2,4)
Sunny (3,4)
Traces (3,4) **2**

Traffic Jam (3)
24 Hours Of Loneliness (2,4)
Waves (2,4)
You Are My Sunshine (1)

CLAY, Andrew Dice   '90
Born Andrew Silverstein on 9/29/57 in Brooklyn, New York. Comedian/actor. Appeared in several movies and TV shows.

4/29/89	94	47	©	1	Dice	[C]	$10	Def American 24214
4/21/90	39	24	©	2	The Day The Laughter Died	[C]	$15	Def American 24287 [2]
5/4/91	81	12	©	3	Dice Rules	[C]	$10	Def American 26555
5/2/92	144	4	©	4	40 Too Long	[C]	$10	Def American 26854

A+ (2)
Action (3)
Apartment Life (3)
Attitude, The (1)
Automatic Pilot (2)
Backwards (3)
Bad Press (3)
Bait, The (1)
Bambi (3)
Birds (3)
Black Chicks (3)
Brooklyn Bad Boy (3)
Car Ride (Goin' To A Party) (3)
Chicks Aren't Funny (Joey Will) (3)
Christmas Presents (3)
Cigarettes (2)
Concave (2)
Couples In Love (1)
Day At The Beach (1)
Debbie Duz Everything (3)
Dice And Truckdrivers (4)
Dice At The Drive Thru (4)

Dice Buys A Suit (4)
Dice Does It Like Dis (4)
Dice Gets Creative In Bed (4)
Dice Goes To The Mall (4)
Dice Greeting Cards (4)
Dice Has Random Thoughts (4)
Dice Jerks Off (4)
Dice Just Says No Leno (4)
Dice Knows When To Say When (4)
Dice Learns To Mambo (4)
Dice On Bodybuilders (4)
Dice On Complaints (4)
Dice On Disasters (4)
Dice On Lasting Relationships (4)
Dice On Manners (4)
Dice On Nutrition (4)
Dice On Orgasms (4)
Dice On Reading Material (4)
Dice On Redheaded Men (4)
Dice On Redheads (4)
Dice Rewrites History (4)

Dice Stops For Gas (4)
Dice Talks To The Salesmen (4)
Dice The Advocate (4)
Dice Vs. PeeWee (4)
Dice's Checklist (4)
Divider, The (2)
Doctors And Nurses (1)
Dogs & Birds (3)
Don't Move (3)
Double Date (2)
Double Parking (3)
Driveway, The (3)
Fat Orgasms (4)
Female Anatomy (2)
Filthy In Bed (4)
First Blow-Job (3)
First Kiss (2)
Frozen Food (2)
Gift, The (2)
Golden Age Of Television (1)
Grocery Store (3)
Handicaps, Cripples (3)

History Lesson (2)
Hoggin' (1)
Hoidy Toidy Chicks (3)
Holiday Season (2)
Hot Mama (1)
Hour Back ... Get It? (2)
How Are Ya? (2,3)
Industrial Size (3)
Japs (3)
Jerkin' Off (2)
Joey (1)
Judy (1)
Kids (2)
Laughter Vs. Comedy (2)
Let Yourself Go (4)
Masturbation (1)
Milk & Shampoo (2)
Moby And The Japs (1)
Mother & Son (2)
Mother Goose (1)
Mothers, Daughters & Sisters (2)
Multiple Sclerosis (3)

News, The (3)
1989 - A Review (3)
1990 (2)
No Guilt (1)
No Pity (1)
Opportunity In America (Al Capone's Safe) (3)
Osmonds, The (2)
People Are Pricks (3)
Personal Delivery Service (2)
Phone Sex (3)
Pizza (2)
Places To Meet Chicks (2)
Rhyme Renditions (2)
Salt & Pepper (3)
Shakin' Hands (3)
Shampoo (1)
Silence Is Golden (2)
Smokin' (3)
Smokin' For Your Health (3)
Something Soft (2)
Speedin' (1)
Subway Travel (3)

Texas (2)
3 Beautiful Dates (3)
Tree, The (2)
True Stories (3)
Turn-On Words (2)
Under 2 Minutes (2)
Urinal, The (3)
Vibrant Beautiful Woman (3)
What A Mess (4)
What Did She Say? (3)
What If The Chick Gets Pregnant... (1)
What'll It Be (2)
When I Was Young (1)
While The Cats Away (2)
Woman's World (3)
Women Comics (2)
Ya Can't Be Nice To Them (3)
Ya Hear? (3)
You May Be Dancing With Me (4)

CLAY, Cassius   '63
Born on 1/18/42 in Louisville, Kentucky. Former world heavyweight boxing champ. Changed name to Muhammad Ali in 1966. Also see **Soundtracks**: *The Greatest*.

| 10/12/63 | 61 | 20 | © | | I Am The Greatest! .... | [C] | $50 | Columbia 2093 / 8893 |

Round 1: I Am The Greatest
Round 2: I Am The Double Greatest

Round 3: Do You Have To Ask?
Round 4: "I Have Written A Drama," He Said Playfully

Round 5: Will The Real Sonny Liston Please Fall Down

Round 6: Funny You Should Ask
Round 7: 2138

Round 8: The Knockout

CLAY, Tom   '71
Born in Binghamton, New York. Died on 11/22/95 (age 66). Was a DJ at KGBS in Los Angeles when he created this recording.

| 8/28/71 | 92 | 5 | | | What The World Needs Now Is Love .... | | $15 | MoWest 103 |

Baby I Need Your Loving
Both Sides Now
Bridge Over Troubled Water

For Years?
Mac Arthur Park
This Guy's In Love With You

Victors, The

What The World Needs Now Is Love/Abraham, Martin And John **8**

What's Going On
Whatever Happened To Love

CLAYDERMAN, Richard   '84
Born Phillipe Pages on 12/28/53 in Paris. Romantic pianist. Known as "The Prince of Romance."

| 11/24/84 | 160 | 9 | | | Amour .... | [I] | $10 | Columbia 39603 |

Ave Maria
Ballade Pour Adeline

Chariots Of Fire
Harmony

Hello
How Deep Is Your Love

Memory
Only You

Up Where We Belong
Way I Loved You

Way We Were

CLAYPOOL, Les, & The Holy Mackerel   '96
Born on 9/29/63 in Richmond, California. Rock singer/bassist. Member of **Primus**. The Holy Mackeral: Joe Gore and Mark Haggard (guitars) and Jay Lane (drums).

| 9/14/96 | 182 | 1 | © | | Highball With The Devil .... | | $10 | Interscope 90085 |

Awakening, The
Calling Kyle
Carolina Rig

Cohibas Esplenditos
Delicate Tendrils
El Sobrante Fortnight

George E. Porge
Granny's Little Yard Gnome
Hendershot

Highball With The Devil
Holy Mackerel
Me And Chuck

Precipitation
Rancor
Running The Gauntlet

CLAYTON, Merry   '75
Born Mary Clayton in New Orleans. Backup vocalist from Los Angeles. In The Raeletts, **Ray Charles**'s backing group. Formed R&B vocal group Sisters Love in 1971. Acted in the 1987 movie *Maid To Order*.

| 11/20/71+ | 180 | 11 | | 1 | Merry Clayton .... | | $15 | Ode 77012 |
| 9/6/75 | 146 | 6 | | 2 | Keep Your Eye On The Sparrow .... | | $15 | Ode 77030 |

After All This Time (1) **71**
Do What You Know (2)
Gets Hard Sometimes (2)
Gold Fever (2)
Grandma's Hands (1)

How'd I Know (2)
If I Lose (2)
Keep Your Eye On The Sparrow (2) **45**
Light On The Hill (1)

Love Me Or Let Me Be Lonely (1)
Loving Grows Up Slow (2)
One More Ride (2)
Rainy Day Women #12 & 35 (2)

Room 205 (2)
Same Old Story (1)
Sho' Nuff (1)
Sink Or Swim (2)
Song For You (1)

Southern Man (1)
Steamroller (2)
Walk On In (1)
Whatever (1)

CLAYTON-THOMAS, David   '69
Born David Thomsett on 9/13/41 in Surrey, England. Lead singer of **Blood, Sweat & Tears**.

9/27/69	159	8		1	David Clayton-Thomas!	[E]	$20	Decca 75146
					recordings prior to **Blood, Sweat & Tears**			
4/15/72	184	3		2	David Clayton-Thomas		$15	Columbia 31000

Boom Boom (1)
Call It Stormy Monday (1)
Caress Me Pretty Music (2)
Don't Let It Bring You Down (2)
Done Somebody Wrong (1)

Dying To Live (2)
Good Lovin' (1)
Howlin' For My Darling (1)
I Got A Woman (1)
Magnificent Sanctuary Band (2)

North Beach Racetrack (2)
Once Burned (2)
Poison Ivy (1)
Say Boss Man (1)
She (2)

Sing A Song (2)
Stealin' In The Name Of The Lord (2)
Tobacco Road (1)

We're All Meat From The Same Bone (2)
Who's Been Talkin' (1)

CLEAR LIGHT '68
Rock group from Los Angeles: Cliff DeYoung (vocals), Bob Seal (guitar), Ralph Schuckett (organ), Michael Ney (percussion), Douglas Lubahn (bass) and Dallas Taylor (drums). DeYoung later pursued a solo music and acting career. Taylor later became a prominent session drummer.

11/25/67+ 126 13   Clear Light .... **$25** Elektra 74011
Ballad Of Freddie & Larry   Child's Smile   Mr. Blue   Sand   They Who Have Nothing   With All In Mind
Black Roses   How Many Days Have Passed   Night Sounds Loud   Street Singer   Think Again

CLEGG, Johnny, & Savuka '90
Born on 7/13/53 in Rochdale, Lancashire, England; raised in South Africa. Singer/guitarist/dancer. Savuka: Steve Mavuso (keyboards), Keith Hutchinson (sax), Solly Letwaba (bass) and Dudu Zulu and Derek De Beer (drums).

9/10/88 155 7 © 1 Shadow Man .... **$10** Capitol 90411
5/12/90 123 13 © 2 Cruel, Crazy, Beautiful World... **$10** Capitol 93446
African Shadow Man (1)   Dela (I Know Why The Dog   Joey Don't Do It (1)   Talk To The People (1)   Woman Be My Country (1)
Bombs Away (2)   Howls At The Moon) (2)   Moliva (2)   Too Early For The Sky (1)
Cruel, Crazy, Beautiful World   Human Rainbow (1)   One (Hu)'Man One Vote (2)   Vezandlebe (2)
(2)   I Call Your Name (1)   Rolling Ocean (2)   Waiting, The (1)
Dance Across The Centuries   It's An Illusion (2)   Siyayilanda (1)   Warsaw 1943 (I Never Betrayed
(1)   Jericho (2)   Take My Heart Away (1)   The Revolution) (2)

CLEMONS, Clarence '86
Born on 1/11/42 in Norfolk, Virginia. Saxophonist with **Bruce Springsteen**'s E Street Band.

11/5/83 174 5   1 Rescue .... **$10** Columbia 38933
11/23/85+ 62 18 © 2 Hero .... **$10** Columbia 40010
Christina (2)   I Wanna Be Your Hero (2)   Kissin' On U (2)   Money To The Rescue (1)   Savin' Up (1)   Temptation (2)
Cross The Line (2)   It's Alright With Me Girl (2)   Liberation Fire (Mokshagun) (2)   Resurrection Shuffle (1)   Sun Ain't Gonna Shine   Woman's Got The Power (1)
Heartache #99 (1)   Jump Start My Heart (1)   Man In Love (1)   Rock 'N' Roll DJ (1)   Anymore (2)   **You're A Friend Of Mine** (2) *18*

CLEOPATRA '98
Teen vocal trio from Manchester, England: sisters Cleopatra, Zainam and Yonah Higgins.

7/25/98 109 14 ©   Comin' Atcha! .... **$10** Maverick 46926
Bird Song   Don't Suffer In Silence   I Want You Back   Thinking About You   Two Timer   World We Live In
Cleopatra's Theme *26*   Dying Rose   Life Ain't Easy *81*   Touch Of Love   What You Gonna Do Boy?

CLEVELAND, James '69
Born on 12/23/32 in Chicago. Died of heart failure on 2/9/91 (age 58). Recorded with more than a dozen different choirs and gospel groups.

12/13/69 12[X] 1 ©   Merry Christmas .... [X] **$20** Savoy 14195
Away In A Manger   Go Tell It On The Mountain   Joy To The World   Pretty Little Boy   Sweet Little Jesus
Behold That Star   Hark The Herald Angels Sing   No Room In The Inn   Silent Night   White Christmas

CLEVELAND ORCHESTRA '75
Conducted by Michael Tilson Thomas.

3/29/75 152 4   Carl Orff: Carmina Burana.. **$15** Columbia 33172

CLIBURN, Van '58
Born Harvey Lavan Cliburn on 7/12/34 in Shreveport, Louisiana. Classical pianist.

8/4/58 ❶[7] 125 ▲ 1 Tchaikovsky: Piano Concerto No. 1   [I] **$30** RCA Victor 2252
7/13/59+ 10 60   2 Rachmaninoff: Piano Concerto No. 3   [I-L] **$30** RCA Victor 2355
   recorded on 5/19/58 at Carnegie Hall
1/9/61 134 13   3 Schumann: Piano Concerto in A Minor .... [I] **$25** RCA Victor 2455
2/3/62 71 29 ● © 4 My Favorite Chopin .... [I] **$25** RCA Victor 2576
3/10/62 25 13   5 Brahms: Piano Concerto No. 2 .... [I] **$25** RCA Victor 2581
Ballade No. 3 In A-Flat, Op. 47   Etude In A Minor, Op. 25, No.   Nocturne No. 17 In B, Op. 62,   Piano Concerto No. 1 In B-Flat   Polonaise No. 6 In A-Flat, Op.   Waltz No. 7 In C-Sharp Minor,
(4)   11 (4)   No. 1 (4)   Minor, Op. 23 (1)   53 (4)   Op. 64, No. 2 (4)
Brahms Concerto No. 2 In   Etude In E, Op. 10, No. 3 (4)   Piano Concerto In A Minor, Op.   Piano Concerto No. 3 In D   Scherzo No. 3 In C-Sharp
B-Flat, Op. 83 (5)   Fantaisie In F Minor, Op. 49 (4)   54 (3)   Minor, Op. 30 (2)   Minor, Op. 39 (4)

CLICK, The '95
All-star rap group: **E-40**, **B-Legit The Savage**, **Suga T** and **D-Shot**.

11/25/95 21 21 ● ©   Game Related .... **$10** Sick Wid' It 41562
Actin' Bad   Get Chopped   **Hurricane** *63*   Out My Body   We Don't Fuck Wit' Dat
Be About Yo' Paper   Hot Ones Echo Thru The   If I Took Your Boyfriend   Rock Up My Birdie   Wolf Tickets
Boss Baller   Ghetto   Learn About It   Scandalous   World Went Crazy

CLIFF, Jimmy '75
Born James Chambers on 4/1/48 in St. James, Jamaica. Reggae singer/composer. Starred in the movies *The Harder They Come* (1975) and *Club Paradise* (1986). Also see *Club Paradise* soundtrack.

3/22/75 140 8   1 The Harder They Come .... [S] **$20** Mango 9202
   includes "Draw Your Brakes" by Scotty, "Rivers Of Babylon" by The Melodians, "Johnny Too Bad" by The Slickers, "Shanty Town" by **Desmond Dekker** and "Sweet And Dandy" and "Pressure Drop" by The Maytals
11/1/75 195 2   2 Follow My Mind .... **$15** Reprise 2218
8/14/82 186 2 © 3 Special .... **$10** Columbia 38099
7/26/86 122 6   4 Club Paradise... [S] **$10** Columbia 40404
   includes "Grenada" by Mighty Sparrow, "Love People" by Blue Riddim Band, and "Sweetie Come From America" by Well Pleased & Satisfied
American Plan (4)   I'm Gonna Live, I'm Gonna   Love Is All (3)   Rock Children (3)   Treat The Youths Right (3)   You Can't Keep A Good Man
Brightest Star (4)   Love (2)   Many Rivers To Cross (1)   Roots Radical (3)   Wahjaka Man (2)   Down (4)
Club Paradise (4)   If I Follow My Mind (2)   News, The (2)   Rub-A-Dub Partner (3)   Where There Is Love (3)   You're The Only One (2)
Dear Mother (2)   Keep On Dancing (4)   No Woman, No Cry (2)   Seven Day Weekend (4)   Who Feels It, Knows It (2)
Going Mad (2)   Lion Awakes (4)   Originator (3)   Sitting In Limbo (1)   You Can Get It If You Really
Harder They Come (1)   Look At The Mountains (2)   Peace Officer (3)   Special (3)   Want (1)
Hypocrites (2)   Love Heights (3)   Remake The World (2)   Third World People (4)

CLIFFORD, Linda '79
Born in 1944 in Brooklyn, New York. Disco singer.

DEBUT	PEAK	WKS	CD	#	Album Title	$	Label & Number
5/20/78	22	22	©	1	If My Friends Could See Me Now	$15	Curtom 5021
4/7/79	26	17	©	2	Let Me Be Your Woman	$20	RSO 3902 [2]
12/1/79	117	9	©	3	Here's My Love	$12	RSO 3067
7/19/80	180	4	©	4	The Right Combination	$12	RSO 3084

LINDA CLIFFORD/CURTIS MAYFIELD

10/4/80	160	6		5	I'm Yours	$12	RSO 3087

Ain't No Love Lost (4)
Bailin' Out (3)
Between You Baby And Me (4)
Bridge Over Troubled Water (2) **41**
Broadway Gypsy Lady (1)
Don't Give It Up (2)

Don't Let Me Have Another Bad Dream (2)
Gypsy Lady (1)
Here's My Love (3)
Hold Me Close (2)
I Can't Let This Good Thing Get Away (2)

I Feel Like Falling In Love Again (1)
I Had A Talk With My Man (5)
I Just Wanna Wanna (3)
I Want To Get Away With You (5)
I'm So Proud (4)
I'm Yours (5)

If My Friends Could See Me Now (1) **54**
If You Let Me (5)
It Don't Hurt No More (5)
It's Lovin' Time (Your Baby's Home) (4)
King For A Night (3)
Let Me Be Your Woman (2)

Lonely Night (3)
Love's Sweet Sensation (4)
Never Gonna Stop (3)
One Of Those Songs (2)
Please Darling, Don't Say Goodbye (1)
Red Light (5) **41**
Repossessed (2)

Right Combination (4)
Rock You To Your Socks (4)
Runaway Love (1) **76**
Shoot Your Best Shot (5)
Sweet Melodies (2)
You Are, You Are (1)

CLIMAX '72
Pop group from Los Angeles: Sonny Geraci (vocals), Walter Nims (guitar), Virgil Weber (keyboards), Steve York (bass) and Robert Neilson (drums). Geraci was a member of **The Outsiders**.

6/24/72	177	7			Climax	$15	Rocky Road 3506

Child Of December
Face The Music

I've Got Everything
If It Feels Good - Do It

It's Coming Today
Life And Breath 52

Merlin
Picnic In The Rain

Precious And Few 3
Rainbow Rides Are Free

CLIMAX BLUES BAND '74
Blues-rock group from Stafford, England: Colin Cooper (vocals, sax), Peter Haycock (guitar, vocals), Derek Holt (bass) and John Cuffley (drums).

DEBUT	PEAK	WKS	CD	#	Album Title	$	Label & Number
11/28/70	197	1	©	1	The Climax Chicago Blues Band Plays On	$20	Sire 97023
2/17/73	150	10	©	2	Rich Man	$20	Sire 7402
12/1/73+	107	30	©	3	FM/Live	[L] $25	Sire 7411 [2]
					recorded at the Academy of Music in New York City; concert broadcast over WNEW-FM in New York City		
6/15/74	37	29	©	4	Sense Of Direction	$15	Sire 7501
9/13/75	69	11	©	5	Stamp Album	$15	Sire 7507
10/23/76+	27	44	©	6	Gold Plated	$15	Sire 7523
4/29/78	71	11		7	Shine On	$15	Sire 6056
6/16/79	170	6		8	Real To Reel	$15	Sire 3334
4/25/81	75	16		9	Flying The Flag	$12	Warner 3493

All The Time In The World (2,3)
Amerita (medley) (4)
Before You Reach The Grave (4)
Berlin Blues (6)
Blackjack And Me (9)
Champagne & Rock 'N Roll (7)
Chasing Change (9)
Children Of The Nightime (8)
City Ways (1)
Cobra (5)
Couldn't Get It Right (6) **3**
Country Hat (3)
Crazy 'Bout My Baby (1)

Crazy World (8)
Cubano Chant (1)
Dance The Night Away (9)
Devil Knows (5)
Extra (6)
Fallen In Love (For The Very Last Time) (8)
Fat City (8)
Flight (1,3)
Goin' To New York (3)
Gospel Singer (7)
Gotta Have More Love (9) **47**
Grinnin' In Your Face (9)

Hey Baby, Everything's Gonna Be Alright, Yeh Yeh Yeh (1)
Hold On To Your Heart (9)
Horizontalized (9)
I Am Constant (3,5)
If You Wanna' Know (2)
Let's Work Together (3)
Like A Movie (7)
Little Girl (1)
Long Distance Love (8)
Loosen Up (5)
Losin' The Humbles (4)
Lovin' Wheel (8)

Makin' Love (7) **91**
Mesopopmania (3)
Mighty Fire (6)
Milwaukee Truckin' Blues (Chipper's Song) (4)
Mistress Moonshine (7)
Mole On The Dole (2)
Money In Your Pocket (8)
Money Talkin' (9)
Mr. Goodtime (5)
Mum's The Word (1)
Nogales (4)
Nothing But Starlight (9)
One For Me And You (9)

Reaching Out (4)
Rich Man (2)
Right Now (4)
Rollin' Home (6)
Running Out Of Time (3)
Sav'ry Gravy (6)
Sense Of Direction (medley) (4)
Seventh Son (3)
Shake Your Love (2,3)
Shopping Bag People (4)
Sky High (5)
So Good After Midnight (9)
So Many Roads (1,3)
Spirit Returning (5)

Standing By A River (2,3)
Summer Rain (8)
Teardrops (4)
Temptation Rag (medley) (1)
Together And Free (4)
Twenty Past Two (medley) (1)
Using The Power (5)
Whatcha Feel (7)
When Talking Is Too Much Trouble (7)
You Make Me Sick (2,3)

CLIMIE FISHER '88
Pop-rock duo. Simon Climie (vocals) was born on 4/7/60 in Fulham, London, England. Rob Fisher (keyboards) was born on 11/5/59 in Cheltenham, Gloucestershire, England; died of complications following stomach surgery on 8/25/99 (age 39). Fisher was also a member of **Naked Eyes**.

5/28/88	120	16	©		Everything	$10	Capitol 48338

Bite The Hand That Feeds
Break The Silence

I Won't Bleed For You
Keeping The Mystery Alive

Love Changes (Everything) 23

Never Let A Chance Go By
Precious Moments

Rise To The Occasion
Room To Move

This Is Me

CLINE, Patsy '63
Born Virginia Patterson Hensley on 9/8/32 in Gore, Virginia. Killed in a plane crash on 3/5/63 (age 30) near Camden, Tennessee. Legendary country singer. Jessica Lange portrayed Cline in the 1985 biographical movie *Sweet Dreams*. Won Grammy's Lifetime Achievement Award in 1995.

DEBUT	PEAK	WKS	RIAA	CD	#	Album Title	Sym	$	Label & Number
3/31/62+	73	21			1	Patsy Cline Showcase		$50	Decca 4202
8/31/63	74	12		©	2	The Patsy Cline Story	[G]	$60	Decca 7176 [2]
11/16/85	29	18	●		3	Sweet Dreams - The Life And Times Of Patsy Cline	[S]	$10	MCA 6149
3/7/87+	5^C	368	▲⁹	©	4	Patsy Cline's Greatest Hits	[G]	$10	MCA 12
11/30/91	24^C	5		©	5	20 Golden Hits	[G]	$10	DeLuxe 7887
1/4/92	166	1	▲		6	The Patsy Cline Collection	[K]	$40	MCA 10421 [4]
6/8/96	31^C	2		©	7	The Legendary Patsy Cline	[G]	$10	Pair 1236
1/29/00+	37^C	9	▲	©	8	Heartaches	[G]	$10	MCA 20265

Always (6)
Anytime (6,8)
Back In Baby's Arms (2,4,6)
Bill Bailey, Won't You Please Come Home (6)
Blue Moon Of Kentucky (3,6)
Church, A Courtroom, And Then Goodbye (6)
Come On In (7)
Come On In (And Make Yourself At Home) (6)
Crazy (1,2,3,4,5,6,8) **9**
Crazy Arms (6)
Crazy Dreams (6)
Cry Not For Me (7)

Does Your Heart Beat For Me (6)
Don't Ever Leave Me (5,7)
Don't Ever Leave Me Again (6)
Faded Love (4,6) **96**
Fingerprints (5)
Foolin' 'Round (1,2,3,6)
For Rent (6)
Gotta Lot Of Rhythm (5,7)
Gotta Lot Of Rhythm In My Soul (6)
Half As Much (3,6)
Have You Ever Been Lonely (Have You Ever Been Blue) (6)
I Cried All The Way To The Altar (1,6)
He Called Me Baby (6)

Heart You Break May Be Your Own (5,6,7)
Heartaches (2,6,8) **73**
Honky Tonk Merry Go Round (6)
How Can I Face Tomorrow (6)
Hungry For Love (5,6)
I Can See An Angel (6)
I Can See An Angel Walking (7)
I Can't Forget (6,7)
I Can't Forget You (5)
I Can't Help It (If I'm Still In Love With You) (6)
I Could See The World (Through The Eyes Of A Child) (6)
I Don't Wanta (6)

I Fall To Pieces (1,2,3,4,5,6,8) **12**
I Love You Honey (6,8)
I Love You So Much It Hurts (1,2,6)
I'll Sail My Ship Alone (6)
I'm Blue Again (5,6,7)
I'm Moving Along (2,6)
I'm Walking The Dog (6)
I've Loved And Lost Again (5,6,7)
If I Could Only Stay Asleep (6)
If I Could See The World (Through The Eyes Of A Child) (6)
If I Could Stay Asleep (5)

Imagine That (2,6) **90**
In Care Of The Blues (5,6,7)
It Wasn't God Who Made Honky Tonk Angels (6)
Just A Closer Walk With Thee (6)
Just Out Of Reach (5,6,7)
Leavin' On Your Mind (2,4,6) **83**
Let The Teardrops Fall (5,6)
Life's Railway To Heaven (6)
Lonely Street (6)
Loose Talk (6)
Love Letters In The Sand (6)
Love, Love, Love Me Honey Do (6)

Love Me, Love Me, Honey Do (7)
Lovesick Blues (6,7)
Lovin' In Vain (6)
Never No More (5,6)
Pick Me Up On Your Way Down (6)
Poor Man's Roses (Or A Rich Man's Gold) (1,2,6)
San Antonio Rose (1,2,3,6)
Seven Lonely Days (1,2,3,6)
She's Got You (2,3,4,6,8) **14**
Shoes (6)
Side By Side (6)
So Wrong (2,4,6) **85**

CLINE, Patsy — Cont'd

Someday (You'll Want Me To Want You) (6)
South Of The Border (Down Mexico Way) (1,2,6)
Stop, Look And Listen (5,6,7)
Strange (2,4,6,8) **97**
Stranger In My Arms (7)
Stupid Cupid (6)

Sweet Dreams (Of You) (2,3,4,6,8) **44**
Tennessee Waltz (6)
That Wonderful Someone (6)
That's How A Heartache Begins (6)
That's My Desire (6)
Then You'll Know (6)

There He Goes (6)
Three Cigarettes In An Ashtray (6,7)
Today, Tomorrow And Forever (5,6)
Today, Tomorrow, Forever (7)
Too Many Secrets (6)
Tra La La Le La Triangle (2,6)
True Love (1,2,6)

Try Again (6)
Turn The Cards Slowly (6,7)
Walkin' After Midnight (1,2,3,6,8) **12**
Walking After Midnight (4,5,7)
Wayward Wind (1,2,6,8)
When I Get Thru With You (You'll Love Me Too) **53**
When You Need A Laugh (6)

When Your House Is Not A Home (6)
Who Can I Count On (6) **99**
Why Can't He Be You (2,4,6)
Yes, I Know Why (6)
Yes, I Understand (6)
You Belong To Me (2,6,8)
You Made Me Love You (I Didn't Want To Do It) (6)

You Took Him Off My Hands (6)
You Were Only Fooling (While I Was Falling In Love) (6)
You're Stronger Than Me (2,4,6)
Your Cheatin' Heart (2,3,6)
Your Kinda Love (6)

CLINTON, George   '83

Born on 7/22/40 in Kannapolis, North Carolina. Highly prolific and influential funk music singer/songwriter/producer. Formed the seminal groups **Parliament** and **Funkadelic**. Those groups featured several influential musicians and spawned several offshoot groups including Bootsy's Rubber Band, **The Brides Of Funkenstein** and the **P-Funk All Stars**.

DEBUT	PEAK	WKS	CD	#	Album Title	$	Label & Number
12/18/82+	40	33	©	1	Computer Games	$10	Capitol 12246
1/7/84	102	18	©	2	You Shouldn't-Nuf Bit Fish	$10	Capitol 12308
8/10/85	163	6	©	3	Some Of My Best Jokes Are Friends	$10	Capitol 12417
5/24/86	81	12	©	4	R&B Skeletons In The Closet	$10	Capitol 12481
9/2/89	192	4	©	5	The Cinderella Theory	$10	Paisley Park 25994
10/30/93	145	3	©	6	Hey Man...Smell My Finger	$10	Paisley Park 25518
6/29/96	121	4	©	7	T.A.P.O.A.F.O.M. - The Awesome Power Of A Fully-Operational Mothership	$10	550 Music 67144
					GEORGE CLINTON & THE P-FUNK ALLSTARS		
11/16/96	138	4	©	8	Greatest Funkin' Hits [K]	$10	Capitol 33911

Airbound (5)
Atomic Dog (1,8)
Banana Boat Song (5)
Bangladesh (3)
Big Pump (6)
Bodyguard (3)
Booty Body Ready For The Plush Funk (8)
Bop Gun (One Nation) (8)
Break My Heart (8)
Bullet Proof (3)
Cinderella Theory (5)
Computer Games (1)
Cool Joe (4)

Dis Beat Disrupts (6)
Do Fries Go With That Shake (4,8)
Double Oh-Oh (3)
Electric Pygmies (4)
Flag Was Still There (6)
Flashlight (8)
Flatman & Bobbin (7)
Free Alterations (1)
French Kiss (5)
Funky Kind (Gonna Knock It Down) (7)
Get Dressed (1)
Get Satisfied (6)

Get Your Funk On (7)
Hard As Steel (7)
Hey Good Lookin' (4,8)
High In My Hello (6)
Hollywood (6)
If Anybody Gets Funked Up (It's Gonna Be You) (7)
If True Love (6)
Intense (4)
Kickback (6)
Knee Deep (8)
Last Dance (2)
Let's Get Funky (7)
Loopzilla (medley) (1)

Man's Best Friend (medley) (1)
Martial Law (6)
Mathematics (6)
Maximumisness (6)
Mixmaster Suite Medley (4)
Mothership Connection Starchild (8)
New Spaceship (7)
Nubian Nut (7)
One Fun At A Time (1)
Paint The White House Black (6)
Pleasures Of Exhaustion (Do It Till I Drop) (3)

Pot Sharing Tots (1)
Quickie (2)
R&B Skeletons (In The Closet) (4)
Rhythm And Rhyme (6)
Rock The Party (7)
Serious Slammin' (5)
(She Got It) Goin' On (5)
Silly Millameter (2)
Sloppy Seconds (7)
Some Of My Best Jokes Are Friends (3)
Stingy (2)
Summer Swim (7)

T.A.P.O.A.F.O.M. (Fly Away) (7)
There I Go Again (5)
Thrashin' (5)
Tweakin' (5)
Underground Angel (7)
Way Up (6)
Why Should I Dog U Out? (5)
You Shouldn't-Nuf Bit Fish (2)

CLIQUE, The   '70

Pop-rock group from Beaumont, Texas: Randy Shaw (vocals), David Dunham, Sid Templeton, Tommy Pena, John Kenesaw and Jerry Cope.

DEBUT	PEAK	WKS	CD		Album Title	$	Label & Number
1/17/70	177	3	©		The Clique	$20	White Whale 7126

Hallelujah!
Holiday

I'll Hold Out My Hand **45**
Judy, Judy, Judy

Little Miss Lucy
My Darkest Hour

Shadow Of Your Love
Soul Mates

Sugar On Sunday **22**
Superman

(There Ain't) No Such Thing As Love

CLIVILLÉS & COLE — see C & C MUSIC FACTORY

CLOONEY, Rosemary   '57

Born on 5/23/28 in Maysville, Kentucky. Sang with her sister Betty in Tony Pastor's orchestra in the late 1940s. Became one of the most popular singers of the early 1950s. Acted in several movies including *White Christmas*. Re-emerged in the late 70's as a successful jazz and ballad singer and as a TV commercial actress. Married for a time to actor Jose Ferrer; their son Gabriel married **Debby Boone**. Her nephew, George Clooney, is a popular TV and movie actor.

DEBUT	PEAK	WKS	CD	#	Album Title	$	Label & Number
7/22/57	14	7	©	1	Ring Around Rosie	$40	Columbia 1006
					ROSEMARY CLOONEY AND THE HI-LO'S		
12/21/96	186	1	©	2	White Christmas [X]	$10	Concord Jazz 4719

Christmas Love Song (2)
Christmas Mem'ries (2)
Christmas Song (2)
Christmas Time Is Here (2)
Christmas Waltz (2)
Coquette (1)

Count Your Blessings (Instead Of Sheep) (2)
Don't Wait Till The Night Before Christmas (2)
Doncha Go 'Way Mad (1)
Everything Happens To Me (1)
First Noël (2)

Have Yourself A Merry Little Christmas (2)
Hey Kris Kringle (medley) (2)
How About You (1)
I Could Write A Book (1)
I'll Be Home For Christmas (2)
I'm Glad There Is You (1)

I'm In The Mood For Love (1)
It's The Most Wonderful Time Of The Year (2)
Joy To The World (2)
Let It Snow (2)
Love Letters (1)
Moonlight Becomes You (1)

O Little Town Of Bethlehem (2)
Rudolph The Red Nosed Reindeer (2)
Santa Claus Is Coming To Town (medley) (2)
Silent Night (2)
Sleep Well, Little Children (2)

Solitude (1)
Spirit Of Christmas (2)
Together (1)
What Is There To Say (1)
White Christmas (2)
Winter Wonderland (2)

CLUB NOUVEAU   '87

R&B group from Sacramento, California: Jay King (producer/owner of King Jay Records; founded the **Timex Social Club**), Valerie Watson, Samuelle Prater, Denzil Foster and Thomas McElroy. Foster and McElroy formed a prolific production duo and also recorded as FMob.

DEBUT	PEAK	WKS	RIAA	CD	#	Album Title	$	Label & Number
12/20/86+	6	44	▲	©	1	Life, Love & Pain	$10	Warner 25531
6/18/88	98	6		©	2	Listen To The Message	$10	Warner 25687

Better Way (2)
Dancin' To Be Free (2)
Envious (2)

For The Love Of Francis (2)
Heavy On My Mind (1)
It's A Cold, Cold World! (2)

Jealousy (1)
Lean On Me (1) **1**
Let Me Go (1)

Listen To The Message (2)
Only The Strong Survive (2)
Promises Promises (1)

Situation #9 (1)
What's Going 'Round? (2)
Why Is It That? (2)

Why You Treat Me So Bad (1) **39**

CLUTCH   '98

Rock group from Germantown, Maryland: Neil Fallon (vocals), Tim Sult (guitar), Dan Maines (bass) and Jean Paul Gaster (drums).

DEBUT	PEAK	WKS	CD	#	Album Title	$	Label & Number
5/2/98	104	1	©	1	The Elephant Riders	$10	Columbia 69113
3/31/01	135	1	©	2	Pure Rock Fury	$10	Atlantic 83433

American Sleep (2)
Brazenhead (2)
Careful With That Mic... (2)
Crackerjack (1)

Dragonfly, The (1)
Drink To The Dead (2)
Eight Times Over Miss October (1)

Elephant Riders (1)
Frankenstein (2)
Great Outdoors! (1)
Green Buckets (1)

Immortal (2)
Muchas Veces (1)
Open Up The Border (2)
Pure Rock Fury (2)

Red Horse Rainbow (2)
Ship Of Gold (1)
Sinkemlow (2)
Smoke Banshee (2)

Soapmakers, The (1)
Spacegrass (1)
Wishbone (1)
Yeti, The (1)

C-MURDER   '99

Born Corey Miller in New Orleans. Male rapper. Brother of **Master P** and **Silkk The Shocker**. Member of **Tru**.

DEBUT	PEAK	WKS	RIAA	CD	#	Album Title	$	Label & Number
4/4/98	3	27	▲	©	1	Life Or Death	$10	No Limit 50723
3/27/99	2[1]	11	●	©	2	Bossalinie	$10	No Limit 50035
9/23/00	9	11		©	3	Trapped In Crime	$10	Tru 50083

C-MURDER — Cont'd

Akickdoe! (1)
Can't Hold Me Back (2)
Closin' Down Shop (2)
Cluckers (1)
Concrete Jungle (3)
Constantly 'N Danger (1)
Damned If They Murder Me (3)
Don't Play No Games (1)
Don't Wanna Be Alone (2)
Down For My N's (3)
Dreams (1)

Duck & Run (1)
Feel My Pain (1)
Forever TRU (3)
Freedom (2)
G's & Macks (2)
Gangsta Walk (2)
Get N Paid (1)
Ghetto Boy (2)
Ghetto Millionaire (2)
Ghetto Ties (1)
How A Thug Like It (3)

Hustlin (3)
I Remember (2)
Life Or Death (1)
Like A Jungle (2)
Lil Nigga (2)
Livin' Legend (2)
Lord Help Us (2)
Makin Moves (1)
Money Talks (2)
Murder And Daz (2)
NL Iggaz (3)

Nasty Chick (2)
On Da Block (3)
On My Enemies (2)
On The Run (1)
Only The Strong Survive (1)
Picture Me (1)
Ride (3)
Ride On Dem Bustas (2)
Riders (1)
2nd Chance (1)
Show Me Luv (1)

Soldiers (1)
Starting At The Walls (3)
Still Makin' Moves (2)
Street Keep Callin (2)
Street Thugs (3)
Survival Of The Fittest (1)
That Calliope (3)
They Don't Really Know You (3)
They Want My Money (3)
Thug In Yo Life (3)
Too Much Noise (3)

Truest Sh... (1)
Want Beef (3)
Watch Yo Enemies (1)
What You Bout (3)
Where Do We Go (3)
Where I'm From (1)
Where We Wanna (2)
Young Thugs (3)

C-NOTE '99
Male vocal group from Orlando, Florida: Jose Martinez, Raul Molina, David Perez and Andrew Rogers.

| 6/12/99 | 163 | 1 | © | | Different Kind Of Love .... | | | | | $10 | Epic 69537 |

Different Kind Of Love
Feels So Good

I Like
Love Of All Time

My Heart Belongs To You
No Dejo De Pensar

One Night With You
Right Next To Me

Spanish Fly
Tear Or Two

Tell Me Where It Hurts
Wait Till I Get Home

COAL CHAMBER '99
Hard-rock group from Los Angeles: Brad Fafara (vocals), Miquel Rascon (guitar), Rayna Rose (bass) and Mike Cox (drums). Fafara is the nephew of actor Stanley Fafara (played "Whitey Whitney" on TV's *Leave It To Beaver*).

| 9/25/99 | 22 | 8 | ● | © | Chamber Music .... | | | | | $10 | Roadrunner 8659 |

Anything But You
Burgundy
El Cu Cuy

Entwined
Feed My Dreams
Mist

My Mercy
No Home
Not Living

Notion
Shari Vegas
Shock The Monkey

Tragedy
Tyler's Song
Untrue

What's In Your Mind?

COBHAM, Billy '74
Born on 5/16/44 in Panama; raised in New York City. Jazz-rock drummer. Formerly with **Miles Davis** and **John McLaughlin**.

11/17/73+	26	43	©	1	Spectrum				[I]	$15	Atlantic 7268
5/4/74	23	21	©	2	**Crosswinds**				[I]	$15	Atlantic 7300
12/21/74+	36	13	©	3	Total Eclipse				[I]	$12	Atlantic 18121
6/28/75	74	8	©	4	Shabazz (Recorded Live In Europe)				[I-L]	$12	Atlantic 18139
					recorded on 7/13/74 at the Rainbow Theatre in London						
11/15/75	79	7	©	5	A Funky Thide Of Sings				[I]	$12	Atlantic 18149
4/10/76	128	8	©	6	Life & Times				[I]	$12	Atlantic 18166
10/23/76	99	9	©	7	"Live"-On Tour In Europe				[L]	$12	Atlantic 18194
					THE BILLY COBHAM/GEORGE DUKE BAND						
6/3/78	172	4	©	8	Inner Conflicts				[I]	$12	Atlantic 19174
10/14/78	166	6		9	Simplicity Of Expression-Depth Of Thought					$12	Columbia 35457

Almustafa The Beloved (7)
Anxiety (medley) (1)
Arroyo (8)
Bandits (3)
Bolinas (9)
Crosswind (2)
Do What Cha Wanna (7)
Early Libra (9)
Earthlings (6)
East Bay (6)
El Barrio (8)

Frankenstein Goes To The
  Disco (7)
Funky Kind Of Thing (5)
Funky Thide Of Sings (5)
Heather (9)
Hip Pockets (7)
Indigo (7)
Inner Conflicts (8)
Ivory Tattoo (7)
Juicy (7)
La Guernica (9)

Last Frontier (3)
Le Lis (medley) (1)
Life & Times (6)
Light At The End Of The Tunnel
  (5)
Lunarputians (3)
Moody Modes (5)
Moon Ain't Made Of Green
  Cheese (3)
Moon Germs (3)
Muffin Talks Back (8)

Nickels And Dimes (8)
On A Natural High (6)
Opelousas (3)
Panhandler (3)
Pleasant Pheasant (2)
Pocket Change (9)
Quadrant 4 (1)
Red Baron (1,4)
Sea Of Tranquility (3)
Searching For The Right Door
  (medley) (1)

Shabazz (4)
Siesta (medley) (6)
Snoopy's Search (medley) (1)
Solarization Medley (3)
Some Skunk Funk (5)
Song For A Friend (Part I & II)
  (6)
Sorcery (5)
Space Lady (7)
Spanish Moss Medley (2)
Spectrum (medley) (1)

Stratus (1)
Sweet Wine (7)
Taurian Matador (1,4)
Tenth Pinn (4)
Thinking Of You (5)
To The Women In My Life
  (medley) (5)
Total Eclipse (3)
29 (6)
Wake Up!!!!!! That's What You
  Said (medley) (6)

COCHRAN, Anita '98
Born on 2/6/67 in Pontiac, Michigan. Country singer/songwriter/guitarist.

| 2/28/98 | 173 | 4 | © | | Back To You .... | | | | | $10 | Warner 46395 |

Back To You
Daddy Can You See Me

Girls Like Fast Cars
I Could Love A Man Like That

One Of Those Days
She Wants To Ride

What If I Said *59*
Will You Be Here

Wrong Side Of Town
You're The Break

COCHRAN, Wayne '68
Born in 1939 in Thompson, Georgia. Flamboyant rock singer.

| 3/30/68 | 167 | 4 | | | Wayne Cochran! .... | | | | | $50 | Chess 1519 |

Big City Woman
Boom Boom
Get Down With It

Get Ready
I'm Leaving It Up To You
I'm Your Hoochie Coochie Man

Little Bitty Pretty One
Peak Of Love
Some-A' Your Sweet Love

When My Baby Cries
You Can't Judge A Book By
  The Cover

You Don't Know Like I Know

COCHRANE, Tom/RED RIDER '92
Born on 5/13/53 in Lynn Lake, Manitoba, Canada. Rock singer/songwriter/guitarist. Formed **Red Rider** in 1976.

					RED RIDER:						
4/26/80	146	5		1	Don't Fight It					$12	Capitol 12028
9/12/81	65	24	©	2	As Far As Siam					$12	Capitol 12145
2/5/83	66	16	©	3	Neruda					$12	Capitol 12226
					dedicated to exiled Chileaen poet Pablo Neruda						
6/23/84	137	8		4	Breaking Curfew					$12	Capitol 12317
					TOM COCHRANE AND RED RIDER:						
8/2/86	112	12	©	5	Tom Cochrane and Red Rider					$10	Capitol 12484
11/12/88	144	13	©	6	Victory Day					$10	RCA 8532
					TOM COCHRANE:						
5/9/92	46	29	●	©	7	Mad Mad World				$10	Capitol 97723

All The King's Men (7)
Among The Ruins (I'll Be Here)
  (4)
Ashes To Diamonds (5)
Avenue "A" (1)
Beacon Hill (4)
Big League (5)
Bigger Man (7)
Boy Inside The Man (5)

Brave And Crazy (7)
Breaking Curfew (4)
Calling America (6)
Can't Turn Back (4)
Caught In The Middle (2)
Citizen Cain (5)
Cowboys In Hong Kong (As Far
  As Siam) (2)
Crack The Sky (Breakaway) (3)

Different Drummer (6)
Don't Fight It (1)
Don't Let Go Of Me (2)
Emotional Truth (7)
Everything Comes Around (1)
Friendly Advice (7)
Get Back Up (7)
Good Man (Feeling Bad) (7)
Good News (1)

Good Times (6)
Hold Tight (4)
How's My Little Girl Tonight (1)
Human Race (3)
Iron In The Soul (5)
Just The Way It Goes (1)
Lasting Song (5)
Laughing Man (2)
Life Is A Highway (7) *6*

Light In The Tunnel (3)
Loading, The (5)
Look Out Again (1)
Love Under Fire (5)
Lunatic Fringe (2)
Mad Mad World (7)
Make Myself Complete (1)
Napoleon Sheds His Skin (3)
No Regrets (7)

Not So Far Away (6)
Ocean Blues (Emotion Blue) (5)
One More Time (Some Old
  Habits) (5)
One Way Out (4)
Only Game In Town (2)
Power (Strength In Numbers)
  (3)
River Of Stone (5)

COCHRANE, Tom/RED RIDER — Cont'd

Saved By The Dawn (6)
Secret Is To Know When To Stop (7)
Shake Monster (4)
Ships (2)

Sights On You (3)
Sinking Like A Sunset (7)
Someone's Watching (4)
Sons Beat Down (6)
Thru The Curtain (2)

Untouchable One (5)
Vacation (In My Mind) (6)
Victory Day (6)
Walking The Fine Line (3)
Washed Away (7) 88

What Have You Got To Do (To Get Off Tonight) (2)
Whipping Boy (4)
White Hot (1) 48
Winner Take All (3)

Work Out (3)
Young Thing, Wild Dreams (Rock Me) (4) 71

COCKBURN, Bruce   '80
Born on 5/27/45 in Ottawa, Canada. Pop-rock singer/songwriter.

2/23/80	**45**	24		© 1	**Dancing In the Dragon's Jaws**		$12	Millennium 7747
10/18/80	**81**	9		© 2	**Humans**		$12	Millennium 7752
5/23/81	**174**	5		© 3	**Bruce Cockburn/Resume**		$12	Millennium 7757
8/25/84+	**74**	31		© 4	**Stealing Fire**		$10	Gold Mountain 80012
7/26/86	**143**	8		© 5	**World Of Wonders**		$10	MCA 5772
2/25/89	**182**	7		© 6	**Big Circumstance**		$10	Gold Castle 71320
3/19/94	**176**	2		© 7	**Dart To The Heart**		$10	Columbia 53831
2/22/97	**178**	1		© 8	**The Charity Of Night**		$10	Rykodisc 10366

After The Rain (1)
All The Ways I Want You (7)
Anything Can Happen (6)
Badlands Flashback (1)
Berlin Tonight (5)
Birmingham Shadows (8)
Bone In My Ear (7)
Burden Of The Angel/Beast (7)
Call It Democracy (5)
Can I Go With You (3)
Charity Of Night (8)
Closer To The Light (7)
Coldest Night Of The Year (3)
Coming Rains (8)
Creation Dream (1)

Dancing In Paradise (5)
Dialogue With The Devil (3)
Don't Feel Your Touch (6)
Down Here Tonight (5)
Dust And Diesel (4)
Facist Architecture (2)
Get Up Jonah (8)
Gift, The (6)
Gospel Of Bondage (6)
Grim Travelers (2)
Guerilla Betrayed (2)
Hills Of Morning (1)
How I Spent My Fall Vacation (2)
If A Tree Falls (6)

If I Had A Rocket Launcher (4) 88
Incandescent Blue (1)
Laughter (3)
Lily Of The Midnight Sky (5)
Listen For The Laugh (7)
Live On My Mind (8)
Lord Of The Starfields (3)
Love Loves You Too (7)
Lovers In A Dangerous Time (4)
Making Contact (4)
Mama Justs Wants To Barrelhouse All Night Long (3)
Maybe The Poet (4)
Mines Of Mozambique (8)

Mistress Of Storms (8)
More/Not More (2)
Nicaragua (4)
Night Rain (8)
No Footprints (1)
Northern Lights (1)
Outside A Broken Phone Booth With Money In My Hand (3)
Pacing The Cage (8)
Pangs Of Love (6)
Peggy's Kitchen Wall (4)
People See Through You (5)
Radium Rain (6)
Rose Above The Sky (2)
Rumours Of Glory (2)

Sahara Gold (4)
Santiago Dawn (5)
Scanning These Crowds (7)
See How I Miss You (5)
Shipwrecked At The Stable Door (6)
Silver Wheels (3)
Someone I Used To Love (7)
Southland Of The Heart (7)
Strange Waters (8)
Sunrise On The Mississippi (7)
Tibetan Side Of Town (6)
Tie Me At The Crossroads (7)
To Raise The Morning Star (4)
Tokyo (2)

Train In The Rain (7)
Understanding Nothing (6)
Water Into Wine (3)
What About The Bond (2)
Where The Death Squad Lives (6)
Whole Night Sky (8)
Wondering Where The Lions Are (1) 21
World Of Wonders (5)
You Get Bigger As You Go (2)

COCKER, Joe   ★197★   '70
Born John Robert Cocker on 5/20/44 in Sheffield, Yorkshire, England. Pop-rock singer. Assembled the **Grease Band** in the mid-1960s. Successful tour with 43-piece revue, Mad Dogs & Englishmen, in 1970. Notable spastic stage antics were based on **Ray Charles**'s movements at the piano.

1)Mad Dogs & Englishmen 2)Joe Cocker! 3)I Can Stand A Little Rain

5/31/69	**35**	37	● © 1	**With A Little Help From My Friends**			$15	A&M 4182
11/22/69+	**11**	53	● © 2	**Joe Cocker!**			$15	A&M 4224
9/5/70	**2**[1]	53	● © 3	**Mad Dogs & Englishmen**	[L-S]		$20	A&M 6002 [2]

recorded on 3/27/70 at the Fillmore East in New York City

12/2/72+	**30**	21	4	**Joe Cocker**			$12	A&M 4368
8/24/74	**11**	36	© 5	**I Can Stand A Little Rain**			$12	A&M 3633
8/30/75	**42**	10	© 6	**Jamaica Say You Will**			$12	A&M 4529
5/15/76	**70**	10	7	**Stingray**			$12	A&M 4574
12/10/77	**114**	8	© 8	**Joe Cocker's Greatest Hits**	[G]		$12	A&M 4670
9/16/78	**76**	13	9	**Luxury You Can Afford**			$12	Asylum 145
7/10/82	**105**	23	© 10	**Sheffield Steel**			$12	Island 9750
5/19/84	**133**	9	© 11	**Civilized Man**			$10	Capitol 12335
4/12/86	**50**	18	© 12	**Cocker**			$10	Capitol 12394
11/14/87+	**89**	27	© 13	**Unchain My Heart**			$10	Capitol 48285
9/16/89+	**52**	30	© 14	**One Night Of Sin**			$10	Capitol 92861
6/23/90	**95**	14	© 15	**Joe Cocker Live**	[L]		$10	Capitol 93416

recorded on 10/15/89 in Lowell, Massachusetts

8/1/92	**111**	10	© 16	**Night Calls**			$10	Capitol 97801

A To Z (12)
All Our Tomorrows (13)
Another Mind Gone (14)
Bad Bad Sign (14)
Bird On The Wire (2,3)
Black-Eyed Blues (4,8) *flip*
Blue Medley (3)
Boogie Baby (9)
Born Thru Indifference (7)
Bye Bye Blackbird (1)
Can't Find My Way Home (16)
Catfish (7)
Change In Louise (1)
Civilized Man (11)
Come On In (11)
Crazy In Love (4)
Cry Me A River (3,8) *11*
Darling Be Home Soon (2,8)
Dear Landlord (2)
Delta Lady (2,3,8) *69*
Do I Still Figure In Your Life? (1)
Do Right Woman (4)
Don't Drink The Water (12)
Don't Forget Me (5)

Don't Let Me Be Misunderstood (1)
Don't Let The Sun Go Down On Me (16)
Don't You Love Me Anymore (12)
Even A Fool Would Let Go (11)
Feeling Alright (1,3,8,15) *33*
Feels Like Forever (16)
Fever (14)
Five Women (16)
Forgive Me Now (6)
Fun Time (9) *43*
Girl From The North Country (3)
Girl Like You (11)
Guilty (5)
Heart Of The Matter (12)
Heaven (12)
Hello Little Friend (2)
High Time We Went (4,8,15) *22*
Hitchcock Railway (2,15)
Hold On (I Feel Our Love Is Changing) (11)
Honky Tonk Women (3)

I Broke Down (7)
I Can Hear The River (16)
I Can Stand A Little Rain (5)
I Can't Say No (9)
I Get Mad (5)
I Heard It Through The Grapevine (11)
I Know (You Don't Want Me No More) (9)
I Love The Night (11)
I Shall Be Released (1)
I Stand In Wonder (13)
I Think It's Going To Rain Today (6,8)
I Will Live For You (14)
I'm Your Man (14)
I've Got To Use My Imagination (14)
If I Love You (6)
Inner City Blues (12)
Isolation (13)
It's A Sin When You Love Somebody (15) *flip*
It's All Over But The Shoutin' (6)
Jack-A-Diamonds (6)

Jamaica Say You Will (6)
Jealous Kind (7,8)
Just Like A Woman (1)
Just Like Always (10)
Just To Keep From Drowning (14)
Lady Put The Light Out (9)
Lawdy Miss Clawdy (2)
Let's Go Get Stoned (3)
Letter, The (3,8,15)
Letting Go (14)
Living In The Promiseland (15)
Living Without Your Love (12)
Long Drag Off A Cigarette (14)
Look What You've Done (9)
Love Is Alive (16)
Love Is On A Fade (12)
Lucinda (6)
Man In Me (7)
Many Rivers To Cross (10)
Marie (13)
Marjorine (1)
Midnight Rider (4) *27*
Moon Dew (7)
Moon Is A Harsh Mistress (5)

Night Calls (16)
Now That The Magic Has Gone (16)
Oh Mama (6)
One, The (13)
One Night Of Sin (14)
Out Of The Rain (16)
Pardon Me Sir (4) *51*
Performance (5)
Please Give Peace A Chance (3)
Please No More (16)
Put Out The Light (5) *46*
River's Rising (13)
Ruby Lee (10)
Sandpaper Cadillac (1)
Satisfied (13)
Seven Days (10)
She Came In Through The Bathroom Window (2,3,15) *30*
She Don't Mind (4)
She Is My Lady (7)
Shelter Me (12,15) *91*
Shocked (10)

Sing Me A Song (5)
So Good So Right (10)
Something (2)
Something To Say (4)
Song For You (7)
Southern Lady (9)
Space Captain (3)
St. James Infirmary Blues (4)
Sticks And Stones (3)
Superstar (7)
Sweet Li'l Woman (10)
Talking Back To The Night (10)
Tempted (11)
(That's What I Like) In My Woman (6)
That's Your Business Now (2)
There Goes My Baby (11)
Trust In Me (13)
Two Wrongs (13)
Unchain My Heart (13,15)
Up Where We Belong (15)
Wasted Years (9)
Watching The River Flow (4)
What Are You Doing With A Fool Like Me (15) *96*

COCKER, Joe — Cont'd

What You Did To Me Last Night (9)
When A Woman Cries (16)
When The Night Comes (14,15) *11*
Where Am I Now (6)
Whiter Shade Of Pale (9)
With A Little Help From My Friends (1,8,15) *68*
Woman Loves A Man (13)
Woman To Woman (4,8) *56*
Worrier (7)
You Are So Beautiful (5,8,15) *5*
You Came Along (7)
You Can Leave Your Hat On (12,15)
You Know We're Gonna Hurt (14)
You've Got To Hide Your Love Away (16)

COCK ROBIN   '85

Pop group from Los Angeles: Peter Kingsbery (vocals, bass), Anna LaCazio (vocals, keyboards), Clive Wright (guitars) and Louis Molino (drums).

DEBUT	PEAK	WKS	CD			$	Label & Number
7/13/85	61	19	©	1	Cock Robin	$10	Columbia 39582
9/5/87	166	3	©	2	After Here Through Midland	$10	Columbia 40375

After Here Through Midland (2)
Another Story (2)
Because It Keeps On Working (1)
Biggest Fool Of All (2)
Born With Teeth (1)
Coward's Courage (2)
El Norte (2)
Every Moment (2)
I'll Send Them Your Way (2)
Just Around The Corner (2)
Just When You're Having Fun (1)
Little Innocence (1)
More Than Willing (1)
Once We Might Have Known (1)
Precious Dreams (2)
Promise You Made (1)
Thought You Were On My Side (1)
When Your Heart Is Weak (1) *35*

COCOA BROVAZ   '98

Rap duo from New York City: Tek and Steele. Formerly known as **Smif-N-Wessun**. Members of **Boot Camp Clik**.

DEBUT	PEAK	WKS	CD			$	Label & Number
1/28/95	59	8	©	1	Dah Shinin'	$10	Wreck 2005
					SMIF-N-WESSUN		
4/18/98	21	7	©	2	The Rude Awakening	$10	Duck Down 50699

Back 2 Life (2)
Black Trump (2)
Blown Away (2)
Bucktown (1) *93*
Bucktown USA (2)
Cash, The (2)
Cession At Da Doghillee (1)
Dry Snitch (2)
Game Of Life (2)
Hellucination (1)
Hold It Down (2)
Home Sweet Home (1)
K.I.M. (1)
Let's Git It On (1)
Live At The Garden (Skit) (2)
Memorial (2)
Money Talks (2)
Myah Angelow (2)
Off The Wall (2)
P.N.C. (1)
Shinin......Next Shit (1)
Sound Bwoy Bureill (1)
Spanish Harlem (2)
Stand Strong (1)
Still Standin Strong (2)
Timz N Hood Chek (1)
Wipe Ya Mouf (1)
Won On Won (2)
Wontime (1)
Wrekonize (1)
Wrektime (1)

COCTEAU TWINS   '90

Pop trio from Grangemouth, Scotland: Elizabeth Fraser (vocals), Robin Guthrie (guitar) and Simon Raymonde (bass). Guthrie and Fraser also recorded in 1984 as This Mortal Coil. Name Cocteau Twins is taken from a **Simple Minds** song.

DEBUT	PEAK	WKS	CD			$	Label & Number
10/15/88	109	18	©	1	Blue Bell Knoll	$10	Capitol 90892
10/6/90	99	19	©	2	Heaven or Las Vegas	$10	Capitol 93669
11/20/93	78	3	©	3	Four-Calendar Cafe	$10	Capitol 99375
6/1/96	99	2	©	4	Milk & Kisses	$10	Capitol 37049

Athol-Brose (1)
Blue Bell Knoll (1)
Bluebeard (3)
Calfskin Smack (4)
Carolyn's Fingers (1)
Cherry-Coloured Funk (2)
Cico Buff (1)
Ella Megalast Burls Forever (1)
Eperdu (4)
Essence (3)
Evangeline (3)
Fifty-Fifty Clown (2)
For Phoebe Still A Baby (1)
Fotzepolitic (2)
Frou-Frou Foxes In Midsummer Fires (2)
Half-Gifts (4)
Heaven Or Las Vegas (2)
I Wear Your Ring (2)
Iceblink Luck (2)
Itchy Glowbo Blow (1)
Kissed Out Red Floatboat (1)
Know who you are at every age (3)
My Truth (3)
Oil of Angels (3)
Pitch The Baby (2)
Pur (3)
Rilkean Heart (4)
Road, River And Rail (2)
Seekers Who Are Lovers (4)
Serpentskirt (4)
Spooning Good Singing Gum (1)
Squeeze-Wax (3)
Suckling The Mender (1)
Summerhead (3)
Theft, and wandering around lost (3)
Tishbite (4)
Treasure Hiding (4)
Ups (4)
Violaine (4)
Wolf In The Breast (2)

COE, David Allan   '83

Born on 9/6/39 in Akron, Ohio. Country singer. Billed as "The Mysterious Rhinestone Cowboy" until 1978. In the movie *Take This Job And Shove It* (also wrote the title tune for **Johnny Paycheck**).

DEBUT	PEAK	WKS	RIAA	CD			Sym	$	Label & Number
6/18/83	39^C	10	▲	©	1	Greatest Hits	[G]	$10	Columbia 35627
7/9/83	179	5			2	Castles In The Sand		$10	Columbia 38535

Castles In The Sand (2)
Cheap Thrills (2)
Divers Do It Deeper (1)
Don't Be A Stranger (2)
Face To Face (1)
Fool Inside Of Me (2)
For Lovers Only (Part 1) (2)
Gotta Serve Somebody (2)
I Can't Let You Be A Memory (2)
Just To Prove My Love For You (1)
Lately I've Been Thinking Too Much Lately (1)
Longhaired Redneck (1)
Missin' The Kid (2)
Ride, The (2)
Sad Country Song (1)
Son Of A Rebel Son (2)
Willie, Waylon And Me (1)
Would You Be My Lady (1)
Would You Lay With Me (In A Field Of Stone) (1)
You Never Even Called Me By My Name (1)

COFFEY, Dennis, And The Detroit Guitar Band   '72

Born in Detroit. Session guitarist for Motown.

DEBUT	PEAK	WKS				Sym	$	Label & Number
11/13/71+	36	25		1	Evolution	[I]	$15	Sussex 7004
3/25/72	90	14		2	Goin' For Myself	[I]	$15	Sussex 7010
1/20/73	189	6		3	Electric Coffey	[I]	$15	Sussex 7021
1/17/76	147	7		4	Finger Lickin Good	[I]	$12	Westbound 212

Big City Funk (1)
Bridge Over Troubled Water (2)
Can You Feel It (2)
Capricorn's Thing (3)
El Tigre (4)
Fame (4)
Finger Lickin Good (4)
Garden Of The Moon (1)
Getting It On (1) *93*
Good Time Rhythm And Blues (1)
Guitar Big Band (3)
Honky Tonk (4)
I've Got A Real Good Feeling (4)
If You Can't Dance To This You Got No Business Havin' Feet (4)
Impressions Of (1)
It's Too Late (2)
Live Wire (4)
Lonely Moon Child (3)
Love And Understanding (4)
Love Song For Libra (3)
Man And Boy (Main Theme) (2)
Midnight Blue (2)
Never Can Say Goodbye (2)
Ride, Sally, Ride (2) *flip*
Sad Angel (1)
Sagittarian, The (3)
Scorpio (1) *6*
Some Like It Hot (4)
Son Of Scorpio (3)
Summer Time Girl (1)
Taurus (2) *18*
Toast And Jam (2)
Twins Of Gemini (3)
Virgo's Song (3)
Whole Lot Of Love (1)
Wild Child (4)
Wild Song (1)

COHEN, Leonard   '69

Born on 9/21/34 in Montreal. Singer/songwriter/poet/novelist. His numerous works include novels *The Favorite Game* and *Beautiful Losers*, six volumes of poetry, several documentaries, and songs recorded by **Judy Collins**, **Tim Hardin** and **Jennifer Warnes**.

DEBUT	PEAK	WKS	CD			Sym	$	Label & Number
3/2/68	83	14	● ©	1	Songs Of Leonard Cohen		$15	Columbia 9533
4/12/69	63	17	©	2	Songs From A Room		$15	Columbia 9767
5/1/71	145	11	©	3	Songs Of Love And Hate		$15	Columbia 30103
5/26/73	156	5		4	Leonard Cohen: Live Songs	[L]	$15	Columbia 31724

Avalanche (3)
Bird On The Wire (2,4)
Bunch Of Lonesome Heros (2)
Butcher, The (2)
Diamonds In The Mine (3)
Dress Rehearsal Rag (3)
Famous Blue Raincoat (3)
Hey, That's No Way To Say Goodbye (1)
Improvisation (4)
Joan Of Arc (3)
Lady Midnight (2)
Last Year's Man (3)
Love Calls You By Your Name (3)
Master Song (1)
Nancy (4)
Old Revolution (2)
One Of Us Cannot Be Wrong (1)
Partisan, The (2)
Passing Thru (4)
Please Don't Pass Me By (A Disgrace) (4)
Queen Victoria (4)
Seems So Long Ago, Nancy (2)
Sing Another Song, Boys (3)
Sisters Of Mercy (1)
So Long, Marianne (1)
Stories Of The Street (1)
Story Of Isaac (2,4)
Stranger Song (1)
Suzanne (1)
Teachers (1)
Tonight Will Be Fine (2)
Winter Lady (1)
You Know Who I Am (2,4)

COHEN, Myron   '66
Born on 7/1/02 in Grodno, Poland; raised in New York City. Died of a heart attack on 3/10/86 (age 83). Comedian.

| 4/2/66 | **102** | 13 | | | **Everybody Gotta Be Someplace** .... [C] | **$20** | RCA Victor 3534 |

Affairs Of The Heart
Assortment Of Yarns
Flies

Foreign Intrigue
Husbands And Wives And
Lovers

Introduction
Life At "The Stage"
Life In The Sun

Long Coat Tale
Parlor Stories
Short Stories

Two Elephant Stories

COHN, Marc   '92
Born on 7/5/59 in Cleveland. Pop-rock singer/songwriter/pianist. Won the 1991 Best New Artist Grammy Award.

4/27/91+	**38**	63	▲	© 1	**Marc Cohn**..	**$10**	Atlantic 82178
6/12/93	**63**	15		© 2	**The Rainy Season**	**$10**	Atlantic 82491
4/4/98	**114**	6		© 3	**Burning The Daze**...	**$10**	Atlantic 82909

Already Home (3)
Baby King (2)
Dig Down Deep (1)
Don't Talk To Her At Night (2)
Ellis Island (3)
From The Station (2)

Ghost Train (1)
Girl Of Mysterious Sorrow (3)
Healing Hands (3)
Lost You In The Canyon (3)
Mama's In The Moon (3)
Medicine Man (2)

Miles Away (1)
Olana (3)
Paper Walls (2)
Perfect Love (1)
Providence (3)
Rainy Season (2)

Rest For The Weary (2)
Saints Preserve Us (3)
Saving The Best For Last (1)
She's Becoming Gold (2)
Silver Thunderbird (1) *63*
Strangers In A Car (1)

Things We've Handed Down (2)
True Companion (1) *80*
Turn On Your Radio (3)
Turn To Me (3)
29 Ways (1)
Valley Of The Kings (3)

Walk On Water (1)
Walk Through The World (2)
Walking In Memphis (1) *13*

COKO   '99
Born Cheryl Gamble on 6/13/74 in the Bronx, New York. R&B singer. Member of **SWV**.

| 8/28/99 | **68** | 6 | | © | **Hot Coko** .... | **$10** | RCA 67766 |

All My Lovin'
Bigger Than We

Don't Take Your Love Away
Everytime

I Ain't Feelin You
If This World Were Mine

So Hard To Say Goodbye
Sunshine *70*

Triflin'
Try-Na Come Home

You And Me

COLD   '01
Rock group from Jacksonville, Florida: Scooter Ward (vocals, guitar), Kelley Hayes (guitar), Jeremy Marshall (bass) and Sam McCandless (drums).

| 9/30/00+ | **98** | 27 | | © | **13 Ways To Bleed On Stage**.. | **$10** | Geffen 490726 |

Anti-Love Song
Bleed
Confession

End Of The World
It's All Good
Just Got Wicked

No One
Outerspace
Same Drug

Send In The Clowns
She Said
Sick Of Man

Witch

COLD BLOOD   '70
Rock group from San Francisco. Core members: Lydia Pense (vocals), Michael Sasaki (guitar), Raul Matute (piano), Rod Ellicott (bass), Max Haskett (trumpet) and Danny Hull (sax).

12/27/69+	**23**	29		© 1	**Cold Blood**	**$20**	San Francisco 200
1/23/71	**60**	13		© 2	**Sisyphus**	**$20**	San Francisco 205
4/22/72	**133**	11		3	**First Taste Of Sin**	**$15**	Reprise 2074
4/28/73	**97**	14		4	**Thriller!**..	**$15**	Reprise 2130
8/10/74	**126**	8		5	**Lydia**	**$15**	Warner 2806
3/13/76	**179**	4		6	**Lydia Pense & Cold Blood**	**$12**	ABC 917

All My Honey (3)
Baby I Love You (4)
Back Here Again (6)
Blinded By Love (6)
Cold Blood Smokin' (medley) (6)
Come Back Into My Life Again (5)
Consideration (5)
Down To The Bone (3)

Drink The Wine (6)
Feel So Bad (4)
Feel The Fire (6)
Funky On My Back (2)
I Can't Stay (2)
I Get Off On You (6)
I Got Happiness (6)
I Just Want To Make Love To You (1)
I Love You More Than You'll Ever Know (6)

I Only Wanted Someone To Hear Me (5)
I Wish I Knew How It Would Feel To Be Free (1)
I'll Be Long Gone (4)
I'm A Good Woman (1)
If You Will (1)
Inside Your Soul (3)
It Takes A Lotta Good Lovin' (6)
Just Like Sunshine (5)
Kissing My Love (4)

Let Me Be The One (6)
Let Me Down Easy (1)
Live Your Dream (4)
Lo And Behold (3)
My Lady Woman (3)
No Way Home (3)
Ready To Live (5)
Shop Talk (2)
Simple Love Life (5)
Sleeping (4)
Too Many People (2)

Under Pressure (5)
Understanding (2)
Valdez In The Country (3)
Visions (3)
Watch Your Step (1)
We Came Down Here (medley) (6)
When It's Over (5)
When My Love Hand Comes Down (5)

You Are The Sunshine Of My Life (4)
You Got Me Hummin (1) *52*
You Had To Know (3)
You're Free Lovin' Me (5)
Your Good Thing (2)

COLD CHISEL   '81
Rock group from Adelaide, Australia: **Jimmy Barnes** (vocals), Ian Moss (guitar), Don Walker (keyboards), Phil Small (bass) and Steven Prestwich (drums).

| 6/13/81 | **171** | 6 | | | **East**.. | **$10** | Elektra 336 |

Best Kept Lies
Cheap Wine

Choirgirl
Khe Sanh

My Baby
My Turn To Cry

Never Before
Rising Sun

Standing On The Outside
Star Hotel

Tomorrow

COLDPLAY   '01
Rock group from Edinburgh, Scotland: Chris Martin (vocals), Jon Buckland (guitar), Guy Barryman (bass) and Will Champion (drums).

| 12/30/00+ | **51** | 40↑ | ● | © | **Parachutes**... | **$10** | Nettwerk 30162 |

Don't Panic
Everything's Not Lost

High Speed
Parachutes

Shiver
Sparks

Spies
Trouble

We Never Change *48*
Yellow

COLE, Jude   '90
Born on 6/18/60 in Carbon Cliff, Illinois; raised in East Moline, Illinois. Male singer/guitarist. Member of **The Records** from 1979-81.

| 5/5/90 | **138** | 12 | | © 1 | **A View From 3rd Street**... | **$10** | Reprise 26164 |
| 10/17/92 | **177** | 3 | | © 2 | **Start The Car**.. | **$10** | Reprise 26898 |

Baby, It's Tonight (1) *16*
Blame It On Fate (2)
Compared To Nothing (1)

First Your Money (Then Your Clothes) (2)
Get Me Through The Night (1)
Hallowed Ground (1)

Heart Of Blues (1)
House Full Of Reasons (1) *69*
It Comes Around (2)
Just Another Night (2)

Open Road (2)
Place In The Line (2)
Prove Me Wrong (1)
Right There Now (2)

Start The Car (2) *71*
Stranger To Myself (1)
Tell The Truth (2) *57*
This Time It's Us (1)

Time For Letting Go (1) *32*
Worlds Apart (2)

COLE, Nat "King" ★36★   '57

Born Nathaniel Adams Coles on 3/17/17 in Montgomery, Alabama; raised in Chicago. Died of cancer on 2/15/65 (age 47). R&B-jazz singer/songwriter/pianist. Father of **Natalie Cole**. Formed The King Cole Trio in 1939. Long series of top-selling records led to his solo career in 1950. Appeared in several movies. Hosted own TV variety series from 1956-57. Won Grammy's Lifetime Achievement Award in 1990. Inducted into the Rock and Roll Hall of Fame in 2000 as an early influence.

1)Love Is The Thing 2)Ramblin' Rose 3)L-O-V-E 4)Wild Is Love 5)Nat 'King' Cole sings

DEBUT	PEAK	WKS	RIAA	CD	#	Album Title	Catalog	Sym	$	Label & Number
11/27/54+	5	20			1	Nat 'King' Cole sings		[EP]	$50	Capitol 9120
7/9/55	9	17			2	Moods In Song		[EP]	$50	Capitol 633
4/28/56	16	2		©	3	Ballads Of The Day			$50	Capitol 680
						also see #30 below				
3/9/57	13	2		©	4	After Midnight			$50	Capitol 782
						with the King Cole Trio				
4/6/57	❶⁸	94	▲	©	5	Love Is The Thing			$40	Capitol 824
9/23/57	18	3			6	This Is Nat "King" Cole			$40	Capitol 870
12/16/57+	18	6		©	7	Just One Of Those Things			$40	Capitol 903
5/5/58	18	3			8	St. Louis Blues		[S]	$40	Capitol 993
						Cole portrayed W.C. Handy in the movie about Handy's life				
9/22/58	12	5		©	9	Cole Espanol		[F]	$40	Capitol 1031
12/1/58	17	2		©	10	The Very Thought Of You			$40	Capitol 1084
6/22/59	45	5		©	11	To Whom It May Concern			$40	Capitol 1190
4/18/60	33	2		©	12	Tell Me All About Yourself			$30	Capitol 1331
10/24/60	4	23		©	13	Wild Is Love			$30	Capitol 1392
5/15/61	79	17		©	14	The Touch Of Your Lips			$30	Capitol 1574
5/5/62	27	16		©	15	Nat King Cole sings/George Shearing plays			$30	Capitol 1675
9/22/62	3	162	▲	©	16	Ramblin' Rose			$30	Capitol 1793
12/29/62+	24	36			17	Dear Lonely Hearts			$30	Capitol 1838
5/25/63	68	6			18	Where Did Everyone Go?			$30	Capitol 1859
7/6/63	14	36			19	Those Lazy-Hazy-Crazy Days Of Summer			$30	Capitol 1932
11/30/63+	❶²ˣ	121	●	©	20	The Christmas Song	C:#4/61	[X]	$30	Capitol 1967
						Christmas charts: 6/'63, 12/'64, 8/'65, 8/'66, 3/'67, 5/'68, 1/'69, 4/'70, 3/'71, 1/'72, 5/'73, 5/'83, 5/'85, 6/'87, 6/'88, 8/'89, 6/'90, 4/'91, 8/'92, 12/'93, 12/'94, 11/'95, 10/'96, 13/'97, 20/'98, 28/'99, 26/'00				
8/1/64	18	45			21	I Don't Want To Be Hurt Anymore			$30	Capitol 2118
9/26/64	74	23			22	My Fair Lady			$30	Capitol 2117
2/6/65	4	38		©	23	L-O-V-E			$30	Capitol 2195
3/20/65	30	39	▲	©	24	Unforgettable	C:#39/7	[E]	$25	Capitol 357
						first released as a 10" album in 1952 ($60)				
7/3/65	77	9			25	Songs From "Cat Ballou" And Other Motion Pictures		[K]	$20	Capitol 2340
9/4/65	60	14			26	Looking Back		[G]	$20	Capitol 2361
2/19/66	74	11			27	Nat King Cole At The Sands		[L]	$20	Capitol 2434
11/26/66	145	3			28	The Great Songs!		[E]	$20	Capitol 2558
						recorded in 1957				
9/14/68	187	5	▲		29	The Best Of Nat King Cole	C:#48/2	[G]	$20	Capitol 2944
8/23/69	197	3			30	Close-Up		[R]	$25	Capitol 252 [2]
						reissue of Ballads Of The Day and Nat King Cole's Top Pops albums				
7/13/91	86	28	●		31	Collectors Series	C:#12/1	[G]	$10	Capitol 93590
12/5/92	8ˣ	39		©	32	It's Christmas Time	C:#6/41	[X]	$10	LaserLight 15152
						BING CROSBY • FRANK SINATRA • NAT KING COLE				
						Christmas charts: 8/'92, 17/'93, 12/'94, 13/'95				
11/27/99+	9ˣ	11		©	33	Christmas Favorites featuring The Christmas Song	C:#7/16	[X]	$10	EMI-Capitol 57729
						an EMI-Capitol Music Special Markets release of 10 selections from #20 above; Christmas charts: 30/'99, 9/'00				

Acercate Mas (Come Closer To Me) (9)
Adelita (9)
Affair To Remember (28)
After The Ball Is Over (19)
Again (26)
(Ah, The Apple Trees) When The World Was Young (18)
Ain't Misbehavin' (5)
All By Myself (17)
All Over The World (17,31) *42*
Alone Too Long (3,30)
Am I Blue? (18)
Angel Eyes (3,30)
Annabelle (6)
Answer Me, My Love (24,29,31)
Around The World (28)
Arrivederci, Roma (Goodbye To Rome) (9)
At Last (5)
Away In A Manger (20,33)
Azure-Te (15)
Ballad Of Cat Ballou (25)
Ballerina (27) *18*
Be Still My Heart (28)
Beale Street Blues (8,25)
Beautiful Friendship (15)

Because You're Mine (30)
Beggar For The Blues (13)
Best Thing For You (12)
Blame It On My Youth (4)
Blossom Fell (2,3,30,31) *2*
Blue Gardenia (3,25,30)
Brush Those Tears From Your Eyes (21)
But Beautiful (10)
Cachito (9)
Can't Help It (11)
Caravan (4)
Careless Love (8)
Caroling Caroling (Christmas Bells Are Ringing) (20,32)
Chantez Les Bas (8)
Cherchez La Femme (10)
Cherie, I Love You (10)
China Gate (25)
Christmas Song (Merry Christmas To You) (20,31,33) *65*
Continental, The (27)
Coquette (30)
Cottage For Sale (7)
Cradle In Bethlehem (20,33)
Crazy She Calls Me (12)
Darling Je Vous Aime Beaucoup (2,3,30,31) *7*

Dear Lonely Hearts (17,29,31) *13*
Deck The Halls (20)
Dedicated To You (12)
Don't Forget (19)
Don't Get Around Much Anymore (7)
Don't Go (15)
Don't Let It Go To Your Head (4)
Don't You Remember? (21)
Dreams Can Tell A Lie (6)
El Bodeguero (Grocer's Cha-Cha) (9)
End Of A Love Affair (18)
Faith Can Move Mountains (30)
Farewell To Arms (15)
Fascination (28)
First Noël (20,32,33)
Fly Me To The Moon (In Other Words) (15)
For All We Know (10)
For The Want Of A Kiss (28)
For You (12)
Forgive My Heart (6) *13*
Friendless Blues (8)
Funny (14,27,30)
Get Me To The Church On Time (22)

Get Out And Get Under The Moon (19)
(Get Your Kicks On) Route 66 ...see: Route 66
Girl From Ipanema (15)
Go, If You're Going (21)
Good Times (16)
Goodnight, Irene, Goodnight (16)
Hajji Baba (25)
Happy New Year (28)
Hark! The Herald Angels Sing (20,33)
Harlem Blues (8)
He Who Hesitates (13)
He'll Have To Go (16)
Hesitating Blues (medley) (8)
Hold My Hand (1)
How I'd Love To Love You (23)
Hundreds And Thousands Of Girls (13)
Hymn To Him (22)
I Could Have Danced All Night (22)
I Don't Want It That Way (16)
I Don't Want To Be Hurt Anymore (21,29) *22*
I Don't Want To See Tomorrow (21) *34*

I Found A Million Dollar Baby (In A Five And Ten Cent Store) (10)
I Got Bad And That Ain't Good (15)
I Had The Craziest Dream (28)
I Just Found Out About Love (4)
I Keep Goin' Back To Joe's (18)
I Know That You Know (4)
(I Love You) For Sentimental Reasons (24,31)
I Must Be Dreaming (26) *69*
I Remember You (14)
I Saw Three Ships (20)
I Should Care (7)
I Thought About Marie (5)
I Understand (7)
I Wish I Knew (10,28)
I Wish You Love (17)
(I Would Do) Anything For You (12)
I'm All Cried Out (21)
I'm Alone Because I Love You (21)
I'm An Ordinary Man (22)
I'm Gonna Laugh You Right Out Of My Life (6) *57*
I'm Lost (15)
I'm Never Satisfied (30)

I've Grown Accustomed To Her Face (22)
If I Give My Heart To You (1,30)
If I May (2,26) *8*
If Love Ain't There (18)
If Love Is Good To Me (3,30)
If You Said No (11)
Illusion (10)
In Love Again (13)
In The Cool Of The Day (25)
In The Good Old Summertime (19)
In The Heart Of Jane Doe (11)
Is It Better To Have Loved And Lost (26)
It Happens To Be Me (3,30)
It's A Beautiful Evening (13)
It's A Lonesome Old Town (When You're Not Around) (7)
It's All In The Game (5)
It's Only A Paper Moon (4)
Joe Turner's Blues (8,27)
Joy To The World (20,32)
Just As Much As Ever (26)
Just For The Fun Of It (7)
Just One Of Those Things (7)
Just You, Just Me (4)
Las Mananitas (9)

173

COLE, Nat "King" — Cont'd

Laughing On The Outside (Crying On The Inside) (18)
Let There Be Love (15)
Lights Out (14)
Lonely One (4)
Lonesome And Sorry (17)
Looking Back (26) *5*
Lost April (15,24)
L-O-V-E (23,29,31) *81*
Love Is The Thing (5)
Love Me As Though There Were No Tomorrow (6)
Love-Wise (11)
Lovesville (11)
Magnificent Obsession (10)
Make Her Mine (24)
Making Believe You're Here (10)
Maria Elena (9)
Memphis Blues (8)
Midnight Flyer (26) *51*
Miss Otis Regrets (She's Unable To Lunch Today) (27)
Miss You (17)
Mona Lisa (24,29,31)
More (23)
More I See You (10)
Morning Star (8)
My First And Only Lover (17)
My Heart Tells Me (Should I Believe My Heart?) (10)
My Heart's Treasure (11)
My Kind Of Girl (23)
My Kind Of Love (27)
My Life (12)
My Need For You (14)

My One Sin (3) *24*
Nature Boy (31)
Near You (17)
Never Let Me Go (6,25) *79*
Night Of The Quarter Moon (25)
Nightingale Sang In Berkeley Square (14)
No, I Don't Want Her (18)
Noche De Ronda (9)
Non Dimenticar (Don't Forget) (31) *45*
Not So Long Ago (14)
Nothing Ever Changes My Love For You (6) *72*
O Holy Night (20,32,33)
O Little Town Of Bethlehem (20,33)
O Tannenbaum (20,32,33)
Oh, How I Miss You Tonight (17)
On A Bicycle Built For Two (19)
On The Sidewalks Of New York (19)
On The Street Where You Live (22)
Once In A While (7)
One Has My Name The Other Has My Heart (16)
Only Forever (14)
Only Yesterday (21)
Our Old Home Team (19)
Papa Loves Mambo (1)
Paradise (10)
Party's Over (7)
Pick-Up (13)
Pick Yourself Up (15)

Poinciana (14)
Portrait Of Jennie (24)
Pretend (24,31)
Quizas, Quizas, Quizas (Perhaps, Perhaps, Perhaps) (9)
Rain In Spain (22)
Ramblin' Rose (16,29,31) *2*
Red Sails In The Sunset (24)
Return To Paradise (3)
Road To Nowhere (21)
Route 66 (4,29,31)
Ruby And The Pearl (30)
Sand And The Sea (2,3,30) *23*
Santa Claus Is Comin' To Town (32)
Say It Isn't So (18)
Send For Me (26,31) *6*
September Song (15)
Serenata (15)
Show Me (22)
Silent Night (20,33)
Sing Another Song (And We'll All Go Home) (16)
Skip To My Lou (16)
Smile (3,30)
Someone To Tell It To (18)
Someone You Love (6) *13*
Somewhere Along The Way (30)
Song Is Ended (But The Melody Lingers On) (7)
Song Of Raintree County (25) *flip*
Spring Is Here (18)
St. Louis Blues (8,25)

Stardust (5) *79*
Stay (8)
Stay As Sweet As You Are (5)
Stay With It (13)
Straighten Up And Fly Right (31)
Sunday, Monday, Or Always (14)
Surrey With The Fringe On Top (27)
Sweet Bird Of Youth (26) *96*
Sweet Lorraine (4,29)
Swiss Retreat (23)
Te Quiero, Dijiste (Magic Is The Moonlight) (9)
Teach Me Tonight (1,30)
Tell Her In The Morning (13)
Tell Me All About Yourself (12)
Thanks To You (23)
That Sunday, That Summer (19) *12*
That's All (6)
That's All There Is (18)
That's What They Meant (By The Good Old Summertime) (19)
There Is A Tavern In The Town (19)
There's A Gold Mine In The Sky (28)
There's A Lull In My Life (15)
There's Love (23)
These Foolish Things Remind Me Of You (7)
They Can't Make Her Cry (25)
This Is All I Ask (10)

This Is Always (12)
This Morning It Was Summer (11)
Those Lazy-Hazy-Crazy Days Of Summer (19,29,31) *6*
Thou Swell (27)
Thousand Thoughts Of You (11)
Three Little Words (23)
Time And The River (26) *30*
To The Ends Of The Earth (6) *25*
To Whom It May Concern (11)
Too Much (11)
Too Young (24,29,31)
Too Young To Go Steady (6) *21*
Touch Of Your Lips (14)
Tu, Mi Delirio (9)
Twilight On The Trail (16)
Unbelievable (3,30)
Unfair (11)
Unforgettable (24,31) *14*
Until The Real Thing Comes Along (12)
Very Thought Of You (10)
Walkin' My Baby Back Home (30,31)
Was That The Human Thing To Do? (21)
Weaver Of Dreams (30)
When I Fall In Love (5)
When Sunny Gets Blue (5)
When You Walked By (12)
When You're Smiling (16)
When Your Lover Has Gone (7)

Where Can I Go Without You? (5)
Where Did Everyone Go? (18)
Where Or When (27)
Who's Next In Line? (17)
Who's Sorry Now? (7)
Why Should I Cry Over You? (17)
Wild Is Love (13)
With A Little Bit Of Luck (22)
Wolverton Mountain (16)
World In My Arms (26)
World Of No Return (11)
Wouldn't It Be Loverly (22)
Wouldn't You Know (Her Name Is Mary) (13)
Yearning (Just For You) (17)
Yellow Dog Blues (8)
You Are My Love (12)
You Did It (22)
You Leave Me Breathless (27)
You Tell Me Your Dream (19)
You're Bringing Out The Dreamer In Me (11)
You're Crying On My Shoulder (21)
You're Looking At Me (4)
You're Mine, You! (14)
You're My Everything (21)
You're My Thrill (28)
You've Got The Indian Sign On Me (12)
Your Cheatin' Heart (16)
Your Love (23)

COLE, Natalie ★134★ '91

Born on 2/6/50 in Los Angeles. R&B singer. Daughter of **Nat "King" Cole**. Professional debut at age 11. Marriages include Marvin Yancey (her producer) and Andre Fischer (former drummer of **Rufus**). Won the 1975 Best New Artist Grammy Award. Hosted own syndicated variety TV show *Big Break* in 1990. Made acting debut in 1993 TV series *I'll Fly Away*. Starred in the 1995 movie *Lily In Winter*.

1)Unforgettable With Love 2)Unpredictable 3)Natalie 4)Thankful 5)Inseparable

DEBUT	PEAK	WKS		CD		ARTIST — Album Title		$	Label & Number
8/30/75	18	56	●	©	1	Inseparable		$12	Capitol 11429
5/29/76	13	30	●	©	2	Natalie		$12	Capitol 11517
3/5/77	8	28	▲		3	Unpredictable		$12	Capitol 11600
12/10/77+	16	39	▲	©	4	Thankful		$12	Capitol 11708
7/15/78	31	16	●	©	5	Natalie...Live!	[L]	$15	Capitol 11709 [2]
4/7/79	52	15	●	©	6	I Love You So		$12	Capitol 11928
12/15/79+	44	19		©	7	We're The Best Of Friends		$12	Capitol 12019
						NATALIE COLE/PEABO BRYSON			
6/14/80	77	22		©	8	Don't Look Back		$12	Capitol 12079
9/26/81	132	4		©	9	Happy Love		$12	Capitol 12165
9/17/83	182	3		©	10	I'm Ready		$10	Epic 38280
6/29/85	140	9		©	11	Dangerous		$10	Modern 90270
8/8/87+	42	58		©	12	Everlasting		$10	Manhattan 53051
5/27/89	59	23		©	13	Good To Be Back		$10	EMI 48902
6/29/91	❶⁵	110	▲⁷	©	14	Unforgettable With Love	C:#36/1	$10	Elektra 61049
7/3/93	26	19	●	©	15	Take A Look		$10	Elektra 61496
11/26/94	36	8	●	©	16	Holly & Ivy	C:#25/16 [X]	$10	Elektra 61704
						Christmas charts: 6/'94, 25/'95			
10/12/96	20	21	●	©	17	Stardust		$10	Elektra 61946
12/21/96	196	2		©	18	A Celebration Of Christmas	[X-L]	$10	Elektra 62000
						JOSÉ CARRERAS-NATALIE COLE-PLÁCIDO DOMINGO			
						recorded on 12/23/95 at the Austria Center in Vienna			
7/10/99	163	3		©	19	Snowfall On The Sahara		$10	Elektra 62401
12/18/99+	157	4		©	20	The Magic Of Christmas	[X]	$10	Elektra 62433
						NATALIE COLE with the London Symphony Orchestra			
						Christmas chart: 21/'99			
12/23/00	154	2		©	21	Greatest Hits Volume I	[G]	$10	Elektra 62582

Across The Nation (9)
Ahmad's Blues (17)
All About Love (15)
Almost Like Being In Love (14)
Amazing Grace (19)
Angel On My Shoulder (21)
Annie Mae (4)
As A Matter Of Fact (13)
As Time Goes By (15)
Autumn Leaves (medley) (14)
Avalon (14)
Be Mine Tonight (3)
Be Thankful (4,5)
Beautiful Dreamer (8)

Billy The Kid Next Door (11)
Calypso Blues (15)
Can We Get Together Again (2,5)
Cantique De Noël (18)
Carol Of The Bells (20)
Caroling, Caroling (16)
Christmas Medley (16)
Christmas Song (Chestnuts Roasting On An Open Fire) (16,18,20)
Christmas Waltz (20)
Cole-Blooded (8)
Corinna (19)

Crazy He Calls Me (15)
Cry Baby (5)
Cry Me A River (15)
Danger Up Ahead (8)
Dangerous (11) *57*
Darling, Je Vous Aime Beaucoup (14)
Dindi (Portuguese) (17)
Don't Explain (15)
Don't Get Around Much Anymore (14)
Don't Look Back (8)
Don't Mention My Heartache (13)

Everlasting (12)
Everyday I Have The Blues (19)
Fiesta In Blue (15)
First Noel (16)
For Sentimental Reasons (medley) (14)
Gift, The (11)
Gimme Some Time (7)
Gonna Make You Mine (13)
Good Morning Heartache (2)
Good To Be Back (13)
Gotta Serve Somebody (19)
Hard To Get Along (2)

Hark The Herald Angels Sing (20)
He Was Too Good To Me (17)
Heaven Is With You (2)
His Eyes, Her Eyes (19)
Hold On (8)
Holly & The Ivy (16,18)
How Come You Won't Stay Here (1)
I Can't Breakaway (3)
I Can't Cry (13)
I Can't Let Go (9)
I Can't Say No (1,5,21)

I Can't Stay Away (4)
I Do (15)
I Live For Your Love (12,21) *13*
I Love Him So Much (1)
I Love You So (6)
I Walked Today Where Jesus Walked (14)
I Want To Be Where You Are (7)
I Wish You Love (15)
I Won't Deny You (10)
I'll Be Home For Christmas (18)

COLE, Natalie — Cont'd

I'm Beginning To See The Light (15)
I'm Catching Hell (3,5,21)
(I'm Coming) Straight From The Heart (10)
I'm Getting In To You (8)
I'm Gonna Laugh You Right Out Of My Life (15)
I'm Ready (10)
I'm The One (12)
I'm Your Mirror (10)
I've Got Love On My Mind (3,5,21) *5*
(I've Seen) Paradise (8)
If Love Ain't There (17)
If You Could See Me Now (17)
In My Reality (12)
Inseparable (1,5,21) *32*
It's Been You (6)
It's Sand Man (15)
Jingle Bells (15)
Joey (1)
Joke Is On You (9)
Joy To The World (16)
Jump Start (12) *13*
Keep It On The Outside (10)
Keep Smiling (2)
Keeping A Light (4)
La Costa (4,21)

Let There Be Love (15)
Let's Face The Music And Dance (17)
Let's Fall In Love (medley) (7)
Like A Lover (17)
Little Bit Of Heaven (11) *81*
Little Boy That Santa Claus Forgot (16)
Livin' For Love (21)
L-O-V-E (17)
Love And Kisses (9)
Love Is On The Way (11)
Love Letters (17)
Love Will Find You (7)
Lovers (4,5,15)
Lucy In The Sky With Diamonds (5,21)
Lush Life (14)
Mary, Did You Know (20)
May Each Day (14)
Merry Christmas Baby (16)
Miss You Like Crazy (13,21) *7*
Mona Lisa (14)
More Than The Stars (12)
More Than You'll Ever Know (19)
Mr. Melody (2,5,21) *49*
My Grown-Up Christmas List (20)

Nature Boy (14)
Needing You (1)
No More Blue Christmas' (16)
No Plans For The Future (2)
Nobody's Soldier (11)
Non Dimenticar (14)
Not Like Mine (2)
Nothin' But A Fool (9)
Nothing Stronger Than Love (4)
O Tanenbaum (20)
Oh, Daddy (6)
Oh, Du Fröhliche (18)
Only Love (9)
Opposites Attract (11)
Orange Colored Sky (14)
Our Love (4,5,21) *10*
Our Love Is Here To Stay (14)
Paper Moon (1)
Party Lights (3,5) *79*
Peaceful Living (3)
Pero Mira Como Beben Los Peces En El Río (18)
Pick Yourself Up (17)
Pink Cadillac (12,21) *5*
Que Sera, Sera (4)
Rest Of The Night (13)
Reverend Lee (19)
Route 66 (14)
Safe (13)

Say You Love Me (19,21)
Secrets (11)
Silent Night (16)
Since You Asked (19)
Sleigh Ride (18,20)
Smile (14)
Smile Like Yours (21) *84*
Snowfall On The Sahara (19,21)
Someone That I Used To Love (8) *21*
Someone's Rockin' My Dreamboat (13)
Something For Nothing (1)
Something's Got A Hold On Me (5)
Song For Christmas (16)
Song For You (19,21)
Sophisticated Lady (She's A Different Lady) (2,5) *25*
Sorry (6)
Split Decision (12)
Stairway To The Stars (8)
Stand By (6)
Stardust (17)
Starting Over Again (13)
Stay With Me (19)
Still In Love (3)
Stille Nacht (18)

Straighten Up And Fly Right (14)
Sweet Little Jesus Boy (20)
Swingin' Shepherd Blues (15)
Take A Look (15)
Teach Me Tonight (17)
Tenderly (medley) (14)
That Sunday That Summer (14)
There's A Lull In My Life (17)
These Eyes (9)
This Can't Be Love (14)
This Heart (3)
This Love Affair (7)
This Morning It Was Summer (17)
This Will Be (1,5,21) *6*
This Will Make You Laugh (15)
Thou Swell (14)
Time (Heals All Wounds) (10)
To Whom It May Concern (17)
Too Close For Comfort (15)
Too Much Mister (10)
Too Young (14)
Touch Me (2)
Twelve Days Of Christmas (20)
Two For The Blues (17)
Undecided (15)
Unforgettable (14,21) *14*
Unpredictable You (3)

Urge To Merge (12)
Very Thought Of You (14)
We're The Best Of Friends (7)
What A Difference A Day Made (17)
What A Wonderful World (18)
What Child Is This? (18)
What You Won't Do For Love (7)
When A Man Loves A Woman (9)
When I Fall In Love (12,17) *95*
Where Can I Go Without You (17)
Where's Your Angel? (10)
White Christmas (18)
Who Will Carry On (6)
Winner, The (6)
Winter Wonderland (18)
With My Eyes Wide Open I'm Dreaming (19)
You (1)
You Send Me (medley) (7)
You Were Right Girl (9)
You're So Good (6)
Your Car (My Garage) (11)
Your Eyes (3)
Your Face Stays In My Mind (1)
Your Lonely Heart (6,7)

COLE, Paula
Born on 4/5/68 in Rockport, Massachusetts. Female singer/songwriter. Won the 1997 Best New Artist Grammy Award. **'98**

2/22/97+	20	77	▲²	©	1 This Fire			$10	Imago 46424
10/16/99	97	4		©	2 Amen.			$10	Imago 47490

PAULA COLE BAND

Amen (2)
Be Somebody (2)
Carmen (1)
Feelin' Love (1)

Free (2)
God Is Watching (2)
Hush, Hush, Hush (1)
I Believe In Love (2)

I Don't Want To Wait (1) *11*
La Tonya (2)
Me (1)
Mississippi (1)

Nietzsche's Eyes (1)
Pearl (2)
Rhythm Of Life (2)
Road To Dead (1)

Suwannee Jo (2)
Throwing Stones (1)
Tiger (1)

Where Have All The Cowboys Gone? (1) *8*

COLEMAN, Durell
Born in Roanoke, Virginia. Male R&B singer. **'85**

9/28/85	155	7			Durell Coleman			$10	Island 90293

Do You Love Me
I Had A Sure Thing

I Should Have Known Better
One False Move

Run To Me
Somebody Took My Love

Take Me Back To My Love In China

Tender Blue
When A Man Loves A Woman

COLLECTIVE SOUL
Rock group from Stockbridge, Georgia: brothers Ed (vocals) and Dean (guitar) Roland with Ross Childress (guitar), Will Turpin (bass) and Shane Evans (drums). **'94**

4/30/94	15	40	▲²	©	1 Hints Allegations And Things Left Unsaid			$10	Atlantic 82596
4/1/95	23	76	▲³	©	2 Collective Soul			$10	Atlantic 82745
3/29/97	16	26	▲	©	3 Disciplined Breakdown			$10	Atlantic 82984
2/27/99	21	35	▲	©	4 Dosage			$10	Atlantic 83162
10/28/00	22	15	●	©	5 Blender			$10	Atlantic 83400

After All (5)
All (1)
Blame (3)
Bleed (2)
Boast (5)
Breathe (1)
Burning Bridges (1)
Collection Of Goods (2)
Compliment (1)
Crowded Head (3)

Crown (4)
Dandy Life (4)
December (2) *20*
Disciplined Breakdown (3)
Everything (3)
Forgiveness (3)
Full Circle (3)
Gel (2)
Generate (4)
Giving (3)

Goodnight, Good Guy (1)
Happiness (5)
Heaven's Already Here (1)
Heavy (4) *73*
In A Moment (1)
In Between (3)
Link (3)
Listen (3) *72*
Love Lifted Me (1)
Maybe (3)

Needs (4)
No More, No Less (4)
Not The One (4)
Over Tokyo (5)
Perfect Day (5)
Precious Declaration (3) *65*
Pretty Donna (5)
Reach (1)
Reunion (1)
Run (4) *76*

Scream (1)
She Gathers Rain (2)
Shine (1) *11*
Simple (2)
Sister Don't Cry (1)
Skin (5)
Slow (4)
Smashing Young Man (2)
10 Yrs. Later (5)
Tremble For My Beloved (4)

Turn Around (5)
Untitled (2)
Vent (5)
Wasting Time (1)
When The Water Falls (2)
Where The River Flows (2)
Why Pt. 2 (5)
World I Know (2) *19*
You Speak My Language (5)

COLLEGE BOYZ, The
Male rap group from Los Angeles: Rom, Squeak, The Q and DJ B-Selector. **'92**

5/2/92	118	11		©	Radio Fusion Radio			$10	Virgin 91658

College Boyz In The House
Funky Quartet

Hollywood Paradox
How Ta Act

Humpin'
Politics Of A Gangster

Real Man
Rigmarole

Underground Blues
Victim Of The Ghetto *68*

COLLIE, Mark
Born on 1/18/56 in Waynesboro, Tennessee. Country singer. **'93**

1/30/93	156	8		©	Mark Collie			$10	MCA 10658

Born To Love You
Even The Man In The Moon Is Cryin'

Heart Of The Matter
Hillbilly Boy With The Rock 'N' Roll Blues

Is That Too Much To Ask?
Keep It Up
Linda Lou

Shame Shame Shame Shame
Something's Gonna Change
Her Mind

Trouble's Comin' Like A Train

COLLINS, Albert
Born on 10/1/32 in Leona, Texas. Died of cancer on 11/24/93 (age 61). Blues singer/guitarist. Cousin of Lightnin' Hopkins. Appeared in the movie *Adventures In Babysitting*. Dubbed "The Master of the Telecaster" and "The Iceman." **'86**

2/12/72	196	2			1 There's Gotta Be A Change			$15	Tumbleweed 103
2/15/86	124	18		©	2 Showdown!			$10	Alligator 4743

ALBERT COLLINS/ROBERT CRAY/JOHNNY COPELAND

Albert's Alley (2)
Black Cat Bone (2)
Blackjack (2)

Bring Your Fine Self Home (2)
Dream, The (2)
Fade Away (1)

Frog Jumpin' (1)
Get Your Business Straight (1)
I Got A Mind To Travel (1)

In Love Wit'cha (1)
Lion's Den (1)
Moon Is Full (2)

She's Into Something (2)
Somethin' On My Mind (1)
Stickin' (1)

T-Bone Shuffle (2)
There's Gotta Be A Change (1)
Today Ain't Like Yesterday (1)

COLLINS, "Bootsy" — see BOOTSY

COLLINS, Edwyn '95
Born on 8/23/59 in Edinburgh, Scotland. Pop-rock singer/songwriter.

| 10/28/95 | 183 | 4 | | © | **Gorgeous George** .... | | | $10 | Bar None 058 |

Campaign For Real Rock   Gorgeous George   If You Could Love Me   Low Expectations   North Of Heaven   Subsidence
Girl Like You *32*   I've Had It Bad   It's Right In Front Of You   Make Me Feel Again   Out Of This World

COLLINS, Judy ★195★ '68
Born on 5/1/39 in Seattle. Contemporary folk singer/songwriter. Moved to Los Angeles, then to Denver at age nine, where her father, Chuck Collins, was a radio personality. **Stephen Stills** wrote "Suite: Judy Blue Eyes" for her. Appeared in the New York Shakespeare Festival's production of *Peer Gynt*. Nominated for a 1974 Academy Award for co-directing *Antonia: A Portrait of the Woman*, a documentary about Judy's former classical mentor and a pioneer female orchestra conductor, Dr. Antonia Brico.

1)Wildflowers   2)Whales & Nightingales   3)Judith

3/28/64	126	10			1 **Judy Collins #3**			$40	Elektra 7243
10/2/65	69	13		©	2 **Judy Collins' Fifth Album**			$40	Elektra 7300
1/7/67	46	34	●	©	3 **In My Life**			$25	Elektra 7320
1/6/68	5	75	●	©	4 **Wildflowers**			$20	Elektra 74012
12/21/68+	29	33	●	©	5 **Who Knows Where The Time Goes**			$20	Elektra 74033
9/20/69	29	29		©	6 **Recollections**		[K]	$15	Elektra 74055
					recordings from 1963-65				
12/5/70+	17	35	●	©	7 **Whales & Nightingales**			$15	Elektra 75010
12/4/71+	64	13		©	8 **Living**			$15	Elektra 75014
5/27/72	37	24	▲	©	9 **Colors Of The Day/The Best Of Judy Collins**		[G]	$15	Elektra 75030
2/10/73	27	20		©	10 **True Stories And Other Dreams**			$15	Elektra 75053
4/12/75	17	34	▲	©	11 **Judith**			$12	Elektra 1032
9/11/76	25	20		©	12 **Bread & Roses**			$12	Elektra 1076
8/6/77	42	27			13 **So Early In The Spring, The First 15 Years**		[K]	$15	Elektra 6002 [2]
3/17/79	54	16		©	14 **Hard Times For Lovers**			$12	Elektra 171
5/3/80	142	6			15 **Running For My Life**			$12	Elektra 253
3/13/82	190	5		©	16 **Times Of Our Lives**			$12	Elektra 60001

Albatross (4,9)
All Things Are Quite Silent (8)
Almost Free (15)
Amazing Grace (7,9) *15*
Anathea (1,6)
Angel On My Side (16)
Angel, Spread Your Wings (11)
Ballata Of Francesco Landini (medley) (4)
Bells Of Rhymney (1,6)
Bird On The Wire (5,13)
Bonnie Ship The Diamond (13)
Born To The Breed (11,13)
Both Sides Now (4,9,13) *8*
Bread And Roses (12,13)
Bright Morning Star (15)
Brother, Can You Spare A Dime (11)
Bullgine Run (1)
Carry It On (2,13)
Che (10)
Chelsea Morning (8) *78*
City Of New Orleans (11)
Coal Tattoo (13)
Come Away Melinda (1)
Come Down In Time (12)
Coming Of The Roads (2)

Cook With Honey (10) *32*
Daddy You've Been On My Mind (2,6)
Dealer (Down And Losin') (10)
Deportee (medley) (1)
Desperado (14)
Don't Say Goodbye Love (16)
Dorothy (14)
Dove, The (1)
Dress Rehearsal Rag (3)
Drink A Round To Ireland (16)
Early Morning Rain (2,6)
Easy Times (8)
Everything Must Change (12)
Farewell (1)
Farewell To Tarwathie (7,9,13)
First Boy I Loved (5)
Fishermen Song (10)
Four Strong Winds (8)
Gene's Song (7)
Golden Apples Of The Sun (3)
Grandaddy (16)
Great Expectations (16)
Green Finch And Linnet Bird (15)
Happy End (14)
Hard Lovin' Loser (3) *97*

Hard Times For Lovers (14) *66*
Hello, Horray (5)
Hey Nelly Nelly (1)
Hey, That's No Way To Say Goodbye (4)
Holly Ann (10,13)
Hostage, The (10,13)
Houses (11,13)
I Could Really Show You Around (11)
I Didn't Know About You (12)
I Remember Sky (14)
I Think It's Going To Rain Today (3)
I'll Be Seeing You (11)
I'll Never Say Goodbye (14)
I've Done Enough Dyin' Today (15)
In My Life (3,9)
In The Heat Of The Summer (2)
In The Hills Of Shiloh (1)
Innisfree (8)
It Isn't Nice (2)
It's Gonna Be One Of Those Nights (16)
Joan Of Arc (8)
Just Like Tom Thumb's Blues (3,8)

King David (12)
La Chanson Des Vieux Amants (The Song Of Old Lovers) (4)
La Colombe (3,13)
Lasso! Di Donna (medley) (4)
Last Thing On My Mind (6)
Liverpool Lullaby (3)
Lord Gregory (2)
Love Hurts (12)
Loving Of The Game (11,13)
Mama Mama (16)
Marat (medley) (3,13)
Marie (14)
Marieke (7,13,15)
Marjorie (14)
Masters Of War (1)
Memory (16)
Michael From Mountains (4)
Moon Is A Harsh Mistress (11)
Mr. Tambourine Man (2,6)
My Father (5,9,13)
Nightingale I & II (7)
Oh Had I A Golden Thread (7)
Open The Door (Song For Judith) (8) *90*
Out Of Control (12)
Pack Up Your Sorrows (2,6)
Patriot Game (7)
Pirate Jenny (3)

Pirate Ships (11)
Plane Wreck At Los Gatos (medley) (1)
Plegaria A Un Labrador (12)
Poor Immigrant (5)
Pretty Polly (5,13)
Pretty Saro (13)
Pretty Women (15)
Priests (4)
Prothalamium (7)
Rainbow Connection (15)
Rest Of Your Life (16)
Running For My Life (15)
Sade (medley) (3,13)
Salt Of The Earth (11)
Secret Gardens (10,13)
Send In The Clowns (11,13) *19*
Settle Down (1)
Simple Gifts (7)
Since You Asked (4,9,13)
Sisters Of Mercy (4)
Sky Fell (4)
So Begins The Task (10)
So Early, Early In The Spring (2,13)
Someday Soon (5,9) *55*
Song For David (7)
Song For Duke (11)

(Song For Judith) ..see: Open The Door
Song For Martin (10)
Sons Of (7,9)
Spanish Is The Loving Tongue (12)
Special Delivery (12,13)
Starmaker (16)
Story Of Isaac (5)
Sun Son (16)
Sunny Goodge Street (3,9)
Suzanne (3,9)
Take This Longing (12)
Ten O'Clock All Is Well (1)
Thirsty Boots (2)
This Is The Day (15)
Through The Eyes Of Love (14)
Time Passes Slowly (7)
Turn! Turn! Turn!/To Everything There Is A Season (1,6) *69*
Vietnam Love Song (8)
Wedding Song (8)
Where Or When (14)
Who Knows Where The Time Goes (5,9)
Winter Sky (6)

COLLINS, Phil ★186★ '85
Born on 1/30/51 in Chiswick, London, England. Pop singer/songwriter/drummer. Stage actor as a young child; played the "Artful Dodger" in the London production of *Oliver*. With group Flaming Youth in 1969. Joined **Genesis** in 1970, became lead singer in 1975. Also with jazz-rock group **Brand X**. Starred in the 1988 movie *Buster* and appeared in *Hook* and *Frauds*. Left Genesis in April 1996.

3/14/81	7	164	▲⁴	©	1 **Face Value**	C:#4/112		$10	Atlantic 16029
11/27/82+	8	141	▲³	©	2 **Hello, I Must Be Going!**	C:#14/28		$10	Atlantic 80035
3/9/85	❶⁷	123	▲¹²	©	3 **No Jacket Required**	C:#13/15		$10	Atlantic 81240
					1985 Grammy winner: Album of the Year				
12/2/89+	❶³	90	▲⁴	©	4 **...But Seriously**			$10	Atlantic 82050
11/24/90+	11	97	▲⁴	©	5 **Serious Hits...Live!**		[L]	$10	Atlantic 82157
11/27/93	13	30	▲	©	6 **Both Sides**			$10	Atlantic 82550
11/9/96	23	20	●	©	7 **Dance Into The Light**			$10	Atlantic 82949
10/24/98	18	102	▲²	©	8 **...Hits**	C:#28/30	[G]	$10	Atlantic 83139

Against All Odds (Take A Look At Me Now) (5,8) *1*
All Of My Life (4)

Another Day In Paradise (4,5,8) *1*
Behind The Lines (1)

Both Sides Of The Story (6,8) *25*
Can't Find My Way (6)

Can't Turn Back The Years (6)
Colours (4)
Dance Into The Light (7,8) *45*

Do You Know, Do You Care? (2)
Do You Remember? (4,5) *4*

Doesn't Anybody Stay Together Anymore (3)

COLLINS, Phil — Cont'd

Don't Let Him Steal Your Heart Away (2)
Don't Lose My Number (3,5) 4
Droned (1)
Easy Lover (5,8) 2
Everyday (6) 24
Father To Son (4)
Find A Way To My Heart (4)
Groovy Kind Of Love (5,8) 1
Hand In Hand (1)
Hang In Long Enough (4) 23

I Cannot Believe It's True
I Don't Care Anymore 39
I Don't Wanna Know (3)
I Missed Again (1) 19
I Wish It Would Rain Down (4,8) 3
I'm Not Moving (1)
I've Forgotten Everything (6)
If Leaving Me Is Easy (1)
In The Air Tonight (1,5,8) 19
Inside Out (3)

It Don't Matter To Me (2)
It's In Your Eyes (7) 77
Just Another Story (7)
Like China (7)
Long Long Way To Go (3)
Lorenzo (7)
Love Police (7)
No Matter Who (7)
One More Night (3,5,8) 1
Only You Know And I Know (3)
Oughta Know By Now (5)

Please Come Out Tonight (6)
River So Wide (7)
Roof Is Leaking (1)
Same Moon (7)
Separate Lives (5,8) 1
Something Happened On The Way To Heaven (4,5,8) 4
Survivors (7)
Sussudio (3,5,8) 1
Take Me Home (3,5,8) 7
That's What You Said (7)

Thats Just The Way It Is (4)
There's A Place For Us (6)
This Must Be Love (1)
Thru These Walls (2)
Thunder And Lightning (1)
Times They Are A-Changin' (7)
Tomorrow Never Knows (1)
True Colors (8)
Two Hearts (5,8) 1
We Fly So Close (6)
We Wait And We Wonder (6)
We're Sons Of Our Fathers (6)

Wear My Hat (7)
West Side (2)
Who Said I Would (3,5) 73
Why Can't It Wait 'Til Morning (2)
You Can't Hurry Love (2,5,8) 10
You Know What I Mean (1)

COLLINS, Tyler   '90
Born in Harlem, New York; raised in Detroit. Female R&B singer.

| 5/26/90 | 85 | 22 | | © | 1 Girls Nite Out | | | $10 | RCA 9642 |

Beyond A Shadow Of A Doubt
Girls Nite Out 6

Give And Take
I Only Wanted

Love Talk
Second Chance 53

Strut
Two In Love

Whatcha Gonna Do
You And Me

COLOR ME BADD   '91
Vocal group from Oklahoma City: Bryan Abrams, Sam Watters, Mark Calderon and Kevin Thornton.

8/10/91	3	77	▲³	©	1 C.M.B.			$10	Giant 24429
1/16/93	189	1		©	2 Young, Gifted And Badd - The Remixes	[K]		$10	Giant 24480
12/4/93	56	17	●	©	3 Time And Chance			$10	Giant 24524
6/1/96	113	4		©	4 Now & Forever			$10	Giant 24622

Ain't Nobody Goin' Home (4)
All 4 Love (1,2) 1
Bells, The (3)
Choose (3) 23
Close To Heaven (3)
Color Me Badd (1,2)
Earth, The Sun, The Rain (4) 21

For All Eternity (3)
Forever Love (2)
From The Back (4)
God Is Love (3)
Groove My Mind (1)
Groovy Now (3)
Heartbreaker (1)
How Deep (3)

I Adore Mi Amor (1,2) 1
I Wanna Sex You Up (1,2) 2
In The Sunshine (3)
Last To Know (3)
Let Love Rule (3)
Let Me Have It All (3)
Let's Start With Forever (3)
Livin' Without Her (3)

On My Mind (4)
Ooh Tonight (4)
Roll The Dice (1,2)
Rosanna's Little Sister (3)
Sexual Capacity (4)
Slow Motion (1,2) 18
Soft N' Easy (4)
Thinkin' Back (1,2) 16

Time And Chance (3) 23
Tonite, Tonite (4)
Trust Me (3)
Wildflower (3)
Your Da One I Onena Love (1,2)

COLOSSEUM   '71
Jazz-rock group from England: Chris Farlowe (vocals; **Atomic Rooster**), Dave Clempson (guitar), Mark Clarke (bass), Dave Greenslade (organ), Dick Heckstall-Smith (sax) and Jon Hiseman (drums). Hiseman and Heckstall-Smith were with **John Mayall**'s Bluesbreakers.

| 11/20/71 | 192 | 3 | | © | Colosseum Live | [L] | | $20 | Warner 1942 [2] |

Lost Angeles
Rope Ladder To The Moon

Skelington

Stormy Monday Blues

Tanglewood '63'

Walking In The Park

COLTER, Jessi   '76
Born Mirriam Johnson on 5/25/43 in Phoenix. Country singer/songwriter. Married to **Duane Eddy** from 1961-68. Married **Waylon Jennings** in October 1969.

| 5/3/75 | 50 | 27 | | | 1 I'm Jessi Colter | | | $15 | Capitol 11363 |
| 2/7/76 | 10 | 51 | ▲² | © | 2 The Outlaws | | | $15 | RCA Victor 1321 |

WAYLON JENNINGS/WILLIE NELSON/JESSI COLTER/TOMPALL GLASER

2/7/76	109	8			3 Jessi			$15	Capitol 11477
8/7/76	79	8			4 Diamond In The Rough			$15	Capitol 11543
3/21/81	43	19	●		5 Leather And Lace			$12	RCA Victor 3931

WAYLON & JESSI

Ain't No Way (4)
All My Life, I've Been Your Lady (3)
Come On In (1)
Darlin' It's Yours (3)
Diamond In The Rough (4)
For The First Time (1)
Get Back (4)
Hand That Rocks The Cradle (3)

Here I Am (3)
Hey Jude (4)
I Ain't The One (1)
I Believe You Can (5)
I Hear A Song (1)
I See Your Face (In The Morning's Window) (3)
I Thought I Heard You Calling My Name (4)
I'll Be Alright (5)

I'm Looking For Blue Eyes (2)
I'm Not Lisa (1) 4
Is There Any Way (You'd Stay Forever) (1)
It's Morning (And I Still Love You) (3)
Love's The Only Chain (1)
Oh Will (Who Made It Rain Last Night) (4)
One Woman Man (3)

Pastels And Harmony (5)
Rainy Seasons (5)
Rounder (3)
Storms Never Last (1,5)
Suspicious Minds (2)
What's Happened To Blue Eyes (1,5) 57
Who Walks Thru Your Memory (Billy Jo) (1)
Wild Side Of Life (5)

Without You (3)
Woman's Heart (Is A Handy Place To Be) (4)
Would You Leave Now (4)
Would You Walk With Me (To The Lilies) (4)
You Ain't Never Been Loved (Like I'm Gonna Love You) (1) 64

You Hung The Moon (Didn't You Waylon?) (4)
You Mean To Say (2)
You Never Can Tell (C'est La Vie) (2)
You're Not My Same Sweet Baby (5)

COLTRANE, Alice   '74
Born Alice McLeod on 8/27/37 in Detroit. Jazz keyboardist. Married to **John Coltrane** until his death on 7/17/67.

| 11/13/71 | 190 | 2 | | | 1 Universal Consciousness | [I] | | $15 | Impulse! 9210 |
| 10/12/74 | 79 | 8 | | | 2 Illuminations | [I] | | $12 | Columbia 32900 |

TURIYA ALICE COLTRANE/DEVADIP CARLOS SANTANA

Angel Of Air (medley) (2)
Angel Of Sunlight (2)

Angel Of Water (medley) (2)
Ankh Of Amen-Ra (1)

Battle At Armageddon (1)
Bliss: The Eternal Now (2)

Guru Sri Chinmoy Aphorism (2)
Hare Krishna (1)

Illuminations (2)
Oh Allah (1)

Sita Ram (1)
Universal Consciousness (1)

COLTRANE, Chi   '72
Born on 11/16/48 in Racine, Wisconsin. Female singer/pianist.

| 9/23/72 | 148 | 10 | | | Chi Coltrane | | | $15 | Columbia 31275 |

Feelin' Good
Go Like Elijah

Goodbye John
I Will Not Dance

It's Really Come To This
Thunder And Lightning 17

Time To Come In
Tree, The

Turn Me Around
Wheel Of Life

You Were My Friend

COLTRANE, John   '71
Born on 9/23/26 in Hamlet, North Carolina. Died of cancer on 7/17/67 (age 40). Legendary jazz tenor saxophonist. With Dizzy Gillespie in the early 1950s, **Miles Davis** in 1955, **Thelonious Monk** in 1957, then solo. Married **Alice Coltrane** in 1966. Awarded Grammy's Lifetime Achievement Award in 1992.

11/18/67	194	3		©	1 Expression	[I]		$25	Impulse! 9120
11/13/71	186	3		©	2 Sun Ship	[E-I]		$20	Impulse! 9211
					recorded on 8/26/65				
2/17/01	21 C	2		©	3 A Love Supreme	[E-I]		$10	Impulse! 050155
					first released in 1965 on Impulse! 77 ($30)				

Acknowledgement (3)
Amen (2)
Ascent (2)

Attaining (2)
Dearly Beloved (2)
Expression (1)

Offering (1)
Ogunde (1)
Part 4 - Psalm (medley) (3)

Pursuance (medley) (3)
Resolution (3)
Sun Ship (2)

To Be (1)

COLVIN, Shawn '96

Born Shanna Colvin on 1/10/58 in Vermillion, South Dakota. Female folk singer. Backing vocalist for **Suzanne Vega**.

12/16/89+	111	24	©	1 **Steady On**		$10	Columbia 45209
11/14/92	142	14	©	2 **Fat City**		$10	Columbia 47122
9/10/94	48	11	©	3 **Cover Girl**		$10	Columbia 57875
10/19/96	39	52 ▲ ©	4 **A Few Small Repairs**		$10	Columbia 67119
12/19/98	181	2	©	5 **Holiday Songs And Lullabies**	[X]	$10	Columbia 69550
				Christmas chart: 18/'98			
4/14/01	101	7	©	6 **Whole New You**		$10	Columbia 69889

All The Pretty Li'l Horses (5)
All Through The Night (5)
Another Long One (1)
Another Plane Went Down (6)
Anywhere You Go (6)
Bonefields (6)
Bound To You (6)
Christ Child's Lullaby (5)
Christmas Time Is Here (5)
Climb On (A Back That's Strong) (2)
Close Your Eyes (5)
Cry Like An Angel (1)
Dead Of The Night (1)

Diamond In The Rough (1)
84,000 Different Delusions (4)
Evening Is A Little Boy (medley) (5)
Every Little Thing (He) Does Is Magic (3)
Facts About Jimmy (4)
Get Out Of This House (4)
I Don't Know Why (2)
I Want It Back (4)
I'll Say I'm Sorry Now (6)
If I Were Brave (4)
If These Walls Could Speak (4)
In The Bleak Mid-Winter (5)

Kill The Messenger (2)
Killing The Blues (3)
Little Road To Bethlehem (5)
(Looking For) The Heart Of Saturday Night (3)
Love Came Down At Christmas (5)
Matter Of Minutes (6)
Monopoly (2)
Mr. Levon (6)
New Thing Now (4)
Night Will Never Stay (medley) (5)
Nothin On Me (4)

Nothing Like You (6)
Now The Day Is Over (5)
Object Of My Affection (2)
One Cool Remove (6)
One Small Year (6)
Orion In The Sky (2)
Polaroids (2)
Ricochet In Time (1)
Rocking (5)
Roger Wilco (6)
Round Of Blues (2)
Satin Sheets (5)
Seal Lullaby (5)
Set The Prairie On Fire (2)

Shotgun Down The Avalanche (1)
Silent Night (5)
Someday (3)
Something To Believe In (1)
Steady On (1)
Story, The (1)
Stranded (1)
Suicide Alley (4)
Sunny Came Home (4) **7**
Tenderness On The Block (2)
Tennessee (2)
There's A Rugged Road (3)

This Must Be The Place (Naive Melody) (3)
Trouble (4)
Twilight (5)
Whole New You (6)
Wichita Skyline (4)
Window To The World (3)
Windy Nights (5)
You And The Mona Lisa (4)
You're Gonna Make Me Lonesome When You Go (3)

COMMAND ALL-STARS — see LIGHT, Enoch

COMMANDER CODY And His Lost Planet Airmen '75

Born George Frayne on 7/19/44 in Boise, Idaho; raised in Brooklyn, New York. Singer/keyboardist. His Lost Planet Airmen consisted of John Tichy, Don Bolton and Bill Kirchen (guitars), Andy Stein (fiddle, sax), Bruce Barlow (bass) and Lance Dickerson (drums).

11/27/71+	82	33	©	1 **Lost In The Ozone**		$15	Paramount 6017
9/9/72	94	13	©	2 **Hot Licks, Cold Steel & Truckers Favorites**		$15	Paramount 6031
6/16/73	104	9	©	3 **Country Casanova**		$15	Paramount 6054
2/16/74	105	14	©	4 **Live From Deep In The Heart Of Texas**	[L]	$15	Paramount 1017
				recorded November 1973 in Austin, Texas			
3/1/75	58	10		5 **Commander Cody & His Lost Planet Airmen**		$12	Warner 2847
10/11/75	168	6		6 **Tales From The Ozone**		$12	Warner 2883
7/31/76	170	3	©	7 **We've Got A Live One Here!**	[L]	$15	Warner 2939 [2]
9/3/77	163	5		8 **Rock 'N Roll Again**		$12	Arista 4125
				COMMANDER CODY BAND			

Armadillo Stomp (4)
Back To Tennessee (1,7)
Beat Me Daddy Eight To The Bar (1) **81**
Big Mammau (7)
Boogie Man Boogie (5)
Cajun Baby (4)
California Okie (5)
Connie (6)
Country Casanova (3)
Cravin' Your Love (2)
Crying Time (4)
Daddy's Gonna Treat You Right (1)
Danny (8)
Devil And Me (5)
Diggy Liggy Lo (2,4)

Don't Let Go (5,7) **56**
Don't Say Nothin' (8)
18 Wheels (7)
Everybody's Doin' It (3)
Family Bible (1)
Four Or Five Times (5)
Git It (4)
Good Rockin' Tonight (4)
Gypsy Fiddle (6)
Hawaii Blues (5)
Honeysuckle Honey (3)
Honky Tonk Music (6)
Hot Rod Lincoln (1,7) **9**
House Of Blue Lights (5)
I Been To Georgia On A Fast Train (6)
I'm Comin' Home (4)

It Should've Been Me (2,7)
It's Gonna Be One Of Those Nights (6,7)
Keep On Lovin' Her (5)
Kentucky Hills Of Tennessee (2)
Lightnin' Bar Blues (6)
Little Sally Walker (4)
Looking At The World Through A Windshield (2,7)
Lost In The Ozone (1,7)
Mama Hated Diesels (2,7)
Mean Woman Blues (4)
Midnight Man (8)
Midnight Shift (1)
Milkcow Blues (7)
Minnie The Moocher (6)

My Home In My Hand (1)
My Window Faces The South (3,7)
Oh Momma Momma (4)
One Man's Meat (Is Another Man's Poison) (3)
One Of Those Nights ..see: It's Gonna Be One Of Those Nights
Paid In Advance (6)
Rave On (3)
Riot In Cell Block #9 (4,7)
Rip It Up (3)
Rock N' Roll Again (8)
Rock That Boogie (3,7)
Roll Your Own (6)
San Antonio Rose (7)

Seeds And Stems (Again) (1,4,7)
Semi-Truck (2,7)
Seven-Eleven (8)
Shadow Knows (4)
Shall We Meet (Beyond The River) (3)
Sister Sue (3)
6 Years On The Road (8)
Smoke! Smoke! Smoke! (That Cigarette) (3,7) **94**
Snooze You Lose (8)
Southbound (5)
Sunset On The Sage (4)
That's What I Like About The South (5)
Tina Louise (7)

Too Much Fun (4,7)
Truck Drivin' Man (2)
Truck Stop Rock (2)
Tutti Fruitti (2)
20 Flight Rock (1)
Watch My .38 (2)
What's The Matter Now? (1)
Where Were You (8)
Widow (8)
Willin' (5)
Wine Do Yer Stuff (1)

COMMITMENTS, The '91

Group of Irish actors/musicians who starred in the movie of the same name: Robert Arkin, Michael Aherne, Angeline Ball, Maria Doyle, Dave Finnegan, Bronagh Gallagher, Glen Hansard, Dick Massey, Kenneth McCluskey, Johnny Murphy and Andrew Strong. All did their own performing.

9/14/91	8	76	▲² ©	1 **The Commitments**	[S]	$10	MCA 10286
4/4/92	118	12	©	2 **The Commitments - Vol. 2**	[S]	$10	MCA 10506

Bring It On Home To Me (2)
Bye Bye Baby (1)
Chain Of Fools (1)
Dark End Of The Street (1)
Destination Anywhere (1)

Do Right Woman Do Right Man (1)
Fa-Fa-Fa-Fa-Fa (Sad Song) (2)
Grits Ain't Groceries (2)
Hard To Handle (2)
I Can't Stand The Rain (1)

I Never Loved A Man (1)
I Thank You (2)
In The Midnight Hour (1)
Land Of A Thousand Dances (2)
Mr. Pitiful (1)

Mustang Sally (1)
Nowhere To Run (2)
Saved (2)
Show Me (2)
Slip Away (1)
Take Me To The River (1)

That's The Way Love Is (2)
Too Many Fish In The Sea (2)
Treat Her Right (1)
Try A Little Tenderness (1) **67**

COMMODORES ★149★ '77

R&B group formed in Tuskegee, Alabama: **Lionel Richie** (vocals, saxophone), Thomas McClary (guitar), William King (trumpet), Milan Williams (keyboards), Ronald LaPread (bass) and Walter "Clyde" Orange (drums). Group appeared in the movie *Thank God It's Friday*. Richie left group in 1982.

1)*Natural High* 2)*Commodores* 3)*Midnight Magic*

8/24/74	138	9		1 **Machine Gun**		$20	Motown 798
3/22/75	26	33	©	2 **Caught In The Act**		$15	Motown 820
11/8/75	29	32		3 **Movin' On**		$15	Motown 848
7/10/76	12	39	©	4 **Hot On The Tracks**		$15	Motown 867
4/2/77	3	53	©	5 **Commodores**		$15	Motown 884
11/12/77	3	28		6 **Commodores Live!**	[L]	$20	Motown 894 [2]

DEBUT	PEAK	WKS	RIAA	CD	ARTIST — Album Title	Catalog	Sym	$	Label & Number

COMMODORES — Cont'd

DEBUT	PEAK	WKS	RIAA	CD	#	ARTIST — Album Title	Sym	$	Label & Number
5/27/78	3	33	▲	©	7	Natural High		$12	Motown 902
11/25/78+	23	20		©	8	Commodores' Greatest Hits	[G]	$12	Motown 912
8/18/79	3	41		©	9	Midnight Magic		$12	Motown 926
6/28/80	7	33	▲	©	10	Heroes		$12	Motown 939
7/11/81	13	40	▲	©	11	In The Pocket		$12	Motown 955
12/4/82+	37	24		©	12	All The Great Hits	[G]	$12	Motown 6028
6/11/83	141	7			13	Commodores Anthology	[G]	$15	Motown 6044 [2]
10/1/83	103	11			14	Commodores 13		$12	Motown 6054
2/16/85	12	37	●		15	Nightshift		$12	Motown 6124
11/22/86	101	15			16	United		$10	Polydor 831194

All The Way Down (10)
Animal Instinct (15) *43*
Assembly Line (1)
Been Loving You (11)
Better Never Than Forever (2)
Brick House (5,6,8,12,13) *5*
Bump, The (1,2)
(Can I) Get A Witness (8)
Can't Dance All Night (16)
Can't Let You Tease Me (4)
Captured (14)
Cebu (3)
Celebrate (10)
Come Inside (4,6)
Don't You Be Worried (13)
Easy (5,6,8,12,13) *4*
Fancy Dancer (4,6,8,13) *39*
Fire Girl (7)
Flying High (7,13) *38*
Free (3)

Funky Situation (5)
Funny Feelings (5,6)
Gettin' It (9)
Gimme My Mule (3)
Girl, I Think The World About You (4)
Goin' To The Bank (16) *65*
Gonna Blow Your Mind (14)
Got To Be Together (10)
Heaven Knows (5)
High On Sunshine (4,13)
Hold On (3)
I Feel Sanctified (1,6,13) *75*
I Keep Running (15)
I Like What You Do (7)
I Wanna Rock You (16)
I'm In Love (14)
I'm Ready (1)
Janet (15) *87*

Jesus Is Love (10)
Just To Be Close To You (4,6,8,13) *7*
Keep On Taking Me Higher (11)
Lady (You Bring Me Up) (11,12) *8*
Land Of The Dreamer (16)
Lay Back (15)
Let's Apologize (16)
Let's Do It Right (2)
Let's Get Started (4)
Lightin' Up The Night (15)
Look What You've Done To Me (2)
Lovin' You (9)
Lucy (11)
Machine Gun (1,8,12,13) *22*
Mary, Mary (3)
Midnight Magic (9,13)
Mighty Spirit (10)

Nightshift (15) *3*
Nothing Like A Woman (14)
Oh No (11,12) *4*
Old-Fashion Love (10) *20*
Only You (14) *54*
Ooo, Woman You (14)
Painted Picture (12) *70*
Patch It Up (5)
Play This Record Twice (15)
Quick Draw (4)
Rapid Fire (1)
Reach High (12)
Sail On (9,12,13) *4*
Saturday Night (11)
Say Yeah (7)
Serious Love (16)
Sexy Lady (9)
Slip Of The Tongue (15)
Slippery When Wet (2,6,8,13) *19*

Sorry To Say (10)
Squeeze The Fruit (5)
Still (9,12,13) *1*
Such A Woman (7)
Superman (1)
Sweet Love (3,6,8,13) *5*
Take It From Me (16)
Talk To Me (14)
There's A Song In My Heart (1)
This Is Your Life (2,8,13)
This Love (11)
Three Times A Lady (7,8,12,13) *1*
Thumpin' Music (4)
Time (3)
Too Hot Ta Trot (6,8,13) *24*
Touchdown (14)
Turn Off The Lights (14)
12:01 A.M. (9)
United In Love (16)

Visions (7)
Wake Up Children (10)
Welcome Home (14)
Why You Wanna Try Me (11) *66*
Wide Open (2)
Woman In My Life (15)
Won't You Come Dance With Me (5,6)
Wonderland (9,13) *25*
X-Rated Movie (7)
You Don't Know That I Know (2)
You're Special (9)
You're The Only Woman I Need (16)
Young Girls Are My Weakness (1,13)
Zoo (The Human Zoo) (1,13)
Zoom (5,6,13)

COMMON '00

Born Lonnie Lynn in 1971 in Chicago. Male rapper.

DEBUT	PEAK	WKS	CD	#	ARTIST — Album Title	$	Label & Number
10/22/94	179	2	©	1	Resurrection	$10	Relativity 1208

COMMON SENSE

10/18/97	62	5	©	2	One Day It'll All Make Sense	$10	Relativity 1535
4/15/00	16	31	● ©	3	Like Water For Chocolate	$10	MCA 111970

All Night Long (2)
Book Of Life (1)
Chapter 13 (Rich Man Vs. Poor Man) (1)
Coldblooded (3)
Communism (1)
Dooinit (3)
Film Called (Pimp) (3)
Food For Funk (2)

Funky For You (3)
Geto Heaven Part Two (3)
Gettin' Down At The Amphitheater (2)
G.O.D. (Gaining One's Definition) (2)
Heat (3)
Hungry (2)
I Used To Love H.E.R. (1)

In My Own World (Check The Method) (1)
Introspective (2)
Invocation (2)
1 2 Many... (2)
Light, The (3) *44*
Maintaining (1)
Making A Name For Ourselves (2)
My City (2)

Nag Champa (Afrodisiac For The World) (3)
Nuthin' To Do (1)
Orange Pineapple Juice (1)
Payback Is A Grandmother (3)
Pop's Rap (1)
Pop's Rap Part 2/Fatherhood (2)

Pops Rap III...All My Children (3)
Questions, The (3)
Real Nigga Quotes (2)
Remind Me (Of Sef) (2)
Resurrection (1)
Retrospect For Life (2)
6th Sense (3)
Song For Assata (3)

Stolen Moments Pt. I, II & III (2)
Sum Shit I Wrote (1)
Thelonius (3)
Thisisme (1)
Time Travelin' (A Tribute To Fela) (3)
Watermelon (1)

COMMUNARDS '87

Dance duo. **Jimmy Somerville** (vocals) was born on 6/22/61 in Glasgow, Scotland. Richard Coles (keyboards) was born on 6/23/62 in Northampton, England. Somerville was also lead singer of **Bronski Beat**.

12/20/86+	90	16	©	1	Communards	$10	MCA 5794
2/6/88	93	9	©	2	Red	$10	MCA 42106

C Minor (2)
Disenchanted (1)
Don't Leave Me This Way (1) *40*
Don't Slip Away (1)

For A Friend (2)
Forbidden Love (1)
Heavens Above (1)
Hold On Tight (2)
If I Could Tell You (2)

La Dolarosa (1)
Lover Man (Oh, Where Can You Be?) (1)
Lovers And Friends (2)
Matter Of Opinion (2)

Never Can Say Goodbye (2) *51*
Reprise (1)
So Cold The Night (1)
T.M.T.♥.T.B.M.G. (2)

Tomorrow (1)
Victims (2)
You Are My World (1)

COMO, Perry ★110★ '57

Born Pierino Como on 5/18/12 in Canonsburg, Pennsylvania. Died on 5/12/2001 (age 88). Owned barbershop in hometown. With Freddy Carlone band in 1933; with Ted Weems from 1936-42. Appeared in several movies. Hosted own TV shows from 1948-63. One of the most popular singers of the 20th century.

1)So Smooth 2)We Get Letters 3)Merry Christmas Music 4)Dream Along With Me 5)When You Come To The End Of The Day

10/15/55	7	15	©	1	So Smooth		$30	RCA Victor 1085

LP: RCA Victor LPM-1085 (#7); EP: RCA Victor EPB-1085 (#10)

9/2/57	8	10	©	2	We Get Letters		$25	RCA Victor 1463
12/16/57	8	5	●	3	Merry Christmas Music	[X]	$25	RCA Victor 1243

charted for six consecutive seasons from 1946-51 on RCA Victor 161; Christmas charts: 17/'63, 15/'64, 53/'65, 63/'66, 16/'68

12/16/57	11	9	©	4	Dream Along With Me		$25	RCA Camden 403
6/23/58	18	2	©	5	Saturday Night With Mr. C.		$25	RCA Victor 1004
9/1/58	24	2	©	6	Como's Golden Records	[G]	$25	RCA Victor 1007

first released as a 10" album on RCA 3224 with a gold cover in April 1954; above 12" version added six more hits from October, 1954 - January, 1958

12/15/58	9	4		7	Merry Christmas Music	[X-R]	$25	RCA Victor 1243
1/5/59	16	7		8	When You Come To The End Of The Day		$25	RCA Victor 1885
11/2/59	17	12	©	9	Como Swings		$25	RCA Victor 2010
1/4/60	22	1	● ©	10	Season's Greetings	[X]	$20	RCA Victor 2066

Christmas charts: 5/'63, 34/'64, 15/'65, 11/'66, 22/'67, 17/'68

12/31/60	27	1	©	11	Season's Greetings	[X-R]	$20	RCA Victor 2066

DEBUT	PEAK	WKS	RIAA	CD	ARTIST — Album Title	Catalog	Sym	$	Label & Number

COMO, Perry — Cont'd

DEBUT	PEAK	WKS	RIAA	CD	ARTIST — Album Title	Sym	$	Label & Number
9/25/61	50	13		© 12	Sing To Me, Mr. C.		$20	RCA Victor 2390
1/6/62	33	3		© 13	Season's Greetings	[X-R]	$20	RCA Victor 2066
9/29/62	32	21		© 14	By Request		$20	RCA Victor 2567
12/8/62	90	6		15	The Best Of Irving Berlin's Songs From "Mr. President"		$20	RCA Victor 2630

includes "Is He The Only Man In The World" by **The Ray Charles Singers**; "The Secret Service" by **Sandy Stewart** and "Song For Belly Dancer" and "They Love Me" by Kaye Ballard

DEBUT	PEAK	WKS	RIAA	CD	ARTIST — Album Title	Sym	$	Label & Number
12/15/62	74	3		© 16	Season's Greetings	[X-R]	$20	RCA Victor 2066
9/21/63	59	18		17	The Songs I Love		$20	RCA Victor 2708
12/21/63+	15^X	15		18	Perry Como Sings Merry Christmas Music	[X]	$15	RCA Camden 660

reissue of album first charted in 1946 on RCA Victor 161 and in 1957 on RCA Victor 1243; Christmas charts: 17/'63, 15/'64, 55/'65, 63/'66, 16/'67, 16/'68

DEBUT	PEAK	WKS	RIAA	CD	ARTIST — Album Title	Sym	$	Label & Number
5/29/65	47	17		19	The Scene Changes		$15	RCA Victor 3396
6/11/66	86	9		20	Lightly Latin		$15	RCA Victor 3552
10/22/66	81	16		21	Perry Como In Italy		$15	RCA Victor 3608
6/21/69	93	11		22	Seattle		$15	RCA Victor 4183
12/5/70	5^X	5	●	© 23	The Perry Como Christmas Album	[X]	$15	RCA Victor 4016

first released in 1968; Christmas charts: 5/'70, 18/'73

DEBUT	PEAK	WKS	RIAA	CD	ARTIST — Album Title	Sym	$	Label & Number
1/16/71	22	27		© 24	It's Impossible		$15	RCA Victor 4473
6/26/71	101	9		25	I Think Of You		$15	RCA Victor 4539
5/26/73	34	19	●	© 26	And I Love You So		$12	RCA Victor 0100
8/17/74	138	10		27	Perry		$12	RCA Victor 0585
12/20/75+	142	9		28	Just Out Of Reach		$12	RCA Victor 0863

Accentuate The Positive (medley) (5)
All By Myself (medley) (12)
All I Do Is Dream Of You (medley) (12)
All Through The Night (8)
Almost Like Being In Love (medley) (5)
And I Love You So (26) *29*
And Roses And Roses (20)
Anema E Core (21)
Angry (2)
Arrivederci Roma (Goodbye To Rome) (21)
As Time Goes By (1)
Aubrey (26)
Ave Maria (23)
Baia (20)
Beady Eyed Buzzard (22)
Because (6)
Begin The Beguine (9)
Behind Closed Doors (27)
Between The Devil And The Deep Blue Sea (5)
Beyond Tomorrow (27)
Birth Of The Blues (5)
Blue Skies (4,12)
Breezin' Along With The Breeze (1)
Brian's Song ..see: Hands Of Time
Bridge Over Troubled Water (25)
Buongiorno Teresa (22)
Can't Help Falling In Love (14)
Carnival (17)
Caroling, Caroling (medley) (23)
Catch A Falling Star (6) *1*
Chincherinchee (4) *59*
Christ Is Born (23)
C-H-R-I-S-T-M-A-S (3,7,18)
Christmas Eve (23)
Christmas Song (Merry Christmas To You) (3,7,10,11,13,16,18)
Come, Come, Come To The Manger (medley) (10,11,13,16)
Come Rain Or Come Shine (5)
Cominciano Ad Amarci (21)
Coo Coo Roo Coo Coo Paloma (20)
Days Of Wine And Roses (17)
Dear Hearts And Gentle People (9)
'Deed I Do (2)
Deep In Your Heart (22)
Dindi (20)
Do You Hear What I Hear? (23)
Don't Let The Stars Get In Your Eyes (6)
Donkey Serenade (9)
Dream Along With Me (I'm On My Way To A Star) (4,5) *85*
Dream Baby (How Long Must I Dream) (25)

Dream On Little Dreamer (19) *25*
E Lei (To You) (21)
El Condor Pasa (24)
Empty Pockets Filled With Love (15)
Everybody Is Looking For An Answer (24)
Fellow Needs A Girl (medley) (12)
First Lady (15)
First Noel (medley) (10,11,13,16,23)
Fly Me To The Moon (In Other Words) (17)
For All We Know (25)
For Me And My Gal (1)
For The Good Times (26)
Forget Domani (21)
Frosty The Snow Man (3,7)
Frosty The Snow Man (18)
Funny How Time Slips Away (19)
Gigi (medley) (12)
Girl Of My Dreams (4)
Give Myself A Party (19)
Glad To Be Home (15)
God Rest Ye Merry Gentlemen (3,7,10,11,13,16,18)
Grass Keeps Right On Growin' (28)
Gringo's Guitar (19)
Gypsy In My Soul (medley) (5)
Hands Of Time (Brian's Song) (27)
Happiness Comes, Happiness Goes (22)
Hark! The Herald Angels Sing (medley) (23)
Hatchet, A Hammer, A Bucket Of Nails (19)
Have Yourself A Merry Little Christmas (23)
Hawaiian Wedding Song (17)
He's Got The Whole World In His Hands (8)
Hearts Will Be Hearts (22)
Here Comes My Baby (19)
Here, There And Everywhere (22)
Here We Come A-Caroling (medley) (10,11,13,16)
Here's That Rainy Day (medley) (12)
Home For The Holidays (10,11,13,16)
Honey, Honey (Bless Your Heart) (2,9)
Hot Diggity (Dog Ziggity Boom) (6) *1*
House Is Not A Home (24)
How Deep Is The Ocean (medley) (12)
How Insensitive (Insensatez) (20)
Hubba-Hubba-Hubba (6)

I Believe In Music (26)
I Don't Know What He Told You (27)
I Gotta Right To Sing The Blues (1)
I Had The Craziest Dream (2)
I Left My Heart In San Francisco (17)
I May Be Wrong (medley) (5)
I May Never Pass This Way Again (8)
I Really Don't Want To Know (19)
I Think I Love You (24)
I Think Of You (25) *53*
I Thought About You (26)
I Wanna Be Around (17)
I Want To Give (26)
I'll Be Home For Christmas (3,7,18)
I'll Remember April (14)
I'm Gonna Get Him (15)
I'm Gonna Sit Right Down And Write Myself A Letter (medley) (12)
I've Got A Feeling I'm Falling (4)
I've Got The World On A String (1)
I've Got You Under My Skin (9)
I've Grown Accustomed To Her Face (medley) (12)
If (25)
If I Loved You (4)
In Our Hide-Away (15)
In The Garden (8)
In The Still Of The Night (1)
Is She The Only Girl In The World (15)
It All Seems To Fall Into Line (26)
It Could Happen To You (5)
It Gets Lonely In The White House (15)
It Had To Be You (5)
It Happened In Monterey (1)
It's A Good Day (1)
It's Easy To Remember (2)
It's Impossible (24) *10*
It's The Talk Of The Town (1)
Jingle Bells (3,7,18) *74*
Joy To The World! (3,7,18)
Just Out Of Reach (28)
Killing Me Softly With Her Song (26)
La Strada, Love Theme From (21)
Let A Smile Be Your Umbrella (On A Rainy Day) (9)
Let It Be Love (28)
Let Me Call You Baby Tonight (28)
Let's Do It Again (28)
Like Someone In Love (medley) (5)
Linda (9)
Little Drummer Boy (23)

Little Man You've Had A Busy Day (medley) (5)
Lollipops And Roses (14)
Love Letters (5)
Love Put A Song In My Heart (28)
Loving Her Was Easier (Than Anything I'll Ever Do Again) (28)
Magic Moments (6) *4*
Make Love To Life (28)
Manha De Carnaval (20)
Maria (14)
May The Good Lord Bless And Keep You (8)
Me And My Shadow (4)
Me And You And A Dog Named Boo (25)
Meditation (Meditacao) (20)
Mi Casa, Su Casa (My House Is Your House) (6) *50*
Mood Indigo (9)
Moon River (14)
Moonglow And Theme From "Picnic" (14)
More Than Likely (14)
More Than You Know (4)
Most Beautiful Girl (27)
My Coloring Book (17)
My Days Of Loving You (25)
My Favorite Things (14)
My Funny Valentine (1)
My Melancholy Baby (4)
My Own Peculiar Way (19)
No Well On Earth (8)
Nobody But You (22)
O Come, All Ye Faithful (Adeste Fideles) (3,7,10,11,13,16,18)
O Holy Night (10,11,13,16,23)
O Little Town Of Bethlehem (medley) (10,11,13,16)
O Marenariello (21)
Oh, How I Miss You Tonight (4)
Oh Marie (21)
Once I Loved (Amor E Paz) (20)
Once Upon A Time (14)
One For My Baby (1)
Only One (8)
Papa Loves Mambo (6)
Pigtails And Freckles (8)
Portrait Of My Love (medley) (12)
Prayer For Peace (8)
Prisoner Of Love (4)
Put Your Hand In The Hand (25)
Quiet Nights Of Quiet Stars (Corcovado) (20)
Raindrops Keep Fallin' On My Head (24)
Red Sails In The Sunset (5)
Round And Round (6) *1*
Route 66 (9)
Rudolph The Red-Nosed Reindeer (3,7,10,11,13,16,18)

Santa Claus Is Comin' To Town (3,7,10,11,13,16)
Santa Lucia (21)
Say It Isn't So (medley) (12)
Scarlet Ribbons (8)
Seattle (22) *38*
Serpico, Love Theme From ..see: Beyond Tomorrow
Shadow Of Your Smile (20)
Silent Night (3,7,10,11,13,16,18,23)
Silver Bells (23)
Sing (26)
Sing To Me, Mr. C (medley) (12)
Sleepy Time Gal (2)
Slightly Out Of Tune (Desafinado) (17)
Smile (medley) (12)
Snowbird (24)
So In Love (medley) (12)
Somebody Cares (14)
Somebody Loves Me (2)
Someone Who Cares (25)
Something (24)
Songs I Love (17)
South Of The Border (2)
Souvenir D'Italie (21)
Sposin' (2)
St. Louis Blues (9)
Stand Beside Me (19)
Stay With Me (20)
Still Small Voice (8)
Sunshine Wine (22)
Sweet Adorable You (19)
Sweetest Sounds (14)
Swinging Down The Lane (2)
Temptation (6,27)
Thank Heaven For Little Girls (medley) (12)
That Ain't All (19)
That Christmas Feeling (3,7,18)
That's All This Old World Needs (22)
That's What I Like (2)
That's You (Eres Tu) (27)
Then You Can Tell Me Goodbye (28)
There Is No Christmas Like A Home Christmas (23)
They Can't Take That Away From Me (2)
(They Long To Be) Close To You (24)
They Say It's Wonderful (4)
This Is A Great Country (15)
This Is All I Ask (17)
This Nearly Was Mine (medley) (12)
Tie A Yellow Ribbon Round The Ole Oak Tree (26)
Till The End Of Time (4)
To Know You Is To Love You (9)
Together Forever (22)

Toselli's Serenade (Dreams And Memories) (21)
Toyland (23)
(Traveling Down A Lonely Road) ..see: La Strada, Love Theme From
Turnaround (22)
'Twas The Night Before Christmas (3,7,18)
Twelve Days Of Christmas (3,7,18)
Twilight On The Trail (medley) (5)
Un Giorno Dopo L'Altro (One Day Is Like Another) (21)
Vaya Con Dios (medley) (5)
Wanted (6)
Way We Were (27)
Way You Look Tonight (medley) (12)
We Three Kings Of Orient Are (medley) (10,11,13,16)
We Wish You A Merry Christmas (medley) (10,11,13,16)
We've Only Just Begun (24)
Weave Me The Sunshine (27)
What Kind Of Fool Am I? (17)
What's New? (14)
When I Fall In Love (5)
When I Lost You (17)
When You Come To The End Of The Day (9)
When You Were Sweet Sixteen (6)
Where Do I Begin (25)
Where Does A Little Tear Come From (19)
Whiffenpoof Song (medley) (5)
White Christmas (3,7,10,11,13,16,18)
Whither Thou Goest (8)
Winter Wonderland (3,7,10,11,13,16,18)
Without A Song (4)
Yesterday (27)
Yesterday I Heard The Rain (25)
You Alone (Solo Tu) (medley) (12)
You Are Never Far Away (5,12)
You Are The Sunshine Of My Life (27)
You Came A Long Way From St. Louis (2)
You Do Something To Me (1)
You Made Me Love You (medley) (12)
You Were Meant For Me (medley) (12)

COMPANY B '87
Female dance trio from Miami: Lori L, Lezlee Livrano and Susan Johnson.

7/18/87 — **143** — 6 — © — **Company B** .... **$10** — Atlantic 81763

Fascinated *21*
Full Circle

| I'm Satisfied | Jam On Me | Signed In Your Book Of Love |
| Infatuate Me | Perfect Lover | Spin Me Around |

COMPANY OF WOLVES '90
Hard-rock group from New York City: Kyf Brewer (vocals), Steve Conte (guitar), John Conte (bass) and Frankie Larocka (drums).

3/17/90 — **166** — 6 — © — **Company Of Wolves** .... **$10** — Mercury 842184

Call Of The Wild
Can't Love Ya, Can't Leave Ya

| Distance, The | Girl | Hell's Kitchen | Jilted! | Romance On The Rocks |
| Everybody's Baby | Hangin' By A Thread | I Don't Wanna Be Loved | My Ship | St. Jane's Infirmary |

COMPTON'S MOST WANTED '94
Rap group from Los Angeles. Fronted by MC Eiht.

7/7/90 — **133** — 7 — © — 1 **It's A Compton Thang** .... **$10** — Orpheus 75627
8/3/91 — **92** — 9 — © — 2 **Straight Checkn 'Em** .... **$10** — Orpheus 47926
10/17/92 — **66** — 9 — © — 3 **Music To Driveby** .... **$10** — Orpheus 52984

MC EIHT Featuring CMW:

8/6/94 — **5** — 14 — ● — © — 4 **We Come Strapped** .... **$10** — Epic Street 57696

4/27/96 — **16** — 8 — © — 5 **Death Threatz** .... **$10** — Epic Street 67139

Ain't Nuthin 2 It (5)	Def Wish III (4)	Goin' Out Like Geez (4)	Jack Mode (3)	Nuthin' But The Gangsta (4)	U's A Bitch (3)
All For The Money (4)	Def Wish IV (Tap That Azz) (5)	Growin' Up In The Hood (2)	Killin Nigguz (3)	One Time Gaffled Em Up (1)	Wanted (2)
Another Victim (3)	Driveby Miss Daisy (2)	Hard Times (4)	Killin Season (5)	Raised In Compton (2)	We Come Strapped (4)
Can I Kill It? (2)	Drugs & Killin (5)	Hit The Floor (3)	Late Night Hype (1)	Rhymes Too Funky Pt. 1 (1)	Who's Xxxxing Who? (3)
Can I Still Kill It (4)	Duck Sick (1)	Hood Took Me Under (1)	Late Nite Hype Part 2 (5)	Run 4 Your Life (5)	You Can't See Me (5)
Collect My Stripez (5)	Duck Sick II (3)	Hoodrat (3)	Love 4 Tha Hood (5)	Set Trippin (5)	
Compton Bomb (4)	8 Iz Enough (3)	I Don't Dance (2)	Mike T's Funky Scratch (1)	Straight Checkn 'Em (2)	
Compton Cyco (4)	Endoness (5)	I Give Up Nuthin (1)	Music To Driveby (3)	Take 2 With Me (4)	
Compton 4 Life (3)	Final Chapter (1)	I Gots Ta Get Over (3)	Niggaz Make The Hood Go	They Still Gafflin (2)	
Compton's Lynchin (2)	Fuc Em All (5)	I Mean Biznez (1)	Round (4)	This Is A Gang (3)	
Dead Men Tell No Lies (3)	Fuc Your Hood (5)	I'm Wit Dat (1)	Niggaz Strugglin (3)	This Is Compton (1)	
Def Wish (2)	Gangsta Shot Out (2)	N 2 Deep (3)	Niggaz That Kill (4)	Thuggin It Up (5)	
Def Wish II (3)	Give It Up (1)	It's A Compton Thang (1)	Nuthin' But High (4)	2 Tha Westside (4)	

COMRADS, The '97
Rap duo from Los Angeles: K-Mac and Gangsta.

7/26/97 — **113** — 2 — © — 1 **The Comrads** .... **$10** — Street Life 75507
7/22/00 — **153** — 2 — © — 2 **Wake Up & Ball** .... **$10** — Hoo-Bangin' 50001

All Nighter (2)	Bustas (1)	Dem Comrads (2)	Get At Me (Call Me) (1)	Playa Hata (1)	Thug Niggaz (2)
Big Ballers (1)	Candy Land (1)	Die Hard (1)	Hey You (1)	Speak On It (2)	Wanna B Gangsta (2)
Bitch Made Niggas (1)	Click Click Bang (1)	Easy Breezy (1)	Homeboyz (1)	Streets Is Talkin' (2)	Westside Connect OG's (1)
Bom Bom (2)	Copped & Dropped (2)	Game Recognize Game (1)	Murder Murder (2)	That There (2)	

CONCENTRATION CAMP II '98
Gathering of solo rappers: **Young Bleed**, C-Loc, Lay Lo, Lucky Knuckles and Boo The Boss Playa.

5/30/98 — **84** — 2 — © — **Da Holocaust** .... **$10** — Priority 53536

Cabbage Savage
Candy And Cream
Comin' Down

Didn't Mean To Do It	Grind	Sickess	What's Love
Dog-Ass Hoes	Nothin' To Lose	Solitaire	When Times Get Rough
Fool (Original)	Outside My Life	Still In All	Where The Playas At

CONCRETE BLONDE '90
Rock group from Los Angeles: Johnette Napolitano (vocals, bass), James Andrew Mankey (guitar) and Harry Rushakoff (drums). Paul Thompson replaced Rushakoff in early 1990; Rushakoff returned in late 1991, replacing Thompson. Group originally known as Dream 6, renamed by Michael Stipe of **R.E.M.**

2/21/87 — **96** — 16 — © — 1 **Concrete Blonde** .... **$10** — I.R.S. 5835
5/13/89 — **148** — 18 — © — 2 **Free** .... **$10** — I.R.S. 82001
6/9/90 — **49** — 44 — ● — © — 3 **Bloodletting** .... **$10** — I.R.S. 82037
3/28/92 — **73** — 15 — © — 4 **Walking In London** .... **$10** — I.R.S. 13137
11/6/93 — **67** — 5 — © — 5 **Mexican Moon** .... **$10** — Capitol 81129

Bajo La Lune Mexicana (5)	Dance Along The Edge (1)	I Call It Love (5)	Jonestown (5)	Over Your Shoulder (1)	Tomorrow, Wendy (3)
Beast, The (3)	Darkening Of The Light (3)	I Don't Need A Hero (3)	Les Coeurs Jumeaux (4)	Rain (5)	True (1)
Beware Of Darkness (1)	Days And Days (3)	I Wanna Be Your Friend Again	Little Conversations (2)	Roses Grow (2)	Walking In London (4)
Bloodletting (The Vampire	End Of The Line (3)	(4)	Little Sister (1)	Run Run Run (2)	When You Smile (5)
Song) (3)	Ghost Of A Texas Ladies' Man	It's A Man's World (4)	...Long Time Ago (4)	Scene Of A Perfect Crime (2)	Why Don't You See Me (4)
Caroline (3)	(4)	It's Only Money (2)	(Love Is A) Blind Ambition (5)	Sky Is A Poisonous Garden (3)	Woman To Woman (4)
Carry Me Away (2)	God Is A Bullet (2)	Jenny I Read (5)	Lullabye (3)	Someday? (4)	Your Haunted Head (1)
City Screaming (4)	Happy Birthday (2)	Jesus Forgive Me (For The	Make Me Cry (1)	Song For Kim (She Said) (1)	
Close To Home (5)	Heal It Up (5)	Things I'm About To Say) (5)	Mexican Moon (5)	Still In Hollywood (1)	
Cold Part Of Town (1)	Help Me (2)	**Joey** (3) *19*	One Of My Kind (5)	Sun (2)	

CONDON, Mark '00
Born in Lancaster, Ohio. Christian choral director.

9/9/00 — **106** — 3 — © — **Marvelous Things** .... **$10** — Hosanna! 17802

All Of Our Praise
Angels (medley)
Giving My Best

His Eye Is On The Sparrow	I'm Loving You More Each Day	Lord You're Worthy	We Seek Your Face
(medley)	Jesus Is The Way	Marvelous Things	You Reign
Holy Is Thy Name	Let Us Come Into This House	My Savior's Love	

CONEY HATCH '83
Rock group from Toronto: Carl Dixon (vocals), Steve Shelski (guitar), Andy Curran (bass) and Dave Ketchum (drums).

9/17/83 — **186** — 2 — **Outa Hand** .... **$10** — Mercury 812869

Don't Say Make Me
Fallen Angel

| First Time For Everything | Music Of The Night | Some Like It Hot | Too Far Gone |
| Love Games | Shake It | To Feel The Feeling Again | |

CONFEDERATE RAILROAD '93

Country-rock group from Marietta, Georgia: Danny Shirley (vocals), Michael Lamb (guitar), Gates Nichols (steel guitar), Chris McDaniel (keyboards), Wayne Secrest (bass) and Mark DuFresne (drums). In 1995, Jimmy Dormire replaced Lamb.

DEBUT	PEAK	WKS	RIAA	CD			$	Label & Number
9/19/92+	53	80	▲²	©	1 Confederate Railroad		$10	Atlantic 82335
4/9/94	52	22	▲	©	2 Notorious		$10	Atlantic 82505
7/8/95	152	5		©	3 When And Where		$10	Atlantic 82774

All I Wanted (3)
Bill's Laundromat, Bar And Grill (3)
Black Label, White Lies (1)
Daddy Never Was The Cadillac Kind (2)
Elvis And Andy (3)
Hunger Pains (2)
I Am Just A Rebel (2)
Jesus And Mama (1)
Long Gone (1)
Move Over Madonna (2)
My Baby's Lovin' (3)
Notorious (2)
Oh No (3)
Queen Of Memphis (1)
Redneck Romeo (2)
Right Track Wrong Train (3)
Roll The Dice (2)
See Ya (3)
She Never Cried (3)
She Took It Like A Man (3)
Sounds Of Home (3)
Summer In Dixie (2)
Three Verses (2)
Time Off For Bad Behavior (1)
Toss A Little Bone (3)
Trashy Women (1)
When And Where (3)
When He Was My Age (3)
When You Leave That Way You Can Never Go Back (1)
You Don't Know What It's Like (1)

★421★ CON FUNK SHUN '80

Funk group from Vallejo, California: **Michael Cooper** (vocals, guitar), Danny Thomas (keyboards), Karl Fuller, Paul Harrell and Felton Pilate (horns), Cedric Martin (bass) and Louis McCall (drums). and Louis McCall (drums).
1)*Spirit Of Love* 2)*Loveshine* 3)*Candy*

DEBUT	PEAK	WKS	RIAA	CD			$	Label & Number
10/15/77	51	28	●	©	1 Secrets		$12	Mercury 1180
7/1/78	32	19	●		2 Loveshine		$12	Mercury 3725
6/2/79	46	22	●		3 Candy		$12	Mercury 3754
4/12/80	30	20	●	©	4 Spirit Of Love		$12	Mercury 3806
12/13/80+	51	19			5 Touch		$12	Mercury 4002
12/12/81+	82	13			6 Con Funk Shun 7		$12	Mercury 4030
12/4/82	115	29			7 To The Max		$12	Mercury 4067
12/3/83+	105	21			8 Fever		$10	Mercury 814447
5/18/85	62	26		©	9 Electric Lady		$10	Mercury 824345
7/19/86	121	11		©	10 Burnin' Love		$10	Mercury 826963

Ain't Nobody, Baby (7)
All Up To You (4)
Baby, I'm Hooked (Right Into Your Love) (8) *76*
Bad Lady (6)
Body Lovers (6)
Burnin' Love (10)
By Your Side (4)
California 1 (6)
Can You Feel The Groove Tonight (4)
Can't Go Away (2)
Can't Say Goodbye (5)
Candy (3)
Chase Me (3)
Circle Of Love (9)
ConFunkShunizeYa (1)
Curtain Call (4)
Da Lady (3)
Do Ya (10)
Don't Go (I Want You Back) (9)
Don't Let Your Love Grow Cold (8)
DooWhaChaWannaDoo (1)
Early Morning Sunshine (4)
Electric Lady (9)
Everlove (7)
Fire When Ready (3)
Give Your Love To Me (5)
Got To Be Enough (4)
Happy Face (4)
Hard Lovin' (8)
Hide And Freak (7)
Honey Wild (4)
How Long (10)
I Think I Found The Answer (2)
I'll Get You Back (8)
I'll Set You Out O.K. (1)
I'm Leaving Baby (9)
If I'm Your Lover (8)
If You're In Need Of Love (6)
Images (3)
Indian Summer Love (1)
Indiscreet Sweet (8)
It's Time Girl (10)
Jo Jo (10)
Juicy (4)
Kidnapped! (5)
Lady's Wild (5)
(Let Me Put) Love On Your Mind (3)
Let's Ride And Slide (7)
Love's Train (7)
Loveshine (2)
Lovestruck 1980 (4)
Lovin' Fever (8)
Magic Woman (4)
Main Slice (3)
Make It Last (3)
Ms. Got The Body (7)
Not Ready (3)
Play Widit (5)
Pretty Lady (9)
Pride And Glory (5)
Promise You Love (6)
Rock It All Night (9)
Secrets (1)
Shake And Dance With Me (2) *60*
She's A Star (10)
She's Sweet (10)
So Easy (2)
Song For You (6)
Spirit Of Love (4)
Straight From The Heart (6)
T.H.E. Freak (7)
Take It To The Max (7)
Tears In My Eyes (1)
Tell Me What You're Gonna Do (9)
Thinking About You, Baby (8)
Too Tight (5) *40*
Touch (5)
Turn The Music Up (9)
Wanna Be There (4)
Welcome Back To Love (5)
When The Feeling's Right (2)
Who Has The Time (1)
You Are The One (7)
You Make Me Wanna Love Again (10)

CONJUNTO PRIMAVERA '01

Latin group from Chihuahua, Mexico: Tony Melendez (vocals), Rolando Perez (guitar), Felix Contreras (keyboards), Juan Dominguez (sax), Oscar Ochoa (bass) and Adan Huerta (drums).

DEBUT	PEAK	WKS	RIAA	CD			Sym	$	Label & Number
2/12/00	153	4	●	©	1 Morir De Amor		[F]	$10	Fonovisa 9926
					title is Spanish for "Love Dies Out"				
4/14/01	139	5		©	2 Ansia De Amar		[F]	$10	Fonovisa 6104
					title is Spanish for "Longing For Love"				

Amiga (2)
Cinco Lagrimas (1)
De Golpe En Golpe (2)
Derecho A La Vida (2)
Dime, Dime, Dime (1)
El Mas Triste (2)
En Cada Gota De Mi Sangre (1)
Enamorado De Ti (1)
Irremediablemente (2)
Jugando Al Amor (1)
Maldita Seas (1)
Mexico Ra, Ra, Ra (1)
Morir De Amor (1)
No Como Amigo (1)
No Se Vivir Sin Ti (1)
No Te Podias Quedar (2)
Quiero Verte Otra Vez (2)
Regresa A Mi Lado (2)
Si Te Vuelvo A Ver (2)
Y Otra Vez (1)

CONLEE, John '83

Born on 8/11/46 in Versailles, Kentucky. Country singer.

DEBUT	PEAK	WKS	RIAA	CD			Sym	$	Label & Number
6/11/83	166	6	●	©	John Conlee's Greatest Hits		[G]	$10	MCA 5405

Baby, You're Something
Backside Of Thirty
Busted
Common Man
Friday Night Blues
I Don't Remember Loving You
Lady Lay Down
Miss Emily's Picture
Rose Colored Glasses
She Can't Say That Anymore

CONLEY, Arthur '67

Born on 4/1/46 in Atlanta. R&B singer.

DEBUT	PEAK	WKS	RIAA	CD			$	Label & Number
5/13/67	93	13			1 Sweet Soul Music		$40	Atco 215
8/19/67	193	2			2 Shake, Rattle & Roll		$40	Atco 220
7/6/68	185	2			3 Soul Directions		$40	Atco 243

Baby What You Want Me To Do (2)
Burning Fire (3)
Change Is Gonna Come (2)
Funky Street (3) *14*
Get Yourself Another Fool (3)
Ha! Ha! Ha! (2)
Hand And Glove (2)
Hear Say (3)
I Can't Stop (No, No, No) (1)
I'll Take The Blame (3)
I'm A Lonely Stranger (1)
I'm Gonna Forget About You (1)
I've Been Loving You Too Long (To Stop Now) (2)
Keep On Talking (2)
Let Nothing Separate Us (1)
Love Comes And Goes (3)
Love Got Me (2)
Otis Sleep On (3)
People Sure Act Funny (3) *58*
Put Our Love Together (3)
Shake, Rattle & Roll (2) *31*
Sweet Soul Music (1) *2*
Take Me (Just As I Am) (1)
There's A Place For Us (1)
This Love Of Mine (3)
Where You Lead Me (1)
Who's Foolin' Who (1)
Wholesale Love (1)
You Don't Have To See Me (2)
You Really Know How To Hurt A Guy (3)

CONNELLS, The '89

Rock group from Raleigh, North Carolina: brothers Mike (guitar) and David (bass) Connell with Doug MacMillan (vocals), Peele Wimberley (drums) and George Huntley (guitar). Steve Potak (keyboards) joined by 1993.

DEBUT	PEAK	WKS	RIAA	CD			$	Label & Number
5/6/89	163	10		©	1 Fun & Games		$10	TVT 2550
11/10/90+	168	18		©	2 One Simple Word		$10	TVT 2580
10/16/93	199	1		©	3 Ring		$10	TVT 2590

All Sinks In (2)
Another Souvenir (2)
Any Day Now (3)
Burden (3)
Carry My Picture (3)
Disappointed (3)
Doin' You (3)
Eyes On The Ground (3)
Find Out (3)
Fun & Games (2)
Get A Gun (2)
Hey Wow (1)
Hey You (3)
Inside My Head (1)
Joke, The (2)
Lay Me Down (1)
Link (2)
Motel (1)
New Boy (3)
One Simple Word (2)
Running Mary (3)
Sal (1)
Sat Nite (USA) (1)
Set The Stage (2)
'74-'75 (3)
Slackjawed (1)
Something To Say (1)
Speak To Me (2)
Spiral (3)
Stone Cold Yesterday (2)
Take A Bow (2)
Ten Pins (1)
Too Gone (2)
Uninspired (1)
Upside Down (1)
Waiting My Turn (2)
What Do You Want? (2)

★275★ CONNICK, Harry Jr. '94

Born on 9/11/67 in New Orleans. Jazz-pop singer/pianist/actor. Acted in several movies. Married model/actress Jill Goodacre in 1994.

1)When My Heart Finds Christmas 2)She 3)Blue Light, Red Light

8/19/89	42	122	▲²	©	1 **When Harry Met Sally...**		[S]	$10	Columbia 45319
7/21/90+	22	96	▲²	©	2 **We Are In Love**	C:#46/1		$10	Columbia 46146
7/21/90	94	11		©	3 **Lofty's Roach Souffle**		[I]	$10	Columbia 46223

HARRY CONNICK, JR. TRIO
trio includes Benjamin Wolfe (bass) and Shannon Powell (drums)

5/25/91+	133	44	▲	©	4 **20**		[E]	$10	Columbia 44369

recorded in 1987

10/12/91+	17	51	▲²	©	5 **Blue Light, Red Light**			$10	Columbia 48685
12/12/92+	19	18	▲	©	6 **25**			$10	Columbia 53172
11/13/93+	13	10	▲²	©	7 **When My Heart Finds Christmas**	C:❶¹/50	[X]	$10	Columbia 57550

Christmas charts: 1/'93, 3/'94, 4/'95, 7/'96, 8/'97, 23/'98, 20/'99, 22/'00

7/30/94	16	33	▲	©	8 **She**			$10	Columbia 64376
7/20/96	38	12		©	9 **Star Turtle**			$10	Columbia 67575
11/29/97	53	15	●	©	10 **To See You**			$10	Columbia 68787
6/19/99	36	13	●	©	11 **Come By Me**			$10	Columbia 69618

After You've Gone (6)
Autumn In New York (1)
Avalon (4)
Ave Maria (7)
Basin Street Blues (4)
Between Us (8)
Blessed Dawn Of Christmas Day (7)
Blessing And A Curse (5)
Blue Light, Red Light (Someone's There) (5)
Blue Skies (4)
Booker (8)
Boozehound (9)
Buried In Blue (2)
But Not For Me (1)
Caravan (6)
Change Partners (11)
Charade (11)
Christmas Dreaming (7)
City Beneath The Sea (9)
Colomby Day (5)
Come By Me (11)
Cry Me A River (11)
Danny Boy (11)
Didn't He Ramble (6)

Do Nothin' Till You Hear From Me (4)
Do You Know What It Means To Miss New Orleans (4)
Don't Get Around Much Anymore (1)
Drifting (2)
Easy For You To Say (11)
Easy To Love (11)
Eyes Of The Seeker (9)
Forever, For Now (2)
Funky Dunky (8)
Harronymous (3)
He Is They Are (5)
Hear Me In The Harmony (9)
Heart Beyond Repair (10)
Heavenly (2)
Here Comes The Big Parade (8)
Honestly Now (Safety's Just Danger...Out Of Place) (8)
How Do Ya'll Know (9)
Hudson Bommer (3)
(I Could Only) Whisper Your Name (8) *67*
I Could Write A Book (1)

I Pray On Christmas (7)
I'll Dream Of You Again (2)
I'm An Old Cowhand (From The Rio Grande) (6)
I've Got A Great Idea (2)
If I Could Give You More (5)
If I Only Had A Brain (4)
Imagination (4)
In Love Again (10)
It Had To Be You (1)
(It Must've Been Ol') Santa Claus (7)
It's Alright With Me (2)
It's Time (5)
Jill (5)
Joe Slam And The Spaceship (8)
Just A Boy (2)
Just Kiss Me (5)
Just Like Me (9)
Last Payday (9)
Lazy River (4)
Lazybones (8)
Learn To Love (10)
Let It Snow! Let It Snow! Let It Snow! (7)
Let Me Love Tonight (10)

Let's Call The Whole Thing Off (1)
Let's Just Kiss (10)
Little Dancing Girl (3)
Little Drummer Boy (7)
Little Farley (9)
Lofty's Roach Souffle (3)
Lonely Side (3)
Love For Sale (11)
Love Is Here To Stay (1)
Love Me Some You (10)
Loved By Me (10)
Mary Ruth (3)
Mind On The Matter (9)
Moment With Me (11)
Moment's Notice (6)
Mr. Spill (3)
Much Love (10)
Music, Maestro, Please (6)
Muskrat Ramble (6)
Never Young (9)
Next Door Blues (11)
Nightingale Sang In Berkeley Square (2)
Nobody Like You To Me (9)
Nowhere With Love (11)
O Holy Night (7)

On The Atchison, Topeka And The Santa Fe (6)
On The Street Where You Live (6)
Once (10)
One Last Pitch (3)
Only 'Cause I Don't Have You (2)
Parade Of The Wooden Soldiers (7)
Please Don't Talk About Me When I'm Gone (4)
Reason To Believe (2)
Recipe For Love (2)
Rudolph The Red-Nosed Reindeer (7)
'S Wonderful (4)
She (8)
She Belongs To Me (5)
She...Blessed Be The One (8)
Sleigh Ride (7)
Sonny Cried (5)
Star Turtle 1-4 (9)
Stardust (6)
Stars Fell On Alabama (4)
Stompin' At The Savoy (1)
Tangerine (6)

That Party (8)
There's No Business Like Show Business (11)
This Time The Dream's On Me (6)
Time After Time (11)
To Love The Language (8)
To See You (10)
Trouble (8)
We Are In Love (2)
What Are You Doing New Year's Eve? (7)
What Child Is This? (7)
When My Heart Finds Christmas (7)
Where Or When (1)
Winter Wonderland (1)
With Imagination (I'll Get There) (5)
You Didn't Know Me When (5)

CONNIFF, Ray, and His Orchestra & Chorus ★12★ '66

Born on 11/6/16 in Attleboro, Massachusetts. Legendary arranger/conductor. Played trombone with Bunny Berigan, Bob Crosby, **Harry James**, Vaughn Monroe and Artie Shaw bands. Conniff's non-instrumental albums feature the Ray Conniff Singers.

1)Somewhere My Love 2)Say It With Music (A Touch Of Latin) 3)Memories Are Made Of This
4)So Much In Love 5)Young At Heart

3/23/57	11	16		©	1 **'S Wonderful!**		[I]	$20	Columbia 925
12/23/57+	10	37	●	©	2 **'S Marvelous**		[I]	$20	Columbia 1074
6/23/58+	9	52		©	3 **'S Awful Nice**		[I]	$20	Columbia 1137 / 8001
9/29/58	9	50	●	©	4 **Concert In Rhythm**		[I]	$20	Columbia 1163 / 8022
5/25/59+	10	20		©	5 **Broadway In Rhythm**		[I]	$20	Columbia 1252 / 8064
6/29/59	29	8		©	6 **Hollywood In Rhythm**		[I]	$20	Columbia 1310 / 8117
11/23/59+	8	36		©	7 **Conniff Meets Butterfield**		[I]	$20	Columbia 1346 / 8155

RAY CONNIFF & BILLY BUTTERFIELD

12/28/59+	14	2	●	©	8 **Christmas With Conniff**		[X]	$20	Columbia 1390 / 8185

Christmas charts: 39/'65, 35/'67, 11/'68, 7/'69

2/15/60	8	54		©	9 **It's The Talk Of The Town**			$20	Columbia 1334 / 8143
3/7/60	13	33		©	10 **Concert In Rhythm - Volume II**		[I]	$20	Columbia 1415 / 8212
8/15/60+	6	28		©	11 **Young At Heart**			$20	Columbia 1489 / 8281
10/10/60	4	58		©	12 **Say It With Music (A Touch Of Latin)**		[I]	$20	Columbia 1490 / 8282
12/31/60	15	1		©	13 **Christmas With Conniff**		[X-R]	$20	Columbia 1390 / 8185
2/13/61	4	34	●	©	14 **Memories Are Made Of This**		[I]	$20	Columbia 1574 / 8374
9/11/61	14	34		©	15 **Somebody Loves Me**			$20	Columbia 1642 / 8442
12/18/61+	16	6		©	16 **Christmas With Conniff**		[X-R]	$20	Columbia 1390 / 8185
2/17/62	5	34	●	©	17 **So Much In Love**			$20	Columbia 1720 / 8520
5/5/62	6	25		©	18 **'S Continental**		[I]	$20	Columbia 1776 / 8576
10/6/62	28	16		©	19 **Rhapsody In Rhythm**		[I]	$20	Columbia 1878 / 8678
12/8/62	32	4	▲	©	20 **We Wish You A Merry Christmas**		[X]	$20	Columbia 1892 / 8692

Christmas charts: 7/'63, 10/'64, 13/'65, 20/'66, 12/'67, 18/'68, 5/'72

CONNIFF, Ray, and His Orchestra & Chorus — Cont'd

DEBUT	PEAK	WKS	CD	#	Title	Sym	$	Label & Number
3/9/63	20	15	©	21	The Happy Beat	[I]	$20	Columbia 1949 / 8749
9/14/63	85	13	©	22	Just Kiddin' Around	[I]	$20	Columbia 2022 / 8822
					RAY CONNIFF & BILLY BUTTERFIELD			
2/15/64	73	17	©	23	You Make Me Feel So Young	[I]	$20	Columbia 2118 / 8918
5/30/64	50	19	©	24	Speak To Me Of Love		$15	Columbia 2150 / 8950
10/3/64	23	27	©	25	Invisible Tears		$15	Columbia 2264 / 9064
4/3/65	141	5	©	26	Friendly Persuasion	[I]	$15	Columbia 2210 / 9010
6/5/65	34	19	©	27	Music From Mary Poppins, The Sound Of Music, My Fair Lady, & Other Great Movie Themes		$15	Columbia 2366 / 9166
9/18/65	54	16	©	28	Love Affair		$15	Columbia 2352 / 9152
12/25/65+	15ˣ	5	©	29	Here We Come A-Caroling	[X]	$20	Columbia 2406 / 9206
					Christmas charts: 17/65, 15/'66; also see #44 below			
4/2/66	80	9	©	30	Happiness Is		$15	Columbia 2461 / 9261
7/16/66	3	90	▲ ©	31	Somewhere My Love		$15	Columbia 2519 / 9319
3/18/67	78	10	©	32	Ray Conniff's World Of Hits	[I]	$15	Columbia 2500 / 9300
					also see #44 below			
5/13/67	180	2	©	33	En Espanol!	[F]	$15	Columbia 2608 / 9408
6/3/67	30	46	©	34	This Is My Song		$15	Columbia 2676 / 9476
10/28/67+	39	15	©	35	Hawaiian Album		$15	Columbia 2747 / 9547
2/17/68	25	41	●	36	It Must Be Him		$15	Columbia 2795 / 9595
6/1/68	22	39	●	37	Honey		$15	Columbia 9661
10/26/68+	70	22		38	Turn Around Look At Me		$15	Columbia 9712
3/8/69	101	14		39	I Love How You Love Me		$15	Columbia 9777
7/12/69	158	5		40	Ray Conniff's Greatest Hits	[G]	$15	Columbia 9839
12/20/69+	103	21		41	Jean		$15	Columbia 9920
4/25/70	47	28		42	Bridge Over Troubled Water		$15	Columbia 1022
9/26/70	177	5		43	Concert In Stereo/Live At The Sahara/Tahoe	[L]	$25	Columbia 30122 [2]
12/12/70+	10ˣ	3		44	Ray Conniff's World Of Hits/Here We Come A-Caroling	[X-R]	$25	Columbia GP 3 [2]
					reissue of albums #29 and #32 above			
12/26/70+	120	13		45	We've Only Just Begun		$15	Columbia 30410
3/27/71	98	15		46	Love Story		$15	Columbia 30498
9/11/71	185	5		47	Great Contemporary Instrumental Hits	[I]	$15	Columbia 30755
2/12/72	138	11		48	I'd Like To Teach The World To Sing		$15	Columbia 31220
6/3/72	114	14		49	Love Theme From "The Godfather"		$15	Columbia 31473
10/7/72	180	10		50	Alone Again (Naturally)		$15	Columbia 31629
2/10/73	165	10		51	I Can See Clearly Now		$15	Columbia 32090
7/7/73	176	5		52	You Are The Sunshine Of My Life		$15	Columbia 32376
10/13/73	194	4		53	Harmony		$15	Columbia 32553

CONNIFF, Ray, and His Orchestra & Chorus — Cont'd

Improvisation On Schubert's "Serenade" (43)
Improvisation On The Fibich "Poeme" (10)
In The Cool, Cool, Cool Of The Evening (23)
In The Still Of The Night (2)
Invisible Tears (25,40) *57*
It Came Upon The Midnight Clear (29,44)
It Had To Be You (3,15)
It Might As Well Be Spring (6)
It Must Be Him (36)
It Never Rains In Southern California (11)
It Was A Very Good Year (38)
It's Been A Long, Long Time (39)
It's Dark On Observatory Hill (11)
It's Impossible (46)
It's Not For Me To Say (17)
It's So Nice To Have A Man Around The House (43)
It's The Talk Of The Town (9)
It's Too Late (47)
Jamaica Farewell (30)
Jean (41)
Jingle Bells (8,13,16)
Jolly Holiday (27)
Jolly Old St. Nicholas (medley) (20)
Joy To The World (29,44)
June In January (3)
June Night (26)
Just Friends (28)
Just Kiddin' Around (22)
Just One Of Those Things (12)
Just Walking In The Rain (17)
Killing Me Softly With His Song (medley) (52)
King Of The Road (31)
Kiss Me Goodbye (37)
Kiss Of Fire (19)
Kisses Sweeter Than Wine (25)
Lady Of Spain (19)
Lagrimas Invisibles (Invisible Tears) (31)
Lamp Is Low (4)
Laura (6)
Leaving On A Jet Plane (42)
Let It Be (45)
Let It Snow! Let It Snow! Let It Snow! (medley) (20)
Let The Sunshine (medley) (41)
Let's Put Out The Lights (9)
Lisbon Antigua (18)
Little Drummer Boy (medley) (20)
Little Green Apples (39)
Live And Let Die (53)
Living In A House Divided (49)
Look Of Love (37)
Louise (32)
Love (Can Make You Happy) (41)
Love Has No Rules (24)
Love Is A Many-Splendored Thing (6,28)
Love Is Blue (L'Amour Est Bleu) (37)
Love Is Born (Song Of The Trumpet) (7)

Love Is The Sweetest Thing (9)
Love Letters (6)
Love Letters In The Sand (14)
Love Me Tender (14)
Love Me Tonight (41,43)
Love Theme From "The Godfather" (Speak Softly Love) (49)
Love Walked In (19)
Lovely To Look At (3)
Lover, Come Back To Me (24)
Lullaby Of Birdland (3)
Lullaby Of The Leaves (23)
Ma, He's Making Eyes At Me (11)
MacArthur Park (38)
Mack The Knife (21,43)
Make It With You (45)
Malaguena (19)
Mam'selle (28)
Mame (34,40,43)
Man And A Woman (36)
Man Without Love (Quando M'Innamoro) (41)
Marianne (25)
Melodie D'Amour (30)
Memories Are Made Of This (14,40,43)
Mi Corazon (Dear Heart) (33)
Midnight Cowboy (42)
Midnight Lace - Part I (30) *92*
Midsummer In Sweden (32,44)
Miss You (30)
Moments To Remember (14)
Moon River (32,38,44)
Moon Song (15)
Moonlight And Roses (19)
Moonlight Serenade (2)
More (32,44)
Morgen (One More Sunrise) (18)
Morning After (53)
Moscow Nights (32,44)
Moulin Rouge (Where Is Your Heart), Song From (21)
Mrs. Robinson (38,43)
Music To Watch Girls By (36)
Muskrat Ramble (43)
My Cup Runneth Over (34)
My Favorite Things (27)
My Foolish Heart (14)
My Heart Cries For You (9)
My Heart Stood Still (6,17)
My Little Grass Shack In Kealakekua, Hawaii (15)
My Old Flame (23)
My Prayer (17)
My Reverie (4)
My Romance (19)
My Special Angel (39)
My Sweet Lord (45)
Neither One Of Us (Wants To Be The First To Say Goodbye) (52)
Never Can Say Goodbye (47)
Never On Sunday (17)
Night And Day (12)
Night The Lights Went Out In Georgia (52)
No Other Love (14)
O Come, All Ye Faithful (medley) (20)

O Holy Night (medley) (20)
O Little Town Of Bethlehem (29,44)
O Tannenbaum (29,44)
Oh Lonesome Me (25)
Oh, What A Beautiful Mornin' (5,7)
Oklahoma! (5,43)
Old Fashioned Love Song (48)
On The Street Where You Live (5,27,40,43)
On The Trail (4)
One Fine Day (10)
One Paddle Two Paddle (35)
Only You (And You Alone) (14)
Our Waltz (19)
Pacific Sunset (6)
Paradise (3)
Pass Me By (27)
Patricia, It's Patricia (23)
Peaceful (52)
Pearly Shells (35)
Peg O' My Heart (22)
People (38)
People Will Say We're In Love (5)
Playground In My Mind (53)
Please (6)
Poor People Of Paris (18)
Popsy (30)
Power Of Love (41)
Precious And Few (49)
Put Your Arms Around Me, Honey (22)
Put Your Hand In The Hand (47)
Raindrops Keep Fallin' On My Head (42)
Real Meaning Of Christmas (29,44)
Red Roses For A Blue Lady (31)
Release Me (36)
Remember (11)
Rhapsody In Blue (4)
Right Thing To Do (52)
Ring Christmas Bells (20)
Rosalie (7,9)
Rosas Rojas Para Una Dama Triste (Red Roses For A Blue Lady) (33)
Rose Garden (46)
Rose Room (26)
Rudolph, The Red-Nosed Reindeer (8,13,16)
Run To Me (50)
S'Posin' (25)
Santa Claus Is Comin' To Town (8,13,16)
Say Has Anybody Seen My Sweet Gypsy Rose (53)
Say It Isn't So (3)
Say It With Music (12)
Scarborough Fair/Canticle (39)
Schubert's Serenade (4)
Second Time Around (28)
Sentimental Journey (1)
September Song (1)
Shadow Of Your Smile (52)
Shadows Of The Night (Quentin's Theme) (41)

Shaft, Theme From (49)
Shangri-La (26)
Sheik Of Araby (30)
Silent Night, Holy Night (29,44)
Silver Bells (8,13,16)
Sing (52)
Singing The Blues (25)
Sleigh Ride (8,13,16)
Slow Poke (24)
Snowbird (45)
So Long, Farewell (31)
So Rare (26)
Softly, As In A Morning Sunrise (12)
Solitude (3)
Some Enchanted Evening (5)
Somebody Loves Me (15)
Someone (42)
Someone To Watch Over Me (2)
Somethin' Stupid (36)
Something (42)
Something To Remember You By (7)
Something's Wrong With Me (51)
Sometimes I'm Happy (1)
Somewhere, My Love (31,40,43) *9*
Song Of Love (28)
Song Sung Blue (50)
Sound Of Music (27)
Sounds Of Silence (37)
South Of The Border (7)
South Rampart Street Parade (43)
Spanish Eyes (37)
Speak Low (1)
Speak To Me Of Love (24)
Spinning Wheel (41)
Spoonful Of Sugar (27)
Stardust (1)
Stella By Starlight (6)
Stompin' At The Savoy (26)
Strange Music (18)
Stranger In Paradise (12)
Strangers In The Night (34)
Summer Breeze (51)
Summer Of '42 (The Summer Knows), Theme From (48)
Summertime (12)
Sunny (39)
Sunrise, Sunset (34)
Supercalifragilisticexpialidocious (27)
Superstar (47)
Surrey With The Fringe On Top (5)
Sweet Caroline (46)
Sweet Leilani (35)
Sweet Sue, Just You (30)
Sweetest Sounds (24)
Swing Little Glow Worm (18)
Take Me In Your Arms (19)
Taking A Chance On Love (28)
Tammy (14)
Taste Of Honey (47)
Tea For Two (43)
Temptation (12)
Thanks For The Memory (6)
That Old Black Magic (1)
That Old Feeling (3)

There Was A Girl (medley) (52)
There's A Kind Of Hush (All Over The World) (36)
These Foolish Things (Remind Me Of You) (11)
They Can't Take That Away From Me (2)
They Long To Be Close To You (45)
They Say It's Wonderful (34)
Third Man Theme (23)
This Guy's In Love With You (38)
This Is My Song (34,40)
This Love Of Mine (38)
This Nearly Was Mine (24)
Those Were The Days (39,43)
Three Coins In The Fountain (14,28)
Threepenny Opera, Theme From The ..see: Mack The Knife
Thrill Is Gone (15)
Tico-Tico (18)
Tie A Yellow Ribbon Round The Ole Oak Tree (52)
Tie Me Kangaroo Down, Sport (31)
Tiger Rag (Hold That Tiger) (26)
Tijuana Taxi (47)
Time For Us (41)
Time On My Hands (You In My Arms) (7)
Tiny Bubbles (35)
To My Love (19)
To You Sweetheart, Aloha (35)
Todos Aman A Alguien (Everybody Loves Somebody) (33)
Too Young (12,50)
Touch Me In The Morning (53)
True Love (17)
Try A Little Tenderness (28)
Try To Remember (32,44)
Turn Around Look At Me (38)
Twelfth Of Never (52)
Twelve Days Of Christmas (20)
Unchained Melody (14)
Under Paris Skies (24)
Up, Up And Away (36)
Usted (Mam'selle) (33)
Valley Of The Dolls, Theme From (37)
Very Thought Of You (3)
Volare (Nel Blu Dipinto Di Blu) (21)
Wagon Wheels (1)
Waitin' For The Evening Train (25)
Warsaw Concerto (10)
Watching Scotty Grow (46)
Way Of Love (49)
Way You Look Tonight (3)
We Three Kings Of Orient Are (medley) (20)
We Wish You A Merry Christmas (medley) (20)
We've Only Just Begun (45)
What A Diff'rence A Day Made (7)

What Child Is This (8,13,16,29,44)
What Have They Done To My Song, Ma? (45)
What Kind Of Fool Am I? (23)
What Now My Love (34)
What The World Needs Now Is Love (36)
Whatever Will Be, Will Be (Que Sera, Sera) (17)
Wheel Of Fortune (21)
When I Grow Too Old To Dream (22)
(When Your Heart's On Fire) Smoke Gets In Your Eyes (3,24,40,43)
(Where Do I Begin) Love Story (46)
Where Is The Love (50)
(Where Is Your Heart) ..see: Moulin Rouge
Where Or When (2)
Whiffenpoof Song (18)
White Christmas (8,13,16)
White Cliffs Of Dover (18)
Who's Sorry Now? (24)
Wichita Lineman (39)
Winchester Cathedral (39)
Windmills Of Your Mind (41)
Winter Wonderland (8,13,16)
With My Eyes Wide Open, I'm Dreaming (23)
Without You (49)
Wonderful Guy (5)
World Will Smile Again (34)
Wouldn't It Be Loverly (31)
Yellow Rose (21)
Yesterday (36)
Yesterday Once More (53)
Yesterdays (6)
You Are The Sunshine Of My Life (52)
You Do Something To Me (2)
You Make Me Feel So Young (23)
You Must Have Been A Beautiful Baby (7)
You Oughta Be In Pictures (22)
You Stepped Out Of A Dream (30)
You'd Be So Nice To Come Home To (15)
You'll Never Know (11,22)
You'll Never Walk Alone (24)
You're An Old Smoothie (9)
You're The Cream In My Coffee (15)
You've Made Me So Very Happy (45)
Young And Foolish (31)
Young At Heart (11)
Young Love (14,53)
Younger Than Springtime (5)
Yours Is My Heart Alone (10)
Zip-A-Dee-Doo-Dah (9)

CONNORS, Norman   '76

Born on 3/1/48 in Philadelphia. Jazz drummer with Archie Shepp, **John Coltrane**, **Pharoah Sanders** and others. Own group on Buddah in 1972. Featured vocalists are **Michael Henderson**, **Jean Carn** and **Phyllis Hyman**. Formed disco group **Aquarian Dream**.

DEBUT	PEAK	WKS	RIAA	CD	#	Album Title	Sym	$	Label & Number
10/11/75	**150**	5		©	1	**Saturday Night Special**		$12	Buddah 5643
7/24/76	**39**	24	●	©	2	**You Are My Starship**		$12	Buddah 5655
4/9/77	**94**	16		©	3	**Romantic Journey**		$12	Buddah 5682
5/27/78	**68**	17		©	4	**This Is Your Life**		$12	Arista 4177
1/13/79	**175**	5		©	5	**The Best Of Norman Connors & Friends**	[G]	$12	Buddah 5716
7/21/79	**137**	7			6	**Invitation**		$12	Arista 4216
9/27/80	**145**	6			7	**Take It To The Limit**		$12	Arista 9534
12/5/81	**197**	2			8	**Mr. C**		$12	Arista 9575

Akia (1)
Anyway You Want (8)
Be There In The Morning (6)
Beijo Partido (6)
Betcha By Golly Wow (2,5)
Black Cow (7)
Bubbles (7)
Butterfly (4)
Captain Connors (4)
Creator, The (4)

Creator Has A Master Plan (2)
Destination Moon (3)
Dindi (1,5)
Disco Land (6)
Everywhere Inside Of Me (7)
For You Everything (3)
Handle Me Gently (6)
I Don't Need Nobody Else (7)
I Have A Dream (6)
Invitation (6)

Just Imagine (2)
Justify (7)
Keep Doin' It (8)
Kingston (6)
Kwasi (1)
Last Tango In Paris (3)
Listen (8)
Love From The Sun (5)
Love's In Your Corner (8)
Maiden Voyage (1)

Melancholy Fire (7)
Mr. C (8)
Once I've Been There (3,5)
Party Town (8)
Romantic Journey (3,5)
Saturday Night Special (1)
Say You Love Me (4)
She's Gone (8)
Sing A Love Song (8)
Skin Diver (1)

So Much Love (2)
Stay With Me (8)
Stella (7)
Take It To The Limit (7)
Thembi (3)
This Is Your Life (4,5)
Together (6)
Valentine Love (1,5) *97*
We Both Need Each Other (2,5)
Wouldn't You Like To See (4,5)

You Are Everything (3)
You Are My Starship (2,5) *27*
You Bring Me Joy (7)
You Make Me Feel Brand New (4)
You've Been On My Mind (7)
Your Love (6)

185

CONSCIOUS DAUGHTERS, The '94
Female rap duo from Oakland: Carla Green and Karryl Smith.

2/26/94 **126** 9 © **Ear To The Street** .... $10 Scarface 53877

Crazybitchmadness   Sh**ty Situation   **Somethin' To Ride To (Fonky**   We Roll Deep
Da Mac Flow   Showdown   **Expedition)** *42*   What's A Girl Do Do?
Princess Of Poetry   TCD In Da Front   Wife Of A Gangsta

CONTRABAND '91
Hard-rock group: Richard Black (vocals; Shark Island), Tracii Guns (guitar; **L.A. Guns**), **Michael Schenker** (guitar), Share Pedersen (bass; **Vixen**) and Bobby Blotzer (drums; **Ratt**).

6/29/91 **187** 1 © **Contraband** .... $10 Impact 10247

All The Way From Memphis   Hang On To Yourself   Kiss By Kiss   Stand
Bad For Each Other   If This Is Love   Loud Guitars, Fast Cars & Wild,   Tonight You're Mine
Good Rockin' Tonight   Intimate Outrage   Wild Livin'

CONTROLLERS, The '78
R&B vocal group from Fairfield, Alabama: brothers Reginald and Larry McArthur, with Lenard Brown and Ricky Lewis.

12/17/77+ **146** 6 **In Control** .... $12 Juana 200,001

Heaven Is Only One Step Away   Reaper, The   Somebody's Gotta Win   You Ain't Fooling Me
People Want Music   Sho Nuff A Blessin   This Train

CONWAY, Julie '61
Born in New York City. Aerobics instructor.

1/9/61 **73** 17 **Good Housekeeping's Plan For Reducing Off-The-Record** .... $20 Harmony 7143
music by The Bob Price Quartet; the first aerobics album

All Or Nothing At All   Heartaches   Little Brown Jug   Pop Goes The Weasel   Under Paris Skies
Blue Scarecrow   Hot Canary   Old Piano Roll   Swanee River   Yellow Rose Of Texas
Domino   I've Found A New Baby   Petite Waltz   Undecided

CONWELL, Tommy, And The Young Rumblers '88
Born in Philadelphia. Rock singer/guitarist. The Young Rumblers: Chris Day (guitar), Rob Miller (keyboards; **Hooters**), Paul Slivka (bass) and Jim Hannum (drums).

9/3/88 **103** 28 © **Rumble** .... $10 Columbia 44186

Everything They Say Is True   I Wanna Make You Happy   Love's On Fire   Walkin' On The Water
Gonna Breakdown   **I'm Not Your Man** *74*   Tell Me What You Want Me To   Workout
Half A Heart   **If We Never Meet Again** *48*   Be

COODER, Ry '81
Born Ryland Cooder on 3/15/47 in Los Angeles. Blues-rock singer/guitarist. Scored several movies. Member of **Little Village**.

2/12/72 **113** 8 © 1 **Into The Purple Valley** .... $15 Reprise 2052
6/8/74 **167** 6 © 2 **Paradise And Lunch** .... $15 Reprise 2179
10/23/76 **177** 5 © 3 **Chicken Skin Music** .... $15 Reprise 2254
9/10/77 **158** 5 4 **Show Time** .... [L] $12 Warner 3059
recorded on 12/14/76 at the Great American Music Hall in San Francisco
8/11/79 **62** 15 © 5 **Bop Till You Drop** .... $12 Warner 3358
1/24/81 **43** 16 © 6 **Borderline** .... $12 Warner 3489
6/12/82 **105** 7 7 **The Slide Area** .... $12 Warner 3651
5/10/86 **85** 9 8 **Crossroads** .... [S] $10 Warner 25399
11/28/87 **177** 12 © 9 **Get Rhythm** .... $10 Warner 25639

Across The Borderline (9)   Don't You Mess Up A Good   He Made A Woman Out Of Me   It's All Over Now (2)   See You In Hell, Blind Boy (8)   UFO Has Landed In The Ghetto
Alimony (4)   Thing (5)   (8)   Jesus On The Mainline (2,4)   634-5789 (6)   (7)
All Shook Up (9)   Down In Hollywood (5)   He'll Have To Go (3)   Johnny Porter (6)   Smack Dab In The Middle (3,4)   Very Thing That Makes You
Always Lift Him Up (3)   Down In Mississippi (8)   Hey Porter (1)   Let's Have A Ball (9)   Somebody's Callin' My Name   Rich (Makes Me Poor) (5)
Billy The Kid (1)   Down In The Boondocks (6)   How Can A Poor Man Stand   Little Sister (5)   (8)   Vigilante Man (1)
Blue Suede Shoes (7)   F.D.R. In Trinidad (1)   Such Times And Live (4)   Look At Granny Run Run (5)   Speedo (8)   Viola Lee Blues (8)
Borderline (6)   Feelin' Bad Blues (8)   How Can You Keep Moving   Low-Commotion (5)   Stand By Me (3)   Viva Sequin (medley) (4)
Bourgeois Blues (3)   Feelin' Good (medley) (2)   (Unless You Migrate Too) (1)   Mama, Don't Treat Your   Tamp 'Em Up Solid (2)   Volver, Volver (4)
Chloe (9)   Fool For A Cigarette (medley)   I Can Tell By The Way You   Daughter Mean (7)   Tattler (2)   Walkin' Away Blues (8)
Cotton Needs Pickin' (8)   (2)   Smell (9)   Married Man's A Fool (2)   Taxes On The Farmer Feeds   Way We Make A Broken Heart
Crazy 'Bout An Automobile   Get Rhythm (9)   I Can't Win (5)   Mexican Divorce (2)   Us All (1)   (6)
(Every Woman I Know) (6)   Girls From Texas (6)   I Got Mine (3)   Money Honey (1)   Teardrops Will Fall (1)   Which Came First (7)
Crossroads (8)   Go Home, Girl (5)   I Need A Woman (7)   Never Make Your Move Too   That's The Way Love Turned   Why Don't You Try Me (6)
Dark End Of The Street (4)   Going Back To Okinawa (9)   I Think It's Going To Work Out   Soon (6)   Out For Me (7)   Willie Brown Blues (8)
Denomination Blues (1)   Goodnight Irene (3)   Fine (5)   Nitty Gritty Mississippi (8)   13 Question Method (9)   Women Will Rule The World (9)
Ditty Wa Ditty (4)   Great Dream From Heaven (1)   I'm Drinking Again (7)   On A Monday (1)   Trouble, You Can't Fool Me (5)   Yellow Roses (3)
Do Re Mi (medley) (4)   Gypsy Woman (7)   If Walls Could Talk (2)   School Is Out (4)

★370★ COOKE, Sam '58
Born on 1/22/31 in Clarksdale, Mississippi; raised in Chicago. Died from a gunshot wound on 12/11/64 (age 33) in Los Angeles; shot by a female motel manager under mysterious circumstances. Son of a Baptist minister. Lead singer of the Soul Stirrers from 1950-56. Uncle of **R.B. Greaves**. Inducted into the Rock and Roll Hall of Fame in 1986. Revered as the definitive soul singer.
1)*Sam Cooke* 2)*The Best Of Sam Cooke* 3)*Sam Cooke At The Copa*

3/10/58 **16** 2 1 **Sam Cooke** .... $200 Keen 2001
6/30/62 **72** 8 2 **Twistin' The Night Away** .... $50 RCA Victor 2555
10/20/62 **22** 35 © 3 **The Best Of Sam Cooke** .... C:#39/4 [G] $40 RCA Victor 2625
3/23/63 **94** 9 4 **Mr. Soul** .... $40 RCA Victor 2673
9/14/63 **62** 19 © 5 **Night Beat** .... $40 RCA Victor 2709
4/4/64 **34** 19 6 **Ain't That Good News** .... $40 RCA Victor 2899
10/31/64+ **29** 55 © 7 **Sam Cooke At The Copa** .... [L] $40 RCA Victor 2970
2/13/65 **44** 23 8 **Shake** .... $40 RCA Victor 3367
7/24/65 **128** 8 9 **The Best Of Sam Cooke, Volume 2** .... [G] $40 RCA Victor 3373
10/30/65 **120** 7 10 **Try A Little Love** .... $40 RCA Victor 3435
6/22/85 **134** 8 © 11 **Live At The Harlem Square Club, 1963** .... [E-L] $12 RCA Victor 5181
recorded on 1/12/63 in Miami
4/5/86 **175** 8 © 12 **The Man And His Music** .... [G] $15 RCA Victor 7127 [2]

COOKE, Sam — Cont'd

Ain't Misbehavin' (1)
Ain't That Good News (6,9,12)
All The Way (4)
Another Saturday Night (6,9,12) 10
Around The World (1)
Baby, Baby, Baby (9) 66
Basin Street Blues (9)
Bells Of St. Mary's (1)
Best Things In Life Are Free (7)
Bill Bailey (7)
Blowin' In The Wind (7)
Bridge Of Tears (10)
Bring It On Home To Me (3,11,12) 13
Camptown Twist (2)
Canadian Sunset (1)
Chain Gang (3,11,12) 2
Chains Of Love (4)
Change Is Gonna Come (6,8,9,12) 31
Comes Love (8)
Cousin Of Mine (9) 31

Cry Me A River (4)
Cupid (3,11,12) 17
Danny Boy (1)
Don't Cry On My Shoulder (10)
Driftin' Blues (4)
Everybody Likes To Cha Cha Cha (3,12) 31
Falling In Love (5)
Feel It (11)
Frankie And Johnny (7,9) 14
Get Yourself Another Fool (5)
Good Times (6,12) 11
Gypsy, The (10)
Having A Party (3,11,12) 17
Home (6)
Houseboat (Almost In Your Arms), Love Song From (10)
I Fall In Love Every Day (10)
I Lost Everything (5)
(I Love You) For Sentimental Reasons (3,4,7,11) 17

I Wish You Love (4)
I'll Come Running Back To You (12) 18
I'm In The Mood For Love (8)
I'm Just A Country Boy (8)
If I Had A Hammer (The Hammer Song) (7)
It's All Right (medley) (11)
It's Got The Whole World Shakin' (8) 41
Just For You (12)
Laughin' And Clownin' (5)
Little Girl (4)
Little Red Rooster (5,9) 11
Little Things You Do (10)
Lonesome Road (1)
Lost And Lookin' (5)
Love Will Find A Way (9,12)
Love You Most Of All (8) 26
Mean Old World (7)
Meet Me At Mary's Place (6,8,12)
Moonlight In Vermont (1)

Movin' And A'Groovin' (2)
No Second Time (6)
Nobody Knows The Trouble I've Seen (5)
Nobody Knows You When You're Down And Out (7)
Nothing Can Change This Love (4,11,12) 12
Ol' Man River (1)
Only Sixteen (3,12) 28
Please Don't Drive Me Away (5)
Riddle Song (6)
Rome Wasn't Built In A Day (6,12)
Sad Mood (3,12) 29
Send Me Some Lovin' (4) 13
Shake (8,9,12) 7
Shake Rattle And Roll (5)
Sittin' On The Sun (6)
Smoke Rings (4)
So Long (1)
(Somebody) Ease My Troublin' Mind (8)

Somebody Have Mercy (2,11,12) 70
Somebody's Gonna Miss Me (2)
Soothe Me (2,12)
Sugar Dumpling (2) 32
Summertime (1,3) 81
Tammy (1,10)
Tennessee Waltz (6,7,9) 35
That Lucky Old Sun (1)
That's Heaven To Me (12)
That's It-I Quit-I'm Movin' On (2) 31
That's Where It's At (9,12) 93
These Foolish Things (4)
This Little Light Of Mine (7)
To Each His Own (10)
Touch The Hem Of His Garment (12)
Trouble Blues (5)
Try A Little Love (10)
Try A Little Tenderness (medley) (7)
Twist, The (2)

Twistin' In The Kitchen With Dinah (2)
Twistin' In The Old Town Tonight (2)
Twistin' The Night Away (2,3,7,11,12) 9
When A Boy Falls In Love (10,12) 52
When I Fall In Love (7)
Whole Lotta Woman (2)
Willow Weep For Me (4)
Win Your Love For Me (8,12) 22
Wonderful World (3,12) 12
Yeah Man (8)
You Gotta Move (5)
You Send Me (1,3,7,10,12) 1
You're Always On My Mind (10)
You're Nobody Till Somebody Loves You (8)

COOL BREEZE   '99
Born Fred Calhoun in Atlanta. Male rapper.

4/10/99	38	6		©	East Points Greatest Hit			$10	Organized Noize 90159

Black Gangster
Butta
Calhouns, The

Cre-A-Tine
Doin' It In The South
E.P.G.H.

Field, The
Ghetto Camelot
Good, Good

Hit Man
Tenn. Points
Watch For The Hook 73

We Get It Crunk
Weeastpointin'

★336★   COOLIDGE, Rita   '77
Born on 5/1/44 in Nashville. Pop-rock singer. Did backup work for **Delaney & Bonnie**, **Leon Russell**, **Joe Cocker** and **Eric Clapton**. With **Kris Kristofferson** from 1971, married to him from 1973-80. Known as "The Delta Lady," for whom Leon Russell wrote the song of the same name. In the 1983 movie *Club Med.*

1)Anytime...Anywhere 2)Full Moon 3)Love Me Again

4/3/71	105	10			1 Rita Coolidge			$15	A&M 4291
12/18/71+	135	8			2 Nice Feelin'			$15	A&M 3130
11/11/72+	46	24			3 The Lady's Not For Sale			$15	A&M 4370
9/22/73	26	33	●		4 Full Moon			$15	A&M 4403
					KRIS KRISTOFFERSON & RITA COOLIDGE				
5/25/74	55	15			5 Fall Into Spring			$15	A&M 3627
12/21/74+	103	12		©	6 Breakaway			$15	Monument 33278
					KRIS KRISTOFFERSON & RITA COOLIDGE				
12/6/75+	85	10			7 It's Only Love			$12	A&M 4531
4/2/77	6	54	▲	©	8 Anytime...Anywhere			$12	A&M 4616
6/17/78	32	22	●		9 Love Me Again			$12	A&M 4699
2/3/79	106	9			10 Natural Act			$12	A&M 4690
					KRIS KRISTOFFERSON & RITA COOLIDGE				
9/22/79	95	16			11 Satisfied			$12	A&M 4781
2/14/81	107	8		©	12 Rita Coolidge/Greatest Hits		[G]	$12	A&M 4836
9/12/81	160	4			13 Heartbreak Radio			$12	A&M 3727

After The Fact (4)
Ain't That Peculiar (1)
Am I Blue (7)
Back In My Baby's Arms (7)
Basic Lady (13)
Better Days (2)
Bird On The Wire (3)
Blue As I Do (9)
Born To Love Me (4)
Born Under A Bad Sign (1,12)
Burden Of Freedom (5)
Bye Bye, Love (9)
Can She Keep You Satisfied (11)
Closer You Get (13)
Cowboys And Indians (5)
Crazy Love (1)
Crime Of Passion (11)
Crippled Crow (6)
Dakota (The Dancing Bear) (6)
Desperados Waiting For The Train (5)
Don't Let Love Pass You By (7)
Donut Man (3)
Everybody Loves A Winner (3)

Family Full Of Soul (2)
Fever (3,12) 76
Fool In Me (11)
Fool That I Am (12) 46
From The Bottle To The Bottom (4)
Good Times (8)
Happy Song (1)
Hard To Be Friends (4)
Heartbreak Radio (13)
Heaven's Dream (5)
Hello Love, Goodbye (9)
Hold An Old Friend's Hand (9)
Hold On (I Feel Our Love Is Changing) (13)
Hoola Hoop (10)
Hungry Years (4)
(I Always Called Them) Mountains (1)
I Believe In You (1)
I Did My Part (13)
I Don't Want To Talk About It (8,12)
I Feel Like Going Home (5)

I Feel The Burden (Being Lifted Off My Shoulders) (8)
I Fought The Law (2)
I Heard The Bluebirds Sing (4)
I Never Had It So Good (4)
I Wanted It All (7)
I'd Rather Be Sorry (6)
I'd Rather Leave While I'm In Love (11,12) 38
I'll Be Here (2)
I'll Be Your Baby Tonight (3)
I'm Down (But I Keep Falling) (4)
I've Got To Have You (6)
If You Were Mine (2)
Inside Of Me (3)
It Just Keeps You Dancing (9)
It's All Over (All Over Again) (4)
It's Only Love (7)
Jealous Kind (9)
Journey Thru The Past (2)
Keep The Candle Burning (7)
Lady's Not For Sale (3)
Late Again (7)
Lay My Burden Down (2)

Let's Go Dancin' (11)
Love Don't Live Here Anymore (10)
Love Has No Pride (5)
Love Me Again (9) 68
Lover Please (6)
Loving Arms (4) 86
Loving You Was Easier (Than Anything I'll Ever Do Again) (10)
Mama Lou (3)
Man And A Woman (13)
Mean To Me (7)
Most Likely You Go Your Way (And I'll Go Mine) (4)
Mud Island (1)
My Crew (13) *flip*
My Rock And Roll Man (7)
Nice Feelin' (2,12)
Nickel For The Fiddler (5)
Not Everyone Knows (10)
Now Your Baby Is A Lady (5)
Number One (10)
One Fine Day (11) 66
One More Heartache (13)

Only You Know And I Know (2,12)
Pain Of Love (11)
Part Of Your Life (4)
Please Don't Tell Me How The Story Ends (10)
Rain (6)
Second Story Window (4)
Seven Bridges Road (1)
Silver Mantis (10)
Slow Dancer (9)
Slow Down (6)
Song I'd Like To Sing (4) 49
Songbird (9)
Southern Lady (8)
Star (7)
Stranger To Me Now (13)
Sweet Emotion (11)
Sweet Inspiration (9)
Sweet Susannah (5)
Take It Home (13)
Take Time To Love (4)
Tennessee Blues (4)
That Man Is My Weakness (1)
That's What Friends Are For (5)

Things I Might Have Been (6)
Trust It All To Somebody (11)
Walk On In (13)
Way You Do The Things You Do (8,12) 20
We Had It All (5)
We Must Have Been Out Of Our Minds (6)
We're All Alone (8,12) 7
What'cha Gonna Do (6)
Whiskey Whiskey (5)
Who's To Bless And Who's To Blame (8)
Wishin' And Hopin' (13)
Woman Left Lonely (3)
Words (8,12)
You (9) 25
You Touched Me In The Morning (2)
You're Gonna Love Yourself (In The Morning) (10)
You're So Fine (9)
(Your Love Has Lifted Me) Higher And Higher (8,12) 2

COOLIO   '96
Born Artis Ivey on 8/1/63 in Los Angeles. Male rapper.

8/6/94	8	30	▲	©	1 It Takes A Thief			$10	Tommy Boy 1083
11/25/95+	9	62	▲²	©	2 Gangsta's Paradise			$10	Tommy Boy 1141
9/13/97	39	9	●	©	3 My Soul			$10	Tommy Boy 1180

Bright As The Sun (2)
Bring Back Somethin Fo Da Hood (1)
C U When U Get There (3) 12
Can I Get Down 1X (3)
Can-O-Corn (1)
Can U Dig It (3)

County Line (1)
Cruisin' (2)
Devil Is Dope (3)
Exercise Yo' Game (2)
Fantastic Voyage (1) 3
For My Sistas (2)
Gangsta's Paradise (2) 1

Get Up Get Down (2)
Geto Highlites (2)
Ghetto Cartoon (1)
Hand On My Nutsac (1)
Hit 'Em (3)
Homeboy (3)
I Remember (1)

Is This Me? (2)
It Takes A Thief (1)
Kinda High Kinda Drunk (2)
Knight Fall (3)
Let's Do It (3)
Mama, I'm In Love Wit A Gangsta (1)

My Soul (3)
N Da Closet (1)
Nature Of The Business (3)
On My Way To Harlem (3)
One Mo (3)
1,2,3,4 (Sumpin' New) (2) 5
Ooh La La (3)

Recoup This (2)
Revolution, The (2)
Smilin' (2)
Smokin' Stix (1)
Sticky Fingers (1)
That's How It Is (2)
Thing Goin' On (2)

187

COOLIO — Cont'd

Thought You Knew (1)
Throwdown 2000 (3)

Too Hot (2) **24**

2 Minutes & 21 Seconds Of
Funk (3)

U Know Hoo! (1)
Ugly Bitches (1)

COOPER, Alice ★125★   '73

Born Vincent Furnier on 2/4/48 in Detroit. Formed hard-rock band, Alice Cooper: Furnier (vocals), Glen Buxton (guitar), Michael Bruce (keyboards), Dennis Dunaway (bass) and Neal Smith (drums). Furnier went on to assume the Alice Cooper name for himself. Band split in 1974. Cooper went solo and became known for his bizarre stage antics. Appeared in the movies *Prince Of Darkness* and *Wayne's World*, among others. Also see **Billion Dollar Babies**.

1) Billion Dollar Babies 2) School's Out 3) Welcome To My Nightmare
4) Alice Cooper's Greatest Hits 5) Muscle Of Love

DEBUT	PEAK	WKS	RIAA	CD	#	Album Title	$	Label & Number
6/28/69	193	6		©	1	Pretties For You	$150	Straight 1051
3/20/71	35	38	▲	©	2	Love It To Death	$30	Warner 1883
12/4/71+	21	54	▲	©	3	Killer	$30	Warner 2567
7/1/72	2³	32	▲	©	4	School's Out	$20	Warner 2623
3/17/73	❶¹	50	▲	©	5	Billion Dollar Babies	$15	Warner 2685
12/8/73+	10	21	●	©	6	Muscle Of Love	$15	Warner 2748
8/31/74	8	23	▲	©	7	Alice Cooper's Greatest Hits	[G] $15	Warner 2803
3/22/75	5	37	▲	©	8	Welcome To My Nightmare	$15	Atlantic 18130
7/17/76	27	32	●	©	9	Alice Cooper Goes To Hell	$12	Warner 2896
5/28/77	42	16		©	10	Lace And Whiskey	$12	Warner 3027
12/17/77+	131	6		©	11	The Alice Cooper Show	[L] $12	Warner 3138
12/16/78+	60	11		©	12	From The Inside	$12	Warner 3263
5/24/80	44	17		©	13	Flush The Fashion	$12	Warner 3436
9/19/81	125	5			14	Special Forces	$12	Warner 3581
10/18/86	59	21			15	Constrictor	$10	MCA 5761
10/24/87	73	15		©	16	Raise Your Fist And Yell	$10	MCA 42091
8/12/89	20	43	▲	©	17	Trash	$10	Epic 45137
7/20/91	47	13		©	18	Hey Stoopid	$10	Epic 46786
7/30/94	68	3		©	19	The Last Temptation	$10	Epic 52771
6/24/00	193	1		©	20	Brutal Planet	$10	Spitfire 5038

Alma Mater (4)
Apple Bush (1)
Aspirin Damage (13)
Awakening, The (4)
B. B. On Mars (1)
Bad Place Alone (1)
Ballad Of Dwight Fry (2)
Be My Lover (3,7) **49**
Bed Of Nails (17)
Big Apple Dreamin' (Hippo) (6)
Billion Dollar Babies (5,7,11) **57**
Black Juju (2)
Black Widow (8,11)
Blow Me A Kiss (20)
Blue Turk (4)
Brutal Planet (20)
Burning Our Bed (18)
Caught In A Dream (2) **94**
Changing, Arranging (1)
Chop, Chop, Chop (16)
Cleansed By Fire (19)
Clones (We're All) (13) **40**
Cold Ethyl (8)
Cold Machines (20)
Crawlin' (15)
Crazy Little Child (6)
Damned If You Do (10)
Dance Yourself To Death (13)
Dangerous Tonight (18)
Dead Babies (3)
Department Of Youth (8) **67**
Desperado (3,7)

Devil's Food (8,11)
Didn't We Meet (9)
Die For You (18)
Dirty Dreams (18)
Don't Talk Old To Me (14)
Earwigs To Eternity (1)
Eat Some More (20)
Eighteen (2,7,11) **21**
Elected (5,7) **26**
Escape (8)
Feed My Frankenstein (18)
Fields Of Regret (1)
For Veronica's Sake (12)
Freedom (18)
From The Inside (12)
Gail (1)
Generation Landslide (5)
Generation Landslide '81 (14)
Gimme (20)
Give It Up (15)
Give The Kid A Break (9)
Give The Radio Back (16)
Go To Hell (9,11)
Going Home (9)
Grande Finale (4)
Great American Success Story (15)
Grim Facts (13)
Guilty (9)
Gutter Cat Vs. The Jets (4)
Hallowed Be My Name (2)
Halo Of Flies (3)
Hard Hearted Alice (6)

He's Back (The Man Behind The Mask) (15)
Headlines (13)
Hell Is Living Without You (17)
Hello Hurray (5,7) **35**
Hey Stoopid (18) **78**
House Of Fire (17) **56**
How You Gonna See Me Now (12) **12**
Hurricane Years (18)
I Love The Dead (5,11)
I Never Cry (9,11) **12**
I Never Wrote Those Songs (10)
I'm Always Chasing Rainbows (9)
I'm The Coolest (9)
I'm Your Gun (17)
Inmates (We're All Crazy) (12)
Is It My Body (2,7,11)
It's Hot Tonight (10)
It's Me (19)
It's The Little Things (20)
Jackknife Johnny (12)
Killer (3)
King Of The Silver Screen (10)
Lace And Whiskey (10)
Leather Boots (13)
Levity Ball (1)
Life And Death Of The Party (15)
Little By Little (18)
Living (1)
Lock Me Up (16)

Long Way To Go (2)
Lost In America (19)
Love's A Loaded Gun (18)
Lullaby (20)
Luney Tune (4)
Man With The Golden Gun (6)
Mary Ann (5)
Might As Well Be On Mars (18)
Millie And Billie (12)
Model Citizen (13)
Muscle Of Love (6,7)
My God (10)
My Stars (4)
Never Been Sold Before (6)
No Longer Umpire (1)
(No More) Love At Your Convenience (10)
No More Mr. Nice Guy (5,7) **25**
Not That Kind Of Love (16)
Nothing's Free (19)
Nuclear Infected (13)
Nurse Rozetta (12)
Only My Heart Talkin' (17) **89**
Only Women (8,11) **12**
Pain (13)
Pessi-Mystic (20)
Pick Up The Bones (20)
Poison (17) **7**
Prettiest Cop On The Block (14)
Prince Of Darkness (16)
Public Animal #9 (4)
Quiet Room (12)
Raped And Freezin' (5)

Reflected (1)
Road Rats (10)
Roses On White Lace (16)
Sanctuary (20)
School's Out (4,7,11) **7**
Second Coming (2)
Serious (12)
Seven & Seven Is (14)
Sick Things (5,11)
Sideshow (19)
Simple Disobedience (15)
Sing Low Sweet Cheerio (1)
Skeletons In The Closet (14)
Snakebite (18)
Some Folks (8)
Spark In The Dark (17)
Step On You (16)
Steven (8)
Stolen Prayer (19)
Street Fight (4)
Sun Arise (2)
Take It Like A Woman (20)
Talk Talk (13)
Teenage Frankenstein (15)
Teenage Lament '74 (6,7) **48**
10 Minutes Before The Worm (1)
This Maniac's In Love With You (17)
Thrill My Gorilla (15)
Time To Kill (16)
Titanic Overture (1)
Today Mueller (1)

Trash (17)
Trick Bag (15)
Ubangi Stomp (10)
Under My Wheels (3,7,11) **59**
Unfinished Sweet (5)
Unholy War (19)
Vicious Rumours (14)
Wake Me Gently (9)
Welcome To My Nightmare (8) **45**
Who Do You Think We Are (14)
Why Trust You (17)
Wicked Young Man (20)
Wind-Up Toy (18)
Wish I Were Born In Beverly Hills (12)
Wish You Were Here (9,11)
Woman Machine (1)
Working Up A Sweat (6)
World Needs Guts (15)
Yeah, Yeah, Yeah (3)
Years Ago (8)
You And Me (10,11) **9**
You Drive Me Nervous (3)
You Gotta Dance (9)
You Look Good In Rags (14)
You Want It, You Got It (14)
You're A Movie (14)
You're My Temptation (19)

COOPER, Michael   '88

Born on 11/15/52 in Vallejo, California. R&B singer/songwriter/guitarist. Leader of **Con Funk Shun**.

| 1/16/88 | 98 | 25 | © | Love Is Such A Funny Game | $10 | Warner 25653 |

Dinner For Two
Just Thinkin' 'Bout Cha

Look Before You Leave
Love Is Such A Funny Game

No Other Lover
Oceans Wide

Quickness
To Prove My Love

You've Got A Friend

COOPER, Pat   '66

Born Pasquale Caputo in Brooklyn, New York. Comedian/actor.

5/28/66	82	42		1	Our Hero...Pat Cooper	[C] $20	United Artists 6446
12/17/66+	84	14		2	Spaghetti Sauce & Other Delights	[C] $20	United Artists 6548
3/22/69	193	2		3	More Saucy Stories From...Pat Cooper	[C] $20	United Artists 6690

And Then The Sun Goes Down (2)
Draft Time (3)
Everyone Is Equal (1)
Family & Holidays (3)

Honeymoon (3)
Honeymoon, The (1)
In My Neighborhood (1)
Italian Wedding (1)
Little Red Scooter (2)

Lu Zampogna (The Italian Bagpipe Man) (2)
Mama (3)
Mama's Moo-Len-Yanna (The Eggplant Song) (1)

Memories (3)
More You Make, The More You Spend (1)
My Father And His Friends (1)
Our Children (3)

Pepperoni Kid (2)
Poppa's Home-Made Wine (2)
Spaghetti Sauce & Other Delights (2)
When I Was A Kid (1)

COPE, Julian '87

Born on 10/21/57 in Bargoed, Wales; raised in Tamworth, England. Former lead singer/songwriter/bassist of British group the **Teardrop Explodes**.

2/21/87	109	6		1 Julian Cope	[M]	$10	Island 90560
4/4/87	105	12	©	2 Saint Julian		$10	Island 90571
12/10/88+	155	13	©	3 My Nation Underground		$10	Island 91025

Charlotte Anne (3)
China Doll (3)
Crack In The Clouds (2)
Easter Everywhere (3)
Eve's Volcano (2)
5 O'Clock World (3)
Great White Hoax (3)
I'm Not Losing Sleep (3)
I've Got Levitation (1)
My Nation Underground (3)
Non-Alignment Pact (1)
Planet Ride (2)
Pulsar (2)
Saint Julian (2)
Screaming Secrets (2)
Shot Down (2)
Someone Like Me (3)
Spacehopper (2)
Trampolene (2)
Transporting (1)
Umpteenth Unnatural Blues (1)
Vegetation (3)
World Shut Your Mouth
  (1,2) **84**

COPELAND, Johnny — see COLLINS, Albert

COPELAND, Stewart '85

Born on 7/16/52 in Alexandria, Egypt. Drummer of **The Police**. Prior to The Police, worked as **Joan Armatrading**'s road manager. Founded **Animal Logic** in 1989.

12/17/83+	157	5	©	1 Rumble Fish	[I-S]	$10	A&M 4983
9/7/85	148	8	©	2 The Rhythmatist		$10	A&M 5084

African Dream (2)
Biff Gets Stomped By Rusty James (1)
Brazzaville (2)
Brothers On Wheels (1)
Cain's Ballroom (medley) (1)
Coco (2)
Don't Box Me In (1)
Father On The Stairs (1)
Franco (2)
Gong Rock (2)
Hostile Bridge To Benny's (1)
Kemba (2)
Koteja (Oh Bolilla) (2)
Liberte (2)
Motorboy's Fate (1)
Our Mother Is Alive (1)
Party At Someone Else's Place (1)
Personal Midget (medley) (1)
Samburu Sunset (2)
Serengeti Long Walk (2)
Tulsa Rags (1)
Tulsa Tango (1)
West Tulsa Story (1)
Your Mother Is Not Crazy (1)

COREA, Chick '76

Born Anthony Armando Corea on 6/11/42 in Chelsea, Massachusetts. Jazz-rock pianist. Worked with **Stan Getz**, Blue Mitchell, **Sarah Vaughan** and Gary Burton before joining the **Miles Davis** band in 1968. Formed group **Return To Forever** in 1973.

3/6/76	42	15	©	1 The Leprechaun	[I]	$12	Polydor 6062
1/15/77	55	12	©	2 My Spanish Heart	[I]	$15	Polydor 9003 [2]
3/11/78	61	14	©	3 The Mad Hatter	[I]	$12	Polydor 6130
8/19/78	86	10	©	4 Friends	[I]	$12	Polydor 6160
3/31/79	100	8	©	5 An Evening With Herbie Hancock & Chick Corea	[I-L]	$15	Columbia 35663 [2]
11/24/79	175	2	©	6 An Evening With Chick Corea & Herbie Hancock	[I-L]	$15	Polydor 6238 [2]
5/10/80	170	3	©	7 Tap Step	[I]	$10	Warner 3425
8/1/81	179	4	©	8 Three Quartets	[I]	$10	Warner 3552

Armando's Rhumba (2)
Bouquet (6)
Button Up (5)
Cappucino (4)
Children's Song #15 (4)
Children's Song #5 (4)
Day Danse (2)
Dear Alice (7)
El Bozo - Parts I-III (2)
Embrace, The (7)
Falling Alice (3)
February Moment (5)
Flamenco (7)
Friends (4)
Gardens, The (2)
Grandpa Blues (7)
Hilltop, The (2)
Homecoming (6)
Hook, The (6)
Humpty Dumpty (3)
Imp's Welcome (1)
La Fiesta (5,6)
Lenore (1)
Leprechaun's Dream (1)
Liza (5)
Looking At The World (1)
Love Castle (2)
Mad Hatter Rhapsody (3)
Magic Carpet (7)
Maiden Voyage (5,6)
My Spanish Heart (2)
Night Streets (2)
Nite Sprite (1)
One Step (4)
Ostinato (6)
Pixiland Rag (1)
Quartet No. 1-3 (8)
Reverie (1)
Samba L.A. (7)
Samba Song (4)
Sicily (4)
Sky Medley (2)
Slide, The (7)
Soft And Gentle (1)
Someday My Prince Will Come (5)
Spanish Fantasy - Parts I-IV (2)
Tap Step (7)
Trial, The (3)
Tweedle Dee (3)
Tweedle Dum (3)
Waltze For Dave (4)
Wind Danse (2)
Woods, The (3)

CORNELIUS BROTHERS & SISTER ROSE '72

R&B family group from Dania, Florida: Edward, Carter and Rose Cornelius. Billie Jo was added in 1973. All 15 Cornelius siblings play instruments or sing. Carter, later known as Gideon Israel, leader of a muslim religious sect; died of a heart attack on 11/7/91 (age 43).

7/29/72	29	25		Cornelius Brothers & Sister Rose		$20	United Artists 5568

Don't Ever Be Lonely (A Poor Little Fool Like Me) 23
Gonna Be Sweet For You
Good Loving Don't Come Easy
I'm Never Gonna Be Alone Anymore **37**
I'm So Glad (To Be Loved By You)
Just Ain't No Love (Like A Lady's)
Let Me Down Easy 96
Let's Stay Together
Lift Your Love Higher
Too Late To Turn Back Now 2
Treat Her Like A Lady 3

CORNELL, Chris '99

Born on 7/20/64 in Seattle. Lead singer of **Soundgarden**.

10/9/99	18	8	©	Euphoria Morning		$10	A&M 490412

Can't Change Me
Disappearing One
Flutter Girl
Follow My Way
Mission
Moonchild
Pillow Of Your Bones
Preaching The End Of The World
Steel Rain
Sweet Euphoria
Wave Goodbye
When I'm Down

CORNERSHOP '98

Rock group based in London: Tjinder Singh (vocals), Ben Ayers (guitar), Anthony Saffrey (sitar), Peter Bengry (percussion) and Nick Simms (drums).

1/24/98	144	5	©	When I Was Born For The 7th Time		$10	Luaka Bop 46576

Brimful Of Asha
Butter The Soul
Candyman
Chocolat
Coming Up
Funky Days Are Back Again
Good Shit
Good To Be On The Road Back Home
It's Indian Tobacco My Friend
Norwegian Wood (This Bird Has Flown)
Sleep On The Left Side
State Troopers (Part I)
We're In Yr Corner
What Is Happening?
When The Light Appears Boy

CORONA '95

Dance duo: Italian producer Francesco Bontempi and Brazilian singer Olga DeSouza.

6/17/95	154	7		The Rhythm Of The Night		$10	EastWest 61817

Baby Baby 57
Baby I Need Your Love
Do You Want Me
Don't Go Breaking My Heart
Get Up And Boogie
I Don't Wanna Be A Star
I Gotta Keep Dancin'
I Want Your Love
In The Name Of Love
Rhythm Of The Night 11
Try Me Out
When I Give My Love
You Gotta Be Movin'

CORPORATION, The '69

Rock group from Milwaukee: Danny Peil (vocals), Gerry Smith (guitar), John Kondos (keyboards), Pat McCarthy (horns), Ken Berdoll (bass) and Nick Kondos (drums).

3/1/69	197	4		The Corporation		$50	Capitol 175

Drifting
Highway
I Want To Get Out Of My Grave
India
Ring That Bell
Smile

CORROSION OF CONFORMITY '96

Hard-rock group from Raleigh, North Carolina: Pepper Keenan (vocals, guitar), Woody Weatherman (guitar), Mike Dean (bass) and Reed Mullin (drums).

10/15/94+	155	15		©	1 **Deliverance**			$10	Columbia 66208
11/2/96	104	2		©	2 **Wiseblood**			$10	Columbia 67583

Albatross (1)
Born Again For The Last Time (2)
Bottom Feeder (El Que Come Abajo) (2)
Broken Man (1)
Clean My Wounds (1)
Deliverance (1)
Door, The (2)
Drowning In A Daydream (2)
Fuel (2)
Goodbye Windows (2)
Heaven's Not Overflowing (1)
King Of The Rotten (1)
Long Whip/Big America (2)
Man Or Ash (2)
Mano De Mono (1)
My Grain (1)
#2121313 (1)
Pearls Before Swine (1)
Redemption City (1)
Senor Limpio (1)
Seven Days (1)
Shake Like You (1)
Shelter (1)
Snake Has No Head (2)
Wiseblood (2)
Wishbone (Some Tomorrow) (2)
Without Wings (1)

CORRS, The '00

Sibling group from Ireland: Andrea (vocals), Jim (guitar), Sharon (violin) and Caroline (drums) Corr.

1/20/96	131	4	●	©	1 **Forgiven, Not Forgotten**			$10	143 92612
3/27/99	72	17	●	©	2 **Talk On Corners - Special Edition**			$10	143 83164
9/30/00	21	44	▲	©	3 **In Blue**			$10	143 83352

All In A Day (3)
All The Love In The World (3)
Along With The Girls (1)
At Your Side (1)
Breathless (3) *34*
Carraroe Jig (1)
Closer (1)
Dreams (2)
Erin Shore (1)
Forgiven Not Forgotten (1)
Give It All Up (3)
Give Me A Reason (3)
Heaven Knows (1)
Hopelessly Addicted (2)
Hurt Before (3)
I Never Loved You Anyway (2)
Irresistible (3)
Leave Me Alone (1)
Little Wing (2)
Love To Love You (1)
Minstrel Boy (1)
No Good For Me (2)
No More Cry (3)
One Night (3)
Only When I Sleep (2)
Paddy McCarthy (3)
Queen Of Hollywood (2)
Radio (3)
Rain (3)
Rebel Heart (3)
Right Time (1)
Runaway (1,2) *68*
Say (3)
Secret Life (1)
So Young (2)
Somebody For Someone (3)
Someday (1)
Toss The Feathers (1)
What Can I Do (2)
When He's Not Around (2)

CORTEZ, Dave "Baby" '62

Born David Cortez Clowney on 8/13/38 in Detroit. Black keyboardist.

9/29/62	107	3			**Rinky Dink**		[I]	$50	Chess 1473

Davy's Shuffle
Gettin' Right
Jammin' Part 1 & 2
Little Paris Melody (Elle Ne Tourne Pas La Terre)
Lost Love
Mr. Gee
Rinky Dink *10*
Skins And Sounds
Wobble Part 1 & 2

CORYELL, Larry '69

Born on 4/2/43 in Galveston, Texas. Jazz/rock guitarist. Founder of **Eleventh House**.

5/31/69	196	3			**Lady Coryell**			$20	Vanguard 6509

Cleo's Mood
Dream Thing
Herman Wright
Lady Coryell
Love Child Is Coming Home
Stiff Neck
Sunday Telephone
Treats Style
Two Minute Classical
You Don't Know What Love Is

COSBY, Bill ★96★ '67

Born on 7/12/38 in Philadelphia. Comedian/actor. Played "Alexander Scott" on TV's *I Spy*. Star of the highly-rated NBC-TV series *The Cosby Show*. Also acted in several other TV shows and movies.

1)Revenge 2)To Russell, My Brother, Whom I Slept With 3)Wonderfulness 4)200 M.P.H.
5)Bill Cosby Sings/Silver Throat

6/27/64+	21	128	▲	©	1 **Bill Cosby Is A Very Funny Fellow, Right!**		[C]	$20	Warner 1518
11/21/64+	32	140	▲	©	2 **I Started Out As A Child**		[C]	$20	Warner 1567
8/28/65+	19	152	▲	©	3 **Why Is There Air?**		[C]	$20	Warner 1606
5/28/66	7	106	▲	©	4 **Wonderfulness**		[C]	$20	Warner 1634
5/13/67	2[1]	73	▲	©	5 **Revenge**		[C]	$20	Warner 1691
9/2/67	18	26			6 **Bill Cosby Sings/Silver Throat**		[N]	$20	Warner 1709
2/24/68	74	11			7 **Bill Cosby Sings/Hooray For The Salvation Army Band!**		[N]	$20	Warner 1728
4/6/68	7	46	●	©	8 **To Russell, My Brother, Whom I Slept With**		[C]	$15	Warner 1734
10/26/68+	16	25	●		9 **200 M.P.H.**		[C]	$15	Warner 1757
2/8/69	37	19			10 **It's True! It's True!**		[C]	$15	Warner 1770
7/12/69	62	16			11 **8:15 12:15**		[C]	$20	Tetragramm. 5100 [2]
					title: times of shows at Harrah's Lake Tahoe; no track titles listed on this album				
9/6/69	51	25	▲		12 **The Best Of Bill Cosby**		[C-K]	$15	Warner 1798
10/18/69+	70	24			13 **Bill Cosby**		[C]	$15	Uni 73066
3/14/70	80	16	©		14 **More Of The Best Of Bill Cosby**		[C-K]	$15	Warner 1836
9/12/70	165	6			15 **"Live" Madison Square Garden Center**		[C]	$15	Uni 73082
3/6/71	72	8			16 **When I Was A Kid**		[C]	$15	Uni 73100
12/11/71+	181	7			17 **For Adults Only**		[C]	$15	Uni 73112
9/30/72	191	4			18 **Inside The Mind Of Bill Cosby**		[C]	$15	Uni 73139
6/16/73	187	4			19 **Fat Albert**		[C]	$15	MCA 333
6/5/76	100	12			20 **Bill Cosby Is Not Himself These Days (Rat Own, Rat Own, Rat Own)**		[N]	$12	Capitol 11530
12/18/82+	64	14	©		21 **Bill Cosby "Himself"**		[C-S]	$12	Motown 6026
6/21/86	26	15	●		22 **Those Of You With Or Without Children, You'll Understand**		[C]	$10	Geffen 24104

American Gambler (10)
Animal Stories (15)
Ants Are Cool (10)
Apple, The (8,12,14)
Aw Shucks, Hush Your Mouth (6)
Baby (3,12)
Baby, What You Want Me To Do (Peepin' 'N' Hidin') (6)
Baseball (8,13)
Basketball (13)
Be Good To Your Wives (17)
Bedroom Slippers (18)
Ben (20)
Big Boss Man (6)
Bill Cosby Fights Back (17)
Bill Cosby Goes To A Football Game (13)
Bill Takes His Daughters To The Zoo (15)
Bill Visits Ray Charles (15)
Bill's Marriage (15,18)
Bill's Two Daughters (17)
Brain Damage (21)
Bright Lights, Big City (6)
Buck, Buck ..see: Fat Albert
Buck Jones (16)
Burlesque Shows (10)
Chick On The Side (20)
Chicken Heart (4)
Chocolate Cake For Breakfast (21)
Christmas Time (2)
Conflict (8,14)
Cool Covers (5)
Cost Of An Egg (17)
Dentist, The (21)
Difference Between Men And Women (1)
Do It To Me (20)
Dogs (16)
Dogs And Cats (9,14)
Don'cha Know (6)
Driving In San Francisco (3,12)
Ennis And His Two Sisters (15)
Ennis' Toilet (18)
Fat Albert (5,12)
Fat Albert Got A Hernia (19)
Fat Albert Plays Dead (19)
Fat Albert's Car (19)
Fernet Branca (1)
Football (13,18)
Foreign Countries (10)
Frogs (16)
"Froofie" The Dog (18)
Funky North Philly (7) *91*
Garbage Truck Lady (20)
Genesis (3)
Get Out Of My Life Woman (7)
Giant, The (2)
Go Carts (4)
Grandfather, The (9)
Grandparents, The (21)
Greasy Kid Stuff (1)
Great Quote (22)
Half Man (1)
Handball Game At The "Y" (15)
Helicopters (10)
His First Baby (15)
Hofstra (3,14)
Hold On I'm A Comin' (7)
Hoof And Mouth (1)
Hooray For The Salvation Army Band (7) *71*
Hush Hush (6)
(I Can't Get No) Satisfaction (7)
I Got A Woman (6)

DEBUT	PEAK	WKS	RIAA	CD	ARTIST — Album Title	Catalog	Sym	$	Label & Number

COSBY, Bill — Cont'd

I Luv Myself Better Than I Luv Myself (20)	Lumps (4)	Niagara Falls (4)	Revenge (5,12)	Stop, Look & Listen (7)	Track And Field - High Jump (13)
(I'm A) Road Runner (7)	Luv Is (20)	9th St. Bridge ..see: Old Weird Harold	Rigor Mortis (2)	Story Of The Chicken (15)	Track And Field - Mile Relay (13)
Invention Of Basketball (18)	Masculinity At Its Finest (17)	Noah: And The Neighbor (1,12)	Same Thing Happens Every Night (21)	Street Football (2,12)	Two Brothers (5)
It's The Women's Fault (10)	Medic (2)	Noah: Me And You, Lord (1,12)	Seattle (2)	Sulphur Fumes (18)	Two Daughters (5,14)
Karate (1,14)	Mojo Workout (6)	Noah: Right! (1,12)	$75 Car (3)	Sunny (7)	200 M.P.H. (9)
Kill The Boy (21)	Mothers And Fathers (9)	Nut In Every Car (1)	Sgt. Pepper's Lonely Hearts Club Band (7)	Superman (1)	Ursalena (7)
Kindergarten (3)	Mr. Ike & The Neighborhood T.V. Set (10)	Old Weird Harold (5,12)	Shift Down (20)	Survival (18)	Wallie, Wallie (17)
Las Vegas-Mirror Over My Bed (17)	My Boy Scout Troop (16)	Oops! (2,14)	Shoelaces (10)	T.V. Football (2)	Water Bottle (2,12)
Little Ole Man (Uptight-Everything's Alright) (6) **4**	My Brother Russell (16,19)	Opening (11)	Shop (3,4,14)	Tank, The (5)	Why Beat On Your Wife (17)
Little Tiny Hairs (1)	My Dad's Car (19)	Pep Talk (1)	Slow Class (18)	Tell Me You Love Me (6)	Wife, The (9)
Lone Ranger (2,12)	My Father (16)	Personal Hygiene (3)	Smoking (5,14)	Time Brings About A Change (7)	Window Of Life (22)
Losers, The (8)	My Hernia (16)	Place In The Sun (6)	Snakes And Alligators (16)	To Russell, My Brother, Whom I Slept With (8)	Wives (5)
Lower Tract (18)	My Pet Rhinoceros (2)	Planes (4)	Sneakers (2)	Tonsils (4)	**Yes, Yes, Yes** (20) **46**
	My Wife And Kids (19)	Playground, The (4)	Spanish Fly (10)	Toothache, The (3)	You're Driving Me Crazy (20)
	Natural Childbirth (21)	Ralph Jameson (2)	Special Class (4)	Toss Of The Coin (1,14)	
	Neanderthal Man (2)	Reach Out I'll Be There (7)			

COSTA, Nikka   '01
Born on 6/4/72 in Los Angeles. Female singer/songwriter. Daughter of prolific producer/arranger Don Costa.

6/9/01	120	9		©	**Everybody Got Their Something**			$10	Cheeba Sound 10096

Corners Of My Mind	Hope It Felt Good	Like A Feather	Nikka Who?	Push & Pull	Some Kind Of Beautiful
Everybody Got Their Something	Just Because	Nikka What?	Nothing	So Have I For You	Tug Of War

COSTANDINOS, Alec R., & The Syncophonic Orchestra '78
Costandinos is a European disco producer who also assembled the studio group **Love And Kisses**.

3/25/78	92	17			**Romeo & Juliet**			$12	Casablanca 7086

Shakespeare play set to a disco beat; side 1: Acts I & II; side 2: Acts III & IV

COSTELLO, Elvis ★109★   '79

Born Declan McManus on 8/25/54 in Paddington, London, England. Leading eclectic rock singer. Changed name to Elvis Costello in 1976; Costello is his mother's maiden name. In 1977, formed backing band The Attractions: Steve "Nieve" Nason (keyboards), Bruce Thomas (bass; **Southerland Brothers & Quiver**) and Peter Thomas (drums). Married Cait O'Riordan, former bassist with **The Pogues**, on 5/16/86. Appeared in the 1987 movie *Straight To Hell*.

1)*Armed Forces* 2)*Get Happy!!* 3)*Punch The Clock* 4)*Trust* 5)*Taking Liberties*

12/3/77+	32	36	▲	©	1	My Aim Is True			$15	Columbia 35037
4/15/78	30	17	●	©	2	This Year's Model	C:#6/174		$15	Columbia 35331
1/27/79	10	25	●	©	3	Armed Forces	C:#31/56		$15	Columbia 35709

ELVIS COSTELLO & THE ATTRACTIONS:

3/22/80	11	15		©	4	Get Happy!!	C:#16/42		$12	Columbia 36347
10/11/80	28	14		©	5	Taking Liberties	[K]		$12	Columbia 36839

ELVIS COSTELLO

2/14/81	28	15		©	6	Trust			$12	Columbia 37051
11/14/81	50	13		©	7	Almost Blue			$12	Columbia 37562
7/24/82	30	24		©	8	Imperial Bedroom			$12	Columbia 38157
8/13/83	24	24		©	9	Punch The Clock			$12	Columbia 38897
7/7/84	35	21		©	10	Goodbye Cruel World			$12	Columbia 39429
11/30/85+	116	16	●	©	11	The Best Of Elvis Costello & The Attractions	[G]		$12	Columbia 40101
3/22/86	39	18		©	12	King Of America			$12	Columbia 40173

ELVIS COSTELLO

10/11/86	84	11		©	13	Blood & Chocolate			$12	Columbia 40518

ELVIS COSTELLO:

2/25/89	32	25	●	©	14	Spike			$10	Warner 25848
6/1/91	55	7		©	15	Mighty Like A Rose			$10	Warner 26575
2/6/93	125	8		©	16	The Juliet Letters			$10	Warner 45180

ELVIS COSTELLO AND THE BRODSKY QUARTET

3/26/94	34	10		©	17	Brutal Youth			$10	Warner 45535
5/27/95	102	7		©	18	Kojak Variety			$10	Warner 45903
6/1/96	53	5		©	19	All This Useless Beauty			$10	Warner 46198

ELVIS COSTELLO & THE ATTRACTIONS

10/17/98	78	6		©	20	Painted From Memory			$10	Mercury 538002

ELVIS COSTELLO WITH BURT BACHARACH

Accidents Will Happen (3,11)	Big Light (12)	Comedians, The (10)	Everyday's Crying Mercy (18)	Great Unknown (10)	I Almost Had A Weakness (16)
After The Fall (15)	Big Sister's Clothes (6)	Complicated Shadows (19)	**Everyday I Write The Book** (9,11) **36**	Greatest Thing (9)	I Can't Stand Up For Falling Down (4,11)
Alison (1,11)	Big Tears (5)	Couldn't Call It Unexpected No. 4 (15)	Expert Rites (16)	Green Shirt (3)	(I Don't Want To Go To) Chelsea (5)
All Grown Up (15)	Birds Will Still Be Singing (16)	Crawling To The U.S.A. (5)	Favourite Hour (17)	Hand In Hand (2)	I Hope You're Happy Now (13)
All The Rage (17)	Black And White World (4,5)	Crimes Of Paris (13)	First To Leave (16)	Harpies Bizarre (15)	I Stand Accused (4)
All This Useless Beauty (19)	Blame It On Cain (1)	Damnation's Cellar (16)	Fish 'N' Chip Paper (6)	Hidden Charms (18)	I Still Have That Other Girl (20)
Almost Blue (8,11)	Blue Chair (13)	Days (4)	5ive Gears In Reverse (4)	High Fidelity (4)	I Thought I'd Write To Juliet (16)
American Without Tears (12)	Boy With A Problem (8)	Dead Letter (16)	For Other Eyes (16)	Home Is Anywhere You Hang Your Head (13)	I Threw It All Away (18)
....And In Every Home (8)	Brilliant Mistake (12)	Dear Sweet Filthy World (16)	From A Whisper To A Scream (6)	Home Truth (10)	I Wanna Be Loved (10,11)
(Angels Wanna Wear My) Red Shoes (1)	Broken (15)	Deep Dark Truthful Mirror (14)	Georgie And Her Rival (15)	Honey, Are You Straight Or Are You Blind? (13)	I Want To Vanish (19)
Any King's Shilling (14)	Brown To Blue (7)	Deliver Us (16)	Getting Mighty Crowded (5)	Honey Hush (7)	I Want You (13)
B Movie (4)	Busy Bodies (3)	Deportees Club (10)	Ghost Train (5)	Hoover Factory (5)	I'll Wear It Proudly (12)
Baby Plays Around (14)	Charm School (9)	Different Finger (6)	Girls Talk (5)	How Much I Lied (7)	I'm Not Angry (1)
Bama Lama Bama Loo (18)	Chemistry Class (3)	Distorted Angel (19)	Glitter Gulch (12)	How To Be Dumb (15)	I'm Your Toy (Hot Burrito #1) (7)
Battered Old Bird (13)	Chewing Gum (14)	Dr. Luther's Assistant (5)	God Give Me Strength (20)	Human Hands (8)	I've Been Wrong Before (18)
Beat, The (2)	Clean Money (5)	Don't Let Me Be Misunderstood (12)	God's Comic (14)	Human Touch (4)	Imposter, The (4)
Beaten To The Punch (4)	Clown Strike (17)	Eisenhower Blues (12)	Good Year For The Roses (7)	Hurry Down Doomsday (The Bugs Are Taking Over) (15)	In The Darkest Place (20)
Beyond Belief (8,11)	Clowntime Is Over (4,5)	Element Within Her (9)	Goon Squad (3)		Inch By Inch (10)
Big Boys (3)	Clubland (6,11)				
	Color Of The Blues (7)				

COSTELLO, Elvis — Cont'd

Indoor Fireworks (12)
Invasion Hit Parade (15)
Invisible Man (9)
It's Time (19)
Jack Of All Parades (12)
Jacksons, Monk And Rowe (16)
Joe Porterhouse (10)
Just A Memory (5)
Just About Glad (17)
Kid About It (8)
Kinder Murder (17)
King Horse (4)
King Of Thieves (9)
Last Boat Leaving (14)
Last Post (16)
Leave My Kitten Alone (18)
Less Than Zero (1)
Let Him Dangle (14)
Let Them All Talk (9)
Letter Home (16)
Lip Service (2)
Lipstick Vogue (2)
Little Atoms (19)
Little Palaces (12)
Little Savage (8)
Little Triggers (2)
Living In Paradise (2)
London's Brilliant Parade (17)
Long Division (20)

Long Honeymoon (8)
Lovable (12)
Love Field (10)
Love For Tender (4)
Love Went Mad (9)
Loved Ones (8)
Lovers Walk (6)
Luxembourg (6)
Man Called Uncle (4)
Man Out Of Time (8)
Miracle Man (1)
Miss Macbeth (14)
Moods For Moderns (3)
Motel Matches (4)
Mouth Almighty (9)
Must You Throw Dirt In My Face (18)
My Funny Valentine (5)
My Science Fiction Twin (17)
My Thief (20)
Mystery Dance (1)
New Amsterdam (4)
New Lace Sleeves (6)
Next Time Round (13)
Night Rally (5)
No Action (2)
No Dancing (1)
Oliver's Army (3,11)
Only Flame In Town (10,11) **56**

Opportunity (4)
Other End Of The Telescope (19)
Other Side Of Summer (15)
Our Little Angel (12)
Pads, Paws And Claws (14)
Painted From Memory (20)
Party Girl (3)
Pay It Back (1)
Payday (18)
Peace In Our Time (10)
Pidgin English (8)
Pills And Soap (9)
Playboy To A Man (15)
Please Stay (18)
Poisoned Rose (12)
Pony St. (17)
Poor Fractured Atlas (19)
Poor Napoleon (13)
Possession (4)
Pouring Water On A Drowning Man (18)
Pretty Words (6)
Pump It Up (2,11)
Radio, Radio (2,11)
Radio Sweetheart (5)
Remove This Doubt (18)
Riot Act (4)
Rocking Horse Road (17)
Romeo's Seance (16)

Room With No Number (10)
Running Out Of Fools (18)
Satellite (14)
Secondary Modern (4)
Senior Service (3)
Shabby Doll (8)
Shallow Grave (19)
Shipbuilding (9,11)
Shot With His Own Gun (6)
Sittin' And Thinkin' (7)
Sleep Of The Just (12)
Sneaky Feelings (1)
So Like Candy (15)
Sour Milk-Cow Blues (10)
Stalin Malone (14)
Starting To Come To Me (19)
Still Too Soon To Know (17)
Strange (18)
Stranger In The House (5)
Strict Time (6)
Success (7)
Such Unlikely Lovers (20)
Suit Of Lights (12)
Sulky Girl (17)
Sunday's Best (5)
Sweet Dreams (7)
Sweet Pear (15)
Sweetest Punch (20)
Swine (16)

T.K.O. (Boxing Day) (9)
Taking My Life In Your Hands (16)
Talking In The Dark (5)
Tears At The Birthday Party (20)
Tears Before Bedtime (8)
13 Steps Lead Down (17)
This House Is Empty Now (20)
This Is Hell (17)
This Offer Is Unrepeatable (16)
This Sad Burlesque (16)
...This Town... (14)
This Year's Girl (2)
Tiny Steps (5)
Tokyo Storm Warning (13)
Toledo (20)
Tonight The Bottle Let Me Down (7)
Too Far Gone (7)
Town Cryer (8)
Tramp The Dirt Down (14)
20% Amnesia (17)
Two Little Hitlers (3)
Uncomplicated (13)
Veronica (14) **19**
Very Thought Of You (18)
Waiting For The End Of The World (1)

Watch Your Step (6,11)
Watching The Detectives (1,11)
Wednesday Week (5)
Welcome To The Working Week (1)
What's Her Name Today? (20)
(What's So Funny 'Bout) Peace, Love And Understanding (3,11)
White Knuckles (9)
Who Do You Think You Are? (16)
Why? (16)
Why Can't A Man Stand Alone? (19)
Why Don't You Love Me (Like You Used To Do) (7)
World And His Wife (9)
Worthless Thing (10)
You Belong To Me (2)
You Bowed Down (19)
You Little Fool (8)
You Tripped At Every Step (17)
You'll Never Be A Man (6)

COTTON, James, Band   '75
Born on 7/1/35 in Tunica, Mississippi. Blues harmonica player.

| 12/16/67 | 194 | 2 | © | 1 | The James Cotton Blues Band | | | $20 | Verve Forecast 3023 |
| 1/18/75 | 146 | 9 | © | 2 | 100% Cotton | | | $12 | Buddah 5620 |

All Walks Of Life (2)
Blues In My Sleep (1)
Boogie Thing (2)
Burner (2)

Creeper Creeps Again (2)
Don't Start Me Talkin' (1)
Fatuation (2)
Feelin' Good (1)

Fever (2)
Good Time Charlie (1)
How Long Can A Fool Go Wrong? (2)

I Don't Know (2)
Jelly, Jelly (1)
Knock On Wood (1)
Off The Wall (1)

Oh Why (1)
One More Mile (2)
Rockett 88 (2)
Something On Your Mind (1)

Sweet Sixteen (1)
Turn On Your Lovelight (1)

COTTON, Josie   '82
Born in Dallas. Singer/actress. Appeared in the movie *Valley Girl*.

| 8/7/82 | 147 | 12 | | | Convertible Music | | | $12 | Elektra 60140 |

Another Girl
Bye, Bye Baby

He Could Be The One 74
I Need The Night, Tonight

Johnny, Are You Queer?
No Pictures Of Dad

Rockin' Love
So Close

Systematic Way
Tell Him

Waitin' For Your Love

COUCHOIS   '79
Rock group: brothers Chris (vocals), Pat (guitar) and Mike (drums) Couchois, with Howard Messer (bass) and Chas Carlson (keyboards). Also see **Ratchell**.

| 4/21/79 | 170 | 4 | | | Couchois | | | $12 | Warner 3289 |

Colonel, The
Cripple
Devil's Triangle

Do It In Darkness
Going To The Races

I Could Never Take Her Away From You
Kalahari Cattle Drive

No Longer Needed
Walkin' The Fence

COUGAR, John — see MELLENCAMP

COULTER, Phil — see GALWAY, James

COUNTDOWN DANCE MASTERS, The   '96
Studio group from Canada.

| 9/7/96 | 93 | 16 | © | | Macarena Tropical Disco | | | $10 | Madacy 0346 |

Bamboleo
Boombastic

Brazil
Dancando Lambada

In The Summertime
La Cumbia

Lambada
Macarena

Oye Como Va
Oye Mi Canto

Ritmo De La Noche
Sweat (Alalalalalong)

COUNTDOWN SINGERS, The   '95
Studio group from Canada.

2/25/95	145	2	©	1	A Time For Romance - Unchained Melodies			$10	Madacy 0338
9/16/95	51	5	©	2	Love Songs From The Movies			$10	Madacy 4902
1/1/00	194	1	©	3	Mambo #5			$10	Madacy 0353

After All (1)
Bailamos (3)
Believe (3)
Boom, Boom, Boom, Boom! (3)
Can You Feel The Love Tonight (1)
End Of The Road (2)

(Everything I Do) I Do It For You (1,2)
Glory Of Love (1)
I Will Always Love You (1,2)
I Will Go With You (Con Te Partiro) (3)
If You Had My Love (3)
It Must Have Been Love (1,2)

It's Not Right But It's Okay (3)
Livin' La Vida Loca (3)
Mambo #5 (A Little Bit Of...) (3)
Memory (1)
Places That Belong To You (2)
Sex On The Beach (3)
Somewhere Out There (1)
Strong Enough (3)

Tears In Heaven (2)
This Used To Be My Playground (2)
Try A Little Tenderness (2)
Unchained Melody (1,2)
We Like To Party (3)
What Becomes Of The Brokenhearted (2)

When I Fall In Love (1,2)
Wild Wild West (3)
Will You Be There (1)
Wind Beneath My Wings (1)
You Gotta Love Someone (2)

COUNT FIVE   '66
Psychedelic-rock group from San Jose, California: Kenn Ellner (vocals), John Michalski and John Byrne (guitars), Ron Chaney (bass) and Craig Atkinson (drums). Atkinson died on 10/13/98 (age 50).

| 12/3/66 | 122 | 6 | © | | Psychotic Reaction | | | $50 | Double Shot 1001 |

Can't Get Your Lovin'
Double-Decker Bus

Morning After
My Generation

Out In The Street
Peace Of Mind

Pretty Big Mouth
Psychotic Reaction 5

She's Fine
They're Gonna Get You

World, The

COUNTING CROWS '96

Rock group from San Francisco: Adam Duritz (vocals), David Bryson (guitar), Charlie Gillingham (piano), Matt Malley (bass) and Steve Bowman (drums). Ben Mize replaced Bowman in 1994. Dan Vickrey (guitar) joined in 1996.

1/1/94	4	93	▲⁷	©	1 August And Everything After	C:#19/38		$10	DGC 24528
11/2/96	❶¹	50	▲²	©	2 Recovering The Satellites			$10	DGC 24975
8/1/98	19	9	●	©	3 Across A Wire - Live In New York		[L]	$15	DGC 25222 [2]

Disc 1: recorded at 8/12/97 at Chelsea Studios; Disc 2: recorded on 11/6/97 at Hammerstein Ballroom

| 11/20/99 | 8 | 23 | ▲ | © | 4 This Desert Life | | | $10 | DGC 490415 |

All My Friends (4)　Children In Bloom (2,3)　Have You Seen Me Lately? (2,3)　Miller's Angels (2)　Rain King (1,3)　Sullivan Street (1,3)
Amy Hit The Atmosphere (4)　Colorblind (4)　High Life (4)　Monkey (2)　Raining In Baltimore (1,3)　Time And Time Again (1)
Angels Of The Silences (2,3)　Daylight Fading (2)　I Wish I Was A Girl (4)　Mr. Jones (1,3)　Recovering The Satellites (2,3)　Walkaways (2,3)
Anna Begins (1,3)　Four Days (4)　I'm Not Sleeping (2,3)　Mrs. Potter's Lullaby (4)　Round Here (1,3)
Another Horsedreamer's Blues (2)　Ghost Train (1,3)　Long December (2,3)　Murder Of One (1,3)　Speedway (4)
Catapult (2,3)　Goodnight Elisabeth (2)　Mercury (2,3)　Omaha (1)　St. Robinson In His Cadillac Dream (4)
　　Hanginaround (4) 28　　Perfect Blue Buildings (1)

COUNTRY JOE AND THE FISH '68

Born Joseph McDonald on 1/1/42 in El Monte, California. Highly political rock singer/guitarist. The Fish: Barry Melton (guitar), David Cohen (guitar), Bruce Barthol (bass) and Chicken Hirsch (drums).

1)Together　2)Electric Music For The Mind And Body　3)Here We Are Again

6/10/67	39	38		©	1 Electric Music For The Mind And Body			$20	Vanguard 79244
12/23/67+	67	28		©	2 I-Feel-Like-I'm-Fixin'-To-Die			$20	Vanguard 79266
7/13/68	23	16		©	3 Together			$20	Vanguard 79277
6/21/69	48	11			4 Here We Are Again			$20	Vanguard 79299
1/3/70	74	9			5 Country Joe & The Fish/Greatest Hits		[G]	$20	Vanguard 6545
5/2/70	111	9		©	6 C.J. Fish			$20	Vanguard 6555

COUNTRY JOE McDONALD:

8/7/71	185	4		©	7 War, War, War			$20	Vanguard 79315
10/30/71	197	2			8 The Life and Times of Country Joe & The Fish from Haight-Ashbury to Woodstock		[K]	$25	Vanguard 27/28 [2]
2/19/72	179	4		©	9 Incredible! Live!		[L]	$20	Vanguard 79316

recorded at the Bitter End in New York City

| 11/1/75+ | 124 | 14 | | © | 10 Paradise With An Ocean View | | | $15 | Fantasy 9495 |

Away Bounce My Bubbles (3)　Eastern Jam (2)　I-Feel-Like-I'm-Fixin'-To-Die-Rag (2,5,8)　Man From Aphabaska (7)　Rock And Soul Music (3,8)　Tricks (10)
Baby Song (6)　Entertainment Is My Business (9)　I'll Survive (4)　Mara (6)　Rock Coast Blues (2)　Tricky Dicky (9)
Baby, You're Driving Me Crazy (4)　Fish Cheer (medley) (2,5)　I'm On The Road Again (9)　March Of The Dead (7)　Rockin' Round The World (6)　Twins, The (7)
Bass Strings (1,5,8)　Fish Moan (3)　It's So Nice To Have Love (4)　Maria (4,5)　Sad And Lonely Times (1)　Untitled Protest (3,8)
Breakfast For Two (10) 92　Flying High (1,8)　Janis (2,8)　Marijuana (8)　Save The Whales! (10)　Walk In Santiago (9)
Bright Suburban Mr. & Mrs. Clean Machine (3)　For No Reason (4)　Jean Desprez (7)　Masked Marauder (1,5,8)　Section 43 (1)　Waltzing In The Moonlight (3,8)
Call, The (7)　Forward (7)　Kiss My Ass (9)　Mojo Navigator (3)　She's A Bird (6)　War Widow (7)
Cetacean (3)　Free Some Day (9)　Limit, The (10)　Munition Maker (7)　Silver And Gold (6)　Who Am I (2,5,8)
Colors For Susan (2)　Grace (1,8)　Living In The Future In A Plastic Dome (9)　My Girl (4)　Sing Sing Sing (6,8)　You Know What I Mean (9)
Crystal Blues (4,8)　Hand Of Man (6)　　**Not So Sweet Martha Lorraine** (1,5,8) 95　Streets Of Your Town (3,5)　Young Fellow, My Lad (7)
Death Sound (1,8)　Hang On (6)　Lonely On The Road (10)　Oh, Jamaica (10)　Super Bird (1,8)
Deep Down In Our Hearts (9)　Harlem Song (3)　Lost My Connection (10)　Oh, My, My (9)　Susan (3)
Doctor Of Electricity (4)　Here I Go Again (4,5)　Love (1,8)　Pat's Song (2)　Sweet Marie (9)
Donovan's Reef (4)　Hey Bobby (6)　Love Machine (6,8)　Porpoise Mouth (1,5,8)　Tear Down The Walls (10)
　　Holy Roller (10)　Magoo (2)　Return Of Sweet Lorraine (6)　Thought Dream (2)
　　　　　　Thursday (2)

COUNTS, The '72

Funk group from Detroit: Mose Davis (vocals), Demetrus Cates, Raoul Keith Mangrum, Andrew Gibson and Leroy Emmanuel.

| 7/1/72 | 193 | 2 | | © | What's Up Front That-Counts | | | $30 | Westbound 2011 |

Bills　Pack Of Lies　Rhythm Changes　Thinking Single　What's Up Front That-Counts　Why Not Start All Over Again

COURTNEY, David '76

Born in England. Singer/songwriter/drummer. Formed a songwriting partnership with **Leo Sayer** in the mid-1970s.

| 2/21/76 | 194 | 4 | | | David Courtney's First Day | | | $12 | United Artists 553 |

Don't Let The Photos Fool You　Everybody Needs A Little Loving　It's All For You　Silverbird　When Your Life Is Your Own
Don't Look Now　If You Wanna Dance　Life Is So They Say　Stranded　You Ain't Got Me
　　My Mind　Take This Mask Away

COVERDALE·PAGE '93

British hard-rock veterans David Coverdale (vocalist of **Deep Purple** and **Whitesnake**) and **Jimmy Page** (guitarist of **The Yardbirds**, **Led Zeppelin** and **The Firm**).

| 4/3/93 | 5 | 24 | ▲ | © | Coverdale-Page | | | $10 | Geffen 24487 |

Absolution Blues　Easy Does It　Over Now　Shake My Tree　Take Me For A Little While　Whisper A Prayer For The Dying
Don't Leave Me This Way　Feeling Hot　Pride And Joy　Take A Look At Yourself　Waiting On You

COVER GIRLS, The '88

Female dance trio from New York City: Louise Sabater, Caroline Jackson and Sunshine Wright (replaced by Margo Urban in 1989).

| 8/15/87+ | 64 | 61 | | © | 1 Show Me | | | $10 | Fever 4 |
| 10/7/89+ | 108 | 19 | | © | 2 We Can't Go Wrong | | | $10 | Capitol 91041 |

All That Glitters Isn't Gold (2) 49　Cute (2)　Love Mission (2)　Nothing Could Be Better (2)　**Promise Me** (1) 40　That Boy Of Mine (1,2)
Because Of You (1) 27　**Inside Outside** (1) 55　**My Heart Skips A Beat** (2) 38　Once Upon A Time (2)　**Show Me** (1) 44　Up On The Roof (2)
　　Love Emergency (1)　One In This World (2)　One Night Affair (1)　**Spring Love** (1) 98　**We Can't Go Wrong** (2) 8

COWARD, Noel '56

Born on 12/16/1899 in Teddington, Middlesex, England. Died of a heart attack on 3/26/73 (age 73). Enormously popular and enduring actor/playwright/personality in England. Knighted by Queen Elizabeth II in 1970.

| 1/28/56 | 14 | 2 | | | Noel Coward At Las Vegas | | [L] | $30 | Columbia 5063 |

recorded at the Desert Inn; Carlton Hayes (orchestra); Peter Matz (piano)

Alice Is At It Again　I'll Follow My Secret Heart (medley)　Let's Do It　Nina　Room With A View
Bar On The Piccola Marina　I'll See You Again (medley)　Loch Lomond　Party's Over Now　Someday I'll Find You (medley)
Dance, Little Lady (medley)　If Love Were All (medley)　Mad Dogs And Englishmen　Play, Orchestra, Play (medley)　Uncle Harry
　　Matelot　Poor Little Rich Girl (medley)　World Weary

COWBOY JUNKIES '89
Country-punk group from Toronto: siblings Margo (vocals), Michael (guitar) and Peter (drums) Timmins, with Alan Anton (bass).

DEBUT	PEAK	WKS	RIAA	CD			$	Label & Number
1/28/89	26	29	▲	©	1	**The Trinity Session**	$10	RCA 8568
3/31/90	47	16		©	2	**The Caution Horses**	$10	RCA 2058
2/29/92	76	15		©	3	**Black Eyed Man**	$10	RCA 61049
12/11/93+	114	14		©	4	**Pale Sun, Crescent Moon**	$10	RCA 66344
3/16/96	55	21		©	5	**Lay It Down**	$10	Geffen 24952
7/18/98	98	5		©	6	**Miles From Our Home**	$10	Geffen 25201
6/2/01	107	2		©	7	**Open**	$10	Latent 431020

Angel Mine (5)
Anniversary Song (4)
Bea's Song (River Song Trilogy: part II) (5)
Beneath The Gate (7)
Black Eyed Man (3)
Blue Guitar (6)
Bread And Wine (7)
'Cause Cheap Is How I Feel (2)
Close My Eyes (7)
Cold Tea Blues (4)
Come Calling (Her Song) (5)
Come Calling (His Song) (5)
Common Disaster (7)
Cowboy Junkies Lament (3)

Crescent Moon (4)
Dark Hole Again (7)
Darkling Days (6)
Dragging Hooks (7)
Dreaming My Dreams With You (1)
Escape Is So Simple (2)
First Recollection (4)
Floorboard Blues (4)
Good Friday (6)
Hard To Explain (4)
Hold On To Me (5)
Hollow As A Bone (6)
Horse In The Country (3)
Hunted (4)

I Did It All For You (7)
I Don't Get It (1)
I'm So Lonesome I Could Cry (1)
I'm So Open (7)
If You Were The Woman And I Was The Man (3)
Just Want To See (5)
Last Spike (3)
Lay It Down (5)
Lonely Sinking Feeling (3)
Mariner's Song (2)
Miles From Our Home (6)
Mining For Gold (1)
Misguided Angel (1)

Murder, Tonight, In The Trailer Park (3)
Musical Key (5)
New Dawn Coming (6)
No Birds Today (6)
Now I Know (5)
Oregon Hill (3)
Pale Sun (4)
Post, The (4)
Postcard Blues (1)
Powderfinger (2)
Ring On The Sill (4)
Rock And Bird (2)
Seven Years (4)
Small Swift Birds (7)

Someone Out There (6)
Something More Besides You (5)
Southern Rain (3)
Speaking Confidentially (5)
Summer Of Discontent (6)
Sun Comes Up, It's Tuesday Morning (2)
Sweet Jane (1)
Thirty Summers (2)
This Street, That Man, This Life (3)
Those Final Feet (6)
Thousand Year Prayer (7)
To Live Is To Fly (3)

To Love Is To Bury (1)
Townes' Blues (3)
200 More Miles (1)
Upon Still Waters (7)
Walking After Midnight (1)
Where Are You Tonight? (2)
White Sail (4)
Winter's Song (3)
Witches (2)
You Will Be Loved Again (2)

COWBOY MOUTH '97
Rock group from New Orleans: John Thomas Griffith (vocals), Paul Sanchez (guitar), Rob Savoy (bass) and Fred LeBlanc (drums).

DEBUT	PEAK	WKS	RIAA	CD			$	Label & Number
6/28/97	192	1		©		**Are You With Me?**	$10	MCA 11447

God Makes The Rain
How Do You Tell Someone

Jenny Says
Laughable

Light It On Fire
Louisiana Lowdown

Love Of My Life
Man On The Run

New Orleans
Peacemaker

So Sad About Me
Take It Out On Me

COWSILLS, The '68
Family pop group from Newport, Rhode Island: brothers Bill, Bob, Paul, Barry and John, with their younger sister Susan and mother Barbara Cowsill (died on 1/31/85, age 56). Susan married Peter Holsapple of **The DB's** on 4/18/93. Group was the inspiration for TV's **The Partridge Family**.

DEBUT	PEAK	WKS	RIAA	CD			Sym	$	Label & Number
11/4/67+	31	17		©	1	**The Cowsills**		$20	MGM 4498
3/9/68	89	14			2	**We Can Fly**		$20	MGM 4534
9/7/68	105	12			3	**Captain Sad And His Ship Of Fools**		$20	MGM 4554
1/18/69	127	9		©	4	**The Best Of The Cowsills**	[G]	$20	MGM 4597
5/10/69	16	24		©	5	**The Cowsills In Concert**	[L]	$20	MGM 4619
5/8/71	200	1			6	**On My Side**		$20	London 587

Act Naturally (5)
Ask The Children (3)
Beautiful Beige (2)
Bridge, The (3)
Can You Love? (6)
Can't Measure The Cost Of A Woman Lost (3)
Captain Sad And His Ship Of Fools (3,4)
Cheatin' On Me (6)
(Come 'Round Here) I'm The One You Need (1)
Contact Mae (6)

Cruel War (5)
Devil With A Blue Dress On (medley) (5)
Dover Mine (6)
Down On The Farm (6)
Dreams Of Linda (1)
Fantasy World Of Harry Faversham (3)
Gettin' Into That Sunny, Sunny Feelin' Again (1)
Good Golly Miss Molly (medley) (5)
Good Ole Rock & Roll Song (6)

Good Vibrations (5)
Gotta Get Away From It All (2,4)
Gray, Sunny Day (2,4)
Hair (5)
Heather Says (6)
Heaven Held (2)
Hello, Hello (5)
How Can I Make You See (1)
If You Can't Have It - Knock It (6)
In Need Of A Friend (2,4) **54**
Indian Lake (3,4) **10**
La Rue Du Sole (1)

Make The Music Flow (3)
Meet Me At The Wishing Well (3)
Mister Flynn (2,4)
Monday, Monday (5)
Mystery Of Life (6)
Newspaper Blanket (3,4)
On My Side (6)
Once There Was A Time (6)
One Man Show (2)
Painting The Day (3)
Paperback Writer (5)
Path Of Love (3,4)

Pennies (1)
Please Mister Postman (5)
Poor Baby (4) **44**
Rain, The Park & Other Things (1,4) **2**
Reach Out (I'll Be There) (5)
River Blue (1)
(Stop, Look) Is Anyone There? (1)
Sunshine Of Your Love (5)
That's My Time Of The Day (1)
There Is A Child (6)

Thinkin' About The Other Side (1)
Time For Remembrance (2,4)
Troubled Roses (1)
Walk Away Renee (5)
We Can Fly (2,4) **21**
What Is Happy? (2)
Who Can Teach A Songbird To Sing (3)
Yesterday's Girl (3)

COX, Deborah '98
Born on 7/13/74 in Toronto. R&B singer/songwriter.

DEBUT	PEAK	WKS	RIAA	CD			$	Label & Number
10/28/95	102	16	▲	©	1	**Deborah Cox**	$10	Arista 18781
10/17/98	72	46	●	©	2	**One Wish**	$10	Arista 19022

Call Me (1)
Couldn't We (2)
I Never Knew (2)
I Won't Give Up (2)
I'm Your Natural Woman (1)

It Could've Been You (1)
It's Over Now (2) **70**
Just Be Good To Me (1)
Just When I Think I'm Over You (2)

Love Is On The Way (2)
My First Night With You (1)
My Radio (1)
Never Gonna Break My Heart Again (1)

Nobody's Supposed To Be Here (2) **2**
One Day You Will (2)
One Wish (2)
Sentimental (1) **20**

September (2)
Sound Of My Tears (1) **97**
Things Just Ain't The Same (2) **56**
We Can't Be Friends (2) **8**

Where Do We Go From Here (1) **48**
Who Do U Love (1) **17**

CRABBY APPLETON '70
Pop-rock group formed in Los Angeles: Michael Fennelly (vocals, guitar), Casey Foutz (keyboards), Flaco Falcon (percussion), Hank Harvey (bass) and Phil Jones (drums).

DEBUT	PEAK	WKS	RIAA	CD			$	Label & Number
6/27/70	175	6				**Crabby Appleton**	$20	Elektra 74067

Can't Live My Life
Catherine

Go Back **36**
How Long Will It Take

Hunger For Love
Other Side

Peace By Peace
Some Madness

To All My Friends
Try

CRACKER '94
Rock trio from Redlands, California: David Lowery (vocals; **Camper Van Beethoven**), John Hickman (guitar) and Dave Faragher (bass). Faragher left in 1995. Bob Rupe (bass) and Charlie Quintana (drums) joined in 1996. Frank Furnaro replaced Quintana in 1997. Kenny Margolis (keyboards) joined in early 1998.

DEBUT	PEAK	WKS	RIAA	CD			$	Label & Number
9/11/93+	59	45	●	©	1	**Kerosene Hat**	$10	Virgin 39012
4/20/96	63	6		©	2	**The Golden Age**	$10	Virgin 41498
9/12/98	182	1		©	3	**Gentleman's Blues**	$10	Virgin 46263

Been Around The World (3)
Bicycle Spaniard (2)
Big Dipper (2)
Dixie Babylon (2)
Gentleman's Blues (3)
Get Off This (1)

Golden Age (2)
Good Life (3)
Hallelujah (3)
Hold Of Myself (3)
How Can I Live Without You (2)
I Can't Forget You (2)

I Hate My Generation (2)
I Want Everything (1)
I Want Out Of The Circus (3)
I'm A Little Rocket Ship (2)
James River (3)
Kerosene Hat (1)

Let's Go For A Ride (1)
Lonesome Johnny Blues (1)
Loser (1)
Low (1) **64**
Lullabye (3)
Movie Star (1)

My Life Is Totally Boring Without You (3)
Nostalgia (1)
Nothing To Believe In (2)
100 Flower Power Maximum (2)

CRACKER — Cont'd

Seven Days (3)	Sweet Potato (1)	Take Me Down To The	Useless Stuff (2)	Wild One (3)
Sick Of Goodbyes (1)	Sweet Thistle Pie (2)	Infirmary (1)	Waiting For You Girl (3)	World Is Mine (3)
Star (3)		Trials & Tribulations (3)	Wedding Day (3)	

CRACK THE SKY '78

Rock group from Steubenville, Ohio: John Palumbo (vocals), Jim Griffiths and Rick Witkowski (guitars), Joe Macre (bass) and Joey D'Amico (drums). In 1977, Gary Lee Chappell replaced Palumbo. Group split in 1979. Palumbo, Witkowski and D'Amico reunited in 1989 with Vince DePaul (keyboards).

DEBUT	PEAK	WKS	CD	#	Title	$	Label & Number
1/24/76	161	6	©	1	**Crack The Sky**	$15	Lifesong 6000
10/30/76	142	5	©	2	**Animal Notes**	$15	Lifesong 6005
3/11/78	124	8	©	3	**Safety In Numbers**	$15	Lifesong 6015
6/24/89	186	5	©	4	**From The Greenhouse**	$10	Grudge 4500
4/7/90	164	10	©	5	**Dog City**	$10	Grudge 4520

All The Things We Do (4)	Dog Redux (5)	I'll Be There (5)	Maybe I Can Fool Everybody	Quicksand (5)	Under Red Skies (4)
Animal Skins (2)	Don't Call Me Brother (5)	Ice (1)	(Tonight) (2)	Rangers At Midnight (2)	Virgin....No (2)
Apathy (3)	Flashlight (3)	Invaders From Mars (2)	Mind Baby (1)	Robots For Ronnie (1)	Waiting For The New World (5)
Big Money (4)	From The Greenhouse (4)	Lighten Up McGraw (3)	Monkeyboy (4)	Safety In Numbers (3)	We Want Mine (2)
Can I Play For You (Ian's Song)	Frozen Rain (4)	Long Nights (3)	Mr. President (5)	Sea Epic (1)	Wet Teenager (2)
(4)	Give Myself To You (3)	Lost Boys (5)	Night On The Town (With Snow	She's A Dancer (1)	
Dog City (5)	Hold On (1)	Lost In America (1)	White) (3)	Sleep (1)	
	I Don't Have A Tie (1)	Love Me Like A Terrorist (1)	Play On (2)	Surf City (1)	

CRADDOCK, Billy "Crash" '74

Born on 6/13/39 in Greensboro, North Carolina. Country-rock singer.

DEBUT	PEAK	WKS	#	Title	$	Label & Number
8/24/74	142	5		**Rub It In**	$12	ABC 817

Arkansas Red	Home Is Such A Lonely Place	It's Hard To Love A Hungry,	Quarter Til Three	**Ruby, Baby** *33*	Walk When Love Walks
Farmer's Daughter	To Go	Worried Man	**Rub It In** *16*	Stop! If You Love Me	Walk Your Kisses

CRAMER, Floyd '61

Born on 10/27/33 in Samti, Louisiana; raised in Huttig, Arkansas. Died of cancer on 12/31/97 (age 64). Legendary country session pianist.

DEBUT	PEAK	WKS	CD	#	Title	Sym	$	Label & Number
8/14/61	70	16	©	1	**On The Rebound**	[I]	$20	RCA Victor 2359
5/26/62	113	6		2	**Floyd Cramer Gets Organ-ized**	[I]	$20	RCA Victor 2488
10/13/62	130	2		3	**I Remember Hank Williams**	[I]	$20	RCA Victor 2544
10/23/65+	107	13		4	**Class Of '65**	[I]	$15	RCA Victor 3405
9/17/66	123	7		5	**Class Of '66**	[I]	$15	RCA Victor 3650
5/6/67	166	6		6	**Here's What's Happening!**	[I]	$15	RCA Victor 3746
12/2/67	26ˣ	5	©	7	**We Wish You a Merry Christmas**	[X-I]	$15	RCA Victor 3828
4/25/70	183	3		8	**The Big Ones, Volume II**	[I]	$15	RCA Victor 4312
5/24/80	170	5		9	**Dallas**	[I]	$12	RCA Victor 3613

Again (2)	First Hurt (2)	I'll Never Fall In Love Again (8)	Lullaby Of Birdland (2)	Santa Claus Is Comin' To Town	When A Man Loves A Woman
All In The Family (Those Were	First Impression (1)	I'm So Lonesome I Could Cry	M*A*S*H (9)	(medley) (7)	(5)
The Days) (9)	First Noël (medley) (7)	(3)	Message To Michael (5)	Sentimental Journey (2)	White Christmas (medley) (7)
Alma Mater (1)	Frosty The Snow Man (medley)	Incredible Hulk (9)	Midnight Cowboy (8)	Silent Night (medley) (7)	Who Am I (6)
Almost Persuaded (6)	(7)	It Came Upon A Midnight Clear	Monday, Monday (5)	Silver Bells (medley) (7)	Why Don't You Love Me (3)
Alone And Forsaken (3)	Good Vibrations (6)	(medley) (7)	Mr. Lonely (4)	Softly, As I Leave You (8)	Willow Weep For Me (4)
Away In A Manger (medley) (7)	Gospel Theme (2)	Jambalaya (3)	My Blue Heaven (2)	Something (8)	Winchester Cathedral (6)
Band Of Gold (5)	Hark! The Herald Angels Sing	Jingle Bell Rock (7)	My Funny Valentine (7)	Somewhere (6)	Winter Wonderland (medley) (7)
Born Free (6)	(medley) (7)	Jingle Bells (medley) (7)	My Way (7)	Spanish Flea (5)	Wonderland By Night (1)
Both Sides Now (8)	Have Yourself A Merry Little	Jordu (2)	O Come, All Ye Faithful	Strangers In The Night (5)	Work Song (6)
Cast Your Fate To The Wind (4)	Christmas (medley) (7)	Joy To The World (medley) (7)	(medley) (7)	String Of Pearls (2)	(You Don't Have To) Paint Me A
Cherish (6)	He (5)	Kaw-Liga (3)	O Little Town Of Bethlehem	Sweet Pea (1)	Picture (6)
Christmas Song (Chestnuts	Here Comes Santa Claus	King Of The Road (4)	(medley) (7)	Tammy (1)	(You're My) Soul And
Roasting on an Open Fire)	(medley) (7)	Knot's Landing (9)	**On The Rebound** (1) *4*	Taxi (9)	Inspiration (5)
(medley) (7)	Hey, Good Lookin' (3)	Laverne And Shirley (Making	Paperback Writer (5)	Those Were The Days ..see: All	You've Lost That Lovin' Feelin'
Cold, Cold Heart (3)	House Of Gold (3)	Our Dreams Come True) (9)	Perdido (2)	In The Family	(4)
Corinna, Corinna (1)	I Can Imagine (1)	Leaving On A Jet Plane (8)	Put A Little Love In Your Heart	Try To Remember (4)	Young And The Restless
Crying (5)	I Can't Help It (3)	**Let's Go** (2) *90*	(8)	Two Of A Kind (1)	(Nadia's Theme), Main Theme
Dallas (9)	I Feel Fine (4)	Little Drummer Boy (medley) (7)	Rain On The Roof (6)	Two-Twenty-Two, Theme From	From (9)
Danny Boy (1)	I Just Don't Know What To Do	Little House On The Prairie	Raindrops Keep Falling On My	(8)	Your Cheatin' Heart (3)
Dear Heart (4)	With Myself (6)	(The Little House) (9)	Head (8)	Up On The Housetop (medley)	
Deck The Halls (medley) (7)	I'll Be Home For Christmas (7)	Louie, Louie (8)	Red Roses For A Blue Lady (4)	(7)	
Downtown (4)	I'll Be There (4)	Love Letters (5)	Rudolph The Red-Nosed	Waltons, The (9)	
Dreamer, The (2)	I'll Follow The Sun (4)	**Lovesick Blues** (3) *87*	Reindeer (medley) (7)	We Have All The Time In The	
Faded Love (1)			**San Antonio Rose** (1) *8*	World (8)	

CRANBERRIES, The '96

Pop-rock group from Limerick, Ireland: Dolores O'Riordan (vocals), brothers Noel (guitar) and Mike (bass) Hogan, and Fergal Lawler (drums).

DEBUT	PEAK	WKS	RIAA	CD	#	Title	$	Label & Number
7/17/93	18	130	▲⁵	©	1	**Everybody Else Is Doing It, So Why Can't We?** ....C:#23/14	$10	Island 514156
10/22/94+	6	90	▲⁷	©	2	**No Need To Argue**	$10	Island 524050
5/18/96	4	51	▲²	©	3	**To The Faithful Departed**	$10	Island 524234
5/15/99	13	10	●	©	4	**Bury The Hatchet**	$10	Island 524611

Animal Instinct (4)	Dying In The Sun (4)	I Can't Be With You (1)	Loud And Clear (4)	Salvation (4)	What's On My Mind (4)
Bosnia (3)	Electric Blue (4)	I Just Shot John Lennon (3)	No Need To Argue (2)	Saving Grace (4)	**When You're Gone** (3) *22*
Copycat (4)	Empty (2)	I Still Do (1)	Not Sorry (1)	Shattered (4)	Will You Remember? (3)
Daffodil Lament (2)	Everything I Said (1)	I Will Always (1)	Ode To My Family (2)	Still Can't... (1)	Yeat's Grave (2)
Delilah (4)	Fee Fi Fo (4)	I'm Still Remembering (3)	Pretty (1)	Sunday (1)	You And Me (4)
Desperate Andy (4)	Forever Yellow Skies (3)	Icicle Melts (1)	Promises (4)	Twenty One (2)	Zombie (2)
Disappointment (2)	**Free To Decide** (3) *48*	Joe (1)	Put Me Down (1)	Waltzing Back (1)	
Dreaming My Dreams (2)	Hollywood (3)	Just My Imagination (4)	Rebels, The (3)	Wanted (1)	
Dreams (1) *42*	How (1)	**Linger** (1) *8*	Ridiculous Thoughts (2)	War Child (3)	

CRANE, Les '72

Born on 12/3/35 in San Francisco. Hosted TV talk show *ABC's Nightlife* in 1964. Married to actress Tina Louise from 1966-70.

| 12/4/71+ | **32** | 11 | | | **Desiderata**.. [T] | **$15** | Warner 2570 |

Beauty - Shining From The Inside Out
Courage - Eyes That See
Desiderata *8*
Esperanza - Hope
Friends
Happiness - I Got No Cares
Independence - A Different Drummer
Love - Children Learn What They Live
Nature - Wilderness
Vision

CRASH TEST DUMMIES '94

Pop-rock group from Winnipeg, Canada: brothers Brad (vocals) and Dan (bass) Roberts, with Ellen Reid (keyboards), Benjamin Darvill (harmonica) and Mitch Dorge (drums).

| 1/29/94 | **9** | 42 | ▲² | © | 1 **God Shuffled His Feet** | C:#29/7 | | **$10** | Arista 16531 |
| 10/19/96 | **78** | 5 | | © | 2 **A Worm's Life** .... | | | **$10** | Arista 39779 |

Afternoons & Coffeespoons (1) *66*
All Of This Ugly (2)
God Shuffled His Feet (1)
He Liked To Feel It (2)
Here I Stand Before Me (1)
How Does A Duck Know? (1)
I Think I'll Disappear Now (1)
I'm A Dog (2)
I'm Outlived By That Thing? (2)
In The Days Of The Caveman (1)
Mmm Mmm Mmm Mmm (1) *4*
My Enemies (2)
My Own Sunrise (2)
Old Scab (2)
Our Driver Gestures (2)
Overachievers (2)
Psychic, The (1)
Swatting Flies (2)
Swimming In Your Ocean (1)
There Are Many Dangers (2)
Two Knights And Maidens (1)
When I Go Out With Artists (1)
Worm's Life (2)

CRAWFORD, Hank '64

Born on 12/21/34 in Memphis. Jazz alto saxophonist. With **Ray Charles**'s band from 1958-63.

8/8/64	**143**	2			1 **True Blue** .... [I]	**$20**	Atlantic 1423
4/17/76	**159**	7			2 **I Hear A Symphony** .... [I]	**$15**	Kudu 26
1/29/77	**167**	3			3 **Hank Crawford's Back** .... [I]	**$15**	Kudu 33

Baby! This Love I Have (2)
Blues In Bloom (1)
Canadian Sunset (3)
Funky Pigeon (3)
Got You On My Mind (1)
Hang It On The Ceiling (2)
I Can't Stop Loving You (3)
I Hear A Symphony (2)
I'll Move You No Mountain (2)
Love Won't Let Me Wait (2)
Madison (Spirit, The Power) (2)
Mellow Down (1)
Merry Christmas Baby (1)
Midnight Over Memphis (3)
Read 'Em And Weep (1)
Save Your Love For Me (1)
Shake A-Plenty (1)
Shooby (1)
Skunky Green (1)
Stripper, The (2)
Sugar Free (2)
Two Years Of Torture (1)
You'll Never Find Another Love Like Mine (3)

CRAWFORD, Johnny '62

Born on 3/26/46 in Los Angeles. One of the original Mouseketeers. Played "Mark McCain" on TV's *The Rifleman*.

| 9/1/62 | **40** | 10 | | | 1 **A Young Man's Fancy** .... | **$40** | Del-Fi 1223 |
| 5/25/63 | **126** | 5 | | | 2 **His Greatest Hits** .... [G] | **$40** | Del-Fi 1229 |

Cindy's Birthday (1,2) *8*
Daydreams (2) *70*
Debbie (1,2)
Donna (1)
I'm Walkin' (1)
In The Wee Small Hours (1)
Little White Cloud (1)
Moon River (1,2)
Mr. Blue (1,2)
Patti Ann (2) *43*
Proud (2) *29*
Rumors (2) *12*
Sittin' And A Watchin' (1,2)
Something Special (1)
We Belong Together (2)
Young At Heart (1)
Your Nose Is Gonna Grow (1,2) *14*

CRAWFORD, Michael '93

Born Michael Dumble-Smith on 1/19/42 in Salisbury, Wiltshire, England. Actor/singer. Starred in several Broadway shows.

7/30/88	**192**	2		©	1 **Songs From The Stage And Screen**	**$10**	Columbia 44321
11/30/91+	**54**	31	▲	©	2 **Michael Crawford Performs Andrew Lloyd Webber**	**$10**	Atlantic 82347
10/16/93	**39**	21	●	©	3 **A Touch Of Music In The Night**	**$10**	Atlantic 82531
3/21/98	**57**	13	●	©	4 **On Eagle's Wings**	**$10**	Atlantic 83076
12/4/99	**98**	6		©	5 **A Christmas Album** .... [X]	**$10**	Atlantic 83222

Christmas chart: 11/'99

| 11/4/00 | **28**ᶜ | 1 | | © | 6 **With Love** .... | **$0** | Atlantic 82403 |

All I Ask Of You (2)
All Is Well (5)
Amazing Grace (4)
And The Money Kept Rolling In (And Out) (2)
Angels We Have Heard On High (medley) (5)
Any Dream Will Do (2)
Ave Maria (4)
Before The Parade Passes By (1)
Being Alive (6)
Bring Him Home (1)
Candlelight Carol (5)
Come Rain Or Come Shine (6)
Eternal Love (4)
Every Time We Say Goodbye (6)
First Man You Remember (medley) (2)
Gethsemane (2)
Holy City (4)
I Dreamed A Dream (6)
I'll Walk With God (4)
If (6)
If I Loved You (1)
If You Could See Me Now (1)
In The Still Of The Night (1)
It Goes Like It Goes (3)
It's The Most Wonderful Time Of The Year (medley) (5)
Joseph's Lullaby (4)
Journey To Bethlehem (A Christmas Medley) (5)
Joy To The World (medley) (5)
Love Changes Everything (2)
Mary Did You Know? (5)
Memory (1,2)
Music Of The Night (2,3)
Not A Day Goes By (1)
Not Too Far From Here (4)
Nothing Like You've Ever Known (2)
Now The Day Is Over (4)
O Holy Night (5)
On Eagle's Wings (4)
On My Own (6)
One Of My Best Friends (3)
Only You (2)
Other Pleasures (medley) (2)
Panis Angelicus (4)
Papa, Can You Hear Me? (medley) (3)
Peace, Peace (medley) (5)
Phantom Of The Opera (3)
Piece Of Sky (medley) (3)
Power Of Love (3)
Scarlet Ribbons (5)
Serenade In Blue (4)
She Used To Be Mine (3)
Silent Night (medley) (5)
Since You Stayed Here (3)
Speak Low (3)
Spirit Of The Living God (4)
Stormy Weather (3)
Story Of My Life (6)
Strange Way To Save The World (5)
Tell Me On A Sunday (2)
Unexpected Song (1)
Very Best Time Of The Year (medley) (5)
West Side Story Medley (1)
What Are You Doing The Rest Of Your Life? (6)
What'll I Do (1)
When I Fall In Love (6)
When You Wish Upon A Star (1)
Why Did I Choose You? (6)
Wishing You Were Somehow Here Again (2)
With You I'm Born Again (6)
With Your Hand Upon My Heart (3)
You Remember (2)
You'll Never Walk Alone (1)

CRAWFORD, Randy '81

Born Veronica Crawford on 2/18/52 in Macon, Georgia; raised in Cincinnati. Female R&B singer.

5/31/80	**180**	7			1 **Now We May Begin**	**$12**	Warner 3421
5/23/81	**71**	19		©	2 **Secret Combination**	**$12**	Warner 3541
6/26/82	**148**	10			3 **Windsong**...	**$10**	Warner 23687
11/5/83	**164**	5			4 **Nightline**	**$10**	Warner 23976
7/26/86	**178**	4			5 **Abstract Emotions**	**$10**	Warner 25423
11/18/89	**159**	13		©	6 **Rich And Poor**	**$10**	Warner 26002

Actual Emotional Love (5)
Ain't No Foolin' (4)
All It Takes Is Love (6)
Almaz (5)
Believe That Love Can Change The World (6)
Betcha (5)
Blue Flame (1)
Bottom Line (4)
Can't Stand The Pain (5)
Cigarette In The Rain (6)
Desire (5)
Don't Come Knockin' (3)
Don't Wanna Be Normal (5)
Every Kind Of People (6)
Gettin' Away With Murder (4)
Go On And Live It Up (4)
Happy Feet (3)
He Reminds Me (3)
Higher Than Anyone Can Count (5)
I Don't Feel Much Like Crying (6)
I Don't Want To Lose Him (3)
I Have Ev'rything But You (3)
In Real Life (4)
Knockin' On Heaven's Door (6)
Last Night At Danceland (1)
Letter Full Of Tears (6)
Lift Me Up (4)
Living On The Outside (4)
Look Who's Lonely Now (3)
Love Is (6)
My Heart Is Not As Young As It Used To Be (1)
Nightline (4)
Now We May Begin (1)
One Day I'll Fly Away (1)
One Hello (3)
Overnight (5)
Rainy Night In Georgia (2)
Rich And Poor (6)
Rio De Janeiro Blue (2)
Same Old Story (Same Old Song) (1)
Secret Combination (2)
Separate Lives (6)
Tender Falls The Rain (1)
That's How Heartaches Are Made (2)
This Is The Love (6)
This Night Won't Last Forever (3)
This 'Ole Heart Of Mine (4)
Time For Love (2)
Trade Winds (2)
Two Lives (2)
We Had A Love So Strong (3)
When I Lose My Way (2)
When I'm Gone (3)
When Your Life Was Low (1)
Why (4)
Windsong (3)
World Of Fools (5)
Wrap-U-Up (5)
You Bring The Sun Out (2)
You Might Need Somebody (2)

CRAWLER — see BACK STREET CRAWLER

CRAY, Robert, Band '87

Born on 8/1/53 in Columbus, Georgia. Blues-rock singer/guitarist. Played bass with fictional band Otis Day & The Knights in the movie *Animal House*. Band formed in 1974 as backing tour group for **Albert Collins**. Lineup from 1986-89: Richard Cousins (bass), Peter Boe (keyboards) and David Olson (drums). Lineup in 1990: Cousins, Tim Kaihatsu (guitar), Jim Pugh (keyboards) and Kevin Hayes (drums). Karl Sevareid (bass) joined in 1992. Cousins and Kaihatsu left in 1996.

1)Strong Persuader 2)Don't Be Afraid Of The Dark 3)Midnight Stroll

2/15/86	124	18		©	1	Showdown!		$10	Alligator 4743
						ALBERT COLLINS/ROBERT CRAY/JOHNNY COPELAND			
4/5/86	141	21		©	2	False Accusations		$10	Hightone 8005
12/20/86+	13	49	▲²	©	3	Strong Persuader		$10	Mercury 830568
3/7/87	143	11		©	4	Bad Influence	[E]	$10	Hightone 8001
						released in 1983			
8/27/88	32	32	●	©	5	Don't Be Afraid Of The Dark		$10	Mercury 834923
10/6/90	51	32	●	©	6	Midnight Stroll		$10	Mercury 846652
						THE ROBERT CRAY BAND FEATURING THE MEMPHIS HORNS			
9/26/92	103	7		©	7	I Was Warned		$10	Mercury 512721
10/23/93	143	3		©	8	Shame + A Sin		$10	Mercury 518237
5/27/95	127	6		©	9	Some Rainy Morning		$10	Mercury 526867
5/24/97	184	3		©	10	Sweet Potato Pie		$10	Mercury 534483
5/15/99	181	2		©	11	Take Your Shoes Off		$10	Rykodisc 10479

Across The Line (5)
Acting This Way (5)
Albert's Alley (1)
All The Way (11)
At Last (5)
Back Home (10)
Bad Influence (4)
Black Cat Bone (1)
Blackjack (1)
Bouncin' Back (6)
Bring Your Fine Self Home (1)
Change Of Heart, Change Of Mind (S.O.F.T.) (2)
Consequences (6)
Do That For Me (10)
Don't Be Afraid Of The Dark (5) *74*
Don't Break This Ring (8)
Don't Touch Me (4)
Don't You Even Care? (5)

Dream, The (1)
Enough For Me (9)
False Accusations (2)
Fantasized (3)
Forecast (Calls For Pain) (6)
Foul Play (3)
Got To Make A Comeback (4)
Gotta Change The Rules (4)
Grinder, The (4)
He Don't Live Here Anymore (7)
Holdin' Court (6)
Holdin' On (9)
I Can't Go Home (5)
I Can't Quit (10)
I Guess I Showed Her (3)
I Shiver (8)
I Was Warned (7)
I Wonder (3)
I'll Go On (9)
I'm A Good Man (7)

I'm Just Lucky That Way (8)
I've Slipped Her Mind (2)
It's All Gone (11)
Jealous Love (9)
Jealous Minds (10)
Just A Loser (7)
Labor Of Love (6)
Last Time (I Get Burned Like This) (2)
Laugh Out Loud (5)
Leave Well Enough Alone (8)
Let Me Know (11)
Lion's Den (5)
Little Birds (10)
Little Boy Big (9)
Living Proof (11)
Love Gone To Waste (11)
March On (4)
Midnight Stroll (6)
Moan (9)

Moon Is Full (1)
More Than I Can Stand (3)
Move A Mountain (6)
My Problem (6)
Never Mattered Much (9)
New Blood (3)
Night Patrol (5)
No Big Deal (4)
Not Bad For Love (10)
Nothin' But A Woman (3)
Nothing Against You (10)
On The Road Down (7)
One In The Middle (10)
Our Last Time (7)
Pardon (11)
Passing By (8)
Payin' For It Now (2)
Phone Booth (4)
Picture Of A Broken Heart (7)
Playin' In The Dirt (2)

Porch Light (2)
Price I Pay (7)
Right Next Door (Because Of Me) (3) *80*
She's Gone (2)
She's Into Something (1)
Simple Things (10)
Smoking Gun (3) *22*
So Many Women, So Little Time (4)
Some Pain, Some Shame (8)
Sonny (2)
Stay Go (8)
Steppin' Out (9)
Still Around (3)
T-Bone Shuffle (1)
Tell The Landlord (9)
1040 Blues (8)
That Wasn't Me (11)
There's Nothing Wrong (11)

These Things (6)
Things You Do To Me (6)
Tollin' Bells (11)
Trick Or Treat (10)
24-7 Man (11)
Up And Down (8)
Waiting For The Tide To Turn (4)
Walk Around Time (6)
What About Me (11)
Where Do I Go From Here (4)
Whole Lotta Pride (7)
Will You Think Of Me (9)
Won The Battle (7)
Won't You Give Him (One More Chance) (11)
You're Gonna Need Me (8)
Your Secret's Safe With Me (5)

CRAZY HORSE '71

Backing band for **Neil Young**. Lineup in 1971: Danny Whitten (vocals, guitar), Jack Nitzsche (piano), Billy Talbot (bass) and Ralph Molina (drums). Lineup in 1972: Talbot, Molina, George Whitsell (vocals, guitar), Greg Leroy (guitar), John Blanton (piano). Whitten died of a heroin overdose on 11/18/72 (age 29). Also see **Neil Young**.

3/27/71	84	11		©	1	Crazy Horse		$15	Reprise 6438
2/5/72	170	6			2	Loose		$15	Reprise 2059

All Alone Now (2)
All The Little Things (2)
And She Won't Even Blow Smoke In My Direction (2)
Beggars Day (1)

Carolay (1)
Crow Jane Lady (1)
Dance, Dance, Dance (1)
Dirty, Dirty (1)
Downtown (1)

Fair Weather Friend (1)
Going Home (2)
Gone Dead Train (1)
Hit And Run (2)
I Don't Believe It (2)

I Don't Want To Talk About It (1)
I'll Get By (1)
Kind Of Woman (2)
Look At All The Things (1)

Move (2)
Nobody (1)
One Sided Love (2)
One Thing I Love (2)
Try (2)

You Won't Miss Me (2)

CRAZY OTTO '55

Born Fritz Schulz-Reichel on 7/4/12 in Germany. Honky-tonk pianist.

4/16/55	❶²	20			1	Crazy Otto	[I]	$30	Decca 8113
4/16/55	2²	24			2	Crazy Otto (Part 1)	[EP-I]	$20	Decca 2201
4/30/55	3	22			3	Crazy Otto (Part 2)	[EP-I]	$20	Decca 2202

Beautiful Ohio (1,3)
Glad Rag Doll (1,2) *19*

In The Mood (1,2)
Lights Out (1,3)

My Melancholy Baby (1,2)
Paddlin' Madelin' Home (1,3)

Red Sails In The Sunset (1)
Rose Of Washington Square (1)

S-H-I-N-E (1,3)
Smiles (1,2) *21*

CRAZY TOWN '01

Rock-rap group from Los Angeles: Seth Binzer and Bret Mazur (vocals), DJ AM (DJ), Craig Tyler and Anthony Valli (guitars), Doug Miller (bass) and James Bradley (drums).

12/9/00+	9	34	▲	©		The Gift Of Game		$10	Columbia 63654

B-Boy 2000
Black Cloud
Butterfly 1

Darkside
Face The Music
Hollywood Babylon

Lollipop Porn
Only When I'm Drunk

Players (Only Love You When They're Playing)
Revolving Door

Think Fast
Toxic

CREACH, Papa John '72

Born on 5/28/17 in Beaver Hills, Pennsylvania. Died on 2/22/94 (age 76). Rock fiddler. Worked with **Jefferson Airplane** from 1970-72 (and later toured and recorded with **Jefferson Starship**) and **Hot Tuna** from 1971-73.

1/1/72	94	14		©		Papa John Creach		$15	Grunt 1003

Danny Boy
Everytime I Hear Her Name

Human Spring
Janitor Drives A Cadillac

Over The Rainbow
Papa John's Down Home Blues

Plunk A Little Funk
Saint Louis Blues

Soul Fever
String Jet Rock

CREAM '68

★304★

All-star rock group from England: **Eric Clapton** (guitar), **Jack Bruce** (bass) and **Ginger Baker** (drums). Baker and Bruce had been in Alexis Korner's Blues Inc. (**C.C.S.**) and the Graham Bond Organization. Clapton and Bruce were in **John Mayall**'s Bluesbreakers. After Cream disbanded, Clapton and Baker formed **Blind Faith**. Cream inducted into the Rock and Roll Hall of Fame in 1993.

1)Wheels Of Fire 2)Goodbye 3)Best Of Cream

5/13/67+	39	92	●	©	1	Fresh Cream		$50	Atco 206
12/9/67+	4	77	▲	©	2	Disraeli Gears		$50	Atco 232
						also see #9 below			
7/13/68	❶⁴	46	●	©	3	Wheels Of Fire	[L]	$60	Atco 700 [2]
						record 1: studio; record 2: Live At The Fillmore; also see #10 below			

DEBUT	PEAK	WKS	RIAA	CD	ARTIST — Album Title	Catalog	Sym	$	Label & Number

CREAM — Cont'd

DEBUT	PEAK	WKS	RIAA	CD	Album Title		$	Label & Number
2/15/69	2²	26	●	© 4	Goodbye		$30	Atco 7001
7/19/69	3	44	●	5	Best Of Cream	[G]	$30	Atco 291
5/2/70	15	21		© 6	Live Cream	[L]	$30	Atco 328
4/1/72	27	16		© 7	Live Cream - Volume II	[L]	$30	Atco 7005
10/28/72	135	10		8	Heavy Cream	[G]	$20	Polydor 3502 [2]
2/19/77	165	6		© 9	Disraeli Gears	[R]	$12	RSO 3010
2/19/77	197	4		© 10	Wheels Of Fire	[R]	$15	RSO 3802 [2]
11/14/87+	20ᶜ	45	▲	© 11	Strange Brew - The Very Best Of Cream	[G]	$10	RSO 811639
5/27/95	49ᶜ	1		© 12	The Very Best Of Cream	[G]	$10	Polydor 3752

Anyone For Tennis (11,12)
As You Said (3,8,10)
Badge (4,5,8,11,12) **60**
Blue Condition (2,9)
Born Under A Bad Sign
(3,5,8,10,11,12)
Cat's Squirrel (1,8)
Crossroads
(3,5,8,10,11,12) **28**

Dance The Night Away (2,9)
Deserted Cities Of The Heart
(3,7,8,10,12)
Doing That Scrapyard Thing
(4,8)
Dreaming (1)
Four Until Late (1)
I Feel Free (1,5,8,11,12)
I'm So Glad (1,4,8,12)

Lawdy Mama (6)
Mother's Lament (2,9)
N.S.U. (1,6,12)
Outside Woman Blues (2,9)
Passing The Time (3,8,10)
Politician (3,4,7,8,10,11,12)
Pressed Rat And Warthog
(3,10)
Rollin' And Tumblin' (1,6,8)

SWLABR (2,5,8,9,12)
Sitting On Top Of The World
(3,4,8,10,12)
Sleepy Time Time (1,6)
Spoonful (3,5,8,10,11,12)
Steppin' Out (7)
Strange Brew (2,5,8,9,11,12)
Sunshine Of Your Love
(2,5,7,8,9,11,12) **5**

Sweet Wine (1,6,12)
Take It Back (2,8,9)
Tales Of Brave Ulysses
(2,5,7,8,9,12)
Those Were The Days
(3,8,10,12)
Toad (1,3,10)
Traintime (3,10)
We're Going Wrong (2,9,12)

What A Bringdown (4,8)
White Room
(3,5,7,8,10,11,12) **6**
World Of Pain (2,9)
Wrapping Paper (12)

CREATIVE SOURCE   '74
R&B vocal group from Los Angeles: Don Wyatt, Celeste Rhodes, Steve Flanagan, Barbara Berryman and Barbara Lewis.

1/19/74	152	10		©	Creative Source		$15	Sussex 8027

Let Me In Your Life
Lovesville

Magic Carpet Ride
Oh Love

Who Is He And What Is He To Wild Flower
You 69

You're Too Good To Be True

You Can't Hide Love

CREATURES, The   '90
Duo from England: Siouxsie Sioux (vocals) and her husband, Peter "Budgie" Clark (percussion). Both are members of **Siouxsie And The Banshees**.

3/3/90	197	2		©	Boomerang		$10	Geffen 24275

Fruitman
Fury Eyes
Killing Time

Manchild
Morrina
Pity

Pluto Drive
Simoom
Solar Choir

Speeding
Standing There
Strolling Wolf

Untiedundone
Venus Sands
Willow

You!

CREED   '99
Rock group from Tallahassee, Florida: Scott Stapp (vocals), Mark Tremonti (guitar), Brian Marshall (bass) and Scott Phillips (drums).

10/18/97+	22	112	▲⁵	© 1	My Own Prison	C:❶⁵⁴/95	$10	Wind-Up 13049
10/16/99	❶²	103↑	▲¹⁰	© 2	Human Clay		$10	Wind-Up 13053

Are You Ready? (2)
Beautiful (2)
Faceless Man (2)
Higher (2) **7**

Illusion (1)
In America (1)
Inside Us All (1)
My Own Prison (1)

Never Die (2)
Ode (1)
One (1) **70**
Pity For A Dime (1)

Say I (2)
Sister (1)
Torn (1)
Unforgiven (1)

Wash Away Those Years (2)
What If (2)
What's This Life For (1)
With Arms Wide Open (2) **1**

Wrong Way (2)

CREEDENCE CLEARWATER REVIVAL   ★106★   '70
Rock group formed in El Cerrito, California: John Fogerty (vocals, guitar), brother **Tom Fogerty** (guitar), Stu Cook (keyboards, bass) and Doug Clifford (drums). First recorded as the Blue Velvets for the Orchestra label in 1959. Recorded as the Golliwogs for Fantasy in 1964. Renamed Creedence Clearwater Revival in 1967. Tom Fogerty left for a solo career in 1971 and group disbanded in October 1972. Cook and Clifford joined the **Don Harrison Band**. Tom Fogerty died of repiratory failure on 9/6/90 (age 48). Group inducted into the Rock and Roll Hall of Fame in 1993.

1)Cosmo's Factory 2)Green River 3)Willy and the Poorboys

7/20/68	52	73	▲	© 1	Creedence Clearwater Revival		$25	Fantasy 8382
2/8/69	7	88	▲²	© 2	Bayou Country		$20	Fantasy 8387
9/13/69	❶⁴	88	▲³	© 3	Green River	C:#24/79	$20	Fantasy 8393
12/13/69+	3	60	▲²	© 4	Willy and the Poorboys	C:#22/80	$20	Fantasy 8397
7/25/70	❶⁹	69	▲⁴	© 5	Cosmo's Factory	C:#11/104	$20	Fantasy 8402
12/26/70+	5	42	▲	© 6	Pendulum		$20	Fantasy 8410
4/29/72	12	24	●	© 7	Mardi Gras		$20	Fantasy 9404
12/2/72+	15	37	▲²	© 8	Creedence Gold	[G]	$15	Fantasy 9418
7/21/73	61	18	●	© 9	More Creedence Gold	[G]	$15	Fantasy 9430
11/24/73	143	10		© 10	Live In Europe	[L]	$20	Fantasy CCR-1 [2]
					recorded in September 1971			
3/6/76	100	30	▲⁴	© 11	Chronicle (The 20 Greatest Hits)	C:#11/415 [G]	$20	Fantasy CCR-2 [2]
12/20/80+	62	20	▲	© 12	The Concert	C:#32/12	$12	Fantasy 4501
					originally titled *The Royal Albert Hall Concert*, the album was actually recorded at the Oakland Coliseum in 1970			

Bad Moon Rising
(3,8,10,11,12) **2**
Before You Accuse Me (5)
Bootleg (2,9)
Born On The Bayou (2,8,10,12)
Born To Move (6)
Chameleon (6)
Commotion (3,10,11,12) **30**
Cotton Fields (4)
Cross-Tie Walker (3)
Don't Look Now (It Ain't You Or
Me) (4,9,12)
Door To Door (7,10)

Down On The Corner
(4,8,11,12) **3**
Effigy (4)
Feelin' Blue (4)
Fortunate Son
(4,9,10,11,12) **14**
Get Down Woman (1)
Gloomy (1)
Good Golly, Miss Molly (2,9)
Graveyard Train (2)
Green River (3,10,11,12) **2**
Have You Ever Seen The Rain
(6,8,11) **8**
Hello Mary Lou (7)

Hey Tonight (6,9,10,11) *flip*
**I Heard It Through The
Grapevine** (5,8,11) **43**
I Put A Spell On You
(1,9,11) **58**
It Came Out Of The Sky (4,10)
It's Just A Thought (6)
Keep On Chooglin' (2,10,12)
Lodi (3,9,10,11) **52**
Long As I Can See The Light
(5,11) *flip*
Lookin' For A Reason (7)
Lookin' Out My Back Door
(5,9,11) **2**

Midnight Special (4,8,12)
Molina (6,9)
My Baby Left Me (5)
Need Someone To Hold (7)
Night Is The Right Time (3,12)
Ninety-Nine And A Half (Won't
Do) (1)
Ooby Dooby (5)
Pagan Baby (6)
Penthouse Pauper (2)
Poorboy Shuffle (4)
Porterville (1,9)
Proud Mary (2,8,10,11,12) **2**
Ramble Tamble (5)

Rude Awakening #2 (6)
Run Through The Jungle
(5,9,11) *flip*
Sail Away (7)
Sailor's Lament (6)
Side Of The Road (4)
Sinister Purpose (3)
Someday Never Comes
(7,11) **25**
Suzie Q. (Part One)
(1,8,10,11) **11**
Sweet Hitch-Hiker
(7,9,10,11) **6**
Take It Like A Friend (7)

Tearin' Up The Country (7)
Tombstone Shadow (3,12)
Travelin' Band (5,10,11,12) **2**
Up Around The Bend
(5,9,10,11) **4**
Walk On The Water (1)
What Are You Gonna Do (7)
Who'll Stop The Rain
(5,9,11,12) *flip*
(Wish I Could) Hideaway (6)
Working Man (1)
Wrote A Song For Everyone (3)

CRENSHAW, Marshall   '82
Born on 11/11/53 in Detroit. Rockabilly singer/guitarist. Played **John Lennon** in the road show of *Beatlemania* in 1976. Appeared in the movie *Peggy Sue Got Married* and portrayed **Buddy Holly** in the 1987 movie *La Bamba*.

5/29/82	50	27		© 1	Marshall Crenshaw		$10	Warner 3673
6/18/83	52	14		© 2	Field Day		$10	Warner 23873

CRENSHAW, Marshall — Cont'd

10/12/85 **110** 18 © 3 **Downtown** .... $10 Warner 25319

All I Know Right Now (2) / Hold It (1) / Mary Anne (1) / Rockin' Around In N.Y.C. (1) / Usual Thing (1)
Blues Is King (3) / I'll Do Anything (1) / Monday Morning Rock (2) / She Can't Dance (1) / (We're Gonna) Shake Up Their
Brand New Lover (1) / I'm Sorry (But So Is Brenda / Not For Me (1) / Soldier Of Love (1) / Minds (3)
Cynical Girl (1) / Lee) (3) / One Day With You (2) / Someday, Someway (1) *36* / What Time Is It? (2)
Distance Between (3) / Lesson Number One (3) / One More Reason (2) / Terrifying Love (3) / Whenever You're On My Mind
For Her Love (2) / Like A Vague Memory (3) / Our Town (2) / There She Goes Again (1) / (2)
Girls... (1) / Little Wild One (No. 5) (3) / Right Now (3) / Try (2) / Yvonne (3)

CRESPO, Elvis '99
Born on 7/30/71 in New York City. Latin singer/songwriter.

5/23/98+ **106** 43 ▲ © 1 **Suavemente** .... [F] $10 Sony Discos 82634
title is Spanish for "Gently"
5/22/99 **49** 10 ● © 2 **Pintame** .... [F] $10 Sony Discos 82917
2/10/00 **155** 1 © 3 **The Remixes** .... [F-K] $10 Sony Discos 83622

Besos De Coral (2) / Llorando (1) / Nuestra Cancion (1) / Princesita (1) / Te Vas (1) / Ven (2)
Come Baby Come (3) / Luna Llena (2) / Pequeño Luis (2) / Si Tu Te Alejas (2) / Tiemblo (2,3) / Vuelve Conmigo (1)
Dame Cariño (2) / Mas Que Una Caricia (2) / Pintame (2) / Solo Me Miro (2) / Tiemblo (A Que No Te Atreves / Yo Me Morire (1)
Enamorado De Ti (2) / Me Arrepiento (1) / Por El Caminito (2) / Suave (Megamix) (3) / - Mix) (3)
Eres Tu (2) / No Comprendo (2) / ¿Porque? (1) / Suavemente (1,3) *84* / Tu Sonrisa (1,3)

CRETONES, The '80
Rock group from Los Angeles: Mark Goldenberg (vocals, guitar), Steve Leonard (keyboards), Peter Bernstein (bass) and Steve Beers (drums).

3/29/80 **125** 10 **Thin Red Line** .... $12 Planet 5

Cost Of Love / Here Comes The Wave / Justine / Mrs. Peel / Thin Red Line
Everybody's Mad At Katherine / I Can't Wait / Mad Love / **Real Love** *79* / Ways Of The Heart

CREWE, Bob, Generation '67
Born on 11/12/37 in Newark, New Jersey. Prolific songwriter/arranger/producer. Assembled The Bob Crewe Generation, an aggregation of studio musicians.

2/25/67 **100** 11 **Music To Watch Girls By** .... [I] $20 DynoVoice 9003

Anna / Girls On The Rocks / Lover's Concerto / **Music To Watch Girls By** *15*
Concrete And Clay / Lazy Girl, Theme For A / Man And A Woman, Theme / Winchester Cathedral
Felicidade, A / Let's Hang On / From A

CRICKETS, The — see HOLLY, Buddy / VEE, Bobby

CRIME BOSS '97
Born Thurston Slaughter in Houston. Male rapper.

3/11/95 **113** 11 © 1 **All In The Game** .... $10 Suave 0003
4/26/97 **25** 5 © 2 **Conflicts & Confusion** .... $10 Suave House 1566

All In The Game (1) / Chick, The (1) / Death Notes (2) / Going Off (1) / Point Of No Return (1) / Warning (2)
Back To The Streets (2) / Close Range (1) / Dreaming (1) / Life Is Crying (2) / Put 'Em Up (1) / What Does It Mean (To Be A
Big Chiefing (1) / Come And Get Some (1) / Fry (1) / No Friends (2) / Recognize (1) / Real Crime Boss) (2)
Chemical Imbalance (2) / Conflicts & Confusion (2) / Get Mine (2) / Please Stop (2) / Story Goes (1)

CRISS, Peter '78
Born Peter Crisscoula on 12/20/47 in New York City. Drummer of **Kiss** (1973-81). Returned to Kiss in 1996.

10/14/78 **43** 20 ▲ © **Peter Criss** .... $20 Casablanca 7122

Don't You Let Me Down / I Can't Stop The Rain / Rock Me Baby / Tossin' And Turnin'
Easy Thing / I'm Gonna Love You / That's The Kind Of Sugar Papa / You Matter To Me
Hooked On Rock And Roll / Kiss The Girl Goodbye / Likes

CRISTIAN '01
Born Cristian Castro in 1975 in Mexico. Latin singer.

6/23/01 **193** 1 © **Azul** .... [F] $10 Ariola 85324
title is Spanish for "Blue"

Amantes De Ocasión / Cupido / Llorar Por Dentro / Nuestro Amor / Yo Quería
Azul / Dos Amantes / Lloviendo Estrellas / Si Pudiera
Con Ella / Gli Amori (medley) / Los Amores (medley) / Solo

CRITTERS, The '66
Pop group from Plainfield, New Jersey: Don Ciccone (vocals, guitar), Jimmy Ryan (guitar), Chris Darway (organ), Kenny Gorka (bass) and Jack Decker (drums). Ciccone later joined **The 4 Seasons**.

9/24/66 **147** 2 **Younger Girl** .... $40 Kapp 3485

Best Love You'll Ever Have / Children And Flowers / Everything But Time / Gone For A While / I Wear A Silly Grin / **Mr. Dieingly Sad** *17*
Blow My Mind / Come Back On A Rainy Day / Forever Or No More / He'll Make You Cry / It Just Won't Be That Way / **Younger Girl** *42*

★466★ CROCE, Jim '73
Born on 1/10/43 in Philadelphia. Killed in a plane crash on 9/20/73 (age 30) in Natchitoches, Louisiana. Singer/songwriter/guitarist.. Recorded with wife Ingrid for Capitol in 1968. Lead guitarist on his hits, Maury Muehleisen, was killed in the same crash.

7/1/72+ **❶**[5] 93 ● 1 **You Don't Mess Around With Jim** $15 ABC 756
2/17/73 **7** 84 ● 2 **Life And Times** $15 ABC 769
12/15/73+ **2**[2] 53 ● © 3 **I Got A Name** $15 ABC 797
10/5/74 **2**[2] 46 ▲ © 4 **Photographs & Memories/His Greatest Hits** C:#19/4 [G] $15 ABC 835
11/1/75+ **87** 18 5 **The Faces I've Been** [E] $20 Lifesong 900 [2]
recordings from 1961-71
2/26/77 **170** 3 © 6 **Time In A Bottle/Jim Croce's Greatest Love Songs** .... [K] $12 Lifesong 6007

Age (3) / Cars And Dates, Chrome And / Good Time Man Like Me Ain't / I Remember Mary (5) / Mississippi Lady (5) / Photographs And Memories
Alabama Rain (2,6) / Clubs (5) / Got No Business (Singin' The / I'll Have To Say I Love You In / New York's Not My Home (1,4) / (1,4,6)
Army, The (5) / **Chain Gang Medley** (5) *63* / Blues) (3,4,6) *9* / A Song (3,4,6) *64* / Next Time, The (2) / Pig's Song (5)
Bad, Bad Leroy Brown (2,4) *1* / Charlie Green Play That Slide / Greenback Dollar (5) / It Doesn't Have To Be That / Old Man River (5) / Railroad Song (5)
Big Fat Woman (5) / Trombone (5) / Gunga Din (5) / Way (2,6) *64* / **One Less Set Of Footsteps** / Railroads And Riverboats (5)
Box #10 (1) / Chinese, The (5) / Hard Time Losin' Man (1) / King's Song (5) / (2,4) *37* / Rapid Roy (The Stock Car Boy)
Careful Man (2) / Country Girl (1) / Hard Way Every Time (3) / Long Time Ago (1,6) / **Operator (That's Not The Way** / (1,4)
Carmella...South Philly (5) / Dreamin' Again (2,6) / Hey Tomorrow (1) / Lover's Cross (3,4,6) / **It Feels)** (1,4,6) *17* / Recently (3)
/ Five Short Minutes (3) / **I Got A Name** (3,4) *10* / Maybe Tomorrow (5) / / Roller Derby Queen (2,4)

CROCE, Jim — Cont'd

Salon And Saloon (3,6)
Speedball Tucker (2)
Stone Walls (5)
Sun Come Up (5)

These Dreams (2,4,6)
This Land Is Your Land (5)
Thursday (3,6)
Time In A Bottle (1,4,6) *1*

Tomorrow's Gonna Be A
  Brighter Day (1)
Top Hat Bar And Grille (3)
Trucks And Ups (5)

Walkin' Back To Georgia (1)
Way We Used To (5)
Which Way Are You Goin' (5)

**Workin' At The Car Wash
  Blues** (3,4) *32*
**You Don't Mess Around With
  Jim** (1,4) *8*

CROSBY, Bing '57

Born Harry Lillis Crosby on 5/3/03 in Tacoma, Washington. Died of a heart attack on 10/14/77 (age 74). One of the most popular entertainers of the 20th century. Charted over 300 hit singles from 1931-54. Starred in several movies (won Academy Award for *Going My Way* in 1944. Married to actress Dixie Lee from 1930 until her death in 1952; their son Gary Crosby began recording in 1950. Married to actress Kathryn Grant from 1957 until his death; their daughter Mary Crosby became an actress. Bing's youngest brother, Bob Crosby, was a popular swing-era bandleader. Bing won Grammy's Lifetime Achievement Award in 1962.

1)Merry Christmas 2)Shillelaghs and Shamrocks 3)A Christmas Sing With Bing Around The World

DEBUT	PEAK	WKS	CD	#	ARTIST — Album Title	Sym	$	Label & Number
12/22/56	21	1		1	**A Christmas Sing With Bing Around The World**	[X]	$40	Decca 8419
12/2/57	❶¹	7	● ©	2	**Merry Christmas** C:#8/25	[X-E]	$40	Decca 8128
					first released in 1945 on Decca 403; #1 for six consecutive seasons from 1945-50 (38 weeks at #1); Christmas charts: 4/'63, 2/'64, 3/'65, 5/'66, 8/'67, 6/'68, 3/'69, 6/'70, 4/'71, 2/'72, 8/'73, 3/'83, 21/'87, 13/'88, 15/'89, 15/'90, 10/'91, 12/'92, 11/'95, 14/'96, 33/'98, 24/'99			
3/31/58	13	2		3	**Shillelaghs and Shamrocks**	[E]	$30	Decca 8207
					first released in 1956			
12/15/58+	2¹	4	©	4	**Merry Christmas**	[X-E-R]	$30	Decca 8128
12/28/59+	17	2	©	5	**Merry Christmas**	[X-E-R]	$30	Decca 8128
12/19/60	9	3	©	6	**Merry Christmas**	[X-E-R]	$30	Decca 8128
12/18/61+	22	7	©	7	**Merry Christmas**	[X-E-R]	$30	Decca 8128
12/22/62	46	2	©	8	**Merry Christmas**	[X-E-R]	$30	Decca 8128
12/22/62	50	2		9	**I Wish You A Merry Christmas**	[X]	$20	Warner 1484
					Christmas chart: 40/'65			
5/30/64	116	7		10	**America, I Hear You Singing** FRANK SINATRA/BING CROSBY/FRED WARING		$20	Reprise 2020
12/12/64	9ˣ	3		11	**12 Songs Of Christmas** BING CROSBY/FRANK SINATRA/FRED WARING And The Pennsylvanians	[X]	$20	Reprise 2022
3/29/69	162	8		12	**Hey Jude/Hey Bing!**		$15	Amos 7001
12/10/77+	98	9	©	13	**Bing Crosby's Greatest Hits**	[G]	$12	MCA 3031
12/5/92	8ˣ	39	©	14	**It's Christmas Time** C:#6/41 BING CROSBY • FRANK SINATRA • NAT KING COLE	[X]	$10	LaserLight 15152
					Christmas charts: 8/'92, 17/'93, 12/'94, 13/'95, 8/'96, 22/'97			
12/4/93+	26ˣ	21	©	15	**White Christmas** C:#24/19	[X]	$10	LaserLight 15444
					Christmas charts: 30/'93, 33/'94, 26/'95, 36/'96, 32/'97			
11/21/98	21ˣ	7	©	16	**It's Christmas Time** C:#13/5 BING CROSBY • FRANK SINATRA • LOUIS ARMSTRONG	[X]	$10	LaserLight 15152
12/4/99	23ˣ	10	©	17	**White Christmas** C:#14/10	[X]	$10	MCA 731143
					Christmas charts: 23/'99, 23/'00			

Ac-Cent-Tchu-Ate The Positive (13)
Adeste Fideles (Oh, Come, All Ye Faithful) (1,2,4,5,6,7,8,14,15,16,17) *45*
Angels We Have Heard On High (Gloria In Excelsis) (1,15)
Away In A Manger (1,15)
Blue Skies (13)
Both Sides Now (12)
Carol Of The Bells (1)
Christmas Candles (11)
Christmas In Killarney (2,4,5,6,7,8,17)
Christmas Song (15)
Dear Old Donegal (3)
Deck The Halls (1,15)
Deep In The Heart Of Texas (13)
Did Your Mother Come From Ireland? (3)

Don't Fence Me In (13)
Donovans, The (3)
Faith Of Our Fathers (2,4,5,6,7,8,17)
First Noel (1,15,16)
Frosty The Snow Man (9)
Go Tell It On The Mountain (1)
God Rest Ye Merry Gentlemen (1,2,4,5,6,7,8,15,16,17)
Good King Wenceslas (1,15)
Happy Holiday (1)
Hark! The Herald Angels Sing (1,9)
Have Yourself A Merry Little Christmas (9)
Hey Jude (12)
Holly And The Ivy (medley) (9)
Home In The Meadow (10)
I Surrender Dear (13)
I Wish You A Merry Christmas (9)

I'll Be Home For Christmas (If Only In My Dreams) (2,4,6,8,15,16,17)
It Came Upon A Midnight Clear (medley) (9)
It's All In The Game (12)
It's Beginning To Look Like Christmas (2,4,5,6,7,8,17)
It's Christmas Time Again (11)
It's The Same Old Shillelagh (3)
Jesus, Sweet Saviour (Jesus, Sauveur Adorable) (1)
Jingle Bells (2,4,5,6,7,8,15,16,17)
Joy To The World (1,15,16)
Just For Tonight (12)
Let It Snow! Let It Snow! Let It Snow! (9,15)
Let Us Break Bread Together (10)
Little Drummer Boy (9,11)

Little Green Apples (12)
Littlest Angel (9)
Livin' On Lovin' (12)
Lonely Street (12)
MacNamara's Band (3)
Mele Kalikimaka (Merry Christmas) (2,4,5,6,7,8,17)
More And More (12)
O Come, All Ye Faithful ..see: Adeste Fideles
O Holy Night (9)
O Little Town Of Bethlehem (1,15)
Pat-A-Pan (medley) (9)
Pistol Packin' Mama (13)
Rose Of Tralee (3)
Santa Claus Is Comin' To Town (2,4,5,6,7,8,17)
Secret Of Christmas (11)
Silent Night (1,2,4,5,6,7,8,14,15,16,17) *54*

Silver Bells (2,4,5,6,7,8,14,15,16,17) *78*
St. Patrick's Day Parade (3)
Straight Life (12)
Swinging On A Star (13)
This Is A Great Country (medley) (10)
This Land Is Your Land (10)
Those Were The Days (12)
Thou Descendeth From The Stars (Tucendi De La Stelli) (1)
Too-Ra-Loo-Ra-Loo-Ral (That's An Irish Lullaby) (13)
Two Shillelagh O'Sullivan (3)
We Three Kings Of Orient Are (1)
We Wish You The Merriest (11)
What Child Is This? (medley) (9)

What Christmas Means To Me (1)
When Irish Eyes Are Smiling (3)
Where The Blue Of The Night Meets The Gold Of The Day (13)
Where The River Shannon Flows (3)
Whiffenpoof Song (13)
While Shepherds Watched Their Sheep (medley) (9)
White Christmas (1,2,4,5,6,7,8,13,14,15,16,17) *7*
Who Threw The Overalls In Mrs. Murphy's Chowder? (3)
Winter Wonderland (9)
With My Shillelagh Under My Arm (3)
You Are My Sunshine (13)
You Never Had It So Good (10)

CROSBY, David '72

Born on 8/14/41 in Los Angeles. Singer/guitarist with **The Byrds** from 1964-68 and later **Crosby, Stills & Nash**. Son of cinematographer Floyd Crosby (*High Noon*). Frequent troubles with the law due to drug charges. Movie cameos in *Backdraft*, *Hook* and *Thunderheart*; appeared on TV's *Roseanne*. Underwent a successful liver transplant on 11/19/94. In early 2000, it was announced that he was the biological father (via artificial insemination) of two children for the couple of **Melissa Etheridge** and Julie Cypher.

DEBUT	PEAK	WKS	RIAA	CD	#	ARTIST — Album Title	Sym	$	Label & Number
3/20/71	12	18	●	©	1	**If I Could Only Remember My Name**		$20	Atlantic 7203
						DAVID CROSBY/GRAHAM NASH:			
4/22/72	4	26	●		2	**Graham Nash/David Crosby**		$15	Atlantic 7220
10/11/75	6	31	●	©	3	**Wind On The Water**		$12	ABC 902
7/24/76	26	15	●	©	4	**Whistling Down The Wire**		$12	ABC 956
11/19/77	52	8			5	**Crosby/Nash - Live**	[L]	$12	ABC 1042
10/28/78	150	4			6	**The Best Of Crosby/Nash**	[G]	$12	ABC 1102
						DAVID CROSBY:			
2/18/89	104	10		©	7	**Oh Yes I Can**		$10	A&M 5232
6/5/93	133	8			8	**Thousand Roads**		$10	Atlantic 82484

Bittersweet (3,6)
Blacknotes (2)
Broken Bird (4)
Carry Me (3,6) *52*
Chicago (6)
Columbus (8)
Coverage (8)
Cowboy Movie (1)

Cowboy Of Dreams (3)
Dancer (4)
Deja Vu (5)
Distances (3)
Drive My Car (7)
Drop Down Mama (7)
Fieldworker (3,5)
Flying Man (7)

Foolish Man (4,5)
Frozen Smiles (2)
Games (8)
Girl To Be On My Mind (2)
Helpless Heart (8)
Hero (8) *44*
Homeward Through The Haze (3)

I Used To Be A King (5)
I'd Swear There Was Somebody Here (1)
Immigration Man (2,5) *36*
In The Wide Ruin (7)
J.B.'s Blues (7)
Lady Of The Harbor (7)
Laughing (1,6)

Leeshore, The (5)
Love Work Out (3,6)
Low Down Payment (3)
Mama Lion (3,5)
Marguerita (4)
Melody (7)
Monkey And The Underdog (7)
Music Is Love (1) *95*

Mutiny (4)
My Country 'Tis Of Thee (7)
Naked In The Rain (3)
Natalie (8)
Oh Yes I Can (7)
Old Soldier (8)
Orleans (1)
Out Of The Darkness (4,6) *89*

CROSBY, David — Cont'd

Page 43 (2,5)
Simple Man (5)
Song With No Words (Tree
  With No Leaves) (1)
Southbound Train (2,6) *99*

Spotlight (4)
Strangers Room (2)
Take The Money And Run (3)
Taken At All (4)
Tamalpais High (At About 3) (1)

Thousand Roads (3)
Through Your Hands (8)
Time After Time (4)
To The Last Whale Medley
  (3,6)

Too Young To Die (8)
Tracks In The Dust (7)
Traction In The Rain (1)
Wall Song (2,6)
What Are Their Names (1)

Where Will I Be? (2)
Whole Cloth (2)
Wild Tales (6)
Yvette In English (8)

CROSBY, STILLS & NASH ★177★ '70

Folk-rock trio formed in Laurel Canyon, California. Consisted of **David Crosby** (guitar), **Stephen Stills** (guitar, keyboards, bass) and **Graham Nash** (guitar). Crosby had been in **The Byrds**, Stills had been in **Buffalo Springfield**, and Nash was with **The Hollies**. Won the 1969 Best New Artist Grammy Award. **Neil Young** (guitar), formerly with Buffalo Springfield, joined group in 1970, left in 1974. Periodic reunions since then. Trio inducted into the Rock and Roll Hall of Fame in 1997.

    1)Deja Vu 2)4 Way Street 3)So Far

DEBUT	PEAK	WKS	RIAA	CD	ARTIST — Album Title	Catalog	Sym	$	Label & Number
6/28/69	6	107	▲⁴	©	1 **Crosby, Stills & Nash**			$20	Atlantic 8229
					CROSBY, STILLS, NASH & YOUNG:				
4/4/70	❶¹	97	▲⁷	©	2 **Deja Vu**	C:#27/4		$15	Atlantic 7200
4/24/71	❶¹	42	▲⁴	©	3 **4 Way Street**	C:#29/5 [L]		$20	Atlantic 902 [2]
9/7/74	❶¹	27	▲⁶	©	4 **So Far**	C:❶⁵/111 [G]		$12	Atlantic 18100
					CROSBY, STILLS & NASH:				
7/9/77	2⁴	33	▲⁴	©	5 **CSN**	C:#21/21		$12	Atlantic 19104
1/10/81	122	5		©	6 **Replay**	[K]		$12	Atlantic 16026
7/17/82	8	41	▲	©	7 **Daylight Again**			$12	Atlantic 19360
7/2/83	43	12		©	8 **Allies**	[L]		$12	Atlantic 80075
12/3/88+	16	22	▲		9 **American Dream**			$10	Atlantic 81888
					CROSBY, STILLS, NASH & YOUNG				
7/14/90	57	11		©	10 **Live It Up**			$10	Atlantic 82107
1/4/92	109	2	▲	©	11 **CSN**	[K]		$40	Atlantic 82319 [4]
9/3/94	98	2		©	12 **After The Storm**			$10	Atlantic 82654
11/13/99	26	9		©	13 **Looking Forward**			$10	Reprise 47436

CROSBY, STILLS, NASH & YOUNG

After The Dolphin (10,11)
After The Storm (12)
Almost Cut My Hair (2,11)
America's Children (medley) (3)
American Dream (9)
Another Sleep Song (11)
Anything At All (5)
Arrows (10)
As I Come Of Age (11)
Bad Boyz (11)
Barrel Of Pain (8)
Barrel Of Pain (Half-Life) (11)
Bittersweet (11)
Black Queen (11)
Blackbird (8,11)
Camera (12)
Carried Away (5)
Carry Me (11) *52*
Carry On (2,3,6)
Cathedral (5,6,11)
Change Partners (6,11) *43*
Chicago (3,11) *35*
Clear Blue Skies (9)
Cold Rain (5,11)
Compass (9)
Country Girl Medley (2)
Cowboy Of Dreams (11)

Cowgirl In The Sand (3)
Dark Star (5,8,11)
Daylight Again (medley) (7,11)
Dear Mr. Fantasy (7)
Deja Vu (2,4,11)
Delta (11)
Don't Let It Bring You Down (3)
Don't Say Goodbye (9)
Dream For Him (13)
Drive My Car (11)
Drivin' Thunder (9)
Everybody I Love You (2)
Fair Game (5) *43*
Faith In Me (13)
Feel Your Love (9)
50/50 (11)
Find A Dream (11)
Find The Cost Of Freedom
  (3,4,7,11)
First Things First (6)
For What It's Worth (8)
49 Bye-Byes (1,3)
4 + 20 (2,11)
Got It Made (9,11) *69*
(Got To Keep) Open (10)
Guinnevere (1,4,11)
Haven't We Lost Enough?
  (10,11)

He Played Real Good For Free
  (8)
Heartland (11)
Helpless (2,4,11)
Helplessly Hoping (1,4,11)
Homeward Through The Haze
  (11)
Horses Through A Rainstorm
  (11)
House Of Broken Dreams (10)
I Give You Give Blind (5,6)
I Used To Be A King (11)
I'd Swear There Was
  Somebody Here (11)
If Anybody Had A Heart (10)
In My Dreams (5,11)
In My Life (12)
Into The Darkness (7)
It Doesn't Matter (11) *61*
It Won't Go Away (12)
Johnny's Garden (11)
Just A Song Before I Go
  (5,6,11) *7*
Lady Of The Island (1,11)
Laughing (11)
Lee Shore (3,11)
Live It Up (10)

Long Time Gone (1,3,11)
Looking Forward (13)
Love The One You're With
  (3,6,11) *14*
Man In The Mirror (11)
Marrakesh Express
  (1,6,11) *28*
Might As Well Have A Good
  Time (7)
Military Madness (11) *73*
Music Is Love (11) *95*
My Love Is A Gentle Thing (11)
Name Of Love (9)
Night Song (9)
Nighttime For The Generals (9)
No Tears Left (13)
Ohio (3,4,11) *14*
Old Times Good Times (11)
On The Way Home (3)
Only Waiting For You (12)
Our House (2,4,11) *30*
Out Of Control (11)
Page 43 (11)
Panama (12)
Pre-Road Downs (1,3,6)
Prison Song (11)
Queen Of Them All (13)
Questions (medley) (11)

Raise A Voice (8)
Right Between The Eyes (3)
Run From Tears (5)
Sanibel (13)
See The Changes (5,11)
Seen Enough (13)
Shadow Captain (5,6,8,11)
Shadowland (9)
Simple Man (11)
Since I Met You (7)
Slowpoke (13)
So Begins The Task (11)
Soldiers Of Peace (9,11)
Someday Soon (13)
Song For Susan (7)
Song With No Words (Tree
  With No Leaves) (11)
Southbound Train (11) *99*
Southern Cross (7,11) *18*
Southern Man (3)
Stand And Be Counted (13)
Straight Line (10)
Street To Lean On (12)
Suite: Judy Blue Eyes
  (1,3,4,11) *21*
Taken At All (11)
Teach Your Children
  (2,3,4,11) *16*

That Girl (9)
These Empty Days (12)
This Old House (9)
Thoroughfare Gap (11)
Till It Shines (11)
To The Last Whale Medley
  (6,11)
Tomboy (10)
Too Much Love To Hide (7) *69*
Tracks In The Dust (11)
Triad (2)
Turn Back The Pages (11) *84*
Turn Your Back On Love (7,8)
Unequal Love (12)
Urge For Going (11)
War Games (8) *45*
Wasted On The Way (7,8,11) *9*
Where Will I Be? (11)
Wild Tales (11)
Woodstock (2,4,11) *11*
Word Game (11)
You Are Alive (7)
You Don't Have To Cry (1,11)
Yours And Mine (10,11)

CROSS, Christopher '80

Born Christopher Geppert on 5/3/51 in San Antonio, Texas. Pop-rock singer/songwriter/guitarist. Won the 1980 Best New Artist Grammy Award.

DEBUT	PEAK	WKS	RIAA	CD	ARTIST — Album Title	Catalog	Sym	$	Label & Number
2/16/80	6	116	▲⁵	©	1 **Christopher Cross**			$10	Warner 3383
					1980 Grammy winner: Album of the Year				
2/19/83	11	31	●	©	2 **Another Page**			$10	Warner 23757
11/30/85	127	6		©	3 **Every Turn Of The World**			$10	Warner 25341

All Right (2) *12*
Baby Says No (2)
Charm The Snake (3) *68*
Deal 'Em Again (2)
Don't Say Goodbye (3)
Every Turn Of The World (3)

I Hear You Call (3)
I Really Don't Know Anymore
  (1)
It's You That Really Matters (3)
Light Is On (1)
Long World (2)

Love Found A Home (3)
Love Is Love (In Any Language)
  (3)
Minstrel Gigolo (1)
Nature Of The Game (2)
Never Be The Same (1) *15*

No Time For Talk (2) *33*
Open Your Heart (3)
Poor Shirley (3)
Ride Like The Wind (1) *2*
Sailing (1) *1*
Say You'll Be Mine (1) *20*

Spinning (1)
Swing Street (3)
Talking In My Sleep (2)
That Girl (3)
Think Of Laura (2) *9*

What Am I Supposed To
  Believe (2)
Words Of Wisdom (2)

CROSS COUNTRY '73

Trio of Jay Siegel (vocals), with brothers Mitch (guitar) and Phil (percussion) Margo. All were members of **The Tokens**.

DEBUT	PEAK	WKS	RIAA	CD	ARTIST — Album Title	Catalog	Sym	$	Label & Number
10/13/73	198	2			**Cross Country**			$15	Atco 7024

Ball Song
Choir Boy

Cross Country
Extended Wings

Fall Song
In The Midnight Hour *30*

Just A Thought
Smile Song

Tastes So Good To Me
Things With Wings

Today

CROSSE, Clay '97

Born Walter Clayton Crossnoe in 1967 in Memphis. Christian singer/songwriter.

DEBUT	PEAK	WKS	RIAA	CD	ARTIST — Album Title	Catalog	Sym	$	Label & Number
7/19/97	141	5		©	**Stained Glass**			$10	Reunion 10005

Consider The Choices
He Ain't Heavy
He Walked A Mile

It Must Have Been Your Hands
Love One Another Right
Saving The World

Sold Out Believer
Somethin' Missin'
Stained Glass Window

When All That's Left Is To
  Believe
Wicked

CROW '70

Rock-blues group from Minneapolis: Dave Waggoner (vocals), Dick Weigand (guitar), Kink Middlemist (organ), Larry Weigand (bass) and Denny Craswell (drums). Craswell was a member of The Castaways.

9/13/69+	69	24			1 Crow Music			$25	Amaret 5002
6/6/70	181	4			2 Crow By Crow			$25	Amaret 5006

Annie Fannie (medley) (2)
Busy Day (1)
Colors (2)
Cottage Cheese (2) 56
Da Da Song (1)

Death Down To Your Soul (medley) (2)
Evil Woman Don't Play Your Games With Me (1) 19
Get Yourself A Number (medley) (2)

Gone, Gone, Gone (2)
Gonna Leave A Mark (1)
Heading North (2)
I Stand To Blame (2)
Last Prayer (medley) (2)

Listen To The Bop (1)
Rollin' (1)
Sleepy Woman (1)
Slow Down (1)
Smokey Joe (2)

Thoughts (1)
Time To Make A Turn (1)
White Eyes (1)

CROW, Sheryl '95

Born on 2/11/63 in Kennett, Missouri. Pop-rock singer/songwriter/guitarist. Worked as backing singer for **Michael Jackson**, **Don Henley**, **George Harrison** and others. Won the 1994 Best New Artist Grammy Award.

3/19/94+	3	100	▲7	©	1 Tuesday Night Music Club	C:#44/4		$10	A&M 540126
10/12/96	6	63	▲3	©	2 Sheryl Crow			$10	A&M 540587
10/17/98	5	53	▲	©	3 The Globe Sessions			$10	A&M 540959
12/25/99	107	11		©	4 Sheryl Crow And Friends: Live From Central Park	[L]		$10	A&M 490574

All I Wanna Do (1,4) 2
Am I Getting Through (Part I & II) (3)
Anything But Down (3) 49
Book, The (2)
Can't Cry Anymore (1) 36
Change Would Do You Good (2,4)

Crash And Burn (3)
Difficult Kind (3,4)
Everyday Is A Winding Road (2,4) 11
Gold Dust Woman (4)
Happy (1)
Hard To Make A Stand (2)
Home (2)

I Shall Believe (1)
If It Makes You Happy (2,4) 10
It Don't Hurt (3,4)
Leaving Las Vegas (1,4) 60
Love Is A Good Thing (2)
Maybe Angels (2)
Maybe That's Something (3)
Members Only (3)

Mississippi (3)
My Favorite Mistake (3,4) 20
Na-Na Song (1)
No One Said It Would Be Easy (1)
Oh Marie (2)
Ordinary Morning (2)
Redemption Day (3,4)

Riverwide (3)
Run, Baby, Run (1)
Solidify (1)
Strong Enough (1,4) 5
Superstar (1)
Sweet Rosalyn (2)
There Goes The Neighborhood (1)

Tombstone Blues (4)
We Do What We Can (1)
What I Can Do For You (1)
White Room (4)

CROWBAR — see KING BISCUIT BOY

CROWDED HOUSE '87

Pop group from New Zealand: Neil Finn (vocals, guitar, piano), Nick Seymour (bass) and Paul Hester (drums). Finn and Hester were members of **Split Enz**. Neil's brother, Tim Finn (also of Split Enz), joined band in 1991; left in 1993, replaced by Mark Hart. Hester left band in April 1994. Group disbanded in June 1996.

8/30/86+	12	58	▲	©	1 Crowded House			$10	Capitol 12485
7/23/88	40	19		©	2 Temple Of Low Men			$10	Capitol 48763
7/20/91	83	17		©	3 Woodface			$10	Capitol 93559
1/29/94	73	7		©	4 Together Alone			$10	Capitol 27048

All I Ask (3)
As Sure As I Am (3)
Better Be Home Soon (2) 42
Black & White Boy (4)
Catherine Wheels (4)
Chocolate Cake (3)
Distant Sun (4)
Don't Dream It's Over (1) 2

Fall At Your Feet (3) 75
Fame Is (3)
Fingers Of Love (4)
Four Seasons In One Day (3)
Hole In The River (1)
How Will You Go (3)
I Feel Possessed (2)
I Walk Away (1)

In My Command (4)
In The Lowlands (4)
Into Temptation (2)
It's Only Natural (3)
Italian Plastic (3)
Kare Kare (4)
Kill Eye (2)
Locked Out (4)

Love This Life (2)
Love You 'Till The Day I Die (1)
Mansion In The Slums (3)
Mean To Me (3)
Nails In My Feet (4)
Never Be The Same (2)
Now We're Getting Somewhere (1)

Pineapple Head (4)
Private Universe (4)
She Goes On (3)
Sister Madly (4)
Skin Feeling (4)
Something So Strong (1) 7
Tall Trees (3)
That's What I Call Love (1)

There Goes God (4)
Together Alone (4)
Tombstone (1)
Walking On The Spot (4)
Weather With You (3)
When You Come (2)
Whispers And Moans (3)
World Where You Live (1) 65

CROWELL, Rodney '81

Born on 8/7/50 in Houston. Country singer/songwriter/guitarist. Married to **Rosanne Cash** from 1979-92.

4/26/80	155	10			1 But What Will The Neighbors Think			$12	Warner 3407
10/3/81	105	8			2 Rodney Crowell			$12	Warner 3587
8/23/86	177	5		©	3 Street Language			$10	Columbia 40116
10/6/90	180	2		©	4 Keys To The Highway			$10	Columbia 45242
6/6/92	155	9		©	5 Life Is Messy			$10	Columbia 47985

Ain't No Money (1)
All You've Got To Do (2)
Alone But Not Alone (5)
Answer Is Yes (5)
Ashes By Now (1) 37
Ballad Of Fast Eddie (3)
Best I Can (3)
Blues In The Daytime (1)
Don't Let Your Feet Slow You Down (4)

Don't Need No Other Now (2)
Faith Is Mine (4)
Heartbroke (1)
Here Come The 80's (1)
I Guess We've Been Together For Too Long (4)
I Hardly Know How To Be (1)
If Looks Could Kill (4)
It Don't Get Better Than This (5)

It's Not For Me To Judge (5)
It's Only Rock 'N' Roll (1)
Just Wanta Dance (2)
Let Freedom Ring (3)
Let's Make Trouble (5)
Life Is Messy (5)
Looking For You (3)
Lovin' All Night (5)
Many A Long & Lonesome Highway (4)

Maybe Next Time (5)
My Past Is Present (4)
Now That We're Alone (4)
Oh King Richard (3)
Old Pipeliner (2)
On A Real Good Night (1)
One About England (1)
Only Two Hearts (2)
Past Like A Mask (3)

Queen Of Hearts (1)
Shame On The Moon (2)
She Ain't Going Nowhere (2)
She Loves The Jerk (3)
Soul Searchin' (4)
Stars On The Water (2)
Stay (Don't Be Cruel) (3)
Tell Me The Truth (4)
Things I Wish I'd Said (4)
'Til I Gain Control Again (2)

Victim Or A Fool (2)
We Gotta Go On Meeting Like This (4)
What Kind Of Love (5)
When I'm Free Again (3)
When The Blue Hour Comes (3)
You Been On My Mind (4)

CROWN HEIGHTS AFFAIR '75

Disco group from New York City: Phil Thomas (vocals), William Anderson (guitar), Howard Young (keyboards), Bert Reid, James Baynard and Ray Reid (horns), Muki Wilson (bass) and Ray Rock (drums).

10/4/75	121	17			1 Dreaming A Dream			$12	De-Lite 2017
3/29/80	148	12			2 Sure Shot			$12	De-Lite 9517

Dreaming A Dream (1) 43
Every Beat Of My Heart (1) 83
Feeling Tall (1)

Foxy (1)
I Am Me (1)
I Don't Want To Change You (2)

I See The Light (2)
Na, Na, Hey, Hey (1)
Picture Show (1)

Sure Shot (2)
Tell Me You Love Me (2)
Use Your Body & Soul (2)

You Gave Me Love (2)
You Smiled (1)
You've Been Gone (2)

CRU '97

Rap trio from New York City: Chadio, Yogi and Mighty Ha.

9/13/97	102	3		©	Da Dirty 30			$10	Violator 537607

Armaggedon
Bluntz & Bakakeemis
Bubblin'
Bulletproof Vest
Dirty 29

Ebonic Plague
Footlong
Fresh, Wild And Bold
Goin' Down
Goines Tale

Hoe 2 Society
Illz, The
Just Another Case 68
Lisa Lipps
Live At The Tunnel

Loungin' Wit My Cru
My Everlovin'
Nuthin' But
O.J.
Pay Attention

Pronto
R.I.P.
Shoot Out
Straight From L.I.P.
Ten To Run

That Sh**
Up North
Wreckgonize
You Used To

CRUCIAL CONFLICT '96

Hip-hop group from Chicago: Corey Johnson, Marrico King, Ralph Leverston and Wondosas Martin.

7/20/96	12	18	●	©	1 The Final Tic			$10	Pallas 53006
11/21/98	38	4		©	2 Good Side Bad Side			$10	Pallas 53163

Airplane (2)

Back Against The Wall (2)

Bidness, The (2)

Come On (2)

Desperado (1)

Faceless Ones (2)

CRUCIAL CONFLICT — Cont'd

Final Tic (1)	I'm Bout To Explode (2)	Like This (2)	Ride The Rodeo (1)	Swing It Over Here (2)	Trigger Happy (1)
Get Up (1)	Just Getting My Money (1)	Lil Advice (1)	Roll Somethin (2)	Tell It To The Judge (1)	Universal Love (2)
Ghetto Queen (2)	Let It Go (2)	Pump It Up (2)	Scummy (2)	To The Left (1)	Young Guns (2)
Hay (1) *18*	Life Ain't The Same (1)	Raw Dope Anthem (2)	Showdown (1)	2 Bogish (2)	

CRUISE, Julee   '90
Born on 12/1/56 in Creston, Iowa. Singer/actress. Joined **The B-52's** on tour in 1992.

6/2/90	74	20	©	Floating Into The Night			$10	Warner 25859

Falling	I Float Alone	Into The Night	Nightingale, The	Swan, The
Floating	I Remember	Mysteries Of Love	Rockin' Back Inside My Heart	World Spins

★208★   CRUSADERS, The   '79
Instrumental jazz-oriented group from Houston: **Joe Sample** (keyboards), **Wilton Felder** (reeds), Nesbert "Stix"Hooper (drums) and Wayne Henderson (trombone). First known as **The Jazz Crusaders**. Henderson left in 1975. **Larry Carlton** was a frequent guitarist from 1972-77. Hooper left in 1983. Sample and Felder reunited with a new lineup in 1991.
1)Street Life 2)Chain Reaction 3)Rhapsody And Blues

THE JAZZ CRUSADERS:

1/4/69	184	2			1 **Powerhouse**	[I]	$20	Pacific Jazz 20136
10/17/70+	90	16	©		2 **Old Socks, New Shoes...New Socks, Old Shoes**	[I]	$15	Chisa 804

THE CRUSADERS:

6/26/71	168	4	©		3 **Pass The Plate**	[I]	$15	Chisa 807
3/4/72	96	29			4 **Crusaders 1**	[I]	$20	Blue Thumb 6001 [2]
3/10/73	45	29			5 **The 2nd Crusade**	[I]	$20	Blue Thumb 7000 [2]
11/24/73	173	14	©		6 **Unsung Heroes**	[I]	$15	Blue Thumb 6007
4/13/74	73	20	©		7 **Scratch**	[I-L]	$15	Blue Thumb 6010
10/26/74	31	23	●	©	8 **Southern Comfort**	[I]	$20	Blue Thumb 9002 [2]
8/23/75	26	17		©	9 **Chain Reaction**	[I]	$15	Blue Thumb 6022
5/22/76	38	18		©	10 **Those Southern Knights**	[I]	$15	Blue Thumb 6024
12/18/76+	122	10			11 **The Best Of The Crusaders**	[G-I]	$20	Blue Thumb 6027 [2]
6/18/77	41	15	©		12 **Free As The Wind**	[I]	$15	Blue Thumb 6029
7/15/78	34	18	●	©	13 **Images**	[I]	$15	Blue Thumb 6030
6/9/79	18	39	●	©	14 **Street Life**	[I]	$12	MCA 3094
7/12/80	29	16		©	15 **Rhapsody And Blues**	[I]	$12	MCA 5124
10/10/81	59	16		©	16 **Standing Tall**	[I]	$12	MCA 5254
7/17/82	144	7		©	17 **Royal Jam**	[I-L]	$15	MCA 8017 [2]
					recorded September 1981 at the Royal Festival Hall in London			
4/21/84	79	22		©	18 **Ghetto Blaster**	[I]	$12	MCA 5429
5/11/91	174	2		©	19 **Healing The Wounds**	[I]	$10	GRP 9638

Ain't Gon' Change A Thang (5)	Feel It (12)	I Just Can't Leave Your Love Alone (17)	Marcella's Dream (13)	Rainbow Visions (9)	Take It Or Leave It (5)
And Then There Was The Blues (10)	Feeling Funky (10)	**I'm So Glad I'm Standing Here Today** (16,17) *97*	Mellow Out (9)	Rainy Night In Georgia (2)	Thank You Falettinme Be Mice Elf Agin (2)
Ballad For Joe (Louis) (8,11)	Fire Water (1)	In The Middle Of The River (6)	Mercy, Mercy, Mercy (19)	Rhapsody And Blues (15)	That's How I Feel (4,11)
Bayou Bottoms (13)	Fly With Wings Of Love (17)	It Happens Everyday (12)	Message From The Inner City (5)	River Rat (12)	This Old World's Too Funky For Me (16)
Better Not Look Down (17)	Free As The Wind (12)	It's Just Gotta Be That Way (4)	Mosadi (Woman) (4)	Rodeo Drive (High Steppin') (14)	Three Children (4)
Burnin' Up The Carnival (17)	Freedom Sound (6)	Jackson! (2)	Mr. Cool (18)	Running Man (19)	Thrill Is Gone (17)
Carnival Of The Night (14)	Full Moon (4)	Jazz! (2)	Mud Hole (4)	Scratch (7,11) *81*	'Til The Sun Shines (10)
Cause We've Ended As Lovers (19)	Funny Shuffle (2)	Journey From Within (5)	My Lady (14)	Search For Soul (5)	Time Bomb (8)
Chain Reaction (9,11)	Georgia Cottonfield (4)	Keep That Same Old Feeling (10,11)	My Mama Told Me So (10)	Serenity (10)	Time Has No Ending (2)
Cookie Man (1)	Get On The Soul Ship (It's Sailing) (8)	Last Call (15,17)	Mystique Blues (4)	Shade Of Blues (4)	Tomorrow Where Are You? (5)
Cosmic Reign (13)	Give It Up (9)	Lay It On The Line (6)	Never Make A Move Too Soon (17)	Shake Dance (19)	Tough Talk (5)
Covert Action (13)	Goin' Down South (3)	Let's Boogie (6)	New Moves (18)	Snowflake (13)	Treat Me Like Ye Treat Yaself (3)
Creole (9)	Golden Slumbers (2)	Lilies Of The Nile (8)	Night Faces (14)	So Far Away (4,7,11)	Unsung Heroes (6)
Crossfire (6)	Gotta Get It On (5)	Listen And You'll See (3)	Night Ladies (18)	Soul Caravan (9,11)	Upstairs (1)
Dead End (18)	Gotta Lotta Shakalada (18)	Little Things Mean A Lot (19)	Night Theme (6)	Soul Shadows (15)	**Way Back Home** (2,7,11) *90*
Do You Remember When? (5,11)	Greasy Spoon (3,8,11)	Longest Night (16)	Nite Crawler (12)	Southern Comfort (8)	Way We Was (12)
Don't Let It Get You Down (5,11) *86*	Hallucinate (9)	Look Beyond The Hill (5)	No Place To Hide (4)	Spiral (10)	Well's Gone Dry (8)
Double Bubble (3)	Hard Times (2,6,7,11)	Love And Peace (1)	Now I Lay Me Down To Sleep (6)	Standing Tall (16)	When There's Love Around (8)
Dream Street (18)	Healing The Wounds (19)	Love Can't Grow Where The Rain Won't Fall (3)	One Day I'll Fly Away (17)	Sting Ray (1)	Where There's A Will There's A Way (5)
Eleanor Rigby (7)	Heavy Up (Don't Get Light With Me) (6)	Love Is Blue (L'Amour Est Bleu) (1)	Pass The Plate Medley (3)	Stomp And Buck Dance (8,11)	Whispering Pines (8)
Elegant Evening (15)	Hey Jude (1)	Luckenbach, Texas (Back To The Basics Of Love) (16)	Pessimisticism (19)	**Street Life** (14,17) *36*	Why Do You Laugh At Me? (2)
Fairy Tales (13)	Hold On (17)	Maputo (19)	Promises, Promises (1)	Sugar Cane (9)	Young Rabbits--'71-'72 (3)
Fancy Dance (1)	Honky Tonk Struttin' (15)		**Put It Where You Want It** (4,11) *52*	Sunshine In Your Eyes (16)	Zalal'e Mini (Take It Easy) (18)
	Hot's It (5)			Super-Stuff (8)	
	Hustler, The (4)			Sweet Gentle Love (15)	
	I Felt The Love (9,12)			Sweet 'N' Sour (12)	
				Sweet Revival (4)	

CRUZADOS   '85
Rock group from Los Angeles: Tito Larriva (vocals), Steven Hufsteter (guitar), Tony Marsico (bass) and Chalo Quintana (drums). Marshall Rohner (guitar) replaced Hufsteter in early 1987. Rohner left in 1989 to join **TSOL**.

11/2/85	76	18	©		1 **Cruzados**			$10	Arista 8383
8/1/87	106	21	©		2 **After Dark**			$10	Arista 8439

Bed Of Lies (2)	Flor De Mal (1)	Last Ride (2)	Road Of Truth (2)	Summer's Come, Summer's Gone (2)	Young And On Fire (2)
Blue Sofa (Still A Fool) (2)	Hanging Out In California (1)	Motorcycle Girl (1)	Seven Summers (2)	Time For Waiting (2)	
Chains Of Freedom (2)	I Want Your World To Turn (2)	1,000 Miles (1)	Small Town Love (2)	Wasted Years (1)	
Cryin' Eyes (1)	Just Like Roses (1)	Rising Sun (1)	Some Day (1)		

CRYAN' SHAMES, The   '68
Rock group from Chicago: Tom Doody (vocals), Jim Fairs (lead guitar), Jerry Stone (rhythm guitar), Jim Pilster (tambourine), Dave Purple (bass) and Dennis Conroy (drums).

5/13/67	192	4			1 **Sugar & Spice**			$25	Columbia 9389
1/13/68	156	5			2 **A Scratch In The Sky**			$25	Columbia 9586
2/15/69	184	9			3 **Synthesis**			$25	Columbia 9719

Baltimore Oriole (3)	Dennis Dupree From Danville (2)	Greenburg, Glickstein, Charles, David Smith & Jones (3)	Hey Joe (Where You Gonna Go) (1)	If I Needed Someone (1)	It's All Right (3)
Ben Franklin's Almanac (1)	First Train To California (3)	Heat Wave (1)	**I Wanna Meet You** (1) *85*	In The Cafe (2)	July (1)
Carol For Lorelei (2)			I Was Lonely When (2)	**It Could Be We're In Love** (2) *85*	Let's Get Together (3)
Cobblestone Road (2)					

CRYAN' SHAMES, The — Cont'd

Master's Fool (3)
Mr. Unreliable (2)
Painter, The (3)
Sailing Ship (2)
She Don't Care About Time (1)
Sugar And Spice (1) *49*
Sunshine Psalm (2)
Sweet Girl Of Mine (3)
Symphony Of The Wind (3)
Town I'd Like To Go Back To (2)
20th Song (3)
Up On The Roof (2) *85*
We Could Be Happy (1)
We Gotta Get Out Of This Place (1)
We'll Meet Again (1)
Your Love (3)

CRYSTAL, Billy '85

Born on 3/14/47 in Long Beach, Long Island, New York. Actor/comedian. Starred in several movies and TV shows.

| 9/21/85 | 65 | 13 | | © | Mahvelous! | [C] | $10 | A&M 5096 |

Buddy Young, Jr.
Face
Fernando's Special Gift
Godammit, You...Bastard
Howard Cosell, Right There!
I Hate When That Happens
"Live" From The Bottom Line
Mind Of Its Own
Now!
Sammy For Africa
Where's Your Messiah Now?
You Look Marvelous *58*

CRYSTAL METHOD, The '97

Electronic-dance duo: Ken Jordan and Scott Kirkland.

| 9/13/97 | 92 | 43 | ● | © | Vegas | [I] | $10 | Outpost 30003 |

Bad Stone
Busy Child
Cherry Twist
Comin' Back
High Roller
Jaded
Keep Hope Alive
She's My Pusher
Trip Like I Do
Vapor Trail

CRYSTALS, The '63

Female vocal group from Brooklyn, New York: Barbara Alston, Delores Kennibrew, Mary Thomas, Pattie Wright and Merna Girard. La La Brooks replaced Girard in 1962. Thomas left in 1962. Wright was replaced by Frances Collins in 1964. Alston died of a heart attack on 5/15/92 (age 48).

| 3/16/63 | 131 | 2 | | © | He's A Rebel | | $600 | Philles 4001 |

Another Country-Another World
Frankenstein Twist
He Hit Me
He's A Rebel *1*
He's Sure The Boy I Love *11*
I Love You Eddie
No One Ever Tells You
Oh Yeah, Maybe Baby
On Broadway
There's No Other (Like My Baby) *20*
Uptown *13*
What A Nice Way To Turn Seventeen

CUBA, Joe, Sextet '66

Born Gilberto Calderon in Harlem, New York. Latin conga player. Other members of his sextet: Jose "Cheo" Feliciano (vocals, not to be confused with the solo star), Tommy Berrios (vibes), Nick Jimenez (piano), Jules Cordero (bass) and Jimmy Sabater (drums).

| 9/17/66 | 119 | 3 | | 1 | We Must Be Doing Something Right! | [F] | $20 | Tico 1133 |
| 1/7/67 | 131 | 6 | | 2 | Wanted Dead Or Alive (Bang! Bang! Push, Push!) | [F] | $20 | Tico 1146 |

Alafia (2)
Arecibo (1)
Asi Soy (2)
"Bang" "Bang" (2) *63*
Bochinchosa (1)
Clave Mambo (2)
Cocinando (2)
El Pito (I'll Never Go Back To Georgia) (1)
Incomparable (1)
La Malanga Brava (2)
Lo Bueno Ya Viene (1)
Mujer Divina (Petite) (2)
My Wonderful You (Baby When I'm Down) (1)
Oh Yeah! (2) *62*
Pruebalo (1)
Push, Push, Push (2)
Que Son Uno (2)
Si Te Dicen (2)
Sock It To Me (2)
Triste (1)
Y Tu Abuela Donde Esta (1)
Ya No Aguanto Mas (1)

CUFF LINKS, The '70

Group is actually the overdubbed voice of Ron Dante (of **The Archies**).

| 12/6/69+ | 138 | 11 | | | Tracy | | $25 | Decca 75160 |

All The Young Women
Early In The Morning
Heather
I Remember
Lay A Little Love On Me
Put A Little Love In Your Heart
Sally Ann (You're Such A Pretty Baby)
Sweet Caroline (Good Times Never Seemed So Good)
Tracy *9*
When Julie Comes Around *41*
Where Do You Go?

CULT, The '89

Rock group from England. Nucleus of evercharging lineup included Ian Astbury (vocals; real name: Ian Lindsay), Billy Duffy (guitar), Jamie Stewart (bass) and Les Warner (drums). Warner left in 1988; replaced by Matt Sorum (**Guns N' Roses**). Stewart left in 1990.

12/28/85+	87	34	●	©	1	Love		$10	Sire 25359
4/25/87	38	32	▲	©	2	Electric		$10	Sire 25555
4/29/89	10	33	▲	©	3	Sonic Temple		$10	Sire 25871
10/12/91	25	12		©	4	Ceremony		$10	Sire 26673
10/29/94	69	4		©	5	The Cult		$10	Sire 45673
6/23/01	37	8		©	6	Beyond Good And Evil		$10	Lava 83440

American Gothic (6)
American Horse (3)
Aphrodisiac Jacket (2)
Ashes And Ghosts (6)
Automatic Blues (3)
Bad Fun (3)
Bangkok Rain (4)
Be Free (5)
Big Neon Glitter (1)
Black Angel (1)
Black Sun (5)
Born To Be Wild (2)
Breathe (6)
Brother Wolf, Sister Moon (1)
Ceremony (4)
Coming Down (Drug Tongue) (5)
Earth Mofo (4)
Edie (Ciao Baby) (3) *93*
Electric Ocean (2)
Emperor's New Horse (5)
Fire Woman (3) *46*
Full Tilt (4)
Gone (5)
Heart Of Soul (4)
Hollow Man (1)
If (4)
Indian (4)
Joy (5)
King Contrary Man (2)
Lil' Devil (2)
Love (1)
Love Removal Machine (2)
Memphis Hip Shake (2)
My Bridges Burn (6)
Naturally High (5)
New York City (4)
Nico (6)
Nirvana (1)
Outlaw (2)
Peace Dog (4)
Phoenix, The (1)
Rain (1)
Real Grrrl (5)
Revolution (1)
Rise (6)
Sacred Life (5)
Saint, The (6)
Saints Are Down (5)
Shape The Sky (4)
She Sells Sanctuary (1)
Soldier Blue (3)
Soul Asylum (1)
Speed Of Light (6)
Star (5)
Sun King (3)
Sweet Salvation (4)
Sweet Soul Sister (3)
Take The Power (6)
True Believers (6)
Universal You (5)
Wake Up Time For Freedom (3)
War (The Process) (6)
White (4)
Wild Flower (2)
Wild Hearted Son (4)
Wonderland (4)

CULTURE CLUB '84

Pop group formed in London: George "**Boy George**" O'Dowd (vocals), Roy Hay (guitar, keyboards), Michael Craig (bass) and Jon Moss (drums). Designer Sue Clowes originated distinctive costuming for the group. Won the 1983 Best New Artist Grammy Award. Boy George went solo in 1987.

1/8/83	14	88	▲	©	1	Kissing To Be Clever		$10	Epic 38398
11/5/83+	2[6]	59	▲[4]	©	2	Colour By Numbers		$10	Epic 39107
11/24/84	26	20	▲	©	3	Waking Up With The House On Fire		$10	Virgin 39881
4/26/86	32	17		©	4	From Luxury To Heartache		$10	Virgin 40345
11/20/93	169	3		©	5	At Worst...The Best Of Boy George And Culture Club	[G]	$10	SBK 39014
8/29/98	148	2		©	6	VH1 Storytellers / Greatest Moments	[G-L]	$15	Virgin 46191 [2]

Disc 1: recorded live; Disc 2: greatest hits

After The Love (5)
Black Money (2,6)
Bow Down Mister (5)
Boy, Boy, (I'm The Boy) (4)
Changing Every Day (2)
Church Of The Poison Mind (2,5,6) *10*
Come Clean (4)
Crime Time (3)
Crying Game (5,6) *15*
Dangerous Man (3)
Dive, The (3)
Do You Really Want To Hurt Me (1,5,6) *2*
Don't Cry (5)
Don't Talk About It (3)
Everything I Own (5,6)
Generations Of Love (5)
God Thank You Woman (4)
Gusto Blusto (4)
Heaven's Children (4)
Hello Goodbye (3)
I Just Wanna Be Loved (6)
I Pray (4)
I'll Tumble 4 Ya (1,5,6) *9*
I'm Afraid Of Me (1)
It's A Miracle (2,5,6) *13*
Karma Chameleon (2,5,6) *1*
Love Hurts (6)
Love Is Love (5,6)
Love Twist (1)
Mannequin (3)
Medal Song (3)
Miss Me Blind (2,5,6) *5*
Mistake No. 3 (3) *33*
Mister Man (3)
More Than Likely (5)
Move Away (4,5,6) *12*
Reasons (4)
Sexuality (4)
Stormkeeper (2)
Strange Voodoo (6)
Sweet Toxic Love (5)
Take Control (1)
That's The Way (I'm Only Trying To Help You) (2,6)
Time (Clock Of The Heart) (1,5,6) *2*

CULTURE CLUB — Cont'd

Too Bad (4)
Unfortunate Thing (3)
Victims (2,5,6)
War Song (3) *17*
What Do You Want (6)
White Boy (1)
White Boys Can't Control It (1)
Work On Me Baby (4)
You Know I'm Not Crazy (1)

CUMMINGS, Burton   '77

Born on 12/31/47 in Winnipeg, Manitoba, Canada. Lead singer of **The Guess Who**.

| 11/6/76+ | 30 | 20 | | © 1 | Burton Cummings .... | | | $12 | Portrait 34261 |
| 7/9/77 | 51 | 6 | | © 2 | My Own Way To Rock | | | $12 | Portrait 34698 |

Burch Magic (1)
Charlemagne (2)
Come On By (2)
Framed (2)
Gotta Find Another Way (2)
I'm Scared (1) *61*
Is It Really Right (1)
My Own Way To Rock (2) *74*
Never Had A Lady Before (2)
Niki Hokey (1)
Nothing Rhymed (1)
Song For Him (2)
Stand Tall (1) *10*
Sugartime Flashback Joys (1)
That's Enough (1)
Timeless Love (2)
Try To Find Another Man (2)
You Ain't Seen Nothin' Yet (1)
Your Back Yard (1)

CURB, Mike, Congregation   '70

Born on 12/24/44 in Savannah, Georgia. Pop music mogul and politician. President of MGM Records from 1969-73. Elected lieutenant governor of California in 1978. Formed own company, Sidewalk Records, in 1964; became Curb Records in 1974.

7/4/70	105	5		1	Come Together			$20	CoBurt 1002
11/21/70	185	2		2	Sweet Gingerbread Man			$20	CoBurt 1003
3/13/71	117	8		3	Burning Bridges and Other Great Motion Picture Themes			$15	MGM 4761

All For The Love Of Sunshine (3)
Arizona (medley) (1)
Bringing In The Sheaves (2)
Burning Bridges (2,3) *34*
Come Together (medley) (1)
Dirty Dingus Magee (3)
Everything Is Beautiful (2)
Games People Play (1)
Give Peace A Chance (medley) (1)
Happy Together (medley) (1)
Hey Jude (medley) (1)
I Was Born In Love With You (3)
It Was A Good Time (Rosy's Theme) (3)
Lead Us On (2)
Let It Be (2,3)
Let's Get Together (medley) (1)
Long And Winding Road (2)
Long Haired Lover From Liverpool (1)
Midnight Special (medley) (1)
My Home Town (2)
No Blade Of Grass (3)
Put A Little Love In Your Heart (1)
Raindrops Keep Fallin' On My Head (1)
Spirit In The Sky (2)
Suspicious Minds (medley) (1)
Sweet Caroline (Good Times Never Seemed So Good) (medley) (1)
Sweet Gingerbread Man (2,3)
Teach Your Children (2)
This Land Is Your Land (2)
Walk A Mile In My Shoes (1)
We'll Sing In The Sunshine (1)
(Where Do I Begin) Love Story (3)
Where Was I When The Parade Went By? (The Major) (3)
You Don't Need A Reason For Love (medley) (1)

★266★   CURE, The   '92

Techno-rock group from England: Robert Smith (vocals, guitar), Porl Thompson (guitar), Laurence "Lol" Tolhurst (keyboards), Simon Gallup (bass) and Boris Williams (drums). Numerous personnel changes with Smith the only constant.

1)Wish 2)Disintegration 3)Wild Mood Swings

8/13/83	179	8			1	The Walk	[M]	$10	Sire 23928
2/25/84	181	5		©	2	Japanese Whispers	[K]	$10	Sire 25076
6/23/84	180	4		©	3	The Top		$10	Sire 25086
10/5/85	59	49	●	©	4	The Head On The Door		$10	Elektra 60435
6/14/86	48	57	▲²		5	Standing On A Beach - The Singles	[K]	$10	Elektra 60477
6/20/87	35	52	▲	©	6	Kiss Me, Kiss Me, Kiss Me		$15	Elektra 60737 [2]
5/20/89	12	55	▲	©	7	Disintegration		$10	Elektra 60855
11/17/90	14	41	▲	©	8	Mixed Up	[K]	$10	Elektra 60978
5/9/92	2¹	26	▲	©	9	Wish		$10	Fiction 61309
10/9/93	42	6		©	10	Show	[L]	$10	Fiction 61551
11/13/93	118	2		©	11	Paris	[L]	$10	Fiction 61552
5/25/96	12	14	●	©	12	Wild Mood Swings		$10	Fiction 61744
11/15/97	32	13		©	13	Galore - The Singles 1987-1997	[G]	$10	Fiction 62117
3/4/00	16	8		©	14	Bloodflowers		$10	Fiction 62236

All I Want (6)
Apart (9,11)
At Night (11)
Baby Screams (4)
Bananafishbones (3)
Bare (12)
Birdmad Girl (3)
Blood, The (4)
Bloodflowers (14)
Boys Don't Cry (5)
Catch (6,11,13)
Caterpillar, The (3,5,8)
Charlotte Sometimes (5,11)
Close To Me (4,5,8,11,13) *24*
Closedown (7)
Club America (12)
Cut (9,10)
Disintegration (7)
Doing The Unstuck (9,10)
Dream, The (1,2)
Dressing Up (3,11)
Empty World (3)
End (9,10)
Fascination Street (7,8,13) *46*
Fight (6)
Figurehead, The (11)
Forest, A (5,8)
Friday I'm In Love (9,10,13) *18*
From The Edge Of The Deep Green Sea (9,10)
Give Me It (3)
Gone! (12)
Hanging Garden (5)
Hey You!!! (6)
High (9,10,13) *42*
Hot Hot Hot!!! (6,8,13) *65*
How Beautiful You Are... (6)
Icing Sugar (6)
If Only Tonight We Could Sleep (6)
In Between Days (Without You) (4,5,8,10) *99*
In Your House (11)
Jumping Someone Else's Train (5)
Jupiter Crash (12)
Just Like Heaven (6,10,13) *40*
Just One Kiss (1,2)
Killing An Arab (5)
Kiss, The (6)
Kyoto Song (4)
La Ment (1,2)
Last Day Of Summer (14)
Let's Go To Bed (1,2,5)
Letter To Elise (9,11,13)
Like Cockatoos (6)
Loudest Sound (14)
Love Cats (2,5)
Love Song (7,8,11,13) *2*
Lullaby (7,8,10,13) *74*
Maybe Someday (14)
Mint Car (12,13) *58*
Never Enough (8,10,13) *72*
Night Like This (4,10)
Numb (12)
One Hundred Years (11)
One More Time (6)
Open (9,10)
Out Of This World (14)
Perfect Girl (6)
Pictures Of You (7,8,10,13) *71*
Piggy In The Mirror (3)
Plainsong (7)
Play For Today (11)
Prayers For Rain (7)
Primary (5)
Push (4)
Return (12)
Round & Round & Round (12)
Same Deep Water As You (7)
Screw (4)
Shake Dog Shake (3)
Shiver And Shake (6)
Sinking (4)
Six Different Ways (4)
Snakepit, The (6)
Speak My Language (2)
Strange Attraction (12,13)
There Is No If... (14)
13th, The (12,13) *44*
39 (14)
This Is A Lie (12)
Thousand Hours (6)
To Wish Impossible Things (9)
Top, The (3)
Torture (4)
Trap (12)
Treasure (12)
Trust (9,10)
Untitled (7)
Upstairs Room (1,2)
Wailing Wall (3)
Walk, The (1,2,5,8)
Want (12)
Watching Me Fall (14)
Wendy Time (9)
Where The Birds Always Sing (14)
Why Can't I Be You? (6,13) *54*
Wrong Number (13)

CURIOSITY KILLED THE CAT   '87

Pop-rock group formed in London: Ben Volpeliere-Pierrot (vocals), Julian Brookhouse (guitar), Nick Thorpe (bass) and Miguel Drummond (drums).

| 8/22/87 | 55 | 29 | | © | Keep Your Distance .... | | | $10 | Mercury 832025 |

Curiosity Killed The Cat
Down To Earth
Free
Know What You Know
Mile High
Misfit *42*
Ordinary Day
Red Lights
Shallow Memory

CURRY, Tim   '79

Born on 4/19/46 in Cheshire, England. Actor/singer. Starred in several movies.

| 9/8/79 | 53 | 24 | | © | 1 | Fearless .... | | | $12 | A&M 4773 |
| 8/29/81 | 112 | 8 | | | 2 | Simplicity .... | | | $12 | A&M 4830 |

Betty Jean (2)
Charge It (1)
Cold Blue Steel And Sweet Fire (1)
Dancing In The Streets (2)
Hide This Face (1)
I Do The Rock (1) *91*
I Put A Spell On You (2)
No Love On The Street (1)
On A Roll (2)
Out Of Pawn (2)
Paradise Garage (1)
Right On The Money (1)
S.O.S. (1)
She's Not There (2)
Simplicity (2)
Something Short Of Paradise (1)
Summer In The City (2)
Take Me I'm Yours (2)
Working On My Tan (2)

CUTLASS, Frankie   '97

Born Francis Parker in Puerto Rico. Hip-hop producer.

| 3/1/97 | 129 | 6 | | © | Politics & Bullsh*t .... | | | $10 | Relativity 1548 |

Boriquas On Da Set
Cypher: Part III
Feel The Vibe
Focus
Games
Know Da Game
Pay Ya Dues
Puerto Rico/Black People
You & You & You

CUTTING CREW '87

Pop-rock group formed in England: Nick Van Eede (vocals), Kevin Scott MacMichael (guitar), Colin Farley (bass) and Martin Beedle (drums).

DEBUT	PEAK	WKS		CD			$	
3/21/87	16	45	● ©	1	Broadcast		$10	Virgin 90573
6/3/89	150	6	©	2	The Scattering		$10	Virgin 91239

Any Colour (1)
(Between A) Rock And A Hard Place (2) 77
Big Noise (2)

Broadcast, The (1)
Don't Look Back (1)
Everything But My Pride (2)
Fear Of Falling (1)

Feel The Wedge (2)
Handcuffs For Houdini (2)
(I Just) Died In Your Arms (1) 1

I've Been In Love Before (1) 9
It Shouldn't Take Too Long (1)
Last Thing (2)
Life In A Dangerous Time (1)

One For The Mockingbird (1) 38
Reach For The Sky (2)
Sahara (1)

Scattering, The (2)
Tip Of Your Tongue (2)
Year In The Wilderness (2)

CYMANDE '73

Black rock group from the West Indies: Ray King (vocals), Pat Patterson (guitar), Peter Serreo (sax), Mike Rose (flute), Pablo Gonsales (congas), Joe Dee (percussion), Derek Gibbs (sax) and Sam Kelly (drums).

				CD			$	
1/13/73	85	17	©	1	Cymande		$15	Janus 3044
6/30/73	180	4		2	Second Time Round		$15	Janus 3054

Anthracite (2)
Bird (2)
Bra (1)
Crawshay (2)

Dove (1)
For Baby Ooh (2)
Fug (2)
Genevieve (2)

Getting It Back (1)
Listen (1)
Message, The (1) 48
One More (2)

Ras Tafarian Folk Song (1)
Rickshaw (1)
Them And Us (2)
To You (2)

Trevorgus (2)
Willies' Headache (2)
Zion I (1)

CYMARRON '71

Male pop vocal trio from Memphis: Richard Mainegra, Rick Yancey and Sherrill Parks.

							$	
10/2/71	187	3			Rings		$15	Entrance 30962

Across The Kansas Sky
Break My Mind
Good Place To Begin

Hello Love
How Can You Mend A Broken Heart

In Your Mind
Rings 17
Table For Two For One

Tennessee Waltz
True Confession
Valerie 96

CYMONE, André '85

Born Andre Simon Anderson in Minneapolis. Former bass player of Prince's band, The Revolution. Went solo in 1981. Much production work for Jody Watley.

							$	
10/15/83	185	4		1	Survivin' In The 80's		$10	Columbia 38902
9/21/85	121	8		2	A.C.		$10	Columbia 40037

Body Thang (1)
Book Of Love (1)
Dance Electric (2)

Don't Let The Future (Come Down On You) (1)
Lipstick Lover (2)

Lovedog (1)
M.O.T.F. (1)
Make Me Wanna Dance (1)

Neon Pussycat (2)
Pretty Wild Girl (2)
Satisfaction (2)

Stay (1)
Survivin' In The 80's (1)
Sweet Sensuality (2)

Vacation (2)
What Are We Doing Here (1)

★449★ CYPRESS HILL '93

Rap trio from Los Angeles: Senen "Sen Dog" Reyes, Louis "B-Real" Freeze and Lawrence "Mixmaster Muggs" Muggerud. Reyes is the brother of Mellow Man Ace. Group appeared in movie The Meteor Man. Freeze was also a member of The Psycho Realm.

				CD			$	
1/4/92	31	89	▲² ©	1	Cypress Hill		$10	Ruffhouse 47889
8/7/93	❶²	56	▲³ ©	2	Black Sunday		$10	Ruffhouse 53931
11/18/95	3	34	▲ ©	3	Cypress Hill III (Temples Of Boom)		$10	Ruffhouse 66991
8/31/96	21	12	● ©	4	Unreleased & Revamped	[E-M]	$10	Ruffhouse 67780
10/24/98	11	16	● ©	5	IV		$10	Ruffhouse 69037
5/13/00	5	26	▲ ©	6	Skull & Bones		$15	Columbia 69990 [2]
12/30/00+	119	6	©	7	Live At The Fillmore	[L]	$10	Columbia 85184

recorded on 8/16/00 in San Francisco

A To The K (2,7)
Another Victory (6)
Audio X (5)
Boom Biddy Bye Bye (3,4) 87
Born To Get Busy (5)
Break It Up (1)
Can I Get A Hit (6)
Can't Get The Best Of Me (6,7)
Certified Bomb (6)
Checkmate (5,7)
Clash Of The Titans (5)
Cock The Hammer (2,7)
Cuban Necktie (2)
Dead Men Tell No Tales (5)
Dr. Greenthumb (5) 72

Dust (6)
Everybody Must Get Stoned (3)
Feature Presentation (5)
From The Window Of My Room (5)
Funk Freakers (4)
Funky Cypress Hill Shit (1)
Get Out Of My Head (6)
(Goin' All Out) Nothin' To Lose (5)
Hand On The Glock (2)
Hand On The Pump (1,4,7)
High Times (5)
Highlife (4)
Hits From The Bong (2,4,7)
Hole In The Head (1)

How I Could Just Kill A Man (1,7) 77
I Ain't Goin' Out Like That (2,7)
I Remember That Freak Bitch (5)
I Wanna Get High (2,7)
Illusions (3,4)
Insane In The Brain (2,7) 19
Intellectual Dons (4)
Intro (6)
Killa Hill Niggas (3)
Killafornia (3)
Latin Lingo (1,4)
Let It Rain (3)
Lick A Shot (2,7)
Light Another (1)

Lightning Strikes (5)
Lil' Putos (2)
Locotes (3)
Looking Through The Eye Of A Pig (5,7)
Make A Move (3)
Man, A (6)
No Rest For The Wicked (3)
Phuncky Feel One (1) 94
Pigs (1,7)
Prelude To A Come Up (5)
Psycobetabuckdown (1)
(Rap) Superstar (6)
Real Estate (1,7)
Red Light Visions (3)
Riot Starter (5,7)

(Rock) Superstar (6,7)
16 Men Till There's No Men Left (5)
Something For The Blunted (1)
Spark Another Owl (3)
Stank Ass Hoe (6)
Steel Magnolia (5)
Stoned Is The Way Of The Walk (1,7)
Stoned Raiders (3)
Strictly Hip Hop (3)
Tequila Sunrise (5) 70
Throw Your Hands In The Air (4)
Throw Your Set In The Air (3) 45

Tres Equis (1)
Ultraviolet Dreams (1)
Valley Of Chrome (6)
We Live This Shit (6)
What Go Around Come Around, Kid (2)
What U Want From Me (6)
Whatta You Know (4)
When The Ship Goes Down (2,4)
Worldwide (6)

CYRKLE, The '66

Pop group formed in Easton, Pennsylvania: Don Dannemann (vocals, guitar), Mike Losekamp (keyboards), Tom Dawes (bass) and Marty Fried (drums).

							$	
8/6/66	47	15		1	Red Rubber Ball		$25	Columbia 2544 / 9344
4/1/67	164	2		2	Neon		$25	Columbia 2632 / 9432

Baby, You're Free (1)
Big, Little Woman (1)
Bony Moronie (1)
Cloudy (1)
Cry (1)

Don't Cry, No Fears, No Tears Comin' Your Way (2)
How Can I Leave Her (1)
I Wish You Could Be Here (2) 70

I'm Happy Just To Dance With You (2)
I'm Not Sure What I Wanna Do (2)
It Doesn't Matter Anymore (2)

Money To Burn (1)
Our Love Affair's In Question (2)
Please Don't Ever Leave Me (2) 59

Problem Child (2)
Red Rubber Ball (1) 2
There's A Fire In The Fireplace (1)
Turn-Down Day (1) 16

Two Rooms (2)
Visit (She Was Here) (2)
Weight Of Your Words (2)
Why Can't You Give Me What I Want (1)

CYRUS, Billy Ray '92

Born on 8/25/61 in Flatwoods, Kentucky. Country singer/songwriter/guitarist.

				CD			$	
6/6/92	❶¹⁷	97	▲⁹ ©	1	Some Gave All		$10	Mercury 510635
7/10/93	3	43	▲ ©	2	It Won't Be The Last		$10	Mercury 514758
11/26/94	73	12	● ©	3	Storm In The Heartland		$10	Mercury 526081
9/7/96	125	4	©	4	Trail Of Tears		$10	Mercury 532829
11/4/00	102	2	©	5	Southern Rain		$10	Monument 62105

Achy Breaky Heart (1) 4
Ain't No Good Goodbye (2)
Ain't Your Dog No More (2)
All I'm Thinking About Is You (5)
Burn Down The Trailer Park (5)

Call Me Daddy (4)
Casualty Of Love (3)
Could've Been Me (1) 72
Crazy 'Bout You Baby (5)
Crazy Mama (4)

Deja Blue (3)
Dreamin' In Color, Livin' In Black And White (2)
Enough Is Enough (3)
Everywhere I Wanna Be (5)

Geronimo (3)
Harper Valley P.T.A. (2)
Heart With Your Name On It (3)
Hey Elvis (5)
How Much (3)

I Ain't Even Left (3)
I Am Here Now (4)
I Will (5)
I'm So Miserable (1)

In The Heart Of A Woman (2) 76
It Won't Be The Last (2)
Love You Back (5)
Need A Little Help (4)

CYRUS, Billy Ray — Cont'd

Never Thought I'd Fall In Love With You (1)
One Last Thrill (3)
Only God Could Stop Me Loving You (3)
Only Time Will Tell (2)
Past, The (3)

Patsy Come Home (3)
Redneck Heaven (3)
Right Face Wrong Time (2)
Roll Me Over (3)
She's Not Cryin' Anymore (1) *70*
Should I Stay (4)

Sing Me Back Home (4)
Some Gave All (1)
Somebody New (2)
Someday, Somewhere, Somehow (1)
Southern Rain (5)
Storm In The Heartland (3)

Talk Some (2)
Tenntucky (4)
These Boots Are Made For Walkin' (1)
Three Little Words (4)
Throwin' Stones (2)
Trail Of Tears (4)

Truth Is I Lied (4)
We The People (5)
When I'm Gone (2)
Wher'm I Gonna Live? (1)
Without You (5)
Words By Heart (2)

You Won't Be Lonely Now (5) *80*

D

DA BRAT   '00
Born Shawntae Harris on 4/14/74 in Chicago. Female rapper.

DEBUT	PEAK	WKS						$	Label & Number
7/16/94	11	46 ▲	©	1	**Funkdafied**			$10	So So Def 66164
11/16/96	20	17 ●	©	2	**Anuthatantrum**			$10	So So Def 67813
4/29/00	5	24 ▲	©	3	**Unrestricted**			$10	So So Def 69772

Ain't No Thang (1)
All My Bitches (3)
Anuthatantrum (2)
Back Up (3)
Breeve On Em (3)
Chi Town (3)

Come And Get Some (1)
Da Shit Ya Can't Fuc Wit (1)
Fa All Y'all (1) *37*
Fire It Up (1)
Fuck You (3)
Funkdafied (1) *6*

Ghetto Love (2) *16*
Give It 2 You (1) *26*
Hands In The Air (3)
High Come Down (3)
Just A Little Bit More (2)
Keepin' It Live (2)

Let's All Get High (2)
Live It Up (2)
Lyrical Molestation (1)
Make It Happen (2)
May Da Funk Be Wit 'Cha (1)
Mind Blowin' (1)

My Beliefs (3)
Pink Lemonade (3)
Runnin' Out Of Time (3)
Sittin' On Top Of The World (2) *30*

That's What I'm Looking For (3) *56*
We Ready (3)
What 'Chu Like (3) *8*
What's On Ya Mind (3)

D.A.D.   '89
Hard-rock group from Copenhagen, Denmark: brothers Jesper (vocals) and Jacob (guitar) Binzer, Stig Pedersen (bass) and Peter Jensen (drums). D.A.D. is abbreviation for Disneyland After Dark.

9/30/89	116	11	©		No Fuel Left For The Pilgrims			$10	Warner 25999

Girl Nation
Ill Will

Jihad
Lords Of The Atlas

Overmuch
Point Of View

Rim Of Hell
Siamese Twin

Sleeping My Day Away
True Believer

Wild Talk
ZCMI

dada   '93
Pop trio from Los Angeles: Joie Calio (vocals, bass), Michael Gurley (guitar) and Phil Leavitt (drums).

1/16/93	111	10	©	1	**Puzzle**			$10	I.R.S. 13141
10/8/94	178	1	©	2	**American Highway Flower**			$10	I.R.S. 27986

All I Am (2)
Ask The Dust (2)
Dim (1)
Dizz Knee Land (1)
Dog (1)

Dorina (1)
8 Track (2)
Feel Me Don't You (2)
Feet To The Sun (2)
Gogo (1)

Green Henry (2)
Heaven And Nowhere (2)
Here Today, Gone Tomorrow (1)
i (2)

Mary Sunshine Rain (1)
Moon (1)
Posters (1)
Pretty Girls Make Graves (2)
Puzzle (1)

Real Soon (2)
S.F. Bar '63 (2)
Scum (2)
Surround (1)
Timothy (1)

Who You Are (1)

DAEMYON, Jerald   '96
Born in Detroit. Classically trained violinist.

2/10/96	195	2	©		Thinking About You		[I]	$10	GRP 9829

Africa
For The Love In Your Eyes

Paradigms
Peace Of Mind

Summer Madness
Thinking About You

"13"
You Make Me Feel Brand New

DAFT PUNK   '01
Dance duo from Paris: Thomas Bangalter and Guy-Manuel de Homem-Christo.

7/26/97	150	18 ●	©	1	**Homework**			$10	Soma 42609
3/31/01	44	17	©	2	**Discovery**			$10	Virgin 49606

Aerodynamic (2)
Alive (1)
Around The World (1) *61*
Burnin' (1)
Crescendolls (2)

Da Funk (1)
Daftendirekt (1)
Digital Love (2)
Face To Face (2)
Fresh (1)

Harder, Better, Faster, Stronger (2)
High Fidelity (1)
High Life (2)
Indo Silver Club (1)

Nightvision (2)
Oh Yeah (1)
One More Time (2) *61*
Phoenix (1)
Revolution 909 (1)

Rock'n Roll (1)
Rollin' & Scratchin' (1)
Short Circuit (1)
Something About Us (2)
Superheroes (1)

Teachers (1)
Too Long (2)
Veridis Quo (2)
Voyager (2)

DA'KRASH   '88
Funk group from St. Louis: Robert Jordan (vocals), Brian Tate, Edgar Hinton, Dee Dee James and Gabriel Acevedo.

4/16/88	184	3	©		Da'Krash			$10	Capitol 48355

Dance With Me
Easy Come, Easy Go

Feeling Like This
Temptation Sensation

Trapped In Phases
Tu Madre

Uptown
Wasn't I Good To Ya?

DALE, Dick, and The Del-Tones   '63
Born Richard Monsour on 5/4/37 in Boston. Influential surf-rock guitarist.

1/26/63	59	17		1	**Surfers' Choice**		[E]	$75	Deltone 1886
					first released in 1962 on Deltone 1001 ($150)				
12/14/63+	106	11		2	**Checkered Flag**			$60	Capitol 2002

Big Black Cadillac (2)
Death Of A Gremmie (1)
Fanny Mae (1)
426 - Super Stock (2)

Grudge Run (2)
Ho-Dad Machine (2)
Hot Rod Racer (2)
It Will Grow On You (2)

Let's Go Trippin' (1) *60*
Lovey Dovey (1)
Mag Wheels (2)
Misirlou Twist (1)

Motion (2)
Night Owl (1)
Night Rider (2)
Peppermint Man (1)

Scavenger, The (2) *98*
Shake N' Stomp (1)
Sloop John B. (1)
Surf Beat (1)

Surf Buggy (1)
Surfing Drums (1)
Take It Off (1)
Wedge, The (2)

DALE & GRACE   '64
Pop vocal duo: Dale Houston (of Ferriday, Louisiana) and Grace Broussard (of Prairieville, Louisiana).

2/1/64	100	7			I'm Leaving It Up To You			$150	Montel 100

Bye Bye Love
Casual Look

Darling It's Wonderful
Gee Baby

Happy, Happy Birthday Baby
Hey Baby

I'm Leaving It Up To You *1*
Let The Good Times Roll

Love Is Strange
Our Teenage Love

Tip Of My Finger
We Belong Together

DA LENCH MOB   '92
Rap trio from Los Angeles: Terry Gray, DeSean Cooper and Jerome Washington. Cooper left in 1993, replaced by Maulkie.

10/10/92	24	21 ●	©	1	**Guerillas In Tha Mist**			$10	Street Know. 92206
11/19/94	81	2	©	2	**Planet Of Da Apes**			$10	Street Know. 53939

Ain't Got No Class (1)
All On My Nut Sac (1)
Ankle Blues (1)
Buck Tha Devil (1)

Capital Punishment In America (1)
Chocolate City (2)
Cut Throats (2)
Environmental Terrorist (2)

Final Call (2)
Freedom Got An A.K. (1)
Goin' Bananas (2)
Guerillas In Tha Mist (1)

Inside Tha Head Of A Black Man (2)
King Of The Jungle (2)
Lenchmob Also In Tha Group (1)

Lord Have Mercy (1)
Lost In Tha System (1)
Mellow Madness (2)
Planet Of Da Apes (1)
Set The Shit Straight (2)

Trapped (2)
Who Ya Gonna Shoot Wit That (1)
You & Your Heroes (1)

DALTON, Kathy   '74
Born in Memphis.

| 11/16/74 | 190 | 3 | | | **Boogie Bands & One Night Stands** .... | | | $15 | DiscReet 2208 |

At The Tropicana   Cannibal Forest   Justine   Musical Chairs
Boogie Bands And One Night   Gypsy Dancer   Light That Shines   Pour Your Wine All Over Me
  Stands *72*   I Need You Tonight   Midnight Creeper   Ride, Ride, Ride

DALTREY, Roger   '75
Born on 3/1/44 in Hammersmith, London, England. Lead singer of **The Who**. Starred in the movies *Tommy, Lisztomania, The Legacy* and *McVicar*.

5/26/73	45	20	©	1	**Daltrey**			$20	Track 328
8/9/75	28	23	©	2	**Ride A Rock Horse**			$15	MCA 2147
7/9/77	46	19	©	3	**One Of The Boys**			$15	MCA 2271
8/16/80	22	15	©	4	**McVicar**		[S]	$12	Polydor 6284
3/27/82	185	5		5	**Best Bits**		[G]	$12	MCA 5301
3/17/84	102	9		6	**Parting Should Be Painless**			$10	Atlantic 80128
10/12/85	42	26	©	7	**Under A Raging Moon**			$10	Atlantic 81269

After The Fire (7) *48*   Free Me (4,5) *53*   It Don't Satisfy Me (7)   One Day (6)   Single Man's Dilemma (3)   **Without Your Love** (4,5) *20*
Avenging Annie (3,5) *88*   Giddy (3)   Just A Dream Away (4)   One Man Band (1)   Somebody Told Me (4)   World Over (2)
Bitter And Twisted (4)   **Giving It All Away** (1,5) *83*   Leon (3)   One Of The Boys (3)   Story So Far (1)   Would A Stranger Do? (6)
Breaking Down Paradise (7)   Going Strong (6)   **Let Me Down Easy** (7) *86*   Parade (3)   Thinking (1)   You And Me (1)
Come And Get Your Love   Hard Life (1,5)   Looking For You (6)   Parting Would Be Painless (6)   Treachery (5)   You Are Yourself (1)
  (2) *68*   Heart-s Right (5)   Martyrs And Madmen (5)   Pride You Hide (7)   Under A Raging Moon (7)   **You Put Something Better**
Doing It All Again (3)   How Does The Cold Wind Cry   McVicar (4)   Prisoner, The (3)   Waiting For A Friend (4)   Inside Of Me (5)
Don't Talk To Strangers (7)   (6)   Milk Train (2)   Proud (2,5)   **Walking In My Sleep** (6) *62*
Don't Wait On The Stairs (6)   I Was Born To Sing Your Song   Move Better In The Night (7)   Reasons (1)   Walking The Dog (2)
Escape Parts 1 & 2 (4)   (2)   My Time Is Gonna Come (4)   Rebel (7)   Way Of The World (1)
Fallen Angel (7)   Is There Anybody Out There?   Near To Surrender (2)   Satin And Lace (3)   When The Music Stops (1)
Feeling (2)   (6)   Oceans Away (2,5)   Say It Ain't So, Joe (3,5)   White City Lights (4)

DAMIAN, Michael   '89
Born Michael Damian Weir on 4/26/62 in San Diego. Pop singer/actor. Played "Danny Romalotti" on the TV soap opera *The Young & The Restless*.

| 6/17/89 | 61 | 26 | © | | **Where Do We Go From Here** .... | | | $10 | Cypress 0130 |

Cover Of Love *31*   My Mistake   Question Of Time   Straight From My Heart   Turn From My Love
Heartbreak Monday   Photograph   **Rock On** *1*   Touch Of Gray   **Was It Nothing At All** *24*

DAMITA JO   '65
Born Damita Jo DuBlanc on 8/5/30 in Austin, Texas. Died of respiratory failure on 12/25/98 (age 68). Female singer. Regular on **Redd Foxx**'s TV variety series in 1977.

| 3/27/65 | 121 | 4 | | 1 | **This Is Damita Jo** .... | | | $20 | Epic 26131 |
| 5/6/67 | 169 | 2 | | 2 | **If You Go Away** .... | | | $20 | Epic 26244 |

Affair To Remember (2)   Happiness Is A Thing Called   I'll Get Along Somehow (1)   My Man's Gone Now (2)   Time To Love And A Time To
Alice Blue Gown (1)   Joe (1)   If You Are But A Dream (1,2)   No Guilty Feelings (2)   Cry (Petite Fleur) (2)
Bye Bye Love (1)   He Loves Me (1)   **If You Go Away** (2) *68*   Nobody Knows You When   What Did I Have That I Don't
Dinner For One Please James   I Could Have Told You (1)   It Could Happen To You (1)   You're Down And Out (1)   Have? (2)
  (2)   I Had Someone Else Before I   Love, I Found You (2)   Silver Dollar (1)   Yellow Days (2)
     Had You (1)   Love Is Here To Stay (1)

DAMNATION OF ADAM BLESSING, The   '70
Rock group: Adam Blessing (vocals), Bob Kalamasz and Jim Quinn (guitars), Ray Benick (bass) and Bill Schwark (drums).

| 3/28/70 | 181 | 2 | | | **The Damnation Of Adam Blessing** .... | | | $20 | United Artists 6738 |

Cookbook   Hold On   Le' Voyage   Morning Dew   You Don't Love Me
Dreams   Last Train To Clarksville   Lonely   Strings And Things

DAMN YANKEES   '91
All-star rock group: **Ted Nugent** (guitar, vocals), **Tommy Shaw** (guitar, vocals), Jack Blades (bass, vocals) and Michael Cartellone (drums). Nugent was with the **Amboy Dukes**. Shaw was with **Styx**. Blades was with **Night Ranger**. Shaw and Blades also recorded as a duo in 1995.

| 3/31/90+ | 13 | 78 | ▲² | © | 1 | **Damn Yankees** .... | | | $10 | Warner 26159 |
| 8/29/92 | 22 | 28 | ● | © | 2 | **Don't Tread** .... | | | $10 | Warner 45025 |

Bad Reputation (1)   Dirty Dog (2)   Firefly (2)   Piledriver (1)   Someone To Believe (2)   **Where You Goin' Now** (2) *20*
Come Again (1) *50*   Don't Tread On Me (2)   **High Enough** (1) *3*   Rock City (1)   Tell Me How You Want It (1)
Coming Of Age (1) *60*   Double Coyote (2)   Mister Please (2)   Runaway (1)   This Side Of Hell (2)
Damn Yankees (1)   Fifteen Minutes Of Fame (2)   Mystified (1)   **Silence Is Broken** (2) *62*   Uprising (2)

DAMON('S), Liz, Orient Express   '71
Damon is the leader of the three-woman, six-man vocal/instrumental group from Hawaii.

| 3/6/71 | 190 | 2 | | | **Liz Damon's Orient Express** .... | | | $15 | White Whale 5003 |

Bring Me Sunshine   Close To You   Let It Be   Something   You Make Me Feel Like   You're Falling In Love
But For Love   Everything Is Beautiful   **1900 Yesterday** *33*   That Same Old Feeling   Someone

DAMONE, Vic   '56
Born Vito Farinola on 6/12/28 in Brooklyn, New York. Pop singer. Appeared in the movies *Kismet, Meet Me In Las Vegas* and *Hell To Eternity*. Hosted own TV series (1956-57). Married actress Diahann Carroll on 1/3/87.

10/13/56	14	8		1	**That Towering Feeling!**			$25	Columbia 900
3/3/62	64	17		2	**Linger Awhile with Vic Damone**			$20	Capitol 1646
10/13/62	57	10		3	**The Lively Ones**			$20	Capitol 1748
7/10/65	86	10		4	**You Were Only Fooling**			$15	Warner 1602

After The Lights Go Down Low   Dearly Beloved (3)   It's Not Unusual (4)   Most Beautiful Girl In The World   Spring Is Here (1)   (When Your Heart's On Fire)
  (2)   Deep Night (2)   Laura (3)   (3)   Stella By Starlight (2)   Smoke Gets In Your Eyes (1)
All The Things You Are (1)   Diane (3)   Let's Face The Music And   Nina Never Knew (3)   Stranger In The World (4)   Why Don't You Believe Me (4)
And Roses And Roses (4)   Dream On Little Dreamer (4)   Dance (2)   One Love (3)   There! I've Said It Again (2)   You Stepped Out Of A Dream
Careless Hands (1)   For Mama (La Mamma) (4)   Let's Fall In Love (1)   Out Of Nowhere (1)   Thrill Of Loving You (4)   (3)
Change Partners (2)   I Want A Little Girl (3)   Linger Awhile (1)   Please Help Me, I'm Falling (In   Time On My Hands (You In My   **You Were Only Fooling**
Charmaine (3)   I'll Never Find Another You (4)   Little Girl (3)   Love With You) (4)   Arms) (1)   (While I Was Falling In Love)
Cheek To Cheek (1)   I'm Glad There Is You (1)   Lively Ones (3)   Ruby (3)   Touch Of Your Lips (1)   (4) *30*
Cherokee (3)   I've Been Looking (4)   Marie (3)   Soft Lights And Sweet Music (2)   Wait Till You See Her (1)
Close Your Eyes (2)   In The Still Of The Night (2)   Song Is You (1)   When Lights Are Low (2)

DANA, Bill — see JIMENEZ, Jose

DANA, Vic '65
Born on 8/26/42 in Buffalo, New York. Pop singer.

11/16/63+	111	9			1 **More**			$25	Dolton 8026
5/16/64	116	5			2 **Shangri-La**			$25	Dolton 8028
4/10/65	13	21			3 **Red Roses For A Blue Lady**			$25	Dolton 8034
12/30/67	114[X]	1			4 **Little Altar Boy & Other Christmas Songs**		[X]	$25	Dolton 8049

Ave Maria (4) · Call Me Irresponsible (2) · Charade (2) · Christmas Song (4) · Danke Schoen (1) · Diane (2) · End Of The World (1) · First Noel (4) · Good News (2) · He Gives Me Love (1) · Hello Dolly! (1) · I Was The One (1) · **I Will** (1) *47* · I'd Trade All Of My Tomorrows (For Just One Yesterday) (3) · I'll Be Around (3) · I'll Be Home For Christmas (4) · I'll Be Seeing You (3) · I'll Get By (3) · I'll See You In My Dreams (3) · I'm In The Mood For Love (3) · It Had To Be You (3) · Little Altar Boy (4) · Little Drummer Boy (4) · Love After Midnight (3) · **More** (1) *42* · More I See You (2) · My Heart Belongs To Only You (2) · My Heart Cries For You (2) · My World (1) · O Come All Ye Faithful (4) · O Holy Night (4) · O Little Town Of Bethlehem (4) · Once In A While (3) · **Red Roses For A Blue Lady** (3) *10* · **Shangri-La** (2) *27* · Shelter Of Your Arms (2) · Silent Night (4) · Silver Bells (4) · So Much In Love (1) · Softly As I Leave You (2) · Stairway To The Stars (2) · That's Why I'm Sorry (1) · Twelve Days Of Christmas (4) · What Good Would It Do (1) · When A Boy Falls In Love (1) · You Were Meant For Me (3) · You're My Everything (3) · You're Nobody 'Till Somebody Loves You (1)

DANA DANE '87
Born in New York City. Male rapper.

| 9/12/87 | 46 | 32 | ● | © | 1 **Dana Dane With Fame** | | | $10 | Profile 1233 |
| 11/10/90 | 150 | 4 | | © | 2 **Dana Dane 4-Ever** | | | $10 | Profile 1298 |

Bedie Boo (2) · Cinderfella Dana Dane (1) · Dana Dane 4-Ever (2) · Dana Dane To It (2) · Dana Dane With Fame (1) · Dedication (1) · Dedication 2 (2) · Delancey Street (1) · Johnny The Dipper (2) · Just Here To Have Fun (2) · Keep The Groove (1) · Little Bit Of Dane Tonight (2) · Lonely Man (2) · Love At First Sight (1) · Makes Me Wanna Sing (2) · Nightmares (1) · Something Special (2) · Tales From The Dane Side (1) · This Be The Def Beat (1) · We Wanna Party (1) · What Dirty Minds U Have (2)

DANDY WARHOLS, The '00
Rock group from Portland, Oregon: Courtney Taylor (vocals), Peter Holmstrom (guitar), Zia McCabe (bass) and Eric Hedford (drums).

| 8/19/00 | 182 | 1 | | © | **Thirteen Tales From Urban Bohemia** | | | $10 | Capitol 57787 |

Big Indian · Bohemian Like You · Cool Scene · Country Leaver · Get Off · Godless · Gospel, The · Horse Pills · Mohammed · Nietzsche · Shakin' · Sleep · Solid

D'ANGELO '00
Born Michael D'Angelo Archer on 2/11/74 in Richmond, Virginia. R&B singer/songwriter.

| 7/22/95+ | 22 | 65 | ▲ | © | 1 **Brown Sugar** | | | $10 | EMI 32629 |
| 2/12/00 | ❶[2] | 33 | ▲ | © | 2 **Voodoo** | | | $10 | Virgin 48499 |

Africa (2) · Alright (1) · **Brown Sugar** (1) *27* · Chicken Grease (2) · **Cruisin'** (1) *53* · Devil's Pie (2) · Feel Like Makin' Love (2) · Greatdayndamornin'/Booty (2) · Higher (1) · Jonz In My Bonz (1) · **Lady** (1) *10* · **Left & Right** (2) *70* · Line, The (2) · **Me And Those Dreamin' Eyes Of Mine** (1) *74* · One Mo'gin (2) · Playa Playa (2) · Root, The (2) · Send It On (2) · Sh*t, Damn, Motherf*cker (1) · Smooth (1) · Spanish Joint (2) · **Untitled (How Does It Feel)** (2) *25* · When We Get By (1)

DANGER DANGER '89
Hard-rock group from Queens, New York: Ted Poley (vocals), Andy Timmons (guitar), Kasey Smith (keyboards), Bruno Ravel (bass) and Steve West (drums).

| 8/19/89 | 88 | 42 | | © | 1 **Danger Danger** | | | $10 | CBS Associated 44342 |
| 10/19/91 | 123 | 5 | | © | 2 **Screw It!** | | | $10 | Epic 46977 |

Bang Bang (1) *49* · Beat The Bullet (2) · Boys Will Be Boys (1) · Comin' Home (2) · Crazy Nites (2) · D.F.N.S. (2) · Don't Blame It On Love (2) · Don't Walk Away (1) · Everybody Wants Some (2) · Feels Like Love (1) · Find Your Way Back Home (2) · Get Your Shit Together (2) · Horny S.O.B. (2) · I Still Think About You (2) · Live It Up (1) · Monkey Business (2) · Naughty Naughty (1) · One Step From Paradise (1) · Puppet Show (2) · Rock America (1) · Saturday Nite (1) · Slipped Her The Big One (2) · Turn It On (1) · Under The Gun (1) · Yeah, You Want It! (2)

DANGERFIELD, Rodney '83
Born Jacob Cohen on 11/22/21 in Babylon, Long Island, New York. Comedian/actor. Starred in several movies.

| 8/2/80 | 48 | 19 | | © | 1 **No Respect** | | [C] | $15 | Casablanca 7229 |
| 11/12/83 | 36 | 20 | | © | 2 **Rappin' Rodney** | | [C] | $12 | RCA Victor 4869 |

No Respect (1) · **Rappin' Rodney** (2) *83* · Rodney Continues Rappin' (2) · Rodney Rappin' (2) · Son Of No Respect (1)

DANGEROUS TOYS '89
Hard-rock group from Austin, Texas: Jason McMaster (vocals), Scott Dalhover and Danny Aaron (guitars), Mike Watson (bass) and Mark Geary (drums).

| 6/17/89 | 65 | 36 | ● | © | 1 **Dangerous Toys** | | | $10 | Columbia 45031 |
| 6/22/91 | 67 | 9 | | © | 2 **Hellacious Acres** | | | $10 | Columbia 46754 |

Angel N U (2) · Bad Guy (2) · Best Of Friends (2) · Bones In The Gutter (1) · Feel Like Makin' Love (2) · Feels Like A Hammer (1) · Gimme' No Lip (2) · Gunfighter (2) · Gypsy (Black-N-Blue Valentine) (2) · Here Comes Trouble (1) · Line 'Em Up (2) · On Top (2) · Outlaw (1) · Queen Of The Nile (1) · Scared (1) · Sport'n A Woody (1) · Sticks & Stones (2) · Sugar, Leather & The Nail (2) · Take Me Drunk (1) · Teas'n, Pleas'n (1) · Ten Boots (Stompin') (1) · That Dog (1)

★307★   DANIELS, Charlie, Band '79
Born on 10/28/36 in Wilmington, North Carolina. Country-rock singer/fiddle player. His band consisted of Tom Crain (guitar), Joe "Taz" DiGregorio (keyboards), Charles Hayward (bass), and James W. Marshall & Fred Edwards (drums). Marshall and Edwards left in 1986; replaced by Jack Gavin. Group appeared in the movie *Urban Cowboy*.

1)Million Mile Reflections 2)Full Moon 3)Windows

| 7/28/73 | 164 | 9 | | | 1 **Honey In The Rock** | | | $15 | Kama Sutra 2071 |

CHARLIE DANIELS

12/28/74+	38	34	▲	©	2 **Fire On The Mountain**			$15	Kama Sutra 2603
10/4/75	57	12		©	3 **Nightrider**			$15	Kama Sutra 2607
5/15/76	35	18	●	©	4 **Saddle Tramp**			$12	Epic 34150
12/4/76	83	10		©	5 **High Lonesome**			$12	Epic 34377
11/12/77	105	11	●		6 **Midnight Wind**			$12	Epic 34970
5/12/79	5	43	▲[3]	©	7 **Million Mile Reflections**			$12	Epic 35751
8/9/80	11	33	▲	©	8 **Full Moon**			$12	Epic 36571
4/3/82	26	19	●	©	9 **Windows**			$12	Epic 37694

DEBUT	PEAK	WKS	RIAA	CD	ARTIST — Album Title	Catalog	Sym	$	Label & Number

DANIELS, Charlie, Band — Cont'd

7/23/83	84	12	▲³	©	10 **A Decade Of Hits**	C:#25/68	[G]	$12	Epic 38795
11/12/88	181	2		©	11 **Homesick Heroes**			$10	Epic 44324
11/25/89+	82	25	▲	©	12 **Simple Man**			$10	Epic 45316
5/25/91	139	3		©	13 **Renegade**			$10	Epic 46835

CHARLIE DANIELS

| 9/20/97+ | 26ᶜ | 5 | ▲ | © | 14 **Super Hits** | | [G] | $8 | Epic 64182 |

Ain't No Ramblers Anymore (9)
Alligator (11)
Behind Your Eyes (7)
Big Bad John (11)
Big Man (1)
Billy The Kid (5)
Birmingham Blues (3)
Black Bayou (6)
Blind Man (2)
Blowing Along With The Wind (9)
Blue Star (7)
Boogie Woogie Fiddle Country Blues (11,14)
Boogie Woogie Man (11)
Caballo Diablo (2)
Carolina (5)
Carolina (I Remember You) (8)
Cowboy Hat In Dallas (11)
Cumberland Mountain Number Nine (4)

Damn Good Cowboy (3)
Dance Gypsy Dance (8)
Devil Went Down To Georgia (7,10,14) **3**
Dixie On My Mind (4)
Drinkin' My Baby Goodbye (14)
El Toreador (8)
Everything Is Kinda' All Right (3)
Everytime I See Him (10)
Evil (3)
Fathers And Sons (13)
Feeling Free (2)
Franklin Limestone (2)
Funky Junky (1,3)
Georgia (2)
Get Me Back To Dixie (11)
Good Ole Boy (6)
Grapes Of Wrath (6)
Heaven Can Be Anywhere (Twin Pines Theme) (6)

High Lonesome (5)
Honky Tonk Avenue (11)
Honky Tonk Life (13)
Ill Wind (11)
In America (8,10,14) **11**
Indian Man (6)
It's My Life (4,12)
Jitterbug (7)
Lady In Red (9)
Layla (13)
Legend Of Wooley Swamp (8,10) **31**
Let Freedom Ring (13)
Let It Roll (10)
Little Folks (13)
Lonesome Boy From Dixie (14)
Long Haired Country Boy (2,10,14) **6**
Makes You Want To Go Home (9)
Maria Teresa (6)

Midnight Lady (1)
Midnight Train (11)
Midnight Wind (6,12)
Mississippi (7)
Mister DJ (12)
Money (8)
Nashville Moon (9)
New York City, King Size Rosewood Bed (2)
No Place To Go (1,2)
No Potion For The Pain (8)
Ode To Sweet Smoky (6)
Oh Atlanta (12)
Old Rock 'N Roller (12)
Orange Blossom Special (2)
Partyin' Gal (9)
Passing Lane (7)
Play Me Some Fiddle (12)
Ragin' Cajun (9)
Rainbow Ride (7)
Redneck Fiddlin' Man (6)

Reflections (7)
Renegade (13)
Revelations (1)
Right Now Tennessee Blues (5)
Roll Mississippi (5)
Running With The Crowd (5)
Saddle Tramp (4)
Saturday Night Down South (12)
Simple Man (12,14)
Slow Song (5)
Somebody Loves You (1)
South Sea Song (8)
South's Gonna Do It (2,10,14) **29**
Still In Saigon (9,10,14) **22**
Stroker's Theme (10)
Sugar Hill Saturday Night (6)
Sweet Louisiana (4)
Sweetwater Texas (4)
Talk To Me Fiddle (13)

Tennessee (5)
Texas (3) **91**
Tomorrow's Gonna' Be Another Day (3)
Trudy (2)
Turned My Head Around (5)
Twang Factor (13)
Uneasy Rider (1,10,14) **9**
Uneasy Rider '88 (11,14)
Universal Hand (9)
Was It 26 (12)
We Had It All One Time (9)
What My Baby Sees In Me (13)
(What This World Needs Is) A Few More Rednecks (12)
Why Can't People (1)
Wichita Jail (9)
Willie Jones (3,13)
You Can't Pick Cotton (11)

DANKO, Rick '78

Born on 12/29/42 in Simcoe, Ontario, Canada. Died on 12/10/99 (age 56). Bassist of **The Band**.

| 12/24/77+ | 119 | 8 | | © | **Rick Danko** | | | $12 | Arista 4141 |

Brainwash
Java Blues

New Mexicoe
Once Upon A Time

Shake It
Sip The Wine

Small Town Talk
Sweet Romance

Tired Of Waiting
What A Town

DANNY WILSON '87

Pop trio from Dundee, Scotland: brothers Gary (vocals, guitar) and Kit (keyboards, drums) Clark, with Ged Grimes (bass). Group named after the 1952 **Frank Sinatra** movie *Meet Danny Wilson*.

| 7/18/87 | 79 | 16 | | © | **Meet Danny Wilson** | | | $10 | Virgin 90596 |

Aberdeen
Broken China
Davy

Five Friendly Aliens
Girl I Used To Know

I Won't Be Here When You Get Home
Lorraine Parade

Mary's Prayer 23
Nothing Ever Goes To Plan
Ruby's Golden Wedding

Spencer-Tracey
Steamtrains To The Milky Way
You Remain An Angel

DANZIG '92

Born Glenn Danzig on 6/23/59 in Lodi, New Jersey. Hard-rock singer/songwriter. His group: John Christ (guitar), Eerie Von (bass) and Chuck Biscuits (drums). Joey Castillo replaced Biscuits in 1994. John Lazie replaced Von in 1996.

10/8/88	125	9	●	©	1 **Danzig**	C:#3/20		$10	Def American 24208
7/14/90	74	13		©	2 **Danzig II - Lucifuge**			$10	Def American 24281
8/1/92	24	7		©	3 **Danzig III - How The Gods Kill**			$10	Def American 26914
6/12/93+	54	20		©	4 **Thrall - Demonsweatlive**		[L-M]	$10	Def American 45286

side 1 titled "Thrall"; side 2 titled "Demonsweatlive" (recorded live on October 31, 1992 at Irvine Meadows, California)

10/22/94	29	8		©	5 **Danzig 4**			$10	American 45647
11/16/96	41	3		©	6 **Danzig 5 - Blackacidevil**			$10	Hollywood 62084
11/20/99	149	1		©	7 **6:66 - Satans Child**			$10	Evilive 61005

Am I Demon (1,4)
Anything (3)
Apokalips (7)
Ashes (6)
Belly Of The Beast (7)
Blackacidevil (6)
Blood And Tears (2)
Bodies (3)
Brand New God (3)
Bringer Of Death (5)
Cantspeak (5)
Cold Eternal (7)
Come To Silver (6)

Cult w/out A Name (7)
Devil's Plaything (2)
Dirty Black Summer (3)
Do You Wear The Mark (3)
Dominion (5)
East Indian Devil (Kali's Song) (7)
End Of Time (1)
Evil Thing (1)
Firemass (7)
Five Finger Crawl (7)
Girl (4)
Godless (3)

Going Down To Die (5)
Hand Of Doom: Version (6)
Heart Of The Devil (7)
Her Black Wings (2)
Hint Of Her Blood (6)
How The Gods Kill (3)
Hunter, The (1)
I Don't Mind The Pain (5)
I'm The One (2)
Into The Mouth Of Abandonement (2)
It's Coming Down (4)
Killer Wolf (2)

Left Hand Black (3)
Let It Be Captured (5)
Lilin (7)
Little Whip (5)
Long Way Back From Hell (2)
Mother (1,4) **43**
Not Of This World (1)
Pain In The World (2)
Possession (3)
Power Of Darkness (6)
Sacrifice (6)
Sadistikal (5)
Satans Child (7)

See All You Were (6)
Serpentia (6)
777 (2)
7th House (6)
She Rides (1)
Sistinas (3,4)
Snakes Of Christ (2,4)
Son Of The Morning Star (5)
Soul On Fire (1)
Stalker Song (5)
Thirteen (7)
Tired Of Being Alive (2)
Trouble (4)

Twist Of Cain (1)
Unspeakable (4)
Until You Call On The Dark (5)
Violet Fire (4)
When The Dying Calls (3)

D'ARBY, Terence Trent '88

Born on 3/15/62 in New York City. R&B-pop singer.

10/24/87+	4	60	▲²	©	1 **Introducing The Hardline According To Terence Trent D'Arby**			$10	Columbia 40964
11/25/89	61	15		©	2 **Terence Trent D'Arby's Neither Fish Nor Flesh**			$10	Columbia 45351
5/29/93	119	7		©	3 **Terence Trent D'Arby's Symphony Or Damn**			$10	Columbia 53616
5/27/95	178	1		©	4 **Terence Trent D'Arby's Vibrator**			$10	Work 67070

...And I Need To Be With Someone Tonight (2)
Are You Happy? (3)
As Yet Untitled (1)
Attracted To You (2)
Baby Let Me Share My Love (3)
Billy Don't Fall (2)
C.Y.F.M.L.A.Y? (4)
Castillian Blue (3)
Dance Little Sister (Part One) (1) **30**
Delicate (3) **74**

Do You Love Me Like You Say? (3)
Holding On To You (4)
I Don't Want To Bring Your Gods Down (2)
I Have Faith In These Desolate Times (2)
I Still Love You (3)
I'll Be Alright (2)
I'll Never Turn My Back On You (Father's Words) (1)
If You All Get To Heaven (4)
If You Go Before Me (1)

If You Let Me Stay (1) **68**
It Feels So Good To Love Someone Like You (2)
It's Been Said (4)
Let Her Down Easy (3)
Let's Go Forward (1)
Neither Fish Nor Flesh (2)
Neon Messiah (2)
Penelope Please (3)
Rain (1)
Read My Lips (I Dig Your Scene) (4)
Resurrection (1)

Roly Poly (2)
Seasons (3)
Seven More Days (4)
She Kissed Me (3)
Sign Your Name (1) **4**
Succumb To Me (3)
Supermodel Sandwich (4)
Supermodel Sandwich w/Cheese (4)
Surrender (4)
"T.I.T.S."/"F&J" (3)
TTD's Recurring Dream (4)

This Side Of Love (2)
To Know Someone Deeply Is To Know Someone Softly (2)
Turn The Page (3)
Undeniably (4)
Vibrator (4)
We Don't Have That Much Time Together (4)
Wet Your Lips (3)
Who's Lovin' You (1)
Wishing Well (1) **1**
You Will Pay Tomorrow (2)

★267★ DARIN, Bobby '60

Born Walden Robert Cassotto on 5/14/36 in the Bronx, New York. Died of heart failure on 12/20/73 (age 37). Singer/pianist/guitarist/drummer. Won the 1959 Best New Artist Grammy Award. Married to actress Sandra Dee from 1960-67. Acted in several movies. Inducted into the Rock and Roll Hall of Fame in 1990.

1)This Is Darin 2)That's All 3)Darin At The Copa

DEBUT	PEAK	WKS	CD	#	Album Title	Sym	$	Label & Number
10/5/59+	7	52	©	1	That's All		$40	Atco 104
3/7/60	6	50	©	2	This Is Darin		$40	Atco 115
10/17/60	9	38	©	3	Darin At The Copa	[L]	$40	Atco 122
5/22/61	18	42	©	4	The Bobby Darin Story	[G]	$40	Atco 131
9/11/61	92	10		5	Love Swings		$40	Atco 134
1/27/62	48	31		6	Twist With Bobby Darin		$40	Atco 138
5/12/62	96	11		7	Bobby Darin Sings Ray Charles		$40	Atco 140
10/6/62	45	10		8	Things & Other Things		$40	Atco 146
11/17/62	100	6		9	Oh! Look At Me Now		$30	Capitol 1791
3/16/63	43	15	©	10	You're The Reason I'm Living		$30	Capitol 1866
8/24/63	98	5		11	18 Yellow Roses		$30	Capitol 1942
12/26/64+	107	8		12	From Hello Dolly To Goodbye Charlie		$30	Capitol 2194
7/10/65	132	4		13	Venice Blue		$30	Capitol 2322
2/11/67	142	5	©	14	If I Were A Carpenter		$25	Atlantic 8135

Ain't That Love (7)
All By Myself (9)
All Nite Long (2)
Alright, O.K., You Win (3)
Always (9)
Amy (14)
Artificial Flowers (4) *20*
Be Honest With Me (10)
Beachcomber (8) *100*
Beyond The Sea (1,4) *6*
Black Coffee (2)
Blue Skies (9)
Bullmoose (6)
By Myself (medley) (3)
Call Me Irresponsible (12)
Can't Get Used To Losing You (11)
Caravan (2)
Charade (12)
Clementine (2,3,4) *21*
Come September, Theme From (8)
Day Dream (14)
Days Of Wine And Roses (12)
Dear Heart (13)
Don't Dream Of Anybody But Me (2)
Don't Make Promises (14)
Down With Love (2)
Dream Lover (3,4) *2*

Drown In My Own Tears (7)
Early In The Morning (4,6) *24*
18 Yellow Roses (11) *10*
End Of Never (12)
End Of The World (11)
For Baby (14)
From A Jack To A King (11)
Gal That Got Away (2)
Girl That Stood Beside Me (14) *66*
Good Life (13)
Goodbye Charlie (12)
Guys And Dolls (4)
Hallelujah I Love Her So (7)
Have You Got Any Castles, Baby (2)
Hello, Dolly! (12) *79*
Here I Am (10)
How About You (5)
I Ain't Sharin' Sharon (6)
I Can't Give You Anything But Love (2,3)
I Didn't Know What Time It Was (5)
I Got A Woman (3,7)
I Guess I'll Have To Change My Plan (2)
I Have Dreamed (3)
(I Heard That) Lonesome Whistle (10)

I Wanna Be Around (13)
I Will Follow Her (11)
I'll Be There (8) *79*
I'll Remember April (1)
I'm Beginning To See The Light (9)
If I Were A Carpenter (14) *8*
In A World Without You (13)
In Love In Vain (5)
Irresistible You (6) *15*
It Ain't Necessarily So (1)
It Had To Be You (5)
It Keeps Right On A-Hurtin' (10)
Jailer Bring Me Water (8)
Just Friends (5)
Keep A Walkin' (6)
Lazy River (4) *14*
Leave My Woman Alone (7)
Lonesome Road (medley) (3)
Long Ago And Far Away (5)
Look At Me (12)
Look For My True Love (8)
Lost Love (8)
Love For Sale (3)
Mack The Knife (1,3,4) *1*
Mighty Mighty Man (6)
Misty Roses (14)
More (12)
More I See You (5)
Multiplication (6) *30*

My Bonnie (7)
My Buddy (9)
My Gal Sal (2)
Nature Boy (8) *40*
Nightingale Sang In Berkeley Square (9)
No Greater Love (5)
Not For Me (11)
Now We're One (8)
Now You're Gone (10)
Oh Lonesome Me (10)
Oh! Look At Me Now (9)
On Broadway (11)
Once In A Lifetime (12)
Oo-Ee-Train (8)
Our Day Will Come (11)
Party's Over (9)
Pete Kelly's Blues (2)
Pity Miss Kitty (6)
Plain Jane (4) *38*
Please Help Me, I'm Falling (10)
Queen Of The Hop (4,6) *9*
Reason To Believe (14)
Red Balloon (1)
Release Me (10)
Reverend Mr. Black (11)
Rhythm Of The Rain (11)
Right Time (7)
Roses Of Picardy (9)
Ruby Baby (11)

Sally Was A Good Old Girl (10)
She Needs Me (1)
Sittin' Here Lovin' You (14)
Skylark (5)
Softly, As I Leave You (13)
Softly As In A Morning Sunrise (1)
Some Of These Days (1,3)
Somebody To Love (4,6) *45*
Something To Remember You By (5)
Somewhere (13)
Sorrow Tomorrow (8)
Splish Splash (4) *3*
Spring Is Here (5)
Sunday In New York (12)
Swing Low Sweet Chariot (medley) (3)
Tell All The World About You (7)
Tell Me How Do You Feel (7)
That's All (1,3)
That's Enough (7)
That's The Way Love Is (1)
There Ain't No Sweet Gal That's Worth The Salt Of My Tears (13)
There's A Rainbow 'Round My Shoulder (9)

Things (8) *3*
Through A Long And Sleepless Night (1)
Under Your Spell Again (10)
Until It's Time For You To Go (14)
Venice Blue (13)
Walk Right In (11)
Was There A Call For Me (1)
What'd I Say (Part 1) (7) *24*
When Your Lover Has Gone (medley) (3)
Where Is The One (1)
Where Love Has Gone (12)
Who Can I Count On (10)
Who Can I Turn To? (13)
Won't You Come Home Bill Bailey (3,4) *19*
You Just Don't Know (13)
You Know How (6)
You Made Me Love You (9)
You Must Have Been A Beautiful Baby (6) *5*
You'd Be So Nice To Come Home To (3)
You'll Never Know (9)
You're Mine (8)
You're The Reason I'm Living (10) *3*

DARK ANGEL '89

Heavy-metal group from Los Angeles: Ron Rinehart (vocals), Jim Durkin and Eric Meyer (guitars), Mike Gonzalez (bass) and Gene Hoglan (drums).

| 4/1/89 | 159 | 6 | © | Leave Scars | $10 | Combat 8264 |

Cauterization
Death Of Innocence

Immigrant Song
Leave Scars

Never To Rise Again
No One Answers

Older Than Time Itself
Promise Of Agony

Worms

DARLING CRUEL '89

Rock group from Los Angeles: Greg Darling (vocals), Danni Bardot (guitar), Janis Massey (sax, flute), Orlando Sims (bass) and Erik Gloege (drums).

| 9/9/89 | 160 | 8 | © | Passion Crimes | $10 | Mika 837920 |

Beautiful One
Everything's Over (Passion Crime)

Legend
Love Child
No Stranger

One By One
Sad Song Jenie
Star Collector

Tales Of Emotion
Weight On My Shoulders

DARRELL, Johnny '69

Born on 7/23/40 in Hopewell, Alabama. Died of diabetes complications on 10/7/97 (age 57). Country singer.

| 9/6/69 | 172 | 3 | | Why You Been Gone So Long | $15 | United Artists 6707 |

Ain't That Livin'
House On The Hill
Hungry Eyes

I Ain't Buying
Jimmy Jacob

Margie's At The Lincoln Park Inn
River Bottom

Why You Been Gone So Long
Woman Without Love
World I Used To Know

You're Always The One

DARREN, James '63

Born James Ercolani on 10/3/36 in Philadelphia. Singer/actor. Starred in several movies. Regular on TV's *The Time Tunnel* from 1966-67 and *T.J. Hooker* from 1983-86.

| 9/25/61 | 132 | 3 | | 1 | Gidget Goes Hawaiian (James Darren Sings The Movies) | $40 | Colpix 418 |
| 5/11/63 | 48 | 18 | © | 2 | Teenage Triangle | $40 | Colpix 426 |

includes 4 cuts by Paul Petersen: "Keep Your Love Locked (Deep In Your Heart) (#58)," "Little Boy Sad," "Lollipops And Roses" (#54) and "She Can't Find Her Keys" (#19)

JAMES DARREN/SHELLEY FABARES/PAUL PETERSEN

| 6/3/67 | 187 | 3 | | 3 | James Darren/All | [G] | $25 | Warner 1688 |

All (3) *35*
Because They're Young (1)
Born Free (3)
Come On My Love (1)
Conscience (2) *11*
Georgy Girl (3)

Gidget (2) *41*
Gidget Goes Hawaiian (1)
Goodbye Cruel World (2) *3*
Goodbye My Lady Love (1)
Hand In Hand (1)
Her Royal Majesty (2) *6*

I Miss You So (3)
Lady (3)
Man And A Woman (Un Homme Et Une Femme) (3)
My Cup Runneth Over (3)
Not Mine (1)

P.S. I Love You (1)
Since I Don't Have You (3)
Sunny (3)
This Is My Song (3)
Traveling Down A Lonely Road (1)

Until The Real Thing Comes Along (1)
Wild About That Girl (1)
You Are My Dream (1)
Your Smile (1)

DARTELLS, The   '63
Rock and roll grouop from Oxnard, California: Doug Phillips (vocals, bass), Dick Burns (guitar), Corky Wilkie and Rich Peil (saxophones), Randy Ray (organ) and Gary Peeler (drums). Phillips died on 5/5/95 (age 50).

| 7/6/63 | 95 | 5 | | | **Hot Pastrami!** .... | | | $50 | Dot 25522 |

Daddy's Home   Dill Pickles   Happy Organ   I Scream, You Scream   One Degree North   Surf Dreams
Dartell Stomp   Fanny Mae   **Hot Pastrami 11**   Night Train   St. James Infirmary   Swiss Cheese

DAS EFX   '92
Rap duo: Andre Weston (born on 9/9/70 in New Jersey) and Willie Hines (born on 11/27/70 in New York City).

4/25/92	16	42	▲	©	1 **Dead Serious**			$10	EastWest 91827
12/4/93	20	12		©	2 **Straight Up Sewaside**			$10	EastWest 92265
10/14/95	22	6		©	3 **Hold It Down**			$10	EastWest 61829
4/11/98	48	3		©	4 **Generation EFX**			$10	EastWest 62063

Alright (3)   Dedicated (3)   Here We Go (3)   Krazy Wit Da Books (2)   Rappaz (2)   Somebody Told Me (4)
Bad News (3)   Dum Dums (1)   Hold It Down (1)   Looseys (1)   Raw Breed (4)   Straight Out The Sewer (1)
Baknaffek (2)   East Coast (1)   Host Wit Da Most (2)   Make Noize (4)   Ready To Rock Rough Rhymes   Take It Back (4)
Brooklyn To T-Neck (1)   40 & A Blunt (3)   If Only (1)   Mic Checka (1)   (3)   **They Want EFX** (1) *25*
Buck-Buck (3)   **Freakit** (2) *43*   It'z Lik Dat (2)   **Microphone Master** (3) *86*   **Real Hip Hop** (3) *61*   Undaground Rappa (2)
Can't Have Nuttin' (3)   Generation EFX (4)   Jussummen (1)   New Stuff (4)   Represent The Real (3)   Whut Goes Around (1)
Change (3)   Gimme Dat Micraphone (2)   Kaught In Da Ak (2)   No Diggedy (3)   Rite Now (4)   Wontu (2)
Check It Out (2)   Hardcore Rap Act (3)   Klap Ya Handz (1)   No Doubt (4)   Set It Off (4)
Comin' Thru (3)   Here It Is (3)   Knockin' Niggaz Off (3)   Rap Scholar (4)   Shine (4)

DASH, Sarah   '79
Born on 8/18/43 in Trenton, New Jersey. R&B singer. Member of **LaBelle**.

| 1/20/79 | 182 | 7 | | | **Sarah Dash** .... | | | $12 | Kirshner 35477 |

Charge It   Do It For Love   I Can't Believe (Someone Like   **Sinner Man** *71*   You
(Come And Take This) Candy   Give Your Man A Helping Hand   You Could Really Love Me)   Touch And Go
  From Your Baby   Look But Don't Touch   We're Lovers After All

DAVE & SUGAR   '77
Country singer Dave Rowland with female duo Vicki Hackeman and Jackie Frantz. Sue Powell replaced Frantz in 1977. Melissa Dean replaced Hackemen in 1979. Jamie Jaye replaced Powell in 1980.

| 9/17/77 | 157 | 4 | | | 1 **That's The Way Love Should Be** .... | | | $12 | RCA Victor 2477 |
| 3/7/81 | 179 | 4 | | | 2 **Dave & Sugar/Greatest Hits** .... | | [G] | $10 | RCA Victor 3915 |

Baby Take Your Coat Off (2)   Got Leavin' On Her Mind (1)   I'm Knee Deep In Loving You   Livin' At The End Of The   That's The Way Love Should
Can't Help But Wonder (2)   Gotta Quit Lookin' At You Baby   (1,2)   Rainbow (1)   Be (1)
Don't Throw It All Away (1,2)   (2)   It's A Beautiful Morning With   My World Begins And Ends   We've Got Everything (1)
Door Is Always Open (2)   I Ain't Leavin' Dallas 'Til The   You (1)   With You (2)
Feel Like A Little Love (1)   Fire Goes Out (1)   It's A Heartache (2)   Queen Of The Silver Dollar (2)
Golden Tears (2)   I Love To Be Loved By You (1)   Tear Time (2)

DAVE DEE, DOZY, BEAKY, MICK AND TICH   '67
Pop group from Wiltshire, England: "Dave Dee" Harmon (vocals), Trevor "Dozy" Davies (guitar), John "Beaky" Dymond (guitar), Michael "Mick" Wilson (bass) and Ian "Tich" Amey (drums).

| 8/5/67 | 155 | 3 | | | **Greatest Hits** .... | | [G] | $40 | Fontana 67567 |

Bend It   Here's A Heart   Hold Tight!   Save Me   You Know What I Want
Hands Off   Hideaway   I'm On The Up   Touch Me, Touch Me   You Make It Move

DAVID & DAVID   '86
Pop-rock duo from Los Angeles: **David Baerwald** and David Ricketts.

| 8/16/86 | 39 | 38 | ● | © | **Boomtown** .... | | | $10 | A&M 5134 |

Ain't So Easy *51*   Being Alone Together   River's Gonna Rise   Swallowed By The Cracks   Welcome To The
All Alone In The Big City   Heroes   Rock For The Forgotten   Swimming In The Ocean   **Boomtown** *37*

DAVIDSON, John   '66
Born on 12/13/41 in Pittsburgh. Singer/actor. Hosted own TV talk show from 1980-82. Co-hosted TV's *That's Incredible* and a version of *Hollywood Squares*.

10/8/66	19	24		©	1 **The Time Of My Life!**			$15	Columbia 9380
4/8/67	125	8			2 **My Best To You**			$15	Columbia 9448
12/2/67	79	12		©	3 **A Kind Of Hush**			$15	Columbia 9534
6/29/68	151	10			4 **Goin' Places**			$15	Columbia 9654
5/17/69	153	7			5 **John Davidson**			$15	Columbia 9795
11/22/69	165	5			6 **My Cherie Amour**			$15	Columbia 9859

Blessed Is The Rain (6)   59th Street Bridge Song (Feelin'   How Come You Do Me Like   Michelle (1)   Suzanne (5)   What Is A Woman? (3)
Blowin' In The Wind (5)   Groovy) (3)   You Do (3)   Minstrel Man (4)   Taste Of Honey (1)   What Now My Love (1)
Both Sides Now (5)   Flame (4)   I Couldn't Live Without Your   More I See You (1)   That's Life (2)   Who Am I (2)
By The Time I Get To Phoenix   Friend, Lover, Woman, Wife (6)   Love (2)   My Cherie Amour (6)   There'll Be Some Changes   Windmills Of Your Mind (6)
  (4)   Games That Lovers Play (2)   I Really Don't Want To Know (3)   My Cup Runneth Over (3)   Made (3)   Woman Helping Man (5)
California Bloodlines (6)   Georgy Girl (3)   I'll Always Remember (2)   My Love (1)   There's A Kind Of Hush (All   Woman, Woman (4)
Can't Take My Eyes Off You   Goin' Out Of My Head (medley)   I've Gotta Be Me (5)   My Way (6)   Over The World) (3)   Words (3)
  (medley) (4)   (4)   If I Gave You (3)   Ob-La-Di Ob-La-Da (5)   Those Were The Days (5)   You Don't Have To Say You
Dakota (1)   Goodnight My Love (Pleasant   If I Were A Carpenter (3)   Shadow Of Your Smile (1)   Time For Us (6)   Love Me (Io Che Non Vivo
Daydream (1)   Dreams) (5)   Just As Much As Ever (4)   Somewhere (2)   Today (3)   Senza Te) (1)
Didn't We (5)   Happiest Guy Alive (4)   Letter, The (6)   Somewhere, My Love (1)   Try To Remember (2)   You've Made Me So Very
Don't Think Twice, It's All Right   Happy Heart (6)   Little Green Apples (5)   Stormy (5)   Valley Of The Dolls, Theme   Happy (6)
  (3)   High Heel Sneakers (6)   Love Is Blue (4)   Strangers In The Night (1)   From (4)
          Mame (2)   Sunny (2)   Visions Of Sugarplums (4)

DAVIES, Dave   '80
Born on 2/3/47 in Muswell Hill, London, England. Lead guitarist of **The Kinks**.

7/26/80	42	14		©	1 **AFL1-3603**			$12	RCA Victor 3603
					title refers to label number bar code				
7/18/81	152	8		©	2 **Glamour**			$12	RCA Victor 4036

Body (2)   Imaginations Real (1)   Nothin' More To Lose (1)   7th Channel (2)   Where Do You Come From (1)
Doing The Best For You (1)   In You I Believe (1)   Reveal Yourself (2)   Telepathy (2)   World Is Changing Hands (1)
Eastern Eyes (2)   Is This The Only Way? (2)   Run (1)   Too Serious (2)   World Of Our Own (1)
Glamour (2)   Move Over (1)   See The Beast (1)   Visionary Dreamer (1)

DAVINA '98

Born in Detroit. Female R&B singer.

| 4/25/98 | 180 | 2 | © | **Best Of Both Worlds** ...... | | | $10 | Loud 67536 |

After The Rain	Getz No Where	Love's Comin' Down	Only One Reason	When It Rains
Come Over To My Place *81*	Give Me Love	Mercy	**So Good** *60*	
Comin' For You	I Can't Help It	My Cryin' Blues	Way I Feel About You	

DAVIS, Alana '98

Born on 5/6/74 in New York City. Female pop-rock singer/songwriter.

| 1/31/98 | 157 | 7 | © | **Blame It On Me** ...... | | | $10 | Elektra 62112 |

| Blame It On Me | Free | Lullaby | One Day | Round & Around | Turtle |
| Crazy | Love & Pride | Murder | Rest Of Yesterday | **32 Flavors** *37* | Weight Of The World |

DAVIS, Chip '96

Born Louis Davis in Sylvania, Ohio. Songwriter/producer/bassoonist/drummer. Founder of **Mannheim Steamroller** and the American Gramaphone record label. Wrote **C.W. McCall**'s "Convoy."

| 11/23/96 | 168 | 1 | © | **Holiday Musik** ...... | [X-I] | | $10 | American Gram. 296 |

Christmas chart: 6/'96

Abblasen: Fanfare	Brandenburg Concerto #5, III,	Brandenburg Concerto #2	E Major, KK 380: Sonata	Op. 3, No. 12: Allegro
Adagio (B Minor)	Allegro	C Major, KK 153: Allegro	Four Seasons: Autumn: Allegro	Recorder Concerto, F Major:
Ancient Airs and Dances, Suite	Brandenburg Concerto #5, II:	Concerto Grosso, Op. 3, No. 4:	Gagliarda	Allegro
No. 3: Italiana	Affettuoso	Allegro	Galliard and Dance	
Ancient Airs and Dances, Suite	Brandenburg Concerto #5, I:	Double Harpsichord Concerto:	Gigue	
No. 3: Siciliana	Allegro	Vivace	La Mourisque	

DAVIS, Danny, & The Nashville Brass '69

Born George Nowlan on 4/29/25 in Dorchester, Massachusetts. Country trumpet player/bandleader. Played and sang in swing bands including Gene Krupa, Bob Crosby, Freddy Martin, Blue Barron, and **Sammy Kaye**. Formed The Nashville Brass in 1968.

1)The Nashville Sound 2)You Ain't Heard Nothin' Yet 3)Down Homers

2/15/69	78	24		1	**The Nashville Sound**	[I]	$15	RCA Victor 4059
7/12/69	143	6		2	**More Nashville Sounds**	[I]	$15	RCA Victor 4176
12/27/69+	141	20		3	**Movin' On**	[I]	$15	RCA Victor 4232
5/30/70	102	12		4	**You Ain't Heard Nothin' Yet**	[I]	$15	RCA Victor 4334
10/31/70	140	12		5	**Down Homers**	[I]	$15	RCA Victor 4424
12/12/70	11ˣ	3		6	**Christmas with Danny Davis and the Nashville Brass**	[X-I]	$15	RCA Victor 4377
4/3/71	161	3		7	**Somethin' Else**	[I]	$15	RCA Victor 4476
9/18/71	184	4		8	**Super Country**	[I]	$15	RCA Victor 4571
11/25/72	193	5		9	**Turn On Some Happy!**	[I]	$15	RCA Victor 4803
3/15/80	150	5		10	**Danny Davis & Willie Nelson with The Nashville Brass**		$12	RCA Victor 3549

new instrumental backing for earlier recordings by Nelson

All I Have To Offer You (Is Me) (3)	Do You Hear What I Hear (6)	Hey, Good Lookin' (3)	Joey's Song (3)	Oh Baby Mine (I Get So Lonely) (4)	Snowbird (7)
Anytime (9)	Don't It Make You Wanta Go Home (1)	Highland Brass (7)	Just One Time (8)	Oh, Lonesome Me (9)	Steel Guitar Rag (4)
Are You From Dixie (Cause I'm From Dixie Too) (7)	Down Yonder (5)	Horny (9)	Kaw-Liga (2)	On The Rebound (1)	Sweet Dreams (3)
Are You Lonesome Tonight (4)	Early Morning Rain (9)	I Can't Stop Loving You (7)	Lappland (2)	Orange Blossom Special (8)	Tennessee Waltz (5)
Big Daddy (8)	Fire Ball Mail (2)	I Fall To Pieces (1)	Lassus Trombone (4)	Raindrops Keep Fallin' On My Head (9)	Turn Your Radio On (9)
Bloody Merry Morning (10)	Foggy Mountain Breakdown (7)	I Love You Because (2)	Let It Be Me (1)	Rainy Day Blues (10)	Under The Double Eagle (8)
Blue Bayou (8)	Four Walls (5)	I Saw The Light (1)	Little Bitty Tear (4)	Release Me (3)	Wabash Cannon Ball (3)
Blue Christmas (6)	Freight Train (2)	I Walk The Line (1)	Local Memory (10)	Ring Of Fire (3)	Wait For The Light To Shine (8)
Bonaparte's Retreat (2)	Funny How Time Slips Away (10)	I Walked Out On Heaven (4)	Lonely Street (2)	Rose Garden (7)	Walking The Floor Over You (5)
Brassy Down Home Rag (5)	Games People Play (9)	I'll Fly Away (9)	Long Gone Lonesome Blues (5)	Ruby, Don't Take Your Love To Town (3)	Ways To Love A Man (3)
Cajun Baby (2)	Give The World A Smile (7)	I'm Movin' On (3)	Maiden's Prayer (4)	San Antonio Rose (4)	White Christmas (6)
Christmas Song (Chestnuts Roasting on an Open Fire) (6)	Good Hearted Woman (10)	I'm So Lonesome I Could Cry (8)	May The Circle Be Unbroken (5)	Santa Claus Is Comin' To Town (6)	Wildwood Brass (2)
Columbus Stockade Blues (2)	Great Speckled Bird (4)	I've Got A New Heartache (1)	Middle Of The Road (1)	Silent Night (6)	Wings Of A Dove (4)
Country Gentleman (2)	Green, Green Grass Of Home (7)	Is Anybody Goin' To San Antone (8)	Mountain Dew (1)	Silver Bells (6)	Winter Wonderland (6)
December Day (10)	Hello Walls (10)	Jambalaya (On The Bayou) (1)	Mule Skinner Blues (1)	Singing My Song (2)	Wolverton Mountain (3)
Difficult (7)	Here Comes My Baby Back Again (1)	Jealous Heart (4)	My Own Peculiar Way (10)	Slowly (8)	Woman (Sensuous Woman) (9)
Distant Drums (5)		Jingle Bell Rock (6)	New Spanish Two-Step (5)		Yakety Axe (2)
		Jingling Brass (8)	Night Life (10)		Yesterday, When I Was Young (3)
		Norman (8)			Yesterday's Wine (10)

DAVIS, Jimmy, & Junction '87

Born in Memphis. Rock singer/guitarist. His band Junction: Tommy Burroughs (guitar), John Scott (piano) and Chuck Reynolds (drums).

| 10/31/87 | 122 | 8 | © | **Kick The Wall** ...... | | | $10 | MCA 42015 |

| Are We Rockin' Yet? | Don't Hold Back The Night | Just Having Touched | Labor Of Love | Shoe Shine Man |
| Catch My Heart | Just A Little Bit | **Kick The Wall** *67* | Over The Top | Why The West Was Won |

DAVIS, Linda '94

Born on 11/26/62 in Dodson, Texas. Country singer.

| 5/14/94 | 124 | 3 | © | 1 | **Shoot For The Moon** ...... | | $10 | Arista 18749 |
| 2/17/96 | 164 | 4 | © | 2 | **Some Things Are Meant To Be** ...... | | $10 | Arista 18804 |

Always Will (2)	Family Tie (1)	If I Could Live Your Life (2)	Love Story In The Making (2)	Some Things Are Meant To Be (2)	What Do I Know (2)
Cast Iron Heart (2)	He's In Dallas (1)	If Promises Were Gold (1)	Neither One Of Us (2)	There Isn't One (2)	When You Took Your Love Away (1)
Company Time (1)	How Can I Make You Love Me (1)	In Pictures (1)	She Doesn't Ask (2)	Walk Away (2)	
Don't You Want My Love (1)		Love Didn't Do It (1)	Shoot For The Moon (1)		

★493★ DAVIS, Mac '72

Born Scott Davis on 1/21/42 in Lubbock, Texas. Country-pop singer/songwriter/actor. Hosted own TV series from 1974-76. Appeared in several movies.

1)Baby Don't Get Hooked On Me 2)Stop And Smell The Roses 3)All The Love In The World

12/25/71+	160	17		1	**I Believe In Music**		$15	Columbia 30926
9/16/72	11	44	▲ ©	2	**Baby Don't Get Hooked On Me**		$15	Columbia 31770
4/21/73	120	13		3	**Mac Davis**		$15	Columbia 32206
5/4/74	13	45	● ©	4	**Stop And Smell The Roses**		$15	Columbia 32582
10/19/74	182	4		5	**Song Painter**	[E]	$15	Columbia 9969

released in 1970

| 2/8/75 | 21 | 14 | ● | 6 | **All The Love In The World** ...... | | $15 | Columbia 32927 |

DAVIS, Mac — Cont'd

DEBUT	PEAK	WKS					$	Label & Number
7/5/75	64	10			7 **Burnin' Thing**		$15	Columbia 33551
4/10/76	156	9			8 **Forever Lovers**		$15	Columbia 34105
5/24/80	69	15	●		9 **It's Hard To Be Humble**		$12	Casablanca 7207
10/18/80	67	9			10 **Texas In My Rear View Mirror**		$12	Casablanca 7239
1/16/82	174	3			11 **Midnight Crazy**		$12	Casablanca 7257

Baby Don't Get Hooked On Me (2) *1*
Baby, I Just Ain't The Man For You (8)
Beginning To Feel The Pain (3) *92*
Biff, The Friendly Purple Bear (6)
Birthday Song (4)
Boogie Woogie Mama (6)
Burnin' Thing (7) *53*
Christmas Carol (1)
Closest I Ever Came (5)
Comfortable (11)
Daddy's Little Man (5)
Dammit Girl (11)
Dream Me Home (2) *3*
Emily Suzanne (6)
Every Now And Then (8)
Every Woman (6)
Everybody Loves A Love Song (2) *63*
Everything A Man Could Ever Need (3)

Fall In Love With Your Wife (6)
Feel Like Crying (3)
Float Away (11)
Forever Lovers (8) *76*
Freedom Trail (6)
Friend, Lover, Woman, Wife (2)
Good Friends And Fireplaces (4)
Good Times We Had (8)
Gravel On The Ground (9)
Greatest Gift Of All (9)
Half And Half (Song For Sarah) (2,5)
Hello Hollywood (10)
Hello L.A., Bye Bye Birmingham (5)
Hits Just Keep On Coming (7)
Hollywood Humpty Dumpty (1)
Home (5)
Honeysuckle Magic (7)
Hooked On Music (10)
(Hope You Didn't) Chop No Wood (3)
Hot Texas Night (10)

I Believe In Music (1)
I Feel The Country Callin' Me (7)
I Got The Hots For You (11)
I Know You're Out There Somewhere (9)
I Still Love You, Still Love Me (6,7)
I Wanta Wake Up With You (9)
I Will Always Love You (9)
I Won't Want To Own You (8)
I'll Paint You A Song (3)
I'm A Survivor (8)
I'm Just In Love (8)
(If You Add) All The Love In The World (6) *54*
In The Eyes Of My People (1,10)
In The Ghetto (5)
It Was Time (9)
It's Hard To Be Humble (9) *43*
Jimmy Brown Song (7)
Kiss It And Make It Better (4,11)
Let's Keep It That Way (9)

Little Less Conversation (1)
Lonesomest Lonesome (2)
Love Lamp (8)
Lovin' You, Lovin' Me (3)
Lucus Was A Redneck (4)
Magic Mystery (6)
Me And Fat Boy (10)
Memories (5)
Midnight Crazy (11)
Naughty Girl (2)
Once You Get Used To It (5)
One Hell Of A Woman (4) *11*
Please Tell Her That I Said Hello (8)
Poem For My Little Lady (1)
Poor Boy Boogie (2)
Poor Man's Gold (4)
Put Another Notch In Your Belt (5)
Remember When (Beverly's Song) (10)
Rock N' Roll (I Gave You The Best Years Of My Life) (6) *15*
Rodeo Clown (10)

Rufus Was A Redneck (7)
Sad Songs (10)
Sarah Between The Lines (1)
Secrets (10) *76*
Smiley (6)
Soft, Sweet Fire (4)
Something's Burning (1,11)
Special Place In Heaven (7)
Spread Your Love On Me (2)
Stop And Smell The Roses (4) *9*
Sunshine (3)
Sweet Dreams And Sarah (7)
Sweetest Song (4)
Tears In Baby's Eyes (8)
(Tell Me Your) Fantasies (11)
Tequila Sheila (9)
Texas In My Rear View Mirror (10) *51*
Two Plus Two (4)
Uncle Boogar Red And Byrdie Nelle (5)
Watching Scotty Grow (1)
Way You Look Today (3)

Whoever Finds This, I Love You (2,5) *53*
Why Don't We Sleep On It (9)
Woman Crying (3)
Words Don't Come Easy (2)
Yesterday And You (1)
You Are So Lovely (11)
You're Gonna Love Yourself (In The Morning) (7)
You're Good For Me (5)
You're My Bestest Friend (11)
Your Side Of The Bed (3) *88*

DAVIS, Martha   '87

Born on 1/15/51 in Berkely, California. Lead singer of **The Motels**.

DEBUT	PEAK	WKS					$	Label & Number
11/14/87	127	13	©		**Policy**		$10	Capitol 48054

Don't Ask Out Loud
Don't Tell Me The Time *80*

Hardest Part Of A Broken Heart
Heaven Outside My Door

Just Like You
Lust

My Promise
Rebecca

Tell It To The Moon
What Money Might Buy

DAVIS, Miles   ★193★   '70

Born on 5/26/26 in Alton, Illinois. Died of a stroke and pneumonia on 9/28/91 (age 65). Innovative jazz trumpeter who influenced the jazz fusion movement. Began career in 1944 with **Billy Eckstine**'s orchestra. With Six Brown Cats group in 1944. With Charlie Parker and Coleman Hawkins. Recorded with Parker on Savoy and Dial from 1945-46. Formed own quintet in 1955. Band members included **Herbie Hancock** and **Wayne Shorter**. Won Grammy's Lifetime Achievement Award in 1990. Married to actress Cicely Tyson from 1981-88.

1)Bitches Brew 2)The Man With The Horn 3)Miles Davis At Carnegie Hall 4)Seven Steps To Heaven
5)Miles Davis In Person

DEBUT	PEAK	WKS				Sym	$	Label & Number
10/2/61	68	19	©	1	**Miles Davis In Person (Friday & Saturday Nights At The Blackhawk, San Francisco)**	[I-L]	$40	Columbia 1669 [2]
3/24/62	116	10		2	**Someday My Prince Will Come**	[I]	$30	Columbia 1656 / 8456
10/6/62	59	7	©	3	**Miles Davis At Carnegie Hall** recorded on 5/19/61	[I-L]	$25	Columbia 1812 / 8612
9/14/63	62	15	©	4	**Seven Steps To Heaven**	[I]	$25	Columbia 2051 / 8851
4/11/64	93	9	©	5	**Quiet Nights**	[I]	$25	Columbia 2106 / 8906
9/26/64	116	10		6	**Miles Davis In Europe** recorded at the Antibes International Jazz Festival in France	[I-L]	$25	Columbia 2183 / 8983
4/24/65	138	9		7	**My Funny Valentine** recorded on 2/12/64 at the Philharmonic Hall in New York City	[I-L]	$25	Columbia 2306 / 9106
9/6/69	134	6	©	8	**In A Silent Way**	[I]	$25	Columbia 9875
5/16/70	35	29	● ©	9	**Bitches Brew**	[I]	$30	Columbia 26 [2]
12/12/70+	123	12	©	10	**Miles Davis At Fillmore** recorded at the Fillmore East in New York City	[I-L]	$30	Columbia 30038 [2]
4/24/71	159	8	©	11	**A Tribute To Jack Johnson** movie is a biography of the world heavyweight boxing champ (1908-1915)	[I-S]	$20	Columbia 30455
12/25/71+	125	13	©	12	**Live-Evil**	[I]	$25	Columbia 30954 [2]
11/18/72	156	11	©	13	**On The Corner**	[I]	$20	Columbia 31906
5/5/73	152	8	©	14	**In Concert** recorded at the Philharmonic Hall in New York City	[I-L]	$25	Columbia 32092 [2]
10/13/73	189	3		15	**Basic Miles - The Classic Performances Of Miles Davis** recordings from 1955-58	[E-I]	$20	Columbia 32025
6/8/74	179	5		16	**Big Fun**	[I]	$25	Columbia 32866 [2]
1/4/75	141	8	©	17	**Get Up With It** tribute to **Duke Ellington**	[I]	$25	Columbia 33236 [2]
3/13/76	168	5	©	18	**Agharta** recorded on 2/1/75 at the Osaka Festival Hall in Japan	[I-L]	$25	Columbia 33967 [2]
5/7/77	190	2		19	**Water Babies** recordings from 1967-69	[I-K]	$15	Columbia 34396
4/11/81	179	2		20	**Directions** unreleased recordings from 1960-70	[I-K]	$20	Columbia 36472 [2]
7/25/81	53	18	©	21	**The Man With The Horn**	[I]	$12	Columbia 36790
5/29/82	159	7	©	22	**We Want Miles**	[I-L]	$15	Columbia 38005 [2]
5/21/83	136	7		23	**Star People**	[I]	$12	Columbia 38657
6/30/84	169	11	©	24	**Decoy**	[I]	$12	Columbia 38991
6/1/85	111	12	©	25	**You're Under Arrest**	[I]	$12	Columbia 40023
10/25/86	141	10	©	26	**Tutu**	[I]	$10	Warner 25490

DEBUT	PEAK	WKS	RIAA	CD	ARTIST — Album Title	Catalog	Sym	$	Label & Number

DAVIS, Miles — Cont'd

| 6/17/89 | 177 | 5 | | | 27 **Amandla** .... | | [I] | $10 | Warner 25873 |

title is Zulu for "Power"

| 7/25/92 | 190 | 4 | | © | 28 **Doo-Bop** .... | | [I] | $10 | Warner 26938 |
| 6/14/97+ | 2[1C] | 125 | ▲[2] | © | 29 **Kind Of Blue** .... | | [E-I] | $10 | Columbia 40579 |

first released in 1959 on Columbia 8163 ($100)

| 2/17/01 | 36[C] | 1 | ● | © | 30 **Sketches Of Spain** .... | | [E-I] | $10 | Columbia 65142 |

first released in 1960 on Columbia 8271 ($100)

Aida (21)
All Blues (7,29)
All Of You (1,6,7)
Amandla (27)
Aos Pes Da Cruz (5)
Ascent (20)
Autumn Leaves (6)
Baby Won't You Please Come Home (4)
Back Seat Betty (21,22)
Backyard Ritual (26)
Basin Street Blues (4)
Big Time (7)
Billy Preston (17)
Bitches Brew (9)
Black Satin (13)
Blow (28)
Blue In Green (29)
Budo (7)
Bye Bye Blackbird (1)
Calypso Frelimo (17)
Capricorn (19)
Catembe (28)
Chocolate Chip (28)
Cobra (27)
Code M.D. (24)
Come Get It (23)
Concierto De Aranjuez (30)
Corcovado (5)
Decoy (24)
Devil May Care (15)
Directions I & II (20)

Don't Lose Your Mind (26)
Doo-Bop Song (28)
Double Image (medley) (12)
Drad-Dog (2)
Dual Mr. Tillman Anthony (19)
Duke Booty (22)
Duran (20)
Fantasy (28)
Fast Track (22)
Fat Time (21)
Flamenco Sketches (29)
Fran-Dance (1,15)
Freaky Deaky (24)
Freddie Freeloader (29)
Friday Miles (10)
Full Nelson (26)
Fun (20)
Funky Tonk (12)
Gemini (medley) (12)
Go Ahead John (16)
Great Expectations (16)
Hannibal (27)
He Loved Him Madly (17)
Helen Butte (medley) (13)
High Speed Chase (28)
Honky Tonk (17)
Human Nature (25)
I Fall In Love Too Easily (4)
I Thought About You (2,7)
If I Were A Bell (1)
Ife (16)
In A Silent Way (medley) (8)

Inamorata (12)
Interlude (18)
Introduction (6)
It Gets Better (23)
It's About That Time (18)
Jack Johnson, Theme From (18)
Jean Pierre (22,25)
Jilli (27)
Jo-Jo (27)
John McLaughlin (9)
Joshua (4,6)
Katia (25)
KIX (22)
Konda (20)
Lament (medley) (3)
Limbo (27)
Little Church (12)
Little Melonae (15)
Lonely Fire (16)
Love, I've Found You (1)
MD 1 & 2 (25)
Maiysha (17,18)
Man With The Horn (21)
Meaning Of The Blues (medley) (3)
Miles Ahead (15)
Miles Davis In Concert (14)
Miles Runs The Voodoo Down (9)
Milestones (6)
Mr. Freedom X (medley) (13)

Mr. Pastorius (27)
Ms. Morrisine (25)
Mtume (17)
My Funny Valentine (7)
My Man's Gone Now (22)
Mystery (28)
Nem Um Talvez (12)
Neo (1)
New Rhumba (medley) (3)
New York Girl (medley) (13)
No Blues (1,3)
Old Folks (2)
Oleo (1,3)
On Green Dolphin Street (15)
On The Corner (medley) (13)
Once Upon A Summertime (5)
One And One (13)
One Phone Call (medley) (25)
Pan Piper (30)
Peaceful (medley) (8)
Perfect Way (26)
Pfrancing (2)
Pharaoh's Dance (9)
Portia (26)
Prelude Parts I & II (18)
Rated X (17)
Red China Blues (17)
Right Off (11)
Robot 415 (24)
Round Midnight (15,20)
Saeta (30)
Sanctuary (9)

Saturday Miles (10)
Selim (12)
Seven Steps To Heaven (4)
Shhh (medley) (8)
Shout (21)
Sivad (12)
So Near, So Far (4,20)
So What (1,3,29)
Solea (30)
Someday My Prince Will Come (2,3)
Something's On Your Mind (medley) (25)
Song #1 (5)
Song #2 (5)
Song Of Our Country (20,30)
Sonya (28)
Spanish Key (9)
Speak (25)
Splatch (26)
Spring Is Here (3)
Star On Cicely (23)
Star People (23)
Stella By Starlight (7,15)
Street Scenes (medley) (25)
Summer Night (5)
Sweet Pea (19)
Sweet Sue, Just You (15)
Teo (2)
That's Right (24)
That's What Happened (24)

Then There Were None (medley) (25)
Thinkin' One Thing And Doin' Another (medley) (13)
Thursday Miles (10)
Time After Time (25)
Tomaas (26)
Tutu (26)
Two Faced (19)
U 'N' I (23)
Ursula (21)
Vote For Miles (medley) (13)
Wait Till You See Her (5)
Walkin' (1,6)
Water Babies (19)
Water On The Pond (20)
Wednesday Miles (10)
Well You Needn't (1)
What I Say (1)
What It Is (24)
Will O' The Wisp (30)
Willie Nelson (21)
Yesternow (11)
You're Under Arrest (25)

DAVIS, Paul   '82

Born on 4/21/48 in Meridian, Mississippi. Singer/songwriter/producer.

1/11/75	148	6			1 **Ride 'Em Cowboy**			$15	Bang 401
1/21/78	82	18			2 **Singer Of Songs - Teller Of Tales**			$15	Bang 410
4/26/80	173	4		©	3 **Paul Davis**			$12	Bang 36094
12/19/81+	52	29			4 **Cool Night**			$10	Arista 9578

All The Way (3)
Bad Dream (2)
Bronco Rider (1)
Can't Get Back To Alabama (medley) (1)
Cool Night (4) **11**
Cry Just A Little (3) **78**
Darlin' (2) **51**
Do Right (3) **23**

Do You Believe In Love (3)
Editorial (2)
Hallelujah Thank You Jesus (3)
He Sang Our Love Songs (3)
I Don't Want To Be Just Another Love (2)
I Go Crazy (2) **7**
I Never Heard The Song At All (2)

I'm The Only Sinner (In Salt Lake City) (1)
Let Me Know If It's Over (3)
Life Of A Cowboy (medley) (1)
Love Or Let Me Be Lonely (4) **40**
Make Her My Baby (1)
Midnight Woman (1)
Nathan Jones (4)

Never Want To Lose Your Love (2)
One More Time For The Lonely (4)
Oriental Eyes (4)
Ride 'Em Cowboy (1) **23**
Simple Country Life (1)
'65 Love Affair (4) **6**
So True (3)

Somebody's Gettin' To You (4)
Southern Man (1)
Sweet Life (2) **17**
Ten Little Indians (medley) (1)
Thank You Shoes (medley) (1)
Too Slow To Disco (3)
We're Still Together (4)
What You Got To Say About Love (4)

When Everything Else Is Gone (3)
You Came To Me (4)
You're Not Just A Rose (1,2)

★302★   **DAVIS, Sammy Jr.**   '55

Born on 12/8/25 in New York City. Died of cancer on 5/16/90 (age 64). Singer/dancer/actor. Starred in several movies and Broadway shows. One of the first black entertainers to gain widespread acclaim from white audiences.

1)Starring Sammy Davis, Jr.   2)Just For Lovers   3)Sammy Davis Jr. Now

| 5/14/55 | ❶[6] | 29 | | | 1 **Starring Sammy Davis, Jr.** | | | $40 | Decca 8118 |

LP: Decca DL-8118 (#1[6]); EP: Decca ED-2214 (#1[2])

| 10/15/55 | 5 | 9 | | | 2 **Just For Lovers** | | | $40 | Decca 8170 |

LP: Decca DL-8170 (#5); EP: Decca ED-2285 (#11)

10/20/62	14	22			3 **What Kind Of Fool Am I And Other Show-Stoppers**			$25	Reprise 6051
3/16/63	96	6		©	4 **Sammy Davis Jr. At The Cocoanut Grove**		[L]	$30	Reprise 6063 [2]
5/25/63	73	15			5 **As Long As She Needs Me**			$25	Reprise 6082
3/14/64	139	3			6 **Sammy Davis Jr. Salutes The Stars Of The London Palladium**			$25	Reprise 6095
4/4/64	26	18			7 **The Shelter Of Your Arms**			$25	Reprise 6114
3/27/65	141	4		©	8 **Our Shining Hour**			$20	Verve 8605

SAMMY DAVIS • COUNT BASIE

9/4/65	104	4			9 **Sammy's Back On Broadway**			$20	Reprise 6169
1/11/69	24	25			10 **I've Gotta Be Me**			$20	Reprise 6324
4/29/72	11	26			11 **Sammy Davis Jr. Now**			$15	MGM 4832
10/14/72	128	15			12 **Portrait Of Sammy Davis, Jr.**			$15	MGM 4852

And This Is My Beloved (1)
April In Paris (8)
As Long As She Needs Me (5) **59**
Back In Your Own Back Yard (5)
Ballin' The Jack (6)
Because Of You (1)
Bee-Bom (4)
Begin The Beguine (4)
Big Bad John (medley) (4)
Bill Basie Won't You Please Come Home (4)
Birth Of The Blues (1,4)

Blues For Mr. Charlie (8)
Body And Soul (2)
Bye Bye Blackbird (3)
Can't We Be Friends (3)
Candy Man (11) **1**
Climb Ev'ry Mountain (5)
Come On Strong (7)
Come Rain Or Come Shine (2)
Do I Hear A Waltz? (9)
Easy To Love (1)
Falling In Love Again (4)
Falling In Love With Love (5)
Get Out Of Town (1)

Girl From Ipanema (5)
Give Me The Moonlight, Give Me The Girl (6)
Glad To Be Unhappy (1)
Gonna Build A Mountain (3)
Guys And Dolls (4)
Happy Ending (2)
Have A Little Talk With Myself (11)
Hello, Dolly! (9)
Here Am I - Broken Hearted (6)
Here I'll Stay (9)
Hey There (1)
Hound Dog (medley) (4)

I Am Over 25-But You Can Trust Me (11)
I Do Not Love You (2)
I Married An Angel (7)
I Want To Be Happy (11)
I Want To Be With You (6)
I'll Begin Again (11)
I'm A Brass Band (10)
I'm Glad There Is You (10)
I've Got You Under My Skin (4,10)
I've Gotta Be Me (10) **11**
If I Loved You (7)

If My Friends Could See Me Now (10)
In My Own Lifetime (11)
In The Still Of The Night (4)
Introduction (6)
It's A Musical World (12)
It's All Right With Me (2)
Jalousie (8)
Jam Session (Sam, By George!) (medley) (5)
John Shaft (11)
Joker, The (4)
Keepin' Out Of Mischief Now (8)
Lazy River (6)

Lonesome Road (1)
Look At That Face (9)
Lost In The Stars (3)
Lot Of Livin' To Do (3)
Love Is All Around (12)
(Love Is) The Tender Trap (5)
MacArthur Park (11)
Make Someone Happy (7)
Man With A Dream (8)
Married Man (9)
Me And My Shadow (4) **64**
Meeting The President (4)
Mr. Bojangles (12)

DAVIS, Sammy Jr. — Cont'd

My Funny Valentine (1)
My Kind Of Girl (6)
My Personal Property (10)
My Romance (3)
My Shining Hour (8)
New York City Blues (8)
Night And Day (medley) (4)
Once In A Lifetime (3,4)
Other Half Of Me (9)
Out Of This World (5)
Over The Rainbow (6)
Party's Over (7)
People (9)
People Tree (12) *92*
River Stay 'Way From My Door (4)

Rock-A-Bye Your Baby With A Dixie Melody (4)
Room Without Windows (9)
Sammy Looks At Old Movies (4)
September Song (1)
She Believes In Me (10)
She's A Woman (8)
Shelter Of Your Arms (7) *17*
Smile (6)
Some Days Everything Goes Wrong (7)
Somebody (10)
Someone Nice Like You (3)
Something's Coming (3)

Sophisticated Lady (6)
Spoken For (1)
Stan' Up An' Fight (1)
Step Out Of That Dream (5)
Sunrise, Sunset (9)
Sweet Gingerbread Man (12)
Sweet November (10)
Take My Hand (11)
Take The Moment (9)
Teach Me Tonight (8)
Tenderly (2)
Tenement Symphony (6)
That's For Me (7)
There Is Nothing Like A Dame (5)

There Was A Tavern In The Town (5)
These Foolish Things (Remind Me Of You) (2)
This Is My Life (11)
This Was My Love (6)
Thou Swell (3)
Thrill Is Gone (7)
Time To Ride (11)
Tomorrow (12)
Too Close For Comfort (3)
Two For The Seesaw (A Second Chance), Song From (5)
We Kiss In A Shadow (5)
West Side Story Medley (4)

What Kind Of Fool Am I (3,4) *17*
What'd I Say (medley) (4)
When The Wind Was Green (12)
When Your Lover Has Gone (2)
Why Try To Change Me Now (8)
Willoughby Grove (11)
Wonderful Day Like Today (9)
Work Song (8)
You Can Have Her (12)
You Do Something To Me (2)
You're My Girl (2)
You're Nobody Till Somebody Loves You (8)

DAVIS, Skeeter   '63

Born Mary Penick on 12/30/31 in Dry Ridge, Kentucky. Country singer. Married to DJ/TV host Ralph Emery (1960-64) and **NRBQ** bassist Joey Spampinato (1983-96).

4/13/63	**61**	15		**The End Of The World**		$30	RCA Victor 2699

Don't Let Me Cross Over
End Of The World *2*
He Called Me Baby

(I Want To Go) Where Nobody Knows Me
Keep Your Hands Off My Baby

Longing To Hold You Again
Mine Is A Lonely Life
My Coloring Book

Once Upon A Time
Silver Threads And Golden Needles

Something Precious
Why I'm Walkin'

DAVIS, Spencer, Group   '67

Born on 7/14/41 in Swansea, South Wales. Singer/rhythm guitarist. Formed his R&B-styled rock group in Birmingham, England, in 1963. Featured **Steve Winwood** (vocals, guitar, keyboards), his brother Muff Winwood (bass) and Pete York (drums). Steve Winwood left in 1967 to form **Traffic**.

3/25/67	**54**	25		1 **Gimme Some Lovin'**		$50	United Artists 6578
7/15/67	**83**	9		2 **I'm A Man**		$50	United Artists 6589
3/30/68	**195**	3		3 **Spencer Davis' Greatest Hits**	[G]	$50	United Artists 6641

Blues In F (3)
Dimples (2)
Don't Want You No More (3)
Every Little Bit Hurts (2)
Georgia On My Mind (2)

Gimme Some Lovin' (1,3) *7*
Goodbye Stevie (1)
Hammer Song (1)
Here Right Now (1)
I Can't Get Enough Of It (2)

I Can't Stand It (2)
I'm A Man (2,3) *10*
It Hurts Me So (1)
Keep On Running (1,3) *76*
Look Away (2)

Midnight Special (1,3)
Midnight Train (2)
My Babe (2)
Nobody Knows You When You're Down And Out (1)

On The Green Light (2,3)
Searchin' (2,3)
Sittin' And Thinkin' (1)
Stevie's Blues (2)

Time Seller (3) *100*
Trampoline (1)
When I Come Home (1)

Somebody Help Me (1,3) *47*

DAVIS, Tyrone   '70

Born on 5/4/38 in Greenville, Mississippi; raised in Saginaw, Michigan. R&B singer. His younger sister, Jean Davis, was a member of **Facts Of Life**.

3/29/69	**146**	6	©	1 **Can I Change My Mind**		$30	Dakar 9005
7/11/70	**90**	11	©	2 **Turn Back The Hands Of Time**		$30	Dakar 9027
7/1/72	**182**	6	©	3 **I Had It All The Time**		$30	Dakar 76901
8/11/73	**174**	6	©	4 **Without You In My Life**		$30	Dakar 76904
10/2/76	**89**	9		5 **Love And Touch**		$15	Columbia 34268
4/7/79	**115**	12		6 **In The Mood With Tyrone Davis**		$15	Columbia 35723
1/8/83	**137**	6		7 **Tyrone Davis**		$12	Highrise 103

After All This Time (3)
Ain't Nothing I Can Do (6)
All The Love I Need (6)
Are You Serious (7) *57*
Beware, Beware (5)
Call On Me (1)
Can I Change My Mind (1) *5*
Close To You (5)
Come And Get This Ring (3)
Fool In Me (7)
Give It Up (Turn It Loose) (5) *38*
Givin' Myself To You (5)

Have You Ever Wondered Why (1)
Honey You Are My Sunshine (4)
How Could I Forget You (3)
I Can't Wait (6)
I Don't Think You Heard Me (6)
I Got A Sure Thing (4)
I Had It All The Time (3,4) *61*
I Keep Coming Back (2)
I'll Be Right Here (2) *53*
I'm Just Your Man (3)
I'm So Excited (7)

If It's Love That You're After (2)
If You Had A Change In Mind (4)
In The Mood (6)
Just Because Of You (2)
Just The One I've Been Looking For (1)
Keep On Dancin' (6)
Knock On Wood (1)
Let Me Back In (2) *58*
Let Me Be The One (7)
Let The Good Times Roll (1)
Little Bit Of Lovin' (7)

Love Bones (2)
Open The Door To Your Heart (1)
Overdue (7)
Put Your Trust In Me (5)
She's Lookin' Good (1)
Slip Away (1)
Something You Got (2)
There It Is (4) *32*
This Time (3)
True Love Is Hard To Find (4)
Turn Back The Hands Of Time (2) *3*

Undying Love (2)
Waiting Was Not In Vain (2)
Was I Just A Fool (3)
Was It Just A Feeling (3)
We Were In Love Then (6)
Where Did We Lose (7)
Why Is It So Hard (To Say You're Sorry) (5)
Without You In My Life (4) *64*
Woman Needs To Be Loved (1)
Wrapped Up In Your Warm And Tender Love (4)
Wrong Doers (5)

You Can't Keep A Good Man Down (1)
You Know What To Do (6)
You Wouldn't Believe (3,4)
You're Too Much (5)
You've Got To (Save Me) (7)
Your Love Keeps Haunting Me (3)

DAVIS, Wild Bill — see HODGES, Johnny

DAWN   ★418★   '75

Pop vocal trio formed in New York City: Tony Orlando (from New York City), Telma Hopkins (from Louisville) and Joyce Vincent (from Detroit). Orlando was manager for April-Blackwood Music at the time of trio's first hit. Own TV show from 1974-76. Hank Medress (**The Tokens**) and Dave Appell (The Applejacks) produced trio's hits. Hopkins acted on TV's *Bosom Buddies*, *Gimme A Break* and *Family Matters*.

1)*Greatest Hits* 2)*Prime Time* 3)*He Don't Love You (Like I Love You)*

12/19/70+	**35**	23	©	1 **Candida**		$15	Bell 6052
				also see #7 below			
				DAWN FEATURING TONY ORLANDO:			
12/18/71	**178**	2		2 **Dawn Featuring Tony Orlando**		$15	Bell 6069
				also see #6 below			
3/24/73	**30**	34	●	3 **Tuneweaving**		$15	Bell 1112
10/20/73+	**43**	58	●	4 **Dawn's New Ragtime Follies**		$15	Bell 1130
				TONY ORLANDO & DAWN:			
12/7/74+	**16**	17		5 **Prime Time**		$15	Bell 1317
1/11/75	**165**	5		6 **Tony Orlando & Dawn II**	[R]	$15	Bell 1322
				reissue of album #2 above			
1/18/75	**170**	4		7 **Candida & Knock Three Times**	[R]	$15	Bell 1320
				reissue of album #1 above			
4/26/75	**20**	17		8 **He Don't Love You (Like I Love You)**		$12	Elektra 1034
6/28/75	**16**	32	●	9 **Greatest Hits**	[G]	$12	Arista 4045
11/1/75	**93**	6		10 **Skybird**		$12	Arista 4059
3/20/76	**94**	6		11 **To Be With You**		$12	Elektra 1049

DEBUT	PEAK	WKS	RIAA	CD	ARTIST — Album Title	Catalog	Sym	$	Label & Number

DAWN — Cont'd

All In The Game (10)
Another Rainy Day In My Life (5)
Atlanta (3)
Candida (1,7,9) *3*
Caress Me Pretty Music (11)
Carmen (2,6)
Carolina In My Mind (1,7)
Come Back Billie Jo (10)
Country (1,7)
Cupid (11) *22*
Dance, Rosie, Dance (8)
Dancing To The Music (10)
Daydream (4)
Did You Ever Think She'd Get Away From You (10)
Dreamboat (5)
Easy Evil (3)

Fancy Meeting You Here Baby (5)
Freedom For The Stallion (3)
Get Out From Where We Are (2,6)
Gimmie A Good Old Mammy Song (5)
Good Life (2,6)
Grandma's Hands (8)
Happy Man (11)
He Don't Love You (Like I Love You) (8) *1*
Here Comes The Spring (5)
Home (1,7)
House Of Strangers (8)
I Can't Believe How Much I Love You (3)

I Didn't Mean To Love You So Good, Juanita (2,6)
I Don't Know You Anymore (3)
I Get Ideas (2,6)
I Play And Sing (2,6) *25*
If It Wasn't For You Dear (4)
If Only (He Would Make Love To Me) (8)
In The Park (2,6)
Jolie (3,10)
Kelly Blye (10)
Knock Three Times (1,7,9) *1*
Lazy Susan (3)
Let's Run Away Girl (1,7)
Little Heads In Bunkbeds (5)
Look At... (1,7)
Look In My Eyes Pretty Woman (5,9) *11*

Love In Your Eyes (1,7)
Love The One You're With (2,6)
Maybe I Should Marry Jamie (8)
Midnight Love Affair (11)
Missin' That Girl (8)
Mornin' Beautiful (8) *14*
My Love Has No Pride (5)
Overture (4)
Perhaps The Joy Of Giving (1,7)
Personality (10)
Pick It Up (8)
Raindrops (4)
Rainy Day Man (1,7)
Runaway/Happy Together (3) *79*
Say, Has Anybody Seen My Sweet Gypsy Rose (4,9) *3*

Selfish One (11)
She Can't Hold A Candle To You (5)
Skybird (10) *49*
Steppin' Out (Gonna Boogie Tonight) (4,9) *7*
Straight Ahead (10)
Summer Sand (2,6,9) *33*
Sweet Soft Sounds Of Love (2,6)
Sweet Summer Days Of My Life (4)
Talk To Me (11)
That's The Way A Wallflower Grows (10)
Tie A Yellow Ribbon Round The Ole Oak Tree (3,9) *1*
To Be With You (11)

Tomorrow's Got To Be Sunny (Far Fitna Di Ess Ere Sani) (8)
Ukulele Man (4)
Up On The Roof (1,7)
Watch A Clown Break Down (3)
What Are You Doing Sunday (1,2,6,7,9) *39*
When The Party's Over (11)
When We All Sang Along (3)
Who Did A Number On Me (2,6)
Who's In The Strawberry Patch With Sally (4,9) *27*
You Say The Sweetest Things (4,9)
You're A Lady (3,9) *70*
You're All I Need To Get By (11) *34*
(You're) Growin' On Me (11)

★472★ DAY, Doris '55

Born Doris Kappelhoff on 4/3/22 in Cincinnati. Lead singer with **Les Brown**'s big band. Starred in several movies. Star of own TV series from 1968-73. Her husband, Marty Melcher, owned Arwin records; their son, Terry, was a member of **The Rip Chords** and Bruce & Terry, and a prolific producer (**The Beach Boys**).

DEBUT	PEAK	WKS							
2/5/55	11	6		1 **Young At Heart**		[S]	**$60**	Columbia 6339

EP: Columbia B-455 (#11); LP: Columbia CL-6339 (#15); includes 2 cuts by **Frank Sinatra**: "One For My Baby (And One More For The Road)" and "Someone To Watch Over Me"

| 6/25/55 | ❶¹⁹ | 28 | | 2 **Love Me Or Leave Me** | | [S] | **$50** | Columbia 710 |

EP: Columbia EPB-540 (#1¹⁹); LP: Columbia CL-710 (#1¹⁷)

2/9/57	11	6		3 **Day By Day**			**$30**	Columbia 942
5/30/60	26	7		4 **Listen To Day**			**$30**	Columbia DD1
10/2/61	97	8		5 **I Have Dreamed**			**$25**	Columbia 1660 / 8460
3/14/64	102	8		6 **Love Him!**			**$25**	Columbia 2131 / 8931
12/30/67	92ˣ	1		7 **The Doris Day Christmas Album**		[X]	**$20**	Columbia 2226 / 9026

first released in 1964

All I Do Is Dream Of You (5)
Anyway The Wind Blows (4) *50*
As Long As He Needs Me (4)
At Sundown (2)
Autumn Leaves (3)
Be A Child At Christmas Time (7)
But Beautiful (3)
But Not For Me (3)
Can't Help Falling In Love (6)
Christmas Present (7)
Christmas Song (Chestnuts Roasting On An Open Fire) (7)
Christmas Waltz (7)

Day By Day (3)
Don't Take Your Love From Me (3)
Everybody Loves My Baby (But My Baby Don't Love Nobody But Me) (2)
Funny (4)
Gone With The Wind (3)
Have Yourself A Merry Little Christmas (7)
He's So Married (4)
Heart Full Of Love (4)
Hello, My Lover, Goodbye (3)
Hold Me In Your Arms (4)
I Believe In Dreams (5)

I Enjoy Being A Girl (4)
I Hadn't Anyone Till You (3)
I Have Dreamed (4)
I'll Be Home For Christmas (7)
I'll Buy That Dream (5)
I'll Never Stop Loving You (2) *13*
Inspiration (4)
It All Depends On You (2)
Just One Of Those Things (1)
Let It Snow! Let It Snow! Let It Snow! (7)
Lollipops And Roses (6)
Losing You (6)
Love Him (6)

Love Me In The Daytime (4) *100*
Love Me Or Leave Me (2)
Mean To Me (2)
More (6)
My Ship (4)
Never Look Back (2)
Night Life (6)
No (4)
(Now And Then There's) A Fool Such As I (4)
Oh What A Beautiful Dream (5)
Oh! What A Lover You'll Be (4)
Periwinkle Blue (5)
Pillow Talk (4)
Possess Me (4)

Ready, Willing And Able (1)
Roly Poly (4)
Sam, The Old Accordion Man (2)
Shaking The Blues Away (4)
Silver Bells (7)
Since I Fell For You (6)
Snowfall (7)
Softly, As I Leave You (6)
Someday I'll Find You (5)
Stay On The Right Side, Sister (2)
Ten Cents A Dance (2)
There'll Never Be Another You (3)

There's A Rising Moon (1)
Till My Love Comes To Me (5)
Time To Say Goodnight (5)
Toyland (7)
Tunnel Of Love (4) *43*
We'll Love Again (5)
When I Grow Too Old To Dream (5)
White Christmas (7)
Winter Wonderland (7)
You Made Me Love You (I Didn't Want To Do It) (3)
You My Love (1)
You Stepped Out Of A Dream (5)

DAY, Morris '85

Born on 12/13/57 in Springfield, Illinois; raised in Minneapolis. Lead singer of **The Time**. Acted in several movies.

DEBUT	PEAK	WKS		CD					
10/19/85	37	31		©	1 **Color Of Success**			**$10**	Warner 25320
3/12/88	41	15		©	2 **Daydreaming**			**$10**	Warner 25651

Addiction (medley) (1)
Are You Ready (2)
Character, The (1)

Color Of Success (1)
Daydreaming (2)
Don't Wait For Me (1)

Fishnet (2) *23*
Love (medley) (1)
Love Is A Game (2)

Love Sign (1)
Man's Pride (1)
Moonlite (Passionlite) (2)

Oak Tree (1) *65*
Sally (2)
Yo' Luv (2)

DAYE, Cory '79

Born on 4/25/52 in the Bronx, New York. Female lead singer of **Dr. Buzzard's Original Savannah Band**.

DEBUT	PEAK	WKS							
10/13/79	171	5			**Cory And Me**			**$12**	New York Int'l. 3408

Be Bop Betty A/K/A Co Co Ree
Green Light
Keep The Ball Rollin'

Pow Wow *76*
Rainy Day Boy
Rhythm Death

Single Again (medley)
What Time Does The Balloon Go Up (medley)

Wiggle & A Giggle All Night

DAYNE, Taylor '88

Born Leslie Wundermann on 3/7/63 in Baldwin, Long Island, New York. Female dance-pop singer.

DEBUT	PEAK	WKS	RIAA	CD					
1/30/88	21	69	▲²	©	1 **Tell It To My Heart**	C:#42/2		**$10**	Arista 8529
11/18/89+	25	55	▲²	©	2 **Can't Fight Fate**			**$10**	Arista 8581
7/31/93	51	22	●	©	3 **Soul Dancing**			**$10**	Arista 18705

Ain't No Good (2)
Can't Get Enough Of Your Love (3) *20*
Carry Your Heart (1)
Dance With A Stranger (3)
Do You Want It Right Now (1)

Don't Rush Me (1) *2*
Door To Your Heart (3)
Heart Of Stone (2) *12*
I Could Be Good For You (3)
I Know The Feeling (2)
I'll Always Love You (1) *3*

I'll Be Your Shelter (2) *4*
I'll Wait (3)
If You Were Mine (3)
In The Darkness (1)
Love Will Lead You Back (2) *1*
Memories (3)

Prove Your Love (1) *7*
Say A Prayer (3)
Send Me A Lover (3) *50*
Someone Like You (3)
Soul Dancing (3)
Tell It To My Heart (1) *7*

Up All Night (3)
Upon The Journey's End (1)
Wait For Me (2)
Want Ads (1)
Where Does That Boy Hang Out (1)

With Every Beat Of My Heart (2) *5*
You Can't Fight Fate (2)
You Meant The World To Me (2)

DA YOUNGSTA'S '93

Rap trio from Philadelphia: brothers Taji and Qur'an Goodman, with Tarik Dawson.

DEBUT	PEAK	WKS		CD					
5/8/93	126	5		©	**The Aftermath**			**$10**	EastWest 92245

Count It Off
Crewz Pop
Da Hood

Handle This
Honeycomb Hide Out
It'z Natural

Iz U Wit Me
Lyrical Stick Up Kids
Rip A Rhyme

Shout It Out
Wake Em Up
Who's The Mic Wrecka

Wild Child

DAYS OF THE NEW '99

Rock group from Louisville, Kentucky: Travis Meeks (vocals), Todd Whitener (guitar), Jesse Vest (bass) and Matt Taul (drums). Whitener, Vest and Taul left in 1999 to form **Tantric**; Meeks continued group name as a solo project.

| 9/13/97 | 54 | 56 | ▲ | © | 1 Days Of The New | | | $10 | Outpost 30004 |
| 9/18/99 | 40 | 10 | | © | 2 Days Of The New | | | $10 | Outpost 30037 |

Bring Yourself (2)　Face Of The Earth (1)　I Think (2)　Phobics Of Tragedy (2)　Skeleton Key (2)　Weapon & The Wound (2)
Cling (1)　Flight Response (2)　Last One (2)　Provider (2)　Solitude (1)　What's Left For Me? (1)
Down Town (1)　Freak (1)　Longfellow (2)　Real, The (2)　Take Me Back Then (2)　Where I Stand (1)
Enemy (2)　How Do You Know You? (1)　Now (1)　Shelf In The Room (1)　Touch, Peel And Stand (1)　Whimsical (1)

DAYTON FAMILY, The '96

Rap group from Flint, Michigan: brothers Eric and Ira ("**Bootleg**") Dorsey, with Matt Hinkle and Raheen Peterson.

| 10/19/96 | 45 | 7 | | © | F.B.I. | | | $10 | Relativity 1544 |

F.B.I.: Fuck Being Indicted

Blood Bath　Ghetto　Newspaper　Real With This　What's On My Mind
Eyes Closed　Hand That Rocks The Cradle　Player Haters　79th & Halstead
F.B.I.　Killer G's　Posse Is Dayton Ave.　Stick & Move

DAZZ BAND '82

Funk group from Cleveland: Skip Martin (vocals), Eric Fearman (guitar), Bobby Harris (sax), Pierre DeMudd (trumpet), Kevin Frederick (keyboards), and brothers Michael (bass) and Isaac (drums) Wiley.

6/27/81	154	11			1 Let The Music Play			$12	Motown 957
4/3/82	14	34	●		2 Keep It Live			$12	Motown 6004
2/12/83	59	16			3 On The One			$12	Motown 6031
12/17/83+	73	33			4 Joystick			$12	Motown 6084
10/20/84	83	29			5 Jukebox			$12	Motown 6117
8/17/85	98	12			6 Hot Spot			$12	Motown 6149
8/30/86	100	11			7 Wild And Free			$10	Geffen 24110

All I Need (7)　Freaky Lovin' (1)　Just Believe In Love (2)　L.O.V.E. M.I.A. (7)　Shake What You Got (2)　Time Will Heal A Broken Heart (7)
All The Way (6)　Gamble With My Love (2)　Just Can't Wait 'Till The Night (2)　Love Song (3)　She Used To Be My Girl (6)　To The Roof (4)
Bad Girl (3)　Heartbeat (5)　Keep It Live (On The K.I.L.) (2)　Main Attraction (5)　She's The One (5)　Undercover Lover (5)
Beat That's Right (7)　Hooks In Me (7)　Keep You Comin' Back For More (5)　Now That I Have You (4)　Slow Rap (6)　Until You (4)
Body And Mind (7)　Hot Spot (6)　Knock! Knock! (1)　On The One For Fun (3)　So Much Love (5)　We Have More Than Love (3)
Can We Dance (2)　I Believe In You (1)　Laughin' At You (4)　Paranoid (3)　Something You Said (7)　What Will I Do Without You (1)
Cheek To Cheek (3)　I'll Keep On Lovin' You (2)　Let It All Blow (5) *84*　Party Right Here (3)　Stay A While With Me (3)　When You Needed Roses (6)
Don't Get Caught In The Middle (3)　I've Been Waiting (5)　Let It Whip (2) *5*　Rock With Me (1)　Straight Out Of School (4)　Wild And Free (7)
Don't Stop (1)　If Only You Were In My Shoes (6)　Let Me Love You Until (2)　S. C. L. & P. (Style, Class, Looks And Personality) (6)　Swoop (I'm Yours) (4)
Dream Girl (5)　It's All Right (7)　Let The Music Play (1)　　T. Mata (3)
Everyday Love (1)　Joystick (4) *61*　Let Me Love You (2)　Satisfying Love (1)　This Time It's Forever (1)

dB's, The '87

Pop-rock group from Chapel Hill, North Carolina: Peter Holsapple (vocals, keyboards), Jeff Beninato (guitar), Gene Holder (bass) and Will Rigby (drums). Holsapple married Susan Cowsill of **The Cowsills** on 4/18/93.

| 11/28/87 | 171 | 8 | | © | The Sound Of Music | | | $10 | I.R.S. 42055 |

Any Old Thing　Change With The Changing Times　Looked At The Sun Too Long　Never Say When　Working For Somebody Else
Better Place　I Lie　Molly Says　Think Too Hard
Bonneville　　Never Before And Never Again　Today Could Be The Day

DC TALK '98

Christian trio from Washington DC: Toby McKeehan, Michael Tait and Kevin Smith.

12/9/95	16	79	▲²	©	1 Jesus Freak			$10	ForeFront 25140
9/13/97	109	11	●	©	2 Live In Concert - Welcome To The Freak Show		[L]	$10	ForeFront 25184
10/10/98	4	38	●	©	3 Supernatural			$10	ForeFront 46525
12/9/00	81	14		©	4 Intermission: The Greatest Hits		[G]	$10	ForeFront 25274
5/12/01	142	3			5 Solo		[M]	$10	ForeFront 25296

Alas My Love (2)　Day By Day (1,2)　I Wish We'd All Been Ready (4)　Like It, Love It, Need It (1,2)　Return Of The Singer (5)　There Is A Treason At Sea (3)
Alibi (5)　Dive (3)　In The Light (1,2,4)　Luv Is A Verb (2,4)　Say The Words (Now) (4)　Time Is (2)
All You Got (5)　Extreme Days (5)　Into Jesus (3)　Mind's Eye (1,2,4)　Since I Met You (3)　Truth, The (3)
Be (5)　Fearless (3)　It's Killing Me (3)　Mr. Morgan (Act I) (4)　So Help Me God (1,2)　Walls (2)
Between You And Me (1,4)　40 Live (5)　It's The End Of The World As We Know It (2)　Mrs. Morgan (Act II) (4)　Socially Acceptable (5)　Wanna Be Loved (3)
Chance (4)　Godsend (5)　Jesus Freak (1,2,4)　My Friend (So Long) (3)　Somebody's Watching (5)　What Have We Become? (1)
Colored People (1,2,4)　Hardway, The (2,4)　Jesus Is Just Alright (2,4)　My Will (4)　SugarCoat It (4)　What If I Stumble? (1,2,4)
Consume Me (3,4)　Help (2)　　Red Letters (3)　Supernatural (3,4)

DEAD BOYS '77

Punk-rock group from Cleveland: Stiv Bators (vocals), Gene Connor (lead guitar), Jimmy Zero (rhythm guitar), Jeff Magnum (bass) and Johnny Blitz (drums). Bators later formed **Lords Of The New Church**. Bators died on 6/4/90 (age 40) after being hit by a car in Paris.

| 10/22/77 | 189 | 4 | | © | Young, Loud And Snotty | | | $25 | Sire 6038 |

Ain't Nothin' To Do　Caught With The Meat In Your Mouth　Down In Flames　High Tension Wire　Not Anymore　What Love Is
All This And More　　Hey Little Girl　I Need Lunch　Sonic Reducer

DEAD CAN DANCE '96

Duo of Brendan Perry (lives in Ireland) and Lisa Gerrard (lives in Australia's Snow River Mountains).

10/2/93	122	11		©	1 Into The Labyrinth			$10	4 A D 45384
11/12/94	131	3		©	2 Toward The Within			$10	4 A D 45769
7/13/96	75	8		©	3 Spiritchaser			$10	4 A D 46230

American Dreaming (2)　Don't Fade Away (2)　Indus (3)　Sanvean (2)　Tell Me About The Forest (You Once Called Home) (1)　Yulunga (Spirit Dance) (1,2)
Ariadne (1)　Emmeleia (3)　Nierika (3)　Snake And The Moon (3)　Towards The Within (1)
Cantara (2)　How Fortunate The Man With None (1)　Oman (2)　Song Of The Dispossessed (3)　Tristan (2)
Carnival Is Over (1)　　Persian Love Song (2)　Song Of The Nile (3)
Dedicacè Outò (3)　I Am Stretched On Your Grave (2)　Piece For Solo Flute (2)　Song Of The Sibyl (2)　Ubiquitous Mr Lovegrove (1)
Desert Song (2)　I Can See Now (2)　Rakim (2)　Song Of The Stars (3)　Wind That Shakes The Barley (1,2)
Devorzhum (3)　　Saldek (1)　Spider's Stratagem (1)

DEAD MILKMEN, The　　'89

Punk-rock group from Philadelphia: Rodney "Anonymous" Linderman (vocals), Anthony "Jasper Thread" Genaro (guitar), David "Lord Maniac" Schulthise (bass) and Dean "Clean" Sabatino (drums).

DEBUT	PEAK	WKS	CD		ARTIST — Album Title	$	Label & Number
8/1/87	163	7	©	1	Bucky Fellini	$10	Enigma 73260
12/24/88+	101	23	©	2	Beelzebubba	$10	Enigma 73351
6/2/90	164	7	©	3	Metaphysical Graffiti	$10	Enigma 73564

Anderson, Walkman, Buttholes And How! (3)
Bad Party (2)
Badger Song (1)
Beige Sunshine (3)
Big Sleazy (3)
Big Time Operator (1)
Bleach Boys (2)
Bloody Orgy Of The Atomic Fern, (Theme From) (1)
Born To Love Volcanos (2)
Brat In The Frat (2)
City Of Mud (1)
Do The Brown Nose (3)
Dollar Signs In Her Eyes (3)
Epic Tales Of Adventure (3)
Everybody's Got Nice Stuff But Me (2)
Going To Graceland (1)
Guitar Song (3)
Howard Beware (2)
I Against Osbourne (2)
I Am The Walrus (3)
I Hate You, I Love You (3)
I Tripped Over The Ottoman (3)
I Walk The Thinnest Line (2)
If You Love Somebody, Set Them On Fire (3)
In Praise Of Sha Na Na (3)
Instant Club Hit (You'll Dance To Anything) (1)
Jellyfish Heaven (1)
Life Is Shit (2)
Little Man In My Head (3)
Methodist Coloring Book (3)
My Many Smells (2)
Nitro Burning Funny Cars (1)
Now Everybody's Me (3)
Part 3 (3)
Pit, The (1)
Punk Rock Girl (2)
RC's Mom (2)
Ringo Buys A Rifle (2)
Rocketship (1)
Smokin' Banana Peels (2)
Sri Lanka Sex Hotel (2)
Stuart (3)
Surfin' Cow (1)
Tacoland (1)
Take Me To The Specialist (1)
Watching Scotty Die (1)

DEAD ON　　'90

Heavy-metal group from Long Island, New York: Mike Raptis (vocals), Michael Caronia and Tony Frazzitta (guitars), John Linder (bass) and Mike Caputo (drums).

DEBUT	PEAK	WKS	CD		ARTIST — Album Title	$	Label & Number
2/10/90	159	6	©		Dead On	$10	SBK 93249

Beat A Dead Horse (1)
Dead On
Different Breed
Escape
Full Moon
Matador's Nightmare
Merry Ship
Salem Girls
Widower, The

DEAD OR ALIVE　　'85

Dance group from Liverpool, England: Pete Burns (vocals), Tim Lever (keyboards), Mike Percy (bass) and Steve Coy (drums).

DEBUT	PEAK	WKS	RIAA	CD		ARTIST — Album Title	Sym	$	Label & Number
7/13/85	31	20	●	©	1	Youthquake		$10	Epic 40119
12/27/86+	52	25		©	2	Mad, Bad, And Dangerous To Know		$10	Epic 40572
7/30/88	195	2		©	3	Rip It Up	[K]	$10	Epic 44255
7/22/89	106	9		©	4	Nude		$10	Epic 45224

Baby Don't Say Goodbye (4)
Big Daddy Of The Rhythm (1)
Brand New Lover (2,3) *15*
Cake And Eat It (1)
Come Home With Me Baby (4) *69*
Come Inside (2)
D.J. Hit That Button (1)
Get Out Of My House (4)
Give It Back That Love Is Mine (4)
Hooked On Love (2,3)
I Cannot Carry On (4)
I Don't Wanna Be Your Boyfriend (4)
I Wanna Be A Toy (1)
I Want You (2)
I'll Save You All My Kisses (2,3)
In Too Deep (1,3)
It's Been A Long Time (1)
Lover Come Back To Me (1,3) *75*
My Forbidden Lover (4)
My Heart Goes Bang (1,3)
Something In My House (2,3) *85*
Son Of A Gun (2)
Special Star (3)
Stop Kicking My Heart Around (4)
Then There Was You (2)
Turn Around And Count 2 Ten (4)
You Spin Me Round (Like A Record) (1,3) *11*

DEAD PREZ　　'00

Male rap duo from Brooklyn, New York: Clayton Gavin and Lavon Alford.

DEBUT	PEAK	WKS	CD		ARTIST — Album Title	$	Label & Number
4/1/00	73	10	©		Lets Get Free	$10	Loud 1867

Animal In Man
Assassination
Be Healthy
Behind Enemy Lines
Discipline
Happiness
Hip-Hop
I'm A African
It's Bigger Than Hip-Hop
Mind Sex
Police State
Psychology
'They' Schools
We Want Freedom
Wolves
You'll Find A Way

DEAL, Bill, & The Rhondels　　'70

Brassy-rock group from Virginia Beach, Virginia: Bill Deal (vocals, organ), Bob Fisher (guitar), Mike Kerwin, Jeff Pollard, Ronny Rosenbaum and Ken Dawson (horn section), Don Queinsenburry (bass) and Ammon Tharp (drums).

DEBUT	PEAK	WKS		ARTIST — Album Title	Sym	$	Label & Number
4/11/70	185	2		The Best Of Bill Deal & The Rhondels	[G]	$30	Heritage 35006

Are You Ready For This
Harlem Shuffle
Hey Bulldog
I've Been Hurt *35*
I've Got My Needs
May I *39*
Nothing Succeeds Like Success *62*
Swingin' Tight *85*
Touch Me
Tuck's Theme
What Kind Of Fool Do You Think I Am *23*
Words

DEAN, Billy　　'93

Born on 4/1/62 in Quincy, Florida. Country singer.

DEBUT	PEAK	WKS	RIAA	CD		ARTIST — Album Title	Sym	$	Label & Number
5/25/91	99	26	●	©	1	Young Man		$10	Capitol 94302
7/4/92	88	37	●	©	2	Billy Dean		$10	Capitol 96728
2/13/93	83	16	●	©	3	Fire In The Dark		$10	Liberty 98947
4/2/94	148	11	●	©	4	Greatest Hits	[G]	$10	Liberty 28357
4/20/96	143	5		©	5	It's What I Do		$10	Capitol 30525

Billy The Kid (2,4)
Brotherly Love (1)
Daddy's Will (2)
Don't Threaten Me With A Good Time (5)
Down To Your Last One More (5)
Give Me All The Pieces (3)
Gone But Not Forgotten (2)
Hammer Down (2)
How Can I Hold You (1)
I Shoulda Listened (2)
I Wanna Take Care Of You (3,4)
I Won't Let You Walk Away (1)
I Wouldn't Be A Man (5)
I'm Not Built That Way (3,4)
If There Hadn't Been You (2,4)
In The Name Of Love (5)
It's What I Do (5)
Leavin' Line (5)
Lowdown Lonely (1)
Mountain Moved (5)
Once In A While (4)
Only A Woman Knows (3)
Only Here For A Little While (1,4)
Only The Wind (2,4)
Play Something We Can Dance To (5)
She's Taken (1)
Simple Things (2)
Small Favors (2)
Somewhere In My Broken Heart (1,4)
Steam Roller (3)
Tear The Wall Down (1)
That Girl's Been Spyin' On Me (5)
That's What I Like About Love (3)
Tryin' To Hide A Fire In The Dark (3,4)
Two Of The Lucky Ones (3)
We Just Disagree (3)
What Have You Got Against Love (1)
When A Woman Cries (4)
When Our Backs Are Against The Wall (5)
You Don't Count The Cost (2,4)
Young Man (1)

DEAN, Jimmy　　'62

Born on 8/10/28 in Plainview, Texas. Country singer/pianist/guitarist. Hosted own CBS-TV series (1957-58); ABC-TV series (1963-66). Business interests include a restaurant chain and a line of pork sausage. Married country singer Donna Meade on 10/27/91.

DEBUT	PEAK	WKS	CD		ARTIST — Album Title	Sym	$	Label & Number
12/4/61+	23	28	©	1	Big Bad John And Other Fabulous Songs And Tales		$25	Columbia 1735 / 8535
11/3/62	144	2		2	Portrait Of Jimmy Dean		$25	Columbia 1894 / 8694
12/11/65	13 [X]	8	©	3	Jimmy Dean's Christmas Card	[X]	$20	Columbia 2404 / 9204

Christmas charts: 13/'65, 37/'66, 80/'67

Basin Street Blues (2)
Big Bad John (1) *1*
Blue Christmas (3)
Cowboy's Prayer (Poem) (3)
Darktown Poker Club (2)
First Noel (medley) (3)
God Rest Ye Merry, Gentlemen (medley) (3)
Gotta Travel On (1)
Grasshopper Mac Clain (1)
Have You Ever Been Lonely (2)
Have Yourself A Merry Little Christmas (3)
I Was Just Walkin' Out The Door (2)
I Won't Go Huntin' With You Jake (But I'll Go Chasin' Wimmin) (1)
It Came Upon The Midnight Clear (3)
Jimmy's Christmas Card (3)
Jingle Bells (3)
Joy To The World (medley) (3)
Kentucky Means Paradise (2)
Little Black Book (2) *29*
Make The Waterwheel Roll (1)
My Christmas Room (3)
Night Train To Memphis (1)
Nobody (2)
O Little Town Of Bethlehem (medley) (3)
Oklahoma Bill (1)
Old Pappy's New Banjo (1)
P.T. 109 (2) *8*
Please Pass The Biscuits (2)
Silent Night, Holy Night (3)
Silver Bells (3)
Sixteen Tons (1)
Smoke, Smoke, Smoke That Cigarette (1)
Steel Men (2) *41*
To A Sleeping Beauty (1) *26*
We Wish You A Merry Christmas (medley) (3)
White Christmas (3)
Yes, Patricia, There Is A Santa Claus (3)
You're Nobody 'Til Somebody Loves You (2)

DEAN, Paul '89
Born on 2/19/46 in Canada. Lead guitarist of **Loverboy**.

| 2/25/89 | 195 | 2 | © | Hard Core | $10 | Columbia 44462 |

Action / Black Sheep / Dirty Fingers / Doctor / Down To The Bottom / Draw The Line / Politics / Sword And Stone / Under The Gun

DEATH ANGEL '88
Heavy-metal group from San Francisco: Mark Osegueda (vocals), Rob Cavestany (guitar), brothers Gus (guitar) and Dennis (bass) Pepa, and Andy Galeon (drums). All members are related.

| 8/6/88 | 143 | 11 | © | Frolic Through The Park | $10 | Enigma 73332 |

Bored / Cold Gin / Confused / Guilty Of Innocence / Mind Rape / Open Up / Road Mutants / Shores Of Sin / 3rd Floor / Why You Do This

DEAUVILLE, Ronnie '57
Lead singer with the **Ray Anthony** band from 1950-51.

| 12/9/57 | 13 | 2 | Smoke Dreams | $50 | Era 20002 |

As Children Do / I Concentrate On You / I Had The Craziest Dream / I Kiss Your Hand, Madame / I'll Close My Eyes / It's Easy To Remember / Love Is Here To Stay / Say It Isn't So / Smoke Dreams / So In Love / Soft Lights And Sweet Music (And Smoke Dreams Theme) / Something To Remember You By / Wonderful One

DeBARGE '85
R&B family group from Grand Rapids, Michigan: **El DeBarge** (keyboards) with brothers Mark (trumpet, saxophone), James (keyboards), Randy (bass) and sister **Bunny DeBarge** (vocals). Their brothers Bobby and Tommy were in **Switch**; brother **Chico DeBarge** also recorded. James was briefly married to **Janet Jackson** in 1984.

9/11/82+	24	48	●©	1 All This Love	$10	Gordy 6012
10/22/83+	36	40	●©	2 In A Special Way	$10	Gordy 6061
3/23/85	19	48	●©	3 Rhythm Of The Night	$10	Gordy 6123

All This Love (1) *17* / Baby, Won't Cha Come Quick (2) / Be My Lady (2) / Can't Stop (1) / Dream, A (2) / Give It Up (3) / **Heart Is Not So Smart** (3) *75* / I Give Up On You (2) / **I Like It** (1) *31* / I'll Never Fall In Love Again (1) / I'm In Love With You (1) / It's Getting Stronger (1) / Life Begins With You (1) / **Love Me In A Special Way** (2) *45* / Need Somebody (2) / Prime Time (3) / Queen Of My Heart (2) / **Rhythm Of The Night** (3) *3* / Share My World (3) / Single Heart (3) / Stay With Me (2) / Stop! Don't Tease Me (1) / **Time Will Reveal** (2) *18* / Walls (Came Tumbling Down) (3) / **Who's Holding Donna Now** (3) *6* / **You Wear It Well** (3) *46*

DeBARGE, Bunny '87
Born on 3/15/55 in Grand Rapids, Michigan. Member of **DeBarge**.

| 3/14/87 | 172 | 5 | In Love | $10 | Motown 6217 |

Dance All Night / Fine Line / I Still Believe / Let's Spend The Night / Life Saver / Never Let Die / Save The Best For Me / So Good For You / Woman In Love

DeBARGE, Chico '99
Born Jonathan DeBarge in 1966 in Grand Rapids, Michigan. DeBarge sibling, but not a member of the group **DeBarge**.

11/15/86+	90	30	1 Chico DeBarge	$10	Motown 6214
12/6/97	86	38	●©	2 Long Time No See	$10	Kedar 53088
11/13/99	41	7	©	3 The Game	$10	Motown 153263

Cross That Line (1) / Desperate (1) / Edge, The (3) / Everybody Knew But Me (3) / Game, The (3) / Girl Next Door (1) / **Give You Want You Want (Fa Sure)** (3) *71* / Heart, Mind & Soul (3) / I Like My Body (1) / I'll Love You For Now (1) / If It Takes All Night (1) / Iggin' Me (2) / Listen To Your Man (3) / Long Time No See (2) / Love Jones (2) / Love Still Good (2) / Ms. Wonderful (2) / No Guarantee (2) / One Love (2) / Physical Train (2) / Sexual (3) / Sorry (3) / Superman (2) / Talk About You (3) / **Talk To Me** (1) *21* / Till Tomorrow (1) / Trouble Man (2) / Virgin (2) / Was It Good (2) / When Can I See You Again (3) / Who Are You Kidding (1) / You Can Make It Better (1) / You're Much Too Fast (1) / Your Way (3)

DeBARGE, El '86
Born Eldra DeBarge on 6/4/61 in Grand Rapids, Michigan. Lead singer of **DeBarge**.

| 6/21/86 | 24 | 23 | ●© | 1 El DeBarge | $10 | Gordy 6181 |
| 6/18/94 | 137 | 7 | © | 2 Heart, Mind & Soul | $10 | Reprise 45375 |

Can't Get Enough (2) / Don't Say It's Over (1) / Heart, Mind & Soul (2) / I Wanna Hear It From My Heart (1) / I'll Be There (2) / It's Got To Be Real (2) / Lost Without Her Love (1) / **Love Always** (1) *43* / Private Line (2) / Secrets Of The Night (1) / Slide (2) / **Someone** (1) *70* / Special Lady (2) / Starlight, Moonlight, Candlelight (2) / Thrill Of The Chase (1) / When Love Has Gone Away (1) / Where Is My Love? (2) / Where You Are (2) / **Who's Johnny** (1) *3* / You Are My Dream (1) / You Got The Love I Want (2)

DeBURGH, Chris '87
Born Christopher Davidson on 10/15/48 of Irish parentage in Buenos Aires, Argentina. Pop-rock singer. DeBurgh was his mother's maiden name.

4/9/83	43	22	©	1 The Getaway	$10	A&M 4929
6/30/84	69	19	©	2 Man On The Line	$10	A&M 5002
9/20/86+	25	32	●©	3 Into The Light	$10	A&M 5121

All The Love I Have Inside (1) / Ballroom Of Romance (3) / Borderline (1) / Crying And Laughing (1) / **Don't Pay The Ferryman** (1) *34* / Ecstasy Of Flight (I Love The Night) (2) / Fatal Hesitation (3) / Fire On The Water (3) / For Rosanna (3) / Getaway, The (1) / Head And The Heart (2) / **High On Emotion** (2) *44* / I'm Counting On You (1) / **Lady In Red** (3) *3* / Last Night (3) / Leader, The (3) / Liberty (3) / Light A Fire (1) / Living On The Island (1) / Man On The Line (1) / Moonlight And Vodka (2) / Much More Than This (2) / One Word (Straight To The Heart) (3) / Revolution, The (1) / Say Goodbye To It All (3) / **Ship To Shore** (1) *71* / Sight And Touch (2) / Sound Of A Gun (2) / Spirit Of Man (3) / Taking It To The Top (2) / Transmission Ends (2) / Vision, The (3) / What About Me? (3) / Where Peaceful Waters Flow (1)

DeCARO, Nick '69
Prolific record producer.

| 4/19/69 | 165 | 5 | Happy Heart | [I] $15 | A&M 4176 |

Amy's Theme / Caroline, No / Happy Heart / Hey Jude / I'll Forget You (Chall-Ha-Dichal) / I'm Gonna Make You Love Me / *If I Only Had Time 95* / Love Is All / Lullaby From Rosemary's Baby / Ob-La-Di, Ob-La-Da / Quiet Sunday

DEE, Dave — see DAVE DEE

DEE, Joey, & the Starliters   '62

Born Joseph DiNicola on 6/11/40 in Passaic, New Jersey. High school classmate of **The Shirelles**. In September 1960, Joey & the Starliters became the house band at the Peppermint Lounge, New York City. Actor Joe Pesci played guitar with band briefly in 1961. After 1964, group included three members who later formed **The Young Rascals**, plus guitarist **Jimi Hendrix**. In the movies *Hey, Let's Twist* and *Two Tickets To Paris*.

| 12/11/61+ | 2[6] | 40 | © | 1 | **Doin' The Twist At The Peppermint Lounge** | | [L] | $50 | Roulette 25166 |
| 2/17/62 | 18 | 23 | | 2 | **Hey, Let's Twist!** | | [S] | $50 | Roulette 25168 |

includes "I Wanna Twist" and "Na Voce, 'Na Chitarra E 'O Poco 'E Luna" by Kay Armen; "It's A Pity To Say Goodnight" and "Mother Goose" by Teddy Randazzo; "Let Me Do My Twist" by Jo-Ann Campbell

| 6/30/62 | 97 | 7 | © | 3 | **Back At The Peppermint Lounge-Twistin'** | | [L] | $50 | Roulette 25173 |

Blue Twister (2)
C C Rider (3)
Fanny Mae (1)
Have You Ever Had The Blues (3)
Hello Josephine (3)

Hey, Let's Twist (2) *20*
Hold It (1)
Honky Tonk (1)
Joey's Blues (3)
Kansas City (3)
Keelee's Twist (2)

Mashed Potatoes (1)
Money (3)
Peppermint Twist - Part I (1,2) *1*
Peppermint Twist - Part II (1)
Rain Drops (3)

Ram-Bunk-Shush (1)
Roly Poly (2) *74*
Shout (2)
Shout - Part I (1) *6*
Slippin' And Slidin' (1)
Sticks And Stones (1)

Talkin' 'Bout You (3)
Will You Love Me Tomorrow (3)
Ya Ya (1)
You Must Have Been A Beautiful Baby (3)

DEE, Kiki   '74

Born Pauline Matthews on 3/6/47 in Yorkshire, England. Female pop singer.

11/16/74	28	18			1 **I've Got The Music In Me**			$15	Rocket 458
					THE KIKI DEE BAND				
5/14/77	159	5			2 **Kiki Dee**			$15	Rocket 2257

Bad Day Child (2)
Chicago (2)
Do It Right (1)

First Thing In The Morning, Last Thing At Night (2)
Heart And Soul (1)
How Much Fun (1)

I've Got The Music In Me (1) *12*
In Return (2)
Into Eternity (1)

Keep Right On (2)
Little Frozen One (1)
Night Hours (2)
Out Of My Head (1)

Someone To Me (1)
Standing Room Only (2)
Step By Step (1)
Sweet Creation (2)

Walking (2)
Water (1)
You Need Help (1)

DEE, Lenny   '55

Born Leonard DeStoppelaire on 1/5/23 in Chicago. Male organist.

7/9/55	11	6			1 **Dee-lightful!**		[I]	$25	Decca 8114
6/8/68	196	3			2 **Gentle On My Mind**		[I]	$15	Decca 74994
3/8/69	199	2			3 **Turn Around, Look At Me**		[I]	$15	Decca 75073
1/3/70	189	3			4 **Spinning Wheel**		[I]	$15	Decca 75152

Apologize (3)
Ballin' The Jack (1)
Birth Of The Blues (1)
By The Time I Get To Phoenix (2)
Can't Take My Eyes Off You (2)
Day In The Life Of A Fool (4)
Donkey Serenade (1)
Dream A Little Dream Of Me (3)

Exactly Like You (1)
Folsom Prison Blues (3)
Gentle On My Mind (2)
Glory Of Love (1)
Hang 'Em High (3)
Happy Barefoot Boy (2)
Hurt So Bad (4)
Jean (2)
Last Waltz (3)
Laura (1)

Little Brown Jug (1)
Love Is Blue (2)
Man Without Love (3)
Odd Couple (3)
Odds And Ends (Of A Beautiful Love Affair) (2)
Quentin's Theme (4)
Remember When (We Made These Memories) (2)

Romeo And Juliet, Love Theme From (4)
Rossana Theme (2)
Ruby Don't Take Your Love To Town (4)
September Song (1)
Siboney (1)
Spinning Wheel (4)
Sunny (2)
Sunshine (3)

Sweet Caroline (Good Times Never Seemed So Good) (4)
Sweet Georgia Brown (1)
Sweet Mouth (3)
True Grit (4)
Turn Around, Look At Me (3)
What Now My Love (Et Maintenant) (2)
Where The Rainbow Ends (3)
With Pen In Hand (3)

World Is Waiting For The Sunrise (1)
Yes Sir, That's My Baby (1)
Yesterday, When I Was Young (4)

DEEE-LITE   '90

Dance trio formed in New York City: Super DJ Dmitry Brill (from Kiev, Soviet Union), Jungle DJ Towa "Towa" Tei (from Tokyo, Japan) and vocalist Lady Miss Kier (Kier Kirby from Youngstown, Ohio). Group's name inspired by the tune "It's De-lovely" from the 1936 Cole Porter musical *Red, Hot & Blue*. Brill and Kier are married. Tei left by 1994, replaced by Ani.

9/15/90	20	41	●	©	1 **World Clique**			$10	Elektra 60957
7/11/92	67	8		©	2 **Infinity Within**			$10	Elektra 61313
8/20/94	127	4		©	3 **Dewdrops In The Garden**			$10	Elektra 61526

Apple Juice Kissing (3)
Bittersweet Loving (3)
Bring Me Your Love (3)
Build The Bridge (1)
Call Me (3)
Come On In, The Dreams Are Fine (2)
DMT (Dance Music Trance) (3)

Deee-Lite Theme (1)
Deep Ending (3)
E.S.P. (1)
Electric Shock (2)
Fuddy Duddy Judge (2)
Good Beat (1)
Groove Is In The Heart (1) *4*
Heart Be Still (2)

I Had A Dream I Was Falling Through A Hole In The Ozone Layer (2)
I Won't Give Up (2)
I.F.O. (Identified Flying Object) (2)
Love Is Everything (2)
Mind Melt [poem] (3)

Music Selector Is The Soul Reflector (3)
Party Happening People (3)
Picnic In The Summertime (3)
Power Of Love (1) *47*
Pussycat Meow (2)
River Of Freedom (3)
Rubber Lover (2)
Runaway (2)

Sampladelic (3)
Say Ahhh... (3)
Smile On (1)
Somebody (3)
Stay In Bed, Forget The Rest (3)
Thank You Everyday (2)
Try Me On ... I'm Very You (1)
Two Clouds Above Nine (2)

Vote, Baby, Vote (2)
What Is Love? (1)
What Is This Music? [poem] (3)
When You Told Me You Loved Me (3)
Who Was That? (1)
World Clique (1)

DEELE, The   '88

R&B group from Cincinnati: Darnell Bristol and Carlos Greene (vocals), Stanley Burke, Kenneth "**Babyface**" Edmonds, Mark "L.A. Reid" Rooney and Kevin Roberson. Babyface and L.A. Reid later formed LaFace Records.

2/4/84	78	19		©	1 **Street Beat**			$10	Solar 60285
7/6/85	155	8			2 **Material Thangz**			$10	Solar 60410
2/27/88	54	25	●	©	3 **Eyes Of A Stranger**			$10	Solar 72555

Body Talk (1) *77*
Can-U-Dance (3)
Crazy 'Bout 'Cha (1)
Eyes Of A Stranger (3)

Hip Chic (3)
I Surrender (1)
I'll Send You Roses (2)
Just My Luck (1)

Let No One Separate Us (3)
Let's Work Tonight (2)
Material Thangz (2)
Sexy Love (1)

She Wanted (3)
Shoot 'Em Up Movies (3)
So Many Thangz (3)
Stimulate (2)

Street Beat (1)
Suspicious (2)
Sweet Nothingz (2)
Sweet November (2)

Two Occasions (3) *10*
Video Villain (2)
Working (9 To 5) (1)
You're All I've Ever Known (2)

DEEP BLUE SOMETHING   '96

Pop-rock group from Dallas: brothers Todd (vocals, bass) and Toby (guitar) Pipes, Kirk Tatom (guitar) and John Kirtland (drums).

| 9/9/95+ | 46 | 35 | ● | © | **Home** | | | $10 | RainMaker 92608 |

Breakfast At Tiffany's *5*
Done

Gammer Gerten's Needle
Halo

Home
I Can Wait

Josey
Kandinsky Prince

Red Light
Song To Make Love To

Water Prayer
Wouldn't Change A Thing

DEEP FOREST   '94

French keyboardist Michel Sanchez and Brussels-based producer Dan Lacksman.

8/21/93+	59	25	●	©	1 **Deep Forest**		[F]	$10	550 Music 57840
7/8/95	62	12		©	2 **Boheme**		[F]	$10	550 Music 67115
3/7/98	127	5		©	3 **Comparsa**		[F]	$10	550 Music 68726

Anasthasia (2)
Boheme (2)
Bohemian Ballet (2)
Bulgarian Melody (2)
Cafe Europa (2)
Comparsa (3)

Deep Folk Song (2)
Deep Forest (1)
Deep Weather (3)
Desert Walk (1)
Earthquake (3)
Ekue Ekue (3)

First Twilight (1)
Forest Hymn (1)
Forest Power (3)
Freedom Cry (2)
Gathering (1)
Green And Blue (3)

Hunting (1)
Katharina (2)
La Lune Se Bat Avec Les Étoiles (3)
Lament (2)
Madazulu (3)

Marta's Song (2)
Media Luna (3)
Night Bird (1)
Noonday Sun (3)
Radio Belize (1)
Savana Dance (1)

Second Twilight (1)
1716 (3)
Sweet Lullaby (1) *78*
Tres Marias (3)
Twosome (2)
White Whisper (1)

DEEP PURPLE ★151★   '73

Hard-rock group from England: Rod Evans (vocals), **Ritchie Blackmore** (guitar), Jon Lord (keyboards), Nicky Simper (bass) and Ian Paice (drums). Evans and Simper left in 1969, replaced by Ian Gillan (vocals) and **Roger Glover** (bass). Evans formed **Captain Beyond**. Gillan and Glover left in late 1973, replaced by **David Coverdale** (vocals) and Glenn Hughes (bass). Blackmore left in early 1975 to form **Rainbow** (which Glover later joined); replaced by American **Tommy Bolin** (ex-**James Gang** guitarist; d: 12/4/76). Band split in July 1976. Coverdale formed **Whitesnake**. Blackmore, Lord, Paice, Gillan and Glover reunited in 1984. Hughes joined **Black Sabbath** as vocalist in 1986. Gillan (who was with Black Sabbath for 1983 *Born Again* album) left in 1989 to form Garth Rockett & The Moonshiners; replaced by **Joe Lynn Turner** (ex-Rainbow), then returned in 1992 to take Turner's place.

1)Made In Japan 2)Machine Head 3)Burn 4)Who Do We Think We Are! 5)Perfect Strangers

9/7/68	24	23	©	1	Shades Of Deep Purple		$30	Tetragrammaton 102
1/11/69	54	14	©	2	The Book Of Taliesyn		$30	Tetragrammaton 107
7/12/69	162	6	©	3	Deep Purple		$30	Tetragrammaton 119
5/16/70	149	8		4	Deep Purple/The Royal Philharmonic Ork. "Concerto For Group And Orchestra" recorded at the Royal Albert Hall	[L]	$20	Warner 1860
9/12/70	143	21	● ©	5	Deep Purple In Rock		$20	Warner 1877
8/21/71	32	18	● ©	6	Fireball		$20	Warner 2564
4/15/72+	7	118	▲² ©	7	Machine Head		$20	Warner 2607
10/21/72	57	20		8	(Purple Passages)	[K]	$25	Warner 2644 [2]
1/20/73	15	49	● ©	9	Who Do We Think We Are!		$20	Warner 2678
4/21/73	6	52	▲ ©	10	Made In Japan recorded on 8/17/72 in Tokyo	[L]	$25	Warner 2701 [2]
3/2/74	9	30	● ©	11	Burn		$20	Warner 2766
12/7/74	20	15	● ©	12	Stormbringer		$20	Warner 2832
12/6/75+	43	14	©	13	Come Taste The Band		$15	Warner 2895
11/27/76	148	6	©	14	Made In Europe	[L]	$15	Warner 2995
11/1/80	148	4	▲ ©	15	Deepest Purple/The Very Best Of Deep Purple	[G]	$15	Warner 3486
12/1/84+	17	32	▲ ©	16	Perfect Strangers		$12	Mercury 824003
1/31/87	34	22	©	17	The House Of Blue Light		$12	Mercury 831318
7/23/88	105	9	©	18	Nobody's Perfect	[L]	$15	Mercury 835897 [2]
11/10/90	87	19	©	19	Slaves And Masters		$10	RCA 2421
8/21/93	192	1		20	The Battle Rages On...		$10	Giant 24517

"A" 200 (11)
And The Address (1,8)
Anthem (2)
Anya (20)
Anyone's Daughter (6)
April (3,8)
Bad Attitude (17,18)
Bird Has Flown (3,8)
Black & White (17)
Black Night (15,18) *66*
Blind
Blistering Hot (5)
Bloodsucker (5)
Breakfast In Bed (19)
Burn (11,14,15)
Call Of The Wild (17)
Chasing Shadows (3,8)
Child In Time (5,10,15,18)
Comin' Home (13)
Concerto For Group And Orchestra (Movements I-III) (4)

Cut Runs Deep (19)
Dead Or Alive (17)
Dealer (13)
Demon's Eye (15)
Drifter (13)
Emmeretta (8)
Exposition (medley) (2)
Faultline (medley) (3)
Fire In The Basement (19)
Fireball (8,15)
Flight Of The Rat (5)
Fools (6)
Fortuneteller (19)
Gettin' Tighter (13)
Gypsy, The (12)
Gypsy's Kiss (16)
Happiness (medley) (1)
Hard Lovin' Man (5)
Hard Lovin' Woman (17,18)
Hard Road (2,8)
Help (5)
Hey Joe (1,8)
High Ball Shooter (12)

Highway Star (7,10,15,18)
Hold On (12)
Holy Man (12)
Hungry Daze (16)
Hush (1,8,18) *4*
I Need Love (13)
I'm So Glad (medley) (1)
Into The Fire (5)
King Of Dreams (19)
Kentucky Woman (2,8) *38*
Knocking At Your Back Door (16,18) *61*
Lady Double Dealer (12,14)
Lady Luck (13)
Lalena (3)
Lay Down, Stay Down (11)
Lazy (7,10,18)
Lick It Up (20)
Listen, Learn, Read On (2)
Living Wreck (5)
Love Child (3)
Love Conquers All (19)
Love Don't Mean A Thing (12)

Love Help Me (1)
Mad Dog (17)
Mandrake Root (1,8)
Mary Long (9)
Maybe I'm A Leo (7)
Mean Streak (16)
Might Just Take Your Life (11) *91*
Mistreated (11,14)
Mitzi Dupree (17)
Mule, The (6,10)
Nasty Piece Of Work (20)
Never Before (7)
No No No (6)
No One Came (6)
Nobody's Home (16)
One Man's Meat (20)
One More Rainy Day (1)
Our Lady (9)
Owed To G (medley) (13)
Painter, The (medley) (3)
Pictures Of Home (7)

Place In Line (19)
Ramshackle Man (20)
Rat Bat Blue (9)
River Deep-Mountain High (2) *53*
Sail Away (11)
Shield, The (2,8)
Smoke On The Water (7,10,15,18) *4*
Smooth Dancer (9)
Soldier Of Fortune (12)
Solitaire (20)
Space Truckin' (7,10,15,18)
Spanish Archer (17)
Speed King (5,15)
Stormbringer (12,14,15)
Strange Kind Of Woman (6,10,15,18)
Strangeways (17)
Super Trouper (9)
Talk About Love (20)
This Time Around (medley) (13)
Time To Kill (20)

Too Much Is Not Enough (19)
Truth Hurts (19)
Twist In The Tale (20)
Under The Gun (16)
Unwritten Law (17)
Wasted Sunsets (16)
We Can Work It Out (medley) (2)
What's Goin' On Here (11)
Why Didn't Rosemary? (3,8)
Wicked Ways (19)
Woman From Tokyo (9,15,18) *60*
You Can't Do It Right (With The One You Love!) (12)
You Fool No One (11,14)
You Keep On Moving (13)

DEES, Rick, And His Cast Of Idiots   '77

Born Rigdon Dees on 3/14/50 in Jacksonville, Florida. One of America's top radio DJs.

3/5/77	157	5		The Original Disco Duck	[N]	$12	RSO 3017

Bad Shark
Barely White (That'll Get It Baby)

Bionic Feet
Dis-Gorilla (Part 1) *56*
Disco Duck (Part 1) *1*

Disco Duck (Part II)
Doctor Disco
Flick The Bick

He Ate Too Many Jelly Donuts
Peanut Prance

DEF LEPPARD ★154★   '88

Hard-rock group from Sheffield, England: Joe Elliott (vocals), Steve Clark and Pete Willis (guitars), Rick Savage (bass) and Rick Allen (drums). Phil Collen replaced Willis in late 1982. Allen lost his left arm in a car crash on 12/31/84. Clark died of alcohol-related respiratory failure on 1/8/91 (age 30). Guitarist Vivian Campbell (**Whitesnake**, **Dio**, Riverdogs, Shadow King) joined in April 1992.

1)Hysteria 2)Adrenalize 3)Pyromania

5/3/80	51	51	▲ ©	1	On Through The Night		$12	Mercury 3828
8/8/81	38	106	▲² ©	2	High 'n' Dry also see #4 below		$12	Mercury 4021
2/5/83	2²	116	▲⁹ ©	3	Pyromania	C:#24/11	$10	Mercury 810308
6/2/84	72	18		4	High 'n' Dry added remixed version of "Bringin' On The Heartbreak" plus "Me & My Wine" (previously unavailable)	[R]	$10	Mercury 818836
8/22/87+	❶⁶	133	▲¹² ©	5	Hysteria	C:#2¹/129	$10	Mercury 830675
4/18/92	❶⁵	65	▲³ ©	6	Adrenalize		$10	Mercury 512185
10/23/93	9	26	▲ ©	7	Retro Active compilation of previously unreleased songs and alternate versions	[K]	$10	Mercury 518305

DEF LEPPARD — Cont'd

11/18/95	15	66	▲³	© 8	**Vault: Greatest Hits 1980-1995** ....C:❶³/183 [G]	$10	Mercury 528815
6/1/96	14	12	●	© 9	**Slang**	$10	Mercury 532486
6/26/99	11	16	●	© 10	**Euphoria**	$10	Mercury 546212

Action (7)
Action! Not Words (3)
All I Want Is Everything (9)
All Night (10)
Animal (5,8) *19*
Another Hit And Run (2,4)
Answer To The Master (1)
Armageddon It (5,8) *3*
Back In Your Face (10)
Billy's Got A Gun (3)
Blood Runs Cold (9)
Breathe A Sigh (9)
Bringin' On The Heartbreak (2,4,8) *61*
Comin' Under Fire (3)
Day After Day (10)

Deliver Me (9)
Demolition Man (10)
Desert Song (7)
Die Hard The Hunter (3)
Disintegrate (10)
Don't Shoot Shotgun (5)
Excitable (5)
Foolin' (3,8) *28*
Fractured Love (7)
From The Inside (7)
Gift Of Flesh (9)
Gods Of War (5)
Goodbye (10)
Guilty (10)
Have You Ever Needed Someone So Bad (6,8) *12*
Heaven Is (9)

Hello America (1)
High 'N' Dry (Saturday Night) (2,4)
Hysteria (5,8) *10*
I Wanna Be Your Hero (7)
I Wanna Touch U (6)
It Could Be You (1)
It Don't Matter (1)
It's Only Love (10)
Kings Of Oblivion (10)
Lady Strange (2,4)
Let It Go (2,4)
Let's Get Rocked (6,8) *15*
Love And Affection (5)
Love Bites (5,8) *1*
Make Love Like A Man (6) *36*
Me & My Wine (4)

Mirror, Mirror (Look Into My Eyes) (2,4)
Miss You In A Heartbeat (7,8) *39*
No No No (2,4)
On Through The Night (2,4)
Only After Dark (7)
Overture (1)
Paper Sun (10)
Pearl Of Euphoria (9)
Personal Property (6)
Photograph (3,8) *12*
Pour Some Sugar On Me (5,8) *2*
Promises (10)
Ride Into The Sun (7)
Ring Of Fire (7)

Rock Brigade (1)
Rock Of Ages (3,8) *16*
Rock! Rock! (Till You Drop) (9)
Rocket (5,8) *12*
Rocks Off (1)
Run Riot (5)
Satellite (10)
She's Too Tough (7)
Slang (9)
Sorrow Is A Woman (1)
Stagefright (3)
Stand Up (Kick Love Into Motion) (6) *34*
Switch 625 (2,4)
Tear It Down (6)
To Be Alive (10)
Tonight (6) *62*

Too Late For Love (3)
Truth? (9)
Turn To Dust (9)
21st Century Sha La La La Girl (10)
Two Steps Behind (7,8) *12*
Wasted (1)
When Love & Hate Collide (8) *58*
When The Walls Came Tumbling Down (1)
Where Does Love Go When It Dies (9)
White Lightning (6)
Women (5) *80*
Work It Out (9)
You Got Me Runnin' (2,4)

DeFRANCO FAMILY Featuring Tony DeFranco '73

Family vocal group from Port Colborne, Ontario, Canada: Tony, Merlina, Nino, Marisa and Benny DeFranco.

| 10/13/73 | 109 | 16 | © 1 | **Heartbeat, It's A Lovebeat** .... | $12 | 20th Century 422 |
| 6/29/74 | 163 | 7 | © 2 | **Save The Last Dance For Me** .... | $12 | 20th Century 442 |

Abra-Ca-Dabra (1) *32*
Baby Blue (2)
Because We Both Are Young (2)

Come A Little Closer (2)
Gorilla (1)
Heartbeat - It's A Lovebeat (1) *3*

Hold Me (2)
I Guess You Already Knew (2)
I Love Everything You Do (1)
I Wanted To Tell You (1)

I'm With You (1)
Love Is Bigger Than Baseball (1)
Love The Way You Do (2)

Maybe It's You (2)
Only One (2)
Poor Boy (2)
Same Kind A' Love (1)

Save The Last Dance For Me (2) *18*
Sweet Sweet Loretta (1)
Write Me A Letter (2)

DEF SQUAD '98

All-star rap trio: **Keith Murray**, **Redman** and **Erick Sermon**.

| 7/18/98 | 2¹ | 11 | © | **El Niño** | $10 | Def Jam 558343 |

Can U Dig It?
Check N' Me Out

Countdown
Def Squad Delite

Full Cooperation
Game (Freestyle)

No Guest List
Rhymin' Wit' Biz

Ride Wit' Us
Say Word!

Ya'll Niggas Ain't Ready
You Do, I Do

DEFTONES '00

Rock group from Sacramento, California: Chino Moreno (vocals), Stephen Carpenter (guitar), Chi Cheng (bass) and Abe Cunningham (drums).

11/15/97	29	17	●	© 1	**Around The Fur**	$10	Maverick 46810
7/8/00	3	38	●	© 2	**White Pony**	$10	Maverick 47667
11/11/00	46ᶜ	1	●	© 3	**Adrenaline** .... [E]	$10	Maverick 46054

released in 1995

Around The Fur (1)
Be Quiet And Drive (Far Away) (1)
Birthmark (3)
Bored (3)

Change (In The House Of Flies) (2)
Dai The Flu (1)
Digital Bath (2)
Elite (2)
Engine No. 9 (3)

Feiticeira (2)
Fireal (3)
Headup (1)
Knife Prty (2)
Korea (2)
Lhabia (1)

Lifter (3)
Lotion (1)
Mascara (1)
Minus Blindfold (3)
Mx (1)
My Own Summer (Shove It) (1)

Nosebleed (3)
One Weak (3)
Passenger (2)
Pink Maggit (2)
RX Queen (2)
Rickets (1)

Root (3)
7 Words (3)
Street Carp (2)
Teenager (2)

DÉJA '88

R&B vocal duo from Dayton, Ohio. Both were members of **Slave** and **Aurra**.

| 12/5/87+ | 186 | 6 | | **Serious** .... | $10 | Virgin 90601 |

Heart Beat
Life

Premonition
Serious

Some Things Turn Around
Straight To The Point

Summer Love
That's Where You'll Find Me

What To Do Now
You And Me Tonight *54*

DEKKER, Desmond, & The Aces '69

Born Desmond Dacris on 7/16/41 in Kingston, Jamaica. Reggae singer.

| 9/6/69 | 153 | 3 | | **Israelites** .... | $30 | Uni 73059 |

For Once In My Life
Intensified

Israelites *9*
It Is Not Easy

It Mek
Nincompoop

Problems
Rude Boy Train

Tip Of My Finger
Too Much Too Soon

DE LA HOYA, Oscar '00

Born on 2/4/73 in Montebello, California. Professional boxer.

| 10/28/00 | 121 | 5 | © | **Oscar De La Hoya** .... [F] | $10 | EMI Latin 21967 |

Amándondos
Estar Sin Ti

Mi Amor
Nunca Imaginé

Para Amarte
Para Qué

Prométeme
Run To Me

Te Amo
Tú Me Completas

Ven A Mi (Run To Me)
With These Hands

DEL AMITRI '90

Pop-rock group from Glasgow, Scotland: Justin Currie (vocals, bass), David Cummings and Iain Harvie (guitars), and Brian McDermott (drums). Cummings and McDermott left in 1996; replaced by Andy Alston, Ashley Sloan and Jon McLaughlin.

4/7/90	95	19	© 1	**Waking Hours**	$10	A&M 5287
9/26/92	178	3	© 2	**Change Everything**	$10	A&M 5385
8/26/95	170	8	© 3	**Twisted**	$10	A&M 540311
7/12/97	160	1	© 4	**Some Other Sucker's Parade**	$10	A&M 540705

Always The Last To Know (2) *30*
As Soon As The Tide Comes In (2)
Be My Downfall (2)
Behind The Fool (2)
Being Somebody Else (3)
Crashing Down (3)
Cruel Light Of Day (4)
Driving With The Brakes On (3)
Empty (1)

First Rule Of Love (2)
Food For Songs (4)
Funny Way To Win (4)
Hatful Of Rain (4)
Here And Now (3)
High Times (4)
I Won't Take The Blame (4)
It Might As Well Be You (3)
It's Never Too Late To Be Alone (3)
Just Like A Man (2)

Kiss This Thing Goodbye (1) *35*
Life Is Full (4)
Lucky Guy (4)
Make It Always Be Too Late (4)
Medicine (4)
Mother Nature's Writing (4)
Move Away Jimmy Blue (1)
Never Enough (3)
No Family Man (4)
Not Where It's At (4)

Nothing Ever Happens (1)
One Thing Left To Do (3)
Ones That You Love Lead You Nowhere (2)
Opposite View (1)
Roll To Me (3) *10*
Some Other Sucker's Parade (4)
Sometimes I Just Have To Say Your Name (2)
Start With Me (3)

Stone Cold Sober (1)
Surface Of The Moon (2)
Tell Her This (3)
This Side Of The Morning (1)
Through All That Nothing (4)
To Last A Lifetime (2)
What I Think She Sees (4)
When I Want You (1)
When You Were Young (2)
Won't Make It Better (4)
You're Gone (1)

DELANEY & BONNIE '70

Vocal duo: Delaney Bramlett (born on 7/1/39 in Pontotoc County, Mississippi) and wife Bonnie Lynn Bramlett (born on 11/8/44 in Acton, Illinois). Married in 1967. Backing artists (Friends) included, at various times, **Leon Russell**, **Rita Coolidge**, **Dave Mason**, **Eric Clapton**, **Duane Allman** (**Allman Brothers Band**) and many others. Friends **Bobby Whitlock**, Carl Radle and Jim Gordon later became Eric Clapton's Dominos. Delaney & Bonnie dissolved their marriage and group in 1972. Their daughter Bekka was the lead singer of **Mick Fleetwood**'s Zoo, then joined **Fleetwood Mac** in 1993. Also see **Eric Clapton**.

7/26/69	175	3			1 Accept No Substitute - The Original Delaney & Bonnie & Friends			$30	Elektra 74039
4/18/70	29	17		©	2 Delaney & Bonnie & Friends On Tour with Eric Clapton		[L]	$25	Atco 326
10/10/70	58	10			3 To Bonnie From Delaney			$25	Atco 341
4/3/71	65	23			4 Motel Shot			$25	Atco 358
4/15/72	133	6			5 D&B Together			$20	Columbia 31377

Alone Together (3)
Big Change Comin' (5)
Come On In My Kitchen (3,4)
Comin' Home (2,5) *84*
Country Life (5)
Dirty Old Man (1)
Do Right Woman (1)
Don't Deceive Me (Please Don't Go) (4)
Faded Love (4)
Free The People (3) *75*

Get Ourselves Together (1)
Ghetto (1)
Gift Of Love (1)
God Knows I Love You (3)
Going Down The Road Feeling Bad (3,4)
Good Thing (I'm On Fire) (5)
Groupie (Superstar) (5)
Hard Luck And Troubles (3)
I Can't Take It Much Longer (1)

I Don't Want To Discuss It (2)
I Know How It Feels To Be Lonely (5)
I Know Something Good About You (5)
Lay Down My Burden (3)
Let Me Be Your Man (3)
Little Richard Medley (2)
Living On The Open Road (3)
Lonesome And A Long Way From Home (4)

Long Road Ahead (4)
Love Me A Little Bit Longer (1)
Love Of My Man (3)
Mama, He Treats Your Daughter Mean (medley) (2)
Miss Ann (3)
Move 'Em Out (5) *59*
Never Ending Song Of Love (4) *13*
Only You Know And I Know (2,5) *20*

Poor Elijah - Tribute To Johnson Medley (2)
Rock Of Ages (4)
Sing My Way Home (4)
Soldiers Of The Cross (1)
Someday (1)
Soul Shake (3) *43*
Sound Of The City (5)
Talkin' About Jesus (2)
That's What My Man Is For (2)

They Call It Rock & Roll Music (3)
Things Get Better (2)
Wade In The River Jordan (5)
Well, Well (5)
When The Battle Is Over (1)
Where The Soul Never Dies (4)
Where There's A Will There's A Way (2) *99*
Will The Circle Be Unbroken (4)

DE LA SOUL '00

Rap trio from Amityville, Long Island, New York: Kelvin Mercer, David Jolicoeur and Vincent Mason.

4/1/89	24	29	▲	©	1 3 Feet High And Rising			$10	Tommy Boy 1019
6/1/91	26	17	●	©	2 De La Soul Is Dead			$10	Tommy Boy 1029
10/9/93	40	7		©	3 Buhloone Mindstate			$10	Tommy Boy 1063
7/20/96	13	9		©	4 Stakes Is High			$10	Tommy Boy 1149
8/26/00	9	12		©	5 Art Official Intelligence: Mosaic Thump			$10	Tommy Boy 1361

Afro Connections At A Hi 5 (In The Eyes Of The Hoodlum) (2)
All Good? (5) *96*
Area (3)
Art Of Getting Jumped (5)
Baby Baby Baby Baby Ooh Baby (4)
Betta Listen (4)
Big Brother Beat (4)
Bitties In The BK Lounge (2)
Bizness, The (4)
Brakes (4)
Breakadawn (3) *76*
Buddy (1)
Can U Keep A Secret? (1)
Change In Speak (1)
Cool Breeze On The Rocks (1)
Copa (Cabanga) (5)

D.A.I.S.Y. Age (1)
De La Orgee (1)
Declaration (5)
Description (1)
Dinninit (4)
Do As De La Does (1)
Dog Eat Dog (4)
Down Syndrome (4)
Ego Trippin' [Part Two] (3)
En Focus (3)
Eye Know (1)
Eye Patch (3)
Fanatic Of The B Word (2)
Foolin' (5)
4 More (4)
Ghetto Thang (1)
I Am I Be (3)
I Be Blowin' (3)

I Can Do Anything (Delacratic) (1)
I.C. Y'all (5)
In The Woods (3)
Itzsoweezee (HOT) (4)
Jenifa Taught Me (Derwin's Revenge) (1)
Johnny's Dead AKA Vincent Mason (2)
Keepin' The Faith (2)
Kicked Out The House (2)
Let, Let Me In (2)
Little Bit Of Soap (1)
Long Island Degrees (4)
Long Island Wildin' (3)
Magic Number (1)
Me Myself And I (1) *34*
Millie Pulled A Pistol On Santa (2)

My Brother's A Basehead (2)
My Writes (5)
Not Over Till The Fat Lady Plays The Demo (2)
Oodles Of O's (2)
Oooh. (5)
Pass The Plugs (2)
Patti Dooke (3)
Pease Porridge (2)
Plug Tunin' (Last Chance To Comprehend) (1)
Pony Ride (4)
Potholes In My Lawn (1)
Rap De Rap Show (2)
Ring Ring Ring (Ha Ha Hey) (2)
Roller Skating Jam Named "Saturdays" (4)
Say No Go (1)
Set The Mood (5)

Shwingalokate (2)
Squat! (5)
Stakes Is High (4)
Stone Age (3)
Sunshine (4)
Supa Emcees (4)
Take It Off (1)
Talkin' Bout Hey Love (2)
This Is A Recording 4 Living In A Full Time Era (L.I.F.E.) (1)
3 Days Later (3)
Thru Ya City (5)
Transmitting Live From Mars (1)
Tread Water (1)
U Can Do (Life) (5)
U Don't Wanna B.D.S. (5)
View (1)
Who Do U Worship? (2)

With Me (5)
Wonce Again Long Island (4)
Words From The Chief Rocker (5)

DELEGATION '79

Disco trio based in England: Ricky Bailey and Ray Patterson (from Jamaica), with Bruce Dunbar (from Texas).

2/17/79	84	16			The Promise Of Love			$12	Shadybrook 010

Back Door Love
Let Me Take You To The Sun

Love Is Like A Fire
Mr. Heartbreak

Oh Honey *45*
Promise Of Love

Someone Oughta Write A Song
Soul Trippin'

Where Is The Love
You've Been Doing Me Wrong

DELFONICS, The '70

R&B vocal group from Philadelphia: brothers William and Wilbert Hart, Ritchie Daniels and Randy Cain. Daniels left for the service in 1968, group continued as a trio. Cain was replaced by **Major Harris** in 1971. Harris went solo in 1974.

6/8/68	100	6		©	1 La La Means I Love You			$80	Philly Groove 1150
3/8/69	155	6		©	2 Sound Of Sexy Soul			$80	Philly Groove 1151
11/29/69+	111	19			3 The Delfonics Super Hits		[G]	$50	Philly Groove 1152
8/15/70	61	18		©	4 The Delfonics			$50	Philly Groove 1153
6/24/72	123	11			5 Tell Me This Is A Dream			$50	Philly Groove 1154

Ain't That Peculiar (2)
Alfie (1)
Baby I Love You (4)
Baby I Miss You (5)
Break Your Promise (1,3) *35*
Can You Remember (1)
Delfonics' Theme (How Could You) (4,5)
Didn't I (Blow Your Mind This Time) (4) *10*

Down Is Up, Up Is Down (4)
Everytime I See My Baby (2)
Face It Girl, It's Over (2)
Funny Feeling (4) *94*
Going Out Of My Head (2)
Hey! Love (5) *52*
Hot Dog Baby (2)
Hurt So Bad (1)
I Gave To You (4)
I'm A Man (3)

I'm Sorry (1,3) *42*
La - La - Means I Love You (1,3) *4*
Let It Be Me (2,3)
Look Of Love (1)
Looking For A Girl (5)
Losing You (1)
Love You Till I Die (5)
Lover's Concerto (1)
Loving Her (2,3)

My New Love (2,3)
Over And Over (4) *58*
Ready Or Not Here I Come (Can't Hide From Love) (2,3) *35*
Round & Round (3)
Scarborough Fair (2)
Shadow Of Your Smile (1)
Somebody Loves You (2,3) *72*
Tell Me This Is A Dream (5) *86*

Think About Me (4)
Too Late (5)
Trying To Make A Fool Of Me (4) *40*
Walk Right Up To The Sun (5) *81*
When You Get Right Down To It (4) *53*
With These Hands (2,3)

You Got Yours And I'll Get Mine (2) *40*
You're Gone (1,3)

DEL FUEGOS, The '85

Rock group from Boston: Dan Zanes (vocals, guitar), Warren Zanes (guitar), Tom Lloyd (bass) and Woody Giessmann (drums). Warren Zanes and Giessmann left in 1988; replaced by Adam Roth and Joe Donnelly.

10/26/85	132	34		©	1 Boston, Mass.			$10	Slash 25339
4/18/87	167	6		©	2 Stand Up			$10	Slash 25540
10/28/89	139	22		©	3 Smoking In The Fields			$10	RCA 9860

Breakaway (3)
Coupe DeVille (1)
Don't Run Wild (1)
Down In Allen's Mills (3)
Dreams Of You (3)
Fade To Blue (1)

Friends Again (3)
Hand In Hand (3)
He Had A Lot To Drink Today (2)
Headlights (3)
Hold Us Down (1)

I Can't Take This Place (2)
I Still Want You (1) *87*
I'll Sleep With You (Cha Cha D'Amour) (1)
I'm Inside You (3)
It's Alright (1)

Long Slide (For An Out) (2)
Lost Weekend (3)
Move With Me Sister (3)
Name Names (2)
New Old World (2)
News From Nowhere (2)

Night On The Town (1)
No No Never (3)
Offer, The (3)
Part Of This Earth (3)
Scratching At Your Door (2)
Shame (1)

Sound Of Our Town (1)
Stand By You (3)
Town Called Love (2)
Wear It Like A Cape (2)

DELINQUENT HABITS '96

Rap trio from Los Angeles: Kemo, Ives and O.G. Style.

6/22/96	74	8	©	Delinquent Habits..................................		$10	Loud 66929

Another Fix · I'm Addicted · Lower Eastside · **Tres Delinquentes** *35* · What's Real Iz Real
Break 'Em Off · If You Want Some · Realm, The · Underground Connection · When The Stakes Are High
Good Times · Juvy · S.A.L.T. (Shit Ain't Like That) · What It Be Like

DELIRIOUS? '99

Christian rock group from Littlehampton, West Sussex, England: Martin Smith (vocals), Stuart Garrard (guitar), Tim Jupp (keyboards), Jon Thatcher (bass) and Stewart Smith (drums).

6/26/99	137	1	©	1	Mezzamorphis.................................	$10	Sparrow 51677
10/28/00	177	1	©	2	Glo..	$10	Sparrow 51739

Awaken The Dawn (2) · Everything (2) · Gravity (1) · It's OK (1) · Mezzanine Floor (1)
Beautiful Sun (1) · Follow (1) · Hang On To You (2) · Jesus' Blood (1,2) · My Glorious (2)
Blindfold (1) · GLO In The Dark (Pts 1-4) (2) · Heaven (1) · Kiss Your Feet (1) · See The Star (1)
Bliss (1) · God You Are My God (2) · Intimate Stranger (2) · Love Falls Down (1) · What Would I Have Done? (2)
Deeper 99 (1) · God's Romance (2) · Investigate (2) · Metamorphis (1) · Years Go By (2)

DELLS, The '68

R&B vocal group from Harvey, Illinois: Johnny Carter, Marvin Junior, Verne Allison, Mickey McGill and Chuck Barksdale. Carter was a member of The Flamingos.

1)There Is 2)Love Is Blue 3)Freedom Means

5/25/68	29	29	©	1	There Is	$50	Cadet 804
3/8/69	146	10		2	The Dells Musical Menu/Always Together...................	$50	Cadet 822
6/14/69	102	22		3	The Dells Greatest Hits................................[G]	$50	Cadet 824
8/23/69	54	24		4	Love Is Blue...	$50	Cadet 829
3/14/70	126	12		5	Like It Is, Like It Was................................	$50	Cadet 837
8/28/71	81	16		6	Freedom Means...	$30	Cadet 50004
6/24/72	162	5		7	The Dells Sing Dionne Warwicke's Greatest Hits........	$30	Cadet 50017
6/23/73	99	9		8	Give Your Baby A Standing Ovation.....................	$30	Cadet 50037
5/4/74	156	6	©	9	The Dells vs. The Dramatics...........................	$30	Cadet 60027
9/21/74	114	8		10	The Mighty Mighty Dells..............................	$30	Cadet 60030
9/23/78	169	3		11	New Beginnings.......................................	$15	ABC 1100
8/30/80	137	12	©	12	I Touched A Dream....................................	$12	20th Century 618

Agatha Van Thurgood (2) · Come Out, Come Out (5) · I Say A Little Prayer (7) · Love Is Missing From Our Lives (9) · One Less Bell To Answer (6) · Summer Place (4)
Ain't No Sunshine (8) · Darling Dear (5) · I Touched A Dream (12) · Love Is So Simple (1,3) · One Mint Julep (4) · Super Woman (11)
Alfie (7) · **Does Anybody Know I'm Here** (2,3) *38* · I Wanna Testify (11) · Love Story (medley) (6) · **Open Up My Heart** (5) *51* · Sweeter As The Days Go By (10)
All About The Paper (12) · Drowning For Your Love (11) · I Want My Momma (2) · **Love We Had (Stays On My Mind)** (6) *30* · Passionate Breezes (12) · That Special Someone (10)
All Your Goodies Are Gone (11) · Free And Easy (6) · **I Wish It Was Me You Loved** (9) *94* · Make It With You (6) · Playin' The Love Game (9) · This Guy's In Love With You (7)
Always Together (2,3) *18* · Freedom Means (6) · I'll Never Fall In Love Again (7) · Make Sure (You Have Someone Who Loves You) (2,3) · Please Don't Change Me Now (1,3) · Trains And Boats And Planes (7)
Be For Real With Me (10) · **Give Your Baby A Standing Ovation** (8) *34* · I'm In Love (9) · Melody Man (6) · Raindrops Keep Fallin' On My Head (7) · Tripped, Slipped, Stumbled And Fell (11)
Believe Me (2) · Glory Of Love (4,8) *92* · I'm Not Afraid Of Tomorrow (5) · My Life Is So Wonderful (When You're Around) (11) · Rather Be With You (6) · Walk On By (7)
Bonified Fool (10) · Good-Bye Mary Ann (2) · If You Go Away (medley) (6) · **Nadine** (5) *flip* · Run For Cover (1) · Way We Were (10)
Bring Back The Love Of Yesterday (10) *87* · Hallelujah Baby! (2) · If You Really Love Your Girl (Show Her) (10) · Nothing Can Stop Me (10) · Share (8) · **Wear It On Our Face** (1,3) *44*
By The Time I Get To Phoenix (medley) (4) · **Higher And Higher** (2,3) *92* · **It's All Up To You** (6) *94* · O-O, I Love You (1,3) *61* · Show Me (1) · When I'm In Your Arms (1)
Call Me (Right By Your Side I'll Be) (11) · Honey (4) · Just A Little Love (12) · Off Shore (5) · Since I Fell For You (5) · Whiter Shade Of Pale (4)
Change We Go Thru (For Love) (1,3) · **I Can Sing A Rainbow/Love Is Blue** (7) · Learning To Love You Was Easy (It's So Hard Trying To Get Over You) (10) · **Oh What A Day** (5) *43* · Since I've Been In Love (10) · Wichita Lineman (medley) (4)
Cherish (7) · **I Can't Do Enough** (2,3) *98* · Little Understanding (4) · **Oh, What A Night** (4) *10* · So You Are Love (12) · Wives And Lovers (7)
Close To You (7) · I Just Don't Know What To Do With Myself (7) · **Long Lonely Nights** (5) *74* · **On The Dock Of The Bay** (4) *42* · Soul Strollin' (8) · You Don't Care (8)
Close Your Eyes (1) · · Look At Us Now (12) · · Stand Up And Show The World (8) · Your Song (10)
Closer (8) · · Love Can Make It Easier (8) · · **Stay In My Corner** (1,3) *10* ·
· · · · Strung Out Over You (9) ·

DEL THA FUNKEE HOMOSAPIEN '00

Born Teren Jones in Oakland. Male rapper. Cousin of **Ice Cube**. Member of **Deltron 3030**.

12/11/93	125	1	©	1	No Need For Alarm..................................	$10	Elektra 61529
4/29/00	118	1	©	2	Both Sides Of The Brain............................	$10	Hiero Imperium 230103

DEL THE FUNKY HOMOSAPIEN

BM's (2) · Don't Forget (1) · Miles To Go (1) · Press Rewind (2) · Style Police (2) · You're In Shambles (1)
Boo Boo Heads (1) · Fake As F**k (2) · No More Worries (1) · Proto Culture (2) · Thank Youse (1)
Catch A Bad One (1) · Heats For The Kiddies (1) · No Need For Alarm (1) · Signature Slogans (2) · Time Is Too Expensive (2)
Catch All This (2) · If You Must (1) · Offspring (2) · Skull & Crossbones (2) · Wack M.C.'s (1)
Check It Ooout (1) · In And Out (1) · Pet Peeves (2) · Soopa Feen (2) · Worldwide (1)
Disastrous (2) · Jaw Gymnastics (2) · Phoney Phranchise (2) · Stay On Your Toes (2) · Wrongplace (1)

DELTRON 3030 '00

Hip-hop trio: **Del Tha Funkee Homosapien**, Dan Nakamura and Kid Koala.

11/4/00	194	1	©		Deltron 3030..	$10	75 Ark 75033

Assmann 640 Speaks · Madness · National Movie Review · St. Catherine St. · Turbulence
Battlesong · Mastermind · New Coke · State Of The Nation · Upgrade (A Brymar College Course)
Fantabulous Rap Extravaganza Part I & II · Meet Cleofis Randolph The Patriarch · News (A Wholly Owned Subsidiary Of Microsoft Inc.) · Things You Can Do · Virus
Love Story · Memory Loss · Positive Contact · 3030 ·
· · · Time Keeps On Slipping ·

DEMIAN, Max — see MAX DEMIAN

DENNIS, Cathy '91

Born on 3/25/69 in Norwich, Norfolk, England. Vocalist for producer Dancin' Danny D's **D-Mob**.

12/15/90+	67	40	©		Move To This...	$10	Polydor 847267

C'mon And Get My Love *10* · **Everybody Move** *90* · Move To This · Tell Me
shown only as D-Mob on single release · Got To Get Your Love · My Beating Heart · **Too Many Walls** *8*
· **Just Another Dream** *9* · Taste My Love · **Touch Me (All Night Long)** *2*

DENNY, Martin (The Exotic Sounds of)   '59

Born on 4/10/11 in New York City. Composer/arranger/pianist. Originated "The Exotic Sounds of Martin Denny" in Hawaii, featuring **Julius Wechter** (**Baja Marimba Band**) on vibes and marimba.

DEBUT	PEAK	WKS			Album	Sym	$	Label & Number
5/4/59	❶⁵	63			1 **Exotica**	[I]	$30	Liberty 7034
					The Exciting Sounds Of MARTIN DENNY			
8/31/59+	8	71			2 **Quiet Village**	[I]	$30	Liberty 7122
11/23/59	50	1			3 **Exotica-Vol. III**..........	[I]	$30	Liberty 7116
					MARTIN DENNY:			
9/29/62	6	27			4 **A Taste Of Honey**	[I]	$20	Liberty 7237
1/16/65	123	7			5 **Hawaii Tattoo**	[I]	$20	Liberty 7394

Ah Me Furi (1)
A-me-ri-ca (4)
Analanie (5)
Bamboo Lullaby (3)
Beautiful Kahana (3)
Beyond The Reef (5)
Black Orchid (4)
Busy Port (1)
Caravan (3)
China Nights (Shina No Yoru) (1)
Clair De Lune (4)

Congo Train (3)
Coronation (2)
Exodus (4)
Firecracker (2)
Happy Talk (2)
Harbor Lights (3)
Hawaii Tattoo (5)
Hawaiian War Chant (2)
Hawaiian Wedding Song (5)
Hello Young Lovers (3)
Hong Kong Blues (1)

I'm In A Dancing Mood (4)
Jungle Flower (1)
Jungle River Boat (3)
Laura (2)
Leah (5)
Limehouse Blues (3)
Lotus Land (1)
Love Dance (1)
Mama Iti E Papa E (3)
Manila (3)
Martinique (2) *88*

Moon Of Manakoora (3)
My Little Grass Shack In Kealakekua, Hawaii - Cha Cha Cha (2)
Now Is The Hour (Maori Farewell Song) (5)
Pagan Love Song (2)
Paradise Found (2)
Pearly Shells (Pupu O Ewa) (5)
Quiet Village (1,2) *4*
Red Sails In The Sunset (5)

Return To Paradise (1)
Ringo Oiwake (3)
Route 66 (4)
Sail Along, Silv'ry Moon (3)
Sake Rock (2)
Similau (1)
Song Of The Islands (Na-Leio Hawaii) (5)
Stone God (1)
Stranger In Paradise (2)
Stranger On The Shore (4)

Sweet Leilani (5)
Sweet Someone (5)
Take Five (4)
Taste Of Honey (4) *50*
Tune From Rangoon (2)
Violetta (4)
Waipio (1)
Walk On The Wild Side (4)
Wild One (4)

DENNY, Sandy   '74

Born Alexandra Denny on 1/6/41 in Wimbledon, London, England. Died of a brain hemorrhage on 4/21/78 (age 37). Lead singer of **Fairport Convention**.

DEBUT	PEAK	WKS			Album	Sym	$	Label & Number
7/20/74	197	2	©		**Like An Old Fashioned Waltz**..........		$15	Island 9340

At The End Of The Day
Carnival
Dark The Night

Friends
(It Will Have To Do) Until The Real Thing Comes Along

Like An Old Fashioned Waltz
No End
Solo

Whispering Grass (Don't Tell The Trees)

DENVER, John ★55★ '74

Born Henry John Deutschendorf on 12/31/43 in Roswell, New Mexico. Died on 10/12/97 (age 53) at the controls of a light plane which crashed off the California coast. Singer/songwriter/guitarist. With the **Chad Mitchell Trio** from 1964-68. Wrote "Leaving On A Jet Plane." Starred in the 1977 movie *Oh, God.*

1)*John Denver's Greatest Hits* 2)*Windsong* 3)*Back Home Again* 4)*An Evening With John Denver* 5)*Rocky Mountain High*

DEBUT	PEAK	WKS	RIAA	CD	Album	Sym	$	Label & Number
10/25/69	148	3			1 **Rhymes & Reasons**..........		$20	RCA Victor 4207
5/2/70	197	2			2 **Take Me To Tomorrow**..........		$20	RCA Victor 4278
4/17/71	15	80	▲	©	3 **Poems, Prayers & Promises**		$15	RCA Victor 4499
12/4/71+	75	16	●		4 **Aerie**		$15	RCA Victor 4607
9/16/72+	4	53	▲²	©	5 **Rocky Mountain High**		$15	RCA Victor 4731
6/16/73	16	35	●	©	6 **Farewell Andromeda**		$15	RCA Victor 0101
12/8/73+	❶³	175	▲⁹	©	7 **John Denver's Greatest Hits**	C:#5/11 [G]	$15	RCA Victor 0374
6/29/74	❶¹	96	▲³	©	8 **Back Home Again**		$15	RCA Victor 0548
3/8/75	2²	50	▲³	©	9 **An Evening With John Denver**	[L]	$20	RCA Victor 0764 [2]
					recorded at the Universal Ampitheater in Los Angeles			
10/4/75	❶²	45	▲²	©	10 **Windsong**		$15	RCA Victor 1183
11/8/75	14	11	▲²	©	11 **Rocky Mountain Christmas**	[X]	$15	RCA Victor 1201
					Christmas chart: 39/'98			
12/20/75+	138	6			12 **John Denver Gift Pak**..........	[X]	$30	RCA Victor 1263 [2]
					consists of albums #10 & 11 in a special Christmas sleeve			
9/4/76	7	30	▲	©	13 **Spirit**		$15	RCA Victor 1694
12/18/76+	115	5		©	14 **Rocky Mountain Christmas**..........	[X-R]	$15	RCA Victor 1201
3/5/77	6	18	▲²	©	15 **John Denver's Greatest Hits, Volume 2**	C:#13/3 [G]	$12	RCA Victor 2195
12/3/77+	45	25	▲	©	16 **I Want To Live**		$12	RCA Victor 2521
1/27/79	25	15	●	©	17 **John Denver**		$12	RCA Victor 3075
11/10/79+	26	12	▲	©	18 **A Christmas Together**..........C:#13/10	[X]	$12	RCA Victor 3451
					JOHN DENVER & THE MUPPETS			
					Christmas charts: 10/'83, 25/'96, 17/'97, 26/'98			
3/1/80	39	17		©	19 **Autograph**..........		$10	RCA Victor 3449
7/4/81	32	30	●	©	20 **Some Days Are Diamonds**		$10	RCA Victor 4055
3/20/82	39	33	●	©	21 **Seasons Of The Heart**		$10	RCA Victor 4256
10/15/83	61	15		©	22 **It's About Time**		$10	RCA Victor 4683
7/6/85	90	19		©	23 **Dreamland Express**..........		$10	RCA Victor 5458
11/10/90	185	6		©	24 **The Flower That Shattered The Stone**		$10	Windstar 53334
12/22/90	28ˣ	5		©	25 **Christmas Like A Lullaby**..........	[X]	$10	Windstar 53335
7/1/95	104	4	●	©	26 **The Wildlife Concert**	[L]	$15	Legacy 64655 [2]
					recorded on 2/23/95 at the Sony Music Studios in New York City			
11/1/97	22ᶜ	1	▲	©	27 **The Rocky Mountain Collection**	[G]	$12	RCA 66837 [2]
11/1/97	52	10		©	28 **The Best Of John Denver Live**	[L]	$10	Legacy 65183
					recorded on 2/23/95 at Sony Studios in New York City			
11/1/97	165	1		©	29 **All Aboard!**		$10	Sony Wonder 63412
12/13/97	130	8		©	30 **A Celebration Of Life (1943-1997) - The Last Recordings**..........	[K]	$10	River North 1360
5/20/00	9ᶜ	14		©	31 **The Best Of John Denver**	[G]	$10	Madacy 4750

DENVER, John — Cont'd

African Sunrise (23)
Alfie, The Christmas Tree (medley) (18)
All Of My Memories (4)
Amazon (26)
American Child (19)
Amsterdam (2)
Ancient Rhymes (24)
Angels From Montgomery (6)
Annie's Other Song (9)
Annie's Song (8,9,15,26,27,28,31) *1*
Anthem - Revelation (2)
Around And Around (3)
Aspenglow (2,11,12,14,27)
Autograph (19,27) *52*
Away In A Manger (11,12,14,25)
Baby Just Like You (11,12,14,18)
Baby, You Look Good To Me Tonight (13) *65*
Back Home Again (8,15,26,27,28,30,31) *5*
Ballad Of Richard Nixon (1)
Ballad Of Spiro Agnew (1)
Ballad Of St. Anne's Reel (19)
Berkeley Woman (6,17)
Bet On The Blues (16,26,28)
Blow Up Your TV (Spanish Pipe Dream) (4)
Blue Christmas (25)
Box, The (3)
Boy From The Country (9,20)
Calypso (10,12,15,26,27,28) *2*
Carolina In My Mind (3)
Casey's Last Ride (4)
Catch Another Butterfly (1)
Children Of Bethlehem (25)
Children Of The Universe (21)
Choo Choo Ch'Boogie (medley) (29)
Christmas For Cowboys (11,12,14,30) *58*
Christmas Is Coming (Round) (18)
Christmas Like A Lullaby (25)
Christmas Song (Chestnuts Roasting On An Open Fire) (11,12,14,25)
Christmas Wish (18)
Circus (1)
City For New Orleans (4,29)
Claudette (23)
(Cold Nights In Canada) ..see: Rocky Mountain Suite

Come And Let Me Look In Your Eyes (13,27)
Cool An' Green An' Shady (8)
Country Love (20)
Coventry Carol (11,12,14)
Cowboy And The Lady (20) *66*
Cowboy's Delight (10,12)
Daddy, What's A Train? (29)
Dancing With The Mountains (19) *97*
Darcy Farrow (5,26,28)
Daydream (1)
Dearest Esmeralda (16)
Deck The Halls (18)
Don't Close Your Eyes, Tonight (23)
Downhill Stuff (17)
Dreamland Express (23,26,30,31)
Dreams (21)
Druthers (16)
Eagle And The Hawk (4,7,9,27)
Eagles And Horses (24,26)
Easy, On Easy Street (20)
Eclipse (8)
Eli's Song (13)
Everyday (4) *81*
Fall (5)
Falling Out Of Love (22,26)
Farewell Andromeda (Welcome To My Morning) (6,9,15,27) *89*
(Farm, The) ..see: Wild Flowers In A Mason Jar
Fire And Rain (3)
First Noel (25)
Flight (The Higher We Fly) (22)
Flower That Shattered The Stone (24)
Fly Away (10,12,15,26,27,28) *13*
Flying For Me (27)
Follow Me (2,7,27)
For Baby (For Bobbie) (5,7)
For You (26,31)
Forest Lawn (2,9)
Freight Train Boogie (medley) (29)
Friends With You (4,27) *47*
Garden Song (17)
Gift You Are (24)
Gimme Your Love (23)
Goodbye Again (5,7,26,27,28) *88*
Gospel Changes (3)
Got My Heart Set On You (23)

Grandma's Feather Bed (8,9,15)
Gravel On The Ground (20)
Harder They Fall (23,26)
Have Yourself A Merry Little Christmas (18,25)
Heart To Heart (21)
High, Wide And Handsome (24)
Hitchhiker (13)
Hold On Tightly (22)
How Can I Leave You Again (16,27) *44*
How Mountain Girls Can Love (19)
I Guess He'd Rather Be In Colorado (3,26,28)
I Remember Romance (22)
I Want To Live (16,27) *55*
I Watch You Sleeping (24)
I Wish I Knew How It Would Feel To Be Free (1)
I'd Rather Be A Cowboy (6,27,28) *62*
I'm In The Mood To Be Desired (23)
I'm Sorry (10,12,15,27,28,30,31) *1*
I've Been Working On The Railroad (29)
If Ever (23)
In My Heart (19)
In The Grand Way (13)
Is It Love? (26)
Isabel (2)
Islands (21)
It Amazes Me (16,27) *59*
It Makes Me Giggle (13) *60*
It's About Time (22)
It's In Everyone Of Us (medley) (18)
It's Up To You (8)
Jenny Dreamed Of Trains (27)
Jimmy Newman (2)
Jingle Bells (25)
Johnny B. Goode (17)
Joseph & Joe (17)
Junk (3)
Last Hobo (29)
Last Train Done Gone Down (29)
Late Nite Radio (10,12)
Late Winter, Early Spring (When Everybody Goes To Mexico) (5)
Leaving, On A Jet Plane (1,7,26,27,28,30,31)

Let It Be (3)
Life Is So Good (17)
Like A Sad Song (13,15,27) *36*
Lining Track (29)
Little Drummer Boy (25)
Little Engine That Could (29)
Little Further North (24)
Little Saint Nick (18)
Looking For Space (10,12,15,27) *29*
Love Again (27,30,31)
Love Is Everywhere (10,12)
Love Of The Common People (1)
Marvelous Toy (25)
Mary's Little Boy Child (25)
Matthew (8,9,26,28)
Me & My Uncle (26)
Molly (2)
Mother Nature's Son (5,9)
Mountain Song (19)
Music Is You (8,9)
My Old Man (1)
My Sweet Lady (3,9,15,27) *32*
Noel: Christmas Eve, 1913 (18)
Nothing But A Breeze (21)
Oh Holy Night (11,12,14)
Old Train (29)
On The Atchison, Topeka And The Santa Fe (29)
On The Road (8)
On The Wings Of A Dream (24)
Opposite Tables (21)
Paradise (5)
Peace Carol (18)
Pegasus (13)
People Get Ready (29)
Perhaps Love (21,27,30,31)
Pickin' The Sun Down (9)
Please, Daddy (6,11,12,14) *69*
Poems, Prayers And Promises (3,7,9,26,27,28)
Polka Dots And Moonbeams (13)
Postcard From Paris (24)
Prisoners (5)
Raven's Child (24)
Readjustment Blues (4)
Relatively Speaking (21)
Rhymes & Reasons (1,7,9,26,27)
Ripplin' Waters (16)
River Of Love (6)
Rocky Mountain High (5,7,9,26,27,28,30,31) *9*

Rocky Mountain Suite (Cold Nights In Canada) (6,9)
Rudolph The Red-Nosed Reindeer (11,12,14,25)
San Antonio Rose (13)
San Francisco Mabel Joy (29)
Saturday Night In Toledo, Ohio (9)
Seasons Of The Heart (21,27,31) *78*
Shanghai Breezes (21,26,27) *31*
She Won't Let Me Fly Away (4)
Shipmates And Cheyenne (10,12)
Silent Night, Holy Night (11,12,14,18)
Silver Bells (11,12,14)
Singing Skies And Dancing Waters (16)
60 Second Song For A Bank, With The Phrase "May We Help You Today?" (4)
Sleepin' Alone (27)
Some Days Are Diamonds (Some Days Are Stone) (20,27) *36*
Somethin' About (22)
Song For All Lovers (26)
Song For The Life (19)
Song Of Wyoming (10,12)
Songs Of... (17)
Southwind (17)
Spirit (10,12)
Spring (5)
Starwood In Aspen (4,7,27)
Steel Rails (29)
Sticky Summer Weather (2)
Stonehaven Sunset (24)
Summer (5,9)
Sunshine On My Shoulders (3,7,26,27,28,30,31) *1*
Sweet Melinda (17)
Sweet Misery (6)
Sweet Surrender (8,9,27) *13*
Take Me Home, Country Roads (3,7,9,26,27,28,30,31) *2*
Take Me To Tomorrow (2)
Thank God I'm A Country Boy (8,9,15,27,31) *1*
Thanks To You (24)
Thirsty Boots (16,27)
This Old Guitar (8,9,15,26,27)
Thought Of You (22)
Till You Opened My Eyes (20)

To The Wild Country (16)
Today (9)
Today Is The First Day Of The Rest Of My Life (Sugacity) (1)
Tools (4)
Tradewinds (16)
Trail Of Tears (23)
Twelve Days Of Christmas (18)
Two Shots (10,12)
Waiting For A Train (29)
We Don't Live Here No More (6)
We Wish You A Merry Christmas (18)
Whalebones And Crosses (19)
What Child Is This (11,12,14)
What One Man Can Do (21)
What's On Your Mind (17)
When I'm Sixty-Four (17)
When The River Meets The Sea (18)
Whiskey Basin Blues (6)
Whispering Jesse (26,30)
White Christmas (25)
Wild Flowers In A Mason Jar (The Farm) (20)
Wild Heart Looking For Home (23)
Wild Montana Skies (22,26,27,28)
Windsong (10,12,27,30,31)
Wings That Fly Us Home (13)
Winter (5)
Wooden Indian (3)
World Game (22)
Wrangle Mountain Song (13,19)
Yellow Cat (1)
(You Dun Stomped) My Heart (1)
You Say That The Battle Is Over (19,26)
You're So Beautiful (17)
Zachary And Jennifer (6)

DEODATO   '73
Born Eumir Deodato on 6/21/42 in Rio de Janeiro, Brazil. Keyboardist/producer/arranger.

DEBUT	PEAK	WKS		CD		ARTIST — Album Title		$	Label & Number
1/20/73	3	26	©	1	**Prelude**	[I]	$15	CTI 6021
8/11/73	19	35	©	2	**Deodato 2**	[I]	$15	CTI 6029
3/23/74	114	9		3	**In Concert**	[I]	$15	CTI 6041

DEODATO/AIRTO

5/4/74	63	16	©	4	**Whirlwinds**	[I]	$12	MCA 410
11/16/74	102	9	©	5	**Artistry**	[I]	$12	MCA 457
9/6/75	110	9		6	**First Cuckoo**	[I]	$12	MCA 491
10/9/76	86	11		7	**Very Together**	[I]	$12	MCA 2219
4/29/78	98	17		8	**Love Island**	[I]	$12	Warner 3132
9/27/80	186	3		9	**Night Cruiser**	[I]	$12	Warner 3467

Adam's Hotel (6)
Also Sprach Zarathustra (2001) (1) *2*
Amani (7)
Area Code 808 (8)
Ave Maria (4)
Baubles, Bangles And Beads (1)
Black Dog (6)
Black Widow (7)

Branches (O Galho Da Roseira) (3)
Caravan (medley) (6)
Carly & Carole (1)
Chariot Of The Gods (8)
Crabwalk (6)
Do It Again (3,4)
East Side Strut (4)
Farewell To A Friend (5)
First Cuckoo (On Hearing The First Cuckoo In Spring) (6)

Funk Yourself (6)
Groovitation (9)
Havana Strut (4)
I Shot The Sheriff (3)
Jivin' (5)
Juanita (7)
Love Island (8)
Love Magic (9)
Moonlight Serenade (4)
Night Cruiser (9)
Nights In White Satin (2)

Parana (3)
Pavane For A Dead Princess (2,5)
Peter Gunn (7) *84*
Pina Colada (9)
Prelude To Afternoon Of A Faun (1)
Rhapsody In Blue (2) *41*
Rio Sangre (3)
San Juan Sunset (8)
September (3) (1)

Skatin' (9)
Skyscrapers (2)
Spanish Boogie (7)
Speak Low (6)
Spirit Of Summer (1,3)
St. Louis Blues (5)
Star Trek, Theme From (7)
Super Strut (2,5)
Tahiti Hut (8)
Take The A Train (8)
Tropea (3)

Uncle Funk (6)
Univac Loves You (7)
Watusi Strut (medley) (6)
West 42nd Street (4)
Whirlwinds (4)
Whistle Bump (8)

★256★   DEPECHE MODE   '93
All-synthesized rock group formed in Basildon, England: singer David Gahan and synthesizer players **Martin L. Gore**, Vince Clarke and Andy Fletcher. Clarke left in 1982 (formed **Yaz**, later **Erasure**), replaced by Alan Wilder (left in 1995). Group name is French for fast fashion.
1)Songs Of Faith And Devotion 2)Violator 3)Ultra

12/26/81+	192	9		©	1	**Speak & Spell**		$12	Sire 3642
12/4/82	177	8		©	2	**A Broken Frame**		$12	Sire 23751
7/28/84+	71	30	●	©	3	**People Are People**		$10	Sire 25124
1/19/85	51	42	▲	©	4	**Some Great Reward**		$10	Sire 25194
12/7/85+	113	18	▲	©	5	**Catching Up With Depeche Mode**	[K]	$10	Sire 25346
4/26/86	90	26	●	©	6	**Black Celebration**		$10	Sire 25429
10/24/87	35	59	▲	©	7	**Music For The Masses**	C:#31/2	$10	Sire 25614

DEBUT	PEAK	WKS	RIAA	CD	ARTIST — Album Title	Catalog	Sym	$	Label & Number

DEPECHE MODE — Cont'd

4/1/89	45	19	●	© 8	101	[L-S]	$15	Sire 25853 [2]

recorded on 6/18/88 at the Rose Bowl in Pasadena

4/7/90	7	74	▲³	© 9	**Violator**	$10	Sire 26081
4/10/93	❶¹	29	▲	© 10	**Songs Of Faith And Devotion**	$10	Sire 45243
12/25/93	193	1		© 11	Songs Of Faith And Devotion/Live...	[L] $10	Sire 45505

recorded in Copenhagen, Milan and New Orleans

5/3/97	5	19	●	© 12	**Ultra**	$10	Mute 46522
10/24/98	38	10		© 13	The Singles 86-98	[G] $15	Mute 47110 [2]
2/6/99	114	3	●	© 14	The Singles 81-85	[G] $10	Mute 47298
6/2/01	8	14		© 15	**Exciter**	$10	Mute 47960

Any Second Now (Voices) (1)
Barrel Of A Gun (12,13) *47*
Behind The Wheel (13)
Big Muff (1)
Black Celebration (6,8)
Blasphemous Rumours (4,5,8,14)
Blue Dress (9)
Bottom Line (12)
Boys Say Go! (1)
Breathe (15)
But Not Tonight (6)
Clean (9)
Comatose (15)
Condemnation (10,11,13)
Dead Of Night (15)
Dream On (15) *85*
Dreaming Of Me (1,5,14)
Dressed In Black (6)
Easy Tiger (15)

Enjoy The Silence (9,13) *8*
Everything Counts (3,8,13,14)
Flexible (5)
Fly On The Windscreen (5,6)
Freelove (15)
Freestate (12)
Get Right With Me (10,11)
Get The Balance Right (3,14)
Goodnight Lovers (15)
Halo (1)
Here Is The House (6)
Higher Love (10,11)
Home (12,13) *88*
I AmYou (15)
I Feel Loved (15)
I Feel You (10,11,13) *37*
I Want You Now (7)
If You Want (4)
In Your Room (10,11,13)
Insight (12)

It Doesn't Matter (4)
It Doesn't Matter Two (6)
It's Called A Heart (5,14)
It's No Good (12,13) *38*
Jazz Thieves (12)
Judas (10,11)
Just Can't Get Enough (1,5,8,14)
Leave In Silence (2,3,14)
Lie To Me (4)
Little 15 (7,13)
Love In Itself (3,5,14)
Love Thieves (12)
Lovetheme (15)
Master And Servant (4,5,8,14) *87*
Meaning Of Love (2,5,14)
Mercy In You (10,11)
Monument (2)
My Secret Garden (2)

Never Let Me Down Again (7,8,13) *63*
New Dress (6)
New Life (1,5,14)
Nodisco (1)
Nothing (7)
Nothing To Fear (2)
Now This Is Fun (3)
One Caress (10,11)
Only When I Lose Myself (13) *61*
People Are People (3,4,8,14) *13*
Personal Jesus (9,13) *28*
Photograph Of You (2)
Photographic (1,14)
Pimpf (7,8)
Pipeline (3)
Pleasure Little Treasure (8)
Policy Of Truth (9,13) *15*

Puppets (1)
Question Of Lust (6,13)
Question Of Time (6,8,13)
Route 66/Behind The Wheel (7,8) *61*
Rush (10,11)
Sacred (7)
Satellite (2)
See You (2,5,14)
Shake The Disease (5,8,14)
Shine (15)
Shouldn't Have Done That (2)
Sister Of Night (12)
Somebody (4,5,8,14)
Something To Do (4,8)
Sometimes (6)
Stories Of Old (4)
Strangelove (7,8,13) *76*
Stripped (6,8,13)
Sun & The Rainfall (2)

Sweetest Condition (15)
Sweetest Perfection (9)
Things You Said (7,8)
To Have And To Hold (7)
Told You So (3)
Tora! Tora! Tora! (1)
Useless (12,13)
Uselink (12)
Waiting For The Night (9)
Walking In My Shoes (10,11,13) *69*
What's Your Name? (1)
When The Body Speaks (15)
Work Hard (3)
World Full Of Nothing (6)
World In My Eyes (9,13) *52*

DEREK AND THE DOMINOS — see CLAPTON, Eric

DERRINGER, Rick '74

Born Richard Zehringer on 8/5/47 in Celina, Ohio. Rock singer/guitarist. Member of **The McCoys** and the **Edgar Winter Group**. Producer for **"Weird Al" Yankovic**.

12/1/73+	25	31	©	1	All American Boy	$15	Blue Sky 32481
4/26/75	141	8		2	Spring Fever	$15	Blue Sky 33423
7/31/76	154	9		3	Derringer	$15	Blue Sky 34181
2/19/77	169	3		4	Sweet Evil	$15	Blue Sky 34470
7/16/77	123	10		5	Derringer Live	[L] $15	Blue Sky 34848

Airport Giveth (The Airport Taketh Away) (1)
Beyond The Universe (3,5)
Cheap Tequila (1)
Comes A Woman (3)
Don't Ever Say Goodbye (2)
Don't Stop Loving Me (4)

Drivin' Sideways (4)
Envy (2)
Gimme More (2)
Goodbye Again (3)
Hang On Sloopy (2) *94*
He Needs Some Answers (2)
Hold (1)

I Didn't Ask To Be Born (4)
It's Raining (1)
Joy Ride (1)
Jump, Jump, Jump (1)
Keep On Makin' Love (4)
Let Me In (3,5) *86*
Let's Make It (4)

Loosen Up Your Grip (3)
One Eyed Jack (4)
Rock (2)
Rock And Roll, Hoochie Koo (1,5) *23*
Roll With Me (2)
Sailor (3,5)

Sittin' By The Pool (4,5)
Skyscraper Blues (2)
Slide On Over Slinky (1)
Still Alive And Well (2,5)
Sweet Evil (4)
Teenage Love Affair (1,5) *80*
Teenage Queen (1)

Time Warp (1)
Tomorrow (2)
Uncomplicated (1,5)
Walkin' The Dog (2)
You Can Have Me (3)

DeSARIO, Teri '80

Born in Miami. Female singer/songwriter.

| 1/19/80 | 80 | 13 | | | Moonlight Madness........... | $12 | Casablanca 7178 |

Dancin' In The Streets *66*
Fallin'

Goin' Thru The Motions
Heart Of Stone

Hold On
Moonlight Madness

Sell My Soul For You
With Your Love

Yes, I'm Ready *2*
You Got What It Takes

DESCENDENTS '96

Punk-rock group from Los Angeles: Milo Aukerman (vocals), Stephen Egerton (guitar), Karl Alvarez (bass) and Bill Stevenson (drums).

| 10/12/96 | 132 | 1 | © | | Everything Sucks .... | $10 | Epitaph 86481 |

Caught
Doghouse
Everything Sux

Hateful Notebook
I Won't Let Me
I'm The One

Rotting Out
She Loves Me
Sick-O-Me

Thank You
This Place
We

When I Get Old

DESERT ROSE BAND, The '90

Country group from California. Core members: **Chris Hillman** (vocals), John Jorgenson (mandolin) and Herb Pedersen (guitar). Hillman was a founding member of **The Byrds** and the **Flying Burrito Brothers**. Jorgenson left in 1992. Disbanded in early 1994.

| 2/17/90 | 187 | 4 | © | | Pages Of Life .... | $10 | MCA/Curb 42332 |

Darkness On The Playground
Desert Rose

Everybody's Hero
God's Plan

In Another Lifetime
Just A Memory

Missing You
Our Baby's Gone

Start All Over Again
Story Of Love

Time Passes Me By

DeSHANNON, Jackie '69

Born Sharon Myers on 8/21/44 in Hazel, Kentucky. Female singer/prolific songwriter.

| 11/1/69 | 81 | 15 | | 1 | Put A Little Love In Your Heart .... | $30 | Imperial 12442 |
| 7/22/72 | 196 | 2 | | 2 | Jackie .... | $20 | Atlantic 7231 |

Always Together (1)
Anna Karina (1)
Brand New Start (2)
Full Time Woman (2)
Heavy Burdens Me Down (2)
I Let Go Completely (1)

I Wanna Roo You (2)
I Won't Try To Put Chains On Your Soul (2)
Keep Me In Mind (1)
Laid Back Days (2)
Live (1)

Love Will Find A Way (1) *40*
Mama's Song (1)
Movin' (1)
Only Love Can Break Your Heart (2)
Paradise (2)

Peaceful In My Soul (2)
Put A Little Love In Your Heart (1) *4*
River Of Love (1)
Vanilla Olay (2) *76*

Would You Like To Learn To Dance (2)
You Are The Real Thing (1)
You Can Come To Me (1)
You Have A Way With Me (1)

DESMOND, Paul '64

Born on 11/25/24 in San Francisco. Died on 5/30/77 (age 52). Jazz alto saxophonist with **Dave Brubeck**.

| 12/28/63+ | 129 | 3 | © | 1 | Take Ten .... | [I] $25 | RCA Victor 2569 |
| 1/10/76 | 167 | 5 | © | 2 | 1975: The Duets .... | [I] $15 | Horizon 703 |

DAVE BRUBECK & PAUL DESMOND

Alice In Wonderland (2)
Alone Together (1)
Balcony Rock (2)

Black Orpheus, Theme From (1)
Blue Dove (2)

El Prince (1)
Embarcadero (1)
Koto Song (2)

Nancy (1)
One I Love (Belongs To Somebody Else) (1)

Samba De Orfeu (1)
Stardust (2)
Summer Song (2)

Take Ten (1)
These Foolish Things (2)
You Go To My Head (2)

DES'REE '95
Born Des'ree Weeks in 1969 in London (West Indian parentage). Female singer.

| 11/19/94+ | 27 | 45 | ▲ | © | 1 **I Ain't Movin'** | | | $10 | 550 Music 64324 |
| 9/5/98 | 185 | 2 | | © | 2 **Supernatural** | | | $10 | 550 Music 69508 |

Best Days (2)	**Feel So High** (1) *67*	I Ain't Movin' (1)	Life (2)	Proud To Be A Dread (2)	What's Your Sign? (2)
Crazy Maze (1)	Fire (2)	I'm Kissing You (2)	Little Child (1)	Strong Enough (1)	**You Gotta Be** (1) *5*
Darwin Star (2)	God Only Knows (2)	In My Dreams (1)	Living In The City (1)	Time (2)	
Down By The River (2)	Herald The Day (1)	Indigo Daisies (2)	Love Is Here (1)	Trip On Love (1)	

DESTINY'S CHILD '01
Female R&B vocal group from Houston: Beyoncé Knowles, Kelly Rowland, LaTavia Roberson and Toya Luckett. Roberson and Luckett left in early 2000, replaced by Farrah Franklin and Michelle Williams. Franklin left shortly thereafter, leaving trio of Knowles, Rowland and Williams.

3/7/98	67	26	▲	©	1 **Destiny's Child**			$10	Columbia 67728
8/14/99+	5	99	▲[7]	©	2 **The Writing's On The Wall**			$10	Columbia 69870
5/19/01	❶[2]	20↑	▲[3]	©	3 **Survivor**			$10	Columbia 61063

Amazing Grace (2)	**Bug A Boo** (2) *33*	Hey Ladies (2)	Killing Time (1)	**Say My Name** (2) *1*	Story Of Beauty (3)
Apple Pie À La Mode (3)	Confessions (2)	If You Leave (2)	My Time Has Come (1)	Second Nature (1)	**Survivor** (3) *2*
Bills, Bills, Bills (2) *1*	Dangerously In Love (3)	Illusion (2)	No, No, No Part 1 (1)	Sexy Daddy (3)	Sweet Sixteen (2)
Birthday (1)	Emotion (3)	**Independent Women Part I** (3) *1*	No, No, No Part 2 (1) *3*	She Can't Love You (2)	Tell Me (1)
Bootylicious (3) *1*	Fancy (3)	Independent Women Part II (3)	**No, No, No Part 2** (1) *3*	Show Me The Way (1)	Temptation (2)
Bridges (1)	Gospel Medley (3)	**Jumpin, Jumpin** (2) *3*	Now That She's Gone (1)	So Good (2)	Where'd You Go (2)
Brown Eyes (3)	Happy Face (3)		Sail On (1)	Stay (2)	With Me Parts I & II (1)

DETECTIVE '78
Rock group from England: Michael Des Barres (vocals), Michael Monarch (guitar), Tony Kaye (keyboards; **Yes**), Bobby Pickett (bass) and Jon Hyde (drums). Des Barres was once married to Pamela Des Barres (author of *I'm With The Band*) and acted on several TV shows. Des Barres later joined **Chequered Past** and was the touring lead singer for **The Power Station**.

| 5/14/77 | 135 | 9 | | | 1 **Detective** | | | $15 | Swan Song 8417 |
| 1/14/78 | 103 | 12 | | | 2 **It Takes One To Know One** | | | $15 | Swan Song 8504 |

Ain't None Of Your Business (1)	Competition (2)	Dynamite (2)	Grim Reaper (2)	One More Heartache (1)	Tear Jerker (2)
Are You Talkin' To Me? (2)	Deep Down (1)	Fever (2)	Help Me Up (2)	Recognition (1)	Warm Love (2)
Betcha Won't Dance (2)	Detective Man (1)	Got Enough Love (1)	Nightingale (1)	Something Beautiful (2)	Wild Hot Summer Nights (1)

DETROIT '72
Rock group from Detroit: Mitch Ryder (vocals), Steve Hunter and Brett Tuggle (guitars), Dirty Ed (congas), Harry Phillips (keyboards), W.R. Cooke (bass) and John Badanjek (drums). Ryder and Badanjek were members of **Mitch Ryder And The Detroit Wheels**. Badanjek later joined the **Rockets**.

| 1/29/72 | 176 | 6 | | | **Detroit** | | | $20 | Paramount 6010 |

Box Of Old Roses	I Found A Love	It Ain't Easy	Long Neck Goose
Drink	Is It You (Or Is It Me)	Let It Rock	Rock 'N Roll

DETROIT EMERALDS '72
R&B vocal trio from Little Rock, Arkansas: brothers Abrim and Ivory Tilmon, with James Mitchell. Abrim Tilmon died of a heart attack in July 1982 (age 37).

6/19/71	151	3			1 **Do Me Right**			$40	Westbound 2006
2/5/72	78	13		©	2 **You Want It, You Got It**			$40	Westbound 2013
4/21/73	181	4			3 **I'm In Love With You**			$40	Westbound 2018

Admit Your Love Is Gone (1)	I Bet You Get The One You Love (2)	If I Lose Your Love (1)	There's A Love For Me Somewhere (2)	Whatcha Gonna Wear Tomorrow (3)
And I Love Her (1)	I Can't See Myself (Doing Without You) (1)	Just Now And Then (1)	Till You Decide To Come Home (2)	You Can't Take This Love For You, From Me (1)
Baby Let Me Take You (In My Arms) (2) *24*	I Think Of You (medley) (3)	Lee (1)	Long Live The King (1)	You Control Me (medley) (3)
Do Me Right (1) *43*	I'll Never Sail The Sea Again (2)	My Dreams Have Got The Best Of Me (3)	**Wear This Ring (With Love)** (1) *91*	**You Want It, You Got It** (2) *36*
Feel The Need In Me (2)	I'm In Love With You (medley) (3)	Shake Your Head (3)	What You Gonna Do About Me (1)	You're Getting A Little Too Smart (3)
Heaven Couldn't Be Like This (medley) (3)	I've Got To Move (2)	So Long (3)		
Holding On (1)		Take My Love (2)		

DeVAUGHN, William '74
Born in 1948 in Washington DC. R&B singer/songwriter/guitarist.

| 8/3/74 | 165 | 11 | | | **Be Thankful For What You Got** | | | $15 | Roxbury 100 |

Be Thankful For What You Got *4*	**Blood Is Thicker Than Water** *43*	Give The Little Man A Great Big Hand	Kiss And Make Up	Something's Being Done	You Can Do It
			Sing A Love Song	We Are His Children	

DEVICE '86
Pop-rock trio formed in Los Angeles: Paul Engemann (vocals), Holly Knight (keyboards, bass) and Gene Black (guitar). Engemann joined Animotion in 1988. Prolific songwriter Knight was also a member of **Spider**.

| 7/12/86 | 73 | 16 | | © | **22B3** | | | $10 | Chrysalis 41526 |

Didn't I Read You Right	I've Got No Room For Your Love	Sand, Stone, Cobwebs And Dust	When Love Is Good
Fall Apart, Golden Heart	Pieces On The Ground	Tough And Tender	**Who Says** *79*
Hanging On A Heart Attack *35*			Who's On The Line

DEVIN '98
Born Devin Copeland in Houston. Male rapper.

| 7/4/98 | 177 | 3 | | © | **The Dude** | | | $10 | Rap-A-Lot 45938 |

Alright	Can't Change Me	Dude, The	Ligole Bips (Southern Girls)	One Day At A Time	Sticky Green
Boo Boo'n	Do Whatcha Wanna Do	Georgy	Like A Sweet	See What I Can Pull	Write & Wrong
Bust One Fa Ya	Don't Wait	I Can't Quit	Mo Fa Me	Show 'Em	

DEVO '80
Robotic-rock group from Akron, Ohio: brothers Mark (synthesizers) and Bob (vocals, guitar) Mothersbaugh, brothers Jerry (bass) and Bob (guitar) Casale, and Alan Myers (drums). David Kendrick replaced Myers by 1988.

10/28/78	78	18	●	©	1 **Q:Are We Not Men? A:We Are Devo!**			$15	Warner 3239
6/30/79	73	10		©	2 **Duty Now For The Future**			$15	Warner 3337
6/14/80	22	51	▲	©	3 **Freedom Of Choice**			$12	Warner 3435
4/18/81	50	12			4 **DEV-O Live**			[L-M]	$12	Warner 3548

DEBUT	PEAK	WKS	RIAA	CD	ARTIST — Album Title	Catalog	Sym	$	Label & Number

DEVO — Cont'd

DEBUT	PEAK	WKS							
10/10/81	23	25		© 5	New Traditionalists			$12	Warner 3595
11/20/82	47	20		© 6	Oh, No! It's Devo			$12	Warner 23741
11/3/84	83	6		© 7	Shout			$12	Warner 25097
7/2/88	189	3		© 8	Total Devo			$10	Enigma 73303

Agitated (8)
Are You Experienced? (7)
Baby Doll (8)
Be Stiff (4)
Beautiful World (5)
Big Mess (6)
Blockhead (2)
Blow Up (8)
Clockout (2)
Cold War (7)
Come Back Jonee (1)
C'mon (7)
Day My Baby Gave Me A Surprize (2)
Deep Sleep (6)

Devo Corporate Anthem (2)
Disco Dancer (8)
Don't Be Cruel (8)
Don't Rescue Me (7)
Don't You Know (3)
Enough Said (5)
Explosions (6)
4th Dimension (7)
Freedom Of Choice (3,4)
Gates Of Steel (3,4)
Girl U Want (3,4)
Going Under (5)
Gut Feeling (medley) (1)
Happy Guy (8)
Here To Go (1)

(I Can't Get No) Satisfaction (1)
I Desire (6)
Id Cry If You Died (8)
It's Not Right (3)
Jerkin' Back 'N' Forth (5)
Jocko Homo (1)
Jurisdiction Of Love (7)
Love Without Anger (5)
Man Turned Inside Out (3)
Mongoloid (1)
Mr. B's Ballroom (3)
Mr. DNA (medley) (2)
Out Of Sync (6)
Patterns (6)
Peek-A-Boo! (6)

Pink Pussycat (2)
Pity You (5)
Plain Truth (8)
Planet Earth (3,4)
Please Please (7)
Praying Hands (1)
Puppet Boy (7)
Race Of Doom (5)
Red Eye (2)
S.I.B. (Swelling Itching Brain) (2)
Satisfied Mind (7)
Secret Agent Man (2)
Shadow, The (8)
Shout (7)

Shrivel-Up (1)
Slap Your Mammy (medley) (1)
Sloppy (I Saw My Baby Gettin') (1)
Smart Patrol (medley) (2)
Snowball (3)
Soft Things (5)
Some Things Never Change (8)
Space Junk (1)
Speed Racer (6)
Strange Pursuit (2)
Super Thing (5)
That's Good (6)
That's Pep! (3)
Through Being Cool (5)

Time Out For Fun (6)
Timing X (2)
Ton O' Luv (3)
Too Much Paranoias (1)
Triumph Of The Will (2)
Uncontrollable Urge (1)
What I Must Do (6)
Whip It (3,4) 14
Wiggly World (2)

DeVOL, Frank, and His Rainbow Strings   '62

Born on 9/20/11 in Moundsville, West Virginia. Died of heart failure on 10/27/99 (age 88). Composer/conductor/arranger for many top singers, radio and TV shows. Composed the TV theme for *My Three Sons*. Married to singer Helen O'Connell until her death in 1993.

DEBUT	PEAK	WKS							
1/6/62	102	2			The Old Sweet Songs Of Christmas		[X-I]	$20	Columbia 1543

Adeste Fideles (O, Come All Ye Faithful) (medley)
Away In A Manger (medley)
Christmas Song (Merry Christmas To You) (medley)
Deck The Hall With Boughs Of Holly (medley)
First Noel (medley)

God Rest Ye Merry, Gentlemen (medley)
Good King Wenceslas (medley)
Hark! The Herald Angels Sing (medley)
Here Comes Santa Claus (medley)
It Came Upon The Midnight Clear (medley)

It's Beginning To Look Like Christmas (medley)
Jingle Bells (medley)
Jolly Old St. Nicholas (medley)
Joy To The World (medley)
March Of The Toys (medley)
O Holy Night (medley)
O Little Town Of Bethlehem (medley)

O Tannenbaum (medley)
Ring Christmas Bells (medley)
Silent Night, Holy Night (medley)
Silver Bells (medley)
Skaters' Waltz (medley)
Toyland (medley)
Twelve Days Of Christmas (medley)

We Three Kings Of Orient Are (medley)
We Wish You A Merry Christmas (medley)
White Christmas (medley)
Winter Wonderland (medley)

DeVORZON, Barry   '77

Born on 7/31/34 in New York City. Prolific songwriter/producer/arranger. Leader of Barry & The Tamerlanes.

DEBUT	PEAK	WKS							
11/6/76+	42	19			1 Nadia's Theme (The Young And The Restless)		[I]	$12	A&M 3412

3 cuts by DeVorzon and Perry Botkin, Jr.; others by various artists: "Bellavia" and "Chase The Clouds Away" by **Chuck Mangione**; "Emmanuel" by Michael Colombier; "Feelings" by Herb Ohta; "My Reverie" by Ira Sullivan; "Rainbow City" by **Tim Weisberg**; "Zero To Sixty In Five" by **Pablo Cruise**

DEBUT	PEAK	WKS							
11/6/76+	133	12			2 Nadia's Theme (The Young And The Restless)		[I]	$12	Arista 4104

cuts by DeVorzon only

All By Myself (2)
Bless The Beasts And Children (1,2) 82

Dancer, The (2)
Down The Line (1)
I Write The Songs (2)

Jelinda's Theme (2)
Midnight (2)

Nadia's Theme (The Young And The Restless) (1,2) 8
Shadows (2)

S.W.A.T., Theme From (2)
This Masquerade (2)
Winter Song (2)

DEXYS MIDNIGHT RUNNERS   '83

Pop-rock group from Birmingham, England: Kevin Rowland (vocals), Billy Adams (guitar), Brian Maurice (sax), Paul Speare (flute), Jimmy Patterson (trombone), Micky Billingham (piano), Giorgio Kilkenny (bass) and Seb Shelton (drums). Billingham was later with **General Public**.

DEBUT	PEAK	WKS							
2/12/83	14	24		©	Too-Rye-Ay			$10	Mercury 4069

All In All (This One Last Wild Waltz)
Celtic Soul Brothers 86

Come On Eileen (1)
I'll Show You (medley)

Jackie Wilson Said (I'm In Heaven When You Smile)
Let's Make This Precious

Liars A To E
Old
Plan B (medley)

Until I Believe In My Soul

DeYOUNG, Dennis   '84

Born on 2/18/47 in Chicago. Lead singer/keyboardist of **Styx**.

DEBUT	PEAK	WKS							
10/6/84	29	25			1 Desert Moon			$10	A&M 5006
3/29/86	108	8			2 Back To The World			$10	A&M 5109

Black Wall (2)
Boys Will Be Boys (1)
Call Me (2) 54

Dear Darling (I'll Be There) (1)
Desert Moon (1) 10
Don't Wait For Heroes (1) 83

Fire (1)
Gravity (1)
I'll Get Lucky (2)

Person To Person (2)
Please (1)
Southbound Ryan (2)

Suspicious (1)
This Is The Time (2) 93
Unanswered Prayers (1)

Warning Shot (2)

DFC   '94

Rap duo from Flint, Michigan: Alpha Breed and T Double E. Formerly with Alpha's cousin **M.C. Breed**. DFC stands for Da Funk Clan.

DEBUT	PEAK	WKS							
8/31/91	142	10		© 1	M.C. Breed & DFC			$10	S.D.E.G. 4103
4/9/94	71	11		© 2	Things In Tha Hood			$10	Assault 92320

Ain't No Future In Yo' Frontin' (1)
Better Terms (1)
Black For Black (1)
Caps Get Peeled (2)

Da Bomb (2)
Death B-4 Dishonesty (2)
Digga Bigga Ditch (2)
Get Loose (1)
Guanja (1)

Hand's On My Nine (2)
I Will Excell (1)
Job Corp (1)
Just Kickin' It (1)
Mo' Love (2)

More Power (1)
Pass The Hooter (2)
Piece Of Mind (2)
Put Your Locs On (2)
Roll With The Clan (2)

That's Life (1)
Things In Tha Hood (2)
2-2 The Chest (2)
Underground Slang (1)
You Can Get The Dick (2)

DFX2   '83

Rock group from San Diego: brothers David (vocals, guitar) and Douglas (guitar) Farage, Eric Gotthelf (bass) and Frank Hailey (drums).

DEBUT	PEAK	WKS							
8/20/83	143	8			Emotion		[M]	$10	MCA 36000

Down To The Bone

Emotion

Maureen

No Dough

Something's Always Happening

DIAMOND, Neil ★11★   '73

Born on 1/24/41 in Brooklyn, New York. Pop-rock singer/guitarist/prolific songwriter. Worked as a staff writer at the Brill Building in New York City. Wrote score for the movie *Jonathan Livingston Seagull*. Starred in and composed the music for *The Jazz Singer* in 1980.

1)Jonathan Livingston Seagull 2)The Jazz Singer 3)Serenade 4)Beautiful Noise
5)You Don't Bring Me Flowers

DEBUT	PEAK	WKS	RIAA	CD	#	Album Title	Catalog	Sym	$	Label & Number
10/29/66	137	4			1	The Feel Of Neil Diamond			$100	Bang 214
9/16/67	80	19			2	Just For You			$50	Bang 217
8/3/68+	100	40			3	Neil Diamond's Greatest Hits		[G]	$40	Bang 219
5/17/69	82	25	●	©	4	Brother Love's Travelling Salvation Show			$30	Uni 73047
12/13/69+	30	47	●	©	5	Touching You Touching Me			$30	Uni 73071
8/22/70	10	56	▲²	©	6	Neil Diamond/Gold	C:#21/32	[L]	$30	Uni 73084
						recorded at the Troubadour in Hollywood				
9/12/70	52	25			7	Shilo		[K]	$40	Bang 221
11/21/70	13	45	▲	©	8	Tap Root Manuscript			$30	Uni 73092
2/27/71	100	6			9	Do It!		[K]	$40	Bang 224
11/13/71	11	25	●	©	10	Stones			$30	Uni 93106
7/15/72	5	41	▲	©	11	Moods			$30	Uni 93136
12/9/72+	5	78	▲²	©	12	Hot August Night		[L]	$25	MCA 8000 [2]
						recorded on 8/24/72 at the Greek Theatre in Los Angeles				
1/20/73	36	21			13	Double Gold		[K]	$40	Bang 227 [2]
9/1/73	35	17	●	©	14	Rainbow		[K]	$20	MCA 2103
11/3/73	2¹	34	▲²	©	15	Jonathan Livingston Seagull		[S]	$15	Columbia 32550
6/8/74	29	42	▲⁴	©	16	Neil Diamond/His 12 Greatest Hits	C:#9/104	[G]	$15	MCA 2106
10/26/74	3	27	▲	©	17	Serenade			$15	Columbia 32919
7/4/76	4	33	▲	©	18	Beautiful Noise			$15	Columbia 33965
						produced by **Robbie Robertson**				
10/9/76	102	5		©	19	And The Singer Sings His Song		[K]	$15	MCA 2227
2/26/77	8	21	▲²	©	20	Love At The Greek		[L]	$20	Columbia 34404 [2]
						recorded August 1976 at the Greek Theatre in Los Angeles				
12/3/77+	6	24	▲²	©	21	I'm Glad You're Here With Me Tonight			$12	Columbia 34990
12/16/78+	4	29	▲²	©	22	You Don't Bring Me Flowers			$12	Columbia 35625
1/12/80	10	20	▲²	©	23	September Morn			$12	Columbia 36121
11/29/80+	3	115	▲⁵	©	24	The Jazz Singer		[S]	$12	Capitol 12120
11/28/81+	17	27	▲	©	25	On The Way To The Sky			$10	Columbia 37628
5/29/82	48	42	▲³	©	26	12 Greatest Hits, Vol. II	C:❶²/9	[G]	$10	Columbia 38068
10/16/82	9	34	▲	©	27	Heartlight			$10	Columbia 38359
6/25/83	171	7	▲	©	28	Classics - The Early Years	C:#16/46	[G]	$10	Columbia 38792
8/18/84	35	25	●	©	29	Primitive			$10	Columbia 39199
5/24/86	20	23	●	©	30	Headed For The Future			$10	Columbia 40368
11/21/87+	59	17	▲	©	31	Hot August Night II		[L]	$15	Columbia 40990 [2]
1/7/89	46	16	●	©	32	The Best Years Of Our Lives			$10	Columbia 45025
9/14/91	44	32	●	©	33	Lovescape			$10	Columbia 48610
6/6/92	90	23	▲³	©	34	The Greatest Hits 1966-1992		[G]	$15	Columbia 52703 [2]
10/24/92	8	15	▲²	©	35	The Christmas Album	C:#4/31	[X]	$10	Columbia 52914
						Christmas charts: 3/'92, 7/'93, 17/'94, 26/'95, 31/'96, 23/'97				
10/16/93	28	15	●	©	36	Up On The Roof - Songs From The Brill Building			$10	Columbia 57529
7/16/94	93	4	●	©	37	Live In America		[L]	$15	Columbia 66321 [2]
11/26/94	51	8	●	©	38	The Christmas Album Volume II	C:#19/10	[X]	$10	Columbia 66465
						Christmas charts: 9/'94, 29/'95, 28/'96				
2/24/96	14	18	●	©	39	Tennessee Moon			$10	Columbia 67382
11/16/96	122	5	●	©	40	In My Lifetime		[K]	$30	Columbia 65013 [3]
11/14/98	31	13	●	©	41	The Movie Album: As Time Goes By			$15	Columbia 69540 [2]

DIAMOND, Neil — Cont'd

Havah Nagilah (37)
Have Yourself A Merry Little Christmas (38)
He Ain't Heavy...He's My Brother (8,14,40) **20**
Headed For The Future (30,31,34,40) **53**
Hear Them Bells (40)
Heartbreak Hotel (34)
Heartlight (27,31,34,37,40) **5**
Heaven Can Wait (40)
Hello Again (24,26,31,34,37,40) **6**
Hey Louise (24)
High Rolling Man (11)
Holly Holy (5,6,12,16,20,31,34,37,40) **6**
Home Is A Wounded Heart (18)
Hooked On The Memory Of You (32,33,37,40)
Hurricane (27)
Hurtin' You Don't Come Easy (4,19)
Husbands And Wives (10,14)
I Am...I Said (10,12,16,31,34,37,40) **4**
I Am The Lion (8)
I Dreamed A Dream (31)
I Feel You (33)
I Got The Feelin' (Oh No No) (1,3,7,13,28,34,40) **16**
I Thank The Lord For The Night Time (2,3,6,7,13,28,31,34) **13**
I Think It's Gonna Rain Today (10,14)
I (Who Have Nothing) (36,37)
I'll Be Home For Christmas (38)
I'll Come Running (1,7,9,13)
I'll See You On The Radio (Laura) (10)
I'm A Believer (2,7,9,13,23,28,34,37,40) **51**
I'm Alive (27,40) **35**
I'm Glad You're Here With Me Tonight (21)
I'm Guilty (27)
I'm Sayin' I'm Sorry (40)
I've Been This Way Before (17,20,40) **34**

If I Couldn't See You Again (32)
If I Lost My Way (39)
If I Never Knew Your Name (4,19)
If There Were No Dreams (33,40)
If You Go Away (10,14)
If You Know What I Mean (18,20,26,34,40) **11**
In Ensenada (31)
In My Lifetime (40)
In The Still Of The Night (41)
It Should Have Been Me (30)
It's A Trip (Go For The Moon) (29)
Jazz Time (23)
Jerusalem (24)
Jingle Bell Rock (35)
Joy To The World (38)
Juliet (4,19)
Jungletime (18)
Just Need To Love You More (40)
Kentucky Woman (3,6,7,13,20,28,34,37,39,40) **2**
Kol Nidre (medley) (24)
La Bamba (1)
Lady Magdelene (17)
Lady-Oh (18,20,37)
Lament In D Minor (medley) (21)
Last Picasso (17,20)
Last Thing On My Mind (10,14) **56**
Let Me Take You In My Arms Again (21)
Let The Little Boy Sing (21)
Like You Do (39)
Little Drummer Boy (35)
Lonely Lady #17 (33)
Lonely Looking Sky (15,20,40)
Long Gone (4)
Long Hard Climb (32)
Long Way Home (2,9,13) **91**
Longfellow Serenade (17,20,26,34,40) **5**
Look Of Love (41)
Lordy (6)

Lost Among The Stars (27)
Lost In Hollywood (30)
Love Burns (25)
Love Doesn't Live Here Anymore (30)
Love On The Rocks (24,26,31,34,37,40) **2**
Love Potion Number Nine (36)
Love To Love (1,9,13)
Love With The Proper Stranger (41)
Love's Own Song (29)
Madrigal (40)
Mama Don't Know (23)
Man You Need (30)
Marry Me (39)
Mary's Little Boy Child (38)
Matter of Love (39)
Me Beside You (30)
Memphis Flyer (22)
Memphis Streets (4)
Merry-Go-Round (19)
Million Miles Away (40)
Missa (8,37)
Monday, Monday (1,7,13)
Moon River (41)
Morning Has Broken (35)
Morningside (11,12,34,40)
Mothers And Daughters, Fathers And Sons (22)
Mountains Of Love (33)
Mr. Bojangles (5,14)
My Heart Will Go On (41)
My Name Is Yussel (medley) (24)
My Time With You (29)
New Orleans (1,3,13) **51**
New York Boy (5)
No Limit (39)
O Come All Ye Faithful (38)
O Come, O Come Emmanuel (medley) (35)
O Holy Night (35)
O Little Town Of Bethlehem (38)
Odyssey Medley (15)
On The Robert E. Lee (24)
On The Way To The Sky (25) **27**

Once In A While (21)
One By One (29)
One Good Love (39)
One Hand, One Heart (33)
Only You (25)
Open Wide These Prison Doors (39)
Play Me (11,12,16,34,37,40) **11**
Porcupine Pie (11,12)
Primitive (29)
Puttin' On The Ritz (41)
Rainy Day Song (25)
Red Red Wine (2,3,7,9,12,13,28,34,37,40) **62**
Red Rubber Ball (1)
Reggae Strut (17)
Remember Me (22)
Reminisce For A While (39)
Right By You (25)
River Deep, Mountain High (36,37)
River Runs, Newgrown Plums (4)
Rosemary's Wine (17)
Ruby (41)
Rudolph The Red-Nosed Reindeer (38)
Sanctus (medley) (20)
Santa Claus Is Comin' Town (35)
Save Me (25)
Save The Last Dance For Me (36)
Say Maybe (22) **55**
Scotch On The Rocks (40)
Secret Love (41)
September Morn' (23,26,31,34,37,40) **17**
Shame (39)
Shelter Of Your Arms (23)
Shilo (2,7,12,13,16,28,34,40) **24**
Shot Down (9,13)
Signs (18)
Silent Night (35)
Silver Bells (35)
Skybird (15,20,40) **75**
Sleep With Me Tonight (29)
Sleigh Ride (38)

Smokey Lady (5)
Soggy Pretzels (12)
Solitary Man (1,2,3,6,7,9,12,13,28,34,37,40) **21**
Someday Baby (1,9,13)
Someone Who Believes In You (33)
Song Of The Whales (Fanfare) (31)
Song Sung Blue (11,12,16,20,31,34,37,40) **1**
Songs Of Life (24)
Soolaimón (African Trilogy II) (8,12,16,31,34,37,40) **30**
Spanish Harlem (36)
Stagger Lee (23)
Stand Up For Love (30)
Star Flight (27)
Stargazer (18,20)
Stones (16,19) **14**
Story Of My Life (30,40)
Straw In The Wind (40)
Street Life (23)
Suite Sinatra (Medley) (41)
Summerlove (24)
Sun Ain't Gonna Shine Anymore (23)
Surviving The Life (18,20)
Suzanne (10,14)
Sweet Caroline (Good Times Never Seemed So Good) (6,12,16,20,31,34,37,40) **4**
Sweet L.A. Days (33)
Sweets For My Sweet (36)
Take Care Of Me (32)
Talking Optimist Blues (Good Day Today) (39)
Ten Lonely Guys (36)
Tennessee Moon (39)
Thank The Lord For The Night Time (40)
That Kind (23)
Theme (11)
This Time (32)
True Love (41)
Turn Around (29) **62**
Unchained Melody (41)

Until It's Time For You To Go (5,14) **53**
Up On The Roof (36,37)
Walk Off (medley) (12)
Walk On Water (11,19) **17**
Way You Look Tonight (41)
We Three Kings Of Orient Are (medley) (35)
We Wish You A Merry Christmas (medley) (38)
What Will I Do? (40)
When You Miss Your Love (33)
When You Wish Upon A Star (41)
White Christmas (35)
Will You Love Me Tomorrow (36)
Win The World (39)
Windmills Of Your Mind (41)
Winter Wonderland (38)
Wish Everything Was Alright (33)
Yes I Will (17)
Yesterday's Songs (25,26,34,40) **37**
You Baby (24)
You Don't Bring Me Flowers (21,22,26,31,34,37,40) **1**
You Got To Me (2,3,7,13,28,34,37,40) **18**
You Make It Feel Like Christmas (29,35,40)
You'll Forget (2,9,13)
You're So Sweet Horseflies Keep Hangin' 'Round Your Face (4,12)
You've Got Your Troubles (22)
You've Lost That Lovin' Feelin' (36,37)

DIAMOND RIO '01

Country group formed in Nashville: Marty Roe (vocals), Jimmy Olander (guitar), Gene Johnson (mandolin), Dan Truman (piano), Dana Williams (bass) and Brian Prout (drums).

DEBUT	PEAK	WKS	RIAA	CD		ARTIST — Album Title	$	Label & Number
6/15/91+	83	85	▲	©	1	Diamond Rio	$10	Arista 8673
11/21/92+	87	21	●	©	2	Close To The Edge	$10	Arista 18656
8/6/94	100	27	▲	©	3	Love A Little Stronger	$10	Arista 18745
3/16/96	92	8	●	©	4	IV	$10	Arista 18812
8/2/97	75	15	●	©	5	Greatest Hits	[G] $10	Arista 18844
8/15/98	70	34	●	©	6	Unbelievable	$10	Arista 18866
2/24/01	36	19	●	©	7	One More Day	$10	Arista 67999

Appalachian Dream (3)
Ballad Of Conley And Billy (The Proof's In The Pickin') (1)
Big (4)
Bubba Hyde (3,5)
Calling All Hearts (Come Back Home) (2)
Close To The Edge (2)
Demons And Angels (2)
Down By The Riverside (3)
Finish What We Started (3)
Gone Out Of My Mind (3)
Hearts Against The Wind (7)
Here I Go Fallin' (7)
Hold Me Now (6)

Holdin' (4,5)
How Your Love Makes Me Feel (5)
I Could Do It With My Eyes Closed (7)
I Know How The River Feels (6)
I Think I Love You (7)
I Thought I'd Seen Everything (6)
I Was Meant To Be With You (2)
(I Will) Start All Over Again (6)
I'm Already Gone (7)
I'm Trying (7)
Imagine That (5)

In A Week Or Two (2,5)
Is That Askin' Too Much (4)
It Does Get Better Than This (2)
It's All In Your Head (4,5)
It's Gone (1)
Just Another Heart (4)
Kentucky Mine (3)
Long Way Back (6)
Love A Little Stronger (3,5)
Love Of A Woman (7)
Love Takes You There (4)
Mama Don't Forget To Pray For Me (1,5)
Meet In The Middle (1,5)
Mirror Mirror (1,5)

Miss That Girl (6)
Night Is Fallin' In My Heart (3,5)
Norma Jean Riley (1,5)
Nothing In This World (2)
Nowhere Bound (1)
Oh Me, Oh My, Sweet Baby (4)
Old Weakness (Coming On Strong) (2)
One More Day (7) **29**
Pick Me Up (1)
Poultry Promenade (1)
Sawmill Road (2)
She Misses Him On Sunday The Most (4,5)
She Sure Did Like To Run (4)

Stuff (7)
Sweet Summer (7)
That's Just That (7)
That's What I Get For Loving You (4)
They Don't Make Hearts (Like They Used To) (1)
This Romeo Ain't Got Julie Yet (2)
This State Of Mind (1)
'Til The Heartache's Gone (7)
Two Pump Texaco (5)
Unbelievable (6) **36**
Walkin' Away (4,5)

What More Do You Want From Me (6)
Who Am I (4)
Wild Blue Yonder (3)
You Ain't In It (3)
You Make Me Feel (6)
You're Gone (6)

DIBANGO, Manu '73

Born on 2/10/34 in Douala, Cameroon, Africa. Jazz-R&B saxophonist/pianist.

DEBUT	PEAK	WKS	CD		ARTIST — Album Title	Sym	$	Label & Number
6/30/73	79	13	©		Soul Makossa	[I]	$15	Atlantic 7267

Dangwa
Hibiscus
Lily
New Bell
Nights In Zeralda
Oboso
Soul Makossa 35

DICKINSON, Bruce '90

Born Paul Bruce Dickinson on 8/7/58 in Worksop, England; raised in Sheffield, England. Lead singer of **Iron Maiden** from 1981-1993.

DEBUT	PEAK	WKS	CD		ARTIST — Album Title	$	Label & Number
5/26/90	100	17	©	1	Tattooed Millionaire	$10	Columbia 46139
8/13/94	185	1	©	2	Balls To Picasso	$10	Mercury 522491

All The Young Dudes (1)
Born In '58 (1)
Change Of Heart (2)
Cyclops (2)

Dive! Dive! Dive! (1)
Fire (2)
Gods Of War (2)
Gypsy Road (1)

Hell No (2)
Hell On Wheels (1)
Laughing In The Hiding Bush (2)

Lickin' The Gun (1)
No Lies (1)
Sacred Cowboys (2)
Shoot All The Clowns (2)

Son Of A Gun (1)
Tattooed Millionaire (1)
Tears Of The Dragon (2)
1000 Points Of Light (2)

Zulu Lulu (1)

DICTATORS '77
Rock group from New York City: Handsome Dick Manitoba (vocals), Ross "The Boss" Funicello (lead guitar), Scott "Top Ten" Kempner (rhythm guitar), Adny Shernoff (keyboards), Mark Mendoza (bass) and Ritchie Teeter (drums). Manitoba, Funicello and Shernoff later formed Manitoba's Wild Kingdom. Mendoza later joined **Twisted Sister**.

| 7/30/77 | 193 | 2 | | | **Manifest Destiny** | | | $15 | Asylum 1109 |

Disease   Heartache   Science Gone Too Far!   Sleepin' With The T.V. On   Young, Fast, Scientific
Exposed   Hey Boys   Search & Destroy   Steppin' Out

DIDDLEY, Bo '62
Born Otha Ellas Bates McDaniel on 12/30/28 in McComb, Mississippi; raised in Chicago. Highly influential singer/songwriter/guitarist. Inducted into the Rock and Roll Hall of Fame in 1987.

| 11/24/62 | 117 | 4 | | | **Bo Diddley** | | | $100 | Checker 2984 |

Babes In The Woods   Diddling   Mama Don't Allow No Twistin'   Who May Your Lover Be   **You Can't Judge A Book By**
Bo's Bounce   Give Me A Break   Mr. Khrushchev   You All Green   **The Cover** 48
Bo's Twist   I Can Tell   Sad Sack

DIDO '01
Born Dido Armstrong on 12/25/71 in London. Female singer.

| 6/3/00+ | 4 | 69 | ▲⁴ | © | **No Angel** | | | $10 | Arista 19025 |

All You Want   Here With Me   Hunter   Isobel   My Lover's Gone   Take My Hand
Don't Think Of Me   Honestly OK   I'm No Angel   My Life   Slide   **Thankyou** 3

DIESEL '81
Rock group from Holland: Rob Vunderink (vocals, guitar), Mark Boon (guitars), Frank Papendrecht (bass) and Pim Koopman (drums).

| 8/8/81 | 68 | 24 | | | **Watts In A Tank** | | | $12 | Regency 19315 |

Alibi   Bite Back   Goin' Back To China   Harness, The   Ready For Love   **Sausalito Summernight** 25
All Because Of You   Down In The Silvermine   Good Mornin' Day   My Kind Of Woman   Remember The Romans

DIFFIE, Joe '94
Born on 12/28/58 in Tulsa; raised in Duncan, Oklahoma. Country singer/guitarist.

2/8/92	132	12	●	©	1	**Regular Joe**			$10	Epic 47477
5/8/93+	67	53	▲	©	2	**Honky Tonk Attitude**			$10	Epic 53002
8/13/94	53	54	▲	©	3	**Third Rock From The Sun**			$10	Epic 64357
12/16/95	129	6		©	4	**Mr. Christmas**		[X]	$10	Epic 67045
						Christmas chart: 32/'95				
1/13/96	167	7	●	©	5	**Life's So Funny**			$10	Epic 67405
6/27/98	131	6		©	6	**Greatest Hits**		[G]	$10	Epic 69137
6/19/99	189	1		©	7	**A Night To Remember**			$10	Epic 69815

Ain't That Bad Enough (1)   Cows Came Home (3)   I'd Like To Have A Problem Like   Leroy The Redneck Reindeer   Praise And Alleluia To The   **Third Rock From The Sun**
All Because Of A Baby Boy (4)   Don't Our Love Look Natural (7)   That (3)   (4)   Savior (4)   (3,6) 84
And That Was The Easy Part   Down In A Ditch (5)   I'm In Love With A Capital "U"   Let It Snow, Let It Snow, Let It   Prop Me Up Beside The   Whole Lotta Gone (5)
(2)   From Here On Out (3)   (3)   Snow (4)   Jukebox (If I Die) (2,6)   Wild Blue Yonder (3)
Are We Even Yet (7)   Good Brown Gravy (3)   I'm Not Through Losin' You (2)   Life's So Funny (5)   **Quittin' Kind** (7) 90   Wrap Me In Your Love (4)
Back To Back Heartaches (1)   Goodnight Sweetheart (1)   I'm The Only Thing I'll Hold   Magazine Angels (4)   She Loves Me (5)   You Can't Go Home (7)
Back To The Cave (5)   Have Yourself A Merry Little   Against You (7)   Mr. Christmas (4)   Ships That Don't Come In (1,6)   You Made Me What I Am (1)
Better Off Gone (7)   Christmas (4)   I'm Willing To Try (5)   My Heart's In Over My Head (2)   Silent Night (4)
Bigger Than The Beatles (5,6)   Here Comes That Train (2)   If I Had Any Pride In Me All (2)   Never Mine To Lose (5)   **So Help Me Girl** (3,6) 84
Christmas Song (Chestnuts   Home (6)   In My Own Backyard (2)   Next Thing Smokin' (1)   Somewhere Under The
Roasting On An Open Fire)   Honky Tonk Attitude (2,6)   Is It Cold In Here (1)   **Night To Remember** (7) 38   Rainbow (2)
(4)   Hurt Me All The Time (6)   **It's Always Somethin'** (7) 57   Not In This Lifetime (7)   Startin' Over Blues (1)
Cold Budweiser And A Sweet   I Can Walk The Line (If It Ain't   **John Deere Green** (2,6) 69   O Holy Night (4)   Tears In The Rain (4)
Tater (2)   Too Straight) (2)   Junior's In Love (3)   **Pickup Man** (3,6) 60   Texas Size Heartache (6)
C-O-U-N-T-R-Y (5)   I Just Don't Know (1)   Just A Regular Joe (1)   Poor Me (6)   That Road Not Taken (3)

DIFFORD & TILBROOK '84
Pop-rock duo from London. Chris Difford was born on 4/11/54. Glenn Tilbrook was born on 8/31/57. Both went on to form **Squeeze**.

| 7/14/84 | 55 | 15 | | © | **Difford & Tilbrook** | | | $10 | A&M 4985 |

Action Speaks Faster   Hope Fell Down   Man For All Seasons   Picking Up The Pieces   Wagon Train
Apple Tree   Love's Crashing Waves   On My Mind Tonight   Tears For Attention   You Can't Hurt Her Girl

DIFRANCO, Ani '98
Born on 9/23/70 in Buffalo, New York. Female singer/songwriter/guitarist. Founded the Righteous Babe record label.

6/8/96	87	4		©	1	**Dilate**			$10	Righteous Babe 008
5/10/97	59	5	●	©	2	**Living In Clip**		[L]	$15	Righteous Babe 011 [2]
3/7/98	22	10		©	3	**Little Plastic Castle**			$10	Righteous Babe 012
2/6/99	29	7		©	4	**Up Up Up Up Up Up**			$10	Righteous Babe 013
12/4/99	76	2		©	5	**To The Teeth**			$10	Righteous Babe 017
4/28/01	50	6		©	6	**Revelling/Reckoning**			$15	Righteous Babe 024 [2]

Adam And Eve (1,2)   Don't Nobody Know (6)   Heartbreak Even (6)   Napoleon (1,2)   Shy (2)   Two Little Girls (3)
Ain't That The Way (6)   Done Wrong (1)   Hello Birmingham (5)   Not So Soft (2)   Sick Of Me (6)   Untouchable Face (1,2)
Amazing Grace (1,2)   Everest (4)   Hide And Seek (2)   O.K. (6)   Slant, The (medley) (2)   Up Up Up Up Up Up (4)
Angel Food (4)   Every State Line (2)   I Know This Bar (5)   Old Old Song (6)   So What (6)   Virtue (4)
Angry Any More (4)   Fierce Flawless (6)   I'm No Heroine (2)   Out Of Habit (2)   Soft Shoulder (5)   We're All Gonna Blow (2)
Anticipate (2)   Fire Door (2)   Imagine That (6)   Out Of Range (2)   Sorry I Am (2)   What How When Where (Why
Arrivals Gate (5)   Flood Waters (6)   In Here (6)   Outta Me, Onto You (1)   Subdivision (6)   Who) (4)
As Is (3)   Freakshow (5)   In Or Out (2)   Overlap (2)   Superhero (1)   Whatall Is Nice (6)
Back Back Back (5)   Fuel (3)   Independence Day (3)   Pixie (3)   Swan Dive (3)   Whatever (2)
Beautiful Night (6)   Garden Of Simple (6)   Joyful Girl (1,2)   Prison Prism (6)   Swing (2)   Willing To Fight (2)
Both Hands (2)   Glass House (3)   Jukebox (2)   Providence (5)   Tamburitza Lingua (6)   Wish I May (5)
Carry You Around (5)   Going Down (1)   Kazoointoit (6)   Pulse (3)   That Was My Love (6)   Wrong With Me (2)
Cloud Blood (5)   Going Once (5)   Know Now Then (4)   Reckoning (6)   32 Flavors (2)   Your Next Bold Move (6)
Come Away From It (4)   Gravel (2,3)   Letter To A John (2)   Revelling (6)   This Box Contains... (6)
Deep Dish (3)   Grey (6)   Little Plastic Castle (3)   Rock Paper Scissors (6)   'Tis Of Thee (4)
Dilate (1)   Harvest (6)   Loom (3)   School Night (6)   To The Teeth (5)
Diner, The (medley) (2)   Hat Shaped Hat (3)   Marrow (6)   Shameless (1,2)   Trickle Down (4)

DEBUT	PEAK	WKS	RIAA	CD	ARTIST — Album Title	Catalog	Sym	$	Label & Number

DIG '94
Rock group from San Diego: Scott Hackwith (vocals, guitar), Jon Morris and Johnny Cornwell (guitars), Phil Friedmann (bass) and Anthony Smedile (drums).

| 2/19/94 | 153 | 6 | | © | **Dig** .... | | | $10 | Radioactive 10916 |

Anymore
Believe

Conversation
Decide

Feet Don't Touch The Ground
Fuck You

Green Room
I'll Stay High

Let Me Know
Ride The Wave

Tight Brain
Unlucky Friend

DIGABLE PLANETS '93
Rap trio from Washington DC: Ishmael Butler, Mary Ann Vierra and Craig Irving.

| 2/27/93 | 15 | 22 | ● | © | 1 **Reachin' (A New Refutation Of Time And Space)** .... | | | $10 | Pendulum 61414 |
| 11/5/94 | 32 | 7 | | © | 2 **Blowout Comb** .... | | | $10 | Pendulum 30654 |

Appointment At The Fat Clinic (1)
Art Of Easing (2)
Black Ego (2)
Blowing Down (2)
Borough Check (2)

Dial 7 (Axioms of Creamy Spies) (2)
Dog It (2)
Escapism (Gettin' Free) (1)
Examination Of What (1)

For Corners (2)
Graffiti (2)
Highing Fly (2)
It's Good To Be Here (1)
Jettin' (2)
Jimmi Diggin Cats (1)

K.B.'s Alley (Mood Dudes Groove) (2)
La Femme Fetal (1)
Last Of The Spiddyocks (1)
May 4th Movement (2)
Nickel Bags (1)

9th Wonder (Blackitolism) (2) *80*
Pacifics (1)
Rebirth Of Slick (Cool Like Dat) (1) *15*
Swoon Units (1)

Time & Space (A New Refutation Of) (1)
What Cool Breezes Do (1)
Where I'm From (1)

DIGGIN' IN THE CRATES — see D.I.T.C.

DIGITAL UNDERGROUND '90
Hip-hop group from Oakland: Eddie Humphrey and Ron Brooks (vocals), Gregory Jacobs (keyboards) and Chopmaster J (samples, percussion). Tupac (**2Pac**) Shakur was a member in 1991. Group appeared in the movie *Nothing But Trouble*.

4/14/90	24	31	▲	©	1 **Sex Packets**	C:#22/11		$10	Tommy Boy 1026
2/2/91	29	27	●	©	2 **This Is An E.P. Release**	[M]		$10	Tommy Boy 964
11/2/91	44	27	●	©	3 **Sons Of The P**			$10	Tommy Boy 1045
10/23/93	79	4		©	4 **The Body-Hat Syndrome**			$10	Tommy Boy 1080
6/22/96	113	3		©	5 **Future Rhythm**			$10	Critique 15452

Arguin' On The Funk (2)
Body-Hats (Part One, Two & Three) (4)
Bran Nu Swetta (4)
Carry The Way (Along Time) (4)
Circus Entrance (4)
DFLO Shuttle (3)
D-Flowstrumental (3)
Danger Zone (1)
digital Lover (4)

Do Ya Like It Dirty? (4)
Doo Woo You (4)
Doowutchyalike (1)
Dope-A-Delic (Do-U-B-Leeve-In-D-Flo?) (4)
Family Of The Underground (3)
Flowin' On The D-Line (3)
Food Fight (5)
Fool Get A Clue (5)
Freaks Of The Industry (1)

Future Rhythm (5)
Glooty-Us-Maximus (5)
Good Thing We're Rappin' (3)
Gutfest '89 (1)
Heartbeat Props (3)
Hella Bump (5)
Higher Heights Of Spirituality (3)
Hokis Pokis (A Classic Case) (5)

Holly Wanstaho (4)
Humpty Dance (1) *11*
Humpty Dance Awards (4)
Jerkit Circus (4)
Kiss You Back (3) *40*
Midnite Snack (5)
New Jazz (One) (1)
No Nose Job (3)
Nuttin' Nis Funky (2)
Oregano Flow (5)

Packet Man (1,2)
Return Of The Crazy One (4)
Rhymin' On The Funk (1)
Rumpty Rump (5)
Same Song (2)
Sex Packets (1)
Shake & Bake (4)
Sons Of The P (3)
Street Scene (4)
Stylin' (5)

Tales Of The Funky (3)
Tie The Knot (2)
Underwater Rimes (1)
Walk Real Kool (5)
Want It All (5)
Way We Swing (1,2)
We Got More (5)
Wheee! (4)
Wussup Wit The Luv (4)

DILATED PEOPLES '00
Rap trio from Los Angeles: Evidence, Iriscience and DJ Babu.

| 6/10/00 | 74 | 7 | | © | **The Platform** .... | | | $10 | Capitol 23310 |

Annihilation
Ear Drums Pop
Expanding Man

Guaranteed
Last Line Of Defense
Main Event

No Retreat
Platform, The
Right On

Service
Shape Of Things To Come
So May I Introduce You

Triple Optics
Work The Angles
Years In The Making

DILLARDS, The '72
Country-rock group from East St. Louis, Illinois: Rodney Dillard (vocals, guitar), Billy Ray Latham (banjo), Dean Webb (mandolin), Mitch Jayne (bass) and Paul York (drums). Also see **The Folkswingers**.

| 6/10/72 | 79 | 18 | | | **Roots And Branches** .... | | | $15 | Anthem 5901 |

Big Bayou
Billy Jack

Forget Me Not
Get Out On The Road

I've Been Hurt
Last Morning

Man Of Constant Sorrow
One A.M.

Redbone Hound
Sunny Day

DILLINGER, Daz '98
Born Delmar Arnaud in Los Angeles. Male rapper. Member of **Tha Dogg Pound**. Cousin of **Snoop Doggy Dogg**.

| 4/18/98 | 8 | 9 | | © | **Retaliation, Revenge And Get Back** .... | | | $10 | Death Row 53524 |

Baby Mama Drama
Gang Bangin Ass Criminal

In California
Initiated
It Might Sound Crazy

Its Going Down
O.G.
Oh No

Only For U
Our Daily Bread
Playa Partners

Retaliation, Revenge And Get Back
Ridin High

Thank God For My Life
Ultimate Come Up

DILLMAN BAND, The '81
Country-rock group: Steve Solmonson (vocals), Pat Frederick (guitar), Michael Wolf (piano), Steve Seamans (bass) and Dan Flaherty (drums). In 1980, Wolf departed; bassist Dik Shopteau joined and Seamans moved from bass to guitar.

| 4/1/78 | 198 | 2 | | | 1 **The Daisy Dillman Band** .... | | | $12 | United Artists 838 |
| 5/16/81 | 145 | 7 | | | 2 **Lovin' The Night Away** .... | | | $12 | RCA Victor 3909 |

Border Bound (1)
Breakdown (2)
C.O.D. (2)
Darlin' Companion (1)

Flyin' Solo (1)
Hoedown (1)
It Doesn't Matter Anymore (1)
Just A Lady (1)

Learn To Fly (1)
Love Don't Run (2)
Lovin' The Night Away (2) *45*
Mexican Nights (1)

Roll Like A Stone (2)
She's Just A Stranger (2)
Slow Ride Home (2)
So Much The Smoother (2)

Spending Time, Making Love And Going Crazy (2)
Turn My Head (1)

DI MEOLA, Al '78
Born on 7/22/54 in Jersey City, New Jersey. Jazz fusion guitarist. Member of **Return To Forever** from 1974-76.

1)Casino 2)Electric Rendezvous 3)Elegant Gypsy

3/27/76	129	10		©	1 **Land Of The Midnight Sun**		[I]	$12	Columbia 34074
5/7/77	58	12	●	©	2 **Elegant Gypsy**		[I]	$12	Columbia 34461
4/29/78	52	17		©	3 **Casino**		[I]	$12	Columbia 35277
7/12/80	119	14		©	4 **Splendido Hotel**		[I]	$15	Columbia 36270 [2]
5/30/81	97	13		©	5 **Friday Night In San Francisco**		[I-L]	$12	Columbia 37152
					JOHN McLAUGHLIN/AL DI MEOLA/PACO DE LUCIA				
2/6/82	55	13		©	6 **Electric Rendezvous**		[I]	$12	Columbia 37654
12/25/82+	165	7		©	7 **Tour De Force - "Live"**		[I-L]	$12	Columbia 38373
					recorded on 2/4/82 at the Tower Theatre in Philadelphia				
8/20/83	171	5		©	8 **Passion, Grace & Fire**		[I]	$12	Columbia 38645
					JOHN McLAUGHLIN/AL DI MEOLA/PACO DE LUCIA				
10/29/83	128	6		©	9 **Scenario**		[I]	$12	Columbia 38944
1/23/88	190	1		©	10 **Tirami Su**		[I]	$10	EMI-Manhattan 46995
					AL DI MEOLA PROJECT				

DI MEOLA, Al — Cont'd

Advantage (7)
African Night (9)
Al Di's Dream Theme (4)
Alien Chase On Arabian Desert (4)
Andonea (10)
Arabella (10)
Aspan (8)
Beijing Demons (10)
Bianca's Midnight Lullaby (4)
Black Cat Shuffle (6)
Cachaca (9)
Calliope (9)

Casino (3)
Chasin' The Voodoo (3)
Chiquito (8)
Cruisin' (6,7)
Dark Eye Tango (3)
David (8)
Dinner Music Of The Gods (4)
Egyptian Danza (3,7)
Electric Rendezvous (6)
Elegant Gypsy Suite (2,7)
Fantasia Suite (5)
Fantasia Suite For Two Guitars Medley (3)

Flight Over Rio (3)
Frevo Rasgado (5)
God Bird Change (6)
Guardian Angel (5)
Hypnotic Conviction (9)
I Can Tell (4)
Isfahan (4)
Island Dreamer (9)
Jewel Inside A Dream (6)
Lady Of Rome, Sister Of Brazil (2)
Land Of The Midnight Sun (1)
Maraba (10)

Mata Hari (9)
Mediterranean Sundance (2,5)
Midnight Tango (2)
Nena (7)
Orient Blue Suite (Part I, II, III) (8)
Passion, Grace & Fire (6,8)
Pictures Of The Sea, Love Theme From (1)
Race With Devil On Spanish Highway (2,7)
Rhapsody Of Fire (10)
Rio Ancho (medley) (5)

Ritmo De La Noche (6)
Roller Jubilee (4)
Sarabande From Violin Sonata In B Minor (1)
Scenario (1)
Scoundrel (9)
Senor Mouse (3)
Sequencer (9)
Short Tales Of The Black Forest (1,5)
Sichia (8)
Silent Story In Her Eyes (4)
Smile From A Stranger (10)

Somalia (6)
Song To The Pharoah Kings (10)
Song With A View (10)
Spanish Eyes (4)
Splendido Sundance (4)
Suite - Golden Dawn Medley (1)
Two To Tango (4)
Wizard, The (1)

DINO '89

Born Dino Esposito on 7/20/63 in Encino, California; raised in Hawaii and Connecticut. Pop-dance singer.

| 3/25/89 | 34 | 48 | ● | © | 1 | 24/7 | $10 | 4th & B'way 4011 |
| 9/8/90 | 82 | 21 | | © | 2 | Swingin' | $10 | Island 846481 |

After The Sun Goes Down (2)
Boyfriend-Girlfriend (1)
Can't Get Away From You (1)
Falling For You (2)

Gentle (2) 31
I Like It (1) 7
In The City (1)
In The Morning (2)

Never 2 Much Of U (1) 61
No More Heartbreak (1)
Real Love (1)
Romeo (2) 6

Summergirls (1) 50
Sunshine (1) 23
Swingin' (2)
Tongue Kiss (2)

24/7 (1) 42
Why Do You Do Me? (2)
Wish On A Star (2)

DINO, DESI & BILLY '65

Vocal trio formed in Los Angeles: Dino Martin, Desi Arnaz Jr. and Billy Hinsche. Martin is the son of **Dean Martin**. Arnaz is the son of Lucille Ball and Desi Arnaz. Dino (formerly married to Olympic skater Dorothy Hamill) was killed on 3/21/87 (age 35) when his Air National Guard jet crashed.

| 9/25/65 | 51 | 24 | | | 1 | I'm A Fool | $25 | Reprise 6176 |
| 2/12/66 | 119 | 6 | | | 2 | Our Time's Coming | $25 | Reprise 6194 |

Act Naturally (2)
Boo-Hoo-Hoo (I Can Tell) (1)
Chimes Of Freedom (1)
Desi's Drums (2)

Everything I Do Is For You (2)
Fun, Fun, Fun (2)
Get Off Of My Cloud (2)
Hang On Sloopy (2)

(I Can't Get No) Satisfaction (1)
I'm A Fool (1) 17
It Ain't Me, Babe (1)
Let Me Be (2)

Like A Rolling Stone (2)
Mr. Tambourine Man (1)
Not The Lovin' Kind (1) 25
Rebel Kind (1)

Seventh Son (1)
She's So Far Out She's In (2)
Sheila (1)
So Many Ways (1)

Turn, Turn, Turn (2)
Yesterday (2)
You've Got To Hide Your Love Away (2)

DINOSAUR JR. '93

Rock trio from Amherst, Massachusetts: Joseph Mascis (vocals, guitar), Mike Johnson (guitar) and Patrick Murphy (drums). Murphy left in late 1993; replaced by George Berz. Mascis acted in the movie *Gas Food Lodging*.

3/30/91	168	6		©	1	Green Mind	$10	Sire 26479
2/27/93	50	15		©	2	Where You Been	$10	Sire 45108
9/17/94	44	8		©	3	Without A Sound	$10	Sire 45719
4/12/97	188	1		©	4	Hand It Over	$10	Reprise 46506

Alone (4)
Blowing It (1)
Can't We Move This (4)
Drawerings (2)
Even You (3)
Feel The Pain (3)
Flying Cloud (1)

Get Me (2)
Get Out Of This (3)
Getting Rough (4)
Goin Home (2)
Gotta Know (4)
Grab It (3)
Green Mind (2)
Hide (2)

How'd You Pin That One On Me (4)
I Ain't Sayin (2)
I Don't Think (4)
I Don't Think So (3)
I Know Yer Insane (4)
I Live For That Look (1)
I'm Insane (4)

Loaded (4)
Mick (4)
Mind Glow (3)
Muck (1)
Never Bought It (4)
Not The Same (2)
Nothin's Goin On (4)
On The Brink (3)

On The Way (2)
Out There (2)
Outta Hand (3)
Over Your Shoulder (3)
Puke + Cry (1)
Seemed Like The Thing To Do (3)
Start Choppin (2)

Sure Not Over You (4)
Thumb (1)
Wagon, The (1)
Water (1)
What Else Is New (2)
Yeah Right (3)

DIO '84

Hard-rock group formed by Ronnie James Dio (born Ronald Padavona on 7/10/49 in Portsmouth, New Hampshire). Former lead singer of **Black Sabbath** and **Rainbow**. Dio consisted of Vivian Campbell (guitar), Jimmy Bain (bass) and Vinny Appice (drums; Black Sabbath). Claude Schnell (keyboards) joined in 1984. Campbell left in 1986, replaced by Craig Goldie. Campbell also with **Whitesnake** and **Def Leppard**.

6/25/83	56	38	▲	©	1	Holy Diver	$10	Warner 23836
7/21/84	23	35	▲	©	2	The Last In Line	$10	Warner 25100
8/31/85	29	29	●	©	3	Sacred Heart	$10	Warner 25292
6/28/86	70	16		©	4	Intermission	[L-M]	$10	Warner 25443
						recorded at the San Diego Sports Arena		
8/15/87	43	11		©	5	Dream Evil	$10	Warner 25612
6/2/90	61	13		©	6	Lock Up The Wolves	$10	Reprise 26212
2/19/94	142	2		©	7	Strange Highways	$10	Reprise 45527

All The Fools Sailed Away (5)
Another Lie (3)
Between Two Hearts (6)
Blood From A Stone (7)
Born On The Sun (6)
Breathless (2)
Bring Down The Rain (7)
Caught In The Middle (1)
Don't Talk To Strangers (1)
Dream Evil (5)
Eat Your Heart Out (2)

Egypt (The Chains Are On) (2)
Evil Eyes (2)
Evil On Queen Street (6)
Evilution (7)
Faces In The Window (5)
Fallen Angels (3)
Firehead (3)
Give Her The Gun (6)
Gypsy (1)
Here's To You (7)
Hey Angel (6)

Hollywood Black (7)
Holy Diver (1)
Hungry For Heaven (3)
I Could Have Been A Dreamer (5)
I Speed At Night (2)
Invisible (3)
Jesus, Mary & The Holy Ghost (7)
Just Another Day (3)
King Of Rock And Roll (3,4)

Last In Line (2)
Like The Beat Of A Heart (3)
Lock Up The Wolves (6)
Long Live Rock 'N' Roll (medley) (4)
Man On The Silver Mountain (medley) (4)
My Eyes (6)
Mystery (2)
Naked In The Rain (6)
Night Music (6)

Night People (5)
One Foot In The Grave (7)
One Night In The City (2)
Overlove (5)
Pain (7)
Rainbow In The Dark (1,4)
Rock 'N' Roll Children (3,4)
Sacred Heart (3,4)
Shame On The Night (1)
Shoot Shoot (3)
Stand Up And Shout (1)

Straight Through The Heart (1)
Strange Highways (7)
Sunset Superman (5)
Time To Burn (4)
Twisted (6)
Walk On Water (6)
We Rock (2,4)
When A Woman Cries (5)
Why Are They Watching Me (6)
Wild One (6)

DION '62

Born Dion DiMucci on 7/18/39 in the Bronx, New York. Formed vocal group, Dion & The Belmonts, in 1958. Consisted of Dion, Angelo D'Aleo, Fred Milano and Carlo Mastrangelo. Named for Belmont Avenue in the Bronx. Dion went solo in 1960 as did **The Belmonts**. Brief reunion with The Belmonts in 1967 and 1972, periodically since then. Inducted into the Rock and Roll Hall of Fame in 1989.

1)Runaround Sue 2)Lovers Who Wander 3)Ruby Baby

11/27/61	11	51			1	Runaround Sue	$100	Laurie 2009
7/14/62	12	22		©	2	Lovers Who Wander	$75	Laurie 2012
12/15/62+	29	22			3	Dion Sings His Greatest Hits	[G]	$75	Laurie 2013
3/23/63	20	21			4	Ruby Baby	$40	Columbia 8810
6/22/63	115	6			5	Dion Sings To Sandy (and all his other girls)	[K]	$50	Laurie 2017
12/21/68+	128	11		©	6	Dion	$50	Laurie 2047
1/1/72	200	2			7	Sanctuary	$20	Warner 1945

DEBUT	PEAK	WKS	RIAA	CD	ARTIST — Album Title	Catalog	Sym	$	Label & Number

DION — Cont'd

| 12/2/72 | 197 | 4 | | | 8 Suite For Late Summer... | | | $20 | Warner 2642 |
| 2/24/73 | 144 | 8 | | © | 9 Reunion-Live At Madison Square Garden 1972 .... | | [L] | $20 | Warner 2664 |

DION & THE BELMONTS
recorded on 6/2/72

| 3/24/73 | 194 | 5 | | | 10 Dion's Greatest Hits .... | | [G] | $20 | Columbia 31942 |
| 5/20/89 | 130 | 19 | | © | 11 Yo Frankie.. | | | $10 | Arista 8549 |

Abraham, Martin And John (6,7) 4
Almond Joy (7)
Always In The Rain (11)
And The Night Stood Still (11) 75
Brand New Morning (7)
Come Go With Me (2) 48
Didn't You Change? (8)
Dolphins, The (6)
Don't Pity Me (3) 40
Dream Lover (1)
Drip, Drop (9)
Drive All Night (11)
End Of The World (7)
Everybody's Talkin' (6)
Fever (4)
From Both Sides Now (6) 91
Go Away Little Girl (4)

Gonna Make It Alone (4)
Gotta Get Up (7)
Harmony Sound (7)
He Looks A Lot Like Me (6)
He'll Only Hurt You (4)
I Can't Go On (Rosalie) (5)
(I Was) Born To Cry (2) 42
I Wonder Why (3,9,10) 22
I've Cried Before (4)
I've Got To Get To You (11)
In The Still Of The Night (1,3) 38
It All Fits Together (8)
Jennifer Knew (8)
Just You (5)
Kansas City (1)
King Of The New York Streets (11)
King Without A Queen (2)

Life Is But A Dream (4)
Little Diane (2,5,9) 8
Little Girl (5)
Little Miss Blue (3) 96
Little Star (1,11)
Loneliest Man In The World (4)
Lonely Teenager (3,10) 12
Lonely World (1)
Lost For Sure (2)
Love Came To Me (5) 10
Lover's Prayer (3,10) 73
Lovers Who Wander (2,10) 3
Loving You Is Killing Me (11)
Loving You Is Sweeter Than Ever (6)
Majestic, The (1) 36
My Mammy (4)
My Private Joy (5)
No One Knows (3,9,10) 19

Please Be My Friend (medley) (7)
Purple Haze (6) 63
Queen Of The Hop (2,5)
Ruby Baby (4,7,9) 2
Runaround Sue (1,9,10) 1
Runaway Girl (1,5)
Running Close Behind You (8)
Sanctuary (7)
Sandy (2,5) 21
Sea Gull (6)
Serenade (11)
Shout (2)
Sisters Of Mercy (6)
Soft Parade Of Years (8)
Somebody Nobody Wants (1)
Stagger Lee (2)
Sun Fun Song (6)
Sunshine Lady (7)

Take A Little Time (medley) (7)
Take Good Care Of My Baby (1)
Teen Angel (3,5)
Teenager In Love (3,9,10) 5
Tennessee Madonna (8)
That's My Desire (3,9)
To Dream Tomorrow (8)
Tomorrow Is A Long Time (medley) (7)
Tonight, Tonight (7)
Tower Of Love (11)
Traveler In The Rain (8)
Twist, The (2)
Unloved, Unwanted Me (4)
Wanderer, The (1,7,9,10) 2
Wedding Song (8)
When You Wish Upon A Star (3,10) 30

Where Or When (3,9,10) 3
Will Love Ever Come My Way (4)
Willigo (7)
Wonderful Girl (5)
Written On The Subway Wall (medley) (11)
Yo Frankie (She's All Right With Me) (11)
You Better Watch Yourself (Sonny Boy) (6)
You Made Me Love You (I Didn't Want To Do It) (4)
You're Nobody 'Til Somebody Loves You (4)

★223★ DION, Celine   **'96**
Born on 3/30/68 in Charlemagne, Quebec, Canada. Pop singer. Married her longtime manager, Rene Angelil, on 12/17/94.

1/19/91	74	26	▲	©	1 Unison..	C:#27/5		$10	Epic 46893
4/18/92	34	76	▲²	©	2 Celine Dion	C:#13/12		$10	Epic 52473
11/27/93+	4	149	▲⁶	©	3 The Colour Of My Love	C:#3/64		$10	550 Music 57555
3/30/96	❶³	113	▲¹⁰	©	4 Falling Into You	C:#4/67		$10	550 Music 67541

1996 Grammy winner: Album of the Year

| 12/6/97+ | ❶¹ | 84 | ▲¹⁰ | © | 5 Let's Talk About Love | C:#46/3 | | $10 | 550 Music 68861 |
| 11/21/98 | 2² | 17 | ▲⁴ | © | 6 These Are Special Times | C:❶⁷/21 | [X] | $10 | 550 Music 69523 |

Christmas charts: 1/'98, 2/'99, 7/'00

| 12/4/99 | ❶³ | 87 | ▲⁶ | © | 7 All The Way...A Decade Of Song | | [G] | $10 | 550 Music 63760 |
| 11/11/00 | 28 | 17 | | © | 8 The Collector's Series Volume One .... | | [K] | $10 | 550 Music 85148 |

Adeste Fideles (O Come All Ye Faithful) (6)
All By Myself (4,8) 4
All The Way (7)
Amar Haciendo El Amor (3)
Another Year Has Gone By (4)
Ave Maria (6)
Be The Man (On This Night) (8)
Beauty And The Beast (2,7) 9
Because You Loved Me (4,7) 1
Blue Christmas (6)
Brahms' Lullaby (6)
Call The Man (4)
Christmas Eve (6)
Christmas Song (Chestnuts Roasting On An Open Fire) (6)
Colour Of My Love (3)

Declaration Of Love (4)
Did You Give Enough Love (3)
Don't Save It All For Christmas Day (6)
Dreamin' Of You (4)
Everybody's Talkin' My Baby Down (3)
Falling Into You (4,8)
Feliz Navidad (6)
First Time Ever I Saw Your Face (7)
Fly (4)
Halfway To Heaven (2)
Happy Xmas (War Is Over) (6)
Have A Heart (1)
I Don't Know (4)
I Feel Too Much (1)
I Hate You Then I Love You (5)
I Love You (4)

I Love You, Goodbye (2)
I Remember L.A. (3)
I Want You To Need Me (7)
I'm Loving Every Moment With You (1)
I'm Your Angel (6,7) 1
If I Were You (2)
If Love Is Out The Question (1)
If That's What It Takes (4)
(If There Was) Any Other Way (1) 35
If Walls Could Talk (7)
If We Could Start Over (1)
If You Asked Me To (2,7) 4
If You Could See Me Now (1)
Immortality (5)
It's All Coming Back To Me Now (4,7) 2
Just A Little Bit Of Love (5)

Last To Know (1)
Les Cloches Du Hameau (6)
Let's Talk About Love (5)
Little Bit Of Love (2)
Live (7)
Love By Another Name (1)
Love Can Move Mountains (2,7) 36
Love Doesn't Ask Why (3)
Love Is On The Way (5)
Lovin' Proof (3)
Magic Of Christmas Day (God Bless Us Everyone) (6)
Make You Happy (4)
Miles To Go (Before I Sleep) (5)
Misled (3) 23
My Heart Will Go On (Love Theme From 'Titanic) (5,7) 1
Next Plane Out (3)

No Living Without Loving You (3)
Nothing Broken But My Heart (2) 29
O Holy Night (6)
Only One Road (3,8) 93
Pour Que Tu M'Aimes Encore (8)
Power Of Love (3,7) 1
Power Of The Dream (8)
Prayer, The (6,8)
Real Emotion (3)
Reason, The (5,8)
Refuse To Dance (3)
River Deep, Mountain High (4)
Seduces Me (4,8)
Show Some Emotion (5)
Tell Him (5,8)
That's The Way It Is (7,8) 6

Then You Look At Me (7)
These Are The Special Times (6)
To Love You More (5,7)
Treat Her Like A Lady (5)
Un Garcon Pas Comme Les Autres (3)
Unison (1)
Us (5,8)
Water From The Moon (2)
When I Fall In Love (3)
When I Need You (5)
Where Does My Heart Beat Now (1,8) 4
Where Is The Love (5)
Why Oh Why (5)
With This Tear (2,8)

★276★ DIRE STRAITS   **'85**
Rock group formed in London: **Mark Knopfler** (vocals, guitar) and his brother David (guitar), with John Illsley (bass) and Pick Withers (drums). David left in mid-1980, replaced by Hal Lindes (left in 1985). Added keyboardist Alan Clark in 1982. Terry Williams replaced drummer Pick Withers in 1983. Guitarist Guy Fletcher added in 1984. Mark and Guy were also members of **The Notting Hillbillies** in 1990. Lineup in 1991: Knopfler, Illsley, Fletcher and Clark, with Chris White (sax), Paul Franklin (pedal steel), Danny Cummings (percussion), Phil Palmer (guitar) and Chris Whitten (drums).
1)Brothers In Arms 2)Dire Straits 3)Communique

1/6/79	2¹	41	▲²	©	1 Dire Straits			$12	Warner 3266
6/30/79	11	19	●	©	2 Communique			$12	Warner 3330
11/15/80	19	31	▲	©	3 Making Movies			$12	Warner 3480
10/16/82	19	32	●	©	4 Love Over Gold			$12	Warner 23728
3/12/83	53	15		©	5 Twisting By The Pool		[M]	$12	Warner 29800
4/21/84	46	18	●	©	6 Dire Straits Live - Alchemy		[L]	$15	Warner 25085 [2]
6/8/85	❶⁹	97	▲⁹	©	7 Brothers In Arms			$10	Warner 25264
11/12/88	62	17	▲	©	8 Money For Nothing.......................................		[G]	$10	Warner 25794
9/28/91	12	32	▲	©	9 On Every Street			$10	Warner 26680
5/29/93	116	5		©	10 On The Night......................................		[L]	$10	Warner 45259

Angel Of Mercy (2)
Badges, Posters, Stickers, T-Shirts (8)
Brothers In Arms (7,8,10)
Bug, The (9)
Calling Elvis (9,10)
Communique (4)
Down To The Waterline (1,8)
Expresso Love (3,6)
Fade To Black (9)
Follow Me Home (2)

Going Home (6)
Hand In Hand (3)
Heavy Fuel (9,10)
How Long (9)
If I Had You (5)
In The Gallery (1)
Industrial Disease (4) 75
Iron Hand (9)
It Never Rains (4)
Lady Writer (2) 45
Les Boys (3)

Lions (1)
Local Hero, Theme From ..see: Going Home
Love Over Gold (4)
Man's Too Strong (7)
Money For Nothing (7,8,10) 1
My Parties (9)
News (2)
On Every Street (9,10)
Once Upon A Time In The West (2,6)

One World (7)
Planet Of New Orleans (9)
Portobello Belle (2,8)
Private Investigation (4,6,8,10)
Ride Across The River (7)
Romeo And Juliet (3,6,8,10)
Setting Me Up (1)
Single-Handed Sailor (2)
Six Blade Knife (1)
Skateaway (3) 58
So Far Away (7) 19

Solid Rock (3,6)
Southbound Again (1)
Sultans Of Swing (1,6,8) 4
Telegraph Road (4,6)
Ticket To Heaven (6)
Tunnel Of Love (3,6,8)
Twisting By The Pool (5,6)
Two Young Lovers (5,6)
Walk Of Life (7,8,10) 7
Water Of Love (1)
When It Comes To You (9)

Where Do You Think You're Going? (2,8)
Why Worry (7)
Wild West End (1)
You And Your Friend (9,10)
Your Latest Trick (7,10)

DIRKSEN, Senator Everett McKinley '67

Born on 1/4/1896 in Pekin, Illinois. Died on 9/7/69 (age 73). U.S. senator from Illinois (1950-69).

1/7/67	**16**	16		©	1 **Gallant Men**		[T]	$20	Capitol 2643
8/5/67	148	3			2 **Man Is Not Alone**		[T]	$20	Capitol 2754
12/23/67	52[X]	2			3 **Everett McKinley Dirksen at Christmas Time**		[X-T]	$20	Capitol 2792

Beatitudes, The (2)
Carpenter Came (2)
Christ Has Come....Joy To The World! (3)
First Time The Christmas Story Was Told (3)
Gallant Men (1) *29*
Gettysburg Address (1)

Greatest Thing In The World (2)
I Heard The Bells On Christmas Day (3)
In The Beginning (2)
Man Is Not Alone (2)
Night Before Christmas (3)
O Little Town Of Bethlehem (3)

Pledge Of Allegiance To The Flag (1)
Prayer Of A Humble Man (2)
Prophecy: He Is Coming (3)
Shepherd And His Flock (2)
Shepherds Are Guided: Away In A Manger (3)
Silent Night (3)

Star Spangled Banner (1)
Story Of Gettysburg (1)
Story Of The Battle For Independence (1)
Story Of The Flag (1)
Story Of The Mayflower And The Mayflower Compact (1)

Story Of The Statue Of Liberty And The New Colossus (1)
Way Is Swift (2)
Wise Men (3)
Word To Guide The Way (2)
You Are The Captain Of Your Soul (2)

DIRT BAND, The — see NITTY GRITTY DIRT BAND

DIRTY '01

Rap duo from Montgomery, Alabama: Daniel Thomas and Tavares Webster.

3/17/01	**88**	17		©	**The Pimp & Da Gangsta**			$10	Universal 13557

Bendin' Corners
Candyman
Da Land

Dipped In Blak
Gimme Sum Mo
Hit Da Floe

Pimp & Da Gangsta
R.I.P.
Ride

Rollin Vogues
6 Deep Creepin
Twinkys

Yean Heard

DIRTY LOOKS '89

Hard-rock group from Pennsylvania: Dutch-born Henrik Ostergaard (vocals, guitar), Paul Lidel (guitar), Jack Pyers (bass) and Gene Barnett (drums).

5/21/88	**134**	14		©	1 **Cool From The Wire**			$10	Atlantic 81836
8/19/89	118	11		©	2 **Turn Of The Screw**			$10	Atlantic 81992

Always A Loser (2)
Can't Take My Eyes Off Of You (1)
C'mon Frenchie (2)

Cool From The Wire (1)
Get It Right (1)
Get Off (1)
Go Away (1)

Have Some Balls (2)
Hot Flash Jelly Roll (2)
It's A Bitch (1)
It's Not The Way You Rock (1)

L.A. Anna (2)
Love Screams (2)
No Brains Child (1)
Nobody Rides For Free (2)

Oh Ruby (1)
Put A Spell On You (1)
Slammin' To The Big Beat (1)
Take What Ya Get (2)

Tokyo (1)
Turn Of The Screw (Who's Screwing You) (2)
Wastin' My Time (1)

DISCO TEX & HIS SEX-O-LETTES '75

Disco studio group assembled by producer **Bob Crewe**. Featuring lead voice Sir Monti Rock III (real name: Joseph Montanez).

5/3/75	**36**	22			**Disco Tex & His Sex-O-Lettes**			$12	Chelsea 505

Around The World (medley)
Boogie Flap

Get Dancin' *10*
(I See Your) Name Up In Lights

I Wanna Dance Wit' Choo
(Doo Dat Dance), Part 1 *23*

Jam Band *80*
Love Is A Killer

Outrageous
Shirley Wood (medley)

DISHWALLA '96

Pop-rock group from Santa Barbara, California: J.R. Richards (vocals), Rodney Browning (guitar), Scot Alexander (bass) and George Pendergast (drums). Jim Wood (keyboards) added in 1997.

5/18/96	**89**	34	●	©	1 **Pet Your Friends**			$10	A&M 540319
8/29/98	164	1		©	2 **And You Think You Know What Life's About**			$10	A&M 540948

All She Can See (1)
Bottom Of The Floor (2)
Bridge Song (2)
Charlie Brown's Parents (1)

Counting Blue Cars (1) *15*
Explode (1)
Feeder, The (1)
5 Star Day (2)

Give (1)
Gone Upside Down (2)
Haze (1)
Healing Star (2)

Miss Emma Peel (1)
Moisture (1)
Once In A While (2)
Only For So Long (1)

Pop Guru (2)
Pretty Babies (1)
So Blind (2)
So Much Time (1)

Stay Awake (2)
Truth Serum (2)
Until I Wake Up (2)

DISTURBED '00

Hard-rock group from Chicago: David Draiman (vocals), Dan Donegan (guitar), Fuzz (bass) and Mike Wengren (drums).

5/13/00	**29**	73↑	▲	©	**The Sickness**			$10	Giant 24738

Conflict
Down With The Sickness

Droppin' Plates
Fear

Game, The
Meaning Of Life

Numb
Shout

Stupify
Violence Fetish

Voices
Want

D.I.T.C. '00

All-star rap group: **Big L**, **Fat Joe**, **O.C.**, Showbiz and AG, Diamond, Lord Finesse and Buckwild. DITC: Diggin' In The Crates.

3/11/00	**141**	2		©	**D.I.T.C.**			$10	Tommy Boy 1304

Champagne Thoughts
Da Enemy
Day One

Drop It Heavy
Ebonics
Foundation

Get Yours
Hey Luv
Stand Strong

Thick
Tribute
Way Of Life

Weekend Nights
Where Ya At

DIVINE '99

Female R&B vocal trio from New Jersey: Nikki Bratcher, Kia Thornton and Tonia Tash.

11/14/98+	**126**	21		©	**Fairy Tales**			$10	Pendulum 12325

All You Need
Fairy Tales
Good 'N Plenty

I Never Thought
I Wish
It's About Time

Lately *1*
Missing U
My Love

One More Try *29*
Sweet Essence (Your Love Is Something)

Tell Me

DIVINYLS '91

Rock group from Australia: Christina Amphlett (vocals), Mark McEntee (guitar), Bjarne Olin (keyboards), Richard Grossman (bass) and J.J. Harris (drums). Grossman joined the **Hoodoo Gurus** in 1989. By 1991, group reduced to a duo of Amphlett and McEntee.

12/7/85+	**91**	18		©	1 **What A Life!**			$10	Chrysalis 41511
2/16/91	15	26	●	©	2 **Divinyls**			$10	Virgin 91397

Bless My Soul (It's Rock-N-Roll) (2)
Bullet (2)
Casual Encounter (1)

Dear Diary (1)
Don't You Go Walking (1)
Follow Through (2)
Good Die Young (1)

Guillotine Day (1)
Heart Telegraph (1)
I Touch Myself (2) *4*
I'm On Your Side (1)

If Love Was A Gun (2)
In My Life (1)
Lay Your Body Down (2)
Love School (2)

Make Out Alright (2)
Motion (1)
Need A Lover (2)
Pleasure And Pain (1) *76*

Sleeping Beauty (1)

DIXIE CHICKS '99

Female country trio from Lubbock, Texas: sisters Emily Robison (guitar, banjo) and Martie Seidel (fiddle, mandolin), with Natalie Maines (lead vocals).

2/14/98+	**4**	134	▲[11]	©	1 **Wide Open Spaces**	C:❶[1]/*56*		$10	Monument 68195
9/18/99	❶[2]	107↑	▲[9]	©	2 **Fly**			$10	Monument 69678

Am I The Only One (Who's Ever Felt This Way) (1)
Cold Day In July (2) *65*
Cowboy Take Me Away (2) *27*
Don't Waste Your Heart (2)
Give It Up Or Let Me Go (1)

Goodbye Earl (2) *19*
Heartbreak Town (2)
Hello Mr. Heartache (2)
Hole In My Head (2)
I Can Love You Better (1) *77*
I'll Take Care Of You (1)

If I Fall You're Going Down With Me (2) *38*
Let 'Er Rip (1)
Let Him Fly (2)
Loving Arms (1)
Never Say Die (1)

Once You've Loved Somebody (1)
Ready To Run (2) *39*
Sin Wagon (2)
Some Days You Gotta Dance (2)

There's Your Trouble (1) *36*
Tonight The Heartache's On Me (2) *41*
Wide Open Spaces (1) *41*
Without You (2) *31*
You Were Mine (1) *34*

DEBUT	PEAK	WKS	RIAA	CD	ARTIST — Album Title	Catalog	Sym	$	Label & Number

DIXIE CUPS, The '64
Female vocal trio from New Orleans: sisters Barbara Ann and Rosa Lee Hawkins, with their cousin Joan Marie Johnson.

| 8/29/64 | 112 | 5 | | | **Chapel Of Love** | | | $75 | Red Bird 100 |

Ain't That Nice
All Grown Up
Another Boy Like Mine
Chapel Of Love *1*
Gee Baby Gee
Gee The Moon Is Shining Bright
Girls Can Tell
I'm Gonna Get You Yet
Iko Iko *20*
People Say *12*
Thank You Mama, Thank You Papa

DIXIE DREGS '82
Instrumental rock quintet: Steve Morse (guitar), T Lavitz (piano), Allen Sloan (violin), Andy West (bass) and Rod Morgenstein (drums). Mark O'Connor (violin) replaced Sloan in late 1981. Morse joined **Kansas** in 1986. Morgenstein later joined **Winger**.

5/27/78	182	4		©	1 **What If**	[I]		$15	Capricorn 0203
5/19/79	111	13		©	2 **Night Of The Living Dregs**	[I-L]		$15	Capricorn 0216
					side 2 recorded live at the Montreux Jazz Festival				
5/10/80	81	17		©	3 **Dregs Of The Earth**	[I]		$12	Arista 9528

DREGS:

| 4/18/81 | 67 | 14 | | © | 4 **Unsung Heroes** | [I] | | $12 | Arista 9548 |
| 3/27/82 | 56 | 15 | | | 5 **Industry Standard** | [I] | | $12 | Arista 9588 |

Assembly Line (5)
Attila The Hun (4)
Bash, The (2)
Bloodsucking Leeches (5)
Broad Street Strut (3)
Chips Ahoy (5)
Conversation Piece (5)
Country House Shuffle (2)
Crank It Up (5)
Cruise Control (4)
Day 444 (4)
Divided We Stand (4)
Gina Lola Breakdown (1)
Go For Baroque (4)
Great Spectacular (3)
Hereafter (3)
I'll Just Pick (4)
I'm Freaking Out (3)
Ice Cakes (1)
Kat Food (4)
Leprechaun Promenade (2)
Little Kids (1)
Long Slow Distance (2)
Night Meets Light (1)
Night Of The Living Dregs (2)
Odyssey (1)
Old World (3)
Patchwork (2)
Pride O' The Farm (3)
Punk Sandwich (2)
Ridin' High (5)
Riff Raff (2)
Road Expense (3)
Rock & Roll Park (4)
Take It Off The Top (1)
Travel Tunes (1)
Twiggs Approved (3)
Up In The Air (5)
Vitamin Q (5)
What If (1)
Where's Dixie? (5)

DIXON, Don '87
Born in Athens, Georgia. Rock singer/guitarist/producer. Produced albums for **R.E.M.** and **The Smithereens**.

| 3/7/87 | 162 | 8 | | © | **Most Of The Girls Like To Dance But Only Some Of The Boys Like To** | | | $10 | Enigma 73239 |

Andy
Cliche
Girls L.T.D.
Ice On The River
Just Rites
Praying Mantis
Renaissance Eyes
Skin Deep
Southside Girl
Talk To Me
Wake Up
(You're A) Big Girl Now
When A Man Loves A Woman

DJ CLUE? '01
Born in Queens, New York. Male rapper/producer.

1/2/99	26	25	▲	©	1 **The Professional**			$10	Roc-A-Fella 558891
9/16/00	6	11	●	©	2 **Backstage Mixtape**			$10	Roc-A-Fella 546641
3/17/01	3	16			3 **The Professional 2**			$10	Roc-A-Fella 542325

Back 2 Life 2001 (3)
Best Of Me (Part 2) (2)
Best Of Queens (It's Us) (3)
Bitch Be A Ho (1)
Brown Paper Bag Thoughts (1)
Change The Game (3)
Chinatown (3)
Come And Get It (2)
Come On (1)
Coming For You (3)
Cops & Robbers (1)
Cream 2001 (3)
Crime Life (2)
Dangerous (3)
Darlin' (2)
Don't Want Beef (2)
Exclusive-New Shit (2)
Fantastic 4 (1)
Fantastic Four Pt. 2 (3)
F**k A B***h (1)
Funkanella (2)
Gangsta Shit (1)
Getting It (3)
Gotta Be A Thug (2)
Hate Music (2)
I Don't Care (3)
I Like Control (1)
If They Want It (1)
In The Club (2)
It's My Thang '99 (1)
It's On (1)
Jay-Z Freestyle (3)
Just Leave Your Love (2)
Keep It Thoro (2)
Live From The Bridge (3)
Made Men (1)
M.A.R.C.Y. (3)
Millionaire (2)
My Mind Right (2)
My N****z Dem (3)
No Love (1)
People's Court (2)
Phone Patch (3)
Professional, The (1)
Queensfinest (1)
RED (3)
Road Dawgs (2)
Ruff Ryders Anthem (1)
Say What U Say (2)
So Hot (3)
That's The Way (1)
Thugged Out Shit (1)
Wanna Take Me Back (2)
What The Beat (3)
Whatever You Want (1)
Who Did You Expect (2)
Who's Next (X-Clue-Sive) (3)

DJ DMD '99
Born Dorie Dorsey in Port Arthur, Texas. Male DJ.

| 7/10/99 | 196 | 1 | | © | **Twenty-Two: P.A. World Wide** | | | $10 | Inner Soul 62428 |

DJ DMD and The Inner Soul Clique

Boonie Loc Off The Dome - Freestyle
Go Back Home
It's The B.U.D.
Landmines
Makin' Moves
Out There On That Corner
Shinin'
'Til The Casket's Closed
Trill Connection
25 Lighters
When You Come Home

D.J. JAZZY JEFF & THE FRESH PRINCE '88
Rap duo from Philadelphia: D.J. Jeff Townes (born on 1/22/65) and rapper/actor **Will Smith** (born on 9/25/68).

4/25/87+	83	35		©	1 **Rock The House**			$10	Jive 1026
4/23/88	4	55	▲3	©	2 **He's The D.J., I'm The Rapper**			$15	Jive 1091 [2]
11/18/89	39	20	●	©	3 **And In This Corner...**			$10	Jive 1188
7/27/91	12	42	▲	©	4 **Homebase**			$10	Jive 1392

JAZZY JEFF & FRESH PRINCE:

| 10/30/93 | 64 | 15 | ● | © | 5 **Code Red** | | | $10 | Jive 41489 |
| 6/6/98 | 144 | 6 | | © | 6 **Greatest Hits** | [G] | | $10 | Jive 41640 |

Ain't No Place Like Home (5)
Another Special Announcement (2)
As We Go (2)
Boom! Shake The Room (5,6) *13*
Brand New Funk (2,6)
Can't Wait To Be With You (5)
Caught In The Middle (Love & Life) (4)
Charlie Mack-The First Out The Limo (2)
Code Red (5)
D.J. On The Wheels (2)
Dog Is A Dog (4)
Don't Even Try It (1)
Dumb Dancin' (4)
Everything That Glitters (Ain't Always Gold) (3)
Fresh Prince Of Bel Air (6)
Girls Ain't Nothing But Trouble (1,6) *57*
Guys Ain't Nothing But Trouble (1)
He's The D.J., I'm The Rapper (2)
Here We Go Again (2)
Hip Hop Dancer's Theme (2)
Human Video Game (2)
I Think I Can Beat Mike Tyson (3,6) *58*
I Wanna Rock (5)
I'm All That (1)
I'm Looking For The One (To Be With Me) (5,6) *79*
Jazzy's Groove (3)
Jazzy's In The House (2)
Just Cruisin' (6)
Just Kickin' It (5)
Just One Of Those Days (1)
Just Rockin' (1)
Let's Get Busy Baby (2)
Live At Union Square, November 1986 (2)
Lovely Daze (6)
Magnificent Jazzy Jeff (1,6)
Megamix (4)
Men In Black (6)
Men Of Your Dreams (3)
My Buddy (2)
Nightmare On My Street (2,6) *15*
Numero Uno (3)
Parents Just Don't Understand (2,6) *12*
Pump Up The Bass (2)
Reverend, The (3)
Rhythm Trax-House Party Style (2)
Ring My Bell (4,6) *20*
Rock The House (1)
Scream (5)
Shadow Dreams (5)
Somethin' Like Dis (5)
Special Announcement (1)
Summertime (4,6) *4*
Summertime '98 (6)
Taking It To The Top (1)
Then She Bit Me (3)
Things That U Do (4)
This Boy Is Smooth (4)
Time To Chill (2)
Too Damn Hype (3)
Touch Of Jazz (1,6)
Trapped On The Dance Floor (4)
Twinkle Twinkle (I'm Not A Star) (5)
Who Stole My Car? (3)
Who Stole The D.J. (4)
You Got It (Donut) (4)
You Saw My Blinker (4,6)

DJ KOOL '96
Born John Bowman in Washington DC. Male rapper.

| 5/18/96 | 161 | 5 | | © | **(Let Me Clear My Throat)** | | | $10 | CLR 7209 |

I Got Dat Feelin'
Let Me Clear My Throat *30*
Music Ain't Loud Enuff
Put That Hump (In Your Back)
Twenty Minute Work-Out
What The Hell Ya Come In Here For

D.J. MAGIC MIKE '93
Born Michael Hampton in Orlando, Florida. Rap producer.

DEBUT	PEAK	WKS				$	Label & Number
7/21/90	157	18	● ©	1	Bass Is The Name Of The Game	$10	Cheetah 9403
1/26/91	153	22	● ©	2	Back To Haunt You!	$10	Cheetah 9404
					VICIOUS BASE Featuring D.J. MAGIC MIKE!		
11/23/91+	72	23	● ©	3	Ain't No Doubt About It	$10	Cheetah 9405
7/25/92	149	7	©	4	Twenty Degrees Below Zero	$10	Cheetah 9412
					D.J. MAGIC MIKE & M.C. MADNESS (above 2)		
3/27/93	67	18	● ©	5	Bass: The Final Frontier	$10	Magic 9413
3/27/93	107	7	©	6	This Is How It Should Be Done	$10	Magic 9411

Abracadabra (3)
Ain't Finished Yet (1)
Ain't No Doubt About It (3,4)
All Wild D.J.'s He Will Tame (2)
Are You Ready (2)
Back To Haunt You (2)
Bass Check I (6)
Bass Check II (5)
Bass To Interprise (5)
Boo-Boo Of Rough J. Rough (3)
Booty Dub (1)
Break, The (2)
Cellular Phone #1 & 2 (3)
Chillin On The DL (5)
Class Is In Session (3,4)
Comin On Strong (2)
Dance All Night (3)
Do You Like Bass? (3)
Do You Like Bass II (6)
Drop The Bass (Live) (5)
Drop The Bass (Pt. 2) (1)
Dynamic Duo (3)
E And The Sea-Gull (3)
Exile Via Freestyle (3)
Feel The Bass Again (1)
Feel The Bass, III (3)
Feel The Bass IV (5)
Feel The Beat (4)
For The Easy Listeners (1)
Fury Who? (4)
Get Laid, Get Funked (2)
Get Wicked (6)
Girls Move Their Butts (5)
Give 'Em An Example How A D.J. Works (3)
Give It To 'Em (1)
Going Home!!! (5)
Hard To Keep A Good Rhyme Down (2)
House Of Magic (1)
How The F*?k Do You Figure? (4)
I'm Gonna Make It Real Funky For You (3)
Intro To The Frontier (5)
It's Automatic (2)
Jeep Jammy (5)
Just Cruisin (3)
Just Get On Down And Rock (1)
Keep It Goin Now (6)
Last Person To F--k With (6)
Lesson, The (5)
Let The Bass Go (5)
Listen To The Bass Go Boom (4)
Lower The Dynamite (1,4)
Lyrical Marathon (5)
M&M's Gettin' Off (1)
Madness To The Brink Of Insanity (3)
Magic & Bartell (6)
Magic And Isaam's Groove (1)
Magic And The Chief (5)
Magic Meets Lace (2)
Magic's Cuttin Up! (6)
Magic's Funky Jeep Beats (6)
Magic's Mixing #3 (6)
Make The Car Go Boom! (5)
Man With The Bass (5)
Meeting, The (2)
Murder In The 1st Degree (3)
My Bass Machine (5)
Nice & Nasty (2)
No Stop To The Madness (2)
Orlando's In The House (3)
Party With Peace Of Mind (2)
Past And Present Times Of A Black Man (6)
Prelude To The Years (6)
Rhyme After Rhyme (6)
Rock The Funky Beat (1)
Royal Brothers In The House (6)
Royalty's Arrived (2)
Sgt. Fester (3)
Shake Your Booty Baby (3)
Slow Draggin (3)
Sorry, Wrong Beat (2)
Speedy And Poncho (3)
Suckers Frontin (3)
This D.J. Cuts Different Ways (5)
This Is For The Bassheads (5)
This Is How It Should Be Done (6)
Through The Years (5,6)
To The Fans I (5)
To The Fans II (6)
Twenty Degrees Below Zero (4)
20 (Degrees) Of Bass (6)
2 For The Bass (6)
Vicious Groove (2)
Why Did You Leave? (5)
Yo! (1)
You Want Bass (2)

DJ POOH '97
Born Mark Jordan in Los Angeles. Rap producer.

DEBUT	PEAK	WKS				$	Label & Number
8/2/97	116	3	©		Bad Newz Travels Fast	$10	Big Beat 92752

Bad Newz Travels Fast
Bump Yo Speakers
Ebonics
Gangsta Vocabulary
Get Money
Get Off
Grow Room
MC's Must Come Down
New World Order
No Idea
Nowhere 2 Hide
Who Cares
Whoop! Whoop!
You Ain't Shit

DJ QUIK '92
Born David Blake on 1/18/70 in Compton, California. Male rapper.

DEBUT	PEAK	WKS				$	Label & Number
3/2/91	29	42	▲ ©	1	Quik Is The Name	$10	Profile 1402
8/8/92	10	14	● ©	2	Way 2 Fonky	$10	Profile 1430
3/11/95	14	16	● ©	3	Safe + Sound	$10	Profile 1462
12/12/98	63	29	©	4	Rhythm-al-ism	$10	Profile 19034
6/3/00	18	13	©	5	Balance & Options	$10	Arista 16419

America'z Most Complete Artist (2)
Bombudd, Tha (1)
Bombudd II (4)
Born And Raised In Compton (1)
Can I Eat It? (3)
Change Da Game (5)
Dedication (1)
Deep (1)
Did Y'all Feel Dat? (5)
Diggin' U Out (3)
Divorce Song (5)
Do I Love Her? (5)
Do Whutcha Want (5)
Dollaz + Sense (5)
Don't You Eat It! (3)
Down, Down, Down (4)
8 Ball (1)
Get At Me (3)
Get 2Getha Again (4)
Hand In Hand (4)
Ho In You (3)
Hoorah 4 Tha Funk (3)
How Come? (5)
I Don't Wanna Party Wit U (5)
I Got That Feelin' (1)
I Useta Know Her (4)
Itz Your Fantasy (3)
Jus Lyke Compton (2) 62
Keep Tha "P" In It (3)
Last Word (2)
Let Me Rip Tonite (2)
Let You Havit (3)
Loked Out Hood (1)
Me Wanna Rip Your Girl (2)
Medley For A "V" (The P***y Medley) (4)
Mo' Pussy (2)
Niggaz Still Trippin' (2)
No Bullshit (2)
No Doubt (4)
Only Fo' Tha Money (2)
Pitch In On A Party (5)
Quik Is The Name (1)
Quik's Groove (1)
Quik'z Groove II (For U 2 Rip 2) (2)
Quik's Groove III (3)
Quik's Groove V (5)
Quikker Said Than Dunn (5)
Roger's Groove (5)
Safe + Sound (3) 81
Sexuality (5)
Skanless (1)
So Many Wayz (4)
Somethin' 4 Tha Mood (3)
Speak On It (3)
Speed (4)
Street Level Entrance (3)
Sucka Free (3)
Summer Breeze (3)
Sweet Black Pussy (1)
Tear It Off (3)
Thinkin' 'Bout U (4)
Tonite (1) 49
U Ain't Fresh (5)
Way 2 Fonky (2)
We Came 2 Play (5)
We Still Party (4)
Well (5)
Whateva U Do (4)
When You're A Gee (2)
You'z A Ganxta (4)

DJ SHADOW '98
Born Josh Davis in 1972 in Los Angeles. Male DJ/producer based in England.

DEBUT	PEAK	WKS				$	Label & Number
1/31/98	118	4	©		Preemptive Strike	$15	Mo Wax 540867 [2]

High Noon
Hindsight
Influx
Organ Donor (Extended Overhaul)
What Does Your Soul Look Like (Parts 1-4)

DJ SKRIBBLE '01
Born Scott Ialacci in New York City. White DJ/producer. Former member of Young Black Teenagers.

DEBUT	PEAK	WKS				$	Label & Number
9/30/00	158	4	©	1	Essential Dance 2000	$10	Big Beat 83343
4/28/01	124	6	©	2	Essential Spring Break - Summer 2001	$10	Big Beat 35065

American Dream (2)
Barber's Adagio For Strings (1)
Beauty Of Silence (2)
Believe (1)
Bodyrock (1)
Desire (1)
Faith (2)
Flowers (1)
Groovejet (1,2)
Happy People (2)
Higher & Higher (1)
House Of God (1)
I Believe In Love (1)
I Do Both Jay And Jane (1)
I Wanna Be You (2)
I'm Not In Love (1)
Kemkraft 400 (1)
Kiss (When The Sun Don't Shine) (1)
9 PM (Till I Come) (1)
Pasilda (2)
Phat Bass (2)
Played A Live (The Bongo Song) (2)
Rocket Base (2)
Salsoul Nugget (If U Wanna) (2)
Sandstorm (2)
Sexual (Li Da Di) (1)
Silence (2)
Somebody (2)
Spaced Invader (2)
Stranger In My House (2)
Sun Is Shining (1)
Take A Picture (1)
That Sound (1)
Toca's Miracle (1)

DLR BAND — see ROTH, David Lee

D-MOB '90
Dance group assembled by producer Danny D. Lead singer Cathy Dennis went solo in late 1990.

DEBUT	PEAK	WKS				$	Label & Number
1/27/90	82	20	©		A Little Bit Of This, A Little Bit Of That	$10	FFRR 828159

All I Do
C'mon And Get My Love 10
It Is Time To Get Funky
It Really Don't Matter
Put Your Hands Together
Rhythm From Within
That's The Way Of The World 59
Trance Dance
We Call It Acieed

DMX '99
Born Earl Simmons on 12/18/73 in Yonkers, New York. Male rapper. Member of Ruff Ryders. DMX is short for Dark Man X. Starred in the movie Exit Wounds.

DEBUT	PEAK	WKS				Catalog	$	Label & Number
6/6/98	❶[1]	101	▲[4] ©	1	It's Dark And Hell Is Hot	C:#8/34	$10	Ruff Ryders 558227
1/9/99	❶[3]	55	▲[3] ©	2	Flesh Of My Flesh Blood Of My Blood		$10	Ruff Ryders 538640
1/8/00	❶[1]	74	▲[5] ©	3	...And Then There Was X		$10	Ruff Ryders 546933

DMX — Cont'd

ATF (1)
Ain't No Way (2)
Angel (3)
Blackout (2)
Bring Your Whole Crew (2)
Comin' For Ya (2)
Coming From (2)
Convo, The (1)

Crime Story (1)
D-X-L (Hard White) (3)
Damien (1)
Dogs For Life (2)
Don't You Ever (3)
Fame (3)
Flesh Of My Flesh, Blood Of My Blood (1)

For My Dogs (1)
Fuckin' Wit' D (1)
Get At Me Dog (1) *39*
Good Girls, Bad Guys (3)
Heat (2)
Here We Go Again (3)
How's It Goin' Down (1) *70*
I Can Feel It (1)

It's All Good (2)
Keep Your Shit The Hardest (2)
Let Me Fly (1)
Look Thru My Eyes (1)
Make A Move (3)
More 2 A Song (3)
Niggaz Done Started Something (1)

No Love 4 Me (2)
Omen, The (2)
One More Road To Cross (3)
Party Up (Up In Here) (3) *27*
Prayer III (3)
Professional, The (3)
Ready To Meet Him (2)
Ruff Ryders' Anthem (1) *94*

Slippin' (2)
Stop Being Greedy (1) *79*
We Don't Give A Fuck (2)
What These B*****s Want (3)
What's My Name? (3) *67*
X-Is Coming (1)

D-NICE '90
Born Derrick Jones on 6/19/70 in the Bronx, New York. Male rapper. Member of **Boogie Down Productions**.

| 8/11/90 | 75 | 13 | | © | 1 **Call Me D-Nice** | | | $10 | Jive 1202 |
| 12/14/91 | 137 | 5 | | © | 2 **To Tha Rescue** | | | $10 | Jive 41466 |

And There U Have It (2)
And You Don't Stop (1)
Call Me D-Nice (1)
Check Yourself (2)

Crumbs On The Table (1)
808 Is Coming (1)
Few Dollars More (1)
Get In Touch With Me (1)

Glory (1)
I Send This Out To... (2)
It's All About Me (1)
It's Over (1)

No, No, No (2)
Pimp Of The Year (1)
Rhymin' Skills (2)
Straight From Tha Bronx (2)

Time To Flow (2)
To Tha Rescue (2)
25 Ta Life (2)
Under Some Budda' (1)

D.O.A. '90
Punk-rock group from Vancouver: Joe Keithley (vocals), Chris Prohom (guitar), Sunny Boy Roy (bass) and Jon Card (drums).

| 6/9/90 | 184 | 5 | | © | **Murder.** | | | $10 | Restless 72376 |

Afrikana Security
Agony And The Ecstasy

Banana Land
Boomtown

Concrete Beach
Guns, Booze & Sex

Midnight Special
No Productivity

Suicidal
Waiting For You - Part 2

Warrior Lives Again
We Know What You Want

D.O.C., The '89
Born Tray Curry in Dallas. Male rapper.

| 8/19/89 | 20 | 34 | ▲ | © | 1 **No One Can Do It Better** | | | $10 | Ruthless 91275 |

produced by Dr. Dre

| 2/10/96 | 30 | 7 | | © | 2 **Helter Skelter** | | | $10 | Giant 24627 |

Beautiful But Deadly (1)
Bitchez (2)
Brand New Formula (2)
Comm. Blues (1)
Comm. 2 (1)

Crazy Bitchez (2)
D.O.C. & The Doctor (2)
Da Hereafter (2)
Erotix Shit (2)
4 My Doggz (2)

Formula, The (1)
.45 Automatic (2)
From Ruthless 2 Death Row (Do We All Part) (2)
Grand Finale (1)

It's Funky Enough (1)
Killa Instinc (2)
Lend Me An Ear (1)
Let The Bass Go (1)
Mind Blowin' (1)

No One Can Do It Better (1)
Portrait Of A Master Piece (1)
Return Of Da Livin' Dead (1)
Secret Plan (2)
Sonz o' Light (2)

Welcome To The New World (2)
Whirlwind Pyramid (1)

DOCTOR AND THE MEDICS '86
Glam-rock group from London: Clive "Doctor" Jackson (vocals), brothers Wendi and Collette Anadin (backing vocals), Steve Maguire (guitar), Richard Searle (bass) and Vom (drums).

| 9/13/86 | 125 | 8 | | © | **Laughing At The Pieces** | | | $10 | I.R.S. 5797 |

Burn
Come On Call Me

Kettle On A Long Chain
Lucky Lord Jim

Miracle Of The Age
Moon Song

No-One Loves You When You've Got No Shoes
Spirit In The Sky *69*

Smallness Of The Mustard Pot
Watermelon Runaway

DR. BUZZARD'S ORIGINAL SAVANNAH BAND '77
Disco group formed in New York City: brothers Stony (guitar) and Thomas "August Darnell" (bass) Browder. Featuring **Cory Daye** (vocals), Andy Hernandez (vibraphone) and Mickey Sevilla (drums). Darnell and Hernandez left in 1980 to form **Kid Creole & The Coconuts**.

| 8/21/76+ | 22 | 49 | ● | © | 1 **Dr. Buzzard's Original Savannah Band** | | | $12 | RCA Victor 1504 |
| 2/11/78 | 36 | 9 | | © | 2 **Dr. Buzzard's Original Savannah Band Meets King Penett** | | | $12 | RCA Victor 2402 |

Auf Wiedersehen, Darrio (2)
Betcha' The Love Bug Bitcha' (medley) (2)
Future D.J. (medley) (2)
Gigolo And I (2)
Hard Times (1)

I'll Always Have A Smile For You (2)
I'll Play The Fool (1) *80*
Lemon In The Honey (medley) (1,2)

March Of The Nignies (medley) (2)
Mister Love (2)
Nocturnal Interludes (2)
Organ Grinder's Tale (2)
Soraya (medley) (2)

Sour And Sweet (medley) (1,2)
Sunshower (1)
Transistor Madness (medley) (2)
We Got It Made (1)

Whispering/Cherchez La Femme/Se Si Bon (1) *27*
You've Got Something (medley) (1)

DR. DEMENTO — see VARIOUS ARTIST COMPILATIONS

DR. DRE '99
Born Andre Young on 2/18/65 in Compton, California. Rapper/producer. Co-founder of **N.W.A.** and **World Class Wreckin' Cru**. Produced several artists. Founded Death Row Records in 1992. Half-brother of **Warren G**.

1/2/93	3	86	▲³	©	1 **The Chronic**	C:#14/26		$10	Death Row 57128
10/8/94	43	8		©	2 **Concrete Roots - Anthology**	[K]		$10	Hitman 51170
6/8/96	52	5		©	3 **First Round Knock Out**	[K]		$10	Triple X 51226
12/4/99	2⁴	93	▲⁶	©	4 **2001**			$10	Aftermath 90486

Ackrite (4)
Another "G" Thang (2)
Bang Bang (4)
Big Ego's (4)
Bitch Niggaz (4)
Bitches Ain't Shit (1)
Bridgette (3)
Chronic, The (1)
Concrete Roots (2)
Day The Niggaz Took Over (1)

Deeez Nuuuts (1)
Deep Cover (2)
Doctor's Office (3)
Dre Day (1) *8*
Dre's Beat (2)
Ed-ucation (4)
Fly, The (3)
Forgot About Dre (4) *25*
Formula (2)
Fuck You (4)

Funky Flute (3)
Grand Finale (2)
He's Bionic (3)
Housewife (4)
It's Funky Enough (3)
It's Not Over (3)
Juice (3)
Let Me Ride (1) *34*
Let's Get High (4)
Light Speed (4)

Lil' Ghetto Boy (1)
Lyrical Gangbang (1)
Message, The (4)
Mo' Juice (3)
Murder Ink (4)
Must Be The Music (2)
Next Episode (4) *23*
Nicety (3)
Nickel Slick Nigga (3)
Nigga Witta Gun (1)

No More Lies (2)
Nuthin' But A "G" Thang (1) *2*
Pause 4 Porno (4)
Planet, The (2)
Rat-Tat-Tat-Tat (1)
Roach, The (1)
Sex Is On (3)
Some L.A. Niggaz (4)
Still D.R.E. (4) *93*
Stranded On Death Row (1)

Surgery II (2)
Turn Off The Lights (3)
$20 Sack Pyramid (1)
Watcher, The (4)
What's The Difference (4)
Xxplosive (4)

DR. HOOK '73
Pop-rock group from Union City, New Jersey: Ray Sawyer (vocals), Dennis Locorriere (vocals, guitar), George Cummings and Rick Elswit (guitars), William Francis (keyboards), Jance Garfat (bass) and Jay David (drums). John Wolters replaced David in 1973. Bob Henke replaced Garfat in 1976. Wolters died of cancer on 6/16/97 (age 52).

1)Sloppy Seconds 2)Dr. Hook & The Medicine Show 3)A Little Bit More

DR. HOOK AND THE MEDICINE SHOW:

4/29/72	45	23		©	1 **Dr. Hook & The Medicine Show**			$15	Columbia 30898
12/2/72+	41	31		©	2 **Sloppy Seconds**			$15	Columbia 31622
10/27/73	141	6			3 **Belly Up!**			$15	Columbia 32270

DR. HOOK:

7/5/75+	141	16			4 **Bankrupt**			$12	Capitol 11397
5/15/76	62	31			5 **A Little Bit More**			$12	Capitol 11522
11/18/78+	66	34	●	©	6 **Pleasure & Pain**			$12	Capitol 11859

DR. HOOK — Cont'd

DEBUT	PEAK	WKS	CD	# ARTIST — Album Title	Sym	$	Label & Number
11/24/79+	71	32		7 Sometimes You Win		$12	Capitol 12018
12/6/80	175	8		8 Rising		$12	Casablanca 7251
12/20/80+	142	12	©	9 Dr. Hook/Greatest Hits	[G]	$12	Capitol 12122
4/3/82	118	7	©	10 Players In The Dark		$12	Casablanca 7264

Acapulco Goldie (3) · **Baby Makes Her Blue Jeans Talk** (2) · Bad Eye Bill (5) · Ballad Of... (3) · Before The Tears (8) · **Better Love Next Time** (7,9) *12* · Blown Away (8) · Body Talking (8) · Bubblin' Up (4) · **Carry Me, Carrie** (2) *71* · Chained To Your Memory (10) · Clyde (6) · Come On In (3) · Cooky And Lila (4) · Couple More Years (5) · **Cover Of "Rolling Stone"** (2,9) *6* · Devil's Daughter (10) · Do Downs (4) · Do You Right Tonight (8) · Doin' It (8) · Dooley Jones (6) · Everybody Loves Me (4) · Everybody's Makin' It Big But Me (4) · Fire In The Night (10) · Four Years Older Than Me (1) · Freakin' At The Freaker's Ball (2) · Get My Rocks Off (2) · **Girls Can Get It** (8) *34* · Hearts Like Yours And Mine (10) · Help Me Mama (7) · Hey, Lady Godiva (1) · Hold Me Like You Never Had Me (8) · I Call That True Love (1) · I Can't Say No To Her (10) · I Can't Touch The Sun (2) · I Don't Feel Much Like Smilin' (7) · I Don't Want To Be Alone Tonight (6) · I Gave Her Comfort (6) · I Got Stoned And I Missed It (4) · I'd If Only Come And Gone (2) · **If Not You** (5) *55* · In Over My Head (7) · Judy (1) · Jungle To The Zoo (5) · Kiss It Away (1) · Knowing She's There (6) · Lady Sundown (10) · Last Mornin' (2) · Let Me Be Your Lover (4) · Levitate (4) · **Life Ain't Easy** (3) *68* · **Little Bit More** (5,9) *11* · Love Monster (7) · **Loveline** (10) *60* · Makin' It Natural (1) · Mama, I'll Sing One Song For You (1) · Marie Lavaux (1) · **Millionaire, The** (4) *95* · Monterey Jack (2) · More Like The Movies (5) · Mountain Mary (7) · 99 And Me (8) · Oh! Jesse (7) · On The Way To The Bottom (5) · **Only Sixteen** (4,5,9) *6* · Penicillin Penny (3) · Pity The Fool (10) · Put A Little Bit On Me (3) · Queen Of The Silver Dollar (2) · Radio, The (5) · **Roland The Roadie And Gertrude The Groupie** (3) *83* · S.O.S. For Love (8) · **Sexy Eyes** (7,9) *5* · **Sharing The Night Together** (6,9) *6* · Sing Me A Rainbow (1) · Stayin' Song (2) · Storms Never Last (6) · Sweetest Of All (6) · **Sylvia's Mother** (1,9) *5* · **That Didn't Hurt Too Bad** (8) *69* · Things I Didn't Say (2) · Turn On (10) · Turn On The World (2) · Up On The Mountain (5) · **Walk Right In** (9) *46* · What About You (5) · What Do You Want? (7) · When Lilly Was Queen (3) · When She Cries (1) · **When You're In Love With A Beautiful Woman** (6,9) *6* · Wonderful Soup Stone (3) · Wups (2) · **Years From Now** (7,9) *51* · You Ain't Got The Right (3) · You Make My Pants Want To Get Up And Dance (6)

DR. JOHN   '73

Born Malcolm Rebennack on 11/20/42 in New Orleans. Swamp-rock singer/pianist.

DEBUT	PEAK	WKS	CD	# ARTIST — Album Title	$	Label & Number
10/9/71	184	5		1 Dr. John, The Night Tripper (The Sun, Moon & Herbs)	$20	Atco 362
5/13/72	112	11	©	2 Dr. John's Gumbo	$20	Atco 7006
3/24/73	24	33	©	3 In The Right Place	$20	Atco 7018
6/16/73	105	12	©	4 Triumvirate	$15	Columbia 32172

MIKE BLOOMFIELD/JOHN PAUL HAMMOND/DR. JOHN

DEBUT	PEAK	WKS	CD	# ARTIST — Album Title	$	Label & Number
5/4/74	105	8	©	5 Desitively Bonnaroo	$15	Atco 7043
5/27/89	142	11	©	6 In A Sentimental Mood	$10	Warner 25889

Accentuate The Positive (6) · Baby Let Me Kiss You (4) · Big Chief (2) · Black John The Conqueror (1) · Black Night (6) · Blow Wind Blow (2) · Can't Git Enuff (5) · Candy (6) · Cha-Dooky-Doo (4) · Cold Cold Cold (3) · Craney Crow (1) · Desitively Bonnaroo (5) · Don't Let The Sun Catch You Cryin' (6) · **(Everybody Wanna Get Rich) Rite Away** (5) *92* · Familiar Reality (1) · Go Tell The People (5) · Ground Hog Blues (4) · Huey Smith Medley (2) · I Been Hoodood (3) · I Yi Yi (4) · **Iko Iko** (2) *71* · In A Sentimental Mood (6) · It Hurts Me Too (4) · Junko Partner (2) · Just The Same (3) · Just To Be With You (4) · Last Night (4) · Let The Good Times Roll (2) · Let's Make A Better World (5) · Life (3) · Little Liza Jane (2) · Love For Sale (6) · Makin' Whoopee! (6) · Me - You = Loneliness (5) · Mess Around (2) · More Than You Know (6) · Mos' Scocious (5) · My Buddy (6) · Peace Brother Peace (3) · Pots On Fiyo (File Gumbo) (medley) (1) · Pretty Thing (4) · Qualified (3) · Quitters Never Win (4) · R U 4 Real (5) · **Right Place Wrong Time** (3) *9* · Rock Me Baby (4) · Same Old Same Old (3) · Sho Bout To Drive Me Wild (4) · Shoo Fly Marches On (3) · Sing Along Song (5) · Somebody Changed The Lock (2) · Stack-A-Lee (5) · Stealin' (5) · **Such A Night** (3) *42* · Those Lonely Lonely Nights (2) · Tipitina (2) · Traveling Mood (3) · What Comes Around (Goes Around) (3) · Where Ya At Mule (1) · Who I Got To Fall On (If The Pot Get Heavy) (medley) (1) · Zu Zu Mamou (1)

DOCTOR J.R. KOOL   '85

Studio group from New York City.

DEBUT	PEAK	WKS	ARTIST — Album Title	$	Label & Number
7/20/85	113	13	The Complete Story Of Roxanne...The Album	$10	Compleat 1014

Queen Of Rox (Shante Rox On) · Rap Your Own Roxanne · Real Roxanne · Roxanne, Roxanne · Roxanne's A Man (The Untold Story - Final Chapter) · Roxanne's Doctor - The Real Man · Roxanne's Revenge · Sparky's Turn (Roxanne You're Through)

DOE, John   '90

Born John Nommensen on 2/25/53 in Decatur, Illinois. Founded the band X with his former wife Exene Cervenka. Appeared in several movies. Took name from the Frank Capra movie *Meet John Doe*.

DEBUT	PEAK	WKS	CD	ARTIST — Album Title	$	Label & Number
6/23/90	193	3	©	Meet John Doe	$10	DGC 24291

By The Light · Dyin' To Get Home · It's Only Love · Knockin' Around · Let's Be Mad · Matter Of Degrees · My Offering · Real One · Take #52 · Touch Me, Baby · With Someone Like You · Worldwide Brotherhood

DOG, Tim   '91

Born Timothy Blair on 1/1/67 in the Bronx, New York. Male rapper.

DEBUT	PEAK	WKS	CD	ARTIST — Album Title	$	Label & Number
11/30/91	155	2	©	Penicillin On Wax	$10	Ruffhouse 48707

Bronx Nigga · Can't Fuck Around · DJ Quick Beat Down · Dog's Gonna Getcha · Fuck Compton · Get Off The Dick · Goin Wild In The Penile · I Ain't Havin It · I Ain't Takin No Shorts · I'll Wax Anybody · Low Down Nigga · Michel'le Conversation · NFL Shit · Patriotic Pimp · Phone Conversation W/Reporter · Robin Harris Shit · Secret Fantasies · Step To Me · You Ain't Shit

DOGG POUND, Tha   '95

Rap duo from Los Angeles: Delmar "**Daz Dillinger**" Arnaud and Ricardo "**Kurupt**" Brown. Arnaud is a cousin of **Snoop Doggy Dogg**. Duo also recorded as **D.P.G.**

DEBUT	PEAK	WKS	RIAA	CD	# ARTIST — Album Title	$	Label & Number
11/18/95	❶1	32	▲2	©	1 Dogg Food	$10	Death Row 50546
5/26/01	124	6		©	2 Dillinger & Young Gotti	$10	D.P.G. 1001

D.P.G.

At Night (2) · Best Run (2) · Big Pimpin 2 (1) · C-Walkin Cha Cha Cha (2) · Coastin (2) · Cyco-Lic-No (Bitch Azz Niggaz) (1) · D.P.G. (2) · Dipp Wit Me (2) · Do What I Feel (1) · Dogg Pound Gangstaz (1) · Doggz Day Afternoon (1) · Gitta Strippin (2) · Here We Are/Go Killem (2) · How Many? (2) · I Don't Like To Dream About Gettin Paid (1) · I'ma Gangsta (2) · If We All Fuc (1) · **Let's Play House** (2) *45* · My Heart Don't Pump No Tear (2) · New York, New York (1) · One By One (1) · Party At My House (2) · Reality (1) · Respect (1) · Ridin', Slippin' And Slidin' (1) · Sh_t Happenz (2) · Smooth (1) · Some Bomb Azz Pussy (1) · Sooo Much Style (1) · There's Someway Out (2) · Treat Her Like A Lady (2) · We About To Get Fucc Up (2) · We Livin Gangsta Like (2) · Work Dat P_ssy (2) · You're Jus A B.I.T.C.H. (2)

DOGGYS ANGELS   '00

Female rap trio assmebled by **Snoop Dogg**: Big Chan, Coniyac and Kola.

DEBUT	PEAK	WKS	CD	ARTIST — Album Title	$	Label & Number
12/9/00	138	2	©	Pleezbaleevit!	$10	Doggy Style 2130

SNOOP DOGG PRESENTS DOGGYS ANGELS

Angels Make The World Go Round · Baby If You're Ready · Bet I Never Slip · Cold Crush Gangsta · Curious · Frontline · Game To Get Over · Gangsta In Me · Hoodtraps · Keep Your Head Up · Pleezbaleevit! · Pop Your Collar 2 Dis · Put Your Hands Up · Ridaz With Me · Told You So · Yac & Koke

DOG'S EYE VIEW '96

Rock group from New York City: Peter Stuart (vocals, guitar), Oren Bloedow (guitar), John Abbey (bass) and Alan Bezozi (drums).

3/16/96	77	19		©	**Happy Nowhere**			$10	Columbia 66882

Bulletproof And Bleeding
Cottonmouth
Everything Falls Apart *14*

Haywire
I Wish I Was Here
Prince's Favorite Son

Shine
Small Wonders *flip*
Speed Of Silence

Subject To Change
Waterline
What I Know Now

Would You Be Willing

DOKKEN '87

Hard-rock group from Los Angeles: Don Dokken (vocals), **George Lynch** (guitar), Juan Croucier (bass) and Mick Brown (drums). Jeff Pilson replaced Croucier in late 1983. Disbanded in 1988. Lynch and Brown formed **Lynch Mob** in 1990. Dokken, Lynch, Pilson and Brown reunited as Dokken in early 1995.

10/15/83	136	13		©	1 **Breaking The Chains**			$10	Elektra 60290
10/13/84+	49	74	▲	©	2 **Tooth And Nail**			$10	Elektra 60376
12/21/85+	32	67	▲	©	3 **Under Lock And Key**			$10	Elektra 60458
12/5/87	13	33	▲	©	4 **Back For The Attack**			$10	Elektra 60735
12/3/88	33	17	●	©	5 **Beast From The East**		[L]	$15	Elektra 60823 [2]
					recorded April 1988 in Japan				
9/15/90	50	11		©	6 **Up From The Ashes**			$10	Geffen 24301
					DON DOKKEN				
6/3/95	47	6		©	7 **Dysfunctional**			$10	Columbia 67075
5/3/97	146	1		©	8 **Shadowlife**			$10	CMC Int'l. 86210

Alone Again (2,5) *64*
Bitter Regret (8)
Breaking The Chains (1,5)
Bullets To Spare (2)
Burning Like A Flame (4) *72*
Convenience Store Messiah (8)
Cracks In The Ground (8)
Crash 'N Burn (8)
Cry Of The Gypsy (4)
Don't Close Your Eyes (2)
Don't Lie To Me (3)
Down In Flames (6)
Dream Warriors (4,5)
Felony (1)

Forever (6)
From The Beginning (7)
Give It Up (6)
Hard To Believe (8)
Heartless Heart (2)
Heaven Sent (4,5)
Hello (8)
Here I Stand (8)
Hole In My Head (2)
Hunger, The (8)
Hunter, The (3)
I Can't See You (1)
I Don't Mind (8)
I Feel (8)

In My Dreams (3,5) *77*
In The Middle (1)
Inside Looking Out (7)
Into The Fire (2,5)
It's Not Love (3,5)
Jaded Heart (3)
Just Got Lucky (2,5)
Kiss Of Death (4,5)
Lesser Of Two Evils (7)
Lightnin' Strikes Again (3)
Live To Rock (Rock To Live) (1)
Living A Lie (6)
Long Way Home (7)
Lost Behind The Wall (4)

Maze, The (7)
Mirror Mirror (6)
Mr. Scary (4,5)
Night By Night (4)
Nightrider (1)
Nothing Left To Say (7)
1000 Miles Away (6)
Paris Is Burning (1)
Prisoner (4)
Puppet On A String (7)
Seven Thunders (1)
Shadows Of Life (7)
Sky Beneath My Feet (8)
Sleepless Nights (4,5)

Slippin' Away (3)
So Many Tears (4)
Standing In The Shadows (4,5)
Stay (6)
Stick To Your Guns (1)
Stop Fighting Love (4)
Sweet Chains (7)
Sweet Life (8)
Til The Livin' End (3)
Too High To Fly (7)
Tooth And Nail (2,5)
Turn On The Action (2,5)
Unchain The Night (3,5)
Until I Know (8)

Walk Away (5)
What Price (7)
When Heaven Comes Down (2,5)
When Love Finds A Fool (6)
When Some Nights (6)
Will The Sun Rise (3)
Without Warning (2)
Young Girls (2)

DOLBY, Thomas '83

Born Thomas Morgan Robertson on 10/14/58 in Cairo, Egypt (of British parentage). Singer/keyboardist. Member of **Bruce Woolley & The Camera Club**. Married to actress Kathleen Beller (Kirby Colby of TV's *Dynasty*).

2/5/83	20	31			1 **Blinded By Science**		[M]	$10	Harvest 15007
3/19/83	13	28		©	2 **The Golden Age Of Wireless**			$10	Capitol 12271
3/17/84	35	18		©	3 **The Flat Earth**			$10	Capitol 12309
5/7/88	70	19		©	4 **Aliens Ate My Buick**			$10	EMI-Manhattan 48075

Ability To Swing (4)
Airhead (4)
Airwaves (1,2)
Budapest By Blimp (4)
Cloudburst At Shingle Street (2)

Commercial Breakup (2)
Dissidents (3)
Europa And The Pirate Twins (2) *67*
Flat Earth (3)

Flying North (1,2)
Hot Sauce (4)
Hyperactive (3) *62*
I Scare Myself (3)
Key To Her Ferrari (4)

Mulu The Rain Forest (3)
My Brain Is Like A Sieve (4)
One Of Our Submarines (1,2)
Pulp Culture (4)
Radio Silence (2)

Screen Kiss (3)
She Blinded Me With Science (1,2) *5*
Weightless (2)
White City (3)

Windpower (1,2)

DOLCE, Joe '81

Born in 1947 in Painesville, Ohio. Novelty singer/songwriter.

6/27/81	181	4			**Shaddap You Face**		[N]	$12	MCA 5211

Ain't Been Missing You
Ain't No U.F.O. Gonna Catch My Diesel

Boat People
How Can Our Love Be Gone
If You Want To Be Happy

Return (Parts 1 & 2)
Shaddap You Face *53*
Stick It Out

Walking The Dog

DOMINGO, Plácido '94

Born on 1/21/41 in Madrid; raised in Mexico. Operatic tenor. Member of **The Three Tenors**.

11/7/81+	18	27	▲	©	1 **Perhaps Love**			$10	CBS 37243
3/13/82	164	6			2 **Domingo-Con Amore**			$10	RCA Victor 4265
4/9/83	117	11		©	3 **My Life For A Song**			$10	CBS 37799
12/15/84	9ˣ	1		©	4 **Christmas With Plácido Domingo**		[X]	$10	CBS 37245
					with the Vienna Symphony Orchestra conducted by Lee Holdridge; first released in 1981; reissued in 1982 with a different album cover				
3/2/91	171	6		©	5 **Be My Love...An Album Of Love**			$10	EMI 95468
12/18/93	154	3		©	6 **Christmas In Vienna**		[X-L]	$10	Sony Classical 53358
					PLÁCIDO DOMINGO-DIANA ROSS-JOSE CARRERAS				
					recorded on 12/23/92 at the Rathaus in Vienna				
12/21/96	196	2		©	7 **A Celebration Of Christmas**		[X-L]	$10	Elektra 62000
					JOSÉ CARRERAS-NATALIE COLE-PLÁCIDO DOMINGO				
					recorded on 12/23/95 at the Austria Center in Vienna				
12/20/97	192	2		©	8 **Merry Christmas From Vienna**		[X-L]	$10	Sony Classical 62970
					PLÁCIDO DOMINGO/YING HUANG/MICHAEL BOLTON				
					recorded on 12/16/96 at the Austria Center in Vienna; includes "Gesú Bambino" by Ying Huang				

Adeste Fideles (6)
Agnes Dei (7)
Aida (Celeste Aida) (2)
Aleluya (medley) (8)
Amazing Grace (7)
American Hymn (1)
Annie's Song (1)
Autumn Leaves (3)
Ave Maria (6)
¡Ay! Para Navidad (7)
Be My Love (5)
Because You're Mine (5)
Besame Mucho (3)
Blue Moon (medley) (3)

Cantique De Noel (O Holy Night) (4,7)
Carmen (Flower Song) (2)
Cavalleria Rusticana (Brindisi) (2)
Che Gelida Manina (2)
Children Of Christmas (8)
Corramos, Corramos (medley) (8)
Dormi, Dormi (medley) (8)
E Lucevan Le Stelle (2)
El Condor Pasa (5)
En Aranjeuz Con Tu Amor (5)
Fanfare (8)
First Noël (4,8)

Follow Me (3)
Fum, Fum, Fum (medley) (8)
Gift Of Love (6)
God Rest Ye Merry, Gentlemen (medley) (4)
Good King Wenceslas (medley) (4)
Have I The Courage To Say I Love You (2)
He Couldn't Love You More (1)
I Couldn't Live Without You For A Day (3)
I Don't Talk To Strangers (3)
I Heard The Bells On Christmas Day (4)

I Walked Today Where Jesus Walked (7)
I Wonder As I Wander (8)
I'll Be Home For Christmas (4,7)
Il Trovatore (Di Quella Pira) (2)
In The Bleak Midwinter (4)
It's Christmas Time This Year (4)
Jealousy Tango (3)
Jingle Bells (6,8)
Joy To The World (4,6,8)
Kling Glöckchen (medley) (8)
La Donna E Mobile (2)
La Golondrina (7)
La Vie En Rose (5)

La Virgen Lava Pañales (4,6)
Love Be My Guiding Star (5)
Love Story (5)
Mamma (5)
Man In The Crowd (Un Uomo Tra La Folla) (2)
Maria Wiegenlied (8)
Mary's Boy Child (4)
May Each Day (7)
Minuit, Chretien (medley) (6)
Moon River (medley) (3)
My Life For A Song (3)
My Treasure (1)
Navidad (7)

Noche De Paz ..see: Silent Night
Now While I Still Remember How (1)
Nu Är Det Jul Igen (medley) (8)
O Joyful Children (4,7)
O Little Town Of Bethlehem (medley) (4,6)
O Sole Mio (5)
O Tannenbaum (medley) (6)
Oh, Du Fröhliche (8)
Perhaps Love (1) *59*
Pero Mira Como Beben Los Peces En El Río (7)

DEBUT	PEAK	WKS	RIAA	CD	ARTIST — Album Title	Catalog	Sym	$	Label & Number

DOMINGO, Plácido — Cont'd

Pujdem Spolu Do Betlema (medley) (8)
Questa O Quella (2)
Quiereme Mucho (5)
Remembering (3)
Silent Night (4)

Sleigh Ride (7)
Sometimes A Day Goes By (1)
Somewhere, My Love (5)
Somewhere Over The Rainbow (5)
Songs Of Summer (3)

Spanish Eyes (5)
Stille Nacht (6,7)
There Will Be Love (3)
Time After Time (1)
To Love (1)

Tu Scendi Dalle Stelle (medley) (6)
Una Furtiva Lagrima (2)
Valencia (5)
Vesti La Giubba (2)
Villancico Yaucano (8)

Weihnachten (8)
What A Wonderful World (7)
What Child Is This? (7)
White Christmas (4,6,7,8)
Wiegenlied, Op. 49 No. 4 (6)
Yesterday (1)

DOMINO   '94

Born Shawn Ivy in 1972 in St. Louis; raised in Long Beach, California. Male rapper.

| 12/25/93+ | 39 | 33 | ● | © | 1 Domino | | | $10 | OutBurst 57701 |
| 6/29/96 | 152 | 1 | | © | 2 Physical Funk | | | $10 | OutBurst 531033 |

A.F.D. (1)
Diggady Domino (1)
Do You Qualify (1,2)
Domino Got Beats (2)

Get Your Groove On (2)
Getto Jam (1) 7
Good Part (2)
Hennessy (2)

Jam (1)
Long Beach Funk (2)
Long Beach Thang (1)
Macadocious (2)

Microphone Musician (2)
Money Is Everything (1)
Physical Funk (2) 87
Raincoat (1)

So Fly (2)
Sweet Potatoe Pie (1) 27
That's Real (1)
Trickin (1)

DOMINO, Fats   '57

Born Antoine Domino on 2/26/28 in New Orleans. Legendary R&B singer/songwriter/pianist. Heavily influenced by Fats Waller and Albert Ammons. Joined the Dave Bartholomew band (mid-1940s). Signed to Imperial record label in 1949. Nicknamed "The Fat Man." Heard on many sessions cut by other R&B artists. In the movies *Shake, Rattle And Rock!*, *Jamboree!*, *The Big Beat* and *The Girl Can't Help It*. Inducted into the Rock and Roll Hall of Fame in 1986. Won Grammy's Hall of Fame and Lifetime Achievement Awards in 1987.

11/10/56+	18	6		©	1 Fats Domino - Rock And Rollin'			$150	Imperial 9009
2/23/57	19	2		©	2 This Is Fats Domino!			$150	Imperial 9028
3/23/57	17	4		©	3 Rock And Rollin' With Fats Domino			$150	Imperial 9004
					released in 1956				
7/21/62	113	6		©	4 Million Sellers By Fats	[G]		$100	Imperial 9195
10/5/63	130	4			5 Here Comes...Fats Domino			$50	ABC-Paramount 455
10/19/68	189	2		©	6 Fats Is Back			$40	Reprise 6304

Ain't Gonna Do It (4)
Ain't That A Shame (3) 10
All By Myself (3)
Are You Going My Way (1)
Blue Monday (2) 5
Blueberry Hill (2) 2
Bo Weevil (3) 35
Bye Baby, Bye, Bye (5)
Can't Go On Without You (4)
Careless Love (1)
Don't Blame It On Me (3)
Fat Man (3)
Fat Man's Hop (2)

Fat's Frenzy (1)
Forever, Forever (5)
Goin' Home (3)
Going To The River (3)
Goodbye (1)
Honest Papas Love Their Mamas Better (6)
Honey Chile (2)
I Got A Right To Cry (5)
I Know (6)
I Love Her (1)
I'm In Love Again (1) 3
I'm Livin' Right (5)

I'm Ready (6)
If You Need Me (1) 98
Jambalaya (On The Bayou) (4) 30
Just A Lonely Man (5)
La La (2)
Land Of 1,000 Dances (4)
Let The Four Winds Blow (4) 15
Lovely Rita (6)
Make Her Belong To You (6)
My Blue Heaven (1) 19

My Girl Josephine (4) 14
My Heart Is Bleeding (4)
My Heart Is In Your Hands (1)
My Old Friend (6)
My Real Name (2) 59
Natural Born Lover (4) 38
One For The Highway (6)
One More Song For You (4)
Please Don't Leave Me (3)
Poor Me (3)
Poor Poor Me (2)
Red Sails In The Sunset (5) 35
Reeling And Rocking (2)

Rose Mary (3)
Second Line Jump (1)
Shu Rah (4) 32
So-Long (2) 44
So Swell When You're Well (6)
Song For Rosemary (5)
Swanee River Hop (1)
Tell Me The Truth, Baby (5)
There Goes (My Heart Again) (5) 59
Three Nights A Week (4) 15
Tired Of Crying (4)
Troubles Of My Own (2)

Trust In Me (2)
Wait Till It Happens To You (6)
Walking To New Orleans (4) 6
What A Price (4) 22
What's The Reason I'm Not Pleasing You (2) 50
When I'm Walking (Let Me Walk) (5)
When My Dreamboat Comes Home (1) 14
You Done Me Wrong (2)
You Said You Love Me (3)
You Win Again (4) 22

DONALDSON, Bo, And The Heywoods   '74

Pop group from Cincinnati: Bo Donaldson (keyboards), Mike Gibbons (vocals), Scott Baker (guitar), Gary Coveyou (reeds), Rick Joswick (percussion), David Krock (bass) and Nicky Brunetti (drums).

| 7/6/74 | 97 | 16 | | | Bo Donaldson And The Heywoods | | | $15 | ABC 824 |

Billy, Don't Be A Hero 1
Deeper And Deeper
Don't Ever Look Back

Fool's Way Of Lovin'
Girl Don't Make Me Wait
Goodbye Holly, Goodbye

Goodnight And Good Morning
Hang Your Lamp In The Window

Keep On Believin' In Love
Last Blues Song

Who Do You Think You Are 15

DONALDSON, Lou   '67

Born on 11/1/26 in Badin, North Carolina. Jazz alto saxophonist.

6/15/63	141	2		©	1 The Natural Soul	[I]		$25	Blue Note 84108
10/7/67	141	11		©	2 Alligator Bogaloo	[I]		$25	Blue Note 84263
10/26/68	182	6		©	3 Midnight Creeper	[I]		$25	Blue Note 84280
4/5/69	153	7			4 Say It Loud!	[I]		$25	Blue Note 84299
10/4/69	158	6		©	5 Hot Dog	[I]		$25	Blue Note 84318
7/11/70	190	2		©	6 Everything I Play Is Funky	[I]		$25	Blue Note 84337
9/22/73	176	4			7 Sassy Soul Strut	[I]		$15	Blue Note 109
9/28/74	185	3			8 Sweet Lou	[I]		$15	Blue Note 259

Alligator Bogaloo (2) 93
Aw Shucks! (2)
Bag Of Jewels (3)
Bonnie (5)
Brother Soul (4)
Caravan (4)
City, Country, City (7)
Dapper Dan (3)
Donkey Walk (6)

Elizabeth (3)
Everything I Do Gonh Be Funky (From Now On) (6)
Funky Mama (1)
Good Morning Heartache (7)
Hamp's Hump (4)
Herman's Mambo (8)
Hip Trip (8)
Hot Dog (5)

I Want A Little Girl (2)
If You Can't Handle It, Give It To Me (8)
Inner Space (7)
It's Your Thing (5)
Lost Love (8)
Love Eyes (8)
Love Power (3)
Love Walked In (1)

Midnight Creeper (3)
Minor Bash (6)
Nice 'N Greasy (1)
One Cylinder (2)
Over The Rainbow (6)
Peepin' (8)
Pillow Talk (7)
Rev. Moses (2)
Sanford And Son Theme (7)

Sassy Soul Strut (7)
Say It Loud (4)
Snake Bone (4)
Sow Belly Blues (1)
Spaceman Twist (1)
Summertime (4)
Thang, The (2)
That's All (1)
This Is Happiness (7)

Turtle Walk (5)
West Indian Daddy (6)
Who's Making Love (5)
You're Welcome, Stop On By (8)

DON AND THE GOODTIMES   '67

Rock group from Portland, Oregon: Don Gallucci (vocals, piano; **The Kingsmen**), Joey Newman (guitar), Jeff Hawks (tambourine), Buzz Overman (bass) and Bobby Holden (drums).

| 8/5/67 | 109 | 4 | | | So Good | | | $20 | Epic 26311 |

And It's So Good
Gimme Some Lovin'
Good Day Sunshine

I Could Be So Good To You 56
I Could Never Be

If You Love Her, Cherish Her And Such
Music Box

My Color Song
Sweet, Sweet, Mama
With A Girl Like You

Captain Beefheart
The Spotlight Kid ('72)

Carpenters
Ticket To Ride ('71)

Gene Chandler
The Duke Of Earl ('62)

Chubby Checker
Twistin' Round The World ('62)

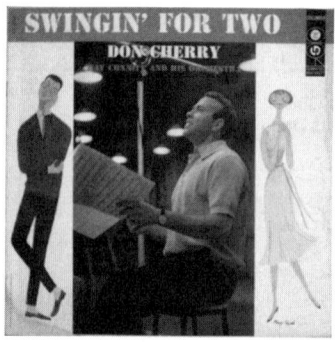

Don Cherry
Swingin' For Two ('56)

The Chieftains
Water From The Well ('00)

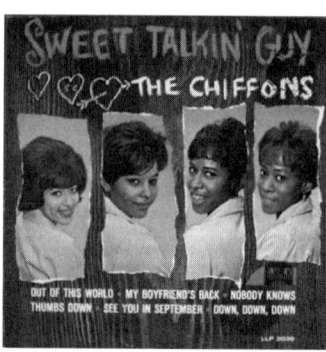

The Chiffons
Sweet Talkin' Guy ('66)

Lou Christie
Lou Christie ('63)

Myron Cohen
Everybody Gotta Be Someplace ('66)

Harry Connick, Jr
When Harry Met Sally ('89)

Chick Corea
The Mad Hatter ('78)

David Crosby/Graham Nash
Wind On The Water ('75)

Dick Dale And His Del-Tones
Checkered Flag ('63)

Bobby Darin
Things & Other Things ('62)

**James Darren/Shelley Fabares/
Paul Petersen...***Teenage Triangle ('63)*

Miles Davis
Doo-Bop ('92)

Sammy Davis-Count Basie
Our Shining Hour ('65)

Spencer Davis Group
Gimme Some Lovin' ('67)

John Denver
John Denver Gift Pak ('75)

Neil Diamond
The Feel Of Neil Diamond ('66)

Dig
Dig ('94)

Dion
Lovers Who Wander ('62)

Divine
Fairy Tales ('98)

D.J. Jazzy Jeff & The Fresh Prince
Rock The House ('87)

245

DONOVAN ★178★   '69

Born Donovan Leitch on 5/10/46 in Glasgow, Scotland; raised in London. Singer/songwriter/guitarist. Appeared in the movies *The Pied Piper of Hamlin* and *Brother Sun, Sister Moon*. Father of actress Ione Skye and actor Donovan Leitch, Jr.

1)*Donovan's Greatest Hits* 2)*Sunshine Superman* 3)*Mellow Yellow* 4)*Open Road* 5)*Donovan In Concert*

DEBUT	PEAK	WKS		CD	#	ARTIST — Album Title	Sym	$	Label & Number
7/17/65	30	23		©	1	**Catch The Wind**		$40	Hickory 123
12/18/65+	85	13		©	2	**Fairytale**		$40	Hickory 127
9/24/66	11	29		©	3	**Sunshine Superman**		$30	Epic 26217
10/1/66	96	7			4	**The Real Donovan**	[K]	$30	Hickory 135
2/18/67	14	21			5	**Mellow Yellow**		$30	Epic 26239
12/30/67+	60	15			6	**Wear Your Love Like Heaven**		$30	Epic 26349
1/6/68	19	22	●	©	7	**A Gift From A Flower To A Garden**		$40	Epic 171 [2]
						deluxe box set of the albums *Wear Your Love Like Heaven* and *For Little Ones*			
1/13/68	185	3			8	**For Little Ones**		$30	Epic 26350
4/6/68	177	4			9	**Like It Is, Was And Evermore Shall Be**	[K]	$30	Hickory 143
7/27/68	18	31		©	10	**Donovan In Concert**	[L]	$20	Epic 26386
10/19/68	20	20		©	11	**The Hurdy Gurdy Man**		$20	Epic 26420
2/22/69	4	56	▲	©	12	**Donovan's Greatest Hits**	[G]	$20	Epic 26439
9/13/69	23	24		©	13	**Barabajagal**		$20	Epic 26481
11/8/69	135	7			14	**The Best Of Donovan**	[K]	$20	Hickory 149
7/18/70	16	19		©	15	**Open Road**		$15	Epic 30125
11/14/70	128	8			16	**Donovan P. Leitch**	[K]	$20	Janus 3022 [2]
3/31/73	25	20			17	**Cosmic Wheels**		$15	Epic 32156
2/2/74	174	5		©	18	**Essence To Essence**		$15	Epic 32800
12/14/74+	135	6			19	**7-Tease**		$15	Epic 33245
6/5/76	174	3			20	**Slow Down World**		$15	Epic 33945

Alamo, The (1,4,16)
Appearances (17)
As I Recall It (11)
Atlantis (13) *7*
Ballad Of Geraldine (2,14)
Ballad Of The Crystal Man (2,4,16)
Belated Forgiveness Plea (2,4,16)
Bert's Blues (3)
Black Widow (20)
Bleak City Woman (5)
Boy For Every Girl (18)
Candy Man (2,14,16)
Car Car (Riding In My Car) (1)
Catch The Wind (1,4,9,12,14,16) *23*
Celeste (3,10)
Celtic Rock (15)
Changes (15)
Children Of The World (20)
Circus Of Sour (2)
Clara Clairvoyant (15)
Colours (2,4,9,12,14,16) *61*
Cosmic Wheels (17)
Cryin' Shame (20)
Curry Land (15)
Cuttin' Out (1)
Dark-Eyed Blue Jean Angel (20)

Dignity Of Man (18)
Divine Daze Of Deathless Delight (18)
Do You Hear Me Now (9)
Donna Donna (1,14)
Earth Sign Man (17)
Enchanted Gypsy (7,8)
Entertaining Of A Shy Girl (11)
Epistle To Derroll (7,8)
Epistle To Dippy (12) *19*
Fat Angel (3,10)
Ferris Wheel (3)
Get Thy Bearings (11)
Goldwatch Blues (1)
Goo Goo Barabajagal (Love Is Hot) (13) *36*
Great Song Of The Sky (19)
Guinevere (3,10)
Hampstead Incident (5)
Happiness Runs (13)
Hey Gyp (4,9,14,16)
Hi It's Been A Long Time (11)
House Of Jansch (5)
How Silly (19)
Hurdy Gurdy Man (11,12) *5*
I Like You (17) *66*
I Love My Shirt (13)
Intergalactic Laxative (17)
Isle Of Islay (7,8,10)
Jennifer Juniper (11,12) *26*

Jersey Thursday (2,14,16)
Joe Bean's Theme (15)
Josie (1,4,9,16)
Keep On Truckin' (1,16)
Lalena (12) *33*
Land That Doesn't Have To Be (6,7)
Lay Of The Last Tinker (7,8)
Lazy Daze (18)
Legend Of A Girl Child Linda (3)
Liberation Rag (10)
Life Goes On (18)
Life Is A Merry-Go-Round (18)
Little Boy In Corduroy (6,7)
Little Tin Soldier (2,14,16)
Love Of My Life (19)
Love Song (13)
Lullaby Of Spring (7,8,10)
Mad John's Escape (6,7)
Magpie, The (19)
Mandolin Man And His Secret (7,8)
Maria Magenta (17)
Mellow Yellow (5,10,12) *2*
Moon Rok (19)
Mountain, The (20)
Museum (17)
Music Makers (17)
My Love Is True (Love Song) (20)

New Year's Resovolution (15)
Observation, The (5)
Oh Deed I Do (4)
Oh Gosh (6,7)
Only The Blues (17)
Operating Manual For Spaceship Earth (18)
Ordinary Family (19)
Pebble Jo (3)
Pebble And The Man (10)
People Used To (15)
Peregrine (11)
Poke At The Pope (15)
Poor Cow (10)
Preachin' Love (10)
Quest, The (19)
Ramblin' Boy (1,4,16)
Ride-A-Mile (19)
Riki Tiki Tavi (15) *55*
River Song (15)
Rock And Roll Souljer (19)
Roots Of Oak (15)
Rules And Regulations (10)
Sadness (19)
Sailing Homeward (18)
Saint Valentines Angel (18)
Salvation Stomp (19)
Sand And Foam (5)
Season Of Farewell (15)
Season Of The Witch (3,12)

Skip-A-Long Sam (6,7)
Sleep (17)
Slow Down World (20)
Someone's Singing (6,7)
Song For John (15)
Song Of The Naturalist's Wife (7,8)
Starfish-On-The-Toast (7,8)
Summer Day Reflection Song (2,9,16)
Sun (6,7)
Sun Is A Very Magic Fellow (11)
Sunny Day (11)
Sunny Goodge Street (2,9,16)
Sunny South Kensington (5)
Sunshine Superman (3,12) *1*
Superlungs My Supergirl (13)
Tangerine Puppet (1,14)
Tangier (11)
Teas (11)
There Is A Mountain (10,12) *11*
There Is An Ocean (18)
There Was A Time (6,7)
Three King Fishers (3)
Tinker And The Crab (7,8)
To Sing For You (1,16)
To Susan On The West Coast Waiting (13) *35*

To Try For The Sun (2,4,9,16)
Trip, The (3)
Trudi (13)
Turquoise (4,16)
Under The Greenwood Tree (6,7)
Universal Soldier (2,9,14,16) *53*
Voice Of Protest (19)
Voyage Into The Golden Screen (7,8)
War Drags On (4,9,16)
Wear Your Love Like Heaven (6,7,12) *23*
Well Known Has-Been (20)
West Indian Lady (11)
Where Is She (13)
Why Do You Treat Me Like You Do (9,16)
Widow With Shawl (A Portrait) (7,8,10)
Wild Witch Lady (17)
Writer In The Sun (5,10)
Yellow Star (18)
You're Gonna Need Somebody On Your Bond (1)
Young Girl Blues (5,10)
Your Broken Heart (19)

DOOBIE BROTHERS, The ★146★   '79

Rock group formed in San Jose, California: **Patrick Simmons** (vocals, guitar), **Tom Johnston** (vocals, guitar), Tiran Porter (bass) and John Hartman (drums). Mike Hossack (percussion) added in 1972 (later replaced by Keith Knudsen). Jeff "Skunk" Baxter (slide guitar), formerly with **Steely Dan**, added in 1974. **Michael McDonald** (lead vocals, keyboards), added in 1975. Johnston left in 1978. Baxter and Hartman replaced by Cornelius Bumpus (keyboards, saxophone), John McFee (guitar) and Chet McCracken (drums) in 1979. Johnston wrote majority of hits from 1972-75; McDonald, from 1976-83. Disbanded in 1983. Re-formed in early 1988 with Johnston, Simmons, Hartman, Porter, Hossack, and Bobby LaKind (percussion). LaKind died of cancer on 12/24/92 (age 47).

1)*Minute By Minute* 2)*One Step Closer* 3)*Stampede*

DEBUT	PEAK	WKS		CD	#	ARTIST — Album Title	Sym	$	Label & Number
8/26/72	21	119	▲	©	1	**Toulouse Street**		$15	Warner 2634
3/31/73	7	102	▲²	©	2	**The Captain And Me**		$15	Warner 2694
3/16/74+	4	62	▲²	©	3	**What Were Once Vices Are Now Habits**		$15	Warner 2750
5/17/75	4	25	●	©	4	**Stampede**		$15	Warner 2835
4/3/76	8	44	▲	©	5	**Takin' It To The Streets**		$15	Warner 2899
11/20/76+	5	93	▲¹⁰	©	6	**Best Of The Doobies**	C:#38/15 [G]	$12	Warner 2978
9/10/77	10	21	●	©	7	**Livin' On The Fault Line**		$12	Warner 3045
12/23/78+	❶⁵	87	▲³	©	8	**Minute By Minute**		$12	Warner 3193
10/11/80	3	28	▲	©	9	**One Step Closer**		$12	Warner 3452
11/21/81	39	15	●	©	10	**Best Of The Doobies, Volume II**	[G]	$12	Warner 3612

DOOBIE BROTHERS, The — Cont'd

DEBUT	PEAK	WKS	RIAA	CD	ARTIST — Album Title	Sym	$	Label & Number
7/23/83	79	9			11 The Doobie Brothers Farewell Tour	[L]	$15	Warner 23772 [2]
6/10/89	17	20	●	© 12	Cycles		$10	Capitol 90371
5/11/91	82	9		© 13	Brotherhood		$10	Capitol 94623

Another Park, Another Sunday (3) *32*
Black Water (3,6,11) *1*
Busted Down Around O Connelly Corners (2)
Can't Let It Get Away (11)
Captain And Me (2)
Carry Me Away (5)
China Grove (2,6,11) *15*
Chinatown (7)
Clear As The Driven Snow (2)
Cotton Mouth (1)
Dangerous (13)
Dark Eyed Cajun Woman (2)
Daughters Of The Sea (3)
Dedicate This Heart (9)
Dependin' On You (8,10) *25*
Disciple (1)
Divided Highway (13)
Doctor, The (12) *9*
Don't Start Me To Talkin' (1,11)

Don't Stop To Watch The Wheels (8)
Double Dealin' Four Flusher (4)
Down In The Track (3)
Echoes Of Love (7,10,11) *66*
8th Avenue Shuffle (5)
Evil Woman (2)
Excited (13)
Eyes Of Silver (3) *52*
Flying Cloud (3)
For Someone Special (5)
Here To Love You (8,10) *65*
How Do The Fools Survive? (4)
I Been Workin' On You (4)
I Can Read Your Mind (12)
I Cheat The Hangman (4) *60*
Is Love Enough (13)
It Keeps You Runnin' (5,6) *37*
Jesus Is Just Alright (1,6,11) *35*
Just In Time (9)

Keep This Train A-Rollin' (9) *62*
Larry The Logger Two-Step (7)
Listen To The Music (1,6,11) *11*
Little Darling (I Need You) (7,10) *48*
Livin' On The Fault Line (7)
Long Train Runnin' (2,6,11) *8*
Losin' End (5)
Mamaloi (1)
Minute By Minute (8,10,11) *14*
Music Man (4)
Natural Thing (2)
Neal's Fandango (4)
Need A Lady (7)
Need A Little Taste Of Love (12) *45*
No Stoppin' Us Now (9)
Nothin' But A Heartache (7)
Olana (11)

One By One (9,10)
One Chain (Don't Make No Prison) (12)
One Step Closer (9,10) *24*
Open Your Eyes (8)
Our Love (13)
Precis (4)
Pursuit On 53rd Street (3)
Rainy Day Crossroad Blues (4)
Real Love (9,10) *5*
Rio (5)
Road Angel (3)
Rockin' Down The Highway (1,6)
Rollin' On (13)
Showdown (13)
Slat Key Soquel Rag (4,11)
Slippery St. Paul (11)
Snake Man (1)
Something You Said (13)
Song To See You Through (3)

South Bay Strut (9)
South City Midnight Lady (2,6,11)
South Of The Border (12)
Spirit (3)
Steamer Lane Breakdown (8,11)
Sweet Feelin' (8)
Sweet Maxine (4) *40*
Take Me In Your Arms (Rock Me) (4,6) *11*
Take Me To The Highway (12)
Takin' It To The Streets (5,6,11) *13*
Tell Me What You Want (And I'll Give You What You Need) (4)
Texas Lullaby (4)
Thank You Love (9)
There's A Light (7)
This Train I'm On (13)
Time Is Here And Gone (12)

Tonight I'm Coming Through (The Border) (12)
Too High A Price (12)
Toulouse Street (1)
Turn It Loose (5)
Ukiah (2)
Under The Spell (13)
What A Fool Believes (8,10,11) *1*
Wheels Of Fortune (5) *87*
White Sun (1)
Without You (2,6)
Wrong Number (12)
You Belong To Me (7,10,11) *79*
You Just Can't Stop It (3)
You Never Change (8)
You're Made That Way (7)

DO OR DIE
Male rap trio: AK 47, N.A.R.D. and Belo Zero.   '98

DEBUT	PEAK	WKS	RIAA	CD	ARTIST — Album Title	$	Label & Number
9/21/96	27	29	●	© 1	Picture This	$10	Rap-A-Lot 42058
4/25/98	13	16	●	© 2	Headz Or Tailz	$10	Rap-A-Lot 45612
9/16/00	13	9		© 3	Victory	$10	Rap-A-Lot 49072

All In The Club (2)
Alpha And Omega (1)
Already Know (3)
Anotha One Dead And Gone (1)
Bounce For Me (3)
Bustin Back (2)
Caine House (2)

Can I (2)
Can U Make It Hot (3)
Choppin Up That Paper (2)
Dead Or Alive (2)
Gangsta Shit (2)
Headz (2)
Heist, Tha (3)
If I Don't Eat (3)

If U Scared (3)
In A Mode (3)
Just Ballin (2)
Keep It Real (3)
Kill Or Be Killed (1)
La, La, La (3)
Lil Sum Sum (2)
Money Flow (1)

Murderers, Pimps + Thugs (3)
Nobody's Home (2)
Paperchase (2)
Pimpology (2)
Playa Like Me And You (1)
Po Pimp (1) *22*
Promise (1)
Ride (3)

Search Warrant (1)
Shut 'Em Down (1)
6 Million (1)
Stay Focused (3)
Still Po Pimpin' (2) *62*
Tailz (2)
Thuggin It Out (3)
Ultimate Shutdown (2)

Under Surveillance (2)
V.I.P. (1)
Victory (3)
Who Am I (2)
Who Knows? (3)

DOORS, The ★69★   '68

Rock group formed in Los Angeles: Jim Morrison (vocals), Robby Krieger (guitar), **Ray Manzarek** (keyboards) and John Densmore (drums). Controversial onstage performances by Morrison caused several arrests and cancellations. Group appeared in the 1969 movie *A Feast of Friends*. Morrison left group on 12/12/70; died of heart failure in Paris on 7/3/71 (age 27). Group disbanded in 1973. 1991 movie based on group's career, *The Doors*, starred Val Kilmer as Morrison. Group inducted into the Rock and Roll Hall of Fame in 1993.

1)Waiting For The Sun 2)The Doors 3)Strange Days 4)Morrison Hotel/Hard Rock Cafe
5)The Soft Parade

DEBUT	PEAK	WKS	RIAA	CD	ARTIST — Album Title	Catalog	Sym	$	Label & Number
3/25/67	2²	121	▲²	© 1	The Doors	C:❶10/40		$50	Elektra 74007
11/4/67	3	63	●	© 2	Strange Days			$40	Elektra 74014
8/10/68	❶4	41	▲	© 3	Waiting For The Sun	C:#3/27		$30	Elektra 74024
8/9/69	6	28	▲	© 4	The Soft Parade	C:#4/27		$30	Elektra 75005
3/7/70	4	27	●	© 5	Morrison Hotel/Hard Rock Cafe			$25	Elektra 75007
8/8/70	8	20	●	© 6	Absolutely Live		[L]	$30	Elektra 9002 [2]
12/19/70+	25	21	▲		7	13		[G]	$25	Elektra 74079
5/8/71	9	34	▲²	© 8	L.A. Woman			$25	Elektra 75011
11/6/71	31	15			9	Other Voices			$20	Elektra 75017
2/12/72	55	11	●		10	Weird Scenes Inside The Gold Mine		[K]	$25	Elektra 6001 [2]
8/5/72	68	15			11	Full Circle			$20	Elektra 75038
9/29/73	158	8			12	The Best Of The Doors		[G]	$20	Elektra 5035
12/16/78+	54	13	●		13	An American Prayer - Jim Morrison	C:❶1/9		$15	Elektra 502
11/1/80	17	99	▲²		14	The Doors Greatest Hits	C:#13/32	[G]	$12	Elektra 515
11/5/83	23	20	●		15	Alive, She Cried		[K-L]	$12	Elektra 60269
6/8/85	124	7			16	Classics		[K]	$12	Elektra 60417
7/11/87	154	11	©		17	Live At The Hollywood Bowl		[L-M]	$12	Elektra 60741
					recorded on 7/5/68				
8/8/87+	32	43	▲³	© 18	The Best Of The Doors	C:#4/259	[G]	$15	Elektra 60345 [2]
3/23/91	8	20	●	© 19	The Doors		[S]	$12	Elektra 61047
					includes "Heroin" by The Velvet Underground				
6/8/91	50	13	▲	© 20	In Concert		[K-L]	$15	Elektra 61082 [2]
11/15/97	65	5	●	© 21	The Doors Box Set		[K]	$40	Elektra 62123 [4]

Alabama Song (Whiskey Bar) (1,6,18,20)
Albinoni's Adagio In G Minor (21)
American Night (13)
American Prayer (13)
Angels And Sailors (medley) (13)
Awake (13)
Back Door Man (1,6,7,20)
Been Down So Long (8)
Black Polished Chrome (medley) (13)

Black Train Song (21)
Blue Sunday (5,10,21)
Break On Through (To The Other Side) (1,6,10,14,18,19,20,21)
Build Me A Woman (6,20,21)
Cars Hiss By My Window (8)
Celebration Of The Lizard (6,21)
Changeling (4,20)
Close To You (6,20)
Crawling King Snake (8,21)
Crystal Ship (1,7,16,18,21)

Curses, Invocations (13)
Dawn's Highway (medley) (13)
Dead Cats, Dead Rats (20)
Do It (4)
Down On The Farm (9)
Easy Ride (4)
End, The (1,10,18,19,20,21)
End Of The Night (1,10,21)
Five To One (3,6,10,16,18,20,21)
4 Billion Souls (11)
Get Up And Dance (11)
Ghost Song (13,19)

Gloria (15,20,21) *71*
Go Insane (21)
Good Rockin' (11)
Hang On To Your Life (9)
Hardwood Floor (11)
Hello, I Love You (3,7,12,14,18,21) *1*
Hill Dwellers (17,20)
Hitchhiker, The (13)
Horse Latitudes (2,10)
Hyacinth House (8)
I Can't See Your Face In My Mind (2,6,21)

I Looked At You (1)
I Will Never Be Untrue (21)
I'm Horny, I'm Stoned (9)
In The Eye Of The Sun (9)
Indian Summer (5)
It Slipped My Mind (11)
L'America (8)
L.A. Woman (8,10,14,18,19,21)
Lament (13)
Land Ho! (5,7,16,21)
Latino Chrome (medley) (13)

Light My Fire (1,7,12,14,15,17,18,19,20,21) *1*
Lions In The Street (20)
Little Game (17,20)
Little Red Rooster (15,20)
Love Her Madly (8,10,12,16,18) *11*
Love Hides (6,20)
Love Street (3,10,19)
Love Me Two Times (2,7,12,14,15,18,20,21) *25*
Love Street (3,10,19)
Maggie M'Gill (5,10)

DOORS, The — Cont'd

Mental Floss (21)
Money (21)
Moonlight Drive (2,7,12,15,20,21)
Mosquito, The (11) *85*
Movie, The (13,19)
My Eyes Have Seen You (2,16,21)
My Wild Love (3)
Names Of The Kingdom (20)
New Born Awakening (medley) (13)
Not To Touch The Earth (3,14,20)
Orange County Suite (21)

Palace Of Exile (20)
Peace Frog (5,10,16,21)
Peking Hand And The New York Queen (11)
People Are Strange (2,7,12,14,18) *12*
Petition The Lord With Prayer (20)
Piano Bird (11)
Poontang Blues (medley) (21)
Queen Of The Highway (5,21)
Riders On The Storm (8,10,12,14,18,19,21) *14*
Roadhouse Blues (5,7,13,14, 16,18,19,20,21) *flip*

Rock Is Dead (21)
Rock Me (21)
Runnin' Blue (4,10) *64*
Severed Garden (19)
Shaman's Blues (4,10,21)
Ship Of Fools (5,10,21)
Ships W/Sails (9)
Soft Parade (4,21)
Someday Soon (21)
Soul Kitchen (1,6,12,20)
Spanish Caravan (3,10,17,18)
Spy, The (5,10)
Stoned Immaculate (13,19)
Strange Days (2,10,16,18)
Summer's Almost Gone (3,21)

Sunday Trucker (medley) (21)
Take It As It Comes (1,10,12,21)
Tell All The People (4) *57*
Texas Radio & The Big Beat (15,20)
Tightrope Ride (9,21) *71*
To Come Of Age (13)
Touch Me (4,7,12,14,18) *3*
Twentieth Century Fox (1)
Unhappy Girl (2)
Universal Mind (6,20)
Unknown Soldier (3,7,16,17,18,20,21) *39*
Variety Is The Spice Of Life (9)

Verdilac (11)
Waiting For The Sun (5,16,18)
Wake Up (17,20)
Wandering Musician (9)
Wasp (Texas Radio & The Big Beat) (8,10,16)
We Could Be So Good Together (3)
When The Music's Over (2,6,10,18,19,20,21)
Whiskey, Mystics And Men (21)
Who Do You Love (6,12,20)
Who Scared You (10,21)
Wild Child (4,7,16,21)
Wintertime Love (3)

Wishful Sinful (4,21) *44*
Yes, The River Knows (3,21)
You Make Me Real (5,15,20) *50*
(You Need Meat) Don't Go No Further (10)
You're Lost Little Girl (2,7,21)

DORATI, Antal '59

Born on 4/9/06 in Budapest, Hungary. Died on 11/13/88 (age 82). Principal conductor of BBC Symphony from 1962-66 and of Stockholm Philharmonic from 1966-74. Music director of Washington National Symphony from 1970-77. Principal conductor of Britain's **Royal Philharmonic Orchestra** from 1975-78. Music director of Detroit Symphony from 1977-81.

| 3/16/59 | 3 | 54 | ● | 1 Tchaikovsky: 1812 Festival Overture/Capriccio Italien | [I] | $30 | Mercury 50054 |
| 2/27/61 | 20 | 16 | | 2 Beethoven: Wellington's Victory/Leonore Overture No. 3/ Prometheus Overture | [I] | $25 | Mercury 9000 |

Capriccio Italien, Op. 45 (1) 1812 - Festival Overture, Op. 49 (1) Leonore Overture No. 3, Opus 72A (2) Prometheus Overture, Opus 43 (2) Wellington's Victory (2)

DORE, Charlie '80

Born in 1956 in London. Female singer/songwriter.

| 4/26/80 | 145 | 7 | | **Where To Now** | | $12 | Island 9559 |

Falling Hula Valley **Pilot Of The Airwaves** *13* Sleepless Where To Now
Fear Of Flying Pickin' Apples Sad Old World Sweetheart Wise Owl

DO-RE-MI CHILDREN'S CHORUS, The '69

Children's chorus that sang with **Tom Glazer** on his 1963 hit single "On Top Of Spaghetti".

| 12/9/67 | 37[X] | 4 | | 1 Do You Hear What I Hear?/Little Drummer Boy, (And More Of The Christmas Songs Children Love To Sing) | [X] | $40 | Kapp 3368 |

first released in 1963

| 12/6/69 | 11[X] | 1 | | 2 Christmas Songs For Children | [X] | $40 | Kapp 3037 |

Come All Ye Faithful (medley) (1)
Deck The Halls (medley) (1)
Do You Hear What I Hear? (1)
First Noel (medley) (1)

God Rest Ye Merry Gentlemen (medley) (1)
Holly Jolly Christmas (1)
It's Beginning To Look Like Christmas (1)

Joy To The World (medley) (1)
Let It Snow! Let It Snow! Let It Snow! (1)
Let's All Sing A Song For Christmas (1)

Little Drummer Boy (1)
Marshmallow World (1)
Oh Christmas Tree (medley) (1)
Oh Little Town Of Bethlehem (medley) (1)

Silver And Gold (1)
Silver Bells (1)
Tell It On The Mountain (1)
We Wish You A Merry Christmas (medley) (1)

DORO '89

Born Dorothee Pesch on 6/3/64 in Dusseldorf, Germany. Female hard-rock singer. Member of **Warlock**.

| 4/29/89 | 154 | 11 | © | **Force Majeure** | | $10 | Mercury 838016 |

Angels With Dirty Faces Cry Wolf I Am What I Am Save My Soul World Gone Wild
Beyond The Trees Hard Times Mission Of Mercy Under The Gun
Bis Aufs Blut Hellraiser River Of Tears Whiter Shade Of Pale

DORSEY, Jimmy, Orchestra '58

Born on 2/29/04 in Shenandoah, Pennsylvania. Died of cancer on 6/12/57 (age 53). Esteemed alto sax and clarinet soloist/bandleader. Recorded with his brother **Tommy Dorsey** in the Dorsey Brothers Orchestra, 1928-35 and 1953-56.

| 10/7/57 | 19 | 4 | | 1 The Fabulous Jimmy Dorsey | | $30 | Fraternity 1008 |
| 5/19/58 | 15 | 6 | © | 2 The Fabulous Dorseys In Hi-Fi | [I] | $25 | Columbia 1190 |

TOMMY DORSEY & JIMMY DORSEY

Amapola (1)
Contrasts (1)
How Far Is It To Jordan (2)
I Dream Of You (2)
It Started All Over Again (2)

It's The Dreamer In Me (1)
Jay-Dee's Boogie Woogie (1) *77*
Judgement Is Coming (2)
June Night (1) *21*

Just Swingin' (1)
Maria Elena (1)
Mombo En Sax (1)
Nevada (2)
No One Ever Lost More (1)

Peace Pipe (2)
Rain (2)
So Rare (1) *2*
Sophisticated Swing (1)
Speak Low (1)

This Is What Gabriel Says (2)
This Love Of Mine (2)
Wagon Wheels (2)
We've Crossed The Widest River (2)

Yesterdays (2)

DORSEY, Lee '66

Born Irving Lee Dorsey on 12/24/24 in New Orleans; raised in Portland, Oregon. Died of emphysema on 12/1/86 (age 61). R&B singer.

| 11/12/66 | 129 | 5 | © | **The New Lee Dorsey** | | $30 | Amy 8011 |

Can You Hear Me **Get Out Of My Life, Woman** *44* **Holy Cow** *23* Mexico **Working In The Coal Mine** *8*
Confusion Little Dab A Do Ya Neighbor's Daughter
Don't You Ever (Leave Me) Greatest Love Mellow Good Time **Ride Your Pony** *28*

DORSEY, Tommy, Orchestra '58

Born on 11/19/05 in Mahanoy Plane, Pennsylvania. Choked to death on 11/26/56 (age 51). Esteemed trombonist/band leader. Tommy and brother **Jimmy Dorsey** recorded together as the Dorsey Brothers Orchestra from 1928-35 and 1953-56. They hosted a musical variety TV show, *Stage Show*, 1954-56. Warren Covington fronted band after Tommy's death.

| 5/19/58 | 15 | 6 | © | 1 The Fabulous Dorseys In Hi-Fi | [I] | $25 | Columbia 1190 |

TOMMY DORSEY & JIMMY DORSEY

| 5/25/59 | 38 | 2 | | 2 Tea For Two Cha Chas | [I] | $20 | Decca 8842 |

Cha Cha For Gia (2)
Corazon De Melon (2)
Dardanella - Cha Cha (2)
Dinah - Cha Cha (2)
How Far Is It To Jordan (1)

I Dream Of You (1)
I Still Get Jealous - Cha Cha (2)
I Want To Be Happy Cha Cha (2) *70*
It Started All Over Again (1)

Judgement Is Coming (1)
Nevada (1)
Patricia (2)
Peace Pipe (1)
Por Favor (Please..) (2)

Rain (1)
Rico Vacilon (2)
Tea For Two Cha Cha (2) *7*
This Is What Gabriel Says (1)
This Love Of Mine (1)

Together I-2-3 (2)
Trumpet Cha-Cha-Cha (2)
Wagon Wheels (1)
We've Crossed The Widest River (1)

Yesterdays (1)

DOUBLE '86

Pop duo from Switzerland: Felix Haug (vocals, guitar) and Kurt Maloo (keyboards).

| 7/26/86 | 30 | 21 | © | **Blue** | | $10 | A&M 5133 |

Captain Of Her Heart *16* Love Is A Plane Tomorrow Woman Of The World
I Know A Place Rangoon Moon Urban Nomads Your Prayer Takes Me Off

DOUBLE EXPOSURE '76
R&B vocal group from Philadelphia: James Williams, Leonard "Butch" Davis, Charles Whittington and Joseph Harris.

8/21/76 **129** 11 © **Ten Percent** .... **$12** Salsoul 5503

| Baby I Need Your Loving | Gonna Give My Love Away | My Love Is Free | Ten Percent 54 |
| Everyman | Just Can't Say Hello | Pick Me | |

DOUBLE TROUBLE '01
Backing duo for **Stevie Ray Vaughan**: Tommy Shannon (bass) and Chris Layton (drums).

2/24/01 **126** 2 © **Been A Long Time** .... **$10** Tone-Cool 471180

| Baby, There's No One Like You | Groundhog Day | In The Middle Of The Night | Say One Thing | Skyscraper |
| Cry Sky | In The Garden | Rock And Roll | She's All Right | Turn Towards The Mirror |

DOUCETTE '78
Rock group from Montreal: Jerry Doucette (vocals, guitar), Mark Olson (keyboards), Donnie Cummings (bass) and Duris Maxwell (drums).

3/25/78 **159** 8 © **Mama Let Him Play** .... **$12** Mushroom 5009

| All I Wanna Do | Down The Road | Keep On Running | **Mama Let Him Play 72** | What's Your Excuse? |
| Back Off | It's Gonna Hurt So Bad | Love Is Gonna Find You | People Say | When She Loves Me |

DOUG E. FRESH & THE GET FRESH CREW '88
Born Douglas Davis on 9/17/66 in New York City. Male rapper. The Get Fresh Crew: Barry Bee, Chill Will and **Slick Rick**.

6/18/88 **88** 13 © **The World's Greatest Entertainer** .... **$10** Reality 9658

| Africa (Goin' Back Home) | Cut That Zero | Ev'rybody Got 2 Get Some | Greatest Entertainer | I'm Gettin' Ready | On The Strength |
| Crazy 'Bout Cars | D.E.F. = Doug E. Fresh | Ev'rybody Loves A Star | Guess? Who? | Keep Risin' To The Top | Plane (So High) |

DOUGLAS, Carl '75
Born in 1942 in Jamaica; raised in California. Disco singer.

12/14/74+ **37** 17 **Kung Fu Fighting And Other Great Love Songs** .... **$15** 20th Century 464

| Blue Eyed Soul | **Dance The Kung Fu 48** | I Want To Give You My | **Kung Fu Fighting 1** | When You Got Love |
| Changing Times | I Don't Care What People Say | Everything | Never Had This Dream Before | Witchfinder General |

DOUGLAS, Carol '77
Born Carol Strickland on 4/7/48 in Brooklyn, New York. Disco singer.

3/29/75 **177** 3 1 **The Carol Douglas Album** .... **$12** Midland Int'l. 0931
11/6/76 **188** 6 2 **Midnight Love Affair** .... **$12** Midland Int'l. 1798
7/16/77 **139** 10 3 **Full Bloom** .... **$12** Midland Int'l. 2222

All Night Long (1)	Dancing Queen (3)	I Fell In Love With Love (1)	Light My Fire (3)	Who, What, When, Where, Why (3)
Baby Don't Let This Good Love	**Doctor's Orders (1) 11**	I Got You On My Mind (3)	Midnight Love Affair (2)	Will We Make It Tonight (1)
Die (1)	Friend In Need (1)	I Want To Stay With You (3)	Take Me (Make Me Lose	
Boy, You Know Just What I'm	Full Bloom Suite #1 & #2 (3)	I'll Take A Chance On Love (3)	Control) (1)	
After (1)	Headline News (2)	In The Morning (2)	We Do It (3)	
Carol's Theme I & II (2)	**Hurricane Is Coming Tonite**	Lie To Me (2)	We're Gonna Make It (3)	
Crime Don't Pay (2)	(1) **81**	Life Time Guarantee (2)		

DOUGLAS, Mike '66
Born Michael Dowd on 8/11/25 in Chicago. Singer for Kay Kyser's band from 1945-50. Hosted own TV talk show from 1961-80.

1/29/66 **46** 15 © **The Men In My Little Girl's Life** .... **$15** Epic 26186

"A" - You're Adorable (The	House I Live In (That's America	I'd Give A Million Tomorrows	Kids!	**Men In My Little Girl's Life 6**
Alphabet Song)	To Me)	(For Just One Yesterday)	Let Her Be A Little Girl (A Little	Sunrise, Sunset
	House Of Love	Is There A Baby In The House	Longer)	While We're Young

DOVE, Ronnie '66
Born on 9/7/35 in Herndon, Virginia; raised in Baltimore. Pop singer.

7/24/65 **119** 41 1 **One Kiss For Old Times' Sake** .... **$25** Diamond 5003
4/2/66 **35** 21 2 **The Best Of Ronnie Dove** .... [G] **$25** Diamond 5005
10/22/66 **122** 5 3 **Ronnie Dove Sings The Hits For You** .... **$25** Diamond 5006
3/4/67 **121** 12 4 **Cry** .... **$25** Diamond 5007

All (1)	I Really Don't Want To Know	Keep It A Secret (2)	One Kiss For Old Times' Sake	That Empty Feeling (3)
All Of Me (1)	(3) **22**	**Kiss Away (2) 25**	(1,2) **14**	Walkin' My Baby Back Home
Almost In Paradise (3)	I Won't Cry Anymore (4)	**Let's Start All Over Again**	One More Mountain To Climb	(4)
Autumn Rhapsody (4)	**I'll Make All Your Dreams**	(3) **20**	(4) **45**	Wheel Of Fortune (4)
Cry (4) 18	**Come True (2) 21**	**Little Bit Of Heaven (1,2) 16**	Right Or Wrong (2) **14**	When Liking Turns To Loving
Happy Summer Days (3) 27	I'm The One Who Taught You	Little White Cloud That Cried	Say You (2) **40**	(2) **18**
Hello Pretty Girl (2) 54	How (3)	(4)	She Only Makes Me Love You	Where In The World (1,2)
I Can't Stop Loving You (4)	If I Cried Everytime You Hurt	Long After (3)	More (1)	Years Of Tears (4)
I Found You (Just In Time) (3)	Me (1)	**Mountain Of Love (3) 67**	Someday (You'll Want Me To	
I Had To Lose You (To Find	If I Live To Be A Hundred (1,2)	Nevertheless (I'm In Love With	Want You) (3)	
That I Need You) (1)	It's Almost Tomorrow (1)	You) (1,2)	Tell The Lady I Said Good-bye	
	It's The Talk Of The Town (4)	On A Slow Boat To China (3)	(4)	

DOVELLS, The '63
Vocal group from Philadelphia: **Len Barry**, Arnie Silver, Jerry Summers and Mike Dennis.

7/13/63 **119** 7 **You Can't Sit Down** .... **$50** Parkway 7025

| Baby Workout | Hey, Beautiful | Lockin' Up My Heart | Miss Daisy De Lite | Summer Job | Wildwood Days |
| Havin' A Good Time | If You Wanna Be Happy | Maybelline | Short Fat Fannie | 36-22-36 | **You Can't Sit Down 3** |

DOVE SHACK '95
Rap trio from Long Beach, California: Mark Makonie, Anthony Blount and Gary Brown.

9/9/95 **68** 8 © **This Is The Shack** .... **$10** G Funk 527933

| Bomb Drop | Freestyle | Ghetto Life | Smoke Out | There'll Come A Day | We Funk (The G Funk) |
| East Side Party | Fuck Ya Mouth | Rollin Wit A Gang | **Summertime In The LBC 54** | This Is The Shack | |

DOWN '95
Hard-rock group: Philip Anselmo (vocals), Pepper Keenan and Kirk Windstein (guitars), Todd Strange (bass), and Jimmy Bower (drums). Anselmo is the lead singer of **Pantera**.

10/7/95 **57** 6 © **Nola** .... **$10** EastWest 61830

Bury Me In Smoke	Jail	Pillars Of Eternity	Stone The Crow	Underneath Everything
Eyes Of The South	Lifer	Pray For The Locust	Swan Song	
Hail The Leaf	Losing All	Rehab	Temptation's Wings	

DOWNING, Will '00

Born in Brooklyn, New York. R&B singer/songwriter/producer.

DEBUT	PEAK	WKS	CD	#	Album Title	$	Label & Number
8/21/93	166	7	©	1	Love's The Place To Be	$10	Mercury 518086
11/25/95	139	2	©	2	Moods	$10	Mercury 528755
11/15/97	127	3	©	3	Invitation Only	$10	Mercury 536350
10/17/98	169	3	©	4	Pleasures Of The Night	$10	Verve Forecast 557613

WILL DOWNING & GERALD ALBRIGHT

| 8/5/00 | 100 | 7 | © | 5 | All The Man You Need | $10 | Motown 157881 |

All About You (3)
All The Man You Need (5)
Angel (3)
Back To The Roots (4)
Before We Say Goodbye (3)
Break Up To Make Up (1)
Come To Me (3) *3*
Do You Still Love Me (1)
Don't Wait For Love (2)
Eternal Love (3)

Everything To Me (1)
Everytime It Rains (5)
Fall In Love Again (2)
Girl Blue (4)
Grandma's Hands (5)
Here's That Rainy Day (4)
Hey Girl (1)
Hold On (2)
I Can't Make You Love Me (2)
I Don't Want To Lose You (3)

If I Could (3)
If She Knew (3)
Inseparable (2)
Island (3)
Just A Game (2)
Just To Be With You (2)
Like A Lover (4)
Look Of Love (4)
Love Of My Life (5)
Love's The Place To Be (1)

Lover's Paradise (1)
Michelle (4)
Moods (2)
Nearness Of You (4)
Nothing Has Ever Felt Like This (1)
One Moment (1)
Only A Moment Away (5)
Personal (3)
Pleasures Of The Night (4)

Real Soon (5)
Sailing On A Dream (1)
Share My World (5)
Sorry, I (2)
Stella By Starlight (2)
Stop, Look, Listen To Your Heart (4)
Summer Day (5)
That Good Morning Love (2)
That's All (1)

There's No Living Without You (1)
These Things (3)
Thinkin' About You (5)
Tired Melody (5)
We'll Be Together Again (4)
When Sunny Gets Blue (3)
When You Need Me (5)
Where Is Love (2)

DOZIER, Lamont '74

Born on 6/16/41 in Detroit. R&B singer/songwriter/producer. With the brothers Brian and Eddie Holland in highly successful songwriting/production team for Motown. Trio left Motown in 1968 and formed own Invictus/Hot Wax label. Trio inducted into the Rock and Roll Hall of Fame in 1990.

DEBUT	PEAK	WKS	#	Album Title	$	Label & Number
1/26/74	136	13	1	Out Here On My Own	$12	ABC 804
1/25/75	186	2	2	Black Bach	$12	ABC 839

All Cried Out (2)
Blue Sky And Silver Bird (2)
Breaking Out All Over (1)
Fish Ain't Bitin' (1) *26*

I Wanna Be With You (2)
Let Me Make Love To You (1)
Let Me Start Tonite (2) *87*
Out Here On My Own (1)

Prelude (2)
Put Out My Fire (2)
Rose (2)
Shine (2)

Take Off Your Make-Up (1)
Thank You For The Dream (2)
Trying To Hold On To My Woman (1) *15*

We Don't Want Nobody To Come Between Us (1)

D.P.G. — see DOGG POUND

DRAG-ON '00

Born Melvin Smalls in New York City. Male rapper. Member of **Ruff Ryders**.

DEBUT	PEAK	WKS		CD	Album Title	$	Label & Number
4/15/00	5	14	●	©	Opposite Of H20	$10	Ruff Ryders 490609

Click, Click, Clack
Drag Shit
Get It Right

Groundhog's Day
Here We Go
Ladies 2000

Life Goes On
Niggas Die 4 Me
Opposite Of H2O

Pop It
Ready For War
Snipe Out

Spit These Bars
Way Life Is
What's It All About

DRAGON, Carmen '62

Born on 7/28/14 in Antioch, California. Died on 3/28/84 (age 69). Conductor of the Capitol Symphony Orchestra. Father of Daryl Dragon (of **Captain & Tennille**). Also see **Leonard Pennario**.

DEBUT	PEAK	WKS	Album Title	Sym	$	Label & Number
4/14/62	36	8	Nightfall	[I]	$20	Capitol 8575

Adagietto
Andante Cantabile

Ases Tod
Berceuse

Brahms Lullaby
Old Creole Days

Pavane For A Dead Princess
Toyland

Vocalise, Op. 34, No. 14

DRAKE, Pete, And His Talking Steel Guitar '64

Born Roddis Franklin Drake on 10/8/32 in Atlanta. Died on 7/29/88 (age 55). Session steel guitarist.

DEBUT	PEAK	WKS	Album Title	$	Label & Number
5/2/64	85	14	Forever	$20	Smash 67053

Danny Boy
For Those That Cry
Forever *25*

I'm Just A Guitar (Everybody Picks On Me)
Making Believe

Melody Of Love
My Bluest Day
Paradise

Red Sails In The Sunset
Sleep Walk
Spook, The

Still

DRAMA '00

Born in 1980 in Atlanta. Male rapper. Drama stands for Drastic Retaliation Against My Adversaries.

DEBUT	PEAK	WKS		CD	Album Title	$	Label & Number
2/26/00	32	26	●	©	Causin' Drama	$10	Atlantic 83306

Double Time (Drama's Cadence)

I'm Ballin' Man
It's Drastic

Left/Right *73*
Let's Go To War

Mama, Mama
My Name Is Drama

Plot, The
Sir. Yes Sir.

DRAMATICS, The '72

R&B vocal group from Detroit: Ron Banks, William Howard, Larry Demps, Willie Ford and Elbert Wilkins. Howard and Wilkins replaced by L.J. Reynolds and Lenny Mayes in 1973.

DEBUT	PEAK	WKS	CD	#	Album Title	$	Label & Number
1/22/72	20	24	©	1	Whatcha See Is Whatcha Get	$25	Volt 6018
10/13/73	86	18	©	2	A Dramatic Experience	$25	Volt 6019
5/4/74	156	6	©	3	The Dells vs. The Dramatics	$30	Cadet 60027
3/22/75	31	18		4	The Dramatic Jackpot	$15	ABC 867
11/15/75	93	12		5	Drama V	$15	ABC 916
10/30/76+	103	25	©	6	Joy Ride	$15	ABC 955
8/13/77	60	19		7	Shake It Well	$15	ABC 1010
5/13/78	44	15	●	8	Do What You Wanna Do	$15	ABC 1072
3/8/80	61	12		9	10 1/2	$12	MCA 3196

After This Dance (6)
Be My Girl (6) *53*
Be With The One You Love (9)
Beautiful People (2)
Beware Of The Man (With The Candy In His Hand) (2)
California Sunshine (8)
Choosing Up On You (3)
Come Inside (7)
Come Out Of Your Thing (6)
Devil Is Dope (2)
Disco Dance Contest (8)
Do What You Want To Do (8)
Don't Make Me No Promises (3)
Door To Your Heart (3) *62*
Dramatic Theme (medley) (5)
Fall In Love, Lady Love (1)

Fell For You (2) *45*
Finger Fever (6)
Get Up And Get Down (1) *78*
Gimme Some (Good Soul Music) (1)
Good Things Don't Come Easy (4)
Hey You! Get Off My Mountain (2) *43*
Hot Pants In The Summertime (1)
How Do You Feel (4)
I Can't Get Over You (6)
I Cried All The Way Home (4)
I Dig Your Music (6)
I Get Carried Away (6)
I Just Wanna Dance The Night Away (9)

(I Like) Makin' You So Happy (7)
I Want You (8)
I Was The Life Of The Party (5)
I'll Make It So Good (5)
I'm Gonna Love You To The Max (5)
I'm In Love (3)
If You Feel Like You Wanna Dance, Dance (9)
In The Rain (1) *5*
It Ain't Rainin' (On Nobody's House But Mine) (9)
Jane (8)
Jim, What's Wrong With Him? (2)

Just Shopping (Not Buying Anything) (5)
Love Is Here (9)
Love Is Missing From Our Lives (3)
Mary Don't Cha Wanna (1)
Me And Mrs. Jones (4) *47*
Me Myself And I (4)
Music Is Forever (7)
Music Is The Peoples Choice (9)
My Ship Won't Sail Without You (7)
Never Let You Go (4)
Now You Got Me Loving You (2)
Ocean Of Thoughts And Dreams (7)

Richest Man Alive (6)
Runnin' From My Love (9)
Say The Word (6)
Shake It Well (7) *76*
She's A Rainmaker (5)
Sing And Dance Your Troubles Away (6)
Spaced Out Over You (7)
Stand Up And Move (6)
Stop Your Weeping (8)
Sundown Is Coming (Hold Back The Night) (6)
Thank You For Your Love (1)
That Heaven Kind Of Feeling (7)
Things Are Changing (5)
Thousand Shades Of Blue (4)

Treat Me Like A Man (medley) (5)
Trying To Get Over Losing You (4)
Tune Up (3)
Welcome Back Home (9)
Whatcha See Is Whatcha Get (1) *9*
Why Do You Want To Do Me Wrong (8)
Yo' Love (Can Only Bring Me Happiness) (8)
You Could Become The Very Heart Of Me (2)
You Make The Music (I Just Dance Along) (7)
You're Fooling You (5) *87*

DREAD ZEPPELIN '90

White reggae group from Pasadena, California: **Elvis Presley** impersonator Greg "Tortelvis" Tortell (vocals), Joe Ramsey and Carl Haasis (guitars), Bryant Fernandez (percussion), Gary Putman (bass) and Paul Masselli (drums). Group specialized in **Led Zeppelin** songs.

8/25/90   **116**   13   ©   **Un-Led-Ed** .... $10   I.R.S. 82048

Black Dog   Heartbreaker (At The End Of   Immigrant Song   Whole Lotta Love
Black Mountain Side   Lonely Street)   Living Loving Maid   Your Time Is Gonna Come
Bring It On Home   I Can't Quit You Baby   Moby Dick

DREAM '01

Female pop vocal group from Los Angeles: Holly, Melissa, Ashley and Diana.

2/10/01   **6**   34↑▲ ©   **It Was All A Dream** $10   Bad Boy 73037

Angel Inside   **He Loves U Not 2**   I Don't Like Anyone   Miss You   Pain   What We Gonna Do About Us
Do You Wanna Dance   How Long   In My Dreams   Mr. Telephone   **This Is Me 39**   When I Get There

DREAM ACADEMY, The '86

Pop-rock trio from England: Nick Laird-Clowes (guitar, vocals), Gilbert Gabriel (keyboards) and Kate St. John (oboe, vocals).

11/9/85+   **20**   37   ©   1   **The Dream Academy**.. $10   Warner 25265
11/14/87   **181**   3   ©   2   **Remembrance Days**... $10   Reprise 25625

Ballad In 4/4 (2)   Everybody's Gotta Learn   Humdrum (2)   Indian Summer (2)   **Love Parade** (1) 36   Power To Believe (2)
Bound To Be (1)   Sometime (2)   In Exile (For Rodrigo Rojas) (2)   Lesson Of Love (2)   Moving On (1)   This World (1)
Doubleminded (2)   Hampstead Girl (2)   In Places On The Run (1)   Life In A Northern Town (1) 7   One Dream (1)
Edge Of Forever (1)   Here (2)   In The Hands Of Love (2)   **Life In A Northern Town** (1) 7   Party, The (1)

DREAMBOY '84

R&B group from Michigan: Jeff Stanton (vocals), Jeff Bass (guitar), Jimi Hunt (keyboards), Paul Stewart (bass) and George Twymon (drums).

1/14/84   **168**   11   **Dreamboy**...   [M] $10   Qwest 23988

Don't Go   Get Off   I Want To Know Your Name   Let's Go Out   Slow Down   Walk The Streets

DREAMS '70

Jazz-rock group: brothers Michael (sax) and Randy (trumpet) Brecker, Edward Vernon (vocals), Jeff Kent (guitar), Barry Rogers (trombone), Doug Lubahn (bass) and **Billy Cobham** (drums). Michael and Randy later recorded as **The Brecker Brothers**.

11/28/70   **146**   6   ©   **Dreams**... $20   Columbia 30225

Devil Lady   15 Miles To Provo   Maryanne, The (2)   Try Me
Dream Suite Medley   Holli Be Home   New York

DREAMS SO REAL '89

Rock trio from Athens, Georgia: Barry Marler (vocals, guitar), Trent Allen (bass) and Drew Worsham (drums).

11/26/88+   **150**   18   ©   **Rough Night In Jericho**.................................. $10   Arista 8555

Bearing Witness   City Of Love   Heart Of Stone   Melanie   Rough Night In Jericho
California   Distance   Love Fall Down   Open Your Eyes   Victim

DREAM SYNDICATE '84

Rock group from Los Angeles: Steve Wynn (vocals, guitar), Karl Precoda (guitar), Dave Provost (bass) and Dennis Duck (drums).

8/4/84   **171**   4   ©   **Medicine Show**.. $10   A&M 4990

Armed With An Empty Gun   Burn   John Coltrane Stereo Blues   Merrittville
Bullet With My Name On It   Daddy's Girl   Medicine Show   Still Holding On To You

DREAM THEATER '94

Hard-rock group from Los Angeles: James LaBrie (vocals), John Petrucci (guitar), Kevin Moore (keyboards), John Myung (bass) and Mike Portnoy (drums). Derek Sherinian replaced Moore in September 1994. Jordan Rudess replaced Sherinian in 1999.

1/9/93	**61**	24	●	©	1	Images And Words....................		$10	Atco 92148
10/22/94	**32**	6		©	2	Awake		$10	EastWest 90126
10/7/95	**58**	3		©	3	A Change Of Seasons	[L-M]	$10	EastWest 61842
10/11/97	**52**	4		©	4	Falling Into Infinity		$10	EastWest 62060
11/14/98	**157**	1		©	5	Once In A Livetime.................	[L]	$15	EastWest 62308 [2]

recorded on 6/25/98 in Paris

11/13/99   **73**   2   ©   6   **Metropolis Pt. 2: Scenes From A Memory** .... $10   EastWest 62448

Achilles Last Stand (medley) (3)   Change Of Seasons VII: The   Innocence Faded (2)   Mike Portnoy Drum Solo (5)   Silent Man (2)   Trial Of Tears (4,5)
Anna Lee (4)   Crimson Sunset (5)   John Petrucci Guitar Solo (5)   Mirror, The (2)   6:00 (2)   Under A Glass Moon (1)
Another Day (1)   Dance Of Eternity (6)   Just Let Me Breathe (4,5)   New Millennium (4)   Song Remains The Same   Voices (2,5)
Beyond This Life (6)   Derek Sherinian Piano Solo (5)   Learning To Live (1,5)   One Last Time (6)   (medley) (3)   Wait For Sleep (1)
Big Medley (3)   Erotomania (2)   Lie (2,5)   Overture 1928 (6)   Space-Dye Vest (2)   YTSE Jam (5)
Burning My Soul (4)   Fatal Tragedy (6)   Lifting Shadows Off A Dream   Perfect Strangers (2)   Spirit Carries On (6)   You Not Me (4)
Caught In A Web (2,5)   Finally Free (6)   (2)   Peruvian Skies (4,5)   Strange Deja Vu (6)
Change Of Seasons (3,5)   Funeral For A Friend (medley)   Lines In The Sand (4,5)   Pull Me Under (1,5)   Surrounded (1)
Change Of Seasons II: (3)   Love Dies Bleeding (medley) (3)   Puppies On Acid (5)   Take Away My Pain (4,5)
Innocence (5)   Hell's Kitchen (4)   Metropolis (5)   Regression (6)   Take The Time (1,5)
Change Of Seasons IV: The   Hollow Years (4,5)   Metropolis-Part I "The Miracle   Rover, The (medley) (3)   Through Her Eyes (6)
Darkest Of Winters (5)   Home (6)   And The Sleeper" (5)   Scarred (2,5)   Through My Words (6)

DREGS — see DIXIE DREGS

D.R.I. '88

Punk-rock group from Houston: Kurt Brecht (vocals), Spike Cassidy (guitar), Josh Pappe (bass) and Felix Griffin (drums). John Menor replaced Pappe in 1989. D.R.I.: Dirty Rotten Imbeciles.

7/23/88   **116**   14   ©   1   **Four Of A Kind** $10   Metal Blade 77304
12/23/89+   **140**   13   ©   2   **Thrash Zone**.. $10   Metal Blade 73407

Abduction (2)   Do The Dream (1)   Gone Too Long (1)   Man Unkind (1)   Slum Lord (1)   Think For Yourself (1)
All For Nothing (1)   Drown You Out (2)   Gun Control (2)   Manifest Destiny (1)   Standing In Line (2)   Thrashard (2)
Beneath The Wheel (2)   Enemy Within (2)   Kill The Words (2)   Modern World (1)   Strategy (2)   Trade, The (2)
Dead In A Ditch (1)   Give A Hoot (2)   Labeled Uncurable (2)   Shut-Up! (1)   Suit And Tie Guy (1)   Worker Bee (2)

DRIFTERS, The '64

R&B vocal group formed in New York City: **Ben E. King**, Charlie Thomas, Doc Green and Elsbearry Hobbs, with Reggie Kimber (guitar). Rudy Lewis replaced King in 1961. Lewis died of a heart attack on 5/20/64 (age 27); replaced by Johnny Moore. Hobbs died on 5/31/96 (age 60). Moore died of respiratory failure on 12/30/98 (age 64). Group inducted into the Rock and Roll Hall of Fame in 1988.

6/8/63	110	9		©	1 Up On The Roof - The Best Of The Drifters		[G]	$150	Atlantic 8073
8/15/64	40	22		©	2 Under The Boardwalk			$100	Atlantic 8099
2/6/65	103	6		©	3 The Good Life With The Drifters			$50	Atlantic 8103
3/16/68	122	8		©	4 The Drifters' Golden Hits		[G]	$50	Atlantic 8153

Another Night With The Boys (1)
As Long As She Needs Me (3)
Dance With Me (4) 15
Desafinado (3)
Didn't It (2)
Good Life (3)
I Count The Tears (4) 17
I Feel Good All Over (2)

I Wish You Love (3)
I'll Take You Home (2) 25
I've Got Sand In My Shoes (4) 33
(If You Cry) True Love, True Love (1,4) 33
If You Don't Come Back (2)
In The Land Of Make Believe

Let The Music Play (3)
Loneliness Or Happiness (1)
Mexican Divorce (1)
More (3)
On Broadway (2,4) 9
On The Street Where You Live (3)
One Way Love (2) 56
Quando Quando Quando (3)

Rat Race (2) 71
Room Full Of Tears (1) 72
Ruby Baby (1)
Saturday Night At The Movies (3,4) 18
Save The Last Dance For Me (1,4) 1
Some Kind Of Wonderful (4) 32

Stranger On The Shore (1) 73
Sweets For My Sweet (1) 16
Temptation (3)
There Goes My Baby (1,4) 2
This Magic Moment (1,4) 16
Tonight (3)
Under The Boardwalk (2,4) 4
Up On The Roof (1,2,4) 5
Vaya Con Dios (2) 43

What Kind Of Fool Am I (3)
What To Do (1)
When My Little Girl Is Smiling (1) 28
Who Can I Turn To (3)

DRISCOLL, Julie — see AUGER, Brian

DRIVIN' N' CRYIN' '91

Rock group from Atlanta: Kevn Kinney (vocals), Buren Fowler (guitar), Tim Nielsen (bass) and Jeff Sullivan (drums).

4/2/88	130	12		©	1 Whisper Tames The Lion			$10	Island 90699
1/26/91	90	38	●	©	2 Fly Me Courageous			$10	Island 848000
3/13/93	95	3		©	3 Smoke			$10	Island 514319

All Around The World (3)
Around The Block Again (2)
Back Against The Wall (3)
Blue Ridge Way (1)
Build A Fire (2)
Can't Promise You The World (1)

Catch The Wind (1)
Chain Reaction (2)
Check Your Tears At The Door (1)
Eastern European Carny Man (3)
Fly Me Courageous (2)

For You (2)
Friend Song (1)
Good Day Every Day (1)
Innocent, The (2)
Legal Gun (1)
Let's Go Dancing (2)
Livin' By The Book (1)

Look What You've Done To Your Brother (2)
Lost In The Shuffle (2)
1988 (3)
On A Clear Daze (1)
Patron Lady Beautiful (3)
Powerhouse (1)

Ridin' On The Soul Road (1)
Rush Hour (2)
She Doesn't Wanna Go (3)
Smoke (3)
1000 Swings (3)
Together (2)
Turn It Up Or Turn It Off (3)

What's The Difference (3)
When You Come Back (3)
Whiskey Soul Woman (3)
Whisper Tames The Lion (1)

DROPKICK MURPHYS '01

Punk-rock group from Boston: Mike McColgan (vocals), Rick Barton (guitar), Ken Casey (bass) and Matt Kelly (drums). McColgan and Barton left in 2000; replaced by Al Barr (vocals) and James Lynch (guitar).

4/3/99	184	1		©	1 The Gang's All Here			$10	Hellcat 80413
2/24/01	144	1		©	2 Sing Loud, Sing Proud!			$10	Hellcat 80430

Amazing Grace (1)
Blood And Whiskey (1)
Boston Asphalt (1)
Caps And Bottles (1)
Curse Of A Fallen Soul (1)
Devil's Brigade (1)

Few Good Men (2)
Fighting 69th (1)
For Boston (1)
Forever (2)
Fortunes Of War (2)
Gang's All Here (1)

Gauntlet, The (2)
Going Strong (1)
Good Rats (2)
Heroes From Our Past (2)
Homeward Bound (1)
Legend Of Finn MacCumhail (1)

New American Way (2)
Only Road (1)
Perfect Stranger (1)
Pipebomb On Lansdowne (1)
Ramble And Roll (2)
Rocky Road To Dublin (2)

Roll Call (1)
Spicy McHaggis Jig (2)
10 Years Of Service (1)
Torch, The (2)
Upstarts And Broken Hearts (1)
Wheel Of Misfortune (1)

Which Side Are You On? (2)
Wild Rover (2)

DROWNING POOL '01

Hard-rock group from Dallas: Dave Williams (vocals), C.J. Pierce (guitar), Stevie Benton (bass) and Mike Luce (drums).

6/23/01	14	15↑	▲	©	Sinner			$10	Wind-Up 13065

All Over Me
Bodies

Follow
I Am

Mute
Pity

Reminded
Sermon

Sinner
Tear Away

Told You So

D.R.S. '93

Male R&B vocal group from Sacramento, California: Endo, Pic, Jail Bait, Deuce Deuce and Blunt. D.R.S.: Dirty Rotten Scoundrels.

11/20/93	34	15	●	©	Gangsta Lean			$10	Capitol 81445

Bonnie & Clyde
Do Me, Baby

44 Ways
Gangsta Lean 4

Make It Rough
Mama Didn't Raise No Punk

Nigga Wit A Badge
Scoundrels Get Lonely

Sickness
Strip

Trust Me

DRU DOWN '96

Born Daniel Robinson in Oakland. Male rapper.

9/21/96	54	7		©	Can You Feel Me			$10	Relativity 1531

Baby Bubba
Breezy
Can You Feel Me 92

Choppin' It Up
Deal Went Bad
500 Mobsters

Freaks Come Out
Game, The
Head & Shoulders

Hustlin' Ain't No Thang
I'm Wondering
Mista Busta

Mobb, The
Playa Fo Real
Suspect One

Underestimated

DRU HILL '98

Male R&B vocal group from Baltimore: Mark **"Sisqo"** Andrews, James **"Woody"** Green, Tamir **"Nokio"** Ruffin and Larry **"Jazz"** Anthony. Green left in March 1999. Group named after Druid Hill Park in Baltimore.

12/7/96+	23	72	▲	©	1 Dru Hill			$10	Island 524306
11/14/98	2[1]	53	▲[2]	©	2 Enter The Dru			$10	Island 524542

All Alone (1)
Angel (2)
Anthem (2)
April Showers (1)
Beauty (2) 79

Do U Believe? (1)
5 Steps (1)
Holding You (2)
How Deep Is Your Love (2) 3
I'll Be The One (2)

I'm Wondering (2)
In My Bed (1) 4
Love We Had (Stays On My Mind) (2)
Love's Train (1)

Never Make A Promise (1) 7
Nothing To Prove (1)
One Good Reason (2)
Real Freak (2)
Satisfied (1)

Share My World (1)
So Special (1)
Tell Me (1) 18
These Are The Times (2) 21
This Is What We Do (2)

What Are We Gonna Do (2)
What Do I Do With The Love (2)
Whatever U Want (1)
You Are Everything (2) 84

D-SHOT '97

Born Donald Stevens in San Francisco. Male rapper. Member of **The Click**. Brother of **E-40**.

8/16/97	81	2		©	Six Figures			$10	Shot 41602

Duck
Great Britain
International...Head/Lee/Own

Huckleberry Hotline
(I'll Be Yo') Huckleberry
I'll Be Your Friend

Is It Cool To Fuck
It's Ma Thang
One More Shot

Out Tha' Pen
Six Figures
They Call Him Shot

True Worldwide Playaz

"D" TRAIN '82

R&B duo from Brooklyn, New York: James "D Train" Williams (vocals) and Hubert Eaves III (keyboards).

6/26/82	128	9			"D" Train			$12	Prelude 14105

"D" Train (Theme)
Keep On

Love Vibrations
Lucky Day

Tryin' To Get Over
Walk On By

You're The One For Me

DUCHIN, Eddy — see MOVIE SOUNDTRACKS: "The Eddy Duchin Story"

DEBUT	PEAK	WKS	RIAA	CD	ARTIST — Album Title	Catalog	Sym	$	Label & Number

DUDEK, Les '78

Born on 8/2/57 in Rhode Island. Prolific session guitarist.

4/23/77	107	12		© 1	**Say No More**			$12	Columbia 34397
5/6/78	100	11		2	**Ghost Town Parade**			$12	Columbia 35088

Avatar (1)　Central Park (2)　Falling Out (2)　Gonna Move (2)　Lady You're Nasty (1)　Tears Turn Into Diamonds (2)
Baby Sweet Baby (1)　Does Anybody Care (2)　Friend Of Mine (1)　I Remember (1)　Old Judge Jones (1)　What's It Gonna Be (1)
Bound To Be A Change (2)　Down To Nothin' (2)　Ghost Town Parade (2)　Jailabamboozle (1)　One To Beam Up (1)　Zorro Rides Again (1)

DUICE '93

Male rap duo: LA Sno (from Los Angeles) and Creo-D (from Barbados).

2/6/93	84	38	● ©		**Dazzey Duks**			$10	TMR 71000

Booty Call　**Dazzey Duks** 12　Feel What I Feel　Pawee, The
Bring The Bass　Duice Is In The House　Pass The Mic　Shitty-Shitty

★388★ DUKE, George '78

Born on 1/12/46 in San Rafael, California. Jazz-rock keyboardist. Own group in San Francisco during the mid-1950s. With the Don Ellis Big Band and **Jean-Luc Ponty**. With **Frank Zappa**'s Mothers Of Invention from 1971-75. Also with **Cannonball Adderley** from 1972-75. Own group from 1977. With **Stanley Clarke** in the Clarke/Duke Project.

1)Reach For It 2)The Clarke/Duke Project 3)Don't Let Go

2/1/75	141	6		1	**Feel**			$15	MPS/BASF 25355
5/31/75	111	10		2	**The Aura Will Prevail**			$15	MPS/BASF 25613
1/24/76	169	6		3	**I Love The Blues, She Heard My Cry**			$15	MPS/BASF 25671
10/23/76	99	9	©	4	**"Live"-On Tour In Europe**		[L]	$12	Atlantic 18194
					THE BILLY COBHAM/GEORGE DUKE BAND				
12/4/76	190	2		5	**Liberated Fantasies**		[I]	$12	MPS/BASF 22835
5/14/77	192	3		6	**From Me To You**			$12	Epic 34469
10/29/77+	25	24	● ©	7	**Reach For It**			$12	Epic 34883
6/3/78	39	14	©	8	**Don't Let Go**			$12	Epic 35366
3/17/79	56	11		9	**Follow The Rainbow**			$12	Epic 35701
11/24/79+	125	11	©	10	**Master Of The Game**			$12	Epic 36263
5/31/80	119	9	©	11	**A Brazilian Love Affair**			$12	Epic 36483
5/9/81	33	23	©	12	**The Clarke/Duke Project**			$10	Epic 36918
					STANLEY CLARKE/GEORGE DUKE				
3/6/82	48	12	©	13	**Dream On**			$10	Epic 37532
4/30/83	147	7	©	14	**Guardian Of The Light**			$10	Epic 38513
11/26/83+	146	10	©	15	**The Clarke/Duke Project II**			$10	Epic 38934
					STANLEY CLARKE/GEORGE DUKE				
4/20/85	183	5		16	**Thief In The Night**			$10	Elektra 60398

After The Love (5)　Dog-Man (10)　Games (10)　Let's Get Started (12)　Remembering The Sixties (16)　Sweet Wine (4)
Alien Challenges The Stick (medley) (10)　Don't Be Shy (5)　Giant Child Within Us - Ego (3)　Liberated Fantasies (5)　Ride (16)　That's What She Said (3)
Alien Succumbs To The Macho Inter-Galactic Funkativity Of The Funkblasters (medley) (10)　Don't Let Go (8)　Give Me Your Love (14)　Light (14)　Ride On Love (13)　Thief In The Night (16)
Almustafa The Beloved (4)　Down In It (6)　Good Times (15)　Look Into Her Eyes (3)　Rokkinrowl, I Don't Know (3)　Touch And Go (12)
Alone-6AM (11)　Dream On (13)　Great Danes (15)　Look What You Find (10)　Say That You Will (9)　Trip You In Love (15)
Ao Que Vai Nascer (11)　Dukey Stick (8)　Heroes (15)　Louie Louie (12)　'Scuse Me Miss (6)　Try Me Baby (15)
Atlanta (15)　Echidna's Arf (2)　Hip Pockets (4)　Love (1)　Searchin' My Mind (7)　Tryin' & Cryin' (5)
Aura, The (2)　End, The (7)　Hot Fire (7)　Love Mission (16)　Seasons (6)　Tzina (1)
Back To Where We Never Left (5)　Every Little Step I Take (10)　I Am For Real (May The Funk Be With You) (9)　Love Reborn (11)　Seeing You (5)　Uncle Remus (2)
Beginning, The (7)　Every Reason To Smile (5)　I C'n Hear That (5)　Malibu (2)　Shane (14)　Up From The Sea It Arose And Ate Rio In One Swift Bite (11)
Born To Love You (14)　Everybody's Talkin' (10)　I Just Want To Love You (12)　Mashavu (3)　**Shine On** (13) 41　Up On It (3)
Brazilian Love Affair (11)　Feel (1)　I Love You More (10)　Morning Sun (8)　Silly Fightin' (14)　Watch Out Baby! (7)
Brazilian Sugar (11)　Festival (9)　I Need You Now (11)　Movin' On (8)　Sing It (6)　Way I Feel (8)
Broken Dreams (6)　Finding My Way (12)　I Surrender (16)　Never Judge A Cover By It's Book (12)　Sister Serene (3)　We Give Our Love (8)
Carry On (6)　Floop De Loop (2)　I Want You For Myself (10)　Old Slipper (1)　Someday (11)　We're Supposed To Have Fun (4)
Celebrate (14)　Fly Away (14)　I Will Always Be Your Friend (13)　Omi (Fresh Water) (7)　Son Of Reach For It (The Funky Dream) (13)　What Do They Really Fear? (6)
Chariot (3)　Follow The Rainbow (9)　In The Distance (10)　Once Over (1)　Soon (14)　What The... (5)
Cora Joberge (1)　Fools (2)　Ivory Tattoo (4)　Overture (14)　Space Lady (4)　Why (16)
Corine (9)　Foosh (2)　Jam (16)　Party Down (9)　Stand (14)　Wild Dog (14)
Cravo E Canela (11)　For Love (I Come Your Friend) (2)　Juicy (4)　Pluck (9)　Starting Again (8)　Winners (12)
Dawn (2)　Framed (12)　Just For You (7)　Positive Energy (13)　Statement (1)　Yana Aminah (1)
Diamonds (7)　Frankenstein Goes To The Disco (4)　La La (16)　Prepare Yourself (3)　Straight From The Heart (9)　Yeah, We Going (8)
Do What Cha Wanna (4)　From Me To You (6)　Lemme At It (7)　Put It On The Line (15)　Sugar Loaf Mountain (11)　You (13)
　Funkin' For The Thrill (9)　Let Your Love Shine (13)　Rashid (1)　Summer Breezin' (11)　You And Me (6)
　Funny Funk (1)　　**Reach For It** (7) 54　Sunrise (9)　You (Are The Light) (14)
　Future, The (8)　　Reach Out (14)　**Sweet Baby** (12) 19　You're Gonna Love It (15)

DUKE, Patty '65

Born Anna Marie Duke on 12/14/46 in Elmhurst, New York. Movie and TV actress. Married to actor John Astin from 1972-85.

9/18/65	90	12			**Don't Just Stand There**			$25	United Artists 3452

Danke Schoen　End Of The World　Save Your Heart For Me　What The World Needs Now Is Love　World Without Love
Don't Just Stand There 8　Everything But Love　**Say Something Funny** 22　World Without Love
Downtown　Ribbons And Roses　Too Young　Why Don't They Understand

DUKE JUPITER '84

Rock group from Rochester, New York: Marshall James Styler (vocals, keyboards), Greg Walker (guitar), Rickey Ellis (bass) and David Corcoran (drums).

6/2/84	122	12			**White Knuckle Ride**			$12	Morocco 6097

Backfire　(I've Got A) Little Black Book　Me And Michelle　She's So Hot　Woman Like You
Don't Turn Your Back　**Little Lady** 68　Rescue Me　Top Of The Bay　Work It Out

DUKES OF DIXIELAND '58

Dixieland jazz group from New Orleans: brothers Frank (trumpet), Fred (trombone) and Joe (banjo) Assunto, Harold Cooper (clarinet), Stanley Mendelson (piano), Bill Porter (tuba) and Paul Ferrara (drums). Fred died on 4/21/66 (age 36). Frank died on 2/25/74 (age 42).

9/9/57+	6	26			**Marching Along With The Dukes Of Dixieland, Vol. 3**		[I]	$20	Audio Fidelity 1851
12/11/61+	10	21	©		**The Best Of The Dukes Of Dixieland**		[G-I]	$20	Audio Fidelity 1956

DUKES OF DIXIELAND — Cont'd

Bill Bailey (2)
Bourbon Street Parade (1,2)
Dixie (2)
Down By The Riverside (2)
Dukes Of Dixieland March (1)
Eyes Of Texas (1,2)

Georgia Camp Meeting (2)
Glory To Old Georgia (1)
Hot Time In The Old Town Tonight (2)
Just A Closer Walk With Thee (1)

Lassus Trombone (1)
McDonough Let The Trombones Blow (1)
Muskrat Ramble (2)
My Home Town (1)
Scobey Strut (1)

South (2)
South Rampart Street Parade (2)
Tromboneum (2)
Wait Till The Sun Shines Nellie (2)

When Johnny Reb Comes Marching Home (1)
When The Saints Go Marching In (2)
With A Pack On My Back (1)

Won't You Come Home Bill Bailey ..see: Bill Bailey

DULFER, Candy   '91
Born on 9/19/69 in Amsterdam. Female saxophonist.

| 6/22/91 | 22 | 36 | ● | © | **Saxuality** .... [I] | | | $10 | Arista 8674 |

Donja
Get The Funk

Heavenly City
Home Is Not A House

Jazzid
Lily Was Here 11

Mr. Lee
Pee Wee

Saxuality
So What

There Goes The Neighbourhood

DUNN, Holly   '91
Born on 8/22/57 in San Antonio, Texas. Country singer/songwriter.

| 8/17/91 | 162 | 1 | ● | © | **Milestones - Greatest Hits** .... [G] | | | $10 | Warner 26630 |

Are You Ever Gonna Love Me
Daddy's Hands
Face In The Crowd

(It's Always Gonna Be)
Someday

Love Someone Like Me
Maybe I Mean Yes

No One Takes The Train Anymore
Only When I Love

Strangers Again
There Goes My Heart Again
You Really Had Me Going

DUPREE, Robbie   '80
Born Robert Dupuis on 12/23/46 in Brooklyn, New York. Singer/songwriter.

| 6/14/80 | 51 | 24 | | | 1 **Robbie Dupree** .... | | | $12 | Elektra 273 |
| 6/13/81 | 169 | 5 | | | 2 **Street Corner Heroes** .... | | | $12 | Elektra 344 |

All Night Long (2)
Are You Ready For Love? (2)
Brooklyn Girls (2) 54
Desperation (2)

Free Fallin' (2)
Hot Rod Hearts (1) 15
I'll Be The Fool Again (1)
I'm No Stranger (1)

It's A Feeling (1)
Lonely Runner (1)
Long Goodbye (2)
Love Is A Mystery (1)

Missin' You (2)
Nobody Else (1)
Saturday Night (2)
Steal Away (1) 6

Street Corner Heroes (2)
Thin Line (1)
We Both Tried (1)

DUPREES, The   '62
Male vocal group from Jersey City, New Jersey: Joey Vann, Mike Arnone, Tom Bialablow, Joe Santollo and John Salvato. Santollo died of a heart attack on 6/3/81 (age 37). Vann died on 2/28/84 (age 40).

| 12/15/62 | 101 | 5 | | © | **You Belong To Me** .... | | | $300 | Coed 905 |

As Time Goes By
Ginny
I Wish I Could Believe You

Let's Make Love Again
My Dearest One
My Own True Love 13

September In The Rain
Take Me As I Am

These Foolish Things Remind Me Of You
Things I Love

Why Don't You Believe Me 37
You Belong To Me 7

DUPRI, Jermaine   '98
Born in 1972 in Atlanta. Rapper/producer.

| 8/8/98 | 3 | 27 | ▲ | © | **Jermaine Dupri Presents Life In 1472 - The Original Soundtrack** | | | $10 | So So Def 69087 |

All That's Got To Go
Don't Hate On Me
Fresh

Get Your Shit Right
Going Home With Me
Jazzy Hoes

Lay You Down
Money Ain't A Thang 52
Party Continues 29

Protector's Of 1472
Sweetheart
Three The Hard Way

Turn It Out
You Get Dealt Wit

★202★   DURAN DURAN   '85
Pop-rock group from Birmingham, England: Simon LeBon (vocals), **Andy Taylor** (guitar), Nick Rhodes (keyboards), John Taylor (bass) and Roger Taylor (drums). None of the Taylors are related. Group named after a villain in the Jane Fonda movie *Barbarella*. In 1984, Andy and Roger left the group. In 1985, Andy and John recorded with supergroup **The Power Station**; Simon, Nick and Roger recorded as Arcadia. Duran Duran reduced to a trio in 1986 of Simon, Nick and John. Expanded to a quintet in 1990 with the addition of Warren Cuccurullo (ex-guitarist of **Missing Persons**) and Sterling Campbell (left by 1993; joined **Soul Asylum** in 1995). John Taylor left in 1996, leaving trio of LeBon, Rhodes and Cuccurullo.

1)Arena 2)Rio 3)Duran Duran

6/5/82+	6	129	▲²	©	1 **Rio**			$10	Harvest 12211
10/2/82	98	15			2 **Carnival** .... [M]			$10	Harvest 15006
					new mixes of previously released material				
2/19/83	10	87	▲	©	3 **Duran Duran** .... [E]			$10	Capitol 12158
					first released in 1981				
12/10/83+	8	64	▲²	©	4 **Seven And The Ragged Tiger**			$10	Capitol 12310
12/1/84+	4	28	▲²	©	5 **Arena**			[L]	$10	Capitol 12374
12/20/86+	12	34	▲	©	6 **Notorious**			$10	Capitol 12540
11/5/88	24	26	●	©	7 **Big Thing**			$10	Capitol 90958
12/9/89+	67	16	▲	©	8 **Decade** .... [G]			$10	Capitol 93178
9/8/90	46	10		©	9 **Liberty**			$10	Capitol 94292
3/13/93	7	47	▲	©	10 **Duran Duran**			$10	Capitol 98876
4/22/95	19	10	●	©	11 **Thank You**			$10	Capitol 29419
11/1/97	58	3		©	12 **Medazzaland**			$10	Capitol 33876
4/24/99	170	1	●	©	13 **Greatest** .... [G]			$10	Capitol 96239
7/1/00	135	1		©	14 **Pop Trash**			$10	Hollywood 62266

All Along The Water (9)
All She Wants Is (7,8,13) 22
American Science (6)
Ball Of Confusion (11)
Be My Icon (12)
Big Bang Generation (12)
Big Thing (7)
Breath After Breath (10)
Buried In The Sand (12)
Can You Deal With It (9)
Careless Memories (3,5)
Chauffeur, The (1,5)
Come Undone (10,13) 7
Crystal Ship (11)
Do You Believe In Shame? (7) 72
Downtown (9)
Drive By (11)
Drowning Man (10)
Drug (It's Just A State Of Mind) (7)

Edge Of America (7)
Electric Barbarella (12,13) 52
Femme Fatale (10)
First Impression (9)
Fragment (14)
Friends Of Mine (3)
Girls On Film (2,3,8,13)
Hallucinating Elvis (14)
Hold Back The Rain (1,2)
Hold Me (6)
Hothead (9)
Hungry Like The Wolf (1,2,5,8,13) 3
I Don't Want Your Love (7,8,13) 4
I Take The Dice (14)
I Wanna Take You Higher (11)
(I'm Looking For) Cracks In The Pavement (4)
Is There Anyone Out There (3)

Is There Something I Should Know (5,8,13) 4
Kiss Goodbye (14)
Lady Xanax (14)
Lake Shore Driving (7)
Land (7)
Last Chance On The Stairway (1)
Last Day On Earth (14)
Lava Lamp (14)
Lay Lady Lay (11)
Liberty (9)
Lonely In Your Nightmare (1)
Love Voodoo (10)
Mars Meets Venus (14)
Matter Of Feeling (6)
Medazzaland (12)
Meet El Presidente (6) 70
Michael You've Got A Lot To Answer For (12)
Midnight Sun (14)

My Antarctica (9)
My Own Way (1,2)
New Moon On Monday (4,13) 10
New Religion (1,5)
911 Is A Joke (11)
None Of The Above (10)
Notorious (6,8,13) 2
Of Crime And Passion (4)
Ordinary World (10,13) 3
Out Of My Mind (12)
Palomino (7)
Perfect Day (11)
Planet Earth (3,5,8,13)
Playing With Uranium (14)
Pop Trash Movie (14)
Proposition (6)
Read My Lips (9)
Reflex, The (4,8,13) 1
Rio (1,8,13) 14
Save A Prayer (1,5,8,13) 16

Serious (9,13)
Seventh Stranger (4,5)
Shadows On Your Side (4)
Shelter (10)
Shotgun (10)
Silva Halo (12)
Sin Of The City (10)
Skin Trade (6,8,13) 39
So Long Suicide (12)
So Misled (6)
Someone Else Not Me (14)
Sound Of Thunder (3)
Starting To Remember (14)
Success (11)
Sun Doesn't Shine Forever (14)
Tel Aviv (3)
Thank You (11)
Tiger Tiger (4)
To Whom It May Concern (10)
Too Late Marlene (7)
Too Much Information (10) 45

UMF (10)
Undergoing Treatment (12)
Union Of The Snake (4,5,8,13) 3
Venice Drowning (9)
Vertigo (Do The Demolition) (6)
View To A Kill (8,13) 1
Violence Of Summer (Love's Taking Over) (9)
(Waiting For The) Night Boat (3)
Watching The Detectives (11)
White Lines (11)
Who Do You Think You Are? (12)
Wild Boys (5,8,13) 2
Winter Marches On (6)

DURANTE, Jimmy '63

Born on 2/10/1893 in New York City. Died of pneumonia on 1/29/80 (age 86). Legendary comedian. Appeared in several movies and TV shows.

| 9/21/63 | 30 | 19 | | © | **September Song** .... | | | $25 | Warner 1506 |

Blue Bird Of Happiness	Don't Lose Your Sense Of	Look Ahead Little Girl	When The Circus Leaves Town
Count Your Blessings Instead	Humor	One Room Home	You'll Never Walk Alone
Of Sheep	I Believe	**September Song** *51*	Young At Heart

DURY, Ian, & The Blockheads '79

Born on 5/12/42 in Upminster, England. Died of cancer on 3/27/2000 (age 57). Crippled by polio during childhood. Known as "The Poet of Punk."

5/6/78	168	5		©	1 **New Boots And Panties!!!**			$12	Stiff 0002
7/21/79	126	6		©	2 **Do It Yourself**			$12	Stiff 36104
2/7/81	159	4			3 **Laughter**			$12	Stiff 36998

Billericay Dickie (1)	Delusions Of Grandeur (3)	Inbetweenies (2)	Pardon (3)	(Take Your Elbow Out Of The	Waiting For Your Taxi (2)
Blackmail Man (1)	Don't Ask Me (2)	Lullaby For Francies (2)	Plaistow Patricia (1)	Soup You're Sitting On The	Wake Up And Make Love With
Blockheads (1)	F----ng Ada (3)	Manic Depression (Jimi) (3)	Quiet (2)	Chicken) (3)	Me (1)
Clevor Trever (1)	Hey, Hey, Take Me Away (3)	Mischief (2)	Sex & Drugs & Rock & Roll (1)	This Is What We Find (2)	What A Waste (1)
Dance Of The Crackpots (3)	I'm Partial To Your Abracadabra	My Old Man (1)	S-------'s Big Sister (3)	Uncoolohol (3)	Yes & No (Paula) (3)
Dance Of The Screamers (2)	(1)	Oh Mr. Peanut (3)	Sink My Boats (2)	Uneasy Sunny Day Hotsy Totsy	
	If I Was With A Woman (1)	Over The Points (3)	Sweet Gene Vincent (1)	(2)	

DYKE AND THE BLAZERS '67

Funk group from Buffalo: Arlester "Dyke" Christian (vocals), Alvester Jacobs (guitar), Bernard Williams and Clarence Towns (saxophones), Alvin Battle (bass) and Willie Earl (drums). Dyke was shot to death on 3/30/71 (age 28).

| 11/4/67 | 186 | 4 | | | **The Funky Broadway** .... | | | $50 | Original Sound 8876 |

Broadway Combination	Don't Bug Me	**Funky Broadway - Parts 1 &**	So Sharp	Wrong House
City Dump		**2** *65*	Uhh, Parts 1 & 2	

DYLAN, Bob ★8★ '74

Born Robert Zimmerman on 5/24/41 in Duluth, Minnesota; raised in Hibbing, Minnesota. Highly influential singer/songwriter/guitarist/harmonica player. Innovator of folk-rock style. Took stage name from poet Dylan Thomas. To New York City in December 1960. Worked Greenwich Village folk clubs. Signed to Columbia Records in October 1961. Motorcycle crash on 7/29/66 led to short retirement. Subject of documentaries *Don't Look Back* (1965) and *Eat The Document* (1969). Published novel *Tarantula* in 1970. Acted in movies *Pat Garrett And Billy The Kid* (1973), *Renaldo And Clara* (1978) and *Hearts Of Fire* (1987). Member of the supergroup **Traveling Wilburys**. His son Jakob is lead singer of **The Wallflowers**. Inducted into the Rock and Roll Hall of Fame in 1988. Won Grammy's Lifetime Achievement Award in 1991.

1)Desire 2)Planet Waves 3)Blood On The Tracks 4)John Wesley Harding 5)Nashville Skyline

9/7/63	22	32	▲	©	1 **The Freewheelin' Bob Dylan**			$50	Columbia 1986 / 8786
3/7/64	20	21	●	©	2 **The Times They Are A-Changin'**			$50	Columbia 2105 / 8905
9/19/64	43	41		©	3 **Another Side Of Bob Dylan**			$40	Columbia 2193 / 8993
5/1/65	6	43	●	©	4 **Bringing It All Back Home**			$40	Columbia 2328 / 9128
10/2/65	3	47	▲	©	5 **Highway 61 Revisited**			$40	Columbia 2389 / 9189
7/23/66	9	34	▲	©	6 **Blonde On Blonde**			$50	Columbia 41 / 841 [2]
5/6/67	10	94	▲⁵	©	7 **Bob Dylan's Greatest Hits**	C:#37/2	[G]	$30	Columbia 2663 / 9463
1/27/68	2⁴	52	▲	©	8 **John Wesley Harding**			$30	Columbia 2804 / 9604
5/3/69	3	47	▲	©	9 **Nashville Skyline**			$30	Columbia 9825
7/4/70	4	22	●	©	10 **Self Portrait**			$40	Columbia 30050 [2]
					album cover painted by Dylan				
11/14/70	7	23	●	©	11 **New Morning**			$20	Columbia 30290
12/11/71+	14	36	▲⁵	©	12 **Bob Dylan's Greatest Hits, Vol. II**		[G]	$25	Columbia 31120 [2]
8/4/73	16	30	●	©	13 **Pat Garrett & Billy The Kid**		[S]	$20	Columbia 32460
12/22/73+	17	15	●		14 **Dylan**		[K]	$20	Columbia 32747
					outtake recordings from 1969-70				
2/9/74	❶⁴	21	●	©	15 **Planet Waves**			$15	Asylum 1003
					BOB DYLAN With The Band				
7/13/74	3	19	▲	©	16 **Before The Flood**		[L]	$20	Asylum 201 [2]
					BOB DYLAN/THE BAND				
2/8/75	❶²	24	▲²	©	17 **Blood On The Tracks**			$15	Columbia 33235
7/26/75	7	14	●	©	18 **The Basement Tapes**		[E]	$20	Columbia 33682 [2]
					BOB DYLAN AND THE BAND				
					recorded in 1967				
1/24/76	❶⁵	35	▲²	©	19 **Desire**			$15	Columbia 33893
10/2/76	17	12	●	©	20 **Hard Rain**		[L]	$15	Columbia 34349
7/8/78	11	23	●	©	21 **Street-Legal**			$15	Columbia 35453
5/12/79	13	25		©	22 **Bob Dylan At Budokan**		[L]	$20	Columbia 36067 [2]
					recorded on 3/1/78 in Japan				
9/8/79	3	26	▲	©	23 **Slow Train Coming**			$15	Columbia 36120
7/12/80	24	11		©	24 **Saved**			$15	Columbia 36553
					album cover painted by Dylan				
9/5/81	33	9		©	25 **Shot Of Love**			$15	Columbia 37496
11/19/83	20	24	●	©	26 **Infidels**			$12	Columbia 38819
1/5/85	115	9		©	27 **Real Live**		[L]	$10	Columbia 39944
6/22/85	33	17		©	28 **Empire Burlesque**			$10	Columbia 40110
12/7/85+	33	22	▲	©	29 **Biograph**		[K]	$50	Columbia 38830 [5]
8/2/86	53	13		©	30 **Knocked Out Loaded**			$10	Columbia 40439
6/18/88	61	10		©	31 **Down In The Groove**			$10	Columbia 40957

DYLAN, Bob — Cont'd

DEBUT	PEAK	WKS		CD	ARTIST — Album Title	Sym	$	Label & Number
2/18/89	37	11	●	© 32	Dylan & The Dead	[L]	$10	Columbia 45056
					BOB DYLAN & GRATEFUL DEAD			
10/7/89	30	23		© 33	Oh Mercy		$10	Columbia 45281
9/29/90	38	11		© 34	Under The Red Sky		$10	Columbia 46794
4/13/91	49	6	●	© 35	The Bootleg Series - Volumes 1-3 [Rare & Unreleased] 1961-1991	[K]	$30	Columbia 47382 [3]
11/21/92	51	8		© 36	Good As I Been To You		$10	Columbia 53200
11/13/93	70	4		© 37	World Gone Wrong		$10	Columbia 57590
12/3/94	126	2	●	© 38	Greatest Hits Volume 3	[G]	$10	Columbia 66783
5/20/95	23	10	●	© 39	MTV Unplugged	[L]	$10	Columbia 67000
10/18/97	10	29	▲	© 40	Time Out Of Mind		$10	Columbia 68556
					1997 Grammy winner: Album of the Year			
10/31/98	31	5		© 41	The Bootleg Series Vol. 4 - Live 1966	[E-L]	$15	Columbia 65759 [2]
					recorded on 5/17/66 at the Free Trade Hall in Manchester, England			
11/18/00	67	18	●	© 42	The Essential Bob Dylan	[G]	$15	Columbia 85168 [2]

Abandoned Love (29)
Absolutely Sweet Marie (6)
Ain't No More Cane (18)
Alberta #1 & #2 (10)
All Along The Watchtower (8,12,16,22,29,32,39,42)
All I Really Want To Do (3,12,22)
All The Tired Horses (10)
Angelina (35)
Apple Suckling Tree (18)
Are You Ready (24)
Arthur McBride (36)
As I Went Out One Morning (8)
Baby, I'm In The Mood For You (29)
Baby, Let Me Follow You Down (29,41)
Baby Stop Crying (21)
Ballad In Plain D (3)
Ballad Of A Thin Man (5,16,22,27,41)
Ballad Of Frankie Lee And Judas Priest (8)
Ballad Of Hollis Brown (2)
Ballad Of Ira Hayes (14)
Belle Isle (10)
Bessie Smith (18)
Big Yellow Taxi (14)
Billy (13)
Black Crow Blues (3)
Black Diamond Bay (19)
Blackjack Davey (36)
Blind Willie McTell (35)
Blood In My Eyes (37)
Blowin' In The Wind (1,7,16,22,29,42)
Blue Moon (10)
Bob Dylan's Blues (1)
Bob Dylan's Dream (1)
Bob Dylan's 115th Dream (4)
Boots Of Spanish Leather (2)
Born In Time (34)
Boxer, The (10)
Broke Down Engine (37)
Brownsville Girl (30,38)
Buckets Of Rain (17)
Bunkhouse Theme (13)
Call Letter Blues (35)
Can You Please Crawl Out Your Window? (29) 58
Can't Help Falling In Love (14)
Can't Wait (40)
Canadee-I-O (36)
Cantina Theme (Workin' For The Law) (13)
Caribbean Wind (29)
Cat's In The Well (34)
Catfish (35)
Changing Of The Guards (21,38)
Chimes Of Freedom (3)
Clean Cut Kid (28)
Clothes Line Saga (18)
Cold Irons Bound (40)
Copper Kettle (The Pale Moonlight) (10)
Corrina, Corrina (1)
Country Pie (9)
Covenant Woman (24)
Crash On The Levee (Down In The Flood) (12,18)
Dark Eyes (28)
Day Of The Locusts (11)
Days Of 49 (10)
Dead Man, Dead Man (25)
Dear Landlord (8,29)
Death Is Not The End (31)
Delia (37)
Desolation Row (5,39,41)
Diamond Joe (36)

Dignity (38,39)
Dirge (41)
Dirt Road Blues (40)
Disease Of Conceit (33)
Do Right To Me Baby (Do Unto Others) (23)
Don't Fall Apart On Me Tonight (26)
Don't Think Twice, It's All Right (1,12,16,22,42)
Don't Ya Tell Henry (18)
Down Along The Cove (8)
Down In The Flood ..see: Crash On The Levee (Down In The Flood)
Down The Highway (1)
Drifter's Escape (8)
Driftin' Too Far From Shore (30)
Early Mornin' Rain (10)
Emotionally Yours (28)
Endless Highway (16)
Eternal Circle (35)
Every Grain Of Sand (25,29,35)
Everything Is Broken (33,42)
Farewell, Angelina (35)
Father Of Night (11)
Final Theme (13)
Fool Such As I (14) 55
Foot Of Pride (35)
Forever Young (15,22,29,38,42)
4th Time Around (6,41)
Frankie & Albert (36)
Froggie Went A Courtin' (36)
From A Buick 6 (5)
Gates Of Eden (4)
Girl From The North Country (1,9,27)
God Knows (34)
Goin' To Acapulco (18)
Going Going Gone (15,22)
Golden Loom (35)
Gonna Change My Way Of Thinking (23)
Got My Mind Made Up (30)
Gotta Serve Somebody (23,29,32,38,42) 24
Gotta Travel On (10)
Groom's Still Waiting At The Altar (29,38)
Had A Dream About You, Baby (31)
Handy Dandy (34)
Hard Rain's A-Gonna Fall (1,12)
Hard Times (36)
Hard Times In New York Town (35)
Hazel (15)
He Was A Friend Of Mine (35)
Heart Of Mine (25,29)
Highlands (40)
Highway 61 Revisited (5,16,27)
Honey, Just Allow Me One More Chance (1)
House Carpenter (35)
Hurricane (Part I) (19,38,42) 33
I Am A Lonesome Hobo (8)
I And I (26,27)
I Believe In You (23,29)
I Don't Believe You (3,29)
I Don't Believe You (She Acts Like We Never Have Met) (41)
I Dreamed I Saw St. Augustine (8)
I Forgot More Than You'll Ever Know (10)
I Pity The Poor Immigrant (8)
I Shall Be Free (1)
I Shall Be Free No. 10 (3)
I Shall Be Released (12,16,22,29,35,42)
I Threw It All Away (9,20) 85

I Wanna Be Your Lover (29)
I Want You (6,7,22,29,32) 20
I'll Be Your Baby Tonight (8,12,29,42)
I'll Keep It With Him (29,35)
I'll Remember You (28)
Idiot Wind (17,20,35)
If Dogs Run Free (11)
If Not For You (11,12,29,35,42)
If You Gotta Go, Go Now (Or Else You Got To Stay All Night) (35)
If You See Her, Say Hello (17,35)
In Search Of Little Sadie (10)
In The Garden (24)
In The Summertime (25)
Is Your Love In Vain? (21,22)
Isis (19,29)
It Ain't Me Babe (3,7,16,27,29,42)
It Hurts Me Too (10)
It Takes A Lot To Laugh, It Takes A Train To Cry (5,35)
It's All Over Now, Baby Blue (4,12,29,41,42)
It's Alright, Ma (I'm Only Bleeding) (4,16,22)
Jack-A-Roe (37)
Jet Pilot (29)
Jim Jones (36)
Joey (19,32)
John Brown (39)
John Wesley Harding (8)
Jokerman (26,38,42)
Just Like A Woman (6,7,16,22,29,41,42) 33
Just Like Tom Thumb's Blues (5,12,41)
Katie's Been Gone (18)
Kingsport Town (35)
Knockin' On Heaven's Door (13,16,22,29,32,38,39,42) 12
Last Thoughts On Woody Guthrie (35)
Lay Down Your Weary Tune (29)
Lay Lady Lay (9,12,16,20,29,42) 7
Lenny Bruce (25)
Leopard-Skin Pill-Box Hat (6,41) 81
Let It Be Me (10)
Let Me Die In My Footsteps (35)
Let's Stick Together (31)
License To Kill (26,27)
Like A Rolling Stone (5,7,10,16,22,29,35,39,41,42) 2
Lily Of The West (14)
Lily, Rosemary And The Jack Of Hearts (17)
Little Maggie (36)
Little Sadie (10)
Living The Blues (10)
Lo And Behold! (18)
Lone Pilgrim (37)
Lonesome Death Of Hattie Carroll (2,29)
Long Distance Operator (18)
Lord Protect My Child (35)
Love Henry (37)
Love Minus Zero/No Limit (4,22)
Love Sick (40)
Maggie's Farm (4,12,20,22,27,42)
Make You Feel My Love (40)
Mama, You Been On My Mind (35)
Man Gave Names To All The Animals (23)
Man In Me (35)
Man In The Long Black Coat (33)

Man Of Peace (26)
Man On The Street (35)
Mary Ann (14)
Masters Of War (1,27,29)
Maybe Someday (30)
Meet Me In The Morning (17)
Mighty Quinn (Quinn, The Eskimo) (10,12,29,42)
Million Dollar Bash (18,29)
Million Miles (40)
Minstrel Boy (10)
Mixed-Up Confusion (29)
Moonshiner (35)
Most Likely You Go Your Way (And I'll Go Mine) (6,16,29) 66
Most Of The Time (33)
Motorpsycho Nitemare (3)
Mozambique (19) 54
Mr. Bojangles (14)
Mr. Tambourine Man (4,7,22,29,41,42)
My Back Pages (3,12)
Nashville Skyline Rag (9)
Need A Woman (35)
Neighborhood Bully (26)
Never Gonna Be The Same Again (24)
Never Say Goodbye (15)
New Morning (11)
New Pony (21)
Night They Drove Old Dixie Down (16)
Ninety Miles An Hour (Down A Dead End Street) (31)
No More Auction Block (35)
No Time To Think (21)
Nobody 'Cept You (35)
North Country Blues (2)
Not Dark Yet (40,42)
Nothing Was Delivered (18)
Obviously 5 Believers (6)
Odds And Ends (18)
Oh, Sister (19,20,22)
On A Night Like This (15,29) 44
On The Road Again (4)
One More Cup Of Coffee (19,22)
One More Night (9)
One More Weekend (11)
One Of Us Must Know (Sooner Or Later) (6)
One Too Many Mornings (2,20,41)
Only A Hobo (35)
Only A Pawn In Their Game (2)
Open The Door, Homer (18)
Orange Juice Blues (Blues For Breakfast) (18)
Outlaw Blues (4)
Oxford Town (1)
Paths Of Victory (35)
Peggy Day (9)
Percy's Song (29)
Please, Mrs. Henry (18)
Pledging My Time (6)
Political World (33)
Positively 4th Street (7,29,42) 7
Precious Angel (23)
Precious Memories (30)
Pressing On (24)
Property Of Jesus (25)
Queen Jane Approximately (5,32)
Quit Your Low Down Ways (35)
Ragged & Dirty (37)
Rainy Day Women #12 & 35 (6,7,16,39,42) 2
Rambling, Gambling Willie (35)
Rank Strangers To Me (31)

Restless Farewell (2)
Ring Them Bells (33,38)
River Theme (13)
Romance In Durango (19,29)
Ruben Remus (18)
Sad Eyed Lady Of The Lowlands (6)
Sally Sue Brown (31)
Santa-Fe (35)
Sara (19)
Sarah Jane (14)
Satisfied Mind (24)
Saved (24)
Saving Grace (24)
Seeing The Real You At Last (28)
Senor (Tales Of Yankee Power) (21,29)
Series Of Dreams (35,38)
Seven Curses (35)
Seven Days (35)
Shape I'm In (16)
She Belongs To Me (4,10,12,41)
She's Your Lover Now (35)
Shelter From The Storm (17,20,22,42)
Shenandoah (31)
Shooting Star (33,39)
Shot Of Love (25)
Sign On The Window (11)
Silvio (31,38,42)
Simple Twist Of Fate (17,22)
Sittin' On Top Of The World (36)
Sitting On A Barbed Wire Fence (35)
Slow Train (23,32)
Solid Rock (24,29)
Someone's Got A Hold Of My Heart (35)
Something There Is About You (15)
Something's Burning, Baby (28)
Spanish Harlem Incident (3)
Spanish Is The Loving Tongue (14)
Stack A Lee (37)
Stage Fright (16)
Standing In The Doorway (40)
Step It Up And Go (36)
Stuck Inside Of Mobile With The Memphis Blues Again (6,12,20)
Subterranean Homesick Blues (4,7,29,35,42) 39
Suze (The Cough Song) (35)
Sweetheart Like You (26) 55
T.V. Talkin' Song (34)
Take A Message To Mary (10)
Take Me As I Am (Or Let Me Go) (10)
Talkin' Bear Mountain Picnic Massacre Blues (35)
Talkin' Hava Negeilah Blues (35)
Talkin' John Birch Paranoid Blues (35)
Talking World War III Blues (1)
Tangled Up In Blue (17,27,29,35,38,42) 31
Tears Of Rage (18)
Tell Me (35)
Tell Me, Momma (41)
Tell Me That It Isn't True (9)
Temporary Like Achilles (6)
10,000 Men (34)
They Killed Him (30)
Things Have Changed (42)
This Wheel's On Fire (18)
Three Angels (11)

Tight Connection To My Heart (Has Anybody Seen My Love) (28)
'Til I Fell In Love With You (40)
Time Passes Slowly (11,29)
Times They Are A-Changin' (2,7,22,29,35,39,42)
Tiny Montgomery (18)
To Be Alone With You (9)
To Ramona (3,29)
Tombstone Blues (5,27,29,39)
Tomorrow Is A Long Time (12)
Tomorrow Night (36)
Tonight I'll Be Staying Here With You (9,12) 50
Too Much Of Nothing (18)
Tough Mama (15)
Trouble (25)
True Love Tends To Forget (21)
Trust Yourself (28)
Tryin' To Get To Heaven (40)
Turkey Chase (13)
2 X 2 (34)
Two Soldiers (37)
Ugliest Girl In The World (31)
Unbelievable (34)
Under The Red Sky (34,38)
Under Your Spell (30)
Union Sundown (26)
Up On Cripple Creek (16)
Up To Me (29)
Visions Of Johanna (6,29,41)
Walkin' Down The Line (35)
Wallflower (35)
Walls Of Red Wing (35)
Watching The River Flow (12) 41
Watered-Down Love (25)
We Better Talk This Over (21)
Wedding Song (15)
Weight, The (16)
Went To See The Gypsy (11)
What Can I Do For You? (24)
What Good Am I? (33)
What Was It You Wanted (33)
When Did You Leave Heaven? (31)
When He Returns (23)
When I Paint My Masterpiece (12)
When The Night Comes Falling From The Sky (28,35)
When The Ship Comes In (2,35)
When You Awake (16)
When You Gonna Wake Up (23)
Where Are You Tonight? (Journey Through Dark Heat) (21)
Where Teardrops Fall (33)
Who Killed Davey Moore? (35)
Wicked Messenger (8)
Wiggle Wiggle (34)
Wigwam (10) 41
Winterlude (11)
With God On Our Side (2,39)
Woogie Boogie (10)
World Gone Wrong (37)
Worried Blues (35)
Yazoo Street Scandal (18)
Ye Shall Be Changed (35)
Yea! Heavy And A Bottle Of Bread (18)
You Ain't Goin' Nowhere (12,18,42)
You Angel You (15,29)
You Changed My Life (35)
You Wanna Ramble (30)
You're A Big Girl Now (17,20,29)
You're Gonna Make Me Lonesome When You Go (17)
You're Gonna Quit Me (36)

DYNAMIC SUPERIORS '75
R&B vocal group from Washington DC: Tony Washington, George Spann, George Peterbark, Michael McCalphin and Maurice Washington.

| 8/9/75 | 130 | 10 | | | **Pure Pleasure** .... | | | $12 | Motown 841 |

Ain't Nothing Like The Real
Thing

Better Way
Deception

Don't Give Up On Me Baby
Face The Music

Feeling Mellow
Hit And Run Lovers

Nobody's Gonna Change Me
Pleasure

DYNAMITE HACK '00
Rock group from Austin, Texas: Mark Morris (vocals, guitar), Mike Vlahakis (guitar), Chad Robinson (bass) and Chase Scott (drums). Group name taken from a line in the movie *Caddyshack*.

| 6/10/00 | 84 | 11 | | © | **Superfast** .... | | | $10 | Woppitzer 157884 |

Alvin
Anyway

Blue Sky
Boyz-N-The Hood

Dear Kate,
G-Force

Granola
Marie...

Pick Up Lines
Slice Of Heaven

Switcheroo
Wussypuff

DYNASTY '80
R&B vocal trio from Los Angeles: Kevin Spencer, Nidra Beard and Linda Carriere.

| 8/2/80 | 43 | 21 | | | 1 **Adventures In The Land Of Music** .... | | | $12 | Solar 3576 |
| 10/10/81 | 119 | 4 | | | 2 **The Second Adventure** .... | | | $12 | Solar 20 |

Adventures In The Land Of
Music (1)
Day And Night (1)
Do Me Right (1)

Give It Up For Love (2)
Give Your Love To Me (2)
Groove Control (1)
Here I Am (2)

High Time (I Left You Baby) (2)
I've Just Begun To Love You
(1) *87*
Ice Breaker (1)

Love In The Fast Lane (2)
Man In Love (2)
Pain, Got A Hold On Me (2)
Revenge (2)

Something To Remember (1)
Take Another Look At Love (1)
That Lovin' Feelin' (2)
You're My Angel (1)

DYSON, Ronnie '70
Born on 6/5/50 in Washington DC; raised in Brooklyn, New York. Died of heart failure on 11/10/90 (age 40). R&B singer. Leading role in the Broadway musical *Hair*. In the movie *Putney Swope*.

| 9/5/70 | 55 | 18 | | | 1 **(If You Let Me Make Love To You Then) Why Can't I Touch You?** .... | | | $15 | Columbia 30223 |
| 4/7/73 | 142 | 7 | | | 2 **One Man Band** .... | | | $15 | Columbia 32211 |

Band Of Gold (1)
Bridge Over Troubled Water (1)
Do What Your Heart Tells You
To Do (1)
Emmie (1)
Fever (1)

Girl Don't Come (2)
Give In To Love (2)
I Don't Wanna Cry (1) *50*
I Just Can't Help Believin' (1)
I Think I'll Tell Her (2)

**(If You Let Me Make Love To
You Then) Why Can't I
Touch You?** (1) *8*
Just Don't Want To Be Lonely
(2) *60*
Love Of A Woman (2)

Make It With You (1)
**One Man Band (Plays All
Alone)** (2)
Point Of No Return (2)
She's Gone (1)
Something (2)

Touch Of Baby (1)
Wednesday In Your Garden (2)
**When You Get Right Down To
It** (2) *94*

E

EAGLES ★72★ '76
Rock group formed in Los Angeles: **Glenn Frey** (vocals, guitar), Bernie Leadon (guitar), **Randy Meisner** (bass) and **Don Henley** (vocals, drums). Meisner was a member of **Poco**. Leadon was a member of the **Flying Burrito Brothers**. Frey and Henley were with **Linda Ronstadt**. Debut album recorded in England in 1972. **Don Felder** (guitar) added in 1975. Leadon replaced by **Joe Walsh** in 1975. Meisner replaced by **Timothy B. Schmit** in 1977. Frey and Henley were the only members to play on all recordings. Disbanded in 1982. Henley, Frey, Felder, Walsh and Schmit reunited in 1994. Group inducted into the Rock and Roll Hall of Fame in 1998.

1) The Long Run 2) Hotel California 3) Eagles/Their Greatest Hits 1971-1975

6/24/72	22	49	▲	©	1 **Eagles**			$15	Asylum 5054
5/5/73	41	70	▲²	©	2 **Desperado**			$15	Asylum 5068
4/20/74	17	87	▲²	©	3 **On The Border** .... C:#10/17			$15	Asylum 1004
6/28/75	❶⁵	56	▲⁴	©	4 **One Of These Nights**			$12	Asylum 1039
3/6/76	❶⁵	133	▲²⁷	©	5 **Eagles/Their Greatest Hits 1971-1975** C:❶¹³/424 [G]			$12	Asylum 1052
12/25/76+	❶⁸	107	▲¹⁶	©	6 **Hotel California** C:#9/158			$12	Asylum 1084
10/20/79	❶⁹	57	▲⁷	©	7 **The Long Run**			$12	Asylum 508
11/29/80	6	26	▲⁷	©	8 **Eagles Live** C:#25/15 [L]			$15	Asylum 705 [2]
11/13/82+	52	15	▲¹⁰	©	9 **Eagles Greatest Hits, Volume 2** .... C:#2⁵/211 [G]			$12	Asylum 60205
11/26/94	❶²	112	▲⁷	©	10 **Hell Freezes Over** C:#6/158 [L]			$10	Geffen 24725

recorded at the Warner Burbank Studios; includes 4 studio cuts

| 12/2/00 | 109 | 10 | ● | © | 11 **Selected Works: 1972-1999** .... [K] | | | $40 | Elektra 62575 [4] |

After The Thrill Is Gone (4,9,11)
All Night Long (8)
All She Wants To Do Is Dance
(11)
Already Gone (3,5,11) *32*
Best Of My Love (3,5,11) *1*
Bitter Creek (2)
Certain Kind Of Fool (2)
Chug All Night (1)
Desperado (2,5,8,10,11)
Dirty Laundry (11)
Disco Strangler (7,11)
Doolin-Dalton (2,8,10,11)
Earlybird (1)
Funk 49 (11)

Funky New Year (11)
Get Over It (10,11) *31*
Girl From Yesterday (10)
Good Day In Hell (3)
Greeks Don't Want No Freaks
(7)
Heartache Tonight (7,8,9,11) *1*
Hollywood Waltz (4,11)
Hotel California (6,8,9,10,11) *1*
I Can't Tell You Why
(7,8,9,10,11) *8*
I Wish You Peace (4)
In The City (7,10,11)
Is It True? (3)
James Dean (3,11) *77*

Journey Of The Sorcerer (4)
King Of Hollywood (7,11)
Last Resort (6,10,11)
Learn To Be Still (10)
Life In The Fast Lane
(6,8,9,10,11) *11*
Life's Been Good (8)
Long Run (7,8,9,11) *8*
Long Run Leftovers (11)
Love Will Keep Us Alive (10,11)
Lyin' Eyes (4,5,11) *2*
Midnight Flyer (3,11)
Most Of Us Are Sad (1)
My Man (3)
New Kid In Town (6,8,9,11) *1*

New York Minute (10)
Nightingale (1)
Ol' '55 (3,11)
On The Border (3,11)
One Of These Nights
(4,5,11) *1*
Out Of Control (2)
Outlaw Man (2,11) *59*
Peaceful Easy Feeling
(1,5,11) *22*
Please Come Home For
Christmas (11)
Pretty Maids All In A Row
(6,10,11)
Random Victims Part 3 (11)

Sad Cafe (7,9,11)
Saturday Night (2,8,11)
Seven Bridges Road (8,9) *21*
Take It Easy (1,5,8,10,11) *12*
Take It To The Limit
(4,5,8,11) *4*
Take The Devil (1)
Teenage Jail (7)
Tequila Sunrise (2,5,10,11) *64*
Those Shoes (7,11)
Too Many Hands (4,11)
Train Leaves Here This
Morning (1,11)
Try And Love Again (6,11)
Tryin' (1)

Twenty-One (2)
Victim Of Love (6,9,11)
Visions (4)
Wasted Time (6,8,10,11)
Witchy Woman (1,5,11) *9*
You Never Cry Like A Lover (3)

EARLAND, Charles '70
Born on 5/24/41 in Philadelphia. R&B-jazz keyboardist/saxophonist. Tenor saxophonist with **Jimmy McGriff**'s trio. Alto saxophonist with **Lou Donaldson** from 1968-70, then formed his own group.

7/11/70	108	19		©	1 **Black Talk!** .... [I]			$15	Prestige 7758
11/21/70+	131	10			2 **Black Drops** .... [I]			$15	Prestige 7815
5/15/71	176	7		©	3 **Living Black!** .... [I-L]			$15	Prestige 10009

recorded at the Key Club in Newark, New Jersey

| 4/3/76 | 155 | 11 | | | 4 **Odyssey** .... | | | $12 | Mercury 1049 |

Aquarius (1)
Black Talk (1)
Buck Green (2)
Cosmic Fever (4)

Don't Say Goodbye (2)
From My Heart To Yours (4)
Here Comes Charlie (1)
Intergalactic Love Song (4)

Journey Of The Soul (4)
Keyclub Cookout (3)
Killer Joe (3)
Lazybird (2)

Letha (4)
Mighty Burner (4)
Milestones (3)
More Today Than Yesterday (1)

Phire (4)
Raindrops Keep Falling On My
Head (2)
Sing A Simple Song (2)

Sons Of The Gods (4)
We All Live In The Jungle (4)
Westbound #9 (3)

EARLE, Steve '89
Born on 1/17/55 in Fort Monroe, Virginia; raised in Schertz, Texas. Country-rock singer/songwriter/guitarist.

DEBUT	PEAK	WKS	RIAA	CD	#	Album Title	$	Label & Number
10/25/86	89	20	●	©	1	Guitar Town	$10	MCA 5713
6/13/87	90	14		©	2	Exit O	$10	MCA 5998
						STEVE EARLE AND THE DUKES		
11/12/88+	56	28	●	©	3	Copperhead Road	$10	Uni 7
7/21/90	100	9		©	4	The Hard Way	$10	MCA 6430
						STEVE EARLE AND THE DUKES		
3/23/96	106	4		©	5	I Feel Alright	$10	Warner 46201
10/25/97	126	2		©	6	El Corazón	$10	Warner 46789
						title is Spanish for "The Heart"		
3/13/99	133	3		©	7	The Mountain	$10	E-Squared 1064
						STEVE EARLE AND THE DEL McCOURY BAND		
6/24/00	66	4		©	8	Transcendental Blues	$10	E-Squared 751033

All My Life (8)
Angry Young Man (2)
Another Town (8)
Back To The Wall (3)
Billy And Bonnie (5)
Billy Austin (4)
Boy Who Never Cried (8)
CCKMP (5)
Carrie Brown (7)
Christmas In Washington (6)
Close Your Eyes (4)
Connemara Breakdown (7)
Copperhead Road (3)
Country Girl (4)
Devil's Right Hand (3)
Dixieland (7)
Down The Road (1)

Esmeralda's Hollywood (4)
Even When I'm Blue (3)
Everyone's In Love With You (8)
Fearless Heart (1)
Feel Alright (5)
Ft. Worth Blues (6)
Galway Girl (8)
Good Ol' Boy (Gettin' Tough) (1)
Goodbye's All We've Got Left (1)
Graveyard Shift (7)
Guitar Town (1)
Halo 'Round The Moon (8)
Hard-Core Troubadour (5)
Harlan Man (7)
Have Mercy (4)

Here I Am (6)
Hillbilly Highway (1)
Hopeless Romantics (4)
Hurtin' Me, Hurtin' You (5)
I Ain't Ever Satisfied (2)
I Can Wait (8)
I Don't Want To Lose You Yet (8)
I Love You Too Much (2)
I Still Carry You Around (6)
I'm Still In Love With You (7)
If You Fall (6)
It's All Up To You (2)
Johnny Come Lately (3)
Justice In Ontario (4)
Leroy's Dustbowl Blues (7)
Little Rock 'N' Roller (1)
Lonelier Than This (8)

Long, Lonesome Highway Blues (7)
More Than I Can Do (5)
Mountain, The (7)
My Old Friend The Blues (1)
N.Y.C. (6)
Nothing But A Child (3)
Now She's Gone (5)
Nowhere Road (2)
No. 29 (2)
Once You Love (3)
Other Kind (4)
Other Side Of Town (6)
Outlaw's Honeymoon (7)
Over Yonder (Jonathan's Song) (8)
Paddy On The Beat (7)
Pilgrim (7)

Poison Lovers (6)
Poor Boy (5)
Promise You Anything (4)
Rain Came Down (2)
Regular Guy (4)
San Antonio Girl (2)
Snake Oil (3)
Someday (1)
Somewhere Out There (8)
South Nashville Blues (5)
Steve's Last Ramble (8)
Sweet Little '66 (2)
Taneytown (6)
Telephone Road (6)
Texas Eagle (7)
Think It Over (1)
This Highway's Mine (Roadmaster) (4)

Transcendental Blues (8)
Until The Day I Die (8)
Valentine's Day (5)
Waiting On You (3)
Week Of Living Dangerously (2)
West Nashville Boogie (4)
When I Fall (8)
When The People Find Out (4)
Wherever I Go (8)
You Belong To Me (3)
You Know The Rest (6)
You're Still Standin' There (5)
Yours Forever Blue (7)

EARTH OPERA '69
Rock group from Boston: Peter Rowan (vocals, guitar), David Grisman (mandolin), John Nagy (bass) and Paul Dillon (drums).

DEBUT	PEAK	WKS			#	Album Title	$	Label & Number
3/22/69	181	4				The Great American Eagle Tragedy	$15	Elektra 74038

Alfie Finney
All Winter Long

American Eagle Tragedy
Home To You 97

It's Love
Mad Lydia's Waltz

Roast Beef Love
Sanctuary From The Law

EARTHQUAKE '76
Rock group from San Francisco: John Doukas (vocals), Robbie Dunbar (guitar), Gary Phillips (piano), Stan Miller (bass) and Steve Nelson (drums).

DEBUT	PEAK	WKS			#	Album Title	$	Label & Number
9/4/76	151	4				8.5	$12	Beserkley 0047

And He Likes To Hurt You
Don't Want To Go Back

Finders Keepers
Girl Named Jesse James

Hit The Floor
Little Cindy

Motivate Me
Same Old Story

Savin' My Love

EARTH, WIND & FIRE ★91★ '76
R&B group formed in Los Angeles by Maurice White (vocals, percussion). In 1969, White, former session drummer for Chess Records and member of The Ramsey Lewis Trio, formed the Salty Peppers; recorded for Capitol. Maurice's brother Verdine White was the group's bassist. Eighteen months later, the brothers hired a new band and recorded as Earth, Wind & Fire (named for the three elements of Maurice's astrological sign). Co-lead singer Philip Bailey joined in 1971. Group generally contained eight to 10 members, with frequent personnel shuffling. Appeared in the movies That's the Way of the World (1975) and Sgt. Pepper's Lonely Hearts Club Band (1978). Inducted into the Rock and Roll Hall of Fame in 2000.

1)That's The Way Of The World 2)Gratitude 3)Spirit 4)All 'N All 5)I Am

DEBUT	PEAK	WKS	RIAA	CD	#	Album Title		$	Label & Number
5/15/71	172	13		©	1	Earth, Wind & Fire		$20	Warner 1905
						also see #6 below			
1/15/72	89	13		©	2	The Need Of Love		$20	Warner 1958
						also see #6 below			
11/25/72+	87	25		©	3	Last Days And Time		$15	Columbia 31702
6/9/73	27	71	▲	©	4	Head To The Sky		$15	Columbia 32194
3/30/74	15	37	▲	©	5	Open Our Eyes		$15	Columbia 32712
9/7/74	97	10			6	Another Time	[R]	$20	Warner 2798 [2]
						reissue of #1 and #2 above			
3/15/75	❶³	55	▲³	©	7	That's The Way Of The World	[S]	$12	Columbia 33280
12/6/75+	❶³	54	▲³	©	8	Gratitude	[L]	$15	Columbia 33694 [2]
10/16/76	2²	30	▲²	©	9	Spirit		$12	Columbia 34241
12/3/77+	3	47	▲³	©	10	All 'N All		$12	Columbia 34905
12/2/78+	6	60	▲⁵	©	11	The Best Of Earth, Wind & Fire, Vol. I	C:#27/12 [G]	$12	ARC 35647
6/16/79	3	38	▲²	©	12	I Am		$12	ARC 35730
11/22/80	10	21	●	©	13	Faces		$15	ARC 36795 [2]
11/14/81	5	25	▲		14	Raise!		$12	ARC 37548
3/12/83	12	21	●	©	15	Powerlight		$10	Columbia 38367
12/3/83+	40	16			16	Electric Universe		$10	Columbia 38980
11/21/87	33	28	●	©	17	Touch The World		$10	Columbia 40596
12/10/88	190	4	●	©	18	The Best Of Earth, Wind & Fire, Vol. II	[G]	$10	Columbia 45013
2/17/90	70	11		©	19	Heritage		$10	Columbia 45268
10/2/93	39	11		©	20	Millennium		$10	Reprise 45274

Africano (7,8)
After The Love Has Gone (12,18) 2
All About Love (7)

And Love Goes On (13) 59
Anything You Want (19)
Back On The Road (13)
Bad Tune (1,6)

Be Ever Wonderful (10)
Beauty (2,6)
Biyo (9)
Blood Brothers (20)

Boogie Wonderland (12,18) 6
Brazilian Rhyme (Interlude) (medley) (10)
Build Your Nest (4)

Burnin' Bush (9)
Can't Hide Love (8,11) 39
Can't Let Go (12)
Caribou (5)

Celebrate (8)
Changing Times (14)
Chicago (Chi-Town) Blues (20)
Close To Home (19)

EARTH, WIND & FIRE — Cont'd

Clover (4)
C'mon Children (1,6)
Could It Be Right (16)
Daydreamin' (1)
Departure (9)
Devotion (5,8,18) *33*
Divine (20)
Drum Song (5)
Earth, Wind & Fire (9)
Electric Nation (16)
Energy (2,6)
Even If You Wonder (20)
Every Now And Then (17)
Everything Is Everything (2,6)
Evil (4) *50*
Evil Roy (17)
Evolution Orange (14)
Faces (13)
Fair But So Uncool (5)
Faith (7)
Fall In Love With Me (15) *17*
Fan The Fire (1,6)
Fantasy (10,11,18) *32*
Feelin' Blue (5)
For The Love Of You (19)

Freedom Of Choice (15)
Getaway (9,11) *12*
Good Time (19)
Got To Get You Into My Life (11) *9*
Gratitude (8)
Handwriting On The Wall (6)
Happy Feelin' (7)
Hearts To Heart (15)
Help Somebody (1,6)
Here Today And Gone Tomorrow (17)
Heritage (8)
Honor The Magic (20)
I Can Feel It In My Bones (4)
I Think About Lovin' You (2,6)
I'd Rather Have You (3)
I'll Write A Song For You (10)
I'm In Love (19)
I've Had Enough (14)
Imagination (9)
In The Marketplace (Interlude) (medley) (10)
In The Stone (12) *58*
In Time (13)

Jupiter (medley) (10)
Just Another Lonely Night (20)
Kalimba Story (5) *55*
Kalimba Tree (medley) (14)
Keep Your Head To The Sky (4) *52*
King Of Groove (19)
"L" Word (20)
Lady Sun (14)
Let Me Talk (13) *44*
Let Your Feelings Show (12)
Let's Groove (14,18) *3*
Love Across The Wire (20)
Love Is Life (1,6)
Love Is The Greatest Story (20)
Love Music (11)
Love's Holiday (10,18)
Magic Mind (10)
Magnetic (16) *57*
Make It With You (3)
Mighty Mighty (5,18) *29*
Miracles (15)
Mom (3)
Moment Of Truth (1,6)
Money Tight (17)

Moonwalk (16)
Motor (19)
My Love (14)
New Horizons (17)
New World Symphony (8)
On Your Face (5)
Open Our Eyes (5)
Power (3,8)
Pride (13)
Reasons (7,8,11)
Remember The Children (3)
Rock That! (7)
Runnin (medley) (10)
Sailaway (13)
Saturday Nite (9,18) *21*
See The Light (7)
September (11) *8*
Serpentine Fire (10,18) *13*
Share Your Love (13)
Shining Star (7,8,11) *1*
Side By Side (15) *76*
Sing A Message To You (8)
Sing A Song (8,11) *5*
Something Special (15)
Song In My Heart (13)

Sparkle (13)
Spasmodic Movements (5)
Speed Of Love (15)
Spend The Night (20)
Spirit (9)
Spirit Of A New World (16)
Spread Your Love (15)
Star (12) *64*
Straight From The Heart (15)
Sun Goddess (8) *44*
Sunday Morning (20) *53*
Sunshine (8)
Super Hero (20)
Sweet Sassy Lady (16)
System Of Survival (17) *60*
Take It To The Sky (8)
Takin' Chances (19)
Tee Nine Chee Bit (5)
That's The Way Of The World (7,11) *12*
They Don't See (3)
Thinking Of You (17) *67*
This World Today (1,6)
Time Is On Your Side (3)
Touch (16)

Touch The World (17)
Turn It Into Something Good (13)
Turn On (The Beat Box) (18)
Two Hearts (20)
Victim Of The Modern Heart (17)
Wait (12)
Wanna Be The Man (19)
Wanna Be With You (14) *51*
We're Living In Our Own Time (16)
Welcome (19)
Where Have All The Flowers Gone (3)
Win Or Lose (13)
World's A Masquerade (4)
Wouldn't Change A Thing About You (20)
Yearnin', Learnin' (7,8)
You (13) *48*
You And I (12,17)
You Are A Winner (medley) (14)
You Went Away (13)
Zanzibar (4)

EAST COAST FAMILY   '92

Grouping of artists assembled by Michael Bivins (**New Edition, Bell Biv DeVoe**). Features Bivins, **Another Bad Creation, Boyz II Men, M.C. Brains**, and **Yo-Yo**, plus newcomers Whytgize, Yvette Brown, Hayden Hajdu, Cali Brock, Tam Rock, Lady V, Tom Boyy, 1010, Fruit Punch, Anthony Velasquez, and Mark Finesse.

| 8/15/92 | 54 | 28 | ● | © | East Coast Family Volume One | | | $10 | Biv 10 6352 |

All These Wanna Be's (Tease)
End Of The Road

It's So Hard To Say Goodbye To Yesterday
Motownphilly

Listen Closely (Bozack)
Playground

1-4-All-4-1 *81*
Sympin'

Pump Ya Fist

Uhh Ahh (The Sequel)

EASTON, Elliot   '85

Born Elliot Shapiro on 12/18/53 in Brooklyn, New York. Lead guitarist of **The Cars**.

| 3/9/85 | 99 | 11 | | © | Change No Change | | | $10 | Elektra 60393 |

Change
Fight My Way To Love

Hard Way
Help Me

I Want You
Shayla

(She Made It) New For Me
Tools Of Your Labor

(Wearing Down) Like A Wheel
Wide Awake

★461★   EASTON, Sheena   '85

Born Sheena Orr on 4/27/59 in Bellshill, Scotland. Pop singer/actress. Won the 1981 Best New Artist Grammy Award. Acted on TV's *Miami Vice*.

3/14/81	24	38	●	©	1 Sheena Easton			$10	EMI America 17049
11/28/81+	47	53	●	©	2 You Could Have Been With Me			$10	EMI America 17061
10/16/82	85	12		©	3 Madness, Money And Music			$10	EMI America 17080
9/17/83	33	38		©	4 Best Kept Secret			$10	EMI America 17101
10/20/84+	15	35	▲	©	5 A Private Heaven			$10	EMI America 17132
11/23/85	40	19	●	©	6 Do You			$10	EMI America 17173
12/3/88+	44	26	●	©	7 The Lover In Me			$10	MCA 42249
4/27/91	90	7		©	8 What Comes Naturally			$10	MCA 10131

All By Myself (5)
Almost Over You (4) *25*
Are You Man Enough (3)
Back In The City (4)
Best Kept Man (4)
Calm Before The Storm (1)
Can't Wait Till Tomorrow (6)
Cool Love (7)
Cry (1)
Days Like This (7)
Devil In A Fast Car (4) *79*
Do It For Love (6) *29*
Don't Break My Heart (6)
Don't Leave Me This Way (4)
Don't Send Flowers (1)

Don't Turn Your Back (6)
Double Standard (5)
Fire And Rain (7)
First Touch Of Love (8)
Follow My Rainbow (7)
Forever Friends (8)
Half A Heart (8)
Hard To Say It's Over (5)
Hungry Eyes (5)
I Like The Fright (4)
I Wouldn't Beg For Water (3) *64*
I'm Not Worth The Hurt (2)
Ice Out In The Rain (3)
If It's Meant To Last (7)

If You Wanna Keep Me (8)
In The Winter (3)
Jimmy Mack (6) *65*
Johnny (2)
Just Another Broken Heart (2)
Just One Smile (4)
Kisses (3)
Let Sleeping Dogs Lie (4)
Letter From Joey (2)
Little Tenderness (2)
Love And Affection (5)
Lover In Me (7) *2*
Machinery (3) *57*
Madness, Money And Music (3)
Magic Of Love (6)

Manic Panic (8)
Modern Girl (1) *18*
Money Back Guarantee (4)
Morning Train (Nine To Five) (1) *1*
Next Time (4)
No Deposit, No Return (7)
One Love (7)
One Man Woman (1)
101 (7)
Prisoner (1)
Savoir Faire (2)
(She's In Love) With Her Radio (4)
So Much In Love (1)

Somebody (8)
Strut (5) *7*
Sugar Walls (5) *9*
Swear (5) *80*
Sweet Talk (4)
Take My Time (1)
Telefone (Long Distance Love Affair) (4) *9*
Telephone Lines (2)
There When I Needed You (3)
Time Bomb (4)
To Anyone (8)
Trouble In The Shadows (2)
Voice On The Radio (1)
Weekend In Paris (3)

What Comes Naturally (8) *19*
When He Shines (2) *30*
When The Lightning Strikes Again (6)
Wind Beneath My Wings (3)
Without You (7)
You Can Swing It (8)
You Could Have Been With Me (2) *15*
You Do It (3)
You Make Me Nervous (5)
Young Lions (6)

EASTSIDAZ, Tha   '00

Rap trio from Long Beach, California: **Snoop Dogg**, Tray Deee and Goldie Loc.

| 2/19/00 | 8 | 31 | ▲ | © | Snoop Dogg Presents Tha Eastsidaz | | | $10 | Dogg House 2040 |

Another Day
Balls Of Steel
Be Thankful
Big Bang Theory

Dogghouse
Eastsidaz, The
G In Deee
G'd Up *47*

Ghetto
Give It 2 'Em Dogg
Got Beef *99*
How You Livin'

LBC Thang
Life Goes On
Mac Bible: Chapter 2:11 Verse 187

Mac Ten Commandments
Nigga 4 Life
Now We Lay 'Em Down
Pussy Sells

Real Talk
Take It Back To '85

EASYBEATS, The   '67

Rock group formed in Sydney, Australia: Steven Wright (vocals), George Young and Harry Vanda (guitars), Dick Diamonde (bass) and Gordon Fleet (drums). Young is the older brother of **AC/DC**'s Angus and Malcolm Young. Young and Vanda went on to form **Flash & The Pan**.

| 6/10/67 | 180 | 5 | | © | Friday On My Mind | | | $50 | United Artists 6588 |

Do You Have A Soul
Friday On My Mind *16*

Happy Is The Man
Made My Bed, Gonna Lie In It

Make You Feel Alright (Women)
Pretty Girl

Remember Sam
River Deep, Mountain High

Saturday Night
See Line Woman

Who'll Be The One
You Me, We Love

EAZY-E   '96

Born Eric Wright on 9/7/63 in Compton, California. Died of AIDS on 3/26/95 (age 31). Rapper/producer. Formerly with **N.W.A.**

| 12/10/88+ | 41 | 90 | ▲² | © | 1 Eazy-Duz-It | C:#22/4 | | $10 | Ruthless 57100 |
| 1/2/93 | 70 | 18 | ● | © | 2 5150 Home 4 Tha Sick | [M] | | $10 | Ruthless 53815 |

5150: police code for the criminally insane

EAZY-E — Cont'd

| 11/6/93 | 5 | 38 | ▲¹ | © 3 | It's On (Dr. Dre) 187um Killa | | [M] | $10 | Ruthless 5503 |

187 is slang for murder

| 12/16/95 | 84 | 12 | | © 4 | Eternal E | | [K] | $10 | Ruthless 50544 |
| 2/17/96 | 3 | 18 | ● | © 5 | Str8 Off Tha Streetz Of Muthaphukkin Compton | | | $10 | Ruthless 5504 |

Any Last Werdz (3)	Eazy Street (4)	Hit The Hooker (5)	Muthaphukkin Real (5)	Nutz On Ya Chin (5)	Sorry Louie (5)
Automobile (4)	Eazy-er Said Than Dunn (1,4)	I'd Rather Fuck You (4)	My Baby'z Mama (5)	Ole School Shit (5)	Still A Nigga (3)
Boyz-N-The Hood (1,3,4)	8 Ball (4)	I'mma Break It Down (1)	Neighborhood Sniper (2,4)	Only If You Want It (2,4)	Still Talkin' (1)
Creep N Crawl (5)	Eternal E (5)	It's On (3)	Niggaz My Height Don't Fight	Radio (1,4)	2 Hard Mutha's (1)
Down 2 Tha Last Roach (3)	Exxtra Special Thankz (3)	Just Tah Let U Know (5) 45	(2,4)	Real Muthaphuckkin G's	We Want Eazy (1,4)
Eazy - Chapter 8 Verse 10 (1)	Gangsta Beat 4 Tha Street (5)	Lickin, Suckin, Phukkin (5)	No More ?'s (1,4)	(3) 42	Wut Would You Do (5)
Eazy-Duz-It (1,4)	Gimmie That Nutt (3)	Merry Mutha****** Xmas (2)	Nobody Move (1,4)	Sippin On A 40 (5)	

EBN/OZN '84
Male duo from New York City: Ned "Ebn" Liben (synthesizer) and "Ozn" Rosen (vocals). Liben died of a heart attack on 2/18/98 (age 44).

| 3/31/84 | 185 | 4 | | | Feeling Cavalier............ | | | $10 | Elektra 60319 |

AEIOU Sometimes Y	Dawn, The	Kuchenga Pamoja	Rockin' Robin	TV Guide
Bag Lady (I Wonder)	I Want Cash	Pop Art Bop	Stop Stop Give It Up	Video D.J.

EBONEE WEBB '81
Funk group from Memphis: Michael Winston (vocals), Thomas Brown (guitar), Gregg Davis and Leon Thomas (keyboards), Ron Coleman (trumpet), Charles Liggins (percussion), Ken Coleman (bass) and Roy Munn (drums).

| 9/12/81 | 157 | 7 | | | Ebonee Webb | | | $12 | Capitol 12148 |

Anybody Wanna Dance	Do Me Right (Everybody Needs	Gonna Get Cha'	Something About You	Throw Down
	A Little Love)	Keep On Steppin'	Stop Teasing Me	Woman

ECHO & THE BUNNYMEN '87
Rock group from Liverpool, England: Ian McCulloch (vocals), Will Sergent (guitar), Les Pattinson (bass) and Pete DeFreitas (drums). DeFreitas died in a motorcycle accident on 6/14/89 (age 27).

7/25/81	184	2		© 1	Heaven Up Here................			$10	Sire 3569
3/26/83	137	9		© 2	Porcupine.........................			$10	Sire 23770
2/11/84	188	3		3	Echo & The Bunnymen..........		[L-M]	$10	Sire 23987

recorded on 7/18/83 at the Royal Albert Hall in London

6/9/84	87	11		© 4	Ocean Rain			$10	Sire 25084
1/11/86	158	9		© 5	Songs To Learn & Sing		[K]	$10	Sire 25360
8/8/87	51	37		© 6	Echo & The Bunnymen..........			$10	Sire 25597

All I Want (1)	Bring On The Dancing Horses	Gods Will Be Gods (2)	Lost And Found (6)	Over The Wall (1)	Seven Seas (4,5)
All In Your Mind (6)	(5)	Heads Will Roll (2)	My Kingdom (4)	Over You (6)	Show Of Strength (1)
All My Colours (1)	Clay (2)	Heaven Up Here (1)	My White Devil (2)	Porcupine (2)	Silver (4,5)
All My Life (6)	Crystal Days (4)	Higher Hell (2)	Never Stop (3,5)	Promise (1,5)	Thorn Of Crowns (4)
Back Of Love (2,3,5)	Cutter, The (2,3,5)	In Bluer Skies (6)	New Direction (6)	Puppet, The (5)	Turquoise Days (1)
Bedbugs And Ballyhoo (6)	Disease, The (1)	It Was A Pleasure (1)	No Dark Things (1)	Rescue (3,5)	With A Hip (1)
Blue Blue Ocean (6)	Do It Clean (3,5)	Killing Moon (4,5)	Nocturnal Me (4)	Ripeness (2)	Yo Yo Man (4)
Bombers Bay (6)	Game, The (6)	Lips Like Sugar (6)	Ocean Rain (4)	Satellite (6)	

ECKSTINE, Billy '62
Born on 7/8/14 in Pittsburgh. Died of heart failure on 3/8/93 (age 78). R&B singer/guitarist/trumpeter. One of the most distinctive baritones in popular music. His son Ed was the president of Mercury Records.

| 11/17/62 | 92 | 6 | | | Don't Worry 'Bout Me............ | | | $25 | Mercury 60736 |

Beauty Of True Love	Exodus Song	I Want To Talk About You	Jeannie	Stranger In Town	Till There Was You
Don't Worry 'Bout Me	Guilty	It Isn't Fair	(Love Is) The Tender Trap	Tender Is The Night	What Kind Of Fool Am I

EDDIE, John '86
Born in 1959 in Virginia; raised in New Jersey. Rock singer.

| 6/21/86 | 83 | 15 | | | John Eddie .... | | | $10 | Columbia 40181 |

Buster	Dream House	Jungle Boy 52	Living Doll	Pretty Little Rebel	Stranded
Cool Walk	Hide Out	Just Some Guy	Please Jodi	Romance	Waste Me

★390★ EDDY, Duane '59
Born on 4/26/38 in Corning, New York; raised in Tucson, Arizona. Highly influential guitarist. Best known for his "twangy" guitar sound. His backing band, The Rebels, included top sessionmen: Al Casey (guitar), Larry Knechtel (piano) and Plas Johnson (sax). Eddy appeared in the movies *Because They're Young*, *A Thunder of Drums*, *The Wild Westerners*, *The Savage Seven* and *Kona Coast*. Married to **Jessi Colter** from 1961-68. Inducted into the Rock and Roll Hall of Fame in 1994.

1)Have 'Twangy' Guitar-Will Travel 2)$1,000,000.00 Worth Of Twang 3)The "Twangs" The "Thang"

1/19/59	5	82		© 1	Have 'Twangy' Guitar-Will Travel		[I]	$100	Jamie 3000
8/3/59	24	24		© 2	Especially For You...		[I]	$60	Jamie 3006
1/25/60	18	24		© 3	The "Twangs" The "Thang"		[I]	$60	Jamie 3009
12/26/60+	10	21		© 4	$1,000,000.00 Worth Of Twang		[G-I]	$60	Jamie 3014
7/17/61	93	15		5	Girls! Girls! Girls!		[I]	$60	Jamie 3019
5/26/62	82	13		6	Twistin' 'N' Twangin'		[I]	$40	RCA Victor 2525
10/27/62	72	6		7	Twangy Guitar-Silky Strings		[I]	$40	RCA Victor 2576
1/19/63	47	17		8	Dance With The Guitar Man		[I]	$40	RCA Victor 2648
10/5/63	93	8		9	"Twangin'" Up A Storm!			$40	RCA Victor 2700
5/16/64	144	2		10	Lonely Guitar			$40	RCA Victor 2798

vocal background on above 3 albums by the **Anita Kerr Singers**

All You Gave To Me (9)	**Because They're Young** (4) 4	Connie (5)	First Love, First Tears (4) 59	High Noon (7)	**Lonely One** (1,4) 23
Along Came Linda (2,10)	Big 'Liza (5)	Country Twist (6)	**Forty Miles Of Bad Road** (4) 9	Home In The Meadow (10)	Lonesome Road (1)
Along The Navajo Trail (2)	Blowin' Up A Storm (9)	Creamy Mashed Potatoes (8)	Fuzz (2)	I'm So Lonesome I Could Cry	Long Lonely Days Of Winter
Angel On My Shoulder (7)	Blueberry Hill (3)	Cryin' Happy Tears (10)	Giddy Goose (9)	(10)	(10)
Annette (5)	**Bonnie Came Back** (4) 26	(Dance With The) Guitar Man	Guitar Child (9)	I'm So Lonesome I Could Cry	Love Me Tender (7)
Annie Laurie (10)	Born To Be With You (7)	(8) 12	Guitar'd And Feathered (9)	(10)	Lover (2)
Anytime (1)	Brenda Medley (5)	Danny Boy (10)	Gunsmoke (10)	I'm So Lonesome I Could Cry	Loving You (1)
Bali Ha'i (7)	**Cannonball** (1,4) 15	Dear Lady Twist (6)	Hard Times (2)	Just Because (2)	Mary Ann (5)
Battle, The (3)	Carol (5)	Detour (1)	He's So Fine (9)	**Kommotion** (4) 78	
Beach Bound (9)	Climb, The (8)	Easy (3)	Hi-Lili, Hi-Lo (7)	Last Minute Of Innocence (3)	
		Exactly Like You (6)		Let's Twist Again (1)	
				Limbo Rock (8)	
				Loco-Locomotion (8)	

DEBUT	PEAK	WKS	RIAA	CD	ARTIST — Album Title	Catalog	Sym	$	Label & Number

EDDY, Duane — Cont'd

Memories Of Madrid (7)
Mirriam (7)
Miss Twist (6)
Moanin' 'N' Twistin' (6)
Mona Lisa (5)
Moon Children, Theme For (4)
Moon River (7)
Moovin' N' Groovin' (1,4) *72*
Mr. Guitar Man (9)

My Baby Plays The Same Old
  Song On His Guitar All Night
  Long (7)
My Blue Heaven (3) *50*
My Destiny (10)
Nashville Stomp (8)
New Hully Gully (8)
Night Train To Memphis (3)
Only Child (2)
Patricia (5)
Peppermint Twist (6)

Peter Gunn (2) *27*
Popeye (The Hitchhiker) (8)
Quiet Three (4) *46*
Quiniela (2)
Ramrod (1) *27*
Rebel-'Rouser (1,4) *6*
Rebel Walk (3)
Route #1 (3)
Scrape, The (8)
Secret Love (7)
Shenandoah (10)

Sioux City Sue (5)
Soldier Boy (9)
Some Kind-A Earthquake
  (4) *37*
Someday The Rainbow (10)
Soul Twist (9)
Spanish Twist (8)
St. Louis Blues (3)
Stalkin' (1)
Sugartime Twist (6)
Summer Kiss (10)

Sweet Cindy (5)
Tammy (5)
Three-30-Blues (1)
Tiger Love & Turnip Greens (3)
Trambone (3)
Trouble In Mind (2)
Tuesday (5)
Tuxedo Junction (2)
Twist, The (6)
Twistin' 'N' Twangin' (6)
Twisting Off A Cliff (6)

Unchained Melody (7)
Walk Right In (9)
Walkin' 'N' Twistin' (I'm Walkin')
  (6)
Waltz Of The Wind (8)
When I Fall In Love (7)
Wild Watusi (8)
"Yep!" (2) *30*
You Are My Sunshine (3)

EDEN'S BRIDGE   '98

Christian group from West Yorkshire, England: Sarah Lacy (vocals), David Bird (guitar), Richard Lacy (keyboards), Jon Large (bass) and Terl Bryant (drums).

| 11/21/98 | 40[X] | 1 | © | | **Celtic Christmas** .... | | [X] | $10 | StraightWay 20204 |

Breath Of Heaven
Christmas Is With Us Again
Coventry Carol

Crying For The World
How Brightly Shone The Moon
It Will Be Well (medley)

Magnificat
O Come Let Us Adore Him
  (medley)

O Come, O Come, Emmanuel
O Little Town Of Bethlehem
  (medley)

Silent Night
Sussex Carol (On Christmas
  Night All Christians Sing)

Unto Us/Triptych

EDEN'S CHILDREN   '68

Rock trio from Boston: Richard Schamach (vocals, guitar), Larry Kiley (bass) and Jimmy Sturman (drums).

| 3/9/68 | 196 | 2 | | | **Eden's Children** .... | | | $40 | ABC 624 |

Don't Tell Me
Goodbye Girl

I Wonder Why
If She's Right

Just Let Go
Knocked Out

My Bad Habit
Out Where The Light Fish Live

Stone Fox

EDEN'S CRUSH

Female vocal group: Ana Maria Lombo (from Columbia), Ivette Sosa (from New Jersey), Maile Misajon (from California), Nicole Scherzinger (from Hawaii) and Rosana Tavarez (from New York). Group assembled for TV series *PopStars*.

| 5/19/01 | 6 | 13 | ● © | | **PopStars** .... | | | $10 | 143 31164 |

Anywhere But Here
Get Over Yourself *8*

Glamorous Life
I Wanna Be Free

It Wasn't Me
Let Me Know

Love This Way
No Drama

1,000 Words (Mil Palabras)
Two Way

What's Good 4 The Goose
You Know I Can

EDER, Linda   '00

Born on 2/3/61 in Tucson, Arizona; raised in Brainerd, Minnesota. Singer/actress. Starred in the Broadway show *Jekyll & Hyde*.

| 3/25/00 | 184 | 2 | © | 1 | **It's No Secret Anymore** .... | | | $10 | Atlantic 83236 |
| 12/16/00 | 158 | 3 | © | 2 | **Christmas Stays The Same** .... | | [X] | $10 | Atlantic 83406 |

LINDA EDER Featuring The Broadway Gospel Choir
Christmas chart: 37/'00

Anything Can Happen (1)
Ave Maria (2)
Bells Of St. Paul (2)
Christmas Medley (2)
Christmas Song (2)
Christmas Stays The Same (2)

Christmas Through A Child's
  Eyes (2)
Do You Hear What I Hear? (2)
Even Now (1)
Havana (1)
Have Yourself A Merry Little
  Christmas (2)

Here Comes Santa Claus
  (medley) (2)
I Guess I Love You (1)
It's No Secret Anymore (1)
Little Drummer Boy (2)
Little Things (1)

Looks Like You Started
  Something (1)
Never Dance (1)
O Come O Come Emmanuel
  (medley) (2)
O Holy Night (2)
One For My Baby (1)

Romancin' The Blues (1)
Santa Claus Is Comin' To Town
  (medley) (2)
Silent Night (2)
This Time Around (1)
Vienna (1)

What Child Is This? (medley) (2)
Why Do People Fall In Love? (1)
You Never Remind Me (1)

EDGE, Graeme, Band Featuring Adrian Gurvitz   '75

Rock trio from England: Graeme Edge (drums; **Moody Blues**), with brothers Adrian (guitar) and Paul (bass) Gurvitz. Also see **Baker Gurvitz Army**.

| 10/11/75 | 107 | 9 | © | 1 | **Kick Off Your Muddy Boots** .... | | | $15 | Threshold 15 |
| 7/9/77 | 164 | 4 | | 2 | **Paradise Ballroom** .... | | | $12 | London 686 |

All Is Fair In Love (2)
Bareback Rider (1)
Caroline (2)

Down, Down, Down (2)
Everybody Needs Somebody
  (2)

Gew Janna Woman (1)
Have You Ever Wondered (1)
Human (2)

In Dreams (1)
In The Night Of The Light (2)
Lost In Space (1)

My Life's Not Wasted (1)
Paradise Ballroom (2)
Shotgun (1)

Somethin' We'd Like To Say (1)
Tunnel, The (1)

EDMONDS, Kevon   '99

Born in Indianapolis. Male R&B singer. Former member of **After 7**. Brother of **Babyface**.

| 11/13/99 | 77 | 30 | © | | **24/7** .... | | | $10 | RCA 67704 |

Anyway
Baby Come To Me

Girl Like You
How Often

I Want You More
Love Will Be Waiting

Never Love You
No Love

Sensitive Mood
Tell Me

24/7
When I'm With You

EDMUNDS, Dave   '82

Born on 4/15/44 in Cardiff, Wales. Singer/songwriter/guitarist/producer. Formed Love Sculpture in 1967. Formed rockabilly band **Rockpile** in 1976. Produced for Shakin' Stevens, Brinsley Schwarz and **Stray Cats**.

8/4/79	54	15	©	1	**Repeat When Necessary**			$12	Swan Song 8507
5/16/81	48	14	©	2	**Twangin..**			$12	Swan Song 16034
1/9/82	163	5	©	3	**The Best Of Dave Edmunds**		[G]	$12	Swan Song 8510
5/1/82	46	14	©	4	**D.E. 7th**			$10	Columbia 37930
5/21/83	51	20	©	5	**Information**			$10	Columbia 38651
10/13/84	140	4		6	**Riff Raff**			$10	Columbia 39273
1/31/87	106	12	©	7	**I Hear You Rockin'**		[L]	$10	Columbia 40603

THE DAVE EDMUNDS BAND

| 3/24/90 | 146 | 6 | © | 8 | **Closer To The Flame** .... | | | $10 | Capitol 90372 |

A. 1. On The Juke Box (3)
Almost Saturday Night (2,3) *54*
Baby Let's Play House (2)
Bad Is Bad (1)
Bail You Out (4)
Breaking Out (6)
Busted Loose (6)
Can't Get Enough (6)
Cheap Talk, Patter And Jive (2)
Closer To The Flame (8)
Crawling From The Wreckage
  (1,3,7)
Creature From The Black
  Lagoon (1,3)

Dear Dad (4)
Deborah (3)
Deep In The Heart Of Texas (4)
Don't Call Me Tonight (5)
Don't Talk To Me (8)
Don't You Double (5)
Dynamite (1)
Every Time I See Her (8)
Fallin' Through A Hole (8)
Far Away (6)
Feel So Right (5)
From Small Things (Big Things
  One Day Come) (4)
Generation Rumble (4)

Girls Talk (1,3,7) *65*
Goodbye Mr. Good Guy (1)
Hang On (6)
Have A Heart (5)
Here Comes The Weekend
  (3,7)
Home In My Hand (1)
How Could I Be So Wrong (4)
I Got Your Number (8)
I Hear You Knocking (7)
I Knew The Bride (When She
  Used To Rock And Roll) (3,7)
I Want You Bad (5)

(I'm Gonna Start) Living Again If
  It Kills Me (2)
I'm Only Human (2)
Information (5,7)
It's Been So Long (2)
Juju Man (3,7)
King Of Love (8)
Louisiana Man (4)
Me And The Boys (4)
Never Take The Place Of You (8)
One More Night (4)
Outa Guys Girls (4)
Paralyzed (7)
Paula Meet Jeanne (4)

Queen Of Hearts (1,3,7)
Race Is On (2,3)
Rules Of The Game (6)
S.O.S. (6)
Shape I'm In (5)
Sincerely (8)
Singin' The Blues (2,3)
Slipping Away (5,7) *39*
Something About You (6)
Something Happens (2)
Stay With Me Tonight (8)
Steel Claw (6)
Stockholm (8)
Sweet Little Lisa (1)

Take Me For A Little While (1)
Test Of Love (8)
Three Time Loser (3)
Trouble Boys (3)
Wait (5)
Wanderer, The (7)
Warmed Over Kisses (Left Over
  Love) (4)
Watch On My Wrist (5)
We Were Both Wrong (1)
What Have I Got To Do To
  Win? (5)
You'll Never Get Me Up (In One
  Of Those) (2)

ED O. G & DA BULLDOGS · '91
Rap group from Boston: Edward Anderson, T-Nyne, Gee Man and DJ Cruz. ED O. G: Every Day, Other Girls. BULLDOGS: Black United Leaders Living Directly On Groovin' Sounds.

| 5/18/91 | 166 | 1 | © | **Life Of A Kid In The Ghetto** .... | $10 | PWL America 848326 |

Be A Father To Your Child · Feel Like A Nut · I Got To Have It · She Said It Was Great
Bug-A-Boo · Gotta Have Money (If You Ain't · I'm Different · Speak Upon It
Dedicated To The Right · Got Money, You Ain't Got · Let Me Tickle Your Fancy · Stop (Think For A Moment)
Wingers · Jack) · Life Of A Kid In The Ghetto

EDWARD BEAR · '73
Pop trio from Toronto: Larry Evoy (vocals, drums), Roger Ellis (guitar) and Paul Weldon (keyboards). Took name from a character in *Winnie The Pooh*.

| 2/10/73 | 63 | 16 | 1 **Edward Bear** .... | $12 | Capitol 11157 |
| 7/7/73 | 183 | 6 | 2 **Close Your Eyes** .... | $12 | Capitol 11192 |

All The Lights (2) · Cachet County (1) · Edgware Station (1) · I Love Her (You Love Me) (2) · Private School Girls (1)
Back Home Again (1) · **Close Your Eyes** (2) *37* · Fly Across The Sea (1) · **Last Song** (1) *3* · Some Sunny Day (2)
Best Friend (1) · Does Your Mother Know (2) · Fool (2) · Masquerade (1) · Walking On Back (2)
Black Pete (1) · Ease Me Down (1) · Haven't You Touched Her (2) · Nowhere Is Karen Around (2) · What You Done (2)

EDWARDS, Dennis · '84
Born on 2/3/43 in Birmingham, Alabama. Lead singer of The Contours until 1968. Lead singer of **The Temptations** from 1968-77, 1980-84 and 1987-present.

| 3/3/84 | 48 | 27 | © | **Don't Look Any Further** .... | $10 | Gordy 6057 |

Another Place In Time · I Thought I Could Handle It · Let's Go Up · (You're My) Aphrodisiac
Can't Fight It · I'm Up For You · Shake Hands (Come Out
Don't Look Any Further *72* · Just Like You · Dancin')

EDWARDS, Jonathan · '72
Born on 7/28/46 in Aitkin, Minnesota; raised in Virginia. Singer/songwriter/guitarist.

| 11/20/71+ | 42 | 20 | © | 1 **Jonathan Edwards** .... | $20 | Capricorn 862 |
| 11/18/72 | 167 | 9 | | 2 **Honky-Tonk Stardust Cowboy** .... | $15 | Atco 7015 |

Athens County (1) · Dues Days Bar (2) · Give Us A Song (2) · King, The (1) · Sometimes (1) · Train Of Glory (1)
Ballad Of Upsy Daisy (2) · Dusty Morning (1) · Honky-Tonk Stardust Cowboy · Longest Ride (2) · Stop And Start It All Again (2)
Cold Snow (1) · Emma (1) · (2) · Morning Train (2) · Sugar Babe (2)
Don't Cry Blue (1) · Everybody Knows Her (1) · It's A Beautiful Day (2) · Paper Doll (2) · **Sunshine** (1) *4*
Dream Song (2) · Everything (2) · Jesse (1) · Shanty (1) · That's What Our Life Is (2)

EDWARDS, Vincent · '62
Born Vincent Edward Zoine on 7/7/28 in Brooklyn, New York. Died of cancer on 3/11/96 (age 67). Actor/singer. Star of TV's *Ben Casey*.

| 7/7/62 | 5 | 21 | 1 Vincent Edwards Sings | $25 | Decca 4311 |
| 12/29/62+ | 125 | 6 | 2 **Sometimes I'm Happy...Sometimes I'm Blue** .... | $25 | Decca 4336 |

And Now (1) · Everybody's Got A Home But · I Got It Bad (And That Ain't · Make Someone Happy (2) · Thrill Is Gone (1) · You've Changed (2)
As Time Goes By (1) · Me (1) · Good) (1) · Polka Dots And Moonbeams (2) · Try A Little Tenderness (1)
Blue Prelude (2) · Glad To Be Unhappy (2) · I Gotta Right To Sing The Blues · Say It Isn't So (2) · Unchained Melody (1)
Cheek To Cheek (2) · Harbor Lights (2) · (2) · Sometimes I'm Happy (2) · When I Fall In Love (1)
Don't Worry 'Bout Me (1) *72* · How Deep Is The Ocean (How · I'll Walk Alone (1) · Stormy Weather (Keeps Rainin' · You Stepped Out Of A Dream
· High Is The Sky) (1) · Lonesome Road (1) · All The Time) (1) · (2)

EELS · '96
Rock trio formed in Los Angeles: Mark Everett (vocals, guitar), Tommy Walter (bass) and Butch Norton (drums).

| 9/7/96 | 114 | 11 | © | **Beautiful Freak** .... | $10 | DreamWorks 50001 |

Beautiful Freak · Guest List · Mental · Not Ready Yet · Rags To Rags · Susan's House
Flower · Manchild · My Beloved Monster · Novocaine For The Soul · Spunky · Your Lucky Day In Hell

E-40 · '96
Born Earl Stevens in Vallejo, California. Male rapper. Member of **The Click**.

10/16/93	131	5	©	1 **The Mail Man**	$10	Sick Wid' It 7340
4/1/95	13	23	● ©	2 **In A Major Way**	$10	Sick Wid' It 41558
11/16/96	4	20	● ©	3 Tha Hall Of Game	$10	Sick Wid' It 41591
8/29/98	13	9	● ©	4 **The Element Of Surprise**	$15	Sick Wid' It 41645 [2]
11/27/99	28	6	©	5 **Charlie Hustle: The BluePrint Of A Self-Made Millionaire**	$10	Sick Wid' It 41691
10/28/00	18	6	©	6 **Loyalty And Betrayal**	$10	Sick Wid' It 41719

All Tha Time (4) · Da Bumble (2) · From The Ground Up (4) · Keep Pimpin' (3) · Nah, Nah... (6) · Seasoned (5)
Back Against The Wall (4) · Dey Ain't No (2) · Fuckin' They Nose (5) · L.I.Q. (5) · Neva Broke (1) · Sideways (5)
Ballaholic (5) · Dirty Deeds (4) · Gangsterous (5) · Lace Me Up (6) · Nigga Shit (6) · Sinister Mob (6)
Ballin' Outta Control (4) · Do It To Me (4) · Get Breaded (5) · Lieutenant Roast A Botch (4) · $999,999 + $1 = A Mealticket · Smebbin' (3)
Behind Gates (6) · Do What You Know Good (5) · Ghetto Celebrity (5) · Like A Jungle (6) · (4) · Smoke 'n' Drank (2)
Big Ballin' With My Homies (5) · Doin' Dirt Bad (4) · Growing Up (3) · Look At Me (5) · 1-Luv (2) *71* · Spittin' (2)
Bootsee (2) · Doin' The Fool (6) · H.I. Double L. (2) · Loyalty And Betrayal (6) · One More Gen (4) · **Sprinkle Me** (2) *44*
Borrow Yo' Broad (5) · Duckin' & Dodgin' (5) · Hope I Don't Go Back (4) · Mack Minister (3) · Outta Bounds (2) · Story, The (3)
Bring The Yellow Tape (1) · Dump, Bust, Blast (4) · I Like What You Do To Me (3) · Mail Man (1) · Personal (4) · **Things'll Never Change** (3) *29*
Broccoli (4) · Dusted 'n' Disgusted (2) · I Wanna Thank U (3) · Mayhem (4) · Pop Ya Collar (4) · To Da Beat (4)
Brownie Points (5) · Earl That's Yo' Life (5) · It Is What It Is (3) · Million Dollar Spot (3) · Practice Lookin' Hard (1) · To Whom This May Concern (6)
Captain Save A Hoe (1) *94* · Element Of Surprise (4) · It's All Bad (2) · Money Scheme (4) · Rappers' Ball (3) · Trump Change (4)
'Cause I Can (5) · Fed (2) · It's On, On Sight (4) · Mouthpiece (5) · Record Haters (3) · Where The Party At (1)
Circumstances (3) · Flamboastin' (6) · It's Pimpin' (5) · My Drinking Club (3) · Ring It (3) · Ya Blind (5)
Clown Wit It (6) · Flashin' (4) · Jump My Bone (4) · My Hoodlums & My Thugs (4) · Rules & Regulations (5) · Zoom (4)

EGAN, Walter · '78
Born on 7/12/48 in Jamaica, New York. Pop-rock singer/songwriter/guitarist.

5/14/77	137	6	1 **Fundamental Roll**	$12	Columbia 34679
4/15/78	44	31	©	2 **Not Shy**	$12	Columbia 35077
5/28/83	187	2	3 **Wild Exhibitions**	$10	Backstreet 5400

Animal Lover (3) · Hot Summer Nights (2) *55* · Magnet And Steel (2) *8* · Star Of My Heart (3) · Too Much Love (3) · Won't You Say You Will (1)
Blonde In The Blue T-Bird (2) · I Wannit (2) · Make It Alone (1) · Stay All Night (3) · Tunnel O' Love (1) · Yes I Guess I Am (1)
Feel So Good (1) · I'd Rather Have Fun (1) · Maybe Maybe (3) · Such A Shame (3) · Unloved (2)
Finally Find A Girlfriend (2) · I'll Be There (3) · **Only The Lucky** (1) *82* · Surfin' & Drivin' (1) · Waitin' (1)
Fool Moon Fire (3) *46* · Just The Wanting (2) · She's So Tough (1) · Sweet South Breeze (2) · When I Get My Wheels (1)
Girl Next Door (3) · Like No Other One (3) · Star In The Dust (2) · Tammy Ann (3) · Where's The Party (1)

EGG CREAM Featuring Andy Adams '77
Rock group from Brooklyn, New York. Led by singer/songwriter Andy Adams.

| 5/28/77 | 197 | 4 | | | **Egg Cream** .... | | | $12 | Pyramid 9008 |

Can I Stay | Good Strong Hearted Band | I Think It's Time We Met | Maybe Tonite | Until The End
Dark Nite Blue Lite Ladies | I Never Wanted To | I Wanna Be With You | My Destruction | Woman

EGYPTIAN LOVER '85
Born Greg Broussard in Los Angeles. Techno-funk singer.

| 2/9/85 | 146 | 10 | | © | **On The Nile** | | | $10 | Egyptian Empire 0663 |

And My Beat Goes Boom | Egypt Egypt | My House (On The Nile) | What Is A D.J. If He Can't
Computer Love (Sweet | Girls | Unreal | Scratch
Dreams) | I Cry (Night After Night)

EIFFEL 65 '00
Male dance trio from Italy: Jeffrey Jey, Maurizio Lobina and Gabry Ponte.

| 12/18/99+ | 4 | 42 | ▲² | © | **Europop** | | | $10 | Republic 157194 |

Another Race | Edge, The | Living In A Bubble | Now Is Forever | Your Clown
Blue (Da Ba Dee) *6* | Europop | Move Your Body | Silicon World
Dub In Life | Hyperlink (Deep Down) | My Console | Too Much Of Heaven

EIGHTBALL & MJG '95
Rap duo from Houston: Rodney Ellis ("**Eightball**") and Marlon Jamal Goodwin ("**MJG**").

6/18/94	106	11		© 1	**On The Outside Looking In**			$10	Suave 0002
11/18/95	8	21	●	© 2	**On Top Of The World**			$10	Suave House 1521
12/6/97	20	13	●	© 3	**No More Glory**			$10	Suave House 53105

MJG

| 6/6/98 | 5 | 13 | ▲² | © 4 | **Lost** | | | $20 | Suave 53127 [3] |

EIGHTBALL
includes "Ill Hill Niggas" by Ill Hill Billies, "Been Done Some Shit" by Psycho Drama, "How We Roll" by **Canibus** & Panama P.I., "Scummie" by **Crucial Conflict**, "What You Weigh Me" by **A+** & **MJG**, "Many Know" by **McGruff**, "Incarcerated Minds" by **MJG**, "Class In Session" by Thorough, "Baby Baby" by Reepz, "The Moocher" by Fa Sho, and "All The Way" by Rodney Ellis

| 6/5/99 | 10 | 12 | | © 5 | **In Our Lifetime** | | | $10 | Suave House 53251 |
| 12/9/00 | 39 | 17 | | © 6 | **Space Age 4 Eva** .... | | | $10 | JCOR 860916 |

All 4 Nuthin' (4) | Buck Bounce (6) | Get Money (4) | Lay It Down (1) | Pimp Shit (4) | Take No Sh*t (3)
All In My Mind (2) | Can't Stop (4) | Gett Bucked (4) | Let's Ride (4) | Pimpin Ain't Easy (3) | 10th Grade (Skit) (3)
All On Me (4) | Coffee Shoppe (4) | Ghetto Luv (4) | Lick'em Up Shot (1) | Players Night Out (1) | Thank God (6)
Alwayz (6) | Collard Greens (6) | Good Damm Man (3) | Lost (4) | Pure Uncut (4) | That Girl (3)
Anotha Day In Tha Hood (1) | Comin' Up (2) | Hand Of The Devil (2) | Love Hurts (5) | Put Tha House On It (4) | Thingz (6)
Armed Robbery (5) | Crumbz 2 Brixx (1) | Hard But Fair (3) | Middle Of The Night (3) | Put Your Hands Up (4) | This Is Dedicated (4)
Artist Pays The Price (4) | Daylight (5) | Hip Hop Voodoo (3) | My First Love (4) | Questions (Skit) (3) | 360° (4)
At Tha Club (6) | Do It How It Go (5) | I Don't Wanna Die (4) | My Homeboy's Girlfriend (4) | Reflections (3) | Throw Your Hands Up (5)
Backyard Mississippi (4) | Don't Flex (5) | I Know U (6) | No Mercy (1) | Sesshead Funk Junky (1) | Time (4)
Ball And Bun (4) | Don't Hold Back (3) | If I Die (4) | No More Glory (3) | Shine And Recline (3) | Top Of The World (2)
Belly (4) | Down And Out (4) | In The Line Of Duty (2) | No Sellout (1) | Slippin' (3) | We Don't Give A Fuk (5)
Black Mac Is Back (3) | Drama In My Life (4) | Intro (5) | Nobody But Me (5) | So What U Sayin' (1) | We Started This (5)
Boom Boom (6) | For Real (2) | It's All Real (6) | On Tha Outside Lookin' In (1) | Space Age 4 Eva (6) | What Can I Do (2)
Bounce Wit Me (4) | Friend Or Foe (4) | Jankie (6) | Paid Dues (5) | Space Age Pimpin' (2) | What Do You See (2)
Break-A-Bitch College (1) | Funk Mission (2) | Keep Your Mind (3) | Pimp Hard (6) | Speed (3) | What Is This (3)
Break'em Off (2) | Get It Crunk (5) | Kick That Shit (4) | Pimp In My Own Rhyme (2) | Stompin' And Pimpin' (4) |

8TH DAY, The '71
R&B session musicians group assembled by production team of Brian Holland, **Lamont Dozier** and Eddie Holland. Consisted of Melvin Davis (vocal, drums), Tony Newton (bass), Michael Anthony and Bruce Nazarian (guitars), Jerry Paul (percussion), Carole Stallings (vocals, violin), Anita Sherman (vibes, vocals) and Lynn Harter (vocals).

| 8/7/71 | 131 | 16 | | | **8th Day** .... | | | $15 | Invictus 7306 |

Enny-Meeny-Miny-Mo (Three's | I'm Worried | Just As Long | **She's Not Just Another** | Too Many Cooks (Spoil The | **You've Got To Crawl (Before**
A Crowd) | I've Come To Save You | La-De-Dah | **Woman** *11* | Soup) | **You Walk)** *28*
I Can't Fool Myself

ELASTICA '95
Rock group from London: Justine Frischmann (vocals), Donna Matthews (guitar), Annie Holland (bass) and Justin Welch (drums). Holland left in late 1995.

| 4/1/95 | 66 | 27 | ● | © | **Elastica** .... | | | $10 | DGC 24728 |

All-Nighter | Car Song | Indian Song | See That Animal | **Stutter** *67* | Waking Up
Annie | **Connection** *53* | Line Up | Smile | 2:1
Blue | Hold Me Now | Never Here | S.O.F.T. | Vaseline

ELBERT, Donnie '72
Born on 5/25/36 in New Orleans. Died on 1/26/89 (age 52). R&B singer.

| 1/1/72 | 153 | 9 | | | **Where Did Our Love Go** .... | | | $25 | All Platinum 3007 |

Can't Get Over Losing You *98* | If I Can't Have You | One Thousand Nine Hundred | **Sweet Baby** *92* | **What Can I Do** *61* | Will You Ever Be Mine
Get Myself Together | Little Piece Of Leather | Seventy Years | That's If You Love Me | **Where Did Our Love Go** *15*

EL CHICANO '70
Latin group formed in Los Angeles. Core members: Mickey Lesperon (guitar), Andre Baeza (congas), Bobby Espinosa (organ), Freddie Sanchez (bass) and Johnny De Luna (drums). Singers included Ersi Arvizu, and brothers Rudy, Steve and Jerry Salas. Rudy and Steve Salas later formed **Tierra**.

6/13/70	51	17		1	**Viva Tirado**	[I]		$15	Kapp 3632
4/17/71	178	9		2	**Revolucion**			$15	Kapp 3640
5/6/72	173	13		3	**Celebration**			$15	Kapp 3663
8/4/73	162	16		4	**El Chicano**			$12	MCA 312
4/6/74	194	3		5	**Cinco**			$12	MCA 401

Ahora Si (5) | El Cayuco (5) | Juntos (3) | Quiet Village (1) | Sunday Kind Of Mood (4) | What's Going On (4)
Brown Eyed Girl (3) *45* | El Grito (3) | Keep On Moving (2) | Sabor A Mi (3) | **Tell Her She's Lovely** (4) *40* | You've Been Wrong So Long
Cantaloupe Island (1) | Eleanor Rigby (3) | La Cucuracha (3) | Satisfy Me Woman (3) | Together (4) | (5)
Chicano Chant (2) | Enchanted Forest (4) | Latin One (5) | (Se Fue Mi) Cha Chita (4) | Un-Mundo (4)
Children (5) | Gringo En Mexico (5) | Light My Fire (1) | Senor Blues (3) | Viva La Raza (2)
Coming Home Baby (1) | Hurt So Bad (4) | Little Sunflower (4) | Sometimes I Feel Like A | **Viva Tirado - Part 1** (1,3) *28*
Cubano Chant (2) | I Feel Free (3) | Look Of Love (1) | Motherless Child (1) | We've Only Just Begun (4)
Don't Put Me Down (If I'm | I'm A Good Woman (2) | Make It All Go (4) | Spanish Grease (2) | What You Don't Know Won't
Brown) (2) | In A Silent Way (3) | Mas Zacate (3) | Sugar Sugar (2) | Hurt You (5)

EL COCO '78

Disco group from Los Angeles: Cleo Kennedy, Merria Ross, Marsha Thacker, Adrienne Williams (vocals), W. Michael Lewis (keyboards) and Laurin Rinder (drums).

| 10/15/77+ | 82 | 23 | | © | **Cocomotion** | | | $12 | AVI 6012 |

Cocomotion *44*

Got That Feeling   I'm Mad As Hell   Love To The World   We Call It Disco   You're My Everything

ELECTRIC BOYS '90

Male rock group from Sweden: Conny Bloom (vocals), Franco Santunione (guitar), Andy Christell (bass) and Niclas Sigevall (drums).

| 6/2/90 | 90 | 20 | | © | **Funk-O-Metal Carpet Ride** .... | | | $10 | Atco 91337 |

All Lips N' Hips *76*

Captain Of My Soul

Change   Electrified   Into The Woods   Rags To Riches
Cheek To Cheek   If I Had A Car   Psychedelic Eyes   Who Are You

ELECTRIC FLAG '68

Rock-blues group formed by **Mike Bloomfield** and **Buddy Miles**.

| 4/20/68 | 31 | 35 | | © 1 | **A Long Time Comin'** .... | | | $20 | Columbia 9597 |
| 1/18/69 | 76 | 12 | | 2 | **The Electric Flag** .... | | | $20 | Columbia 9714 |

Another Country (1)   Killing Floor (1)   Nothing To Do (2)   She Should Have Just (1)   Texas (1)
Easy Rider (1)   My Woman That Hangs Around   Over-Lovin' You (1)   Sittin' In Circles (1)   Wine (1)
Groovin' Is Easy (1)   The House (2)   Qualified (1)   Soul Searchin' (2)   With Time There Is Change (2)
Hey, Little Girl (2)   Mystery (2)   See To Your Neighbor (2)   Sunny (2)   You Don't Realize (1)

ELECTRIC INDIAN, The '69

Instrumental group assembled from top Philadelphia studio musicians. Some members later joined **MFSB**.

| 10/4/69 | 104 | 9 | | | **Keem-O-Sabe** .... | | [I] | $20 | United Artists 6728 |

Geronimo   **Keem-O-Sabe** *16*   Only The Strong Survive   Storm Warning
I Heard It Through The   My Cherie Amour   Rain Dance   What Does It Take To Win Your
Grapevine   1-2-3   Spinning Wheel   Love

ELECTRIC LIGHT ORCHESTRA ★175★ '78

Orchestral rock group formed in Birmingham, England. Core members: **Jeff Lynne** (vocals, guitar), Richard Tandy (keyboards), Kelly Groucutt (bass) and Bev Bevan (drums). Numerous personnel changes. Group first recorded as **The Move**. **Roy Wood** was a member, left after first album. Bevan also recorded with **Black Sabbath** in 1987. Lynne was also a prolific producer and a member of the supergroup **Traveling Wilburys**. Lynne recorded solo as Electric Light Orchestra in 2001.

1)Out Of The Blue 2)Xanadu 3)A New World Record

6/3/72	196	2		© 1	**No Answer**			$15	United Artists 5573
3/3/73	172	8		2	**Split Ends**		[K]	$15	United Artists 5666
					THE MOVE				
4/21/73	62	22		© 3	**Electric Light Orchestra II**			$15	United Artists 040
12/29/73+	52	24		© 4	**On The Third Day**			$15	United Artists 188
10/19/74	16	32	●	© 5	**Eldorado**			$15	United Artists 339
10/25/75+	8	48	●	© 6	**Face The Music**			$15	United Artists 546
7/4/76	32	43	●	© 7	**Ole ELO**		[K]	$15	United Artists 630
10/30/76+	5	69	▲	© 8	**A New World Record**			$15	United Artists 679
11/26/77+	4	58	▲	© 9	**Out Of The Blue**			$15	Jet 823 [2]
6/23/79	5	35	▲²	© 10	**Discovery**			$12	Jet 35769
12/8/79+	30	15	▲⁴	© 11	**ELO's Greatest Hits**		[G]	$12	Jet 36310
7/12/80	4	36	▲²	© 12	**Xanadu**		[S]	$12	MCA 6100

side 1: **Olivia Newton-John**; side 2: Electric Light Orchestra

8/22/81	16	20	●	© 13	**Time**			$12	Jet 37371
7/16/83	36	16		© 14	**Secret Messages**			$12	Jet 38490
3/1/86	49	15		© 15	**Balance Of Power**			$10	CBS Associated 40048
6/30/01	94	2		© 16	**Zoom**			$10	Epic 85336

Above The Clouds (8)   **Don't Bring Me Down** (10) *4*   In My Own Time (16)   Manhattan Rumble (49th Street   Poor Boy (The Greenwood) (5)   **Sweet Talkin' Woman**
Across The Border (9)   Don't Walk Away (12)   In Old England Town (Boogie   Massacre) (1)   Queen Of The Hours (1)   (9,11) *17*
All Over The World (12) *13*   Down Home Town (16)   #2) (3)   Melting In The Sun (16)   Rain Is Falling (13)   Take Me On And On (14)
All She Wanted (16)   Down On The Bay (2)   In The Hall Of The Mountain   Message From The Country (2)   **Rock 'N' Roll Is King** (14) *19*   **Telephone Line** (8,11) *7*
Alright (16)   Dreaming Of 4000 (4)   King (4)   Midnight Blue (10)   Rockaria! (8,11)   Ticket To The Moon (13)
Another Heart Breaks (13)   Easy Money (16)   Is It Alright (15)   Minister, The (2)   **Roll Over Beethoven** (3,7) *42*   Tightrope (8)
Battle Of Marston Moor (July   Eldorado (5)   It Really Doesn't Matter (16)   Mission (A World Record) (8)   Secret Lives (15)   Tonight (2)
2nd, 1644) (1)   Ella James (2)   It Wasn't My Idea To Dance (2)   Moment In Paradise (16)   Secret Messages (14)   Train Of Gold (14)
Believe Me Now (9)   Endless Lies (15)   **It's Over** (9) *75*   **Mr. Blue Sky** (9,11) *35*   Send It (15)   **Turn To Stone** (9,11) *13*
Big Wheels (9)   **Evil Woman** (6,7,11) *10*   Jungle (8)   Mister Kingdom (5)   Shangri-La (8)   21st Century Man (13)
Birmingham Blues (9)   Fall, The (12)   Just For Love (16)   Mr. Radio (1)   **Shine A Little Love** (10) *8*   Twilight (13) *38*
Bluebird (14)   Fire On High (6)   King Of The Universe (medley)   Nellie Takes Her Bow (1)   **Showdown** (4,7,11) *53*   Until Your Mama's Gone (2)
Bluebird Is Dead (4)   First Movement (Jumpin' Biz)   (4)   New World (medley) (4)   So Fine (8)   Waterfall (6)
Boy Blue (5,7)   (1)   Kuiama (3,7)   Night In The City (9)   So Serious (15)   Way Life's Meant To Be (13)
California Man (2)   **Four Little Diamonds** (14) *18*   Laredo Tornado (5)   Nightrider (6)   Sorrow About To Fall (15)   Whale, The (9)
Calling America (15) *18*   From The End Of The World   **Last Train To London** (10) *39*   No Time (2)   Standin' In The Rain (9)   Whisper In The Night (1)
Can't Get It Out Of My Head   (13)   Letter From Spain (14)   Nobody's Child (5)   Starlight (9)   Wild West Hero (9)
(5,7,11) *9*   From The Sun To The World   Lights Go Down (13)   Ocean Breakup (medley) (4)   State Of Mind (16)   Wishing (10)
China Town (2)   (Boogie #1) (3)   **Livin' Thing** (8,11) *13*   Oh No Not Susan (4)   Steppin' Out (9)   Without Someone (15)
Confusion (10) *37*   Getting To The Point (15)   Lonesome Lullaby (16)   On The Run (10)   **Strange Magic** (6,7,11) *14*   Words Of Aaron (2)
Danger Ahead (14)   Heaven Only Knows (15)   Long Time Gone (16)   10538 Overture (1,7)   Stranger (4)   **Xanadu** (12) *8*
Daybreaker (4) *87*   Here Is The News (13)   Look At Me Now (1)   One Summer Dream (6)   Stranger On A Quiet Street (16)   Yours Truly, 2095 (13)
Diary Of Horace Wimp (10)   **Hold On Tight** (13) *10*   Loser Gone Wild (14)   Ordinary Dream (16)   Summer And Lightning (9)
Do Ya (2) *93*   I'm Alive (12) *16*   Ma-Ma-Ma Belle (4,7,11)   Poker (6)   Sweet Is The Night (9)
Do Ya (8) *24*   Illusions In G Major (5)   Mama (3)

ELECTRIC PRUNES, The   '67

Psychedelic-rock group from Seattle: James Lowe (vocals), Ken Williams and James Spagnola (guitars), Mark Tulin (bass) and Preston Ritter (drums).

DEBUT	PEAK	WKS	CD	#	Title	$	Label & Number
4/15/67	113	12	©	1	The Electric Prunes	$50	Reprise 6248
9/2/67	172	4	©	2	Underground	$50	Reprise 6262
1/6/68	135	13	©	3	Mass In F Minor	[F] $40	Reprise 6275

electric rock mass, sung in Latin

About A Quarter To Nine (1)
Antique Doll (2)
Are You Lovin' Me More (But Enjoying It Less) (1)
Bangles (1)
Big City (2)

Capt. Glory (2)
Children Of Rain (2)
Dr. Do-Good (2)
Get Me To The World On Time (1) 27
Great Banana Hoax (2)

Hideaway (2)
I (2)
I Had Too Much To Dream (Last Night) (1) 11
I Happen To Love You (2)
It's Not Fair (2)

King Is In The Counting House (1)
Long Day's Flight (2)
Luvin' (1)
Mass In F Minor (3)
Onie (1)

Sold To The Highest Bidder (1)
Train For Tomorrow (1)
Try Me On For Size (1)
Tunerville Trolley (1)
Wind-Up Toys (2)

ELECTRONIC   '91

Dance duo from Manchester, England: Bernard Sumner (of **New Order**) and Johnny Marr (of **The Smiths**).

DEBUT	PEAK	WKS	CD	#	Title	$	Label & Number
6/15/91	109	15	©	1	Electronic	$10	Warner 26387
7/27/96	143	1	©	2	Raise The Pressure	$10	Warner 45955

Dark Angel (2)
Feel Every Beat (1)
For You (2)
Forbidden City (2)

Freefall (2)
Gangster (1)
Get The Message (1)
Getting Away With It (1) 38

How Long (2)
Idiot Country (1)
If You've Got Love (2)
One Day (2)

Out Of My League (2)
Patience Of A Saint (1)
Reality (1)
Second Nature (2)

Some Distant Memory (1)
Soviet (1)
Tighten Up (1)
Time Can Tell (2)

Try All You Want (1)
Until The End Of Time (2)
Visit Me (2)

ELECTRONIC CONCEPT ORCHESTRA   '69

Studio group directed by Robin McBride. Features Eddie Higgins on the Moog synthesizer.

DEBUT	PEAK	WKS	#	Title	$	Label & Number
10/18/69	175	2		Electric Love	[I] $15	Limelight 86072

Goin' Out Of My Head
I'm Gonna Make You Love Me

Je T'Aime...Moi Non Plus
Like A Lover

Look Of Love
Love Is Blue

Misty
Romeo & Juliet Theme

Stella By Starlight
This Guy's In Love With You

Wichita Lineman

ELEPHANT'S MEMORY   '69

Jazz-rock group from New York City: Michal Shapiro (female vocals), Stan Bronstein (male vocals, sax), Richard Ayers (guitar), Richard Sussman (piano), Myron Yules (trombone), John Ward (bass) and Rick Frank (drums). Backing band on **John Lennon**'s *Some Time In New York City* album, and **Yoko Ono**'s *Approximately Infinite Universe* album.

DEBUT	PEAK	WKS	#	Title	$	Label & Number
5/10/69	200	2		Elephant's Memory	$20	Buddah 5033

Band Of Love
Brief Encounter

Crossroads Of The Stepping Stones
Don't Put Me On Trial No More

Hot Dog Man
Jungle Gym At The Zoo
Old Man Willow

R.I.P.
Super Heep
Takin' A Walk

Yogurt Song

ELEVENTH HOUSE WITH LARRY CORYELL   '74

Jazz-rock group: **Larry Coryell** (guitar), Randy Brecker (trumpet; **Dreams**, **The Brecker Brothers**), Mike Mandel (piano), Danny Trifan (bass) and **Alphonse Mouzan** (drums). In early 1975, Michael Lawrence replaced Brecker and John Lee replaced Trifan.

DEBUT	PEAK	WKS	CD	#	Title	$	Label & Number
4/13/74	163	11	©	1	Introducing The Eleventh House With Larry Coryell	[I] $15	Vanguard 79342
8/9/75	163	4		2	Level One	[I] $12	Arista 4052

Adam Smasher (1)
Birdfingers (1)
Diedra (2)
Dream, Theme For A (1)

Eyes Of Love (2)
Funky Waltz (1)
Gratitude "A So Low" (1)
Ism-Ejercicio (1)

Joy Ride (1)
Level One (2)
Low-Lee-Tah (1)
Nyctabobia (2)

Other Side (2)
Right On Y'all (1)
Some Greasy Stuff (2)
Struttin' With Sunshine (2)

Suite Medley (2)
That's The Joint (2)
Yin (1)

ELFMAN, Danny   '89

Born on 5/29/53 in Los Angeles. Lead singer of **Oingo Boingo**. Prolific composer of movie soundtracks since 1984.

DEBUT	PEAK	WKS	CD	#	Title	$	Label & Number
6/25/88	118	6	©	1	Beetlejuice	[I-S] $10	Geffen 24202

includes "Day-O" and "Jump In Line (Shake, Shake Senora)" by Harry Belafonte

8/26/89	30	12	©	2	Batman Original Motion Picture Score	[I-S] $10	Warner 25977
8/4/90	194	1	©	3	Dick Tracy Original Score	[I-S] $10	Sire 26264
1/26/91	174	3	©	4	Edward Scissorhands	[I-S] $10	MCA 10133

includes "With These Hands" by Tom Jones

| 7/11/92 | 61 | 5 | © | 5 | Batman Returns | [I-S] $10 | Warner 26972 |

includes "Face To Face" by Siouxsie And The Banshees

| 11/6/93 | 98 | 9 | © | 6 | Tim Burton's The Nightmare Before Christmas | [X-S] $10 | Walt Disney 60855 |

Christmas chart: 12/'93

After The "Kid" (3)
Aftermath, The (1)
Attack Of The Batwing (2)
Ballet De Suburbia (Suite) (4)
Bat Cave (2)
Batman Returns, End Credits (5)
Batman Theme (2)
Batman To The Rescue (2)
Batman vs. The Circus (5)
Beautiful Dreamer (medley) (2)
Beautiful New World (medley) (4)
Beetle-Snake (1)
Beetlejuice, End Credits From (1)
Beetlejuice, Main Titles From (1)
Big Boy/Bad Boys (3)

Birth Of A Penguin (5)
Blank Gets The Boogie (3)
Book!, The (medley) (1)
Breathless Comes On (3)
Breathless' Theme (1)
Castle On The Hill (4)
Cat Suite (3)
Cemetery, The (5)
Charge Of The Batmobile (2)
Chase, The (3)
Children's Hour (5)
Christmas Eve Montage (6)
Clown Attack (2)
Cookie Factory (4)
Crime Spree (3)
Death! (4)
Descent Into Mystery (2)
Dick Tracy, Main Titles From (3)
Doctor Finklestein (medley) (1)

Edwardo The Barber (4)
End, The (4)
Enter..."The Family" (medley) (1)
Esmeralda (4)
Etiquette Lesson (4)
Farewell (4)
Final Confrontation [Batman] (2)
Final Confrontation [Batman Returns] (5)
Final Confrontation [Edward Scissorhands] (4)
Finale [Batman] (2)
Finale, The [Batman Returns] (5)
Finale [Nightmare Before Christmas] (6)
First Confrontation (2)
Flier, The (medley) (1)

Flowers (2)
Fly, The (5)
Home Sweet Home (medley) (4)
Ice Dance (4)
In The Forest (medley) (6)
In The Model (1)
Incantation, The (1)
Jack And Sally Montage (6)
Jack's Lament (6)
Jack's Obsession (6)
Joker's Poem (2)
Juno's Theme (1)
Kidnap The Sandy Claws (6)
Lair, The (5)
Laughs (3)
Love Theme (2)
Lydia Discovers? (1)
Lydia Strikes A Bargain... (1)

Lydia's Pep Talk (medley) (1)
Making Christmas (6)
Meet The Blank (3)
Nabbed (6)
Obituaries (medley) (1)
Oogie Boogie's Song (6)
Photos (medley) (2)
Poor Jack (6)
Reunited (medley) (3)
Rise And Fall From Grace (5)
Roasted Dude (2)
Roof Fight (2)
Rooftops [Dick Tracy] (3)
Rooftops (medley) [Batman Returns] (5)
Sally's Song (6)
Sand Worm Planet (medley) (6)
Selina Transforms (5)
Showdown (medley) (5)

Showtime! (1)
Slimy D.A. (3)
Sold (1)
Sore Spots (5)
Story Unfolds (3)
Storytime (4)
Tess' Theme (3)
This Is Halloween (6)
Tide Turns (Suite) (4)
To The Rescue (2)
Town Meeting Song (6)
Travel Music (1)
Up The Cathedral (2)
Waltz To The Death (5)
Wedding, The (1)
What's This? (6)
Wild Ride (medley) (5)

ELGART, Larry, And His Manhattan Swing Orchestra   '82

Born on 3/20/22 in New London, Connecticut. Alto saxophonist. Brother of **Les Elgart**.

DEBUT	PEAK	WKS	RIAA	CD	#	Title	$	Label & Number
10/10/64	128	5			1	Command Performance! Les & Larry Elgart Play The Great Dance Hits..	[I] $20	Columbia 2221 / 9021

LES & LARRY ELGART

| 6/19/82 | 24 | 41 | ▲ | © | 2 | Hooked On Swing | [I] $10 | RCA Victor 4343 |
| 2/12/83 | 89 | 14 | | © | 3 | Hooked On Swing 2 | [I] $10 | RCA Victor 4589 |

Blues In The Night (1)
Hooked On A Star Medley (2)
Hooked On Astaire Medley (2)

Hooked On Big Bands Medley (2)

Hooked On Broadway Medley (2)
Hooked On Dixie Medley (3)

Hooked On Swing Medley (2) 31
Hooked On Swing 2 Medley (3)

Hooked On The Blue(s) Medley (2)

Hooked On The Roaring '20s Medley (3)
Jersey Bounce (1)

DEBUT	PEAK	WKS	RIAA	CD	ARTIST — Album Title	Catalog	Sym	$	Label & Number

ELGART, Larry, And His Manhattan Swing Orchestra — Cont'd

Mood Indigo (1)
My Heart Belongs To Daddy (1)
One O'Clock Jump (1)

Save The Last Dance For Me Medley (3)
Sentimental Journey (1)

Skyliner (1)
So Rare (1)
Song Of India (1)

Swing With Bing Medley (3)
Swingin' The Classics Medley (3)

Tuxedo Junction (1)
Woodchopper's Ball (1)

You Made Me Love You (I Didn't Want To Do It) (1)

ELGART, Les, And His Orchestra   '56
Born on 8/3/18 in New Haven, Connecticut. Died on 7/29/95 (age 76). Trumpeter/bandleader. Brother of **Larry Elgart**.

9/3/55	15	2			1 The Dancing Sound .... [EP-I]			$20	Columbia 314
11/3/56	13	7		©	2 The Elgart Touch .... [I]			$25	Columbia 875
8/19/57	14	7		©	3 For Dancers Also .... [I]			$25	Columbia 1008
10/10/64	128	5			4 Command Performance! Les & Larry Elgart Play The Great Dance Hits.. [I]			$20	Columbia 2221 / 9021

LES & LARRY ELGART

Alice Blue Gown (1)
Autumn Serenade (2)
Blues In The Night (4)
Boy Next Door (1)
Dancing Sound (2)
Don't Be That Way (2)
Fascinatin' Rhythm (2)

For Dancers Also (3)
Green Satin (3)
High On A Windy Hill (3)
How Long Has This Been Going On? (3)
I Had The Craziest Dream (2)
I Hear A Rhapsody (3)

Jersey Bounce (4)
Makin' Whoopee (1)
Melancholy Serenade (1)
Mood Indigo (4)
My Heart Belongs To Daddy (4)
One O'Clock Jump (4)
Paradise (3)

'S Too Much (3)
Seems Like Old Times (1)
Sentimental Journey (4)
Skyliner (4)
Slo Roll (2)
So Rare (4)
Song Of India (4)

Stompin' At The Savoy (2)
Street Of Dreams (2)
Swingin' Down The Lane (2)
Swingy Swan (4)
Three To Get Ready (2)
Tuxedo Junction (4)
Where Or When (2)

Who Cares (3)
Why Do I Love You? (2)
Woodchopper's Ball (4)
You Go To My Head (3)
You Made Me Love You (I Didn't Want To Do It) (4)
You Walk By (3)

ELLIMAN, Yvonne   '78
Born on 12/29/51 in Honolulu. Portrayed Mary Magdalene on the concept album and in the rock opera and movie *Jesus Christ Superstar*. Backing singer for **Eric Clapton**.

3/12/77	68	16			1 Love Me			$12	RSO 3018
3/11/78	40	17			2 Night Flight			$12	RSO 3031
11/10/79	174	6			3 Yvonne			$12	RSO 3038

Baby Don't Let It Mess Your Mind (2)
Cold Wind Across My Heart (3)
Down The Backstairs Of My Life (2)
Everything Must Change (3)

Good Sign (1)
Greenlight (3)
Hello Stranger (1) *15*
Hit The Road Jack (medley) (3)
How Long (3)
I Can't Get You Outa My Mind (1)

(I Don't Know Why) I Keep Hangin' On (1)
I Know (1)
I'd Do It Again (1)
I'll Be Around (2)
I'm Gonna Use What I Got To Get What I Need (3)

If I Can't Have You (3) *1*
In A Stranger's Arms (2)
Lady Of The Silver Spoon (2)
Love Me (1) *14*
Love Pains (3) *34*
Nowhere To Hide (3)
Prince Of Fools (2)

Rock Me Slowly (3)
Sailing Ships (2)
Sally Go 'Round The Roses (2)
Savannah (3)
She'll Be Home (1)
Sticks And Stones (medley) (3)
Up To The Man In You (2)

Uphill Peace Of Mind (1)
Without You (There Ain't No Love At All) (1)

ELLINGTON, Duke   '57
Born Edward Kennedy Ellington on 4/29/1899 in Washington DC. Died of cancer on 5/24/74 (age 75). Legendary jazz bandleader/composer/arranger. Won Grammy's Lifetime Achievement Award in 1966 and the Grammy Trustees Award in 1968.

| 6/24/57 | 14 | 1 | | © | 1 Ellington At Newport .... [I-L] | | | $40 | Columbia 934 |

recorded on July 7, 1956 at the Newport Jazz Festival

| 10/3/64 | 133 | 7 | | | 2 Ellington '65: Hits Of The 60's/This Time By Ellington .... [I] | | | $30 | Reprise 6122 |
| 5/14/66 | 145 | 3 | | | 3 The Duke At Tanglewood .... [I-L] | | | $25 | RCA Victor 2857 |

DUKE ELLINGTON/BOSTON POPS/ARTHUR FIEDLER

| 2/24/68 | 78 | 13 | | © | 4 Francis A. & Edward K. .... | | | $20 | Reprise 1024 |

FRANK SINATRA & DUKE ELLINGTON

All I Need Is The Girl (4)
Blowin' In The Wind (2)
Call Me Irresponsible (2)
Caravan (3)
Come Back To Me (4)
Danke Schoen (2)
Diminuendo And Crescendo In Blue (1)

Do Nothin' 'Til You Hear From Me (3)
Fly Me To The Moon (In Other Words) (2)
Follow Me (4)
Hello, Dolly! (2)
I Got It Bad And That Ain't Good (3)

I Left My Heart In San Francisco (2)
I Let A Song Go Out Of My Heart (3)
I Like The Sunrise (4)
I'm Beginning To See The Light (3)
Indian Summer (4)

Jeep's Blues (1)
Love Scene (3)
Mooch, The (3)
Mood Indigo (3)
More (2)
Never On Sunday (2)
Newport Jazz Festival Suite Medley (1)

Peking Theme (So Little Time) (2)
Poor Butterfly (4)
Satin Doll (3)
Second Time Around (2)
Solitude (3)
Sophisticated Lady (3)
Stranger On The Shore (2)

Sunny (4)
Timon Of Athens March (3)
Yellow Days (4)

ELLIOT, Cass — see MAMA CASS

ELLIOTT, Alecia   '00
Born on 12/25/82 in Muscle Shoals, Alabama. Female country singer.

| 2/12/00 | 172 | 5 | | © | I'm Diggin' It.. | | | $10 | MCA 170087 |

Ain't No Ordinary Love
Every Heart
I Don't Understand

I'm Diggin' It
I'm Waiting For You
Say You Will

Some People Fall, Some People Fly
Some Say I'm Running

Stay Awhile
That's The Only Way
You Wanna What?

ELLIOTT, Missy "Misdemeanor"   '01
Born in 1971 in Portsmouth, Virginia. Female rapper/songwriter.

8/2/97	3	37	▲	©	1 Supa Dupa Fly			$10	The Gold Mind 62062
7/10/99	10	39	▲	©	2 Da Real World			$10	The Gold Mind 62232
6/2/01	2[1]	18↑	▲	©	3 Miss E... So Addictive			$10	The Gold Mind 62639

All N My Grill (2) *64*
Beat Biters (2)
Beep Me 911 (1)
Best Friends (1)
Busa Rhyme (2)
Crazy Feelings (2)
Dangerous Mouths (2)

Dog In Heat (3)
Don't Be Commin' (In My Face) (1)
4 My People (3)
Friendly Skies (1)
Get Ur Freak On (3) *7*
Gettaway (1)

Hit 'Em Wit Da Hee (1)
Hot Boyz (2) *5*
I'm Talkin' (1)
Izzy Izzy Ahh (1)
Lick Shots (3)
Mr. D.J. (2)
Old School Joint (3)

One Minute Man (3)
Pass Da Blunt (1)
Rain (Supa Dupa Fly) (1)
Scream A.K.A. Itchin' (3)
She's A Bitch (2) *90*
Slap! Slap! Slap! (3)
Smooth Chick (2)

Sock It 2 Me (1) *12*
Step Off (3)
Stickin' Chickens (2)
Take Away (3)
They Don't Wanna F*** Wit Me (1)
U Can't Resist (2)

We Did It (2)
Whatcha Gon' Do (3)
Why You Hurt Me (1)
X-tasy (3)
You Don't Know (2)

ELLIS, Terry   '95
Born on 9/5/63 in Houston. Female singer. Member of **En Vogue**.

| 12/2/95 | 116 | 5 | | © | Southern Gal.. | | | $10 | EastWest 61857 |

Back Down Memory Lane (1)
I Don't Mind

I Don't Want To Wait Till Tomorrow
It Ain't Over

It's You That I Need
She's A Lady
Sista Sista

Slow Dance
Southern Gal Interlude
What Did I Do To You?

Where Ever You Are *52*
You Make Me High

ELMO & PATSY   '87
Husband-and-wife team of Elmo Shropshire and Patsy Trigg. Divorced in 1985.

| 12/19/87 | 8[X] | 10 | ▲ | © | Grandma Got Run Over By A Reindeer | C:#42/2 [X] | | $10 | Epic 39931 |

Christmas charts: 8/87, 12/88, 24/89, 28/91

Christmas
Grandma Got Run Over By A Reindeer *87*

Here's To The Lonely
Jingle Bell Rock
Jingle Bells

Joy To The World
Percy, The Puny Poinsettia

Rudolph The Red-Nosed Reindeer
Senor Santa Claus

Silent Night

EL RAYO-X — see LINDLEY, David

ELY, Joe   '81
Born on 9/2/47 in Amarillo, Texas; raised in Lubbock, Texas. Country-rock singer/songwriter/guitarist.

| 4/11/81 | 135 | 11 | | © | 1 **Musta Notta Gotta Lotta** .... | | | $12 | SouthCoast 5183 |
| 10/24/81 | 159 | 3 | | © | 2 **Live Shots** .... | | [L] | $12 | SouthCoast 5262 |

Bet Me (1)
Boxcars (2)
Dallas (1)
Dam Of My Heart (1)

Fingernails (2)
Fools Fall In Love (2)
Good Rockin' Tonight (1)
Hard Livin' (1)

Hold On (1)
Honky Tonk Masquerade (2)
Honky Tonkin' (2)
I Had My Hopes Up High (2)

I Keep Gettin' Paid The Same (1)
Johnny's Blues (2)
Long Snake Moan (2)

Midnight Shift (2)
Musta Notta Gotta Lotta (1)
Road Hawg (1)
Rock Me My Baby (1)

She Never Spoke Spanish To Me (2)
Wishin' For You (1)

EMERSON, Keith   '81
Born on 11/1/44 in Todmorden, Lancashire, England. Keyboardist of **Emerson, Lake & Palmer** and **The Nice**.

| 5/2/81 | 183 | 3 | | | **Nighthawks** .... | | [I-S] | $12 | Backstreet 5196 |

Bust, The
Chase, The

Chopper, The
Face To Face

Flight Of A Hawk
I'm A Man

I'm Comin' In
Mean Stalkin'

Nighthawking
Nighthawks - Main Title Theme

Tramway

★227★ EMERSON, LAKE & PALMER   '72
Classical-oriented rock trio from England: **Keith Emerson** (keyboards; **The Nice**), **Greg Lake** (vocals, bass, guitars; **King Crimson**) and Carl Palmer (drums; **Atomic Rooster, Crazy World of Arthur Brown**). Group split up in 1979, with Palmer joining supergroup **Asia**. Emerson and Lake re-grouped in 1986 with new drummer Cozy Powell (**Whitesnake**). Palmer returned in 1987, replacing Powell who joined **Black Sabbath** in 1990. Powell died in a car crash on 4/5/98 (age 50).
1)Welcome back, my friends, to the show that never ends-Ladies and Gentlemen 2)Trilogy 3)Tarkus

2/6/71	18	42	●	©	1 **Emerson, Lake & Palmer**			$15	Cotillion 9040
7/3/71	9	26	●	©	2 **Tarkus**			$15	Cotillion 9900
1/22/72	10	23	●	©	3 **Pictures At An Exhibition**		[L]	$15	Cotillion 66666
					based on Mussorgsky's classical composition				
7/29/72	5	37	●	©	4 **Trilogy**			$15	Cotillion 9903
12/15/73+	11	47	●	©	5 **Brain Salad Surgery**			$15	Manticore 66669
9/7/74+	4	24	●	©	6 **Welcome back, my friends, to the show that never ends - Ladies and Gentlemen**		[L]	$15	Manticore 200 [3]
4/9/77	12	26	●	©	7 **Works, Volume 1**			$20	Atlantic 7000 [2]
12/10/77+	37	14	●	©	8 **Works, Volume 2**			$12	Atlantic 19147
					above 2 albums feature mostly solo material				
12/9/78+	55	9	●	©	9 **Love Beach**			$12	Atlantic 19211
12/1/79	73	10		©	10 **Emerson, Lake & Palmer In Concert**		[L]	$12	Atlantic 19255
11/29/80	108	7		©	11 **The Best Of Emerson, Lake & Palmer**		[G]	$12	Atlantic 19283
6/14/86	23	26		©	12 **Emerson, Lake & Powell**			$10	Polydor 829297
6/27/92	78	4			13 **Black Moon**			$10	Victory 480003

Abaddon's Bolero (4)
Affairs Of The Heart (13)
All I Want Is You (9)
Aquatarkus (2)
Are You Ready Eddy? (2)
Barbarian, The (1)
Barrelhouse Shake-Down (8)
Battlefield (2)
Benny The Bouncer (5)
Better Days (13)
Bitches Crystal (2)
Black Moon (13)
Blues Variation (3)
Brain Salad Surgery (8)
Bullfrog (8)
Burning Bridges (13)
C'est La Vie (7,10) **91**
Canario (9)

Changing States (13)
Close But Not Touching (8)
Close To Home (13)
Closer To Believing (7)
Curse Of Baba Yaga (3)
End, The (medley) (3)
Endless Enigma (Parts 1 & 2) (4)
Enemy God Dances With The Black Spirits (7,10)
Eruption (2)
Fanfare For The Common Man (7,11)
Farewell To Arms (13)
Food For Your Soul (7)
Footprints In The Snow (13)
For You (8)
From The Beginning (4) **39**

Fugue (4)
Gambler, The (9)
Gnome, The (3)
Great Gates Of Kiev (medley) (3)
Hallowed Be Thy Name (7)
Hoedown (4,6,11)
Honky Tonk Train Blues (8)
Hut Of Baba Yaga (3)
Iconoclast (2)
Infinite Space (2)
Jeremy Bender (2,6)
Jerusalem (5,6,11)
Karn Evil 9 (5,6,11)
Knife Edge (1,10)
L.A. Nights (7)

Lay Down Your Guns (12)
Learning To Fly (12)
Lend Your Love To Me Tonight (7)
Living Sin (4)
Love Beach (9)
Love Blind (12)
Lucky Man (1,11) **48**
Manticore (2)
Maple Leaf Rag (8)
Mars, The Bringer Of War (12)
Mass (2)
Memoirs Of An Officer And A Gentleman Medley (9)
Miracle, The (12)
New Orleans (7)
Nobody Loves You Like I Do (7)
Nutrocker (medley) (3) **70**

Old Castle (3)
Only Way (2)
Paper Blood (13)
Peter Gunn (10,11)
Piano Concerto No. 1 (7,10)
Piano Improvisations (6)
Pictures At An Exhibition (10)
Pirates (7)
Promenade (3)
Romeo And Juliet (13)
Sage, The (3)
Score, The (13)
Sheriff, The (4,6)
Show Me The Way To Go Home (8)
So Far To Fall (8)
Step Aside (9)
Still....You Turn Me On (5,11)

Stones Of Years (2)
Take A Pebble (1,6)
Tank (1,7)
Tarkus (6)
Taste Of My Love (9)
Three Fates Medley (1)
Tiger In A Spotlight (8,10,11)
Time And A Place (7)
Toccata (5,6)
Touch & Go (12) **60**
Trilogy (4,11)
Two Part Invention In D Minor (7)
Watching Over You (8)
When The Apple Blossoms Bloom In The Windmills Of Your Mind I'll Be Your Valentine (8)

I Believe In Father Christmas (8) **95**

EMF   '91
Techno-funk group from Forest of Dean, Gloucestershire, England: James Atkin (vocals), Ian Dench (guitar), Derry Brownson (keyboards, percussion), Zac Foley (bass) and Mark Decloedt (drums).

| 6/1/91 | 12 | 36 | ▲ | © | **Schubert Dip** .... | | | $10 | EMI 96238 |

Admit It
Children

Girl Of An Age
I Believe

Lies **18**
Long Summer Days

Longtime
Travelling Not Running

Unbelievable 1
When You're Mine

EMILIO   '95
Born Emilio Navaira on 8/23/62 in San Antonio, Texas. Country singer.

| 10/14/95 | 82 | 5 | | © | **Life Is Good** .... | | | $10 | Capitol 32392 |

Any Little Lie
Even If I Tried

Hace Cuanto He Dicho Que Te Amo (Have I Told You Lately)
Have I Told You Lately

Honky Tonk Habits
I Think We're On To Something
I Was There

It's Not The End Of The World
Life Is Good
Long As I Got You

No Es El Fin Del Mundo (It's Not The End Of The World)
There'll Be No More Crying

EMINEM   '00
Born Marshall Mathers on 10/17/73 in Kansas City; raised in Detroit. White male rapper.

| 3/13/99 | 2³ | 100 | ▲⁴ | © | 1 **The Slim Shady LP** .... | C:#15/9 | | $10 | Aftermath 90287 |
| 6/10/00 | ❶⁸ | 67 | ▲⁸ | © | 2 **The Marshall Mathers LP** .... | | | $10 | Aftermath 490629 |

Amityville (2)
As The World Turns (1)
Bad Meets Evil (1)
Bitch Please II (2)
Brain Damage (1)

Criminal (2)
Cum On Everybody (1)
Drug Ballad (2)
Guilty Conscience (1)
I'm Back (2)

I'm Shady (1)
If I Had (1)
Just Don't Give A Fuck (1)
Kill You (2)
Kim (2)

Marshall Mathers (2)
My Fault (1)
My Name Is (1) **36**
97' Bonnie & Clyde (1)
Real Slim Shady (2) **4**

Remember Me? (2)
Rock Bottom (1)
Rode Model (1)
Stan (2) **51**
Steve Berman (2)

Still Don't Give A Fuck (1)
Under The Influence (2)
Way I Am (2) **58**
Who Knew (2)

EMOTIONS, The   '77
Female R&B vocal trio from Chicago: sisters Wanda, Sheila and Jeanette Hutchinson.

DEBUT	PEAK	WKS	RIAA	CD	Album	Sym	$	Label & Number
8/28/76	45	27	●		1 Flowers		$12	Columbia 34163
6/25/77	7	33	▲	©	2 Rejoice		$12	Columbia 34762
12/3/77+	88	15		©	3 Sunshine	[E]	$12	Stax 4100
8/26/78	40	12	●	©	4 Sunbeam		$12	Columbia 35385
12/8/79	96	10			5 Come Into Our World		$12	ARC 36149
9/26/81	168	4			6 New Affair		$12	ARC 37456

Ain't No Doubt About It (4)
Ain't No Sunshine (3)
All Night, Alright (6)
Anyway You Look At It (3)
Baby, I'm Through (3)
Best Of My Love (2) 1
Blessed (2)
Cause I Love You (5)
Come Into My World (5)
Don't Ask My Neighbors (2) 44
Feeling Is (2)

Flowers (1) 87
Gee Whiz (Look At His Eyes) (3)
God Will Take Care Of You (1)
Here You Come Again (6)
How Can You Stop Loving Someone (1)
How'd I Know That Love Would Slip Away (2)
I Don't Wanna Lose Your Love (1) 51

I Really Miss You (3)
I Should Be Dancing (5)
I Wouldn't Lie (4)
Innocent (3)
Key To My Heart (2)
Layed Back (5)
Love Is Right On (4)
Love Lies (6)
Love Vibes (4)
Love's What's Happenin' (2)

Me For You (1)
Movie, The (5)
Music Box (4)
My Everything (4)
New Affair (6)
No Plans For Tomorrow (1)
Now That I Know (6)
On & On (5)
Put A Little Love Away (3) 73
Rejoice (2)
Runnin' Back (And Forth) (3)

Shouting Out Love (3)
Smile (4)
Special Part (1)
Spirit Of Summer (4)
There'll Never Be Another Moment (6)
Time Is Passing By (4)
Turn It Out (6)
Walking The Line (4)
We Go Through Changes (1)

What's The Name Of Your Love? (3)
When You Gonna Wake Up (6)
Where Is Your Love? (5)
Whole Lot Of Shakin' (4)
Yes, I Am (5)
You've Got The Right To Know (1)

ENCHANTMENT   '78
R&B vocal group from Detroit: Ed Clanton, Bobby Green, Davis Banks, Emanuel Johnson and Joe Thomas.

DEBUT	PEAK	WKS	RIAA	CD	Album	Sym	$	Label & Number
3/5/77	104	19			1 Enchantment		$12	United Artists 682
1/21/78	46	21			2 Once Upon A Dream		$12	Roadshow 811
3/17/79	145	8			3 Journey To The Land Of...Enchantment		$12	Roadshow 3269

Angel In My Life (2)
Anyway You Want It (3)
Come On And Ride (1)
Dance To The Music (3)
Forever More (3)
Fun (3)

Future Gonna Get You (3)
Gloria (1) 25
Hold On (1)
I Wanna Boogie (3)
If You're Ready (Here It Comes) (2)

It's You That I Need (2) 33
Journey (3)
Let Me Entertain You (3)
Love Melodies (3)
Magnetic Feel (3)
My Rose (1)

Oasis Of Love (3)
Sexy Lady (1)
Silly Love Song (2)
Sunny Shine Feeling (1)
Sunshine (1) 45

Thank You Girl For Loving Me (1)
Trying To Get Over (With You) (2)
Up Higher (2)

Where Do We Go From Here (3)
You Must Be An Angel (2)
You're The One (2)

ENGLAND, Ty   '95
Born on 12/5/63 in Oklahoma City. Country singer/songwriter/guitarist.

DEBUT	PEAK	WKS	RIAA	CD	Album	Sym	$	Label & Number
9/2/95	95	6		©	Ty England		$10	RCA 66522

Blues Ain't News To Me
Her Only Bad Habit Is Me

Is That You
It's Lonesome Everywhere

New Faces In The Fields
Redneck Son

Should've Asked Her Faster
Smoke In Her Eyes

Swing Like That
You'll Find Somebody New

ENGLAND DAN & JOHN FORD COLEY   '76
Pop duo from Austin, Texas: **Dan Seals** (born on 2/8/50) and Coley (born on 10/13/51). In the late '60s, both were members of group Southwest F.O.B. Dan is the brother of Jim Seals of **Seals & Crofts** and cousin of country singers Johnny Duncan, Troy Seals and Brady Seals (of **Little Texas**). Coley appeared in the 1987 movie *Scenes From The Goldmine*.

DEBUT	PEAK	WKS	RIAA	CD	Album	Sym	$	Label & Number
8/21/76	17	31	●		1 Nights Are Forever		$12	Big Tree 89517
4/23/77	80	15			2 Dowdy Ferry Road		$12	Big Tree 76000
4/8/78	61	14			3 Some Things Don't Come Easy		$12	Big Tree 76006
4/14/79	106	12			4 Dr. Heckle And Mr. Jive		$12	Big Tree 76015
1/5/80	194	2		©	5 Best Of England Dan & John Ford Coley	[G]	$12	Big Tree 76018

Another Golden Oldie Night For Wendy (4)
Beyond The Tears (3)
Broken Hearted Me (4)
Calling For You Again (3)
Caught Up In The Middle (4)
Children Of The Half-Light (4)
Don't Feel That Way No More (2)

Dowdy Ferry Road (2,4)
Everything's Gonna Be Alright (1)
Falling Stars (2,5)
Gone Too Far (2,5) 23
Hold Me (3)
Hollywood Heckle & Jive (4)
Holocaust (2)
I'd Really Love To See You Tonight (1,5) 2

I'll Stay (1)
If The World Ran Out Of Love Tonight (3)
In It For Love (5) 75
It's Not The Same (1)
It's Sad To Belong (2,5) 21
Just The Two Of Us (3)
Lady (1)
Long Way Home (1)
Love Is The Answer (4,5) 10

Love Is The One Thing We Hide (2)
Lovin' Somebody On A Rainy Night (3)
Nights Are Forever Without You (1,5) 10
Only A Matter Of Time (4)
Prisoner, The (1)
Rolling Fever (4)
Running After You (4)

Showboat Gambler (1)
Soldier In The Rain (2,5)
Some Things Don't Come Easy (3)
There'll Never Be Another For Me (1)
Wanting You Desperately (3)
We'll Never Have To Say Goodbye Again (3,5) 9
Westward Wind (1)

What Can I Do With This Broken Heart (4,5) 50
What's Forever For (4)
Where Do I Go From Here (2)
Who's Lonely Now (3,5)
Why Is It Me (5)
You Can't Dance (3) 49
You Know We Belong Together (2)

ENGLISH BEAT   '83
Ska-rock group formed in Birmingham, England: Dave Wakeling and **Ranking Roger** (vocals), Andy Cox (guitar), Saxa (sax), Dave Steele (bass) and Everett Martin (drums). Split in 1983. Wakeling and Roger formed **General Public**. Cox and Steele formed **Fine Young Cannibals**.

DEBUT	PEAK	WKS	RIAA	CD	Album	Sym	$	Label & Number
8/9/80	142	14		©	1 I Just Can't Stop It		$12	Sire 6091
6/27/81	126	6		©	2 Wha'ppen?		$12	Sire 3567
11/13/82+	39	44		©	3 Special Beat Service		$10	I.R.S. 70032
12/17/83+	87	22		©	4 What Is Beat?	[K]	$10	I.R.S. 70040

Ackee 1 2 3 (3)
All Out To Get You (2)
Best Friend (1,4)
Big Shot (1)
Can't Get Used To Losing You (1,4)
Cheated (2)
Click Click (1)

Doors Of Your Heart (2,4)
Dream Home In NZ (2)
Drowning (2)
End Of The Party (3)
French Toast (Soleil Trop Chaud) (2)
Get-A-Job (2,4)
Hands Off...She's Mine (1)

Hit It (4)
I Am Your Flag (2)
I Confess (3,4)
Jackpot (1)
Jeanette (1)
Limits We Set (2)
Mirror In The Bathroom (1,4)
Monkey Murders (4)

Noise In This World (3)
Over And Over (2)
Pato And Roger A Go Talk (3)
Ranking Full Stop (1)
Rotating Heads (3)
Rough Rider (1)
Save It For Later (3,4)
She's Going (3)

Sole Salvation (3)
Sorry (3)
Spar Wid Me (3)
Stand Down Margaret (1,4)
Sugar & Stress (3)
Tears Of A Clown (1,4)
Too Nice To Talk To (4)
Twist & Crawl (1,4)

Two Swords (1)
Walk Away (2)
What's Your Best Thing? (4)
Whine & Grine (medley) (1)

ENGVALL, Bill   '97
Born on 7/27/57 in Galveston, Texas. Country comedian/actor. Played "Bill Pelton" on TV's *The* Jeff Foxworthy *Show*.

DEBUT	PEAK	WKS	RIAA	CD	Album	Sym	$	Label & Number
3/1/97	50	30	▲	©	1 Here's Your Sign	[C]	$10	Warner 46263
10/31/98	119	11		©	2 Dorkfish	[C]	$10	Warner 47090
11/20/99	33 [X]	1		©	3 Here's Your Christmas Album	[X-N]	$10	Warner 47488
					Christmas chart: 33/'99			
9/9/00	133	5		©	4 Now That's Awesome!	[C]	$10	BNA 69311

Baby Barf And The Turkey Hunt (1)
Bar Scene In California (4)
Bike, The (3)
Broke Food (2)
Bronc Busting (2)

Bungee Jumping And Parachuting (2)
Caught Big Time (1)
Christmas In The Country Holiday (3)
Christmas Sign (3)

Deer Hunting (2)
Discovery Channel (2)
Dog Had To Be Trained (4)
Dorkfish (2)
Factory Outlet Malls (2)
Flying (2)

Fruitcake Makes Me Puke (3)
Gift Emergency (3)
Gift That She Don't Want (3)
Going To The Fair (1)
Here's Your Sign (Get The Picture) (1) 43

Here's Your Sign Christmas (3)
How's Your Sign Christmas (3)
I'm A Cowboy (2)
I'm Getting Sued By Santa Claus (3)

I.G. Joe (1)
Love Magic (1)
Minivan (2)
More Here's Your Sign (2)
My Daughter's Growing Up (2)
90's, The (4)

DEBUT	PEAK	WKS	RIAA	CD	ARTIST — Album Title	Catalog	Sym	$	Label & Number

ENGVALL, Bill — cont'd

Nobody Disciplines Their Kids Anymore (1)	Pound Puppies (4)	Surfing Lesson (4)	Too Much Information (Cause I'm The Dad) (4)	When Did Shrapnel Become A Fashion Accessory? (4)
Now That's Awesome (4)	Rudolph Got A DUI (3)	T-Ball And Indian Guides (2)	We've Got A Full House (1)	White Trash Road Race (4)
Pads (4)	Shoulda Shut Up (4)	Tell Me What I'm Thinking (1)	Weather And News (2)	
People Amaze Me (Here's Your Sign) (4)	Smoker Aquarium (4)	That's What's Wrong With Christmas (3)	Whale Watching (2)	
	Smokers (2)	Things Have Changed (1)		
	Snake In The Toilet (4)			

ENIGMA '91

Born Michael Cretu on 5/18/57 in Bucharest, Romania. Producer. Moved to Germany in 1975. Worked with **Vangelis** and **The Art Of Noise**. Featured vocalist is Cretu's wife, Sandra.

DEBUT	PEAK	WKS	RIAA	CD		Catalog		$	Label & Number
3/2/91	6	282	▲⁴	©	1 **MCMXC A.D.**	C:#4/50		$10	Charisma 91642
					title is the Roman numeral for the year 1990				
2/26/94	9	63	▲²	©	2 **Enigma 2: The Cross of Changes**	C:#14/53		$10	Charisma 39236
12/14/96	25	29	▲	©	3 **Enigma 3: Le Roi Est Mort, Vive Le Roi!**			$10	Virgin 42066
					title is French for "The King Is Dead, Long Live The King!"				
2/5/00	33	17	●	©	4 **The Screen Behind The Mirror**			$10	Virgin 48616

Age Of Loneliness (Carly's Song) (2)	Camera Obscura (4)	Gravity Of Love (4)	Morphing Thru Time (4)	Screen Behind The Mirror (4)	Traces (Light And Weight) (4)
Almost Full Moon (3)	Child In Us (3)	I Love You ... I'll Kill You (2)	Odyssey Of The Mind (3)	Second Chapter (2)	Voice & The Snake (1)
Back To The Rivers Of Belief Medley (1)	CROSS Of Changes (2)	Knocking On Forbidden Doors (1)	Out From The Deep (2)	Shadows In Silence (3)	Voice Of Enigma (1)
Between Mind & Heart (4)	Dream Of The Dolphin (2)	Le Roi Est Mort, Vive Le Roi! (3)	Prism Of Life (3)	Silence Must Be Heard (4)	Why!... (3)
Beyond The Invisible (3) 81	Endless Quest (4)	Mea Culpa (1)	Push The Limits (4)	Silent Warrior (2)	
Callas Went Away (1)	Eyes Of Truth (2)	Modern Crusaders (4)	Return To Innocence (2) 4	Smell Of Desire (4)	
	Find Love (1)		Roundabout, The (3)	T.N.T. For The Brain (3)	
	Gate, The (4)		Sadeness Part 1 (1) 5	Third Of Its Kind (3)	

ENNIS, Ethel '64

Born on 11/28/32 in Baltimore. Jazz singer/pianist.

DEBUT	PEAK	WKS						$	Label & Number
3/21/64	147	2			**This Is Ethel Ennis**			$25	RCA Victor 2786

As You Desire Me	Joey, Joey, Joey	Moon Was Yellow (And The Night Was Young)	Nobody Told Me	When Did I Fall In Love
Dear Friend	Love, Don't Turn Away	Night Club	Occasional Man	Who Will Buy?
He Loves Me		Starry-Eyed And Breathless		

ENO, Brian '81

Born on 5/15/48 in Woodbridge, Suffolk, England. Rock producer/keyboardist. Founding member of **Roxy Music**. Production work for **David Bowie**, **Devo**, **Ultravox** and **Talking Heads**. Also see **Passengers**.

DEBUT	PEAK	WKS		CD		Catalog		$	Label & Number
8/24/74	151	6		©	1 **Here Come The Warm Jets**			$12	Island 9268
5/27/78	171	5		©	2 **Before And After Science**			$12	Island 9478
3/21/81	44	13		©	3 **My Life In The Bush Of Ghosts**		[I]	$10	Sire 6093
					BRIAN ENO-DAVID BYRNE				

America Is Waiting (3)	Cindy Tells Me (1)	Here Come The Warm Jets (1)	Mea Culpa (3)	Paw Paw Negro Blowtorch (1)	Through Hollow Lands (2)
Baby's On Fire (1)	Come With Us (3)	Here He Comes (2)	Moonlight In Glory (3)	Qu'Ran (3)	
Backwater (2)	Dead Finks Don't Talk (1)	Jezebel Spirit (3)	Mountain Of Needles (3)	Regiment (3)	
Blank Frank (1)	Driving Me Backwards (1)	Julie With... (2)	Needles In The Camel's Eye (1)	Secret Life (3)	
By This River (2)	Energy Fools The Magician (2)	King's Lead Hat (2)	No One Receiving (2)	Some Of Them Are Old (1)	
Carrier, The (3)	Help Me Somebody (3)	Kurt's Rejoinder (2)	On Some Faraway Beach (1)	Spider And I (2)	

ENRIQUEZ, Jocelyn '97

Born on 12/28/74 in San Francisco. Female dance singer.

DEBUT	PEAK	WKS		CD				$	Label & Number
5/31/97	182	1		©	**Jocelyn**			$10	Classified 3049

Can You Feel It (Rock It Don't Stop It)	Even If	If I'm Falling In Love part 1 & 2	Lovely People	Stay With Me
Do You Miss Me 49	Everything I Need	Kailanman	Only You	
	Get Into The Rhythm	Little Bit Of Ecstasy 55	Save Me From Being Alone	

ENTOUCH '90

Male R&B vocal duo of Eric McCain (from Mt. Vernon, New York) and Free (from the Bronx, New York).

DEBUT	PEAK	WKS		CD				$	Label & Number
2/10/90	177	4		©	**All Nite**			$10	Vintertainment 60858

All Nite 71	4Ever	Scratch My Back	II Steps 2 The Right	
Crazay 4/U	Just A Little Bit Of Luv	II Hype	Whatchagonnado	

ENTWISTLE, John '81

Born on 10/9/44 in Chiswick, London. Bass guitarist of **The Who**.

DEBUT	PEAK	WKS		CD				$	Label & Number
10/23/71	126	9		©	1 **Smash Your Head Against The Wall**			$20	Decca 79183
11/18/72+	138	13		©	2 **Whistle Rymes**			$15	Track 79190
7/7/73	174	7		©	3 **Rigor Mortis Sets In**			$15	Track 321
3/1/75	192	1		©	4 **Mad Dog**			$15	Track 2129
					JOHN ENTWISTLE'S OX				
10/10/81	71	9		©	5 **Too Late The Hero**			$12	Atco 142

Apron Strings (2)	I Believe In Everything (1)	Love Is A Heart Attack (5)	Peg Leg Peggy (3)	What Are We Doing Here? (1)
Big Black Cadillac (3)	I Fall To Pieces (4)	Lovebird (5)	Pick Me Up (Big Chicken) (1)	What Kind Of People Are They? (1)
Cell Number Seven (4)	I Feel Better (2)	Lucille (3)	Roller Skate Kate (3)	Who Cares? (2)
Dancin' Master (5)	I Found Out (2)	Mad Dog (4)	Sleepin Man (5)	Who In The Hell? (4)
Do The Dangle (3)	I Was Just Being Friendly (2)	Made In Japan (3)	Talk Dirty (5)	Window Shopper (2)
Drowning (4)	I Wonder (2)	Mr. Bass Man (3)	Ted End (1)	You Can Be So Mean (4)
Fallen Angel (5)	I'm Coming Back (5)	My Size (1)	Ten Little Friends (2)	You're Mine (1)
Gimme That Rock N' Roll (4)	I'm So Scared (4)	My Wife (3)	Thinkin' It Over (2)	
Heaven And Hell (1)	Jungle Bunny (4)	Nightmare (Please Wake Me Up) (2)	Too Late The Hero (5)	
Hound Dog (3)	Lady Killer (4)	No. 29 (External Youth) (1)	Try Me (5)	

ENUFF Z'NUFF '89

Rock group from Chicago: Chip Z'Nuff (bass), Donnie Vie (vocals), Derek Frigo (guitar) and Vikki Foxx (drums).

DEBUT	PEAK	WKS		CD				$	Label & Number
9/30/89	74	34		©	1 **Enuff Z'nuff**			$10	Atco 91262
4/13/91	143	6		©	2 **Strength**			$10	Atco 91638

Baby Loves You (2)	For Now (1)	I Could Never Be Without You (1)	Little Indian Angel (1)	She Wants More (1)	World Is A Gutter (2)
Blue Island (2)	Goodbye (2)	Long Way To Go (2)	Something For Free (2)	
Coming Home (medley) (2)	Heaven Or Hell (2)	In Crowd (2)	Missing You (2)	Strength (2)	
Finger On The Trigger (1)	Holly Wood Ya (2)	In The Groove (1)	Mother's Eyes (2)	Time To Let You Go (2)	
Fly High Michelle (1) 47	Hot Little Summer Girl (1)	Kiss The Clown (1)	New Thing (1) 67	Way Home (medley) (2)	

EN VOGUE '92

Female R&B vocal group from San Francisco: Dawn Robinson, Terry Ellis, Cindy Herron and Maxine Jones. Herron married pro baseball player Glenn Braggs in June of 1993 and acted in the movie *Juice*. Robinson left in early 1997.

DEBUT	PEAK	WKS	RIAA	CD	Album Title	Sym	$	Label & Number
4/28/90	21	69	▲	© 1	Born To Sing		$10	Atlantic 82084
4/11/92	8	86	▲³	© 2	Funky Divas		$10	EastWest 92121
10/9/93	49	19		© 3	Runaway Love	[M]	$10	EastWest 92296
					3 of 6 songs are remixes from the above album			
7/5/97	8	20	▲	© 4	EV3		$10	EastWest 62057
6/10/00	67	5		© 5	Masterpiece Theatre		$10	EastWest 62416

Beat Of Love (5)
Damn I Wanna Be Your Lover (4)
Desire (2,3)
Does Anybody Hear Me (4)
Don't Go (1)
Don't Let Go (Love) (4) *2*
Eyes Of A Child (4)
Falling In Love (5)
Free Your Mind (2) *8*
Give It Up, Turn It Loose (2) *15*

Giving Him Something He Can Feel (2) *6*
Hip Hop Bugle Boy (1)
Hip Hop Lover (2,3)
Hold On (1) *2*
Hooked On Your Love (2)
It Ain't Over Till The Fat Lady Sings (2)
Just Can't Stay Away (1)
Latin Soul (5)
Let It Flow (4)
Lies (1) *38*

Love Don't Love You (2) *36*
Love Makes You Do Thangs (4)
Love U Crazay (5)
Love Won't Take Me Out (5)
Luv Lines (1)
My Lovin' (You're Never Gonna Get It) (2) *2*
No No No (Can't Come Back) (5)
Number One Man (5)
Part Of Me (1)
Party (1)

Riddle (5) *92*
Right Direction (4)
Runaway Love (3) *51*
Sad But True (5)
Sitting By Heaven's Door (4)
Strange (1)
This Is Your Life (2)
Those Dogs (5)
Time Goes On (1)
Too Gone, Too Long (4) *33*
Waitin' On You (1)

What A Difference A Day Makes (4)
What Is Love (2,3)
Whatever (4) *16*
Whatever Will Be Will Be (5)
Whatta Man (3) *3*
Work It Out (5)
Yesterday (2)
You Don't Have To Worry (1)
You're All I Need (4)

★319★ ENYA '96

Born Eithne Ni Brennan on 5/17/61 in Gweedore, County Donegal, Ireland. Female singer. Member of the **Clannad** from 1980-82.

DEBUT	PEAK	WKS	RIAA	CD	Album Title	Catalog	Sym	$	Label & Number
2/4/89	25	39	▲⁴	© 1	Watermark	C:❶¹⁷/299		$10	Geffen 24233
12/7/91+	17	238	▲⁵	© 2	Shepherd Moons	C:#22/20		$10	Reprise 26775
2/15/92+	6ᶜ	148	▲	© 3	Enya			$10	Atlantic 81842
					later released as *The Celts* on Reprise 45681				
12/23/95+	9	66	▲³	© 4	The Memory Of Trees			$10	Reprise 46106
11/29/97+	30	40	▲²	© 5	Paint The Sky With Stars - The Best Of Enya	C:#2⁷/39	[G]	$10	Reprise 46835
12/9/00	17	43†	▲²	© 6	A Day Without Rain			$10	Reprise 47426

Afer Ventus (2)
Aldebaran (3)
Angeles (2)
Anywhere Is (4,5)
Athair Ar Neamh (4)
Bard Dance (3)
Boadicea (3,5)
Book Of Days (2,5)
Caribbean Blue (2,5) *79*
Celts, The (3,5)
China Roses (4,5)

Cù Chulainn (medley) (3)
Cursum Perficio (3)
Dan Y Dwr (3)
Day Without Rain (6)
Deireadh An Tuath (3)
Deora Ar Mo Chroí (6)
Ebudae (2,5)
Epona (3)
Evacuee (2)
Evening Falls... (1)
Exile (1)

Fairytale (3)
Fallen Embers (6)
Flora's Secret (6)
From Where I Am (4)
Hope Has A Place (4)
How Can I Keep From Singing? (2)
I Want Tomorrow (3)
La Sonadora (4)
Lazy Days (6)
Longships, The (1)

Lothlorien (2)
Marble Halls (2,5)
March Of The Celts (3)
Memory Of Trees (4,5)
Miss Clare Remembers (1)
Na Laetha Geal M'oige (1)
No Holly For Miss Quinn (2)
Oisin (medley) (3)
On My Way Home (4,5)
On Your Shore (1)
Once You Had Gold (4)

One By One (6)
Only If... (5) *88*
Only Time (6)
Orinoco Flow (Sail Away) (1,5) *24*
Paint The Sky With Stars (5)
Pax Deorum (4)
Pilgrim (6)
Portrait (Out Of The Blue) (3)
River (1)
St. Patrick (medley) (3)

Shepherd Moons (2,5)
Silver Inches (6)
Smaointe (5)
Storms In Africa (1,5)
Sun In The Stream (3)
Tea-House Moon (4)
Tempus Vernum (6)
To Go Beyond (I & II) (3)
Watermark (1,5)
Wild Child (6)

★419★ EPMD '99

Rap duo from Long Island, New York: **Erick Sermon** and Parrish Smith. EPMD: Erick and Parrish Making Dollars. Smith recorded solo as **PMD**.

1)Out Of Business 2)Business Never Personal 3)Back In Business

DEBUT	PEAK	WKS	RIAA	CD	Album Title	Sym	$	Label & Number
7/9/88	80	23	●	© 1	Strictly Business		$10	Fresh 82006
8/19/89	53	14	●	© 2	Unfinished Business		$10	Fresh 92012
2/2/91	36	21	●	© 3	Business As Usual		$10	Def Jam 47067
8/15/92	14	18	●	© 4	Business Never Personal		$10	RAL 52848
11/6/93	16	6		© 5	No Pressure		$10	Def Jam 57460
					ERICK SERMON			
10/15/94	65	3		© 6	Shade Business		$10	PMD 66475
					PMD			
11/25/95	35	4		© 7	Double Or Nothing		$10	Def Jam 529286
					ERICK SERMON			
11/9/96	180	1		© 8	Bu$ine$$ I$ Bu$ine$$		$10	Relativity 1569
					PMD			
10/11/97	16	11	●	© 9	Back In Business		$10	Def Jam 536389
8/7/99	13	8		© 10	Out Of Business		$10	Def Jam 558928

All In The Mind (5)
Back To The Rap (6)
Back Up Or Get Smacked Up (6)
Big Payback (7)
Bomdigi (7) *84*
Boon Dox (4)
Boy Meets World (7)
Brothers On My Jock (3)
Bu$ine$$ I$ Bu$ine$$ (8)
Can't Hear Nothing But The Music (3)
Check 1,2 (10)
Chill (6)
Crossover (4) *42*
Cummin' At Cha (4)
D.J. K La Boss (1)
Da Joint (9) *94*
Do It Again (9)
Do It Up (5)
Do Your Thing (7)

Draw (10)
Dungeon Master (9)
Erick Sermon (5)
Fake Homeyz (6)
Fan, The (10)
Female Species (5)
Focus (7)
For My People (3)
Freak Out (7)
Funk, The (10)
Funky Piano (3)
Get Off The Bandwagon (1)
Get The Bozack (2)
Get The Zone (6)
Get Wit This (9)
Give The People (3)
Gold Digger (3)
Hardcore (3)
Head Banger (4)
Here They Cum (6)
Hit Squad Heist (9)
Hittin' Switches (5)

Hold Me Down (10)
Hostile (5)
House Party (10)
Hype, The (5)
I Saw It Cummin' (6) *89*
I'll Wait (6)
I'm A B- Boy (8)
I'm Housin' (1)
I'm Mad (4)
Ill Shit (5)
Imma Gitz Mine (6)
In The Heat (7)
In The Zone (6)
Intrigued (9)
It Wasn't Me, It Was The Fame (2)
It's Going Down (4)
It's My Thing (1)
It's The Ones (8)
It's The Pee (8)
It's Time To Party (2)

Jane (1)
Jane II (2)
Jane 3 (3)
Jane 5 (9)
Jane 6 (10)
K.I.M. (9)
Knick Knack Patty Wack (2)
Kool Kat (8)
Last Man Standing (9)
Leave Your Style Cramped (8)
Let The Funk Flow (1)
Lil Crazy (5)
Man Above (7)
Manslaughter (3)
Move On (7)
Mr. Bozack (3)
Never Seen Before (3)
Never Watered Down (8)
No Shorts And No Sleep (6)
Nobody's Safe Chump (4)
Nuttin Move (8)

Open Fire (7)
Payback II (5)
Phuck It Up Scratch (6)
Pioneers (10)
Play The Next Man (4)
Please Listen To My Demo (2)
Put On (9)
Rampage (3)
Rap Is Outta Control (3)
Rap Is Still Outta Control (10)
Respect Mine (6)
Richter Scale (9)
Right Now (10)
Rugged-N-Raw (8)
Safe Sex (5)
Scratch Bring It Back (Part 2-Mic Doc) (4)
Set It Off (7)
Shade Business (6)
So Wat Cha Sayin' (2)
Stay Real (5) *92*

Steppin' Thru Hardcore (6)
Steve Martin (5)
Strictly Business (1)
Strictly Snappin' Necks (6)
Swing It Over Here (5)
Swing Your Own Thing (6)
Symphony (4)
Symphony 2000 (10)
Tell 'Em (7)
Total Kaos (2)
U Got Shot (10)
Underground (3)
Welcome (9)
What Cha Gonna Do (8)
Who Killed Jane (4)
Who's Booty (2)
You Got 2 Chill '97 (9)
You Gots To Chill (1)
You Had Too Much To Drink (2)
You're A Customer (1)

EPPS, Preston '60

Born in 1931 in Oakland. Bongo player.

DEBUT	PEAK	WKS	CD	Album Title	Sym	$	Label & Number
8/15/60	35	3		Bongo Bongo Bongo	[I]	$50	Original Sound 5002

Bongo Bongo Bongo *78*
Bongo In The Congo

Bongo Rock *14*
Bongos In Pastel

Call Of The Jungle
Doin' The Cha Cha Cha

Jungle Drums

DEBUT	PEAK	WKS	RIAA	CD	ARTIST — Album Title	Catalog	Sym	$	Label & Number

★446★ ERASURE '94
Dance duo formed in England: Andy Bell (vocals) and Vince Clarke (instruments). Clarke was a member of **Depeche Mode** and **Yaz**.

1)I Say I Say I Say 2)Chorus 3)Cowboy

7/18/87	190	3		©	1 **The Circus**			$10	Sire 25554
1/16/88	186	3		©	2 **The Two Ring Circus**	[K]		$15	Sire 25667 [2]
6/18/88	49	50	▲	©	3 **The Innocents** .... C:#49/1			$10	Sire 25730
5/13/89	73	10		©	4 **Crackers International**			$10	Sire 25904
11/11/89	57	23		©	5 **Wild!**			$10	Sire 26026
11/2/91	29	17		©	6 **Chorus**			$10	Sire 26668
7/18/92	85	22		©	7 **Abba-esque**	[M]		$10	Mute 61386
12/12/92+	112	15	●	©	8 **Pop! - The First 20 Hits**	[G]		$10	Sire 45153
6/4/94	18	17		©	9 **I Say I Say I Say**			$10	Mute 61633
11/11/95	82	3		©	10 **"Erasure"**			$10	Elektra 61852
5/10/97	43	8		©	11 **Cowboy**			$10	Maverick 46631

All Through The Years (9)
Always (9) *20*
Am I Right? (6,8)
Angel (10)
Because You're So Sweet (9)
Blue Savannah (5,8)
Blues Away (9)
Boy (10)
Breath Of Life (6,8)
Brother And Sister (5)
Chains Of Love (3,8) *12*
Chorus (Fishes In The Sea) (6,8) *83*
Circus, The (1,8)
Crown Of Thorns (5)

Don't Dance (1,2)
Don't Say Your Love Is Killing Me (11)
Drama! (5,8)
Fingers & Thumbs (Cold Summer's Day) (10)
Grace (10)
Guess I'm Into Feeling (10)
Hallowed Ground (3)
Hardest Part (4)
Heart Of Stone (3)
Heavenly Action (8)
Hideaway (1,2)
Home (6)
How Can I Say (11)

How Many Times? (5)
I Love Saturday (9)
I Love You (10)
If I Could (1,2)
Imagination (3)
In My Arms (11) *55*
It Doesn't Have To Be (1,2,8)
Joan (9)
Knocking On Your Door (4)
La Gloria (5)
Lay All Your Love On Me (7)
Leave Me To Bleed (1,2)
Little Respect (3,8) *14*
Long Goodbye (10)
Love Affair (11)

Love The Way You Do So (10)
Love To Hate You (6,8)
Magic Moments (11)
Man In The Moon (9)
Miracle (9)
My Heart...So Blue (2)
Oh L'amour (8)
Perfect Stranger (6)
Phantom Bride (1)
Piano Song (5)
Precious (11)
Rain (11)
Rapture (11)
Reach Out (11)
Rescue Me (10)

Rock Me Gently (10)
Run To The Sun (9)
S.O.S. (7)
Save Me Darling (11)
Sexuality (1)
She Won't Be Home (4)
Ship Of Fools (3,8)
Siren Song (6)
Sixty-Five Thousand (3)
So The Story Goes (9)
Sometimes (1,2,8)
Sono Luminus (10)
Spiralling (1,2)
Star (5,8)
Stay With Me (10)

Stop! (4,8) *97*
Take A Chance On Me (7,8)
Take Me Back (9)
Treasure (11)
Turns The Love To Anger (6)
2,000 Miles (5)
Victim Of Love (1,2,8)
Voulez Vous (7)
Waiting For The Day (6)
Weight Of The World (3)
Who Needs Love (Like That) (8)
Witch In The Ditch (3)
Worlds On Fire (11)
Yahoo! (3)
You Surround Me (5,8)

ERIC B. & RAKIM '97
Rap duo: DJ Eric Barrier (from Elmhurst, New York) and rapper William "**Rakim**" Griffin (from Long Island, New York).

9/12/87	58	38	▲	©	1 **Paid In Full**			$10	4th & B'way 4005
8/13/88	22	16	●	©	2 **Follow The Leader**			$10	Uni 3
7/7/90	32	14	●	©	3 **Let The Rhythm Hit 'Em**			$10	MCA 6416
7/11/92	22	11		©	4 **Don't Sweat The Technique**			$10	MCA 10594
					RAKIM:				
11/22/97	4	17	●	©	5 **The 18th Letter**			$10	Universal 53113
12/18/99	72	2		©	6 **The Master**			$10	Universal 542082

All Night Long (6)
As The Rhyme Goes On (1)
Beats For The Listeners (2)
Casualties Of War (4)
Chinese Arithmetic (1)
Don't Sweat The Technique (4)
18th Letter (Always And Forever) (5)
Eric B. Is On The Cut (1)
Eric B. Is President (1)
Eric B. Made My Day (3)
Eric B. Never Scared (2)

Extended Beat (1)
Finest Ones (6)
Flow Forever (6)
Follow The Leader (2)
Guess Who's Back (5)
How I Get Down (6)
I Ain't No Joke (1)
I Know (6)
I Know You Got Soul (1)
I'll Be There (6)
In The Ghetto (3)
It's A Must (6)

It's Been A Long Time (5)
It's The R (6)
Juice (Know The Ledge) (4) *96*
Just A Beat (2)
Keep 'Em Eager To Listen (3)
Keep The Beat (4)
Kick Along (4)
Let The Rhythm Hit 'Em (3)
Lyrics Of Fury (1)
Mahogany (3)
Microphone Fiend (2)

Move The Crowd (1)
Musical Massacre (2)
My Melody (1)
Mystery (Who Is God?) (5)
New York (Ya Out There) (5)
No Competition (2)
No Omega (3)
Paid In Full (1)
Pass The Hand Grenade (4)
Punisher, The (4)
Put Your Hands Together (2)
R, The (2)

Real Shit (6)
Relax With Pep (4)
Remember That (5)
Rest Assured (4)
Run For Cover (4)
Saga Begins (5)
Set 'Em Straight (3)
Show Me Love (5)
Stay A While (5)
Step Back (5)
Strong Island (6)
Teach The Children (4)

To The Listeners (2)
Untouchables (3)
Uplift (6)
Waiting For The World To End (6)
We'll Never Stop (6)
What's Going On (4)
What's On Your Mind (4)
When I B On Tha Mic (6)
When I'm Flowin (5)

ERUPTION '78
Techno-funk group of Jamaican natives based in London: Precious Wilson and Lintel (vocals), brothers Gregory and Morgan Petrineau (guitars), Horatio McKay (keyboards) and Eric Kingsley (drums).

4/1/78	133	13			**Eruption**			$12	Ariola 50033

Be Yourself
Computer Love

Do You Know What It Feels Like
Like

I Can't Carry On
I Can't Stand The Rain *18*

I'll Take You There
Movin'

Party, Party
Way We Were

Wayward Love

ESCAPE CLUB, The '88
Rock group formed in London: Trevor Steel (vocals), John Holliday (guitar), Johnnie Christo (bass) and Milan Zekavica (drums).

8/27/88	27	38	●	©	1 **Wild Wild West**			$10	Atlantic 81871
4/6/91	145	12		©	2 **Dollars And Sex**			$10	Atlantic 82198

Blast Off To Heaven (2)
Call It Poison (2) *44*
Come Alive (2)
Edge Of Your Bed (2)

Freedom (2)
Goodbye Joey Rae (1)
I'll Be There (2) *8*
Jealousy (1)

Longest Day (1)
Only The Rain (1)
Shake For The Sheik (1) *28*
Shout The Walls Down (2)

So Fashionable (2)
Staring At The Sun (1)
Sugar Man (2)
This City (2)

Walking Through Walls (1) *81*
Who Do You Love? (2)
Wild, Wild West (1) *1*
Working For The Fatman (1)

ESCOVEDO, Coke '76
Born Thomas Escovedo on 4/30/41 in Los Angeles. Died on 7/13/86 (age 45). Latin singer/percussionist. Member of **Azteca**. Uncle of **Sheila E.**

3/13/76	195	2			1 **Coke**			$12	Mercury 1041
5/29/76	190	3			2 **Comin' At Ya!**			$12	Mercury 1085
2/12/77	195	1			3 **Disco Fantasy**			$12	Mercury 1132

Backseat (2)
Breeze And I (2)
Diamond Dust (medley) (2)
Disco Fantasy (3)
Doesn't Anybody Want To Hear A Love Song (3)

Easy Come, Easy Go (1)
Everything Is Coming Our Way (2)
Fried Neck Bones And Home Fries (2)
Hall's Delight (1)

Hangin' On (2)
Hot Soul Single (3)
I Wouldn't Change A Thing (2)
If I Ever Lose This Heaven (1)
Life Is A Tortured Love Affair (1)
Love Letters (1)

Make It Sweet (1)
No One To Depend On (1)
Rebirth (3)
Runaway (2)
Somebody's Callin' (2)
Something So Simple (2)

Something Special (3)
Soul Support (3)
Stay With Me (2)
Trash Man (3)
Vida (medley) (2)
What Are You Under (1)

Who Do You Want To Love (1)
Why Can't We Be Lovers (1)
Won't You Gimme The Funk (3)
Your Kind Of Loving (3)

ESQUIRE '87
Rock trio from England: Nikki Squire (vocals), Nigel McLaren (bass) and Charles Olins (keyboards). Nikki is married to **Chris Squire** of **Yes**.

3/28/87	165	4		©	**Esquire**			$10	Geffen 24101

Blossomtime
Hourglass

Knock Twice For Heaven
Moving Together

Silent Future
Special Greeting

Sunshine
To The Rescue

Up Down Turnaround
What You've Been Saying

ESSEX, The '63

R&B vocal group formed in North Carolina: Anita Humes, Walter Vickers, Rodney Taylor, Billy Hill and Rudolph Johnson.

8/3/63	119	5	©	**Easier Said Than Done**			$40	Roulette 25234

All In My Mind / Been So Long / Conga La Ya / Every Night / I Love Her / Whenever I Need My Baby
Are You Going My Way / Come On To My Party / **Easier Said Than Done** 1 / I Have To Cry / We Belong Together / Where Is He

ESSEX, David '74

Born David Cook on 7/23/47 in London. Portrayed Christ in the London production of *Godspell*. Star of British movies since 1970.

1/5/74	32	21	©	**Rock On**			$20	Columbia 32560

Bring In The Sun / Lamplight 71 / **Rock On** 5 / Tell Him No
For Emily, Whenever I May / Ocean Girl / Sept. 15th / Turn Me Loose
Find Her / On And On / Streetfight / We All Insane

ESTÉBAN '00

Born Stephen Paul in Arizona. Flamenco guitarist.

7/22/00	10 C	2	©	1 **Flamenco Y Rosas**	[I]	$15	Daystar 0010 [2]
7/29/00	53	1	©	2 **Heart Of Gold**	[I]	$10	Daystar 0028
7/29/00	54	2	©	3 **All My Love**	[I]	$10	Daystar 0022
8/19/00	5 C	2	©	4 **Pasión**	[I]	$10	Daystar 0014
8/19/00	23 C	2	©	5 **Enter The Heart**	[I]	$10	Daystar 0016
11/4/00	159	3	©	6 **At Home With Estéban**	[I]	$15	Daystar 8830 [2]
11/25/00+	8 X	1	©	7 **What Child Is This?**	C:#5/3 [X-E-I]	$10	Daystar 0007

first released in 1995

| 4/14/01 | 105 | 2 | © | 8 **Live!** .... | [I-L] | $15 | Daystar 8832 [2] |

Alicante (8) / Caundo Calienta el Sol (3) / Für Elise (6) / La Paloma (3,4) / O Come O Come Emmanuel (7) / Soleares (1)
All I Ask Of You (3) / City Girls (8) / God Rest Ye Merry Gentleman (7) / Lady In Red (3) / O Mio Bambino Caro (6) / Some Children See Him (7)
Amazing Grace (6,8) / Coventry Carol (medley) (7) / Largo From The New World Symphony (6) / Pachebel's Canon (medley) (7) / Spanish Eyes (1)
Angel Of The Morning (3) / Dance Of The Blessed Spirits (6) / Golden Earrings (1) / Lonely Bull (1,8) / Perfidia (1) / Speak Softly Love (3)
Angels We Have Heard On High (medley) (7) / Don't Cry For Me Argentina (3,4) / Guajiras (1) / Malaguena (1,3) / Play Me (2) / Stay (8)
Argentina (8) / Down The Long Road (6) / Hark The Herald Angels Sing (7) / Malaguena Rhumba (4,8) / Rumba Riastro (2) / Tarantas (1)
Avenida Concha Espiña (5) / Duende (8) / Here Comes The Sun (2,8) / Maria Elena (1,4) / Runaway (1,2,3,4,8) / Time For Us (3,8)
Bag Jam (5) / Edelweiss (6) / In The Garden Of Joy (6) / Mary's Little Boy Child (7) / San Antonio Sunset (5) / Unchained Melody (3,8)
Besame Mucho (1,4,8) / El Rio De Vida (1) / In The Hall Of The Mountain King (6) / Mediterana (5) / Scarboro Fair (2) / Veracruz Express (5)
Blue Lotus (8) / Eleanor Rigby (2,8) / Jesu Joy Of Man's Desire (7) / Minuet (6) / Sedona Sunrise (5) / Walk Don't Run (medley) (2)
Bulerias (1) / Enter The Heart (5) / Jolly Old St. Nicholas (medley) (7) / My Favorite Things (6) / Sevillanas (1) / What Child Is This? (7)
Can't Help Falling In Love (8) / Fernando (3,4,8) / Never My Love (3) / Silver Raine (5) / Zorro (6,8)
Carnival Manha de Carnival (2) / Flamenco Wind (5) / Nights In White Satin (6,8) / Simple Gifts (6)
Carol Of The Bells (7) / Norwegian Wood (2,8) / Sleeping Beauty Waltz (6)

ESTEFAN, Gloria/Miami Sound Machine ★179★ '91

Latin-pop group from Miami: **Gloria Estefan** (born Gloria Fajardo on 12/1/57 in Havana, Cuba; raised in Miami), her husband Emilio Estefan (keyboards), Juan Avila (bass) and Enrique Garcia (drums). Group later grew to nine members. Gloria and Emilio married on 9/2/78; both were involved in a serious bus crash on 3/20/90. Gloria played "Isabel Vasquez" in the movie *Music of the Heart*.

1)Into The Light 2)Let It Loose 3)Cuts Both Ways

MIAMI SOUND MACHINE:

11/23/85+	21	75	▲3	©	1 **Primitive Love**	C:#32/9	$10	Epic 40131

GLORIA ESTEFAN AND MIAMI SOUND MACHINE:

6/20/87+	6	97	▲3	©	2 **Let It Loose**		$10	Epic 40769

GLORIA ESTEFAN:

7/29/89	8	69	▲3	©	3 **Cuts Both Ways**		$10	Epic 45217
2/16/91	5	68	▲2	©	4 **Into The Light**		$10	Epic 46988
11/21/92	15	77	▲4	©	5 **Greatest Hits**	C:#8/40	[G] $10	Epic 53046
7/10/93	27	46	▲	©	6 **Mi Tierra**		[F] $10	Epic 53807

title is Spanish for "My Country"

| 11/20/93 | 43 | 8 | ▲ | © | 7 **Christmas Through Your Eyes** .... | C:#12/18 | [X] $10 | Epic 57567 |

Christmas charts: 9/'93, 18/'94, 22/'95, 28/'96, 40/'97

11/5/94	9	44	▲2	©	8 **Hold Me, Thrill Me, Kiss Me**		$10	Epic 66205
10/14/95	67	16	●	©	9 **Abriendo Puertas**		[F] $10	Epic 67284

title is Spanish for "Opening Doors"

6/22/96	23	40	▲	©	10 **Destiny**		$10	Epic 67283
6/20/98	23	16	●	©	11 **Gloria!**		$10	Epic 69200
6/10/00	50	9	●	©	12 **Alma Caribeña - Caribbean Soul**		[F] $10	Epic 62163
2/24/01	92	3		©	13 **Greatest Hits Vol. II**		[G] $10	Epic 85396

Abriendo Puertas (Opening Doors) (9) / Cherchez La Femme (8) / **Cuts Both Ways** (3) 44 / Farolito (Little Star) (9) / Higher (10) / Lejos De Ti (Far From You) (9)
Along Came You (A Song For Emily) (10) / Christmas Auld Lang Syne (7) / Dame Otra Oportunidad (Give Me Another Chance) (12) / Feelin' (11) / Hold Me, Thrill Me, Kiss Me (8) / Let It Loose (2)
Always Tomorrow (5) 81 / Christmas Song (Chestnuts Roasting On An Open Fire) (7) / Desde La Oscuridad (Coming Out Of The Dark) (4) / Felicidad (Happiness) (9) / How Can I Be Sure (8) / Let It Snow, Let It Snow, Let It Snow (7)
Anything For You (2,5) 1 / **Get On Your Feet** (3,5) 11 / I Got No Love (13) / Light Of Love (4)
Arbolito De Navidad (7) / Christmas Through Your Eyes (5,7) / Destiny (10) / Give It Up (2) / I Just Wanna Be Happy (11) / **Live For Loving You** (4) 22
Ay, Ay, I (3) / Close My Eyes (4) / Don't Let The Sun Catch You Crying (8) / Go Away (5) / I Know You Too Well (10) / Love On A Two Way Street (8)
Ayer (3) / **Coming Out Of The Dark** (4,5) 1 / Goodnight My Love (8) / I See Your Smile (5) 48 / Love Toy (2)
Bad Boy (1) 8 / Don't Let This Moment End (11) 76 / Hablas De Mí (6) / I Want You So Bad (2) / Lucky Girl (11)
Betcha Say That (2) 36 / Como Me Duele Perderte (How It Hurts To Lose You) (12) / Don't Release Me (11) / Hablemos El Mismo Idioma (6) / I'll Be Home For Christmas (7) / Mama Yo Can't Go (4)
Body To Body (1) / Don't Stop (11) / Have Yourself A Merry Little Christmas (7) / **I'm Not Giving You Up** (10,13) 40 / Mas Alla (Beyond) (9)
Breaking Up Is Hard To Do (8) / Con Los Años Que Me Quedan (6) / **Don't Wanna Lose You** (3,5) 1 / Heart Never Learns (10) / If We Were Lovers (13) / Me Voy (I'm Leaving) (12)
Can't Forget You (4) 43 / Dulce Amor (Sweet Love) (9) / Heart With Your Name On It (4) / It's Too Late (8) / Mi Buen Amor (6)
Can't Stay Away From You (2,5) 6 / **Conga** (1,5) 10 / **Everlasting Love** (8,13) 27 / **Heaven's What I Feel** (11,13) 27 / La Flor Y Tu Amor (The Flower And Your Love) (12) / Mi Tierra (6)
Cuba Libre (11) / **Falling In Love (Uh-Oh)** (1) 25 / **Here We Are** (3,5) 6 / La Parranda (The Big Party) (9) / Milagro (Miracle) (6)
Montuno (6)

ESTEFAN, Gloria/Miami Sound Machine — Cont'd

Movies (1)
Mucho Money (1)
Music Of My Heart (13) *2*
Nayib's Song (I Am Here For You) (4)
No Hay Mal Que Por Bien No Venga (6)
No Me Dejes De Querer (12) *77*
Nothin' New (3)
Nuestra Felicidad (Our Happiness) (12)

Nuevo Dia (New Day) (9)
1-2-3 (2,5) *3*
Out Of Nowhere (13)
Oye (11,13)
Oye Mi Canto (Hear My Voice) (3) *48*
Path Of The Right Love (10)
Por Un Beso (For A Kiss) (12)
Primitive Love (1)
Punto De Referencia (Point Of Reference) (12)
Reach (10,13) *42*

Real Woman (11)
Remember Me With Love (4)
Rhythm Is Gonna Get You (2,5) *5*
Say (3)
Seal Our Fate (4) *53*
Sex In The 90's (4)
Show Me The Way Back To Your Heart (10)
¡Si Señor!... (6)
Silent Night (7)
Silver Bells (7)

Solo Por Tu Amor (Only For Your Love) (12)
Steal Your Heart (10)
Surrender (2)
Surrender Paradise (1)
Te Tengo A Ti (If I Have You) (12)
Tengo Que Decirte Algo (I Have To Tell You Something) (12)
Think About You Now (3)
This Christmas (7)
Touched By An Angel (11)

Traces (8)
Tradición (6)
Tres Deseos (Three Wishes) (9)
Tres Gotas De Agua Bendita (Three Drops Of Holy Water) (12)
Turn The Beat Around (8,13) *13*
Tus Ojos (6)
Volverás (6)
What Goes Around (4)

White Christmas (7)
Words Get In The Way (1,5) *5*
Y-Tu-Conga (13)
You Can't Walk Away From Love (13)
You Made A Fool Of Me (1)
You'll Be Mine (Party Time) (10,13) *70*
You've Made Me So Very Happy (8)
Your Love Is Bad For Me (3)

ESTUS, Deon '89
Born in Detroit. R&B singer/bassist.

4/1/89	89	15		©	Spell............			$10	Mika 835713

Blue Envelope
False Start

Heaven Help Me *5*
Love Can't Wait

Love Me Over
Me Or The Rumours

Solid Ground
Spell

You're The Only One

ETERNAL '94
Female R&B vocal group from London: sisters Easther and Vernie Bennett, with Louise Nurding and Kelle Bryan.

3/26/94	152	7		©	Always & Forever............			$10	EMI 28212

Amazing Grace
Crazy
Don't Say Goodbye

I'll Be There
If You Need Me Tonight
Just A Step From Heaven

Let's Stay Together
Never Gonna Give You Up
Oh Baby, I...

Save Our Love
So Good
Stay *19*

Sweet Funky Thing
This Love's For Real

★470★ ETHERIDGE, Melissa '95
Born on 5/29/61 in Leavenworth, Kansas. Pop-rock singer/songwriter/guitarist.

6/18/88+	22	65	▲2	©	1 Melissa Etheridge............ C:#23/41			$10	Island 90875
10/7/89	22	58	▲	©	2 Brave And Crazy............ C:#50/1			$10	Island 91285
4/4/92	21	26	▲	©	3 Never Enough............			$10	Island 512120
10/9/93+	15	138	▲6	©	4 Yes I Am............			$10	Island 848660
12/2/95	6	41	▲2	©	5 Your Little Secret			$10	Island 524154
10/23/99	12	18		©	6 Breakdown............			$10	Island 546518

Ain't It Heavy (3)
All American Girl (4)
All The Way To Heaven (5)
Angels, The (2)
Angels Would Fall (6) *51*
Boy Feels Strange (3)
Brave And Crazy (2)
Breakdown (6)
Bring Me Some Water (1)
Change (5)
Chrome Plated Heart (1)

Come To My Window (4) *25*
Dance Without Sleeping (3)
Don't You Need (1)
Enough Of Me (6)
How Would I Know (6)
I Could Have Been You (5)
I Really Like You (5)
I Want To Come Over (5) *22*
I Want You (1)
I Will Never Be The Same (4)
I'm The Only One (4) *8*

If I Wanted To (4) *16*
Into The Dark (6)
It's For You (3)
Keep It Precious (3)
Late September Dogs (1)
Let Me Go (2)
Letting Go (3)
Like The Way I Do (1) *42*
Mama I'm Strange (6)
Meet Me In The Back (3)
Must Be Crazy For Me (3)

My Back Door (2)
My Lover (6)
No Souvenirs (2) *95*
Nowhere To Go (5) *40*
Occasionally (1)
Place Your Hand (3)
Precious Pain (1)
Resist (4)
Royal Station 4/16 (2)
Ruins (4)
Scarecrow (6)

Shriner's Park (5)
Silent Legacy (4)
Similar Features (1) *94*
Skin Deep (2)
Sleep (6)
Stronger Than Me (6)
Talking To My Angel (4)
Testify (5)
This War Is Over (5)
Truth Of The Heart (6)
2001 (3)

Unusual Kiss (5)
Watching You (1)
Yes I Am (4)
You Can Sleep While I Drive (2)
You Used To Love To Dance (2)
Your Little Secret (5)

ETZEL, Roy '65
Born in Germany. Trumpet player.

12/18/65	140	5			The Silence (Il Silenzio)............		[I]	$20	MGM 4330

El Amor
Goldfinger

La Mama
Melancholy

More
Non Ho L'eta (Per Amarti)

Oh, Warum?
Puerto Rico

Silence (Il Silenzio)
Sonny Boy

Stardust
Sunrise

E.U. '89
Funk group from Washington DC. Led by singer/bassist Gregory Elliott. E.U.: Experience Unlimited.

4/22/89	158	9			Livin' Large............			$10	Virgin 91021

Buck Wild
Come To The Go-Go

Da Butt '89
Don't Turn Around

Express
Livin' Large

Shaka Zulu
Shake It Like A White Girl

Shake Your Thang
Taste Of Your Love

EUROGLIDERS '85
Pop-rock group from Perth, Australia: Grace Knight (vocals), Crispin Akerman (guitar), Amanda Vincent and Bernie Lynch (keyboards), Ron Francois (bass) and John Bennetts (drums).

12/22/84+	140	11		©	This Island............			$10	Columbia 39588

Another Day In The Big World
Cold Comfort

Heaven (Must Be There) *65*
It's The Way

Judy's World
Keep It Quiet

Maybe Only I Dream
Never Say

No Action
Nothing To Say

Someone
Waiting For You

EUROPE '87
Hard-rock group from Stockholm, Sweden: Joey Tempest (vocals), Kee Marcello (guitar), John Leven (bass), Mic Michaeli (keyboards) and Ian Haugland (drums).

11/1/86+	8	78	▲3	©	1 The Final Countdown			$10	Epic 40241
8/27/88	19	25	▲	©	2 Out Of This World............			$10	Epic 44185

Carrie (1) *3*
Cherokee (1) *72*
Coast To Coast (2)
Danger On The Track (1)

Final Countdown (1) *8*
Heart Of Stone (1)
Just The Beginning (2)
Let The Good Times Rock (2)

Lights And Shadows (2)
Love Chaser (1)
More Than Meets The Eye (2)
Never Say Die (2)

Ninja (1)
On The Loose (1)
Open Your Heart (2)
Ready Or Not (2)

Rock The Night (1) *30*
Sign Of The Times (2)
Superstitious (2) *31*
Time Has Come (1)

Tomorrow (2)
Tower's Callin' (2)

★342★ EURYTHMICS '84
Pop-rock duo: **Annie Lennox** (vocals, keyboards) and **David A. Stewart** (guitar). Lennox was born on 12/25/54 in Aberdeen, Scotland. Stewart was born on 9/9/52 in Sunderland, England. Both had been in The Tourists from 1977-80. Stewart married Siobhan Fahey of **Bananarama** on 8/1/87. Lennox appeared in the TV movie "The Room."

1)Touch 2)Be Yourself Tonight 3)Revenge

5/28/83	15	59	●	©	1 Sweet Dreams (Are Made Of This)............			$10	RCA Victor 4681
2/4/84	7	37	▲	©	2 Touch			$10	RCA Victor 4917
7/7/84	115	11		©	3 Touch Dance............		[K]	$10	RCA Victor 5086
					vocal and instrumental dance remixes of some cuts from above album				
1/5/85	93	14		©	4 1984 (for the love of big brother)............		[S]	$10	RCA Victor 5349
5/25/85	9	45	▲	©	5 Be Yourself Tonight			$10	RCA Victor 5429

EURYTHMICS — Cont'd

8/9/86	12	33	●	©	6 **Revenge**			$10	RCA Victor 5847
12/26/87+	41	19		©	7 **Savage**			$10	RCA Victor 6794
9/30/89	34	28		©	8 **We Too Are One**			$10	Arista 8606
6/15/91	72	23	▲³	©	9 **Greatest Hits**	C:#33/2	[G]	$10	Arista 8680
11/6/99	25	12	●	©	10 **Peace**			$10	Arista 14617

Adrian (5)
Angel (8,9)
Anything But Strong (10)
Aqua (2)
Beautiful Child (10)
Beethoven (I Love To Listen To) (7)
Better To Have Lost In Love (Than Never To Have Loved At All) (5)
Brand New Day (7)
Conditioned Soul (5)
Cool Blue (2,3)
Do You Want To Break Up? (7)
Don't Ask Me Why (8,9) 40
Doubleplusgood (4)
First Cut (2,3)

For The Love Of Big Brother (4)
Forever (10)
Greetings From A Dead Man (4)
Heaven (7)
Here Comes That Sinking Feeling (5)
Here Comes The Rain Again (2,9) 4
How Long? (8)
I Could Give You (A Mirror) (1)
I Did It Just The Same (1)
I Love You Like A Ball And Chain (5)
I Need A Man (7,9) 46
I Need You (7)
I Remember You (6)

I Saved The World Today (10)
I Want It All (10)
I've Got A Lover (Back In Japan) (7)
I've Got An Angel (1)
I've Tried Everything (10)
In This Town (4)
It's Alright (Baby's Coming Back) (5) 78
Jennifer (4)
Julia (4)
King & Queen Of America (8,9)
Last Time (6)
Let's Go! (6)
Lifted (10)
Little Of You (6)
Love Is A Stranger (1,9) 23

Ministry Of Love (4)
Miracle Of Love (6)
Missionary Man (6,9) 14
(My My) Baby's Gonna Cry (8)
My True Love (10)
No Fear, No Hate, No Pain (No Broken Hearts) (2)
Paint A Rumour (2,3)
Peace Is Just A Word (10)
Power To The Meek (10)
Put The Blame On Me (7)
Regrets (2,3)
Revival (8)
Right By Your Side (2) 29
Room 101 (4)
Savage (7)
17 Again (10)

Sexcrime (Nineteen Eighty-Four) (4) 81
Shame (7)
Sisters Are Doin' It For Themselves (5,9) 18
Somebody Told Me (1)
Sweet Dreams (Are Made Of This) (1,9) 1
Sylvia (8)
Take Your Pain Away (6)
There Must Be An Angel (Playing With My Heart) (5,9) 22
This City Never Sleeps (1)
This Is The House (1)
Thorn In My Side (6,9) 68
Walk, The (1)

We Two Are One (8)
When The Day Goes Down (8)
When Tomorrow Comes (6,9)
Who's That Girl? (2,9) 21
Wide Eyed Girl (7)
Winston's Diary (4)
Would I Lie To You? (5,9) 5
Wrap It Up (1)
You Have Placed A Chill In My Heart (7) 64
You Hurt Me (And I Hate You) (8)

EVAN AND JARON   '01

Duo of identical twin brothers: Evan and Jaron Lowenstein. Born on 3/18/74 in Atlanta.

1/13/01	156	7		©	**Evan And Jaron**			$10	Columbia 69937

Crazy For This Girl 15
Distance, The
Done Hangin' On Maybe

From My Head To My Heart
I Could Fall
Make It Better

On The Bus
Outerspace
Pick Up The Phone

Ready Or Not
Wouldn't It Be Nice To Be Proud

You Don't Know Me

EVANS, Faith   '98

Born on 6/10/73 in Newark, New Jersey. Female R&B singer. Married **The Notorious B.I.G.** in 1995.

9/16/95	22	32	▲	©	1 **Faith**			$10	Bad Boy 73003
11/14/98	6	45	●	©	2 **Keep The Faith**			$10	Bad Boy 73016

Ain't Nobody (1) 67
All Night Long (2) 9
All This Love (1)
Anthing You Need (2)
Caramel Kisses (2)

Come Over (1)
Don't Be Afraid (1)
Fallin' In Love (1)
Give It To Me (1)
Keep The Faith (2)

Lately I (2)
Life Will Pass You By (2)
Love Don't Live Here Anymore (1)
Love Like This (2) 7

My First Love (2)
Never Gonna Let You Go (2) 17
No Other Love (1)
No Way (2)

Reasons (1)
Soon As I Get Home (1) 21
Sunny Days (2)
You Don't Understand (1)
You Used To Love Me (1) 24

EVANS, Sara   '01

Born on 2/5/71 in Boonesboro, Missouri. Country singer.

1/23/99	116	13	●	©	1 **No Place That Far**			$10	RCA 67653
10/28/00+	55	49↑		©	2 **Born To Fly**			$10	RCA 67964

Born To Fly (2) 34
Cryin' Game (1)
Cupid (1)
Every Little Kiss (2)
Fool, I'm A Woman (1)

Four-Thirty (2)
Great Unknown (1)
I Could Not Ask For More (2) 35

I Keep Looking (2)
I Learned That From You (2)
I Thought I'd See Your Face Again (1)

Knot Comes Untied (1)
Let's Dance (2)
Love, Don't Be A Stranger (1)
No Place That Far (1) 37
Saints & Angels (2)

Show Me The Way To Your Heart (2)
There's Only One (1)
These Days (1)
Time Won't Tell (1)

Why Should I Care (2)
You Don't (2)

EVE   '99

Born Eve Jeffers in 1979 in Philadelphia. Female rapper. Member of **Ruff Ryders**.

10/2/99	❶¹	38	▲	©	1 **Ruff Ryders' First Lady**			$10	Ruff Ryders 490453
3/24/01	4	28↑	▲	©	2 **Scorpion**			$10	Ruff Ryders 490845

Ain't Got No Dough (1)
Be Me (2)
Cowboy (2)
Dog Match (1)
Gangsta Bitch (2)

Got What You Need (2)
Gotta Man (1) 26
Heaven Only Knows (1)
Let Me Blow Ya Mind (2) 2
Let's Talk About (1)

Life Is So Hard (2)
Love Is Blind (1) 34
Maniac (1)
No, No, No (2)
Philly, Philly (1)

Scenario 2000 (1)
Scream Double R (2)
Stuck Up (1)
That's What It Is (2)
Thug In The Street (2)

We On That Shit! (1)
What You Want (1) 29
Who's That Girl? (2) 47
You Ain't Gettin' None (2)
You Had Me, You Lost Me (2)

EVERCLEAR   '00

Rock trio formed in Portland, Oregon: Art Alexakis (vocals, guitar), Craig Montoya (bass) and Greg Eklund (drums).

1/13/96	25	38	▲	©	1 **Sparkle And Fade**			$10	Capitol 30929
10/25/97	33	88	▲	©	2 **So Much For The Afterglow**			$10	Capitol 36503
7/29/00	9	36	▲	©	3 **Songs From An American Movie Vol. One: Learning How To Smile**			$10	Capitol 97061
12/9/00	66	10		©	4 **Songs From An American Movie Vol. Two: Good Time For A Bad Attitude**			$10	Capitol 95873

AM Radio (3)
All Fucked Up (4)
Amphetamine (2)
Annabella's Song (3)
Ataraxia (2)
Babytalk (4)
Brown Eyed Girl (3)
Chemical Smile (1)
El Distorto De Melodica (2)
Electra Made Me Blind (1)

Everything To Everyone (2)
Father Of Mine (2) 70
Good Witch Of The North (4)
Halloween Americana (4)
Heartspark Dollarsign (1) 85
Her Brand New Skin (1)
Here We Go Again (3)
Heroin Girl (1)
Honeymoon Song (3)
I Will Buy You A New Life (2)

Learning How To Smile (3)
Like A California King (2)
Misery Whip (4)
My Sexual Life (1)
Nehalem (2)
Normal Like You (2)
Now That It's Over (3)
One Hit Wonder (2)
Otis Redding (3)
Out Of My Depth (4)

Overwhelming (4)
Pale Green Stars (1)
Queen Of The Air (1)
Rock Star (4)
Santa Monica (1)
Short Blonde Hair (4)
Slide (4)
So Much For The Afterglow (2)
Song From An American Movie pt. I (3)

Song From An American Movie pt. 2 (4)
Strawberry (1)
Summerland (1)
Sunflowers (2)
Thrift Store Chair (3)
Twistinside, The (1)
Unemployed Boyfriend (3)
When It All Goes Wrong Again (4)

White Men In Black Suits (2)
Why I Don't Believe In God (2)
Wonderful (3) 11
You Make Me Feel Like A Whore (1)

EVERETT, Betty — see BUTLER, Jerry

EVERLAST   '99

Born Erik Schrody on 8/18/69 in Valley Stream, New York. Former member of **House Of Pain**. Played "Rhodes" in the movie Judgment Night.

10/17/98+	9	55	▲²	©	1 **Whitey Ford Sings The Blues**			$10	Tommy Boy 1236
11/4/00	20	15	●	©	2 **Eat At Whitey's**			$10	Tommy Boy 1411

Babylon Feeling (2)
Black Coffee (2)
Black Jesus (2)
Children's Story (2)
Deadly Assassins (2)

Death Comes Callin' (1)
Ends (1)
Funky Beat (1)
Get Down (1)
Graves To Dig (2)

Hot To Death (1)
I Can't Move (2)
Letter, The (1)
Love For Real (2)
Mercy On My Soul (2)

Money (Dollar Bill) (1)
Next Man (1)
One And The Same (2)
One, Two (2)
Painkillers (1)

Praise The Lord (1)
7 Years (1)
Tired (1)
Today (Watch Me Shine) (1)
We're All Gonna Die (2)

What It's Like (1) 13
Whitey (2)

★486★ EVERLY BROTHERS, The '60

Vocal duo/guitarists/songwriters. Don was born on 2/1/37 in Brownie, Kentucky. Phil was born on 1/19/39 in Chicago. Parents were folk and Country singers. Don (beginning at age eight) and Phil (age six) sang with parents through high school. Invited to Nashville by **Chet Atkins** and first recorded there for Columbia in 1955. Signed to Archie Bleyer's Cadence Records in 1957. Phil married for a time to the daughter of Janet Bleyer (Chordettes). Duo split up in July 1973 and reunited in September 1983. Inducted into the Rock and Roll Hall of Fame in 1986. Don's daughter Erin was married for a short time to Axl Rose of **Guns N' Roses** in 1990.

1)A Date With The Everly Brothers 2)It's Everly Time! 3)The Everly Brothers

2/10/58	16	3	©	1	The Everly Brothers			$100	Cadence 3003
5/23/60	9	10		2	It's Everly Time!			$50	Warner 1381
8/22/60	23	19	©	3	The Fabulous Style Of The Everly Brothers		[K]	$100	Cadence 3040
12/5/60+	9	24		4	A Date With The Everly Brothers			$50	Warner 1395
8/25/62	35	17	©	5	The Golden Hits Of The Everly Brothers		[G]	$50	Warner 1471
9/25/65	141	3		6	Beat & Soul			$50	Warner 1605
7/18/70	180	8		7	The Everly Brothers' Original Greatest Hits		[G]	$30	Barnaby 350 [2]
3/10/84	162	5	©	8	The Everly Brothers Reunion Concert		[L]	$15	Passport 11001 [2]
					recorded September 1983 at the Royal Albert Hall in London				
10/13/84	38	17	©	9	EB 84			$12	Mercury 822431
2/8/86	83	19	©	10	Born Yesterday			$12	Mercury 826142

Abandoned Love (10)
All I Have To Do Is Dream (7,8) *1*
Always Drive A Cadillac (10)
Always It's You (4) *56*
Amanda Ruth (10)
Arms Of Mary (10)
Asleep (9)
Baby What You Want Me To Do (4)
Be Bop A-Lula (1,3,7,8) *74*
Bird Dog (7,8) *1*
Born Yesterday (10)
Brand New Heartache (1,3,7)
Bye Bye Love (1,7,8) *2*
Carol Jane (2)
Cathy's Clown (4,5,8) *1*
Change Of Heart (4)

Claudette (8)
Crying In The Rain (5,8) *6 flip*
Danger Danger (9)
Devoted To You (medley) (8)
Don't Blame Me (5) *20*
Don't Say Goodnight (10)
Donna, Donna (4)
Ebony Eyes (5,8) *8*
First In Line (9)
Following The Sun (9)
Girl Can't Help It (6)
Gone Gone Gone (8)
Good Golly Miss Molly (8)
Hey Doll Baby (1,3)
Hi Heel Sneakers (6)
How Can I Meet Her? (5) *75*
I Almost Lost My Mind (6)
I Know Love (10)
I Want You To Know (2)

I Wonder If I Care As Much (1,8) *flip*
I'm Not Angry (5)
I'm Takin' My Time (9)
Just In Case (2)
Keep A Knockin' (1,7)
Lay, Lady, Lay (9)
Leave My Woman Alone (1,7)
Let It Be Me (3,7,8) *7*
Lightning Express (7,8)
Like Strangers (3,7) *22*
Lonely Avenue (6)
Long Time Gone (7)
Love Hurts (4,8)
Love Is Strange (6,8)
Love Of My Life (7) *40*
Lucille (4,5,8) *21*
Made To Love (4)
Man With Money (6)

Maybe Tomorrow (1,7,8)
Memories Are Made Of This (2)
Money (That's What I Want) (6)
More Than I Can Handle (9)
Muskrat (5) *82*
My Babe (6)
Nashville Blues (2)
Oh, True Love (2)
Oh, What A Feeling (3)
On The Wings Of A Nightingale (9) *50*
People Get Ready (6)
Poor Jenny (3,7) *22*
Price Of Love (8)
Problems (7) *2*
Put My Little Shoes Away (8)
Rip It Up (1,3,7)
Rockin' Alone (In An Old Rocking Chair) (7)

See See Rider (6)
Should We Tell Him (1,7) *flip*
Sigh, Cry, Almost Die (4)
Since You Broke My Heart (3)
Sleepless Nights (2)
So How Come (No One Loves Me) (4)
So Sad (To Watch Good Love Go Bad) (2,5,8) *7*
Some Sweet Day (2)
Step It Up And Go (8)
Stick With Me Baby (4) *41*
Story Of Me (9)
Take A Message To Mary (3,8) *16*
Temptation (5,8) *27*
That Uncertain Feeling (10)
That's Just Too Much (4)

That's Old Fashioned (That's The Way Love Should Be) (5) *9*
That's What You Do To Me (2)
These Shoes (10)
Thinkin' 'Bout You (10)
This Little Girl Of Mine (1) *26*
('Til) I Kissed You (3,7,8) *4*
Wake Up Little Susie (1,7,8) *1*
Walk Right Back (5,8) *7*
Walking The Dog (6)
What Am I Living For (6)
What Kind Of Girl Are You (2)
When Will I Be Loved (3,8) *8*
Why Worry (10)
You Make It Seem So Easy (9)
You Thrill Me (Through And Through) (2)

EVERY MOTHER'S NIGHTMARE '91

Hard-rock group formed in Nashville: Rick Ruhl (vocals), Steve Malone (guitar), Mark McMurtry (bass) and Jim Phipps (drums).

11/17/90+	146	15	©		Every Mother's Nightmare			$10	Arista 8633

Bad On Love
Dues To Pay

EZ Come, EZ Go
Hard To Hold

Listen Up
Long Haired Country Boy

Lord Willin'
Love Can Make You Blind

Nobody Knows
Walls Come Down

EVERY MOTHERS' SON '67

Pop-rock group from New York City: brothers Dennis (vocals) and Larry (guitar) (bass) and Christopher Augustine (drums). Larden, Bruce Milner (organ), Schuyler Larsen

6/10/67	117	10			Every Mothers' Son			$20	MGM 4471

Ain't It A Drag
Ain't No Use

Allison Dozer
Come On Down To My Boat *6*

Come On Queenie
Didn't She Lie

For Brandy
I Believe In You

I Won't
Sittin' Here (Peter's Tune)

What Became Of Mary

EVERYTHING '98

Ska-rock group from Sperryville, Virginia: Craig Honeycutt (vocals, guitar), Rich Bradley, Wolfe Quinn and Steve Van Dam (horns), David Slankard (bass) and Nate Brown (drums).

9/5/98	173	8	©		Super Natural			$10	Blackbird 38003

Be Gone
Big D's Playground

Good Thing (St. Luicia)
Hooch *69*

Ladybug
Real, The

Spent
Super Natural

Time Will Heal Me
Upon These Dreams

EVERYTHING BUT THE GIRL '95

Pop duo formed in London: Tracey Thorn (vocals) and Ben Watt (instruments). Group name taken from a furniture store on England's Hull University campus.

3/17/90	77	18	©	1	The Language Of Life			$10	Atlantic 82057
8/6/94+	46	32	● ©	2	Amplified Heart			$10	Atlantic 82605
6/8/96	37	16	©	3	Walking Wounded			$10	Atlantic 82912
10/16/99	65	7	©	4	Temperamental			$10	Atlantic 83214

Before Today (3)
Big Deal (3)
Blame (4)
Compression (4)
Disenchanted (2)
Downhill Racer (4)
Driving (1)

Five Fathoms (4)
Flipside (3)
Future Of The Future (Stay Gold) (4)
Get Back Together (1)
Get Me (2)
Good Cop Bad Cop (3)

Hatfield 1980 (4)
Heart Remains A Child (3)
I Don't Understand Anything (2)
Imagining America (1)
Language Of Life (1)
Letting Love Go (1)
Low Tide Of The Night (4)

Lullaby Of Clubland (4)
Me And Bobby D (1)
Meet Me In The Morning (1)
Mirrorball (3)
Missing (2) *2*
My Baby Don't Love Me (1)
No Difference (4)

Road, The (1)
Rollercoaster (2)
Single (3)
Take Me (1)
Temperamental (4)
Troubled Mind (2)
25th December (2)

Two Star (2)
Walking To You (2)
Walking Wounded (3)
We Walk The Same Line (2)
Wrong (3) *68*

EVE 6 '98

Rock trio from Los Angeles: Jon Siebels (vocals, guitar), Max Collins (bass) and Tony Fagenson (drums).

6/27/98	33	47	▲ ©	1	Eve 6			$10	RCA 67617
8/12/00	34	28	● ©	2	Horrorscope			$10	RCA 67713

Amphetamines (2)
Bang (2)
Enemy (2)
Girl Eyes (2)

Here's To The Night (2)
How Much Longer (2)
Inside Out (1) *28*
Jesus Nitelite (1)

Jet Pack (2)
Leech (2)
Nightmare (2)
Nocturnal (2)

On The Roof Again (2)
Open Road Song (1)
Promise (2)
Rescue (2)

Saturday Night (1)
Showerhead (1)
Small Town Trap (1)
Sunset Strip Bitch (2)

Superhero Girl (1)
There's A Face (1)
Tongue Tied (1)

EVORA, Cesaria '01

Born in Cape Verde. Female singer.

6/30/01	188	2	©		São Vincente		[F]	$10	Windham Hill 11590

Bondade E Maldade
Crepuscular Solidão
Dor Di Amor

Esperança Irisada
Fada
Homem Na Meio Di' Homem

Linda Mimosa
Negue
Nutridinha

Pic Nic Na Salamansa
Ponta De Fi
Regresso

Sabôr De Pecado
São Vicente Di Longe
Tiempo Y Silencio

EXILE '78

Pop group formed in Lexington, Kentucky: J.P. Pennington (vocals, guitar), Les Taylor (guitar), Marlon Hargis (keyboards), Sonny Lemaire (bass) and Steve Goetzman (drums). Group had a highly successful country career from 1983-91.

| 8/19/78 | 14 | 26 | ● | © | **Mixed Emotions** | | | $12 | Warner/Curb 3205 |

Ain't Got No Time
Don't Do It

Kiss You All Over *1*
Never Gonna Stop

One Step At A Time
Stay With Me

There's Been A Change
You And Me

You Thrill Me 40

EXODUS '88

Heavy-metal group from San Francisco: Steve Souza (vocals), Rick Hunolt and Gary Holt (guitars), Rob McKillop (bass) and Tom Hunting (drums). Kirk Hammet of **Metallica** was a member in the early 1980s.

11/28/87+	82	20		©	1 **Pleasures Of The Flesh**			$10	Combat 8169
2/25/89	82	17		©	2 **Fabulous Disaster**			$10	Combat 2001
8/11/90	137	9		©	3 **Impact Is Imminent**			$10	Capitol 90379

A.W.O.L. (3)
Brain Dead (1)
Cajun Hell (2)
Changing Of The Guard (3)
Chemi-Kill (1)
Choose Your Weapon (1)
Corruption (2)

Deranged (1)
Fabulous Disaster (2)
Faster Than You'll Ever Live To Be (1)
Heads They Win (Tails You Lose) (3)
Impact Is Imminent (3)

Last Act Of Defiance (2)
Like Father, Like Son (2)
Low Rider (2)
Lunatic Parade (3)
Objection Overruled (3)
Only Death Decides (3)
Open Season (3)

Parasite (1)
Pleasures Of The Flesh (1)
Seeds Of Hate (3)
30 Seconds (1)
Thrash Under Pressure (3)
'Til Death Do Us Part (1)
Toxic Waltz (2)

Verbal Razors (2)
Within The Walls Of Chaos (3)

EXOTIC GUITARS, The '69

Studio group featuring the lead guitar of Al Casey.

8/3/68	155	5			1 **The Exotic Guitars**		[I]	$15	Ranwood 8002
1/4/69	167	11			2 **Those Were The Days**		[I]	$15	Ranwood 8040
5/31/69	162	6			3 **Indian Love Call**		[I]	$15	Ranwood 8051

Alley Cat (1)
Autumn Leaves (2)
Battle Hymn Of The Republic (3)
Bells That Ring For No One (1)
Blue Velvet (2)
Blueberry Hill (1)

C'est Si Bon (1)
Galveston (3)
Green Door (3)
Heartaches (1)
I Walk Alone (2)
I Will Wait For You (1)
Indian Love Call (3)

La Paloma (3)
Love Is Blue (2)
Man And A Woman (2)
Melody Of Love (1)
Moon River (3)
Music To Watch Girls By (2)
My Happiness (1)

Only You (2)
Pearly Shells (3)
Petite Fleur (3)
Red Roses For A Blue Lady (3)
Sabre Dance (from Ballet Gayne) (3)
Sound Of Music (2)

Spanish Eyes (1)
Strangers On The Shore (1)
Taste Of Honey (2)
Those Were The Days (2)
Trying (3)
Twilight Time (2)
Vaya Con Dios (3)

Wonderland By Night (1)
Yellow Bird (1)

EXPOSÉ '88

Female dance vocal group: Ann Curless (from Miami), Jeanette Jurado (from Los Angeles) and Gioia Bruno (born in Italy; raised in New York City). Kelly Moneymaker (from Fairbanks, Alaska) replaced Bruno in 1992.

2/21/87+	16	74	▲²	©	1 **Exposure**			$10	Arista 8441
7/1/89	33	50	●	©	2 **What You Don't Know**			$10	Arista 8532
11/21/92+	135	13	●	©	3 **Exposé**			$10	Arista 18577

Angel (1)
As Long As I Can Dream (3) *55*
Come Go With Me (1) *5*
December (1)
Didn't It Hurt To Hurt Me (2)
Exposed To Love (1)
Extra Extra (1)

Face To Face (3)
Give Me All Your Love (3)
I Know You Know (1)
I Specialize In Love (3)
I Think I'm In Trouble (3)
I Wish The Phone Would Ring (3)

I'll Never Get Over You Getting Over Me (3) *8*
In Walked Love (3) *84*
Let Me Be The One (1) *7*
Let Me Down Easy (2)
Love Don't Hurt (Until You Fall) (2)
Love Is Our Destiny (1)

Now That I Found You (2)
Point Of No Return (1) *5*
Same Love (3)
Seasons Change (1) *1*
Still Hung Up On You (2)
Stop, Listen, Look & Think (2)
Tell Me Why (2) *9*
Touch And Go (3)

Walk Along With Me (2)
What You Don't Know (2) *8*
When I Looked At Him (2) *10*
You Don't Know What You Got (3)
You're The One I Need (1)
Your Baby Never Looked Good In Blue (2) *17*

EXTREME '91

Rock group from Boston: Gary Cherone (vocals), Nuno Bettencourt (guitar), Pat Badger (bass) and Paul Geary (drums). Geary replaced by Mike Mangini by 1995. Cherone became lead singer of **Van Halen** in September 1996.

4/8/89	80	32		©	1 **Extreme**			$10	A&M 5238
8/25/90+	10	75	▲²	©	2 **Pornograffitti**			$10	A&M 5313
10/10/92	10	23	●	©	3 **III Sides To Every Story**			$10	A&M 540006
2/25/95	40	5		©	4 **Waiting For The Punchline**			$10	A&M 540327

Am I Ever Gonna Change (3)
Big Boys Don't Cry (1)
Color Me Blind (3)
Cupid's Dead (3)
Cynical (4)
Decadence Dance (2)
Evilangelist (4)
Flesh 'N' Blood (1)
Get The Funk Out (2)

God Isn't Dead? (3)
He-Man Woman Hater (2)
Hip Today (4)
Hole Hearted (2) *4*
It's A Monster (3)
Kid Ego (1)
Leave Me Alone (4)
Li'l Jack Horny (2)
Little Girls (1)

Midnight Express (4)
Money (In God We Trust) (2)
More Than Words (2) *1*
Mutha (Don't Wanna Go To School Today) (1)
Naked (2)
No Respect (4)
Our Father (3)
Peacemaker Die (3)

Politicalamity (3)
Pornograffitti (2)
Rest In Peace (3) *96*
Rise 'N Shine (3)
Rock A Bye Bye (1)
Seven Sundays (3)
Shadow Boxing (4)
Smoke Signals (1)
Song For Love (2)

Stop The World (3) *95*
Suzi (Wants Her All Day What?) (2)
Teacher's Pet (1)
Tell Me Something I Don't Know (4)
There Is No God (4)
Tragic Comic (3)
Unconditionally (4)

Warheads (3)
Watching, Waiting (1)
When I First Kissed You (2)
When I'm President (2)
Who Cares? (3)
Wind Me Up (1)

EYE TO EYE '82

Pop duo: singer Deborah Berg (from Seattle) and pianist Julian Marshall (from England).

| 6/19/82 | 99 | 15 | | | **Eye To Eye** | | | $12 | Warner 3570 |

Hunger Pains
Life In Motion

More Hopeless Knowledge
Nice Girls *37*

On The Mend
Physical Attraction

Progress Ahead
Time Flys

EZO '87

Hard-rock group from Sapporo, Japan: Masaki Yamada (vocals), Shoyo Iida (guitar), Taro Takahashi (bass) and Hiro Homma (drums).

| 6/13/87 | 150 | 9 | | | **E-Z-O** | | | $10 | Geffen 24143 |

produced by **Gene Simmons** (of **Kiss**)

Big Changes
Desiree

Destroyer
Flashback Heart Attack

Here It Comes
House Of 1,000 Pleasures

I Walk Alone
Kiss Of Fire

Mr. Midnight

F

FABARES, Shelley '62

Born Michele Fabares on 1/19/44 in Santa Monica, California. Pop singer/actress. Niece of actress Nanette Fabray. Starred in several movies and TV shows. Married to record producer Lou Adler from 1964-67. Married actor Mike Farrell on 1/31/84.

7/21/62	106	11	©	1 Shelley!	$150 Colpix 426
10/27/62	121	5	©	2 The Things We Did Last Summer	$100 Colpix 431
5/11/63	48	18	©	3 Teen-Age Triangle	[G] $40 Colpix 444

JAMES DARREN/SHELLEY FABARES/PAUL PETERSEN
includes 4 cuts by Paul Petersen: "Keep Your Love Locked (Deep In Your Heart)," "Little Boy Sad," "Lollipops And Roses" and "She Can't Find Her Keys"

Boy Of My Own (1)
Breaking Up Is Hard To Do (2)
Conscience *[Darren]* (3) 11
Funny Face (1)
Gidget *[Darren]* (3) 41

Goodbye Cruel World *[Darren]* (3) 3
It Keeps Right On A Hurtin' (2)
Her Royal Majesty *[Darren]* (3) 6
Hi Lilli, Hi-Lo (1)

I'm Growing Up (1,2,3)
It Keeps Right On A Hurtin' (2)
It's Been A Long, Long Time (1)
Johnny Angel (1,3) 1
Johnny Get Angry (2)

Johnny Loves Me (2,3) 21
Loco-Motion (2)
Love Letters (1)
Palisades Park (2)
Picnic (1)

Roses Are Red (2)
Sealed With A Kiss (2)
See You In September (2)
Things We Did Last Summer (2,3) 46

True Love (1)
Vacation (2)
Very Unlikely (1)
Where's It Gonna Get Me? (1)

FABIAN '60

Born Fabiano Forte on 2/6/43 in Philadelphia. Pop singer. Acted in several movies.

| 5/18/59 | 5 | 21 | | 1 Hold That Tiger! | $100 Chancellor 5003 |
| 12/28/59+ | 3 | 19 | | 2 Fabulous Fabian | $100 Chancellor 5005 |

Ain't Misbehavin' (2)
Any Ole Time (2)
Cuddle Up A Little Closer (1)
Don't You Think It's Time? (1)
Everything Is Just Right (2)

Gimme A Little Kiss (2)
Give (2)
Gonna Get You (1)
Gonna Make You Mine (2)
Gotta Tell Somebody (2)

Hold Me (In Your Arms) (1)
I Don't Know Why (1)
I'm Sincere (2)
Just One More Time (1)
Lovin' (2)

Love Me, Love My Tiger (1)
Lovesick (1)
Ohh What You Do! (1)
Please Don't Stop (1)
Remember Me (2)

Steady Date (1)
Tiger Rag (1)
Turn Me Loose (1) 9
You Excite Me (2)
You'll Never Tame Me (2)

FABIAN, Lara '00

Born in January 1970 in Etterbeek, Belgium; raised in Italy. Female singer/songwriter.

| 6/17/00 | 85 | 16 | © | Lara Fabian | $10 Columbia 69053 |

Adagio
Broken Vow

Givin' Up On You
I Am Who I Am

I Will Love Again 32
Love By Grace

Part Of Me
Till I Get Over You

To Love Again (Si Tu M'Aimes)
Yeliel (My Angel)

You Are My Heart
You're Not From Here

FABRIC, Bent, and His Piano '63

Born Bent Fabricius-Bjerre on 12/7/24 in Copenhagen, Denmark. Male pianist.

| 10/27/62+ | 13 | 39 | | Alley Cat | [I] $25 Atco 148 |

Across The Alley From The Alamo
Alley Cat 7

Baby Won't You Please Come Home
Catsanova Walk

Comme Ci, Comme Ca
Delilah
Early Morning In Copenhagen

In The Arms Of My Love
Markin' Time
Symphony

Trudie
You Made Me Love You

FABULOUS POODLES '79

Rock group from England: Tony DeMeur (vocals, guitar), Bobby Valentino (violin), Richie Robertson (bass) and Bryn Burrows (drums).

| 2/10/79 | 61 | 17 | | 1 Mirror Stars | $12 Epic 35666 |
| 12/1/79 | 185 | 3 | | 2 Think Pink | $12 Epic 36256 |

Anna Rexia (2)
Any Port In A Storm (2)
B Movies (1)
Bike Blood (2)

Bionic Man (2)
Cherchez La Femme (1)
Chicago Boxcar (1)
Cossack Cowboy (1)

(Hollywood) Dragnet (2)
Man With Money (2)
Mirror Star (1) 81
Mr. Mike (1)

Oh Cheryl (1)
Pink City Twist (2)
Roll Your Own (1)
Suicide Bridge (2)

Tit Photographer Blues (1)
Toytown People (1)
Vampire Rock (2)
Work Shy (1)

You Wouldn't Listen (2)

FABULOUS RHINESTONES, The '72

Rock trio from Chicago: Kal David (vocals, guitar), Harvey Brooks (bass) and Martin Grebb (vocals, keyboards). David was with **Illinois Speed Press**. Grebb was with **The Buckinghams**.

| 7/29/72 | 193 | 6 | | 1 The Fabulous Rhinestones | $15 Just Sunshine 1 |
| 9/22/73 | 193 | 3 | | 2 Freewheelin' | $15 Just Sunshine 9 |

Big Indian (1)
Do It Like Ya' Mean It (2)
Down To The City (2)
Easy As You Make It (1)

Free (1)
Freewheelin' (2)
Go With Change (2)
Harmonize (1)

Hurt Somebody (2)
Just Can't Turn My Back On You (1)
Live It Out To The End (1)

Living On My Own Time (1)
Nothing New (1)
Positive Direction (1)
Roots With You, Girl (2)

Vicious Circle (2)
What A Wonderful Thing We Have (1) 78
What Becomes Of Your Life (2)

Whitecaps (2)

FABULOUS THUNDERBIRDS, The '86

Male blues-rock group from Austin, Texas: Kim Wilson (vocals, harmonica), **Jimmie Vaughan** (guitar; older brother of **Stevie Ray Vaughan**), Keith Ferguson (bass) and Fran Christina (drums). Preston Hubbard replaced Ferguson in late 1981. Jimmie appeared in the 1989 movie *Great Balls Of Fire* and recorded in **The Vaughan Brothers** in 1990. Disbanded in June 1990. Reorganized in 1991 with Wilson, Hubbard, Christina and guitarists Duke Robillard and Kid Bangham. Ferguson died of liver failure on 4/29/97 (age 49).

3/28/81	176	7	©	1 Butt Rockin'	$12 Chrysalis 1319
3/15/86	13	53	▲ ©	2 Tuff Enuff	$10 CBS Associated 40304
7/18/87	49	15	©	3 Hot Number	$10 CBS Associated 40818
5/6/89	118	7	©	4 Powerful Stuff	$10 CBS Associated 45094

Amnesia (2)
Cherry Pink And Apple Blossom White (1)
Close Together (4)
Don't Bother Tryin' To Steal Her Love (3)
Down At Antones (2)
Emergency (4)
Give Me All Your Lovin' (1)

Hot Number (3)
How Do You Spell Love (3)
I Believe I'm In Love (1)
I Don't Care (2)
I Hear You Knockin' (1)
I'm Sorry (1)
In Orbit (1)
It Comes To Me Naturally (3)
It Takes A Big Man To Cry (3)

Knock Yourself Out (4)
Look At That (2)
Love In Common (3)
Mathilda (1)
Mistake Number 1 (4)
Now Loosen Up Baby (4)
One Night Stand (4)
One's Too Many (1)
Powerful Stuff (4) 65

Rainin' In My Heart (4)
Rock This Place (4)
Roll, Roll, Roll (1)
She's Hot (4)
Sofa Circuit (3)
Stand Back (3) 76
Streets Of Gold (3)
Tell Me (2)
Tell Me Why (1)

Tip On In (1)
True Love (2)
Tuff Enuff (2) 10
Two Time My Lovin' (2)
Wasted Tears (3)
Why Get Up (2)
Wrap It Up (2) 50

FACEMOB '96

Rap group from Houston: Harold Armstrong, Devon Copeland, Gene Dorcy, Loretta Dorsey and Rod Smith.

| 8/24/96 | 51 | 7 | © | The Other Side Of The Law | $10 Interface 41336 |

Bank Robbery
Black Woman

Da Coldest
In The Flesh

Millions
Other Side

Respect Rude
Rivals

Stay True
Tales From Tha Hood

FACES '72

British rock group formed in 1969 by former **Small Faces** members **Ronnie Lane** (bass), **Ian McLagan** (organ) and Kenney Jones (drums) with former **Jeff Beck** Group members **Rod Stewart** (vocals) and **Ronnie Wood** (bass). Lane left in 1973; replaced by Tetsu Yamauchi (**Free**). Disbanded in late 1975. Wood joined **The Rolling Stones** in 1976. Jones joined **The Who** in 1978 and formed **The Law** in 1991. Lane died on 6/4/97 (age 51) of multiple sclerosis.

DEBUT	PEAK	WKS	RIAA	CD				$	Label & Number
4/18/70	119	12		© 1	First Step			$20	Warner 1851

SMALL FACES

3/13/71	29	19		© 2	Long Player			$20	Warner 1892
12/18/71+	6	24	● © 3	A Nod Is As Good As A Wink...To A Blind Horse			$20	Warner 2574
4/21/73	21	16		© 4	Ooh La La			$15	Warner 2665
1/5/74	63	11		© 5	Rod Stewart/Faces Live - Coast To Coast Overture and Beginners [L]			$15	Mercury 697

ROD STEWART/FACES

Amazing Grace (medley) (5)
Angel (5)
Around The Plynth (1)
Bad 'N' Ruin (2)
Borstal Boys (4,5)
Cindy Incidentally (4) *48*
Cut Across Shorty (5)
Debris (3)
Devotion (1)
Every Picture Tells A Story (medley) (5)
Flags And Banners (4)
Fly In The Ointment (4)
Flying (1)
Glad And Sorry (4)
Had Me A Real Good Time (2)
I Feel So Good (2)
I Wish It Would Rain (5)
I'd Rather Go Blind (5)
If I'm On The Late Side (4)
It's All Over Now (5)
Jealous Guy (5)
Jerusalem (2)
Just Another Honky (4)
Last Orders Please (3)
Looking Out The Window (1)
Love Lives Here (3)
Maybe I'm Amazed (2)
Memphis (3)
Miss Judy's Farm (3)
My Fault (4)
Nobody Knows (1)
On The Beach (2)
Ooh La La (4)
Pineapple And The Monkey (1)
Richmond (2)
Shake, Shudder, Shiver (1)
Silicone Grown (4)
Stay With Me (3,5) *17*
Stone (1)
Sweet Lady Mary (2)
Tell Everyone (2)
That's All You Need (3)
Three Button Hand Me Down (1)
Too Bad (3,5)
Wicked Messenger (1)
You're So Rude (3)

FACE TO FACE '84

Rock group from Boston: Laurie Sargent (vocals), brothers Angelo and Stuart Kimball (guitars), John Ryder (bass) and William Beard (drums).

| 6/16/84 | 126 | 16 | | 1 | Face To Face | | | $10 | Epic 38857 |
| 6/18/88 | 176 | 7 | | © 2 | One Big Day | | | $10 | Mercury 834376 |

All Because Of You (1)
As Forever As You (2)
Change In The Wind (2)
Day I Was Born (2)
Don't Talk Like That (1)
Ever Since Eve (Blood Gone Bad) (2)
Face In Front Of Mine (1)
Grass Grows Greener (2)
Heaven On Earth (1)
I Believe In You (2)
Never Had A Reason (2)
Out Of My Hands (1)
Over The Edge (1)
Pictures Of You (1)
Place Called Home (2)
She's A Contradiction (2)
Some Stories (2)
10-9-8 (1) *38*
Under The Gun (1)
Wreckless Heart (1)

FACE TO FACE '96

Punk-rock group from Los Angeles: Trevor Keith (vocals), Chad Yaro (guitar), Scott Shiflett (bass) and Rob Kurth (drums). Pete Parada replaced Kurth in 1999.

| 9/28/96 | 139 | 2 | | © 1 | Face To Face | | | $10 | A&M 540601 |
| 8/14/99 | 162 | 1 | | © 2 | Ignorance Is Bliss | | | $10 | Lady Luck 78048 |

(a)Pathetic (2)
Blind (1)
Burden (1)
Can't Change The World (1)
Complicated (1)
Devil You Know (God Is A Man) (2)
Everyone Hates A Know-It-All (2)
Everything's Your Fault (1)
Falling (1)
Handout (1)
Heart Of Hearts (2)
I Know What You Are (2)
I Won't Lie Down (1)
In Harms Way (2)
Lost (2)
Maybe Next Time (2)
Nearly Impossible (2)
Ordinary (1)
Overcome (2)
Prodigal (2)
Put You In Your Place (1)
Resignation (1)
Run In Circles (2)
Take It Back (1)
Walk The Walk (1)

FACTS OF LIFE '77

R&B vocal trio: Jean Davis (younger sister of **Tyrone Davis**), Keith William (of The Flamingos) and Chuck Carter.

| 4/9/77 | 146 | 7 | | | Sometimes | | | $12 | Kayvette 802 |

Bitter Woman
Caught In The Act (Of Getting It On)
Givin' Me Your Love
Hundred Pounds Of Pain
Looks Like We Made It
Lost Inside Of You
Love Is The Final Truth
Sometimes *31*
That Kind Of Fire
Uphill Places Of Mind
What Would Your Mama Say?

FAGEN, Donald '93

Born on 1/10/48 in Passaic, New Jersey. Pop-rock singer/keyboardist. Member of **Steely Dan**.

| 10/30/82 | 11 | 27 | ▲ © 1 | The Nightfly | | | $10 | Warner 23696 |

an account of one night at the fictional jazz radio station WJAZ

| 6/12/93 | 10 | 19 | ● © 2 | Kamakiriad | | | $10 | Reprise 45230 |

Countermoon (2)
Florida Room (2)
Goodbye Look (1)
Green Flower Street (1)
I.G.Y. (What A Beautiful World) (1) *26*
Maxine (1)
New Frontier (1) *70*
Nightfly, The (1)
On The Dunes (2)
Ruby Baby (1)
Snowbound (2)
Springtime (2)
Teahouse On The Tracks (2)
Tomorrow's Girls (2)
Trans-Island Skyway (2)
Walk Between Raindrops (1)

FAIRGROUND ATTRACTION '89

Pop group from England: Eddi Reader (female vocals), Mark Nevin (guitar), Simon Edwards (bass) and Roy Dodds (drums).

| 1/21/89 | 137 | 11 | | © | The First Of A Million Kisses | | | $10 | RCA 8596 |

Allelujah
Clare
Comedy Waltz
Fairground Attraction
Find My Love
Moon Is Mine
Moon On The Rain
Perfect *80*
Smile In A Whisper
Station Street
Whispers
Wind Knows My Name

FAIRPORT CONVENTION '75

Folk-rock group from London. Varying membership included vocalists **Sandy Denny** and **Ian Matthews** (1967-69) and guitarist **Richard Thompson** (1967-71). Denny died of a brain hemorrhage on 4/21/78 (age 37).

| 12/4/71 | 200 | 1 | | 1 | Angel Delight | | | $20 | A&M 4319 |
| 3/25/72 | 195 | 3 | | 2 | "Babbacombe" Lee | | | $20 | A&M 4333 |

based on the story of condemned prisoner John Lee

| 8/16/75 | 143 | 8 | | 3 | Rising For The Moon | | | $15 | Island 9313 |

After Halloween (3)
Angel Delight (1)
Banks Of The Sweet Primroses (1)
Bonny Black Hare (1)
Bridge Over The River Ash (1)
Cuckoo's Nest (medley) (1)
Dawn (3)
Hardiman The Fiddler (medley) (1)
Iron Lion (3)
John Babbacombe Lee (2)
Journeyman's Grace (1)
Let It Go (3)
Lord Marlborough (1)
Night-Time Girl (3)
One More Chance (3)
Papa Stoor (medley) (1)
Restless (3)
Rising For The Moon (3)
Sickness & Diseases (1)
Sir William Gower (1)
Stranger To Himself (3)
What Is True? (3)
White Dress (3)
Wizard Of The Worldly Game (1)

FAITH, Percy ★124★   '61

Born on 4/7/08 in Toronto. Died of cancer on 2/9/76 (age 67). Orchestra leader. Moved to the U.S. in 1940. Joined Columbia Records in 1950 as conductor/arranger. Also see **Mary Stuart**

1)Camelot 2)Bouquet 3)Jealousy 4)My Fair Lady 5)Themes For Young Lovers

DEBUT	PEAK	WKS		CD	#	Album Title	Sym	$	Label & Number
7/28/56	18	2		©	1	Passport To Romance	[I]	$20	Columbia 880
5/6/57	8	2		©	2	My Fair Lady	[I]	$20	Columbia 895
5/25/59	17	14			3	Porgy And Bess	[I]	$15	Columbia 1298 / 8105
1/11/60	7	17	●	©	4	Bouquet	[I]	$15	Columbia 1322 / 8124
11/28/60+	7	15		©	5	Jealousy	[I]	$15	Columbia 1501 / 8292
1/9/61	6	23		©	6	Camelot	[I]	$15	Columbia 1570 / 8370
10/9/61	38	7		©	7	Mucho Gusto! More Music Of Mexico	[I]	$15	Columbia 1639 / 8439
4/14/62	26	6		©	8	Bouquet Of Love	[I]	$15	Columbia 1681 / 8481
9/29/62	105	5			9	The Music Of Brazil!	[I]	$15	Columbia 1822 / 8622
6/22/63	12	36	●	©	10	Themes For Young Lovers	[I]	$15	Columbia 2023 / 8823
10/19/63	80	15			11	Shangri-La!	[I]	$15	Columbia 2024 / 8824
2/15/64	103	12			12	Great Folk Themes	[I]	$15	Columbia 2108 / 8908
5/30/64	110	7			13	More Themes for Young Lovers	[I]	$15	Columbia 2167 / 8967
12/19/64	34[X]	2			14	Music Of Christmas	[X-I]	$15	Columbia 1381 / 8176

first released in 1954 on Columbia 588; above release issued in 1959 with a new album cover

DEBUT	PEAK	WKS		CD	#	Album Title	Sym	$	Label & Number
12/4/65	101	5			15	Broadway Bouquet	[I]	$15	Columbia 2356 / 9156
12/17/66	24[X]	7		©	16	Christmas Is...	[X]	$15	Columbia 2577 / 9377

Christmas charts: 24/'66, 46/'67, 27/'68

DEBUT	PEAK	WKS		CD	#	Album Title	Sym	$	Label & Number
5/27/67	152	5			17	The Academy Award Winner and Other Great Movie Themes	[I]	$15	Columbia 2650 / 9450
9/16/67	111	17			18	Today's Themes For Young Lovers		$15	Columbia 2704 / 9504
3/23/68	121	22			19	For Those In Love		$15	Columbia 2810 / 9610
9/21/68	95	11			20	Angel Of The Morning (Hit Themes For Young Lovers)		$15	Columbia 9706
2/15/69	88	14			21	Those Were The Days		$15	Columbia 9762
5/31/69	194	4			22	Windmills Of Your Mind	[I]	$15	Columbia 9835
9/27/69	134	11			23	Love Theme From "Romeo & Juliet"		$15	Columbia 9906
2/14/70	88	14			24	Leaving On A Jet Plane		$15	Columbia 9983
6/13/70	196	2			25	Held Over! Today's Great Movie Themes	[I]	$15	Columbia 1019
10/17/70	179	4			26	The Beatles Album	[I]	$15	Columbia 30097
1/23/71	200	2			27	A Time For Love	[K]	$20	Columbia 30330 [2]
2/27/71	198	2			28	I Think I Love You	[I]	$15	Columbia 30502
7/31/71	184	5			29	Black Magic Woman	[I]	$15	Columbia 30800
12/18/71+	186	6			30	Jesus Christ, Superstar	[I]	$15	Columbia 31042
4/1/72	176	6			31	Joy	[I]	$15	Columbia 31301
9/23/72	197	4			32	Day By Day		$15	Columbia 31627

FAITH, Percy — Cont'd

Man And A Woman (17,27)
Man Without Love (Quando M'Innamoro) (20)
March (6)
March Of Siamese Children (11)
Maria Elena (7)
Mary In The Morning (18)
Mary, Queen Of Scots (This Way Mary), Love Theme From (31)
Maxixe (Dengoza) (9)
Merry-Go-Round (Complainte De La Butte) (1)
Michael Row The Boat (12)
Michelle (26)
Midnight Cowboy (25)
Minute Samba (9)
Moon Of Manakoora (11)
More Than You Know (5)
Most Beautiful Girl In The World (5)
Moulin Rouge, Song From (4)
Mountain High, Valley Low (11)
Mrs. Robinson (20)
Mucho Gusto (7)
Music Until Midnight (Lullaby For Adults Only) (8)
My Coloring Book (10)
My Man's Gone Now (3)
My Special Angel (21)
My Sweet Lord (28)
Never Can Say Goodbye (29)
Never My Love (19)

Norwegian Wood (26)
O Come, All Ye Faithful (Adeste Fideles) (14)
O Holy Night (14)
O Lawd I'm On My Way (3)
O Little Town Of Bethlehem (medley) (14)
Oh I Can't Sit Down (3)
Old Fashioned Love Song (31)
On Broadway (10,27)
On The Street Where You Live (2)
Once Upon A Time (15)
One (23)
Oscar (Maybe September), Song From The (17)
Our Day Will Come (10,27)
Out Of This World (8)
Oye Como Va (29)
Patton Theme (25)
Perfidia (7)
Pilate's Dream (30)
Popsicles And Icicles (13)
Portuguese Washerwomen (Les Lavandieres Du Portugal) (1)
Promises, Promises (21)
Quiet Day (21)
Quiet Thing (15)
Rain In Spain (2)
Raindrops Keep Fallin' On My Head (24,25)
Release Me (18)
Return To Paradise (11)

Reza (Ray-za) (29)
Rhythm Of The Rain (10)
Right As The Rain (5)
Romeo And Juliet, Love Theme From (23)
Rose Garden (28)
Rudolph, The Red-Nosed Reindeer (16)
Sand Pebbles (And We Were Lovers), Theme From The (17)
Sayonara (11)
Scalinatella (Stay After School) (1)
Scarborough Fair/Canticle (20)
See The Funny Little Clown (13)
Shaft, Theme From (31)
Shangri-La (11)
Show Me (2)
Sierra Madre (Luna Gitana) (1)
Silent Night, Holy Night (14)
Silver Bells (16)
Simon Zealotes (30)
Simple Joys Of Maidenhood (6)
Since I Fell For You (13)
Sloop John B. (12)
Soft Lights And Sweet Music (8)
Solitude (4)
Sombra (Merveilleux) (1)
Somethin' Stupid (18)
Something (24,26)
Somewhere (15)
Somewhere, My Love (17)

Song Of India (11)
Song Sung Blue (32)
Sophisticated Lady (5)
Spanish Harlem (27)
Speak Low (4)
Spinning Wheel (23)
Star! (22)
Stella By Starlight (8)
Stormy (21)
Stranger In Paradise (11)
Strawberry Woman And The Crab Man (3)
Sugar Shack (13)
Summer Of '42 (The Summer Knows), Theme From (31)
Summer Place, Theme From A (23) *1*
Summertime (3)
Sun King (29)
Sunny (19,27)
Sunrise, Sunset (medley) (15,27,31)
Superstar (30)
Sweetest Sounds (15)
Tell Her (Every Girl Likes To Be Told) (20)
Temple, The (30)
Temptation (5)
Tenderly (4)
That Old Black Magic (5)
Then You May Take Me To The Fair (6)
There's A Boat That's Leavin' Soon For New York (3)

There's A Kind Of Hush (All Over The World) (18)
This Guy's In Love With You (20)
This Hotel (17)
This Is My Song (17)
This Land Is Your Land (12)
This Train (12)
Those Were The Days (21)
Threepenny Opera (Moritat), Theme From The (1)
Through The Eyes Of A Child (Un Jour, Un Enfant) (23)
Tia Juana (5)
Tico-Tico (9)
Time For Livin' (20)
Time For Love (17,27)
Too Young (32)
Tres (29)
Trial Before Pilate (30)
True Grit (25)
Tu Sabes (29)
Um, Um, Um, Um, Um, Um (13)
Up On The Roof (10,27)
Viva Tirado (29)
Wailing Of The Willow (29)
Waitin' ('Round The Bend) (19)
Wanting You (24)
Wave (29)
We Need A Little Christmas (16)
Wedding Bell Blues (24)
What Are You Doing The Rest Of Your Life (25)

What Do The Simple Folks Do (6)
What Kind Of Fool Am I? (15,27)
What's The Buzz (30)
Where Or When (5)
White Christmas (16)
Who Can I Turn To (When Nobody Needs Me) (15)
Windmills Of Your Mind (22)
Windy (18,27)
Wishing Doll (17)
With A Little Bit Of Luck (2) *82*
Without Her (23)
Without You (3)
Wives And Lovers (13)
Woman Is A Sometime Thing (3)
World Of Whispers (18)
Wouldn't It Be Lovely (2)
Yellow Days (18)
Yester-Me, Yester-You, Yesterday (24)
Yesterday (26)
You Don't Own Me (13)
Young Lovers, Theme For (10) *35*
"Z" (To Yelasto Pedi), Theme From (25)
Zorba (21)

FAITH — see EVANS, Faith

FAITHFULL, Marianne '65

Born on 12/29/46 in Hampstead, London. Singer/actress. Involved in a long, tumultuous relationship with **Mick Jagger**. Acted in several stage and screen productions.

DEBUT	PEAK	WKS	CD	#	Album Title	$	Label & Number
6/5/65	12	31		1	Marianne Faithfull	$25	London 423
12/25/65+	81	16		2	Go Away From My World	$25	London 452
11/19/66	147	2		3	Faithful Forever...	$25	London 482
4/5/69	171	10	©	4	Marianne Faithfull's Greatest Hits	[G] $20	London 547
2/2/80	82	15	©	5	Broken English	$12	Island 9570
10/17/81	104	9		6	Dangerous Acquaintances	$12	Island 9648
3/26/83	107	7	©	7	A Child's Adventure	$12	Island 90066
7/7/90	160	9	©	8	Blazing Away	[L] $10	Island 842794

recorded on 11/25/89 at St. Anne's Cathedral in New York City

As Tears Go By (1,4,8) *22*
Ashes In My Hand (7)
Ballad Of Lucy Jordan (5,8)
Blazing Away (8)
Blue Millionaire (7)
Brain Drain (5)
Broken English (5,8)
Come And Stay With Me (1,4) *26*
Come My Way (2)
Counting (7)
Easy In The City (6)
Eye Communication (6)

Falling From Grace (7)
First Time (3)
For Beautie's Sake (6)
Go Away From My World (2,4) *89*
Guilt (5,8)
He'll Come Back To Me (1)
How Should True Love (2)
I Have A Love (3)
I'm A Loser (1)
I'm The Sky (3)
If I Never Get To Love You (1)
In My Time Of Sorrow (1,4)

In The Night Time (3)
Intrigue (6)
Ireland (7)
Is This What I Get For Loving You? (4)
Last Thing On My Mind (2)
Les Prisons Du Roy (8)
Lucky Girl (3)
Lullabye (2)
Mary Ann (2)
Monday Monday (3,4)
Morning Come (7)
Ne Me Quitte Pas (3)

North Country Maid (2)
Paris Bells (1)
Plaisir D'Amour (1)
Running For Our Lives (7)
Sally Free And Easy (2)
Scarborough Fair (2,4)
She Moved Through The Fair (8)
She's Got A Problem (7)
Sister Morphine (8)
So Sad (4)
Some Other Spring (3)
Strange One (6)

Strange Weather (8)
Summer Nights (2,4) *24*
Sweetheart (6)
Tenderness (6)
That's Right Baby (3)
This Little Bird (1,4) *32*
Time Takes Time (1)
Times Square (7)
Tomorrow's Calling (3,4)
Truth Bitter Truth (6)
What Have I Done Wrong (1)
What Have They Done To The Rain (1)

What's The Hurry? (5)
When I Find My Life (8)
Why'd Ya Do It? (5,8)
Wild Mountain Tyme (2)
Witches' Song (5)
With You In Mind (3)
Working Class Hero (5,8)
Yesterday (2,4)

FAITH, HOPE & CHARITY '75

R&B vocal trio from Tampa, Florida: Brenda Hilliard, Albert Bailey and Diane Destry.

DEBUT	PEAK	WKS	#	Album Title	$	Label & Number
8/30/75	100	14		Faith, Hope & Charity	$12	RCA Victor 1100

Disco Dan
Don't Go Looking For Love

Find A Way
Just One Look

Let's Go To The Disco
Little Bit Of Love

Mellow Me
Rescue Me

To Each His Own *50*

FAITH NO MORE '90

Rock group from San Francisco: Michael Patton (vocals), Jim Martin (guitar), Roddy Bottum (keyboards), Billy Gould (bass) and Mike Bordin (drums). Dean Menta replaced Martin in 1994. Jon Hudson replaced Menta in 1995. Patton is also leader of **Mr. Bungle**.

DEBUT	PEAK	WKS	RIAA	CD	#	Album Title	$	Label & Number
2/24/90	11	60	▲	©	1	The Real Thing	$10	Slash 25878
7/4/92	10	19	●	©	2	Angel Dust	$10	Slash 26785
4/15/95	31	8		©	3	King For A Day/Fool For A Lifetime	$10	Slash 45723
6/21/97	41	8		©	4	Album Of The Year	$10	Slash 46629

Ashes To Ashes (4)
Be Aggressive (2)
Caffeine (2)
Caralho Voador (3)
Collision (4)
Crack Hitler (2)
Cuckoo For Caca (3)
Digging The Grave (3)
Edge Of The World (1)

Epic (1) *9*
Everything's Ruined (2)
Evidence (3)
Falling To Pieces (1) *92*
From Out Of Nowhere (1)
Gentle Art Of Making Enemies (3)
Get Out (3)
Got That Feeling (4)

Helpless (3)
Home Sick Home (4)
Jizzlobber (2)
Just A Man (3)
Kindergarten (2)
King For A Day (3)
Land Of Sunshine (2)
Last Cup Of Sorrow (4)
Last To Know (3)

Malpractice (2)
MidLife Crisis (2)
Midnight Cowboy (2)
Morning After (1)
Mouth To Mouth (4)
Naked In Front Of The Computer (4)
Paths Of Glory (4)
Pristina (4)

RV (2)
Real Thing (1)
Ricochet (4)
She Loves Me Not (4)
Small Victory (2)
Smaller And Smaller (2)
Star A.D. (3)
Stripsearch (4)
Surprise! You're Dead! (1)

Take This Bottle (3)
Ugly In The Morning (3)
Underwater Love (1)
War Pigs (1)
What A Day (3)
Woodpecker From Mars (1)
Zombie Eaters (1)

FALCO '86

Born Johann Holzel on 2/19/57 in Vienna, Austria. Died in a car crash on 2/6/98 (age 40). Male singer/songwriter.

5/7/83	64	13			1 Einzelhaft			$10	A&M 4951
3/1/86	3	27	●	©	2 **Falco 3**			$10	A&M 5105

America (2) Ganz Wien (2) Jeanny (2) Maschine Brennt (1) Nothin' Sweeter Than Arabia (2) **Vienna Calling** (2) *18*
Auf Der Flucht (1) Helden Von Heute (1) Macho Macho (1) Munich Girls (Looking For Love) **Rock Me Amadeus** (2) *1* Zuviel Hitze (1)
Der Kommissar (1) Hinter Uns Die Sintflut (1) Manner Des Westens - Any (2) Siebzehn Jahr (1)
Einzelhaft (1) It's All Over Now, Baby Blue (2) Kind Of Land (1) Nie Mehr Schule (1) Tango The Night (2)

FÄLTSKOG, Agnetha '83

Born on 4/5/50 in Jonkoping, Sweden. Member of **Abba**.

9/17/83	102	11		©	Wrap Your Arms Around Me			$10	Polydor 813242

Can't Shake Loose *29* Man Stand By My Side To Love
Heat Is On Mr. Persuasion Stay Wrap Your Arms Around Me
I Wish Tonight Could Last Once Burned, Twice Shy Take Good Care Of Your
Forever Shame Children

FAME, Georgie '65

Born Clive Powell on 6/26/43 in Leigh, Lancashire, England. Began as a pianist with Billy Fury's backup group, The Blue Flames.

5/1/65	137	3			1 Yeh Yeh			$30	Imperial 12282
5/11/68	185	4			2 The Ballad Of Bonnie And Clyde			$25	Epic 26368
1/27/96	55	11		©	3 How Long Has This Been Going On		[L]	$10	Verve 529136

VAN MORRISON with Georgie Fame & Friends
recorded on 5/3/95 at Ronnie Scott's Club in London

All Saint's Day (3) Centerpiece (3) Heathrow Shuffle (3) Mellow Yellow (2) Preach And Teach (1) That's Life (3)
Ask Me Nice (2) Don't Worry About A Thing (3) How Long Has This Been Monkey Time (1) Pride And Joy (1) This Is Always (2)
Ballad Of Bonnie And Clyde Early In The Morning (3) Going On? (3) Monkeying Around (1) Sack O' Woe (3) When I'm Sixty-Four (1)
(2) *7* Exactly Like You (2) I Love The Life I Live (1) Moondance (3) Side By Side (2) Who Can I Turn To? (2)
Blue Prelude (2) Get On The Right Track, Baby I Will Be There (3) New Symphony Sid (3) Someone To Watch Over Me **Yeh, Yeh** (1) *21*
Blues In The Night (3) (1) I'm In The Mood For Love (1) Pink Champagne (1) (2) Your Mind Is On Vacation (3)
Bullets La Verne (2) Gimme That Wine (1) Let The Sun Shine In (1) Point Of No Return (1) St. James Infirmary (2)

FAMILY '72

Rock group from England: Roger Chapman (vocals), John Wetton (guitar, keyboards; **King Crimson**, **Uriah Heep**, **U.K.**, **Asia**), Charlie Whitney (guitar), John Palmer (keyboards) and Rob Townsend (drums).

2/5/72	177	7		©	1 Fearless			$15	United Artists 5562
10/28/72	183	5		©	2 Bandstand			$15	United Artists 5644

Between Blue And Me (1) Burlesque (2) Crinkly Grin (1) My Friend The Sun (2) Spanish Tide (1)
Blind (1) Burning Bridges (1) Dark Eyes (2) Ready To Go (2) Take Your Partners (1)
Bolero Babe (2) Children (1) Glove (2) Sat'd'y Barfly (1) Top Of The Hill (2)
Broken Nose (2) Coronation (2) Larf And Sing (1) Save Some For Thee (1)

FAMILY, The '85

Dance group from Minneapolis: Susannah Melvoin (female vocals), Paul Peterson (vocals, keyboards), Jerome Benton (percussion), Eric Leeds (sax) and Jellybean Johnson (drums). Melvoin is the twin sister of Wendy Melvoin (**Prince**'s Revolution, **Wendy & Lisa**); their father is jazz pianist Mike Melvoin (**The Plastic Cow**) and their brother was the late Jonathan Melvoin (**The Smashing Pumpkins**). Peterson, Benton and Johnson were members of **The Time**.

9/7/85	62	22			The Family			$10	Paisley Park 25322

Desire Mutiny River Run Dry Susannah's Pajamas
High Fashion Nothing Compares 2 U **Screams Of Passion** *63* Yes

FANNY '72

Female rock group from Los Angeles: sisters June (vocals, guitar) and Jean (vocals, bass) Millington, Nicole Barclay (keyboards) and Alice DeBuhr (drums).

10/23/71	150	7			1 Charity Ball			$15	Reprise 6456
4/1/72	135	6			2 Fanny Hill			$15	Reprise 2058

Ain't That Peculiar (2) *85* **Charity Ball** (1) *40* Little While Later (1) Soul Child (1) Thinking Of You (1) You're The One (1)
Blind Alley (2) First Time (2) Person Like You (1) Sound And The Fury (2) What Kind Of Lover (1) You've Got A Home (2)
Borrowed Time (2) Hey Bulldog (2) Place In The Country (1) Special Care (1) What's Wrong With Me? (1)
Cat Fever (1) Knock On My Door (2) Rock Bottom Blues (2) Think About The Children (2) Wonderful Feeling (1)

FANTASTIC FOUR '75

R&B vocal group from Detroit: James Epps, Joseph Pruitt, Cleveland Horne and Ernest Newsome. Horne died of a heart attack on 4/13/2000.

6/21/75	99	16			Alvin Stone (The Birth And Death Of A Gangster)			$15	Westbound 201

Alvin Stone (The Birth & County Line Let This Moment Last Forever Words
Death Of A Gangster) *74* Have A Little Mercy My Love Won't Stop At Nothing

FANTASY '70

Rock group from Miami: Vincent DeMeo (male vocals, guitar), Lydia Miller (female vocals), Mario Russo (organ), David Robbins (bass) and Greg Kimple (drums).

8/15/70	194	3			Fantasy			$20	Liberty 7643

Circus Of Invisible Men Happy Understand What's Next
Come **Stoned Cowboy** *77* Wages Of Sin

FARGO, Donna '72

Born Yvonne Vaughan on 11/10/45 in Mt. Airy, North Carolina. Country singer/songwriter.

7/15/72	47	43	●	©	1 The Happiest Girl In The Whole U.S.A.			$15	Dot 26000
3/17/73	104	11			2 My Second Album			$15	Dot 26006

Awareness Of Nothing (1) **Funny Face** (1) *5* Hot Diggity Dog (2) It Would Have Been Just Manhattan, Kansas (1) You Don't Mess Around With
Daddy Dumplin' (1) **Happiest Girl In The Whole** How Close You Came (To Perfect (1) Society's Got Us (1) Jim (1)
Don't Be Angry (2) **U.S.A.** (1) *11* Being Gone) (1) Johnny B. Goode (1) Song I Can Sing (2) **You Were Always There** (2) *93*
Forever Is As Far As I Could Go Have Yourself A Time (2) How Would I (2) Little Somethin' (To Hang On **Superman** (2) *41*
(2) He Can Have All He Wants (2) I'd Love You To Want Me (2) To) (1)

FARQUAHR '70

Rock group from New Haven, Connecticut: brothers Barnswallow, Hummingbird, Condor and Flamingo Farquahr. All play guitar and all share vocals.

12/5/70	195	3			Farquahr			$15	Elektra 74083

Babe In The Woods Hanging On By A Thread Just For Kings Much Too Nice A Day Peace In Mind
Dear John Deere Holy Moses Moonrider My Island Silver Spoons Start Living
  Streets Of Montreal

DEBUT	PEAK	WKS	RIAA	CD	ARTIST — Album Title	Catalog	Sym	$	Label & Number

FARRELL, Eileen '61
Born on 2/13/20 in Willimantic, Connecticut. Opera singer.

| 2/13/61 | 15 | 17 | | © | I've Got A Right To Sing The Blues | | | $25 | Columbia 1465 |

Blues In The Night / Ev'rytime / Glad To Be Unhappy / He Was Too Good To Me / I Gotta Right To Sing The Blues / I'm Old Fashioned / Looking For A Boy / Old Devil Moon / On The Sunny Side Of The Street / September Song / Supper Time / Ten Cents A Dance

FARRELL, Joe — see BENSON, George

FARRENHEIT '87
Rock trio from Boston: Charlie Farren (vocals, guitar), David Heit (bass) and Muzz (drums). Farren was lead singer of the **Joe Perry Project**.

| 5/9/87 | 179 | 7 | | © | Farrenheit | | | $10 | Warner 25564 |

Bad Habit / Fool In Love / Goofy Boy / Impossible World / Lost In Loveland / New Days / Shine / Stand Out / Staying Together / Time Won't Wait / Wildness

FARRIS, Dionne '95
Born in Bordentown, New Jersey. R&B singer. Former member of **Arrested Development**.

| 3/4/95 | 57 | 20 | | © | Wild Seed - Wild Flower | | | $10 | Columbia 57359 |

Audition, The / Blackbird / Don't Ever Touch Me (Again) / 11th Hour / Find Your Way / Food For Thought / Human / **I Know 4** / Now Or Later / Old Ladies / Passion / Reality / Stop To Think / Water

FASTBALL '98
Rock trio from Austin, Texas: Miles Zuniga (vocals, guitar), Tony Scalzo (vocals, bass) and Joey Shuffield (drums).

| 3/28/98 | 29 | 52 | ▲ | © | 1 All The Pain Money Can Buy | | | $10 | Hollywood 62130 |
| 10/7/00 | 97 | 3 | | © | 2 The Harsh Light Of Day | | | $10 | Hollywood 62237 |

Better Than It Was (1) / Charlie, The Methadone Man (1) / Damaged Goods (1) / Dark Street (2) / Don't Give Up On Me (2) / Fire Escape (1) **86** / Funny How It Fades Away (2) / G.O.D. (Good Old Days) (1) / Goodbye (2) / Love Is Expensive And Free (2) / Morning Star (2) / Nowhere Road (1) / **Out Of My Head** (1) **20** / Slow Drag (1) / Sooner Or Later (1) / Sweetwater, Texas (1) / This Is Not My Life (2) / Time (2) / Vampires (2) / Warm Fuzzy Feeling (1) / Way, The (1) / Whatever Gets You On (2) / Which Way To The Top? (1) / Wind Me Up (2) / You're An Ocean (2)

FASTER PUSSYCAT '90
Hard-rock group from Los Angeles: Taime Downe (vocals), Greg Steele and Brent Muscat (guitars), Eric Stacy (bass) and Mark Michals (drums). Michals was replaced by Brett Bradshaw in early 1992. Group name taken from the 1965 action movie *Faster Pussycat! Kill! Kill!*.

8/29/87	97	35		©	1 Faster Pussycat			$10	Elektra 60730
9/23/89+	48	41	●	©	2 Wake Me When It's Over			$10	Elektra 60883
8/22/92	90	4		©	3 Whipped!			$10	Elektra 61124

Ain't No Way Around It (2) / Arizona Indian Doll (2) / Babylon (1) / Bathroom Wall (1) / Big Dictionary (3) / Body Thief (3) / Bottle In Front Of Me (1) / Cat Bash (3) / Cathouse (1) / City Has No Heart (1) / Cryin' Shame (1) / Don't Change That Song (1) / Friends (3) / Gonna Walk (2) / House Of Pain (2) **28** / Jack The Bastard (3) / Little Dove (2) / Loose Booty (3) / Madam Ruby's Love Boutique (3) / Maid In Wonderland (3) / Mr. Lovedog (3) / No Room For Emotion (1) / Nonstop To Nowhere (3) / Only Way Out (3) / Out With A Bang (3) / Poison Ivy (2) / Pulling Weeds (2) / Ship Rolls In (1) / Shooting You Down (1) / Slip Of The Tongue (2) / Smash Alley (1) / Tattoo (2) / Where There's A Whip There's A Way (2)

FASTWAY '83
Hard-rock group from England: David King (vocals), Fast Eddie Clarke (guitar), Charlie McCracken (bass) and Jerry Shirley (drums). Clarke was with **Motorhead**. Shirley was with **Humble Pie**.

5/28/83	31	32		©	1 Fastway			$10	Columbia 38662
7/21/84	59	14		©	2 All Fired Up			$10	Columbia 39373
11/22/86+	156	12		©	3 Trick Or Treat		C:#32/24 [S]	$10	Columbia 40549
4/22/89	135	10		©	4 On Target			$10	GWR 75411

After Midnight (3) / All Fired Up (2) / All I Need Is Your Love (1) / Another Day (1) / Change Of Heart (4) / Close Your Eyes (4) / Dead Or Alive (4) / Don't Stop The Fight (3) / Easy Livin' (1) / Feel Me, Touch Me (Do Anything You Want) (1) / Fine Line (4) / Get Tough (3) / Give It All You Got (1) / Give It Some Action (1) / Heft! (1,3) / Hold On To The Night (1) / Hung Up On Love (2) / Hurtin' Me (2) / If You Could See (2,3) / Let Him Rock (4) / Misunderstood (2) / Non-Stop Love (2) / Say What You Will (1) / She Is Danger (4) / Show Some Emotion (4) / Stand Up (1) / Station (2) / Steal The Show (2) / Stranger, The (2) / Tear Down The Walls (3) / Telephone (2) / Tell Me (2) / These Dreams (4) / Trick Or Treat (3) / Two Hearts (4) / We Become One (1) / You (4) / You Got Me Runnin' (1)

FATAL '98
Born Bruce Washington in New York City. Male rapper.

| 4/18/98 | 50 | 4 | | © | In The Line Of Fire | | | $10 | Relativity 1622 |

Everyday / Friday / Getto Star / I Know The Rules / M.O.B. / Outlaws / Take Your Time / Time's Wastin' / What's Your Life Worth? / World Is Changing

FATBACK '80
Funk group: Bill Curtis (vocals, drums), Johnny King (guitar), Saunders McCrae (keyboards), Earl Shelton, George Williams, George Adam and Richard Cromwell (horns) and Johnny Flippin (bass).

| 2/28/76 | 158 | 8 | | © | 1 Raising Hell | | | $15 | Event 6905 |
| 8/28/76 | 182 | 5 | | © | 2 Night Fever | | | $15 | Spring 6711 |

THE FATBACK BAND (above 2)

8/12/78	73	12			3 Fired Up 'N' Kickin'			$12	Spring 6718
9/29/79	89	12		©	4 Fatback XII			$12	Spring 6723
4/19/80	44	27	●	©	5 Hot Box			$12	Spring 6726
11/1/80	91	7		©	6 14 Karat			$12	Spring 6729
6/20/81	102	8		©	7 Tasty Jam			$12	Spring 6731
1/9/82	148	4		©	8 Gigolo			$12	Spring 6734

All Day (1) / Angel (6) / (Are You Ready) Do The Bus Stop (1) / At Last (3) / Backstrokin' (5) / Boogie Freak (3) / Booty, The (2) / Can't You See (3) / Chillin' Out (6) / Come And Get The Love (5) / Concrete Jungle (6) / December 1963 (Oh, What A Night) (2) / Disco Bass (4) / Disco Crazy (2) / Disco Queen (4) / Do It ('Til The Feelin' Runs Out) (8) / Get Out On The Dance Floor (3) / Get Ready For The Night (7) / Gigolo (8) / Gimme That Sweet Sweet Lovin' (4) / Gotta Get My Hands On Some (Money) (2) / Groovy Kind Of Day (1) / High Steppin' Lady (7) / Higher (8) / Hot Box (5) / I Can't Help Myself (Sugar Pie, Honey Bunch) (1) / I Like Girls (3) / I'm Fired Up (3) / I'm So In Love (8) / If That's The Way You Want It (2) / Joint (You And Me) (3) / Keep Your Fingers Out The Jam (7) / King Tim III (Personality Jock) (4) / Kool Whip (7) / Lady Groove (6) / Let's Do It Again (6) / Little Funky Dance (2) / Love In Perfect Harmony (4) / Love Spell (5) / Na Na, Hey Hey, Kiss Her Goodbye (8) / Night Fever (2) / No More Room For Dancing (2) / Oh Girl (8) / Party Time (1) / Put Your Love (In My Tender Care) (1) / Rockin' To The Beat (8) / Rub Down (8) / Snake (3) / Spanish Hustle (1) / Street Band (5) / Take It Any Way You Want It (7) / (To Be) Without Your Love (6) / Wanna Dance (Keep Up The Dance) (4) / You're My Candy Sweet (4) / Your Love Is Strange (6)

FAT BOYS '87
Rap trio from Brooklyn, New York: Mark "Prince Markie Dee" Morales, Darren "The Human Beat Box" Robinson and Damon "Kool Rock" Wimbley. Group starred in the 1987 movie *Disorderlies*. Robinson died of heart failure on 12/10/95 (age 28).

DEBUT	PEAK	WKS		CD	#	Album Title		$	Label & Number
1/5/85	48	40	●	©	1	Fat Boys		$10	Sutra 1015
8/31/85	63	33	●		2	The Fat Boys Are Back!		$10	Sutra 1016
5/24/86	62	19			3	Big & Beautiful		$10	Sutra 1017
6/13/87	8	49	▲	©	4	Crushin'		$10	Tin Pan Apple 831948
10/3/87	108	10		©	5	The Best Part Of The Fat Boys	[K]	$10	Sutra 1018
7/9/88	33	24	●	©	6	Coming Back Hard Again		$10	Tin Pan Apple 835809
10/28/89	175	3		©	7	On And On		$10	Tin Pan Apple 838867

All Day Lover (6) / All You Can Eat (5) / Are You Ready For Freddy (6) / Back & Forth (4) / Beat Box Is Rockin' (3) / Between The Sheets (4) / Big And Beautiful (3) / Big Daddy (6) / Boys Will Be Boys (4) / Braggin' (7) / Breakdown (3) / Can You Feel It (1) / Comin' Back Hard Again (6) / Crushin' (4) / Don't Be Stupid (2) / Don't Dog Me (1) / Double-O Fat Boys (7) / Falling In Love (4) / Fat Boys (1,5) / Fat Boys Are Back (2,5) / Fat Boys Dance (4) / Fat Boys Scratch (2) / Get Down (7) / Go For It (3) / Hard Core Reggae (2,5) / Hell, No! (4) / Human Beat Box (1,5) / Human Beat Box #2 (2) / Human Beat Box, Part 3 (3) / If It Ain't One Thing It's Anuddah (Bruddah) (7) / In The House (3,5) / It's Getting Hot (7) / Jail House Rap (1,5) / Jellyroll (6) / Just Loungin' (7) / Knock 'Em Out The Box (7) / Lie-z (7) / Louie, Louie (6) 89 / Making Noise (4) / My Nuts (medley) (4) / On And On (7) / Pig Feet (6) / Place To Be (1) / Powerlord (6) / Protect Yourself (medley) (4) / Pump It Up (2) / Rainy, Rainy (7) / Rap Symphony (In C-Minor) (4) / Rock 'N' Roll (2,5) / Rock Ruling (2) / Rock The House, Y'all (6) / School Days (7) / Sex Machine (3,5) / She's Hookin' (7) / Stick 'Em (1,5) / T'ings Nah Go So (7) / Trouble (7) / **Twist (Yo, Twist!)** (6) 16 / We Can Do This (6) / Wipeout (4) 12 / Yes, Yes, Y'all (2)

FATBOY SLIM '99
Born Norman Cook on 7/31/63 in Brighton, Sussex, England. Techno-house instrumentalist. Former member of **The Housemartins** and **Beats International**.

DEBUT	PEAK	WKS		CD	#	Album Title		$	Label & Number
11/7/98+	34	63	▲	©	1	You've Come A Long Way, Baby		$10	Skint 66247
4/8/00	195	1		©	2	The Fatboy Slim/Norman Cook Collection	[K]	$10	Hip-O 564787
4/15/00	173	3		©	3	On The Floor At The Boutique		$10	Skint 49130
11/25/00	51	5		©	4	Halfway Between The Gutter And The Stars		$10	Skint 50460

Acid 8000 (1) / Acid Enlightenment (3) / Apache (3) / Because I Got It Like That (3) / Break In (3) / Build It Up - Tear It Down (1,3) / Can You Feel It? (3) / Deaf Mick's Throwdown (3) / Demons (4) / Discositdown (3) / Drop The Hate (4) / Dub Be Good To Me (2) / E.V.A. (2) / Echo Chamber (2) / Everybody In The House (3) / Forget It (3) / Gangster Tripping (1) / Give Me My Auger Back (3) / I Left My Wallet In El Segundo (2) / I'm A Disco Dancer (3) / In Heaven (1) / Kalifornia (1) / Love Island (1) / Love Life (4) / Mad Flava (4) / Michael Jackson (3) / Payback (2) / Phun-Ky (3) / Post Punk Progression (3) / Praise You (1) 36 / Psyché Rock (2) / Psychopath (3) / Renegade Master (2) / Retox (4) / Right Here, Right Now (1) / **Rockafeller Skank** (1,3) 76 / Roll The Dice (2) / Song For Shelter (4) / Soul Surfing (1) / Star 69 (4) / Start An Avalanche (2) / Sun Doesn't Shine (2) / Sunset (Bird Of Prey) (4) / Talking Bout My Baby (4) / That Green Jesus (3) / Tribute To King Tubby (2) / Vol 1 Side 2 Track 2 (3) / Weapon Of Choice (4) / Won't Talk About It (2) / World Is Made Up Of This & That (2) / World's Made Up Of This & That (3) / Ya Mama (4) / You're Not From Brighton (1)

F.A.T.E. '00
Female R&B vocal trio from Jersey City, New Jersey: Tiffany Chisolm, Shaunesa Walker and Patricia McKelvin. F.A.T.E.: For All That's Endured.

DEBUT	PEAK	WKS		CD		Album Title		$	Label & Number
6/24/00	196	1		©		For All That's Endured		$10	Warner 47591

Bring Your Love / Fallin' / For Sure / Get Wit' Me / Hooked / I Don't Need Your Money / If I Tell You Yes / Just Because / No More Games / Soon As You Get Paid / They'll Never Be / Why Am I Holding On

FATES WARNING '88
Hard-rock group from Hartford, Connecticut: John Arch (vocals), Jim Matheos and Frank Aresti (guitars), Joe DiBiase (bass) and Steve Zimmerman (drums). By 1988, Ray Adler replaced Arch. By 1989, Mark Zonder replaced Zimmerman.

DEBUT	PEAK	WKS		CD	#	Album Title		$	Label & Number
2/7/87	191	4		©	1	Awaken The Guardian		$10	Enigma 73231
4/23/88	111	13		©	2	No Exit		$10	Enigma 73330
9/16/89	141	9		©	3	Perfect Symmetry		$10	Enigma 73408

Anarchy Divine (2) / Arena, The (3) / At Fates Hands (3) / Chasing Time (3) / Exodus (1) / Fata Morgana (1) / Giant's Lore (Heart Of Winter) (1) / Guardian (1) / In A Word (2) / Ivory Gate Of Dreams Medley (2) / No Exit (2) / Nothing Left To Say (3) / Part Of The Machine (3) / Prelude To Ruin (1) / Shades Of Heavenly Death (2) / Silent Cries (2) / Sorcerer, The (1) / Static Acts (3) / Through Different Eyes (3) / Time Long Past (1) / Valley Of The Dolls (1) / World Apart (3)

FATHER MC '91
Born Timothy Brown in New York City. Dancehall reggae singer.

DEBUT	PEAK	WKS		CD	#	Album Title		$	Label & Number
12/1/90+	62	30		©	1	Father's Day		$10	Uptown 10061
9/12/92+	185	3		©	2	Close To You		$10	Uptown 10542

Ain't It Funky (1) / All I Want (2) / Baby We Can Do It (2) / Close To You (2) / Dance 4 Me (1) / Do The One, Two (2) / **Everything's Gonna Be Alright** (2) 37 / Father's Day (1) / Go Natalie (2) / I Come Correct (1) / I'll Do 4 U (1) 20 / I've Been Watching You (1) / Ladies, I Luv 'Em (2) / Lisa Baby (1) / My Body (2) / On The Road Again (2) / One Nite Stand (2) / Red Lace Lingerie (2) / Tell Me Something Good (1) / Treat Them Like They Want To Be Treated (1) / Why U Wanna Hurt Me (1)

FAT JOE '98
Born Joseph Cartagena in the Bronx, New York. Male rapper. Member of **Terror Squad**.

DEBUT	PEAK	WKS		CD	#	Album Title		$	Label & Number
11/11/95	71	3		©	1	Jealous One's Envy		$10	Relativity 1239
9/19/98	7	10	●	©	2	Don Cartagena		$10	Mystic 92805

Bet Ya Man Can't (Triz) (2) / Bronx Keeps Creating It (1) / Bronx Tale (1) / Crack Attack (2) / Dat Gangsta Shit (2) / Dedication (1) / Don Cartagena (2) / **Envy** (1) 85 / Fat Joe's In Town (1) / Find Out (2) / Good Times (2) / Hidden Hand (2) / John Blaze (2) / Misery Needs Company (2) / My Prerogative (2) / My World (2) / Part Deux (1) / Respect Mine (1) / Say Word (1) / Shit Is Real (1) / Success (1) / Terror Squadians (2) / Triplets (2) / Walk On By (2) / Watch Out (1)

FAT MATTRESS '69
Rock group from England: Neil Landon (vocals), Noel Redding (guitar), Jimmy Leverton (bass) and Eric Dillon (drums). Redding played bass with the **Jimi Hendrix** Experience.

DEBUT	PEAK	WKS		CD		Album Title		$	Label & Number
11/15/69	134	10		©		Fat Mattress		$20	Atco 309

All Night Drinker / Bright New Way / Everything's Blue / How Can I Live / I Don't Mind / Magic Forest / Mr. Moonshine / Petrol Pump Assistant / She Came In The Morning / Walking Through A Garden

FAZE-O '78

Funk group from Chicago: Robert Neal (vocals), Ralph Aikens (guitar), Keith Harrison (keyboards), Fred Crum (bass) and Roger Parker (drums).

3/4/78	98	17	1 **Riding High**	$12	She 740
11/11/78	145	3	2 **Good Thang**	$12	She 741

Funky Lady (2)　　Good Thang (2)　　Riding High (1)　　Toe Jam (1)　　You And I (Belong Together) (1)
Funky Reputation (1)　Love Me Girl (2)　Space People (2)　True Love (1)
Get Some Booty (1)　Party Time (2)　Test-This Is Faze-O (1)　Who Loves You (2)

FCC [Funky Communication Committee] '79

Country-pop group: Jim "Be-Bop" Evans (drums), Dennis Clifton (vocals, guitar), J.B. Christman (vocals, keyboards), Steve Gooch (guitar) and Lonnie Ledford (bass).

9/8/79	192	2	**Baby I Want You**	$12	Free Flight 3405

Ain't Givin' Up No Love　Dreamer　How Great A Love Can Be　Shot From The Saddle　That Didn't Hurt Too Bad
Baby I Want You 47　Ghost Of Love　It Took A Woman Like You　Sunshine　Woman

FEAR FACTORY '01

Hard-rock group from Los Angeles: Burton Bell (vocals), Dino Cazares (guitar), Christian Olde Wolbers (bass) and Ray Herrera (drums).

6/7/97	158	1	©	1 **Remanufacture (Cloning Technology)**	$10	Roadrunner 8834
8/15/98	77	9	● ©	2 **Obsolete**	$10	Roadrunner 8752
5/12/01	32	5	©	3 **Digimortal**	$10	Roadrunner 8487

Acres Of Skin (3)　Dead Man Walking (3)　Genetic Blueprint (New Breed)　Machines Of Hate (Self Bias　Refinery (1)　Strain Vs. Resistance (3)
Back The F*** Up (3)　Descent (2)　　(1)　Resistor) (1)　Remanufacture (1)　T-1000 (H-K) (1)
Bionic Chronic (1)　Digimortal (3)　Hi-Tech Hate (2)　(Memory Imprints) Never End　Repentance (3)　Timelessness (2)
Bound For Forgiveness (A　Edgecrusher (2)　Hurt Conveyor (3)　(3)　Resurrection (2)　21st Century Jesus (P*sschrist)
　Therapy For Pain) (1)　Faithless (Zero Signal) (1)　Invisible Wounds (Dark Bodies)　National Panel Beating (Body　Securitron [Police State 2000]　(1)
Burn (Flashpoint) (1)　Freedom Or Fire (2)　(3)　Hammer) (1)　(2)　What Will Become? (3)
Byte Block (3)　Full Metal Contact (3)　Linchpin (3)　No One (3)　Shock (2)
Damaged (3)　　　Obsolete (2)　Smasher/Devourer (2)

FEELIES, The '88

Rock group from Hoboken, New Jersey: Glenn Mercer (vocals), Bill Million (guitar), Dave Weckerman (percussion), Brenda Sauter (bass) and Stan Demeski (drums).

11/19/88	173	5	©	**Only Life**	$10	A&M 5214

Away　Final Word　Higher Ground　Too Far Gone　Undertow, The
Deep Fascination　For Awhile　It's Only Life　Too Much　What Goes On

FEITEN, Buzz — see LARSEN/FEITEN BAND

FELDER, Don '84

Born on 9/21/47 in Gainesville, Florida. Singer/songwriter/guitarist. Member of the **Eagles**.

12/3/83+	178	8	**Airborne**	$10	Elektra 60295

Asphalt Jungle　Haywire　Night Owl　Who Tonight
Bad Girls　Never Surrender　Still Alive　Winners

FELDER, Wilton '85

Born on 8/31/40 in Houston. Reed player. Co-founder of **The Crusaders**.

12/9/78+	173	14	1 **We All Have A Star**	$12	ABC 1109
11/8/80	142	13	2 **Inherit The Wind**	$10	MCA 5144
3/9/85	81	16	3 **Secrets**	[I]	$10	MCA 5510

Cycles Of Time (1)　Inherit The Wind (2)　Mr. Scoots (3)　Secrets (3)　Why Believe (1)
I Found You (3)　Insight (2)　My Name Is Love (1)　Someday We'll All Be Free (2)　You And Me And Ecstasy (1)
I Know Who I Am (1)　L.A. Light (2)　(No Matter How High I Get) I'll　Truth Song (3)
I've Got A Secret I'm Gonna　La Luz (3)　Still Be Lookin' Up To You (3)　Until The Morning Comes (2)
　Tell (2)　Let's Dance Together (1)　Ride On (1)　We All Have A Star (1)

★456★ FELICIANO, José '68

Born on 9/8/45 in Lares, Puerto Rico; raised in New York City. Blind since birth. Singer/guitarist. Appeared as himself in the movie *Fargo*. Won the 1968 Best New Artist Grammy Award.

1)Feliciano! 2)Feliciano/10 To 23 3)Souled

7/20/68	2³	59	● ©	1 **Feliciano!**	$20	RCA Victor 3957
12/7/68+	24	19		2 **Souled**	$20	RCA Victor 4045
7/5/69	16	36	●	3 **Feliciano/10 To 23**	$20	RCA Victor 4185
12/20/69+	29	14	●	4 **Alive Alive-O!**	[L]	$25	RCA Victor 6021 [2]
				recorded at the London Palladium		
5/30/70	57	20		5 **Fireworks**	$15	RCA Victor 4370
4/17/71	92	10		6 **Encore! José Feliciano's Finest Performances**	[G]	$15	RCA Victor LSP-1005
11/13/71	173	9		7 **That The Spirit Needs**	$15	RCA Victor 4573
5/19/73	156	8		8 **Compartments**	$15	RCA Victor 0141
12/1/73	3ˣ	4		9 **José Feliciano**	[X]	$15	RCA Victor 4421
				first released in 1970		
12/21/74+	136	7		10 **And The Feeling's Good**	$15	RCA Victor 0407
9/6/75	165	4		11 **Just Wanna Rock 'N' Roll**	$15	RCA Victor APL-1005

Affirmation (11)　Comedy Bit (4)　Find Somebody (8)　Hey Jude (3)　La Entrada de Bilboa (Battle of　Me And Baby Jane (8)
Ain't That Peculiar (11)　Compartments (8)　Fireworks (5)　Hey Look At The Sun (4)　Entrada) (4)　Mellow Feeling (5)
Amor Jibaro (3)　Day In The Life (4)　First Noel (9)　**Hi-Heel Sneakers** (2,4,6) 25　Lady Madonna (3)　Miss Otis Regrets (3)
And I Love Her (1)　Day Tripper (4)　First Of May (3)　**Hitchcock Railway** (2,6) 77　Last Thing On My Mind (1)　Must Be The Breeze (11)
And The Feeling's Good (10)　Daytime Dreams (7)　God Save The Queen (4)　I Can't Get Next To You (11)　Let It Be (5)　My Last Farewell (7)
And The Sun Will Shine (2)　Destiny (5,6) 83　Golden Lady (10)　(I Can't Get No) Satisfaction (5)　Life Is That Way (6)　**My World Is Empty Without**
Blackbird (3)　Differently (10)　Gotta Get A Message To You　I'll Be Your Baby Tonight (2)　**Light My Fire** (1,4,6) 3　**You** (2) 87
Border Song (7)　Don't Fail (8)　(3)　I'm Leavin' (8)　Little Drummer Boy (9)　Nature Boy (6)
By The Time I Get To Phoenix　Don't Let The Sun Catch You　Guantanamera (4)　I've Got To Convince Myself　Little Red Rooster (9)　Nena Na Na (1)
　(3)　Crying (1,4)　Hard Times In El Barrio (10)　(10)　Malaguena (4,6)　No Dogs Allowed (4)
California Dreamin' (1,4,6)　El Jenite (4)　Hark, The Herald Angels Sing　In My Life (1)　Mama Don't Allow It (4)　No Jive (11)
Cherry Tree Carol (9)　El Voh (4)　(9)　It Came Upon A Midnight Clear　Manha de Carnaval (medley)　Nobody Knows You When
Chico And The Man (10) 96　Essence Of Your Love (10)　Here, There And Everywhere　(9)　(4)　You're Down And Out (4)
Christmas Song (9)　Felicidade (medley) (9)　(1)　Jingle Bells (9)　Marie (11)　Norwegian Wood (5)
Come Down Jesus (7)　Feliz Navidad (9)　**Hey! Baby** (2) 71　Just A Little Bit Of Rain (1)　Mary's Little Boy Child (9)

284

FELICIANO, José — Cont'd

Not That Kind Of Guy (Hot Burrito #1) (11)
Once There Was A Love (5)
Only Once (7)
Pay Day (7)
Peace Of Mind (8)
Pegao (5,6)
Rain (3,4,6) *76*

Rock 'N' Roll (11)
Sad Gypsy (2)
Samba de Orfeu (medley) (4)
Sea Cruise (8)
She Came In Through The Bathroom Window (5)
She Let Me Down (7)
She's A Woman (3)

She's Too Good To Me (2)
Silent Night (9)
Simple Song (8)
Sleep Late, My Lady Friend (2)
Spirit, The (7)
Stay With Me (10)
Sunny (1)
Susie-Q (5,6) *84*

Suspicions (11)
Take Me To The Pilot (7)
Thank God (11)
(There's) Always Something There To Remind Me (1)
Things Are Changing (8)
Twilight Time (11)
Virgo (10)

We Three Kings Of Orient Are (9)
White Christmas (9)
Wichita Lineman (6)
Wild World (7)
Windmills Of Your Mind (3)
Yes We Can Can (8)
Yesterday (5)

You're No Good (10)
You've Got A Lot Of Style (2)
Younger Generation (2)

FELONY '83
Rock group from Los Angeles: brothers Jeffrey Scott (vocals) and Curly Joe (guitar) Spry, Danny Sands (keyboards), Louis Ruiz (bass) and Arty Blea (drums).

3/26/83	185	5		©	**The Fanatic**			$10	Rock 'n' Roll 38453

Aggravated Man
Fanatic, The *42*

Girl Ain't Straight
Kristine

No Room In Heaven
One Step

Positively Negative
666 Beware

Teaser
What A Way To Go

FELONY, Jayo '98
Born James Savage in New York City. Male rapper.

9/12/98	46	5		©	**Whatcha Gonna Do**			$10	Def Jam 558792

Bumpin' Bullet Loco
Easy To Get In

End Of The World
Finna S**t On 'Em
Gettin' Loop Loop (Skit)

How Angry
Hustle In My Genes
I'm Deadly

J.A.Y.O. - Justice Against Y'all Oppressors
Love Don't Love

Lovely
Nitty Gritty
Nobody On Dry Land

On The Way To 47 Block (Skit)
Whatcha Gonna Do

FEMME FATALE '89
Hard-rock group: Lorraine Lewis (vocals), Mazzi Rawd and Bill D'Angelo (guitars), Rick Rael (bass) and Bobby Murray (drums).

1/28/89	141	5		©	**Femme Fatale**			$10	MCA 42155

Back In Your Arms Again
Cradle's Rockin'

Falling In & Out Of Love
Fortune & Fame

Heat The Fire
If

My Baby's Gun
Rebel

Touch And Go
Waiting For The Big One

FENDER, Freddy '75
Born Baldemar Huerta on 6/4/37 in San Benito, Texas. Country singer/guitarist. Played "Sammy Cantu" in the movie *The Milagro Beanfield War*. Joined the **Texas Tornados** in 1990.

4/19/75	20	43	●		1 **Before The Next Teardrop Falls**			$12	ABC/Dot 2020
10/18/75	41	18			2 **Are You Ready For Freddy**			$12	ABC/Dot 2044
2/28/76	59	11			3 **Rock 'N' Country**			$12	ABC/Dot 2050
11/6/76	170	3			4 **If You're Ever In Texas**			$12	ABC/Dot 2061
5/21/77	155	7			5 **The Best Of Freddy Fender**		[G]	$12	ABC/Dot 2079

After The Fire Is Gone (1)
Before The Next Teardrop Falls (1,5) *1*
Begging To You (2)
Big Boss Man (3)
Cielito Lindo Is My Lady (2)
Don't Do It Darling (4)
50's Medley (4)
Goodbye Clothes (2)
How Much Is That Doggie In The Window (2)

I Almost Called Your Name (1)
I Can't Help It (If I'm Still In Love With You) (3)
I Can't Put My Arms Around A Memory (2)
I Love My Rancho Grande (1,5)
I Need You So (3)
I'm Not A Fool Anymore (1)
I'm Not Through Loving You Yet (2)
If You're Ever In Texas (4)
It's All In The Game (4)

It's Too Late (4)
Just One Time (4)
Just Out Of Reach Of My Two Open Arms (3)
Living It Down (4,5) *72*
Loving Cajun Style (2)
Mathilda (3,5)
My Happiness (3)
Pass Me By (If You're Only Passing Through) (4)
Please Don't Tell Me How The Story Ends (1)

Rains Came (3,5)
Roses Are Red (1)
San Antonio Lady (4)
Secret Love (2,5) *20*
Since I Met You Baby (3,5) *45*
Sometimes (4)
Sugar Coated Love (5)
Take Her A Message! I'm Lonely (3)
Take Your Time (2)
Teardrops In My Heart (2)

Then You Can Tell Me Goodbye (1)
Vaya Con Dios (3,5) *59*
Wasted Days And Wasted Nights (1,5) *8*
What A Difference A Day Made (4)
What'd I Say (2)
Wild Side Of Life (1,5)
(You Came In) The Winter Of My Life (2)

You Can't Get Here From There (1)
You'll Lose A Good Thing (3,5) *32*

FENIX*TX '00
Punk-rock group from Houston: Willie Salazar (vocals, guitar), Damon De La Paz (guitar), Adam Lewis (bass) and Donnie Vomit (drums). Vomit left after first album, guitarist James Love joined and De La Paz moved to drums.

6/3/00	115	8		©	1 **Fenix*TX**			$10	Drive-Thru 12013
6/9/01	87	3		©	2 **Lechuza**			$10	Drive-Thru 112484

Abba Zabba (2)
All My Fault (1)
Apple Pie Cowboy Toothpaste (1)
Beating A Dead Horse (2)

Ben (1)
El Borracho (2)
Flight 601 (All I've Got Is Time) (1)
G.B.O.H. (1)

Jean Claude Trans Am (1)
Jolly Green Dumbass (1)
Katie W. (2)
Manufactured Inspirato (2)
Minimum Wage (1)

No Lie (1)
Pasture Of Muppets (2)
Philosophy (1)
Phoebe Cates (1)
Rooster Song (1)

Something Bad Is Gonna Happen (2)
Song For Everyone (2)
Speechless (1)
Surf Song (1)

Tearjerker (2)
Threesome (2)

FENN, Rick — see MASON, Nick

FERGUSON, Jay '78
Born John Ferguson on 5/10/43 in Burbank, California. Pop-rock singer. Member of **Spirit** and **Jo Jo Gunne**.

3/25/78	72	12			1 **Thunder Island**			$12	Asylum 1115
4/21/79	86	16			2 **Real Life Ain't This Way**			$12	Asylum 158
4/17/82	178	5			3 **White Noise**			$10	Capitol 12196

Baby Come Back (3)
Babylon (1)
City Of Angels (2)
Cozumel (1)
Davey (2)
Do It Again (2)

Empty Sky (3)
Happy Birthday, Baby (1)
Happy Too! (1)
Have You Seen Your Mother, Baby, Standing In The Shadow? (medley) (2)

Heat Of The Night (3)
I Come Alive (3)
I'm Down (3)
Inside Out (3)
Let's Spend The Night Together (medley) (2)

Losing Control (1)
Love Is Cold (1)
Magic Moment (1)
Million $ (3)
Night Shift (1)
No Secrets (2)

Paying Time (2)
Real Life Ain't That Way (2)
Shakedown Cruise (2) *31*
She's Mine Tonight (3)
Soulin' (1)
Thunder Island (1) *9*

Tonite (Fallin' For Ya') (3)
Too Late To Save Your Heart (2)
Turn Yourself In (2)
White Noise (3)

FERGUSON, Maynard '77
Born on 5/4/28 in Verdun, Quebec, Canada. Jazz trumpeter.

7/28/73	128	8			1 **M.F. Horn/3**		[I]	$15	Columbia 32403
4/17/76	75	14			2 **Primal Scream**		[I]	$12	Columbia 33953
4/2/77	22	26	●	©	3 **Conquistador**		[I]	$12	Columbia 34457
11/26/77	124	8			4 **New Vintage**		[I]	$12	Columbia 34971
10/7/78	113	9			5 **Carnival**		[I]	$12	Columbia 35480
9/1/79	188	3			6 **Hot**		[I]	$12	Columbia 36124
9/27/80	188	2			7 **It's My Time**		[I]	$12	Columbia 36766
5/22/82	185	4			8 **Hollywood**		[I]	$12	Columbia 37713

Airegin (4)
Awright, Awright (1)
Baker Street (5)

Battlestar Galactica, Theme From (5)
Birdland (5)
Cheshire Cat Walk (2)

Conquistador (3)
Dance To Your Heart (7)
Dayride (6)
Deja Vu (8)

Don't Stop 'Til You Get Enough (8)
El Vuelo (The Flight) (4)
Everybody Loves The Blues (7)

Fantasy (5)
Fly, The (5)
For Your Eyes Only (8)
Gabriel (6)

Gonna Fly Now (Theme From "Rocky") (3) *28*
Here Today (4)
Hollywood (8)

FERGUSON, Maynard — Cont'd

How Ya Doin' Baby? (5)
Invitation (2)
It's My Time (7)
M.F. Carnival (5)
Maria (4)
Mister Mellow (3)

Mother Fingers (1)
Naima (6)
Nice 'N Juicy (1)
Nine To Five (8)
Oasis (4)
Offering Of Love - Part 1 (7)

Om Sai Ram (6)
Over The Rainbow (5)
Pagliacci (2)
Pocahontas (1)
Portuguese Love (8)
Primal Scream (2)

Red Creek (7)
Rocky II Disco (6) *82*
'Round Midnight (1)
S.O.M.F. (1)
Scheherazade (4)
Soar Like An Eagle (3)

Spirit Of St. Frederick (7)
Star (7)
Star Trek, Theme From (3,6)
Star Wars, Main Title From (4)
Stella By Starlight (5)
Swamp (2)

Topa-Topa Woman (6)
Touch And Go (8)
Valachi Papers, Love Theme From The (1)
You Can Have Me Anytime (7)

FERNÁNDEZ, Alejandro
Born in Mexico. Latin singer.
'97

10/11/97	125	26	▲	©	1 **Me Estoy Enamorando**	[F]	$10	Sony Discos 82446
					title is Spanish for "Love Me In The Morning"				
5/29/99	148	3		©	2 **Mi Verdad**	[F]	$10	Sony Discos 83182
					title is Spanish for "My Truth"				
5/13/00	144	5		©	3 **Entre Tus Brazos**	[F]	$10	Sony Discos 83812
					title is Spanish for "Within Your Arms"				

A Una Señora (2)
Agua De Mar (3)
Amante Torero (2)
Así Como Soy, Yo Soy (2)
Avísame (2)
Cada Mañana (3)

Como El Sol Y El Trigo (1)
En El Jardín (1)
Enséñame (3)
Entre Tus Brazos (3)
Esta Noche (2)
Estás Aquí (1)

Háblame (3)
Hoy Que Estás Ausente (2)
La Lluvia Sigue Cayendo (2)
Loco (2)
Me Estoy Enamorando (1)
Mentirosos (2)

Mi Verdad (2)
Nadie Simplemente Nadie (2)
No Sé Olvidar (1)
No Será Igual (3)
Noche Triste (1)
Nunca Me Arrepiento (3)

¿Por Qué? (2)
Promesa (1)
Quiéreme (3)
Quisiera (3)
Si He Sabido Amor (2)
Si Te Vas (3)

Si Tú Supieras (1)
Siento (3)
Te Juro (1)
Te Llevo Guardada (3)
Volverás (1)
Yo Nací Para Amarte (1)

FERRANTE & TEICHER ★108★
'62
Piano duo: Arthur Ferrante (b: 9/7/21, New York City) and Louis Teicher (b: 8/24/24, Wilkes-Barre, Pennsylvania). Met as children while attending Manhattan's performing arts academy Juilliard School. First recorded for Columbia in 1953.

1)West Side Story & Other Motion Picture & Broadway Hits 2)Tonight 3)Love Themes
4)Love Themes From Cleopatra 5)Golden Piano Hits

11/20/61+	10	47	1 **West Side Story & Other Motion Picture & Broadway Hits**	[I]	$20	United Artists 6166
12/18/61+	23	16	2 **Love Themes**	[I]	$20	United Artists 8514
2/10/62	30	27	3 **Golden Piano Hits**	[I]	$20	United Artists 8505
3/17/62	11	38	4 **Tonight**	[I]	$20	United Artists 6171
6/16/62	61	11	5 **Golden Themes From Motion Pictures**	[I]	$20	United Artists 6210
9/29/62	43	7	6 **Pianos In Paradise**	[I]	$20	United Artists 6230
12/15/62+	60	11	7 **Snowbound**	[I]	$20	United Artists 6233
6/29/63	23	13	8 **Love Themes From Cleopatra**	[I]	$20	United Artists 6290
12/14/63+	63	17	9 **Concert For Lovers**	[I]	$20	United Artists 6315
3/21/64	128	7	10 **50 Fabulous Piano Favorites**	[I]	$20	United Artists 6343
7/18/64	128	5	11 **The Enchanted World Of Ferrante & Teicher**	[I]	$20	United Artists 6375
11/14/64	145	9	12 **My Fair Lady**	[I]	$20	United Artists 6361
11/28/64+	35	20	13 **The People's Choice**	[I]	$15	United Artists 6385
4/24/65	130	6	14 **Springtime**	[I]	$15	United Artists 6406
6/12/65	120	4	15 **By Popular Demand**	[I]	$15	United Artists 6416
9/11/65	49	13	16 **Only The Best**	[I]	$15	United Artists 6434
1/1/66	134	5	17 **The Ferrante And Teicher Concert**	[I-L]	$15	United Artists 6444
6/25/66	119	5	18 **For Lovers Of All Ages**	[I]	$15	United Artists 6483
9/24/66	57	21	19 **You Asked For It!**	[I]	$15	United Artists 6526
12/24/66	52 X	4	20 **We Wish You A Merry Christmas**	[X-I]	$15	United Artists 6536
			Christmas charts: 52/'66, 102/'67, 57/'68			
2/18/67	133	5	21 **A Man And A Woman & Other Motion Picture Themes**	[I]	$15	United Artists 6572
12/2/67	177	2	22 **Our Golden Favorites**	[I]	$15	United Artists 6556
12/21/68+	198	4	23 **A Bouquet Of Hits**	[I]	$15	United Artists 6659
10/11/69	93	27 ●	24 **10th Anniversary - Golden Piano Hits**	[G-I]	$20	United Artists 70 [2]
11/22/69+	61	26	25 **Midnight Cowboy**	[I]	$15	United Artists 6725
5/30/70	97	10	26 **Getting Together**	[I]	$15	United Artists 5501
12/5/70	188	2	27 **Love Is A Soft Touch**	[I]	$15	United Artists 6771
3/6/71	134	9	28 **The Best Of Ferrante & Teicher**	[I-K]	$20	United Artists 73 [2]
			recordings from 1967-70			
5/8/71	172	4	29 **The Music Lovers**	[I]	$15	United Artists 6792
10/9/71	172	5	30 **It's Too Late**	[I]	$15	United Artists 5531
1/1/72	186	3	31 **Fiddler On The Roof**	[I]	$15	United Artists 5552

Ac-cent-tchu-ate The Positive (medley) (10)
Adventures In Paradise (6)
African Echoes (6)
After The Fox (21)
Alfie (24)
All The Way (5)
Alley Cat (22)
Aloha Oe (11)
And I Love Her (13)
Angels We Have Heard On High (medley) (20)
Anniversary Song (9)
Antony And Cleopatra Theme (8) *83*
Apartment, Theme From The (24) *10*
Applause (30)
April In Paris (14)

Aquarius (24,25)
Around The World In 80 Days (1)
As Long As He Needs Me (15)
As Time Goes By (5)
Autumn Leaves (8)
Away In A Manger (medley) (20)
Ballad Of Easy Rider (26)
Ballad Of The Green Berets (19)
Basin Street Blues (medley) (10)
Be My Love (5)
Beautiful (9)
Begin The Beguine (3)
Bewitched (5)
Beyond The Blue Horizon (medley) (10)

Bible...In The Beginning, Song Of The (21)
Blue Moon (18)
Born Free (21,22,28)
Brazilian Sleigh Bells (7)
Breeze & I (6)
Bridge Over Troubled Water (27)
Buttons And Bows (medley) (10)
By The Time I Get To Phoenix (23,28)
Caesar & Cleopatra Theme (8)
Call Me Irresponsible (13)
Camelot (1)
Can't Help Lovin' Dat Man (2)
Can't Stop Loving You (28)
Canadian Sunset (3)

Caravan (8)
Carnival, Theme From (1)
Cast Your Fate To The Wind (16)
Champagne Waltz (medley) (10)
Charade (13)
Chim Chim Cher-ee (16)
Chopsticks (Bossa Nouveau) (22)
Christmas Song (Chestnuts Roasting On An Open Fire) (20)
Claire De Lune (6,24)
Close To You ...see: (They Long To Be)
Colonel Bogie March (26)
Comedy Tonight (21)

Concerto For A Love's Ending (29)
Country Boy (16)
Crystal Fingers (17)
Days Of Wine And Roses (9)
Dear Heart (15)
Dear Hearts And Gentle People (medley) (10)
Debutante Waltz (15)
Deck The Halls With Boughs Of Holly (medley) (20)
Devotion (8)
Do I Hear A Waltz? (16)
Do You Love Me? (31)
Dolores (medley) (10)
Dominique (22)
Downtown (16)

Dream Of Love (Liebestraum) (2,11)
Drifting And Dreaming (medley) (10)
Easter Parade (14)
Ebb Tide (6,18)
El Condor Pasa (28)
Eleventh Hour, Theme From The (9)
Enjoy Yourself (medley) (10)
Everybody Loves Somebody (13)
Exodus (3,17,24) *2*
Familiar Concerto (26,28,29)
Fanny (1)
Fascination (9)
Fiddler On The Roof (16,31)
Finale (12)

FERRANTE & TEICHER — Cont'd

Firebird (19)
First Noel (medley) (20)
Five Minutes More (medley) (10)
Flamingo (6)
Fly Me To The Moon (9)
For All We Know (30)
For Every Man There Is A Woman (medley) (10)
For Once In My Life (26,28)
Gentle On My Mind (25)
Georgia On My Mind (13)
Get Me To The Church On Time (12)
Gigi (1)
Girl From Ipanema (13,24)
Gitchie Goomie (30)
God Rest Ye Merry Gentlemen (medley) (20)
Goin' Out Of My Head (23,28)
Golden Earrings (18)
Goldfinger (15)
Good King Wenceslas (medley) (20)
Good Morning Starshine (26)
Good, The Bad And The Ugly (23)
Goodbye Again, Theme From (2) *85*
Greatest Story Ever Told (15)
Greensleeves (9,24)
Hair (26)
Half A Sixpence (16)
Happy Sleigh Ride (7,11)
Hark! The Herald Angels Sing (medley) (20)
Hawaii (21)
He (19)
He Ain't Heavy, He's My Brother (28)
Heart And Soul (medley) (10)
Hello Dolly (13)
Her Concerto (9)
Hey Look Me Over (medley) (10)
High And The Mighty (5)
Highlights From Borodin (17)
Honey (23,28)
Hooray For Love (medley) (10)
Hush...Hush, Sweet Charlotte (16)
I Could Have Danced All Night (12)
I Feel Pretty (1)
I Hear Music (medley) (10)
I Left My Heart In San Francisco (10)
I Remember You (medley) (10)
I Will Wait For You (15)
I'll Be Seeing You (4)
I'll Never Fall In Love Again (27)
I'll Remember April (14)
I'll Walk Alone (medley) (10)

I'm Always Chasing Rainbows (22)
I'm Glad There Is You (medley) (10)
I'm In The Mood For Love (2)
I've Got A Crush On You (2)
I've Got My Love To Keep Me Warm (7)
I've Grown Accustomed To Her Face (12)
I've Heard That Song Before (medley) (10)
If I Ruled The World (16)
If I Were A Rich Man (31)
Imagination (2)
Impossible Dream (The Quest) (22,24)
In A Persian Market (8)
In The Cool Cool Cool Of The Evening (medley) (10)
Is Paris Burning, Love Theme From (21)
Is That All There Is (27)
It Came Upon The Midnight Clear (medley) (10)
It Might As Well Be Spring (14)
It's Been A Long Long Time (medley) (10)
It's Impossible (Somos Novios) (30)
It's So Nice To Have A Man Around The House (medley) (10)
It's Too Late (30)
Italian Caprice (The Happy Italian) (29)
James Bond Theme (13)
Japanese Garden (11)
Jean (27)
Jessica (15)
Jingle Bells (7)
Jingle, Jangle, Jingle (medley) (10)
Joy To The World (medley) (20)
Judith (21)
June In January (7)
Jungle Rhumba (6)
Just One More Chance (medley) (10)
Khartoum (19)
Kids (medley) (10)
King Of Kings (4)
Knack, Main Theme From The (21)
La Strada (4)
Lara's Theme (19,24)
Last Time I Saw Paris (17)
Late Show (18)
Laura (2)
Lay Lady Lay (26,28) *99*
Leaving On A Jet Plane (26)
Let It Be (27)
Let It Snow (7)

Letter To My Secret Love (18)
Lili Marlene (4)
Little Drummer Boy (20)
Little Green Apples (25,28)
Little Hands (18)
Loch Lomond (11)
Louise (medley) (10)
Love Is A Many Splendored Thing (2)
Love Is A Soft Touch (27)
Love Is Blue (L'Amour Est Bleu) (23)
Love Is Just Around The Corner (medley) (10)
Love Is Now (Tchaikovsky 5th Symphony - 2nd Movement) (29)
Love Me With All Your Heart (13)
Love Story, Theme From (29,30)
Love's Old Sweet Song (25)
Lover (medley) (10)
Lover's Lullaby (4)
Mac Arthur Park (23,28)
Magical Connection (27)
Magnificent Seven (21)
Make Believe Ballroom (medley) (10)
Malaguena (22)
Mame (19)
Man And A Woman (21,24)
Man That Got Away (medley) (10)
Man Without Love (Quando M'Innamoro) (23)
March From The River Kwai ..see: Colonel Bogie March
Maria (1)
Matchmaker (15,31)
Mexican Hat Dance (11)
Midnight Cowboy (25,28) *10*
Miracle Of Miracles (31)
Misirlou (3)
Misty (6,24)
Mona Lisa (5)
Moon Of Manakoora (6)
Moon River (4,24)
Moonlight In Vermont (7)
Moonlight On The Ganges (8)
Moonlight Serenade (7)
More (9,24)
More I See You (19)
Moulin Rouge (5)
Music Lovers (Piano Concerto In B Flat Minor) (29)
My Fair Lady Overture (12)
My Foolish Heart (5)
My Funny Valentine (2)
My Ideal (medley) (10)
My Love, Forgive Me (15)
My Silent Love (2)
My Way (25)

Near You (3)
Nearness Of You (medley) (10)
Negligee (6)
Nocturne In E Flat (3)
Now I Have Everything (31)
O Come, All Ye Faithful (medley) (20)
O Little Town Of Bethlehem (medley) (20)
O Tannenbaum (medley) (20)
Ode To Joy (Symphony No. 9 In D Minor) (29)
Oh! Calcutta! (26)
Oh To Be Young Again (27)
Ole Buttermilk Sky (medley) (10)
Oliver (24)
On A Clear Day (You Can See Forever) (18)
On The Street Where You Live (12)
Once Around The World (30)
One Dozen Roses (medley) (10)
One Eyed Jacks, Love Theme From (2) *37*
Orientale (10)
Out Of Nowhere (medley) (10)
Out Of This World (medley) (10)
Paper Mache (27)
Paris In The Spring (14)
Penthouse Serenade (medley) (10)
People (13)
Phaedra, Love Theme From (21)
Piano Concerto In A Minor (29)
Piano Concerto No. 1 In B Flat Minor - (1st Movement) (29)
Piano Concerto No. 21 In C Major - K.467 (23,24,28)
Piano Concerto No. 2 (29)
Picnic (2)
Pieces Of Dreams (27)
Playboy's Theme (medley) (10)
Please (medley) (10)
Polonaise (22)
Popi (25)
Possessed (2,11)
Procession Of Sardar (8,11)
Proud Mary (30)
Put Your Hand In The Hand (30)
Quiet Village (3)
Rage To Live (18,21)
Rain In Spain (12)
Raindrops Keep Fallin' On My Head (26,28)
Rainy Days And Mondays (30)
Red Roses For A Blue Lady (16)
Reverie (15)
Rock-A-Bye Baby (25)

Romeo & Juliet, Love Theme From (28)
Rose By Any Other Name (16)
Route 66! (medley) (10)
Rudolph, The Red-Nosed Reindeer (20)
S'posin (medley) (10)
Samson & Delilah (8,11)
Sands Of Time (8)
Santa Claus Is Comin' To Town (20)
Scarborough Fair (25)
Scheherazade (8,11)
Schubert's Serenade (18)
Secret Love (5)
Sentimental Journey (medley) (10)
Seventh Dawn (13)
Shadow Of Your Smile (19)
Shalom (4)
Shangri-La (6)
Show Me (12)
Silent Night (medley) (20)
Silver Bells (20)
Sirocco (8,11)
Skaters Waltz (7,11)
Sleighride (7)
Smile (4) *94*
Smile A Little Smile For Me (27)
Snowbird (27)
Snowbound (7)
Something (26,28)
Somewhere (1)
Somewhere, My Love ..see: Lara's Theme
Sound Of Music (15)
Sound Of Silence (25,28)
Spanish Eyes (24)
Spellbound (7)
Spring Is Here (14)
Spring-Song (14)
Spring Will Be A Little Late This Year (14)
Springtime (14)
Stella By Starlight (medley) (10)
Stephen Foster Medley (17)
Strangers In The Night (19)
Summer Place, Theme From A (18)
Sunny (23,28)
Sunrise, Sunset (31)
Swan Lake (Swan Lake Suite, No. 1) (29)
Symphony No. 5, E Minor (3rd Movement) (29)
Symphony No. 40 In G Minor, K550 (1st Movement) (30)
Taboo (6)
Tammy (7)
Tangerine (medley) (10)
Tara's Theme (2,24)
Taste Of Honey (9)

Tchaikovsky Concerto (3)
Temptation (22)
That's Amore (medley) (10)
Theme From Grieg's Piano Concerto (Eddie's Tune) (22)
(They Long To Be) Close To You (28)
Those Were The Days (24,25)
Thousand And One Nights (4)
Three Coins In The Fountain (1)
Three Over Four (19)
Tiger Rag (17)
Till (3)
To Life (31)
To Spring (14)
Tonight (1,4,17,24) *8*
True Love (5)
Twelve Days Of Christmas (20)
Twilight (15)
Two Different Worlds (23)
Two Sleepy People (medley) (10)
Unchained Melody (17)
Valley Of The Dolls, Theme From (23)
Walk In The Black Forest (22)
Warsaw Concerto (3)
Way You Look Tonight (4)
We Wish You A Merry Christmas (medley) (20)
What Child Is This (medley) (20)
What Kind Of Fool Am I (9)
What Now My Love (18,24)
When It's Springtime In The Rockies (14)
When Your Hair Has Turned To Silver (medley) (10)
White Christmas (20)
Who Can I Turn To (15)
Why (23)
Windmills Of Your Mind (24,25)
Winter Wonderland (7)
Witchcraft (medley) (10)
With A Little Bit Of Luck (12)
With The Wind And The Rain In Your Hair (medley) (10)
Wives And Lovers (13)
Work Song (19)
Wouldn't It Be Loverly (12)
Yellow Bird (22)
Yellow Rolls-Royce, Theme From The (16)
Yesterday (18,24)
You Did It (12)
You Don't Have To Say You Love Me (Lo Che Non Vivo [Senza Te]) (19)
You've Got A Friend (30)
Younger Than Springtime (14)
Z (To Yelasto Pedi), Theme From (26)

FERRELL, Rachelle

'00

Born in Philadelphia. Female R&B singer/keyboardist.

DEBUT	PEAK	WKS	RIAA	CD	ARTIST — Album Title	$	Label & Number
7/16/94	161	8	●	© 1	**Rachelle Ferrell**	$10	Manhattan 93769
4/22/95	151	8		© 2	**First Instrument**	[E] $10	Blue Note 27820
					recorded in 1990		
9/30/00	71	9		© 3	**Individuality (Can I Be Me?)**	$10	Capitol 94980

Autumn Leaves (2)
Bye Bye Blackbird (2)
Could've Fooled Me (1)
Don't Waste Your Time (2)
Extensions (2)
Gaia (3)
I Can Explain (3)

I Forgive You (3)
I Gotta Go (3)
I Know You Love Me (1)
I'm Special (1)
Inchworm (2)
Individuality (Can I Be Me?) (3)
It Only Took A Minute (1)

My Funny Valentine (2)
Nothing Has Ever Felt Like This (1)
Peace On Earth (1)
Prayer Dance (2)
Reflections Of My Heart (3)
Run To Me (3)

Satisfied (3)
Sentimental (1)
Sista (3)
'Til You Come Back To Me (1)
Too Late (1)
Waiting (1)
Welcome To My Love (1)

What Is This Thing Called Love (2)
Why You Wanna Mess It All Up? (3)
Will You Remember Me? (3)
With Every Breath I Take (2)
With Open Arms (1)

You Can't Get (Until You Learn To Start Giving) (1)
You Don't Know What Love Is (2)
You Send Me (2)

FERRER, Ibrahim

'99

Born on 2/20/27 in Santiago, Cuba. Singer with the **Buena Vista Social Club**.

DEBUT	PEAK	WKS	RIAA	CD	ARTIST — Album Title	$	Label & Number
6/26/99	137	16	● ©		**Buena Vista Social Club Presents Ibrahim Ferrer**	[F] $10	World Circuit 79532

Aquellos Ojos Verdes
Bruca Maniguá

Cienfuegos Tiene Su Guaguancó
Como Fue

Guateque Campesino
Herido De Sombras
Mamí Me Gustó

Marieta
Nuestra Ultima Cita
Qué Bueno Baila Usted

Silencio

FERRY, Bryan

'88

Born on 9/26/45 in County Durham, England. Lead singer of **Roxy Music**.

DEBUT	PEAK	WKS	RIAA	CD	ARTIST — Album Title	$	Label & Number
10/16/76	160	5		© 1	**Let's Stick Together**	$12	Atlantic 18187
4/23/77	126	5		© 2	**In Your Mind**	$12	Atlantic 18216
11/4/78	159	5		© 3	**The Bride Stripped Bare**	$12	Atlantic 19205
6/29/85	63	25	●	© 4	**Boys And Girls**	$10	Warner 25082
11/21/87+	63	31		© 5	**Bete Noire**	$10	Reprise 25598

title is French for "Black Beast"

DEBUT	PEAK	WKS	RIAA	CD	ARTIST — Album Title	Catalog	Sym	$	Label & Number

FERRY, Bryan — Cont'd

| 8/26/89 | 100 | 11 | | © 6 | Street Life-20 Great Hits .... | [G] | $15 | Reprise 25857 [2] |

BRYAN FERRY/ROXY MUSIC
6 Bryan Ferry solos and 14 **Roxy Music** hits (see Roxy Music for tracks) from 1972-85

5/1/93	79	8		© 7	Taxi	$10	Reprise 45246
10/8/94	94	5		© 8	Mamouna	$10	Virgin 39838
11/6/99	195	1		© 9	As Time Goes By	$10	Virgin 48270

All Night Operator (2)
All Tomorrow's Parties (7)
Amazing Grace (7)
Answer Me (7)
As Time Goes By (9)
Because You're Mine (7)
Bete Noire (5)
Boys And Girls (4)
Can't Let Go (3)
Carrickfergus (3)
Casanova (1)
Chain Reaction (8)
Chance Meeting (1)
Chosen One (4)
Day For Night (5)
Don't Stop The Dance (4)

Don't Want To Know (8)
Easy Living (9)
Falling In Love Again (9)
Gemini Moon (8)
Girl Of My Best Friend (7)
Hard Rain's A-Gonna Fall (6)
Heart On My Sleeve (1) *86*
Hold On (I'm Coming) (3)
I Put A Spell On You (9)
I'm In The Mood For Love (9)
In Your Mind (2)
It's Only Love (1)
Just One Look (7)
Just One Of Those Things (9)
Kiss And Tell (5) *31*
Let's Stick Together (1,6)

Limbo (5)
Love Me Madly Again (2)
Love Me Or Leave Me (9)
Lover Come Back To Me (9)
Mamouna (8)
Miss Otis Regrets (She's
   Unable To Have Lunch
   Today) (9)
N.Y.C. (8)
Name Of The Game (5)
New Town (5)
One Kiss (2)
Only Face (8)
Party Doll (9)
Price Of Love (1)
Re-Make/Re-Model (1)

Rescue Me (7)
Right Stuff (5)
Rock Of Ages (2)
Same Old Blues (3)
Sea Breezes (1)
Sensation (4)
September Song (9)
Seven Deadly Sins (5)
Shame, Shame, Shame (1)
Sign Of The Times (3,6)
Slave To Love (4,6)
Smoke Gets In Your Eyes (6)
Stone Woman (4)
Sweet And Lovely (9)
Take Me To The River (3)
Taxi (7)

That's How Strong My Love Is
   (3)
These Foolish Things (6)
39 Steps (8)
This Is Tomorrow (2)
This Island Earth (3)
Time On My Hands (9)
Tokyo Joe (2)
2 HB (1)
Valentine (4)
Waste Land (9)
Way You Look Tonight (9)
What Goes On (3)
When She Walks In The Room
   (3)

When Somebody Thinks You're
   Wonderful (9)
Where Or When (9)
Which Way To Turn (8)
Wildcat Days (8)
Will You Love Me Tomorrow (7)
Windswept (4)
You Do Something To Me (9)
You Go To My Head (1)
Your Painted Smile (8)
Zamba (5)

FESTIVAL '80

Disco studio group assembled by producer Boris Midney.

| 2/9/80 | 50 | 18 | | © | Evita.. | $12 | RSO 3061 |

Buenos Aires

**Don't Cry For Me
Argentina** *72*

Eva's Theme: Lady Woman
High Flying, Adored

I'd Be Surprisingly Good For
You

Rainbow High
She Is A Diamond

FETCHIN BONES '89

Rock group from Los Angeles: Hope Nicholls (vocals), Aaron Pitkin and Errol Stewart (guitars), Danna Pentes (bass) and Clay Richardson (drums).

| 11/18/89 | 175 | 8 | | © | Monster .... | $10 | Capitol 90661 |

Bonework
Cross

Deep Blue
I Dig You

(I Feel Like An) Astronaut
Love Crushing

Mr. Bad
Say The Word

Spot
You're So Much

FEVER TREE '69

Psychedelic-rock group from Houston: Dennis Keller (vocals), Michael Knust (guitar), Rob Landes (piano), E.E. Wolfe (bass) and John Tuttle (drums).

5/18/68	156	21		© 1	Fever Tree	$25	Uni 73024
12/28/68+	83	13		© 2	Another Time, Another Place	$25	Uni 73040
2/7/70	97	6		3	Creation	$25	Uni 73067

Catcher In The Rye (3)
Come With Me (Rainsong) (1)
Day Tripper (medley) (1)
Death Is The Dancer (2)
Don't Come Crying To Me Girl
   (2)
Fever (2)
Fever Blue (3)

Filligree & Shadow (1)
God Game (3)
Grand Candy Young Sweet (2)
I've Never Seen Evergreen (2)
Imitation Situation 1 (1,3)
Jokes Are For Sad People (2)
Love Makes The Sunrise (3)

Man Who Paints The Pictures
   (1)
Man Who Paints The Pictures -
   Part II (2)
Ninety-Nine And One Half (1)
Nowadays Clancy Can't Even
   Sing (1)
Peace Of Mind (2)

Run Past My Window (3)
**San Francisco Girls (Return
   Of The Native)** (1) *91*
Sun Also Rises (1)
Time Is Now (3)
Unlock My Door (1)
We Can Work It Out (medley)
   (1)

What Time Did You Say It Is In
   Salt Lake City? (2)
Where Do You Go? (medley)
   (1)
Wild Woman Ways (3)
Woman, Woman (Woman) (3)

FFH '99

Christian vocal group: husband-and wife Jeromy and Jennifer Deibler, with Steve Croyle and Brian Smith. Michael Boggs replaced Croyle after first album. FFH: Far From Home.

| 12/11/99 | 64 | 1 | | © 1 | I Want To Be Like You .... | $10 | Essential 0498 |
| 3/25/00 | 154 | 2 | | © 2 | Found A Place .... | $10 | Essential 0529 |

Be My Glory (2)
Because Of Who You Are (2)
Big Fish (1)
Breathe In Me (1)

Daniel (2)
Every Now And Then (2)
Fall To You (1)
Found A Place (2)

I Want To Be Like You (1)
I'm Alright (1)
I'm Not Afraid To Love You (2)
It's Been A Long Time (2)

Little Change (1)
Lord Move, Or Move Me (2)
One Of These Days (1)
Only You (1)

Power In His Blood (1)
So Is His Love (1)
Take Me As I Am (1)
When I Praise (2)

Wholly To You (1)
Why Do I (2)
Your Love Is Life To Me (2)

FIEDLER, Arthur — see BOSTON POPS

FIELD, Sally '68

Born on 11/6/46 in Pasadena, California. Prolific TV/movie actress.

| 12/23/67+ | 172 | 4 | | | The Flying Nun .... | $30 | Colgems 106 |

Count To Ten
Darkest Before Dawn
Felicidad *94*

Find Yourself A Rainbow
Flying Nun Theme ..see: Who
   Needs Wings To Fly

Follow The Star
I'm On My Way
I'm So Glad I Can Fly

Louder I Sing (The Braver I
   Get)
Musicians, The

Optimize
Paint Me A Picture
Turn On The Sunshine

Who Needs Wings To Fly?

FIELD MOB '01

Male rap duo from Albany, Georgia: Boondox Blax and Kalage.

| 1/20/01 | 194 | 2 | | © | 613: Ashy To Classy .... | $10 | MCA 112348 |

Can't Stop Us
Channel 613, Part 1

Cheatin' On We
Crutch

Da' Durty
Dead In Your Chevy

Dimez (Jazzy B's)
Hey Shawty

My Main Roni
Project Dreamz

Shake Sumpthin'
Waiting

FIELDS, Richard "Dimples" '81

Born in San Francisco. Died of a stroke on 1/15/2000 (age 52). R&B singer/songwriter/producer.

| 7/25/81 | 33 | 17 | | 1 | Dimples .... | $12 | Boardwalk 33232 |
| 3/6/82 | 63 | 20 | | 2 | Mr. Look So Good! .... | $12 | Boardwalk 33249 |

After I Put My Lovin' On You (2)
Baby Work Out (2)
Don't Ever Take Your Love (1)
Earth Angel (1)
I Like Your Lovin (1)

I've Got To Learn To Say No!
   (1)
**If It Ain't One Thing...It's
   Another** (2) *47*

In The Still Of The Night (I'll
   Remember) (1)
Lady Is Bad (2)
Let Me Take You In My Arms
   Tonight (1)

Let The Lady Dance (1)
Lovely Lady (1)
Mr. Look So Good (2)
She's Got Papers On Me (1)
Sincerely (1)

Taking Applications (2)
(Woman At Home And) A Freak
   On The Side (2)

FIELDS, W.C.   '69
Born on 1/29/1880 in Philadelphia. Died of pneumonia on 12/25/46 (age 66). Legendary movie comedian.

DEBUT	PEAK	WKS	RIAA	CD	ARTIST — Album Title	Sym	$	Label & Number
1/4/69	30	29		© 1	The Original Voice Tracks From His Greatest Movies	[C]	$15	Decca 79164
10/18/69	197	2		2	W. C. Fields On Radio	[C]	$15	Columbia 9890

Chicanery Of W.C. Fields (1)
Children (2)
Feathered Friends (2)
Moths (2)
Old Friends And Old Wine (2)

Pharmacist, The (2)
Philosophy Of W.C. Fields (1)
Promotions Unlimited (2)
Rascality Of W.C. Fields (1)
Skunk Trap (2)

Snake Story (A Commercial) (2)
"Sound" Of W.C. Fields (1)
Spirit Of W.C. Fields (1)
Swim To Catalina Island (2)
Temperance Lecture (2)

W.C. Fields - A Man Against Children, Motherhood, Fatherhood And Brotherhood (1)

W.C. Fields - Creator Of Weird Names (1)
W.C. Fields - The Braggart And Teller Of Tall Tales (1)

FIEND   '98
Born Rickey Jones in New Orleans. Male rapper.

DEBUT	PEAK	WKS	RIAA	CD	ARTIST — Album Title	$	Label & Number
5/23/98	8	16	●	© 1	There's One In Every Family	$10	No Limit 50715
7/24/99	15	12		© 2	Street Life	$10	No Limit 50107

Ak'n Bad (2)
All I Know (1)
All In A Week (1)
At All Times (1)
Baddest, The (1)
Been Thru It All (2)
Big Timer (1)

Do You Know? (1)
Do You Wanna Be A Rider (2)
For The N.O. (1)
Get In 2 It (2)
Going Out With A Blast (1)
Heart Of A Ghetto Boy (2)
I Swore (1)

I Was Placed Here (2)
I'm Losing My Mind (2)
If They Don't Know (2)
Live Me Long (1)
Mr. Whomp Whomp (2)
On A Mission (1)
Only A Few (1)

Rock Show (2)
Slangin' (1)
Street Life (2)
Streets Ain't Safe (1)
Take My Pain (1)
Talk It How I Bring It (2)
They Don't Hear Me (2)

Trip To London (2)
Truth Is (2)
Waiting On God (2)
Walk Like A "G" (1)
Walk That Line (2)
War 4 Reason (2)
We Survivors (1)

What Cha Mean (1)
Who Got The Fire (1)

FIFTH ANGEL   '88
Hard-rock group from Bellevue, Washington: Ted Pilot (vocals), James Byrd and Ed Archer (guitars), John Macko (bass) and Ken Mary (drums).

DEBUT	PEAK	WKS	RIAA	CD	ARTIST — Album Title	$	Label & Number
4/16/88	117	13		© 1	Fifth Angel	$10	Epic 44201

Call Out The Warning
Cry Out The Fools

Fade To Flames
Fifth Angel

In The Fallout
Night, The

Only The Strong Survive
Shout It Out

Wings Of Destiny

★207★   5TH DIMENSION, The   '69
Vocal group from Los Angeles: **Marilyn McCoo, Billy Davis, Jr.,** Florence LaRue, Lamont McLemore and Ron Townson. McLemore and McCoo had been in the Hi-Fi's; Townson and Davis had been with groups in St. Louis. First called the Versatiles. McCoo and Davis were married in 1969 and recorded as a duo since 1976. Townson died of kidney failure on 8/2/2001 (age 68).

1)The Age Of Aquarius 2)The 5th Dimension/Greatest Hits 3)Up, Up And Away

DEBUT	PEAK	WKS	RIAA	CD	ARTIST — Album Title	Sym	$	Label & Number
6/17/67	8	83	●	© 1	Up, Up And Away		$15	Soul City 92000
1/13/68	105	31		© 2	The Magic Garden		$15	Soul City 92001
8/24/68	21	21		© 3	Stoned Soul Picnic		$15	Soul City 92002
5/31/69	2²	72	●	© 4	The Age Of Aquarius		$15	Soul City 92005
5/9/70+	20	50	●	© 5	Portrait		$15	Bell 6045
5/16/70	5	55	●	6	The 5th Dimension/Greatest Hits	[G]	$15	Soul City 33900
8/15/70	63	8		7	The July 5th Album	[K]	$15	Soul City 33901
3/13/71	17	23	●	8	Love's Lines, Angles And Rhymes		$15	Bell 6060
10/23/71	32	18	●	9	The 5th Dimension/Live!!	[L]	$20	Bell 9000 [2]
11/6/71	112	7		10	Reflections	[K]	$15	Bell 6065
4/1/72	58	32		11	Individually & Collectively		$15	Bell 6073
9/30/72	14	24	●	© 12	Greatest Hits On Earth	[G]	$15	Bell 1106
3/24/73	108	11		13	Living Together, Growing Together		$15	Bell 1116
8/23/75	136	8		14	Earthbound		$12	ABC 897

All Kinds Of People (11)
Another Day, Another Heartache (1) 45
Aquarius/Let The Sunshine In (4,6,9,12) 1
Ashes To Ashes (13) 52
Band Of Gold (11)
Be Here How (medley) (14)
Black Patch (11)
Blowing Away (4,6,10) 37
Bobbie's Blues (Who Do You Think Of?) (3,7)
Border Song (11)
Broken Wing Bird (3)
California My Way (1,7,10)
California Soul (3,6,10) 25
Carpet Man (2,6,10) 29
Change Is Gonna Come & People Gotta Be Free (5) 60
Day By Day (13)
Declaration, The (medley) (5) 64

Dimension 5ive (5)
Don't Stop For Nothing (14)
Don'tcha Hear Me Callin' To Ya (4,7)
Dreams/Pax/Nepenthe (2)
Earthbound (14)
Eleventh Song (What A Groovy Day!) (7)
Eli's Coming (9)
Every Night (8)
Everything's Been Changed (13) 70
Feelin' Alright? (7)
Girls' Song (2,6,9) 43
Go Where You Wanna Go (1,7) 16
Good News (3)
Guess Who (8)
He's A Runner (8)
Hideaway, The (8)
I Just Wanta Be Your Friend (9)

I Want To Take You Higher (9)
I've Got A Feeling (14)
If I Could Reach You (11,12) 10
It'll Never Be The Same Again (3,7,10)
It's A Great Life (3)
(Last Night) I Didn't Get To Sleep At All (11,12) 8
Lean On Me Always (14)
Learn How To Fly (1)
Leave A Little Room (11)
Let It Be Me (4,7,10)
Let Me Be Lonely (13)
Light Sings (8) 44
Living Together, Growing Together (13) 32
Love Like Ours (5)
Love Medley (9)
Love's Lines, Angles And Rhymes (8,12) 19
Lovin' Stew (3,7)
Magic Garden (2)

Magic In My Life (14)
Misty Roses (1)
Moonlight Mile (12)
Never Gonna Be The Same (1)
Never My Love (9,12) 12
Ode To Billy Joe (9)
One Less Bell To Answer (5,12) 2
Open Your Window (13)
Orange Air (2)
Paper Cup (2,6,9) 34
Pattern People (1)
Poor Side Of Town (1,7,10)
Puppet Man (5,12) 24
Rainmaker, The (8)
Requiem: 820 Latham (2)
Riverwitch, The (11)
Rosecrans Blvd. (1)
Sailboat Song (3,7)
Save The Country (5,9,12) 27
Shake Your Tambourine (9)
Singer, The (8)

Skinny Man (4)
Sky & Sea (11)
Speaking With My Heart (14)
Stoned Soul Picnic (3,6,9,12) 3
Stoney End (medley) (9)
Summer's Daughter (2)
Sunshine Of Your Love (4,7,10)
Sweet Blindness (3,6,9) 13
There Never Was A Day (13)
There's Nothin' Like Music (13)
This Is Your Life (5,9)
Those Were The Days (4,7,10)
Ticket To Ride (2,7,10)
Time And Love (8)
Together Let's Find Love (9,12) 37
Tomorrow Belongs To The Children (11)
Turn Around To Me (11)
Up-Up And Away (1,6,9,12) 7
Viva Tirado (8)

Walk Your Feet In The Sunshine (14)
Wedding Bell Blues (4,6,9,12) 1
What Do I Need To Be Me (13)
What Does It Take (To Win Your Love)? (8)
When Did I Lose Your Love (14)
Which Way To Nowhere (1)
Winds Of Heaven (4)
Workin' On A Groovy Thing (4,6,10) 20
Worst That Could Happen (2,6,9)
Woyaya (13)

5TH WARD BOYZ   '94
Rap trio from Houston: Andre Barnes, Eric Taylor and Richard Nash.

DEBUT	PEAK	WKS	RIAA	CD	ARTIST — Album Title	$	Label & Number
6/5/93	176	3		© 1	Ghetto Dope	$10	Rap-A-Lot 53859
3/12/94	105	8		© 2	Gangsta Funk	$10	Rap-A-Lot 53844
12/2/95	189	1		© 3	Rated G	$10	Rap-A-Lot 40758
12/6/97	180	1		© 4	Usual Suspects	$10	Rap-A-Lot 45117
9/18/99	125	3		© 5	P.W.A. The Album...Keep It Poppin'	$10	Rap-A-Lot 50125

Act A Donkey (5)
All The Same (5)
Anotha Ho (5)
Big Faces (4)
Bitch Pleeze (1)
Blood, Sweat & Glory (1)
Bringing Hats (1)
Buckin' (1)
Busta Free (3)
Concrete Hell (3)

Death Is Calling (4)
Dirty (3)
Don't Nuttin Change (4)
Down Azz Zaggin (4)
Fear No Man (5)
5th Of Ghetto (1)
5th Ward (4)
Fuck Strugglin' (4)
Gangsta Funk (2)
Gangsta Shit (4)

Get Wit U (5)
Ghetto Curse Words (1,2)
Got II Be Down II Die (4)
Gotta Be Down To Die (1)
Heat (4)
Hedpusefingtip'nlips (5)
Ho Shit (1)
Hollywood (4)
Hustlin' (4)
I Know (4)

Immortal 2K (5)
Jealous (5)
Live Your Life (4)
Lo Life In The Street (2)
Mama's Praying (4)
My Life (3)
Once Again Its On (2)
One Night Stand (3)
P.W.A. (4,5)
Punks And Guns (1)

Pussy Poppin' (5)
Raisin Cain (3)
Reason (2)
Rhyme Or Crime (5)
S.A. Partner (5)
Same Ole Shit (1,2)
See Us Ball (5)
Situations (3)
Somethin' To Ride To (4)
Step Into My Hood (3)

Streets (3)
Studio Gangster (1)
Swing Wide (3)
Thanks For The Blessing (1)
Thug & Dangerous (5)
Til The World Blow Up (4)
Til' They Kill Me (5)
Undercover Gangstas (1)
Underground G's (4)
Your Life (3)

DEBUT	PEAK	WKS	RIAA	CD	ARTIST — Album Title			Catalog	Sym	$	Label & Number

5TH WARD JUVENILEZ '95
Rap trio from Houston.

| 7/15/95 | 200 | 1 | | © | **Deadly Groundz**.......... | | | | | $10 | Rap-A-Lot 40531 |

Bad Newz	5th Ward Juvenilez	Gangsta N My Hood	Kar Phreak	No Conscious
Busta Azz Niggaz	G-Groove	Ghetto Talez	Menace	Not 2 Young
Deadly Groundz	G-ing N Tha Nickel	Gotsta Get Paid	Mr. Slimm	Nut Check

50 GUITARS OF TOMMY GARRETT — see GARRETT, Tommy

FIGHT '93
Hard-rock group from England: Rob **Halford** (vocals), Russ Parrish and Brian Tilse (guitars), Jay Jay (bass) and Scott Travis (drums). Mark Chaussee replaced Parrish in 1994. Halford was lead singer of **Judas Priest**.

| 10/2/93 | 83 | 5 | | © | 1 | **War Of Words**.......... | | | | $10 | Epic 57372 |
| 5/6/95 | 120 | 1 | | © | 2 | **A Small Deadly Space**.......... | | | | $10 | Epic 66649 |

Beneath The Violence (2)	Gretna Greene (2)	In A World Of My Own Making	Laid To Rest (1)	Mouthpiece (2)	Small Deadly Space (2)
Blowout In The Radio Room (2)	Human Crate (2)	(2)	Legacy Of Hate (2)	Nailed To The Gun (1)	Vicious (1)
Contortion (1)	I Am Alive (2)	Into The Pit (1)	Life In Black (1)	Never Again (2)	War Of Words (1)
For All Eternity (1)	Immortal Sin (1)	Kill It (1)	Little Crazy (1)	Reality, A New Beginning (1)	

FILTER '99
Industrial rock duo from Cleveland: Richard Patrick (vocals, guitar, bass) and Brian Liesegang (keyboards, drums). Both worked with Trent Reznor in **Nine Inch Nails**.

| 5/13/95 | 59 | 27 | ▲ | © | 1 | **Short Bus**.......... | | | | $10 | Reprise 45864 |
| 9/11/99 | 30 | 35 | ▲ | © | 2 | **Title Of Record**.......... | | | | $10 | Reprise 47388 |

Best Things (2)	Dose (1)	I'm Not The Only One (2)	Sand (2)	Stuck In Here (1)	Welcome To The Fold (2)
Cancer (1)	Gerbil (1)	It's Gonna Kill Me (2)	Skinny (2)	Take A Picture (2) 12	White Like That (1)
Captain Bligh (2)	**Hey Man Nice Shot** (1) 76	It's Over (1)	So Cool (1)	Take Another (1)	
Consider This (1)	I Will Lead You (2)	Miss Blue (2)	Spent (1)	Under (1)	

FINE YOUNG CANNIBALS '89
Pop-rock trio formed in Birmingham, England: Roland Gift (vocals), Andy Cox (guitar) and David Steele (bass). Cox and Steele were with **English Beat**. Group name taken from the 1960 movie *All The Fine Young Cannibals*. Group appeared in the movie *Tin Men*. Gift acted in the movies *Sammy And Rosie Get Laid* and *Scandal*.

| 1/25/86 | 49 | 28 | | © | 1 | **Fine Young Cannibals**.......... | | | | $10 | I.R.S. 5683 |
| 3/11/89 | ❶[7] | 63 | ▲[2] | © | 2 | **The Raw & The Cooked**.......... | | | | $10 | I.R.S. 6273 |

As Hard As It Is (2)	Don't Let It Get You Down (2)	**Good Thing** (2) 1	It's OK (It's Alright) (2)	On A Promise (1)	Time Isn't Kind (1)
Blue (1)	**Don't Look Back** (2) 11	I'm Not Satisfied (2) 90	**Johnny Come Home** (1) 76	**She Drives Me Crazy** (2) 1	
Couldn't Care More (1)	Ever Fallen In Love (1)	**I'm Not The Man I Used To Be**	Like A Stranger (1)	Suspicious Minds (1)	
Don't Ask Me To Choose (1)	Funny How Love Is (1)	(2) 54	Move To Work (1)	Tell Me What (2)	

FINN, Tim '83
Born on 6/25/52 in Te Awamutu, New Zealand. Singer/songwriter/guitarist. Member of **Split Enz** and **Crowded House** (with brother Neil Finn).

| 9/17/83 | 161 | 5 | | | | **Escapade** .... | | | | $10 | A&M 4972 |

Below The Belt	Growing Pains	In A Minor Key	Not For Nothing	Through The Years
Fraction Too Much Friction	I Only Want To Know	Made My Day	Staring At The Embers	Wait And See

FINNEY, Albert '77
Born on 5/9/36 in Salford, Manchester, England. Prolific movie actor.

| 9/3/77 | 199 | 1 | | | | **Albert Finney's Album**.......... | | | | $12 | Motown 889 |

Bird Of Paradise	How Do You Know?	Stream Of Life	We'll Be Okay	When It's Gone
But I Was A Child	I'd Like It To Be Me	They Say	What Have They Done (To My	
Crazy Song	State Of Grace	Those Other Men	Home Town?)	

FIONA '85
Born Fiona Flanagan on 9/13/61 in New York City. Co-starred in the 1987 movie *Hearts Of Fire*.

| 3/30/85 | 71 | 18 | | | 1 | **Fiona**.......... | | | | $10 | Atlantic 81242 |
| 11/25/89+ | 150 | 16 | | © | 2 | **Heart Like A Gun**.......... | | | | $10 | Atlantic 81903 |

Bringing In The Beast (2)	Here It Comes Again (2)	Love Makes You Blind (1)	**Talk To Me** (1) 64
Draw The Line (2)	James (1)	Mariel (2)	Victoria Cross (2)
Everything You Do (You're Sexing Me) (2) 52	Little Jeannie (Got The Look Of Love) (2)	Na Na Song (1)	When Pink Turns To Blue (2)
		Over Now (1)	Where The Cowboys Go (2)
Hang Your Heart On Me (1)	Look At Me Now (2)	Rescue You (1)	You're No Angel (1)

FIORILLO, Elisa '88
Born in 1970 in Philadelphia. Female dance singer.

| 2/20/88 | 163 | 8 | | © | | **Elisa Fiorillo**.......... | | | | $10 | Chrysalis 41608 |

Do Something Foolish	Gimme Special Love	**How Can I Forget You** 60	Lover's Prayer	Two Times Love
Forgive Me For Dreaming 49	Headin' For A Heartache	Little Too Good To Me	More Than Love	You Don't Know

FIREBALLET '75
Rock group from New Jersey: Jim Como (vocals), Ryche Chlanda (guitar), Bryan Howe (keyboards), Frank Petto (piano) and Martyn Biglin (bass).

| 9/6/75 | 151 | 8 | | | | **Night On Bald Mountain**.......... | | | | $15 | Passport 98010 |

Atmospheres	Centurion (Tales Of Fireball Kids)	Fireballet, The	Night On Bald Mountain (Suite)
		Les Cathedrales	

FIREBALLS, The — see GILMER, Jimmy

FIREFALL '76
Soft-rock group formed in Boulder, Colorado: Rick Roberts (vocals), Larry Burnett and Jack Bartley (guitars), Mark Andes (bass) and Mike Clarke (drums). David Muse (keyboards) joined in 1977. Andes was a member of **Spirit** and **Jo Jo Gunne**; joined **Heart** in 1980. Calrke was a member of **The Byrds**. Roberts and Clarke were members of **Flying Burrito Brothers**. Clarke died of liver failure on 12/19/93 (age 49).

5/8/76	28	67	●	©	1	**Firefall**..........				$12	Atlantic 18174
8/20/77	27	28	●	©	2	**Luna Sea**				$12	Atlantic 19101
10/28/78+	27	24	▲	©	3	**Elan**..........				$12	Atlantic 19183
4/12/80	68	15		©	4	**Undertow**..........				$12	Atlantic 16006
1/10/81	102	13			5	**Clouds Across The Sun**..........				$12	Atlantic 16024

DEBUT	PEAK	WKS	RIAA	CD	ARTIST — Album Title	Catalog	Sym	$	Label & Number

FIREFALL — Cont'd

| 12/26/81+ | 186 | 4 | | | 6 The Best Of Firefall | | [G] | $12 | Atlantic 19316 |
| 3/12/83 | 199 | 3 | | | 7 Break Of Dawn | | | $10 | Atlantic 80017 |

Always (7) *59*
Anymore (3)
Baby (3)
Be In Love Tonight (5)
Body And Soul (7)
Break Of Dawn (7)
Business Is Business (4)
Cinderella (1,6) *34*
Clouds Across The Sun (5)
Count Your Blessings (3)
Do What You Want (1)

Dolphin's Lullaby (1)
Don't It Feel Empty (5)
Don't Tell Me Why (7)
Dreamers (5)
Even Steven (2)
Fall For You (7)
Falling In Love (7)
Get You Back (3)
Getaway (2)
Goodbye, I Love You (3,6) *43*
Head On Home (2)

Headed For A Fall (4,6) *35*
I Don't Want To Hear It (5)
If You Only Knew (4)
In The Dead Of Night (7)
It Doesn't Matter (1)
It's Not Too Late (7)
Just Remember I Love You (2,6) *11*
Just Think (2)
Laugh Or Cry (4)
Leave It Alone (4)

Livin' Ain't Livin' (1) *42*
Love Ain't What It Seems (5)
Love Isn't All (1)
Love That Got Away (4,6) *50*
Mexico (1,6)
No Class (5)
No Way Out (1)
Old Wing Mouth (5)
Only A Fool (2)
Only Time Will Tell (4)
Piece Of Paper (2)

Quite Like You (5)
Sad Ol' Love Song (1)
So Long (2,6) *48*
Sold On You (2)
Some Things Never Change (4)
Someday Soon (2)
Stardust (4)
Staying With It (5,6) *37*
Strange Way (3,6) *11*
Suddenly (7)
Sweet And Sour (3)

Sweet Ann (3)
Take Me Back (7)
Undertow (4)
Winds Of Change (3)
Wrong Side Of Town (3)
You Are The Woman (1,6) *9*

FIREHOUSE '91

Pop-rock group from North Carolina: C.J. Snare (vocals), Bill Leverty (guitar), Perry Richardson (bass) and Michael Foster (drums).

3/9/91	21	76	▲²	©	1 Firehouse			$10	Epic 46186
7/4/92	23	30	●	©	2 Hold Your Fire			$10	Epic 48615
4/29/95	66	9		©	3 3			$10	Epic 57459

All She Wrote (1) *58*
Don't Treat Me Bad (1) *19*
Don't Walk Away (1)
Get A Life (3)
Get In Touch (2)
Helpless (1)

Here For You (3)
Hold The Dream (2)
Hold Your Fire (2)
Home Is Where The Heart Is (1)
I Live My Life For You (3) *26*
Life In The Real World (2)

Love Is A Dangerous Thing (3)
Love Of A Lifetime (1) *5*
Lover's Lane (1)
Mama Didn't Raise No Fool (2)
Meaning Of Love (2)
No One At All (3)

Oughta Be A Law (1)
Overnight Sensation (1)
Reach For The Sky (2) *83*
Rock On The Radio (1)
Rock You Tonight (2)
Seasons Of Change (1)

Shake & Tumble (1)
Sleeping With You (2) *78*
Somethin' 'Bout Your Body (3)
Talk Of The Town (2)
Temptation (3)
Trying To Make A Living (3)

Two Sides (3)
What's Wrong (3)
When I Look Into Your Eyes (2) *8*
You're Too Bad (2)

FIRESIGN THEATRE '71

Satirical comedy group from Los Angeles: Phil Austin, Peter Bergman, David Ossman and Philip Proctor.

10/18/69	195	2		©	1 How Can You Be In Two Places At Once When You're Not Anywhere At All		[C]	$15	Columbia 9884
9/19/70	106	10			2 Don't Crush That Dwarf, Hand Me The Pliers		[C]	$15	Columbia 30102
9/25/71	50	14		©	3 I Think We're All Bozos On This Bus		[C]	$15	Columbia 30737
2/26/72	75	11		©	4 Dear Friends		[C-K]	$20	Columbia 31099 [2]
11/25/72	115	8			5 Not Insane Or Anything You Want To		[C]	$15	Columbia 31585
3/2/74	172	5			6 The Tale Of The Giant Rat Of Sumatra		[C]	$15	Columbia 32730
11/2/74	147	6			7 Everything You Know Is Wrong		[C]	$15	Columbia 33141
6/11/77	184	2			8 Just Folks...A Firesign Chat		[C]	$12	Butterfly 001

Any More Rocket Fuel For You
Hardhats? (8)
Balliol Bros. (4)
Ben Bland's All-Day Matinee,
Part One (8)
Ben Bland's All-Night Matinee,
Part Two (8)
Bob's Brazerko Lounge (4)
Brickbreaking (4)
Chinchilla Show (4)
Coal! (4)
Deputy Dan Has No Friends (4)

Dr. Whiplash (4)
Driving For Dopers (4)
Duke Of Madness Motors (4)
Echo Poem (4)
Electrician Exposes Himself (6)
Everything You Know Is Wrong
(7)
40 Great Unclaimed Melodies!
(4)
Freezing Mr. Foster (4)
Funny Thing Happened On The
Way To The Inquisition (4)

Further Adventures Of Nick
Danger (1)
Giant Toad (4)
Hello, What's Happening? I Die
Every Night (8)
How Can You Be In Two Places
At Once When You're Not
Anywhere At All (1)
I Think We're All Bozos On This
Bus (3)
I Was A Cock-Teaser For
Roosterama! (4)

International Youth-Sex On
Parade (4)
Live From The Senate Bar (If
You Call That Living!) (4)
Mark Time! (4)
Minority Street (4)
Not Insane (5)
Not Quite The Solution He
Expected (6)
Not Responsible (5)
$100.00 Ben (4)
Other Side (2)

Outrageously Disgusting
Disguise (6)
Pass The Indian, Please (8)
Pickles Down The Rat Hole! (6)
Poop's Principles (4)
Praise The Hoove! (4)
Sleep (4)
Small Animal Administration (4)
Sodom And Jubilee (4)
Someday Funnies (4)
Stiff Idiot Is The Worst Kind! (8)

T.B. Guide (4)
T.V. Glide (4)
This Side (2)
Toad Away (4)
Truck Stops Here (8)
Where Did Jonas Go When The
Lights Went Out? (6)
Where There's Smoke, There's
Work (6)

FIRM, The '85

All-star rock group from England: **Paul Rodgers** (vocals), **Jimmy Page** (guitar), Tony Franklin (keyboards) and Chris Slade (drums). Rodgers was with **Free** and **Bad Company**. Page was with **The Yardbirds** and **Led Zeppelin**. Disbanded in 1986. Franklin joined **Blue Murder** in 1989. Slade joined **AC/DC** in 1990. Rodgers joined **The Law** in 1991.

| 3/2/85 | 17 | 33 | ● | © | 1 The Firm | | | $10 | Atlantic 81239 |
| 2/22/86 | 22 | 19 | | © | 2 Mean Business | | | $10 | Atlantic 81628 |

All The Kings Horses (2) *61*
Cadillac (2)
Closer (1)
Dreaming (2)

Fortune Hunter (2)
Free To Live (2)
Live In Peace (2)
Make Or Break (1)

Midnight Moonlight (1)
Money Can't Buy (1)
Radioactive (1) *28*

Satisfaction Guaranteed
(1) *73*
Someone To Love (1)
Spirit Of Love (2)

Tear Down The Walls (2)
Together (1)
You've Lost That Lovin' Feeling
(1)

FIRM, The '97

All-star rap group: **Nas**, **Foxy Brown**, **AZ** and **Nature**.

| 11/8/97 | ❶¹ | 22 | | © | The Firm - The Album | | | $10 | Aftermath 90136 |

Desparados
Executive Decision
Firm All Stars

Firm Biz
Firm Family
Firm Fiasco

Five Minutes To Flush
Fuck Somebody Else
Hardcore

I'm Leaving
Phone Tap
Throw Your Guns

Untouchable

FIRST CHOICE '77

Female R&B vocal trio from Philadelphia: Rochelle Fleming, Annette Guest and Joyce Jones. By 1977, Jones left and Ursula Herring joined. Herring left by 1979 and Debbie Martin joined.

10/27/73	184	4			1 Armed And Extremely Dangerous			$15	Philly Groove 1400
10/26/74	143	7			2 The Player			$15	Philly Groove 1502
10/1/77	103	8			3 Delusions			$12	Gold Mind 7501
3/31/79	135	12			4 Hold Your Horses			$12	Gold Mind 9502

All I Need Is Time (2)
**Armed And Extremely
Dangerous** (1) *28*
Boy Named Junior (1)
Chances Go Around (3)
Do Me Again (3)
Doctor Love (3) *41*

Double Cross (3)
Gamble On Love (3)
Good Morning Midnight
(medley) (4)
Great Expectations (medley) (4)
Guess What Mary Jones Did (2)
Guilty (2)

Hold Your Horses (4)
Hustler Bill (2)
I Love You More Than Before
(3)
Indian Giver (3)
Jimmy "D" (3)
Let Me Down Easy (medley) (4)

Let No Man Put Asunder (3)
Love And Happiness (1)
Love Having You Around (3)
Love Thang (4)
Newsy Neighbors (1) *97*
One Step Away (1)
Player - Part 1 (2) *70*

Runnin' Out Of Fools (1)
Smarty Pants (1) *56*
This Is The House (1)
This Little Woman (1)
Wake Up To Me (1)
You Took The Words Right Out
Of My Mouth (2)

You've Been Doin' Wrong For
So Long (2)

FIRST EDITION, The — see ROGERS, Kenny

FISCHER, Lisa '91

Born in Brooklyn, New York. R&B singer.

| 5/18/91 | 100 | 14 | | © | So Intense | | | $10 | Elektra 60889 |

Chain Of Broken Hearts
Get Back To Love

How Can I Ease The Pain *11*
Last Goodbye

Save Me *74*
Send The Message Of Love

So Intense
So Tender

Some Girls
Wildflower

FISHBONE   '91

Funk-rock group from Los Angeles: Angelo Moore (vocals, sax), Kendall Jones and Charlie Down (guitars), Christopher Dowd (keyboards), Walter Kibby (trumpet), John Fisher (bass) and Phillip Fisher (drums). Down left in 1991, replaced by John Bigham. Jones left in 1993. Group appeared in several movies.

10/1/88	153	9	©	1 Truth And Soul	$10	Columbia 40891
5/11/91	49	10	©	2 The Reality Of My Surroundings	$10	Columbia 46142
6/12/93	99	4	©	3 Give A Monkey A Brain And He'll Swear He's The Center Of The Universe	$10	Columbia 52764
6/8/96	158	1	©	4 Chim Chim's Badass Revenge	$10	Rowdy 37010

Alcoholic (4)
Asswhippin' (2)
Babyhead (2)
Beergut (4)
Behavior Control Technician (2)
Black Flowers (3)
Bonin' In The Boneyard (1)
Change (1)
Chim Chim's Badass Revenge (4)

Deathmarch (2)
Deep Inside (1)
Drunk Skitzo (3)
End The Reign (3)
Everyday Sunshine (4)
Fight The Youth (2)
Freddie's Dead (1)
Ghetto Soundwave (1)
Housework (2)
If I Were A ... I'd (2)

In The Cube (4)
Junkies Prayer (2)
Lemon Meringue (3)
Love...Hate (4)
Ma And Pa (1)
Mighty Long Way (1)
Monkey Dick (4)
Naz-tee May'en (2)
No Fear (3)
Nutmeg (2)

Nutt Megalomaniac (3)
One Day (1)
Pouring Rain (1)
Pray To The Junkiemaker (2)
Pre Nut (4)
Pressure (2)
Properties Of Propaganda (Fuk This Shit On Up) (3)
Psychological Overcast (4)
Question Of Life (1)

Rock Star (4)
Servitude (3)
Slow Bus Movin' (Howard Beach Party) (1)
So Many Millions (2)
Sourpuss (4)
Subliminal Fascism (1)
Sunless Saturday (2)
Swim (3)

They All Have Abandoned Their Hopes (3)
Those Days Are Gone (2)
Unyielding Conditioning (3)
Warmth Of Your Breath (3)

FISHER, Climie — see CLIMIE

FISHER, Eddie   '55

Born on 8/10/28 in Philadelphia. Pop singer/actor. Married to **Debbie Reynolds** (1955-59), Elizabeth Taylor (1959-64) and Connie Stevens (1967-69). Daughter with Debbie is actress/author Carrie Fisher. Daughters with Connie are singer Tricia Leigh Fisher and actress Joely Fisher. Own "Coke Time" 15-minute TV series (1953-57). Acted in several movies.

| 4/30/55 | 5 | 14 | | 1 I Love You | $30 | RCA Victor 1097 |

EP: RCA Victor EPB-1097 (#5); LP RCA Victor LPM-1097 (#8)

| 3/30/63 | 128 | 3 | © | 2 Eddie Fisher At The Winter Garden.. [L] | $25 | Ramrod 1 [2] |

recorded on 10/2/62 in New York City

7/24/65	52	10		3 Eddie Fisher Today!	$20	Dot 25631
11/26/66+	72	10		4 Games That Lovers Play	$15	RCA Victor 3726
7/1/67	193	3		5 People Like You	$15	RCA Victor 3820

Back In Your Own Backyard (2)
Born Free (5)
Call Me Irresponsible (3)
Carnival (Manha De Carnaval) (4)
Come Love! (5)
Dear Heart (3)
Dr. Zhivago ..see: Lara's Theme
Don't Let It Get You Down (2)
Downtown (3)
Games That Lovers Play (4) 45
Girl That I Marry (1)
Hava Naguila (Dance Everyone Dance) (2)

Heart (medley) (2)
Hello, Dolly! (3)
Hit Medley (2)
How Insensitive (Insensatez) (4)
I Can't Give You Anything But Love (1)
I Get Along Without You Very Well (4)
I Haven't Got Anything Better To Do (5)
I Surrender, Dear (1)
I Will Wait For You (5)
If I Loved You (3)
If She Walked Into My Life (5)

It Never Entered My Mind (4)
Jolson Medley No. 1 & 2 (2)
Just Let Me Look At You (4)
Lara's Theme (4)
Let's Fall In Love (1)
Love Sends A Little Gift Of Roses (1)
Love Somebody (1)
Mack The Knife (2)
Makin' Whoopee (4)
Mame (5)
Maybe Today (Le Coeur Trop Tendre) (5)
Mein Shtetele Belz (That Wonderful Girl Of Mine) (2)

Moon River (2)
My Best Girl (5)
My One And Only Love (1)
My Romance (1)
Never On Sunday (2)
Oh My Papa (O Mein Papa) (medley) (2)
Once I Loved (4)
Once Upon A Time (3)
People (3)
People Like You (5) 97
Pretty Baby (1)
Red Roses For A Blue Lady (3)
So In Love (1)
Somebody Loves Me (1)

Somewhere, My Love ..see: Lara's Theme
Sonny Boy (2)
Sunrise, Sunset (3)
Sweetest Sounds (2)
This Nearly Was Mine (2)
Try To Remember (3)
Watch What Happens (5)
West Side Story Medley (2)
What Is This Thing Called Love? (1)
What Kind Of Fool Am I (2)
What Now My Love (Et Maintenant) (3)
Where's That Rainbow (4)

Who Can I Turn To (When Nobody Needs Me) (3)
Wish You Were Here (medley) (2)
Yesterday (4)
You Don't Have To Say You Love Me (Io Che Non Vivo [Senza Te]) (1)
You Made Me Love You (2)
You're Devastating (4)

★425★   FITZGERALD, Ella   '61

Born on 4/25/18 in Newport News, Virginia. Died of diabetes on 6/15/96 (age 78). Legendary jazz singer. Won Grammy's Lifetime Achievement Award in 1967.

1)*Songs From Pete Kelly's Blues* 2)*Ella Fitzgerald Sings The Rodgers And Hart Song Book* 3)*Mack The Knife - Ella In Berlin*

| 9/17/55 | 7 | 10 | | 1 Songs from Pete Kelly's Blues | $60 | Decca 8166 |

PEGGY LEE and ELLA FITZGERALD

| 7/28/56 | 15 | 1 | © | 2 Ella Fitzgerald sings the Cole Porter Song Book................................ | $50 | Verve 4001 [2] |
| 12/15/56 | 12 | 2 | © | 3 Ella And Louis .... | $50 | Verve 4003 |

ELLA FITZGERALD and LOUIS ARMSTRONG backing by the Oscar Peterson Trio and Buddy Rich

| 3/16/57 | 11 | 4 | © | 4 Ella Fitzgerald sings the Rodgers and Hart Song Book............... | $50 | Verve 4002 [2] |
| 9/12/60+ | 11 | 51 | © | 5 Mack The Knife - Ella In Berlin.. [L] | $30 | Verve 4041 |

accompanied by the Paul Smith Quartet

| 11/13/61+ | 35 | 34 | © | 6 Ella In Hollywood .... [L] | $30 | Verve 4052 |
| 10/19/63 | 69 | 20 | © | 7 Ella And Basie! .... | $30 | Verve 4061 |

ELLA FITZGERALD/COUNT BASIE arranged by Quincy Jones

| 3/28/64 | 111 | 5 | © | 8 Ella Fitzgerald sings the George and Ira Gershwin Song Books .... | $60 | Verve V-29-5 [5] |

recorded 1958-59; arranged and conducted by Nelson Riddle

8/22/64	146	2		9 Hello, Dolly!	$30	Verve 4064
8/19/67	172	2	©	10 Brighten The Corner	$25	Capitol 2685
12/9/67	27[X]	4	©	11 Ella Fitzgerald's Christmas .... [X]	$25	Capitol 2805
10/18/69	196	2		12 Ella	$15	Reprise 6354

Abide With Me (10)
Ace In The Hole (4)
Ain't Misbehavin' (7)
Airmail Special (6)
All Of You (2)
All Through The Night (2)
Always True To You In My Fashion (2)
Angels We Have Heard On High (11)
Anything Goes (2)
April In Paris (3)
Aren't You Kind Of Glad We Did? (8)
Away In A Manger (11)

Baby, Won't You Please Come Home (6)
Begin The Beguine (2)
Beginner's Luck (8)
Bewitched (4)
Bidin' My Time (8)
Blue Moon (4,6)
Blue Room (4)
Boy Wanted (8)
Boy! What Love Has Done To Me! (8)
Brighten The Corner (Where You Are) (10)
But Not For Me (8)
By Strauss (8)
Can't Buy Me Love (9)

Can't We Be Friends (3)
Cheek To Cheek (3)
Church In The Wildwood (10)
Clap Yo' Hands (8)
Dancing On The Ceiling (4)
'Deed I Do (7)
Do I Love You (2)
Don't Fence Me In (2)
Dream A Little Dream Of Me (7)
Easy To Love (2)
Ella Hums The Blues (1)
Embraceable You (8)
Ev'ry Time We Say Good-bye (2)
Ev'rything I've Got (4)

Fascinating Rhythm (8)
First Noël (11)
Foggy Day (3,8)
For You, For Me, For Evermore (8)
From This Moment On (2)
Funny Face (8)
Get Out Of Town (2)
Get Ready (12)
Give It Back To The Indians (4)
God Be With You Till We Meet Again (10)
God Rest Ye Merry Gentlemen (11)
God Will Take Care Of You (10)
Gone With The Wind (5)

Got To Get You Into My Life (12)
Half Of It, Dearie Blues (8)
Hard Hearted Hannah (The Vamp Of Savannah) (1)
Hark The Herald Angels Sing (11)
Have You Met Miss Jones? (4)
He Loves And She Loves (8)
Hello, Dolly! (9)
Here In My Arms (4)
Honeysuckle Rose (7)
How High The Moon (Part 1) (5,9) 76
How Long Has This Been Going On? (8)

Hunter Gets Captured By The Game (12)
I Am In Love (2)
I Can't Be Bothered Now (8)
I Concentrate On You (2)
I Could Write A Book (4)
I Didn't Know What Time It Was (4)
I Get A Kick Out Of You (2)
I Got Rhythm (8)
I Love Paris (2)
I Need Thee Every Hour (10)
I Shall Not Be Moved (10)

FITZGERALD, Ella — Cont'd

I Was Doing All Right (8)
I Wish I Were In Love Again (4)
I Wonder Why (12)
I'll Never Fall In Love Again (12)
I'm Beginning To See The Light (7)
I've Got A Crush On You (8)
I've Got Five Dollars (8)
I've Got The World On A String (6)
I've Got You Under My Skin (6)
In The Garden (10)
In The Still Of The Night (2)
Into Each Life Some Rain Must Fall (7)
Isn't It A Pity? (8)
Isn't It Romantic (4)
Isn't This A Lovely Day (3)
It Came Upon A Midnight Clear (11)
It Might As Well Be Spring (6)
It Never Entered My Mind (4)
It's All Right With Me (4)
It's Delovely (2)
Johnny One Note (4)

Joy To The World (11)
Just A Closer Walk With Thee (10)
Just Another Rhumba (8)
Just In Time (6)
Just One Of Those Things (2)
Knock On Wood (12)
Lady Is A Tramp (4,5)
Let The Lower Lights Be Burning (10)
Let's Call The Whole Thing Off (8)
Let's Do It (2)
Let's Kiss And Make Up (8)
Little Girl Blue (4)
Looking For A Boy (8)
Lorelei (5,8)
Love For Sale (2)
Love Is Here To Stay (8)
Love Is Sweeping The Country (8)
Love Walked In (8)
Lover (4)
Lullaby Of The Leaves (9)
Mack The Knife (5) *27*

Man I Love (5,8)
Manhattan (4)
Memories Of You (9)
Miss Otis Regrets (2,9)
Misty (5)
Moonlight In Vermont (3)
Mountain Greenery (4)
My Cousin In Milwaukee (8)
My Funny Valentine (4)
My Heart Stood Still (4)
My Last Affair (7)
My Man (9)
My One And Only (8)
My Romance (4)
Nearness Of You (3)
Nice Work If You Can Get It (8)
Night And Day (2)
O Come All Ye Faithful (11)
O Holy Night (11)
O Little Town Of Bethlehem (11)
Of Thee I Sing (Baby) (8)
Oh, Lady Be Good! (8)
Oh, So Nice (8)
Old Rugged Cross (10)

On The Sunny Side Of The Street (7)
Ooo Baby Baby (12)
Open Your Window (12)
People (9)
Pete Kelly's Blues (1,9)
Real American Folk Song (8)
Ridin' High (2)
Rock Of Ages, Cleft For Me (10)
'S Wonderful (8)
Sam And Delilah (8)
Satin Doll (6,7)
Savoy Truffle (12)
Shall We Dance? (8)
Ship Without A Sail (4)
Shiny Stockings (7)
Silent Night (11)
Slap That Bass (8)
Sleep My Little Lord Jesus (11)
So In Love (2)
Somebody From Somewhere (8)
Someone To Watch Over Me (8)

Soon (8)
Spring Is Here (4)
Stairway To The Stars (6)
Stars Fell On Alabama (3)
Stiff Upper Lip (8)
Strike Up The Band (8)
Summertime (5)
Sweetest Sounds (9)
Take The "A" Train (6)
Tea For Two (7)
Ten Cents A Dance (4)
Tenderly (3)
That Certain Feeling (8)
Them There Eyes (7)
There's A Small Hotel (4)
They All Laughed (8)
They Can't Take That Away From Me (3,8)
Things Are Looking Up (8)
This Can't Be Love (4)
This Could Be The Start Of Something Big (6)
Thou Swell (8)
Thrill Is Gone (4)
Throw Out The Lifeline (10)

To Keep My Love Alive (4)
Too Darn Hot (2,5)
Treat Me Rough (8)
Under A Blanket Of Blue (3)
Volare (Nel Blu Dipinto Di Blu) (9)
Wait Till You See Her (4)
We Three Kings (11)
What A Friend We Have In Jesus (11)
What Is This Thing Called Love (2)
Where Or When (4)
Who Cares? (8)
Why Can't You Behave (2)
With A Song In My Heart (4)
Yellow Man (12)
You Do Something To Me (2)
You Took Advantage Of Me (4)
You'll Have To Swing It Mr. Paganini (6)
You're Driving Me Crazy (6)
You're The Top (2)
You've Got What Gets Me (8)

FIVE · '99

Male vocal group from England: Rich Neville, Scott Robinson, Richard Breen, Jason Brown and Sean Conlon.

DEBUT	PEAK	WKS	RIAA	CD	ARTIST — Album Title	$	Label & Number
8/22/98+	27	54	▲	©	1 **Five**	$10	Arista 19003
6/3/00	108	3		©	2 **Invincible**	$10	Arista 14620

Don't Fight It Baby (2)
Don't Wanna Let You Go (2)
Everybody Get Up (1)
Everyday (1)
Got The Feelin' (1)

How Do Ya Feel (2)
If Ya Gettin' Down (2)
Invincible (2)
It's All Over (1)
It's Alright (2)

It's The Things You Do (1) *53*
Keep On Movin' (2)
My Song (1)
Partyline 555-On-Line (1)
Satisfied (1)

Serious (2)
Slam Dunk (Da Funk) (1) *86*
That's What You Told Me (1)
Two Sides To Every Story (2)
Until The Time Is Through (1)

We Will Rock You (2)
When I Remember When (1)
When The Lights Go Out (1) *10*
You Make Me A Better Man (2)

FIVE AMERICANS, The · '67

Pop-rock group from Dallas: Michael Rabon (vocals), Norman Ezell (guitar), John Durrill (keyboards), James Grant (bass) and James Wright (drums).

DEBUT	PEAK	WKS	RIAA	CD	ARTIST — Album Title	$	Label & Number
4/30/66	136	5		©	1 **I See The Light**	$40	HBR 9503
7/8/67	121	10			2 **Western Union**	$30	Abnak 2067

Big Cities (2)
Don't You Dare Blame Me (1)
Gimme Some Lovin' (2)
Goodbye (1)

Husbands And Wives (2)
I Know They Lie (1)
I Put A Spell On You (2)
I See The Light (1) *26*

I'm So Glad (1)
If I Could (2)
It's A Crying Shame (1)
Losing Game (1)

Now That It's Over (2)
Outcast, The (1)
Reality (1)
See-Saw-Man (2)

She's-A-My Own (1)
Sound Of Love (2) *36*
Sympathy (2)
Tell Ann I Love Her (2)

Train, The (1)
Twist And Shout (1)
Western Union (2) *5*
What'd I Say (1)

FIVE IRON FRENZY · '00

Christian ska-rock group from Denver: Reese Roper (vocals), Scott Kerr and Micah Ortega (guitars), Dennis Culp and Nathanael Dunham (horns), Keith Hoerig (bass) and Andrew Verdecchio (drums). Sonnie Johnston replaced Kerr in 1998.

DEBUT	PEAK	WKS	RIAA	CD	ARTIST — Album Title		$	Label & Number
11/29/97	176	1		©	1 **Our Newest Album Ever!**		$10	Sarabellum 46815
11/20/99	190	1		©	2 **Live: Proof That The Youth Are Revolting**	[L]	$10	Five Minute Walk 25248
5/13/00	146	1		©	3 **All The Hype That Money Can Buy**		$10	Five Minute Walk 22401

All That Is Good (2)
All The Hype (3)
Anthem (2)
Arnold & Willis & Mr. Drumond (2)
Banner Year (1)
Blue Comb '78 (1,2)

Dandelions (2)
Every New Day (1,2)
Fahrenheit (3)
Fistful Of Sand (2)
Flowery Song (3)
Four-Fifty-One (3)
Giants (3)

Greatest Story Ever Told (3)
Handbook For The Sellout (1,2)
Hurricanes (3)
I Still Like Larry (3)
It's Not Unusual (2,3)
Litmus (1)
Me Oh My (3)

Most Likely To Succeed (1)
New Hope (2,3)
Oh, Canada (1,2)
One Girl Army (2)
Phantom Mullet (3)
Receive Him (3)
Second Season (1)

Solidarity (3)
Suckerpunch (1,2)
Superpowers (1,2)
Ugly Day (2,3)
Where Is Micah? (1)
Where 0 Meets 15 (2)
World Without End (3)

You Probably Shouldn't Move Here (3)

FIVE MAN ELECTRICAL BAND · '71

Rock group from Ontario, Canada: Les Emmerson (vocals, guitar), Ted Gerow (piano), Brian Rading (bass) and brothers Rick (percussion) and Mike (drums) Belanger.

DEBUT	PEAK	WKS	RIAA	CD	ARTIST — Album Title	$	Label & Number
7/31/71	148	9			1 **Good-Byes & Butterflies**	$30	Lionel 1100
2/12/72	199	2			2 **Coming Of Age**	$20	Lionel 1101

Absolutely Right (2) *26*
All Is Right (With The World) (1)
Coming Of Age (2)
Country Girl (Suite) Medley (2)

Dance Of The Swamp Woman (1)
Find The One (2)
Forever Together (1)

Friends & Family (2)
Hello Melinda Goodbye (1)
Isn't It A Long Hard Road (2)
Julianna (2)

Mama's Baby Child (1)
Man With The Horse And Wagon (1)
Me & Harley Davidson (2)

Moonshine (Friend Of Mine) (1)
Safe And Sound (With Jesus) (1)
Signs (1) *3*

Variations On A Theme Of Lepidoptera (1)
Whole Lotta Heavy (2)
(You And I) Butterfly (1)

504 BOYZ · '00

All-star rap trio from New Orleans: **Master P** ("Nino Brown"), **Silkk The Shocker** ("Vito") and **Mystikal** ("G Money"). 504 is the area code for New Orleans.

DEBUT	PEAK	WKS	RIAA	CD	ARTIST — Album Title	$	Label & Number
5/20/00	2¹	26	●	©	**Goodfellas**	$10	No Limit 50722

Beefing
Big Toys
Check'em
D-Game

Enemies
I Can Tell
If You Real, Keep It Real
Life Is Serious

Moving Things
No Limit
Roll, Roll
Say Brah

Souljas
Them Boyz
Thug Girl II
Up Town

We Bust
Whodi
Wobble Wobble *17*

FIVE SPECIAL · '79

R&B vocal group from Detroit: Bryan Banks, Steve Harris, Greg Finley, Mike Pettilo and Steve Boyd. Banks is brother of Ron Banks of **The Dramatics**.

DEBUT	PEAK	WKS	RIAA	CD	ARTIST — Album Title	$	Label & Number
8/11/79	118	11			**Five Special**	$12	Elektra 206

Baby
Do It Baby

It's A Wonderful Day

It's Such A Groove Part II - Whatcha Got For Music!

Rock Dancin'
Why Leave Us Alone *55*

You're Something Special

FIVE STAIRSTEPS, The   '70

R&B group from Chicago: brothers Clarence (vocals), James (guitar), Kenny (bass) and Dennis (drums) Burke, with their sister Alohe (vocals). Later joined by their five-year-old brother Cubie. Later became **The Invisible Man's Band**.

DEBUT	PEAK	WKS				$	Label & Number
3/25/67	**139**	4			1 The Five Stairsteps	$25	Windy C 6000

5 STAIRSTEPS & CUBIE:

| 1/27/68 | **195** | 3 | | | 2 Our Family Portrait .... | $20 | Buddah 5008 |
| 4/26/69 | **198** | 2 | | | 3 Love's Happening .... | $20 | Curtom 8002 |

STAIRSTEPS:

6/13/70	**83**	12			4 Stairsteps	$15	Buddah 5061
12/12/70	**199**	2			5 Step by Step by Step	[K] $15	Buddah 5068
5/31/80	**90**	14			6 The Invisible Man's Band	$12	Mango 9537

All Night Thing (6) *45* — (Baby) Make Me Feel So Good (3,5) — Bad News (2) — **Because I Love You** (4,5) *flip* — Behind Curtains (1,5) — **Come Back** (1,5) *61* — X-Country (6) — **Danger! She's A Stranger** (1,5) *89* — Dear Prudence (4) *66* — **Don't Change Your Love** (3) *59* — Don't Waste Your Time (1,5) — Find Me (2) — Full Moon (6) — Getting Better (4) — Girl I Love (1) — I Made A Mistake (3) — I Remember You (2) — I'm The One Who Loves You (3) — Little Boy Blue (3) — Little Young Lover (3) — Look Of Love (2) — Love Can't Come/Love Has Come (6) — Loves Happening (3) — **Million To One** (2) *68* — New Dance Craze (2,3) — 9 X's Out Of Ten (6) — **O-o-h Child** (4,5) *8* — **Oooh, Baby Baby** (1,5) *63* — Playgirl's Love (1,5) — Rent Strike (6) — **Something's Missing** (2) *88* — **Stay Close To Me** (3,5) *91* — Sweet As A Peach (4) — Tell Me Who (2) — Touch Of You (1,5) — Under The Spell (2) — Up & Down (4) — Vice The Lights (4) — **We Must Be In Love** (5) *88* — What About Your Wife (4) — Who Do You Belong To (4) — Windows Of The World (2) — **World Of Fantasy** (1,5) *49* — You Don't Love Me (1) — You Make Me So Mad (2) — **You Waited Too Long** (1,5) *94* — Your Love Has Changed (3)

FIVE STAR   '86

Family vocal group from Romford, Essex, England: siblings Deniece, Stedman, Doris, Lorraine and Delroy Pearson.

DEBUT	PEAK	WKS		CD		$	Label & Number
9/21/85+	**57**	47		©	1 Luxury Of Life	$10	RCA Victor 8052
10/4/86	**80**	25		©	2 Silk & Steel	$10	RCA Victor 5901

All Fall Down (1) *65* — Are You Man Enough? (2) — **Can't Wait Another Minute** (2) *41* — Crazy (1) — Don't You Know I Love It (2) — Find The Time (2) — Hide And Seek (1) — **If I Say Yes** (2) *67* — **Let Me Be The One** (1) *59* — Love Take Over (1) — Now I'm In Control (1) — Please Don't Say Goodnight (2) — R.S.V.P. (1) — Rain Or Shine (2) — Say Goodbye (1) — Show Me What You've Got For Me (2) — Slightest Touch (2) — Stay Out Of My Life (2) — System Addict (1) — Winning (1)

FIXX, The   '83

Techno-pop group formed in London: Cy Curnin (vocals), Jamie West-Oram (guitar), Rupert Greenall (keyboards), Dan Brown (bass) and Adam Woods (drums).

DEBUT	PEAK	WKS	RIAA	CD		Sym	$	Label & Number
11/13/82+	**106**	51		©	1 Shuttered Room		$10	MCA 5345
5/28/83	**8**	54	▲	©	2 Reach The Beach		$10	MCA 39001
9/8/84	**19**	29	●	©	3 Phantoms		$10	MCA 5507
6/14/86	**30**	21		©	4 Walkabout		$10	MCA 5705
7/18/87	**110**	7		©	5 React	[L]	$10	MCA 42008
2/11/89	**72**	18		©	6 Calm Animals		$10	RCA 8566
3/16/91	**111**	10		©	7 Ink		$10	MCA 10205

All Is Fair (7) — All The Best Things (7) — **Are We Ourselves?** (3,5) *15* — Big Wall (5) — Built For The Future (4,5) — Calm Animals (6) — Cameras In Paris (1) — Camphor (4) — Can't Finish (4) — Cause To Be Alarmed (6) — Changing (2) — Chase The Fire (4) — Climb The Hill (7) — Crucified (7) — Deeper And Deeper (5) — Don't Be Scared (5) — **Driven Out** (6) *55* — Facing The Wind (3) — Falling In Love (7) — Flow, The (6) — Fool, The (1) — Gypsy Feet (6) — **How Much Is Enough** (7) *35* — I Found You (1) — I Live (1) — I Will (3) — I'm Life (6) — In Suspense (3) — Less Cities, More Moving People (3) — Liner (2) — Lose Face (3) — Lost In Battle Overseas (3) — Lost Planes (1) — Make No Plans (7) — No One Has To Cry (7) — One Jungle (7) — One Look Up (4) — **One Thing Leads To Another** (2,5) *4* — Opinions (2) — Outside (2) — Phantom Living (3) — Precious Stone (6) — Privilege (2) — Question (3) — Reach The Beach (2) — Read Between The Lines (4) — Red Skies (1,5) — Rules And Schemes (5) — Running (2) — **Saved By Zero** (2,5) *20* — **Secret Separation** (4) *19* — Sense The Adventure (4) — Shred Of Evidence (6) — Shut It Out (7) — Shuttered Room (1) — **Sign Of Fire** (2) *32* — Some People (1) — **Stand Or Fall** (1,5) *76* — Still Around (7) — Strain, The (1) — Subterranean (6) — **Sunshine In The Shade** (3) *69* — Treasure It (4) — Walkabout (4) — Wish (3) — Woman On A Train (3) — World Weary (6) — Yesterday, Today (7)

FLACK, Roberta   ★169★   '71

Born on 2/10/39 in Asheville, North Carolina; raised in Arlington, Virginia. Played piano from an early age. Music scholarship to Howard University at age 15; classmate of **Donny Hathaway**. Worked as a high school music teacher in North Carolina. Discovered by jazz musician **Les McCann**. Signed to Atlantic in 1969.

1)First Take 2)Killing Me Softly 3)Roberta Flack & Donny Hathaway

DEBUT	PEAK	WKS	RIAA	CD		Sym	$	Label & Number
1/31/70+	**❶**[5]	54	●	©	1 First Take		$15	Atlantic 8230
8/29/70	**33**	82	●	©	2 Chapter Two		$15	Atlantic 1569
12/11/71+	**18**	48	●	©	3 Quiet Fire		$15	Atlantic 1594
5/13/72	**3**	39	●	©	4 Roberta Flack & Donny Hathaway		$15	Atlantic 7216
9/1/73	**3**	53	●	©	5 Killing Me Softly		$15	Atlantic 7271
3/29/75	**24**	26		©	6 Feel Like Makin' Love		$12	Atlantic 18131
1/7/78	**8**	32	●	©	7 Blue Lights In The Basement		$12	Atlantic 19149
9/30/78	**74**	10			8 Roberta Flack		$12	Atlantic 19186
3/29/80	**25**	24	●		9 Roberta Flack Featuring Donny Hathaway		$12	Atlantic 16013
12/20/80+	**52**	19		©	10 Live & More	[L]	$15	Atlantic 7004 [2]

ROBERTA FLACK & PEABO BRYSON
recorded at the Holiday Star Theater in Merrillville, Indiana

6/27/81	**161**	11			11 Bustin' Loose	[S]	$10	MCA 5141
6/19/82	**59**	21		©	12 I'm The One		$10	Atlantic 19354
8/13/83	**25**	42	●	©	13 Born To Love		$10	Capitol 12284

PEABO BRYSON/ROBERTA FLACK

| 1/14/89 | **159** | 8 | | © | 14 Oasis .... | | $10 | Atlantic 81916 |
| 11/9/91 | **110** | 10 | | © | 15 Set The Night To Music .... | | $10 | Atlantic 82321 |

FLACK, Roberta — Cont'd

After You (7)
All Caught Up In Love (14)
Always (15)
And So It Goes (14)
And The Feeling's Good (8)
Angelitos Negros (1)
Baby I Love You (4)
Baby I Love You So (8)
Back Together Again (9,10) *56*
Ballad For D. (11)
Ballad Of The Sad Young Men (1)
Be Real Black For Me (4)
Blame It On Me (13)
Born To Love (13)
Bridge Over Troubled Water (3)
Business Goes On As Usual (2)
Can We Find Love Again (13)
Children's Song (11)
Closer I Get To You (7) *2*
Come Share My Love (8)
Come Ye Disconsolate (4)
Comin' Alive (13)
Compared To What (1)
Conversation Love (5)
Disguises (9)

Do What You Gotta Do (2)
Don't Make Me Wait Too Long (9,10)
Early Ev'ry Midnite (6)
Feel Like Makin' Love (6,10) *1*
Feel The Fire (10)
Feelin' That Glow (6) *76*
Fine, Fine Day (7)
First Time Ever I Saw Your Face (1) *1*
For All We Know (4)
Friend (15)
Go Up Moses (3)
God Don't Like Ugly (9,10)
Gone Away (2)
Happiness (12)
Heaven Above Me (13)
Hey, That's No Way To Say Goodbye (1)
(His Name) Brazil (14)
Hittin' Me Where It Hurts (11)
I Believe In You (medley) (10)
I Can See The Sun In Late December (6)
I Just Came Here To Dance (13)
I Told Jesus (1)

I Wanted It Too (6)
I (Who Have Nothing) (4)
I'd Like To Be Baby To You (7)
I'm The Girl (5)
I'm The One (12) *42*
If Ever I See You Again (8) *24*
If Only For One Night (10)
Impossible Dream (2)
In The Name Of Love (12)
Independent Man (8)
Jesse (5) *30*
Just Like A Woman (2)
Just When I Needed You (11)
Knowing That We're Made For Each Other (8)
Let It Be Me (2)
Let Them Talk (3)
Love (Always Commands) (11)
Love And Let Love (12)
Love In Every Season (medley) (10)
Love Is A Waiting Game (10)
Love Is The Healing (7)
Lovin' You (Is Such An Easy Thang To Do) (11)

Make The World Stand Still (10)
Making Love (12) *13*
Maybe (13)
Mood (4)
More Than Everything (10)
Mr. Magic (6)
My Foolish Heart (15)
My Love For You (12)
My Someone To Love (14)
Natural Thing (15)
Never Loved Before (12)
No Tears (In The End) (10)
Oasis (14)
Old Heartbreak Top Ten (6)
Only Heaven Can Wait (For Love) (9,10)
Ordinary Man (12)
Our Ages Or Our Hearts (1)
Qual E Malindrinho (Why Are You So Bad) (11)
Reachin' For The Sky (10)
Reverend Lee (2)
River (5)
Rollin' On (11)
See You Then (3)
Set The Night To Music (15) *6*
She's Not Blind (6)

Shock To My System (14)
Some Gospel According To Matthew (6)
Something Magic (14)
Something Your Heart Has Been Telling Me (15)
Soul Deep (7)
Stay With Me (9)
Summertime (15)
Sunday And Sister Jones (3)
Suzanne (3)
Sweet Bitter Love (3)
This Time I'll Be Sweeter (7)
'Til The Morning Comes (12)
To Love Somebody (3)
Tonight, I Celebrate My Love (13) *16*
Tryin' Times (1)
25th Of Last December (7)
Uh-Uh Ooh-Ooh Look Out (Here It Comes) (14)
Unforgettable (15)
Until It's Time For You To Go (2)
Waiting Game (15)
What A Woman Really Means (8)

When It's Over (8)
When Love Has Grown (4)
When Someone Tears Your Heart In Two (15)
When Will I Learn (10)
When You Smile (15)
Where I'll Find You (7)
Where Is The Love (4) *5*
Why Don't You Move In With Me (7)
Will You Still Love Me Tomorrow (3) *76*
You Are Everything (8)
You Are My Heaven (9,10) *47*
You Know What It's Like (14)
You Make Me Feel Brand New (15)
You Stopped Loving Me (11)
You Who Brought Me Love (14)
You're Looking Like Love To Me (13) *58*
You've Got A Friend (4) *29*
You've Lost That Lovin' Feelin' (4) *71*

FLAGG, Fannie '67

Born Patricia Neal on 9/21/44 in Birmingham, Alabama. TV and movie comedienne/author. Her novel was made into the 1992 movie *Fried Green Tomatoes.*

| 9/23/67 | 183 | 3 | | | Rally 'Round The Flagg .... [C] | | | $20 | RCA Victor 3856 |

Baseball
Beauty Contest
Bingo
Check Out

Don't Do That John
Let's Cook
Mrs. Johnson Speaks
New Teacher

Renting Agent
Spelling Bee
Susie Sweetwater Local Wedding

Susie Sweetwater Society Wedding
Susie Sweetwater Theatre Review

Telephone Operator
Weather Girl
Winchester Cathedral

FLAME, The '77

Rock group from Brooklyn, New York: Marge Raymond (vocals), Jimmy Crespo and Frank Ruby (guitars), Bob Leone (piano), John Paul Fetta (bass) and Eddie Barbato (drums). Crespo was a member of **Aerosmith** from 1979-83.

| 5/14/77 | 147 | 5 | | | Queen Of The Neighborhood .... | | | $12 | RCA Victor 2160 |

All My Love To You
Angry Times

Beg Me
Everybody Loves A Winner

Grown Up Man
Laugh My Tears Away

Long Time Gone
Queen Of The Neighborhood

You Sit In Darkness

FLAMING EMBER, The '70

White R&B-rock group from Detroit: Joe Sladich (vocals, guitar), Bill Ellis (piano), Jim Bugnel (bass) and Jerry Plunk (drums).

| 8/29/70 | 188 | 3 | | | Westbound #9 .... | | | $15 | Hot Wax 702 |

Empty Crowded Room
Flashbacks And Reruns

Going In Circles
Heart On (Loving You)

Mind, Body And Soul *26*
Shades Of Green *88*

Spinning Wheel
Stop The World And Let Me Off

This Girl Is A Woman Now
Westbound #9 *24*

Where's All The Joy
Why Don't You Stay

FLAMING LIPS, The '95

Rock group from Oklahoma City: Wayne Coyne (vocals), Ron Jones (guitar), Michael Ivins (bass) and Steven Drozd (drums).

| 1/21/95 | 108 | 11 | | © | Transmissions From The Satellite Heart .... | | | $10 | Warner 45334 |

Be My Head
Chewin The Apple Of Your Eye
Moth In The Incubator

Oh My Pregnant Head
Pilot Can At The Queer Of God
She Don't Use Jelly *55*

Slow Nerve Action
"Song From Cool Hand Luke"-Plastic Jesus (*******)

Superhumans
Turn It On
When Yer Twenty Two

FLAMIN' GROOVIES '76

Rock group from San Francisco: Cyril Jordan and Chris Wilson (vocals, guitars), James Farrell (guitar), George Alexander (bass) and David Wright (drums).

| 8/21/76 | 142 | 7 | | © | Shake Some Action .... | | | $15 | Sire 7521 |

produced by **Dave Edmunds**

Don't You Lie To Me
I Can't Hide
I Saw Her

I'll Cry Alone
Let The Boy Rock 'N' Roll
Misery

Please Please Girl
Shake Some Action
She Said Yeah

Sometimes
St. Louis Blues
Teenage Confidential

Yes It's True
You Tore Me Down

FLASH '72

Rock group from England: Colin Carter (vocals), **Peter Banks** (guitar), Ray Bennett (bass) and Michael Hough (drums). Banks had been in **Yes**; later with **After The Fire**.

5/20/72	33	29		©	1 Flash			$15	Capitol 11040
12/9/72+	121	13		©	2 Flash In The Can			$15	Capitol 11115
9/1/73	135	8		©	3 Out Of Our Hands			$15	Capitol 11218

Bishop (3)
Black And White (2)
Children Of The Universe (1)
Dead Ahead (Queen) (3)

Dreams Of Heaven (1)
Farewell Number One (Pawn) (3)

Lifetime (1)
Man Of Honour (Knight) (3)
Manhattan Morning (Christmas '72) (3)

Monday Morning Eyes (2)
Morning Haze (1)
None The Wiser (King) (3)
Open Sky (3)

Psychosync (Escape) (Farewell Number Two) (3)
Shadows (It's You) (3)
Small Beginnings (1) *29*

There No More (2)
Time It Takes (1)

(also see: Psychosync)

FLASH AND THE PAN '79

Pop duo formed in Australia: George Young and Harry Vanda (both formerly with **The Easybeats**). George's younger brothers, Angus and Malcolm Young, are members of **AC/DC**.

| 5/26/79 | 80 | 16 | | © | 1 Flash And The Pan .... | | | $12 | Epic 36018 |
| 5/31/80 | 159 | 6 | | © | 2 Lights In The Night .... | | | $12 | Epic 36432 |

African Shuffle (1)
Atlantis Calling (2)
California (1)
Captain Beware (2)

Down Among The Dead Men (1)
First And Last (1)
Headhunter (2)

Hey, St. Peter (1) *76*
Hole In The Middle (1)
Lady Killer (1)
Lights In The Night (2)

Make Your Own Cross (2)
Man In The Middle (1)
Man Who Knew The Answer (1)
Media Man (2)

Restless (2)
Walking In The Rain (1)
Welcome To The Universe (2)

FLATT & SCRUGGS '63

Bluegrass duo of Lester Flatt (guitar) and Earl Scruggs (banjo). Flatt was born on 6/19/14 in Overton County, Tennessee. Died of a heart attack on 5/11/79 (age 64). Scruggs was born on 1/6/24 in Flintville, North Carolina. Duo formed in 1948 while both were members of Bill Monroe's band. Regulars on TV's *Beverly Hillbillies*.

DEBUT	PEAK	WKS			#	Album Title		Sym	$	Label & Number
4/13/63	115	4		©	1	Hard Travelin' featuring The Ballad Of Jed Clampett			$25	Columbia 1951 / 8751
9/28/63	134	6		©	2	Flatt And Scruggs At Carnegie Hall!		[L]	$25	Columbia 2045 / 8845
						recorded on 12/8/62				
3/30/68	194	4		©	3	Changin' Times featuring Foggy Mountain Breakdown			$20	Columbia 9596
6/8/68	161	4			4	Original Theme From Bonnie & Clyde		[E]	$20	Mercury 61162
						recordings from 1948-50				
7/6/68	187	5			5	The Story Of Bonnie & Clyde			$20	Columbia 9649

Another Ride With Clyde (5)
Ballad Of Jed Clampett (1) 44
Bang, You're Alive (5)
Barrow Gang Will Get You Little Man (5)
Blowin' In The Wind (3)
Bound To Ride (1)
Bouquet In Heaven (4)
Buddy, Don't Roll So Slow (3)
Chase, The (5)
Coal Miner's Blues (1)
Cora Is Gone (4)
Dig A Hole In The Meadow (2)

Dixie Home (1)
Doin' My Time (4)
Don't Think Twice, It's All Right (3)
Down In The Flood (3)
Drowned In The Deep Blue Sea (1)
Durham's Reel (2)
Fiddle And Banjo (2)
Flint Hill Special (2)
Foggy Mountain Breakdown (3,4,5) 55
Footprints In The Snow (2)

Four Strong Winds (3)
Get-Away (5)
Hard Travelin' (1)
Highway's End (5)
Hot Corn, Cold Corn (2)
I Wonder Where You Are Tonight (2)
I'll Be Going To Heaven Some Time (4)
It Ain't Me Babe (3)
Let The Church Roll On (2)
Mama Blues (2)
Martha White Theme (2)

Mr. Tambourine Man (3)
My Cabin In Caroline (4)
My Little Girl In Tennessee (4)
My Native Home (1)
99 Years Is Almost For Life (3)
No Mother Or Dad (4)
Ode To Billie Joe (3)
Over The Hill To The Poorhouse (1)
Pastures Of Plenty (1)
Picture Of Bonnie (5)
Pike County Breakdown (4)
Reunion (5)

Roll In My Sweet Baby's Arms (4)
Salty Dog Blues (2)
See Bonnie Die, See Clyde Die (See Bonnie And Clyde Die) (5)
Story Of Bonnie And Clyde (5)
Take Me In A Lifeboat (4)
Take This Hammer (4)
This Land Is Your Land (3)
When I Let East Virginia (1)
Where Have All The Flowers Gone (3)

Why Don't You Tell Me So (4)
Wreck Of The Old 97 (1)
Yonder Stands Little Maggie (2)

FLECK, Bela, & The Flecktones '98

Born on 7/10/59 in New York City. Male banjo player. The Flecktones: Victor Wooten (bass) and Jeff Coffin (drums).

DEBUT	PEAK	WKS			#	Album Title		Sym	$	Label & Number
6/27/98	191	1		©		Left Of Cool		[I]	$10	Warner 46896

Almost 12
Big Blink
Big Country

Communication
Let Me Be The One
Oddity

Prelude To Silence
shanti
Sleeping Dogs Lie

Slow Walker
Sojourn Of Arjuna
Step Quiet

Throwdown At The Hoedown
Trane To Conamarra
Trouble And Strife

FLEETWOOD, Mick '81

Born on 6/24/42 in London. Blues-rock drummer. Member of **John Mayall**'s Bluesbreakers and **Fleetwood Mac**. Played "Mic" in the 1987 movie *The Running Man*.

DEBUT	PEAK	WKS			#	Album Title		Sym	$	Label & Number
7/18/81	43	14		©		The Visitor			$12	RCA Victor 4080

Amelle (Come On Show Me Your Heart)

Cassiopeia Surrender
Don't Be Sorry (Just Be Happy)

Not Fade Away
O' Niamali

Rattlesnake Shake
Super Brains

Visitor, The
Walk A Thin Line

You Weren't In Love

FLEETWOOD MAC ★48★ '77

Formed as a British blues band in 1967 by ex-**John Mayall**'s Bluesbreakers **Peter Green** (guitar), **Mick Fleetwood** (drums) and John McVie (bass), along with guitarist Jeremy Spencer. Many lineup changes followed as group headed toward rock superstardom. Green and Spencer left in 1970. **Christine McVie** (keyboards) joined in August 1970. **Bob Welch** (guitar) joined in April 1971, stayed through 1974. Group relocated to California in 1974, whereupon Americans **Lindsey Buckingham** (guitar) and **Stevie Nicks** (vocals) joined in January 1975. Buckingham left in summer of 1987. Guitarists/vocalists Billy Burnette (son of Dorsey Burnette) and Rick Vito joined in July 1987. Christine McVie and Nicks quit touring with the band at the end of 1990. Vito left in 1991. In early 1993, Nicks and Burnette left. In late 1993, Bekka Bramlett (leader of The Zoo and daughter of **Delaney & Bonnie** Bramlett) and **Dave Mason** joined Mick, John and Christine in band. The classic lineup of Fleetwood, John and Christine McVie, Buckingham and Nicks reunited in May 1997. Inducted into the Rock and Roll Hall of Fame in 1998.

1)Rumours 2)Mirage 3)Fleetwood Mac 4)The Dance 5)Tusk

DEBUT	PEAK	WKS	RIAA	CD	#	Album Title	Catalog	Sym	$	Label & Number
8/17/68	198	3		©	1	Fleetwood Mac			$30	Epic 26402
						also see #6 below				
2/8/69	184	6		©	2	English Rose			$30	Epic 26446
						also see #6 below				
12/13/69+	109	22		©	3	Then Play On			$25	Reprise 6368
10/31/70	69	14		©	4	Kiln House			$25	Reprise 6408
7/3/71	190	6		©	5	Fleetwood Mac In Chicago		[E]	$30	Blue Horizon 3801 [2]
						recorded in January 1969; also see #14 below				
10/16/71	143	7			6	Black Magic Woman		[R]	$30	Epic 30632 [2]
						reissue of albums #1 and #2 above				
10/30/71	91	12	● ©	7	Future Games			$20	Reprise 6465
4/22/72	70	27	▲		8	Bare Trees			$20	Reprise 2080
4/28/73	49	13		©	9	Penguin			$20	Reprise 2138
11/17/73	67	26	● ©	10	Mystery To Me			$20	Reprise 2158
10/5/74	34	26		©	11	Heroes Are Hard To Find			$20	Reprise 2196
3/1/75	138	9			12	Vintage Years		[K]	$25	Sire 3706 [2]
						recordings from 1967-69				
8/2/75+	❶¹	148	▲⁵ ©	13	Fleetwood Mac			$15	Reprise 2225
12/6/75+	118	16			14	Fleetwood Mac In Chicago		[E-R]	$20	Sire 3715 [2]
						new cover is eggplant-colored and not the side of a car door				
2/26/77	❶³¹	134	▲¹⁸ ©	15	Rumours	C:#4/126		$12	Warner 3010
						1977 Grammy winner: Album of the Year				
11/3/79	4	37	▲² ©	16	Tusk			$15	Warner 3350 [2]
12/27/80+	14	18	● ©	17	Fleetwood Mac Live		[L]	$15	Warner 3500 [2]
7/17/82	❶⁵	45	▲² ©	18	Mirage			$10	Warner 23607
5/2/87	7	57	▲³ ©	19	Tango In The Night			$10	Warner 25471
12/10/88+	14	26	▲⁸ ©	20	Greatest Hits	C:❶³/408	[G]	$10	Warner 25801
4/28/90	18	19	● ©	21	Behind The Mask			$10	Warner 26111
9/6/97	❶¹	77	▲⁵ ©	22	The Dance	C:#40/9	[L]	$10	Reprise 46702
						recorded in June 1997 on a soundstage in Burbank, California				

Affairs Of The Heart (21)
Albatross (2,6,12)
Although The Sun Is Shining (3)
Angel (11,16)

As Long As You Follow (20) 43
Bad Loser (11)
Bare Trees (8)

Beautiful Child (16)
Before The Beginning (3)
Behind The Mask (21)
Believe Me (10)

Bermuda Triangle (11)
Big Boat (3)
Big Love (19,22) 5
Black Jack Blues (5,14)

Black Magic Woman (2,6,12)
Bleed To Love Her (22)
Blood On The Floor (4)
Blue Letter (13)

Book Of Love (18)
Born Enchanter (11)
Bright Fire (9)
Brown Eyes (16)

FLEETWOOD MAC — Cont'd

Buddy's Song (4)	**Fireflies** (17) *60*	In The Back Of My Mind (21)	Never Going Back Again
Can't Go Back (18)	For Your Love (10)	Isn't It Midnight (19)	(15,17)
Caroline (19)	Forever (10)	Jewel Eyed Judy (4)	Never Make Me Cry (16)
Caught In The Rain (9)	Freedom (21)	Jigsaw Puzzle Blues (2,6,12)	Night Watch (9)
Chain, The (15,22)	Future Games (7)	Just Crazy Love (10)	No Place To Go (1,6)
Child Of Mine (10)	Ghost, The (8)	Just The Blues (12)	No Questions Asked (20)
City, The (10)	**Go Your Own Way**	Keep On Going (10)	Not That Funny (16,17)
Closing My Eyes (3)	(15,17,20,22) *10*	**Landslide** (13,17,22) *51*	Oh Daddy (15)
Cold Black Night (1,6)	Gold Dust Woman (15)	Last Night (5,14)	Oh Diane (18)
Come A Little Bit Closer (11)	Got To Move (1,6)	Lay It All Down (7)	**Oh Well - Pt. 1** (3,17) *55*
Coming Home (2,6,11,12)	**Gypsy** (18,20) *12*	Lazy Poker Blues (12)	One More Night (17)
Coming Your Way (3)	Hard Feelings (10)	Ledge, The (16)	One Sunny Day (2,6)
Crystal (13)	Hellhound On My Trail (1,6)	Like Crying (9)	One Together (4)
Danny's Chant (8)	Heroes Are Hard To Find (11)	Like It This Way (5,14)	Only Over You (18)
Derelect, The (9)	Hi Ho Silver (4)	**Little Lies** (19,20) *4*	Ooh Baby (15)
Did You Ever Love Me (9)	**Hold Me** (18,20) *4*	Long Grey Mare (1,6)	Over & Over (16,17)
Dissatisfied (9)	Homeward Bound (8)	Looking For Somebody (1,6,12)	**Over My Head** (13,17) *20*
Do You Know (21)	Homework (5,14)	**Love In Store** (18) *22*	Prove Your Love (11)
Doctor Brown (2,6,12)	Honey Hi (16)	Love Is Dangerous (21)	Rambling Pony (12)
Don't Let Me Down Again (17)	Hungry Country Girl (5,14)	Love That Burns (2,6,12)	Rattlesnake Shake (3)
Don't Stop (15,17,20,22) *3*	Hypnotized (10)	Madison Blues (5,14)	Red Hot Jam (5,14)
Dreams (15,17,20,22) *1*	I Can't Hold Out (5,14)	Man Of The World (12)	Remember Me (9)
Dust (8)	I Don't Want To Know (15)	Merry Go Round (1,6)	Revelation (9)
Dust My Broom (12)	I Got The Blues (5,14)	Miles Away (10)	**Rhiannon (Will You Ever Win)**
Earl Gray (4)	I Held My Baby Last Night	Mission Bell (4)	(13,17,20,22) *11*
Emerald Eyes (10)	(5,14)	Monday Morning (13,17)	Rockin' Boogie (5,14)
Empire State (18)	I Know I'm Not Wrong (16)	Morning Rain (7)	Rollin' Man (12)
Evenin' Boogie (2,6,12)	I Need Your Love (5,14)	My Baby's Good To Me (1,6)	Safe Harbour (11)
Everyday I Have The Blues	(I'm A) Road Runner (9)	My Heart Beat Like A Hammer	Sands Of Time (7)
(5,14)	I'm So Afraid (13,17,22)	(1,6)	**Sara** (16,17,20) *7*
Everywhere (19,20,22) *14*	I'm Worried (5,14)	My Little Demon (22)	**Save Me** (21) *33*
Eyes Of The World (18)	I've Lost My Baby (2,6,12)	Mystified (19)	Save Me A Place (7)
Family Man (19) *90*	If I Loved Another Woman (1,6)	Need Your Love So Bad (12)	**Say You Love Me**
Farmer's Daughter (17)	If You Want To Be My Baby	Need Your Love Tonight (12)	(13,17,20,22) *11*
Fighting For Madge (3)	(12)	Never Forget (16)	Searching For Madge (3)

Second Hand News (15)	Tell Me All The Things You Do
Second Time (21)	(4)
Sentimental Lady (8)	Temporary One (22)
Seven Wonders (19) *19*	That's All For Everyone (16)
Shake Your Moneymaker	That's Alright (18)
(1,6,12)	That's Enough For Me (16)
She's Changing Me (11)	**Think About Me** (16) *20*
Show-Biz Blues (3)	This Is The Rock (4)
Show Me A Smile (7)	Thoughts On A Grey Day (8)
Silver Heels (11)	Trying So Hard To Forget (12)
Silver Springs (22)	**Tusk** (16,20,22) *8*
Sisters Of The Moon (16) *86*	Underway (3)
Skies The Limit (21)	Walk A Thin Line (16)
Somebody (10)	Warm Ways (13)
Someday Soon Baby (5,14)	Watch Out (5,14)
Something Inside Of Me	Way I Feel (10)
(2,6,12)	Welcome To The Room...Sara
Sometimes (7)	(19)
Songbird (15)	What A Shame (7)
South Indiana (5,14)	What Makes You Think You're
Spare Me A Little Of Your Love	The One (16)
(8)	When I See You Again (19)
Stand On The Rock (21)	When It Comes To Love (21)
Stop Messin' 'Round (2,6,12)	When The Sun Goes Down (21)
Storms (16)	Why (10)
Straight Back (18)	Wish You Were Here (18)
Sugar Daddy (13)	Without You (2,6)
Sugar Mama (5,14)	Woman Of 1000 Years (7)
Sun Is Shining (12)	World Keep On Turning (1,6)
Sunny Side Of Heaven (8)	World Turning (13)
Sweet Girl (22)	Worlds In A Tangle (5,14)
Talk With You (5,14)	You And I, Part II (19)
Tango In The Night (19)	**You Make Loving Fun**
	(15,22) *9*

FLEETWOODS, The '63
Pop vocal trio from Olympia, Washington: Gary Troxel, Gretchen Christopher and Barbara Ellis.

12/29/62+	**71**	6			The Fleetwoods' Greatest Hits	[G]	**$50**	Dolton 8018

Come Softly To Me *1*	Graduation's Here *39*	Last One To Know *96*	Outside My Window *28*	Runaround *23*	Truly Do
Confidential	(He's) The Great Impostor *30*	Mr. Blue *1*	Poor Little Girl	Tragedy *10*	**You Mean Everything To Me** *84*

FLESH FOR LULU '88
Punk-rock group from England: Nick Marsh (vocals), Rocco Barker (guitar), Derek Greening (keyboards), Mike Steed (bass) and Hans Perrson (drums).

12/12/87+	**89**	24	©	Long Live The New Flesh	**$10**	Capitol 48217

Crash	Good For You	I Go Crazy	Postcards From Paradise	Sleeping Dogs	Way To Go
Dream On Cowboy	Hammer Of Love	Lucky Day	Siamese Twist	Sooner Or Later	

FLESH-N-BONE '96
Born Stanley Howse in Cleveland. Male rapper. Member of **Bone Thugs-N-Harmony**.

12/7/96	**23**	16	● ©	1	T.H.U.G.S. - Trues Humbly United Gatherin' Souls	**$10**	Def Jam 533938
10/28/00	**98**	3	©	2	5th Dog Let Loose	**$10**	Koch 8196

Amen (2)	Empty The Clip (1)	Live Soil (1)	Northcoast (2)	Silence Isn't Over (1)	Word To The Wise (2)
Come F#!k With Me (2)	Havin' A Ball (2)	Master, The (2)	Nothin But Da Bone In Me (1)	Silent Night (2)	World So Cruel (1)
Coming 2 Serve You (1)	Hero (2)	Mystic Spirits (2)	Playa Hater (1)	Sticks And Stones (1)	
Crazy By The Flesh (1)	If You Could See (2)	No Mercy (1)	Reverend Run Sermon (1)	T.H.U.G.S. (2)	
Deadly (2)	Kurupted Flesh (2)	No Other Like My Kind (2)	Say A Little Prayer (2)	Way Back (1)	

FLESHTONES '82
Rock group from New York City: Peter Zaremba (vocals), Keith Streng (guitar), Jan Merek Pakulski (bass) and Bill Milhizer (drums).

3/6/82	**174**	5			Roman Gods	**$12**	I.R.S. 70018

Chinese Kitchen	Hope Come Back	Let's See The Sun	R-I-G-H-T-S	Shadow-line (To J. Conrad)	World Has Changed
Dreg (Fleshtone-77)	I've Gotta Change My Life	Ride Your Pony	Roman Gods	Stop Fooling Around!	

FLIPMODE SQUAD '98
Rap collective from New York City: **Busta Rhymes**, **Rampage**, **Rah Digga**, Serious and Spliff Star.

10/10/98	**15**	8	● ©	The Imperial	**$10**	Elektra 62238

Cha Cha Cha	Everything	Last Night	Settin' It Off	To My People
Do For Self	Hit Em Wit Da Heat	Money Talks	Straight Spittin	We Got U Opin (Part 2)
Everybody On The Line Outside	I Got Your Back	Run For Cover	This Is What Happens	Where You Think You Goin'

FLOATERS, The '77
R&B vocal group from Detroit: brothers Paul and Ralph Mitchell, Charles Clarke and Larry Cunningham.

6/25/77	**10**	25	▲	1	Floaters	**$12**	ABC 1030
4/22/78	**131**	8		2	Magic	**$12**	ABC 1047

Anything That Keeps You	**Float On** (1) *2*	I Bet You Get The One You	Let's Try Love (One More Time)	Take One Step At A Time (1)	You Don't Have To Say You
Satisfied (2)	Got To Find A Way (1)	Love (1)	(2)	Time Is Now (2)	Love Me (1)
Everything Happens For A	I Am So Glad I Took My Time	I Dedicate My Love To You (2)	Magic (We Thank You) (2)	What Ever Your Sign (2)	
Reason (1)	(1)	I Just Want To Be With You (2)	No Stronger Love (1)		

FLOCK, The '69
Rock group from Chicago: Fred Glickstein (vocals, guitar), Jerry Goodman (violin), Rick Canoff, Tom Webb and Frank Posa (horns), Jerry Smith (bass) and Ron Karpman (drums). Canoff died on 6/18/88 (age 40).

9/20/69	**48**	20	©	1	The Flock	**$20**	Columbia 9911
10/17/70	**96**	9	©	2	Dinosaur Swamps	**$20**	Columbia 30007

Big Bird (2)	Green Slice (2)	Introduction (1)	Store Bought - Store Thought	Truth (1)
Clown (2)	Hornschmeyer's Island (2)	Lighthouse (2)	(1)	Uranian Sircus (2)
Crabfoot (2)	I Am The Tall Tree (1)	Mermaid (2)	Tired Of Waiting (1)	

FLOCK OF SEAGULLS, A '82

New-wave group from Liverpool, England: brothers Mike (vocals, keyboards) and Ali (drums) Score, with Paul Reynolds (guitar) and Frank Maudsley (bass).

DEBUT	PEAK	WKS	RIAA	CD		$	Label & Number
5/22/82	10	50	● ©	1	**A Flock Of Seagulls**	$10	Jive 66000
5/28/83	16	23		2	**Listen**..	$10	Jive 8013
8/25/84	66	10		3	**The Story Of A Young Heart**....................	$10	Jive 8250

D.N.A. (1)
Don't Ask Me (1)
Electrics (2)
End, The (3)
European (I Wish I Was) (3)
Fall, The (2)

Heart Of Steel (3)
I Ran (So Far Away) (1) *9*
(It's Not Me) Talking (2)
Man Made (1)
Messages (1)
Modern Love Is Automatic (1)

More You Live, The More You Love (3) *56*
Never Again (The Dancer) (3)
Nightmares (2)
Over My Head (3)
Over The Border (2)

Remember David (3)
Space Age Love Song (1) *30*
Standing In The Doorway (1)
Story Of A Young Heart (3)
Suicide Day (3)
Telecommunication (1)

Transfer Affection (2)
Traveller, The (2)
2:30 (2)
What Am I Supposed To Do (2)
Wishing (If I Had A Photograph Of You) (2) *26*

You Can Run (1)

FLOTSAM AND JETSAM '88

Hard-rock group from Phoenix: Eric Knutson (vocals), Ed Carlson and Mike Gilbert (guitars), Troy Gregory (bass) and Kelly Smith (drums).

DEBUT	PEAK	WKS	RIAA	CD		$	Label & Number
6/18/88	143	8	©	1	**No Place For Disgrace**	$10	Elektra 60777
7/7/90	174	7	©	2	**When The Storm Comes Down**	$10	MCA 6382

Burned Device (2)
Deviation (2)
Dreams Of Death (1)
E.M.T.E.K. (2)

Escape From Within (1)
Greed (2)
Hard On You (1)
I Live You Die (1)

Jones, The (1)
K.A.B. (2)
Master Sleeps (2)
Misguided Fortune (1)

N.E. Terror (1)
No More Fun (2)
No Place For Disgrace (1)
October Thorns (2)

P.A.A.B. (1)
Saturday Night's Alright For Fighting (1)
Scars (2)

6, Six, VI (2)
Suffer The Masses (2)

FLOYD, King '71

Born on 2/13/45 in New Orleans. R&B singer/songwriter.

DEBUT	PEAK	WKS	RIAA	CD		$	Label & Number
5/29/71	130	5			**King Floyd**	$15	Cotillion 9047

Baby Let Me Kiss You *29*
Day In The Life Of A Fool

Don't Leave Me Lonely
Groove Me *6*

It's Wonderful
Let Us Be

Messing Up My Mind
So Glad I Found You

What Our Love Needs
Woman Don't Go Astray *53*

FLYING BURRITO BROTHERS '75

Country-rock group from Los Angeles. Various members included **Gram Parsons**, **Chris Hillman** and Mike Clarke (all from **The Byrds**), **Bernie Leadon** (later with the **Eagles**) and Rick Roberts (later with **Firefall**). Parsons died of a drug overdose on 9/19/73 (age 26). Clarke died of liver failure on 12/19/93 (age 49).

DEBUT	PEAK	WKS	RIAA	CD		$	Label & Number
5/3/69	164	7	©	1	**The Gilded Palace Of Sin**..............................	$15	A&M 4175
6/12/71	176	9	©	2	**The Flying Burrito Bros.**..............................	$15	A&M 4295
6/3/72	171	7	©	3	**Last Of The Red Hot Burritos**.................... [L]	$15	A&M 4343
7/13/74	158	5		4	**Close Up The Honky Tonks**............ [K]	$20	A&M 3631 [2]
					recordings from 1968-72		
10/25/75	138	3	©	5	**Flying Again**	$12	Columbia 33817
5/22/76	185	4		6	**Sleepless Nights** .... [E]	$12	A&M 4578

GRAM PARSONS/THE FLYING BURRITO BROS.

Ain't That A Lot Of Love (3)
All Alone (2)
Angels Rejoiced Last Night (6)
Beat The Heat (4)
Bon Soir Blues (5)
Bony Moronie (4)
Brand New Heartache (6)
Break My Mind (4)
Building Fires (5)
Can't You Hear Me Calling (2)
Christine's Tune (1,4)

Close Up The Honky Tonks (4,6)
Cody, Cody (4)
Colorado (2)
Crazy Arms (4)
Dark End Of The Street (1)
Devil In Disguise (4)
Did You See (4)
Dim Lights, Thick Smoke (And Loud, Loud Music) (5,6)
Dixie Breakdown (3)
Do Right Woman (1,4)

Do You Know How It Feels (1)
Don't Fight It (3)
Don't Let Your Deal Go Down (3)
Easy To Get On (5)
Four Days Of Rain (2)
God's Own Singer (4)
Green, Green Grass Of Home (6)
Hand To Mouth (2)
Here Tonight (4)
High Fashion Queen (3,4)

Hippie Boy (1)
Honky Tonk Women (6)
Hot Burrito #1 (1,4)
Hot Burrito #2 (1,3,4)
Hot Burrito #3 (5)
If You Gotta Go (4)
Juanita (1)
Just Can't Be (2)
Losing Game (3)
Money Honey (4)
My Uncle (1,3)
Orange Blossom Special (3)

River Road (5)
Roll Over Beethoven (4)
Sin City (1,4)
Sing Me Back Home (4,6)
Six Days On The Road (3)
Sleepless Nights (6)
Sweet Desert Childhood (5)
To Love Somebody (4)
To Ramona (2)
Together Again (6)
Tonight The Bottle Let Me Down (6)

Train Song (4)
Tried So Hard (2)
Wake Up Little Susie (4)
Wheels (1,4)
White Line Fever (2)
Why Are You Crying (2)
Why Baby Why (5)
Wild Horses (4)
Wind And Rain (5)
You Left The Water Running (5)
Your Angel Steps Out Of Heaven (6)

FLYING LIZARDS, The '80

Electronic group from England: Patti Palladin (vocals), David Cunningham (guitar, keyboards), Steve Beresford (bass) and J.J. Johnson (drums).

DEBUT	PEAK	WKS	RIAA	CD		$	Label & Number
2/23/80	99	8			**The Flying Lizards**..................................	$12	Virgin 13137

Der Song Von Mandelay
Events During Flood

Flood, The
Her Story

Money *50*
Russia

Summertime Blues
TV

Trouble
Window, The

FLYING MACHINE, The '70

Studio project of British songwriters/producers Tony MacAuley and Geoff Stephens. Touring group featured Tony Newman as lead vocalist. Not to be confused with James Taylor's group.

DEBUT	PEAK	WKS	RIAA	CD		$	Label & Number
12/27/69+	179	7			**The Flying Machine**..................................	$15	Janus 3007

Baby Make It Soon *87*
Broken Hearted Me, Evil Hearted You

Marie Take A Chance
My Baby's Coming Home
Send My Baby Home Again

Smile A Little Smile For Me *5*
That Same Old Feeling
There She Goes

Thing Called Love
Waiting On The Shores Of Nowhere

FLYS, The '99

Rock group from Los Angeles: brothers Adam and Joshua Paskowitz (vocals), Peter Perdichizzi (guitar), James Book (bass) and Nick Lucero (drums).

DEBUT	PEAK	WKS	RIAA	CD		$	Label & Number
10/31/98+	109	21	©		**Holiday Man**....................................	$10	Trauma 74006

Afraid
Family, The

Girls Are The Cruelest
Give You My Car

Gods Of Basketball
Got You (Where I Want You)

Groove Is Where You Find It
Holiday Man

Sexual Sandwich
She's So Huge

Superfly
Take U There

FOCUS '73

Progressive-rock group formed in Amsterdam, Holland: **Jan Akkerman** (guitar), Thijs van Leer (keyboards, flute), Martin Dresdan (bass) and Hans Cleuver (drums).

DEBUT	PEAK	WKS	RIAA	CD		$	Label & Number
1/20/73	8	38	● ©	1	**Moving Waves** [I]	$15	Sire 7401
4/14/73	35	22	● ©	2	**Focus 3**.. [I]	$20	Sire 3901 [2]
6/30/73	104	9	©	3	**In And Out Of Focus**........................ [E]	$15	Sire 7404
					recorded in 1970		
11/17/73	132	10		4	**Live At The Rainbow**........................ [I-L]	$15	Sire 7408
					recorded on 5/5/73 at the Rainbow Theatre in London		
8/3/74	66	19		5	**Hamburger Concerto** .... [I]	$15	Atco 100

DEBUT	PEAK	WKS	RIAA	CD	ARTIST — Album Title	Catalog	Sym	$	Label & Number

FOCUS — Cont'd

3/1/75	120	9			6 Dutch Masters - A Selection Of Their Finest Recordings 1969-1973 ..... [I-K]			$15	Sire 7505
9/27/75	152	6			7 Mother Focus .... [I]			$10	Atco 117
6/4/77	163	7			8 Ship Of Memories .... [K]			$12	Sire 7531

All Together!.....Oh That! (7)
Anonymous (3)
Anonymus II (2)
Answers? Questions?
  Questions? Answers! (2,4)
Bennie Helder (7)
Birth (5)
Black Beauty (3)
Can't Believe My Eyes (8)

Carnival Fugue (2,6)
Crackers (8)
Delitiae Musicae (5)
Elspeth Of Nottingham (2)
Eruption Medley (1,4)
Father Bach (7)
Focus (3,6)
Focus II (1,4,6)
Focus III (2,4,6)

Focus IV (7)
Focus V (8)
Glider (8)
Hamburger Concerto Medley
  (5)
Happy Nightmare (Mescaline)
  (3)
Hard Vanilla (7)
Harem Scarem (5)

Hocus Pocus (1,4,6) *9*
House Of The King (2,6)
I Need A Bathroom (7)
Janis (1)
La Cathedrale De Strasbourg
  (5)
Le Clochard (Bread) (1)
Love Remembered (2,6)
Mother Focus (7)

Moving Waves (1,6)
My Sweetheart (7)
No Hang Ups (7)
Out Of Vesuvius (8)
P'S March (8)
Red Sky At Night (8)
Round Goes The Gossip (2)
Ship Of Memories (8)
Soft Vanilla (7)

Someone's Crying.....What! (7)
Spoke To The Lord Creator (8)
Sylvia (2,4,6) *89*
Tropic Bird (7)
Why Dream (3)

FOGELBERG, Dan ★170★ '80

Born on 8/13/51 in Peoria, Illinois. Singer/songwriter/guitarist. Worked as a folk singer in Los Angeles. With **Van Morrison** in the early 1970s. Session work in Nashville. Also see **Fools Gold**.

1)Phoenix 2)The Innocent Age 3)Twin Sons Of Different Mothers

12/7/74+	17	27	▲²	©	1 Souvenirs C:❶²/185			$12	Full Moon 33137
					produced by Joe Walsh				
10/4/75	23	19	▲	©	2 Captured Angel .... C:#5/104			$12	Full Moon 33499
6/4/77	13	39	▲²	©	3 Nether Lands .... C:#3/117			$12	Full Moon 34185
9/16/78	8	35	▲	©	4 Twin Sons Of Different Mothers			$12	Full Moon 35339
					DAN FOGELBERG & TIM WEISBERG				
12/8/79+	3	39	▲²	©	5 Phoenix			$12	Full Moon 35634
9/12/81	6	62	▲²	©	6 The Innocent Age			$15	Full Moon 37393 [2]
7/24/82	2²ᶜ	97	▲	©	7 Home Free [E]			$15	Columbia 31751
					released in 1973				
11/13/82	15	35	▲³	©	8 Dan Fogelberg/Greatest Hits .... [G]			$10	Full Moon 38308
2/18/84	15	27	●	©	9 Windows And Walls			$10	Full Moon 39004
5/11/85	30	23	●	©	10 High Country Snows			$10	Full Moon 39616
6/20/87	48	19		©	11 Exiles			$10	Full Moon 40271
9/22/90	103	13		©	12 The Wild Places			$10	Full Moon 45059
10/16/93	164	3		©	13 River Of Souls			$10	Full Moon 46934

Aireshire Lament (6)
All There Is (13)
Along The Road (5)
Anastasia's Eyes (12)
Anyway I Love You (7)
As The Raven Flies (1)
Aspen (medley) (2)
Be On Your Way (7)
Beggar's Game (5)
Believe In Me (9) *48*
Below The Surface (medley) (2)
Better Change (1)
Blind To The Truth (12)
Bones In The Sky (12)
Captured Angel (2)
Changing Horses (1)
Comes And Goes (2)
Crow (2)
Dancing Shoes (3)
Down The Road (10)
Empty Cages (6)
Ever On (12)
Exiles (11)

Face The Fire (5)
Faces Of America (13)
False Faces (3)
Forefathers (12)
Ghosts (6)
Give Me Some Time (3)
Go Down Easy (10) *85*
Gone Too Far (9)
Guitar Etude No. 3 (4)
Gypsy Wind (5)
Hard To Say (6,8) *7*
Heart Hotels (5,8) *21*
Hearts In Decline (11)
Hickory Grove (7)
High Country Snows (10)
Higher Ground (13)
Higher You Climb (10)
Holy Road (13)
Hurtwood Alley (4)
Illinois (1)
In The Passage (6)
Innocent Age (6)
Intimidation (4)

It Doesn't Matter (11)
Lahaina Luna (4)
Language Of Love (9) *13*
Last Nail (2)
Last To Know (5)
Lazy Susan (4)
Leader Of The Band (6,8) *9*
Lessons Learned (2)
Let Her Go (9)
Lion's Share (6)
Lonely In Love (11)
Long Way (1)
Long Way Home (Live In The
  Country) (7)
Longer (5,8) *2*
Looking For A Lady (7)
Loose Ends (3)
Lost In The Sun (6)
Love Gone By (3)
Love Like This (13)
Lovers In A Dangerous Time
  (12)
Loving Cup (9)

Magic Every Moment (13)
Make Love Stay (8) *29*
Man In The Mirror (medley) (2)
Minstrel, The (13)
Missing You (8) *23*
More Than Ever (7)
Morning Sky (1)
Mountain Pass (10)
Nether Lands (3)
Next Time (2)
Nexus (6)
Old Tennessee (2)
Once Upon A Time (3)
Only The Heart May Know (6)
Our Last Farewell (11)
Outlaw, The (10)
Paris Nocturne (4)
Part Of The Plan (1,8) *31*
Phoenix (5)
Power Of Gold (4,8) *24*
Promises Made (3)
Reach, The (6)
Rhythm Of The Rain (12)

River (7)
River Of Souls (13)
Run For The Roses (6,8) *18*
Same Old Lang Syne (6,8) *9*
Sand And The Foam (6)
Scarecrow's Dream (3)
Seeing You Again (11)
Serengeti Moon (13)
Shallow Rivers (10)
She Don't Look Back (11) *84*
Since You've Asked (4)
Sketches (3)
(Someone's Been) Telling You
  Stories (1)
Song From Half Mountain (1)
Song Of The Sea (12)
Souvenirs (1)
Spirit Trail (12)
Stars (7)
Stolen Moments (6)
Sutter's Mill (10)
Sweet Magnolia (And The
  Travelling Salesman) (9)

Tell Me To My Face (4)
There's A Place In The World
  For A Gambler (1)
These Days (medley) (2)
Think Of What You've Done
  (10)
Times Like These (6)
To The Morning (7)
Tucson, Arizona (Gazette) (9)
Tullamore Dew (5)
Twins Theme (4)
Voice For Peace (13)
Wandering Shepherd (10)
Washington Post March
  (medley) (4)
Way It Must Be (11)
What You're Doing (11)
Wild Places (12)
Windows And Walls (4)
Wishing On The Moon (5)
Wolf Creek (10)
Wysteria (7)

FOGERTY, John '85

Born on 5/28/45 in Berkeley, California. Singer/songwriter/multi-instrumentalist. Leader of **Creedence Clearwater Revival**. Brother of **Tom Fogerty**. Went solo in 1972 and recorded as **The Blue Ridge Rangers**.

5/5/73	47	15		©	1 The Blue Ridge Rangers			$15	Fantasy 9415
10/4/75	78	7			2 John Fogerty			$12	Asylum 1046
1/26/85	❶¹	51	▲²	©	3 Centerfield			$10	Warner 25203
10/11/86	26	19	●	©	4 Eye Of The Zombie			$10	Warner 25449
6/7/97	37	31	●	©	5 Blue Moon Swamp			$10	Warner 45426
6/27/98	29	16	●	©	6 Premonition .... [L]			$10	Reprise 46908
					recorded at The Burbank Studio				

Almost Saturday Night
  (2,6) *78*
Bad Bad Boy (5)
Bad Moon Rising (6)
Big Train (From Memphis) (3)
Blue Moon Nights (5)
Blue Ridge Mountain Blues (1)
Blueboy (5)
Born On The Bayou (6)
Bring It Down To Jelly Roll (5)
California Blues (Blue Yodel #4)
  (1)
Centerfield (3,6) *44*
Change In The Weather (4)

Down On The Corner (6)
Dream (medley) (2)
Eye Of The Zombie (4) *81*
Flyin' Away (4)
Fortunate Son (6)
Goin' Back Home (4)
Green River (6)
Have Thine Own Way, Lord (1)
Headlines (4)
Hearts Of Stone (1) *37*
Hot Rod Heart (5,6)
Hundred And Ten In The Shade
  (5)
I Ain't Never (1)

I Can't Help Myself (3)
I Put A Spell On You (6)
I Saw It On T.V. (3)
Jambalaya (On The Bayou)
  (1) *16*
Joy Of My Life (5,6)
Knockin' On Your Door (4)
Lonely Teardrops (2)
Mr. Greed (3)
Old Man Down The Road
  (3,6) *10*
Please Help Me I'm Falling (1)
Premonition (6)
Proud Mary (6)

Rambunctious Boy (5)
Rattlesnake Highway (5)
Rock And Roll Girls (3) *20*
Rockin' All Over The World
  (2,6) *27*
Sail Away (4)
Sea Cruise (2)
Searchlight (3)
She Thinks I Still Care (1)
Soda Pop (4)
Somewhere Listening (For My
  Name) (1)
Song (medley) (2)
Southern Streamline (5)

Susie Q. (6)
Swamp River Days (5,6)
Today I Started Loving You
  Again (1)
Travelin' Band (6)
Travelin' High (2)
Violence Is Golden (4)
Walking In A Hurricane (5)
Wall, The (2)
Wasn't That A Woman (4)
Where The River Flows (2)
Who'll Stop The Rain (6)
Workin' On A Building (1)
You Rascal You (2)

You're The Reason (1)
Zanz Kant Danz (3)
*appeared as "Vanz Kant
  Danz" on most copies due to
  legal conflict*

FOGERTY, Tom '72

Born on 11/9/41 in Berkeley, California. Died of respiratory failure on 9/6/90 (age 48). Guitarist of **Creedence Clearwater Revival**. Brother of **John Fogerty**. Went solo in 1970.

| 6/3/72 | 180 | 6 | | | Tom Fogerty .... | | | $15 | Fantasy 9407 |

Beauty Is Under The Skin   Everyman   Lady Of Fatima   Me Song   Train To Nowhere
Cast The First Stone   Here Stands The Clown   Legend Of Alcatraz   My Pretty Baby   Wondering

★315★ FOGHAT '77

Rock group formed in England: "Lonesome" Dave Peverett (vocals, guitar; formerly with **Savoy Brown**), Rod Price (guitar), Tony Stevens (bass) and Roger Earl (drums). Settled in New York City in 1975, many bass player changes since. Price replaced by Erik Cartwright in 1981. Peverett died of pneumonia on 2/7/2000 (age 57).

1)Foghat Live 2)Fool For The City 3)Stone Blue

7/15/72	127	22		©	1 Foghat			$15	Bearsville 2077
3/31/73	67	19	●	©	2 Foghat			$15	Bearsville 2136
					above 2 are different albums				
2/2/74	34	30	●	©	3 Energized			$12	Bearsville 6950
11/9/74	40	19	●	©	4 Rock And Roll Outlaws			$12	Bearsville 6956
10/11/75+	23	52	▲	©	5 Fool For The City			$12	Bearsville 6959
11/20/76	36	21	●	©	6 Night Shift			$12	Bearsville 6962
9/10/77	11	29	▲²	©	7 Foghat Live		[L]	$12	Bearsville 6971
5/20/78	25	23	●	©	8 Stone Blue			$12	Bearsville 6977
10/13/79	35	21		©	9 Boogie Motel			$12	Bearsville 6990
6/21/80	106	10		©	10 Tight Shoes			$12	Bearsville 6999
7/25/81	92	9		©	11 Girls To Chat & Boys To Bounce			$12	Bearsville 3578
11/13/82	162	5		©	12 In The Mood For Something Rude			$10	Bearsville 23747
6/25/83	192	2		©	13 Zig-Zag Walk			$10	Bearsville 23888

Ain't Livin' Long Like This (12)   And I Do Just What I Want (12)   Baby Can I Change Your Mind (10)   Back For A Taste Of Your Love (12)   Be My Woman (10)   Blue Spruce Woman (4)   Boogie Motel (9)   Burnin' The Midnight Oil (9)   Bustin' Up Or Bustin' Out (12)   Chateau Lafitte '59 Boogie (4)   Chevrolet (8)   Choo Choo Ch'Boogie (13)   Comin' Down With Love (9)   Couldn't Make Her Stay (2)   Dead End Street (10)   Delayed Reaction (11)

Don't Run Me Down (6)   Down The Road A Piece (13)   Dreamer (4)   Drive Me Home (5)   **Drivin' Wheel** (6) *34*   Easy Money (8)   Eight Days On The Road (4)   Feel So Bad (2)   Fly By Night (3)   **Fool For The City** (5,7) *45*   Fool's Hall Of Fame (1)   Full Time Lover (10)   Golden Arrow (3)   Gotta Get To Know You (1)   Hate To See You Go (4)   Helping Hand (2)   High On Love (8)   Highway (Killing Me) (1)

Hole To Hide In (1)   Home In My Hand (3,7)   Honey Hush (3,7)   Hot Shot Love (6)   **I Just Want To Make Love To You** (1) *83*   **I Just Want To Make Love To You** [live] (7) *33*   I'll Be Standing By (6) *67*   It Hurts Me Too (8)   It'll Be Me (13)   It's Too Late (2)   Jenny Don't Mind (13)   Leavin' Again (Again!) (1)   Let Me Get Close To You (11)   Linda Lou (13)   Live Now - Pay Later (11)   Long Way To Go (2)

Loose Ends (10)   Love In Motion (9)   Love Rustler (12)   Love Zone (11)   Maybelline (1)   Midnight Madness (8)   My Babe (5)   Nervous Release (9)   Night Shift (6)   No Hard Feelings (10)   Nothin' I Won't Do (3)   Paradise Alley (1)   Ride, Ride, Ride (2)   Road Fever (2,7)   Rock & Roll Outlaw (4)   Sarah Lee (1)   Save Your Loving (For Me) (5)   Second Childhood (11)

Seven Day Weekend (13)   She's Gone (2)   Shirley Jean (4)   Silent Treatment (13)   Sing About Love (11)   Slipped, Tripped, Fell In Love (12)   **Slow Ride** (5,7) *20*   Somebody's Been Sleepin' In My Bed (9)   Stay With Me (8)   Step Outside (3)   **Stone Blue** (8) *36*   **Stranger In My Home Town** (10) *81*   Sweet Home Chicago (8)   Take It Or Leave It (5)   Take Me To The River (6)

Take This Heart Of Mine (12)   Terraplane Blues (5)   That'll Be The Day (3)   That's What Love Can Do (13)   There Ain't No Man That Can't Be Caught (12)   **Third Time Lucky (First Time I Was A Fool)** (9) *23*   Three Wheel Cadillac (13)   Too Late The Hero (10)   Trouble In My Way (4)   Trouble, Trouble (1)   Weekend Driver (11)   What A Shame (2) *82*   Wide Boy (11)   Wild Cherry (3)   Zig-Zag Walk (13)

FOLDS, Ben, Five '99

Pop-rock trio from Chapel Hill, North Carolina: Ben Folds (vocals, piano), Robert Sledge (bass) and Darren Jessee (drums).

4/5/97+	42	40	▲	©	1 Whatever And Ever Amen			$10	550 Music 67762
1/31/98	94	4		©	2 Naked Baby Photos		[E-L]	$10	Caroline 7554
					includes recordings from 1995-97				
5/15/99	35	9		©	3 The Unauthorized Biography Of Reinhold Messner			$10	550 Music 69808

Alice Childress (2)   Army (3)   Bad Idea (2)   Battle Of Who Could Care Less (1)   Boxing (2)   Brick (1)   Cigarette (1)   Dick Holster (2)

Don't Change Your Plans (3)   Eddie Walker (2)   Emaline (2)   Evaporated (1)   Fair (1)   For Those Of Ya'll Who Wear Fannie Packs (2)   Hospital Song (3)   Jackson Cannery (2)

Jane (3)   Julianne (2)   Kate (1)   Lullabye (3)   Magic (3)   Mess (3)   Missing The War (1)   Narcolepsy (3)

One Angry Dwarf And 200 Solemn Faces (1)   Philosophy (2)   Regrets (3)   Satan Is My Master (2)   Selfless, Cold And Composed (1)   Smoke (1)   Song For The Dumped (1,2)

Stevens Last Night In Town (1)   Tom & Mary (2)   Twin Falls (2)   Ultimate Sacrifice (2)   Underground (2)   Your Most Valuable Possession (3)   Your Redneck Past (3)

FOLEY, Ellen '79

Born in 1951 in St. Louis. Singer/actress. Vocalist on **Meat Loaf**'s *Bat Out Of Hell* album. Acted in several movies and TV shows.

| 9/29/79 | 137 | 6 | | | 1 Nightout .... | | | $12 | Cleveland Int'l. 36052 |
| 4/4/81 | 152 | 4 | | | 2 Spirit Of St. Louis .... | | | $12 | Cleveland Int'l. 36984 |

Beautiful Waste Of Time (2)   Death Of The Psychoanalyst Of Salvador Dali (2)   Don't Let Go (1)

Game Of A Man (2)   Hideaway (1)   How Glad I Am (1)   In The Killing Hour (2)

Indestructible (2)   M.P.H. (2)   My Legionnaire (2)   Night Out (1)

Phases Of Travel (2)   Sad Song (1)   Shuttered Palace (2)   Stupid Girl (1)

Theatre Of Cruelty (2)   Thunder And Rain (1)   Torchlight (2)   We Belong To The Night (1)

What's A Matter Baby (1) *92*   Young Lust (1)

FOLKSWINGERS, The '63

Instrumental group formed in Los Angeles: **Glen Campbell** (12-string guitar), brothers Rod (guitar) and Doug (banjo) Dillard, and Dean Webb (bass). The latter three were also in **The Dillards**.

| 9/28/63 | 132 | 4 | | | 12 String Guitar! .... | | [I] | $30 | World Pacific 1812 |

Answer Is Blowin' In The Wind   Black Mountain Rag   Bull Durham

Columbus Stockade Blues   Cottonfields   Dark As A Dungeon

If I Had A Hammer (Hammer Song)   Midnight Special

Rye Whiskey   This Train   Wabash Cannonball

Walk Right In   Wildwood Flower

FONDA, Jane '83

Born on 12/21/37 in New York City. Prolific actress. Daughter of legendary actor Henry Fonda. Albums below contain instructions for aerobic exercises.

5/29/82+	15	120	▲²		1 Jane Fonda's Workout Record			$10	Columbia 38054 [2]
					all cuts also done as instrumentals				
5/21/83	117	7			2 Jane Fonda's Workout Record For Pregnancy, Birth And Recovery			$10	Columbia 38675 [2]
					music by a special studio group; no track titles listed				
8/18/84	135	10	●		3 Jane Fonda's Workout Record - New And Improved			$10	Columbia 39287 [2]
					all cuts also done as instrumentals				

FONDA, Jane — Cont'd

Bridge Over Troubled Water [Linda Clifford] (1)
Can You Feel It [Jacksons] (1)
Changes In Latitudes, Changes In Attitudes [Jimmy Buffett] (1)
Dance For Me (medley) [Dean Correa] (3)
Do Ya Wanna Funk [Sylvester] (3)
Harbor Lights [Boz Scaggs] (1)
In Your Letter [REO Speedwagon] (1)
Keep The Fire Burnin' [REO Speedwagon] (3)
Megatron Man [Patrick Cowley] (3)
Night (Feeling Like Getting Down) [Billy Ocean] (1)
One Hundred Ways [Quincy Jones feat. James Ingram] (3)
Rhythm Part I (medley) [Dean Correa] (3)
Stomp! [Brothers Johnson] (1)
Wanna Be Startin' Somethin' [Michael Jackson] (3)
X-Cit-Mental (medley) [Dean Correa] (3)

FONTAINE, Frank '63

Born on 4/19/20 in Cambridge, Massachusetts. Died of a heart attack on 8/4/78 (age 58). Comedian/singer/actor. Played "Crazy Guggenheim" on **Jackie Gleason**'s TV show.

2/9/63	❶⁵	53	●		1 Songs I Sing On The Jackie Gleason Show			$20	ABC-Paramount 442
8/24/63	44	25			2 Sings Like Crazy			$20	ABC-Paramount 460
3/7/64	92	12			3 How Sweet It Is			$20	ABC-Paramount 470

All I Do Is Dream Of You (3)
Always (1)
Beautiful (1)
Carolina Moon (2)
Daddy's Little Girl (1)
Easter Parade (1)
For All We Know (3)
Galway Bay (3)
(Gang That Sang) Heart Of My Heart (1)
Girl Of My Dreams (2)
Have You Ever Been Lonely (2)
How Sweet It Is (3)
I Don't Know Why (2)
I Want A Girl (2)
I Wonder Who's Kissing Her Now (1)
I'll Get By (2)
I'm Afraid To Love You (3)
I'm Forever Blowing Bubbles (1)
If I Had My Way (1)
If You Were The Only Girl In The World (1)
It's The Talk Of The Town (3)
Let Me Call You Sweetheart (2)
Let The Rest Of The World Go By (3)
Love Letters In The Sand (2)
Mary's A Grand Old Name (1)
Miss You (3)
Oh How I Miss You Tonight (2)
Pretty Baby (3)
R.S.V.P. (3)
Shine On Harvest Moon (2)
Sweet And Lovely (2)
That Old Gang Of Mine (1)
Till We Meet Again (2)
When I Grow Too Old To Dream (3)
When Your Hair Has Turned To Silver (1)
When Your Old Wedding Ring Was New (3)

FONTANA, Wayne — see MINDBENDERS, The

FOO FIGHTERS '97

Rock group formed in Seattle: Dave Grohl (vocals, guitar), Pat Smear (guitar), Nate Mendel (bass) and William Goldsmith (drums). Taylor Hawkins replaced Goldsmith in 1997. Franz Stahl replaced Smear in 1998. Grohl was drummer for **Nirvana**. Group name taken from the fiery UFO-like apparitions seen by U.S. pilots during World War II.

7/22/95	23	51	▲	©	1 Foo Fighters			$10	Roswell 34027
5/11/96	175	1		©	2 Big Me		[M]	$10	Roswell 58530
6/7/97	10	74	▲	©	3 The Colour And The Shape		C:#35/1	$10	Roswell 55832
11/20/99	10	41	▲	©	4 There Is Nothing Left To Lose			$10	Roswell 67892

Ain't It The Life (4)
Alone + Easy Target (1)
Aurora (4)
Big Me (1,2)
Breakout (4)
Doll (3)
Enough Space (3)
Everlong (3)
Exhausted (1)
February Stars (3)
Floaty (1)
For All The Cows (1,2)
Generator (4)
Gimme Stitches (4)
Good Grief (1)
Headwires (4)
Hey, Johnny Park! (3)
How I Miss You (2)
I'll Stick Around (1)
Learn To Fly (4) **19**
Live-In Skin (4)
M.I.A. (4)
Monkey Wrench (3)
My Hero (3)
My Poor Brain (3)
New Way Home (3)
Next Year (4)
Oh, George (1)
Ozone (2)
Podunk (2)
See You (3)
Stacked Actors (4)
This Is A Call (1)
Up In Arms (3)
Walking After You (3)
Wattershed (1,2)
Weenie Beenie (1)
Wind Up (3)
Winnebago (2)
X-Static (1)

FOOLS, The '80

Rock group from Boston: Mike Girard (vocals), brothers Stacey (guitar) and Chris (drums) Pedrick, Rich Bartlett (guitar) and Doug Forman (bass).

4/5/80	151	8			1 Sold Out			$12	EMI America 17024
3/28/81	158	4			2 Heavy Mental			$12	EMI America 17046

Alibi (2)
Around The Block (2)
Coming Home With Me (2)
Don't Tell Me (1)
Dressed In White (2)
Easy For You (1)
Fine With Me (1)
I Won't Grow Up (1)
It's A Night For Beautiful Girls (1) **67**
Last Cadillac On Earth (2)
Local Talent (2)
Lost Number (2)
Mind Control (2)
Mutual Of Omaha (1)
Night Out (1)
Running Scared (2) **50**
Sad Story (1)
Sold Out (1)
Spent The Rent (1)
Tell Me You Love Me (2)
What I Tell Myself (2)

FOOLS GOLD '76

Backing group for **Dan Fogelberg**: Denny Henson (vocals, guitar), Doug Livingston (piano), Tom Kelly (bass) and Ron Grinel (drums).

4/24/76	100	13			Fools Gold			$12	Morning Sky 5500

Choices
Coming Out Of Hiding
I Will Run
Love Me Through And Through
Old Tennessee
One By One
Rain, Oh Rain 76
Rollin' Fields And Meadows
Sailing To Monterey
Way Love Grows

FORBERT, Steve '80

Born in 1955 in Meridian, Mississippi. Singer/songwriter/guitarist.

2/10/79	82	15		©	1 Alive On Arrival			$12	Nemperor 35538
11/10/79+	20	26		©	2 Jackrabbit Slim			$12	Nemperor 36191
10/11/80	70	9			3 Little Stevie Orbit			$12	Nemperor 36595
7/24/82	159	6			4 Steve Forbert			$12	Nemperor 37434

Baby (2)
Beautiful Diana (4)
Big City Cat (1)
Cellophane City (3)
Complications (2)
Get Well Soon (3)
Goin' Down To Laurel (1)
Grand Central Station, March 18, 1977 (1)
He's Gotta Live Up To His Shoes (1)
I'm An Automobile (3)
I'm In Love With You (2)
If You Gotta Ask You'll Never Know (3)
It Isn't Gonna Be That Way (1)
It Takes A Whole Lotta Help (To Make It On Your Own) (4)
January 23-30, 1978 (2)
Laughter Lou (Who Needs You?) (3)
Listen To Me (4)
Lonely Girl (3)
Lost (4)
Lucky (3)
Make It All So Real (2)
Oh So Close (And Yet So Far Away) (4)
On The Beach (4)
One More Glass Of Beer (3)
Prisoner Of Stardom (4)
Rain (3)
Romeo's Tune (2) **11**
Sadly Sorta Like A Soap Opera (2)
Say Goodbye To Little Jo (2) **85**
Schoolgirl (3)
Settle Down (1)
Song For Katrina (3)
Song for Carmelita (3)
Steve Forbert's Midsummer Night's Toast (1)
Sweet Love That You Give (Sure Goes A Long, Long Way) (2)
Thinkin' (1)
Tonight I Feel So Far Away From Home (1)
Visitor, A (3)
Wait (2)
What Kinda Guy? (1)
When You Walk In The Room (4)
Ya Ya (Next To Me) (4)
You Cannot Win If You Do Not Play (1)
You're Darn Right (4)

FORCE M.D.'S '86

R&B vocal group from Staten Island, New York: brothers Stevie and Antoine Lundy, Jesse Daniels, Trisco Pearson and Charles Nelson. Nelson died of a heart attack on 3/10/95 (age 30). Antoine Lundy died of ALS on 1/18/98 (age 33). M.D.: Musical Diversity.

12/15/84	185	4			1 Love Letters			$10	Tommy Boy 1003
2/22/86	69	25			2 Chillin'			$10	Tommy Boy 1010
8/15/87	67	16		©	3 Touch And Go			$10	Tommy Boy 25631

Be Mine Girl (1)
Chillin' (2)
Couldn't Care Less (3)
Don't Make Me Dance (All Night Long) (1)
Force M.D.'S Meet The Fat Boys (2)
Forgive Me Girl (1)
Here I Go Again (2)
I Just Wanna Love You (1)
Itchin' For A Scratch (1)
Let Me Love You (1)
Let's Stay Together (1)
Love Is A House (3) **78**
Midnite Lover (3)
One Plus One (2)
Sweet Dreams (3)
Take Your Love Back (3)
Tears (1)
Tender Love (2) **10**
Touch And Go (3)
Uh Oh! (2)
Walking On Air (2)
Will You Be My Girlfriend? (2)
Would You Love Me? (3)
Your Love Drives Me Crazy (3)

FORD, Lita '88

Born on 9/23/59 in London; raised in Los Angeles. Rock singer/guitarist. Member of **The Runaways** from 1975-79.

8/4/84	66	16	©	1 **Dancin' On The Edge**		**$10**	Mercury 818864
2/20/88	29	62	▲	©	2 **Lita**	C:#50/1	**$10**	RCA 6397
6/16/90	52	16	©	3 **Stiletto**		**$10**	RCA 2090
11/30/91	132	4	©	4 **Dangerous Curves**		**$10**	RCA 61025

Aces & Eights (3) — Back To The Cave (2) — Bad Boy (3) — Bad Love (4) — Big Gun (3) — Black Widow (4) — Blueberry (2) — Broken Dreams (2) — Can't Catch Me (2) — Cherry Red (3) — Close My Eyes Forever (2) 8 — Dancin' On The Edge (1) — Dedication (3) — Don't Let Me Down Tonight (1) — Dressed To Kill (1) — Falling In And Out Of Love (2) — Fatal Passion (2) — Fire In My Heart (1) — Gotta Let Go (1) — Hellbound Train (2) — Hit 'N Run (1) — Holy Man (4) — **Hungry** (3) 98 — **Kiss Me Deadly** (2) 12 — Lady Killer (1) — Larger Than Life (4) — Lisa (3) — Little Black Spider (4) — Little Too Early (4) — Only Women Bleed (3) — Playin' With Fire (4) — Ripper, The (3) — Run With The $ (1) — **Shot Of Poison** (4) 45 — Stiletto (3) — Still Waitin' (1) — Tambourine Dream (4) — Under The Gun (2) — What Do Ya Know About Love (4) — Your Wake Up Call (3)

FORD, Rita [Music Boxes] '72

Born in New York City. Opened own music box shop in 1947. All songs played on Rita Ford's collection of authentic 19th century music boxes, which were an early ancestor of phonographs and juke boxes.

12/21/63	26[X]	8	©	1 **A Music Box Christmas**	[X-I]	**$20**	Columbia 1698 / 8498

Christmas charts: 26/'63, 29/'67, 29/'68

12/23/72	14[X]	1		2 **Christmas With Rita Ford's Music Boxes**	[X-I]	**$15**	Harmony 31577

Adeste Fideles (1,2) — Ave Maria (1) — Christmas Lights (2) — Each Year The Christ Child Is Reborn (2) — First Noël (1) — Hark! The Herald Angels Sing (1,2) — Holy City (1,2) — Ihr Kinderlein Kommet (1,2) — Jesus, Lover Of My Soul (1) — Jingle Bells (1) — Lobe Den Herren (1) — Monastery Bells (1,2) — Nazareth (2) — Nun Danket Alle Gott (2) — O Holy Night (1) — O Sanctissima (1,2) — O Tannenbaum (1,2) — Old Hundred (2) — Ora Pro Nobis (2) — Silent Night, Holy Night (1,2) — Spin, Spin (1) — Star Of Bethlehem (2) — Still, Still, Holy Melody (1) — Zu Bethlehem Geboren (1)

FORD, Robben '88

Born on 12/16/51 in Ukiah, California. Male session guitarist. Member of **Jimmy Witherspoon**'s band, **Tom Scott**'s L.A. Express and the **Yellowjackets**.

8/6/88	120	13	©	**Talk To Your Daughter**	**$10**	Warner 25647

Ain't Got Nothin' But The Blues — Born Under A Bad Sign — Can't Let Her Go — Getaway — Help The Poor — I Got Over It — Revelation — Talk To Your Daughter — Wild About You (Can't Hold Out Much Longer)

★255★ FORD, "Tennessee" Ernie '57

Born on 2/13/19 in Bristol, Tennessee. Died of liver failure on 10/17/91 (age 72). Legendary country singer. Hosted own TV variety show from 1955-65. Known as "The Old Pea Picker."

1)Hymns 2)The Star Carol 3)Nearer The Cross

4/28/56	12	3		1 **This Lusty Land!**		**$30**	Capitol 700
1/5/57	2[3]	277	▲	©	2 **Hymns**	**$25**	Capitol 756
5/6/57	5	68	●	©	3 **Spirituals**	**$25**	Capitol 818
6/9/58	5	77	●	4 **Nearer The Cross**	**$25**	Capitol 1005
12/22/58+	4	3	▲	©	5 **The Star Carol**	[X]	**$20**	Capitol 1071

Christmas charts: 15/'64, 25/'65, 56/'66, 41/'67

12/28/59+	7	2	©	6 **The Star Carol**	[X-R]	**$20**	Capitol 1071
5/2/60	23	26		7 **Sing A Hymn With Me**		**$20**	Capitol 1332
12/31/60	28	1	©	8 **The Star Carol**	[X-R]	**$20**	Capitol 1071
12/25/61+	110	3	©	9 **The Star Carol**	[X-R]	**$20**	Capitol 1071
1/27/62	67	19		10 **Hymns At Home**		**$20**	Capitol 1604
5/26/62	110	12		11 **Here Comes The Mississippi Showboat**		**$20**	Capitol 1684
11/10/62	43	2		12 **I Love To Tell The Story**		**$20**	Capitol 1751
12/22/62	48	2	©	13 **The Star Carol**	[X-R]	**$20**	Capitol 1071
1/5/63	71	12		14 **Book Of Favorite Hymns**	[K]	**$20**	Capitol 1794
12/14/63	14[X]	8		15 **The Story Of Christmas**	[X-TV]	**$20**	Capitol 1964

TENNESSEE ERNIE FORD & THE ROGER WAGNER CHORALE
Christmas charts: 14/'63, 19/'64, 28/'68

12/25/65	31[X]	1	16 **Sing We Now Of Christmas**	[X]	**$20**	Capitol 2394
4/25/70	192	17 **America The Beautiful**		**$15**	Capitol 412

Adeste Fideles (5,6,8,9,13,15) — All Hail The Power (7,14) — America (17) — America, I Love You (17) — America, The Beautiful (17) — Angels We Have Heard On High (15,16) — Asleep In Jesus (12) — Away In A Manger (16) — Band Played On (11) — Battle Hymn Of The Republic (17) — Beautiful Isle Of Somewhere (4,14) — Blessed Assurance (12) — Blest Be The Tie That Binds (10) — Break Thou The Bread Of Life (10) — Brighten The Corner Where You Are (7) — Bringing In The Sheaves (7) — Caroling, Caroling (16) — Cherry Flower (15) — Chicken Road (1) — Church In The Wildwood (7) — Comin' Home (10) — Count Your Blessings (7) — Dark As A Dungeon (1) — Day Is Dying In The West (10) — Deck The Halls (medley) (15) — Did You Think To Pray? (10) — Drifting Too Far From The Shore (14) — El Rorro (15) — Face To Face (12) — Fairest Lord Jesus (12) — False Hearted Girl (1) — Farther Along (12) — First Noel (5,6,8,9,13) — Floatin' Down To Cotton Town (11) — Gaily The Troubador (1) — Gesu Bambino (medley) (15) — Get On Board, Little Children (3) — Give To The Winds Thy Fears (12) — God Be With You (4) — God Bless America (17) — God Rest Ye Merry, Gentlemen (5,6,8,9,13,15) — Good King Wenceslas (16) — Hark! The Herald Angels Sing (5,6,8,9,13) — He Is Born (medley) (15) — He'll Understand And Say "Well Done" (3) — His Amazing Grace (10) — His Eye Is On The Sparrow (4,12) — Holy Spirit, Faithful Guide (10) — Home Over There (7) — How Great Thou Art (12) — I Gave My Love A Cherry (1) — I Know The Lord Laid His Hands On Me (3) — I Love To Tell The Story (7,12) — I Need Thee Every Hour (4) — I Want To Be Ready (3) — If I Can Help Somebody (12) — In The Garden (2) — In The Pines (1) — In The Shade Of The Old Apple Tree (11) — It Came Upon A Midnight Clear (5,15) — It Is Well With My Soul (10) — Ivory Palaces (2) — Jesus Loves Me (7) — Jesus Paid It All (10) — Jesus, Savior, Pilot Me (4) — John Henry (1) — Joy To The World (5,6,8,9,13,15) — Just A Closer Walk With Thee (3) — Last Letter (1) — Let The Lower Lights Be Burning (2) — Little Drummer Boy (16) — Little Gray Donkey (15,16) — Lord, I'm Coming Home (1) — Mary's A Grand Old Name (1) — My Faith Looks Up To Thee (10) — My Jesus, I Love Thee (10) — My Task (2,12) — Nearer, My God, To Thee (4) — Nine Pound Hammer (1) — Ninety And Nine (2,14) — Noah Found Grace In The Eyes Of The Lord (3) — Now The Day Is Over (4) — O Christmas Tree (O Tannenbaum) (16) — O Come, All Ye Faithful ..see: Silent Night (5,6,8,9,13) — O Come, All Ye Faithful ..see: Sing We Now Of Christmas (15,16) — O Come, All Ye Faithful ..see: Adeste Fideles (5,6,8,9,13) — O Come, All Ye Faithful ..see: Adeste Fideles — O Come, All Ye Faithful ..see: Adeste Fideles — O Come, All Ye Faithful ..see: Adeste Fideles — O Hearken Ye (5,6,8,9,13) — O Holy Night (5,6,8,9,13,15) — O Little Town Of Bethlehem (5,6,8,9,13,15) — O Tannenbaum (15) — Oh How I Love Jesus (7) — Old Piano Roll Blues (11) — Old Rugged Cross (2) — Onward Christian Soldiers (7,14) — Others (2,12) — Our Land, O Lord (17) — Paddlin' Madelin' Home (11) — Peace In The Valley (3) — Pledge Of Allegiance (17) — Precious Memories (14) — Rock Of Ages (2,14) — **Rovin' Gambler** (1) 60 — Row, Row, Row (11) — Saved By Grace (11) — Shall We Gather At The River (7) — Silent Night (5,6,8,9,13) — Sing We Now Of Christmas (15,16) — Sleep, My Little Lord Jesus (5,6,8,9,13) — Soft Shoe Song (11) — Softly And Tenderly (2,14) — Some Children See Him (5,6,8,9,13,15) — Stand By Me (3) — Star Carol (5,6,8,9,13) — Star-Spangled Banner (17) — Story Of The Christmas Tree (15) — Straw Hat And A Cane (11) — Sweet Hour Of Prayer (2,10) — Sweet Peace The Gift Of God's Love (4) — Take My Hand, Precious Lord (3) — Take Time To Be Holy (4) — Take Your Girlie To The Movies (11) — There Is Power In The Blood (7) — There'll Be No New Tunes On This Old Piano (11) — This Is My Country (17) — This Land Is Your Land (17) — Trouble In Mind (1) — Twelve Days Of Christmas (16) — Virgin's Slumber Song (15,16) — Waiting For The Robert E. Lee (11) — Wayfaring Pilgrim (3) — We Three Kings (5,6,8,9,13,15) — Were You There? (3) — What A Friend (7) — What A Friend We Have In Jesus (4,14) — What Child Is This? (15,16) — When God Dips His Love In My Heart (3) — When The Roll Is Called Up Yonder (7,14) — When They Ring The Golden Bells (2,14) — Whispering Hope (4,14) — Who At My Door Is Standing (2) — Who Will Shoe Your Pretty Little Foot (1) — Xhosa Lullaby (15)

DEBUT	PEAK	WKS	RIAA	CD	ARTIST — Album Title	Catalog	Sym	$	Label & Number

FORDHAM, Julia '90
Born on 8/10/62 in Portsmouth, Hampshire, England.

| 12/3/88+ | 118 | 25 | © | 1 Julia Fordham | $10 | Virgin 90955 |
| 2/17/90 | 74 | 20 | © | 2 Porcelain | $10 | Virgin 91325 |

Behind Closed Doors (1) · Few Too Many (1) · Happy Ever After (1) · Manhattan Skyline (2) · Towerblock (2) · Your Lovely Face (2)
Cocooned (1) · For You Only For You (2) · Invisible War (1) · My Lover's Keeper (1) · Unconditional Love (1)
Comfort Of Strangers (1) · Genius (2) · Island (2) · Other Woman (1) · Where Does The Time Go? (1)
Did I Happen To Mention? (2) · Girlfriend (2) · Lock And Key (2) · Porcelain (2) · Woman Of The 80's (1)

★228★ FOREIGNER '81
British-American rock group formed in New York City: **Lou Gramm** (vocals), **Mick Jones** (guitar), Ian McDonald (guitar, keyboards), Al Greenwood (keyboards), Ed Gagliardi (bass) and Dennis Elliott (drums). Gagliardi, Gramm and Greenwood are from New York. Most of material written by Jones (**Spooky Tooth**) and Gramm. Rick Wills (**Roxy Music**, **Small Faces**) replaced Gagliardi in 1979. Greenwood and McDonald (**King Crimson**) left in 1980. Gramm left in 1991 to form Shadow King; replaced by Johnny Edwards (**Montrose**). Gramm returned in mid-1992. Wills left in 1992 to join **Bad Company**; Elliott left to open woodworking business. Jones not to be confused with Mick Jones of The Clash and Big Audio Dynamite.

1)4 2)Double Vision 3)Foreigner

3/26/77	4	113	▲5	©	1 Foreigner	$12	Atlantic 18215
7/8/78	3	88	▲6	©	2 Double Vision	$12	Atlantic 19999
9/29/79	5	41	▲3	©	3 Head Games	$12	Atlantic 29999
7/25/81	❶10	81	▲6	©	4 4	$10	Atlantic 16999
12/25/82+	10	25	▲5	©	5 Foreigner Records	C:#20/42 [G]	$10	Atlantic 80999
1/5/85	4	45	▲3	©	6 Agent Provocateur	$10	Atlantic 81999
12/26/87+	15	37	▲	©	7 Inside Information	$10	Atlantic 81808
7/6/91	117	9		©	8 Unusual Heat	$10	Atlantic 82299
10/10/92	123	20	▲2	©	9 The Very Best...And Beyond	[G]	$10	Atlantic 89999
3/11/95	136	6		©	10 Mr. Moonlight	$10	Generama 53961

All I Need To Know (10) · **Double Vision** (2,5,9) *2* · **I Don't Want To Live Without You** (7,9) *5* · Love In Vain (6) · Ready For The Rain (8) · Two Different Worlds (6)
At War With The World (1) · **Down On Love** (6) *54* · I Have Waited So Long (2) · Love On The Telephone (3) · Real World (10) · **Until The End Of Time** (10) *42*
Back Where You Belong (7) · Face To Face (2) · I Keep Hoping (10) · Lowdown And Dirty (8) · Rev On The Red Line (3,9) · Unusual Heat (8)
Beat Of My Heart (7) · **Feels Like The First Time** · I Need You (1) · Luanne (4) *75* · Running The Risk (10) · **Urgent** (4,5,9) *4*
Big Dog (10) · (1,5,9) *4* · **I Want To Know What Love Is** · Modern Day (3) · Safe In My Heart (8) · **Waiting For A Girl Like You**
Blinded By Science (3) · Flesh Wound (8) · (6,9) *1* · Moment Of Truth (8) · **Say You Will** (7,9) *6* · (4,5,9) *2*
Blue Morning, Blue Day (1) *15* · Fool For You Anyway (1) · I'll Fight For You (8) · Mountain Of Love (8) · Seventeen (3) · When The Night Comes Down
Break It Up (4) *26* · Girl On The Moon (4) · I'll Get Even With You (3) · Night Life (4) · She's Too Tough (6) · (8)
Can't Wait (7) · Growing Up The Hard Way (6) · I'm Gonna Win (4) · Night To Remember (7) · Soul Doctor (9) · White Lie (10)
Cold As Ice (1,5,9) *6* · Hand On My Heart (10) · Inside Information (7) · No Hiding Place (8) · Spellbinder (2) · With Heaven On Our Side (9)
Counting Every Minute (7) · **Head Games** (3,5,9) *14* · **Juke Box Hero** (4,5,9) *26* · Only Heaven Knows (8) · Starrider (1) · Woman In Black (4)
Damage Is Done (1) · Headknocker (1) · Lonely Children (2) · Out Of The Blue (7) · Stranger In My Own House (6) · Woman Oh Woman (1)
Dirty White Boy (3,5,9) *12* · **Heart Turns To Stone** (7) *56* · **Long, Long Way From Home** · Prisoner Of Love (9) · That Was Yesterday (6,9) *12* · **Women** (3) *41*
Do What You Like (3) · Hole In My Soul (10) · (1,5) *20* · Rain (10) · Tooth And Nail (6) · You're All I Am (2)
Don't Let Go (4) · **Hot Blooded** (2,5,9) *3* · Love Has Taken Its Toll (2) · **Reaction To Action** (6) *54* · Tramontane (2)

FORESTER SISTERS, The '91
Country family vocal group from Lookout Mountain, Georgia: Kathy, Kim, June and Christy Forester.

| 4/20/91 | 137 | 7 | © | Talkin' 'Bout Men | $10 | Warner 26500 |

Blues Don't Stand A Chance · Let Not Your Heart Be Troubled · Somebody Else's Moon · That Makes One Of Us · What About Tonight
It's Gettin' Around · Men · Step In The Right Direction · Too Much Fun · You Take Me For Granted

FOREST FOR THE TREES '97
Group is actually solo singer/songwriter/producer Carl Stephenson (co-writer of **Beck**'s "Loser").

| 9/27/97 | 190 | 1 | © | Forest For The Trees | $10 | DreamWorks 50002 |

Algorithm · Fall · Infinite Cow · Planet Unknown · Thoughts In My Head · Wet Paint
Dream *72* · Green Light Street · Ohm · Stream · Tree · You Create The Reason

FOREVER MORE '70
Rock group from Scotland: Alan Gorrie (vocals, bass), Mick "Travis" Strode (vocals, guitar), Onnie "Mair" McIntyre (guitar, vocals) and Stuart Francis (drums). Strode had been in Band Of Joy with **Robert Plant**. Gorrie and McIntyre later formed **AWB**.

| 3/7/70 | 180 | 3 | | Yours Forever More | $15 | RCA Victor 4272 |

Back In The States Again · Good To Me · Mean Pappie Blues · You Too Can Have A Body Like
Beautiful Afternoon · Home Country Blues · Sylvester's Last Voyage · Mine
8 O'Clock & All's Well · It's Home · We Sing · Yours

FOR SQUIRRELS '96
Rock group from Gainesville, Florida: John Francis Vigliatura (vocals), Travis Michael Tooke (guitar), William Richard White (bass) and Thomas Jacob Griego (drums). Vigliatura and White were killed in a car crash on 9/8/95. Took and Griego went on to form Subrosa.

| 2/3/96 | 171 | 4 | © | Example | $10 | 550 Music 67150 |

Disenchanted · Eskimo Sandune · Long Live The King · Orangeworker · Superstar
8:02 PM · Immortal Dog And Pony Show · Mighty K.C. · Stark Pretty · Under Smithville

FORTÉ, John '98
Born in Brooklyn, New York. Male rapper.

| 8/1/98 | 84 | 3 | © | Poly Sci | $10 | Ruffhouse 68639 |

All F#cked Up · Flash The Message · Ninety Nine (Flash The · P.B.E. (Powerful, Beautiful, · Right One
All You Gotta Do · God Is Love God Is War · Message) *59* · Excellent) · They Got Me
Born To Win · Madina Passage · Poly Sci · We Got This

FORTUNES, The '71
Pop group formed in England: Shel MacRae and Barry Pritchard (vocals, guitars), David Carr (keyboards), Rod Allen (bass) and Andy Brown (drums). Pritchard died of heart failure on 1/12/99 (age 54).

| 7/10/71 | 134 | 10 | © | Here Comes That Rainy Day Feeling Again | $20 | Capitol 809 |

All My Calendar Is You · **Here Comes That Rainy Day** · Just A Line To Let You Know · Oh! Babe
Eye For The Main Chance · **Feeling Again** *15* · Night Started To Cry · Thoughts
Hear The Band · I Gotta Dream · Noises (In My Head)

FOSTER, David '93

Born in Victoria, British Columbia, Canada. Prolific producer/keyboardist. Member of the groups **Skylark** and **Attitudes**.

7/19/86	195	3	©	1	David Foster	....			$10	Atlantic 81642
2/20/88	111	8	©	2	The Symphony Sessions	....		[I-L]	$10	Atlantic 81799
					recorded on 6/26/87 at the Orpheum Theater in Vancouver					
12/11/93	48	5	©	3	The Christmas Album	....		[X]	$10	Interscope 92295

Christmas chart: 13/'93

All That My Heart Can Hold (1)
Away In A Manger *[Tammy Wynette]* (3)
Ballet, The (2)
Best Of Me (1) *80*
Blue Christmas *[Wynonna]* (3)
Carol Of The Bells *[Instrumental]* (3)
Christmas Song (Chestnuts Roasting On An Open Fire) *[Celine Dion]* (3)
Color Purple (Mailbox/Proud Theme), Theme From The (1)
Conscience (2)
Elizabeth (1)
Firedance (2)
First Noel *[BeBe & CeCe Winans]* (3)
Flight Of The Snowbirds (3)
Go Tell It On The Mountain (medley) *[Vanessa Williams]* (3)
Grown-Up Christmas List *[Natalie Cole]* (3)
I'll Be Home For Christmas *[Peabo Bryson & Roberta Flack]* (3)
It's The Most Wonderful Time Of The Year *[Johnny Mathis]* (3)
Just Out Of Reach (2)
Mary Had A Baby (medley) *[Vanessa Williams]* (3)
Mary's Boy Child *[Tom Jones]* (3)
Morning To Morning (2)
O Holy Night *[Michael Crawford]* (3)
Piano Concerto In G (2)
Playing With Fire (1)
Saje (1)
St. Elmo's Fire, Love Theme From (1) *15*
TapDance (1)
Time Passing (2)
Water Fountain (2)
We Were So Close (2)
White Christmas *[All Artists]* (3)
Who's Gonna Love You Tonight (1)
Winter Games (2) *85*

FOSTER & LLOYD '89

Country vocal duo of songwriters Radney Foster and Bill Lloyd.

5/13/89	142	6	©		Faster & Llouder	....			$10	RCA 9587

Before The Heartache Rolls In
Fair Shake
Faster And Louder
Fat Lady Sings
Happy For Awhile
I'll Always Be Here Loving You
Lie To Yourself
She Knows What She Wants
Suzette

FOTOMAKER '78

Pop-rock group from New York: Wally Bryson and Lex Marchesi (guitars), Frankie Vinci (keyboards), Gene Cornish (bass) and Dino Danelli (drums). All share vocals. Bryson was a member of **The Raspberries**. Cornish and Danelli were members of **The Rascals**.

3/25/78	88	13			Fotomaker	....			$12	Atlantic 19165

All There In Her Eyes
All These Years
Can I Please Have Some More
Lose At Love
Other Side
Pain
Plaything
Say The Same For You
Two Can Make It Work
Where Have You Been All My Life *81*

FOUNDATIONS, The '69

R&B-pop group formed in England: Colin Young (vocals), Alan Warner (guitar), Eric Allendale, Pat Burke and Michael Elliott (horns), Anthony Gomez (keybaords), Peter McBeth (bass) and Tim Harris (drums).

3/8/69	92	11			Build Me Up Buttercup	....		[L]	$30	Uni 73043

side 1: live; side 2: studio

Am I Groovin' You
Any Old Time (You're Lonely And Sad)
Back On My Feet Again *59*
Build Me Up Buttercup *3*
Comin' Home Baby
Harlem Shuffle
I Can Take Or Leave Your Loving
I'm A Whole New Thing
Love Is All Right
New Direction
People Are Funny
Tomorrow

★341★ FOUNTAIN, Pete '60

Born on 7/3/30 in New Orleans. Jazz clarinet player. Member of **Al Hirt**'s band from 1956-57.

1)Pete Fountain's New Orleans 2)Music From Dixie 3)Pete Fountain Day

2/22/60	8	87	©	1	Pete Fountain's New Orleans		[I]	$20	Coral 57282
5/9/60	31	4		2	Pete Fountain Day	....	[I-L]	$20	Coral 57313
					recorded on 10/29/59 at the Municipal Auditorium in New Orleans				
9/11/61	43	4		3	Pete Fountain's French Quarter	....	[I]	$20	Coral 57359
					Fountain's nightclub at 231 Bourbon St. in New Orleans				
2/3/62	41	2		4	Bourbon Street	....	[I]	$20	Coral 57389
					PETE FOUNTAIN/AL HIRT				
7/28/62	30	6		5	Music From Dixie	....	[I]	$20	Coral 57401
9/7/63	91	9		6	South Rampart Street Parade	....	[I]	$20	Coral 57440
6/13/64	53	14		7	New Orleans At Midnight	....	[I]	$20	Coral 57429
8/22/64	48	44		8	Licorice Stick	....	[I]	$20	Coral 57460
1/2/65	121	7		9	Pete's Place	....	[I-L]	$20	Coral 57453
					recorded at Fountain's French Quarter Inn				
5/8/65	64	14		10	Mr. Stick Man	....	[I]	$20	Coral 57473
4/23/66	100	8		11	A Taste Of Honey	....		$20	Coral 57486
12/23/67	100 X	2		12	"Candy Clarinet" Merry Christmas from Pete Fountain	....	[X]	$20	Coral 57487
6/15/68	187	2		13	For The First Time	....		$15	Decca 74955
					BRENDA LEE & PETE FOUNTAIN				
3/22/69	186	6		14	Those Were The Days	....	[I]	$15	Coral 57505

Amazon (10)
American Boys (14)
Another World (10)
Anything Goes (13)
At The Jazz Band Ball (4)
Avalon (2)
Ballin' The Jack (7)
Basin Street Blues (1,6,9,13)
Battle Hymn Of The Republic (7)
Birth Of The Blues (3)
Blue Christmas (12)
Blues On Bourbon Street (4)
Born To Lose (8)
Bourbon Street Parade (7)
Bye Bye Bill Bailey (5)
Bye Bye Blackbird (5)
Cabaret (13)
California Summer (People Movin' West) (14)
Can't Take My Eyes Off You (13)
Candy Clarinet (12)
Careless Love (6)
Cast Your Fate To The Wind (11)
China Boy (Go Sleep) (2)
Chlo-E (Song Of The Swamp) (5)
Christmas Is A-Comin' (May God Bless You) (12)
Christmas Song (Merry Christmas To You) (12)
Clarinet Strip (8)
Closer Walk (1) *93*
Cotton Fields (1)
Creole Love Call (7)
Cycles (14)
Darktown Strutters' Ball (6)
Dear Old Southland (3)
Dear World (14)
Dixie (3)
Dixie Jubilee (5)
Do You Know What It Means To Miss New Orleans (1)
Don't Be That Way (2)
Estrellita (8)
Farewell Blues (4,6)
Fascination (medley) (9)
59th Street Bridge Song (Feelin' Groovy) (13)
Folsom Prison Blues (14)
Fountain Blue (8)
Fountain In The Rain (11)
French Quarter, Theme From The (3)
Goodbye (10)
Gotta Travel On (10)
Gravy Waltz (8)
Hallelujah (5)
Hello, Dolly! (8)
High Society (5)
Honey-Wind Blows (8)
Humbug (10)
I Got Rhythm (2)
I Gotta Right To Sing The Blues (13)
I Know A Place (13)
I Love You So Much It Hurts (8)
I Want To Be Happy (7)
I Wish I Could Shimmy Like My Sister Kate (5)
I'll Be Home For Christmas (12)
I'm Henry VIII, I Am (11)
"In" Crowd (11)
It's Been A Long, Long Time (11)
It's Just A Little While (To Stay Here) (9)
Ja-Da (2)
Jambalaya (On The Bayou) (10)
Jazz Me Blues (4)
Jingle Bell Rock (12)
Jingle Bells (medley) (12)
King Of The Road (11)
Lazy Bones (3)
Lazy River (1,4)
Les Bicyclettes De Belsize (14)
Let It Snow! Let It Snow! Let It Snow! (12)
Licorice Stick (8)
Little Drummer Boy (12)
Lucky Pierre (11)
March Of The Bob Cats (4)
March Through The Streets Of Their City (7)
March To Peruna (9)
Marching 'Round The Mountain (6)
Maria Elena (8)
Midnight Boogie (7)
Midnight Pete (7)
Milenberg Joys (5)
Mood Indigo (13)
Moonglow (7)
Mr. Stick Man (10)
My Special Angel (14)
Night And Day (13)
Oh, Didn't He Ramble (3)
Oh, Lady Be Good! (9)
Ol' Man River (1)
On The South Side Of Chicago (14)
On The Street Where You Live (10)
One Of Those Songs (Le Bal De Madame De Mortemouille) (13)
Over The Waves (6)
Poor Butterfly (2)
Preacher, The (9)
Puddin' (14)
Put On Your Old Grey Bonnet (6)
Rockin' Chair (7)
S' Wonderful (2)
Santa Claus Is Comin' To Town (medley) (12)
Second Line (6)
Shadow Of Your Smile (11)
Sheik Of Araby (9)
Shine (2,5)
Show Me A City Like New Orleans (10)
Shrimp Boats (3)
Silver Bells (12)
Song Of The Wanderer (Where Shall I Go?) (5)
Sound Of Music (10)
South Rampart Street Parade (6)
St. James Infirmary (4)
Stand By Me (11)
Struttin' With Some Barbecue (5)
Sugar Bowl Parade (6)
Summertime (3)

FOUNTAIN, Pete — Cont'd

Sweethearts On Parade (1)
Swing Low (7)
Taste Of Honey (11)
That Da Da Strain (3)
That's A Plenty (9)
There's A Kind Of Hush (All Over The World) (13)
Those Were The Days (14)

Tiger Rag (2)
Tin Roof Blues (1,9)
Tippin' In (8)
Walking Through New Orleans (6)
Washington And Lee Swing (6)
Way Down Yonder In New Orleans (1,9)

(What Did I Do To Be So) Black And Blue (9)
(When It's) Darkness On The Delta (5)
When It's Sleepy Time Down South (1)
When The Saints Come Marching In March (1)

When You're Smiling (The Whole World Smiles With You) (5)
Whiffenpoof Song (Baa Baa Baa) (10)
While We Danced At The Mardi Gras (1)
Whipped Cream (10)

White Christmas (12)
Wichita Lineman (14)
Windy (13)
Winter Wonderland (12)
Yearling, Theme From The (11)
Young Maiden's Prayer (8)

4 BY FOUR '87

Soul quartet from Queens, New York: Damen and Lance Heyward, Steve Gray and Jeraude Jackson.

6/27/87	141	7	©		4 By Four	12560		$10	Capitol 12560

Come Over
Don't Put The Blame On Me

Fingertips
Mommy - Daddy

Problems Too
She's Alright

Smokin'
This Time I Know It's Real

Want You For My Girlfriend 79
You Changed

FOUR FRESHMEN, The '56

Vocal group from Indianapolis: brothers Ross and Don Barbour, their cousin Bob Flanigan and Ken Albers. Don Barbour died in a car crash on 10/5/61 (age 32).

Debut	Peak	Wks	CD	#	Album Title		Sym	$	Label & Number
2/25/56	6	33	©	1	Four Freshmen and 5 Trombones			$40	Capitol 683
10/13/56	11	8		2	Freshmen Favorites		[G]	$30	Capitol 743
3/2/57	9	7	©	3	4 Freshmen and 5 Trumpets			$30	Capitol 763
11/18/57	25	1		4	Four Freshmen and Five Saxes			$30	Capitol 844
9/29/58	17	1		5	The Four Freshmen In Person		[L]	$25	Capitol 1008
11/3/58	11	6	©	6	Voices In Love			$25	Capitol 1074

sequel to their first album in 1954 *Voices In Modern* (#8)

1/11/60	40	1		7	The Four Freshmen and Five Guitars			$25	Capitol 1255

After You've Gone (3)
Angel Eyes (1)
Charmaine (2) *69*
Circus (3)
Come Rain Or Come Shine (7)
Day By Day (2,5) *42*
Day Isn't Long Enough (2)
Don't Worry 'Bout Me (7)
East Of The Sun (4)
Easy Street (3)
Ev'ry Time We Say Goodbye (3)
For All We Know (4)
Give Me The Simple Life (3)
Good Night Sweetheart (3)
Good-bye (3)

Got A Date With An Angel (3)
Graduation Day (2) *17*
Guilty (1)
Holiday (5)
How Can I Tell Her (2)
I Get Along Without You Very Well (4)
I Heard You Cried Last Night (And So Did I) (6)
I May Be Wrong (4)
I Never Knew (7)
I Remember You (1)
I Understand (7)
I'll Remember April (6)
I'm Always Chasing Rainbows (6)

In The Still Of The Night (4)
In This Whole Wide World (2,5)
Indian Summer (5)
Invitation (7)
It All Depends On You (7)
It Could Happen To You (6)
It Never Occurred To Me (3)
It's A Blue World (6)
It's A Pity To Say Goodnight (7)
Last Time I Saw Paris (1)
Laughing On The Outside (Crying On The Inside) (3)
Liza (4)
Lonely Night In Paris (2)
Love (1)
Love Is Here To Stay (1)

Love Is Just Around The Corner (1)
Love Turns Winter To Spring (2)
Lullaby In Rhythm (4)
Malaya (5)
Mam'selle (1)
Moonlight (6)
More I See You (7)
Mr. B's Blues (5)
My Heart Stood Still (5)
Nancy (7)
Night We Called It A Day (3)
Now You Know (2)
Oh Lonely Winter (7)
Old Folks (5)

Out Of Nowhere (6)
Poinciana (Song Of The Tree) (2)
Rain (7)
Seems Like Old Times (2)
Somebody Loves Me (1,5)
Someone Like You (3)
Something In The Wind (3)
Sometimes I'm Happy (4)
Speak Low (1)
Sweet Lorraine (3)
Them There Eyes (5)
There Is No Greater Love (6)
There Will Never Be Another You (3)
There's No One But You (4)

This Can't Be Love (4)
This Love Of Mine (4)
This October (7)
Time Was (Duerme) (6)
Very Thought Of You (4)
Warm (6)
While You Are Gone (6)
You Made Me Love You (I Didn't Want To Do It) (1)
You Stepped Out Of A Dream (1)
You're All I See (6)
You've Got Me Cryin' Again (4,5)

4 HIM '98

Christian vocal group from Mobile, Alabama: Mark Harris, Marty Magehee, Kirk Sullivan and Andy Chrisman.

7/13/96	115	4	©	1	The Message			$10	Benson 4321
4/25/98	95	5	©	2	Obvious			$10	Benson 2205
4/10/99	123	1	©	3	Best Ones		[G]	$10	Benson 2395

All The Evidence I Need (1)
Basics Of Life (3)
Before The River Came (2,3)
Can't Get Past The Evidence (2)
Center Of The Mark (1,3)

Couldn't We Stand (3)
For Future Generations (3)
Great Awakening (2,3)
Greatest Story Ever Told (1)
Hand Of God (2)
He Never Changes (3)

King And I (1)
Land Of Mercy (1)
Lay It All On The Line (1,3)
Let The Lion Run Free (2)
Lot Like You (1)
Measure Of A Man (1,3)

Message, The (1,3)
Mystery Of Grace (2)
Obvious (2)
Real Thing (3)
Sacred Hideaway (1)
Signs And Wonders (2)

That Kind Of Love (2)
Voice In The Wilderness (2)
Where There Is Faith (3)
Who's At The Wheel (3)
Why (3)
Window With A View (1)

Wings (3)

FOUR JACKS AND A JILL '68

Pop group from South Africa: Glenys Lynne (vocals), Bruce Bark (guitar), Till Hannamann (organ), Clive Harding (bass) and Tony Hughes (drums).

6/22/68	155	6			Master Jack			$20	RCA Victor 4019

Bobby Blows A Blue Note
Fifi The Flea

Hamba Liliwam
I Looked Back

La La Song
Lonely Desert Boy

Master Jack *18*
Mister Nico *96*

Penny Paper
Sunny Side Of Somewhere

Timothy

FOUR LADS, The '56

Vocal group from Toronto: Bernie Toorish, Jimmie Arnold, Frankie Busseri and Connie Codarini.

10/6/56	14	2			On The Sunny Side			$50	Columbia 912

Bidin' My Time
Dancing In The Dark
Lazy River

Makin' Whoopee
On The Sunny Side Of The Street

Sentimental Journey
Side By Side
Taking A Chance On Love

These Foolish Things (Remind Me Of You)
Things We Did Last Summer

Way You Look Tonight

Wrap Your Troubles In Dreams (And Dream Your Troubles Away)

4 NON BLONDES '93

Pop-rock group from San Francisco: Linda Perry (vocals), Roger Rocha (guitar), Christa Hillhouse (bass) and Dawn Richardson (drums).

4/3/93	13	59	▲ ©		Bigger, Better, Faster, More!			$10	Interscope 92112

Calling All The People
Dear Mr. President

Drifting
Morphine & Chocolate

No Place Like Home
Old Mr. Heffer

Pleasantly Blue
Spaceman

Superfly
Train

What's Up *14*

FOURPLAY '91

All-star jazz group: **Lee Ritenour** (guitar), **Bob James** (keyboards), **Nathan East** (bass) and **Harvey Mason** (drums). **Larry Carlton** replaced Ritenour in 1997.

10/12/91	97	33	● ©	1	Fourplay		[I]	$10	Warner 26656
9/4/93	70	17	● ©	2	Between The Sheets		[I]	$10	Warner 45340
9/9/95	90	10	● ©	3	Elixir		[I]	$10	Warner 45922
6/27/98	146	5	©	4	4		[I]	$10	Warner 46921
9/9/00	135	5	©	5	Fourplay...Yes, Please!		[I]	$10	Warner 47694

After The Dance (1)
Amoroso (2)
Anthem (2)
Bali Run (1)
Between The Sheets (2)

Blues Force (5)
Chant (2)
Charmed, I'm Sure (4)
Closer I Get To You (3)
Double Trouble (5)

Dream Come True (3)
East 2 West (3)
Elixir (3)
Fannie Mae (3)
Flying East (2)

Foreplay (1)
Fortress (5)
Free Range (5)
Go With Your Heart (5)
Gulliver (2)

In My Corner (3)
Licorice (3)
Li'l Darlin' (2)
Little Fourplay (5)
Little Foxes (4)

Lucky (5)
Magic Carpet Ride (3)
Max-O-Man (1)
Midnight Stroll (1)
Monterey (2)

FOURPLAY — Cont'd

Moonjogger (1)	Piece Of My Heart (4)	Rio Rush (4)	Someone To Love (4)	Vest Pocket (4)
October Morning (1)	Play Lady Play (3)	Robo Bop (5)	Song For Somalia (2)	Whisper In My Ear (3)
Once In The A.M. (2)	Poco A Poco (5)	Save Some Love For Me (5)	Still The One (4)	Why Can't It Wait Till Morning
Once Upon A Love (5)	Quadrille (1)	Sexual Healing (4)	Summer Child (2)	(3)
101 Eastbound (1)	Rain Forest (1)	Slow Slide (4)	Swamp Jazz (4)	Wish You Were Here (1)

4 P.M.   '95

Male vocal quartet formed in Baltimore: brothers Rene and Roberto Pena, with Larry McFarland and Marty Ware.

2/4/95	126	9	© Now's The Time	$10	Next Plateau 828579

Father and Child	Forever In My Heart	Glad You Said the Words	Lay Down Your Love	Sukiyaki 8	Time (Clock Of The Heart)
For What More	Gift of Perfect Love	In This Life	Naturally	Then Came You	Yes

FOUR PREPS, The   '61

Vocal group from Hollywood: Bruce Belland, Ed Cobb, Marvin Ingram and Glen Larson. Ingram died of a heart attack on 3/7/99 (age 62). Cobb died of leukemia on 9/19/04 (age 61).

8/21/61	8	26	© 1	The Four Preps On Campus .... [L]	$30	Capitol 1566
3/24/62	40	17	© 2	Campus Encore .... [L]	$30	Capitol 1647

Big Draft (2) 61	In The Good Old Summer Time	Moon River (2)	Opening (1)	Sphinx Won't Tell (2)	Their Hearts Were Full Of
Come To The Dance (2)	(1)	More Money For You And Me	Preps Hit Medley (1)	Suzy Cocroach (2)	Spring (1)
He's Goin' Away (1)	Lonesome Town (2)	(1) 17	Rememb'ring (2)	Swing Down Chariot (2)	Young And Foolish (1)
Heart And Soul (1)	Lullaby (2)	Next Man Told His Tale (2)	Rock 'N Roll (1)		

4 RUNNER   '95

Country vocal group: Craig Morris, Billy Crittenden, Lee Hilliard and Jim Chapman.

5/27/95	144	5	© 4 Runner	$10	Polydor 527379

Cain's Blood	Heart With 4 Wheel Drive	House At The End Of The Road	Oh No	Southern Wind
Good Lookin'	Home Alone	Let The Good Times Roll	Ripples	You Make The Moonlight

4 SEASONS, The ★99★   '64

Vocal group formed in Newark, New Jersey: **Frankie Valli**, Bob Gaudio, Nick Massi and Tommy DeVito. In 1965, Nick Massi was replaced by Charlie Calello and then by Joe Long. Group disbanded in the early 1970s. Re-formed in 1975: Valli (vocals), Gerry Polci (vocals, drums), John Pavia (guitar), Lee Shapiro (keyboards) and Don Ciccone (bass; formerly with **The Critters**). Group inducted into the Rock and Roll Hall of Fame in 1990. Also recorded as The Wonder Who?.

1)Dawn (Go Away) and 11 other great songs 2)Sherry & 11 others 3)Rag Doll
4)Big Girls Don't Cry and twelve others 5)The 4 Seasons' Gold Vault of Hits

10/27/62	6	27		1	Sherry & 11 others		$50	Vee-Jay 1053
3/2/63	8	19		2	Big Girls Don't Cry and Twelve others		$50	Vee-Jay 1056
7/13/63	47	12		3	Ain't That A Shame and 11 others		$50	Vee-Jay 1059
9/7/63	15	56		4	Golden Hits of the 4 Seasons	[G]	$50	Vee-Jay 1065
					also see #11 below			
12/7/63	13[X]	1		5	The 4 Seasons Greetings	[X]	$50	Vee-Jay 1055
					also see #18 below			
2/29/64	84	9	©	6	Born To Wander		$40	Philips 129
3/28/64	6	25		7	Dawn (Go Away) and 11 other great songs		$40	Philips 124
6/6/64	100	5		8	Stay & Other Great Hits	[K]	$40	Vee-Jay 1082
					originally titled Folk-Nanny			
8/8/64	7	26		9	Rag Doll		$40	Philips 146
9/5/64	105	5		10	More Golden Hits By The Four Seasons	[K]	$40	Vee-Jay 1088
10/10/64	142	3		11	The Beatles vs. The Four Seasons	[R]	$800	Vee-Jay 30 [2]
					reissue of album #4 above and Introducing...The Beatles			
4/10/65	77	13		12	The 4 Seasons Entertain You		$30	Philips 164
12/11/65+	10	88	● ©	13	The 4 Seasons' Gold Vault of Hits	[G]	$30	Philips 196
12/18/65+	106	10	©	14	Big Hits by Burt Bacharach...Hal David...Bob Dylan...		$30	Philips 193
1/29/66	50	15	©	15	Working My Way Back To You		$30	Philips 201
12/3/66+	22	53	● ©	16	2nd Vault Of Golden Hits	[G]	$30	Philips 221
12/17/66+	107	9		17	Lookin' Back	[K]	$30	Philips 222
					recordings from the group's first 3 Vee-Jay albums			
12/24/66+	28[X]	6	©	18	The 4 Seasons' Christmas Album	[X-R]	$30	Philips 600223
					reissue of #5 above; Christmas charts: 72/'66, 28/'67			
6/24/67	37	25		19	New Gold Hits		$30	Philips 243
12/28/68+	37	21	●	20	Edizione D'Oro (The 4 Seasons Gold Edition-29 Gold Hits)	[G]	$40	Philips 6501 [2]
2/15/69	85	11		21	The Genuine Imitation Life Gazette		$25	Philips 290
6/13/70	190	2		22	Half & Half		$20	Philips 600341
					half the songs by Frankie Valli (see Valli for tracks), half by The 4 Seasons			
11/29/75+	38	31		23	Who Loves You		$15	Warner/Curb 2900
12/13/75+	51	17		24	The Four Seasons Story	[G]	$20	Private Stock 7000 [2]
5/14/77	168	5		25	Helicon		$15	Warner/Curb 3016

Ain't That A Shame! (3,4,11,20,24) 22	Angels From The Realms Of Glory (medley) (5,18)	**Beggin'** (19,20,24) 16	Can't Get Enough Of You Baby (15)	**Dawn (Go Away)** (7,13,20,24) 3	Earth Angel (7)
All I Really Want To Do (14)	Any Day Now (medley) (22)	Betrayed (12,13)	**Candy Girl** (3,4,11,16,20,24) 3	**December, 1963 (Oh, What A Night)** (23) 1	Electric Stories (24) 61
Alone (2,10,16,20,24) 28	Anyone Who Had A Heart (14)	**Big Girls Don't Cry** (1,2,4,11,16,20,24) 1	Carol Of The Bells (5,18)	Deck The Halls (medley) (5,18)	Emily's (Salle De Danse) (23)
Always Something There To Remind Me (14)	Apple Of My Eye ..see: You're The Apple Of My Eye	**Big Man In Town** (12,13,20,24) 12	Christmas Song (5,18)	Do You Want To Dance (7)	Everybody Knows My Name (15)
American Crucifixion Resurrection (21)	Around And Around (Andaroundandaroundandaro undandaround) (19)	Big Man's World (7)	Christmas Tears (5,18)	Dody (19)	Excelsis Deo (medley) (5,18)
And That Reminds Me (My Heart Reminds Me) (22,24) 45	Away In A Manger (medley) (5,18)	Blowin' In The Wind (14)	Church Bells May Ring (7)	Don't Cry, Elena (6)	First Noel (medley) (5,18)
Angel Cried (9)	Ballad For Our Time (6)	Born To Wander (6)	C'mon Marianne (19,20,24) 9	Don't Let Go (7)	Funny Face (9)
	Beggars Parade (15)	Breaking Up Is Hard To Do (7)	Comin' Up In The World (15)	**Don't Think Twice** (14,20,24) 12	Genuine Imitation Life (21)
		Bye, Bye, Baby (Baby Goodbye) (12,13,20,24) 12	Connie-O (4,8,11,16,20)	**Down The Hall** (25) 65	**Girl Come Running** (13,20) 30
			Cry Myself To Sleep (6,13)	Dumb Drum (3,10)	Girl In My Dreams (1)
			Danger (9)		God Rest Ye Merry Gentlemen (medley) (5,18)

4 SEASONS, The — Cont'd

Golden Ribbon (6)
Good-bye Girl (19)
Goodnight My Love (2,8,17)
Happy, Happy Birthday Baby (3,10,17)
Hark The Herald Angels Sing (medley) (5,18)
Harmony, Perfect Harmony (23)
Helicon (25)
Hi-Lili, Hi-Lo (2,8,10)
Honey Love (3,10,17)
Huggin' My Pillow (9)
I Believe In You (25)
I Can't Give You Anything But Love (1)
I Saw Mommy Kissing Santa Claus (5,18)
I Woke Up (15)
I'm Gonna Change (19)
I've Cried Before (4,11)
I've Got You Under My Skin (16,20,24) *9*
Idaho (21) *95*
If We Should Lose Our Love (25)

It Came Upon A Midnight Clear (medley) (5,18)
Joy To The World (5,18)
Jungle Bells (5,18)
La Dee Dah (1)
Let's Get It Right (25)
Let's Hang On! (13,20,24) *3*
Let's Ride Again (19)
Life Is But A Dream (7)
Like A Rolling Stone (14)
Little Angel (12)
Little Darlin' (12)
Little Drummer Boy (5,18)
Little Pony (Get Along) (6)
Living Just For You (12,15)
Lonesome Road (19) *89*
Long Ago (25)
Long Lonely Nights (3,8,10,17)
Look Up Look Over (21)
Lost Lullabye (1,8)
Lucky Ladybug (2,17)
Make It Easy On Yourself (14)
Marcie (9)
Marlena (3,4,11,16,20,24) *36*
Melancholy (3,8)

Millie (6)
Mountain High (7)
Mr. Tambourine Man (14)
Mrs. Stately's Garden (21)
My Prayer (12)
My Sugar (2)
Mystic Mr. Sam (23)
Never On Sunday (1)
New Mexican Rose (3,10) *36*
New Town (6)
New York Street Song (No Easy Way) (25)
No One Cares (9)
No Surfin' Today (6)
O Come All Ye Faithful (medley) (5,18)
Oh Holy Night (medley) (5,18)
Oh, Carol (1,10)
Oh Happy Day (medley) (22)
On Broadway Tonight (9)
One Clown Cried (12,15)
One Song (2,8)
Only Yesterday (7)
Opus 17 (Don't You Worry 'Bout Me) (16,20,24) *13*

Patch Of Blue (22) *94*
Peanuts (1,4,11,16,20)
Pity (15)
Puppet Song (19)
Put A Little Away (25)
Queen Jane Approximately (14)
Rag Doll (9,13,20,24) *1*
Rhapsody (25)
Ronnie (9,13,20,24) *6*
Santa Claus Is Coming To Town (5,18)
Saturday's Father (21)
Save It For Me (9,13,20,24) *10*
Searching Wind (6)
Setting Sun (9)
She Gives Me Light (22)
Sherry (1,4,11,16,20,24) *1*
Show Girl (12,15)
Silence Is Golden (6,13,20,24)
Silent Night (medley) (5,18)
Silhouettes (2,10,17)
Silver Star (23) *38*
Silver Wings (4,8,11)
Since I Don't Have You (2,17)
Sincerely (2,17) *75*

16 Candles (7)
Slip Away (23)
Something's On Her Mind (21) *98*
Somewhere (12)
Soon (I'll Be Home Again) (3,4,8,11) *77*
Sorry (25)
Soul Of A Woman (21)
Starmaker (4,8,11)
Stay (3,8,10,16,20,24) *16*
Storybook Lovers (23)
Sundown (15)
Teardrops (1,8,17)
Tell It To The Rain (19,20,24) *10*
That's The Only Way (3) *88*
Tonite, Tonite (2,17)
Too Many Memories (15)
Touch Of You (9)
Toy Soldier (12,13,20,24) *64*
Walk Like A Man (2,4,11,16,20,24) *1*
Walk On By (14)
Wall Street Village Day (21)

Watch The Flowers Grow (20,24) *30*
We Wish You A Merry Christmas (medley) (5,18)
What Child Is This (5,18)
What The World Needs Now Is Love (14)
What's New Pussycat? (14)
Where Have All The Flowers Gone (6)
Where Is Love? (12)
White Christmas (5,18)
Who Loves You (23) *3*
Why Do Fools Fall In Love (2,10,17)
Will You Love Me Tomorrow (20,24) *24*
Wonder What You'll Be (21)
Working My Way Back To You (15,16,20,24) *9*
Yes Sir, That's My Baby (1,10,17)
You Send Me (1)
You're The Apple Of My Eye (1) *62*

FOUR TOPS ★94★   '67

Legendary R&B vocal group from Detroit: Levi Stubbs (lead singer), Renaldo "Obie" Benson, Lawrence Payton and Abdul "Duke" Fakir. Stubbs was the voice of the killer plant in the 1986 movie *Little Shop of Horrors*. Stubbs is the brother of Joe Stubbs (of **100 Proof Aged In Soul**). Payton died on 6/20/97 (age 59). Group inducted into the Rock and Roll Hall of Fame in 1990.

1)The Four Tops Greatest Hits 2)Four Tops Reach Out 3)Four Tops Live! 4)Four Tops Second Album
5)Still Waters Run Deep

DEBUT	PEAK	WKS	CD	#	Album Title	Sym	$	Label & Number
2/27/65	63	27	©	1	Four Tops		$40	Motown 622
11/13/65+	20	35	©	2	Four Tops Second Album		$30	Motown 634
8/27/66	32	22	©	3	4 Tops On Top		$30	Motown 647
12/17/66+	17	43	©	4	Four Tops Live!	[L]	$30	Motown 654
					recorded at the Roostertail in Detroit			
4/8/67	79	15		5	4 Tops On Broadway		$30	Motown 657
8/12/67	11	59	©	6	Four Tops Reach Out		$30	Motown 660
9/30/67	4	73	©	7	The Four Tops Greatest Hits	[G]	$25	Motown 662
9/28/68	91	16		8	Yesterday's Dreams		$25	Motown 669
7/5/69	74	10	©	9	Four Tops Now!		$25	Motown 675
12/13/69+	163	6		10	Soul Spin		$25	Motown 695
4/11/70	21	42	©	11	Still Waters Run Deep		$25	Motown 704
10/17/70	109	12	©	12	Changing Times		$25	Motown 721
10/17/70	113	16	©	13	The Magnificent 7		$25	Motown 717
6/26/71	154	6		14	The Return Of The Magnificent Seven		$25	Motown 736
					SUPREMES & FOUR TOPS (above 2)			
9/25/71	106	10		15	Four Tops Greatest Hits, Vol. 2	[G]	$25	Motown 740
1/8/72	160	6		16	Dynamite		$25	Motown 745
					SUPREMES & FOUR TOPS			
5/27/72	50	28	©	17	Nature Planned It		$25	Motown 748
11/11/72+	33	31	©	18	Keeper Of The Castle		$15	Dunhill/ABC 50129
5/12/73	103	9		19	The Best Of The 4 Tops	[G]	$20	Motown 764 [2]
9/22/73	66	14		20	Main Street People		$15	Dunhill/ABC 50144
4/27/74	118	11		21	Meeting Of The Minds		$15	Dunhill/ABC 50166
10/26/74	92	9		22	Live & In Concert	[L]	$15	Dunhill/ABC 50188
6/14/75	148	5		23	Night Lights Harmony		$15	ABC 862
11/13/76	124	8		24	Catfish		$15	ABC 968
9/12/81	37	21	©	25	Tonight!		$12	Casablanca 7258
6/29/85	140	9		26	Magic		$10	Motown 6130
9/24/88	149	7	©	27	Indestructible		$10	Arista 8492

Again (26)
Ain't No Woman (Like The One I've Got) (18,22) *4*
Ain't Nothing Like The Real Thing (13)
All I Do (25)
All My Love (21)
Am I My Brother's Keeper (20)
Are You Man Enough (20,22) *15*
Are You With Me (27)
Ask The Lonely (1,4,7,19) *24*
Baby I Need Your Loving (1,4,7,19,22) *11*
Baby, (You've Got What It Takes) (13)
Barbara's Boy (10)
Bernadette (6,7,19) *4*
Bigger Than Love (The Harder You Fall) (16)
Bluesette (3)

Brenda (3)
Bring Me Together (11)
By The Time I Get To Phoenix (8)
California Dreamin' (10)
Call Me (14)
Call On Me (1)
Can't Seem To Get You Out Of My Mind (8)
Catfish (24) *71*
Change Of Heart (27)
Cherish (6)
Climb Ev'ry Mountain (4,5)
Darling, I Hum Our Song (2)
Daydream Believer (8)
Disco Daddy (24)
Do What You Gotta Do (9)
Do You Love Me Just A Little, Honey (16)
Don't Bring Back Memories (9)

Don't Let Him Take Your Love From Me (9,15) *45*
Don't Let Me Lose This Dream (16)
Don't Tell Me That It's Over (26)
Don't Turn Away (1,26)
Don't Walk Away (25)
Easier Said Than Done (26)
Eleanor Rigby (9)
Elusive Butterfly (11)
Everybody's Talking (11)
Everyday People (13)
Feel Free (24)
Fool On The Hill (9)
For Once In My Life (5)
For Your Love (13)
From A Distance (25)
Girl From Ipanema (4)
Good Lord Knows (18)

Good Lovin' Ain't Easy To Come By (16)
Got To Get You Into My Life (10)
Happy (Is A Bumpy Road) (17)
Hello Broadway (5)
Hello Stranger (16)
Helpless (4)
Hey Man (medley) (17)
Honey (10)
How Will I Forget You (17)
I Almost Had Her (But She Got Away) (12)
I Am Your Man (17,22)
I Can Feel The Magic (26)
I Can't Believe You Love Me (14)
I Can't Help Myself (2,4,7,19,22) *1*
I Can't Hold On Much Longer (23)

I Can't Quit Your Love (17)
I Found The Spirit (21)
I Got A Feeling (3)
I Just Can't Get You Out Of My Mind (20) *62*
I Know You Like It (24)
I Left My Heart In San Francisco (4)
I Like Everything About You (2,4)
(I Think I Must Be) Dreaming (18)
I Want To Be With You (5)
I Wish I Were Your Mirror (11)
I Wonder Where We're Going (14)
I'll Never Change (17)
I'll Never Ever Leave Again (25)
I'll Turn To Stone (4,6,19) *76*
I'm A Believer (6)

I'm Glad About It (14)
I'm Glad You Walked Into My Life (23)
I'm Grateful (2)
I'm In A Different World (8,15,19) *51*
I'm Only Wounded (27)
I'm Ready For Love (26)
I've Got What You Need (23)
If (16)
If Ever A Love There Was (27)
If I Could Build The Whole World Around You (16)
If I Had A Hammer (4)
If I Were A Carpenter (6,15,19) *20*
If You Could See Me Now (14)
If You Let Me (17)
In The Still Of The Night (4)
In These Changing Times (12,15,19) *70*

FOUR TOPS — Cont'd

Indestructible (27) *35*
Introduction (4)
Is There Anything That I Can Do (2)
Is This The Price? (23)
It Won't Be The First Time (10)
(It Would Almost) Drive Me Out Of My Mind (23)
It's All In The Game (11,15,19) *24*
It's Got To Be A Miracle (This Thing Called Love) (13)
It's Impossible (16)
It's Not Unusual (4)
It's The Same Old Song (2,4,7,19) *5*
(It's The Way) Nature Planned It (17,19) *53*
Jubilee With Soul (18)
Just As Long As You Need Me (2)
Just Seven Numbers (Can Straighten Out My Life) (12,15,19) *40*
Keeper Of The Castle (18,22) *10*
Key, The (9)
Knock On My Door (13)
L.A. (My Town) (11)
Last Train To Clarksville (6)
Left With A Broken Heart (1)
Let Me Know The Truth (23)
Let Me Set You Free (25)
Let's Jam (27)

Let's Make Love Now (14)
Light My Fire (10)
Little Green Apples (9)
Loco In Acapulco (27)
Long And Winding Road (medley) (12)
Look At My Baby (24)
Look Of Love (10)
Look Out Your Window (10)
Lost In A Pool Of Red (10)
Love Ain't Easy To Come By (21,22)
Love Don't Come Easy (24)
Love Feels Like Fire (2)
Love Has Gone (1)
Love Is The Answer (11)
Love Makes You Human (18)
Love Music (18,22)
Love The One You're With (16)
Loving You Is Sweeter Than Ever (3,7,19) *45*
MacArthur Park (Part II) (9,19) *38*
Main Street People (20)
Make Someone Happy (5)
Mama You're All Right With Me (23)
Mame (5)
Maria (5)
Matchmaker (3)
Maybe Tomorrow (26)
Meeting Of The Minds (21)
Melodie (16)
Michelle (3)

Midnight Flower (21,22) *55*
My Past Just Crossed My Future (9)
My Way (5)
Never My Love (8)
Next Time (27)
Nice 'N' Easy (5)
No Sad Songs (21)
Nothing (10)
On The Street Where You Live (5)
Once Upon A Time (8)
One Chain Don't Make No Prison (21,22) *41*
One More Bridge To Cross (14)
One Woman Man (20)
Opportunity Knock (For Me) (9)
Peace Of Mind (20)
Place In The Sun (8)
Put A Little Love Away (18)
Quiet Nights Of Quiet Stars (3)
Raindrops Keep Fallin' On My Head (12)
Reach Out And Touch (Somebody's Hand) (13)
Reach Out I'll Be There (4,6,7,19,22) *1*
Reflections (11)
Remember Me (26)
Remember What I Told You To Forget (18)
Remember When (8)
Right Before My Eyes (12)
Right On Brother (21)

River Deep - Mountain High (13) *14*
Sad Souvenirs (1)
Seven Lonely Nights (23) *71*
7 Rooms Of Gloom (6,7,19) *14*
Sexy Ways (26)
Shake Me, Wake Me (When It's Over) (3,7,19) *18*
She's An Understanding Woman (17)
Since You've Been Gone (2)
Sing A Song Of Yesterday (12)
Something About You (2,7,19) *19*
Something To Remember (3)
Something's Tearing At The Edges Of Time (12)
Sound Of Music (5)
Standing In The Shadows Of Love (6,7,19,22) *6*
Stay In My Lonely Arms (2)
Still Water (Love) (11,15,19) *11*
Still Water (Peace) (11,15)
Stoned Soul Picnic (13)
Stop The World (10)
Strung Out For Your Love (24)
Sun Ain't Gonna Shine (27)
Sunny (8)
Sweet Understanding Love (20) *33*
Sweetheart Tree (8)
Taste Of Honey (13)
Tea House In China Town (1)

Tell Me You Love Me (Love Sounds) (21)
Then (3)
There's No Left Love (3)
This Guy's In Love With You (10)
Together We Can Make Such Sweet Music (13)
Tonight I'm Gonna Love You All Over (25)
Too Little Too Late (20)
Try To Remember (12)
Turn On The Light Of Your Love (18)
Until You Love Someone (3)
Walk Away Renee (6,15,19) *14*
Walk With Me, Talk With Me, Darling (17)
We All Gotta Stick Together (23) *97*
We Got To Get You A Woman (medley) (17)
We've Got A Strong Love (On Our Side) (8)
Well Is Dry (21)
What Did I Have That I Don't Have (5)
What Do You Have To Do (To Stay On The Right Side Of Love) (14)
What Else Is There To Do (But Think About You) (6)
What Is A Man (9,15) *53*

When She Was My Girl (25) *11*
When Tonight Meets Tomorrow (18)
When You Dance (27)
Whenever There's Blue (20)
Where Did You Go (1)
Where Would I Be Without You, Baby (14)
Who's Right, Who's Wrong (25)
Wish I Didn't Love You So (9)
Without The One You Love (Life's Not Worth While) (1,7,13,19) *43*
Wonderful Baby (6)
Yesterday's Dreams (8,15,19) *49*
You Can't Hold Back On Love (24)
You Can't Hurry Love (4)
You Gotta Forget Him Darling (17)
You Gotta Have Love In Your Heart (14) *55*
You Keep Running Away (15,19) *19*
Your Love Is Amazing (1)

FOWLEY, Kim '69

Born on 7/21/39 in Manila; raised in Los Angeles. Male producer/songwriter/manager.

DEBUT	PEAK	WKS			ARTIST — Album Title	$	Label & Number
4/19/69	198	3			**Outrageous**	$40	Imperial 12423

Animal Man
Barefoot Country Boy
Bubble Gum
California Hayride
Caught In The Middle
Chinese Water Torture
Down
Hide And Seek
Inner Space Discovery
Nightrider
Up
Wildfire

FOX, Samantha '87

Born on 4/15/66 in London. Dance singer. Former topless model.

DEBUT	PEAK	WKS		CD	#	ARTIST — Album Title	$	Label & Number
11/29/86+	24	28	●	©	1	**Touch Me**	$10	Jive 1012
10/24/87+	51	25	●	©	2	**Samantha Fox**	$10	Jive 1061
11/26/88+	37	34	●	©	3	**I Wanna Have Some Fun**	$10	Jive 1150

Baby I'm Lost For Words (1)
Best Is Yet To Come (2)
Confession (2)
Do Ya Do Ya (Wanna Please Me) (1) *87*
Dream City (2)
He's Got Sex (1)
Hold On Tight (1)
Hot For You (3)
(I Can't Get No) Satisfaction (2)
I Only Wanna Be With You (3) *31*
I Promise You (2)
I Surrender (To The Spirit Of The Night) (2)
I Wanna Have Some Fun (3) *8*
I'm All You Need (1)
If Music Be The Food Of Love (2)
Love House (3)
Naughty Girls (Need Love Too) (2) *3*
Next To Me (3)
Nothing's Gonna Stop Me Now (2) *80*
One In A Million (3)
Out Of Our Hands (3)
Ready For This Love (3)
Rockin' In The City (1)
Suzie, Don't Leave Me With Your Boyfriend (1)
That Sensation (2)
Touch Me (I Want Your Body) (1) *4*
True Devotion (2)
Walking On Air (3)
Want You To Want Me (1)
Wild Kinda Love (1)
You Started Something (3)
Your House Or My House (3)

FOX, Virgil '71

Born on 5/3/12 in New York City. Died of cancer on 10/25/80 (age 68). Male organist.

DEBUT	PEAK	WKS			#	ARTIST — Album Title	Sym	$	Label & Number
12/24/66	69[X]	1			1	**The Christmas Album**	[X-I]	$15	Command 11032
5/29/71	183	2			2	**Bach Live At Fillmore East**	[I-L]	$15	Decca 75263

recorded on 12/1/70 in New York City

Adeste Fideles (1)
Air For The G String (2)
Divinum Mysterium (1)
Fanfare: Toccata In D Minor (2)
First Noel (1)
Fugue In A Minor (2)
God Rest Ye Merry, Gentlemen (1)
I Saw Three Ships (1)
I Wonder As I Wander (1)
In Dulci Jubilo (1)
Now Thank We All Our God (2)
O Holy Night (1)
Passacaglia And Fugue In C Minor (2)
Perpetuum Mobile (2)
Prelude And Fugue In D Major (2)
Vers La Creche (1)
Virgin's Slumber Song (1)
Vivace: Trio Sonata No. 6 In G Major (2)

FOXWORTHY, Jeff '95

Born on 9/6/58 in Atlanta; raised in Hapeville, Georgia. Comedian/actor. Starred in own TV sitcom.

DEBUT	PEAK	WKS	RIAA	CD	#	ARTIST — Album Title	Sym	$	Label & Number
8/27/94+	38	75	▲[3]	©	1	**You Might Be A Redneck If...**	[C]	$10	Warner 45314
8/5/95	8	59	▲[3]	©	2	**Games Rednecks Play**	[C]	$10	Warner 45856
8/12/95	155	7		©	3	**The Redneck Test - Volume 43**	[C-E]	$10	Laughing Hyena 2043
8/19/95	184	2		©	4	**The Original - Volume 79**	[C-E]	$10	Laughing Hyena 2079
9/14/96	21	20	▲	©	5	**Crank It Up - The Music Album**	[N]	$10	Warner 46361
6/6/98	50	13		©	6	**Totally Committed**	[C]	$10	Warner 46861
11/6/99	189	1		©	7	**Greatest Bits**	[C-G]	$10	Warner 47427
5/13/00	143	7		©	8	**Big Funny**	[C]	$10	DreamWorks 50200

Back In The South (4)
Big O' Moon (5)
Bikini Season (7)
Blue Collar Dollar (8)
Bubble Wrap (7)
Clampets Go To Maui (7)
Commemorative Plates (7)
Copenhagen (5)
Dad Goes Driving (4)
Designated Drivers (3)
Don't Drink And Drive (2)
Encore (4)
Every Single Hair On Her Body (6)
Faded Genes (4)
First Single's Apartment (7)
Fragrances (3)
Games Rednecks Play (2)
House Full Of Girls (4)
Howdy From Maui (5,7)
I Don't Need To Know That (8)
I Don't Want To Be Single Again (6)
I Love Being A Parent (2)
I Love Being Married (1)
I Need Some Space (7)
I Still Don't Know... (6)
I'd Thought I'd Heard Every Redneck Thing (8)
I'm From Georgia (7)
It's A Different World (8)
It's OK That I'm This Way (8)
Jeff Gordon Enunciates (8)
Let Me Drive (5)
Life As A Father (1)
Men's/Women's Magazines (7)
Money Fights (3)
More You Might Be A Redneck If... (2)
Morning After (7)
Mothers Against Drunk Driving (4)
My Favorite Southern Word (7)
My Wife's Family (8)
NASA & Alabama (8)
NASA & Alabama & Fishing Shows (2)
Out Of The Gene Pool (2)
Party All Night (2,5,7)
Poor Old Fluffy (7)
Practical Jokes (3)
Protect Our Stuff (6)
Pure Bred Redneck (5)
Redneck Games (5,7) *66*
Redneck Stomp (5,7) *75*
Redneck Test (3,4)
Redneck 12 Days Of Christmas (5,7)
Rednecks And Shiny Stuff (7)
Rednecks Play The Lottery (7)
Rules Of Marriage (6)
Security Deposit (7)
Seeing Things On The Road (8)
Seek And Destroy (2)
She Has A Boyfriend (7)
S.I.N.G.L.E. (5)
Single Life Is Just Too Hard (1)
Sophisticated People Vs. Rednecks (6)
Southern Accent (2,7)
Southern Words (3,4)
Speaking Of Words (8)
Still More You Might Be A Redneck If... (5)
Stuffed Animal (3)
Super-Size Them Fries (7)
Telephones In The Bathroom (8)
Thanks Y'all - Encore (8)
Throwing A Party (4)
Totally Committed (6,7)
Towing Dad's Boat (3,4)
'Twas The Night After Christmas (3)
Victoria's Secret (3)
Wallhangings (8)
Way I Grew Up (8)
Wedding Reception (4)
Women Want To Talk (8)
Words In The South (1,7)
Worried Mothers (4)
You Are Being Trained (8)
You Can't Give Rednecks Money (6)
You Might Be A Redneck (3)
You Might Be A Redneck If... (1,7)
You Might Be A Redneck If...Part II (1)
You Will Get Remarried (7)

FOXX, Jamie '94

Born Eric Bishop on 12/13/67 in Terrell, Texas. R&B singer/actor/comedian. Acted in several movies and TV shows.

| 8/6/94 | 78 | 10 | | © | Peep This | | | $10 | Fox 66436 |

Baby Don't Cry · Dog House · Don't Let The Sun (Go Down On Our Love) · Experiment · If You Love Me · **Infatuation 92** · Light A Candle · Miss You · Peep This · Precious · Summertime · Your Love

FOXX, Redd '76

Born John Elroy Sanford on 12/9/22 in St. Louis. Died of a heart attack on 10/11/91 (age 68). Actor/comedian. Starred in several movies and TV shows.

| 6/3/72 | 198 | 3 | | | 1 Sanford & Foxx | | [C] | $20 | Dooto 853 |
| 7/29/72 | 155 | 8 | | | 2 Sanford and Son | | [C-TV] | $15 | RCA Victor 4739 |

includes "Sanford And Son Theme" by **Quincy Jones**

| 1/3/76 | 87 | 13 | | | 3 You Gotta Wash Your Ass | | [C] | $12 | Atlantic 18157 |

no track titles listed on this album

Alligator Dog (1) · Beret, The (2) · Bravery (1) · Cheap Accident (1) · Childless Couple (1) · Chinese Restaurant (2) · Christmas Hardtimes (1) · Cigarettes (2) · Dental Care (1) · Festive Dinner With Donna (2) · Fiddler On The Roof (2) · Fred's Birthday (2) · Funerals (1) · Gift Pajamas (1) · Happy Couple (1) · Lamont's Wedding (2) · Lost Wallet (1) · Luau Layaway Furniture Company (1) · Missionary On The Menu (1) · My Son (1) · Parlay, The (1) · Private Eye (1) · Sales Manners (1) · Scarce Dogmeat (1) · Shower Stall (1) · Sleepy Deacon (1) · Social Security (2) · Television (1) · That's Poor (2) · Ugly White Woman (2) · Ugly Women (1) · Union Man (1) · Voting (1) · We Were Robbed (2) · Whiskey Sales (1) · Wino DTs (1)

FOXXX, Freddie '00

Born Fred Campbell in 1969 in Westbury, New York. Male rapper. Member of The Flavor Unit MCs. Also records as **Bumpy Knuckles**.

| 7/15/00 | 179 | 4 | | © | Industry Shakedown | | | $10 | Kjac 2000 |

FREDDIE FOXXX (BUMPY KNUCKLES)

Bumpy Bring It Home · Bumpy Knuckles Baby · Feel Like I Been Here · Industry Shakedown · Inside Your Head · Intelligent Thug-Bumpy's Theory · Live @ The Roxy 2000 · MCs Come And MCs Go · Mastas, The · Never Bow Down · Part Of My Life · R.N.S. · Searchin' · Stock In The Game · Tell 'Em I'm Here · 24 Hrs. · Who Knows Why?

FOXY '78

Latin dance group from Miami: Ish "Angel" Ledesma (vocals, guitar), Richie Puente (percussion), Charlie Murciano (keyboards), Arnold Pasiero (bass) and Joe Galdo (drums). Puente is the son of famous bandleader Tito Puente. Ledesma later formed **Oxo**.

| 7/22/78 | 12 | 27 | | © | 1 Get Off | | | $12 | Dash 30005 |
| 4/14/79 | 29 | 16 | | © | 2 Hot Numbers | | | $12 | Dash 30010 |

Chicapon-Chicapbon (2) · Devil Boogie (2) · **Get Off** (1) *9* · Give Me A Break (2) · Give Me That Groove (2) · Goin' Back To You (1) · Head Hunter (2) · **Hot Number** (2) *21* · It's Happening (1) · Lady (2) · Lady Of The Streets (2) · Lucky Me (1) · Madamoiselle (1) · Nobody Will Ever Take Me Away From You (2) · Ready For Love (1) · Tena's Song (1) · You (1)

★317★ FRAMPTON, Peter '76

Born on 4/22/50 in Beckenham, Kent, England. Rock singer/songwriter/guitarist. Former member of **Humble Pie**. Played "Billy Shears" in the 1978 movie *Sgt. Pepper's Lonely Hearts Club Band*.

1)*Frampton Comes Alive!* 2)*I'm In You* 3)*Where I Should Be*

10/7/72	177	6		©	1 Wind Of Change			$15	A&M 4348
6/9/73	110	22		©	2 Frampton's Camel			$15	A&M 4389
3/30/74	125	9		©	3 Somethin's Happening			$15	A&M 3619
3/29/75	32	64	●	©	4 Frampton			$15	A&M 4512
1/31/76	❶[10]	97	▲[6]	©	5 Frampton Comes Alive!		[L]	$20	A&M 3703 [2]
6/25/77	2[4]	32	▲	©	6 I'm In You			$12	A&M 4704
6/23/79	19	16	●		7 Where I Should Be			$12	A&M 3710
6/13/81	43	13			8 Breaking All The Rules			$12	A&M 3722
8/28/82	174	8			9 The Art Of Control			$12	A&M 4905
2/8/86	80	14		©	10 Premonition			$10	Atlantic 81290
10/14/89	152	6		©	11 When All The Pieces Fit			$10	Atlantic 82030

All Eyes On You (10) · All I Want To Be (Is By Your Side) (1,5) · All Night Long (2) · Alright (1) · Apple Of Your Eye (4) · **Baby, I Love Your Way** (4,5) *12* · Baby (Somethin's Happening) (3) · Back To Eden (9) · Back To The Start (11) · Barbara's Vacation (9) · Breaking All The Rules (8) · Call Of The Wild (9) · Crying Clown (4) · Day's Dawning (4) · Dig What I Say (8) · Do You Feel Like We Do (2,5) *10* · Don't Fade Away (2) · Don't Think About Me (9) · Doobie Wah (3,5) · Everything I Need (7) · Eye For An Eye (9) · Fanfare (4) · Fig Tree Bay (1) · Friday On My Mind (8) · Going To L.A. (8) · Golden Goose (3) · Got My Feet Back On The Ground (7) · Hard (1) · Hard Earned Love (11) · Heart In The Fire (9) · Here Comes Caroline (9) · Hiding From A Heartache (10) · Hold Tight (1) · Holding On To You (11) · I Believe (When I Fall In Love With You It Will Be Forever) · **I Can't Stand It No More** (7) *14* · I Don't Wanna Let You Go (8) · I Got My Eyes On You (2) · I Read The News (9) · I Wanna Go To The Sun (3,5) · (I'll Give You) Money (4,5) · (I'm A) Road Runner (6) · **I'm In You** (6) *2* · Into View (10) · It's A Plain Shame (1,5) · It's A Sad Affair (7) · Jumping Jack Flash (1,5) · Just The Time Of Year (2) · Lady Lieright (1) · Lines On My Face (2,5) · Lodger, The (1) · Lost A Part Of You (8) · **Lying** (10) *74* · Magic Moon (Da Da Da Da!) (3) · May I Baby (7) · Mind Over Matter (11) · More Ways Than One (11) · Moving A Mountain (10) · My Heart Goes Out To You (11) · Nassau (medley) (4) · Now And Again (11) · Nowhere's Too Far (For My Baby) (4) · Oh For Another Day (1) · One More Time (4) · Penny For Your Thoughts (4,5) · People All Over The World (11) · Premonition (10) · (Putting My) Heart On The Line (6) · Rise Up (8) · Rocky's Hot Club (6) · Sail Away (3) · Save Me (9) · She Don't Reply (7) · Shine On (5) · **Show Me The Way** (4,5) *6* · **Signed, Sealed, Delivered (I'm Yours)** (6) *18* · Sleepwalk (9) · Something's Happening (5) · St. Thomas (Don't You Know How I Feel) (6) · Stop (10) · Take Me By The Hand (7) · This Time Around (11) · **Tried To Love** (6) *41* · Underhand (3) · Wasting The Night Away (8) · Waterfall (1) · We've Just Begun (7) · Where I Should Be (Monkey's Song) (7) · Which Way The Wind Blows (2) · White Sugar (2) · Wind Of Change (1,5) · Won't You Be My Friend (6) · You Don't Have To Worry (6) · You Don't Know Like I Know (7) · You Kill Me (8) · You Know So Well (10)

FRANCHI, Sergio '62

Born in 1933 in Cremona, Italy. Died of cancer on 5/1/90 (age 57). Romantic tenor.

| 11/24/62 | 17 | 18 | | © | 1 Romantic Italian Songs | | [F] | $20 | RCA Victor 2640 |

also see #7 below

2/9/63	66	21			2 Our Man From Italy			$20	RCA Victor 2657
7/6/63	103	5			3 Broadway...I Love You			$20	RCA Victor 2674
1/25/64	97	7			4 The Dream Duet			$20	RCA Victor 2675

ANNA MOFFO/SERGIO FRANCHI

| 3/27/65 | 114 | 4 | | | 5 Live At The Cocoanut Grove | | [L] | $15 | RCA Victor 3310 |

recorded on 10/15/64

FRANCHI, Sergio — Cont'd

12/18/65	25ˣ	7	© 6 The Heart of Christmas (Cuor' di Natale)	[X]	$15	RCA 3437

Christmas charts: 25/'65, 48/'66, 108/'67, 55/'68

9/5/98	167	1	© 7 Romantic Italian Songs	[F-R]	$10	RCA Victor 68902

'A Vucchella (1,7)
Ah! Sweet Mystery Of Life (4)
And This Is My Beloved (medley) (5)
Anema E Core (How Wonderful To Know) (2)
Arrivederci, Roma (Goodbye To Rome) (2)
As Long As She Needs Me (3)
Autumn In Rome (2)
Ave Maria (6)
Away In A Manger (6)
Buon Natale (Christmastime in Rome) (6)
Chicago (5)
Clair De Lune (medley) (5)
Comme Facette Mammeta (1,7)

Core 'Ngrato (1,5,7)
Dicitencello Vuie (You Should Tell Her) (2)
E Lucevan Le Stelle (5)
Fenesta Che Lucive (1,7)
First Noël (6)
Funiculi-Funicula (1,7)
Gypsies (Les Gitans) (5)
Heart Of Christmas (Cuor' di Natale) (6)
Hootenanny Medley (5)
I Left My Heart In San Francisco (5)
I Wish You Love (Que Reste-t-il De Nos Amours?) (5)
I'Te Vurria Vasa! (I Want To Kiss You!) (2)

I'll See You Again (4)
I've Grown Accustomed To Her Face (3)
If Ever I Would Leave You (3)
In The Still Of The Night (medley) (5)
Indian Love Call (4)
It Came Upon A Midnight Clear (6)
Just Say I Love Her (Dicitencello Vuie) (5)
Kiss In The Dark (4)
La Strada (Traveling Down A Lonely Road), Love Theme From (2)
La Vilanella (1,7)
Lord's Prayer (6)

Lover, Come Back To Me! (4)
Luna Rossa (Blushing Moon) (2)
Make Someone Happy (3)
Mamma (2)
Mamma Mia Che Vo'Sape (1,7)
Marechiare (1,7)
Mattinata (1,7)
My Hero (4)
O Bambino (One Cold And Blessed Winter) (medley) (6)
O Come, All Ye Faithful (Adeste Fideles) (6)
O Sole Mio (1,7)
O Surdato 'Namorato (1,7)
Oh Little Town Of Bethlehem (6)

One Alone (4)
Panis Angelicus (6)
Quando-Quando-Quando (5)
Santa Lucia (2)
Shalom (3)
She's My Love (3)
Silent Night (6)
Some Day (4)
Somebody, Somewhere (3)
Sound Of Music (3,5)
Souvenir D'Italie (Souvenir Of Italy) (2)
Stella By Starlight (5)
Summertime In Venice (2,5)
Sweetest Sounds (3)
Sweethearts (4)
This Is All I Ask (medley) (5)

Till There Was You (3)
Tonight (3)
Torna A Surriento (1,7)
Torna, Piccina! (Come Back, My Little Girl) (2)
Tu Scendi Dalle Stelle (medley) (6)
What Kind Of Fool Am I? (3)
Will You Remember (4)
Woman In Love (5)
You Are Love (4)
Yours Is My Heart Alone (4)

FRANCIS, Connie   ★127★   '60

Born Concetta Rosa Maria Franconero on 12/12/38 in Newark, New Jersey. Pop singer/actress. Appeared in the movies *Where The Boys Are*, *Follow The Boys*, *Looking For Love* and *When The Boys Meet The Girls*. Pop music's top female vocalist from 1958-64.

1)*Italian Favorites* 2)*More Italian Favorites* 3)*Never On Sunday* 4)*Connie's Greatest Hits*
5)*Country Music Connie Style*

2/8/60	4	81	1 Italian Favorites	[F]	$40	MGM 3791
2/22/60	17	100	2 Connie's Greatest Hits	[G]	$40	MGM 3793
12/12/60+	9	20	3 More Italian Favorites	[F]	$40	MGM 3871
5/8/61	65	19	4 Connie Francis At The Copa	[L]	$30	MGM 3913
5/29/61	69	10	5 Jewish Favorites	[F]	$30	MGM 3869
7/3/61	39	17	6 More Greatest Hits	[G]	$30	MGM 3942
10/30/61	11	34	7 Never On Sunday and other title songs from motion pictures		$30	MGM 3965
4/14/62	47	17	8 Do The Twist		$30	MGM 4022
8/25/62	111	9	9 Connie Francis sings	[G]	$30	MGM 4049
10/13/62	22	14	10 Country Music Connie Style		$30	MGM 4079
2/16/63	103	5	11 Modern Italian Hits	[F]	$30	MGM 4102
3/30/63	66	11	12 Follow The Boys	[S]	$30	MGM 4123
6/15/63	108	5	13 Award Winning Motion Picture Hits		$30	MGM 4048
10/5/63	94	17	14 Greatest American Waltzes		$30	MGM 4145
10/19/63	70	13	15 Mala Femmena & Connie's Big Hits From Italy	[F-K]	$30	MGM 4161
11/2/63+	68	23 ●	16 The Very Best Of Connie Francis	[G]	$30	MGM 4167
12/14/63	16ˣ	5	© 17 Christmas In My Heart	[X]	$30	MGM 3792

first released in 1959; Christmas charts: 16/'63, 33/'64

2/1/64	126	2	18 In The Summer Of His Years		$30	MGM 4210

a tribute to President John F. Kennedy

8/1/64	122	9	19 Looking For Love	[S]	$30	MGM 4229

includes "Whoever You Are I Love You" by Claus Ogerman

12/5/64	149	2	20 A New Kind Of Connie...		$30	MGM 4253
5/1/65	78	15	21 Connie Francis sings For Mama		$30	MGM 4294
1/29/66	61	9	22 When The Boys Meet The Girls	[S]	$30	MGM 4334

includes "Aruba Liberace" by Liberace, "Bidin' My Time" and "Listen People" by Herman's Hermits, "Embraceable You" by Harve Presnell, "I Got Rhythm" and "Throw It Out Your Mind" by Louis Armstrong and "Monkey See, Monkey Do" by Sam The Sham & The Pharoahs

Addio Addio (11)
Adeste Fidelis (17)
Ain't That Better Baby (8)
Al Di La (11) 90
Al Jolson Medley (4)
All The Way (13)
Always (14)
Among My Souvenirs (6,16) 7
Anema E Core (1)
Anna (7)
Anniversary Song (5)
Anniversary Waltz (14)
April Love (7)
Around The World (7)
Arrivederci Roma (1,11)
Aura Lee (18)
Ave Maria (17,18)
Baby's First Christmas (9) 26
Be My Love (19)
Beautiful Ohio (14)
Bells Of Saint Mary's (18)
Bill Baily, Won't You Please Come Home (medley) (4)
Breakin' In A Brand New Broken Heart (9,16) 7
But Not For Me (22)
C'e Qualcuno ..see: Where The Boys Are

Carolina Moon (2)
Che Bella Notte! ..see: Tonight's My Night
Christmas Song (Chestnuts Roasting On An Open Fire) (17)
Ciao, Ciao, Bambina (1)
Come Back To Sorrento (1)
Come Prima (For The First Time) (11)
Come Sinfonia (11)
Comm'e Bella A Stagione (1)
Connie Francis-Lady Valet Theme (19)
Danny Boy (18)
Days Of Wine And Roses (13)
Do You Love Me Like You Kiss Me? (Scapricciatiello) (1)
Does Ol' Broadway Ever Sleep (8)
Don't Break The Heart That Loves You (9,15,16) 1
Drop It (14)
Embraceable You (22)
Every Night (18)
Everybody's Somebody's Fool (6,16) 1
Fallin' (2) 30
Fascination (14)

First Noel (17)
Follow The Boys (12,16) 17
For Every Young Heart (12)
For Mama (La Mamma) (21) 48
Frankie (2,16) 9
Funiculi, Funicula (3)
God Bless America (6,18) 36
Gonna Git That Man (9)
Guaglione (3)
Happy Days And Lonely Nights (2)
Hava Nagila (Dance Everyone Dance) (4,5)
Have Yourself A Merry Little Christmas (17)
He Thinks I Still Care (10) 57
(He's My) Dreamboat (9) 14
Heartaches By The Number (10)
Hey Ring-A-Ding (4)
High Hopes (13)
High Noon (7)
I Can't Believe That You're In Love With Me (19)
I Can't Reach Your Heart (12)
I Can't Stop Loving You (10)
I Don't Hurt Anymore (10)
In Your Arms (12)

I Fall To Pieces (10)
I Found Myself A Guy (20)
I Got Rhythm (22)
I Have But One Heart (1)
I Love You Much Too Much (5)
I Really Don't Want To Know (10)
I Walk The Line (10)
I Was Such A Fool (To Fall In Love With You) (21) 24
I Won't Be Home To You (8)
I'll Be Home For Christmas (17)
(I'll Be With You) In Apple Blossom Time (14)
I'm A Fool To Care (10)
I'm Glad There Is You (20)
I'm Gonna Be Warm This Winter (16) 18
I'm Movin' On (10)
I'm Sorry I Made You Cry (2) 36
I've Got A Crush On New York Town (20)
If I Didn't Care (2) 22
Il Cielo In Una Stanza (This World We Live In) (11)
In The Summer Of His Years (18) 46

Intrigue (12)
It All Depends On You (4)
It Happened Last Night (9)
It Takes More (21)
It's Gonna Take Me Some Time (21)
Italian Lullaby (12,15)
Jealous Of You (Tango Della Gelosia) (4,6,15) 19
Johnny Darlin' (8)
Just Say I Love Him (3)
Kiss 'N' Twist (Tarantella) (8)
La Paloma (Your Love) (15)
Last Time I Saw Paris (13)
Let's Have A Party (19)
Like Someone In Love (20)
Lipstick On Your Collar (2,16) 5
Looking For Love (19) 45
Lord's Prayer (17,18)
Love Is A Many Splendored Thing (7)
Love Me Tender (7)
Loveliest Night Of The Year (3)
Lullaby Of Broadway (13)
Luna Caprese (15)
Ma (He's Making Eyes At Me) (20)

Mail Call (22)
Mala Femmena (15)
Malaguena (6) 42
Mama (1,4,6) 8
Many Tears Ago (4,6) 7
Mein Shtetele Belz (5)
Melody Of Love (14)
Mom-E-Le (Mother Dear) (5)
Mommy Your Daughter's Fallin' In Love (8)
Moon River (13)
Moonglow And Picnic (7)
More (20)
Moulin Rouge (Where Is Your Heart), Song From (7)
Mr. Twister (8)
My Buddy (14,18)
My Dearest Possession (12)
My Happiness (2,16) 2
My Heart Has A Mind Of Its Own (6,16) 1
My Kind Of Guy (20)
My Man (20)
My Real Happiness (8)
My Yiddishe Momme (5)
Nessuno Al Mondo (No Arms Can Ever Hold You) (11)

FRANCIS, Connie — cont'd

Nessuno E' Solo (No One Is Alone) (15)
Never On Sunday (7)
Nights Of Splendor (3)
No One (6,21) *34*
No One Ever Sends Me Roses (21)
Non Dimenticar (Don't Forget) (T'Ho Voluto Bene) (1)
Nun E Peccato (11)
O Little Town Of Bethlehem (17)
O Mein Papa (Oh! My Pa-Pa) (5)
Oh, Lonesome Me (10)
Oifen Pripetchik (5)
Ol' Man Mose (4)
On A Little Street In Venice (12)
Over The Rainbow (13)
Picnic ..see: Moonglow
Playin' Games (21)
Plenty Good Lovin' (2) *69*
Portami Con Te (Fly Me To The Moon) (In Other Words) (15)

Pretty Little Baby (9)
Quando Quando Quando (Tell Me When) (11)
Red River Valley (18)
Remember (14)
Return To Me (3)
Rock Dem Bells (19)
Roman Guitar (3)
Romantica (11)
Santa Lucia (1)
Second Hand Love (9,16) *7*
Secret Love (13)
Senza Mamma (With No One) (3,6) *87*
She'll Have To Go (10)
Shein Vi De Levone (4,5)
Silent Night! Holy Night! (17)
Smack Dab In The Middle (4)
Someday (You'll Want Me To Want You) (10)
Someone Else's Boy (9)
Somewhere Near Someplace (12)
Souvenirs (21)
Stupid Cupid (2,16) *14*

Summertime In Venice (3)
Sweetest Sounds (20)
Tammy (11)
Tango Della Gelosia ..see: Jealous Of You
Tango Italiano (11)
Teach Me How To Twist (8)
Telephone Lover (8)
Tell Me You're Mine (8)
That's Amore (That's Love) (3)
There's No Tomorrow (1)
This Is My Happiest Moment (19)
Three Coins In The Fountain (7)
Three O'Clock In The Morning (14)
Till We Meet Again (14)
Tonight's My Night (12,15)
Too Many Rules (9) *72*
Too-Ra-Loo-Ra-Loo-Ral (That's An Irish Lullaby) (18)
Torero (3)
Toward The End Of The Day (1)

True Love (14)
True Love, True Love (18)
Twelve Days Of Christmas (17)
24 Mila Baci (11)
Tzena Tzena (5)
Un Desiderio Folle ..see: Don't Break The Heart That Loves You
Un Violina Nel Mio Cuor (A Violin In My Heart) (15)
Vacation (16) *9*
Valentino (6)
Violina Tsigano (Gypsy Violin) (15)
Volare (Nel Blu, Dipinto Di Blu) (1)
Vus Geven Is Geven (5)
Waiting For Billy (12)
Way You Look Tonight (13)
What Kind Of Fool Am I? (21)
Whatever Will Be Will Be (Que Sera Sera) (13)
When The Boy In Your Arms (Is The Boy In Your Heart) (9) *10*

When The Boys Meet The Girls (22)
When The Clock Strikes Midnight (19)
When The Saints Go Marching In (medley) (4)
When You Wish Upon A Star (13)
Where Can I Go Without You (20)
Where Did Ev'ryone Go? (20)
(Where Is Your Heart) ..see: Moulin Rouge
Where The Boys Are (6,15,16) *4*
White Christmas (17)
Who's Sorry Now (2,16) *4*
Whoever You Are I Love You (19)
Whose Heart Are You Breaking Tonight (21) *43*
Will You Still Be Mine? (20)
Winter Wonderland (17)
Won't You Come Home Bill Bailey ..see: Bill Bailey
Yossel, Yossel (1)

You Alone (Solo Tu) (1)
You Always Hurt The One You Love (4)
You Can Take It From Me (20)
You Can't Be True, Dear (14)
You'll Never Know (13)
You're Gonna Miss Me (2) *34*
You're The Only One Can Hurt Me (21)
Young At Heart (7)
Zip-A-Dee Doo-Dah (13)

FRANKE & THE KNOCKOUTS   '81

Soft-rock group from New Brunswick, New Jersey: Franke Previte (vocals), Billy Elworthy (guitar), Blake Levinsohn (keyboards), Leigh Foxx (bass) and Claude LeHenaff (drums).

3/28/81	**31**	27		1 **Franke & The Knockouts**	$12	Millennium 7755
4/10/82	**48**	18		2 **Below The Belt**	$12	Millennium 7763

Annie Goes Hollywood (1)
Any Way That You Want Me (2)
Come Back (1)
Don't Stop (1)

Gina (2)
Have No Fear (2)
Just What I Want (2)
Keep On Fighting (2)

Morning Sun (Dream On) (2)
Never Had It Better (2)
One For All (1)
Running Into The Night (1)

Shakedown (2)
She's A Runner (1)
Sweetheart (1) *10*
Tell Me Why (1)

Tonight (1)
Without You (Not Another Lonely Night) (2) *24*
You're My Girl (1) *87*

FRANKIE GOES TO HOLLYWOOD   '84

Dance-rock group from Liverpool, England: William "Holly" Johnson and Paul Rutherford (vocals), Brian Nash (guitar), Mark O'Toole (bass) and Peter Gill (drums). Group's name inspired by publicity recounting **Frank Sinatra**'s move into the movie industry.

11/24/84	**33**	41	©	1 **Welcome To The Pleasuredome**	$15	Island 90232 [2]
11/15/86	**88**	13	©	2 **Liverpool**	$10	Island 90546

Bang... (1)
Black Night White Light (1)
Born To Run (1)
Ferry (1)
For Heaven's Sake (2)

Is Anybody Out There? (2)
Kill The Pain (2)
Krisco Kisses (1)
Lunar Bay (2)
Maximum Joy (2)

Only Star In Heaven (1)
Power Of Love (1)
Rage Hard (2)
Relax (1) *10*
San Jose (1)

Snatch Of Fury (1)
Two Tribes (1) *43*
War (1)
Warriors Of The Wasteland (2)
Watching The Wildlife (2)

Welcome To The Pleasure Dome (1)
Well... (1)
Wish The Lads Were Here (1)
World Is My Oyster (1)

FRANKLIN, Aretha   ★16★   '67

Born on 3/25/42 in Memphis; raised in Buffalo and Detroit. Legendary R&B singer/songwriter/pianist. Known as "The Queen of Soul." Daughter of famous gospel preacher Rev. Cecil L. Franklin, pastor of Detroit's New Bethel Baptist Church. Signed to Columbia Records in 1960 as a jazz-styled singer. Dramatic turn in style and success after signing with Atlantic in 1966 and working with producer Jerry Wexler. Her sisters Carolyn and **Erma Franklin** also recorded. Married to her manager/cowriter Ted White (1961-69) and actor Glynn Turman (1978-84). Appeared in the 1980 movie *The Blues Brothers*. Won Grammy's Living Legends Award (1990) and Lifetime Achievement Award (1994). Inducted into the Rock and Roll Hall of Fame in 1987.

1)*I Never Loved A Man The Way I Love You* 2)*Aretha: Lady Soul* 3)*Aretha Now* 4)*Aretha Arrives* 5)*Aretha Live At Fillmore West*

11/17/62	**69**	12			1 **The Tender, The Moving, The Swinging Aretha Franklin**		$50	Columbia 1876 / 8676
12/19/64+	**84**	13			2 **Runnin' Out Of Fools**		$40	Columbia 2281 / 9081
7/10/65	**101**	8			3 **Yeah!!!**	[L]	$40	Columbia 2351 / 9151
8/6/66	**132**	4			4 **Soul Sister**		$40	Columbia 2521 / 9321
4/8/67	**2**[3]	79	●	©	5 **I Never Loved A Man The Way I Love You**		$30	Atlantic 8139
6/10/67	**94**	14			6 **Aretha Franklin's Greatest Hits**	[G]	$30	Columbia 2673 / 9473
8/26/67	**5**	41	©		7 **Aretha Arrives**		$30	Atlantic 8150
10/21/67	**173**	8			8 **Take A Look**	[K]	$30	Columbia 2754 / 9554
2/24/68	**2**[2]	52	●	©	9 **Aretha: Lady Soul**		$30	Atlantic 8176
7/13/68	**3**	35	●	©	10 **Aretha Now**		$20	Atlantic 8186
11/23/68+	**13**	20	©		11 **Aretha In Paris**	[L]	$20	Atlantic 8207
					recorded on 5/7/68 at the Olympia Theatre			
2/15/69	**15**	32	©		12 **Aretha Franklin: Soul '69**		$20	Atlantic 8212
7/19/69	**18**	33	©		13 **Aretha's Gold**	[G]	$20	Atlantic 8227
2/14/70	**17**	30	©		14 **This Girl's In Love With You**		$20	Atlantic 8248
9/12/70	**25**	22	©		15 **Spirit In The Dark**		$20	Atlantic 8265
6/5/71	**7**	34	●	©	16 **Aretha Live At Fillmore West**	[L]	$20	Atlantic 7205
9/25/71	**19**	34			17 **Aretha's Greatest Hits**	[G]	$20	Atlantic 8295
2/19/72	**11**	31	●	©	18 **Young, Gifted & Black**		$20	Atlantic 7213
6/17/72	**7**	23	▲[2]	©	19 **Amazing Grace**	[L]	$25	Atlantic 906 [2]
					recorded at the New Temple Missionary Baptist Church in Los Angeles			
6/24/72	**160**	9			20 **In The Beginning/The World Of Aretha Franklin 1960-1967**	[K]	$25	Columbia 31355 [2]
7/14/73	**30**	20	©		21 **Hey Now Hey (The Other Side Of The Sky)**		$15	Atlantic 7265
3/16/74	**14**	25	©		22 **Let Me In Your Life**		$15	Atlantic 7292
12/21/74+	**57**	13			23 **With Everything I Feel In Me**		$15	Atlantic 18116
11/15/75	**83**	11			24 **You**		$15	Atlantic 18151
6/19/76	**18**	24	●		25 **Sparkle**	[S]	$15	Atlantic 18176

FRANKLIN, Aretha — Cont'd

DEBUT	PEAK	WKS	RIAA	CD	Album Title	Sym	$	Label & Number
12/25/76+	135	8			26 Ten Years Of Gold	[G]	$15	Atlantic 18204
6/18/77	49	19			27 Sweet Passion		$15	Atlantic 19102
5/13/78	63	11			28 Almighty Fire		$15	Atlantic 19161
10/13/79	146	6			29 La Diva		$15	Atlantic 19248
10/25/80	47	30		©	30 Aretha		$12	Arista 9538
8/29/81	36	17		©	31 Love All The Hurt Away		$12	Arista 9552
8/14/82	23	30	●	©	32 Jump To It		$12	Arista 9602
7/30/83	36	18		©	33 Get It Right		$12	Arista 8019

above 2 produced by **Luther Vandross**

DEBUT	PEAK	WKS	RIAA	CD	Album Title	Sym	$	Label & Number
7/27/85	13	51	▲	©	34 Who's Zoomin' Who?		$10	Arista 8286
11/15/86+	32	39	●	©	35 Aretha		$10	Arista 8442
12/26/87+	106	16		©	36 One Lord, One Faith, One Baptism	[L]	$15	Arista 8497 [2]

recorded in July 1987 at the New Bethel Baptist Church in Detroit

DEBUT	PEAK	WKS	RIAA	CD	Album Title	Sym	$	Label & Number
5/20/89	55	18		©	37 Through The Storm		$10	Arista 8572
8/10/91	153	7		©	38 What You See Is What You Sweat		$10	Arista 8628
3/12/94	85	29	▲	©	39 Greatest Hits (1980-1994)	[G]	$10	Arista 18722
4/11/98	30	15	●	©	40 A Rose Is Still A Rose		$10	Arista 18987
11/11/00	45ᶜ	1	●	℗ ©	41 The Very Best Of Aretha Franklin, Vol. 1	[G]	$10	Rhino 71598

Ain't No Way (9,13,41) *16*
Ain't Nobody Ever Loved You (34)
Ain't Nobody (Gonna Turn Me Around) (7)
Ain't Nothing Like The Real Thing (22) *47*
All Of These Things (23)
All The King's Horses (18) *26*
Almighty Fire (Woman Of The Future) (28)
Amazing Grace (19)
Angel (21,26) *20*
Angel Cries (35)
Another Night (34,39) *22*
April Fools (18)
As Long As You Are There (24)
Ave Maria (36)
Baby, Baby, Baby (5)
Baby I Love You (7,11,13,17,26,41) *4*
Better Friends Than Lovers (23)
Bill Bailey, Won't You Please Come Home? (8)
Blue Holiday (8)
Border Song (Holy Moses) (18) *37*
Brand New Me (18) *flip*
Break It To Me Gently (27) *85*
Bridge Over Troubled Water (16,17) *6*
Bring It On Home To Me (12)
Call Me (14,17,41) *13*
Can't Turn You Loose (30)
Can't You Just See Me (4) *96*
Chain Of Fools (9,11,13,17,41) *2*
Change, A (10)
Change Is Gonna Come (5)
Climbing Higher Mountains (19)
Close To You (28)
Come Back Baby (9,11)
Come To Me (30,37) *84*
Crazy He Calls Me (12)
Cry Like A Baby (4,6,20)
Dark End Of The Street (14)
Day Dreaming (28,26) *5*
Deeper Love (39) *63*
Didn't I (Blow Your Mind This Time) (18)
Do Right Woman - Do Right Man (5,13,17,41)
Doctor's Orders (38,39)
Don't Cry, Baby (11,20) *92*
Don't Go Breaking My Heart (23)
Don't Let Me Lose This Dream (5,11)
Don't Play That Song (15,16,17) *11*
Drown In My Own Tears (5)
Eight Days On The Road (22)
Eleanor Rigby (14,16,41) *17*
Elusive Butterfly (12)
Ever Changing Times (38,39)
Every Girl (Wants My Guy) (33)
Every Little Bit Hurts (2,20,40)
Every Natural Thing (22)
Everyday People (38)
Evil Gal Blues (6,20)
Feeling, The (29)
First Snow In Kokomo (18)
Follow Your Heart (4,8)

Freeway Of Love (34,39) *3*
Gentle On My Mind (12) *76*
Get It Right (33,39) *61*
Gimme Your Love (37)
Give Yourself To Jesus (19)
Giving In (33)
God Bless The Child (1,6,20)
God Will Take Care Of You (19)
Going Down Slow (7)
Good Times (5)
Good To Me As I Am To You (9)
Groovin' (9,11)
Half A Love (29)
He'll Come Along (35)
He's The Boy (37)
Hello Sunshine (10)
Here We Go Again (40) *76*
Hey Now Hey (The Other Side Of The Sky) (21)
Higher Ground (36)
Hold On I'm Comin' (31)
Honest I Do (15)
Honey (39)
Honey I Need Your Love (29)
Hooked On Your Love (25)
House That Jack Built (13,41) *6*
How Deep Is The Ocean (1)
How Glad I Am (2)
How I Got Over (19)
How Many Times (40)
I Apologize (1)
(I Can't Get No) Satisfaction (7,11)
I Can't See Myself Leaving You (10) *28*
I Can't Wait Until I See My Baby's Face (2)
I Don't Know You Anymore (1)
I Dreamed A Dream (38,39)
I Get High (25)
I Got Your Love (33)
I Knew You Were Waiting (For Me) (35,39) *1*
I Love Every Little Thing About You (23)
I Needed You Baby (28)
I Never Loved A Man (The Way I Love You) (5,11,13,17,26,41) *9*
I Say A Little Prayer (10,13,17,41) *10*
I Take What I Want (30)
I Wanna Make It Up To You (32)
I Was Made For You (29)
I Wish It Would Rain (33)
I Won't Cry Anymore (8)
I Wonder (7)
I'll Dip (40)
I'll Keep On Smiling (8)
I'll Never Be Free (12)
I'm In Love (22) *19*
I'm Not Strong Enough To Love You Again (24)
I'm Sitting On Top Of The World (1)
I'm Wandering (1)
In Your Speed (3)
I've Been In The Storm Too Long (36)
I've Been Loving You Too Long (18)
I've Got The Music In Me (medley) (27)

If Ever A Love There Was (37)
If Ever I Would Leave You (6,20)
If I Had A Hammer (3)
If She Don't Want Your Lovin' (32)
If You Don't Think (22)
If You Gotta Make A Fool Of Somebody (12)
If You Need My Love Tonight (35)
Impossible (3)
In Case You Forgot (40)
In The Morning (40)
Integrity (34)
It Ain't Fair (14)
It Isn't, It Wasn't, It Ain't Never Gonna Be (37) *41*
It Only Happens (When I Look At You) (24)
It's Gonna Get A Bit Better (29)
It's Just A Matter Of Time (2)
(It's Just) Your Love (32)
It's My Turn (31)
It's Your Thing (32)
Jesus Hears Every Prayer (36)
Jimmy Lee (35,39) *28*
Jump (25) *72*
Jump To It (32,39) *24*
Jumpin' Jack Flash (35) *21*
Just For A Thrill (1,20)
Just My Daydream (32)
Just Right Tonight (21)
Keep On Loving You (38)
Kind Of Man (31)
Ladies Only (29)
Lady, Lady (28)
Lee Cross (8,20)
Let It Be (14,17)
Let Me In Your Life (2)
Living In The Streets (31)
Long And Winding Road (18)
Look For The Silver Lining (1)
Look Into Your Heart (25) *82*
Look To The Rainbow (35)
Lord's Prayer (36)
Love All The Hurt Away (31) *46*
Love For Sale (4)
Love Me Forever (30)
Love Me Right (32)
Love Pang (40)
Love The One You're With (16)
Lover Come Back To Me (1)
Loving You Baby (25)
Make It With You (16)
Mary, Don't You Weep (19)
Mary Goes Round (38)
Masquerade Is Over (22)
Meadows Of Springtime (27)
Mercy (37)
Mister Spain (21)
Misty (3)
Mockingbird (2,20) *94*
Money Won't Change You (19)
Moody's Mood (21)
More (3)
More Than Just A Joy (28)
Mother's Love (4)
Mr. D.J. (5 For The D.J.) (24) *53*
Muddy Water (3)
Mumbles (medley) (27)
My Guy (2)

Natural Woman (You Make Me Feel Like) (9,11,13,17,26,39,41) *8*
Never Grow Old (19)
Never Leave You Again (40)
Never Let Me Go (7)
Night Life (7,11)
Night Time Is The Right Time (10)
Niki Hoeky (9)
96 Tears (7)
No Matter Who You Love (28)
(No, No) I'm Losing You (4)
No One Could Ever Love You More (27)
Oh Baby (22)
Oh Happy Day (36)
Oh Me Oh My (I'm A Fool For You Baby) (18) *73*
Oh No Not My Baby (15)
Ol' Man River (4)
Old Landmark (19)
Once In A Lifetime (2)
One Room Paradise (2)
One Step Ahead (6,20)
One Way Ticket (15)
Only Star (7)
Operation Heartbreak (8)
Packing Up, Getting Ready To Go (36)
People (20)
People Get Ready (9)
Pitiful (37)
Precious Lord, Take My Hand (medley) (19)
Precious Memories (19)
Pretender (33)
Prove It (15)
Pullin' (15)
Push (34)
Ramblin' (12)
Reach Out And Touch (Somebody's Hand) (16)
Reasons Why (29)
Respect (5,11,13,16,17,26,41) *1*
River's Invitation (12)
Rock-A-Bye Your Baby With A Dixie Melody (6) *37*
Rock-A-Lott (35) *82*
Rock Steady (18,26) *9*
Rock With Me (25)
Rose Is Still A Rose (40) *26*
Runnin' Out Of Fools (2,6,20) *57*
Satisfaction ..see: (I Can't Get No)
Save Me (5)
School Days (30)
Search On (31)
See Saw (10,13,26,41) *14*
Sha-La Bandit (24)
Share Your Love With Me (14,41) *13*
Shoop Shoop Song (It's In His Kiss) (2)
Since You've Been Gone ..see: (Sweet Sweet Baby)
Sing It Again - Say It Again (23)
Sister From Texas (31)
Sisters Are Doin' It For Themselves (34) *18*
Sit Down And Cry (14)
Skylark (20)
So Long (12)
So Swell When You're Well (21)

Someone Else's Eyes (38)
Something He Can Feel (25,26) *28*
Somewhere (21)
Son Of A Preacher Man (14) *flip*
Song For You (22)
Soul Serenade (5,11)
Soulville (20) *83*
Spanish Harlem (17,26) *2*
Sparkle (21)
Spirit In The Dark (15,16) *23*
Sunshine Will Never Be The Same (27)
Surely God Is Able (36)
Swanee (4)
Sweet Bitter Love (2)
Sweet Passion (27)
(Sweet Sweet Baby) Since You've Been Gone (9,11,13,41) *5*
Take A Look (4,8,20) *56*
Take It Like You Give It (20)
Take Me With You (30)
Tender Touch (27)
That's All I Want From You (15)
That's Life (7)
That's The Way I Feel About Cha (21)
There Is No Greater Love (3)
There's A Star For Everyone (31)
Think (10,13,26,41) *7*
Think (1989) (37)
This Could Be The Start Of Something (3)
This Girl's In Love With You (14)
This Is For Real (32)
This You Can Believe (28)
Thrill Is Gone (From Yesterday's Kiss) (15)
Through The Storm (37) *16*
Today I Love Ev'rybody (3)
Today I Sing The Blues (6,12,20)
Together Again (40)
Touch Me Up (27)
Tracks Of My Tears (12) *71*
Trouble In Mind (3) *86*
Truth And Honesty (31)
Try A Little Tenderness (1,6,20) *100*
Try Matty's (15)
Two Sides Of Love (2)
United Together (30,39) *56*
Until You Come Back To Me (That's What I'm Gonna Do) (22,26) *3*
Until You Say You Love Me (34)
Until You Were Gone (4,8)
Walk In The Light (36)
Walk On By (2)
Walk Softly (24)
Watch My Back (40)
We Need Power (36)
Weight, The (14,41) *19*
What A Fool Believes (30)
What A Friend We Have In Jesus (19)
What Did You Give (38)
What I Did For Love (27)
What If I Should Ever Need You (29)

What You See Is What You Sweat (38)
Whatever It Is (30)
When I Think About You (27)
When The Battle Is Over (15)
When You Get Right Down To It (23)
When You Love Me Like That (33)
Who's Zoomin' Who (34,39) *7*
Whole Lot Of Me (31)
Wholy Holy (19) *81*
Why I Sing The Blues (15)
Willing To Forgive (39) *26*
With Everything I Feel In Me (23)
With Pen In Hand (22)
Without Love (23) *45*
Without The One You Love (1,3,6,20)
Without You (24)
Woman, The (40)
Won't Be Long (8) *76*
Won't You Come Home Bill Bailey ..see: Bill Bailey
You (24)
You And Me (15) *flip*
You Are My Sunshine (7)
You Brought Me Back To Life (29)
You Can't Always Get What You Want (31)
You Can't Take Me For Granted (38)
You Got All The Aces (24)
You Made Me Love You (I Didn't Want To Do It) (4)
You Make My Life (24)
You Move Me (23)
You Send Me (10,13) *56*
You'll Lose A Good Thing (2)
You'll Never Get To Heaven (23)
You'll Never Walk Alone (19)
You're A Sweet Sweet Man (10)
You're All I Need To Get By (17) *19*
You've Got A Friend (medley) (19)
Young, Gifted And Black (18)

FRANKLIN, Erma '69
Born in 1943 in Memphis. Sister of **Aretha Franklin**.

| 10/18/69 | 199 | 2 | | | **Soul Sister** | | | $20 | Brunswick 754147 |

Baby I Love You
By The Time I Get To Phoenix
Can't See My Way

Change My Thoughts From You
For Once In My Life

Gotta Find Me A Lover (24 Hours A Day)
Hold On, I'm Comin'

Light My Fire
Saving My Love For You
Son Of A Preacher Man

You've Been Cancelled

FRANKLIN, Kirk, and The Family '98
Born on 1/26/70 in Fort Worth, Texas. Gospel singer/choir leader. Also see **God's Property**.

3/12/94+	58	36	▲	©	1 **Kirk Franklin and The Family**		[L]	$10	GospoCentric 2119
					recorded on 7/25/92 at Grace Temple Church in Fort Worth, Texas				
11/25/95	60	8	●	©	2 **Christmas**	C:#30/5	[X]	$10	GospoCentric 2130
					Christmas charts: 9/'95, 25/'96, 26/'97				
5/18/96	23	58	▲	©	3 **Whatcha Lookin' 4**		[L]	$10	GospoCentric 72127
					recorded at the Calvary Temple in Dallas				
10/17/98	7	49	▲²	©	4 **The Nu Nation Project**			$10	GospoCentric 90178

KIRK FRANKLIN

Anything 4 U (3)
Blessing In The Storm (4)
Call On The Lord (1)
Conquerors (3)
Don't Take Your Joy Away (4)
Family Worship Medley (1)
Go Tell It On The Mountain (2)
Gonna Be A Lovely Day (4)
He Can Handle It (1)

He Loves Me (4)
He's Able (1)
Hold Me Now (4)
I Can (4)
I Love You Jesus (4)
If You've Been Delivered (4)
Jesus Is The Reason For The Season (2)
Jesus Paid It All (3)

Lean On Me (4) 79
Let Me Touch You (3)
Letter From My Friend (1)
Love (4)
Love Song (2)
Mama's Song (3)
Melodies From Heaven (3)
My Desire (4)
Night That Christ Was Born (2)

Now Behold The Lamb (2)
O Come All Ye Faithful (2)
Praise Joint (4)
Real Love (1)
Revolution (4)
Riverside (4)
Savior More Than Life (3)
Silent Night (2)
Silver & Gold (1,2)

Smile Again (4)
Something About The Name Jesus (4)
Speak To Me (1)
Thank You For Your Child (2)
There's No Christmas Without You (2)
They Need To Know (2)
Till We Meet Again (1)

Washed Away (3)
Whatcha Lookin' 4 (3)
When I Think About Jesus (3)
Where The Spirit Is (3)
Why We Sing (1)
You Are (4)

FRANKLIN, Rodney '80
Born on 9/16/58 in Berkeley, California. Jazz pianist.

4/19/80	104	13			1 **You'll Never Know**		[I]	$10	Columbia 36122
1/22/83	190	3			2 **Learning To Love**			$10	Columbia 38198
2/25/84	187	3			3 **Marathon**			$10	Columbia 38953

Don't Wanna Let You Go (2)
Early Morning (medley) (2)
Enuff Is Enuff (1)
Felix Leo (1)
Genesis (medley) (2)

God Bless The Blues (1)
Groove, The (1)
Journey (1)
Learning To Love (2)
Let There Be Light (medley) (2)

Let's Talk (3)
Love Is The Answer (3)
Lumiere (3)
Marathon (3)
Nature's Way (medley) (2)

New Day (medley) (2)
Parkay Man (1)
Reflection Of A Dream (3)
Return (1)
Sailing (3)

Searchin' For (3)
Sonshine (2)
Stay On In The Groove (3)
That's The Way I Feel 'Bout Your Love (2)

Watcher, The (1)
You'll Never Know (1)

FRANKS, Michael '82
Born on 9/18/44 in La Jolla, California. Jazz-pop singer/songwriter.
1)Objects Of Desire 2)Tiger In The Rain 3)One Bad Habit

7/31/76	131	13	●	©	1 **The Art Of Tea**	C:#13/8		$12	Reprise 2230
2/19/77	119	9	●	©	2 **Sleeping Gypsy**			$12	Warner 3004
4/8/78	90	10		©	3 **Burchfield Nines**			$12	Warner 3167
3/17/79	68	16		©	4 **Tiger In The Rain**			$12	Warner 3294
5/10/80	83	21		©	5 **One Bad Habit**			$12	Warner 3427
1/30/82	45	14		©	6 **Objects Of Desire**			$12	Warner 3648
10/29/83	141	11		©	7 **Passionfruit**			$10	Warner 23962
6/15/85	137	27		©	8 **Skin Dive**			$10	Warner 25275
8/1/87	147	11		©	9 **The Camera Never Lies**			$10	Warner 25570
7/7/90	121	17		©	10 **Blue Pacific**			$10	Reprise 26183

All Dressed Up With Nowhere To Go (5)
All I Need (10)
Alone At Night (7)
Amazon (7)
Antonio's Song (The Rainbow) (2)
Art Of Love (10)
B'wana-He No Home (2)
Baseball (5)
Blue Pacific (10)
Burchfield Nines (3)
Camera Never Lies (9)
Chain Reaction (2)
Chez Nous (10)
Crayon Sun (Safe At Home) (10)

Dear Little Nightingale (3)
Doctor Sax (9)
Don't Be Blue (2)
Don't Be Shy (8)
Down In Brazil (2)
Eggplant (1)
Face To Face (9)
Flirtation (6)
He Tells Himself He's Happy (5)
Hideaway (4)
How The Garden Grows (7)
I Don't Know Why I'm So Happy I'm Sad (1)
I Really Hope It's You (2)
I Surrender (3)
In Search Of The Perfect Shampoo (3)

In The Eye Of The Storm (2)
Innuendo (9)
Inside You (5)
Island Life (9)
Jardin Botanico (4)
Jealousy (6)
Jive (1)
Ladies' Nite (6)
Lady Wants To Know (2)
Laughing Gas (6)
Let Me Count The Ways (8)
Lifeline (4)
Lip Service (9)
Living On The Inside (4)
Long Slow Distance (10)
Lotus Blossom (5)
Love Duet (6)

Loving You More And More (5)
Meet Me In The Deerpark (3)
Monkey See-Monkey Do (1)
Mr. Blue (1)
Never Satisfied (7)
Never Say Die (7)
Nightmoves (1)
No-Deposit Love (6)
No One But You (6)
Now I Know Why (They Call It Falling) (8)
Now That Your Joystick's Broke (7)
Now You're In My Dreams (4)
On My Way Home To You (5)
On The Inside (10)
One Bad Habit (5)

Please Don't Say Goodnight (8)
Popsicle Toes (1) 43
Queen Of The Underground (8)
Rainy Night In Tokyo (7)
Read My Lips (8)
Robinsong, A (3)
Sanpaku (4)
Satisfaction Guaranteed (4)
Sometimes I Just Forget To Smile (1)
Speak To Me (10)
St. Elmo's Fire (1)
Still Life (5)
Sunday Morning Here With You (7)
Tahitian Moon (6)
Tell Me All About It (7)

Tiger In The Rain (4)
Underneath The Apple Tree (4)
Vincent's Ear (10)
Vivaldi's Song (3)
When I Give My Love To You (8)
When I Think Of Us (9)
When She Is Mine (4)
When It's Over (4)
When Sly Calls (Don't Touch That Phone) (7)
When The Cookie Jar Is Empty (3)
Woman In The Waves (10)
Wonderland (6)
Wrestle A Live Nude Girl (3)
Your Secret's Safe With Me (8)

FRATIANNE, Linda '82
Born on 8/2/60 in Northridge, California. World champion figure skater.

| 2/20/82 | 174 | 7 | | | **Dance & Exercise With The Hits** | | | $10 | Columbia 37653 |
| | | | | | music performed by The Beachwood All-Stars (studio group) | | | | |

Bette Davis Eyes
Games People Play

Hot Rod Hearts
How Do I Survive

I'm In Love
Kiss On My List

Real Love
Slow Hand

Sweetheart

FREAK NASTY '97
Born Carlito Timmons in Puerto Rico; raised in New Orleans. Male rapper.

| 4/19/97 | 132 | 12 | | © | **Controversee...That's Life...And That's The Way It Is** | | | $10 | Power 2111 |

Boom Boom Bomb
Boot Up (Who Ya Wit)
Bump That Rump

Controversee (Start)
Cut Up
Da' Dip 15

Deep Deep South
Dirty Mouth
Down Low

F-ckie S-ckie (At Freaknasty Party)
I Want 2 F-ck

P.G.P.B.
Respect
Rumors Pt. 1 & 2

FREBERG, Stan '61
Born on 8/7/26 in Pasadena, California. Top pop music satirist. Did several cartoon voices. Later had a highly successful advertising career.

| 7/3/61 | 34 | 24 | | © | **Stan Freberg Presents The United States Of America** | | [C] | $30 | Capitol 1573 |

Battle Of Yorktown
Betsy Ross And The Flag

Boston Tea Party
Columbus Discovers America

Declaration Of Independence
Pilgrim's Progress

Sale Of Manhattan
Thanksgiving Story

Washington Crosses The Delaware

Yankee Doodle Go Home

FRED, John, & His Playboy Band '68
Born John Fred Gourrier on 5/8/41 in Baton Rouge, Louisiana. Pop-rock singer/songwriter.

| 2/3/68 | 154 | 10 | | | **Agnes English** | | | $25 | Paula 2197 |

later released as Judy In Disguise With Glasses

AcHenall Riot · **Judy In Disguise (With** · No Good To Cry · Sad Story · Up And Down
Agnes English · **Glasses)** *1* · Off The Wall · She Shot A Hole In My Soul · When The Lights Go Out
· Most Unlikely To Succeed · Out Of Left Field · Sometimes You Just Can't Win

FREDDIE AND THE DREAMERS '65
Pop group from Manchester, England: Freddie Garrity (vocals; born on 11/14/40), Derek Quinn and Roy Crewsdon (guitars), Peter Birrell (bass) and Bernie Dwyer (drums).

| 4/17/65 | 19 | 19 | | | 1 **Freddie & The Dreamers** | | | $30 | Mercury 61017 |
| 5/8/65 | 86 | 10 | | | 2 **I'm Telling You Now** | | | $30 | Tower 5003 |

includes "After Today" and "Low Grades And High Fever" by Linda Laine & The Sinners, "The Beating Of My Heart" and "Questions I Can't Answer" by Heinz, "Bye Bye Bird" and "I'm Gonna Jump" by Toggery Five, "Head Over Heels" and "I'm Leaving You" by Mike Rabon & The Demons and "That's My Baby" and "Things Will Never Be The Same" by Four Just Men

| 6/19/65 | 85 | 12 | | | 3 **Do The Freddie** | | | $30 | Mercury 61026 |

Do The Freddie (3) *18* · I Understand (Just How You · In My Baby's Arms (3) · Little Bitty Pretty One (3) · Sally Anne (1) · Things I'd Like To Say (3)
Don't Do That To Me (3) · Feel) (1) *36* · It Doesn't Matter Anymore (1) · **Little You** (3) *48* · Say It Isn't True (1) · What Have I Done To You (2)
Early In The Morning (1) · **I'm Telling You Now** (2) *1* · Johnny B. Goode (1) · Love Like You (3) · She Belongs To You (3) · Yes I Do (1)
Feel So Blue (3) · If You Gotta Make A Fool Of · Just For You (3) · Money (That's What I Want) (1) · Silly Girl (3)
I Don't Love You Anymore (1) · Somebody (1) · Kansas City (1) · Over You (3) · Tell Me When (1)

FREDDY JONES BAND, The '95
Rock group formed in South Bend, Indiana: Marty Lloyd and Wayne Healy (vocals, guitars), brothers Rob (guitar) and Jim (bass) Bonaccorsi and Simon Horrocks (drums).

| 8/26/95 | 186 | 1 | | © | **North Avenue Wake Up Call** | | | $10 | Capricorn 42040 |

Alone · Goodbye · Rain · Turn · Warm Like Home
Deep In The Flow · Hold On To Midnight · Rietiem · Under The Tree · Wherever You Roam
Ferris Wheel · Old Angels · This Could Be Soon · Waitress

FREE '70
Rock group formed in England: **Paul Rodgers** (vocals), **Paul Kossoff** (guitar), Andy Fraser (bass) and Simon Kirke (drums). Kossoff and Fraser left in 1972, replaced by Tetsu Yamauchi (bass, later with **Faces**) and John "Rabbit" Bundrick (keyboards). Kossoff (died on 3/19/76 of heart failure) formed **Back Street Crawler**. Rodgers and Kirke formed **Bad Company** in 1974. Rodgers was also lead singer of **The Firm** and **The Law**.

9/13/69	197	2			1 **Tons Of Sobs**			$20	A&M 4198
9/5/70	17	27		©	2 **Fire And Water**			$20	A&M 4268
2/27/71	190	2			3 **Highway**			$20	A&M 4287
9/11/71	89	8		©	4 **Free Live!**		[L]	$20	A&M 4306
5/27/72	69	16			5 **Free At Last**			$20	A&M 4349
2/3/73	47	16		©	6 **Heartbreaker**			$15	Island 9217
5/24/75	120	7		©	7 **Best Of Free**		[G]	$12	A&M 3663

All Right Now (2,4,7) *4* · Don't Say You Love Me (2) · Heavy Load (2) · Mouthful Of Grass (7) · Remember (2) · Sweet Tooth (1)
Be My Friend (3,4) · Easy On My Soul (6) · Highway Song (3,7) · Mr. Big (2,4) · Ride On Pony (3,4) · Travellin In Style (6)
Bodie (3) · Fire And Water (2,4,7) · Hunter, The (1,4,7) · Muddy Water (6) · Sail On (5) · Travellin' Man (5)
Catch A Train (5,7) · Get Where I Belong (4) · I'm A Mover (1,4,7) · My Brother Jake (4,7) · Seven Angels (6) · Walk In My Shadow (1)
Child (5) · Goin' Down Slow (1) · Little Bit Of Love (5,7) · Oh I Wept (2) · Soldier Boy (1) · Wild Indian Woman (1)
Come Together In The Morning · Goodbye (5,7) · Love You So (3) · On My Way (3) · Soon I Will Be Gone (3) · Wishing Well (6)
(6) · Guardian Of The Universe (5) · Magic Ship (5) · Over The Green Hills - Parts I & · Stealer (3,7) *49* · Woman (7)
Common Mortal Man (6) · Heartbreaker (6) · Moonshine (1) · II (1) · Sunny Day (1) · Worry (1)

FREED, Alan — see VARIOUS ARTIST COMPILATIONS

FREEMAN, Russ — see RIPPINGTONS, The

FREE MOVEMENT, The '72
R&B vocal group from Los Angeles: brothers Adrian and Claude Jefferson, Godoy Colbert, Cheryl Conley, Josephine Brown and Jennifer Gates.

| 1/29/72 | 167 | 8 | | | **I've Found Someone Of My Own** | | | $15 | Columbia 31136 |

Coming Home · I Know I Could Love You Better · If Only You Believe · Where Do We Go From Here
Could You Believe In A Dream · (The Second Time Around) · Land Where I Live · Your Love Has Grown Cold
Harder I Try (The Bluer I · **I've Found Someone Of My** · Love The One You're With
Get) *50* · Own *5* · Son Of The Zulu King

FREHLEY, Ace '79
Born Paul Frehley on 4/27/51 in the Bronx, New York. Rock guitarist. Member of **Kiss**.

10/14/78+	26	23	▲	©	1 **Ace Frehley**			$20	Casablanca 7121
5/23/87	43	25		©	2 **Frehley's Comet**			$10	Megaforce 81749
2/27/88	84	10		©	3 **Live + 1**		[L]	$10	Megaforce 81826

recorded on 9/4/87 at the Aragon Ballroom in Chicago

| 6/11/88 | 81 | 13 | | © | 4 **Second Sighting** | | | $10 | Megaforce 81862 |

FREHLEY'S COMET (above 2)

| 11/11/89 | 102 | 9 | | © | 5 **Trouble Walkin'** | | | $10 | Megaforce 82042 |

Acorn Is Spinning (4) · Fallen Angel (4) · Insane (4) · New Kind Of Lover (4) · Separate (4) · 2 Young 2 Die (5)
Back To School (5) · Five Card Stud (4) · Into The Night (2) · **New York Groove** (1) *13* · Shot Full Of Rock (5) · Trouble Walkin' (5)
Breakout (2,3) · Fractured Mirror (1) · It's Over Now (4) · Ozone (1) · Snow Blind (1) · We Got Your Rock (2)
Calling To You (2) · Fractured Too (2) · Juvenile Delinquent (4) · Remember Me (5) · Something Moved (2,3) · What's On Your Mind? (1)
Dancin' With Danger (4) · Fractured III (5) · Loser In A Fight (4) · Rip It Out (1,3) · Speedin' Back To My Baby (1) · Wiped-Out (1)
Do Ya (5) · Hide Your Heart (5) · Lost In Limbo (5) · Rock Soldiers (2) · Stranger In A Strange Land (2) · Words Are Not Enough (3)
Dolls (2) · I'm In Need Of Love (1) · Love Me Right (2) · Rocket Ride (3) · Time Ain't Runnin' Out (4)

FREIBERG, David — see KANTNER, Paul / SLICK, Grace

FRENCH, Nicki '95
Born in Carlisle, England. Female dance singer.

| 7/8/95 | 151 | 4 | | © | **Secrets** | | | $10 | Critique 15436 |

Did You Ever Really Love Me? · Forever And A Day · Is There Anybody Out There? · Secrets
For All We Know · I'll Be Waiting · Never In A Million Years · Something About You · **Total Eclipse Of The Heart** *2* · Voice Of America

FRENTE! '94
Pop-rock group from Melbourne, Australia: Angie Hart (vocals), Simon Austin (guitar), Tim O'Connor (bass) and Mark Picton (drums). Band name is Spanish for "Front."

| 5/14/94 | 75 | 20 | | © | **Marvin The Album** .... | | $10 | Mammoth 92390 |

Accidently Kelly Street · **Bizarre Love Triangle** *49* · Cuscutlan · Dangerous · Explode · Girl · Labour Of Love · Lonely · Most Beautiful · No Time · Ordinary Angels · Pretty Friend · Reflect · See/Believe

FRESH PRINCE — see D.J. JAZZY JEFF

FREY, Glenn '85
Born on 11/6/48 in Detroit. Singer/songwriter/guitarist. Founding member of the **Eagles**. Played "Cody McMahon" on the 1993 TV series *South of Sunset*.

6/26/82	32	38	●	© 1	**No Fun Aloud**		$12	Asylum 60129
7/14/84+	22	65	●	© 2	**The Allnighter**		$10	MCA 5501
9/3/88	36	19		© 3	**Soul Searchin'**		$10	MCA 6239

All Those Lies (1) *41* · Allnighter, The (2) *54* · Better In The U.S.A. (2) · Can't Put Out This Fire (3) · Don't Give Up (1) · I Did It For Your Love (3) · I Found Somebody (1) *31* · I Got Love (2) · I Volunteer (1) · I've Been Born Again (1) · It's Your Life (3) · Let's Go Home (2) · Let's Pretend We're Still In Love (3) · Livin' Right (3) *90* · Living In Darkness (2) · Lover's Moon (2) · New Love (2) · One You Love (1) *15* · Partytown (1) · Sea Cruise (1) · **Sexy Girl** (2) *20* · She Can't Let Go (1) · **Smuggler's Blues** (2) *12* · Some Kind Of Blue (3) · Somebody Else (2) · Soul Searchin' (3) · That Girl (1) · **True Love** (3) *13* · Two Hearts (3) · Working Man (3)

FRIDA '83
Born Anni-Frid Lyngstad on 11/15/45 in Narvik, Sweden. Member of **Abba**.

| 11/13/82+ | 41 | 28 | | | **Something's Going On** .... | | $10 | Atlantic 80018 |

produced by **Phil Collins**

Baby Don't You Cry No More · Here We'll Stay · I Got Something · **I Know There's Something Going On** *13* · I See Red · Strangers · Tell Me It's Over · Threnody · To Turn The Stone · Way You Do · You Know What I Mean

FRIEDMAN, Dean '77
Born in 1955 in Paramus, New Jersey. Pop singer/songwriter.

| 6/4/77 | 192 | 6 | | | **Dean Friedman** .... | | $12 | Lifesong 6008 |

Ariel *26* · Company · Funny Papers · Humor Me · I May Be Young · Letter, The · Love Is Not Enough · Solitaire · Song For My Mother · Woman Of Mine

FRIEDMAN, Kinky '75
Born Richard Friedman on 10/31/44 in Rio Duckworth, Texas. Country singer/satirist.

| 2/1/75 | 132 | 6 | | © | **Kinky Friedman** .... | | $15 | ABC 829 |

Autograph · Before All Hell Breaks Loose · Homo Erectus · Lover Please · Miss Nickelodeon · Popeye The Sailor Man · Rapid City South Dakota · Somethin's Wrong With The Beaver · They Ain't Makin' Jews Like Jesus Anymore · When The Lord Closes The Door (He Opens A Little Window) · Wild Man From Borneo

FRIENDS OF DISTINCTION, The '69
R&B vocal group from Los Angeles: Floyd Butler, Harry Elston, Jessica Cleaves and Barbara Jean Love. Butler died of a heart attack on 4/29/90 (age 49).

5/3/69	35	25		© 1	**Grazin'**		$15	RCA Victor 4149
10/25/69	173	6		© 2	**Highly Distinct**		$15	RCA Victor 4212
3/28/70	68	21		3	**Real Friends**		$15	RCA Victor 4313
10/31/70	179	3		4	**Whatever**		$15	RCA Victor 4408
8/7/71	166	7		5	**Friends & People**		$15	RCA Victor 4492

And I Love Him (1) · Any Way You Want Me (3) · Baby I Could Be So Good At Loving You (1) · Bring Us A Better Day (4) · Check It Out (4) · Crazy Mary (3) · Didn't We (4) · Down I Go (5) · Dying To Live (5) · Eli's Comin (1) · Faces On The Bus (5) · Going In Circles (1) *15* · Great Day (1) · Help Yourself (To All Of My Lovin') (1) · I Can't Get You Out Of My Mind (5) · **I Need You** (5) *79* · I Really Hope You Do (1) · I've Never Found A Girl (To Love Me Like You Do) (1) · Impressions (2) · It Don't Matter To Me (3) · It's A Wonderful World (2) · It's Just A Game Love (2) · It's Sunday (2) · It's Time To See Each Other (5) · Jenny Wants To Know (5) · Just A Little Lovin' (3) · Lady Mae (3) · Let Me Be (5) · **Let Yourself Go** (2) *63* · Light My Fire (2) · Lonesome Mood (1) · Long Time Comin' My Way (3) · **Love Or Let Me Be Lonely** (3) *6* · My Mind Is A Camera (3) · New Mother Nature (4) · Oh, How I Miss You (5) · On & On (3) · Out In The Country (3) · Peaceful (1) · People (5) · People Talkin' And Sayin' Nothin' (4) · Soulful Anthem (4) · Sweet Young Thing Like You (1) · This Generation (2) · **Time Waits For No One** (4) *60* · We Got A Good Thing Goin' (2) · Why Did I Lose You (2) · Willa Faye (3) · Workin' On A Groovy Thing (2) · You And I (4)

FRIJID PINK '70
Rock group formed in Detroit: Kelly Green (lead singer), Gary Thompson (guitar), Tom Beaudry (bass) and Rich Stevens (drums).

| 1/24/70 | 11 | 30 | | 1 | **Frijid Pink** .... | | $25 | Parrot 71033 |
| 10/31/70 | 149 | 12 | | 2 | **Defrosted** .... | | $25 | Parrot 71041 |

Black Lace (2) · Boozin' Blues (1) · Bye Bye Blues (2) · Crying Shame (1) · Drivin' Blues (1) · End Of The Line (1) · God Gave Me You (1) · **House Of The Rising Sun** (1) *7* · I Haven't Got The Time (2) · I Want To Be Your Lover (1) · I'll Never Be Lonely (2) · I'm Movin' (2) · I'm On My Way (1) · Pain In My Heart (2) · **Sing A Song For Freedom** (2) *55* · Sloony (2) · Tell Me Why (1)

FRIPP, Robert '82
Born on 5/16/46 in Wimbourne, Dorset, England. Rock guitarist. Founder of **King Crimson**.

5/26/79	79	14		© 1	**Exposure**		$12	EG 6201
4/26/80	110	6		2	**God Save The Queen/Under Heavy Manners**	[I]	$12	Polydor 6266
4/4/81	90	7		3	**The League Of Gentlemen**	[I]	$12	Polydor 6317
11/6/82	60	11		© 4	**I Advance Masked**	[I]	$10	A&M 4913
10/20/84	155	5		© 5	**Bewitched**	[I]	$10	A&M 5011

Aquarelle (medley) (4) · Begin The Day (5) · Bewitched (5) · Breathless (3) · Chicago (1) · China - Yellow Leader (4) · Cognitive Dissonance (3) · Disengage (1) · Dislocated (3) · Exposure (1) · Eye Needles (3) · Forgotten Steps (5) · Girl On A Swing (4) · God Save The Queen (2) · Guide (5) · H.G. Wells (3) · Haaden Two (1) · Hardy Country (4) · Heptaparaparshinokh (3) · Here Comes The Flood (1) · I Advance Masked (4) · I May Not Have Had Enough Of Me But I've Had Enough Of You (1) · Image And Likeness (5) · In The Cloud Forest (4) · Indiscreet, I, II & III (3) · Inductive Resonance (3) · Lakeland (medley) (5) · Maquillage (5) · Mary (1) · Minor Man (3) · NY3 (1) · New Marimba (4) · 1983 (2) · North Star (4) · Ochre (3) · Painting And Dance (4) · Parade (5) · Pareto Optimum I & II (3) · Postscript (1) · Red Two Scorer (2) · Seven On Seven (4) · Still Point (4) · Stultified (4) · Train (5) · Trap (3) · Tribe (3) · Truth Of Skies (4) · Under Bridges Of Silence (4) · Under Heavy Manners (2) · Urban Landscape (1) · Water Music I & II (1) · What Kind Of Man Reads Playboy (5) · You Burn Me Up I'm A Cigarette (1) · Zero Of The Signified (2)

FRONT, The '90

Hard-rock group from Kansas City: brothers Michael (vocals) and Bobby (keyboards) Franano, Mike Greene (guitar), Randy Jordan (bass) and Shane (drums).

2/3/90	118	14		©	The Front			$10	Columbia 45260

Fire   Le Motion   Ritual   Sister Moon   Sweet Addiction
In The Garden   Pain   Sin   Sunshine Girl   Violent World

FRONT 242 '91

Industrial dance group from Brussels, Belgium: vocalists Jean-Luc De Meyer and Richard Jonckheere with instrumentalists Daniel Bressanutti and Patrick Codenys.

2/16/91	95	12		© 1	Tyranny For You			$10	Epic 46998
6/12/93	166	1		© 2	06:21:03:11 Up Evil			$10	Epic 53433

Crapage (2)   Leitmotiv 136 (1)   Neurobashing (1)   Skin (2)   Trigger 2 (Anatomy Of A Shot)
Flag (2)   Melt (2)   Religion (1)   Soul Manager (1)   (1)
Fuel (2)   Moldavia (1)   Rhythm Of Time (1)   Stratoscape (2)   Untold (1)
Gripped By Fear (1)   Motion (2)   (S)Crapage (2)   Tragedy For You (1)   Waste (2)
Hymn (2)   Mutilate (1)   Sacrifice (1)

FROST '70

Rock group from Detroit: Dick Wagner (vocals, guitar), Don Hartman (guitar), Gordy Garris (bass) and Bob Riggs (drums).

6/21/69	168	10		1	Frost Music			$20	Vanguard 6520
11/29/69+	148	8		2	Rock And Roll Music		[L]	$20	Vanguard 6541

recorded at the Grande Ballroom in Detroit

10/17/70	197	2		3	Through The Eyes Of Love			$20	Vanguard 6556

Baby Once You Got It (1)   Fifteen Hundred Miles (Through   Linda (2)   Mystery Man (1)   Through The Eyes Of Love
Big Time Spender (3)   The Eye Of A Beatle) (3)   Little Susie Singer (1)   Rock And Roll Music (2)   (God Help Us Please) (3)
Black As Night (3)   First Day Of May (1)   Long Way Down From Mobile   Stand In The Shadows (1)   We Got To Get Out Of This
Black Train (2)   Help Me Baby (2)   (1)   Sweet Lady Love (2)   Place (2)
Donny's Blues (2)   It's So Hard (3)   Long Way From Home (3)   Take My Hand (1)   Who Are You? (1)
Family, The (1)   Jennie Lee (1)   Maybe Tomorrow (3)

FROST — see KID FROST

FROZEN GHOST '87

Pop-rock duo from Canada: Arnold Lanni (vocals, guitar, keyboards) and Wolf Hassel (bass). Both were members of the group **Sheriff**.

4/11/87	107	13		©	Frozen Ghost			$10	Atlantic 81736

Beware The Masque   Love Like A Fire   Promises   Soldiers Cry   Truth In Lies
End Of The Line   Love Without Lies   **Should I See** *69*   Time Is The Answer   Yum Bai Ya

FRYE, David '70

Comedian/impressionist. Best known for his impression of President Nixon.

12/27/69+	19	18		1	I Am The President		[C]	$15	Elektra 75006
3/27/71	123	6		2	Radio Free Nixon		[C]	$15	Elektra 74085
12/11/71+	60	13		3	Richard Nixon Superstar		[C]	$12	Buddah 5097
8/11/73	45	15		4	Richard Nixon: A Fantasy		[C]	$12	Buddah 1600

Addressing The Nation (4)   Dear Dick (1)   Foreign Affairs (2)   Loyal Opposition (3)   Prison Break (4)   Ten O'Clock Shadow (1)
Advisors, The (3)   Dear Henry Cabot (1)   Funnies, The (2)   Message, The (2)   Prison Reform (4)   Thought For Tomorrow (2)
And The Winner Is (1)   Dick Nixon Show (2)   Golda Goes Washington (1)   My Way (2)   Prologue (2)   Trial, The (4)
Big Four (2)   Dick Nixon's Solid Gold (4)   Historic Words (1)   New Tenants (2)   Public Servant Number 1 (3)   Trip, The (4)
Big House (4)   Dr. Kissinger (2)   Hush, Hush, Sweet Spiro (2)   Nixon Meets The Godfather (4)   Rocky Reports (1)   Victory Speech (1)
Bill Buckley Show (4)   Early Nixon Medley (3)   Inauguration, The (3)   Nixon Sings The Blues (4)   Sesame Street (3)   WNIX Sports (2)
Blessed Event (1)   Echoes Of His Mind (1)   Inside Hubert (1)   Oh Dad, Poor Dad (1)   Soap Opera (2)   Weather Report (2)
Boss, The (3)   Economy, The (3)   It's A Gas (1)   Parable, The (3)   Southern Strategy (3)
Break In (4)   Editorial, An (2)   Last Mile (4)   Power Politics (3)   Special Bulletin (2)
Cellmates, The (4)   Face The Country (2)   Late Night At The Office (1)   Presidential Trip (2)   State Of The Union (3)
Critics Medley (3)   Farm Report (2)   Listen To Martha (2)   Press Conference (2)   Swing Vote (3)

FUEL '00

Rock group from Harrisburg, Pennsylvania: Brett Scallions (vocals), Carl Bell (guitar), Jeff Abercrombie (bass) and Kevin Miller (drums).

4/18/98	77	35	▲	© 1	Sunburn			$10	550 Music 68554
10/7/00	17	52↑	▲²	© 2	Something Like Human			$10	550 Music 69436

Bad Day (2) *64*   Hemorrhage (In My Hands)   Jesus Or A Gun (1)   Ozone (1)   Solace (2)
Bittersweet (1)   (2) *30*   Knives (1)   Prove (1)   Song For You (1)
Down (2)   Hideaway (1)   Last Time (2)   Scar (2)   Sunburn (1)
Easy (2)   Innocent (2)   Mary Pretends (1)   **Shimmer** (1) *42*   Untitled (1)
Empty Spaces (2)   It's Come To This (1)   New Thing (1)   Slow (2)

FUGAZI '95

Punk-rock group from Washington DC: Ian MacKaye (vocals, guitar), Guy Picciotto (guitar), Joe Lally (bass) and Brendan Canty (drums).

7/3/93	153	4		© 1	In On The Kill Taker			$10	Dischord 70
7/1/95	126	5		© 2	Red Medicine			$10	Dischord 90
5/16/98	138	2		© 3	End Hits			$10	Dischord 110

Arpeggiator (3)   Caustic Acrostic (3)   Fell, Destroyed (2)   Instrument (1)   Place Position (3)   Target (2)
Back To Base (2)   Closed Captioned (3)   Five Corporations (3)   Last Chance For A Slow Dance   Public Witness Program (1)   23 Beats Off (1)
Bed For The Scraping (2)   Combination Lock (2)   Floating Boy (3)   (1)   Recap Modotti (3)   Version (1)
Birthday Pony (2)   Do You Like Me (2)   Foreman's Dog (2)   Latest Disgrace (2)   Rend It (1)   Walken's Syndrome (1)
Break (3)   Downed City (3)   Forensic Scene (2)   Long Distance Runner (2)   Returning The Screw (1)
By You (2)   F/D (3)   Great Cop (1)   No Surprise (3)   Smallpox Champion (1)
Cassavetes (1)   Facet Squared (1)   Guilford Fall (3)   Pink Frosty (3)   Sweet And Low (1)

FUGEES (REFUGEE CAMP) '96

Hip-hop trio from East Orange, New Jersey: **Lauryn Hill**, **Wyclef Jean** and **Pras Michel**. Fugees is short for refugees.

3/2/96	❶⁴	64	▲⁶	© 1	The Score	C:#40/4		$10	Ruffhouse 67147
12/14/96+	127	13		© 2	Bootleg Versions		[K]	$10	Ruffhouse 67904

Beast, The (1)   Family Business (1)   Killing Me Softly (1,2)   Mista Mista (1)   Ready Or Not (1,2)   Zealots (1)
Cowboys (1)   **Fu-Gee-La** (1) *29*   Manifest (1)   Nappy Heads (2)   Score, The (1)
Don't Cry Dry Your Eyes (2)   How Many Mics (1)   Mask, The (1)   No Woman, No Cry (1,2)   Vocab (2)

FUGS, The '66
Rock trio formed in New York City: Tuli Kupferberg (vocals), Ed Sanders (guitar) and Ken Weaver (drums).

7/2/66	95	26		1 The Fugs	$50	ESP 1028
10/29/66	142	4	©	2 The Fugs First Album	$50	ESP 1018
10/19/68	167	10		3 It Crawled Into My Hand, Honest	$30	Reprise 6305

Ah! Sunflower, Weary Of Time (2)
Boobs A Lot (2)
Burial Waltz (3)
Claude Pelieu And J.J. Lebel Discuss The Early Verlaine Bread Crust Fragments (3)
Coming Down (1)

Crystal Liaison (3)
Dirty Old Man (1)
Divine Toe (Part I & II) (medley) (3)
Doin' All Right (1)
Frenzy (1)
Grope Need (Part I & II) (medley) (3)
Group Grope (1)

How Sweet I Roamed From Field To Field (2)
I Couldn't Get High (2)
I Feel Like Homemade Shit (2)
I Want To Know (1)
Irene (medley) (3)
Johnny Pissoff Meets The Red Angel (medley) (3)
Kill For Peace (1)

Leprechaun (medley) (3)
Life Is Funny (medley) (3)
Life Is Strange (3)
Marijuana (medley) (3)
Morning, Morning (1)
National Haiku Contest (medley) (3)
Nothing (2)
Ramses II Is Dead, My Love (3)

Robinson Crusoe (medley) (3)
Seize The Day (2)
Skin Flowers (1)
Slum Goddess (2)
Supergirl (1)
Swinburne Stomp (2)
Tuli Visited By Ghost Of Plotinus (medley) (3)
Virgin Forest (1)

We're Both Dead Now, Alice (medley) (3)
When The Mode Of The Music Changes (medley) (3)
Whimpers From The Jello (medley) (3)
Wide Wide River (3)

FULL BLOODED '98
Born in New Orleans. Male rapper.

12/19/98	112	1	©	Memorial Day	$10	No Limit 50027

Bad Dreams
Count Down
Dog Fight

Dog Shit
Foes Bleed Bullets
Full Blooded

Gangsta Shit
Give 'Em Some
Head Busting

I'm Gonna Hustle
My Day Gon Come
Out Of Sight, Out Of Mind

Quickest Way To Die
Red Rum
Same Ole Nigga

Sleep No More

FULLER, Bobby, Four '66
Born on 10/22/43 in Baytown, Texas. Died mysteriously of asphyxiation in Los Angeles on 7/18/66 (age 22). Rock singer/guitarist. His group included his brother Randy Fuller (bass), Jim Reese (guitar) and DeWayne Quirico (drums).

4/2/66	144	2		The Bobby Fuller Four	$100	Mustang 901

Another Sad And Lonely Night
Fool Of Love

I Fought The Law 9
Julie

Let Her Dance
Little Annie Lou

Never To Be Forgotten
New Shade Of Blue

Only When I Dream
Saturday Night

Take My Word
You Kiss Me

FULL FORCE '86
Rap group from Brooklyn, New York: brothers Brian, Paul and Lou George, with their cousins Gerry Charles, Junior Clark and Curt Bedeau. Assembled and produced **Lisa Lisa & Cult Jam**. Production work for numerous others.

2/15/86	160	8		1 Full Force	$10	Columbia 40117
8/30/86	141	13		2 Full Force get busy 1 time!	$10	Columbia 40395
12/5/87	126	11	©	3 Guess Who's Comin' To The Crib?	$10	Columbia 40894

Alice, I Want You Just For Me! (1)
All In My Mind (3)
Black Radio (3)
Body Heavenly (2)

Chain Me To The Night (2)
Child's Play (Part I & II) (2)
Child's Play (Part 3) (3)
Dream Believer (1)
Full Force Git Money $ (3)
Girl If You Take Me Home (1)

Half A Chance (1)
Katty Women (3)
Let's Dance Against The Wall (1)
Love Is For Suckers (Like Me And You) (3)

Love Scene (2)
Low Blow Brenda (3)
Man Upstairs (1)
Never Had Another Lover (2)
Old Flames Never Die (1)
Please Stay (1)

So Much (2)
Take Care Of Homework (3)
Temporary Love Thing (2)
3: O'Clock...School's Out! (3)
Unfaithful (2)
United (1)

Unselfish Lover (1)
Your Love Is So Def (3)

FUN BOY THREE '83
Rock trio from England: Neville Staples and Terry Hall (vocals), with Lynval Golding (guitar). All were members of the **Specials**.

7/30/83	104	7	©	Waiting	$10	Chrysalis 41417

Farm Yard Connection
Going Home
More I See (The Less I Believe)

Murder She Said
Our Lips Are Sealed

Pressure Of Life (Takes Weight Off The Body)
Things We Do

Tunnel Of Love
We're Having All The Fun
Well Fancy That!

FUNKADELIC '78
★439★

Ensemble of nearly 40 musicians assembled by **George Clinton** (producer/songwriter/lead singer) that also recorded as **Parliament**. In 1968, Clinton formed Funkadelic with rhythm section of his soul group The Parliaments. Although on different labels, Funkadelic and Parliament shared the same personnel which included former members of **The JB's**: brothers Phelps "Catfish" (guitar) and William "Bootsy" Collins (bass), Frank "Kash" Waddy (drums) and horn players Maceo Parker and Fred Wesley. Known as "A Parliafunkadelicament Thang," this funk ensemble fostered various offshoot bands, including **The Brides Of Funkenstein**. Concert tours featured elaborate stagings and characters. In 1977, vocalists Clarence "Fuzzy" Haskins, Calvin Simon and Grady Thomas split from Clinton and recorded as Funkadelic for LAX in 1981. The corporation disassembled in the early 1980s. Clinton signed his first solo recording contract in 1982.

1)One Nation Under A Groove 2)Uncle Jam Wants You 3)Free Your Mind...And Your Ass Will Follow

3/21/70	126	17	©	1 Funkadelic	$50	Westbound 2000
10/31/70	92	11	©	2 Free Your Mind...And Your Ass Will Follow	$50	Westbound 2001
8/14/71	108	16	©	3 Maggot Brain	$50	Westbound 2007
6/17/72	123	15	©	4 America Eats Its Young	$50	Westbound 2020 [2]
7/21/73	112	13	©	5 Cosmic Slop	$50	Westbound 2022
9/7/74	163	5	©	6 Standing On The Verge Of Getting It On	$50	Westbound 1001
7/19/75	102	16	©	7 Let's Take It To The Stage	$50	Westbound 215
10/9/76	103	10	©	8 Tales Of Kidd Funkadelic	$50	Westbound 227
11/27/76	96	12	©	9 Hardcore Jollies	$25	Warner 2973
10/7/78	16	22	▲ ©	10 One Nation Under A Groove	$25	Warner 3209
10/13/79	18	17	● ©	11 Uncle Jam Wants You	$25	Warner 3371
8/29/81	105	4	©	12 The Electric Spanking Of War Babies	$25	Warner 3482

Adolescent Funk (9)
Alice In My Fantasies (6)
America Eats Its Young (4)
Atmosphere (7)
Back In Our Minds (3)
Balance (4)
Be My Beach (7)
Better By The Pound (7) 99
Biological Speculation (4)
Brettino's Bounce (12)
Butt-To-Buttresuscitation (9)
Can You Get To That (3) 93
Can't Stand The Strain (5)
Cholly (Funk Getting Ready To Roll!) (10)
Comin' Round The Mountain (9)
Cosmic Slop (5,9)

Electric Spanking Of War Babies (12)
Electro-Cuties (12)
Eulogy And Light (2)
Everybody Is Going To Make It This Time (4)
Field Maneuvers (11)
Foot Soldiers (Star-Spangled Funky) (4)
Freak Of The Week (11)
Free Your Mind And Your Ass Will Follow (2)
Friday Night, August 14th (2)
Funk Gets Stronger (Part I) (12)
Funky Dollar Bill (2)
Get Off Your Ass And Jam (7)
Good Old Music (1)

Good Thoughts, Bad Thoughts (6)
Good To Your Earhole (7)
Groovallegiance (10)
Hardcore Jollies (9)
Hit It And Quit It (3)
Holly Wants To Go To California (11)
How Do Yeaw View You? (8)
I Got A Thing, You Got A Thing, Everybody's Got A Thing (1) 80
I Wanna Know If It's Good To You? (2) 81
I'll Bet You (1) 63
I'll Stay (6)

I'm Never Gonna Tell It (8)
Icka Prick (12)
If You Don't Like The Effects, Don't Produce The Cause (4)
If You Got Funk, You Got Style (9)
Into You (10)
Jimmy's Got A Little Bit Of Bitch In Him (6)
Joyful Process (4)
Let's Make It Last (5)
Let's Take It To The People (8)
Let's Take It To The Stage (7)
Loose Booty (4)
Lunchmeataphobia (Think! It Ain't Illegal Yet!) (10)
Maggot Brain (3,10)

March To The Witch's Castle (4)
Miss Lucifer's Love (4)
Mommy, What's A Funkadelic? (1)
Music For My Mother (1)
Nappy Dugout (5)
No Compute (5)
No Head, No Backstage Pass (7)
(Not Just) Knee Deep - Part 1 (11) 77
One Nation Under A Groove - Part 1 (10) 28
P.E. Squad (Doo Doo Chasers) (10)

Philmore (4)
Pussy (4)
Qualify & Satisfy (1)
Red Hot Momma (6)
Sexy Ways (6)
She Loves You (medley) (12)
Shockwaves (9)
Smokey (9)
Some More (2)
Song Is Familiar (7)
Soul Mate (9)
Standing On The Verge Of Getting It On (6)
Stuffs And Things (7)
Super Stupid (3)
Take Your Dead Ass Home! (Say Som'n Nasty) (8)

FUNKADELIC — Cont'd

Tales Of Kidd Funkadelic (Opusdelite Years) (8)	Uncle Jam (11)
That Was My Girl (4)	Undisco Kidd (8)
This Broken Heart (5)	Wake Up (4)
Trash-A-Go-Go (5)	Wars Of Armageddon (3)
	We Hurt Too (4)

What Is Soul (3)
Who Says A Funk Band Can't Play Rock?! (10)
You And Your Folks, Me And My Folks (3) *91*

You Can't Miss What You Can't Measure (5)
You Hit The Nail On The Head (4)

You Scared The Lovin' Outta Me (9)

FUNKADELIC '81

Group features three original vocalists of The Parliaments: Clarence "Fuzzy" Haskins, Calvin Simon and Grady Thomas. Split from **George Clinton's Parliament/Funkadelic** corporation in 1977.

| 4/11/81 | 151 | 4 | **Connections & Disconnections** | $12 | LAX 37087 |

Call The Doctor
Come Back

Connections And Disconnections

Phunklords
Who's A Funkadelic

Witch Medley
You'll Like It Too

FUNKDOOBIEST '93

Rap trio from Los Angeles: Ralph Medrano, Jason Vasquez and Tyrone Pachenco.

| 5/22/93 | 56 | 9 | © | 1 **Which Doobie U B?** | $10 | Immortal 53212 |
| 7/22/95 | 115 | 3 | © | 2 **Brothas Doobie** | $10 | Immortal 64195 |

Bow Wow Wow (1) *89*
Dedicated (2)
Doobie To The Head (1)
Freak Mode (1)

Funk's On Me (1)
Funkiest, The (1)
Here I Am (1)
I'm Shittin' On 'Em (1)

It Ain't Going Down (2)
Ka Sera Sera (2)
Lost In Thought (2)
Pussy Ain't Shit (2)

Rock On (2)
Superhoes (2)
This Is It (2)
Tomahawk Bang (2)

'Uh C'mon Yeah! (1)
What The Deal (2)
Where's It At (1)
Who Ra Ra (2)

Who's The Doobiest (1)
Wopbabalubop (1)
XXX Funk (2)
You're Dummin' (2)

FUNKMASTER FLEX '98

Born Aston Taylor in New York City. Rap DJ/producer.

11/25/95	108	14	©	1 **Funkmaster Flex Presents The Mix Tape Volume 1**	$10	Loud 66805
3/1/97	19	16	● ©	2 **Funkmaster Flex: The Mix Tape Volume II**	$10	Loud 67472
8/29/98	4	11	● ©	3 **Funkmaster Flex: The Mix Tape Volume III**	$10	Loud 67647
12/25/99	35	15	● ©	4 **The Tunnel**	$10	Def Jam 538258

FUNKMASTER FLEX & BIG KAP

| 12/23/00 | 26 | 17 | ● © | 5 **60 Minutes Of Funk, Volume IV: The Mixtape** | $10 | Loud 1961 |

Ain't No Nigga (3)
Akinyele - Freestyle (2)
All For One (1)
Ante Up (5)
Award Tour (1)
Back To Life (However Do You Want Me) (2)
Bad (5)
Biggie/Tupac Live Freestyle (4)
Block Lockdown (5)
Boot Camp Click - Freestyle (4)
Bounce (4)
Break Da Law 2001 (5)
Busta Rhymes - Freestyle (1)
Call Me Drag-On (5)
Clear My Throat (2)
Come Over (5)
Confrontation (4)
Cormega - Freestyle (2)
Crowd Participation (4)
DAV - Freestyle (2)
Das EFX & PMD - Freestyle (2)
Deadman Walking (4)
Def Jam 2000 (4)
Dem Want War (4)
Did She Say (5)
Do That (3)
Do You (5) *91*
Droppin' Science (1)
Duck Down (5)

Eric B. Is President (1)
Erick Sermon - Freestyle (1)
Everyday & Everynight (1)
Fat Joe & Punisher - Freestyle (1)
Feelin The Hate (5)
Fine Line (5)
Flashlight (2)
For My Thugs (4)
Foxy Brown - Freestyle (2)
Freestyle Over Chic "Good Times" & "Take Me To The Mardi Gras" (3)
Freestyle Over Instrumental (3)
Freestyle Over Mobb Deep "Drop A Gem On Em" (3)
Freestyle Over Mobb Deep "Give Up The Goods (Just Step)" (3)
Freestyle Over Mobb Deep "Hell On Earth" (3)
Freestyle Over Mobb Deep "Shook Ones Pt. II" (3)
Freestyle Over "Mona Lisa" (3)
Freestyle Over Raekwon "Glaciers Of Ice" (3)
Freestyle Over Raekwon "Ice Cream" (3)
Freestyle Over Raekwon "Incarcerated Scarfaces" (3)

Freestyle Over Sadat X "Lump Lump" (3)
Freestyle Over Tha Alkaholiks "Next Level" (3)
Freestyle Over Wu-Tang Clan "It's Yourz" (3)
Freestyle Over Wu-Tang Clan "MGM" (3)
Freestyle Over Wu-Tang Clan "Triumph" (3)
Freestyle Over Xzibit "At The Speed Of Life" (3)
Freestyle Over Xzibit "Los Angeles Times" (3)
Fugees - Freestyle (1)
Get Money (3)
Get Up (1)
Give Up The Goods (Just Step) (1)
Good Life (5)
Here We Go (2,3) *72*
Hip Hop Hooray (2)
How About Some Hardcore (2)
How I Could Just Kill A Man (2)
How Would You Like It (5)
I Don't Care (5)
I Got It Made (1)
I'm Not Feeling You (2)
If I Get Locked Up (2)

I-ight (1)
Ill Bomb (4)
Incarcerated Scarfaces (1)
Jay-Z - Freestyle (2)
Jump Around (3)
KRS-One Speech (1)
Kaotic Style - Freestyle (1)
Keith Murray & Redman - Freestyle (1)
Lady Saw - Freestyle (2)
Let's Be Specific (1)
Lil' Kim - Freestyle (2)
Live At The Tunnel (1)
Lost Boyz - Freestyle (2)
Loud Hangover (1)
Make The Music With Your Mouth (1)
Mary J. Blige - Freestyle (1)
Method Man (2)
Michelob - Freestyle (2)
Millennium Thug (4)
Mobb Deep Blend (2)
Mona Lisa (2)
Nas - Freestyle (2)
Needle, The (5)
900 Number (1)
No Joke/Follow Me (2)
Nobody Beats The Biz (1)
Notorious B.I.G. & Da Lox - Freestyle (2)

OPP (3)
Okay (4)
Outstanding (2)
Party Groove (1)
Peter Piper (1)
Prime Time (3)
Puerto Rico (1)
Puff Daddy & Mase - Freestyle (2)
Put Your Hammer Down (3)
Q-Tip - Freestyle (1)
QBG (3)
Ras T - Freestyle (2)
Rasta T - Freestyle (1)
Real G's (4)
Redman - Freestyle (2)
Redman & Method Man - Freestyle (1)
Relax & Party (2)
Release Yo Delf (2)
Respect (4)
Rising To The Top (2)
Rock The Bells (1)
Rockin (5)
Rush (5)
Set If Off (2)
Shake Whatcha Mama Gave Ya (3)
Shimmy Shimmy Ya (3)
Shook Ones Pt. II (medley) (1)

Show Down (3)
Show Me Love (3)
Sucker MC's (2)
Talkin' Shit (2)
10% DIS (3)
That Shit (3)
Thug Brothers (3)
Thuun (4)
Time 4 Sum Aksion (2)
Tour (3)
True (4)
Uhhnnh (5)
Uptown Anthem (2)
We In Here (4)
What Son What (5)
Whoop Whoop (3)
Wickedest, The (5)
Wild For The Night (3)
Words Are Weapons (5)
Wow (4)
Wu-Tang Clan Ain't Nuthing Ta F' Wit (medley) (1)
Wu-Tang Cream Team Line-Up (3)
Xzibit - Freestyle (2)
You Will Never Find (5)
Zulu War Chant (1)

FUNKY COMMUNICATION COMMITTEE — see FCC

FUN LOVIN' CRIMINALS '96

Eclectic hip-hop trio from New York City: Huey Morgan (vocals, guitar), Brian Leiser (bass, keyboards) and Steve Borgovini (drums).

| 10/5/96 | 144 | 12 | © | **Come Find Yourself** | $10 | EMI 35703 |

Bear Hug
Bombin' The L
Come Find Yourself

Crime And Punishment
Fun Lovin' Criminal
I Can't Get With That

King Of New York
Methadonia
Passive/Aggressive

Scooby Snacks
Smoke 'Em
Grave & The Constant

We Have All The Time in the World

FURAY, Richie '76

Born on 5/9/44 in Yellow Springs, Ohio. Member of **Buffalo Springfield**, **Poco**, and **The Souther, Hillman, Furay Band**.

| 8/7/76 | 130 | 8 | | **I've Got A Reason** | $12 | Asylum 1067 |

Gettin' Through
I've Got A Reason

Look At The Sun
Mighty Maker

Over And Over Again
Starlight

Still Rolling Stones
We'll See

You're The One I Love

FURTADO, Nelly '01

Born in 1979 in Victoria, British Columbia, Canada. Female singer/songwriter.

| 1/13/01 | 26 | 38↑▲ | © | **Whoa, Nelly!** | $10 | DreamWorks 450217 |

Baby Girl
Hey, Man!
I Will Make U Cry

I'm Like A Bird *9*
Legend
My Love Grows Deeper Part 1

...On The Radio (Remember the Days)
Party

Scared Of You
Trynna Finda Way
Turn Off The Light

Well, Well

FU-SCHNICKENS '92

Rap trio from Brooklyn, New York: Larry "Poc Fu" Maturine, Rod "Chip Fu" Roachford and James "Moc Fu" Jones.

| 4/4/92 | 64 | 20 | ● © | 1 **F.U. "Don't Take It Personal"** | $10 | Jive 41472 |
| 11/12/94 | 81 | 4 | | 2 **Nervous Breakdown** | $10 | Jive 41519 |

Aaahh Oooohhh! (2)
Back Off (1)
Bebo (1)
Breakdown (2) *67*

Check It Out (1)
Generals (1)
Got It Covered (2)
Heavenly Father (1)

Hi Lo (2)
La Schmoove (1)
Movie Scene (1)
Props (1)

Ring The Alarm (1)
Sneakin' Up On Ya (2)
Sum Dum Munkey (2)
True Fuschnick (1)

Visions (20/20) (2)
Watch Ya Back Door (2)
What's Up Doc (Can We Rock) (2) *39*

Who Stole The Pebble (2)

FUSE ONE '82
All-star jazz group: **George Benson**, **Tom Browne**, **Stanley Clarke**, Ronnie Foster, **Eric Gale**, **Wynton Marsalis**, Ndugu, **Stanley Turrentine** and **Dave Valentin**.

| 2/13/82 | **139** | 8 | | | **Silk** .... | | [I] | **$12** | CTI 9006 |

Hot Fire

In Celebration Of The Human Spirit   Silk   Sunwalk

FUZZ, The '71
Female R&B vocal trio from Washington DC: Sheila Young, Barbara Gilliam and Val Williams.

| 10/2/71 | **196** | 3 | | | **The Fuzz** .... | | | **$20** | Calla 2001 |

All About Love
I Love You For All Seasons *21*

I Think I Got The Making Of A True Love Affair
I'm So Glad *95*

It's All Over
Leave It All Behind Me
Like An Open Door *77*

Ooh Baby Baby
Search Your Mind

G

GABRIEL, Juan, & Rocio Dúrcal '97
Male singer Gabriel was born as Alberto Aguilera Valdez in 1950 in Mexico. Female singer Dúrcal is also from Mexico.

| 5/24/97 | **152** | 3 | © | | **Juntos Otra Vez** .... | | [F] | **$15** | Ariola 47805 [2] |

title is Spanish for "Together Again"

Así Son Los Hombres
Donde Hay Celos
Dos Favores
El Destino

El Final
El México De Rocío
El Principio
El Verdadero Amor

Juntos
La Gitana
La Incertidumbre
Me Refugié En Tu Juventud

Nena Que Pena
No Me Digas
Que Bonito Es Santa Fé
Que Rechula Es Katy

¿Sabes Por Qué?
Santo Niñito
Te He Escrito Otra Canción
Te Sigo Amando

★277★   GABRIEL, Peter '86
Born on 2/13/50 in London. Pop-rock singer/songwriter. Lead singer of **Genesis** from 1966-75.
1)So 2)Us 3)Peter Gabriel

3/12/77	**38**	17	©	1	**Peter Gabriel** .... C:#28/33	**$15**	Atco 147
7/22/78	**45**	10	©	2	**Peter Gabriel**	**$12**	Atlantic 19181
6/21/80	**22**	29	©	3	**Peter Gabriel**	**$12**	Mercury 3848
10/2/82	**28**	31	● ©	4	**Peter Gabriel (Security)**	**$12**	Geffen 2011
6/25/83	**44**	16	● ©	5	**Peter Gabriel/Plays Live** .... [L]	**$15**	Geffen 4012 [2]
4/20/85	**162**	7	©	6	**Birdy** .... [I-S]	**$10**	Geffen 24070
6/14/86	**2**³	93	▲⁵ ©	7	**So** .... C:#14/32	**$10**	Geffen 24088
7/1/89	**60**	14	●	8	**Passion: Music For The Last Temptation Of Christ** .... [I-S]	**$10**	Geffen 24206 [2]
12/22/90+	**48**	28	▲² ©	9	**Shaking The Tree - Sixteen Golden Greats** .... C:#33/9 [G]	**$10**	Geffen 24326
10/17/92	**2**¹	53	▲ ©	10	**Us**	**$10**	Geffen 24473
10/1/94	**23**	12	● ©	11	**Secret World Live** .... [L]	**$15**	Geffen 24722 [2]

recorded on 11/16/93 in Modena, Italy

Across The River (11)
And Through The Wire (3)
Animal Magic (2)
At Night (6)
Before Night Falls (8)
Big Time (7,9) *8*
Biko (3,5,9)
Birdy's Flight (6)
Blood Of Eden (10,11)
Bread And Wine (8)
Close Up (6)
Come Talk To Me (10,11)
D.I.Y. (2,5)
Different Drum (5)
Digging In The Dirt (10,11) *52*
Disturbed (8)

Don't Give Up (7,9,11) *72*
Down The Dolce Vita (1)
Dressing The Wound (6)
Excuse Me (1)
Exposure (2)
Family And The Fishing Net (4,5)
Family Snapshot (3,5,9)
Feeling Begins (8)
Floating Dogs (6)
Flotsam And Jetsam (2)
Fourteen Black Paintings (10)
Games Without Frontiers (3,9) *48*
Gethsemane (8)
Heat, The (6)

Here Comes The Flood (1,9)
Home Sweet Home (2)
Humdrum (1,5)
I Don't Remember (3,5,9)
I Go Swimming (5)
I Have The Touch (4,5,9)
In Doubt (8)
In Your Eyes (7,11) *26*
Indigo (2)
Intruder (3,5)
It Is Accomplished (8)
Kiss Of Life (4)
Kiss That Frog (10,11)
Lay Your Hands On Me (4)
Lazarus Raised (8)
Lead A Normal Life (3)

Love To Be Loved (10)
Mercy Street (7,9)
Modern Love (1)
Moribund The Burgermeister (1)
Mother Of Violence (2)
No Self Control (3,5)
Not One Of Us (3,5)
Of These, Hope (8)
On The Air (2,5)
Only Us (10)
Open (8)
Passion (8)
Perspective (2)
Powerhouse At The Foot Of The Mountain (6)
Promise Of Shadows (8)

Quiet And Alone (6)
Red Rain (7,9,11)
Rhythm Of The Heat (4,5)
San Jacinto (4,5,9)
Sandstorm (8)
Secret World (10,11)
Shaking The Tree (9,11)
Shock The Monkey (4,5,9) *29*
Sketchpad With Trumpet And Voice (6)
Sledgehammer (7,9,11) *1*
Slow Marimbas (6,11)
Slow Water (6)
Slowburn (1)
Solsbury Hill (1,9) *68*
Solsbury Hill [live] (5,11) *84*

Start (3)
Steam (10,11) *32*
Stigmata (8)
That Voice Again (7)
Troubled (8)
Under Lock And Key (6)
Waiting For The Big One (1)
Wall Of Breath (8)
Wallflower (4)
Washing Of The Water (10,11)
We Do What We're Told (7)
White Shadow (2)
With This Love (8)
Wonderful Day In A One-Way World (2)
Zaar (8,9)

GAITHER, Bill & Gloria, & Their Homecoming Friends '99
Gospel group. Bill Gaither was born on 3/28/36 in Alexandria, Indiana. Gloria Sickal was born in 1942. They were married in 1962.
1)Kennedy Center Homecoming 2)Mountain Homecoming 3)Christmas In The Country

11/30/96	**36**ˣ	1	©	1	**Joy To The World** .... [X-L]	**$10**	Spring House 25388
4/10/99	**93**	2	©	2	**Kennedy Center Homecoming** .... [L]	**$10**	Spring House 42213
11/13/99	**98**	3	©	3	**Mountain Homecoming** .... [L]	**$10**	Spring House 42220
11/13/99	**122**	2	©	4	**I'll Meet You On The Mountain** .... [L]	**$10**	Spring House 42221
3/4/00	**163**	5	©	5	**Good News** .... [L]	**$10**	Spring House 42253
5/13/00	**126**	3	©	6	**Memphis Homecoming** .... [L]	**$10**	Spring House 42266
5/13/00	**145**	2	©	7	**Oh, My, Glory!** .... [L]	**$10**	Spring House 42267
8/26/00	**116**	1	©	8	**Homecoming Hymns With The Homecoming Friends**	**$10**	Spring House 42272
11/11/00	**141**	1	©	9	**Irish Homecoming** .... [L]	**$10**	Spring House 42268
11/11/00	**157**	1	©	10	**Whispering Hope** .... [L]	**$10**	Spring House 42269
12/2/00	**105**	3	©	11	**Christmas In The Country** .... [X-L]	**$10**	Spring House 42316

Christmas chart: 29/'00

| 3/3/01 | **149** | 2 | © | 12 | **What A Time!** .... [L] | **$10** | Spring House 42322 |

America, The Beautiful (2)
Away In A Manger (1,11)
Battle Hymn Of The Republic (2)
Beautiful Star Of Bethlehem (1)
Beyond The Sunset (medley) (6)
Bless His Holy Name (2,8)
Blood-Bought Church (9)
Body And Blood (2)

Bread Upon The Water (2)
Build An Ark (6)
Child, You're Forgiven (10)
Christ Is Born (11)
C-H-R-I-S-T-M-A-S (1)
Christmas In The Country (11)
Climbing Jacob's Ladder (12)
Come And See What's Happenin' (11)
Come On Ring Those Bells (1)

Come Out Of The Wilderness (7)
Come See Me (9)
Come To The River (6)
Dearest Friend I Ever Had (7)
Did You Ever Go Sailin' (3)
Does Jesus Care? (8)
Doesn't Get Any Better Than This (10)
Don't Wanna Miss A Thing (6)

Down By The Riverside (medley) (2)
Every Time I Feel The Spirit (2)
Except For Grace (medley) (5)
Faith Like That (3)
For Those Tears I Died (7)
Gentle Shepherd (8)
Give Them All To Jesus (10)
Glory Road (7)

Glory To God In The Highest (11)
Go Ask (9)
Go Rest High On That Mountain (3)
Go Tell It On The Mountain (1)
God Bless America (2)
God Is Good All The Time (6)
God Leads Us Along (4,8)
God On The Mountain (3)

God Took Away My Yesterdays (3)
God Will Make A Way (12)
Good, Good News (5)
Good News (5)
Grace Greater Than Our Sin (medley) (12)
Great Is Thy Faithfulness (medley) (12)
Hand In Hand With Jesus (7)

GAITHER, Bill & Gloria, & Their Homecoming Friends — Cont'd

Hark! The Herald Angels Sing (medley) (11)
He Drew The Line (11)
He Hideth My Soul (2,8)
He'd Still Been God (10)
He'll Be Holdin' His Own (4)
He's Worthy (Song Of The Redeemed) (6)
Hear The Voice Of My Beloved (10)
Heaven Will Surely Be Worth It All (4)
Heaven's Joy Awaits (2)
Heavenly Love (10)
Heavenly Parade (12)
Here We Are (12)
Hold To God's Unchanging Hand (4,8)
Holy Ground (6,8)
Holy Hills Of Heaven Call Me (10)
How Are Things At Home (7)
How Big Is God (4,12)
How Great Thou Art (medley) (12)
I Am Loved (4)
I Came Here To Stay (4)
I Can Call Jesus Anytime (4)
I Have Returned (3)
I Hold His Hand (9)
I Just Can't Make It By Myself (9)
I Saw The Light (6)
I Shall Wear A Crown (7)
I Stood On The Banks Of Jordan (4)
I Was There When The Spirit Came (3)
I Will Glory In The Cross (4,8)
I Will Go On (7)

I Wouldn't Take Nothin' For My Journey (12)
I'd Still Like To Go To Grandma's House For Christmas (1)
I'll Be Home With Bells On (1)
I'll Live Again (3)
I'll Meet You On The Mountain (4)
I'm A Citizen Of Two Worlds (7)
I'm Bound For The Promised Land (medley) (2)
I'm Feeling Fine (9)
I'm Free (5)
I'm Free Again (4)
I'm Going Higher Someday (12)
I'm Longing For Jesus To Come Back (1)
I've Got Me A Home (12)
I've Just Seen Jesus (2)
In The Garden (4)
In Time, On Time, Every Time (12)
Is Not This The Land Of Beulah (3,8)
It All Belongs To My Father (4)
It Is Finished (9)
It Won't Be Long (4)
It's All Right (4)
It's Gonna Be A Good Day (3)
Jesu, Joy Of Man's Desiring (1)
Jesus Is Coming Soon (4)
Jesus Is Mine (9)
Jesus Saves (3)
Jesus, The Light Of The World (1)
Jesus, The Waymaker (2)
Jesus, What A Wonderful Child (1)
Jewels (When He Cometh) (8)

Jingle Bells (11)
Joy Of Heaven (7)
Joy To The World (1,11)
Just A Closer Walk With Thee (4,8)
Lead Me Gently Home, Father (8)
Lead Me To That Rock (3)
Let Freedom Ring (7)
Lifeboat, The (10)
Lift Me Up Above The Shadows (4)
Little Is Much When God Is In It (9)
Little Old Wooden Church On The Hill (4)
Little One (1)
Lord, Feed Your Children (5)
Lord, I'm Coming Home (3)
Lord, Send Your Angels (6)
Love In Any Language (11)
Love Is Like A River (7)
Love Of God (3)
Mary, Did You Know? (1)
Mary Was The First One To Carry The Gospel (11)
Master The Tempest Is Raging (10)
Midnight Cry (9)
Mind Over Matter (10)
My Burdens Have Rolled Away (5)
My God Is Real (6)
My Mother's Faith (9)
My Soul Is Gonna Live On (1)
New Star Shining (1)
Ninety And Nine (5)
No Fishin' (9)
No Tears In Heaven (12)

O Come All Ye Faithful (medley) (11)
O Holy Night (1,11)
O Little Town Of Bethlehem (1,11)
O Say, But I'm Glad (10)
Oh, How Much He Cares For Me (8)
Oh, My, Glory, Glory, Glory (7)
Oh, What A Time (12)
Old Gospel Ship (2)
On Jordan's Stormy Banks (8)
One Day At A Time (2)
One More Time (2)
Only A Look (8)
Only Real Peace (9)
Our Debts Will Be Paid (7)
Pass Me Not (2,8)
Peace Shall Come (3)
Peace In The Valley (8)
Perfect Heart (3)
Please Forgive Me (12)
Praise His Name (9)
Precious Jesus (10)
Promise, The (9)
Promises One By One (2)
Redemption Draweth Nigh (7)
Rejoice With Exceeding Great Joy (1)
Right Place, Right Time (2)
Rise Again (12)
Road To Forgiveness (7)
Rolling, Riding, Rocking (7)
Satisfied (9)
Scatter Sunshine (12)
Searchin' (6)
Shall We Gather At The River (medley) (2)
Sheltered In The Arms Of God (8)

Should You Go First And I Remain (Reading) (medley) (6)
Silent Night, Holy Night (11)
Singing For The Bus (12)
Singing With The Saints (10)
Sitting By The Fire (11)
Sleep, Baby, Sleep (1)
Somebody Loves Me (2)
Something To Shout About (11)
Soon And Very Soon (2)
Star Spangled Banner (2)
Stepping On The Clouds (10)
Sweeter Each Day (10)
Sweetest Words He Ever Said (2)
Take This Trial Trip Beside Me (3)
Tennessee Christmas (11)
Thank You, Jesus (5)
That Glad Reunion Day (6)
That Old-Time Religion (5)
That's No Hill For A Climber (4)
Then Came The Morning (10)
There Is A Mountain (4)
(There's No Place Like) Home For The Holidays (11)
There's Something About A Mountain (3)
There's Something About That Name (1)
Thinkin' About Home (6)
This Could Be The Dawning Of That Day (9)
This Flight That Is Leavin' Soon (12)
'Til The Storm Passes By (10)
To The Other Side (7)
Trying To Get A Glimpse (5)
Unspeakable Joy (11)

Up Above My Head (6)
Virgin Mary Had A Baby Boy (1)
Wait Till You See Me In My New Home (6)
We'll Soon Be Done With Troubles And Trials (6)
We'll Work 'Til Jesus Comes (3)
What A Friend We Have In Jesus (9)
What A Meeting In The Air (5)
What A Wonderful World (11)
What Child Is This? (1)
What Did You Say Was The Baby's Name? (1)
When All God's Singers Get Home (6)
When God Dips His Love In My Heart (10)
When He Set Me Free (5)
When He Was On The Cross (I Was On His Mind) (9)
When I Meet You (7)
When I Reach That City (3)
Whenever We Agree Together (9)
Where No One Stands Alone (6)
Where The Soul Never Dies (10)
While Ages Roll (4)
Whispering Hope (10)
Why Me (3)
Winter Wonderland (1)
You Can Have A Song In Your Heart (12)
You Can Lean On Me (5)
You Sure Do Need Him Now (12)

GAITHER VOCAL BAND, The   '01
Gospel group: **Bill Gaither**, Mark Lowry, Guy Penrod and David Phelps.

6/5/99	162	1	©	1	God Is Good			$10	Spring Hill 25475
3/3/01	121	2	©	2	I Do Believe			$10	Spring Hill 21009

Baptism Of Jesse Taylor (1)
Child, You're Forgiven (1)
God Is Good All The Time (1)
Good, Good News (1)
He Came Down To My Level (1)

He Touched Me (1)
He's Watching Me (1)
Hide Thou Me (2)
I Do Believe (2)
I Heard It First On The Radio (1)

Let Freedom Ring (1)
Love Of God (2)
Make It Real (2)
Mercy (1)
More Than Ever (2)
Oh, What A Time (2)

On The Authority (2)
One Good Song (2)
Satisfied (1)
Sinner Saved By Grace (2)
Something To Say (2)
Star Spangled Banner (1)

Steel On Steel (2)
Whenever We Agree Together (1)
Where No One Stands Alone (2)
Where The River Flows (2)

GALE, Eric   '77
Born on 9/20/38 in Brooklyn, New York. Died of cancer on 5/25/94 (age 55). Jazz guitarist. Member of **Fuse One** and **Stuff**.

4/9/77	148	12	©	1	Ginseng Woman		[I]	$12	Columbia 34421
7/21/79	154	5		2	Part Of You		[I]	$12	Columbia 35715

De Rabbit (1)
East End, West End (1)

Ginseng Woman (1)
Holding On To Love (2)

Let-Me-Slip-It-To-You (2)
Lookin' Good (2)

Nezumi (2)
Part Of You (2)

Red Ground (1)
Sara Smile (1)

She Is My Lady (1)
Trio (2)

GALLAGHER, Rory   '72
Born on 3/2/49 in Ballyshannon, Ireland; raised in Cork, Ireland. Died of liver failure on 6/14/95 (age 46). Blues-rock singer/guitarist. Leader of **Taste**.

8/26/72	101	15	©	1	Rory Gallagher/Live!		[L]	$15	Polydor 5513
4/21/73	147	7	©	2	Blueprint			$15	Polydor 5522
12/1/73+	186	7	©	3	Tattoo			$15	Polydor 5539
9/14/74	110	11	©	4	Irish Tour '74		[L]	$20	Polydor 9501 [2]
2/22/75	156	5		5	Sinner...And Saint			$15	Polydor 6510
11/29/75+	121	13	©	6	Against The Grain			$12	Chrysalis 1098
10/30/76+	163	11	©	7	Calling Card			$12	Chrysalis 1124
11/4/78+	116	15	©	8	Photo-Finish			$12	Chrysalis 1170
10/6/79	140	4	©	9	Top Priority			$12	Chrysalis 1235

Admit It (3)
Ain't Too Good (6)
All Around Man (6)
As The Crow Flies (4)
At The Bottom (6)
At The Depot (9)
Back On My (Stompin' Ground) (4)
Bad Penny (9)
Banker's Blues (7)
Barley And Grape Rag (7)
Bought And Sold (6)
Brute Force And Ignorance (8)
Bullfrog Blues (1)

Calling Card (7)
Cloak And Dagger (8)
Country Mile (7)
Cradle Rock (3,4)
Crest Of A Wave (5)
Cross Me Off Your List (8)
Cruise On Out (4)
Daughter Of The Everglades (2)
Do You Read Me (7)
Don't Know Where I'm Going (5)
Edged In Blue (7)
Follow Me (9)
For The Last Time (5)

Fuel To The Fire (8)
Going To My Home Town (1)
Hands Off (2)
Hands Up (5)
I Could've Had Religion (1)
I Fall Apart (5)
I Take What I Want (6)
I Wonder Who (Who's Gonna Be Your Sweet Man) (4)
I'll Admit You're Gone (7)
I'm Not Awake Yet (5)
If I Had A Reason (2)
In Your Town (1)
Jackknife Beat (7)

Just A Little Bit (4)
Just Hit Town (9)
Just The Smile (5)
Keychain (9)
Last Of The Independants (8)
Laundromat (1)
Let Me In (6)
Livin' Like A Trucker (3)
Lost At Sea (6)
Messin' With The Kid (1)
Million Miles Away (3,4)
Mississippi Sheiks (8)
Moonchild (1)
Off The Handle (9)

Out On The Western Plain (6)
Overnight Bag (8)
Philby (9)
Pistol Slapper Blues (1)
Public Enemy No. 1 (9)
Race The Breeze (3)
Secret Agent (7)
Seventh Son Of A Seventh Son (2)
Shadow Play (8)
Shin Kicker (8)
Sinner Boy (5)
Sleep On A Clothes-Line (3)
Souped-Up Ford (6)

Tattoo'd Lady (3,4)
There's A Light (5)
They Don't Make Them Like You Anymore (3)
Too Much Alcohol (4)
20:20 Vision (9)
Unmilitary Two-Step (2)
Used To Be (3)
Walk On Hot Coals (2,4)
Wayward Child (9)
Who's That Coming (3,4)

GALLERY   '72
Pop group from Detroit: Jim Gold (vocals), Brent Anderson and Cal Freeman (guitars), Bill Nova (percussion), Dennis Kovarik (bass) and Danny Brucato (drums).

8/5/72	75	15			Nice To Be With You			$15	Sussex 7017

Big City Miss Ruth Ann 23
Gee Whiz

Ginger Haired Man
He Will Break Your Heart

I Believe In Music 22
Louisiana Line

Lover's Hideaway
Nice To Be With You 4

Someone
Sunday And Me

There's An Island
You're Always On My Mind

DEBUT	PEAK	WKS	RIAA	CD	ARTIST — Album Title	Catalog	Sym	$	Label & Number

GALWAY, James '91

Born on 12/8/39 in Belfast, Ireland. Classical flutist.

DEBUT	PEAK	WKS						$	Label & Number
3/3/79	153	5			1 Annie's Song And Other Galway Favorites		[I]	$12	RCA Victor 3061
7/26/80	150	6	©		2 Sometimes When We Touch			$12	RCA Victor 3628

CLEO LAINE & JAMES GALWAY

12/14/91	144	1	©		3 The Wind Beneath My Wings		[I]	$10	RCA Victor 60862
3/30/96	199	1	©		4 The Celtic Minstrel		[I]	$10	RCA Victor 68393
4/5/97	186	1	©		5 Legends		[I]	$10	RCA Victor 68776

JAMES GALWAY & PHIL COULTER

Angel Of Music (3)
Annie's Song (1)
Anyone Can Whistle (2)
Ashokan Farewell (5)
Bachianas Brasileiras No. 5: Aria (1)
Basque (3)
Battle Of Kinsale (The Valley Of Tears) (5)
Belfast Hornpipe (1)
Believe Me If All Those Endearing Young Charms (medley) (5)
Berceuse (1)
Brian Boru's March (1)

Cail n Fionn (Natasha) (5)
Carmen Fantasy (1)
Carrickfergus (Air) (4)
Cath Cheim An Fhia (The Battle Of Deer's Leap) (4)
Ceremony, The (3)
Come To My Garden (3)
Consuelo's Love Theme (2)
Danny Boy (4,5)
Dark Island (4)
Down By The Salley Gardens (4)
Drifting, Dreaming (Gymnopedie No. 1) (2)
El Condor Pasa (If I Could) (3)

Fields Of Athenry (4)
Fluter's Ball (2)
From A Distance (3)
Gentle Maiden (medley) (4)
Harry's Game (5)
Hoedown (5)
How, Where, When? (2)
I Dreamt I Dwelt In Marble Halls (4)
I'll Take You Home Again, Kathleen (4)
Irish Medley (3)
Keep Loving Me (2)
Kerry Dances (medley) (5)
La Plus Que Lente (1)

La Vie En Rose (3)
Lament For The Wild Geese (5)
Lannigan's Ball (medley) (4)
Last Rose Of Summer (4)
Le Basque (1)
Liebesfreud (1)
Like A Sad Song (2)
Lo! Hear The Gentle Lark (2)
Memory (3)
Minstrel Boy (4)
Mná na h-Eireann (Women Of Ireland) (5)
Music For A Found Harmonium (5)
My Lagan Love (5)

Over The Sea To Skye (4)
Perhaps Love (3)
Piano Sonata In C.K. 545 - Allegro (1)
Play It Again, Sam (2)
Riverdance (5)
Send In The Clowns (3)
She Moved Through The Fair (4)
Shoheen Sholyoh (4)
Skylark (2)
Slievenamon (4)
Smoke Gets In Your Eyes (3)
Sometimes When We Touch (2)
Spanish Love Song (1)

Still Was The Night (2)
Tambourin (1)
Thornbirds, The (5)
Unchained Melody (3)
When You And I Were Young, Maggie (4)
Wind Beneath My Wings (3)
Windmills Of Your Mind (3)

GAMBINO FAMILY '98

Male rap duo from New Orleans: Gotti and Feno.

| 11/7/98 | 17 | 4 | © | | Ghetto Organized | | | $10 | No Limit 50718 |

Childhood Years
Clean Sweep
Desperado

Don't Cry
Drama In My City
Ghetto Wayz

I'm A Baller
Losing My Faith
Mafiosos

Make'm Bleed
Memories
Only G's Ride

So Much Drama
Studio B
2 All My Thug N...

Trapped In A Storm
U Neva Know
Young Gunz

GAMMA '80

Rock group formed in San Francisco: Davey Pattison (vocals), Ronnie **Montrose** (guitar), Mitchell Froom (keyboards), Glenn Letsch (bass) and Denny Carmassi (drums). Carmassi later joined **Heart**. Pattison later recorded with **Robin Trower**. Froom, also a producer, married **Suzanne Vega** on 3/17/95.

9/22/79	131	17			1 Gamma 1			$15	Elektra 219
9/13/80	65	19			2 Gamma 2			$15	Elektra 288
3/20/82	72	12			3 Gamma 3			$15	Elektra 60034

Cat On A Leash (2)
Condition Yellow (3)
Dirty City (2)
Fight To The Finish (1)
Four Horsemen (2)

I'm Alive (1) 60
Mayday (2)
Mean Streak (2)
Mobile Devotion (3)
Modern Girl (2)

Moving Violation (3)
No Tears (1)
No Way Out (3)
Razor King (1)
Ready For Action (1)

Right The First Time (3) 77
Skin And Bone (2)
Solar Heat (1)
Something In The Air (2)
Stranger (3)

Third Degree (3)
Thunder And Lightning (1)
Voyager (3)
What's Gone Is Gone (3)
Wish I Was (1)

GANG OF FOUR '83

New-wave group from Leeds, England: Jon King (vocals), Andy Gill (guitar), Dave Allen (bass) and Hugo Burnham (drums).

6/6/81	190	2	©		1 Solid Gold			$10	Warner 3565
2/13/82	195	2	©		2 Another Day/Another Dollar		[M]	$10	Warner 3646
6/26/82	175	3	©		3 Songs Of The Free			$10	Warner 23683
10/8/83	168	4			4 Hard			$10	Warner 23936

Arabic (4)
Call Me Up (3)
Capital (It Fails Us Now) (2)
Cheeseburger (1,2)
He'd Send In The Army (1)
History Of The World (3)

History's Bunk! (2)
Hole In The Wallet (1)
I Fled (4)
I Love A Man In A Uniform (3)
I Will Be A Good Boy (1)
If I Could Keep It For Myself (1)

In The Ditch (1)
Independence (4)
Is It Love (4)
It Don't Matter (4)
It Is Not Enough (3)
Life! It's A Shame (1)

Man With A Good Car (4)
Muscle For Brains (3)
Of The Instant (3)
Outside The Trains Don't Run On Time (1)
Paralysed (1)

Piece Of My Heart (4)
Republic, The (1)
Silver Lining (4)
To Hell With Poverty (2)
We Live As We Dream, Alone (3)

What We All Want (1,2)
Why Theory? (4)
Woman Town (4)

GANGSTA BOO '98

Female rapper. Member of **Prophet Posse**, **Three 6 Mafia** and **Hypnotize Camp Posse**.

| 10/17/98 | 46 | 6 | © | | Enquiring Minds | | | $10 | Relativity 1685 |

Be Real
Da Ones Close, Know Most
Don't Stand So Close
Enquiring Minds
Fuck You

High Off That Weed
I'll Be The Other Woman
Kill, Kill, Kill, Murder, Murder, Murder
Life In The Metro

Money And The Powder
Nasty Trick
Nigga Yeah Know
Oh No
Only You

Suck A Little Dick
This Is Personal
Wanna Go To War
Where Dem Dollas At
Who We Be

GANG STARR '98

Rap duo from Brooklyn, New York: Christopher "DJ Premier" Martin and Keith "**Guru**" Elam.

3/16/91	121	12	©		1 Step In The Arena			$10	Chrysalis 21798
5/23/92	65	10	©		2 Daily Operation			$10	Chrysalis 21910
3/26/94	25	12	©		3 Hard To Earn			$10	Chrysalis 28435
4/18/98	6	13	● ©		4 Moment Of Truth			$10	Noo Trybe 45585
7/31/99	33	7	● ©		5 Full Clip: A Decade Of Gang Starr		[K]	$15	Noo Trybe 47279 [2]

Above The Clouds (4,5)
Aiiight Chill... (3)
All 4 Tha Ca$h (5)
ALONGWAYTOGO (4)
As I Read My S-A (1)
B.I. Vs. Friendship (4)
B.Y.S. (2,5)
Betrayal (4,5)
Beyond Comprehension (1)
Blowin' Up The Spot (3)
Brainstorm (3)
Check The Technique (4)
Code Of The Streets (3,5)
Comin' For Datazz (3)
Conspiracy (2)

Credit Is Due (5)
DWYCK (3)
Daily Operation (Intro) (2)
Discipline (5)
Dwyck (5)
Ex Girl To Next Girl (2,5)
Execution Of A Chump (No More Mr. Nice Guy Pt. 2) (1)
F.A.L.A. (3)
Flip The Script (2)
Form Of Intellect (1)
Full Clip (5)
Game Plan (1)
Gotta Get Over (Taking Loot) (5)

Hardcore Composer (2)
Here Today, Gone Tomorrow (1)
I'm The Man (2,5)
Illest Brother (2)
In Memory Of... (4)
Itz A Set Up (4)
JFK 2 LAX (4)
Jazz Thing (5)
Just To Get A Rep (1,5)
Lovesick (1)
Make 'Em Pay (4)
Mall, The (4)
Mass Appeal (3,5) 67
Meaning Of The Name (1)

Militia, The (4,5)
Militia II (5)
Moment Of Truth (4)
Mostly Tha Voice (3)
Much Too Much (Mack A Mil) (2)
My Advice 2 You (4)
Name Tag (Premier & The Guru) (1)
New York Strait Talk (4)
Next Time (4)
No Shame In My Game (2)
Now You're Mine (3,5)
1/2 & 1/2 (5)
Place Where We Dwell (2)

Planet, The (3)
Precisely The Right Rhymes (1)
? Remainz (5)
Rep Grows Bigga (4)
Robbin Hood Theory (4)
Royalty (4,5)
Say Your Prayers (1)
She Knowz What She Wantz (4)
So Wassup?! (5)
Soliloquy Of Chaos (2,5)
Speak Ya Clout (3,5)
Stay Tuned (5)
Step In The Arena (1,5)
Street Ministry (1)

Suckas Need Bodyguards (3)
Take A Rest (1)
Take It Personal (2,5)
Take Two And Pass (4)
Tonz 'O' Gunz (3,5)
2 Deep (3)
24-7/365 (2)
What I'm Here 4 (4)
What You Want This Time? (1)
Who's Gonna Take The Weight? (1,5)
Words From The Nutcracker (4)
Words I Manifest (5)
Work (4,5)
You Know My Steez (4,5) 76

GANKSTA NIP '93

Born Rowdy Lewayne on 8/28/69 in Houston. Male rapper.

7/24/93	151	2		©	**Psychic Thoughts (Are What I Conceive?)**			$10	Rap-A-Lot 53860

Come Into My World · Now Watch 'Em Drop · Psychic Thoughts · SPC Shoutout · Strictly For The Club · Trance
Fuck You · Only NIP Can Do It · Reporter From Hell · Set Up Bitches · That's How It Is: Psychic Part II

★498★ GAP BAND, The '82

Funk trio of brothers from Tulsa, Oklahoma: Ronnie (vocals, horns, keyboards), Robert (vocals, bass) and **Charlie Wilson** (vocals, drums). Group named for three streets in Tulsa: Greenwood, Archer and Pine.

5/19/79	77	18		© 1	The Gap Band			$12	Mercury 3758
12/22/79+	42	28	●	© 2	The Gap Band II			$12	Mercury 3804
12/27/80+	16	37	▲	© 3	The Gap Band III			$12	Mercury 4003
6/12/82	14	52	▲	© 4	Gap Band IV			$10	Total Experience 3001
9/10/83	28	43	●	© 5	Gap Band V - Jammin'			$10	Total Experience 3004
1/19/85	58	23		6	Gap Band VI			$10	Total Experience 5705
3/9/85	103	16	▲	© 7	Gap Gold/Best Of The Gap Band		[G]	$10	Total Exper. 824343
2/1/86	159	15		8	Gap Band VII			$10	Total Experience 5714
12/9/89+	189	7		© 9	Round Trip			$10	Capitol 90799

Addicted To Your Love (9) · Don't You Leave Me (6) · I Found My Baby (6) · Lonely Like Me (4) · Shake A Leg (5) · When I Look In Your Eyes (3)
All Of My Love (9) · **Early In The Morning** (4,7) *24* · I Know We'll Make It (8) · Messin' With My Mind (1) · Smile (5) · Where Are We Going? (5)
Antidote (To Love) (9) · Gash Gash Gash (3) · I Like It (9) · No Easy Out (9) · Someday (5) · Who Do You Call (2)
Are You Living (3) · Going In Circles (8) · I Need Your Love (8) · No Hiding Place (2) · Stay With Me (4,7) · **Yearning For Your Love** (3,7) *60*
Automatic Brain (5) · Got To Get Away (1) · I Want A Real Love (8) · Nothin' Comes To Sleepers (3) · Steppin' (Out) (2) · You Are My High (2)
Baby Baba Boogie (1) · Humpin' (3) · I'm Dreaming (9) · Ooh, What A Feeling (8) · Sun Don't Shine Everyday (6) · You Can Count On Me (1)
Beep A Freak (6) · I Believe (6) · I'm In Love (1) · Open Up Your Mind (Wide) (1) · Sweet Caroline (4) · **You Dropped A Bomb On Me** (4,7) *31*
Boys Are Back In Town (2) · I Can Sing (1) · I'm Ready (If You're Ready) (5) · **Outstanding** (4,7) *51* · Talkin' Back (4) · You're My Everything (5)
Bumpin' Gum People (8) · I Can't Get Over You (4) · It's Our Duty (9) · Party Lights (2) · Video Junkie (6) · You're Something Special (5)
Burn Rubber (Why You · I Don't Believe You Want To · Jam (3) · Party Train (5,7) · Way, The (3)
Wanna Hurt Me) (3,7) *84* · Get Up And Dance (Oops!) · Jam The Motha' (5) · Season's No Reason To · We Can Make It Alright (9)
Desire (8) · (2,7) · Jammin' In America (5) · Change (4,7) · Weak Spot (6)
Disrespect (6) · I Expect More (5) · L'il Red Funkin' Hood (8) · Shake (1,7) · Wednesday Lover (9)

GARBAGE '96

Rock group formed in Madison, Wisconsin: Shirley Manson (vocals, guitar; native of Edinburgh, Scotland), Doug Erikson (guitar, bass, keyboards), Steve Marker (guitar, samples) and Butch Vig (drums). Vig produced albums for **Nirvana**, **Soul Asylum**, **Sonic Youth** and **Smashing Pumpkins**.

9/30/95+	20	81	▲²	© 1	Garbage			$10	Almo Sounds 80004
5/30/98	13	70	▲	© 2	Version 2.0			$10	Almo Sounds 80018

As Heaven Is Wide (1) · I Think I'm Paranoid (2) · **Only Happy When It Rains** · Special (2) *52* · Trick Is To Keep Breathing (2)
Dog New Tricks (2) · Medication (2) · (1) *55* · Stroke Of Luck (1) · Vow (1) *97*
Dumb (2) · Milk (1) · **Push It** (2) *52* · **Stupid Girl** (1) *24* · When I Grow Up (2)
Fix Me Now (1) · My Lover's Box (1) · Queer (1) · Supervixen (1) · Wicked Ways (2)
Hammering In My Head (2) · Not My Idea (1) · Sleep Together (2) · Temptation Waits (2) · You Look So Fine (2)

GARCIA, Jerry '72

Born on 8/1/42 in San Francisco. Died of a heart attack on 8/9/95 (age 53). Rock singer/guitarist. Member of the **Grateful Dead** and **Old & In The Way**.

1)Garcia 2)Reflections 3)Garcia

1/29/72	35	14		© 1	Garcia			$40	Warner 2582
6/22/74	49	15		2	Garcia			$25	Round 102
2/14/76	42	14		© 3	Reflections			$25	Round 565
4/15/78	114	5		© 4	Cats Under The Stars			$15	Arista 4160
11/20/82	100	8		© 5	Run For The Roses			$15	Arista 9603
9/14/91	97	5		© 6	Jerry Garcia Band		[L]	$15	Arista 18690 [2]
11/16/96	135	1		© 7	Shady Grove			$10	Acoustic Disc 21

JERRY GARCIA - DAVID GRISMAN

5/3/97	81	5		© 8	How Sweet It Is		[L]	$10	14051

recorded in 1990 at the Warfield Theater in San Francisco

2/10/01	137	2		© 9	Don't Let Go		[E-L]	$15	Grateful Dead 14078 [2]

recorded on 5/21/76 at the Orpheum Theatre in San Francisco

4/7/01	194	1		© 10	Shining Star		[L]	$15	Grateful Dead 14079 [2]

JERRY GARCIA BAND (above 3)

After Midnight (9) · Fair Ellender (7) · Let It Rock (2,10) · My Sisters And Brothers (6,9) · Sitting In Limbo (9) · Tough Mama (8)
Ain't No Bread In The Breadbox · Get Out Of My Life (6) · Let's Spend The Night Together · Night They Drove Old Dixie · Someday Baby (8) · Turn On The Bright Lights (2)
(10) · Gomorrah (4,8) · (2,10) · Down (6) · Spidergawd (1) · Valerie (5)
Bird Song (1) · Handsome Cabin Boy (7) · Like A Road (8) · Odd Little Place (1) · Stealin' (7) · Waiting For A Miracle (6)
Casey Jones (7) · He Ain't Give You None (2,10) · Lonesome And A Long Way · Off To Sea Once More (7) · Stop That Train (6) · Way You Do The Things You
Catfish John (3) · How Sweet It Is (To Be Loved · From Home (9) · Palm Sunday (4) · Strange Man (9) · Do (6,9)
Cats Under The Stars (4,8) · By You) (8) · Loser (1) · Positively 4th Street (10) · Struggling Man (10) · What Goes Around (2)
Comes A Time (3) · I Saw Her Standing There (5) · Louis Collins (7) · Rain (4) · **Sugaree** (1,9) *94* · Wheel, The (1)
Deal (1) · I Shall Be Released (6) · Love In The Afternoon (4) · Rhapsody In Red (4) · Sweet Sunny South (7) · When The Hunter Gets
Dear Prudence (6) · I Truly Understand (7) · Maker, The (10) · Rubin And Cherise (4) · Tangled Up In Blue (6) · Captured By The Game (2,10)
Don't Let Go (6,9) · I'll Take A Melody (3,9) · Midnight Getaway (5) · Run For The Roses (8) · Tears Of Rage (8) · Whiskey In The Jar (7)
Down Home (4) · It Must Have Been The Roses · Midnight Moonlight (10) · Russian Lullaby (2,10) · That Lucky Old Sun (6) · Without Love (5)
Down In The Valley (9) · (3) · Midnight Town (2) · Second That Emotion (10) · That's What Love Will Make
Dreadful Wind And Rain (7) · Jackaroo (7) · Might As Well (3) · Senor (Tales Of Yankee Power) · You Do (2,8,9)
Eep Hour (1) · Knockin' On Heaven's Door · Mighty High (9) · (6) · They Love Each Other (3,9)
Evangeline (3) · (5,9) · Mission In The Rain (3,9) · Shady Grove (7) · Think (8)
Everybody Needs Somebody · Late For Supper (1) · Mississippi Moon (2,10) · Shining Star (10) · To Lay Me Down (1)
To Love (10) · Leave The Little Girl Alone (5) · Money Honey (10) · Simple Twist Of Fate (6) · Tore Up Over You (3,8,9)

GARDNER, Dave '60

Born on 6/11/26 in Jackson, Tennessee. Died of a heart attack on 9/22/83 (age 57). Comedian known as "Brother Dave."

6/20/60	5	69		© 1	Rejoice, Dear Hearts!	[C]		$25	RCA Victor 2083
8/29/60	5	56		© 2	Kick Thy Own Self	[C]		$25	RCA Victor 2239
9/18/61	15	30		3	Ain't That Weird?	[C]		$25	RCA Victor 2335
9/1/62	49	13		4	Did You Ever?	[C]		$25	RCA Victor 2498

GARDNER, Dave — Cont'd

3/9/63	52	10			5 All Seriousness Aside .... [C]	$25	RCA Victor 2628
5/4/63	28	13			6 It Don't Make No Difference .... [C]	$25	Capitol 1867

no track titles listed on any of the albums above

GARFUNKEL, Art   '73

Born on 11/5/41 in Forest Hills, New York. Half of **Simon & Garfunkel** duo. Appeared in movies *Catch 22, Carnal Knowledge* and *Bad Timing*. Has Master's degree in mathematics from Columbia University.

9/29/73	5	25	●	©	1 **Angel Clare**	$15	Columbia 31474
10/25/75	7	28	▲	©	2 **Breakaway**	$12	Columbia 33700
2/4/78	19	16	●	©	3 **Watermark**	$12	Columbia 34975
4/7/79	67	14		©	4 **Fate For Breakfast**	$12	Columbia 35780
9/12/81	113	8		©	5 **Scissors Cut**	$12	Columbia 37392
4/16/88	134	8		©	6 **Lefty**	$10	Columbia 40942

All I Know (1) *9*	Do Space Men Pass Dead	**I Only Have Eyes For You**
All My Love's Laughter (3)	Souls On Their Way To The	(2) *18*
And I Know (4)	Moon? (medley) (1)	**I Shall Sing** (1) *38*
Another Lullaby (1)	Down In The Willow Garden (1)	Under Why (6)
Barbara Allen (1)	Feuilles-Oh (medley) (1)	If Love Takes You Away (6)
Beyond The Tears (4)	Finally Found A Reason (4)	In A Little While (I'll Be On My
Break Away (2) *39*	French Waltz (5)	Way) (4)
Bright Eyes (5)	Hang On In (5)	In Cars (5)
Can't Turn My Heart Away (5)	**Heart In New York** (5) *66*	King Of Tonga (6)
Crying In My Sleep (3)	I Believe (When I Fall In Love It	Looking For The Right One (3)
Disney Girls (2)	Will Be Forever) (2)	Love Is The Only Chain (6)
	I Have A Love (6)	Marionette (3)
		Mary Was An Only Child (1)

Miss You Nights (4)	Saturday Suit (3)	Traveling Boy (1)
Mr. Shuck 'N' Jive (3)	Scissors Cut (5)	Up In The World (5)
My Little Town *[Simon &*	She Moved Through The Fair	Watermark (3)
Garfunkel] (2) *9*	(3)	Waters Of March (2)
99 Miles From L.A. (2)	Shine It On Me (3)	**(What A) Wonderful World**
Oh How Happy (4)	**Since I Don't Have You** (4) *53*	(3) *17*
Old Man (1)	Slow Breakup (6)	When A Man Loves A Woman
Paper Chase (4)	So Easy To Begin (5)	(6)
Promise, The (6)	So Much In Love (6)	When Someone Doesn't Want
Rag Doll (3)	Someone Else (1958) (3)	You (4)
Sail On A Rainbow (4)	That's All I've Got To Say (5)	Wooden Planes (1)
Same Old Tears On A New	This Is The Moment (6)	Woyaya (1)
Background (2)		

★338★   GARLAND, Judy   '61

Born Frances Gumm on 6/10/22 in Grand Rapids, Minnesota. Died of an accidental sleeping pill overdose on 6/22/69 (age 47). Legendary actress/singer. Hosted own TV variety series (1963-64). Married to movie director Vincente Minnelli from 1945-51. Mother of **Liza Minnelli**.

1)Judy At Carnegie Hall 2)Miss Show Business 3)Judy

10/29/55	5	7		©	1 **Miss Show Business**	$40	Capitol 676
11/10/56	17	5		©	2 **Judy**	$40	Capitol 734
6/17/57	17	3		©	3 **Alone**	$40	Capitol 835
7/31/61	❶¹³	95	●	©	4 **Judy At Carnegie Hall** C:#26/1 [L]	$50	Capitol 1569 [2]

recorded on 4/23/61; 1961 Grammy winner: Album of the Year

8/25/62	33	14			5 **The Garland Touch**	$40	Capitol 1710
5/11/63	45	6			6 **I Could Go On Singing** .... [S]	$40	Capitol 1861

includes "Overture," "Interlude: Matt's Dilemma" and "Helicopter Ride" by Mort Lindsey

1/4/64	136	2			7 **The Best Of Judy Garland** .... [G]	$30	Decca 7172 [2]
9/4/65	41	14			8 **"Live" At The London Palladium** .... [L]	$30	Capitol 2295 [2]

JUDY GARLAND & LIZA MINNELLI
recorded on 11/8/64

9/16/67	174	3			9 **Judy Garland At Home At The Palace - Opening Night** .... [L]	$25	ABC 620

recorded at the Palace Theatre in New York City

8/16/69	161	3			10 **Judy Garland's Greatest Hits** .... [G]	$20	Decca 75150
6/9/73	164	8			11 **"Live" At The London Palladium** .... [L-R]	$20	Capitol 11191

JUDY GARLAND & LIZA MINNELLI
condensation of album #8 above

After You've Gone (1,4,8,11)	Dirty Hands, Dirty Face (2)	I Feel A Song Coming On (2,9)	Last Night When We Were	Poor Little Rich Girl (7)	When The Saints Go Marching
Almost Like Being In Love	Do I Love You? (5)	I Get The Blues When It Rains	Young (2)	Pretty Girl Milking Her Cow	In (medley) (1)
(medley) (4,9)	Do It Again (4)	(3)	Life Is Just A Bowl Of Cherries	(1,7,10)	When You Wore A Tulip (And I
Alone Together (4)	F.D.R. Jones (7)	I Happen To Like New York (5)	(2)	Puttin' On The Ritz (4)	Wore A Big Red Rose) (7,10)
Among My Souvenirs (3)	Foggy Day (4)	I Loved Him, But He Didn't Love	Little Girl Blue (3)	Rock-A-Bye Your Baby With A	When You're Smiling (The
Any Place I Hang My Hat Is	For Me And My Gal (1,4,7,9,10)	Me (9)	Love (7)	Dixie Melody (1,4,9)	Whole World Smiles With
Home (2)	Happiness Is A Thing Called	I Never Knew (I Could Love	Lucky Day (2,5)	'S Wonderful (medley) (8,11)	You) (4)
April Showers (2)	Joe (1,5)	Anybody Like I'm Loving	Make Someone Happy (8)	San Francisco (4,8)	While We're Young (medley) (1)
Blue Prelude (3)	Happy New Year (3)	You) (7)	Man That Got Away (4,8,9,11)	Smile (8)	Who Cares? (So Long As You
Bob White (Whatcha Gonna	Have Yourself A Merry Little	I Will Come Back (2)	Me And My Shadow (3)	Stormy Weather (4)	Care For Me) (4)
Swing Tonight?) (medley)	Christmas (7,10)	I'm Always Chasing Rainbows	Mean To Me (3)	Swanee (4,8,11)	You And The Night And The
(8,9)	He's Got The Whole World In	(7,10)	Meet Me In St. Louis, Louis	Sweet Danger (5)	Music (medley) (8,11)
Boy Next Door (1,7,10)	His Hands (8,11)	I'm Nobody's Baby (7,10)	(7,10)	Sweet Sixteen (7)	You Go To My Head (4)
Brotherhood Of Man (medley)	Hello Bluebird (6)	If Love Were All (4)	Memories Of You (2)	That Old Black Magic (7)	You Made Me Love You
(11)	Hello, Dolly! (8,11)	In-Between (7)	More Than You Know (5)	That's Entertainment (4,9)	(I Didn't Want To Do It)
But Not For Me (7)	Hooray For Love (medley)	It All Depends On You (medley)	Music That Makes Me	This Can't Be Love (medley)	(1,4,7,9,10)
By Myself (3,6,11)	(8,11)	(8,11)	Dance (8)	(4,9)	You'll Never Walk Alone (5,7)
Carolina In The Morning (1)	How About Me (3)	It Never Was You (6)	Never Will I Marry (8)	This Is The Time Of The	You're Nearer (4)
Chicago (4,8)	How About You (medley) (8,11)	It's A Great Day For The	Ol' Man River (medley) (9)	Evening (medley) (1)	Zing! Went The Strings Of My
Come Rain Or Come Shine	How Long Has This Been	Irish (5)	On The Atchison, Topeka And	Together (Wherever We Go)	Heart (4,7)
(2,4)	Going On? (4)	Jamboree Jones (medley) (9)	The Santa Fe (7,10)	(8,9,11)	
Comes Once In A Lifetime (5)	I Am The Monarch Of The	Judy At The Palace Medley	On The Sunny Side Of The	Trolley Song (1,4,7,9,10)	
Danny Boy (1)	Sea (6)	(1,5)	Street (7)	We Could Make Such Beautiful	
(Dear Mr. Gable) ..see: You	I Can't Give You Anything But	Just A Memory (3)	Our Love Affair (7)	Music (medley) (8)	
Made Me Love You (I Didn't	Love (4)	Just Imagine (2)	Over The Rainbow	What Now My Love (8,9,11)	
Want To Do It)	I Could Go On Singing (6)	Just You, Just Me (4)	(1,4,7,8,9,10,11)		

GARNER, Erroll   '58

Born on 6/15/23 in Pittsburgh. Died on 1/2/77 (age 53). Jazz pianist/songwriter.

11/25/57	16	2			1 **Other Voices** .... [I]	$40	Columbia 1014
3/10/58	12	7			2 **Concert By The Sea** .... [I-L]	$40	Columbia 883

recorded in 1956 in Carmel, California

6/26/61	35	31			3 **Dreamstreet** .... [I]	$30	ABC-Paramount 365
7/6/63	94	6			4 **One World Concert** .... [I-L]	$25	Reprise 6080

recorded at Seattle World's Fair

April In Paris (2)	Dancing Tambourine (4)	Happiness Is A Thing Called	I Didn't Know What Time It Was	It Might As Well Be Spring (1)	Lover Came Back To Me (4)
Autumn Leaves (2)	Dreamstreet (3)	Joe (1)	(1)	It's All Right With Me (3)	Mack The Knife (4)
Blue Lou (3)	Dreamy (1)	How Could You Do A Thing	I'll Remember April (2)	Just One Of Those Things (3)	Mambo Carmel (2)
Come Rain Or Come Shine (3)	Erroll's Theme (4)	Like That To Me (2)	I'm Getting Sentimental Over	Lady Is A Tramp (3)	Mambo Gotham (1)
			You (3)		

DEBUT	PEAK	WKS	RIAA	CD	ARTIST — Album Title	Catalog	Sym	$	Label & Number

GARNER, Erroll — Cont'd

Misty (1,4)	On The Street Where You Live (1)	Thanks For The Memory (4)	Very Thought Of You (1)	When You're Smiling (The Whole World Smiles With You) (3)
Moment's Delight (1)	Other Voices (1)	They Can't Take That Away From Me (2)	Way You Look Tonight (4)	
Movin' Blues (4)	Red Top (2)	Sweet Lorraine (3)	This Is Always (1)	Where Or When (2)
Oklahoma! Medley (3)	Sweet And Lovely (4)			
	Solitaire (1)			

(note: columns) Misty (1,4); Moment's Delight (1); Movin' Blues (4); Oklahoma! Medley (3) | On The Street Where You Live (1); Other Voices (1); Red Top (2) | Solitaire (1); Sweet And Lovely (4); Sweet Lorraine (3); Teach Me Tonight (2) | Thanks For The Memory (4); They Can't Take That Away From Me (2); This Is Always (1) | Very Thought Of You (1); Way You Look Tonight (4) | When You're Smiling (The Whole World Smiles With You) (3); Where Or When (2)

GARNETT, Gale   '64

Born on 7/17/42 in Auckland, New Zealand. Female singer/songwriter.

DEBUT	PEAK	WKS			ARTIST — Album Title			$	Label & Number
9/26/64	43	22		©	My Kind Of Folk Songs			$40	RCA Victor 2833

Fly Bird | I Know You Rider | Malaika | Pretty Boy | Sleep You Now | Wanderin'
I Came To The City | Little Man, Nine Years Old | Oh Brandy Leave Me Alone | Prism Song | Take This Hammer | We'll Sing In The Sunshine 4

GARRETT, Leif   '78

Born on 11/8/61 in Hollywood. Pop singer/actor. Acted in several movies.

DEBUT	PEAK	WKS	RIAA		#	ARTIST — Album Title			$	Label & Number
12/17/77+	37	24	●		1	Leif Garrett			$12	Atlantic 19152
11/25/78+	34	19	●		2	Feel The Need			$12	Scotti Brothers 7100
12/15/79+	129	22			3	Same Goes For You			$12	Scotti Brothers 16008
12/12/81+	185	7			4	My Movie Of You			$12	Scotti Brothers 37625

Bad To Me (1) | Give In (3) | I Was Looking For Someone To Love (3) 78 | Little Things You Do (3) | Put Your Head On My Shoulder (1) 58 | Special Kind Of Girl (1)
California Girls (1) | Groovin' (2) | I Was Made For Dancin' (2) 10 | Living Without Your Love (3) | Runaround Sue (1) 13 | Surfin' USA (1) 20
Every Night With You (4) | Guilty (3) | If I Were A Carpenter (3) | Memorize Your Number (3) 60 | Runaway Rita (4) 84 | That's All (1)
Feel The Need (2) 57 | Hungry For Your Love Tonight (3) | Missin' You (4) | This Time (2)
Feels So Right (4) | Johnny B. Goode (1) | Mo Mo Way (Momoe) (4) | Same Goes For You (3) | Uptown Girl (4)
Forget About You (2) | I Don't Want To Want You (4) | Just Like A Brother (4) | Moonlight Dancin' (4) | Santa Monica Bay (4) | Wanderer, The (1) 49
Fun, Fun, Fun (2) | I Wanna Share A Dream With You (1) | Kicks (3) | Movie Of You (4) | Sheila (2) | When I Think Of You (2,3) 78
| | | Once A Fool (2) | Singin' In The Rain (3) |

GARRETT, Tommy, 50 Guitars Of   '62

Born on 7/5/39 in Dallas. Prolific producer. Better known as "Snuff" Garrett. 50 Guitars featured guitar solos by Tommy Tedesco. Also see **Midnight String Quartet** and **The Renaissance**.

DEBUT	PEAK	WKS	CD	#	ARTIST — Album Title	Sym	$	Label & Number
12/18/61+	36	6	©	1	50 Guitars Go South Of The Border	[I]	$15	Liberty 14005
12/14/63+	94	8		2	Maria Elena	[I]	$15	Liberty 14030
6/13/64	142	2		3	50 Guitars Go Italiano	[I]	$15	Liberty 14028
11/26/66	99	5		4	50 Guitars In Love	[I]	$15	Liberty 14037
7/8/67	168	3		5	More 50 Guitars In Love	[I]	$15	Liberty 14039
5/3/69	147	9		6	The Best Of The 50 Guitars Of Tommy Garrett	[G-I]	$15	Liberty 14045

Adios (1) | Granada (1) | Lara's Theme (4) | Old Cape Cod (5) | Summertime In Venice (3)
Al-Di-La (3) | Come Back To Sorrento (3) | Guadalajara (1,6) | Love Me With All Your Heart (6) | Our Day Will Come (4) | Sure Gonna Miss Her (4)
Amapola (2) | Come Closer To Me (1) | Guantanamera (6) | Malaguena (4) | Perfidia (1) | Taboo (2)
Anema E Core (3) | Courtin' (5) | Guitar Serenade (5) | Man And A Woman (5) | Poinciana (2) | Volare (2)
Anna (2) | Dr. Zhivago ..see: Lara's Theme | Hung Up In Your Eyes (5) | Maria Elena (2,6) | Return To Me (3) | What Now My Love (4)
Arrivederci, Roma (3) | Dream Theme (4) | I Left My Heart In San Francisco (4) | Mattinata (3) | Shadow Of Your Smile (4) | Without You (2)
Be Mine Tonight (1) | El Choclo (2) | If You Go Away (5) | Mexican Hat Dance (6) | Softly, As I Leave You (5) | You Belong To My Heart (1)
Besame Mucho (1) | El Relicario (5) | Jungle Drums (2) | Michelle (4) | Someone In Love, Theme For (5) | You Don't Have To Say You Love Me (4)
Brazil (2) | Escape To Love (4) | La Bamba (1,6) | Moon Guitar (4) | Somewhere, My Love ..see: Lara's Theme | You've Lost That Lovin' Feelin' (5)
Breeze And I (2) | Flamenco Love (2) | La Negra (6) | My Cup Runneth Over (5) |
Cherry Pink And Apple Blossom White (2) | Frenesi (1) | La Strada, Love Theme From (3) | My Love, Forgive Me (5) | South Of The Border (1) |
Ciao, Ciao Bambina (3) | Girl From Ipanema (6) | La Virgen De La Macarena (1) | My Special Angel (5) | Spanish Eyes (6) |
| Good, The Bad, And The Ugly (6) | | Non Dimenticar (4) | Strangers In The Night (4) |
| | | O Sole Mio (3) |

★259★   GARY, John   '65

Born on 11/29/32 in Watertown, New York. Died of cancer on 1/4/98 (age 65). Singer on Don McNeill's radio program, *Breakfast Club*.
1)The Nearness Of You 2)Encore 3)A Little Bit Of Heaven

DEBUT	PEAK	WKS	#	ARTIST — Album Title	Sym	$	Label & Number
11/9/63+	19	63	1	Catch A Rising Star		$20	RCA Victor 2745
2/22/64	16	46	2	Encore		$20	RCA Victor 2804
8/15/64	42	28	3	So Tenderly		$20	RCA Victor 2922
11/14/64	141	4	4	David Merrick presents Hits From His Broadway Hits		$20	RCA Victor 2947

JOHN GARY/ANN-MARGRET
includes "Hello, Dolly!," "Comes Once In A Lifetime," "Make Someone Happy" and "Take Me Along" by Merrill Staton Voices

DEBUT	PEAK	WKS	#	ARTIST — Album Title	Sym	$	Label & Number
12/5/64	3[X]	17	5	The John Gary Christmas Album	[X]	$15	RCA Victor 2940

Christmas charts: 3/'64, 11/'65, 18/'66, 32/'67, 20/'67

1/23/65	17	33	6	A Little Bit Of Heaven		$15	RCA Victor 2994
7/24/65	11	29	7	The Nearness Of You		$15	RCA Victor 3349
10/30/65	21	25	8	Your All-Time Favorite Songs		$15	RCA Victor 3411
3/12/66	51	20	9	Choice		$15	RCA Victor 3501
7/9/66	65	12	10	Your All-Time Country Favorites		$15	RCA Victor 3570
10/8/66	73	17	11	A Heart Filled With Song		$15	RCA Victor 3666
2/11/67	117	14	12	Especially For You		$15	RCA Victor 3695
5/13/67	90	11	13	Spanish Moonlight		$15	RCA Victor 3785
10/7/67	76	19	14	The John Gary Carnegie Hall Concert	[L]	$15	RCA Victor 1139
4/19/69	192	3	15	Love Of A Gentle Woman		$15	RCA Victor 4134

All The Things You Are (8) | Brown Eyed Baby Boy (3) | Ebb Tide (1) | Have I Told You Lately That I Love You? (10) | I Ain't Down Yet (9) | I'm Sitting On Top Of The World (14)
And This Is My Beloved (2) | Charade (9) | Fanny (4) | Have Yourself A Merry Little Christmas (11) | I Can't Stop Loving You (10) | If (2)
Any Time (10) | Christmas Song (Chestnuts Roasting On An Open Fire) (5) | Far Away Places (2) | | I Left My Heart In San Francisco (3) | If Ever I Would Leave You (11)
Anyone Would Love You (4) | Fascination (8) | Hawaiian Wedding Song (Ke Kali Nei Au) (7) | I Really Don't Want To Know (10) | If You Go Away (Ne Me Quitte Pas) (15)
Anywhere I Wander (2) | First Noël (medley) (5) | He'll Have To Go (10) | I Wish You Love (Que Reste-t-il De Nos Amours) (7) | If You Love Me (Really Love Me) (3)
As Time Goes By (8) | Cockles And Mussels (Molly Malone) (6) | Fly Me To The Moon (In Other Words) (11) | Here I'll Stay (3) | I'll Be Home For Christmas (5)
Autumn Leaves (8) | Cold, Cold Heart (10) | Galway Bay (6) | Here In My Heart (15) | I'll Be Seeing You (9) | Impossible Dream (The Quest) (9)
Be My Love (11) | Come To Me, Bend To Me (3) | Georgia On My Mind (9) | How Are Things In Glocca Morra (3) | I'll Never Fall In Love Again (15) | (It's Been) Grand Knowing You (2)
Beautiful (7) | Cu-Cu-Rru-Cu-Cu, Paloma (13) | Granada (Fantasia Espagnola) (13) | How Deep Is The Ocean (How High Is The Sky) (9) | I'll Remember Her (9) | Kathleen Mavourneen (6)
Beautiful Thing (2) | Danny Boy (3) | Guantanamera (13) | How I Learned To Sing Medley (14) | I'll Rock You In My Mind (15) |
Because Of You (11) | Dear Heart (7) | Half As Much (1) | | I'll Take You Home Again, Kathleen (6) |
Believe Me If All Those Endearing Young Charms (6) | Deep Purple (8) | Hark! The Herald Angels Sing (medley) (5) |
Black Is The Color Of My True Love's Hair (12) | Do You Hear What I Hear (5) | Don't Blame Me (9) |

GARY, John — Cont'd

La Malaguena (Son Huasteco) (13,14)
Let There Be Peace On Earth (Let It Begin With Me) (12)
Little Bit Of Heaven (6)
Little Snow Girl (5)
Love Is A Many Splendored Thing (7)
Love Is Here To Stay (9)
Love Me Tender (10)
Love Me With All Your Heart (Cuando Calienta El Sol) (13)
Love Of A Gentle Woman (15)
Luck Be A Lady (9)
Macushla (6)
Made For Each Other (Tu Felicidad) (13)
Make The World Go Away (10)
Maria Elena (3)
Medley (Finale) (14)
Melodie D'Amour (Melody Of Love) (2)
Michelle (12)
More (1,14)
Most Beautiful Girl In The World (14)

Mother Machree (6)
My Cup Runneth Over (14)
My Foolish Heart (7)
My Kind Of Girl (1)
My Wild Irish Rose (6)
Nearness Of You (7)
Night And Day (8)
No Arms Can Ever Hold You (Like These Arms Of Mine) (11)
O Come, All Ye Faithful (medley) (5)
O Holy Night (medley) (5)
O Little Town Of Bethlehem (medley) (5)
Oh, Lonesome Me (10)
Ol' Man River (2)
On The Street Where You Live (7)
Once Upon A Summertime (La Valse Des Lilas) (12)
Once Upon A Time (1)
Opportunity (Poem) (14)
Perfect Day (12)
Poinciana (13)
Possum Song (1)

Red Rosey Bush (3)
Scarborough Fair (15)
Shadow Of Your Smile (14)
She Loves Me (14)
Silent Night (medley) (5)
Small World (4)
Smilin' Through (3)
Smoke Gets In Your Eyes (3)
Softly, As I Leave You (7)
Some Enchanted Evening (8)
Someday (You'll Want Me To Want You) (10)
Something Simple (3)
Somewhere (9)
Somewhere Along The Way (1)
Song Of The Cuckoo (3)
Sound Of Music (2)
Spanish Moonlight (13)
Star Dust (8)
Stella By Starlight (2)
Straight Life (15)
Stranger In Paradise (2)
Sunrise, Sunset (14)
Sweet Little Jesus Boy (5)
Take Me In Your Arms (2)

Take My Love (3)
Tammy (9)
Ten Girls Ago (3)
Tender Is The Night (2)
Tenderly (3)
Tennessee Waltz (2)
Thank Heaven For Little Girls (12)
That's An Irish Lullaby (Too-Ra-Loo-Ra-Loo-Ral) (6)
They Don't Make Love Like They Used To (15)
This Is All I Ask (1)
'Til Tomorrow (12)
Till (11)
Till The Birds Sing In The Morning (1)
Till There Was You (12)
Till We Meet Again (12)
Time After Time (7)
Tonight (8)
Try To Remember (12)
Two Different Worlds (12)
Unchained Melody (1)
What Kind Of Fool Am I? (4)
What Now My Love (11)

When Irish Eyes Are Smiling (6)
While We're Young (11)
White Christmas (5)
Who Can I Turn To (When Nobody Needs Me) (7)
Windmills Of Your Mind (15)
Winter Wonderland (5)
Wintertime And Christmas Time (5)
Without A Song (13)
Without You (Tres Palabras) (13)
Yellow Bird (1)
Yesterday (11)
You Belong To My Heart (Solamente Una Vez) (13)
You Don't Have To Say You Love Me (15)
You Don't Know Me (10)
You Stepped Out Of A Dream (7)
You'll Never Walk Alone (8)
Young At Heart (12)
Younger Than Springtime (9)
Your Cheatin' Heart (1)
Yours (Quiereme Mucho) (13)

GARY'S GANG   '79

Disco group from Queens, New York: Gary Turnier (drums), Eric Matthew (vocals, guitar), Al Lauricella and Rino Minetti (keyboards), Bill Catalano (percussion), Bob Forman (sax) and Jay Leon (trombone).

| 3/31/79 | 42 | 10 | | | **Keep On Dancin'** .... | | | $12 | Columbia 35793 |

Do It At The Disco   **Keep On Dancin'** *41*   Let's Lovedance Tonight   Party Tonight!   Showtime   You'll Always Be My Everything

GASCA, Luis   '72

Born on 3/3/40 in Houston. Jazz trumpet player.

| 5/27/72 | 195 | 3 | | | **Luis Gasca** .... | [I] | | $15 | Blue Thumb 37 |

La Raza   Little Mama   Spanish Gypsy   Street Dude

GATES, David   '75

Born on 12/11/40 in Tulsa, Oklahoma. Pop singer/songwriter. Lead singer of **Bread**.

10/27/73	107	10			1 **First**			$15	Elektra 75066
2/15/75	102	9			2 **Never Let Her Go**			$12	Elektra 1028
8/12/78	165	4			3 **Goodbye Girl**			$12	Elektra 148

Angel (2)
Ann (1,3)
California Lady (3)
Chain Me (2)
Clouds (medley) (1,3) *47*
Do You Believe He's Comin' (1)

Drifter (3)
Goodbye Girl (3) *15*
Greener Days (2)
He Don't Know How To Love You (3)
Help Is On The Way (1)

Light Of My Life (2)
Lorilee (1,3)
Never Let Her Go (2,3) *29*
Overnight Sensation (3)
Part Time Love (2,3)
Playin' On My Guitar (2)

Rain (medley) (1,3)
Sail Around The World (1) *50*
Sight & Sound (1)
Soap (I Use The) (1)
Someday (2)
Strangers (2)

Sunday Rider (1,3)
Took The Last Train (3) *30*
Watch Out (2)

GATLIN, Larry   '80

Born on 5/2/48 in Seminole, Texas. Country singer/songwriter/guitarist.

4/1/78	175	5			1 **Love Is Just A Game**			$15	Monument 7616
7/22/78	140	8			2 **Oh! Brother**			$15	Monument 7626
12/23/78+	171	9	●	©	3 **Larry Gatlin's Greatest Hits**	[G]		$15	Monument 7628

LARRY GATLIN & THE GATLIN BROTHERS BAND:

11/17/79+	102	16	▲	©	4 **Straight Ahead**			$12	Columbia 36250
11/1/80	118	4			5 **Help Yourself**			$12	Columbia 36582
10/17/81	184	2		©	6 **Not Guilty**...			$12	Columbia 37464

All The Gold In California (4)
Alleluia (1)
Anything But Leavin' (1)
Bitter They Are, Harder They Fall (3)
Broken Lady (3)
Can't Cry Anymore (4)
Can't Take It With You (6)
Cold Day In Hell (2)
Daytime Heroes (5)
Delta Dirt (3) *84*
Do It Again Tonight (2,3)

Everything I Know About Cheatin' (2)
Everytime A Plane Flies Over Our House (1)
Good Wilbur (6)
Gypsy Flower Child (4)
Hard Workin' Hands (6)
Heart, The (3)
Help Yourself To Me (5)
Hold Me Closer (4)
How Much Is A Man Supposed To Take (4)

I Don't Wanna Cry (1,3)
I Just Wish You Were Someone I Love (1,3)
I Still Don't Love You Anymore (5)
I've Done Enough Dyin' Today (2)
I've Got You (2)
If Practice Makes Perfect (1)
In Like With Each Other (6)
It Don't Get No Better Than This (5)

It's Love At Last (1)
Kiss It All Goodbye (1)
L.A. You're A Killer (2)
Love Is Just A Game (1,3)
Midnight Choir (Mogen David) (4)
Must Be All The Same To You (5)
My Last Love Song (6)
Night Time Magic (2,3)
Nothin' You Do (2)
Piece By Piece (3)

Rain (6)
She Used To Sing On Sunday (6)
Someone Else's Day (6)
Songwriters Trilogy (4)
Standin' By Me (2)
Statues Without Hearts (3)
Straight To My Heart (5)
Sweet Becky Walker (3)
Take Me To Your Lovin' Place (5)

Taking Somebody With Me When I Fall (4)
Tomorrow (1)
Until She Said Goodbye (5)
Way I Did Before (4)
We're Number One (4)
What Are We Doin' Lonesome (6)
Wind Is Bound To Change (5)
You Happened To Me (2)
You Wouldn't Know Love (6)

GATTON, Danny   '91

Born on 9/4/45 in Washington DC. Died of self-inflicted gunshot wound on 10/4/94 (age 49). Rock guitarist.

| 4/27/91 | 121 | 4 | | © | **88 Elmira St.** .... | [I] | | $10 | Elektra 61032 |

Blues Newburg   Fandingus   In My Room   Pretty Blue   Red Label   Slidin' Home
Elmira St. Boogie   Funky Mama   Muthaship   Quiet Village   Simpsons, The

GAYE, Marvin ★62★   '73

Born on 4/2/39 in Washington DC. Fatally shot by his father after a quarrel on 4/1/84 (one day before his 45th birthday) in Los Angeles. Sang in his father's Apostolic church. In vocal groups the Rainbows, Marquees and **Moonglows**. Session work as a drummer at Motown; married to Berry Gordy's sister Anna, 1961-75. First recorded under own name for Tamla in 1961. In seclusion for several months following the death of Tammi Terrell in 1970. Problems with drugs and the IRS led to his moving to Europe for three years. Inducted into the Rock and Roll Hall of Fame in 1987. Won Grammy's Lifetime Achievement Award in 1996.

1)Let's Get It On 2)Marvin Gaye Live At The London Palladium 3)I Want You 4)What's Going On
5)Midnight Love

DEBUT	PEAK	WKS	CD	#	ARTIST — Album Title	Catalog	Sym	$	Label & Number
5/16/64	42	16	©	1	**Together**..			$50	Motown 613
					MARVIN GAYE & MARY WELLS				
5/30/64	72	14		2	Marvin Gaye/Greatest Hits		[G]	$40	Tamla 252
2/27/65	128	10	©	3	How Sweet It Is To Be Loved By You			$40	Tamla 258
7/16/66	118	10	©	4	Moods Of Marvin Gaye			$40	Tamla 266
9/30/67	178	5		5	Marvin Gaye/Greatest Hits, Vol. 2		[G]	$30	Tamla 278
10/7/67	69	44	©	6	United			$25	Tamla 277
9/21/68	60	21	©	7	You're All I Need			$25	Tamla 284
					MARVIN GAYE & TAMMI TERRELL (above 2)				
11/2/68+	63	27		8	In The Groove			$25	Tamla 285
6/14/69	33	18	©	9	M.P.G.			$25	Tamla 292
6/14/69	183	7	©	10	Marvin Gaye And His Girls		[K]	$25	Tamla 293
10/18/69	184	2	©	11	Easy			$25	Tamla 294
					MARVIN GAYE & TAMMI TERRELL				
11/1/69+	189	3	©	12	That's The Way Love Is			$25	Tamla 299
6/13/70	171	3		13	Marvin Gaye & Tammi Terrell Greatest Hits		[G]	$25	Tamla 302
11/7/70	117	6	©	14	Marvin Gaye Super Hits		[G]	$25	Tamla 300
6/12/71	6	53	● ©	15	**What's Going On** .... C:#39/28			$20	Tamla 310
12/30/72+	14	21	©	16	Trouble Man		[I-S]	$20	Tamla 322
9/15/73	2¹	61	©	17	**Let's Get It On** .... C:#7/36			$20	Tamla 329
11/17/73	26	47	©	18	Diana & Marvin			$20	Motown 803
					DIANA ROSS & MARVIN GAYE				
4/20/74	61	29	©	19	Marvin Gaye Anthology		[G]	$30	Motown 791 [3]
7/13/74	8	28	©	20	**Marvin Gaye Live!**		[L]	$20	Tamla 333
					recorded at the Alameda County Coliseum in Oakland				
4/3/76	4	28	©	21	**I Want You**			$20	Tamla 342
10/2/76	44	8		22	Marvin Gaye's Greatest Hits .... C:#4/188		[G]	$20	Tamla 348
4/2/77	3	26	©	23	**Marvin Gaye Live At The London Palladium**		[L]	$25	Tamla 352 [2]
1/6/79	26	21	©	24	Here, My Dear			$25	Tamla 364 [2]
2/7/81	32	17	©	25	In Our Lifetime			$12	Tamla 374
11/20/82	7	41	▲³ ©	26	**Midnight Love**			$10	Columbia 38197
10/22/83+	80	16	▲ ©	27	Every Great Motown Hit Of Marvin Gaye ▲ .... C:#11/61		[G]	$10	Motown 6058
6/2/84	18ᶜ	20		28	Motown Superstar Series Volume 15.................		[K]	$10	Motown 115
6/8/85	41	15	©	29	Dream Of A Lifetime		[K]	$10	Columbia 39916
5/3/86	193	2		30	Motown Remembers Marvin Gaye		[E]	$10	Tamla 6172

GAYE, Marvin — Cont'd

This Magic Moment (9)
This Poor Heart Of Mine (11)
'Til Tomorrow (26)
Time To Get It Together (24)
Together (1,10)
Too Busy Thinking About My Baby (9,14,19,23,27) *4*
Trouble Man (16,19,20,22,23,27) *7*
Trouble Man, Theme From (16)

Try It Baby (3,5,14,19,20) *15*
Try My True Love (9)
Turn On Some Music (26)
Two Can Have A Party (6)
Until I Met You (1)
What Good Am I Without You (10,19) *61*
What You Gave Me (11,13) *49*
What's Going On (15,19,20,22,23,27,28) *2*

What's Happening Brother (15)
What's The Matter With You Baby (1,10,19) *17*
When Did I Stop Loving Me, When Did I Stop Loving You (24)
When Love Comes Knocking At My Heart (7)
Wholy Holy (15)
World Is Rated X (30)

Yesterday (12)
You (8,14,19,23) *34*
You Ain't Livin' 'Till You're Lovin' (7,13)
You Are Everything (18)
You Came A Long Way From St. Louis (1)
You Can Leave, But It's Going To Cost You (24)
You Got What It Takes (6)

You Sure Love To Ball (17) *50*
You're A Special Part Of Me (18) *12*
You're A Wonderful One (2,3,14,19,20,23) *15*
You're All I Need To Get By (7,13,19,23,27) *7*
You're The Man (19) *50*
You're The One For Me (4)

You're What's Happening (In The World Today) (8)
You've Been A Long Time Coming (4)
Your Precious Love (6,10,13,19,23,27) *5*
Your Unchanging Love (4,5,19) *33*

★485★

GAYLE, Crystal '77

Born as Brenda Gail Webb on 1/9/51 in Paintsville, Kentucky; raised in Wabash, Indiana. Country singer. Youngest sister of **Loretta Lynn**.
1)We Must Believe In Magic 2)Miss The Mississippi 3)When I Dream

DEBUT	PEAK	WKS	RIAA	CD	#	Album Title	Sym	$	Label & Number
9/3/77	12	35	▲	©	1	We Must Believe In Magic		$12	United Artists 771
7/15/78	52	39	▲	©	2	When I Dream		$12	United Artists 858
8/11/79	128	8			3	We Should Be Together		$12	United Artists 969
9/29/79	36	28	●		4	Miss The Mississippi		$12	Columbia 36203
11/17/79+	62	22		©	5	Classic Crystal	[G]	$12	United Artists 982
5/3/80	149	6		©	6	Favorites	[K]	$12	United Artists 1034
9/27/80	79	11	●	©	7	These Days		$10	Columbia 36512
9/19/81	99	16		©	8	Hollywood, Tennessee		$10	Columbia 37438
12/4/82+	120	12			9	True Love		$10	Elektra 60200
9/10/83	169	8	●	©	10	Crystal Gayle's Greatest Hits	[G]	$10	Columbia 38803
11/12/83	171	6			11	Cage The Songbird		$10	Warner 23958

Ain't No Love In The Heart Of The City (7)
Ain't No Sunshine (8)
All I Want To Do In Life (1,6)
Baby, What About You (9) *83*
Beyond You (3)
Blue Side (4,10) *81*
Cage The Songbird (11)
Come Back (When You Can Stay Forever) (11)
Come Home Daddy (6)
Cry Me A River (2)
Crying In The Rain (8)
Dancing The Night Away (4)
Danger Zone (4)
Deeper In The Fire (9)
Don't Go My Love (4)
Don't It Make My Brown Eyes Blue (1,5) *2*
Don't Treat Me Like A Stranger (2,6)

Easier Said Than Done (9)
Everything I Own (9)
Funny (1)
Going Down Slow (1)
Green Door (1)
Half The Way (4,10) *15*
He Is Beautiful To Me (9)
Heart Mender (2,6)
Hello I Love You (2)
Help Yourselves To Each Other (7)
Hollywood (3)
I Don't Wanna Lose Your Love (11)
I Just Can't Leave Your Love Alone (7)
I Still Miss Someone (2)
I Wanna Come Back To You (1,6)
I'll Do It All Over Again (5)
I'll Get Over You (5) *71*

If You Ever Change Your Mind (7,10)
It's All Right With Me (1)
It's Like We Never Said Goodbye (4,10) *63*
Keepin' Power (8,10)
Lean On Me (8)
Let Your Feelings Show (9)
Little Bit Of The Rain (4)
Livin' In These Troubled Times (8,10)
Love Crazy Love (8)
Lover Man (7)
Make A Dream Come True (1)
Me Against The Night (11)
Miss The Mississippi And You (4)
On Our Way To Love (11)
Other Side Of Me (4)
Our Love Is On The Faultline (9)

Paintin' This Old Town Blue (2)
Ready For The Times To Get Better (5) *52*
Right In The Palm Of Your Hand (6)
River Road (1,6)
Room For One More (4)
Same Old Story (Same Old Song) (7)
Sneakin' Out The Back Door (3)
Somebody Loves You (5)
Someday Soon (2)
Sound Of Goodbye (11) *84*
Take It Easy (7,10)
Take Me Home (11)
Talking In Your Sleep (2,5) *18*
Through Believing In Love Songs (3)
'Til I Gain Control Again (9)

Time Will Prove That I'm Right (3)
Too Deep For Tears (3)
Too Good To Throw Away (2)
Too Many Lovers (7,10)
True Love (9)
Turning Away (11)
Victim Or A Fool (11)
Wayward Wind (2,6)
We Must Believe In Magic (1)
We Should Be Together (3)
What A Little Moonlight Can Do (7)
What I've Been Needin' (6)
When I Dream (2,5) *84*
Why Have You Left The One You Left Me For (2,5)
Woman In Me (8,10) *76*
Wrong Road Again (5)
You (6)

You Bring Out The Lover In Me (9)
You Made A Fool Of Me (11)
You Never Gave Up On Me (8,10)
You Never Miss A Real Good Thing ('Till He Says Goodbye) (5)
You'll Be Loved Someday (3)
You're The Best Thing In My Life (3)
You've Almost Got Me Believin' (3)
Your Kisses Will (3)
Your Old Cold Shoulder (3)

GAYLORD & HOLIDAY '76

Italian-American duo: Ronnie "Gaylord" Fredianelli and Burt "Holiday" Bonaldi. With pianist/arranger Don Rea. Recorded in the late '50s as The Gaylords.

DEBUT	PEAK	WKS				Album Title		$	Label & Number
2/21/76	180	8				Second Generation		$15	Prodigal 10009

Dio Como Ti Amo
Dormi, Dormi, Dormi
Eh! Cumpari *72*

From The Vine Came The Grape
Godfather (Speak Softly Love), Love Theme From The

I Will Never Pass This Way Again
Italian Wedding Song
Little Shoemaker

Sempre Tu
Tell Me You're Mine
To The Door Of The Sun

GAYNOR, Gloria '79

Born on 9/7/49 in Newark, New Jersey. Disco singer.

DEBUT	PEAK	WKS			#	Album Title		$	Label & Number
2/1/75	25	15			1	Never Can Say Goodbye		$15	MGM 4982
10/11/75	64	21			2	Experience Gloria Gaynor		$15	MGM 4997
8/14/76	107	14			3	I've Got You		$12	Polydor 6063
3/19/77	183	4			4	Glorious		$12	Polydor 6095
1/6/79	4	34	▲		5	Love Tracks		$12	Polydor 6184
10/20/79	58	11			6	I Have A Right		$12	Polydor 6231
5/24/80	178	4			7	Stories		$12	Polydor 6274

Ain't No Bigger Fool (7)
All I Need Is Your Sweet Lovin' (1)
All My Life (7)
Anybody Wanna Party? (5)
As Time Goes By (4)
Be Mine (3)
Can't Fight The Feelin' (6)
Casanova Brown (2)
Do It Right (3)
Don't Read Me Wrong (7)
Don't Stop Us (6)

False Alarm (1)
Goin' Out Of My Head (5)
Honey Bee (1)
How High The Moon (2) *75*
I Let Love Slip Right Through My Hands (7)
I Said Yes (5)
I Will Survive (5) *1*
I'm Still Yours (2)
I've Got You Under My Skin (3)
(If You Want It) Do It Yourself (2) *98*

Let Me Know (I Have A Right) (6) *42*
Let's Make A Deal (3)
Let's Make Love (3)
Life Ain't Worth Living (4)
Lock Me Up (7)
Luckiest Girl In The World (7)
Make Me Yours (7)
Midnight Rocker (6)
Most Of All (4)
Never Can Say Goodbye (1) *9*
Nothing In This World (3)

On A Diet Of You (7)
One Number One (6)
Please, Be There (5)
Prettiest Face I've Ever Seen (2)
Real Good People (1)
Reach Out, I'll Be There (1) *60*
Say Somethin' (6)
Searchin' (1)
So Much Love (4)
Stoplight (5)
Substitute (5)

Sweet Sweet Melody (4)
Talk, Talk, Talk (3)
Tell Me How (2)
This Side Of The Pain (4)
Tonight (4)
Touch Of Lightning (3)
Walk On By (2) *98*
We Belong Together (1)
We Can Start All Over Again (4)
What'll I Do (2)
Why Should I Pay (4)
You Can Exit (5)

You Took Me In Again (6)

★201★

GEILS, J., Band '82

Rock group from Boston: Jerome Geils (guitar), **Peter Wolf** (vocals), Magic Dick Salwitz (harmonica), Seth Justman (keyboards, vocals), Danny Klein (bass) and Stephen Jo Bladd (drums). Wolf left for a solo career in the fall of 1983.
1)Freeze-Frame 2)Bloodshot 3)Love Stinks

DEBUT	PEAK	WKS	RIAA	CD	#	Album Title	Sym	$	Label & Number
1/30/71	195	2		©	1	The J. Geils Band		$15	Atlantic 8275
11/6/71	64	17		©	2	The Morning After		$15	Atlantic 8297
10/21/72	54	26	●	©	3	"Live" - Full House	[L]	$15	Atlantic 7241

recorded on 4/21/72 at the Cinderella Ballroom in Detroit

GEILS, J., Band — Cont'd

DEBUT	PEAK	WKS					$	Label & Number
4/28/73	10	44	● ©	4	**Bloodshot**		$15	Atlantic 7260
12/1/73+	51	18	©	5	Ladies Invited		$15	Atlantic 7286
10/19/74	26	22	©	6	Nightmares...and other tales from the vinyl jungle		$15	Atlantic 18107
9/27/75	36	9	©	7	Hotline		$15	Atlantic 18147
5/22/76	40	11	©	8	Live - Blow Your Face Out	[L]	$20	Atlantic 507 [2]
					recorded on 11/15/75 at the Boston Garden and on 11/19/75 at Cobo Hall in Detroit			
7/9/77	51	17	©	9	Monkey Island		$15	Atlantic 19103
12/16/78+	49	22	● ©	10	Sanctuary		$12	EMI America 17006
7/21/79	129	5	©	11	Best of the J. Geils Band	C:#20/8 [G]	$12	Atlantic 19234
2/9/80	18	42	©	12	Love Stinks		$12	EMI America 17016
11/14/81+	❶⁴	70	▲ ©	13	**Freeze-Frame**		$12	EMI America 17062
12/4/82+	23	19	●	14	Showtime!	[L]	$12	EMI America 17087
					recorded September 1982 at the Pine Knob Music Theater in Detroit			
11/24/84	80	10		15	You're Gettin' Even While I'm Gettin' Odd		$12	EMI America 17137

(Ain't Nothin' But A) House Party (4,8,11)
Angel In Blue (13) *40*
Back To Get Ya (4,8)
Be Careful (What You Do) (7)
Believe In Me (7)
Bite From Inside (15)
Californicatin' (15)
Centerfold (13,14) *1*
Chimes (5,8)
Come Back (12) *32*
Concealed Weapons (15) *63*
Cruisin' For A Love (1,3)
Cry One More Time (2)
Desire (Please Don't Turn Away) (12)
Detroit Breakdown (6,8,11)
Did You No Wrong (5)
Diddyboppin' (5)
Do You Remember When (13)
Don't Try To Hide It (4)
Easy Way Out (7)

Eenie Meenie Minie Moe (15)
Fancy Footwork (7)
First I Look At The Purse (1,3)
Flamethrower (13)
Floyd's Hotel (2)
Freeze-Frame (13) *4*
Funky Judge (6)
Gettin' Out (6)
Give It To Me (4,8,11) *30*
Givin' It All Up (6)
Gonna Find Me A New Love (2)
Gotta Have Your Love (2)
Hard Drivin' Man (1,3)
Heavy Petting (15)
Hold Your Loving (4)
Homework (1,3)
I Can't Believe You (10)
I Can't Go On (5)
I Could Hurt You (10)
I Do (9,11,14) *24*
I Don't Hang Around Much Anymore (10)

I Don't Need You No More (2)
I Will Carry You Home (15)
I'll Be Coming Home (6)
I'm Falling (9,14)
I'm Not Rough (9)
Ice Breaker (For The Big "M") (1)
Insane, Insane Again (13)
It Ain't What You Do (It's How You Do It!) (2)
Jealous Love (7)
Jus' Can't Stop Me (10,14)
Just Can't Wait (12,14) *78*
Lady Makes Demands (5)
Land Of A Thousand Dances (14) *60*
Lay Your Good Thing Down (5)
Look Me In The Eye (6)
Looking For A Love (2,3,8,11) *39*
Love Rap (Rap) (14)
Love Stinks (12,14) *38*

Love-itis (7,8)
Make Up Your Mind (4) *98*
Mean Love (7)
Monkey Island (9)
Must Of Got Lost (6,8,11) *12*
My Baby Don't Love Me (5)
Night Time (12)
Nightmares (6)
No Anchovies, Please (12)
No Doubt About It (5)
On Borrowed Time (1)
One Last Kiss (10,14) *35*
Orange Driver (7)
Pack Fair And Square (1,3)
Piss On The Wall (13)
Rage In The Cage (13)
Raise Your Hand (8)
River Blindness (13)
Sanctuary (10,14)
Serves You Right To Suffer (1,3)
Shoot Your Shot (8)

Sno-Cone (1,8)
So Good (9)
So Sharp (2,8)
Somebody (9)
Southside Shuffle (4,8,11)
Start All Over Again (4,8)
Stoop Down #39 (6,14)
Struttin' With My Baby (4)
Surrender (9)
Take A Chance (On Romance) (5)
Take It Back (10) *67*
Takin' You Down (12)
Tell 'Em Jonesy (15)
Teresa (10)
That's Why I'm Thinking Of You (5)
Think It Over (7)
Till The Walls Come Tumblin' Down (12,14)
Truck Drivin' Man (8)
Tryin' Not To Think About It (12)

Usual Place (2)
Wait (1,8)
Wasted Youth (15)
Whammer Jammer (2,3,11)
What's Your Hurry (1)
Where Did Our Love Go (8,11) *68*
Wild Man (10)
Wreckage (9)
You're Gettin' Even While I'm Gettin' Odd (15)
You're The Only One (9) *83*

GELDOF, Bob   '87

Born on 10/5/54 in Dublin, Ireland. Leader of **The Boomtown Rats**. Played "Pink" in the **Pink Floyd** movie *The Wall*. Organized British superstar benefit group **Band Aid** and earned a Nobel Peace Prize nomination.

							$	Label & Number
12/13/86+	130	12	©		Deep In The Heart Of Nowhere		$10	Atlantic 81687

August Was A Heavy Month
Beat Of The Night
Deep In The Heart Of Nowhere
I Cry Too
In The Pouring Rain
Love Like A Rocket
Night Turns To Day
This Heartless Heart
This Is The World Calling *82*
When I Was Young
Words From Heaven

GENE LOVES JEZEBEL   '88

Techno-rock group formed in England: twin brothers Jay and Michael Aston (vocals), James Stevenson (guitar), Peter Rizzo (bass) and Chris Bell (drums) joined. Michael Aston left in early 1989.

							$	Label & Number
10/18/86+	155	19	©	1	Discover		$10	Geffen 24118
11/14/87+	108	22	©	2	The House Of Dolls		$10	Geffen 24171
8/18/90	123	14	©	3	Kiss Of Life		$10	Geffen 24260

Beyond Doubt (1)
Brand New Moon (1)
Desire (1)
Drowning Crazy (2)
Evening Star (3)

Every Door (2)
Gorgeous (2)
Heartache (1)
I Die For You (3)
It'll End In Tears (3)

Jealous (3) *68*
Kick (1)
Kiss Of Life (3)
Maid Of Sker (1)
Message (1)

Motion Of Love (2) *87*
Over The Rooftops (1)
Set Me Free (2)
Suspicion (2)
Sweetest Thing (1)

Syzygy (3)
Tangled Up In You (3)
Treasure (2)
Twenty Killer Hurts (2)
Two Shadows (2)

Up There (2)
Wait And See (1)
Walk Away (3)
White Horse (1)
Why Can't I? (3)

GENERAL PUBLIC   '85

Pop group formed in Birmingham, England: Dave Wakeling (vocals, guitar), **Ranking Roger** (vocals, keyboards), Kevin White (guitar), Micky Billingham (keyboards), Horace Panter (bass) and Stoker (drums). Wakeling and Roger had been in **English Beat**. Billingham was with **Dexys Midnight Runners**. General Public disbanded in March 1987. Wakeling and Roger reunited in 1994.

							$	Label & Number
10/27/84+	26	39	©	1	...All The Rage		$10	I.R.S. 70046
10/25/86	83	16	©	2	Hand To Mouth		$10	I.R.S. 5782

Anxious (1)
Are You Leading Me On? (1)
As A Matter Of Fact (1)
Burning Bright (1)

Cheque In The Post (2)
Come Again (1)
Cry On Your Shoulder (2)
Day-To-Day (1)

Faults And All (2)
Forward As One (2)
General Public (1)
Hot You're Cool (1)

In Conversation (2)
Love Without The Fun (2)
Murder (2)
Never All There (2)

Never You Done That (1)
Tenderness (1) *27*
Too Much Or Nothing (2)
Where's The Line? (1)

GENESIS ★114★   '86

Formed as a progressive-rock group in England in 1967. Consisted of **Peter Gabriel** (lead vocals), **Anthony Phillips** (guitar), **Tony Banks** (keyboards), **Mike Rutherford** (guitar, bass) and Chris Stewart (drums; replaced by John Silver in 1968, then John Mayhew in 1969). Phillips and Mayhew left in 1970, replaced by **Steve Hackett** (guitar) and **Phil Collins** (drums). Gabriel left in June 1975, with Collins replacing him as new lead singer. Hackett went solo in 1977, leaving group as a trio: Collins, Rutherford and Banks. Added regular members for touring: Americans Chester Thompson (drums), in 1977, and guitarist Daryl Stuermer, in 1978. Collins also recorded in jazz-fusion group **Brand X**. Rutherford also in own group, **Mike + The Mechanics**, formed in 1985. Hackett later formed group **GTR**. Collins announced his departure from the group in April 1996; Ray Wilson joined as lead singer in June 1997.

1)Invisible Touch 2)We Can't Dance 3)Abacab

							$	Label & Number
12/15/73+	70	29	● ©	1	Selling England By The Pound		$20	Charisma 6060
5/18/74	105	14	©	2	Genesis Live	[L]	$20	Charisma 1666
					recorded February 1973 in Manchester, England			
10/12/74	170	4	©	3	From Genesis To Revelation	[E]	$30	London 643
					released in 1969			
12/14/74+	41	16	● ©	4	The Lamb Lies Down On Broadway		$20	Atco 401 [2]
3/20/76	31	19	● ©	5	A Trick Of The Tail		$15	Atco 129
1/22/77	26	21	● ©	6	Wind & Wuthering	C:#22/22	$15	Atco 144

GENESIS — Cont'd

DEBUT	PEAK	WKS	RIAA	CD	ARTIST — Album Title	Catalog	Sym	$	Label & Number
12/3/77	47	16		© 7	Seconds Out		[L]	$15	Atlantic 9002 [2]
4/15/78	14	33	▲	© 8	And Then There Were Three...	C:#25/20		$12	Atlantic 19173
4/26/80	11	31	▲	© 9	Duke			$12	Atlantic 16014
10/17/81	7	64	▲²	© 10	Abacab			$12	Atlantic 19313
6/26/82	10	25	●	© 11	Three Sides Live		[L]	$12	Atlantic 2000 [2]
					side 4: studio cuts from 1979-81				
10/29/83	9	50	▲⁴	© 12	Genesis	C:#18/33		$10	Atlantic 80116
6/28/86	3	85	▲⁶	© 13	Invisible Touch	C:#23/4		$10	Atlantic 81641
11/30/91	4	72	▲⁴	© 14	We Can't Dance			$10	Atlantic 82344
12/5/92	35	23	●	© 15	Live/The Way We Walk - Volume One: The Shorts		[L]	$10	Atlantic 82452
2/27/93	20	9		© 16	Live/The Way We Walk - Volume Two: The Longs		[L]	$10	Atlantic 82461
9/20/97	54	5		© 17	Calling All Stations			$10	Atlantic 83037
11/13/99	65	9	●	© 18	Turn It On Again - The Hits		[G]	$10	Atlantic 83244

Abacab (10,11,18) 26
After The Ordeal (1)
Afterglow (6,7,11)
Aisle Of Plenty (medley) (1)
Alien Afternoon (17)
All In A Mouse's Night (6)
Alone Tonight (9)
Am I Very Wrong (3)
Another Record (10)
Anything She Does (13)
Anyway (4)
Back In N.Y.C. (4)
Ballad Of Big (8)
Battle Of Epping Forest (1)
Behind The Lines (9,11)
Blood On The Rooftops (6)
Brazilian, The (13)
Broadway Melody Of 1974 (4)
Burning Rope (8)
Calling All Stations (17)
Carpet Crawlers (4,7)
Carpet Crawlers 1999 (18)
Chamber Of 32 Doors (4)
Cinema Show (1,7,11)
Colony Of Slippermen Medley (4,11)
Congo (17,18)
Conqueror, The (3)

Counting Out Time (4)
Cuckoo Cocoon (4)
Cul-De-Sac (9)
Dance On A Volcano (5,7,16)
Dancing With The Moonlit Knight (1)
Deep In The Motherlode (8)
Dividing Line (17)
DoDo (10,11)
Domino Medley (13,16)
Down And Out (8)
Dreaming While You Sleep (14)
Driving The Last Spike (14,16)
Drum Duet (16)
Duchess (9,11)
Duke's End (9)
Duke's Travels (9)
Eleventh Earl Of Mar (6)
Entangled (4)
Evidence Of Autumn (11)
Fading Lights (14,16)
Fireside Song (3)
Firth Of Fifth (1,7,16)
Fly On A Windshield (4)
Follow You Follow Me (8,11,18) 23
Get 'Em Out By Friday (2)
Grand Parade Of Lifeless Packaging (4)

Guide Vocal (9)
Hairless Heart (4)
Heathaze (9)
Hold On My Heart (14,15,18) 12
Home By The Sea (12,16)
I Can't Dance (14,15,18) 7
I Know What I Like (In Your Wardrobe) (1,7,16,18)
If That's What You Need (17)
Illegal Alien (12) 44
In Hiding (3)
In Limbo (3)
...In That Quiet Earth (medley) (6)
In The Beginning (3)
In The Cage (4,11)
In The Rapids (4)
In The Wilderness (3)
In Too Deep (13,15,18) 3
Invisible Touch (13,15,18) 1
It (4)
It's Gonna Get Better (12)
Jesus He Knows Me (14,15,18) 23
Just A Job To Do (12)
Keep It Dark (10)
Knife, The (2)
Lady Lies (8)

Lamb Lies Down On Broadway (4,7,16)
Lamia, The (4)
Land Of Confusion (13,15,18) 4
Light Dies Down On Broadway (4)
Like It Or Not (10)
Lilywhite Lilith (4)
Living Forever (14)
Los Endos (5,7)
Lurker (10)
Mad Man Moon (5)
Mama (12,15,18) 73
Man On The Corner (10) 40
Many Too Many (8)
Me And Sarah Jane (10,11)
Me And Virgil (11)
Misunderstanding (9,11,18) 14
More Fool Me (1)
Musical Box (2,7,16)
Never A Time (14) 21
No Reply At All (10) 29
No Son Of Mine (14,15,18) 12
Not About Us (17)
One Day (3)
One For The Vine (6)

One Man's Fool (17)
Open Door (11)
Paperlate (11) 32
Place To Call My Own (11)
Please Don't Ask (9)
Ravine (4)
Return Of The Giant Hogweed (2)
Riding The Scree (4)
Ripples (5)
Robbery, Assault & Battery (5,7)
Say It's Alright Joe (8)
Scenes From A Night's Dream (12,16)
Second Home By The Sea (12,16)
Serpent, The (3)
Shipwrecked (17)
Silent Sorrow In Empty Boats (4)
Silent Sun (3)
Silver Rainbow (12)
Since I Lost You (14)
Small Talk (17)
Snowbound (8)
Squonk (5,7)
Supernatural Anaesthetist (4)
Supper's Ready (7)

Taking It All Too Hard (12) 50
Tell Me Why (14)
That's All! (12,15,18) 6
There Must Be Some Other Way (17)
Throwing It All Away (13,15,18) 4
Tonight, Tonight, Tonight (13,15,18) 3
Trick Of The Tail (5)
Turn It On Again (9,11,18) 58
Uncertain Weather (17)
Undertow (8)
Unquiet Slumbers For The Sleepers... (medley) (6)
Waiting Room (4)
Watcher Of The Skies (2)
Way Of The World (14)
Where The Sour Turns To Sweet (3)
Who Dunnit? (10)
Window (3)
Wot Gorilla? (6)
You Might Recall (11)
Your Own Special Way (6) 62

GENIUS/GZA '95

Born Gary Grice on 8/22/66 in Brooklyn, New York. Male rapper. Member of **Wu-Tang Clan**.

DEBUT	PEAK	WKS	RIAA	CD	ARTIST — Album Title	$	Label & Number
11/25/95	9	24	●	© 1	Liquid Swords	$10	Geffen 24813
7/17/99	9	10	●	© 2	Beneath The Surface	$10	Wu-Tang 11969

GZA/GENIUS

Amplified Sample (2)
Beneath The Surface (2)
B.I.B.L.E. (Basic Instructions Before Leaving Earth) (1)
Breaker, Breaker (2)

Cold World (1) 97
Crash Your Crew (2)
Duel Of The Iron Mic (1)
Feel Like An Enemy (2)

4th Chamber (1)
Gold (1)
Hell's Wind Staff (1)
High Price, Small Reward (2)
Hip Hop Fury (2)

I Gotcha Back (1)
Investigative Reports (1)
Killah Hills 10304 (1)
Labels (1)
Liquid Swords (1) 48

Living In The World Today (1)
Mic Trippin (2)
Publicity (2)
Shadowboxin' (1) 67

Stringplay (Like This, Like That) (2)
Victim (2)

GENTLE GIANT '75

Progressive-rock group formed in England: brothers Ray (bass, guitar), Derek (sax, vocals) and Phil (sax, trumpet) Shulman, with Kerry Minnear (keyboards), Gary Green (guitar) and John Weathers (drums). Phil Shulman left after second album.

DEBUT	PEAK	WKS	RIAA	CD	ARTIST — Album Title	$	Label & Number
10/21/72	197	5		© 1	Three Friends	$15	Columbia 31649
3/31/73	170	9		© 2	Octopus	$15	Columbia 32022
10/12/74	78	13		© 3	The Power And The Glory	$12	Capitol 11337
8/16/75	48	11		© 4	Free Hand	$12	Capitol 11428
5/29/76	137	5		© 5	Interview........	$12	Capitol 11532
2/19/77	89	6		© 6	The Official "Live" Gentle Giant - Playing The Fool	$12	Capitol 11592 [2]
10/15/77	81	7		© 7	The Missing Piece	$12	Capitol 11696

Advent Of Panurge (2)
Another Show (5)
As Old As You're Young (7)
Aspirations (4)
Betcha Thought We Couldn't Do It (7)
Boys In The Band (2)
Cogs In Cogs (3)
Cry For Everyone (2)

Design (5)
Dog's Life (2)
Empty City (5)
Excerpts From Octopus (6)
Experience (6)
Face, The (3)
For Nobody (7)
Free Hand (4,6)
Funny Ways (6)

Give It Back (5)
His Last Voyage (4)
I Lost My Head (5,6)
I'm Turning Around (7)
Interview (5)
Just The Same (4,6)
Knots (2)
Memories Of Old Days (7)
Mister Class And Quality? (1)

Mobile (4)
Mountain Time (7)
No God's A Man (3)
On Reflection (4,6)
Peel The Paint (1,6)
Playing The Game (3)
Proclamation (3,6)
Raconteur Troubadour (2)
River (2)

Runaway, The (6)
Schooldays (1)
So Sincere (3,6)
Sweet Georgia Brown (Breakdown In Brussels) (6)
Talybont (4)
Think Of Me With Kindness (2)
Three Friends (1)
Time To Kill (3)

Timing (5)
Two Weeks In Spain (7)
Valedictory (3)
Who Do You Think You Are? (7)
Winning (7)
Working All Day (1)

GENTRY, Bobbie '67

Born Roberta Streeter on 7/27/44 in Chickasaw County, Mississippi; raised in Greenwood, Mississippi. Singer/songwriter. Won the 1967 Best New Artist Grammy Award. Married to **Jim Stafford** (1978-79).

DEBUT	PEAK	WKS	RIAA	CD	ARTIST — Album Title	$	Label & Number
9/16/67	❶²	30	●	1	Ode To Billie Joe	$20	Capitol 2830
3/23/68	132	12		2	The Delta Sweete	$20	Capitol 2842
10/12/68	11	47	●	3	Bobbie Gentry & Glen Campbell........	$20	Capitol 2928
8/9/69	164	4		4	Touch 'Em With Love	$15	Capitol 155
12/27/69+	180	2	©	5	Bobbie Gentry's Greatest!	[G]	$15	Capitol 381
5/9/70	96	17		6	Fancy	$15	Capitol 428

Ace Insurance Man (5)
Big Boss Man (2)
Bugs (1)

Canticle ..see: Scarborough Fair
Chickasaw County Child (1)

Courtyard (2)
Delta Man (6)
Fancy (6) 31

Find 'Em, Fool 'Em And Forget 'Em (6)
Gentle On My Mind (3)

Glory Hallelujah, How They'll Sing (4,5)

Greyhound Goin' Somewhere (4)

329

GENTRY, Bobbie — Cont'd

He Made A Woman Out Of Me (6) 71	(It's Only Your) Imagination (3)	Natural To Be Gone (4)	Raindrops Keep Fallin' On My Head (6)	Something In The Way He Moves (6)	Where's The Playground, Johnny (4)
Heart To Heart Talk (3)	Jessye' Lisabeth (2)	Niki Hoeky (1)	Rainmaker (6)	Son Of A Preacher Man (4)	You've Made Me So Very Happy (4)
Hurry, Tuesday Child (1)	Lazy Willie (1)	Ode To Billie Joe (1,5) 1	Refractions (2)	Sunday Best (1)
I Saw An Angel Die (1)	Less Of Me (3)	Okolona River Bottom Band (2,5) 54	Reunion (2)	Sunday Mornin' (3)
I Wouldn't Be Surprised (4)	Let It Be Me (3) 36	Papa, Won't You Let Me Go To Town With You (1)	Scarborough Fair/Canticle (3)	Sweet Peony (5)
I'll Never Fall In Love Again (4,6)	Little Green Apples (3)	Papa's Medicine Show (5)	Seasons Come, Seasons Go (4)	Terrible Tangled Web (3)
If You Gotta Make A Fool Of Somebody (6)	Louisiana Man (2) 100	Parchman Farm (2)	Sermon (2)	Tobacco Road (2)
	Mississippi Delta (1,5)	Penduli Pendulum (2,5)	Sittin' Pretty (5)	Touch 'Em With Love (4,5)
	Mornin' Glory (2,3) 74			Wedding Bell Blues (6)
	My Elusive Dreams (3)			

GENTRYS, The '66

Pop-rock group from memphis: Larry Raspberry, Jimmy Hart and Bruce Bowles (vocals), Bobby Fisher (guitar), Jimmy Johnson (trumpet), Pat Neal (bass) and Larry Wall (drums). Hart later became a professional wrestling manager, known as "The Mouth of The South."

| 12/18/65+ | 99 | 10 | | | Keep On Dancing .... | | | $30 | MGM 4336 |

Brown Paper Sack	Everybody To Their Own Kick	Hey Girl Don't Bother Me	Make Up Your Mind	Sometimes
Do You Love Me	Hand Jive	Keep On Dancing 4	So Sad (To Watch Good Love Go Bad)	
Don't Send Me No Flowers	Hang On Sloopy	Little Girl Next Door		

GEORGE, Lowell '79

Born on 4/13/45 in Hollywood. Died of drug-related heart failure on 6/29/79 (age 34). Lead singer of **Little Feat**.

| 4/14/79 | 71 | 9 | | | Thanks I'll Eat It Here .... | | | $12 | Warner 3194 |

Can't Stand The Rain	Easy Money	Himmler's Ring	20 Million Things	What Do You Want The Girl To Do
Cheek To Cheek	Find A River	Honest Man	Two Trains	

GEORGIA SATELLITES '87

Rock group from Atlanta: Dan Baird (vocals, guitar) Rick Richards (guitar), Rich Price (bass) and Mauro Magellan (drummer). Richards later joined **Izzy Stradlin And The Ju Ju Hounds**.

11/1/86+	5	42	▲	© 1	Georgia Satellites			$10	Elektra 60496
7/2/88	77	13		© 2	Open All Night			$10	Elektra 60793
11/1/89	130	13		© 3	In The Land Of Salvation And Sin			$10	Elektra 60887

All Over But The Cryin' (3)	Can't Stand The Pain (1)	Down And Down (2)	I Dunno (3)	Nights Of Mystery (1)	Sheila (2)
Another Chance (3)	Cool Inside (2)	Dunk 'N' Dine (2)	Keep Your Hands To Yourself (1) 2	Open All Night (2)	Six Years Gone (3)
Baby So Fine (2)	Crazy (3)	Every Picture Tells A Story (1)	Mon Cheri (2)	Over And Over (1)	Slaughterhouse (3)
Battleship Chains (1) 86	Dan Takes Five (3)	Games People Play (3)	My Baby (2)	Railroad Steel (1)	Stellazine Blues (3)
Bottle O' Tears (3)	Days Gone By (3)	Golden Light (1)	Myth Of Love (1)	Red Light (1)	Sweet Blue Midnight (3)
Bring Down The Hammer (3)	Don't Pass Me By (2)	Hand To Mouth (2)		Shake That Thing (3)	Whole Lotta Shakin' (2)

GEORGIO '88

Born Georgio Allentini in San Francisco. Singer/songwriter/keyboardist/guitarist.

| 4/25/87+ | 117 | 52 | | © | Sexappeal .... | | | $10 | Motown 6229 |

Bed Rock	I Won't Change	Menage A Trois	Sexappeal 58	
Hey U	Lover's Lane 59	1/4 2 9	Tina Cherry 96	

GERARDO '91

Born Gerardo Mejia on 4/16/65 in Guayaquil, Ecuador; raised in Glendale, California. Rapper/actor. Raps in Spanglish (half Spanish, half English). Appeared in the movies *Can't Buy Me Love* and *Colors*.

| 2/23/91 | 36 | 32 | ● | © | Mo' Ritmo .... | | | $10 | Interscope 91619 |

Ritmo is Spanish for "Rhythm"

Brother To Brother	En Mi Barrio	Groove Remains The Same (Mo' Ritmo)	Latin Till I Die (Oye Como Va)	We Want The Funk 16	You Gotta Hold Of My Soul
Christina	Fandango		Rico Suave 7	When The Lights Go Out 98	

GERONIMO, Mic '97

Born in Queens, New York. Male rapper.

| 11/22/97 | 112 | 2 | | © | Vendetta .... | | | $10 | Blunt 4930 |

Be Like Mic	Life N Lessons	Single Life	Things Ain't What They Used	Usual Suspects	
For Tha Family	Nothin' Move But The Money 70	Street Life	To Be	Vendetta	
How You Been?		Survival	Unstoppable		

GERRY AND THE PACEMAKERS '65

Pop group from Liverpool, England: brothers Gerry (vocals, guitar; born on 9/24/42) and Freddie (drums) Marsden, with Leslie Maguire (piano) and Les Chadwick (bass).

7/11/64	29	12		© 1	Don't Let The Sun Catch You Crying			$30	Laurie 2024
11/21/64	129	9		© 2	Gerry & The Pacemakers Second Album			$30	Laurie 2027
2/27/65	13	20		3	Ferry Cross The Mersey		[S]	$40	United Artists 6387

includes "I Gotta Woman" by The Black Knights, "Shake A Tail Feather" by Earl Royce & The Olympics and "Why Don't You Love Me" by The Blackwells

| 2/27/65 | 120 | 7 | | 4 | I'll Be There! .... | | | $30 | Laurie 2030 |
| 5/15/65 | 44 | 22 | | 5 | Gerry & The Pacemakers Greatest Hits ...... | | [G] | $30 | Laurie 2031 |

Away From You (1,5)	Here's Hoping (2)	It's Gonna Be Alright (3,5) 23	She's The Only Girl For Me (3)	Where Have You Been (2)	You'll Never Walk Alone
Baby You're So Good To Me (3)	How Do You Do It? (1,5) 9	It's Happened To Me (2)	Shot Of Rhythm And Blues (2)	Whole Lotta Shakin' Goin' On (4)	(1) 48
Chills (2,5)	I Count The Tears (4)	Jambalaya (1,2)	Show Me That You Care (1)	Why Oh Why (3)	You're The Reason (1)
Don't Let The Sun Catch You Crying (1,5) 4	I Like It (2,5) 17	Mabellene (1)	Skinny Minnie (4)	Wrong Yo Yo (2)	
Don't You Ever (1)	I'll Be There (4,5) 14	My Babe (4,5)	Slow Down (1,2)	You Can't Fool Me (2)	
Fall In Love (3)	I'll Wait For You (3)	Now I'm Alone (4)	Summertime (3)	You Win Again (4)	
Ferry Cross The Mersey (3,5) 6	I'm The One (1,5) 82	Pretend (2,5)	Think About Love (3)	You You You (4)	
	It'll Be Me (4,5)	Reelin' And A Rockin' (4)	This Thing Called Love (3)		
	It's All Right (2)	Rip It Up (4)	What'd I Say (4)		

GERSHWIN, George '94

Born on 9/26/1898 in New York City. Died of a brain tumor on 7/11/37 (age 38). Legendary composer of numerous Broadway and movie scores, most with brother Ira's help. George and Ira won the Grammy's Trustees Award in 1986.

| 2/12/94 | 156 | 4 | | © | Gershwin Plays Gershwin: The Piano Rolls .... | | [I] | $10 | Nonesuch 79287 |

digital recordings of 12 of Gershwin's original player piano rolls; realized by Artis Wodehouse

American In Paris	Novelette In Fourths	Rhapsody In Blue	Swanee	When You Want 'Em, You Can't
Idle Dreams	On My Mind The Whole Night Long	Scandal Walk	Sweet And Lowdown	Get 'Em, When You've Got
Kickin' The Clouds Away		So Am I	That Certain Feeling	'Em, You Don't Want 'Em

GETO BOYS, The '96

Rap group from Houston: Richard "**Bushwick Bill**" Shaw, William "**Willie D**" Dennis, Brad "**Scarface**" Jordan, and "**Big Mike**" Barnett.

DEBUT	PEAK	WKS	RIAA	CD	ARTIST — Album Title	$	Label & Number
3/24/90	166	10		© 1	Grip It! On That Other Level	$10	Rap-A-Lot 103
					GHETTO BOYS		
10/20/90	171	7		© 2	The Geto Boys	$10	Rap-A-Lot 24306
7/27/91	24	42	▲ © 3		We Can't Be Stopped	$10	Rap-A-Lot 57161
12/5/92	147	9		© 4	Best Uncut Dope [K]	$10	Rap-A-Lot 57183
3/27/93	11	27	● © 5		Till Death Do Us Part	$10	Rap-A-Lot 57191
4/20/96	6	18	● © 6		The Resurrection	$10	Rap-A-Lot 41555
12/5/98	26	12		© 7	Da Good Da Bad & Da Ugly	$10	Rap-A-Lot 46780

Action Speaks Louder Than Words (4)
Ain't With Being Broke (3)
And My Word (4)
Another Nigger In The Morgue (3)
Assassins (2,4)
Big Faces (7)
Bitches & Ho's (7)
Blind Leading The Blind (6)
Bring It On (5)
Cereal Killer (5)
Chuckie (3,4)
City Under Siege (2)

Crooked Officer (5)
Damn It Feels Good To Be A Gangsta (4)
Dawn 2 Dusk (7)
Do It Like A G.O. (1,2,4)
Do Yo Time (7)
Eye 4 An Eye (7)
First Light Of The Day (6)
Free (7)
F___ A War (3)
F#@* 'Em (2)
Gangsta (Put Me Down) (7)
Gangster Of Love (1,2)
G.E.T.O. (5)

Geto Boys and Girls (6)
Geto Fantasy (6)
Ghetto Prisoner (6)
Gota Let Your Nuts Hang (3,4)
Gun In My Mouth (7)
Hold It Down (4)
Homie Don't Play That (3)
I Don't Fuck With You (7)
I Just Wanna Die (6)
I'm Not A Gentleman (3)
It Ain't (5)
Let A Ho Be A Ho (1,2)
Life In The Fast Lane (1,2)
Like Some Ho's (7)

Livin' 4 The Moment (7)
Mind Of A Lunatic (1,2,4)
Mind Playing Tricks On Me (3,4) *23*
Murder After Midnight (5)
Murder Avenue (5)
Niggas Ain't Doin' Shit (7)
Niggas And Flies (6)
No Nuts No Glory (5)
No Sell Out (1)
Open Minded (6)
Other Level (3)
Point Of No Return (6)
Punk-B____ Game (1)

Quickie (3)
Raise Up (5)
Read These Nikes (1,2)
Rebel Rap Family (3)
Retaliation (7)
Scarface (1,2,4)
Seek And Destroy (1)
Six Feet Deep (5) *40*
Size Ain't Shit (1,2,4)
Still (5)
Straight Gangstaism (5)
Street Game (7)
Street Life (5)

Talkin' Loud Ain't Saying Nothin' (1,2)
They Bitches (7)
This 's For You (5)
Thugg Niggaz (7)
Time Taker (6)
Trigga Happy Nigga (1,2)
Trophy (3)
Unseen, The (4)
Visit With Larry Hoover (6)
We Can't Be Stopped (6)
Why U Playin' (7)
World Is A Ghetto (6) *82*

GETZ, Stan '63

Born Stan Gayetsky on 2/2/27 in Philadelphia. Died of cancer on 6/6/91 (age 64). Jazz tenor saxophonist. With **Stan Kenton** (1944-45), **Jimmy Dorsey** (1945-46), **Benny Goodman** (1946) and **Woody Herman** (1947-49).

DEBUT	PEAK	WKS	RIAA	CD	ARTIST — Album Title	Sym	$	Label & Number
9/15/62+	❶[1]	70		© 1	Jazz Samba	[I]	$25	Verve 8432
					STAN GETZ/CHARLIE BYRD			
12/22/62+	13	23		© 2	Big Band Bossa Nova	[I]	$25	Verve 8494
5/18/63	88	11		© 3	Jazz Samba Encore!	[I]	$25	Verve 8523
4/11/64	122	6		© 4	Reflections	[I]	$20	Verve 8554
6/6/64	2[2]	96	● © 5		Getz/Gilberto		$20	Verve 8545
					STAN GETZ/JOAO GILBERTO			
					1964 Grammy winner: Album of the Year			
12/19/64+	24	46		© 6	Getz Au Go Go	[L]	$20	Verve 8600
					THE NEW STAN GETZ QUARTET Featuring Astrud Gilberto			
					recorded on 8/19/64 at the Cafe Au Go Go in Greenwich Village			
9/2/67	195	2		© 7	Sweet Rain	[I]	$20	Verve 8693
3/1/75	191	1		© 8	Captain Marvel	[I]	$15	Columbia 32706

Baia (1)
Balanco No Samba (Street Dance) (2)
Bim Bom (2)
Blowin' In The Wind (4)
Captain Marvel (8)
Charade (2)
Chega De Saudade (Too Much Longing) (2)
Con Alma (7)
Corcovado (5,6)
Day Waves (8)
Desafinado (1,5) *15*

Doralice (2)
E Luxo So (1)
Early Autumn (4)
Ebony Samba (3)
Entre Amigos (Sympathy Between Friends) (2)
Five Hundred Miles High (8)
Girl From Ipanema (5) *5*
Here's That Rainy Day (6)
If Ever I Would Leave You (4)
Insensatez (3)
It Might As Well Be Spring (6)
La Fiesta (8)

Litha (7)
Love (4)
Lush Life (8)
Manha De Carnival (Morning Of Carnival) (2)
Mania De Maria (3)
Melancolico (Melancholy) (2)
Menina Flor (3)
Moonlight In Vermont (4)
Nitetime (3)
Noite Triste (Night Sadness) (2)
O Grande Amor (5,7)
O Morro Nao Tem Vez (3)

O Pato (1)
One Note Samba ..see: Samba De Uma Nota So
Only Trust Your Heart (6)
Para Machuchar Meu Coracao (To Hurt My Heart) (5)
Penthouse Serenade (4)
Quiet Nights Of Quiet Stars ..see: Corcovado
Reflections (4)
Samba De Duas Notas (Two Note Samba) (3)
Samba De Uma Nota So (One Note Samba) (1,2,6)

Samba Dees Days (1)
Samba Triste (1)
Sambalero (2)
Saudade Vem Correndo (3)
Singing Song (6)
Six, Nix Quix, Flix (6)
Sleeping Bee (4)
So Danco Samba (Jazz Samba) (3,5)
Spring Can Really Hang You Up The Most (4)
Summertime (6)
Sweet Rain (7)

Telephone Song (6)
Times Lie (8)
Um Abraco No Getz (A Tribute To Getz) (8)
Vivo Sohando (5)
Voce E Eu (6)
Windows (7)

GHETTO BOYS — see GETO

GHETTO COMMISSION '98

Rap group from New Orleans: Gary Arnold, Byron Dolliole, Dwayne Lawrence, Carlos Stephens and Walter Valerio.

DEBUT	PEAK	WKS	CD	ARTIST — Album Title	$	Label & Number
11/28/98	59	2	©	Wise Guys	$10	No Limit 50011

Bad Weather
Blood Line
Devil's Playground

Get 'Em Up
Ghost In The Dark
How Could You Blame Us

Hustla Baller
I'm A Soulja
Lost Thugs

Our Thing
Run Quickly
Shackled

These Eyes Of Mine
Thug Luv
Thug 'Til I Die

Trying To Change
Trying To Make It
Wise Guys

GHETTO MAFIA '98

Rap duo from Decatur, Georgia: Rod Barber and Fred Pilgrim.

DEBUT	PEAK	WKS	ARTIST — Album Title	$	Label & Number
11/7/98	169	2	On Da Grind	$10	Rap Artist 2061
					P.A.N.

Boyz In Blue
Cell Block G

Chaos
Dot My Doe

Down Goes My Beeper
F.T.K.

Ghetto Mafia
Goin Out With This Gauge

In Decatur
On Da Grind

GHETTO TWIINZ '98

Rap duo from New Orleans: twin sisters Tonya and Tremethia Jupiter.

DEBUT	PEAK	WKS	CD	ARTIST — Album Title	$	Label & Number
10/10/98	191	1	©	No Pain/No Gain	$10	Rap-A-Lot 46259

B's Jack Too
Bout Dat Gangsta Gangsta
Die "MF" Die

Gonna Be A Murda
Got It On My Mind
Livin' Ghetto

Mil Don't Make U Real
Ms. Ghetto News
No Pain No Gain

No Sunshine
Responsibility
Small Time

Smokin' Love
Soldier Song
Stop Playin'

You Don't Wanna (Go To War)

GHOSTFACE KILLAH '96

Born Dennis Coles on 5/9/70 in Brooklyn, New York. Male rapper. Member of **Wu-Tang Clan**.

DEBUT	PEAK	WKS	RIAA	CD	ARTIST — Album Title	$	Label & Number
11/16/96	2[1]	26	● © 1		Ironman	$10	Razor Sharp 67729
2/26/00	7	19	● © 2		Supreme Clientele	$10	Razor Sharp 69325
							Wu Banga (2)

After The Smoke Is Clear (1)
All That I Got Is You (1)
Apollo Kids (2)
Assassination Day (1)
Black Jesus (1)
Box In Hand (1)

Buck 50 (2)
Camay (1)
Cherchez LaGhost (2) *98*
Child's Play (1)
Daytona 500 (1)
Deck's Beat (2)

Faster Blade (1)
Fish (2)
G-Dini (2)
In The Rain (2)
Iron Maiden (1)
Malcolm (2)

Marvel (1)
Mighty Healthy (2)
Motherless Child (1)
Nutmeg (2)
One (2)
Poisonous Darts (1)

Saturday Nite (2)
Soul Controller (1)
260 (1)
We Made It (2)
Wildflower (1)
Winter Warz (1)

GIANT '90
Rock group formed in Nashville: brothers Dan (vocals, guitar) and David (drums) Huff, with Alan Pasqua (keyboards) and Mike Brignardello (bass).

| 10/14/89+ | 80 | 36 | | © | **Last Of The Runaways**... | | | $10 | A&M 5272 |

| Big Pitch | I Can't Get Close Enough | I'm A Believer *56* | It Takes Two | No Way Out | Stranger To Me |
| Hold Back The Night | I'll See You In My Dreams *20* | Innocent Days | Love Welcome Home | Shake Me Up | |

GIANT STEPS '88
Duo from England: Campsie (vocals) and George McFarlane (instruments).

| 11/12/88 | 184 | 5 | | © | **The Book Of Pride**... | | | $10 | A&M 5190 |

| Another Lover *13* | Dance Away | Dream Wonderful | Golden Hours | Same Planet Different World |
| Book Of Pride | Do You Still Care | End Of The War | Into You *58* | Steamy |

GIBB, Andy '78
Born on 3/5/58 in Manchester, England. Died of heart failure on 3/10/88 (age 30). Pop singer/songwriter. Youngest brother of Robin, Maurice and **Barry** Gibb (**The Bee Gees**). Hosted TV's *Solid Gold* from 1981-82.

7/2/77	19	68	▲	©	1	**Flowing Rivers**...			$12	RSO 3019
6/17/78	7	43	▲	©	2	Shadow Dancing			$12	RSO 3034
3/1/80	21	15	●	©	3	**After Dark**...			$12	RSO 3069
12/6/80+	46	18			4	**Andy Gibb's Greatest Hits**.......................... [G]			$12	RSO 3091

After Dark (3,4)	Everlasting Love (2,4) *5*	I Just Want To Be Your	Melody (2)	Someone I Ain't (3)	Wherever You Are (3)
Come Home For The Winter (1)	Falling In Love With You (3)	Everything (1,4) *1*	One Love (3)	Starlight (1)	Why (2)
Dance To The Light Of The	Flowing Rivers (1)	In The End (1)	One More Look At The Night (2)	Time Is Time (4) *15*	Will You Love Me Tomorrow (4)
Morning (1)	Fool For A Night (2)	Let It Be Me (1)	(Our Love) Don't Throw It All	Too Many Looks In Your Eyes	Words And Music (1)
Desire (3,4) *4*	Good Feeling (2)	(Love Is) Thicker Than Water	Away (2,4) *1*	(1)	
Dreamin' On (3)	I Can't Help It (3) *12*	(1,4) *1*	Rest Your Love On Me (3)	Waiting For You (2)	
	I Go For You (2)	Me (Without You) (4) *40*	Shadow Dancing (2,4) *1*	Warm Ride (3)	

GIBB, Barry '84
Born on 9/1/46 in Manchester, England. Member of the **Bee Gees**.

| 10/20/84 | 72 | 8 | | © | **Now Voyager**... | | | $10 | MCA 5506 |

| Face To Face | Hunter | Lesson In Love | Shatterproof | **Shine Shine** *37* | Temptation |
| Fine Line | I Am Your Driver | One Night (For Lovers) | She Says | Stay Alone | |

GIBBS, Terri '81
Born on 6/15/54 in Augusta, Georgia. Female country singer/pianist. Blind since birth.

| 2/14/81 | 53 | 25 | | | **Somebody's Knockin'**... | | | $12 | MCA 5173 |

I Won't Cry In Dallas Anymore	Plans	Some Days It Rains All Night	Tell Me That You Love Me
It's True	**Rich Man** *89*	Long	Wasted Love
Magic Time		**Somebody's Knockin'** *13*	Wishing Well

GIBSON, Debbie '89
Born on 8/31/70 on Long Island, New York. Singer/songwriter/pianist. Playing piano since age five and songwriting since age six. Played "Eponine" in Broadway's *Les Misérables*.

9/5/87+	7	89	▲³	©	1	Out Of The Blue			$10	Atlantic 81780
2/11/89	❶⁵	51	▲²	©	2	Electric Youth			$10	Atlantic 81932
12/1/90	41	17	●	©	3	**Anything Is Possible**...			$10	Atlantic 82167
2/6/93	109	3		©	4	**Body Mind Soul**...			$10	Atlantic 82451

Another Brick Falls (3)	Free Me (4)	Little Birdie (4)	One Step Ahead (3)	Shock Your Mama (4)	Try (3)
Anything Is Possible (3) *26*	Goodbye (4)	**Losin' Myself** (4) *86*	Only In My Dreams (1) *4*	Should've Been The One (2)	Wake Up To Love (1)
Between The Lines (1)	Helplessly In Love (2)	Lost In Your Eyes (2) *1*	Out Of The Blue (1) *3*	Silence Speaks (A Thousand	**We Could Be Together** (2) *71*
Deep Down (3)	How Can This Be? (4)	Love In Disguise (2)	Over The Wall (2)	Words) (2)	When I Say No (4)
Do You Have It In Your Heart?	In His Mind (3)	Love Or Money (4)	Play The Field (1)	Stand Your Ground (3)	Where Have You Been? (3)
(4)	It Must've Been My Boy (3)	Mood Swings (3)	Red Hot (1)	**Staying Together** (1) *22*	Who Loves Ya Baby? (2)
Electric Youth (2) *11*	Kisses 4 One (4)	Negative Energy (3)	Reverse Psychology (3)	Sure (3)	
Fallen Angel (1)	Lead Them Home My Dreams	**No More Rhyme** (2) *17*	Shades Of The Past (2)	Tear Down These Walls (4)	
Foolish Beat (1) *1*	(3)	One Hand, One Heart (3)	Shake Your Love (1) *4*	This So-Called Miracle (3)	

GIBSON, Don '63
Born on 4/3/28 in Shelby, North Carolina. Country singer/songwriter/guitarist.

| 11/2/63 | 134 | 3 | | | **I Wrote A Song...**... | | | $30 | RCA Victor 2702 |
featuring new versions of Gibson's biggest hits

After The Heartache	Blue, Blue Day	I Can't Stop Loving You	Lonesome Number One	Oh Such A Stranger
Anything New Gets Old (Except	Don't Tell Me Your Troubles	(I'd Be) A Legend In My Time	Love Has Come My Way	
My Love For You)	Give Myself A Party	Just One Time	Oh Lonesome Me	

GIBSON BROTHERS '79
Disco trio from the West Indies: brothers Chris (guitar), Alex (keyboards) and Patrick (drums) Gibson. All share vocals.

| 7/28/79 | 185 | 2 | | | **Cuba**... | | | $12 | Island 9579 |

| Better Do It Salsa! | Ooh, What A Life... | Que Sera Mi Vida (If You | West Indies |
| **Cuba** *81* | | Should Go) | You |

GIFFORD, Kathie Lee '93
Born Kathie Epstein on 8/16/53 in Paris; raised in Bowie, Maryland. TV personality. Married to former pro football player/sportscaster Frank Gifford. Co-hostess of TV show *Live With Regis & Kathie Lee* from 1989-2000.

5/15/93	108	3		©	1	**Sentimental**...			$10	Warner 45084
12/11/93+	125	5		©	2	**It's Christmastime**.................................... [X]			$10	Warner 45346
						Christmas chart: 23/'93				
5/20/00	139	2		©	3	**Born For You**...			$10	On The Lamb 15115
11/11/00	170	1		©	4	**Heart Of A Woman**...			$10	Universal 159690

KATHIE LEE

Always Been You (4)	Child In Me (3)	Hardest Part (4)	Help Is On The Way (3)	(I Love You) For Sentimental	It Goes Like It Goes (medley)
Angels We Have Heard On	Christmas Waltz (medley) (2)	Hark! The Herald Angels Sing	Here's That Rainy Day (3)	Reasons (1)	(3)
High (medley) (2)	Circle Game (medley) (3)	(medley) (2)	Hey There (1)	I'll Be Home For Christmas (2)	It Had To Be You (1)
Away In A Manger (medley) (2)	Don't Rain On My Parade	Have Yourself A Merry Little	I Don't Know Why (I Just Do)	If Only Then Was Now (4)	It's Beginning To Look Like
Before The Parade Passes By	(medley) (3)	Christmas (2)	(1)	In This Life (4)	Christmas (2)
(medley) (3)	First Noel (medley) (2)	Heart Of A Woman (4)	I Don't Wanna Say Goodbye (4)	It Came Upon A Midnight Clear	It's Christmas Time (2)
Best Gift (2)	First Time (medley) (3)	Heartache, Heartache (4)	I Got Lost In His Arms (4)	(medley) (2)	Journey, The (3)
Born For You (3)					Love Never Fails (4)

GIFFORD, Kathie Lee — Cont'd

Make My Day (4)
Moondance (3)
Most Of All I Wish You Were Here (2)

Most Wonderful Time Of The Year (medley) (2)
Not Exactly Paris (medley) (3)
O Little Town Of Bethlehem (medley) (2)

On My Way To You (3)
Only My Pillow Knows (3)
Over The Rainbow (1)
Reason Enough (4)
Silver Bells (2)

Sleep Well Little Children (medley) (2)
Sunrise Sunset (medley) (3)
Sweet Dreams (medley) (3)
That Sunday, That Summer (1)
That's All (1)

There I've Said It Again (1)
Try To Remember (medley) (3)
Very Thought Of You (1)
We Don't Make Love Anymore (4)
What Child Is This (2)

When I Fall In Love (1)
White Christmas (2)
Winter Wonderland (2)

GILBERTO, Astrud   '65

Born on 3/30/40 in Salvador, Brazil. Wife of composer/guitarist **Joao Gilberto**.

12/19/64+	24	46		©	1 Getg Au Go Go .... [L]			$20	Verve 8600

THE NEW STAN GETZ QUARTET Featuring Astrud Gilberto
recorded on 8/19/64 at the Cafe Au Go Go in Greenwich Village

5/15/65	41	18			2 The Astrud Gilberto Album			$20	Verve 8608
10/9/65	68	18			3 The Shadow Of Your Smile			$20	Verve 8629

Agua De Beber (2)
All That's Left Is To Say Goodbye (2)
And Roses And Roses (2)
Corcovado (1)
Day By Day (3)

Dindi (2)
Dreamer (2)
Funny World (3)
Gentle Rain (3)
How Insensitive (2)

(In Other Words) Fly Me To The Moon (1)
It Might As Well Be Spring (1)
Manha De Carnaval (3)
Meditation (2)
Non-Stop To Brazil (3)

O Ganso (3)
O Morro (Nao Tem Vez) (2)
Once I Loved (2)
One Note Samba ..see: Samba De Uma Nota So
Only Trust Your Heart (1)
Photograph (2)

Sambe De Uma Nota So (One Note Samba) (1)
Sandpiper (The Shadow Of Your Smile), Love Theme From The (3)
So Finha De Ser Com Voce (2)
(Take Me To) Aruanda (3)

Telephone Song (1)
Tristeza (2)
Voce E Eu (1)
Who Can I Turn To? (When Nobody Needs Me) (3)

GILBERTO, Joao — see GETZ, Stan

GILDER, Nick   '78

Born on 11/7/51 in London; raised in Vancouver, Canada. Singer/songwriter.

9/23/78	33	20			1 City Nights			$12	Chrysalis 1202
7/7/79	127	8			2 Frequency			$12	Chrysalis 1219

All Because Of Love (1)
Brightest Star (2)
Electric Love (2)
Fly High (1)

Frustration (1)
Got To Get Out (1)
Here Comes The Night (1) *44*
Hold On Me Tonight (1)

Hot Child In The City (1) *1*
Into The 80's (1)
Metro Jets (2)
Rock Me (2) *57*

Rockaway (1)
(She's) One Of The Boys (1)
Time After Time (1)
21st Century (1)

Watcher Of The Night (2)
We'll Work It Out (1)
Worlds Collide (2)

GILL, Johnny   '90

Born on 5/22/66 in Washington DC. R&B singer. Joined **New Edition** in 1988. His brother Randy and cousin Jermaine Mickey are members of **II D Extreme**. Member of **LSG**.

3/31/84	139	8		©	1 Perfect Combination			$12	Cotillion 90136

STACY LATTISAW & JOHNNY GILL

5/5/90	8	60	▲²	©	2 Johnny Gill			$10	Motown 6283
6/26/93	14	20	●	©	3 Provocative			$10	Motown 6355
10/26/96	32	26	●	©	4 Let's Get The Mood Right			$10	Motown 0646

Baby It's You (1)
Block Party (1)
Bring It On (4)
Come Out Of The Shadows (1)
Cute, Sweet, Love Addiction (3)
Fairweather Friend (2) *28*
Falling In Love Again (1)
Feels So Much Better (2)

50/50 Love (1)
Floor, The (3) *56*
4 U Alone (4)
Fun 'N' Games (1)
Giving My All To You (2)
Having Illusions (4)
Heartbreak Look (1)
I Got You (3)

I Know Where I Stand (3)
I Know You Want Me (4)
It's Your Body (4) *43*
Just Another Lonely Night (2)
Lady Dujour (2)
Let's Get The Mood Right (4) *53*
Let's Spend The Night (2)

Long Way From Home (3)
Love In An Elevator (4)
Love U Right (4)
Mastersuite (3)
Maybe (4)
My, My, My (2) *10*
Never Know Love (2)
Perfect Combination (1) *75*

Provocative (3)
Quiet Time To Play (3)
Rub You The Right Way (2) *3*
Simply Say I Love U (4)
So Gentle (4)
Someone To Love (4)
Take Me (I'm Yours) (4)
Tell Me How U Want It (3)

Touch (4)
Where No Man Has Gone Before (3)
Wrap My Body Tight (2) *84*

★248★   GILL, Vince   '94

Born on 4/12/57 in Norman, Oklahoma. Country singer/guitarist. Member of **Pure Prairie League** from 1979-83. Married to Janis Oliver of the Sweethearts Of The Rodeo from 1980-97. Married **Amy Grant** on 3/10/2000.

1)When Love Finds You 2)I Still Believe In You 3)Souvenirs

7/28/90	67	78	▲²	©	1 When I Call Your Name .... C:#44/1			$10	MCA 42321
3/23/91+	37	98	▲²	©	2 Pocket Full Of Gold			$10	MCA 10140
10/19/91	19ᶜ	11	▲	©	3 The Best Of Vince Gill .... [G]			$10	RCA 9814
9/19/92	10	100	▲⁵	©	4 I Still Believe In You			$10	MCA 10630
10/9/93	14	16	▲²	©	5 Let There Be Peace On Earth .... C:#4/33 [X]			$10	MCA 10877

Christmas charts: 1/'93, 6/'94, 9/'95, 9/'96, 29/'97, 25/'99, 34/'00

6/25/94	6	112	▲⁴	©	6 When Love Finds You	C:#42/6		$10	MCA 11047
12/9/95	11	36	▲²	©	7 Souvenirs .... [G]			$10	MCA 11394
6/15/96	24	44	▲	©	8 High Lonesome Sound			$10	MCA 11422
8/29/98	11	27	●	©	9 The Key			$10	MCA 70017
11/14/98	39	9		©	10 Breath Of Heaven .... C:#9/8 [X]			$10	MCA 70038

with Patrick Williams & His Orchestra; Christmas charts: 3/'98, 13/'99

5/6/00	39	7		©	11 Let's Make Sure We Kiss Goodbye			$10	MCA 70098

All Those Years (9)
Baby Please Don't Go (11)
Blue Christmas (10)
Breath Of Heaven (Mary's Song) (10)
Christmas Song (10)
Cinderella (3)
Cradle In Bethlehem (10)
Do You Hear What I Hear (5)
Don't Come Cryin' To Me (9)
Don't Let Our Love Start Slippin' Away (4,7)
Down To New Orleans (8)
Feels Like Love (11) *52*
For The Last Time (11)
Given More Time (8)
Go Rest High On That Mountain (6)
Have Yourself A Merry Little Christmas (5)
Heart Won't Lie (7)
Hey God (A Song For Payne) (11)

High Lonesome Sound (8)
Hills Of Caroline (9)
I Can't Tell You Why (9)
I Never Knew Lonely (3)
I Never Really Knew You (9)
I Quit (2)
I Still Believe In You (4,7)
I Will Always Love You (7)
I'll Be Home For Christmas (5)
I'll Take Texas (9)
I've Been Hearing Things About You (3)
If I Didn't Have You In My World (9)
If I Had My Way (8)
If There's Anything I Can Do (6)
If You Ever Have Forever In Mind (6) *60*
It Won't Be The Same This Year (5)
It's The Most Wonderful Time Of The Year (10)
Jenny Dreamed Of Trains (8)

Key To Life (9)
Kindly Keep It Country (9)
Let Her In (9)
Let It Snow, Let It Snow, Let It Snow (10)
Let There Be Peace On Earth (5)
Let's Do Something (3)
Let's Make Sure We Kiss Goodbye (11)
Little Left Over (2)
Little More Love (8)
Little Things (11)
Live To Tell It All (9)
Liza Jane (2,7)
Look At Us (2,7)
Look What Love's Revealing (11)
Love Never Broke Anyone's Heart (4)
Luckiest Guy In The World (11)
Lucy Dee (3)
Maybe Tonight (6)

My Kind Of Woman/My Kind Of Man (7)
Never Alone (1,7)
Never Knew Lonely (1,7)
No Future In The Past (4,7)
Nothing Like A Woman (4)
O Come All Ye Faithful (10)
O Holy Night (10)
O Little Town Of Bethlehem (10)
Oh Carolina (3)
Oh Girl (You Know Where To Find Me) (11)
Oklahoma Borderline (3)
Oklahoma Swing (1)
One (11)
One Bright Star (5)
One Dance With You (8)
One More Last Chance (4,7)
Pocket Full Of Gold (2,7)
Pretty Little Adriana (8)
Pretty Words (4)
Radio, The (3)

Real Lady's Man (6)
Ridin' The Rodeo (1)
Rita Ballou (1)
Santa Claus Is Coming To Town (5)
Say Hello (4)
Shoot Straight From Your Heart (11)
Sight For Sore Eyes (1)
Silver Bells (10)
South Side Of Dixie (6)
Sparkle (2)
Strings That Tie You Down (2,7)
Take Your Memory With You (2,7)
Tell Me Lover (8)
That Friend Of Mine (11)
There's Not Much Love Here Anymore (8)
Til The Season Comes Around Again (5)
Tryin' To Get Over You (4,7) *88*

Turn Me Loose (3)
Under These Conditions (4)
Victim Of Life's Circumstances (3)
We Could Have Been (1)
We Won't Dance (1)
What Child Is This (5)
What They All Call Love (9)
What The Cowgirls Do (6)
What's A Man To Do (2)
When I Call Your Name (1)
When I Look Into Your Heart (11)
When Love Finds You (6)
Whenever You Come Around (6) *72*
Which Bridge To Cross (Which Bridge To Burn) (6)
White Christmas (6)
Winter Wonderland (10)
Worlds Apart (8)
You And You Alone (8)
You Better Think Twice (6)

GILLAN '80

Born Ian Gillan on 8/19/45 in Hounslow, Middlesex, England. Lead singer of **Deep Purple**. Portrayed Jesus in the rock opera *Jesus Christ Superstar*. Joined **Black Sabbath** for *Born Again* album.

| 12/6/80 | 183 | 3 | | © | Glory Road... | | | $12 | RSO 1001 |

Are You Sure?   Nervous   On The Rocks   Time And Again   Your Mother Was Right
If You Believe Me   No Easy Way   Running, White Face, City Boy   Unchain Your Brain

GILLETTE '95

Born Sandra Gillette on 9/16/73 in Chicago. Female rapper.

| 4/15/95 | 155 | 4 | | © | On The Attack.. | | | $10 | SOS 11102 |

Bad Boys   Move Too Fast   Short, Short Man   Wanna Wild Thing
Coochie Dance   **Mr. Personality** *42*   *hit #14 on "Hot 100" as "Short*   Whatcha Gonna Do
I'm On The Attack   Pay Back   *Dick Man"*   You're A Dog

GILLEY, Mickey '81

Born on 3/9/36 in Natchez, Mississippi; raised in Ferriday, Louisiana. Country singer/pianist. First cousin to both **Jerry Lee Lewis** and Reverend Jimmy Swaggart. Owner of Gilleys nightclub in Pasadena, Texas. Gilley and the club were featured in the movie *Urban Cowboy*. The club closed in 1989.

| 8/30/80 | 177 | 3 | | 1 | That's All That Matters To Me .... | | | $12 | Epic 36492 |
| 8/22/81 | 170 | 6 | | 2 | You Don't Know Me .... | | | $12 | Epic 37416 |

Blame Lies With Me (1)   Headache Tomorrow (Or A   Lonely Nights (2)   She Left You (A Long Time   We've Watched Another
Blues Don't Care Who's Got   Heartache Tonight) (1)   Lyin' Again (1)   Ago) (2)   Evening Waste Away (2)
  'Em (1)   Jukebox Argument (1)   Million Dollar Memories (1)   So Easy To Begin (1)   **You Don't Know Me** (2) *55*
Clinging To A Memory (2)   Ladies Night (2)   More I Turn The Bottle Up (1)   Tears Of The Lonely (2)
Drinking Old Memories Down   Learning To Live Without You   My Affection (2)   That's All That Matters (1)
  (2)   (2)   **True Love Ways** (1) *66*

GILMAN, Billy '00

Born on 5/24/88 in Westerly, Rhode Island; raised in Hope Valley, Rhode Island. Country singer.

| 7/8/00 | 22 | 48 | ▲ | © 1 | One Voice... | | | $10 | Epic 62086 |
| 11/4/00 | 42 | 10 | ● | © 2 | Classic Christmas.. | | [X] | $10 | Epic 61594 |

Christmas chart: 5/'00

| 5/26/01 | 45 | 11 | ● | © 3 | Dare To Dream... | | | $10 | Epic 62087 |

Almost Love (3)   I Think She Likes Me (1)   My Time On Earth (3)   Shamey, Shamey, Shame (3)   Spend Another Night (1)   White Christmas (2)
Angels We Have Heard On   I Wanna Get To Ya (1)   O Holy Night (2)   She's Everything You Want (3)   There's A Hero (1)   Winter Wonderland (2)
  High (2)   I've Got To Make It To Summer   **Oklahoma** (1) *63*   She's My Girl (3)   There's A New Kid In Town (2)   Woman In My Life (3)
Away In A Manger (2)   (2)   **One Voice** (1) *38*   Silent Night (2)   'Til I Can Make It On My Own   You Don't You Won't (3)
Christmas Song (2)   Jingle Bell Rock (2)   Our First Kiss (3)   Sleigh Ride (2)   (1)
Elisabeth (2)   Little Bitty Pretty One (1)   Rockin' Around The Christmas   Snake Song (1)   Warm & Fuzzy (2)
God's Alive And Well (3)   Little Things (1)   Tree (2)   Some Things I Know (3)   What's Forever For (1)

GILMER, Jimmy, & The Fireballs '63

Rock and roll group formed in Raton, New Mexico: Jimmy Gilmer (vocals, piano; b: 1940 in LaGrange, Illinois), George Tomsco and Dan Trammell (guitars), Stan Lark (bass) and Doug Roberts (drums). Roberts died on 11/18/81.

| 11/16/63 | 26 | 14 | | © | Sugar Shack .... | | | $60 | Dot 25545 |

Almost Eighteen   Let's Talk   Lonesome Tears   Red Cadillac And A Black   Suzie Q
I Wonder Why   Linda Lu   Pretend   Mustache   Won't Be Long
Let The Good Times Roll   Little Baby   **Sugar Shack** *1*

GILMOUR, David '84

Born on 3/6/44 in Cambridge, England. Rock singer/guitarist. Member of **Pink Floyd**.

| 7/1/78 | 29 | 18 | ● | © 1 | David Gilmour.. | | | $12 | Columbia 35388 |
| 3/17/84 | 32 | 28 | ● | © 2 | About Face.. | | | $10 | Columbia 39296 |

All Lovers Are Deranged (2)   I Can't Breathe Anymore (1)   Mihalis (1)   Out Of The Blue (2)   There's No Way Out Of Here
Blue Light (2) *62*   It's Deafinitely (1)   Murder (2)   Raise My Rent (1)   (1)
Cruise (2)   Let's Get Metaphysical (2)   Near The End (2)   Short And Sweet (1)   Until We Sleep (2)
Cry From The Street (1)   Love On The Air (2)   No Way (1)   So Far Away (1)   You Know I'm Right (2)

GILSTRAP, Jim '75

Born in Texas. R&B singer.

| 8/30/75 | 179 | 7 | | | Swing Your Daddy... | | | $15 | Roxbury 102 |

Ain't That Peculiar   One More Heartache   Special Occasion   Swing Your Daddy, Part II
House Of Strangers *93*   Put Out The Fire   **Swing Your Daddy** *55*   Take Your Daddy For A Ride

GIN BLOSSOMS '96

Pop-rock group from Tempe, Arizona: Robin Wilson (vocals), Jesse Valenzuela and Scott Johnson (guitars), Bill Leen (bass) and Phillip Rhodes (drums). Early guitarist Doug Hopkins died of a self-inflicted bullet wound on 12/5/93 (age 32).

| 5/1/93+ | 30 | 102 | ▲⁴ | © 1 | New Miserable Experience ....C:#36/3 | | | $10 | A&M 5403 |
| 3/2/96 | 10 | 20 | ▲ | © 2 | Congratulations I'm Sorry | | | $10 | A&M 540469 |

Allison Road (1)   Competition Smile (2)   Hands Are Tied (1)   I Can't Figure You Out (2)   My Car (2)   29 (1)
As Long As It Matters (2) *75*   Day Job (2)   **Hey Jealousy** (1) *25*   Lost Horizons (1)   Not Only Numb (2)   Until I Fall Away (1)
Cajun Song (1)   **Follow You Down** (2) *9*   Highwire (2)   Memphis Time (2)   Perfectly Still (2)   Virginia (2)
Cheatin' (1)   **Found Out About You** (1) *25*   Hold Me Down (1)   Mrs. Rita (1)   Pieces Of The Night (1)   Whitewash (2)

GINUWINE '01

Born Elgin Lumpkin on 10/15/75 in Washington DC. Male R&B singer.

10/26/96+	26	68	▲²	© 1	Ginuwine...The Bachelor			$10	550 Music 67685
4/3/99	5	54	▲²	© 2	100% Ginuwine			$10	550 Music 69598
4/21/01	3	24	●	© 3	The Life			$10	Epic 69622

All Nite All Day (2)   Hello (1)   None Of Ur Friends Business   She's Out Of My Life (2)   That's How I Get Down (3)   **What's So Different?** (2) *49*
Differences (3)   Holler (1)   (2) *48*   Show After The Show (3)   **There It Is** (3) *66*   When Doves Cry (1)
Do You Remember (2)   How Deep Is Your Love (3)   No. 1 Fan (2)   **So Anxious** (2) *16*   Toe 2 Toe (2)   Why Did You Go (3)
Final Warning (2)   I Know (2)   Only When U R Lonely (1)   So Anxious (Timbaland's   Tribute To A Woman (3)   Why Not Me (3)
550 What? (1)   I'll Do Anything/I'm Sorry (1)   Open Arms (3)   Anxiety Pt. 2) (3)   Two Reasons I Cry (3)   World Is So Cold (1)
G. Thang (2)   I'm Crying Out (2)   **Pony** (1) *6*   So Fine (3)   Two Sides To A Story (2)
G's Got A Thing For You (3)   Just Because (3)   Role Play (3)   Superhuman (3)   2 Way (3)
Ginuwine 4 Ur Mind (1)   Lonely Daze (1)   Same Ol' G (2)   Tell Me Do U Wanna (1)   Wait A Minute (2)

GIORGIO — see MORODER, Giorgio

DEBUG	PEAK	WKS	RIAA	CD	ARTIST — Album Title	Catalog	Sym	$	Label & Number

GIOVANNI '97
Born Giovanni Marradi in Italy. Classically-trained pianist.

| 3/1/97 | 170 | 2 | | © | **Romance** .... | | [I] | $10 | NewCastle 5527 |

Amazing Grace
Death Theme "Untouchables"
Greensleeves
Hymne
I Want To Live
Midnight Express
Moonlight Sonata
Once Upon A Time In America
Phantom Of The Opera
Somewhere In Time
Una Lagrima Furtiva
Wind Beneath My Wing

GIOVANNI, Nikki, & The New York Community Choir '71
Born on 6/7/43 in Knoxville, Tennessee. Female poet.

| 8/21/71 | 165 | 13 | | | **Truth Is On Its Way** .... | | [T] | $15 | Right-On 5001 |

Giovanni recites her poems to the music of famous spirituals performed by various gospel artists

Alabama Poem
All I Gotta Do (poem)
Amazing Grace [New York Community Choir]
Ego Tripping (poem)
Great Pax Whitey (poem)
I Stood On The Banks Of Jordan [Arthur Freeman]
I've Decided To Make Jesus My Choice [New York Community Choir]
It Is Well [Isaac Douglas]
Must Jesus Bear The Cross Alone [Edgar Kendricks]
My Tower (poem)
Nikki Rosa (poem)
Nobody Knows The Trouble I've Seen [Wilbert Johnson]
Peace Be Still [Isaac Douglas]
Poem For A Lady Of Leisure
Now Retired
Poem For Aretha
Pretty Little Baby [Edgar Kendricks]
Second Rap Poem
This Little Light Of Mine [New York Community Choir]
Woman Poem

GIPSY KINGS '89
Flamenco guitar group: brothers Andre, Chico and Nicolas Reyes, with brothers Diego, Paci and Tonino Baliardo.

12/17/88+	57	42	▲	©	1 **Gipsy Kings**		[F]	$10	Elektra Musician 60845
12/16/89+	95	19	●	©	2 **Mosaique**		[F]	$10	Elektra Musician 60892
8/3/91	120	7		©	3 **Este Mundo**		[F]	$10	Elektra Musician 61179
					title is Spanish for "This World"				
4/22/95	105	22	▲	©	4 **The Best Of The Gipsy Kings**		[F-G]	$10	Nonesuch 79358
3/30/96	143	3		©	5 **Tierra Gitana**		[F]	$10	Nonesuch 79399
8/30/97	97	7		©	6 **Compas**		[F]	$10	Nonesuch 79466

A Mi Manera (My Way) (1)
A Ti A Ti (5)
A Tu Vera (4,5)
Ami Wa Wa (Solo Por Ti) (6)
Amor, Amor (1)
Amor Gitano (6)
Baila Me (3,4)
Bamboleo (1,4)
Bem, Bem, Maria (1,4)
Caminando Por La Calle (2)
Campesino (5)
Canto A Brazil (6)
Cataluna (5)
Di Me (6)
Djobi Djoba (1,4)
Duende (1)
El Camino (2)
El Mauro (3)
Escucha Me (4)
Este Mundo (3)
Estrellas (5)
Faena (1)
Furia (3)
Galaxia (4)
Habla Me (3)
Igual Se Entonces (5)
Inspiration (5)
La Dona (4)
La Fiesta Comenza (6)
La Rumba De Nicolas (5)
Lagrimas (3)
Liberte (2)
Lo Mal Y Lo Bien (6)
Los Peces En El Rio (5)
Love & Liberte (4)
Mi Corazon (5)
Mi Nino (6)
Mi Vida (3)
Mira La Itana Mora (6)
Montana (4)
Moorea (1,4)
Mosaique (2)
Mujer (5)
Nina Morena (2)
No Volvere (3)
Obsesion De Amor (6)
Oh Mai (3)
Oy (3)
Pajarito (5)
Passion (2)
Pida Me La (medley) (4)
Que Si Que No (Funiculi Funicula) (6)
Quiero Saber (1,4)
Recuerdo Apasionado (6)
Salsa De Noche (6)
Serana (2)
Siempre Acaba Tu Vida (5)
Sin Ella (3)
Soy (2)
Ternuras (3)
Tierra Gitana (5)
Trista Pena (2,4)
Tu Quieres Volver (1)
Un Amor (1,4)
Una Rumba Por Aqui (6)
Vamos A Bailar (2,4)
Viento Del Arena (4)
Volare (2,4)

GIRLSCHOOL '82
Female hard-rock group from England: Kelly Johnson and Kim McAuliffe (vocals, guitars), with Enid Williams (bass) and Denise Dufort (drums).

| 5/22/82 | 182 | 5 | | | **Hit And Run** .... | | | $12 | Stiff 18 |

C'mon Let's Go
Future Flash
Hit And Run
Hunter
Kick It Down
Not For Sale
Race With The Devil
Take It All Away
Watch Your Step
Yeah Right

GIUFFRIA '85
Rock group from California: Gregg Giuffria (keyboards; **Angel**), David Glen Eisley (vocals), Craig Goldy (guitar), Chuck Wright (bass) and Alan Krigger (drums). Lanny Cordola and David Sikes replaced Goldy and Wright in late 1985. Giuffria, Wright and Cordola joined **House Of Lords** in 1988.

| 12/8/84+ | 26 | 29 | | © | 1 **Giuffria** .... | | | $10 | MCA 5524 |
| 5/24/86 | 60 | 14 | | © | 2 **Silk + Steel** .... | | | $10 | MCA 5742 |

Awakening (1)
Call To The Heart (1) *15*
Change Of Heart (2)
Dance (1)
Dirty Secrets (2)
Do Me Right (1)
Don't Tear Me Down (1)
Girl (2)
Heartache (2)
I Must Be Dreaming (2) *52*
Lethal Lover (2)
Line Of Fire (1)
Lonely In Love (1) *57*
Love You Forever (1)
No Escape (2)
Out Of The Blue (Too Far Gone) (1)
Radio (2)
Tell It Like It Is (2)
Trouble Again (1)
Turn Me On (1)

GLASER, Tompall — see JENNINGS, Waylon

GLASS, Philip '86
Born on 1/31/37 in Baltimore. New Age composer.

| 4/10/82 | 121 | 6 | | | 1 **Glassworks** .... | | [I] | $10 | CBS 37265 |
| 4/12/86 | 91 | 13 | | | 2 **Songs From Liquid Days** .... | | | $10 | CBS 39564 |

Changing Opinion (2)
Facades (1)
Floe (1)
Forgetting (2)
Freezing (2)
Islands (1)
Lightning (2)
Liquid Days (Part I) (2)
Open The Kingdom (Liquid Days, Part II) (2)
Rubric (1)

GLASS HARP '71
Rock trio from Youngstown, Ohio: Phil Keaggy (vocals, guitar), Dan Pecchio (bass) and John Sferra (drums).

| 11/27/71 | 192 | 3 | | | **Synergy** .... | | | $25 | Decca 75306 |

Answer
Child Of The Universe
Coming Home
Dawn Of A New Day
Just Always
Mountains
Never Is A Long Time
One Day At A Time
Song Of Hope
Special Friends

GLASS MOON '80
Pop-rock group: Dave Adams (vocals, keyboards), Jaime Glaser (guitar), Nestor Nunez (bass) and Chris Jones (drums).

| 5/10/80 | 148 | 9 | | | **Glass Moon** .... | | | $12 | Radio 2003 |

Blue Windows
Dreamer
Easy Life
Follow Me
(I Like) The Way You Play
Killer At 25
Only Have To Cry One Time
Solsbury Hill
Sundays And Mondays

GLASS TIGER '87
Pop-rock group from Canada: Alan Frew (vocals), Al Connelly (guitar), Sam Reid (keyboards), Wayne Parker (bass) and Michael Hanson (drums).

| 7/19/86+ | 27 | 51 | ● | © | 1 **The Thin Red Line** .... | | | $10 | Manhattan 53032 |
| 5/7/88 | 82 | 15 | | © | 2 **Diamond Sun** .... | | | $10 | EMI-Manhattan 48684 |

Ancient Evenings (1)
Closer To You (1)
Diamond Sun (2)
Don't Forget Me (When I'm Gone) (1) *2*
Ecstacy (1)
Far Away From Here (2)
I Will Be There (1) *34*
I'm Still Searching (2) *31*
It's Love U Feel (2)
Lifetime Of Moments (2)
Looking At A Picture (1)
My Song (2)
Secret, The (1)
Send Your Love (2)
Someday (1) *7*
Suffer In Silence (2)
Thin Red Line (1)
This Island Earth (2)
Vanishing Tribe (1)
(Watching) Worlds Crumble (2)
You're What I Look For (1)

GLAZER, Tom, And The Do-Re-Mi Children's Chorus   '63
Born on 9/3/14 in Philadelphia. Folk singer. Hosted own ABC radio program (1945-47).

| 7/27/63 | **114** | 8 | | | **On Top Of Spaghetti** .... | | [N] | $20 | Kapp 3331 |

Barbers Anthem / Dance With A Dolly (With A / From The Halls Of Montezuma / **On Top Of Spaghetti 14** / Webfooted Friends
Battle Hymn Of The Children / Hole In Her Stocking) / (To The Shores Of P.T.A.) / Puff (The Magic Dragon) / When The Dust Mops Go
Capital Ship / Dunderbeck / Oh, How I Hate To Get Up In / There's A Hole In The Bottom / Rolling Along
The Morning / Of The Sea

GLEASON, Jackie   ★198★   '55
Born Herbert John Gleason on 2/26/16 in Brooklyn, New York. Died of cancer on 6/24/87 (age 71). Legendary movie and TV comedian. Father of actress Linda Miller. Grandfather of actor Jason Patric. His albums featured dreamy "mood music" played by studio orchestras, conducted by Gleason with trumpet solos by Bobby Hackett and Pee Wee Erwin; much of the music was written by Gleason.

1)Lonesome Echo 2)Romantic Jazz 3)Music To Remember Her

3/5/55	**5**	16		1	**Music To Remember Her**		[I]	$25	Capitol 570
					LP: Capitol W-570 (#5); EP: Capitol EBF-570 (#6)				
6/25/55	**❶²**	23	©	2	**Lonesome Echo**		[I]	$25	Capitol 627
					LP: Capitol W-627 (#1); EP: Capitol EAP-627 (#2)				
11/12/55	**2²**	11		3	**Romantic Jazz**		[I]	$25	Capitol 568
					LP: Capitol W-568 (#2); EP: Capitol EBF-568 (#6)				
1/28/56	**7**	7	©	4	**Music For Lovers Only/Music To Make You Misty**		[E-I]	$25	Capitol 475 [2]
					reissue of 2 albums: *Music For Lovers Only* (#1 for 23 weeks in 1953 on Capitol 352) and *Music To Make You Misty* (#2 in 1954 on Capitol 455)				
2/25/56	**8**	5		5	**Music To Change Her Mind**		[I]	$25	Capitol 632
6/9/56	**10**	10		6	**Night Winds**		[I]	$25	Capitol 717
12/8/56	**16**	3	©	7	Merry Christmas		[X-I]	$25	Capitol 758
					also see #19 below; Christmas charts: 25/'63, 70/'66, 32/'67				
8/26/57	**13**	2	●	8	Music For The Love Hours		[I]	$20	Capitol 816
9/9/57	**16**	10		9	Velvet Brass		[I]	$20	Capitol 859
12/9/57	**14**	4		10	Jackie Gleason presents "Oooo!"		[I]	$20	Capitol 905
8/10/63	**82**	5		11	Movie Themes - For Lovers Only		[I]	$20	Capitol 1877
12/7/63	**115**	8		12	Today's Romantic Hits/for lovers only		[I]	$20	Capitol 1978
6/6/64	**82**	10		13	Today's Romantic Hits/for lovers only, Vol. 2		[I]	$20	Capitol 2056
2/5/66	**141**	4		14	Silk 'N' Brass		[I]	$20	Capitol 2409
11/26/66	**71**	11		15	How Sweet It Is for lovers		[I]	$20	Capitol 2582
6/24/67	**200**	2		16	A Taste Of Brass for lovers only		[I]	$20	Capitol 2684
12/23/67	**37ˣ**	2	©	17	'Tis The Season		[X-I]	$20	Capitol 2791
					also see #19 below				
8/23/69	**192**	2		18	Close-Up		[E-I]	$20	Capitol 255 [2]
					reissue of *Music For Lovers Only* (see #4 above) and *Music, Martinis and Memories* (#1 in 1954 on Capitol 509)				
12/20/69	**13ˣ**	3		19	All I Want For Christmas		[X-I-R]	$20	Capitol 346 [2]
					reissue of albums #7 and #17 above; Christmas charts: 13/'69, 21/'70				

African Waltz (16) / All By Myself (5) / Alone (6) / Alone Together (4) / Am I Blue? (9) / Are You Lonesome Tonight (6) / Art Of Love (16) / As Long As He Needs Me (12) / Au Revoir (15) / Autumn Waltz (15) / Begin To Love (14) / Best Things In Life Are Free (3) / Beyond The Blue Horizon (10) / Blue Christmas (17,19) / Blue Velvet (13) / Body And Soul (4,18) / But Not For Me (4,9,18) / By The Beautiful Sea (9) / By The Fireside (7) / Call Me (16) / Call Me Irresponsible (11) / Cardinal, Theme From The (13) / Charade (13) / Charmaine (1) / Cherokee (Indian Love Song) (9) / Cherry (1) / Chinatown, My Chinatown (9) / Christmas In Paris (7) / Christmas Island (17,19) / Christmas Moon (17,19) / Christmas Song (Merry Christmas To You) (7,19) / Close As Pages In A Book (6) / Colette (1) / Come Rain Or Come Shine (2) / Coquette (7) / Crazy Rhythm (3) / Dancing In The Dark (5) / Dancing On The Ceiling (2) / Dancing With Tears In My Eyes (6)

Danke Schoen (12) / Darling, Je Vous Aime Beaucoup (2) / Darn That Dream (8) / Days Of Wine And Roses (11) / December (17,19) / Deep Purple (2,13) / Desafinado (12) / Diane (1) / Did I Remember (5) / Dinah (1) / Dr. Zhivago ..see: Lara's Theme / Don't Blame Me (3) / Everything's Coming Up Roses (14) / Fly Me To The Moon (12) / Fools Rush In (13) / For You (13) / From Russia With Love (13) / Garden In The Rain (2) / Get Out Of Town (8) / Girl From Ipanema (14) / Girl Of My Dreams (9) / Girls Of The Folies Bergere (14) / Good Life (12) / Good Night, Sweet Nightingale (6) / Guilty (5) / Happy Holiday (7,19) / Have You Heard (13) / Have Yourself A Merry Little Christmas (7,19) / Here Lies Love (10) / High On A Windy Hill (10) / Home (7) / Home In The Meadow (11) / House Is Haunted (By The Echo Of Your Last Goodbye) (8) / How About Me (10) / How About You? (3) / How Deep Is The Ocean (2)

How Did She Look (8) / How Sweet It Is (15) / I Apologize (6) / I Can't Believe That You're In Love With Me (9) / I Can't Get Started (18) / I Cover The Waterfront (18) / I Don't Know Why (I Just Do) (2) / I Don't Stand A Ghost Of A Chance With You (8) / I Got It Bad And That Ain't Good (18) / I Guess I'll Have To Change My Plan (4) / I Hadn't Anyone Till You (4) / I Left My Heart In San Francisco (12) / I Love You Much Too Much (8) / I Never Knew (3) / I Only Have Eyes For You (4,18) / I Remember You (18) / I Saw Mommy Kissing Santa Claus (17,19) / I Still Got A Thrill (2) / I Wanna Be Loved By You (15) / I Will Wait For You (15) / I Wished On The Moon (2) / I'll Be Around (10) / I'll Be Home For Christmas (If Only In My Dreams) (7,19) / I'm Always Chasing Rainbows (2) / I'm Glad There Is You (5) / I'm In The Mood For Love (4,18) / I've Got A Crush On You (10) / I've Got My Eyes On You (3) / I've Got My Love To Keep Me Warm (7,19) / I've Got You Under My Skin (8) / If He Walked Into My Life (15)

If I Had You (18) / If I Ruled The World (14) / If I Should Lose You (6) / Imagination (4) / It All Depends On You (4,16) / It Could Happen To You (18) / It Happened In Monterey (4) / It Was So Beautiful (5) / It's All Right With Me (10) / It's Christmas Time All Over The World (17,19) / It's Such A Happy Day (14) / It's The Talk Of The Town (5) / Jeannine, I Dream Of Lilac Time (1) / Jingle Bells (7,19) / Jo Anne (1) / Just A Memory (8) / La Dolce Vita (The Sweet Life) (11) / La Terre (The Earth) (16) / Lady Is A Tramp (3) / Lara's Theme (15) / Late In December (17) / Laura (1) / Lawrence Of Arabia (11) / Leaves Of Grass (14) / Let It Snow, Let It Snow, Let It Snow (17,19) / Little Girl (18) / Louise (1) / Love Is Here To Stay (4,16,18) / Love Letters In The Sand (6) / Love Locked Out (6) / Love Nest (3) / Love (Your Spell Is Everywhere) (1) / Mad About The Boy (2) / Make Someone Happy (12) / Mame (16) / Man I Love (4,9) / Man That Got Away (11)

Maria Elena (13) / Marie (1) / Marilyn (1) / Me And My Shadow (9) / Memories Of You (6) / Mickey (4) / Midnight Sun (12) / Misty (12) / Moonlight Becomes You (8) / More I See You (10) / More (Theme from Mondo Cane) (12) / Most Beautiful Girl In The World (3) / Mutiny On The Bounty (Follow Me), Love Theme From (11) / My Blue Heaven (3) / My Buddy (9) / My Devotion (10) / My Funny Valentine (4) / My Ideal (18) / My Love For Carmen (16,18) / My Romance (11) / My Sin (5) / Once In A While (18) / Out Of Nowhere (18) / Petite Waltz (2) / Real Live Girl (14) / Remember (2) / Rosanne (1) / Ruby (1) / Santa Claus Is Comin' To Town (7,19) / Say It Isn't So (4) / Second Time Around (15) / September Song (9) / Serenade In Blue (8) / Shadow Of Your Smile (15) / Shangri-La (14,18) / She's Funny That Way (5) / Since I Fell For You (13) / Skyliner (9)

Sleepy Time Gal (6) / Snowbound For Christmas (17,19) / Snowfall (7) / Some Day (3) / Somebody Else Is Taking My Place (4) / Someday I'll Find You (2) / Somewhere, My Love ..see: Lara's Theme / Song Is Ended (18) / Soon (3) / Speak Low (2) / Starry Eyed And Breathless (14) / Stella By Starlight (1) / Story Of A Starry Night (7,19) / Strangers In The Night (15) / Sweet Lorraine (1) / Sweet Sue Just You (1) / Take Me In Your Arms (9) / Take The "A" Train (9) / Tangerine (1) / Taras Bulba (The Wishing Star), Theme From (11) / Taste Of Honey (16) / That's What I Want For Christmas (17,19) / There I've Said It Again (13) / There Must Be A Way (2) / There'll Be Some Changes Made (3) / Third Man Theme (11) / Thousand Goodnights (6) / Thrill Is Gone (4) / Time On My Hands (18) / Touch Of Your Lips (6) / Unforgiven, Theme From The (12) / What Can I Say After I Say I'm Sorry (6) / What Kind Of Fool Am I? (12) / What's New? (9)

DEBUT	PEAK	WKS	RIAA	CD	ARTIST — Album Title	Catalog	Sym	$	Label & Number

GLEASON, Jackie — Cont'd

When You're Away (6)
White Christmas (7,19)
Who Cares? (So Long As You Care For Me) (3)
Willow Weep For Me (10)
Winter Wonderland (7,19)

World Is Waiting For The Sunrise (3)
Yesterdays (18)
You And The Night And The Music (5)
You Are Too Beautiful (6)

You Brought A New Kind Of Love To Me (10)
You Call It Madness (5)
You Can't Pull The Wool Over My Eyes (3)
You Hit The Spot (16)
You Were Meant For Me (4)

You're All I Want For Christmas (17,19)
You're All The World To Me (11)
You're Driving Me Crazy! (What Did I Do?) (9)

You're Gonna Hear From Me (15)
You're My Greatest Love (5)
You're Nobody Till Somebody Loves You (14)
You've Changed (5)

GLITTER, Gary   '72
Born Paul Gadd on 5/8/44 in Banbury, Oxfordshire, England. Glam-rock singer.

| 10/28/72 | 186 | 8 | | | Glitter.. | | | $15 | Bell 1108 |

Ain't That A Shame
Baby Please Don't Go
Clapping Song
Donna

Famous Instigator
I Didn't Know I Loved You (Till I Saw You Rock And Roll) *35*

Rock And Roll Part 1
Rock And Roll Part 2 *7*
Rock On

School Day (Ring! Ring! Goes The Bell)
Shakey Sue
Wanderer, The

GLOVER, Roger   '84
Born on 11/30/45 in Brecon, Powys, Wales. Rock singer/bassist. Member of **Deep Purple** and **Rainbow**.

| 1/24/76 | 142 | 8 | © | 1 | The Butterfly Ball and the Grasshopper's Feast .... | | | $15 | UK 56000 |
| 6/16/84 | 101 | 12 | | 2 | Mask .... | | | $12 | 21 Records 9009 |

Aranea (1)
Behind The Smile (1)
Dancin' Again (2)
Dawn (1)
Divided World (2)

Don't Look Down (2)
Dreams Of Sir Bedivere (1)
Fake It (2)
Feast (2)
Fly Away (1)

Get Ready (1)
Getting Stranger (2)
Harlequin Hare (1)
Hip Level (2)
Homeward (1)

Love Is All (1)
Magician Moth (1)
Mask (2)
No Solution (1)
Old Blind Mole (1)

Saffron Dormouse And Lizzy Bee (1)
Sir Maximus Mouse (1)
Sitting In A Dream (1)
Together Again (1)

Waiting (1)
Watch Out For The Bat (1)
(You're So) Remote (2)

GOANNA   '83
Rock group from Australia: Shane Howard (vocals), Warrick Harwood and Graham Davidge (guitars), Peter Coughlan (bass) and Robert Ross (drums).

| 6/25/83 | 179 | 5 | | | Spirit Of Place.. | | | $10 | Atco 90081 |

Borderline
Cheatin' Man
Children Of The Southern Land

Factory Man
Four Weeks Gone
On The Platform

Razor's Edge
Scenes (From An Occasional Window)

Solid Rock *71*
Stand Yr' Ground

GODFATHERS, The   '88
Rock group formed in London: brothers Peter (vocals) and Chris (bass) Coyne, Mike Gibson and Kris Dollimore (guitars), and George Mazur (drums).

| 2/20/88 | 91 | 16 | © | 1 | Birth, School, Work, Death .... | | | $10 | Epic 40946 |
| 5/20/89 | 174 | 6 | © | 2 | More Songs About Love & Hate .... | | | $10 | Epic 45023 |

Another You (2)
Birth, School, Work, Death (1)
'Cause I Said So (1)
Halfway Paralysed (2)

How Low Is Low (2)
I Don't Believe In You (2)
I'm Lost And Then I'm Found (2)

If I Only Had Time (1)
It's So Hard (1)
Just Like You (1)
Life Has Passed Us By (2)

Love Is Dead (1)
Obsession (1)
Pretty Girl (2)
S.T.B. (2)

She Gives Me Love (2)
Strangest Boy (1)
Tell Me Why (1)
This Is Your Life (2)

Those Days Are Over (2)
Walking Talking Johnny Cash Blues (2)
When Am I Coming Down (1)

GODFREY, Arthur — see QUINN, Carmel

GODHEAD   '01
Hard-rock group from Washington DC: Jason Miller (vocals, guitar), Mike Miller (guitar), Method (bass) and James O'Connor (drums).

| 2/10/01 | 153 | 1 | © | | 2000 Years Of Human Error .... | | | $10 | Posthuman 27289 |

Backstander
Break You Down

Eleanor Rigby
I Hate Today

I Sell Society
Inside You

Penetrate
Reckoning, The

Sinking
Tired Old Man

2000 Years Of Human Error

GODLEY & CREME   '85
Duo from Manchester, England: Kevin Godley (born on 10/7/45) and Lol Creme (born on 9/19/47). Both were members of Hotlegs and 10cc.

| 8/17/85 | 37 | 15 | © | | The History Mix Volume 1 .... | | | $10 | Polydor 825981 |

Cry *16*

Englishman In New York

Golden Boy

Light Me Up

Save A Mountain For Me

Wet Rubber Soup Medley

GOD LIVES UNDERWATER   '98
Techno-rock duo from Los Angeles: David Reilly and Jeff Turzo.

| 4/11/98 | 137 | 2 | © | | Life In The So-Called Space Age .... | | | $10 | A&M 540871 |

Alone Again
Behavior Modification
Can't Come Down

Dress Rehearsal For Reproduction
From Your Mouth

Happy?
Medicated To The One I Love

Rush Is Loud
Vapors

Rearrange

GODSMACK   '00
Hard-rock group from Methuen, Massachusetts: Sully Erna (vocals), Tony Rombola (guitar), Robbie Merrill (bass) and Tommy Stewart (drums).

| 1/23/99 | 22 | 92 | ▲³ © | 1 | Godsmack ....C:❶³/49 | | | $10 | Republic 53190 |
| 11/18/00 | 5 | 46↑ | ▲ © | 2 | Awake | | | $10 | Republic 159688 |

Awake (2)
Bad Magick (2)
Bad Religion (1)
Forgive Me (2)

Get Up, Get Out! (1)
Goin' Down (2)
Greed (2)
Immune (1)

Journey, The (2)
Keep Away (1)
Mistakes (2)
Moon Baby (1)

Now Or Never (1)
Sick Of Life (2)
Situation (1)
Someone In London (1)

Spiral (2)
Stress (1)
Time Bomb (1)
Trippin' (2)

Vampires (2)
Voodoo (2)
Whatever (1)

GOD'S PROPERTY   '97
Funk-rap-gospel collective of 50 young singers (ages 16-26) founded in Dallas by Linda Searight. Members of mentor **Kirk Franklin**'s Nu Nation.

| 6/14/97 | 3 | 54 | ▲² © | | God's Property | | | $10 | B-Rite 90093 |

Faith
He Will Take The Pain Away

It's Rainin'
Love

More Than I Can Bear
My Life Is In Your Hands

So Good
Stomp

Storm Is Over Now
Sweet Spirit

Up Above My Head
You Are The Only One

GODZ, The   '79
Rock group from Columbus, Ohio: Bob Hill and Mark Chatfield (guitars), Eric Moore (bass) and Glen Cataline (drums). All share vocals.

| 4/8/78 | 191 | 5 | | 1 | The Godz .... | | | $12 | Millennium 8003 |
| 2/17/79 | 189 | 2 | | 2 | Nothing Is Sacred .... | | | $12 | Casablanca 7134 |

Baby I Love You (1)
Candy's Going Bad (1)
Cross Country (1)

Festyvul Seasun (2)
Go Away (1)
Gotta Keep A Runnin' (1)

Gotta Muv (2)
Guaranteed (1)
He's A Fool (2)

Hey Mama (2)
I Don't Wanna Go Home (2)
I'll Bi Yer Luv (2)

Luv Kage (2)
Rock Yer Sox Auf (2)
714 (2)

Snakin' (2)
Under The Table (1)

GOFFIN, Louise '79

Born in New York City. Singer/songwriter. Daughter of one of pop music's most prolific songwriting teams, Gerry Goffin and **Carole King**.

| 8/4/79 | 87 | 13 | | | Kid Blue.. | | | $12 | Asylum 203 |

All I've Got To Do · Jimmy And The Tough Kids · Red Lite Fever · Singing Out Alone
Angels Ain't For Keeping · Kid Blue · **Remember (Walking In The** · Trapeze
Hurt By Love · Long Distance · **Sand)** *43*

GO-GO'S '82

Female rock group formed in Los Angeles: **Belinda Carlisle** (vocals), **Jane Wiedlin** (guitar), Charlotte Caffey (guitar), Kathy Valentine (bass) and Gina Schock (drums). Disbanded in 1984. Reunions in 1990, 1994 and 2001. Caffey formed **The Graces** in 1989.

8/1/81+	❶[6]	72	▲[2]	© 1	**Beauty And The Beat**			$10	I.R.S. 70021
8/14/82	8	28	●	© 2	**Vacation**	C:#28/36		$10	I.R.S. 70031
4/7/84	18	32		© 3	**Talk Show**			$10	I.R.S. 70041
11/17/90	127	4		© 4	**Greatest**		[G]	$10	I.R.S. 44797
6/2/01	57	3		© 5	**God Bless The Go-Go's**			$10	Beyond 578182

Apology (5) · Daisy Chain (5) · How Much More (1,4) · Lust To Love (1,4) · This Town (1,4) · We Don't Get Along (2)
Automatic (1) · Fading Fast (2) · I Think It's Me (2) · Mercenary (3,4) · Throw Me A Curve (5) · **We Got The Beat** (1,4) *2*
Automatic Rainy Day (5) · Forget That Day (3) · I'm The Only One (3,4) · **Our Lips Are Sealed** (1,4) *20* · Tonite (1) · Worlds Away (2)
Beatnik Beach (2,4) · **Get Up And Go** (2,4) *50* · I'm With You (3) · Skidmarks On My Heart (1) · **Turn To You** (3,4) *32* · **Yes Or No** (3) *84*
Beneath The Blue Sky (3) · Girl Of 100 Lists (2) · Insincere (5) · Sonic Superslide (5) · Unforgiven (5) · You Can't Walk In Your Sleep
Can't Stop The World (1) · He's So Strange (2) · It's Everything But Partytime (2) · Stuck In My Car (5) · **Vacation** (2,4) *8* · (If You Can't Sleep) (1)
Capture The Light (3) · Head Over Heels (3,4) *11* · Kissing Asphalt (5) · Talking Myself Down (5) · Vision Of Nowness (5) · You Thought (3,4)
Cool Jerk (2,4) · Here You Are (5) · La La Land (5) · This Old Feeling (2) · Way You Dance (2)

GOLD, Andrew '78

Born on 8/2/51 in Burbank, California. Son of soundtrack composer Ernest Gold and singer Marni Nixon. Member of pop duo **Wax** in 1986.

1/10/76	190	2		1	**Andrew Gold**			$12	Asylum 1047
5/7/77	95	16		2	**What's Wrong With This Picture?**			$12	Asylum 1086
2/25/78	81	14		3	**All This And Heaven Too**..			$12	Asylum 116

Always For You (3) · Go Back Home Again (2) · I'm Coming Home (1) · Must Be Crazy (2) · Passing Thing (2) · **Thank You For Being A**
Angel Woman (2) · Hang My Picture Straight (1) · I'm On My Way (3) · Never Let Her Slip Away · Resting In Your Arms (1) · **Friend** (3) *25*
Do Wah Diddy (2) · Heartaches In Heartaches (1) · Learning The Game (2) · (3) *67* · Stay (2) · **That's Why I Love You** (1) *68*
Endless Flight (1) · Hope You Feel Good (3) · **Lonely Boy** (2) *7* · Note From You (1) · Still You Linger On (3) · You're Free (3)
Firefly (2) · How Can This Be Love (3) · Looking For My Love (3) · Oh Urania (Take Me Away) (3) · Ten Years Behind Me (1)
Genevieve (3) · I'm A Gambler (1) · Love Hurts (1) · One Of Them Is Me (2)

GOLD, Marty '63

Born on 12/26/15 in New York City. Composer/conductor/pianist.

| 4/13/63 | 10 | 18 | | | **Soundpower!** | | [I] | $20 | RCA Victor 2620 |

Harlem Nocturne · I Left My Heart In San · Misty · Stella By Starlight · Till There Was You
I Concentrate On You · Francisco · Moon Was Yellow · String Of Pearls · Without A Song
· I'll Remember April · Shangri-La · Terry Theme From Limelight

GOLDDIGGERS, The '69

Female singing/dancing troupe from **Dean Martin**'s TV show: Pauline Antony, Wanda Bailey, Jackie Chidsey, Paula Cinko, Rosetta Cox, Michelle Fave, Tara Leigh, Susan Lund, Micki McGlone and Patricia Mickey.

| 8/2/69 | 142 | 7 | | | **The Golddiggers**.. | | | $15 | Metromedia 1009 |

Blame It On My Youth · Come Rain Or Come Shine · I Wanna Be Loved · Kumquat Tree · There's A Place For Lovers
Can't Take My Eyes Off Of You · (medley) · It Seems Like Yesterday · Montage From How Sweet It Is
(medley) · 59th Street Bridge Song (Feelin' · It's Fun To Be Young · One Person
· Groovy) · Just Another Old Time Movie · Shuffle Off To Buffalo

GOLDEN EARRING '74

Rock group formed in Amsterdam, Holland: Barry Hay (vocals), George Kooymans (guitar), Rinus Gerritsen (bass) and Cesar Zuiderwijk (drums).

5/4/74	12	29	●	© 1	**Moontan**			$15	Track 396
4/12/75	108	8		2	**Switch**...			$15	Track 2139
2/28/76	156	4		3	**To The Hilt**..			$12	MCA 2183
5/28/77	182	2		4	**Mad Love**..			$12	MCA 2254
12/11/82+	24	30		5	**Cut**			$10	21 Records 9004
3/17/84	107	9		6	**N.E.W.S.**			$10	21 Records 9008
11/24/84	158	6		7	**Something Heavy Going Down - Live From The Twilight Zone**		[L]	$10	21 Records 823717
7/12/86	196	2		© 8	**The Hole**			$10	21 Records 90514

Are You Receiving Me (1) · Facedancer (3) · Last Of The Mohicans (5) · Plus Minus Absurdio (2) · Time's Up (4)
Baby Dynamite (5) · Fightin' Windmills (4) · Latin Lightnin' (3) · Quiet Eyes (8) · To The Hilt (3)
Big Tree, Blue Sea (1) · Fist In Glove (6) · Lonesome D.J. (2) · **Radar Love** (1,7) *13* · Tons Of Time (2)
Bombay (4) · Future (5,7) · Long Blond Animal (7) · Save The Best For Later (8) · Troubles & Hassles (2)
Candy's Going Bad (1) *91* · Have A Heart (8) · Lost And Found (5) · Secrets (5) · **Twilight Zone** (5,7) *10*
Chargin' Up My Batteries (5) · I Need Love (4) · Love In Motion (8) · Shout In The Dark (8) · Vanilla Queen (1)
Clear Night Moonlight (6) · I'll Make It All Up To You (6) · Love Is A Rodeo (2) · Sleep Walkin' (3) · Violins (3)
Con Man (4) · It's Over Now (6) · Mad Love's Comin' (4) · Something Heavy Going Down · **When The Lady Smiles** (6) *76*
Daddy's Gonna Save My Soul · Jane Jane (8) · Mission Impossible (6,7) · (7) · Why Do I (8)
(2) · Jump And Run (8) · N.E.W.S. (6) · Sueleen (Sweden) (4) · Why Me? (3)
Devil Made Me Do It (5) *79* · Kill Me (Ce Soir) (2) · Switch (2)
Enough Is Enough (6,7) · They Dance (8)

GOLDEN GATE STRINGS '67

Studio group produced by Stu Phillips and conducted by Sid Feller. Phillips earlier conducted **The Hollyridge Strings**.

| 5/27/67 | 200 | 2 | | | **The Monkees Song Book** .... | | [I] | $15 | Epic 26248 |

Auntie Grizelda · (I'm Not Your) Steppin' Stone · Monkees, (Theme From) The · This Just Doesn't Seem To Be
I Wanna Be Free · Last Train To Clarksville · Saturday's Child · My Day
I'm A Believer · Mary, Mary · She

GOLDFINGER   '97
Rock group from Santa Monica, California: John Feldman (vocals, guitar), Charlie Paulson (guitar), Simon Williams (bass) and Darrin Pfeiffer (drums). Kelly LeMieux replaced Williams in 1999.

DEBUT	PEAK	WKS		CD	Title	$	Label & Number
5/11/96	110	14	©	1	Goldfinger	$10	Mojo 53007
9/27/97	85	4	©	2	Hang-Ups	$10	Mojo 53079
4/15/00	109	2	©	3	Stomping Ground	$10	Mojo 157531

Answers (1) · Anxiety (1) · Anything (1) · Authority (2) · Bro (2) · Carlita (2) · Carry On (3) · Chris Cayton (2) · City With Two Faces (1) · Counting The Days (3) · Disorder (2) · Don't Say Goodbye (3) · Donut Dan (3) · End Of The Day (3) · Forgiveness (3) · Get Away (3) · Here In Your Bedroom (1) · I Need To Know (2) · I'm Down (3) · If Only (2) · King For A Day (1) · Last Time (2) · Mable (1) · Margaret Ann (3) · Miles Away (1) · Minds Eye (1) · My Girlfriend's Shower Sucks (1) · My Head (2) · 99 Red Balloons (3) · Nothing To Prove (1) · Only A Day (1) · Pick A Fight (3) · Pictures (1) · Question (2) · S.M.P. (2) · San Simeon (3) · Stay (1) · Superman (2) · This Lonely Place (2) · Too Late (2) · 20¢ Goodbye (2) · You Think It's A Joke (3)

GOLDIE   '98
Born in 1964 in Wolverhampton, Warwickshire, England. Male techno performer.

DEBUT	PEAK	WKS		CD	Title	$	Label & Number
2/21/98	178	1	©		Saturnzreturn	$15	London 828983 [2]

Believe · Chico-Death Of A Rockstar · Crystal Clear · Demonz · Digital · Dragonfly · Fury-The Origin · I'll Be There For You · Letter Of Fate · Mother · Temper Temper · Truth

GOLDSBORO, Bobby   '68
Born on 1/18/41 in Marianna, Florida. Singer/songwriter/guitarist. Hosted own TV variety show from 1972-75.
1)Honey 2)Today 3)Bobby Goldsboro's Greatest Hits

DEBUT	PEAK	WKS	RIAA	CD	#	Title	Sym	$	Label & Number
5/6/67	165	3			1	Solid Goldsboro - Bobby Goldsboro's Greatest Hits	[G]	$20	United Artists 6561
4/20/68	5	48	●	©	2	**Honey**		$20	United Artists 6642
9/21/68	116	13			3	Word Pictures featuring Autumn Of My Life		$20	United Artists 6657
6/7/69	60	13			4	Today		$20	United Artists 6704
1/17/70	139	11			5	Muddy Mississippi Line		$20	United Artists 6735
7/4/70	103	10			6	Bobby Goldsboro's Greatest Hits	[G]	$20	United Artists 5502
1/23/71	120	13			7	We Gotta Start Lovin'		$15	United Artists 6777
						also released as *Watching Scotty Grow*			
8/28/71	142	5			8	Come Back Home		$15	United Artists 5516
9/29/73	150	11		©	9	Summer (The First Time)		$15	United Artists 124
11/16/74	174	3			10	Bobby Goldsboro's 10th Anniversary Album	[G]	$20	United Artists 311 [2]

About Time (7) · Ain't That Livin' (4) · **And I Love You So** (8) *83* · **Autumn Of My Life** (3,6,10) *19* · Beautiful People (2) · Brand New Kind Of Love (10) · **Broomstick Cowboy** (1,5,10) *53* · By The Time I Get To Phoenix (2) · **California Wine** (10) · **Can You Feel It** (6,10) *75* · **Come Back Home** (8,10) *69* · Danny (3) · Danny Is A Mirror To Me (8) · Dissatisfied Man (3) · Don't It Make You Wanta Go Home (5) · Down On The Bayou (7) · Everybody's Talkin' (5) · For The Very First Time (7) · Gentle Of A Man (8) · **Glad She's A Woman** (4,6) *61* · Gold Hill Hotel (8) · Graveyard Of My Mind (5) · Hard Luck Joe (3) · He Ain't Heavy, He's My Brother (7) · He's Part Of Us (9) · Heaven Here On Earth (7) · Hoboes And Kings (4) · **Honey** (2,6,10) *1* · I Am A Rock (3) · **I Know You Better Than That** (1) *56* · I'll Remember You (8) · **I'm A Drifter** (4,6,10) *46* · If You Go Away (Ne Me Quitte Pas) (3) · If You Got A Heart (1) · **If You Wait For Love** (1) *75* · **If You've Got A Heart** (10) *60* · If'n I Was God (9) · **It Hurts Me** (1) *70* · It's Gonna Change (7) · **It's Too Late** (1,6,10) *23* · It's Up To Us (8) · Jean (5) · Killing Me Softly With Her Song (9) · L&N Don't Stop Here Anymore (9) · Letter To Emily (3) · Lisa Was (5) · Little Green Apples (2) · **Little Things** (1,10) *13* · Lodi (5) · Look Around You (It's Christmas Time) (3) · Love Arrestor (2) · Maggie (3) · Marlena (9,10) · Mary Jackson (7) · **Me Japanese Boy I Love You** (1) *74* · Mississippi Delta Queen (9) · **Mornin Mornin** (5) *78* · **Muddy Mississippi Line** (5,6,10) *53* · My God And I (7) · Next Girl That I Marry (8) · Pardon Me Miss (2) · Pledge Of Love (2) · Poem For My Little Lady (8) · Proud Mary (5) · Requiem (7) · Richer Men Than I (4) · Run To Me (2) · Saturdays Only (8) · Say It's Not Over (4) · **See The Funny Little Clown** (1,6,10) *9* · She (9) · Sing Me A Smile (9) · Spread My Wings And Fly (9) · **Straight Life** (3,6,10) *36* · Summer (The First Time) (9,10) *21* · Sweet Caroline (5) · Throwback (8) · Time Good, Time Bad (5) · Today (4) · Tomorrow Is Forgotten (4) · **Voodoo Woman** (1,10) *27* · **Watching Scotty Grow** (7,10) *11* · Water Color Days (7) · We Gotta Start Lovin' (7) · What A Wonderful World (4) · **Whenever He Holds You** (1) *39* · **With Pen In Hand** (2,6,10) *94* · Woman (2) · Woman Without Love (4) · World Beyond (8) · World I Used To Know (4) · You're Here (4) · Your Song (8)

GOMM, Ian   '79
Born on 3/17/47 in Ealing, London, England. Pop-rock singer/songwriter/guitarist.

DEBUT	PEAK	WKS			Title	$	Label & Number
9/22/79	104	12			Gomm With The Wind	$12	Stiff 36103

Airplane · Another Year · Black And White · Chicken Run · Come On · Dirty Lies · **Hold On** *18* · Hooked On Love · Sad Affair · That's The Way I Rock 'N' Roll · 24 Hour Service · You Can't Do That

GONZALEZ   '79
Disco group from England featuring vocals by Linda Taylor and Alan Marshall.

DEBUT	PEAK	WKS			Title	$	Label & Number
1/20/79	67	14			Shipwrecked	$12	Capitol 11855

Baby, Baby, Baby · Bob Gropes Blues · **Haven't Stopped Dancing Yet** *26* · Just Let It Lay · Oh I · Rockmaninoff · Shipwrecked · Tear Down The Business

GOOD CHARLOTTE   '00
Rock group from New York City: Joel (vocals), Benji and Billy (guitars), Paul (bass) and Aaron (drums).

DEBUT	PEAK	WKS		CD	Title	$	Label & Number
10/14/00	185	2		©	Good Charlotte	$10	Daylight 61452

Change · Complicated · East Coast Anthem · Festival Song · I Don't Wanna Stop · I Heard You · Let Me Go · Little Things · Motivation Proclamation · Screamer · Seasons · Waldorfworldwide · Walk By

GOODIE MOB   '98
Male rap group from Atlanta: Cee-Lo, Khujo, T-Mo and Big Gipp.

DEBUT	PEAK	WKS	RIAA	CD	#	Title	$	Label & Number
11/25/95	45	29	●	©	1	Soul Food	$10	LaFace 26018
4/25/98	6	20	●	©	2	**Still Standing**	$10	LaFace 26047
1/8/00	48	12	●	©	3	World Party	$10	LaFace 26064

All A's (3) · Beautiful Skin (2) · **Black Ice (Sky High)** (2) *50* · **Cell Therapy** (1) *39* · Chain Swang (3) · Coming, The (1) · Cutty Buddy (3) · Damm, The (2) · Day After (1) · Dip, The (3) · **Dirty South** (1) *92* · Distant Wilderness (2) · Experience, The (3) · Fie Fie Delish (3) · Fighting (1) · Fly Away (2) · Free (1) · Get Rich To This (3) · Ghetto-ology (2) · Goodie Bag (1) · Greeny Green (2) · Guess Who (1) · Gutta Butta (2) · I Didn't Ask To Come (1) · I Refuse Limitation (2) · I.C.U. (3) · Inshallah (2) · Just About Over (2) · Just Do It (3) · Live At The O.M.N.I. (1) · Rebuilding (3) · See You When I See You (2) · Sesame Street (1) · **Soul Food** (1) *64* · Still Standing (2) · Street Corner (3) · They Don't Dance No Mo' (2) · Thought Process (1) · What It Ain't (Ghetto Enuff) (3) · World Party (3)

GOODMAN, Benny '56

Born on 5/30/09 in Chicago. Died of a heart attack on 6/13/86 (age 77). Nicknamed "The King of Swing." Legendary clarinetist/orchestra leader. Won Grammy's Lifetime Achievement Award in 1986.

3/19/55	7	16	©	1	**B.G. In Hi-Fi**		[I]	$30	Capitol 565

LP: Capitol W-565 (#7); EP: Capitol EAP-565 (#11)

3/24/56	4	10	©	2	**The Benny Goodman Story**		[I-S]	$40	Decca 8252/3 [2]
11/10/62	80	6		3	Benny Goodman In Moscow		[I-L]	$30	RCA Victor 6008 [2]
3/7/64	90	10	©	4	Together Again!		[I]	$20	RCA Victor 2698
4/3/71	189	7	©	5	Benny Goodman Today		[I-L]	$25	London Phase 4 21 [2]

recorded in Stockholm

Air Mail Special (1)
And The Angels Sing (2)
Avalon (2,3)
Baubles, Bangles And Beads (5)
Bei Mir Bist Du Schoen (3)
Big John's Special (1,5)
Blue Lou (1)
Blue Skies (5)
Body And Soul (3,5)
Bugle Call Rag (2)
Bye Bye Blackbird (3)
China Boy (1)
Dear Dave (5)
Dearest (4)
Don't Be That Way (2,5)
Down South Camp Meetin' (2)
Feathers (3)
Fontainebleau (3)
Four Once More (4)
Get Happy (1)
Goodbye (3,5)
Goody Goody (2)
I Got It Bad And That Ain't Good (3,4)
I Would Do Most Anything For You (5)
I'll Get By (4)
I've Found A New Baby (4)
If I Had You (5)
It's Been So Long (2)
Jersey Bounce (1,2)
Jumpin' At The Woodside (1)
King Porter Stomp (2)
Let's Dance (1,2,3,5)
Meadowland (3)
Meet The Band (3)
Memories Of You (2)
Midgets (3)
Mission To Moscow (3)
Moonglow (3)
On The Alamo (3)
One O'Clock Jump (2,3,5)
Poor Butterfly (5)
Rock Rimmon (1)
Roll 'Em (2,5)
Rose Room (medley) (3)
Runnin' Wild (4)
Say It Isn't So (4)
Sent For You Yesterday And Here You Come Today (1)
Seven Come Eleven (4)
Shine (2)
Sing, Sing, Sing (With A Swing) (2,5)
Slipped Disc (2)
Somebody Loves Me (4)
Somebody Stole My Gal (1)
Sometimes I'm Happy (2)
Stealin' Apples (3,5)
Stompin' At The Savoy (1,2)
String Of Pearls (3)
Sweet Georgia Brown (5)
Swift As The Wind (3)
Titter Pipes (3)
Venus H.B. (Turkish March) (5)
What Can I Say After I Say I'm Sorry? (1)
When I Grow Too Old To Dream (1)
Who Cares (4)
Why You? (3)
Willow Weep For Me (5)
World Is Waiting For The Sunrise (medley) (3)
You Brought A New Kind Of Love To Me (1)
You Turned The Tables On Me (2)
You're A Sweetheart (1)

GOODMAN, Dickie '76

Born Richard Goodman on 4/19/34 in Brooklyn, New York. Died of a self-inflicted gunshot on 11/6/89 (age 55). Goodman and partner Bill Buchanan originated the novelty "break-in" recordings featuring bits of the original versions of Top 40 hits interwoven throughout the recording. Buchanan died of cancer on 8/1/96 (age 66).

12/6/75+	144	8			Mr. Jaws and other Fables		[G-N]	$30	Cash 6000

includes "Super Fly Meets Shaft" (#31) by John & Ernest

Energy Crisis '74 *33*
Flying Saucer (Parts 1 & 2) *3*
Flying Saucer The 2nd *18*
Mr. Jaws *4*
Santa And The Satellite (Parts I & II) *32*
Touchables, The *60*
Touchables In Brooklyn *42*

GOODMAN, Jerry, & Jan Hammer '75

Jazz-rock duo. Violinist Goodman and keyboardist Hammer were formerly with **John McLaughlin**.

2/8/75	150	3			Like Children			$15	Nemperor 430

Country And Eastern Music
Earth (Still Our Only Home)
Full Moon Boogie
Giving In Gently (medley)
I Remember Me
I Wonder (medley)
Night
No Fear
Steppings Tones
Topeka

GOODMAN, Steve '75

Born on 7/25/48 in Chicago. Died of leukemia on 9/20/84 (age 36). Singer/songwriter/guitarist.

8/23/75	144	6		1	Jessie's Jig & Other Favorites			$15	Asylum 1037
5/15/76	175	4		2	Words We Can Dance To			$15	Asylum 1061

Banana Republics (2)
Between The Lines (2)
Blue Umbrella (1)
Can't Go Back (2)
Death Of A Salesman (2)
Door Number Three (1)
Glory Of Love (2)
I Can't Sleep (1)
It's A Sin To Tell A Lie (1)
Jessie's Jig (Rob's Romp, Beth's Bounce) (1)
Lookin' For Trouble (1)
Mama Don't Allow It (1)
Moby Book (1)
That's What Friends Are For (2)
Old Fashioned (2)
Roving Cowboy (Ballad Of Dan Moody) (2)
Spoon River (1)
This Hotel Room (1)
Tossin' And Turnin' (2)
Unemployed (2)

GOODMAN, Vestal '00

Born in Alabama. Mother of the Happy Goodman Family gospel group. Known as the "Queen of Gospel."

5/27/00	177	1	©		Vestal & Friends			$10	Pamplin 2058

Angel Band
Big Homecoming
Friends
Giver Of Life
Great Is Thy Faithfulness
He Touched Me
Jesus Made A Way
Oh, Happy Day
Satisfied
With You
You're Able

GOO GOO DOLLS '96

Rock trio from Buffalo, New York: Johnny Rzeznik (vocals, guitar), Robby Takac (bass) and Mike Malinin (drums).

9/9/95+	27	54	▲² ©	1	A Boy Named Goo			$10	Warner 45750
10/10/98	15	104	▲² ©	2	Dizzy Up The Girl		C:#20/7	$10	Warner 47058
6/16/01	164	1	©	3	What I Learned About Ego, Opinion, Art & Commerce (1987-2000)		[K]	$10	Warner 47945

Acoustic #3 (2,3)
Ain't That Unusual (1,3)
All Eyes On Me (2,3)
Amigone (2,3)
Another Second Time Around (3)
Black Balloon (2) *16*
Broadway (2) *24*
Bullet Proof (2,3)
Burnin' Up (1,3)
Cuz You're Gone (3)
Disconnected (3)
Dizzy (2)
Extra Pale (2)
Eyes Wide Open (1,3)
Fallin' Down (3)
Flat Top (1,3)
Full Forever (2)
Girl Right Next To Me (3)
Hate This Place (2)
I'm Addicted (3)
Impersonality (1)
Iris (3) *9*
January Friend (2)
Just The Way You Are (3)
Laughing (3)
Long Way Down (1)
Lucky Star (3)
Naked (1,3)
Name (1) *5*
On The Lie (3)
Only One (1)
Slave Girl (1)
Slide (2) *8*
So Long (1)
Somethin' Bad (1)
There You Are (3)
Two Days In February (3)
Up Yours (3)
We Are The Normal (3)

GOOSE CREEK SYMPHONY '72

Country rock group: Ritchie Hart (vocals, guitar), Paul Howard (guitar), Bob Henke (keyboards), Ellis Schweid (fiddle), Chris Mostert (sax), Dave Birkett (bass) and Dennis Kenmore (drums).

6/3/72	167	8	©		Words Of Earnest			$20	Capitol 11044

Broken Creek Goose Down
Gearheart And God
Gospel, The
Guitars Pickin', Fiddles Playin'
Me And Him
Rush On Love
(Oh Lord Won't You Buy Me A) Mercedes Benz *64*
Speakin' Of
Whupin' It
Words Of Earnest

GORDON, Nina '00

Born in Chicago. Female singer/songwriter/guitarist. Former member of **Veruca Salt**.

8/12/00	123	10	©		Tonight And The Rest Of My Life			$10	Warner 47746

Badway
End Of The World
Fade To Black
Got Me Down
Hate Your Way
Hold On To Me
Horses In The City
New Year's Eve
Now I Can Die
Number One Camera
Tonight And The Rest Of My Life
2003
Too Slow To Ride

GORDON, Robert '79

Born in 1947 in Washington DC. Rockabilly singer. Member of **Tuff Darts** until 1976.

10/1/77	142	8	©	1	Robert Gordon with Link Wray			$12	Private Stock 2030
3/18/78	124	7	©	2	Fresh Fish Special			$12	Private Stock 7008

above 2 feature guitarist **Link Wray**

GORDON, Robert — Cont'd

DEBUT	PEAK	WKS			Album Title			$	Label & Number
3/24/79	106	12	©	3	Rock Billy Boogie			$12	RCA Victor 3294
2/2/80	150	9	©	4	Bad Boy			$12	RCA Victor 3523
4/18/81	117	15	©	5	Are You Gonna Be The One			$12	RCA Victor 3773

All By Myself (3)
Am I Blue (3)
Are You Gonna Be The One (5)
Bad Boy (4)
Black Slacks (3)
Blue Christmas (3)
Blue Eyes (Don't Run Away) (2)
Boppin' The Blues (1)
Born To Lose (4)
But, But (5)

Catman, The (3)
Crazy Man Crazy (4)
Drivin' Wheel (5)
Fire (2)
Five Days, Five Days (2)
Flyin' Saucers Rock & Roll (1)
Fool (1)
I Just Found Out (3)
I Just Met A Memory (3)
I Sure Miss You (1)

I Want To Be Free (2)
If This Is Wrong (2)
Is It Wrong (For Loving You) (4)
Is This The Way (1)
It's In The Bottle (1)
It's Only Make Believe (3)
Lonesome Train (On A Lonesome Track) (2)
Look Who's Blue (5)
Love My Baby (3)

Lover Boy (5)
Need You (4)
Nervous (4)
Picture Of You (4)
Red Cadillac, And A Black Mustache (2)
Red Hot (1) *83*
Rock Billy Boogie (3)
Sea Cruise (2)
She's Not Mine Anymore (5)

Someday, Someway (5) *76*
Standing On The Outside Of Her Door (5)
Summertime Blues (1)
Sweet Love On My Mind (4)
Sweet Surrender (1)
Take Me Back (5)
Too Fast To Live, Too Young To Die (5)
Torture (4)

Twenty Flight Rock (2)
Uptown (4)
Walk On By (3)
Way I Walk (2)
Wheel Of Fortune (3)
Woman (You're My Woman) (1)
Worrying Kind (4)

GORE, Lesley '63

Born on 5/2/46 in New York City; raised in Tenafly, New Jersey. Pop singer. Appeared in the movies *Girls On The Beach*, *Ski Party* and *The T.A.M.I. Show*.

DEBUT	PEAK	WKS			Album Title			$	Label & Number
7/13/63	24	15	©	1	I'll Cry If I Want To			$40	Mercury 60805
1/25/64	125	8	©	2	Lesley Gore Sings Of Mixed-Up Hearts			$40	Mercury 60849
7/18/64	127	6		3	Boys, Boys, Boys			$40	Mercury 60901
12/12/64	146	2		4	Girl Talk			$40	Mercury 60943
7/17/65	95	24	©	5	The Golden Hits Of Lesley Gore	[G]		$40	Mercury 61024
12/4/65	120	4	©	6	My Town, My Guy & Me			$40	Mercury 61042
5/13/67	169	5		7	California Nights			$40	Mercury 61120

All Of My Life (5) *71*
Baby That's Me (6)
Bad (7)
Before And After (6)
Boys (3)
Bubble Broke (7)
California Nights (7) *16*
Cry (1)
Cry And You Cry Alone (1)
Cry Like A Baby (7)
Cry Me A River (1)
Danny (3)
Don't Call Me (3)
Fools Rush In (Where Angels Fear To Tread) (2)

Girl In Love (6)
Hey Now (4,5) *76*
I Died Inside (4)
I Don't Care (6)
I Don't Wanna Be A Loser (3,5) *37*
I Struck A Match (2)
I Understand (1)
I Would (1)
I'll Make It Up To You (3)
I'm Coolin', No Foolin' (3)
I'm Going Out (The Same Way I Came In) (7)
If That's The Way You Want It (2)
It's Gotta Be You (3)

It's Just About That Time (4)
It's My Party (1,5) *1*
Judy's Turn To Cry (1,5) *5*
Just Another Fool (6)
Just Let Me Cry (1,5)
Leave Me Alone (3)
Let Me Dream (6)
Lilacs And Violets (7)
Little Girl Go Home (4)
Live And Learn (4)
Look Of Love (4,5) *27*
Love Goes On Forever (7)
Maybe I Know (4,5) *14*
Maybe Now (7)
Misty (1)
Movin' Away (4)

My Foolish Heart (7)
My Town, My Guy And Me (6) *32*
No Matter What You Do (6)
No More Tears (1)
Off And Running (7)
Old Crowd (2)
Party's Over (1)
Run Bobby, Run (2)
She's A Fool (2,5) *5*
Something Wonderful (3)
Sometimes I Wish I Were A Boy (4) *86*
Sunshine, Lollipops And Rainbows (2,5) *13*

That's The Way Boys Are (3,5) *12*
That's The Way The Ball Bounces (3)
Things We Did Last Summer (6)
Time To Go (2)
Treat Me Like A Lady (7)
What Am I Gonna Do With You (6)
What Kind Of Fool Am I (1)
What's A Girl Supposed To Do (6)
Wonder Boy (4)
You Didn't Look 'Round (6)

You Don't Own Me (2,5) *2*
You Name It (3)
You've Come Back (4)
Young And Foolish (4)
Young Lover (2)

GORE, Martin L. '89

Born on 7/23/61 in Basildon, England. Member of **Depeche Mode**.

DEBUT	PEAK	WKS			Album Title		Sym	$	Label & Number
8/12/89	156	5	©		Counterfeit e.p.		[M]	$10	Sire 25980

Compulsion
Gone

In A Manner Of Speaking
Motherless Child

Never Turn Your Back On Mother Earth

Smile In The Crowd

GORKY PARK '89

Rock group from Russia: Nikolai Noskov (vocals), Alexei Belov and Jan Ianenkov (guitars), "Big" Sasha Minkov (bass) and "Little" Sasha Lvov (drums). Group named after a famous park in Moscow.

DEBUT	PEAK	WKS			Album Title			$	Label & Number
9/9/89	80	21	©		Gorky Park			$10	Mercury 838628

Bang
Child Of The Wind

Danger
Fortress

Hit Me With The News
My Generation

Peace In Our Time
Sometimes At Night

Try To Find Me *81*
Within Your Eyes

★293★ GORME, Eydie '57

Born on 8/16/31 in New York City. Vocalist with the big bands of Tommy Tucker and Tex Beneke in the late 1940s. Featured on **Steve Allen**'s *Tonight Show*. Married **Steve Lawrence** on 12/29/57.

1)Eydie Gorme 2)Eydie Swings The Blues 3)Eydie Gorme Vamps The Roaring 20's

DEBUT	PEAK	WKS			Album Title			$	Label & Number
5/6/57	14	10	©	1	Eydie Gorme			$30	ABC-Paramount 150
10/28/57	19	4	©	2	Eydie Swings The Blues			$30	ABC-Paramount 192
3/31/58	19	4		3	Eydie Gorme Vamps The Roaring 20's			$30	ABC-Paramount 218
11/3/58	20	1		4	Eydie In Love			$30	ABC-Paramount 246
4/6/63	22	22		5	Blame It On The Bossa Nova			$20	Columbia 2012 / 8812
2/15/64	143	3		6	Gorme Country Style			$20	Columbia 2120 / 8920
9/12/64	54	22		7	Amor	[F]		$20	Columbia 2203 / 9003
8/28/65	53	11		8	More Amor	[F]		$20	Columbia 2376 / 9176
6/4/66	22	37		9	Don't Go To Strangers			$20	Columbia 2476 / 9276
12/3/66	9ˣ	4		10	Navidad means Christmas	[X-F]		$20	Columbia 2557 / 9357
2/18/67	85	18		11	Softly, As I Leave You			$20	Columbia 2594 / 9394
5/20/67	136	6		12	Together On Broadway			$20	Columbia 2636 / 9436
					STEVE LAWRENCE & EYDIE GORME				
12/2/67+	148	9		13	Eydie Gorme's Greatest Hits	[G]		$20	Columbia 2764 / 9564
3/8/69	141	6		14	What It Was, Was Love			$15	RCA Victor 4115
5/10/69	188	3		15	Real True Lovin'			$15	RCA Victor 4107
					STEVE LAWRENCE & EYDIE GORME (above 2)				
3/7/70	105	12		16	Tonight I'll Say A Prayer			$15	RCA Victor 4303

After You've Gone (2)
Aguinaldo No. 1 (Christmas Gift) (10)
Alegre Navidad (Merry Christmas) (10)
All Alone (11)
Almost Like Being In Love (5)
Amor (7,13)
Back In Your Own Back Yard (3)

Be Careful, It's My Heart (1)
Blame It On The Bossa Nova (5,13) *7*
Blanca Navidad (White Christmas) (10)
Blues In The Night (2)
Boys And Girls (14)
Button Up Your Overcoat (3)
Cabaret (12)
Call Me (15)

Caminito (7)
Can't Help Lovin' Dat Man (2)
Can't Take My Eyes Off You (15)
Cancion Para Meditar (Song For Meditation) (10)
Chapter One (15)
Chicago (That Toddling Town) (3)

Coffee Song (They've Got An Awful Lot Of Coffee In Brazil) (5)
Come Back To Me (12)
Crazy (4)
Cuando Vuelva A Tu Lado (5)
Cuatro Vidas (Four Lives) (8)
Curtain Falls (12)
Dansero (5)
Day By Day (1)

Desafinado (Slightly Out Of Tune) (5)
Desesperadamente (Desperately) (8)
Di Que No Es Verdad (7)
Didn't We (16)
Don't Get Around Much Anymore (2)
Don't Go To Strangers (9,13)
Don't Worry 'Bout Me (11)

End Of The World (6)
Every Time We Say Goodbye (11)

GORME, Eydie — Cont'd

Felices Pascuas (A Happy Christmas) (10)
Fine And Dandy (1)
First Impression (1)
Flores Negras (Black Flowers) (8)
For All We Know (1)
Fuego Bajo Tu Piel (Fire Under Your Skin) (8)
Gentleman Is A Dope (1)
Gift! (Recado Bossa Nova) (5)
Glad To Be Unhappy (11)
Gloria A Dios En Las Alturas (Glory To God In The Highest) (10)
Gracias A Dios (Thank God) (10)
Guess I Should Have Loved Him More (11)
Guess Who I Saw Today (1)
Guitarra Romana (Roman Guitar) (8)
Gypsy In My Soul (1)
Happy Together (15)
Here I Am In Love Again (4)
Historia De Un Amor (7)
Honeymoon Is Over (12)
How About Me (9)
How Did He Look (9)
How Long Has This Been Going On (1)

I Believe In You (12)
I Can't Help It (If I'm Still In Love With You) (6)
I Can't Stop Loving You (6)
I Got It Bad And That Ain't Good (2)
I Gotta Right To Sing The Blues (2)
I Really Don't Want To Know (6)
I Remember You (5)
I Walk The Line (6)
I Wanna Be Around (4)
I Wanna Be Loved By You (3)
I Wish You Love (9,13)
I'll Be Around (9)
I'll Take Romance (1) **65**
I'm Sorry (6)
Idle Conversation (4)
If He Walked Into My Life (9,13)
Impossible (4)
In Love In Vain (4)
In Other Words (4)
In The Wee Small Hours Of The Morning (4)
It Could Happen To You (4)
It Takes A Fool Like Me (16)
It's Not Unusual (15)
Knowing When To Leave (16)
La Ultima Noche (7)
Let's Do It (Let's Fall In Love) (3)

Love Letters (4)
Luna Lunera (Bright Moon) (8)
Make The World Go Away (6)
Mala Noche (Evil Night) (8)
Mame (12)
Man, A (14)
Man I Love (2)
Mas Amor (More Love) (8,13)
Matchmaker (13)
Media Vuelta (7)
Melchor, Gaspar Y Baltazar (The Three Kings) (10)
Melodie D'Amour (5)
Message, The (5)
Moon River (5)
My Buddy (3)
My Mama Done 'Tol Me (2)
My Man (3)
Navidad Y Ano Nuevo (Christmas And The New Year) (10)
Never My Love (15)
Nice People (16)
Nightingale Can Sing The Blues (2)
No One To Cry To (6)
No Te Vayas Sin Mi (Don't Leave Without Me) (8)
Noche De Paz (Silent Night) (10)
Noche De Ronda (7)

Nochecita (Little Night) (8)
Nosotros (7)
Oh Lonesome Me (6)
Old Fashioned Wedding (12)
Old Man (14)
One Note Samba (5)
Oracion Caribe (Caribbean Prayer) (8)
Piel Canela (7)
Quiet Soul (16)
Real True Lovin' (15)
Romeo & Juliet, Love Theme From ..see: Time For Us
Room With The View Inside (14)
Sabor A Mi (7,13)
Saturday Night (Is The Loneliest Night Of The Week) (1)
Save The Last Dance For Me (15)
Secret Place (14)
Singin' In The Rain (2)
Softly, As I Leave You (11,13)
Someday (You'll Want Me To Want You) (16)
Stormy Weather (2)
Sunrise, Sunset (12)
Sweetest Sounds (5)
Tell Him I Said Hello (9)
There Goes The Bride (14)

This Is No Laughing Matter (1)
Time (16)
Time For Us (Love Theme from Romeo And Juliet) (16)
Tip Toe Through The Tulips With Me (3)
To Be In Love (14)
Together Forever (12)
Tonight I'll Say A Prayer (16) **45**
Too Close For Comfort (1) **39**
Toot Toot Tootsie, Goodbye (3)
Vereda Tropical (Tropical Trail) (7)
Walk On By (15)
Walking Happy (12)
We Had It All (14)
What Did I Have That I Don't Have? (9,13)
What Is A Woman? (11)
What It Was, Was Love (14)
What The World Needs Now (15)
What You Say (14)
What's Good About Goodbye? (11)
What's New (9)
When He Leaves You (9)
When I Fall In Love (4)

When The Red Red Robin Comes Bob Bob Bobbin' Along (3)
When The Sun Comes Out (2)
When The World Was Young (4)
When Your Lover Has Gone (2)
Who's Sorry Now (3)
Why Shouldn't I? (4)
Why Try To Change Me Now (4)
With A Little Help From My Friends (15)
Without You (16)
Y... (7)
Yeah, But What If? (14)
Yesterday, When I Was Young (16)
You Don't Know Me (6)
You Don't Know What Love Is (2)
You've Changed (11)
You've Made Me So Very Happy (16)

GOUDREAU, Barry   '80

Born on 11/29/51 in Lynn, Massachusetts. Rock guitarist. Member of **Boston**, **Orion The Hunter** and **RTZ**.

| 9/20/80 | 88 | 8 | © | | Barry Goudreau | | | $12 | Portrait 36542 |

Cold Cold World
Dreams

Hard Luck
Leavin' Tonight

Life Is What We Make It
Mean Woman Blues

Nothin' To Lose
Sailin' Away

What's A Fella To Do?

GOULD, Morton, and His Orchestra   '60

Born on 12/10/13 in Richmond Hill, New York. Died on 2/21/96 (age 82). Conductor/arranger.

| 11/9/59 | 5 | 52 | | 1 | Tchaikovsky: 1812 Overture/Ravel: Bolero | [I] | $25 | RCA Victor 2345 |
| 7/18/60 | 3 | 41 | | 2 | Grofe: Grand Canyon Suite/Beethoven: Wellington's Victory | [I] | $25 | RCA Victor 2433 |

Bolero (1)

Grand Canyon Suite (2)

Overture 1812, Op. 49 (1)

Wellington's Victory (2)

GOULET, Robert ★200★   '65

Born on 11/26/33 in Lawrence, Massachusetts. Singer/actor. Launched career as Sir Lancelot in the hit Broadway musical *Camelot*. Won the 1962 Best New Artist Grammy Award.

1)My Love Forgive Me 2)Sincerely Yours... 3)The Wonderful World Of Love

3/17/62+	43	65		1	Always You		$20	Columbia 1676 / 8476
9/1/62	20	55		2	Two Of Us		$20	Columbia 1826 / 8626
1/5/63	9	48	©	3	Sincerely Yours...		$20	Columbia 1931 / 8731
4/27/63	11	29		4	The Wonderful World Of Love		$20	Columbia 1993 / 8793
10/19/63	16	23		5	Robert Goulet In Person	[L]	$20	Columbia 2088 / 8888
					recorded at the Chicago Opera House			
11/30/63	4[X]	16	©	6	This Christmas I Spend With You	[X]	$20	Columbia 2076 / 8876
					Christmas charts: 4/'63, 5/'64, 17/'65, 90/'67, 30/'68			
5/2/64	31	22		7	Manhattan Tower/The Man Who Loves Manhattan		$20	Columbia 6050 / 2450
					composed and conducted by **Gordon Jenkins**			
10/17/64	72	16		8	Without You		$20	Columbia 2200 / 9000
12/26/64+	5	29	● ©	9	My Love Forgive Me		$20	Columbia 2296 / 9096
6/5/65	69	16		10	Begin To Love		$20	Columbia 2342 / 9142
8/14/65	31	19		11	Summer Sounds		$20	Columbia 2380 / 9180
12/11/65+	33	22		12	Robert Goulet On Broadway		$20	Columbia 2418 / 9218
4/30/66	73	12		13	I Remember You		$20	Columbia 2482 / 9282
3/11/67	145	3		14	Robert Goulet On Broadway, Volume 2		$15	Columbia 2586 / 9386
9/14/68	162	15		15	Woman, Woman		$15	Columbia 9695
4/12/69	135	13		16	Both Sides Now		$15	Columbia 9763
9/6/69	174	3		17	Souvenir d'Italie		$15	Columbia 9874
11/14/70	198	2		18	I Wish You Love	[K]	$20	Columbia 30011 [2]

All I Do Is Dream Of You (4,18)
All Of Me (4)
All Of You (2)
All Or Nothing At All (5)
Almost Like Being In Love (medley) (12)
Always You (1)
And This Is My Beloved (1)
Another Time, Another Place (3)
As Time Goes By (10,18)
Autumn In Rome (17)
Autumn Leaves (8)

Ave Maria (6)
Begin To Love (Cominciamo Ad Amarci) (10)
Blues Are Marching In (5)
Bon Soir Dame (16)
Both Sides Now (16)
Breeze And I (1)
But Beautiful (2)
By The Time I Get To Phoenix (15)
Cabaret (16)
Call Me Irresponsible (13,18)
Choose (9)

Christmas Song (Chestnuts Roasting On An Open Fire) (6)
Ciao Compare (14)
Come Back To Me (12)
Come Back To Sorrento (17)
Come Prima (17)
Concentrate On One Thing At A Time (5)
Core'Ngrato (17)
Cycles (16)
Dear Love (12)
December Time (6)

Didn't We (18)
Do It Again (11)
Do You Know The Way To San Jose (15)
Don't Blame Me (2)
Don't Worry 'Bout Me (8)
Ebb Tide (3)
Fall Of Love (10)
For Once In My Life (16)
Full Moon And Empty Arms (1)
Gigi (3,5)
Gone With The Wind (13)

Goodbye (2)
Have Yourself A Merry Little Christmas (6)
Hello, Dolly! (12)
Here (1)
Here In My Heart (16,18)
Here's That Rainy Day (2)
Honey (I Miss You) (15,18)
How Small We Are How Little We Know (16)
I Hadn't Anyone Till You (13)
I Never Got To Paris (10)
I Remember You (13)

I Talk To The Trees (3)
(I Wanna Go Where You Go, Do What You Do) Then I'll Be Happy (4)
I Wish You Love (Que Reste-t-il De Nos Amours?) (2,18)
I'll Be Seeing You (8)
I'll Catch The Sun (16)
I'll Get By (As Long As I Have You) (11)

GOULET, Robert — Cont'd

I'll Remember April (13)
I'll Take Romance (4)
I'm A Fool To Want You (8,18)
I've Got The World On A String (11)
If Ever I Would Leave You (5)
If I Ruled The World (12)
If She Walked Into My Life (If He Walked Into My Life) (14)
If You Are But A Dream (1)
If You Love Me (Really Love Me) (Hymne A L'Amour) (11)
Imagination (13)
Impossible Dream (The Quest) (14)
In The Still Of The Night (10)
It Had To Be You (medley) (5)
It's A Blue World (13)
It's All In The Game (1)
Just Say I Love Her (Dicitencello Vuie) (9,17,18)
La Strada (Gelsomina), Love Theme From (17)
Lamp Is Low (1)
Lazy River (medley) (5)
Learnin' My Latin (medley) (7)
Les Bicyclettes De Belsize (16)
Let It Snow! Let It Snow! Let It Snow! (6)

Life Is Just A Bowl Of Cherries (4)
Little White Lies (2)
Live For Life (15)
Long Ago (12)
Long Ago And Far Away (10)
Look For Small Pleasures (12)
Love In A Tower (Never Leave Me) (medley) (7)
Love Is Blue (15)
Lush Life (3)
Magical City (medley) (7)
Make Someone Happy (2)
Mala Femmina (17)
Mam'selle (11)
Mame (14)
Man Without Love (Quando M'Innamoro) (15)
Maria (3)
Married I Can Always Get (medley) (7)
Mean To Me (4)
Melinda (5)
Moon Was Yellow (3)
More I See Of Mimi (10)
My Cup Runneth Over (14)
My Ideal (13,18)
My Lady Won't Be Here Tonight (8)

My Love, Forgive Me (Amore, Scusami) (9) *16*
My Melancholy Baby (medley) (5)
Nearness Of You (3,18)
Never Leave Me (medley) (7)
New York's My Home (medley) (7)
Night Song (12)
Night They Raided Minsky's (Wait For Me), Love Theme From (16)
No Moon At All (4)
Non Dimenticar (17)
Now That It's Ended (medley) (7)
O Come All Ye Faithful (6)
O Holy Night (Cantique De Noel) (6)
Old Cape Cod (11)
Old Songs Are Really Like Old Friends (medley) (7)
On A Clear Day You Can See Forever (12,18)
Once Upon A Dream (medley) (7)
Once Upon A Summertime (La Valse Des Lilas) (11)
Once Upon A Time (18)
Out Of This World (4)
Panis Angelicus (6)
Party, The (medley) (7)

People (12)
Poinciana (Song Of The Tree) (3)
Quiet Nights Of Quiet Stars (Corcovado) (9)
Real Live Girl (10)
Repeat After Me (medley) (7)
S'posin' (4)
Sad Songs (8)
Shalom (11)
She Touched Me (12)
Silver Bells (6)
Skylark (13)
Smile (10)
Softly, As I Leave You (9)
Soliloquy (5)
Something's Gotta Give (2)
Somewhere, My Love (18)
Souvenir D'Italie (17)
Stella By Starlight (3)
Story Of A Starry Night (1)
Strange Music (1)
Summer Sounds (11) *58*
Summertime (11)
Sunny (15)
Sunrise, Sunset (12)
Take Me In Your Arms (3)
There But For You Go I (14)
These Foolish Things (Remind Me Of You) (13)

They Call The Wind Maria (medley) (5)
Things I Love (1)
Thirty Days Hath September (16)
This Christmas I Spend With You (6)
This Guy's In Love With You (15)
This Is All I Ask (5,9,18)
Those Were The Days (16)
Till (11)
Time After Time (10,18)
Time For Love (18)
Today (10)
Tonight (3)
Too Good (9)
Two Different Worlds (9)
Two Of Us (2)
Two People (3)
Unicorn (5)
Wake Up (5)
Walk Into The Dawn (11)
Walking Happy (14)
Welcome Home Angelina (9)
What A Wonderful World (15)
What Can You Do? (9)
What Is A Woman? (14)
What Kind Of Fool Am I? (5,9) *89*

What Now My Love (Et Maintenant) (11,18)
What's New? (8)
When Did I Fall In Love? (14)
When The Red, Red Robin Comes Bob, Bob, Bobbin' Along (medley) (5)
Where Are You? (8)
Where Do I Go From Here? (2)
Where Is The One (8)
White Christmas (6)
Who Can I Turn To (When Nobody Needs Me) (12,18)
Winter Wonderland (6)
With These Hands (10)
Without You (8)
Woman, Woman (15)
Wonderful World Of Love (4)
You Don't Have To Say You Love Me (Io Che Non Vivo [Senza Te]) (17)
You Stepped Out Of A Dream (3)
You're Breaking My Heart (1,18)
You're Nobody 'Till Somebody Loves You (4,18)
Young Only Yesterday (13)

GO WEST '85
Pop-rock duo from England: Peter Cox (vocals) and Richard Drummie (guitar, vocals).

DEBUT	PEAK	WKS	CD	#	Album Title	$	Label & Number
3/23/85	60	35	©	1	Go West	$10	Chrysalis 41495
8/22/87	172	9	©	2	Dancing On The Couch	$10	Chrysalis 41550
1/30/93	154	11	©	3	Indian Summer	$10	EMI 94230

Bluebeat (3)
Call Me (1) *54*
Chinese Whispers (2)
Count Me Out (3)
Crossfire (2)
Crystal Ball (3)

Dangerous (2)
Don't Look Down (1)
Don't Look Down - The Sequel (2) *39*
Eye To Eye (1) *73*
Faithful (3) *14*

Forget That Girl (3)
From Baltimore To Paris (2)
Goodbye Girl (1)
Haunted (1)
I Want To Hear It From You (2)
I Want You Back (3)

Innocence (1)
King Is Dead (2)
King Of Wishful Thinking (3) *8*
Little Caesar (1)
Masque Of Love (2)

Missing Persons (1)
S.O.S. (1)
Still In Love (3)
Sun And The Moon (3)
Taste Of Things To Come (3)
Tell Me (3)

That's What Love Can Do (3)
True Colours (2)
We Close Our Eyes (1) *41*
What You Won't Do For Love (3) *55*

GQ '79
Disco group from the Bronx, New York: Emmanuel LeBlanc (vocals, guitar), Herb Lane (keyboards), Keith Crier (bass) and Paul Service (drums).

DEBUT	PEAK	WKS	RIAA	#	Album Title	$	Label & Number
4/7/79	13	35	▲	1	Disco Nights	$12	Arista 4225
4/5/80	46	20		2	Two	$12	Arista 9511
11/14/81	140	8		3	Face To Face	$12	Arista 9547

Boogie Oogie Oogie (1)
Boogie Shoogie Feelin' (3)
Dark Side Of The Sun (3)
Disco Nights (Rock-Freak) (1) *12*

Don't Stop This Feeling (3)
Face To Face (3)
GQ Down (2)
I Do Love You (1) *20*
I Love (The Skin You're In) (3)

Is It Cool (2)
It's Like That (2)
It's Your Love (1)
Lies (2)
Make My Dream A Reality (1)

Reason For The Season (2)
Sad Girl (3) *93*
Shake (3)
Shy Baby (3)
Sitting In The Park (2)

Someday (In Your Life) (3)
Spirit (1)
Standing Ovation (2)
This Happy Feeling (1)
Wonderful (1)

You Put Some Love In My Life (3)
You've Got The Floor (3)

GRACES, The '89
Female vocal trio formed in Los Angeles: Charlotte Caffey (guitarist of the **Go-Go's**), **Meredith Brooks** and Gia Ciambotti.

DEBUT	PEAK	WKS	CD		Album Title	$	Label & Number
9/9/89	147	9	©		Perfect View	$10	A&M 5265

Fear No Love
50,000 Candles Burning

Lay Down Your Arms *56*
Out In These Fields

Perfect View
Should I Let You In

Time Waits For No One
Tomorrow

We Never Met
When The Sun Goes Down

★438★ GRAHAM, Larry/GRAHAM CENTRAL STATION '75
Born on 8/14/46 in Beaumont, Texas; raised in Oakland. R&B singer/bassist. Member of **Sly & The Family Stone** from 1966-72. Formed **Graham Central Station** in 1973: Hershall Kennedy and Robert Sam (keyboards), Willie Sparks and Patrice Banks (percussion), and David Vega (guitar). Graham went solo in 1980.

1)Ain't No 'Bout-A-Doubt It 2)One In A Million You 3)Mirror

GRAHAM CENTRAL STATION:

DEBUT	PEAK	WKS	RIAA	#	Album Title	$	Label & Number
2/9/74	48	26		1	Graham Central Station	$15	Warner 2763
10/5/74	51	18		2	Release Yourself	$15	Warner 2814
8/2/75	22	24	●	3	Ain't No 'Bout-A-Doubt It	$15	Warner 2876
6/26/76	46	16		4	Mirror	$15	Warner 2937
4/23/77	67	10		5	Now Do U Wanta Dance	$15	Warner 3041

LARRY GRAHAM & GRAHAM CENTRAL STATION:

7/1/78	105	11		6	My Radio Sure Sounds Good To Me	$12	Warner 3175
7/14/79	136	4		7	Star Walk	$12	Warner 3322

LARRY GRAHAM:

6/21/80	26	24	●	8	One In A Million You	$10	Warner 3447
8/8/81	46	13		9	Just Be My Lady	$10	Warner 3554
6/26/82	142	9		10	Sooner Or Later	$10	Warner 3668
7/30/83	173	4		11	Victory	$10	Warner 23878

Are You Happy? (6)
Baby (11)
Baby, You Are My Sunshine (9)
Boogie Witcha, Baby (6)
Can You Handle It? (1) *49*
Can't Nobody Take Your Place (9)

Crazy Chicken (5)
Do Yah (4)
Don't Stop When You're Hot (10)
Don't Think Too Long (11)
Earthquake (5)
Easy Love (10)

Easy Rider (3)
Entertainer, The (7)
Entrow (4)
Feel The Need (2)
Feels Like Love (9)
Forever (4)
Forever Yours (8)

G.C.S. (2)
Ghetto (1)
Got To Go Through It To Get To It (2)
Guess Who (9)
Hair (1)
Happ-E-2-C-U-A-Ginn (5)

Have Faith In Me (5)
Hey Mr. Writer (2)
Hold Up Your Hand (10)
I Believe In You (2)
I Can't Stand The Rain (3)
I Feel Good (10)
I Got A Reason (4)

I Just Can't Stop Dancing (8)
I Just Love You (9)
I Never Forgot Your Eyes (11)
I'd Rather Be Loving You (11)
I'm Sick And Tired (11)
I'm So Glad It's Summer Again (8)

GRAHAM, Larry/GRAHAM CENTRAL STATION — Cont'd

Is It Love? (6)
It Ain't No Fun To Me (1)
It Ain't Nothing But A Warner
  Brothers Party (3)
It's Alright (3) **92**
It's The Engine In Me (6)
Jam, The (3) **63**
Just Be My Lady (9) **67**
Just Call My Name (11)
Last Train (5)
Lead Me On (5)

Let Me Come Into Your Life
  (10)
Love And Happiness (5)
Love (Covers A Multitude Of
  Sin) (4)
Loving You Is Beautiful (9)
Luckiest People (3)
Mirror (4)
Movin' Inside Your Love (11)
Mr. Friend (6)
My Radio Sure Sounds Good
  To Me (6)

No Place Like Home (9)
Now Do-U-Wanta Dance (5)
Ole Smokey (3)
One In A Million You (8) **9**
Our Love Keeps Growing
  Strong (9)
People (1)
Pow (6)
Priscilla (4)
Release Yourself (2)
Remember When (9)
Save Me (4)

Saving My Love For You (5)
Scream (7)
Sneaky Freak (7)
Sooner Or Later (10)
Stand Up And Shout About
  Love (8)
Star Walk (7)
Still Thinkin' Of You (10)
Stomped Beat-Up And
  Whooped (3)
Sunshine, Love And Music (8)
Sweetheart (8)

Tell Me What It Is (1)
There's Something About You
  (8)
Time For You And Me (8)
'Tis Your Kind Of Music (2)
Today (2)
Tonight (7)
Turn It Out (6)
Victory (11)
Walk Baby Walk (10)
Water (7)
We Be's Gettin' Down (1)

We've Been Waiting (1)
When We Get Married (8) **76**
Why? (1)
(You're A) Foxy Lady (7)
You're My Girl (10)
You've Been (1)
Your Love (3) **38**

GRAMM, Lou '87

Born Lou Grammatico on 5/2/50 in Rochester, New York. Lead singer of **Foreigner**.

| 2/28/87 | 27 | 26 | | © | 1 Ready Or Not | | | $10 | Atlantic 81728 |
| 11/11/89+ | 85 | 23 | | © | 2 Long Hard Look | | | $10 | Atlantic 81915 |

Angel With A Dirty Face (2)
Arrow Thru Your Heart (1)
Broken Dreams (2)
Chain Of Love (1)

Day One (2)
Hangin' On My Hip (2)
Heartache (1)
I'll Come Running (2)

I'll Know When It's Over (2)
If I Don't Have You (1)
Just Between You And Me
  (2) **6**

Lover Come Back (1)
Midnight Blue (1) **5**
Ready Or Not (1) **54**
She's Got To Know (1)

Time (1)
Tin Soldier (2)
True Blue Love (2) **40**
Until I Make You Mine (1)

Warmest Rising Sun (2)

GRAND FUNK RAILROAD ★140★ '70

Hard-rock group formed in Flint, Michigan: Mark Farner (guitar), Mel Schacher (bass) and Don Brewer (drums). All share vocals. Brewer and Farner had been in **Terry Knight and The Pack**; Schacher was bassist with **? & The Mysterians**. Knight became producer/manager for Grand Funk, until his firing in March 1972. Craig Frost (keyboards) added in 1973. Disbanded in 1976. Re-formed in 1981, with Farner, Brewer and Dennis Bellinger (bass). Disbanded again shortly thereafter.

1)We're An American Band 2)Live Album 3)E Pluribus Funk

10/11/69	27	55	●	©	1 On Time			$15	Capitol 307
1/31/70	11	67	▲		2 Grand Funk			$15	Capitol 406
7/11/70	6	63	▲²	©	3 Closer To Home			$15	Capitol 471
12/5/70	5	62	▲²		4 Live Album	[L]		$20	Capitol 633 [2]
5/1/71	6	40	▲	©	5 Survival			$15	Capitol 764
12/4/71+	5	30	▲	©	6 E Pluribus Funk			$15	Capitol 853
5/13/72	17	27	●		7 Mark, Don & Mel 1969-71	[K]		$15	Capitol 11042 [2]
10/14/72	7	27	●	©	8 Phoenix			$15	Capitol 11099
8/18/73	2²	35	▲	©	9 We're An American Band			$15	Capitol 11207
3/30/74	5	29	●	©	10 Shinin' On			$15	Capitol 11278
12/21/74+	10	24	●	©	11 All The Girls In The World Beware!!!			$15	Capitol 11356

GRAND FUNK (above 3)

9/13/75	21	10		©	12 Caught In The Act	[L]		$20	Capitol 11445 [2]
1/31/76	47	11			13 Born To Die			$12	Capitol 11482
8/28/76	52	9		©	14 Good Singin' Good Playin'			$12	MCA 2216
11/20/76	126	5		©	15 Grand Funk Hits	[G]		$12	Capitol 11579
10/17/81	149	5			16 Grand Funk Lives			$12	Full Moon 3625
3/27/99	40ᶜ	1		©	17 Capitol Collectors Series	[G]		$10	Capitol 90608

Aimless Lady (3)
Ain't Got Nobody (9)
All The Girls In The World
  Beware (11)
All You've Got Is Money (5)
Anybody's Answer (1)
Bad Time (11,15,17) **4**
Big Buns (14)
Black Licorice (9,12)
Born To Die (13)
Call Yourself A Man (1)
Can You Do It (14) **48**
Can't Be Too Long (1)
Can't Be With You Tonight (16)
Carry Me Through (10)
Closer To Home (3,7,12,17) **22**
Comfort Me (5)
Country Road (5)
Creepin' (9)
Crossfire (14)

Don't Let 'Em Take Your Gun
  (14)
Dues (13)
Feelin' Alright (5,7,17) **54**
Flight Of The Phoenix (8)
Footstompin' Music
  (6,7,12,17) **29**
Freedom Is For Children (8)
Genevieve (13)
Get It Together (3)
Gettin' Over You (10)
Gimme Shelter (5,12,17) **61**
Goin' For The Pastor (14)
Good & Evil (11)
Good Things (13)
Good Times (16)
Got This Thing On The Move
  (2)
Gotta Find Me A Better Day (8)
Greed Of Man (16)
Heartbreaker (1,4,7,12,17) **72**

High Falootin' Woman (2)
High On A Horse (1)
Hooked On Love (3)
I Can Feel Him In The Morning
  (5)
I Come Tumblin' (6)
I Don't Have To Sing The Blues
  (3)
I Fell For Your Love (13)
I Just Gotta Know (8)
I Want Freedom (5)
I'm Your Captain ..see: Closer
  To Home
In Need (2,4)
Inside Looking Out
  (2,4,7,12,17)
Into The Sun (1,4,7)
Introduction (1)
Just Couldn't Wait (14)
Life (11)
Little Johnny Hooker (10)

Loco-Motion, The
  (10,12,15,17) **1**
Loneliest Rider (9)
Loneliness (6,7)
Look At Granny Run Run (11)
Love Is Dyin' (13)
Mark Say's Alright (4)
Mean Mistreater (3,4,7,17) **47**
Memories (11)
Miss My Baby (14)
Mr. Limousine Driver (2) **97**
Mr. Pretty Boy (10)
No Lies (6)
No Reason Why (16)
Nothing Is The Same (3)
Out To Get You (14)
Paranoid (2,4,7)
Pass It Around (14)
People, Let's Stop The War (6)
Please Don't Worry (2)

Please Me (10)
Politician (13)
Queen Bee (16)
Railroad, The (9,12)
Rain Keeps Fallin' (8)
Release Your Love (14)
Responsibility (11)
Rock 'N Roll Soul
  (8,12,15,17) **29**
Runnin' (11)
Sally (13,15) **69**
Save The Land (6)
She Got To Move Me (8)
Shinin' On (10,12,15,17) **11**
Sin's A Good Man's Brother (3)
So You Won't Have To Die (8)
Some Kind Of Wonderful
  (11,12,15,17) **3**
Someone (8)
Stop Lookin' Back (9)
Stuck In The Middle (16)

Take Me (13,15) **53**
Talk To The People (13)
Testify (16)
Time Machine (1,7,17) **48**
To Get Back In (10,15)
Trying To Get Away (8)
Ups And Downs (1)
Upsetter (6) **73**
Wait For Me (16)
Walk Like A Man (9,15,17) **19**
We Gotta Get Out Of This
  Place (16)
We're An American Band
  (9,12,15,17) **1**
Wild (11)
Winter And My Soul (2)
Words Of Wisdom (4)
Y.O.U. (16)

GRANDMASTER FLASH & THE FURIOUS FIVE '82

Born Joseph Saddler in Barbados; raised in the Bronx, New York. Pioneer rap DJ/producer. The Furious Five consisted of Melvin "Grandmaster Melle Mel" Glover, Nathaniel Glover, Guy WIlliams, Keith Wiggins and Eddie Morris. Wiggins died on 9/8/89 (age 28).

10/16/82	53	24			1 The Message			$12	SugarHill 268
5/17/86	145	6			2 The Source			$10	Elektra 60476
4/25/87	197	1		©	3 Ba-Dop-Boom-Bang			$10	Elektra 60723

GRANDMASTER FLASH (above 2)

| 4/30/88 | 189 | 3 | | © | 4 On The Strength | | | $10 | Elektra 60769 |

Ain't We Funkin' Now (3)
All Wrapped Up (3)
Behind Closed Doors (2)
Big Black Caddy (3)
Boy Is Dope (4)
Bus Dis (Wooo) (4)
Cold In Effect (4)
Dreamin' (1)
Fastest Man Alive (2)

Fly Life (4)
Freelance (3)
Get Yours (3)
Gold (4)
House That Rocked (3)
I Am Somebody (3)
It's A Shame (Mt. Airy Groove)
  (1)
It's Nasty (2)

Kid Named Flash (3)
King, The (4)
Larry's Dance Theme (Part 2)
  (2)
Leave Here (4)
Lies (2)
Magic Carpet Ride (4)
Message, The (1) **62**
Ms. Thang (2)

On The Strength (4)
P.L.U. (Peace, Love And Unity)
  (4)
Scorpio (1)
She's Fresh (1)
Street Scene (2)
Style (Peter Gunn Theme) (2)
Tear The Roof Off (3)
Them Jeans (3)

This Is Where You Got It From
  (4)
Throwin' Down (2)
U Know What Time It Is (3)
Underarms (3)
We Will Rock You (3)
Yo Baby (4)
You Are (1)

GRAND PUBA '92

Born Maxwell Dixon on 3/4/66 in the Bronx; raised in New Rochelle, New York. Male rapper. Former member of **Brand Nubian**.

11/7/92	28	14		© 1	Reel To Reel			$10	Elektra 61314
7/8/95	48	8		© 2	2000			$10	Elektra 61619

Amazing (2)
Baby What's Your Name? (1)
Back It Up (1)
Back Stabbers (2)
Big Kids Don't Play (1)

Change Gonna Come (2)
Check It Out (1)
Check Tha Resume (1)
Don't Waste My Time (2)
Honey Don't Front (1)

I Like It (I Wanna Be Where You Are) (2) 91
Keep On (2)
Lickshot (1)
Little Of This (2)

Play It Cool (2)
Playin The Game (2)
Proper Education (1)
Reel To Reel (1)
Soul Controller (1)

That's How We Move It (1)
360° (What Goes Around) (1) 68
2000 (2)
Very Special (2)

Who Makes The Loot? (1)
Ya Know How It Goes (1)

★322★ GRANT, Amy '92

Born on 11/25/60 in Augusta, Georgia. Pop singer/songwriter. Began career as a top Christian singer. Married to **Gary Chapman** from 1982-99. Married **Vince Gill** on 3/10/2000.

1)Home For Christmas 2)Behind The Eyes 3)Heart In Motion

4/20/85	133	20	● © 1	Straight Ahead			$10	A&M 5058
6/15/85	35	38	▲ © 2	Unguarded			$10	A&M 5060
12/21/85+	5ˣ	23	▲ © 3	A Christmas Album	C:#5/20 [X]		$10	A&M 5057

Christmas charts: 9/'85, 12/'87, 13/'88, 25/'89, 5/'91, 16/'92, 28/'93, 37/'94

9/20/86+	66	33	▲ © 4	Amy Grant - The Collection		[G]	$10	A&M 3900
7/23/88	71	13	● © 5	Lead Me On			$10	A&M 5199
3/23/91	10	105	▲5 © 6	Heart In Motion			$10	A&M 5321
10/24/92	2¹	14	▲3 © 7	Home For Christmas	C:#3/45 [X]		$10	A&M 540001

Christmas charts: 1/'92, 6/'93, 7/'94, 8/'95, 13/'96, 13/'97, 18/'98

9/10/94	13	52	▲2 © 8	House Of Love	C:#13/5		$10	A&M 540230
9/27/97	8	24	● © 9	Behind The Eyes			$10	A&M 540760
11/6/99	36	12	● © 10	A Christmas To Remember	C:#10/8 [X]		$10	A&M 490462

Christmas charts: 3/'99, 9/'00

Agnus Dei (10)
All Right (5)
Angels (1,4)
Angels We Have Heard On High (medley) (3)
Ask Me (6)
Baby Baby (6) 1
Big Yellow Taxi (8) 67
Breath Of Heaven (Mary's Song) (7)
Children Of The World (8)
Christmas Can't Be Very Far Away (10)
Christmas Hymn (3)
Christmas Lullaby (I Will Lead You Home) (10)
Christmas Song (Chestnuts) (3)
Christmas To Remember (10)
Cry A River (9)
Curious Thing (9)

Doubly Good To You (1)
El Shaddai (4)
Emmanuel (3,4)
Emmanuel, God With Us (3)
Every Heartbeat (6) 2
Every Road (9)
Everywhere I Go (2,4)
Faithless Heart (5)
Father's Eyes (4)
Feeling I Had (9)
Fight (2)
Find A Way (2,4) 29
For Unto Us A Child Is Born (medley) (7)
Gabriel's Oboe (10)
Galileo (6)
Good For Me (6) 8
Grown-Up Christmas List (7)
Hark! The Herald Angels Sing (3)

Hats (6)
Have Yourself A Merry Little Christmas (7)
Heirlooms (3)
Helping Hand (8)
Highland Cathedral (10)
Hope Set High (6)
House Of Love (8) 37
How Can We See That Far (6)
I Love You (2)
I Will Be Your Friend (9)
I Will Remember You (6) 20
I'll Be Home For Christmas (7)
If These Walls Could Speak (5)
It's Not A Song (1)
It's The Most Wonderful Time Of The Year (7)
Jehovah (1)
Jesu, Joy Of Man's Desiring (7)
Jingle Bell Rock (10)

Joy To The World (medley) (7)
Lead Me On (5) 96
Leave It All Behind (9)
Like I Love You (9)
Little Town (3)
Love Can Do (4)
Love Has A Hold On Me (8)
Love Has Come (3)
Love Of Another Kind (2)
Lucky One (8) 18
Mighty Fortress (medley) (3)
Missing You (9)
Mister Santa (10)
Night Before Christmas (7)
1974 (5)
Nobody Home (9)
Now And The Not Yet (1)
O' Come All Ye Faithful (7)
Oh How The Years Go By (8)
Open Arms (1)

Our Love (8)
Power, The (8)
Preiset Dem Konig! (Praise The King) (3)
Prodigal, The (2)
Rockin' Around The Christmas Tree (7)
Saved By Love (5)
Say Once More (5)
Say You'll Be Mine (8)
Shadows (5)
Sharayah (2)
Silent Night (10)
Sing Your Praise To The Lord (4)
Sleigh Ride (3)
Somewhere Down The Road (9)
Stay For Awhile (4)
Stepping In Your Shoes (2)

Straight Ahead (1)
Sure Enough (5)
Takes A Little Time (9)
Tennessee Christmas (3)
That's What Love Is For (6) 7
Thy Word (1,4)
'Til The Season Comes 'Round Again (10)
Tomorrow (1)
Turn This World Around (9)
Welcome To Our World (10)
What About The Love (5)
Whatever It Takes (8)
Where Do You Hide Your Heart (1)
Who To Listen To (2)
Winter Wonderland (7)
Wise Up (2) 66
You're Not Alone (6)

GRANT, Earl '61

Born on 1/2/31 in Idabelle, Oklahoma. Died in a car crash on 6/10/70 (age 39). Singer/songwriter/pianist.

8/21/61	7	45	● © 1	Ebb Tide		[I]	$20	Decca 74165
4/7/62	17	32	2	Beyond The Reef		[I]	$20	Decca 74231
12/1/62	92	10	3	Earl Grant At Basin Street East		[L]	$20	Decca 74299
				recorded in New York City				
1/4/64	139	5	4	Fly Me To The Moon		[I]	$20	Decca 74454
7/11/64	149	2	5	Just For A Thrill		[I]	$20	Decca 74506
5/15/65	143	4	6	Trade Winds		[I]	$20	Decca 74623
12/17/66+	14ˣ	11	7	Winter Wonderland		[X-I]	$20	Decca 74677

Christmas charts: 35/'66, 16/'67, 16/'68, 14/'69

3/23/68	192	2	8	Gently Swingin'		[I]	$20	Decca 74937

Alfie (8)
Angel Eyes (2)
Because Of Rain (3)
Bewitched (1)
Beyond The Reef (2)
Blue Velvet (5)
Breeze And I (4)
Canadian Sunset (1)
Carol Of The Drum (7)
(Carol's Theme) The Eyes Of Love (8)
Christmas Song (Merry Christmas To You) (7)
Climb Ev'ry Mountain (2)
Count Your Blessings Instead Of Sheep (3)
Days Of Wine And Roses (5)
Deep Purple (1)
Don't Sleep In The Subway (8)

Dreamy (1)
Ebb Tide (1)
El Cid, Love Theme From (4)
Eternally (6)
Evening Rain (1) 63
Exodus, Theme From (1)
Fever (3)
Fly Me To The Moon (In Other Words) (4)
Girl From Ipanema (Garota De Ipanema) (5)
Goin' Out Of My Head (8)
Gotta Be This Or That (3)
Hallelujah, I Love Her So (3)
Hava Nagillah (3)
High And The Mighty (4)
How Are Things In Glocca Morra (1)
How High The Moon (6)

I Miss You So (4)
I'll Build A Stairway To Paradise (3)
I'll Never Smile Again (5)
I'm In The Mood For Love (1)
I've Got My Love To Keep Me Warm (7)
It Came Upon The Midnight Clear (7)
Jingle Bells (7)
Just For A Thrill (5)
Learnin' The Blues (3)
Let It Be Me (8)
Londonderry Air (1)
Make Someone Happy (2)
Meditation (Meditacao) (6)
Misty (1)
Mood Indigo (2)
Moon Of Manakoora (6)

Moon River (3)
More (4)
My Foolish Heart (1)
Off Shore (4)
One Note Samba (8)
Over The Rainbow (4)
Quiet Village (6)
Release Me (8)
Ruby (6)
Rudolph The Red-Nosed Reindeer (7)
Santa Claus Is Comin' Town (7)
Satin Doll (5)
Second Time Around (2)
Silent Night (7)
Silver Bells (7)
Snowfall (4)

Someone To Watch Over Me (5)
Something You Got (8)
Spring Is Here (4)
Star Dust (5)
Stella By Starlight (4)
Stormy Weather (Keeps Rainin' All The Time) (1)
Street Of Dreams (6)
Sukiyaki (4)
Summertime In Venice (6)
Sunny (8)
Sweet Leilani (6)
Sweet Sixteen Bars (3) 55
Sweetest Sounds (5)
Swingin' Gently (2) 44
Tender Is The Night (2)
That's All (1)

That's Life (8)
Too Close For Comfort (3)
Trade Winds (6)
Very Thought Of You (2)
Walk On By (8)
When My Sugar Walks Down The Street (3)
When Sunny Gets Blue (2)
Where Are You (5)
White Christmas (7)
Willow Weep For Me (7)
Winter Wonderland (7)
Without A Song (5)
Yellow Bird (2)
You Stepped Out Of A Dream (5)

GRANT, Eddy '83

Born Edmond Grant on 3/5/48 in Plaisance, Guyana; raised in London. Rock-reggae singer. Member of The Equals.

4/23/83	10	30	● © 1	Killer On The Rampage			$10	Portrait 38554
6/23/84	64	17	2	Going For Broke			$10	Portrait 39261

Another Revolutionary (1)
Blue Wave (2)
Boys In The Street (2)
Come On Let Me Love You (2)

Drop Baby Drop (1)
Electric Avenue (1) 2
Funky Rock 'N' Roll (1)
I Don't Wanna Dance (1) 53

Ire Harry (2)
It's All In You (1)
Killer On The Rampage (1)
Latin Love Affair (1)

Only Heaven Knows (2)
Political Bassa-Bassa (2)
Rock You Good (2)
Romancing The Stone (2) 26

Telepathy (2)
Till I Can't Take Love No More (2)
Too Young To Fall (1)

War Party (1)

345

GRAPPELLI, Stephane '81

Born on 1/26/08 in Paris. Died on 12/1/97 (age 89). Jazz violinist.

6/6/81	108	10		©	Live..		[I-L]	$12	Warner 3550

STEPHANE GRAPPELLI/DAVID GRISMAN
recorded on 9/20/79 at the Berklee Center in Boston

| Fisztorza (medley) | Misty | Satin Doll | Sweet Georgia Brown | Tiger Rag |
| Fulginiti (medley) | Pent-Up House | Shine | Swing '42 | Tzigani (medley) |

GRASS ROOTS, The '69

Pop-rock group formed in San Francisco: Rob Grill (vocals, bass), Warren Entner and Creed Bratton (guitars), and Rick Coonce (drums). New lineup in 1971 included Grill, Entner, Reed Kailing and Virgil Webber (guitars), and Joel Larson (drums).

8/19/67	75	15		©	1 Let's Live For Today			$25	Dunhill 50020
11/23/68+	25	43	●		2 Golden Grass		[G]	$20	Dunhill/ABC 50047
3/29/69	73	16			3 Lovin' Things			$20	Dunhill/ABC 50052
12/6/69	36	21			4 Leaving It All Behind			$20	Dunhill/ABC 50067
10/24/70+	152	27			5 More Golden Grass		[G]	$20	Dunhill/ABC 50087
10/2/71	58	20	●		6 Their 16 Greatest Hits		[G]	$20	Dunhill/ABC 50107
6/24/72	86	14			7 Move Along			$20	Dunhill/ABC 50112

Anyway The Wind Blows (7)	Feelings (2,6)	I'd Wait A Million Years (4,5,6) 15	Monday Love (7)	Someone To Love (7)	Wake Up, Wake Up (1,2) 68
Baby Hold On (5,6) *35*	Fly Me To Havanna (3)	I'm Livin' For You Girl (4)	Move Along (7)	Something's Comin' Over Me (4)	**Walking Through The Country** (4,5,6) *44*
Baby, You Do It So Well (3)	Get It Together (5)	Is It Any Wonder (1)	No Exit (1)	**Sooner Or Later** (6) *9*	What Love Is Made Of (3)
Back To Dreamin' Again (4)	**Glory Bound** (7) *34*	Keepin' Me Down (5)	One Word (7)	Take Him While You Can (4)	**Where Were You When I Needed You** (1,2,6) *28*
Beatin' Round The Bush (1)	**Heaven Knows** (4,5,6) *24*	Lady Pleasure (2)	Only One (7)	**Temptation Eyes** (5,6) *15*	
Bella Linda (2,6) *28*	Here's Where You Belong (2)	Let It Go (5)	Out Of This World (4)	**Things I Should Have Said** (1,2,6) *23*	Won't You See Me (1)
City Women (3)	Hot Bright Lights (2)	**Let's Live For Today** (1,2,6) *8*	Out Of Touch (1)	This Precious Time (1)	(You Gotta) Live For Love (3)
Come On And Say It (5,6) *61*	House Of Stone (1)	**Lovin' Things** (3,5,6) *49*	Pain (3)	Tip Of My Tongue (1)	
Days Of Pearly Spencer (3)	I Can Turn Off The Rain (5,6)	Melinda Love (4)	**River Is Wide** (3,5,6) *31*	Truck Drivin' Man (4)	
Don't Remind Me (4)	I Can't Help But Wonder, Elisabeth (3)	Melody For You (2)	Runnin' Just To Get Her Home Again (7)	**Two Divided By Love** (7) *16*	
Face The Music (7)	I Get So Excited (3)	**Midnight Confessions** (2,6) *5*	Runway (7) *39*		

GRATEFUL DEAD ★41★ '87

Legendary rock group formed in San Francisco: **Jerry Garcia** (vocals, guitar), **Bob Weir** (vocals, guitar), Ron "Pigpen" McKernan (organ, harmonica), Phil Lesh (bass) and Bill Kreutzmann (drums). **Mickey Hart** (2nd drummer) and Tom Constanten (keyboards) added in 1968. Constanten left in 1970; Hart in 1971. Keith Godchaux (piano) and his wife Donna (vocals) joined in 1972. Pigpen died of liver failure on 3/8/73 (age 27). Hart returned in 1975. Brent Mydland (keyboards) added in 1979, replacing Keith and Donna Godchaux. Mydland was a member of **Silver**. Keith Godchaux died in a motorcycle crash on 7/23/80 (age 32). Weir and Mydland also recorded as **Bobby & The Midnites**. Mydland died of a drug overdose on 7/26/90 (age 37); **Bruce Hornsby** then took over keyboards on tour until **Tubes** keyboardist Vince Welnick joined band. Garcia died of a heart attack on 8/9/95 (age 53). Incessant touring band with faithful followers known as "Deadheads." Weir, Lesh, Hart and Hornsby formed **The Other Ones**. Inducted into the Rock and Roll Hall of Fame in 1994.

1)In The Dark 2)Blues For Allah 3)Grateful Dead From The Mars Hotel 4)Wake Of The Flood 5)Go To Heaven

5/6/67	73	28	●	©	1 The Grateful Dead			$80	Warner 1689
8/31/68	87	17		©	2 Anthem Of The Sun			$40	Warner 1749
6/21/69	73	11	●	©	3 Aoxomoxoa			$40	Warner 1790
1/3/70	64	15		©	4 Live/Dead		[L]	$50	Warner 1830 [2]
6/27/70	27	26	▲	©	5 Workingman's Dead	C:#35/1		$40	Warner 1869
10/31/70	127	10			6 Vintage Dead		[E-L]	$40	Sunflower 5001
					recorded in 1966 at the Avalon Ballroom in San Francisco				
12/12/70+	30	19	▲²	©	7 American Beauty	C:#6/8		$40	Warner 1893
6/26/71	154	7			8 Historic Dead		[E-L]	$40	Sunflower 5004
					more recordings from 1966				
10/16/71	25	12		©	9 Grateful Dead	C:#21/4	[L]	$50	Warner 1935 [2]
12/2/72+	24	24	▲²	©	10 Europe '72		[L]	$50	Warner 2668 [3]
7/28/73	60	11		©	11 History Of The Grateful Dead, Vol. 1 (Bear's Choice)		[L]	$30	Warner 2721
					recorded February 1970 at the Fillmore East in New York City				
10/27/73	18	19		©	12 Wake Of The Flood			$25	Grateful Dead 01
3/9/74	75	10	▲³	©	13 The Best Of/Skeletons From The Closet	C:❶³/205	[G]	$25	Warner 2764
7/13/74	16	20		©	14 Grateful Dead From The Mars Hotel			$25	Grateful Dead 102
9/6/75	12	13		©	15 Blues For Allah			$25	Grateful Dead 494
7/4/76	56	9		©	16 Steal Your Face		[L]	$30	Grateful Dead 620 [2]
					recorded October 1974 at Winterland in San Francisco				
8/20/77	28	16	●	©	17 Terrapin Station			$15	Arista 7001
11/12/77	121	8	▲	©	18 What A Long Strange Trip It's Been: The Best Of The Grateful Dead	C:#40/1	[G]	$20	Warner 3091 [2]
12/9/78+	41	19	●	©	19 Shakedown Street			$15	Arista 4198
5/17/80	23	21		©	20 Go To Heaven			$15	Arista 9508
4/18/81	43	16		©	21 Reckoning		[L]	$20	Arista 8604 [2]
9/19/81	29	11		©	22 Dead Set		[L]	$20	Arista 8606 [2]
7/25/87	6	34	▲²	©	23 In The Dark	C:#22/5		$10	Arista 8452
2/18/89	37	11	●	©	24 Dylan & The Dead		[L]	$10	Columbia 45056
					BOB DYLAN & GRATEFUL DEAD				
11/18/89	27	15	●	©	25 Built To Last			$10	Arista 8575
10/13/90	43	12	●	©	26 Without A Net	C:#41/1	[L]	$15	Arista 8634 [2]
5/11/91	106	2		©	27 One From The Vault		[E-L]	$10	Grateful Dead 40132
					recorded on 8/13/75 at the Great American Music Hall in San Francisco				
5/30/92	119	3		©	28 Two From The Vault		[E-L]	$15	Grateful Dead 40162 [2]
					recorded on 8/23/68 at the Shrine Auditorium in Los Angeles				
10/14/95	26	13	●	©	29 Hundred Year Hall		[E-L]	$15	Grateful Dead 40202 [2]
					recorded on 4/26/72 in Frankfurt, Germany				
11/2/96	95	2		©	30 The Arista Years		[G]	$15	Arista 18934 [2]
11/16/96	74	4	●	©	31 Dozin' At The Knick		[L]	$25	Arista 4025 [3]
					recorded on 3/25/90 at the Knickerbocker Arena in Albany, New York				

DEBUT	PEAK	WKS	RIAA	CD	ARTIST — Album Title	Catalog	Sym	$	Label & Number

GRATEFUL DEAD — Cont'd

7/5/97	83	3		© 32	**Fallout From The Phil Zone**		[K-L]	$15	Grateful Dead 4052 [2]
					recorded from 1967-1995				
11/15/97	77	2		© 33	**Fillmore East 2-11-69**..		[E-L]	$15	Grateful Dead 4054 [2]
11/27/99	170	1	●	© 34	**So Many Roads (1965-1995)**		[K-L]	$50	Grateful Dead 14066 [5]
10/28/00	165	2		© 35	**Ladies And Gentlemen...Filmore East: New York City: April 1971** ...		[E-L]	$40	Grateful Dead 14075 [4]

Ain't It Crazy (The Rub) (35)
Alabama Getaway (20,30) **68**
All Along The Watchtower (24,31)
Alligator (2,35)
Althea (20,26)
And We Bid You Goodnight (4,31)
Antwerp's Placebo (The Plumber) (20)
Around And Around (16,27,31)
Attics Of My Life (7)
Beat It On Down The Line (1,16,35)
Beautiful Jam (34)
Been All Around This World (21)
Believe It Or Not (34)
Bertha (9,29,35)
Big Boss Man (9)
Big Railroad Blues (9,29)
Big River (16,27)
Bird Song (21,26,34,35)
Black Muddy River (23,30)
Black Peter (5,11,18,31)
Black-Throated Wind (16)
Blow Away (25,31)
Blues For Allah (15,27)
Born Cross-Eyed (2,18)
Box Of Rain (7,32)
Brokedown Palace (7,22,31)
Brown-Eyed Woman (10,18)
Built To Last (25,30)
Can't Come Down (34)
Candyman (7,22)
Casey Jones (5,13,16,35)
Cassidy (21,26,30,34)
Caution (Do Not Stop On Tracks) (2,33,34)
China Cat Sunflower (3,10,26,29,34,35)
China Doll (14,21)
Chinatown Shuffle (34)
Clementine (34)
Cold Rain And Snow (1,16,35)

Comes A Time (29)
Cosmic Charlie (3,18)
Crazy Fingers (15,27)
Cream Puff War (1,34)
Cryptical Envelopment (29,33)
Cumberland Blues (5,10,18,35)
Dancing In The Street (6,17,32)
Dark Hollow (11,21,35)
Dark Star (4,18,28,33,34,35)
Days Between (34)
Deal (22)
Dear Mr. Fantasy (26)
Death Don't Have No Mercy (4,28,34)
Deep Elem Blues (21)
Dire Wolf (5,21,30)
Doin' That Rag (3,18,33)
Don't Ease Me In (20)
Drums (27,31,33,35)
Dupree's Diamond Blues (3,31,33)
Easy To Love You (20)
Easy Wind (5,32)
El Paso (16,35)
Eleven, The (4,28,33,34)
Epilogue (10)
Estimated Prophet (17,30,34)
Eternity (34)
Eyes Of The World (12,26,27,30,34)
Far From Me (20,30)
Feedback (4,33)
Feel Like A Stranger (20,22,26,30)
Fire On The Mountain (19,22,30,34)
Foolish Heart (25,30)
France (19)
Franklin's Tower (15,22,26,27,30)
Friend Of The Devil (7,13,22)
From The Heart Of Me (19)
Gentlemen, Start Your Engines (34)

Goin' Down The Road Feeling Bad (9,27,29,31,35)
Golden Road (To Unlimited Devotion) (1,13)
Good Lovin' (19,30,35)
Good Morning, Little School Girl (1,8,28,33)
Gotta Serve Somebody (24)
Greatest Story Ever Told (24)
Hard To Handle (11,32,35)
He's Gone (10)
Hell In A Bucket (23,30,31)
Help On The Way (15,26,27)
Here Comes Sunshine (12)
Hey Jude (33)
Hey Pocky Way (34)
High Time (5,18)
Hurts Me Too (10)
I Know You Rider (6,10,26,29,34,35)
I Need A Miracle (19,30)
I Want You (24)
I Will Take You Home (25,31)
I'm A King Bee (33,35)
I've Been All Around This World (11)
If I Had The World To Give (19)
In The Midnight Hour (6,32,35)
Introduction (27)
It Hurts Me Too (6,35)
It Must Have Been The Roses (16,21,27)
It's All Over Now Baby Blue (6)
Jack-A-Roe (21,31,32)
Jack Straw (10,18,29)
Jam (35)
Jam Into Days Between (34)
Jam Out Of Foolish Heart (34)
Jam Out Of Terrapin (34)
Joey (24)
Johnny B. Goode (9)
Just A Little Light (25,30,31)
Katie Mae (11)
King Solomon's Marbles (15,27)

Knockin' On Heaven's Door (24)
Lady With A Fan (31)
Lazy River Road (34)
Let It Grow (26)
Let Me Sing Your Blues Away (12)
Liberty (34)
Lindy (8)
Little Red Rooster (22)
Looks Like Rain (26)
Loose Lucy (14)
Loser (22,35)
Lost Sailor (20)
Mama Tried (9)
Mason's Children (32,34)
Me & Bobby McGee (9,35)
Me & My Uncle (9,18,29,35)
Mexicali Blues (13)
Mississippi Half-Step Uptown Toodeloo (12,16,26)
Money Money (14)
Monkey And The Engineer (21)
Morning Dew (1,10,28,35)
Mountains Of The Moon (3,33)
Mr. Charlie (10)
Mud Love Buddy Jam (31)
Music Never Stopped (15,27,32,34) **81**
Never Trust A Woman (31)
New, New Minglewood Blues (1,18,19,22,35)
New Potato Caboose (2,28)
New Speedway Boogie (5,18,32)
Next Time You See Me (29,35)
Not Fade Away (9,31,35)
Oh Babe It Ain't No Lie (21)
On The Road Again (21,34)
One More Saturday Night (10,13,26,29)
Operator (7)
Other One (9,27,28,33)
Passenger (17,22,30)

Picasso Moon (25,30)
Playing In The Band (9,18,29,31,34)
Prelude (10)
Pride Of Cucamonga (14)
Promised Land (16)
Queen Jane Approximately (24)
Race Is On (21)
Ramble On Rose (10,18)
Rhythm Devils (22)
Ripple (7,18,21,35)
Rosalie McFall (21)
Rosemary (3,13)
Row Jimmy (12,31)
Sage & Spirit (15,27)
Saint Of Circumstance (20,30)
Same Thing (8,34)
Samson & Delilah (17,22,30)
Sand Castles & Glass Camels (15)
Scarlet Begonias (14,34)
Second That Emotion (15)
Serengetti (19)
Shakedown Street (19,30,34)
Ship Of Fools (14,16)
Sing Me Back Home (34,35)
Sitting On Top Of The World (1)
Slipknot! (15,26)
Slow Train (34)
Smokestack Lightnin (11)
So Many Roads (1,18,19,22,35)
Space (22,31)
Spanish Jam (medley) (34)
St. Stephen (3,4,13,18,28,33,35)
Stagger Lee (19)
Standing On The Moon (25,30)
Stealin' (8)
Stella Blue (12,16,31,34)
Stronger Than Dirt Or Milkin' The Turkey (15)
Sugar Magnolia (7,10,13,29,35) **91**
Sugaree (16,27)

Sunrise (17)
Tennessee Jed (10,18)
Terrapin Station (17,30,31,34)
That's It For The Other One Medley (2,34)
Throwing Stones (23,30)
Till The Morning Comes (7)
To Lay Me Down (21,34)
Tons Of Steel (23)
Touch Of Grey (23,30) **9**
Truckin' (7,10,13,18,29,35) **64**
Turn On Your Love Light (4,13,28,29,33,35)
U.S. Blues (14,16,27,34)
Unbroken Chain (14)
Uncle John's Band (5,13,31,35) **69**
Unusual Occurances In The Desert (15)
Victim Or The Crime (25,26)
Viola Lee Blues (1,32)
Visions Of Johanna (32)
Wake Up Little Susie (11)
(Walk Me Out In The) ..see: Morning Dew
Walkin' Blues (26,31)
Watkins Glen Soundcheck Jam (34)
Way To Go Home (34)
We Bid You Goodnight (33,35)
Weather Report Suite Medley (12)
West L.A. Fadeaway (23,30)
Wharf Rat (9,35)
What's Become Of The Baby (3)
Wheel, The (31,34)
When I Paint My Masterpiece (31)
When Push Comes To Shove (23)
Whiskey In The Jar (34)
You Don't Have To Ask (34)
You Win Again (10)

GRAVEDIGGAZ '97

Male rap group: Robert "**RZA**" Diggs (of **Wu-Tang Clan**), Anthony Berkeley, Paul Huston and Arnold Hamilton. Berkeley died of cancer on 7/15/2001 (age 35).

8/27/94	36	11		© 1	**6 Feet Deep**		$10	Gee Street 524016
11/1/97	20	6		© 2	**The Pick, The Sickle And The Shovel**		$10	Gee Street 32501

Bang Your Head (1)
Blood Brothers (1)
Constant Elevation (1)
Da Bomb (2)

Dangerous Mindz (2)

Deadliest Biz (1)
Deathtrap (1)
Defective Trip (Trippin') (1)
Diary Of A Madman (1) **82**
Elimination Process (2)
Fairytalez (2)

Graveyard Chamber (1)
Here Comes The Gravediggaz (1)
Hidden Emotions (2)
Mommy, What's A Gravediggaz? (1)
Never Gonna Come Back (2)

Night The Earth Cried (2)
Nowhere To Run, Nowhere To Hide (1)
1-800 Suicide (1)
Pit Of Snakes (2)
Repentance Day (2)

6 Feet Deep (1)
360 Questions (1)
Twelve Jewelz (2)
2 Cups Of Blood (1)
Unexplained (2)
What's Goin' On (2)

GRAVITY KILLS '96

Techno-rock group from Jefferson City, Missouri: Jeff Scheel (vocals), Matt Dudenhoeffer (guitar), Douglas Firley (keyboards) and Kurt Kerns (bass, drums).

3/23/96	89	25		© 1	**Gravity Kills**		$10	TVT 5910
6/27/98	107	4		© 2	**Perversion**..		$10	TVT 5920

Alive (2)
Always (2)
Belief (To Rust) (2)
Blame (1)

Crashing (2)
Disintegrate (2)
Down (1)
Drown (2)

Enough (1)
Falling (2)
Forward (1)
Goodbye (1)

Guilty (1) **86**
Here (1)
Hold (1)
If (2)

Inside (1)
Last (1)
Never (1)
One (2)

Wanted (2)

GRAY, David '01

Born in 1968 in Manchester, England; raised in Solva, Wales. Rock singer/songwriter/guitarist.

9/2/00+	35	57↑▲	© 1	**White Ladder**			$10	ATO 69351
5/5/01	153	3	© 2	**Lost Songs 95-98**		[E]	$10	ATO 69375

As I'm Leaving (2)
Babylon (1) **57**
Babylon II (1)
Clean Pair Of Eyes (2)

Falling Down the Mountainside (2)
Flame Turns Blue (2)
Hold On (2)

If Your Love Is Real (2)
January Rain (1)
My Oh My (1)
Nightblindness (1)

Please Forgive Me (1)
Red Moon (2)
Sail Away (1)
Say Hello Wave Goodbye (1)

Silver Lining (1)
This Year's Love (1)
Tidal Wave (2)
Twilight (1)

We're Not Right (1)
White Ladder (1)
Wurlitzer (2)

GRAY, Dobie '73

Born Lawrence Darrow Brown on 7/26/40 in Brookshire, Texas. Singer/songwriter. Acted in the Los Angeles production of *Hair*.

3/10/73	64	21		1	**Drift Away**		$15	Decca 75397
11/10/73	188	3		2	**Loving Arms**		$15	MCA 371
2/17/79	174	4		3	**Midnight Diamond**...		$12	Infinity 9001

Caddo Queen (1)
City Stars (1)
Drift Away (1) **5**
Eddie's Song (1)
Good Old Song (2)
I Can See Clearly Now (3)

I Never Had It So Good (2)
I'll Be Your Hold Me Tight (3)
L.A. Lady (1)
Lay Back (1)
Let This Man Take Hold Of Your Life (3)

Love Is On The Line (2)
Lovin' The Easy Way (2)
Loving Arms (2) **61**
Miss You Nights (2)
Mississippi Rolling Stone (2)
Now That I'm Without You (1)

Reachin' For The Feeling (2)
Rockin' Chair (1)
Rose (2)
Sharing The Night Together (3)
Sweet Lovin' Woman (1)
Thank You For Tonight (2)

There's A Honky Tonk Angel (Who'll Take Me Back In) (2)
Time I Love You The Most (1)
We Had It All (1)
We've Got To Get It On Again (3)
Weekend Friend (3)

Who's Lovin' You (3)
You And Me (2)
You Can Do It (3) **37**

GRAY, Glen, & The Casa Loma Orchestra　　'57

Born Glen Gray Knoblaugh on 6/7/06 in Metamora, Illinois. Died on 8/23/63 (age 57). Alto saxophonist/bandleader. Formed the Casa Loma Orchestra in 1927.

DEBUT	PEAK	WKS				$	Label & Number
2/23/57	18	9		1	Casa Loma In Hi-Fi!.................................... [I]	$25	Capitol 747
6/29/59	28	2		2	Sounds Of The Great Bands!..................... [I]	$20	Capitol 1022
2/2/63	63	13		3	Themes Of The Great Bands...................... [I]	$20	Capitol 1812
10/19/63	69	15		4	Today's Best.. [I]	$20	Capitol 1938

Alley Cat (4)　Artistry In Rhythm (3)　Begin The Beguine (2)　Black Jazz (1)　Blue Flame (3)　Casa Loma Stomp (1)　Ciribiribin (3)　Come And Get It (1)　Contrasts (2)　Dance Of The Lame Duck (1)　Days Of Wine And Roses (4)　Desafinado (4)　Elks' Parade (2)　Fly Me To The Moon (In Other Words) (4)　Flying Home (2)　For You (1)　Good Life (4)　I Can't Get Started (3)　I Cried For You (1)　I Left My Heart In San Francisco (4)　I Will Follow You (Chariot) (4)　I'm Gettin' Sentimental Over You (3)　Just An Old Manuscript (1)　Leap Frog (3)　Let's Dance (3)　Maniac's Ball (1)　Memories Of You (1)　Moonlight Serenade (3)　Nightmare (3)　No Name Jive (1)　Our Day Will Come (4)　Quaker City Jazz (3)　Redskin Rhumba (3)　720 In The Books (2)　Sleepy Time Gal (1)　Smoke Rings (1)　Snowfall (2)　Song Of India (2)　Stranger On The Shore (4)　String Of Pearls (2)　Sunrise Serenade (1)　Sweetest Sounds (2)　Symphony In Riffs (2)　Take The A Train (3)　Tenderly (2)　Those Lazy-Hazy-Crazy Days Of Summer (4)　Tuxedo Junction (3)　What Kind Of Fool Am I? (4)　White Jazz (1)　Woodchopper's Ball (2)

GRAY, Macy　　'00

Born Natalie McIntyre in 1969 in Canton, Ohio. Female R&B singer/songwriter.

8/14/99+	4	89	▲³		On How Life Is	$10	Epic 69490

Caligula　Do Something　I Can't Wait To Meetchu　I Try 5　I've Committed Murder　Letter, The　Moment To Myself　Sex-O-Matic Venus Freak　Still　Why Didn't You Call Me

GREAN, Charles Randolph, Sounde　　'69

Born on 10/1/13 in New York City. Conductor/arranger. Married singer Betty Johnson.

7/26/69	23	15			Quentin's Theme...................................... [I]	$15	Ranwood 8055

Deep Purple　Forgotten Dreams　La Golandrina　Manolito　#1 At The "Blue Whale"　On The Trail　Perfect Song　Quentin's Theme 13　Serenade To Summertime　Sunset

GREASE BAND　　'71

Backing band for **Joe Cocker**: Henry McCullough (vocals, guitar), Neil Hubbard (guitar), Phil Plunk (keyboards), Alan Spenner (bass) and Bruce Rowland (drums). McCullough was a member of **Paul McCartney**'s Wings from 1972-1973. Hubbard and Spenner later joined **Kokomo**.

4/17/71	190	3	©		Grease Band..	$15	Shelter 8904

All I Wanna Do　Down Home Mama　Jessie James　Laugh At The Judge　Let It Be Gone　Mistake No Doubt　My Baby Left Me　To The Lord　Visitor　Willie And The Pig

GREAT SOCIETY — see SLICK, Grace

GREAT WHITE　　'89

Hard-rock group formed in Los Angeles: Jack Russell (vocals), Mark Kendall (guitar), Lorne Black (bass) and Gary Holland (drums). Audie Desbrow replaced Holland in 1986. Michael Lardie (keyboards) joined in 1987. Tony Montana replaced Black in 1987. Teddy Cook replaced Montana in 1993. Sean McNabb replaced Cook in 1998.

3/24/84	144	12		©	1 Great White..	$10	EMI America 17111
8/16/86	82	13		©	2 Shot In The Dark.......................................	$10	Capitol 12525
7/18/87	23	53	▲	©	3 Once Bitten..	$10	Capitol 12565
2/13/88	99	12		©	4 Recovery: Live!..................................... [L]	$10	Enigma 73295
5/6/89	9	50	▲²	©	5 ...Twice Shy	$10	Capitol 90640
3/16/91	18	25	●	©	6 Hooked...	$10	Capitol 95330
10/10/92	107	6		©	7 Psycho City..	$10	Capitol 98835
5/28/94	168	1		©	8 Sail Away..	$15	Zoo 11080 [2]
7/24/99	192	1		©	9 Can't Get There From Here......................	$10	Portrait 69547

Afterglow (6)　Ain't No Shame (9)　All Over Now (3,8)　All Right (8)　Alone (8)　**Angel Song** (5) 30　Babe (I'm Gonna Leave You) (8)　Baby's On Fire (5)　Bad Boys (1,4)　Big Goodbye (7)　**Call It Rock N' Roll** (6,8) 53　Can't Shake It (6)　Cold Hearted Lovin' (6)　Congo Square (6)　Cryin' (8)　Dead End (1)　Desert Moon (6)　Doctor Me (7)　Face The Day (2)　Fast Road (3)　Freedom Song (9)　Get On Home (7)　Gimme Some Lovin' (2)　Gone To The Dogs (9)　Gone With The Wind (8)　Gonna Getcha (3)　Hard And Cold (4)　Heart The Hunter (5)　Heartbreaker (6)　Hey Mister (9)　Hiway Nights (5)　Hold On (1)　**House Of Broken Love** (5) 83　I Don't Need No Doctor (4)　I Want You (7)　If I Ever Saw A Good Thing (8)　Immigrant Song (4)　In The Tradition (9)　Is Anybody There (2)　Lady Red Light (3)　Livin' In The U.S.A. (8)　Love Is A Lie (7,8)　Loveless Age (9)　Lovin' Kind (6)　Maybe Someday (7)　Mista Bone (5)　Mistreater (3)　Momma Don't Stop (8)　Money (That's What I Want) (4)　Mother's Eyes (8)　Move It (5)　Never Change Heart (3)　Never Trust A Pretty Face (7)　Nightmares (1)　No Better Than Hell (1)　Old Rose Motel (7,8)　On The Edge (3)　On Your Knees (1)　**Once Bitten Twice Shy** (5,8) 5　Original Queen Of Sheba (6)　Out Of The Night (1)　Psychedelic Hurricane (9)　Psycho City (7)　Red House (4)　**Rock Me** (3,8) 60　Rock N Roll (4)　Rollin' Stoned (9)　Run Away (2)　Sail Away (8)　Saint Lorraine (9)　**Save Your Love** (3) 57　She Only (5)　She Shakes Me (2)　Shot In The Dark (2)　Silent Night (9)　Sister Mary (9)　South Bay Cities (6)　Step On You (7)　Stick It (1,4)　Streetkiller (1,4)　Substitute (1,4)　Waiting For Love (2)　What Do You Do (3)　Wooden Jesus (9)

GREAVES, R.B.　　'70

Born Ronald Bertram Greaves on 11/28/44 at the U.S. Air Force base in Georgetown, British Guyana. R&B singer. Nephew of **Sam Cooke**.

1/3/70	85	14			R.B. Greaves..	$20	Atco 311

Ain't That Good News　**Always Something There To Remind Me** 27　Ballad Of Leroy　Birmingham, Alabama　Cupid　Don't Play That Song (You Lied)　Home To Stay　Oh When I Was A Boy　**Take A Letter Maria** 2　This Is Soul

GREBENSHIKOV, Boris　　'89

Born on 11/27/53 in Leningrad. Rock singer/songwriter/guitarist.

8/26/89	198	2	©		Radio Silence..	$10	Columbia 44364

China　Death Of King Arthur　Fields Of My Love　Mother　Postcard, The　Radio Silence　Real Slow Today　That Voice Again　Time, The　Wind, The　Winter　Young Lions

GRECH, Rick　　'73

Born on 11/1/46 in Bordeaux, France. Died of liver failure on 3/17/90 (age 43). Rock bassist. Member of **Family**, **Traffic**, **Blind Faith**, **Ginger Baker's Air Force** and **KGB**.

9/29/73	195	3			The Last Five Years................................... [K]	$15	RSO 876

Doin' It　Face In The Cloud　Hey Mr. Policeman　How-Hi-The-Li　Just A Guest　Kiss The Children　Rock 'N' Roll Stew　Sea Of Joy　Second Generation Woman

GREELEY, George
'61

Born on 7/23/17 in Westerly, Rhode Island. Conductor/pianist.

The Best Of The Popular Piano Concertos .... [I-K] $20 Warner 1410

5/22/61 **29** 16

Affair To Remember (Our Love Affair)
Aloha Oe (Farewell To Thee)
Come Back To Sorrento
Hawaiian War Chant
Laura
Love Is A Many Splendored Thing
Moonlight Sonata
On The Trail
Street Scene
Three Coins In The Fountain
Tristan And Isolde, Love Music From

GREEN, Al ★165★
'72

Born on 4/13/46 in Forrest City, Arkansas. R&B singer/songwriter. Began career as a gospel singer; returned to gospel music in 1980. Inducted into the Rock and Roll Hall of Fame in 1995.

1)I'm Still In Love With You 2)Let's Stay Together 3)Call Me

8/28/71+	**58**	43		©	1	Al Green Gets Next To You	$20	Hi 32062
2/12/72	**8**	56	●	©	2	**Let's Stay Together**	$15	Hi 32070
9/16/72	**162**	9			3	**Al Green** .... [E]	$15	Bell 6076
						recordings from 1967-68		
10/21/72	**4**	67	▲	©	4	**I'm Still In Love With You** C:#50/1	$15	Hi 32074
1/6/73	**19**	28		©	5	Green Is Blues.......................[E]	$15	Hi 32055
						released in 1969		
5/19/73	**10**	41	●	©	6	**Call Me**	$15	Hi 32077
12/29/73+	**24**	30	●	©	7	**Livin' For You**	$15	Hi 32082
11/23/74+	**15**	33	●	©	8	Al Green Explores Your Mind	$15	Hi 32087
3/22/75	**17**	21		©	9	Al Green/Greatest Hits.......................C:#20/82 [G]	$15	Hi 32089
						also see #16 below		
9/13/75	**28**	23		©	10	**Al Green Is Love**	$15	Hi 32092
3/20/76	**59**	16		©	11	**Full Of Fire**	$15	Hi 32097
11/27/76+	**93**	14		©	12	Have A Good Time	$15	Hi 32103
7/2/77	**134**	9		©	13	Al Green's Greatest Hits, Volume II ....[G]	$15	Hi 32105
12/24/77+	**103**	12		©	14	The Belle Album	$15	Hi 6004
5/2/87	**131**	14		©	15	Soul Survivor	$10	A&M 5150
8/19/95	**127**	29	▲	©	16	Al Green/Greatest Hits .... C:#12/106 [G-R]	$10	Right Stuff 30800
10/7/00	**186**	1		©	17	Take Me To The River .... [G]	$15	Right Stuff 28679 [2]

All Because (1)
All N All (14)
Always (11)
Are You Lonely For Me Baby (1)
Back Up Train (3) *41*
Belle (14,16,17) *83*
Beware (7)
Call Me (Come Back Home) (6,9,16,17) *10*
Chariots Of Fire (14)
City, The (8)
Could I Be The One (10)
Don't Hurt Me No More (3)
Don't Leave Me (3)
Dream (14)
Drivin' Wheel (1)
Everything's Gonna Be Alright (15)
Feels Like Summer (14)
For The Good Times (4,13,17)
Free At Last (7)
Full Of Fire (11,13,16) *28*
Funny How Time Slips Away (6)
Georgia Boy (14)
Get Back (5)

Get Back Baby (1)
Get Yourself Together (3)
Glory Glory (11)
God Blessed Our Love (8,17)
God Is Standing By (1)
Gotta Find A New World (5)
Guilty (3) *69*
Hangin' On (8,17)
Happy (12)
Have A Good Time (12)
Have You Been Making Out O.K. (6)
He Ain't Heavy (15)
Here I Am (Come And Take Me) (6,9,16,17) *10*
Hold On Forever (12)
Home Again (7)
Hot Wire (3) *71*
How Can You Mend A Broken Heart (2,9,17)
I Can't Get Next To You (1,9,16,17) *60*
I Didn't Know (10)
I Feel Good (14)
I Gotta Be More (Take Me Higher) (10)

I Stand Accused (5)
I Tried To Tell Myself (12,17)
I Wish You Were Here (10)
I'd Fly Away (11)
I'll Be Good To You (3)
I'm A Ram (1)
I'm Glad You're Mine (4,17)
I'm Hooked On You (8)
I'm Reachin' Out (3)
I'm So Lonesome I Could Cry (6)
I'm Still In Love With You (4,9,16,17) *3*
I've Never Found A Girl (Who Loves Me Like You Do) (2)
It Ain't No Fun To Me (2)
Jesus Is Waiting (6)
Jesus Will Fix It (15)
Judy (2)
Keep Me Cryin' (12,13) *37*
La-La For You (2)
Lean On Me (17)
Let It Shine (11,17)
Let Me Help You (3)
Let's Get Married (7,9,16,17) *32*

Let's Stay Together (2,9,16,17) *1*
Letter, The (5)
Light My Fire (1)
Livin' For You (7,13,16,17) *19*
Look What You Done For Me (4,9,16,17) *4*
Love And Happiness (4,13,16,17)
L-O-V-E (Love) (10,13,16,17) *13*
Love Ritual (10)
Love Sermon (10)
Loving You (14)
My Girl (5)
My God Is Real (7)
My Sweet Sixteen (7)
Nothing Takes The Place Of You (12,17)
Oh Me, Oh My (Dreams In My Arms) (10) *48*
Oh, Pretty Woman (4)
Old Time Lovin (2)
One Nite Stand (8)
One Of These Good Old Days (4)
One Woman (5)

Rhymes (10,13)
Right Now Right Now (1,17)
School Days (8)
Sha-La-La (Make Me Happy) (8,13,16,17) *7*
Simply Beautiful (4)
Smile A Little Bit More (12)
So Good To Be Here (7,17)
So Real To Me (15)
So You're Leaving (2)
Something (12)
Soon As I Get Home (11)
Soul Survivor (15)
Spirit Might Come - On And On (17)
Stand Up (6)
Stay With Me Forever (8)
Stop And Check Myself (3)
Strong As Death (Sweet As Love) (17)
Summertime (5)
Take Me To The River (8,13,17)
Talk To Me (5)
That's All It Takes (Lady) (3)
That's The Way It Is (11)
There Is Love (10)

There's No Way (11,17)
Tired Of Being Alone (1,9,16,17) *11*
Together Again (11)
Tomorrow's Dream (5)
Truth Marches On (12)
23rd Psalm (15)
Unchained Melody (7)
What A Wonderful Thing Love Is (4)
What Am I Gonna Do With Myself (5,17)
What Is This Feeling (2)
Yield Not To Temptation (15)
You Know And I Know (15)
You Ought To Be With Me (6,9,16,17) *3*
You Say It (1)
You've Got A Friend (15)
Your Love Is Like The Morning Sun (6)

GREEN, Grant
'71

Born on 6/6/31 in St. Louis. Jazz guitarist.

Visions .... [I] $15 Blue Note 84373

10/16/71 **151** 9

Blues For Abraham
Cantaloupe Woman
Does Anybody Really Know What Time It Is
Love On A Two Way Street
Maybe Tomorrow
Never Can Say Goodbye
Symphony No. 40 In G Minor, K550, 1st Movement
We've Only Just Begun

GREEN, Jack
'80

Born on 3/12/51 in Glasgow, Scotland. Rock guitarist. Former member of **T. Rex** and **Pretty Things**.

Humanesque.. $12 RCA Victor 3639

10/18/80 **121** 8

Babe
Bout That Girl
Can't Stand It
Factory Girl
I Call, No Answer
Life On The Line
Murder
So Much
This Is Japan
Thought It Was Easy
Valentina

GREEN, Peter
'80

Born Peter Greenbaum on 10/29/46 in London. Blues-rock guitarist. Member of **John Mayall**'s Bluesbreakers and **Fleetwood Mac**.

Little Dreamer .... $12 Sail 0112

10/25/80 **186** 5

Baby When The Sun Goes Down
Born Under A Bad Sign
Cryin' Won't Bring You Back
I Could Not Ask For More
Little Dreamer
Loser Two Times
Momma Don'tcha Cry
One Woman Love
Walkin' The Road

GREEN, Steve   '96
Born in 1956 in Costa Rica (parents were American missionaries). Christian singer/songwriter.

| 11/23/96 | 40[X] | 1 | © | The First Noel | [X] | $10 | Sparrow 51585 |

All My Heart Rejoices · Angels We Have Heard On High (medley) · Away In A Manger (medley) · Come, Thou Long-Expected Jesus · First Noel · Good News · Holy Child · It Came Upon The Midnight Clear (medley) · Jesu, Light Of Lights · O Come, All Ye Faithful (medley) · O Little Town Of Bethlehem (medley) · Rose Of Bethlehem · What Child Is This

GREENBAUM, Norman   '70
Born on 11/20/42 in Malden, Massachusetts. Pop-rock singer/songwriter.

| 2/28/70 | 23 | 25 | © | Spirit In The Sky | $20 | Reprise 6365 |

Alice Bodine · Good Lookin' Woman · Jubilee · Junior Cadillac · Marcy · Milk Cow · Power, The · Skyline · **Spirit In The Sky 3** · Tars Of India

GREEN DAY   '95
Punk-rock trio formed in Berkeley, California: Billie Joe Armstrong (vocals, guitar), Mike Dirnt (bass) and Frank "Tre Cool" Wright (drums).

2/19/94+	2[2]	113	▲10 ©	1 Dookie	C:#27/3	$10	Reprise 45529
10/1/94+	❶2C	43	● ©	2 Kerplunk!	[E]	$10	Lookout 46
				released in 1992			
10/8/94+	4[C]	34	● ©	3 1,039/Smoothed Out Slappy Hours	[E]	$10	Lookout 22
				released in 1990			
10/28/95	2[1]	39	▲2 ©	4 Insomniac		$10	Reprise 46046
11/1/97	10	70	▲2 ©	5 Nimrod		$10	Reprise 46794
10/21/00	4	25	● ©	6 Warning:		$10	Reprise 47613

All The Time (5) · Android (2) · Armatage Shanks (4) · At The Library (3) · Bab's Uvula Who? (4) · Basket Case (1) · Best Thing In Town (2) · Blood, Sex And Booze (6) · Brain Stew (4) · Brat (4) · Burnout (1) · Castaway (6) · Christie Road (2) · Chump (1) · Church On Sunday (6) · Coming Clean (1) · Deadbeat Holiday (6) · Disappearing Boy (3) · Dominated Love Slave (2) · Don't Leave Me (3) · Dry Ice (3) · 80 (2) · 86 (4) · Emenius Sleepus (1) · F.O.D. (1) · Fashion Victim (6) · 409 In Your Coffeemaker (3) · Geek Stink Breath (4) · Going To Pasalacqua (3) · Good Riddance (Time Of Your Life) (5) · Green Day (3) · Grouch, The (5) · Haushinka (5) · Having A Blast (1) · Hitchin' A Ride (5) · Hold On (6) · I Want To Be Alone (3) · I Was There (4) · In The End (1) · Jackass (6) · Jaded (4) · Jinx (5) · Judge's Daughter (3) · King For A Day (5) · Knowledge (3) · Last Ride In (5) · Long View (1) · Macy's Day Parade (6) · Minority (6) · Misery (6) · My Generation (2) · Nice Guys Finish Last (5) · No One Knows (2) · No Pride (4) · One For The Razorbacks (2) · One I Want (3) · One Of My Lies (2) · 1,000 Hours (3) · Only Of You (3) · Panic Song (4) · Paper Lanterns (3) · Platypus (I Hate You) (5) · Private Ale (2) · Prosthetic Head (5) · Pulling Teeth (1) · Redundant (5) · Reject (5) · Rest (3) · Road To Acceptance (3) · Sassafras Roots (1) · Scattered (5) · She (1) · 16 (3) · Strangeland (4) · Stuart and the Ave. (4) · Stuck With Me (4) · Sweet Children (3) · Take Back (5) · Tight Wad Hill (4) · 2000 Light Years Away (2) · Uptight (5) · Waiting (6) · Walking Alone (5) · Walking Contradiction (4) · Warning (6) · Welcome To Paradise (1,2) · Westbound Sign (4) · When I Come Around (1) · Who Wrote Holden Caulfield? (2) · Why Do You Want Him (3) · Words I Might Have Ate (2) · Worry Rock (5)

GREENE, Jack   '67
Born on 1/7/30 in Maryville, Tennessee. Country singer/songwriter/guitarist. Nicknamed the "Jolly Green Giant."

| 2/25/67 | 66 | 21 | | 1 There Goes My Everything | $20 | Decca 74845 |
| 7/22/67 | 151 | 12 | | 2 All The Time | $20 | Decca 74904 |

All The Time (2) · Almost Persuaded (1) · Crazy (2) · Cryin' Time (2) · Don't You Ever Get Tired (Of Hurting Me) (1) · Ever Since My Baby Went Away (1) · Happy Tracks (2) · Hardest Easy Thing (2) · Here Comes My Baby (1) · Hurt's On Me (1) · I Can't Help It (If I'm Still In Love With You) (1) · I'm A Lonesome Fugitive (2) · Make The World Go Away (1) · Room For One More Heartache (2) · She's Gone, Gone, Gone (2) · Tender Years (1) · **There Goes My Everything (1) 65** · Think I'll Go Somewhere And Cry Myself To Sleep (1) · Together Again (1) · Touch My Heart (2) · Walk Through This World With Me (2) · Walking On New Grass (1) · Wanting You But Never Having You (2) · Wound Time Can't Erase (1)

GREENE, Lorne   '65
Born on 2/12/14 in Ottawa, Canada. Died of heart failure on 9/11/87 (age 73). Acted in several movies. Starred on TV's *Bonanza* and *Battlestar Galactica*.

| 11/28/64+ | 35 | 19 | | 1 Welcome To The Ponderosa | $25 | RCA Victor 2843 |
| 12/25/65 | 54[X] | 1 | | 2 Have a Happy Holiday | [X] | $25 | RCA Victor 3410 |

Alamo (1) · Blue Guitar (1) · Bonanza (1) · Christmas Is A-Comin' (May God Bless You) (2) · Endless Prairie (1) · Ghost Riders In The Sky (1) · Gift Of The Magi (2) · Holy Night (A Christmas Cantata) (2) · Jingle Bells (2) · Ol' Tin Cup (And A Battered Ol' Coffee Pot) (1) · Pony Express (1) · **Ringo (1) 1** · Saga Of The Ponderosa (1) · Sand (1) · (There's No Place Like) Home For The Holidays (2) · 'Twas The Night Before Christmas (A Visit fro St. Nicholas) (2) · We Wish You A Merry Christmas (2)

GREEN JELLY   '93
Novelty hard-rock group formed in Kenmore, New York: Moronic Dicktator (lead vocals), Joey Blowey, Rootin', Jesus Quisp, Coy Roy, Sadistica, Hotsy Menshot, Tin Titty, Sven Seven, Reason Clean, Mother Eucker, Roof D.H. and Daddy Longlegs. Group originally known as Green Jello.

| 4/3/93 | 23 | 26 | ● | Cereal Killer Soundtrack | $10 | Zoo 11038 |

Anarchy In The U.K. · Cereal Killer · Electric Harley House (Of Love) · Flight Of The Skajaquada · Green Jello Theme Song · House Me Teenage Rave · Misadventures Of Shitman · Obey The Cowgod · Rock-N-Roll Pumpkihn · **Three Little Pigs 17** · Trippin' On XTC

GREEN ON RED   '86
Country-rock group from Tucson, Arizona: Dan Stuart (vocals), Chuck Prophet (guitar), Alex MacNicol (keyboards), Jack Waterson (bass) and Chris Cacavas (drums).

| 5/3/86 | 177 | 6 | © | No Free Lunch | $10 | Mercury 826346 |

Ballad Of Guy Fawkes · Funny How Time Slips Away · Honest Man · Jimmy Boy · Keep On Moving · No Free Lunch · Time Ain't Nothing

GREENWOOD, Lee   '83
Born on 10/27/42 in Los Angeles. Country singer/songwriter/multi-instrumentalist.

5/28/83	73	21	●	1 Somebody's Gonna Love You	$10	MCA 5403
6/9/84	150	20	●	2 You've Got A Good Love Comin'	$10	MCA 5488
9/8/84	89	13	©	3 Meant For Each Other	$10	MCA 5477
				BARBARA MANDRELL/LEE GREENWOOD			
5/18/85	163	8	▲ ©	4 Greatest Hits	[G]	$10	MCA 5582

Ain't No Trick (It Takes Magic) (4) · Barely Holding On (1) · Call It What You Want To (It's Still Love) (1) · Can't Get Too Much Of A Good Thing (3) · Dixie Road (4) · Even Love Can't Save Us Now (2) · Fool's Gold (2,4) · God Bless The USA (2,4) · Going, Going, Gone (1,4) · Held Over (3) · I Don't Want To Wake You (2) · I Found Love In Time (2) · I'll Never Stop Loving You (3)

GREENWOOD, Lee — Cont'd

I.O.U. (1,4) *53*
It Should Have Been Love By Now (3)
It Turns Me Inside Out (4)
Ladies Love (1)
Lean, Mean, Lovin' Machine (2)

Love Me Like I'm Leavin' Tonight (2)
Love Won't Let Us Say Goodbye (1)
Now You See Us, Now You Don't (3)

One On One, Eye To Eye, Heart To Heart (3)
Ring On Her Finger, Time On Her Hands (4)
She's Lying (4)
Soft Shoulder (3)

Somebody's Gonna Love You (1,4) *96*
Someone Who Remembers (1)
Think About The Good Times (1)
To Me (3)

Two Heart Serenade (2)
We Were Meant For Each Other (3)
We're A Perfect Match (1)
Wind Beneath My Wings (1)
Worth It For The Ride (2)

You've Got A Good Love Comin' (2)

GREGG, Ricky Lynn
Born on 8/22/62 in Longview, Texas. Country-rock singer/songwriter/guitarist. **'93**

| 5/15/93 | 190 | 1 | © | **Ricky Lynn Gregg** | | | $10 | Liberty 80135 |

Alright Already
Bring On The Neon
Can You Feel It

Change (Is Gonna Do Me Good)
Cheyenne

Good Habit Is Hard To Break
If I Had A Cheatin' Heart
No Place Left To Go

That's What Happens
Three Nickels And A Dime

GREGGAINS, Joanie
Born in Los Angeles. Fitness instructor. **'83**

| 6/18/83 | 177 | 4 | | | **Aerobic Shape-Up II** | | | $10 | Parade 106 |

music by studio musicians

Do I Do
Don't It Make You Wanna Dance

Double Dutch Bus
E. T. Theme
Ebony & Ivory

Get Down On It
Let It Whip

Love's Been A Little Bit Hard On Me
Other Woman

Wake Up Little Susie
Work That Body

GREGORY, Dick
Born on 10/12/32 in St. Louis. Comedian/civil rights activist. **'61**

| 6/5/61 | 23 | 27 | | 1 | **In Living Black & White** | [C] | | $25 | Colpix 417 |
| 8/16/69+ | 182 | 8 | © | 2 | **The Light Side: The Dark Side** | [C] | | $20 | Poppy 60001 [2] |

American History (2)
Assassinations (2)
Atmosphere Of Trust (2)
Black Attitudes (2)
Black Progress (2)

Black Rioters (2)
Comedians Of The '60's (1)
Commentary On Affairs Political (1)
Concerned Honky Law (2)

Congo Daily Tribune (1)
Draft Resisters (2)
50,000 Ft. - And No Insurance (1)
Learning To Live (2)

Middle East (1)
Moral Gap (2)
Not Poor - Just Busted (1)
100 Proof (1)
Presidential Campaign (2)

Property Rights-Human Rights (2)
Thoughts On Outer Space (1)
White Brother (1)
White Racists Institutions (2)

Young Moral Dedication (2)

GREY & HANKS
R&B vocal duo from Chicago: Zane Grey and Len Ron Hanks. **'79**

| 2/3/79 | 97 | 11 | | 1 | **You Fooled Me** | | | $12 | RCA Victor 3069 |
| 2/23/80 | 195 | 3 | | 2 | **Prime Time** | | | $12 | RCA Victor 3477 |

Closer To Something Real (1)
Dancin' (1) *83*
For The People (2)
Gotta Put Something In (1)

How Can You Live Without Love (1)
I Can Tell Where Your Head Is (1)

I'm Calling On You (2)
Love's In Command (2)
Never Let You Down (1)
Now I'm Fine (2)

Prime Time (2)
Since I Found You (Love Is Better Than Ever) (2)
Single Girls (2)

Tired Of Taking Chances (2)
Way Out To Get In (1)
We Need More (2)
You Fooled Me (1)

GRIFFITH, Andy
Born on 6/1/26 in Mount Airy, North Carolina. Actor/comedian. Starred in several movies and Broadway shows. Star of TV's *The Andy Griffith Show* and *Matlock*. **'96**

| 4/20/96 | 55 | 28 | ▲ | © | 1 | **I Love To Tell The Story - 25 Timeless Hymns** | | | $10 | Sparrow 51440 |
| 5/16/98 | 143 | 3 | | © | 2 | **Just As I Am - 30 Favorite Old Time Hymns** | | | $10 | Sparrow 51666 |

All The Way My Savior Leads Me (medley) (2)
Amazing Grace (medley) (1)
Beautiful Isle (medley) (2)
Beulah Land (medley) (2)
Church In The Wildwood (medley) (2)
Does Jesus Care (medley) (2)
Down At The Cross (Glory To His Name) (medley) (1)
God Will Take Care Of You (medley) (2)
Grace Greater Than All Our Sin (medley) (1)
He Leadeth Me (medley) (2)
His Eye Is On The Sparrow (medley) (2)
How Great Thou Art (1)

I Am Bound For The Promised Land (medley) (2)
I Love To Tell The Story (1)
I Need Thee Every Hour (medley) (2)
I'll Fly Away (medley) (2)
In The Sweet By And By (medley) (1)
It Is No Secret (2)
Jesus, I Come (medley) (2)
Jesus, Lover Of My Soul (medley) (2)
Jesus, Savior, Pilot Me (medley) (2)
Just A Little Talk With Jesus (medley) (2)
Just As I Am (medley) (2)

Leaning On The Everlasting Arms (medley) (2)
Near The Cross (medley) (1)
Near To The Heart Of God (medley) (2)
New Name Written Down In Glory (medley) (2)
No Not One (medley) (2)
Old Rugged Cross (medley) (1)
Onward, Christian Soldiers (medley) (2)
Pass Me Not (medley) (1)
Precious Memories (1)
Shall We Gather At The River (medley) (1)
Softly And Tenderly (medley) (1)

Stand Up, Stand Up For Jesus (medley) (2)
Surrender All (medley) (1)
Sweet Hour Of Prayer (medley) (1)
Sweet Prospect (medley) (1)
Take The Name Of Jesus With You (medley) (2)
Take Time To Be Holy (medley) (2)
There's Power In The Blood (medley) (2)
'Tis So Sweet To Trust In Jesus (medley) (2)
Unclouded Day (medley) (2)
Wayfaring Stranger (1)

We'll Understand It Better By And By (medley) (1)
We're Marching To Zion (medley) (2)
What A Friend We Have In Jesus (medley) (1)
What Wondrous Love Is This (medley) (2)
When I Can Read My Title Clear (2)
When The Roll Is Called Up Yonder (medley) (1)
When The Saints Go Marching In (medley) (1)
When They Ring The Golden Bells (medley) (1)

When We All Get To Heaven (medley) (1)
Whispering Hope (1)
Will The Circle Be Unbroken (medley) (1)

GRIFFITH, Nanci
Born on 7/16/54 in Seguin, Texas; raised in Austin, Texas. Country singer/songwriter/guitarist. **'94**

9/16/89	99	14	©	1	**Storms**			$10	MCA 6319
10/12/91	185	1	©	2	**Late Night Grande Hotel**			$10	MCA 10306
3/20/93	54	14	©	3	**Other Voices - Other Rooms**			$10	Elektra 61464
10/1/94	48	8	©	4	**Flyer**			$10	Elektra 61681
4/12/97	119	6	©	5	**Blue Roses From The Moons**			$10	Elektra 62015
8/8/98	85	7	©	6	**Other Voices, Too (A Trip Back To Bountiful)**			$10	Elektra 62235

Across The Great Divide (3)
Always Will (4)
Anything You Need But Me (4)
Are You Tired Of Me Darling (3)
Battlefield (5)
Boots Of Spanish Leather (3)
Brave Companion Of The Road (1)
Can't Help But Wonder Where I'm Bound (3)
Canadian Whiskey (6)
Comin' Down In The Rain (3)
Darcy Farrow (6)
Deportee (Plane Wreck At Los Gatos) (6)
Desperadoes Waiting For A Train (6)
Do Re Mi (3)
Don't Forget About Me (4)

Down 'N' Outer (2)
Dress Of Laces (6)
Drive-In Movies And Dashboard Lights (1)
Everything's Comin' Up Roses (5)
Fields Of Summer (2)
Flyer, The (4)
Fragile (4)
From Clare To Here (3)
Going Back To Georgia (4)
Goodnight To A Mother's Dream (4)
Gulf Coast Highway (5)
Hard Times Come Again No More (2)
He Was A Friend Of Mine (6)
Heaven (2)
Hometown Streets (2)

I Don't Wanna Talk About Love (1)
I Fought The Law (5)
I Still Miss Someone (6)
I'll Move Along (5)
If I Had A Hammer (The Hammer Song) (6)
If Wishes Were Changes (1)
Is This All There Is? (5)
It's A Hard Life Wherever You Go (1)
It's Just Another Morning Here (2)
It's Too Late (2)
Late Night Grande Hotel (2)
Leaving The Harbor (1)
Listen To The Radio (1)
Maybe Tomorrow (5)
Morning Song For Sally (3)

Morning Train (5)
Night Rider's Lament (3)
Nobody's Angel (4)
Not My Way Home (5)
On Grafton Street (4)
One Blade Shy Of A Sharp Edge (2)
Power Lines (2)
Radio Fragile (1)
Saint Teresa Of Avila (5)
San Diego Serenade (2)
Say It Isn't So (4)
She Ain't Goin' Nowhere (5)
Southbound Train (4)
Speed Of The Sound Of Loneliness (3)
Storms (1)
Streets Of Baltimore (6)
Summer Wages (6)

Sun, Moon, And Stars (2)
Talk To Me While I'm Listening (4)
Tecumseh Valley (3)
Ten Degrees And Getting Colder (3)
These Days In An Open Book (4)
This Heart (2)
This Old Town (3)
Three Flights Up (3)
Time Of Inconvenience (4)
Try The Love (6)
Turn Around (3)
Two For The Road (5)
Waiting For Love (5)
Walk Right Back (6)
Wall Of Death (6)
Wasn't That A Mighty Storm (6)

Who Knows Where The Time Goes (6)
Wimoweh (3)
Wings Of A Dove (6)
Woman Of The Phoenix (4)
Wouldn't That Be Fine (5)
Yarrington Town (6)
You Made This Love A Teardrop (6)
You Were On My Mind (3)

GRIGGS, Andy '99

Born on 8/13/73 in Monroe, Louisiana. Counrty singer/songwriter/guitarist.

| 5/1/99 | 142 | 16 | ● | © | You Won't Ever Be Lonely .... | | | $10 | RCA 67596 |

Ain't Done Nothin' Wrong   I Don't Know A Thing   **I'll Go Crazy** 65   Shine On Me   Waitin' On Sundown   **You Won't Ever Be Lonely** 28
Ain't Livin' Long Like This   I Miss You The Most   **She's More** 37   Side Of Me   You Made Me That Way

GRIM REAPER '84

Hard-rock group from Droitwich, England: Steve Grimmett (vocals), Nick Bowcott (guitar), Dave Wanklin (bass) and Lee Harris (drums). In 1985, Mark Simon replaced Harris.

8/25/84	73	27		©	1 See You In Hell			$10	RCA Victor 8038
7/6/85	108	14		©	2 Fear No Evil			$10	RCA Victor 5431
8/1/87	93	21		©	3 Rock You To Hell			$10	RCA Victor 6250

All Hell Let Loose (1)   Lay It On The Line (2)   Matter Of Time (2)   Rock You To Hell (3)   When Heaven Comes Down (3)
Dead On Arrival (1)   Let The Thunder Roar (2)   Never Coming Back (2)   Run For Your Life (1)   Wrath Of The Ripper (1)
Fear No Evil (2)   Liar (1)   Night Of The Vampire (3)   See You In Hell (1)   You'll Wish That You Were
Fight For The Last (2)   Lord Of Darkness (Your Living   Now Or Never (1)   Show Must Go On (1)   Never Born (3)
Final Scream (2)   Hell) (2)   Rock & Roll Tonight (2)   Suck It And See (3)
I Want More (3)   Lust For Freedom (3)   Rock Me 'Till I Die (3)   Waysted Love (3)

GRIN '72

Rock group formed in New York City: **Nils Lofgren** (vocals, guitar), Bob Gordon (bass) and Bob Berberich (drums). Lofgren's brother, guitarist Tom, joined in mid-1972. Disbanded in 1973.

8/7/71	192	3			1 Grin			$15	Spindizzy 30321
2/5/72	180	6			2 1 + 1			$15	Spindizzy 31038
3/10/73	186	7			3 All Out			$15	Spindizzy 31701

Ain't Love Nice (3)   Everybody's Missin' The Sun   If I Were A Song (1)   Moon Tears (2)   Sad Letter (3)   Take You To The Movies
All Out (3)   (1)   Just A Poem (2)   Open Wide (1)   See What A Love Can Do (1)   Tonight (1)
Direction (1)   Heart On Fire (3)   Like Rain (1)   Outlaw (1)   She Ain't Right (3)   We All Sung Together (1)
Don't Be Long (3)   Heavy Chevy (3)   Lost A Number (2)   Pioneer Mary (1)   Slippery Fingers (3)   **White Lies** (2) 75
18 Faced Lover (1)   Hi, Hello Home (2)   Love Again (3)   Please Don't Hide (2)   Soft Fun (2)
End Unkind (2)   I Had Too Much (Miss Dazi) (1)   Love Or Else (3)   Rusty Gun (3)   Sometimes (2)

GRINDER SWITCH '77

Rock group from Macon, Georgia: Dru Lombar (vocals, guitar), Larry Howard (guitar), Stephen Miller (keyboards), Joe Dan Petty (bass) and Rick Burnett (drums). Petty died in a plane crash on 1/8/2000 (age 52).

| 11/19/77 | 144 | 8 | | | Redwing .... | | | $12 | Atco 152 |

Faster And Faster   Redwing   That Special Woman   Watermelon Time In Georgia   You And Me
I Bought All The Lies   Taste Of Love   This Road   Wings Of An Angel

GRISMAN, David '81

Born on 3/23/45 in Hackensack, New Jersey. Jazz-bluegrass mandolin player. Member of **Earth Opera** and **Old & In The Way**.

| 9/13/80 | 152 | 8 | | | 1 David Grisman - Quintet '80 .... | | [I] | $12 | Warner 3469 |
| 6/6/81 | 108 | 10 | | © | 2 Live .... | | [I-L] | $12 | Warner 3550 |

STEPHANE GRAPPELLI/DAVID GRISMAN
recorded on 9/20/79 at the Berklee Center in Boston

| 10/24/81 | 174 | 3 | | © | 3 Mondo Mando .... | | [I] | $12 | Warner 3618 |
| 11/16/96 | 135 | 1 | | © | 4 Shady Grove .... | | | $10 | Acoustic Disc 21 |

JERRY GARCIA - DAVID GRISMAN

Albuquerque Turkey (3)   Dawg Funk (3)   Fisztorza (medley) (2)   Misty (2)   Sea Of Cortez (1)   Thailand (1)
Anouman (3)   Dawgma (1)   Fulginiti (medley) (2)   Mondo Mando (3)   Shady Grove (4)   Tiger Rag (2)
Barkley's Bug (1)   Dawgmatism (1)   Handsome Cabin Boy (1)   Mugavero (1)   Shine (2)   Tzigani (medley) (2)
Bow Wow (1)   Down In The Valley (4)   I Truly Understand (4)   Naima (1)   Stealin' (4)   Whiskey In The Jar (4)
Calinete (3)   Dreadful Wind And Rain (4)   Jackaroo (1)   Off To Sea Once More (4)   Sweet Georgia Brown (2)
Casey Jones (4)   Fair Ellender (4)   Japan (Op. 23) (3)   Pent-Up House (2)   Sweet Sunny South (4)
Cedar Hill (3)   Fanny Hill (3)   Louis Collins (4)   Satin Doll (2)   Swing '42 (2)

GROCE, Larry '76

Born on 4/22/48 in Dallas. Pop-folk singer/songwriter.

| 3/27/76 | 187 | 2 | | | Junkfood Junkie .... | | [L] | $12 | Warner/Curb 2933 |

At The End Of The Long,   Calhoun County   **Junk Food Junkie** 9   Muddy Boggy Banjo Man
Lonely Day   Coal Tattoo   Like The Trout Dart About   Old Home Place
Biggest Whatever   I Still Miss Someone   Little Old Lady In Cowboy Boots   You Ain't Goin' Nowhere

GROOVE THEORY '95

Male-female R&B duo: Bryce Wilson and **Amel Larrieux**. Wilson, then known as Bryce Luvah, was a member of **Mantronix**.

| 11/11/95 | 69 | 20 | ● | © | Groove Theory .... | | | $10 | Epic 57421 |

Angel   Come Home   Hello It's Me   Ride   Time Flies
Baby Luv 65   Didja Know   Hey U   **Tell Me** 5   You're Not The 1
Boy At The Window   Good 2 Me   **Keep Tryin'** 64   10 Minute High

GROSS, Henry '75

Born on 4/1/51 in Brooklyn, New York. Pop-rock singer/songwriter/guitarist.

2/8/75	26	23			1 Plug Me Into Something			$12	A&M 4502
2/14/76	64	28		©	2 Release			$12	Lifesong 6002
3/12/77	176	7		©	3 Show Me To The Stage			$12	Lifesong 6010

All My Love (1)   Hideaway (3)   Moonshine Alley (2)   Pokey (2)   Southern Band (1)
Come Along (3)   I Can't Believe (3)   One Last Time (2)   **Shannon** (2) 6   **Springtime Mama** (2) 37
Dixie Spider Man (1)   I'll Love Her (1)   **One More Tomorrow** (1) 93   Show Me To The Stage (3)   String Of Hearts (3)
Driver's Engine (1)   If We Tie Our Ships Together   Only One (1)   Showboat (3)   Tomorrow's Memory Lane (1)
Evergreen (1)   (3)   Overton Square (2)   **Someday (I Didn't Want To**   Travelin' Time (1)
Help (3)   Juke Box Song (2)   Painting My Love Song (3)   **Have To Be The One)** (2) 85   What A Sound (3)
   Lincoln Road (2)   Something In Between (2)

GRUSIN, Dave   '80

Born on 6/26/34 in Littleton, Colorado. Jazz pianist. Composer/producer of numerous movie and TV soundtracks.

1)The Electric Horseman 2)The Fabulous Baker Boys 3)Mountain Dance

1/12/80	52	25	●		1 **The Electric Horseman**	[S]	$12	Columbia 36327

side 1: songs performed by **Willie Nelson**; side 2: instrumental score by Grusin

3/21/81	74	18	©	2 **Mountain Dance**..	[I]	$12	GRP 5010
7/18/81	140	7	©	3 **Dave Grusin and the GRP All-Stars/Live In Japan**....................	[I-L]	$12	GRP 5506

recorded on 3/16/80 in Osaka, Japan

8/7/82	88	9	©	4 **Out Of The Shadows**..	[I]	$12	GRP 5510
4/16/83	181	6	©	5 **Dave Grusin and the NY/LA Dream Band**	[I-L]	$12	GRP 1001
10/5/85	192	2	©	6 **Harlequin**...	[I]	$10	GRP 1015

DAVE GRUSIN/LEE RITENOUR

includes "Before It's Too Late (Antes Que Seja Tarde)" and "Harlequin (Arlequim Desconhecido)" by Ivan Lins

2/25/89	110	12	©	7 **Dave Grusin Collection**..	[G-I]	$10	GRP 9579
10/21/89	145	8	©	8 **Migration**	[I]	$10	GRP 9592
11/18/89	74	13	©	9 **The Fabulous Baker Boys**	[I-S]	$10	GRP 2002

includes "Makin' Whoopee" and "My Funny Valentine" by Michelle Pfeiffer, "Do Nothin' Till You Hear From Me" by Duke Ellington, "Lullaby Of Birdland" by the Earl Palmer Trio and "Moonglow" by **Benny Goodman**

12/14/91	170	2	©	10 **The Gershwin Connection**..	[I]	$10	GRP 2005

Actor's Life (7)
Anthem Internationale (4)
Bess You Is My Woman (medley) (10)
Bird, The (6)
Captain Caribe (2,3)
Cats Of Rio (6)
Champ (What Matters Most), Theme From The (5)
City Lights (2)
Count Down (5)
Crystal Morning (4)
Dancing In The Township (8)
Disco Magic (1)

Don And Dave (3)
Early A.M. Attitude (6)
Either Way (2)
Electro-Phantasma (4)
Electric Horseman (1)
Fabulous Baker Boys ..see: Jack's Theme
Fascinating Rhythm (10)
First-Time Love (8)
Five Brothers (4)
Freedom Epilogue (1)
Friends and Strangers (2,3)
Grid-Lock (6)
Hokkaido (4)

How Long Has This Been Going On? (10)
I Loves You Porgy (medley) (10)
I've Got Plenty O' Nuthin' (10)
In The Middle Of The Night (8)
Jack's Theme (9)
Last Train To Paradiso (4)
Maybe (10)
Milagro Beanfield War Suite Medley (8)
Modaji (3)
Moment Of Truth (9)
Mountain Dance (2,7)

My Man's Gone Now (10)
Nice Work If You Can Get It (10)
Number 8 (5)
Our Love Is Here To Stay (10)
Playera (7)
Prelude II (10)
Punta Del Soul (8)
Rag Bag (2)
Rising Star (Love Theme) (1)
River Song (7)
Rondo - "If You Hold Out Your Hand" (2)
'S Wonderful (10)

San Ysidro (6)
Serengeti Walk (Slippin' In The Back Door) (4,5,7)
Shamballa (3)
She Could Be Mine (4,7)
Shop Till You Bop (9)
Shuffle City (5)
Silent Message (6)
Soft On Me (9)
Soon (10)
Southwest Passage (8)
St. Elsewhere (7)
Summer Sketches '82 (5)
Suzie And Jack (9)

Sweetwater Nights (4)
Thankful 'N Thoughtful (7)
Thanksong (2)
That Certain Feeling (10)
There's A Boat Dat's Leavin' Soon For New York (10)
Three Days Of The Condor (5)
Trade Winds (3)
Uh, Oh! (3)
Welcome To The Road (9)
Western Women (8)

GTR   '86

Rock group formed in England: Max Bacon (vocals), **Steve Hackett** and **Steve Howe** (guitars), Phil Spalding (bass) and Jonathan Mover (drums). Hackett was with **Genesis**. Howe was with **Yes** and **Asia**. Name is short for guitar.

5/17/86	11	26	●	©	**GTR**..	$10	Arista 8400

Hackett To Bits
Here I Wait

Hunter, The *85*
Imagining

Jekyll And Hyde
Reach Out (Never Say No)

Sketches In The Sun
Toe The Line

When The Heart Rules The Mind *14*

You Can Still Get Through

GUADALCANAL DIARY   '89

Rock group formed in Marietta, Georgia: Murray Attaway (vocals), Jeff Walls (guitar), Rhett Crowe (bass) and John Poe (drums). Group named after a 1943 war movie.

1/16/88	183	7	©	1 **2 X 4**	$10	Elektra 60752
3/25/89	132	13	©	2 **Flip-Flop**	$10	Elektra 60848

Always Saturday (2)
Barometer (2)
Everything But Good Luck (2)
Fade Out (2)

Get Over It (1)
Happy Home (2)
Let The Big Wheel Roll (1)
Likes Of You (2)

Lips Of Steel (1)
Litany (Life Goes On) (1)
Little Birds (1)
Look Up! (2)

Newborn (1)
Pretty Is As Pretty Does (2)
Say Please (1)
Ten Laws (2)

Things Fall Apart (1)
3 AM (1)
Under The Yoke (1)
...Vista (2)

Where Angels Fear To Tread (1)
Whiskey Talk (2)
Winds Of Change (1)

GUARALDI, Vince, Trio   '63

Born on 7/17/32 in San Francisco. Died of a heart attack on 2/6/76 (age 43). Jazz pianist. Formerly with **Woody Herman** and **Cal Tjader**. Wrote the music for the *Peanuts* TV specials.

2/2/63	24	28	©	1 **Jazz Impressions of Black Orpheus**..	[I]	$30	Fantasy 3337
12/19/87+	9^X	64	▲	©	2 **A Charlie Brown Christmas**	C:#9/44 [X-I-TV]	$15	Fantasy 8431

soundtrack of the classic Christmas TV special; first released in 1965 on Fantasy 5019; Christmas charts: 13/'87, 9/'88, 9/'89, 9/'90, 18/'91, 16/'92, 23/'93, 22/'94, 17/'95, 17/'96, 15/'97, 18/'98, 25/'99

Alma-Ville (1)
Cast Your Fate To The Wind (1) *22*
Christmas Is Coming (2)

Christmas Song (2)
Christmas Time Is Here (2)
For Elise (2)
Generique (1)

Hark, The Herald Angels Sing (2)
Linus And Lucy (2)
Manha De Carnaval (1)

Moon River (1)
My Little Drum (2)
O Nusso Amor (1)
O Tannenbaum (2)

Samba De Orpheus (1)
Since I Fell For You (1)
Skating (2)
What Child Is This (2)

GUARD, Dave, & The Whiskeyhill Singers   '62

Born on 11/19/34 in Honolulu. Died of cancer on 3/22/91 (age 56). Member of **The Kingston Trio** from 1957-61.

6/30/62	92	11	©	**Dave Guard & The Whiskeyhill Singers**	$25	Capitol 1728

Banks Of The Ohio
Bonnie Ship, The Diamond
Brady And Duncan
Isa Lei

Nobody Knows You When You're Down And Out
Plane Wreck At Los Gatos (Deportees)

Ride On Railroad Bill
Shine The Light On Me (Salomila)
Soy Libre

We're The World's Last Authentic Playboys
When The War Breaks Out In Mexico

Wild Rippling Water

GUCCI CREW II   '89

Rap trio from Miami: Rick Taylor, Cleveland Bell and Victor May.

9/23/89	173	6	©	**Everybody Wants Some**	$10	Gucci 3314

Beepers
Can We Get Funky

Everybody Wants Some
Five Dollar High ($5)

It's All About The Money
N.T.S.

Return The Burn
Straight From The Bottom

Vic's Story
Who's Cadillac

★224★   GUESS WHO, The   '70

Rock group formed in Winnipeg, Canada: Chad Allan (vocals, guitar), Randy Bachman (guitar), Bob Ashley (piano), Jim Kale (bass) and Garry Peterson (drums). Recorded as Chad Allan & The Expressions. Ashley replaced by new lead singer **Burton Cummings** in 1966. Allan left shortly thereafter. Bachman left in 1970 to form **Bachman-Turner Overdrive**; replaced by Kurt Winter and Greg Leskiw. Leskiw and Kale left in 1972, replaced by Don McDougall and Bill Wallace. Domenic Troiano replaced both Winter and McDougall in 1973. Group disbanded in 1975; several reunions since then. Winter died of a bleeding ulcer on 12/14/97 (age 51).

1)American Woman 2)The Best of The Guess Who 3)Share The Land

4/26/69	45	19	©	1 **Wheatfield Soul**	$25	RCA Victor 4141
10/4/69	91	17	©	2 **Canned Wheat Packed by The Guess Who**	$25	RCA Victor 4157

GUESS WHO, The — Cont'd

DEBUT	PEAK	WKS	RIAA	CD	ARTIST — Album Title	Catalog	Sym	$	Label & Number
2/14/70	9	55	●	© 3	American Woman			$20	RCA Victor 4266
10/17/70	14	25	●	© 4	Share The Land			$20	RCA Victor 4359
4/17/71	12	45	●	© 5	The Best of The Guess Who	C:#10/227	[G]	$20	RCA Victor 1004
8/21/71	52	16		6	So Long, Bannatyne			$20	RCA Victor 4574
3/18/72	79	10		7	Rockin'			$20	RCA Victor 4602
8/19/72	39	21		© 8	Live At The Paramount (Seattle)		[L]	$15	RCA Victor 4779
					recorded on 5/22/72				
1/20/73	110	12		9	Artificial Paradise			$15	RCA Victor 4830
7/14/73	155	8		10	#10			$15	RCA Victor 0130
1/12/74	186	4		11	The Best of The Guess Who, Volume II		[G]	$15	RCA Victor 0269
5/11/74	60	26		12	Road Food			$15	RCA Victor 0405
2/1/75	48	9		13	Flavours			$15	RCA Victor 0636
7/26/75	87	7		14	Power In The Music			$15	RCA Victor 0995
4/30/77	173	4		© 15	The Greatest of The Guess Who		[G]	$15	RCA Victor 2253

Albert Flasher (8,11,15) 29
All Hashed Out (9)
American Woman (3,5,8,15) 1
Arrivederci Girl (7)
Attila's Blues (12)
Back To The City (7)
Ballad Of The Last Five Years (12)
Broken (11) 55
Bus Rider (4,5)
Bye Bye Babe (9)
Cardboard Empire (10)
Clap For The Wolfman (12,15) 6
Coming Down Off The Money Bag (medley) (4)
Coors For Sunday (14)
Dancin' Fool (13,15) 28
Diggin' Yourself (13)
Dirty (13)
Do You Miss Me Darlin' (4,5)

Don't You Want Me (7,12)
Down And Out Woman (14)
Dreams (14)
8:15 (3)
Eye (13)
Fair Warning (2)
Fiddlin' (6)
Follow Your Daughter Home (9,11) 61
Friends Of Mine (1)
Get Your Ribbons On (7)
Glace Bay Blues (8)
Glamour Boy (10,11,15)
Goin' A Little Crazy (6)
Grey Day (6)
Guns, Guns, Guns (7,11) 70
Hamba Gahle-Usalang Gahle (9)
Hand Me Down World (4,5,15) 17
Hang On To Your Life (4,5) 43

Heartbroken Bopper (7,11) 47
Heaven Only Moved Once Yesterday (medley) (7)
Herbert's A Loser (7)
Hoe Down Time (13)
Humpty's Blues (medley) (3)
I Found Her In A Star (1)
Just Let Me Sing (10)
Key (2)
Laughing (2,5,15) 10
Lie Down (10)
Life In The Bloodstream (6,11)
Lightfoot (1)
Long Gone (13)
Lost And Found Town (9)
Love And A Yellow Rose (1)
Loves Me Like A Brother (13)
Maple Fudge (1)
Minstrel Boy (2)
Miss Frizzy (10)
Moan For You Joe (4)

Musicione (10)
New Mother Nature (3,5,8)
969 (The Oldest Man) (3)
No Sugar Tonight (medley) (3,5) flip
No Time (2,3,5,15) 5
Nobody Knows His Name (13)
Of A Dropping Pin (2)
Old Joe (2)
One Divided (6)
One Man Army (6)
One Way Road To Hell (12)
Orly (9,11)
Pain Train (6,8)
Pink Wine Sparkles In The Glass (1)
Pleasin' For Reason (12)
Power In The Music (14)
Proper Stranger (3)
Rain Dance (6,11) 19
Rich World - Poor World (14)

Road Food (12)
Rock And Roller Steam (9)
Rosanne (14)
Runnin' Back To Saskatoon (8,11) 96
Running Bear (7)
Samantha's Living Room (9)
Sea Of Love (medley) (7)
Seems Like I Can't Live With You, But I Can't Live Without You (13)
Self Pity (10)
Share The Land (4,5) 10
She Might Have Been A Nice Girl (4)
Shopping Bag Lady (14)
6 A.M. Or Nearer (2)
Smoke Big Factory (7)
So Long Bannatyne (6)
Song Of The Dog (medley) (4)
Sour Suite (6,11) 50

Star Baby (12,15) 39
Straighten Out (12)
Take It Off My Shoulders (10)
Talisman (3)
These Eyes (1,5,15) 6
Those Show Biz Shoes (9)
Three More Days (4)
Truckin' Off Across The Sky (8)
Undun (2,5,15) 22
Watcher, The (9)
We're Coming To Dinner (1)
Wednesday In Your Garden (1)
When Friends Fall Out (3)
When The Band Was Singin' "Shakin' All Over" (14,15)
When You Touch Me (1)
Women (14)
Your Nashville Sneakers (7)

GUIDED BY VOICES   '01

Rock group from Dayton, Ohio: Robert Pollard (vocals), Doug Gillard and Nate Farley (guitars), Tim Tobias (bass) and Jim MacPherson (drums).

DEBUT	PEAK	WKS	RIAA	CD	ARTIST — Album Title	Catalog	Sym	$	Label & Number
4/21/01	168	1		©	Isolation Drill			$10	TVT 2160

Brides Have Hit Glass
Chasing Heather Crazy
Enemy, The

Fair Touching
Fine To See You
Frostman

Glad Girls
How's My Drinking?
Pivotal Film

Privately
Run Wild
Sister I Need Wine

Skills Like This
Twilight Campfighter
Unspirited

Want One?

GUIDRY, Greg   '82

Born on 1/23/50 in St. Louis. Singer/songwriter/pianist.

DEBUT	PEAK	WKS	RIAA	CD	ARTIST — Album Title	Catalog	Sym	$	Label & Number
4/17/82	147	7			Over The Line			$12	Columbia 37735

Are You Ready For Love
Darlin' It's You

Goin' Down 17
Gotta Have More Love

(I'm) Givin' It Up
If Love Doesn't Find Us

Into My Love 92
Over The Line

Show Me Your Love
(That's) How Long

GUN   '90

Rock group from Glasgow, Scotland: Mark Rankin (vocals), Giuliano Gizzi and Baby Stafford (guitars), Dante Gizzi (bass) and Scott Shields (drums).

DEBUT	PEAK	WKS	RIAA	CD	ARTIST — Album Title	Catalog	Sym	$	Label & Number
3/31/90	134	8		©	Taking On The World			$10	A&M 5285

Better Days
Can't Get Any Lower

Feeling Within
Girls In Love

I Will Be Waiting
Inside Out

Money (Everybody Loves Her)
Shame On You

Something To Believe In
Taking On The World

GUNNE, Jo Jo — see JO JO

★262★   GUNS N' ROSES   '88

Hard-rock group formed in Los Angeles: William "Axl Rose" Bailey (vocals), Saul "Slash" Hudson and Jeffrey "Izzy Stradlin'" Isbell (guitars), Michael "Duff" McKagen (bass) and Steven Adler (drums). Rose married Erin Everly (daughter of Don Everly of The Everly Brothers) briefly in 1990. Matt Sorum replaced Adler in 1990. Keyboardist Dizzy Reed joined in 1990. Gilby Clarke replaced Stradlin' in late 1991. Slash married model Renee Surran in November 1992. Clarke left band in January 1995. Slash, Sorum and Clarke recorded in 1995 in Slash's Snakepit.

DEBUT	PEAK	WKS	RIAA	CD	ARTIST — Album Title	Catalog	Sym	$	Label & Number
8/29/87+	❶[5]	147	▲[15]	© 1	Appetite For Destruction	C:❶[1]/342		$10	Geffen 24148
12/17/88+	2[1]	53	▲[5]	© 2	G N' R Lies	C:#21/40		$10	Geffen 24198
					side A: reissue of their 4-song EP, Live Like A Suicide; side B: 4 tracks recorded in 1988				
10/5/91	❶[2]	106	▲[7]	© 3	Use Your Illusion II			$10	Geffen 24420
10/5/91	2[2]	108	▲[7]	© 4	Use Your Illusion I			$10	Geffen 24415
12/11/93	4	22	▲	© 5	The Spaghetti Incident?			$10	Geffen 24617
12/18/99	45	13	●	© 6	Live Era '87-'93		[L]	$15	Geffen 490514 [2]

Ain't It Fun (5)
Anything Goes (1)
Attitude (5)
Back Off Bitch (4)
Bad Apples (4)
Bad Obsession (4)
Black Leather (5)
Breakdown (3)
Buick Makane (5)
Civil War (3)
Coma (4)

Dead Horse (4)
Don't Cry (3,4,6) 10
Don't Damn Me (4)
Double Talkin' Jive (4)
Down On The Farm (5)
Dust N' Bones (4,6)
Estranged (3,6)
14 Years (3)
Garden, The (4)
Garden Of Eden (4)
Get In The Ring (3)

Hair Of The Dog (5)
Human Being (5)
I Don't Care About You (5)
It's Alright (6)
It's So Easy (1,6)
Knockin' On Heaven's Door (3,6)
Live And Let Die (4) 33
Locomotive (4)
Look At Your Game Girl (5)
Mama Kin (2)

Move To The City (2,6)
Mr. Brownstone (1,6)
My Michelle (1,6)
My World (3)
New Rose (5)
Nice Boys (2)
Nightrain (1,6) 93
November Rain (4,6) 3
One In A Million (2)
Out Ta Get Me (1,6)
Paradise City (1,6) 5

Patience (2,6) 4
Perfect Crime (4)
Pretty Tied Up (3,6)
Raw Power (5)
Reckless Life (2)
Right Next Door To Hell (4)
Rocket Queen (1,6)
Shotgun Blues (3)
Since I Don't Have You (5) 69
So Fine (5)
Sweet Child O' Mine (1,6) 1

Think About You (1)
Used To Love Her (2,6)
Welcome To The Jungle (1,6) 7
Yesterdays (3,6) 72
You Ain't The First (4)
You Can't Put Your Arms Around A Memory (5)
You Could Be Mine (3,6) 29
You're Crazy (1,2,6)

GURU '95

Born Keith Elam on 7/18/66 in Boston. Rapper from the duo **Gang Starr**. Guru stands for Gifted Unlimited Rhymes Universal.

6/5/93	94	19		©	1 **Jazzmatazz Volume I**			$10	Chrysalis 21998
8/5/95	71	9		©	2 **Jazzmatazz Volume II: The New Reality**			$10	Chrysalis 34290
10/21/00	32	7		©	3 **Jazzmatazz Streetsoul**			$10	Virgin 50189

All I Said (3)
Certified (2)
Choice Of Weapons (2)
Count Your Blessings (2)
Defining Purpose (2)
Down The Backstreets (1)
Feel The Music (2)
For You (2)
Guidance (3)
Hip Hop As A Way Of Life (3)
Hustlin' Daze (3)
Keep Your Worries (3)
Le Bien, Le Mal (1)
Lift Your Fist (3)
LiveSaver (2)
Living In This World (2)
Looking Through Darkness (2)
Lost Souls (3)
Loungin' (1)
Maintaining Focus (2)
Mashin' Up Da World (3)
Medicine (2)
New Reality Style (2)
Night Vision (3)
No More (3)
No Time To Play (1)
Nobody Knows (2)
Plenty (3)
Respect The Architect (2)
Revelation (2)
Sights In The City (1)
Slicker Than Most (1)
Something In The Past (2)
Supa Love (3)
Take A Look (At Yourself) (1)
Timeless (2)
Transit Ride (1)
Traveler, The (2)
Trust Me (1)
Watch What You Say (2)
When You're Near (1)
Where's My Ladies? (3)
Who's There? (3)
Young Ladies (2)

GURVITZ, Adrian — see BAKER GURVITZ ARMY / EDGE, Graeme, Band

GUSTER '99

Rock trio from Boston: Adam Gardner (vocals, guitar), Ryan Miller (guitar) and Brian Rosenworcel (drums).

| 10/16/99 | 169 | 1 | | © | **Lost And Gone Forever** | | | $10 | Hybrid 31064 |

All The Way Up To Heaven
Barrel Of A Gun
Center Of Attention
Either Way
Fa Fa
Happier
I Spy
Rainy Day
So Long
Two Points For Honesty
What You Wish For

★471★ GUTHRIE, Arlo '68

Born on 7/10/47 in Coney Island, New York. Folk singer/songwriter. Son of **Woody Guthrie**. Starred as himself in the 1969 movie *Alice's Restaurant* which was based on his 1967 song "Alice's Restaurant Massacree." Often performed in concert with **Pete Seeger**.

1)*Alice's Restaurant* 2)*Washington County* 3)*Hobo's Lullabye*

11/18/67+	17	99	▲	©	1 **Alice's Restaurant**			$20	Reprise 6267
10/26/68	100	12		©	2 **Arlo**	[L]		$20	Reprise 6299
					recorded at the Bitter End in New York City				
10/18/69	63	17			3 **Alice's Restaurant**	[S]		$20	United Artists 5195
					includes "Amazing Grace" by Garry Sherman Chorus, "Songs To Aging Children" by Tigger Outlaw and "You're A Fink" by Al Schackman				
10/25/69	54	19		©	4 **Running Down The Road**			$20	Reprise 6346
11/7/70	33	17		©	5 **Washington County**			$15	Reprise 6411
6/10/72	52	38		©	6 **Hobo's Lullabye**			$15	Reprise 2060
4/28/73	87	14		©	7 **Last Of The Brooklyn Cowboys**			$15	Reprise 2142
6/8/74	165	10		©	8 **Arlo Guthrie**			$15	Reprise 2183
5/17/75	181	4			9 **Together In Concert**	[L]		$20	Reprise 2214 [2]
					PETE SEEGER & ARLO GUTHRIE				
10/2/76	133	6		©	10 **Amigo**			$15	Reprise 2239
					title is Spanish for "Friend"				
6/27/81	184	3		©	11 **Power Of Love**			$12	Warner 3558

Alice's Restaurant Massacree (1,3)
hit POS 97 on "Hot 100" as Alice's Rock & Roll Restaurant
Anytime (6)
Bling Blang (8)
Children Of Abraham (8)
Chilling Of The Evening (1)
City Of New Orleans (6,9) *18*
Coming In To Los Angeles (4)
Connection (10)
Cooper's Lament (7)
Cowboy Song (7)
Crash Pad Improvs (3)
Creole Belle (4)
Darkest Hour (10)
Days Are Short (6)
Declaration Of Independence (9)
Deportee (Plane Wreck At Los Gatos) (8,9)
Don't Think Twice, It's All Right (9)
Estadio Chile (9)
Every Hand In The Land (4)
Farrell O'Gara (7)
Fence Post Blues (9)
Gabriel's Mother's Hiway Ballad #16 Blues (5)
Garden Song (11)
Gates Of Eden (7)
Get Up And Go (9)
Give It All You Got (11)
Go Down Moses (8)
Golden Vanity (9)
Grocery Blues (10)
Guabi, Guabi (9)
Guantanamera (9)
Gypsy Davy (7)
Hard Times (8)
Harps And Marriage (3)
Henry My Son (9)
Highway In The Wind (1)
Hobo's Lullaby (6)
I Could Be Singing (9)
I Want To Be Around (5)
I'm Going Home (1)
If I Could Only Touch Your Life (11)
If You Would Just Drop By (5)
Introduction (5)
Jamaica Farewell (11)
Joe Hill (9)
John Looked Down (2)
Last To Leave (8)
Last Train (7)
Lay Down Little Doggies (5)
Let Down (3)
Lightning Bar Blues (6)
Living In The Country (4)
Living Like A Legend (11)
Lonesome Valley (9)
Lovesick Blues (7)
Manzanillo Bay (10)
Mapleview (20%) Rag (6)
Massachusetts (10)
May There Always Be Sunshine (9)
Me And My Goose (8)
Meditation (Wave Upon Wave) (2)
Miss The Mississippi & You (7)
Mother, The Queen Of My Heart (9)
Motorcycle Song (1,2)
My Front Pages (4)
My Love (10)
1913 Massacre (6)
Nostalgia Rag (8)
Now And Then (1)
Ocean Crossing (10)
Oh, In The Morning (4)
Oklahoma Hills (4)
Oklahoma Nights (11)
On A Monday (9)
Patriots' Dream (10)
Pause Of Mr. Claus (2)
Percy's Song (5)
Power Of Love (11)
Presidential Rag (8,9)
Quite Early Morning (9)
Ramblin' 'Round (7)
Ring-Around-A-Rosy Rag (1)
Roving Gambler (9)
Running Down The Road (4)
Sailor's Bonnett (7)
Shackles & Chains (6)
Slow Boat (11)
Somebody Turned On The Light (6)
Standing At The Threshold (2)
Stealin' (4,9)
Sweet Rosyanne (9)
This Troubled Mind Of Mine (7)
Three Rules Of Discipline And The Eight Rules Of Attention (9)
Traveling Music (3)
Trip To The City (3)
Try Me One More Time (2)
Ukulele Lady (6)
Uncle Jeff (7)
Valley To Pray (5)
Victor Jara (10)
Waimanalo Blues (11)
Walkin' Down The Line (9)
Walking Song (10)
Washington County (5)
Way Out There (9)
Week On The Rag (7)
Well May The World Go (9)
Wheel Of Fortune (4)
When I Get To The Border (11)
When The Cactus Is In Bloom (8)
When The Ship Comes In (6)
Won't Be Long (8)
Wouldn't You Believe It (2)
Yodeling (9)

GUTHRIE, Gwen '86

Born on 7/9/50 in Newark, New Jersey. Died of cancer on 2/4/99 (age 48). R&B singer/songwriter.

| 8/30/86 | 89 | 13 | | © | **Good To Go Lover** | | | $10 | Polydor 829532 |

Ain't Nothin' Goin' On But The Rent *42*
Good To Go Lover
I Still Want You
Outside In The Rain
Passion Eyes
Stop Holding Back
(They Long To Be) Close To You
You Touched My Life

GUTHRIE, Woody — see VARIOUS ARTIST COMPILATIONS

GUY '00

R&B vocal trio from New York City: brothers **Aaron Hall** and **Damion Hall**, with Teddy Riley. Riley also formed **BLACKstreet**.

7/30/88+	27	70	▲²	©	1 **Guy**			$10	Uptown 42176
12/1/90+	16	46	▲	©	2 **The Future**			$10	MCA 10115
2/12/00	13	10		©	3 **III**			$10	MCA 112054

Dancin' (3) *19*
Do It (3)
Do Me Right (2)
D-O-G Me Out (2)
Don't Clap...Just Dance (2)
Don't U Miss Me (3)
Fly Away (3)
Future, The (2)
Goodbye Love (1)
Gotta Be A Leader (2)
Groove Me (1)
Her (2)
I Like (1) *70*
I Wanna Get With U (2) *50*
Let's Chill (2) *41*
Let's Stay Together (2)
Long Gone (2)
Love Online (3)
My Business (1)
Not A Day (3)
Piece Of My Love (1)
Rescue Me (3)
'Round And 'Round (Merry Go 'Round Of Love) (1)
Smile (2)
Someday (3)
Spend The Night (1)
Spend Time (3)
Tease Me Tonite (2)
Teddy's Jam (1)
Teddy's Jam 2 (2)
Teddy's Jam III (3)
Tellin Me No (3)
Total Control (2)
2004 (3)
We're Comin (3)
Where Did The Love Go (2)
Why You Wanna Keep Me From My Baby (3)
Yearning For Your Love (2)
You Can Call Me Crazy (1)

GUY, Buddy   '91

Born George Guy on 7/30/36 in Lettsworth, Louisiana. Blues singer/guitarist. Recipient of *Billboard's* Century Award in 1993.

DEBUT	PEAK	WKS	RIAA	CD	Album	$	Label & Number
10/19/91	136	6	●	© 1	Damn Right, I've Got The Blues	$10	Silvertone 41462
3/27/93	145	7		© 2	Feels Like Rain	$10	Silvertone 41498
11/12/94	180	1		© 3	Slippin' In	$10	Silvertone 41542
5/4/96	186	1		© 4	Live! The Real Deal [L]	$10	Silvertone 41543

BUDDY GUY WITH G.E. SMITH & THE SATURDAY NIGHT LIVE BAND
recorded at Irving Plaza in New York City and at Legend's in Chicago

DEBUT	PEAK	WKS	RIAA	CD	Album	$	Label & Number
6/20/98	163	1		© 5	Heavy Love	$10	Silvertone 41632
6/2/01	162	1		© 6	Sweet Tea	$10	Silvertone 41751

Ain't That Lovin' You (4)
Are You Lonely For Me Baby (5)
Baby Please Don't Leave Me (6)
Black Night (1)
Change In The Weather (2)
Cities Need Help (3)
Country Man (2)
Damn Right, I've Got The Blues (1,4)
Did Somebody Make A Fool Out Of You (5)

Don't Tell Me About The Blues (3)
Done Got Old (6)
Early In The Morning (1)
Feels Like Rain (2)
First Time I Met The Blues (4)
Five Long Years (1)
Had A Bad Night (5)
Heavy Love (5)
I Could Cry (2)
I Go Crazy (2)
I Got A Problem (5)
I Gotta Try You Girl (6)

I Just Want To Make Love To You (5)
I Need You Tonight (5)
I Smell Trouble (3)
I've Got My Eyes On You (4)
I've Got News For You (4)
It's A Jungle Out There (6)
Let Me Love You Baby (1,4)
Let Me Show You (5)
Little Dab-A-Doo (3)
Look What All You Got (6)
Love Her With A Feeling (3)
Man Of Many Words (3)

Mary Ann (2)
Midnight Train (5)
Mustang Sally (1)
My Time After Awhile (4)
Please Don't Drive Me Away (3)
Rememberin' Stevie (1)
Saturday Night Fish Fry (5)
7-11 (3)
Shame, Shame, Shame (3)
She Got The Devil In Her (6)
She's A Superstar (2)
She's Nineteen Years Old (2)
Some Kind Of Wonderful (2)

Someone Else Is Steppin' In (Slippin' Out, Slippin' In) (3)
Stay All Night (6)
Sufferin' Mind (2)
Sweet Black Angel (Black Angel Blues) (4)
Talk To Me Baby (4)
There Is Something On Your Mind (1)
Too Broke To Spend The Night (1)
Tramp (6)
Trouble Blues (3)

Trouble Man (2)
When The Time Is Right (5)
Where Is The Next One Coming From (1)
Who's Been Foolin' You (6)

GUY, Jasmine   '90

Born on 3/10/64 in Boston; raised in Atlanta. Singer/actress. Acted in several movies. Played "Whitley Gilbert" on TV's *A Different World*.

DEBUT	PEAK	WKS	RIAA	CD	Album	$	Label & Number
11/3/90	143	13		©	Jasmine Guy	$10	Warner 26021

Another Like My Lover *66*
Don't Want Money

Everybody Knows My Name
I Don't Have To Justify

I Wish You Well
Johnny Come Lately

Just Want To Hold You *34*
More Love

Try Me
Tuff Boy

GWAR   '92

Hard-rock group formed in Richmond, Virginia: David "Odorus Urungus" Brockie (vocals), Michael "Balsac the Jaws of Death" Derks and Peter "Flattus Maximus" Lee (guitars), Danyelle "Slymenstra Hymen" Stampe (whips), Charles "Sexicutioner" Varga (chains), Michael "Beefcake the Mighty" Bishop (bass) and Brad "Jizmak the Gusha" Roberts (drums). Group name stands for "God What an Awful Racket."

DEBUT	PEAK	WKS	RIAA	CD	Album	$	Label & Number
4/18/92	177	1		©	America Must Be Destroyed	$10	Metal Blade 26807

America Must Be Destroyed
Blimey
Crack In The Egg

Gilded Lily
Gor-Gor
Ham On The Bone

Have You Seen Me?
Morality Squad
Poor Ole Tom

Pussy Planet
Road Behind

Rock N Roll Never Felt So Good

GYPSY   '70

Rock group formed in Los Angeles: James "Owl" Walsh (vocals, keyboards), James Johnson and Enrico Rosenbaum (guitars), Doni Larson (bass) and Jay Epstein (drums). In early 1971, Willie Weeks replaced Larson and William Lordan replaced Epstein.

DEBUT	PEAK	WKS	RIAA	CD	Album	$	Label & Number
10/10/70	44	20		© 1	Gypsy	$20	Metromedia 1031 [2]
8/7/71	173	8		© 2	In The Garden	$15	Metromedia 1044

Around You (2)
As Far As You Can See, As Much As You Can Feel (2)
Blind Man (2)

Dead And Gone (1)
Decisions (1)
Dream If You Can (1)
Gypsy Queen - Part 1 (1) *62*

Gypsy Queen - Part 2 (1)
Here In My Loneliness (1)
Here (In The Garden) Part I & II (2)

I Was So Young (1)
Late December (1)
Man Of Reason (1)
More Time (1)

Reach Out Your Hand (2)
Third Eye (1)
Time Will Make It Better (1)

Tomorrow Is The Last To Be Heard (1)
Vision, The (1)

H

HACKETT, Steve   '78

Born on 2/12/50 in London. Rock guitarist. Former member of **Genesis** (1970-77). Formed **GTR** in 1986.

DEBUT	PEAK	WKS	RIAA	CD	Album	$	Label & Number
4/17/76	191	4		© 1	Voyage Of The Acolyte	$12	Chrysalis 1112
4/29/78	103	14		© 2	Please Don't Touch	$12	Chrysalis 1176
7/7/79	138	4		© 3	Spectral Mornings	$12	Chrysalis 1223
8/30/80	144	6		© 4	Defector	$12	Charisma 3103
10/24/81	169	3		© 5	Cured	$12	Epic 37632

Ace Of Wands (1)
Air-Conditioned Nightmare (5)
Ballad Of The Decomposing Man (3)
Can't Let Go (5)
Carry On Up The Vicarage (2)
Clocks - The Angel Of Mons (3)
Cradle Of Swans (5)

Every Day (3)
Funny Feeling (5)
Hammer In The Sand (4)
Hands Of The Priestess Part 1 & 2 (1)
Hermit, The (1)
Hope I Don't Wake (5)
Hoping Love Will Last (2)

How Can I (2)
Icarus Ascending (2)
Jacuzzi (4)
Kim (2)
Land Of A Thousand Autumns (2)
Leaving (4)
Lost Time In Cordoba (3)

Lovers, The (1)
Narnia (2)
Overnight Sleeper (5)
Picture Postcard (5)
Please Don't Touch (2)
Racing In A (2)
Red Flower Of Tachai Blooms Everywhere (3)

Sentimental Institution (4)
Shadow Of The Hierophant (1)
Show, The (4)
Slogans (4)
Spectral Mornings (3)
Star Of Sirius (1)
Steppes, The (4)
Tigermoth (3)

Time To Get Out (4)
Toast, The (4)
Tower Struck Down (1)
Turn Back Time (3)
Two Vamps As Guests (4)
Virgin And The Gypsy (3)
Voice Of Necan (2)

HADDAWAY   '94

Born Nestor Haddaway in 1966 in Tobago, West Indies; raised in Chicago. Singer/dancer/choreographer.

DEBUT	PEAK	WKS	RIAA	CD	Album	$	Label & Number
1/15/94	111	12		©	Haddaway	$10	Arista 18743

Come Back (Love Has Got A Hold On Me)
I Miss You

Life (Everybody Needs Somebody To Love) *41*
Mama's House

Rock My Heart
Shout
Sing About Love

Stir It Up
Tell Me Where It Hurts
What Is Love *11*

Yeah

★285★   HAGAR, Sammy   '87

Born on 10/13/47 in Monterey, California. Rock singer/songwriter/guitarist. Nicknamed "The Red Rocker." Lead singer of **Montrose** (1973-75) and **Van Halen** (1985-96). Also see **Hagar, Schon, Aaronson, Shrieve**.

1)Sammy Hagar 2)Three Lock Box 3)Marching To Mars

DEBUT	PEAK	WKS	RIAA	CD	Album	$	Label & Number
2/26/77	167	9		© 1	Sammy Hagar	$12	Capitol 11599
1/21/78	100	11		© 2	Musical Chairs	$12	Capitol 11706
8/19/78	89	9		© 3	All Night Long [L]	$12	Capitol 11812
9/8/79	71	13		© 4	Street Machine	$12	Capitol 11983
6/21/80	85	12		© 5	Danger Zone	$12	Capitol 12069
1/30/82	28	32	▲	© 6	Standing Hampton	$10	Geffen 2006
12/25/82+	17	34	●	© 7	Three Lock Box	$10	Geffen 2021

DEBUT	PEAK	WKS	RIAA	CD	ARTIST — Album Title	Catalog Sym	$	Label & Number
1/8/83	171	9		8	Rematch	[K]	$10	Capitol 12238
8/11/84	32	36	▲ ©	9	VOA		$10	Geffen 24043
7/11/87	14	23	● ©	10	Sammy Hagar		$10	Geffen 24144

as a result of an MTV contest, album title changed to *I Never Said Goodbye*; however, no vinyl copies were pressed with the new title

DEBUT	PEAK	WKS	RIAA	CD	ARTIST — Album Title	Catalog Sym	$	Label & Number
4/2/94	51	11	● ©	11	Unboxed	[G]	$10	Geffen 24702
6/7/97	18	17	©	12	Marching To Mars		$10	MCA 11627
4/10/99	22	14	©	13	Red Voodoo		$10	MCA 11872

SAMMY HAGAR and The Waboritas

| 11/11/00 | 52 | 2 | © | 14 | Ten 13 | | $10 | Cabo Wabo 78110 |

Amnesty Is Granted (12)
Baby, It's You (6)
Baby's On Fire (6,11)
Back Into You (10)
Bad Motor Scooter (3)
Bad Reputation (5,8)
Both Sides Now (12)
Boys' Night Out (14)
Burnin' Down The City (9)
Buying My Way Into Heaven (11)
Can't Get Loose (6)
Catch The Wind (1)
Child To Man (4)
Crack In The World (2)
Cruisin' & Boozin' (1,8)
Danger Zone (5)
Deeper Kinda Love (14)
Dick In The Dirt (9)
Don't Fight It (Feel It) (13)
Don't Make Me Wait (9)
Don't Stop Me Now (2)

Eagles Fly (10,11) *82*
Eclipse (medley) (1)
Falling In Love (4)
Feels Like Love (4)
Fillmore Shuffle (1)
Free Money (1)
Give To Live (10,11) *23*
Growing Pains (4)
Growing Up (7)
Hands And Knees (10)
Heartbeat (5)
Heavy Metal (6,11)
Hey Boys (2)
High And Dry Again (13)
High Hopes (11)
Hungry (1)
I Can't Drive 55 (9,11) *26*
I Don't Need Love (7,11)
I Wouldn't Change A Thing (7)
I'll Fall In Love Again (6,11) *43*
I've Done Everything For You (3,8)

Iceman, The (5)
In The Night (Entering The Danger Zone) (5)
In The Room (1)
Inside Lookin' In (6)
It's Gonna Be All Right (2)
Kama (12)
Lay Your Hand On Me (13)
Leaving The Warmth Of The Womb (2)
Let Sally Drive (14)
Little Bit More (14)
Little Star (medley) (1)
Little White Lie (12)
Love, The (13)
Love Has Found Me (1)
Love Or Money (5,8)
Make It Last (medley) (3)
Marching To Mars (12)
Mas Tequila (13)
Message, The (14)
Miles From Boredom (5)

Mommy Says, Daddy Says (5)
Never Give Up (7) *46*
Never Say Die (4)
On The Other Hand (12)
Piece Of My Heart (6) *73*
Pits, The (1)
Plain Jane (4,8) *77*
Privacy (10)
Protection (14)
Real Deal (14)
Reckless (2,3)
Red (1,3,8)
Red Voodoo (13)
Remember The Heroes (7)
Remote Love (7)
Returning Home (10)
Returning Of The Wish (13)
Revival, The (13)
Right On Right (13)
Rise Of The Animal (7)
Rock 'N' Roll Weekend (1,3,8)
Rock Is In My Blood (9)

Run For Your Life (5)
Salvation On Sand Hill (12)
Serious Juju (14)
Shag (13)
Shaka Doobie (The Limit) (14)
Someone Out There (2)
Standin' At The Same Old Crossroads (12)
Straight From The Hip Kid (7)
Straight To The Top (4)
Surrender (6)
Sweet Hitchhiker (6)
Swept Away (9)
Sympathy For The Human (13)
Ten 13 (14)
There's Only One Way To Rock (6,11)
This Planet's On Fire (Burn In Hell) (4,8)
3 In The Middle (14)
Three Lock Box (7,11)

Trans Am (Highway Wonderland) (4,8)
Tropic Of Capricorn (14)
Try (Try To Fall In Love) (2)
Turn Up The Music (2,3,8)
20th Century Man (5)
Two Sides Of Love (9,11) *38*
VOA (9)
What They Gonna Say Now (10)
When The Hammer Falls (10)
Who Has The Right? (12)
Would You Do It For Free? (12)
Wounded In Love (4)
Yogi's So High (I'm Stoned) (12)
You Make Me Crazy (2) *62*
Young Girl Blues (3)
Your Love Is Driving Me Crazy (7) *13*

HAGAR, SCHON, AARONSON, SHRIEVE '84

All-star rock group: **Sammy Hagar** (vocals), **Neal Schon** (guitar), Kenny Aaronson (bass) and **Michael Shrieve** (drums).

| 3/31/84 | 42 | 18 | © | | Through The Fire | [L] | $10 | Geffen 4023 |

Animation
Giza

He Will Understand
Hot And Dirty

Missing You
My Home Town

Top Of The Rock
Valley Of The Kings

Whiter Shade Of Pale *94*

HAGEN, Nina '84

Born on 3/11/55 in East Berlin. Dance-punk singer/actress.

| 6/5/82 | 184 | 3 | © | 1 | Nunsexmonkrock | | $10 | Columbia 38008 |
| 1/28/84 | 151 | 8 | © | 2 | Fearless | | $10 | Columbia 39214 |

Antiworld (1)
Born In Xixax (1)
Change, The (2)
Cosma Shiva (1)

Dr. Art (1)
Dread Love (1)
Flying Saucers (2)
Future Is Now (1)

I Love Paul (2)
Iki Maska (1)
My Sensation (2)
New York New York (2)

Silent Love (2)
Smack Jack (1)
Springtime In Paris (2)
T.V. Snooze (2)

Taitschi - Tarot (1)
UFO (1)
What It Is (2)
Zarah (2)

★268★ HAGGARD, Merle '70

Born on 4/6/37 in Bakersfield, California. Country singer/songwriter/guitarist.

1)Pancho & Lefty 2)Okie From Muskogee 3)A Tribute To The Best Damn Fiddle Player In The World 4)Hag 5)Same Train, A Different Time

DEBUT	PEAK	WKS	RIAA	CD	ARTIST — Album Title	Catalog Sym	$	Label & Number
5/13/67	165	10	©	1	I'm A Lonesome Fugitive		$30	Capitol 2702
10/21/67	167	4	©	2	Branded Man		$30	Capitol 2789
3/15/69	189	7		3	Pride In What I Am		$25	Capitol 168
6/14/69	67	18	©	4	Same Train, A Different Time		$30	Capitol 223 [2]
8/23/69	140	6		5	Close-Up		$30	Capitol 259 [2]

reissue of *Strangers* and *Swinging Doors* albums

| 10/18/69 | 99 | 11 | © | 6 | A Portrait Of Merle Haggard | | $20 | Capitol 319 |
| 1/24/70 | 46 | 52 | ▲ © | 7 | Okie From Muskogee | [L] | $20 | Capitol 384 |

recorded in Muskogee, Oklahoma

| 7/25/70 | 68 | 33 | ● © | 8 | The Fightin' Side Of Me | [L] | $20 | Capitol 451 |

recorded at the Civic Center Hall in Philadelphia

12/19/70+	58	9	©	9	A Tribute To The Best Damn Fiddle Player In The World (or, My Salute To Bob Wills)		$20	Capitol 638
4/17/71	66	15		10	Hag		$15	Capitol 735
9/18/71	108	10		11	Someday We'll Look Back		$15	Capitol 835
4/8/72	166	8		12	Let Me Tell You About A Song		$15	Capitol 882
10/7/72	137	9	▲	13	The Best Of The Best Of Merle Haggard	[G]	$15	Capitol 11082
8/25/73	126	11	©	14	I Love Dixie Blues...so I recorded "Live" in New Orleans	[L]	$15	Capitol 11200
12/8/73	4[X]	3	©	15	Merle Haggard's Christmas Present (Something Old, Something New)	[X]	$15	Capitol 11230
3/23/74	190	3		16	If We Make It Through December		$15	Capitol 11276
6/28/75	129	9		17	Keep Movin' On		$15	Capitol 11365
11/19/77	133	5	©	18	My Farewell To Elvis		$15	MCA 2314
11/7/81+	161	28	● ©	19	Big City		$12	Epic 37593
9/25/82	123	12	©	20	A Taste Of Yesterday's Wine		$12	Epic 38203

MERLE HAGGARD & GEORGE JONES

| 2/12/83 | 37 | 53 | ▲ © | 21 | Pancho & Lefty | | $12 | Epic 37958 |

MERLE HAGGARD/WILLIE NELSON

After I Sing All My Songs (20)
All Of Me Belongs To You (1)
All The Soft Places To Fall (21)
Always Wanting You (17)
Are The Good Times Really Over (I Wish A Buck Was Still Silver) (19)

Are You Lonesome Tonight (18)
Better Off When I Was Hungry (16)
Big Bad Bill (Is Sweet William Now) (14)
Big City (19)
Big Time Annie's Square (11)

Bill Woods From Bakersfield (11)
Billy Overcame His Size (7)
Blue Christmas (18)
Blue Rock (7)
Blue Suede Shoes (18)
Blue Yodel No. 6 (4)

Bobby Wants A Puppy Dog For Christmas (15)
Bottle Let Me Down (5)
Brain Cloudy Blues (9)
Branded Man (2,7)
Bring It On Down To My House, Honey (12)

Brothers, The (20)
Brown Skinned Gal (9)
C.C. Waterback (20)
California Blues (3,4)
California Cottonfields (11)
Carolyn (11,14) *58*
Champagne (14)

Come On Into My Arms (16)
Corrine Corrina (8,9)
Daddy Frank (The Guitar Man) (12,13)
Daddy Won't Be Home Again For Christmas (15)
Day The Rains Came (3)

357

HAGGARD, Merle — Cont'd

Devil Woman (medley) (8)
Don't Be Cruel (18)
Don't Get Married (2)
Down The Old Road To Home (4)
Drink Up And Be Somebody (1)
Emptiest Arms In The World (14)
Every Fool Has A Rainbow (6,8,13)
Everybody's Had The Blues (14) *62*
Falling For You (5)
Farmer's Daughter (10,13)
Fightin' Side Of Me (8,13) *92*
Finale (14)
Folsom Prison Blues (medley) (8)
Frankie And Johnny (4)
From Graceland To The Promised Land (18) *58*
Funeral, The (12)
Go Home (2)
Gone Crazy (2)
Good Old American Guest (19)
Grandma Harp (12)
Grandma's Christmas Card (15)
Half A Man (21)
Hammin' It Up (8,14)
Harold's Super Service (8)
Heartbreak Hotel (18)
Here In Frisco (17)
High On A Hilltop (5)
Hobo Bill's Last Ride (4,7)
Hobo's Meditation (4)
House Of Memories (1)
Hungry Eyes (6,13)
Huntsville (11)
I Ain't Got Nobody (And Nobody Cares For Me) (14)
I Always Get Lucky With You (19)
I Came So Close To Living Alone (6)

I Can't Be Myself (10)
I Can't Hold Myself In Line (3)
I Can't Stand Me (5)
I Die Ten Thousand Times A Day (6)
I Forget Every Day (14)
I Haven't Found Her Yet (20)
I Just Want To Look At You One More Time (3)
I Knew The Moment I Lost You (9)
I Made The Prison Band (2)
I Take A Lot Of Pride In What I Am (3,8)
I Think I'm Gonna Live Forever (19)
I Think I've Found A Way (To Live Without You) (20)
I Think We're Livin' In The Good Old Days (3)
I Threw Away The Rose (2)
I Wonder If They Ever Think Of Me (14)
I'd Rather Be Gone (11)
I'd Trade All Of My Tomorrows (5)
I'll Break Out Again Tonight (16)
I'll Look Over You (5)
I'm A Good Loser (10)
I'm A Lonesome Fugitive (1,7)
I'm An Old, Old Man (Tryin' To Live While I Can) (16)
I'm Bringin' Home Good News (3)
I'm Free (3)
I'm Gonna Break Every Heart I Can (5)
I'm Movin' On (medley) (8)
I've Done It All (10)
I've Got A Darlin' (For A Wife) (17)
I've Got A Yearning (17)
If I Could Be Him (5)
If I Had Left It Up To You (5,7)

If We Make It Through December (15,16) *28*
If You Want To Be My Woman (1)
If You've Got Time (To Say Goodbye) (10)
In The Arms Of Love (7)
In The Ghetto (18)
Irma Jackson (12)
It Meant Goodbye To Me When You Said Hello To Him (3)
It's My Lazy Day (21)
Jackson (medley) (8)
Jailhouse Rock (18)
Jesus, Take A Hold (10)
Jimmie Rodgers' Last Blue Yodel (The Women Make A Fool Out Of Me) (4)
Jimmie's Texas Blues (4)
Jingle Bells (15)
Keep Me From Cryin' Today (3)
Kentucky Gambler (17)
Life In Prison (1)
Life's Like Poetry (17)
Loneliness Is Eating Me Alive (2)
Long Black Limousine (2)
Longer You Wait (13)
Love And Honor (16)
Love Me Tender (18)
Love's Gonna Live Here (medley) (8)
Lovesick Blues (14)
Mama Tried (7,13)
Man Who Picked The Wildwood Flower (12)
Man's Gotta Give Up A Lot (17)
Mary's Mine (1)
Misery (9)
Miss The Mississippi And You (4)
Mixed Up Mess Of A Heart (1)
Mobile Bay (Magnolia Blossoms) (20)

Montego Bay (6)
Mother, The Queen Of My Heart (4)
Movin' On (17)
Mule Skinner Blues (Blue Yodel No. 8) (4)
Must've Been Drunk (20)
My Carolina Sunshine Girl (4)
My Favorite Memory (19)
(My Friends Are Gonna Be) Strangers (5)
My Hands Are Tied (2)
My Life's Been A Pleasure (I Still Love You As I Did In Yesterday) (21)
My Mary (21)
My Old Pal (4)
My Rough And Rowdy Ways (1)
No Hard Times (4,7)
No More You And Me (3)
No Reason To Quit (10,13,21)
No Show Jones (20)
Nobody Knows But Me (4)
Nobody Knows I'm Hurtin' (14)
Okie From Muskogee (7,8,13,14) *41*
Old Doc Brown (12)
Old Fashioned Love (9)
One Row At A Time (3)
One Sweet Hello (11)
Only Trouble With Me (11)
Opportunity To Cry (21)
Orange Blossom Special (medley) (8)
Pancho And Lefty (21)
Peach Picking Time Down In Georgia (4)
Philadelphia Lawyer (8)
Please Mr. D.J. (5)
Proudest Fiddle In The World (A Maiden's Prayer) (12)
Reasons To Quit (21)
Right Or Wrong (9)
Roly Poly (9)

Sam Hill (5)
San Antonio Rose (9)
Santa Claus And Popcorn (15)
September In Miami (17)
Shade Tree (Fix-It Man) (5)
She Thinks I Still Care (6)
Shelly's Winter Love (10)
Sidewalks Of Chicago (10)
Silent Night (15)
Silver Bells (15)
Silver Eagle (20)
Silver Wings (6,7,13)
Sing A Sad Song (5)
Sing Me Back Home (medley) (7)
Skid Row (1)
Soldier's Last Letter (10) *90*
Some Of Us Never Learn (2)
Someday We'll Look Back (11)
Someone Else You've Known (5)
Someone Told My Story (1)
Somewhere Between (2)
Somewhere On Skid Row (3)
Stay A Little Longer (9)
Stealin' Corn (8)
Still Water Runs The Deepest (21)
Stop The World (And Let Me Off) (19)
Swinging Doors (5,7)
T.B. Blues (8)
Take Me Back To Tulsa (9)
Texas Fiddle Song (19)
That's All Right (Mama) (18)
There's Just One Way (16)
These Mem'ries We're Making Tonight (17)
They're Tearin' The Labor Camps Down (12)
This Cold War (16)
This Song Is Mine (19)
Time Changes Everything (9)

To Each His Own (16)
Today I Started Loving You Again (8,13)
Train Of Life (11)
Train Whistle Blues (4)
Travelin' Blues (4)
Tulare Dust (11)
Turnin' Off A Memory (12)
Uncle Lem (16)
Waitin' For A Train (4)
Walking The Floor Over You (5)
'Way Down Yonder In New Orleans (14)
What's Wrong With Stayin' Home (6)
Whatever Happened To Me (1)
When Did Right Become Wrong (8)
White Christmas (15)
White Line Fever (7)
Who Do I Know In Dallas (6)
Who'll Buy The Wine (3)
Why Should I Be Lonely? (4)
Winter Wonderland (15)
Workin' Man Blues (6,7,13,19)
Yesterday's Wine (20)
You Don't Have Very Far To Go (2,5,19)
You'll Always Be Special (17)
You're The Only Girl In The Game (16)

HAIRCUT ONE HUNDRED '82

Pop-rock group from Beckenham, Kent, England: **Nick Heyward** (vocals), Graham Jones (guitar), Phil Smith (sax), Mark Fox (percussion), Les Nemes (bass) and Blair Cunningham (drums).

| 4/24/82 | 31 | 37 | © | Pelican West .... | $12 Arista 6600 |

Baked Bean
Calling Captain Autumn
Fantastic Day
Favourite Shirts (Boy Meets Girl)
Kingsize (You're My Little Steam Whistle)
Lemon Firebrigade
Love Plus One *37*
Love's Got Me In Triangles
Marine Boy
Milk Farm
Snow Girl
Surprise Me Again

HALEY, Bill, And His Comets '55

Born on 7/6/25 in Highland Park, Michigan. Died of a heart attack on 2/9/81 (age 55). Began career as a country singer. His Comets consisted of Billy Williamson (guitar), Joey D'Ambrose (sax), Johnny Grande (piano), Marshall Lytle (bass) and Billy Guesack (drums). D'Ambrose, Richards and Lytle left in September 1955 to form the Jodimars. Comets lineup on subsequent recordings included Williamson, Grande, Frank Beecher (guitar), Rudy Pompilli (sax), Al Rex (bass), Ralph Jones (drums). Pompilli died of cancer on 2/5/76 (age 47). Group inducted into the Rock and Roll Hall of Fame in 1987.

2/19/55	5	32	1 Shake Rattle and Roll	[EP] $100 Decca 2168
1/28/56	12	4	2 Rock Around the Clock	[G] $150 Decca 8225
10/13/56	18	5	3 Rock 'n Roll Stage Show	$150 Decca 8345

A.B.C. Boogie (1,2)
Birth Of The Boogie (2) *17*
Blue Comet Blues (3)
Burn That Candle (2) *9*
Calling All Comets (3)
Choo Choo Ch'Boogie (3)
Dim, Dim The Lights (I Want Some Atmosphere) (2) *11*
Goofin' Around (3)
Happy Baby (2)
Hey Then, There Now (3)
Hide And Seek (3)
Hook, Line And Sinker (3)
Hot Dog Buddy Buddy (3) *60*
Mambo Rock (2) *18*
Razzle-Dazzle (2) *15*
Rock-A-Beatin' Boogie (2) *23*
Rockin' Through The Rye (3) *78*
Rocking Little Tune (3)
Rudy's Rock (3) *34*
Shake, Rattle And Roll (1,2)
Thirteen Women (And Only One Man In Town) (1,2)
Tonight's The Night (3)
Two Hound Dogs (2) *flip*
(We're Gonna) Rock Around The Clock (1,2) *1*

HALFORD '00

Born Rob Halford on 8/25/51 in Walsall, England. Hard-rock singer. Former lead singer of **Judas Priest**, **Fight** and **Two**.

| 8/26/00 | 140 | 1 | © | Resurrection .... | $10 Metal-Is 85200 |

Cyberworld
Drive
Locked And Loaded
Made In Hell
Night Fall
One You Love To Hate
Resurrection
Saviour
Silent Screams
Slow Down
Temptation
Twist

HALL, Aaron '93

Born on 8/10/64 in Brooklyn, New York. Member of **Guy** with younger brother **Damion Hall**.

| 10/16/93 | 47 | 55 | ▲ | © | 1 The Truth .... | $10 Silas 10810 |
| 11/7/98 | 55 | 5 | © | 2 Inside Of You .... | $10 Silas 11778 |

All The Places (I Will Kiss You) (2) *26*
Baby I'll Be By Your Side (2)
Do Anything (1)
Don't Be Afraid (1)
Don't Rush The Night (2)
Get A Little Freaky With Me (1)
Going Down (2)
I Miss You (1) *14*
I Want Your Body (2)
I'll Do Anything (2)
If You Leave Me (1)
Let's Make Love (1)
Move It Girl (2)
None But The Righteous (2)
None Like You (2)
Open Up (1)
Pick Up The Phone (1)
Thinkin' Of You (2)
Until I Found You (1)
Until The End Of Time (1)
What Did I Do (2)
When You Need Me (1)
You Keep Me Crying (1)
You Make Me Feel Good Inside (2)

HALL, Arsenio — see CHUNKY A

HALL, Damion "Crazy Legs" '94

Born Albert Damion Hall on 6/6/68 in Brooklyn, New York. Member of **Guy** with older brother **Aaron Hall**.

| 5/14/94 | 147 | 2 | © | Straight To The Point .... | $10 Silas 10996 |

Black As You Wanna Be
Crazy About You
Do Me Like You Wanna Be Done
Holdin' On
Let's Get It Going On
Long Lasting Love Affair
Lost Inside Of You
Love's Knockin'
Never Enough
Now Or Never
Satisfy You
Second Chance
Song For You

HALL, Daryl '86

Born Daryl Franklin Hohl on 10/11/48 in Philadelphia. Half of **Hall & Oates** duo.

3/29/80	**58**	12	© 1	**Sacred Songs**	$12	RCA Victor 3573
9/6/86	**29**	26	© 2	**Three Hearts in the Happy Ending Machine**	$10	RCA Victor 7196
9/25/93	**177**	3	© 3	**Soul Alone**	$10	Epic 53937

Babs And Babs (1)
Borderline (3)
Don't Leave Me Alone With Her (1)
Dreamtime (2) *5*
Farther Away I Am (1)

Foolish Pride (2) *33*
Help Me Find A Way To Your Heart (3)
I Wasn't Born Yesterday (2)

I'm In A Philly Mood (3) *82*
Let It Out (2)
Love Revelation (3)
Money Changes Everything (3)
NYCNY (1)
Next Step (2)

Only A Vision (2)
Power Of Seduction (3)
Right As Rain (2)
Sacred Songs (1)
Send Me (3)
Someone Like You (2) *57*

Something In 4/4 Time (1)
Stop Loving Me, Stop Loving You (3)
Survive (1)
This Time (3)
Urban Landscape (1)

What's Gonna Happen To Us (2)
Why Was It So Easy (1)
Wildfire (3)
Without Tears (1)
Written In Stone (3)

HALL, Daryl, & John Oates ★101★ '83

Daryl Hall (see previous entry) and John Oates (born on 4/7/49 in New York City) met while students at Temple University in 1967. Hall sang backup for many top soul groups before teaming up with Oates in 1972. They passed **The Everly Brothers** as the #1 charting duo of the rock era.

1)H₂O 2)Private Eyes 3)Big Bam Boom

2/23/74+	**33**	38	● © 1	**Abandoned Luncheonette**	$15	Atlantic 7269
10/26/74	**86**	10	2	**War Babies**	$15	Atlantic 18109
				produced by **Todd Rundgren**		
9/13/75+	**17**	76	● © 3	**Daryl Hall & John Oates**	$12	RCA Victor 1144
8/28/76	**13**	57	● © 4	**Bigger Than Both Of Us**	$12	RCA Victor 1467
3/26/77	**92**	6	5	**No Goodbyes**	[K] $12	Atlantic 18213
9/17/77	**30**	17	● © 6	**Beauty On A Back Street**	$12	RCA Victor 2300
5/27/78	**42**	10	7	**Livetime**	[L] $12	RCA Victor 2802
9/9/78	**27**	22	● © 8	**Along The Red Ledge**	$12	RCA Victor 2804
10/27/79	**33**	24	© 9	**X-Static**	$12	RCA Victor 3494
8/16/80+	**17**	100	▲ © 10	**Voices**	$10	RCA Victor 3646
9/26/81+	**5**	61	▲ © 11	**Private Eyes**	$10	RCA Victor 4028
10/30/82+	**3**	68	▲² © 12	**H₂O**	$10	RCA Victor 4383
11/19/83+	**7**	44	▲² © 13	**Rock 'N Soul, Part 1**	C:#45/5 [G] $10	RCA Victor 4858
10/27/84	**5**	51	▲² © 14	**Big Bam Boom**	$10	RCA Victor 5309
9/28/85	**21**	18	● © 15	**Live At The Apollo with David Ruffin & Eddie Kendrick**	[L] $10	RCA Victor 7035
				recorded at the re-opening of New York's Apollo Theater; side 1 features guest vocalists Ruffin and Kendrick		
5/21/88	**24**	26	▲ © 16	**ooh yeah!**	$10	Arista 8539
10/27/90	**60**	29	● © 17	**Change Of Season**	$10	Arista 8614
10/18/97	**95**	5	© 18	**Marigold Sky**	$10	Push 90200

Abandoned Luncheonette (1,7)
Adult Education (13,15) *8*
Africa (10)
Ain't Too Proud To Beg (medley) (15)
All You Want Is Heaven (9)
All American Girl (14)
Alley Katz (8)
Alone Too Long (3)
Art Of Heartbreak (12)
At Tension (12)
August Day (8)
Back Together Again (4) *28*
Bad Habits And Infections (6)
Bank On Your Love (14)
Beanie G. And The Rose Tattoo (2,5)
Bebop/Drop (9)
Better Watch Your Back (2)
Big Kids (10)
Bigger Than Both Of Us (6)
Camellia (3)
Can't Stop The Music (He Played It Much Too Long) (2,5)
Change Of Season (17)
Cold Dark And Yesterday (14)
Crazy Eyes (4)
Crime Pays (12)
Dance On Your Knees (14)
Delayed Reaction (12)
Did It In A Minute (11) *9*
Diddy Doo Wop (I Hear The Voices) (10)

Do What You Want, Be What You Are (4,7) *39*
Don't Blame It On Love (8)
Don't Change (6)
Don't Hold Back Your Love (17) *41*
Downtown Life (16) *31*
Emptyness, The (6,7)
Ennui On The Mountain (3)
Everything Your Heart Desires (16) *3*
Everytime I Look At You (1)
Everytime You Go Away (10,15)
Everywhere I Look (17)
Falling (4)
Family Man (12) *6*
Friday Let Me Down (11)
Get Ready (medley) (15)
Gino (The Manager) (3)
Girl Who Used To Be (6)
Give It Up (Old Habits) (17)
Go Solo (12)
Going Thru The Motions (14)
Gotta Lotta Nerve (Perfect Perfect) (10)
Grounds For Separation (3)
Guessing Games (12)
Had I Known You Better Then (1)
Halfway There (17)
Hallofon (9)
Hard To Be In Love With You (10)

Have I Been Away Too Long (8)
Head Above Water (11)
Heavy Rain (17)
Hold On To Yourself (18)
How Does It Feel To Be Back (10) *30*
I Ain't Gonna Take It This Time (17)
I Can't Go For That (No Can Do) (11,13,15) *1*
I Don't Think So (18)
I Don't Wanna Lose You (8) *42*
I Want To Know You For A Long Time (5)
I'm In Pieces (16)
I'm Just A Kid (Don't Make Me Feel Like A Man) (1,7)
I'm Watching You (A Mutant Romance) (2)
Intravino (9)
Is It A Star (2)
It's A Laugh (8) *20*
It's Uncanny (5) *80*
Italian Girls (12)
Johnny Gore And The "C" Eaters (2)
Keep On Pushin' Love (16)
Kerry (4)
Kiss On My List (10,13) *1*
Lady Rain (1)
Las Vegas Turnaround (The Stewardess Song) (1,5)
Last Time (8)

Laughing Boy (1)
Lilly (Are You Happy) (5)
London Luck, & Love (4)
Looking For A Good Sign (11)
Love Hurts (Love Heals) (6)
Love You Like A Brother (5)
Love Out Loud (18)
Maneater (12,13) *1*
Mano A Mano (11)
Marigold Sky (18)
Melody For A Memory (8)
Method Of Modern Love (14) *5*
Missed Opportunity (16) *29*
My Girl ..see: Nite At The Apollo Live!
Nite At The Apollo Live! The Way You Do The Things You Do/My Girl (15) *20*
Nothing At All (3)
Number One (9)
One On One (12,13,15) *7*
Only Love (17)
Open All Night (12)
Out Of Me, Out Of You (3)
Out Of The Blue (18)
Out Of Touch (14) *1*
Pleasure Beach (8)
Portable Radio (9)
Possession Obsession (14,15) *30*
Private Eyes (11,13) *1*
Promise Ain't Enough (18)
ReaLove (16)

Rich Girl (4,7,13) *1*
Rockability (16)
Rocket To God (16)
Romeo Is Bleeding (18)
Room To Breathe (4,7)
Running From Paradise (9)
Sara Smile (3,7,13) *4*
Say It Isn't So (13) *2*
Screaming Through December (2)
Serious Music (8)
70's Scenario (2,5)
She's Gone (1,5,13) *7*
Sky Is Falling (18)
So Close (17) *11*
Soldering (3)
Some Men (11)
Some Things Are Better Left Unsaid (14) *18*
Sometimes A Mind Changes (17)
Soul Love (16)
Starting All Over Again (17)
Talking All Night (16)
Tell Me What You Want (11)
Throw The Roses Away (18)
Time Won't Pass Me By (18)
Unguarded Minute (11)
United State (10)
Wait For Me (9,13) *18*
Want To (18)
War Baby Son Of Zorro (2)
War Of Words (18)

Way You Do The Things You Do ..see: Nite At The Apollo Live!
When Something Is Wrong With My Baby (15)
When The Morning Comes (1,5)
Who Said The World Was Fair (9)
Why Do Lovers (Break Each Others Heart?) (6) *73*
Winged Bull (4)
Woman Comes And Goes (9)
(You Know) It Doesn't Matter Anymore (3)
You Make My Dreams (10,13) *5*
You Must Be Good For Something (6)
You'll Never Learn (4)
You're Much Too Soon (2)
You've Lost That Lovin' Feeling (12) *12*
Your Imagination (11) *33*

HALL, Jimmy '80

Born on 4/26/49 in Mobile, Alabama. Lead singer of **Wet Willie**.

11/22/80	**183**	2		**Touch You**	$12	Epic 36516

Bad News
Eazy Street

I'm Happy That Love Has Found You *27*

Midnight To Daylight
Never Again

Private Number
Rock & Roll Soldier

Same Old Moon
634-5789

Touch You

HALL, John, Band '83
Born on 10/25/47 in Baltimore. Rock singer/guitarist. Leader of **Orleans**. Band includes Bob Leinbach (keyboards), John Troy (bass) and Eric Parker (drums).

| 12/5/81 | **158** | 13 | | | 1 **All Of The Above** .... | | | **$12** | EMI America 17058 |
| 3/5/83 | **147** | 5 | | | 2 **Searchparty** .... | | | **$12** | EMI America 17082 |

Can't Stand To See You Go (1) — Don't Treat Your Woman Like That (2) — Ipso Facto (2) — Open Up The Door (2) — Star In Your Sky (1) — You Sure Fooled Me (1)
Clouds (1) — Little Miss Maybe (2) — Original Sin (2) — Touch, The (1)
Crazy (Keep On Falling) (1) 42 — Earth Out Tonight (1) — **Love Me Again** (2) 64 — Security (2) — What You Do To Me (1)
Don't Hurt Me (1) — I'm The One (2) — On Hold (2) — Somebody's Calling (1) — Woman Of The Water (2)

HALL, Tom T. '71
Born on 5/25/36 in Olive Hill, Kentucky. Country singer/songwriter/guitarist.

10/9/71	**137**	6			1 **In Search Of A Song**			**$15**	Mercury 61350
6/9/73	**181**	4			2 **The Rhymer And Other Five And Dimers**			**$15**	Mercury 668
1/26/74	**149**	11			3 **For The People In The Last Hard Town**			**$15**	Mercury 687
4/19/75	**180**	2			4 **Songs Of Fox Hollow**			**$15**	Mercury 500

Another Town (2) — I Care (3) — Joe, Don't Let Your Music Kill You (3) — Mysterious Fox Of Fox Hollow (4) — Second Handed Flowers (1) — Who's Gonna Feed Them Hogs (1)
Back When We Were Young (3) — I Flew Over Our House Last Night (2) — Kentucky Feb. 27, '71 (1) — Never Having You (3) — **Sneaky Snake** (4) 55 — **Year That Clayton Delaney Died** (1) 42
Barn Dance (4) — I Know Who I'll Be Seeing In New Zealand (3) — L.A. Blues (1) — Old Five And Dimers Like Me (2) — Song For Uncle Curt (2)
Candy In The Window (2) — I Like To Feel Pretty Inside (4) — Last Hard Town (3) — Ole Lonesome George The Basset (4) — Song Of The One Legged Chicken (4)
Don't Forget The Coffee Billy Joe (2) — **I Love** (3,4) 12 — Little Lady Preacher (4) — Pay No Attention To Alice (3) — Spokane Motel Blues (2)
Everybody Loves To Hear A Bird Sing (4) — I Wish I Had A Million Friends (4) — Looking Forward To Seeing You Again (2) — Ramona's Revenge (2) — Subdivision Blues (3)
How To Talk To A Little Baby Goat (4) — It Sure Can Get Cold In Des Moines (1) — Love's Been Good To Me (3) — Ravishing Ruby (2) — Too Many Do-Goods (2)
— — Man Who Hated Freckles (2) — Running Wild (3) — Trip To Hyden (1)
— Million Miles To The City (1) — — Tulsa Telephone Book (1)

HALLIWELL, Geri '99
Born on 8/18/70 in Watford, Hertfordshire, England. Former member of the **Spice Girls** (as "Ginger Spice").

| 7/3/99 | **42** | 7 | ● | © | **Schizophonic** .... | | | **$10** | Capitol 21009 |

Bag It Up — Let Me Love You — Look At Me — Someone's Watching Over Me — Walkaway
Goodnight Kiss — Lift Me Up — Mi Chico Latino — Sometime — You're In A Bubble

HAMILTON, Chico '65
Born Foreststorn Hamilton on 9/21/21 in Los Angeles. Jazz drummer.

| 12/19/64+ | **145** | 4 | | © | **Man From Two Worlds** .... | | [I] | **$30** | Impulse! 59 |

Blues For O.T. — Child's Play — Forest Flower - Sunset — Mallet Dance
Blues Medley — Forest Flower - Sunrise — Love Song To A Baby — Man From Two Worlds

HAMILTON, George IV '63
Born on 7/19/37 in Winston-Salem, North Carolina. Country singer/songwriter/guitarist. Hosted own TV series in 1959.

| 10/5/63 | **77** | 8 | | © | **Abilene** .... | | | **$30** | RCA Victor 2778 |

Abilene **15** — Everglades, The — If You Don't Know I Ain't Gonna Tell You — Little Lunch Box — Tender Hearted Baby
China Doll — (I Want To Go) Where Nobody Knows Me — — Oh So Many Years — You Are My Sunshine
Come On Home Boy — — Jimmy Brown The News Boy — Roving Gambler —

HAMILTON, JOE FRANK & REYNOLDS '71
Pop vocal trio: Dan Hamilton, Joe Frank Carollo and Tommy Reynolds. All were members of **The T-Bones**. Reynolds left group in 1972 and was replaced by Alan Dennison. Although Reynolds had left, group still recorded as Hamilton, Joe Frank & Reynolds until July 1976. Hamilton died on 12/23/94 (age 48).

6/19/71	**59**	15			1 **Hamilton, Joe Frank & Reynolds**			**$15**	Dunhill/ABC 50103
2/19/72	**191**	4			2 **Hallway Symphony**			**$15**	Dunhill/ABC 50113
12/13/75+	**82**	14			3 **Fallin' In Love**			**$12**	Playboy 407

Ain't No Woman (Like The One I've Got) (2) — Bridge Over Troubled Water (medley) (2) — **Fallin' Love** (3) 1 — Love Is (3) — What Can You Say (1)
Anna, No Can Do (2) — C'est La Vie (2) — Goin' Down (1) — Nora (1) — What Kind Of Love Is This (3)
Annabella (1) 46 — Don't Be Afraid Of The World (2) — Hallway Symphony (2) — On The Other Hand (2) — Who Do You Love (3)
Badman (3) — — If Every Man (2) — One Good Woman (2) — **Winners And Losers** (3) 21
Barroom Blues (3) — **Don't Pull Your Love** (1) 4 — It Takes The Best (1) — Only Love (Will Break Your Heart) (3) — You've Got A Friend (medley) (2)
Behold (1) — Don't Refuse My Love (1) — Like Monday Follows Sunday (2) — So Good At Lovin' You (3) — Young, Wild And Free (1)
— **Everyday Without You** (3) 62 — Long Road (1) — Sweet Pain (1) —

HAMLISCH, Marvin '74
Born on 6/2/44 in New York City. Pianist/composer/conductor. Won the 1974 Best New Artist Grammy Award.

| 1/26/74 | **❶**[5] | 41 | ● | | 1 **The Sting** .... | | [I-S] | **$12** | MCA 390 |
| 8/31/74 | **170** | 5 | | | 2 **The Entertainer** .... | | [I] | **$12** | MCA 2115 |

Bethena (2) — Glove, The (1) — I Love A Piano (2) — Merry-Go-Round Music Medley (1) — Rag Time Dance (medley) (1) — Stoptime Rag (2)
Easy Winners (1) — Grandpa's Spells (2) — Little Girl (1) — Mexican Dreams (2) — Ragtime Nightingale (2)
Entertainer, The (1,2) **3** — Heliotrope Bouquet (2) — Luther (1) — Pine Apple Rag (1) — Rialto Ripples (2)
Gladiolus Rag (medley) (1) — Hooker's Hooker (1) — Maple Leaf Rag (2) — — Solace (1)

HAMMER — see M.C. HAMMER

HAMMER, Jan — see BECK, Jeff / GOODMAN, Jerry / SCHON, Neal / TELEVISION SOUNDTRACKS: "Miami Vice"

HAMMOND, Albert '73
Born on 5/18/42 in London; raised in Gibraltar, Spain. Pop-rock singer/songwriter.

| 12/9/72+ | **77** | 15 | | © | 1 **It Never Rains In Southern California** .... | | | **$15** | Mums 31905 |
| 9/1/73 | **193** | 4 | | | 2 **The Free Electric Band** .... | | | **$15** | Mums 32267 |

Air That I Breathe (1) — Down By The River (1) **91** — I Think I'll Go That Way (2) — Names, Tags, Numbers & Labels (1) — Who's For Lunch Today? (2)
Anyone Here In The Audience (1) — Everything I Want To Do (2) — **If You Gotta Break Another Heart** (1) **63** — **Peacemaker, The** (2) **80** — Woman Of The World (2)
Brand New Day (1) — For The Peace Of All Mankind (2) — **It Never Rains In Southern California** (1) **5** — Rebecca (2) —
Day The British Army Lost The War (2) — **Free Electric Band** (2) **48** — Listen To The World (1) — Road To Understanding (1) —
— From Great Britain To L.A. (1) — — Smokey Factory Blues (2) —

HAMMOND, Fred, & Radical For Christ '00
Born in Detroit. Gospel singer. Former lead singer of Commissioned.

| 5/16/98 | 51 | 21 | ▲ | © | 1 **Pages Of Life - Chapters I & II** .... | | | $15 | Verity 43110 [2] |
| 4/8/00 | 46 | 17 | ● | © | 2 **Purpose By Design** .... | | | $10 | Verity 43140 |

All Things Are Working (1) · Dwell (1) · Give Me A Clean Heart (2) · Glory To Glory To Glory (1) · He's God (1) · I Know It Was The Blood (2) · I Press (2) · I Wanna Be Yours (1) · I Wanna Know Your Ways (1) · I Want My Destiny (2) · I Will Bless His Holy Name (1) · Jesus Be A Fence Around Me (2) · Jesus Is All (1) · Just To Be Close To You (1) · Let Me Praise You Now (2) · Let The Praise Begin (1) · My Father Was/Is (2) · No Way, No Way (You Won't Lose) (1) · No Weapon (1) · Our Father (2) · Please Don't Pass Me By (1) · Thank You Lord (For Being There For Me) (2) · When The Spirit Of The Lord (1) · When You Praise (1) · Willing To Follow You (2) · Yes He Will (2) · You Are My Song (1) · You Are The Living Word (2) · You Called Me Friend (1) · You Were Much Closer (1) · Your Love (1) · Your Steps Are Ordered (1)

HAMMOND, John Paul — see BLOOMFIELD, Mike

HAMMOND, Johnny '71
Born John Robert Smith on 12/16/33 in Louisville, Kentucky. Jazz organist.

| 9/11/71 | 125 | 14 | | | 1 **Breakout** .... | [I] | | $15 | Kudu 01 |
| 5/20/72 | 174 | 6 | | | 2 **Wild Horses/Rock Steady** .... | [I] | | $15 | Kudu 04 |

Blues Selah (1) · Breakout (1) · I Don't Know How To Love Him (2) · It's Impossible (2) · It's Too Late (1) · Never Can Say Goodbye (1) · Peace Train (2) · Rock Steady (2) · Who Is Sylvia? (2) · Wild Horses (2) · Workin' On A Groovy Thing (1)

★251★ HANCOCK, Herbie '74
Born on 4/12/40 in Chicago. Jazz electronic keyboardist. Pianist with the **Miles Davis** band from 1963-68. Scored several movies. Also see **Headhunters** and **V.S.O.P.**

1)Head Hunters 2)Thrust 3)Man-Child

| 5/13/67 | 192 | 2 | | © | 1 **Blow-Up** .... | [I-S] | | $25 | MGM 4447 |

includes "Stroll On" by The Yardbirds

6/2/73	176	6		©	2 **Sextant**	[I]		$15	Columbia 32212
1/12/74	13	47	▲	©	3 **Head Hunters**	[I]		$15	Columbia 32731
10/5/74	13	23		©	4 **Thrust**	[I]		$15	Columbia 32965
10/12/74	158	3			5 **Treasure Chest**	[E-I]		$20	Warner 2807 [2]
10/18/75	21	24		©	6 **Man-Child**	[I]		$15	Columbia 33812
9/11/76	49	17		©	7 **Secrets**	[I]		$15	Columbia 34280
5/7/77	79	7			8 **V.S.O.P.**	[I-L]		$15	Columbia 34688 [2]

V.S.O.P.: Very Special Onetime Performance; recorded on 6/29/76 at the Newport Jazz Festival

7/8/78	58	13		©	9 **Sunlight**			$15	Columbia 34907
3/17/79	38	22		©	10 **Feets Don't Fail Me Now**			$15	Columbia 35764
3/31/79	100	8		©	11 **An Evening With Herbie Hancock & Chick Corea**	[I-L]		$15	Columbia 35663 [2]
11/24/79	175	2		©	12 **An Evening With Chick Corea & Herbie Hancock**	[I-L]		$15	Polydor 6238 [2]
4/19/80	94	18		©	13 **Monster**			$12	Columbia 36415
11/29/80	117	6			14 **Mr. Hands**	[I]		$12	Columbia 36578
10/3/81	140	6		©	15 **Magic Windows**			$12	Columbia 37387
5/29/82	151	6		©	16 **Lite Me Up**			$12	Columbia 37928
9/3/83	43	65	▲	©	17 **Future Shock**	[I]		$12	Columbia 38814
9/1/84	71	14		©	18 **Sound-System**	[I]		$12	Columbia 39478

Actual Proof (4) · Autodrive (17) · Bed, The (1) · Blow Up (1) · Bomb (16) · Bouquet (12) · Bring Down The Birds (1) · Bubbles (6) · Butterfly (4) · Button Up (11) · Calypso (14) · Can't Hide Your Love (16) · Cantelope Island (7) · **Chameleon** (3) *42* · Come Running To Me (9) · Crossings (5) · Curiosity (1) · Doin' It (7) · Don't Hold It In (13) · Earth Beat (17) · Everybody's Broke (15) · Eye Of The Hurricane (8) · February Moment (11) · 4 AM (14) · Fun Tracks (16) · Future Shock (17) · Gentle Thoughts (7) · Gettin' To The Good Part (16) · Give It All Your Heart (16) · Go For It (13) · Good Question (9) · Hang Up Your Hang Ups (6,8) · Hardrock (18) · Heartbeat (6) · Help Yourself (15) · Hidden Shadows (2) · Homecoming (12) · Honey From The Jar (10) · Hook, The (14) · Hornets (2) · I Thought It Was You (9) · It All Comes Round (13) · Jane's Theme (1) · Junku (18) · Just Around The Corner (14) · Karabali (18) · Kiss, The (1) · Knee Deep (10) · La Fiesta (11,12) · Li'l Brother (5) · Lite Me Up! (16) · Liza (11) · Magic Number (15) · Maiden Voyage (8,11,12) · Making Love (13) · Metal Beat (18) · Motor Mouth (16) · Naked Camera (1) · Nefertiti (8) · No Means Yes (9) · Ostinato (5,12) · Palm Grease (4) · Paradise (16) · People Are Changing (18) · People Music (7) · Quasar (5) · Rain Dance (2) · Ready Or Not (10) · **Rockit** (17) *71* · Rough (17) · Sansho Shima (4) · Satisfied With Love (15) · Saturday Night (13) · Shiftless Shuffle (14) · Sleeping Giant (5) · Sly (3) · Someday My Prince Will Come (11) · Sound-System (18) · Spank-A-Lee (4) · Spider (7,8) · Spiraling Prism (14) · Stars In Your Eyes (13) · Steppin' In It (6) · Sun Touch (6) · Sunlight (17) · Swamp Rat (7) · TFS (17) · Tell Everybody (10) · Tell Me A Bedtime Story (5) · Textures (14) · Thief, The (1) · Thomas Studies Photos (1) · Tonight's The Night (15) · Toys (8) · Traitor, The (6) · Trust Me (11) · Twilight Clone (15) · Vein Melter (3) · Verushka Part I & II (1) · Watermelon Man (3) · Wiggle Waggle (5) · You Bet Your Love (10) · You'll Know When You Get There (5,8)

HANDY, John '76
Born on 2/3/33 in Dallas. Jazz saxophonist.

| 6/5/76 | 43 | 21 | | | 1 **Hard Work** .... | [I] | | $12 | ABC/Impulse 9314 |
| 4/16/77 | 200 | 2 | | | 2 **Carnival** .... | [I] | | $12 | ABC/Impulse 9324 |

Afro Wiggle (1) · All The Things You Are (2) · Alvina (2) · Blues For Louis Jordan (1) · Carnival (2) · Christina's Little Song (2) · Didn't I Tell You (1) · **Hard Work** (1) *46* · I Will Leave You (2) · Love For Brother Jack (1) · Love's Rejoicing (2) · Make Her Mine (1) · Watch Your Money Go (2) · You Don't Know (1) · Young Enough To Dream (1)

HANSON '97
Pop trio of brothers from Tulsa, Oklahoma: Isaac (guitar), Taylor (keyboards) and Zac (drums) Hanson. All share vocals.

| 5/24/97 | 2[1] | 58 | ▲4 | © | 1 **Middle Of Nowhere** | | | $10 | Mercury 534615 |
| 12/6/97 | 7 | 9 | ▲ | © | 2 **Snowed In** | C:#23/7 | [X] | $10 | Mercury 536717 |

Christmas charts: 1/'97, 12/'98

| 5/30/98 | 6 | 19 | ▲ | © | 3 **3 Car Garage: The Indie Recordings '95-'96** | | [E] | $10 | Mercury 558399 |
| 11/21/98 | 32 | 9 | ● | © | 4 **Live From Albertane** .... | | [L] | $10 | Mercury 538240 |

recorded on 7/21/98 at the Key Arena in Seattle

| 5/27/00 | 19 | 16 | ● | © | 5 **This Time Around** .... | | | $10 | Island 542383 |

At Christmas (2) · Can't Stop (5) · Christmas (Baby Please Come Home) (2) · Christmas Time (2) · Day Has Come (3) · Dying To Be Alive (5) · Ever Lonely (4) · Everybody Knows The Claus (2) · Gimme Some Lovin' (medley) (4) · Hand In Hand (5) · **I Will Come To You** (1,4) *9* · If Only (5) · In The City (5) · Little Saint Nick (2) · Look At You (1) · Love Song (5) · Lucy (1) · **MMMBop** (1,3,4) *1* · Madeline (1) · Man From Milwaukee (1,4) · Merry Christmas Baby (2)

HANSON — Cont'd

Minute Without You (1,4)
Money (That's What I Want) (4)
More Than Anything (4)
Pictures (3)
River (3,4)

Rockin' Around The Christmas Tree (2)
Run Rudolph Run (2)
Runaway Run (5)
Save Me (5)

Shake A Tail Feather (medley) (4)
Silent Night Medley (2)
Soldier (3)
Sometimes (3)
Song To Sing (5)

Speechless (1,4)
Stories (3)
Sure About It (5)
Surely As The Sun (3)
Thinking Of You (1,3)
This Time Around (5) *20*

Two Tears (3)
Weird (1)
What Christmas Means To Me (2)
Where's The Love (1,4)
White Christmas (2)

Wish That I Was There (5)
With You In Your Dreams (1,3,4)
Yearbook (1)
You Never Know (5)

HANSSON, Bo   '73
Born in 1943 in Sweden. Male organist.

| 5/5/73 | 154 | 8 | | © | Lord Of The Rings .... [I] | | | $15 | Charisma 1059 |

At The House Of Elrond (medley)
Battle Of The Pelennor Fields (medley)

Black Riders (medley)
Dreams In The Houses Of Healing
Flight To The Ford (medley)

Fog On The Barrow-Downs (medley)
Great Havens
Homeward Bound (medley)
Horns Of Rohan (medley)

Journey In The Dark
Leaving Shire
Lothlorien
Old Forest (medley)

Ring Goes South (medley)
Scouring Out Shire (medley)
Shadowfax
Tom Bombadil (medley)

HAPPENINGS, The   '66
Vocal group from Paterson, New Jersey: Bob Miranda, Tom Giuliano, Ralph DiVito and Dave Libert.

| 10/15/66 | 61 | 12 | | | 1 The Happenings .... | | | $40 | B.T. Puppy 1001 |
| 7/22/67 | 134 | 6 | | | 2 Back To Back .... | | | $40 | B.T. Puppy 1002 |

THE TOKENS/THE HAPPENINGS
side 1: The Tokens; side 2: The Happenings

| 8/10/68 | 156 | 4 | | | 3 The Happenings Golden Hits! .... [G] | | | $40 | B.T. Puppy 1004 |
| 9/6/69 | 181 | 2 | | | 4 Piece Of Mind .... | | | $30 | Jubilee 8028 |

Be My Brother (4)
Breaking Up Is Hard To Do (3) *67*
Cold Water (4)
Don't You Think It's Time (4)
Girl On A Swing (1,3)
Girls On The Go (1)
Go Away Little Girl (1,3) *12*

Goodnight My Love (2,3) *51*
He Thinks He's A Hero (2)
Heartbeat (2)
I Believe In Nothing (2)
If You Love Me, Really Love Me (1)
Imagine (4)

Impatient Girl (2)
Let's Do Something (4)
Lillies By Monet (2)
Living In Darkness (4)
Music Music Music (3) *96*
My Mammy (3) *13*
New Day Comin' (4)
Piece Of Mind (4)

Randy (3)
Same Old Story (1)
Sealed With A Kiss (1,3)
See You In September (1,3) *3*
Tea For Two (3)
Tea Time (1)
Tonight I Fell In Love (1)

We're Gonna Make Them Care (4)
What To Do (1)
Where Do I Go/Be-In/Hare Krishna (4) *66*
Why Do Fools Fall In Love (3) *41*

You're Coming On Strong, Babe (1)
You're In A Bad Way (1)

HAPPY MONDAYS   '91
Dance-rock group formed in Manchester, England: brothers Shaun (vocals) and Paul (bass) Ryder, Mark Day (guitar), Paul Davis (keyboards), Mark Berry (percussion) and Gary Whelan (drums).

| 2/23/91 | 89 | 13 | | © | Pills 'N' Thrills And Bellyaches .... | | | $10 | Elektra 60986 |

Bob's Yer Uncle
Dennis And Lois

Donovan
God's Cop

Grandbag's Funeral
Harmony

Holiday
Kinky Afro

Loose Fit
Step On

HARBOR, Pearl — see PEARL

HARDCASTLE, Paul   '85
Born on 12/10/57 in London. Keyboardist/producer. Also see **The Jazzmasters**.

| 3/23/85 | 63 | 25 | | | 1 Rain Forest .... [I] | | | $12 | Profile 1206 |
| 4/30/94 | 182 | 6 | | © | 2 Hardcastle .... | | | $10 | JVC 2033 |

A.M. (1)
Can't Stop Now (2)
Cruisin' To Midnight (2)
Do It Again (2)

Don't Be Shy (2)
Driftin' Away (2)
Feel The Breeze (2)
Forest Fire (1)

Forever Dreamin' (2)
It Must Be Love (2)
King Tut (1)
Lazy Days (2)

Loitering With Intent (1)
Never Let You Go (2)
Only One (1)
Panic (1)

Rain Forest (1,2) *57*
Sound Chaser (1)
You May Be Gone (2)

HARDEN TRIO, The   '66
Country vocal group from England, Kansas: siblings Bobby, Robbie and Arlene Harden.

| 6/25/66 | 146 | 5 | | | Tippy Toeing .... | | | $25 | Columbia 9306 |

Dear Brother
Hey Pinnoch

How Long Does It Take
Is It Really Over

Little Boy Walk Like A Man
Little White House

Make The World Go Away
Poor Boy

Race Is On
Tall Green Pines

Tippy Toeing *44*

HARDIN, Tim   '69
Born on 12/23/41 in Eugene, Oregon. Died of a drug overdose on 12/29/80 (age 39). Folk-blues singer/songwriter. Relative of notorious outlaw John Wesley Hardin.

| 4/26/69 | 129 | 8 | | © | 1 Suite For Susan Moore And Damion-We Are-One, One, All In One .... | | | $25 | Columbia 9787 |
| 7/31/71 | 189 | 1 | | © | 2 Bird On A Wire .... | | | $20 | Columbia 30551 |

Andre Johray (2)
Bird On The Wire (2)
Country I'm Living In (1)
Everything Good Become More True (1)

First Love Song (1)
Georgia On My Mind (2)
Hoboin' (2)
If I Knew (2)
Last Sweet Moments (1)

Loneliness She Knows (1)
Love Hymn (2)
Magician (1)
Moonshiner (2)
Once-Touched By Flame (1)

One, One, The Perfect Sum (1)
Question Of Birth (1)
Satisfied Mind (1)
Soft Summer Breeze (2)
Southern Butterfly (2)

Susan (1)

HARDY, Hagood   '76
Born in 1937 in Angola, Indiana. Died of cancer on 1/1/97 (age 59). Vibraphonist based in Toronto. Sideman for **Herbie Mann** and **George Shearing**.

| 1/3/76 | 112 | 14 | | © | The Homecoming .... [I] | | | $12 | Capitol 11468 |

Balloons
Clouds

Cold On The Shoulder
Homecoming, The *41*

I Won't Last A Day Without You
Jennifer's Song

My Elusive Dreams
Quorum

Travellin' On
Trouble With Hello Is Goodbye

Wintertime
You And Me Against The World

HARDY BOYS, The   '69
Group used in the animated cartoon TV series *The Hardy Boys*: brothers Frank (guitar) and Joe (bass) Hardy, Wanda Kay (piano), Chubby Morton (sax) and Pete Jones (drums). All share vocals.

| 11/15/69 | 199 | 2 | | | Here Come The Hardy Boys .... | | | $20 | RCA Victor 4217 |

Feels So Good
Here Come The Hardys

(I Want You To) Be My Baby
Love And Let Love

My Little Sweetpea
Namby-Pamby

One Time In A Million
Sha-La-La

Sink Or Swim
That's That

Those Country Girls

HARLEM WORLD   '99
Rap group from Harlem, New York: Baby Stase (twin sister of **Mase**), Blinky-Blink (brother of Mase), Cardan, Meeno, Loon and Huddy.

| 3/27/99 | 11 | 9 | ● | © | The Movement .... | | | $10 | All Out 69503 |

includes "A Change Is Gon' Come" by the Harlem Boys Choir

Across The Border
Cali Chronic
Crew Of The Year

Family Crisis
I Really Like It
Meaning Of Family

Minute Man
Not The Kids
One Big Fiesta

100 Shiesty's
Pointing Fingers
We Both Frontin'

You Made Me

HARMONICATS '61

Harmonica trio formed in Chicago: Jerry Murad (died on 5/11/96, age 80), Al Fiore (died on 10/25/96, age 73) and Don Les (died on 8/25/94, age 79).

| 3/27/61 | 17 | 4 | | | **Cherry Pink And Apple Blossom White** .... | | [I] | $20 | Columbia 8356 |

Jerry Murad's "Fabulous" HARMONICATS

Cherry Pink And Apple Blossom White *56*
Fascination

I'll Never Smile Again
It Happened In Monterey
It's A Sin To Tell A Lie

Kiss Of Fire
Lonely Love
Mack The Knife

Paradise
Polka Dots And Moonbeams
Ramona

Ruby

HARNELL, Joe, His Piano And Orchestra '63

Born on 8/2/24 in the Bronx, New York. Conductor/arranger.

| 1/26/63 | 3 | 36 | | | **Fly Me To The Moon and the Bossa Nova Pops** | | [I] | $25 | Kapp 3318 |

Cry Me A River
Early Autumn
Eso Beso

Fly Me To The Moon-Bossa Nova *14*
Loads Of Love

I Left My Heart In San Francisco
Midnight Sun
One Note Samba

Midnight Sun
My One And Only Love

Senza Fine
What Kind Of Fool Am I?

You'd Be So Nice To Come Home To

HARPER, Ben, & The Innocent Criminals '99

Born on 10/28/69 in Empire, California. Folk-rock singer/guitarist. The Innocent Criminals: Juan Nelson (bass) and Dean Butterworth (drums).

7/5/97	89	11	©	1	**The Will To Live**			$10	Virgin 44178
					BEN HARPER				
10/9/99	67	22	©	2	**Burn To Shine**			$10	Virgin 48151
4/14/01	70	9	©	3	**Live From Mars**		[L]	$15	Virgin 10079 [2]

Alone (2,3)
Another Lonely Day (3)
Ashes (1)
Beloved One (2,3)
Burn One Down (3)
Burn To Shine (2)
Drugs Don't Work (3)

Excuse Me Mr. (3)
Faded (1,3)
Forgiven (2,3)
Glory & Consequence (1,3)
Ground On Down (3)
Homeless Child (1)
I Shall Not Walk Alone (1)

I Want To Be Ready (1)
I'll Rise (medley) (3)
In The Lord's Arms (2,3)
Jah Work (1)
Less (2)
Like A King (medley) (3)
Mama's Got A Girlfriend (3)

Mama's Trippin' (1)
Not Fire, Not Ice (3)
Number Three (1,3)
Please Bleed (2,3)
Pleasure And Pain (3)
Power Of The Gospel (3)
Roses From My Friends (1,3)

Sexual Healing (3)
Show Me A Little Shame (2)
Steal My Kisses (2,3)
Suzie Blue (2)
Two Hands Of A Prayer (3)
Waiting On An Angel (3)
Walk Away (3)

Welcome To The Cruel World (3)
Whole Lotta Love (medley) (3)
Widow Of A Living Man (1)
Will To Live (1)
Woman In You (2,3)

HARPERS BIZARRE '68

Vocal group from Santa Cruz, California: Ted Templeman, Eddie James, Dick Yount, John Petersen and Dick Scoppettone. Petersen was a member of **The Beau Brummels**. Templeman later produced many albums for **The Doobie Brothers** and **Van Halen**.

| 5/6/67 | 108 | 7 | | 1 | **Feelin' Groovy** .... | | | $25 | Warner 1693 |
| 12/9/67+ | 76 | 13 | | 2 | **Anything Goes** .... | | | $25 | Warner 1716 |

Anything Goes (medley) (2) *43*
Biggest Night Of Her Life (2)
Chattanooga Choo Choo (2) *45*
Come Love (1)

Come To The Sunshine (1) *37*
Debutante's Ball (1)
59th Street Bridge Song (Feelin' Groovy) (1) *13*
Happy Talk (1)
Happyland (1)

Hey, You In The Crowd (2)
High Coin (2)
I Can Hear The Darkness (1)
Jessie (2)
Louisiana Man (2)
Milord (1)

Peter And The Wolf (1)
Pocketful Of Miracles (2)
Raspberry Rug (1)
Simon Smith And The Amazing Dancing Bear (1)
Snow (2)

This Is Only The Beginning (medley) (2)
Two Little Babes In The Wood (2)
Virginia City (2)
You Need A Change (2)

★415★ HARRIS, Eddie '61

Born on 10/20/36 in Chicago. Died of cancer on 11/5/96 (age 60). Jazz tenor saxophonist.

1)Exodus To Jazz 2)Swiss Movement 3)The Electrifying Eddie Harris

5/29/61	2[1]	37	©	1	**Exodus To Jazz**		[I]	$40	Vee-Jay 3016
4/13/68	36	41	©	2	**The Electrifying Eddie Harris**		[I]	$20	Atlantic 1495
8/3/68	120	16	©	3	**Plug Me In**		[I]	$20	Atlantic 1506
2/22/69	199	2		4	**Silver Cycles**		[I]	$20	Atlantic 1517
8/16/69	122	9	©	5	**High Voltage**		[I-L]	$20	Atlantic 1529
					recorded at the Village Gate in New York City and at Shelly's Manne-Hole in Hollywood				
12/13/69+	29	38	©	6	**Swiss Movement**		[I-L]	$20	Atlantic 1537
					LES McCANN & EDDIE HARRIS				
					recorded June 1969 at the Montreaux Jazz Festival in Switzerland				
4/18/70	191	3	©	7	**The Best Of Eddie Harris**		[G-I]	$20	Atlantic 1545
5/29/71	41	27	©	8	**Second Movement**		[I]	$20	Atlantic 1583
					EDDIE HARRIS & LES McCANN				
11/27/71	164	10	©	9	**Eddie Harris Live At Newport**		[I-L]	$15	Atlantic 1595
7/22/72	185	7	©	10	**Instant Death**		[I]	$15	Atlantic 1611
2/16/74	150	11	©	11	**E.H. in the U.K.**		[I]	$15	Atlantic 1647
10/12/74	100	11	©	12	**Is It In**		[I]	$15	Atlantic 1659
4/19/75	125	9	©	13	**I Need Some Money**		[I]	$15	Atlantic 1669
9/27/75	133	6	©	14	**Bad Luck Is All I Have**		[I]	$15	Atlantic 1675

A.M. Blues (1)
A.T.C. (1)
Abstractions (14)
Alicia (1)
Baby (11)
Bad Luck Is All I Have (14)
Ballad (For My Love) (3,5)
Bumpin (13)
Carnival (13)
Carry On Brother (8,9)
Children's Song (5,9)
Cold Duck Time (6)
Coltrane's View (4)
Compared To What (6) *85*
Conversations Of Everything And Nothing (11)
Don't You Know The Future's In Space (9)

Electric Ballad (4)
Exodus (1) *36*
Free At Last (4)
Freedom Jazz Dance (7)
Funkaroma (12)
Funky Doo (5)
Generation Gap (6)
Get On Down (13)
Get On Up And Dance (14)
Gone Home (1)
Happy Gemini (12)
He's Island Man (11)
House Party Blues (12)
I Don't Want No One But You (2)
I Don't Want Nobody (13)
I Need Some Money (13)
I Waited For You (11)

I'm Gonna Leave You By Yourself (4)
I've Tried Everything (11)
Infrapolations (4)
Instant Death (10)
Is It In (12)
Is There A Place For Us (5)
It Feels So Good (14)
It's Crazy (3) *88*
It's War (12)
Judie's Theme (2)
Kathleen's Theme (6)
Listen Here (2,5,7) *45*
Little Bit (4)
Little Girl Blue (1)
Little Wes (10)
Live Right Now (3,7)
Look Ahere (12)

Lovely Is Today (3)
Movin' On Out (5,7)
Nightcap (10)
1974 Blues (9)
Obnoxious (14)
Samia (3)
Sandpiper, Love Theme From The (7)
Set Us Free (8)
Shadow Of Your Smile ..see: Sandpiper, Love Theme From The
Sham Time (8)
Shorty Rides Again (8)
Silent Majority (9)
Silver Cycles (4)
Smoke Signals (4)
South Side (9)

Space Commercial (12)
Spanish Bull (2)
Summer's On Its Way (10)
Superfluous (10)
Tampion (10)
That's It (13)
Theme In Search Of A Movie (2,7)
Theme In Search Of A T.V. Commercial (3)
These Lonely Nights (12)
Time To Do Your Thing (13)
Tranquility & Antagonistic (12)
Universal Prisoner (8)
Velocity (9)
W.P. (1)
Wait A Little Longer (11)
Walk Soft (9)

Why Must We Part (14)
Winter Meeting (3)
You Got It In Your Soulness (6)
Zambezi Dance (10)

HARRIS, Emmylou ★143★   '87

Born on 4/2/47 in Birmingham, Alabama. Country singer/songwriter/guitarist. Worked as a folk singer in Washington DC in the late '60s. First recorded for Jubilee in 1969. Toured with the **Flying Burrito Brothers** and **Gram Parsons** until 1973. Own band from 1975. Married to producer Brian Ahern from 1977-84. Married to British songwriter Paul Kennerley from 1985-93. Recipient of *Billboard's* Century Award in 1999.

1)Trio 2)Luxury Liner 3)Evangeline 4)Elite Hotel 5)Roses In The Snow

DEBUT	PEAK	WKS	RIAA	CD	#	Album Title	Sym	$	Label & Number
3/15/75	45	15	●	©	1	Pieces Of The Sky		$15	Reprise 2213
1/24/76	25	23	●	©	2	Elite Hotel		$15	Reprise 2236
1/22/77	21	21	●	©	3	Luxury Liner		$12	Warner 3115
2/4/78	29	18	●	©	4	Quarter Moon In A Ten Cent Town		$12	Warner 3141
12/2/78+	81	17	●	©	5	Profile/Best Of Emmylou Harris	[G]	$12	Warner 3258
5/5/79	43	22	●	©	6	Blue Kentucky Girl		$12	Warner 3318
5/24/80	26	34	●	©	7	Roses In The Snow		$12	Warner 3422
11/29/80	102	9		©	8	Light Of The Stable	[X]	$12	Warner 3484
2/21/81	22	24	●		9	Evangeline		$12	Warner 3508
12/12/81+	46	20		©	10	Cimarron		$12	Warner 3603
11/13/82	65	17		©	11	Last Date	[L]	$10	Warner 23740
11/19/83+	116	13		©	12	White Shoes		$10	Warner 23961
10/6/84	176	6		©	13	Profile II - The Best Of Emmylou Harris	[G]	$10	Warner 25161
5/25/85	171	4		©	14	The Ballad Of Sally Rose		$10	Warner 25205
3/8/86	157	6			15	Thirteen		$10	Warner 25352
3/28/87	6	48	▲	©	16	Trio		$10	Warner 25491

DOLLY PARTON, LINDA RONSTADT, EMMYLOU HARRIS

DEBUT	PEAK	WKS	RIAA	CD	#	Album Title	Sym	$	Label & Number
8/1/87	166	4		©	17	Angel Band		$10	Warner 25585
2/1/92	174	3		©	18	At The Ryman	[L]	$10	Reprise 26664

EMMYLOU HARRIS & THE NASH RAMBLERS
recorded on 4/30/91 in Nashville

DEBUT	PEAK	WKS	RIAA	CD	#	Album Title	Sym	$	Label & Number
10/16/93	152	5		©	19	Cowgirl's Prayer		$10	Asylum 61541
10/14/95	94	7		©	20	Wrecking Ball		$10	Asylum 61854
8/29/98	180	2		©	21	Spyboy		$10	Eminent 25001
2/27/99	62	14		©	22	Trio II		$10	Asylum 62275

EMMYLOU HARRIS, LINDA RONSTADT, DOLLY PARTON

DEBUT	PEAK	WKS	RIAA	CD	#	Album Title	Sym	$	Label & Number
9/11/99	73	7		©	23	Western Wall - The Tucson Sessions		$10	Asylum 62408

LINDA RONSTADT & EMMYLOU HARRIS

DEBUT	PEAK	WKS	RIAA	CD	#	Album Title	Sym	$	Label & Number
9/30/00	54	18		©	24	Red Dirt Girl		$10	Nonesuch 79616

Abraham, Martin And John (medley) (18)
Across The Border (23)
After The Gold Rush (22)
All I Left Behind (23)
All My Tears (20,21)
Amarillo (1)
Angel Band (17)
Angel Eyes (Angel Eyes) (8)
Another Lonesome Morning (10)
Ashes By Now (9)
Away In A Manger (8)
Baby, Better Start Turnin' 'Em Down (12)
Bad Moon Rising (9)
Bad News (14)
Ballad Of A Runaway Horse (19)
Ballad Of Sally Rose (14)
Bang The Drum Slowly (24)
Beautiful Star Of Bethlehem (8)
Before Believing (1)
Beneath Still Waters (6,13)
Blackhawk (19)
Blue Kentucky Girl (6,13)
Blue Train (22)
Bluebird Wine (1)
Born To Run (10,13,21)
Bottle Let Me Down (1)
Boulder To Birmingham (1,5,21)
Boxer (1)
Boy From Tupelo (24)
Bright Morning Stars (17)
Buckaroo (medley) (11)
Burn That Candle (4)
C'est La Vie ..see: (You Never Can Tell)
Calling My Children Home (18,21)
Cattle Call (18)
Christmas Time's A-Coming (8)
Coat Of Many Colors (1)
Crescent City (19)
Darkest Hour Is Just Before Dawn (7)
Deeper Well (20,21)
Defying Gravity (4)
Devil In Disguise (11)
Diamond In My Crown (14)

Diamonds Are A Girl's Best Friend (12)
Do I Ever Cross Your Mind (22)
Drifting Too Far (17)
Drivin' Wheel (12)
Easy From Now On (4,5)
Evangeline (3)
Even Cowgirls Get The Blues (6)
Everytime You Leave (6)
Falling Down (23)
Farther Along (16)
Feelin' Single - Seein' Double (2)
Feels Like Home (22)
First Noel (8)
For A Dancer (23)
For No One (1)
Get Up John (18)
Goin' Back To Harlan (20)
Gold Watch And Chain (7)
Golden Cradle (8)
Good News (12)
Goodbye (20)
Green Pastures (7,21)
Green Rolling Hills (4)
Grievous Angel (11)
Guess Things Happen That Way (18)
Guitar Town (18)
Half As Much (18)
Hard Times (18)
He Rode All The Way To Texas (22)
He Was Mine (23)
Heart To Heart (medley) (14)
Hello Stranger (3,5)
Here, There And Everywhere (2) 65
Hickory Wind (6)
High Powered Love (19)
High Sierra (22)
Hobo's Meditation (16)
Hot Burrito #2 (9)
Hour Of Gold (24)
How High The Moon (9)
I Ain't Living Long Like This (4,21)
I Don't Have To Crawl (9)

I Don't Wanna Talk About It Now (24)
I Feel The Blues Movin In (22)
I Had My Heart Set On You (15)
I Hear A Call (19)
I Think I Love Him (medley) (14)
I'll Be Your San Antone Rose (11)
I'll Go Stepping Too (7)
I'm Movin' On (11,13)
I've Had Enough (16)
If I Be Lifted Up (17)
If I Could Be There (18)
If I Could Only Win Your Love (1,5) 58
If I Needed You (10)
In My Dreams (12)
It's A Hard Life Wherever You Go (medley) (18)
It's Not Love (But It's Not Bad) (11)
It's Only Rock 'N Roll (12)
J'ai Fait Tout (24)
Jambalaya (2)
Jerusalem Tomorrow (19)
Jordan (7)
Juanita (11)
Just Someone I Used To Know (15)
K-S-O-S Medley (14)
Lacassine Special (15)
Last Cheater's Waltz (10)
Leaving Louisiana In The Broad Daylight (4)
Light, The (19)
Light Of The Stable (8)
Like An Old Fashioned Waltz (12)
Like Strangers (18)
Little Drummer Boy (8)
Lodi (18)
Long May You Run (11)
Long Tall Sally Rose (14)
(Lost His Love) On Our Last Date (11,13)
Love Hurts (4)
Love's Gonna Live Here (medley) (11)
Lover's Return (22)

Lovin' You Again (19)
Loving The Highway Man (23)
Luxury Liner (3)
Maker, The (21)
Making Believe (3,5)
Making Plans (16)
Mansion On The Hill (18)
May This Be Love (20)
Michelangelo (24)
Millworker (9)
Miss The Mississippi (7)
Mister Sandman (9,13) 37
Montana Cowgirl (18)
My Antonia (24)
My Baby Needs A Shepherd (24)
My Dear Companion (16)
My Father's House (15)
My Songbird (4,21)
Mystery Train (15)
1917 (23)
O Little Town Of Bethlehem (8)
Oh Atlanta (9)
On The Radio (12)
One Big Love (24)
One Of These Days (2,5)
One Paper Kid (4)
Ooh Las Vegas (2)
Orphan Girl (20)
Other Side Of Life (17)
Pain Of Loving You (16)
Pancho & Lefty (3)
Pearl, The (24)
Pledging My Love (12,13)
Poncho & Lefty ..see: Pancho And Lefty
Prayer In Open D (19,21)
Precious Memories (17)
Price You Pay (10)
Queen Of The Silver Dollar (1)
Racing In The Streets (11)
Raise The Dead (23)
Red Dirt Girl (24)
Restless (11)
Rhythm Guitar (14)
Rose Of Cimarron (10)
Roses In The Snow (7)
Rosewood Casket (16)
Rough And Rocky (6)

Satan's Jewel Crown (2)
Save The Last Dance For Me (6,13)
Scotland (18)
She (3)
Silent Night (8)
Sin City (2)
Sister's Coming Home (6)
Sisters Of Mercy (3)
Sleepless Nights (1)
Smoke Along The Track (14)
So Sad (To Watch Good Love Go Bad) (11)
Someday My Ship Will Sail (17)
Someone Like You (13)
Son Of A Rotten Gambler (10)
Sorrow In The Wind (6)
Spanish Is A Loving Tongue (10)
Spanish Johnny (9)
Sweet Dreams (2,5)
Sweet Chariot (14)
Sweet Old World (20)
Sweet Spot (23)
Sweetheart Of The Pines (15)
Sweetheart Of The Rodeo (14)
Telling Me Lies (16)
Tennessee Rose (10)
Tennessee Waltz (10)
Thanks To You (19)
They'll Never Take His Love From Me (6)
This Is To Mother You (23)
Those Memories Of You (16)
Till I Gain Control Again (2)
Timberline (14)
To Daddy (4,5)
To Know Him Is To Love Him (16)
Today I Started Loving You Again (15)
Together Again (2,5)
Too Far Gone (1,5)
Tragedy (24)
Tulsa Queen (3,21)
Two More Bottles Of Wine (4,5)
Valerie (23)
Walls Of Time (18)
Waltz Across Texas Tonight (20)

Wayfaring Stranger (7,13)
Ways To Go (19)
We Shall Rise (17)
We'll Sweep Out The Ashes (In The Morning) (11)
Western Wall (23)
Wheels (2,21)
When He Calls (17)
When I Stop Dreaming (3)
When I Was Yours (15)
When They Ring Those Golden Bells (17)
When We're Gone, Long Gone (22)
Where Could I Go But To The Lord (17)
Where Will I Be (20,21)
White Line (18)
White Shoes (12)
Who Will Sing For Me (17)
Wildflowers (16)
Woman Walk The Line (14)
Wrecking Ball (20)
You Don't Know Me (19)
(You Never Can Tell) C'est La Vie (3,5)
You'll Never Be The Sun (22)
You're Free To Go (15)
You're Learning (7)
You're Supposed To Be Feeling Good (3)
Your Long Journey (15)

HARRIS, Major '75
Born on 2/9/47 in Richmond, Virginia. R&B singer. Member of **The Delfonics** from 1971-74.

3/29/75	28	22			1 **My Way**			$15	Atlantic 18119
2/28/76	153	6			2 **Jealousy**			$15	Atlantic 18160

After Loving You (1) — It's Got To Be Magic (2) — **Love Won't Let Me Wait** (1) *5* — Ruby Lee (2) — Talking To Myself (2) — Walkin' In The Footsteps (2)
Each Morning I Wake Up (1) — **Jealousy** (2) *73* — Loving You Is Mellow (1) — Sideshow (1) — Two Wrongs (1) — What's The Use In The Truth
I Got Over Love (2) — Just A Thing That I Do (1) — My Way (1) — Sweet Tomorrow (1) — Tynisa (Goddess Of Love) (2) — (2)

HARRIS, Richard '68
Born on 10/1/30 in Limerick, Ireland. Began prolific acting career in 1958. Portrayed "King Arthur" in the long-running stage production and movie version of *Camelot*.

5/18/68	4	42		©	1 **A Tramp Shining**			$15	Dunhill/ABC 50032
11/16/68+	27	15			2 **The Yard Went On Forever**			$15	Dunhill/ABC 50042
12/18/71+	71	14			3 **My Boy**			$15	Dunhill/ABC 50116
12/16/72+	181	6			4 **Slides**			$15	Dunhill/ABC 50133
9/8/73	25	27			5 **Jonathan Livingston Seagull**		[T]	$15	Dunhill/ABC 50160
					narration from the book; music composed by Terry James				
12/28/74+	29	15		©	6 **The Prophet by Kahlil Gibran**		[T]	$12	Atlantic 18120
					Harris recites Gibran's classic work				

All The Broken Children (3) — Hive (2) — Lovers Such As I (1) — On Friendship (6) — Prophet (Pleasure Is A — This Is Our Child (3)
Ballad To An Unborn Child (3) — How I Spent My Summer (4) — Lucky Me (2) — On Giving (6) — Freedom Song), Theme From — This Is The Way (3)
Best Way To See America (4) — Hymns From The Grand — **MacArthur Park** (1) *2* — On Laws (6) — The (6) — This Is Where I Came In (3)
Beth (3) — Terrace (2) — **My Boy** (3) *41* — On Love (6) — Proposal (3) — Tramp Shining (1)
Blue Canadian Rocky Dream — I Don't Have To Tell You (4) — Name Of My Sorrow (1) — On Marriage (6) — Requiem (3) — Trilogy From The Prophet
(4) — I'm Comin' Home (4) — November Song (4) — On Pleasure (6) — Roy (4) — (Love, Marriage, Children) (6)
Coming Of The Ship (6) — If You Must Leave My Life (1) — On Children (6) — On Religion (6) — Sidewalk Song (3) — Watermark (2)
Dancing Girl (1) — In The Final Hours (1) — On Clothes (6) — On Teaching And — Slides (4) — Why Did You Leave Me (3)
Didn't We (1) *63* — Interim (2) — On Crime And Punishment (6) — Self-Knowledge (6) — Sunny Jo (4) — **Yard Went On Forever** (2) *64*
Farewell, The (6) — Jonathan Livingston Seagull (5) — On Death (6) — On Work (6) — That's The Way It Was (2)
Gayla (2) — Like Father Like Son (3) — On Eating And Drinking (6) — Once Upon A Dusty Road (4) — There Are Too Many Saviours
Gin Buddy (4) — Paper Chase (1) — On My Cross (4)

HARRIS, Rolf '63
Born on 3/30/30 in Perth, Australia. Played piano from age nine. Moved to England in the mid-1950s. Developed his unique "wobble board" sound out of a sheet of masonite. Own BBC-TV series from 1970.

8/3/63	29	9			**Tie Me Kangaroo Down, Sport & Sun Arise**		[N]	$40	Epic 26053

Big Black Hat — I've Been Everywhere — Living It Up — Someone's Pinched My Winkles — Tie Me Kangaroo Down,
Ground Hog — In The Wet — Mighty Thunderer — **Sun Arise** *61* — Sport *3*
Hair Oil On My Ears — Johnny Day — Nick Teen And Al K. Hall *95*

HARRIS, Sam '84
Born on 6/4/61 in Cushing, Oklahoma. Singer/actor.

9/29/84	35	29	● ©		1 **Sam Harris**			$10	Motown 6103
2/15/86	69	14			2 **Sam-I-Am**			$10	Motown 6165

Always (medley) (2) — Don't Want To Give Up On — Hearts On Fire (1) — I've Heard It All Before (1) — Over The Rainbow (1) — Suffer The Innocent (2)
Ba-Doom Ba-Doom (2) — Love (2) — I Need You (medley) (2) — In Your Eyes (2) — Pretender (1) — **Sugar Don't Bite** (1) *36*
Bells (medley) (2) — Forever For You (2) — I Will Not Wait For You (1) — Inside Of Me (1) — Rescue (2) — You Keep Me Hangin' On (1)
Don't Look In My Eyes (1) — Heart Of The Machine (2) — **I'd Do It All Again** (2) *52* — Out Of Control (1) — Stay With Me (2)

HARRISON, Don, Band '76
Rock group: Don Harrison (vocals), Russell DaShiell (guitar), Stu Cook (bass) and Doug Clifford (drums). Cook and Clifford were members of **Creedence Clearwater Revival**.

5/1/76	159	6			**The Don Harrison Band**			$12	Atlantic 18171

Barroom Dancing Girl — Fame And Fortune — Rock 'N' Roll Records — **Sixteen Tons** *47* — Sweetwater William
Bit Of Love — Living Another Day — Romance — Sometimes Loving You — Who I Really Am

HARRISON, George ★166★ '71
Born on 2/24/43 in Liverpool, England. Singer/songwriter/guitarist. Formed his first group, the Rebels, at age 13. Joined **John Lennon** and **Paul McCartney** in The Quarrymen in 1958; group later evolved into **The Beatles**, with Harrison as lead guitarist. Organized the Bangladesh benefit concerts at Madison Square Garden in 1971. Member of the 1988 supergroup **Traveling Wilburys**. Recipient of *Billboard*'s Century Award in 1992.

1)All Things Must Pass 2)Living In The Material World 3)The Concert For Bangla Desh

1/11/69	49	16		©	1 **Wonderwall Music**		[I-S]	$40	Apple 3350
					Indian-influenced instrumentals for the unreleased movie *Wonderwall*				
7/5/69	191	2		©	2 **Electronic Sound**		[I]	$40	Zapple 3358
					sounds made by a Moog synthesizer				
12/19/70+	❶⁷	38	▲⁶	©	3 **All Things Must Pass**		C:#4/8	$50	Apple 639 [3]
1/8/72	2⁶	41	●	©	4 **The Concert For Bangla Desh**		[L]	$50	Apple 3385 [3]
					recorded on 8/1/71 at Madison Square Garden; 1972 Grammy winner: Album of the Year				
6/16/73	❶⁵	26	●	©	5 **Living In The Material World**			$20	Apple 3410
12/28/74+	4	17	●	©	6 **Dark Horse**			$20	Apple 3418
10/11/75	8	11	●	©	7 **Extra Texture (Read All About It)**			$20	Apple 3420
11/27/76	31	15	●		8 **The Best of George Harrison**		[G]	$15	Capitol 11578
					includes "For You Blue," "Here Comes The Sun," "If I Needed Someone," "Something," "Taxman," "Think For Yourself" and "While My Guitar Gently Weeps" by **The Beatles**				
12/11/76+	11	21	●	©	9 **Thirty-Three & 1/3**			$15	Dark Horse 3005
3/17/79	14	18	●	©	10 **George Harrison**			$12	Dark Horse 3255
6/20/81	11	13		©	11 **Somewhere In England**			$12	Dark Horse 3492
11/27/82	108	7		©	12 **Gone Troppo**			$12	Dark Horse 23734
11/21/87+	8	31	▲	©	13 **Cloud Nine**			$10	Dark Horse 25643

HARRISON, George — Cont'd

11/4/89	132	6	© 14 **Best Of Dark Horse 1976-1989** .... [G]	$10	Dark Horse 25726
8/1/92	126	2	© 15 **Live In Japan** .... [L]	$15	Dark Horse 26964 [2]

All Things Must Pass (3)
All Those Years Ago (11,14,15) *2*
Answer's At The End (7)
Apple Scruffs (3)
Art Of Dying (3)
Awaiting On You All (3,4)
Baby Don't Run Away (12)
Ballad Of Sir Frankie Crisp (Let It Roll) (3)
Baltimore Oriole (11)
Bangla-Desh (4,8) *23*
Bangla Dhun (4)
Be Here Now (5)
Beautiful Girl (9)
Behind That Locked Door (3)
Beware Of Darkness (3,4)
Bit More Of You (7)
Blood From A Clone (11)
Blow Away (10,14) *16*
Blowin' In The Wind (4)
Breath Away From Heaven (13)
Bye Bye, Love (6)
Can't Stop Thinking About You (7)
Cheer Down (14,15)
Circles (12)
Cloud 9 (13,14,15)

Cockamamie Business (14)
Congratulations (3)
Cowboy Museum (1)
Crackerbox Palace (9,14) *19*
Crying (medley) (1)
Dark Horse (6,8,15) *15*
Dark Sweet Lady (10)
Day The World Gets 'Round (5)
Dear One (9)
Devil's Radio (13,15)
Ding Dong; Ding Dong (6) *36*
Don't Let Me Wait Too Long (5)
Dream Away (12)
Dream Scene (medley) (1)
Drilling A Home (medley) (1)
Fantasy Sequins (medley) (1)
Far East Man (6)
Faster (10)
Fish On The Sand (13)
Give Me Love - (Give Me Peace On Earth) (5,8,15) *1*
Glass Box (medley) (1)
Gone Troppo (12)
Got My Mind Set On You (13,14,15) *1*
Greasy Legs (medley) (1)

Greece (12)
Grey Cloudy Lies (7)
Guru Vandana (medley) (1)
Hard Rain's Gonna Fall (4)
Hari's On Tour (Express) (6)
Hear Me Lord (3)
Here Comes The Moon (10,14)
Here Comes The Sun (4,15)
His Name Is Legs (Ladies & Gentlemen) (7)
Hong Kong Blues (11)
I Dig Love (3)
I Really Love You (12)
I Remember Jeep (3)
I Want To Tell You (15)
I'd Have You Anytime (3)
If I Needed Someone (15)
If Not For You (3)
If You Believe (10)
In The Park (medley) (1)
Isn't It A Pity (3,15) *flip*
It Don't Come Easy (4)
It Is "He" (Jai Sri Krishna) (4)
It Takes A Lot To Laugh, It Takes A Train To Cry (4)
It's What You Value (9)
Jumping Jack Flash (medley) (4)

Just For Today (13)
Just Like A Woman (4)
Learning How To Love You (9)
Let It Down (3)
Life Itself (11,14)
Light That Has Lighted The World (5)
Living In The Material World (5)
Lord Loves The One (That Loves The Lord) (5)
Love Comes To Everyone (10,14)
Love Scene (medley) (1)
Maya Love (6)
Microbes (1)
Mr. Tambourine Man (4)
My Sweet Lord (3,4,8,15) *1*
Mystical One (12)
No Time Or Space (2)
Not Guilty (10)
Old Brown Shoe (15)
On The Bed (1)
Ooh Baby (You Know That I Love You) (7)
Out Of The Blue (3)
Party Seacombe (1)
Piggies (15)
Plug Me In (3)

Poor Little Girl (14)
Pure Smokey (9)
Red Lady Too (1)
Roll Over Beethoven (15)
Run Of The Mill (3)
Save The World (11)
See Yourself (9)
Simply Shady (6)
Singing OM (1)
Ski-ing And Gat Kirwani (medley) (1)
So Sad (6)
Soft-Hearted Hana (10)
Soft Touch (10)
Someplace Else (13)
Something (4,15)
Sue Me, Sue You Blues (5)
Tabla And Pakavaj (medley) (1)
Taxman (15)
Teardrops (11)
Thanks For The Pepperoni (3)
That Is All (5)
That Which I Have Lost (11)
That's The Way God Planned It (4)
That's The Way It Goes (12,14)
That's What It Takes (13)

This Guitar (Can't Keep From Crying) (7)
This Is Love (13)
This Song (9) *25*
Tired Of Midnight Blue (7)
True Love (9)
Try Some Buy Some (5)
Unconsciousness Rules (11)
Under The Mersey Wall (2)
Unknown Delight (12)
Wah-Wah (3,4)
Wake Up My Love (12,14) *53*
What Is Life (3,8,15) *10*
When We Was Fab (13,14) *23*
While My Guitar Gently Weeps (4,15)
Who Can See It (5)
Woman Don't You Cry For Me (9)
Wonderwall To Be Here (1)
World Of Stone (7)
Wreck Of The Hesperus (13)
Writing's On The Wall (11)
You (7,8) *20*
Youngblood (medley) (4)
Your Love Is Forever (10)

HARRISON, Jerry: Casual Gods   '88

Born on 2/21/49 in Milwaukee. Rock keyboardist/producer. Member of **Talking Heads**. The Casual Gods are 13 backing musicians.

2/6/88	78	20	© 1 **Casual Gods**	$10	Sire 25663
6/9/90	188	3	© 2 **Walk On Water**	$10	Sire 25943

A.K.A. Love (1)
Are You Running? (1)
Big Mouth (2)
Bobby (1)

Cherokee Chief (1)
Confess (1)
Cowboy's Got To Go (2)
Doctors Lie (2)

Facing The Fire (2)
Flying Under Radar (2)
I Cry For Iran (2)
I Don't Mind (1)

If The Rains Return (2)
Kick Start (2)
Let It Come Down (1)
Man With A Gun (1)

Never Let It Slip (2)
Perfect Lie (1)
Remain Calm (2)
Rev It Up (1)

Sleep Angel (1)
Song Of Angels (1)
We're Always Talking (1)

HARRISON, Noel   '68

Born on 1/29/34 in London. Singer/actor. Son of actor Rex Harrison.

12/9/67+	135	9	**Collage**	$20	Reprise 6263

Go Ask Your Man
Just Like A Woman

Lucy In The Sky With Diamonds
Mrs. Williams' Rose

Museum
People In The Rain

Sign Of The Queen
Strawberry Fields Forever

Suzanne *56*
When I'm 64

Whiter Shade Of Pale
Woman

HARRISON, Wes   '63

Born on 1/31/25 in Spartanburg, South Carolina. Sound effects comedian.

11/2/63	83	5	**You Won't Believe Your Ears** .... [C]	$30	Philips 103

Better Late Than Never

Father, Oh Father

Out At The Outhouse

Saga Of The Duck Hunt

Wes' Car

HARRISON, Wilbert   '70

Born on 1/5/29 in Charlotte, North Carolina. Died of a stroke on 10/26/94 (age 65). R&B singer.

1/24/70	190	2	**Let's Work Together**	$50	Sue 8801

Blue Monday
Forgive Me
Kansas City

Let's Work Together (Part 1) *32*
Louie-Louie

Peepin' & Hidin'
Soul Rattler
Stagger Lee

Stand By Me
Tropical Shakedown
What Am I Living For

HARRY, Debbie   '81

Born on 7/1/45 in Miami; raised in New Jersey. Singer/actress. Member of **The Wind In The Willows**. Lead singer of **Blondie**. Acted in several movies.

8/29/81	25	12	● © 1 **KooKoo**	$12	Chrysalis 1347
12/13/86+	97	13	© 2 **Rockbird**	$10	Geffen 24123
10/14/89	123	8	© 3 **Def, Dumb & Blonde**	$10	Sire 25938

DEBORAH HARRY

Backfired (1) *43*
Beyond The Limit (2)
Brite Side (3)
Buckle Up (2)
Bugeye (3)

Calmarie (3)
Chrome (1)
End Of The Run (3)
Free To Fall (2)
French Kissin (2) *57*

Get Your Way (3)
He Is So (3)
I Want That Man (3)
I Want You (2)
In Love With Love (2) *70*

Inner City Spillover (1)
Jam Was Moving (1) *82*
Jump Jump (1)
Kiss It Better (3)
Lovelight (3)

Maybe For Sure (3)
Military Rap (1)
Now I Know You Know (1)
Oasis (1)
Rockbird (2)

Secret Life (2)
Surrender (1)
Sweet And Low (3)
Under Arrest (1)
You Got Me In Trouble (2)

HART, Beth   '00

Born in Santa Monica, California. Female singer/songwriter.

1/29/00	143	6	© **Screamin' For My Supper**	$10	143 83192

By Her
Delicious Surprise
Favorite Things

G.O.P.
Get Your Sh-t Together
Girls Say

Is That Too Much To Ask
Just A Little Hole
L.A. Song *90*

Mama
Skin
Sky Is Falling

Stay

HART, Corey   '85

Born on 5/31/62 in Montreal, Canada; raised in Malaga, Spain and Mexico City. Male singer/songwriter/keyboardist.

7/14/84	31	36	● © 1 **First Offense**	$10	EMI America 17117
7/20/85	20	37	● © 2 **Boy In The Box**	$10	EMI America 17161
10/18/86	55	27	● © 3 **Fields Of Fire**	$10	EMI America 17217
7/9/88	121	8	© 4 **Young Man Running**	$10	EMI-Manhattan 48752
4/28/90	134	5	© 5 **Bang!**	$10	EMI 92513

Angry Young Man (3)
Art Of Color (5)
At The Dance (1)
Ballade For Nien Cheng (5)

BANG! (Starting Over) (5)
Blind Faith (3)
Boy In The Box (2) *26*
Broken Arrow (3)

Can't Help Falling In Love (3) *24*
Can't Lose Stalin' Us (3)
Chase The Sun (4,5)

Cheatin' In School (1)
Chippin' Away (4)
Crossroad Caravan (4)
Dancin' With My Mirror (3) *88*

Diamond Cowboy (5)
Does She Love You (1)
Don't Take Me To The Racetrack (4)

Eurasian Eyes (2)
Everything In My Heart (2) *30*
Goin' Home (3)
I Am By Your Side (3) *18*

HART, Corey — Cont'd

Icon (5)
In Your Soul (4) 38
Is It Too Late? (3)
It Ain't Enough (1) 17
Jenny Fey (1)

Jimmy Rae (3)
Kisses On The Train (5)
Komrade Kiev (2)
Lamp At Midnite (1)
Little Love (5) 37

Lone Wolf (4)
Never Surrender (2) 3
No Love Lost (4)
Peruvian Lady (1)
Political Cry (3)

Rain On Me (5)
She Got The Radio (1)
Silent Talking (2)
Slowburn (5)
So It Goes... (4)

Spot You In A Coalmine (4)
Still In Love (4)
Sunglasses At Night (1) 7
Sunny Place - Shady People (2)
Take My Heart (3)

Truth Will Set You Free (4)
Waiting For You (2)
Water From The Moon (2)
World Is Fire (1)

HART, Freddie '71
Born Fred Segrest on 12/21/26 in Lochapoka, Alabama. Country singer/songwriter/guitarist.

DEBUT	PEAK	WKS				$	
10/9/71	37	20	●	1	Easy Loving	$15	Capitol 838
3/18/72	89	11		2	My Hang-Up Is You	$15	Capitol 11014
7/1/72	93	16		3	Bless Your Heart	$15	Capitol 11073
9/22/73	188	6		4	Trip To Heaven	$15	Capitol 11197

Bless Your Heart (3)
California Grapevine (1)
Cinderella (3)
Coldest Bed (4)
Conscience Makes Cowards (Of Us All) (3)
Cravin' (3)
Easy Loving (1) 17

Everytime He Touches You (3)
Greatest Gift Of All (2)
Heart (2)
House Of Sand (1)
Human Rat Race (3)
Hungry Row (3)
I'm Afraid To Love You ('Fraid I Might Like It) (3)

I'm In Love (3)
I'm No Angel (4)
I'm Not Going Hungry (3)
If Fingerprints Showed Up On Skin (1)
In The Arms Of Love (1)
Jesus Is My Kind Of People (3)
Key's In The Mailbox (2)

Living On Leftovers Of You (4)
Look-A-Here (4)
Love Did This To Me (4)
Love Makes The Difference (2)
Loving Her Through You (4)
My Hang-Up Is You (2)
One More Mountain To Climb (1)

She Belongs To Me (2)
Skid Row Street (4)
That Hurtin' Feeling (1)
Trip To Heaven (4)
Twin Of An Angel (4)
Ugly Duckling (4)
Until Now (3)
Whole World Holding Hands (1)

Without You (1)
Would You Settle For Roses (2)
Write It All In (Put It All In) (1)
You Belong To Me (4)

HART, Mickey '72
Born in 1950 in Long Island, New York. Rock drummer. Member of the Grateful Dead.

DEBUT	PEAK	WKS				$	
10/21/72	190	4	©		Rolling Thunder	$40	Warner 2635

Blind John
Chase (Progress)

Deep, Wide And Frequent
Fletcher Carnaby

Granma's Cookies
Hangin' On

Main Ten (Playing In The Band)
Pump Song

Rolling Thunder (medley)
Shoshone Invocation (medley)

Young Man

HARTFORD, John '69
Born on 12/30/37 in New York City; raised in St. Louis. Died of cancer on 6/4/2001 (age 63). Singer/songwriter/banjo player. Regular on The Smothers Brothers TV show.

DEBUT	PEAK	WKS				$	
6/14/69	137	9		1	John Hartford	$20	RCA Victor 4156
11/27/71	193	4	©	2	Aereo-Plain	$15	Warner 1916

Back In The Goodle Days (2)
Because Of You (2)
Boogie (2)
Collector, The (1)
Dusty Miller Hornpipe And Fugue In A Major For Strings, Brass And 5-String Banjo (1)

First Girl I Loved (2)
Holding (2)
I Didn't Know The World Would Last This Long (1)
I've Heard That Tearstained Monologue You Do There By The Door Before You Go (1)

Leather Britches (2)
Little Old Lonesome Little Circle Song (1)
Little Piece In A (2)
Mr. Jackson's Got Nothing To Do (1)
Open Road Ode (1)

Orphan Of World War Two (1)
Poor Old Prurient Interest Blues (1)
Presbyterian Guitar (2)
Railroad Street (1)
Short Sentimental Interlude (1)
Station Break (2)

Steam Powered Aereo Plane (2)
Steamboat Whistle Blues (2)
Symphony Hall Rag (2)
Tear Down The Grand Ole Opry (2)
Turn Your Radio On (2)

Up On The Hill Where They Do The Boogie (2)
Wart, The (1)
With A Vamp In The Middle (2)

HARTLEY, Keef, Band '70
Born on 3/8/44 in Preston, Lancashire, England. Jazz-rock drummer. Member of John Mayall's Bluesbreakers.

DEBUT	PEAK	WKS				$	
11/28/70	191	3			The Time Is Near	$20	Deram 18047

Another Time, Another Place
Change

From A Window
Morning Rain

Premonition
Time Is Near

You Can't Take It With You

HARTMAN, Dan '84
Born on 12/8/50 in Harrisburg, Pennsylvania. Died of a brain tumor on 3/22/94 (age 43). Pop-disco singer/songwriter/producer/multi-instrumentalist. Member of the Edgar Winter Group from 1972-76.

DEBUT	PEAK	WKS				$	
12/16/78+	80	19		1	Instant Replay	$12	Blue Sky 35641
3/15/80	189	2		2	Relight My Fire	$12	Blue Sky 36302
11/3/84	55	28	©	3	I Can Dream About You	$10	MCA 5525

Chocolate Box (1)
Countdown (medley) (1)
Double-O-Love (1)
Electricity (3)

Free Ride (2)
Hands Down (2)
I Can Dream About You (3) 6
I Can't Get Enough (3)

I Love Makin' Music (2)
I'm Not A Rolling Stone (3)
Instant Replay (1) 29
Just For Fun (2)

Love Is A Natural (1)
Love Strong (2)
Name Of The Game (3)
Power Of A Good Love (3)

Rage To Live (3)
Relight My Fire (medley) (2)
Second Nature (3) 39
Shy Hearts (3)

This Is It (medley) (1) 91
Time And Space (1)
Vertigo (medley) (2)
We Are The Young (3) 25

HARVEY, PJ '95
Born Polly Jean Harvey on 10/9/69 in Yeovil, England. Female singer/guitarist. Had own trio, also named PJ Harvey, which included bassist Stephen Vaughan and drummer Rob Ellis.

DEBUT	PEAK	WKS				$	
5/22/93	158	1	©	1	Rid Of Me	$10	Island 514696
3/18/95	40	15	©	2	To Bring You My Love	$10	Island 524085
10/12/96	178	1	©	3	Dance Hall At Louse Point	$10	Island 524278
					JOHN PARISH & POLLY JEAN HARVEY		
10/17/98	54	4	©	4	Is This Desire?	$10	Island 524563
11/18/00	42	9	©	5	Stories From The City, Stories From The Sea	$10	Island 548144

Angelene (4)
Beautiful Feeling (5)
Big Exit (5)
Catherine (4)
City Of No Sun (3)
Civil War Correspondent (3)
C'Mon Billy (3)
Dance Hall At Louse Point (3)
Dancer, The (2)
Down By The Water (2)
Dry (1)

Ecstasy (1)
Electric Light (4)
50Ft Queenie (1)
Garden, The (4)
Girl (1)
Good Fortune (5)
Heela (2)
Highway '61 Revisited (1)
Hook (1)
Horses In My Dreams (5)
I Think I'm A Mother (2)

Is That All There Is? (3)
Is This Desire? (4)
Joy (4)
Kamikaze (5)
Legs (1)
Long Snake Moan (2)
Lost Fun Zone (3)
Man-Size (1)
Man-Size Sextet (1)
Me-Jane (1)
Meet Ze Monsta (2)

Missed (1)
My Beautiful Leah (4)
No Girl So Sweet (4)
One Line (5)
Perfect Day Elise (4)
Place Called Home (5)
Rid Of Me (1)
River, The (4)
Rope Bridge Crossing (3)
Rub 'Til It Bleeds (1)
Send His Love To Me (2)

Sky Lit Up (4)
Snake (1)
Taut (3)
Teclo (2)
That Was My Veil (3)
This Is Love (5)
This Mess We're In (5)
To Bring You My Love (2)
Un Cercle Autour Du Soleil (2)
Urn With Dead Flowers In A Drained Pool (2)

We Float (5)
Whores Hustle And The Hustlers Whore (5)
Wind, The (4)
Working For The Man (2)
You Said Something (5)
Yuri-G (1)

HARVEY, Sensational Alex, Band '75
Born on 2/5/35 in Glasgow, Scotland. Died of a heart attack on 2/4/82 (one day before his 47th birthday). His band: Zal Cleminson (guitar), Hugh McKenna (keyboards), Chris Glen (bass) and Ted McKenna (drums).

DEBUT	PEAK	WKS				$	
3/1/75	197	1		1	The Impossible Dream	$15	Vertigo 2000
11/1/75	100	4		2	"Live"	[L] $12	Atlantic 18148

recorded on 5/24/75 at the Hammersmith Odeon in London

Anthem (1)
Delilah (2)
Faith Healer (2)

Fanfare (Justly, Skillfully, Magnanimously) (2)
Framed (2)

Give My Compliments To The Chef (2)
Impossible Dream (medley) (1)

Long Hair Music (1)
Man In The Jar (medley) (1)
Money Honey (medley) (1)

River Of Love (1)
Sergeant Fury (1)
Tomahawk Kid (1,2)

Vambo (1,2)
Weights Made Of Lead (1)

The Do-Re-Mi Children's Chorus
Do You Hear What I Hear? ('67)

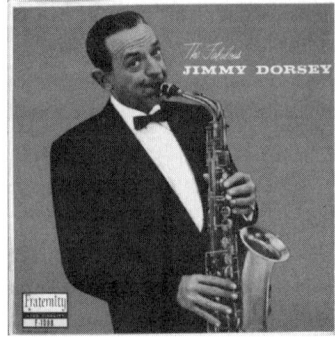

Jimmy Dorsey
The Fabulous Jimmy Dorsey ('57)

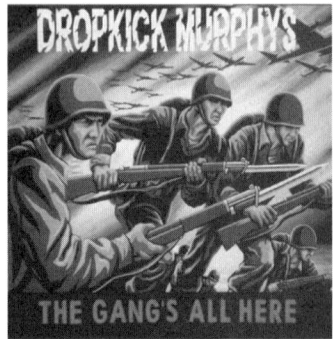

Dropkick Murphys
The Gang's All Here ('99)

Patty Duke
Don't Just Stand There ('65)

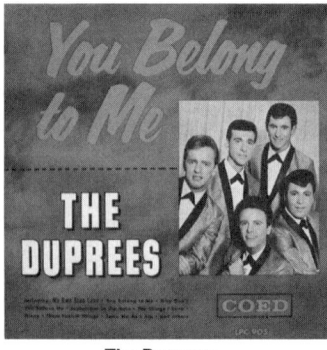

The Duprees
You Belong To Me ('62)

Bob Dylan
MTV Unplugged ('95)

Danny Elfman
Edward Scissorhands ('91)

Bent Fabric
Alley Cat ('62)

Fastway
All Fired Up ('84)

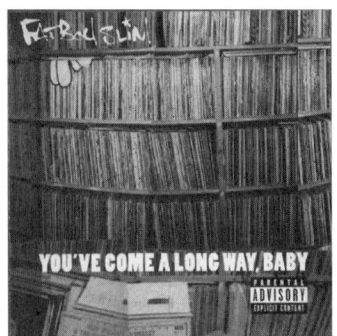

Fatboy Slim
You've Come A Long Way, Baby ('98)

Ella Fitzgerald...*Ella Fitzgerald sings the
Rodgers and Hart Song Book ('57)*

Lester Flatt & Earl Scruggs
The Story of Bonnie & Clyde ('68)

A Flock Of Seagulls
The Story Of A Young Heart ('84)

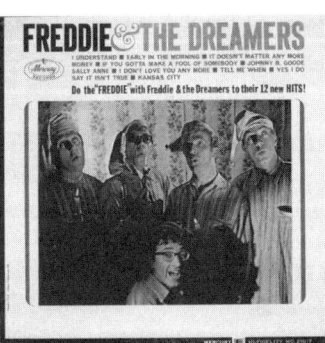

Freddie & The Dreamers
Freddie & The Dreamers ('65)

Funkadelic
Uncle Jam Wants You ('79)

Gaither Vocal Band
God Is Good ('99)

Nikki Giovanni
Truth Is On Its Way ('71)

Goodie Mob
World Party ('00)

Dickie Goodman
Mr. Jaws and other Fables ('75)

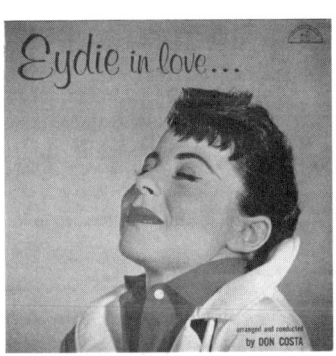

Eydie Gorme
Eydie In Love ('58)

Vince Guaraldi Trio
Jazz Impressions of Black Orpheus ('63)

Buddy Guy
Feels Like Rain ('93)

Bill Haley and his Comets
Shake Rattle and Roll ('55)

The Happenings
The Happenings ('66)

HARVEY DANGER   '98
Rock group from Seattle: Sean Nelson (vocals), Jeff Lin (guitar), Aaron Huffman (bass) and Evan Sult (drums).

| 6/20/98 | 70 | 20 | ● | ● | Where Have All The Merrymakers Gone? | | | $10 | Slash 556000 |

Carlotta Valdez   Flagpole Sitta
Jack The Lion   Old Hat   Private Helicopter   Problems And Bigger Ones   Radio Silence   Terminal Annex   Woolly Muffler   Wrecking Ball

HASLAM, Annie   '78
Born in Bolton, Lancashire, England. Lead singer of **Renaissance**.

| 12/24/77+ | 167 | 13 | | | Annie In Wonderland | | | $15 | Sire 6046 |

Going Home   Hunioco
I Never Believed In Love   If I Loved You   If I Were Made Of Music   Inside My Life   Nature Boy   Rockalise

HATFIELD, Juliana, Three   '95
Born on 7/2/67 in Wiscasset, Maine. Female rock singer/guitarist. Group also included bassist Dean Fisher and drummer Todd Philips. Former member of **The Lemonheads**.

| 8/21/93 | 119 | 12 | © | 1 | Become What You Are | | | $10 | Atlantic 92278 |
| 4/15/95 | 96 | 7 | © | 2 | Only Everything | | | $10 | Mammoth 92540 |

JULIANA HATFIELD

Addicted (1)   Bottles And Flowers (2)   Congratulations (2)   Dame With A Rod (1)   Dumb Fun (2)
Dying Proof (1)   Feelin' Massachusetts (1)   Fleur De Lys (2)   For The Birds (1)   Hang Down From Heaven (2)
I Got No Idols (1)   Little Pieces (1)   Live On Tomorrow (2)   Mabel (1)   My Darling (2)
My Sister (1)   OK OK (2)   Outsider (2)   President Garfield (1)   Simplicity Is Beautiful (2)
Spin The Bottle (1)   Supermodel (1)   This Is The Sound (1)   Universal Heart-Beat (2)   What A Life (2)
You Blues (2)

HATHAWAY, Donny   '72
Born on 10/1/45 in Chicago; raised in St. Louis. Committed suicide on 1/13/79 (age 33). R&B singer/songwriter/keyboardist. Father of **Lalah Hathaway**.

| 5/15/71 | 89 | 21 | © | 1 | Donny Hathaway | | | $15 | Atco 360 |
| 5/29/71 | 73 | 25 | © | 2 | Everything Is Everything | | [E] | $15 | Atco 332 |

released in 1970

| 3/4/72 | 18 | 38 | ● | 3 | Donny Hathaway Live | | [L] | $15 | Atco 386 |

recorded at the Bitter End in New York City

| 5/13/72 | 3 | 39 | ● | © | 4 | Roberta Flack & Donny Hathaway | | | $15 | Atlantic 7216 |
| 7/21/73 | 69 | 13 | | | 5 | Extension Of A Man | | | $15 | Atco 7029 |

Baby I Love You (4)   Be Real Black For Me (4)   Come Little Children (5)   Come Ye Disconsolate (4)   Flying Easy (5)   For All We Know (4)   **Ghetto-Part One** (2,3) *87*   **Giving Up** (1) *81*
He Ain't Heavy, He's My Brother (1)   Hey Girl (3)   I Believe In Music (1)   I Believe To My Soul (2)   I Know It's You (5)   I Love The Lord; He Heard My Cry (Parts I & II) (5)
I Love You More Than You'll Ever Know (5) *60*   I (Who Have Nothing) (4)   Je Vous Aime (I Love You) (2)   Jealous Guy (3)   Little Ghetto Boy (3)   Little Girl (1)   **Love, Love, Love** (5) *44*   Magdalena (5)
Magnificent Sanctuary Band (1)   Misty (4)   Mood (4)   Put Your Hand In The Hand (1)   She Is My Lady (1)   Slums, The (5)   Someday We'll All Be Free (5)   Song For You (1)   Sugar Lee (2)
Take A Love Song (1)   Thank You Master (For My Soul) (2)   To Be Young, Gifted And Black (1)   Tryin' Times (2)   Valdez In The Country (5)   Voices Inside (Everything Is Everything) (2,3)
We're Still Friends (3)   What's Goin' On (3)   When Love Has Grown (4)   **Where Is The Love** (3,4) *5*   **You've Got A Friend** (3,4) *29*   **You've Lost That Lovin' Feelin'** (4) *71*

HATHAWAY, Lalah   '90
Born in 1969 in Chicago. R&B singer. Daughter of **Donny Hathaway**.

| 10/20/90 | 191 | 2 | © | 1 | Lalah Hathaway | | | $10 | Virgin 91382 |
| 5/29/99 | 196 | 1 | © | 2 | The Song Lives On | | | $10 | GRP 9956 |

JOE SAMPLE Featuring Lalah Hathaway

Baby Don't Cry (1)   Bitter Sweet (2)   Come Along With Me (2)   Fever (2)
For All We Know (1)   Heaven Knows (1)   I Gotta Move On (1)   I'm Coming Back (1)
Living In Blue (2)   Long Way From Home (2)   Obvious (2)   One Day I'll Fly Away (2)
Sentimental (1)   Smile (1)   Somethin' (1)   Song Lives On (2)
Stay Home Tonight (1)   Street Life (2)   U-Godit Gowin On (1)   When The World Turns Blue (2)
When Your Life Was Low (2)

HAVANA 3 A.M.   '91
Rock group formed in England: Nigel Dixon (vocals, guitar), **Gary Myrick** (guitar), Paul Simonon (bass) and Travis Williams (drums). Simonon was a member of **The Clash**.

| 5/4/91 | 169 | 3 | © | | Havana 3 A.M. | | | $10 | I.R.S. 13069 |

Blue Gene Vincent   Blue Motorcycle Eyes
Death In The Afternoon   Hardest Game   Hey Amigo   Hole In The Sky   Joyride   Life On The Line   Living In This Town   Reach The Rock   Surf In The City   What About Your Future

HAVENS, Richie   '71
Born on 1/21/41 in Brooklyn, New York. Black folk singer/guitarist.
1)Alarm Clock 2)Richie Havens On Stage 3)Richard P. Havens, 1983

| 2/24/68 | 184 | 7 | © | 1 | Something Else Again | | | $20 | Verve Forecast 3034 |
| 7/6/68 | 182 | 2 | © | 2 | Mixed Bag | | [E] | $20 | Verve Forecast 3006 |

released in 1967; also see #6 below

| 11/30/68 | 192 | 3 | | 3 | Electric Havens | | [E] | $20 | Douglas 780 |

released in 1966

1/11/69	80	11		4	Richard P. Havens, 1983			$25	Verve Forecast 3047 [2]
1/10/70	155	14		5	Stonehenge			$15	Stormy Forest 6001
11/7/70	190	2		6	Mixed Bag		[R]	$15	MGM 4698
1/9/71	29	34		7	Alarm Clock			$15	Stormy Forest 6005
11/13/71	126	11		8	The Great Blind Degree			$15	Stormy Forest 6010
9/23/72	55	18		9	Richie Havens On Stage		[L]	$20	Stormy Forest 6012 [2]
6/9/73	182	4		10	Portfolio			$15	Stormy Forest 6013
10/12/74	186	3		11	Mixed Bag II			$15	Stormy Forest 6201
10/2/76	157	4		12	The End Of The Beginning			$12	A&M 4598
10/3/87	173	4	©	13	Simple Things			$10	RBI 400

Adam (2,6)   Alarm Clock (7)   Arrow Through Me (13)   Baby Blue (5)   Band On The Run (11)   Boots And Spanish Leather (3)   C.C. Rider (3)
Cautiously (4)   Daughter Of The Night (12)   Do It Again (12)   Do You Feel Good (medley) (4)   Dolphins, The (9)   Don't Listen To Me (1)   Dreaming As One (12)
Dreaming My Life Away (10)   Drivin' (12)   Eleanor Rigby (2,6)   End Of The Season (7)   Fathers And Sons (8)   Fire And Rain (8)   Follow (2,6)
For Haven's Sake (4)   From The Prison (1,9)   Girls Don't Run Away (7)   God Bless The Child (9)   Handsome Johnny (2,6)   Headkeeper (11)   **Here Comes The Sun** (7) *16*
High Flyin' Bird (2,6,9)   I Can't Make It Anymore (2,6)   I Don't Need Nobody (10)   I Don't Wanna Know (13)   I Know I Won't Be There (10)   I Pity The Poor Immigrant (4)   I Started A Joke (5)
I Was Educated By Myself (12)   I'm A Stranger Here (3)   I'm Not In Love (12)   If Not For You (12)   In These Flames (8)   Indian Prayer (11)   Indian Rope Man (4)

HAVENS, Richie — Cont'd

Inside Of Him (1)
It Could Be The First Day (5)
It Was A Very Good Year (10)
Just Above My Hobby Horse's Head (4)
Just Like A Woman (2,6,9)
Klan, The (1)
Lady Madonna (4)
Little Help From My Friends (4)
Loner, The (1)
Long Train Running (12)
Maggie's Farm (1)
Makings Of You (11)
Mama Loves You (10)
Minstrel From Gault (5,9)

Missing Train (7)
Morning, Morning (2,6)
My Own Way (3)
My Sweet Lord (9)
New City (1)
900 Miles (3)
No Opportunity Necessary, No Experience Needed (1,9)
Nobody Knows (9)
Old Friends (9)
Ooh Child (11)
Open Our Eyes (5)
Oxford Town (3)
Parable Of Ramon (4)
Passin' By (13)

Patient Lady (7)
Prayer (5)
Priests (4)
Putting Out The Vibration, And Hoping It Comes Home (4)
Ring Around The Moon (5)
Rocky Raccoon (9)
Run, Shaker Life (1,4)
Runner In The Night (13)
Sad Eyed Lady (Of The Lowlands) (11)
San Francisco Bay Blues (2,6,9)
Sandy (2,6)
Shadow Town (3)
She's Leaving Home (4)

Shouldn't All The World Be Dancing (5)
Shouldn't We All Be Having A Good Time (13)
Simple Things (13)
Some Will Wait (7)
Someone Suite (11)
Somethin' Else Again (1)
Songwriter (13)
Stop Pulling And Pushing Me (4)
Strawberry Fields Forever (4)
Sugarplums (1)
Teach Your Children (8,9)
There's A Hole In The Future (5)

Think About The Children (8)
Three Day Eternity (2,6)
3:10 To Yuma (3)
Tight Rope (10)
Tiny Little Blues (5)
To Give All Your Love Away (7)
Tommy (8)
Tupelo Honey (9)
23 Days In September (10)
Wake Up & Dream (13)
Wandering Angus (11)
We Can't Hide It Anymore (12)
Wear Your Love Like Heaven (4)
What About Me (8)

What Have We Done (8)
What More Can I Say John (4)
What's Going On (10)
Where Have All The Flowers Gone (9)
Wild Night (12)
With A Little Help From My Friends ..see: Little Help From My Friends
Woman (10)
You Can Close Your Eyes (12)
Younger Men Grow Older (7,9)

HAWKINS, Edwin, Singers   '69

Born in August 1943 in Oakland. Formed gospel group with Betty Watson in 1967 as the Northern California State Youth Choir. Member Dorothy Morrison went on to a solo career.

5/3/69	15	23	1 Let Us Go Into The House Of The Lord	$20 Pavilion 10001
10/18/69	169	4	2 Live At Yankee Stadium ..... [L]	$30 T-Neck 3004 [2]

side A: **Isley Brothers**; side B: Edwin Hawkins Singers; side C: **Brooklyn Bridge**; side D: "Don't Change Your Love" by **The Five Stairsteps**, "Somebody's Been Messin'" by Judy White and "Love Is What You Make It" by Sweet Cherries; recorded on 6/21/69

10/2/71	180	8	3 Children (Get Together)	$15 Buddah 5086
5/27/72	171	4	4 I'd Like To Teach The World To Sing	$15 Buddah 5101

Children Get Together (3)
Deeper Love (3)
Early In The Morning (1)
Give Me A Star (4)
Grove Of Eucalyptus (4)

Here's The Reason (4)
His Way (3)
I Don't Know How To Love Him (4)
I Hear The Voice Of Jesus (1)
I Shall Be Free (3)

I'd Like To Teach The World To Sing (4)
I'm Going Through (1)
Jesus, Lover Of My Soul (1,2)
Joy, Joy (1,2)
Late In The Evening (4)

Let Us Go Into The House Of The Lord (1)
Long Way To Go (3)
Lord We Try (4)
Oh Happy Day (1,2) **4**
Ooh Child (4)

Shine (4)
Someday (3)
There's A Place For Me (3)
To My Father's House (1)
Together In Peace (3)
Trouble The World Is In (3)

Wake Up To What's Happening (4)
When We Love (4)
World Is Going To Be A Better Place (3)

HAWKINS, Sophie B.   '92

Born Sophie Ballantine Hawkins on 11/1/67 in Manhattan, New York. Female singer/songwriter.

5/16/92	51	24	●	©	1 Tongues And Tails	$10 Columbia 46797
8/26/95	65	32	●	©	2 Whaler	$10 Columbia 53300

As I Lay Me Down (2) **6**
Ballad Of Sleeping Beauty..see: Only Love
Before I Walk On Fire (1)
California Here I Come (1)
Carry Me (1)

Damn I Wish I Was Your Lover (1) **5**
Did We Not Choose Each Other (2)
Don't Don't Tell Me No (2)
Don't Stop Swaying (1)

I Need Nothing Else (2)
I Want You (1)
Let Me Love You Up (2)
Listen (1)
Live And Let Love (1)
Mr. Tugboat Hello (2)

Mysteries We Understand (1)
Only Love (The Battle Of Sleeping Beauty) (2) **49**
Right Beside You (2) **56**
Saviour Child (1)
Sometimes I See (2)

Swing From Limb To Limb (My Home Is In Your Jungle) (2)
True Romance (2)
We Are One Body (1)

HAWKWIND   '74

Space-rock group formed in London by lead singer/guitarist Dave Brock. Fluctuating lineup included **Ginger Baker** and **Motorhead**'s Ian "Lemmy" Kilminster.

11/24/73	179	8	©	1 Space Ritual/Alive In Liverpool And London ..... [L]	$20 United Artists 120 [2]
10/5/74	110	12	©	2 Hall Of The Mountain Grill	$15 United Artists 328
6/14/75	150	5	©	3 Warrior On The Edge Of Time	$15 Atco 115

Assault & Battery Part I (3)
Awakening, The (1)
Black Corridor (1)
Born To Go (medley) (1)
Brainstorm (1)
D-Rider (2)
Demented Man (3)

Down Through The Night (1)
Dying Seas (3)
Earth Calling (medley) (1)
Electronic No. 1 (1)
Goat Willow (3)
Golden Void Part II (3)
Hall Of The Mountain Grill (2)

Kings Of Speed (3)
Lord Of Light (3)
Lost Johnnie (2)
Magnu (3)
Master Of The Universe (1)
Opa-Loka (3)
Orgone Accumulator (1)

Paradox (2)
Psychedelic Warlocks (Disappear In Smoke) (2)
7 X 7 (1)
Sonic Attack (1)
Space Is Deep (1)
Spiral Galaxy 28948 (3)

Standing At The Edge (3)
10 Seconds Of Forever (1)
Time We Left This World Today (1)
Upside Down (1)
Warriors (3)
Web Weaver (2)

Welcome To The Future (1)
Wind Of Change (2)
Wizard Blew His Horn (3)
You'd Better Believe It (2)

HAY, Colin James   '87

Born on 6/29/53 in Scotland; raised in Melbourne, Australia. Lead singer/guitarist of **Men At Work**.

2/21/87	126	9	©	Looking For Jack	$10 Columbia 40611

Can I Hold You?
Circles Erratica

Fisherman's Friend
Hold Me 99

I Don't Need You Anymore
Looking For Jack

Master Of Crime
Puerto Rico

These Are Our Finest Days
Ways Of The World

HAYES, Isaac   ★112★   '71

Born on 8/20/42 in Covington, Tennessee. R&B singer/songwriter/keyboardist/actor. Session musician for the Stax label. Teamed with songwriter **David Porter** to write many classic songs. Acted in several movies. Supplies the voice of "Chef" for TV's *South Park*.

1)Shaft 2)Hot Buttered Soul 3)The Isaac Hayes Movement 4)Black Moses 5)To Be Continued

7/12/69	8	81	●	©	1 Hot Buttered Soul	$20	Enterprise 1001
4/18/70	8	75		©	2 The Isaac Hayes Movement	$20	Enterprise 1010
12/5/70	11	56		©	3 To Be Continued	$20	Enterprise 1014
8/21/71	❶¹	60	●	©	4 Shaft ..... [I-S]	$25	Enterprise 5002 [2]
12/11/71+	10	34		©	5 Black Moses	$25	Enterprise 5003 [2]
2/26/72	102	12		©	6 In The Beginning ..... [E]	$15	Atlantic 1599
					first released in 1968 as *Presenting Isaac Hayes* on Enterprise 100 ($30)		
5/19/73	14	26	●	©	7 Live At The Sahara Tahoe ..... [L]	$20	Enterprise 5005 [2]
10/27/73	16	27	●	©	8 Joy	$15	Enterprise 5007
6/15/74	146	8		©	9 Tough Guys ..... [I-S]	$15	Enterprise 7504
					music from the movie *Three Tough Guys*		
8/3/74	156	9		©	10 Truck Turner ..... [I-S]	$20	Enterprise 7507 [2]
6/21/75	18	19	●	©	11 Chocolate Chip	$15	HBS 874

HAYES, Isaac — Cont'd

DEBUT	PEAK	WKS	CD	ARTIST — Album Title		$	Label & Number
8/23/75	165	4		12 The Best Of Isaac Hayes	[G]	$15	Enterprise 7510
1/17/76	85	17		13 Disco Connection		$15	HBS 923
2/21/76	45	12		14 Groove-A-Thon		$15	HBS 925
7/24/76	124	7		15 Juicy Fruit (Disco Freak)		$15	HBS 953
2/19/77	49	13		16 A Man And A Woman	[L]	$20	HBS 996 [2]

ISAAC HAYES & DIONNE WARWICK

DEBUT	PEAK	WKS	CD	ARTIST — Album Title	$	Label & Number
12/17/77+	78	12		17 New Horizon	$12	Polydor 6120
11/18/78+	75	18		18 For The Sake Of Love	$12	Polydor 6164
9/29/79+	39	30	●	19 Don't Let Go	$12	Polydor 6224
10/20/79	80	19	©	20 Royal Rappin's	$12	Polydor 6229

MILLIE JACKSON & ISAAC HAYES

DEBUT	PEAK	WKS	CD	ARTIST — Album Title	$	Label & Number
5/17/80	59	15		21 And Once Again	$12	Polydor 6269

After Five (13)
Ain't No Sunshine (7)
Aruba (13)
Be Yourself (4)
Believe In Me (18)
Blue's Crib (10)
Body Language (11,16)
Brand New Me (medley) (5)
Breakthrough (10)
Bumpy's Blues (4)
Bumpy's Lament (4)
Buns O'Plenty (3)
By The Time I Get To Phoenix (1,12,16) *37*
Cafe Regio's (4)
Can't Hide Love (16)
Chocolate Chip (11,16) *92*
Choppers (13)
Close To You ..see: (They Long To Be)
Come Live With Me (11,16)
Come On (medley) (7)
Disco Connection (13)
Disco Shuffle (13)
Do You Wanna Make Love (20)
Do Your Thing (4,7,12) *30*
Don't Let Go (19) *18*
Don't Let Me Be Lonely Tonight (18)
Don't Take Your Love Away (17)
Dorinda's Party (10)
Drinking (3)
Driving In The Sun (10)

Duke, The (10)
Early Sunday Morning (4)
Ellie's Love Theme (4,7,12)
Feelin' Alright (7)
Feeling Keeps On Coming (8)
I Love Music (medley) (16)
Feelings (medley) (16)
Feels Like The First Time (20)
Fever (19)
Few More Kisses To Go (19)
First Day Of Forever (13)
First Time Ever I Saw Your Face (7)
For The Good Times (5)
Friend's Place (4)
Get Down Tonight (medley) (16)
Give It To Me (10)
Going In Circles (5)
Going To Chicago Blues (medley) (6)
Good Love 6-9969 (15)
Groove-A-Thon (14)
Have You Never Been Mellow (medley) (16)
Help Me Love (medley) (5)
Hospital Shootout (10)
House Full Of Girls (10)
House Of Beauty (10)
Hung Up On My Baby (9)
Hyperbolicsyllabicsequedalymistic (1)
I Ain't Never (21)
I Can't Turn Around (11)
I Changed My Mind (20)

I Just Don't Know What To Do With Myself (2,16)
I Just Want To Make Love To You (medley) (6)
I Love You That's All (8)
I Say A Little Prayer (medley) (16)
I Stand Accused (2,12) *42*
I Want To Make Love To You So Bad (11)
I'll Never Fall In Love Again (5)
I'm Gonna Make It (Without You) (8)
If I Had My Way (20)
If We Ever Needed Peace (18)
If You Had Your Way (20)
Ike's Mood I (3)
Ike's Rap I (3)
Ike's Rap II, III & IV (medley) (5)
Ike's Rap V & VI (medley) (16)
Ike's Rap VII (medley) (21)
Insurance Company (10)
It's All In The Game (21)
It's Heaven To Me (17)
It's Too Late (7)
Joe Bell (9)
Joy - Pt. 1 (8,12) *30*
Juicy Fruit (Disco Freak) (15)
Just The Way You Are (18)
Kidnapped (9)
Lady Of The Night (15)
Let's Don't Ever Blow Our Thing (15)

Light My Fire (medley) (7)
Look Of Love (3,7) *79*
Love Changes (20)
Love Has Been Good To Us (21)
Love Me Or Lose Me (15)
Love Will Keep Us Together (medley) (16)
Make A Little Love To Me (14)
Man Will Be A Man (8)
Man's Temptation (5)
Men, Theme From The (7)
Misty (medley) (6)
Moonlight Lovin' (Menage A Trois) (17)
Music To Make Love By (15)
My Eyes Adored You (medley) (16)
My Love (16)
Need To Belong To Someone (5)
Never Can Say Goodbye (5,7,12) *22*
Never Gonna Give You Up (5)
No Name Bar (4)
Nothing Takes The Place Of You (5)
Now We're One (10)
Once You Hit The Road (16)
One Big Unhappy Family (2)
One Woman (1)
Our Day Will Come (3)
Out Of The Ghetto (17)
Part-Time Love (5)

Precious, Precious (6)
Pursuit Of The Pimpmobile (10)
Randolph & Dearborn (9)
Red Rooster (9)
Rock Me Baby (6,7)
Rock Me Easy Baby (14)
Run Fay Run (9)
Runnin' Out Of Fools (3)
Shaft, Theme From (4,7,9,12) *1*
Shaft II (18)
Shaft Strikes Again (4)
Shaft's Cab Ride (4)
Someone Who Will Take The Place Of You (19)
Something (2)
Soulsville (4)
St. Thomas Square (13)
Storm Is Over (15)
Stormy Monday Blues (7)
Stranger In Paradise (4)
Sweet Music, Soft Lights, And You (20)
Thank You Love (15)
That Loving Feeling (11)
That's The Way I Like It (medley) (16)
Then Came You (16)
(They Long To Be) Close To You (5)
This Time I'll Be Sweeter (medley) (21)
This Will Be (An Everlasting Love) (medley) (16)

Truck Turner (10)
Type Thang (7)
Unity (16)
Use Me (7)
Vykkii (13)
Walk From Regio's (4)
Walk On By (1,12,16) *30*
Way I Want To Touch You (medley) (16)
We Need Each Other Girl (10)
We've Got A Whole Lot Of Love (14)
What Does It Take (19)
When I Fall In Love (6)
Wherever You Are (21)
Windows Of The World (7)
Wish You Were Here (medley) (16)
You Don't Know Like I Know (6)
You Needed Me (20)
You Never Cross My Mind (10)
You're In My Arms Again (10)
You've Lost That Lovin' Feelin' (3)
Your Love Is So Doggone Good (medley) (5)
Your Loving Is Much Too Strong (14)
Zeke The Freak (18)

HAYES, Wade '96

Born on 4/20/69 in Bethel Acres, Oklahoma. Country singer/songwriter.

DEBUT	PEAK	WKS	RIAA	CD	ARTIST — Album Title	$	Label & Number
1/28/95	99	44	●	©	1 Old Enough To Know Better	$10	Columbia 66412
7/13/96	91	10		©	2 On A Good Night	$10	Columbia 67563
2/14/98	92	6		©	3 When The Wrong One Loves You Right	$10	Columbia 68037

Are We Having Fun Yet (3)
Day That She Left Tulsa (In A Chevy) (3) *86*
Don't Make Me Come To Tulsa (1)
Don't Stop (1)
Family Reunion (1)

How Do You Sleep At Night (3) *67*
Hurts Don't It (2)
I Still Do (2)
I'm Still Dancin' With You (1)
If I Wanted To Forget (3)
It's Gonna Take A Miracle (1)

It's Over My Head (2)
Kentucky Bluebird (1)
Mine To Lose (3)
My Side Of Town (2)
Old Enough To Know Better (1)
On A Good Night (2)
One More Night With You (3)

Our Time Is Coming (2)
Room, The (2)
Someone Had To Teach You (1)
Steady As She Goes (1)
Summer Was A Bummer (3)

This Is My Heart Talking Now (3)
This Is The Life For Me (2)
Tore Up From The Floor Up (3)
Undo The Right (2)
What I Meant To Say (1)

When The Wrong One Loves You Right (2)
Where Do I Go To Start All Over (2)

HAYWARD, Justin '75

Born on 10/14/46 in Swindon, Wiltshire, England. Lead singer/guitarist of **The Moody Blues**.

DEBUT	PEAK	WKS	CD	ARTIST — Album Title	$	Label & Number
3/29/75	16	23	©	1 Blue Jays	$20	Threshold 14

JUSTIN HAYWARD/JOHN LODGE

DEBUT	PEAK	WKS	CD	ARTIST — Album Title	$	Label & Number
3/12/77	37	16	©	2 Songwriter	$20	Deram 18073
8/9/80	166	5	©	3 Night Flight	$15	Deram 4801

Bedtime Stories (3)
Country Girl (3)
Crazy Lovers (3)
Doin' Time (2)
Face In The Crowd (3)

I Dreamed Last Night (1) *47*
I'm Sorry (3)
It's Not On (3)
Lay It On Me (3)
Maybe (1)

Maybe It's Just Love (3)
My Brother (1)
Nearer To You (3)
Night Flight (3)
Nights, Winters, Years (1)

Nostradamus (2)
One Lonely Room (2)
Penumbra Moon (3)
Raised On Love (2)
Remember Me, My Friend (1)

Saved By The Music (1)
Songwriter (Part 1 & 2) (2)
Stage Door (2)
Suitcase (2)
This Morning (1)

Tight Rope (3)
When You Wake Up (1)
Who Are You Now (1)
You (1)

HAYWOOD, Leon '80

Born on 2/11/42 in Houston. R&B singer/keyboardist.

DEBUT	PEAK	WKS	CD	ARTIST — Album Title	$	Label & Number
8/16/75	140	13		1 Come And Get Yourself Some	$12	20th Century 476
5/17/80	92	10		2 Naturally	$12	20th Century 613

Believe Half Of What You See (And None Of What You Hear) (1) *94*
Come An' Get Yourself Some (1) *83*

Consider The Source (1)
Daydream (2)
Don't Push It Don't Force It (2) *49*
I Know What Love Is (1)

I Want'a Do Something Freaky To You (1) *15*
If You're Lookin' For A Night Of Fun (Look Past Me, I'm Not The One) (2)

Just Your Fool (1)
Love Is What We Came Here For (2)
Lover's Rap (2)
That's What Time It Is (2)

This Feeling's Rated Extra (1)
Who You Been Giving It Up To (1,2)
You Need A Friend Like Mine (1)

HAZA, Ofra '89

Born on 11/19/57 in Tel Aviv, Israel. Died of AIDS on 2/23/2000 (age 42). Female singer/songwriter/actress.

DEBUT	PEAK	WKS	CD	ARTIST — Album Title	$	Label & Number
1/21/89	130	9	©	1 Shaday	$10	Sire 25816
2/10/90	156	5	©	2 Desert Wind	$10	Sire 25976

Da'Ale Da'Ale (1)
Da'asa (2)
Eshal (1)
Face To Face (1)
Fatamorgana (Mirage) (2)

Galbi (1)
I Want To Fly (2)
Im Nin'Alu (1)
In-Ta (2)
Kaddish (2)

Love Song (1)
MM'MMA (My Brothers Are There) (2)
Middle East (2)
My Aching Heart (1)

Shaday (1)
Slave Dream (2)
Take Me To Paradise (1)
Taw Shi (2)
Wish Me Luck (2)

Ya Ba Ye (2)

HAZARD, Robert '83
Born in Philadelphia. Rock singer/songwriter. Wrote **Cyndi Lauper**'s "Girls Just Want To Have Fun."

| 3/26/83 | 102 | 11 | | | Robert Hazard .... [M] | | | $10 | RCA Victor 8500 |

Blowin' In The Wind   Change Reaction   Escalator Of Life *58*   Hang Around With You   Out Of The Blue

HAZLEWOOD, Lee — see SINATRA, Nancy

HEAD, Roy '66
Born on 9/1/41 in Perkins, Oklahoma. Rock-country singer/guitarist.

| 12/4/65+ | 122 | 8 | | | Treat Me Right .... | | | $40 | Scepter 532 |

Convicted   Get Back *88*   Money   Night Train   Treat Me Right
Feelings Gone   **Just A Little Bit** *39*   My Babe *99*   One More Time

HEADBOYS, The '79
Rock group from Edinburgh, Scotland: Lou Lewis (guitar), Calum Malcolm (keyboards), George Boyter (bass) and Davy Ross (drums). All share vocals.

| 11/10/79 | 113 | 15 | | | The Headboys .... | | | $12 | RSO 3068 |

Breakout, The   Experiments   Kickin' The Kans   Ripper, The   **Shape Of Things To Come** *67*   Stepping Stones
Changing With The Times   Gonna Do It Like This   My Favourite D.J.   Schoolgirls   Silver Lining   Take It All Down

HEAD EAST '79
Rock group from St. Louis: John Schlitt (vocals), Michael Sommerville (guitar), Roger Boyd (keyboards), Dan Birney (bass) and Steve Huston (drums). Schlitt, Sommerville and Birney were replaced by Dan Odum, Tony Gross and Mark Boatman in early 1980.

8/30/75	126	17	●	© 1	Flat As A Pancake			$12	A&M 4537
5/22/76	161	6		2	Get Yourself Up			$12	A&M 4579
4/2/77	136	7		3	Gettin' Lucky			$12	A&M 4624
3/11/78	78	14		4	Head East			$12	A&M 4680
2/3/79	65	14		5	Head East Live! .... [L]			$15	A&M 6007 [2]
11/17/79	96	16		6	A Different Kind Of Crazy			$12	A&M 4795
11/8/80	137	6		7	U.S. 1			$12	A&M 4826

Babie Ruth (7)   Every Little Bit Of My Heart   I Surrender (7)   Love My Blues Away (2)   Pictures (4)   This Woman's In Love (2)
Back In My Own Hands (3)   (3,5)   I'm Feelin' Fine (4,5)   Lovin' Me Along (1)   Sailor (2)   Ticket Back To Georgia (1)
Brother Jacob (1)   Feelin' Is Right (6)   If You Knew Me Better (6)   Man I Wanna Be (4,5)   Sands Of Time (3)   Time Has A Way (3)
Call To Arms And Legs (3)   Fight For Your Life (7)   It's For You (5)   Monkey Shine (2,5)   Separate Ways (2)   Too Late (6)
City Of Gold (1,5)   Fly By Night Lady (1,5)   Jailer (2)   Morning (6)   Show Me I'm Alive (3)   Trouble (2)
Dance Away Lover (4)   Get Up & Enjoy Yourself (4,5)   Jefftown Creek (1,5)   **Never Been Any Reason**   **Since You Been Gone** (4,5) *46*   Victim, The (2)
Dancer Road (3)   Gettin' Lucky (3,5)   Keep A Secret (4)   (1,5) *68*   Sister Sister (7)   When I Get Ready (2,5)
Don't Let Me Sleep In The   Got To Be Real (6)   Lonelier Now (6)   Nothing To Lose (4)   Specialty (6)   You'll Be The One (7)
   Morning (3)   Hard Drivin' Days (6)   Look To The Sky (7)   One Against The Other (1)   Susan (7)
Elijah (4,5)   I Don't Want The Chance (2)   Love Me Now (7)   Open Up The Door (4)   Take A Hand (5)
   Love Me Tonight (1,5) *54*   Out Of The Blue (7)   Take It On Home (3)

HEADHUNTERS '75
Backing band for **Herbie Hancock**: Blackbird McKnight (guitar), Bennie Maupin (sax), **Bill Summers** (percussion), Paul Jackson (bass) and Mike Clark (drums).

| 4/19/75 | 126 | 10 | | | Survival Of The Fittest .... [I] | | | $12 | Arista 4038 |

Daffy's Dance   God Make Me Funky   Here And Now   If You've Got It, You'll Get It   Mugic   Rima

HEADPINS '84
Rock group from Canada: Darby Mills (female vocals), Brian MacLeod (guitar), Ab Bryant (bass) and Bernie Aubin (drums). MacLeod and Bryant were with **Chilliwack**. Bryant was also with **Prism**. MacLeod died of cancer on 4/25/92.

| 1/21/84 | 114 | 9 | | | Line Of Fire .... | | | $12 | Solid Gold 9031 |

Celebration   Double Trouble   I Know What You're Thinking   **Just One More Time** *70*
Don't Stand In The Line Of Fire   Feel It (Feel My Body)   I've Heard It All Before   Mine, All Mine

HEALEY, Jeff, Band '89
Born on 3/25/66 in Toronto. Blues-rock singer/guitarist. Blind since age one. Formed own group with Joe Rockman (bass) and Tom Stephen (drums). Group appeared in the 1989 movie *Road House*.

10/8/88+	22	69	▲	© 1	See The Light			$10	Arista 8553
6/16/90	27	39	●	© 2	Hell To Pay			$10	Arista 8632
11/28/92	174	2		© 3	Feel This			$10	Arista 18706

Angel Eyes (1) *5*   Dreams Of Love (3)   House That Love Built (3)   I Think I Love You Too Much   Life Beyond The Sky (2)   Someday, Someway (1)
Baby's Lookin' Hot (3)   Evil And Here To Stay (3)   How Long Can A Man Be   (2)   **Lost In Your Eyes** (3) *91*   Something To Hold On To (2)
Blue Jean Blues (1)   Full Circle (2)   Strong (2)   If You Can't Feel Anything Else   My Kinda Lover (3)   That's What They Say (1)
Confidence Man (1)   Heart Of An Angel (1)   How Much (2)   (3)   My Little Girl (1)   While My Guitar Gently Weeps
Cruel Little Number (3)   Hell To Pay (2)   I Can't Get My Hands On You   It Could All Get Blown Away (3)   Nice Problem To Have (1)   (2)
Don't Let Your Chance Go By   Hideaway (1)   (2)   Leave The Light On (3)   River Of No Return (1)   You're Coming Home (3)
   (1)   Highway Of Dreams (2)   I Need To Be Loved (1)   Let It All Go (2)   See The Light (1)

HEAR 'N AID '86
Collection of 40 hard-rock artists formed to raise money for famine relief efforts in Africa and around the world.

| 7/5/86 | 80 | 7 | | | Hear 'N Aid .... | | | $10 | Mercury 826044 |

Can You See Me *[Jimi Hendrix]*   Go For The Throat *[Y&T]*   Hungry For Heaven *[Dio]*   Stars   Zoo, The *[Scorpions]*
Distant Early Warning *[Rush]*   Heaven's On Fire *[Kiss]*   On The Road *[Motorhead]*   Up To The Limit *[Accept]*

HEART ★138★   '85

Rock group formed in Seattle: sisters Ann (vocals) and Nancy (guitar) Wilson, brothers Roger and Mike Fisher (guitars), Steve Fossen (bass) and Mike DeRosier (drums). The Fishers left in 1979. Howard Leese (guitar) joined in 1980. Fossen and DeRosier left by 1982, replaced by Mark Andes (of **Spirit**, **Jo Jo Gunne** and **Firefall**) and Denny Carmassi (of **Montrose** and **Gamma**). In 1990, former members Fossen, DeRosier and Roger Fisher joined **Alias**. Andes left by 1993. Carmassi left in 1994 to join **Whitesnake**. Nancy married movie director Cameron Crowe.

1)Heart 2)Bad Animals 3)Brigade

4/10/76	7	100	▲	© 1	**Dreamboat Annie**			$12	Mushroom 5005
5/28/77	9	41	▲³	© 2	**Little Queen**	C:#18/59		$12	Portrait 34799
4/22/78	17	25	▲	© 3	**Magazine**			$12	Mushroom 5008
10/7/78+	17	36	▲²	© 4	**Dog & Butterfly**	C:#26/64		$12	Portrait 35555
3/8/80	5	22	●	© 5	**Bebe Le Strange**			$12	Epic 36371
12/6/80	13	25	▲²	© 6	**Greatest Hits/Live**		[G-L]	$15	Epic 36888 [2]
					6 of 18 tracks are live				
6/12/82	25	14		© 7	**Private Audition**			$12	Epic 38049
9/17/83	39	21		© 8	**Passionworks**			$12	Epic 38800
7/13/85	❶¹	92	▲⁵	© 9	**Heart**			$10	Capitol 12410
6/13/87	2³	50	▲³	© 10	**Bad Animals**			$10	Capitol 12546
4/21/90	3	49	▲²	© 11	**Brigade**			$10	Capitol 91820
10/12/91	107	7		© 12	**Rock The House Live!**		[L]	$10	Capitol 95797
					recorded on 11/28/90 in Worcester, Massachusetts				
12/4/93	48	17	●	© 13	**Desire Walks On**			$10	Capitol 99627
9/16/95	87	6	●	© 14	**The Road Home**		[L]	$10	Capitol 30489
					recorded on 8/12/94 at The Backstage in Seattle				
3/29/97	131	13		© 15	**Greatest Hits**		[G]	$10	Capitol 53376

All Eyes (9)
All I Wanna Do Is Make Love To You (11,14,15) **2**
Allies (8) **83**
Alone (10,14,15) **1**
Ambush (8)
America (7)
Angels (7)
Anything Is Possible (13)
Back To Avalon (13,14)
Bad Animals (10)
Barracuda (2,6,12,14,15) **11**
(Beat By) Jealousy (8)
Bebe Le Strange (5,6)
Black On Black II (13)
Blue Guitar (8)
Break (5)
Bright Light Girl (7)
Call Of The Wild (11,12)
City's Burning (7)
Cook With Fire (4)
Crazy On You (1,6,14,15) **35**
Cruel Nights (11)

Cry To Me (9)
Desire (13)
Desire Walks On (13)
Devil Delight (3)
Dog & Butterfly (4,6,14,15) **34**
Down On Me (5)
Dream Of The Archer (2,14)
Dreamboat Annie (1,6,14,15) **42**
Easy Target (10)
Even It Up (5,6) **33**
Fallen From Grace (11,12)
Fast Times (7)
Go On Cry (3)
Heartless (3,6,15) **24**
Heavy Heart (8)
Here Song (3)
Hey Darlin Darlin (5)
High Time (4)
Hijinx (4)
Hit Single (6)
How Can I Refuse (8,12) **44**
How Deep It Goes (1)

I Didn't Want To Need You (11) **23**
I Love You (11)
I Want You So Bad (10) **49**
I Want Your World To Turn (11)
I'm Down (medley) (6)
I've Got The Music In Me (3)
If Looks Could Kill (9,12,15) **54**
In Walks The Night (13)
Johnny Moon (8)
Just The Wine (3)
Kick It Out (2) **79**
Language Of Love (8)
Lighter Touch (4)
Little Queen (2) **62**
Long Tall Sally (medley) (6)
Love Alive (2,12)
Love Hurts (14)
(Love Me Like Music) I'll Be Your Song (1)
Love Mistake (8)
Magazine (3)

Magic Man (1,6,15) **9**
Mistral Wind (4,6)
Mother Earth Blues (3)
My Crazy Head (13)
Nada One (4)
Never (9,15) **4**
Night, The (11,12)
Nobody Home (9)
Nothin' At All (9,15) **10**
One Word (7)
Perfect Stranger (7)
Pilot (5)
Private Audition (7)
RSVP (10)
Rage (13)
Raised On You (5)
Ring Them Bells (13)
River (14)
Rock And Roll (6)
Rockin Heaven Down (5)
Say Hello (14)
Seasons (14)
Secret (11) **64**

Shell Shock (9,12)
Silver Wheels (5,6)
Sing Child (1)
Situation, The (7)
Sleep Alone (8)
Soul Of The Sea (1)
Straight On (4,6,14,15) **15**
Stranded (11,15) **13**
Strange Euphoria (6)
Strange Night (5)
Strangers Of The Heart (10)
Sweet Darlin (5,6)
Sylvan Song (2)
Tall, Dark Handsome Stranger (11,12)
Tell It Like It Is (6) **8**
There's The Girl (10) **12**
These Dreams (9,14,15) **1**
This Man Is Mine (7) **33**
Together Now (8)
Treat Me Well (2)
Unchained Melody (6) **83**
Under The Sky (11,12)

(Up On) Cherry Blossom Road (14)
Voodoo Doll (13)
Wait For An Answer (10)
Way Back Machine (12)
What About Love? (9,15) **10**
What He Don't Know (9)
White Lightning & Wine (1)
Who Will You Run To (10,12,15) **7**
Wild Child (11,12)
Will You Be There (In The Morning) (13,15) **39**
Without You (3)
Wolf (9)
Woman In Me (13)
You Ain't So Tough (10)
You're The Voice (12)

HEARTSFIELD   '75

Rock group from Chicago: J.C. Heartsfield (vocals), Fred Dobbs, Perry Cordell and Phil Lucafo (guitars), Greg Biela (bass) and Artie Baldacci (drums).

8/16/75	159	7		©	**Foolish Pleasures**		$12	Mercury 1034

Another Man Down
As I Look Into The Fire

Drummer Boy
Honest Junkie

Magic Mood
Nashville

Needing Her
Rocking Chair

HEAT, Reverend Horton — see REVEREND HORTON HEAT

HEATH, Ted, And His Music   '61

Born Edward Heath on 3/30/1900 in London. Died on 11/18/69 (age 69). Trombonist/bandleader.

10/9/61	28	10		© 1	**Big Band Percussion**	[I]	$20	London Phase 4 44002
9/15/62	36	2		© 2	**Big Band Bash**	[I]	$20	London Phase 4 44017

A-Tisket A-Tasket (2)
Blues In The Night (1)
But Not For Me (1)
Capuccina (2)

Cherokee (2)
Clopin-Clopant (2)
Daddy (1)
Drum Crazy (1)

Harlem Nocturne (2)
Hernando's Hideaway (2)
Hindustan (2)
I Don't Know Why (2)

In A Persian Market (2)
It Ain't Necessarily So (1)
Johnny One Note (1)
Mood Indigo (1)

More Than You Know (1)
Out Of Nowhere (1)
Peanut Vendor (1)
Poinciana (1)

Sabre Dance (2)
Taking A Chance On Love (1)
Thou Swell (1)

HEATHERLY, Eric   '00

Born on 2/21/73 in Chattanooga, Tennessee. Country singer/guitarist.

5/6/00	157	15		©	**Swimming In Champagne**		$10	Mercury 170124

Didn't Mean A Thing
Flowers On The Wall **50**

Freedom Chain
I Just Break'em

Let Me
One Night

She's So Hot
Someone Else's Cadillac

Swimming In Champagne
WhyDon'tCha

Wrong Five O'clock

HEATHERTON, Joey   '72

Born Johanna Heatherton on 9/14/44 in Rockville Centre, Long Island, New York. Movie/TV actress.

10/21/72	154	13			**The Joey Heatherton Album**		$20	MGM 4858

Crazy
God Only Knows

Gone **24**
I'm Sorry **87**

It's Not Easy
Right Or Wrong

Road I Took To You (Pieces)
Say Hello

Shake-A-Hand
Someone To Watch Over Me

HEATWAVE '78

Multi-national, interracial group formed in Germany. Core members: brothers Johnnie and Keith Wilder (vocals), Eric Johns and William Jones (guitars), Rod Temperton (keyboards), Derek Bramblz (bass) and Ernest Berger (drums).

8/6/77	11	45	▲	©	1 Too Hot To Handle	$12	Epic 34761
4/22/78	10	26	▲	©	2 Central Heating	$12	Epic 35260
5/12/79	38	14	●		3 Hot Property	$12	Epic 35970
12/13/80+	71	10			4 Candles	$12	Epic 36873
7/10/82	156	6			5 Current	$12	Epic 38065

Ain't No Half Steppin' (1)
All I Am (4)
All Talked Out (3)
All You Do Is Dial (1)
Always And Forever (1) *18*
Beat Your Booty (1)
Big Guns (5)
Boogie Nights (1) *2*

Central Heating (2)
Disco (4)
Dreamin' You (4)
Eyeballin' (3)
Find It In Your Heart (5)
First Day Of Snow (3)
Gangsters Of The Groove (4)
Goin' Crazy (4)

Groove Line (2) *7*
Happiness Togetherness (4)
Hold On To The One (5)
Jitterbuggin' (4)
Lay It On Me (1)
Leavin' For A Dream (2)
Lettin' It Loose (5)
Look After Love (5)

Mind Blowing Decisions (2)
Mind What You Find (5)
Naturally (5)
One Night Tan (3)
Party Poops (2)
Party Suite (4)
Posin' 'Til Closin' (4)
Put The Word Out (2)

Raise A Blaze (3)
Razzle Dazzle (3)
Send Out For Sunshine (2)
Sho'nuff Must Be Luv (1)
Star Of A Story (2)
State To State (5)
Super Soul Sister (1)

That's The Way We'll Always Say Goodnight (3)
Therm Warfare (3)
This Night We Fell (3)
Too Hot To Handle (1)
Turn Around (4)
Where Did I Go Wrong (4)

HEAVENS EDGE '90

Rock group from Philadelphia: Mark Evans (vocals), Reggie Wu and Steven Parry (guitars), G.G. Guidotti (bass) and David Rath (drums).

| 6/23/90 | 141 | 12 | | © | 1 Heavens Edge | $10 | Columbia 45262 |

Bad Reputation
Can't Catch Me

Come Play The Game
Daddy's Little Girl

Don't Stop, Don't Go
Find Another Way

Hold On To Tonight
Is That All You Want?

Play Dirty
Skin To Skin

Up Against The Wall

HEAVEN 17 '83

Electro-pop trio from England: Glenn Gregory (vocals), Martyn Ware and Ian Craig Marsh (synthesizers). Ware and Marsh were founding members of **Human League**.

2/12/83	68	28			1 Heaven 17	$12	Arista 6606
6/4/83	72	13		©	2 The Luxury Gap	$12	Arista 8020
4/4/87	177	3		©	3 Pleasure One	$10	Virgin 90569

Best Kept Secret (2)
Come Live With Me (2)
Contenders (3)
Crushed By The Wheels Of Industry (2)
Free (3)

Geisha Boys And Temple Girls (1)
Height Of The Fighting (1)
I'm Your Money (1)
If I Were You (3)
Key To The World (2)

Lady Ice And Mr. Hex (2)
Let Me Go (1) *74*
Let's All Make A Bomb (2)
Look At Me (3)
Low Society (3)
Move Out (3)

Penthouse And Pavement (1)
Play To Win (1)
Red (3)
Somebody (3)
Song With No Name (2)
Temptation (2)

Trouble (3)
(We Don't Need This) Fascist Groove Thang (1)
We Live So Fast (2)
We're Going To Live For A Very Long Time (1)

Who Will Stop The Rain (1)

HEAVY D & THE BOYZ '97

Born Dwight Meyers on 5/24/67 in Jamaica, raised in Mt. Vernon, New York. Male rapper. Former president of Uptown Records. Acted in the movie *The Cider House Rules*. The Boyz consisted Glen Parrish, Troy Dixon and Edward Ferrell. Dixon died on 7/15/90 (age 22) from an accidental fall in Indianapolis.

11/14/87	92	16		©	1 Living Large	$10	MCA 5986
7/1/89	19	51	▲	©	2 Big Tyme	$10	Uptown 42302
7/20/91	21	41	▲	©	3 Peaceful Journey	$10	Uptown 10289
1/30/93	40	18	●	©	4 Blue Funk	$10	Uptown 10734
6/11/94	11	25	▲	©	5 Nuttin' But Love	$10	Uptown 10998

HEAVY D:

| 5/10/97 | 9 | 22 | ● | © | 6 Waterbed Hev | $10 | Uptown 53033 |
| 7/3/99 | 60 | 6 | | © | 7 Heavy | $10 | Uptown 53260 |

Ask Heaven (7)
Better Land (2)
Big Daddy (6) *18*
Big Tyme (2)
Black Coffee (5) *57*
Blue Funk (4)
Body And Mind (3)
Buncha Niggas (4)
Can You Handle It (6)
Chunky But Funky (1)
Cuz He'z Alwayz Around (3)
Dancin' In The Night (7)
Dedicated (7)
Do Me, Do Me (3)
Don't Be Afraid (6)

Don't Curse (3)
Don't Stop (7)
Don't You Know (1)
Ez Duz It, Do It Ez (2)
Flexin' (2)
Friends & Respect (5)
Get Fresh Hev (6)
Girl (4)
Got Me Waiting (5) *20*
Gyrlz, They Love Me (2)
Here Comes The Heavster (4)
Here We Go (1)
Here We Go Again, Y'all (2)
I Can Make You Go Oooh (3)
I Don't Think So (7)

I Know You Love Me (7)
I'll Do Anything (6)
I'm Getting Paid (1)
I'm Gonna Make You Love Me (1)
Imagine That (7)
Is It Good To You (3) *32*
It's A New Day (4)
Keep It Comin (3)
Keep It Goin' (5)
Let It Flow (2)
Let It Rain (3)
Letter To The Future (5)
Like Dat Dhere (1)
Listen (7)

Love Sexy (4)
Lover's Got What U Need (3)
Moneyearnin' Mount Vernon (1)
Mood For Love (2)
More Bounce (2)
Move On (5)
Mr. Big Stuff (1)
Nike (1)
Now That We Found Love (3) *11*
Nuttin' But Love (5) *40*
On Point (7)
On The Dance Floor (1)
Overweight Lovers In The House (1)

Overweighter (1)
Peaceful Journey (3)
Rock The Bass (1)
Sex Wit You (5)
Shake It (6)
Silky (4)
Sister Sister (3)
Slow Down (4)
Somebody For Me (2,3)
Something Goin' On (5)
Spanish Fly (7)
Spend A Little Time On Top (5)
Swinging With Da Hevster (3)
Take Your Time (5)
Talk Is Cheap (4)

This Is Your Night (5)
Truthful (4)
Wanna Be A Player (6)
Waterbed Hev (6)
We Got Our Own Thang (2)
Who's In The House (4)
Who's The Man? (4)
Yes Y'All (4)
You Ain't Heard Nuttin Yet (2)
You Can Get It (6)
You Know (7)
You Nasty Hev (7)

HEBB, Bobby '66

Born on 7/26/41 in Nashville. R&B singer/songwriter.

| 9/10/66 | 103 | 12 | | | Sunny | $25 | Philips 212 |

Bread
Crazy Baby
For You

Good Good Lovin'
Got You On My Mind
I Am Your Man

Love Love Love
Satisfied Mind *39*
Sunny *2*

Where Are You
Yes Or No Or Maybe Not

You Don't Know What You Got Until You Lose It

(HED)PLANET EARTH '00

Rap-rock group from Huntington Beach, California: Jahred Shaine (vocals), DJ Product (DJ), Wesstyle and Chizad (guitars), Mawk (bass) and B.C. (drums).

| 9/9/00 | 63 | 8 | | © | Broke | $10 | Volcano 41710 |

Bartender
Boom (How You Like That)

Crazy Legs
Feel Good

I Got You
Jesus (Of Nazareth)

Killing Time
Meadow, The

Pac Bell
Stevie

Swan Dive
Waiting To Die

HEFTI, Neal '55

Born on 10/29/22 in Hastings, Nebraska. Conductor/trumpeter.

| 2/5/55 | 8 | 2 | | | 1 Music Of Rudolf Friml | [I] | $30 | RCA Victor 3021 |

NEAL HEFTI AND HIS ORCHESTRA
10" album

| 3/12/66 | 41 | 21 | | | 2 Batman Theme | [I] | $30 | RCA Victor 3573 |

Allah's Holiday (1)
Batman Chase (2)
Batman Theme (2) *35*
Batusi, The (2)
Donkey Serenade (1)

Eivol Ekdol, The Albanian Genius (2)
Evil Plot To Blow Up Batman (2)
Giannina Mia (1)

Holy Diploma, Batman - Straight A's! (2)
Indian Love Call (1)
Jervis (2)
Just A Simple Millionaire (2)

L'Amour-Toujours-L'Amour (Love Everlasting) (1)
Mafista, The (2)
Mr. Freeze (2)
My Fine Feathered Finks (2)

Only A Rose (1)
Rose Marie (1)
Sewer Lady (2)
Sympathy (1)

HEIGHTS, The '92

Band made up of cast members from the Fox network prime time TV show of the same name. Show is based on fictional adventures featuring the band. Led by actors/vocalists Shawn Thompson and **Jamie Walters**.

| 11/7/92 | 40 | 15 | ● © | The Heights .... [TV] | $10 | Capitol 80328 |

Battleground
Children Of The Night
Common Ground
Feelin' Alright

Friendship
How Do You Talk To An Angel 1
I'm Still On Your Side

Joanne
Man You Used To Be (A Song For Dad)
Natalie

Rear View Mirror
So Hot
Strongest Man Alive

What Does It Take (To Win Your Love)

HEINDORF, Ray/Matty Matlock '55

Ray Heindorf was born on 8/25/08 in Haverstraw, New York. Died on 2/3/80 (age 71). Longtime musical director for the Warner Brothers Orchestra. Julian "Matty" Matlock was born on 4/27/09 in Paducah, Kentucky. Died on 6/14/78 (age 69). Clarinet player with numerous TV and radio appearances.

| 9/3/55 | 9 | 8 | | Pete Kelly's Blues | [I] | $30 | Columbia 690 |

LP: Columbia CL-690 (#9); EP: Columbia B-2103; songs from the movie; also see vocal recording by **Peggy Lee** and **Ella Fitzgerald**, and narrated recording by **Jack Webb**

Breezin' Along With The Breeze
Bye Bye, Blackbird
Hard-Hearted Hannah (The Vamp Of Savannah)

He Needs Me
I Never Knew
I'm Gonna Meet My Sweetie Now

Oh, Didn't He Ramble
Pete Kelly's Blues
Smiles
Somebody Loves Me

Sugar (That Sugar Baby O'Mine)
(What Can I Say) After I Say I'm Sorry?

HEINTJE '71

Born Hendrik Simons on 8/12/55 in Heerlen, Holland. Male singer.

| 12/5/70+ | 108 | 11 | | Mama .... | $15 | MGM 4739 |

Happiest Day
I Would Like To Have A Little Fiddle

I'm Your Little Boy
In Grandma's Rocking Chair
Let The Sun Shine

Little Children, Little Sorrows
Mama
Mother's Tears

Only Memories Are Our Friends
Two Little Stars

When High From The Sky
Gleaming Stars Look Down

HELFGOTT, David '97

Born on 5/19/47 in Melbourne, Australia. Classical pianist. The 1996 movie *Shine* was based on his life.

| 2/15/97 | 103 | 8 | © | David Helfgott Plays Rachmaninov .... [I] | $10 | RCA Victor 40378 |

Piano Concerto No. 3, Op. 30, in D Minor: Allegro Ma Non Tanto
Piano Concerto No. 3, Op. 30, in D Minor: Finale: Alla Breve

Piano Concerto No. 3, Op. 30, in D Minor: Intermezzo Adagio
Prelude in C Sharp Minor, Op. 3 No. 2

Prelude in G Major, Op. 32 No. 5
Prelude in G Minor, Op. 23 No. 5

Prelude in G Sharp Minor, Op. 32 No. 12
Sonata No. 2 in B Flat Minor, Op. 36: Allegro Moderato

Sonata No. 2 in B Flat Minor, Op. 36: Allegro Motto
Sonata No. 2 in B Flat Minor, Op. 36: Lento

HELIX '84

Hard-rock group from Waterloo, Canada: Brian Vollmer (vocals), Brent Doerner and Paul Hackman (guitars), Mike Uzelac (bass; replaced by Daryl Gray in 1984) and Greg Hinz (drums). Doerner left in mid-1990. Hackman was killed in a car crash on 7/6/92 (age 39).

10/22/83	186	4	© 1	No Rest For The Wicked..	$10	Capitol 12281
8/18/84	69	16	2	Walkin' The Razor's Edge	$10	Capitol 12362
6/29/85	103	17	3	Long Way To Heaven	$10	Capitol 12411
11/7/87	179	2	© 4	Wild In The Streets	$10	Capitol 46920
8/18/90	179	6	5	Back For Another Taste..	$10	Grudge 4521

Ain't No High Like Rock 'N Roll (1)
Animal House (2)
Back For Another Taste (5)
Bangin' Off-A-The Bricks (3)
Breakdown (5)
Check Out The Love (1)
Christine (3)
Deep Cuts The Knife (3)
Dirty Dog (1)
Does A Fool Ever Learn (1)

Don't Get Mad Get Even (1)
Don't Touch The Merchandise (3)
Dream On (4)
Feel The Fire (2)
Gimme Gimme Good Lovin' (2)
Give 'Em Hell (4)
Give It To You (5)
Good To The Last Drop (5)
Heavy Metal Cowboys (5)
Heavy Metal Love (1)

High Voltage Kicks (4)
House On Fire (3)
Kids Are All Shakin' (3)
Kiss It Goodbye (4)
Let's All Do It Tonight (1)
Long Way To Heaven (3)
Love Hungry Eyes (4)
(Make Me Do) Anything You Want (2)
Midnight Express (5)
My Kind Of Rock (2)

Never Gonna Stop The Rock (4)
Never Want To Lose You (1)
No Rest For The Wicked (1)
Ride The Rocket (3)
Rock You (2)
Rockin' Rollercoaster (5)
Running Wild In The 21st Century (5)
School Of Hard Knocks (3)
She's Too Tough (4)

Shot Full Of Love (4)
Six Strings, Nine Lives (2)
Storm, The (5)
That's Life (5)
What Ya Bringin' To The Party (4)
Wheels Of Thunder (5)
When The Hammer Falls (2)
White Lace And Black Leather (1)
Wild In The Streets (4)

Without You (Jasmine's Song) (3)
You Keep Me Rockin' (2)
Young & Wreckless (2)

HELLO PEOPLE '74

White-faced, mime-rock group: Greg Geddes, Robert Sedita, N.D. Smart and Laurence Tasse.

| 11/30/74 | 145 | 13 | | The Handsome Devils.. | $15 | Dunhill/ABC 50184 |

produced by **Todd Rundgren**

Cry Baby
Destiny

Finger Poppin' Time
Future Shock 71

Greego
How High Is The Moon

Just One Victory
Listen To Your Heart

Ripped Again
Save A Dance For Me

Take The Love In Your Body

HELLOWEEN '87

Hard-rock group from Hamburg, Germany: Michael Kiske (vocals), Kai Hansen and Michael Weikath (guitars), Markus Grosskopf (bass) and Ingo Schwichtenberg (drums). Schwichtenberg committed suicide on 3/8/95 (age 29).

7/4/87	104	21	© 1	Keeper Of The Seven Keys - Part I	$10	RCA Victor 6399
10/29/88	108	16	© 2	Keeper Of The Seven Keys - Part II	$10	RCA 8529
4/22/89	123	7	© 3	I Want Out - Live .... [L]	$10	RCA 9709

Dr. Stein (2,3)
Eagle Fly Free (2,3)
Follow The Sign (1)
Future World (1,3)

Halloween (1)
Happy Helloween (medley) (3)
How Many Tears (3)
I Want Out (2,3)

I'm Alive (1)
Initiation (1)
Invitation (2)
Keeper Of The Seven Keys (2)

Little Time (1,3)
March Of Time (2)
Rise And Fall (2)
Save Us (2)

Tale That Wasn't Right (1)
Twilight Of The Gods (1)
We Got The Right (2,3)
You Always Walk Alone (2)

HELM, Levon, & The RCO All-Stars '77

Born on 5/26/42 in Marvell, Arkansas. Singer/drummer/actor. Member of **The Band**. Portrayed **Loretta Lynn**'s father in the movie *Coal Miner's Daughter*. The RCO All-Stars: **Booker T.**, **Paul Butterfield**, **Steve Cropper**, **Dr. John** and Duck Dunn.

| 11/19/77 | 142 | 10 | © | Levon Helm & The RCO All-Stars .... | $15 | ABC 1017 |

Blues So Bad
Havana Moon
Milk Cow Boogie

Mood I Was In
Rain Down Tears

Sing, Sing, Sing (Let's Make A Better World)
That's My Home

Tie That Binds
Washer Woman
You Got Me

HELMET '94

Rock group from New York: Page Hamilton (vocals, guitar), Peter Mengede (guitar), Henry Bogdan (bass) and John Stanier (drums). Rob Echeverria replaced Mengede in 1993. Chris Traynor replaced Echeverria in 1996.

8/22/92	68	29	● © 1	Meantime..	$10	Interscope 92162
7/9/94	45	12	© 2	Betty	$10	Interscope 92404
4/5/97	47	5	© 3	Aftertaste	$10	Interscope 90073

HELMET — Cont'd

Beautiful Love (2)
Better (1)
Birth Defect (3)
Biscuits For Smut (2)
Broadcast Emotion (3)
Clean (2)
Crisis King (3)

Diet Aftertaste (3)
Driving Nowhere (3)
Exactly What You Wanted (3)
FBLA II (1)
Give It (1)
Harmless (3)
He Feels Bad (1)

(High) Visibility (3)
I Know (2)
In The Meantime (1)
Insatiable (3)
Ironhead (1)
It's Easy To Get Bored (3)
Like I Care (3)

Milquetoast (2)
Overrated (2)
Pure (3)
Renovation (3)
Role Model (1)
Rollo (2)
Sam Hell (2)

Silver Hawaiian (2)
Speechless (2)
Street Crab (2)
Tic (2)
Turned Out (1)
Unsung (1)
Vaccination (2)

Wilma's Rainbow (2)
You Borrowed (1)

HELTAH SKELTAH   '98

Male rap duo from Brooklyn, New York: Rock and Ruck. Members of **Boot Camp Clik**.

| 7/6/96 | 35 | 11 | © | 1 Nocturnal | | | $10 | Duck Down 50532 |
| 10/31/98 | 34 | 4 | © | 2 Magnum Force | | | $10 | Duck Down 53543 |

Black Fonzirelliz (2)
Brownsville II Long Beach (2)
Call Of The Wild (2)
Chicka Woo (2)
Clan's, Posse's, Crew's & Clik's (1)

Da Wiggy (1)
Forget Me Knots (2)
Gang's All Here (2)
Grate Unknown (1)
Gunz 'N Onez (Iz U Wit Me) (2)
Here We Come (1)

Hold Your Head Up (2)
I Ain't Havin That (2) 80
LeFlaur LeFlah Eshkoshka (1) 75
Letha Brainz Blo (1)
MFC Lawz (2)

Magnum Force (2)
Operation Lock Down (1)
Perfect Jab (2)
Place To Be (1)
Prowl (1)
Sean Price (1)

Sean Wigginz (2)
Soldiers Gone Psyco (1)
Square, The (1)
Therapy (1)
Undastand (1)
Who Dat? (1)

Worldwide (Rock The World) (2)

HENDERSON, Joe   '62

Born in 1937 in Como, Mississippi; raised in Gary, Indiana. Died on 10/24/64 (age 27). R&B singer.

| 10/13/62 | 93 | 5 | | Snap Your Fingers | | | $50 | Todd 2701 |

After Loving You
Baby Don't Leave Me

Big Love 74
Cause We're In Love

If You See Me Cry
Just Call Me

Love Me
Right Now

Sad Teardrops At Dawn
Snap Your Fingers 8

Three Steps
You Can't Lose

HENDERSON, Michael   '80

Born on 7/7/51 in Yazoo City, Mississippi. R&B singer/bassist. Featured vocalist with **Norman Connors**.

12/4/76+	173	7	©	1 Solid			$12	Buddah 5662
8/27/77	49	13	©	2 Goin' Places			$12	Buddah 5693
7/8/78	38	28	● ©	3 In The Night-Time			$12	Buddah 5712
8/4/79	64	12	©	4 Do It All			$12	Buddah 5719
8/30/80	35	18	©	5 Wide Receiver			$12	Buddah 6001
9/19/81	86	11	©	6 Slingshot			$12	Buddah 6002
6/4/83	169	5		7 Fickle			$12	Buddah 6004

Am I Special (3)
Ask The Lonely (5)
Assault With A Friendly Weapon (7)
At The Concert (2)
Be My Girl (1)
Can't We Fall In Love Again (6)
Come To Me (6)
Do It All (4)
Everybody Wants To Know Why (4)

Feeling Like Myself Once Again (7)
Fickle (7)
Goin' Places (2)
Happy (3)
I Can't Help It (2)
I'll Be Understanding (2)
In It For The Goodies (6)
In The Night-Time (3)
In The Summertime (4)

Let Love Enter (1)
Let Me Love You (2)
Love Will Find A Way (7)
Make It Easy On Yourself (6)
Make Me Feel Better (2)
Make Me Feel Like (5)
Never Gonna Give You Up (6)
One Step At A Time (7)
One To One (3)
Playing On The Real Thing (4)
Prove It (5)

Reach Out For Me (5)
Riding (4)
Slingshot (6)
Solid (1)
Stay With Me This Summer (1)
Take Care (6)
There's No One Like You (5)
Thin Walls (7)
Time (1)
To Be Loved (4)

Treat Me Like A Man (1)
Valentine Love (1)
Wait Until The Rain (4)
(We Are Here To) Geek You Up (6)
We Can Go On (3)
What I'm Feeling (For You) (5)
Whip It (2,7)
Whisper In My Ear (3)
Wide Receiver (5)
Won't You Be Mine (2)

You Haven't Made It To The Top (1)
You Wouldn't Have To Work At All (7)
You're My Choice (5)
Yours Truly, Indiscreetly (3)

HENDERSON, Skitch   '65

Born Lyle Henderson on 1/27/18 in Halstad, Minnesota. Conductor for TV's *The Tonight Show* from 1962-66.

| 10/9/65 | 103 | 8 | | Skitch...Tonight! | | [I] | $20 | Columbia 9167 |

Bill's Blues
Cleopatra's Asp

Come Thursday
Curacao

Heart And Soul
Night Life

Night-Lights
See-Saw

So What Else Is New?
30 Rockefeller Plaza

Tootie Flutie
Try Again

HENDRIX, Jimi   ★32★   '68

Born on 11/27/42 in Seattle. Died of a drug overdose in London on 9/18/70 (age 27). Legendary psychedelic-blues guitarist. Began career as a studio guitarist. Created The Jimi Hendrix Experience with Noel Redding (bass) and Mitch Mitchell (drums). Formed new group in 1969, Band of Gypsys, with **Buddy Miles** (drums) and Billy Cox (bass). The Jimi Hendrix Experience was inducted into the Rock and Roll Hall of Fame in 1992. Won Grammy's Lifetime Achievement Award in 1992.

1)*Electric Ladyland* 2)*Axis: Bold As Love* 3)*The Cry Of Love* 4)*Band Of Gypsys* 5)*Are You Experienced?*

THE JIMI HENDRIX EXPERIENCE:

| 8/26/67+ | 5 | 106 | ▲⁴ | © | 1 Are You Experienced? | C:#11/5 | | $50 | Reprise 6261 |
| 12/30/67+ | 75 | 12 | | | 2 Get That Feeling | | [E] | $40 | Capitol 2856 |

JIMI HENDRIX

2/10/68	3	53	▲ ©		3 Axis: Bold As Love	C:#11/21		$40	Reprise 6281
10/19/68	❶²	37	▲² ©		4 Electric Ladyland	C:#18/1		$50	Reprise 6307 [2]
8/2/69	6	35	▲² ©		5 Smash Hits	C:#16/76	[G]	$40	Reprise 2025

JIMI HENDRIX:

| 5/2/70 | 5 | 61 | ▲² © | | 6 Band Of Gypsys | C:#13/5 | [L] | $40 | Capitol 472 |

recorded on 12/31/69 at the Fillmore East in New York City; also see #33 below

| 9/19/70 | 16 | 20 | ● | | 7 Monterey International Pop Festival | | [L-S] | $40 | Reprise 2029 |

OTIS REDDING/THE JIMI HENDRIX EXPERIENCE
recorded June 1967 and featured in the movie *Monterey Pop*; side 1: songs performed by The Jimi Hendrix Experience; side 2: songs performed by **Otis Redding**

| 3/6/71 | 3 | 39 | ▲ © | | 8 The Cry Of Love | | | $40 | Reprise 2034 |
| 3/20/71 | 127 | 4 | | | 9 Two Great Experiences Together! | | [E-I] | $40 | Maple 6004 |

JIMI HENDRIX and LONNIE YOUNGBLOOD
recorded in 1965

10/9/71	15	21	●		10 Rainbow Bridge		[S]	$30	Reprise 2040
3/4/72	12	19	●		11 Hendrix In The West		[K-L]	$30	Reprise 2049
9/2/72	82	11			12 Rare Hendrix		[E]	$20	Trip 9500

recorded on 6/10/66 with Lonnie Youngblood

| 12/9/72+ | 48 | 18 | | | 13 War Heroes | | [K] | $20 | Reprise 2103 |

HENDRIX, Jimi — Cont'd

DEBUT	PEAK	WKS	RIAA	CD	ARTIST — Album Title	Catalog	Sym	$	Label & Number
7/14/73	89	18			14 sound track recordings from the film Jimi Hendrix	[L-S]		$25	Reprise 6481 [2]
3/22/75	5	20	● ©		15 Crash Landing	[K]		$20	Reprise 2204
11/29/75	43	11			16 Midnight Lightning	[K]		$20	Reprise 2229
8/12/78	114	15			17 The Essential Jimi Hendrix	[K]		$25	Reprise 2245 [2]
8/18/79	156	7			18 The Essential Jimi Hendrix, Volume Two	[K]		$15	Reprise 2293
4/26/80	127	7			19 Nine To The Universe	[I-K]		$15	Reprise 2299
9/25/82	79	8	©		20 The Jimi Hendrix Concerts	[K-L]		$20	Reprise 22306 [2]
11/17/84	148	5	©		21 Kiss The Sky	[K]		$15	Reprise 25119
3/8/86	192	3	©		22 Jimi Plays Monterey	[L-S]		$15	Reprise 25358
					recorded on 6/18/67				
12/3/88+	119	17	©		23 Radio One	[K]		$15	Rykodisc 0078 [2]
					THE JIMI HENDRIX EXPERIENCE				
					3-sided album compiled from 5 sessions broadcast on BBC Radio in 1967				
1/5/91	174	5	©		24 Lifelines/The Jimi Hendrix Story	[K]		$40	Reprise 26435 [4]
5/15/93	72	77	▲3 ©		25 The Ultimate Experience	C:#4/170	[G]	$10	MCA 10829
5/14/94	45	18	▲ ©		26 Blues	[K]		$10	MCA 11060
8/20/94	37	8	©		27 Jimi Hendrix: Woodstock	[L]		$10	MCA 11063
					recorded on 8/18/69; also see #34 below				
4/29/95	66	7	©		28 Voodoo Soup	[K]		$10	MCA 11236
5/10/97	49	11	©		29 First Rays Of The New Rising Sun	[K]		$10	Exp. Hendrix 11599
10/25/97	51	6	©		30 South Saturn Delta	[K]		$10	Exp. Hendrix 11684
6/20/98	50	9	● ©		31 BBC Sessions	[E-L]		$15	Exp. Hendrix 11742 [2]
					THE JIMI HENDRIX EXPERIENCE				
11/21/98+	133	40	● ©		32 Experience Hendrix: The Best Of Jimi Hendrix	C:#27/18	[G]	$10	Exp. Hendrix 11671
3/13/99	65	4	©		33 Live At The Fillmore East	[L]		$15	Exp. Hendrix 11931 [2]
					recorded on 12/31/69 (same concert as #6 above)				
7/24/99	90	3	©		34 Live At Woodstock	[L]		$15	Exp. Hendrix 11987 [2]
					recorded on 8/18/69 (same concert as #27 above)				
9/30/00	78	3	● ©		35 The Jimi Hendrix Experience	[K]		$40	Exp. Hendrix 112316 [4]
5/26/01	112	4	©		36 Voodoo Child: The Jimi Hendrix Collection	[K]		$15	Exp. Hendrix 112603 [2]
					disc 1: studio recordings; disc 2: live recordings				

Ain't No Telling (3)
All Along The Watchtower (4, 5,17,21,24,25,30,32,35,36) 20
All I Want (9)
...And The Gods Made Love (4)
Angel (8,24,25,28,29,32,36)
Are You Experienced? (1,17,20,21,36)
Astro Man (8,29,35)
Auld Lang Syne (33)
Beginning (13)
Beginnings (Jam Back At The House) (16,27,29,34)
Belly Button Window (8,28,29)
Bleeding Heart (13,20,26,30)
Blue Suede Shoes (11,16,35)
Bold As Love (3,17,24,32,35)
Born Under A Bad Sign (26)
Bring My Baby Back (12)
Burning Desire (33)
Burning Of The Midnight Lamp (4,17,23,24,25,31,35,36)
Can You Please Crawl Out Your Window? (31)
Can You See Me (5,7,22)
Captain Coconut (15)
Castles Made Of Sand (3,17,21,25,32)
Catfish Blues (23,26,31,35)
Changes (6,33)
Cherokee Mist (24,35)
Come Down Hard On Me (15,35)
Come On (Part 1) (4,24)
Country Blues (35)
Crash Landing (15)
Crosstown Traffic (4,5,18,21,25,32,36) 52

Day Tripper (23,31)
Dolly Dagger (10,17,24,29,32,36) 74
Drifter's Escape (24,30)
Drifting (8,17,28,29)
Drivin' South (23,24,31)
Drone Blues (19)
Earth Blues (10,29,33,35)
Easy Blues (19)
Electric Church Red House (26)
Ezy Ryder (8,17,28,29,35)
Farewell (27)
Fire (1,5,18,20,23,25,27,31,32,34,35,36)
Foxey Lady (1,5,18,22,23,24,25,31,32,34,35,36) 67
Freedom (8,17,28,29,32,35,36) 59
Get That Feeling (2)
Gloria (35)
Go Go Shoes, Part 1 & 2 (12)
Good Feeling (12)
Good Times (12)
Goodbye (Bessie Mae) (9)
Gotta Have A New Dress (2)
Gypsy Boy (New Rising Sun) (16)
Gypsy Eyes (4,17,25,35)
Have You Ever Been (To Electric Ladyland) (4,17,35)
Hear My Train A Comin' (10,14,16,20,23,26,27,31,33,34,35,36)
Here He Comes (Lover Man) (30,35)
Hey Baby (New Rising Sun) (10,29,35,36)

Hey Joe (1,5,14,18,20,22,23,24,25,31,32,34,35,36)
Highway Chile (13,25,35,36)
Hoochie Koochie Man (23,24,31)
Hot Trigger (12)
Hound Dog (23,31)
House Burning Down (4,17)
How Would You Feel (2)
Hush Now (2)
I Don't Live Today (1,18,20,21,24,35,36)
I Was Made To Love Her (31)
I'm A Man (24)
If 6 Was 9 (3,17,32,35)
In From The Storm (8,14,28,29,35)
It's Too Bad (35)
Izabella (13,17,27,29,33,34,35,36)
Jammin' (31)
Jelly 292 (26)
Jimi/Jimmy Jam (19)
Johnny B. Goode (11,14,35,36)
Killing Floor (21,22,23,31,35)
Lawdy Miss Clawdy (24)
Like A Rolling Stone (7,14,22,24,35)
Little Miss Lover (3,17,31,35)
Little Miss Strange (4)
Little Wing (3,11,17,20,24,25,30,32,35,36)
Long Hot Summer Night (4,25)
Look Over Yonder (10,24,30)
Love Or Confusion (1,23,31)
Lover Man (11,34,35)
Machine Gun (6,14,16,18,24,33,36)

Manic Depression (1,5,24,25,31,32)
Mannish Boy (26)
May This Be Love (1)
Message To Love (6,15,28,30,34,35)
Midnight (13,28,30)
Midnight Lightning (16,30)
Mister Bad Luck (medley) (24)
Moon, Turn The Tides...Gently Gently Away (4)
My Friend (8,29)
New Rising Sun (28)
Night Bird Flying (8,24,28,29,32,35)
Nine To The Universe (19)
1983...(A Merman I Should Turn To Be) (4,24)
No Business (2)
Once I Had A Woman (16,26)
One Rainy Wish (3,24)
Pali Gap (10,28,30)
Peace In Mississippi (15,28)
Peter Gunn (13)
Power Of Soul (6,30,33)
Psycho (9)
Queen, The (11)
Radio One Theme (23,31)
Rainy Day, Dream Away (4)
Rainy Day Shuffle (24)
Red House (5,11,14,20,21,24,25,26,27,32,34,35,36)
Remember (5)
Rock Me, Baby (7,14,22,24,35)
Room Full Of Mirrors (10,17,24,28,29,35)

Send My Love To Linda (24)
Sgt. Pepper's Lonely Hearts Club Band (11,35)
She's So Fine (3)
Simon Says (2)
Slow Blues (35)
Somewhere (35)
Somewhere Over The Rainbow (15)
South Saturn Delta (24,30)
Spanish Castle Magic (3,23,24,31,34,35,36)
Star Spangled Banner (10,14,18,24,25,27,32,34,35,36)
Stars That Play With Laughing Sam's Dice (35)
Stepping Stone (13,17,21,27,28,29,33,36)
Still Raining, Still Dreaming (4,17)
Stone Free (5,20,23,31,32,33,35,36)
Stone Free Again (15)
Stop (33)
Straight Ahead (8,29)
Strange Things (2)
Sunshine Of Your Love (24,31)
Suspicious (32)
Sweat Segway II & III (9)
Sweet Angel (Angel) (30,35)
Table II & III (9)
Taking Care Of No Business (35)
Tax Free (13,24,30)
Testify (24)
Things That I Used To Do (24)
Third Stone From The Sun (1,17,21,24,35)

3 Little Bears (13)
Title #3 (35)
Trash Man (16)
Traveling With The Experience (31)
Two In One Goes (9)
Under The Table (9)
Up From The Skies (3) 82
Valley Of Neptune (24)
Villanova Junction (27,34)
Voice In The Wind (12)
Voodoo Child (Slight Return) (4,17,20,21,24,25,27,31,32,33,34,35,36)
Voodoo Chile (4,11,24)
Voodoo Chile Blues (26)
Wait Until Tomorrow (3,23,25,31)
We Gotta Live Together (6,33)
Welcome Home (2)
Who Knows (6,33)
Wild Thing (7,14,18,20,22,25,33,36)
Wind Cries Mary (1,5,18,22,24,25,32,35,36)
Wipe The Sweat (9)
With The Power (15)
Woodstock Improvisation (27,34)
You Got Me Floatin' (3)
Young/Hendrix (19)

HENDRYX, Nona   '83

Born on 8/18/45 in Trenton, New Jersey. R&B singer. Member of Patti LaBelle & The Blue-Belles from 1961-77.

DEBUT	PEAK	WKS	RIAA	CD	ARTIST — Album Title	$	Label & Number
4/23/83	83	19			1 Nona	$12	RCA Victor 4565
5/5/84	167	7			2 The Art Of Defense	$12	RCA Victor 4999
5/23/87	96	13		©	3 Female Trouble	$10	EMI America 17248

B-Boys (1)
Baby Go-Go (3)
Big Fun (3)
Design For Living (1)
Drive Me Wild (3)
Dummy Up (1)

Electricity (2)
Female Trouble (2)
Ghost Love (2)
I Know What You Need (Pygmy's Confession) (3)

I Sweat (Going Through The Motions) (2)
I Want You (3)
Keep It Confidential (1) 91
Life, The (2)
Living On The Border (1)

Rhythm Of Change (3)
Run For Cover (1)
Soft Targets (1)
Steady Action (1)
To The Bone (2)
Too Hot To Handle (3)

Transformation (1)
Why Should I Cry? (3) 58
Winds Of Change (Mandela to Mandela) (3)

HENLEY, Don   '00

Born on 7/22/47 in Gilmer, Texas. Rock singer/songwriter/drummer. Member of the Eagles. Married model Sharon Summerall on 5/20/95.

DEBUT	PEAK	WKS	RIAA	CD	ARTIST — Album Title	Catalog	Sym	$	Label & Number
9/4/82	24	35	● ©		1 I Can't Stand Still			$12	Asylum 60048
12/15/84+	13	63	▲3 ©		2 Building The Perfect Beast			$10	Geffen 24026
7/15/89	8	148	▲6 ©		3 The End Of The Innocence	C:#36/2		$10	Geffen 24217

HENLEY, Don — Cont'd

DEBUT	PEAK	WKS	RIAA	CD	ARTIST — Album Title	$	Label & Number
12/9/95	48	26	▲	© 4	Actual Miles - Henley's Greatest Hits .... [G]	$10	Geffen 24834
6/10/00	7	32	▲	© 5	Inside Job	$10	Warner 47083

All She Wants To Do Is Dance (2,4) *9*
Annabel (5)
Boys Of Summer (2,4) *5*
Building The Perfect Beast (2)
Damn It, Rose (5)
Dirty Laundry (1,4) *3*
Drivin' With Your Eyes Closed (2)
End Of The Innocence (3,4) *8*
Everybody Knows (4)

Everything Is Different Now (5)
For My Wedding (5)
Garden Of Allah (4)
Genie, The (5)
Gimme What You Got (5)
Goodbye To A River (5)
Heart Of The Matter (3,4) *21*
How Bad Do You Want It? (3) *48*
I Can't Stand Still (1) *48*
I Will Not Go Quietly (3,4)

If Dirt Were Dollars (3)
Inside Job (5)
Johnny Can't Read (1) *42*
La Eile (1)
Land Of The Living (2)
Last Worthless Evening (3,4) *21*
Lilah (1)
Little Tin God (3)
Long Way Home (1)
Man With A Mission (2)

Miss Ghost (5)
My Thanksgiving (5)
New York Minute (3,4) *48*
Nobody Else In The World But You (5)
Nobody's Business (1)
Not Enough Love In The World (2,4) *34*
Shangri-La (3)
Sunset Grill (2,4) *22*
Taking You Home (5) *58*

Talking To The Moon (1)
Them And Us (1)
They're Not Here, They're Not Coming (5)
Unclouded Day (1)
Workin' It (5)
You Better Hang Up (1)
You Can't Make Love (2)
You Don't Know Me At All (4)
You're Not Drinking Enough (2)

HENSEL, Carol   '81
Born in New York City. Fitness instructor.

DEBUT	PEAK	WKS			ARTIST — Album Title	$	Label & Number
3/21/81	56	55		1	Carol Hensel's Exercise & Dance Program	$10	Vintage 7713
					originally titled Dancersize on Vintage 7701; music by a studio group		
12/19/81+	70	28		2	Carol Hensel's Exercise & Dance Program, Volume 2	$10	Vintage 7733
					music performed by The Beachwood All-Star (studio group)		
1/22/83	104	12		3	Carol Hensel's Exercise & Dance Program, Volume 3	$10	Vintage 30004
					music by a studio group		

Ain't No Stoppin Us Now (1)
Bobbie Sue (3)
Celebration (2)
Chariots Of Fire - Titles (3)

De Do Do Do, De Da Da Da (2)
Freeze Frame (3)
I Go To Rio (3)
I Just Wanna Stop (1)

I Will Survive (1)
Jessie's Girl (3)
(Just Like) Starting Over (3)
Just The Two Of Us (2)

Just The Way You Are (1)
Let's Groove (3)
Mama Used To Say (3)
Morning Train (9 To 5) (2)

9 To 5 (2)
Sailing (2)
Shake It Up (3)
Summer Nights (1)

Turn Your Love Around (3)
What A Fool Believes (1)
Whip It (2)
You May Be Right (2)

HENSLEY, Ken   '73
*Born on 8/24/45 in London. Rock keyboardist. Member of **Uriah Heep**.*

DEBUT	PEAK	WKS			ARTIST — Album Title	$	Label & Number
4/7/73	173	7	©		Proud Words On A Dusty Shelf	$15	Mercury 661

Black-Hearted Lady
Cold Autumn Sunday

Fortune
From Time To Time

Go Down
King Without A Throne

Last Time
Proud Words

Rain
When Evening Comes

HERMAN, Woody   '55
Born on 5/16/13 in Milwaukee. Died of heart failure on 10/29/87 (age 74). Legendary saxophonist/clarinetist/bandleader. Won Grammy's Lifetime Achievement Award in 1987.

DEBUT	PEAK	WKS			ARTIST — Album Title	$	Label & Number
2/19/55	11	2		1	The 3 Herds .... [I-K]	$30	Columbia 592
					recordings from 1945-54		
8/17/63	136	4		2	Encore: Woody Herman - 1963 .... [I-L]	$20	Philips 092
					recorded at the Basin Street in Hollywood		
3/21/64	148	2		3	Woody Herman: 1964 .... [I]	$20	Philips 118

After You've Gone (3)
Better Get It In Your Soul (2)
Blame Boehm (1)
Body And Soul (2)
Caldonia (1,2)

Cousins (3)
Days Of Wine And Roses (2)
Deep Purple (3)
Early Autumn (1)
El Toro Grande (2)

Four Brothers (1)
Four Others (1)
Good Earth (1)
Goof And I (1)
Hallelujah Time (1)

Jazz Hoot (3)
Jazz Me Blues (2)
Keen And Peachy (1)
Mulligan Tawny (1)
My Wish (3)

Non-Alcoholic (3)
Satin Doll (3)
Sidewalks Of Cuba (1)
Strut, The (3)
Taste Of Honey (3)

That's Where It Is (2)
Third Herd (1)
Watermelon Man (2)

★305★ HERMAN'S HERMITS   '65
Pop group formed in Manchester, England: Peter "Herman" Noone (vocals, born on 11/5/47), Derek Leckenby and Keith Hopwood (guitars), Karl Green (bass) and Barry Whitwam (drums). Group name derived from cartoon character "Sherman" of TV's The Bullwinkle Show. Leckenby died of cancer on 6/4/94 (age 48).

1)Herman's Hermits On Tour 2)Introducing Herman's Hermits 3)The Best Of Herman's Hermits

DEBUT	PEAK	WKS		CD	ARTIST — Album Title	$	Label & Number
2/20/65	2⁴	40		● 1	Introducing Herman's Hermits	$25	MGM 4282
6/19/65	2⁶	39		● 2	Herman's Hermits On Tour	$25	MGM 4295
11/20/65	5	105		● 3	The Best Of Herman's Hermits .... [G]	$25	MGM 4315
3/26/66	14	26		4	Hold On! .... [S]	$25	MGM 4342
8/20/66	48	21		5	Both Sides Of Herman's Hermits	$25	MGM 4386
12/3/66+	20	32		● 6	The Best Of Herman's Hermits, Volume 2 .... [G]	$25	MGM 4416
3/18/67	13	35		7	There's A Kind Of Hush All Over The World .... [G]	$25	MGM 4438
10/7/67	75	9		8	Blaze	$25	MGM 4478
1/13/68	102	8		9	The Best Of Herman's Hermits, Volume III .... [G]	$25	MGM 4505
9/28/68	182	3		10	Mrs. Brown, You've Got A Lovely Daughter .... [S]	$25	MGM 4548

Ace, King, Queen, Jack (8)
Big Man (9)
Bus Stop (5,6)
Busy Line (8)
Can't You Hear My Heartbeat (2,3) *2*
Dandy (6,7) *5*
Dial My Number (5)
Don't Go Out Into The Rain (You're Going To Melt) (8,9) *18*
Don't Try To Hurt Me (2)
East West (7,9) *27*
End Of The World (2,3)
For Love (5)
For Your Love (2,6)
Future Mrs. 'Awkins (5)

Gas Light Street (7)
George And Dragon (4)
Got A Feeling (4)
Gotta Get Away (4)
Green Street Green (8)
Heartbeat (2)
Hold On! (4,6)
Holiday Inn (10)
I Call Out Her Name (8)
I Gotta Dream On (2,3)
I Know Why (1)
I Understand (Just How You Feel) (1)
I Wonder (1)
I'll Never Dance Again (2)
I'm Henry VIII, I Am (2,3) *1*
I'm Into Something Good (1,3) *1*

If You're Thinkin' What I'm Thinkin' (7)
It's Nice To Be Out In The Morning (10)
Jezebel (7)
Just A Little Bit Better (3) *7*
Kansas City Loving (1)
L'Autre Jour (5)
Last Bus Home (8,9)
Leaning On The Lamp Post (4,6)
Lemon And Lime (10)
Listen People (6) *3*
Little Boy Sad (6)
Little Miss Sorrow Child Of Tomorrow (7)
Make Me Happy (4)
Man With The Cigar (5)

Moonshine Man (8,9)
Most Beautiful Thing In My Life (10)
Mother-In-Law (1,3)
Mrs. Brown You've Got A Lovely Daughter (1,3,10) *1*
Museum (8,9) *39*
Must To Avoid (4,6) *8*
My Old Dutch (5)
My Reservation's Been Confirmed (5)
No Milk Today (7,9) *35*
Oh Mr. Porter (5)
One Little Packet Of Cigarettes (8)
Ooh, She's Done It Again (10)
Rattler (7)

Saturday's Child (7)
Sea Cruise (1,3)
Show Me Girl (1)
Silhouettes (2,3) *5*
Story Of My Life (6)
Take Love, Give Love (6)
Tell Me Baby (2)
There's A Kind Of Hush (7,9,10) *4*
Things I Do For You Baby (4)
Thinking Of You (1)
This Door Swings Both Ways (5,6) *12*
Traveling Light (2)
Two Lovely Black Eyes (5)
Upstairs, Downstairs (8)
Walkin' With My Angel (1)

What Is Wrong What Is Right (9)
Where Were You When I Needed You (4)
Wild Love (4)
Wings Of Love (9)
Wonderful World (3) *4*
World Is For The Young (10)
You Won't Be Leaving (7)
Your Hand In Mine (1)

HERNANDEZ, Patrick   '79
Born on 4/6/49 in Paris. Disco singer.

DEBUT	PEAK	WKS			ARTIST — Album Title	$	Label & Number
7/28/79	61	15			Born To Be Alive	$12	Columbia 36100

Born To Be Alive *16*

Disco Queen

I Give You Rendezvous

It Comes So Easy

Show Me The Way You Kiss

You Turn Me On

HERNDON, Ty   '96
Born Boyd Tyrone Herndon on 5/2/62 in Meridian, Mississippi; raised in Butler, Alabama. Country singer/songwriter/guitarist.

5/6/95	68	13	●	©	1 What Mattered Most		$10	Epic 66397
8/31/96	65	10	●	©	2 Living In A Moment		$10	Epic 67564
6/13/98	140	3		©	3 Big Hopes		$10	Epic 68167
11/20/99	124	2		©	4 Steam		$10	Epic 69899

Before There Was You (2)
Big Hopes (3)
Big Time Dreamer (3)
Don't Tell Mama (2)
Hands Of A Working Man (3) *47*
Hat Full Of Rain (1)
Heart Half Empty (1)

Her Heart Is Only Human (2)
How Much Can One Man Love You (3)
I Can't Do It All (4)
I Have To Surrender (2)
I Know How The River Feels (2)
I Want My Goodbye Back (1)
In A New York Second (4)

In Your Face (1)
It Must Be Love (3) *38*
Living In A Moment (2)
Lookin' For The Good Life (4)
Love At 90 Miles An Hour (1)
Love Don't Work That Way (2)
Love Like That (3)
Loved Too Much (2)

Man Holdin' On (To A Woman
Lettin' Go) (3) *81*
No Brakes (3)
No Mercy (4) *92*
Only Way I Know (3)
Pray For Me (4)
Pretty Good Thing (1)
Putting The Brakes On Time (4)

Returning The Faith (2)
She Wants To Be Wanted Again (2)
Somewhere A Lover (3)
Steam (4) *83*
Summer Was A Bummer (1)
Tears In God's Eyes (3)
That's What I Call Love (4)

Thinkin' With My Heart Again (3)
What Mattered Most (1) *90*
You Can Leave Your Hat On (4)
You Don't Mess Around With Jim (1)
You Just Get One (1)

HERSH, Kristin   '94
Born on 8/7/66 in Atlanta. Singer/guitarist. Member of **Throwing Muses**. Stepsister of Tanya Donnelly (of **Belly**).

2/19/94	197	1		©	Hips And Makers		$10	Sire 45413

Beestung
Close Your Eyes
Cuckoo, The

Hips And Makers
Houdini Blues
Letter, The

Loon, A
Lurch
Me And My Charms

Sparky
Sundrops
Teeth

Tuesday Night
Velvet Days
Your Ghost

HESITATIONS, The   '68
R&B vocal group from Cleveland. Lead singer George "King" Scott was accidentally killed in February 1968.

2/24/68	193	3			The new Born Free		$20	Kapp 3548

Born Free *38*
Don't Go

I Believe In Love
I Wish It Could Be Me

I've Gotta Find Her
Let's Groove

Love Is Everywhere
Overworked And Underpaid

Push A Little Bit Harder
We Can Do It

We Only Have One Life
Without Your Love

HEWETT, Howard   '90
Born on 10/1/57 in Akron, Ohio. R&B singer. Member of **Shalamar** (1979-85). Married to **Nia Peeples** from 1989-93.

11/1/86+	159	16		©	1 I Commit To Love		$10	Elektra 60487
4/16/88	110	12		©	2 Forever and Ever		$10	Elektra 60779
4/14/90	54	21		©	3 Howard Hewett		$10	Elektra 60904
2/25/95	181	2		©	4 It's Time		$10	Caliber 1008

Call His Name (4)
Challenge (4)
Crystal Clear (4)
Don't Give In (3)
Eye On You (1)
For The Lover In You (4)
Forever And Ever (2)
Good-bye Good Friend (2)

How Do I Know I Love You (4)
I Commit To Love (1)
I Do (3)
I Got 2 Go (1)
I Know You'll Be Comin' Back (3)
I Wanna Know You (4)
I'm For Real (1) *90*

If I Could Only Have That Day Back (3)
In A Crazy Way (1)
Jesus (3)
Just To Keep You Satisfied (4)
Last Forever (1)
Let Me Show You How To Fall In Love (3)

Let's Get Deeper (3)
Let's Try It All Over Again (1)
Love Don't Wanna Wait (1)
Love Of Your Own (4)
More I Get (The More I Want) (3)
Natural Love (2)
On & On (4)

Once, Twice, Three Times (2)
Say Amen (1)
Say Good-bye (4)
Shadow (3)
Shakin' My Emotion (2)
Share A Love (2)
Show Me (3) *62*
Stay (1)

Strange Relationship (2)
This Love Is Forever (4)
This Time (2)
When Will It Be (3)
You'll Find Another Man (2)
Your Body Needs Healin' (4)

HEYWARD, Nick   '84
Born on 5/20/61 in Beckenham, Kent, England. Pop-rock singer/guitarist. Member of **Haircut One Hundred** (1981-83).

1/14/84	178	4		©	North of a Miracle		$12	Arista 8106

Atlantic Monday
Blue Hat For A Blue Day

Club Boy At Sea
Day It Rained Forever

Kick Of Love
On A Sunday

Take That Situation
Two Make It True

When It Started To Begin
Whistle Down The Wind

HEYWOOD, Eddie   '59
Born on 12/4/15 in Atlanta. Died on 1/2/89 (age 73). Jazz pianist.

5/25/59	16	4		©	Canadian Sunset		[I]	$30	RCA Victor 1529

All About You
Blues In A Happy Mood

Canadian Sunset
Dearest Darling

Heywood's Beguine
I'm Saving Myself For You

Lies
Now You're Mine

Rain
Rendezvous For Two

Subway Serenade
Time To Go Home

HEYWOODS — see DONALDSON, Bo

HIATT, John   '93
Born on 8/20/52 in Indianapolis. Singer/songwriter/guitarist. Member of **Little Village**.

7/4/87	107	17		©	1 Bring The Family		$10	A&M 5158
9/24/88	98	31		©	2 Slow Turning		$10	A&M 5206
7/7/90	61	19		©	3 Stolen Moments		$10	A&M 5310
9/25/93	47	11		©	4 Perfectly Good Guitar		$10	A&M 540135
11/11/95	48	9		©	5 Walk On		$10	Capitol 33416
7/19/97	111	4		©	6 Little Head		$10	Capitol 54672
10/14/00	110	4		©	7 Crossing Muddy Waters		$10	Vanguard 79576

After All This Time (6)
Alone In The Dark (1)
Angel (4)
Back Of My Mind (3)
Before I Go (7)
Blue Telescope (4)
Bring Back Your Love To Me (3)
Buffalo River Home (4)
Child Of The Wild Blue Yonder (3)
Cross My Fingers (4)
Crossing Muddy Waters (7)
Cry Love (5)

Drive South (2)
Dust Down A Country Road (5)
Ethylene (5)
Far As We Go (6)
Feelin' Again (5)
Feels Like Rain (2)
Friend Of Mine (5)
Georgia Rae (2)
God's Golden Eyes (7)
Gone (7)
Good As She Could Be (5)
Graduated (6)
Have A Little Faith In Me (1)
I Can't Wait (5)

Icy Blue Heart (2)
Is Anybody There? (2)
It'll Come To You (2)
Learning How To Love You (1)
Lift Up Every Stone (7)
Lincoln Town (7)
Lipstick Sunset (1)
Listening To Old Voices (3)
Little Head (6)
Loving A Hurricane (4)
Memphis In The Meantime (1)
Mr. Stanley (7)
My Sweet Girl (6)
Native Son (5)

Old Habits (4)
One Kiss (3)
Only The Song Survives (7)
Paper Thin (2)
Perfectly Good Guitar (4)
Permanent Hurt (4)
Pirate Radio (6)
Real Fine Love (3)
Rest Of The Dream (3)
Ride Along (2)
River Knows Your Name (5)
Rock Back Billy (3)
Runaway (6)
Seven Little Indians (3)

Shredding The Document (5)
Slow Turning (2)
Something Wild (4)
Sometime Other Than Now (2)
Stolen Moments (3)
Stood Up (1)
Straight Outta Time (4)
Sure Pinocchio (6)
Take It Back (7)
Take It Down (7)
Tennessee Plates (2)
Thank You Girl (1)
Thing Called Love (1)
Thirty Years Of Tears (3)

Through Your Hands (3)
Tip Of My Tongue (1)
Trudy And Dave (2)
Walk On (5)
What Do We Do Now (7)
When You Hold Me Tight (4)
Woman Sawed In Half (6)
Wreck Of The Barbie Ferrari (4)
Wrote It Down And Burned It (5)
You Must Go (5)
Your Dad Did (1)
Your Love Is My Rest (5)

HIBBLER, Al   '56
Born on 8/16/15 in Little Rock, Arkansas. Died on 4/24/2001 (age 85). Blind since birth. R&B singer.

8/4/56	20	2		©	Starring Al Hibbler		$30	Decca 8328

After The Lights Go Down Low *10*
Count Every Star

I Don't Stand A Ghost Of A Chance With You
Night And Day

Pennies From Heaven
September In The Rain
Shanghai Lil

Stella By Starlight
There Are Such Things
Where Are You

Where Or When
You'll Never Know

HI-C   '92
Born in 1972 in Louisiana; raised in California. Male rapper.

| 1/25/92 | **152** | 12 | © | **Skanless**.. | | | $10 | Skanless 61235 |

Bullshit
Compton Hoochies
Ding-A-Ling
Froggy Style
Funky Rap Sanga
I'm Not Your Puppet 63
Jack Move
Leave My Curl Alone
Punk Shit
Request Line
Sitting In The Park
2 Drunk Ta F__k
Too Greasy
2 Skanless
2 Ada Time
Yo Dick

HICKS, Dan, & His Hot Licks   '73
Born on 12/9/41 in Little Rock, Arkansas; raised in Santa Rosa, California. Singer/songwriter/guitarist.

10/2/71	**195**	8	©	1	**Where's The Money?** .... [L]			$15	Blue Thumb 29
					recorded at the Troubadour in Los Angeles				
5/20/72	**170**	5	©	2	**Striking It Rich!**..			$15	Blue Thumb 36
6/9/73	**67**	18	©	3	**Last Train To Hicksville...the home of happy feet**...............................			$15	Blue Thumb 51
3/25/78	**165**	3		4	**It Happened One Bite**...			$12	Warner 3158

DAN HICKS

Boogaloo Jones (4)
Boogaloo Plays Guitar (4)
Buzzard Was Their Friend (1)
By Hook Or By Crook (1)
Canned Music (2)
Caught In The Rain (1)
Cheaters Don't Win (3)
Cloud My Sunny Mood (3)
Coast To Coast (1)
Collared Blues (4)
Cowboy's Dream No. 19 (3)
Crazy - 'Cause He Is (4)
Cruizin' (4)
Dig A Little Deeper (1)
Dizzy Dogs (4)
Euphonius Whale (3)
Flight Of The Fly (2)
Fujiyama (3)
Garden In The Rain (4)
I Asked My Doctor (3)
I Feel Like Singing (1)
I Scare Myself (2)
I'm An Old Cowhand (From The Rio Grand) (2)
Is This My Happy Home? (1)
It's Not My Time To Go (3)
Laughing Song (2)
Lonely Madman (3)
'Long Come A Viper (3)
Lovers For Life (4)
Mama, I'm An Outlaw (4)
Moody Richard (The Innocent Bystander) (2)
My Old Timey Baby (3)
News From Up The Street (3)
O'Reilly At The Bar (2)
Payday Blues (3)
Philly Rag (2)
Presently In The Past (2)
Reelin' Down (1)
Reveille Revisited (4)
Shorty Falls In Love (3)
Skippy's Farewell (2)
Success (3)
Sure Beats Me (3)
Sweetheart (3)
Traffic Jam (1)
Vinnie's Lookin' Good (4)
Vivando (3)
Waitin' (4)
Walkin' One And Only (2)
Where's The Money? (1)
Woe, The Luck (2)
You Got To Believe (2)

HI-FIVE   '91
R&B vocal group from Waco, Texas: **Tony Thompson**, Roderick Clark, Russell Neal, Marcus Sanders and Toriano Easley (left after release of first album, replaced by Treston Irby). Clark and Neal left by 1993; Shannon and Terrance joined.

12/8/90+	**38**	45	● ©	1	**Hi-Five**			$10	Jive 1328
8/29/92	**82**	28	● ©	2	**Keep It Goin' On**			$10	Jive 41474
11/13/93	**105**	4	©	3	**Faithful**			$10	Jive 41528

As One (3)
Faithful (3)
Fly Away (2)
I Can't Wait Another Minute (1) 8
I Just Can't Handle It (1)
I Like The Way (The Kissing Game) (1) 1
I'm In Need (3)
Just Another Girlfriend (1) 88
Know Love (1)
Let's Get It Started (Keep It Goin' On) (2)
Little Bit Older Now (1)
Mary, Mary (3)
Merry-Go-Round (1)
Miss U Girl (3)
Never Should've Let You Go (3) 30
Quality Time (2) 38
Rag Doll (1)
Ready 4 U 2 Love (3)
She Said (2)
She's Playing Hard To Get (2) 5
Sweetheart (1)
Too Young (1)
Unconditional Love (3)
Video Girl (2)
Way You Said Goodbye (1)
What Can I Say To You (To Justify My Love) (3)
Whenever You Say (2)

HIGGINS, Bertie   '82
Born Elbert Higgins on 12/8/44 in Tarpon Springs, Florida. Singer/songwriter.

| 2/27/82 | **38** | 25 | | | **Just Another Day In Paradise** .... | | | $12 | Kat Family 37901 |

Candle Dancer
Casablanca
Down At The Blue Moon
Heart Is The Hunter
Just Another Day in Paradise 46
Key Largo 8
Port O Call (Savannah '55)
She's Gone To Live On The Mountain
Tropics, The
White Line Fever

HIGH & MIGHTY, The   '99
Rap duo from New York City: Mighty Mi and Mr. Eon.

| 9/11/99 | **193** | 2 | © | | **Home Field Advantage** .... | | | $10 | Rawkus 50121 |

B-Boy Document '99
Dick Starbuck "Porno Detective"
Dirty Decibels
Friendly Game Of Football
Half, The
Hands On Experience Pt. II
Hot Spittable
In-Outs
Last Hit
Meaning, The
Mind, Soul And Body
Open Mic Night Remix
Shaquan & Eon
Tip Off Time
Top Prospects
Weed

HIGH INERGY   '78
R&B vocal group from Pasadena, California: sisters Barbara and Vernessa Mitchell, Linda Howard and Michelle Rumph. Vernessa left in 1978; group continued as a trio.

11/5/77+	**28**	25		1	**Turnin' On**			$12	Gordy 978
7/22/78	**42**	13		2	**Steppin' Out**			$12	Gordy 982
5/26/79	**147**	5		3	**Shoulda Gone Dancin'**			$12	Gordy 987

Ain't No Love Left (In My Heart For You) (1)
Beware (2)
Come And Get It (3)
Could This Be Love (1)
Didn't Wanna Tell You (2)
Everytime I See You I Go Wild (1)
Fly Little Blackbird (2)
Hi! (2)
High School (1)
I've Got What You Need (3)
Let Me Get Close To You (1)
Let Yourself Go (3)
Love Is All You Need (1) 89
Love Of My Life (3)
Lovin' Fever (2)
Midnight Music Man (3)
Peaceland (2)
Save It For A Rainy Day (1)
Searchin' (I've Got To Find My Love) (1)
Shoulda Gone Dancin' (3)
Some Kinda Magic (1)
Too Late (The Damage Is Done) (3)
We Are The Future (2)
You Can't Turn Me Off (In The Middle Of Turning Me On) (1) 12
You Captured My Heart (2)

HIGHWAYMEN, The   '61
Folk group formed in Middletown, Connecticut: Dave Fisher, Bob Burnett, Chan Daniels, Steve Trott and Steve Butts. Daniels died of pneumonia on 8/2/75 (age 35).

10/9/61	**42**	22	©	1	**The Highwaymen**			$20	United Artists 3125
3/24/62	**99**	14	©	2	**Standing Room Only!**			$20	United Artists 6168
9/7/63	**79**	9		3	**Hootenanny with The Highwaymen** .... [L]			$20	United Artists 6294

A La Claire Fontaine (1)
Ah Si Mon Moina (1)
Au Claire De La Lune (1)
Big Rock Candy Mountain (1)
Black Eyed Suzie (2)
Calton Weaver (2)
Can Ye Sew Cushions? (3)
Carni Valito (1)
Chanson De Chagrin (3)
Cindy Oh Cindy (1)
Cotton Fields (2,3) 13
Great Silkie (2)
Greenland Fisheries (1)
Gypsy Rover (2) 42
Irish Work Song (Pat Works On The Railway) (1)
Johnny With The Bandy Legs (2)
La Cansone Del Vino (3)
Michael (1,3) 1
Mister Noah (3)
Nostalgias Tucumanas (2)
Old Maid's Song (3)
One For The Money (3)
Passing Through (3)
Pollerita (2)
Raise A Ruckus Tonight (3)
Rise Up Shepherd (2)
Roll On, Columbia, Roll On (3)
Run Come See Jerusalem (3)
Santiano (1)
Shaggy Dog Songs (3)
Sinner Man (1)
Take This Hammer (1)
Tale Of Michael Flynn (3)
Three Jolly Rogues (1)
Turtle Dove (3)
Wildwood Flower (2)
You're Always Welcome At Our House (medley) (3)

HILL, Dan   '78
Born on 6/3/54 in Toronto. Pop singer/songwriter.

12/6/75+	**104**	17		1	**Dan Hill**			$12	20th Century 500
12/10/77+	**21**	24	●	2	**Longer Fuse** _____			$12	20th Century 547
1/21/78	**79**	14		3	**Hold On**			$12	20th Century 526
9/23/78	**118**	6		4	**Frozen In The Night**			$12	20th Century 558
8/8/87	**90**	19	©	5	**Dan Hill**			$10	Columbia 40456

HILL, Dan — Cont'd

All Alone In California (3)
All I See Is Your Face (4) *41*
Blood In My Veins (5)
Can't We Try (5) *6*
Canada (3)
Carmelia (5)
Caroline (3)
City Madness (3)
Conscience (5)
Crazy (2)

Dark Side Of Atlanta (4)
Every Boys Fantasy (5)
Fountain (1)
14 Today (1)
Friends (4)
Frozen In The Night (4)
Growin' Up (1) *67*
Hold On (3)
I Dreamt I Saw Your Face Last Night (1)

I've Been Alone (3)
In The Name Of Love (2)
Indian Woman (4)
Jean (2)
Let The Song Last Forever (4) *91*
Longer Fuse (2)
Looking Back (1)
Lose Control (5)
McCarthy's Day (2)

Never Thought (That I Could Love) (5) *43*
No One Taught Me How To Lie (4)
Nobody's Right (1)
People (1)
Perfect Love (5)
Phonecall (3)
Pleasure Centre (5)
Proposal (3)

Question Marks In Time (3)
Rain (3)
Seed Of Music (1)
Sometimes When We Touch (2) *3*
Sour Whiskey (3)
Southern California (2)
Still Not Used To (2)
Till The Day I Die (4)
USA/USSR (5)

Welcome (1)
When The Hurt Comes (4)
(Why Did You Have To Go And) Pick On Me (4)
You Are All I See (2)
You Make Me Want To Be (1)
You Say You're Free (1)
Your Only Friend (1)

HILL, Faith   '99

Born on 9/21/67 in Jackson, Mississippi. Country singer. Adopted at less than a week old and raised as Audrey Faith Perry in Star, Mississippi. Married **Tim McGraw** on 10/6/96.

DEBUT	PEAK	WKS	RIAA	CD	Album Title	Catalog	$	Label & Number
1/29/94	59	54	▲²	©	1 Take Me As I Am	C:#32/1	$10	Warner 45389
9/16/95+	29	80	▲³	©	2 It Matters To Me	C:#43/1	$10	Warner 45872
5/9/98	7	99	▲⁵	©	3 Faith	C:#16/38	$10	Warner 46790
11/27/99	❶¹	97↑	▲⁷	©	4 Breathe		$10	Warner 47373

Bed Of Roses (2)
Better Days (3)
Breathe (4) *2*
Bringing Out The Elvis (4)
But I Will (1)
Go The Distance (1)
Hard Way (3)
I Can't Do That Anymore (2)

I Got My Baby (4)
I Love You (3)
I Would Be Stronger Than That (1)
I've Got This Friend (1)
If I Should Fall Behind (4)
If I'm Not In Love (2)
If My Heart Had Wings (4) *39*

It Matters To Me (2) *74*
It Will Be Me (4)
Just About Now (1)
Just Around The Eyes (1)
Just To Hear You Say That You Love Me (3)
Keep Walkin' On (2)
Let Me Let Go (3) *33*

Let's Go To Vegas (2)
Let's Make Love (4) *54*
Life's Too Short To Love Like That (1)
Love Ain't Like That (3) *68*
Love Is A Sweet Thing (4)
Man's Home Is His Castle (2)
Me (3)

My Wild Frontier (3)
Piece Of My Heart (3)
Room In My Heart (2)
Secret Of Life (3) *46*
Somebody Stand By Me (3)
Someone Else's Dream (2)
Take Me As I Am (1)
That's How Love Moves (4)

There Will Come A Day (4)
This Kiss (3) *7*
Way You Love Me (4) *6*
What's In It For Me (4)
Wild One (3)
You Can't Lose Me (3)
You Give Me Love (3)
You Will Be Mine (2)

HILL, Lauryn   '98

Born on 5/25/75 in South Orange, New Jersey. Singer/actress. Member of **The Fugees**. Acted on TV's *As The World Turns* and in the movie *Sister Act 2*.

9/12/98	❶⁴	81	▲⁷	©	The Miseducation Of Lauryn Hill	$10	Ruffhouse 69035

1998 Grammy winner: Album of the Year

Can't Take My Eyes Off Of You
Doo Wop (That Thing) *1*
Every Ghetto, Every City

Everything Is Everything *35*
Ex-Factor *21*
Final Hour

Forgive Them Father
I Used To Love Him
Lost Ones

Miseducation Of Lauryn Hill
Nothing Even Matters
Superstar

Tell Him
To Zion
When It Hurts So Bad

HILL, Z.Z.   '84

Born on Arzel Hill on 9/30/35 in Naples, Texas. Died of a heart attack on 4/27/84 (age 48). Blues singer.

1/22/72	194	2			1 The Brand New Z.Z. Hill	$20	Mankind 201
2/5/83	165	5			2 The Rhythm & The Blues	$12	Malaco 7411
1/7/84	170	9		©	3 I'm A Blues Man	$12	Malaco 7415

Been So Long (3)
Blind Side (3)
Blues At The Opera (Communication In Regard To Circumstances) Medley (1)
Cheatin' Love (3)
Chokin' Kind (1)

Early In The Morning (1)
Get A Little, Give A Little (3)
Get You Some Business (2)
Help Me, I'm In Need (2)
Hold Back (One Man At A Time) (1)

I Ain't Buying What You're Selling (3)
I Think I'd Do It (1)
I'm A Blues Man (3)
Man Needs A Woman (A Woman Needs A Man) (1)
Open House At My House (2)

Outside Thang (2)
Please Don't Let Our Good Thing End (3)
Shade Tree Mechanic (3)
Someone Else Is Steppin' In (2)
Steal Away (3)
That Fire Is Hot (2)

Three Into Two Won't Go (3)
Wang Dang Doodle (2)
What Am I Gonna Tell Her (2)
Who You Been Giving It To (2)
You're Gonna Be A Woman (2)

HILLAGE, Steve   '77

Born on 8/2/51 in England. Rock guitarist.

1/15/77	130	9		©	L	$12	Atlantic 18205

produced by **Todd Rundgren**

Electrick Gypsies

Hurdy Gurdy Glissando
Hurdy Gurdy Man

It's All Too Much

Lunar Musick Suite

Om Nama Shivaya

HILLMAN, Chris   '76

Born on 12/4/42 in Los Angeles. Rock singer/bassist. Member of **The Byrds**, **Flying Burrito Brothers**, **The Souther, Hillman, Furay Band**, **McGuinn, Clark & Hillman** and **The Desert Rose Band**.

6/19/76	152	6		©	1 Slippin' Away	$12	Asylum 1062
9/17/77	188	3			2 Clear Sailin'	$12	Asylum 1104

Ain't That Peculiar (2)
Blue Morning (1)
Clear Sailin' (2)
Down In The Churchyard (1)

Fallen Favorite (2)
Falling Again (1)
Heartbreaker (2)
Hot Dusty Roads (2)

Love Is The Sweetest Amnesty (1)
Lucky In Love (2)
Midnight Again (1)

Nothing Gets Through (2)
Playing The Fool (2)
Quits (2)
Rollin' And Tumblin' (2)

Slippin' Away (1)
Step On Out (1)
Take It On The Run (1)
(Take Me In Your) Lifeboat (1)

Witching Hour (1)

HILLSIDE SINGERS, The   '72

Pop vocal group: Lori Ham, Mary Mayo, Joelle Marino, Bill Marino, Frank Marino, Laura Marino, Rick Shaw and Susan Wiedenmann. The Marinos are siblings. Mary Mayo was the wife of producer Al Ham; Lori Ham is their daughter. Rick and Ron Shaw are brothers.

1/8/72	71	16			I'd Like To Teach The World To Sing	$15	Metromedia 1051

Amen
Day By Day

I'd Like To Teach The World To Sing (In Perfect Harmony) *13*
Kum Ba Yah

Last Night I Had The Strangest Dream
Night They Drove Old Dixie Down

Old Fashioned Love Song
One Man's Hands
Take Me Home, Country Roads
Tomorrow Belongs To Me

We're Together *100*

HI-LO'S, The   '57

Vocal group formed in Chicago: Gene Puerling, Clark Burroughs, Bob Morse and Bob Strasen. Numerous appearances on **Rosemary Clooney**'s TV show.

4/13/57	13	3		©	1 Suddenly It's The Hi-Lo's	$40	Columbia 952
7/22/57	14	7		©	2 Ring Around Rosie	$40	Columbia 1006

ROSEMARY CLOONEY AND THE HI-LO'S

10/14/57	19	4		©	3 Now Hear This	$40	Columbia 1023

Basin Street Blues (1)
Brahms' Lullaby (1)
Brown-Skin Gal In The Calico Gown (1)
Camptown Races (3)
Coquette (2)
Deep Purple (1)

Desert Song (1)
Doncha Go 'Way Mad (2)
Down The Old Ox Road (1)
Everything Happens To Me (2)
Heather On The Hill (3)
How About You (1)
I Could Write A Book (2)

I Married An Angel (1)
I'm Glad There Is You (2)
I'm In The Mood For Love (2)
Laura (3)
Life Is Just A Bowl Of Cherries (1)
Little Girl Blue (3)

Love Letters (2)
Love Walked In (1)
My Melancholy Baby (2)
My Sugar Is So Refined (1)
My Time Is Your Time (3)
Quiet Girl (3)

Shine On Your Shoes (3)
Solitude (2)
Stormy Weather (1)
Sunnyside Up (2)
Swing Low, Sweet Chariot (1)
Tenderly (1)
There's No You (3)

Together (2)
Two Ladies In De Shade Of De Banana Tree (3)
What Is There To Say (2)

HINDU LOVE GODS '90

One-time gathering: **Warren Zevon** (vocals) with **R.E.M.** members: Peter Buck (guitar), Mike Mills (bass) and Bill Berry (drums).

| 11/10/90 | 168 | 10 | | © | **Hindu Love Gods** .... | | | $10 | Giant 24406 |

Battleship Chains
Crosscut Saw

| I'm A One Woman Man | Mannish Boy | Travelin' Riverside Blues | Walkin' Blues |
| Junko Pardner | Raspberry Beret | Vigilante Man | Wang Dang Doodle |

HIPSWAY '87

Pop group from Scotland: Graham Skinner (vocals), Pim Jones (guitar), John McElhone (bass) and Harry Travers (drums). McElhone later joined **Texas**.

| 2/21/87 | 55 | 18 | | © | **Hipsway** .... | | | $10 | Columbia 40522 |

Ask The Lord
Bad Thing Longing

| Broken Years | **Honeythief, The** 19 | Set This Day Apart | Upon A Thread |
| Forbidden | Long White Car | Tinder | |

HIROSHIMA '80

Jazz-pop group from Los Angeles: Teri Koide (vocals), Dan Kuramoto and Kimo Cornwell (keyboards), Dean Cortez (bass) and Danny Yamamoto (drums).

12/22/79+	51	27		© 1	**Hiroshima**			$12	Arista 4252
11/15/80	72	18		© 2	**Odori**			$12	Arista 9541
8/20/83	142	9		© 3	**Third Generation**		[I]	$10	Epic 38708
11/30/85+	79	45	●	© 4	**Another Place**			$10	Epic 39938
8/15/87	75	32	●	© 5	**Go**			$10	Epic 40679
3/25/89	105	19		© 6	**East**			$10	Epic 45022

All I Want (2)	Echoes (2)	Heavenly Angel (3)	Midtown Higashi (6)	Save Yourself For Me (4)	Touch And Go (4)
Another Place (4)	Even Then (5)	Holidays (1)	Never, Ever (1)	Shinto (2)	Undercover (4)
Come To Me (6)	Fifths (4)	I Do Remember (4)	No. 9 (5)	Stay Away (4)	Warriors (2)
Crusin' J-Town (2)	Fortune Teller (2)	I've Been Here Before (5)	Obon (5)	Streetcorner Paradise (6)	We Are (3)
Da-Da (1)	From The Heart (3)	Kokoro (1)	Odori (2)	Sukoshi Bit (3)	What's It To Ya (4)
Daydreamer (4)	Game, The (4)	Lion Dance (1)	One Wish (4)	Tabo (6)	Why Can't I Love You (5)
Distant Thoughts (3)	Go (5)	Living In America (6)	Ren (3)	Taiko Song (1)	Winds Of Change (Henka Non
Do What You Can (3)	Golden Age (6)	Long Time Love (1)	Roomful Of Mirrors (1)	Thousand Cranes (6)	Nagare) (2)
East (6)	Hawaiian Electric (5)	Long Walks (3)	San Say (3)	311 (5)	You And Me (6)

HIRT, AL ★135★ '64

Born on 11/7/22 in New Orleans. Died of liver failure on 4/27/99 (age 76). Legendary trumpet player. Toured with **Jimmy & Tommy Dorsey**, Ray McKinley and Horace Heidt. Formed own Dixieland Combo (with **Pete Fountain**) in the late 1950s.

1)*Honey In The Horn* 2)*Cotton Candy* 3)*Sugar Lips*

5/15/61	21	32			1 **The Greatest Horn In The World**		[I]	$20	RCA Victor 2366
10/9/61	61	11			2 **Al (He's the King) Hirt and His Band**		[I]	$20	RCA Victor 2354
2/3/62	41	2			3 **Bourbon Street**		[I]	$20	Coral 57389
					PETE FOUNTAIN/AL HIRT				
2/10/62	24	25			4 **Horn A-Plenty**		[I]	$20	RCA Victor 2446
1/19/63	96	7			5 **Trumpet And Strings**		[I]	$20	RCA Victor 2584
3/23/63	44	3		©	6 **Our Man In New Orleans**		[I]	$20	RCA Victor 2607
9/21/63+	3	104	●	©	7 **Honey In The Horn**			$20	RCA Victor 2733
2/29/64	83	9			8 **Beauty And The Beard**			$20	RCA Victor 2690
					AL HIRT/ANN-MARGRET				
5/23/64	6	53	●	©	9 **Cotton Candy**		[I]	$20	RCA Victor 2917
8/22/64	9	48	●	©	10 **Sugar Lips**			$20	RCA Victor 2965
9/26/64	18	31			11 **"Pops" Goes The Trumpet**		[I]	$25	RCA Victor 2729
					AL HIRT/BOSTON POPS/ARTHUR FIEDLER				
1/30/65	13	43	●		12 **The Best Of Al Hirt**		[G-I]	$15	RCA Victor 3309
3/13/65	28	27		©	13 **That Honey Horn Sound**			$15	RCA Victor 3337
7/24/65	47	22			14 **Live At Carnegie Hall**		[I-L]	$15	RCA Victor 3416
					recorded on 4/22/65				
12/11/65	12[X]	8		©	15 **The Sound Of Christmas**		[X]	$15	RCA Victor 3417
					Christmas charts: 12/'65, 57/'66, 48/'67				
2/12/66	39	18			16 **They're Playing Our Song**		[I]	$15	RCA Victor 3492
7/30/66	125	6			17 **The Happy Trumpet**		[I]	$15	RCA Victor 3579
3/18/67	127	5		©	18 **Music To Watch Girls By**		[I]	$15	RCA Victor 3773
2/10/68	116	13			19 **Al Hirt Plays Bert Kaempfert**		[I]	$15	RCA Victor 3917

Afrikaan Beat (19)	Bourbon Street Parade (12)	Cornet Chop Suey (2)	Everybody Loves My Baby (But	Hark! The Herald Angels Sing	I'll Take Romance (19)
Al Di La (7)	Bugler's Holiday (11)	**Cotton Candy** (9,12) 15	My Baby Don't Love Nobody	(medley) (15)	I'm Movin' On (7)
Alley Cat (13)	Butterball (13)	Danke Schoen (19)	But Me) (8)	Hello, Dolly! (9)	I'm On My Way (1)
As Time Goes By (5)	Bye Bye Blues (14,19)	Danny Boy (13)	**Fancy Pants** (13) 47	Here Comes Santa Claus	I've Heard That Song Before
At The Jazz Band Ball (3)	Candy Man Jones (17)	Dear Old Southland (6)	Farewell Blues (3)	(Right Down Santa	(16)
Autumn Leaves (16)	Love Makes The World Go	Deck The Halls (medley) (15)	Fiddler On The Roof (13)	Lane) (medley) (15)	If You Go Away (Ne Me Quitte
Ave Maria (15)	'Round (Theme from Carnival)	Deep Purple (16)	First Noël (medley) (15)	His Girl (18)	Pas) (18)
Baby, It's Cold Outside (8)	(12)	Django's Castle (9)	Flowers And Candy (13)	Holiday For Trumpet (4,12)	It Came Upon A Midnight Clear
Baby Won't You Please Come	Carnival (Love Makes The	Do Nothin' Till You Hear From	Fly Me To The Moon (In Other	How Deep Is The Ocean (How	(medley) (15)
Home (4)	World Go 'Round), Theme	Me (4)	Words) (7)	High Is The Sky) (9)	It's Been A Long, Long Time
Back Home Again In Indiana	From (4)	Down By The Riverside (2,14)	Fools Rush In (5)	I Can't Get Started (7)	(16)
(10)	Carnival Of Venice (11,14)	Dream, Theme From A (7)	Fox, The (17)	I Cried For You (5)	Ja-Da (6)
Bad Man (17)	Cherry Pink And Apple Blossom	East Of The Sun (And West Of	Georgia On My Mind (1)	I Had The Craziest Dream (16)	**Java** (7,11,12,14) 4
Begin The Beguine (1)	White (16)	The Moon) (3)	Girl From Ipanema (10)	I Love Paris (2,12)	Jazz Me Blues (2,3)
Best Man (8,12)	Christmas Song (Merry	Easy Street (4)	Going To Chicago Blues (14)	I Saw Mommy Kissing Santa	Jitterbug Waltz (2)
Big Man (9)	Christmas To You) (15)	Easy To Love (5)	Good King Wenceslas (medley)	Claus (medley) (15)	Joy To The World (medley) (15)
Bill Bailey (8)	Christopher Columbus (2)	Eili, Eili (11)	(15)	I'll Be Seeing You (16)	Just Because (8)
Birth Of The Blues (6)	Clarinet Marmalade (6)	Elmer's Tune (18)	Gypsy In My Soul (14)	I'll Get By (16)	Kansas City (14)
Blow Your Own Horn (18)	Contrary Waltz (13)		Happy Trumpet (17)	I'll Never Smile Again (5)	

HIRT, Al — Cont'd

King's Blues (2)
La Virgen De La Macarena (11)
Lady (19)
Last Date (9)
Laura (2)
Let's Do It (Let's Fall In Love) (1)
Limelight (14)
Little Boy (Little Girl) (8)
Little Gold Ring (17)
Long Walk Home (13)
Lookin' For The Blues (10)
Lost Chord (11)
Love For Sale (14)
Lover Come Back To Me (2)
Ma (He's Making Eyes At Me) (8)
Magic Trumpet (19)
Malibu (7)
Man With A Horn (7)
March Of The Bob Cats (3)
Mardi Gras (17)
Margie (4)
Mas Que Nada (18)
Melissa (9)

Memories Of You (4)
Milano (10)
Moo Moo (9)
Moulin Rouge (Where Is Your Heart), Song From (16)
Music To Watch Girls By (18)
Muskrat Ramble (6)
Mutual Admiration Society (8)
My Baby Just Cares For Me (8)
Nature Boy (18)
New Orleans (6)
New Orleans, My Home Town (10)
Night Life (10)
Night Theme (7)
None But The Lonely Heart (13)
Nutty Jingle Bells (15)
O Come, All Ye Faithful (Adeste Fideles) (medley) (15)
O Holy Night (15)
Oh Dem Golden Slippers (6)
Oh Little Town Of Bethlehem (medley) (15)
Ol' Man River (6)
Old Folks At Home (2)

One O'Clock Jump (2)
Out Of Nowhere (1)
Over The Rainbow (13)
Panama (6)
Paper Doll (16)
Pavanne (11)
Personality (8)
Pink Confetti (10)
Pitty Pat (17)
Poor Butterfly (5,12)
Poupee Brisee (Broken Doll) (10)
Pussy Cat (17)
Red Roses For A Blue Lady (19)
Row, Row, Row (8)
Rudolph, The Red-Nosed Reindeer (15)
Rumpus (4,9)
Sand Pebbles, Theme From The (14)
Santa Claus Is Comin' To Town (15)
September Song (10)
Silent Night (15)

Silver Bells (15)
Six Long Days (Sechs Tage Lang) (18)
Skokiaan (17)
Sleepless Hours (5)
Sleepy Lagoon (5)
Sleigh Ride (15)
Spanish Eyes (19)
Star Dust (13)
Stella By Starlight (1,12)
Stompin' At The Savoy (1)
Stranger In Paradise (5,12)
Strangers In The Night (19)
Sugar Lips (10,12) *30*
Sweet Maria (19)
Sweet Sue - Just You (1)
Swing Low, Sweet Chariot (4)
Swingin' Safari (19)
Syncopated Clock (17)
'Tain't What You Do (8)
Talkin' 'Bout That River (7)
Tansy (7)
Tenderly (10)
Tennessee Waltz (14)
That Old Feeling (15)

There, I've Said It Again (16)
Three Little Words (2)
Till There Was You (4)
To Ava (1)
To Be In Love (7)
Too Late (Trop Tard) (9)
Toy Trumpet (11)
True Love (5)
Trumpet Concerto (11)
Trumpet's Lullaby (11)
12th Street Rag (9)
Twentieth Century Drawing Room (21)
Undecided (1)
Up Above My Head (I Hear Music In The Air) (10,14) *85*
Walk Right In (14)
Walkin' (9)
Walkin' With Mr. Lee (9)
We Three Kings Of Orient Are (medley) (15)
We Wish You A Merry Christmas (medley) (15)
What Child Is This (medley) (15)

What The World Needs Now Is Love (17)
What's New (1)
When I'm Feelin' Kinda Blue (14)
When It's Sleepy Time Down South (6)
When The Saints Go Marching In (6,12)
(Where Is Your Heart) ..see: Moulin Rouge
Wilkommen (Welcome) (18)
Willow Weep For Me (1)
Wolverine Blues (6)
Won't You Come Home Bill Bailey ..see: Bill Bailey
Wonderland By Night (19)
World We Knew (Over And Over) (19)
Yo-Yo (Puppet Song) (18)
You Took Advantage Of Me (13)
You'll Never Know (16)

HITCHCOCK, Robyn, & The Egyptians   '88
Born on 3/3/52 in London. Male rock singer/guitarist. The Egyptians: Andy Metcalfe (bass) and Morris Windsor (drums).

3/5/88	111	15		©	1 Globe Of Frogs			$10	A&M 5182
4/1/89	139	9		©	2 Queen Elvis			$10	A&M 5241

Autumn Sea (2)
Balloon Man (1)
Chinese Bones (1)
Devils Coachman (2)

Flesh Number One (Beatle Dennis) (1)
Freeze (2)
Globe Of Frogs (1)

Knife (2)
Luminous Rose (1)
Madonna Of The Wasps (2)
One Long Pair Of Eyes (2)

Shapes Between Us Turn Into Animals (1)
Sleeping With Your Devil Mask (1)

Superman (2)
Swirling (2)
Tropical Flesh Mandala (1)
Unsettled (1)

Veins Of The Queen (2)
Vibrating (1)
Wax Doll (2)

HI-TEK — see KWELI, Talib

HO, Don, and The Aliis   '67
Born on 8/13/30 in Kakaako, Oahu, Hawaii. Singer/actor. Father of **Hoku**.

3/5/66	117	5			1 Don Ho-Again!	[L]		$15	Reprise 6186
12/17/66+	15	50			2 Tiny Bubbles			$15	Reprise 6232
5/27/67	115	5			3 East Coast/West Coast	[L]		$15	Reprise 6244
3/22/69	199	3			4 Suck 'Em Up	[L]		$15	Reprise 6331
8/23/69	162	6	●	©	5 Don Ho-Greatest Hits!	[G]		$15	Reprise 6357
10/18/69	188	2			6 The Don Ho TV Show	[TV]		$15	Reprise 6367

Ain't No Big Thing (1,5)
All That's Left Is The Lemon Tree (3)
Aloha Means (4)
Aquarius (medley) (6)
Beautiful Kauai (2,5)
Beyond The Reef (4)
Born Free (3)
Bring Back The Good Times (6)
Cycles (6)
Day Is Done (6)
Didn't We (4)

Do I Love You? (3)
Down By The Shack, By The Sea (4,5)
E Lei Ka Lei Lei (Beach Party Song) (5)
Following Sea (1,5)
Geev'um (2)
Gentle On My Mind (6)
Girls Of The Island (2)
Goin' Out Of My Head (3)
Hang On Sloopy (1)
Happy Me (2)

Hawaii (4)
I Love The Simple Folk (2)
I Wish They Didn't Mean Goodbye (1)
I'll Remember You (5)
I'm A Drifter (6)
If I Had It To Do Over Again (1)
Kanaka Pete (4)
Lahaina Luna (1)
Let The Sunshine In (medley) (6)
Lights Of Home (2)

Lover's Prayer (1,3,5)
Macao (3)
Maka Hilahila (1)
Molokai Nui Ahina (4)
More I Know About You (4)
My Way (6)
Night Life (1,5)
One Paddle, Two Paddle (2,3)
Pearly Shells (2)
Please Wait For Me (2)
Remembering (4)
Sands Of Waikiki (4,6)

She's Gone Again (I'll Remember You) (2,3)
Soon It's Gonna Rain (3)
Straight Life (6)
Suck 'Em Up (1)
Sunny Days, Starry Nights (Ke La La) (4)
Sweet Someone (1,5)
This Could Be The Start Of Something (3)
This Town (3)
Tiny Bubbles (2,3,5) *57*

Turn Around, Look At Me (6)
Ukelele Talk (6)
Welcome Pretty Lady (4)
What Now My Love (3)
Windward Side (Of The Island) (5)
You Are Beautiful (1)
You May Go (1)
You'll Never Go Home (2)
You're Gonna Hear From Me (4)
Young Land (2)

HODGES, Johnny, & Wild Bill Davis   '65
Jazz saxophonist Hodges was born on 7/25/06 in Cambridge, Massachusetts. Died of a heart attack on 5/11/70 (age 63). Jazz organist Davis was born on 11/24/18 in Glasgow, Missouri; raised in Parsons, Kansas. Died of a stroke on 8/17/95 (age 76).

2/20/65	148	2			Blue Rabbit	[I]		$30	Verve 8599

Blues O'Mighty
Creole Love Call
Fiddler's Fancy

I Let A Song Go Out Of My Heart
Mud Pie

Satin Doll
Tangerine

Things Ain't What They Used To Be
Wisteria

HODGSON, Roger   '84
Born on 5/21/50 in London. Lead singer of **Supertramp**.

10/27/84	46	22		©	1 In The Eye Of The Storm			$10	A&M 5004
10/31/87	163	6		©	2 Hai Hai			$10	A&M 5112

Desert Love (2)
Give Me Love, Give Me Life (1)
Had A Dream (Sleeping With The Enemy) (1) *48*

Hai Hai (2)
Hooked On A Problem (1)
House On The Corner (2)
I'm Not Afraid (1)

In Jeopardy (2)
Land Ho (2)
London (2)
Lovers In The Wind (1)

My Magazine (2)
Only Because Of You (1)
Puppet Dance (2)
Right Place (2)

Who's Afraid (2)
You Make Me Love You (2)

HOFFS, Susanna   '91
Born on 1/17/59 in Newport Beach, California. Lead singer of **The Bangles**. Starred in the 1987 movie *The Allnighter*. Her mother is movie director Tamara Hoffs. Married movie director Jay Roach on 4/17/93.

2/16/91	83	11		©	When You're A Boy			$10	Columbia 46076

Boys Keep Swinging
It's Lonely Out Here

Made Of Stone
My Side Of The Bed *30*

No Kind Of Love
Only Love

So Much For Love
Something New

That's Why Girls Cry
This Time

Unconditional Love
Wishing On Telstar

HOKU   '00
Born Hoku Ho on 6/10/81 in Oahu, Hawaii. Daughter of **Don Ho**.

5/20/00	151	3		©	Hoku			$10	Geffen 490646

Another Dumb Blonde *27*
Every Time

How Do I Feel (The Burrito Song)

I'm Scared
In The First Place

Just Enough
Nothing In This World

Oxygen
We Will Follow The Sun

What You Need
You First Believed

HOLE '98

Rock group formed in Los Angeles: Courtney Love (vocals, guitar), Eric Erlandson (guitar), Kristen Pfaff (bass) and Patty Schemel (drums). Love acted in several movies; married to Kurt Cobain (of **Nirvana**) from 2/24/92 until his death on 4/8/94. Pfaff was found dead in her bathtub on 6/16/94 (age 27). Melissa Auf Der Maur replaced Pfaff.

4/30/94+	52	68	▲	©	1 **Live Through This**			$10	DGC 24631
10/14/95	172	2		©	2 **Ask For It**	[E-M]		$10	Caroline 1470
					recordings from 1991-92				
9/26/98	9	41	▲	©	3 **Celebrity Skin**			$10	DGC 25164

Asking For It (1)
Awful (3)
Boys On The Radio (3)
Celebrity Skin (3) *85*
Credit In The Straight World (1)

Doll Parts (1,2) *58*
Drown Soda (2)
Dying (3)
Forming (medley) (2)
Gutless (1)

Heaven Tonight (3)
Hit So Hard (3)
Hot Chocolate Boy (medley) (2)
I Think That I Would Die (1)
Jennifer's Body (1)

Malibu (3) *81*
Miss World (1)
Northern Star (3)
Over The Edge (3)
Pale Blue Eyes (2)

Petals (3)
Playing Your Song (3)
Plump (1)
Reasons To Be Beautiful (3)
Rock Star (1)

She Walks On Me (1)
Softer, Softest (1)
Use Once & Destroy (3)
Violet (1,2)

HOLIDAY, Billie '73

Born Eleanor Gough on 4/7/15 in Philadelphia. Died on 7/17/59 (age 44). Legendary jazz singer. Nicknamed "Lady Day." Subject of the 1972 movie *Lady Sings The Blues* starring **Diana Ross**. Won Grammy's Lifetime Achievement Award in 1987. Inducted into the Rock and Roll Hall of Fame in 2000 as an early influence.

12/23/72+	85	21			1 **The Billie Holiday Story**	[K]		$20	Decca 161 [2]
					recordings from 1944-50				
1/13/73	108	16			2 **Strange Fruit**	[K]		$15	Atlantic 1614
					recordings from 1939 and 1944				
2/24/73	135	9			3 **The Original Recordings**	[K]		$15	Columbia 32060
					recordings from 1935-58				
2/10/01	174	2		©	4 **Ken Burns Jazz - The Definitive Billie Holiday**	[K-TV]		$10	Verve 549081

Ain't Nobody's Business If I Do (1)
All Of Me (3)
As Time Goes By (2)
Autumn In New York (4)
Baby Get Lost (1)
(Billie's Blues) I Love My Man (2)
Crazy He Calls Me (1)
Deep Song (1)
Do Your Duty (1)

Don't Explain (1,4)
Easy Living (1)
Embraceable You (2)
Fine And Mellow (2,4)
Gimme A Pigfoot And A Bottle Of Beer (1)
Gloomy Sunday (3,4)
God Bless The Child (1,3,4)
Good Morning Heartache (1,4)
How Am I To Know (2)
I Cover The Waterfront (2,4)

I Cried For You (3,4)
(I Got A Man Crazy For Me) He's Funny That Way (2)
I Gotta Right To Sing The Blues (2)
I'll Be Seeing You (2)
I'll Get By (2)
I'll Look Around (1)
I'm Yours (2)
Keeps On Rainin' (1)
Lady Sings The Blues (4)

Lover Come Back To Me (2)
Lover Man (Oh, Where Can You Be?) (1,4)
Man I Love (3)
Me, Myself And I (4)
Mean To Me (3)
Miss Brown To You (3)
My Man (1,3)
My Old Flame (2)
No More (1)
Now Or Never (1)

On The Sunny Side Of The Street (2)
Porgy (1)
Solitude (1,4)
Some Other Spring (4)
Somebody's On My Mind (1)
Strange Fruit (2,4)
That Ole Devil Called Love (1)
Them There Eyes (1,3)
There Is No Greater Love (1)
This Is Heaven To Me (1)

Trav'lin' Light (4)
What A Little Moonlight Can Do (3,4)
Without Your Love (4)
Yesterdays (2,4)
You're My Thrill (1)
You've Changed (3,4)

HOLIDAY EXPRESS '01

All-volunteer, nonprofit, nonsectarian organization, whose royalties go toward helping the needy.

| 1/20/01 | 16ˣ | 1 | | © | **Greatest Hits** | [X] | | $10 | Oglio 89120 |

All Alone On Christmas
Disco Santa
Do You Hear What I Hear?
Feliz Navidad

Frosty The Snowman
Have Yourself A Merry Little Christmas

Jesus Was Born On Christmas Day
One Little Christmas Tree

Santa Bring My Baby Back (To Me)
Silent Night
Sleigh Ride

HOLLAND, Amy '80

Pop singer. Daughter of country singer Esmereldy and opera singer Harry Boersma. Married to **Michael McDonald**.

| 8/30/80 | 146 | 14 | | | **Amy Holland** | | | $12 | Capitol 12071 |

Don't Kid Yourself
Forgetting You

Here In The Light
Holding On To You

How Do I Survive *22*
I'm Wondering

Looking For Love
Show Me The Way Home

Stars
Strengthen My Love

HOLLIDAY, Jennifer '83

Born on 10/19/60 in Riverside, Texas. R&B singer/actress. Appeared in several Broadway musicals.

10/22/83	31	22		©	1 **Feel My Soul**			$12	Geffen 4014
9/14/85	110	14			2 **Say You Love Me**			$12	Geffen 24073
11/9/91	184	1		©	3 **I'm On Your Side**			$10	Arista 18578

Change Is Gonna Come (1)
Come Sunday (2)
Dream With Your Name On It (3)
Dreams Never Die (2)
Guilty (3)

Hard Times For Lovers (2) *69*
He's A Pretender (2)
I Am Love (1) *49*
I Am Ready Now (1)
I Fall Apart (3)
I Rest My Case (2)

I'm On Your Side (3)
Is It Love (3)
It Will Haunt Me (3)
It's In There (3)
Just A Matter Of Time (2)
Just For A While (1)

Just Let Me Wait (1)
Love Stories (3)
More 'N' More (3)
My Sweet Delight (1)
No Frills Love (2) *87*
Raise The Roof (3)

Say You Love Me (2)
Shine A Light (1)
This Day (1)
This Game Of Love (I'm Never Coming Down) (1)
What Kind Of Love Is This? (2)

You're The One (1)

★364★ HOLLIES, The '67

Pop-rock group from Manchester, England: Allan Clarke (vocals), **Graham Nash** and Tony Hicks (guitars), Eric Haydock (bass) and Bobby Elliott (drums). Haydock left in 1966, replaced by Bernie Calvert (first heard on "Bus Stop"). Nash left in December 1968 to join **David Crosby** and **Stephen Stills** in new trio, replaced by Terry Sylvester, formerly of **The Swinging Blue Jeans**. Shuffling personnel since then. Clarke, Nash, Hicks and Elliott regrouped briefly in 1983.

1)The Hollies' Greatest Hits 2)Distant Light 3)Hollies

2/12/66	145	3			1 **Hear! Here!**			$50	Imperial 12299
10/22/66	75	11			2 **Bus Stop**			$40	Imperial 12330
2/25/67	91	8			3 **Stop! Stop! Stop!**			$40	Imperial 12339
6/3/67	11	40			4 **The Hollies' Greatest Hits**	[G]		$40	Imperial 12350
8/5/67	43	14		©	5 **Evolution**			$30	Epic 26315
4/4/70	32	14			6 **He Ain't Heavy, He's My Brother**			$20	Epic 26538
2/13/71	183	2		©	7 **Moving Finger**			$20	Epic 30255
7/15/72	21	21		©	8 **Distant Light**			$20	Epic 30958
1/27/73	84	12			9 **Romany**			$15	Epic 31992
10/20/73	157	7		©	10 **The Hollies' Greatest Hits**	[G]		$15	Epic 32061
5/11/74	28	23	●	©	11 **Hollies**			$15	Epic 32574
3/29/75	123	10			12 **Another Night**			$15	Epic 33387
7/9/83	90	9			13 **What Goes Around**			$12	Atlantic 80076

Air That I Breathe (11) *6*
Another Night (12) *71*
Baby That's All (2)
Blue In The Morning (9)
Bus Stop (2,4,10) *5*
Cable Car (8)

Candy Man (2)
Carrie-Anne (5,10) *9*
Casualty (13)
Clown (3)
Confessions Of A Mind (7)

Courage Of Your Convictions (9)
Crusader (3)
Day That Curly Billy Shot Down Crazy Sam McGee (11)
Dear Eloise (10) *50*

Delaware Taggett And The Outlaw Boys (9)
Do You Believe In Love? (6)
Don't Even Think About Changing (3)
Don't Give Up Easily (6)

Don't Let Me Down (11)
Don't Run And Hide (2)
Down On The Run (11)
Down River (9)
Down The Line (1)
Falling Calling (11)

Frightened Lady (7)
Games We Play (5)
Gasoline Alley Bred (7)
Give Me Time (12)
Goodbye Tomorrow (6)

385

HOLLIES, The — Cont'd

Have You Ever Loved Somebody (5)
Having A Good Time (13)
He Ain't Heavy, He's My Brother (6,10) **7**
Heading For A Fall (5)
Here I Go Again (4)
High Classed (3)
Hold On (8)
I Am A Rock (2)
I Can't Let Go (4) **42**
I Got What I Want (13)
I'm Alive (1,4)
I'm Down (12)
I've Been Wrong (1)
If The Lights Go Out (13)
Isn't It Nice (7)
It's A Shame, It's A Game (11)
It's You (3)

Jesus Was A Crossmaker (9)
Just One Look (4,10,13) **44**
King Midas In Reverse (10) **51**
Lady Please (7)
Lawdy Miss Clawdy (1)
Life I've Led (8)
Little Girl (7)
Little Love (2)
Little Thing Like Love (8)
Lonely Hobo Lullabye (12)
Long Cool Woman (In A Black Dress) (8,10) **2**
Long Dark Road (8,10) **26**
Look At Life (6)
Look Out Johnny (There's A Monkey On Your Back) (12)
Look Through Any Window (1,4,10) **32**
Look What We've Got (8)

Love Makes The World Go Round (11)
Lullaby To Tim (5)
Lucy (12)
Magic Woman Touch (9) **60**
Man Without A Heart (7)
Marigold Gloria Swansong (7)
Memphis (4)
Mickey's Monkey (2)
My Life Is Over With You (6)
On A Carousel (4,10) **11**
Oriental Sadness (I'll Never Trust In Anybody No More) (2)
Out On The Road (11)
Pay You Back With Interest (3,4,10) **28**
Peculiar Situation (3)
Perfect Lady Housewife (7)
Pick Up The Pieces Again (11)

Please Let Me Please (6)
Please Sign Your Letters (6)
Promised Land (8)
Pull Down The Blind (8)
Put Yourself In My Place (1)
Rain On The Window (5)
Reflections Of A Time Long Past (6)
Romany (9)
Rubber Lucy (11)
Sandy (12) **85**
Say You'll Be Mine (13)
Second Hand Hangups (12)
Slow Down (7)
So Lonely (1)
Someone Else's Eyes (13)
Something Ain't Right (13)
Stop In The Name Of Love (13) **29**

Stop Right There (5)
Stop Stop Stop (3,4,10) **7**
Survival Of The Fittest (7)
Suspicious Look In Your Eyes (3)
Sweet Little Sixteen (2)
Take My Love And Run (13)
Tell Me To My Face (3,4)
That's My Desire (1)
Then The Heartaches Begin (5)
Time Machine Jive (12)
To Do With Love (8)
Too Many People (1)
Too Young To Be Married (7)
Touch (9)
Transatlantic Westbound Jet (11)
Very Last Day (1)
We're Through (2)

What Went Wrong (3)
What's Wrong With The Way I Live (3)
Whatcha Gonna Do About It (2,4)
When I Come Home To You (1)
Why Didn't You Believe (6)
Won't We Feel Good That Morning (9)
Words Don't Come Easy (9)
Ye Olde Toffee Shoppe (5)
You Gave Me Life (With That Look In Your Eyes) (12)
You Know He Did (2)
You Know The Score (8)
You Love 'Cos You Like It (6)
You Must Believe Me (1)
You Need Love (5)

HOLLISTER, Dave '99
Born in Chicago. Former member of **Blackstreet**.

6/12/99	34	28	●	©	1	Ghetto Hymns		$10	Def Squad 50047
12/9/00	49	28	●	©	2	Chicago '85... The Movie		$10	Def Squad 50278

Baby Mama Drama (1)
Call On Me (1)
Came In The Door Pimpin' (1)
Can't Stay (1) **84**
Destiny (2)

Doin' Wrong (2)
Don't Take My Girl Away (2)
Ghetto Hymns (1)
I Don't Want To Be A Hustler (2)

I'm Not Complete (2)
I'm Sorry (1)
It's Alright (1)
Keep Forgettin' (1)
Keep On Lovin' (2)

Missin' You (1)
My Favorite Girl (1) **39**
My Feelin's (1)
On The Side (2)
One Woman Man (2) **44**

Program, The (1)
Respect 2 Him (1)
Round And Round (1)
Take Care Of Home (2)
We've Come Too Far (2)

Woman Will (2)
Yo Baby's Daddy (2)
You Can't Say (2)

HOLLOWAY, Loleatta '78
Born on 11/11/46 in Chicago. Female disco singer.

12/2/78	187	2		Queen Of The Night		$12	Gold Mind 9501

Catch Me On The Rebound
Good Good Feeling

I May Not Be There When You Want Me (But I'm Right On Time)

I'm In Love
Mama Don't, Papa Won't
Only You 87

Two Sides To Every Story
You Light Up My Life

HOLLY, Buddy/The Crickets '59
Born Charles Hardin Holley on 9/7/36 in Lubbock, Texas. One of rock and roll's most original and innovative performers. In February 1957, Holly assembled his backing group, **The Crickets**: Niki Sullivan (rhythm guitar), Joe B. Mauldin (bass) and Jerry Ivan Allison (drums). Signed to Brunswick and Coral labels (subsidiaries of Decca Records). Because of contract arrangements, all Brunswick records were released as The Crickets, and all Coral records were released as Buddy Holly. Holly split from The Crickets in Fall 1958. Holly (age 22), **Ritchie Valens** and the Big Bopper were killed in a plane crash near Mason City, Iowa, on 2/3/59. Gary Busey starred in the 1978 biographical movie *The Buddy Holly Story*. Holly was inducted into the Rock and Roll Hall of Fame in 1986. Also see **Bobby Vee**.

4/27/59	11	181	●	1	The Buddy Holly Story	[G]	$200	Coral 57279

includes 4 songs with **The Crickets**

3/16/63	40	17		2	Reminiscing	[K]	$100	Coral 57426

BUDDY HOLLY
instrumental backing by **The Fireballs** dubbed in (1962)

8/5/78	55	12	●	3	Buddy Holly/The Crickets 20 Golden Greats	C:#35/12 [G]	$20	MCA 3040

Baby, Won't You Come Out Tonight (3)
Because I Love You (2)
Bo Diddley (2,3)
Brown Eyed Handsome Man (2,3)
Changing All Those Changes (2)

Early In The Morning (1) **32**
Everyday (1,3)
Heartbeat (1,3) **82**
I'm Gonna Set My Foot Down (2)
It Doesn't Matter Anymore (1,3) **13**

It's Not My Fault (2)
It's So Easy (1,3)
Listen To Me (3)
Maybe Baby (1,3) **17**
Not Fade Away (3)
Oh, Boy! (1,3) **10**
Peggy Sue (1,3) **3**

Peggy Sue Got Married (3)
Raining In My Heart (1,3) **88**
Rave On (1,3) **37**
Reminiscing (2)
Rock-A-Bye-Rock (2)
Slippin' And Slidin' (2)
That'll Be The Day (1,3) **1**

Think It Over (1,3) **27**
True Love Ways (3)
Wait Till The Sun Shines Nellie (2)
Well...Alright (3)
Wishing (3)
Words Of Love (3)

HOLLY & THE ITALIANS '81
Rock group from Los Angeles: Holly Vincent (vocals, guitar), Mark Sidgwick (bass) and Steve Young and Mike Osborn (drums).

7/11/81	177	3		The Right To Be Italian		$12	Virgin 37359

Baby Gets It All
Do You Say Love

I Wanna Go Home
Just For Tonight

Just Young
Means To A Den

Miles Away
Rock Against Romance

Tell That Girl To Shut Up
Youth Coup

HOLLYRIDGE STRINGS, The '64
Arranged and conducted by Stu Phillips, later of the **Golden Gate Strings**.

6/20/64	15	25		1	The Beatles Song Book	[I]	$20	Capitol 2116
10/10/64	82	12		2	The Beach Boys Song Book	[I]	$20	Capitol 2156
2/13/65	144	3		3	Hits Made Famous By Elvis Presley	[I]	$20	Capitol 2221
4/24/65	136	3		4	The Nat King Cole Song Book	[I]	$20	Capitol 2310
6/4/66	142	3		5	The New Beatles Song Book	[I]	$20	Capitol 2429

All My Loving (1) **93**
And I Love Her (5)
Answer Me, My Love (4)
Are You Lonesome Tonight? (3)
Ask Me (3)
Bossa Nova, Baby (3)
Can't Buy Me Love (1)
Can't Help Falling In Love (3)
Christmas Song (Merry Christmas To You) (4)
Day Tripper (5)

Do You Want To Know A Secret? (1)
Don't Be Cruel (3)
Don't Worry Baby (2)
From Me To You (1)
Fun, Fun, Fun (2)
Girl (5)
Girls On The Beach (2)
Good Luck Charm (3)
Heartbreak Hotel (3)
Help! (5)

I Get Around (2)
I Saw Her Standing There (1)
I Want To Hold Your Hand (1)
In My Room (2)
It's Only A Paper Moon (4)
Kiss Me Quick (3)
(Let Me Be Your) Teddy Bear (3)
Little Saint Nick (2)
Love (4)
Love Me Do (1)

Love Me Tender (3)
Michelle (5)
Mona Lisa (4)
Nature Boy (4)
Night Before (5)
Norwegian Wood (This Bird Has Flown) (5)
Nowhere Man (5)
P.S. I Love You (1)
Please Please Me (1)
Pretend (4)

Ramblin' Rose (4)
Return To Sender (3)
She Knows Me Too Well (2)
She Loves You (1)
Shut Down (2)
Somewhere Along The Way (4)
Surfin' U.S.A. (2)
Taste Of Honey (1)
Those Lazy-Hazy-Crazy Days Of Summer (4)
Ticket To Ride (5)

Too Young (4)
Unforgettable (4)
Warmth Of The Sun (2)
We Can Work It Out (5)
Wendy (2)
Yesterday (5)

HOLLYWOOD STUDIO ORCHESTRA, The '61
Conducted by Mitchell Powell.

1/23/61	23	17		Exodus	[I]	$25	United Artists 6123

Ari
Brothers, The
Conspiracy

Dawn
Escape
Exodus, Theme Of

Fight For Peace
Fight For Survival
Hatikvah

In Jerusalem
Karen
Prison Break

Summer In Cyprus
Valley Of Jezreel

HOLMAN, Eddie '70
Born on 6/3/46 in Norfolk, Virginia. R&B singer/songwriter.

2/21/70 75 13 © I Love You .... $30 ABC 701

Am I A Loser	Four Walls	I Cried	I'll Be Forever Loving You	Let Me Into Your Life	Since My Love Has Gone
Don't Stop Now 48	**Hey There Lonely Girl** 2	I Love You	It's All In The Game	**Since I Don't Have You** flip	

HOLMES, Cecil, Soulful Sounds '73
Born in New York City. R&B songwriter/producer. Former executive with Buddah record label.

4/28/73 141 10 The Black Motion Picture Experience .... [I] $15 Buddah 5129

Across 110th Street	Ben	Lady Sings The Blues, Love	Shaft	Superfly	Trouble Man (medley)
Also Sprach Zarathustra (2001)	Freddie's Dead	Theme From	Slaughter	T Stands For Trouble (medley)	

HOLMES, Clint '73
Born on 5/9/46 in Bournemouth, Dorset, England; raised in Farnham, England. Pop singer.

5/26/73 122 12 Playground In My Mind .... $15 Epic 32269

Come Hell Or High Water	Me And America	Neither One Of Us (Wants To	**Playground In My Mind** 2	What Will My Mary Say
Killing Me Softly With His Song	Miss Lady Loretta	Be The First To Say	Sneaking Around Corners	
Like The Fellow Once Said		Goodbye)	There's No Future In My Future	

HOLMES, Jake '70
Born on 12/28/39 in San Francisco. Singer/songwriter.

11/14/70 135 6 So Close, So Very Far To Go .... $15 Polydor 4034

Django & Friend	I Remember Sunshine	Little Comfort	Population	So Very Far To Go
Her Song	I Sure Like Her Song	Paris Song	**So Close** 49	We're All We've Got

HOLMES, LeRoy '67
Born Alvin Holmes on 9/22/13 in Pittsburgh. Died on 7/27/86 (age 72). Orchestra conductor/arranger.

9/9/67 42 29 1 For A Few Dollars More and other Motion Picture Themes .... [I] $20 United Artists 6608
6/1/68 138 8 2 The Good, The Bad And The Ugly and other Motion Picture Themes .... [I] $20 United Artists 6633

Aces High (1)	Finale (1)	Here We Go Round The	Thoroughly Modern Millie (2)	Valley Of The Dolls, Theme
Around The World (2)	Fistful Of Dollars (1)	Mulberry Bush (2)	To Sir, With Love (2)	From (2)
Bonnie And Clyde (2)	For A Few Dollars More (1)	Live For Life (Vivre Pour Vivre)	Tom Jones (1)	Vice Of Killing (1)
Camelot (2)	Good, The Bad And The Ugly	(2)	Topkapi (1)	Viva Maria (1)
Doctor Dolittle (2)	(2)	Sixty Seconds To What (1)	Train, Theme From The (1)	Zorba The Greek, Theme From
Down Here On The Ground (2)	Goodbye Colonel (1)	Tara Theme (2)		(1)

HOLMES, Richard "Groove" '66
Born on 5/2/31 in Camden, New Jersey. Died of cancer on 6/29/91 (age 60). Jazz organist.

5/14/66 89 26 © 1 Soul Message .... [I] $20 Prestige 7435
10/29/66 143 3 © 2 Living Soul .... [I-L] $20 Prestige 7468
12/24/66+ 134 6 © 3 Misty .... $20 Prestige 7485

Blues For Yna Yna (2)	Groove's Groove (1)	On The Street Where You Live	Song For My Father (1)	There Will Never Be Another	**What Now My Love** (3) 96
Dahoud (1)	Living Soul (2)	(3)	Soul Message (1)	You (3)	
Gemini (2)	**Misty** (1,3) 44	Over The Rainbow (2)	Strangers In The Night (3)	Things We Did Last Summer	
Girl From Ipanema (2)	More I See You (3)	Shadow Of Your Smile (3)	Summertime (3)	(1)	

HOLMES, Rupert '80
Born on 2/24/47 in Northwich, Cheshire, England; raised in Manhattan, New York. Pop singer/songwriter. Wrote the Broadway musical Drood.

11/10/79+ 33 31 ● © Partners In Crime .... $12 Infinity 9020

Answering Machine 32	Escape (The Pina Colada	Get Outta Yourself	In You I Trust	Nearsighted	People That You Never Get To
Drop It	Song) 1	Him 6	Lunch Hour	Partners In Crime	Love

HOMBRES, The '67
Rock group from Memphis: B.B. Cunningham (vocals, organ), Gary McEwen (guitar), Jerry Masters (bass) and Johnny Hunter (drums). Hunter committed suicide in February 1976 (age 34). Cunningham's brother, Bill, was a member of **The Box Tops**.

12/9/67 180 4 Let It Out (Let It All Hang Out) .... $30 Verve Forecast 3036

Am I High	It's A Gas	Little 2 Plus 2	Sorry 'Bout That	
Gloria	**Let It Out (Let It All Hang**	Mau Mau Mau	This Little Girl	
Hey Little Girl	**Out)** 12	So Sad	Ya Ya	

HONDELLS, The '64
Producer Gary Usher recorded various studio musicians in Southern California under different group names. "Little Honda" featured Usher, Chuck Girard (vocals), **Glen Campbell** and Richie Podolor (guitars), Hal Blaine (drums) and Ritchie Burns (backing vocals). Usher died of cancer on 5/25/90 (age 51).

11/28/64 119 4 Go Little Honda .... $50 Mercury 60940

Black Boots And Bikes	Guy Without Wheels	Hon-da Beach Party	**Little Honda** 9	Ridin' Trails	Two Wheel Show Stopper
Death Valley Run	Haulin' Honda	Hot Rod High	Mean Streak	Rip's Bike	Wild One

HONEYCOMBS, The '65
Pop-rock group from London: Dennis D'ell (vocals), Allan Ward and Martin Murray (guitars), John Lantree (bass) and his sister Ann "Honey" Lantree (drums).

1/2/65 147 2 Here Are The Honeycombs .... $50 Interphon 88001

Color Slide	I Want To Be Free	Leslie Anne	Once You Know	This Too Shall Pass Away
Have I The Right? 5	It Ain't Necessarily So	Me From You	She's Too Way Out	Without You It Is Night
How The Mighty Have Fallen	Just A Face In The Crowd	Nice While It Lasted	That's The Way	

HONEY CONE, The '72
R&B vocal trio from Los Angeles: Carolyn Willis, Edna Wright (sister of Darlene Love) and Shellie Clark.

6/19/71 137 8 1 Sweet Replies .... $15 Hot Wax 706
12/11/71+ 72 20 2 Soulful Tapestry .... $15 Hot Wax 707
9/23/72 189 4 3 Love, Peace & Soul .... $15 Hot Wax 713

Ace In The Hole (3)	Don't Count Your Chickens	My Mind's On Leaving, But My	**Sittin' On A Time Bomb**	**Want Ads** (1,2) 1	You Made Me Come To You (1)
All The King's Horses (All The	(Before They Hatch) (2)	Heart Won't Let Me Go (1)	**(Waitin' For The Hurt To**	We Belong Together (1)	
King's Men) (2)	Don't Send Me An Invitation (3)	O-O-O Baby, Baby (3)	**Come)** (3) 96	When Will It End (1)	
Are You Man Enough, Are You	Feeling's Gone (1)	**One Monkey Don't Stop No**	Stay In My Corner (3)	Who's It Gonna Be (2)	
Strong Enough (1)	How Does It Feel (2)	**Show Part I** (2) 15	**Stick-Up** (2) 11	Who's Lovin' You (3)	
Blessed Be Our Love (1)	I Lost My Rainbow (3)	One Monkey Don't Stop No	Sunday Morning People (3)	Woman Can't Live By Bread	
Day I Found Myself (1,2) 23	Innocent 'Til Proven Guilty (3)	Show Part II (2)	Take Me With You (1)	Alone (3)	
Deaf, Blind, Paralyzed (1)	Little More (2)		V.I.P. (2)	Woman's Prayer (3)	

387

HONEYDRIPPERS, The   '84

All-star rock group: **Robert Plant** (vocals), **Jimmy Page** and **Jeff Beck** (guitars), and Nile Rodgers (bass). Plant and Page are from **Led Zeppelin** and Rodgers is from **Chic**.

| 10/20/84 | 4 | 31 | ▲ | © | Volume One | [M] | $10 | Es Paranza 90220 |

I Get A Thrill · I Got A Woman · **Rockin' At Midnight** 25 · Sea Of Love 3 · Young Boy Blues

HONEYMOON SUITE   '86

Rock group from Toronto: Johnnie Dee (vocals), Dermot Grehan (guitar), Ray Coburn (keyboards), Garry Lalonde (bass) and Dave Betts (drums). Coburn left in 1987, replaced by Rob Preuss.

8/25/84	60	17		© 1	Honeymoon Suite	$10	Warner 25098
3/15/86	61	35		© 2	The Big Prize	$10	Warner 25293
5/14/88	86	10		© 3	Racing After Midnight	$10	Warner 25652

All Along You Knew (2) · Bad Attitude (2) · Burning In Love (1) · Cold Look (3) · Face To Face (1) · Fast Company (3) · **Feel It Again** (2) 34 · Funny Business (1) · Heart On Fire (1) · It's Over Now (3) · It's Your Heart (1) · Lethal Weapon (3) · Long Way Back (3) · Lookin' Out For Number One (3) · Lost And Found (2) · **Love Changes Everything** (3) 91 · Love Fever (3) · **New Girl Now** (1) 57 · Now That You Got Me (1) · Once The Feeling (2) · One By One (2) · Other Side Of Midnight (3) · Stay In The Light (1) · Take My Hand (2) · Tears On The Page (3) · Turn My Head (1) · Wave Babies (1) · **What Does It Take** (2) 52 · Words In The Wind (2) · Wounded (2)

HOODOO GURUS   '89

Pop-rock group from Sydney, Australia: Dave Faulkner (vocals), Brad Shepherd (guitar), Clyde Bramley (bass) and Mark Kingsmill (drums). Rick Grossman (of the **Divinyls**) replaced Bramley in 1989.

5/10/86	140	7		© 1	Mars Needs Guitars!	$10	Elektra 60485
5/2/87	120	13		© 2	Blow Your Cool!	$10	Elektra 60728
8/12/89	101	15		© 3	Magnum Cum Louder	$10	RCA 9781
5/18/91	172	1		© 4	Kinky	$10	RCA 3009

All The Way (3) · Another World (3) · Axe Grinder (3) · Baby Can Dance (Parts II-IV) (3) · Bittersweet (1) · Brainscan (4) · Castles In The Air (4) · Come Anytime (3) · Come On (2) · Death Defying (3) · Death In The Afternoon (3) · Desiree (4) · Dressed In Black (4) · Glamourpuss (3) · Good Times (2) · Hallucination (3) · Hayride To Hell (3) · Head In The Sand (4) · Hell For Leather (2) · I Don't Know Anything (3) · I Don't Mind (4) · I Was The One (3) · In The Middle Of The Land (3) · In The Wild (1) · Like Wow - Wipeout (1) · Mars Needs Guitars! (1) · Miss Freelove '69 (4) · My Caravan (2) · On My Street (2) · 1000 Miles Away (4) · Other Side Of Paradise (1) · Out That Door (2) · Party Machine (2) · Place In The Sun (4) · Poison Pen (1) · Shadow Me (3) · She (1) · Show Some Emotion (1) · Something's Coming (4) · Too Much Fun (4) · What's My Scene (2) · Where Nowhere Is (2) · Where's That Hit? (3)

HOOKER, John Lee   '90

Born on 8/22/17 in Clarksdale, Mississippi. Died on 6/21/2001 (age 83). Legendary blues singer/guitarist. Inducted into the Rock and Roll Hall of Fame in 1991.

| 2/27/71 | 73 | 16 | | © 1 | Hooker 'N Heat | $20 | Liberty 35002 [2] |

CANNED HEAT & JOHN LEE HOOKER

3/27/71	126	13		© 2	Endless Boogie	$20	ABC 720 [2]
3/18/72	130	6		© 3	Never Get Out Of These Blues Alive	$15	ABC 736
10/7/89+	62	38		© 4	The Healer	$10	Chameleon 74808
9/28/91	101	11		© 5	Mr. Lucky	$10	Charisma 91724
3/11/95	135	8		© 6	Chill Out	$10	Pointblank 40107
3/22/97	163	3		© 7	Don't Look Back	$10	Pointblank 42771

Ain't No Big Thing (7) · Alimonia Blues (1) · Annie Mae (6) · Baby Lee (4) · Backstabbers (5) · Blues Before Sunrise (7) · Boogie Chillen No. 2 (1) · Boogie With The Hook (3) · Bottle Up And Go (1) · Bumblebee, Bumblebee (3) · Burning Hell (1) · Chill Out (Things Gonna Change) (6) · Country Boy (3) · Crawlin' Kingsnake (5) · Cuttin' Out (4) · Deep Blue Sea (6) · Dimples (7) · Doin' The Shout (2) · Don't Look Back (7) · Drifter (1) · Endless Boogie, Parts 27 And 28 (2) · Father Was A Jockey (5) · Feelin' Is Gone (1) · Frisco Blues (7) · Good 'Un ..see: (I Got) A Healer, The (4) · Healing Game (7) · Highway 13 (5) · Hit The Road (3) · House Rent Boogie (2) · I Cover The Waterfront (5) · I Don't Need No Steam Heat (2) · (I Got) A Good 'Un (1) · I Got My Eyes On You (1) · I Love You Honey (7) · I Want To Hug You (5) · I'm In The Mood (1) · If You've Never Been In Love (6) · Just You And Me (1) · Kick Hit 4 Hit Kix U (Blues For Jimi And Janis) (2) · Kiddio (4) · Let's Make It (1) · Letter To My Baby (3) · Meet Me In The Bottom (1) · Messin' With The Hook (1) · Mr. Lucky (5) · My Dream (4) · Never Get Out Of These Blues Alive (3) · No Substitute (4) · One Bourbon, One Scotch, One Beer (6) · Peavine (1) · Pots On, Gas On High (2) · Rainy Day (7) · Red House (7) · Rockin' Chair (4) · Sally Mae (4) · Send Me Your Pillow (1) · Serves Me Right To Suffer (medley) (6) · Sheep Out On The Foam (2) · Sittin' Here Thinkin' (1) · Sittin' In My Dark Room (2) · Spellbound (7) · Standin' At The Crossroads (2) · Stripped Me Naked (5) · Susie (5) · Syndicator (medley) (6) · T.B. Sheets (5) · Talkin' The Blues (6) · That's Alright (4) · Think Twice Before You Go (4) · This Is Hip (5) · Too Young (6) · Travellin' Blues (7) · Tupelo (6) · We Might As Well Call It Through (I Didn't Get Married To Your Two-Timing Mother (2) · We'll Meet Again (6) · Whiskey And Wimmen' (1) · Woman On My Mind (6) · World Today (1) · You Talk Too Much (1)

HOOPER, Stix   '79

Born Nesbert Hooper on 8/15/38 in Houston. Drummer with **The Crusaders**.

| 11/10/79 | 166 | 5 | | | The World Within | [I] | $12 | MCA 3180 |

African Spirit · Brazos River Breakdown · Cordon Bleu · Jasmine Breeze · Little Drummer Boy · Passion · Rum Or Tequila??

HOOTERS   '86

Pop-rock group from Philadelphia: Eric Bazilian (vocals, guitar), Rob Hyman (vocals, keyboards), John Lilley (guitar), Andy King (bass) and David Uosikkinen (drums). Fran Smith replaced King in early 1989.

5/25/85+	12	74	▲2	© 1	Nervous Night	$10	Columbia 39912
8/8/87	27	26	●	© 2	One Way Home	$10	Columbia 40659
12/2/89+	115	16		© 3	Zig Zag	$10	Columbia 45058

All You Zombies (1) 58 · Always A Place (3) · **And We Danced** (1) 21 · Beat Up Guitar (3) · Blood From A Stone (1) · Brother, Don't You Walk Away (3) · **Day By Day** (1) 18 · Deliver Me (3) · Don't Knock 'Til You Try It (3) · Don't Take My Car Out Tonight (1) · Engine 999 (2) · Fightin' On The Same Side (2) · **500 Miles** (3) 97 · Give The Music Back (3) · Graveyard Waltz (2) · Hanging On A Heartbeat (1) · Hard Rockin' Summer (3) · Heaven Laughs (3) · Johnny B (2) 61 · Karla With A K (3) · Mr. Big Baboon (3) · One Way Home (2) · **Satellite** (2) 61 · She Comes In Colors (1) · South Ferry Road (1) · Washington's Day (2) · **Where Do The Children Go** (1) 38 · You Never Know Who Your Friends Are (3)

HOOTIE & THE BLOWFISH   '95

Pop-rock group formed in South Carolina: Darius Rucker (vocals), Mark Bryan (guitar), Dean Felber (bass) and Jim Sonefeld (drums). Won the 1995 Best New Artist Grammy Award.

7/23/94+	❶8	129	▲16	© 1	Cracked Rear View	C:#10/18	$10	Atlantic 82613
5/11/96	❶2	44	▲3	© 2	Fairweather Johnson		$10	Atlantic 82886
10/3/98	4	23	▲	© 3	Musical Chairs		$10	Atlantic 83136

DEBUT	PEAK	WKS	RIAA	CD	ARTIST — Album Title	Catalog	Sym	$	Label & Number

HOOTIE & THE BLOWFISH — Cont'd

11/11/00	71	3	©	4	Scattered, Smothered & Covered.. [K]	$10	Atlantic 83408

Almost Home (4)	Drowning (1)	Hold My Hand (1) 10	Let Her Cry (1) 9	Only Wanna Be With You	Time (1) 14
Answer Man (3)	Earth Stopped Cold At Dawn	Home Again (3)	Let It Breathe (2)	(1) 6	Tootie (2)
Araby (4)	(2)	Honeyscrew (2)	Let Me Be Your Man (2)	Please, Please, Please Let Me	Tucker's Town (2) 38
Be The One (2)	Fairweather Johnson (2)	I Go Blind (4)	Look Away (1)	Get What I Want (4)	Use Me (4)
Before The Heartache Rolls In	Fine Line (4)	I Hope That I Don't Fall In Love	Michelle Post (3)	Renaissance Eyes (4)	What Do You Want From Me
(4)	Fool (2)	With You (4)	Not Even The Trees (1)	Running From An Angel (1)	Now (3)
Bluesy Revolution (3)	Goodbye (1)	I Will Wait (2)	Old Man & Me (When I Get To	Sad Caper (2)	What's Going On Here (3)
Desert Mountain Showdown (3)	Gravity Of The Situation (4)	I'm Goin' Home (1)	Heaven) (2) 13	She Crawls Away (2)	When I'm Lonely (2)
Dream Baby (4)	Hannah Jane (1)	I'm Over You (4)	One By One (3)	Silly Little Pop Song (2)	Wishing (3)
Driver 8 (4)	Hey Hey What Can I Do (4)	Las Vegas Nights (3)	Only Lonely (3)	So Strange (2)	

HOPE, Bob   '76

Born Leslie Townes Hope on 5/29/03 in Eltham, London, England; raised in Cleveland. Legendary movie/TV/radio comedian. Starred in several movies with **Bing Crosby**.

7/4/76	175	4			America Is 200 Years Old...And There's Still Hope! .... [C]	$15	Capitol 11538

comedy sketches featuring Jim Backus, Phyllis Diller and Dudley Moore

Betsy Ross - Song: Young	Bunker Hill - Song: You Can't	Declaration Of Independence -	Washington Crosses The
Glory	Win A War Without A War	Song: Freedom Policy	Delaware - Song: Drink It
Boston Commons - Songs:	Song	Paul Revere's Ride - Song:	Down Boys
Rapid Robert/The Boston Tea	Burning Tree	Paul Revere	
Party	Cornwallis' Surrender	Prince En Avignon	

HOPKIN, Mary   '69

Born on 5/3/50 in Pontardawe, Glamorganshire, Wales. Pop singer. Married to producer Tony Visconti from 1971-81.

3/29/69	28	20	©		Post Card	$25	Apple 3351

produced by **Paul McCartney**

Game, The	Lord Of The Reedy River	Pebble And The Man	Puppy Song	Those Were The Days 2	Young Love
Honeymoon Song	Love Is The Sweetest Thing	(Happiness Runs)	There's No Business Like Show	Voyage Of The Moon	
Inch Worm	Lullaby Of The Leaves	Prince En Avignon	Business	Y Blodyn Gwyn	

HOPKINS, Nicky   '72

Born on 2/24/44 in London. Died of an intestinal disorder on 9/6/94 (age 50). Session pianist. Member of **Night**.

2/12/72	33	11		1	Jamming With Edward! .... [I]	$20	Rolling Stones 39100
5/5/73	108	10		2	The Tin Man Was A Dreamer..	$15	Columbia 32074

Banana Anna (2)	Dolly (2)	Edward's Thrump Up (1)	It Hurts Me Too (1)	Shout It Out (2)	Waiting For The Band (2)
Blow With Ry (1)	Dreamer, The (2)	Highland Fling (1)	Lawyer's Lament (2)	Speed On (2)	
Boudoir Stomp (1)	Edward (2)	Interlude A La El Hopo (1)	Pig's Boogie (2)	Sundown In Mexico (2)	

HORNE, Jimmy "Bo"   '78

Born on 9/28/49 in West Palm Beach, Florida. Disco singer.

7/1/78	122	10			Dance Across The Floor	$12	Sunshine Sound 7801

Ask The Birds And The Bees	Don't Worry About It	Gimme Some	It's Your Sweet Love
Dance Across The Floor 38	Get Happy	I Wanna Go Home With You	Let Me (Let Me Be Your Lover)

HORNE, Lena   '59

Born on 6/30/17 in Brooklyn, New York. Singer/actress. Starred in several movies and Broadway shows. Won Grammy's Lifetime Achievement Award in 1989.

9/16/57	24	2		1	Lena Horne at the Waldorf Astoria .... [L]	$40	RCA Victor 1028
					recorded on 12/31/56		
11/17/58	20	1		2	Give The Lady What She Wants	$40	RCA Victor 1879
6/22/59	13	22		3	Porgy & Bess	$30	RCA Victor 1507
					LENA HORNE/HARRY BELAFONTE		
4/14/62	102	8		4	Lena On The Blue Side	$25	RCA Victor 2465
2/9/63	102	5		5	Lena...Lovely And Alive	$25	RCA Victor 2587
12/24/66	74ˣ	1	©	6	Merry - from Lena .... [X]	$20	United Artists 6546
5/16/70	162	10	©	7	Lena & Gabor	$20	Skye 15
					LENA HORNE & GABOR SZABO		
9/26/81	112	9	©	8	Lena Horne: The Lady And Her Music.. [OC]	$15	Qwest 3597 [2]

includes "Cotton Club Revue Medley" which contains titles performed by various cast members

As Long As I Live (8)	Everybody's Talkin' (7)	I Love To Love (1)	It's A Lonesome Old Town (4)	Oh, I Got Plenty Of Nothin' (3)	That's What Miracles Are All
As You Desire Me (4)	Fly (8)	I Only Have Eyes For You (5)	Jingle All The Way (6)	Paradise (4)	About (8)
At Long Last Love (2)	Fool On The Hill (7)	I Surrender Dear (5)	Just In Time (2)	People Will Say We're In Love	There's A Boat That's Leavin'
Baubles, Bangles And Beads	From This Moment On (1,8)	I Understand (5)	Just One Of Those Things (8)	(2)	Soon For New York (3)
(2)	Get Out Of Town (2)	I Wanna Be Loved (4)	Lady Is A Tramp (8)	Push De Button (8)	They Didn't Believe Me (4)
Bess, Oh Where's My Bess (3)	Have Yourself A Very Merry	I Want To Be Happy (5,8)	Lady Must Live (8)	Raisin' The Rent (8)	Today I Love Everybody (1)
Bess, You Is My Woman (3)	Christmas (6)	I Wants To Stay Here (3)	Lady With The Fan (8)	Rocky Raccoon (8)	Watch What Happens (7,8)
Bewitched (2)	Honey In The Honeycomb (2)	I'm Beginning To See The Light	Let It Snow! Let It Snow! Let It	Rudolph, The Red Nosed	What Are You Doing New
Bewitched, Bothered And	Honeysuckle Rose (1)	(medley) (1)	Snow! (6)	Reindeer (6)	Year's Eve (6)
Bewildered (8)	How You Say It (1)	I'm Confessin' (That I Love You)	Let Me Love You (1)	Rules Of The Road (4)	What'll I Do (4)
Can't Help Lovin' Dat Man (8)	I Ain't Got Nobody (And Nobody	(5)	Let's Put Out The Lights And	Silent Night! (6)	Where Or When (8)
Christmas Song (Chestnuts	Cares For Me) (5)	I'm Glad There Is You (8)	Go To Sleep (5)	Someone To Watch Over Me	White Christmas (6)
Roasting On An Open Fire)	I Concentrate On You (4)	I'm Gonna Sit Right Down And	Life Goes On (8)	(4)	Winter Wonderland (6)
(6)	I Found A New Baby (5)	Write Myself A Letter (8)	Little Drummer Boy (6)	Something (7)	Woman Is A Sometime Thing
Cole Porter Medley (1)	I Get The Blues When It Rains	I'm Through With Love (4)	Love (2,8)	Speak Low (2)	(8)
Come Runnin' (1)	(5)	I've Grown Accustomed To His	Message To Michael (7)	Stormy Weather (Part I & II) (8)	Yesterday When I Was Young
Darn That Dream (4)	I Got A Name (8)	Face (7)	Mood Indigo (medley) (1)	Street Calls Medley (3)	(7,8)
Day In - Day Out (1)	I Got Rhythm (5)	If You Believe (8)	My Man's Gone Now (3)	Summertime (3)	You'd Better Know It (2)
Deed I Do (8)	I Hadn't Anyone Till You (4)	In My Life (7)	My Mood Is You (7)	Surrey With The Fringe On Top	
Diamonds Are A Girl's Best	I Let A Song Go Out Of My	It Ain't Necessarily So (3)	New-Fangled Tango (1)	(8)	
Friend (2)	Heart (5)	It Might As Well Be Spring (4)	Nightwind (7)		

HORNSBY, Bruce, And The Range   '87

Born on 11/23/54 in Williamsburg, Virginia. Singer/songwriter/pianist. The Range: George Marinelli and David Mansfield (guitars), Joe Puerta (bass) and John Molo (drums). Puerta was a member of **Ambrosia**. Hornsby later toured as a member of the **Grateful Dead** and **The Other Ones**. Won 1986 Best New Artist Grammy Award.

6/21/86+	3	73	▲³	©	1	The Way It Is	C:#38/1	$10	RCA Victor 5904
5/21/88	5	27	▲	©	2	scenes from the southside		$10	RCA 6686
7/7/90	20	21	●	©	3	A Night On The Town		$10	RCA 2041

BRUCE HORNSBY:

DEBUT	PEAK	WKS						$	Label & Number
4/24/93	46	16	● ©	4	Harbor Lights			$10	RCA 66114
8/5/95	68	12	©	5	Hot House			$10	RCA 66584
10/31/98	148	2	©	6	Spirit Trail			$15	RCA 67468 [2]
11/11/00	167	1	©	7	Here Come The Noise Makers		[L]	$15	RCA 69308 [2]

Across The River (3) *18*   Every Little Kiss (1) *14*   Lady With A Fan (7)   Pete & Manny (6)   Song D (6)   Till The Dreaming's Done (2)
Another Day (3)   Fields Of Gray (4) *69*   Line In The Dust (6)   Preacher In The Ring Pt. I & II (6)   Special Night (3)   Twelve Tone Tune (medley) (7)
Barren Ground (3)   Fire On The Cross (3)   Listen To The Silence (6)   Spider Fingers (5,7)   Valley Road (2,7) *5*
Big Rumble (5)   Fortunate Son (6,7)   Long Race (1)   Rainbow's Cadillac (4,7)   Stander On The Mountain (3,7)   Variations On Swan Song &
Black Muddy River (medley) (7)   Funhouse (6)   Long Tall Cool One (4,7)   Red Plains (1,7)   Stranded On Easy Street (3)   Song D (6)
Blackberry Blossom (medley) (7)   Great Divide (6,7)   Longest Night (5)   Resting Place (6)   Sunflower Cat (Some Dour Cat)   Walk In The Sun (5) *54*
Carry The Water (3)   Harbor Lights (4)   Look Out Any Window (2) *35*   River Runs Low (1)   (Down With That) (6,7)   Way It Is (1,7) *1*
Changes, The (5)   Hot House Ball (5)   Lost Soul (3) *84*   Road Not Taken (2,7)   Sunlight Moon (6)   What A Time (4)
China Doll (4)   I Loves You Porgy (medley) (7)   Mandolin Rain (1,7) *4*   Sad Moon (6)   Swan Song (6)   White Wheeled Limousine (5)
Country Doctor (5)   I Will Walk With You (2)   Night On The Town (3)   See The Same Way (6)   Swing Street (5)   Wild Frontier (1)
Cruise Control (5)   It Takes A Lot To Laugh, It   Nocturne (medley) (7)   Shadow Hand (6)   Talk Of The Town (4)
Defenders Of The Flag (2)   Takes A Train To Cry   Old PlayGround (2)   Show Goes On (2)   Tango King (5)
Down The Road Tonight (1)   (medley) (7)   On The Western Skyline (1)   Sneaking Up On Boo Radley   Tempus Fugit (medley) (7)
End Of The Innocence (7)   Jacob's Ladder (2,7)   Passing Through (4)   (6,7)   These Arms Of Mine (3)
   King Of The Hill (6,7)   Pastures Of Plenty (4)   Song C (6)   Tide Will Rise (4)

HOROWITZ, Vladimir   '62

Born Vladimir Gorowicz on 10/3/03 in Kiev, Russia. Died of a heart attack on 11/5/89 (age 86). Legendary classical pianist. Moved to the United States in 1928. Won Grammy's Lifetime Achievement Award in 1990.

DEBUT	PEAK	WKS					$	Label & Number
11/10/62	14	22		1	Vladimir Horowitz (Chopin, Schumann, Rachmaninoff, Liszt)	[I]	$25	Columbia 6371
6/22/63	129	8		2	The Sound Of Horowitz	[I]	$25	Columbia 6411
7/24/65	22	32		3	Horowitz at Carnegie Hall - An Historic Return	[I-L]	$30	Columbia 728 [2]
					recorded on 5/9/65			
11/16/68	185	4		4	Horowitz On Television	[I-L]	$20	Columbia 7106
					recorded on 2/1/68 at Carnegie Hall			
4/29/78	102	14		5	Golden Jubilee Concert - Rachmaninoff Concerto No. 3	[I-L]	$15	RCA Victor 2633

recorded on 1/8/78 at Carnegie Hall; with **Eugene Ormandy & The New York Philharmonic**

Arabesque, Op. 18 (1,4)   Etude-Tableau In C Major, Op.   Nocturne In F Minor, Op. 55,   Scenes Of Childhood, Op. 15   Sonata No. 9, Op. 68 (3)
Ballade In G Minor, Op. 23 (3,4)   33, No. 2 (1)   No. 1 (4)   (2)   Sonata No. 2 In B-Flat Minor,
Etude In A-Flat Major, Op. 72,   Etude-Tableau In E-Flat Minor,   Organ Toccata In C Major (3)   Serenade For The Doll from   Op. 35 (1)
No. 11 (3)   Op. 39, No. 5 (1)   Piano Concerto No. 3 In   Children's Corner (3)   Toccata, Op. 7 (2)
Etude In C-Sharp Minor, Op. 2,   Fantasy In C Major, Op. 17 (3)   D-Minor, Op. 30 (5)   Sonata In A Major, Longo 483   Traumerei (Dream) from
No. 1 (2,3)   Hungarian Rhapsody No. 19 (1)   Poem In F-Sharp Major, Op. 32,   (2)   Kinderszenen, Op. 15 (3,4)
Etude In D-Sharp Minor, Op. 8,   Impromptu In G-Flat Major, Op.   No. 1 (2,3)   Sonata In E Major, Longo 430   Two Sonatas - E Major (L. 23)
No. 12 (2,4)   90, No. 3 (2)   Polonaise In F-Sharp Minor,   (2)   G Major (L. 335) (4)
Etude In F Major, Op. 10, No. 8   Mazurka In C-Sharp Minor, Op.   Op. 44 (4)   Sonata In G Major, Longo 209   Variations On A Theme from
(3)   30, No. 4 (3)   (2)   Bizet's Carmen (4)

HORSLIPS   '78

Rock group from Dublin, Ireland: John Fean (vocals, guitar), Jim Lockhart (keyboards), Charles O'Connor (fiddle), Barry Devlin (bass) and Eamon Carr (drums).

DEBUT	PEAK	WKS					$	Label & Number
2/25/78	98	9		1	Aliens		$12	DJM 16
3/10/79	155	9	©	2	The Man Who Built America		$12	DJM 20

Before The Storm (1)   Green Star Liner (2)   Letters From Home (2)   Long Week-End (2)   Speed The Plough (1)   Wrath Of The Rain (1)
Come Summer (1)   Homesick (2)   Lifetime To Pay (1)   Man Who Built America (2)   Stowaway (1)
Exiles (1)   I'll Be Waiting (2)   Loneliness (2)   New York Wakes (1)   Sure The Boy Was Green (1)
Ghosts (1)   If It Takes All Night (2)   Long Time Ago (2)   Second Avenue (1)   Tonight (You're With Me) (2)

HORTON, Johnny   '61

Born on 4/30/25 in Los Angeles; raised in Tyler, Texas. Died in a car crash on 11/5/60 (age 35). Country singer.

DEBUT	PEAK	WKS					$	Label & Number
2/27/61	8	34	▲ ©	1	Johnny Horton's Greatest Hits	[G]	$40	Columbia 8396
4/28/62	104	10		2	Honky-Tonk Man	[K]	$40	Columbia 8779

All For The Love Of A Girl (1)   Goodbye, Lonesome, Hello,   I'm A One-Woman Man (2)   Johnny Reb (1) *54*   Sink The Bismarck (1) *3*   When It's Springtime In Alaska
Battle Of New Orleans (1) *1*   Baby Doll (2)   I'm Coming Home (2)   Mansion You Stole (1)   Sleepy-Eyed John (2) *54*   (It's Forty Below) (1)
Comanche (The Brave Horse)   Honky Tonk Hardwood Floor (2)   I'm Ready, If You're Willing (1)   North To Alaska (1) *4*   They'll Never Take Her Love   Whispering Pines (1)
(1)   Honky-Tonk Man (2) *96*   Jim Bridger (1)   Ole Slew-Foot (2)   From Me (2)   Wild One (2)
Everytime I'm Kissing You (2)   I Got A Hole In My Pirogue (2)   Johnny Freedom (1) *69*   She Knows Why (2)

HOT   '77

Female vocal trio from Los Angeles: Gwen Owens, Cathy Carson and Juanita Curiel.

DEBUT	PEAK	WKS					$	Label & Number
5/28/77	125	15			Hot		$12	Big Tree 89522

Angel In Your Arms *6*   Just 'Cause I'm Guilty   Who's Gonna Love You   You Brought The Woman Out   You're The Reason For All The
Don't Let Me Leave You Behind   Mama's Girl   Why Don't You Believe In Your   Of Me *71*   Songs
If You Don't Love Her (When   Right Feeling At The Wrong   Man   You Can Do It
You Gonna Leave Her?)   Time *65*

HOT BOY$ '99

All-star rap group from New Orleans: **B.G.**, **Juvenile**, **Lil' Wayne** and **Turk**.

DEBUT	PEAK	WKS					$	Label & Number
8/14/99	5	44	● ©		Guerilla Warfare		$10	Cash Money 53264

Bout Whatever   Get Out Tha Way   I Need A Hot Girl *65*   Ridin   Too Hot   You Dig
Boys At War   Help   Off Tha Porch   Shoot 1st   Tuesday & Thursday
Clear Tha Set   I Feel   Respect My Mind   Sick Uncle   We On Fire

HOT BUTTER   '72

Group is actually Stan Free (Moog synthesizer player).

DEBUT	PEAK	WKS					$	Label & Number
10/21/72	137	7			Popcorn	[I]	$20	Musicor 3242

Amazing Grace   At The Movies   Hot Butter   Popcorn *9*   Telestar   Tristana
Apache   Day By Day   Pipeline   Song Of The Narobi Trio   Tomatoes

HOT CHOCOLATE   '79

Interracial group formed in London: Errol Brown (vocals), Harvey Hinsley (guitar), Larry Ferguson (keyboards), Patrick Olive (bass) and Tony Connor (drums).

DEBUT	PEAK	WKS			ARTIST — Album Title			$	Label & Number
3/1/75	55	17			1 **Cicero Park**			$15	Big Tree 89503
11/22/75+	41	21			2 **Hot Chocolate**			$15	Big Tree 89512
9/18/76	172	6			3 **Man To Man**			$15	Big Tree 89519
1/6/79	31	16			4 **Every 1's A Winner**			$12	Infinity 9002
7/28/79	112	6			5 **Going Through The Motions**			$12	Infinity 9010

Amazing Skin Song (2) — Brother Louie (1) — Call The Police (2) — Changing World (1) — Child's Prayer (2) — Cicero Park (1) — Confetti Day (4) — Congas Man (5) — Could Have Been Born In The Ghetto (Theme from Love Head) (1) — Dance (Get Down To It) (5) — Disco Queen (1) *28* — Dollar Sign (2) — Don't Stop It Now (3) *42* — Dreaming Of You (5) — **Emma** (1) *8* — Every 1's A Winner (4) *6* — Funky Rock 'N' Roll (1) — Going Through The Motions (5) *53* — Harry (3) — Heaven Is In The Back Seat Of My Cadillac (3) — Hello America (2) — I Just Love What You're Doing (5) — I'll Put You Together Again (4) — I'm Going To Make You Feel Like A Woman (4) — Lay Me Down (2) — Living On A Shoe String (3) — Love Is The Answer One More Time (4) — Love Like Yours (1) — Love's Coming On Strong (2) — Makin' Music (1) — Man To Man (3) — Mindless Boogie (5) — Night Ride (5) — Put Your Love In Me (4) — Seventeen Years Of Age (3) — Sex Appeal (3) — **So You Win Again** (4) *31* — Sometimes It Hurts To Be A Friend (4) — Stay With Me (4) — Street, The (2) — Sugar Daddy (3) — Warm Smile (3) — You Could've Been A Lady (3) — **You Sexy Thing** (2) *3* — You're A Natural High (1)

HOTHOUSE FLOWERS   '88

Folk-rock group from Dublin, Ireland: Liam O'Maonlai (vocals), Fiachna O'Braonain (guitar), Peter O'Toole (bass) and Jerry Fehily (drums).

DEBUT	PEAK	WKS		CD	ARTIST — Album Title			$	Label & Number
8/27/88	88	33		©	1 **people**			$10	London 828101
7/14/90	122	16		©	2 **Home**			$10	London 828197
4/10/93	156	3		©	3 **Songs From The Rain**			$10	London 828350

Ballad Of Katie (1) — Be Good (3) — Christchurch Bells (2) — Dance To The Storm (3) — Don't Go (1) — Emotional Time (3) — Eyes Wide Open (2) — Feet On The Ground (1) — Forgiven (1) — Give It Up (2) — Giving It All Away (2) — Good For You (3) — Gypsy Fair (3) — Hallelujah Jordan (1) — Hardstone City (1) — Home (2) — I Can See Clearly Now (2) — I'm Sorry (1) — If You Go (1) — Isn't It Amazing (3) — It'll Be Easier In The Morning (1) — Love Don't Work This Way (1) — Movies (2) — Older We Get (1) — One Tongue (3) — Seoladh na nGamhna (2) — Shut Up And Listen (2) — Spirit Of The Land (3) — Stand Beside Me (3) — Sweet Marie (2) — Thing Of Beauty (3) — This Is It (Your Soul) (3) — Trying To Get Through (2) — Water (2) — Yes I Was (1) — Your Nature (3)

HOT TUNA   '70

Rock group formed in San Francisco by **Jefferson Airplane** members **Jorma Kaukonen** (guitar) and Jack Casady (bass). Numerous personnel changes with Kaukonen and Casady the only constants.

DEBUT	PEAK	WKS		CD	ARTIST — Album Title		Sym	$	Label & Number
7/18/70	30	19		©	1 **Hot Tuna**		[L]	$15	RCA Victor 4353
					recorded at New Orleans House in Berkeley, California				
6/26/71	43	13		©	2 **First Pull Up Then Pull Down**		[L]	$15	RCA Victor 4550
3/18/72	68	23		©	3 **Burgers**			$15	Grunt 1004
2/9/74	148	7		©	4 **The Phosphorescent Rat**			$15	Grunt 0348
5/10/74	75	11		©	5 **America's Choice**			$15	Grunt 0820
11/29/75	97	9		©	6 **Yellow Fever**			$15	Grunt 1238
11/20/76	116	10		©	7 **Hoppkorv**			$15	Grunt 1920
4/15/78	92	10		©	8 **Double Dose**		[L]	$20	Grunt 2545 [2]
					recorded at Theatre 1839 in San Francisco				

Baby What You Want Me To Do (6) — Bar Room Crystal Ball (6) — Been So Long (2) — Bowlegged Woman, Knock Kneed Man (7,8) — Candy Man (2) — Come Back Baby (2) — Corners Without Exits (4) — Day To Day Out The Window Blues (4) — Death Don't Have No Mercy (1) — Don't You Leave Me Here (1) — Drivin' Around (7) — Easy Now (4) — Embryonic Journey (8) — Extrication Love Song (7,8) — Free Rein (6) — Funky #7 (5,8) — Genesis (4) — Great Divide: Revisited (5) — Half/Time Saturation (6) — Hesitation Blues (1) — Highway Song (3) — Hot Jelly Roll Blues (6) — Hit Single #1 (4) — How Long Blues (1) — I Can't Be Satisfied (7,8) — I Don't Wanna Go (5) — I See The Light (4,8) — I Wish You Would (7,8) — In The Kingdom (5) — Invitation (5) — It's So Easy (7) — John's Other (2) — Keep On Truckin' (3) — Keep Your Lamps Trimmed And Burning (2,8) — Killing Time In The Crystal City (8) — Know You Rider (1) — Let Us Get Together Right Down Here (3) — Letter To The North Star (4) — Living Just For You (4) — Mann's Fate (1) — Never Happen No More (2) — New Song (For The Morning) (1) — 99 Year Blues (3) — Ode For Billy Dean (3) — Oh Lord, Search My Heart (1) — Sally, Where'd You Get Your Liquor From? (4) — Santa Claus Retreat (7) — Sea Child (3) — Seeweed Strut (4) — Serpent Of Dreams (5,8) — Sleep Song (3) — Soliloquy For 2 (4) — Song For The Fire Maiden (6) — Song From The Stainless Cymbal (7) — Sunny Day Strut (3) — Sunrise Dance With The Devil (6,8) — Surphase Tension (6) — Talking 'Bout You (7,8) — True Religion (3) — Uncle Sam Blues (1) — Walkin' Blues (5) — Want You To Know (2) — Watch The North Wind Rise (7,8) — Water Song (3) — Winin' Boy Blues (1,8)

HOUSEMARTINS, The   '87

Pop-rock group from Hull, Humberside, England: Paul Heaton (vocals), Norman Cook (guitar), Stan Collimore (bass) and Hugh Whitaker (drums). Dave Hemmingway replaced Whitaker in late 1987. Cook formed **Beats International** and later recorded as **Fatboy Slim**.

DEBUT	PEAK	WKS		CD	ARTIST — Album Title			$	Label & Number
2/7/87	124	14		©	1 **London 0 Hull 4**			$10	Elektra 60501
1/16/88	177	6		©	2 **The People Who Grinned Themselves To Death**			$10	Elektra 60761

Anxious (1) — Bow Down (2) — Build (2) — Five Get Over Excited (2) — Flag Day (1) — Freedom (1) — Get Up Off Our Knees (1) — Happy Hour (1) — I Can't Put My Finger On It (2) — Johannesburg (2) — Lean On Me (1) — Light Is Always Green (2) — Me And The Farmer (2) — Over There (1) — People Who Grinned Themselves To Death (2) — Pirate Aggro (2) — Reverends Revenge (1) — Sheep (1) — Sitting On A Fence (1) — Think For A Minute (1) — We're Not Deep (1) — We're Not Going Back (2) — World's On Fire (2) — You Better Be Doubtful (2)

HOUSE OF FREAKS   '89

Rock duo from Richmond, Virginia: singer/guitarist Bryan Harvey and drummer Johnny Hott.

DEBUT	PEAK	WKS		CD	ARTIST — Album Title			$	Label & Number
5/6/89	154	10		©	**Tantilla**			$10	Rhino 70846

Big Houses — Birds Of Prey — Broken Bones — Family Tree — I Want Answers — Kill The Mockingbird — King Of Kings — Righteous Will Fall — Sun Gone Down — When The Hammer Came Down — White Folks' Blood — World Of Tomorrow

HOUSE OF LORDS   '89

Hard-rock group: James Christian (vocals), Lanny Cordola (guitar), Gregg Giuffria (keyboards), Chuck Wright (bass) and Ken Mary (drums). Cordola was with **Ozzy Osbourne**. Giuffria was with **Angel**. Giuffria and Wright were both with **Giuffria**; Wright was also with **Quiet Riot**. Mary was with **Alice Cooper**. Michael Guy replaced Cordola in 1990.

DEBUT	PEAK	WKS		CD	ARTIST — Album Title			$	Label & Number
11/19/88+	78	27		©	1 **House Of Lords**			$10	RCA 8530
10/20/90+	121	18		©	2 **Sahara**			$10	RCA 2170

American Babylon (2) — Call My Name (1) — Can't Find My Way Home (2) — Chains Of Love (2) — Edge Of Your Life (1) — Heart On The Line (2) — Hearts Of The World (1) — **I Wanna Be Loved** (1) *58* — It Ain't Love (2) — Jealous Heart (1) — Kiss Of Fire (2) — Laydown Staydown (2) — Lookin' For Strange (1) — Love Don't Lie (1) — Pleasure Palace (1) — **Remember My Name** (2) *72* — Sahara (2) — Shoot (2) — Slip Of The Tongue (1) — Under Blue Skies (1)

HOUSE OF LOVE, The   '90
Pop-rock group from England: Guy Chadwick (vocals, guitar), Simon Walker (guitar), Chris Groothuizen (bass) and Pete Evans (drums).

| 9/17/88 | 156 | 7 | © | 1 | The House Of Love | $10 | Relativity 8245 |
| 5/5/90 | 148 | 8 | © | 2 | The House Of Love | $10 | Fontana 842293 |

Beatles And The Stones (2)
Blind (2)
Christine (1)
Fisherman's Tale (1)
Hannah (2)

Happy (1)
Hedonist (2)
Hope (1)
I Don't Know Why I Love You (2)

In A Room (2)
Love In A Car (1)
Man To Child (1)
Never (2)
Road (1)

Salome (1)
Se Dest (2)
Shake And Crawl (2)
Shine On (2)

Someone's Got To Love You (2)
Sulphur (1)
32nd Floor (2)
Touch Me (1)

HOUSE OF PAIN   '92
White rap group from Los Angeles: Erik Schrody, Dan O'Connor and Leor DiMant. Schrody later recorded solo as **Everlast**.

8/15/92	14	58	▲	©	1	House Of Pain	$10	Tommy Boy 1056
7/16/94	12	15	●	©	2	Same As It Ever Was	$10	Tommy Boy 1089
11/9/96	47	4		©	3	Truth Crushed To Earth Shall Rise Again	$10	Tommy Boy 1161

All My Love (1)
All That (2)
Back From The Dead (2)
Choose Your Poison (3)
Come And Get Some Of This (1)
Danny Boy, Danny Boy (1)
Earthquake (3)

Fed Up (3)
Feel It (1)
Guess Who's Back (1)
Have Nots (3)
Heart Full Of Sorrow (3)
House And The Rising Sun (1)
House Of Pain Anthem (1)

I'm A Swing It (2)
It Ain't A Crime (2)
Jump Around (1) 3
Keep It Comin' (2)
Killa Rhyme Klik (2)
Life Goes On (1)
No Doubt (3)
On Point (2) 85

One For The Road (1)
Over There Shit (2)
Pass The Jinn (3)
Put On Your Shit Kickers (1)
Put Your Head Out (1)
Runnin' Up On Ya (2)
Salutations (1)
Same As It Ever Was (2)

Shamrocks And Shenanigans
(Boom Shalock Lock Boom)
(1) 65
Shut The Door (3)
Still Got A Lotta Love (2)
Top O' The Morning To Ya (1)
What's That Smell (3)
Where I'm From (2)

While I'm Here (3)
Who's The Man (2)
Word Is Bond (2)
X-Files (3)

HOUSTON, David   '66
Born on 12/9/38 in Bossier City, Louisiana. Died of an aneurysm on 11/30/93 (age 54). Country singer/songwriter/guitarist.

8/6/66	57	20			1	Almost Persuaded	$20	Epic 26213
9/13/69	143	5			2	David	$20	Epic 26482
4/18/70	194	2			3	Baby, Baby	$20	Epic 26539
9/26/70	170	3			4	Wonders Of The Wine	$20	Epic 30108

Almost Persuaded (1) 24
Baby, Baby (I Know You're A
Lady) (3)
Bridge Over Troubled Water (4)
China Doll (1)
Don't Mention Tomorrow (1,3)
From A Jack To A King (1)
Give All Your Love (3)

Gonna Lay Down My Burdens
(2)
Heart, We Did All That We
Could (1)
Heavenly Sunshine (4)
Hold That Tear (3)
Homecoming (3)
I Do My Swinging At Home (4)
I Thought I'd Die (3)

I'm Not Man Enough (To Make
My Heart Stop Loving You) (4)
(I'm So) Afraid Of Losing You
Again (3)
I've Been Had (1)
If God Can Forgive Me (Why
Can't You?) (4)
If I Had My Way (3)
Little Pedro (1)

Livin' In A House Full Of Love
(1)
Long Lonesome Highway (4)
Mama, Take Me Home (4)
Milky White Way (2)
My Love (4)
Oh Happy Day (2)
Okie From Muskogee (4)
Old Blind Barnabas (2)

Old Time Religion (2)
Ramblin' Rose (1)
Swing Low, Sweet Chariot (2)
This Train (2)
Tonight You Belong To Me (1)
True Love's A Lasting Thing (3)
Watching My World Walk Away
(3)
We Got Love (1)

Were You There (2)
When The Saints Go Marching
In (2)
Will The Circle Be Unbroken?
(2)
Wonders Of The Wine (4)
You're Always The One (3)

HOUSTON, Thelma   '77
Born on 5/7/46 in Leland, Mississippi. R&B singer/actress.

12/25/76+	11	37		©	1	Any Way You Like It	$15	Tamla 345
6/18/77	53	12		©	2	Thelma & Jerry	$15	Motown 887
						THELMA HOUSTON & JERRY BUTLER		
11/12/77	64	11			3	The Devil In Me	$15	Tamla 358
5/30/81	144	6			4	Never Gonna Be Another One	$12	RCA Victor 3842

And You've Got Me (2)
Any Way You Like It (1)
Baby, I Love You Too Much (3)
Come To Me (1)
Differently (1)
Don't Know Why I Love You (1)
Don't Leave Me This Way (1) 1
Don't Make Me Over (4)

Don't Make Me Pay (For
Another Girl's Mistake) (1)
Give Me Something To Believe
In (3)
Hollywood (4)
I Can't Go On Living Without
Your Love (3)

I Love You Through Windows
(2)
I'm Here Again (3)
I've Got The Devil In Me (3)
If It's The Last Thing I Do
(1) 47
If You Feel It (4)

If You Leave Me Now (medley)
(2)
It's A Lifetime Thing (2)
It's Just Me Feeling Good (3)
Joy Inside My Tears (2)
Let's Get Together (2)
Let's Pretend ..see (Play The
Game Of)

Love So Right (medley) (2)
Memories (2)
Never Give You Up (4)
Never Gonna Be Another One (4)
96 Tears (4)
Only The Beginning (2)
(Play The Game Of) Let's
Pretend (2)

Sharing Something Perfect
Between Ourselves (1)
Sweet Love I've Found (1)
There's No Runnin' Away From
Love (4)
Too Many Teardrops (4)
Triflin' (3)
Your Eyes (3)

HOUSTON, Whitney   ★155★   '92
Born on 8/9/63 in Newark, New Jersey. R&B singer/actress. Daughter of Cissy Houston and cousin of **Dionne Warwick**. Former fashion model. Married **Bobby Brown** on 7/18/92. Starred in the movies The Bodyguard, Waiting To Exhale and The Preacher's Wife.

3/30/85+	❶ 14	162	▲ 12	©	1	Whitney Houston		$10	Arista 8212
6/27/87	❶ 11	85	▲ 9	©	2	Whitney		$10	Arista 8405
11/24/90	3	51	▲ 4	©	3	I'm Your Baby Tonight		$10	Arista 8616
12/5/92	❶ 20	141	▲ 16	©	4	The Bodyguard	C:#17/16 [S]	$10	Arista 18699

includes "Even If My Heart Would Break" by **Kenny G** & **Aaron Neville**; "Someday (I'm Coming Back)" by **Lisa Stansfield**, "It's Gonna Be A Lovely Day" by The **S.O.U.L. S.Y.S.T.E.M.**; "(What's So Funny 'Bout) Peace, Love And Understanding by **Curtis Stigers**; "Theme From The Bodyguard" by Alan Silvestri; and "Trust In Me" by **Joe Cocker** & **Sass Jordan**; 1993 Grammy winner: ALbum of the Year

| 12/14/96 | 3 | 38 | ▲ 3 | © | 5 | The Preacher's Wife | [S] | $10 | Arista 18951 |

includes "The Lord Is My Shepherd" by Cissy Houston

| 12/5/98 | 13 | 75 | ▲ 4 | © | 6 | My Love Is Your Love | | $10 | Arista 19037 |
| 6/3/00 | 5 | 29 | ▲ 2 | © | 7 | The Greatest Hits | [G] | $15 | Arista 14626 [2] |

After We Make Love (3)
All At Once (1,7)
All The Man That I Need
(3,7) 1
Anymore (3)
**Could I Have This Kiss
Forever** (7) 52
Didn't We Almost Have It All
(2,7) 1

Exhale (Shoop Shoop) (7) 1
Fine (7)
For The Love Of You (2)
Get It Back (6)
Greatest Love Of All (1,7) 1
He's All Over Me (5)
Heartbreak Hotel (6,7) 2
Hold Me (1) 46

Hold On, Help Is On The Way
(5)
How Will I Know (1,7) 1
I Believe In You And Me
(5,7) 4
I Belong To You (3)
I Bow Out (6)
I Go To The Rock (5)
I Have Nothing (4,7) 1

I Know Him So Well (2)
I Learned From The Best
(6,7) 27
I Love The Lord (5)
**I Wanna Dance With
Somebody (Who Loves Me)**
(2,7) 1
I Will Always Love You (4,7) 1
I'm Every Woman (4,7) 4

I'm Knockin' (3)
I'm Your Baby Tonight (3,7) 1
If I Told You That (6,7)
If You Say My Eyes Are
Beautiful (2)
In My Business (6)
It's Not Right But It's Okay
(6,7) 4
Jesus Loves Me (4)

Joy (5)
Joy To The World (5)
Just The Lonely Talking Again (2)
Love Is A Contact Sport (2)
Love Will Save The Day
(2,7) 9
Lover For Life (3)
Miracle (3) 9
My Heart Is Calling (5) 77

DEBUT	PEAK	WKS	RIAA	CD	ARTIST — Album Title	Catalog	Sym	$	Label & Number

HOUSTON, Whitney — Cont'd

My Love Is Your Love (6,7) *4*
My Name Is Not Susan (3) *20*
Nobody Loves Me Like You Do (1)
Oh Yes (6)
One Moment In Time (7) *5*
Queen Of The Night (4,7)
Run To You (4,7) *31*

Same Script, Different Cast (7) *70*
Saving All My Love For You (1,7) *1*
So Emotional (2,7) *1*
Somebody Bigger Than You And I (5)
Someone For Me (1)

Star Spangled Banner (7) *20*
Step By Step (5,7) *15*
Take Good Care Of My Heart (1)
Thinking About You (1)
Until You Come Back (6)
We Didn't Know (3)
When You Believe (6) *15*

Where Do Broken Hearts Go (2,7) *1*
Where You Are (2)
Who Do You Love (3)
Who Would Imagine A King (5)
Why Does It Hurt So Bad (7) *26*
You Give Good Love (1,7) *3*

You Were Loved (5)
You'll Never Stand Alone (6)
You're Still My Man (2)

HOWARD, Adina   '95
Born on 11/14/74 in Grand Rapids, Michigan. Female R&B singer.

| 3/18/95 | 39 | 26 | ● | © | Do You Wanna Ride? .... | | | $10 | Mecca Don 61757 |

Baby Come Over
Coolin' In The Studio

Do You Wanna Ride?
Freak Like Me *2*

Horny For Your Love
If We Make Love Tonight

It's All About You
Let's Go To Da Sugar Shack

My Up And Down *68*
You Can Be My Nigga

You Don't Have To Cry
You Got Me Humpin'

HOWARD, George   '87
Born on 9/15/56 in Philadelphia. Died of cancer on 3/22/98 (age 41). Jazz saxophonist.

9/1/84	178	4		©	1 Steppin' Out	[I]		$10	TBA 201
7/27/85	169	4		©	2 Dancing In The Sun	[I]		$10	TBA 205
4/19/86	142	11		©	3 Love Will Follow	[I]		$10	TBA 210
12/27/86+	109	26		©	4 A Nice Place To Be	[I]		$10	MCA 5855
6/18/88	109	8		©	5 Reflections	[I]		$10	MCA 42145
3/24/90	128	11		©	6 Personal	[I]		$10	MCA 6335
3/16/91	131	10		©	7 Love And Understanding	[I]		$10	GRP 9629
5/2/92	137	9		©	8 Do I Ever Cross Your Mind	[I]		$10	GRP 9669
8/20/94	180	4		©	9 A Home Far Away	[I]		$10	GRP 9780

Attitude (5)
Baby Come To Me (7)
Broad Street Strut (7)
Come With Me (3)
Cross Your Mind (8)
Dancing In The Sun (2)
Dr. Rock (1)
Doria (9)
Dream Ride (1)
Everything I Miss At Home (1)
Fakin' The Feeling (6)
For Our Fathers (9)
Funk It Out (5)
Got It Goin' On (6)

Grover's Groove (9)
Home Far Away (9)
Hopscotch (7)
Human Nature (1)
I Want You For Myself (6)
I'm In Effect (6)
If You Were Mine (9)
In Love (2)
It Can't Be Forever (2)
Jade's World (4)
Jo Jo (8)
Just The Way I Feel (8)
Late Night (5)
Let's Live In Harmony (4)

Let's Pretend (5)
Love And Understanding (7)
Love Struck (7)
Love Will Conquer All (5)
Love Will Find A Way (9)
Love Will Follow (3)
Mind Bender (8)
Miracle (9)
Modern Love (8)
Moods (2)
Nice Place To Be (4)
No No (4)
No Ordinary Love (9)
One Love (5)

Only Here For A Minute (7)
Partly Cloudy (8)
Personally (6)
Philly Talk (1)
Piano In The Dark (6)
Pretty Face (4)
Quiet As It's Kept (6)
Raiders, The (3)
Red, Black, 'N' Blue (7)
Reflections (5)
Renewal (9)
September Rain (9)
Shadow (8)
Shower You With Love (6)

Slow Walking (3)
Spenser For Hire (4)
Spirit (8)
Stanley's Groove (4)
Stay Here With Me (8)
Stay With Me (2)
Steppin' Out (1)
Sweet Dreams (Are Made Of This) (1)
Sweetest Taboo (4)
Talk To The Drum (7)
Tear Of Spring (1)
Telephone (2)
That's Just What It Is (3)

Too Bad (5)
Try Again (8)
Until Tomorrow (9)
Uptown (6)
You And Me (6)
You Can Make The Story Right (9)
You Only Come Out At Night (6)

HOWARD, Miki   '92
Born in 1962 in Chicago. R&B singer/actress. Portrayed **Billie Holiday** in the movie *Malcolm X*.

3/14/87	171	6			1 Come Share My Love			$10	Atlantic 81688
2/20/88	145	16		©	2 Love Confessions			$10	Atlantic 81810
3/3/90	112	16		©	3 Miki Howard			$10	Atlantic 82024
10/3/92	110	11		©	4 Femme Fatale			$10	Giant 24452

Ain't Nobody Like You (4)
Ain't Nuthin' In The World (3)
Baby, Be Mine (2)
Bitter Love (2)
But I Love You (4)
Cigarette Ashes On The Floor (4)
Come Back To Me Lover (1)
Come Home To Me (3)

Come Share My Love (1)
Crazy (4)
Do You Want My Love (1)
Good Morning Heartache (4)
Hope That We Can Be Together Soon (4)
I Can't Wait (To See You Alone) (1)
I Surrender (1)

I Wanna Be There (2)
I'll Be Your Shoulder (3)
I've Been Through It (4)
If You Still Love Her (3)
Imagination (1)
In Too Deep (2)
Just The Way You Want Me To (3)
Love Confession (2)

Love Me All Over (3)
Love Under New Management (3)
Love Will Find A Way (1)
Mister (3)
My Friend (1)
New Fire From An Old Flame (3)
Reasons (2)

Release Me (4)
Shining Through (4)
Thank You For Talkin' To Me Africa (4)
That's What Love Is (2)
This Bitter Earth (4)
Until You Come Back To Me (That's What I'm Gonna Do) (3)

Who Ever Said It Was Love (3)
You Better Be Ready To Love Me (1)
You've Changed (2)

HOWE, Steve   '76
Born on 4/8/47 in London. Rock guitarist. Member of **Yes**, **Asia** and **GTR**.

| 12/20/75+ | 63 | 11 | | © | 1 Beginnings .... | | | $12 | Atlantic 18154 |
| 2/16/80 | 164 | 4 | | © | 2 The Steve Howe Album .... | [I] | | $12 | Atlantic 19243 |

All's A Chord (2)
Australia (1)
Beginnings (1)
Break Away From It All (1)

Cactus Boogie (2)
Concerto In D (Second Movement) (2)
Continental, The (2)

Diary Of A Man Who Vanished (2)
Doors Of Sleep (1)
Double Rondo (2)

Look Over Your Shoulder (2)
Lost Symphony (1)
Meadow Rag (2)
Nature Of The Sea (1)

Pennants (2)
Pleasure Stole The Night (1)
Ram (1)
Surface Tension (2)

Will O' The Wisp (1)

HOWLIN' WOLF   '71
Born Chester Arthur Burnett on 6/10/10 in West Point, Mississippi. Died of cancer on 1/10/76 (age 65). Legendary blues singer/guitarist. Inducted into the Rock and Roll Hall of Fame in 1991 as an early influence.

| 8/21/71 | 79 | 15 | | © | The London Howlin' Wolf Sessions .... | | | $20 | Chess 60008 |

Built For Comfort
Do The Do

Highway 49
I Ain't Superstitious

Poor Boy
Red Rooster

Rockin' Daddy
Sittin' On Top Of The World

Wang-Dang-Doodle
What A Woman!

Who's Been Talking?
Worried About My Baby

H-TOWN   '93
R&B vocal trio from Houston: brothers Shazam and John Conner with Darryl Jackson.

4/24/93	16	27	▲	©	1 Fever For Da Flavor			$10	Luke 126
11/26/94+	98	23	●	©	2 Beggin' After Dark			$10	Luke 212
11/15/97	53	11		©	3 Ladies Edition			$10	Relativity 1596

Baby I Love Ya' (2)
Baby I Wanna (1)
Back Seat (Wit No Sheets) (2)
Beggars Can't Be Choosey (3)
Beggin' After Dark (2)
Buss One (2)
Can't Fade Da H (1)
Cruisin' Fo' Honeys (2)

Die For You (3)
Don't Hold Back The Rain (3)
Don't Sleep On The Female (3)
Emotions (2) *51*
Fever For Da Flavor (1)
Full Time (2)
H-Town Bounce (1)
I Sleep U I Wear U (3)

Indo Love (2)
Jezebel (3)
Julie Rain (3)
Keepin' My Composure (1)
Knockin' Da Boots (1) *3*
Last Record (2)
Lick U Up (1) *67*
Married Man (3)

Mindtaker (3)
Much Feelin' (And It Tastes Great) (2)
Natural Woman (3)
One Night Gigolo (2)
1-900-Call GI (2)
Rockit Steady (2)
Sex Bowl (2)

Sex Me (1)
Shoot 'Em Up (3)
Special Kinda Fool (3)
They Like It Slow (3) *35*
Toon Girl (3)
Treat U Right (1)
Tumble & Rumble (2)
Visions In My Mind (3)

Ways To Treat A Woman (3)
Woman's Anthem (3)
Woman's World (3)
Won't U Come Back (1)

DEBUT	PEAK	WKS	RIAA	CD	ARTIST — Album Title	Catalog	Sym	$	Label & Number

HUBBARD, Freddie '76
Born on 4/7/38 in Indianapolis. Jazz trumpeter.

DEBUT	PEAK	WKS	CD	# Album Title	Sym	$	Label & Number
3/10/73	165	7	©	1 **Sky Dive**	[I]	$12	CTI 6018
1/19/74	186	5	©	2 **Keep Your Soul Together**	[I]	$12	CTI 6036
9/14/74	153	7		3 **High Energy**	[I]	$12	Columbia 33048
1/11/75	127	7		4 **The Baddest Hubbard**	[I-K]	$12	CTI 6047
5/17/75	167	4		5 **Polar AC**	[I]	$12	CTI 6056
7/19/75	149	6		6 **Liquid Love**	[I]	$12	Columbia 33556
9/4/76	85	9		7 **Windjammer**	[I]	$12	Columbia 34166
10/29/77	149	6		8 **Bundle Of Joy**	[I]	$12	Columbia 34902
7/15/78	131	5		9 **Super Blue**	[I]	$12	Columbia 35386

Baraka Sasa (3)	Ebony Moonbeams (3)	In A Mist (1,4)	People Make The World Go Round (5)
Betcha By Golly, Wow (5)	Feelings (7)	Kareem, Theme For (9)	Polar AC (5)
Black Maybe (3)	First Light (4)	Keep Your Soul Together (2)	Portrait Of Jenny (8)
Brigitte (2)	From Behind (8)	Kuntu (6)	Povo (1)
Bundle Of Joy (8)	From Now On (8)	Liquid Love (6)	Put It In The Pocket (6)
Camel Rise (3)	Godfather, The (1)	Lost Dreams (6)	Rahsann (8)
Crisis (3)	Gospel Truth (9)	Midnight At The Oasis (6)	Rainy Day Song (8)
Destiny's Children (2)	Here's That Rainy Day (4)	Naturally (5)	Red Clay (4)
Dream Weaver (7)	I Don't Want To Lose You (8)	Neo Terra (New Land) (7)	

Rock Me Arms (7)	Touch Me Baby (7)
Sky Dive (1)	Tucson Stomp (8)
Son Of Sky Dive (5)	Windjammer (7)
Spirits Of Trane (2)	Yesterday's Thoughts (6)
Super Blue (9)	
Surest Things Can Change (1)	
Take It To The Ozone (9)	
To Her Ladyship (9)	
Too High (3)	

HUDSON, David '80
Born in Miami. R&B singer.

DEBUT	PEAK	WKS	Album Title	$	Label & Number
8/23/80	184	2	**To You Honey, Honey With Love**	$12	Alston 4412

Ease Up
Honey, Honey 59

I Have Never Loved A Woman (The Way I Love You)	I Must Have Your Love	Pump It	When I'm Lovin' You
	Let Me Wrap You In My Love	Scratch My Back	

HUDSON AND LANDRY '71
Comedy duo of Los Angeles DJs Bob Hudson and Ron Landry. Split up in 1976. Hudson died on 9/20/97 (age 66).

DEBUT	PEAK	WKS	# Album Title	Sym	$	Label & Number
4/10/71	30	26	1 **Hanging In There**	[C]	$20	Dore 324
11/27/71+	33	23	2 **Losing Their Heads**	[C]	$20	Dore 326
1/6/73	147	9	3 **Right-Off!**	[C]	$20	Dore 329

Ajax Airlines (2) *68*	Bruiser LaRue (2)	Fredericksim (2)	Hippo, The (3)
Ajax Liquor Store (1) *43*	Bruiser LaRue Meets Count Dracula (3)	Friar Shuck (1,2)	Impossible Dreams (1)
Ajax Mortuary (1)	Charlie Chin (3)	Frontier Christmas (Harlow & The Mrs.) (3)	Kearsarge (1)
Ajax Pet Store (3)	Doctors, The (1)	Heads, The (3)	Loch Ness Monster (1)
Ajax Travel Bureau (2)	Five Points (1)	Hippie & The Redneck (1)	Murph Almighty (3)
Astro Nut (2)			Obscene Phone Bust (2)

Pierre's Restaurant (1)	Soul Bowl (3)
Porno Flicks (1)	Top Forty D.J.'s (1)
Prospectors, The (2)	
Rising & Falling Of Adolph Hitler (3)	
Sir Basil (1)	

HUDSON BROTHERS '74
Pop vocal trio from Portland, Oregon: Bill, Brett and Mark Hudson. Hosted own TV variety show during the summer of 1974; also hosted kiddie TV show *The Hudson Brothers Razzle Dazzle Comedy Show*. Bill was married to actress Goldie Hawn from 1976-79; their daughter is actress Kate Hudson.

DEBUT	PEAK	WKS	# Album Title	$	Label & Number
11/30/74	179	4	1 **Totally Out Of Control**	$12	Rocket 460
12/7/74	176	4	2 **Hollywood Situation**	$12	Casablanca 7004
12/13/75+	165	6	3 **Ba-Fa**	$12	Rocket 2169

Adventures Of Chucky Margolis (2)	Dolly Day (1)	La La Layna (1)	Oh Gabriel (3)
Apple Pie Hero (3)	Find Me A Woman (medley) (1)	Little Brown Box (medley) (1)	One And The Same (medley) (1)
Be A Man (1)	Hard On Me (3)	**Lonely School Year** (3) *57*	Out Of The Rainbow (medley) (2)
Bernie Was A Friend Of Ours (3)	Hollywood Situation (2)	Long Long Day (1)	Playmate (3)
Coochie Coochie Coo (2)	Home (medley) (1)	Lover Come Back To Me (1)	Razzle Dazzle (2)
Cry, Cry, Cry (2)	If You Really Need Me (1)	Ma Ma Ma Baby (2)	**Rendezvous** (3) *26*
	Isn't It Lovely (1)	My Career (3)	
	Killer On The Road (1)	My Heart Can't Take It (3)	

Smooth Talker (3)	Strike Up The Boys In The Band (2)
So You Are A Star (2) *21*	Sunday Driver (1)
Sometimes The Rain Will Fall (2)	These Things We Do (medley) (1)
Song For Stephanie (2)	Three Of Us (2)
Spinning The Wheel (With The Girl You Love) (1)	Truth Of The Matter (1)
Straight Up And Tall (1)	With Somebody Else (3)

HUES CORPORATION, The '74
R&B vocal trio from Los Angeles: H. Ann Kelly, Bernard Henderson and Fleming Williams.

DEBUT	PEAK	WKS	# Album Title	$	Label & Number
6/29/74	20	18	1 **Freedom For The Stallion**	$12	RCA Victor 0323
7/5/75	147	5	2 **Love Corporation**	$12	RCA Victor 0938

All Goin' Down Together (1)	**Freedom For The Stallion** (1) *1*	He's My Home (2)	Miracle Maker (Sweet Soul Shaker) (1)
Bound On A Reason (1)	Go To The Poet (1)	Live A Lie (1)	Off My Cloud (1)
Family, The (1)	Gold Rush (2)	Long Road (2)	One Good Night Together (2)
Follow The Spirit (2)		**Love Corporation** (2) *62*	

Rock The Boat (1) *1*	When You Look Down The Road (2)
Salvation Lady (1-3-5) (1)	You Showed Me What Love Is (2)
Sing To Your Song (2)	
Soul Sailin' (2)	

HUGH, Grayson '89
Born in Connecticut. Singer/songwriter/pianist.

DEBUT	PEAK	WKS	CD	Album Title	$	Label & Number
10/15/88+	71	24	©	**Blind To Reason**	$10	RCA 7661

Blind Return
Blind To Reason

Bring It All Back *87*	Finally Found A Friend	Romantic Heart	Tears Of Love
Empty As The Wind	Hard Life	**Talk It Over** *19*	That's Cool
			Two Hearts

HUGO & LUIGI '63
Producers/songwriters/label executives. Hugo Peretti was born on 12/6/16; died on 5/1/86 (age 69). Luigi Creatore was born on 12/21/20. Owned record labels Roulette and Avco/Embassy.

DEBUT	PEAK	WKS	# Album Title	$	Label & Number
4/27/63	14	13	1 **The Cascading Voices of the Hugo & Luigi Chorus**	$20	RCA Victor 2641
10/26/63	125	2	2 **Let's Fall In Love**	$20	RCA Victor 2717

Always (2)	For You (1)	I'll See You In My Dreams (1)	Look For The Silver Lining (1)
Anniversary Song (2)	Good Night Sweetheart (2)	I'm In The Mood For Love (2)	Marcheta (1)
As Time Goes By (2)	I Don't Know Why (I Just Do) (2)	It Happened In Monterey (1)	Melody Of Love (2)
Can't Help Falling In Love (2)	I Love You (1)	Let Me Call You Sweetheart (2)	Moonlight And Roses (1)
Falling In Love With Love (2)		Let's Fall In Love (2)	Paradise (1)

Remembering Time (1)	When Day Is Done (1)
Three O'Clock In The Morning (1)	
True Love (2)	

HUM '95
Rock group from Champaign, Illinois: Matt Talbott (vocals), Tim Lash (guitar), Jeff Dimpsey (bass) and Bryan St. Pere (drums).

DEBUT	PEAK	WKS	CD	# Album Title	$	Label & Number
7/15/95	105	12	©	1 **You'd Prefer An Astronaut**	$10	RCA 66577
2/14/98	150	1	©	2 **Downward Is Heavenward**	$10	RCA 67446

Afternoon With The Axolotls (2)	Green To Me (2)	Inuit Promise (2)	Pod, The (1)
Apollo (2)	I Hate it Too (1)	Isle Of The Cheetah (2)	Scientists, The (2)
Comin' Home (2)	I'd Like Your Hair Long (2)	Little Dipper (2)	Songs of Farewell and Departure (1)
Dreamboat (2)	If You Are To Bloom (1)	Ms. Lazarus (2)	

Stars (1)	
Suicide Machine (1)	
Very Old Man (1)	
Why I Like the Robins (1)	

HUMAN BEINZ, The '68

Rock group from Youngstown, Ohio: Dick Belly (vocals, guitar), Joe Markulin (guitar), John Pachuta (bass) and Mike Tatum (drums).

| 3/9/68 | 65 | 10 | | © | Nobody But Me........ | | | $30 | Capitol 2906 |

Black Is The Color Of My True Love's Hair
Dance On Through
Flower Grave
Foxey Lady
It's Fun To Be Clean
Nobody But Me *8*
Serenade To Sarah
Shaman, The
Sueno
This Lonely Town
Turn On Your Love Light *80*

HUMAN LEAGUE, The '82

Electro-pop trio from Sheffield, England: lead singer/synthesist Philip Oakey, with female vocalists Joanne Catherall and Susanne Sulley. Early members Martyn Ware and Ian Craig Marsh left to form **Heaven 17**.

| 2/27/82 | 3 | 38 | ● | © | 1 Dare | | | $12 | A&M 4892 |
| 9/18/82 | 135 | 7 | | | 2 Love And Dancing............ | | [I] | $12 | A&M 3209 |

THE LEAGUE UNLIMITED ORCHESTRA
instrumental versions of songs from album #1 above

6/18/83	22	29			3 Fascination!...........		[M]	$10	A&M 2501
6/16/84	62	13		©	4 Hysteria................			$10	A&M 4923
10/4/86	24	25		©	5 Crash................			$10	A&M 5129

Are You Ever Coming Back? (5)
Betrayed (4)
Darkness (1)
Do Or Die (1,2)
Don't You Know I Want You (4)
Don't You Want Me (1,2) *1*
Get Carter (1)
Hard Times (2,3)
Human (5) *1*
I Am The Law (1)
I Love You Too Much (3,4)
I Need Your Loving (5) *44*
I'm Coming Back (4)
Jam (5)
(Keep Feeling) Fascination (3) *8*
Lebanon, The (4) *64*
Life On Your Own (4)
Louise (4)
Love Action (I Believe In Love) (1,2)
Love Is All That Matters (5)
Love On The Run (5)
Mirror Man (3) *30*
Money (5)
Open Your Heart (1,2)
Party (5)
Real Thing (5)
Rock Me Again And Again And Again And Again And Again (Six Times) (4)
Seconds (1,2)
Sign, The (4)
So Hurt (4)
Sound Of The Crowd (1,2)
Swang (5)
Things That Dreams Are Made Of (1,2)
You Remind Me Of Gold (3)

★475★ HUMBLE PIE '72

Rock group from England: **Peter Frampton** and Steve Marriott (vocals, guitars; **Small Faces**), Greg Ridley (bass; **Spooky Tooth**) and Jerry Shirley (drums). Frampton left in October 1971, replaced by Clem Clempson (**Rough Diamond**). Disbanded in 1975. Reunited from 1980-81 with Marriott, Shirley, Bobby Tench (guitar) and Anthony Jones (bass). Shirley later joined **Fastway**. Marriott died on 4/20/91 (age 44).

5/8/71	118	23		©	1 Rock On...........			$15	A&M 4301
11/6/71	21	32	●	©	2 Performance-Rockin' The Fillmore........		[L]	$20	A&M 3506 [2]
4/1/72	6	34	●	©	3 Smokin'........			$15	A&M 4342
9/30/72	37	20			4 Lost And Found........		[E]	$20	A&M 3513 [2]
3/24/73	13	21			5 Eat It........			$20	A&M 3701 [2]
3/9/74	52	14			6 Thunderbox........			$15	A&M 3611
4/26/75	100	8			7 Street Rats........			$15	A&M 4514
4/12/80	60	14		©	8 On To Victory........			$12	Atco 122
5/9/81	154	6		©	9 Go For The Throat........			$12	Atco 131

Alabama '69 (4)
All Shook Up (9)
Anna (Go To Him) (6)
As Safe As Yesterday (4)
Baby Don't You Do It (8)
Bang? (4)
Beckton Dumps (5)
Big George (1)
Black Coffee (5)
Buttermilk Boy (4)
Chip Away (The Stone) (9)
Cold Lady (4)
C'mon Everybody (3)
Countryman Stomp (7)
Desperation (4)
Don't Worry, Be Happy (4)
Down Home Again (4)
Drift Away (9)
Drive My Car (7)
Driver (9)
Drugstore Cowboy (5)
Every Mothers Son (4)
Every Single Day (6)
Fixer, The (3)
Fool For A Pretty Face (Hurt By Love) (8) *52*
Four Day Creep (2)
Further Down The Road (8)
Get Down To It (5)
Get It In The End (8)
Go For The Throat (9)
Good Booze And Bad Women (5)
Groovin' With Jesus (6)
Hallelujah (I Love Her So) (2)
Heartbeat (4)
Home And Away (4)
Honky Tonk Woman (5)
Hot 'N' Nasty (3) *52*
I Believe To My Soul (5)
I Can't Stand The Rain (6)
I Don't Need No Doctor (2) *73*
I Walk On Gilded Splinters (2)
I Wonder (3)
I'll Go Alone (4)
(I'm A) Road Runner (3,5)
I'm Ready (2)
Infatuation (8)
Is It For Love? (5)
Keep It On The Island (9)
Let Me Be Your Lovemaker (7)
Light, The (1)
Light Of Love (4)
Lottie And The Charcoal Queen (9)
My Lover's Prayer (8)
Natural Born Woman (4)
Nifty Little Number Like You (4)
Ninety-Nine Pounds (6)
No Money Down (6)
No Way (6)
Oh, Bella (All That's Hers) (6)
Oh La-De-Da (6)
Old Time Feelin' (3)
Ollie, Ollie (4)
Only You Can Say (4)
Over You (8)
Queens And Nuns (7)
Rain (7)
Rally With Ali (6)
Red Neck Jump (1)
Restless Blood (9)
Road Hog (7)
Road Runner ..see: (I'm A)
Rock And Roll Music (7)
Rollin' Stone (1,2)
Sad Bag Of Shaky Jake (4)
Savin' It (8)
Say No More (5)
Scored Out (7)
79th And Sunset (1)
Shine On (1)
Shut Up And Don't Interrupt Me (5)
Silver Tongue (4)
Song For Jenny (1)
Sour Grain (1)
Stick Shift (4)
Stone Cold Fever (1,2)
Strange Days (1)
Street Rat (7)
Summer Song (5)
Sweet Peace And Time (3)
Take It From Here (8)
Take Me Back (4)
Teenage Anxiety (9)
That's How Strong My Love Is (5)
There 'Tis (7)
30 Days In The Hole (3)
Thunderbox (6)
Tin Soldier (9)
Up Our Sleeve (5)
We Can Work It Out (7)
What You Will (4)
You Soppy Pratt (8)
You're So Good For Me (3)

HUMPERDINCK, Engelbert ★182★ '70

Born Arnold Dorsey on 5/2/36 in Madras, India; raised in Leicester, England. Pop singer. First recorded for Decca in 1958. Met **Tom Jones**'s manager, Gordon Mills, in 1965, who suggested his name change to Engelbert Humperdinck (a famous German opera composer). Starred in his own musical variety TV series in 1970.

1)Engelbert Humperdinck 2)Release Me 3)The Last Waltz

6/17/67	7	118	●		1 Release Me			$20	Parrot 71012
12/23/67+	10	60	●		2 The Last Waltz			$20	Parrot 71015
8/24/68	12	78	●		3 A Man Without Love........			$15	Parrot 71022
3/22/69	12	33	●		4 Engelbert........			$15	Parrot 71026
1/3/70	5	41	●		5 Engelbert Humperdinck			$15	Parrot 71030
7/11/70	19	40	●		6 We Made It Happen........			$15	Parrot 71038
2/20/71	22	24	●		7 Sweetheart........			$15	Parrot 71043
9/11/71	25	15	●		8 Another Time, Another Place........			$15	Parrot 71048
1/1/72	45	13		©	9 Live At The Riviera, Las Vegas........		[L]	$15	Parrot 71051
8/19/72	72	14			10 In Time........			$15	Parrot 71056
8/11/73	113	10			11 King Of Hearts........			$15	Parrot 71061
12/21/74+	103	14		©	12 His Greatest Hits........		[G]	$15	Parrot 71067
11/27/76+	17	28	▲²		13 After The Lovin'........			$12	Epic 34381
7/16/77	167	5			14 Miracles by Engelbert Humperdinck........			$12	Epic 34730

DEBUT	PEAK	WKS	RIAA	CD	ARTIST — Album Title	Catalog	Sym	$	Label & Number

HUMPERDINCK, Engelbert — Cont'd

DEBUT	PEAK	WKS			Album Title	Catalog	$	Label & Number
12/24/77+	156	4	●	15	Christmas Tyme	[X]	$12	Epic 35031
5/19/79	164	4		16	This Moment In Time		$12	Epic 35791
11/25/95	23ˣ	1	©	17	The Magic of Christmas	[X]	$10	Core 9462

ENGELBERT

After The Lovin' (13) **8**
All This World And The Seven Seas (2)
All You've Gotta Do Is Ask (Una Volta Nella Vita) (5)
Am I That Easy To Forget (2,9,12) **18**
Another Time, Another Place (8) **43**
Aquarius (medley) (5)
Around The World In 80 Days (medley) (9)
Baby I'm A Want You (10)
Blue Christmas (17)
By The Time I Get To Phoenix (3)
Cafe (Cosa Hai Messo Nel Caffe) (5)
California Maiden (7)
Call On Me (3)
Can't Help Falling In Love (16)
Can't Smile Without You (13)
Can't Take My Eyes Off You (3)
Carol Tyme Medley (15)
Christmas Song (15,17)
Christmas Time Again (15)
Day After Day (10)
Days Of Icy Fingers (8)
Deck The Halls (medley) (17)
Didn't We (5)
Do I Love You (11)
Don't Say No (Again) (4)
Eternally (11)
Everybody Knows (2)
Everybody's Talkin' (6)

First Noel (medley) (17)
First Time Ever I Saw Your Face (7,10)
First Time In My Life (16)
For The Good Times (7)
From Me To You (14)
From Here To Eternity (3)
Gentle On My Mind (5)
Girl Of Mine (10)
Good Thing Going (4)
Goodbye My Friend (14) **97**
Have Yourself A Very Merry Christmas (17)
Help Me Make It Through The Night (8,9)
Home Tyme Medley (15)
How Near Is Love (3)
Hungry Years (13)
I Believe In Miracles (14)
I Believe In You (16)
I Can't Live A Dream (13)
I Love Making Love To You (3)
I Never Said Goodbye (10) **61**
I Wish You Love (5)
I'll Be Your Baby Tonight (7)
I'm A Better Man (5) **38**
I'm Holding Your Memory (But He's Holding You) (8)
I'm Leavin' You (11) **99**
I'm Stone In Love With You (11)
If I Were You (2)
If It Comes To That (2)
Il Mondo (1)
In Time (10) **69**

It's Impossible (9)
Jingle Bell Tyme Medley (15)
Just A Little Bit Of You (9)
Just Say I Love Her (6)
Last Waltz (2,9,12) **25**
Leavin' On A Jet Plane (6)
Les Bicyclettes De Belsize (4,9,12) **31**
Let Me Happen To You (13)
Let Me Into Your Life (4)
Let The Sunshine In (medley) (5)
Let's Kiss Tomorrow Goodbye (Un Nuovo Mondo) (5)
Let's Remember The Good Times (13)
Life Goes On (10)
Live And Just Let Live (7)
Long Gone (2)
Look At Me (14)
Lord's Prayer (17)
Love Can Fly (4)
Love For Love (Ciao, My Love) (6)
Love Letters (5)
Love Me With All Your Heart (Quando Caliente El Sol) (4)
Love The One You're With (9)
Love Was Here Before The Stars (4)
Lover's Holiday (17)
Lovin' You Too Long (16)
Loving You, Losing You (14)
Man And A Woman (3)
Man Without Love (3,9,12) **19**

Marry Me (4)
Maybe Tomorrow (16)
Miss Elaine E.S. Jones (2)
Misty Blue (2)
Morning (8)
Most Beautiful Girl (11)
Much, Much Greater Love (16)
My Cherie Amour (8)
My Prayer (9)
My Summer Song (11)
My Wife The Dancer (6,9)
Nashville Lady (8)
Night To Remember (15,17)
O' Come All Ye Faithful (17)
O' Little Town Of Bethlehem (17)
Only Your Love (11)
Our Love Will Rise Again (8)
Peace Of Mind (14)
Place In The Sun (2)
Put A Light In Your Window (14)
Put Your Hand In The Hand (7)
Quando, Quando, Quando (3,12)
Quiet Nights (1)
Raindrops Keep Fallin' On My Head (6)
Release Me (And Let Me Love Again) (1,9,12) **4**
Revivin' Old Emotions (8)
Rudolph The Red Nose Reindeer (medley) (17)
Santa Claus Is Coming To Town (medley) (17)

Santa Lija (Sogno D'Amore) (7)
Shadow Of Your Smile (3)
Signs Of Love (3)
Silent Night (15,17)
Silver Bells (15,17)
Sing-A-Long Tyme Medley (15)
Somebody Waiting (11)
Something (6)
Songs We Sang Together (11)
Spanish Eyes (3,12)
Summer Of My Life (14)
Sweetheart (7) **47**
Take Me For Now Love (7)
Take My Heart (1)
Talk It Over In The Morning (8)
Talking Love (1)
Ten Guitars (1)
That's What It's All About (11)
There Goes My Everything (1,9,12) **20**
There's A Kind Of Hush (1)
There's An Island (7)
(They Long To Be) Close To You (10)
This I Find Is Beautiful (13)
This Is My Song (1)
This Is What You Mean To Me (13)
This Moment In Time (16) **58**
Through The Eyes Of Love (4)
Till (medley) (9)
Time After Time (10)
Time For Us (Love Theme from Romeo & Juliet) (7)

To Get To You (4)
To The Ends Of The Earth (2)
Too Beautiful To Last (10) **86**
Travelin' Boy (16)
True (4)
Twenty Miles From Home (8)
Two Different Worlds (2)
Up, Up And Away (3)
Walk Through This World With Me (1)
Way It Used To Be (4,9,12) **42**
We Made It Happen (6)
We Three Kings (medley) (17)
We Wish You A Merry Christmas (medley) (17)
What A Wonderful World (3)
What I Did For Love (14)
When There's No You (7,9) **45**
White Christmas (15,17)
Winter Wonderland (17)
Winter World Of Love (5,12) **16**
Without You (10,14)
Woman In My Life (7)
Wonderland By Night (3)
Words (6)
World Without Music (13)
You Are There (14)
You Know Me (16)
You'll Never Walk Alone (9)
You're Easy To Love (4)
You're Something Special (16)
Yours Until Tomorrow (1)

HUMPHREY, Bobbi   '75

Born Barbara Ann Humphrey on 4/25/50 in Dallas. Jazz flutist.

DEBUT	PEAK	WKS			Album Title	Catalog	$	Label & Number
3/30/74	84	21	©	1	Blacks and Blues	[I]	$15	Blue Note 142
12/7/74+	30	18		2	Satin Doll		$15	Blue Note 344
11/29/74	133	5		3	Fancy Dancer	[I]	$15	Blue Note 550
7/1/78	89	14		4	Freestyle		$12	Epic 35338

Baby's Gone (1)
Blacks And Blues (1)
Chicago, Damn (1)
Fancy Dancer (3)
Freestyle (4)

Fun House (2)
Good Times (4)
Harlem River Drive (1)
Home-Made Jam (1)
I Could Love You More (4)

If You Let Me (4)
If You Want It (4)
Jasper Country Man (1)
Just A Love Child (1)
Ladies Day (2)

Mestizo Eyes (3)
My Destiny (4)
My Little Girl (4)
New York Times (2)
Please Set Me At Ease (3)

Rain Again (2)
San Francisco Lights (2)
Satin Doll (2)
Sunset Burgundy (4)
Sweeter Than Sugar (3)

Trip, The (3)
Uno Esta (2)
You Are The Sunshine Of My Life (2)
You Make Me Feel So Good (3)

HUMPHREY, Paul, & The Cool Aid Chemists   '71

Born on 10/12/35 in Detroit. R&B drummer. The Cool Aid Chemists were Clarence MacDonald, **David T. Walker** and Bill Upchurch.

DEBUT	PEAK	WKS		Album Title	Catalog	$	Label & Number
6/12/71	170	6		Paul Humphrey & The Cool Aid Chemists	[I]	$20	Lizard 20106

Ain't That Peculiar
Baby Rice

Cool Aid *29*
Detroit

Dreams
Funky L.A.

Music Talk
Sack Full Of Dreams

Something
Them Changes

HUNTER, Ian   '79

Born on 6/3/46 in Shrewsbury, Shropshire, England. Rock singer/guitarist. Leader of **Mott The Hoople** from 1969-74.

DEBUT	PEAK	WKS			Album Title	Catalog	$	Label & Number
5/17/75	50	14	©	1	Ian Hunter		$12	Columbia 33480
5/22/76	177	7	©	2	All-American Alien Boy		$12	Columbia 34142
4/28/79	35	24	©	3	You're Never Alone With A Schizophrenic		$12	Chrysalis 1214
4/26/80	69	17		4	Ian Hunter Live/Welcome To The Club	[L]	$15	Chrysalis 1269 [2]
8/29/81	62	11	©	5	Short Back N' Sides		$12	Chrysalis 1326
8/6/83	125	8		6	All Of The Good Ones Are Taken		$12	Columbia 38628
10/28/89+	157	20	©	7	Y U I ORTA		$10	Mercury 838973

IAN HUNTER/MICK RONSON

All American Alien Boy (2)
All Of The Good Ones Are Taken (6)
All The Way From Memphis (4)
All The Young Dudes (4)
American Music (7)
Angeline (4)
Apathy 83 (2)
Bastard (3,4)
Beg A Little Love (7)
Big Time (7)
Boy (1)
Captain Void 'N' The Video Jets (6)

Central Park N' West (5)
Cleveland Rocks (3,4)
Cool (7)
Death 'N' Glory Boys (6)
Every Step Of The Way (6)
F.B.I. (4)
Fun (6)
God (Take 1) (2)
Gun Control (5)
I Get So Excited (4)
I Need Your Love (5)
I Wish I Was Your Mother (4)
Irene Wilde (2,4)

It Ain't Easy When You Fall (medley) (1)
Just Another Night (3,4) **68**
Keep On Burning (5)
Laugh At Me (4)
Leave Me Alone (5)
Letter To Brittania From The Union Jack (2)
Life After Death (3)
Lisa Likes Rock N' Roll (5)
Livin' In A Heart (5)
Loner, The (7)
Lounge Lizard (5)
Man 'O' War (4)

Noises (5)
Old Records Never Die (5)
Once Bitten Twice Shy (1,4)
Outsider, The (3)
Rain (5)
Rape (2)
Restless Youth (2)
Rock 'N' Roll Queen (medley) (4)
Seeing Double (4)
Shades Off (medley) (1)
Ships (3)
Silver Needles (4)

Slaughter On Tenth Avenue (4)
Somethin's Goin' On (6)
Sons And Daughters (4)
Sons 'N' Lovers (7)
Speechless (6)
Standin' In My Light (3,4)
Sweet Dreamer (7)
Tell It Like It Is (7)
That Girl Is Rock 'N' Roll (6)
Theatre Of The Absurd (7)
3,000 Miles From Here (1)
Truth, The Whole Truth, Nuthin' But The Truth (1)

Walkin' With A Mountain (medley) (4)
We Gotta' Get Out Of Here (4)
When The Daylight Comes (4)
Who Do You Love (1)
Wild East (3)
Womens Intuition (7)
You Nearly Did Me In (2)

HUNTER, John   '85

Born in Chicago. Rock singer/keyboardist.

DEBUT	PEAK	WKS		Album Title	Catalog	$	Label & Number
2/9/85	148	9		Famous At Night		$10	Private I 39626

Crimes Of Passion
Horses

Losin' You Again
Put Yourself On The Line

Sad Songs On The Radio
She Advertises

Take Your Chances
This Is Forever

Tragedy *39*
Valentine

HUNTLEY, Chet, & David Brinkley '64

Co-anchors of TV's *NBC Nightly News* from 1955-70. Brinkley was born on 7/10/20 in Wilmington, North Carolina. Huntley was born on 12/10/11 in Cardwell, Montana; died on 3/20/74 (age 62).

3/14/64 | 115 | 7 | **A Time To Keep: 1963** .... [T] $20 RCA Victor 1088
a recall of the voices and events of 1963

| Eventful Summer | People And Providence | Torch Is Passed | World Politics |
| Negro Revolution | Terrible Weekend | World Mourns | |

HURRICANE '88

Hard-rock group from Los Angeles: Kelly Hansen (vocals), Robert Sarzo (guitar), Tony Cavazo (bass) and Jay Schellen (drums). Sarzo is the brother of **Whitesnake**'s Rudy Sarzo. Cavazo is the brother of **Quiet Riot**'s Carlos Cavazo. Sarzo left the band in 1989, replaced by Doug Aldrich.

4/30/88 | 92 | 36 | © | 1 **Over The Edge** .... $10 Enigma 73320
4/14/90 | 125 | 10 | © | 2 **Slave To The Thrill** .... $10 Enigma 73511

Baby Snakes (1)	I'm Eighteen (1)	Let It Slide (2)	Next To You (2)	Spark In My Heart (1)	Young Man (2)
Dance Little Sister (2)	I'm Onto You (1)	Livin' Over The Edge (1)	Reign Of Love (2)	Temptation (2)	
Don't Wanna Dream (2)	In The Fire (2)	Lock Me Up (2)	Shout (1)	10,000 Years (2)	
Give Me An Inch (1)	Insane (1)	Messin' With A Hurricane (1)	Smiles Like A Child (2)	We Are Strong (1)	

HÜSKER DÜ '87

Rock trio from Minneapolis: **Bob Mould** (vocals, guitar), Greg Norton (bass) and Grant Hart (drums). Mould later formed **Sugar**.

4/12/86 | 140 | 10 | © | 1 **Candy Apple Grey** .... $10 Warner 25385
2/14/87 | 117 | 10 | © | 2 **Warehouse: Songs And Stories** .... $15 Warner 25544 [2]

Actual Condition (2)	Could You Be The One? (2)	Friend, You've Got To Fall (2)	No Reservations (2)	Tell You Why Tomorrow (2)	Visionary (2)
All This I've Done For You (1)	Crystal (1)	Hardly Getting Over It (1)	She Floated Away (1)	These Important Years (2)	You Can Live At Home (2)
Back From Somewhere (2)	Dead Set On Destruction (1)	I Don't Know For Sure (1)	She's A Woman (And Now He	Too Far Down (1)	You're A Soldier (2)
Bed Of Nails (2)	Don't Want To Know If You Are	Ice Cold Ice (2)	Is A Man) (1)	Too Much Spice (1)	
Charity, Chastity, Prudence,	Lonely (1)	It's Not Peculiar (2)	Sorry Somehow (1)	Turn It Around (2)	
And Hope (2)	Eiffel Tower High (1)	No Promise Have I Made (1)	Standing In The Rain (2)	Up In The Air (2)	

HUTCH, Willie '73

Born Willie Hutchinson in 1946 in Los Angeles; raised in Dallas. R&B producer/songwriter. Uncle of Don Hutchinson of **Above The Law**.

6/2/73 | 114 | 16 | © | 1 **The Mack** .... [S] $15 Motown 766

10/13/73 | 183 | 6 | 2 **Fully Exposed** .... $15 Motown 784
5/18/74 | 179 | 4 | 3 **Foxy Brown** .... [S] $15 Motown 811
11/15/75 | 150 | 6 | 4 **Ode To My Lady** .... $15 Motown 838
4/3/76 | 163 | 6 | 5 **Concert In Blues** .... $15 Motown 854

Ain't Nothing Like Togetherness	Don't Let A Little Money Keep	Hospital Prelude Of Love	If You Ain't Got No Money (You	Out There (3)	Tell Me Who Has Our Love
(2)	You Acting Funny (5)	Theme (3)	Can't Get No Honey) (2)	Overture Of Foxy Brown (3)	Turned Cold (2)
Ain't That (Mellow, Mellow) (3)	Foxy Brown, Theme Of (3)	I Choose You (1)	Just Another Day (4)	Party Down (4,5)	Vampin (1)
Baby Come Home (5)	Foxy Lady (3)	I Finally Made The Headlines	Love Me Back (4)	Precious Pearl (5)	Way We Were (4)
Brother's Gonna Work It Out	Getaway (Chase Scene)	(5)	**Love Power** (4) *41*	Shake, Rattle And Roll (5)	Whatever You Do (Do It Good)
(1) *67*	(medley) (3)	I Just Wanted To Make Her	Mack, Theme Of The (1)	Since I Found You Everything's	(3)
California My Way (2)	Give Me Some Of That Good	Happy (2)	Mack Man (Got To Get Over)	Alright (4)	You Gotta Give Love Up (4)
Can't Get Ready For Losing	Old Love (3)	I Wanna Be Where You Are (2)	(1)	**Slick** (1) *65*	You Sure Know How To Love
You (2)	Have You Ever Asked Yourself	I Wish You Love (5)	Mack's Stroll (medley) (1)	Stormy Monday (5)	Your Man (3)
Chase (3)	Why (All About Money Game)	I'll Be There (2)	Mother's Theme (Mama) (1)	Stormy Weather (5)	
Come On Let's Do The Thang	(3)	(I'm Gonna) Hold On (4)	Now That It's All Over (1)	Sunshine Lady (2)	
(5)			Ode To My Lady (4)	Talk To Me (4)	

HUTCHENCE, Michael '00

Born on 1/22/60 in Sydney, Australia. Committed suicide on 11/22/97 (age 37). Lead singer of **INXS**.

3/11/00 | 200 | 1 | © | **Michael Hutchence** $10 V2 27064
recorded shortly before his death in 1997

All I'm Saying	Don't Save Me From Myself	Get On The Inside	Put The Pieces Back Together	Straight Line
Baby It's Alright	Fear	Let Me Show You	She Flirts For England	
Breathe	Flesh And Blood	Possibilities	Slide Away	

HUTSON, Leroy '76

Born on 6/4/45 in Newark, New Jersey. R&B singer. Member of **The Impressions** from 1971-73.

3/6/76 | 170 | 8 | © | **Feel The Spirit** .... $12 Curtom 5010

| Butterfat | Feel The Spirit ('76) | Let's Be Lonely Together | Never Know What You Can Do |
| Don't Let It Get Next To You | It's The Music | Lover's Holiday | (Give It A Try) |

HYDE, Paul, And The Payolas '85

Pop-rock group from Canada: Paul Hyde (vocals), Bob Rock (guitar), Alex Boynton (bass) and Chris Taylor (drums). Hyde and Rock later recorded as the duo **Rock And Hyde**.

6/8/85 | 144 | 10 | **Here's The World For Ya** .... $10 A&M 5025

| All That I Want | Here's The World | It Won't Be You | Never Leave This Place | Stuck In The Rain |
| Cruel Hearted Lovers | It Must Be Love | Little Boys | Rhythm Slaves | **You're The Only Love** *84* |

HYLAND, Brian '69

Born on 11/12/43 in Queens, New York. Pop singer.

4/19/69 | 160 | 5 | 1 **Tragedy/A Million To One** .... $20 Dot 25926
1/30/71 | 171 | 4 | 2 **Brian Hyland** .... $15 Uni 73097
produced by Del Shannon

Be That Someone (1)	**Lonely Teardrops** (2) *54*	On The East Side (2)	Thrill Is Gone (2)	You & Me (2)
Drivin' Me Crazy (2)	Lonesome Town (1)	See The Funny Little Clown (1)	**Tragedy** (1) *56*	You'd Better Stop - And Think It
Gypsy Woman (2) *3*	Lorrayne (2)	Slow Down (2)	Walk Right Back (1)	Over (1)
I'm Without You (2)	Mail Order Gun (2)	So Sad (To Watch Good Love	When I Fall In Love (1)	
It Could All Begin Again (In	Maria (medley) (2)	Go Bad) (1)	Will You Love Me Tomorrow (1)	
You) (1)	**Million To One** (1) *90*	Somewhere (medley) (2)	You (1)	

HYMAN, Dick '69

Born on 3/8/27 in New York City. Pianist/conductor/arranger.

11/25/57 | 21 | 2 | 1 **60 Great All Time Songs, Vol. 3** .... [I] $25 MGM 3537

11/9/63 | 117 | 7 | 2 **Electrodynamics** .... [I] $20 Command 856
4/4/64 | 132 | 5 | 3 **Fabulous** .... [I] $20 Command 862
4/27/68 | 179 | 2 | 4 **Mirrors - Reflections Of Today** .... [I] $15 Command 924
DICK HYMAN AND "THE GROUP"

HYMAN, Dick — Cont'd

DEBUT	PEAK	WKS	CD	ARTIST — Album Title	Catalog	$	Label & Number
4/19/69	30	30	©	5 Moog - The Electric Eclectics Of Dick Hyman	[I]	$15	Command 938
9/27/69	110	11		6 The Age Of Electronicus	[I]	$15	Command 946

Ain't She Sweet Medley (1)
Ain't We Got Fun Medley (1)
Alfie (6)
Aquarius (6)
As Time Goes By Medley (1)
Band Played On Medley (1)
Best Is Yet To Come (3)
Big Ben Bossa (2)
Birth Of The Blues Medley (1)
Blackbird (6)
Both Sides Now (6)
Cuddle Up A Little Closer Medley (1)

Danke Schoen (3)
Do Nothin' Till You Hear From Me (4)
Evening Thoughts (5)
Flower Road (4)
Fly Me To The Moon (2)
Four Duets In Odd Meter (5)
Give It Up Or Turn It Loose (6)
Green Onions (6)
Groovin' (6)
Hit The Road Jack (4)
House Of Mirrors (4)
I Got Rhythm Medley (1)

I Left My Heart In San Francisco (2)
I'll Be Around (3)
I'll Remember April (3)
Improvisation In Fourths (5)
In The Heat Of The Night (4)
In The Wee Small Hours (Of The Morning) (4)
Kolumbo (5)
Legend Of Johnny Pot (5)
Living On Borrowed Time (3)
Mack The Knife (2)
Mercy, Mercy, Mercy (4)

Minotaur, The (5) *38*
Moog And Me (5)
Mr. Lucky (3)
Ob-La-Di, Ob-La-Da (6)
Ode To Billy Joe (4)
Paradise (2)
Respect (4)
S'posin' (3)
Satin Doll (2)
Shadowland (2)
Side By Side (2)
Sing Something Simple Medley (1)

So Easy (3)
Sonny Boy (3)
South America Take It Away Medley (1)
Stompin' At The Savoy (2)
Sweetest Sounds (2)
Tap Dance In The Memory Banks (5)
This Is All I Ask (2)
Till We Meet Again (2)
Time Is Tight (6)
Topless Dancers Of Corfu (5)
Total Bells And Tony (5)

Up, Up And Away (4)
Washington Square (3)
Week End Blues (4)
What'd I Say (3)
Wives & Lovers (3)

HYMAN, Phyllis   '80

Born on 7/6/50 in Philadelphia; raised in Pittsburgh. Committed suicide on 6/30/95 (age 45). R&B singer/actress/model.

DEBUT	PEAK	WKS	CD	ARTIST — Album Title	$	Label & Number
4/30/77	107	14	©	1 Phyllis Hyman	$12	Buddah 5681
2/3/79	70	17	©	2 Somewhere In My Lifetime	$12	Arista 4202
12/8/79+	50	21		3 You Know How To Love Me	$12	Arista 9509
8/1/81	57	13		4 Can't We Fall In Love Again	$12	Arista 9544
6/18/83	112	12		5 Goddess Of Love	$12	Arista 8021
10/11/86+	78	41	©	6 Living All Alone	$10	Philadelphia Int'l. 53029
8/10/91	117	12	©	7 Prime Of My Life	$10	Philadelphia Int'l. 11006
11/25/95	67	9	©	8 I Refuse To Be Lonely	$10	Philadelphia Int'l. 11040

Ain't You Had Enough Love (6)
Answer Is You (2)
Back To Paradise (8)
Be Careful (How You Treat My Love) (2)
Beautiful Man Of Mine (1)
But I Love You (3)
Can't We Fall In Love Again (4)
Children Of The World (4)
Complete Me (3)
Deliver The Love (1)
Don't Tell Me, Tell Her (4)
Don't Wanna Change The World (7)
Falling Star (5)
First Time Together (6)

Give A Little More (3)
Give Me One Good Reason To Stay (3)
Goddess Of Love (5)
Gonna Make Changes (2)
Heavenly (3)
Here's That Rainy Day (2)
Hold On (3)
I Ain't Asking (4)
I Can't Take It Anymore (7)
I Don't Want To Lose You (1)
I Found Love (7)
I Refuse To Be Lonely (8)
I'm Calling You (8)
I'm Truly Yours (8)
If You Want Me (6)

It Takes Two (8)
It's Not About You (It's About Me) (8)
Just Another Face In The Crowd (4)
Just Me And You (5)
Just Twenty Five Miles To Anywhere (5)
Kiss You All Over (2)
Let Somebody Love You (5)
Living All Alone (6)
Living In Confusion (7)
Living Inside Your Love (2)
Lookin' For A Lovin' (2)
Love Too Good To Last (4)
Loving You-Losing You (1)

Meet Me On The Moon (7)
Night Bird Gets The Love (1)
No One Can Love You More (1)
Old Friend (6)
One Thing On My Mind (1)
Prime Of My Life (7)
Riding The Tiger (5)
Screaming At The Moon (6)
Slow Dancin' (6)
So Strange (2)
Some Way (3)
Somewhere In My Lifetime (2)
Soon Come Again (2)
Sunshine In My Life (4)
This Feeling Must Be Love (3)

This Too Shall Pass (8)
Tonight You And Me (4)
Under Your Spell (3)
Waiting For The Last Tear To Fall (8)
Walk Away (1)
Was Yesterday Such A Long Time Ago (1)
We Should Be Lovers (5)
What Ever Happened To Our Love (7)
What You Won't Do For Love (6)
When I Give My Love (This Time) (7)

When You Get Right Down To It (7)
Why Did You Turn Me On (5)
Why Not Me (8)
You Just Don't Know (6)
You Know How To Love Me (3)
You Sure Look Good To Me (4)
Your Move, My Heart (5)

HYPNOTIZE CAMP POSSE   '00

Gathering of rappers from Memphis: **Gangsta Boo**, **Project Pat**, **Three 6 Mafia** and T-Rock.

DEBUT	PEAK	WKS	CD	ARTIST — Album Title	$	Label & Number
2/12/00	36	15	©	Three 6 Mafia Presents Hypnotize Camp Posse	$10	Hypnotize Minds 1883

Azz & Tittiez
Big Mouth, Big Talk
D-Suckin'-H

Da First Date
Die A Soldier
Don't Make Me Kill

Don't Trust 'Em
Drive By
Fie It On Up

Hoes Can Be Like Niggaz
Project Hoes
We Ain't Playin'

We 'Bout To Ride
Who Run It

I

IAN, Janis   '75

Born Janis Eddy Fink on 4/7/51 in New York City. Singer/songwriter/pianist/guitarist.

DEBUT	PEAK	WKS	CD	ARTIST — Album Title	$	Label & Number
6/17/67	29	28		1 Janis Ian	$20	Verve Forecast 3017
12/30/67+	179	5		2 For All The Seasons Of Your Mind	$20	Verve Forecast 3024
6/1/74+	83	20	©	3 Stars	$12	Columbia 32857
3/22/75	❶[1]	64	▲ ©	4 Between The Lines	$12	Columbia 33394
1/24/76	12	19		5 Aftertones	$12	Columbia 33919
1/29/77	45	12		6 Miracle Row	$12	Columbia 34440
9/16/78	120	11		7 Janis Ian	$12	Columbia 35325
7/4/81	156	3		8 Restless Eyes	$12	Columbia 37360

Aftertones (5)
And I Did Ma (2)
Applause (3)
At Seventeen (4) *3*
Bahimsa (2)
Belle Of The Blues (5)
Between The Lines (4)
Bigger Than Real (4)
Boy I Really Tied One On (5)
Bridge, The (7)
Bright Lights And Promises (4)
Candlelight (6)
Come On (4)
Dance With Me (3)
Dear Billy (8)
Do You Wanna Dance? (7)
Don't Cry, Old Man (5)

Down And Away (8)
Evening Star (2)
From Me To You (4)
Get Ready To Roll (8)
Goodbye To Morning (5)
Hair Of Spun Gold (1)
Honey D'Ya Think? (2)
Hopper Painting (7)
Hotels & One-Night Stands (7)
Hymn (5)
I Believe I'm Myself Again (8)
I Need To Live Alone Again (7)
I Remember Yesterday (8)
I Want To Make You Love Me (6)
I Would Like To Dance (5)
I'll Cry Tonight (6)

I'll Give You A Stone If You'll Throw It (Changing Tymes) (1)
In The Winter (4)
Insanity Comes Quietly To The Structured Mind (2)
Janey's Blues (1)
Jesse (3)
Let Me Be Lonely (6)
Light A Light (4)
Lonely One (2)
Love Is Blind (5)
Lover Be Kindly (1)
Lover's Lullaby (4)
Man You Are In Me (3)
Maria (medley) (6)
Miracle Row (medley) (6)
Mrs. McKenzie (1)

My Mama's House (7)
New Christ Cardiac Hero (1)
Page Nine (3)
Party Lights (6)
Passion Play (8)
Pro-Girl (1)
Queen Merka & Me (2)
Restless Eyes (8)
Roses (5)
Shady Acres (2)
Silly Habits (7)
Slow Dance Romance (6)
Society's Child (Baby I've Been Thinking) (1) *14*
Some People (7)
Song For All The Seasons Of Your Mind (2)

Stars (3)
Streetlife Serenaders (7)
Sugar Mountain (8)
Sunflakes Fall, Snowrays Call (2)
Sunset Of Your Life (6)
Sweet Sympathy (3)
Take To The Sky (6)
Tea & Sympathy (4)
Thankyous (3)
That Grand Illusion (7)
Then Tangles Of My Mind (1)
There Are Times (2)
This Must Be Wrong (5)
Tonight Will Last Forever (7)
Too Old To Go 'Way Little Girl (1)

Under The Covers (8) *71*
Water Colors (4)
When The Party's Over (4)
Will You Dance? (6)
Without You (3)
You've Got Me On A String (3)
Younger Generation Blues (1)

IAN & SYLVIA   '64

Folk duo from Canada: Ian Tyson (born on 9/25/33 in Victoria, British Columbia) and wife Sylvia Fricker (born on 9/19/40 in Chatham, Ontario). Began performing together in 1959. Married from 1964-73.

DEBUT	PEAK	WKS	CD	ARTIST — Album Title	$	Label & Number
9/28/63	115	6	©	1 Four Strong Winds	$25	Vanguard 79133
9/5/64	70	12	©	2 Northern Journey	$25	Vanguard 79154

DEBUG	PEAK	WKS	RIAA	CD	ARTIST — Album Title	Catalog	Sym	$	Label & Number

IAN & SYLVIA — Cont'd

6/19/65	77	18		© 3	Early Morning Rain			$25	Vanguard 79175
5/28/66	142	6		© 4	Play One More			$25	Vanguard 79225
4/1/67	130	7		© 5	So Much For Dreaming			$25	Vanguard 79241
7/8/67	148	10		6	Lovin' Sound			$20	MGM 4388

Awake Ye Drowsy Sleepers (3) · Big River (6) · Brave Wolfe (2) · Captain Woodstock's Courtship (2) · Catfish Blues (5) · Changes (4) · Child Apart (5) · Circle Game (5) · Come All Ye Fair And Tender Ladies (2) · Come In Stranger (3) · Cutty Wren (5) · Darcy Farrow (3) · Early Morning Rain (3) · Ella Speed (1) · Every Night When The Sun Goes Down (1) · Every Time I Feel The Spirit (1) · (Find A) Reason To Believe (6) · For Lovin' Me (3) · Four Rode By (2) · Four Strong Winds (1) · French Girl (4) · Friends Of Mine (4) · Ghost Lover (2) · Gifts Are For Giving (4) · Green Valley (2) · Greenwood Sidie (The Cruel Mother) (1) · Grey Morning (5) · Hang On To A Dream (6) · Hey What About Me (4) · Hold Tight (5) · I Don't Believe You (6) · I'll Bid My Heart Be Still (3) · January Morning (5) · Jealous Lover (2) · Jesus Met The Woman At The Well (1) · Katy Dear (1) · Lady Of Carlisle (1) · Little Beggarman (2) · Lonely Girls (4) · Long Lonesome Road (1) · Lovin' Sound (6) · Marlborough Street Blues (3) · Maude's Blues (3) · Molly And Tenbrooks (4) · Moonshine Can (2) · Mr. Spoons (6) · Nancy Whiskey (3) · National Hotel (6) · Nova Scotia Farewell (2) · Pilgrimage To Paradise (6) · Play One More (4) · Poor Lazarus (1) · Red Velvet (3) · Royal Canal (1) · Satisfied Mind (4) · Short Grass (4) · Si Les Bateaux (5) · So Much For Dreaming (5) · Some Day Soon (2) · Song For Canada (3) · Spanish Is A Loving Tongue (1) · Summer Wages (4) · Sunday (6) · Swing Down, Chariot (3) · Texas Rangers (4) · Tomorrow Is A Long Time (1) · Traveling Drummer (3) · Trilogy (6) · Twenty-Four Hours From Tulsa (4) · V'La L'bon Vent (1) · When I Was A Cowboy (4) · Where Did All The Love Go? (6) · Wild Geese (3) · Windy Weather (6) · You Were On My Mind (2)

★318★ **ICE CUBE** '92

Born O'Shea Jackson on 6/15/69 in Los Angeles. Male rapper/actor. Former member of **N.W.A.** Acted in several movies. Cousin of **Del The Funkyhomosapien.**

6/2/90	19	26	▲ © 1	AmeriKKKa's Most Wanted			$10	Priority 57120
1/5/91	34	43	▲ © 2	Kill At Will .... [M]			$10	Priority 7230
11/16/91	2¹	33	▲ © 3	Death Certificate			$10	Priority 57155
12/5/92	❶¹	52	▲ © 4	The Predator			$10	Priority 57185
12/25/93	5	48	▲ © 5	Lethal Injection			$10	Priority 53876
12/10/94	19	24	● © 6	Bootlegs & B-Sides .... [K]			$10	Priority 53921
1/3/98	116	14	© 7	Featuring...Ice Cube .... [K]			$10	Priority 51037
12/5/98	7	20	▲ © 8	War & Peace Vol. 1 (The War Disc)			$10	Priority 50700
4/8/00	3	25	● © 9	War & Peace Vol. 2 (The Peace Disc)			$10	Best Side 50015

Alive On Arrival (3) · AmeriKKKa's Most Wanted (1) · Ask About Me (8) · Bend A Corner Wit Me (7) · Better Off Dead (1) · Bird In The Hand (3) · Birth, The (3) · Black Korea (3) · Bomb, The (1) · **Bop Gun (One Nation)** (5,7) *23* · Bow Down (7) · Can You Bounce? (9) · Cash Over Ass (8) · Cave Bitch (5) · **Check Yo Self** (4,6,7) *20* · Color Blind (3) · Curse Of Money (8) · D'Voidofpopniggafiedmegamix (6) · Dead Homiez (2) · Death (3) · Dirty Mack (4) · Dr. Frankenstein (8) · Doing Dumb Shit (3) · Don't Trust 'Em (4) · Drive-By, The (1) · Endangered Species (Tales From The Darkside) (1,2,7) · Enemy (5) · Extradition (8) · Fuck Dying (8) · Funeral, The (3) · Game Over (7) · Gangsta's Fairytale (1) · Gangsta's Fairytale 2 (4) · Get Off My Dick And Tell Yo Bitch To Come Here (1,2) · Ghetto Bird (3) · Ghetto Vet (8) · Givin' Up The Nappy Dug Out (3) · Gotta Be Insanity (9) · Greed (8) · Gutter S*** (9) · Hello (9) · Horny Lil' Devil (3) · I Gotta Say What Up!!! (2) · I Wanna Kill Sam (3) · I'm Only Out For One Thang (1) · If I Was Fuckin' You (8) · **It Was A Good Day** (4,6) *15* · It's A Man's World (1,7) · JD's Gafflin' (Part 2) (2) · Jackin' For Beats (2) · Lil Ass Gee (5,6) · Limos, Demos & Bimbos (8) · Look Who's Burnin' (3) · Make It Ruff, Make It Smooth (5) · Man's Best Friend (3) · My Skin Is My Sin (6) · My Summer Vacation (3) · Natural Born Killaz (7) · N**** Of The Century (9) · Nigga Ya Love To Hate (1) · No Vaseline (3) · Now I Gotta Wet 'Cha (4) · Once Upon A Time In The Projects (1) · Once Upon A Time In The Projects 2 (8) · Peckin' Order (8) · Penitentiary (8) · Predator, The (4) · Product, The (2) · **Pushin' Weight** (8) *26* · **Really Doe** (5) *54* · Record Company Pimpin' (9) · Robbin' Hood (Cause It Ain't All Good) (6) · Robin Lench (3) · Roll All Day (9) · Rollin' Wit The Lench Mob (1) · Say Hi To The Bad Guy (4) · Steady Mobbin' (3) · Supreme Hustle (9) · 3 Strikes You In (8) · Trespass (7) · True To The Game (3) · Turn Off The Radio (1) · 24 Mo' Hours (9) · 24 Wit An L (6) · 2 N The Morning (6) · Two To The Head (7) · U Ain't Gonna Take My Life (6) · Until We Rich (9) · Us (3) · Waitin' Ta Hate (9) · War & Peace (8) · We Had To Tear This Mothafucka Up (2) · West Up! (7) · What Can I Do? (5,6) · What They Hittin' Foe? (1) · When I Get To Heaven (5,6) · When Will They Shoot? (4) · Who Got The Camera? (4) · Who's The Mack? (4) · **Wicked** (4) *55* · Wicked Wayz (7) · Wrong Nigga To Fuck Wit (3) · X-Bitches (8) · You Ain't Gotta Lie (Ta Kick It) (9) · **You Can Do It** (9) *35* · You Can't Fade Me (1) · You Don't Wanna Fuck Wit These (6) · **You Know How We Do It** (5,6) *30*

ICEHOUSE '88

Rock group formed in Sydney, Australia: Iva Davies (vocals, guitar), Anthony Smith (keyboards), Keith Welsh (bass) and John Lloyd (drums). Numerous personnel changes through the '80s, with Davies the only constant. Group name is Australian slang for an insane asylum.

7/25/81	82	15	© 1	Icehouse			$12	Chrysalis 1350
10/9/82	129	6	© 2	Primitive Man			$12	Chrysalis 1390
5/24/86	55	24	© 3	Measure For Measure			$10	Chrysalis 41527
10/17/87+	43	44	© 4	Man Of Colours			$10	Chrysalis 41592

Angel Street (3) · Anybody's War (4) · Baby, You're So Strange (3) · Boulevarde (1) · Can't Help Myself (1) · **Crazy** (4) *14* · Cross The Border (3) · **Electric Blue** (4) *7* · Fatman (1) · Flame, The (4) · Girl In The Moon (4) · Glam (2) · Goodnight, Mr. Matthews (2) · Great Southern Land (2) · Heartbreak Kid (4) · Hey' Little Girl (2) · Icehouse (1) · Kingdom, The (4) · Love In Motion (2) · Lucky Me (3) · Man Of Colours (4) · Mr. Big (3) · **My Obsession** (4) *88* · Mysterious Thing (2) · No Kind (1) · **No Promises** (3) *79* · Not My Kind (1) · Nothing Too Serious (4) · One By One (2) · Paradise (4) · Regular Boys (3) · Sister (1) · Skin (1) · Sons (1) · Spanish Gold (3) · Street Cafe (3) · Sunrise (4) · Trojan Blue (3) · Uniform (2) · Walls (1) · **We Can Get Together** (1) *62*

ICE-T '93

Born Tracy Morrow on 2/16/58 in Newark, New Jersey. Male rapper/actor. Formed group **Body Count.** Acted in several movies.

8/15/87	93	27	● © 1	Rhyme Pays			$10	Sire 25602
10/1/88	35	33	● © 2	Power			$10	Sire 25765
10/28/89	37	28	● © 3	Freedom Of Speech...Just Watch What You Say			$10	Sire 26028
6/1/91	15	33	● © 4	O.G. Original Gangster			$10	Sire 26492
4/10/93	14	11	● © 5	Home Invasion			$10	Rhyme Syndicate 53858
6/22/96	89	4	© VI	Return Of The Real			$10	Rhyme Syndicate 53933

Addicted To Danger (5) · Bitches 2 (4) · Black 'N' Decker (3) · Body Count (4) · Bouncin' Down The Streezet (3) · Cramp Your Style (6) · Dear Homie (6) · Depths Of Hell (5) · Drama (2) · Ed (4) · Escape From The Killing Fields (4) · Evil E-What About Sex? (4) · 5th, The (6) · First Impression (4) · Fly By (4) · Forced To Do Dirt (4) · 409 (1) · Freedom Of Speech (3) · Fried Chicken (4) · Funky Gripsta (5) · G Style (5) · Girl Tried To Kill Me (3) · Girls L.G.B.N.A.F. (2) · Gotta Lotta Love (5) · Grand Larceny (2) · Heartbeat (2) · High Rollers (2) · Hit The Deck (3) · Home Invasion (5) · Home Of The Bodyhag (5) · House, The (4) · How Does It Feel (5) · Hunted Child (3) · I Ain't New Ta This (5) · I Love Ladies (1) · I Must Stand (4) · I'm Your Pusher (2) · Ice M.F. T (5) · Iceberg, The (3) · Inside Of A Gangsta (6) · It's On (5) · Lane, The (6) · Lethal Weapon (3) · Lifestyles Of The Rich And Infamous (4) · M.V.P.s (4) · Make It Funky (3) · Make The Loot Loop (6) · Message To The Soldier (5) · Mic Contract (4) · Midnight (4) · Mind Over Matter (4) · **New Jack Hustler (Nino's Theme)** (4) *67* · 99 Problems (4) · O.G. Original Gangster (4) · Pain (1) · Peel Their Caps Back (3) · Personal (2)

ICE-T — Cont'd

Pimp Anthem (6)
Pimp Behind The Wheels (DJ Evil E The Great) (5)
Power (2)
Prepared To Die (4)
Pulse Of The Rhyme (4)

Race War (5)
Radio Suckers (2)
Rap Game's Hijacked (6)
Return Of The Real (6)
Rhyme Pays (1)
Sex (1)

Shit Hit The Fan (5)
Shut Up, Be Happy (3)
6 'N The Mornin' (1)
Somebody Gotta Do It (Pimpin' Ain't Easy!!!) (1)
Soul On Ice (2)

Squeeze The Trigger (1)
Straight Up Nigga (4)
Street Killer (4)
Syndicate, The (2)
Syndicate 4 Ever (6)
That's How I'm Livin' (5)

They Want Me Back In (6)
This One's For Me (3)
Tower, The (4)
Watch The Ice Break (5)
What Ya Wanna Do? (3)
Where The Shit Goes Down (6)

Ya Shoulda Killed Me Last Year (4)
You Played Yourself (3)
Ziplock (4)

ICICLE WORKS '84

Rock trio from Liverpool, England: Robert Ian McNabb (vocals, guitar), Chris Layhe (bass) and Chris Sharrock (drums).

4/21/84	40	18		©	**Icicle Works**			$10	Arista 8202

As The Dragonfly Flies

Chop The Tree
Factory In The Desert

In The Cauldron Of Love
Love Is A Wonderful Colour

Lovers' Day
Nirvana

Out Of Season
Waterline

Whisper To A Scream (Birds Fly) *37*

ICON '84

Rock group from Phoenix: Stephen Clifford (vocals), Dan Wexler and John Aquilino (guitars), Tracy Wallach (bass) and Pat Dixon (drums).

6/9/84	190	2		©	**Icon**			$10	Capitol 12336

Hot Desert Night
I'm Alive

Iconoclast
It's Up To You

Killer Machine
On Your Feet

Rock 'N' Roll Maniac
(Rock On) Through The Night

Under My Gun
World War

ICONZ '01

Rap group from Miami: Luc Duc, Stage McCloud, Bull Dog, Chapter, Tony Manshino, Screwface and Supastar.

3/3/01	64	10		©	**Street Money**			$10	Landmark 62617

Doggy Style
Get Crunked Up *93*
Home-Vade

I Represent
Ignorance
In This B%#@h

Laughin' At Ya
Let's Roll
Lick Shot

Ni#%a What!
Representin' Da South
We Ain't Goin' Home Tonite

What Y'all Know 'Bout Dat?
You're A Trick

IDEAL '00

R&B vocal group from Houston: J-Dante, Maverick, PZ and Swab.

10/9/99+	83	37	●	©	**Ideal**			$10	Noontime 47882

All About You
Break Your Plans
Creep Inn

Get Down With Me
Get Gone *13*
I Don't Mind

Ideally Yours
Jealous Skies
Never Let You Go

No More
Sexy Dancer
Skit - "Pigeon"

Tell Me Why
There's No Way
Things You Can't Do

IDES OF MARCH, The '70

Rock group from Chicago: Jim Peterik (vocals, guitar), Ray Herr (guitar), Larry Millas (keyboards), John Larson and Chuck Soumar (horns), Bob Bergland (bass) and Mike Borch (drums). Group named after a line in Shakespeare's *Julius Caesar*. Peterik later formed **Survivor**.

6/27/70	55	12			**Vehicle**			$20	Warner 1863

Aire Of Good Feeling
Bald Medusa
Dharma For One (medley)

Factory Band
Home
One Woman Man

Sky Is Falling
Symphony For Eleanor (Eleanor Rigby)

Time For Thinking
Vehicle *2*
Wooden Ships (medley)

★371★ IDOL, Billy '84

Born William Broad on 11/30/55 in Stanmore, Middlesex, England. Rock singer. Leader of the punk group Generation X from 1977-81. Appeared in the movie *The Wedding Singer*.

10/24/81+	71	68		© 1	**Don't Stop**	[M]		$10	Chrysalis 4000
7/31/82+	45	104	●	© 2	**Billy Idol**			$10	Chrysalis 41377
12/3/83+	6	82	▲²	© 3	**Rebel Yell**			$10	Chrysalis 41450
11/8/86	6	47	▲	© 4	**Whiplash Smile**			$10	Chrysalis 41514
10/10/87	10	29	▲	© 5	**Vital Idol**	[K]		$10	Chrysalis 41620
5/19/90	11	39	▲	© 6	**Charmed Life**			$10	Chrysalis 21735
7/17/93	48	7		© 7	**Cyberpunk**			$10	Chrysalis 26000
4/14/01	74	24		© 8	**Greatest Hits**	[G]		$10	Chrysalis 28812

Adam In Chains (7)
All Summer Single (4)
Baby Talk (1)
Beyond Belief (4)
Blue Highway (3)
Catch My Fall (3,5,8) *50*
Come On, Come On (2)
Concrete Kingdom (7)
Congo Man (7)
Cradle Of Love (6,8) *2*

Crank Call (3)
Dancing With Myself (1,5,8)
Daytime Drama (3)
Dead Next Door (3)
Dead On Arrival (2)
(Do Not) Stand In The Shadows (3)
Don't Need A Gun (4,8) *37*
Don't You (Forget About Me) (8)
Endless Sleep (6)

Eyes Without A Face (3,8) *4*
Fatal Charm (4)
Flesh For Fantasy (3,5,8) *29*
Heroin (7)
Hole In The Wall (2)
Hot In The City (2,5,8) *23*
It's So Cruel (2)
L.A. Woman (6,8) *52*
License To Thrill (6)
Love Calling (2,5)

Love Labours On (7)
Love Unchained (6)
Loveless, The (6)
Man For All Seasons (4)
Mark Of Caine (6)
Mony Mony (1,5,8)
Mother Dawn (7)
Neuromancer (7)
Nobody's Business (2)
One Night, One Chance (4)

Power Junkie (7)
Prodigal Blues (6)
Pumping On Steel (6)
Rebel Yell (3,8) *46*
Right Way (6)
Shangrila (7)
Shock To The System (7,8)
Shooting Stars (2)
Soul Standing By (4)
Sweet Sixteen (4,8) *20*

Then The Night Comes (7)
To Be A Lover (4,5,8) *6*
Tomorrow People (7)
Trouble With The Sweet Stuff (6)
Untouchables (1)
Venus (7)
Wasteland (7)
White Wedding (2,5,8) *36*
Worlds Forgotten Boy (4)

IF '71

Jazz-rock group from England: J.W. Hodkinson (vocals), Terry Smith (guitar), Dick Morrissey and Dave Quincy (reeds), John Mealing (keyboards), Jim Richardson (bass) and Dennis Elliot (drums).

10/31/70	187	2		© 1	**If**			$20	Capitol 539
9/25/71	171	3		2	**If 3**			$20	Capitol 820
10/28/72	195	4		3	**Waterfall**			$15	Metromedia 1057

Cast No Shadows (3)
Child Of Storm (2)
Dockland (1)
Far Beyond (2)

Fibonacci's Number (2)
Forgotten Roads (2)
Here Comes Mr. Time (2)
I'm Reaching Out On All Sides (1)

Light Still Shines (3)
Paint Your Pictures (3)
Promised Land (1)
Raise The Level Of Your Conscious Mind (1)

Sector 17 (3)
Seldom Seen Jam (3)
Sweet January (2)
Throw Myself To The Wind (3)
Upstairs (2)

Waterfall (3)
What Can A Friend Say? (1)
What Did I Say About The Box, Jack? (1)

Woman Can You See (What This Big Thing Is All About?) (1)

IFIELD, Frank — see BEATLES, The

IGGY & THE STOOGES — see POP, Iggy

IGLESIAS, Enrique '99

Born on 5/8/75 in Madrid; raised in Miami. Latin singer. Son of **Julio Iglesias**.

5/25/96	148	18	▲	© 1	**Enrique Iglesias**	[F]		$10	Fonovisa 0506
2/15/97	33	18	▲	© 2	**Vivir**	[F]		$10	Fonovisa 0001
					title is Spanish for "To Live"				
10/10/98	64	16	●	© 3	**Cosas Del Amor**	[F]		$10	Fonovisa 80002
					title is Spanish for "Things Of Love"				
6/19/99	65	22	●	© 4	**Bailamos - Greatest Hits**	[F-G]		$10	Fonovisa 0517

DEBUT	PEAK	WKS	RIAA	CD	ARTIST — Album Title	Catalog	Sym	$	Label & Number

IGLESIAS, Enrique — Cont'd

| 12/11/99 | 33 | 49 | ▲ | © 5 | **Enrique** | | | $10 | Interscope 490540 |
| 3/4/00 | 175 | 2 | | © 6 | **The Best Hits** .... [F-G] | | | $10 | Fonovisa 0518 |

Al Despertar (2,6)
Alabao (5)
Alguien Como Tú (3)
Bailamos (4,5,6) *1*
Be With You (5) *1*
Contigo (3)
Cosas Del Amor (3,6)
Could I Have This Kiss Forever (5) *52*
Desnudo (3)

Dicen Por Ahí (3)
El Muro (2,4)
Enamorado Por Primera Vez (2,6)
Esperanza (3,4,6)
Experiencia Religiosa (1,6)
Falta Tanto Amor (1,4,6)
I Have Always Loved You (5)
I'm Your Man (5)
Inalcanzable (1,4)

Inventame (1)
Lluvia Cae (5)
Mas Es Amar (Sad Eyes) (5)
Miente (2,6)
Muneca Cruel (1)
No Llores Por Mi (1,6)
No Puedo Mas Sin Ti (I'm Your Man) (5)
Nunca Te Olvidaré (3,4,6)
Only You (Solo En Ti) (4)

Oyeme (5)
Para De Jugar (3)
Por Amarte (1,6)
Revolucion (2)
Rhythm Divine (5) *32*
Ritmo Total (Rhythm Divine) (5)
Ruleta Rusa (3)
Sad Eyes (5)
Si Juras Regresar (1,4,6)
Si Tu Te Vas (1,6)

Sirena (3)
Solo En Ti (Only You) (2)
Trapecista (1,6)
Tu Vacio (2,4)
Vivire Y Morire (2,4)
Volvere (2,6)
You're My #1 (5)

★451★ IGLESIAS, Julio '84
Born on 9/23/43 in Madrid. Latin singer. Father of **Enrique Iglesias**.
1)1100 Bel Air Place 2)Crazy 3)Julio

4/2/83	32	89	▲²	© 1	**Julio**.. [F]			$10	Columbia 38640
8/25/84	159	9		© 2	**In Concert**.. [F-L]			$15	Columbia 39570 [2]
9/1/84	5	34	▲⁴	© 3	**1100 Bel Air Place**			$10	Columbia 39157
9/1/84	179	6	●	© 4	**Hey!**.. [E-F]			$10	Columbia 39567
					recorded in 1980				
9/1/84	181	6		© 5	**From A Child To A Woman**............... [E-F]			$10	Columbia 39569
					recorded in 1981				
9/15/84	191	4		© 6	**Moments**.. [E-F]			$10	Columbia 39568
					recorded in 1982				
8/24/85	92	12	●	© 7	**Libra**... [F]			$10	Columbia 40180
6/4/88	52	17	●	© 8	**Non Stop**			$10	Columbia 40995
12/1/90+	37	31	●	© 9	**Starry Night**			$10	Columbia 46857
6/6/92	186	2		© 10	**Calor**... [F]			$10	Sony Discos 80763
					title is Spanish for "Hot"				
6/4/94	30	19	●	© 11	**Crazy**			$10	Columbia 57584
12/7/96+	81	18	●	© 12	**Tango**.. [F]			$10	Columbia 67899

Cana Y A Cafe (10)
A Media Luz (12)
Abracame (Wrap Your Arms Around Me) (1)
Abril En Portugal (Coimbra) (7)
Adios, Pampa Mia (12)
Ae, Ao (8)
Air That I Breathe (3)
All Of You (3) *19*
Amantes (Lovers) (4)
Amor (1,6)
And I Love Her (9)
As Time Goes By (De La Pelicula Casablanca) (2)
Bambou Medley (1)
Begin The Beguine (1,2,5)
Cambalache (12)
Caminito (12)
Can't Help Falling In Love (9)
Cantando A Francia (Singing To France Medley) (2)
Cantando A Latinoamerica-I & II (Singing To Latin American Medley) (2)
Cantando A Mexico (Singing To Mexico Medley) (2)
Caruso (11)
Como Tu (Like You) (5)

Con La Misma Piedra (With The Same Stone) (6)
Coracao Apaixonado (7)
Crazy (11)
Cryin' Time (9)
De Domingo A Domingo (10)
De Nina A Mujer (From A Child To A Woman) (1,2,5)
Despues De Ti (After You) (5)
Dire (7)
El Choclo (12)
El Dia Que Me Quieras (12)
Esa Mujer (That Woman) (6)
Esos Amores (10)
Esta Cobardia (7)
Everytime We Fall In Love (8)
Feelings (2)
Felicidades (Duo Con D. Pedro Vargas) (7)
Fidele (Amantes) (2)
Fragile (11)
Grande, Grande, Grande (Great, Great, Great) (2,5,8)
Guajira (medley) (11)
Hey (1,2,4)
Homenaje A Cole Porter (Homage To Cole Porter) Medley (2)

I Keep Telling Myself (11)
I Know It's Over (8)
I've Got You Under My Skin (7)
If (E Poi) (3)
If I Ever Needed You (I Need You Now) (8)
If You Go Away (9)
Isla En El Sol (Island In The Sun) (5)
La Cumparsita (12)
La Nave Del Olvido (The Ship Of Forgetfulness) (4)
La Paloma (The Dove) (1,6)
La Quiero Como Es (10)
Las Cosas Que Tiene La Vida (The Things Life Has) (6)
Last Time (3)
Let It Be Me (11)
Lia (10)
Love Has Been A Friend To Me (9)
Love Is On Our Side Again (8)
Mammy Blue (11)
Mano A Mano (12)
Me Ama Mo (10)
Me Olvide De Vivir (I Forgot To Live) (2)
Me Va, Me Va (3)

Mi Buenos Aires Querido (12)
Milonga Medley (10)
Momentos (Moments) (2,6)
Mona Lisa (9)
Moonlight Lady (3)
Morrinas (Homesickness) (4)
My Love (8) *80*
Nathalie (2,6)
Never, Never, Never ..see: Grande, Grande, Grande
Ni Te Tengo, Ni Te Olvido (7)
Ni Tu Gato Gris, Ni Tu Perro Fiel (7)
99 Miles From L.A. (9)
No Me Vuelvo A Enamorar (I Won't Fall In Love Again) (6)
Non Si Vive Cosi (Can't Live Like This) (1)
Nostalgie (Nostalgia) (1)
O Me Quieres O Me Dejas (Devaneos) (Love Me Or Leave Me) (6)
Ou Est Passee Ma Boheme? (Carefree Days) (1,2)
Oye Como Va (medley) (11)
Pajaro Chogui (Chogui Bird) (7)
Paloma Blanca (White Dove) (2,4)

Pelo Amor De Uma Mulher (Por El Amor De Una Mujer) (11)
Pensami (Jurame) (Think Of Me) (2)
Por Ella (Because Of Her) (4)
Quand Tu N'es Plus La (Caminito) (When You Are Not Here Anymore) (2)
Que Nadie Sepa Mi Sufrir (I Don't Want Anyone To Know My Suffering) (5)
Quijote (Quixote) (2,6)
Ron Y Coca Cola (Rum And Coca Cola) (4)
Samba Da Minha Terra (Samba Of My Land) (2)
Si El Amor Llama A Tu Puerta (If Love Knocks On Your Door) (6)
Si, Madame (Yes, Madame) (5)
Somos (10)
Song Of Joy (11)
To All The Girls I've Loved Before (3) *5*
Todo Y Nada (7)
Too Many Women (8)
Tu Y Yo (7)
Two Lovers (3)

Un Canto A Galicia (A Song To Galicia) (2)
Un Sentimental (A Sentimental) (2,4)
Uno (10,12)
Viejas Tradiciones (Old Traditions) (4)
Vincent (Starry Starry Night) (9)
Vivir A Dos (Live Together) (2)
Volver (12)
Volver A Empezar ..see: Begin The Beguine
When I Fall In Love (3)
When I Need You (9)
When You Tell Me That You Love Me (11)
Wo Best Du (Where Are You) (1)
Words And Music (8)
Y Aunque Te Haga Calor (10)
Y Pensar...(And To Think...) (5)
Yesterday When I Was Young (9)
Yira...Yira (12)

IHA, James '98
Born on 3/26/68 in Elk Grove, Illinois. Rock guitarist. Member of **Smashing Pumpkins**.

| 2/28/98 | 171 | 1 | | © | **Let It Come Down**.................................. | | | $10 | Virgin 45411 |

Be Strong Now
Beauty

Country Girl
Jealousy

Lover, Lover
No One's Gonna Hurt You

One And Two
See The Sun

Silver String
Sound Of Love

Winter

ILL AL SKRATCH '94
Male rap duo from New York City: ILL (I Lyrical Lord) and Al Skratch.

| 8/20/94 | 137 | 12 | | © | **Creep Wit' Me**.. | | | $10 | Mercury 522661 |

Brooklyn Uptown Connection
Chill With That
Classic Shit

Creep Wit' Me
Get Dough
I'll Take Her *62*

Summertime (It's All Good)
They Got Love For Us
This Is For My Homiez

Where My Homiez? (Come Around My Way)

ILLEGAL '93
Male rap duo from Atlanta: Malik Edwards and **Jamal** Phillips.

| 9/11/93 | 119 | 8 | | © | **The Untold Truth** .... | | | $10 | Rowdy 37002 |
| | | | | | | | | | **We Getz Buzy 95** |

Back In The Day
Ban Da Iggidy

CrumbSnatcher
Head Or Gut

If U Want It
Illegal Will Rock

Lights, Camera, Action
On Da M.I.C.

Stick 'Em Up
Understand The Flow

ILLINOIS SPEED PRESS, The '69
Rock group from Chicago: Kal David (vocals, guitar; **The Fabulous Rhinestones**), Paul Cotton (guitar; **Poco**), Mike Anthony (organ), Rob Lewine (bass) and Fred Page (drums).

| 5/24/69 | 144 | 4 | | | **The Illinois Speed Press**.................... | | | $20 | Columbia 9792 |

Be A Woman
Beauty
Free Ride

Get In The Wind
Hard Luck Story
Here Today

Overture
P.N.S. (When You Come Around)

Pay The Price
Sky Song

ILLUSION '77

Jazz-rock group formed in England: Jane Relf (vocals), Jim McCarty (vocals, guitar; **The Yardbirds**), John Knightsbridge (guitar), John Hawken (keyboards), Louis Cennamo (bass) and Eddie McNeil (drums). Relf, McCarty and Hawken were also members of **Renaissance**.

7/2/77	163	7		©	Out Of The Mist			$12	Island 9489

Beautiful Country   Everywhere You Go   Isadora   Solo Flight
Candles Are Burning   Face Of Yesterday   Roads To Freedom

ILLUSION, The '69

Rock group from Long Island, New York: John Vinci (vocals), Richie Cerniglia (guitar), Mike Maniscalco (keyboards), Chuck Adler (bass) and Mike Ricciardella (drums).

5/10/69	69	27			The Illusion			$20	Steed 37003

Alone   I Love You, Yes I Do   Run, Run, Run (medley)   Willy Gee (Miss Holy Lady)
Charlena   Just Imagine   Talkin' Sweet Talkin' Soul   (medley)
Did You See Her Eyes 32   Real Thing (medley)   Why, Tell Me Why (medley)   You Made Me What I Am

IMBRUGLIA, Natalie '98

Born on 2/4/75 in Sydney, Australia. Female singer/songwriter.

3/28/98	10	52	▲²	©	Left Of The Middle			$10	RCA 67634

Big Mistake   Don't You Think?   Intuition   Left Of The Middle   Pigeons And Crumbs   **Torn** 42
City   Impressed   Leave Me Alone   One More Addiction   Smoke   Wishing I Was There

IMMATURE '96

Male R&B vocal trio from Los Angeles: Marques Houston, Jerome Jones and Kelton Kessee. Later shortened group name to **IMx**.

8/27/94+	88	37	●	© 1	Playtyme Is Over			$10	MCA 11068
12/23/95+	76	30	●	© 2	We Got It			$10	MCA 11385
10/11/97	92	3		© 3	The Journey			$10	MCA 11668
11/13/99	101	4		© 4	Introducing IMx			$10	MCA 112061

IMx

All Alone (3)   Constantly (1) 16   I Can't Wait (3)   Look Into Your Eyes (1)   Pager (2)   Trick (4)
Beautiful (4)   Crazy (2)   I Don't Know (2)   Love Me In A Special Way (4)   Pay You Back (2)   24/7 (3)
Boy Like Me (2)   Don't Ever Say Never (3)   **I Don't Mind** (1) 95   Lover's Groove (2)   **Please Don't Go** (2) 36   Walk You Home (1)
Bring Your Lovin' Home (3)   Everytime (4)   I'll Give You Everything (3)   **Never Lie** (1) 5   Stay The Night (4) 23   **We Got It** (2) 37
Broken Heart (1)   Extra, Extra (3)   **I'm Not A Fool** (3) 69   Nothing But A Party (1)   Summertime (1)   What I Gotta Do (4)
Bubbling (4)   Feel The Funk (2)   In & Out Of Love (4)   Old School Love (4)   Sweetest Love (1)   When It's Love (2)
Can't You See (3)   Give Up The Ghost (3)   Just A Little Bit (1,2)   One Last Chance (4)   Tamika (3)   Where Do We Go (3)
Candy (2)   I Can't Stop The Rain (2)   Keep It On The Low (4)   Ooh Wee Baby (3)   Temptations (4)

IMPELLITTERI '88

Hard-rock group: Chris Impellitteri (guitar), Graham Bonnet (vocals; **Rainbow** and **Alacatraz**), Phil Wolfe (keyboards), Chuck Wright (bass; **Quiet Riot**), Pat Torpey (drums; **Ted Nugent** and **Mr. Big**).

6/25/88	91	20		©	Stand In Line			$10	Relativity 8225

Goodnight And Goodbye   Playing With Fire   Since You've Been Gone   Stand In Line   White And Perfect
Leviathan   Secret Lover   Somewhere Over The Rainbow   Tonight I Fly

★308★ IMPRESSIONS, The '64

R&B vocal group from Chicago: **Jerry Butler**, **Curtis Mayfield**, Sam Gooden and brothers Arthur and Richard Brooks. Butler left for a solo career in 1958, replaced by Fred Cash. The Brooks brothers left in 1962, leaving Mayfield as the trio's leader. Mayfield left in 1970 for a solo career, replaced by **Leroy Hutson**. In 1973, Hutson was replaced by Reggie Torian and Ralph Johnson. Mayfield died on 12/26/99 (age 57). Group inducted into the Rock and Roll Hall of Fame in 1991.

1)Keep On Pushing   2)People Get Ready   3)We're A Winner

8/31/63+	43	33		© 1	The Impressions			$40	ABC-Paramount 450
3/28/64	52	22		© 2	The Never Ending Impressions			$40	ABC-Paramount 468
8/8/64	8	34		© 3	Keep On Pushing			$40	ABC-Paramount 493
3/6/65	23	19		© 4	People Get Ready			$40	ABC-Paramount 505
3/20/65	83	15		5	The Impressions Greatest Hits		[G]	$30	ABC-Paramount 515
9/18/65	104	9		© 6	One By One			$30	ABC-Paramount 523
3/5/66	79	10		© 7	Ridin' High			$30	ABC-Paramount 545
7/15/67	184	11		© 8	The Fabulous Impressions			$25	ABC 606
3/2/68	35	27		© 9	We're A Winner			$25	ABC 635
9/21/68+	172	15		10	The Best Of The Impressions		[G]	$25	ABC 654
12/7/68+	107	13		© 11	This Is My Country			$20	Curtom 8001
5/24/69	104	18		© 12	The Young Mods' Forgotten Story			$20	Curtom 8003
3/20/71	180	6		13	16 Greatest Hits		[G]	$20	ABC 727
4/29/72	192	2		© 14	Times Have Changed			$20	Curtom 8012
3/3/73	180	6		15	Curtis Mayfield/His Early Years With The Impressions		[G]	$25	ABC 780 [2]
7/6/74	176	3		16	Finally Got Myself Together			$15	Curtom 8019
8/9/75	115	5		17	First Impressions			$15	Curtom 5003
3/13/76	195	3		18	Loving Power			$15	Curtom 5009
2/5/77	199	2		19	The Vintage Years		[G]	$20	Sire 3717 [2]

featuring 13 hits by **Jerry Butler** (see Butler for cuts), 13 by The Impressions and 2 by **Curtis Mayfield**: "Freddie's Dead" and "Superfly"

Amen (3,5,10,13,15,19) 7   First Impressions (17)   Hard To Believe (4)   I Wanna Be Around (6)   I've Found That I've Lost (4)   Lemon Tree (2)
Answer Me, My Love (6)   **Fool For You** (11) 22   How High Is High (17)   I Want To Be With You (6)   If It's In You To Do Wrong (16)   Let It Be Me (7)
As Long As You Love Me (1)   **For Your Precious Love**   I Ain't Supposed To (3)   I Wish I'd Stayed In Bed (18)   If You Have To Ask (18)   Let Me Tell The World (9)
Aware Of Love (8)   (19) 11   **I Can't Stay Away From You**   I'll Always Be Here (16)   Inner City Blues (14)   Little Boy Blue (2)
Can't Satisfy (10) 65   Get Up And Move (4,15)   (8) 80   (I'm A Changed Man) ..see: Isle Of Sirens (8)   Little Brown Boy (9)
Can't Work No Longer (4,15)   Girl I Find (12)   I Can't Wait To See You (18)   Finally Got Myself Together   It's All Over (8)   Little Girl (4)
Choice Of Colors (12) 21   Girl You Don't Know Me (2)   I Gotta Keep On Movin' (2)   I'm A Tellin' You (7)   **It's All Right** (1,5,13,15,19) 4   **Little Young Lover** (1) 96
Dedicate My Song To You (3)   Gone Away (11)   I Love You (Yeah) (3)   I'm Gettin' Ready (9)   It's Not Unusual (6)   Lonely Man (6)
Don't Forget What I Told You   Gotta Get Away (7)   **I Loved And I Lost** (9,10) 61   I'm Loving Nothing (11)   Jealous Man (1)   Long Long Winter (3)
(16)   Groove (17)   I Made A Mistake (3)   **I'm So Glad** (17)   Just Another Dance (4)   **Love Me** (14) 94
Don't Let It Hide (3)   **Grow Closer Together**   I Need A Love (7)   **I'm So Proud** (2,5,13,15,19) 14   **Just One Kiss From You**   Love's A Comin' (8)
Emotions (4,15)   (1,5,13,15) 99   I Need To Belong To Someone   I'm Still Waitin' (8)   (6) 76   Love's Miracle (12)
Falling In Love With You (5)   Guess What I've Got (16)   (7,14)   **I'm The One Who Loves You**   **Keep On Pushing**   Loves Happening (11)
Finally Got Myself Together   **Gypsy Woman**   I Need Your Love (1)   (1,5,13,15) 73   (3,5,13,15,19) 10   Loving Power (18)
(I'm A Changed Man) (16) 17   (1,5,13,15,19) 20   I Thank Heaven (3)   I've Been Trying (3,10)   Keep On Trying (18)   Man's Temptation (7)

IMPRESSIONS, The — Cont'd

Meeting Over Yonder (19) *48*
Mighty Mighty (Spade & Whitey) (12)
Minstrel And Queen (1,5)
Miracle Woman (16)
Mona Lisa (6)
Moonlight Shadows (9)
My Deceiving Heart (12)
My Prayer (6)
My Woman's Love (11)
Nature Boy (6)
Never Let Me Go (1,5,13,15)
No One Else (7)
No One To Love (9)
Nothing Can Stop Me (9)

Old Before My Time (17)
100 Lbs. Of Clay (8)
Our Love Goes On And On (14)
People Get Ready (4,10,13,15,19) *14*
Potent Love (14)
Ridin' High (7,13,15)
Right On Time (7)
Romancing To The Folk Song (9)
Sad, Sad Girl And Boy (1,5,13,15) *84*
Same Thing It Took (17) *75*
Satin Doll (2)
See The Real Me (4)

September Song (17)
Seven Years (12) *84*
Sister Love (2)
So Unusual (11)
Somebody Help Me (3)
Sometimes I Wonder (4,15)
Sooner Or Later (17) *68*
Soulful Love (12)
Stay Close To Me (11)
Stop The War (14)
Sunshine (18)
Talking About My Baby (3,5,13,15,19) *12*
Ten To One (2)

That's What Love Will Do (2)
That's What Mama Say (7)
They Don't Know (11)
This Is My Country (11) *25*
This Loves For Real (14)
This Must End (10)
Times Have Changed (14)
Too Slow (7,10) *91*
Try Me (16)
Twilight Time (6)
Twist And Limbo (1)
Up Up And Away (9)
We Go Back A Ways (16)
We're A Winner (9,10,13,15,19) *14*

We're In Love (4)
We're Rolling On (Part 1) (10,13,15) *59*
Wherever You Leadeth Me (12)
Why Must A Love Song Be A Sad Song (17)
Without A Song (6)
Woman Who Loves Me (2)
Woman's Got Soul (4,13,15,19) *29*
You Always Hurt Me (8) *96*
You Always Hurt The One You Love (2)
You Can't Be Wrong (All The Time) (18)

You Must Believe Me (4,5,13,15,19) *15*
You Ought To Be In Heaven (8)
You Want Somebody Else (11)
You've Been Cheatin' (10,19) *33*
You've Come Home (1)
Young Mods' Forgotten Story (12)

IMx — see IMMATURE

INCOGNITO '95
Jazz-funk trio from England: Maysa Leak (female vocals), Jean Paul Maunick (guitar) and Patrick Clahar (sax).

| 6/24/95 | 149 | 6 | © | | 100 Degrees And Rising .... | | | $10 | Talkin Loud 528000 |

After The Fall
Barumba
Everyday

Good Love
I Hear Your Name
Jacob's Ladder

Millenium
One Hundred And Rising
Roots (Back To A Way Of Life)

Spellbound And Speechless
Time Has Come
Too Far Gone

Where Did We Go Wrong

INCREDIBLE BONGO BAND, The '73
Studio group assembled by producer Michael Viner.

| 8/18/73 | 197 | 2 | | | Bongo Rock .... | [I] | | $15 | Pride 0028 |

Apache
Bongo Rock *57*

Bongolia
Dueling Bongos

In-A-Gadda-Da-Vida
Last Bongo In Belgium

Let There Be Drums
Raunchy '73

INCREDIBLE STRING BAND '69
Folk group from Scotland. Formed by Mike Heron and Robin Williamson. Numerous personnel changes with Heron and Williamson the only constants.

7/20/68	161	9	©	1	The Hangman's Beautiful Daughter			$20	Elektra 74021
3/22/69	174	3	©	2	Wee Tam			$20	Elektra 74036
3/22/69	180	3	©	3	The Big Huge			$20	Elektra 74037
12/6/69	166	3	©	4	Changing Horses			$20	Elektra 74057
7/25/70	196	2	©	5	I Looked Up			$20	Elektra 74061
1/23/71	183	3		6	'U'			$25	Elektra 2002 [2]
2/19/72	189	3		7	Liquid Acrobat As Regards The Air			$20	Elektra 74112

Adam And Eve (7)
Air (2)
Astral Plane Theme (6)
Bad Sadie Lee (6)
Beyond The See (2)
Big Ted (4)
Black Jack Davy (5)
Bridge Song (6)
Bridge Theme (6)
Circle Is Unbroken (3)
Cosmic Boy (7)
Cousin Caterpillar (3)
Creation (4)
Cutting The Strings (6)
Darling Belle (7)

Dear Old Battlefield (7)
Douglas Traherne Harding (3)
Ducks On A Pond (2)
Dust Be Diamonds (4)
El Wool Suite (6)
Evolution Rag (7)
Fair As You (5)
Fairies' Hornpipe (medley) (6)
Glad To See You (medley) (6)
Greatest Friend (3)
Half-Remarkable Question (2)
Here Till Here Is There (7)
Hiram Pawnitof (medley) (6)
I Know You (6)
Iron Stone (3)

Jigs Medley (7)
Job's Tears (2)
Juggler's Song (6)
Koeeoaddi There (1)
Letter, The (5)
Light In Time Of Darkness (medley) (6)
Log Cabin Home In The Sky (2)
Lordly Nightshade (3)
Maya (3)
Mercy I Cry City (1)
Minotaur's Song (1)
Mountain Of God (3)
Mr. & Mrs. (4)
Nightfall (1)

Painted Chariot (7)
Partial Belated Overture (6)
Pictures In A Mirror (5)
Puppet Song (6)
Puppies (2)
Queen Of Love (6)
Rainbow (6)
Red Hair (7)
Robot Blues (6)
Sleepers, Awake! (4)
Son Of Noah's Brother (3)
Swift As The Wind (1)
Talking Of The End (7)
This Moment (5)
Three Is A Green Crown (1)

Time (6)
Tree (7)
Very Cellular Song (1)
Walking Along With You (6)
Waltz Of The New Moon (1)
Water Song (1)
When You Find Out Who You Are (5)
White Bird (4)
Witches Hat (1)
Worlds They Rise And Fall (7)
Yellow Snake (2)
You Get Brighter (2)

INCUBUS '00
Hard-rock group from Calabasas, California: Brandon Boyd (vocals), Mike Einziger (guitar), Chris Kilmore (DJ), Dirk Lance (bass) and Jose Pasillas (drums).

11/13/99+	47	94↑	▲²	©	1	Make Yourself			$10	Immortal 63652
9/9/00	41	5		©	2	When Incubus Attacks Vol. 1	[M]		$10	Immortal 61395
11/25/00	116	1			3	Fungus Amongus	[E]		$10	Immortal 61497

Answer, The (1)
Battlestar Scralatchtica (1)
Clean (1)
Consequence (1)
Crowded Elevator (2)

Drive (1)
Favorite Things (2)
Hilikus (3)
I Miss You (1)
Make Yourself (1,2)

Medium (3)
Nowhere Fast (1)
Out From Under (1)
Pardon Me (1,2)
Privilege (1)

Psychopsilocybin (3)
Shaft (3)
Sink Beneath The Line (3)
Speak Free (3)
Stellar (1,2)

Take Me To Your Leader (3)
Trouble In 421 (3)
Warmth, The (1)
When It Comes (1)
You Will Be A Hot Dancer (3)

INDECENT OBSESSION '90
Pop group from Brisbane, Australia: David Dixon (vocals), Andrew Coyne (guitar), Michael Szumowski (keyboards) and Darryl Sims (drums).

| 9/1/90 | 148 | 6 | © | | Indecent Obsession .... | | | $10 | MCA 6426 |

Believe
Come Back To Me

Dream After Dream
Going Down

Never Gonna Stop
Nowhere To Hide

Say Goodbye
Spoken Words

Survive The Heat
Tell Me Something *31*

INDEPENDENTS, The '73
R&B vocal group from Chicago: Chuck Jackson, Maurice Jackson, Helen Curry and Eric Thomas. Chuck Jackson, not to be confused with the same-named solo singer, is the brother of civil rights leader Jesse Jackson.

| 5/19/73 | 127 | 9 | | | The First Time We Met .... | | | $15 | Wand 694 |

Baby I've Been Missing You *41*
Can't Understand It

Couldn't Hear Nobody Say (I Love You Like You Do)
Here I Am

I Just Want To Be There
I Love You, Yes I Do

Just As Long As You Need Me, Part 1 *84*
Leaving Me *21*

Our Love Has Got To Come Together

INDIA.ARIE '01
Born India Arie Simpson in 1976 in Denver; raised in Atlanta. Female R&B singer/songwriter/guitarist.

| 4/14/01 | 10 | 25↑ | ● | © | Acoustic Soul | | | $10 | Motown 013770 |

Always In My Head
Back To The Middle
Beautiful

Brown Skin
I See God In You
Nature

Part Of My Life
Promises
Ready For Love

Simple
Strength, Courage & Wisdom
Video *47*

Wonderful (Stevie Wonder Dedication)

★437★ INDIGO GIRLS '97

Folk-rock duo from Decatur, Georgia: singers/songwriters/guitarists Amy Ray (born on 4/12/64) and Emily Saliers (born on 7/22/63).

DEBUT	PEAK	WKS	RIAA	CD	#	Album Title	Sym	$	Label & Number
4/15/89	22	35	▲²	©	1	Indigo Girls	C:#18/31	$10	Epic 45044
11/25/89+	159	14	●	©	2	Strange Fire	[E]	$10	Epic 45427
						songs recorded in 1987			
10/13/90	43	29	●	©	3	Nomads-Indians-Saints		$10	Epic 46820
5/30/92	21	34	▲	©	4	Rites Of Passage		$10	Epic 48865
5/28/94	9	26	▲	©	5	Swamp Ophelia		$10	Epic 57621
10/28/95	40	14	▲	©	6	1200 Curfews	[L]	$15	Epic 67229 [2]
5/17/97	7	22	●	©	7	Shaming Of The Sun		$10	Epic 67891
10/16/99	34	7		©	8	Come On Now Social		$10	Epic 69914
10/21/00	128	4		©	9	Retrospective	[G]	$10	Epic 61602

Airplane (4)
Andy (8)
Back Together Again (6)
Blood And Fire (1)
Burn All The Letters (7)
Bury My Heart At Wounded Knee (6)
Caramia (7)
Cedar Tree (4)
Center Stage (1)
Chickenman (4,6)
Closer To Fine (1,6,9) *52*
Cold Beer And Remote Control (8)
Compromise (8)
Crazy Game (2)

Cut It Out (7)
Dead Man's Hill (5,6)
Devotion (9)
Don't Give That Girl A Gun (7)
Down By The River (6)
Everything In Its Own Time (7)
Fare Thee Well (5)
Faye Tucker (8)
Fugitive (5)
Galileo (4,6,9) *89*
Get Out The Map (7,9)
Get Together (2)
Ghost (4,6,9)
Girl With The Weight Of The World In Her Hands (3)
Go (8,9)

Gone Again (8)
Hammer And A Nail (3)
Hand Me Downs (3)
Hey Jesus (2)
Hey Kind Friend (7)
History Of Us (1)
I Don't Wanna Know (2,6)
It's Alright (7)
Joking (4,6)
Jonas & Ezekial (4,6)
Keeper Of My Heart (3)
Kid Fears (1,9)
Land Of Canaan (1,2,6)
Language Or The Kiss (5,6)
Least Complicated (5,6,9)
Leaving (9)

Leeds (7)
Left Me A Fool (2)
Let It Be Me (4)
Love Will Come To You (4)
Love's Recovery (1,6)
Make It Easier (2)
Midnight Train To Georgia (6)
Mystery (5,6)
Nashville (4)
1 2 3 (3)
Ozilline (8)
Peace Tonight (8)
Power Of Two (5,6,9)
Prince Of Darkness (1)
Pushing The Needle Too Far (3,6)

Reunion (5,9)
River (6)
Romeo And Juliet (4)
Scooter Boys (7)
Secure Yourself (1)
Shame On You (7,9)
Shed Your Skin (7)
Sister (8)
Soon Be To Nothing (8)
Southland In The Springtime (3)
Strange Fire (2,6,9)
Tangled Up In Blue (6)
Thin Line (6)
This Train Revised (5,6)
Three Hits (4,9)
Touch Me Fall (5)

Tried To Be True (1)
Trouble (8,9)
Virginia Woolf (4,6)
Walk Away (9)
Watershed (3,9)
We Are Together (8)
Welcome Me (3)
Wood Song (5)
World Falls (3,6)
You And Me Of The 10,000 Wars (3)
You Left It Up To Me (2)

INDO G '98

Born in Memphis. Male rapper. Former member of **Prophet Posse**.

DEBUT	PEAK	WKS	CD	#	Album Title	$	Label & Number
9/12/98	105	3	©		Angel Dust	$10	Relativity 1683

Ain't No Bitch In My Blood
Ashes To Ashes
Big Boy Shit

Break The Law '98
Can You Feel Me?
Cleopatra

Dead Men Don't Talk
Fall Up Off Me Ho
Fly Straight

Fuck What Ya Heard
Ghetto Party
My Nigga's Crazy

Prophet Hataz
Remember Me Ballin'
Throw Them Thangs

Will A Nigga Make It

INFECTIOUS GROOVES '93

Rock-funk group from Los Angeles: Mike Muir (vocals), Dean Pleasants and Adam Siegel (guitars), Dave Dunn (keyboards), Robert Trujillo (bass) and Stephen Perkins (drums). Muir and Trujillo were formerly with **Suicidal Tendencies**.

DEBUT	PEAK	WKS	CD	#	Album Title	$	Label & Number
2/22/92	198	1	©	1	The Plague That Makes Your Booty Move...It's The Infectious Grooves	$10	Epic 47402
3/6/93	109	5	©	2	Sarsippius' Ark	$10	Epic 53131

Back To The People (1)
Closed Session (1)
Do The Sinister (1,2)
Don't Stop, Spread The Jam! (2)
Fame (2)

I Look Funny? (1)
I'm Gonna Be My King (1)
Immigrant Song (2)
Infectious Blues (1)
Infectious Grooves (1,2)
Infecto Groovalistic (1)

Mandatory Love Song (1)
Monster Skank (1)
Punk It Up (1)
Savor Da Flavor (2)
Slo-Motion Slam (2)
Stop Funk'N With My Head (1)

Thanx But No Thanx (1)
Therapy (1)
These Freaks Are Here To Party (1)
Three Headed Mind Pollution (2)

Turn Your Head (1)
Turtle Wax (Funkaholics Anonymous) (2)
You Lie...And Yo Breath Stank (1)

You Pick Me Up (Just To Throw Me Down) "Therapy" (2)

INFORMATION SOCIETY '88

Techno-dance group from Minneapolis: Kurt Valaquen (singer), Paul Robb (songwriter), Amanda Kramer (keyboards) and Jack Cassidy (bass). Kramer left in early 1990.

DEBUT	PEAK	WKS	RIAA	CD	#	Album Title	$	Label & Number
8/20/88	25	38	●	©	1	Information Society	$10	Tommy Boy 25691
11/3/90	77	14		©	2	Hack	$10	Tommy Boy 26258

Attitude (1)
Can't Slow Down (2)
Chemistry (2)
Come With Me (2)
Fire Tonight (2)

Hack 1 (2)
Hard Currency (2)
How Long (2)
If Only (2)
Knife And A Fork (2)

Lay All Your Love On Me (1) *83*
Make It Funky (1)
Mirrorshades (2)
Move Out (1)

Now That I Have You (2)
Over The Sea (1)
Repetition (1) *76*
Running (1)
Seek 200 (2)

Slipping Away (2)
Something In The Air (1)
Think (2) *28*
Tomorrow (1)
Walking Away (1) *9*

What's On Your Mind (Pure Energy) (1) *3*

INGRAM, James '84

Born on 2/16/56 in Akron, Ohio. R&B singer/songwriter/pianist.

DEBUT	PEAK	WKS	RIAA	CD	#	Album Title	Sym	$	Label & Number
11/12/83+	46	42	●	©	1	It's Your Night		$10	Qwest 23970
9/13/86	123	9		©	2	Never Felt So Good		$10	Qwest 25424
10/6/90	117	10		©	3	It's Real		$10	Warner 25924
10/19/91	168	3	●	©	4	The Power Of Great Music	[G]	$10	Warner 26700
5/1/99	165	1		©	5	Forever More (Love Songs, Hits & Duets)	[G]	$10	Private Music 82174

Always (2)
Baby Be Mine (3)
Baby, Come To Me (4,5) *1*
Call On Me (3)
Day I Fall In Love (5)
Everything Must Change (5)
Forever More (Love Songs, Hits & Duets) (5)
Get Ready (4)

How Do You Keep The Music Playing? (4) *45*
I Believe I Can Fly (5)
I Believe In Those Love Songs (5)
I Don't Have The Heart (3,4,5)
I Wanna Come Back (3)
It's Real (3)

It's Your Night (1)
Just Once (4,5) *17*
Lately (2)
Love Come Down (3)
Love 1 Day At A Time (3)
Love's Been Here And Gone (2)
My Funny Valentine (5)
Never Felt So Good (2)
No Need To Say Goodbye (5)

One Hundred Ways (4,5) *14*
One More Rhythm (1)
Party Animal (1)
Red Hot Lover (2)
Remember The Dream (4)
Right Back (2)
Say Hey (2)
She Loves Me (The Best That I Can Be) (1)

So Fine (3)
Someday We'll All Be Free (3)
Somewhere Out There (4,5) *2*
There's No Easy Way (1,4) *58*
Trust Me (2)
Try Your Love Again (1)
Tuff (2)
Whatever We Imagine (1,4)

When Was The Last Time Music Made You Cry (3)
Where Did My Heart Go? (4)
Wings Of My Heart (2)
Wish You Were Here (5)
Yah Mo B There (1,4,5) *19*
(You Make Me Feel Like) A Natural Man (3)

INGRAM, Luther '72

Born on 11/30/44 in Jackson, Tennessee. R&B singer/songwriter.

DEBUT	PEAK	WKS	CD	#	Album Title	$	Label & Number
1/15/72	175	11		1	I've Been Here All The Time	$15	Koko 2201
9/30/72	39	21	©	2	If Loving You Is Wrong I Don't Want To Be Right	$15	Koko 2202

Ain't That Loving You (For More Reasons Than One) (1) *45*
Always (2) *64*
Be Good To Me Baby (1) *97*
Dying & Crying (2)

Ghetto Train (1)
Help Me Love (1)
I Can't Stop (2)
I Remember (2)
I'll Be Your Shelter (In Time Of Storm) (2) *40*

I'll Just Call You Honey (1)
I'll Love You Until The End (1,2)
I'm Trying To Sing A Message To You (2)
(If Loving You Is Wrong) I Don't Want To Be Right (2) *3*

Love Ain't Gonna Run Me Away (1)
Missing You (1)
My Honey And Me (1) *55*
Oh Baby, You Can Depend On Me (1)

Pity For The Lonely (1)
Since You Don't Want Me (1)
To The Other Man (1)
You Were Made For Me (1) *93*

INMATES, The '80
Rock group from England: Bill Hurley (vocals), Peter "Gunn" Staines and Tony Oliver (guitars), Ben Donnelly (bass) and Jim Russell (drums).

| 12/1/79+ | **49** | 17 | | | **First Offence** .... | | | $12 | Polydor 6241 |

Back In History · **Dirty Water 51** | I Can't Sleep · If Time Could Turn Backwards · Jealousy · Love Got Me · Midnight To Six Man · Mr. Unreliable · Three Time Loser · Walk, The · You're The One That Done It

INNER CIRCLE '93
Reggae group formed in Kingston, Jamaica: Calton Coffie (vocals), Touter Harvey, Lancelot Hall, brothers Ian and Roger Lewis, and Lester Adderly.

| 5/22/93 | **64** | 49 | ▲ | | **Bad Boys** .... | | | $10 | Big Beat 92261 |

Bad Boys 8 · Bad To The Bone | Cops, Theme From ...see: Bad Boys · Down By The River · Hey Love · Living It Up · Looking For A Better Way · **Rock With You 98** · Slow It Down · Sunglasses At Nite · **Sweat (A La La La La Long) 16** · Tear Down These Walls · Wrapped Up In Your Love

INNER CITY '89
Techno-funk group led by Detroit producer/songwriter/mixer Kevin Saunderson and female vocalist Paris Grey (from Glencove, Illinois).

| 6/24/89 | **162** | 4 | | © | **Big Fun** .... | | | $10 | Virgin 91242 |

Ain't Nobody Better · And I Do | Big Fun · Do You Love What You Feel · **Good Life 73** · Inner City Theme · Power Of Passion · Paradise · **Secrets Of The Mind** · Set Your Body Free

INNOCENCE MISSION, The '90
Rock group from Lancaster, Pennsylvania: Karen Peris (vocals), her husband Don Peris (guitar), Mike Bitts (bass) and Steve Brown (drums).

| 3/24/90 | **167** | 10 | | © | **The Innocence Mission** .... | | | $10 | A&M 5274 |

Black Sheep Wall · Broken Circle · Clear To You | Come Around And See Me · Curious · I Remember Me · Medjugorje · Mercy · Notebook · Paper Dolls · Surreal · Wonder Of Birds · You Chase The Light

INSANE CLOWN POSSE '99
White rap duo from Detroit: Joe "Violent J" Bruce and Joe "Shaggy 2 Dope" Utsler. Both wear clown makeup.

7/12/97	**63**	88	▲	©	1 **The Great Milenko**	C:#22/15		$10	Island 524442
9/5/98	**46**	5		©	2 **Forgotten Freshness Volumes 1 & 2**		[K]	$15	Island 524552 [2]
6/12/99	**4**	18	●	©	3 The Amazing Jeckel Brothers			$10	Island 524661
11/18/00	**20**	6		©	4 **Bizaar**			$10	Psychopathic 548174
11/18/00	**21**	5		©	5 **Bizzar**			$10	Psychopathic 548175

above 2 are different albums

Another Love Song (3) · Assassins (3) · Behind The Paint (4) · B*tches (3) · Bizzar (4) · Boogie Woogie Wu (1) · Bring It On (3) · Cherry Pie (I Need A Freak) (5) · Clown Love (2) · Crystal Ball (5) · Dead Pumpkins (2) · Dog Beats (2) · Down With The Clown (1) · Echo Side (3) · 85 Bucks An Hour (2) · Everybody Rize (3) · Fat Sweaty Betty (2) · Fearless (4) · F*ck The World (3) · Fxck Off! (2) · Graveyard (2) · Great Milenko (1) · Halloween On Military Street (2) · Halls Of Illusions (1) · Hellalujah (1) · Hey Vato (2) · Hokus Pokus (1,2) · House Of Horrors (1) · House Of Wonders (2) · How Many Times? (1) · I Didn't Mean To Kill 'Em (2) · I Stab People (3) · I Want My Sh*t (3) · I'm Not Alone (2) · If (5) · Jake Jeckel (3) · Juggalo Paradise (5) · Just Like That (1) · Let A Killa (5) · Let's Go All The Way (5) · Mad Professor (3) · Mental Warp (2) · Mr. Happy (5) · Mr. Johnson's Head (2) · Mr. Rotten Treats (2) · My Axe (5) · My Homie Baby Mama (4) · Neden Game (1) · Nothing's Left (3) · Pass Me By (1) · Pendulum's Promise (4) · Piggy Pie (1,2) · Play With Me (3) · Please Don't Hate Me (4) · Questions (5) · Radio Stars (5) · Rainbows & Stuff (4) · Red Christmas (3) · **Santa's A Fat Bitch (2) 67** · Shaggy Show (3) · Southwest Strangla (2) · Southwest Voodoo (1) · Still Stabbin' (4) · Take Me Away (4) · Terrible (3) · Tilt-A-Whirl (4) · Under The Moon (1) · We Gives No F**k (4) · What Is A Juggalo? (1) · Whut (4) · Willy Bubba (2) · Witching Hour (2)

INSIDERS '87
Rock group from Chicago: John Siegle (vocals), Jay O'Rourke and Gary Yerkins (guitars), Jim DeMonte (bass) and Ed Breckenfeld (drums).

| 10/10/87 | **167** | 5 | | © | **Ghost On The Beach** .... | | | $10 | Epic 40630 |

Ghost On The Beach · Love Like Candy | Memory Row · Moondog Howl · Our Last Day · Peace In Time · Price Of Love · Sad Songs · Stand In Chains · 35,000

INSPECTAH DECK '99
Born Jason Hunter in New York City. Male rapper. Member of **Wu-Tang Clan**.

| 10/23/99 | **19** | 5 | | © | **Uncontrolled Substance** .... | | | $10 | Loud 1865 |

Cause, The · Elevation · Femme Fatale | Forget Me Not · Friction · Grand Prix · Hyperdermix · Longevity · Lovin You · Movas & Shakers · 9th Chamber · R.E.C. Room · Show N Prove · Trouble Man · Uncontrolled Substance · Word On The Street

INSTANT FUNK '79
Funk group from Philadelphia: James Carmichael (vocals), brothers Kim (guitar) and Scotty (drums) Miller, George Bell (guitar), Dennis Richardson (keyboards), Charles Williams (percussion), Larry Davis (trumpet), Johnny Onderline (sax) and Raymond Earl (bass).

2/17/79	**12**	22	●	©	1 **Instant Funk**			$12	Salsoul 8513
12/8/79+	**129**	13			2 **Witch Doctor**			$12	Salsoul 8529
10/18/80	**130**	6			3 **The Funk Is On**			$12	Salsoul 8536
4/10/82	**147**	7			4 **Looks So Fine**			$12	Salsoul 8545

Bodyshine (2) · Can You See Where I'm Coming From (3) · Crying (1) · Dark Vader (1) · Don't You Wanna Party (1) · Everybody (3) | Funk Is On (3) · Funk-N-Roll (3) · Give It To You Baby (4) · Gotta Like That (4) · **I Got My Mind Made Up (You Can Get It Girl) (1) 20** · I Had A Dream (2) | I Want To Love You (2) · I'll Be Doggone (1) · It's Cool (3) · It's Your Love On My Mind (2) · Jumpin' To Conclusions (4) · Looks So Fine (4) · Never Let It Go Away (1) | Punk Rockin' (4) · Scream And Shout (2) · Slam Dunk The Funk (4) · Slap, Slap, Lickedy Lap (2) · What Can I Do For You (3) · Why Don't You Think About Me (4) | Wide World Of Sports (1) · Witch Doctor (2) · You Say You Want Me To Stay (1) · You Want My Love (3) · You're Not Getting Older (3)

INSYDERZ, The '98
Christian ska-rock group from Detroit: Joe Yerke (vocals), Kyle Wasil (guitar), Bram Roberts and Mike Rowland (horns), Beau McCarthy (bass) and Nate Sjogren (drums).

| 3/21/98 | **200** | 1 | | © | **The Insyderz Present...Skalleluia!** .... | | | $10 | Squint 7035 |

Ancient Of Days · Awesome God · He Has Made Me Glad | Jesus Draw Me Close · Jesus, Name Above All Names (medley) · Joy · Lord, I Lift Your Name On High · More Precious Than Silver (medley) · Mourning Into Dancing · Oh, Lord, You're Beautiful · We Will Glorify · You Are My All In All

INTERNATIONAL ALL STARS '61
Directed by Harry Frekin.

| 12/4/61 | 47 | 2 | | | Percussion Around The World .... | [I] | $20 | London Phase 4 44010 |

April In Portugal   Children's Marching Song   Japanese Sandman   Poor People Of Paris (Jean's   Volare
Auf Wiederseh'n Sweetheart   Cielito Lindo   La Montana   Song)
Calcutta   Frenesi   Never On Sunday   Third Man Theme

INTERNATIONAL CHILDRENS' CHOIR '95
Children's choir from Germany.

| 11/25/95 | 34[X] | 2 | © | | Frosty The Snowman ....C:#45/2 | [X] | $10 | LaserLight 15307 |

recorded in 1990

Angels We Have Heard On   Deck The Halls   Good King Wenceslas   Must Be Santa   Rudolph, The Red-Nosed   Up On The House-Top
High   Frosty The Snowman   Jingle Bells   O Little Town Of Bethlehem   Reindeer   What Child Is This
Away In A Manger   Good Christian Men Rejoice   Jolly Old Saint Nicholas   O Tannenbaum   Silent Night   Winter Wonderland

INTOCABLE '99
Latin group from Zapata, Texas: Ricardo Munoz, Daniel Sanchez, Rene Martinez, Felix Salinas, Sergio Serna and Juan Hernandez.

| 8/14/99 | 173 | 1 | © | | Contigo .... | [F] | $10 | EMI Latin 21502 |

Agradecimiento   Costumbre   Estoy Enamorado   Soñador Eterno   Vuelvo A Creer En El Amor
Contigo   El Amigo Que Se Fué   Fuerte No Soy   Te Quiero   Ya Estoy Cansado
Contigo He Fallado   Es Tan Bello   Hoy Duele   Un Desengaño

INTRO '93
R&B vocal trio from Brooklyn, New York: Kenny Greene, Clinton Wike and Jeff Sanders.

| 4/24/93 | 65 | 45 | ● © | 1 | Intro .... | | $10 | Atlantic 82463 |
| 11/18/95 | 86 | 2 | © | 2 | New Life .... | | $10 | Atlantic 82662 |

Anything For You (1)   Feels Like The First Time (2)   Love Me Better (2)   New Life (2)   Somebody Loves You (2)   What You Won't Do For Love
Come Inside (1) 33   **Funny How Time Flies** (2) 90   Love Thang (1)   One Of A Kind Love (1)   Spending My Life With You (2)   (2)
Don't Leave Me (1)   It's All About You (1)   My Love's On The Way (2)   Ribbon In The Sky (1)   Strung Out On Your Lovin' (2)   Why Don't You Love Me (1)
Ecstasy Of Love (1)   Let Me Be The One (1)   My Song (2)   So Many Reasons (1)   There Is A Way (2)

INTRUDERS, The '68
R&B vocal group from Philadelphia: Sam Brown, Eugene Daughtry, Phil Terry and Robert Edwards. Daughtry died on 12/25/94 (age 55).

7/27/68	112	9		1	Cowboys To Girls		$50	Gamble 5004
1/25/69	144	6		2	The Intruders Greatest Hits	[G]	$40	Gamble 5005
5/19/73	133	18		3	Save The Children		$25	Gamble 31991

By The Time I Get To Phoenix   Good For Me Girl (1)   **(Love Is Like A) Baseball**   Save The Children (3)   Turn The Hands Of Time (1)
  (1)   Hang On In There (3)   **Game** (1,2) 26   **Slow Drag** (2) 54   **(We'll Be) United** (2) 78
Call Me (1)   **I Wanna Know Your Name**   Love That's Real (2) 82   (So Glad I'm) Yours (1)   (Who's Your) Favorite
Cowboys To Girls (1,2) 6   (3) 60   Me Tarzan You Jane (2)   Teardrops (3)   Candidate (2)
Everyday Is A Holiday (1)   **I'll Always Love My Mama**   Memories Are Here To Stay (3)   To Be Happy Is The Real Thing
Friends No More (1,2)   **(Part 1)** (3) 36   Mother And Child Reunion (3)   (3)
Girls Girls Girls (2)   It Must Be Love (1)   **Sad Girl** (1) 47   **Together** (2) 48

★287★ INXS '88
Rock group from Sydney, Australia: **Michael Hutchence** (vocals), Kirk Pengilly (guitar, saxophone), Garry Beers (bass) and brothers Tim (guitar), Andy (keyboards, guitar) and Jon (drums) Farriss. Hutchence starred in the movies *Dogs In Space* and *Frankenstein Unbound*; formed the group **Max Q**. Jon Farriss married actress Leslie Bega (TV's *Head Of The Class*) on 2/14/92. Hutchence committed suicide on 11/22/97 (age 37).

1)Kick 2)X 3)Listen Like Thieves

| 3/19/83 | 46 | 31 | ● © | 1 | Shabooh Shoobah .... | | $10 | Atco 90072 |
| 10/1/83 | 148 | 6 | | 2 | Dekadance .... | [M] | $10 | Atco 90115 |

4 extended tracks from above album

| 5/26/84 | 52 | 28 | ▲ © | 3 | The Swing ....C:#39/20 | | $10 | Atco 90160 |
| 8/18/84 | 164 | 3 | © | 4 | INXS .... | [E] | $10 | Atco 90184 |

recorded in 1980

11/2/85+	11	55	▲² ©	5	Listen Like Thieves ....C:#13/50		$10	Atlantic 81277
11/14/87+	3	81	▲⁶ ©	6	Kick C:#15/17		$10	Atlantic 81796
10/6/90	5	43	▲² ©	7	X		$10	Atlantic 82140
11/23/91	72	11	▲ ©	8	Live Baby Live	[L]	$10	Atlantic 82294
8/22/92	16	31	▲ ©	9	Welcome To Wherever You Are		$10	Atlantic 82394
11/20/93	53	5	©	10	Full Moon, Dirty Hearts		$10	Atlantic 82541
11/19/94	112	3	▲ ©	11	The Greatest Hits	[G]	$10	Atlantic 82622
5/3/97	41	8	©	12	Elegantly Wasted		$10	Mercury 534531

All Around (9)   **Devil Inside** (6,11) 2   Here Comes (1,2)   Loved One (6)   Please (You Got That...) (10)   Swing, The (3)
All The Voices (3)   **Disappear** (7,11) 8   **I Send A Message** (3) 77   Make Your Peace (10)   Questions (9)   Taste It (9)
Baby Don't Cry (9)   Doctor (4)   I'm Just A Man (12)   Mediate (6,8)   Red Red Sun (5)   **This Time** (5,8) 81
Back On Line (9)   **Don't Change** (1) 80   I'm Only Looking (10)   Melting In The Sun (3)   Roller Skating (4)   Three Sisters (5)
Beautiful Girl (9,11) 46   Don't Lose Your Head (12)   In Vain (4)   Men And Women (9)   Same Direction (5)   Time (10)
Biting Bullets (5)   Elegantly Wasted (12)   Jan's Song (1)   Messenger, The (10)   Searching (12)   Tiny Daggers (6)
Bitter Tears (7) 46   Everything (1)   Johnson's Aeroplane (3)   Mystify (6,8)   Shake The Tree (12)   To Look At You (1,2)
Black And White (1,2)   Face The Change (3)   Jumping (4)   **Need You Tonight** (6,8,11) 1   She Is Rising (12)   Viking Juice (10)
Body Language (4)   Faith In Each Other (7)   Just Keep Walking (4)   **Never Tear Us Apart** (6,8,11) 7   Shine Like It Does (5,11)   We Are Thrown Together (12)
Building Bridges (12)   Freedom Deep (10)   Kick (6)   **New Sensation** (6,8,11) 3   Shining Star (8)   **What You Need** (5,8,11) 5
Burn For You (3,8)   Full Moon Dirty Hearts (10)   Kill The Pain (10)   Newsreel Babies (4)   Show Me (Cherry Baby) (12)   Who Pays The Price (7)
By My Side (7,8)   Gift, The (10)   Kiss The Dirt (Falling Down The   **Not Enough Time** (9) 28   Soul Mistake (1)   Wild Life (6)
Calling All Nations (6)   Girl On Fire (12)   Mountain) (5)   Old World New World (1)   Spy Of Love (1)   Wishing Well (9)
Communication (9)   Golden Playpen (1)   Know The Difference (4)   On A Bus (4)   Stairs, The (7,8,11)   Wishy Washy (4)
Cut Your Roses Down (10)   Good + Bad Times (5)   Lately (7)   On My Way (7)   Strange Desire (9)
Dancing On The Jetty (3)   Guns In The Sky (6,8)   Learn To Smile (4)   One X One (5,8)   Strangest Party (These Are The
Days Of Rust (10)   Hear That Sound (7,8)   **Listen Like Thieves** (5,11) 54   **One Thing** (1,2,8,11) 30   Times) (11)
Deliver Me (11)   Heaven Sent (9,11)   Love Is (What I Say) (3)   **Original Sin** (3,11) 58   **Suicide Blonde** (7,8,11) 9

IOMMI '00
Born Tony Iommi on 2/19/48 in Birmingham, England. Lead guitarist of **Black Sabbath**.

| 11/4/00 | 129 | 1 | © | | Iommi .... | | $10 | Divine 27857 |

Black Oblivion   Goodbye Lament   Just Say No To Love   Laughing Man (In The Devil   Meat   Time Is Mine
Flame On   Into The Night   Mask)   Patterns   Who's Fooling Who

IRIS, Donnie　'81

Born Dominic Ierace on 2/28/47 in Beaver Falls, Pennsylvania. Rock singer/songwriter/guitarist. Former member of **The Jaggerz**.

12/13/80+	57	23	© 1	**Back On The Streets**	$12	MCA 3272
9/26/81	84	31	© 2	**King Cool**	$12	MCA 5237
11/27/82	180	4	3	**The High And The Mighty**	$12	MCA 5358
7/2/83	127	12	4	**Fortune 410**	$12	MCA 5427
3/16/85	115	15	5	**No Muss...No Fuss**	$10	HME 39949

Agnes (1)
Ah! Leah! (1) *29*
Back On The Streets (1)
Broken Promises (2)
Color Me Blue (2)
Cry If You Want To (4)
Daddy Don't Live Here Anymore (1)
Do You Compute? (4) *64*
Don't Cry Baby (5)
Follow That Car (5)
Glad All Over (3)
Headed For A Breakdown (5)
High And The Mighty (3)
Human Evolution (4)
I Belong (4)
I Can't Hear You (1)
I Wanna Tell Her (3)
I Want You Back (5)
I'm A User (4)
Injured In The Game Of Love (5) *91*
Joking (1)
King Cool (2)
Last To Know (2)
L.O.V.E. (5)
Love Is Like A Rock (2) *37*
Love Is Magic (3)
My Girl (2) *25*
Never Did I (4)
Parallel Time (3)
Pretender (2)
Promise, The (2)
Ridin' Thunder (5)
She's So European (3)
She's So Wild (1)
Shock Treatment (1)
Somebody (4)
Stagedoor Johnny (4)
State Of The Heart (5)
Sweet Merilee (2) *80*
Tell Me What You Want (4)
10th Street (5)
That's The Way Love Ought To Be (2)
This Time It Must Be Love (3)
Too Young To Love (1)
Tough World (3) *57*
You're Gonna Miss Me (3)
You're My Serenity (5)
You're Only Dreaming (1)

IRISH ROVERS, The　'68

Irish-born folk group formed in Calgary, Alberta, Canada: Jimmy Ferguson (vocals), brothers Will (vocals, guitar) and George (guitar) Millar, their cousin Joe Millar (bass) and Wilcil McDowell (accordian). Ferguson died in October 1997 (age 57).

4/6/68	24	43	© 1	**The Unicorn**	$20	Decca 74951
11/9/68	119	8	2	**All Hung Up**	$20	Decca 75037
5/10/69	182	5	3	**Tales To Warm Your Mind**	$20	Decca 75081
4/25/81	157	8	4	**Wasn't That A Party**	$12	Cleveland Int'l. 37107

THE ROVERS

Ally-Bally (3)
Bare Legged Joe (2)
Biplane, Ever More (2) *91*
Black Velvet Band (1)
Bonnie Kellswater (1)
Bridget Flynn (1)
Cold Winter Shadows (2)
Come In (1)
Does Your Chewing Gum Lose Its Flavor On The Bedpost Over Night? (2)
Fireflyte (4)
First Love In Life (1)
Goodbye Mrs. Durkin (1)
Goodnight Irene (2)
Happy Trails (medley) (4)
Henry Joy McCracken (2)
Here's To The Horses (4)
Hiring Fair (1)
Lily The Pink (3)
Liverpool Lou (2)
Matchstalk Men And Matchstalk Cats And Dogs (4)
Mexican Girl (4)
Minstrel Of Cranberry Lane (3)
Movie Medley (medley) (4)
Mrs. Crandall's Boardinghouse (3)
My Little Maureen (2)
Oh You Mucky Kid (Liverpool Lullaby) (3)
Orange And The Green (1)
Our Little Boy Blue (3)
Pat Of Mullingar (1)
Penny Whistle Peddler (3)
Pheasant Plucker's Son (4)
Pigs Can't Fly (3)
(Puppet Song) Whiskey On A Sunday (2) *75*
Rovers Fancy (2)
Shamrock Shore (2)
Stolen Child (3)
Stop, Look, Listen (3)
Tara, The Ice Cream Girl (4)
Unicorn, The (1) *7*
Up Among The Heather (2)
Victory Chimes (4)
Village Of Brambleshire Wood (3)
Wasn't That A Party (4) *37*
Wind That Shakes The Corn (1)
Yo Yo Man (4)

IRISH TENORS, The　'01

All-star vocal trio: John McDermott, Anthony Kearns and Ronan Tynan.

| 4/3/99 | 151 | 10 | ● © 1 | **The Irish Tenors** | [L] | $10 | Mastertone 8552 |

recorded at the Royal Dublin Society Hall in Dublin, Ireland

| 12/4/99 | 111 | 6 | © 2 | **Home For Christmas** | C:#44/2 | [X] | $10 | Mastertone 8870 |

Christmas charts: 20/99, 35/00

| 3/25/00 | 122 | 3 | © 3 | **Live In Belfast** | [L] | $10 | Point 9018 |

recorded on 2/5/00 at Waterfront Hall in Belfast, Ireland

| 3/24/01 | 107 | 3 | © 4 | **Ellis Island** | | $10 | Music Matters 9020 |

Adeste Fideles (O Come All Ye Faithful) (2)
Amazing Grace (2)
Angels We Have Heard On High (medley) (2)
As I Sit Here (3)
Ave Maria (2)
Away In A Manger (2)
Bantry Bay (3)
Believe Me (1)
Boolavogue (1)
Carrickfergus (3)
Come Back Paddy Reilly (medley) (3)
Courtin' Medley (4)
Croppy Boy (4)
Danny Boy (1,4)
Darling Girl From Clare (1)
Ding Dong Merrily On High (medley) (2)
Dublin In The Rare Old Times (medley) (3)
Eileen Óg (1)
Fields Of Athenry (3)
First Noel (2)
Forty Shades Of Green (4)
Galway Bay (1)
God Bless America (4)
Good King Wenceslas (medley) (2)
Grace (1)
Green Fields Of France (4)
Green Isle Of Erin (3)
Holy City (2)
How Are Things In Glocco Morra (4)
I'll Take You Home Again Kathleen (1)
Ireland, Mother Ireland (3)
Irish Medley (4)
Isle Of Hope, Isle Of Tears (4)
Isle Of Inisfree (3)
It Came Upon A Midnight Clear (2)
Joy To The World (2)
Kerry Dance (3)
Last Rose Of Summer (3)
Lay Of The West Clare Railway (Are Ye Right There Michael?) (medley) (3)
Let There Be Peace (4)
Lift The Wings (3)
Love Thee Dearest (4)
Love's Old Sweet Song (1)
Macushla (4)
Mary From Dungloe (3)
Minstrel Boy (1)
Molly Malone (medley) (3)
Mountains Of Mourne (1)
My Wild Irish Rose (4)
Nation Once Again (4)
O Holy Night (2)
Old Bog Road (4)
Old Man (1)
Only Our Rivers Run Free (1)
Phil The Fluther's Ball (medley) (3)
Red Is The Rose (3)
Rose Of Tralee (3)
Scorn Not His Simplicity (3)
She Is Far From The Land (3)
Silent Night (2)
Slievenamon (4)
Spanish Lady (1)
Star Of The County Down (3)
Suo Gan (2)
Sweet Little Jesus Boy (2)
There Is A Flower That Bloometh (3)
Toora-Loora-Looral (1)
Town I Loved So Well (1)
Voyage (1)
Wexford Carol (2)
What Child Is This? (2)
When Irish Eyes Are Smiling (1)
When You Were Sweet Sixteen (1)
While Shepherds Watch Their Flocks (2)
Will Ye Go, Lassie, Go? (1,3)

IRON BUTTERFLY　'69

Hard-rock group from San Diego: Doug Ingle (vocals, keyboards), Erik Braunn (guitar), Lee Dorman (bass) and Ron Bushy (drums). Braunn left in late 1969, replaced by Mike Pinera (leader of **Blues Image**) and Larry Reinhardt. Split in mid-1971. Braunn and Bushy regrouped in early 1975 with Phil Kramer (bass) and Howard Reitzes (keyboards). Kramer, who later earned a physics degree and became a mutimedia executive, mysteriously disappeared on 2/12/95; his remains were found at the bottom of a Malibu canyon on 5/29/99.

3/9/68	78	49	© 1	**Heavy**	$30	Atco 227
7/20/68+	4	140	▲4 © 2	In-A-Gadda-Da-Vida	$25	Atco 250
2/15/69	3	44	● © 3	Ball	$25	Atco 280
5/23/70	20	23	© 4	**Iron Butterfly Live**	[L]	$25	Atco 318
8/29/70	16	23	© 5	**Metamorphosis**	$25	Atco 339
12/25/71+	137	6	6	**The Best Of Iron Butterfly/Evolution**	[G]	$25	Atco 369
2/15/75	138	6	© 7	**Scorching Beauty**	$20	MCA 465

Am I Down (7)
Are You Happy (2,4)
Before You Go (7)
Belda-Beast (3,6)
Best Years Of Our Life (5)
Butterfly Bleu (7)
Easy Rider (Let The Wind Pay The Way) (5,6) *66*
Fields Of Sun (7)
Filled With Fear (3,4)
Flowers And Beads (2,6)
Free Flight (5)
Gentle As It May Seem (1)
Get Out Of My Life, Woman (1)
Hard Miserae (7)
Her Favorite Style (3)
High On A Mountain Top (7)
In-A-Gadda-Da-Vida (2,4,6) *30*
In The Crowds (3)
In The Time Of Our Lives (3,4) *96*
Iron Butterfly Theme (1,6)
It Must Be Love (3)
Lonely Boy (3)
Lonely Hearts (7)
Look For The Sun (1)
Most Anything You Want (2)
My Mirage (4)
New Day (5)
1975 Overture (7)
Pearly Gates (7)
People Of The World (7)
Possession (1,6)
Real Fright (3)
Searchin' Circles (7)
Shady Lady (4)
Slower Than Guns (5,6)
So-Lo (1)
Soldier In Our Town (5)
Soul Experience (3,4,6) *75*
Stamped Ideas (1)
Stone Believer (5,6)
Termination (2,6)
Unconscious Power (1,6)
You Can't Win (1,4)

IRONHORSE　'79

Rock group: Randy Bachman (vocals, guitar), Tom Sparks (guitar), John Pierce (bass) and Mike Baird (drums). Bachman was a member of **Guess Who** and **Bachman-Turner Overdrive**.

| 4/7/79 | 153 | 10 | | **Ironhorse** | $12 | Scotti Brothers 7103 |

Jump Back In The Light
Old Fashioned
One And Only
She's Got It
Stateline Blues
Sweet Lui-Louise *36*
There Ain't No Cure
Tumbleweed
Watch Me Fly
You Gotta Let Go

★220★ IRON MAIDEN — '86

Hard-rock group formed in London: Paul Di'anno (vocals), Dave Murray and Adrian Smith (guitars), Steve Harris (bass) and Clive Burr (drums). **Bruce Dickinson** replaced Di'anno in early 1982. Nick McBrain replaced Burr in early 1983. Blaze Bayley replaced Dickinson in September 1993. Janick Gers replaced Smith in 1994. Dickinson returned to replace Bayley in 1999; Adrian Smith returned that same year.

1)Somewhere In Time 2)Seventh Son Of A Seventh Son 3)Fear Of The Dark

DEBUT	PEAK	WKS	RIAA	CD	ARTIST — Album Title	Sym	$	Label & Number
6/6/81	78	23	●	©	1 Killers		$12	Harvest 12141
10/31/81	89	30			2 Maiden Japan	[L-M]	$12	Harvest 15000
					recorded on May 23, 1981 at Kosei Nenkin Hall in Nagoya, Japan			
4/10/82	33	65	▲	©	3 The Number Of The Beast		$12	Harvest 12202
6/11/83	14	45	▲	©	4 Piece Of Mind		$10	Capitol 12274
9/29/84	21	34	▲	©	5 Powerslave		$10	Capitol 12321
11/16/85	19	22	▲	©	6 Live After Death	[L]	$15	Capitol 12441 [2]
10/11/86	11	39	▲	©	7 Somewhere In Time		$10	Capitol 12524
4/30/88	12	23	●	©	8 Seventh Son Of A Seventh Son		$10	Capitol 90258
10/20/90	17	18	●	©	9 No Prayer For The Dying		$10	Epic 46905
5/30/92	12	13		©	10 Fear Of The Dark		$10	Epic 48993
4/10/93	106	2		©	11 A Real Live One	[L]	$10	Capitol 81456
11/20/93	140	1		©	12 A Real Dead One	[L]	$10	Capitol 89248
10/28/95	147	3		©	13 The X Factor		$10	CMC Int'l. 8003
4/11/98	124	1		©	14 Virtual XI		$10	CMC Int'l. 86240
6/17/00	39	10		©	15 Brave New World		$10	Portrait 62208

Aces High (5,6)
Afraid To Shoot Strangers (10,11)
Aftermath, The (13)
Alexander The Great (7)
Angel And The Gambler (14)
Another Life (1)
Apparition, The (14)
Assassin, The (9)
Back In The Village (5)
Be Quick Or Be Dead (10,11)
Blood Brothers (15)
Blood On The World's Hands (13)
Brave New World (15)
Bring Your Daughter ... To The Slaughter (9,11)
Can I Play With Madness (8,11)
Caught Somewhere In Time (7)
Chains Of Misery (10)

Childhood's End (10)
Children Of The Damned (3,6)
Clairvoyant, The (8,11)
Clansman, The (14)
Como Estais Amigos (14)
Deja Vu (1)
Die With Your Boots On (4,6)
Don't Look To The Eyes Of A Stranger (14)
Dream Of Mirrors (15)
Drifter (1)
Duellists, The (5)
Edge Of Darkness (13)
Educated Fool (14)
Evil That Men Do (8,11)
Fallen Angel (15)
Fates Warning (9)
Fear Is The Key (10)
Fear Of The Dark (10,11)
Flash Of The Blade (5)

Flight Of Icarus (4,6)
Fortunes Of War (13)
From Here To Eternity (10,11)
Fugitive, The (10)
Futureal (14)
Gangland (3)
Genghis Khan (1)
Ghost Of The Navigator (15)
Hallowed Be Thy Name (3,6,12)
Heaven Can Wait (7,11)
Holy Smoke (9)
Hooks In You (9)
Ides Of March (1)
Infinite Dreams (8)
Innocent Exile (1,2)
Invaders (1)
Iron Maiden (6,12)
Judas Be My Guide (10)
Judgement Of Heaven (13)
Killers (1,2)

Lightning Strikes Twice (14)
Loneliness Of The Long Distance Runner (7)
Look For The Truth (13)
Lord Of The Flies (13)
Losfer Words (Big 'Orra) (5)
Man On The Edge (13)
Mercenary, The (15)
Moonchild (8)
Mother Russia (9)
Murders In The Rue Morgue (1)
No Prayer For The Dying (9)
Nomad, The (15)
Number Of The Beast (3,6,12)
Only The Good Die Young (8)
Out Of The Silent Planet (15)
Phantom Of The Opera (6)
Powerslave (5,6)
Prisoner, The (3)
Prodigal Son (1)

Prophecy, The (8)
Prowler (12)
Public Enema Number One (9)
Purgatory (1)
Quest For Fire (4)
Remember Tomorrow (2,12)
Revelations (4,6)
Rime Of The Ancient Mariner (5,6)
Run Silent Run Deep (9)
Run To The Hills (3,6,12)
Running Free (2,6,12)
Sanctuary (12)
Sea Of Madness (7)
Seventh Son Of A Seventh Son (8)
Sign Of The Cross (13)
Still Life (4)
Stranger In A Strange Land (7)
Sun And Steel (4)

Tailgunner (9,11)
Thin Line Between Love And Hate (15)
To Tame A Land (4)
Transylvania (12)
Trooper, The (4,6,12)
22, Acacia Avenue (3,6)
Twilight Zone (1)
2 A.M. (13)
2 Minutes To Midnight (5,6,12)
Unbeliever, The (13)
Wasted Years (7)
Wasting Love (10,11)
Weekend Warrior (10)
When Two Worlds Collide (14)
Where Eagles Dare (4,12)
Wicker Man (15)
Wrathchild (1,2,6)

ISAAK, Chris — '91

Born on 6/26/56 in Stockton, California. Singer/songwriter/guitarist/actor. Acted in several movies.

DEBUT	PEAK	WKS	RIAA	CD	ARTIST — Album Title	Sym	$	Label & Number
4/11/87	194	2		©	1 Chris Isaak		$10	Warner 25536
7/15/89+	7	74	▲²	©	2 Heart Shaped World		$10	Reprise 25837
5/1/93	35	24	●	©	3 San Francisco Days		$10	Reprise 45116
6/10/95	31	41	▲	©	4 Forever Blue	C:#41/3	$10	Reprise 45845
10/26/96	33	17	●	©	5 Baja Sessions		$10	Reprise 46325
10/10/98	41	9		©	6 Speak Of The Devil		$10	Reprise 46849

Baby Did A Bad Bad Thing (4)
Back On Your Side (5)
Beautiful Homes (3)
Black Flowers (6)
Blue Hotel (1)
Blue Spanish Sky (2)
Breaking Apart (6)
Can't Do A Thing (To Stop Me) (3)
Changed Your Mind (4)
Cryin' (1)
Dancin' (1)
Don't Get So Down On Yourself (6)

Don't Leave Me On My Own (4)
Don't Make Me Dream About You (2)
End Of Everything (4)
Except The New Girl (3)
Fade Away (1)
5:15 (3)
Flying (6)
Forever Blue (4)
Forever Young (2)
Go Walking Down There (4)
Goin' Nowhere (4)
Graduation Day (4)
Heart Full Of Soul (1)

Heart Shaped World (2)
I Believe (4)
I Want Your Love (3)
I Wonder (5)
I'm Not Sleepy (6)
I'm Not Waiting (2)
In The Heat Of The Jungle (2)
Kings Of The Highway (2)
Lie To Me (1)
Like The Way She Moves (6)
Lonely Nights (6)
Lonely With A Broken Heart (3)
Lovers Game (1)
Move Along (3)

Nothing's Changed (2)
Only The Lonely (5)
Please (6)
Pretty Girls Don't Cry (5)
Return To Me (5)
Round 'N' Round (3)
San Francisco Days (3)
Shadows In A Mirror (4)
Solitary Man (3)
Somebody's Crying (4) 45
South Of The Border (Down Mexico Way) (5)
Speak Of The Devil (6)
Super Magic 2000 (3)

Sweet Leilani (5)
Talkin' 'Bout A Home (6)
There She Goes (4)
Things Go Wrong (4)
Think Of Tomorrow (5)
This Love Will Last (1)
This Time (6)
Two Hearts (3,5)
Waiting (3)
Waiting For My Lucky Day (5)
Waiting For The Rain To Fall (1)
Walk Slow (6)
Wanderin' (4)

Wicked Game (2) 6
Wild Love (3)
Wrong To Love You (2,5)
Yellow Bird (5)
You Owe Me Some Kind Of Love (1)
You Took My Heart (1)

ISLE OF MAN — '86

Multi-ethnic pop group (members are from France, Nicaragua, Italy and U.S.): Robere Parlez (vocals), Raun (guitar), Jamie Roberto (bass) and Ronnie Lee Sage (drums).

DEBUT	PEAK	WKS	RIAA	CD	ARTIST — Album Title	$	Label & Number
7/19/86	110	18			Isle Of Man	$10	Pasha 40319

Afraid Of Heights
Am I Forgiven 90
Building Bridges

Desperate Surrender (Amor Moriendo)
Land Of The Heroes

Only The Brave
Rock Of Ages
Skin Trade

Speaking English
Tenderness

ISLEY, Ernie — '90

Born on 3/7/52 in Cincinnati. Member of **The Isley Brothers** and Isley, Jasper, Isley.

DEBUT	PEAK	WKS	RIAA	CD	ARTIST — Album Title	$	Label & Number
3/31/90	174	11		©	High Wire	$10	Elektra 60902

Back To Square One
Deal With It
Deep Water

Diamond In The Rough
Fare Thee Well, Fair-Weather Friend

High Wire
In Deep
Love Situation

Muses, The
Rising From The Ashes
She Takes Me Up

Song For The Muses

ISLEY, Ronald — see ISLEY BROTHERS, The

ISLEY BROTHERS, The ★83★   '75

R&B vocal trio of brothers from Cincinnati: O'Kelly, Ronald and Rudolph Isley. Added their younger brothers Marvin (bass, percussion) and **Ernie Isley** (guitar, drums) and brother-in-law Chris Jasper (keyboards) in September 1969. Formed own T-Neck label the same year. Ernie, Marvin and Chris began recording as the trio **Isley, Jasper, Isley** in 1984. O'Kelly died of a heart attack on 3/31/86 (age 48); Ronald and Rudolph continued on as The Isley Brothers through 1990. Ernie, Marvin and Ronald reunited as The Isley Brothers in 1991. Ronald married **Angela Winbush** on 6/26/93. Group inducted into the Rock and Roll Hall of Fame in 1992.

1)The Heat Is On 2)Showdown 3)Go For Your Guns 4)Go All The Way 5)3 + 3

DEBUT	PEAK	WKS	RIAA	CD			$	Label & Number
9/29/62	61	13		©	1	Twist & Shout	$100	Wand 653
6/18/66	140	5		©	2	This Old Heart Of Mine	$30	Tamla 269
5/3/69	22	18			3	It's Our Thing	$20	T-Neck 3001
10/18/69	169	4			4	Live At Yankee Stadium	[L] $30	T-Neck 3004 [2]

side A: Isley Brothers; side B: **Edwin Hawkins Singers**; side C: **Brooklyn Bridge**; side D: "Don't Change Your Love" by **The Five Stairsteps**, "Somebody's Been Messin'" by Judy White and "Love Is What You Make It" by Sweet Cherries; recorded on 6/21/69

10/18/69	180	3		©	5	The Brothers: Isley	$20	T-Neck 3002
9/25/71	71	25		©	6	Givin' It Back	$15	T-Neck 3008
7/1/72	29	33		©	7	Brother, Brother, Brother	$15	T-Neck 3009
3/17/73	139	13		©	8	The Isleys Live	[L] $20	T-Neck 3010 [2]
9/8/73	8	37	▲	©	9	3 + 3	$15	T-Neck 32453
12/22/73	195	3			10	Isleys' Greatest Hits	[G] $15	T-Neck 3011
9/7/74	14	28	●		11	Live It Up	$12	T-Neck 33070
6/14/75	❶[1]	40	▲[2]	©	12	The Heat Is On	$12	T-Neck 33536
5/29/76	9	26	●	©	13	Harvest For The World	$12	T-Neck 33809
4/16/77	6	34	▲[2]	©	14	Go For Your Guns	$12	T-Neck 34432
8/27/77	58	11			15	Forever Gold	[G] $12	T-Neck 34452
4/22/78	4	21	▲		16	Showdown	$12	T-Neck 34930
6/16/79	14	20	●	©	17	Winner Takes All	$15	T-Neck 36077 [2]
4/19/80	8	22	▲		18	Go All The Way	$12	T-Neck 36305
3/21/81	28	17	●		19	Grand Slam	$12	T-Neck 37080
10/31/81	45	13			20	Inside You	$12	T-Neck 37533
8/21/82	87	12			21	The Real Deal	$12	T-Neck 38047
6/4/83	19	23	▲	©	22	Between The Sheets	$12	T-Neck 38674
12/7/85+	140	12			23	Masterpiece	$10	Warner 25347
6/20/87	64	17		©	24	Smooth Sailin'	$10	Warner 25586

THE ISLEY BROTHERS FEATURING RONALD ISLEY:

9/2/89	89	13		©	25	Spend The Night	$10	Warner 25940
6/13/92	140	3		©	26	Tracks Of Life	$10	Warner 26620
3/26/94	48[C]	2	▲[2]		27	Isley's Greatest Hits, Vol. 1	[G] $10	T-Neck 39240

THE ISLEY BROTHERS

6/1/96	31	45	▲	©	28	Mission To Please	$10	Island 524214

Ain't Givin' Up No Love (16)
Ain't I Been Good To You (Part 1 & 2) (11)
All In My Lover's Eyes (21)
Are You With Me? (21)
(At Your Best) You Are Love (13,15)
Baby Come Back Home (25)
Baby Don't You Do It (2)
Baby Hold On (20)
Ballad For The Fallen Soldier (22)
Bedroom Eyes (26)
Belly Dancer (Parts 1 & 2) (18)
Between The Sheets (22,27)
Black Berries - Pt 1 (5) *79*
Brazilian Wedding Song (Setembro) (26)
Brother, Brother (7,10)
Brown Eyed Girl (11)
Can I Have A Kiss (For Old Times' Sake)? (28)
(Can't You See) What You Do To Me? (17)
Choosey Lover (22)
Climbin' Up The Ladder (Part 1 & 2) (14)
Cold Bologna (6)
Colder Are My Nights (23)
Come My Way (24)
Come To Me (23)
Come Together (25)
Coolin' Me Out (Part 1 & 2) (16)
Dedicate This Song (26)
Dish It Out (24)
Don't Give It Away (3)
Don't Hold Back Your Love (Part I & II) (20)
Don't Let Me Be Lonely Tonight (9)
Don't Let Up (19)
Don't Say Goodnight (It's Time For Love) (Parts 1 & 2) (18) *39*

Don't You Feel (1)
Everything Is Alright (24)
Feel Like The World (3,5)
Fight The Power Part 1 (12,15,27) *4*
Fire And Rain (6)
First Love (20)
Floatin' On Your Love (28) *47*
Footsteps In The Dark (Part 1 & 2) (14,27)
For The Love Of You (Part 1&2) (12,15,27) *22*
Freedom (10) *72*
Fun And Games (16)
Get Down Off The Train (5)
Get Into Something (10) *89*
Get My Licks In (26)
Gettin' Over (22)
Give The Women What They Want (3)
Go All The Way (Parts 1 & 2) (18)
Go For What You Know (17)
Go For Your Guns (14)
Groove With You (16,27)
Harvest For The World (13,15) *63*
He's Got Your Love (3)
Heat Is On (Part 1 & 2) (12)
Hello It's Me (11,15)
Here We Go Again (Parts 1 & 2) (18)
Highways Of My Life (9)
Hold On Baby (1)
Holding Back The Years (28)
Holding On (5)
Hope You Feel Better Love (Part 1 & 2) (12,15)
How Lucky I Am (Part 1 & 2) (9)
Hurry Up And Wait (19) *58*
I Got To Get Myself Together (5)

I Guess I'll Always Love You (2) *61*
I Hear A Symphony (2)
I Know Who You Been Socking It To (3,4,10)
I Must Be Losing My Touch (3)
I Need Your Body (22)
I Once Had Your Love (And I Can't Let Go) (19)
I Say Love (1)
I Turned You On (4,5,10) *23*
I Wanna Be With You (Parts 1 & 2) (17)
I Wish (24)
I'll Be There 4 U (26)
I'll Do It All For You (21)
If Leaving Me Is Easy (23)
If You Ever Need Somebody (25)
If You Were There (1)
Inside You (Part I & II) (20)
It Takes A Good Woman (24)
It's A Disco Night (Rock Don't Stop) (17) *90*
It's Alright With Me (21)
It's Too Late (7,8)
It's Your Thing (3,4,8,10,27) *2*
Just Ain't Enough Love (2)
Keep On Doin' (10) *75*
Keep On Walkin' (7)
Koolin' Out (26)
Lay-Away (7,8,10) *54*
Lay Lady Lay (6,8) *71*
Let Me Down Easy (13)
Let Me In Your Life (Parts 1 & 2) (17)
Let's Fall In Love (Parts 1 & 2) (17)
Let's Get Intimate (28)
Let's Lay Together (28) *93*
Let's Make Love Tonight (22)
Lets Twist Again (1)
Life In The City (Parts 1 & 2) (17)

Liquid Love (Parts 1 & 2) (17)
Listen To The Music (9)
Live It Up Part 1 (11,15,27) *52*
Livin' In The Life (14) *40*
Lost In Your Love (26)
Love Comes And Goes (Parts 1 & 2) (17)
Love Fever (Floatin' 1 & 2) (16)
Love Is What You Make It (16)
Love Merry-Go-Round (20)
Love Put Me On The Corner (7)
Love The One You're With (6,8,10) *18*
Love Zone (20)
Lover's Eve (11)
Machine Gun (6,8)
Make Me Say It Again Girl (Part 1 & 2) (12)
Make Your Body Sing (28)
May I? (23)
Midnight Sky (Part 1) (11) *73*
Mind Over Matter (Parts 1 & 2) (17)
Mission To Please (28)
Morning Love (26)
Most Beautiful Girl (23)
My Best Was Good Enough (23)
My Little Girl (5)
Need A Little Taste Of Love (11)
Never Leave Me Baby (1)
No Axe To Grind (26)
Nothing To Do But Today (6)
Nowhere To Run (2)
Ohio (6,8)
One Of A Kind (25)
Party Night (19)
Pass It On (Parts 1 & 2) (18)
People Of Today (13)
Pop That Thang (7,8,10) *24*
Pride (Part 1) (14) *63*
Put A Little Love In Your Heart (7)

Put Yourself In My Place (3)
Real Deal (Part I And II) (21)
Real Woman (25)
Red Hot (26)
Release Your Love (23)
Right Now (1)
Rock You Good (22)
Rockin' With Fire (Part 1 & 2) (16)
Rubber Leg Twist (1)
Say You Will (Parts 1 & 2) (18)
Searching For A Miracle (26)
Seek And You Shall Find (2)
Send A Message (24)
Sensitive Lover (26)
Sensuality (Part 1 & 2) (12)
Shout - Part 1 (4,10) *47*
Showdown (Parts 1 & 2) (16)
Slow Down Children (22)
Slow Is The Way (28)
Smooth Sailin' Tonight (24)
Snake, The (1)
So You Wanna Stay Down (13)
Somebody Been Messin' (3)
Somebody I Used To Know (24)
Spanish Twist (1)
Spend The Night (Ce Soir) (25)
Spill The Wine (6,10) *49*
Stay Gold (13)
Stone Cold Lover (21)
Stop! In The Name Of Love (2)
Summer Breeze (Part 1) (9,15) *62*
Sunshine (Go Away Today) (9)
Sweet Seasons (7)
Take Me To The Next Phase (Part 1 & 2) (16)
Take Some Time Out For Love (2) *66*
Tears (28) *28*
Tell Me When You Need It Again (Part 1 & 2) (14)
That Lady (Part 1) (9,15,27) *6*

There's No Love Left (2)
This Old Heart Of Mine (Is Weak For You) (2) *12*
Time After Time (1)
Tonight Is The Night (If I Had You) (19)
Touch Me (22)
Turn On The Demon (26)
Twist And Shout (1) *17*
Under The Influence (21)
Vacuum Cleaner (5,10)
Voyage To Atlantis (14)
Was It Good To You (5) *83*
Way Out Love (22)
Welcome Into My Heart (20)
What It Comes Down To (9) *55*
Whatever Turns You On (26)
Whenever You're Ready (28)
Who Could Ever Doubt My Love (2)
Who Loves You Better-Part 1 (13) *47*
Who Said? (19)
Winner Takes All (17)
Work To Do (7,8,10) *51*
You Better Come Home (1)
You Never Know When You're Gonna Fall In Love (23)
You Still Feel The Need (13)
You Walk Your Way (9)
You'll Never Walk Alone (25)
You're Beside Me (Parts 1 & 2) (17)
You're The Key To My Heart (17)
Young Girls (19)

ISLEY, JASPER, ISLEY '85

R&B trio: Ernie Isley, Chris Jasper, Marvin Isley. See above Isley Brothers biography.

2/9/85	135	10			1 Broadway's Closer To Sunset Blvd.			$10	CBS Associated 39873
11/2/85	77	26		©	2 Caravan Of Love			$10	CBS Associated 40118

Break This Chain (1)   Caravan Of Love (2) 51   I Can Hardly Wait (2)   Insatiable Woman (2)   Look The Other Way (1)   Sex Drive (1)
Broadway's Closer To Sunset   Dancin' Around The World (2)   I Can't Get Over Losin' You (1)   Kiss And Tell (1) 63   Love Is Gonna Last Forever (1)
Blvd. (1)   High Heel Syndrome (2)   If You Believe In Love (2)   Liberation (2)   Serve You Right (1)

IT'S A BEAUTIFUL DAY '69

Folk-rock group from San Francisco. Core members: David LaFlamme (male vocals, violin), Pattie Santos (female vocals), Fred Webb (keyboards) and Val Fuentes (drums). LaFlamme left in 1973. Bassist Bud Cockrell later joined Pablo Cruise. Santos died in a car crash on 12/14/89 (age 40).

6/14/69	47	70	● ©		1 It's A Beautiful Day			$40	Columbia 9768
7/4/70	28	21	©		2 Marrying Maiden			$30	Columbia 1058
12/11/71+	130	16			3 Choice Quality Stuff/Anytime			$25	Columbia 30734
11/11/72	144	9			4 It's A Beautiful Day At Carnegie Hall		[L]	$25	Columbia 31338
4/7/73	114	10			5 It's A Beautiful Day...Today			$25	Columbia 32181

Ain't That Lovin' You Baby (5)   Child (2)   Galileo (5)   Hot Summer Day (1,4)   No Word For Glad (3)   Wasted Union Blues (1)
Angels And Animals (4)   Creator (5)   Girl With No Eyes (1)   It Comes Right Down To You   Oranges & Apples (3)   Watching You, Watching Me (5)
Anytime (3)   Creed Of Love (3)   Give Your Woman What She   (2)   Place Of Dreams (3)   White Bird (1,4)
Bitter Wine (3)   Do You Remember The Sun (2)   Wants (4)   Lady Love (3)   Ridin' Thumb (5)   Words (3)
Bombay Calling (1,4)   Dolphins, The (2)   Going To Another Party (4)   Let A Woman Flow (2)   Soapstone Mountain (2)
Bulgaria (1)   Don And Dewey (2)   Good Lovin' (2,4)   Lie To Me (5)   Time (5)
Burning Low (5)   Down On The Bayou (5)   Grand Camel Suite (3,4)   Misery Loves Company (3)   Time Is (1)
Bye Bye Baby (3)   Essence Of Now (2)   Hoedown (2)   Mississippi Delta (5)   Waiting For The Song (3)

IVES, Burl '62

Born on 6/14/09 in Huntington Township, Illinois. Died of cancer on 4/14/95 (age 85). Folk singer/actor. Acted in several movies. Narrated the animated TV classic *Rudolph The Red-Nosed Reindeer.*

2/17/62	35	34			1 The Versatile Burl Ives!			$20	Decca 4152
6/2/62	24	36			2 It's Just My Funny Way Of Laughin'			$20	Decca 4279
12/5/64+	65	15			3 Pearly Shells			$20	Decca 74578
12/25/65	32[X]	1		©	4 Have A Holly Jolly Christmas		[X]	$15	Decca 74689
12/23/67	93[X]	2		©	5 Christmas Eve with Burl Ives		[X]	$15	Decca 78391
11/21/98+	23[X]	11		©	6 Rudolph The Red-Nosed Reindeer	C:#29/10	[X-TV]	$10	MCA 22177

soundtrack of the classic Christmas TV show; first released in 1966 on Decca 74815; Christmas charts: 30/'98, 32/'99, 23/'00

Almighty Dollar Bill (1)   Holly Jolly Christmas (4,6)   Little Bitty Tear (1) 9   Oh, Little Town Of Bethlehem   Silver And Gold (6)   What You Gonna Do, Leroy?
Brooklyn Bridge (2)   I Ain't Comin' Home Tonight (2)   Little Drummer Boy (4)   (5)   Silver Bells (4)   (2)
Call Me Mr. In-Between (2) 19   I Ain't Missing Nobody (3)   Long Black Veil (1)   Oh, My Side (1)   Sixteen Fathoms Down (2)   When Santa Claus Gets Your
Christmas Can't Be Far Away   I Heard The Bells On Christmas   Lower Forty (3)   Okeechobee Ocean (3)   Snow For Johnny (4)   Letter (medley) (6)
(4)   Day (4,6)   Lynching Party (3)   Pearly Shells (3) 60   That's All I Can Remember (2)   White Christmas (4)
Christmas Child (Loo, Loo, Loo)   I Walk The Line (1)   Mama Don't Want No Peas An'   Poor Little Jimmie (2)   There Were Three Ships (5)   Who Done It? (3)
(4)   In Foggy Old London (2)   Rice An' Cocoanut Oil (1)   Rockin' Around The Christmas   There's Always Tomorrow (6)   Winter Wonderland (4)
Christmas Is A Birthday (4)   It Came Upon The Midnight   Merry Merry Christmas   Tree (medley) (6)   Thumbin' Johnny Brown (2)
Delia (1)   Clear (5)   (medley) (6)   Royal Telephone (1)   Twelve Days Of Christmas (5)
Don't Let Love Die (1)   Jesous Ahatonia (5)   Mockin' Bird Hill (1)   Rudolph The Red-Nosed   Two Of The Usual (3)
Down In Yon Forest (5)   Jingle Jingle Jingle (6)   Most Wonderful Day Of The   Reindeer (4,6)   We Are Santa's Elves (6)
Forty Hour Week (1)   Kentucky Turkey Buzzard (3)   Year (6)   Santa Claus Is Comin' To Town   We're A Couple Of Misfits (6)
Friendly Beasts (5)   King Herod And The Cock (5)   Mother Wouldn't Do That (2)   (4)   What Child Is This? (5)
Funny Way Of Laughin' (2) 10   Legend Of The "T" (3)   Night Before Christmas   Seven Joys Of Mary (5)   What Little Tears Are Made Of
Hard Luck And Misery (3)   Lenora, Let Your Hair Hang   (medley) (6)   Shanghied (1)   (3)
   Down (1)   Ninety-Nine (2)   Silent Night (5)

J

JACKS, Terry '74

Born on 3/29/44 in Winnipeg, Canada. Pop singer/songwriter/guitarist. Recorded with wife Susan Jacks as The Poppy Family.

3/16/74	81	9			Seasons In The Sun			$15	Bell 1307

Again And Again   Fire On The Skyline   I'm So Lonely Here Today   Love Game   Sail Away   Since You Broke My Heart
Concrete Sea   I'm Gonna Love You Too   It's Been There From The Start   Pumpkin Eater   Seasons In The Sun 1

JACKSON, Alan ★196★ '98

Born on 10/17/58 in Newnan, Georgia. Country singer/guitarist. Former car salesman and construction worker. Formed own band, Dixie Steel. Signed to Glen Campbell's publishing company in 1985.

1)High Mileage 2)The Greatest Hits Collection 3)Who I Am

3/31/90+	57	110	▲² ©		1 Here In The Real World			$10	Arista 8623
6/1/91	17	118	▲⁴ ©		2 Don't Rock The Jukebox			$10	Arista 8681
10/24/92+	13	122	▲⁶ ©		3 A Lot About Livin' (And A Little 'Bout Love)			$10	Arista 18711
11/6/93	42	12	▲ ©		4 Honky Tonk Christmas	C:#17/13	[X]	$10	Arista 18736
					Christmas charts: 4/'93, 15/'94, 31/'95				
7/16/94	5	69	▲⁴ ©		5 Who I Am			$10	Arista 18759
11/11/95	5	104	▲⁴ ©		6 The Greatest Hits Collection	C:#11/97	[G]	$10	Arista 18801
11/16/96	12	73	▲³ ©		7 Everything I Love			$10	Arista 18813
9/19/98	4	40	▲ ©		8 High Mileage			$10	Arista 18864
11/13/99	9	51	▲ ©		9 Under The Influence			$10	Arista 18892
11/25/00	15	31↑	▲ ©		10 When Somebody Loves You			$10	Arista 69335

JACKSON, Alan — Cont'd

Ace Of Hearts (1)
All American Country Boy (5)
Amarillo (8)
Angels Cried (4)
Another Good Reason (8)
Between The Devil And Me (7)
Blue Blooded Woman (1)
Blues Man (A Tribute To Hank Williams, Jr.) (9)
Buicks To The Moon (7)
Chasin' That Neon Rainbow (1,6)
Chattahoochee (3,6) **46**
Dallas (2,6)
Dancin' All Around It (8)
Dog River Blues (1)
Don't Rock The Jukebox (2,6)
Everything I Love (7)
Farewell Party (9)
From A Distance (2)

Gone Country (5,6)
Gone Crazy (8) **43**
Here In The Real World (1,6)
Hole In The Wall (5)
Holly Jolly Christmas (4)
Home (1,6)
Honky Tonk Christmas (4)
House With No Curtains (7)
Hurtin' Comes Easy (8)
I Don't Even Know Your Name (5,6)
I Don't Need The Booze (To Get A Buzz On) (3)
I Only Want You For Christmas (4)
I Still Love You (10)
I'd Love You All Over Again (1,6)
I'll Go On Loving You (8)
I'll Try (8)

If I Had You (5)
If It Ain't One Thing (It's You) (3)
If We Make It Through December (4)
If You Don't Wanna See Santa Claus Cry (4)
It Must Be Love (9) **37**
It's Alright To Be A Redneck (10)
It's Time You Learned About Good-Bye (7)
Job Description (5)
Just Playin' Possum (2)
Kiss An Angel Good Mornin' (9)
Let's Get Back To Me And You (5)
Life Or Love (10)
Little Bitty (7) **58**
Little Man (8) **39**
Livin' On Love (5,6)

Love Like That (10)
Love's Got A Hold On You (2,6)
Margaritaville (9)
Maybe I Should Stay Here (10)
Meat and Potato Man (10)
Mercury Blues (3,6)
Merry Christmas To Me (4)
Midnight In Montgomery (2,6)
Must've Had A Ball (7)
My Own Kind Of Hat (9)
Once You've Had The Best (9)
Please Daddy (Don't Get Drunk This Christmas) (4)
Pop A Top (9) **43**
Revenooer Man (9)
Right In The Palm Of Your Hand (9)
Right On The Money (8) **43**
Santa's Gonna Come In A Pickup Truck (4)

She Don't Get The Blues (1)
She Just Started Liking Cheatin' Songs (9)
She Likes It Too (3)
She's Got The Rhythm (And I Got The Blues) (3,6)
Short Sweet Ride (1)
Someday (2,6)
Song For The Life (5)
Summertime Blues (5,6)
Tall, Tall Trees (6)
Thank God For The Radio (5)
That's All I Need To Know (2)
There Goes (7)
There's A New Kid In Town (1)
Three Minute Positive Not Too Country Up-tempo Love Song (10)
Thrill Is Back (10)
Tonight I Climbed The Wall (3)

Tropical Depression (3)
Up To My Ears In Tears (3)
www.memory (10) **45**
Walk On The Rocks (7)
Walkin' The Floor Over Me (2)
Wanted (1,6)
Way I Am (7)
What A Day Yesterday Was (8)
When Somebody Loves You (10) **52**
Where I Come From (10)
Who I Am (5)
(Who Says) You Can't Have It All (3,6)
Who's Cheatin' Who (7)
Woman's Love (8)
Working Class Hero (5)
You Can't Give Up On Love (5)

JACKSON, Brian — see SCOTT-HERON, Gil

JACKSON, Freddie — '85

Born on 10/2/56 in Harlem, New York. R&B singer/songwriter.

DEBUT	PEAK	WKS	RIAA	CD	ALBUM	$	Label & Number
5/25/85	10	62	▲	© 1	**Rock Me Tonight**	$10	Capitol 12404
11/15/86+	23	51	▲	© 2	**Just Like The First Time**	$10	Capitol 12495
8/13/88	48	30	●	© 3	**Don't Let Love Slip Away**	$10	Capitol 48987
11/24/90	59	30	●	© 4	**Do Me Again**	$10	Capitol 92217
8/29/92	83	12		© 5	**Time For Love**	$10	Capitol 96859
2/5/94	66	8		© 6	**Here It Is**	$10	Orpheus 66318
3/18/95	187	2		© 7	**Private Party**	$10	Street Life 75457

Addictive 2 Touch (6)
All I'll Ever Ask (5)
All Over You (4)
Calling (1)
Can I Touch You (5)
Can We Try (5)
Chivalry (5)
Come Home II U (6)
Come With Me Tonight (5)
Crazy (For Me) (3)
Do Me Again (4)
Don't It Feel Good (4)
Don't Let Love Slip Away (4)
Don't Say You Love Me (4)

Giving My Love To You (6)
Good Morning Heartache (1)
Have You Ever Loved Somebody (2) **69**
He'll Never Love You (Like I Do) (1) **25**
Here It Is (6)
Hey Lover (3)
How Does It Feel (6)
I Can't Let You Go (2)
I Can't Take It (4)
I Could Use A Little Love (Right Now) (1)
I Don't Want To Lose Your Love (2)

I Love (6)
I Tried My Best (7)
I Wanna Say I Love You (1)
(I Want) To Thank You (7)
I'll Be Waiting For You (4)
If You Don't Know Me By Now (3)
It Takes Two (4)
It's Gonna Take A Long, Long Time (3)
Jam Tonight (2) **32**
Janay (2)
Just Like The First Time (2)
Lay Your Love On Me (7)

Live For The Moment (4)
Live My Life Without You (5)
Look Around (2)
Love Is Just A Touch Away (1)
Love Me Down (4)
Love You All Over (7)
Main Course (4)
Make Love Easy (6)
Me & Mrs. Jones (5)
My Family (6)
Nice 'N' Slow (3) **61**
No One Else (7)
Once In A While (7)
One Heart Too Many (3)

Paradise (6)
Private Party (7)
Rock Me Tonight (For Old Times Sake) (1) **18**
Rub Up Against You (7)
Second Time For Love (4)
Sing A Song Of Love (1)
Special Lady (3)
Still Waiting (2)
Tasty Love (2) **41**
Teach Me (7)
Thank You ...see: (I Want To)
Time For Love Tonight (5)
Trouble (5)

Was It Something (6)
Will You Be There (5)
Yes, I Need You (3)
You And I Got A Thang (3)
You Are My Lady (1) **12**
You Are My Love (2)
Your Lovin' (Is A Good Thang) (7)

★260★

JACKSON, Janet — '93

Born on 5/16/66 in Gary, Indiana. R&B singer/actress. Sister of **The Jacksons** (youngest of nine children). Acted in several movies and TV shows. Married to James DeBarge (of **DeBarge**) from 1984-85. Secretly married to producer Rene Elizondo from 1991-2000.

DEBUT	PEAK	WKS	RIAA	CD	ALBUM	Catalog	Sym	$	Label & Number
11/20/82+	63	25		© 1	Janet Jackson			$12	A&M 4907
10/27/84	147	6		2	Dream Street			$12	A&M 4962
3/8/86	❶²	106	▲⁵	© 3	Control			$10	A&M 5106
10/7/89	❶⁴	108	▲⁶	© 4	Janet Jackson's Rhythm Nation 1814			$10	A&M 3920
6/5/93	❶⁶	106	▲⁶	© 5	janet.	C:#35/2		$10	Virgin 87825
10/28/95	3	29	▲²	© 6	Design Of A Decade 1986/1996	C:#3/11	[G]	$10	A&M 540399
10/25/97	❶¹	74	▲³	© 7	The Velvet Rope	C:#30/2		$10	Virgin 44762
5/12/01	❶¹	21↑	▲²	© 8	All For You			$10	Virgin 10144

Again (5) **1**
All For You (8) **1**
All My Love To You (2)
Alright (4,6) **4**
Any Time, Any Place (5) **2**
Anything (7)
Are You Still Up (5)
Because Of Love (5) **10**
Better Days (8)
Black Cat (4,6) **1**
Body That Loves You (5)
China Love (8)
Come Back To Me (4,6) **2**
Come Give Your Love To Me (1) **58**

Come On Get Up (8)
Communication (2)
Control (3,6) **5**
Doesn't Really Matter (8) **1**
Don't Mess Up This Good Thing (1)
Don't Stand Another Chance (2)
Dream Street (2)
Empty (5)
Escapade (4,6) **1**
Every Time (7)
Fast Girls (2)
Feels So Right (8)
Forever Yours (1)
Free Xone (7)

Funky Big Band (5)
Funny How Time Flies (When You're Having Fun) (3)
Go Deep (7)
Got 'Til It's Gone (7)
He Doesn't Know I'm Alive (3)
Hold Back The Tears (2)
I Get Lonely (7) **3**
If (5) **4**
If It Takes All Night (2)
Knowledge, The (4)
Let's Wait Awhile (3,6) **2**
Livin' In A World (They Didn't Make) (4)
Lonely (4)
Love And My Best Friend (1)

Love Scene (Ooh Baby) (8)
Love Will Never Do (Without You) (4,6) **1**
Magic Is Working (1)
Miss You Much (4,6) **1**
My Need (7)
Nasty (3,6) **3**
New Agenda (5)
Pleasure Principle (3,6) **14**
Pretty Boy (2)
Rhythm Nation (4,6) **2**
Rope Burn (7)
Runaway (6) **3**
Say You Do (1)
Someday Is Tonight (4)
Someone To Call My Lover (8)

Son Of A Gun (I Betcha Think This Song Is About You) (8)
Special (7)
State Of The World (4)
That's The Way Love Goes (5,6) **1**
This Time (5)
Throb (5)
Together Again (7) **1**
Tonight's The Night (7)
Trust A Try (8)
Truth (8)
Twenty Foreplay (6)
Two To The Power Of Love (2)
Velvet Rope (7)
What About (7)

What Have You Done For Me Lately (3,6) **4**
What'll I Do (5)
When I Think Of You (3,6) **1**
When We Wooo (8)
Where Are You Now (5)
Would You Mind (5)
You (7)
You Ain't Right (8)
You Can Be Mine (3)
You Want This (5) **8**
You'll Never Find (A Love Like Mine) (1)
Young Love (1) **64**

★417★

JACKSON, Jermaine — '80

Born on 12/11/54 in Gary, Indiana. Singer/bassist. **The Jackson 5** until group left Motown in 1976. Married Hazel Joy Gordy, daughter of Berry Gordy, on 12/15/73; later divorced. Rejoined The Jacksons in 1984 for the group's *Victory* album and tour.

1)Let's Get Serious 2)Jermaine Jackson 3)Jermaine

DEBUT	PEAK	WKS	RIAA	CD	ALBUM	$	Label & Number
8/12/72	27	36		1	Jermaine	$15	Motown 752
6/16/73	152	6		2	Come Into My Life	$15	Motown 775
9/25/76	164	11		3	My Name Is Jermaine	$12	Motown 842
8/27/77	174	3		4	Feel The Fire	$12	Motown 888
4/12/80	6	29	●	© 5	Let's Get Serious	$12	Motown 928
12/6/80+	44	23		6	Jermaine	$12	Motown 948
9/26/81	86	10		7	I Like Your Style	$12	Motown 952

JACKSON, Jermaine — Cont'd

8/21/82	46	16			8 Let Me Tickle Your Fancy			$12	Motown 6017
5/19/84	19	49	●	©	9 Jermaine Jackson			$10	Arista 8203
3/22/86	46	22		©	10 Precious Moments			$10	Arista 8277
12/2/89+	115	16		©	11 Don't Take It Personal			$10	Arista 8493

Ain't That Peculiar (1)
All Because Of You (6)
Bass Odyssey (3)
Beautiful Morning (6)
Bigger You Love (The Harder You Fall) (2)
Burnin' Hot (5)
Can I Change My Mind (6)
Climb Out (11)
Come Into My Life (2)
(C'mon) Feel The Need (5)
Come To Me (One Way Or Another) (9)
Daddy's Home (1) 9
Do What You Do (9) 13
Do You Remember Me? (10) 71
Does Your Mama Know About Me (2)
Don't Make Me Wait (11)
Don't Take It Personal (11) 64

Dynamite (9) 15
Escape From The Planet Of The Ant Men (9)
Faithful (3)
Feel The Fire (Burning From Me To You) (4)
Feelin' Free (5)
First You Laugh, Then You Cry (6)
Git Up And Dance (4)
Give A Little Love (10)
Got To Get To You Girl (4)
Happiness Is (4)
Homeward Bound (1)
I Can't Take No More (7)
I Gotta Have Ya (7)
I Hear Heartbeat (10)
I Just Want To Take This Time (3)
I Let Love Pass Me By (1)
I Like Your Style (8)

I Love You More (4)
I Miss You So (6)
I Need You More Now Than Ever (2)
I Only Have Eyes For You (1)
I Think It's Love (10) 16
I'd Like To Get To Know You (11)
I'm In A Different World (1)
I'm Just Too Shy (7) 60
I'm My Brother's Keeper (7)
If You Don't Love Me (2)
If You Say My Eyes Are Beautiful (10)
If You Were My Woman (1)
Is It Always Gonna Be Like This (7)
It's Still Undone (7)
Let Me Tickle Your Fancy (8) 18
Let's Be Young Tonight (3) 55

Let's Get Serious (5) 9
Little Girl Don't You Worry (6)
Live It Up (1)
Lonely Won't Leave Me Alone (10)
Look Past My Life (3)
Lovely You're The One (3)
Ma (2)
Make It Easy On Love (11)
Maybe Next Time (7)
Messing Around (3)
Million To One (2)
My Touch Of Madness (3)
Next To You (11)
Oh Mother (9)
Our Love Story (10)
Paradise In Your Eyes (7)
Pieces Fit (6)
Precious Moments (10)
Rise To The Occasion (11)
Running (8)

Signed, Sealed, Delivered I'm Yours (7)
Sitting On The Edge Of My Mind (2)
So In Love (2)
So Right (11)
Some Kind Of Woman (4)
Some Things Are Private (9)
Stay With Me (3)
Strong Love (4)
Sweetest Sweetest (9)
Take Good Care Of My Heart (9)
Take Me In Your Arms (Rock Me For A Little While) (1)
Take Time (4)
Tell Me I'm Not Dreamin' (Too Good To Be True) (9)
That's How Love Goes (1) 46
There's A Better Way (8)
This Time (8)

Two Ships (In The Night) (11)
Uh, Uh, I Didn't Do It (8)
Very Special Part (8)
Voices In The Dark (10)
We Can Put It Back Together (5)
Where Are You Now (5)
Who's That Lady (3)
Words Into Action (10)
You Belong To Me (8)
You Got To Hurry Girl (5)
You Like Me Don't You (6) 50
You Moved A Mountain (8)
You Need To Be Loved (4)
You're Givin' Me The Runaround (7)
You're In Good Hands (2) 79
You're Supposed To Keep Your Love For Me (5) 34
You've Changed (6)

★264★ ## JACKSON, Joe '82

Born on 8/11/55 in Burton-on-Trent, Staffordshire, England. Singer/songwriter/pianist.
1)Night And Day 2)Body And Soul 3)Look Sharp!

4/7/79	20	39	●	©	1 Look Sharp! .... C:#2⁶/211			$12	A&M 4743
10/27/79	22	25		©	2 I'm The Man			$12	A&M 4794
11/8/80	41	16		©	3 Beat Crazy..			$12	A&M 4837
8/1/81	42	13		©	4 Joe Jackson's Jumpin' Jive			$12	A&M 4871
7/17/82	4	57	●	©	5 Night And Day			$10	A&M 4906
9/24/83	64	13			6 Mike's Murder	[S]		$10	A&M 4931
4/7/84	20	29		©	7 Body And Soul			$10	A&M 5000
4/19/86	34	25			8 Big World...	[L]		$15	A&M 6021 [2]
5/2/87	131	8		©	9 Will Power	[I]		$10	A&M 3908
5/21/88	91	12		©	10 Live 1980/86	[L]		$15	A&M 6706 [2]
5/6/89	61	21		©	11 Blaze Of Glory			$10	A&M 5249
5/18/91	116	4		©	12 Laughter & Lust...			$10	Virgin 91628

Acropolis Now (11)
Amateur Hour (2)
Another World (5)
Baby Stick Around (1)
Band Wore Blue Shirts (2)
Battleground (3)
Be My Number Two (7,10)
Beat Crazy (3,10)
Best I Can Do (11)
Biology (3)
Blaze Of Glory (11)
Breakdown (6)
Breaking Us In Two (5,10) 18
Cancer (5,10)
Cha Cha Loco (7)
Chinatown (5)
Cosmopolitan (6)
Crime Don't Pay (3)
Discipline (11)
(Do The) Instant Mash (1)
Don't Wanna Be Like That (2,10)

Down To London (11)
Drowning (12)
Evil Empire (11)
Evil Eye (3)
Fifty Dollar Love Affair (8)
Fit (3)
Five Guys Named Moe (4)
Fools In Love (1,10)
Forty Years (8)
Friday (2)
Geraldine And John (2)
Get That Girl (2)
Go For It (7)
Goin' Downtown (12)
Got The Time (1,10)
Happy Ending (7) 57
Happy Loving Couples (1)
Heart Of Ice (7)
Hit Single (12)
Home Town (8)
How Long Must I Wait For You (4)

Human Touch (5)
I'm The Man (2,10)
In Every Dream Home (A Nightmare) (3)
Is She Really Going Out With Him? (1,10) 21
Is You Is Or Is You Ain't My Baby (4)
(It's A) Big World (8)
It's All Too Much (12)
It's Different For Girls (2,10)
Jack, You're Dead (4)
Jamie G. (12)
Jet Set (3)
Jumpin' Jive (4,10)
Jumpin' With Symphony Sid (4)
Kinda Kute (2)
Laundromat Monday (6)
Loisaida (7)
Look Sharp! (1,10)
Mad At You (3)
Man In The Street (8)

Me And You (Against The World) (11)
Memphis (6,10) 85
Moonlight (3)
Moonlight Theme (6)
My House (12)
Nineteen Forever (11)
No Pasaran (9)
Nocturne (9)
Not Here, Not Now (7)
Obvious Song (12)
Oh Well (12)
On Your Radio (2,10)
One More Time (3)
One To One (3,10)
1-2-3- Go (This Town's A Fairground) (6)
Other Me (12)
Precious Time (8)
Pretty Boys (3)
Pretty Girls (1)

Rant And Rave (11)
Real Men (5,10)
Right And Wrong (8)
San Francisco Fan (4)
Sentimental Thing (11)
Shanghai Sky (8)
Slow Song (5,10)
Solitude (9)
Someone Up There (3)
Soul Kiss (8)
Steppin' Out (5,10) 6
Stranger Than Fiction (12)
Sunday Papers (1,10)
Survival (9)
Symphony In One Movement (9)
T.V. Age (5)
Tango Atlantico (8)
Target (5)
Throw It Away (1)
Tomorrow's World (11)
Tonight And Forever (8)

Trying To Cry (12)
Tuxedo Junction (4)
Verdict, The (7)
We Can't Live Together (8)
We The Cats (Shall Hep Ya) (4)
What's The Use Of Getting Sober (When You're Gonna Get Drunk Again) (4)
When You're Not Around (12)
Wild West (8)
Will Power (9)
You Can't Get What You Want (Till You Know What You Want) (7,10) 15
You Run Your Mouth (And I'll Run My Business) (4)
You're My Meat (4)
Zemeo (6)

JACKSON, LaToya '80

Born on 5/29/56 in Gary, Indiana. Sister of **The Jacksons**.

10/18/80	116	13			1 LaToya Jackson			$12	Polydor 6291
9/12/81	175	3			2 My Special Love			$12	Polydor 6328
6/9/84	149	6			3 Heart Don't Lie			$10	Private 1 39361

Are You Ready? (1)
Bet'cha Gonna Need My Lovin' (3)
Camp Kuchi Kaiai (2)
Fill You Up (2)

Frustration (3)
Giving You Up (2)
Heart Don't Lie (3) 56
Hot Potato (3)
I Don't Want You To Go (2)

I Like Everything You're Doin' (3)
If I Ain't Got It (1)
If You Feel The Funk (1)
Love Song (2)

Lovely Is She (1)
My Love Has Passed You By (1)
Night Time Lover (1)
Private Joy (3)

Save Your Love (1)
Special Love (2)
Stay The Night (2)
Summertime With You (2)

Taste Of You (Is A Taste Of Love) (1)
Think Twice (3)
Without You (3)

JACKSON, Luscious — see LUSCIOUS JACKSON

JACKSON, Mahalia '62

Born on 10/26/11 in New Orleans. Died of heart failure on 1/27/72 (age 60). Legendary gospel singer. Won Grammy's Lifetime Achievement Award in 1972. Inducted into the Rock and Roll Hall of Fame in 1997 as an early influence.

1/6/62	130	2			1 Sweet Little Jesus Boy	[X]		$25	Columbia 702
					first released in 1955				
12/14/63+	11ˣ	17		©	2 Silent Night - Songs For Christmas	[X]		$20	Columbia 1903 / 8703
					Christmas charts: 16/'63, 34/'64, 17/'65, 11/'66, 15/'67, 13/'68				
12/21/68+	2¹ˣ			©	3 Christmas with Mahalia	[X]		$15	Columbia 9727
					Christmas charts: 18/'68, 2/'69				
12/18/93	35ᶜ	1		©	4 Silent Night Gospel Christmas With Mahalia Jackson	[X]		$10	LaserLight 15300

Amazing Grace (4)
Child Of The King (4)

Christmas Comes To Us All (4)
Once A Year (2)

Come To Jesus (4)
Do You Hear What I Hear? (3)

First Noel (3)
Go Tell It On The Mountain (1,2,4)

God Spoke To Me (4)

JACKSON, Mahalia — Cont'd

Happy Birthday To You, Our Lord (3)
Hark! The Herald Angels Sing (2)
He's My Light (4)
Holy Babe (1)
I Believe (4)
I Wonder As I Wander (1)
In The Upper Room (4)
It Came Upon The Midnight Clear (3)
Jesus Is With Me (4)
Joy To The World! (1,2)
Lo, How A Rose E'er Blooming (3)
No Room At The Inn (1,3)
Nobody Knows The Trouble I've Seen (4)
O Come, All Ye Faithful (Adeste Fideles) (1,2)
O Holy Night (3)
O Little Town Of Bethlehem (1,2)
Silent Night, Holy Night (1,2,4)
Silver Bells (3)
Star Stood Still (Song Of The Nativity) (2)
Sweet Little Jesus Boy (1,2)
Walk With Me (4)
What Can I Give (2)
What Child Is This (3)
White Christmas (1,3)

JACKSON, Marlon   '87
Born on 3/12/57 in Gary, Indiana. Member of **The Jacksons**.

| 11/28/87 | 175 | 7 | © | Baby Tonight .... | | | $10 | Capitol 46942 |

Baby Tonight
Don't Go
Life
Lovely Eyes
She Never Cried
Something Coming Down
Talk-2-U
To Get Away
When Will You Surrender
Where Do I Stand

JACKSON, Michael   ★86★   '83

Born on 8/29/58 in Gary, Indiana. Self-proclaimed "King of Pop." Lead singer of **The Jackson 5**. Played "The Scarecrow" in the 1978 movie musical *The Wiz*. Starred in the 15-minute movie *Captain Eo*, which was shown exclusively at Disneyland and Disneyworld. His 1988 autobiography, *Moonwalker*, became a movie the same year. Won Grammy's Living Legends Award in 1993. Married to **Elvis Presley**'s daughter, Lisa Marie, from 1994-96. Inducted into the Rock and Roll Hall of Fame in 2001.

1)Thriller 2)Bad 3)Dangerous

2/19/72	14	23	©	1	Got To Be There			$15	Motown 747
8/26/72	5	32	©	2	Ben			$15	Motown 755
5/5/73	92	12		3	Music & Me			$15	Motown 767
2/15/75	101	9		4	Forever, Michael			$15	Motown 825
9/27/75	156	5		5	The Best Of Michael Jackson ....C:#12/24 [G]			$15	Motown 851
9/1/79+	3	169	▲7 ©	6	Off The Wall ....C:#19/18			$12	Epic 35745
4/25/81	144	10	©	7	One Day In Your Life			[E-K]	$12	Motown 956
					recordings from 1973-75; 4 of 10 tracks with **The Jackson 5**				
12/25/82+	❶37	122	▲26 ©	8	Thriller ....C:#2²/50			$12	Epic 38112
					1983 Grammy winner: Album of the Year				
12/3/83+	7C	50		9	Great Songs And Performances That Inspired The Motown 25th Anniversary Television Special [G]			$12	Motown 5312
					MICHAEL JACKSON & THE JACKSON 5				
6/2/84	46	15		10	Farewell My Summer Love 1984 .... [E]			$12	Motown 6101
					recordings from 1973				
6/23/84	168	7		11	Michael Jackson And The Jackson 5 - 14 Greatest Hits .... [G]			$12	Motown 6099
					picture disc; 9 cuts by **The Jackson 5**; 5 cuts by Michael Jackson				
9/26/87	❶6	87	▲8 ©	12	Bad ....C:#10/19			$10	Epic 40600
12/14/91	❶4	117	▲7 ©	13	Dangerous ....C:#47/1			$10	Epic 45400
7/8/95	❶2	36	▲7 ©	14	HIStory: Past, Present And Future - Book I [G]			$15	Epic 59000 [2]
					disc 1: greatest hits; disc 2: new recordings				
6/7/97	24	9	▲ ©	15	Blood On The Dance Floor - HIStory In The Mix .... [K]			$10	MJJ Music 68000
					contains remixes from #14 above				

ABC (9,11) *1*
Ain't No Sunshine (1)
All The Things You Are (3)
Another Part Of Me (12) *11*
Baby Be Mine (8)
Bad (2,5,9,11) *1*
Beat It (8,14) *1*
Ben (8,14) *1*
Billie Jean (8,14) *1*
Black Or White (13,14) *1*
Blood On The Dance Floor (15) *42*
Burn This Disco Out (6)
Call On Me (10)
Can't Let Her Get Away (13)
Childhood (14) *flip*
Cinderella Stay Awhile (4)
Come Together (14)
D.S. (14)
Dancing Machine (9,11) *2*
Dangerous (13)
Dapper-Dan (4)
Dear Michael (4,7)
Dirty Diana (12) *1*
Doggin' Around (3)
Don't Let It Get You Down (10)
Don't Say Goodbye Again (7)
Don't Stop 'Til You Get Enough (6,14) *1*
Earth Song (14,15)
Euphoria (7)
Everybody's Somebody's Fool (2)
Farewell My Summer Love (10) *38*
Get On The Floor (6)
Ghosts (15)
Girl Don't Take Your Love From Me (1)
Girl Is Mine (8,14) *2*
Girl You're So Together (10)
Girlfriend (6)
Give In To Me (13)
Gone Too Soon (13)
Got To Be There (1,5,9,11) *4*
Greatest Show On Earth (2)
Happy (3,5)
Heal The World (13,14) *27*
Here I Am (Come And Take Me) (10)
HIStory (14,15)
Human Nature (8) *7*
I Can't Help It (6)
I Just Can't Stop Loving You (12,14) *1*
I Wanna Be Where You Are (1,5,9,11) *16*
I Want You Back (9,11) *1*
I'll Be There (9,11) *1*
I'll Come Home To You (4,7)
In Our Small Way (1,2)
In The Closet (13) *6*
Is It Scary (15)
It's The Falling In Love (6)
It's Too Late To Change The Time (7)
Jam (13) *26*
Johnny Raven (3)
Just A Little Bit Of You (4) *23*
Just Good Friends (8)
Keep The Faith (13)
Lady In The Life (8)
Liberian Girl (12)
Little Susie (14)
Lookin' Through The Windows (11) *16*
Love Is Here And Now You're Gone (1)
Love You Save (9,11) *1*
Make Tonight All Mine (7)
Mama's Pearl (11) *2*
Man In The Mirror (12,14) *1*
Maria (You Were The Only One) (1)
Maybe Tomorrow (9,11) *20*
Melodie (14)
Money (14,15)
Morning Glow (3,5)
Morphine (15)
My Girl (2)
Never Can Say Goodbye (11) *2*
Off The Wall (6) *10*
One Day In Your Life (4,5,7,11) *55*
P.Y.T. (Pretty Young Thing) (8) *10*
People Make The World Go Round (2)
Remember The Time (13,14) *3*
Rock With You (6,14) *1*
Rockin' Robin (1,5,9,11) *2*
Scream (14) *5*
Scream Louder (15)
She Drives Me Wild (13)
She's Out Of My Life (6,14) *10*
Shoo Be Doo Be Doo Da Day (2)
Smile (14)
Smooth Criminal (12) *7*
Speed Demon (14)
Stranger In Moscow (14,15) *91*
Superfly Sister (15)
Tabloid Junkie (14)
Take Me Back (4,7)
They Don't Care About Us (14) *30*
This Time Around (14,15)
To Make My Father Proud (10)
2 Bad (14,15)
Too Young (3)
Touch The One You Love (10)
We're Almost There (4,5) *54*
We've Got A Good Thing Going (2)
We've Got Forever (4,7)
What Goes Around Comes Around (2)
Who Is It (13) *14*
Why You Wanna Trip On Me (13)
Will You Be There (13) *7*
Wings Of My Love (1)
With A Child's Heart (3,5) *50*
Working Day And Night (6)
You Are Not Alone (14,15) *1*
You Are There (4,7)
You Can Cry On My Shoulder (2)
You're My Best Friend, My Love (7)
You've Got A Friend (1)
You've Really Got A Hold On Me (10)
Up Again (3)
Wanna Be Startin' Somethin' (8,14) *1*
Way You Make Me Feel (12,14) *1*

★401★   JACKSON, Millie   '74
Born on 7/15/44 in Thomson, Georgia. R&B singer/songwriter.

1)Caught Up 2)Feelin' Bitchy 3)Get It Out'cha System

9/16/72	166	11	©	1	Millie Jackson			$15	Spring 5703
9/29/73	175	6	©	2	It Hurts So Good			$15	Spring 5706
11/2/74	21	21	● ©	3	Caught Up			$12	Spring 6703
7/26/75	112	16	©	4	Still Caught Up			$12	Spring 6708
2/19/77	175	6	©	5	Lovingly Yours			$12	Spring 6712
10/22/77+	34	23	● ©	6	Feelin' Bitchy			$12	Spring 6715
7/22/78	55	14	● ©	7	Get It Out'cha System			$12	Spring 6719
4/21/79	144	6	©	8	A Moment's Pleasure			$12	Spring 6722

JACKSON, Millie — Cont'd

DEBUT	PEAK	WKS		$	Label & Number
10/20/79	80	19	© 9 Royal Rappin's	$12	Polydor 6229
			MILLIE JACKSON & ISAAC HAYES		
12/22/79+	94	18	© 10 Live & Uncensored [L]	$15	Spring 6725 [2]
			recorded at The Roxy in Los Angeles		
6/21/80	100	10	© 11 For Men Only	$12	Spring 6727
2/7/81	137	4	© 12 I Had To Say It	$12	Spring 6730
3/13/82	113	13	13 Live And Outrageous (Rated XXX) [L]	$12	Spring 6735
			recorded at Mr. Vees Figure 8 in Atlanta		
12/27/86+	119	17	14 An Imitation Of Love	$10	Jive 1016

Ain't No Comin' Back (11)
All I Want Is A Fighting Chance (3)
All The Way Lover (6,10)
Angel In Your Arms (6)
Ask Me What You Want (1) 27
Be A Sweetheart (10)
Body Movements (5)
Breakaway (2)
Cheatin' Is (6)
Child Of God (It's Hard To Believe) (1)
Close My Eyes (2)
Da Ya Think I'm Sexy? (10)
Despair (11)
Didn't I Blow Your Mind (10)
Do What Makes You Satisfied (4)
Do You Wanna Make Love (9)
Don't Send Nobody Else (2)
Don't You Ever Stop Lovin' Me (13)
Fancy This (12)
Feelin' Like A Woman (6)
Feels Like The First Time (9)
Fool's Affair (11)
From Her Arms To Mine (5)

Give It Up (10)
Go Out And Get Some (Get It Out'cha System) (7)
Good To The Very Last Drop (2)
He Wants To Hear The Words (7)
Help Me Finish My Song (5)
Help Yourself (2)
Here You Come Again (7)
Hold The Line (10)
Horse Or Mule (13)
Hot! Wild! Unrestricted! Crazy Love (14)
Hurts So Good (2,10) 24
Hypocrisy (2)
I Ain't Giving Up (1)
I Ain't No Glory Story (12)
I Can't Say Goodbye (5)
I Changed My Mind (9)
I Cry (2)
I Fell In Love (14)
I Gotta Get Away (From My Own Self) (1)
I Had To Say It (12,13)
I Just Can't Stand It (1)

I Just Wanna Be With You (7)
I Miss You Baby (1) 95
I Need To Be By Myself (14)
I Still Love You (You Still Love Me) (4,10)
I Wanna Be Your Lover (14)
I Wish That I Could Hurt That Way Again (11)
I'll Be Rolling (With The Punches) (9)
I'll Continue To Love You (5)
I'll Live My Love For You (5)
I'm Through Trying To Prove My Love To You (3)
I'm Tired Of Hiding (3)
If I Had My Way (9)
If Loving You Is Wrong I Don't Want To Be Right (3,10) 42
If That Don't Turn You On (11)
If This Is Love (1)
If You Had Your Way (9)
If You're Not Back In Love By Monday (6) 43
Imitation Of Love (14)
It Hurts So Good ..see: Hurts So Good
It's A Thang (14)

It's All Over But The Shouting (3)
It's Easy Going (3)
It's Gonna Take Some Time This Time (12)
Just When I Needed You Most (10)
Keep The Home Fire Burnin' (7,10)
Kiss You All Over (8)
Ladies First (12)
Little Taste Of Outside Love (6)
Logs And Thangs (7,10)
Love Changes (9)
Love Doctor (1)
Love Is A Dangerous Game (14)
Love Of Your Own (5)
Lovers And Girlfriends (13)
Lovin' Your Good Thing Away (6)
Loving Arms (4)
Loving Arms '81 (12)
Making The Best Of A Bad Situation (4)
Memory Of A Wife (4)

Mind Over Matter (14)
Moment's Pleasure (8,10)
My Man, A Sweet Man (1) 42
Never Change Lovers In The Middle Of The Night (8,10)
Not On Your Life (11)
Now That You Got It (2)
Once You've Had It (8)
Passion (13)
Phuck U Symphony (10)
Put Something Down On It (7,10)
Rap, The (3,10)
Rap '81 (medley) (12)
Rising Cost Of Love (8)
Seeing You Again (8)
Soaps, The (10)
Somebody's Love Died Here Last Night (12)
Somethin' Bout Cha (5)
Still (13)
Strange Things (1)
Stranger (medley) (12)
Summer (The First Time) (3)
Sweet Music Man (7,10)
Sweet Music, Soft Lights, And You (9)

Tell Her It's Over (4)
This Is It (11,13)
This Is Where I Came In (11)
Ugly Men (13)
We Got To Hit It Off (8)
What Am I Waiting For (10)
What Went Wrong Last Night (Part I & II) (8)
Why Say You're Sorry (7)
You Can't Stand The Thought (4)
You Can't Turn Me Off (In The Middle Of Turning Me On) (5)
You Created A Monster (6)
You Must Have Known I Needed Love (11)
You Needed Me (9)
You Never Cross My Mind (9)
You Owe Me That Much (12)
You're The Joy Of My Life (1)

JACKSON, Rebbie   '84
Born Maureen Jackson on 5/29/50 in Gary, Indiana. Sister of **The Jacksons**.

DEBUT	PEAK	WKS		$	Label & Number
10/27/84	63	18	Centipede	$10	Columbia 39238

Centipede 24
Come Alive It's Saturday Night
Fork In The Road
Hey Boy
I Feel For You
Open Up My Love
Play Me (I'm A Jukebox)
Ready For Love

JACKSON, Walter   '76
Born on 3/19/38 in Pensacola, Florida. Died of a cerebral hemorrhage on 6/20/83 (age 45). R&B singer.

DEBUT	PEAK	WKS		$	Label & Number
6/24/67	194	5	1 Speak Her Name	$30	Okeh 14120
10/9/76	113	18	© 2 Feeling Good	$15	Chi-Sound 656
4/30/77	141	5	© 3 I Want To Come Back As A Song	$15	Chi-Sound 733

After You There Can Be Nothing (1)
Baby, I Love Your Way (3)
Corner In The Sun (1) 83
Everything Must Change (3)
Feelings (2) 93
Gotta Find Me An Angel (3)
I Want To Come Back As A Song (3)
I'll Keep On Trying (1)
I've Got It Bad Feelin' Good (2)
I've Never Been To Me (3)
If You Walked Away (3)
It's All Over (3) 67
It's An Uphill Climb To The Bottom (1) 88
Love Is Lovelier (3)
Love Woke Me Up This Morning (2)
My One Chance To Make It (1)
Not You (1)
Player In The Band (2)
Please Pardon Me (You Remind Me Of A Friend) (2)
She's A Woman (1)
Someone Saved My Life Tonight (2)
Sorry Seems To Be The Hardest Word (3)
Speak Her Name (1) 89
Stay A While With Me (3)
Tear For Tear (1)
They Don't Give Medals (To Yesterday's Heroes) (1)
Too Shy To Say (2)
Welcome Home (2) 95
What Would You Do (3)
Words (Are Impossible) (2)

JACKSON, Willis   '66
Born on 4/25/32 in Miami. Died of heart failure on 10/25/87 (age 55). Jazz tenor saxophonist.

DEBUT	PEAK	WKS		$	Label & Number
7/23/66	137	4	1 Together Again! [I]	$25	Prestige 7364
			WILLIS JACKSON with JACK McDUFF		
8/30/75	182	3	2 The Way We Were [I]	$15	Atlantic 18145

Brown Eyed Girl (2)
Fire (2)
Glad 'A See Ya' (1)
It Might As Well Be Spring (1)
Lady Marmalade (2)
Love's Theme (2)
Lover's Eve (2)
Pick Up The Pieces (2)
Shame, Shame, Shame (2)
Sideshow (2)
Then Came You (2)
This'll Get To Ya' (1)
Three Little Words (1)
Tu'Gether (1)
Way We Were (2)

JACKSON 5/JACKSONS ★88★   '70
Group of brothers from Gary, Indiana: **Michael Jackson** (vocals) **Jermaine Jackson**, **Marlon Jackson**, Tito Jackson and Jackie Jackson. Known as **The Jackson 5** from 1968-75. Randy Jackson replaced Jermaine in 1976. Jermaine rejoined the group for 1984's highly publicized *Victory* album and tour. Marlon left for a solo career in 1987. Their sisters **Rebbie Jackson**, **La Toya Jackson** and **Janet Jackson** backed the group; each had solo hits. Michael and Janet emerged with superstar solo careers in the '80s. Group lineup since 1989: Jackie, Tito, Jermaine and Randy Jackson. Tito's sons recorded as **3T**. Group inducted into the Rock and Roll Hall of Fame in 1997.

1)Third Album 2)Victory 3)ABC 4)Diana Ross Presents The Jackson 5 5)Lookin' Through The Windows

THE JACKSON 5:

DEBUT	PEAK	WKS		$	Label & Number
1/17/70	5	32	© 1 Diana Ross Presents The Jackson 5	$25	Motown 700
6/6/70	4	50	© 2 ABC	$25	Motown 709
9/26/70	4	50	© 3 Third Album	$25	Motown 718
12/5/70	❶6X	16	© 4 Christmas Album [X]	$25	Motown 713
			Christmas charts: 1/70, 2/71, 1/72, 1/73		
5/1/71	11	41	© 5 Maybe Tomorrow	$20	Motown 735
10/9/71	16	26	© 6 Goin' Back To Indiana [TV]	$20	Motown 742
1/1/72	12	41	© 7 Jackson 5 Greatest Hits C:#4/69 [G]	$20	Motown 741
6/3/72	7	33	© 8 Lookin' Through The Windows	$20	Motown 750
4/14/73	44	16	© 9 Skywriter	$15	Motown 761
10/6/73	100	29	© 10 Get It Together	$15	Motown 783
10/5/74	16	21	© 11 Dancing Machine	$15	Motown 780

JACKSON 5/JACKSONS — Cont'd

DEBUT	PEAK	WKS	CD		ARTIST — Album Title	Sym	$	Label & Number
6/14/75	36	15	© 12		Moving Violation		$15	Motown 829
7/17/76	84	9	© 13		Jackson Five Anthology	[G]	$30	Motown 868 [3]
12/4/76+	36	27	● © 14		The Jacksons		$12	Epic 34229
10/29/77	63	11	© 15		Goin' Places		$12	Epic 34835
12/16/78+	11	41	▲ © 16		Destiny		$12	Epic 35552
10/18/80	10	29	▲ © 17		Triumph		$12	Epic 36424
11/28/81+	30	19	© 18		Jacksons Live	[L]	$15	Epic 37545 [2]
12/3/83+	7C	50	19		Great Songs And Performances That Inspired The Motown 25th Anniversary Television Special MICHAEL JACKSON & THE JACKSON 5	[G]	$12	Motown 5312
6/23/84	168	7	20		Michael Jackson And The Jackson 5 - 14 Greatest Hits picture disc; 9 cuts by The Jackson 5; 5 cuts by Michael Jackson	[G]	$12	Motown 6099
7/21/84	4	30	▲2 © 21		Victory		$10	Epic 38946
6/17/89	59	11	© 22		2300 Jackson Street		$10	Epic 40911

ABC (2,7,13,18,19,20) 1
Ain't Nothing Like The Real Thing (1)
All I Do Is Think Of You (12,13)
All Night Dancin' (16)
Alright With Me (22)
Art Of Madness (22)
Be Not Always (21)
Ben (13,18,19,20) 1
Blame It On The Boogie (16) 54
Bless His Soul (16)
Blues Away (14)
Body (21) 47
Body Language (Do The Love Dance) (12,13)
Boogie Man (9,13)
Born To Love You (1)
Breezy (12)
Bridge Over Troubled Water (3)
Call Of The Wild (1)
Can I See You In The Morning (3)
Can You Feel It (17,18) 77
Can You Remember (1)
Chained (1)
Children Of The Light (8)
Christmas Song (Merry Christmas To You) (4)
Christmas Won't Be The Same This Year (1)
(Come Round Here) I'm The One You Need (2)
Corner Of The Sky (9,13) 18
Daddy's Home (13) 9
Dancing Machine (10,11,13,19,20) 2
Darling Dear (3)
Day Basketball Was Saved (6)

Destiny (16)
Different Kind Of Lady (15)
Do What You Wanna (15)
Doctor My Eyes (8)
Don't Know Why I Love You (2,13)
Don't Let Your Baby Catch You (8)
Don't Say Good Bye Again (10)
Don't Stop 'Til You Get Enough (18)
Don't Want To See Tomorrow (8)
Dreamer (14)
E-Ne-Me-Ne-Mi-Ne-Moe (The Choice Is Yours To Pull) (8)
Enjoy Yourself (14) 6
Even Though You're Gone (15)
Everybody (17)
Feeling Alright (6)
Find Me A Girl (15)
Forever Came Today (12,13)
Frosty The Snowman (4)
Get It Together (10,13) 28
Give It Up (17)
Give Love On Christmas Day (4)
Goin' Back To Indiana (3,6,7,13)
Goin' Places (15) 52
Good Times (14)
Got To Be There (13,19,20) 4
Hallelujah Day (9,13) 28
Harley (22)
Have Yourself A Merry Little Christmas (4)
Heartbreak Hotel (17,18) 22

Heaven Knows I Love You, Girl (15)
Honey Chile (5)
Honey Love (12)
How Funky Is Your Chicken (3)
Hum Along And Dance (10)
Hurt, The (21)
I Am Love (Parts I & II) (11,13) 15
I Can Only Give You Love (2)
I Can't Quit Your Love (9)
I Found That Girl (2,7,13) flip
(I Know) I'm Losing You (1)
I Saw Mommy Kissing Santa Claus (4)
I Wanna Be Where You Are (13,19,20) 16
I Want To Take You Higher (6)
I Want You Back (1,6,7,13,18,19,20) 1
I Will Find A Way (5)
I'll Be There (3,7,13,18,19,20) 1
I'll Bet You (2)
If I Don't Love You This Way (11)
If I Have To Move A Mountain (8)
If You'd Only Believe (22)
It All Begins And Ends With Love (11)
It's Great To Be Here (5)
It's Too Late To Change The Time (10)
Jump For Joy (15)
Just A Little Bit Of You (13) 23
Keep On Dancing (14)
La-La Means I Love You (2)

Life Of The Party (11)
Little Bitty Pretty One (8,13) 13
Little Drummer Boy (4)
Living Together (14)
Lookin' Through The Windows (8,13,20) 16
Love Don't Want To Leave (13)
Love I Saw In You Was Just A Mirage (3)
Love You Save (2,6,7,13,18,19,20) 1
Lovely One (17,18) 12
Mama I Gotta Brand New Thing (Don't Say No) (10)
Mama's Pearl (3,7,13,20) 2
Man Of War (15)
Maria (22)
Maybe Tomorrow (5,6,7,13,20) 20
Midnight Rendezvous (22)
Mirrors Of My Mind (11)
Moving Violation (12)
Music's Takin' Over (15)
My Cherie Amour (19)
My Little Baby (5)
Never Can Say Goodbye (5,7,13,20) 2
Never Had A Dream Come True (1)
Nobody (1)
Nothin (That Compares 2 U) (22) 77
Off The Wall (18)
Oh How Happy (3)
One Day In Your Life (20) 55
One More Chance (2)
One More Chance (21)
Ooh, I'd Love To Be With You (9)

Petals (5)
Play It Up (22)
Private Affair (22)
Push Me Away (16)
Reach In (3)
Ready Or Not Here I Come (Can't Hide From Love) (3)
Reflections (1)
Rock With You (18)
Rockin' Robin (13,19,20) 2
Rudolph The Red-Nosed Reindeer (4)
Santa Claus Is Comin' To Town (1)
Shake Your Body (Down To The Ground) (16,18) 7
She (22)
She's A Rhythm Child (11)
She's Good (5)
She's Out Of My Life (18)
Show You The Way To Go (14) 28
Sixteen Candles (5)
Skywriter (9,13)
Someday At Christmas (4)
Stand (1,6)
Standing In The Shadows Of Love (1)
State Of Shock (21) 3
Strength Of One Man (14)
Style Of Life (14)
Sugar Daddy (7,13) 10
That's How Love Goes (13) 46
That's What You Get (For Being Polite) (16)
Things I Do For You (16,18)
Think Happy (14)
Time Explosion (12)
Time Waits For No One (17)

To Know (8)
Torture (21) 17
Touch (9)
True Love Can Be Beautiful (2)
2300 Jackson Street (22)
2-4-6-8 (2)
Up On The Housetop (4)
Uppermost (9)
Wait (21)
Walk On (medley) (6)
Walk Right Now (17) 73
Wall (5)
We Can Change The World (21)
We're Almost There (13) 54
(We've Got) Blue Skies (5)
What You Don't Know (11)
Whatever You Got, I Want (11,13) 38
Who's Lovin' You (1,7)
Wondering Who (17)
Working Day And Night (18)
World Of Sunshine (19)
You Made Me What I Am (9)
You Need Love Like I Do (Don't You?) (10)
(You Were Made) Especially For Me (12)
You've Changed (1)
Young Folks (2)
Your Ways (17)
Zip-A-Dee-Doo-Dah (1)

JACKYL '94

Hard-rock group from Atlanta: Jesse James Dupree (vocals), Jimmy Stiff and Jeff Worley (guitars), Tom Bettini (bass) and Chris Worley (drums).

DEBUT	PEAK	WKS		CD		ARTIST — Album Title	$	Label & Number
10/10/92+	76	65	▲	© 1		Jackyl	$10	Geffen 24489
8/20/94	46	11	●	© 2		Push Comes To Shove	$10	Geffen 24710
8/9/97	133	1		© 3		Cut The Crap	$10	Epic 67948

Back Down In The Dirt (2)
Back Off Brother (1)
Brain Drain (1)
Chinatown (2)
Cut The Crap (3)
Dirty Little Mind (1)

Dixieland (2)
Down On Me (1)
Dumb Ass Country Boy (3)
God Strike Me Dead (3)
Headed For Destruction (2)
I Am The I Am (2)

I Could Never Touch Like You Do (2)
I Stand Alone (1)
I Want It (2)
Just Like A Devil (1)
Let's Don't Go There (1)

Locked & Loaded (2)
Lumberjack, The (1)
Misery Loves Company (3)
My Life (2)
Open Up (3)
Private Hell (2)

Push Comes To Shove (2)
Push Pull (3)
Reach For Me (1)
Redneck Punk (1)
Rock-A-Ho (2)
Secret Of The Bottle (2)

She Loves My Cock (1)
Speak Of The Devil (3)
Thanks For The Grammy (3)
Twice As Ugly (2)
When Will It Rain (1)

JACOBI, Lou '66

Born on 12/28/13 in Toronto. Actor/comedian. Acted in several movies and TV shows.

DEBUT	PEAK	WKS		ARTIST — Album Title	Sym	$	Label & Number
11/12/66	134	3		Al Tijuana And His Jewish Brass	[I-N]	$20	Capitol 2596

Chicken Fat
Downtown

It's Not Unusual
Malaguena

Never On Sunday
People

Peter Gunn
Strangers In The Night

Taste Of Honey
Tsena, Tsena

What Now My Love
Yellow Rose Of Texas

JACOBS, Debbie '79

Born in Baltimore. Disco singer.

DEBUT	PEAK	WKS		ARTIST — Album Title	$	Label & Number
9/1/79	153	8	1	Undercover Lover	$12	MCA 3156
2/9/80	178	7	2	High On Your Love	$12	MCA 3202

All The Way (1)
Burnin' Desire (1)
Don't You Want My Love (1)

High On Your Love (2) 70
Hot Hot (Give It All You Got) (1,2)

I Can Never Forget A Friend (2)
Lovin' Spree (2)
Make It Love (2)

Think I'm Fallin' In Love (1)
Undercover Lover (1)
What Goes Up (2)

JADE '93

Female R&B vocal trio: Joi Marshall, Tonya Kelly and Diane Reed.

DEBUT	PEAK	WKS		CD		ARTIST — Album Title	$	Label & Number
1/23/93	56	37	▲	© 1		Jade To The Max	$10	Giant 24466
10/15/94	80	22		© 2		Mind, Body & Song	$10	Giant 24558

Bedroom (2)
Blessed (1)
Do You Want Me (2)
Don't Ask My Neighbor (1)
Don't Walk Away (1) 4

Every Day Of The Week (2) 20
Everything (2)
5-4-3-2 (Yo! Time Is Up) (2) 72
Give Me What I'm Missing (2)
Hangin' (2)

Hold Me Close (1)
I Like The Way (1)
I Wanna Love You (1)
I Want 'Cha Baby (1)
If The Lovin' Ain't Good (2)

If The Mood Is Right (2)
It's On (1)
Looking For Mr. Do Right (1) 69
Mind, Body & Song (2)

One Woman (1) 22
Out With The Girls (1)
That Boy (1)
There's Not A Man (2)
What's Goin' On (2)

JADE WARRIOR '72

Progressive-rock trio from England: Glyn Havard (vocals, bass), Tony Duhig (guitar) and Jon Field (percussion). Duhig died of a heart attack in November 1990 (age 44).

| 5/6/72 | 194 | 2 | © | | Released | | | $15 | Vertigo 1009 |

Barazinbar / Bride Of Summer / Eyes On You / Minnamoto's Dream / Three-Horned Dragon King / Water Curtain Cave / We Have Reason To Believe / Yellow Eyes

JAGGED EDGE '00

Male R&B vocal group from Atlanta: identical twin brothers Brian and Brandon Casey, with Richard Wingo and Kyle Smith.

| 3/7/98 | 104 | 36 | ● | © | 1 A Jagged Era | | | $10 | So So Def 68181 |
| 2/5/00 | 8 | 74 | ▲² | © | 2 J.E. Heartbreak | | | $10 | So So Def 69862 |

Addicted To Your Love (1) / Ain't No Stoppin' (1) / Can I Get With You (2) / Did She Say (2) / Funny How (1) / Girl Is Mine (2) / Gotta Be (1) 23 / He Can't Love U (2) 15 / Healing (2) / Heartbreak (2) / I'll Be Right There (1) / Keys To The Range (2) / Lace You (2) / Let's Get Married (2) 11 / Promise (2) 9 / Ready & Willing (1) / Rest Of Our Lives (1) / Slow Motion (1) / True Man (2) / Way That You Talk (1) 65 / Wednesday Lover (1) / What You Tryin' To Do (2)

JAGGER, Chris '73

Born on 12/19/47 in Dartford, Kent, England. Younger brother of **Mick Jagger**.

| 11/3/73 | 186 | 4 | | | Chris Jagger | | | $15 | Asylum 5069 |

All Souls / Going Nowhere (medley) / Handful Of Dust / Hold On / Joy Of The Ride / King Of The Fishes / Let Me Down Easy / My Friend John / Riddle Song / Something New (medley)

JAGGER, Mick '85

Born Michael Phillip Jagger on 7/26/43 in Dartford, Kent, England. Lead singer of **The Rolling Stones**. Appeared in the movies *Ned Kelly* and *Freejack*. Married to model Bianca Jagger from 1971-80. Married to actress/model Jerry Hall from 1990-99. Older brother of **Chris Jagger**.

3/16/85	13	29	▲	©	1 She's The Boss			$10	Columbia 39940
10/3/87	41	20		©	2 Primitive Cool			$10	Columbia 40919
2/27/93	11	16	●	©	3 Wandering Spirit			$10	Atlantic 82436

Angel In My Heart (3) / Don't Tear Me Up (3) / Evening Gown (3) / 1/2 A Loaf (1) / Handsome Molly (3) / Hang On To Me Tonight (3) / Hard Woman (1) / I've Been Lonely For So Long (3) / Just Another Night (1) 12 / Kow Tow (2) / Let's Work (2) 39 / Lonely At The Top (1) / Lucky In Love (1) 38 / Mother Of A Man (3) / Out Of Focus (3) / Party Doll (2) / Peace For The Wicked (2) / Primitive Cool (2) / Put Me In The Trash (3) / Radio Control (1) / Running Out Of Luck (1) / Say You Will (2) / Secrets (1) / She's The Boss (1) / Shoot Off Your Mouth (2) / Sweet Thing (3) 84 / Think (3) / Throwaway (2) 67 / Turn The Girl Loose (1) / Use Me (3) / Wandering Spirit (3) / War Baby (2) / Wired All Night (3)

JAGGERZ, The '70

Pop-rock group formed in Pittsburgh: **Donnie Iris** (vocals, trumpet), Jimmy Ross (vocals, trombone), Billy Maybray (vocals, bass), Benny Faiella (guitar), Thom Davis (organ) and Jim Pugliano (drums).

| 4/11/70 | 62 | 11 | | | We Went To Different Schools Together | | | $20 | Kama Sutra 2017 |

At My Window / Carousel / Don't Make My Sky Cry / I Call My Baby Candy 75 / Looking Glass / Memoirs Of The Traveler / Rapper, The 2 / That's My World / Things Gotta Get Better / With A Little Help From My Friends

JAHEIM '01

Born Jaheim Hoagland in 1979 in New Brunswick, New Jersey. Male rapper.

| 3/31/01 | 9 | 27↑ | ● | © | Ghetto Love | | | $10 | Divine Mill 47452 |

Anything / Could It Be 26 / Finders Keepers / For Moms / Forever / Ghetto Love / Happiness / Heaven In My Eyes / Just In Case / Let It Go / Lil' Nigga Ain't Mine / Looking For Love / Love Is Still Here / Ready, Willing & Able / Remarkable / Waitin' On You

JAKES, T.D. '01

Born Thomas Dexter Jakes on 6/9/57 in South Charleston, West Virginia. Gospel singer.

| 3/29/97 | 183 | 2 | | © | 1 T.D. Jakes Presents Music From Woman, Thou Art Loosed! | | [L] | $10 | Integrity 10502 |

recorded at the Superdome in New Orleans

| 4/24/99 | 118 | 10 | | © | 2 Sacred Love Songs | | | $10 | Island 524630 |
| 3/31/01 | 56 | 10 | | © | 3 The Storm Is Over | | [L] | $10 | Dexterity Sounds 20303 |

BISHOP T.D. JAKES & THE POTTER'S HOUSE MASS CHOIR
recorded on 12/3/00 at The Potter's House in Dallas

Bless The Lord (3) / Born Again To Win (3) / Come To Me (1) / Devil's Already Defeated (3) / From Mother To Daughter (2) / Give Thanks (medley) (1) / He Teaches Me To Love (Passage Of Reading) (2) / Holding You Close (2) / I Worship You Almighty God (1) / I'm Your First Husband (1) / Lady, Her Lover And Lord (2) / Let Your Glory Fill This Place (3) / Lord I Lift Her Up To You (2) / Lord Of All (3) / Marvelous (3) / Mercy Saw Me (1) / Now I Only Dance For You (2) / Sanctuary (medley) (1) / Satin Sheets (2) / Storm Is Over Now (3) / Taking It Back (1) / Talitha Cumi (2) / Thou Art My Help (3) / Trust And Obey (3) / Usher Me (2) / What A Mighty God We Serve (medley) (1) / What A Mighty God We Serve Chorale (medley) (1) / When God Gave Me You (2) / When My Season Comes (3) / Woman, Thou Art Loosed! (1) / You Are My Ministry (2)

JAM, The '81

New-wave trio from England: Paul Weller (vocals, bass), Bruce Foxton (guitar) and Rick Buckler (drums). Disbanded in 1982. Weller formed **The Style Council**.

2/16/80	137	8		©	1 Setting Sons			$12	Polydor 6249
2/7/81	72	11		©	2 Sound Affects			$12	Polydor 6315
12/19/81	176	7			3 The Jam		[M]	$12	Polydor 503
3/27/82	82	16		©	4 The Gift			$12	Polydor 6349
11/27/82	135	14			5 The Bitterest Pill (I ever had to swallow)		[M]	$12	Polydor 506
1/15/83	131	9		©	6 Dig The New Breed		[L]	$12	Polydor 6365
4/9/83	171	4			7 Beat Surrender		[M]	$12	Polydor 810751

Absolute Beginners (3) / All Mod Cons (6) / Beat Surrender (7) / Big Bird (6) / Bitterest Pill (I Ever Had To Swallow) (5) / Boy About Town (2) / Burning Sky (1) / But I'm Different Now (2) / Carnation (4) / Circus (4) / Disguises (3) / Dream Time (2) / Dreams Of Children (6) / Eton Rifles (1) / Fever (medley) (5) / Funeral Pyre (3) / Ghosts (4,6) / Gift (4) / Girl On The Phone (1) / Going Underground (6) / Great Depression (5) / Happy Together (4) / In The City (6) / In The Crowd (6) / It's Too Bad (6) / Just Who Is The 5 O'Clock Hero? (4) / Little Boy Soldiers (1) / Liza Radley (3) / (Love Is Like A) Heat Wave (1) / Man In The Corner Shop (2) / Monday (2) / Move On Up (7) / Music For The Last Couple (2) / Pity Poor Alfie (medley) (5) / Planner's Dream Goes Wrong (4) / Precious (4) / Pretty Green (2) / Private Hell (1,6) / Running On The Spot (4) / Saturday's Kids (1) / Scrape Away (2) / Set The House Ablaze (2,6) / Shopping (2) / Smithers-Jones (1) / Standards (6) / Start! (2,6) / Stoned Out Of My Mind (7) / Strange Town (1) / Tales From The Riverbank (3) / That's Entertainment (2,6) / Thick As Thieves (1) / To Be Someone (6) / Town Called Malice (4) / Trans-Global Express (4) / War (5,7) / Wasteland (1)

JAMAL '95

Born Jamal Phillips in Atlanta. Male rapper. Member of **Illegal**.

11/25/95	198	1		©	**Last Chance, No Breaks**			$10	Rowdy 37008

| Da Come Up | Fades Em All | Genetic For Terror | Keep It Live | Live Illegal | Unf**kwittable |
| Don't Trust No | Game, The | Insane Creation | Keep It Real | Situation | |

JAMAL, Ahmad '58

Born Fritz Jones on 7/2/30 in Pittsburgh. Jazz pianist.

9/22/58	3	107		© 1	**But Not For Me/Ahmad Jamal at the Pershing**		[I-L]	$40	Argo 628
11/17/58	11	18		2	**Ahmad Jamal, Volume IV**		[I-L]	$40	Argo 636
					recorded on 9/6/58 at the Spotlite Club in Washington DC				
2/1/60	32	7		3	**Jamal At The Penthouse**		[I]	$40	Argo 646
12/30/67+	168	8		4	**Cry Young**			$20	Cadet 792
					vocals by the Howard Roberts Chorale				
3/15/80	173	5		5	**Genetic Walk**		[I-K]	$12	20th Century 600

Ahmad's Blues (3)	Cry Young (4)	Minor Moods (4)	Should I (2)	Time For Love (5)
Autumn In New York (2)	Don't Ask My Neighbors (5)	Moonlight In Vermont (1)	Sophisticated Gentleman (3)	Tropical Breeze (4)
Beautiful Friendship (4)	Genetic Walk (5)	Music, Music, Music (1)	Spartacus Love Theme (5)	What's New (1)
Bellows (5)	Girl Next Door (2)	Nature Boy (4)	Squatty Roo (2)	Where Is Love (4)
But Not For Me (1)	I Like To Recognize The Tune (3)	Never Never Land (3)	Stompin At The Savoy (2)	Who Needs Manhattan (4)
C'est Si Bon (4)	I Wish I Knew (2)	No Greater Love (1)	Surrey With The Fringe On Top (1)	Wood'yn You (1)
Call Me Irresponsible (4)	I'm Alone With You (3)	Pablo Sierra (5)	Taboo (2)	
Chaser (5)	Ivy (3)	Poinciana (1)	Tangerine (3)	
Cheek To Cheek (2)	La Costa (5)	Secret Love (2)	That's All (2)	
Comme Ci, Comme Ca (3)	Little Ditty (4)	Seleritus (3)	There Are Such Things (4)	

JAMES '94

Rock group from Manchester, England: Tim Booth (vocals), James Gott (guitar), Mark Hunter (keyboards), Saul Davies (violin), Andy Diagram (trumpet), Jim Glennie (bass) and David Baynton-Power (drums).

1/29/94	72	26	●	© 1	**Laid**			$10	Fontana 514943
3/15/97	158	1		© 2	**Whiplash**			$10	Fontana 534354

Avalanche (2)	Five-O (1)	Knuckle Too Far (1)	Lullaby (1)	Play Dead (2)	Sometimes (Lester Piggott) (1)
Blue Pastures (2)	Go To The Bank (2)	**Laid** (1) *61*	One Of The Three (1)	Say Something (1)	Tomorrow (2)
Dream Thrum (1)	Greenpeace (2)	Lost A Friend (2)	Out To Get You (1)	She's A Star (2)	Waltzing Along (2)
Everybody Knows (1)	Homeboy (2)	Low Low Low (1)	P.S. (1)	Skindiving (1)	Watering Hole (2)

JAMES, Bob ★160★ '79

Born on 12/25/39 in Marshall, Missouri. Jazz fusion keyboardist. Discovered by **Quincy Jones** in 1962. Was **Sarah Vaughan**'s musical director for four years. In 1973, became arranger of CTI records. In 1976, appointed director of progressive A&R at CBS Records. Formed own label, Tappan Zee, in 1977. Wrote/ performed theme for the TV show *Taxi*. Joined the jazz quartet **Fourplay** in 1991.

1)*One On One* 2)*Touchdown* 3)*BJ4* 4)*Lucky Seven* 5)*Two Of A Kind*

11/2/74	85	14		© 1	**One**		[I]	$15	CTI 6043
4/12/75	75	14		© 2	**Two**		[I]	$15	CTI 6057
7/4/76	49	27		© 3	**Three**		[I]	$15	CTI 6063
4/9/77	38	17		© 4	**BJ4**		[I]	$15	CTI 7074
11/26/77+	47	31		© 5	**Heads**		[I]	$12	Tappan Zee 34896
12/16/78+	37	29	●	© 6	**Touchdown**		[I]	$12	Tappan Zee 35594
8/25/79	42	14		© 7	**Lucky Seven**		[I]	$12	Tappan Zee 36056
11/3/79	23	33	●	© 8	**One On One**		[I]	$12	Tappan Zee 36241

BOB JAMES AND EARL KLUGH

7/12/80	47	18		© 9	**"H"**		[I]	$12	Tappan Zee 36422
2/21/81	66	16		© 10	**All Around The Town**		[I-L]	$15	Tappan Zee 36786 [2]
9/12/81	56	14		© 11	**Sign Of The Times**			$12	Tappan Zee 37495
7/17/82	72	17		© 12	**Hands Down**		[I]	$12	Tappan Zee 38067
11/6/82	44	29		© 13	**Two Of A Kind**		[I]	$12	Capitol 12244

EARL KLUGH & BOB JAMES

6/4/83	77	11		© 14	**The Genie (Themes & Variations From The TV Series "Taxi")**		[I]	$12	Columbia 38678
10/8/83	106	13		© 15	**Foxie**		[I]	$12	Tappan Zee 38801
10/27/84	136	10		© 16	**12**		[I]	$12	Tappan Zee 39580
6/14/86	50	64	▲	© 17	**Double Vision**		[I]	$10	Warner 25393

BOB JAMES/DAVID SANBORN

11/22/86+	142	27		© 18	**Obsession**		[I]	$10	Warner 25495
9/10/88	196	2		© 19	**Ivory Coast**		[I]	$10	Warner 25757
8/29/92	170	3		© 20	**Cool**		[I]	$10	Warner 26939

BOB JAMES/EARL KLUGH

3/26/94	168	2		© 21	**Restless**		[I]	$10	Warner 45536

Adult Situations (19)	Calaban (15)	Friends (7)	I Want To Thank You (Very Much) (6)	Kissing Cross (21)	Midnight (16)
Afterglow, The (8)	Caribbean Nights (6)	Fugitive Life (20)	I'll Never See You Smile Again (8)	Last Chance (14)	Miniature (20)
Angela (6,10,14)	Courtship (16)	Genie (14)		Legacy (16)	Miranda (15)
Animal Dreams (21)	Dream Journey (2)	Golden Apple (2,10)	I'm In You (5)	Look-Alike (7)	Moodstar (19)
As It Happens (20)	El Verano (4)	Gone Hollywood (18)	In The Garden (1)	Lotus Leaves (21)	Moon Tune (17)
Ashanti (19)	Enchanted Forest (11)	Groove For Julie (14)	Ingenue (13)	Love Lips (8)	Moonbop (16)
Awaken Us To The Blue (21)	Falcon, The (13)	Handara (20)	Into The Light (21)	Love Power (11)	More Than Friends (17)
Back To Bali (21)	Farandole (L'Arlesienne Suite #2) (2,10)	Heads (5)	It's Only Me (12)	Ludwig (15)	Movin' On (20)
Ballade (14)		Hello Nardo (14)	It's You (17)	Macumba (12)	Nautilus (13)
Big Stone City (7)	Feel Like Making Love (1) *88*	Hypnotique (11)	Jamaica Farewell (3)	Mallorca (8)	Never Enough (17)
Blue Lick (7)	Feel The Fire (18)	I Feel A Song (In My Heart) (2)	Janus (12)	Maputo (17)	New York Mellow (14)
Brighton By The Sea (9)	Fireball (15)	I Need More Of You (16)	Kari (8,10)	Marco Polo (15)	New York Samba (20)
Brooklyn Heights Boogie (14)	Fly Away (7)			Marilu (14)	Night Crawler (5)

DEBUT	PEAK	WKS	RIAA	CD	ARTIST — Album Title	Catalog	Sym	$	Label & Number

JAMES, Bob — Cont'd

Night Moods (14)
Night On Bald Mountain (1)
Night That Love Came Back (20)
Nights Are Forever Without You (4)
No Pay, No Play (16)
Obsession (18)
One Loving Night (5)
One Mint Julep (3)
Orpheus (19)
Pure Imagination (4)

Rain (18)
Restless (21)
Reunited (9)
Roberta (12)
Rosalie (19)
Rousseau (18)
Ruby, Ruby, Ruby (16)
Rush Hour (7)
San Diego Stomp (20)
Sandstorm (13)
Secret Wishes (20)
Serenissima (21)

Shamboozie (12)
Shepherd's Song (9)
Sign Of The Times (11)
Since I Fell For You (17)
Snowbird Fantasy (9)
So Much In Common (20)
Soulero (1)
Sponge, The (20)
Spunky (12)
Steady (18)
Steamin' Feelin' (11)
Stompin' At The Savoy (10)

Storm King (3)
Storm Warning (21)
Sun Runner (6)
Take Me To The Mardi Gras (2)
Tappan Zee (4)
Taxi, Theme From ..see: Angela
Terpsichore (20)
Thoroughbred (9)
3 A.M. (18)
Touchdown (6,10)
Treasure Island (4)

Under Me (21)
Unicorn (11)
Valley Of The Shadows (1)
Walkman, The (9)
We're All Alone (5,10)
Wes (13)
Westchester Lady (3,10)
Where I Wander (13)
Where The Wind Blows Free (4)
Whiplash (13)
Winding River (8)

Women Of Ireland (3)
Yogi's Dream (19)
You Are So Beautiful (5)
You Don't Know Me (17)
You're As Right As Rain (2)
Zebra Man (15)

JAMES, Etta   '61

Born Jamesetta Hawkins on 1/25/38 in Los Angeles. R&B singer. Nicknamed "Miss Peaches." Inducted into the Rock and Roll Hall of Fame in 1993.

DEBUT	PEAK	WKS	CD	#	Album Title	Sym	$	Label & Number
8/21/61	68	12	©	1	At Last!		$50	Argo 4003
8/24/63	117	4		2	Etta James Top Ten	[G]	$50	Argo 4025
2/1/64	96	10	©	3	Etta James Rocks The House	[L]	$50	Argo 4032
					recorded on 9/27/63 at the New Era Club in Nashville			
3/9/68	82	13	©	4	Tell Mama		$25	Cadet 802
9/15/73	154	9		5	Etta James		$20	Chess 50042

All I Could Do Was Cry (1,2) 33
All The Way Down (5)
Anything To Say You're Mine (1)
At Last (1,2) 47
Baby What You Want Me To Do (3) 82
Don't Lose Your Good Thing (4)

Down So Low (5)
Fool That I Am (2) 50
Girl Of My Dreams (4)
God's Song (5)
I Just Want To Make Love To You (1)
I'd Rather Go Blind (4)
I'm Gonna Take What He's Got (4)

It Hurts Me So Much (4)
Just A Little Bit (4)
Just One More Day (5)
Lay Back Daddy (5)
Leave Your Hat On (5)
Love Of My Man (4)
Money (3)
My Dearest Darling (1,2) 34
My Mother-In-Law (4)

Only A Fool (5)
Ooh Poo Pah Doo (3)
Pushover (2) 25
Sail Away (5)
Same Rope (4)
Security (4) 35
Seven Day Fool (5) 95
Something's Got A Hold On Me (2,3) 37

Steal Away (4)
Stop The Wedding (2) 34
Stormy Weather (1)
Sunday Kind Of Love (1,2)
Sweet Little Angel (3)
Tell Mama (4) 23
Tough Mary (1)
Trust In Me (1,2) 30
Watch Dog (4)

What I Say (3)
Woke Up This Morning (3)
Would It Make Any Difference To You (2) 64
Yesterday's Music (5)

JAMES, Harry   '55

Born on 3/15/16 in Albany, Georgia. Died of cancer on 7/5/83 (age 67). Legendary trumpet player/bandleader. Achieved fame playing with **Benny Goodman** in the late 1930s. Married to actress Betty Grable from 1943-65.

DEBUT	PEAK	WKS	Album Title	Sym	$	Label & Number
11/12/55	10	2	Harry James In Hi-Fi	[I]	$30	Capitol 654

Cherry
Ciribiribin
I Cried For You (Now It's Your Turn To Cry Over Me)

I'm Beginning To See The Light
I've Heard That Song Before
It's Been A Long, Long Time
Jalousie

James Session
Music Makers
My Silent Love
Sleepy Lagoon

Trumpet Blues
Two O'Clock Jump
Velvet Moon

You Made Me Love You (I Didn't Want To Do It)

JAMES, Jimmy, & The Vagabonds   '76

Born in September 1940 in Jamaica. R&B singer. The Vagabonds: Count Prince Miller (vocals), Wallace Wilson (guitar), Carl Noel (keyboards), Matt Fredericks and Milton James (horns), Phil Chen (bass) and Rupert Balgobin (drums).

DEBUT	PEAK	WKS	Album Title	$	Label & Number
11/29/75+	139	16	You Don't Stand A Chance If You Can't Dance	$12	Pye 12111

Chains Of Love
Come Lay Some Lovin' On Me
Dancin' To The Music Of Love

Hey Girl
I Am Somebody 94

I Know You Don't Love Me But You Got Me Anyway
Let's Have Fun

Suspicious Love
You Don't Stand A Chance (If You Can't Dance) (Pt. 1 & 2)

JAMES, Joni   '55

Born Joan Carmello Babbo on 9/22/30 in Chicago. Pop singer.

DEBUT	PEAK	WKS	Album Title	Sym	$	Label & Number
4/2/55	15	4	Little Girl Blue	[EP]	$100	MGM 272 [2]

Autumn Leaves
I'm Thru With Love

In Love In Vain
It's The Talk Of The Town

Little Girl Blue
That Old Feeling

These Foolish Things (Remind Me Of You)

Too Late Now

JAMES, Melvin   '87

Born in Des Moines, Iowa. Rock singer/songwriter/guitarist.

DEBUT	PEAK	WKS	CD	Album Title	$	Label & Number
10/3/87	146	8	©	The Passenger	$10	MCA 5663

Devil With A Halo
Loving You Is Strange

Passenger
She's So Sorry

Sugar Candy
Telephone

Twisted
We Hear The Thunder

Why Won't You Stay (Come In, Come Out Of The Rain)

JAMES, Rick   '81

★295★

Born James Johnson on 2/1/52 in Buffalo. Funk-rock singer/songwriter/guitarist/producer. Also see **Stone City Band**.

1)Street Songs 2)Throwin' Down 3)Come Get It!

DEBUT	PEAK	WKS	RIAA	CD	#	Album Title	Sym	$	Label & Number
6/24/78	13	36	●	©	1	Come Get It!		$12	Gordy 981
2/10/79	16	27		©	2	Bustin' Out Of L Seven		$12	Gordy 984
11/3/79	34	20			3	Fire It Up		$12	Gordy 990
8/23/80	83	10			4	Garden Of Love		$12	Gordy 995
5/2/81	3	74	▲	©	5	Street Songs		$12	Gordy 1002
6/5/82	13	23	●	©	6	Throwin' Down		$12	Gordy 6005
8/27/83	16	29	●	©	7	Cold Blooded		$12	Gordy 6043
8/25/84	41	19		©	8	Reflections	[G]	$12	Gordy 6095
5/11/85	50	26			9	Glow		$12	Gordy 6135
7/5/86	95	12			10	The Flag		$12	Gordy 6185
7/23/88	148	8		©	11	Wonderful		$10	Reprise 25659
11/8/97	170	1		©	12	Urban Rapsody		$10	Private I 417070

Are You ..see: R U
Back In You Again (12)
Be My Lady (5)
Below The Funk (Pass The J) (5)
Big Time (4)
Bring On The Love (12)
Bustin' Out (2,8) 71
Call Me Up (5)
Can't Stop (9) 50
Cold Blooded (7) 40

Come Into My Life (3)
Cop 'N' Blow (2)
Dance Wit' Me - Part 1 (6,8) 64
Doin' It (7)
Don't Give Up On Love (4)
Dream Maker (1)
Ebony Eyes (7) 43
Favorite Flava (12)
Fire And Desire (5,8)
Fire It Up (3)
Fool On The Street (2)

Forever And A Day (10)
Free To Be Me (10)
Funk In America (medley) (10)
Gettin' It On (In The Sunshine) (4)
Ghetto Life (5)
Give It To Me Baby (5,8) 40
Glow (9)
Good Ol Days (12)
Happy (6)
Hard To Get (6)

High On Your Love Suite (2) 72
Hollywood (1)
Hypnotize (11)
I Believe In U (11)
In The Girls' Room (11)
Island Lady (4)
It's Time (12)
Jefferson Ball (2)
Judy (11)
Loosey's Rap (11)

Love Gun (3)
Love In The Night (3)
Love Interlude (2)
Love's Fire (11)
Lovin' You Is A Pleasure (3)
Make Love To Me (5)
Mama's Eyes (12)
Mary-Go-Round (4)
Mary Jane (1,8) 41
Melody Make Me Dance (9)
Money Talks (6)

Moonchild (9)
Mr. Policeman (5)
My Love (6)
Never Say You Love Me (12)
New York Town (7)
Oh What A Night (4 Luv) (8)
One Mo Hit (Of Your Love) (medley) (2)
1,2,3 (Her And Me) (7)
Painted Pictures (10)
P.I.M.P. The S.I.M.P. (7)

418

DEBUT	PEAK	WKS	RIAA	CD	ARTIST — Album Title	Catalog	Sym	$	Label & Number

JAMES, Rick — Cont'd

Player's Way (12)
R U Experienced (10)
Rick's Raga (10)
Rock And Roll Control (9)
Save It For Me (10)
17 (8) **36**
Sexual Luv Affair (11)

Sexy Lady (1)
Sha La La La La (Come Back Home) (9)
Sherry Baby (11)
Silly Little Man (medley) (10)
69 Times (6)
Slow And Easy (10)

So Soft So Wet (12)
So Tight (11)
Somebody (The Girl's Got) (9)
Somebody's Watching You (12)
Soul Sista (12)
Spacey Love (2)
Spend The Night With Me (9)

Standing On The Top-Part 1 (6) **66**
Stone City Band (1)
Stormy Love (3)
Summer Love (4)
Super Freak (Part 1) (5,8) **16**
Sweet And Sexy Thing (10)

Teardrops (6)
Tell Me (What You Want) (7)
Throwdown (6)
Turn It Out (12)
U Bring The Freak Out (7)
Unity (7)
Urban Rapsody (12)

West Coast Thang (12)
When Love Is Gone (3)
Wonderful (11)
You And I (1,8) **13**
You Turn Me On (8)

JAMES, Sonny '69
Born James Loden on 5/1/29 in Hackleburg, Alabama. Country singer/songwriter/guitarist. Nicknamed "The Southern Gentleman."
1)The Astrodome Presents In Person Sonny James 2)The Best Of Sonny James 3)Empty Arms

DEBUT	PEAK	WKS						$	Label & Number
12/24/66	73[X]	1		1	My Christmas Dream		[X]	$20	Capitol 2589
12/24/66+	141	4		2	The Best of Sonny James		[G]	$20	Capitol 2615
4/12/69	161	3		3	Only The Lonely			$15	Capitol 193
8/23/69	184	3		4	Close-Up			$20	Capitol 258 [2]
					reissue of *True Love's A Blessing* and *I'll Never Find Another You* albums				
10/18/69	83	13		5	The Astrodome Presents In Person Sonny James		[L]	$15	Capitol 320
4/11/70	177	4		6	It's Just A Matter Of Time			$15	Capitol 432
9/19/70	197	2		7	My Love/Don't Keep Me Hangin' On			$15	Capitol 478
11/28/70+	187	4		8	#1			$15	Capitol 629
4/24/71	150	5		9	Empty Arms			$15	Capitol 734
9/11/71	197	2		10	The Sensational Sonny James			$15	Capitol 804
9/23/72	190	5		11	When The Snow Is On The Roses			$15	Columbia 31646

All My Love, All My Life (4)
Amazin' Love (6)
Any Time (8)
Back Door To Heaven (4)
Barefoot Santa Claus (1)
Behind The Tear (2)
Blue For You (7)
Born To Be With You (medley) (5)
Born To Lose (8)
Bright Lights, Big City (10) **91**
Christmas In My Hometown (1)
Christmas Letter (1)
Deep In The Heart Of Texas (medley) (5)
Do You Hear What I Hear (1)
Don't Ask For Tomorrow (4)
Don't Cut Timber On A Windy Day (4)
Don't Keep Me Hangin' On (7)
Empty Arms (9) **93**
Endlessly
Every Day Every Night (11)
Everything Begins And Ends With You (9)

Eyes Of Texas Are Upon You (medley) (5)
First Noel (medley) (1)
Fool #1 (3)
For The Love Of A Woman Like You (9)
Free Roamin' Mind (6)
Going Through The Motions (Of Living) (2)
Goodbye, Maggie, Goodbye (4)
Happiness Bound (10)
Happy Memories (7)
He'll Have To Go (8)
Heaven On Earth (10)
How Great Thou Art (medley) (5)
I Can't Stop Loving You (8)
I Get Fooled, Don't I (4)
I Know (4)
I Walk The Line (8)
I'll Do The Same Thing For You (6)
I'll Keep Holding On (Just To Your Love) (2)
I'll Never Find Another You (4,5) **97**

I'll Think About That Tomorrow (11)
I'll Watch Over You (6)
I'm Movin' On (medley) (5)
I've Just Got To Keep On Keepin' On (6)
Is It Wrong (For Loving You) (11)
It Keeps Right On A Hurtin' (10)
It's Gonna Rain Some In My Heart (4)
It's Just A Matter Of Time (6) **87**
It's Worth It All (3)
Jesus Knows (10)
Just A Closer Walk With Thee (medley) (5)
Just Keep On Thinking Of Me (9)
Keep Me In Mind (3)
King Of The Road (8)
Kiss In The Sunshine (7)
Last Time (4)
Let Me Live And Love With You (7)
Little Drummer Boy (1)

Love Is A Rainbow (4)
Love Is You (9)
Love Me Like That (4)
Mean Ole Mississippi (3)
Minute You're Gone (2) **95**
Miracles Still Happen (10)
Missing You (11)
My Christmas Dream (1)
My Love (7)
Old Sweetheart Of Mine (4)
On The Fingers Of One Hand (4)
One Day By And By (3)
Only Ones We Truly Hurt (10)
Only The Lonely (3,5) **92**
Out Of This World (3)
Pocketful Of Mistletoe (1)
Rally 'Round Your Love (6)
Ramblin' Rose (7)
Reach Out Your Hand And Touch Me (9)
Room In Your Heart (2)
Roses Are Red (3)
Running Bear (5) **94**
Scars (4)
She Believes In Me (10)

She Will, I Know (3)
She's Comin' Home (11)
Silent Night (medley) (1)
Silver Bells (1)
Since I Met You, Baby (5) **65**
'68 Rock Island Line (medley) (5)
Somehow Your Name Comes Up Again (6)
Star Still Shines (1)
Suddenly There's A Valley (11)
Take Good Care Of Her (2,4)
Tennessee Waltz (4)
There's Always Another Day (4)
This Time (11)
This World Of Ours (6)
Till The Last Leaf Shall Fall (2)
Today Is The End Of The World (4)
Traces (9)
Train Special '69 (5)
True Love Lasts Forever (10)
True Love's A Blessing (2,4,5)
Wake Up To Me Gentle (3)
Waterloo (7)
We're On Our Way (4)

What Am I Living For (9)
When The Snow Is On The Roses (11)
When Your World Stops Turning (4)
Where Did My Love Go (3)
Where Forgotten Things Belong (3)
Where The Tree Is (1)
White Silver Sands (1)
Why Is It I'm The Last To Know (11)
Woodbine Valley (7)
World Of Our Own (5)
You Are All I Love (7)
You Are My Sunshine (8)
You're The Only World I Know (2) **91**
You're The Reason I'm Living (10)
Young Love (2,5,8) **1**
Your Cheatin' Heart (8)

JAMES, Tommy, And The Shondells '69
Born Thomas Jackson on 4/29/47 in Dayton, Ohio; raised in Niles, Michigan. Pop-rock singer/songwriter. The Shondells: Eddie Gray (guitar), Ronnie Rosman (organ), Mike Vale (bass) and Pete Lucia (drums).
1)Crimson & Clover 2)The Best Of Tommy James & The Shondells 3)Hanky Panky

DEBUT	PEAK	WKS	CD				Sym	$	Label & Number
7/30/66	46	15	©	1	Hanky Panky			$30	Roulette 25336
4/29/67	74	18		2	I Think We're Alone Now			$30	Roulette 25353
2/24/68	174	5		3	Something Special! The Best Of Tommy James & The Shondells		[G]	$30	Roulette 25355
7/27/68	193	2	©	4	Mony Mony			$25	Roulette 42012
2/1/69	8	35	©	5	Crimson & Clover			$25	Roulette 42023
10/25/69	141	6	©	6	Cellophane Symphony			$25	Roulette 42030
12/13/69+	21	41		7	The Best Of Tommy James & The Shondells		[G]	$25	Roulette 42040
4/11/70	91	9		8	Travelin'			$25	Roulette 42044
				TOMMY JAMES:					
9/11/71	131	8	©	9	Christian Of The World			$20	Roulette 3001
3/22/80	134	7		10	Three Times In Love			$12	Millennium 7748

Adrienne (9) **93**
Another Hill To Climb (9)
(Baby, Baby) I Can't Take It No More (2,7)
Baby Let Me Down (2)
Ball Of Fire (7) **19**
Bits & Pieces (9)
Bloody Water (8)
Breakaway (9)
California Sun (2)
Candy Maker (8)
Cellophane Symphony (6)
Changes (6)
Christian Of The World (9)
Church Street Soul Revival (9) **62**
Cleo's Mood (1)

Crimson And Clover (5,7) **1**
Crystal Blue Persuasion (5,7) **2**
Do Something To Me (5) **38**
Do Unto Me (4)
Don't Let My Love Pass You By (3)
Don't Throw Our Love Away (1)
Draggin' The Line (9) **4**
Early In The Mornin' (8)
Evergreen (1)
Everything I Am (10)
Get Out Now (4) **48**
Gettin' Together (3) **18**
Gingerbread Man (4)
Gone, Gone, Gone (2)
Good Lovin' (1)

Gotta Get Back To You (8) **45**
Hanky Panky (1,3,7) **1**
I Am A Tangerine (5)
I Believe In People (9)
I Can't Go Back To Denver (4)
I Just Wanna Play Music (1)
I Know Who I Am (6)
I Like The Way (2,3) **25**
I Think We're Alone Now (2,3,7) **4**
I'll Go Crazy (1)
I'm Alive (5)
I'm Comin' Home (9) **40**
I'm So Proud (1)
(I'm) Taken (4)
It's All Right (For Now) (10)

It's Magic (10)
It's Only Love (3) **31**
Kathleen McArthur (5)
Kelly Told Ann (8)
Lady In White (10)
Let It Slide (10)
Let's Be Lovers (2)
Light Of Day (9)
Long Way Down (10)
Lot's Of Pretty Girls (1)
Love Makes The World Go Round (1)
Love Of A Woman (6)
Love's Closin' In On Me (3)
Loved One (8)
Lover, The (1)
Makin' Good Time (6)

Mirage (2,3,7) **10**
Money Money (4,7) **3**
Moses And Me (9)
Nightime (I'm A Lover) (4)
On Behalf Of The Entire Staff & Management (6)
One Two Three And I Fell (4)
Out Of The Blue (3) **43**
Papa Rolled His Own (6)
Real Girl (9)
Red Rover (8)
Rings And Things (9)
Run Away With Me (4)
Run, Run, Baby, Run (2,3)
Sail A Happy Ship (9)
Say I Am (What I Am) (1,3) **21**
Shake A Tail Feather (1)

She (8) **23**
Shout (2)
Silk, Satin, Carriage Waiting (9)
Sing, Sing, Sing (9)
Smokey Roads (5)
Some Kind Of Love (4)
Somebody Cares (4) **53**
Soul Searchin' Baby (1)
Sugar On Sunday (5,7)
Sweet Cherry Wine (6,7) **7**
Talkin' And Signifyin' (8)
Three Times In Love (10) **19**
Travelin' (8)
Trust Each Other In Love (2)
What I'd Give To See Your Face Again (2)
You Got Me (10)

★394★ JAMES GANG, The · '70

Rock group from Cleveland: **Joe Walsh** (guitar, keyboards, vocals), Jim Fox (drums) and Tom Kriss (bass; replaced by Dale Peters in 1970). Walsh left in late 1971, replaced by Dominic Troiano and Roy Kenner. Troiano left in 1973 to join **The Guess Who**, replaced by **Tommy Bolin** (died on 12/4/76, age 25). Many personnel changes from 1974 until group disbanded in 1976.

1)James Gang Rides Again 2)James Gang Live In Concert 3)Thirds

DEBUT	PEAK	WKS		CD	ALBUM		$	Label & Number
11/1/69+	83	24		© 1	Yer' Album		$20	BluesWay 6034
7/25/70	20	66	●	© 2	James Gang Rides Again		$15	ABC 711
4/17/71	27	30	●	© 3	Thirds		$15	ABC 721
9/11/71	24	16	●	© 4	James Gang Live In Concert	[L]	$15	ABC 733
					recorded on 5/15/71 at Carnegie Hall			
3/18/72+	58	19		© 5	Straight Shooter		$15	ABC 741
10/7/72	72	15		© 6	Passin' Thru		$15	ABC 760
2/10/73	79	16		7	The Best Of The James Gang featuring Joe Walsh	[G]	$15	ABC 774
12/8/73	181	5		© 8	16 Greatest Hits	[G]	$20	ABC 801 [2]
1/5/74	122	18		© 9	Bang		$12	Atco 7037
9/14/74	97	10		© 10	Miami		$12	Atco 102
5/31/75	109	9		11	Newborn		$12	Atco 112

Again (3,8)
Ain't Seen Nothin' Yet (6)
Alexis (9)
All I Have (11)
Ashes The Rain And I (2,4,7,8)
Asshtonpark (2)
Bluebird (1)
Bomber Medley (2,7,8)
Cold Wind (11)
Collage (1,8)
Come With Me (11)
Cruisin' Down The Highway (10)
Devil Is Singing Our Song (9)
Do It (10)
Dreamin' In The Country (3)
Driftin' Dreamer (11)
Drifting Girl (6)
Earthshaker (11)
Everybody Needs A Hero (4)
Fred (medley) (1)
From Another Time (9)
Funk (medley) (1)
Funk #48 (1,7,8)
Funk #49 (2,7,8) *59*
Garden Gate (2)
Get Her Back Again (5)
Getting Old (5)
Gonna Get By (11)
Got No Time For Trouble (9)
Had Enough (6)
Hairy Hypochondriac (5)
Head Above The Water (10)
Heartbreak Hotel (11)
I Don't Have The Time (1)
I'll Tell You Why (5)
It's All The Same (3)
Kick Back Man (5)
Let Me Come Home (5)
Live My Life Again (3)
Looking For My Lady (5)
Lost Woman (1,4)
Madness (5)
Merry-Go-Round (11)
Miami Two-Step (10)
Midnight Man (3,7,8) *80*
Must Be Love (9) *54*
My Door Is Open (5)
Mystery (9)
One Way Street (6)
Out Of Control (6)
Praylude (medley) (10)
Rather Be Alone With You (A.K.A. Song For Dale) (9)
Red Satin Lover (11)
Red Skies (medley) (10)
Ride The Wind (9)
Run, Run, Run (6)
Shoulda' Seen Your Face (11)
Sleepwalker (3)
Spanish Lover (10)
Standing In The Rain (9)
Stone Rap (1)
Stop (1,4,7,8)
Summer Breezes (10)
Take A Look Around (1,4,7,8)
Tend My Garden (2,4,8)
Thanks (2,8)
There I Go Again (2,8)
Things I Could Be (3)
Things I Want To Say To You (6)
Tuning Part One (1)
Up To Yourself (6)
Walk Away (3,4,7,8) *51*
Watch It (1)
White Man/Black Man (3,8)
Wildfire (10)
Woman (2,7,8)
Wrapcity In English (medley) (1)
Yadig? (3,7,8)
You're Gonna Need Me (4)

JAMIROQUAI · '97

Group is actually singer/songwriter Jason Kay (born in 1969 in London).

DEBUT	PEAK	WKS		CD	ALBUM	$	Label & Number
2/1/97	24	62	▲	© 1	Travelling Without Moving	$10	Work 67903
6/26/99	28	11		© 2	Synkronized	$10	Work 69973

Alright (1) *78*
Black Capricorn Day (2)
Butterfly (2)
Canned Heat (2)
Cosmic Girl (1)
Destitute Illusion (2)
Didjerama (1)
Didjital Vibrations (1)
Drifting Along (1)
Everyday (1)
Falling (2)
High Times (1)
King For A Day (2)
Planet Home (2)
Soul Education (2)
Spend A Lifetime (2)
Supersonic (2)
Travelling Without Moving (1)
Use The Force (1)
Virtual Insanity (1)
Where Do We Go From Here (2)
You Are My Love (1)

★464★ JAN & DEAN · '64

Surf-rock male vocal duo from Los Angeles: Jan Berry (born on 4/3/41) and Dean Torrence (born on 3/10/40). Jan was critically injured in a car crash on 4/19/66. Their biographical movie *Dead Man's Curve* aired on TV in 1978.

1)Drag City 2)Surf City And Other Swingin' Cities 3)Command Performance/Live In Person

DEBUT	PEAK	WKS		CD	ALBUM		$	Label & Number
6/22/63	71	10		© 1	Jan & Dean take Linda Surfin'		$80	Liberty 7294
8/10/63	32	21		© 2	Surf City And Other Swingin' Cities		$50	Liberty 7314
1/18/64	22	14		© 3	Drag City		$50	Liberty 7339
5/23/64	80	21		© 4	Dead Man's Curve/The New Girl In School		$50	Liberty 7361
10/10/64+	40	20		© 5	The Little Old Lady From Pasadena		$40	Liberty 7377
10/17/64+	66	19		© 6	Ride The Wild Surf	[S]	$40	Liberty 7368
2/27/65	33	16		7	Command Performance/Live In Person	[L]	$40	Liberty 7403
10/2/65	107	6		8	Jan & Dean Golden Hits, Volume 2	[G]	$40	Liberty 7417
1/15/66	145	3		© 9	Folk 'N Roll		$40	Liberty 7431
5/14/66	127	5		10	Filet Of Soul	[L]	$40	Liberty 7441

All I Have To Do Is Dream (7)
Anaheim, Azusa & Cucamonga Sewing Circle, Book Review And Timing Association (5,8) *77*
"B" Gas Rickshaw (4)
Barons, West L.A. (4)
Beginning From An End (9)
Best Friend I Ever Had (1)
Bucket "T" (4)
Dead Man's Curve (3,4,7,8,10) *8*
Detroit City (2)
Do Wah Diddy Diddy (7)
Down At Malibu Beach (6)
Drag City (3,8) *10*
Drag Strip Girl (3)
Eve Of Destruction (9)
Everybody Loves A Clown (10)
Folk City (9)
Gonna Hustle You (10)
Gypsy Cried (1)
Hang On Sloopy (My Girl Sloopy) (9)
(Here They Come) From All Over The World (7,8) *56*
Hey Little Cobra (4)
Honolulu Lulu (2,8,10) *11*
Horace The Swingin' School-Bus Driver (5)
Hot Stocker (3)
I Can't Wait To Love You (9)
I Found A Girl (9,10) *30*
I Get Around (7)
I Gotta Drive (3)
I Left My Heart In San Francisco (2)
I Should Have Known Better (7)
It Ain't Me Babe (9)
It's A Shame To Say Goodbye (9)
It's As Easy As 1,2,3 (4,5)
Kansas City (2)
Let's Hang On (10)
Let's Turkey Trot (1)
Lightnin' Strikes (10)
Linda (1,4,8) *28*
Little Deuce Coupe (3)
Little Honda (7)
Little Old Lady (From Pasadena) (5,7,8) *3*
Louie, Louie (7)
Manhattan (2)
Memphis (2,5)
Michelle (10)
Move Out Little Mustang (5)
Mr. Bassman (1)
My Foolish Heart (1)
My Mighty G.T.O. (4)
New Girl In School (4,8) *37*
Norwegian Wood (This Bird Has Flown) (10)
Old Ladies Seldom Power Shift (5)
One-Piece Topless Bathingsuit (5)
1-2-3 (10)
Philadelphia, Pa. (2)
Popsicle Truck (3)
Rhythm Of The Rain (1)
Ride The Wild Surf (6,8) *16*
Rock And Roll Music (7)
Rockin' Little Roadster (4)
Schlock Rod (Part 1 & 2) (3)
School Day (4)
She's My Summer Girl (6)
Sidewalk Surfin' (5,6,7,8) *25*
Skateboarding - Part 1 (6)
Skateboarding - Part 2 (5)
Soul City (2)
Sting Ray (3)
Submarine Races (6)
Summer Means Fun (5)
Surf City (2,7,8) *1*
Surf Route 101 (3)
Surfer's Dream (6)
Surfin' (1)
Surfin' Hearse (3)
Surfin' Safari (1)
Surfin' Wild (6)
T.A.M.I. Show, Theme From ...see: (Here They Come) From All Over The World
Tallahassee Lassie (2)
Tell 'Em I'm Surfin' (6)
Three Window Coupe (4)
Turn! Turn! Turn! (9)
Universal Coward (9)
Waimea Bay (6)
Walk Like A Man (1)
Walk On The Wet Side (6)
Walk Right In (1)
Way Down Yonder In New Orleans (2)
When I Learn How To Cry (1)
When It's Over (5)
Where Were You When I Needed You (4)
Yesterday (9)
You Came A Long Way From St. Louis (2)
You Really Know How To Hurt A Guy (8) *27*
You've Got To Hide Your Love Away (10)

JANE'S ADDICTION · '90

Rock group from Los Angeles: Perry Farrell (vocals), Dave Navarro (guitar), Eric Avery (bass) and Stephen Perkins (drums). Farrell and Perkins later formed **Porno For Pyros**. Navarro later joined **Red Hot Chili Peppers**.

DEBUT	PEAK	WKS		CD	ALBUM		$	Label & Number
9/17/88+	103	35	▲	© 1	Nothing's Shocking	C:#36/6	$10	Warner 25727
9/8/90	19	60	▲²	© 2	Ritual de lo Habitual		$10	Warner 25993
11/22/97	21	17		© 3	Kettle Whistle		$10	Warner 46752

Ain't No Right (2,3)
Been Caught Stealing (2,3)
City (3)
Classic Girl (2)
Had A Dad (1,3)
Idiots Rule (1)
Jane Says (1,3)
Kettle Whistle (3)
Mountain Song (1,3)
My Cat's Name Is Maceo (3)
No One's Leaving (2)
Obvious (2)
Ocean Size (1,3)
Of Course (3)
Slow Divers (3)
So What! (3)
Standing In The Shower...Thinking (1)
Stop! (2,3)
Summertime Rolls (1)
Ted, Just Admit It... (1)
Thank You Boys (1)
Then She Did... (2)
Three Days (2,3)
Up The Beach (1,3)
Whores (3)

JANKEL, Chas '82
Born on 4/16/52 in England. Former keyboardist/guitarist with **Ian Dury & The Blockheads**.

3/6/82	126	14			Questionnaire			$10	A&M 4885

Boy
Glad To Know You

Johnny Funk
Magic Of Music

Now You're Dancing
109

Questionnaire
3,000,000 Synths

JANKOWSKI, Horst '65
Born on 1/30/36 in Berlin. Died of cancer on 6/29/98 (age 62). Jazz pianist.

5/22/65	18	31			1 The Genius Of Jankowski!		[I]	$20	Mercury 60993
12/4/65+	65	13			2 More Genius Of Jankowski		[I]	$20	Mercury 61054
12/3/66	107	2			3 So What's New?		[I]	$20	Mercury 61093

All My Happiness (3)
Bald Klopft Das Gluck Auch Mal
An Deine Tur (Soon Luck Will
Also Knock On Your Door) (1)
Berlin Stroll (3)
Bossa Novissima (3)
Canadian Sunset (2)
Caroline - Denise (1)

Charming Vienna (2)
Clair de Lune (1)
Cruising Down The Rhine (2)
Donkey Serenade (1)
Dreamers Concerto (3)
Eine Schwarzwaldfahrt ..see:
Walk In The Black Forest
Exactly You (3)

Grand Amour (3)
Happy Frankfurt (2)
Heide (2)
Highway At Night (3)
Moonlight Cocktail (3)
My Roman Love Song (3)
My Yiddishe Momme (1)
Nola (1)

Paris Parade (3)
Parlez-Moi D'Amour (Speak To
Me Of Love) (1)
Place In The Sun (3)
Play A Simple Melody (2)
Simpel Gimpel (1) 91
Sing-Song (1)
So What's New? (3)

Strangers In The Night (3)
Sunrise Serenade (2)
Then The Girls Go Marching In
(1)
3rd Man Theme (2)
Toselli Serenade (1)
Walk In Bavaria (2)

Walk In The Black Forest
(1) 12

JARRE, Jean-Michel '86
Born on 8/24/48 in Lyon, France. Electronic keyboardist.

10/15/77	78	19		©	1 Oxygene		[I]	$12	Polydor 6112
2/3/79	126	8		©	2 Equinoxe		[I]	$12	Polydor 6175
7/11/81	98	12		©	3 Magnetic Fields		[I]	$12	Polydor 6325
5/3/86	52	20		©	4 Rendez-Vous		[I]	$10	Dreyfus 829125

Equinoxe Part 1-8 (2)
Magnetic Fields Part 1-5 (3)

Oxygene (Part 1-6) (1)
Rendez-Vous (First-Last) (4)

Ron's Piece ..see:
Rendez-Vous

★291★ JARREAU, Al '81
Born on 3/12/40 in Milwaukee. R&B/jazz-styled singer.
1)Breakin' Away 2)Jarreau 3)This Time

8/28/76	132	11		©	1 Glow			$12	Reprise 2248
6/25/77	49	15	●	©	2 Look To The Rainbow/Live In Europe		[L]	$15	Warner 3052 [2]
10/14/78	78	28		©	3 All Fly Home			$12	Warner 3229
6/21/80	27	35	●	©	4 This Time			$12	Warner 3434
8/22/81	9	103	▲	©	5 Breakin' Away			$12	Warner 3576
4/16/83	13	43	▲	©	6 Jarreau			$10	Warner 23801
11/24/84	49	35		©	7 High Crime			$10	Warner 25106
9/21/85	125	9		©	8 Al Jarreau In London		[L]	$10	Warner 25331
					recorded November 1984 at Wembley Arena				
10/4/86	81	28	●	©	9 L Is For Lover			$10	Warner 25477
12/3/88+	75	23		©	10 Heart's Horizon			$10	Reprise 25778
7/4/92	105	9		©	11 Heaven And Earth			$10	Reprise 26849
6/11/94	114	8		©	12 Tenderness			$10	Reprise 45422
3/25/00	137	6		©	13 Tomorrow Today			$10	GRP 547884

Across The Midnight Sky (9)
After All (7) 69
Agua De Beber (1)
All (3)
All Of My Love (10)
All Or Nothing At All (10)
Alonzo (4)
Better Than Anything (2)
Black And Blues (6,8)
Blue Angel (7)
Blue In Green (Tapestry)-Part I
& II (11)
Blue Rondo A La Turk ..see:
(Round, Round, Round)
Boogie Down (6) 77
Breakin' Away (5) 43
Brite 'N' Sunny Babe (1)
Burst In With The Dawn (4)
Closer To Your Love (5)
Could You Believe (2)
Dinosaur (12)
Distracted (4)

Easy (7)
Fallin' (7)
Fire And Rain (1)
Flame (13)
Fly (3)
Gimme What You Got (4)
Give A Little More Lovin' (9)
Glow (1)
Go Away Little Girl (12)
God's Gift To The World (10)
Golden Girl (9)
Have You Seen The Child (1)
Heart's Horizon (10)
Heaven And Earth (11)
High Crime (7,8)
Hold On Me (1)
I Do (3)
I Must Have Been A Fool (10)
I Will Be Here For You
(Nitakungodea Milele) (6,8)
I'm Home (3)
If I Break (11)

(If I Could Only) Change Your
Mind (4)
Imagination (7)
In My Music (13)
It's How You Say It (11)
It's Not Hard To Love You (11)
Just To Be Loved (13)
Killer Love (10)
L Is For Lover (9)
Last Night (13)
Let Me Love You (13)
Let's Pretend (7,8)
Letter Perfect (2)
Look To The Rainbow (2)
Love Is Real (4)
Love Is Waiting (6)
Love Of My Life (11)
Love Speaks Louder Than
Words (7)
Loving You (2)
Mas Que Nada (12)
Milwaukee (1)

More Love (10)
Mornin' (6) 21
Murphy's Law (7)
My Favorite Things (12)
My Old Friend (5)
Never Givin' Up (4)
No Ordinary Romance (9)
Not Like This (6)
One Good Turn (2)
One Way (10)
Our Love (5)
Pleasure (9)
Pleasure Over Pain (10)
Puddit (Put It Where You Want
It) (13)
Raging Waters (7,8)
Rainbow In Your Eyes (1,2)
Real Tight (9)
(Rhyme) This Time (4)
Roof Garden (5,8)
(Round, Round, Round) Blue
Rondo A La Turk (5)

Save Me (6)
Save Your Love For Me (12)
Says (9)
She's Leaving Home (3,12)
(Sittin' On) The Dock Of The
Bay (3)
So Good (10)
So Long Girl (9)
Somebody's Watching You (1)
Something That You Said (13)
Spain (I Can Recall) (4)
Step By Step (6)
Sticky Wicket (7)
Summertime (2)
Superfine Love (11)
Take Five (2)
Teach Me Tonight (5,8) 70
Tell Me (7)
Tell Me What I Gotta Do (9)
10K Hi (10)
Thinkin' About It Too (3)
Through It All (13)

Tomorrow Today (13)
Trouble In Paradise (6) 63
Try A Little Tenderness (12)
Wait A Little While (3)
Wait For The Magic (10)
Way To Your Heart (10)
We Got By (2,12)
(We Got) Telepathy (9)
We're In This Love Together
(5,8) 15
What You Do To Me (11)
Whenever I Hear Your Name
(11)
Yo' Jeans (10)
You Don't See Me (2,12)
Your Song (1,12)
Your Sweet Love (4)

JARRETT, Keith '77
Born on 5/8/45 in Allentown, Pennsylvania. Jazz pianist.

8/2/75	160	5			1 El Juicio (The Judgement)		[I]	$12	Atlantic 1673
3/13/76	195	1		©	2 In The Light		[I]	$15	ECM 1033 [2]
7/10/76	179	3		©	3 Arbour Zena		[I]	$12	ECM 1070
7/17/76	184	2		©	4 Mysteries		[I]	$12	ABC/Impulse 9315
2/12/77	174	4		©	5 Shades		[I]	$12	ABC/Impulse 9322
8/6/77	141	12		©	6 Staircase/Hourglass/Sundial/Sand		[I]	$15	ECM 1090 [2]
10/1/77	117	6			7 Byablue		[I]	$12	ABC/Impulse 9331
9/2/78	174	2		©	8 My Song		[I]	$12	ECM 1115

Brass Quintet (2)
Byablue (7)
Country (8)
Crystal Moment (2)
Diatribe (5)
El Juicio (1)
Everything That Lives Laments
(4)

Fantasm (7)
Flame (1)
Fughata For Harpsichord (2)
Gypsy Moth (1)
Hourglass (Part 1 & 2) (6)
In The Cave, In The Light (2)
Journey Home (8)
Konya (7)

Mandala (8)
Metamorphosis (2)
Mirrors (3)
My Song (8)
Mysteries (4)
Pagan Hymn (2)
Pardon My Rags (1)
Piece For Ornette (1)

Pre-Judgement Atmosphere (1)
Questar (8)
Rainbow (7)
Rose Petals (5)
Rotation (4)
Runes (3)
Sand (Parts 1, 2 & 3) (6)
Shades Of Jazz (5)

Short Piece For Guitar And
Strings (2)
Solara March (3)
Southern Smiles (5)
Staircase (Parts 1-3) (6)
String Quartet (2)
Sundial (Parts 1-3) (6)
Tabarka (8)

Toll Road (1)
Trieste (7)
Yahllah (7)

DEBUT	PEAK	WKS	RIAA	CD	ARTIST — Album Title	Catalog	Sym	$	Label & Number

JARS OF CLAY   '97
Christian pop group formed in Illinois: Dan Haseltine (vocals), Steve Mason and Matt Odmark (guitars), and Charlie Lowell (keyboards).

| 9/23/95+ | 46 | 70 | ▲² | © | 1 Jars Of Clay | C:#19/13 | | $10 | Essential 5573 |
| 12/9/95 | 101 | 4 | | © | 2 Drummer Boy | C:#32/2 | [X-M] | $10 | Essential 5622 |

Christmas charts: 29/'96, 19/'99

| 10/4/97 | 8 | 19 | ▲ | © | 3 **Much Afraid** | | | $10 | Essential 41612 |
| 11/27/99 | 44 | 12 | ● | © | 4 If I Left The Zoo | | | $10 | Essential 0499 |

Art In Me (1)
Blind (1)
Boy On A String (1)
Can't Erase It (4)
Collide (4)
Crazy Times (3)

Fade To Grey (3)
Famous Last Words (4)
Five Candles (You Were There) (3)
Flood (1) 37
Frail (3)

God Rest Ye Merry Gentlemen (2)
Goodbye, Goodnight (4)
Grace (4)
Hand (4)
He (1,2)
Hymn (3)

I'm Alright (4)
Like A Child (1)
Liquid (1)
Little Drummer Boy (2)
Love Song For A Savior (1)
Much Afraid (3)
No One Loves Me Like You (4)

Overjoyed (3)
Portrait Of An Apology (4)
River Constantine (4)
Sad Clown (4)
Sinking (1)
Tea And Sympathy (3)
Truce (3)

Unforgetful You (4)
Weighed Down (3)
Worlds Apart (1)

JA RULE   '00
Born Jeffrey Atkins on 2/29/76 in New York City. Male rapper. Member of **The Murderers**.

| 6/19/99 | 3 | 31 | ▲ | © | 1 **Venni Vetti Vecci** | | | $10 | Def Jam 538920 |
| 10/28/00 | ❶¹ | 49 | ▲³ | © | 2 **Rule 3:36** | | | $10 | Murder Inc. 542934 |

Between Me And You (2) 11
Chris Black (Skit) (1)
Count On Your Nigga (2)
Daddy's Little Baby (1)
Die (2)
E-Dub & Ja (1)

Extasy (2)
F*** You (2)
Grey Box (Skit) (2)
Holla Holla (1) 35
I Cry (2) 40
It's Murda (1)

It's Your Life (2)
Kill 'Em All (1)
Let's Ride (1)
Love Me, Hate Me (2)
March Prelude (1)
Murda 4 Life (1)

Murderers, The (1)
Nigguz Theme (1)
One Of Us (2)
Only Begotten Son (1)
Put It On Me (2) 8
Race Against Time (1)

Rule Won't Die (2)
6 Feet Underground (2)
Story To Tell (1)
Suicide Freestyle (1)
Watching Me (2)
We Here Now (1)

World's Most Dangerous (1)

JASON & THE SCORCHERS   '87
Rock group from Nashville: Jason Ringenberg (vocals), Warner Hodges (guitar), Jeff Johnson (bass) and Perry Baggs (drums).

3/10/84	116	23		©	1 Fervor	[M]		$10	EMI America 19008
3/30/85	96	15		©	2 Lost & Found			$10	EMI America 17153
11/22/86+	91	19		©	3 Still Standing			$10	EMI America 17219

Absolutely Sweet Marie (1)
Blanket Of Sorrow (2)
Both Sides Of The Line (1)
Broken Whiskey Glass (2)
Change The Tune (2)

Crashin' Down (3)
Far Behind (2)
Ghost Town (3)
Golden Ball And Chain (3)
Good Things Come To Those Who Wait (3)

Harvest Moon (3)
Help There's A Fire (1)
Hot Nights In Georgia (1)
I Can't Help Myself (1)
I Really Don't Want To Know (2)
If Money Talks (2)

Last Time Around (2)
Lost Highway (2)
My Heart Still Stands With You (3)
19th Nervous Breakdown (3)
Ocean Of Doubt (3)

Pray For Me, Mama (I'm A Gypsy Now) (1)
Shop It Around (2)
Shotgun Blues (3)
Still Tied (2)

Take Me To Your Promised Land (3)
White Lies (2)

JASPER, Chris   '88
Born in Cincinnati. R&B singer. Member of **The Isley Brothers** from 1969-84. Formed trio (**Isley, Jasper, Isley**) with cousins Marvin and **Ernie Isley**.

| 3/5/88 | 182 | 3 | | © | Superbad | | | $10 | CBS Associated 44053 |

Dance For The Dollar
Earthquake

Givin' My All
Like I Do

My Soul Train
One Time Love

Son Of Man
Superbad

JAY & THE AMERICANS   '66
Vocal group formed in New York City: John "Jay" Traynor, Sandy Yaguda, Kenny Vance and Howie Kane, with Marty Sanders (guitar). Traynor left in 1962 and was replaced by lead singer Jay Black (born David Blatt on 11/2/38).

12/12/64	131	4		©	1 **Come A Little Bit Closer**			$30	United Artists 6407
6/12/65	113	17			2 **Blockbusters**			$25	United Artists 6417
11/20/65+	21	20		©	3 **Jay & The Americans Greatest Hits!**		[G]	$25	United Artists 6453
3/19/66	141	4		©	4 **Sunday And Me**			$25	United Artists 6474
3/15/69	51	21		©	5 **Sands Of Time**			$25	United Artists 6671
2/28/70	105	11		©	6 **Wax Museum**			$25	United Artists 6719

Baby Stop Your Cryin' (4)
Can't We Be Sweethearts (5)
Cara, Mia (2,3) 4
Chilly Winds (4)
Come A Little Bit Closer (1,3) 3
Come Dance With Me (1) 76
Crying (4) 25
Do I Love You (6)
Friday (1)
Girl (3)
Good Lovin' (4)

Goodbye Boys Goodbye (1,3)
Goodnight My Love (5)
Granada (4)
Gypsy Woman (5)
Hang Around (2)
Hushabye (5) 62
I Don't Need A Friend (4)
I Don't Want To Cry (6)
I Miss You (When I Kiss You) (4)
If You Were Mine, Girl (2,3)
Johnny B. Goode (6)
Let It Be Me (6)

Let's Lock The Door (And Throw Away The Key) (2,3) 11
Life Is But A Dream (5)
Lonely Teardrops (6)
Look In My Eyes Maria (1)
Lover's Question (6)
Maria (4)
Mean Woman Blues (5)
Message To Martha (6)
My Prayer (5)
Only In America (1,3) 25
Please Let Me Dream (2)

Pledging My Love (5)
Room Full Of Tears (6)
Run To My Lovin' Arms (2,3)
She Doesn't Know It (1)
She's The Girl (That's Messin' Up My Mind) (4)
Silly Girl, Silly Boy (2)
Since I Don't Have You (5)
So Much In Love (5)
Some Enchanted Evening (3) 13
Some Kind-A Wonderful (6)
Somebody's Gonna Cry (2)

Something In My Eye! (2,3)
Strangers Tomorrow (1)
Sunday And Me (4) 18
Think Of The Good Times (2,3) 57
This Is It (1)
This Is My Love (6)
Through This Doorway (3)
To Wait For Love (1)
Tomorrow (1)

Twenty Four Hours From Tulsa (2)
Walkin' In The Rain (4) 19
What's The Use (1)
When It's All Over (2,3)
When You Dance (5) 70
Why Can't You Bring Me Home (4) 63
You Were On My Mind (6)

JAY AND THE TECHNIQUES   '68
Interracial R&B-rock group from Allentown, Pennsylvania: Jay Proctor (born on 10/28/40), Karl Landis, Ronnie Goosly, John Walsh, George Lloyd, Chuck Crowl and Dante Dancho.

| 10/28/67+ | 129 | 13 | | © | Apples, Peaches, Pumpkin Pie | | | $30 | Smash 67095 |

Ain't No Soul (Left In These Old Shoes)

Apples, Peaches, Pumpkin Pie 6
Been So Long (Since I Loved You)
Contact

Here We Go Again
Hey Diddle Diddle
Keep The Ball Rollin' 14

Lovin' For Money
Power Of Love
Stronger Than Dirt

Victory!

JAYE, Jerry   '67
Born Gerald Jaye Hatley on 10/19/37 in Manila, Arkansas.

| 7/29/67 | 195 | 2 | | | My Girl Josephine | | | $20 | Hi 32038 |

Ain't Got No Home
Ain't That A Shame
Don't Be Cruel

I'm Gonna Be A Wheel
Someday
Kansas City

Let The Four Winds Blow
My Girl Josephine 29
Singing The Blues

What Am I Living For
When My Dreamboat Comes Home

White Silver Sands
Whole Lot Of Shakin' Going On

JAYE, Miles   '88
Born Miles Davis in Brooklyn, New York. R&B singer/songwriter.

| 12/12/87+ | 125 | 12 | | © | 1 Miles | | | $10 | Island 90615 |
| 6/10/89 | 160 | 9 | | © | 2 Irresistible | | | $10 | Island 91235 |

Come Home (1)
Desiree (1)
Happy 2 Have U (1)

Heaven (1)
I Cry For You (2)
I'll Be There (2)

I've Been A Fool For You (1)
Irresistible (2)
Lazy Love (1)

Let's Start Love Over (1)
Love In The Night (2)
Message (2)

Neither One Of Us (2)
Next Time (2)
Objective (2)

Slo-Dance (2)
Special Thing (1)

JAYHAWKS, The '95

Rock group from Minneapolis: Mark Olson (vocals), Gary Louris (guitar), Marc Perlman (bass) and Ken Callahan (drums). Olson left in 1996. Louris took over lead vocals.

2/27/93	192	2		©	1 Hollywood Town Hall			$10	Def American 26829
3/4/95	92	9		©	2 Tomorrow The Green Grass			$10	American 43006
5/10/97	112	1		©	3 Sound Of Lies			$10	American 43114
5/27/00	129	2		©	4 Smile			$10	Columbia 69522

Ann Jane (2)
Baby, Baby, Baby (4)
Bad Time (2)
Better Days (4)
Big Star (3)
Blue (2)
Bottomless Cup (3)
Break In The Clouds (4)
Broken Harpoon (4)
Clouds (1)
Crowded In The Wings (1)
Dying On The Vine (3)
Haywire (3)
I'd Run Away (2)
I'm Gonna Make You Love Me (4)
(In My) Wildest Dreams (4)
It's Up To You (3)
Life Floats By (4)
Man Who Loved Life (3)
Martin's Song (1)
Miss Williams' Guitar (2)
Mr. Wilson (4)
Nevada, California (1)
Nothing Left To Borrow (2)
Over My Shoulder (2)
Poor Little Fish (3)
Pray For Me (2)
Pretty Thing (4)
Queen Of The World (4)
Real Light (2)
Red's Song (3)
See Him On The Street (2)
Settled Down Like Rain (1)
Sister Cry (1)
Sixteen Down (3)
Smile (4)
Somewhere In Ohio (4)
Sound Of Lies (3)
Stick In The Mud (3)
Take Me With You (When You Go) (1)
Ten Little Kids (2)
Think About It (3)
Trouble (3)
Two Angels (1)
Two Hearts (2)
Waiting For The Sun (1)
What Led Me To This Town (4)
Wichita (1)

JAY-Z '98

Born Shawn Carter on 12/4/69 in New York City. Male rapper. Founded the Roc-A-Fella record label.

7/13/96	23	18	●	©	1 Reasonable Doubt	C:#2^1/11		$10	Roc-A-Fella 50592
11/22/97	3	24	▲	©	2 In My Lifetime, Vol. 1			$10	Roc-A-Fella 536392
10/17/98	❶^5	69	▲^{5}	©	3 Vol. 2...Hard Knock Life			$10	Roc-A-Fella 558902
1/15/00	❶^1	47	▲^{3}	©	4 Vol. 3...Life And Times Of S. Carter			$10	Roc-A-Fella 546822
11/18/00	❶^1	33	▲^{2}	©	5 The Dynasty Roc La Familia (2000 —)			$10	Roc-A-Fella 548203

Ain't No Nigga (1) 50
(Always Be My) Sunshine (2)
Big Pimpin' (4) 18
Bring It On (1)
Brooklyn's Finest (1)
Can I Get A... (3) 19
Can I Live (1)
Can't Knock The Hustle (1) 51
Cashmere Thoughts (1)
Change The Game (5) 86
City Is Mine (2) 52
Come And Get Me (4)
Coming Of Age (1)
Coming Of Age (Da Sequel) (3)
D'Evils (1)
Dead Presidents II (1) flip
Do It Again (Put Ya Hands Up) (4) 65
Dope Man (4)
Face Off (4)
Feelin' It (1) 79
Friend Or Foe (1)
Friend Or Foe '98 (2)
Get Your Mind Right Mami (5)
Guilty Until Proven Innocent (5) 82
Hard Knock Life (Ghetto Anthem) (3) 15
Holla (5)
I Just Wanna Love U (Give It 2 Me) (5) 11
I Know What Girls Like (2)
If I Should Die (3)
Imaginary Player (2)
It's Alright (4)
It's Hot (Some Like It Hot) (4)
It's Like That (3)
Lucky Me (2)
Million And One Questions (medley) (2)
Money Ain't A Thang (3) 52
Money, Cash, Hoes (3)
NYMP (4)
Nigga What, Nigga Who (Originator 99) (3)
1-900-Hustler (5)
Paper Chase (3)
Parking Lot Pimpin' (5)
Politics As Usual (1)
Pop 4 Roc (4)
R.O.C., The (5)
Rap Game/Crack Game (2)
Real Niggaz (2)
Regrets (1)
Reservoir Dogs (3)
Rhyme No More (medley) (2)
Ride Or Die (3)
S. Carter (4)
Snoopy Track (4)
So Ghetto (4)
Soon You'll Understand (5)
Squeeze 1st (5)
Stick 2 The Script (5)
Streets Is Talking (5)
Streets Is Watching (2)
There's Been A Murder (4)
Things That U Do (4)
This Can't Be Life (5)
22 Two's (1)
Watch Me (4)
Week Ago (3)
Where Have You Been (5)
Where I'm From (5)
Who You Wit (2) 84
You, Me, Him And Her (5)
You Must Love Me (2)

JAZZ CRUSADERS — see CRUSADERS, The

JAZZMASTERS, The '95

Studio project featuring multi-instrumentalist **Paul Hardcastle** and vocalist Helen Rogers.

8/12/95	132	8		©	The Jazzmasters II			$10	JVC 2049

Can You Hear Me?
Do You Remember
Good Lovin'
Inner Changes
Just Can't Understand
Slomotion
Smooth Groove
So Much In Love
Summer Rain
Time To Move On
Walkin' To Freedom
Wonderland

JB's, The '73

Funk group led by **Fred Wesley**. Backing group for **James Brown**.

7/28/73	77	13			1 Doing It To Death			$80	People 5603
6/29/74	197	3			2 Damn Right I Am Somebody			$25	People 6602

FRED WESLEY & THE J.B.'s

Blow Your Head (2)
Damn Right I'm Somebody (2)
Doing It To Death (1) 22
Going To Get A Thrill (2)
I'm Payin' Taxes, What Am I Buyin' (2)
If You Don't Get It The First Time, Back Up And Try It Again, Parrty (2)
La Di Da La Di Day (1)
Make Me What You Want Me To Be (2)
More Peas (1)
Same Beat - Part 1 (2)
Sucker (1)
You Can Have Watergate Just Gimme Some Bucks And I'll Be Straight (1)
You Sure Love To Ball (2)

JEAN, Wyclef '00

Born on 10/17/70 in Haiti. Member of **The Fugees**.

7/12/97	16	67	▲^{2}	©	1 Wyclef Jean Presents The Carnival Featuring Refugee Allstars			$10	Ruffhouse 67974
9/9/00	9	30	▲	©	2 The Ecleftic: 2 Sides II A Book			$10	Columbia 62180

Anything Can Happen (1)
Apocalypse (1)
Bubblegoose (1)
Bus Search (2)
Carnival (1)
Columbia Records (2)
Da Cypha (2)
Diallo (2)
Gone Till November (1) 7
Guantanamera (1)
Gunpowder (1)
Hollyhood To Hollywood (2)
However You Want It (2)
It Doesn't Matter (2)
Jaspora (1)
Kenny Rogers - Pharoahe Monch Dub Plate (2)
Low Income (2)
Mona Lisa (2)
911 (2) 38
Perfect Gentleman (2)
Pullin' Me In (2)
Red Light District (2)
Runaway (2)
Sang Fézi (1)
Something About Mary (2)
Street Jeopardy (1)
Thug Angels (2)
To All The Girls (1)
We Trying To Stay Alive (1) 45
Where Fugees At? (2)
Whitney Houston Dub Plate (2)
Wish You Were Here (2)
Year Of The Dragon (1)
Yelé (1)

JEFFERSON AIRPLANE/STARSHIP ★43★ '75

Pop-rock group formed as **Jefferson Airplane** in San Francisco: **Marty Balin** and **Grace Slick** (vocals), **Paul Kantner** (vocals, guitar), **Jorma Kaukonen** (guitar), Jack Casady (bass) and Spencer Dryden (drums). Original drummer Skip Spence formed **Moby Grape**. Dryden left in 1970 to join **New Riders Of The Purple Sage**; replaced by Joey Covington. Casady and Kaukonen left by 1974 to go full time with **Hot Tuna**. Balin left in 1971, rejoined in 1975, by which time group was renamed **Jefferson Starship** and consisted of Slick, Kantner, **Papa John Creach** (violin; died on 2/22/94, age 76), David Freiberg (bass), Craig Chaquico (guitar), Pete Sears (bass) and John Barbata (drums). Balin left group from June 1978 to January 1981. In 1979, singer Mickey Thomas joined (replaced Balin), along with Aynsley Dunbar (**John Mayall**'s Bluesbreakers, **Frank Zappa**'s Mothers Of Invention, **Journey**) who replaced Barbata. Don Baldwin (formerly with **Snail**) replaced Dunbar (later with **Whitesnake**) in 1982. Kantner left in 1984, and, due to legal difficulties, band's name was shortened to **Starship**, whose lineup included Slick, Thomas, Sears, Chaquico, Baldwin, Brett Bloomfield (bass) and Mark Morgan (keyboards). Starship disbanded in 1990. Group inducted into the Rock and Roll Hall of Fame in 1996. In 1989, the original 1966 lineup of Balin, Slick, Kantner, Kaukonen and Casady reunited as Jefferson Airplane with Kenny Aronoff (from **John Cougar Mellencamp**'s band) replacing Dryden. Continuing as Starship were Thomas, Chaquico, Baldwin, Brett Bloomfield (bass) and Mark Morgan (keyboards). Starship disbanded in 1990. Group inducted into the Rock and Roll Hall of Fame in 1996.

1)Red Octopus 2)Spitfire 3)Surrealistic Pillow 4)Earth 5)Crown Of Creation

JEFFERSON AIRPLANE:

9/17/66	128	11		©	1 Jefferson Airplane Takes Off			$50	RCA Victor 3584
3/25/67	3	56	●	©	2 Surrealistic Pillow			$30	RCA Victor 3766
12/23/67+	17	23		©	3 After Bathing At Baxter's			$30	RCA Victor 1511
9/7/68	6	25	●	©	4 Crown Of Creation			$25	RCA Victor 4058

DEBUT	PEAK	WKS	RIAA	CD	ARTIST — Album Title	Catalog	Sym	$	Label & Number

JEFFERSON AIRPLANE/STARSHIP — Cont'd

DEBUT	PEAK	WKS	RIAA	CD	ARTIST — Album Title	Catalog	Sym	$	Label & Number
3/1/69	17	20		© 5	Bless Its Pointed Little Head		[L]	$25	RCA Victor 4133
11/22/69	13	44	●	© 6	Volunteers			$20	RCA Victor 4238
12/12/70+	12	40	▲	© 7	The Worst Of Jefferson Airplane	C:#16/18	[G]	$20	RCA Victor 4459
12/19/70+	20	23	●	© 8	Blows Against The Empire			$20	RCA Victor 4448

PAUL KANTNER/JEFFERSON STARSHIP

DEBUT	PEAK	WKS	RIAA	CD	ARTIST — Album Title	Catalog	Sym	$	Label & Number
9/18/71	11	21	●	© 9	Bark			$20	Grunt 1001
8/19/72	20	21	●	© 10	Long John Silver			$20	Grunt 1007
4/14/73	52	16		© 11	Thirty Seconds Over Winterland		[L]	$20	Grunt 0147
5/4/74	110	8		© 12	Early Flight		[K]	$20	Grunt 0437

JEFFERSON STARSHIP:

DEBUT	PEAK	WKS	RIAA	CD	ARTIST — Album Title	Catalog	Sym	$	Label & Number
10/26/74	11	37	●	© 13	Dragon Fly			$15	Grunt 0717
7/19/75	❶⁴	87	▲²	© 14	Red Octopus			$15	Grunt 0999
7/10/76	3	38	▲	© 15	Spitfire			$15	Grunt 1557
1/29/77	37	15	●	16	Flight Log (1966-1976)		[K]	$20	Grunt 1255 [2]

includes "Hesitation Blues" and "Ja Da (Keep On Truckin')" by **Hot Tuna**, "¿Come Again? Toucan" by **Grace Slick**, "Silver Spoon" and "Sketches Of China" by **Paul Kantner/Grace Slick**, and "Genesis" by **Jorma Kaukonen** & Tom Hobson

DEBUT	PEAK	WKS	RIAA	CD	ARTIST — Album Title	Catalog	Sym	$	Label & Number
3/18/78	5	34	▲	© 17	Earth			$12	Grunt 2515
2/17/79	20	14	●	© 18	Gold		[G]	$12	Grunt 3247
12/1/79+	10	28	●	© 19	Freedom At Point Zero			$12	Grunt 3452
4/18/81	26	33	●	20	Modern Times			$12	Grunt 3848
10/30/82	26	31	●	© 21	Winds Of Change			$12	Grunt 4372
6/16/84	28	23	●	© 22	Nuclear Furniture			$12	Grunt 4921

STARSHIP:

DEBUT	PEAK	WKS	RIAA	CD	ARTIST — Album Title	Catalog	Sym	$	Label & Number
10/5/85+	7	50	▲	© 23	Knee Deep In The Hoopla			$10	Grunt 5488
4/18/87	138	9		© 24	2400 Fulton Street - An Anthology		[K]	$15	RCA Victor 5724 [2]

JEFFERSON AIRPLANE

DEBUT	PEAK	WKS	RIAA	CD	ARTIST — Album Title	Catalog	Sym	$	Label & Number
7/25/87	12	25	●	© 25	No Protection			$10	Grunt 6413
8/19/89	64	18		© 26	Love Among The Cannibals			$10	RCA 9693
9/23/89	85	7		© 27	Jefferson Airplane			$10	Epic 45271

reunion of the 1966-74 lineup

Aerie (Gang Of Eagles) (10)
Ai Garimasu (There Is Love) (14)
Alexander The Medium (10)
Alien (20)
All Fly Away (13)
All Nite Long (17)
And I Like It (1)
Assassin (22)
Awakening (19)
Baby Tree (8)
Babylon (22)
Ballad Of You & Me & Pooneil (3,7,24) **42**
Be My Lady (21) **28**
Be Young You (13)
Bear Melt (5)
Beat Patrol (25) **46**
Before I Go (23) **68**
Big City (15)
Black Widow (21)
Blaze Of Love (26)
Blues From An Airplane (1,7)
Bringing Me Down (1)
Burn, The (26)
Can't Find Love (21)
Caroline (13,18)
Champion (22)
Chauffeur Blues (1)
Child Is Coming (8)
Children, The (25)
Chushingura (4,7)
Clergy (5)
Come To Life (13)
Come Up The Years (1,16,24)
Comin' Back To Me (2,16,24)
Common Market Madrigal (27)
Connection (22)
Count On Me (17,18) **8**
Crazy Feelin' (17) **54**
Crazy Miranda (9)

Crown Of Creation (4,7,11,24) **64**
Cruisin' (15)
D.C.B.A.- 25 (2)
Dance With The Dragon (15)
Desperate Heart (23)
Devils Den (13)
Don't Slip Away (1)
Easter? (10)
Eat Starch Mom (10)
Embryonic Journey (2,7,24)
Eskimo Blue Day (6)
Fading Lady Light (19)
Farm, The (6)
Fast Buck Freddie (14,18)
Fat Angel (5)
Feel So Good (9,11,16)
Find Your Way Back (20) **29**
Fire (17)
Free (20)
Freedom (27)
Freedom At Point Zero (19)
Girl With The Hungry Eyes (19) **55**
Girls Like You (25)
Git Fiddler (14)
Go To Her (12)
Good Shepherd (6,7)
Greasy Heart (4,16) **98**
Have You Seen The Saucers (11,12)
Have You Seen The Stars Tonite (8,16)
Healing Waters (26)
Hearts Of The World (Will Understand) (26)
Hey Fredrick (6)
High Flyin' Bird (12)
Hijack (8)
Home (8)
Hot Water (15)

House At Pooneil Corners (4)
How Do You Feel (2)
How Suite It Is Medley (3)
Hyperdrive (13)
I Came Back From The Jaws Of The Dragon (21)
I Didn't Mean To Stay All Night (26) **75**
I Don't Know Why (25)
I Want To See Another World (14)
I Will Stay (21)
I'll Be There (26)
Ice Age (27)
Ice Cream Phoenix (4)
If You Feel (4,16)
In The Morning (1)
In Time (4)
It's Alright (12)
It's No Secret (1,5,7,24)
It's Not Enough (26) **12**
It's Not Over ('Til It's Over) (25) **9**
J.P.P. McStep B. Blues (12)
Jane (19) **14**
Just The Same (19)
Keep On Dreamin' (21)
Last Wall Of The Castle (medley) (3)
Lather (4,7,24)
Law Man (9)
Layin' It On The Line (22) **66**
Let Me In (1)
Let's Get Together (1)
Lets Go Together (8)
Lightning Rose (19)
Live And Let Live (22)
Long John Silver (10)
Love Among The Cannibals (26)
Love Lovely Love (15)

Love Rusts (23)
Love Too Good (17,18)
Madeleine Street (27)
Magician (22)
Martha (3,7,24)
Mary (20)
Mau Mau (Amerikon) (8)
Meadowlands (6)
Mexico (12,24)
Milk Train (10,11,16)
Miracles (14,18) **3**
Modern Times (20)
My Best Friend (2,24)
Never Argue With A German If You're Tired Or European Song (9)
No Way Out (22) **23**
Nothing's Gonna Stop Us Now (25) **1**
Now Is The Time (27)
Other Side Of This Life (5)
Out Of Control (21)
Panda (27)
Planes (27)
Plastic Fantastic Lover (2,5,7,24)
Play On Love (14,18) **49**
Please Come Back (16)
Pretty As You Feel (9,16,24)
Private Room (23)
Quit Wasting Time (21)
Rejoyce (3,24)
Ride The Tiger (13,16,18) **84**
Rock And Roll Island (9)
Rock Me Baby (1)
Rock Music (19)
Rock Myself To Sleep (23)
Rose Goes To Yale (22)
Run Around (1)
Runaway (17,18) **12**

Runnin' 'Round This World (12)
Sandalphon (14)
Sara (23) **1**
Save Your Love (20)
Send A Message (26)
Set The Night To Music (27)
Share A Little Joke (4)
She Has Funny Cars (2,24)
Shining In The Moonlight (22)
Show Yourself (17)
Showdown (22)
Skateboard (17)
Small Package Of Value Will Come To You, Shortly (3,24)
Solidarity (27)
Somebody To Love (5)
Son Of Jesus (10)
Song For All Seasons (6)
Song To The Sun Medley (15)
Sorry Me, Sorry You (22)
St. Charles (15,18) **64**
Stairway To Cleveland (20)
Star Track (4)
Starship (27)
Stranger (20) **48**
Summer Of Love (27)
Sunrise (8)
Sweeter Than Honey (14)
Switchblade (15)
Take Your Time (17)
Thats For Sure (13)
There Will Be Love (14)
Things To Come (19)
Third Week In The Chelsea (9,24)
3/5 Of A Mile In 10 Seconds (2,5)
Thunk (9)
Tobacco Road (1)
Today (2,7,24)

Tomorrow Doesn't Matter Tonight (23) **26**
Too Many Years (27)
Transatlantic (27)
Triad (4,24)
Trial By Fire (10,11)
Trouble In Mind (26)
True Love (27)
Tumblin (14)
Turn My Life Down (6)
Turn Out The Lights (5)
Twilight Double Leader (10,11)
Two Heads (medley) (3)
Up Or Down (12)
Upfront Blues (27)
Volunteers (6,7,16,24) **65**
War Movie (9)
We Built This City (23) **1**
We Can Be Together (6,7,24)
We Dream In Color (26)
Wheel, The (27)
When The Earth Moves Again (9,11)
White Rabbit (2,7,16,24) **8**
Wild Eyes (20)
Wild Turkey (9)
Wild Tyme (3,24)
Winds Of Change (21) **38**
Wings Of A Lie (25)
With Your Love (15,18) **12**
Won't You Try Saturday Afternoon (3,16,24)
Wooden Ships (6,16,24)
X M (8)
Young Girl Sunday Blues (medley) (3)

JEFFREYS, Garland '81

Born in 1944 in Brooklyn, New York. Black rock singer.

DEBUT	PEAK	WKS	RIAA	CD	ARTIST — Album Title	Catalog	Sym	$	Label & Number
3/26/77	140	10			1 Ghost Writer			$12	A&M 4629
4/15/78	99	10			2 One-Eyed Jack			$12	A&M 4681
9/22/79	151	5			3 American Boy & Girl			$12	A&M 4778
3/21/81	59	18		©	4 Escape Artist			$10	Epic 36983
10/31/81	163	4			5 Rock & Roll Adult		[L]	$10	Epic 37436
2/26/83	176	4			6 Guts For Love			$10	Epic 38190

American Backslide (6)
American Boy & Girl (3)
Bad Dream (3)
Been There And Back (2)
Bound To Get Ahead Someday (5)

Bring Back The Love (3)
Christine (4)
City Kids (2)
Cool Down Boy (1,5)
Dance Up (6)

Desperation Drive (2)
El Salvador (6)
Fidelity (6)
Ghost Of A Chance (4)
Ghost Writer (1)

Graveyard Rock (4)
Guts For Love (6)
Haunted House (2)
I May Not Be Your Kind (1,5)
If Mao Could See Me Now (3)

Innocent (4)
Jump Jump (4)
Keep On Trying (2)
Lift Me Up (1)
Livin' For Me (3)

Loneliness (6)
Matador (3,5)
Modern Lovers (4)
Mystery Kids (4)
New York Skyline (1)

424

DEBUT	PEAK	WKS	RIAA	CD	ARTIST — Album Title	Catalog	Sym	$	Label & Number

JEFFREYS, Garland

Night Of The Living Dead (3)	Real Man (6)	Scream In The Night (2)	Spanish Town (1)	What Does It Take (To Win
96 Tears (4,5) *66*	Rebel Love (6)	She Didn't Lie (2)	Surrender (6)	Your Love) (6)
No Woman No Cry (2)	Reelin' (2)	Ship Of Fools (3)	35 Millimeter Dreams (1,5)	Why-O (1)
Oh My Soul (2)	R.O.C.K. (4,5)	Shoot The Moonlight Out (3)	True Confessions (4)	Wild In The Streets (1,5)
One-Eyed Jack (2)	Rough And Ready (1)	Shout (6)		

JELLYBEAN   **'87**

Born John Benitez on 11/7/57 in the Bronx, New York. Renowned club DJ/remixer/producer.

9/5/87	101	11		©	**Just Visiting This Planet**			$10	Chrysalis 41569

Am I Dreaming	Jingo	Little Too Good To Me	Walking In My Sleep
Hypnotized (By Your Touch)	Just A Mirage	**Real Thing** *82*	**Who Found Who** *16*

JELLYFISH   **'91**

Rock group from San Francisco: Andy Sturmer (vocals, drums), Jason Falkner (guitar), and brothers Chris (bass) and Roger (keyboards) Manning. Falkner and Chris Manning left by 1993; bassist Tim Smith joined.

11/17/90+	124	27		© 1	**Bellybutton**			$10	Charisma 91400
2/27/93	164	1		© 2	**Spilt Milk**			$10	Charisma 86459

All I Want Is Everything (1)	Brighter Day (2)	Glutton Of Sympathy (2)	Joining A Fan Club (2)	Now She Knows She's Wrong
All Is Forgiven (2)	Bye, Bye, Bye (2)	He's My Best Friend (2)	King Is Half-Undressed (1)	(1)
Baby's Coming Back (1) *62*	Calling Sarah (1)	Hush (2)	Man I Used To Be (1)	Russian Hill (2)
Bedspring Kiss (1)	Ghost At Number One (2)	I Wanna Stay Home (1)	New Mistake (2)	Sebrina Paste And Plato (2)

She Still Loves Him (1) / That Is Why (1) / Too Much, Too Little, Too Late (2)

JENKINS, Gordon   **'56**

Born on 5/12/10 in Webster Groves, Missouri. Died of ALS (Lou Gehrig's disease) on 5/1/84 (age 73). Pianist/arranger/composer.

11/24/56	13	4			**Gordon Jenkins Complete Manhattan Tower**			$30	Capitol 766

a musical narrative originally composed by Jenkins in 1945 and first released in 1949 on Decca 723

Happiness Cocktail	Magic Fire	Married I Can Always Get	New York's My Home	Party, The	Statue Of Liberty
I'm Learnin' My Latin	Magical City	Never Leave Me	Once Upon A Dream	Repeat After Me	This Close To The Dawn

JENNINGS, Waylon ★115★   **'79**

Born on 6/15/37 in Littlefield, Texas. Legendary country singer/songwriter/guitarist. Bass player for **Buddy Holly** on the fateful "Winter Dance Party" tour in 1959 (gave up his plane seat to the Big Bopper). Established himself in the mid-1970s as a leader of the "outlaw" movement in country music. Married to **Jessi Colter** since 1969. Narrator for TV's *The Dukes Of Hazzard*.

1)The Outlaws 2)Waylon & Willie 3)Ol' Waylon 4)Greatest Hits 5)Are You Ready For The Country

10/4/69	169	4		1	**Country-Folk**			$25	RCA Victor 4180
					WAYLON JENNINGS & THE KIMBERLYS				
5/16/70	192	2		2	**Waylon**			$20	RCA Victor 4260
8/11/73	185	5		© 3	**Honky Tonk Heroes**			$20	RCA Victor 0240
10/5/74	105	17		© 4	**The Ramblin' Man**			$20	RCA Victor 0734
7/5/75	49	21	●	© 5	**Dreaming My Dreams**			$15	RCA Victor 1062
2/7/76	10	51	▲²	© 6	**The Outlaws**			$15	RCA Victor 1321
					WAYLON JENNINGS/WILLIE NELSON/JESSI COLTER/TOMPALL GLASER includes "Put Another Log On The Fire" and "T For Texas" by Tompall Glaser				
4/17/76	189	4		7	**Mackintosh & T.J.**		[S]	$15	RCA Victor 1520
					includes "(Stay All Night) Stay A Little Longer" by **Willie Nelson**; "Back In The Saddle Again," "Crazy Arms," "Gardenia Waltz" and "Shopping" by The Waylors				
7/17/76	34	35	●	8	**Are You Ready For The Country**			$15	RCA Victor 1816
12/18/76+	46	17	●	© 9	**Waylon Live**		[L]	$15	RCA Victor 1108
5/21/77	15	33	▲	© 10	**Ol' Waylon**			$12	RCA Victor 2317
2/4/78	12	29	▲²	© 11	**Waylon & Willie**			$12	RCA Victor 2686
					WAYLON JENNINGS & WILLIE NELSON				
10/21/78	48	24	●	12	**I've Always Been Crazy**			$12	RCA Victor 2979
5/5/79	28	115	▲⁴	© 13	**Greatest Hits**		[G]	$12	RCA Victor 3378
11/10/79	49	28	●	14	**What Goes Around Comes Around**			$12	RCA Victor 3493
6/7/80	36	43	●	15	**Music Man**			$12	RCA Victor 3602
3/21/81	43	19	●	16	**Leather And Lace**			$12	RCA Victor 3931
					WAYLON & JESSI				
3/6/82	39	23		17	**Black On Black**			$12	RCA Victor 4247
10/30/82	57	22	●	© 18	**WWII**			$12	RCA Victor 4455
					WAYLON & WILLIE				
4/30/83	109	11		19	**It's Only Rock & Roll**			$12	RCA Victor 4673
5/21/83	60	16	●	© 20	**Take It To The Limit**			$10	Columbia 38562
					WILLIE NELSON with WAYLON JENNINGS				
6/1/85	92	35	▲	© 21	**Highwayman**			$10	Columbia 40056
3/17/90	79	13		© 22	**Highwayman 2**			$10	Columbia 45240
					WILLIE NELSON/JOHNNY CASH/WAYLON JENNINGS/KRIS KRISTOFFERSON (above 2)				
8/18/90	172	5		© 23	**The Eagle**			$10	Epic 46104
8/3/91	193	3		© 24	**Clean Shirt**			$10	Epic 47462
					WAYLON & WILLIE				

Against The Wind (21)	Are You Ready For The	Bob Wills Is Still The King	Cindy, Oh Cindy (21)	Desperados Waiting For A	Dreaming My Dreams With You
Ain't No God In Mexico (3)	Country (8)	(5,7,9)	Cloudy Days (4)	Train (21)	(5)
All Around Cowboy (7)	**Are You Sure Hank Done It**	Born And Raised In Black And	Clyde (15,19)	Do It Again (15)	**Drivin' Nails In The Wall** (1)
All Of Me Belongs To You (2)	**This Way** (5,13) *60*	White (22)	Come Stay With Me (1)	Don't Cuss The Fiddle (11)	**Dukes Of Hazzard (Good Ol'**
Amanda (4,13) *54*	As The 'Billy World Turns (12)	Brand New Goodbye Song (10)	Come With Me (14)	Don't Play The Game (2)	**Boys), Theme From** (15) *21*
American Remains (22)	Belle Of The Ball (10)	Breakin' Down (19)	Committed To Parkview (21)	Don't You Think This Outlaw	Eagle, The (23)
Angel Eyes (Angel Eyes) (19)	Big River (21)	Brown Eyed Handsome Man (2)	Couple More Years (8)	Bit's Done Get Out Of Hand	Elvis Hits Medley (10)
Angels Love Bad Men (22)	Billy (12)	Buddy Holly Hits Medley (12)	Deportee (Plane Wreck At Los	(12,19)	Folsom Prison Blues (17)
Another Man's Fool (14)	Black Rose (3)	But You Know I Love You (1)	Gatos) (21)	Door Is Always Open (5)	Games People Play (1)
Anthem '84 (22)	Blackjack County Chains (20)	**Can't You See** (8) *97*			Get Naked With Me (17)

425

JENNINGS, Waylon — Cont'd

Girl I Can Tell (You're Trying To Work It Out) (12)
Gold Dust Woman (11)
Gonna Write A Letter (17)
Good Hearted Woman (6,9,13,19) 25
(Good Ol' Boys) ..see: Dukes Of Hazzard
Good Ol' Nights (24)
Guitars That Won't Stay In Tune (24)
He Went To Paris (15)
Heaven Or Hell (6)
Her Man (23)
Heroes (18)
High Time (You Quit Your Lowdown Ways) (5)
Highwayman (21)
Homeward Bound (20)
Honky Tonk Blues (17)
Honky Tonk Heroes (3,6,13)
House Of The Rising Sun (9)
Hunger, The (4)
I Ain't Living Long Like This (14)
I Ain't The One (16)
I Believe You Can (16)
I Can Get Off On You (11)
I Can't Keep My Hands Off Of You (4)
I Could Write A Book About You (24)
I Got The Train Sittin' Waitin' (14)
I May Never Pass This Way Again (2)

I Recall A Gypsy Woman (5)
I Think I'm Gonna Kill Myself (10)
I Walk The Line (12)
I'll Be Alright (16)
I'll Go Back To Her (8)
I'm A Ramblin' Man (4,9,13,19) 75
I've Always Been Crazy (12,13,19)
I've Been A Long Time Leaving (But I'll Be A Long Time Gone) (5)
If I Can Find A Clean Shirt (24)
If You See Her (14)
If You See Me Getting Smaller (10)
It'll Be Her (4)
It's Alright (15)
It's Only Rock & Roll (19)
It's The World's Gone Crazy (14)
Ivory Tower (14)
Jack A Diamonds (8)
Jim, I Wore A Tie Today (21)
Just Across The Way (2)
Just To Satisfy You (17) 52
Ladies Love Outlaws (13,19)
Lady In The Harbor (4)
Last Cowboy Song (18,21)
Last Letter (9)
Let Her Do The Walking (19)
Let Me Tell You My Mind (1)
Let's All Help The Cowboys (Sing The Blues)

Let's Turn Back The Years (5)
Living Legend (22)
Living Legends (A Dyin' Breed) (19)
Lonesome, On'ry And Mean (13)
Long Time Ago (12)
Long Way Back Home (1)
Lookin' For A Feeling (11)
Loves' Legalities (3)
Low Down Freedom (3)
Lucille (10,19)
Luckenbach, Texas (Back To The Basics Of Love) (10,13,19) 25
MacArthur Park (1,8) 93
Makin's Of A Song (24)
Mammas Don't Let Your Babies Grow Up To Be Cowboys (11,13) 42
Mary Ann Regrets (1)
May I Borrow Some Sugar From You (17,18)
Me And Bobby McGee (14)
Me And Paul (9)
Memories Of You And I (4)
Mental Revenge (19)
Midnight Rider (4)
Mr. Shuck And Jive (18)
My Heroes Have Always Been Cowboys (6)
Nashville Wimmin (15)
No Love At All (20)
No Middle Ground (19)
Oklahoma Sunshine (4)

Old Age And Treachery (24)
Old Church Hymns And Nursery Rhymes (23)
Old Five And Dimers (Like Me) (3)
Old Friend (8,20)
Old Love, New Eyes (14)
Old Mother's Locket Trick (18)
Omaha (3)
Only Daddy That'll Walk The Line (13)
Out Among The Stars (14)
Pastels And Harmony (16)
Pick Up The Tempo (9,11)
Precious Memories (8)
Put Me On A Train Back To Texas (24)
Rainy Day Woman (4,9)
Rainy Seasons (16)
Reno And Me (23)
Ride Me Down Easy (3,7)
Rocks From Rolling Stones (24)
Roman Candles (18)
Satin Sheets (10)
She's Looking Good (5)
Shine (17)
Shutting Out The Light (2)
Silver Stallion (22)
(Sittin' On) The Dock Of The Bay (18)
So Good Woman (8)
Song For The Life (17)
Songs That Make A Difference (22)
Storms Never Last (15,16)

Suspicious Minds (6)
Sweet Caroline (10)
Sweet Music Man (15)
T For Texas (9)
Take It To The Limit (20)
Teddy Bear Song (18)
Texas (22)
Them Old Love Songs (8)
These New Changing Times (1)
Thirty Third Of August (2)
This Is Getting Funny (But There Ain't Nobody Laughing) (10)
This Time (9,19)
This Time Tomorrow (I'll Be Gone) (2)
Till I Gain Control Again (10,20)
Tonight The Bottle Let Me Down (12)
Too Close To Call (23)
Tryin' To Outrun The Wind (24)
Twentieth Century Is Almost Over (21)
Two Old Sidewinders (3)
Two Stories Wide (22)
Waking Up With You (23)
Waltz Across Texas (15)
Waymore's Blues (5)
We Had It All (3,20)
We Made It As Lovers (We Just Couldn't Make It As Friends) (17)
We're All In Your Corner (22)
Welfare Line (21)
What About You (15)

What Bothers Me Most (23)
What Goes Around (14)
What's Happened To Blue Eyes (16)
Where Corn Don't Grow (23)
Where Love Has Died (2)
Whistlers And Jugglers (12)
Why Baby Why (20)
Why Do I Have To Choose (20)
Wild Side Of Life (16)
Willy The Wandering Gypsy And Me (3)
Women Do Know How To Carry On (17)
Workin' Cheap (23)
World Of Our Own (1)
Would You Lay With Me (In A Field Of Stone) (20)
Write Your Own Songs (18)
Wrong (23)
Wurlitzer Prize (I Don't Want To Get Over You) (11)
Year That Clayton Delaney Died (18)
Year 2003 Minus 25 (11)
Yellow Haired Woman (2)
Yes, Virginia (3)
You Ask Me To (3)
You Never Can Tell (C'est La Vie) (16)
You're Not My Same Sweet Baby (16)

JERKY BOYS, The   '94

Prank telephone callers from New York City: John Brennan and Kamal Ahmed. Duo starred in the 1995 movie *The Jerky Boys*.

DEBUT	PEAK	WKS	RIAA	CD	#	Album Title	Sym	$	Label & Number
4/17/93+	75	95	▲	©	1	The Jerky Boys	[C]	$10	Select 61495
9/3/94	12	34	▲	©	2	The Jerky Boys 2	[C]	$10	Select 92411
9/7/96	18	12	●	©	3	The Jerky Boys 3	[C]	$10	Ratchet 532893
10/25/97	63	8		©	4	The Jerky Boys 4	[C]	$10	Ratchet 536357
6/5/99	117	4		©	5	Stop Staring At Me!	[C]	$10	Ratchet 546063

Angry Camper's Dad (3)
Auto Mechanic (1)
Bacon (4)
Bad Ass Massage (3)
Bad Tomatoes (3)
Ball Game Beating (2)
Balloon Rides (5)
Bamm! (3)
Big Hock (5)
Bird Feed (3)
Boats Express (4)
Body Building (3)
Breast Enlargement (2)
Burial Vaults (5)
Car Salesman (1)
Chainsaw Shock (Part 1 & 2) (3)
Civil War Memorabilia (Parts 1 & 2) (3)
Cold Feet (4)
Cremation Services (2)

Dead Pet Removal (4)
Dental Malpractice (1)
Diamond Dealer (2)
Dresser, The (3)
Drinking Problem (2)
Duck Cleaning (5)
Egyptian Magician (1)
Facelift Without Surgery (3)
Fava Beans (2)
Firecracker Mishap (1)
Florida, The Tropical State (3)
Food & Drug Complaint (4)
Frank's Pickles (5)
Gay Hairdresser (2)
Gay Hard Hat (1)
Gay Model (1)
Hair Vitamins (5)
Hello Ray (The Phone Man) (4)
Herman (3)
Hey Sir! (4)
Home Wrecker (1)

Hot Rod Mover (1)
Hucklebuck (5)
Hurt At Work (1)
Husband Beating (2)
I Pickle They (5)
I'm A Diva (4)
Insulator Job (1)
Irate Tile Man (1)
Jerk Baby Jerk (4)
Kissel Crooner (3)
Kissel Sails (4)
Laser Surgery (1)
Laundromat (4)
Lawn Equipment Debate (3)
Lawnmower Sale (3)
Little Elves (4)
Little Emergency (2)
Little Information (4)
Mariposa (4)
Marriage Insurance (5)
Masturbation Box (5)

Mattress King (2)
Mining For Scotty (4)
Nam Hu? (5)
Need To Dance (4)
New Awnings (3)
No! (3)
Nuts To You (5)
1-800-How's My Driving? (3)
One Thousand Chickens Trilogy (Parts 1-3) (5)
Pablo Honey (2)
Paradise (3)
Pet Cobra (2)
Piano Tuner (1)
Pick Up Pie (5)
Pico's Mexican Hairpiece (2)
Pizza Lawyer (2)
Pork Fried Rice (5)
Punitive Damages (1)
Rizzo The Rainmaker (4)
Roofing (2)

Rosine Likes Balloons (5)
Safety Gates (3)
Santa's Delivery (3)
Scaffolding (2)
Security Service (2)
Send A Salami To Your Boy In The Army (5)
Sex Therapy (2)
Signin' (3)
Silly Food (3)
Sol's Glasses (1)
Sol's Naked Photo (2)
Sol's Nude Beach (2)
Sol's Phobia (2)
Sol's Thermometer Mishap (4)
Sol's Turnstile (4)
Sol's Warts (2)
Sparky The Clown (2)
Special Delivery (3)
Spider Monkey (4)
Sporting Goods (2)

Starter Motor Repair (1)
Stop That (3)
Super Across The Way (1)
Super Gay (5)
Sushi Chef (1)
Synchronized Swimming (5)
TV Repair (3)
Tandem Bicycles (3)
Tarbash's Cab Trouble (3)
Tarbash's New Shoes (3)
Terrorist Pizza (2)
Testing For Jeopardy (4)
Trains (4)
Truck Registration (4)
Uncle Freddie (1)
Unemployed Painter (1)
Volunteer (1)
Willie The Jackass (5)
You Wanna Scrap? (5)

JEROME, Henry   '61

Born on 11/12/17 in New York City. Bandleader/composer.

DEBUT	PEAK	WKS	RIAA	CD	#	Album Title	Sym	$	Label & Number
10/9/61	42	2				Brazen Brass Goes Hollywood	[I]	$20	Decca 4085

Around The World
Colonel Bogey
Gigi

High Noon (Do Not Forsake Me)
Love Is A Many-Splendored Thing

Man With The Golden Arm, Main Title From
Moonglow And Theme From "Picnic"

Moulin Rouge (Where Is Your Heart), Song From
Summer Place, Theme From A
Tammy - Cha Cha Cha

Third Man Theme
Three Coins In The Fountain - Cha Cha

JERU THE DAMAJA   '94

Born Kendrick Jeru Davis in Brooklyn, New York. Male rapper.

DEBUT	PEAK	WKS	CD	#	Album Title	Sym	$	Label & Number
6/11/94	36	9	©	1	The Sun Rises In The East		$10	Payday 124011
11/2/96	35	5	©	2	Wrath Of The Math		$10	Payday 124119

Ain't The Devil Happy (1)
Black Cowboys (2)
Brooklyn Took It (1)
Bullshit, Tha (2)
Come Clean (1) 88
D. Original (1)

Da Bichez (1)
Frustrated Nigga (2)
Invasion (2)
Jungle Music (1)
Me Or The Papes (2)
Mental Stamina (1)

My Mind Spray (1)
Not The Average (2)
Now I'm Livin' (2)
One Day (2)
Perverted Monks In Tha House (1)

Physical Stamina (2)
Revenge Of The Prophet (Part 5) (2)
Scientifical Madness (2)
Statik (1)
Too Perverted (2)

Whatever (2)
Wrath Of The Math (2)
Ya Playin' Yoself (2)
You Can't Stop The Prophet (1)

JESUS & MARY CHAIN, The   '94

Rock group from Glasgow, Scotland: brothers William and Jim Reid (vocals, guitars), Douglas Hart (bass) and Murray Dalglish (drums). Numerous personnel changes with the Reid brothers the only constants.

DEBUT	PEAK	WKS	CD	#	Album Title	Sym	$	Label & Number
2/22/86	188	4	©	1	Psycho Candy		$10	Reprise 25383
10/17/87	161	4	©	2	Darklands		$10	Warner 25656
6/18/88	192	3	©	3	Barbed Wire Kisses		$10	Warner 25729
11/25/89+	105	25	©	4	Automatic		$10	Warner 26015
5/2/92	158	2	©	5	Honey's Dead		$10	Def American 26830

DEBUT	PEAK	WKS	RIAA	CD	ARTIST — Album Title	Catalog	Sym	$	Label & Number

JESUS & MARY CHAIN, The — Cont'd

| 9/10/94 | 98 | 6 | | © 6 | **Stoned & Dethroned** | | | $10 | American 45573 |

About You (2)
Almost Gold (5)
April Skies (2)
Between Planets (4)
Between Us (6)
Blues From A Gun (4)
Bullet Lovers (6)
Catchfire (6)
Cherry Came Too (2)
Coast To Coast (4)
Come On (6)
Cut Dead (1)
Darklands (2)
Deep One Perfect Morning (2)

Dirty Water (6)
Don't Ever Change (3)
Down On Me (2)
Everybody I Know (6)
Everything's Alright When You're Down (3)
Fall (2)
Far Gone And Out (5)
Feeling Lucky (6)
Frequency (5)
Gimme Hell (4)
Girlfriend (6)
God Help Me (6)
Good For My Soul (5)

Half Way To Crazy (4)
Happy Place (3)
Happy When It Rains (2)
Hardest Walk (1)
Head (3)
Head On (4)
Her Way Of Praying (4)
Here Comes Alice (4)
Hit (3)
Hole (6)
I Can't Get Enough (5)
In A Hole (1)
Inside Me (1)
It's So Hard (1)

Just Like Honey (1)
Just Out Of Reach (3)
Kill Surf City (3)
Living End (1)
My Little Underground (1)
Never Saw It Coming (6)
Never Understand (1)
Nine Million Rainy Days (2)
On The Wall (2,3)
Psycho Candy (3)
Reverence (5)
Rider (3)
Rollercoaster (5)
Save Me (6)

She (6)
Sidewalking (3)
Something's Wrong (1)
Sometimes Always (6) *96*
Sowing Seeds (1)
Sugar Ray (5)
Sundown (5)
Surfin' USA (3)
Swing (3)
Take It (4)
Taste Of Cindy (1,3)
Taste The Floor (1)
Teenage Lust (5)
These Days (5)

Till It Shines (6)
Tumbledown (5)
UV Ray (4)
Upside Down (3)
Who Do You Love (3)
Wish I Could (6)
You Trip Me Up (1)
You've Been A Friend (6)

JESUS JONES '91

Pop-rock group formed in London: Mike Edwards (vocals, guitar), Jerry DeBorg (guitar), Iain Baker (keyboards), Al Jaworski (bass) and Simon Matthews (drums).

| 2/23/91 | 25 | 52 | ▲ | © 1 | **Doubt** | | | $10 | Food 95715 |
| 2/13/93 | 59 | 6 | | © 2 | **Perverse** | | | $10 | Food 80647 |

Are You Satisfied (1)
Blissed (1)
Devil You Know (2)
Don't Believe It (2)
From Love To War (2)

Get A Good Thing (2)
I'm Burning (1)
Idiot Stare (2)
International Bright Young Thing (1)

Magazine (2)
Nothing To Hold Me (1)
Real, Real, Real (1) *4*
Right Decision (2)
Right Here, Right Now (1) *2*

Spiral (2)
Stripped (1)
Tongue Tied (2)
Trust Me (1)
Two And Two (1)

Welcome Back Victoria (1)
Who? Where? Why? (1)
Yellow Brown (2)
Your Crusade (1)
Zeroes And Ones (1)

JETBOY '88

Hard-rock group from San Francisco: Mickey Finn (vocals), Fernie Rod and Billy Rowe (guitars), Sam Yaffa (bass) and Ron Tostenson (drums).

| 11/12/88 | 135 | 10 | | © | **Feel The Shake** | | | $10 | MCA 42235 |

Bad Disease
Bloodstone

Feel The Shake
Fire In My Heart

Hard Climb
Hometown Blues

Locked In A Cage
Make Some Noise

Snakebite
Talkin'

JETHRO TULL ★61★ '72

Progressive-rock group formed in Blackpool, England: Ian Anderson (vocals, flute), Mick Abrahams (guitar), Glenn Cornick (bass) and Clive Bunker (drums). Group named after 18th-century agriculturist/inventor of seed drill. Abrahams left after recording of first album (in 1968) to form **Blodwyn Pig**, replaced by Martin Barre. Added keyboardist John Evan in 1970. Cornick replaced by Jeffrey Hammond-Hammond in 1971. Bunker left in late 1971, replaced by Barriemore Barlow. John Glascock replaced Hammond-Hammond by 1976. Glascock died in 1979, replaced by bassist David Pegg. Since 1980, Anderson and Barre have fronted several lineups that have included Pegg and drummer Doane Perry.

1)Thick As A Brick 2)A Passion Play 3)War Child 4)Living In The Past 5)Aqualung

3/1/69	62	17		© 1	**This Was**			$20	Reprise 6336
10/11/69	20	40	●	© 2	**Stand Up**			$20	Reprise 6360
5/9/70	11	41	●	© 3	**Benefit**			$15	Reprise 6400
5/15/71	7	76	▲³	© 4	**Aqualung**			$15	Reprise 2035
5/20/72	❶²	46	●	© 5	**Thick As A Brick**			$15	Reprise 2072
11/11/72	3	31	●	© 6	**Living In The Past**		[K]	$20	Chrysalis 1035 [2]
7/21/73	❶¹	32	●	© 7	**A Passion Play**			$15	Chrysalis 1040
10/26/74	2³	31	●	© 8	**War Child**			$15	Chrysalis 1067
9/27/75	7	14	●	© 9	**Minstrel In The Gallery**			$15	Chrysalis 1082
1/24/76	13	23	▲	© 10	**M.U. - The Best Of Jethro Tull**		[G]	$15	Chrysalis 1078
5/29/76	14	21		© 11	**Too Old To Rock 'N' Roll: Too Young To Die!**			$15	Chrysalis 1111
3/5/77	8	22	●	© 12	**Songs From The Wood**			$12	Chrysalis 1132
12/3/77	94	6		© 13	**Repeat-The Best Of Jethro Tull, Vol. II**		[G]	$12	Chrysalis 1135
4/29/78	19	17		© 14	**Heavy Horses**			$12	Chrysalis 1175
10/21/78	21	15	●	© 15	**Jethro Tull Live - Bursting Out**		[L]	$15	Chrysalis 1201 [2]
10/6/79	22	17		© 16	**Stormwatch**			$12	Chrysalis 1238
9/13/80	30	12		© 17	**"A"**			$12	Chrysalis 1301
5/1/82	19	17		© 18	**The Broadsword And The Beast**			$12	Chrysalis 1380
10/27/84	76	12		© 19	**Under Wraps**			$12	Chrysalis 41461
10/10/87	32	28	●	© 20	**Crest Of A Knave**			$12	Chrysalis 41590
8/13/88	97	15		© 21	**20 Years Of Jethro Tull**		[K]	$50	Chrysalis 41653 [5]
9/30/89	56	18		© 22	**Rock Island**			$10	Chrysalis 21708
9/28/91	88	5		© 23	**Catfish Rising**			$10	Chrysalis 21863
10/10/92	150	2		© 24	**A Little Light Music**		[L]	$10	Chrysalis 21954
9/30/95	114	1		© 25	**Roots To Branches**			$10	Chrysalis 35418
9/11/99	161	1		© 26	**J-Tull Dot Com**			$10	Fuel 2000 1043

AWOL (26)
Acres Wild (14)
Aeroplane (21)
Alive And Well And Living In (6)
And Further On (17)
And The Mouse Police Never Sleeps (14)
Another Christmas Song (22)
Another Harry's Bar (25)
Apogee (17)
Aqualung (4,10,15,21)
At Last, Forever (25)
Back-Door Angels (8)
Back To Family (2)

Bad-Eyed And Loveless (11)
Baker St. Muse Medley (9)
Batteries Not Included (17)
Beastie (18)
Beggar's Farm (1)
Beltane (21)
Bends Like A Willow (26)
Beside Myself (25)
Big Dipper (11)
Big Riff And Mando (22)
Black Mamba (26)
Black Satin Dancer (9,21)
Black Sunday (17)

Blues Instrumental (Untitled) (21)
Bouree (2,6,13,15,21,24)
Broadsword (18)
Budapest (20)
Bungle In The Jungle (8,10,21) *12*
By Kind Permission Of (6)
Cat's Squirrel (1)
Chateau D'Isaster Tapes Medley (21)
Cheap Day Return (4,21)
Cheerio (18)

Chequered Flag (Dead Or Alive) (11)
Christmas Song (6,24)
Clasp, The (18,21)
Cold Wind To Valhalla (9,21)
Conundrum (15)
Coronach (21)
Crazed Institution (11)
Cross-Eyed Mary (4,13,15)
Crossfire (17)
Crossword (21)
Cup Of Wonder (12)
Dambusters March/Medley (15)
Dangerous Veils (25)

Dark Ages (16)
Dharma For One (1,6)
Dr. Bogenbroom (6)
Doctor To My Disease (23)
Dog-Ear Years (26)
Dot Com (26)
Down At The End Of Your Road (21)
Driving Song (6)
Dun Ringill (16,21)
Ears Of Tin (22)
El Niño (26)
Elegy (16)
European Legacy (19)

Fallen On Hard Times (18,21)
Far Alaska (26)
Farm On The Freeway (20,21)
Fat Man (2,10,21)
Fire At Midnight (12)
Flute Solo Improvisation (medley) (15)
Flying Colours (18)
Flying Dutchman (16)
For A Thousand Mothers (2)
For Michael Collins, Jeffrey And Me (3)
4.W.D. (Low Ratio) (17)

JETHRO TULL — Cont'd

From A Dead Beat To An Old Greaser (11,24)
From Later (6)
Fylingdale Flyer (17)
Gift Of Roses (26)
Glory Row (13)
God Rest Ye Merry Gentlemen (medley) (15)
Gold-Tipped Boots, Black Jacket And Tie (23)
Grace (9,21)
Heat (19)
Heavy Horses (14)
Heavy Water (22)
Home (16)
Hot Mango Flush (26)
Hunt By Numbers (26)
Hunting Girl (12,15)
Hymn 43 (4,6) *91*
I'm Your Gun (21)
Inside (3)
It's Breaking Me Up (1)
Jack-A-Lynn (21)
Jack Frost And The Hooded Crow (21)
Jack-In-The-Green (12,15)
Jeffrey Goes To Leicester Square (2)
John Barleycorn (24)
Journey Man (14)
Jump Start (20)
Just Trying To Be (6)
Kelpie (21)

King Henry's Madrigal (21)
Kissing Willie (22)
Ladies (8)
Lap Of Luxury (19)
Later, That Same Evening (19)
Lick Your Fingers Clean (21)
Life Is A Long Song (6,21,24)
Like A Tall Thin Girl (19)
Living In The Past (6,10,21,24) *77*
Living In These Hard Times (21)
Locomotive Breath (4,10,15,21,24) *62*
Look Into The Sun (2,24)
Love Story (6,21)
Mango Surprise (26)
March The Mad Scientist (21)
Mayhem, Maybe (21)
Minstrel In The Gallery (9,13,15,21) *79*
Mother Goose (4)
Moths (14,21)
Motoreyes (21)
Mountain Men (20)
Move On Alone (1)
My God (4)
My Sunday Feeling (1)
New Day Yesterday (2,13,15,21,24)
No Lullaby (14,15)
Nobody's Car (19)
North Sea Oil (16)

Nothing Is Easy (2,10)
Nothing To Say (3)
Nursie (6,21,24)
Occasional Demons (23)
Old Ghosts (16)
One Brown Mouse (14,15)
One For John Gee (21)
One White Duck (9,21,24)
Only Solitaire (8,21)
Orion (16)
Out Of The Noise (25)
Overhang (21)
Pan Dance (21)
Paparazzi (21)
Part Of The Machine (21)
Passion Play (7)
Passion Play (Edit #8) (10) *80*
Passion Play Edit #9 (13)
Pibroch (Cap In Hand) (12,21)
Pied Piper (11)
Pine Marten's Jig (17)
Play In Time (3)
Protect And Survive (17)
Pussy Willow (18,24)
Quatrain (15)
Queen And Country (8)
Quizz Kid (11)
Radio Free Moscow (19)
Rainbow Blues (10)
Raising Steam (20)
Rare And Precious Chain (25)
Rattlesnake Trail (22)
Reasons For Waiting (2)

Requiem (9)
Rhythm In Gold (21)
Ring Out, Solstice Bells (12)
Rock Island (22)
Rocks On The Road (23,24)
Roll Yer Own (23)
Roots To Branches (25)
Round (1)
Rover (1)
Saboteur (19)
Said She Was A Dancer (20)
Salamander (11,21)
Saturation (21)
SeaLion (8)
Seal Driver (18)
Serenade To A Cuckoo (1)
Singing All Day (6)
Skating Away On The Thin Ice Of The New Day (8,10,15)
Sleeping With The Dog (23)
Slipstream (4)
Slow Marching Band (18)
Some Day The Sun Won't Shine For You (1,24)
Something's On The Move (16)
Son (3)
Song For Jeffrey (1,6,21)
Songs From The Wood (12,15,21)
Sossity; You're A Woman (3)
Sparrow On The Schoolyard Wall (23)

Spiral (26)
Steel Monkey (20)
Still Loving You Tonight (23)
Stitch In Time (21)
Stormy Monday Blues (21)
Story Of The Hare Who Lost His Spectacles (7)
Strange Avenues (22)
Strip Cartoon (21)
Stuck In The August Rain (25)
Summerday Sands (21)
Sunshine Day (21)
Sweet Dream (6,15,21)
Taxi Grab (11)
Teacher (3,6,10,21)
Thick As A Brick (5,15,21)
Thick As A Brick Edit #1 (10)
Thick As A Brick Edit #4 (13)
Thinking Round Corners (23)
Third Hoorah (8)
This Free Will (25)
This Is Not Love (23,24)
Time For Everything (3)
To Cry You A Song (3,13)
Too Many Too (21)
Too Old To Rock 'N' Roll: Too Young To Die (11,13,15,24)
Two Fingers (8)
Under Wraps #1 & 2 (19,21,24)
Undressed To Kill (22)
Uniform (17)
Up The 'Pool (6)
Up To Me (4)

Valley (25)
Velvet Green (12,21)
WarChild (8,13)
Warm Sporran (16)
Watching Me Watching You (18)
We Used To Know (2)
Weathercock (14)
Whalers Dues (22)
When Jesus Came To Play (23)
Whistler, The (12) *59*
White Innocence (23)
Wicked Windows (26)
Wind-Up (8)
Witch's Promise (6,21)
With You There To Help Me (1)
Wond'ring Again (6)
Wond'ring Aloud (4,21)
Working John - Working Joe (17)
Wounded, Old And Treacherous (25)
0 = Nothing At All (medley) (9,21)

JETS, The '86

Family group from Minneapolis: siblings Leroy, Eddie, Eugene, Haini, Rudy, Kathi, Elizabeth and Moana Wolfgramm. Their parents are from the South Pacific country of Tonga. All members play at least two instruments. Eugene left group and formed duo **Boys Club** in 1988.

DEBUT	PEAK	WKS	RIAA	CD	#	Album	Sym	$	Label
4/5/86	21	70	▲	©	1	**The Jets**		$10	MCA 5667
11/7/87+	35	50	●	©	2	**Magic**		$10	MCA 42085
12/10/88	30ˣ	2		©	3	**Christmas with The Jets**	[X]	$10	MCA 5856
9/2/89	107	7		©	4	**Believe**		$10	MCA 6313

All Alone On Christmas Eve (3)
Anytime (2)
Believe In Love (4)
Believe It Or Not, It's Magic (2)
Christmas In My Heart (3)
Christmas Is My Favorite Time Of Year (3)
Cross My Broken Heart (2) *7*

Crush On You (1) *3*
Curiosity (1)
Do You Remember (4)
Emotional (4)
First Time In Love (2)
Heart On The Line (1)
How Can I Be Sure (4)
I Do You (2) *20*

I'm Home For Christmas (3)
In My Dreams (4)
La La Means I Love You (1)
Leave It To Me (4)
Love So Rare (3)
Love Umbrella (1)
Make It Real (2) *4*
Mesmerized (4)

On Christmas Night (3)
Only Dance (2)
Private Number (1) *47*
Right Before My Eyes (1)
Rocket 2 U (2) *6*
Same Love (4) *87*
Sendin' All My Love (2) *88*
Somebody To Love Me (4)

Somewhere Out There (3)
This Christmas (2)
This Christmas, This Year (3)
Under Any Moon (1)
When You're Young And In Love (2)
You Better Dance (4) *59*
You Got It All (1) *3*

You Make It Christmas (3)
You've Got Another Boyfriend (4)

JETT, Joan, & The Blackhearts '82

Born Joan Larkin on 9/22/60 in Philadelphia. Rock singer/guitarist. Member of **The Runaways** from 1975-78. The Blackhearts: Ricky Byrd (guitar; **Susan**), Gary Ryan (bass) and Lee Crystal (drums). **Kasim Sulton** and Thommy Price replaced Ryan and Crystal in 1987. Jett starred in the 1987 movie *Light Of Day* as the leader of a rock band called The Barbusters.

DEBUT	PEAK	WKS	RIAA	CD	#	Album	$	Label
3/14/81+	51	21		©	1	**Bad Reputation**	$12	Boardwalk 37065
12/19/81+	2³	59	▲	©	2	**I Love Rock-N-Roll**	$12	Boardwalk 33243
7/16/83	20	20	●	©	3	**Album**	$10	Blackheart 5437
10/27/84	67	21		©	4	**Glorious Results Of A Misspent Youth**	$10	Blackheart 5476
10/25/86	105	16		©	5	**Good Music**	$10	Blackheart 40544
5/28/88	19	46	▲	©	6	**Up Your Alley**	$10	Blackheart 44146
2/3/90	36	18		©	7	**The Hit List**	$10	Blackheart 45473

JOAN JETT

Back It Up (6)
Bad Reputation (1)
Be Straight (2)
Bits And Pieces (2)
Black Leather (5)
Celluloid Heroes (7)
Cherry Bomb (4)
Coney Island Whitefish (3)
Contact (5)
Crimson And Clover (2) *7*
Desire (6)
Dirty Deeds (7) *36*
Do You Wanna Touch Me (Oh Yeah) (1) *20*

Doing All Right With The Boys (1)
Don't Abuse Me (1)
Everyday People (3) *37*
Fake Friends (3) *35*
French Song (3)
Frustrated (4)
Fun, Fun, Fun (5)
Good Music (5) *83*
Had Enough (3)
Handyman (3)
Have You Ever Seen The Rain? (7)
Hold On (5)

Hundred Feet Away (3)
I Got No Answers (4)
I Hate Myself For Loving You (6) *8*
I Love Playin' With Fire (3)
I Love You Love Me Love (4)
I Need Someone (4)
I Still Dream About You (6)
I Wanna Be Your Dog (6)
(I'm Gonna) Run Away (2)
If Ya Want My Luv (5)
Jezebel (1)
Just Like In The Movies (6)

Just Lust (5)
Let Me Go (1)
Little Drummer Boy (2)
Little Liar (6) *19*
Long Time (4)
Love Hurts (7)
Love Is Pain (2)
Love Like Mine (4)
Love Me Two Times (7)
Make Believe (1)
Nag (2)
New Orleans (4)
Outlaw (5)
Play That Song Again (6)

Pretty Vacant (7)
Push And Stomp (4)
Ridin' With James Dean (5)
Roadrunner (5)
Roadrunner USA (7)
Secret Love (3)
Shout (1)
Someday (4)
Talkin Bout My Baby (4)
This Means War (5)
Time Has Come Today (7)
Too Bad On Your Birthday (1)
Tossin' & Turnin' (4)
Tulane (6)

Tush (7)
Up From The Skies (7)
Victim Of Circumstance (2)
Why Can't We Be Happy (3)
Wooly Bully (1)
You Don't Know What You've Got (1)
You Don't Own Me (1)
You Got Me Floatin' (5)
You Want In I Want Out (5)
You're Too Possessive (2)

JEWEL '98

Born Jewel Kilcher on 5/23/74 in Payson, Utah; raised in Homer, Alaska. Singer/songwriter/guitarist. Wrote own book of poetry. Played "Sue Lee Shelley" in the movie *Ride With The Devil*.

DEBUT	PEAK	WKS	RIAA	CD	#	Album	Chart	Sym	$	Label
2/17/96+	4	114	▲¹¹	©	1	**Pieces Of You**	C:#4/61		$10	Atlantic 82700
12/5/98	3	51	▲⁴	©	2	**Spirit**			$10	Atlantic 82950
11/20/99	32	9	▲	©	3	**Joy: A Holiday Collection**	C:#5/8	[X]	$10	Atlantic 83250

Christmas charts: 2/'99, 11/'00

Absence Of Fear (2)
Adrian (1)
Amen (1)
Angel Standing By (1)
Ave Maria (3)
Barcelona (2)
Daddy (1)
Deep Water (2)

Do You (2)
Don't (1)
Down So Long (2) *59*
Enter From The East (2)
Face Of Love (3)
Fat Boy (3)
Foolish Games (1) *7*
From A Distance (medley) (3)

Gloria (3)
Go Tell It On The Mountain (medley) (3)
Hands (2,3) *6*
Hark! The Herald Angels Sing (3)
I Wonder As I Wander (3)
I'm Sensitive (1)

Innocence Maintained (2)
Joy To The World (3)
Jupiter (2)
Kiss The Flame (2)
Life Uncommon (2,3)
Little Sister (1)
Morning Song (1)
Near You Always (1)

O Holy Night (3)
O Little Town Of Bethlehem (3)
Painters (1)
Pieces Of You (1)
Rudolph The Red-Nosed Reindeer (3)
Silent Night (3)
This Little Bird (2)

What's Simple Is True (2)
Who Will Save Your Soul (1) *11*
Winter Wonderland (3)
You Were Meant For Me (1) *2*

JIGSAW '76

Pop group from England: Des Dyer (vocals, drums), Tony Campbell (guitar), Clive Scott (keyboards) and Barrie Bernard (bass).

| 12/13/75+ | 55 | 19 | | | Sky High .... | | | $12 | Chelsea 509 |

Baby Don't Do It
Call Collect
Have You Heard The News

I've Seen The Film, I've Read
  The Book
Listen To The Joker

Love Fire *30*
Mention My Name
Mystic Harmony

Sky High *3*
Tell Me Why
That's The Way It Goes

JIMENEZ, Jose '61

Born William Szarthmary on 10/5/24 in Quincy, Massachusetts. Stage name: Bill Dana. Head writer for **Steve Allen**'s TV show. Star of own TV series from 1963-65. Created the Latin American comic character "Jose Jimenez."

8/1/60	15	29			1 My Name...Jose Jimenez		[C]	$25	Signature 1013
7/17/61	5	51			2 Jose Jimenez - The Astronaut (The First Man In Space)		[C]	$20	Kapp 1238
12/25/61+	109	9			3 More...Jose Jimenez		[C]	$20	Kapp 1215
1/13/62	32	22			4 Jose Jimenez In Orbit/Bill Dana On Earth		[C]	$20	Kapp 1257
10/13/62	16	20			5 Jose Jimenez Talks To Teenagers Of All Ages		[C]	$20	Kapp 1304
2/23/63	30	14			6 Jose Jimenez - Our Secret Weapon		[C]	$20	Kapp 1320
12/14/63	128	4			7 Jose Jimenez In Jollywood		[C]	$20	Kapp 1332

Admiral, The (6)
Another History Lesson -
  George Washington (5)
Any Questions? (2)
Artist, The (3)
Astronaut (Parts 1 & 2) (2) 19
Baseball Star (5)
Bob Sled Racer (1)
Broadway Writer (3)
Burgemeister, The (1)
Cheerleader, The (5)

Child Star (7)
Civil Defense Director (6)
Coast Guardsman (6)
Darling, Je Vous Aime
  Beaucoup (2)
Deep Sea Diver (1)
Dialogue Director (7)
Director Of The Central
  Intelligence Agency (6)
Etiquette Expert (5)
Everything's A OK (4)
General, The (6)

History Lesson - Christopher
  Columbus (5)
Hollywood Agent (7)
Hollywood Columnist (7)
Infantryman, The (6)
J.J.J. Salesman (3)
Jingle Bells (4)
Jose And Cleopatra (7)
Judo Expert (3)
K-9 Corps (6)
King Of The Surf (7)
Lance Playboy (7)

Lion Tamer (4)
Look Award (1)
Mail Call (6)
Man In The Pub (1)
Marine Drill Instructor (6)
Marriage Counselor (5)
Musical Director (1)
My Alma Mater (5)
My Funny Valentine (4)
My Night Club Act (2)
Paratrooper, The (6)
Piano Tuner (3)

Presenting Bill Dana (2)
Presidential Trip (1)
Press Conference (1)
Psychiatrist, The (7)
Rancher, The (4)
Sailor, The (6)
Santa Claus (1)
Shakespeare (1)
Shakespearean Actor (7)
Shine On Harvest Moon (4)
Skin Diver (4)
Smog Expert (7)

Submarine Officer (3)
Teenage Problems (5)
Television Engineer (5)
U.S. Senator (1,4)
Vocational Guidance Counselor
  (5)
Warmup From Spike Jones
  Show (3)
What Kind Of Fool Am I (7)
With Steve (1)

JIMMIE'S CHICKEN SHACK '99

Rock group from Bowie, Maryland: Jimmie HaHa (vocals), Jimmy McD (guitar), Che Colovita Lemon (bass) and Jimmy Chaney (drums).

| 9/11/99 | 153 | 7 | | © | Bring Your Own Stereo.. | | | $10 | Rocket 546382 |

Do Right
Face It
Fill In The Blank

Lazy Boy Dash
Let's Get Flat
Ooh

Pure
Silence Again
Spiraling

String Of Pearls
30 Days
Trash

Waiting

JINGLE CATS, The '93

The sounds of real cats digitally mastered into song by Mike Spalla. The cats are Cheese Puff, Max, Sprocket, Binky, Clara, Cueball, Graymer, Twizzler and Petunia.

| 12/25/93+ | 86 | 3 | | © | 1 Meowy Christmas .... | C:#10/6 | [X-N] | $10 | Jingle Cats 41226 |

Christmas charts: 19/'93, 14/'94, 40/'95

| 12/31/94 | 182 | 1 | | © | 2 Here Comes Santa Claws .... | | [X-N] | $10 | Jingle Cats 41229 |

Christmas chart: 39/'94

Angels We Have Heard On
  High (1)
Auld Lang Syne (1)
Ave Maria (2)
Bird In A Gilded Cage (2)
Blue Christmas (1)
Blue Danube Waltz (2)
Carol Of The Bells (1)

Chipmunk Song (2)
Christmas Song (2)
Dance Of The Reed Flutes (1)
Dance Of The Sugarplum
  Fairies (2)
Deck The Halls (1)
Frosty The Snowman (2)
Go Tell It On The Mountain (1)

God Rest Ye Merry Gentlemen
  (1)
Good King Wenceslas (1)
Hatikva (2)
Here Comes Santa Claus (2)
I'll Be Home For Christmas (2)
It Came Upon The Midnight
  Clear (2)

Jesu, Joy Of Man's Desiring (1)
Jingle Cats Legend (2)
Jingle Cats Medley (1)
Joy To The World (2)
Little Drummer Boy (2)
My Favorite Things (2)
Ode To Joy (1)
Oh Christmas Tree (1)

Oh Come All Ye Faithful (1)
Oh Holy Night (2)
Oh Little Town Of Bethlehem
  (1)
Rudolph The Red Nosed
  Reindeer (2)
Silent Night (1)
Up On The Housetop (1)

Waltz Of The Flowers (1)
We Three Kings Of Orient Are
  (1)
What Child Is This? (1)
White Christmas (2)

JIVE BUNNY AND THE MASTERMIXERS '90

Group from England: DJ Les Hemstock and mixers John Pickles, his son Andy Pickles and Ian Morgan.

| 1/6/90 | 26 | 18 | ● | © | The Album.. | | | $10 | Music Factory 91322 |

Do You Wanna Rock
Glen Miller Medley

Hopping Mad
Lover's Mix

Rock And Roll Party Mix
Swing Sisters Swing

Swing The Mood *11*
That's What I Like *69*

J.J. FAD '88

Female rap trio from Los Angeles: Juana Burns, Dania Birks and Michelle Franklin. J.J. Fad stands for Just Jammin' Fresh And Def.

| 7/23/88 | 49 | 30 | ● | © | Supersonic - The Album.. | | | $10 | Ruthless 90959 |

produced by **Dr. Dre**

Blame It On The Muzick
Eenie Meenie Beats

In The Mix
Is It Love *92*

Let's Get Hyped
Now Really

Supersonic *30*
Time Tah Get Stupid

Way Out *61*

JO, Damita — see DAMITA JO

JOBIM, Antonio Carlos '67

Born on 1/25/27 in Rio de Janerio. Died on 12/8/94 (age 67). Singer/songwriter/guitarist.

9/11/65	57	14		©	1 The Wonderful World Of Antonio Carlos Jobim			$20	Warner 1611
4/15/67	19	28		©	2 Francis Albert Sinatra & Antonio Carlos Jobim.............			$20	Reprise 1021
1/13/68	114	11		©	3 Wave		[I]	$15	A&M 3002
1/9/71	196	2		©	4 Stone Flower		[I]	$15	CTI 6002

Amparo (4)
Andorinha (4)
Antigua (3)
Aqua De Beber (1)
Batidinha (3)
Baubles, Bangles And Beads
  (2)
Bonita (1)

Brazil (4)
Captain Bacardi (3)
Change Partners (2)
Children's Games (4)
Choro (4)
Dialogo (3)
Dindi (1,2)
Favela (1)

Felicidade (1)
Girl From Ipanema (2)
God And The Devil In The Land
  Of The Sun (4)
How Insensitive (2)
I Concentrate On You (2)
If You Never Come To Me (2)
Lamento (3)

Look To The Sky (3)
Meditation (2)
Mojave (3)
Once I Loved (2)
Por Toda A Minha Vida (1)
Quiet Nights Of Quiet Stars
  (Corcovado) (2)
Red Blouse (3)

Sabia (4)
Samba Do Aviao (1)
She's A Carioca (1)
So' Tinha De Ser Com Voce (1)
Stone Flower (4)
Surfboard (1)
Tereza My Love (4)
Triste (3)

Useless Landscape (1)
Valsa De Porto Das Caixas (1)
Wave (3)

JoBOXERS '83

Pop group formed in London: Dig Wayne (vocals), Rob Marche (guitar), Dave Collard (keybaords), Chris Bostock (bass) and Sean McLusky (drums).

| 10/15/83 | 70 | 15 | | | Like Gangbusters.. | | | $10 | RCA Victor 4847 |

Boxerbeat
Crime Of Passion

Crosstown Walk Up
Curious George

Fully Booked
Hide Nor Hair

Johnny Friendly
Just Got Lucky *36*

Not My Night
She's Got Sex

JODECI '95

R&B vocal group. Two pairs of brothers from Tiny Grove, North Carolina: Joel "JoJo" and Cedric "K-Ci" Hailey, with Dalvin and Donald "DeVante Swing" DeGrate. Also see K-Ci & JoJo.

9/14/91+	18	83	▲³	©	1 Forever My Lady			$10	Uptown 10198
1/8/94	3	36	▲²	©	2 Diary Of A Mad Band			$10	Uptown 10915
8/5/95	2¹	46	▲	©	3 The Show - The After-Party - The Hotel			$10	Uptown 11258

Alone (2)
Bring On Da' Funk (3)
Can We Flo? (3)
Come & Talk To Me (1) *11*
Cry For You (3) *15*
Fallin' (3)
Feenin' (2) *25*

(553-NASTY) (1)
Forever My Lady (1) *25*
Freek'n You (3) *14*
Fun 2Nite (3)
Get On Up (3) *22*
Gimme All You Got (2)
Good Luv (3)

Gotta Love (1)
I'm Still Waiting (3) *85*
In The Meanwhile (2)
It's Alright (1)
Jodecial Hotline (2)
Let's Do It (3)
Love U 4 Life (3) *31*

My Heart Belongs To U (2)
My Phone (1)
Play Thang (1)
Pump It Back (3)
Ride & Slide (2)
S-More (3)
Show, The (3)

Stay (1) *41*
Success (2)
Sweaty (2)
Time & Place (3)
Xs We Share (1)
Treat U (1)
U & I (1)

What About Us (2)
Won't Waste You (3)
You Got It (2)
Zipper (3)

JOE '00

Born Joseph Thomas in 1972 in Cuthbert, Georgia. R&B singer/songwriter/guitarist.

9/11/93	105	11		©	1 Everything			$10	Mercury 518016
8/16/97	13	46	▲	©	2 All That I Am	C:#44/2		$10	Jive 41603
5/6/00	2¹	60	▲³	©	3 My Name Is Joe			$10	Jive 41703

All Or Nothing (1)
All That I Am (2)
All The Things (Your Man Won't Do) (2) *11*
Baby Don't Stop (1)
Black Hawk (3)
Come Around (2)

Don't Wanna Be A Player (2) *21*
Everything (1)
Finally Back (1)
Get A Little Closer (1)
Get Crunk Tonight (3)

Good Girls (2)
How Soon (2)
I Believe In You (3)
I Can Do It Right (1)
I Wanna Know (3) *4*
I'm In Luv (1) *64*
If Loving You Is Wrong (1)

It's Alright (1)
Love Don't Make No Sense (2)
Love Scene (2)
No One Else Comes Close (2)
One For Me (1)
One Life Stand (3)
Peep Show (3)

Sanctified Girl (Can't Fight This Feeling) (2)
So Beautiful (3)
Somebody Gotta Be On Top (3)
Stutter (3) *1*
Table For Two (3)
Thank God I Found You (3) *1*

Treat Her Like A Lady (3) *63*
U Shoulda Told Me (U Had A Man) (2)
What's On Your Mind (1)

JOE & EDDIE '64

Black folk duo from Berkeley, California: Joe Gilbert and Eddie Brown. Joe died on 8/6/66 (age 25).

1/18/64	119	7			1 There's A Meetin' Here Tonite		[L]	$20	Crescendo 86
2/15/64	140	4			2 Coast To Coast		[L]	$20	Crescendo 96

Amen! (2)
Children Go! (1)
Crawfish (1)
Drinking Gourd (1)
Farewell My Cindy Jane (2)

First Time (2)
I Laid Around (1)
I Loved A Lass (2)
Joshua (2)
Kisses Sweeter Than Wine (1)

Laurie (2)
Lonely And A Lonesome Traveler (1)
Make A Long Time Man Feel Bad (2)

Mariah (1)
Muddy Old River (1)
Old Man (1)
San Francisco Bay Blues (2)
Scarlet Ribbons (1)

Sing Hallelujah! (1)
Summer's Over (1)
There's A Meetin' Here Tonite (1)
Water Is Wide (2)

JOEL, Billy ★58★ '78

Born William Martin Joel on 5/9/49 in the Bronx, New York; raised in Hicksville, Long Island, New York. Pop-rock singer/songwriter/pianist. Member of The Hassles in the late 1960s. Involved in a serious motorcycle accident in Long Island in 1982. Married to supermodel Christie Brinkley from 1985-94. Recipient of Grammy's Living Legends Award in 1990 and Billboard's Century Award in 1994. Inducted into the Rock and Roll Hall of Fame in 1999.

1)52nd Street 2)Glass Houses 3)River Of Dreams

1/5/74	27	40	▲⁴	©	1 Piano Man	C:❶⁴/257		$15	Columbia 32544
11/2/74	35	18	▲	©	2 Streetlife Serenade			$15	Columbia 33146
6/5/76	122	12	▲	©	3 Turnstiles	C:#28/40		$15	Columbia 33848
10/8/77+	2⁶	137	▲⁹	©	4 The Stranger	C:#32/13		$12	Columbia 34987
10/28/78	❶⁸	76	▲⁷	©	5 52nd Street			$12	Columbia 35609
					1979 Grammy winner: Album of the Year				
3/22/80	❶⁶	73	▲⁷	©	6 Glass Houses			$12	Columbia 36384
10/3/81	8	27	▲³	©	7 Songs In The Attic		[L]	$12	Columbia 37461
10/16/82	7	35	▲²	©	8 The Nylon Curtain			$12	Columbia 38200
8/20/83	4	111	▲⁷	©	9 An Innocent Man			$12	Columbia 38837
1/14/84	158	8		©	10 Cold Spring Harbor		[E]	$12	Columbia 38984
					remix of his first album (released in 1971 on Family 2700)				
7/20/85	6	65	▲²¹	©	11 Greatest Hits, Volume I & Volume II	C:#8/224	[G]	$15	Columbia 40121 [2]
8/16/86	7	47	▲²	©	12 The Bridge			$10	Columbia 40402
11/7/87	38	18	▲	©	13 Kohu,ept.		[L]	$15	Columbia 40996 [2]
					recorded in Leningrad (St. Petersburg), Russia; title translates roughly to: "In Concert"				
11/4/89	❶¹	69	▲⁴	©	14 Storm Front			$10	Columbia 44366
8/28/93	❶³	56	▲⁵	©	15 River Of Dreams			$10	Columbia 53003
9/6/97	9	28	▲	©	16 Greatest Hits Volume III		[G]	$10	Columbia 67347
5/20/00	40	8	●		2000 Years - The Millennium Concert		[L]	$15	Columbia 63792 [2]
					recorded on 12/31/99 at Madison Square Garden				

A Minor Variation (15)
Ain't No Crime (1)
All About Soul (15,16) *29*
All For Leyna (6)
All You Wanna Do Is Dance (3)
Allentown (8,11,13,17) *17*
And So It Goes (14,16) *37*
Angry Young Man (3,13,17)
Auld Lang Syne (17)
Baby Grand (12,13,16) *75*
Back In The U.S.S.R. (13)
Ballad Of Billy The Kid (1,7,17)
Beethoven's Ninth Symphony (17)

Big Man On Mulberry Street (12,13,17)
Big Shot (5,11,13,17) *14*
Blonde Over Blue (15)
C'Etait Toi (You Were The One) (6)
Captain Jack (1,7)
Careless Talk (9)
Christie Lee (9)
Close To The Borderline (6)
Code Of Silence (12)
Dance To The Music (13)
Don't Ask Me Why (6,11,17) *19*
Downeaster "Alexa" (14,16) *57*

Easy Money (9)
Entertainer, The (2) *34*
Everybody Has A Dream (4)
Everybody Loves You Now (7,10)
Falling Of The Rain (10)
Famous Last Words (15)
52nd Street (5)
Get It Right The First Time (4)
Getting Closer (14)
Goodnight Saigon (8,11,13,17) *56*
Got To Begin Again (10)
Great Suburban Showdown (2)
Great Wall Of China (15)

Half A Mile Away (5)
Hey Girl (16)
Honesty (5,13) *24*
Honky Tonk Women (17)
I Don't Want To Be Alone (6)
I Go To Extremes (14,16,17) *6*
I've Loved These Days (3,7,17)
If I Only Had The Words (To Tell You) (1)
Innocent Man (9,13,16) *10*
It's Still Rock And Roll To Me (6,11,17) *1*
James (3)
Just The Way You Are (4,11) *3*
Keeping The Faith (9,16) *18*

Last Of The Big Time Spenders (2)
Laura (8)
Leave A Tender Moment Alone (9) *27*
Leningrad (14,16)
Light As The Breeze (16)
Longest Time (9,11) *14*
Los Angelenos (2,7)
Lullabye (Goodnight, My Angel) (15,16) *77*
Matter Of Trust (12,13,16) *10*
Mexican Connection (3)
Miami 2017 (Seen The Lights Go Out On Broadway) (3,7)
Modern Woman (12) *10*

Movin' Out (Anthony's Song) (4,11,17) *17*
My Life (5,11,17) *3*
New York State Of Mind (3,11,17)
Night Is Still Young (11) *34*
No Man's Land (15)
Nocturne (10)
Odoya (13)
Only The Good Die Young (4,11,13,17) *24*

JOEL, Billy — Cont'd

Piano Man (1,11) *25*
Pressure (8,11) *20*
River Of Dreams (15,16,17) *3*
Roberta (2)
Room Of Our Own (8)
Root Beer Rag (2)
Rosalinda's Eyes (5)
Running On Ice (12)
Say Goodbye To Hollywood (3,7,11) *17*
Scandinavian Skies (8)

Scenes From An Italian Restaurant (4,17)
Shades Of Grey (15)
Shameless (14,16)
She's Always A Woman (4,11) *17*
She's Got A Way (7,10) *23*
She's Right On Time (8)
Sleeping With The Television On (6)
Sometimes A Fantasy (6,13) *36*

Somewhere Along The Line (1)
Souvenir (2)
State Of Grace (14)
Stiletto (5,13)
Stop In Nevada (1)
Storm Front (14)
Stranger, The (4,11)
Streetlife Serenader (2,7)
Summer, Highland Falls (3,7,17)
Surprises (8)
Tell Her About It (9,11) *1*

Temptation (12)
That's Not Her Style (14) *77*
This Is The Time (12,16) *18*
This Night (9,17)
Through The Long Night (6)
Times They Are A Changin' (13)
To Make You Feel My Love (16) *50*
Tomorrow Is Today (10)
Travelin' Prayer (1) *77*
Turn Around (2)
Two Thousand Years (15,17)

Until The Night (5)
Uptown Girl (9,11,13) *3*
Vienna (4)
We Didn't Start The Fire (14,16,17) *1*
Weekend Song (2)
When In Rome (14)
Where's The Orchestra? (8)
Why Judy Why (10)
Worse Comes To Worst (1) *80*
You Can Make Me Free (10)
You Look So Good To Me (10)

You May Be Right (6,11,17) *7*
You're My Home (1,7)
You're Only Human (Second Wind) (11) *9*
Zanzibar (5)

JOE PUBLIC   '92
R&B vocal group from Buffalo, New York: Kevin Scott, Joe Carter, Joe Sayles and Dwight Wyatt.

| 4/11/92 | 111 | 17 | | © | Joe Public .... | | | $10 | Columbia 48628 |

Anything
Do You Everynite *98*

I Gotta Thang
I Like It

I Miss You *55*
I've Been Watchin'

Live And Learn *4*
This One's For You

Touch You
When I Look In Your Eyes

JOHANSEN, David   '88
Born on 1/9/50 in Staten Island, New York. Rock singer/actor. Leader of the **New York Dolls** from 1971-75. Recorded jazz-pop as **Buster Poindexter**. Acted in several movies.

9/29/79	177	4		©	1	In Style			$12	Blue Sky 36082
7/11/81	160	3		©	2	Here Comes The Night			$12	Blue Sky 36589
7/3/82	148	15		©	3	Live It Up		[L]	$12	Blue Sky 38004
1/9/88	90	15		©	4	Buster Poindexter			$10	RCA 6633

BUSTER POINDEXTER AND HIS BANSHEES OF BLUE

Are You Lonely For Me Baby (4)
Bad Boy (4)
Big City (1)
Bohemian Love Pad (2,3)
Build Me Up Buttercup (3)
Cannibal (4)

Don't Bring Me Down (medley) (3)
Donna (3)
Flamingo Road (1)
Frenchette (3)
Funky But Chic (3)
Good Morning Judge (4)
Havin' So Much Fun (2)

Heart Of Gold (2,4)
Here Comes The Night (2)
Hot Hot Hot (4) *45*
House Of The Rising Sun (4)
In Style (1)
Is This What I Get For Loving You (3)
It's My Life (medley) (3)

Justine (1)
Marquesa De Sade (2)
Melody (1,3)
My Obsession (2)
Party Tonight (2)
Personality Crisis (3)
Reach Out I'll Be There (3)
Rollin' Job (2)

Screwy Music (4)
She (1)
She Knew She Was Falling In Love (1)
She Loves Strangers (2)
Smack Dab In The Middle (4)
Stranded In The Jungle (3)
Suspicion (2)

Swaheto Woman (1)
We Gotta Get Out Of This Place (medley) (3)
Whadaya Want? (4)
Wreckless Crazy (1)
You Fool You (2)
You Touched Me Too (1)

JOHN, Elton   ★7★   '74

Born Reginald Kenneth Dwight on 3/25/47 in Pinner, Middlesex, England. Pop-rock singer/songwriter/pianist. Formed his first group Bluesology. Took the name of Elton John from the first names of Bluesology members Elton Dean and **Long John Baldry**. Teamed up with lyricist Bernie Taupin beginning in 1969. Formed Rocket Records in 1973. Played the "Pinball Wizard" in the movie version of *Tommy*. Elton was the #1 pop artist of the '70s. Inducted into the Rock and Roll Hall of Fame in 1994.

1)Elton John - Greatest Hits 2)Goodbye Yellow Brick Road 3)Captain Fantastic And The Brown Dirt Cowboy 4)Honky Chateau 5)Caribou

10/3/70+	4	51	●	©	1	Elton John			$25	Uni 73090
1/23/71	5	37	▲	©	2	Tumbleweed Connection			$25	Uni 73096
3/27/71	36	19	●		3	"Friends"		[S]	$25	Paramount 6004
5/29/71	11	23		©	4	11-17-70		[L]	$25	Uni 93105
						title is date of a New York City concert broadcast on WPLJ-FM				
11/27/71+	8	51	▲²	©	5	Madman Across The Water			$20	Uni 93120
6/17/72	❶⁵	61	▲	©	6	Honky Chateau			$20	Uni 93135
2/10/73	❶²	89	▲³	©	7	Don't Shoot Me I'm Only The Piano Player			$15	MCA 2100
10/20/73	❶⁸	103	▲⁷	©	8	Goodbye Yellow Brick Road	C:#3/16		$20	MCA 10003 [2]
7/6/74	❶⁴	54	▲²	©	9	Caribou			$15	MCA 2116
11/23/74	❶¹⁰	104	▲¹⁵	©	10	Elton John - Greatest Hits	C:❶¹⁰¹/638	[G]	$15	MCA 2128
2/1/75	6	18		©	11	Empty Sky		[E]	$15	MCA 2130
						his first album, originally released in 1969				
6/7/75	❶⁷	43	▲³	©	12	Captain Fantastic And The Brown Dirt Cowboy			$15	MCA 2142
11/8/75	❶³	26	▲	©	13	Rock Of The Westies			$15	MCA 2163
5/22/76	4	20	▲	©	14	Here And There		[L]	$15	MCA 2197
11/13/76	3	22	▲	©	15	Blue Moves			$20	MCA/Rocket 11004 [2]
10/22/77	21	20	▲⁵	©	16	Elton John's Greatest Hits, Volume II .... C:#3/282		[G]	$12	MCA 3027
11/11/78	15	18	▲	©	17	A Single Man			$12	MCA 3065
6/30/79	51	18		©	18	The Thom Bell Sessions		[M]	$12	MCA 13921
10/27/79	35	10		©	19	Victim Of Love			$12	MCA 5104
5/31/80	13	21	●	©	20	21 At 33			$12	MCA 5121
6/6/81	21	19		©	21	The Fox			$10	Geffen 2002
5/8/82	17	33	●	©	22	Jump Up!			$10	Geffen 2013
6/11/83+	25	54	●	©	23	Too Low For Zero			$10	Geffen 4006
7/21/84	20	34	▲	©	24	Breaking Hearts			$10	Geffen 24031
11/30/85+	48	28	●	©	25	Ice On Fire			$10	Geffen 24077
12/6/86	91	9		©	26	Leather Jackets			$10	Geffen 24114
7/25/87+	24	41	▲	©	27	Live In Australia		[L]	$15	MCA 8022 [2]
						recorded on 12/14/86 in Sydney with the Melbourne Symphony Orchestra				
10/3/87	84	23	▲²	©	28	Elton John's Greatest Hits, Volume III, 1979-1987 .... C:#26/6		[G]	$10	Geffen 24153
7/9/88	16	29	●	©	29	Reg Strikes Back			$10	MCA 6240
9/16/89	23	53	▲	©	30	Sleeping With The Past			$10	MCA 6321
11/24/90	82	13	●	©	31	To Be Continued...		[K]	$40	MCA 10110 [4]

431

JOHN, Elton — Cont'd

DEBUT	PEAK	WKS	RIAA	CD	ARTIST — Album Title	Catalog	Sym	$	Label & Number
7/11/92	8	53	▲²	© 32	**The One**			$10	MCA 10614
11/28/92+	4ᶜ	71	▲²	© 33	**Greatest Hits 1976-1986**		[G]	$10	MCA 10693
12/11/93	25	22	▲	© 34	**Duets**			$10	MCA 10926
4/8/95	13	46	▲	© 35	**Made In England**			$10	Rocket 526185
10/12/96	24	76	▲³	© 36	**Love Songs**	C:#17/26	[G]	$10	MCA 11481
10/11/97	9	23	▲	© 37	**The Big Picture**			$10	Rocket 536266
4/1/00	63	8		© 38	**The Road To El Dorado**		[S]	$10	DreamWorks 50219
12/9/00	65	18	●	© 39	**One Night Only–The Greatest Hits**		[G-L]	$10	Universal 13050

recorded in October 2000 at Madison Square Garden

Act Of War (31)
Ain't Nothing Like The Real Thing (34)
All Quiet On The Western Front (22)
All The Girls Love Alice (8,31)
All The Nasties (5)
Amazes Me (30)
Amoreena (2)
Amy (6)
Angeline (26)
Are You Ready For Love (18)
Bad Side Of The Moon (4,31)
Ball & Chain (22)
Ballad Of A Well-Known Gun (2)
Ballad Of Danny Bailey (1909-34) (8)
Belfast (35)
Believe (35,36) *13*
Bennie And The Jets (8,10,14,31,39) *1*
Better Off Dead (12)
Between Seventeen And Twenty (15)
Big Dipper (17)
Big Picture (37)
Billy Bones And The White Bird (13)
Bitch Is Back (9,16,31,39) *4*
Bite Your Lip (Get Up And Dance!) (15) *28*
Bitter Fingers (12)
Blessed (35,36) *34*
Blue Avenue (30)
Blue Eyes (22,28,31,33,36) *12*
Blues For Baby And Me (7)
Boogie Pilgrim (15)
Border Song (1,10,14,31) *92*
Born Bad (19)
Born To Lose (34)
Breaking Down Barriers (21)
Breaking Hearts (Ain't What It Used To Be) (24)
Brig, The (37)
Burn Down The Mission (2,4,27)
Burning Buildings (24)
Cage, The (1)
Cage The Songbird (15)
Camera Never Lies (29)
Can I Put You On (3,4)
Can You Feel The Love Tonight (8,27,31,36,39) *4*
Candle In The Wind (8,27,31,36,39) *6*
Candy By The Pound (25)
Captain Fantastic And The Brown Dirt Cowboy (12)
Carla Etude (21,31)
Cartier (31)
Chameleon (15)
Chasing The Crown (20)
Cheldorado (38)
Chloe (21,31) *34*
Circle Of Life (36) *18*
Club At The End Of The Street (30) *28*
Cold (35)
Cold As Christmas (In The Middle Of The Year) (23)

Come Back Baby (31)
Come Down In Time (2)
Country Comfort (2,31)
Crazy Water (15)
Crocodile Rock (7,10,14,31,39) *1*
Cry To Heaven (25)
Crystal (23)
Curtains (12)
Dan Dare (Pilot Of The Future) (13)
Daniel (7,10,31,36,39) *2*
Dear God (20)
Dear John (22)
Did He Shoot Her? (24)
Dirty Little Girl (8)
Dixie Lily (9)
Don't Go Breaking My Heart (16,31,33,34,39) *92*
Don't Let The Sun Go Down On Me (9,10,27,31,34,36,39) *2*
Don't Trust That Woman (26)
Donner Pour Donner (31)
Duets For One (34)
Durban Deep (30)
Easier To Walk Away (31)
Ego (31) *34*
El Dorado (38)
Elderberry Wine (7)
Elton's Song (21)
Emily (32)
Empty Garden (Hey Hey Johnny) (22,28,31,33) *13*
Empty Sky (11)
End Will Come (37)
Fanfare (21,31)
Fascist Faces (21)
Feed Me (13)
First Episode At Hienton (1)
Four Moods (3)
Fox, The (21)
Friends (3,31) *34*
(also see Variations)
Friends Never Say Goodbye (38)
Funeral For A Friend (medley) (8,14,31)
Georgia (17)
Get Back (medley) (4)
Give Me The Love (20)
Give Peace A Chance (31)
Go It Alone (26)
Go On And On (34)
Goodbye (5)
Goodbye Marlon Brando (20)
Goodbye Yellow Brick Road (8,10,31,39) *2*
(Gotta Get A) Meal Ticket (12)
Greatest Discovery (1,27)
Grey Seal (8,31)
Grimsby (9)
Grow Some Funk Of Your Own (13,16) *14*
Gulliver (medley) (11)
Gypsy Heart (3)
Hard Luck Story (13)
Harmony (8,31)
Have Mercy On The Criminal (7,27)
Hay Chewed (medley) (11)

Healing Hands (30) *13*
Heart In The Right Place (21)
Heartache All Over The World (26,28) *55*
Heavy Traffic (29)
Heels Of The Wind (21)
Hercules (6)
High Flying Bird (7)
Holiday Inn (1)
Honey Roll (29)
Honky Cat (6,10,14,31) *8*
Honky Tonk Women (4)
Hoop Of Fire (26)
House (35)
Hymn 2000 (11)
I Am Your Robot (22)
I Can't Steer My Heart Clear Of You (37)
I Don't Care (17)
I Don't Wanna Go On With You Like That (29,31) *2*
I Fall Apart (26)
I Feel Like A Bullet (In The Gun Of Robert Ford) (13,31) *flip*
I Guess That's Why They Call It The Blues (23,28,31,33,39) *4*
I Meant To Do My Work Today (3)
I Need You To Turn To (1,27)
I Never Knew Her Name (30)
I Saw Her Standing There (31)
I Swear I Heard The Night Talkin' (31)
I Think I'm Gonna Kill Myself (6)
I'm Going To Be A Teenage Idol (7)
I'm Still Standing (23,28,31,33,39) *12*
I'm Your Puppet (34)
I've Seen That Movie Too (8)
I've Seen The Saucers (9)
Idol (31)
If The River Can Bend (37)
If There's A God In Heaven (What's He Waiting For?) (15)
If You Were Me (34)
In Neon (24) *38*
Indian Sunset (5)
Island Girl (13,16,31) *1*
It Ain't Gonna Be Easy (17)
It's Me That You Need (31)
It's Tough To Be A God (38)
Jack Rabbit (31)
Jamaica Jerk-Off (8)
January (37)
Japanese Hands (29)
Johnny B. Goode (19)
Just Like Belgium (21)
King Must Die (1,27)
Kiss The Bride (23,28,33) *25*
Lady Samantha (31)
Lady What's Tomorrow (11)
Last Song (32) *23*
Latitude (35)
Leather Jackets (26)
Legal Boys (22)
Levon (5,16,31) *24*
Li'l 'Frigerator (24)
Lies (31)

Little Jeannie (20,28,31,33) *3*
Live Like Horses (37)
Long Way From Happiness (37)
Love Letters (34)
Love Lies Bleeding (medley) (8,14,31)
Love Song (2,14)
Love's Got A Lot To Answer For (37)
Lucy In The Sky With Diamonds (16,31) *1*
Made For Me (31)
Made In England (35) *52*
Madman Across The Water (5,27,31)
Madness (17)
Mama Can't Buy You Love (18,28,31,33) *9*
Man (35)
Mellow (6)
Memory Of Love (26)
Michelle's Song (3)
(also see: Variations)
Midnight Creeper (7)
Mona Lisas And Mad Hatters (6,29,31)
My Baby Left Me (medley) (8)
My Father's Gun (2)
My Heart Dances (38)
Never Gonna Fall In Love Again (20)
Nikita (25,28,31,33) *7*
No Shoe Strings On Louise (1)
No Valentines (36)
Nobody Wins (21) *21*
North, The (32)
On Dark Street (32)
One, The (32,36) *9*
One Day At A Time (31)
One Horse Town (15)
One More Arrow (23)
Out Of The Blue (15)
Pain (35)
Panic In Me (38)
Paris (26)
Part-Time Love (17) *22*
Passengers (24)
Philadelphia Freedom (16,31,39) *1*
Pinball Wizard (16,31)
Pinky (9)
Please (35)
Poor Cow (29)
Power, The (34)
Princess (22)
Queen Of Cities (37)
Razor Face (5)
Recover Your Soul (37) *55*
Religion (23)
Restless (24)
Retreat, The (31)
Return To Paradise (17)
Reverie (17)
Rock And Roll Madonna (31)
Rocket Man (6,10,14,31,39) *6*
Rotten Peaches (5)
Roy Rogers (31)
Runaway Train (32)
Sacrifice (30,31,36,39) *18*

Sad Songs (Say So Much) (24,28,31,33,39) *5*
Sails (11)
Saint (23)
Salvation (6)
(Sartorial Eloquence) Don't Ya Wanna Play This Game No More? (20) *39*
Satellite (25)
Saturday Night's Alright For Fighting (8,10,31,39) *12*
Scaffold, The (11)
Seasons (4)
Shakey Ground (34)
Shine On Through (17)
Shoot Down The Moon (25)
Shooting Star (17)
Shoulder Holster (15)
Simple Life (32) *30*
Since God Invented Girls (29)
16th Century Man (38)
Sixty Years On (1,4,27,31)
Skyline Pigeon (11,14)
Slave (6)
Sleeping With The Past (30)
Slow Down Georgie (She's Poison) (24)
Slow Rivers (26)
Social Disease (8)
Solar Prestige A Gammon (9)
Someday Out Of The Blue (Theme From El Dorado) (38) *49*
Someone Saved My Life Tonight (12,16,31,36) *4*
Someone's Final Song (15)
Something About The Way You Look Tonight (37) *flip*
Son Of Your Father (2)
Song For Guy (17,31)
Sorry Seems To Be The Hardest Word (15,16,27,31,33,36) *6*
Soul Glove (25)
Spiteful Child (22)
Spotlight (19)
Step Into Christmas (31)
Stinker (8)
Stones Throw From Hurtin' (30)
Street Boogie (19)
Street Kids (13)
Suzie (Dramas) (6)
Sweat It Out (32)
Sweet Painted Lady (8)
Take Me Back (20)
Take Me To The Pilot (1,4,14,27,31)
Talking Old Soldiers (2)
Teacher I Need You (7)
Teardrops (34)
Tell Me What The Papers Say (25)
Tell Me When The Whistle Blows (12)
Texan Love Song (7)
Theme From A Non-Existent TV Series (31)
This Song Has No Title (8)
This Town (25)
Three Way Love Affair (18)
Thunder In The Night (19)

Ticking (9)
Tiny Dancer (5,27,31) *41*
Tonight (15,27)
Too Low For Zero (23,28)
Too Young (25)
Tower Of Babel (12)
Town Of Plenty (29)
Trail We Blaze (38)
True Love (34) *56*
Trust Me (38)
Two Rooms At The End Of The World (20)
Ugly (medley) (13)
Understanding Women (32)
Valhalla (11)
Variations On "Friends" Theme (The First Kiss) (3)
Variations On Michelle's Song (3)
Victim Of Love (19) *31*
Warm Love In A Cold World (12)
We All Fall In Love Sometimes (12)
Wednesday Night (medley) (13)
Western Ford Gateway (11)
When A Woman Doesn't Want You (32)
When I Think About Love (I Think About You) (34)
Whenever You're Ready (We'll Go Steady Again) (31)
Where Have All The Good Times Gone? (22)
Where To Now St. Peter? (2)
Where's The Shoorah? (15)
Whipping Boy (23)
Whispers (30)
White Lady White Powder (20)
Whitewash County (32)
Who Wears These Shoes? (24,33) *16*
Wicked Dreams (37)
Wide-Eyed And Laughing (15)
Without Question (38)
Woman's Needs (34)
Wonders Of The New World (38)
Word In Spanish (29) *19*
Wrap Her Up (25,28,33) *20*
Writing (12)
Yell Help (medley) (13)
You Can Make History (Young Again) (36) *70*
You Gotta Love Someone (31) *43*
You're So Static (9)
Young Man's Blues (31)
Your Sister Can't Twist (But She Can Rock 'N' Roll) (8)
Your Song (1,10,27,31,36,39) *8*
Your Starter For... (15)

JOHN, Robert   '79

Born Robert John Pedrick in 1946 in in Brooklyn, New York. Pop singer.

DEBUT	PEAK	WKS	RIAA	CD	ARTIST — Album Title	Catalog	Sym	$	Label & Number
8/25/79	68	14			**Robert John**			$12	EMI America 17007

Am I Ever Gonna Hold You Again
Dance The Night Away
Give A Little More
Lonely Eyes *41*
Love Of A Woman
Only Time
Sad Eyes *1*
Stay A Little Longer
Takin' My Love For Granted
That's What Keeps Us Together

JOHNNY & THE DISTRACTIONS   '82

Rock group from Portland, Oregon: Johnny Koonce (vocals), Mark Spangler (guitar), Gregg Perry (keyboards), Laure Todd (bass) and Kevin Jarvis (drums).

DEBUT	PEAK	WKS	RIAA	CD	ARTIST — Album Title	Catalog	Sym	$	Label & Number
2/20/82	152	9			**Let It Rock**			$10	A&M 4884

Break These Chains
City Of Angels
Complicated Now
Forever
Guys Like Me
In The Street
Let It Rock
My Desire
Octane Twilight
Shoulder Of The Road

JOHNNY AND THE HURRICANES   '60
Instrumental group from Toledo, Ohio: leader Johnny Paris (saxophone), Dave Yorko (guitar), Paul Tesluk (organ), Lionel Mattice (bass) and Bo Savich (drums).

| 4/18/60 | **34** | 3 | | | Stormsville... | | [I] | **$200** | Warwick 2010 |

Beanbag   Corn Bread   "Hep" Canary (The Hot Canary)   Hungry Eye   **Reveille Rock 25**   Time Bomb
Catnip   Cyclone   Hot Fudge   Milk Shake   Rockin' "T"   Travelin'

JOHNNY HATES JAZZ   '88
Pop trio formed in England: Clark Datchler (vocals), Calvin Hayes (keyboards, drums) and Mike Nocito (guitar, bass). Hayes is the son of producer Mickie Most.

| 4/16/88 | **56** | 25 | | © | Turn Back The Clock .... | | | **$10** | Virgin 90860 |

Different Seasons   Don't Say It's Love   Heart Of Gold   Listen   Turn Back The Clock
Don't Let It End This Way   Foolish Heart   **I Don't Want To Be A Hero 31 Shattered Dreams 2**   What Other Reason

JOHNS, Sammy   '75
Born on 2/7/46 in Charlotte, North Carolina. Singer/songwriter/guitarist.

| 3/29/75 | **148** | 12 | | | Sammy Johns .... | | | **$12** | GRC 5003 |

America   **Early Morning Love 68**   Hang My Head And Moan   Jenny   Way Out Jesus
Chevy Van 5   Friends Of Mine   Holy Mother, Aging Father   **Rag Doll 52**   We Will Shine

JOHNSON, Don   '86
Born on 12/15/49 in Flatt Creek, Missouri. Actor/singer. Played "Sonny Crockett" on TV's *Miami Vice* and title role in TV's *Nash Bridges*. Starred in several movies. Twice married to and divorced from actress Melanie Griffith.

| 9/13/86 | **17** | 27 | ● | © | Heartbeat .... | | | **$10** | Epic 40366 |

Can't Take Your Memory   Gotta Get Away   **Heartbeat 5**   Lost In Your Eyes   Star Tonight
Coco Don't   **Heartache Away 56**   Last Sound Love Makes   Love Roulette   Voice On A Hotline

JOHNSON, Eric   '96
Born on 8/17/54 in Austin, Texas. Rock guitarist.

4/21/90+	**67**	60	●	©	1 Ah Via Musicom		[I]	**$10**	Capitol 90517
9/21/96	**51**	6		©	2 Venus Isle		[I]	**$10**	Capitol 98331
6/21/97	**108**	3		©	3 G3 - Live In Concert		[I-L]	**$10**	Epic 67920

JOE SATRIANI/ERIC JOHNSON/STEVE VAI

Ah Via Musicom (1)   East Wes (1)   My Guitar Wants To Kill Your   Righteous (1)   Venus Isle (2)
All About You (1)   Forty Mile Town (1)   Mama (3)   S.R.V. (2)   Venus Reprise (2)
Battle We Have Won (2)   Going Down (3)   Nothing Can Keep Me From   Song For George (1)   When The Sun Meets The Sky
Camel's Night Out (2,3)   High Landrons (3)   You (1)   Song For Lynette (2)   (2)
Cliffs Of Dover (1)   Lonely In The Night (2)   Pavilion (2)   Steve's Boogie (1)   Zap (3)
Desert Rose (1)   Manhattan (2,3)   Red House (1)   Trademark (1)

JOHNSON, Howard   '82
Born in Miami. R&B singer.

| 9/11/82 | **122** | 9 | | | Keepin' Love New .... | | | **$10** | A&M 4895 |

Forever Falling In Love   Keepin' Love New   So Fine   Take Me Through The Night
Jam Song   Say You Wanna   So Glad You're My Lady   This Is Heaven

JOHNSON, Jesse   '85
Born on 5/29/60 in Rock Island, Illinois. R&B guitarist. Member of **The Time**.

3/16/85	**43**	43	●	©	1 Jesse Johnson's Revue			**$10**	A&M 5024
10/18/86	**70**	20		©	2 Shockadelica			**$10**	A&M 5122
4/16/88	**79**	13		©	3 Every Shade Of Love			**$10**	A&M 5188

Addiction (2)   Burn You Up (2)   Do Yourself A Favor (2)   I'm Just Wanting You (3)   She (I Can't Resist) (2)   Stop-Look-Listen (3)
Baby Let's Kiss (2)   Can You Help Me (1)   Every Shade Of Love (3)   I'm The One (3)   She Won't Let Go (1)   Tonite (2)
Be Your Man (1) **61**   Change Your Mind (2)   Everybody Wants Somebody   Just Too Much (1)   She's A Doll (1)
Better Way (2)   Color Shock (3)   To Love (3)   Let's Have Some Fun (1)   So Misunderstood (3)
Black In America (2)   **Crazay** (2) **53**   **I Want My Girl** (1) **76**   **Love Struck** (3) **78**   Special Love (1)

JOHNSON, Michael   '78
Born on 8/8/44 in Alamosa, Colorado; raised in Denver. Singer/guitarist.

| 7/15/78 | **81** | 17 | | | 1 The Michael Johnson Album .... | | | **$12** | EMI America 17002 |
| 9/15/79 | **157** | 12 | | | 2 Dialogue .... | | | **$12** | EMI America 17010 |

Almost Like Being In Love   Dancin' Tonight (1)   Foolish (1)   Let This Be A Lesson To You   She Put The Sad In All His   25 Words Or Less (1)
(1) **32**   Dialogue (2)   Gypsy Woman (1)   (2)   Songs (2)   Two In Love (1)
Blackmail (2)   Doors (2)   I Just Can't Say No To You (2)   Ridin' In The Sky (1)   **This Night Won't Last Forever**   Very First Time (2)
Bluer Than Blue (1) **12**   Drops Of Water (2)   I'll Always Love You (2)   Sailing Without A Sail (1)   (2) **19**   When You Come Home (1)

JOHNSON, Robert   '79
Born in Memphis. Session guitarist. Member of **John Entwistle**'s group Ox in 1974.

| 1/13/79 | **174** | 8 | | | Close Personal Friend .... | | | **$12** | Infinity 9000 |

Debbie's Theme   I'll Be Waiting   Leslie   Say Girl   Wish Upon A Star
Guide My Energy (Parts 1 & 2)   Kerri   Responsibility   Tell Me About It, "Slim"   Wreck My Mind

JOHNSON, Robert   '91
Born on 5/8/11 in Hazlehurst, Mississippi. Died of strychnine poisoning on 8/16/38 (age 27). Legendary blues singer/guitarist. Inducted into the Rock and Roll Hall of Fame in 1986 as an early influence.

| 12/12/87 | **34**[C] | 5 | | © | 1 King Of The Delta Blues Singers............................... | | [K] | **$10** | Columbia 1654 |
| 10/13/90+ | **80** | 31 | ▲ | © | 2 The Complete Recordings .... | | [K] | **$20** | Columbia 46222 [2] |

Come On In My Kitchen (1,2)   Honeymoon Blues (2)   Last Fair Deal Gone Down (1,2)   Phonograph Blues (2)   Sweet Home Chicago (1,2)   When You Got A Good Friend
Cross Road Blues (1,2)   I Believe I'll Dust My Broom (2)   Little Queen Of Spades (2)   Preaching Blues (Up Jumped   Terraplane Blues (1,2)   (1,2)
Dead Shrimp Blues (2)   I'm A Steady Rollin' Man (2)   Love In Vain (2)   The Devil) (2)   They're Red Hot (2)
Drunken Hearted Man (2)   If I Had Possession Over   Malted Milk (2)   Rambling On My Mind (1,2)   32-20 Blues (1,2)
From Four Till Late (2)   Judgment Day (2)   Me And The Devil Blues (1,2)   Stones In My Passway (1,2)   Traveling Riverside Blues (1,2)
Hellhound On My Trail (1,2)   Kindhearted Woman Blues (1,2)   Milkcow's Calf Blues (2)   Stop Breakin' Down Blues (2)   Walking Blues (1,2)

JOHNSON, Syleena '01
Born in 1976 in Chicago. Female R&B singer.

| 6/2/01 | 101 | 9 | | © | Chapter 1: Love, Pain & Forgiveness | | | $10 | Jive 41700 |

Ain't No Love
All Of Me
Baby I'm So Confused
Everybody Wants Something
He's Gonna Do You In
Hit On Me
I Am Your Woman
I'd Rather Be Wrong
One Day
You Ain't Right
You Got Me Spinnin'
You Said

JOHNSTON, Freedy '97
Born in 1961 in Kinsley, Kansas. Male rock singer/songwriter.

| 3/15/97 | 184 | 1 | | © | Never Home | | | $10 | Elektra 61920 |

Gone To See The Fire
He Wasn't Murdered
Hotel Seventeen
I'm Not Hypnotized
If It's True
On The Way Out
One More Thing To Break
Seventies Girl
Something's Out There
Western Sky
You Get Me Lost

JOHNSTON, Tom '79
Born in Visalia, California. Lead singer/guitarist of **The Doobie Brothers**.

| 10/20/79 | 100 | 13 | | 1 | Everything You've Heard Is True | | | $12 | Warner 3304 |
| 5/16/81 | 158 | 7 | | 2 | Still Feels Good | | | $12 | Warner 3527 |

Baby, Take Me In (2)
Down Along The River (1)
Excuse Me Ma'am (2)
I Can Count On You (1)
Last Desperado (2)
Madman (2)
Man On The Stage (1)
One-Way Ticket (2)
Outlaw (1)
Reachin' Out For Lovin' From You (1)
Savannah Nights (1) *34*
Show Me (1)
Small Time Talk (1)
Up On The Stage (2)
Wastin' Time (2)
Wishing (2)

JO JO GUNNE '72
Pop-rock group from Los Angeles: **Jay Ferguson** (keyboards), brothers Matthew (guitar) and Mark (bass) Andes and Curly Smith (drums). Both Ferguson and Mark Andes had been in **Spirit**. By 1973, Jimmie Randall had replaced Mark Andes. By 1974, John Staehely had replaced Matthew Andes. Group named after the 1958 **Chuck Berry** hit. Mark Andes was later with **Firefall** and **Heart**.

2/26/72	57	22		1	Jo Jo Gunne			$15	Asylum 5053
3/17/73	75	17		2	Bite Down Hard			$15	Asylum 5065
12/22/73+	169	7		3	Jumpin' The Gunne			$15	Asylum 5071
12/28/74	198	1		4	So...Where's The Show?			$15	Asylum 1022

Academy Award (1)
Around The World (4)
At The Spa (3)
Babylon (1)
Barstow Blue Eyes (1)
Before You Get Your Breakfast (3)
Big, Busted Bombshell From Bermuda (4)
Broken Down Man (2)
Couldn't Love You Better (3)
Falling Angel (4)
Flying Home (1)
Getaway (3)
High School Drool (3)
I Make Love (1)
I Wanna Love You (3)
I'm Your Shoe (4)
Into My Life (4)
Monkey Music (3)
Neon City (3)
99 Days (1)
Ready Freddy (2)
Red Meat (3)
Rhoda (2)
Rock Around The Symbol (2)
Roll Over Me (2)
Run Run Run (1) *27*
S & M Blvd. (4)
Shake That Fat (1)
She Said Allright (4)
Single Man (4)
60 Minutes To Go (2)
Special Situations (4)
Take It Easy (1)
Take Me Down Easy (2)
To The Island (3)
Turn The Boy Loose (3)
Wait A Lifetime (2)
Where Is The Show? (4)

JOLI, France '79
Born in 1963 in Montreal. Female dance singer.

| 9/8/79 | 26 | 17 | | 1 | France Joli | | | $12 | Prelude 12170 |
| 6/28/80 | 175 | 3 | | 2 | Tonight | | | $12 | Prelude 12179 |

Come To Me (1) *15*
Don't Stop Dancing (1)
Feel Like Dancing (2)
Heart To Break The Heart (2)
Let Go (1)
Playboy (1)
Stoned In Love (2)
This Time (I'm Giving All I've Got) (2)
Tonight (2)
Tough Luck (2)
When Love Hurts Inside (2)

JOLLY, Pete, Trio and Friends '63
Born Peter Ceragioli on 6/5/32 in New Haven, Connecticut. Jazz pianist.

| 6/8/63 | 139 | 2 | | | Little Bird | | [I] | $25 | Ava 22 |

Alone Together
Falling In Love With Love
Little Bird
My Favorite Things
Never Never Land
Spring Can Really Hang You Up The Most
Three-Four-Five
To Kill A Mocking Bird
Toot, Toot, Tootsie (Goodbye)

JOLSON, Al '62
Born Asa Yoelson on 3/26/1886 in St. Petersburg, Russia; raised in Washington DC. Died on 10/23/50 (age 64). One of the most popular entertainers of the 20th century. Starred in several movies and Broadway shows. Married to actress Ruby Keeler from 1928-39.

| 9/22/62+ | 40 | 42 | | | The Best Of Jolson | | [G] | $20 | Decca 169 [2] |

About A Quarter To Nine
Anniversary Song
April Showers
Avalon
Baby Face (medley)
California, Here I Come
Carolina In The Morning
Dinah (medley)
Easter Parade
I Wish I Had A Girl
I'm Always Chasing Rainbows
I'm Looking Over A Four Leaf Clover (medley)
If I Only Had A Match
Let Me Sing And I'm Happy
Liza (All The Clouds'll Roll Away)
Ma Blushin' Rosie (Ma Posie Sweet)
Ma (She's Makin' Eyes At Me) (medley)
Margie
My Blue Heaven (medley)
My Mammy
My Melancholy Baby (medley)
Ol' Man River
Rockabye Your Baby With A Dixie Melody
She's A Latin From Manhattan
Sonny Boy
Swanee
There's A Rainbow 'Round My Shoulder
Toot, Toot, Tootsie! (Goo'Bye)
When The Red, Red, Robin Comes Bob, Bob, Bobbin' Along
When You Were Sweet Sixteen
You Made Me Love You (I Didn't Want To Do It)

JON & VANGELIS '81
Duo of Jon Anderson (lead singer of **Yes**; born on 10/25/44 in Lancashire, England) and **Vangelis** (born on 3/29/43 in Valos, Greece).

5/31/80	125	15		© 1	Short Stories			$12	Polydor 6272
8/8/81	64	34		© 2	The Friends Of Mr. Cairo			$12	Polydor 6326
8/13/83	148	7		© 3	Private Collection			$12	Polydor 813174

And When The Night Comes (3)
Back To School (2)
Beside (2)
Bird Song (medley) (1)
Curious Electric (1)
Deborah (3)
Each And Everyday (medley) (1)
Far Away In Baagad (1)
Friends Of Mr. Cairo (2)
He Is Sailing (3)
Horizon (3)
I Hear You Now (1) *58*
Italian Song (3)
Love Is (medley) (1)
Mayflower (2)
One More Time (medley) (1)
Outside Of This (Inside Of That) (2)
Play Within A Play (1)
Polonaise (1)
Road, The (1)
State Of Independence (2)
Thunder (1)

JON B '01
Born Jonathan Buck on 11/11/74 in Rhode Island. R&B singer/songwriter.

6/10/95	79	24	●	© 1	Bonafide			$10	Yab Yum 66436
10/4/97+	33	59	▲	© 2	Cool Relax			$10	Yab Yum 67805
4/7/01	6	13		© 3	Pleasures U Like			$10	Edmonds 69998

All I Want Is You (1)
Are U Still Down (2) *29*
Bad Girl (2)
Bonafide (1)
Boy Is Not A Man (3)
Burning 4 You (1)
Calling On You (3)
Can We Get Down (2)
Can't Help It (2)
Cocoa Brown (3)
Cool Relax (2)
Do It All Again (3)
Don't Say (2) *68*
Don't Talk (3) *58*
Finer Things (3)
Gone Before Light (1)
I Ain't Going Out (2)
I Do (Whatcha Say Boo) (2)
Inside (3)
Isn't It Scary (1)
Layaway (3)
Let Me Know (2)
Lonely Girl (3)
Love Don't Do (1)
Love Hurts (2)
Love Is Candi (1)
Mystery 4 Two (1)
Now That I'm With You (1)
Overflow (1)
Overjoyed (3)
Pants Off (1)
Pleasures U Like (3)
Pretty Girl (1) *25*
Pride & Joy (2)
Shine (2)
Simple Melody (1)
Sof'n Sweet (3)
Someone To Love (1) *10*
Tell Me (3)
They Don't Know (2) *7*
Time After Time (1)
Tu Amor (2)
Vibezelect Café (3)

JONES, Davy '67
Born on 12/30/45 in Manchester, England. Member of **The Monkees**.

| 5/27/67 | 185 | 6 | | | David Jones .... | | | $40 | Colpix 493 |

Any Old Iron	Face Up To It	Maybe It's Because I'm A	Put Me Amongst The Girls	What Are We Going To
Baby It's Me	It Ain't Me Babe	Londoner	Theme For A New Love	Do? 93
Dream Girl		My Dad	This Bouquet	

JONES, Donell '99
Born in Chicago. R&B singer/songwriter.

| 10/19/96 | 180 | 4 | | © 1 | My Heart .... | | | $10 | LaFace 26025 |
| 10/30/99 | 35 | 51 | ▲ | © 2 | Where I Wanna Be .... | | | $10 | LaFace 26060 |

All About You (1)	He Won't Hurt You (2)	**Knocks Me Off My Feet** (1) 49	Pushin' (2)	This Luv (2)	Wish You Were Here (1)
All Her Love (2)	I Wanna Luv U (2)	My Heart (1)	Shorty (Got Her Eyes On Me)	U Know What's Up (2) 7	Yearnin' (1)
Believe In Me (1)	I Want You To Know (1)	Natural Thang (1)	(2)	Waiting On You (1)	You Should Know (1)
Don't Cry (1)	**In The Hood** (1) 79	No Interruptions (1)	Think About It (Don't Call My	When I Was Down (2)	
Have You Seen Her (2)	It's Alright (1)	Only One You Need (1)	Crib) (2)	**Where I Wanna Be** (2) 29	

JONES, Freddy, Band — see FREDDY JONES BAND

JONES, George '99
Born on 9/12/31 in Saratoga, Texas. Legendary country singer/songwriter/guitarist. Married to **Tammy Wynette** from 1969-75. Known as "No Show Jones" (due to several missed shows in the late 1970s) and "Possum."

1)Cold Hard Truth 2)Walls Can Fall 3)Still The Same Ole Me

3/20/65	141	4		© 1	George Jones & Gene Pitney			$40	Musicor 3044
6/26/65	149	2		© 2	The Race Is On			$30	United Artists 3422
8/2/69	185	5		3	I'll Share My World With You			$30	Musicor 3177
11/13/71	169	6		4	We Go Together			$20	Epic 30802
					TAMMY WYNETTE & GEORGE JONES				
6/13/81	132	14	▲	© 5	I Am What I Am			$12	Epic 36586
11/28/81+	115	14	●	6	Still The Same Ole Me			$12	Epic 37106
9/25/82	123	12		© 7	A Taste Of Yesterday's Wine			$12	Epic 38203
					MERLE HAGGARD & GEORGE JONES				
11/2/91	148	10		© 8	And Along Came Jones			$10	MCA 10398
10/10/92+	25^C	15	▲	© 9	Super Hits	[G]		$10	Epic 40776
11/14/92+	77	20	●	© 10	Walls Can Fall			$10	MCA 10652
12/18/93+	124	11	●	© 11	High-Tech Redneck			$10	MCA 10910
1/28/95	142	4		© 12	The Bradley Barn Sessions			$10	MCA 11096
7/8/95	117	13		© 13	One			$10	MCA 11248
					GEORGE JONES & TAMMY WYNETTE				
9/7/96	171	2		© 14	I Lived To Tell It All			$10	MCA 11478
7/10/99	53	25	●	© 15	Cold Hard Truth			$10	Asylum 62368

After Closing Time (4)
After I Sing All My Songs (7)
Ain't It Funny What A Fool Will
Do (2)
Ain't Love A Lot Like That (15)
All I Have To Offer You Is Me
(13)
Angels Don't Fly (8)
Back Down To Hung Up On
You (14)
Bartender's Blues (9,12)
Billy B. Bad (14)
Bone Dry (5)
Bottle Let Me Down (10)
Brother To The Blues (5)
Brothers, The (7)
C.C. Waterback (7)
Choices (15)
Cold Hard Truth (15)
Come Home To Me (8)
Couldn't Love Have Picked A
Better Place To Die (6)
Daddy Come Home (6)
Day After Forever (15)
Do What You Think's Best (3)
Don't Let The Stars Get In Your
Eyes (2)
Don't Rob Another Man's Castle
(1)
Don't Send Me No Angels (10)
Drive Me To Drink (10)
Finally Friday (10)
Forever's Here To Stay (11)

Girl, You Sure Know How To
Say Goodbye (6)
Golden Ring (12)
Good Hearted Woman (5)
Good Ones And Bad Ones
(6,12)
Good Year For The Roses (12)
Grand Tour (9)
Hard Act To Follow (5)
He Stopped Loving Her Today
(5,9)
Heartaches And Hangovers (3)
Heckel And Jeckel (8)
Hello Darlin' (11)
Hello Heart (14)
High-Tech Redneck (11)
His Lovin' Her Is Gettin' In My
Way (5)
Honky Tonk Myself To Death
(8)
Honky Tonk Song (14)
Hundred Proof Memories (14)
I Don't Go Back Anymore (8)
I Don't Have Sense Enough (To
Come In Out Of The Rain) (3)
I Don't Need Your Rockin' Chair
(10)
I Haven't Found Her Yet (7)
I Must Have Done Something
Bad (14)
I Think I've Found A Way (To
Live Without You) (7)

I Won't Need You Anymore (6)
I'll Give You Something To
Drink About (14)
I'll Never Let Go Of You (2)
I'll Share My World With You (3)
I'm A Fool To Care (1)
I'm Not Ready Yet (5)
I'm The One She Missed Him
With Today (5)
I've Aged Twenty Years In Five
(5)
I've Got A New Heartache (1)
I've Got Five Dollars And It's
Saturday Night (1) 99
I've Still Got Some Hurtin' Left
To Do (11)
If Drinkin' Don't Kill Me (Her
Memory Will) (5)
If God Met You (13)
It Ain't Gonna Worry My Mind
(14)
It Scares Me Half To Death (2)
It's An Old Love Thing (13)
It's So Sweet (4)
Just Look What We've Started
Again (13)
King Of The Mountain (8)
Lifetime Left Together (4)
Livin' On Easy Street (4)
Lone Ranger (14)
Love Bug (12)
Love In Your Eyes (11)
Milwaukee Here I Come (3)

Mobile Bay (Magnolia
Blossoms) (7)
Must've Been Drunk (7)
My Shoes Keep Walking Back
To You (1)
Never Bit A Bullet Like This (11)
Never Grow Cold (4)
No Show Jones (7)
One (13)
One Has My Name (1)
One I Loved Back Then (The
Corvette Song) (9)
One Woman Man (12)
Our Bed Of Roses (15)
Our Happy Home (3)
Picture Of Me (Without You) (9)
Race Is On (2,3,12) 96
Real Deal (15)
Same Ole Me (6)
Say It's Not You (12)
She Loved A Lot In Her Time
(8)
(She's Just) An Old Love
Turned Memory (13)
She's Mine (2)
Silent Partners (11)
Silver Eagle (7)
Sinners & Saints (15)
Solid As A Rock (13)
Someday My Day Will Come (6)
Someone I Used To Know (4)
Something To Brag About (4)
Still Doin' Time (6)

Sweeter Than The Flowers (1)
Take Me (4)
Take Me As I Am (2)
Tear Me Out Of The Picture
(11)
Tennessee Whiskey (9)
There's The Door (10)
They'll Never Take Her Love
From Me (2)
They're Playing Our Song (13)
Things Have Gone To Pieces
(1)
This Wanting You (15)
Thousand Times A Day (11)
Three's A Crowd (2)
Tied To A Stone (14)
Time Changes Everything (2)
Together Alone (4)
Visit, The (11)
Walls Can Fall (10)
We Go Together (2)
Wearing My Heart Away (1)
What Am I Doing There (10)
What Ever Happened To Us
(13)
When The Grass Grows Over
Me (3)
When The Last Curtain Falls
(15)
When The Wife Runs Off (3)
When True Love Steps In (4)
Where Grass Won't Grow (12)

Where The Tall Grass Grows
(8)
White Lightning (9,12) 73
Who's Gonna Fill Their Shoes
(9)
Why Baby Why (9,12)
Will You Travel Down This
Road With Me (13)
Window Up Above (9)
World's Worse Loser (2)
Wreck On The Highway (11)
Wrong's What I Do Best (10)
Yesterday's Wine (7)
You Can't Get The Hell Out Of
Texas (6)
You Couldn't Get The Picture
(8)
You Done Me Wrong (8)
You Must Have Walked Across
My Mind (12)
You Never Know Just How
Good You've Got It (15)
You're Everything (4)
You've Become My Everything
(3)
Your Heart Turned Left (2)

JONES, Glenn '87
Born in 1961 in Jacksonville, Florida. R&B singer/actor.

| 10/10/87 | 94 | 17 | | © | Glenn Jones .... | | | $10 | Jive 1062 |

All I Need To Know	I Love You	It's All In The Game	Oh Girl	We've Only Just Begun (The
At Last	It Must Be Love	Living In The Limelight	That Night Mood	Romance Is Not Over) 66

JONES, Grace '81
Born Grace Mendoza on 5/19/52 in Spanishtown, Jamaica; raised in Syracuse, New York. Dance singer/actress/model. Acted in several movies.

10/22/77	109	20		© 1	Portfolio			$12	Island 9470
8/5/78	97	8		2	Fame			$12	Island 9525
9/1/79	156	7		3	Muse			$12	Island 9538
6/21/80	132	10		© 4	Warm Leatherette			$12	Island 9592
5/23/81	32	20		© 5	Nightclubbing			$12	Island 9624

JONES, Grace — Cont'd

12/11/82	86	20	©	6	Living My Life			$12	Island 90018
11/23/85	73	20	©	7	Slave To The Rhythm			$12	Manhattan 53021
1/18/86	161	7	©	8	Island Life		[G]	$12	Island 90491
12/13/86+	81	16	©	9	Inside Story			$12	Manhattan 53038

All On A Summers Night (2)
Am I Ever Gonna Fall In Love In NYC (2)
Apple Stretching (6)
Art Groupie (5)
Atlantic City Gambler (3)
Autumn Leaves (2)
Barefoot In Beverly Hills (9)
Below The Belt (La Vieille Fille) (2)
Breakdown (4)
Bullshit (4)

Chan Hitchhikes To Shanghai (9)
Crossing (Ooh The Action...) (7)
Crush (9)
Cry Now, Laugh Later (6)
Demolition Man (5)
Do Or Die (2,8)
Don't Cry - It's Only The Rhythm (7)
Don't Mess With The Messer (3)
Everybody Hold Still (6)
Fame (2)

Fashion Show (7)
Feel Up (5)
Frog And The Princess (7)
Hollywood Liar (9)
Hunter Gets Captured By The Game (4)
I Need A Man (1,8) *83*
I'll Find My Way To You (3)
I'm Not Perfect (But I'm Perfect For You) (9) *69*
I've Done It Again (5)
I've Seen That Face Before (Libertango) (5,8)

Inside Story (9)
Inspiration (6)
Jones The Rhythm (7)
La Vie En Rose (1,8)
Ladies And Gentlemen: Miss Grace Jones (7)
Love Is The Drug (4,8)
My Jamaican Guy (6,8)
Nightclubbing (5)
Nipple To The Bottle (6)
On Your Knees (3)
Operattack (7)
Pars (4)

Party Girl (9)
Pride (2)
Private Life (4,8)
Pull Up To The Bumper (5,8)
Repentence (Forgive Me) (3)
Rolling Stone (4)
Saved (3)
Scary But Fun (9)
Send In The Clowns (1)
Sinning (3)
Slave To The Rhythm (7,8)
Sorry (1) *71*
Suffer (3)

That's The Trouble (1) *flip*
Tomorrow (1)
Unlimited Capacity For Love (6)
Use Me (5)
Victor Should Have Been A Jazz Musician (9)
Walking In The Rain (5,8)
Warm Leatherette (4)
What I Did For Love (1)
White Collar Crime (9)

JONES, Howard   '85

Born on 2/23/55 in Southampton, Hampshire, England. Pop singer/songwriter/keyboardist.

3/24/84	59	43	©	1	Human's Lib			$10	Elektra 60346
4/20/85	10	45	▲ ©	2	Dream Into Action			$10	Elektra 60390
5/3/86	34	24		3	Action Replay		[K-M]	$10	Elektra 60466
11/1/86	56	21	©	4	One To One			$10	Elektra 60499
4/15/89	65	22	©	5	Cross That Line			$10	Elektra 60794

All I Want (4) *76*
Always Asking Questions (3)
Assault And Battery (2)
Automaton (2)
Balance Of Love (Give And Take) (4)
Bounce Right Back (2,3)
Conditioning (1)
Cross That Line (5)

Don't Always Look At The Rain (1)
Don't Want To Fight Anymore (4)
Dream Into Action (2)
Elegy (2)
Equality (1)
Everlasting Love (5) *12*
Fresh Air Waltz (5)

Give Me Strength (4)
Good Luck, Bad Luck (4)
Guardians Of The Breath (5)
Hide And Seek (1,3)
Human's Lib (1)
Hunger For The Flesh (4)
Hunt The Self (1)
Is There A Difference? (2)
Last Supper (5)

Life In One Day (2) *19*
Like To Get To Know You Well (2) *49*
Little Bit Of Snow (4)
Look Mama (2,3)
Natural (1)
New Song (1) *27*
No One Is To Blame (2,3) *4*
Out Of Thin Air (5)

Pearl In The Shell (1)
Powerhouse (5)
Prisoner, The (5) *30*
Specialty (3)
Step Into These Shoes (4)
Things Can Only Get Better (2) *5*
Those Who Move Clouds (5)
Wanders To You (5)

What Is Love? (1) *33*
Where Are We Going? (4)
Will You Still Be There? (4)
You Know I Love You...Don't You? (4) *17*

★270★   JONES, Jack   '66

Born on 1/14/38 in Los Angeles. Pop singer. Son of actress Irene Hervey and actor/singer Allan Jones. Performed the theme for TV's *Love Boat*. Married to actress Jill St. John from 1967-69.

1)The Impossible Dream 2)Dear Heart 3)Wives And Lovers

6/29/63+	98	25		1	Call Me Irresponsible			$20	Kapp 3328
12/28/63+	18	53		2	Wives And Lovers			$20	Kapp 3352
6/20/64	43	19		3	Bewitched			$20	Kapp 3365
8/29/64	62	23		4	Where Love Has Gone			$20	Kapp 3396
12/19/64+	15ˣ	11		5	The Jack Jones Christmas Album		[X]	$20	Kapp 3399
					Christmas charts: 17/'64, 30/'65, 15/'66, 26/'67				
1/9/65	11	25		6	Dear Heart			$20	Kapp 3415
5/8/65	29	22		7	My Kind Of Town			$20	Kapp 3433
9/18/65	86	13		8	There's Love & There's Love & There's Love			$20	Kapp 3435
3/26/66	147	2		9	For The "In" Crowd			$20	Kapp 3465
7/16/66	9	64		10	The Impossible Dream			$20	Kapp 3486
11/26/66+	75	12		11	Jack Jones Sings			$20	Kapp 3500
3/25/67	23	25		12	Lady			$20	Kapp 3511
10/14/67	148	7		13	Our Song			$20	Kapp 3531
12/16/67+	146	7		14	Without Her			$15	RCA Victor 3911
2/24/68	167	6		15	What The World Needs Now Is Love!		[K]	$15	RCA Victor 3551
4/27/68	198	3		16	If You Ever Leave Me			$15	RCA Victor 3969
9/21/68	195	3		17	Where Is Love?			$15	RCA Victor 4048
8/16/68	183	4		18	A Time For Us			$15	RCA Victor 4209

Adeste Fideles (O Come All Ye Faithful) (medley) (5)
Afraid To Love (12)
After Today (13)
Afterthoughts (15)
Alfie (10)
All Or Nothing At All (10)
All The Things You Are (6)
Along The Way (13)
And I Love Her (8)
And I'll Go (18)
Angel Eyes (2)
Angels We Have Heard On High (medley) (5)
As Time Goes By (13)
Autumn Leaves (11)
Baby, Don't You Quit Now (16)
Baby I'm Yours (9)
Beautiful Friendship (12)
Bewitched (3)
Brother, Where Are You (12)
By Myself (4)
By The Time I Get To Phoenix (16)
Call Me Irresponsible (1) *75*
'Cause I Got So Much Lovin' In Me (13)
Charade (2)
Christmas Song (5)

Christmas Waltz (5)
Come Rain Or Come Shine (2)
Day In The Life Of A Fool (11) *62*
Dear Heart (6) *30*
Do You Hear What I Hear (5)
Don't Give Your Love Away (13)
Don't Rain On My Parade (1)
Don't Talk To Me (14)
Dreams Are All I Have Of You (17)
Easy To Be Hard (18)
Embraceable You (8)
Emily (6)
Ev'ry Time We Say Goodbye (4)
Eyes Of Love (15)
Face I Love (11)
Far Away (3)
Feeling Good (10)
First Noel (medley) (5)
Fly Me To The Moon (In Other Words) (2)
For All We Know (14)
Free Again (12)
From Russia With Love (3)
Girl Talk (12)
God Rest Ye Merry Gentlemen (medley) (5)

Goin' Out Of My Head (16)
Good Times (17)
Guess I'll Hang My Tears Out To Dry (15)
Gypsies, The Jugglers, And The Clowns (15)
Here's That Rainy Day (4)
Home (18)
Homeward Bound (14)
Hushed Whispers (14)
I Can't Believe I'm Losing You (7)
I Can't Believe That You're In Love With Me (8)
I Can't Get Started (14)
I Don't Care Much (11)
I Keep Leavin' Houses Behind (18)
I Must Know (7)
I Never Go There Anymore (15)
I Only Have Eyes For You (15)
I Really Want To Know You (17)
I See Your Face Before Me (2)
I Want To Meet Her (9)
I Will Wait For You (10)
I Wish You Love (2)
I'll Be Home For Christmas (5)
I'll Get By (As Long As I Have You) (6)

I'll Never Fall In Love Again (18)
I'm All Smiles (7)
I'm Falling In Love Again (16)
I'm Getting Sentimental Over You (16)
I'm Glad There Is You (In This World Of Ordinary People) (6)
I'm Indestructible (15) *81*
I'm Moody (2)
I'm Old Fashioned (3)
I've Grown Accustomed To Her Face (3)
If You Ever Leave Me (16) *92*
If You Go Away (12)
If You Never Come To Me (12)
Impossible Dream (The Quest) (10) *35*
"In" Crowd (9)
Isn't It Lonely Together (18)
Isn't It Romantic? (14)
It Came Upon A Midnight Clear (medley) (5)
It Only Takes A Moment (3)
It's Easy To Remember (12)
It's Nice To Be With You (17)
Josephine For Better Or For Worse (18)
Julie (1)
Just Yesterday (9) *73*

King Of The Road (7)
Lady (12) *39*
(Lara's Theme) ..see: Somewhere, My Love
Last Seven Days (18)
Letter (16)
Light My Fire (17)
Live For Life (15) *99*
Lollipops And Roses (1) *66*
Lonely Afternoon (17)
Long Ago, Last Night (16)
Look Of Love (14)
Lorelei (4)
Love After Midnight (11)
Love Bug (9) *71*
Love Is Here To Stay (6)
Love Letters (1)
Love With The Proper Stranger (3) *62*
Lovely Way To Spend An Evening (3)
Luck Be A Lady (3)
Lullaby For Christmas Eve (5)
Lush Life (4)
Mean To Me (14)
Michelle (13)
Mistletoe And Holly (5)
Mood I'm In (3)
Moonlight Becomes You (1)

More (7)
More And More (13)
My Best Girl (10)
My Favorite Things (5)
My Kind Of Town (7)
My Romance (1)
Nice 'N' Easy (12)
Night Is Young And You're So Beautiful (8)
Nina Never Knew (2)
Now I Know (13) *73*
Oh How Much I Love You (Dio Come Ti Amo!) (13)
Old Man River (17)
Once Upon A Time (12)
One I Love Belongs To Somebody Else (7,15)
1 - 2 - 3 (9)
Our Song (13) *92*
People (2)
People Will Say We're In Love (11)
Pretty (16)
Race Is On (7) *15*
Right As The Rain (3)
Rosalie (3)
Sand Pebbles (And We Were Lovers), Theme From The (12)

JONES, Jack — Cont'd

Seein' The Right Love Go Wrong (15) *46*
Shadow Of Your Smile (10)
Shining Sea (11)
Silent Night (medley) (5)
Sleigh Ride (5)
Snows Of Yesteryear (11)
Something's Gotta Give (6)
Somewhere (16)
Somewhere Along The Way (7)
Somewhere, My Love (Lara's Theme) (11)
Somewhere There's Someone (11)

Song About Love (2)
Spinning Wheel (18)
Strangers In The Night (10)
Street Of Dreams (11)
Summertime Promises (2)
Sunshine, Lollipops And Rainbows (9)
Suzanne (17)
Sweet Child (18)
Tenderly (8)
Thank Heaven For Little Girls (6)
Then Was Then And Now Is Now (10)

There Comes A Time (16)
There Will Never Be Another You (1)
There's Love & There's Love & There's Love (8)
They Didn't Believe Me (1)
This Is All I Ask (10)
This Was My Love (1)
Time After Time (7)
Time For Us (Love Theme From Romeo And Juliet) (18)
To Love And Be Loved (4)
Toys In The Attic (2) *92*
Travellin' On (7)

True Love (8,15)
True Picture (13)
Valley Of The Dolls (17)
Village Of St. Bernadette (5)
(Waitin') 'Round The Bend (17)
Watch What Happens (11)
Weekend, The (9)
What Now My Love (10)
What The World Needs Now Is Love (9,15)
What's New? (4)
When I Look In Your Eyes (13)
When She Makes Music (6)
Where Is Love? (17)

Where Love Has Gone (4) *62*
While We're Young (8)
White Christmas (5)
Wildflower (9)
Willow Weep For Me (4)
Without Her (14)
Wives And Lovers (2) *14*
Yes, I Can! (7)
Yesterday (9,15)
You And The Night And The Music (14)
You Better Go Now (10)
You Do Something To Me (8)

You Made Me Love You (I Didn't Want To Do It) (8)
You Stepped Out Of A Dream (1)
You'd Better Love Me (6)
You're My Girl (6)
You're Sensational (6)
You've Got Your Troubles (9)
Young At Heart (8)

JONES, Jesus — see JESUS

JONES, Jonah   '58
Born Robert Jones on 10/31/09 in Louisville, Kentucky. Died on 4/30/2000 (age 90). Jazz trumpeter.

| 3/10/58 | 7 | 17 | | 1 Muted Jazz | [I] | $40 | Capitol 839 |

THE JONAH JONES QUARTET:

| 4/28/58 | 7 | 19 | | 2 Swingin' On Broadway | [I] | $40 | Capitol 963 |
| 9/8/58 | 14 | 5 | © 3 | Jumpin' With Jonah | [I] | $30 | Capitol 1039 |

Baby, Won't You Please Come Home (3)
Baubles, Bangles And Beads (2)
Bill Bailey Won't You Please Come Home? (3)
Blues Don't Care (Who's Got 'Em) (3)

Dance Only With Me (3)
Hey There (2)
I Can't Get Started (1)
I Could Have Danced All Night (2)
It's A Good Day (3)
Jumpin' With Jonah (3)
Just A Gigolo (3)

Just In Time (2)
Just My Luck (2)
Kiss To Build A Dream On (3)
Lots Of Luck Charley (3)
Mack The Knife (1)
Man With The Golden Arm, Main Title From (1)
My Blue Heaven (1)

Night Train (3)
No Moon At All (3)
On The Street Where You Live (1)
Party's Over (2)
Rose Room (1)
Royal Garden Blues (1)
Seventy Six Trombones (2)

St. James Infirmary (1)
Surrey With The Fringe On Top (2)
That's A Plenty (3)
Till There Was You (2)
Too Close For Comfort (1)
Undecided (1)
Whatever Lola Wants (2)

You're Just In Love (2)
You're So Right For Me (2)

JONES, Mick   '89
Born on 12/27/44 in London. Rock guitarist. Member of **Spooky Tooth** and **Foreigner**. Not to be confused with Mick Jones of The Clash and Big Audio Dynamite.

| 9/23/89 | 184 | 3 | © | Mick Jones | | $10 | Atlantic 81991 |

Danielle
Everything That Comes Around

4 Wheels Turnin'
Johnny (Part 1)

Just Wanna Hold
Save Me Tonight

That's The Way My Love Is
Write Tonight

Wrong Side Of The Law
You Are My Friend

JONES, Oran "Juice"   '86
Born on 3/28/57 in Houston; raised in Harlem, New York. R&B singer/rapper.

| 9/20/86 | 44 | 22 | © | Oran "Juice" Jones | | $10 | Def Jam 40367 |

Curiosity
Here I Go Again

It's Yours
Love Will Find A Way

1.2.1
Rain, The *9*

Two Faces
You Can't Hide From Love

Your Song

JONES, Quincy ★176★   '74
Born on 3/14/33 in Chicago; raised in Seattle. Composer/producer/conductor/arranger. Began as a jazz trumpeter with Lionel Hampton (1950-53). Music director for Mercury Records in 1961, then vice president in 1964. Wrote scores for many movies. Scored TV series *Roots* in 1977. Arranger/producer for hundreds of successful singers and orchestras. Produced **Michael Jackson**'s mega-albums *Off The Wall*, *Thriller* and *Bad*. Established own Qwest label in 1981. Married to actress Peggy Lipton (TV's *Mod Squad*) from 1974-89. Won the Grammy's Trustees Award in 1989. Won Grammy's Living Legends Award in 1990. His biographical movie *Listen Up: The Lives Of Quincy Jones* was released in 1990.

1)Body Heat 2)Back On The Block 3)The Dude

12/29/62+	112	8	© 1	Big Band Bossa Nova	[I]	$40	Mercury 60751
11/22/69+	56	39	© 2	Walking In Space	[I]	$15	A&M 3023
9/5/70	63	16	© 3	Gula Matari	[I]	$15	A&M 3030
10/16/71	56	33	© 4	Smackwater Jack	[I]	$15	A&M 3037
3/4/72	173	9		5 Ndeda	[I-K]	$20	Mercury 623 [2]
6/2/73	94	24		6 You've Got It Bad Girl	[	$15	A&M 3041
5/25/74	6	43	● © 7	Body Heat		$15	A&M 3617
8/23/75	16	30	© 8	Mellow Madness		$15	A&M 4526
10/2/76	43	15		9 I Heard That!!	[K]	$20	A&M 3705 [2]
2/19/77	21	14	●	10 Roots	[TV]	$15	A&M 4626
6/24/78	15	20	▲ © 11	Sounds...And Stuff Like That!!		$15	A&M 4685
4/4/81+	10	80	▲ © 12	The Dude	C:#23/89	$12	A&M 3721
7/17/82	122	17	© 13	The Best	[G]	$12	A&M 3200
12/9/89+	9	40	▲ © 14	Back On The Block		$10	Qwest 26020
11/25/95	32	38	▲ © 15	Q's Jook Joint		$10	Qwest 45875
2/20/99	72	8	© 16	From Q, With Love	[K]	$15	Qwest 46490 [2]

Ai No Corrida (12,13) *28*
Air Mail Special (9)
Along Came Betty (7)
Anderson Tapes, Theme From The (4,9)
At The End Of The Day (Grace) (15,16)
Baby, Come To Me (16)
Back At The Chicken Shack (5)
Back On The Block (14)
Beautiful Black Girl (8)
Behold, The Only Thing Greater Than Yourself (Birth) (10)

Betcha' Wouldn't Hurt Me (12,13)
Birdland (14)
Birth Of A Band (5)
Bluesette (8)
Body Heat (7,9,13)
Boogie Bossa Nova (1)
Boogie Joe, The Grinder (7)
Boy In The Tree (4)
Boyhood To Manhood (10)
(Brazilian Wedding Song) ..see: Setembro
Bridge Over Troubled Water (3)

Brown Ballad (4)
Brown Soft Shoe (9)
Carnival (Manha De Carnaval) (1)
Cast Your Fate To The Wind (4)
Chega De Saudade (No More Blues) (1)
Chump Change (6)
Cool Joe, Mean Joe (Killer Joe) (15)
Cry Baby (8)
Dead End (2)
Desafinado (1)

Do Nothin' Till You Hear From Me (15)
Dreamsville (5)
Dude, The (12)
Everything (16)
Everything Must Change (7,13,16)
Eyes Of Love (6)
Free At Last? (The Civil War) (10)
Getaway, Love Theme From The (6)
Golden Boy, Theme From (5)

Gravy Waltz (5)
Guitar Blues Odyssey: From Roots To Fruits (9)
Gula Matari (3,9)
Harlem Drive (5)
Heaven's Girl (15,16)
Hikky-Burr (4)
How Do You Keep The Music Playing? (16)
Human Nature (16)
Hummin' (3)
(I Can't Get No) Satisfaction (5)
I Don't Go For That (14)

I Had A Ball (5)
I Heard That!! (9)
I Never Told You (2)
I'll Be Good To You (14) *18*
I'm Gonna Miss You In The Morning (11,13,16)
I'm Yours (16)
If I Ever Lose This Heaven (7,9,13)
If This Time Is The Last Time (16)
Ironside (4)

JONES, Quincy — Cont'd

Is It Love That We're Missin' (8,9,15) **70**
Jazz Corner Of The Word (14)
Jive Samba (5)
Jumpin' De Broom (Marriage Ceremony) (6)
Just A Little Taste Of Me (8)
Just A Man (7)
Just Once (12,13,16) **17**
Killer Joe (2,9,13) **74**
Lady In My Life (16)
Lalo Bossa Nova (1,5)
Let The Good Times Roll (15)
Liberian Girl (16)
Listen (What It Is) (8)
Love And Peace (2)
Love Dance (16)
Love, I Never Had It So Good (11)
Love Me By Name (11)

Manteca (6)
Many Rains Ago (Oluwa) (10)
Mellow Madness (8)
Middle Passage (Slaveship Crossing) (10)
Midnight Soul Patrol (9)
Midnight Sun Will Never Set (5)
Mirage (5)
Moody's Mood For Love (15,16)
Motherland (10)
Mr. Lucky (5)
My Cherie Amour (8)
Oh Happy Day (2)
Oh Lord, Come By Here (10)
Ole Fiddler (10)
On The Street Where You Live (1)
One Hundred Ways (12,16) **14**
One Man Woman (14)

One Track Mind (7)
Paranoid (8)
Pawnbroker, Theme From The (5)
Peter Gunn (5)
Places You Find Love (14)
Rack 'Em Up (5)
Razzamatazz (12)
Rock With You (15,16)
"Roots" Medley (10) **57**
Roots (Mama Aifambeni), Main Title (10)
Samba De Uma Nota So (One Note Samba) (1)
Sanford & Son Theme (The Streetbeater) (6)
Sax In The Garden (16)
Se E Tarde Me, Pardoa (Forgive Me If I'm Late) (1)
Seaweed (5)

Secret Garden (Sweet Seduction Suite) (14,16) **31**
Serenata (1)
Setembro (Brazilian Wedding Song) (14,16)
Shadow Of Your Smile (Love Theme From The Sandpiper) (16)
Slender Thread (5)
Slow Jams (15) **68**
Smackwater Jack (4)
Somethin' Special (12)
Something I Cannot Have (16)
Somewhere (16)
Soul Bossa Nova (1,5)
Soul Saga (Song Of The Buffalo Soldier) (7)
Stomp (15)
Stuff Like That (11,13,15) **21**
Summer In The City (6,9)

Superstition (6,9)
Superwoman (Where Were You When I Needed You) (5)
Takin' It To The Streets (11)
Tell Me A Bedtime Story (11)
There's A Train Leavin' (9)
Things Could Be Worse For Me (9)
Tomorrow (A Better You, A Better Me) (14) **75**
Touboo Is Here! (The Capture) (10)
Tribute To A.F. - RO Medley (5)
Tryin' To Find Out About You (8)
Turn On The Action (12)
Velas (12,16)
Verb To Be (14)
Walkin' (3)
Walking In Space (2,9)

Wee B. Dooinit (14)
What Good Is A Song (9)
What Shall I Do? (Hush, Hush, Somebody's Calling My Name) (10)
What's Going On? (4,13)
Witching Hour (5)
You Have To Do It Yourself (9)
You In Americuh Now, African (10)
You Put A Move On My Heart (15,16) **98**
You've Got It Bad Girl (6)

★484★ JONES, Rickie Lee '79
Born on 11/8/54 in Chicago. Female singer/songwriter. Won the 1979 Best New Artist Grammy Award.
1)Rickie Lee Jones 2)Pirates 3)Flying Cowboys

DEBUT	PEAK	WKS	RIAA	CD	#	Album Title	Sym	$	Label & Number
4/7/79	3	36	▲	©	1	Rickie Lee Jones		$12	Warner 3296
8/8/81	5	29	●	©	2	Pirates		$12	Warner 3432
7/2/83	39	16			3	Girl At Her Volcano	[M]	$12	Warner 23805
10/13/84	44	21		©	4	The Magazine		$12	Warner 25117
10/14/89	39	25	●	©	5	Flying Cowboys		$10	Geffen 24246
10/12/91	121	5		©	6	Pop Pop		$10	Geffen 24426
10/2/93	111	7		©	7	Traffic From Paradise		$10	Geffen 24602
10/7/95	121	2		©	8	Naked Songs - Live And Acoustic	[L]	$10	Reprise 45950
7/5/97	159	1		©	9	Ghosthead		$10	Reprise 46557
9/30/00	148	2		©	10	It's Like This		$10	Artemis 751054

After Hours (Twelve Bars Past Goodnight) (1)
Albatross, The (7)
Altar Boy (7,8)
Atlas' Marker (5)
Autumn Leaves (8)
Away From The Sky (5)
Ballad Of The Sad Young Men (6)
Beat Angels (7)
Bye Bye Blackbird (6)
Chuck E.'s In Love (1,8) **4**
Cloud Of Unknowing (9)
Comin' Back To Me (6)
Company (1)
Coolsville (1,8)
Cycles (5)
Danny's All-Star Joint (1)
Dat Dere (6)

Deep Space (5)
Don't Let The Sun Catch You Crying (5)
Easy Money (1)
Firewalker (9)
Flying Cowboys (5,8)
For No One (10)
Ghetto Of My Mind (5)
Ghost Train (5)
Ghostyhead (9)
Gravity (4)
Hey, Bub (3)
Hi-Lili Hi-Lo (6)
Horses, The (5,8)
Howard (9)
I Can't Get Started (10)
I Won't Grow Up (6)
I'll Be Seeing You (6)
It Must Be Love (4,8)

Jolie Jolie (7)
Juke Box Fury (4)
Just My Baby (5)
Last Chance Texaco (1,8)
Letters From The 9th Ward (medley) (3)
Little Yellow Town (9)
Living It Up (2,8)
Love Is Gonna Bring Us Back Alive (5)
Love Junkyard (6)
Low Spark Of High Heeled Boys (10)
Lucky Guy (2) **64**
Lush Life (3)
Magazine (4,8)
Matters (9)
My Funny Valentine (3)
My One And Only Love (6)

Night Train (1)
On Saturday Afternoons In 1963 (1)
On The Street Where You Live (10)
One Hand, One Heart (10)
Pink Flamingos (7)
Pirates (So Long Lonely Avenue) (2)
Rainbow Sleeves (3)
Real End (4) **83**
Rebel Rebel (7)
Returns, The (2)
Road Kill (9)
Rodeo Girl (9)
Rorschachs (medley) (4)
Runaround (4)
Running From Mercy (7)
Satellites (5)

Scary Chinese Movie (3)
Second Time Around (6)
Show Biz Kids (10)
Skeletons (2,8)
Smile (10)
So Long (3)
Someone To Watch Over Me (10)
Spring Can Really Hang You Up The Most (6)
Stewart's Coat (7,8)
Stranger's Car (7)
Sunny Afternoon (9)
Theme For The Pope (medley) (4)
Tigers (7)
Traces Of The Western Slopes (2)
Trouble Man (10)

Under The Boardwalk (3)
Unsigned Painting (medley) (4)
Up A Lazy River (10)
Up From The Skies (6)
Vessel Of Light (9)
Walk Away Rene (medley) (3)
We Belong Together (2,8)
Weasel And The White Boys Cool (1,8)
Weird Beast (medley) (4)
Woody And Dutch On The Slow Train To Peking (2)
Young Blood (1,8) **40**

JONES, Shirley '86
Born in Detroit. Lead singer of **The Jones Girls**.

DEBUT	PEAK	WKS				Album Title		$	Label & Number
8/23/86	128	10				Always In The Mood		$10	Philadelphia Int'l. 53031

Always In The Mood
Breaking Up

Caught Me With My Guard Down

Do You Get Enough Love
I'll Do Anything For You

Last Night I Needed Somebody
She Knew About Me

Surrender

JONES, Spike, & His City Slickers '63
Born Lindley Armstrong Jones on 12/14/11 in Long Beach, California. Died of emphysema on 5/1/65 (age 53). Novelty bandleader. Known as "The King of Corn."

DEBUT	PEAK	WKS				Album Title		$	Label & Number
11/23/63	113	4				Washington Square	[I]	$25	Liberty 3338

Alley Cat
Ballad Of Jed Clampett

Blowin' In The Wind
Frankie And Johnnie

Green, Green
If I Had A Hammer

Maria Elena
Puff (The Magic Dragon)

Red Sails In The Sunset
September Song

Washington Square
Whistler's Muddah

JONES, Steve '89
Born on 9/3/55 in London. Rock guitarist. Member of the **Sex Pistols**.

DEBUT	PEAK	WKS				Album Title		$	Label & Number
10/21/89	169	4		©		Fire And Gasoline		$10	MCA 6298

Fire And Gasoline
Freedom Fighter

Get Ready
Gimme Love

God In Louisiana
Hold On

I Did U No Wrong
Leave Your Shoes On

Trouble Maker
We're Not Saints

Wild Wheels

JONES, Tom ★153★ '69
Born Thomas Jones Woodward on 6/7/40 in Pontypridd, South Wales. Pop singer. Won the 1965 Best New Artist Grammy Award. Host of own TV musical variety series from 1969-71.

1)Tom Jones Live In Las Vegas 2)This Is Tom Jones 3)Help Yourself

DEBUT	PEAK	WKS	RIAA	CD	#	Album Title		$	Label & Number
7/3/65	54	42			1	It's Not Unusual		$20	Parrot 71004
9/18/65	114	5		©	2	What's New Pussycat?		$20	Parrot 71006
3/4/67+	65	45	●	©	3	Green, Green Grass Of Home		$20	Parrot 71009
6/15/68+	14	82	●		4	The Tom Jones Fever Zone		$20	Parrot 71019
2/1/69	5	54	●		5	Help Yourself		$20	Parrot 71025

DEBUT	PEAK	WKS	RIAA	CD	ARTIST — Album Title	Catalog	Sym	$	Label & Number

JONES, Tom — Cont'd

DEBUT	PEAK	WKS			Album Title		Sym	$	Label & Number
3/15/69	13	58	●	© 6	Tom Jones Live!		[L]	$20	Parrot 71014
					originally recorded and released in 1967				
6/14/69	4	43	●	7	This Is Tom Jones			$20	Parrot 71028
11/15/69	3	51	●	8	Tom Jones Live In Las Vegas		[L]	$20	Parrot 71031
					recorded at The Flamingo hotel				
5/9/70	6	26	●	9	Tom			$20	Parrot 71037
11/14/70	23	40	●	© 10	I (Who Have Nothing)			$20	Parrot 71039
5/22/71	17	20	●	11	She's A Lady			$20	Parrot 71046
11/6/71	43	14	●	12	Tom Jones Live At Caesars Palace		[L]	$25	Parrot 71049 [2]
6/17/72	64	20		13	Close Up			$20	Parrot 71055
6/16/73	93	10		14	The Body And Soul Of Tom Jones			$15	Parrot 71060
1/5/74	185	4		15	Tom Jones' Greatest Hits		[G]	$15	Parrot 71062
3/5/77	76	16		16	Say You'll Stay Until Tomorrow			$12	Epic 34468
3/5/77	191	3		17	Tom Jones Greatest Hits		[G]	$12	London 50002
5/23/81	179	3		© 18	Darlin'			$12	Mercury 4010

Ain't No Sunshine (14)
All I Can Say Is Goodbye (5)
All I Ever Need Is You (13)
And I Tell The Sea (2)
Anniversary Song (16)
Any Day Now (3)
At Every End There's A Beginning (16)
Autumn Leaves (1)
Ballad Of Billy Joe (14)
Bama Lama Bama Loo (2)
Bed, The (5)
Bridge Over Troubled Water (12)
Bright Lights And You Girl (8)
Brother Can You Spare A Dime (10)
But I Do (18)
Cabaret (12)
Can't Stop Loving You (10) *25*
Come Home Rhondda Boy (18)
Come To Me (16)
Dance Of Love (7,12)
Danny Boy (4,8)
Darlin' (18)
Daughter Of Darkness (10,12,15) *13*
Daughter's Question (18)
Dime Queen Of Nevada (18)
Do What You Gotta Do (11)
Don't Fight It (4)
Ebb Tide (The Sea) (11)
Elusive Dreams (5)
Endlessly (2)

Fly Me To The Moon (In Other Words) (7)
Funny Familiar Forgotten Feelings (15,17) *49*
Funny How Time Slips Away (4)
Georgia On My Mind (3)
Get Ready (4)
God Bless The Children (12)
Good News (6)
Green, Green Grass Of Home (3,6,15,17) *11*
Hard To Handle (8)
Have You Ever Been Lonely (16)
Hello Young Lovers (6)
Help Yourself (5,8,15,17) *35*
Hey Jude (7,8)
Hi Heel Sneakers (14)
Hold On, I'm Coming (4)
House Song (5)
I Believe (6)
I Can't Break The News To Myself (11)
I Can't Stop Loving You (6,8)
I Can't Turn You Loose (9)
I Don't Want To Know You That Well (14)
I Get Carried Away (5)
I Have Dreamed (10)
I Know (4)
I Need Your Loving (1)
I Still Love You Enough (To Love You All Over Again) (14)
I Thank You (9)
I Wake Up Crying (4)
I Was Made To Love Her (4)

I (Who Have Nothing) (10,12) *14*
I Won't Be Sorry To See Suzanne Again (13)
I'll Never Fall In Love Again (8,12,15,17) *6*
I'll Share My World With You (14)
I'm A Fool To Want You (7)
I'm Coming Home (17) *57*
I've Got A Heart (2)
If (13)
If Ever I Would Leave You (3)
If I Promise (5)
If I Ruled The World (9)
If Loving You Is Wrong (I Don't Wanna Be Right) (14)
If You Go Away (5)
If You Need Me (1)
Impossible Dream (9)
In Dreams (11)
It's A Man's Man's World (4)
It's Just A Matter Of Time (1)
It's Not Unusual (1,6,8,12,15,17) *10*
It's Up To The Woman (11)
Kansas City (3)
Keep On Running (4)
Kiss An Angel Good Morning (13)
Lady Lay Down (18)
Land Of A Thousand Dances (6)
Laura (5)
Lean On Me (14)
Let It Be Me (7)

Let There Be Love (9)
Letter To Lucille (14) *60*
Little By Little (2)
Little Green Apples (7)
Lodi (10)
Love Me Tonight (8,12,15,17) *13*
Love's Been Good To Me (10)
Memphis Tennessee (1)
My Girl Maria (5)
My Mother's Eyes (3)
My Prayer (7)
My Way (12)
My Yiddische Momme (6)
No Guarantee (18)
Not Responsible (6) *58*
Nothing Rhymed (11)
Once Upon A Time (1)
One Man Woman (16)
One More Chance (2)
One Night (18)
One Night Only Love Maker (11)
Only Once (7)
Papa (6)
Polk Salad Annie (9)
Proud Mary (9)
Puppet Man (11) *26*
Resurrection Shuffle (11,12) *38*
Rock N' Roll Medley (12)
Rose, The (2)
Runnin' Bear (14)
Say You'll Stay Until Tomorrow (16) *15*

See-Saw (10)
Set Me Free (5)
Shake (6)
She's A Lady (11,12,15) *2*
Since I Loved You Last (14)
(Sitting On) The Dock Of The Bay (7)
Skye Boat Song (1)
So Afraid (5)
Some Day (You'll Want Me) (3)
Some Other Guy (2)
Soul Man (12)
Spanish Harlem (1)
Sugar Sugar (9)
Take Me Tonight (16)
Taste Of Honey (3)
That Lucky Old Sun (6)
That Old Black Magic (3)
That Wonderful Sound (7)
That's All Any Man Can Say (7)
Things That Matter Most To Me (18)
Til I Can't Take It Anymore (11)
Till (12) *41*
Time To Get It Together (13)
Tired Of Being Alone (13)
To Love Somebody (10)
To Wait For Love (Is To Waste Your Life Away) (2)
Today I Started Loving You (14)
Try A Little Tenderness (10)
Turn On Your Love Light (8)
Twist And Shout (4)
Untrue (2)
Venus (9)

Watcha Gonna Do (1)
We Had It All (16)
What In The World's Come Over You (18)
What The World Needs Now (10)
What's New Pussycat? (2,6,15,17) *3*
When I Fall In Love (3)
When It's Just You And Me (16)
When The World Was Beautiful (1)
Wichita Lineman (7)
Witch Queen Of New Orleans (13)
With These Hands (2) *27*
Without Love (There Is Nothing) (9,17) *5*
Without You (Non C'E' Che Lei) (7)
Woman You Took My Life (13)
Worried Man (1)
Yesterday (8)
You Came A Long Way From St. Louis (3)
You Keep Me Hanging On (4)
You're My World (Il Mio Mondo) (11)
You've Got A Friend (3)
You've Lost That Lovin' Feelin' (9)
Young New Mexican Puppeteer (13) *80*

JONES GIRLS, The   '79

R&B vocal trio from Detroit: sisters Brenda, Valorie and **Shirley Jones**.

DEBUT	PEAK	WKS			Album Title			$	Label & Number
6/9/79	50	16		1	The Jones Girls			$12	Philadelphia Int'l. 35757
10/18/80	96	24		2	At Peace With Woman			$12	Philadelphia Int'l. 36767
12/5/81+	155	15		3	Get As Much Love As You Can			$12	Philadelphia Int'l. 37627

ASAP (As Soon As Possible) (3)
At Peace With Woman (2)
Back In The Day (2)
Children Of The Night (2)
Dance Turned Into A Romance (2)

Get As Much Love As You Can (3)
I Close My Eyes (2)
(I Found) That Man Of Mine (3)
I Just Love The Man (2)
I'm At Your Mercy (1)

Let's Be Friends First (Then Lovers) (3)
Let's Celebrate (Sittin' On Top Of The World) (2)
Life Goes On (1)
Love Don't Ever Say Goodbye (3)

Nights Over Egypt (3)
Show Love Today (1)
This Feeling's Killing Me (1)
We're A Melody (1)
When I'm Gone (2)
Who Can I Run To (1)
World Will Sing Our Song (3)

You Gonna Make Me Love Somebody Else (1) *38*
You Made Me Love You (1)
You're Breakin' My Heart (3)

JONZUN CREW, The   '83

Funk group from Boston: brothers Michael (vocals) and Soni (keyboards) Johnson, with Gordy Worthy (bass) and Steve Thorpe (drums).

DEBUT	PEAK	WKS			Album Title			$	Label & Number
5/14/83	66	20	©		Lost In Space			$10	Tommy Boy 1001

Electro Boogie Encounter   Ground Control   Pack Jam   Space Cowboy   Space Is The Place   We Are The Jonzun Crew

★328★   **JOPLIN, Janis**   '71

Born on 1/19/43 in Port Arthur, Texas. Died of a heroin overdose on 10/4/70 (age 27). White blues-rock singer. Nicknamed "Pearl." To San Francisco in 1966, joined **Big Brother & The Holding Company**. Left band to go solo in 1968. **Bette Midler** movie *The Rose* was inspired by Joplin's life. Inducted into the Rock and Roll Hall of Fame in 1995.

DEBUT	PEAK	WKS	RIAA	CD	Album Title	Catalog	Sym	$	Label & Number
10/11/69	5	28	▲	© 1	I Got Dem Ol' Kozmic Blues Again Mama!			$20	Columbia 9913
1/30/71	❶⁹	42	▲⁴	© 2	Pearl	C:#18/38		$20	Columbia 30322
5/13/72	4	27	●	© 3	Joplin In Concert		[L]	$25	Columbia 31160 [2]
					side 1: with Big Brother & The Holding Company; side 2: with Full Tilt Boogie Band				
7/14/73	37	22	▲⁷	© 4	Janis Joplin's Greatest Hits	C:#2¹/445	[G]	$15	Columbia 32168
5/17/75	54	9		© 5	Janis	C:#39/2	[S]	$15	Columbia 33345 [2]
2/13/82	104	11		© 6	Farewell Song		[K]	$12	Columbia 37569

All Is Loneliness (3)
Amazing Grace (medley) (6)
As Good As You've Been To This World (1)
Ball And Chain (3,4,5)
Black Mountain Blues (5)

Buried Alive In The Blues (2)
Bye, Bye Baby (3,4)
Careless Love (5)
Catch Me Daddy (6)
Cry Baby (2,4,5) *42*
Daddy, Daddy, Daddy (5)

Down On Me (3,4) *91*
Ego Rock (3)
Farewell Song (6)
Flower In The Sun (3)
Get It While You Can (2,3,4) *78*

Half Moon (2,3)
Harry (6)
Hi Heel Sneakers (medley) (6)
I'll Drown In My Own Tears (5)
K.C. Blues (5)
Kozmic Blues (1,3) *41*

Little Girl Blue (1)
Magic Of Love (6)
Mary Jane (5)
Maybe (1,5)
Me And Bobby McGee (2,4,5) *1*

Mercedes Benz (2,5)
Misery'N (4)
Mississippi River (5)
Move Over (2,3,4,5)
My Baby (3)
No Reason For Livin' (5)

JOPLIN, Janis — Cont'd

One Good Man (1)	River Jordan (5)	Silver Threads And Golden	Tell Mama (6)	Try (Just A Little Bit Harder)	Winin' Boy (5)
One Night Stand (6)	Road Block (3)	Needles (5)	To Love Somebody (1)	(1,3,4,5)	Woman Left Lonely (2)
Piece Of My Heart (3,4,5) *12*	San Francisco Bay Blues (5)	Stealin' (5)	Trouble In Mind (5)	Walk Right In (5)	Work Me, Lord (1)
Raise Your Hand (6)	See See Rider (5)	Summertime (3,4,5)	Trust Me (2)	What Good Can Drinkin' Do (5)	

JORDAN, Jeremy   '93

Born Don Henson on 9/19/73 in Hammond, Indiana: raised in Calumet City, Illinois.

DEBUT	PEAK	WKS	CD	Title	$	Label & Number
5/15/93	176	2	©	Try My Love	$10	Giant 24483

Different Man	I Wanna Be With You	Lovin' On Hold	**Right Kind Of Love** *14*	**Wannagirl** *28*
Do It To The Music	It's Alright (This Love Is For	My Love Is Good Enough	Show Me Where It Hurts	
Girl You Got It Goin' On	Real)	My Name Is J.J.	Try My Love	

JORDAN, Jerry   '75

Born in Texas. Country/religious comedian.

DEBUT	PEAK	WKS	CD	Title	Sym	$	Label & Number
5/31/75	79	12	©	Phone Call From God	[C]	$12	MCA 473

Air-Conditioned Cars	It All Depends	Overdrawn At The Bank	Prejudiced People
Hog Story	No Hand To Dismiss	Phone Call From God	Tell Me The Story

JORDAN, Lonnie   '78

Born LeRoy Jordan on 11/21/48 in San Diego. R&B singer/keyboardist. Member of **War**.

DEBUT	PEAK	WKS	Title	$	Label & Number
2/25/78	158	5	Different Moods Of Me	$12	MCA 2329

Best Way I Can	Discoland	He Used To Be A Friend Of	Jungle Dancin'	Nasty
Different Moods Of Me	Grey Rainy Days	Mine	Junkie To My Music	

JORDAN, Montell   '95

Born on 12/3/68 in Los Angeles. R&B singer.

DEBUT	PEAK	WKS	RIAA	CD	#	Title	$	Label & Number
4/22/95	12	36	▲	©	1	This Is How We Do It	$10	Def Jam 527179
9/14/96	47	24	●	©	2	More...	$10	Def Jam 533191
4/18/98	20	26	●	©	3	Let's Ride	$10	Def Jam 536987
11/27/99	32	26	●	©	4	Get It On...Tonite	$10	Def Soul 546714

Against All Odds (4)	Daddy's Home (1)	**Get It On Tonite** (4) *4*	Last Night (Can We Move On?)	Once Upon A Time (4)	What's It Feel Like? (Is It
All I Need (2)	Do You? (4)	Gotta' Get My Roll On (1)	(4)	One Last Chance (3)	Good?) (4)
Anything And Everything (3)	Don't Call Me (3)	**I Can Do That** (3) *14*	Let Me Be The One (Come	One Last Time (Break Up Sex)	**What's On Tonight** (2) *21*
Body Ah (3)	Don't Keep Me Waiting (1)	**I Like** (2) *28*	Runnin') (2)	(4)	When You Get Home (3)
Bounce 2 This (2)	Down On My Knees (1)	I Say Yes (2,3)	Let's Cuddle Up (4)	Payback (1)	Why You Wanna Do That?
Can I? (3)	Everybody (Get Down) (4)	I Wanna (1)	**Let's Ride** (3) *2*	**Somethin' 4 Da Honeyz** (1) *21*	(Ooh Girl) (4)
Can't Get Enough (4)	Everything Is Gonna Be Alright	I'll Do Anything (1)	Longest Night (3)	Superlover Man (2)	
Close The Door (1)	(2)	Introducing Shaunta (1)	Maybe She Will (4)	**This Is How We Do It** (1) *1*	
Come Home (4)	**Falling** (2) *18*	Irresistible (3)	Missing You (3)	Time To Say Goodbye (4)	
Comin' Home (1)	4 You (3)	It's Over (1)	Never Alone (2)	Tricks On My Mind (4)	

JORDAN, Sass   '94

Born in 1962 in Montreal. Female rock singer.

DEBUT	PEAK	WKS	CD	#	Title	$	Label & Number
8/29/92	174	7	©	1	Racine	$10	Impact 10524
3/19/94	158	4	©	2	Rats	$10	Impact 10980

Breakin' (2)	Give (2)	Honey (2)	Make You A Believer (1)	Time Flies (1)	Windin' Me Up (1)
Cry Baby (1)	Goin' Back Again (1)	I Want To Believe (1)	Pissin' Down (2)	Ugly (2)	Wish (2)
Damaged (2)	Head (2)	I'm Not (2)	Slave (2)	Where There's A Will (1)	You Don't Have To Remind Me
Do What Ya Want (1)	High Road Easy (2)	If You're Gonna Love Me (1)	**Sun's Gonna Rise** (2) *86*	Who Do You Think You Are (1)	(1)

JORDAN, Stanley   '85

Born on 7/31/59 in Chicago. Jazz guitarist.

DEBUT	PEAK	WKS	CD	#	Title	Sym	$	Label & Number
5/25/85	64	66	©	1	Magic Touch	[I]	$10	Blue Note 85101
2/14/87	116	18	©	2	Standards, Volume 1	[I]	$10	Blue Note 85130
10/15/88	131	9	©	3	Flying Home	[I]	$10	EMI 48682

All The Children (1)	Child Is Born (1)	Georgia On My Mind (2)	My Favorite Things (2)	Silent Night (2)	Time Is Now (3)
Angel (1)	Eleanor Rigby (1)	Guitar Man (2)	One Less Bell To Answer (2)	Sound Of Silence (2)	Tropical Storm (3)
Because (2)	Flying Home (3)	Lady In My Life (1)	Return Expedition (1)	Stairway To Heaven (3)	When Julia Smiles (3)
Brooklyn At Midnight (3)	Freddie Freeloader (1)	Moon River (2)	Round Midnight (1)	Street Talk (3)	
Can't Sit Down (3)	Fundance (1)	Music's Gonna Change (3)	Send One Your Love (2)	Sunny (2)	

JOSEPH, Margie   '71

Born in 1950 in Gautier, Mississippi. R&B singer.

DEBUT	PEAK	WKS	CD	#	Title	$	Label & Number
2/6/71	67	14	©	1	Margie Joseph Makes A New Impression	$20	Volt 6012
8/17/74	165	3		2	Sweet Surrender	$15	Atlantic 7277

Baby I'm-A Want You (2)	He's Got A Way (2)	Medicine Bend (1)	**Stop! In The Name Of Love**	Temptation's About To Take
Come Lay Some Lovin' On Me	How Beautiful The Rain (1)	**My Love** (2) *69*	(1) *96*	Your Love (1)
(2)	I'm Fed Up (1)	Punish Me (1)	(Strange) I Still Love You (2)	To Know You Is To Love You
Come Tomorrow (1)	If I'm Still Around Tomorrow (1)	Ridin' High (2)	Sweet Surrender (2)	(2)
Come With Me (2)	Make Me Believe You'll Stay (1)	Same Thing (1)	Sweeter Tomorrow (1)	

JOURNEY   ★90★   '81

Rock group formed in San Francisco: **Neal Schon** and George Tickner (guitars), Gregg Rolie (keyboards, vocals), Ross Valory (bass) and Aynsley Dunbar (drums; **John Mayall** and **Frank Zappa**'s Mothers Of Invention). Schon and Rolie had been in **Santana**. Tickner left in 1975. **Steve Perry** (lead vocals) added by 1978. In 1979, Steve Smith replaced Dunbar, who later joined **Jefferson Starship**, then **Whitesnake**. **Jonathan Cain** (keyboards; **The Babys**) added in 1981, replacing Rolie. In 1986 group pared down to a three-man core: Perry, Schon and Cain. The latter two hooked up with **Bad English** in 1989. Smith, Valory and Rolie joined **The Storm** in 1991. Schon with Hardline in 1992. Reunion in 1996 of Perry, Schon, Cain, Valory and Smith. Steve Augeri replaced Perry in 2001.

1)Escape 2)Frontiers 3)Trial By Fire

DEBUT	PEAK	WKS	RIAA	CD	#	Title	Sym	$	Label & Number
5/3/75	138	9		©	1	Journey		$15	Columbia 33388
2/14/76	100	15		©	2	Look Into The Future		$15	Columbia 33904
2/19/77	85	10		©	3	Next		$15	Columbia 34311
2/11/78	21	123	▲³	©	4	Infinity		$12	Columbia 34912
4/14/79	20	96	▲³	©	5	Evolution		$12	Columbia 35797
1/5/80	152	8			6	In The Beginning	[K]	$15	Columbia 36324 [2]

DEBUT	PEAK	WKS	RIAA	CD	ARTIST — Album Title	Catalog	Sym	$	Label & Number

JOURNEY — Cont'd

3/22/80	8	57	▲³	© 7	Departure			$12	Columbia 36339
2/21/81	9	69	▲²	© 8	Captured		[L]	$15	Columbia 37016 [2]
8/8/81	❶¹	146	▲⁹	© 9	Escape	C:#17/16		$10	Columbia 37408
2/19/83	2⁹	85	▲⁶	© 10	Frontiers			$10	Columbia 38504
5/10/86	4	67	▲²	© 11	Raised On Radio			$10	Columbia 39936
12/3/88+	10	92	▲¹⁰	© 12	Greatest Hits	C:#2⁵/419	[G]	$10	Columbia 44493
12/26/92+	90	4	●	© 13	Time³		[K]	$30	Columbia 48937 [3]
11/9/96	3	27	▲	© 14	Trial By Fire			$10	Columbia 67514
4/11/98	79	7		© 15	Greatest Hits Live		[G-L]	$10	Columbia 69139
					recorded from 1981-83				
4/21/01	56	6		© 16	Arrival			$10	Columbia 69864

After The Fall (10,13,15) 23
All That Really Matters (13)
All The Things (16)
All The Way (16)
Any Way You Want It (7,8,12,13,15) 23
Anytime (4,8,13) 83
Anyway (2,6)
Ask The Lonely (12,13)
Back Talk (10)
Be Good To Yourself (11,12,13) 9
Can Do (4)
Can't Tame The Lion (14)
Castles Burning (14)
Chain Reaction (10)
City Of The Angels (14)
Colors Of The Spirit (14)
Conversations (medley) (1,6)
Cookie Duster (13)
Daydream (5)
Dead Or Alive (9)
Departure (7)
Dixie Highway (8,13)
Do You Recall (5,8)
Don't Be Down On Me Baby (14)

Don't Stop Believin' (9,12,13,15) 9
Easy To Fall (14)
Edge Of The Blade (10)
Escape (9,15)
Eyes Of A Woman (11,13)
Faithfully (10,12,13,15) 12
Feeling That Way (4,8,13)
For You (13)
Forever In Blue (14)
Frontiers (10)
Girl Can't Help It (11,12,13) 17
Good Morning Girl (7,13)
hit "Hot 100" as a medley with "Stay Awhile"
Good Times (13)
Happy To Give (11,13)
Here We Are (13)
Higher Place (14)
Homemade Love (7,13)
Hustler (3)
I Got A Reason (16)
I Would Find You (3)
I'll Be Alright Without You (11,12,13) 14
I'm Cryin' (14)
I'm Gonna Leave You (2,6,13)

If He Should Break Your Heart (14)
In My Lonely Feeling (medley) (1,6)
In The Morning Day (1)
Into Your Arms (13)
It Could Have Been You (11)
It's All Too Much (2,6)
It's Just The Rain (14)
Just The Same Way (5,8,13) 58
Karma (3)
Keep On Runnin' (9,13)
Kiss Me Softly (16)
Kohoutek (1,6,13)
La Do Da (4,8)
La Raza Del Sol (13)
Lady Luck (5)
Lay It Down (9)
Liberty (13)
Lifetime Of Dreams (16)
Lights (4,8,12,13,15) 74
Line Of Fire (7,8,13,15)
Little Girl (13)
Live And Breathe (16)
Livin' To Do (16)
Look Into The Future (2,6)

Loved By You (16)
Lovin', Touchin', Squeezin' (5,8,12,13,15) 16
Lovin' You Is Easy (5)
Majestic (5,8,13)
Message Of Love (14)
Midnight Dreamer (2)
Mother, Father (9,13)
Mystery Mountain (1,6)
Natural Thing (13)
Next (3)
Nickel & Dime (3,6,13)
Nothin' Comes Close (16)
Of A Lifetime (1,6,13)
On A Saturday Nite (2)
Once You Love Somebody (11,13)
One More (14)
Only Solutions (13)
Only The Young (12,13) 9
Open Arms (9,12,13,15) 2
Opened The Door (4)
Party's Over (Hopelessly In Love) (8,13) 34
Patiently (4,13)
People (3,6)
People And Places (7)

Positive Touch (11)
Precious Time (7)
Raised On Radio (11)
Rubicon (10)
Send Her My Love (10,12,13,15) 23
Separate Ways (Worlds Apart) (10,12,13,15) 8
She Makes Me (Feel Alright) (2)
Signs Of Life (16)
Someday Soon (7,13)
Somethin' To Hide (4)
Spaceman (3,6)
Stay Awhile (7,8,13,15) 55
hit "Hot 100" as a medley with "Good Morning Girl"
Still She Cries (14)
Still They Ride (9,13,15) 19
Stone In Love (9,13,15)
Suzanne (11) 17
Sweet And Simple (5,13)
To Be Alive Again (16)
To Play Some Music (1)
Too Late (5,8,13) 70
Topaz (1,6)
Trial By Fire (14)
Troubled Child (10)

Velvet Curtain (medley) (13)
Walks Like A Lady (7,8,13) 32
We Will Meet Again (16)
Wheel In The Sky (4,8,12,13,15) 57
When I Think Of You (14)
When You Love A Woman (14) 12
When You're Alone (It Ain't Easy) (5)
Where Were You (7,8,13)
Who's Crying Now (9,12,13,15) 4
Why Can't This Night Go On Forever (11,13) 60
Winds Of March (4)
With A Tear (13)
With Your Love (16)
World Gone Wild (16)
You're On Your Own (2,6)

JOY DIVISION '88

Industrial-rock group formed in Manchester, England: Ian Curtis (vocals), Bernard Albrecht (guitar), Peter Hook (bass) and Stephen Morris (drums). Curtis committed suicide on 5/18/80 (age 23). Group became **New Order**, recruiting keyboardist/guitarist Gillian Gilbert in December 1980.

| 8/27/88 | 146 | 8 | | © | Substance | | [K] | $10 | Qwest 25747 |

Atmosphere
Autosuggestion
Dead Souls
Digital
Incubation
Leaders Of Men
Love Will Tear Us Apart
She's Lost Control
Transmission
Warsaw

JOY OF COOKING '71

Country-rock group from Berkeley, California: Terry Garthwaite (vocals), Toni Brown (vocals, keyboards), Ron Wilson (percussion), Jeff Neighbor (bass) and Fritz Kasten (drums).

3/6/71	100	17			1 Joy Of Cooking			$15	Capitol 661
10/9/71	136	7			2 Closer To The Ground			$15	Capitol 828
6/10/72	174	6			3 Castles			$15	Capitol 11050

All Around The Sun And The Moon (3)
Bad Luck Blues (3)
Beginning Tomorrow (3)
Blues For A Friend (2)
Brownsville (medley) (1) 66
Castles (3)
Children's House (1)
Closer To The Ground (2)
Dancing Couple (1)
Did You Go Downtown (1)
Don't The Moon Look Fat And Lonesome (3)
Down My Dream (1)
First Time, Last Time (3)
Home Town Man (3)
Humpty Dumpty (2)
Hush (1)
If Some God (Sometimes You Gotta Go Home) (1)
Lady Called Love (3)
Laugh, Don't Laugh (2)
Let Love Carry You Along (3)
Mockingbird (medley) (1)
New Colorado Blues (2)
Only Time Will Tell Me (1)
Pilot (2)
Red Wine At Noon (1)
Sometimes Like A River (Loving You) (2)
Thousand Miles (2)
Three-Day Loser (3)
Too Late, But Not Forgotten (1)
Waiting For The Last Plane (3)
War You Left (2)

J-SHIN '00

Born in Miami. Male R&B singer.

| 3/18/00 | 71 | 6 | | © | My Soul, My Life | | | $10 | Slip-N-Slide 83256 |

Ghetto Life (Interlude)
Givin' U Luv
I'll Do It
One Night Stand 34
Player Hater
Pony Ride
Sex Is Not
Sleepin' With Friends
Tell Me Why
3Some (Interlude)
Treat U Better
U, Me & She
What's On My Mind
Whatever U Want

JT THE BIGGA FIGGA '95

Born in San Francisco. Male rapper.

| 10/28/95 | 168 | 1 | | © | Dwellin' In Tha Labb | | | $10 | Get Low 53981 |

Ain't Something Wrong
Bay Area Playaz
Beware Of Those
Critical
Did You Get Yo Geez
Dwellin' In Tha Labb
Flypn' Nygaz Lyke Ounces
It's Going Down
Lost In A Massacarade
Mack Hand
Representing
Root Of All Evil
Scrilla, Scratch, Paper
Young G's And OG's

★283★ JUDAS PRIEST '82

Hard-rock group formed in Birmingham, England: Rob **Halford** (vocals), K.K. Downing and Glenn Tipton (guitars), Ian Hill (bass) and Dave Holland (drums). Scott Travis replaced Holland in 1990. Halford left in 1992 to form **Fight**. New lead singer Tim "Ripper" Owens joined in 1996.

1)Screaming For Vengeance 2)Turbo 3)Defenders Of The Faith

4/8/78	173	3	●	© 1	Stained Class			$12	Columbia 35296
3/31/79	128	7	●	© 2	Hell Bent For Leather			$12	Columbia 35706
10/6/79	70	11	▲	© 3	Unleashed In The East (Live In Japan)		[L]	$12	Columbia 36179
5/31/80	34	18	▲	© 4	British Steel			$12	Columbia 36443
4/4/81	39	25	●	© 5	Point Of Entry			$12	Columbia 37052
7/24/82	17	53	▲	© 6	Screaming For Vengeance			$12	Columbia 38160

441

JUDAS PRIEST — Cont'd

DEBUT	PEAK	WKS			Album		Sym	$	Label & Number
7/30/83+	15^C	108	●	©	7 Sin After Sin			$12	Columbia 34787
11/5/83+	10^C	83		©	8 Sad Wings Of Destiny			$15	Ovation 1751
2/4/84	18	37	▲	©	9 Defenders Of The Faith			$12	Columbia 39219
4/12/86	17	36	▲	©	10 Turbo			$12	Columbia 40158
6/20/87	38	15		©	11 Priest...Live!		[L]	$15	Columbia 40794 [2]
6/4/88	31	19	●	©	12 Ram It Down			$10	Columbia 44244
10/6/90	26	20	●	©	13 Painkiller			$10	Columbia 46891
6/5/93	155	2		©	14 Metal Works '73-'93		[K]	$15	Columbia 53932 [2]
11/15/97	82	2		©	15 Jugulator			$10	CMC Int'l. 86224

Abductors (15)
All Guns Blazing (13)
All The Way (5)
Battle Hymn (13)
Before The Dawn (2,14)
Better By You Better Than Me (1)
Between The Hammer & The Anvil (13)
Beyond The Realms Of Death (1,14)
Blood Red Skies (12,14)
Blood Stained (15)
Bloodstone (6,14)
Brain Dead (15)
Breaking The Law (4,11,14)
Bullet Train (15)
Burn In Hell (15)
Burnin' Up (2)
Call For The Priest (medley) (7)
Cathedral Spires (15)
Come And Get It (12)
Dead Meat (15)
Death Row (15)

Decapitate (15)
Deceiver (8)
Defenders Of The Faith (9)
Delivering The Goods (2,14)
Desert Plains (5,14)
Devil's Child (6,14)
Diamonds And Rust (3,7)
Dissident Aggressor (7,14)
Don't Go (5)
Don't Have To Be Old To Be Wise (4)
Dreamer Deceiver (8)
Eat Me Alive (9,14)
Electric Eye (6,11,14)
Epitaph (8)
Evening Star (2)
Evil Fantasies (14)
Exciter (1,3,14)
Fever (8)
Freewheel Burning (9,11,14)
Genocide (3,8)
Green Manalishi (With The Two-Pronged Crown) (2,3)
Grinder (4)

Hard As Iron (15)
Heading Out To The Highway (5,11,14)
Heavy Duty (9)
Heavy Metal (12)
Hell Bent For Leather (2,14)
Hell Patrol (13)
Hellion, The (6,14)
Here Come The Tears (7)
Heroes End (1)
Hot For Love (10)
Hot Rockin' (5)
I'm A Rocker (12)
Invader (1)
Island Of Domination (8)
Jawbreaker (9)
Johnny B. Goode (12)
Jugulator (15)
Killing Machine (2)
Last Rose Of Summer (1)
Leather Rebel (13)
Let Us Prey (7)
Living After Midnight (4,11,14)
Locked In (10)

Love Bites (9,11)
Love You To Death (12)
Love Zone (12)
Metal Gods (4,11,14)
Metal Meltdown (13,14)
Monsters Of Rock (12)
Night Comes Down (9,14)
Night Crawler (13,14)
On The Run (5)
One Shot At Glory (13)
Out In The Cold (10,11)
Pain And Pleasure (6)
Painkiller (13,14)
Parental Guidance (10,11)
Prelude (8)
Private Property (10,11)
Rage, The (4,14)
Ram It Down (12,14)
Rapid Fire (4)
Raw Deal (medley) (7)
Reckless (10)
Riding On The Wind (6)
Ripper (3,8)
Rock Forever (2)

Rock Hard Ride Free (9)
Rock You All Around The World (10,11)
Running Wild (2,3)
Saints In Hell (1)
Savage (1)
Screaming For Vengeance (6,14)
Sentinel, The (9,11)
Sinner (3,7,14)
Solar Angels (5,14)
Some Heads Are Gonna Roll (9,11)
Stained Class (1)
Starbreaker (2)
Steeler (4)
Take On The World (2)
(Take These) Chains (6)
Touch Of Evil (13,14)
Troubleshooter (5)
Turbo Lover (10,11,14)
Turning Circles (5)
Tyrant (3,8)
United (4)

Victim Of Changes (3,8,14)
White Heat, Red Hot (1)
Wild Nights, Hot & Crazy Days (10,14)
You Say Yes (5)
You've Got Another Thing Comin' (6,11,14) *67*

JUDD, Cledus T.
Born Barry Poole on 12/18/64 in Crowe Springs, Georgia. Country novelty singer.   **'97**

DEBUT	PEAK	WKS			Album		Sym	$	Label & Number
9/21/96+	173	9		©	1 I Stoled This Record		[N]	$10	Razor & Tie 2825
4/18/98	181	2		©	2 Did I Shave My Back For This?		[N]	$10	Razor & Tie 82835
12/2/00	198	2		©	3 Just Another Day In Parodies		[N]	$10	Monument 85106

Cadirac Style (1)
Change, The (1)
Cledus BUSTED! (1)
Cledus Don't Stop Eatin' For Nuthin' (2)
Cledus Went Down To Florida (1)
Did I Shave My Back For This? (2)

Every Bulb In The House Is Blown (2)
First Redneck On The Internet (2)
Goodbye Squirrel (3)
Grandpa Got Runned Over By A John Deere (1)
Hankenstein (2)
Hip Hop & Honky Tonk (2)

How Do You Milk A Cow (3)
I'm Not In Here For Love (Just Yer Beer) (1)
If Shania Was Mine (1)
Jackson (Alan That Is) (1)
Merry Christmas From The Whole Fam Damily (3)
Mindy McCready (3)
Momma's Boy (3)

More Beaver (3)
My Cellmate Thinks I'm Sexy (3)
Night I Can't Remember (3)
1-900-SHEILA (1)
Plowboy (3)
Psychic To The Stars (3)
Quit Teasin' Me Ed (1)
Record Deal (3)

(She's Got A Butt) Bigger Than The Beatles (1)
Skoal: The Grundy County Spitting Incident (1)
Stoled: The Copyright Infringement Incident (1)
Third Rock From Her Thumb (2)
What The *$@# Did You Say (3)

Wife Naggin' (3)
Wives Do It All The Time (2)
You Have No Right To Remain Violent (1)

JUDD, Wynonna — see WYNONNA

★395★   **JUDDS, The**   **'89**

Country vocal duo from Ashland, Kentucky: Naomi (born on 1/11/46) and her daughter **Wynonna** (born on 5/30/64) Judd.

1)River Of Time 2)Heartland 3)Greatest Hits Volume Two

DEBUT	PEAK	WKS			Album		Sym	$	Label & Number
12/1/84+	71	26	▲²	©	1 Why Not Me			$10	RCA/Curb 5319
12/8/84+	153	15		©	2 The Judds		[M]	$10	RCA/Curb 8515
11/16/85+	66	57	▲	©	3 Rockin' With The Rhythm			$10	RCA/Curb 7042
4/4/87	52	31	▲	©	4 Heartland	C:#34/7		$10	RCA/Curb 5916
12/19/87	9^X	20		©	5 Christmas Time with The Judds	C:#21/12	[X]	$10	RCA/Curb 6422
					Christmas charts: 9/87, 9/88, 29/89, 26/90, 12/91, 24/92, 29/93, 36/99				
8/27/88	76	97	▲²	©	6 Greatest Hits	C:#10/2	[G]	$10	RCA/Curb 8318
4/22/89	51	20	●	©	7 River Of Time			$10	RCA/Curb 9595
9/29/90+	62	53	▲	©	8 Love Can Build A Bridge			$10	RCA/Curb 2070
6/1/91+	25^C	3	●	©	9 Collector's Series		[G]	$10	RCA 2278
9/28/91+	54	32	●	©	10 Greatest Hits Volume Two	C:#14/2	[G]	$10	RCA/Curb 61018
6/3/95	187	1		©	11 Number One Hits	C:#22/3	[G]	$10	RCA/Curb 66489
5/27/00	107	2		©	12 Reunion Live		[L]	$15	Curb 170134 [2]

recorded 12/31/99 at America West Arena in Phoenix

Are The Roses Not Blooming (8)
Auld Lang Syne (12)
Away In A Manger (5)
Beautiful Star Of Bethlehem (5)
Blue Nun Cafe (2)
Born To Be Blue (8,10)
Bye Bye Baby Blues (1)
Cadillac Red (7)
Calling In The Wind (8)
Can't Nobody Love You (Like I Do) (12)
Change Of Heart (2,6,11)
Come Some Rainy Day (12)
Cow Cow Boogie (4)

Cry Myself To Sleep (3,6,9)
Don't Be Cruel (4)
Dream Chaser (3)
Drops Of Water (1)
Endless Sleep (1)
Freedom (12)
Girls Night Out (1,6,11,12)
Give A Little Love (6,12)
Grandpa (Tell Me 'Bout The Good Old Days) (3,6,11,12)
Guardian Angel (7,10)
Had A Dream (For The Heart) (2,10,12)
Have Mercy (3,6,9,11,12)

I Know Where I'm Going (4,10,11,12)
I Saw The Light (12)
I Wish She Wouldn't Treat You That Way (3,9)
I'm Falling In Love Tonight (4)
If I Were You (3)
In My Dreams (8)
Isn't He A Strange One (2,9)
John Deere Tractor (2,8,10)
Let Me Tell You About Love (7,10,11)
Love Can Build A Bridge (8,10,12)

Love Is Alive (1,6,9,11,12)
Mama He's Crazy (1,2,6,11,12)
Maybe Your Baby's Got The Blues (4,10)
Mr. Pain (1)
My Baby's Gone (1)
My Strongest Weakness (12)
Not My Baby (7)
Oh Holy Night (5)
Old Pictures (4)
One Hundred And Two (8)
One Man Woman (7)
River Of Time (7,12)
River Roll On (3)

Rock Bottom (12)
Rockin' With The Rhythm Of The Rain (3,6,11,12)
Rompin' Stompin' Blues (8)
Santa Claus Is Comin' To Town (5)
She Is His Only Need (12)
Silent Night (5)
Silver Bells (5)
Sleeping Heart (1)
Sleepless Nights (7,9)
Sweetest Gift (4)
Talk About Love (8)
Tears For You (3,9)

This Country's Rockin' (8)
Tuff Enuff (12)
Turn It Loose (4,10,11,12)
Water Of Love (7,9)
What Child Is This (5)
Who Is This Babe (5)
Why Don't You Believe Me (4)
Why Not Me (1,6,11,12)
Winter Wonderland (5)
Working In The Coal Mine (1)
Wyld Unknown (12)
Young Love (7,10,11)

DEBUT	PEAK	WKS	RIAA	CD	ARTIST — Album Title	Catalog	Sym	$	Label & Number

JULUKA '83
Interracial pop group from South Africa: **Johnny Clegg** and Sipho Mchunu (vocals, guitars), Cyril Mnculwane and Glenda Miller (keyboards), Scorpion Madondo (horns), Gary Van Zyl (bass) and Derrick DeBeer (drums).

8/13/83 | 186 | 5 | © | **Scatterlings**.. | | | $12 | Warner 23898

Digging For Some Words | Kwela Man | Shake My Way | Siyayilanda | Two Humans On The Run
Ijwanasibeki | Scatterlings Of Africa | Simple Things | Spirit Is The Journey | Umbaqanga Music

JUNGKLAS, Rob '86
Born in Boston. Rock singer/songwriter/guitarist.

6/14/86 | 102 | 22 | © | **Closer To The Flame**.. | | | $10 | Manhattan 53017

Back To 17 | Boystown | Hello Heaven | Memphis Thing | See That Girl
Big Bouffant | Dizzy Blonde | **Make It Mean Something** 86 | Not Like The Other Boys | When You Hold Me

JUNIOR '82
Born Norman Giscombe on 11/10/61 in London. R&B singer/songwriter.

5/8/82 | 71 | 16 | 1 | **"Ji"**.. | | | $12 | Mercury 4043
7/23/83 | 177 | 6 | 2 | **Inside Lookin' Out**.. | | | $12 | Mercury 812325

Baby I Want You Back (2) | Down Down (1) | Let Me Know (2) | Sayin' Something (2) | Women Say It (2)
Communication Breakdown (2) | F.B. Eye (2) | Love Dies (1) | Story Teller (2) | You're The One (2)
Darling You (Don't You Know) | I Can't Help It (1) | **Mama Used To Say** (1) 30 | Tell Me (2) |
(1) | Is This Love (1) | Runnin' (2) | Too Late (1) |

JUNIOR M.A.F.I.A. '95
Rap group from New York City: **Lil' Kim**, Klepto, Trife, Larceny, **Lil' Cease**, Chico and Nino Brown. Proteges of **The Notorious B.I.G.** M.A.F.I.A.: Masters At Finding Intelligent Attitudes.

9/16/95 | 8 | 31 | ● © | **Conspiracy** | | | $10 | Undeas 92614

Back Stabbers | **Get Money** 17 | Lyrical Wizardry | Oh My Lord | Realms Of Junior M.A.F.I.A.
Crazaay | I Need You Tonight | Murder Onze | **Player's Anthem** 13 | White Chalk

JUNKYARD '89
Hard-rock group formed in Los Angeles: David Roach (vocals), Chris Gates and Brian Baker (guitars), Clay Anthony (bass) and Pat Muzingo (drums).

8/12/89 | 105 | 11 | © | **Junkyard**.. | | | $10 | Geffen 24227

Blooze | Hands Off | Hot Rod | Long Way Home | Simple Man
Can't Hold Back | Hollywood | Life Sentence | Shot In The Dark | Texas

JUPITER, Duke — see DUKE

JURASSIC 5 '00
Rap group from Los Angeles: rappers Chali 2NA, Zaakir, Akil and Marc 7, with DJ's Cut Chemist and Nu-Mark.

7/8/00 | 43 | 15 | © | **Quality Control** .... | | | $10 | Rawkus 490664

Contact | Great Expectations | Influence, The | Monkey Bars | Twelve
Contribution | How We Get Along | Jurass Finish First | Quality Control | World Of Entertainment (Woe Is
Game, The | Improvise | Lausd | Swing Set | Me)

JUSTIS, Bill '63
Born on 10/14/26 in Birmingham, Alabama. Died on 7/15/82 (age 55). Session saxophonist/arranger/producer. Led house band for Sun Records.

11/24/62 | 94 | 8 | 1 | **Bill Justis plays 12 big instrumental hits (Alley Cat/Green Onions)**......... [I] | | | $25 | Smash 67021
2/23/63 | 89 | 6 | 2 | **Bill Justis plays 12 more big instrumental hits (Telstar/The Lonely Bull)** [I] | | | $25 | Smash 67030

Alley Cat (1) | I Got A Woman - Part 1 (2) | Near You (2) | Stripper, The (1) | Wheels (2)
Calcutta (1) | Last Date (1) | **Raunchy** 2 | Summer Place, Theme From | Wonderland By Night (1)
(Dance With) The Guitar Man | Last Night (2) | Rebel Rouser (2) | (1) |
(2) | Lonely Bull (2) | Rinky-Dink (1) | Swingin' Safari (1) |
Desafinado (2) | Melody Of Love (2) | Sail Along Silvery Moon (2) | Take Five (1) |
Green Onions (1) | Mexico (1) | Stranger On The Shore (1) | Tel-Star (2) |

JUVENILE '99
Born Terius Gray in 1975 in New Orleans. Male rapper. Member of **Cash Money Millionaires** and **Hot Boy$**.

11/21/98+ | 9 | 100 | ▲⁴ © | 1 | **400 Degreez** | | C:#37/2 | $10 | Cash Money 53162
6/5/99 | 137 | 2 | © | 2 | **Being Myself (Remixed)** .... [E] | | | $10 | Warlock 2809
1/1/00 | 10 | 26 | ▲ © | 3 | **Tha G-Code** | | | $10 | Cash Money 542179

After Cash Money Concert (1) | Da Magnolia (3) | Gone Ride With Me (1) | March Nigga Step (3) | Sling It To Tha Back (2) | Welcome 2 Tha Nolia (1)
Back That Thang Up (1) 19 | Flossin Season (1) | Guerrilla (3) | Million And One Things (3) | Solja Rag (1)
Betcha' 20 Dollars (Bounce II) | 400 Degreez (1) | **"Ha"** (1) 68 | Never Had S*** (3) | Somethin' I Forgot (2)
(2) | F*** That Nigga (3) | I Got That Fire (3) | Off Top (1) | Something Got 2 Shake (3)
Cash Money Concert (1) | G-Code (3) | If You're A Player (2) | Pass Azz 'Nigga (2) | Take Them 5 (3)
Catch Your Cut (3) | G-ing Men (2) | Juvenile On Fire (1) | Powder Bag (2) | U Can't Come Around (2)
Conversation With Tha Man | Get It Right (3) | Lil Boyz (3) | Rich Niggaz (1) | **U Understand** (3) 83
Above (2) | Ghetto Children (1) | Man, Tha (3) | Run For It (1) | U.P.T. (1)

JUVET, Patrick '78
Born on 8/21/50 in Montreux, Switzerland. Disco singer.

7/1/78 | 125 | 14 | | **Got A Feeling**... | | | $12 | Casablanca 7101

Another Lonely Man | Got A Feeling | I Love America | Where Is My Woman

K

KADISON, Joshua '94
Born on 2/8/63 in Los Angeles. Singer/songwriter/pianist.

1/29/94 | 69 | 52 | ▲ © | **Painted Desert Serenade**...................................... | | | $10 | SBK 80920

Beau's All Night Radio Love | **Beautiful In My Eyes** 19 | Invisible Man | Mama's Arms | **Picture Postcards From** | When A Woman Cries
Line | Georgia Rain | **Jessie** 26 | Painted Desert Serenade | **L.A.** 84

DEBUT	PEAK	WKS	RIAA	CD	ARTIST — Album Title	Catalog	Sym	$	Label & Number

KAEMPFERT, Bert, And His Orchestra ★171★ '61

Born on 10/16/23 in Hamburg, Germany. Died on 6/21/80 (age 56). Multi-instrumentalist/bandleader/producer/arranger. Composed such songs as "Strangers In The Night" and "Spanish Eyes." Produced first **Beatles** recording session.

1)Wonderland By Night 2)Blue Midnight 3)That Happy Feeling 4)The Magic Music Of Far Away Places
5)Bert Kaempfert's Greatest Hits

DEBUT	PEAK	WKS			ARTIST — Album Title		Sym	$	Label & Number
12/31/60+	❶⁵	40	●	©	1 **Wonderland By Night**		[I]	$20	Decca 74101
11/20/61	92	6			2 **Dancing In Wonderland**		[I]	$20	Decca 74161
4/21/62	82	13		©	3 **Afrikaan Beat and other favorites**		[I]	$15	Decca 74273
9/29/62	14	17		©	4 **That Happy Feeling**		[I]	$15	Decca 74305
7/6/63	87	12		©	5 **Living It Up!**		[I]	$15	Decca 74374
11/30/63	6ˣ	16		©	6 **Christmas Wonderland**		[X-I]	$15	Decca 74441
					Christmas charts: 6/'63, 34/'64, 38/'65, 21/'66, 62/'67, 38/'68				
11/30/63	79	6		©	7 **Lights Out, Sweet Dreams**		[I]	$15	Decca 74265
1/23/65	5	55	●	©	8 **Blue Midnight**		[I]	$15	Decca 74569
7/10/65	42	22		©	9 **Three O'Clock In The Morning**		[I]	$15	Decca 74670
9/4/65	27	23		©	10 **The Magic Music Of Far Away Places**		[I]	$15	Decca 74616
3/12/66	46	28		©	11 **Bye Bye Blues**		[I]	$15	Decca 74693
7/9/66	39	21		©	12 **Strangers In The Night**		[I]	$15	Decca 74795
10/8/66	30	40	●		13 **Bert Kaempfert's Greatest Hits**		[G-I]	$15	Decca 74810
5/13/67	122	7		©	14 **Hold Me**		[I]	$15	Decca 74860
10/7/67	136	7		©	15 **The World We Knew**		[I]	$15	Decca 74925
11/2/68	186	2		©	16 **My Way Of Life**		[I]	$15	Decca 75059
3/29/69	194	5		©	17 **Warm and Wonderful**		[I]	$15	Decca 75089
11/1/69	153	10		©	18 **Traces Of Love**		[I]	$15	Decca 75140
3/28/70	87	7		©	19 **The Kaempfert Touch**		[I]	$15	Decca 75175
2/13/71	140	6			20 **Orange Colored Sky**		[I]	$15	Decca 75256
9/25/71	188	2			21 **Bert Kaempfert Now!**		[I]	$15	Decca 75305

Afrikaan Beat (3,13) *42*
Aim Of My Desires (1)
All For You (19)
Almost There (8)
Are We Becoming Strangers (18)
As I Love You (1)
Autumn Leaves (Les Feuilles Mortes) (10)
Balkan Melody (10)
Bell Bottoms (21)
Bert's Tune (3)
Black Beauty (4)
Blue Midnight (8)
Blue Moon (12)
Body And Soul (7)
Boo Hoo (12)
But Not Today (12)
Bye Bye Blackbird (20)
Bye Bye Blues (11,13) *54*
Can't Take My Eyes Off You (17)
Cherokee (Indian Love Call) (3)
Children's Christmas Dream (6)
Christmas Wonderland (6)
Cotton Candy (20)
Cracklin' Rosie (20)
Dancing In The Dark (3)
Danke Schoen (5,13)
Daybreak Serenade (7)
Didn't We (19)
Don't Go (20)
Don't Talk To Me (5)
Dream (7)
Dream Baby (How Long Must I Dream) (21)
Dreaming The Blues (1)
Drifting And Dreaming (Sweet Paradise) (1)
Dutch Treat (5)
Easy Going (5)
Every Sunday Morning (12)
Falling Free (21)
Fascination (16)
Fluter's Holiday (5)
Forgive Me (12)
Free As A Bird (8)

Friends (20)
Funny Talk (2)
Games People Play (18)
Gemma (7)
Gentleman Jim (5)
Give And Take (5)
Goodnight Sweet Dreams (8)
Gray Eyes Make Me Blue (1)
Happiness Never Comes Too Late (1)
Happy Trumpeter (4)
Hava Nagila (10)
Headin' Home (19)
Here's My Life (Here's My Love) (18)
Hi-De-Ho (That Old Sweet Roll) (20)
Highland Dream (7)
Hold Back The Dawn (14)
Hold Me (14)
Holiday For Bells (6)
How Deep Is The Ocean (How High Is The Sky) (2)
I Can't Give You Anything But Love (12) *100*
I Can't Help Remembering You (15)
I Heard The Bells On Christmas Day (6)
I Love How You Love Me (18)
I May Be Wrong (But I Think You're Wonderful) (18)
I'll Get By (As Long As I Have You) (2)
I'm Beginning To See The Light (11)
I've Gotta Be Me (18)
If I Give My Heart To You (9)
If I Had You (7)
In Apple Blossom Time (20)
In Our Time (A Musical Prayer For Peace) (21)
In The Mood (5)
It Makes No Difference (11)
It's The Talk Of The Town (1)
Japanese Farewell Song (10)
Java (8)

Jean (19)
Jingo Jango (6)
Jumpin' Jiminy Christmas (6)
Just As Much As Ever (3)
Kiss Her Once With Feeling (21)
La Cumparsita (10)
La Vie En Rose (1)
Lady (14)
Let A Smile Be Your Umbrella (On A Rainy Day) (9)
Let's Go Home (9)
Little Drummer Boy (6)
Living Easy (5)
Living It Up (5)
Lonely Nightingale (8)
Lonesome (15)
Love (8,13)
Love Comes But Once (8)
Love Letters (7)
Love Me Happy (18)
Lover (15)
Lullaby For Lovers (1)
Magic Trumpet (13)
Magnolia Blossoms (7)
Malaysian Melody (16)
Maltese Melody (17)
Mambossa (10)
Manhattan After Dark (16)
Marjoram (14)
Market Day (4)
Me And My Shadow (21)
Melina (11)
Memories Of Mexico (16)
Mexican Shuffle (12)
Midnight In Moscow (10)
Milica (12)
Mister Sandman (16)
Monte Carlo (10)
Moon Is Making Eyes (9)
Moon Over Naples (10,13) *59*
Moonglow (3)
Moonlight Serenade (15)
My Love (20)
Nightingale Sang In Berkeley Square (9)

Nothing's New (9)
Now And Forever (2) *48*
Oh Woman, Oh Why? (21)
On A Little Street In Singapore (10)
On My Lonely Way (16)
On The Alamo (1)
Once In A While (11)
One Day With You (19)
One Lonely Night (17)
One Morning In May (17)
Only A Fool (Would Lose You) (18)
Only In Your Arms (17)
Only Those In Love (2)
Orange Colored Sky (20)
Our Street Of Love (17)
Out Of Nowhere (11)
Petula (17)
Pony Violins (3)
Proud Mary (21)
Pussy Footin' (14)
Put Your Hand In The Hand (21)
Rain (15)
Rainbow Melody (9)
Raindrops Keep Fallin' On My Head (19)
Red Roses For A Blue Lady (8,13) *11*
Red Sky At Morning (21)
Remember When (We Made These Memories) (11)
Reminiscing (17)
Ridin' Rainbows (16)
Rose Of Washington Square (9)
Rose Room (14)
Santa Claus Is Comin' To Town (6)
Send Me Home (18)
Sentimental Journey (7)
Serenade In Blue (15)
Sermonette (14)
She Lets Her Hair Down (Early In The Morning) (19)
Show Me The Way To Go Home (12)
Similau (4)

Skokiaan (South African Song) (4)
Sleepy Lagoon (2)
Sleigh Ride (6)
Snowbird (20)
So What's New (14)
Solitude (3)
Some Of These Days (17)
Somebody Loves Me (2)
Somebody Loves You (14)
Someday We'll Be Together (19)
Something (19)
Soul Time (16)
Spanish Eyes ..see: Moon Over Naples
Stardust (3,10)
Stay With Me (1)
Stay With The Happy People (15)
Steady Does It (11)
Stompin' At The Savoy (16)
Strangers In The Night (12,13)
Sunday In Madrid (4)
Sweet Dreams (7)
Sweet Maria (14)
Swingin' Safari (4,13)
Swissy Missy (10)
Tahitian Sunset (11)
Take Me (4)
Take My Heart (9)
Take Seven (14)
Talk (15)
Tammy (1)
Tea And Trumpets (20)
Tell Me Why (7)
That Happy Feeling (4,13) *67*
There I've Said It Again (2)
(There'll Be Bluebirds Over) The White Cliffs Of Dover (9)
This Guy's In Love With You (17)
This Song Is Yours Alone (1)
This Woman Is Mine (19)
Three O'Clock In The Morning (8,9) *33*
Tijuana Taxi (12)
Time (18)

Time On My Hands (You In My Arms) (12)
Tipsy Gypsy (5)
Tootie Flutie (4)
Toy Parade (6)
Traces (20)
Treat For Trumpet (8)
Tricky Trombone (5)
Trumpet In The Night (3)
Twilight Time (2)
Two Can Live On Love Alone (12)
Two On A Tune (5)
Unchained Melody (2)
Vat 96 (19)
Wake Up And Live (20)
Way It Used To Be (18)
We Can Make It Girl (19)
Welcome To My Heart (16)
When I Fall In Love (2)
When You're Smiling (The Whole World Smiles With You) (11)
Where Flamingos Fly (3)
Where Or When (3)
While The Children Sleep (20)
Whispering (7)
White Christmas (6)
Wiederseh'n (11,13)
Wimoweh (4)
Winter Wonderland (6)
Wonderland By Night (1,13) *1*
World We Knew (15)
You Are My Sunshine (15)
(You Are) My Way Of Life (16)
You Stepped Out Of A Dream (11)
You You You (9)
You're Mine (19)
You're Worth It All (18)
Zambesi (4)

KAJAGOOGOO '83

Pop group formed in London: Chris "**Limahl**" Hamill (vocals), Steve Askew (guitar), Stuart Neale (keyboards), Nick Beggs (bass) and Jez Strode (drums). Limahl left in late 1983; Beggs took over lead vocals.

DEBUT	PEAK	WKS			ARTIST — Album Title		Sym	$	Label & Number
6/11/83	38	20		©	1 **White Feathers**			$10	EMI America 17094
4/27/85	185	4			2 **Extra Play**			$10	EMI America 17157

Big Apple (2)
Ergonomics (1)
Frayo (1)
Hang On Now (1) *78*

Islands (2)
Kajagoogoo (1)
Lies And Promises (1)
Lion's Mouth (2)

Loop, The (2)
Magician Man (1)
Melting The Ice Away (2)
On A Plane (2)

Ooh To Be Ah (2)
Part Of Me (Is You) (2)
Power To Forgive (2)
This Car Is Fast (1)

Too Shy (1) *5*
Turn Your Back On Me (2)
White Feathers (1)

KALEIDOSCOPE '69
Folk-rock group from Los Angeles: **David Lindley** (vocals, guitar), Solomon Feldthouse (clarinet), Templeton Parcely (violin), Stuart Brotman (bass) and Paul Lagos (drums).

| 6/14/69 | 139 | 8 | | © | Incredible Kaleidoscope | | | $30 | Epic 26467 |

Banjo
Cuckoo
Let The Good Love Flow
Lie To Me
Petite Fleur
Seven-Ate Sweet
Tempe Arizona

KALLMANN, Gunter, Chorus '65
Born on 11/19/30 in Berlin, Germany. Choral director.

5/1/65	97	10			1 Serenade For Elisabeth	[F]		$15	4 Corners 4209
12/24/66+	126	8			2 Wish Me A Rainbow			$15	4 Corners 4235
12/30/67	76^X	1			3 The Gunter Kallman Chorus Sings 28 Christmas Songs	[X-F]		$15	4 Corners 4245

Annabelle (1)
Bell Serenade (1)
Bells Never Rang Sweeter (3)
Bells Ring To The Stars (1)
Beyond The Sea (2)
Children Are Coming (medley) (3)
Christmas Tree Candles (medley) (3)
Come, Shepherds (medley) (3)
Day The Rains Came (2)
Do You Hear The Bells Ringing (medley) (3)
Dream Melody (1)
Every Year (medley) (3)
Falling Snow (medley) (3)
From Heaven (medley) (3)
Holy Night (medley) (3)
I'll Be Home For Christmas (medley) (3)
I'm Always Chasing Rainbows (2)
If You Are But A Dream (1)
Impossible Dream (2)
In The Evenings I Will Sleep (medley) (3)
Jingle Bells (medley) (3)
La Montanara (1)
Let Us Listen (medley) (3)
Let's Be Happy And Gay (medley) (3)
Lollipops And Roses (2)
Mary's Boy Child (medley) (3)
More I See You (2)
Music For Falling In Love (1)
O Christmas Tree (medley) (3)
O, Mein Papa (1)
Oh Happy Christmas Time (medley) (3)
Open Up Heaven's Door (medley) (3)
Ring Bells (medley) (3)
Romantica (2)
Rose Is Blooming (medley) (3)
Round Dance (1)
Serenade For Elisabeth (1)
Serenade From The Millions Of Harlequins (1)
Shepherds Awake (medley) (3)
Silent Night (medley) (3)
Sleep My Prince, Sleep (medley) (3)
Somewhere, My Love (Lara's Theme) (2)
Star Shone In Bethlehem (medley) (3)
Strangers In The Night (2)
Tomorrow The Children Get Presents (medley) (3)
Toselli Serenade (1)
Waltz Music (1)
White Christmas (medley) (3)
Wish Me A Rainbow (2) *63*
You're Nobody 'Til Somebody Loves You (2)

KALYAN '77
Disco-reggae group from Trinidad. Led by singer Olsop David.

| 4/16/77 | 173 | 4 | | | Kalyan | | | $12 | MCA 2245 |

Disco Reggae (Tony's Groove)
Hello Africa
Hosannah
La La Jam Back
Neighbour, Neighbour
Nice 'N' Slow
Sweet Music
What We Gonna Do Next

KAM '93
Born Craig Miller in Los Angeles. Male rapper.

| 3/6/93 | 110 | 7 | | © | 1 Neva Again | | | $10 | Street Know. 92208 |
| 4/1/95 | 158 | 1 | | © | 2 Made In America | | | $10 | EastWest 61754 |

Ain't That A Bitch (1)
Down Fa Mine (2)
Drama (1)
Givin' It Up (2)
Hang 'Um High (1)
Holiday Madness (1)
In Traffic (2)
Keep Tha Peace (2)
Neva Again (1)
Nut'n Nice (2)
Peace Treaty (1)
Pull Ya Hoe Card (2)
Represent (2)
Stereotype (1)
Still Got Love 4 'Um (1)
That's My Nigga (2)
Trust Nobody (2)
Watts Riot (1)
Way'a Life (2)
Who Ridin' (2)
Y'all Don't Hear Me Dough (1)

KANDI '00
Born Kandi Burruss in Atlanta. Female R&B singer/songwriter. Former member of **Xscape**.

| 10/7/00 | 72 | 8 | | © | Hey Kandi | | | $10 | Columbia 63753 |

Can't Come Back
Cheatin' On Me
Don't Think I'm Not *24*
Easier
Hey Kandi
I Wanna Know
I Won't Bite My Tongue
Just So You Know
Pants On Fire
Sucka For You
Talking 'Bout Me
What I'm Gon' Do To You

KANE, Big Daddy '89
Born Antonio Hardy on 9/10/68 in Brooklyn, New York. Male rapper. Acted in the movies *The Meteor Man* and *Posse*.

7/16/88	116	19	●	©	1 Long Live The Kane			$10	Cold Chillin' 25731
10/7/89	33	30	●	©	2 It's A Big Daddy Thing			$10	Cold Chillin' 25941
11/17/90	37	16		©	3 Taste Of Chocolate			$10	Cold Chillin' 26303
11/16/91	57	8		©	4 Prince Of Darkness			$10	Cold Chillin' 26715
6/12/93	52	9		©	5 Looks Like A Job For...			$10	Cold Chillin' 45128
10/1/94	155	1		©	6 Daddy's Home			$10	MCA 11102

Ain't No Half-Steppin' (1)
Ain't No Stoppin' Us Now (2)
All Of Me (3)
Another Victory (2)
Beef Is On (5)
Big Daddy Vs. Dolemite (3)
Big Daddy's Theme (2)
Brooklyn Style...Laid Out (6)
Brother, Brother (4)
Brother Man, Brother Man (5)
Calling Mr. Welfare (2)
Cause I Can Do It Right (3)
Children R The Future (2)
Chocolate City (5)
Come On Down (4)
D.J.s Get No Credit (4)
Daddy's Home (6)
Dance With The Devil (3)
Day You're Mine (1)
Death Sentence (4)
Don't Do It To Yourself (6)
Down The Line (3)
Float (4)
Get Down (4)
Git Bizzy (4)
Give It To Me (5)
Groove With It (4)
Here Comes Kane, Scoob And Scrap (5)
House That Cee Built (2)
How U Get A Record Deal? (5)
I Get The Job Done (2)
I'll Take You There (1)
I'm Not Ashamed (4)
In The PJ's (6)
It's A Big Daddy Thing (2)
It's Hard Being The Kane (3)
Just Rhymin' With Biz (1)
Keep 'Em On The Floor (3)
Let Yourself Go (6)
Long Live The Kane (1)
Looks Like A Job For... (5)
Lover In You (4)
Lyrical Gymnastics (6)
Mister Cee's Master Plan (1)
Mortal Combat (2)
Mr. Pitiful (3)
Niggaz Never Learn (5)
No Damn Good (3)
'Nuff Respect (5)
On The Bugged Tip (1)
On The Move (1)
Ooh, Aah, Nah-Nah-Nah (4)
Pimpin' Ain't Easy (2)
Prince Of Darkness (4)
Put Your Weight On It (3)
Raw (1)
Raw '91 (4)
Rest In Peace (3)
Set It Off (1)
Sex According To The Prince Of Darkness (6)
Show & Prove (2)
Smooth Operator (2)
Somebody's Been Sleeping In My Bed (4)
Stop Shammin' (5)
T.L.C. (4)
Taste Of Chocolate (3)
That's How I Did 'Em (6)
3 Forties And A Bottle Of Moet (6)
To Be Your Man (2)
Troubled Man (2)
Very Special (5) *31*
W.G.O.N.R.S. (6)
Warm It Up, Kane (2)
Way It's Goin' Down (4)
Who Am I (3)
Word To The Mother(Land) (1)
Young, Gifted And Black (2)

KANE & ABEL '98
Male rap duo from Oakland: twin brothers David and Daniel Garcia.

11/9/96	179	1		©	1 The 7 Sins			$10	No Limit 50634
7/25/98	5	13	●	©	2 Am I My Brothers Keeper			$10	No Limit 50720
10/9/99	61	6		©	3 Rise To Power			$10	EastWest 62450
10/14/00	194	2		©	4 Most Wanted			$10	Most Wanted 0001

AKZ (4)
Abortion (1)
Am I My Brothers Keeper (2)
Basement Session (1)
Beat It Up (3)
Betta Kill Me (2)
Between Us (1)
Black Jesus (1)
Bout That Combat (2)
Brave N's (3)
Call Me When You Need Some (2)
Count Your Ones (4)
Don't Give A F*ck About Cha (4)
Drama (4)
Game, The (2)
Gangstafied (1)
Gangstafied Forever (2)
Get Cha Mind Right (3)
Get Cha Weight Up (3)
Get Right! (4)
Ghetto Day (2)
Git'n Paid (1)
God & Gunz (4)
Greens, Cornbread & Cabbage (2)
Hit The Block (3)
Hydroponix (3)
I Ain't Runnin (2)
I Don't Care (3)
Jealous Again (1)
Kane & Abel (4)
Lemme Get Up In Ya (4)
Let 'Em Come (3)
Let Them Hands Go (3)
Let's Go Get Em (2)
My Hood To Yo Hood (2)
No Limit N....'s (4)
No Turnin Back (2)
Only God Knows (2)
Out Of Town B's (2)
Possibility, The (3)
Quick 2 Buss (4)
Rise To Power (Illegal Business) (3)
Shake It Like A Dog (4)
Show Me What Cha Workin' Wit (3)
Snakes (4)
Soldier Story (2)
Somebody Gotta Pay (4)
State's Evidence (3)
Straight Thuggin' (3)
Stress (2)
That's How It's Gon' Happen 2 U (1)
This Is For The Smokers (2)
This Is The Life (1)
This Life (3)
3/2 Murder 1 (1)
Throw Them Thangs (2)
Time After Time (2)
Tryin 2 Have Sumthin' (2)
Watch Me (2)
We Don't Care (2)
We Got That Candy (4)

KANE GANG, The '87

Pop trio formed in England: vocalists Martin Brammer and Paul Woods with guitarist David Brewis.

11/21/87	115	20		©	Miracle			$10	Capitol 48176

Closest Thing To Heaven   Finer Place   Let's Get Wet   Motortown 36   Take Me To The World
Don't Look Any Further 64   King Street Blues   Looking For Gold   Strictly Love (It Ain't)   What Time Is It

KANO '82

Disco studio group from Italy.

1/9/82	189	4			New York Cake			$12	Mirage 19327

Baby Not Tonight   Can't Hold Back (Your Loving) 89   Don't Try To Stop Me   Round And Round   She's A Star
     Party

★281★ KANSAS '77

Pop-rock group from Topeka, Kansas: **Steve Walsh** (vocals, keyboards), Kerry Livgren (guitar, keyboards), Rich Williams (guitar), Robby Steinhardt (violin), Dave Hope (bass) and Phil Ehart (drums). Walsh left in 1981 and was replaced by John Elefante. Revised lineup in 1986: Walsh, Ehart, Williams, **Steve Morse** (guitar; **Dixie Dregs**) and Billy Greer (bass).

1)Point Of Know Return 2)Leftoverture 3)Monolith

6/15/74	174	10	● ©	1	Kansas			$15	Kirshner 32817
3/22/75	57	15	● ©	2	Song For America			$15	Kirshner 33385
12/27/75+	70	20	● ©	3	Masque			$15	Kirshner 33806
11/6/76+	5	42	▲⁴ ©	4	Leftoverture			$12	Kirshner 34224
10/15/77+	4	51	▲⁴ ©	5	Point Of Know Return			$12	Kirshner 34929
11/18/78+	32	19	▲ ©	6	Two For The Show		[L]	$15	Kirshner 35660 [2]
6/9/79	10	24	● ©	7	Monolith			$12	Kirshner 36008
10/4/80	26	21	● ©	8	Audio-Visions			$12	Kirshner 36588
6/12/82	16	20	©	9	Vinyl Confessions			$12	Kirshner 38002
8/13/83	41	21	©	10	Drastic Measures			$10	CBS Associated 38733
9/8/84	154	5	▲³ ©	11	The Best of Kansas		C:#37/6 [G]	$10	CBS Associated 39283
11/15/86+	35	27	©	12	Power			$10	MCA 5838
11/5/88	114	6	©	13	In The Spirit Of Things			$10	MCA 6254

All I Wanted (12) *19*
All The World (3)
Andi (10)
Angels Have Fallen (7)
Anything For You (8)
Apercu (1)
Away From You (7)
Back Door (8)
Belexes (1)
Bells Of Saint James (13)
Borderline (9)
Bringing It Back (1)
Can I Tell You (1)
Can't Cry Anymore (12)
Carry On Wayward Son (4,6,11) *11*
Chasing Shadows (9)
Cheyenne Anthem (4)
Child Of Innocence (3)

Closet Chronicles (5,6)
Crossfire (9)
Curtain Of Iron (8)
Death Of Mother Nature Suite (1)
Devil Game (2)
Diamonds And Pearls (9)
Don't Open Your Eyes (8)
Don't Take Your Love Away (10)
Down The Road (2)
Dust In The Wind (5,6,11) *6*
End Of The Age (10)
Everybody's My Friend (10)
Face It (9)
Fair Exchange (9)
Fight Fire With Fire (10,11) *58*
Get Rich (10)
Ghosts (13)

Glimpse Of Home (7)
Going Through The Motions (10)
Got To Rock On (8) *76*
Hold On (8,11) *40*
Hopelessly Human (5)
House On Fire (13)
How My Soul Cries Out For You (7)
I Counted On Love (13)
Icarus - Borne On Wings Of Steel (3,6)
Incident On A Bridge (10)
Incomudro-Hymn To The Atman (2)
Inside Of Me (13)
It Takes A Woman's Love (To Make A Man) (3)
It's You (3)

Journey From Mariabronn (1,6)
Lamplight Symphony (2,6)
Lightning's Hand (5)
Lonely Street (2)
Lonely Wind (1,6) *60*
Loner (8)
Magnum Opus Medley (4,6)
Mainstream (10)
Miracles Out Of Nowhere (4)
Musicatto (12)
Mysteries And Mayhem (3,6)
No One Together (8,11)
No Room For A Stranger (8)
Nobody's Home (5)
On The Other Side (7)
Once In A Lifetime (13)
One Big Sky (13)
One Man, One Heart (13)
Opus Insert (4)

Paradox (5,6)
People Of The South Wind (7) *23*
Perfect Lover (11)
Pilgrimage, The (1)
Pinnacle, The (3)
Play The Game Tonight (9,11) *17*
Point Of Know Return (5,6,11) *28*
Portrait (He Knew) (5,6) *64*
Power (12) *84*
Preacher, The (13)
Questions Of My Childhood (4)
Rainmaker (13)
Reason To Be (7) *52*
Relentless (8)
Right Away (9) *73*

Secret Service (12)
Silhouettes In Disguise (12)
Song For America (2,6,11)
Sparks Of The Tempest (5)
Spider, The (5)
Stand Beside Me (13)
Stay Out Of Trouble (7)
T.O. Witcher (13)
Taking In The View (12)
Three Pretenders (12)
Tomb 19 (12)
Two Cents Worth (8)
Wall, The (4,11)
We're Not Alone Anymore (12)
What's On My Mind (4)
Windows (9)

KANTNER, Paul '71

Born on 3/17/41 in San Francisco. Rock guitarist. Member of **Jefferson Airplane/Starship** and **KBC Band**.

12/19/70+	20	23	● ©	1	Blows Against The Empire			$20	RCA Victor 4448

     PAUL KANTNER/JEFFERSON STARSHIP

12/25/71+	89	9	©	2	Sunfighter			$15	Grunt 1002

     PAUL KANTNER/GRACE SLICK

6/23/73	120	12	©	3	Baron von Tollbooth & The Chrome Nun			$15	Grunt 0148

     PAUL KANTNER, GRACE SLICK & DAVID FREIBERG

Across The Board (3)
Baby Tree (1)
Ballad Of The Chrome Nun (3)
Child Is Coming (1)
China (2)

Diana - Part 1 & 2 (2)
Earth Mother (2)
Fat (3)
Fishman (3)
Flowers Of The Night (3)
Harp Tree Lament (3)

Have You Seen The Stars Tonite (1)
Hijack (1)
Holding Together (2)
Home (1)
Lets Go Together (1)

Look At The Wood (2)
Mau Mau (Amerikon) (1)
Million (2)
Silver Spoon (2)
Sketches Of China (3)
Starship (1)

Sunfighter (2)
Sunrise (1)
Titanic (2)
Universal Copernican Mumbles (2)
Walkin (3)

When I Was A Boy I Watched The Wolves (2)
White Boy (Transcaucasian Airmachine Blues) (3)
X M (1)
Your Mind Has Left Your Body (3)

KAOMA '90

Dance group assembled in Paris by keyboardist/arranger Jean-Claude Bonaventure.

1/27/90	40	21	● ©		World Beat		[F]	$10	Epic 46010

Dancando Lambada (1)   Lamba Caribe   Lambamor   Melodie D'Amour   Sindiang
Jambe Finete (Grille)   **Lambada** 46   Lambareggae   Salsa Nuestra   Sopenala

KaSANDRA '68

Born John Anderson on 7/30/36 in Panama City, Florida. R&B singer/songwriter.

11/23/68	142	8			John W. Anderson Presents KaSandra			$20	Capitol 2957

Don't Pat Me On The Back And Call Me Brother 91   Flag, The   Just Look In My Face   My Neighborhood   Wilderness
     If A Storm Wind Blows   Mose   Preacher Man

KASHIF '83

Born Michael Jones in 1959 in Brooklyn, New York. Techno-funk singer/musician. Member of **B.T. Express** from 1976-79.

4/9/83	54	33		1	Kashif			$10	Arista 9620
7/21/84	51	21	©	2	Send Me Your Love			$10	Arista 8205
12/21/85+	144	14	©	3	Condition Of The Heart			$10	Arista 8385
12/5/87	118	19	©	4	Love Changes			$10	Arista 8447

All (1)
Are You The Woman (2)
Baby Don't Break Your Baby's Heart (2)

Botha Botha (The Apartheid Song) (3)
Call Me Tonight (2)
Condition Of The Heart (3)

Dancing In The Dark (Heart To Heart) (3)
Don't Stop My Love (1)
Edgartown Groove (2)

Fifty Ways (To Fall In Love) (4)
Help Yourself To My Love (1)
I Just Gotta Have You (Lover Turn Me On) (1)

I Wanna Have Love With You (3)
I've Been Missin' You (2)
It All Begins Again (4)

Love Changes (4)
Love Has No End (2)
Love Me All Over (4)
Loving You Only (4)

KASHIF — Cont'd

Midnight Mood (4)　　Ooh Love (2)　　Say Something Love (1)　　Somebody (4)　　That's How It Goes (2)　　Who's Getting Serious? (4)
Mood, The (1)　　**Reservations For Two** (4) *62*　　Say You Love Me (3)　　Stay The Night (3)　　Vacant Heart (4)
Movie Song (3)　　Rumors (1)　　Send Me Your Love (2)　　Stone Love (1)　　Weakness (3)

KATRINA AND THE WAVES　　'85

Pop-rock group formed in London: Katrina Leskanich (vocals; born in Topeka, Kansas), Kimberley Rew (guitar), Vince Dela Cruz (bass) and Alex Cooper (drums).

4/13/85	25	32	©	1	**Katrina And The Waves**			$10	Capitol 12400
4/12/86	49	16	©	2	**Waves**			$10	Capitol 12478
9/2/89	122	8	©	3	**Break Of Hearts**			$10	SBK 92649

Break Of Hearts (3)　　I Can Dream About It (3)　　Lovely Lindsey (2)　　Red Wine And Whiskey (1)　　Stop Trying To Prove (How　　To Have And To Hold (3)
Can't Tame My Love (3)　　(I've Got A) Crush On You (3)　　Machine Gun Smith (1)　　Riding Shotgun (2)　　　　Much Of A Man Is) (2)　　**Walking On Sunshine** (1) *9*
Cry For Me (1)　　Is That It? (2) *70*　　Mexico (1)　　Rock Myself To Sleep (3)　　Sun Street (2)
Do You Want Crying (1) *37*　　Keep Running To Me (3)　　Money Chain (2)　　Rock N' Roll Girl (3)　　Sun Won't Shine Without You (1)
Game Of Love (1)　　Love Calculator (3)　　Mr. Star (2)　　Sleep On My Pillow (2)　　Tears For Me (2)
Going Down To Liverpool (1)　　Love That Boy (2)　　Que Te Quiero (1) *71*　　　　**That's The Way** (3) *16*

KAUKONEN, Jorma, & Vital Parts　　'81

Born on 12/23/40 in Washington DC. Rock guitarist. Member of **Jefferson Airplane** and **Hot Tuna**. Vital Parts: Denny DeGorio (bass) and John Stench (drums).

| 2/14/81 | 163 | 6 | © | | **Barbeque King** | | | $12 | RCA Victor 3725 |

Barbeque King　　Man For All Seasons　　Roads And Roads &　　Runnin' With The Fast Crowd　　Starting Over Again
Love Is Strange　　Milkcow Blues Boogie　　Rockabilly Shuffle　　Snout Psalm　　To Hate Is To Stay Young

KAY, John　　'72

Born Joachim Krauledat on 4/12/44 in Tilsit, Germany. Leader of **Steppenwolf**.

| 4/29/72 | 113 | 11 | | 1 | **Forgotten Songs & Unsung Heroes** | | | $15 | Dunhill/ABC 50120 |
| 7/14/73 | 200 | 2 | | 2 | **My Sportin' Life** | | | $15 | Dunhill/ABC 50147 |

Bold Marauder (1)　　Giles Of The River (2)　　Moonshine (Friend Of Mine) (2)　　Sing With The Children (2)　　Walk Beside Me (1)
Dance To My Song (2)　　Heroes And Devils (2)　　My Sportin' Life (2)　　Somebody (1)　　Walkin' Blues (1)
Drift Away (2)　　**I'm Movin' On** (1) *52*　　Nobody Lives Here Anymore　　To Be Alive (1)　　You Win Again (1)
Easy Evil (2)　　Many A Mile (1)　　(2)　　Two Of A Kind (1)

KAYAK　　'78

Rock group from Holland: Max Werner (vocals), Johan Slager (guitar), Ton Scherpenzeel (keyboards), Theo DeJong (bass) and Charles Schouten (drums).

1/17/76	199	2		1	**Royal Bed Bouncer**			$12	Janus 7023
3/4/78	117	9		2	**Starlight Dancer**			$12	Janus 7034
3/3/79	145	7		3	**Phantom Of The Night**			$12	Janus 7039

Back To The Front (2)　　Do You Care (2)　　Keep The Change (3)　　No Man's Land (3)　　Royal Bed Bouncer (1)　　Winning Ways (3)
Ballad For A Lost Friend (2)　　First Signs Of Spring (3)　　Land On The Water (2)　　Nothingness (2)　　Ruthless Queen (3)　　(You're So) Bizarre (1)
Bury The World (1)　　**I Want You To Be Mine** (1) *55*　　Life Of Gold (1)　　Patricia Anglaia (1)　　Said No Word (1)
Chance For A Lifetime (1)　　If This Is Your Welcome (1)　　Love Of A Victim (2)　　Phantom Of The Night (3)　　Starlight Dancer (2)
Crime Of Passion (3)　　Irene (2)　　Moments Of Joy (1)　　Poet And The One Man Band　　Still My Heart Cries For You (2)
Daphine (Laurel Tree) (3)　　Journey Through Time (3)　　My Heart Never Changed (1)　　(3)　　Turn The Tide (2)

KAYE, Sammy　　'56[1]

Born on 3/13/10 in Rocky River, Ohio. Died of cancer on 6/2/87 (age 77). Leader of popular "sweet" dance band with the slogan "Swing and Sway with Sammy Kaye." Also played clarinet and alto sax.

8/4/56	20	1		1	**My Fair Lady (For Dancing)**		[I]	$30	Columbia 885
11/17/56	19	1		2	**What Makes Sammy Swing and Sway**		[I]	$30	Columbia 891
5/30/64	97	9		3	**Come Dance To The Hits**		[I]	$20	Decca 74502

Alley Cat (3)　　Deep Purple (3)　　I Could Have Danced All Night　　Little Brown Jug (2)　　Red Sails In The Sunset (3)　　Tuxedo Junction (3)
Ascot Gavotte (1)　　Dominique (3)　　(1)　　Maria Elena (3)　　720 In The Books (2)　　Washington Square (3)
Begin The Beguine (2)　　Fools Rush In (3)　　I've Grown Accustomed To Her　　Mood Indigo (2)　　She Loves Me (3)　　With A Little Bit Of Luck (1)
Blue Velvet (3)　　Get Me To The Church On　　Face (1)　　On The Street Where You Live　　Show Me (1)　　Without You (1)
Charade (3) *36*　　Time (1)　　In The Mood (2)　　(1)　　Stompin' At The Savoy (2)　　Wouldn't It Be Lovely (1)
Cherokee (2)　　I Can't Get Started (2)　　Jersey Bounce (3)　　One O'Clock Jump (3)　　String Of Pearls (3)　　You Did It (1)
Danke Schoen (3)　　　　Just You Wait (1)　　Rain In Spain (1)　　There I've Said It Again (3)

KAY-GEES, The　　'75

Disco group from Jersey City, New Jersey: Kevin Bell (guitar), Kevin Lassiter (keyboards), Wilson Beckett (percussion), Peter Duarte, Ray Wright and Dennis White (horns), Michael Cheek (bass) and Callie Cheek (drums). Bell is the brother of Ronald Bell of **Kool & The Gang**, band is named for that group.

| 3/1/75 | 199 | 1 | | | **Keep On Bumpin' & Masterplan** | | | $12 | Gang 101 |

Ain't No Time (Part 1 & 2)　　Get Down　　Master Plan　　Who's The Man? (With The　　Wondering
Anthology　　Let's Boogie　　My Favorite Song　　Master Plan)　　You've Got To Keep On
　　　　　　Bumpin'

KBC BAND　　'87

Rock trio of former **Jefferson Airplane** bandmates: Paul Kantner (guitar), Marty Balin (vocals) and Jack Casady (bass).

| 11/8/86+ | 75 | 24 | © | | **KBC Band** | | | $10 | Arista 8440 |

America　　Hold Me　　Mariel　　Sayonara　　Wrecking Crew
Dream Motorcycle　　It's Not You, It's Not Me *89*　　No More Heartaches　　When Love Comes

KC AND THE SUNSHINE BAND　　'75

Disco group from Hialeah, Florida. Formed by Harry "KC" Casey (vocals, keyboards; born on 1/31/51) and Richard Finch (bass). Other members included Jerome Smith (guitar), Fermin Coytisolo (congas), Robert Johnson (drums), and Ronnie Smith, Denvil Liptrot, James Weaver, and Charles Williams (horn section). Smith died in a construction accident on 7/28/2000 (age 47).

8/2/75	4	47	©	1	**KC And The Sunshine Band**			$12	TK 603
10/4/75	131	8		2	**The Sound Of Sunshine**		[I]	$12	TK 604
					THE SUNSHINE BAND				
10/23/76	13	77	©	3	**Part 3**			$12	TK 605
8/19/78	36	13		4	**Who Do Ya (Love)**			$12	TK 607
7/7/79	50	37		5	**Do You Wanna Go Party**			$12	TK 611
3/22/80	132	11		6	**Greatest Hits**		[G]	$12	TK 612
2/4/84	93	18		7	**KC Ten**			$10	Meca 8301

KC AND THE SUNSHINE BAND — Cont'd

Ain't Nothin' Wrong (1)
All I Want (6)
Are You Ready? (7)
Baby I Love You (Yes, I Do) (3)
Boogie Shoes (1,6) *35*
Come On In (3)
Come To My Island (4)
Do You Feel All Right (4) *63*
Do You Wanna Go Party (5) *50*

Don't Break My Heart (7)
Don't Let Go (7)
Funky '75 (2)
Get Down Tonight (1,6) *1*
Give It Up (7) *18*
Hey J (2)
Hooked On Your Love (5)
How About A Little Love (4)
I Betcha Didn't Know That (5)
I Get Lifted (1)

I Like To Do It (3) *37*
I Love You (2)
I Will Love You Tomorrow (4)
I'm So Crazy ('Bout You) (1)
I'm Your Boogie Man (3,6) *1*
I've Got The Feeling (5)
In My World (7)
It's The Same Old Song (4) *35*
Just A Groove (2)
Keep It Comin' Love (3,6) *2*

Let It Go (Part One & Two) (1)
Let's Get Together (7)
Let's Go Party (3)
Let's Go Rock And Roll (4)
Miss B. (2)
Nobody Knows (7)
On The Top (7)
Ooh, I Like It (5)
Please Don't Go (5,6) *1*
Que Pasa? (5)

Queen Of Clubs (6) *66*
Rock Your Baby (2)
S.O.S. (2)
(Shake, Shake, Shake) Shake Your Booty (3,6) *1*
Sho-Nuff' (4)
Shotgun Shuffle (2) *88*
So Glad (4)
Sound Your Funky Horn (6)
Sunshine City (2)

Thank You (Falettinme Be Mice Elf Agin) (7)
That's The Way (I Like It) (1,6) *1*
Too High (7)
What Makes You Happy (1)
Who Do Ya Love (4) *68*
Wrap Your Arms Around Me (3) *48*

K-CI & JOJO   '98

Brothers Cedric "K-Ci" and Joel "JoJo" Hailey from Charlotte, North Carolina. K-Ci was born on 9/2/69. JoJo was born on 6/10/71. Both were founding members of **Jodeci**.

DEBUT	PEAK	WKS	RIAA	CD		Album Title			$	Label & Number
7/5/97+	6	90	▲³	©	1	Love Always			$10	MCA 11613
7/10/99	8	29	▲	©	2	It's Real			$10	MCA 11937
12/23/00+	20	30	▲	©	3	X			$10	MCA 112398

All My Life (1) *1*
All The Things I Should Have Known (3)
Baby Come Back (1)
Crazy (3) *11*
Don't Rush (Take Love Slowly) (1)

Fee Fie Foe Fum (2)
Game Face (3)
Get Back (3)
Girl (2)
HBI (1)
Hello Darlin' (2)
Here He Comes Again (2)

Honest Lover (3)
How Could You (1) *53*
How Long Must I Cry (2)
How Many Times (Will You Let Him Break Your Heart) (1)
I Can't Find The Words (3)
I Wanna Get To Know You (2)

I Wanna Make Love To You (2)
If It's Going To Work (3)
Just For Your Love (1)
Last Night's Letter (1) *46*
Life (2) *60*
Love Ballad (3)
Makin Me Say Goodbye (2)

Momma's Song (2)
Now And Forever (1)
One Last Time (3)
Ooh Yeah (3)
Something Inside Of Me (3)
Still Waiting (1)
Suicide (3)

Tell Me It's Real (2) *2*
Thug N U Thug N Me (3)
Wanna Do You Right (3)
What Am I Gonna Do (3)
You Bring Me Up (1) *26*

KEB' MO'   '96

Born Kevin Moore in Los Angeles. Blues singer/songwriter/guitarist.

DEBUT	PEAK	WKS		CD		Album Title			$	Label & Number
7/6/96	197	1		©	1	Just Like You			$10	Okeh 67316
9/12/98	109	6		©	2	Slow Down			$10	Okeh 69376
10/28/00	122	4		©	3	The Door			$10	Okeh 61428
6/30/01	199	1		©	4	Big Wide Grin			$10	Okeh 63829

Action, The (1)
America The Beautiful (4)
Anyway (3)
Beginning, The (3)
Better Man (2)
Big Yellow Taxi (4)
Change (3)
Color Him Father (4)
Come On Back (3)

Dangerous Mood (1)
Don't Say No (4)
Don't You Know (3)
Door, The (3)
Everybody Be Yoself (4)
Everything I Need (2)
Family Affair (4)
Flat Foot Floogie (4)
Gimme What You Got (3)

God Trying To Get Your Attention (2)
Grandma's Hands (4)
Hand It Over (1)
Henry (2)
I Am Your Mother Too (4)
I Don't Know (2)
I Was Wrong (2)
I'm On Your Side (1)

I'm Telling You Now (2)
Infinite Eyes (4)
Isn't She Lovely (4)
It Hurts Me Too (3)
It's All Coming Back (3)
Just Like You (1)
Last Fair Deal Gone Down (1)
Letter To Tracy (2)
Loola Loo (3)

Love In Vain (2)
Love Train (4)
Lullaby Baby Blues (1)
Momma, Where's My Daddy (1)
Mommy Can I Come Home (3)
More Than One Way Home (1)
Muddy Water (2)
Perpetual Blues Machine (1)
Rainmaker (2)

Slow Down (2)
Soon As I Get Paid (2)
Stand Up (And Be Strong) (3)
Standin' At The Station (1)
That's Not Love (1)
You Can Love Yourself (1)

KEEL   '86

Hard-rock group from New York City: Ron Keel (vocals), Bryan Jay and Marc Ferrari (guitars), Kenny Chaisson (bass) and Dwain Miller (drums).

DEBUT	PEAK	WKS		CD		Album Title			$	Label & Number
3/9/85	99	21		©	1	The Right To Rock			$10	Gold Mountain 5041
4/19/86	53	18		©	2	The Final Frontier			$10	MCA 5727

above 2 produced by **Gene Simmons (Kiss)**

| 6/27/87 | 79 | 13 | | © | 3 | Keel | | | $10 | MCA 42005 |

Arm And A Leg (2)
Back To The City (1)
Because The Night (2)
Calm Before The Storm (3)
Cherry Lane (3)
Don't Say You Love Me (3)

Easier Said Than Done (1)
Electric Love (1)
Final Frontier (2)
4th Of July (3)
Get Down (1)

Here Today, Gone Tomorrow (2)
I Said The Wrong Thing To The Right Girl (1)
If Love Is A Crime (I Wanna Be Convicted) (3)
It's A Jungle Out There (3)

Just Another Girl (2)
King Of The Rock (3)
Let's Spend The Night Together (1)
Nightfall (2)
No Pain No Gain (2)

Raised On Rock (2)
Right To Rock (1)
Rock And Roll Animal (2)
So Many Girls, So Little Time (1)
Somebody's Waiting (3)

Speed Demon (1)
Tears Of Fire (2)
United Nations (3)
You're The Victim (I'm The Crime) (1)

KEEN, Robert Earl   '98

Born on 1/11/56 in Houston. Singer/songwriter/guitarist. Cousin of **Lee Roy Parnell**.

DEBUT	PEAK	WKS		CD		Album Title			$	Label & Number
5/17/97	160	1		©	1	Picnic			$10	Arista 18834
11/14/98	149	1		©	2	Walking Distance			$10	Arista 18876

Billy Gray (2)
Carolina (medley) (2)
Coming Home Of The Son And Brother (1)
Down That Dusty Trail (2)

Feelin' Good Again (2)
Fourth Of July (1)
Happy Holidays Y'All (2)
I Wonder Where My Baby Is Tonight (1)

I'll Be Here For You (2)
Levelland (1)
New Life In Old Mexico (2)
Oh Rosie (1)
Over The Waterfall (1)

Road To No Return (medley) (2)
Runnin' With The Night (1)
Shades Of Gray (1)
Still Without You (medley) (2)

That Buckin' Song (1)
Then Came Lo Mein (1)
Travelin' Light (2)
Undone (1)

KEENE, Tommy   '86

Born in Bethesda, Maryland. Rock singer/songwriter/guitarist.

DEBUT	PEAK	WKS		CD		Album Title			$	Label & Number
3/29/86	148	17		©		Songs From The Film			$10	Geffen 24090

As Life Goes By
Astronomy
Call On Me

Gold Town
In Our Lives
Kill Your Sons

Listen To Me
My Mother Looked Like Marilyn Monroe

Paper Words And Lies
Places That Are Gone
Story Ends

Underworld

KEITH   '67

Born James Barry Keefer on 5/7/49 in Philadelphia. Pop singer/songwriter.

DEBUT	PEAK	WKS				Album Title			$	Label & Number
3/25/67	124	5				98.6/Ain't Gonna Lie			$20	Mercury 61102

Ain't Gonna Lie *39*
I Can't Go Wrong
Mind If I Hang Around

98.6 *7*
Our Love Started All Over Again

Pretty Little Shy One
Sweet Dreams (Do Come True)
Teeny Bopper Song

Tell Me To My Face *37*
To Whom It Concerns
White Lightin'

You'll Come Running Back To Me

KEITH, Toby   '94

Born Toby Keith Covel on 7/8/61 in Clinton, Oklahoma. Country singer/songwriter/guitarist.

DEBUT	PEAK	WKS	RIAA	CD		Album Title			$	Label & Number
5/15/93	99	62	▲	©	1	Toby Keith			$10	Mercury 514421
10/15/94	46	30	●	©	2	Boomtown			$10	Polydor 523407
5/4/96	51	18	▲	©	3	Blue Moon			$10	A&M 531192
7/12/97	107	12	●	©	4	Dream Walkin'			$10	Mercury 534836
11/7/98	61	20	▲	©	5	Greatest Hits Volume One		C:#18/8 [G]	$10	Mercury 558962
1/22/00+	56	89↑	▲	©	6	How Do You Like Me Now?!			$10	DreamWorks 50209

KEITH, Toby — Cont'd

Ain't No Thang (1)
Big Ol' Truck (2,5)
Blue Bedroom (6)
Boomtown (2)
Close But No Guitar (1)
Closin' Time At Home (3)
Country Comes To Town (6) *54*
Die With Your Boots On (6)
Do I Know You (Bottom Of My Heart) (6)
Does That Blue Moon Ever Shine On You (3,5)

Double Wide Paradise (4)
Dream Walkin' (4,5)
Every Night (3)
Getcha Some (5)
He Ain't Worth Missing (1,5)
Heart To Heart (Stelen's Song) (6)
Hello (3)
Hold You, Kiss You, Love You (6)
How Do You Like Me Now?! (6) *31*

I Don't Understand My Girlfriend (6)
I Know A Wall When I See One (6)
I'm So Happy I Can't Stop Crying (4,5) *84*
If A Man Answers (5)
In Other Words (2)
Jacky Don Tucker (Play By The Rules Miss All The Fun) (4)
Life Was A Play (The World A Stage) (2)

Little Less Talk And A Lot More Action (1,5)
Lonely, The (3)
Lucky Me (3)
Mama Come Quick (1)
Me Too (3,5)
New Orleans (6)
No Honor Among Thieves (2)
She Only Gets That Way With Me (6)
She Ran Away With A Rodeo Clown (4)

She's Gonna Get It (3)
She's Perfect (3)
Should've Been A Cowboy (1,5) *93*
Some Kinda Good Kinda Hold On Me (1)
Strangers Again (4)
Tired (4)
Under The Fall (1)
Upstairs Downtown (2)
Valentine (1)
Victoria's Secret (2)

We Were In Love (4,5)
When Love Fades (6)
Who's That Man (2,5)
Wish I Didn't Know Now (1,5)
Woman Behind The Man (2)
Woman's Touch (3)
Yet (4)
You Ain't Much Fun (2,5)
You Don't Anymore (4)
You Shouldn't Kiss Me Like This (6) *32*

KELIS   '00
Born Kelis Rogers in Harlem, New York. Female R&B singer.

| 1/22/00 | **144** | 6 | | © | Kaleidoscope .... | | | $10 | Virgin 47911 |

Caught Out There *54*
Game Show
Get Along With You

Ghetto Children
Good Stuff
I Want Your Love

In The Morning
Mafia
Mars

No Turning Back
Roller Rink
Suspended

Wouldn't You Agree

KELLEM, Manny   '68
Born in Philadelphia. Prolific record producer.

| 4/13/68 | **197** | 2 | | | Love Is Blue .... | | | $15 | Epic 26367 |

And I Love Her
Claudine

Free Again
Here, There And Everywhere

I Will Wait For You
It's Not Unusual

Love Is Blue *96*
Man And A Woman

My Love
Trains And Boats And Planes

What A Wonderful World

KELLY, R.   '95
Born Robert Kelly on 1/8/67 in Chicago. R&B singer/songwriter/multi-instrumentalist. **Public Announcement** was his backing group.

2/15/92	**42**	62	▲	©	1	Born Into The 90's			$10	Jive 41469
						R. KELLY and Public Announcement				
11/27/93+	**2**[1]	65	▲[6]	©	2	12 Play			$10	Jive 41527
12/2/95	**❶**[1]	68	▲[5]	©	3	R. Kelly			$10	Jive 41579
11/28/98	**2**[1]	51	▲[7]	©	4	R.			$15	Jive 41625 [2]
11/25/00	**❶**[1]	45↑	▲[3]	©	5	TP-2.com			$10	Jive 41705

All I Really Want (5)
As I Look Into My Life (3)
Baby, Baby, Baby, Baby... (3)
Back To The Hood Of Things (2)
Born Into The 90's (1)
Bump N' Grind (2) *1*
Chase, The (4)
Dancing With A Rich Man (4)
Dedicated (1) *31*
Definition Of A Hotti (1)
Dollar Bill (4)
Don't Put Me Out (4)
Don't You Say No (5)

Down Low Double Life (4)
Down Low (Nobody Has To Know) (4)
Etcetera (4)
Feelin' On Yo Booty (5)
Fiesta Remix (5) *6*
For You (2)
Freak Dat Body (2)
Get Up On A Room (4)
Ghetto Queen (4)
Greatest Sex (5)
Half On A Baby (4)
Hangin' Out (1)
Heaven If You Hear Me (3)
Hey Love (Can I Have A Word) (1)

Home Alone (4) *65*
Homie Lover Friend (2)
Honey Love (1) *39*
Hump Bounce (3)
I Believe I Can Fly (4) *2*
I Can't Sleep Baby (If I) (3) *5*
I Decided (5)
I Don't Mean It (5)
I Know What You Need (1)
I Like The Crotch On You (2)
I Mean (I Don't Mean It) (5)
I Wish (5) *14*
I'm Your Angel (4) *1*
If I Could Turn Back The Hands Of Time (4) *12*
If I'm Wit You (4)

It Seems Like You're Ready (2)
Just Like That (5)
Keep It Street (1)
Like A Real Freak (5)
Looking For Love (4)
Love Is On The Way (3)
Money Makes The World Go Round (4)
Not Gonna Hold On (4)
One Man (4)
One Me (5)
Only The Loot Can Make Me Happy (4)
Opera, The (4)
R&B Thug (4)
Reality (4)

Religious Love (3)
Sadie (2)
2nd Kelly (4)
Sermon, The (3)
Sex (Part I & II) (2)
She's Got That Vibe (1) *59*
She's Loving Me (1)
Slow Dance (Hey Mr. DJ) (1) *43*
Spendin' Money (4)
Step In My Room (3)
Storm Is Over Now (5)
Strip For You (5)
Suicide (4)
Summer Bunnies (2) *55*
TP-2 (5)

Tempo Slow (5)
Thank God It's Friday (3)
Trade In My Life (4)
V.I.P. (4)
We Ride (4)
What I Feel/Issues (4)
When A Woman's Fed Up (4) *22*
Woman's Threat (5)
You Remind Me Of Something (3) *4*
(You To Be) Be Happy (3)
Your Body's Callin' (2) *13*

KEMP, Johnny   '88
Born in Nassau, Bahamas; raised in Harlem, New York. R&B singer/dancer/actor/songwriter.

| 6/11/88 | **68** | 19 | | © | Secrets Of Flying .... | | | $10 | Columbia 40770 |

Dancin' With Myself
Feeling Without Touching

Just Got Paid *10*
Just Like Flyin'

My Only Want Is You
One Thing Led To Another

Urban Times Medley

KEMP, Tara   '91
Born on 5/11/64 in San Francisco. R&B singer/songwriter/pianist.

| 2/16/91 | **109** | 14 | | © | Tara Kemp .... | | | $10 | Giant 24408 |

Be My Lover
Hold You Tight *3*

Monday Love
One Love

Piece Of My Heart *7*
Something To Groove To

Tara By The Way
Together

Too Much *95*
Way You Make Me Feel

KENDRICKS, Eddie   '73
Born on 12/17/39 in Union Springs, Alabama; raised in Birmingham. Died of cancer on 10/5/92 (age 52). Lead singer of **The Temptations** from 1960-71. Kendricks later dropped letter "s" from his last name. Also see **Hall & Oates**.

5/22/71	**80**	32			1	All By Myself			$15	Tamla 309
6/3/72	**131**	14		©	2	People...Hold On			$15	Tamla 315
6/16/73	**18**	40			3	Eddie Kendricks			$15	Tamla 327
3/16/74	**30**	17			4	Boogie Down!			$15	Tamla 330
12/7/74+	**108**	14			5	For You			$15	Tamla 335
7/12/75	**63**	25			6	The Hit Man			$15	Tamla 338
1/31/76	**38**	19			7	He's A Friend			$15	Tamla 343
10/9/76	**144**	7			8	Goin' Up In Smoke			$15	Tamla 346
4/22/78	**180**	3		©		Vintage '78			$12	Arista 4170

Ain't No Smoke Without Fire (9)
All Of My Love (7)
Any Day Now (3)
Best Of Strangers Now (9)
Body Talk (6)
Boogie Down (4) *2*
Born Again (8)
Can I (1)
Can't Help What I Am (3)
Chains (7)
Darling Come Back Home (3) *67*

Date With The Rain (4)
Day By Day (4)
Deep And Quiet Love (5)
Didn't We (1)
Don't Put Off Till Tomorrow (4)
Don't Underestimate The Power Of Love (9)
Don't You Want Light (8)
Each Day I Cry A Little (3)
Eddie's Love (2) *77*
Fortune Teller (6)
Get It While It's Hot (7)

Get The Cream Off The Top (6) *50*
Girl Of My Dreams (4)
Girl You Need A Change Of Mind (Part 1) (2) *87*
Goin' Up In Smoke (8)
Happy (6) (4)
He's A Friend (7) *36*
Honey Brown (4)
Hooked On Your Love (4)
How's Your Love Life Baby (3)
I Did It All For You (1)

I Won't Take No (7)
I'm On The Sideline (2)
I've Got To Be (6)
If (5)
If Anyone Can (6)
If It Takes All Night (9)
If You Let Me (2) *66*
If You Think (You Can) (5)
It's Not What You Got (7)
It's So Hard For Me To Say Good-Bye (1) *88*
Just Memories (2)

Keep On Truckin' (Part 1) (3) *1*
Let Me Run Into Your Lonely Heart (2)
Let Yourself Go (5)
Let's Go Back To Day One (1)
Love Love Love (5)
Loving You The Second Time Around (4)
Maybe I'm A Fool To Love You (9)
Music Man (8)

My People...Hold On (2)
Never Gonna Leave You (7)
Newness Is Gone (8)
Not On The Outside (3)
On My Way Home (7)
One Of The Poorest People (9)
One Tear (5) *71*
Only Room For Two (3)
Part Of Me (7)
Please Don't Go Away (5)
Shoeshine Boy (5) *18*
Skeleton In Your Closet (8)

KENDRICKS, Eddie — Cont'd

Skippin' Work Today (6)
Someday We'll Have A Better World (2)
Something's Burning (1)
Son Of Sagittarius (4) *28*

Sweet Tenderoni (8)
Sweeter You Treat Her (7)
Tell Her Love Has Felt The Need (4) *50*
Thanks For The Memories (8)

Thin Man (4)
This Used To Be The Home Of Johnnie Mae (1)
Time In A Bottle (5)
To You From Me (8)

Trust Your Heart (4)
Where Do You Go (Baby) (3)
Whip (9)
You Are The Melody Of My Life (4)

You Loved Me Then (6)
Your Wish Is My Command (9)

KENEALLY, Mike, and Beer For Dolphins   '00

Born in San Diego. Rock singer/guitarist. Beer For Dolphins: Rick Musallam (guitar), Evan Francis (sax), Chris Opperman (trumpet), Tricia Williams (percussion), Marc Ziegenhagen (keyboards), Bryan Beller (bass) and Jason Smith (drums).

10/14/00	167	1	©	**Dancing**			$10	Exowax 2404

Ankle Bracelet
Backwards Deb
Brown Triangles
Dancing

Friends And Family
I Was Not Ready For You
Joe
Kedgeree

Lhai Sal
Live In Japan
MM
Mystery Music

Only Mondays
Poo-Tee-Weet?
Pretty Enough For Girls
Ragged Ass

Selfish Otter
Skull Bubbles
Taster
We'll Be Right Back

★429★   KENNEDY, John Fitzgerald   '64

Born on 5/29/17 in Brookline, Massachusetts. Assassinated in Dallas on 11/22/63 (age 46). Elected president of the United States in 1960. Albums below are tributes to his life and career. Also see **Leonard Bernstein** and the **Boston Symphony Orchestra**.

1)That Was The Week That Was 2)The Presidential Years 1960-1963 3)A Memorial Album

12/28/63+	5	15		1	**That Was The Week That Was**		[T]	$25	Decca 9116

the BBC telecast tribute to Kennedy on 11/23/63

| 12/28/63+ | 8 | 14 | | 2 | **The Presidential Years 1960-1963** | | [T] | $25 | 20th Century Fox 3127 |

narrated by David Teig

| 1/11/64 | 42 | 8 | | 3 | **JFK The Man, The President** .... | | [T] | $25 | Documentaries Un. |

narrated by Barry Gray; no record label number

| 1/18/64 | 18 | 9 | ● | 4 | **A Memorial Album** .... | | [T] | $25 | Premier 2099 |

narrated by Ed Brown; a broadcast on 11/22/63 by WMCA in New York

| 1/18/64 | 109 | 5 | | 5 | **Actual Speeches of Franklin D. Roosevelt and John F. Kennedy** .... | | [T] | $20 | Somerset 16100 |

side 1: Kennedy's complete Inaugural Address (1/20/61); side 2: Roosevelt speeches

1/25/64	101	4		6	**John F. Kennedy - A Memorial Album**		[T]	$20	Diplomat 10000
1/25/64	119	4		7	**The Presidential Years (1960-1963)**		[T]	$20	Pickwick 169
2/8/64	29	10		8	**Four Days That Shocked The World**		[T]	$20	Colpix 2500

narrated by Reid Collins

| 12/26/64+ | 49 | 11 | | 9 | **The Kennedy Wit** .... | | [T] | $20 | RCA Victor 101 |

narrated by **David Brinkley**; introduction by Adlai E. Stevenson

| 12/11/65+ | 93 | 8 | | 10 | **John Fitzgerald Kennedy...As We Remember Him** .... | | [T] | $25 | Legacy 1017 [2] |

narrated by Charles Kuralt; includes a 240-page book

Alliance For Progress (7)
Ambassador Adlai Stevenson (6)
American Labor Movement, May, 1963 (2)
Another Prayer Breakfast, Feb., 1963 (2)
Berlin Speech (7)
Birmingham, May, 1963 (2,7)
Campaign In New York, Oct., 1960 (2)
Complete Story - Nov. 22-25, 1963 (8)
Cuba - Another Crisis, Oct., 1962 (2,6,7)
Election Eve (7)

Election Night, Nov., 1960 (2)
Equal Job Opportunities, Nov., 1962 (2)
Eulogy - Taps (6)
Eye Witness Account Of Assassination (6)
Family, The (9)
Final Address, Fort Worth, Nov. 22, 1963 (2,7)
General Dwight D. Eisenhower (6)
His Holiness Pope Paul VI (6)
Houston Speech (2)
In The Summer Of His Years (1)

Inaugural Address, Jan., 1961 (2,5,6,7)
J.F.K. Speech Of Space Flight (6)
Newscast Of Assassination (6)
1917 - 1942: John F. Kennedy's Boyhood And Education (10)
1942-1953: Service In The Pacific; Entry Into Politics; Marriage To Jacqueline B. (10)
1952 - 1961: The Senator And Campaigner; The Inauguration (10)
1960 Campaign (9)

1961 - 1963: John Fitzgerald Kennedy, President Of The United States (10)
Nomination Acceptance, July, 1960 (2)
Nuclear Test Speech (7)
Nuclear Tests, Nov., 1961 (2)
Oath Of Office For Presidency By J.F.K. (6,7)
On Labor (7)
Peace Corps Speech (7)
Prayer Breakfast, Feb., 1961 (2)
Pre-Election Speech Of Senator Kennedy (6,7)

Pres. Franklin D. Roosevelt Highlights Of Speeches (5)
Presidency, The (9)
President Johnson's Tribute At Andrews A.F.B., November 22, 1963 (6,7)
Presidential Press Conference (6)
Press Conferences (9)
Prime Minister Sir Alec Home (6)
Report On Berlin, July, 1961 (2)
Senator Barry Goldwater (6)
"So I Go To Khrushchev In Vienna", May, 1961 (2)

State Of The Union Message, Jan., 1961 (2,7)
Steel Crisis, April, 1962 (2,7)
Still Greater Crisis, Feb., 1963 (2)
To Jackie (7)
Tomb Of The Unknown Soldier, Nov., 1961 (2)
U.N. Address, Sept., 1961 (2,7)
Unspoken Credo, Nov. 22, 1963 (2)
Yale Graduation Address, June, 1962 (2)

KENNEDY, Joyce   '84

Born in Chicago. R&B singer. Member of **Mother's Finest**.

9/8/84	79	13			**Lookin' For Trouble**			$10	A&M 4996

Chain Reaction
Chase The Night

Last Time I Made Love *40*
Lookin' For Trouble

Love Is A Bet
Stronger Than Before

Tailor Made
Watch My Body

You Can Bet Your Life

KENNEDY, Robert Francis   '69

Born on 11/20/25 in Brookline, Massachusetts. Assassinated in Los Angeles on 6/5/68 (pronounced dead one day later; age 42). Senator from New York. Was running for president when he was killed.

1/11/69	187	4			**A Memorial**		[T]	$25	Columbia 792 [2]

record 1: highlights of speeches 1964-68; record 2: excerpts from the High Requiem Mass at St. Patrick's Cathedral on 6/9/68; includes "Battle Hymn Of The Republic" by **Andy Williams**

Excerpts from the High Requiem Mass
Humor

Measure Of A Nation
Memorial To Another Kennedy
On Vietnam

On Violence
On Youth And Its Responsibilities

Presidential Campaign Of 1968
To The Deprived
Toward A Better World

KENNY G ★158★   '93

Born Kenny Gorelick on 7/6/56 in Seattle. Alto saxophonist. Member of **Jeff Lorber**'s fusion group. Joined **Barry White**'s **Love Unlimited Orchestra** at age 17. Graduated from the University of Washington with an accounting degree.

1)Miracles - The Holiday Album 2)Breathless 3)The Moment

3/24/84	62	21	▲	©	1	G Force		[I]	$12	Arista 8192
6/1/85	97	12	▲	©	2	Gravity		[I]	$12	Arista 8282
						KENNY G & G FORCE				
9/6/86+	6	102	▲⁵	©	3	**Duotones**	C:#37/21	[I]	$10	Arista 8427
10/22/88	8	57	▲⁴	©	4	**Silhouette**	C:#33/10	[I]	$10	Arista 8457
12/9/89+	16	122	▲⁴	©	5	Live	C:#33/32	[I-L]	$15	Arista 8613 [2]

recorded on 8/26/89 in Seattle

DEBUT	PEAK	WKS	RIAA	CD	ARTIST — Album Title	Catalog	Sym	$	Label & Number

KENNY G — Cont'd

| 12/5/92+ | 2[11] | 214 | ▲[12] | © | 6 **Breathless** | C:#6/14 | [I] | $10 | Arista 18646 |
| 11/19/94 | ❶[3] | 14 | ▲[8] | © | 7 **Miracles - The Holiday Album** | C:❶[27]/60 | [X-I] | $10 | Arista 18767 |

Christmas charts: 1/'94, 1/'95, 1/'96, 3/'97, 5/'98, 9/'99, 11/'00

10/19/96	2[1]	51	▲[4]	©	8 **The Moment**		[I]	$10	Arista 18935
12/6/97	19	37	▲[3]	©	9 **Greatest Hits**	C:#24/8	[G-I]	$10	Arista 18991
7/17/99	17	33	▲	©	10 **Classics In The Key Of G**		[I]	$10	Arista 19085
12/4/99+	6	9	▲[2]	©	11 **Faith - A Holiday Album**	C:❶[6]/9	[X-I]	$10	Arista 19090

Christmas charts: 1/'99, 2/'00

Against Doctor's Orders (4)
All In One Night (4)
All The Way (medley) (9)
Alone (6)
Always (8)
Auld Lang Syne (The Millennium Mix) (11) *7*
Ave Maria (11)
Away In A Manger (7)
Baby G (9)
Body And Soul (10)
Brahms Lullaby (7)
By The Time This Night Is Over (9) *25*
Carol Of The Bells (medley) (11)
Champagne (3)
Champion's Theme (9)
Chanukah Song (7)
Christmas Song (11)
Desafinado (10)

Do Me Right (1)
Don't Make Me Wait For Love (3,5,9) *15*
Eastside Jam (8)
End Of The Night (6)
Esther (3,5)
Eternal Light (A Chanukah Song) (11)
Even If My Heart Would Break (6)
Everytime I Close My Eyes (8,9)
First Noel (11)
Forever In Love (6,9) *18*
G-Bop (6)
G Force (1)
Gettin' On The Step (8)
Girl From Ipanema (10)
Going Home (5,9) *56*
Gravity (2)

Greensleeves (7)
Havana (8,9) *66*
Have Yourself A Merry Little Christmas (7)
Help Yourself To My Love (1)
Hi, How Ya Doin'? (1)
Home (4,5)
Homeland (6)
How Could An Angel Break My Heart (9)
I Wanna Be Yours (1)
I'll Be Alright (4)
I'll Be Home For Christmas (11)
I've Been Missin' You (1,5)
In A Sentimental Mood (10)
In The Rain (6)
Innocence (8,9)
Japan (2)
Joy Of Life (6)
Last Night Of The Year (2)
Let Go (4)

Let It Snow! Let It Snow! Let It Snow! (11)
Little Drummer Boy (7)
Look Of Love (11)
Love On The Rise (2)
Loving You (9)
Midnight Motion (3,5)
Miracles (7)
Moment, The (8,9) *63*
Moonlight (9)
Morning (6)
Northern Lights (8)
O Christmas Tree (11)
One For My Baby (And One More For The Road) (medley) (9)
One Man's Poison (Another Man's Sweetness) (2)
One Night Stand (9)
Over The Rainbow (10)
Passages (8)

Pastel (4)
'Round Midnight (10)
Sade (3,5)
Santa Claus Is Coming To Town (11)
Sax Attack (2)
Sentimental (6,9) *72*
Silent Night (7)
Silhouette (4,5,9) *13*
Silver Bells (7)
Sister Rose (6)
Sleigh Ride (11)
Slip Of The Tongue (3)
Songbird (3,5,9) *4*
Stranger On The Shore (10)
Summer Song (4)
Summertime (10)
Sunset At Noon (1)
That Somebody Was You (8)
Theme From Dying Young (9)
Three Of A Kind (3)

Tradewinds (4)
Tribeca (1,5)
Uncle Al (5)
Virgin Island (2)
We Three Kings (medley) (11)
We've Saved The Best For Last (4) *47*
Wedding Song (6)
What A Wonderful World (10)
What Does It Take (To Win Your Love) (3)
Where Do We Take It (From Here) (2)
White Christmas (7)
Winter Wonderland (7)
Year Ago (6)
You Make Me Believe (3)
You Send Me (9)

KENOLY, Ron   '95

Born in 1944 in Coffeyville, Kansas. Gospel singer.

| 9/9/95 | 134 | 4 | | © | **Sing Out With One Voice** | | [L] | $10 | Integrity 02392 |

recorded at Carpenter's Home Church in Lakeland, Florida

Ain't Gonna Let No Rock
Come Into This House (medley)
For The Lord Is Good

Give To The Lord
God Is So Good
I Will Come And Bow Down

Joyfully, Joyfully
(Let Your Glory Fill) This Place
Lord Be Magnified

Oh The Glory Of Your Presence
Praise From Every Nation
Sing Out

We Dedicate This Time
Welcome Rap (medley)
With One Voice

KENTON, Stan   '56

Born on 2/19/12 in Wichita, Kansas. Died of a stroke on 8/25/79 (age 67). Jazz bandleader/pianist/composer.

9/8/56	13	2		©	1 **Kenton In Hi-Fi**		[I]	$40	Capitol 724
9/15/56	17	4		©	2 **Cuban Fire!**		[I]	$40	Capitol 731
10/23/61	16	28		©	3 **Kenton's West Side Story**		[I]	$25	Capitol 1609
7/1/72	146	14			4 **Stan Kenton Today**		[I-L]	$20	London Ph. 4 44179 [2]

recorded in London

Ambivalence (4)
America (3)
Artistry In Boogie (1)
Artistry In Percussion (4)
Artistry In Rhythm (1)
Artistry Jumps (1)
Bogota (4)
Chiapas (3)
Collaboration (1)

Concerto To End All Concertos (1)
Cool (3)
Eager Beaver (1)
El Congo Valiente (Valiant Congo) (2)
Fringe Benefit (4)
Fuego Cubano (Cuban Fire) (2)
Gee, Officer Krupke (3)

God Save The Queen (4)
I Feel Pretty (3)
Intermission Riff (1,4)
La Guera Baila (The Fair One Dances) (2)
La Suerte De Los Tontos (Fortune Of Fools) (2)
Lover (3)
Malaga (4)

Malaguena (4)
Maria (3)
Minor Riff (1)
Opus In Pastels (4)
Painted Rhythm (1)
Peanut Vendor (1,4)
Prologue (4)
Quien Sabe (Who Knows) (2)
Recuerdos (Reminiscences) (2)

Something's Coming (3)
Somewhere (3)
Southern Scandal (1)
Take The "A" Train (4)
Taunting Scene (3)
Tonight (3)
Unison Riff (1)
Walk Softly (4)

What Are You Doing The Rest Of Your Life (4)
Yesterdays (4)

KENTUCKY HEADHUNTERS, The   '90

Country group from Edmonton, Kentucky: brothers Ricky Lee (vocals) and Doug (bass) Phelps, brothers Richard (guitar) and Fred (drums) Young, and their cousin Greg Martin (guitar). The Phelps brothers left in 1992 to form Brother Phelps; replaced by Mark Orr (vocals) and Anthony Kenney (bass).

12/16/89+	41	96	▲[2]	©	1 **Pickin' On Nashville**			$10	Mercury 838744
4/20/91	29	30	●	©	2 **Electric Barnyard**			$10	Mercury 848054
3/13/93	102	6		©	3 **Rave On!!**			$10	Mercury 512568

Always Makin' Love (2)
Ballad Of Davy Crockett (2)
Big Mexican Dinner (2)
Blue Moon Of Kentucky (3)
Celina Tennessee (3)
Diane (2)
Dixiefried (3)

Dizzie Miss Daisy (3)
Dumas Walker (1)
Freedom Stomp (3)
Ghost Of Hank Williams (3)
High Steppin' Daddy (1)
Honky Tonk Walkin' (3)
It's Chitlin' Time (2)

Just Ask Fo' Lucy (3)
Kickin' Them Blues Around (2)
Love Bug Crawl (2)
Muddy Water (3)
My Daddy Was A Milkman (1)
My Gal (3)
Oh Lonesome Me (1)

Only Daddy That'll Walk The Line (2)
Rag Top (1)
Redneck Girl (3)
Rock 'N' Roll Angel (1)
16 And Single (2)
Skip A Rope (1)

Smooth (1)
Some Folks Like To Steal (1)
Spirit In The Sky (2)
Take Me Back (2)
Underground (3)
Walk Softly On This Heart Of Mine (1)

Wishin' Well (2)
With Body And Soul (2)

KERR, Anita, Singers   '69

Born Anita Jean Grob on 10/13/27 in Memphis. Formed her group of session singers in 1949. Also see **The San Sebastian Strings**.

| 3/22/69 | 162 | 6 | | © | 1 **The Anita Kerr Singers Reflect on the hits of Burt Bacharach & Hal David** | | | $15 | Dot 25906 |
| 9/20/69 | 172 | 3 | | © | 2 **Velvet Voices And Bold Brass** | | | $15 | Dot 25951 |

Alfie (1)
Are You There (With Another Girl) (1)
Do You Know The Way To San Jose (1)

Don't Make Me Over (1)
God Bless The Child (2)
Goodbye (2)
Happy Heart (2)
House Is Not A Home (1)

I Say A Little Prayer (1)
In Between The Heartaches (1)
Lalena (2)
Look Of Love (1)
My Way (2)

Ob-La-Di, Ob-La-Da (2)
Suppose (2)
Walk On By (1)
What The World Needs Now Is Love (1)

What's New Pussycat? (1)
When The World Was Young (2)
Whoever You Are, I Love You (1)

Windmills Of Your Mind (2)
Windows Of The World (1)
You And I (2)
You've Made Me So Very Happy (2)

KERSH, David   '98

Born on 12/9/70 in Humble, Texas. Country singer/songwriter.

| 3/15/97 | 169 | 10 | | © | 1 **Goodnight Sweetheart** | | | $10 | Curb 77848 |
| 3/7/98 | 134 | 6 | | © | 2 **If I Never Stop Loving You** | | | $10 | Curb 77905 |

Another You (1)
Anything With Wheels (2)
As If I Didn't Know (2)

Boys Will Be Boys (1)
Breaking Hearts And Taking Names (1)

Day In, Day Out (1)
Faster I Go (2)
Goodnight Sweetheart (1)

Hello Walls (2)
I Breathe In, I Breathe Out (2)

If I Never Stop Loving You (2) *67*
It's Out Of My Hands (2)

Louisiana Country Mile (1)
Love Of A Man (1)
Need, The (2)

KERSH, David — Cont'd

One Good Reason (1)   She Wants Me To Stay (Stay Gone) (1)   Something To Think About (2)   Things Your Daddy Wouldn't Want Us To Do (1)   Until Now (1)   Wonderful Tonight (2)

Sudden Stop (2)

KERSHAW, Nik '84

Born on 3/1/58 in Bristol, Somerset, England. Pop singer/songwriter/guitarist.

DEBUT	PEAK	WKS		CD	#	Album Title		$	Label & Number
5/5/84	70	20			1	Human Racing		$10	MCA 39020
4/27/85	113	10		©	2	The Riddle		$10	MCA 5548

Bogart (1)   Drum Talk (1)   Human Racing (1)   Riddle, The (2)   Wide Boy (2)
Cloak And Dagger (1)   Easy (2)   I Won't Let The Sun Go Down On Me (1)   Roses (2)   Wild Horses (2)
Dancing Girls (1)   Faces (1)   Save The Whale (2)   Wouldn't It Be Good (1,2) *46*
Don Quixote (2)   Gone To Pieces (1)   Know How (2)   Shame On You (1)   You Might (2)

KERSHAW, Sammy '98

Born Samuel Cashat on 2/24/58 in Abbeville, Louisiana; raised in Kaplan, Louisiana. Country singer/songwriter/guitarist.

DEBUT	PEAK	WKS	RIAA	CD	#	Album Title		$	Label & Number
1/25/92	95	57	▲	©	1	Don't Go Near The Water		$10	Mercury 510161
3/27/93	57	59	▲	©	2	Haunted Heart		$10	Mercury 514332
7/9/94	73	27	●	©	3	Feelin' Good Train		$10	Mercury 522125
9/30/95	131	18	●	©	4	The Hits/Chapter 1	[G]	$10	Mercury 528536
5/25/96	115	36	●	©	5	Politics, Religion And Her		$10	Mercury 528893
11/22/97+	49	30	▲	©	6	Labor Of Love		$10	Mercury 536318
5/1/99	99	7		©	7	Maybe Not Tonight		$10	Mercury 538889
5/5/01	114	3		©	8	I Finally Found Someone		$10	RCA 67004

LORRIE MORGAN & SAMMY KERSHAW

Anywhere But Here (1,4)   He Drinks Tequila (8)   If You Ever Come This Way Again (3)   Memory That Just Won't Quit (2)   Sad City (8)   What A Wonderful World (8)
Arms Length Away (6)   Heart That Time Forgot (3)   If You're Gonna Walk, I'm Gonna Crawl (3)   Memphis, Tennessee (5)   Same Place (5)   What Am I Worth (1)
Be My Reason (8)   Here She Comes (5)   More Than I Can Say (7)   She Don't Know She's Beautiful   What Might Have Been (2)
Better Call A Preacher (3)   Honky Tonk America (6)   Kickin' In (1)   National Working Woman's Holiday (3,4)   (2,4)   When You Love Someone (7)
Big Time (8)   How Can I Say No (7)   Labor Of Love (3)   Neon Leon (2)   Shootin' The Bull (In An Old Cowtown) (6)   Without Strings (7)
Cadillac Style (1,4)   How Much Does The World Weigh (7)   Little Bitty Crack In Her Heart (5)   Never Bit A Bullet Like This (3)   Southbound (3)   Yard Sale (1,4)
Chevy Van (5)   I Buy Her Roses (1)   Little Did I Know (6)   One Day Left To Live (6)   Still Lovin' You (2,4)   You've Got A Lock On My Love (2)
Cotton County Queen (6)   I Can't Reach Her Anymore (2,4)   Look What I Did To Us (7)   Ouch (7)   Sugar (8)   Your Tattoo (4)
Cry, Cry Darlin' (2)   Louisiana Hot Sauce (7)   Paradise From Nine To One (3)   Thank God You're Gone (6)
Don't Go Near The Water (1,4)   I Can't Think Of Anything But You (8)   Love Me, Loving You (7)   Politics, Religion And Her (5)   That's Where I'll Be (8)
Every Third Monday (1)   Love Of My Life (6) *85*   Queen Of My Double Wide Trailer (2,4)   These Flowers (5)
Feelin' Good Train (3)   I Finally Found Someone (8)   Matches (6)   Third Rate Romance (3,4)
Fit To Be Tied Down (5)   I Must Be Gettin' Older (8)   **Maybe Not Tonight** (7) *86*   Real Old-Fashioned Broken Heart (1)   3 Seconds (8)
For Years (8)   I Saw You Today (5)   Me And Maxine (7)   Too Far Gone To Leave (3)
Harbor For A Lonely Heart (1)   I've Never Gone This Far Before (7)   Meant To Be (5)   Roamin' Love (6)   29 Again (8)
Haunted Heart (2,4)   Vidalia (5)

KESNER, Dick, & His Stradivarius Violin '59

Born in New York City. Violin player. Regular on **Lawrence Welk**'s TV show (1955-59).

DEBUT	PEAK	WKS				Album Title		$	Label & Number
1/12/59	22	2				Lawrence Welk Presents Dick Kesner	[I]	$25	Brunswick 54044

All I Want Is Just Your Love   I'll Be With You When The Roses Bloom In Spring   Lullaby Of Love   Play Fiddle Play   When The Harvest Moon Is Shining
Farewell Juanita   Melody Of Love   Silver Moon
I Love You Truly   Kiss In Your Eyes   My Heart Still Remembers   Zigeuner

KETCHUM, Hal '92

Born on 4/9/53 in Greenwich, New York. Country singer/guitarist.

DEBUT	PEAK	WKS	RIAA	CD	#	Album Title		$	Label & Number
2/1/92	45	39	●	©	1	Past The Point Of Rescue		$10	Curb 77450
10/10/92	151	10		©	2	Sure Love		$10	Curb 77581
6/18/94	146	6		©	3	Every Little Word		$10	Curb 77660

Another Day Gone (3)   Five O'Clock World (1)   Mama Knows The Highway (2)   Softer Than A Whisper (2)   That's What I Get For Losin' You (3)   Veil Of Tears (3)
Daddy's Oldsmobile (2)   Ghost Town (2)   No Easy Road (3)   Some Place Far Away (2)   Walk Away (3)
Don't Strike A Match (To The Book Of Love) (1)   Hearts Are Gonna Roll (2)   Old Soldiers (1)   Somebody's Love (1)   Till The Coast Is Clear (2)   You Lovin' Me (2)
I Know Where Love Lives (1)   Past The Point Of Rescue (1)   Stay Forever (3)   (Tonight We Just Might) Fall In Love Again (3)
Drive On (3)   I Miss My Mary (1)   She Found The Place (1)   Sure Love (2)
Every Little Word (3)   Long Day Comin' (1)   Small Town Saturday Night (1)   Swing Low (3)   Trail Of Tears (2)

KEVIN & BEAN '94

Morning show DJ team from Los Angeles: Kevin Ryder and Gene "Bean" Baxter.

DEBUT	PEAK	WKS				Album Title		$	Label & Number
12/24/94	57	1				Kevin & Bean/No Toys For OJ	[X-C]	$10	KROQ 59337

available only on cassette; comedy bits by Kevin & Bean, and songs by alternative artists; proceeds benefit the Starlight Foundation of Southern California; 50,000 copies manufactured and sold only at The Wherehouse chain of music stores in Southern California; Christmas chart: 17/'94

Christmas Song   Holiday Greetings   Let It Snow   Merry Christmas   Silent Night
Cindy's Christmas Gift   Holly Jolly Christmas   Let Me Sleep (It's Christmastime)   My Christmas Memory   Snow Miser Won
Dingo Boy Christmas   I'll Be Home For Christmas   Rudolph The Red Nosed Reindeer   Storytime With Bobcat
Father Christmas   Jimmy's Christmas Wish   Me And Mrs. Claus

KGB '76

All-star rock group: Ray Kennedy (vocals), **Rick Grech** (bass; **Family**, **Traffic**, **Blind Faith**, **Ginger Baker**), **Mike Bloomfield** (guitar; **Paul Butterfield**, **Electric Flag**; d: 2/15/81, age 36), Carmine Appice (drums; **Cactus**, **Vanilla Fudge**, **Blue Murder**) and Barry Goldberg (keyboards).

DEBUT	PEAK	WKS				Album Title		$	Label & Number
3/6/76	124	6				KGB		$12	MCA 2166

Baby Should I Stay Or Go   I've Got A Feeling   Let Me Love You   Midnight Traveler   Workin' For The Children
High Roller   It's Gonna Be A Hard Night   Magic In Your Touch   Sail On Sailor   You Got The Notion

★453★ KHAN, Chaka '78

Born Yvette Marie Stevens on 3/23/53 in Great Lakes, Illinois. R&B singer. Became lead singer of **Rufus** in 1972. Sister of **Taka Boom**.

DEBUT	PEAK	WKS	RIAA	CD	#	Album Title		$	Label & Number
11/4/78	12	21	●	©	1	Chaka		$12	Warner 3245
6/21/80	43	16		©	2	Naughty		$12	Warner 3385
5/9/81	17	18	●		3	What Cha' Gonna Do For Me		$12	Warner 3526
12/18/82+	52	18			4	Chaka Khan		$10	Warner 23729
10/20/84	14	49	▲	©	5	I Feel For You		$10	Warner 25162
8/23/86	67	12			6	Destiny		$10	Warner 25425
12/17/88	125	12		©	7	C.K.		$10	Warner 25707

DEBUT	PEAK	WKS	RIAA	CD	ARTIST — Album Title	Catalog	Sym	$	Label & Number

KHAN, Chaka — Cont'd

| 5/2/92 | 92 | 9 | | © | 8 **The Woman I Am** | | | $10 | Warner 26296 |
| 11/30/96 | 84 | 10 | | © | 9 **Epiphany: The Best Of Chaka Khan Volume One** | | [G] | $10 | Reprise 45865 |

Ain't Nobody (9) 22 / All Night's All Right (2) / And The Melody Still Lingers On (Night In Tunisia) (3,9) / Any Old Sunday (9) / Baby Me (7) / Be Bop Medley (4) / Be My Eyes (8) / Best In The West (4) / Caught In The Act (5) / Chinatown (5) / Clouds (2) / Coltrane Dreams (6) / Don't Look At Me That Way (8) / Earth To Mickey (6) / End Of A Love Affair (7,9) / Eternity (7)

Every Little Thing (9) / Everything Changes (8) / Everywhere (9) / Eye To Eye (5) / Facts Of Love (8) / Fate (3) / Father He Said (3) / Get Ready, Get Set (2) / Give Me All (8) / Got To Be There (4) 67 / Heed The Warning (3) / Hold Her (5) / I Can't Be Loved (8) / I Feel For You (5,9) 3 / I Know You, I Live You (3,9) / I Want (8) / I Was Made To Love Him (1)

I'll Be Around (7) / I'm Every Woman (1,9) 21 / It's My Party (7) / It's You (6) / Keep Givin' Me Lovin' (8) / La Flamme (3) / Life Is A Dance (1) / Love Has Fallen On Me (1) / Love Me Still (9) / Love Of A Lifetime (6) 53 / Love With No Strings (8) / Love You All My Lifetime (8) 68 / Make It Last (7) / Message In The Middle Of The Bottom (1) / Move Me No Mountain (2)

My Destiny (6) / My Love Is Alive (5) / Never Miss The Water (9) / Night Moods (3) / Nothing's Gonna Take You Away (2) / Other Side Of The World (6) / Our Love's In Danger (2) / Papillon (aka Hot Butterfly) (2,9) / Pass It On (A Sure Thing) (Pasa Lo Esta Seguro) (4) / Roll Me Through The Rushes (1) / Signed, Sealed, Delivered (I'm Yours) (7) / Sleep On It (1) / Slow Dancin' (4)

So Close (6) / So Naughty (2) / So Not To Worry (4) / Some Love (1) / Somethin' Deep (9) / Soul Talkin' (7) / Sticky Wicked (7) / Stronger Than Before (5) / Tearin' It Up (4) / Telephone (8) / Tell Me Something Good (9) / This Is My Night (5) 60 / This Time (8) / Through The Fire (5,9) 60 / Tight Fit (6) / Too Much Love (2) / Twisted (7)

Watching The World (6) / We Can Work It Out (3) / We Got Each Other (3) / We Got The Love (1) / What Cha' Gonna Do For Me (3,9) 53 / What You Did (2) / Where Are You Tonite (7) / Who's It Gonna Be (6) / Woman I Am (8) / Woman In A Man's World (1) / You Can Make The Story Right (8) / Your Love Is All I Know (9)

KHAN, Steve '78
Born on 4/28/47 in Los Angeles. Jazz guitarist/producer. Son of famed songwriter Sammy Cahn.

| 2/4/78 | 157 | 5 | | | **Tightrope** | | [I] | $12 | Tappan Zee 34857 |

Big Ones

Darlin' Darlin' Baby (Sweet, Tender, Love) / Soft Summer Breeze / Some Punk Funk / Star Chamber / Tightrope (For Folon) / Where Shadows Meet

KICK AXE '84
Hard-rock group from Canada: George Criston (vocals), Raymond Harvey and Larry Gillstrom (guitars), Victor Langen (bass) and Brian Gillstrom (drums).

| 6/30/84 | 126 | 15 | | © | **Vices** | | | $10 | Pasha 39297 |

Alive & Kickin' / All The Right Moves

Cause For Alarm / Dreamin' About You / Heavy Metal Shuffle / Just Passin' Through / Maneater / On The Road To Rock / Stay On Top / Vices

KID CAPRI '98
Born David Love in 1968 in the Bronx, New York. DJ/rapper.

| 12/5/98 | 135 | 1 | | © | **Soundtrack To The Streets** | | | $10 | Track Masters 68781 |

Be Alright / Block Party / Do Or Die

Follow Me / Freestyle (Camp Lo) / Freestyle (Ranjah)

Hit Off / Hot This Year / Like That

Loud & Clear / My Niggaz / One On One

Soundtrack To The Streets / Unify / We're Unified

When We Party

KID CREOLE & THE COCONUTS '82
Born August Darnell Browder on 8/12/50 in Montreal. Singer/songwriter/producer. With his brother Stony Browder in **Dr. Buzzard's Original Savannah Band** during the mid-1970s. Formed The Coconuts with his wife, Adriana "Addy" Kaegi, and Andy "Coati Mundi" Hernandez (also in Dr. Buzzard's; appeared in the movie *Who's That Girl*). Group appeared in the movie *Against All Odds*.

| 7/18/81 | 180 | 2 | | | 1 **Fresh Fruit In Foreign Places** | | | $12 | Sire 3534 |
| 7/3/82 | 145 | 12 | | | 2 **Wise Guy** | | | $12 | Sire 3681 |

Animal Crackers (1) / Annie, I'm Not Your Daddy (2) / Dear Addy (1) / Gina, Gina (1)

Going Places (1) / I Am (1) / I Stand Accused (1) / I'm A Wonderful Thing, Baby (2)

I'm Corrupt (2) / Imitation (2) / In The Jungle (1) / Latin Music (1)

Love We Have (2) / Loving You Made A Fool Out Of Me (2) / Musica Americana (1)

No Fish Today (2) / Schweinerei (1) / Stool Pigeon (1) / Table Manners (1)

With A Girl Like Mimi (1)

KID FROST '90
Born Arturo Molina on 5/31/64 in Los Angeles. Male rapper. Later shortened name to **Frost**. Member of **Latin Alliance**.

| 7/28/90 | 67 | 14 | | © | 1 **Hispanic Causing Panic** | | | $10 | Virgin 91377 |
| 5/9/92 | 73 | 10 | | © | 2 **East Side Story** | | | $10 | Virgin 92097 |

FROST:

| 11/11/95 | 119 | 3 | | © | 3 **Smile Now, Die Later** | | | $10 | Ruthless 1504 |
| 7/19/97 | 154 | 3 | | © | 4 **When HELL.A. Freezes Over** | | | $10 | Ruthless 1578 |

Anotha Day Anotha Dolla (4) / Another Firme Rola (Bad Cause I'm Brown) (2) / Bamseeya (3) / Chema Otro Leno Mas (4) / Come Together (1) / East Side Rendezvous (3) 73 / East Side Story (2) / From My Block To Your Block (4)

Get Down (Make It Hot Big Daddy, Make It Hot) (4) / Heaven & Hell (4) / Heaven Sent (4) / Hispanic Causing Panic (1) / Hold Your Own (1) / Home Boyz (2) / Homicide (1) / How Many Ways Can You Lose A Body (3)

I Got Pulled Over (2) / In The City (1) / La Familia (3) 77 / La Raza (1) 42 / La Raza Part II (3) / Last Days (3) / Loco (4) / Look At What I See (3) / Man, The (2) / Mari (3)

Mexican Border (4) / Mi Vida Loca (2) / No More Wars (2) / No Sunshine (2) 95 / Nothing But Love For The Neighborhood (3) / Nothing In This World (4) / Penitentiary (3) / Rest In Peace (3) / Reunited (Lo Riding) (4)

Rock On (4) / Smiling Faces (2) / Smoke (1) / Straight To The Bank (1) / These Stories Have To Be Told (2) / Thin Line (2) / Throwing Q-VO's (2) / Tombstone (4) / Volo, The (2)

What's Your Name (Time Of The Season) (4) / Ya Estuvo (1) / You Ain't Right (3) / You're A Big Girl Now (4) / Youseemurda (3)

KID 'N PLAY '90
Rap duo from New York City: Christopher "Kid" Reid and Christopher "Play" Martin. Starred in the *House Party* movies.

12/17/88+	96	47	●	©	1 **2 Hype**			$10	Select 21628
3/31/90	58	12	●	©	2 **Kid 'N Play's Funhouse**			$10	Select 21638
10/19/91	144	11		©	3 **Face The Nation**			$10	Select 61206

Ain't Gonna Hurt Nobody (3) 51 / Back On Wax (3) / Back To Basix (2) / Bill's At The Door (3) / Brother Man Get Hip (1)

Can You Dig That (1) / Can't Get Enuff (2) / Damn That DJ (The Wizard M.E.) (1) / Decisions (2) / Do This My Way (1)

Do Whatcha Want 2 (2) / Energy (2) / Face The Nation (3) / Foreplay (3) / Funhouse (3) / Gittin' Funky (1)

Give It Here (3) / Got A Good Thing Going On (3) / I Don't Know (2) / It's Alright Y'All (3) / Kid 'N Play Kick Step (1) / Last Night (1)

Next Question (3) / Rollin' With Kid 'N Play (1) / Show 'Em How It's Done (2) / Slippin' (2) / Soul Man (1) / Strokin' (2)

Toe To Toe (2,3) / 2 Hype (1) / Undercover (1) / Y U Jellin' Me (2)

KID ROCK '00
Born Robert Ritchie on 1/17/71 in Dearborn, Michigan. Hip-hop/rock singer.

| 1/16/99+ | 4 | 95 | ▲10 | © | 1 **Devil Without A Cause** | C:#3/47 | | $10 | Lava 83119 |
| 6/17/00 | 2¹ | 41 | ▲2 | © | 2 **The History Of Rock** | | [K] | $10 | Lava 83314 |
recordings from 1991-2000

Abortion (2) / American Bad Ass (2) / Bawitdaba (2) / Black Chic, White Guy (1) / Born 2 B A Hick (2)

Cowboy (1) 82 / Dark & Grey (2) / Devil Without A Cause (2) / Early Mornin' Stoned Pimp (2) / Fist Of Rage (1)

F-ck Off (1) / F**k That (2) / F**k You Blind (2) / I Am The Bullgod (1) / I Got One For Ya' (1)

I Wanna Go Back (2) / My Oedipus Complex (2) / Only God Knows Why (1) 19 / Paid (2) / Prodigal Son (1)

Roving Gangster (Rollin') (1) / Somebody's Gotta Feel This (1) / 3 Sheets To The Wind (What's My Name) (2) / Wasting Time (2)

Welcome 2 The Party (Ode 2 The Old School) (1) / Where U At Rock (1) / Ya' Keep On (1)

KID SENSATION — '90
Born Steven Spence in Seattle. DJ/keyboardist.

DEBUT	PEAK	WKS		CD				$	Label & Number
8/4/90	175	8		©	Rollin' With Number One			$10	Nastymix 70180

Back To Boom   Flowin'   I S.P.I.T.   Maxin' With E.C.P.   Prisoner Of Ignorance   Skin To Skin
Emergency   Hype It Up   Legal   Partners In Rhyme   Seatown Ballers   Two Minutes

KIDS FROM "FAME", The — '83
Studio musicians featuring cast members of the TV series *Fame*: Debbie Allen, Erica Gimpel, Gene Anthony Ray, Valerie Landsburg, Lee Curreri, Lori Singer, Albert Hague and Carlo Imperato. Singer/actress/director Allen's sister is actress Phylicia Rashad and husband is former basketball player Norm Nixon.

DEBUT	PEAK	WKS				Catalog	Sym	$	Label & Number
4/3/82	146	8		1	The Kids From "Fame"			$10	RCA Victor 4249
1/15/83	181	4		2	Songs			$10	RCA Victor 4525
3/26/83	98	11		3	The Kids From "Fame" Live!		[L]	$10	RCA Victor 4674

recorded at the Royal Albert Hall in London

Be My Music (1,3)   Could We Be Magic Like You (2,3)   Friday Night (3)   It's Gonna Be A Long Night (1,3)   Mannequin (2,3)   Step Up To The Mike (1)
Be Your Own Hero (3)   Dancing Endlessly (2)   Hi-Fidelity (1,3)   Just Like You (2)   Secret, The (medley) (3)   There's A Train (2)
Beautiful Dreamer (2)   Desdemona (1,3)   I Can Do Anything Better Than You Can (1)   Lay Back And Be Cool (2)   Songs (2)   We Got The Power (1,3)
Bet Your Life It's Me (2)   Fame (3)   I Still Believe In Me (1,3)   Life Is A Celebration (1,3)   Special Place (medley) (3)
Body Language (2,3)   Starmaker (1,3)

KIHN, Greg, Band — '83
Born on 7/10/50 in Baltimore. Rock singer/songwriter/guitarist. His band consisted of Dave Carpender (guitar), Gary Phillips (keyboards), Steve Wright (bass) and Larry Lynch (drums). Greg Douglas replaced Carpender in late 1982. Kihn went solo in late 1984.

DEBUT	PEAK	WKS		CD				$	Label & Number
9/16/78	145	12		©	1 Next Of Kihn			$12	Beserkley 0056
8/11/79	114	10			2 With The Naked Eye			$12	Beserkley 10063
4/26/80	167	5			3 Glass House Rock			$12	Beserkley 10068
4/11/81	32	32			4 Rockihnroll			$12	Beserkley 10069
4/10/82	33	17			5 Kihntinued			$12	Beserkley 60101
3/12/83	15	24		©	6 Kihnspiracy			$12	Beserkley 60224
6/16/84	121	9			7 Kihntagious			$12	Beserkley 60354
3/23/85	51	13		©	8 Citizen Kihn			$10	EMI America 17152

GREG KIHN

Anna Belle Lee (3)   Cold Hard Cash (4)   Girl Most Likely (4)   Make Up (7)   Rock (7)   Testify (5)
Another Lonely Saturday Night (2)   Confrontation Music (7)   Go Back (8)   Man Who Shot Liberty Valance (3)   Secret Meetings (1)   They Rock By Night (8)
Beside Myself (2)   Curious (6)   Good Life (8)   Moulin Rouge (2)   Seeing Is Believing (5)   Things To Come (3)
Boy's Won't (8)   Dedication (5)   **Happy Man** (5) *62*   Museum (1)   Serenade Her (3)   Trouble In Paradise (4)
Breakup Song (They Don't Write 'Em) (4) *15*   Desire Me (3)   Hard Times (7)   Night After Night (3)   Sheila (4)   Trouble With The Girl (7)
   Every Love Song (5) *82*   Higher And Higher (5)   Nothing's Gonna Change (4)   Small Change (3)   True Confessions (1)
Can't Have The Highs (Without The Lows) (2)   Everybody Else (1)   How Long (6)   One Thing About Love (7)   Someday (6)   Understander (1)
Can't Love Them All (6)   Everyday/Saturday (5)   I Fall To Pieces (6)   Only Dance There Is (3)   Sorry (1)   Valerie (2)
Can't Stop Hurtin' Myself (4)   Fallen Idol (2)   I'm In Love Again (8)   Privacy (8)   Sound System (5)   When The Music Starts (4)
Castaway (3)   Family (2)   Imitation Love (8)   Remember (1)   Stand Together (7)   Whenever (8)
Cheri Baby (7)   Fascination (6)   In The Naked Eye (2)   Rendezvous (4)   Talkin' To Myself (6)   Womankind (4)
Chinatown (1)   For Your Love (3)   **Jeopardy** (6) *2*   Reunited (7)   Tear That City Down (6)   Work, Work, Work (7)
   Free Country (8)   **Love Never Fails** (6) *59*   Roadrunner (2)   Tell Me Lies (3)   Worst That Could Happen (7)
   Getting Away With Murder (2)   **Lucky** (8) *30*   Temper, Temper (8)

KILLAH PRIEST — '98
Born William Reed in New York City. Male rapper. Member of **Sunz Of Man**.

DEBUT	PEAK	WKS		CD				$	Label & Number
3/28/98	24	6		©	1 Heavy Mental			$10	Geffen 24971
5/27/00	73	3		©	2 View From Masada			$10	MCA 112177

Almost There (1)   Crusaids (1)   High Explosives (1)   Live By The Gun (2)   Rap Legend (2)   Wisdom (1)
Atoms To Adam (1)   Fake MC's (1)   I'm Wit That (2)   Maccabean Revolt (2)   Science Project (1)
B.I.B.L.E. (1)   From Then Till Now (1)   If I Die (2)   Mystic City (1)   Tai Chi (1)
Blessed Are Those (1)   Gotta Eat (2)   If You Don't Know (1)   One Step (1)   View From Masada (2)
Bop Your Head (2)   Hard Times (2)   Information (1)   Places I've Been (2)   When Will We Learn (2)
Cross My Heart (1)   Heavy Mental (1)   It's Over (1)   Professional, The (1)   Whut Part Of The Game? (2)

KILLARMY — '97
Male rap group from New York City: Killa Sin, Shogun Assassin, Ninth Prince, Baretta Nine, Islord and Dom Pachino.

DEBUT	PEAK	WKS		CD				$	Label & Number
8/23/97	34	8		©	1 Silent Weapons For Quiet Wars			$10	Wu-Tang 50633
8/29/98	40	5		©	2 Dirty Weaponry			$10	Wu-Tang 50014

Allah Sees Everything (2)   Clash Of The Titans (1)   5 Stars (1)   Pain (2)   Shoot Out (2)   Wake Up (1)
Bastard Swordsman (2)   Doomsday (2)   Full Moon (1)   Red Dawn (2)   Swinging Swords (1)   War Face (1)
Blood For Blood (1)   Dress To Kill (1)   Galactics (2)   Seems It Never Fails (1)   Under Siege (1)   Where I Rest At (2)
Burning Season (1)   Fair, Love & War (1)   Last Poet (2)   Serving Justice (2)   Unite To Fight (2)   Wu-Renegades (1)
Camouflage Ninjas (1)   5 Stages Of Consciousness (2)   Murder Venue (2)   Shelter (1)   Universal Soldiers (1)

KILLER DWARFS — '90
Hard-rock group from Toronto: Russ (vocals), Mike (guitar), Ron (bass) and Darrell (drums) Dwarf. Mike was replaced by Jerry Dwarf by 1992.

DEBUT	PEAK	WKS		CD				$	Label & Number
5/28/88	165	6		©	1 Big Deal			$10	Epic 44098
4/28/90	151	9		©	2 Dirty Weapons			$10	Epic 45139

All That We Dream (2)   Comin' Through (2)   I'm Alive (1)   Nothin' Gets Nothin' (2)   Tell Me Please (1)
Appeal (2)   Desperados (1)   Last Laugh (2)   One Way Out (1)   Union Of Pride (1)
Breakaway (2)   Dirty Weapons (2)   Lifetime (1)   Power (1)   Want It Bad (2)
Burn It Down (1)   Doesn't Matter (2)   Not Foolin' (2)   Startin' To Shine (1)   We Stand Alone (1)

KILLING JOKE — '87
Dance-rock group from England: Jeremy Coleman (vocals), Geordie Walker (guitar), Paul Raven (bass) and Paul Ferguson (drums).

DEBUT	PEAK	WKS		CD				$	Label & Number
4/11/87	194	1		©	Brighter Than A Thousand Suns			$10	Virgin 90568

Adorations   Love Of The Masses   Sanity   Twilight Of The Mortal
Chessboard   Rubicon   Southern Sky   Wintergardens

KILO ALI — '97
Born in 1972 in Atlanta. Male rapper.

DEBUT	PEAK	WKS		CD				$	Label & Number
8/16/97	173	1		©	Organized Bass			$10	Death Row 90128

Ali   Bottom To The Top   Hit Me   Loot Chi Chi   Love In Ya Mouth   Save Me
Baby, Baby   Girls All Dance   It's Tricky   Lost Y'All Mind   Organized Bass   Show Me Love

KILZER, John   '88

Born in Jackson, Tennessee; raised in Memphis. Rock singer/songwriter/guitarist.

6/11/88	110	15		©	**Memory In The Making**			$10	Geffen 24190

Dirty Dishes   Give Me A Highway   Heart And Soul   If Sidewalks Talked   Memory In The Making   Red Blue Jeans
Dream Queen   Green, Yellow And Red   I Love You   Loaded Dice   Pick Me Up   When Fools Say Love

KIM, Andy   '74

Born Androwis Jovakim on 12/5/52 in Montreal. Pop singer/songwriter.

8/2/69	82	14			1 **Baby I Love You**			$20	Steed 37004
9/14/74	21	17			2 **Andy Kim**			$15	Capitol 11318
12/21/74	190	6			3 **Andy Kim's Greatest Hits**		[G]	$15	Dunhill/ABC 50193

And I Will Sing You To Sleep (2)   Didn't Have To Tell Her (1)   Here Comes The Mornin' (2)   I'll Be Loving You (1)   **Shoot 'Em Up, Baby** (3) *31*   Tricia Tell Your Daddy (3)
Baby, I Love You (1,3) *9*   **Fire, Baby I'm On Fire** (2) *28*   **How'd We Ever Get This Way** (3) *21*   If I Were A Carpenter (1)   **So Good Together** (1,3) *36*   Walkin' My La De Da (1)
Be My Baby (3) *17*   **Friend In The City** (3) *90*   **It's Your Life** (3) *85*   Songs I Can Sing Ya (2)   You Are My Everything (2)
By The Time I Get To Phoenix (1)   Good Good Mornin' (2)   **I Been Moved** (3) *97*   Let's Get Married (1)   Sunshine (2)
   Hang Up Those Rock 'N Roll Shoes (2)   I Got To Know (1)   **Rainbow Ride** (3) *49*   This Guy's In Love With You (1)
   I Wish I Were (3) *62*   **Rock Me Gently** (2) *1*   This Is The Girl (1)

KIMBERLYS, The — see JENNINGS, Waylon

KIME, Warren, & His Brass Impact Orchestra   '67

Born in Chicago. Orchestra leader/arranger/flugelhorn player.

| 4/15/67 | 89 | 12 | | | 1 **Brass Impact** .... | | [I] | $15 | Command 910 |
| 11/11/67+ | 177 | 7 | | | 2 **Explosive Brass Impact** .... | | [I] | $15 | Command 919 |

Baubles, Bangles & Beads (1)   Eleanor Rigby (1)   Georgy Girl (2)   Man And A Woman (2)   One Note Samba (Samba De Uma Nota So) (1)   Sweetest Sounds (1)
Brasilia (1)   Everybody Loves My Baby (2)   Get Out Of Town (2)   Mas Que Nada (Pow, Pow, Pow) (1)   Prelude To A Kiss (1)   What Now My Love (1)
Breeze And I (1)   Feeling Good (2)   In The Still Of The Night (1)   Mr. Lucky (1)   So In Love (2)
Constant Rain (Chove Chuva) (2)   Foggy Day (1)   It's All Right With Me (2)   No Moon At All (2)   So What's New (2)
   Gentle Rain (2)   Laia Ladaia (Reza) (2)

KIMMEL, Tom   '87

Born in Memphis. Rock singer/songwriter.

| 7/4/87 | 104 | 15 | | © | **5 To 1** .... | | | $10 | Mercury 832248 |

A To Z   Heroes   On The Defensive   **That's Freedom** *64*   Tryin' To Dance
5 To 1   No Tech   Shake   True Love   Violet Eyes

KING   '85

Pop-rock group from Coventry, England: Paul King (vocals), Jim Lantsbery (guitar), Mick Roberts (keyboards), Tony Wall (bass) and Adrian Lillywhite (drums).

| 8/17/85 | 140 | 9 | | © | **Steps In Time** .... | | | $10 | Epic 40061 |

And As For Myself   Fish   **Love & Pride** *55*   Trouble   Won't You Hold My Hand Now
Cherry   I Kissed The Spikey Fridge   Soul On My Boots   Unity Song

KING, Albert   '69

Born Albert Nelson on 4/25/23 in Indianola, Mississippi. Died of a heart attack on 12/21/92 (age 69). Blues singer/guitarist.

| 11/16/68 | 150 | 10 | | © | 1 **Live Wire/Blues Power** .... | | [I-L] | $50 | Stax 2003 |

recorded at the Fillmore in San Francisco

3/1/69	194	5		©	2 **King Of The Blues Guitar**			$25	Atlantic 8213
5/24/69	133	4			3 **Years Gone By**			$25	Stax 2010
7/12/69	171	5		©	4 **Jammed Together**		[I]	$25	Stax 2020

ALBERT KING/STEVE CROPPER/POP STAPLES

7/3/71	188	6			5 **Lovejoy**			$20	Stax 2040
10/7/72	140	8		©	6 **I'll Play The Blues For You**			$20	Stax 3009
3/20/76	166	6		©	7 **Truckload Of Lovin'**			$15	Utopia 1387
3/12/77	182	3			8 **Albert Live**		[L]	$20	Utopia 2205 [2]

Angel Of Mercy (6)   Cockroach (3)   Gonna Make It Somehow (7)   Jam In A Flat (8)   Overall Junction (2,8)   Watermelon Man (1,8)
Answer To The Laundromat Blues (6)   **Cold Feet** (2) *67*   Heart Fixing Business (3)   Kansas City (8)   Personal Manager (2)   What'd I Say (4)
As The Years Go Passing By (8)   Cold Women With Warm Hearts (7)   High Cost Of Loving (6)   Killing Floor (3)   Please Love Me (1)   Wrapped Up In Love Again (3)
Baby, What You Want Me To Do (4)   Corina Corina (2)   Hold Hands With One Another (7)   Knock On Wood (4)   Sensation, Communication Together (7)   You Don't Love Me (3)
Bay Area Blues (5)   Crosscut Saw (2)   Homer's Theme (4)   Laundromat Blues (2)   She Caught The Katy & Left Me A Mule To Ride (5)   You Sure Drive A Hard Bargain (2)
Big Bird (4)   Don't Burn Down The Bridge (6,8)   Honky Tonk Woman (5)   Like A Road Leading Home (5)   Sky Is Crying (3)   You Threw Your Love On Me Too Strong (3)
Blues At Sunrise (1,8)   Don't Turn Your Heater Down (4)   I Love Lucy (4)   Little Brother (Make A Way) (6)   Stormy Monday (8)   You're Gonna Need Me (2)
Blues Power (1)   Drowning On Dry Land (3)   I'll Be Doggone (6)   Lonely Man (3)   That's What The Blues Is All About (8)
Born Under A Bad Sign (2)   Everybody Wants To Go To Heaven (5)   I'll Play The Blues For You (6,8)   Look Out (1)   Trashy Dog (4)
Breaking Up Somebody's Home (6) *91*   For The Love Of A Woman (5)   I'm Gonna Call You As Soon As The Sun Goes Down (8)   Lovejoy, III. (5)   Truckload Of Lovin' (7)
Cadillac Assembly Line (7)   Funk-Shun (2)   I'm Your Mate (7)   Matchbox Holds My Clothes (3)   Tupelo (4)
   Going Back To Iuka (5)   If The Washing Don't Get You, The Rinsing Will (3)   Night Stomp (1)   Water (4)
   Nobody Wants A Loser (7)
   Oh, Pretty Woman (2)
   Opus De Soul (4)

KING, B.B.   ★139★   '00

Born Riley King on 9/16/25 in Itta Bena, Mississippi. Legendary blues singer/guitarist. His guitar named "Lucille." Moved to Memphis in 1946. Own radio show on WDIA-Memphis, 1949-50, where he was dubbed "The Beale Street Blues Boy," later shortened to "Blues Boy," then simply "B.B." First recorded for Bullet in 1949. Inducted into the Rock and Roll Hall of Fame in 1987. Won Grammy's Lifetime Achievement Award in 1987. Appeared in the movies *Into The Night* and *Amazon Women On The Moon*

    1) *Riding With The King* 2)*Live In Cook County Jail* 3)*Indianola Mississippi Seeds* 4)*Completely Well*
    5)*Together For The First Time...Live*

| 10/12/68 | 192 | 3 | | © | 1 **Lucille** .... | | | $25 | BluesWay 6016 |
| 6/14/69 | 56 | 34 | | © | 2 **Live & Well** .... | | [L] | $20 | BluesWay 6031 |

side 1: live; side 2: studio

12/27/69+	38	30		©	3 **Completely Well**			$20	BluesWay 6037
4/11/70	193	2			4 **The Incredible Soul Of B.B. King**		[E]	$20	Kent 539
10/17/70	26	28		©	5 **Indianola Mississippi Seeds**			$15	ABC 713

KING, B.B. — Cont'd

DEBUT	PEAK	WKS	CD	#	Title	Sym	$	Label & Number
2/20/71	25	33	©	6	Live In Cook County Jail	[L]	$15	ABC 723
					recorded on 9/10/70 in Chicago			
9/25/71	78	8	©	7	Live At The Regal	[E-L]	$15	ABC 724
					recorded on 11/21/64 in Chicago			
10/16/71	57	17	©	8	B.B. King In London		$15	ABC 730
2/26/72	53	17		9	L.A. Midnight		$15	ABC 743
9/9/72	65	20	©	10	Guess Who		$15	ABC 759
2/24/73	101	11		11	The Best Of B.B. King	[G]	$15	ABC 767
9/8/73	71	25	©	12	To Know You Is To Love You		$15	ABC 794
8/17/74	153	6		13	Friends		$15	ABC 825
10/26/74+	43	20	●	14	Together For The First Time...Live	[L]	$20	Dunhill/ABC 50190 [2]
					B.B. KING & BOBBY BLAND			
11/8/75	140	5	©	15	Lucille Talks Back		$15	ABC 898
7/17/76	73	14	©	16	Together Again...Live	[L]	$12	ABC/Impulse 9317
					BOBBY BLAND & B.B. KING			
2/12/77	154	7		17	King Size		$12	ABC 977
5/20/78	124	24	©	18	Midnight Believer		$12	ABC 1061
8/25/79	112	12	©	19	Take It Home		$12	MCA 3151
4/26/80	162	4	©	20	"Now Appearing" At Ole Miss	[L]	$15	MCA 8016 [2]
					recorded at the University of Mississippi			
2/28/81	131	10	©	21	There Must Be A Better World Somewhere		$12	MCA 5162
5/15/82	179	5	©	22	Love Me Tender		$12	MCA 5307
7/2/83	172	4	©	23	Blues 'N' Jazz		$12	MCA 5413
9/11/93	182	1	©	24	Blues Summit		$10	MCA 10710
11/22/97+	73	30	●	25	Deuces Wild		$10	MCA 11711
11/7/98	186	2	©	26	Blues On The Bayou		$10	MCA 11879
7/1/00	3	43	▲2 ©	27	Riding With The King		$10	Reprise 47612
					B.B. KING & ERIC CLAPTON			
1/13/01	145	2	©	28	The Best Of B.B. King: The Millennium Collection ...C:#16/6	[G]	$10	MCA 111939

Ain't Gonna Worry My Life Anymore (5)
Ain't Nobody Home (8,11,25,28) **46**
Alexis' Boogie (8)
Any Other Way (10)
Ask Me No Questions (5) **40**
B.B. King Blues Theme (20)
Baby I Love You (6)
Baby I'm Yours (13)
Bad Case Of Love (26)
Beginning Of The End (19)
Better Lovin' Man (10)
Better Not Look Down (19)
Black Night (medley) (14)
Blue Shadows (8)
Blues Boys Tune (26)
Blues In "G" (26)
Blues Man (26)
Blues We Like (26)
Born Again Human (21)
Breaking Up Somebody's Home (15)
Broken Heart (23)
Broken Promise (26)
Caldonia (14)
Call It Stormy Monday (24)
Can't You Hear Me Talking To You? (9)
Chains And Things (5) **45**
Chains Of Love (medley) (14)
Cherry Red (medley) (14)
Come By Here (4)
Come Rain Or Come Shine (27)
Confessin' The Blues (3,25)
Country Girl (7)
Cryin' Won't Help You Babe (25)
Cryin' Won't Help You Now (3)
Dangerous Mood (25)
Darlin' What Happened (26)
Darlin' You Know I Love You (6,20,23)
Days Of Old (27)
Don't Answer The Door (2,14,20,28)
Don't Change On Me (22)

Don't Cry No More (14)
Don't Make Me Pay For His Mistakes (15)
Don't You Lie To Me (17)
Driftin' Blues (14)
Driving Wheel (medley) (14)
Every Day I Have The Blues (6,7,16)
Everybody Lies A Little (15)
Everybody's Had The Blues (24)
Feel So Bad (16)
Five Long Years (10)
Fool Too Long (4)
Found What I Need (10)
Friends (2)
Friends (13)
Get Off My Back Woman (2) **74**
Ghetto Woman (8) **68**
Go Underground (5)
Goin' Down Slow (14)
Gonna Get Me An Old Woman (medley) (14)
Good Man Gone Bad (26)
Good To Be Back Home (medley) (14)
Got My Mojo Working (17)
Guess Who (10,20,28) **62**
Happy Birthday Blues (19)
Have Faith (15)
Heed My Warning (23)
Help The Poor (7,9,27) **90**
Hold On (I Feel Our Love Is Changing) (18,20)
Hold On I'm Coming (27)
How Blue Can You Get (6,7,11) **97**
Hummingbird (5,11) **48**
I Ain't Gonna Be The First To Cry (medley) (16)
(I Believe) I've Been Blue Too Long (9)
I Can't Leave (12)
I Can't Let You Go (23)
I Got Some Help I Don't Need (9,20,28) **92**

I Got Some Outside Help I Don't Need (26)
I Got Them Blues (13)
I Gotta Move Out Of This Neighborhood (medley) (14)
I Just Can't Leave Your Love Alone (18,20)
I Just Want To Make Love To You (medley) (17)
I Know The Price (15)
I Like To Live The Love (12,14,28) **28**
I Love You So (4)
I Need Love So Bad (medley) (20)
I Need Your Love (1)
I Pity The Fool (24)
I Wanna Be (27)
I Want You So Bad (2)
I Wonder Why (17)
(I'd Be) A Legend In My Time (22)
I'll Survive (26)
I'll Take Care Of You (14)
I'm Cracking Up Over You (4)
I'm Sorry (14)
I'm With You (1)
I've Always Been Lonely (19)
I've Got Papers On You Baby (4)
If I Lost You (26)
If That Ain't It I Quit (26)
If You Love Me (25)
Inflation Blues (23)
Into The Night (28)
Introduction (6)
It Takes A Young Girl (10)
It's Just A Matter Of Time (17)
It's My Own Fault (7,14)
Just A Little Love (3) **76**
Just Can't Please You (10)
Keep It Coming (25)
Key To My Kingdom (4)
Key To The Highway (27)
King's Special (5)
Let Me Make You Cry A Little Longer (18)

Let The Good Times Roll (16,28)
Let's Get Down To Business (2)
Life Ain't Nothing But A Party (21)
Little By Little (24)
Love (12)
Love Me Tender (22)
Lucille (1)
Lucille Talks Back (Copulation) (15)
Lucille's Granny (9)
Make Love To Me (23)
Marry You (27)
Mean Old World (16,26)
Midnight (9)
Midnight Believer (18)
More, More, More (21)
Mother Fuyer (17)
Mother-In-Law Blues (medley) (16)
My Mood (2)
My Silent Prayer (4)
My Song (13)
Neighborhood Affair (10)
Never Make A Move Too Soon (18,20)
Night Life (22,25)
No Good (3)
No Money No Luck (1)
Nobody Loves Me But My Mother (5,11,20,24)
Oh To Me (12)
One Of Those Nights (22)
Part-Time Love (8)
Paying The Cost To Be The Boss (25,28)
Power Of The Blues (8)
Philadelphia (13) **64**
Playin' With My Friends (24)
Please Accept My Love (2,6)
Please Love Me (7)
Please Send Me Someone To Love (22,25)
Rainbow Riot (23)
Rainin' All The Time (1)
Reconsider Baby (15)

Respect Yourself (12)
Riding With The King (27)
Rock Me Baby (14,20,25) **34**
Same Love That Made Me Laugh (17)
Same Old Story (Same Old Song) (19)
Second Hand Woman (23)
Sell My Monkey (23)
Shake It Up And Go (26)
Shouldn't Have Left Me (10)
Since I Met You Baby (22,24)
Slow And Easy (17)
So Excited (3) **54**
Something You Got (24)
Stop Putting The Hurt On Me (1)
Stormy Monday Blues (medley) (16)
Story Everybody Knows (19)
Strange Things Happen (medley) (16)
Summer In The City (10)
Sweet Little Angel (2)
Sweet Sixteen (6,9,11,28) **93**
Sweet Thing (4)
Take It Home (19)
Teardrops From My Eyes (23)
Tell Me Baby (26)
Ten Long Years (27)
Thank You For Loving The Blues (12)
That's The Way Love Is (14)
There Must Be A Better World Somewhere (21,25)
There's Something On Your Mind (24)
3 O'Clock Blues (6,14,20,27)
Thrill Is Gone (3,6,11,16,20,25,28) **15**
Time Is A Thief (22)
Time To Say Goodbye (4)
To Know You Is To Love You (12) **38**
Tomorrow Is Another Day (4)
Tonight I'm Gonna Make You A Star (19)

Treat Me Right (4)
Until I'm Dead And Cold (5)
Up At 5 AM (13)
Victim, The (21)
Walkin' In The Sun (17)
Watch Yourself (1)
We Can't Agree (8)
We Can't Make It (4)
We're Gonna Make It (24)
Wet Hayshark (8)
What Happened (3)
When Everything Else Is Gone (13)
When I'm Wrong (15,20)
When It All Comes Down (I'll Still Be Around) (18)
When My Heart Beats Like A Hammer (27)
Who Are You (12) **78**
Why I Sing The Blues (2,11,14) **61**
Woke Up This Mornin' (7)
Woman I Love (4) **94**
World Full Of Strangers (18)
World I Never Made (22)
Worried Life Blues (14,27)
Worry, Worry, Worry (6,7)
You And Me, Me And You (22)
You Don't Know Nothin' About Love (10)
You Done Lost Your Good Thing Now (7,20)
You Move Me So (1)
You Shook Me (24)
You Upset Me Baby (7)
You're Going With Me (21)
You're Losin' Me (3)
You're Mean (3)
You're Still My Woman (5)
You're The Boss (24)
You've Always Got The Blues (22)
Your Lovin' Turns Me On (medley) (17)

KING, Ben E.   '77

Born Benjamin Earl Nelson on 9/23/38 in Henderson, North Carolina; raised in New York City. Lead singer of **The Drifters** from 1959-60.

DEBUT	PEAK	WKS	CD	#	Title	$	Label & Number
8/7/61	57	7	©	1	Spanish Harlem	$50	Atco 133
5/3/75	39	14		2	Supernatural	$12	Atlantic 18132
7/23/77	33	21		3	Benny And Us	$12	Atlantic 19105
					AVERAGE WHITE BAND & BEN E. KING		

Amor (1) **18**
Besame Mucho (1)
Come Closer To Me (1)
Do It In The Name Of Love (2) **60**
Do You Wanna Do A Thing (2)

Drop My Heart Off (2)
Extra-Extra (2)
Fool For You Anyway (3)
Frenesi (1)
Get It Up For Love (3)
Granada (1)

Happiness Is Where You Find It (2)
Imagination (2)
Imagine (3)
Keepin' It To Myself (3)
Love Me, Love Me (1)

Message, The (3)
Perfidia (1)
Quizas, Quizas, Quizas (Perhaps, Perhaps, Perhaps) (1)
Someday We'll All Be Free (3)

Souvenir Of Mexico (1)
Spanish Harlem (1) **10**
Star In The Ghetto (3)
Supernatural Thing-Part I (2) **5**
Supernatural Thing-Part II (2)

Sway (1)
Sweet And Gentle (1)
What Do You Want Me To Do (2)
What Is Soul (3)
Your Lovin' Ain't Good Enough (2)

KING, Carole ★97★   '71
Born Carole Klein on 2/9/42 in Brooklyn, New York. Singer/songwriter/pianist. Married to songwriting partner Gerry Goffin from 1958-68; their daughter is **Louise Goffin**. One of the most successful female songwriters of the rock era. She and Goffin were inducted as a songwriting team into the Rock and Roll Hall of Fame in 1990.

1)Tapestry 2)Music 3)Wrap Around Joy

4/10/71	❶¹⁵	302	▲¹⁰	©	1 Tapestry	C:❶¹²/235		$15	Ode 77009
					1971 Grammy winner: Album of the Year				
5/1/71	84	27		©	2 Writer: Carole King			$15	Ode 77006
12/11/71+	❶³	44	▲	©	3 Music			$15	Ode 77013
11/4/72	2⁵	31	●	©	4 Rhymes & Reasons			$15	Ode 77016
6/23/73	6	37	●	©	5 Fantasy			$15	Ode 77018
9/28/74	❶¹	29	●	©	6 Wrap Around Joy			$15	Ode 77024
3/8/75	20	15		©	7 Really Rosie	[TV]		$15	Ode 77027
2/7/76	3	21	●	©	8 Thoroughbred			$15	Ode 77034
8/6/77	17	14	●		9 Simple Things..........................			$12	Capitol 11667
4/1/78	47	13	▲	©	10 Her Greatest Hits	[G]		$12	Ode 34967
6/17/78	104	8			11 Welcome Home			$12	Avatar 11785
6/23/79	104	9			12 Touch The Sky			$12	Capitol 11953
6/7/80	44	17	©		13 Pearls-Songs of Goffin and King........			$12	Capitol 12073
4/3/82	119	11			14 One To One			$12	Atlantic 19344
5/6/89	111	16		©	15 City Streets			$10	Capitol 90885
4/2/94	160	3	©		16 In Concert	[L]		$10	King's X 53878

Ain't That The Way (15)
Alligators All Around (7)
Ambrosia (8)
Ave. P (7)
Awful Truth (7)
Back To California (3)
Ballad Of Chicken Soup (7)
Beautiful (1,16)
Been To Canaan (4,10) **24**
Being At War With Each Other (5)
Believe In Humanity (5,10) **28**
Best Is Yet To Come (6)
Bitter With The Sweet (4)
Brighter (3)
Brother, Brother (3,10)
Can't You Be Real (2)
Carry Your Load (3)
Chains (13,16)
Change In Mind, Change Of Heart (6)
Changes (11)
Chicken Soup With Rice (7)
Child Of Mine (2)
City Streets (15)
Come Down Easy (4)
Corazon (5,10) **37**
Crazy (12)
Dancin' With Tears In My Eyes (13)

Daughter Of Light (8)
Directions (11)
Disco Tech (11)
Down To The Darkness (15)
Dreamlike I Wander (12)
Eagle (12)
Eventually (2)
Everybody's Got The Spirit (11)
Fantasy Beginning (5)
Fantasy End (5)
Feeling Sad Tonight (4)
Ferguson Road (4)
First Day In August (4)
Goat Annie (14)
God Only Knows (9)
Goin' Back (2,13)
Golden Man (14)
Good Mountain People (12)
Goodbye Don't Mean I'm Gone (4)
Gotta Get Through Another Day (4)
Growing Away From Me (3)
Hard Rock Cafe (9,16) **30**
Haywood (5)
Hey Girl (13)
Hi De Ho (13)
High Out Of Time (8) **76**
Hold On (7)
Hold Out For Love (16)

Home Again (1)
Homeless Heart (15)
I Can't Hear You No More (2)
I Can't Stop Thinking About You (15)
I Feel The Earth Move (1,10,16) **flip**
I Think I Can Hear You (4)
I'd Like To Know You Better (9)
In The Name Of Love (9)
It's A War (14)
It's Going To Take Some Time (3)
It's Gonna Work Out Fine (8)
It's Too Late (1,10,16) **1**
Jazzman (6,10,16) **2**
Labyrinth (9)
Legacy (15)
Life Without Love (14)
Little Prince (14)
Locomotion (13,16)
Lookin' Out For Number One (14)
(Love Is Like A) Boomerang (14)
Lovelight (15)
Main Street Saturday Night (11)
Midnight Flyer (15)
Morning Sun (11)
Move Lightly (12)

Music (3)
My Lovin' Eyes (6)
My My She Cries (4)
My Simple Humble Neighborhood (7)
Night This Side Of Dying (6)
Nightingale (6,10) **9**
No Easy Way Down (2)
Oh No Not My Baby (13)
One (9)
One Fine Day (13) **12**
One To One (14) **45**
One Was Johnny (7)
Only Love Is Real (8,10) **28**
Passing Of The Days (12)
Peace In The Valley (4)
Pierre (7)
Quiet Place To Live (5)
Raspberry Jam (2)
Read Between The Lines (14)
Really Rosie (7)
Ride The Music (11)
Screaming And Yelling (7)
Seeing Red (12)
Simple Things (9)
Smackwater Jack (1,10,16) **flip**
Snow Queen (13)
So Far Away (1,10,16) **14**
So Many Ways (8)

Some Kind Of Wonderful (3)
Someone Who Believes In You (15)
Someone You Never Met Before (14)
Song Of Long Ago (3)
Spaceship Races (2)
Stand Behind Me (4)
Still Here Thinking Of You (8)
Such Sufferin' (7)
Sunbird (11)
Surely (2)
Sweet Adonis (6)
Sweet Life (15)
Sweet Seasons (3,10) **9**
Sweet Sweetheart (2)
Tapestry (1)
That's How Things Go Down (15)
There's A Space Between Us (8)
Time Alone (9)
Time Gone By (12)
To Know That I Love You (9)
To Love (2)
Too Much Rain (3)
Venusian Diamond (11)
Walk With Me (I'll Be Your Companion) (12)
Wasn't Born To Follow (13)

Way Over Yonder (1)
We All Have To Be Alone (8)
We Are All In This Together (6)
Weekdays (5)
Welcome Home (11)
Welfare Symphony (5)
What Have You Got To Lose (2)
Where You Lead (1)
Will You Love Me Tomorrow? (1,16)
Wings Of Love (11)
Wrap Around Joy (6)
You Gentle Me (6)
You Go Your Way, I'll Go Mine (6)
You Light Up My Life (5) **67**
(You Make Me Feel Like) A Natural Woman (1,16)
You Still Want Her (12)
You're Something New (6)
You're The One Who Knows (7)
You've Been Around Too Long (5)
You've Got A Friend (1,16)

KING, Claude   '62
Born on 2/5/33 in Shreveport, Louisiana. Country singer/songwriter/guitarist.

8/11/62	80	7			Meet Claude King			$25	Columbia 8610

Big River, Big Man **82**
Comancheros, The **71**
Give Me Your Love And I'll Give You Mine

I Backed Out
I Can't Get Over The Way You Got Over Me

I'm Here To Get My Baby Out Of Jail
Little Bitty Heart
Pistol Packin' Papa

Sweet Lovin'
Tell Me Darlin', Would You Care?
Wolverton Mountain **6**

You're Breaking My Heart

KING, Diana   '95
Born on 11/8/70 in St. Catherine, Jamaica. Reggae singer.

8/19/95	179	4	●	©	Tougher Than Love			$10	Work 64189

Ain't Nobody **94**
Black Roses

Can't Do Without You
Love Me Thru The Night

Love Triangle
Shy Guy **13**

Slow Rush
Tougher Than Love

Treat Her Like A Lady
Tumble Down

KING, Evelyn "Champagne"   '78
Born on 6/29/60 in the Bronx, New York; raised in Philadelphia. R&B singer.

5/27/78	14	45	●		1 Smooth Talk			$12	RCA Victor 2466
4/14/79	35	17	●		2 Music Box			$12	RCA Victor 3033
10/11/80	124	7			3 Call On Me			$12	RCA Victor 3543
7/25/81	28	18			4 I'm In Love			$12	RCA Victor 3962
9/11/82	27	32	●	©	5 Get Loose			$12	RCA Victor 4337
					EVELYN KING (above 2)				
12/24/83+	91	20			6 Face To Face			$12	RCA Victor 4725
6/25/88	192	3		©	7 Flirt			$10	EMI-Manhattan 46968

Action (6) **75**
Back To Love (5)
Bedroom Eyes (3)

Before The Date (7)
Best Is Yet To Come (5)

Betcha She Don't Love You (5) **49**
Call On Me (3)

Dancin', Dancin', Dancin' (1)
Don't Hide Our Love (4)
Don't It Feel Good (6)

Face To Face (6)
Flirt (7)
Get Loose (5)

Get Up Off Your Love (5)
Givin' You My Love (What Cha Gonna Do With It) (6)

DEBUT	PEAK	WKS	RIAA	CD	ARTIST — Album Title	Catalog	Sym	$	Label & Number

KING, Evelyn "Champagne" — Cont'd

Hold On To What You've Got (7)
I Can't Stand It (5)
I Can't Take It (4)
I Don't Know If It's Right (1) *23*
I Need Your Love (3)
I Think My Heart Is Telling (2)
I'm In Love (4) *40*
I'm Just Warmin' Up (5)
If You Want My Lovin' (4)
It's OK (2)
Just A Little Bit Of Love (3)
Kisses Don't Lie (7)
Let's Get Crazy (6)
Let's Get Funky Tonight (3)
Let's Start All Over Again (2)
Love Come Down (5) *17*
Make Up Your Mind (2)
Makin' Me So Proud (6)
Music Box (2) *75*
No Time For Fooling Around (2)
Nobody Knows (1)
Other Side Of Love (4)
Out There (2)
Shake Down (6)
Shame (1) *9*
Show Is Over (1)
Smooth Talk (1)
Spirit Of The Dancer (4)
Steppin' Out (Part I & II) (2)
Stop It (7)
Stop That (5)
Talk Don't Hurt Nobody (3)
Teenager (6)
Tell Me Something Good (6)
Til I Come Off The Road (1)
Universal Girl (3)
We're Going To A Party (1)
What Are You Waiting For (4)
When Your Heart Says Yes (7)
Whenever You Touch Me (7)
You Can Turn Me On (7)
Your Kind Of Loving (3)

KING, Freddie '73
Born Freddie Christian on 9/3/34 in Gilmer, Texas. Died of a heart attack on 12/28/76 (age 42). Blues singer/guitarist.

| 7/21/73 | 158 | 8 | | © | Woman Across The River | | | $15 | Shelter 8919 |

Boogie Man
Danger Zone
Help Me Through The Day
Hootchie Cootchie Man
I'm Ready
Just A Little Bit
Leave My Woman Alone
Trouble In Mind
Woman Across The River
Yonder Wall
You Don't Have To Go

KING, Morgana '64
Born on 6/4/30 in Pleasantville, New York. Jazz singer/actress. Played "Mama Corleone" in the movie *The Godfather*.

| 8/22/64 | 118 | 15 | | © 1 | With A Taste Of Honey | | | $25 | Mainstream 6015 |
| 10/27/73 | 184 | 5 | | 2 | New Beginnings... | | | $15 | Paramount 6067 |

All In All (2)
As Long As He Will Stay (2)
Corcavado (1)
Desert Hush (medley) (2)
Easy To Love (1)
Fascinating Rhythm (1)
I Am A Leaf (medley) (2)
I Love Paris (1)
Jennifer Had (2)
Lady Is A Tramp (1)
Lazy Afternoon (1)
Like A Seed (2)
Prelude To A Kiss (1)
Sands Of Time And Changes (2)
Song For You (2)
Taste Of Honey (1)
We Could Be Flying (2)
When The World Was Young (medley) (2)
You Are The Sunshine Of My Life (2)
Young And Foolish (medley) (1)

KING, Rev. Martin Luther '68
Born on 1/15/29 in Atlanta. Assassinated in Memphis on 4/4/68 (age 39). America's civil rights leader. The third Monday in January is a principal U.S. holiday: Martin Luther King Day.

10/26/63	141	9		1	The Great March To Freedom		[T]	$40	Gordy 906
					recorded on 6/23/63 at Detroit's Freedom Rally				
11/2/63	102	5		2	The March On Washington		[T]	$30	Mr. Maestro 1000
					side 1: History of Negro Contributions; side 2: recorded on 8/28/63 in Washington DC				
11/9/63	119	5		3	Freedom March On Washington		[T]	$30	20th Century Fox 3110
					recorded on 8/28/63				
5/4/68	69	8		© 4	I Have A Dream		[T]	$20	Creed 3201
					recorded on 8/28/63 in Washington DC				
5/18/68	173	4		5	The American Dream		[T]	$20	Dooto 841
					recorded during a Freedom Rally at the Los Angeles Coliseum; no track titles listed on above 3 albums				
6/8/68	150	3		6	In Search Of Freedom		[T]	$20	Mercury 61170
					speeches from 1964-68				
6/8/68	154	3		7	In The Struggle For Freedom And Human Dignity		[T]	$20	Unart 21033
					recorded on 12/17/64 in New York City				

Address To American Jewish Committee (6)
Chronological History Of Negro Contributions (2)
Commitment To Non-Violence (6)
Dr. King's Entrance Into Civil Rights Movement (6)
Eulogy (A Preacher Leading His Flock) (6)
Faith In America (6)
Ground Crew And Mississippi (7)
I Believe I've Got To Go Back To The Valley (7)
I Have A Dream (1,6) *88*
I've Been To The Mountain Top (excerpt from speech the day before his death) (6)
Introduction (2)
Love Your Enemy (1)
March On Washington (2)
Militant Negro (1)
Must Establish Priorities (6)
Non-Violent Approach (1)
100 Years Later (1)
Pilots Of The Movement (7)
Police Brutality Will Backfire (6)
Price Of Freedom (1)
Segregation In The North (1)
Segregation Is Wrong (1)
Sense Of Dignity (1)
Urgency Of The Moment (1)
Who Is The Least Of These (7)

KINGBEES, The '80
Rock trio from Los Angeles: Jamie James (vocals, guitar), Michael Rummons (bass) and Rex Roberts (drums).

| 5/31/80 | 160 | 12 | | © | The Kingbees | | | $12 | RSO 3075 |

Everybody's Gone
Fast Girls
Follow Your Heart
Man Made For Love
My Mistake *81*
No Respect
Once Is Not Enough
Shake-Bop
Sweet Sweet Girl To Me
Ting-A-Ling

KING BISCUIT BOY WITH CROWBAR '71
Born Richard Newell on 3/9/44 in Hamilton, Ontario, Canada. Blues-rock singer/guitarist. Crowbar: Rheal Lanthier (guitar), Richard Bell (piano), Roland Greenway (bass) and Larry Atamanuik (drums).

| 12/26/70+ | 194 | 2 | | © | Official Music | | | $15 | Paramount 5030 |

Badly Bent
Biscuit's Boogie
Cookin' Little Baby
Corrina, Corrina
Don't Go No Further
Highway 61
Hoy Hoy Hoy
I'm Just A Lonely Guy
Key To The Highway
Shout Bama Lama
Unseen Eye

★350★ KING CRIMSON '70
Progressive-rock formed in England by guitarist **Robert Fripp**. Group featured an everchanging lineup of top British artists, among them Ian McDonald (sax; **Foreigner**), **Greg Lake** (bass, vocals; **Emerson, Lake & Palmer**), Bill Bruford (drums; **Yes**), Boz Burrell (bass, vocals; **Bad Company**), John Wetton (bass, vocals; **Family, Uriah Heep, U.K., Asia**) and American **Adrian Belew** (vocals, guitar).
1)*In The Court Of The Crimson King* 2)*In The Wake Of Poseidon* 3)*Discipline*

12/13/69	28	25	●	© 1	In The Court Of The Crimson King - An Observtion By King Crimson	C:#9/16		$20	Atlantic 8245
9/12/70	31	13		© 2	In The Wake Of Poseidon			$20	Atlantic 8266
3/20/71	113	10		© 3	Lizard			$20	Atlantic 8278
2/5/72	76	12		© 4	Islands			$20	Atlantic 7212
5/5/73	61	14		© 5	Larks' Tongues In Aspic			$20	Atlantic 7263
5/4/74	64	11		© 6	Starless And Bible Black			$20	Atlantic 7298
11/23/74	66	11		© 7	Red			$15	Atlantic 18110
5/24/75	125	5		8	USA		[L]	$15	Atlantic 18136
10/31/81	45	17		© 9	Discipline			$12	Warner 3629
7/3/82	52	14		© 10	Beat			$12	Warner 23692
4/7/84	58	17		© 11	Three of a Perfect Pair			$12	Warner 25071
5/13/95	83	2		© 12	THRAK		[I]	$10	Virgin 40313

Asbury Park (8)
B'Boom (12)
Book Of Saturday (5)
Cadence And Cascade (2)
Cat Food (2)
Cirkus (3)
Coda: Marine 475 (12)
Court Of The Crimson King-Part 1 (1) *80*
Devil's Triangle (2)
Dig Me (11)
Dinosaur (12)
Discipline (9)
Easy Money (5,8)
Elephant Talk (9)
Epitaph (1,8)
Exiles (5,8)
Fallen Angel (7)
Formentera Lady (4)
Fracture (6)
Frame By Frame (9)
Great Deceiver (6)
Happy Family (3)
Heartbeat (10)
Howler, The (10)
I Talk To The Wind (1)
In The Wake Of Poseidon (2)
Indiscipline (9)
Indoor Games (3)
Industry (11)
Inner Garden I & II (12)
Islands (medley) (4)
Ladies Of The Road (4)
Lady Of The Dancing Water (3)
Lament (6,8)

KING CRIMSON — Cont'd

Larks' Tongues In Aspic, Part One (5)
Larks' Tongues In Aspic, Part Two (5,8)
Larks' Tongues In Aspic, Part Three (11)
Letters, The (4)
Lizard Medley (3)
Man With An Open Heart (11)

Matte Kudasai (9)
Mincer, The (6)
Model Man (11)
Moonchild (1)
Neal And Jack And Me (10)
Neurotica (10)
Night Watch (6)
No Warning (11)

Nuages (That Which Passes, Passes Like Clouds) (11)
One More Red Nightmare (7)
One Time (12)
Peace (Parts 1-3) (2)
People (12)
Pictures Of A City (2)
Providence (7)
Red (7)

Requiem (10)
Sailor's Tale (4)
Sartori In Tangier (10)
Sex Sleep Eat Drink Dream (12)
Sheltering Sky (9)
Sleepless (11)
Song Of The Gulls (medley) (4)
Starless (7)

Starless And Bible Black (6)
THRAK (12)
Talking Drum (5)
Thela Hun Ginjeet (9)
Three Of A Perfect Pair (11)
Trio (6)
21st Century Schizoid Man (1,8)
Two Hands (10)

VROOOM (12)
VROOOM VROOOM (12)
VROOOM VROOOM: Coda (12)
Waiting Man (10)
Walking On Air (12)
We'll Let You Know (6)

KING CURTIS '71

Born Curtis Ousley on 2/7/34 in Fort Worth, Texas. Stabbed to death in New York City on 8/13/71 (age 37). Prolific R&B session saxophonist.

DEBUT	PEAK	WKS	CD	#	Album Title	Sym	$	Label & Number
6/13/64	103	12	©	1	Soul Serenade	[I]	$30	Capitol 2095
6/3/67	185	12	©	2	The Great Memphis Hits	[I]	$25	Atco 211
12/9/67+	168	9	©	3	King Size Soul	[I]	$25	Atco 231
8/17/68	198	2	©	4	Sweet Soul	[I]	$20	Atco 247
12/21/68	190	4	©	5	The Best of King Curtis	[G-I]	$20	Atco 266
7/19/69	160	3	©	6	Instant Groove	[I]	$20	Atco 293
8/29/70	198	2		7	Get Ready	[I]	$20	Atco 338
8/21/71	54	15	©	8	Live At Fillmore West	[I-L]	$20	Atco 359
3/25/72	189	3		9	Everybody's Talkin'	[I]	$20	Atco 385

Alexander's Ragtime Band (9)
Bridge Over Troubled Water (7)
By The Time I Get To Phoenix (4)
C.C. Rider (3)
Central Park (9)
Changes (8)
Dock Of The Bay ..see: (Sittin' On)
Dog, The (2)
Everybody's Talkin' (9)
Fa-Fa-Fa-Fa-Fa (Sad Song) (2)
Floatin' (7)
Foot Pattin' (6)
For What It's Worth (3) 87
Games People Play (6)

Get Ready (7)
Good To Me (2)
Green Onions (2)
Groove Me (9)
Harlem Nocturne (1)
Harper Valley P.T.A. (5) 93
Hey Joe (6)
Hey Jude (6)
Hold Me Tight (6)
Hold On, I'm Comin' (2)
Honey (4)
Honky Tonk (Parts 1 & 2) (1,9)
I Heard It Thru The Grapevine (4,5) 83
I Never Loved A Man (The Way I Love You) (3)

I Stand Accused (8)
I Was Made To Love Her (3,5) 76
I've Been Loving You Too Long (2)
If I Were A Carpenter (9)
In The Midnight Hour (2)
Instant Groove (6)
Jump Back (2,5) 63
Knock On Wood (2)
La Jeanne (6)
Last Night (2)
Let It Be (7)
Little Green Apples (6)
Live For Life (Vivre Pour Vivre) (3)

Look Of Love (4)
Love The One You're With (9)
Makin' Hey (5)
Memphis (1)
Memphis Soul Stew (3,5,8) 33
Mr. Bojangles (8)
Night Train (1)
Ode To Billie Joe (3,5,8) 28
Promenade (7)
Ridin' Thumb (2)
Signed Sealed Delivered I'm Yours (8)
Sing A Simple Song (6)
(Sittin' On) The Dock Of The Bay (4,5) 84
Someday We'll Be Together (7)

Something (7)
Something On Your Mind (5)
Somewhere (6)
Soul Serenade (1,4,5,8) 51
Soul Twist (1) 17
Soulin' (7)
Spanish Harlem (5) 89
Spooky (4)
Sugar Foot (7)
Sweet Inspiration (4)
Swingin' Shepherd Blues (1)
Teasin' (7)
Tequila (1)
To Sir, With Love (3)
Up - Up And Away (4)
Valley Of The Dolls (4) 83

Watermelon Man (1)
Weight, The (6)
Wet Funk (Low Down And Dirty) (9)
When A Man Loves A Woman (3)
When Something Is Wrong With My Baby (2)
Whiter Shade Of Pale (3,8)
Whole Lotta Love (8)
Wichita Lineman (6)
Wiggle Wobble (1)
You Don't Miss Your Water (2)
You're The One (9)
You've Lost That Lovin' Feelin' (5)

KING DIAMOND '88

Hard-rock group from Denmark: King Diamond (vocals), Andy LaRocque and Michael Denner (guitars), Timi Hansen (bass) and Mikkey Dee (drums). By 1988, Pete Blakk had replaced Denner and Hal Patino had replaced Hansen.

DEBUT	PEAK	WKS	CD	#	Album Title	$	Label & Number
7/11/87	123	13	©	1	Abigail	$10	Roadracer 9622
7/23/88	89	12	©	2	Them	$10	Roadracer 9550
9/30/89	111	8	©	3	Conspiracy	$10	Roadracer 9461
12/15/90+	179	8	©	4	"The Eye"	$10	Roadracer 9346

Abigail (1)
Accusation Chair (1)
"Amon" Belongs To "Them" (2)
Arrival (1)
At The Graves (3)
Behind These Walls (4)
Black Horsemen (1)

Broken Spell (2)
Burn (4)
Bye, Bye Missy (2)
Coming Home (2)
Cremation (4)
Curse, The (4)
Eye Of The Witch (4)

Family Ghost (1)
Father Picard (4)
Funeral (1)
Insanity (4)
Into The Convent (4)
Invisible Guests (2)
Let It Be Done (3)

Lies (3)
Mansion In Darkness (1)
Meetings, The (4)
Mother's Getting Weaker (2)
Omens (2)
Out From The Asylum (2)
Possession, The (1)

7th Day Of July 1777 (1)
1642 Imprisonment (4)
Sleepless Nights (3)
Something Weird (3)
Tea (2)
Them (2)
Trial (Chambre Ardente) (4)

Twilight Symphony (2)
Two Little Girls (4)
Victimized (3)
Visit From The Dead (3)
Wedding Dream (3)
Welcome Home (2)

KINGDOM COME '88

Hard-rock group formed in America: Lenny Wolf (vocals; from Hamburg, Germany), with Danny Stag and Rick Steier (guitars), Johnny Frank (bass), and James Kottak (drums; Montrose). In 1984, Wolf formed and fronted Stone Fury.

DEBUT	PEAK	WKS	RIAA	CD	#	Album Title	$	Label & Number
3/19/88	12	29	●	©	1	Kingdom Come	$10	Polydor 835368
5/13/89	49	15		©	2	In Your Face	$10	Polydor 839192

Do You Like It (2)
Get It On (1) 69
Gotta Go (Can't Wage A War) (2)

Hideaway (1)
Highway 6 (2)
Just Like A Wild Rose (2)
Living Out Of Touch (1)

Loving You (1)
Mean Dirty Joe (2)
Now "Forever After" (1)
Overrated (2)

Perfect 'O' (2)
Pushin' Hard (1)
17 (1)
Shout It Out (1)

Shuffle, The (1)
Stargazer (2)
What Love Can Be (1)
Who Do You Love (2)

Wind, The (2)

KING FAMILY, The '65

The daughters of William King Driggs, with their families, numbering nearly 40. The extended family had own variety TV series in 1965. Included the Four King Sisters (Alyce, Yvonne, Donna and Louise Driggs). Accompanied by the Alvino Rey Orchestra (the husband of Luise Driggs).

DEBUT	PEAK	WKS	#	Album Title	Sym	$	Label & Number
7/10/65	34	16	1	The King Family Show!		$20	Warner 1601
10/2/65	142	3	2	The King Family Album		$20	Warner 1613
12/18/65	8ˣ	2	3	Christmas With The King Family	[X]	$20	Warner 1627

Amen (1)
America The Beautiful (2)
Auld Lang Syne (medley) (3)
Battle Hymn Of The Republic (2)
Bluebird Of Happiness (2)
Caroling, Caroling (medley) (3)
Climb Ev'ry Mountain (1)
Come Dear Children (medley) (3)
Every Man Has A Castle (2)

First Noel (medley) (3)
Go Tell It On The Mountain (medley) (3)
God Bless The Child (3)
Hark The Herald Angels Sing (medley) (3)
He's Got The Whole World In His Hands (2)
Hear The Sledges With The Bells (3)
Holiday Of Love (3)

I Don't Know Why (I Just Do) (1)
I Used To Love You (But It's All Over Now) (1)
Irving Berlin Medley (1)
It Came Upon A Midnight Clear (medley) (3)
Jingle Bells (medley) (3)
Jolly Old St. Nicholas (medley) (3)
Joy To The World (medley) (3)

Line The Track (1)
Little Drummer Boy (3)
Make Someone Happy (1)
My Favorite Things (1)
O Come All Ye Faithful (medley) (3)
O Little Town Of Bethlehem (medley) (3)
Open Up Your Heart (And Let The Sunshine In) (2)
Pass Me By (1)

Shenandoah (3)
Silent Night (3)
Some Children See Him (3)
Square, The (1)
Star Carol (medley) (3)
Stardust (1)
Sunrise, Sunset (1)
Swing Low, Sweet Chariot (2)
Very Last Day (2)
We Wish You A Merry Christmas (medley) (3)

What Child Is This? (3)
When Are You Going To Learn? (1)
When The Saints Come Marching In (2)
(When There's) Love At Home (1)
White Christmas (3)
You'll Never Walk Alone (2)

KINGFISH '76

Rock group formed in San Francisco: Bob Weir (vocals, guitar; Grateful Dead), Robby Hoddinott and Matthew Kelly (guitars), Dave Torbert (bass; New Riders Of The Purple Sage) and Chris Herold (drums).

DEBUT	PEAK	WKS	CD	#	Album Title	Sym	$	Label & Number
3/27/76	50	9	©	1	Kingfish		$20	Round 564
5/21/77	103	10	©	2	Live 'N' Kickin'	[L]	$15	Jet 732

recorded at the Roxy in Hollywood

KINGFISH — Cont'd

Around And Around (2)	Bye And Bye (1)	Hypnotize (1,2)	Jump Back (2)	Mule Skinner Blues (2)	Supplication (1)
Asia Minor (1)	Good-Bye Yer Honor (1,2)	I Hear You Knocking (2)	Jump For Joy (1,2)	Overnight Bag (2)	This Time (1)
Big Iron (1)	Home To Dixie (1)	Juke (2)	Lazy Lightnin' (1)	Shake And Fingerpop (2)	Wild Northland (1)

KING HARVEST   '73

Pop-rock group from Olcott, New York: Ron Altback (vocals, piano), Eddie Tuleja (guitar), Rod Novack (sax), Dave Robinson (trombone), Tony Cahill (bass) and David Montgomery (drums).

| 1/27/73 | 136 | 10 | © | Dancing In The Moonlight .... | $15 | Perception 36 |

Dancing In The Moonlight 13	Lady, Come On Home	Motor Job	She Keeps Me High	Think I Better Wait Till	You And I
I Can Tell	Marty And The Captain	Roosevelt And Ira Lee	Smile On Her Face	Tomorrow	

KINGOFTHEHILL   '91

Rock-funk group from St. Louis: Frankie (vocals), Jimmy Griffin (guitar), George Potsos (bass) and Vito Bono (drums).

| 4/13/91 | 139 | 6 | © | Kingofthehill .... | $10 | SBK 95827 |

Big Groove	Freak Show	If I Say 63	Place In My Heart	Something 'Bout You
Electric Riot	I Do U	Party In My Pocket	Roses	Take It Or Leave It (Kingadahill)

KING RICHARD'S FLUEGEL KNIGHTS   '68

Instrumental group led by Dick "King Richard" Behrke.

| 1/27/68 | 198 | 2 | | Something Super! .... | [I] $15 | MTA 5005 |

Bye, Bye Blues	Georgy Girl	Lay Some Happiness On Me	There's A Kind Of Hush	Yes Sir That's My Baby
Come On Over	Goin' Outta My Head	Some Day My Prince Will Come	Who's Afraid Of The Big Bad	
Don't Sleep In The Subway	Horn Duey	Somethin' Stupid	Wolf	

KINGS, The   '80

Rock group from Toronto: David Diamond (vocals, bass), Aryan Zero (guitar), Sonny Keyes (keyboards) and Max Styles (drums).

| 8/16/80 | 74 | 26 | | 1 | The Kings Are Here .... | $15 | Elektra 274 |
| 9/26/81 | 170 | 4 | | 2 | Amazon Beach .... | $12 | Elektra 543 |

All The Way (2)	Don't Let Me Know (1)	Go Away (1)	Loading Zone (2)	Partyitis (1)	Switchin' To Glide (1) 43
Amazon Beach (2)	Equal Noise (2)	Got Two Girlfriends (2)	Love Store (1)	Run Shoes Running (1)	This Beat Goes On (1) flip
Anti Hero Man (1)	Fools Are In Love (2)	It's Okay (1)	My Habit (1)	Surprises (2)	Why Don't Love Do (2)

KINGSMEN, The   '64

Rock group from Portland, Oregon: Jack Ely (vocals, guitar), Lynn Easton (drums), Mike Mitchell (guitar), Bob Nordby (bass) and Don Gallucci (keyboards). After release of "Louie Louie" (featuring lead vocal by Ely), Easton took over leadership of band and replaced Ely as lead singer.

1/18/64	20	131	©	1	The Kingsmen In Person	[L] $40	Wand 657
9/26/64	15	37	©	2	The Kingsmen, Volume II	[L] $40	Wand 659
2/20/65	22	18	©	3	The Kingsmen, Volume 3	[L] $40	Wand 662
10/30/65+	68	17	©	4	The Kingsmen On Campus	[L] $40	Wand 670
8/20/66	87	8		5	15 Great Hits	[K] $40	Wand 674

Annie Fanny (4)	Genevieve (4)	Killer Joe (5) 77	Mother In Law (3)	Searching For Love (3)	Waiting, The (1)
Bent Scepter (1)	Good Lovin' (5)	La-Do-Dada (3)	New Orleans (2,5)	Shotgun (4)	Walking The Dog (2)
Climb, The (4) 65	Great Balls Of Fire (2)	Linda Lu (2)	Night Train (1)	Shout (3,5)	You Can't Sit Down (1)
Come On Baby, Let The Good	Hang On Sloopy (5)	Little Green Thing (4)	Ooh Poo Pah Doo (2,5)	Something's Got A Hold On Me	
Times Roll (2)	Hard Day's Night (4)	Little Latin Lupe Lu (2)	Over You (3)	(2)	
Comin' Home Baby (3)	I Go Crazy (3)	Long Green (2,3)	Peter Gunn (4)	Sometimes (4)	
David's Mood (2)	I Like It Like That (4)	Long Tall Texan (1)	Poison Ivy (5)	Stand By Me (4)	
Death Of An Angel (2)	J.A.J. (1)	Louie Louie (1) 2	Quarter To Three (5)	Sticks And Stones (4)	
Do You Love Me (2,5)	Jenny Take A Ride (C.C. Rider)	Mashed Potatoes (1)	Rosalie (4)	Tall Cool One (3)	
Don't You Just Know It (3)	(5)	Mojo Workout (1)	Satisfaction (5)	That's Cool, That's Trash (3)	
Fever (1,5)	Jolly Green Giant (3)	Money (1,5) 16	Searchin' (5)	Twist & Shout (1,5)	

KINGS OF THE SUN   '88

Hard-rock group from Sydney, Australia: brothers Jeffrey (vocals) and Clifford (drums) Hoad, Glen Morris (guitar) and Anthony Ragg (bass).

| 4/30/88 | 136 | 16 | © | 1 | Kings Of The Sun .... | $10 | RCA 6826 |
| 6/9/90 | 130 | 7 | © | 2 | Full Frontal Attack .... | $10 | RCA 9889 |

Bad Love (1)	Cry 4 Love (1)	Haunt You Baby (2)	I Get Lonely (2)	Overdrive (2)	Tom Boy (1)
Black Leather (1) 98	Drop The Gun (2)	Hooked On It (1)	Jealous (1)	Rescue Me (2)	Vampire (2)
Bottom Of My Heart (1)	Full Frontal Attack (2)	Hot To Trot (1)	Lock Me Up (2)	Serpentine (1)	Vicious Delicious (1)
Crazy (2)	Get On Up (1)	Howling Wind (2)	Medicine Man (1)	There Is Danger (2)	

KINGSTON TRIO, The ★21★   '59

Folk trio formed in San Francisco: Dave Guard (banjo), Bob Shane and Nick Reynolds (guitars). Big break came at San Francisco's Purple Onion, where the group stayed for eight months. Guard left in 1961 to form the Whiskeyhill Singers; John Stewart replaced him. Disbanded in 1968, Shane formed New Kingston Trio. Guard died of cancer on 3/22/91 (age 56). Current trio consists of Shane, Reynolds and George Grove (joined group in 1972). Originators of the folk music craze of the 1960s.

1)The Kingston Trio At Large 2)Sold Out 3)String Along 4)Here We Go Again! 5)The Kingston Trio

11/3/58	❶[1]	195	●	©	1	The Kingston Trio	$40	Capitol 996
2/16/59	2[4]	178	●	©	2	From The Hungry i	[L] $40	Capitol 1107
						recorded in San Francisco		
6/22/59	❶[15]	118	●	©	3	The Kingston Trio At Large	$30	Capitol 1199
11/9/59	❶[8]	126	●	©	4	Here We Go Again!	$30	Capitol 1258
4/25/60	❶[12]	73	●	©	5	Sold Out	$30	Capitol 1352
8/15/60	❶[10]	60	●	©	6	String Along	$30	Capitol 1407
9/5/60	15	15			7	Stereo Concert	[L] $30	Capitol 1183
						recorded at Liberty Hall in El Paso, Texas		
12/5/60	11	4		©	8	The Last Month Of The Year	[X] $30	Capitol 1446
2/27/61	2[1]	39		©	9	Make Way!	$30	Capitol 1474

DEBUT	PEAK	WKS	RIAA	CD	ARTIST — Album Title		$	Label & Number
					KINGSTON TRIO, The — Cont'd			
7/3/61	3	41		© 10	Goin' Places		$30	Capitol 1564
10/9/61	3	46		© 11	Close-Up		$30	Capitol 1642
3/10/62	3	51		© 12	College Concert	[L]	$25	Capitol 1658
					recorded at UCLA			
6/9/62	7	105	●	© 13	The Best Of The Kingston Trio	[G]	$25	Capitol 1705
8/18/62	7	37		© 14	Something Special		$25	Capitol 1747
12/15/62+	16	36		© 15	New Frontier		$25	Capitol 1809
3/30/63	4	29		© 16	The Kingston Trio #16		$25	Capitol 1871
8/17/63	7	25		© 17	Sunny Side!		$25	Capitol 1935
1/11/64	69	14		18	Sing A Song with The Kingston Trio	[I]	$25	Capitol 2005
2/1/64	18	21		© 19	Time To Think		$25	Capitol 2011
5/30/64	22	20		© 20	Back In Town	[L]	$25	Capitol 2081
					recorded at the Hungy i in San Francisco			
1/16/65	53	13		© 21	The Kingston Trio (Nick-Bob-John)		$25	Decca 74613
6/19/65	126	10		© 22	Stay Awhile		$25	Decca 74656
7/12/69	163	6		23	Once Upon A Time	[E-L]	$30	Tetragramm. 5101 [2]
					recorded at the Sahara-Tahoe Hotel in Las Vegas			

Across The Wide Missouri (4)
Adios Farewell (15)
Ah, Woe, Ah, Me (20)
All My Sorrows (3)
All Through The Night (8)
Ally Ally Oxen Free (19) *61*
Ann (20)
Away Rio (14)
Babe, You've Been On My Mind (Mama, You Been On My Mind) (23)
Baby Boy (11)
Bad Man Blunder (6,13) *37*
Ballad Of The Quiet Fighter (16)
Ballad Of The Shape Of Things (12,23)
Ballad Of The Thresher (17)
Banua (1,7)
Bay Of Mexico (1)
Beneath The Willow (11)
Big Ball In Town (16)
Billy Goat Hill (10)
Bimini (5)
Blind Date (23)
Blow The Candle Out (9)
Blow Ye Winds (3)
Blowin' In The Wind (17,18)
Blue Eyed Gal (9)
Bonny Hielan' Laddie (19)
Bottle Of Wine (22)
Brown Mountain Light (14)
Buddy Better Get On Down The Line (6)
Bye, Bye, Thou Little Tiny Child (8)
Carrier Pigeon (5)
Chilly Winds (12,18)
Coal Tattoo (19)
Coast Of California (10)
Colorado Trail (6)
Colours (23)
Come All You Fair And Tender Ladies (9)
Coplas (1,7)
Coplas Revisited (12)

Corey, Corey (3,18)
Day In Our Room (23)
Deportee (19)
Desert Pete (17) *33*
Dogie's Lament (15)
Don't Cry Katie (5)
Don't You Weep, Mary (11)
Dooley (22)
Dorie (2)
E Inu Tatou E (4)
Early Mornin' (3)
Early Mornin' Rain (23)
El Matador (5) *32*
En El Agua (9)
Everglades (6) *60*
Farewell Adelita (5)
Farewell Captain (20)
Farewell (Fare Thee Well My Own True Love) (21)
Fast Freight (1)
First Time (15)
500 Miles (12,18)
Follow Now, Oh Shepherds (8)
Genny Glenn (15)
Georgia Stockade (20)
Getaway John (3,23)
Go Where I Send Thee (8)
Goin' Away For To Leave You (12)
Gonna Go Down The River (22)
Goo Ga Gee (17)
Goober Peas (4)
Good News (3)
Goodnight Irene (23)
Goodnight My Baby (8)
Gotta Travel On (21)
Greenback Dollar (15,18,23) *21*
Guardo El Lobo (10)
Gue, Gue (2)
Gypsy Rover (11)
Hangman (9)
Hanna Lee (22)
Hard, Ain't It Hard (1,23)

Hard Travelin' (9,23)
Haul Away (4)
Hobo's Lullaby (19)
Honey, Are You Mad At Your Man? (15)
Hope You Understand (21)
Hunter, The (5)
I Bawled (3)
I'm Going Home (21,23)
If I Had A Ship (22)
If You Don't Look Around (19)
If You See Me Go (22)
Isle In The Water (20)
It Was A Very Good Year (10)
Jackson (17)
Jane, Jane, Jane (14) *93*
Jesse James (11)
Jug Of Punch (5)
Karu (11)
La Bamba (16)
Laredo? (12)
Last Month Of The Year (What Month Was Jesus Born In) (8)
Last Night I Had The Strangest Dream (19)
Leave My Woman Alone (6)
Lemon Tree (4)
Let's Get Together (20)
Little Boy (14)
Little Maggie (1)
Little Play Soldiers (21)
Lonesome Traveler (medley) (2)
Long Black Rifle (3)
Long Black Veil (15)
Love Comes A Trickling Down (21)
Love's Been Good To Me (21)
Low Bridge (16)
M.T.A. (3,12,13,23) *15*
Mangwani Mpulele (5)
Marcelle Vahine (17)
Mark Twain (16)
Mary Mild (8)
Merry Minuet (2,7,13)

Midnight Special (21)
Molly Dee (4)
More Poems (21)
Mountains O'Mourne (5)
My Lord What A Mornin' (15)
My Ramblin' Boy (21)
New Frontier (15)
New York Girls (2)
No One To Talk My Troubles To (19)
O Ken Karenge (11,12)
O Willow Waly (14)
Oh Joe Hannah (16)
Oh, Miss Mary (12)
Oh, Yes, Oh! (9)
Old Joe Clark (14)
Oleanna (4)
One More Round (16)
One More Town (14,18) *97*
One Too Many Mornings (23)
Pastures Of Plenty (10)
Patriot Game (19)
Police Brutality (23)
Poor Ellen Smith (15)
Portland Town (14)
Poverty Hill (21)
Pullin' Away (14,18)
Raspberries, Strawberries (5,7,13) *70*
Razors In The Air (10)
Remember The Alamo (3)
Reverend Mr. Black (16) *8*
Rider (17)
River Is Wide (9)
River Run Down (16)
Road To Freedom (16)
Roddy McCorley (12)
Rollin' Stone (4)
Round About Christmas (8)
'Round About The Mountain (4)
Rovin' Gambler (medley) (23)
Ruben James (11,18)
Run Molly, Run (10)
Run The Ridges (16)
Rusting In The Rain (22)

Sail Away (11)
Salty Dog (20)
San Miguel (4)
Santy Anno (1)
Saro Jane (1)
Scarlet Ribbons (3)
Seasons In The Sun (19)
Seine, The (3)
Senora (10)
Shady Grove (medley) (2)
She Was Too Good To Me (14)
Silicone Bust (23)
Sing Out (17)
Sing We Noel (8)
Sloop John B ..see: Wreck Of The John B
So Hi (20)
Some Day Soon (21)
Some Fool Made A Soldier Of Me (15)
Somerset Gloucestershire Wassail (8)
Song For A Friend (19)
South Coast (2,7)
South Wind (6)
Speckled Roan (9)
Stay Awhile (22)
Stories Of Old (22)
Strange Day (14)
Take Her Out Of Pity (11,13)
Tanga Tika (medley) (5)
Tattooed Lady (6)
Tell It On The Mountain (14)
Them Poems Medley (20)
These Seven Men (13)
They Call The Wind Maria (2,7)
This Land Is Your Land (19)
This Little Light (12)
This Mornin', This Evenin', So Soon (6)
This Train (medley) (23)
Those Brown Eyes (17)
Those Who Are Wise (17)
Three Jolly Coachmen (1,7)

Three Song (22)
Tic, Tic, Tic (2)
Tijuana Jail (13,23) *12*
To Be Redeemed (15)
To Morrow (6)
Toerau (medley) (5)
Tom Dooley (1,7,13,18,20,23) *1*
Tomorrow Is A Long Time (23)
Try To Remember (16)
Turn Around (19)
Two-Ten, Six Eighteen (17)
Unfortunate Miss Bailey (4)
Utawena (9)
Walkin' This Road To My Town (20)
Wanderer, The (4)
We Wish You A Merry Christmas (8)
When I Was Young (6)
When My Love Was Here (11)
When The Saints Go Marching In (2,7,18,23)
Where Have All The Flowers Gone (12,13,18,23) *21*
Where I'm Bound (22)
Wherever We May Go (11)
White Snows Of Winter (8)
Who's Gonna Hold Her Hand (6)
Wimoweh (2,23)
With Her Head Tucked Underneath Her Arm (5)
With You My Johnny (5)
World I Used To Know (20)
Worried Man (4,13,18) *20*
Wreck Of The John B (1)
Yes I Can Feel It (22)
You Don't Knock (10)
You're Gonna Miss Me (Frankie And Johnny) (4)
Zombie Jamboree (2,7)

KING SWAMP '89

Rock group formed in London: Walter Wray (vocals), Steve Halliwell and Dominic Miller (guitars), Dave Allen (bass) and Martin Barker (drums). Halliwell, Allen and Barker were members of **Shriekback**. Miller, who was replaced by Nick Lashley in 1989, was a member of **World Party**.

DEBUT	PEAK	WKS	RIAA	CD	ARTIST — Album Title	$	Label & Number
6/3/89	159	14		©	King Swamp	$10	Virgin 91069

Blown Away
Is This Love?
Louisiana Bride
Man Behind The Gun
Mirror, The
Motherlode
Original Man
Sacrament, The
Widders Dump
Year Zero

KING'S X '91

Rock trio from Houston: Douglas Pinnick (vocals, bass), Ty Tabor (guitar) and Jerry Gaskill (drums).

DEBUT	PEAK	WKS	RIAA	CD	ARTIST — Album Title	$	Label & Number
5/7/88	144	11		© 1	Out Of The Silent Planet	$10	Megaforce 81825
8/5/89	123	18		© 2	Gretchen Goes To Nebraska	$10	Megaforce 81997
11/10/90+	85	24		© 3	Faith Hope Love By King's X	$10	Megaforce 82145
3/28/92	138	3		© 4	King's X	$10	Atlantic 82372
2/5/94	88	4		© 5	Dogman	$10	Atlantic 82558
6/8/96	105	1		© 6	Ear Candy	$10	Atlantic 82880

American Cheese (Jerry's Pianto) (6)
Big Picture (4)
Black Flag (4)
Black The Sky (5)
Box, A (6)
Burning Down (2)
Chariot Song (4)
Cigarettes (5)
Complain (5)

Difference (In The Garden Of St. Anne's-On-The-Hill) (2)
Dogman (5)
Don't Believe It (It's Easier Said Than Done) (4)
Don't Care (5)
Dream In My Life (4)
Everybody Knows A Little Bit Of Something (2)
Everywhere I Go (3)

Faith Hope Love (3)
Fall On Me (2)
Far, Far Away (1)
Fathers (6)
Fine Art Of Friendship (3)
Flies And Blue Skies (5)
Fool You (5)
Goldilox (4)
Human Behavior (5)
I Can't Help It (3)

I'll Never Be The Same (3)
I'll Never Get Tired Of You (3)
In The New Age (1)
It's Love (3)
King (1)
Legal Kill (3)
Lies In The Sand (The Ballad Of...) (4)
Life Going By (6)
Looking For Love (6)

Lost In Germany (4)
Manic Depression (5)
Mission (2)
Mississippi Moon (6)
Moanjam (3)
Mr. Wilson (3)
Not Just For The Dead (4)
Ooh Song (4)
Out Of The Silent Planet (2)
Over My Head (2)

Picture (6)
Pillow (6)
Pleiades (2)
Power Of Love (1)
Pretend (5)
Prisoner (5)
Run (6)

KING'S X — Cont'd

Send A Message (2)
Shoes (5)
Shot Of Love (1)
Silent Wind (4)
Six Broken Soldiers (3)

67 (6)
Sometime (6)
Sometimes (1)
Summerland (2)
Sunshine Rain (5)

Talk To You (3)
(Thinking And Wondering) What
  I'm Gonna Do (6)
Train, The (6)
Visions (1)

We Are Finding Who We Are
  (3)
We Were Born To Be Loved (3)
What I Know About Love (4)
What Is This? (1)

Wonder (1)
World Around Me (4)

KING TEE '93

Born Roger McBride on 12/14/68 in Los Angeles. Male rapper.

1/21/89	125	15	©		1 **Act A Fool**			$10	Capitol 90544
10/20/90	175	4	©		2 **At Your Own Risk**			$10	Capitol 92359
2/13/93	95	6	©		3 **Tha Triflin' Album**			$10	Capitol 99354
4/15/95	171	1	©		4 **IV Life**			$10	MCA 11146

Act A Fool (1)
Advertisement (4)
At Your Own Risk (2,3)
Baggin' On Moms (1)
Bass (1)
Black Togetha Again (3)
Blow My Sox Off (3)
Bus Dat Ass (3)
Can This Be Real (2)

Check The Flow (4)
Coolest, The (1)
Dippin' (4)
Diss You (2)
Do Your Thing (2)
Down Ass Loc (4)
Drunk Tekneek (3)
Duck (4)
E Get Swift (2)

Flirt (1)
Free Style Ghetto (4)
Got It Bad Y'all (3)
Great, Tha (3)
Guitar Playin' (1)
Hoe B-4 Tha Homie (3)
I Got A Cold (1)
Introduction (4)
Jay Fay Dray (2)

Just Clowning (1)
Just Flauntin' (3)
King Tee Production (2)
King Tee's Beer Stand (3)
Ko Rock Stuff (1)
Let's Dance (1)
Let's Get It On (4)
On Tha Rox (3)
On The Dance Tip (2)

Payback's A Mutha (1)
Played Like A Piano (2)
Ruff Rhyme (Back Again) (2)
Skanless (2)
Super Nigga (4)
Take You Home (2)
3 Strikes Ya' Out (4)
Time To Get Out (2)
Triflin' Nigga (2)

Way Out There (4)
We Got Tha Fat Joint (3)
Where'sa Hoe Sat (3)
You Can't See Me (4)

KINISON, Sam '88

Born on 12/8/53 in Peoria, Illinois. Died in a car crash on 4/10/92 (age 38). Shock comedian/actor. Acted in the movie *Back To School* and the TV show *Charlie Hoover*.

11/8/86	175	5			1 **Louder Than Hell**		[C]	$10	Warner 25503
11/26/88	43	17	● ©		2 **Have You Seen Me Lately?**		[C]	$10	Warner 25748
4/14/90	95	8	©		3 **Leader Of The Banned**		[C]	$10	Warner 26073

Alphabet (1)
Big Menu (1)
Blind (1)
Buddies (2)
Butt And The Bible (2)
Casual Users Of Terrorism (3)
Detox This (3)

Devil (1)
Gonna Raise Hell (3)
Grilled Cheese Sandwich (3)
Heart-Stoppers (2)
Highway To Hell (3)
Jerry's Bastard Kid (3)
Jesus (1)

Jesus The Miracle Caterer (2)
Lenny Bruce's Mom (3)
Lesbians Are Our Friends (2)
Letter From Home (1)
Libya (1)
Love Song (1)
Manson (1)

Mississippi Queen (3)
Mother Mary's Mystery Date (2)
Old People Must Die (3)
Parties With The Dead (3)
Phone Call From Hell (3)
Pocket Toys (2)
Relationships (1)

Robo-Pope (2)
Rock Against Drugs? (2)
Rubber Love (2)
Sex, Videotape And Zoo
  Animals (3)
Sexual Diaries (2)
Sexual Therapy (1)

Shopping For Pets (3)
Story Of Jim (Bakker) (2)
Under My Thumb (2)
Wild Thing (2)
World Hunger (1)

KINKS, The ★68★ '65

Rock group formed in London: Ray Davies (vocals, guitar) and his brother **Dave Davies** (guitar, vocals). Original lineup also included Peter Quaife (bass) and Mike Avory (drums). Numerous personnel changes during the '70s. Ray appeared in the 1986 movie *Absolute Beginners*. Longtime members included the Davies brothers, Ian Gibbons (keyboards, 1979-88), Jim Rodford (bass; from 1978) and Bob Henrit (drums; from 1984; **Charlie**). Henrit and Rodford were members of **Argent**. Group inducted into the Rock and Roll Hall of Fame in 1990.

1)The Kinks Greatest Hits! 2)Low Budget 3)State of Confusion 4)Kinks-Size 5)One For The Road

12/12/64+	29	26	©		1 **You Really Got Me**			$50	Reprise 6143
4/3/65	13	29	©		2 **Kinks-Size**			$50	Reprise 6158
8/28/65	60	9	©		3 **Kinda Kinks**			$50	Reprise 6173
12/25/65+	47	17	©		4 **Kinks Kinkdom**			$50	Reprise 6184
4/30/66	95	12	©		5 **The Kink Kontroversy**			$50	Reprise 6197
8/27/66	9	64	●		6 **The Kinks Greatest Hits!**		[G]	$50	Reprise 6217
2/11/67	135	3	©		7 **Face To Face**			$50	Reprise 6228
9/9/67	162	4	©		8 **The Live Kinks**		[L]	$50	Reprise 6260
					recorded in Scotland				
3/2/68	153	2	©		9 **Something Else By The Kinks**			$50	Reprise 6279
11/22/69	105	20	©		10 **Arthur (or the decline and fall of The British Empire)**			$40	Reprise 6366
					rock opera written for a British TV show				
12/26/70+	35	12	©		11 **Lola Versus Powerman and The Moneygoround, Part One**			$40	Reprise 6423
12/18/71+	100	14	©		12 **Muswell Hillbillies**			$30	RCA Victor 4644
4/15/72	94	13	©		13 **The Kink Kronikles**		[K]	$40	Reprise 6454 [2]
9/23/72	70	14	©		14 **Everybody's In Show-Biz**		[L]	$40	RCA Victor 6065 [2]
					record 1: studio recordings; record 2: live recordings				
2/24/73	145	5			15 **The Great Lost Kinks Album**		[K]	$40	Reprise 2127
					recordings which were never released in the U.S.				
12/15/73+	177	6	©		16 **Preservation Act 1**			$20	RCA Victor 5002
6/15/74	114	11	©		17 **Preservation Act 2**			$25	RCA Victor 5040 [2]
5/17/75	51	13	©		18 **Soap Opera**			$20	RCA Victor 5081
12/6/75+	45	14	©		19 **Schoolboys In Disgrace**			$20	RCA Victor 5102
6/26/76	144	5			20 **The Kink's Greatest-Celluloid Heroes**		[K]	$20	RCA Victor 1743
2/26/77	21	16	©		21 **Sleepwalker**	C:#47/4		$12	Arista 4106
6/3/78	40	21	©		22 **Misfits**	C:#28/4		$12	Arista 4167
7/28/79	11	18	● ©		23 **Low Budget**			$12	Arista 4240
6/28/80	14	33	●		24 **One For The Road**		[L]	$15	Arista 8401 [2]
9/20/80	177	4			25 **Second Time Around**		[K]	$12	RCA Victor 3520
9/12/81	15	36	● ©		26 **Give The People What They Want**			$12	Arista 9567
6/11/83	12	25	©		27 **State Of Confusion**			$12	Arista 8018
12/15/84+	57	20	©		28 **Word Of Mouth**			$12	Arista 8264
7/19/86	159	4			29 **Come Dancing With The Kinks - The Best Of The Kinks 1977-1986**		[G]	$15	Arista 8428 [2]
12/20/86+	81	16	©		30 **Think Visual**			$10	MCA 5822
2/6/88	110	7	©		31 **The Road**		[L]	$10	MCA 42107
11/25/89	122	8	©		32 **UK Jive**			$10	MCA 6337

KINKS, The — Cont'd

| 5/1/93 | 166 | 1 | | © 33 | **Phobia** .... | | | $10 | Columbia 48724 |

Acute Schizophrenia Paranoia Blues (12,14,25)
Add It Up (26)
Afternoon Tea (9)
Aggravation (32)
Alcohol (12,14,20)
All Day And All Of The Night (2,6,24) **7**
Apeman (11,13,31) **45**
Around The Dial (26,31)
Art Lover (26,31)
Arthur (17)
Artificial Man (17)
Attitude (23,24)
Australia (10)
Autumn Almanac (13)
Babies (33)
Baby Face (14)
Back To Front (26)
Bald Headed Woman (1)
Banana Boat Song (14)
Batman Theme (medley) (8)
Beautiful Delilah (1)
Berkeley Mews (13)
Bernadette (27)
Better Things (26,29) **92**
Big Black Smoke (13)
Black Messiah (22)
Brainwashed (10,14)
Brother (21)
Cadillac (1)
Catch Me Now I'm Falling (23,24,29)
Celluloid Heroes (14,20,24,25,29)
Cliches Of The World (B Movie) (27,31)
Close To The Wire (33)
Come Dancing (27,29,31) **6**
Come On Now (2,8)
Complicated Life (12)
Contenders, The (11)
Cricket (16)
Dancing In The Street (3)
Dandy (7,8)
David Watts (9,13,24)
Daylight (16)
Days (13)
Deadend Street (13) **73**
Dear Margaret (32)
Death Of A Clown (9,13)
Dedicated Follower Of Fashion (6) **36**
Definite Maybe (27)
Demolition (16)
Denmark Street (11)
Destroyer (26,29,31) **85**
Did You See His Name? (13)
Do It Again (28,29) **41**
Don't (33)
Don't Ever Change (3)
Don't Forget To Dance (27,29) **29**

Don't You Fret (4)
Down All The Days (To 1992) (32)
Drift Away (33)
Drivin' (13)
Ducks On The Wall (18)
Education (19)
End Of The Season (9)
Entertainment (32)
Ev'rybody's Gonna Be Happy (3,6)
Everybody's A Star (Starmaker) (18,20)
Face In The Crowd (18,20,25)
Fancy (7,13)
Father Christmas (29)
Finale (19)
First Time We Fall In Love (19)
Flash's Confession (17)
Flash's Dream (The Final Elbow) (17)
Full Moon (21)
Funny Face (9)
Gallon Of Gas (23)
Get Back In Line (11,13)
Get Up (22)
Give The People What They Want (26,31)
God's Children (13)
Going Solo (28)
Good Day (28)
Got Love If You Want It (1)
Got My Feet On The Ground (3)
Got To Be Free (11)
Gotta Get The First Plane Home (7)
Groovy Movies (15)
Guilty (28)
Hard Way (19,24,25)
Harry Rag (7)
Hatred (A Duet) (33)
Have A Cuppa Tea (12)
Have Another Drink (18)
Hay Fever (22)
He's Evil (17)
Headmaster (19)
Heart Of Gold (27,29)
Here Come The People In Grey (12)
Here Comes Flash (16)
Here Comes Yet Another Day (14,20)
Holiday (12,14,20)
Holiday In Waikiki (7,13)
Holiday Romance (18)
Hollaway Jail (12)
Hot Potatoes (14,25)
House In The Country (7)
How Are You (30)
How Do I Get Close (32)
I Am Free (5)
I Am Your Man (medley) (16)
I Gotta Go Now (2)

I Gotta Move (2)
I Need You (4)
I'll Remember (7)
I'm A Lover Not A Fighter (2)
I'm In Disgrace (19)
I'm Not Like Everybody Else (15)
I'm On An Island (5,8)
I've Been Driving On Bald Mountain (7)
I've Got That Feeling (2)
In A Foreign Land (22)
In A Space (23)
Informer, The (23)
Introduction To Solution (1)
It (31)
It's All Right (4)
It's Alright (Don't Think About It) (33)
It's Too Late (5)
Jack The Idiot Dunce (19)
Juke Box Music (21,29)
Just Can't Go To Sleep (1)
King Kong (13)
Labour Of Love (27)
Last Assembly (19)
Lavender Hill (15)
Lazy Old Sun (9)
Life Goes On (21)
Life On The Road (21)
Little Bit Of Abuse (26)
Little Bit Of Emotion (23)
Little Miss Queen Of Darkness (7)
Live Life (22)
Living On A Thin Line (28,29,31)
Lola (11,13,14,25) **9**
Lola [live] (24,29) **81**
Long Distance (29)
Long Tall Shorty (1)
Long Way From Home (11)
Look A Little On The Sunny Side (14)
Look For Me Baby (3)
Loony Balloon (32)
Lost And Found (30,31)
Louie Louie (2,4)
Love Me Till The Sun Shines (9)
Low Budget (23,24,29)
Massive Reductions (28)
Maximum Consumption (14)
Milk Cow Blues (5,8)
Mindless Child Of Motherhood (13)
Mirror Of Love (17)
Misery (23)
Misfits (22,24,29)
Missing Persons (28)
Misty Water (15)

Money & Corruption (medley) (16)
Money Talks (17)
Moneygoround, The (11)
Morning Song (16)
Most Exclusive Residence For Sale (7)
Motorway (14,25)
Moving Pictures (23)
Mr. Big Man (21)
Mr. Churchill Says (10)
Mr. Pleasant (13) **80**
Mr. Songbird (15)
Mr. Wonderful (14)
Muswell Hillbilly (12,14,20)
Naggin' Woman (4)
National Health (23,24)
Natural Gift (30)
Never Met A Girl Like You Before (4)
Nine To Five (18)
No More Looking Back (19,25)
No Return (9)
Nobody Gives (17)
Nothin' In The World Can Stop Me Worryin' 'Bout That Girl (3)
Nothing Lasts Forever (17)
Nothing To Say (10)
Now And Then (32)
Oh Where Oh Where Is Love? (17)
Oklahoma U.S.A. (12)
One Of The Survivors (16,20)
Only A Dream (33)
Opening (24)
Ordinary People (18)
Out Of The Wardrobe (22)
Over The Edge (17)
Party Line (7)
Permanent Waves (22)
Phobia (33)
Pictures In The Sand (15)
Plastic Man (15)
Polly (13)
Powerman (11)
Predictable (24)
Pressure (23,24)
Prince Of The Punks (24)
Property (27)
Rainy Day In June (7)
Rats (11)
Repetition (30)
Revenge (2)
Ring The Bells (5)
Road, The (31)
Rock 'N' Roll Cities (30)
Rock 'N' Roll Fantasy (22,29) **30**
Rosemary Rose (15)
Rosy Won't You Please Come Home (7)
Rush Hour Blues (18)
Salvation Road (17)

Scattered (33)
Schooldays (19,25)
Scrapheap City (17)
Scum Of The Earth (17)
Second-Hand Car Spiv (17)
See My Friends (4)
Session Man (7)
Set Me Free (3,6) **23**
Shangri-La (10,13)
She Bought A Hat Like Princess Marina (10)
She's Got Everything (13)
Shepherds Of The Nation (17)
Sitting In My Hotel (14,20)
Sitting In The Midday Sun (16,20)
Situation Vacant (9)
Skin And Bone (12,14,20)
Sleepless Night (21)
Sleepwalker (21,29) **48**
So Long (33)
So Mystifying (1)
Sold Me Out (28)
Some Mother's Son (10)
Somebody Stole My Car (33)
Something Better Beginning (3,6)
State Of Confusion (27)
Still Searching (33)
Stop Your Sobbing (1,24)
Stormy Sky (21)
Strangers (11)
Such A Shame (4)
Summer's Gone (28)
Sunny Afternoon (7,8,13) **14**
Superman ..see: (Wish I Could Fly Like)
Supersonic Rocket Ship (14)
Surviving (13)
Susannah's Still Alive (13)
Sweet Lady Genevieve (16)
There Is No Life Without Love (15)
There's A Change In The Weather (14)
Things Are Getting Better (2)
Think Visual (30,31)
This Is Where I Belong (13)
This Man He Weeps Tonight (15)
This Time Tomorrow (11)
Til Death Do Us Part (15)
Till The End Of The Day (5,6,8,24) **50**
Tin Soldier Man (9)
Tired Of Waiting For You (2,6,8) **6**
Too Hot (28)
Too Much Monkey Business (1)
Too Much On My Mind (7)
Top Of The Pops (11,14)
Trust Your Heart (22)
20th Century Man (12,20,24)

Two Sisters (9)
UK Jive (32)
Uncle Son (12)
Underneath The Neon Sign (18)
Unreal Reality (14)
Victoria (10,13,24) **62**
Video Shop (30)
Village Green Preservation Society (13)
Wait Till The Summer Comes Along (4)
Wall Of Fire (33)
War Is Over (32)
Waterloo Sunset (9,13)
Way Love Used To Be (15)
Welcome To Sleazy Town (30)
Well Respected Man (4,6,8) **13**
What Are We Doing (32)
What's In Store For Me (5)
When A Solution Comes (5)
When I See That Girl Of Mine (5)
When I Turn Off The Living Room Light (5)
When Work Is Over (18)
When You Were A Child (30)
Where Are They Now? (16)
Where Did The Spring Go (15)
Where Have All The Good Times Gone (5,24)
Who'll Be The Next In Line (4,6) **34**
Willesden Green (13)
(Wish I Could Fly Like) Superman (23,24,29) **41**
Wonder Where My Baby Is Tonight (3)
Wonderboy (13)
Word Of Mouth (28)
Working At The Factory (30)
World Keeps Going 'Round (5)
Yes Sir No Sir (10)
Yo-Yo (26)
You Can't Stop The Music (19)
You Can't Win (5)
You Don't Know My Name (14)
You Make It All Worthwhile (18)
You Really Got Me (1,6,8,24,29) **7**
You Shouldn't Be Sad (3)
You're Lookin' Fine (7,8)
Young And Innocent Days (10)
Young Conservatives (27)

KINLEYS, The   '97

Country vocal duo of identical twin sisters Heather and Jennifer Kinley (born on 11/5/70 in Philadelphia).

| 10/18/97 | 153 | 14 | ● | © 1 | **Just Between You And Me** .... | | | $10 | Epic 67965 |
| 8/5/00 | 177 | 1 | | © 2 | **II** .... | | | $10 | Epic 69593 |

Contradiction (1)
Dance In The Boat (1)
Here (2)
I Need You Now (2)
I'm In (2)

I'm Me With You (2)
If Ever I Needed You (2)
Just Between You And Me (1)
Love Rules (1)
Lovers (2)

Me Too (1)
(Ooh, Aah) Crazy Kind Of Love Thing (1)
Please (1) **67**
Real Thing (1)

She Ain't The Girl For You (2)
Somebody's Out There Watching (2) **64**
Takin' Our Own Sweet Time (1)
Talk To Me (1)

That's Gonna Mess You Up (2)
When The Blues And My Baby Collide (2)
Yeah, Yeah, Yeah (2)
You Make It Seem So Easy (1)

You're Still Here (2)

KISS ★47★   '98

Hard-rock group formed in New York City: **Paul Stanley** (vocals, guitar), **Gene Simmons** (vocals, bass), **Ace Frehley** (guitar) and **Peter Criss** (drums). Noted for elaborate makeup and highly theatrical stage shows; Simmons was made up as "The Bat Lizard," Stanley as "Star Child," Frehley as "Space Man" and Criss as "The Cat." Criss replaced by Eric Carr in 1981. Frehley replaced by **Vinnie Vincent** in 1982. Group appeared without makeup for the first time in 1983 on album cover *Lick It Up*. Mark St. John replaced Vincent in 1984. Bruce Kulick, brother of Bob Kulick of **Balance**, replaced St. John in 1985. Carr died of cancer on 11/25/91 (age 41). Drummer Eric Singer joined in 1991. The original group reunited in 1996.

1)Psycho-Circus 2)Love Gun 3)Revenge 4)Alive II 5)Alive!

4/20/74	87	23	●	© 1	**Kiss**			$40	Casablanca 9001
11/16/74	100	15	●	© 2	**Hotter Than Hell**			$30	Casablanca 7006
4/19/75	32	29	●	© 3	**Dressed To Kill**			$30	Casablanca 7016
10/11/75	9	110	●	© 4	**Alive!**	[L]		$40	Casablanca 7020 [2]
4/3/76	11	78	▲	© 5	**Destroyer**			$25	Casablanca 7025
8/21/76	36	17		6	**The Originals**	[R]		$100	Casablanca 7032 [3]

reissue of albums #1-3 above

DEBUT	PEAK	WKS	RIAA	CD	ARTIST — Album Title	Catalog	Sym	$	Label & Number

KISS — Cont'd

DEBUT	PEAK	WKS	RIAA	CD	ARTIST — Album Title	Sym	$	Label & Number
11/20/76	11	45	▲	©	7 Rock And Roll Over		$25	Casablanca 7037
7/9/77	4	26	▲	©	8 Love Gun		$25	Casablanca 7057
11/26/77+	7	33	▲²	©	9 Alive II	[L]	$30	Casablanca 7076 [2]
5/20/78	22	24	▲	©	10 Double Platinum	[G]	$30	Casablanca 7100 [2]
6/23/79	9	25	▲	©	11 Dynasty		$15	Casablanca 7152
6/21/80	35	14	●	©	12 Kiss Unmasked		$15	Casablanca 7225
12/5/81+	75	11		©	13 Music From The Elder		$15	Casablanca 7261
11/20/82+	45	19	●	©	14 Creatures Of The Night		$15	Casablanca 7270
10/15/83	24	30	▲	©	15 Lick It Up		$12	Mercury 814297
10/6/84	19	38	●	©	16 Animalize		$12	Mercury 822495
10/5/85	20	29	●	©	17 Asylum		$12	Mercury 826099
10/10/87	18	34	▲	©	18 Crazy Nights		$12	Mercury 832626
12/3/88+	21	27	▲²	©	19 Smashes, Thrashes & Hits	[G]	$10	Mercury 836427
11/4/89	29	36	●	©	20 Hot In The Shade		$10	Mercury 838913
6/6/92	6	23		©	21 Revenge		$10	Mercury 848037
6/5/93	9	12		©	22 Alive III	[L]	$10	Mercury 514777
3/30/96	15	10		©	23 MTV Unplugged	[L]	$10	Mercury 528950
7/13/96	17	11	●	©	24 You Wanted The Best, You Got The Best!!	[K-L]	$10	Mercury 532741
4/26/97	77	4		©	25 Greatest Kiss	[G]	$10	Mercury 534725
11/15/97	27	4		©	26 Carnival Of Souls - The Final Sessions		$10	Mercury 536323
10/10/98	3	14	●	©	27 Psycho-Circus		$10	Mercury 558992

All American Man (9)
All Hell's Breakin' Loose (15)
All The Way (2,6)
Almost Human (8)
And On The 8th Day (15)
Any Way You Slice It (17)
Any Way You Want It (9)
Anything For My Baby (3,6)
Baby Driver (7)
Bang Bang You (8)
Beth (5,9,10,19,23,24,25) 7
Betrayed (20)
Black Diamond (1,4,6,10)
Boomerang (20)
Burn Bitch Burn (16)
Cadillac Dreams (20)
Calling Dr. Love (7,9,10,19,24,25) 16
Carr Jam 1981 (21)
Charisma (11)
Childhood's End (26)
Christine Sixteen (8,9,25) 25
Cold Gin (1,4,6,10,25)
C'mon And Love Me (3,4,6,10)
Comin' Home (2,6,23)
Crazy Crazy Nights (18) 65
Creatures Of The Night (14,22)
Dance All Over Your Face (15)
Danger (14)
Dark Light (13)
Detroit Rock City (5,9,10,19,22,25) flip
Deuce (1,4,6,10,19,22,25)
Dirty Livin' (11)
Do You Love Me (5,10,23,25)
Domino (21,22,23)
Dreamin' (27)

Easy As It Seems (12)
Escape From The Island (13)
Every Time I Look At You (21,23)
Exciter (15)
Fanfare (13)
Firehouse (1,4,6,10,24)
Fits Like A Glove (15)
Flaming Youth (5,25) 74
Forever (20,22) 8
Get All You Can Take (16)
Getaway (3,6)
Gimme More (15)
God Gave Rock 'N' Roll To You II (21,22)
God Of Thunder (5,9,10)
Goin' Blind (2,6,23)
Good Girl Gone Bad (18)
Got Love For Sale (8)
Got To Choose (2,4,6)
Great Expectations (5)
Hard Luck Woman (7,9,10,25) 15
Hard Times (11)
Hate (26)
Heart Of Chrome (21)
Heaven's On Fire (16,19,22) 49
Hell Or High Water (18)
Hide Your Heart (20) 66
Hooligan (8)
Hotter Than Hell (2,4,6,10)
I (13)
I Confess (26)
I Finally Found My Way (27)
I Just Wanna (21,22)
I Love It Loud (14,19,22)

I Pledge Allegiance To The State Of Rock & Roll (27)
I Still Love You (14,22,23)
I Stole Your Love (8,9,24)
I Walk Alone (26)
I Want You (7,9,10)
I Was Made For Lovin' You (11,19,22,25) 11
I Will Be There (26)
I'll Fight Hell To Hold You (11)
I'm Alive (17)
I've Had Enough (Into The Fire) (16)
In My Head (26)
In The Mirror (26)
Into The Void (27)
Is That You? (12)
It Never Goes Away (26)
Journey Of 1,000 Years (27)
Jungle (26)
Just A Boy (13)
Keep Me Comin' (14)
Killer (14)
King Of Hearts (20)
King Of The Mountain (17)
King Of The Night Time World (5,9)
Kiss, Love Theme From (1,6)
Kissin' Time (6) 83
Ladies In Waiting (3,6)
Ladies Room (7,9)
Larger Than Life (9)
Let Me Go, Rock 'N Roll (2,4,6,10)
Let Me Know (1,6,24)
Let's Put The X In Sex (19) 97
Lick It Up (15,19,22) 66

Little Caesar (20)
Lonely Is The Hunter (16)
Love 'Em And Leave 'Em (7)
Love Gun (8,9,10,19) 61
Love Her All I Can (3,6)
Love's A Deadly Weapon (17)
Love's A Slap In The Face (20)
Magic Touch (11)
Mainline (2,6)
Makin' Love (7,9,10)
Master & Slave (26)
Million To One (15)
Mr. Blackwell (13)
Mr. Speed (7)
Murder In High-Heels (16)
My Way (18)
Naked City (12)
No, No, No (18)
Not For The Innocent (15)
Nothin' To Lose (1,4,6,23)
Oath, The (13)
Odyssey (13)
100,000 Years (1,4,6,10)
Only You (13)
Paralyzed (21)
Parasite (2,4,6,24)
Plaster Caster (8,23,25)
Prisoner Of Love (20)
Psycho Circus (27)
Radar For Love (17)
Rain (26)
Raise Your Glasses (27)
Read My Body (20)
Reason To Live (18) 64
Rise To It (20) 81
Rock And Roll All Nite (3,6,10,19,25) 68

Rock And Roll All Nite [live] (4,22,23,24) 12
Rock And Roll Hell (14)
Rock Bottom (3,4,6,23,24)
Rock Hard ...see: (You Make Me)
Rocket Ride (9) 39
Rockin' In The USA (9)
Room Service (3,6,24)
Saint And Sinner (14)
Save Your Love (11)
Secretly Cruel (17)
Seduction Of The Innocent (26)
See You In Your Dreams (7)
See You Tonight (23)
Shandi (12) 47
She (3,4,6,10)
She's So European (12)
Shock Me (8,9)
Shout It Out Loud (5,19,25) 31
Shout It Out Loud [live] (9,24) 54
Silver Spoon (20)
Somewhere Between (Heaven And Hell) (20)
Spit (21)
Star Spangled Banner (22)
Strange Ways (2,6)
Street Giveth And The Street Taketh Away (20)
Strutter (1,4,6,19,25)
Strutter '78 (10)
Sure Know Something (11,23,25) 47
Sweet Pain (5)
Take It Off (21)
Take Me (7,24)

Talk To Me (12)
Tears Are Falling (17,19) 51
Then She Kissed Me (8)
Thief In The Night (18)
Thou Shalt Not (21)
Thrills In The Night (16)
Tomorrow (12)
Tomorrow And Tonight (8,9)
Torpedo Girl (9)
Tough Love (21)
Trial By Fire (17)
Turn On The Night (18)
Two Sides Of The Coin (12,25)
2,000 Man (11,23)
Two Timer (3,6,24)
Uh! All Night (17)
Under The Gun (16)
Under The Rose (13)
Unholy (21,22)
War Machine (14)
Watchin' You (2,4,6,22)
We Are One (27)
What Makes The World Go 'Round (12)
When Your Walls Come Down (18)
While The City Sleeps (16)
Who Wants To Be Lonely (17)
Within (27)
World Without Heroes (13,23) 56
X-Ray Eyes (11)
You Love Me To Hate You (20)
(You Make Me) Rock Hard (19)
You Wanted The Best (27)
You're All That I Want (12)
Young And Wasted (15)

KITARO '86

Born Masanori Takahashi on 2/4/53 in Toyohashi City, Japan. New Age synthesizer player.

DEBUT	PEAK	WKS	CD	ARTIST — Album Title	Sym	$	Label & Number
11/30/85	191	2	©	1 Asia	[I-L]	$10	Geffen 24087
				recorded in Shanghai, China			
5/10/86	141	10	©	2 My Best	[I-K]	$10	Gramavision 7016
4/4/87	183	1	©	3 Tenku	[I]	$10	Geffen 24112
5/12/90	159	5	©	4 Kojiki	[I]	$10	Geffen 24255
9/9/95	199	1	©	5 An Enchanted Evening	[I-L]	$10	DOMO 71005
12/28/96	185	1	©	6 Peace On Earth	[X-I]	$10	DOMO 71014

A La Nanita Nana (6)
Angels We Have Heard On High (6)
Aqua (2)
Aura (3)
Caravansary (1)
Chant From The Heart (5)
Cloud (1)
Cosmic Love (1)
Dance Of Sarasvati (5)
Dawn In Malaysia (1)

Earth Born (1)
First Noel (medley) (6)
Four Changes (2)
God Rest Ye Merry Gentlemen (6)
Great Spirit (6)
Hajimari (4)
Heaven & Earth (5)
It Came Upon A Midnight Clear (6)
Japanese Drums (1)

Jesu Joy Of Man's Desiring (6)
Jingle Bells (6)
Joy To The World (medley) (6)
Koi (4)
Kokoro (5)
Legend Of The Road (3)
Little Drummer Boy (6)
Mandala (5)
Matsuri (4)
Message From The Cosmos (3)
Milky Way (3)

Nageki (4)
O Holy Night (6)
Oasis (2)
Orochi (4)
Planet (5)
Reimei (4)
Return To Russia (1)
Revelation (2)
Rising Sun (4)
Romance (3)
Rosa Mystica (6)

Sacred Journey II (2)
Shimmering Light (2)
Silent Night (6)
Silk Road (5)
Silk Road Fantasy (2)
Silver Moon (2)
Sozo (4)
Spirit Of Taiko (5)
Straightaway To Orion (1)
Tenku (3)
Theme Of Silk Road (1)

Time (2)
Time Traveller (3)
Westbound (2)
Wings (3)

KITTIE '00

Female rock group from London, Ontario, Canada: sisters Morgan (vocals, guitar) and Mercedes (drums) Lander, with Fallon Bowman (guitar) and Talena Atfield (bass).

DEBUT	PEAK	WKS	RIAA	CD	ARTIST — Album Title	$	Label & Number
1/29/00	79	37	●	©	Spit	$10	Artemis 1002

Brackish
Charlotte
Choke
Do You Think I'm A Whore
Get Off (You Can Eat A Dick)
Immortal
Jonny
Paperdoll
Raven
Spit
Suck
Trippin'

DEBUT	PEAK	WKS	RIAA	CD	ARTIST — Album Title	Catalog	Sym	$	Label & Number

KIX '89

Hard-rock group from Hagerstown, Maryland: Steve Whiteman (vocals), Ronnie Younkins and Brian Forsythe (guitars), Donnie Purnell (bass) and Jimmy Chalfant (drums).

5/28/83	177	8		©	1 Cool Kids			$10	Atlantic 80056
10/15/88+	46	60	▲	©	2 Blow My Fuse			$10	Atlantic 81877
7/27/91	64	11		©	3 Hot Wire			$10	EastWest 91714

Blow My Fuse (2)
Body Talk (1)
Boomerang (2)
Bump The La La (3)
Burning Love (1)

Cold Blood (2)
Cold Chills (3)
Cool Kids (1)
Dirty Boys (2)
Don't Close Your Eyes (2) 11

For Shame (1)
Get It While It's Hot (2)
Get Your Monkeys Out (1)
Girl Money (1)
Hee Bee Jee Bee Crush (3)

Hot Wire (3)
Loco-Emotion (1)
Love Pollution (1)
Luv-A-Holic (3)
Mighty Mouth (1)

Nice On Ice (1)
No Ring Around Rosie (2)
Pants On Fire (Liar, Liar) (2)
Piece Of The Pie (2)
Red Lite, Green Lite, TNT (2)

Restless Blood (1)
Rock & Roll Overdose (3)
Same Jane (3)
She Dropped Me The Bomb (2)
Tear Down The Walls (3)

KLAATU '77

Rock trio from Canada: Dee Long (vocals, guitar), Terry Draper (keyboards) and John Woloschuck (drums). Anonymous first release led to speculation that they were **The Beatles**. Name taken from alien character in the classic 1951 sci-fi movie *The Day The Earth Stood Still*.

| 4/2/77 | 32 | 11 | | © | 1 Klaatu | | | $15 | Capitol 11542 |
| 10/15/77 | 83 | 7 | | © | 2 Hope | | | $15 | Capitol 11633 |

Anus Of Uranus (1)
Around The Universe In Eighty Days (2)

California Jam (1)
Calling Occupants (1) flip
Doctor Marvello (1)

Hope (2)
Little Neutrino (1)
Loneliest Of Creatures (2)

Long Live Politzania (2)
Madman (2)
Prelude Song (2)

Sir Bodsworth Rugglesby III (2)
So Said The Lighthouse Keeper (2)

Sub-Rosa Subway (1) 62
True Life Hero (1)
We're Off You Know (2)

KLEEER '81

R&B group from New York City: Paul Crutchfield (vocals, percussion), Richard Lee (guitar), Norman Durham (bass) and Woody Cunningham (drums).

4/26/80	140	10			1 Winners			$12	Atlantic 19262
3/7/81	81	16			2 License To Dream			$12	Atlantic 19288
2/20/82	139	8			3 Taste The Music			$12	Atlantic 19334

Affirmative Mood (3)
Close To You (1)
De Kleeer Ting (2)
De Ting Continues (3)
Fella (3)

Get Tough (2)
Hunger For Your Love (1)
Hypnotized (2)
I Shall Get Over (3)
I Still Love You (1)

I've Had Enough (Can't Take Anymore) (3)
License To Dream (2)
Nothin' Said (1)
Open Your Mind (1)

Rollin' On (1)
Running Back To You (2)
Say You Love Me (2)
Sippin' & Kissin' (2)
Swann (3)

Taste The Music (3)
Wall To Wall (3)
Where Would I Be (Without Your Love) (2)
Winners (1)

Your Way (1)

KLEIN, Robert '73

Born on 2/8/42 in New York City. Comedian/actor/writer. Appeared in several movies and TV shows. Married to opera singer Brenda Boozer from 1973-90.

| 4/28/73 | 191 | 3 | | © | Child Of The 50's | | [C] | $15 | Brut 6001 |

All Night Groceries
Athletics
Childhood Myth
Civil Defense (No Talking)

Commercials
F.M. Disc Jockey
Fabulous 50's
Foreigner, The

James Abram Garfield
Middle Class Educated Blues
Musical Instruments
My Last Movie

My Little Margie
New York City Animals
Our Gang
Panhandler, The

Public School
Public Service Commercials
School Assembly
School Lunch

Sex Impulse
Starting Your Car
Substitute School Teacher
Words

KLEMMER, John '76

Born on 7/3/46 in Chicago. Jazz saxophonist/flutist.
1)LifeStyle (Living & Loving) 2)Barefoot Ballet 3)Arabesque

9/13/69	176	5		©	1 Blowin' Gold		[I]	$20	Cadet Concept 321
12/27/75+	90	40		©	2 Touch		[I]	$15	ABC 922
9/18/76	66	16		©	3 Barefoot Ballet		[I]	$12	ABC 950
6/18/77	51	17		©	4 LifeStyle (Living & Loving)		[I]	$12	ABC 1007
6/17/78	83	10		©	5 Arabesque		[I]	$12	ABC 1068
11/18/78	178	3		©	6 Cry		[I]	$12	ABC 1106
6/2/79	172	9		©	7 Brazilia		[I]	$12	ABC 1116
11/24/79	187	2		©	8 The Best Of John Klemmer, Volume One/Mosaic		[I-K]	$15	MCA 8014 [2]
8/9/80	146	11			9 Magnificent Madness		[I]	$12	Elektra 284
6/13/81	99	9			10 Hush		[I]	$12	Elektra 527

Adventures In Paradise (9)
Arabesque (5)
At 17 (3,8)
Bahia (7)
Barefoot Ballet (3,8)
Body Pulse (2,8)
Brazilia (7)
Caress (4,8)
Children Of The Earth: Flames! (1)
Copacabana (7)
Cry (6)
Crystal Fingers (3)
Deja Vu (9)

Desire (5)
Don't Take Your Love Away (9)
Ecstasy (5)
Excursion #2 (1)
Falling (5)
Feelin' Free (10)
Forest Child (3,8)
Forever (4)
Free Fall Lover (2,8)
Free Soul (1)
Glass Dolphins (2)
Happiness (6)
Heart (Summer Song) (9)
Heartbreak (7,8)

Hey Jude (1)
Hot (10)
Hummingbird Bay (10)
Hush (10)
I Am (6)
I Can't Help It (9)
Infinity (6)
Intimacy (6)
Let's Make Love (10)
Life Is So Beautiful (10)
Lifesong (3)
Lifestyle (4)
Love (6)
Love Affair (5,8)

Love You Madly (10)
Lovin' Feelings (4)
Magic (10)
Magnificent Madness (9)
Mardi Gras (5)
My Heart Sings (1)
My Love Has Butterfly Wings (1,7)
Naked (3)
Nothing Will Ever Be The Same Again Forever (5,8)
Paradise (5)
Picasso (5)
Poem Painter (3,8)

Pure Love (4)
Purity (4,8)
Quiet Afternoon (4,8)
Rain Dancer (3)
'Round Midnight (6)
Sleeping Eyes (2)
Summertime (7)
Taboo (8)
Talking Hands (3,8)
Tender Storm (7,8)
Third Stone From The Sun (1)
Tone Row Weaver (2)
Touch (3,8)

Tropical Snowflakes (7)
Walk In Love (5)
Walk With Me My Love And Dream (2,8)
Waterfalls (7)
Waterwheels (2)
We Couldn't Start Over (9)
Whisper To The Wind (3,8)

KLF, The '91

Dance duo formed in England: Bill Drummond and Jim Cauty (formerly with **Zodiac Mindwarp**). KLF: Kopyright Liberation Front.

| 6/29/91 | 39 | 50 | ● | © | The White Room | | | $10 | Arista 8657 |

Build A Fire
Church Of The KLF

Justified And Ancient
Last Train To Trancentral

Make It Rain
No More Tears

3 A.M. Eternal 5
What Time Is Love? 57

White Room

KLIQUE '83

R&B vocal trio: Howard Huntsberry, Isaac Suthers and his sister Deborah Hunter.

| 10/8/83 | 70 | 14 | | | Try It Out | | | $12 | MCA 39008 |

Burning Hot
Flashback

Honey (I Want To Be Your Lover)

Inside Me
Sarah

Stop Doggin' Me Around 50
Tender Footed

Try It Out

KLOWNS, The '70

Four-man, two-woman group produced by Jeff Barry. Actor Barry Bostwick was a member. Group hosted own ABC-TV special on 11/15/70.

| 12/12/70 | 184 | 2 | | | The Klowns | | | $15 | RCA Victor 4438 |

Be A Kid
Dream On

Fish Tales
Good News

Honey Bunny Day
If You Can't Be A Clown

Lady Love 95
Love Is The Answer

Movin'
River Cruisin'

Whole Lotta Love
Yellow Sunglasses

465

★216★ KLUGH, Earl '79

Born on 9/16/53 in Detroit. Jazz acoustic guitarist/pianist. Taught guitar from age 15. Worked Baker's Keyboard Lounge. Toured with **Return To Forever** and **George Benson**. First solo recording for Blue Note in 1976.

1)One On One 2)Low Ride 3)Dream Come True 4)Two Of A Kind 5)Heart String

7/10/76	124	6		© 1	**Earl Klugh**		[I]	$12	Blue Note 596
12/11/76	188	2		© 2	**Living Inside Your Love**		[I]	$12	Blue Note 667
7/9/77	84	8		© 3	**Finger Paintings**		[I]	$12	Blue Note 737
7/1/78	139	9		© 4	**Magic In Your Eyes**		[I]	$12	United Artists 877
5/19/79	49	21		© 5	**Heart String**		[I]	$12	United Artists 942
11/3/79	23	33	●	© 6	**One On One**		[I]	$12	Tappan Zee 36241

BOB JAMES AND EARL KLUGH

4/19/80	42	19		© 7	**Dream Come True**		[I]	$12	United Artists 1026
9/27/80	134	4		8	**How To Beat The High Cost Of Living**		[I-S]	$12	Columbia 36741

HUBERT LAWS & EARL KLUGH

12/6/80+	98	23		© 9	**Late Night Guitar**		[I]	$12	Liberty 1079
11/14/81	53	27		© 10	**Crazy For You**		[I]	$12	Liberty 51113
11/6/82	44	29		© 11	**Two Of A Kind**		[I]	$12	Capitol 12244

EARL KLUGH & BOB JAMES

5/7/83	38	24		© 12	**Low Ride**		[I]	$12	Capitol 12253
3/31/84	69	23		© 13	**Wishful Thinking**		[I]	$12	Capitol 12323
10/27/84	107	17		© 14	**Nightsongs**		[I]	$12	Capitol 12372
5/11/85	110	17		© 15	**Soda Fountain Shuffle**		[I]	$10	Warner 25262
8/30/86	143	11		© 16	**Life Stories**		[I]	$10	Warner 25478
7/11/87	59	31	●	© 17	**Collaboration**		[I]	$10	Warner 25580

GEORGE BENSON/EARL KLUGH

5/20/89	150	5		© 18	**Whispers And Promises**		[I]	$10	Warner 25902
4/6/91	189	3		© 19	**Midnight In San Juan**		[I]	$10	Warner 26293
8/29/92	170	3		© 20	**Cool**		[I]	$10	Warner 26939

BOB JAMES/EARL KLUGH

Acoustic Lady Part I & II (5)
Afterglow, The (6)
Ain't Misbehavin' (14)
Alicia (4)
All The Time (13)
Amazon (7)
Angelina (7)
Another Time, Another Place (2)
April Fools (2)
April Love (15)
As It Happens (20)
Baby Cakes (15)
Back In Central Park (12)
Balladina (10)
Brazilian Stomp (17)
Broadway Ramble (10)
Cabo Frio (3)
Calypso Getaway (10)
Caper, The (8)
Captain Caribe (2)
Cast Your Fate To The Wind (4)
Catherine (3)
Certain Smile (14)
Christina (12)
Close To Your Heart (15)
Collaboration (17)
Could It Be I'm Falling In Love (1)
Crazy For You (10)
Cry A Little While (4)
Dance With Me (3)
Debra Anne (16)

Doc (7)
Dr. Macumba (3)
Down River (8)
Dream Come True (7)
Dream Something (8)
Dreamin' (17)
Edge, The (8)
Every Moment With You (19)
Falcon, The (11)
Fall In Love (18)
Felicia (2)
For The Love Of You (16)
Frisky Biscuits (18)
Fugitive Life (20)
Good Time Charlie's Got The Blues (4)
Handara (20)
Heart String (5)
I Don't Want To Leave You Alone Anymore (7)
I Heard It Through The Grapevine (2)
I Never Thought I'd Leave You (12)
I'll Never Say Goodbye (The Promise) (9)
I'll Never See You Smile Again (6)
I'll See You Again (5)
I'm Ready For Your Love (10)
If It's In Your Heart (It's In Your Smile) (7)
(If You Want To) Be My Love (12)

If You're Still In Love With Me (12)
Incognito (15)
Ingenue (11)
It's So Easy Loving You (8)
Jamaica (17)
Jamaican Farewell (9)
Jamaican Winds (19)
Jolanta (3)
Julie (4)
Just For Your Love (16)
Just Like Yesterday (12)
Just Pretend (15)
Just You And Me (18)
Kari (6)
Keep Your Eye On The Sparrow (Baretta's Theme) (9)
Kiko (2)
Kissin' On The Beach (19)
Las Manos De Fuego (Hands Of Fire) (11)
Laughter In The Rain (1)
Laura (9)
Like A Lover (9)
Lisbon Antiqua (9)
Living Inside Your Love (2)
Lode Star (4)
Long Ago And Far Away (3)
Look Of Love (14)
Love Lips (6)
Low Ride (12)
Magic In Your Eyes (4)
Mallorca (6)

Master Of Suspense (18)
Mayaguez (4)
Message To Michael (7)
Midnight In San Juan (19)
Mimosa (17)
Miniature (20)
Mirabella (9)
Mobimientos Del Alma (Rhythms Of The Soul) (19)
Mona Lisa (7)
Moon And The Stars (16)
Moonlight Dancing (15)
Mt. Airy Road (17)
Movin' On (20)
Natural Thing (13)
Nature Boy (14)
New York Samba (20)
Nice To Be Around (Nice To Have Around) (9)
Night Drive (12)
Night Moves (3)
Night Song (14)
Night That Love Came Back (20)
Once Again (13)
One Night (Alone With You) (15)
Only One For Me (13)
Outsiders, Theme From The ...see: Stay Gold
Pawnbroker, Theme From The (14)
Piccolo Boogie (8)
Picnic, Theme From (14)

Pretty World (5)
Rainbow Man (15)
Rainmaker (10)
Rainy Day, Theme For A (19)
Rayna (5)
Ready To Run (8)
Return Of The Rainmaker (16)
Right From The Start (13)
Rose Hips (4)
San Diego Stomp (20)
Sandman (16)
Sandstorm (11)
Santiago Sunset (16)
Scuffle, The (8)
Second Chances (16)
Secret Wishes (20)
See See Rider (14)
Shadow Of Your Smile (14)
She Never Said Why (19)
Since You're Gone (17)
Slippin' In The Back Door (1)
Smoke Gets In Your Eyes (9)
So Much In Common (20)
Soda Fountain Shuffle (15)
Soft Stuff (And Other Sweet Delights) (10)
Some Other Time (15)
Song For A Pretty Girl (8)
Spanish Night (5)
Spellbound (3)
Sponge, The (20)
Stay Gold (14)
Strawberry Avenue (18)

Summer Nights (18)
Summer Song (3)
Sweet Rum And Starlight (7)
Take It From The Top (13)
Take You There (19)
Tango Classico (18)
Tenderly (9)
Terpsichore (20)
This Time (3)
Time For Love (9)
Traveler (Part I & II) (16)
Triste (9)
Tropical Legs (13)
Twinkle (10)
Two For The Road (9)
Vonetta (1)
Waiting For Cathy (5)
Waltz For Debby (1)
Water Song (18)
Wes (11)
What Love Can Do (18)
Where I Wander (11)
Whiplash (11)
Whispers And Promises (18)
Wind And The Sea (1)
Winding River (6)
Wishful Thinking (13)

KLYMAXX '86

Female R&B group from Los Angeles: Lorena Porter (vocals), Cheryl Cooley (guitar), Lynn Malsby and Robbin Grider (keyboards), Joyce Irby (bass) and Bernadette Cooper (drums).

2/2/85+	18	67	●	© 1	**Meeting In The Ladies Room**			$10	Constellation 5529
12/6/86+	98	31		© 2	**Klymaxx**			$10	Constellation 5832
6/23/90	168	4		© 3	**The Maxx Is Back**			$10	MCA 6376

Ask Me No Questions (1)
Come Back (2)
Danger Zone (2)
Divas Need Love Too (2)
Don't Mess With My Man (3)

Don't Run Away (3)
Fab Attack (2)
Fashion (2)
Finishing Touch (3)
Girls Chasing Boys (3)

Good Love (3)
I Betcha (1)
I Miss You (1) *5*
I'd Still Say Yes (2) *18*
Just Our Luck (1)

Lock And Key (1)
Long Distance Love Affair (2)
Love Bandit (1)
Man Size Love (2) *15*
Maxx Is Back (3)

Meeting In The Ladies Room (1) *59*
Men All Pause (1) *80*
Private Party (3)
Sexy (2)

Shame (3)
She's A User (3)
Video Kid (1)
When You Kiss Me (3)

KMFDM '96

Industrial rock group from Germany and based in Chicago: Cheryl Wilson, Chris Connelly, Dorona Alberti, Nicole Blackman and Jennifer Ginsberg (vocals), Gunter Schulz, En Esch and Mark Durante (guitars), Sascha Konietzko (bass), F.M. Einheit and John Van Eaton (various instruments) and William Rieflin (drums). KMFDM is an acronym for: Kein Mehrheit Fur Die Mitleid, which is German for: No Pity For The Majority. Konietzko left to form **MDFMK**.

7/13/96	92	3		© 1	**Xtort**			$10	Wax Trax! 7242
10/11/97	137	2		© 2	**KMFDM**			$10	Wax Trax! 7245
5/8/99	189	1		© 3	**Adios**			$10	Wax Trax! 7258

Adios (3)
Anarchy (2)
Apathy (1)
Bereit (2)
Blame (1)

Craze (1)
D.I.Y (3)
Dogma (3)
Down And Out (2)
Full Worm Garden (3)

Ikons (1)
Inane (1)
Leid Und Elend (2)
Megalomaniac (2)
Mercy (3)

Power (1)
R.U.OK? (3)
Rubicon (3)
Rules (1)
Son Of A Gun (1)

Spit Sperm (2)
Stray Bullet (2)
Sycophant (3)
That's All (3)
Today (3)

Torture (2)
Unfit (2)
Waste (2)
Witness (3)
Wrath (1)

KNACK, The '79

Rock group formed in Los Angeles: Doug Fieger (vocals, guitar), Berton Averre (guitar), Prescott Niles (bass) and Bruce Gary (drums). Fieger was a member of the Detroit rock trio **Sky**.

6/30/79	❶⁵	40	▲²	©	1 Get The Knack			$12	Capitol 11948
3/1/80	15	14	●	©	2 But The Little Girls Understand			$12	Capitol 12045
11/7/81	93	6			3 Round Trip			$12	Capitol 12168

Africa (3)
Another Lousy Day In Paradise (3)
Art War (3)
Baby Talks Dirty (2) *38*
Boys Go Crazy (3)
Can't Put A Price On Love (2) *62*
End Of The Game (2)
Feeling I Get (2)
Frustrated (1)
Good Girls Don't (1) *11*
Hard Way (2)
(Havin' A) Rave Up (2)
Heartbeat (1)
Hold On Tight And Don't Let Go (2)
How Can Love Hurt So Much (2)
I Want Ya (2)
It's You (2)
Just Wait And See (3)
Let Me Out (1)
Lil' Cals Big Mistake (3)
Lucinda (2)
Maybe Tonight (1)
Mr. Handleman (2)
My Sharona (1) *1*
Oh Tara (1)
Pay The Devil (Ooo, Baby, Ooo) (3) *67*
Radiating Love (3)
She Likes The Beat (3)
(She's So) Selfish (1)
Siamese Twins (The Monkey And Me) (1)
Soul Kissin' (3)
Sweet Dreams (3)
Tell Me You're Mine (2)
That's What The Little Girls Do (1)
We Are Waiting (3)
Your Number Or Your Name (1)

KNAPP, Jennifer '00

Born in 1975 in Kansas. Christian singer/songwriter/guitarist.

3/18/00	77	7		©	Lay It Down			$10	Gotee 2816

All Consuming Fire
Diamond In The Rough
Into You
Lay It Down
Little More
Peace
Usher Me Down
When Nothing Satisfies
You Answer Me
You Remain

KNICKERBOCKERS, The '66

Rock group formed in Bergenfield, New Jersey: Buddy Randell (vocals, sax), brothers Beau (guitar) and Johnny (bass) Charles, and Jimmy Walker (drums).

2/12/66	134	5		©	Lies			$150	Challenge 622

Can't You See I'm Trying
Harlem Nocturne
I Believe In Her
I Can Do It Better
Just One Girl
Lies *20*
Please Don't Fight It
Wishful Thinking
You'll Never Walk Alone
Your Kind Of Lovin'

KNIGHT, Gladys, & The Pips ★79★ '73

R&B family group from Atlanta: Gladys Knight (born on 5/28/44), her brother Merald "Bubba" Knight, and cousins William Guest and Edward Patten. Named "Pips" for their manager, cousin James "Pip" Woods. First recorded for Brunswick in 1958. Due to legal problems, Gladys could not record with the Pips from 1977-80. Gladys was a cast member of the 1985 TV series *Charlie & Co.* Group inducted into the Rock and Roll Hall of Fame in 1996.

1)Imagination 2)Neither One Of Us 3)I Feel A Song 4)2nd Anniversary 5)Visions

10/14/67	60	24		©	1 Everybody Needs Love			$30	Soul 706
6/8/68	158	13		©	2 Feelin' Bluesy			$30	Soul 707
1/11/69	136	16		©	3 Silk N' Soul			$30	Soul 711
10/25/69	81	10		©	4 Nitty Gritty			$30	Soul 713
4/4/70	55	16			5 Gladys Knight & The Pips Greatest Hits		[G]	$20	Soul 723
5/15/71	35	26		©	6 If I Were Your Woman			$20	Soul 731
1/8/72	60	24		©	7 Standing Ovation			$20	Soul 736
3/10/73	9	30		©	8 Neither One Of Us			$20	Soul 737
7/14/73	70	21		©	9 All I Need Is Time			$20	Soul 739
10/27/73	9	61	●	©	10 Imagination			$15	Buddah 5141
2/16/74	77	23		©	11 Anthology		[G]	$20	Motown 792 [2]
3/16/74	139	11			12 Knight Time		[K]	$15	Soul 741
3/23/74	35	34	●	©	13 Claudine		[S]	$15	Buddah 5602
					includes "Claudine Theme" by **Curtis Mayfield**				
11/16/74	17	41	●	©	14 I Feel A Song			$15	Buddah 5612
4/26/75	164	4			15 A Little Knight Music		[K]	$15	Soul 744
10/18/75	24	16	●	©	16 2nd Anniversary			$15	Buddah 5639
2/7/76	36	15			17 The Best Of Gladys Knight & The Pips		[G]	$15	Buddah 5653
11/27/76	94	12			18 Pipe Dreams		[S]	$15	Buddah 5676
4/23/77	51	21			19 Still Together			$15	Buddah 5689
9/16/78	145	6			20 The One And Only			$15	Buddah 5701
5/31/80	48	18			21 About Love			$12	Columbia 36387
9/5/81	109	8		©	22 Touch			$12	Columbia 37086
5/21/83	34	33	●	©	23 Visions			$12	Columbia 38205
3/23/85	126	12			24 Life			$12	Columbia 39423
12/12/87+	39	27	●	©	25 All Our Love			$10	MCA 42004
					GLADYS KNIGHT:				
7/20/91	45	15		©	26 Good Woman			$10	MCA 10329
10/1/94	53	24	●	©	27 Just For You			$10	MCA 10946
3/17/01	98	5		©	28 At Last			$10	MCA 112397

Add It Up (21)
Ain't No Greater Love (23)
Ain't No Sun Since You've Been Gone (1,4)
Ain't You Glad You Chose Love (2)
Alaskan Pipeline (18)
All I Could Do Was Cry (4)
All I Need Is Time (9) *61*
All The Time (20)
All We Need Is A Miracle (15)
And This Is Love (8)
At Every End There's A Beginning (16)
Baby, Baby Don't Waste My Time (22)
Baby Don't Change Your Mind (19) *52*
Baby I Need Your Loving (3)
Be Yourself (20)
Best Thing That Ever Happened To Me (10,17) *3*
Better Love Next Time (28)
Better You Go Your Way (14)
Between Her Goodbye And My Hello (12) *57*
Billy, Come On Back As Quick As You Can (12)
Bourgie', Bourgie' (21)
Boy From Crosstown (2)
Bridge Over Troubled Water (medley) (7)
Butterfly (19) *52*
Can You Give Me Love With A Guarantee (7,15)
Can't Give It Up No More (8)
Changed (22)
Choice Of Colors (27)
Cloud Nine (4)
Come Back And Finish What You Started (20)
Come Together (15)
Complete Recovery (25)
Daddy Could Swear, I Declare (8,11) *19*
Didn't You Know (You'd Have To Cry Sometime) (4,5,11) *63*
Do You Love Me Just A Little, Honey (1)
Do You Really Want To Know (What Makes Me Fall In Love) (28)
Do You Wanna Have Some Fun (24)
Don't Burn Down The Bridge (14) *flip*
Don't It Make You Feel Guilty (8)
Don't Let Her Take Your Love From Me (2)
Don't Make Me Run Away (23)
Don't Say No To Me Tonight (20)
Don't Tell Me I'm Crazy (15)
Don't Turn Me Away (2)
Don't You Miss Me A Little Bit Baby (2)
Ease Me To The Ground (12)
End Of Our Road (2,5,11) *15*
End Of The Road Medley (27)
Every Beat Of My Heart (5,11) *45*
Every Little Bit Hurts (3,11)
Everybody Is A Star (6)
Everybody Needs Love (1,5,11) *39*
Everybody's Got To Find A Way (18)
Feel Like Makin' Love (16)
Feeling Alright (6)
Fire And Rain (7)
For Once In My Life (8,11)
Forever (24)
Friend Of Mine (22)
Friendly Persuasion (21)

KNIGHT, Gladys, & The Pips — Cont'd

Friendship Train (5,11) 17
Georgia On My Mind (16)
Get The Love (21)
Give Me A Chance (26)
Giving Up (5,11) 38
Glitter (22)
Goin' Out Of My Head (3)
God Is (22)
Going Ups And The Coming Downs (14,17)
Good Woman (26)
Got Myself A Good Man (4)
Grandma's Hands (28)
Greatest Love Of All (28)
Groovin' (3)
Guilty (27)
He Ain't Heavy, He's My Brother (medley) (7)
He's My Kind Of Fellow (1)
Heaven Sent (23)
Heavy Makes You Happy (9)
Help Me Make It Through The Night (7,11) 33
Here I Am Again (6,9)
Hero (23)
Hold On (13)
Home Alone (27)
Home Is Where The Heart Is (19)
How Can You Say That Ain't Love (6,12)
I Can See Clearly Now (10,17)
I Don't Want To Do Wrong (6,11) 17
I Don't Want To Know (27)
I Feel A Song (In My Heart) (14,17) 21
I Hate Myself For Loving You (15)
I Heard It Through The Grapevine (1,5,11) 2
I Know Better (2)
(I Know) I'm Losing You (4)

I Love To Feel That Feeling (19)
I Said You Lied (28)
I Wanna Be Loved (28)
I Want Him To Say It Again (4)
I Will Fight (22)
I Will Follow My Dream (18)
I Will Survive (22)
I Wish It Would Rain (3,5,11) 41
I'll Be Here (When You Get Home) (9)
I'll Be Standing By (1)
I'll Fall In Love If You Hang Around (7)
I'll Miss You (18)
I've Got To Use My Imagination (10,17) 4
If I Were Your Woman (6,11) 9
If I Were Your Woman II (28)
If That'll Make You Happy (22)
If You Gonna Leave (Just Leave) (7)
If You Only Knew (26)
In The Middle Of The Road (15)
In This Life (26)
Is There A Place (In His Heart For Me) (6)
It Should Have Been Me (2,5,11) 40
It Takes A Whole Lot Of Human Feeling (12)
It Takes A Whole Lotta Man For A Woman Like Me (7)
It's A Better Than Good Time (20)
It's All Over But The Shoutin' (12)
It's Gonna Take All Our Love (25)
It's Gotta Be That Way (8)
It's Summer (4)
It's Time To Go Now (2)

Just Be My Lover (23)
Just Let Me Love You (24)
Just Take Me (28)
Just Walk In My Shoes (1,11)
Keep An Eye (4)
Keep Givin' Me Love (24)
Landlord (21) 46
Let It Be (6)
Let Me Be The One (25)
Letter Full Of Tears (5,11) 19
Life (24)
Little Bit Of Love (19)
Long And Winding Road (7)
Look Of Love (3)
Love Finds It's Own Way (14) 47
Love Hurts (28)
Love Is Always On Your Mind (19)
Love Is Fire (Love Is Ice) (25)
Love Overboard (25) 13
Love Was Made For Two (22)
Lovin' On Next To Nothin' (25)
Make Me The Woman That You Go Home To (7,11) 27
Make Yours A Happy Home (13,17)
Makings Of You (13)
Master Of My Mind (7,12)
Meet Me In The Middle (26)
Men (26)
Midnight Train To Georgia (10,17) 1
Money (16) 50
Mr. Love (26)
Mr. Welfare Man (13)
My Bed Of Thorns (1)
My Time (24)
Need To Be (14)
Neither One Of Us (Wants To Be The First To Say Goodbye) (8,11) 2
Next Time (27)

Nitty Gritty (4,5,11) 19
No One Could Love You More (7,15)
Nobody But You (18)
Oh La De Da (23)
Oh! What A Love I Have Found (9)
On And On (13,17) 5
Once In A Lifetime Thing (10)
One And Only (20)
One Less Bell To Answer (6)
One Step Away (6)
Only Time You Love Me Is When You're Losing Me (9)
Our Love (27)
Overnight Success (25)
Part Time Love (16) 22
Perfect Love (14)
Pipe Dreams (18)
Please Help Me I'm Falling (In Love With You) (28)
Point Of View (25)
Pot Of Jazz (18)
Put A Little Love In Your Heart (15)
Reach High (22)
Rose Bouquet (28)
Runnin' Out (4)
Save The Overtime (For Me) (23) 66
Saved By The Grace Of Your Love (20)
Say What You Mean (25)
Seconds (14,23)
Signed Gladys (6)
Since I've Lost You (1)
Singer, The (4)
So Sad The Song (18) 47
Somebody Stole The Sunshine (12)
Somehow He Loves Me (27)
Something Blue (28)
Sorry Doesn't Make It Right (20)

Still Such A Thing (21)
Storms Of Troubled Times (10)
Straight Up (24)
Stranger, The (4)
Street Brother (16)
Strivin' (24)
Sugar Sugar (15)
Summer Sun (16)
Superwoman (26)
Take Me In Your Arms And Love Me (1,11) 98
Taste Of Bitter Love (21)
Tenderness Is His Way (14)
Thank You (Falletin Me Be Mice Elf Agin) (9)
That's The Way Love Is (2)
That's Why They Call It Love (28)
There's A Lesson To Be Learned (9)
Thief In Paradise (25)
This Child Needs Its Father (8)
This Is Love (28)
Till I See You Again (24)
To Be Invisible (13)
To Make A Long Story Short (19)
Together (3)
Tracks Of My Tears (3,11)
Try To Remember ..see: Way We Were
Valley Of The Dolls, Theme From (3)
Waiting On You (26)
Walk Softly (19)
Way We Were/Try To Remember (14,17) 11
We Need Hearts (21)
We've Got Such A Mellow Love (12)
What Good Am I Without You (2)

What If I Should Ever Need You (20)
When You're Far Away (23)
Where Do I Put His Memory (16)
Where Peaceful Waters Flow (10,17) 28
Where Would I Be (26)
Who Is She (And What Is She To You) (8)
Window Raisin' Granny (10)
Yes, I'm Ready (1)
Yesterday (3)
You (25)
You And Me Against The World (16)
You Don't Love Me No More (1)
You Need Love Like I Do (Don't You) (5,11) 25
You Put A New Life In My Body (19)
You're My Everything (3)
You're Number One (In My Book) (23)
You've Lost That Lovin' Feelin' (3)
Your Heartaches I Can Surely Heal (12)
Your Love's Been Good For Me (6)
Your Old Standby (2)

KNIGHT, Jean   '71
Born on 1/26/43 in New Orleans. Female R&B singer.

| 8/21/71 | 60 | 11 | © | 1 | Mr. Big Stuff .... | | | $40 | Stax 2045 |
| 8/3/85 | 180 | 4 | | 2 | My Toot Toot .... | | | $12 | Mirage 90282 |

Call Me Your Fool (If You Want To) (1)
Don't Talk About Jody (1)
Funny Bone (2)
Isn't Life So Wonderful (2)

Let The Good Times Roll (2)
Little Bit Of Something (Is Better Than All Of Nothing) (1)
Magic (2)
Mr. Big Stuff (1,2) 2

My Heart Is Willing (2)
My Toot Toot (2) 50
One Monkey Don't Stop The Show (2)

One-Way Ticket To Nowhere (It's The End Of The Ride) (1)
Take Him (You Can Have My Man) (1)
Think It Over (1)

Why I Keep Living These Memories (1)
Working Your Mojo (2)
You City Slicker (1)
Your Six-Bit Change (1)

KNIGHT, Jerry   '81
Born in 1955 in Los Angeles. R&B singer/bassist. Former member of **Raydio**.

| 5/24/80 | 165 | 7 | | 1 | Jerry Knight .... | | | $12 | A&M 4788 |
| 4/11/81 | 146 | 6 | | 2 | Perfect Fit .... | | | $12 | A&M 4843 |

Easier To Run Away (2)
Freek Show (1)
Good Times (1)

Higher (2)
Joy Ride (2)
Let Me Be The Reason (1)

Monopoly (2)
Now That She's Rockin' (1)
Overnight Sensation (1)

Perfect Fit (2)
Play Sista' (2)
Rainbow (2)

Sweetest Love (1)
Too Busy (2)
Turn It Out (2)

Twilight (2)

KNIGHT, Jordan   '99
Born on 5/15/70 in Worcester, Massachusetts. Former member of **New Kids On The Block**.

| 6/12/99 | 29 | 16 | ● | © | Jordan Knight .... | | | $10 | Interscope 90322 |

Broken By You
Change My Ways
Close My Eyes

Different Party
Don't Run
Finally Finding Out

Give It To You 10
I Could Never Take The Place Of Your Man

Separate Ways
When You're Lonely

KNIGHT, Robert   '67
Born on 4/21/45 in Franklin, Tennessee. R&B singer.

| 12/16/67 | 196 | 2 | © | | Everlasting Love .... | | | $40 | Rising Sons 17000 |

Branded!
Dance Of Love

Everlasting Love 13
It's Been Worth It All

Letter, The
My Rainbow Valley

Never My Love
Rachel The Stranger

Sandy
Somebody's Baby

Somewhere My Love (Lara's Theme from Dr. Zhivago)

KNIGHT, Terry, and The Pack   '67
Rock group from Flint, Michigan: Terry Knight (vocals), Curt Johnson (guitar), Bob Caldwell (organ), Mark Farner (bass) and Don Brewer (drums). Knight formed, managed and produced **Grand Funk Railroad**, which included Farner and Brewer.

| 11/26/66+ | 127 | 13 | | 1 | Terry Knight And The Pack .... | | | $40 | Lucky Eleven 8000 |
| 11/4/72 | 192 | 3 | | 2 | Mark, Don & Terry 1966-67 .... | [K] | | $20 | Abkco 4217 [2] |

Mark Farner, Don Brewer (both of **Grand Funk**) and Terry Knight

Change On The Way (1,2)
Come With Me (2)
Dimestore Debutante (2)
Dirty Lady (2)
Forever And A Day (2)

Got Love (1,2)
He's A Bad Boy (2)
I (Who Have Nothing) (1,2) 46
I've Been Told (1,2)
Lady Jane (1,2)

Lizabeth Peach (2)
Love Goddess Of Sunset Strip (2)
Love Love Love (2)
Lovin' Kind (1,2)

Numbers (1,2)
One Monkey Don't Stop No Show (2)
Satisfaction (2)
Shut-In (1,2)

Sleep Talkin' (1,2)
This Precious Time (2)
What's On Your Mind (1)
Where Do You Go (1)

You're A Better Man Than I (1,2)

K-9 POSSE   '89
Rap duo from Teaneck, New Jersey: Vernon Lynch and Wardell Mahone.

| 3/4/89 | 98 | 14 | © | | K-9 Posse .... | | | $10 | Arista 8569 |

Ain't Nothin To It
It Gets No Deeper
No Sell Out

No Stoppin Or Standin Between The Rhyme
Say Who Say What

Somebody's Brother
This Beat Is Military
Tough Cookie

This Is The Way The Quick Cut Goes
Turn That Down

KNOBLOCK, Fred '80
Born J. Fred Knobloch on 4/28/53 in Jackson, Mississippi. Pop-country singer/songwriter.

| 10/4/80 | 179 | 5 | | | **Why Not Me** | | | $12 | Scotti Brothers 7109 |

Bigger Fool   Can't Keep From Crying   It's Over   Let Me Love You   Still Feel The Same Way   **Why Not Me** *18*
Can I Get A Wish   Father   Laugh It Off   Love Isn't Easy   Take A Flight Tonight

KNOPFLER, Mark '00
Born on 8/12/49 in Glasgow, Scotland; raised in Newcastle, England. Rock singer/guitarist. Leader of **Dire Straits** and **The Notting Hillbillies**.

| 11/3/90 | 127 | 25 | © | 1 | **Neck And Neck** | | [I] | $10 | Columbia 45307 |

CHET ATKINS/MARK KNOPFLER

| 4/13/96 | 105 | 12 | © | 2 | **Golden Heart** | | | $10 | Warner 46026 |
| 10/14/00 | 60 | 22 | © | 3 | **Sailing To Philadelphia** | | | $10 | Warner 47753 |

Are We In Trouble Now (2)   El Macho (3)   Just One Time (1)   Prairie Wedding (3)   Sweet Dreams (1)   What It Is (3)
Baloney Again (3)   Golden Heart (2)   Last Laugh (3)   Rudiger (2)   Tahitian Skies (1)   Who's Your Baby Now (3)
Cannibals (2)   I'll See You In My Dreams (1)   Next Time I'm In Town (1)   Sailing To Philadelphia (3)   Tears (1)   Yakety Axe (1)
Darling Pretty (2)   I'm The Fool (2)   Night In Summer Long Ago (1)   Sands Of Nevada (3)   There'll Be Some Changes
Do America (3)   Imelda (2)   No Can Do (2)   Silvertown Blues (3)   Made (1)
Don't You Get It (3)   Je Suis Desole (2)   Nobody's Got The Gun (2)   So Soft, Your Goodbye (1)   Vic And Ray (2)
Done With Bonaparte (2)   Junkie Doll (3)   Poor Boy Blues (1)   Speedway At Nazareth (3)   Wanderlust (3)

KOFFEE BROWN '01
Male-female R&B duo from Minneapolis: Fonz and Vee.

| 3/24/01 | 32 | 11 | © | | **Mars/Venus** | | | $10 | Arista 14662 |

After Party *44*   Blackout   Do U See   I Got Love (Scars)   Weekend Thing
All I Need (Bonnie & Clyde)   Chick On Da Side   Fingerpointing   Qualified
All Those Fancy Things   Didn't Mean To Turn You On   Hater's Disease   Quickie

KOKOMO '75
Jazz-rock group from England: Dyan Birch, Paddie McHugh and Frank Collins (vocals), Neil Hubbard and Jim Mullen (guitars), Tony O'Malley (piano), Joan Linscott (percussion), Mel Collins (sax), Alan Spenner (bass) and Terry Stannard (drums). Hubbard and Spenner were members of **Grease Band**.

| 6/7/75 | 159 | 9 | | 1 | **Kokomo** | | | $12 | Columbia 33442 |
| 4/17/76 | 194 | 2 | | 2 | **Rise And Shine!** | | | $12 | Columbia 34031 |

Angel (1)   Feelin' Good (2)   I Can Understand It (1)   Kitty Sittin' Pretty (1)   That's Enough (2)
Angel Love (2)   Feeling This Way (1)   I'm Sorry Babe (1)   Little Girl (2)   Use Your Imagination (2)
Anytime (1)   Forever (1)   It Ain't Cool (To Be Cool No   Rise And Shine (2)   Without Me (2)
Do It Right (2)   Happy Birthday (2)   More) (1)   Sweet Sugar Thing (1)

KONGAS '78
Disco studio group assembled by **Cerrone**.

| 3/18/78 | 120 | 8 | © | | **Africansim** | | | $12 | Polydor 6138 |

Africanism/Gimme Some   Dr. Doo-Dah
   Lovin' *84*   Tatoo Woman

KOOL & THE GANG ★148★ '81
R&B group formed in Jersey City, New Jersey. Nucleus of group: Robert "Kool" Bell (bass), his brother Ronald Bell (sax), Claydes Smith (guitar), Rick Westfield (keyboards), Dennis Thomas (sax), Robert Mickens (trumpet) and George Brown (drums). All shared vocals. Added lead singer James "J.T." Taylor in 1978. Earl Toon replaced Westfield in 1978. Taylor left in 1988.

1)Celebrate! 2)Something Special 3)Ladies' Night 4)Emergency 5)Forever

2/27/71	122	19	©	1	**Live At The Sex Machine**		[I-L]	$15	De-Lite 2008
9/25/71	157	8		2	**The Best Of Kool And The Gang**		[G]	$15	De-Lite 2009
1/1/72	171	7	©	3	**Live At P.J.'S**		[I-L]	$15	De-Lite 2010
					recorded on 5/29/71 in Hollywood				
3/17/73	142	7	©	4	**Good Times**			$15	De-Lite 2012
10/13/73+	33	60	●	5	**Wild And Peaceful**			$12	De-Lite 2013
1/12/74	187	4		6	**Kool Jazz**		[I-K]	$12	De-Lite 4001
10/5/74	63	34	● ©	7	**Light Of Worlds**			$12	De-Lite 2014
3/8/75	81	23		8	**Kool & The Gang Greatest Hits!**		[G]	$12	De-Lite 2015
8/30/75	48	14	©	9	**Spirit Of The Boogie**			$12	De-Lite 2016
3/20/76	68	20	©	10	**Love & Understanding**			$12	De-Lite 2018
11/20/76+	110	18		11	**Open Sesame**			$12	De-Lite 2023
1/28/77	142	7		12	**The Force**			$12	De-Lite 9501
9/22/79	13	45	▲ ©	13	**Ladies' Night**			$12	De-Lite 9513
10/18/80+	10	44	▲ ©	14	Celebrate!			$12	De-Lite 9518
10/17/81	12	67	▲ ©	15	**Something Special**			$10	De-Lite 8502
10/9/82	29	24	●	16	**As One**			$10	De-Lite 8505
12/10/83+	29	37	● ©	17	**In The Heart**			$10	De-Lite 8508
12/15/84+	13	74	▲[2] ©	18	**Emergency**			$10	De-Lite 822943
12/6/86+	25	42	● ©	19	**Forever**			$10	Mercury 830398
8/20/88	109	11	©	20	**Everything's Kool & The Gang: Greatest Hits & More**		[G]	$10	Mercury 834780

All Night Long (11)   **Caribbean Festival** (9) *55*   Dujii (3,6)   **Funky Stuff** (5,8,20) *29*   Hangin' Out (13)   Home Is Where The Heart Is
Ancestral Ceremony (9)   **Celebration** (14,20) *1*   **Emergency** (18) *18*   **Gangs Back Again** (2) *85*   Heaven At Once (5)   (17)
As One (16)   **Cherish** (18,20) *2*   Father, Father (4)   **Get Down On It** (15) *10*   Here After (7)   I.B.M.C. (19)
Bad Woman (18)   Chocolate Buttermilk (1,2)   Force, The (12)   Gift Of Love (19)   Hi De Hi, Hi De Ho (16)   I Remember John W. Coltrane
Be My Lady (15)   Come Together ..see: Love And   Forever (19)   God's Country (19)   **Higher Plane** (7,8) *37*   (4,6)
Big Fun (16) *21*   Understanding   Free (12)   Good Time Tonight (15)   **Holiday** (19) *66*   I Want To Take You Higher (1)
Blowin' With The Wind (6)   Cosmic Energy (10)   **Fresh** (18,20) *9*   Good Times (4,8)   **Hollywood Swinging**   If You Feel Like Dancin' (13)
Breeze & Soul (6)   Country Junkey (4)   Fruitman (7)   Got You Into My Life (13)   (5,8,10,20) *6*   Ike's Mood (medley) (3)
Broadway (19)   Do It Right Now (10)   **Funky Man** (1,2) *87*   In The Heart (17)

KOOL & THE GANG — Cont'd

Joanna (17,20) **2**
Jones Vs. Jones (14) **39**
Jungle Boogie (5,8,20) **4**
Jungle Jazz (9)
Just Be True (12)
Just Friends (14)
Kool And The Gang (2) **59**
Kool It (Here Comes The Fuzz) (2)
Kools Back Again (2)
Ladies Night (13) **8**
Let The Music Take Your Mind (1,2) **78**
Let's Go Dancin' (Ooh La La, La) (16) **30**
Life Is What You Make It (5)
Life's A Song (12)
Light Of Worlds (7)

Little Children (11)
L-O-V-E (11)
Love Affair (14)
Love And Understanding (Come Together) (10) **77**
Love Festival (14)
Lucky For Me (3,6)
Making Merry Music (4)
Mighty, Mighty High (12)
Misled (18) **10**
Money And Power (20)
More Funky Stuff (5,8)
Morning Star (14)
Mother Earth (9)
Music Is The Message (8)
N.T. (3)
Night People (14)
No Show (15)

North, East, South, West (4,6)
Oasis (12)
Open Sesame - Part 1 (11,20) **55**
Pass It On (15)
Peace Maker (19)
Penguin, The (2)
Place For Us (11)
Place In Space (12)
Pneumonia (1,2)
Pretty Baby (16)
Rags To Riches (10)
Rated X (4,8)
Raw Hamburger (2)
Rhyme Tyme People (7) **63**
Ricksonata (3)
Ride The Rhythm (9)
Rollin' (17)

Ronnie's Groove (3)
Sea Of Tranquility (6)
September Love (17)
Slick Superchick (12)
Sombrero Sam (3,6)
Soul Vibrations (8)
Special Way (19) **72**
Spirit Of The Boogie (9) **35**
Stand Up And Sing (15)
Steppin' Out (15) **89**
Stone Love (19,20) **10**
Straight Ahead (17)
Street Corner Symphony (7)
Street Kids (16)
Strong (20)
Sugar (10)
Summer Madness (7,10) flip
Sunshine (11)

Sunshine And Love (9)
Super Band (11)
Surrender (18)
Take It To The Top (14)
Take My Heart (You Can Have It If You Want It) (15) **17**
Think It Over (16)
This Is You, This Is Me (5)
Tonight (17) **13**
Tonights The Night (13)
Too Hot (13,20) **5**
Touch Of You (1)
Trying To Make A Fool Of Me (1)
Universal Sound (10)
Victory (19) **10**
Walk On By (1)

What Would The World Be Like Without Music (medley) (1)
Whisper Softly (11)
Whiting H. & G. (7)
Who's Gonna Take The Weight - Part 1 & 2 (1,2)
Wichita Lineman (1)
Wild And Peaceful (5)
Wild Is Love (4,6)
Winter Sadness (9)
You Are The One (18)
You Can Do It (17)
You Don't Have To Change (7)
You've Lost That Lovin' Feeling (medley) (3)

KOOL G RAP & D.J. POLO '95

Rap duo. Kool G Rap (Kool Genius Of Rap) was born Nathaniel Wilson on 7/20/68 in Elmhurst, Queens, New York.

DEBUT	PEAK	WKS	RIAA	CD	ARTIST — Album Title		$	Label & Number
12/12/92	185	1		© 1	Live And Let Die		$10	Cold Chillin' 5001
10/14/95	24	6		© 2	4,5,6		$10	Cold Chillin' 57808

KOOL G RAP

Blowin' Up In The World (1)
Crime Pays (1)
Edge Of Sanity (1)
Executioner Style (1)
Fast Life (2) **74**

For Da Brothaz (2)
4,5,6 (2)
Fuck U Man (1)
Ghetto Knows (2)
Go For Your Guns (1)

Home Sweet Home (1)
Ill Street Blues (1)
It's A Shame (2)
Letters (1)
Live And Let Die (1)

Money On My Brain (2)
Nuff Said (1)
#1 With A Bullet (1)
On The Run (1)
Operation CB (1)

Still Wanted Dead Or Alive (1)
Straight Jacket (1)
Take 'Em To War (2)
Train Robbery (1)
Two To The Head (1)

KOOL KEITH '99

Born Keith Thornton in the Bronx, New York. Male rapper.

DEBUT	PEAK	WKS	RIAA	CD	ARTIST — Album Title		$	Label & Number
8/28/99	180	1		©	Black Elvis/Lost In Space		$10	Ruffhouse 52000

All The Time
Black Elvis
Clifton

Fine Girls
Girls Don't Like The Job
I Don't Play

I'm Seein' Robots
Keith Turbo
Livin' Astro

Lost In Space
Master Of The Game
Maxi Curls

Rockets On The Battlefield
Static
Supergalactic Lover

KOOL MOE DEE '88

Born Mohanndas DeWese on 8/8/67 in Harlem, New York. Male rapper.

DEBUT	PEAK	WKS	RIAA	CD	ARTIST — Album Title		$	Label & Number
4/18/87	83	21		© 1	Kool Moe Dee		$10	Jive 1025
11/28/87+	35	50	▲	© 2	How Ya Like Me Now		$10	Jive 1079
6/17/89	25	23	●	© 3	Knowledge Is King		$10	Jive 1182
6/29/91	72	9		© 4	Funke Funke Wisdom		$10	Jive 1388

All Night Long (3)
Avenue, The (3)
Bad, Bad, Bad (4)
Bad Mutha (1)
Best, The (1)
Death Blow (4)
Do You Know What Time It Is? (1)

Don, The (3)
Don't Dance (2)
Dumb Dick (Richard) (1)
50 Ways (2)
Funke Wisdom (4)
Gangster Boogie (4)
Get Paid (2)
Get The Picture (3)

Go See The Doctor (1) **89**
Here We Go Again (4)
How Kool Can One Blackman Be (4)
How Ya Like Me Now (2)
I Go To Work (3)
I Like It Nasty (4)
I'm A Player (4)

I'm Blowin' Up (3)
I'm Hittin' Hard (3)
I'm Kool Moe Dee (3)
Knowledge Is King (3)
Let's Get Serious (4)
Little Jon (1)
Mo' Better (4)
Monster Crack (1)

No Respect (2)
Poetic Justice (4)
Pump Your Fist (3)
Rise 'N' Shine (4)
Rock Steady (1)
Rock You (2)
Stupid (2)
Suckers (2)

They Want Money (3)
Times Up (4)
To The Beat Y'all (1)
Way Way Back (2)
Wild, Wild West (2) **62**

KOOPER, AL '68

Born on 2/5/44 in Brooklyn, New York. Top session keyboardist/guitarist/vocalist. Founded **Blood, Sweat & Tears** in 1968, left in 1969. A member of The Royal Teens in 1959. Founded **The Blues Project** in 1967.

DEBUT	PEAK	WKS	RIAA	CD	ARTIST — Album Title		$	Label & Number
8/31/68	12	37	●	© 1	Super Session		$20	Columbia 9701
					MIKE BLOOMFIELD/AL KOOPER/STEVE STILLS			
2/8/69	18	20		© 2	The Live Adventures Of Mike Bloomfield And Al Kooper [L]		$25	Columbia 6 [2]
					MIKE BLOOMFIELD & AL KOOPER recorded on 9/27/68 at the Fillmore in San Francisco			
2/8/69	54	13			3 I Stand Alone		$15	Columbia 9718
10/11/69	125	6			4 You Never Know Who Your Friends Are		$15	Columbia 9855
1/24/70	182	5			5 Kooper Session		$15	Columbia 9951
					AL KOOPER Introduces SHUGGIE OTIS			
9/19/70	105	6			6 Easy Does It		$20	Columbia 30031 [2]
7/3/71	198	3			7 New York City (You're A Woman)		$15	Columbia 30506
5/6/72	200	2			8 A Possible Projection Of The Future/Childhood's End		$15	Columbia 31159
1/8/77	182	5		©	9 Act Like Nothing's Wrong		$12	United Artists 702

Albert's Shuffle (1)
Anna Lee (What Can I Do For You) (4)
Baby Please Don't Go (6)
Back On My Feet (7)
Ballad Of The Hard Rock Kid (7)
Bended Knees (Please Don't Leave Me Now) (8)
Blue Moon Of Kentucky (3)
Blues, Part IV (4)
Brand New Day (Main Theme from The Landlord) (6)
Buckskin Boy (6)
Bury My Body (5)
Camille (1)
Can You Hear It Now (500 Miles) (7)
Childhood's End (8)
Coloured Rain (3)
Come Down In Time (7)
Country Road (6)
Dear Mr. Fantasy (2)

Dearest Darling (4)
Don't Know Why I Love You (4)
Don't Throw Your Love On Me So Strong (2)
Double Or Nothing (5)
Easy Does It (6)
59th Street Bridge Song (Feelin' Groovy) (2)
First Time Around (4)
Fly On (8)
God Sheds His Grace On Thee (6)
Going Quietly Mad (7)
Great American Marriage (medley) (7)
Green Onions (2)
Harvey's Tune (1)
Her Holy Modal Highness (2)
Hey, Western Union Man (3)
His Holy Modal Majesty (1)
Hollywood Vampire (9)
I Bought You The Shoes (You're Walking Away In) (6)

I Can Love A Woman (3)
I Forgot To Be Your Lover (9)
I Got A Woman (6)
I Stand Alone (3)
I Wonder Who (2)
I'm Never Gonna Let You Down (4)
In My Own Sweet Way (9)
Introduction (6)
Is We On The Downbeat? (9)
It Takes A Lot To Laugh, It Takes A Train To Cry (1)
John The Baptist (Holy John) (7)
Landlord, Love Theme From The (6)
Let The Duchess No (6)
Let Your Love Shine (4)
Lookin' For A Home (5)
Loretta (Union Turnpike Eulogy) (4)
Love Is A Man's Best Friend (medley) (7)

Love Trap (8)
Lucille (2)
Magic In My Socks (4)
Man In Me (8)
Man's Temptation (1)
Mary Ann (2)
Missing You (9)
Monkey Time (3)
Mourning Glory Story (4)
New York City (You're A Woman) (7)
Nightmare No. 5 (7)
No More Lonely Nights (2)
Nothing (medley) (1)
One (3)
One Room Country Shack (5)
Oo Wee Baby, I Love You (medley) (7)
Out Of Left Field (9)
Overture (3)
(Please Not) One More Time (9)
Please Tell Me Why (8)

Possible Projection Of The Future (8)
Really (1)
Refugee (2)
Right Now For You (3)
Rose And A Baby Ruth (6)
Sad, Sad Sunshine (4)
Season Of The Witch (1)
She Don't Ever Lose Her Groove (9)
She Gets Me Where I Live (6)
Shuggie's Old Time Dee-Dee-Di-Leet-Deet Slide Boogie (5)
Shuggie's Shuffle (5)
Soft Landing On The Moon (3)
Song And Dance For The Unborn, Frightened Child (4)
Sonny Boy Williamson (2)
Stop (1)
Swept For You Baby (8)
That's All Right (2)
This Diamond Ring (9)

Toe Hold (3)
Together 'Til The End Of Time (2)
Too Busy Thinking About My Baby (4)
Turn My Head Towards Home (9)
12:15 Slow Goonbash Blues (5)
Visit To The Rainbow Bar & Grill (9)
Warning (Someone's On The Cross Again) (7)
Weight, The (2)
You Don't Love Me (1)
You Never Know Who Your Friends Are (4)

KORGIS, The '80

Pop trio formed in England: James Warren (vocals, bass), Stuart Gordon (guitar) and Andy Davis (drums). Warren and Davis were with Stackridge.

| 11/8/80 | 113 | 12 | | © | **Dumb Waiters** .... | | | **$12** | Asylum 290 |

Drawn And Quartered
Dumb Waiters

Everybody's Got To Learn Sometime *18*
If It's Alright With You Baby
Intimate

It's No Good Unless You Love Me
Love Ain't Too Far Away
Perfect Hostess

Rovers Return
Silent Running

KORN '98

Techno-rock group from Huntington Beach, California: Jonathan Davis (vocals), Brian Welch and James Munkey (guitars), Reggie Fieldy Arvizu (bass) and David Silveria (drums).

8/26/95+	72	64	▲²	©	1 **Korn**	C:#5/92		**$10**	Immortal 66633
11/2/96	3	50	▲²	©	2 **Life Is Peachy**	C:#8/51		**$10**	Immortal 67554
9/5/98	❶¹	89	▲⁴	©	3 **Follow The Leader**			**$10**	Immortal 69001
12/4/99	❶¹	47	▲²	©	4 **Issues**			**$10**	Immortal 63710

A.D.I.D.A.S. (2)
All In The Family (3)
Am I Going Crazy (4)
Ass Itch (2)
B.B.K. (3)
Ball Tongue (1)
Beg For Me (4)
Blind (1)
Cameltosis (3)
Chi (2)

Children Of The Korn (3)
Clown (4)
Counting (4)
Daddy (1)
Dead (4)
Dead Bodies Everywhere (3)
Dirty (4)
Divine (1)
Faget (1)
Fake (1)

Falling Away From Me (4)
4 U (4)
Freak On A Leash (3)
Good God (2)
Got The Life (3)
Helmet In The Bush (1)
Hey Daddy (4)
It's Gonna Go Away (4)
It's On! (3)
Justin (3)

K@#ø%! (2)
Kill You (2)
Let's Get This Party Started (4)
Lies (1)
Lost (2)
Lowrider (2)
Make Me Bad (4)
Mr. Rogers (2)
My Gift To You (3)
Need To (1)

No Place To Hide (2)
No Way (4)
Porno Creep (2)
Predictable (1)
Pretty (3)
Reclaim My Place (3)
Seed (3)
Shoots And Ladders (1)
Somebody Someone (4)
Swallow (2)

Trash (4)
Twist (2)
Wake Up (4)
Wicked (2)
Wish You Could Be Me (4)

KOSSOFF, Paul '75

Born on 9/14/50 in Hampstead, London, England. Died of heart failure on 3/19/76 (age 25). Rock guitarist. Member of **Free** and **Back Street Crawler**.

| 9/6/75 | 191 | 2 | | | **Back Street Crawler** .... | [E-I] | | **$15** | Island 9264 |

recorded in 1973; Kossoff formed new band (named after album title) in 1975

Back Street Crawler (Don't Need You No More)
I'm Ready
Molten Gold
Time Away
Tuesday Morning

KOSTELANETZ, Andre, & His Orchestra '55

Born on 12/22/01 in St. Petersburg, Russia. Died on 1/13/80 (age 78). Conductor/arranger.

| 10/1/55 | 4 | 11 | | | 1 **Meet Andre Kostelanetz** .... | [I-K] | | **$20** | Columbia KZ 1 |
| 12/28/63 | 30ˣ | 2 | | | 2 **Wonderland Of Christmas** .... | [X-I] | | **$15** | Columbia 2068 / 8868 |

Christmas charts: 30/'63, 52/'65

| 5/23/64 | 68 | 7 | | | 3 **New York Wonderland** .... | [I] | | **$15** | Columbia 2138 / 8938 |
| 12/17/66 | 36ˣ | 2 | | | 4 **Wishing You A Merry Christmas** .... | [X] | | **$15** | Columbia 6779 |

with The St. Kilian Boychoir and Phyllis Curtin, soloist

| 12/2/67 | 30ˣ | 5 | | | 5 **Joy To The World (Music For Christmas)** .... | [X] | | **$15** | Harmony 7432 / 11232 |

with Earl Wrightson, baritone; originally released in 1960 on Columbia 1528 / 8328

6/7/69	200	2			6 **Traces**	[I]		**$15**	Columbia 9823
11/1/69	194	2			7 **Sounds Of Love**	[I-K]		**$15**	Columbia 10 [2]
4/10/71	183	2			8 **Love Story**	[I]		**$15**	Columbia 30501

Alfie (7)
Angels We Have Heard On High (medley) (4)
Autumn In New York (3)
Away In A Manger (4,5)
Bowery, The (medley) (3)
(Carol's Theme) The Eyes Of Love (7)
Celeste Aida (1)
Chitty Chitty Bang Bang (6)
Christmas Chimes (4)
Christmas Chopsticks (2)
Christmas Song (Merry Christmas To You) (2)
Days Of Wine And Roses (7)
Deck The Halls With Boughs Of Holly (medley) (2,4)
Don't Blame Me (7)
Easy To Love (1)
Ebb Tide (7)
Eyes Of Love ..see: (Carol's Theme)
First Noel (medley) (2,4,5)

Fool On The Hill (6)
Funny Girl (7)
Galveston (6)
Games That Lovers Play (7)
Give My Regards To Broadway (medley) (3)
Green Grass Starts To Grow (8)
Hark! The Herald Angels Sing (medley) (4,5)
Have Yourself A Merry Little Christmas (medley) (2)
I Cover The Waterfront (8)
I Don't Know Why (I Just Do) (7)
I Love You (1)
I Saw Mommy Kissing Santa Claus (medley) (2)
I Want To Be Happy (medley) (8)
I'll Begin Again (medley) (8)
I'll Catch The Sun (6)
I'll Follow My Secret Heart (1)
I'm In The Mood For Love (7)

I've Gotta Be Me (6)
In The Still Of The Night (1)
It Came Upon The Midnight Clear (2,4,5)
It's Beginning To Look Like Christmas (2)
It's Impossible (8)
Jingle Bells (medley) (2,4)
Joy To The World (medley) (2,4,5)
Let It Snow! Let It Snow! Let It Snow! (2)
Love For Three Oranges - March (1)
Love Is A Many-Splendored Thing (7)
Love Story, Theme From (8)
Lullaby Of Birdland (3)
Lullaby Of Broadway (3)
Man And A Woman (7)
Manhattan (3)
Manhattan Serenade (3)
March Of The Toys (medley) (5)

Moon River (7)
Mr. Bojangles (8)
Nearness Of You (7)
New York, New York (3)
Oh Come, All Ye Faithful (2,4,5)
O Holy Night (4,5)
O Little Town Of Bethlehem (4,5)
Oh Tannenbaum (4)
One Less Bell To Answer (8)
Overture From Carmen (1)
People (7)
Romeo And Juliet, Theme From (6)
Rose Garden (8)
Rudolph, The Red-Nosed Reindeer (medley) (2)
Santa Claus Is Comin' To Town (medley) (2)
Shake Me I Rattle (Squeeze Me I Cry) (medley) (2)
She's A Latin From Manhattan (3)

Silent Night, Holy Night (2,4,5)
Silver Bells (medley) (2)
Skaters' Waltz (5)
Sleigh Ride (2,5)
So In Love (1)
Someone To Watch Over Me (7)
Something Doesn't Happen (8)
Somewhere, My Love (Lara's Theme) (7)
Song Of India (1)
Spanish Harlem (3)
Stella By Starlight (7)
Street Scene (3)
Tales From The Vienna Woods (1)
Tara Theme (7)
Tea For Two (medley) (8)
Thank You Very Much (medley) (8)
This Guy's In Love With You (6)
This Is My Song (7)

Thomas Crown Affair (Windmills Of Your Mind), Theme From The (6)
Toyland (medley) (5)
Traces (6)
Try A Little Tenderness (6)
Valse De Rothschild (7)
Waltz Of The Flowers (1,5)
Washington Square (3)
We Three Kings Of Orient Are (4,5)
We Wish You A Merry Christmas (2)
We've Only Just Begun (8)
What Child Is This? (4,5)
What Now My Love (7)
Where Or When (1)
White Christmas (2,5)
(Windmills Of Your Mind) ..see: Thomas Crown Affair
Winter Wonderland (medley) (2)
Zorba Theme (Life Is) (6)

KOTTKE, Leo '74

Born on 9/11/45 in Athens, Georgia. Acoustic guitarist.

6/19/71	168	7		©	1 **Mudlark**			**$15**	Capitol 682
2/12/72	127	9		©	2 **Greenhouse**			**$12**	Capitol 11000
4/7/73	108	11		©	3 **My Feet Are Smiling**	[I-L]		**$12**	Capitol 11164

recorded on 12/19/72 at the Guthrie Theater in Minneapolis

2/2/74	69	18		©	4 **Ice Water**			**$12**	Capitol 11262
11/9/74	45	12		©	5 **Dreams and all that stuff**	[I]		**$12**	Capitol 11335
10/25/75	114	7		©	6 **Chewing Pine**			**$12**	Capitol 11446
11/27/76	153	4			7 **Leo Kottke 1971-1976 - Did You Hear Me?**	[I-K]		**$12**	Capitol 11576
1/29/77	107	9			8 **Leo Kottke**	[I]		**$12**	Chrysalis 1106
9/2/78	143	12		©	9 **Burnt Lips**			**$12**	Chrysalis 1191

Airproofing (8)
All Through The Night (4,7)
America, The Beautiful (medley) (5)
Bean Time (2,3)

Bill Cheatham (5)
Blue Dot (3)
Born To Be With You (4)
Bourree (1)
Buckaroo (8)

Bumblebee (1)
Burnt Lips (9)
Busted Bicycle (3)
Can't Quite Put It Into Words (6)
Child Should Be A Fish (4)

Constant Traveler (5)
Cool Water (9)
Credits: Out-Takes From Terry's Movie (9)
Cripple Creek (1,7)

Crow River Waltz (medley) (3)
Death By Reputation (8)
Don't You Think (6)
Easter (3)
Eggtooth (3)

Eight Miles High (1)
Endless Sleep (9)
Everybody Lies (9)
Fisherman, The (3)
Frank Forgets (9)

KOTTKE, Leo — Cont'd

From The Cradle To The Grave (2)
Good Egg (4)
Grim To The Brim (6,7)
Hayseed Suede (8)
Hear The Wind Howl (1,3)
Hole In The Day (5)
I Called Back (9)
Ice Miner (1)
In Christ There Is No East Or West (2)
Introduction (3)
Jack Fig (medley) (3)

Jesu, Joy Of Man's Desiring (medley) (3)
June Bug (1,3,7)
Last Steam Engine Train (2)
Living In The Country (3)
Lost John (2)
Louise (2,3)
Low Thud (9)
Lullaby (1)
Machine #2 (1)
Maroon (8)
Mona Ray (5)
Mona Roy (5)

Monkey Lust (3)
Monkey Money (6)
Morning Is The Long Way Home (4,7)
Open Country Joy (Constant Traveler) (7)
Orange Room (9)
Owls (3)
Pamela Brown (4,7)
Poor Boy (1)
Power Failure (6,7)
Quiet Man (9)
Range (8)

Rebecca (6)
Regards From Chuck Pink (6)
Rio Leo (8)
Room 8 (1,7)
San Antonio Rose (medley) (5)
Sand Street (9)
Scarlatti Rip-Off (6,7)
Shadowland (8)
Short Stories (4)
Song Of The Swamp (2)
Sonora's Death Row (9)
Spanish Entomologist (2)
Standing In My Shoes (1,3)

Standing On The Outside (6,7)
Stealing (1,3)
Taking A Sandwich To A Feast (5)
Tilt Billings And The Student Prince (4)
Tiny Island (2)
Train And The Gate: From Terry's Movie (9)
Trombone (4)
Twilight Property (5)
Up Tempo (8)
Venezuela, There You Go (6)

Vertical Trees (5)
Voluntary Target (9)
Waltz (8)
Wheels (6)
When Shrimps Learn To Whistle (5,7)
White Ape (8)
Why Ask Why? (5,7)
You Don't Have To Need Me (2)
You Know I Know You Know (4)
You Tell Me Why (4,7)

KOTTONMOUTH KINGS   '00

Rock group from Los Angeles: Saint, D-Loc, Bobby B, Pakelika and Daddy X.

7/15/00	65	9		©	**High Society**			$10	Suburban Noize 21480

B-Dubb's Blend
Coffee Shop
Crucial

Day Dreamin' Fazes
Elevated Sounds
Face Facts

First Class
Good As Gold
Here We Go Again

Joint, The
King's Blend
Lottery, The

Peace Not Greed
Round & Round
Size Of An Ant

Unxplanetory
We The People
Wickit Klowns

KOZ, Dave   '91

Born on 3/27/63 in Los Angeles. Saxophonist.

3/23/91	128	9		©	1	**Dave Koz**	[I]	$10	Capitol 91643
8/14/93	176	5	●	©	2	**Lucky Man**	[I]	$10	Capitol 98892
9/21/96	182	2		©	3	**Off The Beaten Path**	[I]	$10	Capitol 32798
10/16/99	190	1		©	4	**The Dance**	[I]	$10	Capitol 99458

After Dark (2)
Art Of Key Noise (1)
Awakenings (3)
Bright Side (4)
Can't Let You Go (The Sha La Song) (4)
Careless Whisper (4)
Castle Of Dreams (1)
Cuban Hideaway (4)

Dance, The (4)
Don't Give Up (4)
Don't Look Any Further (2)
Don't Look Back (3)
Emily (1)
Endless Summer Nights (1)
Faces Of The Heart (2)
Flat Feet (3)
Follow Me Home (3)

Give It Up (1)
I'll Be There (4)
I'm Ready (3)
I'm Waiting For You (4)
If Love Is All We Have (1)
Know You By Heart (4)
Leave The Light On (3)
Let Me Count The Ways (3)
Love Is On The Way (4)

Love Of My Life (1)
Lucky Man (2)
Lullaby For A Rainy Night (3)
Misty (2)
My Back Porch (3)
Nothing But The Radio On (1)
Perfect Stranger (1)
Remembrance (3)
Right By Your Side (4)

Saxman (2)
Shakin' The Shack (2)
Show Me The Way (2)
Silverlining (2)
So Far From Home (1)
Surrender (4)
Tender Is The Night (2)
That's The Way I Feel About You (3)

Together Again (4)
Under The Spell Of The Moon (3)
Wait A Little While (2)
Wake Up Call (3)
Yesterday's Rain (1)
You Are Me, I Am You (4)
You Make Me Smile (2)

KRAFTWERK   '75

Progressive-rock group formed in Dusseldorf, Germany: Ralf Hutter (keyboards), Florian Schneider (woodwinds), Klaus Roeder (guitar) and Wolfgang Flur (drums).

2/8/75	5	22		©	1	**Autobahn**	[I]	$15	Vertigo 2003
9/20/75	160	5			2	**Ralf And Florian**	[I]	$15	Vertigo 2006
12/13/75+	140	8		©	3	**Radio-Activity**		$12	Capitol 11457
4/16/77	119	10		©	4	**Trans-Europe Express**		$12	Capitol 11603
5/13/78	130	9		©	5	**The Man-Machine**	[I]	$12	Capitol 11728
6/6/81	72	42		©	6	**Computer-World**	[I]	$10	Warner 3549
11/29/86	156	14		©	7	**Electric Cafe**		$10	Warner 25525

Airwaves (3)
Ananas Symphonie (Pineapple Symphony) (2)
Antenna (3)
Autobahn (1) *25*
Boing Boom Tschak (7)
Computer Love (6)
Computer-World (6)
Electric Cafe (7)

Elektrisches Roulette (Electric Roulette) (2)
Endless Endless (4)
Europe Endless (4)
Franz Schubert (4)
Geiger Counter (3)
Hall Of Mirrors (4)
Heimatklange (The Bells Of Home) (2)

Home Computer (6)
It's More Fun To Compute (6)
Kometenmelodie 1 & 2 (Comet Melody 1 & 2) (1)
Kristallo (Crystals) (2)
Man-Machine (5)
Metal On Metal (4)
Metropolis (5)
Mitternacht (Midnight) (1)

Model, The (5)
Morgenspaziergang (Morning Walk) (1)
Musique Non Stop (7)
Neon Lights (5)
News (3)
Numbers (6)
Ohm Sweet Ohm (3)
Pocket Calculator (6)

Radio Stars (3)
Radioactivity (3)
Radioland (3)
Robots, The (5)
Sex Object (7)
Showroom Dummies (4)
Spacelab (5)
Tanzmusik (Dance Music) (2)
Techno Pop (7)

Telephone Call (7)
Terminal Board (6)
Tongebirge (Mountain Of Sound) (2)
Trans-Europe Express (4) *67*
Transistor (3)
Uranium (3)
Voice Of Energy (3)

KRALL, Diana   '00

Born on 11/16/64 in Nanaimo, British Columbia, Canada. Jazz singer/pianist.

9/13/97+	109	8	●	©	1	**Love Scenes**	C:#29/2	$10	Impulse! 233
11/21/98	35[X]	1		©	2	**Have yourself a merry little Christmas**	[X-M]	$10	Impulse! 3111
6/26/99+	56	60	▲	©	3	**When I Look In Your Eyes**		$10	Verve 304

All Or Nothing At All (1)
Best Thing For You (3)
Christmas Time Is Here (2)
Devil May Care (3)
Do It Again (3)
East Of The Sun (And West Of The Moon) (3)
Garden In The Rain (1)

Gentle Rain (1)
Have Yourself A Merry Little Christmas (2)
How Deep Is The Ocean (How High Is The Sky) (1)
I Can't Give You Anything But Love (3)

I Don't Know Enough About You (1)
I Don't Stand A Ghost Of A Chance With You (1)
I Miss You So (1)
I'll String Along With You (3)
I've Got You Under My Skin (3)
Jingle Bells (2)

Let's Face The Music And Dance (3)
Let's Fall In Love (3)
Lost Mind (1)
My Love Is (1)
Peel Me A Grape (1)
Pick Yourself Up (3)
Popsicle Toes (3)

They Can't Take That Away From Me (1)
When I Look In Your Eyes (3)
You're Getting To Be A Habit With Me (1)

KRAMER, Billy J., With The Dakotas   '64

Born William Ashton on 8/19/43 in Bootle, Merseyside, England. Pop singer. The Dakotas consisted of Mike Maxfield and Robin McDonald (guitars), Ray Jones (bass) and Tony Mansfield (drums).

6/20/64	48	15		©		**Little Children**		$50	Imperial 12267

Bad To Me *9*
Da Doo Ron Ron
Dance With Me

Do You Want To Know A Secret
Great Balls Of Fire

I Know
I'll Keep You Satisfied *30*
It's Up To You

Little Children *7*
Pride
Tell Me Girl

They Remind Me Of You

KRAUSS, Alison   '95

Born on 7/23/71 in Champaign, Illinois. Country singer/bluegrass fiddler.

2/25/95	13	66	▲[2]	©	1	**Now That I've Found You: A Collection**	[K]	$10	Rounder 0325
4/12/97	45	14	●	©	2	**So Long So Wrong**		$10	Rounder 0365
						ALISON KRAUSS & UNION STATION			
8/21/99	60	8		©	3	**Forget About It**		$10	Rounder 610465

Baby, Now That I've Found You (1)
Blue Trail Of Sorrow (2)
Broadway (1)

Could You Lie (3)
Deeper Than Crying (2)
Dreaming My Dreams With You (3)

Empty Hearts (3)
Every Time You Say Goodbye (1)
Forget About It (3)

Find My Way Back To My Heart (2)
Ghost In This House (3)

Happiness (2)
I Can Let Go Now (2)

KRAUSS, Alison

I Don't Believe You've Met My Baby (1)
I Will (1)
I'll Remember You, Love, In My Prayers (2)
In the Palm of Your Hand (1)
It Doesn't Matter (2)

It Don't Matter Now (3)
It Wouldn't Have Made Any Difference (3)
Little Liza Jane (2)
Looking In The Eyes Of Love (2)
Maybe (3)

Never Got Off The Ground (3)
No Place To Hide (2)
Oh, Atlanta (1)
Pain Of A Troubled Life (2)
Road Is A Lover (2)
Sleep On (1)
So Long, So Wrong (2)

Stay (3)
Teardrops Will Kiss the Morning Dew (1)
That Kind Of Love (3)
There Is A Reason (2)
Tonight I'll Be Lonely Too (1)

When God Dips His Pen of Love In My Heart (1)
When You Say Nothing At All (1) *53*

KRAVITZ, Lenny   '00

Born on 5/26/64 in New York City. Pop-rock singer/songwriter/guitarist. Married to actress Lisa Bonet from 1989-91. Son of actress Roxie Roker (played "Helen Willis" on TV's *The Jeffersons*).

DEBUT	PEAK	WKS	RIAA	CD	#	Album Title	Catalog	$	Label & Number
11/25/89+	61	28	●	©	1	Let Love Rule		$10	Virgin 91290
4/20/91	39	40	▲	©	2	Mama Said	C:#17/2	$10	Virgin 91610
3/27/93	12	60	▲²	©	3	Are You Gonna Go My Way		$10	Virgin 86984
9/30/95	10	16	●	©	4	Circus		$10	Virgin 40696
5/30/98+	28	110	▲²	©	5	5	C:#3/19	$10	Virgin 45605
11/11/00	2¹	47↑	▲³	©	6	Greatest Hits	[G]	$10	Virgin 50316

Again (6) *4*
All I Ever Wanted (2)
Always On The Run (2,6)
American Woman (6) *49*
Are You Gonna Go My Way (3,6)
Be (1)
Believe (3,6) *60*
Beyond The 7th Sky (4)
Black Girl (3)
Black Velveteen (5,6)
Butterfly (2)

Can We Find A Reason (5)
Can't Get You Off My Mind (4,6) *62*
Circus (4)
Come On And Love Me (3)
Difference Is Why (2)
Does Anybody Out There Even Care (1)
Don't Go And Put A Bullet In Your Head (4)
Eleutheria (3)
Fear (1)

Fields Of Joy (2)
Flowers For Zoe (2)
Fly Away (5,6) *12*
Freedom Train (1)
God Is Love (4)
Heaven Help (3,6) *80*
I Belong To You (5,6) *71*
I Build This Garden For Us (1)
If You Can't Say No (5)
In My Life Today (4)
Is There Any Love In Your Heart (2)

It Ain't Over 'Til It's Over (2,6) *2*
It's Your Life (5)
Just Be A Woman (3)
Let Love Rule (1,6) *89*
Little Girl's Eyes (5)
Live (5)
Magdalene (4)
More Than Anything In This World (2)
Mr. Cab Driver (1,6)
My Love (3)

My Precious Love (1)
Resurrection, The (4)
Rock And Roll Is Dead (4,6) *75*
Rosemary (1)
Sister (3)
Sittin' On Top Of The World (1)
Stand By My Woman (2,6) *76*
Stop Draggin' Around (2)
Straight Cold Player (5)
Sugar (3)
Super Soul Fighter (5)

Take Time (5)
Thin Ice (4)
Thinking Of You (5)
Tunnel Vision (4)
What Goes Around Comes Around (2)
What The .... Are We Saying? (2)
When The Morning Turns To Night (2)
You're My Flavor (5)

KRAYZIE BONE   '99

Born Anthony Henderson in Cleveland. Male rapper. Member of **Bone Thugs-N-Harmony**.

DEBUT	PEAK	WKS	RIAA	CD	#	Album Title	$	Label & Number
4/24/99	4	13	▲	©	1	Thug Mentality 1999	$15	Mo Thugs 1671 [2]

Armageddon
Drama
Dummy Man
Heated Heavy
I Still Believe
Knieght Rieduz (Here We Come)

Murda Mo
Paper
Payback Iz A Bitch
Pimpz, Thugz, Hustlaz & Gangstaz
Power
(Relay) Thugline

Revolution
Shoot The Club Up
Silence
Silent Warrior
Smoke & Burn
Smokin' Budda
Street People

That's The Way
Theze Dayz
Thug Alwayz
Thug Mentality
Thugz All Ova Da World
Try Me
War Iz On

We Starvin'
When I Die
Where My Thugz At
Won't Ez Up Tonight
World War

KRIS KROSS   '92

Rap duo from Atlanta: Chris "Mack Daddy" Kelly (born on 5/1/78) and Chris "Daddy Mack" Smith (born on 1/10/79). Appeared in the movie *Who's The Man?*

DEBUT	PEAK	WKS	RIAA	CD	#	Album Title	$	Label & Number
4/18/92	❶²	65	▲⁴	©	1	Totally Krossed Out	$10	Ruffhouse 48710
8/21/93	13	25	▲	©	2	Da Bomb	$10	Ruffhouse 57278
1/27/96	15	22	●	©	3	Young, Rich & Dangerous	$10	Ruffhouse 67441

Alright (2) *19*
Can't Stop The Bum Rush (1)
D.J. Nabs Break (2)
Da Bomb (2)
Da Streets Ain't Right (3)

Freak Da Funk (2)
Hey Sexy (3)
I Missed The Bus (1) *63*
I'm Real (2) *84*
It Don't Stop (2)
It's A Shame (1)

Jump (1) *1*
Lil' Boys In Da Hood (1)
Live And Die For Hip Hop (3) *72*
Lot 2 Live 4 (2)
Mackin' Ain't Easy (3)

Money, Power And Fame (Three Thangs Thats Necessities) (3)
Party (1)
Real Bad Dream (1)
Some Cut Up (3)

Sound Of My Hood (2)
Take Um Out (2)
2 Da Beat Ch'yall (2)
Tonite's Tha Night (3) *12*
Warm It Up (1) *13*
Way Of Rhyme (1)

We're In Da House (1)
You Can't Get With This (1)
Young, Rich And Dangerous (3)

★252★ KRISTOFFERSON, Kris   '71

Born on 6/22/36 in Brownsville, Texas. Country singer/songwriter/actor. Starred in several movies. Married to **Rita Coolidge** from 1973-80.

1)The Silver Tongued Devil And I 2)Full Moon 3)Jesus Was A Capricorn

DEBUT	PEAK	WKS	RIAA	CD	#	Album Title	Sym	$	Label & Number
7/31/71	21	28	●	©	1	The Silver Tongued Devil And I		$15	Monument 30679
9/11/71	43	22	●	©	2	Me And Bobby McGee		$15	Monument 30817
3/18/72	41	16		©	3	Border Lord		$15	Monument 31302
11/25/72+	31	54	●	©	4	Jesus Was A Capricorn		$15	Monument 31909
9/22/73	26	33	●		5	Full Moon		$15	A&M 4403
						KRIS KRISTOFFERSON & RITA COOLIDGE			
5/25/74	78	14		©	6	Spooky Lady's Sideshow		$15	Monument 32914
12/21/74+	103	12		©	7	Breakaway		$15	Monument 33278
						KRIS KRISTOFFERSON & RITA COOLIDGE			
12/6/75+	105	11		©	8	Who's To Bless...And Who's To Blame		$15	Monument 33379
8/21/76	180	2		©	9	Surreal Thing		$15	Monument 34254
5/7/77	45	18	●	©	10	Songs Of Kristofferson	[K]	$15	Monument 34687
4/1/78	86	7		©	11	Easter Island		$15	Monument 35310
2/3/79	106	9			12	Natural Act		$12	A&M 4690
						KRIS KRISTOFFERSON & RITA COOLIDGE			
1/15/83	109	14		©	13	Kris, Willie, Dolly & Brenda...the winning hand		$15	Monument 38389 [2]
						KRIS KRISTOFFERSON, WILLIE NELSON, DOLLY PARTON & BRENDA LEE			
11/10/84	152	5			14	Music from SongWriter	[S]	$12	Columbia 39531
						WILLIE NELSON & KRIS KRISTOFFERSON			
6/1/85	92	35	▲	©	15	Highwayman		$10	Columbia 40056
3/17/90	79	13		©	16	Highwayman 2		$10	Columbia 45240
						WILLIE NELSON/JOHNNY CASH/WAYLON JENNINGS/KRIS KRISTOFFERSON (above 2)			

After The Fact (5)
Against The Wind (15)
American Remains (16)
Angels Love Bad Men (16)
Anthem '84 (16)
Back In My Baby's Arms (12)
Bad Love Story (9)

Bandits Of Beverly Hills (13)
Best Of All Possible Worlds (2)
Big River (15)
Bigger The Fool (The Harder The Fall) (11,13)
Billy Dee (1)
Blame It On The Stones (2)

Blue As I Do (12)
Border Lord (3)
Born And Raised In Black And White (16)
Born To Love Me (13)
Breakdown (A Long Way From Home) (1)

Bring On The Sunshine (13)
Broken Freedom Song (6)
Burden Of Freedom (3)
Casey's Last Ride (2,13)
Committed To Parkview (15)
Crippled Crow (7)
Crossing The Border (14)

Dakota (The Dancing Bear) (7)
Darby's Castle (2)
Deportee (Plane Wreck At Los Gatos) (15)
Desperados Waiting For A Train (15)
Don't Cuss The Fiddle (8)

Down To Her Socks (14)
Duvalier's Dream (2)
Easter Island (11)
Easy, Come On (8)
Eddie The Eunuch (9)
Enough For You (4)
Epitaph (Black And Blue) (1)

KRISTOFFERSON, Kris — Cont'd

Everything's Beautiful (In It's Own Way) (13)
Eye Of The Storm (14)
Fighter, The (11)
Final Attraction (14)
For The Good Times (2,10)
Forever In Your Love (11)
From The Bottle To The Bottom (5)
Gettin' By, High And Strange (3)
Give It Time To Be Tender (4)
Golden Idol (9)
Good Christian Soldier (1)
Happy Happy Birthday Baby (13)
Hard To Be Friends (5)
Help Me (4)
Help Me Make It Through The Night (2,10,13)
Here Comes That Rainbow Again (13)
Highwayman (15)
Hoola Hoop (12)
How Do You Feel (About Foolin' Around) (11,14)
I Fought The Law (12)

I Got A Life Of My Own (9,10)
I Heard The Bluebirds Sing (5)
I May Smoke Too Much (6)
I Never Cared For You (13)
I Never Had It So Good (5)
I'd Rather Be Sorry (7)
I'm Down (But I Keep Falling) (5)
I've Got To Have You (7)
If It's All The Same To You (8)
If You Don't Like Hank Williams (9)
It Sure Was (Love) (4)
It's All Over (All Over Again) (5)
It's Never Gonna Be The Same Again (9)
Jesse Younger (4)
Jesus Was A Capricorn (9) **91**
Jim, I Wore A Tie Today (15)
Jody And The Kid (1)
Josie (3) **63**
Just The Other Side Of Nowhere (2)
Killing Time (9)
King Of A Lonely Castle (13)
Kiss The World Goodbye (9)

Last Cowboy Song (15)
Late Again (Gettin' Over You) (6)
Law Is For Protection Of The People (2)
Lay Me Down (And Love The World Away) (11)
Lights Of Magdala (6)
Little Girl Lost (3)
Little Things (13)
Living Legend (11,16)
Love Don't Live Here Anymore (12)
Lover Please (7)
Loving Arms (5) **86**
Loving Her Was Easier (Than Anything I'll Ever Do Again) (1,10,12) **26**
Me And Bobby McGee (2,10)
Nobody Wins (4)
Not Everyone Knows (12)
Number One (12)
One For The Money (6)
Out Of Mind, Out Of Sight (4)
Part Of Your Life (5)
Pilgrim - Chapter 33 (1,10)

Ping Pong (13)
Please Don't Tell Me How The Story Ends (12)
Prisoner, The (9)
Put It Off Until Tomorrow (13)
Rain (7)
Rescue Mission (6)
Risky Bizness (11)
Rock And Roll Time (6)
Rocket To Stardom (8)
Sabre And The Rose (11)
Same Old Song (4)
Shandy (The Perfect Disguise) (6)
Silver Mantis (12)
Silver Stallion (16)
Silver (The Hunger) (8)
Silver Tongued Devil And I (1,10)
Slow Down (7)
Smile At Me Again (6)
Smokey Put The Sweat On Me (3)
Somebody Nobody Knows (3)
Someone Loves You Honey (13)

Song I'd Like To Sing (5) **49**
Songs That Make A Difference (16)
Spooky Lady's Revenge (11)
Stagger Mountain Tragedy (3)
Stairway To The Bottom (6)
Stallion (8)
Star-Spangled Bummer (Whores Die Hard) (6)
Stranger (8,10)
Stranger I Love (9)
Sugar Man (4)
Sunday Mornin' Comin' Down (2,10)
Sweet Susannah (7)
Take Time To Love (5)
Taker, The (1)
Tennessee Blues (5)
Texas (16)
Things I Might Have Been (7)
To Beat The Devil (2)
To Make A Long Story Short, She's Gone (13)
Twentieth Century Is Almost Over (15)
Two Stories Wide (16)

Under The Gun (14)
We Must Have Been Out Of Our Minds (7)
We're All In Your Corner (16)
Welfare Line (15)
What Do You Think About Lovin' (13)
What'cha Gonna Do (7)
When I Loved Her (1)
When She's Wrong (3)
Who's To Bless And Who's To Blame (8,10)
Why Me (4,10) **16**
Year 2000 Minus 25 (8)
You Left Me A Long, Long Time Ago (13)
You Show Me Yours (And I'll Show You Mine) (9,10)
You'll Always Have Someone (13)
You're Gonna Love Yourself (In The Morning) (12,13)

KROKUS '83

Hard-rock group from Zurich, Switzerland: Marc Storace (vocals), Fernando Von Arb and Tommy Kiefer (guitars), Chris Von Rohr (bass) and Freddy Steady (drums). Kiefer was replaced by Mark Kohler in late 1981. Steady was replaced by Steve Pace in late 1982. Pace was replaced by Jeff Klaven in 1984. Von Rohr left in 1984.

DEBUT	PEAK	WKS	RIAA	CD	ARTIST — Album Title	$	Label & Number
4/4/81	103	12			1 Hardware	$10	Ariola 1508
4/10/82	53	20			2 One Vice At A Time	$10	Arista 9591
4/16/83	25	41	●	©	3 Headhunter	$10	Arista 9623
9/8/84	31	27	●	©	5 The Blitz	$10	Arista 8243
5/3/86	45	17		©	5 Change Of Address	$10	Arista 8402
11/22/86	97	12		©	6 Alive And Screamin'	[L] $10	Arista 8445
5/7/88	87	11		©	7 Heart Attack	$10	MCA 42087

American Woman (2)
Axx Attack (7)
Bad, Bad Girl (7)
Bad Boys Rag Dolls (2)
Ballroom Blitz (4)
Bedside Radio (6)
Boys Nite Out (4)
Burning Bones (1)
Burning Up The Night (5)
Celebration (1)

Down The Drain (2)
Easy Rocker (1)
Eat The Rich (3,6)
Everybody Rocks (4)
Flyin' High (7)
Hard Luck Hero (5)
Headhunter (3,6)
Hot Shot City (5,6)
Hot Stuff (6)
I'm On The Run (2)

Lay Me Down (6)
Let It Go (7)
Let This Love Begin (5)
Long Stick Goes Boom (2,6)
Long Way From Home (5)
Mad Racket (1)
Midnite Maniac (4,6) **71**
Mr. Sixty Nine (1)
Night Wolf (3)
Now (All Through The Night) (5)

Our Love (4)
Out Of Control (4)
Out To Lunch (4)
Playin' The Outlaw (5)
Ready To Burn (3)
Ready To Rock (4)
Rock City (1)
Rock N' Roll (2)
Rock 'N' Roll Tonight (7)
Rock The Nation (4)

Russian Winter (3)
Save Me (2)
Say Goodbye (5)
School's Out (5) **67**
Screaming In The Night (3,6)
She's Got Everything (1)
Shoot Down The Night (7)
Smelly Nelly (1)
Speed Up (7)
Stand And Be Counted (3)

Stayed Awake All Night (3,6)
To The Top (2)
White Din (3)
Wild Love (7)
Winning Man (1,7)
World On Fire (5)

KRS-ONE '97

Born Lawrence "Kris" Parker in 1966 in New York City. Male rapper. Co-founder of **Boogie Down Productions**.

DEBUT	PEAK	WKS	RIAA	CD	ARTIST — Album Title	$	Label & Number
10/16/93	37	8		©	1 Return Of The Boom Bap	$10	Jive 41517
10/28/95	19	6		©	2 KRS One	$10	Jive 41570
6/7/97	3	13	●	©	3 I Got Next	$10	Jive 41601
9/9/00	200	1		©	4 A Retrospective	[G] $10	Jive 41718
5/12/01	43	6		©	5 The Sneak Attack	$10	Front Page 8242

Ah-Yeah (2)
Attendance (1)
Black Cop (1,4)
Blowe (3)
Bridge Is Over (4)
Brown Skin Woman (1)
Build Ya Skillz (2)
Can't Stop, Won't Stop (3)
Come To Da Party (3)
Criminal Minded (4)
De Automatic (1)
Essays On BDP-ism (4)
False Pride (5)

Free Mumia (2)
Friend, A (3)
Get Your Self Up (5)
Ghetto Lifestyles (5)
Health, Wealth, Self (2)
Heartbeat (3)
Higher Level (1)
H.I.P.H.O.P. (3)
Hiphop Knowledge (5)
Hold (3)
Hot (5)
Hush (5)
I Can't Wake Up (1)

I Got Next (medley) (3)
I Will Make It (5)
I'm Still #1 (4)
Jack Of Spades (4)
Jimmy (4)
Just To Prove A Point (3)
KRS-ONE Attacks (1)
Krush Them (5)
Lessin, The (5)
Love's Gonna Get'cha (Material Love) (4)
MC, The (3)
MC's Act Like They Don't Know (2,4) **57**

Mad Crew (1)
Mind, The (5)
Mortal Thought (1)
My Philosophy (4)
Neva Hadda Gun (medley) (3)
Out For Fame (2)
Over Ya Head (3)
"P" Is Still Free (1)
Rappaz R. N. Dainja (2)
Raptism, The (5)
Real Hip-Hop - Part II (3)
R.E.A.L.I.T.Y. (2)

Represent The Real Hip Hop (2)
Return Of The Boom Bap (1)
Shutupayouface (5)
Slap Them Up (5)
Sneak Attack (5)
Sound Of Da Police (1,4) **89**
South Bronx (1)
Squash All Beef (2)
Step Into A World (Rapture's Delight) (3,4) **70**
Stop Frontin' (1)
Truth, The (2)
Uh Oh (1)

Wannabemceez (2)
What Kinda World (5)
Why (5)
Why Is That? (4)
You Must Learn (4)

K'S CHOICE '97

Rock group from Belgium: Sarah Bettens (vocals), her brother Gert Bettens (vocals, keyboards), Jan Van Sichem (guitar) and Bart Van Der Zeeuw (drums).

DEBUT	PEAK	WKS	RIAA	CD	ARTIST — Album Title	$	Label & Number
5/24/97	121	16		©	Paradise In Me	$10	550 Music 67720

Dad
Iron Flower
Mr. Freeze

My Record Company
Not An Addict
Old Woman

Only Dreaming
Paradise In Me
Something's Wrong

Song For Catherine
Sound That Only You Can Hear
To This Day

Wait
White Kite Fauna

K7 '94

Born Louis Sharpe in New York City. Male rapper.

DEBUT	PEAK	WKS	RIAA	CD	ARTIST — Album Title	$	Label & Number
1/29/94	96	33	●	©	Swing Batta Swing	$10	Tommy Boy 1071

Beep Me
Body Rock *flip*

Come Baby Come *18*
Hang On In There Baby

Hi De Ho
Hotel Motel

I'll Make You Feel Good
Let's Bang

Little Help From My Friends
Move It Like This *54*

Zunga Zeng *61*

K-SOLO '92

Born Kevin Madison in Central Islip, New York. Male rapper. K-Solo stands for Kevin Self Organization Left Others.

DEBUT	PEAK	WKS	RIAA	CD	ARTIST — Album Title	$	Label & Number
6/20/92	135	2			Times Up	$10	Atlantic 82388

Baby Doesn't Look Like Me
Formula (House Party)
Household Maid

I Can't Hold It Back
King Of The Mountain
Letterman

Long Live The Fugitive
Premonition Of A Black Man
Prisoner

Rock Bottom
Sneak Tip
Who's Killin' Who?

KUBAN, Bob, And The In-Men · '66
Pop-rock group from St. Louis: Bob Kuban (drums), Walter Scott (vocals), Ray Schulte (guitar), Greg Hoeltzel (keyboards), Pat Hixton (trumpet), Harry Simon (sax), Skip Weisser (trombone) and Mike Krenski (bass). Scott disappeared on 12/27/83; his ex-wife and her husband were charged with Scott's murder after his body was found three years later with a gunshot wound to the back.

4/23/66	129	5			**Look Out For The Cheater**			$50	Musicland 3500

All I Want
Batman Theme
Cheater, The *12*

Get Out
Harlem Shuffle
In The Midnight Hour

Stop Her On Sight (S.O.S.)
These Boots Were Made For
Walking

Try Me Baby
Virginia Wolfe, Theme From

You've Got Your Troubles (I've
Got Mine)

KULA SHAKER · '97
Rock group from London: Crispian Mills (vocals, guitar), Jay Darlington (keyboards), Alonza Bevan (bass) and Paul Winter-Hart (drums). Mills is the son of actress/singer Hayley Mills.

2/1/97	200	1	©		**K**			$10	Columbia 67822

Govinda
Grateful When You're Dead
(medley)

Hey Dude
Hollow Man (Parts 1 & 2)
Into The Deep

Jerry Was There (medley)
Knight On The Town
Magic Theatre

Sleeping Jiva
Smart Dogs
Start All Over

Tattva
Temple Of Everlasting Light
303

KUMBIA KINGS FEATURING A.B. QUINTANILLA · '01
Latin group: Jason Cano, Roy Ramirez and Andrew Maes (vocals), Jorge Pena (percussion), Alex Ramirez and Cruz Martinez (keyboards), A.B. Quintanilla (bass) and Robert Del Moral (drums). Quintanilla is the brother of **Selena**.

3/17/01	92	14	©		**Shhh!**	[F]		$10	EMI Latin 29745

A.B. QUINTANILLA Y LOS KUMBIA KINGS

Boom Boom
Desde Que No Estas Aqui
Dime Porque

I Need Your Love
I Never Knew
In Da Zone

Me Enamore
Me Estoy Muriendo
Say It (A Million Times)

Sshh
Te Di
Think'n About U

Why Did You

KURUPT · '98
Born Ricardo Brown in Los Angeles. Male rapper. Member of **Tha Dogg Pound**.

10/24/98	8	6	©	1	**Kuruption!**			$15	A&M 540963 [2]
12/4/99	31	15	©	2	**Tha Streetz Iz A Mutha**			$10	Antra 2001

Another Day (1)
Ask Yourself A Question (1)
C-Walk (1)
Can't Let That Slide (1)
Fresh (1)
Game (1)
Gimmewhutchagot (1)

Girls All Pause (2)
Ho's A Housewife (1,2)
I Ain't Sh%t Without My
Homeboyz (2)
I Call Shots (2)
I Wanna... (1)
If You See Me (1)

It Ain't About You (2)
It's A Set Up (1)
It's Time (1)
Life, The (1)
Light Shit Up (1)
Live On The Mic (1)
Loose Cannons (2)

Make Some Noize (1)
Neva Gonna Give It Up (2)
No Feelings (1)
Play My Cards (1)
Put That On Something (1)
Represent Dat G.C. (1)
Step Up (1)

Streetz Iz A Mutha (2)
Tequilla (2)
That's Gangsta (1)
This One's For U (1)
Trylogy (2)
We Can Freak It (1)
Welcome Home (2)

Who Do U Be (1)
Who Ride Wit Us (2)
Ya Can't Trust Nobody (2)
Your Gyrl Friend (2)

KUT KLOSE · '95
Female R&B vocal trio from Atlanta: Tabitha Duncan, Athena Cage and LaVonn Battle.

4/1/95	66	20	©		**Surrender**			$10	Elektra 61668

Do Me
Don't Change

Get Up On It
Giving You My Love Again

I Like *34*
Keep On

Lay My Body Down
Like You've Never Been Done

Lovely Thang
Sexual Baby

Surrender

KWAMÉ AND A NEW BEGINNING · '89
Born Kwamé Holland in Queens, New York. Male rapper.

5/27/89	114	18	©	1	**The Boy Genius Featuring A New Beginning**			$10	Atlantic 81941
6/16/90	113	15	©	2	**"A Day In The Life" A Pokadelick Adventure**			$10	Atlantic 82100

Boy Genius (1)
Da' Man (2)
Day In The Life (2)
Doin' Ma Thang (2)

Hai (2)
Itz Oh Kay (2)
Keep On Doin' (What You're
Doin' Baby) (1)

Man We All Know And Love (1)
Mic Is Mine (1)
Oneovdabigboiz (2)
Ownlee Eue (2)

Pushthepanicbutton!!! (1)
Rhythm, The (1)
Skinee Muva (2)
Sweet Thing (1)

Therez A Partee Goinz On (2)
U Gotz 2 Get Down! (1)
Whoz Dat Guy (2)
Yes Yes Yall (2)

KWELI, Talib, & Hi-Tek · '00
Duo from Brooklyn, New York: rapper Talib Kweli (of **Black Star**) with DJ **Hi-Tek**.

11/4/00	17	21	©	1	**Reflection Eternal**			$10	Rawkus 26143
5/26/01	66	10	©	2	**Hi-Teknology**			$10	Rawkus 50171

HI-TEK

Africa Dream (1)
All I Need Is You (2)
Big Del From Da Natti (1)
Blast, The (1)
Breakin' Bread (2)
Down For The Count (1)

Eternalists (1)
Experience Dedication (1)
For Women (1)
Get Back Pt. II (2)
Get Ta Steppin' (1)
Ghetto Afterlife (1)

Good Mourning (1)
Hi-Teknology (2)
Illest It Gets (2)
L.T.A.H. (2)
Love Language (1)
Love Speakeasy (1)

Memories Live (1)
Move Somethin' (1)
Name Of The Game (1)
On My Way (1)
Round & Round (2)
Scratch Rappin (2)

Some Kind Of Wonderful (1)
Soul Rebels (1)
Suddenly (2)
Sun God (2)
Theme From Hi-Tek (2)
This Means You (1)

Tony Guitar Watson (2)
Too Late (1)
Touch You (1)
Where I'm From (2)

KWICK · '80
R&B vocal group from Memphis: Terry Bartlett, Bertram Brown, William Sumlin and Vince Williams.

6/7/80	197	2			**Kwick**			$12	EMI America 17025

Can't Help Myself

Here I Go Again (Another
Weekend)

I Want To Dance With You
Let This Moment Be Forever

Serious Business
Tonight Is The Night

We Ought To Be Dancing
Why Don't We Love Each Other

K.W.S. · '92
Dance trio from Nottingham, England: Chris King, Winnie Williams and Meg St. Joseph.

10/17/92	143	5	©		**Please Don't Go (The Album)**			$10	Next Plateau 828368

Different Man
Hold Back The Night

I Guess I'll Try It Again
Keep It Comin' Love

Please Don't Go *6*
Reach For The Sky

Rock Your Baby
This Time

Where Will You Go When The
Party's Over

KYPER · '90
Born Randall Kyper in Baton Rouge, Louisiana. Male rapper.

8/4/90	82	12	©		**Tic Tac Toe**			$10	Atlantic 82116

Conceited
Dangerous

Do It
I Wanna Freak

Let's Rock This Party
Satisfaction

Throw Down
Tic-Tac-Toe *14*

What Gets Your Body Hyped
(XTC)

What Is This World Comin' To
Work It

L

★204★ LaBELLE, Patti   '86

Born Patricia Holt on 5/24/44 in Philadelphia. Female R&B singer. The LaBelle trio also consisted of **Nona Hendryx** and **Sarah Dash**. In 1977, group disbanded and Patti recorded solo.

1)*Winner In You* 2)*Nightbirds* 3)*Flame*

LaBELLE:

12/21/74+	7	28	●	©	1 Nightbirds	$15	Epic 33075
9/20/75	44	13			2 Phoenix	$15	Epic 33579
9/25/76	94	10		©	3 Chameleon	$15	Epic 34189

PATTI LaBELLE:

9/24/77	62	16		©	4 Patti LaBelle	$12	Epic 34847
6/24/78	129	7			5 Tasty	$12	Epic 35335
3/31/79	145	16			6 It's Alright With Me	$12	Epic 35772
4/12/80	114	13			7 Released	$12	Epic 36381
10/3/81	156	4		©	8 The Spirit's In It	$10	Philadelphia Int'l. 37380
1/7/84	40	35	●	©	9 I'm In Love Again	$10	Philadelphia Int'l. 38539
8/10/85	72	29		©	10 Patti	$10	Philadelphia Int'l. 40020
5/24/86	❶¹	30	▲	©	11 Winner In You	$10	MCA 5737
7/22/89	86	26		©	12 Be Yourself	$10	MCA 6292
12/22/90+	18ˣ	5		©	13 This Christmas .... [X]	$10	MCA 10113
10/19/91+	71	36		©	14 Burnin'	$10	MCA 10439
11/28/92	135	3		©	15 Live! .... [L]	$10	MCA 10691

recorded at the Apollo Theatre in New York City

6/25/94	48	22	●	©	16 Gems	$10	MCA 10870
7/12/97	39	21	●	©	17 Flame	$10	MCA 11642
10/10/98	182	1		©	18 Live! One Night Only .... [L]	$15	MCA 11814 [2]

recorded at the Hammerstein Ballroom in New York City

| 11/11/00 | 63 | 5 | | © | 19 When A Woman Loves .... | $10 | MCA 112267 |

Action Time (2)
Addicted To You (17)
Ain't That Enough (7)
All Girl Band (1)
All Right Now (15)
All This Love (16)
Are You Lonely? (1)
Be Yourself (12)
Beat My Heart Like A Drum (11)
Bells, The (18)
Black Holes In The Sky (2)
Boats Against The Current (8)
Body Language (9)
Born In A Manger (13)
Burnin' (The Fire Is Still) Burnin' For You (14)
Call Me Gone (19)
Can't Bring Me Down (12)
Chameleon (3)
Chances Go Round (2)
Change Is Gonna Come (18)
Come And Dance With Me (7)
Come As You Are (16)
Come Into My Life (3)
Come What May (6)
Cosmic Dancer (2)
Country Christmas (13)
Crazy Love (4)
Dan Swit Me (4)
Deliver The Funk (6)
Do I Stand A Chance (4)
Does He Love You (17)
Don't Block The Blessings (17)
Don't Bring Me Down (1)
Don't Let Go (5)
Don't Make Me Over (18)
Don't Make Your Angel Cry (7)

Eyes In The Back Of My Head (5)
Family (8)
Far As We Felt Like Goin' (2)
Feels Like Another One (14,15)
Finally We're Back Together Again (11)
Find The Love (7)
Flame (17,18)
Funky Music (4)
Get Ready (Lookin' For Loving) (7)
Get You Somebody New (3)
Give It Up (The Dawning Of Rejection) (7)
Going Down Makes Me Shiver (3)
Good Intentions (2)
Got To Be Real (18)
Gypsy Moths (3)
He Doesn't Love You (18)
Here You Come Again (8)
Hold On (18)
I Believe (18)
I Believe I Can Fly (18)
I Can Fly (12)
I Can't Complain (12)
I Can't Forget (10)
I Can't Tell My Heart What To Do (16)
I Don't Do Duets (14)
I Don't Go Shopping (7)
I Don't Like Goodbyes (medley) (15)
I Fell In Love Without Warning (8)
I Got It Like That (12)
I Hear Your Voice (14)

I Like The Way It Feels (17)
I Never Stopped Loving You (16)
I See Home (5)
I Think About You (4)
I'll Never, Never Give Up (9)
I'll Still Love You More (19)
I'm Christmasing With You (13)
I'm In Love (16)
I'm In Love Again (9)
I'm Scared Of You (12)
If By Chance (17)
If Everyday Could Be Like Christmas (13)
If I Didn't Have You (16)
If I Was A River (19)
If Only You Knew (9,15,18) *46*
If You Asked Me To (12,18) *79*
If You Don't Know Me By Now (10)
If You Love Me (18)
Is It Still Good To You (18)
Isn't It A Shame (3)
It Took A Long Time (1)
It's Alright With Me (6)
Joy To Have Your Love (4)
Kiss Away The Pain (11)
Kitchen, The (19)
Lady Marmalade (1,15,18) *1*
Let Me Be There For You (17)
Let Me Be Your Lady (17)
Little Girls (5)
Living Double (10)
Look To The Rainbow (10)
Lord's Side (18)
Love And Learn (6)
Love Bankrupt (9)

Love 89 (12)
Love Has Finally Come (7)
Love Is Just A Touch Away (6)
Love Is Just A Whisper Away (17)
Love Lives (8)
Love, Need And Want You (9)
Love Never Dies (14)
Love Symphony (10)
Love Will Lead You Back (19)
Lover Man (Oh, Where Can You Be?) (9)
Make Tonight Beautiful (19)
Man In A Trenchcoat (Voodoo) (3)
Messin' With My Mind (2)
Monkey See - Monkey Do (5)
Most Likely You Go Your Way (And I'll Go Mine) (4)
Music Is My Way Of Life (6)
My Best Was Good Enough (6)
Need A Little Faith (12)
New Attitude (15,18)
Nightbird (1)
Nothing Could Be Better (13)
O Holy Night (13)
Oh, People (11) *29*
On My Own (11,18) *1*
Our World (16)
Over The Rainbow (8,15)
Patti Talk (18)
Phoenix (The Amazing Flight Of A Lone Star) (2)
Quiet Time (5)
Reason For The Season (13)
Release (7)
Release Yourself (14,15)

Right Kinda Lover (16) *61*
Rocking Pneumonia And The Boogie Woogie Flu (8)
Save The Last Dance For Me (5)
Shoe Was On The Other Foot (17)
Shoot Him On Sight (8)
Shy (10)
Since I Don't Have You (4)
Sleep With Me Tonight (11)
Slow Burn (2)
Somebody Loves You Baby (You Know Who It Is) (14,15)
Somebody Somewhere (1)
Someone Like You (17)
Something Special (Is Gonna Happen Tonight) (11)
Somewhere Over The Rainbow (18)
Space Children (1)
Sparkle (18)
Spirit's In It (8)
Stay In My Corner (16)
Still In Love (12)
Take The Night Off (2)
Teach Me Tonight (Me Gusta Tu Baile) (5)
Tell Me Where It Hurts (19)
Temptation (4)
There's A Winner In You (11)
This Christmas (13)
This Word Is All (16)
Time Will (19)
Time Will Tell (16)
Too Good To Be Through (16)
Too Many Tears, Too Many Times (7)

'Twas Love (13)
Twisted (11)
Up There With You (15)
We're Not Makin' Love Anymore (14)
What Are You Doing New Year's Eve (13)
What Can I Do For You? (1) *48*
What Can I Do For You (10)
What'cha Doing To Me (6)
When A Woman Loves (19)
When Am I Gonna Find True Love (9)
When You Love Somebody (I'm Saving My Love For You) (14)
When You Talk About Love (17,18) *56*
When You've Been Blessed (Feels Like Heaven) (14,15)
Where I Wanna Be (10)
Who's Watching The Watcher? (3)
Why Do We Hurt Each Other (19)
Wind Beneath My Wings (15)
Wouldn't It Be Beautiful (13)
Yo Mister (12)
You And Me (6)
You Are My Friend (4,15,18)
You Are My Solid Ground (17)
You Can't Judge A Book By The Cover (4)
You Make It So Hard (To Say No) (5)
You Saved My Life (17)
You Turn Me On (1)
You're Mine Tonight (11)

LABOE, Art — see VARIOUS ARTIST COMPILATIONS

L.A. BOPPERS   '80

R&B group from Los Angeles: Vance Tennort (vocals, drums), Kenny Styles (guitar), Stan Martin (trumpet) and Ed Reddick (bass).

| 3/15/80 | 85 | 11 | | | L.A. Boppers .... | $12 | Mercury 3816 |

Are We Wrong
Be-Bop Dancin'
Funk It Out
I Can't Stay
Is This The Best (Bop-Doo-Wah)
Life Is What You Make It
Saturday
Watching Life
You Did It Good

LA BOUCHE   '96

Male/female dance duo: Melanie Thornton and Lane McCray. La Bouche is French for "mouth."

| 2/3/96 | 28 | 55 | ▲ | © | 1 Sweet Dreams .... | $10 | RCA 66759 |
| 7/11/98 | 194 | 1 | | © | 2 S.O.S. .... | $10 | RCA 67439 |

Be My Lover (1) *6*
Body & Soul (2)
Bolingo (2)
Do You Still Need Me (1)
Don't Let The Rain (2)

Fallin' In Love (1)
Heat Is On (1)
I Can't Stand The Rain (2)
I Love To Love (1)
I'll Be There (1)

Moment Of Love (2)
Nice 'N' Slow (1)
On A Night Like This (2)
Poetry In Motion (1)
SOS (2)

Say It With Love (2)
Say You'll Be Mine (2)
Shoo Bee Do Bee Do (I Like That Way) (1)
Sweet Dreams (1) *13*

Sweet Little Persuader (2)
Tonight Is The Night (1)
Unexpected Lovers (2)
Whenever You Want (2)
Where Do You Go (1)

You Won't Forget Me (2) *48*

LACE   '88
R&B vocal trio: Lisa Frazier, Vivian Ross and Kathy Merrick.

| 1/23/88 | 187 | 5 | | © | **Shades Of Lace** .... | | | $10 | Wing 833451 |

Don't Get So Emotional   How Could It Be   My Love Is Deep   Still In Love
Falling In Love   Keep It Comin'   Since You Came Over Me   Triple Threat

LADD, Cheryl   '78
Born Cheryl Stoppelmoor on 7/2/51 in Huron, South Dakota. Singer/actress. Starred in several movies and TV shows. Married to David Ladd (son of actor Alan Ladd) from 1973-79. Married producer/songwriter Brian Russell (Brian & Brenda) in 1981.

| 8/12/78 | 129 | 11 | | 1 | **Cheryl Ladd** .... | | | $12 | Capitol 11808 |
| 4/28/79 | 179 | 3 | | 2 | **Dance Forever** .... | | | $12 | Capitol 11927 |

Better Days (2)   I Know I'll Never Love This Way Missing You (2)   Skinnydippin' (1)   Thunder In The Distance (2)   You Turn Me Around (1)
Dance Forever (2)   Again (1) On The Run (2)   Still Awake (2)   Walking In The Rain (1)   You're The Only One I Ever
Good Good Lovin' (1)   I'll Come Runnin' (1) Rock And Roll Slave (2) Teach Me Tonight (2)   Whatever Would I Do Without   Needed (2)
Here Is A Song (1)   Lady Gray (1) Rose Nobody Knows (1) **Think It Over** (1) *34*   You (2)

L.A. DREAM TEAM   '86
Rap group led by Rudy Pardee (from Cleveland) and Chris Wilson (from Los Angeles).

| 9/13/86 | 138 | 7 | | 1 | **Kings Of The West Coast** .... | | | $10 | MCA 5779 |
| 11/14/87 | 162 | 4 | | 2 | **Bad To The Bone** .... | | | $10 | MCA 42042 |

And The Orchestra Plays (1) Don't Push Me (2)   For Lisa For Love (2)   Kings Of The West Coast (1) Rudy And Snake (2)   Uhh! Song (2)
Calling On The Dream Team Dream Team Is In The House Hollywood Boulevard (1) Nursery Rhymes (1) She Only Rock And Rolls (2) What's A Skeezer? (2)
(1) (1)   Just Chill'n (2)   Rockberry Jam (1) Stop To Start (2)   You're Just Too Young (1)

LADY OF RAGE, The   '97
Born Robin Allen in Farmville, Virginia. Female rapper.

| 7/12/97 | 32 | 6 | | © | **Necessary Roughness** .... | | | $10 | Death Row 90109 |

Big Bad Lady   Get With Da Wickedness (Flow Necessary Roughness   Rough Rugged & Raw   Super Supreme
Breakdown   Like That) No Shorts   Sho Shot
Confessions   Microphone Pon Cok Raw Deal   Some Shit

L.A. EXPRESS   '76
Backing group for **Tom Scott**: **Robben Ford** (guitar), David Luell (sax), Victor Feldman (keyboards), Max Bennett (bass) and John Guerin (drums).

| 3/6/76 | 167 | 8 | | | **L.A. Express** .... | | [I] | $12 | Caribou 33940 |

Cry Of The Eagle   It's Happening Right Now Shrug   Suavements (Gently)   Western Horizon
Down The Middle   Midnite Flite Stairs   Transylvania Choo Choo

LAFLAMME, David   '77
Born on 4/5/41 in Salt Lake City. Electric violinist/singer. Leader of **It's A Beautiful Day**.

| 12/25/76+ | 159 | 6 | | © | **White Bird** .... | | | $12 | Amherst 1007 |

Baby Be Wise   Hot Summer Day Swept Away   **White Bird** *89*
Easy Woman   Spirit Of America This Man

L.A. GUNS   '90
Hard-rock group from Los Angeles: Philip Lewis (vocals), Tracii Guns and Mick Cripps (guitars), Kelly Nickels (bass), and Steve Riley (drums). Guns was also a member of **Contraband** in 1991.

2/6/88	50	33	●	©	1 **L.A. Guns**			$10	Vertigo 834144
9/16/89+	38	56	●	©	2 **Cocked & Loaded**			$10	Vertigo 838592
7/13/91	42	18		©	3 **Hollywood Vampires**			$10	Polydor 849485

Ballad Of Jayne (2) *33* Down In The City (1)   I'm Addicted (3)   My Koo Ka Choo (3) Over The Edge (2)   Slap In The Face (1)
Big House (3)   Electric Gypsy (1) **It's Over Now** (3) *62* Never Enough (2)   Rip And Tear (2)   Sleazy Come Easy Go (2)
Bitch Is Back (1)   Give A Little (2) Kiss My Love Goodbye (3) No Mercy (1)   17 Crash (2)   Snake Eyes Boogie (3)
Cry No More (1)   Here It Comes (3) Letting Go (2)   Nothing To Lose (1)   Sex Action (1)   Some Lie 4 Love (3)
Crystal Eyes (3)   Hollywood Tease (1) Magdalaine (2)   One More Reason (1) Shoot For Thrills (1) Wheels Of Fire (2)
Dirty Luv (3)   I Found You (3) Malaria (2)   One Way Ticket (1)   Showdown (Riot On Sunset) (2) Wild Obsession (3)

LAID BACK   '84
Synth-pop duo from Denmark: Tim Stahl (keyboards) and John Guldberg (guitar).

| 3/31/84 | 67 | 15 | | | **...Keep Smiling** .... | | | $10 | Sire 25058 |

Don't Be Mean   High Society Girl Sunshine Reggae   **White Horse** *26*
Elevator Boy   Slowmotion Girl Walking In The Sunshine
Fly Away (medley)   So Wie So (medley)

LAINE, Cleo   '76
Born Clementina Campbell on 10/28/27 in Southall, Middlesex, England (Jamaican father and British mother). Jazz singer. Married bandleader Johnny Dankworth in 1958.

4/6/74	157	8		©	1 **Cleo Laine Live!!! at Carnegie Hall**		[L]	$15	RCA Victor 5015
					recorded on 10/17/73				
7/20/74	199	1			2 **Day By Day**			$15	Buddah 5607
12/21/74+	168	5		©	3 **A Beautiful Thing**			$15	RCA Victor 5059
2/7/76	158	10		©	4 **Born On A Friday**			$15	RCA Victor 5113
12/4/76	138	11		©	5 **Porgy & Bess** ============================			$20	RCA Victor 1831 [2]

RAY CHARLES/CLEO LAINE
includes "Summertime," "I Got Plenty 'Nuttin'," "Strawberry Woman," "It Ain't Necessarily So," "There's a Boat Dat's Leavin' Soon For New York," "I Loves You, Porgy" and "Oh, Bess, O Where's My Bess" by Frank DeVol

| 7/26/80 | 150 | 6 | | © | 6 **Sometimes When We Touch** .... | | | $12 | RCA Victor 3628 |

CLEO LAINE & JAMES GALWAY

All In Love Is Fair (3)   Both Sides Now (2) Drifting, Dreaming   I Got Plenty O'Nuttin' (5) Let Me Be The One (4)   Perdido (1)
Any Place I Hang My Hat Is Can It Be True (3) (Gymnopedie No. 1) (6) I Know Where I'm Going (1) Life Is A Wheel (3)   Play It Again, Sam (6)
Home (4)   Colours Ran (4) Feel The Warm (2)   I Loves You Porgy (3,5) Like A Sad Song (6)   Please Don't Talk About Me
Anyone Can Whistle (6) Come Back To Me (4) Fluter's Ball (6)   I Think It's Gonna Rain Living Is Easy (4)   When I'm Gone (1)
Beautiful Thing (3)   Consuelo's Love Theme (6) Gimme A Pig Foot & A Bottle Of Today (4)   Lo! Hear The Gentle Lark (6) Prepare Ye The Way Of The
Bess, You Is My Woman (5) Control Yourself (1) Beer (1)   It Ain't Necessarily So (5) Make It With You (2)   Lord (medley) (2)
Big Best Shoes (1)   Day By Day (medley) (2) Good, Bad But Beautiful (2) Keep Loving Me (6)   Music (1)   Rainy Day Man (2)
Bill (1)   Do You Really Want Him (4) Here Come De Honeyman (5) Least You Can Do Is The Best My Man's Gone Now (5) Ridin' High (1)
Birdsong (Sambalaya) (4) Don't Talk Now (2) How, Where, When? (6) You Can (3)   Oh, Doctor Jesus (5)   Send In The Clowns (1,3)

LAINE, Cleo — Cont'd

Skip-A-Long Sam (3)
Skylark (6)
Slow Motion (2)
Something's Wrong (2)

Sometimes When We Touch (6)
Still Was The Night (6)
Stop And Smell The Roses (1,2)

Strawberry Woman (5)
Streets Of London (4)
Summer Knows (3)
Summertime (5)

Sunday (4)
They Needed Each Other (3)
They Pass By Singin' (5)
Traces (2)

Unlucky Woman (Born On A Friday) (4)
Until It's Time For You To Go (3)

What You Want Wid Bess? (5)
Wish You Were Here (I Do Miss You) (1)
You Must Believe In Spring (1)

LAINE, Frankie '57
Born Frank LoVecchio on 3/30/13 in Chicago. Pop singer.

DEBUT	PEAK	WKS		CD	ARTIST — Album Title	$	Label & Number
4/20/57	13	12		© 1	**Rockin'**	$40	Columbia 975
10/23/61	71	37		© 2	**Hell Bent For Leather!**	$30	Columbia 8415
5/13/67	16	29		3	**I'll Take Care Of Your Cares**	$20	ABC 604
10/14/67	162	2		4	**I Wanted Someone To Love**	$20	ABC 608
3/23/68	127	9		5	**To Each His Own**	$20	ABC 628
4/19/69	55	11		6	**You Gave Me A Mountain**	$20	ABC 682

Allegra (6)
Along The Navajo Trail (2)
Blue Turning Grey Over You (1)
Born To Be With You (6)
Bowie Knife (2)
By The River Sainte Marie (1)
City Boy (2)
Cool Water (2)
Cry Of The Wild Goose (2)
Don't Make Promises (6)
Ev'ry Street's A Boulevard (In Old New York) (4)
Fresh Out Of Tears (6)
Give Me A Kiss For Tomorrow (1)
Give Me Your Kisses (I'll Give You My Heart) (4)

Green, Green Grass Of Home (5)
Gunfight At O.K. Corral (2)
Gypsy (4)
Hanging Tree (2)
Heartless One (3)
High Noon (Do Not Forsake Me) (2)
I Don't Want To Set The World On Fire (5)
I Found You (5)
I Heard You Cried Last Night (4)
I Need You (5)
I Wish I Had Someone Like You (5)

I Wish You Were Jealous Of Me (3)
I'll Take Care Of Your Cares (3) *39*
I'm Free (3)
I'm Happy To Hear You're Sorry (5)
I've Got A Right To Cry (5)
If I Didn't Care (3)
It Don't Mean A Thing To Me (5)
Laughing On The Outside (Crying On The Inside) (5)
Laura, What's He Got That I Ain't Got (4) *66*
Making Memories (3) *35*
Maybe (3)
Meet Me Half Way (5)

Moment Of Truth (5)
Mule Train (2)
On The Sunny Side Of The Street (1)
Place In The Shade (6)
Rawhide (2)
Real True Meaning Of Love (4)
Rockin' Chair (1)
Secret Of Happiness (6)
Shine (1)
Sing An Italian Song (6)
Sometimes (I Just Can't Stand You) (4)
Somewhere There's Someone (3)
Story Of My Life (6)
That Ain't Right (1)

That Lucky Old Sun (1)
That's My Desire (1)
There's Not A Moment To Spare (4)
3:10 To Yuma (2)
To Each His Own (5) *82*
Walk On Out Of My Mind (6)
Wanted Man (2)
We'll Be Together Again (1)
West End Blues (1)
(What Did I Do To Be So) Black And Blue (1)
What Do You Do With An Old Old Song? (3)
You Always Hurt The One You Love (5)

You Gave Me A Mountain (6) *24*
You, No One But You (4) *83*
You Taught Me How To Love
You Now Teach Me To Forget (4)
You Wanted Someone To Play With (I Wanted Someone To Love) (4) *48*
You're Breaking My Heart (3)

LAKE '77
Progressive-rock group from Hamburg, Germany: James Hopkins-Harrison (vocals), Alex Conti (guitar), Geoffrey Peacey (keyboards), Martin Tiefensee (bass) and Dieter Ahrendt (drums).

DEBUT	PEAK	WKS		CD	ARTIST — Album Title	$	Label & Number
8/20/77	92	15		©	**Lake**	$12	Columbia 34763

Between The Lines
Chasing Colours

Do I Love You
Jesus Came Down

Key To The Rhyme
On The Run

Sorry To Say
Time Bomb *83*

LAKE, Greg '81
Born on 11/10/48 in Bournemouth, Dorset, England. Guitarist/bassist with **King Crimson** and **Emerson, Lake & Palmer**.

DEBUT	PEAK	WKS		CD	ARTIST — Album Title	$	Label & Number
10/31/81	62	17			**Greg Lake**	$12	Chrysalis 1357

Black And Blue
For Those Who Dare

It Hurts
Let Me Love You Once *48*

Lie, The
Long Goodbye

Love You Too Much
Nuclear Attack

Retribution Drive
Someone

LAKESIDE '81
Funk group from Dayton, Ohio: Tiemeyer McCain, Thomas Shelby, Otis Stokes and Mark Wood (vocals), Steve Shockley (guitar), Fred Lewis (percussion), Norman Beavers (keyboards), Marvin Craig (bass) and Fred Alexander (drums).

DEBUT	PEAK	WKS		CD	ARTIST — Album Title	$	Label & Number
1/6/79	74	19		© 1	**Shot Of Love**	$12	Solar 2937
11/3/79	141	18		© 2	**Rough Riders**	$12	Solar 3490
11/29/80+	16	35	●	© 3	**Fantastic Voyage**	$12	Solar 3720
12/12/81	109	10		4	**Keep On Moving Straight Ahead**	$12	Solar 3974
1/9/82	58	23		© 5	**Your Wish Is My Command**	$12	Solar 26
5/28/83	42	18		© 6	**Untouchables**	$12	Solar 60204
7/28/84	68	15		7	**Outrageous**	$12	Solar 60355

Alibi (6)
All For You (4)
All In My Mind (2)
Anything For You (4)
Baby I'm Lonely (7)
Back Together Again (4)
Be My Lady (4)
Eveready Man (3)
Fantastic Voyage (3) *55*
From 9:00 Until (2)

Given In To Love (1)
Hold On Tight (1)
Hollywood Story ..see: Tinsel Town Theory
I Can't Get You Out Of My Head (2)
I Love Everything You Do (3)
I Need You (3)
I Want To Hold Your Hand (5)
I'll Be Standing By (5)

I'll Never Leave You (2)
If You Like Our Music (Get On Up And Move) (2)
It's All The Way Live (1)
It's Got To Be Love (4)
It's You (4)
Keep On Moving Straight Ahead (4)
Magic Moments (5)
Make It Right (7)

Make My Day (7)
One Minute After Midnight (1)
Outrageous (7)
Pull My Strings (2)
Raid (6)
Real Love (6)
Restrictions (7)
Rough Rider (2)
Say Yes (3)
Shot Of Love (1)

Show You The Way (7)
So Let's Love (6)
Something About That Woman (5)
Something About You (7)
Songwriter (5)
Special (5)
Strung Out (3)
Time (1)
Tinsel Town Theory (6)

Turn The Music Up (6)
Untouchable (6)
Urban Man (5)
Visions Of My Mind (1)
We Want You (On The Floor) (4)
Worn 'N Torn (7)
Your Love Is On The One (3)
Your Wish Is My Command (5)

LaMOND, George '90
Born George Garcia on 2/25/67 in Washington DC; raised in the Bronx, New York. Pop singer.

DEBUT	PEAK	WKS		CD	ARTIST — Album Title	$	Label & Number
8/18/90	104	10		©	**Bad Of The Heart**	$10	Columbia 45488

Bad Of The Heart *25*
Look Into My Eyes *63*

Love's Contagious
No Matter What *49*

Passing Time
Serenade You

Stop That Girl
What Could've Been

Who Needs Love
Without You

LAMPA, Rachael '00
Born in 1985 in Louisville, Colorado. Christian pop singer.

DEBUT	PEAK	WKS		CD	ARTIST — Album Title	$	Label & Number
8/19/00	120	5		©	**Live For You**	$10	Word 61068

Always Be My Home
Blessed

Day Of Freedom
Free

God Loves You
Hide Me

Live For You
My Father's Heart

Secret Place
Shaken

You Lift Me Up

LANCE, Major '64
Born on 4/4/42 in Chicago. Died of heart disease on 9/3/94 (age 52). R&B singer.

DEBUT	PEAK	WKS		CD	ARTIST — Album Title	$	Label & Number
10/5/63	113	3		1	**The Monkey Time**	$50	Okeh 12105
3/28/64	100	9		2	**Um, Um, Um, Um, Um, Um/The Best Of Major Lance**	[G] $50	Okeh 12106
9/4/65	109	6		3	**Major's Greatest Hits**	[G] $50	Okeh 12110

Ain't It A Shame (3) *91*
Bird, The (1)
Come See (3) *40*
Delilah (1)
Girls (3) *68*
Gotta Get Away (3)

Gotta Right To Cry (2)
Gypsy Woman (2)
Hey Little Girl (2,3) *13*
Hitchhike (1)
I'm The One (2)
It Ain't No Use (3) *68*

It's All Right (2)
Just One Look (1)
Keep On Loving You (1)
Land Of A Thousand Dances (1)
Little Young Lover (2)

Mama Didn't Know (1,2)
Matador, The (3) *20*
Monkey Time (1,2,3) *8*
Pride And Joy (1)
Rhythm (3) *24*
Soldierboy (1)

Sometimes I Wonder (3) *64*
Sweet Music (3)
That's What Mama Say (2)
Think Nothing About It (2)
Um, Um, Um, Um, Um, Um (2,3) *5*

Watusi (3)
What's Happening (1)
You'll Want Me Back (2)

LANE, Robin, & The Chartbusters '81

Rock group formed in Boston by female vocalist Lane, with Asa Brebner (guitar), Leroy Radcliffe (keyboards), Scott Baerenwald (bass) and Tim Jackson (drums). Lane is the daughter of **Dean Martin**'s pianist, Ken Lane.

| 4/25/81 | 172 | 4 | | | Imitation Life.. | | | $12 | Warner 3537 |

For You
Idiot

Imitation Life
No Control

Pretty Mala
Rather Be Blind

Say Goodbye
Send Me An Angel

Solid Rock
What The People Are Doing

LANE, Ronnie — see TOWNSHEND, Pete

LANG, Jonny '98

Born Jon Langseth on 1/29/81 in Fargo, North Dakota. Blues-rock singer/guitarist.

| 2/15/97 | 44 | 62 | ▲ | © 1 | Lie To Me.. | | | $10 | A&M 540640 |
| 11/7/98 | 28 | 29 | ▲ | © 2 | Wander This World .... | | | $10 | A&M 540984 |

Angel Of Mercy (2)
Back For A Taste Of Your Love (1)
Before You Hit The Ground (2)
Breakin' Me (2)

Cherry Red Wine (2)
Darker Side (2)
Good Morning Little School Girl (1)
Hit The Ground Running (1)

I Am (2)
Leaving To Stay (2)
Levee, The (2)
Lie To Me (1)
Matchbox (1)

Missing Your Love (1)
Quitter Never Wins (1)
Rack 'Em Up (1)
Right Back (2)
Second Guessing (2)

Still Rainin' (1)
Still Wonder (1)
There's Gotta Be A Change (1)
Walking Away (1)
Wander This World (2)

When I Come To You (1)

lang, k.d. '93

Born Kathryn Dawn Lang on 11/2/61 in Consort, Alberta, Canada. Eclectic singer/songwriter.

| 5/28/88 | 73 | 25 | ● | © 1 | Shadowland .... | | | $10 | Sire 25724 |
| 6/17/89+ | 69 | 56 | ● | © 2 | Absolute Torch And Twang .... | | | $10 | Sire 25877 |

k.d. lang and THE RECLINES

4/4/92+	18	90	▲²	© 3	Ingénue			$10	Sire 26840
11/20/93	82	14		© 4	Even Cowgirls Get The Blues	[S]		$10	Sire 45433
10/28/95	37	20	●	© 5	All You Can Eat			$10	Warner 46034
6/28/97	29	16	●	© 6	Drag			$10	Warner 46623
7/8/00	58	11		© 7	Invincible Summer			$10	Warner 47605

Acquiesce (5)
Air That I Breathe (6)
Big Big Love (2)
Big Boned Gal (2)
Black Coffee (1)
Busy Being Blue (1)
Consequences Of Falling (7)
Constant Craving (3) *38*
Cowgirl Pride (4)
Curiosity (5)
Curious Soul Astray (4)
Didn't I (2)
Don't Be A Lemming Polka (4)
Don't Let The Stars Get In Your Eyes (1)

Don't Smoke In Bed (6)
Extraordinary Thing (7)
Full Moon Full Of Love (2)
Get Some (5)
Hain't It Funny? (6)
Honkey Tonk Angels' Medley (1)
Hush Sweet Lover (4)
I Want It All (5)
I Wish I Didn't Love You So (1)
I'm Down To My Last Cigarette (1)
If I Were You (5)
In Perfect Dreams (4)
Infinite And Unforeseen (5)

It's Happening With You (7)
It's Me (2)
Joker, The (6)
Just Keep Me Moving (4)
Kundalini Yoga Waltz (4)
Lifted By Love (4)
Lock, Stock And Teardrops (1)
Love Is Like A Cigarette (6)
Love's Great Ocean (7)
Luck In My Eyes (2)
Maybe (3)
Mind Of Love (3)
Miss Chatelaine (3)
My Last Cigarette (2)
My Old Addiction (6)

Myth (4)
Nowhere To Stand (2)
Only Love (7)
Or Was I (4)
Outside Myself (3)
Overture (4)
Pullin' Back The Reins (2)
Ride Of Bonanza Jellybean (4)
Save Me (3)
Season Of Hollow Soul (3)
Sexuality (5)
Shadowland (1)
Simple (7)
Smoke Dreams (6)
Smoke Rings (6)

So It Shall Be (3)
Still Thrives This Love (3)
Suddenly (7)
Sugar Moon (1)
Summerfling (7)
Sweet Little Cherokee (4)
Tears Don't Care Who Cries Them (1)
Tears Of Love's Recall (3)
Theme From The Valley Of The Dolls (6)
This (5)
Three Days (2)
Till The Heart Caves In (6)
Trail Of Broken Hearts (2)

Walkin' In And Out Of Your Arms (2)
Wallflower Waltz (2)
(Waltz Me) Once Again Around The Dance Floor (1)
Wash Me Clean (3)
Western Stars (1)
What Better Said (7)
When We Collide (4)
World Of Love (5)
You're OK (5)
Your Smoke Screen (6)

LANIN, Lester, And His Orchestra '57

Born on 8/26/11 in Philadelphia. Orchestra leader.

6/24/57	7	10		1	**Dance To The Music Of Lester Lanin**	[I]		$20	Epic 3340
11/11/57	18	2		2	Lester Lanin And His Orchestra	[I]		$20	Epic 3242
2/3/58	17	2		3	Lester Lanin At The Tiffany Ball	[I]		$20	Epic 3410
6/9/58	19	3		4	Lester Lanin Goes To College	[I]		$20	Epic 3474
11/17/58	12	4		5	Have Band, Will Travel...	[I]		$20	Epic 3520
1/20/62	37	20	©	6	Twistin' In High Society!...	[I]		$15	Epic 3825

Acceleration Waltz (medley) (2)
Adios Muchachos (5)
After The Ball (medley) (1)
After You've Gone (medley) (4)
Alexander's Ragtime Band (medley) (4)
All Of You (medley) (4)
All The Things You Are (medley) (1)
Always (medley) (5)
Always True To You In My Fashion (medley) (3)
Anything Can Happen - Mambo (medley) (4)
Anything Goes (medley) (1)
April In Portugal (medley) (3)
Arrivederci Roma (medley) (5)
Artist's Life (medley) (1)
At The Darktown Strutters' Ball (1,6)
Babes In The Wood (medley) (1)
Bali Ha'i (medley) (5)
Ballin' The Jack (medley) (1)
Baubles, Bangles And Beads (medley) (5)
Best Things In Life Are Free (medley) (1)
Bewitched (medley) (3)
Big "D" (medley) (5)
Bill Bailey, Won't You Please Come Home? (medley) (1)
Blue Moon (4,6)
Blue Skies (medley) (4)
Buckle Down, Winsocki (medley) (3)
Button Up Your Overcoat (medley) (1)
C'est Magnifique (medley) (2)

Carioca (4)
Charleston (4,6)
Cheek To Cheek (medley) (2)
Chicago (medley) (5)
Colonel Bogey (medley) (4)
Continental, The (medley) (2)
Dancing In The Dark (medley) (2)
Dancing On The Ceiling (medley) (2)
Deep Purple (medley) (4)
Die Schoenbrunner (3)
Dirty Lady! (medley) (1)
Dixie (medley) (3)
Do I Love You Because You're Beautiful? (medley) (4)
Down Home Rag (medley) (3)
Easy To Love (medley) (4)
Ev'rything I've Got (medley) (5)
Fidgety Feet (medley) (5)
Fine Romance (medley) (5)
Five Foot Two, Eyes Of Blue (medley) (5)
Foggy Day (medley) (1)
Frankie & Johnny (medley) (5)
From This Moment On (medley) (2)
Gang That Sang "Heart Of My Heart" (medley) (5)
Get Me To The Church On Time (medley) (3)
Getting To Know You (medley) (3)
Greensleeves (medley) (1)
Guitar Boogie Twist (6)
Guys And Dolls (medley) (5)
Hawaiian War Chant (medley) (4)
Heart (medley) (5)

Hello Ma Baby (medley) (1)
Hello Young Lovers (medley) (3)
Hey, There (medley) (5)
Hot Time In The Old Town Tonight (medley) (5)
How High The Moon (medley) (4)
I Can't Give You Anything But Love (medley) (4)
I Could Have Danced All Night (medley) (1)
I Could Write A Book (medley) (3)
I Don't Know Why (I Just Do) (5,6)
I Love Paris (medley) (2)
I Want My Mama (5)
I Wish I Were In Love Again (medley) (4)
I Won't Dance (medley) (3)
I'm In The Mood For Love (medley) (4)
I've Got A Crush On You (medley) (2)
I've Grown Accustomed To Her Face (medley) (5)
If I Loved You (medley) (3)
If I Were A Bell (medley) (5)
If You Knew Susie Like I Know Susie (medley) (2)
In The Mood (medley) (4)
In The Still Of The Night (medley) (3)
It's A Lovely Day Today (medley) (5)
It's All Right With Me (medley) (2)
It's Delovely (medley) (4)

It's Good To Be Alive (medley) (3)
Ja-Da (medley) (5)
Jazz Me Blues (medley) (1)
Johnson Rag (medley) (5)
Josephine (6)
Jubilation T. Cornpone (medley) (5)
June Is Bustin' Out All Over (medley) (3)
Just In Time (medley) (5)
Just One Of Those Things (medley) (2)
La Mer (Beyond The Sea) (medley) (1)
Lady Is A Tramp (medley) (2)
Last Time I Saw Paris (medley) (5)
Laura (medley) (4)
Lester Lanin Cha-Cha (medley) (4)
Linda Mujer (5)
Little Brown Jug (medley) (4)
Love For Sale (medley) (1)
Love Is A Many-Splendored Thing (medley) (4)
Love Is Here To Stay (medley) (4)
Love Walked In (medley) (4)
Mack The Knife (medley) (3)
Make Believe (medley) (3)
Mambo Jumbo Samba (1)
March From The River Kwai ...see: Colonel Bogey
Marianne (medley) (1)
Mine (medley) (2)
Mississippi Mud (medley) (2)
Mister Sandman (medley) (4)
Moonglow (medley) (4)

Mountain Greenery (medley) (2)
Music Goes 'Round And 'Round (medley) (2)
Muskrat Ramble (2,6)
My Blue Heaven (medley) (3)
My Funny Valentine (medley) (1)
My Heart Belongs To Daddy (medley) (3)
Namely You (medley) (5)
Night And Day (medley) (1)
O Sole Mio (medley) (5)
Oh What A Beautiful Mornin'! (medley) (3)
Oklahoma (medley) (1)
Ol' Man River (medley) (3)
Old Devil Moon (medley) (3)
On The Street Where You Live (medley) (1)
On The Sunny Side Of The Street (medley) (4)
Once In Love With Amy (medley) (5)
Orchids In The Moonlight (3)
Organ Twist (6)
Over The Rainbow (5)
Panama (medley) (1)
Party's Over (medley) (5)
Peg O' My Heart (medley) (5)
People Will Say We're In Love (medley) (3)
Poor People Of Paris (medley) (5)
Por Favor (medley) (4)
Puttin' On The Ritz (medley) (5)
Rain In Spain (medley) (3)
Rhode Island Is Famous For You (medley) (3)
Ridin' High (medley) (4)

'S Wonderful (medley) (4)
Say Darling (medley) (5)
Sentimental Journey (medley) (4)
September Song (medley) (1)
Seventy-Six Trombones (medley) (5)
Shall We Dance (medley) (3)
Short'nin' Bread (medley) (5)
Smoke Gets In Your Eyes (medley) (3)
So In Love (medley) (3)
Something's Gotta Give (medley) (1)
Sophisticated Swing (medley) (4)
South Pacific Medley (3)
St. Louis Blues (medley) (3)
Standing On The Corner (medley) (5)
Stardust (medley) (4)
Steppin' In Society (medley) (2)
Stumbling (medley) (5)
Sunny (medley) (1)
Sunshine Girl (medley) (3)
Surrey With The Fringe On Top (medley) (3)
Sweet Georgia Brown (2,6)
Taking A Chance On Love (medley) (4)
Tenderly (medley) (4)
That Old Black Magic (medley) (4)
There's A Small Hotel (medley) (1)
They Can't Take That Away From Me (medley) (4)
They Say It's Wonderful (medley) (5)
Till There Was You (medley) (5)

LANIN, Lester, And His Orchestra — Cont'd

Tin Roof Blues (medley) (4)
Too Darn Hot (medley) (3)
Toot, Toot, Tootsie, Goo'bye (medley) (2)
Top Hat, White Tie And Tails (medley) (5)
Toreador Song (medley) (3)

True Love (medley) (4)
Twelfth Street Rag (medley) (3)
Twisting Saints (5)
Waltz From "Der Rosenkavalier" (medley) (2)
Waltz From Eugen Onegin (1)
Wang, Wang Blues (medley) (3)

'Way Down Yonder In New Orleans (3,6)
Wedding Bells Are Breaking Up That Old Gang Of Mine (medley) (5)
When The Saints Go Marching In (medley) (2)
Whiffenpoof Song (medley) (5)

Who? (medley) (3)
Why Do I Love You (medley) (3)
Wine, Women And Song (medley) (1)
With A Little Bit Of Luck (medley) (1)
Wonderful Guy (medley) (5)

Wouldn't It Be Loverly (medley) (5)
Wunderbar (medley) (5)
You're Just In Love (medley) (5)
You're Sensational (medley) (4)
You're So Right For Me (medley) (5)

LANOIS, Daniel   '90
Born on 9/19/51 in Hull, Canada. Prolific producer.

| 1/20/90 | 166 | 5 | © | | Acadie .... | | | $10 | Opal 25969 |

Amazing Grace
Fisherman's Daughter

Ice
Jolie Louise

Maker, The
O Marie

Silium's Hill
St. Ann's Gold

Still Water
Under A Stormy Sky

Where The Hawkwind Kills
White Mustang II

LANZ, David   '88
Born in 1950 in Seattle. New Age pianist.

| 1/30/88 | 125 | 12 | © | 1 | Natural States .... | | [I] | $10 | Narada Equinox 63001 |

DAVID LANZ & PAUL SPEER

| 11/5/88 | 180 | 6 | ● © | 2 | Cristofori's Dream .... | | [I] | $10 | Narada Lotus 61021 |
| 11/26/94 | 39[X] | 1 | © | 3 | Christmas Eve.. | | [X-I] | $10 | Narada Lotus 61046 |

Allegro/985 (1)
Angel At Midnight (3)
Angel King (3)
Angel Of Hope (3)
Angel Of Joy (3)
Angels We Have Heard On High (3)

Behind The Waterfall (1)
Christmas Eve Waltz (medley) (3)
Cristofori's Dream (2)
Faces Of The Forest Part 1 & 2 (1)
First Light (1)

First Noël (medley) (3)
Free Fall (2)
God Rest Ye Merry Gentlemen (3)
Green Into Gold (2)
I Saw The Path Of The Angels (3)

Joy To The World (3)
Lento/984 (1)
Miranova (1)
Mountain (1)
O Come All Ye Faithful (3)
O Come, O Come, Emmanuel (3)

O Holy Night (3)
O Little Town Of Bethlehem (3)
Rain Forest (1)
Silent Night (3)
Spiral Dance (2)
Summer's Child (2)
What Child Is This (3)

Whiter Shade Of Pale (1)
Wings To Altair (2)

★473★   LANZA, Mario   '60
Born Alfredo Cocozza on 1/31/21 in Philadelphia. Died of a heart attack on 10/7/59 (age 38). Operatic tenor/actor.

4/28/56	9	6		1	Serenade	[S]	$40	RCA Victor 1996
3/17/58	7	8		2	Seven Hills Of Rome	[S]	$40	RCA Victor 2211
11/2/59	5	46		3	For The First Time	[S]	$40	RCA Victor 2338
12/14/59+	4	4		4	Lanza Sings Christmas Carols	[X]	$30	RCA Victor 2333

first released in 1956 on RCA Victor 2029, an expanded version of his 1951 album *Mario Lanza Sings Christmas Songs* on RCA Victor 1649

5/16/60	4	53		5	Mario Lanza Sings Caruso Favorites	[F]	$30	RCA Victor 2393
12/18/61+	67	5		6	Lanza Sings Christmas Carols	[X-R]	$30	RCA Victor 2333
10/6/62+	64	41		7	I'll Walk With God	[E]	$30	RCA Victor 2607
12/21/63+	15[X]	12	©	8	Christmas Hymns and Carols	[X]	$20	RCA Camden 777

first released in 1951 as *Mario Lanza Sings Christmas Songs* on RCA Victor 155; reissued in 1956 on RCA 2029 and in 1959 on RCA 2333 (each issue featured a slightly different song selection); Christmas charts: 24/'63, 15/'64, 56/'65, 51/'66, 36/'67

| 8/8/64 | 87 | 15 | | 9 | The Best Of Mario Lanza | [G] | $20 | RCA Victor 2748 |

Addio Alla Madre (7)
Aida: Act I (3)
Amor Ti Vieta (1)
And This Is My Beloved (9)
Ave Maria (1,3,7)
Away In A Manger (4,6,8)
Be My Love (9)
Because (7)
Because You're Mine (9)
Come Dance With Me (2)
Come Prima (3)
Deck The Halls (4,6)
Di Quella Pira (1)
Di Rigori Armato (1)
Dio Ti Giocondi (1)
Do You Wonder (2)

Earthbound (2) *53*
First Noel (4,6,8)
Funiculi' Funicula' (9)
God Rest Ye Merry, Gentlemen (4,6,8)
Guardian Angels (4,6,7,8)
Hark! The Herald Angels Sing (4,6,8)
Hofbrauhaus Song (3)
I Love Thee (7)
I Saw Three Ships (4,6,8)
I'll Walk With God (7)
Ich Liebe Dich (3)
Ideale (5)
It Came Upon A Midnight Clear (4,6)
Jezebel (medley) (2)

Joy To The World (4,6,8)
Kiss, A (9)
L'Alba Separa Dalla Luce L'Ombra (5)
La Danza (1)
La Mia Canzone (5)
Lamento Di Federico (1)
Lolita (2,5)
Lord's Prayer (7,8)
Love In A Home (2)
Loveliest Night Of The Year (9)
Luna D'Estate (5)
Mazurka (3)
Memories Are Made Of This (medley) (2)
Musica Proibita (5)
My Destiny (1,2)

Neapolitan Dance (3)
Nessun Dorma (1)
Never Till Now (2)
None But The Lonely Heart (7)
O Christmas Tree (4,6,8)
O Come, All Ye Faithful (Adeste Fideles) (4,6,8)
O Holy Night (7,8)
O Little Town Of Bethlehem (4,6,8)
O, Mon Amour (3)
O Paradiso (1)
O Soave Fanciulla (1)
O Sole Mio (3)
One Alone (9)
Only A Rose (9)
Otello: Finale (3)

Pineapple Pickers (3)
Pour Un Baiser (5)
Questa O Quella (2)
Santa Lucia (5,9)
Senza Nisciuno (5)
Serenade (1,2,9)
Serenata (5)
Seven Hills Of Rome (2)
Silent Night (4,6,8)
Somebody Bigger Than You And I (7)
Tarantella (3)
Temptation (medley) (2)
There's Gonna Be A Party Tonight (3)
Through The Years (7)
Torna A Surriento (3)

Trees (7)
Trembling Of A Leaf (2)
Vaghissima Sembianza (5)
Vesti La Giubba (3,9)
Vieni Sul Mar (5)
Virgin's Slumber Song (7)
We Three Kings Of Orient Are (4,6,8)
When The Saints Go Marching In (medley) (2)

LARKIN, Billy, & The Delegates   '66
Born in Huntland, Tennessee. Jazz pianist.

| 4/2/66 | 148 | 2 | | | Hole In The Wall .... | [I] | $25 | World Pacific 1837 |

Agent Double-O-Soul
And I Love Her

Blue Satin
Close Your Eyes

Hole In The Wall
Hot Sauce

Hot Toddy
"In" Crowd

In The Midnight Hour
Little Mama

Soul Beat
Taste Of Honey

LARKS, The   '65
R&B vocal trio from Los Angeles: Don Julian, Ted Walters and Charles Morrison. Julian died of pneumonia on 11/6/98 (age 61).

| 1/23/65 | 143 | 4 | | | The Jerk .... | | $50 | Money 1102 |

Do The Jerk
Jerk, The *7*

Jerk Once More
Jerkin' U.S.A.

Keep Jerkin'
Mickey's East Coast Jerk

Slauson Shuffle #1 & 2
Soul Jerk

You Must Believe Me

LARRIEUX, Amel   '00
Born in Manhattan, New York. Female singer. Former member of **Groove Theory**.

| 3/4/00 | 79 | 9 | © | | Infinite Possibilities .... | | $10 | 550 Music 69741 |

Down
Even If

Get Up *97*
Infinite Possibilities

Ini
Make Me Whole

Searchin' For My Soul
Shine

Sweet Misery
Weather

LARSEN, Neil   '79
Born on 8/7/48 in Cleveland; raised in Siesta Key, Florida. Session keyboardist. Member of **Larsen-Feiten Band**.

| 9/1/79 | 139 | 7 | | | High Gear .... | [I] | $12 | Horizon 738 |

Demonette
Futurama

High Gear
Night Letter

Nile Crescent
Rio Este

This Time Tomorrow

LARSEN-FEITEN BAND '80
Duo of session musicians: **Neil Larsen** (keyboards) and Buzz Feiten (guitar).

| 9/13/80 | 142 | 10 | | | Larsen-Feiten Band.. | | | $12 | Warner 3468 |

Aztec Legend / Danger Zone | Further Notice / Make It | Morning Star / Over | She's Not In Love | Who'll Be The Fool Tonight *29* | Talk To Me (4)

LARSON, Nicolette '79
Born on 7/17/52 in Helena, Montana; raised in Kansas City. Died of a cerebral edema on on 12/16/97 (age 45). Former session singer. Married session drummer Russ Kunkel.

11/18/78+	15	37	●		1 Nicolette...			$12	Warner 3243
11/3/79	47	21			2 In The Nick Of Time..			$12	Warner 3370
1/24/81	62	12			3 Radioland..			$12	Warner 3502
8/14/82	75	10			4 All Dressed Up & No Place To Go			$12	Warner 3678

Angels Rejoiced (1)
Baby, Don't You Do It (1)
Back In My Arms (2)
Been Gone Too Long (3)
Breaking Too Many Hearts (2)
Can't Get Away From You (1)
Come Early Mornin' (1)

Daddy (1)
Dancin' Jones (2)
Fallen (2)
Fool For Love (3)
French Waltz (1)
Give A Little (1)
How Can We Go On (3)

I Only Want To Be With You (4) *53*
I Want You So Bad (4)
I'll Fly Away (Without You) (4)
Isn't It Always Love (2)
Just In The Nick Of Time (4)
Just Say I Love You (4)

Last In Love (1)
Let Me Go, Love (2) *35*
Long Distance Love (3)
Lotta Love (1) *8*
Love, Sweet, Love (4)
Mexican Divorce (1)
Nathan Jones (4)

Ooo-eee (3)
Radioland (3)
Rhumba Girl (1) *47*
Rio De Janeiro Blue (4)
Say You Will (4)
Still You Linger On (4)
Straight From The Heart (3)

Talk To Me (4)
Tears, Tears And More Tears (3)
Trouble (2)
Two Trains (4)
When You Come Around (3)
You Send Me (1)

LaRUE, D.C. '77
Born David Charles L'Heureux on 4/26/48 in Meriden, Connecticut. Disco singer.

| 6/26/76 | 139 | 13 | | | 1 Cathedrals.. | | | $12 | Pyramid 9003 |
| 1/8/77 | 115 | 11 | | | 2 The Tea Dance... | | | $12 | Pyramid 9006 |

Bad News (2)
Broadway Melody (2)
Cathedrals (1) *94*

Deep, Dark, Delicious Night (1)
Don't Keep It In The Shadows (2)

Face Of Love (2)
Fanfare (2)
Going Hollywood (2)

I Don't Want To Lose You (1)
I'll Still Be Here For You (1)
Indiscreet (2)

O Ba Ba (No Reino Da Mae Do Ouro) (2)
Overture (2)

Tea Dance (2)

LA'S, The '91
Rock group from Liverpool, England: brothers Lee (vocals) and Neil (drums) Mavers, with Peter Camell (guitar), and John Power (bass). Group name is slang for lads.

| 7/6/91 | 196 | 1 | | © | The La's... | | | $10 | London 828202 |

Doledrum
Failure

Feelin'
Freedom Song

I Can't Sleep
I.O.U.

Liberty Ship
Looking Glass

Son Of A Gun
There She Goes *49*

Timeless Melody
Way Out

LaSALLE, Denise '72
Born Denise Craig on 7/16/39 in LeFlore County, Mississippi. R&B singer/songwriter.

| 2/5/72 | 120 | 9 | | | Trapped By A Thing Called Love..................................... | | | $20 | Westbound 2012 |

Catch Me If You Can
Deeper I Go (The Better It Gets)

Do Me Right
Good Goody Getter
Heartbreaker Of The Year

Hung Up, Strung Out
If You Should Loose Me
It's Too Late

Keep It Coming
Now Run And Tell That *46*

Trapped By A Thing Called Love *13*

LAST, James '80
Born on 4/17/29 in Bremen, Germany. Producer/arranger/conductor.

2/19/72	160	5			1 Music From Across The Way			$15	Polydor 5505
8/16/75	172	3			2 Well Kept Secret...		[I]	$15	Polydor 6040
6/28/80	148	8			3 Seduction...		[I]	$12	Polydor 6283

JAMES LAST BAND

Bolero '75 (2)
Chirpy Chirpy Cheep Cheep (1)
Dancing Shadows (3)
Dock Of The Bay (1)
Falling Star (3)
Fantasy (3)
Glow (3)
Here Comes The Sun (1)

Hot Love (2)
I Am...I Said (1)
I Can't Move No Mountains (2)
Infight (3)
It's Over (3)
Jamaica Farewell (1)
Joy To The World (1)
Jubilation (2)

Love For Sale (2)
Me And You And A Dog Named Boo (1)
Music From Across The Way (1) *84*
Night Drive (3)
On The Beach (1)
Power To The People (1)

Prisoner Of Second Avenue, Theme From (2)
Question (2)
Related To What (3)
Seduction (Love Theme) (3) *28*
Slaughter On 10th Avenue (2)
So Excited (3)

South Of The Border Down Mexico Way (1)
Summertime (2)
Vibrations (3)

LAST POETS, The '70
Black protest group from Harlem, New York: Abiodun Oyewole, Alafia Pudim, Omar Ben Hassen, Nilaja, David Nelson, Felipe Luciano and Gylan Kain. Nelson, Luciano and Kain split from the others to record as **The Original Last Poets**.

| 6/20/70 | 29 | 30 | © | | 1 The Last Poets... | | | $50 | Douglas 3 |
| 3/6/71 | 106 | 6 | © | | 2 Right On!.. | | [S] | $50 | Juggernaut 8802 |

THE ORIGINAL LAST POETS

| 4/3/71 | 104 | 15 | | | 3 This Is Madness .... | | | $50 | Douglas 30583 |

Alley (1)
Been Done Already (2)
Black Is (3)
Black People What Y'all Gon' Do (3)
Black Thighs (1)
Black Wish (1)
Black Woman (2)

Die Nigga!!! (2)
Gashman (1)
Hey Now (2)
Into The Streets (2)
James Brown (2)
Jazz (2)
Jibaro/My Pretty Nigger (2)
Jones Comin' Down (1)

Just Because (1)
Library, The (2)
Little Willie Armstrong Jones (2)
Mean Machine (3)
New York, New York (1)
O.D. (3)
On The Subway (1)
Opposites (3)

Poetry Is Black (2)
Puerto Rican Rhythms (2)
Related To What (3)
Run Nigger (1)
Scared Of Revolution (1)
Shalimar, The (2)
Soul (2)
Surprises (1)

Tell Me Brother (2)
This Is Madness (3)
Time (3)
Today Is A Killer (2)
True Blues (3)
Two Little Boys (1)
Un Rifle/Oracion Rifle Prayer (2)

Wake Up Niggers (1)
When The Revolution Comes (1)
White Man's Got A God Complex (3)

LATEEF, Yusef '69
Born William Evans on 10/9/20 in Chattanooga, Tennessee; raised in Detroit. Jazz tenor saxophonist/flutist. After high school graduation, played with Lucky Millinder. Worked with Dizzy Gillespie in 1949, then Charlie Mingus in the early 1960s.

| 8/16/69 | 183 | 5 | | | Yusef Lateef's Detroit... | | [I] | $20 | Atlantic 1525 |

Belle Isle
Bishop School

Eastern Market
Livingston Playground

Raymond Winchester
Russell And Eliot

That Lucky Old Sun
Woodward Avenue

LATIMORE '77
Born Benjamin Latimore on 9/7/39 in Charleston, Tennessee. R&B singer.

| 3/26/77 | 181 | 5 | | | It Ain't Where You Been... .... | | | $12 | Glades 7509 |

All The Way Lover
I Get Lifted

It Ain't Where You Been
Let Me Go

Let's Do It In Slow Motion
Somethin' 'Bout 'Cha *37*

Sweet Vibrations

The Edwin Hawkins Singers
Children (Get Together) ('71)

Head East
Get Yourself Up ('76)

Eric Heatherly
Swimming In Champagne ('00)

Al Hirt
The Happy Trumpet ('66)

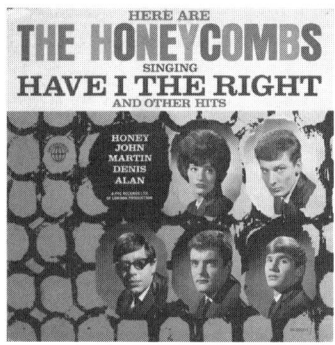

The Honeycombs
Here Are The Honeycombs ('65)

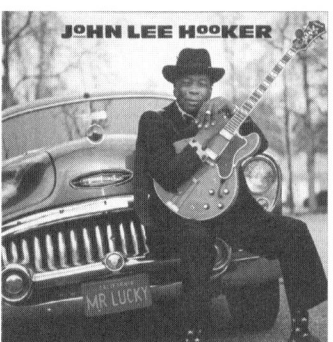

John Lee Hooker
Mr. Lucky ('91)

Humble Pie
Rock On ('71)

Ian & Sylvia
Early Morning Rain ('65)

Instant Funk
The Funk Is On ('80)

The Isley Bros.
This Old Heart Of Mine ('66)

Alan Jackson...*A Lot About Livin'*
(And A Little 'Bout Love) ('92)

Bob James
Lucky Seven ('79)

Etta James
At Last! ('61)

Jingle Cats
Here Comes Santa Claws ('94)

Antonio Carlos Jobim
Stone Flower ('71)

George Jones
I'll Share My World With You ('69)

Quincy Jones
Smackwater Jack ('71)

John F. Kennedy
A Memorial Album ('64)

B.B. King & Eric Clapton
Riding With The King ('00)

The Kingston Trio
Stay Awhile ('65)

Terry Knight And The Pack
Terry Knight And The Pack ('66)

Bob Kuban and the In-Men
Look Out For The Cheater ('66)

Patti LaBelle
Burnin' ('91)

Frankie Laine
Rockin' ('57)

LATIN ALLIANCE '91
All-star rap trio: **Kid Frost**, **Mellow Man Ace** and ALT.

| 8/24/91 | 133 | 8 | © | **Latin Alliance** | $10 | Virgin 91625 |

Can U Feel It
Know What I'm Sayin'?
Latinos Unidos (United Latins)

Low Rider (On The Boulevard) *54*
No Man's Land

Runnin'
Smooth Roughness
Valla En Paz (Go In Peace)

What Is An American?
What You See Is What You Get

LaTOUR '91
Born William LaTour in Chicago. Techno-dance artist.

| 5/11/91 | 145 | 4 | © | **LaTour** | $10 | Smash 848323 |

Allen's Got A New Hi-Fi
Amazing You

Blue
Cold

Dark Sunglasses
Fantasy Soldiers

Involved
Laurie Monster

People Are Still Having Sex *35*
Psych

LATTIMORE, Kenny '98
Born in Washington DC. R&B singer.

| 7/20/96+ | 92 | 34 | ● © | 1 **Kenny Lattimore** | $10 | Columbia 67125 |
| 11/7/98 | 71 | 8 | © | 2 **From The Soul Of Man** | $10 | Columbia 68854 |

All I Want (1)
All My Tomorrows (2)
Always Remember (1)
Climb The Mountain (1)
Days Like This (2)

Destiny (2)
For You (1) *33*
Forever (1)
Forgiveness (1)
Heaven And Earth (2)

I Love You More Than You'll Ever Know (2)
I Won't Forget (Whose I Am) (1)
I Won't Let You Down (1)
If I Lose My Woman (2)

If You Could See You (Through My Eyes) (2)
Joy (1)
Just Can't Get Over You (2)
Just What It Takes (1)

Love Will Find A Way (2)
Make Believe (2)
Never Too Busy (1) *89*
Tomorrow (2)
Trial Separation (2)

Well Done (2)
Where Did Love Go (1)
While My Guitar Gently Weeps (2)

LATTISAW, Stacy '80
Born on 11/25/66 in Washington DC. R&B singer.

7/5/80	44	28	©	1 **Let Me Be Your Angel**	$12	Cotillion 5219
7/25/81	46	15	©	2 **With You**	$12	Cotillion 16049
8/28/82	55	16	©	3 **Sneakin' Out**	$12	Cotillion 90002
8/27/83	160	8	©	4 **Sixteen**	$12	Cotillion 90106
3/31/84	139	8	©	5 **Perfect Combination**	$12	Cotillion 90136

STACY LATTISAW & JOHNNY GILL

| 10/11/86 | 131 | 22 | | 6 **Take Me All The Way** | $10 | Motown 6212 |
| 3/5/88 | 153 | 10 | © | 7 **Personal Attention** | $10 | Motown 6247 |

Ain't No Mountain High Enough (7)
Attack Of The Name Game (3) *70*
Baby I Love You (2)
Baby It's You (5)
Black Pumps And Pink Lipstick (4)
Block Party (5)
Call Me (7)
Changes (7)
Come Out Of The Shadows (5)
Don't Throw It All Away (3)

Don't You Want To Feel It (For Yourself) (1)
Dreaming (1)
Dynamite! (1)
Electronic Eyes (7)
Every Drop Of Your Love (7)
Falling In Love Again (5)
Feel My Love Tonight (medley) (2)
50/50 Love (5)
Find Another Lover (7)
Fun 'N' Games (5)

Guys Like You (Give Love A Bad Name) (3)
Hard Way (6)
He's Got A Hold On Me (7)
Heartbreak Look (5)
Hey There Lonely Boy (3)
I Could Love You So Divine (3)
I'm Down For You (3)
I've Loved You Somewhere Before (2)
It Was So Easy (2)
Johey! (4)

Jump Into My Life (6)
Jump To The Beat (1)
Let Me Be Your Angel (1) *21*
Let Me Take You Down (7)
Little Bit Of Heaven (6)
Longshot (6)
Love Me Like The First Time (1)
Love On A Two Way Street (2) *26*
Love Town (7)
Memories (3)
Million Dollar Babe (4)

My Love (1)
Nail It To The Wall (6) *48*
One More Night (6)
Over The Top (6)
Perfect Combination (5) *75*
Personal Attention (7)
Screamin' Off The Top (2)
16 (4)
Sneakin' Out (3)
Spotlight (2)
Stacy Rap (medley) (2)
Take Me All The Way (6)

Tonight I'm Gonna Make You Mine (3)
Ways Of Love (4)
What's So Hot 'Bout Bad Boys (4)
With You (2)
You Ain't Leavin' (6)
You Don't Love Me Anymore (1)
You Know I Like It (1)
You Take Me To Heaven (2)
Young Girl (2)

LAUPER, Cyndi '84
Born on 6/20/53 in Queens, New York. Pop-rock singer. Won the 1984 Best New Artist Grammy Award. In the movies *Vibes* and *Life With Mikey*. Married actor David Thornton on 11/24/91.

12/24/83+	4	96	▲6 ©	1 **She's So Unusual**	$10	Portrait 38930
10/4/86	4	44	▲2 ©	2 **True Colors**	$10	Portrait 40313
5/27/89	37	21	©	3 **A Night To Remember**	$10	Epic 44318
7/3/93	112	4	©	4 **Hat Full Of Stars**	$10	Epic 52878
8/5/95	81	12	●	5 **Twelve Deadly Cyns...And Then Some**	[G]	$10	Epic 66100
4/19/97	188	1	©	6 **Sisters Of Avalon**	$10	Epic 66433

All Through The Night (1,5) *5*
Ballad Of Cleo & Joe (6)
Boy Blue (2) *71*
Brimstone And Fire (6)
Broken Glass (4)
Calm Inside The Storm (2)
Change Of Heart (2,5) *3*
Come On Home (5)
Dancing With A Stranger (3)
Dear John (4)
Fall Into Your Dreams (6)

Faraway Nearby (2)
Fearless (6)
Feels Like Christmas (4)
Girls Just Want To Have Fun (1,5) *2*
Hat Full Of Stars (4)
He's So Unusual (1)
Heading West (3)
Hey Now (Girls Just Want To Have Fun) (5) *87*
Hot Gets A Little Cold (6)

I Don't Want To Be Your Friend (3)
I Drove All Night (3,5) *6*
I'll Kiss You (1)
I'm Gonna Be Strong (5)
Iko Iko (2)
Insecurious (3)
Kindred Spirit (3)
Lies (4)
Like A Cat (3)
Like I Used To (4)

Love To Hate (6)
Maybe He'll Know (2)
Money Changes Everything (1,5) *27*
Mother (6)
My First Night Without You (3) *62*
Night To Remember (3)
911 (2)
One Track Mind (2)
Part Hate (4)

Primitive (3)
Product Of Misery (4)
Sally's Pigeons (4,5)
Say A Prayer (6)
Searching (6)
She Bop (1,5) *3*
Sisters Of Avalon (6)
Someone Like Me (4)
That's What I Think (4,5)
Time After Time (1,5) *1*
True Colors (2,5) *1*

Unconditional Love (3)
Unhook The Stars (6)
What's Going On (2,5) *12*
When You Were Mine (1)
Who Let In The Rain (4)
Witness (1)
Yeah Yeah (1)
You Don't Know (6)

LAW, The '91
Rock duo from England: vocalist **Paul Rodgers** (**Free**, **Bad Company**, **The Firm**) and drummer Kenney Jones (**Small Faces**, **Faces**, **The Who**).

| 4/13/91 | 126 | 6 | © | **The Law** | $10 | Atlantic 82195 |

Anything For You
Best Of My Love

Come Save Me (Julianne)
For A Little Ride

Laying Down The Law
Miss You In A Heartbeat

Missing You Bad Girl
Nature Of The Beast

Stone
Stone Cold

Tough Love

LAWRENCE, Joey '93
Born on 4/20/76 in Montgomery, Pennsylvania. Actor/singer. Played "Joey Russo" on TV's *Blossom*.

| 3/6/93 | 74 | 22 | © | **Joey Lawrence** | $10 | Impact 10659 |

Anything For Love
I Can't Help Myself

I Like The Way (Kick Da Smoove Groove)
In These Times

Justa 'Nother Love Song
My Girl
Night By Night

Nothin' My Love Can't Fix *19*
Read My Eyes
Stay Forever *52*

Ways Of Love
Where Does That Leave Me

LAWRENCE, Martin '93
Born on 4/16/65 in Frankfurt, Germany; raised in New York City. Actor/comedian. Starred in several movies and TV shows.

| 10/9/93 | 76 | 9 | © | **Talkin' Shit** | [C] | $10 | EastWest 92289 |

Boxin'
Braggin' On Their Dicks
Drivin' Cross Country

Eddie's House
Fartin' & Shitin'
Head

I Love Sex
Ilaldo
Michael Jackson

Smokin' Weed
Talking During Sex
White Kids/Black Kids

Worrying About Your Weight

LAWRENCE, Steve — '63

Born Sidney Leibowitz on 7/8/35 in Brooklyn, New York. Pop singer. Regular performer on **Steve Allen**'s *Tonight Show*. Married **Eydie Gorme** on 12/29/57.

DEBUT	PEAK	WKS		ARTIST — Album Title	$	Label & Number
6/2/58	19	2	1	Here's Steve Lawrence	$50	Coral 57204
8/14/61	76	10	2	Portrait Of My Love	$25	United Artists 6150
2/9/63	27	29	3	Winners!	$20	Columbia 1953 / 8753
2/15/64	135	5	4	Academy Award Losers	$20	Columbia 2121 / 8921
9/12/64	73	9	5	Everybody Knows	$20	Columbia 2227 / 9027
12/11/65	133	2	6	The Steve Lawrence Show	$20	Columbia 2419 / 9219

STEVE LAWRENCE & EYDIE GORME:

DEBUT	PEAK	WKS		ARTIST — Album Title	$	Label & Number
5/20/67	136	6	7	Together On Broadway	$20	Columbia 2636 / 9436
3/8/69	141	6	8	What It Was, Was Love	$15	RCA Victor 4115
5/10/69	188	3	9	Real True Lovin'	$15	RCA Victor 4107

All The Way (3)
Around The World (3)
Bluesette (5)
Boys And Girls (8)
Cabaret (7)
Call Me (9)
Can't Get Over (The Bossa Nova) (5)
Can't Take My Eyes Off You (9)
Change Partners (4)
Chapter One (9)
Chattanooga Choo Choo (4)
Cheek To Cheek (4)
Come Back To Me (7)
Come Rain Or Come Shine (1)
Cotton Fields (3)
Curtain Falls (7)
Day In Day Out (1)
Don't Blame Me (2)
Don't Let The Sun Catch You Crying (5)

Don't Take Your Love From Me (2)
Easy To Love (1)
Everybody Knows (5) *72*
Exactly Like You (2)
For You (2)
Girl From Ipanema (5)
Go Away Little Girl (3) *1*
Happy Together (9)
Hello, Dolly! (5)
Here's That Rainy Day (5)
Honeymoon Is Over (7)
How About You (4)
I Believe In You (7)
I'll Remember April (4)
I'm Glad There Is You (2)
I've Got You Under My Skin (1,4)
I've Grown Accustomed To Her Face (2)
It's Not For Me To Say (3)

It's Not Unusual (9)
Kansas City (3)
Lazy River (3)
Lollipops And Roses (3)
Long Ago (And Far Away) (4)
Love Letters (4)
Love Me With All Your Heart (5)
Makin' Whoopee (1)
Mame (7)
Millions Of Roses (6)
Misty (3)
Moon River (3)
More Than You Know (2)
More (Theme from Mondo Cane) (5)
Music, Maestro, Please! (1)
My Foolish Heart (4)
Never My Love (9)
Old Fashioned Wedding (7)
Old Man (8)
Once In A Lifetime (6)

People (5)
Portrait Of My Love (2) *9*
Put 'Em In A Box, Tie 'Em With A Ribbon (And Throw 'Em In The Deep Blue Sea) (1)
Real True Lovin' (9)
Remember (6)
Room With The View Inside (8)
Room Without Windows (6)
Sandpiper, Love Theme From The ..see: Shadow Of Your Smile
Save The Last Dance For Me (9)
Second Time Around (2)
Shadow Of Your Smile (6)
Sunny Side Up (1)
Sunrise, Sunset (7)
Sweetheart Tree (6)
Teach Me Tonight (3)
That Old Feeling (4)

There Will Never Be Another You (2)
They Can't Take That Away From Me (4)
Time Has Come To Say Goodnight (6)
To Be In Love (8)
Together Forever (7)
Volare (3)
Walk On By (9)
Walkin' My Baby Back Home (1)
Walking Happy (7)
Warm Hours (6)
What Now My Love (6)
What The World Needs Now (9)
What You Say (8)
What's New Pussycat? (6)
When She Leaves You (2)
When You're In Love (2)

Where Can I Go (6)
Where You Are (8)
Which Way Is Yesterday? (8)
Who's Sorry Now (3)
With A Little Help From My Friends (9)
Wives And Lovers (5)
Yeah, But What If? (8)
Yet...I Know (5) *77*
You Made Me Love You (I Didn't Want To Do It) (1)
You Took Advantage Of Me (1)
You'd Be So Nice To Come Home To (4)
You'll Never Know (6)

LAWRENCE, Tracy — '96

Born on 1/27/68 in Atlanta, Texas; raised in Foreman, Arkansas. Male country singer.

DEBUT	PEAK	WKS	RIAA	CD		ARTIST — Album Title	$	Label & Number
1/18/92	71	40	▲	©	1	Sticks And Stones	$10	Atlantic 82326
3/27/93	25	48	▲²	©	2	Alibis	$10	Atlantic 82483
10/8/94	28	54	▲	©	3	I See It Now	$10	Atlantic 82656
10/7/95	151	4		©	4	Live [L]	$10	Atlantic 82847
2/10/96	25	56	▲²	©	5	Time Marches On	$10	Atlantic 82866
4/5/97	45	22	●	©	6	The Coast Is Clear	$10	Atlantic 82985
9/19/98	92	6	●	©	7	The Best Of Tracy Lawrence [G]	$10	Atlantic 83137
2/19/00	69	6		©	8	Lessons Learned	$10	Atlantic 83269

Alibis (2,4,7) *72*
Any Minute Now (6)
April's Fool (1)
As Any Fool Can See (3)
As Lonesome As It Gets (6)
Back To Back (2)
Better Man, Better Off (6,7)
Between Us (1)
Can't Break It To My Heart (2,4,7)
Cards, The (3)
Coast Is Clear (6)
Crying Ain't Dying (2)

Dancin' To Sweet 17 (1)
Different Man (5)
Don't Talk To Me That Way (1)
Excitable Boy (5)
From Here To Kingdom Come (8)
From The Inside Out (8)
From What We Give (5)
Froze Over (4)
God Made Woman On A Good Day (3)
Guilt Trip (3)
Her Old Stompin' Ground (7)

Hillbilly With A Heartache (3)
Holes That He Dug (8)
How A Cowgirl Says Goodbye (6)
I Got A Feelin' (3)
I Hit The Ground Crawlin' (6)
I Hope Heaven Has A Honky Tonk (1)
I Know That Hurt By Heart (5)
I Threw The Rest Away (2,4)
I'd Give Anything To Be Your Everything Again (3)

If The Good Die Young (2,4,7)
If The World Had A Front Porch (3,7)
If You Loved Me (5)
In A Moment Of Weakness (6)
Is That A Tear (5,7)
It Only Takes One Bar (To Make A Prison) (2)
Just You And Me (8)
Lessons Learned (8) *40*
Livin' In Black And White (6)
Lonely (8)
Long Wet Kiss (8)

Man I Was (8)
My Second Home (2)
One Step Ahead Of The Storm (6)
Paris, Tennessee (1)
Renegades, Rebels and Rogues (4)
Runnin' Behind (1,4)
Somebody Paints The Wall (1,4)
Somewhere Between The Moon And You (5)
Speed Of A Fool (5)

Stars Over Texas (5,7)
Steps (8)
Sticks And Stones (1,4,7)
Texas Tornado (3)
Time Marches On (5,7)
Today's Lonely Fool (1,4)
Unforgiven (8)
Up All Night (8)
We Don't Love Here Anymore (2)
While You Sleep (6,7)

LAWRENCE, Vicki — '73

Born on 5/26/49 in Inglewood, California. Singer/actress. With **The Young Americans** from 1964-67. Regular on **Carol Burnett**'s CBS-TV series from 1967-78. Also starred in TV's *Mama's Family* (1982-87). Married to **Bobby Russell** from 1972-74.

DEBUT	PEAK	WKS		ARTIST — Album Title	$	Label & Number
4/28/73	51	14		The Night The Lights Went Out In Georgia	$15	Bell 1120

Dime A Dance
(For A While) We Helped Each Other Out

Gypsys, Tramps, And Thieves
He Did With Me *75*
How You Gonna Stand It

It Could Have Been Me
Killing Me Softly With His Song
Little Green Apples

Mr. Allison
Night The Lights Went Out In Georgia *1*

Sensual Man

LAWS, Debra — '81

Born on 9/10/56 in Houston. R&B singer. Sister of **Eloise Laws**, **Hubert Laws** and **Ronnie Laws**.

DEBUT	PEAK	WKS		ARTIST — Album Title	$	Label & Number
4/11/81	70	27		Very Special	$12	Elektra 300

All The Things I Love
Be Yourself

How Long
Long As We're Together

Meant For You
On My Own

Very Special *90*
Your Love

LAWS, Eloise — '78

Born on 11/6/43 in Houston. R&B singer. Sister of **Debra Laws**, **Hubert Laws** and **Ronnie Laws**.

DEBUT	PEAK	WKS		ARTIST — Album Title	$	Label & Number
2/4/78	156	5	1	Eloise	$12	ABC 1022
2/14/81	175	7	2	Eloise Laws	$12	Liberty 1063

Almost All The Way To Love (2)
Baby You Lied (1)
Forever Now (1)
Got You Into My Life (2)
His House And Me (1)

I'm Just Warmin' Up (2)
If I Don't Watch Out (2)
Let's Find Those Two People Again (1)
Love Comes Easy (1)

Love Is Feeling (1)
Moment To Moment (2)
Number One (1) *97*
Search, Find (2)

Someone Who Still Needs Me (1)
Strength Of A Woman (2)
1,000 Laughs (1) *91*
You Are Everything (2)

You're Incredible (1)

LAWS, Hubert — '75

Born on 11/10/39 in Houston. Jazz flutist. Brother of **Ronnie Laws**, **Eloise Laws** and **Debra Laws**.

DEBUT	PEAK	WKS		ARTIST — Album Title	$	Label & Number
2/24/73	148	9	1	Morning Star [I]	$15	CTI 6022
6/30/73	175	6	2	Carnegie Hall [I-L]	$15	CTI 6025
				recorded on 1/12/73		

LAWS, Hubert — Cont'd

DEBUT	PEAK	WKS			Album	Sym	$	Label & Number
6/21/75	42	18		3	The Chicago Theme	[I]	$15	CTI 6058
11/6/76	139	6	©	4	Romeo & Juliet	[I]	$12	Columbia 34330
4/8/78	71	18		5	Say It With Silence	[I]	$12	Columbia 35022
4/28/79	93	8		6	Land Of Passion		$12	Columbia 35708
9/27/80	134	4		7	How To Beat The High Cost Of Living	[I-S]	$12	Columbia 36741

HUBERT LAWS & EARL KLUGH

| 11/8/80 | 133 | 13 | | 8 | Family | [I] | $12 | Columbia 36396 |

Amazing Grace (1) — Baron, The (5) — Caper, The (7) — Chicago Theme (3) — Down River (7) — Dream Something (7) — Edge, The (7) — False Faces (5) — Family (8) — Fire & Rain (medley) (2) — Forlane (4) — Going Home (3) — Guatemala Connection (4) — Heartbeats (6) — I Had A Dream (3) — Inflation Chaser (3) — It Happens Every Day (5) — It's So Easy Loving You (7) — Key, The (6) — Land Of Passion (6) — Let Her Go (1) — Love Gets Better (5) — Memory Of Minnie (Riperton) (8) — Midnight At The Oasis (3) — Morning Star (1) — Music Forever (6) — Night Moves (7) — No More (1) — Passacaglia In C Minor (2) — Piccolo Boogie (7) — Ravel's Bolero (8) — Ready To Run (7) — Romeo & Juliet (4) — Say It With Silence (5) — Say You're Mine (8) — Scuffle, The (7) — Song For A Pretty Girl (7) — Tryin' To Get The Feeling Again (4) — Undecided (4) — We Will Be (6) — We're In Ecstasy (6) — What A Night! (8) — What Are We Gonna Do (4) — What Do You Think Of This World Now? (1) — Where Is The Love (1) — Wildfire (8) — Windows (medley) (2) — You Make Me Feel Brand New (3)

LAWS, Ronnie '77

Born on 10/3/50 in Houston. Jazz saxophonist. Brother of **Debra Laws**, **Eloise Laws** and **Hubert Laws**. With **Earth, Wind & Fire** from 1972-73.

9/27/75	73	29	©	1	Pressure Sensitive	[I]	$15	Blue Note 452
6/12/76	46	21	©	2	Fever	[I]	$15	Blue Note 628
5/7/77	37	28	● ©	3	Friends And Strangers	[I]	$15	Blue Note 730
11/4/78	51	22	©	4	Flame		$12	United Artists 881
2/16/80	24	19		5	Every Generation		$12	United Artists 1001
10/10/81	51	19	©	6	Solid Ground		$12	Liberty 51087
8/13/83	98	11	©	7	Mr. Nice Guy		$12	Capitol 12261

All For You (4) — All The Time (2) — Always There (1) — As One (5) — Big Stars (7) — Can't Save Tomorrow (7) — Captain Midnite (2) — Every Generation (5) — Fever (2) — Flame (4) — Friends And Strangers (3) — From Ronnie With Love (2) — Good Feelings (6) — Goodtime Ride (3) — Grace (4) — Heavy On Easy (6) — In The Groove (7) — Joy (4) — Just As You Are (6) — Just Love (3) — Karmen (2) — Let's Keep It Together (2) — Life In Paradise (3) — Live Your Life Away (4) — Living Love (4) — Love Is Here (4) — Love's Victory (5) — Mis' Mary's Place (1) — Momma (2) — Mr. Nice Guy (7) — Never Be The Same (1) — Never Get Back To Houston (5) — New Day (3) — Night Breeze (2) — Nothing To Lose (1) — Nuthin' 'Bout Nuthin' (3) — O.T.B.A. Law (Outta Be A Law) (5) — Off And On Again (7) — Rolling (7) — Same Old Story (3) — Saturday Evening (3) — Segue (6) — Solid Ground (6) — **Stay Awake (6) 60** — Stay Still (And Let Me Love You) (2) — Strugglin' (2) — Summer Fool (6) — Tell Me Something Good (1) — There's A Way (6) — These Days (4) — Third Hour (7) — Thoughts & Memories (5) — Tidal Wave (1) — Tomorrow (4) — What Does It Take (7) — Why Do You Laugh At Me (1) — You (7) — Young Child (5) — Your Stuff (6)

L-BURNA A.K.A. LAYZIE BONE '01

Born Steven Howse in Cleveland. Male rapper. Member of **Bone Thugs-N-Harmony**.

| 4/7/01 | 43 | 6 | © | | Thug By Nature | | $10 | Ruthless 85173 |

As The Rain — Battlefield — Connectin' The Plots — Deadly Musical — Fear No Man — How Long Will It Last — Listen — Lock-N-Load — Make My Day — My Niggaz — Smoke On — Still The Greatest — There They Go — Thug By Nature — Time Will Tell — Up Against The Wall

LEADERS OF THE NEW SCHOOL '93

Rap group from Uniondale, New York: **Busta Rhymes**, Charlie Brown, Dinco D and Cut Monitor Milo.

| 8/17/91 | 128 | 6 | | 1 | A Future Without A Past... | | $10 | Elektra 60976 |
| 10/30/93 | 66 | 4 | © | 2 | T.I.M.E. - The Inner Mind's Eye - The Endless Dispute With Reality | | $10 | Elektra 61382 |

Bass Is Loaded (2) — Case Of The P.T.A. (1) — Classic Material (2) — Connections (2) — Daily Reminder (2) — Difference, The (2) — End Is Near (2) — Eternal (2) — Feminine Fatt (1) — International Zone Coaster (1) — Just When You Thought It Was Safe... (1) — My Ding-A-Ling (1) — Noisy Meditation (2) — Quarter To Cutthroat (2) — Show Me A Hero (1) — Sobb Story (1) — Sound Of The Zeekers @#^*?! (1) — Spontaneous (13 MC's Deep!) (2) — Syntax Era (2) — Teachers, Don't Teach Us Nonsense!! (1) — Time Will Tell (2) — Too Much On My Mind (1) — Trains, Planes And Automobiles (1) — Transformers (1) — Understanding The Inner Mind's Eye (2) — What's Next? (2) — What's The Pinocchio's Theory? (1) — Where Do We Go From Here? (1) — Zearocks (2)

LEADON, Bernie/Michael Georgiades Band '77

Leadon was born on 7/19/47 in Minneapolis. Rock guitarist. Member of the **Flying Burrito Brothers** and the **Eagles**. With Georgiades on vocals/guitar.

| 8/20/77 | 91 | 6 | | | Natural Progressions | | $12 | Asylum 1107 |

As Time Goes On — At Love Again — Breath — Callin' For Your Love — Glass Off — How Can You Live Without Love? — Rotation — Sparrow, The — Tropical Winter — You're The Singer

LEAGUE UNLIMITED ORCHESTRA — see HUMAN LEAGUE, The

LEAPY LEE '69

Born Lee Graham on 7/2/42 in Eastbourne, England. Male singer/actor.

| 1/18/69 | 71 | 12 | | | Little Arrows | | $20 | Decca 75076 |

Harper Valley P.T.A. — I'll Be Your Baby Tonight — If I Ever Get To Saginaw Again — **Little Arrows 16** — Little Green Apples — My Girl Maria — Roly — Senorita Jones — So Afraid — Teresa — Where Has All The Love Gone

LEARY, Denis '93

Born on 4/20/57 in Boston. Comedian/actor. Acted in several movies and TV shows.

| 2/13/93 | 85 | 13 | © | 1 | No Cure For Cancer | [C] | $10 | A&M 540055 |
| 12/6/97 | 169 | 1 | © | 2 | Lock 'N Load | [C] | $10 | A&M 540832 |

Asshole (1) — Asshole Of The Dance (2) — Beer (2) — Coffee (2) — Deaf Mute Cocktail Party (2) — Death (1) — Downtrodden Song (1) — Drugs (1) — Elvis And I (2) — Fat Fucks (2) — Fuck Santa (2) — Fuck The Kennedys (2) — Fuck The Pope (2) — Fuck This (2) — I'm Happy (2) — Insane Cowboy (In Africa) (2) — Life's Gonna Suck (2) — Lock 'N Load (2) — Love Barge (2) — Marv Marv Marv (2) — Meat (1) — More Drugs (1) — My Kids (2) — President Leary (2) — Reading From The Book Of Apple (2) — Rehab (1) — Save This (2) — Smoke (1) — Traditional Irish Folk Song (1) — Voices In My Head (1)

LEATHERWOLF '88

Hard-rock group from Los Angeles: Michael Oliveri (vocals), Carey Howe and Geoffrey Gayer (guitars), Paul Carman (bass) and Dean Roberts (drums).

| 3/5/88 | 105 | 12 | | © | 1 **Leatherwolf** | | | $10 | Island 90660 |
| 4/29/89 | 123 | 8 | | © | 2 **Street Ready** | | | $10 | Island 91072 |

Bad Moon Rising (1) Black Knight (2) Calling, The (1) Cry Out (1) Gypsies And Thieves (1) Hideaway (2) Lonely Road (2) Magical Eyes (1) Princess Of Love (1) Rise Or Fall (1) Rule The Night (1) Share A Dream (1) Spirits In The Wind (2) Street Ready (2) Take A Chance (2) Thunder (2) Too Much (2) Way I Feel (2) Wicked Ways (2)

LEAVES, The '66

Garage-rock group from Northridge, California: Robert Arlin (vocals), John Beck and Robert Lee Reiner (guitars), Jim Pons (bass), and Tom Ray (drums). Pons was later a brief member of **The Turtles**.

| 7/30/66 | 127 | 5 | | © | **Hey Joe** | | | $50 | Mira 3005 |

Back On The Avenue Dr. Stone Get Out Of My Life Woman Girl From The East Good-Bye My Lover He Was A Friend Of Mine **Hey Joe** *31* Just A Memory Tobacco Road Too Many People War Of Distortion Words

LeBLANC & CARR '78

Soft-rock duo: Lenny LeBlanc (born on 6/17/51 in Leominster, Massachusetts) and Pete Carr (born on 4/22/50 in Daytona Beach).

| 3/18/78 | 145 | 7 | | | **Midnight Light** | | | $12 | Big Tree 89521 |

Coming And Going Desperado **Falling** *13* How Does It Feel (To Be In Love) I Believe That We I Need To Know Johnny Too Bad **Midnight Light** *91* Something About You Stronger Love

LeDOUX, Chris '92

Born on 10/2/48 in Biloxi, Mississippi. Country singer/songwriter/guitarist. Former rodeo champion.

8/15/92	65	38	●	©	1 **Whatcha Gonna Do With A Cowboy**			$10	Liberty 98818
7/31/93	131	8		©	2 **Under This Old Hat**			$10	Liberty 80892
9/24/94	128	3		©	3 **Haywire**			$10	Liberty 28770
8/1/98	180	1		©	4 **One Road Man**			$10	Capitol 21942
6/26/99	145	7		©	5 **20 Greatest Hits**		[G]	$10	Capitol 99781
8/19/00	134	5		©	6 **Cowboy**			$10	Capitol 26601

Bang A Drum (4,5) Big Love (3) Billy The Kid (3) Blue Eyes And Freckles (3) Borderline, The (4) Caballo Diablo (4) Cadillac Cowboy (5) Cadillac Ranch (1,2,5) Call Of The Wild (1) Copenhagen (5) County Fair (5) Cowboy's Got To Ride (6) Cowboys Like A Little Rock And Roll (2) Dallas Days And Fort Worth Nights (3,5) Even Cowboys Like A Little Rock And Roll (5) Every Time I Roll The Dice (2) Fever, The (4) Five Dollar Fine (5) For Your Love (2,5) Get Back On That Pony (4) Gravitational Pull (5) Hairtrigger Colts (3) He Rides The Wild Horses (6) Hippies In Calgary (6) Honky Tonk World (3,5) Hooked On An 8 Second Ride (1,5) I'm Country (6) I'm Ready If You're Willing (1) Life Is A Highway (4,5) Light Of The World (4) Little Long-Haired Outlaw (6) Look At You Girl (1,5) Love Needs A Fool (3) Making Ends Meet (1) Old Paint (4) Ole Slew Foot (4) One Ride In Vegas (4) One Road Man (4) One Tonight (4) Our First Year (6) Powder River Home (2) Runaway Love (4) Running Through The Rain (6) She's Tough (2) Silence On The Line (6) Slow Down (3) Soft Place To Fall (2) Sometimes You've Just Gotta Ride (4) Song Of Wyoming (6) Sons Of The Pioneers (3) Stampede (5) Strugglin' Years (2) Ten Seconds In The Saddle (6) This Cowboy's Hat (5) Tougher Than The Rest (3,5) Under This Old Hat (2) Western Skies (1,5) Whatcha Gonna Do With A Cowboy (1,5) Wild And Wooly (2) Yellow Stud (2) You Just Can't See Him From The Road (1)

LED ZEPPELIN ★45★ '71

Hard-rock group formed in England: **Robert Plant** (vocals), **Jimmy Page** (guitar), John Paul Jones (bass, keyboards) and John Bonham (drums). First known as the New Yardbirds. Page had been in **The Yardbirds** from 1966-68. Plant and Bonham had been in a group called Band of Joy. Group formed own Swan Song label in 1974. In concert movie *The Song Remains The Same* in 1976. Bonham died of asphyxiation on 9/25/80 (age 33). Group disbanded in December 1980. Plant and Page formed **The Honeydrippers** in 1984. Page also with **The Firm** (1984-86). "**Bonham**" is the name of group formed by Jason Bonham, John's son, in 1989. Led Zeppelin's most famous recording, "Stairway To Heaven" (on album *Led Zeppelin IV*), was never released as a commercial single. Group inducted into the Rock and Roll Hall of Fame in 1995.

1)Led Zeppelin II 2)In Through The Out Door 3)Physical Graffiti

2/15/69	10	95	▲⁸	©	1 **Led Zeppelin**	C:#10/105		$20	Atlantic 8216
11/8/69	❶⁷	98	▲¹²	©	2 **Led Zeppelin II**	C:#6/149		$20	Atlantic 8236
10/24/70	❶⁴	42	▲⁶	©	3 **Led Zeppelin III**			$15	Atlantic 7201
11/27/71	2⁴	259	▲²²	©	4 **Led Zeppelin IV (untitled)**	C:❶⁴⁹/344		$15	Atlantic 7208
4/14/73	❶²	99	▲¹¹	©	5 **Houses Of The Holy**	C:#17/70		$15	Atlantic 7255
3/15/75	❶⁶	41	▲¹⁵	©	6 **Physical Graffiti**			$20	Swan Song 200 [2]
4/24/76	❶²	30	▲³	©	7 **Presence**	C:#14/19		$15	Swan Song 8416
11/6/76	2³	48	▲⁴	©	8 **The Soundtrack From The Film "The Song Remains The Same"** recorded at Madison Square Garden		[L-S]	$20	Swan Song 201 [2]
9/8/79	❶⁷	41	▲⁷	©	9 **In Through The Out Door**			$15	Swan Song 16002
12/18/82+	6	16	▲	©	10 **Coda** previously unreleased recordings from 1969-78		[K]	$15	Swan Song 90051
11/10/90	18	20	▲¹⁰	©	11 **Led Zeppelin (Boxed Set)**	C:#18/12	[K]	$40	Atlantic 82144 [4]
3/28/92	47	12	▲²	©	12 **Remasters**		[K]	$30	Atlantic 82371 [3]
10/9/93	87	2	▲²	©	13 **Boxed Set 2**		[K]	$20	Atlantic 82477 [2]
12/6/97	12	20	▲²	©	14 **BBC Sessions** recorded from 1969-71		[E-L]	$15	Atlantic 83061 [2]
12/11/99	71	26	▲	©	15 **Early Days - The Best Of Led Zeppelin Volume One**		[G]	$10	Atlantic 83268
4/8/00	81	6		©	16 **Latter Days - The Best Of Led Zeppelin Volume Two**		[G]	$10	Atlantic 83278

Achilles Last Stand (7,11,12,16) All My Love (9,11,12,16) Babe I'm Gonna Leave You (1,11,12,15) Baby Come On Home (13) Battle Of Evermore (4,11,12,15) Black Country Woman (6,13) **Black Dog** (4,11,12,14,15) *15* Black Mountain Side (1,11,13) Bonzo's Montreux (10,11,13) Boogie With Stu (6,13) Bring It On Home (2,13) Bron-Y-Aur Stomp (3,11) Bron-Yr-Aur (6,13) Candy Store Rock (7,11) Carousel Ambra (3) Celebration Day (3,8,11,12) Communication Breakdown (1,11,12,14,15) Crunge, The (5,13) Custard Pie (6,11) **D'yer Mak'er** (5,11,12) *20* Dancing Days (5,11) Darlene (10,13) Dazed And Confused (1,8,11,12,14,15) Down By The Seaside (6,13) **Fool In The Rain** (9,11) *21* For Your Life (7,13) Four Sticks (4,13) Friends (3,11) Gallows Pole (3,11) Girl I Love She Got Long Black Wavy Hair (14) Going To California (4,11,14) **Good Times Bad Times** (1,12,13,15) *80* Hats Off To (Roy) Harper (3,13) Heartbreaker (2,11,12,14) Hey Hey What Can I Do (11) Hot Dog (9,13) Hots On For Nowhere (7,13) Houses Of The Holy (6,11,12,16) How Many More Times (1,13,14) I Can't Quit You Baby (1,10,11,13,14) I'm Gonna Crawl (9,11) **Immigrant Song** (3,11,12,14,15) *16* In My Time Of Dying (6,13) In The Evening (9,11,12,16) In The Light (6,11) Kashmir (6,11,12,16) Lemon Song (2,13) **Living Loving Maid (She's Just A Woman)** (2,13) *65* Misty Mountain Hop (4,11,12) Moby Dick (2,8,11,13) Night Flight (6,13) No Quarter (5,8,11,12,16) Nobody's Fault But Mine (7,11,12,16) Ocean, The (5,11) **Over The Hills And Far Away** (5,11) *51* Ozone Baby (10,11) Poor Tom (10,11)

LED ZEPPELIN — Cont'd

Rain Song (5,8,11,12)
Ramble On (2,11,12)
Rock And Roll
(4,8,11,12,15) **47**
Rover, The (6,13)
Royal Orleans (7,13)
(She's Just A Woman) ..see:
Living Loving Maid

Sick Again (6,13)
Since I've Been Loving You (3,11,12,14,15)
Somethin' Else (14)
Song Remains The Same (5,8,11,12,16)
South Bound Saurez (9,13)

Stairway To Heaven (4,8,11,12,14,15)
Tangerine (3,11)
Tea For One (7,13)
Ten Years Gone (6,11,16)
Thank You (2,11,14)
That's The Way (3,13,14)

Trampled Under Foot (6,11,12,16) **38**
Travelling Riverside Blues (11,14)
Walter's Walk (10,13)
Wanton Song (6,11)
We're Gonna Groove (10,13)

Wearing And Tearing (10,11)
What Is And What Should Never Be (2,11,14,15)
When The Levee Breaks (4,11,15)
White Summer (medley) (11)

Whole Lotta Love (2,8,11,12,14,15) **4**
Whole Lotta Love (Medley) (14)
You Shook Me (1,13,14)
Your Time Is Gonna Come (1,11)

LEE, Alvin   '75

Born on 12/19/44 in Nottingham, England. Rock singer/guitarist. Leader of **Ten Years After**.

DEBUT	PEAK	WKS	CD	#	Title	Sym	$	Label
1/12/74	138	8		1	On The Road To Freedom		$12	Columbia 32729
					ALVIN LEE & MYLON LeFEVRE			
1/4/75	65	12	©	2	In Flight	[L]	$15	Columbia 33187 [2]
9/6/75	131	5	©	3	Pump Iron!		$12	Columbia 33796
6/3/78	115	11		4	Rocket Fuel		$12	RSO 3033
5/26/79	158	5		5	Ride On		$12	RSO 3049
12/20/80+	198	4		6	Free Fall		$12	Atlantic 19287
8/23/86	124	9	©	7	Detroit Diesel		$10	21 Records 90517

Ain't Nothin' Shakin' (4,5)
All Life's Trials (2)
Alvin's Blue Thing (4)
Baby, Don't You Cry (4)
Back In My Arms Again (7)
(Battle, The) ..see: Devil's Screaming
Burnt Fungus (3)
Can't Sleep At Nite (5)
Carry My Load (1)
City Lights (6)
Darkest Night (3)
Detroit Diesel (7)
Devil's Screaming - Part 1 & 2 (4)

Don't Be Cruel (2)
Don't Want To Fight (7)
Dustbin City (6)
Every Blues You've Ever Heard (2)
Fallen Angel (1)
Freedom For The Stallion (2)
Friday The 13th (4)
Funny (1)
Going Home (5)
Going Through The Door (2)
Gonna Turn U On (4)
Got To Keep Moving (2)
Have Mercy (3)
Heart Of Stone (7)

Heartache (6)
Hey Joe (5)
How Many Times (2)
I Can't Take It (1)
I Don't Wanna Stop (6)
I'm Writing You A Letter (2)
I've Got Eyes For You Baby (2)
It's A Gaz (3)
It's All Right Now (3)
Julian Rice (3)
Keep A Knockin' (2)
Lay Me Back (1)
Let 'Em Say What They Will (1)
Let The Sea Burn Down (3)
Let's Get Back (2)

Let's Go (7)
Money Honey (2)
Mystery Train (2)
No More Lonely Nights (6)
On The Road To Freedom (1)
One Lonely Hour (6)
One More Chance (3)
Ordinary Man (7)
Ride My Train (3)
Ride On Cowboy (5)
Ridin' Truckin' (6)
Riffin (1)
Rocket Fuel (4)
Rockin' Till The Sun Goes Down (1)

Running Round (2)
Scat Encounter (5)
She's So Cute (7)
Shot In The Dark (7)
Sittin' Here (5)
Slow Down (2)
So Sad (No Love Of His Own) (1)
Somebody Callin' Me (4)
Somebody's Waltz (4)
Sooner Or Later (6)
Stealin' (6)
Take The Money And Run (6)
Talk Don't Bother Me (7)
There's A Feeling (2)

Time And Space (3)
Too Late To Run For Cover (7)
Too Much (5)
Truckin' Down The Other Way (3)
Try To Be Righteous (1)
We Will Shine (1)
World Is Changing (1)
You Need Love Love Love (2)
You Told Me (3)

LEE, Brenda   ★185★   '61

Born Brenda Mae Tarpley on 12/11/44 in Lithonia, Georgia. Professional singer since age six. Signed to Decca Records in 1956. Became known as "Little Miss Dynamite." Successful country singer from 1971-85.

1)This Is.....Brenda 2)Brenda Lee 3)All The Way

DEBUT	PEAK	WKS	#	Title	Sym	$	Label
8/22/60	5	57	1	Brenda Lee		$40	Decca 74039
11/21/60+	4	41	2	This Is.....Brenda		$40	Decca 74082
5/8/61	24	33	3	Emotions		$30	Decca 74104
8/28/61	17	39	4	All The Way		$30	Decca 74176
3/24/62	29	23	5	Sincerely		$30	Decca 74216
11/3/62	20	22	6	Brenda, That's All		$30	Decca 74326
3/9/63	25	31	7	All Alone Am I		$30	Decca 74370
12/21/63+	39	13	8	Let Me Sing		$30	Decca 74439
6/13/64	90	11	9	By Request		$30	Decca 74509
12/5/64+	7[X]	18	10	Merry Christmas from Brenda Lee	[X]	$30	Decca 74583
				Christmas charts: 15/'64, 17/'65, 20/'66, 58/'67, 33/'68, 7/'72			
9/25/65	36	14	11	Too Many Rivers		$25	Decca 74684
4/9/66	94	13	12	Bye Bye Blues		$25	Decca 74755
6/25/66	70	14	13	10 Golden Years	[G]	$20	Decca 74757
12/24/66+	94	12	14	Coming On Strong		$15	Decca 74825
6/15/68	187	2	15	For The First Time		$15	Decca 74955
				BRENDA LEE & PETE FOUNTAIN			
5/24/69	98	9	16	Johnny One Time		$15	Decca 75111
1/15/83	109	14	©	17	Kris, Willie, Dolly & Brenda...the winning hand		$15	Monument 38389 [2]
				KRIS KRISTOFFERSON, WILLIE NELSON, DOLLY PARTON & BRENDA LEE			

All Alone Am I (7,13) **3**
All By Myself (7)
All The Way (4)
Angel And The Little Blue Bell (10)
Anything Goes (15)
Around The World (3)
As Usual (9,13) **12**
At Last (8)
Bandits Of Beverly Hills (17)
Basin Street Blues (15)
Be My Love Again (1)
Big Chance (4)
Bigger The Fool, The Harder The Fall (17)
Bill Bailey, Won't You Please Come Home (13)
Blue Christmas (10)
Blue Velvet (9)
Blueberry Hill (2)
Born To Love Me (17)
Break It To Me Gently (8) **4**
Bring Me Sunshine (16)

Bring On The Sunshine (17)
Build A Big Fence (2)
By Myself (7)
Bye Bye Blues (12)
Cabaret (15)
Call Me (14)
Call Me Irresponsible (11)
Can't Take My Eyes Off You (15)
Casey's Last Ride (17)
Christmas Will Be Just Another Lonely Day (10)
Coming On Strong (14) **11**
Crazy Talk (3)
Cry (3)
Crying Time (14)
Danke Schoen (9)
Days Of Wine And Roses (9)
Do I Worry (Yes I Do) (4)
Dum Dum (4,13) **4**
Dynamite (1,13) **72**
Emotions (3) **7**

End Of The World (8)
Eventually (4) **56**
Everybody Loves Somebody (11)
Everything's Beautiful (In It's Own Way) (17)
59th Street Bridge Song (Feelin' Groovy) (15)
Flowers On The Wall (12)
Fly Me To The Moon (In Other Words) (7)
Fool #1 (6,13) **3**
Fools Rush In (Where Angels Fear To Tread) (6)
For Once In My Life (16)
Frosty The Snowman (10)
Georgia On My Mind (3)
Gonna Find Me A Bluebird (6)
Good Life (12)
Grass Is Greener (9) **17**
Hallelujah I Love Him So (2)
Happy Happy Birthday Baby (17)

Heading Home (1)
Hello, Dolly! (11)
Help Me Make It Through The Night (17)
Help Yourself (16)
Here Comes That Rainbow Again (17)
Hold Me (5)
How Deep Is The Ocean (How High Is The Sky) (5)
I Gotta Right To Sing The Blues (15)
I Hadn't Anyone Till You (7)
I Left My Heart In San Francisco (7)
I Love You Because (9)
I Miss You (5)
I Never Cared For You (17)
I Wanna Be Around (8)
I Want To Be Wanted (2) **1**
I Wonder (9) **25**
I'll Always Be In Love With You (5)

I'll Be Seeing You (5)
I'm Confessin' (That I Love You) (9)
I'm In The Mood For Love (3)
I'm Learning About Love (3) **33**
I'm Sitting On Top Of The World (17)
I'm Sorry (1,13) **1**
If I Didn't Care (2)
(If I'm Dreaming) Just Let Me Dream (1)
If You Go Away (16)
If You Love Me (Really Love Me) (3)
It's A Lonesome Old Town (When You're Not Around) (6)
It's All Right With Me (7)
It's Not Unusual (11)
It's The Talk Of The Town (5)
Jambalaya (On The Bayou) (1,13)
Jingle Bell Rock (10)

Johnny One Time (16) **41**
Just A Little (2) **40**
Just Another Lie (3)
Just Out Of Reach (6)
Kansas City (4)
King Of A Lonely Castle (17)
Kiss Away (14)
Lazy River (5)
Let It Be Me (16)
Let's Jump The Broomstick (1)
Letter, The (16)
Little Things (17)
Losing You (8) **6**
Love And Learn (2)
Lover (7)
Lover, Come Back To Me (4)
Make The World Go Away (12)
Marshmallow World (10)
Matelot (16)
Mood Indigo (15)
More (9)
My Baby Likes Western Guys (1)

488

LEE, Brenda — Cont'd

My Coloring Book (7)
My Prayer (7)
My Whole World Is Falling Down (9) *24*
Night And Day (8,15)
No One (11) *98*
On The Sunny Side Of The Street (4)
One Of Those Songs (Le Bal De Madame De Mortemouille) (15)
Only You (And Only Me) (5)
Organ Grinder's Swing (6)
Our Day Will Come (8)
Out In The Cold Again (8)
Ping Pong (17)
Pretend (2)
Put It Off Until Tomorrow (17)
Remember When (We Made These Memories) (12)

Rockin' Around The Christmas Tree (10) *14*
Rusty Bells (12) *33*
Sandpiper, Love Theme From The ..see: Shadow Of Your Smile
Santa Claus Is Comin' To Town (10)
Send Me Some Lovin' (5)
September In The Rain (11)
Shadow Of Your Smile (12)
Silver Bells (10)
Softly, As I Leave You (12)
Someday You'll Want Me To Want You (6)
Someone Loves You Honey (17)
Someone To Love Me (The Prisoner's Song) (4)
Somewhere (14)

Speak To Me Pretty (4)
Stormy Weather (Keeps Raining All The Time) (11)
Strangers In The Night (14)
Strawberry Snow (10)
Summer Wind (14)
Swanee River Rock (3)
Sweet Dreams (14)
Sweet Nothin's (1,13) *4*
Sweethearts On Parade (6)
Talkin' 'Bout You (4)
Tammy (4)
Taste Of Honey (12)
Teach Me Tonight (2)
That's All You Gotta Do (1) *6*
There Goes My Heart (8)
There's A Kind Of Hush (All Over The World) (15)
Think (11) *25*
This Girl's In Love With You (16)

This Time Of The Year (10)
To Make A Long Story Short, She's Gone (17)
Too Many Rivers (11,13) *13*
Traces (16)
Tragedy (4)
Truer Than True (11)
Unforgettable (11)
Uptight (Everything's Alright) (14)
Valley Of Tears (6)
Walk Away (16)
Walkin' To New Orleans (2)
We Three (My Echo, My Shadow And Me) (2)
Wee Wee Willies (1)
Weep No More My Baby (1)
What A Diff'rence A Day Made (12)
What Do You Think About Lovin' (17)

What Kind Of Fool Am I? (7)
What Now My Love (14)
When I Fall In Love (3)
When My Dreamboat Comes Home (2)
When Your Lover Has Gone (8)
Where Are You (8)
Whispering (11)
White Silver Sands (6)
Who Can I Turn To (When Nobody Needs Me) (11)
Why Don't You Believe Me (9)
Why Me? (6)
Will You Love Me Tomorrow (3)
Windy (15)
Winter Wonderland (10)
Yesterday (12)
You Always Hurt The One You Love (5)
You Can Depend On Me (6) *6*

You Don't Have To Say You Love Me (14)
You Left Me A Long, Long Time Ago (17)
You'll Always Have Someone (17)
You're Gonna Love Yourself (In The Morning) (17)
You're The Reason I'm Living (8)
You've Got Me Crying Again (5)
You've Got Your Troubles (14)

LEE, Dickey   '62

Born Dickey Lipscomb on 9/21/36 in Memphis. Pop-country singer/songwriter.

| 11/10/62 | 50 | 12 | | | **The Tale Of Patches** | | | $40 | Smash 67020 |

Ballad Of A Teenage Queen
Devil Woman
Ebony Eyes
Little Bitty Tear
Miller's Cave
Patches *6*
Roses Are Red
Running Bear
Teen Angel
Tell Laura I Love Her
Travelin' Man
Wolverton Mountain

LEE, Geddy   '00

Born Gary Lee Weinrib on 7/29/53 in Toronto. Lead singer/bassist of **Rush**.

| 12/2/00 | 52 | 3 | | © | **My Favorite Headache** | | | $10 | Anthem 83384 |

Angels' Share
Grace To Grace
Home On The Strange
Moving To Bohemia
My Favorite Headache
Present Tense
Runaway Train
Slipping
Still
Window To The World
Working At Perfekt

LEE, Jackie   '66

Born Earl Nelson on 9/8/28 in Lake Charles, Louisiana. R&B singer.

| 2/5/66 | 85 | 9 | | | **The Duck** | | | $30 | Mirwood 7000 |

Bounce, The
Dancin' In The Street
Do The Temptation Walk
Do You Love Me
Duck, The *14*
Duck - Part II, The
Everybody Jerk
Harlem Shuffle
Hully Gully
Land Of A Thousand Dances
Neighborhood, The
Shotgun And The Duck

LEE, Johnny   '80

Born John Lee Ham on 7/3/46 in Texas City; raised in Alta Loma, Texas. Country singer/songwriter. Married to actress Charlene Tilton from 1982-84.

| 11/15/80 | 132 | 21 | ● | 1 | **Lookin' For Love** | | | $12 | Asylum 309 |
| 10/24/81 | 147 | 8 | | 2 | **Bet Your Heart On Me** | | | $12 | Full Moon 541 |

Anni (1)
Be There For Me Baby (2)
Bet Your Heart On Me (2) *54*
Crossfire (2)
Do You Love As Good As You Look (1)
Down And Dirty (1)
Dreams Die Hard (1)
Finally Fallin' (2)
Fool For Love (1)
Highways Run On Forever (2)
How Deep In Love Am I (2)
I've Come A Long Way (But I Got A Long Way To Go) (2)
Little Bit Of Lovin' (2)
Lookin' For Love (1) *5*
Never Lay My Lovin' Down (1)
One In A Million (1)
Prisoner Of Hope (1)
Somebody Love You (2)
Too Damned Old (1)
When You Fall In Love (2)

LEE, Laura   '72

Born Laura Lee Rundless on 3/9/45 in Chicago. R&B singer.

| 1/29/72 | 117 | 11 | | | **Women's Love Rights** | | | $20 | Hot Wax 708 |

(Don't Be Sorry) Be Careful If You Can't Be Good
Her Picture Matches Mine
I Don't Want Nothing Old (But Money)
It's Not What You Fall For, It's What You Stand For
Love And Liberty *94*
Since I Fell For You *76*
That's How Strong My Love Is
Two Lovely Pillows
Wedlock Is A Padlock
Women's Love Rights *36*

LEE, Leapy — see LEAPY LEE

★249★ LEE, Peggy   '60

Born Norma Jean Egstrom on 5/26/20 in Jamestown, North Dakota. Jazz singer with Jack Wardlow (1936-40), Will Osborne (1940-41) and **Benny Goodman** (1941-43). Went solo in March 1943. In movies *Mister Music* (1950), *The Jazz Singer* (1953) and *Pete Kelly's Blues* (1955). Co-wrote many songs with husband Dave Barbour (married from 1943-52). Awarded nearly $4 million in court for her singing in the animated movie *Lady And The Tramp*. Won Grammy's Lifetime Achievement Award in 1995.

1)*Songs from Pete Kelly's Blues* 2)*Latin ala Lee!* 3)*Jump For Joy*

| 9/17/55 | 7 | 10 | | 1 | **Songs from Pete Kelly's Blues** | | | $60 | Decca 8166 |

PEGGY LEE and ELLA FITZGERALD
LP: Decca DL-8166 (#7); EP: Decca ED-2269 (#7)

9/23/57	20	1	©	2	**The Man I Love**			$50	Capitol 864
7/14/58	15	2	©	3	**Jump For Joy**			$40	Capitol 979
12/8/58	16	1	©	4	**Things Are Swingin'**			$30	Capitol 1049
4/11/60	11	59	©	5	**Latin ala Lee!**			$25	Capitol 1290
9/11/61	77	22	©	6	**Basin Street East**		[L]	$25	Capitol 1520
					recorded on 1/12/61				
8/25/62	85	6		7	**Bewitching-Lee!**		[G]	$25	Capitol 1743
11/17/62+	40	21	©	8	**Sugar 'N' Spice**			$25	Capitol 1772
3/9/63	18	26		9	**I'm A Woman**			$25	Capitol 1857
7/27/63	42	9	©	10	**Mink Jazz**			$25	Capitol 1850
9/26/64	97	6		11	**In The Name Of Love**			$20	Capitol 2096
5/22/65	145	4		12	**Pass Me By**			$20	Capitol 2320
7/30/66	130	3		13	**Big $pender**			$20	Capitol 2475
12/30/67	115[X]	1		14	**Happy Holiday**		[X]	$20	Capitol 2390
12/13/69+	55	18		15	**Is That All There Is?**			$15	Capitol 386
6/6/70	142	9		16	**Bridge Over Troubled Water**			$15	Capitol 463
12/19/70	194	2		17	**Make It With You**			$15	Capitol 622

LEE, Peggy — Cont'd

After You've Gone (11)
Ain't That Love (8)
Ain't We Got Fun (3)
Alley Cat Song (9)
Alone Together (4)
Alright, Okay, You Win (4,7,13) **68**
As Long As I Live (10)
Back In Your Own Back Yard (3)
Best Is Yet To Come (8)
Bewitched (12)
Big Bad Bill (Is Sweet William Now) (8)
Big Spender (13)
Boy From Ipanema (Garota De Ipanema) (11)
Bridge Over Troubled Water (16)
Brother Love's Traveling Salvation Show (15)
Bye, Bye, Blackbird (1)
C'est Magnifique (5)
Cheek To Cheek (3)
Christmas Carousel (14)
Christmas List (14)
Christmas Song (Merry Christmas To You) (14)
Christmas Waltz (14)
Close Your Eyes (10)
Cloudy Morning (10)
Come Back To Me (13)
Come Rain Or Come Shine (9)
Dance Only With Me (5)
Day In - Day Out (6)
Days Of Wine And Roses (10)
Dear Heart (12)
Deck The Hall (14)
Don't Smoke In Bed (7,15)

Embrasse Moi (8)
Fever (6,7) **8**
Folks Who Live On The Hill (2)
Four Or Five Times (3)
Glory Of Love (3)
Golden Earrings (7)
Good-bye (17)
Gotta Travel On (13)
Hallelujah, I Love Him So (7) **77**
Happiness Is A Thing Called Joe (2)
Happy Holiday (14)
Hard Day's Night (12)
Have You Seen My Baby (16)
He Needs Me (1)
He Used Me (16)
He's My Guy (2)
Heart (5)
Hey There (5)
I Am In Love (5)
I Believe In You (8)
I Could Have Danced All Night (5)
I Could Write A Book (10)
I Don't Know Enough About You (7)
I Don't Wanna Leave You Now (8)
I Enjoy Being A Girl (5)
I Got A Man (6)
I Hear Music (3)
I Left My Heart In San Francisco (9)
I Like A Sleighride (Jingle Bells) (14)
I Love Being Here With You (6)
I Must Know (13)
I Never Had A Chance (10)

I Never Knew (1)
I See Your Face Before Me (16)
I Wanna Be Around (12)
I Won't Dance (10)
I'll Get By (As Long As I Have You) (9)
I'll Only Miss Him When I Think Of Him (13)
I'm A Woman (9,15) **54**
I'm Beginning To See The Light (4)
I'm Gonna Meet My Sweetie Now (1)
I'm Walkin' (2)
I've Got The World On A String (8)
I've Never Been So Happy In My Life (17)
If I Should Lose You (2)
In The Name Of Love (11)
Is That All There Is (15) **11**
It's A Big Wide Wonderful World (10)
It's A Good Day (7)
It's A Good, Good Night (4)
It's A Wonderful World (4,13)
It's Been A Long, Long Time (4)
Johnny (Linda) (15)
Joy House (Just Call Me Love Bird), Theme From (11)
Jump For Joy (5)
Just In Time (3)
Just One Way To Say I Love You (2)
Lady Is A Tramp (10)
Let's Fall In Love (13)
Let's Get Lost In Now (17)
Life Is For Livin' (4)
Little Drummer Boy (14)

Long And Winding Road (17)
Love (12)
Love Story (15)
Lullaby In Rhythm (4)
Mack The Knife (4)
Make It With You (17)
Mama's Gone, Goodbye (9)
Man I Love (2)
Manana (7)
Me And My Shadow (15)
Moments Like This (6)
Music! Music! Music! (1)
My Heart Stood Still (2)
My Love, Forgive Me (Amore, Scusami) (12)
My Man (7) **81**
My Old Flame (15)
My Romance (medley) (6)
My Silent Love (10)
My Sin (11)
No-Color Time Of The Day (17)
Oh Didn't He Ramble (1)
Old Devil Moon (3)
On The Street Where You Live (5)
One Kiss (medley) (6)
One More Ride On The Merry-Go-Round (17)
One Note Samba (Samba De Una Nota So) (9)
Party's Over (5)
Pass Me By (12) **93**
Passenger Of The Rain (Le Passager De La Pluie) (17)
Peggy Lee Bow Music (6)
Please Be Kind (2)
Quiet Nights (Corcovado) (12)
Raindrops Keep Fallin' On My Head (16)

Ridin' High (4)
Right To Love (Reflections) (11)
Santa Claus Is Coming To Town (14)
See See Rider (8)
Senza Fine (11)
Shangri-La (11)
Sing A Rainbow (1)
Sneakin' Up On You (12)
Somebody Loves Me (1)
Something (15)
Something Strange (14)
Something Wonderful (2)
Sugar (That Sugar Baby Of Mine) (1)
Surrey With The Fringe On Top (5)
Sweetest Sounds (8)
Talk To Me Baby (11)
Taste Of Honey (9)
Teach Me Tonight (8)
Tell All The World About You (8)
That's All (2)
That's What It Takes (12)
That's What Living's About (17)
Them There Eyes (6,7)
Then I'll Be Tired Of You (2)
There Ain't No Sweet Man That's Worth The Salt Of My Tears (9)
There Is No Greater Love (2)
There'll Be Some Changes Made (11)
(There's) Always Something There To Remind Me (16)
Things Are Swingin' (4)
Thrill Is Gone (From Yesterday's Kiss) (16)

Till There Was You (5)
Tree, The (14)
Tribute To Ray Charles Medley (6)
Vagabond King Waltz (medley) (6)
Watch What Happens (13)
What A Little Moonlight Can Do (3)
What Are You Doing The Rest Of Your Life? (16)
What Can I Say After I Say I'm Sorry? (1)
When In Rome (11)
When My Sugar Walks Down The Street (All The Little Birdies Go Tweet-Tweet-Tweet) (3)
When The Sun Comes Out (8)
Where Can I Go Without You? (10)
While We're Young (7)
Whisper Not (10)
Whistle For Happiness (15)
White Christmas (14)
Why Don't You Do Right (7)
Winter Wonderland (14)
Wish You Were Here (5)
You Always Hurt The One You Love (12)
You Don't Know (13)
You'll Remember Me (16,17)
You're Getting To Be A Habit With Me (4)
You're Mine, You (4)
You're Nobody 'Til Somebody Loves You (9)
You've Got Possibilities (13)

LEE, Tracey ... '97
Born in Philadelphia. Male rapper.

4/26/97	111	6	©	**Many Facez** .... $10 Universal 53036

After Party (The Theme II)
Big Will
Clue (Who Shot LR?)

Give It Up Baby
Keep Your Hands High
Many Facez

On The Edge
Professionals, The
Repent

Rugged One
Stars In The East
Theme (It's Party Time) **55**

Who's Crew

LEFEVRE, Raymond ... '68
Born in 1922 in Paris. Conductor/pianist/flutist.

3/30/68	117	16	**Soul Coaxing (Ame Caline)** .... [I] $15 4 Corners 4244

Adios Amor
Ame Caline (Soul Coaxing) **37**
Dommage, Dommage

Groovin'
If I Were A Carpenter
L'Important De La Rose

Puppet On A String
Quand On Revient
Release Me

Soul Coaxing ..see: Ame Caline
This Is My Song

Time Alone Will Tell (Non Pensare A Me)
Whiter Shade Of Pale

LEFT BANKE, The ... '67
Rock group from New York City: Steve Martin (vocals), Rick Brand (guitar), Mike Brown (piano), Tom Finn (bass) and George Cameron (drums). Brown later joined **Stories**.

3/25/67	67	11	**Walk Away Renee/Pretty Ballerina** .... $40 Smash 67088

Barterers And Their Wives
Evening Gown
I Haven't Got The Nerve

I've Got Something On My Mind
Lazy Day
Let Go Of You Girl

Pretty Ballerina **15**
Shadows Breaking Over My Head

She May Call You Up Tonight
Walk Away Renee **5**
What Do You Know

LeGRAND, Michel ... '55
Born on 2/24/32 in Paris. Pianist/composer/conductor/arranger. Scored several movies.

5/28/55	5	16	1	**Holiday In Rome** .... [I] $20 Columbia 647

LP: Columbia CL-647 (#5); EP: Columbia B-497 (#13)

9/17/55	13	2	2	**Vienna Holiday** .... [I] $20 Columbia 706
6/30/56	9	4	3	**Castles In Spain** .... [I] $20 Columbia 888
3/11/72	127	10	4	**"Brian's Song" themes & variations** .... [I] $15 Bell 6071
7/1/72	173	12	© 5	**Sarah Vaughan/Michel Legrand** .... $15 Mainstream 361

Addormentarmi Cosi (1)
Andalucia (3)
Andaluza (3)
Artist's Life Waltz (2)
Aveva Un Bavero (1)
Blue Danube Waltz (2)
Blue, Green, Grey And Gone (5)
Brian's Song (4,5) **56**
Cafe Mozart Waltz (2)
Caprice Viennois (2)
Deep Blue C (4)
Dicitencello Vuie! (You Tell Her) (1)

Dis-Moi (4)
El Choclo (3)
El Gato Montes (3)
Emperor Waltz (2)
Espana (3)
Espana Cani (3)
Fiorin Fiorello (In Love) (1)
Funiculi Funicula (1)
Go-Between, Theme From The (4)
Grazie Dei Fiori (1)
Hands Of Time ..see: Brian's Song

His Eyes, Her Eyes (5)
I Was Born In Love With You ..see: Wuthering Heights
I Was Born In Love With You (Theme From Wuthering Heights) (5)
I Will Say Goodbye (4,5)
Jungle Drums (3)
La Danse Du Feu (3)
La Violetera (3)
Luna Lunera (1)
Luna Rossa (Blushing Moon) (1)
Malaguena (3)

Mattinata (1)
Merry Widow Waltz (2)
Munasterio 'E Santa Chiara (1)
Neapolitan Nights (3)
Non Dimenticar (Don't Forget) (1)
O Sole Mio (My Sunshine) (1)
Old Refrain (2)
Once You've Been In Love (5)
Oriental (3)
Picasso Summer (4)
Pieces Of Dreams (4,5)
Pizzicato Polka (2)

Rondella Aragonesa (3)
Sant Marti Del Canigo (3)
Sentir De La Alhambra (3)
Serenade (2)
Summer Knows (Theme From Summer Of '42) (5)
Summer Me, Winter Me (5)
Summer Of '42 (The Summer Knows), Theme From (4)
Tales From The Vienna Woods (2)
Tango (3)
Third Man Theme (2)

Torna A Surriento (Come Back To Sorrento) (1)
Vieni, Vieni (1)
Vienna, City Of My Dreams (2)
Vilia (2)
Vola, Colomba (1)
What Are You Doing The Rest Of Your Life (4,5)
Windmills Of Your Mind (4)
Wuthering Heights, Theme From (4)

LEHRER, Tom ... '66
Born on 4/9/28 in New York City. Satirical singer/songwriter/pianist.

11/6/65+	18	51	● © 1	**That Was The Year That Was** .... [C] $25 Reprise 6179
3/26/66	133	8	© 2	**An Evening wasted With Tom Lehrer** .... [C] $25 Reprise 6199

recorded March 1959 in Cambridge, Massachusetts

Alma (2)
Bright College Days (2)
Christmas Carol (2)
Clementine (2)

Elements, The (2)
Folk Song Army (2)
George Murphy (1)
In Old Mexico (2)

It Makes A Fellow Proud To Be A Soldier (2)
MLF Lullaby (1)
Masochism Tango (2)

National Brotherhood Week (1)
New Math (1)
Oedipus Rex (2)

Poisoning Pigeons In The Park (1)
Pollution (1)
Send The Marines (1)

She's My Girl (2)
Smut (1)
So Long, Mom (A Song For World War III) (1)

DEBUT	PEAK	WKS	RIAA	CD	ARTIST — Album Title	Catalog	Sym	$	Label & Number

LEHRER, Tom — Cont'd

Vatican Rag (1)	We Will All Go Together When We Go (2)	Wernher Von Braun (1)	Whatever Became Of Hubert? (1)	Who's Next? (1)

LEMONHEADS, The '93

Rock group formed in Boston by Evan Dando (vocals, guitar) with numerous lineup changes. **Juliana Hatfield** played bass on *It's A Shame About Ray* album. Until 1994, David Ryan (drums; from 1990) and Australian Nic Dalton (bass; from 1992) were members.

1/9/93	68	19	●	©	1 It's A Shame About Ray	$10	Atlantic 82460
10/30/93	56	17	●	©	2 Come On Feel The Lemonheads	$10	Atlantic 82537
11/2/96	130	2		©	3 Car Button Cloth	$10	Atlantic 92726

Alison's Starting To Happen (1)	C'mon Daddy (3)	Hannah & Gabi (1)	It's All True (3)	Outdoor Type (3)	6ix (3)
Being Around (2)	Confetti (1)	Hospital (3)	Jello Fund (2)	Paid To Smile (2)	Something's Missing (3)
Big Gay Heart (2)	Dawn Can't Decide (2)	I'll Do It Anyway (2)	Kitchen (1)	Rest Assured (3)	Style (2)
Bit Part (1)	Down About It (2)	If I Could Talk I'd Tell You (3)	Knoxville Girl (3)	Rick James Style (2)	Tenderfoot (3)
Break Me (3)	Favorite T (2)	Into Your Arms (2) 67	Losing Your Mind (3)	Rockin Stroll (1)	Turnpike Down (1)
Buddy (1)	Frank Mills (1)	It's A Shame About Ray (1)	Mrs. Robinson (1)	Rudderless (1)	You Can Take It With You (2)
Ceiling Fan In My Spoon (1)	Great Big NO (2)	It's About Time (2)	One More Time (3)	Secular Rockulidge (3)	

LEMON PIPERS, The '68

Pop-rock group from Oxford, Ohio: Ivan Browne (vocals, guitar), Bill Bartlett (guitar), R.G. Nave (organ), Steve Walmsley (bass) and Bill Albaugh (drums). Bartlett later joined **Ram Jam**. Albaugh died on 1/20/99 (age 53).

| 2/17/68 | 90 | 18 | | © | Green Tambourine | $25 | Buddah 5009 |

Ask Me If I Care	**Green Tambourine 1**	Shoemaker Of Leatherwear	Straglin' Behind
Blueberry Blue	Rainbow Tree	Square	Through With You
Fifty Year Void	**Rice Is Nice 46**	Shoeshine Boy	Turn Around Take A Look

LEN '99

Rock group from Toronto: Marc Costanzo (vocals), his sister Sharon Costanzo, D. Rock, DJ Moves, Planet Pea and Drunkness Monster.

| 7/3/99 | 46 | 27 | ● | © | You Can't Stop The Bum Rush | $10 | Work 69528 |

Beautiful Day	Cold Chillin'	Cryptik Souls Crew	Hot Rod Monster Jam	**Steal My Sunshine 9**
Big Meanie	Crazy 'Cause I Believe (Early	Feelin' Alright	Junebug	
Cheekybugger	Morning Sunshine)	Hard Disk Approach	Man Of The Year	

LENNON, John ★102★ '80

Born on 10/9/40 in Woolton, Liverpool, England. Shot to death in New York City on 12/8/80 (age 40). Founding member of **The Beatles**. Married to Cynthia Powell from 8/23/62 to 11/8/68; their son is **Julian Lennon**. Met **Yoko Ono** in 1966; married her on 3/20/69; their son **Sean Lennon**. Formed Plastic Ono Band in 1969. To New York City in 1971. Fought deportation from the U.S., 1972-76, until he was granted a permanent visa. Won Grammy's Lifetime Achievement Award in 1991. Inducted into the Rock and Roll Hall of Fame in 1994.

1)*Double Fantasy* 2)*Imagine* 3)*Walls And Bridges* 4)*John Lennon/Plastic Ono Band*
5)*Rock 'N' Roll*

JOHN LENNON & YOKO ONO:

2/8/69	124	8		©	1 Unfinished Music No. 1: Two Virgins	$150	Apple 5001
6/28/69	174	8		©	2 Unfinished Music No. 2: Life With The Lions	$50	Zapple 3357
12/13/69	178	3		©	3 Wedding Album	$150	Apple 3361

JOHN LENNON/PLASTIC ONO BAND:

| 1/10/70 | 10 | 32 | ● | © | 4 The Plastic Ono Band - Live Peace In Toronto 1969 | [L] | $50 | Apple 3362 |

recorded on 9/13/69

12/26/70+	6	33	●	©	5 John Lennon/Plastic Ono Band	$25	Apple 3372
9/18/71	❶¹	45	▲²	©	6 Imagine	C:#28/1	$25	Apple 3379
7/1/72	48	17		©	7 Some Time In New York City	[L]	$30	Apple 3392 [2]

record 1: studio recordings backed by **Elephants Memory**; record 2: *Live Jam* featuring concert recordings with **Frank Zappa**'s Mothers of Invention

JOHN LENNON:

11/24/73	9	31	●	©	8 Mind Games	C:#14/45	$20	Apple 3414
10/12/74	❶¹	35	●	©	9 Walls And Bridges		$20	Apple 3416
3/8/75	6	15	●	©	10 Rock 'N' Roll	C:#17/28	$20	Apple 3419
11/8/75	12	32	▲	©	11 Shaved Fish	[G]	$20	Apple 3421

JOHN LENNON & YOKO ONO:

| 12/6/80 | ❶⁸ | 74 | ▲³ | © | 12 Double Fantasy | $15 | Geffen 2001 |

1981 Grammy winner: Album of the Year

| 12/4/82+ | 33 | 16 | ▲³ | © | 13 The John Lennon Collection | [G] | $15 | Geffen 2023 |
| 1/14/84 | 94 | 12 | | | 14 Heart Play - unfinished dialogue | [T] | $12 | Polydor 817238 |

excerpts from a *Playboy* magazine interview done shortly before Lennon's death

| 2/11/84 | 11 | 19 | ● | © | 15 Milk and Honey | $12 | Polydor 817160 |

recorded in 1980

JOHN LENNON:

| 3/22/86 | 41 | 11 | ● | | 16 Live In New York City | [L] | $12 | Capitol 12451 |

recorded on 8/30/72 at Madison Square Garden

| 11/22/86 | 127 | 4 | | © | 17 Menlove Ave. | [K] | $12 | Capitol 12533 |

Liverpool street Lennon lived on as a child; comprised of outtakes from *Rock 'N' Roll* and *Walls And Bridges* album sessions

| 10/22/88 | 31 | 18 | ● | © | 18 Imagine: John Lennon | [S] | $15 | Capitol 90803 [2] |

from the movie documentary of Lennon's life; includes 9 cuts by **The Beatles**: "Ballad Of John & Yoko," "A Day In The Life," "Don't Let Me Down," "Help!," "In My Life," "Julia," "Revolution," "Twist And Shout," and "Strawberry Fields Forever"

| 3/14/98 | 65 | 9 | | © | 19 Lennon Legend - The Very Best Of John Lennon | [G] | $10 | Parlophone 21954 |
| 11/21/98 | 99 | 2 | ● | © | 20 Anthology | [K] | $40 | Capitol 30614 [4] |

Ain't She Sweet (20)	Attica State (7,20)	Beautiful Boy (Darling Boy)	Born In A Prison (7)	Cleanup Time (12)	Dear Yoko (12,13,20)
Ain't That A Shame (10)	Au (7)	(12,13,18,19,20)	Borrowed Time (15,19,20)	**Cold Turkey** (4,7,11,16,19) **30**	Dizzy Miss Lizzie (4)
Aisumasen (I'm Sorry) (8)	Baby Please Don't Go (20)	Beef Jerky (9)	Bring It On Home To Me	Come Together (16,20)	Do The Oz (20)
Amsterdam (7)	Baby's Heartbeat (2)	Bless You (9,17,20)	(medley) (10,20)	Crippled Inside (6)	Do You Want To Dance (10)
Angel Baby (17)	Be-Bop-A-Lula (10,20)	Blue Suede Shoes (4)	Bring On The Lucie (8,20)	David Frost Show (20)	
Angela (7)	Be My Baby (20)	Bony Moronie (10)	Cambridge 1969 (2)	Dear John (20)	

491

LENNON, John — Cont'd

Don't Worry Kyoko (Mummy's Only Looking For Her Hand In The Snow) (4,7)
(Forgive Me) My Little Flower Princess (15)
"Fortunately" (20)
Geraldo Rivera-One To One Concert (20)
Give Me Some Truth (6)
Give Peace A Chance (4,11,13,16,18,19,20) **14**
God (5,18,20)
God Save Oz (20)
Going Down On Love (9,20)
Goodnight Vienna (20)
Great Wok (20)
Grow Old With Me (15,20)
Happy Xmas (War Is Over) (11,19,20)
Here We Go Again (17)
Hold On (5,20)
Hound Dog (16)
How? (6,18)
How Do You Sleep? (6,20)
I Don't Wanna Face It (15,20)
I Don't Want To Be A Soldier (6,20)

I Found Out (5,20)
I Know (I Know) (8,20)
I'm Losing You (12,13,20)
I'm Stepping Out (15,20) **55**
I'm The Greatest (20)
Imagine (6,11,13,16,18,19,20) **3**
Instant Karma (We All Shine On) (11,13,16,19) **3**
Intuition (8)
Isolation (5,20)
It's Real (20)
It's So Hard (6,16,20)
Jamrag (7)
Jealous Guy (6,13,18,19,20) **80**
Jerry Lewis Telethon (20)
John & Yoko (3)
John John (Let's Hope For Peace) (4)
John Sinclair (7,20)
Just Because (10)
(Just Like) Starting Over (12,13,18,19) **1**
"Kiss Is Just A Kiss" (20)
Life Begins At 40 (20)
Long Lost John (20)

Look At Me (5,20)
Love (5,13,19,20)
Luck Of The Irish (7,20)
Maggie Mae (20)
Meat City (8)
Mind Games (8,11,13,19,20) **18**
Money (4)
Mother (5,11,16,18,19,20) **43**
Move Over Ms. L (20)
Mr. Hyde's Gone (Don't Be Afraid) (20)
Mucho Mungo (20)
My Life (20)
My Mummy's Dead (5)
New York City (7,16,20)
No Bed For Beatle John (2)
Nobody Loves You (When You're Down And Out) (9,17,20)
Nobody Told Me (15,19,20) **5**
#9 Dream (9,11,13,19) **9**
Nutopian International Anthem (8)
Oh My Love (6,20)
Oh Yoko! (1)
Old Dirt Road (9,17,20)

One Day (At A Time) (8,20)
Only People (8)
Only You (20)
Out The Blue (8)
Peggy Sue (10,20)
Phil And John 1, 2 & 3 (20)
Power To The People (11,13,19) **11**
Radio Play (2)
Ready Teddy (medley) (10,20)
Real Love (18,20)
Remember (5,20)
Rip It Up (medley) (10,20)
Rishi Kesh Song (20)
Rock And Roll People (17)
Satire 1, 2 & 3 (20)
Scared (9,17,20)
Scumbag (7)
Sean's "In The Sky" (20)
Sean's "Little Help" (20)
Sean's "Loud" (20)
Send Me Some Lovin' (medley) (10,20)
Serve Yourself (20)
Since My Baby Left Me (17)
Sisters O Sisters (7)
Slippin' And Slidin' (10,20)

Stand By Me (10,18,19) **20**
Steel And Glass (9,17,20)
Stranger's Room (20)
Sunday Bloody Sunday (7)
Surprise, Surprise (Sweet Bird Of Paradox) (9,20)
Sweet Little Sixteen (10)
Tight A$ (8)
To Know Her Is To Love Her (17)
Two Minutes Silence (2)
Two Virgins (1)
Watching The Wheels (12,13,19,20) **10**
We're All Water (7)
Well (Baby Please Don't Go) (7)
Well Well Well (5,16)
What You Got (9,20)
Whatever Gets You Thru The Night (9,11,13,19,20) **1**
"When In Doubt, Fuck It" (20)
Woman (12,13,18,19,20) **2**
Woman Is The Nigger Of The World (7,11,16,20) **57**
Working Class Hero (5,19,20)
Ya Ya (9,10)
Yer Blues (7)

Yesterday (20)
You Are Here (8,20)
You Can't Catch Me (10)

LENNON, Julian   '85
Born John Charles Julian Lennon on 4/8/63 in Liverpool, England. Pop-rock singer/songwriter/keyboardist. Son of Cynthia and **John** Lennon.

DEBUT	PEAK	WKS	RIAA	CD	#	Title	Sym	$	Label & Number
11/10/84+	17	46	●	©	1	Valotte		$10	Atlantic 80184
4/12/86	32	18	●	©	2	The Secret Value of DayDreaming		$10	Atlantic 81640
4/1/89	87	15		©	3	Mr. Jordan		$10	Atlantic 81928

Always Think Twice (2)
Angillette (3)
Coward Till The End? (2)
Everyday (2)
I Get Up (3)

I Want You To Know (3)
I've Seen Your Face (2)
Jesse (1) **54**
Let Me Be (1)
Let Me Tell You (2)

Lonely (1)
Make It Up To You (3)
Mother Mary (3)
Now You're In Heaven (3) **93**
O.K. For You (1)

On The Phone (1)
Open Your Eyes (3)
Say You're Wrong (1) **21**
Second Time (3)
Space (1)

Stick Around (2) **32**
Sunday Morning (3)
This Is My Day (2)
Too Late For Goodbyes (1) **5**
Valotte (1) **9**

Want Your Body (2)
Well I Don't Know (1)
You Don't Have To Tell Me (2)
You Get What You Want (2)
You're The One (3)

LENNON, Sean   '98
Born on 10/9/75 in New York City. Rock singer/songwriter/guitarist. Son of **John Lennon** and **Yoko Ono**.

DEBUT	PEAK	WKS	RIAA	CD	#	Title	Sym	$	Label & Number
6/6/98	153	1		©		Into The Sun		$10	Grand Royal 94551

Bathtub
Breeze
Home

Into The Sun
Mystery Juice

Part One Of The Cowboy Trilogy
One Night

Photosynthesis
Queue
Sean's Theme

Spaceship
Two Fine Lovers
Wasted

LENNON SISTERS, The   '67
Vocal group from Venice, California: sisters Dianne (born on 12/1/39), Peggy (born on 4/8/41), Kathy (born on 8/2/43) and Janet (born on 6/15/46) Lennon. With **Lawrence Welk** from 1955-68.

DEBUT	PEAK	WKS	RIAA	CD	#	Title	Sym	$	Label & Number
12/25/61+	95	4			1	Christmas With The Lennon Sisters	[X]	$15	Dot 25343

Christmas charts: 40/'63, 31/'67

| 5/27/67 | 77 | 18 | | | 2 | Somethin' Stupid | | $15 | Dot 25797 |

Adeste Fideles (1)
Away In A Manger (1)
Christmas Island (1)
Dedicated To The One I Love (2)

Georgy Girl (2)
Hark! The Herald Angels Sing (1)
I Saw Mommy Kissing Santa Claus (1)

I'll Be Home For Christmas (1)
Jingle Bells (1)
Joy To The World (1)
Little Drummer Boy (1)
Lover's Concerto (2)

My Cup Runneth Over (2)
O Little Town Of Bethlehem (1)
Rudolph The Red-Nosed Reindeer (1)
Silent Night (1)

Single Girl (2)
Somethin' Stupid (2)
Sure Gonna Miss Him (2)
There's A Kind Of Hush (2)
This Is My Song (2)

White Christmas (1)
Winter Wonderland (1)
You Don't Have To Say You Love Me (2)

LENNOX, Annie   '95
Born on 12/25/54 in Aberdeen, Scotland. Lead singer of the **Eurythmics**. Appeared in the movie *Edward II* and TV movie *The Room*.

DEBUT	PEAK	WKS	RIAA	CD	#	Title	Sym	$	Label & Number
5/30/92	23	72	▲²	©	1	Diva	C:#25/26	$10	Arista 18704
4/1/95	11	60	▲²	©	2	Medusa		$10	Arista 25717

Cold (1)
Don't Let It Bring You Down (2)
Downtown Lights (2)
Gift, The (1)
I Can't Get Next To You (2)

Keep Young And Beautiful (1)
Legend In My Living Room (1)
Little Bird (1) **49**
Money Can't Buy It (1)
No More "I Love You's" (2) **23**

Precious (1)
Primitive (1)
Something So Right (2)
Stay By Me (1)
Take Me To The River (2)

Thin Line Between Love And Hate (2)
Train In Vain (2)
Waiting In Vain (2)

Walking On Broken Glass (1) **14**
Whiter Shade Of Pale (2)
Why (1) **34**

LEONTI, Nikki   '98
Born in 1981. Contemporary Christian singer.

DEBUT	PEAK	WKS	RIAA	CD	#	Title	Sym	$	Label & Number
10/3/98	179	1		©		Shelter Me		$10	Pamplin 9829

Everlasting Place
Every Moment

It Will Come To You
It'll Be Alright

Love One Another
Now I Believe In Miracles

One World
Shelter Me

Shoelaces
What You Did For Me

LE PAMPLEMOUSSE   '78
Disco studio group led by producers Laurin Rinder and W. Michael Lewis. Group name is French for "The Grapefruit."

DEBUT	PEAK	WKS	RIAA	CD	#	Title	Sym	$	Label & Number
1/21/78	116	11				Le Spank		$12	AVI 6032

Cafe Au Lait
Come On Inside

Get Your Boom Boom (Around The Room Room)

Le Spank **58**
Monkey See, Monkey Do

When She Smiles

LEROI BROTHERS, The   '87
Rock group from Austin, Texas: Steve Doerr (vocals, guitar), Rick Rawls (guitar), Jackie Newhouse (bass) and Mike Buck (drums).

DEBUT	PEAK	WKS	RIAA	CD	#	Title	Sym	$	Label & Number
3/28/87	181	5		©		Open All Night		$10	Profile 1224

Alligator Man
Ballad Of The Leroi Brothers

Beat Don't Ever Stop
Chain Of Love

Cindy Cindy
Gusano

Hard Luck Blues
Hey Baby

Maybe Little Baby
Pretty Girls Everywhere

So Much To Say
Wicked Prayer

LE ROUX '82

Rock group from Louisiana: Jeff Pollard (vocals), Tony Haseldon (guitar), Rod Roddy (piano), Bobby Campo (horns), Leon Medica (bass) and David Peters (drums).

7/8/78	135	15	1 **Louisiana's Le Roux**	$12 Capitol 11734
6/9/79	162	4	2 **Keep The Fire Burnin'**	$12 Capitol 11926
			LOUISIANA'S LeROUX (above 2)	
8/23/80	145	6	3 **Up**	$12 Capitol 12092
2/6/82	64	21	4 **Last Safe Place**	$12 RCA Victor 4195

Addicted (4)
Back To The Levee (2)
Backslider (1)
Bridge Of Silence (1)
Call Home The Heart (2)
Crazy In Love (1)
Crying Inside (3)
Fa-Fa-Fa-Fa (Sad Song) (2)

Feel It (2)
Get It Right The First Time (3)
Heavenly Days (1)
I Can't Do One More Two-Step (1)
I Know Trouble When I See It (3)
I Won't Be Staying (3)

Inspiration (4)
It Could Be The Fever (3)
It Doesn't Matter (4)
Keep The Fire Burnin' (2)
Last Safe Place On Earth (4) *77*
Let Me Be Your Fantasy (3)
Long Distance Lover (4)

Love Abductor (1)
Make Believe (4)
Midnight Summer Dream (4)
Mystery (3)
New Orleans Ladies (1) *59*
Nobody Said It Was Easy (Lookin' For The Lights) (4) *18*

Rock 'N' Roll Woman (4)
Roll Away The Stone (3)
Say It (With Your Heart) (2)
Slow Burn (1)
Snake Eyes (1)
Take A Ride On A Riverboat (1)
Thunder N' Lightnin' (2)
Waiting For Your Love (3)

When I Get Home (3)
Window Eyes (2)
You Be My Vision (2)
You Know How Those Boys Are (4)

LES NUBIANS '99

Vocal duo of sisters from Bordeaux, France: Helene and Celia Faussart.

3/27/99	100	16	© **Princesses Nubiennes**	[F] $10 Omtown 45997

Bebela
Demain (Jazz)

Désolée
Embrasse-Moi

Les Portes Du Souvenir
Makeda

Princesse Nubienne
Si Je T'Avais Écouté

Sourire
Sugar Cane

Tabou
Voyager

LESS THAN JAKE '98

Rock trio from Gainesville, Florida: Chris DeMakes (vocals, guitar), Roger Manganelli (bass) and Vinnie Fiorello (drums).

10/24/98	80	3	© 1 **Hello Rockview**	$10 Capitol 57663
11/11/00	103	1	© 2 **Borders & Boundaries**	$10 Fat Wreck Chords 616

Al's War (1)
All My Best Friends Are Metalheads (1)
Bad Scene And A Basement Show (2)
Big Crash (1)
Bigger Picture (2)

Danny Says (1)
Faction (2)
Five State Drive (1)
Gainesville Rock City (2)
Great American Sharpshooter (1)
Hell Looks A Lot Like L.A. (2)

Help Save The Youth Of America From Exploding (1)
History Of A Boring Town (1)
Is This Thing On? (2)
Kehoe (2)
Last Hour Of The Last Day Of Work (2)

Last One Out Of Liberty City (1)
Look What Happened (2)
Magnetic North (2)
Malt Liquor Tastes Better When You've Got Problems (2)
Motto (1)
Mr. Chevy Celebrity (2)

Nervous In The Alley (1)
1989 (2)
Pete Jackson Is Getting Married (2)
Richard Allen George...No, It's Just Cheez (1)

Scott Farcas Takes It On The Chin (1)
Suburban Myth (2)
Theme Song For H Street (1)

LESTER, Ketty '62

Born Revoyda Frierson on 8/16/34 in Hope, Arkansas. R&B singer/actress. Acted in several movies and TV shows.

6/9/62	53	11	© **Love Letters**	$50 Era 108

Fallen Angel
Gloomy Sunday

Goin' Home
I'll Never Stop Loving You

I'm A Fool To Want You
Love Letters *5*

Moscow Nights
Once Upon A Time

P.S. I Love You
Porgy, I's Your Woman Now

When I Fall In Love
Where Or When

LET'S ACTIVE '84

Pop-rock trio formed in North Carolina: Mitch Easter (vocals, guitar), Faye Hunter (bass) and Sara Romweber (drums).

2/18/84	154	11	© 1 **Afoot**	[M] $10 I.R.S. 70505
11/10/84	138	16	© 2 **Cypress**	$10 I.R.S. 70648
4/26/86	111	10	© 3 **Big Plans For Everybody**	$10 I.R.S. 5703

Badger (3)
Blue Line (2)
Co-star (2)
Counting Down (2)
Crows On A Phone Line (2)

Easy Does (2)
Edge Of The World (1)
Every Word Means No (1)
Fell (3)
Flags For Everything (2)

Gravel Truck (2)
In Between (2)
In Little Ways (3)
Last Chance Town (3)
Leader Of Men (1)

Lowdown (2)
Make Up With Me (1)
Ornamental (2)
Prey (3)
Reflecting Pool (3)

Ring True (2)
Room With A View (1)
Route (1)
Still Dark Out (3)
Talking To Myself (3)

Waters Part (2)
Whispered News (3)
Won't Go Wrong (3)
Writing The Book Of Last Pages (3)

LETTERMEN, The ★57★ '62

Vocal trio formed in Los Angeles: Tony Butala (born on 11/20/40), Jim Pike (born on 11/6/38) and Bob Engemann (born on 2/19/36). Engemann replaced by Gary Pike (Jim's brother) in 1968. The #1 Adult Contemporary vocal group of the 1960s.

1)A Song For Young Love 2)The Lettermen!!!...and "Live!" 3)Goin' Out Of My Head 4)The Hit Sounds Of The Lettermen 5)Hurt So Bad

2/24/62	6	55	1 **A Song For Young Love**	$20 Capitol 1669
6/9/62	30	24	2 **Once Upon A Time**	$20 Capitol 1711
10/13/62+	59	19	3 **Jim, Tony And Bob**	$20 Capitol 1761
4/13/63	65	10	4 **College Standards**	$20 Capitol 1829
8/31/63	76	10	5 **The Lettermen In Concert**	[L] $15 Capitol 1936
			recorded at Iona College in New Rochelle	
2/8/64	31	32	6 **A Lettermen Kind Of Love**	$15 Capitol 2013
			also see #24 below	
6/20/64	94	10	7 **The Lettermen Look At Love**	$15 Capitol 2083
			also see #24 below	
11/14/64	41	20	8 **She Cried**	$15 Capitol 2142
3/13/65	27	23	9 **Portrait Of My Love**	$15 Capitol 2270
8/21/65	13	24	10 **The Hit Sounds Of The Lettermen**	$15 Capitol 2359
10/30/65	73	13	11 **You'll Never Walk Alone**	$15 Capitol 2213
2/19/66	57	17	12 **More Hit Sounds Of The Lettermen!**	$15 Capitol 2428
6/25/66	52	15	13 **A New Song For Young Love**	$15 Capitol 2496
10/8/66+	17	27	● © 14 **The Best Of The Lettermen**	[G] $15 Capitol 2554
12/17/66+	18[X]	10	15 **For Christmas This Year**	[X] $15 Capitol 2587
			Christmas charts: 25/66, 41/67, 47/68, 18/70	
2/4/67	58	17	16 **Warm**	$15 Capitol 2633
7/8/67	31	26	17 **Spring!**	$15 Capitol 2711
11/25/67+	10	48	● 18 **The Lettermen!!!...and "Live!"**	[L] $15 Capitol 2758

DEBUT	PEAK	WKS	RIAA	CD	ARTIST — Album Title	Catalog	Sym	$	Label & Number

LETTERMEN, The — Cont'd

DEBUT	PEAK	WKS						$	
4/13/68	13	44	●		19 **Goin' Out Of My Head**			$15	Capitol 2865
9/14/68	82	14			20 **Special Request**		[K]	$15	Capitol 2934
12/14/68+	43	21			21 **Put Your Head On My Shoulder**			$15	Capitol 147
2/22/69	128	10		©	22 **The Best Of The Lettermen, Vol. 2**		[G]	$15	Capitol 138
4/5/69	74	18			23 **I Have Dreamed**			$15	Capitol 202
8/23/69	90	8			24 **Close-Up**		[R]	$15	Capitol 251 [2]
					reissue of albums #6 and #7 above				
9/6/69	17	30	●		25 **Hurt So Bad**			$15	Capitol 269
2/7/70	42	23			26 **Traces/Memories**			$15	Capitol 390
9/5/70	134	11			27 **Reflections**			$15	Capitol 496
2/6/71	119	10			28 **Everything's Good About You**			$15	Capitol 634
6/26/71	192	6			29 **Feelings**			$15	Capitol 781
10/9/71	88	13			30 **Love Book**			$15	Capitol 836
3/18/72	136	6			31 **Lettermen 1**			$12	Capitol 11010
6/23/73	193	7			32 **"Alive" Again...Naturally**		[L]	$12	Capitol 11183
2/23/74	186	4		©	33 **All-Time Greatest Hits**		[G]	$12	Capitol 11249

Again (3)
Ain't No Sunshine (30)
All I Do Is Dream Of You (4)
All I Have To Do Is Dream (7,24)
(All Of A Sudden) My Heart Sings (25)
Almost There (9)
Alone Again (Naturally) (32)
And I Love Her (12)
Ane Lisle (4)
Anticipation (31)
Anyone Who Had A Heart (19)
Are You Lonesome Tonight (8)
Baby Don't Get Hooked On Me (32)
Baby, It's You (25)
Be My Girl (6,24)
Big Hurt (28)
Black And White (medley) (32)
Blue Moon (7,24)
Blue Velvet (12)
Blueberry Hill (1)
Born Free (17)
Bridge Over Troubled Water (medley) (17)
By The Time I Get To Phoenix (19)
California Dreamin' (23)
Can't Help Falling In Love With You (6,24)
Canticle ..see: Scarborough Fair
Catch The Wind (26)
Chanson D'Amour (16,22)
Cherish (17,20)
Christmas All Alone (15)
Christmas Song (Chestnuts Roasting On An Open Fire) (15)
Christmas Waltz (15)
Climb Ev'ry Mountain (11)
Come Back Silly Girl (1) *17*
Come Softly To Me (9)
Crimson And Clover (29)
Crying (8)
Crying In The Chapel (12)
Day After Day (31)
Dear Heart (10)
Dearly Beloved (6)
Dedicated To The One I Love (17)
Don't Blame It On Me (16)
Don't Let The Sun Catch You Crying (8)
Don't Make Me Over (29)
Don't Pull Your Love (30)
Don't You Know? (26)
Downtown (10)
Dream (4)
Dream Lover (26)

Dreamer (1)
Dreamin' (10)
Elusive Butterfly (25)
End, The (11)
End Of The World (19)
Evening Rain (2)
Everybody Loves Somebody (9)
Everyone's Gone To The Moon (29)
Everything Is Good About You (28) *74*
Exodus (11)
Fast Freight (5)
Feelings (29)
First Time Ever I Saw Your Face (32)
Folk Medley (5)
For Love (26)
For No One (16)
For Your Love (26)
Forget Him (7)
Friendly Persuasion (6,24)
Gentle On My Mind (21)
Georgy Girl (17)
Go Away Little Girl (7,24)
Goin' Out Of My Head/Can't Take My Eyes Off You (18,19,22,33) *7*
Graduation Day (4)
Graduation Girl (13)
Greatest Discovery (29)
Greensleeves (medley) (19)
Groups Are Nothing New Medley (5)
Halls Of Ivy (4)
Hang On Sloopy (26) *93*
Happy Together (17)
Harper Valley PTA (21)
Have Yourself A Merry Little Christmas (15)
Hawaiian Wedding Song (10)
Heartache Oh Heartache (8)
Hello, I Love You (21)
Here, There And Everywhere (16,25)
Hey, Girl (27)
Hey Jude (21)
Hey, Look Me Over (5)
Holly (19)
How Can You Mend A Broken Heart (30)
How Is Julie? (2) *42*
Hurt So Bad (25,33) *12*
I Believe (11,18,22,33)
I Believe In Music (medley) (32)
I Have Dreamed (23)
I Love How You Love Me (23)
I Only Have Eyes For You (13,20) *72*
I Told The Stars (3)
I Wanna Be Free (19)

I Will Love You (3)
I'll Be Home For Christmas (15)
I'll Be Seeing You (1)
I'll Never Stop Loving You (6,24)
I'll See You In My Dreams (4)
I'm Gonna Make You Love Me (23)
I'm Leavin' (30)
I'm Only Sleeping (31)
I'm Sorry (9)
If (30)
If Ever I Would Leave You (10)
If I Loved You (13)
If She Walked Into My Life (18)
Impossible Dream (The Quest) (22)
In The Still Of The Night (1)
It Happened Once Before (1)
It Never Rains In Southern California (32)
It's All In The Game (8)
It's Dark On Observatory Hill (4)
It's One Of Those Nights (31)
It's Over (28)
Jean (26)
Just Say Goodbye (29)
Let It Be Me (3,22)
Light My Fire (21)
Listen People (13)
Listen To The Music (medley) (32)
Little Drummer Boy (15)
Lonely Little Girl (3)
Look Of Love (19)
Look To Your Soul (28)
Love (30,33) *42*
Love Is A Hurtin' Thing (29)
Love Is A Many-Splendored Thing (6,14)
Love Is Blue (medley) (19)
Love Is Here And Now You're Gone (25)
Love Letters (13)
Love Letters In The Sand (7,24)
Love Me Tender (3)
Love Means (You Never Have To Say You're Sorry) (30)
Love On A Two Way Street (29)
Love Story, Theme From (30)
Lover's Beach (2)
MacArthur Park (32)
Make It With You (27)
Mary's Little Boy Child (15)
Mary's Rainbow (21)
Maybe Tomorrow (30)
Me About You (23)
Meditation (medley) (18)
Michael (2)
Michelle (13)

Moments To Remember (4)
Moon River (13)
More (17,20)
Morning Girl (28)
Mr. Lonely (9)
Mr. Sun (17)
Mr. Tambourine Man (12)
My Cup Runneth Over (17)
My Funny Valentine (2)
My Girl (27)
Never Been To Spain (31)
Never My Love (19)
No Man Is An Island (11)
No Other Love (4,23)
O Holy Night (Cantique de Noel) (15)
Oh My Love (31)
Ol' Man River (11)
Old Fashioned Love Song (31)
On Broadway (25)
Once Upon A Time (2)
Only Friends (29)
Only You (7,24)
Our Day Will Come (19)
Our Winter Love (16) *72*
Party's Over (4)
People (9)
Place For The Winter (16)
Polka Dots And Moonbeams (2)
Poor Side Of Town (28)
Portrait Of My Love (9,14)
Pretty Blue Eyes (6,24)
Put A Little Love In Your Heart (medley) (32)
Put Away Your Tear Drops (8)
Put Your Head On My Shoulder (21,33) *44*
Quiet Nights (medley) (18)
Red Roses For A Blue Lady (10)
Reflections (27)
Remembering Last Summer (2)
Run To Him (8)
Running Scared (9)
Sally Was A Good Old Girl (18)
Save Your Heart For Me (12)
Scarborough Fair/Canticle (21)
Sealed With A Kiss (10,22)
Secret Love (7,20,24)
Secretly (12,14) *64*
Seventh Dawn Theme (8)
Shangri-La (25,33) *64*
She Cried (8,14) *73*
She Don't Want Me Now (16)
Shelter Of Your Arms (7,24)
Sherry Don't Go (20) *52*
Silent Night, Holy Night (15)
Silly Boy (She Doesn't Love You) (3) *81*
Since I'm Alone (13)

Sincerely (7,24)
Sixteen Reasons (Why I Love You) (2)
Smile (1,14)
Smoke Gets In Your Eyes (16)
Softly, As I Leave You (8,20)
Something (28)
Somewhere My Love (17)
Song For Young Love (1,20)
Song From Sleep Walk (16)
Spinning Wheel (26)
Spooky (19)
Suddenly There's A Valley (11)
Summer Place, Theme From (10,14,33) *16*
Summer Song (10,20,32)
Summer's Come And Gone (3)
Summer's Gone (2)
Sun Ain't Gonna Shine Any More (27)
Sunny (25)
Sweet September (12)
(Sweet, Sweet Baby) Since You've Been Gone (27)
Sweetheart Of Sigma Chi (4)
Symphony For Susan (16)
T.K.E. Sweetheart Song (Of All The Girls That I Have Known) (23)
Take Good Care Of My Baby (9)
That Lucky Old Sun (11)
That's Enough For Me (31)
There's Got To Be A Girl (1)
(They Long To Be) Close To You (27)
Things We Did Last Summer (12)
This Guy's In Love With You (31)
This Is My Song (18)
Three Bells (17)
Through A Long And Sleepless Night (7,24)
Till (6,24)
Till Then (7,24)
Time For Us (Love Theme from Romeo And Juliet) (25)
Time To Cry (8)
Time Was (Duerme) (2)
To Know Her Is To Love Her (9)
Too Young (6,24)
Touch Me (27,31)
Traces/Memories Medley (23,26,33) *47*
Tree In The Meadow (3)
Try To Remember (13)
Turn Around, Look At Me (2,22)
Turn! Turn! Turn! (12)
Unchained Melody (3)

Until It's Time For You To Go (28)
Up On The Roof (27)
Up, Up And Away (18)
Valley High (1)
Venus (9,20)
Volare (17,22)
Walk Hand In Hand (11)
Walk On By (8,20)
Warm (16,20)
Way You Look Tonight (1,14,33) *13*
Wedding Song (There Is Love) (30)
West Side Story Medley (5)
What Can I Give You This Christmas? (15)
What Child Is This? (15)
What Kind Of Fool Am I? (5)
What Now, My Love? (13,18,22)
When I Fall In Love (1,5,14,33) *7*
When Summer Ends (10)
When You Wish Upon A Star (3)
Where Did Our Love Go (28)
(Where Do I Begin) ..see: Love Story
Where Is Love? (26)
Where Or When (6,24) *98*
Whiffenpoof Song (4)
White Christmas (15)
White Lies, Blue Eyes (31)
Wichita Lineman (23)
Willow Weep For Me (9)
Windy (18)
Woman, Woman (21)
Wonder Of You (6,24)
Worlds (28)
Worst That Could Happen (23)
Yes, I'm Ready (29)
Yesterday (12,14)
(You Make Me Feel Like) A Natural Man (27)
You Showed Me (23)
You Were On My Mind (12)
You'll Be Needin' Me (13)
You'll Never Walk Alone (5,11,14)
You've Got A Friend (medley) (32)
You've Lost That Lovin' Feelin' (10,22)
Young And Foolish (2)
Young Girl (21)
Young Love (6,24)

LETTERS TO CLEO   '95

Pop-rock group from Boston: Kay Hanley (vocals), Michael Eisenstein and Greg McKenna (guitars), Scott Riebling (bass) and Stacy Jones (drums). Jones later became lead singer with **American Hi-Fi**.

DEBUT	PEAK	WKS						$	
4/8/95	123	9		©	1 **Aurora Gory Alice**			$10	Giant 24598
8/26/95	188	1		©	2 **Wholesale Meats And Fish**			$10	Giant 24613

Acid Jed (2)
Awake (2) *88*
Big Star (1)
Come Around (1)
Demon Rock (2)

Do What You Want, Yeah (2)
Fast Way (2)
From Under The Dust (1)
Get On With It (1)
He's Got An Answer (2)

Here & Now (1) *56*
I Could Sleep (The Wuss Song) (2)
I See (1)
Jennifer (2)

Laudanum (2)
Little Rosa (2)
Mellie's Comin' Over (1)
Pizza Cutter (2)
Rim Shak (1)

St. Peter (2)
Step Back (1)
Wasted (1)

LEVEL 42   '86

Pop-rock group formed in Manchester, England: Mark King (vocals, bass), brothers Boon (guitar) and Phil (drums) Gould, and Mike Lindup (keyboards). The Goulds left in October 1987; replaced by Alan Murphy (guitar) and Gary Husband (drums). Murphy died of AIDS on 10/19/89 (age 35).

DEBUT	PEAK	WKS	CD	#	Album Title	$	Label & Number
3/22/86	18	36	©	1	World Machine	$10	Polydor 827487
4/11/87	23	34	©	2	Running In The Family	$10	Polydor 831593
10/29/88	128	7	©	3	Staring At The Sun	$10	Polydor 837247

Chant Has Begun (1)
Children Say (2)
Fashion Fever (2)
Good Man In A Storm (1)
Heaven In My Hands (3)
Hot Water (1) *87*
I Don't Know Why (3)
It's Not The Same For Us (1)
It's Over (2)
Leaving Me Now (1)
Lessons In Love (2) *12*
Lying Still (1)
Man (3)
Over There (3)
Physical Presence (1)
Running In The Family (2) *83*
Silence (3)
Sleepwalkers (2)
Something About You (1) *7*
Staring At The Sun (3)
Take A Look... (3)
To Be With You Again (2)
Tracie (2)
Two Hearts Collide (1)
Two Solitudes (1)
World Machine (1)

LEVERT   '87

R&B vocal trio from Ohio: Gerald Levert, Sean Levert and Marc Gordon.

DEBUT	PEAK	WKS	RIAA	CD	#	Album Title	$	Label & Number
10/25/86	192	3		©	1	Bloodline	$10	Atlantic 81669
9/5/87	32	24	●	©	2	The Big Throwdown	$10	Atlantic 81773
11/26/88+	79	31	●	©	3	Just Coolin'	$10	Atlantic 81926
12/1/90	122	34	●	©	4	Rope A Dope Style	$10	Atlantic 82164
4/10/93	35	27	●	©	5	For Real Tho'	$10	Atlantic 82462
3/29/97	49	8		©	6	The Whole Scenario	$10	Atlantic 82986

ABC-123 (5) *46*
Absolutely Positive (4)
Ain't No Thang (6)
All Season (4)
Baby I'm Ready (4)
Casanova (2) *5*
Clap Your Hands (5)
Do It Right Here (6)
Do The Thangs (5)
Don't U Think It's Time (2)
Fascination (1)
Feel Real (3)
For Real Tho' (5)
Give A Little Love (4)
Good Ol' Days (5) *78*
Good Stuff (2)
Gotta Get The Money (3)
Grip (1)
Hey Girl (4)
I Start You Up, You Turn Me On (1)
I'll Get It Done (6)
I've Been Waiting (4)
In N Out (2)
Join In The Fun (3)
Just Coolin' (3)
Keys To My House (4)
Kiss And Make Up (1)
Let's Get Romantic (3)
Let's Go Out Tonight (1)
Like Water (6)
Looking For Love (1)
Love The Way U Love Me (2)
Loveable (3)
Mama's House (6)
Me 'N' You (3)
My Forever Love (2)
My Place (Your Place) (5)
Nobody Does It Better (4)
Now You Know (4)
Playground (6)
(Pop, Pop, Pop, Pop) Goes My Mind (1)
Pose (1)
Pull Over (3)
Quiet Storm (5)
Rain (4)
Rope A Dope Style (4)
Say You Will (5)
She's All That (I've Been Looking For) (5)
Smilin' (3)
Sorry Is (6)
Start Me Up Again (3)
Sweet Sensation (2)
Swing My Way (6)
Take Your Time (3)
Temptation (2)
Throwdown (5)
Tribute Song (5)
Tru Dat (6)
Whole Scenario (6)
You Keep Me Comin' (6)

LEVERT, Gerald   '00

Born on 7/13/66 in Cleveland. R&B singer. Member of Levert. Son of Eddie Levert (of The O'Jays). Member of LSG.

DEBUT	PEAK	WKS	RIAA	CD	#	Album Title	$	Label & Number
11/2/91+	48	40	▲	©	1	Private Line	$10	EastWest 91777
9/24/94	18	34	▲	©	2	Groove On	$10	EastWest 92416
10/14/95	20	30	●	©	3	Father And Son	$10	EastWest 61859
						GERALD LEVERT & EDDIE LEVERT SR.		
8/8/98	17	32	▲	©	4	Love & Consequences	$10	EastWest 62261
3/25/00	8	28	●	©	5	G	$10	EastWest 62417

Already Missing You (3) *75*
Answering Service (2)
Apple Don't Fall (3)
Application (I'm Looking 4 A New Love) (5)
Baby Hold On To Me (1) *37*
Baby U Are (5) *89*
Breaking My Heart (4)
Callin Me (5)
Can You Handle It (1)
Can't Help Myself (2) *98*
Definition Of A Man (4)
Don't Make Me Beg (4)
Don't Take It Away (5)
For The Love (3)
Get Your Thing Off (3)
Groove On (2)
Have Mercy (2)
Heart Don't (5)
How Many Times (2)
Hugs & Kisses (4)
Humble Me (4)
Hurting For You (1)
I Got You (3)
I Got Your Back (3)
I Wanna Be Bad (1)
I'd Give Anything (2) *28*
I'm Savin' Your Place (3)
It Hurts Too Much To Stay (5)
It's Your Turn (4)
Just A Little Something (1)
Just Because I'm Wrong (1)
Let The Juices Flow (2)
Love Street (2)
Men Like Us (4)
Misery (5)
Mr. Too Damn Good (5) *76*
Nice & Wet (2)
No I'm Not The Blame (4)
No Man's Land (4)
No Sense (4)
Nothin To Somethin (5)
Point The Finger (4)
Private Line (1)
Rock Me (All Nite Long) (2)
Same Place, Same Time (2)
School Me (1)
Second Time Around (5)
She Done Been (5)
Shootin' The Breeze (1)
Someone (2)
Strings, Strings (5)
Taking Everything (4) *11*
That's The Way I Feel About You (4)
These (5)
Thinkin' Bout It (4) *12*
What About Me (4)
Wind Beneath My Wings (3)
You Got Your Hooks In Me (3)
You Need Love (3)
You Oughta Be With Me (1)
You're Hurting Me (3)

LEVERT, Sean   '95

Born on 9/28/68 in Cleveland. R&B singer. Member of Levert. Son of Eddie Levert (of The O'Jays).

DEBUT	PEAK	WKS	CD	Album Title	$	Label & Number
7/15/95	146	1	©	The Other Side	$10	Atlantic 82663

I'm In A Freaky Mood
I'm Ready
Just Can't Get Enough
Just For The Fun Of It
Only You
Other Side
Place To Be
Put Your Body Where Your Mouth Is
Same One
Tasty Love

LEWIS, Barbara   '65

Born on 2/9/43 in South Lyon, Michigan. R&B singer/songwriter.

DEBUT	PEAK	WKS	Album Title	Sym	$	Label & Number
9/25/65	118	7	Baby, I'm Yours	[G]	$50	Atlantic 8110

Baby, I'm Yours *11*
Come Home
Hello Stranger *3*
How Can I Say Goodbye
If You Love Her
My Heart Went Do Da Dat
Puppy Love *38*
Snap Your Fingers *71*
Someday We're Gonna Love Again
Stop That Girl
Straighten Up Your Heart *43*
Think A Little Sugar

LEWIS, Crystal   '96

Born on 4/29/70 in Newport Beach, California. Christian singer/songwriter.

DEBUT	PEAK	WKS	CD	#	Album Title	$	Label & Number
10/26/96	134	2	©	1	Beauty For Ashes	$10	Myrrh 5036
3/21/98	188	1	©	2	Gold	$10	Myrrh 5041

Be With Him (2)
Beauty For Ashes (1)
Beauty Of The Cross (1)
Dyer Road (2)
For Such A Time As This (2)
God And I (2)
God's Been Good To Me (1)
Gold (2)
Healing Oil (1)
In Return (1)
It's Heaven (1)
Lion And The Lamb (1)
Lord I Believe In You (2)
Not The Same (1)
Over Me (1)
People Get Ready...Jesus Is Comin' (1)
Remember Who You Are (2)
Return To Me (2)
Seasons Change (1)
Tomorrow (2)
What About God (2)
Why? (2)

LEWIS, Donna   '96

Born in Cardiff, Wales. Female singer/songwriter.

DEBUT	PEAK	WKS	RIAA	CD	Album Title	$	Label & Number
7/27/96	31	39	▲	©	Now In A Minute	$10	Atlantic 82762

Agenais
Fools Paradise
I Love You Always Forever *2*
Lights Of Life
Love & Affection
Mother
Nothing Ever Changes
Silent World
Simone
Without Love *41*

LEWIS, Gary, And The Playboys   '66

Born Gary Levitch on 7/31/45 in New York City. Pop singer/drummer. Son of comedian Jerry Lewis. The Playboys consisted Al Ramsey and John West (guitars), David Walker (keyboards) and David Costell (bass). Also see Mae West.

DEBUT	PEAK	WKS	CD	#	Album Title	$	Label & Number
3/27/65	26	25	©	1	This Diamond Ring	$30	Liberty 7408
9/18/65	18	20	©	2	A Session With Gary Lewis And The Playboys	$30	Liberty 7419

LEWIS, Gary, And The Playboys — Cont'd

DEBUT	PEAK	WKS	CD	#	Album Title	Sym	$	Label & Number
12/4/65+	44	16		3	Everybody Loves A Clown		$30	Liberty 7428
3/12/66	71	17		4	She's Just My Style		$25	Liberty 7435
5/28/66	47	24		5	Hits Again!		$25	Liberty 7452
10/22/66	10	46	● ©	6	Golden Greats	[G]	$25	Liberty 7468
2/11/67	79	16		7	(You Don't Have To) Paint Me A Picture		$20	Liberty 7487
7/8/67	185	4		8	New Directions		$20	Liberty 7519
8/17/68	150	9		9	Gary Lewis Now!		$20	Liberty 7568

All Day And All Of The Night (1) · All I Have To Do Is Dream (4) · Autumn (5) · Barefootin' (7) · Best Man (1) · Birds And The Bees (1) · Chip Chip (3) · Concrete And Clay (2) · **Count Me In** (2,6) *2* · Daydream (5) · Double Good Feeling (8) · Down In The Boondocks (7) · Down On The Sloop John B. (7) · Dream Lover (1) · Dreamin' (3) · Elusive Butterfly (9) · **Everybody Loves A Clown** (3,6) *4* · Face In The Crowd (5)

For Your Love (2) · Forget Him (1) · Free Like Me (2) · **Girls In Love** (8) *39* · Go To Him (1) · **Green Grass** (5,6) *8* · Heart Full Of Soul (4) · Hello Sunshine (8) · Here I Am (8) · How Can I Thank You (9) · Hundred Pounds Of Clay (9) · I Can Read Between The Lines (5) · I Gotta Find Cupid (3) · I Won't Make That Mistake Again (4,6) · I Wonder What She's Doing Tonight? (9) · It's Too Late (5)

Judy In Disguise (With Glasses) (9) · Keep Searchin' (1) · Keepin' Company (8) · Let Me Tell Your Fortune (3) · Let's Be More Than Friends (8) · Lies (4) · Linda Lu (7) · Little Love From You (8) · Little Miss Go-Go (2,6) · Look Through Any Window (5) · Looking For The Stars (7) · Love Potion Number Nine (1) · Me About You (8) · Moonshine (8) · Mr. Blue (3) · **My Heart's Symphony** (7) *13* · My Special Angel (3) · Needles And Pins (1)

Neighborhood Rock 'N Roll Band (8) · New In Town (8) · Night Has A Thousand Eyes (1) · One Track Mind (5) · Palisades Park (7) · Pretty Thing (9) · Rubber Ball (5) · Run For Your Life (4) · Runaway (2) · Sara Jane (9) · **Save Your Heart For Me** (2,6) *2* · **Sealed With A Kiss** (9) *19* · Sha La La (3) · **She's Just My Style** (4,6) *3* · Sloop John B ...see: Down On The Sloop John B. · Slow Movin' Man (8)

Someone I Used To Know (4) · String Along (7) · Sunny (9) · **Sure Gonna Miss Her** (5,6) *9* · Sweet Little Rock And Roller (1) · Take Good Care Of My Baby (4) · **This Diamond Ring** (1,6) *1* · (Till) I Kissed You (3) · Time Stands Still (3,6) · Tina (I Held You In My Arms) (6,7) · Tossin' And Turnin' (3) · Travelin' Man (2) · Voodoo Woman (2) · Walk Right Back (2) · We'll Work It Out (3) · Well Respected Man (5) · What Am I Gonna Do (9)

When Summer Is Gone (7) · **Where Will The Words Come From** (7) *21* · Wild Thing (7) · Windy (9) · Without A Word Of Warning (2,6) · You Baby (5) · You Didn't Have To Be So Nice (4) · **(You Don't Have To) Paint Me A Picture** (7) *15* · You're Sixteen (7) · You've Got To Hide Your Love Away (1) · Young Girl (9)

★440★ **LEWIS, Huey, and The News** '84

Born Hugh Cregg III on 7/5/50 in New York City. Pop-rock singer/songwriter. Formed the News in San Francisco: Chris Hayes (guitar), Sean Hopper (keyboards), Johnny Colla (sax), Mario Cipollina (bass) and Bill Gibson (drums). Lewis acted in the movies *Back To The Future* and *Short Cuts*.

DEBUT	PEAK	WKS	RIAA	CD	#	Album Title	Sym	$	Label & Number
2/27/82	13	59	● ©		1	Picture This		$10	Chrysalis 1340
10/8/83+	❶¹	158	▲⁷ ©		2	Sports		$10	Chrysalis 41412
9/13/86	❶¹	61	▲³ ©		3	Fore!		$10	Chrysalis 41534
8/20/88	11	30	▲ ©		4	Small World		$10	Chrysalis 41622
5/25/91	27	27	● ©		5	Hard At Play		$10	EMI 93355
5/28/94	55	21	©		6	Four Chords & Several Years Ago		$10	Elektra 61500
11/16/96	185	1	©		7	Time Flies...The Best Of Huey Lewis & The News	[G]	$10	Elektra 61977

Attitude (5) · Bad Is Bad (2,7) · Best Of Me (5) · Better Be True (4) · Better To Have And Not Need (6) · Blue Monday (6) · Bobo Tempo (4) · Build Me Up (5) · **But It's Alright** (7) *54* · Buzz Buzz Buzz (1) · Change Of Heart (1) · **Couple Days Off** (5) *11* · **Do You Believe In Love** (1,7) *7*

Do You Love Me, Or What? (5) · **Doing It All For My Baby** (3,7) *6* · Don't Look Back (5) · Finally Found A Home (2) · Forest For The Trees (3) · Function At The Junction (6) · **Give Me The Keys (And I'll Drive You Crazy)** (4) *47* · Giving It All Up For Love (1) · Going Down Slow (6) · Good Morning Little School Girl (6) · He Don't Know (5)

Heart And Soul (2,7) *8* · Heart Of Rock & Roll (2,7) *6* · Hip To Be Square (3) *3* · Honky Tonk Blues (2) · **Hope You Love Me Like You Say You Do** (1) *36* · 100 Years From Now (7) · **I Know What I Like** (3) *9* · I Never Walk Alone (3) · **I Want A New Drug** (2,7) *6* · **If This Is It** (2,7) *6* · If You Gotta Make A Fool Of Somebody (6) · Is It Me (1)

It Hit Me Like A Hammer (5) *21* · It's Alright (3) · Jacob's Ladder (3) *1* · Little Bitty Pretty One (6) · Mother In Law (6) · Naturally (6) · Old Antone's (4) · Only One (1) · **Perfect World** (4) *3* · **Power Of Love** (7) *1* · Searching For My Love (6) · Shake Rattle And Roll (6) · She Shot A Hole In My Soul (6) · Time Ain't Money (5)

(She's) Some Kind Of Wonderful (6) *44* · Simple As That (3) · Slammin' (4) · **Small World** (4) *25* · Small World (Part Two) (4) · So Little Kindness (4) · Stagger Lee (6) · **Stuck With You** (3,7) *1* · Surely I Love You (6) · Tell Me A Little Lie (1) · That's Not Me (5) · 'Til The Day After (7) · Time Ain't Money (5)

Trouble In Paradise (7) · **Walking On A Thin Line** (2) *18* · Walking With The Kid (4) · We Should Be Making Love (5) · Whatever Happened To True Love (1) · When The Time Has Come (7) · Whole Lotta Lovin' (3) · **Workin' For A Livin'** (1,7) *41* · World To Me (4) · You Crack Me Up (2) · You Left The Water Running (6) · Your Cash Ain't Nothin' But Trash (6)

LEWIS, Jerry '57

Born Joseph Levitch on 3/16/25 in Newark, New Jersey. Comedian/actor. Father of **Gary Lewis**. Formed comedy duo with **Dean Martin** in 1946. Starred in several movies.

DEBUT	PEAK	WKS	CD	Album Title	$	Label & Number
12/22/56+	3	19	©	Jerry Lewis Just Sings	$60	Decca 8410

Back In Your Own Back Yard · Birth Of The Blues · By Myself · Bye Bye Baby · Come Rain Or Come Shine · Get Happy · How Long Has This Been Going On · I'm Sitting On Top Of The World · I've Got The World On A String · **Rock-A-Bye Your Baby With A Dixie Melody** *10* · Shine On Your Shoes · Sometimes I'm Happy

---

★298★ **LEWIS, Jerry Lee** '69

Born on 9/29/35 in Ferriday, Louisiana. Rock and roll singer/pianist. Appeared in the movie *Jamboree!* in 1957. Career waned in 1958 after marriage to 13-year-old cousin, Myra Gale Brown, daughter of his bass player. Made comeback in country music beginning in 1968. Nicknamed "The Killer." Cousin to country singer **Mickey Gilley** and TV evangelist Jimmy Swaggart. Inducted into the Rock and Roll Hall of Fame in 1986. Jerry's early career is documented in the 1989 movie *Great Balls Of Fire* starring Dennis Quaid.

1)The Session 2)Great Balls Of Fire! 3)The Greatest Live Show On Earth
4)Class Of '55 (Memphis Rock & Roll Homecoming) 5)The "Killer" Rocks On

DEBUT	PEAK	WKS	CD	#	Album Title	Sym	$	Label & Number
3/28/64	116	8		1	The Golden Hits Of Jerry Lee Lewis		$30	Smash 67040
					new recordings of his Sun label hits			
12/5/64+	71	17		2	The Greatest Live Show On Earth	[L]	$30	Smash 67056
					recorded on 7/1/64 in Birmingham, Alabama			
6/5/65	121	5		3	The Return Of Rock		$30	Smash 67063
5/14/66	145	3		4	Memphis Beat		$30	Smash 67079
6/29/68	160	12		5	Another Place Another Time		$15	Smash 67104
2/8/69	149	7		6	She Still Comes Around (To Love What's Left Of Me)		$15	Smash 67112
5/10/69	127	10		7	Jerry Lee Lewis Sings The Country Music Hall Of Fame Hits, Vol. 1		$15	Smash 67117
5/10/69	124	10		8	Jerry Lee Lewis Sings The Country Music Hall Of Fame Hits, Vol. 2		$15	Smash 67118
9/27/69	119	4	©	9	Original Golden Hits - Volume 1	[G]	$15	Sun 102
9/27/69	122	5	©	10	Original Golden Hits - Volume 2	[G]	$15	Sun 103
2/28/70	186	2		11	She Even Woke Me Up To Say Goodbye		$15	Smash 67128
5/9/70	114	14		12	The Best Of Jerry Lee Lewis	[G]	$15	Smash 67131
10/10/70	149	6		13	Live At The International, Las Vegas	[L]	$15	Mercury 61278
					includes "Take These Chains From My Heart" by Linda Gail Lewis			
1/30/71	190	6		14	There Must Be More To Love Than This		$15	Mercury 61323

LEWIS, Jerry Lee — Cont'd

DEBUT	PEAK	WKS	CD	#	Album Title	Sym	$	Label & Number
7/24/71	152	3		15	Touching Home		$15	Mercury 61343
11/27/71	115	12		16	Would You Take Another Chance On Me?		$15	Mercury 61346
4/22/72	105	12		17	The "Killer" Rocks On		$15	Mercury 637
3/17/73	37	19	©	18	The Session		$20	Mercury 803 [2]
4/28/79	186	3		19	Jerry Lee Lewis		$12	Elektra 184
6/21/86	87	12	©	20	Class Of '55 (Memphis Rock & Roll Homecoming)	C:#13/2	$10	America Smash 830002

CARL PERKINS/JERRY LEE LEWIS/ROY ORBISON/JOHNNY CASH

DEBUT	PEAK	WKS	CD	#	Album Title	Sym	$	Label & Number
7/22/89	62	10	©	21	Great Balls Of Fire!	[S]	$8	Polydor 839516

includes "Big Legged Woman" by Booker T. Laury, "Rocket 88" by Jackie Brenston and "Whole Lot Of Shakin' Going On" by Valerie Wellington

All Night Long (5)
All The Good Is Gone (5,12)
Another Hand Shakin' Goodbye (16)
Another Place Another Time (5,12) *97*
Baby, Hold Me Close (3)
Baby What You Want Me To Do (18)
Bad Moon Rising (18)
Ballad Of Forty Dollars (13)
Before The Next Teardrop Falls (5)
Big Blon' Baby (16)
Big Boss Man (4,18)
Big Train (From Memphis) (20)
Birth Of Rock And Roll (20)
Born To Lose (7)
Bottles And Barstools (14)
Break My Mind (5)
Break-Up (10) *52*
Breathless (1,9,21) *7*
Brown-Eyed Handsome Man (11)
Burning Memories (8)
C.C. Rider (17)
Chantilly Lace (17) *43*
Class Of '55 (20)
Cold Cold Heart (8)
Comin' Back For More (15)
Coming Home (20)
Corine, Corina (3)
Crazy Arms (1,9,21)
Don't Be Cruel (19)
Don't Let Go (3,19)
Drinkin' Champagne (13)
Drinking Wine Spo-Dee O'Dee (4,18) *41*
Early Morning Rain (18)
Echoes (6,11)
End Of The Road (1,9)
Every Day I Have To Cry (19)

Flip, Flop And Fly (3,13)
Foolaid (19)
Foolish Kind Of Man (15)
Fools Like Me (1,10)
For The Good Times (16)
Four Walls (7)
Fraulein (8)
Games People Play (17)
Good Golly Miss Molly (medley) (18)
Goodbye Of The Year (16)
Got You On My Mind (3)
Great Balls Of Fire (1,9,21) *2*
Hallelujah, I Love Her So (4)
He'll Have To Go (8)
Heartaches By The Number (7)
Hearts Were Made For Beating (15)
Help Me Make It Through The Night (15)
Herman The Hermit (3)
High Heel Sneakers (21) *91*
High School Confidential (1,10,18,21) *21*
Home Away From Home (14)
Hound Dog (3)
How's My Ex Treating You (10)
Hurtin' Part (16)
I Believe In You (3)
I Can't Get Over You (6)
I Can't Stop Loving You (8)
I Could Never Be Ashamed Of You (10)
I Forgot More Than You'll Ever Know (14)
I Get The Blues When It Rains (8)
I Got A Woman (2)
I Like It Like That (9)
I Love You Because (7)
I Will Rock And Roll With You (20)

I Wish I Was Eighteen Again (19)
I Wonder Where You Are Tonight (7)
I'd Be Talkin' All The Time (14)
I'll Make It All Up To You (1,10) *85*
I'll Sail My Ship Alone (10) *93*
I'm A Lonesome Fugitive (5)
I'm On Fire (21) *98*
I'm So Lonesome I Could Cry (7)
I'm Walkin' (17)
It Makes No Difference Now (8)
It'll Be Me (9)
Jackson (7)
Jambalaya (7,13)
Jenny Jenny (2,18)
Johnny B. Goode (3,18)
Jukebox (18)
Just Because (4)
Keep My Motor Running (20)
Let's Talk About Us (6,12)
Lewis Boogie (9)
Life's Little Ups And Downs (14)
Lincoln Limousine (4)
Listen, They're Playing My Song (6)
Little Queenie (9)
Lonely Weekends (17)
Lonesome Fiddle Man (16)
Long Tall Sally (2,18)
Louisiana Man (6,12)
Mathilda (4)
Maybelline (3)
Me And Bobby McGee (16,17) *40*
Mean Woman Blues (10)
Memphis (2,18)
Memphis Beat (4)
Mom And Dad's Waltz (7)
Money (10)

More And More (8)
Mother, The Queen Of My Heart (15)
Move On Down The Line (9,18)
Music To The Man (18)
My Only Claim To Fame (11)
No Headstone On My Grave (18)
No Particular Place To Go (2)
Number One Lovin' Man (19)
Oh Lonesome Me (7)
On The Back Row (5)
Once More With Feeling (11,12,13)
One Has My Name (The Other Has My Heart) (8,12)
One More Time (14)
Out Of My Mind (6)
Pick Me Up On Your Way Down (8)
Play Me A Song I Can Cry To (5)
Please Don't Talk About Me When I'm Gone (15)
Pledging My Love (18)
Release Me (6)
Reuben James (14)
Rita May (19)
Rock And Roll (Fais-Do-Do) (20)
Rockin' My Life Away (19)
Rocking Little Angel (19)
Roll Over Beethoven (3)
San Antonio Rose (13)
Save The Last Dance For Me (10)
Sea Cruise (18)
Sexy Ways (3)
She Even Woke Me Up To Say Goodbye (11,12,13)
She Still Comes Around (To Love What's Left Of Me) (6,12,13)

She Thinks I Still Care (4)
Shotgun Man (17)
Since I Met You Baby (11)
Sixteen Candles (20)
Sixty-Minute Man (18)
Slipping Around (12)
Sticks And Stones (4)
Sweet Dreams (7)
Sweet Georgia Brown (14)
Sweet Thang (8)
Swinging Doors (16)
Teen-Age Letter (9)
That Lucky Old Sun (21)
There Must Be More To Love Than This (14)
There Stands The Glass (6)
Things That Matter Most To Me (16)
Thirteen At The Table (16)
Time Changes Everything (15)
To Make Love Sweeter For You (6,12)
Today I Started Loving You Again (6)
Together Again (2)
Too Young (4)
Touching Home (15)
Trouble In Mind (18)
Turn On Your Love Light (17) *95*
Tutti Frutti (medley) (18)
Urge, The (4)
Waiting For A Train (11)
Walk A Mile In My Shoes (17)
Walking The Floor Over You (5)
Waymore's Blues (20)
We Live In Two Different Worlds (5)
We Remember The King (20)
What'd I Say (10,18) *30*

What's Made Milwaukee Famous (Has Made A Loser Out Of Me) (5,12) *94*
When Baby Gets The Blues (15)
When He Walks On You (Like You Have Walked On Me) (15)
When The Grass Grows Over Me (1)
When You Wore A Tulip And I Wore A Big Red Rose (13)
Whenever You're Ready (4)
Who Will The Next Fool Be (2,19)
Whole Lot Of Shakin' Going On (1,2,9,18,21) *3*
Why Don't You Love Me (Like You Used To Do) (8)
Wild One (21)
Wine Me Up (11)
Woman, Woman (Get Out Of Our Way) (14)
Workin' Man Blues (11)
Would You Take Another Chance On Me (16)
You Can Have Her (17)
You Don't Miss Your Water (17)
You Helped Me Up (When The World Let Me Down) (15)
You Went Back On Your Word (3)
You Went Out Of Your Way (To Walk On Me) (11)
You Win Again (1,9) *95*
(You've Got) Personality (19)
You've Still Got A Place In My Heart (7)
Your Cheating Heart (1)

LEWIS, Linda Gail — see MORRISON, Van

LEWIS, Ramsey ★105★   '65

Born on 5/27/35 in Chicago. R&B-jazz pianist. His trio included Eldee Young (bass) and Isaac "Red" Holt (drums). Disbanded in 1965. Young and Holt then formed **The Young-Holt Trio**. Lewis re-formed his trio with Cleveland Eaton (bass) and **Maurice White** (drums; later with **Earth, Wind & Fire**). Reunited with Young and Holt in 1983.

1)The In Crowd 2)Sun Goddess 3)Hang On Ramsey! 4)Wade In The Water 5)Don't It Feel Good

RAMSEY LEWIS TRIO:

DEBUT	PEAK	WKS	CD	#	Album Title	Sym	$	Label & Number
12/22/62	129	2	©	1	Sound Of Christmas	[X-I]	$50	Argo 687

Christmas charts: 20/'63, 7/'64, 4/'65, 8/'66, 8/'67, 13/'68, 6/'69

DEBUT	PEAK	WKS	CD	#	Album Title	Sym	$	Label & Number
7/4/64	125	7		2	Bach To The Blues	[I]	$40	Argo 732
10/17/64	103	13		3	The Ramsey Lewis Trio At The Bohemian Caverns	[I-L]	$40	Argo 741
12/19/64	8[X]	15		4	More Sounds Of Christmas	[X]	$40	Argo 745

Christmas charts: 16/'65, 14/'66, 49/'67, 41/'68

DEBUT	PEAK	WKS	CD	#	Album Title	Sym	$	Label & Number
8/14/65	2[1]	47	©	5	The In Crowd	[I-L]	$40	Argo 757

recorded on 5/14/65 at The Bohemian Caverns in Washington DC

DEBUT	PEAK	WKS	CD	#	Album Title	Sym	$	Label & Number
11/6/65+	54	19		6	Choice! The Best Of The Ramsey Lewis Trio	[G-I]	$20	Cadet 755
2/19/66	15	27		7	Hang On Ramsey!	[I-L]	$20	Cadet 761

recorded on 10/15/65 at The Lighthouse in Hermosa Beach, California

RAMSEY LEWIS:

DEBUT	PEAK	WKS	CD	#	Album Title	Sym	$	Label & Number
9/10/66	16	34	©	8	Wade In The Water	[I]	$20	Cadet 774
3/25/67	95	16		9	Goin' Latin	[I]	$20	Cadet 790
7/22/67	124	5		10	The Movie Album	[I]	$20	Cadet 782
10/28/67+	59	16		11	Dancing In The Street	[I-L]	$20	Cadet 794
3/9/68	52	31		12	Up Pops Ramsey Lewis	[I]	$20	Cadet 799
7/20/68	55	20	©	13	Maiden Voyage	[I]	$20	Cadet 811
3/29/69	156	14		14	Mother Nature's Son	[I]	$20	Cadet 821
9/6/69	139	14		15	Another Voyage	[I]	$20	Cadet 827
3/14/70	172	12		16	The Best Of Ramsey Lewis	[G-I]	$20	Cadet 839

LEWIS, Ramsey — Cont'd

DEBUT	PEAK	WKS	RIAA	CD	ARTIST — Album Title		$	Label & Number
3/21/70	157	8			17 **Ramsey Lewis, The Piano Player**	[I]	$20	Cadet 836
10/24/70	177	7			18 **Them Changes**	[I-L]	$20	Cadet 844
					recorded on 5/8/70 at The Depot in Minneapolis			
6/19/71	163	9			19 **Back To The Roots**	[I]	$20	Cadet 6001
6/24/72	79	21		©	20 **Upendo Ni Pamoja**	[I]	$15	Columbia 31096
3/3/73	117	10		©	21 **Funky Serenity**	[I]	$15	Columbia 32030
10/13/73	198	3		©	22 **Ramsey Lewis' Newly Recorded All-Time, Non-Stop Golden Hits**	[I]	$15	Columbia 32490
12/28/74+	12	30	●	©	23 **Sun Goddess**		$12	Columbia 33194
10/4/75	46	22			24 **Don't It Feel Good**		$12	Columbia 33800
5/22/76	77	11			25 **Salongo**	[I]	$12	Columbia 34173
5/28/77	79	10			26 **Love Notes**	[I]	$12	Columbia 34696
12/24/77+	111	9		©	27 **Tequila Mockingbird**	[I]	$12	Columbia 35018
10/28/78	149	5			28 **Legacy**	[I]	$12	Columbia 35483
8/23/80	173	8			29 **Routes**	[I]	$12	Columbia 36423
6/20/81	152	5			30 **Three Piece Suite**	[I]	$12	Columbia 37153
9/8/84	144	9		©	31 **The Two Of Us**		$12	Columbia 39326

RAMSEY LEWIS & NANCY WILSON

African Boogaloo Twist (13)
Ain't That Peculiar (8)
Alfie (12)
All My Love Belongs To You (7)
All The Way Live (28)
And I Love Her (7)
Aufu Oodu (25)
Bach To The Blues (2)
Back In The USSR (14)
Back To The Roots (19)
Bearmash (12)
Betcha By Golly Wow! (21)
Billy Boy (medley) (7)
Black Bird (14)
Blue Bongo (9)
Blue Spring (6)
Blues For The Night Owls (6,22)
Bold And Black (15)
Brazilica (25)
Breaker Beat (31)
C C Rider (6)
Camino El Bueno (27)
Can't Function (24)
Can't Wait Till Summer (30)
Candida (31)
Caribbean Blue (29)
Caring For You (27)
Carmen (6,22)
Cast Your Fate To The Wind (9)
Caves, The (3)
Cecile (15)
Chili Today, Hot Tamale (26)
China Gate (10)
Christmas Blues (1)
Christmas Song (1)
Close Your Eyes And Remember (17)
Closer Than Close (31)
Collage (20)
Colors In Space (29)
Come Back Jack (29)
Come Sunday (5)
Concierto De Aranjuez (20)
Crescent Noon (19)
Cry Baby Cry (14)
Crystals 'N Sequence (29)
Dance Mystique (2)
Dancing In The Street (11,16) **84**
Day Tripper (8) **74**

Dear Prudence (14)
Delilah (6,22)
Didn't We (17)
Distant Dreamer (17)
Django (11)
Do I Love Her (17)
Do What You Wanna (15)
Do Whatever Sets You Free (18)
Do You Know The Way To San Jose (11)
Don't Ever Go Away (30)
Don't It Feel Good (24)
Don't Look Back (28)
Down By The Riverside (9)
Dreams (21)
Drown In My Own Tears (18)
Egg Nog (4)
Emily (10)
Eternal Journey (13)
Everybody's Got Something To Hide Except Me And My Monkey (1)
Everybody's Talkin' (17)
Expansions (8)
Felicidade (Happiness) (5,11)
Fish Bite (24)
Fly Me To The Moon (In Other Words) (3)
Fool On The Hill (19)
For The Love Of A Princess (27)
Free Again (9)
From Russia With Love (10)
Function At The Junction (9,16)
Gemini Rising (23)
Gentle Rain (10)
Girl Talk (10)
God Rest Ye Merry Gentlemen (1)
Goin' Hollywood (10)
Goin' Out Of My Head (12)
Golden Slumber (17)
Good Night (14)
Got To Be There (20)
Hang On Sloopy (7,16,22) **11**
Hard Day's Night (7) **29**
He Ain't Heavy, He's My Brother (17)
He's A Real Gone Guy (7)
Hell On Wheels (29)
Hello, Cello! (6)

Here Comes Santa Claus (1)
Hey Mrs. Jones (9)
Hi-Heel Sneakers Pt. 1 (7,22) **70**
High Point (29)
Hold It Right There (8)
Hot Dawgit (23) **50**
How Beautiful Is Spring (15)
Hurt So Bad (8)
I Dig You (24)
I Love To Please You (28)
I Was Made To Love Her (12)
I'll Wait For You (9)
If Loving You Is Wrong I Don't Want To Be Right (21)
If You've Got It, Flaunt It (Part 1 & 2) (15)
"In" Crowd (5,16,22) **5**
In The Heat Of The Night (13)
Intimacy (27)
Jade East (12,16)
Jingle Bells (4)
Juaacklyn (24)
Julia (14,16) **76**
Jungle Strut (23)
Kufanya Mapenzi (Making Love) (21) **93**
Lady Madonna (13)
Lakeshore Cowboy (30)
Lara's Theme ..see: Somewhere, My Love
Legacy (28)
Les Fleur (13,16)
Little Drummer Boy (4)
Little Liza Jane (6)
Living For The City (23)
Lonely Avenue (6)
Look-A-Here (6)
Look Of Love (12)
Looking Glass (29)
Love I Feel For You (17)
Love Is (30)
Love Notes (26)
Love Now On (19)
Love Song (23)
Maiden Voyage (13,16)
Manha De Carnaval (medley) (11)
Matchmaker, Matchmaker (10)
Memphis In June (6)
Merry Christmas Baby (1)

Message To Michael (8)
Messenger, The (26)
Mi Compasion (8)
Michelle (30)
Midnight Rendezvous (31)
Mighty Quinn (Quinn The Eskimo) (13)
Misty Days, Lonely Nights (2)
Money In The Pocket (8)
Mood For Mendes (11)
Moogin' On (28)
More I See You (7)
Mother Nature's Son (14)
Movin' Easy (7)
My Angel's Smile (27)
My Babe (8)
My Bucket's Got A Hole In It (6)
My Cherie Amour (15)
My Love For You (21)
Never Wanna Say Goodnight (31)
Nicole (25)
Nights In White Satin (21)
Ode (13)
Oh Happy Day (18)
One, Two, Three (9) 67
Only When I'm Dreaming (13)
Opus V (15)
Party Time (12)
Pawnbroker (10,16)
Peace And Tranquility (2)
People (3)
People Make The World Go Round (20)
Please Send Me Someone To Love (20)
Plum Puddin' (4)
Put Your Hand In The Hand (20)
Quiet Nights (Corcovado) (11)
Quiet Storm (31)
Rainy Day In Centerville (17)
Ram (31)
Respect (12)
Return To Paradise (10,16)
Rocky Raccoon (14)
Romance Me (30)
Rubato (25)
Rudolph, The Red Nosed Reindeer (4)
Sadness Done Come (2)

Salongo (25)
Samba De Orpheus (medley) (11)
Santa Claus Is Coming To Town (1)
Satin Doll (7)
Saturday Night After The Movies (10)
See The End From The Beginning, Look Afar (18)
Serene Funk (31)
Seventh Fold (25)
Sexy Sadie (14)
Shadow Of Your Smile (19)
She's Out Of My Life (30)
Shelter Of Your Arms (3)
Shining (2)
Since I Fell For You (5,19)
Since You've Been Gone (13) **98**
Skippin' (27)
Sleigh Ride (1)
Slick (25)
Slippin' Away (31)
Slipping Into Darkness (20,22)
Sloopy Downtown (5)
Snowbound (4)
Snowfall (4)
So Much More (30)
Something (18)
Something About You (24)
Something You Got (3,6,22) **63**
Somewhere, My Love (9)
(Song Of) Delilah ..see: Delilah
Song Without Words (Remembering) (31)
Soul Man (12,16) **49**
Sound Of Christmas (1)
Spanish Grease (9)
Spartacus, Love Theme From (5)
Spring High (26)
Star Is Born (Evergreen), Love Theme From A (26)
Stash Dash (24)
Struttin' Lightly (11)
Summer Samba (9)
Sun Goddess (23) **44**
Sweet Rain (13)
Tambura (25)
Tennessee Waltz (5)

Tequila Mockingbird (27)
That Ole Bach Magic (27)
That's The Way Of The World (24)
(Them) Changes (18)
Time And Space (17)
Tobacco Road (8)
Tondelayo (29)
Travel On (2,6)
Trilogy Medley (20)
Twelve Days Of Christmas (4)
Two Of Us (31)
Uhuru (15)
Unsilent Minority (18)
Up In Yonder (19)
Up Tight (8,16) **49**
Upendo Ni Pamoja (Love Is Together) (20)
Wade In The Water (8,16,22) **19**
Wanderin' Rose (15,27)
We Three Kings (4)
We've Only Just Begun (19)
Well, Well, Well! (28)
West Side Story Medley (3)
What Are You Doing New Year's Eve (1)
What It Is! (21)
What Now My Love (11)
What's The Name Of This Funk (Spider Man) (24) **69**
Whenever, Wherever (17)
Where Is The Love (21)
Whisper Zone (29)
White Christmas (4)
Why Am I Treated So Bad (12)
Why Don't You Do Right (2)
Will You (30)
Winter Wonderland (1)
You Are The Reason (29)
You Been Talkin' 'Bout Me Baby (5)
You Don't Know Me (11)
You'll Love Me Yet (2)
You've Made Me So Very Happy (17)

LEWIS, Webster
Born in Baltimore. R&B keyboardist.

DEBUT	PEAK	WKS			ARTIST — Album Title		$	Label & Number		
3/15/80	114	9			**8 For The 80's**		$12	Epic 36197		'80

Fire
Give Me Some Emotion
Go For It
Heavenly
I Want To Blow (My Horn)
Love You Give To Me
Mild Wind
You Deserve To Dance

LFO
Vocal trio from Sheffield, England: Rich Cronin, Brad Fischetti and Devin Lima. LFO: Lyte Funky Ones.

DEBUT	PEAK	WKS	RIAA	CD	ARTIST — Album Title		$	Label & Number	'99
9/11/99	21	52	▲	©	**LFO**		$10	Arista 14605	

All I Need To Know
Baby Be Mine
Can't Have You
Cross My Heart
Forever
Girl On TV 10
I Don't Wanna Kiss You Goodnight 61
I Will Show You Mine
My Block
Summer Girls 3
Think About You
West Side Story 84
Your Heart Is Safe With Me

LFT CHURCH CHOIR
Gospel group assembled by **Hezekiah Walker**. LFT: Love Fellowship Tabernacle.

DEBUT	PEAK	WKS		CD	ARTIST — Album Title		$	Label & Number	'01
4/7/01	180	1		©	**Love Is Live!**	[L]	$10	Verity 43157	

Battle, The
He Made A Way
I Praise God
I'm A Newborn Soul
Lamb Of God
Let Go, Let God
Lord Do It
Lord Lift Me Up
Praise Break (The Ma-Shon-Da!) (Let The Church Be The Church)
Thank You, You Died For Me
Wait On God
You Have Been Right There

LIEBERMAN, Lori
Born on 11/18/49 in Los Angeles. Folk singer/songwriter. **'73**

| 8/18/73 | 192 | 6 | | | **Becoming** .... | | | $15 | Capitol 11203 |

Becoming · House Full Of Women · It Didn't Come Easy · Seed First · Song Of The Seventies
Eleazar · I Go Along · No Way Of Knowing · Someone Come And Take It · Sweet Morning After

LIEBERT, Ottmar
Born in 1963 in Cologne, Germany (Chinese-German father and Hungarian mother). Flamenco guitarist. Luna Negra (Spanish for Black Moon) are bassist Jon Gagan and drummer Dave Bryant. **'92**

| 5/26/90 | 134 | 18 | ▲ | © 1 | **Nouveau Flamenco** .... | [I] | | $10 | Higher Octave 7026 |
| 1/5/91 | 170 | 2 | | © 2 | **Poets & Angels** .... | [X-I] | | $10 | Higher Octave 7030 |

Christmas chart: 22/'90

OTTMAR LIEBERT + LUNA NEGRA:

| 7/6/91 | 176 | 5 | ● | © 3 | **Borrasca** .... | [I] | | $10 | Higher Octave 7036 |
| 4/11/92 | 94 | 25 | ● | © 4 | **Solo Para Ti** .... | [I] | | $10 | Epic 47848 |

title is Spanish for "Only For You"

| 9/4/93 | 132 | 12 | ● | © 5 | **The Hours Between Night + Day** .... | [I] | | $10 | Epic 53804 |

Adrift In Tangier (5) · Dancing Under The Moon (3) · 1st Rain (medley) (3) · Lone Rider 4 Slick (5) · Promise (Beyond The Mountains) (4) · Summantra (5)
After The Rain (1) · Flowers Of Romance (4 Bok Yun) (1) · Luna Negra Beat (medley) (2) · Surrender 2 Love (1)
Albatross (5) · Danza De Los Sentidos (5) · Lush Sea Of Sound (5) · Reaching Out 2 U (Todos Bajo La Misma Luna) (4) · Temple Dawn Ultravivid Clouds (5)
Angels We Have Heard On High (medley) (2) · Danza Viva (My Heart Grows Wings) (4) · Fullmoonbeachwalk 4 Jon (5) · Merengue De Alegrias (Candy 4 My Soul) (4) · Road 2 Her (medley) (1) · Ten Piedad De Mi Mercy Mercy Me (The Ecology) (5)
Arrow W/O Destination (4) · Dawn In A New World (4) · Havana Club (5) · Moon Over Trees (1) · Samba Pa Ti (Thru Every Step In Life U Find Freedom From Within) (4) · 3 Women Walking (1)
August Moon (3) · Deck The Halls (2) · Heart Still (medley) (1) · Morning Arrival In Goa · Thru The Trees (medley) (3)
Away In A Manger (medley) (2) · Deep In Your Heart (4) · High On Hope (medley) (2) · Lighthouse Flash Over The Sea (5) · Santa Fe (1) · 2 The Night (Fast Cars/4 Frank) (1)
Bajo La Luna Mix (3) · Dream I Just Want 2 Drown In U (5) · Home (Bulerias) (medley) (1) · Morning Glory (2) · Santa Fe X'mas (medley) (2) · Twilight In Galisteo (3)
Barcelona Nights (1) · In The Hands Of Love (3) · Neon Ghost Sensei Overflowing (5) · Shadows (1) · Waiting 4 Stars 2 Fall (1)
Beating (4 Berlin) (medley) (1) · Driving 2 Madrid (B4 The Storm) (3) · Isla Del Sol (3) · Shepherd's Nite Watch (2) · We 3 Kings (Of Orient R) (medley) (2)
Black Hair In The Wind (4) · Island X'mas (4 Bok Yun) (medley) (2) · Night In Granada (3) · Silent Nite (2) · When I'm With U (medley) (4)
Bombay Night Of Dreams (5) · Duende Del Amor (Day) (4) · Jingle Bells (2) · O X'mas Tree (4 Anna + Barthelomaus) (2) · Sleepless Distortion/System Crash (5) · Whispering Hills (4)
Borrasca (3) · Duende Del Amor (Night) (4) · La Aurora (3) · O Holy Nite (2) · Snakecharmer (5)
Buddha's Flower 4 My Sister (5) · Everything I Ever Needed (medley) (4) · La Rosa Negra (3) · Passing Storm (1) · Starry Nite (March Of Kings) (2)
Bullfighter's Dream (3) · Festival (Of 7 Lights) (2) · Like Fire 2 Straw (5) · Poets + Angels (2) · Storm Sings (3)
Cloudless Sky (medley) (3) · 1st Nowell (2) · Lilac Sun (4)
Cry Of Faith (medley) (3) · Little Drummer Boy (medley) (2)

LIFEHOUSE
Rock trio from Malibu, California: Jason Wade (vocals, guitar), Sergio Andrade (bass) and Rick Woolstenhulme (drums). **'01**

| 11/18/00+ | 6 | 46↑ | ▲2 | © | **No Name Face** | | | $10 | DreamWorks 50231 |

Breathing · Everything · Only One · Sick Cycle Carousel · Somebody Else's Song · Trying
Cling And Clatter · **Hanging By A Moment 2** · Quasimodo · Simon · Somewhere In Between · Unknown

LIFE OF AGONY
Rock group from Brooklyn, New York: Keith Caputo (vocals), Joey Z (guitar), Alan Robert (bass) and Sal Abruscato (drums). Dan Richardson replaced Abruscato in 1997. Joey Z and Richardson later joined **Stereomud**. **'95**

| 10/28/95 | 153 | 1 | | © 1 | **Ugly** .... | | | $10 | Roadrunner 8924 |
| 9/27/97 | 157 | 1 | | © 2 | **Soul Searching Sun** .... | | | $10 | Roadrunner 8816 |

Angry Tree (2) · Fears (1) · How It Would Be (1) · My Mind Is Dangerous (2) · Tangerine (2)
Damned If I Do (1) · Gently Sentimental (2) · I Regret (1) · Neg (2) · Ugly (1)
Desire (2) · Hemophiliac In Me (2) · Lead You Astray (2) · None (2) · Unstable (1)
Don't You (Forget About Me) (1) · Heroin Dreams (2) · Let's Pretend (1) · Other Side Of The River (1) · Weeds (2)
Drained (1) · Hope (2) · Lost At 22 (1) · Seasons (1) · Whispers (2)

LIGHT, Enoch, & The Light Brigade ★84★ **'60**
Born on 8/18/07 in Canton, Ohio. Died on 7/31/78 (age 70). Conductor of own orchestra, The Light Brigade, since 1935. President of Grand Award label and managing director for Command Records, for whom he produced a long string of hit stereo percussion albums in the 1960s. Enoch's studio musicians variously billed as Terry Snyder And The All-Stars (Terry died on 3/15/63, age 47), and The Command All-Stars. Also see **Charleston City All-Stars**, **Los Admiradores**, and **Tony Mottola**.

1)Persuasive Percussion 2)Stereo 35/MM 3)Provocative Percussion 4)Persuasive Percussion, Volume 2
5)Persuasive Percussion, Volume 3

| 6/15/59 | 38 | 4 | | 1 | **I Want To Be Happy Cha Cha's** .... | [I] | | $25 | Grand Award 388 |
| 1/25/60 | ❶13 | 124 | ● | © 2 | **Persuasive Percussion** | [I] | | $20 | Command 800 |

TERRY SNYDER & THE ALL-STARS

| 1/25/60 | 2⁵ | 97 | | © 3 | **Provocative Percussion** | [I] | | $20 | Command 806 |

THE COMMAND ALL-STARS

| 8/22/60 | 3 | 53 | | 4 | **Persuasive Percussion, Volume 2** | [I] | | $20 | Command 808 |

TERRY SNYDER & THE ALL-STARS

| 9/19/60 | 4 | 46 | | 5 | **Provocative Percussion, Volume 2** | [I] | | $20 | Command 810 |
| 4/24/61 | 3 | 20 | | 6 | **Persuasive Percussion, Volume 3** | [I] | | $20 | Command 817 |

THE COMMAND ALL-STARS

10/9/61	❶7	57		7	**Stereo 35/MM**	[I]		$20	Command 826
2/17/62	8	27		8	**Stereo 35/MM, Volume Two**	[I]		$20	Command 831
2/24/62	34	8		9	**Persuasive Percussion, Volume 4**	[I]		$20	Command 830

ENOCH LIGHT & THE COMMAND ALL-STARS

4/21/62	27	13		10	**Great Themes From Hit Films**	[I]		$20	Command 835
11/3/62	44	4		11	**Enoch Light And His Orchestra At Carnegie Hall Play Irving Berlin**	[I]		$20	Command 840
12/15/62+	8	33		12	**Big Band Bossa Nova**	[I]		$20	Command 844
11/2/63	133	3		13	**1963-The Year's Most Popular Themes**	[I]		$20	Command 854
4/4/64	121	7		14	**Rome 35/MM**	[I]		$20	Command 863
5/30/64	78	9		15	**Dimension "3"**	[I]		$20	Command 867
6/13/64	129	4		16	**Command Performances**	[I-K]		$20	Command 868

DEBUT	PEAK	WKS	RIAA	CD	ARTIST — Album Title	Catalog	Sym	$	Label & Number

LIGHT, Enoch, & The Light Brigade — Cont'd

DEBUT	PEAK	WKS			Title		Sym	$	Label & Number
10/3/64	143	4			17 Great Themes From Hit Films		[I]	$20	Command 871
11/7/64+	84	15			18 Discotheque Dance...Dance...Dance		[I]	$20	Command 873
9/11/65	105	10			19 Magnificent Movie Themes		[I]	$20	Command 887
5/21/66	144	6			20 Persuasive Percussion 1966		[I]	$20	Command 895
4/15/67	173	2			21 Film On Film - Great Movie Themes		[I]	$15	Project 3 5005
4/22/67	163	4			22 Spanish Strings		[I]	$15	Project 3 5000
4/26/69	192	7			23 Enoch Light & The Brass Menagerie		[I]	$15	Project 3 5036
3/21/70	191	4			24 Spaced Out		[I]	$15	Project 3 5043
7/24/71	176	5	©		25 Big Band Hits Of The 30's & 40's!		[I]	$15	Project 3 5056

Adios (15)
Ain't Misbehavin' (3)
Alexander's Ragtime Band (11)
Alfie (21)
All I Do Is Dream Of You (15)
All The Way (6,7)
All The Way Home (17)
Aloha Oe (2)
Alphabet Murders (21)
Always (11)
Am I Blue (9)
Amorous Adventures Of Moll Flanders, Theme From (19)
And I Love Her (18)
Anna (14)
Antony And Cleopatra Theme (13)
April In Paris (25)
April In Portugal (22)
Army Medley (11,16)
Arrivederci, Roma (14)
Autumn In New York (6)
Autumn Leaves (20)
Besame Mucho (9,12)
Bingo Bango Bongo Baby (6)
Blowin' In The Wind (23)
Blue Is The Night (4)
Blue Max, Love Theme From The (21)
Blue Skies (11)
Blue Tango (4,22)
Blues In The Night (3)
Bond Street (24)
Born Free (21)
Both Sides Now (23)
Brazil (4,12)
Breeze And I (2)
Bye Bye Blues (medley) (21)
California Dreamin' (23)
Call Me Irresponsible (17)
Can't Get Enough For My Baby (1)
Cara Mia Cha Cha (Ciribiribin) (1)
Caravan (20)
Carpetbaggers, Love Theme From The (17)
Carribe (15)
Cheek To Cheek (11)
Cherokee (25)
Chim Chim Cher-ee (19)
Ciumachella (14)
C'mon And Swim (18)
Come On, Come On, Come On, Don't Be Timido (22)
Come Rain Or Come Shine (6)
Days Of Wine And Roses (13)
Dear Heart (19)
Dearly Beloved (4)

Deep Purple (8)
Desafinado (12)
Diga Diga Doo (8)
Do It Again (8)
Don't Get Around Much Anymore (25)
Don't Worry 'Bout Me (8)
Down By The Riverside (18)
Dream Lover (18)
E Luxo So (12)
El Cid, Love Theme From (10)
Eleanor Rigby (24)
Everything's Coming Up Roses (20)
Exodus (10)
Fascinating Rhythm (3)
Fate Is The Hunter (17)
Fly Me To The Moon (16)
Flying Home (25)
Foggy Day Cha Cha (5)
Fool On The Hill (23)
For All We Know (15)
Forget Domani (Forget Tomorrow) (19)
Four Brothers (25)
Four Horsemen Of The Apocalypse, Theme From (10)
From Russia With Love (17)
Galanura (1)
Get Back (24)
Goldfinger (19)
Goodnight Sweetheart-Cha Cha (5)
Got A Date With An Angel (9)
Guaglione (1)
Gypsy In My Soul (8)
Happy Ever After (23)
Hard Day's Night (17)
Hawaii (21)
Hawaiian War Chant (6)
Hawaiian Wedding Song (15)
Heat Wave (7)
Hello, Dolly! (Bossa Nova) (8)
Hello Young Lovers (9)
Hernando's Hideaway (5)
Hey There (15)
Hold Me (9)
How Deep Is The Ocean? (11)
How High The Moon (1)
How Insensitive (22)
How The West Was Won (13)
Hud (13)
Hustler, Theme From The (10)
I Can't Get Started With You (25)
I Could Go On Singing (13)
I Could Have Danced All Night (17)
I Love, I Live, I Love (22)

I Love Paris (2)
I May Be Wrong (9)
I Remember Her So Well (19)
I See Your Face Before Me (7)
I Still Get A Thrill (8)
I Surrender Dear (2)
I Want To Be Happy (8,18)
I Want To Be Happy Cha Cha (1) 48
I Want To Hold Your Hand (24)
I'll Never Smile Again (25)
I'll See You Again (17)
I'm Gonna Make You Love Me (23)
I'm In The Mood For Love (2)
I've Got A Crush On You (7)
I've Got A Right To Sing The Blues (5)
I've Got My Love To Keep Me Warm (11)
I've Gotta Be Me (23)
If I Had A Hammer (18)
In A Little Spanish Town (8)
In A Persian Market (4)
In The Mood (9)
Istanbul (20)
It Had Better Be Tonight (17)
It's De Lovely (9)
It's Only A Paper Moon (15)
Japanese Sandman (2)
Jersey Bounce (25)
Just One Of Those Things (8)
Kashmiri Song (6)
Khartoum (21)
King Of Kings, Theme From (10)
Knowing When To Leave (24)
La Cucaracha (4)
La Dolce Vita (10,16)
La Mentira (22)
La Puerta Del Sol (12)
Lady Is A Tramp (5)
Lady L., Theme From (21)
Lady Of Spain (4)
Lawrence Of Arabia Theme (13)
Lemon Merengue (18)
Life Is Just A Bowl Of Cherries (15)
Light In The Piazza (10)
Lisbon Antigua (22)
Little Fugue For You And Me (24)
Lolita Cha Cha (1)
Love And Marriage (15)
Love For Sale (3,7)
Love Is A Many-Splendored Thing (2)
Love Me Now (19)

Lover (1)
Lover's Concerto (24)
Lullaby Of Birdland (12)
Mack The Knife (5)
Mad About The Boy (3)
Mambo Jambo (4)
Man I Love (3,7)
Maria My Own (22)
Marie (25)
Matilda (5)
Miami Beach Rhumba (4)
Mirror, Mirror, Mirror (21)
Misirlou (2)
Moments To Remember (6)
Mondo Cane No. 2 (17)
Mood Indigo (3)
Moon River (10)
Moonlight Sonata (25)
More (Theme From Mondo Cane) (13)
Mutiny On The Bounty, Theme From (13)
My Blue Heaven (9)
My Favorite Things (23)
My Heart Belongs To Daddy (2)
My Old Flame (15)
My Romance (7)
My Silent Song (24)
'Na Voce, 'Na Chitarra, E'O Poco 'E Luna (14)
Natives Are Restless Tonight (5)
Never On Sunday (10,20)
Night Train (18)
Nina (14)
Non Dimenticar (Don't Forget) (14)
Norwegian Wood (24)
O Sole Mio (14)
Ob-La-Di, Ob-La-Da (24)
Of Thee I Sing (8)
Oh Lady Be Good (9,16)
One For My Baby (6)
One Note Samba (12)
Orchids In The Moonlight (2)
Out Of Nowhere (4)
Paris Smiles (21)
Parlami D'Amore, Mariu (Tell Me That You Love Me) (14)
Patricia (1)
Peking Theme (So Little Time) (13)
People (2)
Per Tutta La Vita (I Want To Be Wanted) (14)
Perdido (6,12)
Perhaps, Perhaps, Perhaps (3,22)
Petite Paulette (24)

Polovetzian Dances, Theme From (6)
Pretty Girl Is Like A Melody (11)
Put On A Happy Face (17)
Put Your Head On My Shoulder (23)
Rain (medley) (20)
Red Roses For A Blue Lady (20)
Remember (11)
Rio Junction (Bossa Nova) (12,16)
Rock-A-Bongo Boogie (4)
S'Wonderful (3)
Sand Pebbles, Theme From The (21)
Sandpiper (The Shadow Of Your Smile), Love Theme From The (19)
Satan Never Sleeps (10)
Say It Isn't So (11)
Scalinatella (Stairway To The Sea) (14,16)
Sem Saudades De Voce (12)
Sentimental Journey (17)
September In The Rain (20)
September Song (8,16)
Seventh Dawn (17)
Sheik, The (1)
Ship Of Fools (19)
Sing, Sing, Sing Part 1 & 2 (25)
Somebody Loves Me (3)
Someone To Light Up My Life (22)
Someone To Watch Over Me (7)
Song Of India (3)
Soulful Strut (Am I The Same Girl) (23)
Sound Of Music (19)
Speak Low (5)
Speak Not A Word (13)
Speak To Me Of Love-Cha Cha (5)
Spencer's Mountain (13)
Swamp-Fire (11)
Sweet And Gentle (1)
Tabu (2)
Take The "A" Train (12)
Tango Delle Rose (14)
Tea For Two Cha Cha (1)
Temptation (5)
Tender Is The Night (10)
That Old Black Magic (16)
That's My Desire (11)
There's No Business Like Show Business (11)
Third Man Theme (16)
This Can't Be Love (20)

Thrill Is Gone (7)
Tintarella Di Luna (Magic Color Of The Moonlight) (18)
Tom Jones (Main Theme & Love Song) (17)
Tonight (10,16,20)
Top Hat, White Tie And Tails (11)
Touch Me (23)
Tremendo Cha Cha (1)
Tuxedo Junction (25)
Two Lovers (21)
Very Thought Of You (8)
Via Veneto (14)
Von Ryan March (19)
Walk On By (24)
Was She Prettier Than I? (15)
Watermelon Man (18)
What A Difference A Day Made (22)
What Is This Thing Called Love (5)
What The World Needs Now Is Love (24)
Whatever Lola Wants (2)
When Your Lover Has Gone (6)
Who Can I Turn To (When Nobody Needs Me) (20)
Who's Afraid Of Virginia Woolf? (21)
Wichita Lineman (23)
With A Song In My Heart (7)
Without You (Tres Palabras) (20)
Ya Ya (18)
Yes Sir, That's My Baby (1)
You Brought A New Kind Of Love To Me (9)
You Do Something To Me (8)
You're The Top (3)
Yours Is My Heart Alone (4)
Zing Went The Strings Of My Heart (7,16)
Zorba The Greek, Theme From (19)

LIGHTER SHADE OF BROWN   '94

Hispanic rap duo from Riverside, California: Robert Gutierrez and Bobby Ramirez.

DEBUT	PEAK	WKS		CD	Title		Sym	$	Label & Number
2/8/92	184	4	©		1 Brown & Proud			$10	Pump 15154
8/13/94	169	2	©		2 Layin' In The Cut			$10	Mercury 522479

Bouncin' (1)
Brown & Proud (1)
Dip Into My Ride (2)
Doin' The Same Thing (2)

El Varrio (1)
Everyday All Day (2)
Hey D.J. (2) 43
I Like It (2)

If You Wanna Groove (2)
Latin Active (1) 59
On A Sunday Afternoon (1) 39
Pancho Villa (1)

Paquito Soul (1)
Playin' In The Shade (2)
Spill The Wine (2)
T.J. Nights (1)

Talkin' 'Bout (Gettin' It On) (2)
Things Ain't The Same (2)
Where Ya At (2)

★244★   LIGHTFOOT, Gordon   '74

Born on 11/17/38 in Orillia, Ontario, Canada. Folk-pop singer/songwriter/guitarist.

1)Sundown 2)Cold On The Shoulder 3)Summertime Dream

DEBUT	PEAK	WKS	RIAA	CD	Title		Sym	$	Label & Number
11/15/69	143	6		©	1 Sunday Concert		[L]	$20	United Artists 6714
					recorded at Massey Hall in Toronto				
5/30/70+	12	37	●	©	2 Sit Down Young Stranger			$15	Reprise 6392
					later reissued as If You Could Read My Mind				
5/29/71	38	20		©	3 Summer Side Of Life			$15	Reprise 2037
6/26/71	178	5			4 Classic Lightfoot (The Best Of Lightfoot/Volume 2)		[K]	$15	United Artists 5510
3/25/72	42	17		©	5 Don Quixote			$15	Reprise 2056
11/18/72	95	12			6 Old Dan's Records			$15	Reprise 2116
2/2/74	❶²	42	▲	©	7 Sundown			$15	Reprise 2177
7/27/74+	155	9			8 The Very Best Of Gordon Lightfoot		[K]	$12	United Artists 243

LIGHTFOOT, Gordon — Cont'd

DEBUT	PEAK	WKS	RIAA	CD	Album Title	$	Label & Number
3/1/75	10	20		© 9	Cold On The Shoulder	$12	Reprise 2206
11/22/75+	34	24	▲²	© 10	Gord's Gold .... [G]	$15	Reprise 2237 [2]
6/26/76	12	41	▲	© 11	Summertime Dream	$12	Reprise 2246
2/4/78	22	20	●	© 12	Endless Wire	$12	Warner 3149
4/5/80	60	11		13	Dream Street Rose	$12	Warner 3426
2/20/82	87	12		14	Shadows	$12	Warner 3633
8/13/83	175	5		15	Salute	$10	Warner 23901
8/9/86	165	6		© 16	East Of Midnight	$10	Warner 25482

Affair On Eighth Avenue (4,8,10)
Alberta Bound (5)
All I'm After (14)
All The Lovely Ladies (9)
Anything For Love (16)
Apology (1)
Approaching Lavender (2)
Auctioneer, The (13)
Baby It's Alright (2)
Baby Step Back (14) *50*
Ballad Of Yarmouth Castle (1,4)
Beautiful (5,10) *58*
Bells Of The Evening (9)
Bend In The Water (9)
Biscuit City (15)
Bitter Green (1,10)
Black Day In July (8)
Blackberry Wine (14)
Boss Man (1)
Brave Mountaineers (5)
Broken Dreams (15)
Cabaret (3)
Can't Depend On Love (6)
Canadian Railroad Trilogy (1,8,10)
Carefree Highway (7,10) *10*
Cherokee Bend (9)
Christian Island (Georgian Bay) (5)
Circle Is Small (I Can See It In Your Eyes) (12) *33*

Circle Of Steel (7,10)
Cobwebs & Dust (2)
Cold On The Shoulder (9,10)
Cotton Jenny (3,10)
Daylight Katy (12)
Did She Mention My Name (8,10)
Don Quixote (5,10)
Dream Street Rose (13)
Dreamland (12)
Early Morning Rain (8,10)
East Of Midnight (16)
Ecstasy Made Easy (16)
Endless Wire (16)
Farewell To Annabel (6)
Fine As Fine Can Be (9)
For Lovin' Me (8,10)
14 Karat Gold (14)
Ghosts Of Cape Horn (13)
Go My Way (3)
Gotta Get Away (15)
Hangdog Hotel Room (12)
Heaven Help The Devil (14)
Hey You (13)
High And Dry (7)
Hi'Way Songs (6)
Home From The Forest (14)
House You Live In (11)
I'd Do It Again (11)
I'll Do Anything (14)
I'll Tag Along (16)

I'm Not Sayin' (1,8,10)
I'm Not Supposed To Care (11)
If Children Had Wings (12)
If I Could (4,8)
If There's A Reason (12)
If You Could Read My Mind (2,10) *5*
If You Need Me (13)
In A Windowpane (1)
In My Fashion (14)
Is There Anyone Home (7)
It's Worth Believin' (6)
Knotty Pine (15)
Last Time I Saw Her (4,8)
Lazy Mornin' (6)
Leaves Of Grass (1)
Lesson In Love (16)
Let It Ride (16)
List, The (7)
Long Way Back Home (4)
Looking At The Rain (5)
Lost Children (1)
Love & Maple Syrup (3)
Make Way For The Lady (13)
Me And Bobby McGee (2)
Miguel (3)
Minstrel Of The Dawn (2,10)
Mister Rock Of Ages (13)
Morning Glory (16)
Mother Of A Miner's Child (6)
Mountains And Marian (4)

My Pony Won't Go (6)
Never Too Close (11)
Nous Vivons Ensemble (3)
Now And Then (9)
Ode To Big Blue (5)
Old Dan's Records (6,10)
On Susan's Floor (5)
On The High Seas (13)
Ordinary Man (5)
Passing Ship (16)
Patriot's Dream (5)
Pony Man (1)
Poor Little Allison (2)
Protocol (11)
Pussy Willows, Cat-Tails (1)
Race Among The Ruins (11) *65*
Rainbow Trout (9)
Rainy Day People (9,10) *26*
Redwood Hill (3)
Ribbon Of Darkness (medley) (1,10)
Romance (15)
Rosanna (4)
Salute (A Lot More Livin' To Do) (15)
Same Old Loverman (3)
Saturday Clothes (2)
Sea Of Tranquility (15)
Second Cup Of Coffee (5)
Seven Island Suite (7)

Shadows (14)
She's Not The Same (14)
Sit Down Young Stranger (2)
Slide On Over (9)
Softly (1,10)
Someone To Believe In (15)
Something Very Special (4)
Sometimes I Don't Mind (12)
Somewhere U.S.A. (7)
Song For A Winter's Night (10)
Songs The Minstrel Sang (12)
Soul Is The Rock (9)
Spanish Moss (11)
Stay Loose (16)
Steel Rail Blues (10)
Summer Side Of Life (3,10) *98*
Summertime Dream (11)
Sundown (7,10) *1*
Sweet Guinevere (12)
Talking In Your Sleep (3) *64*
Tattoo (15)
10 Degrees & Getting Colder (3)
Thank You For The Promises (14)
That Same Old Obsession (6)
Too Late For Prayin' (7)
Too Many Clues In This Room (11)
Tree Too Weak To Stand (9)
Triangle (14)

Walls (4,8)
Watchman's Gone (7)
Way I Feel (8)
Wherefore And Why (8,10)
Whisper My Name (13)
Whispers Of The North (3)
Without You (15)
Wreck Of The Edmund Fitzgerald (11) *2*
You Are What I Am (6)
You Just Gotta Be (16)
Your Love's Return (Song For Stephen Foster) (2)

LIGHTHOUSE   '71

Rock group from Toronto: Bob McBride (vocals), Ralph Cole (guitar), Paul Hoffert (keyboards), Howard Shore (sax), Don Dinovo (viola), Dick Armin (cello), Louie Yacknin (bass) and Skip Prokop (drums). Prokop was a member of **The Paupers**. Shore went on to become the original musical director of TV's *Saturday Night Live*. McBride died on 2/20/98 (age 51).

DEBUT	PEAK	WKS		CD	Album Title	$	Label & Number
5/9/70	133	3		1	Peacing It All Together	$15	RCA Victor 4325
7/24/71	80	21		2	One Fine Morning	$15	Evolution 3007
1/29/72	157	7		3	Thoughts Of Movin' On	$15	Evolution 3010
7/29/72	178	7		4	Lighthouse Live! .... [L]	$20	Evolution 3014 [2]
					recorded on 2/6/72 at Carnegie Hall		
1/13/73	190	9	©	5	Sunny Days	$15	Evolution 3016

Beneath My Woman (5)
Broken Guitar Blues (5)
Country Song (1)
Daughters And Sons (1)
Eight Miles High (4)
1849 (2,4)
Every Day I Am Reminded (1)
Fiction Of Twenty-Six Million (1)

Fly My Airplane (3)
Hats Off (To The Stranger) (2)
I Just Wanna Be Your Friend (3,4) *93*
I'd Be So Happy (3)
I'm Gonna Try To Make It (3)
Insane (1)
Just A Little More Time (1)

Let The Happiness Begin (medley) (1)
Letter Home (5)
Little Kind Words (2)
Little People (medley) (1)
Lonely Places (5)
Love Of A Woman (2)
Merlin (5)

Mr. Candleman (1)
Nam Myoho Renge' Kyo (1)
Old Man (2,4)
On My Way To L.A. (1)
One Fine Morning (2,4) *24*
Rockin' Chair (3,4)
Sausalito (1)
Show Me The Way (2)

Silver Bird (5)
Sing, Sing, Sing (2)
Step Out On The Sea (2)
Sunny Days (5) *34*
Sweet Lullabye (2,4)
Take It Slow (Out In The Country) (3,4) *64*
Walk Me Down (3)

What Gives You The Right (3)
You And Me (3,4)
You Girl (5)
You Give To Me (5)

LIGHTNING SEEDS, The   '90

Group is actually singer/producer Ian Broudie (born on 8/4/58 in Liverpool, England).

DEBUT	PEAK	WKS		CD	Album Title	$	Label & Number
5/5/90	46	27		© 1	Cloudcuckooland	$10	MCA 6404
3/14/92	154	6		© 2	Sense	$10	MCA 10388

All I Want (1)
Blowing Bubbles (2)
Bound In A Nutshell (1)
Control The Flame (1)

Cool Place (2)
Don't Let Go (1)
Fools (1)
Frenzy (1)

Happy (2)
Joy (1)
Life Of Riley (2) *98*
Love Explosion (1)

Marooned (2)
Nearly Man (1)
Price, The (1)
Pure (1) *31*

Sense (2)
Small Slice Of Heaven (2)
Sweet Dreams (1)
Thinking Up Looking Down (2)

Tingle Tangle (2)
Where Flowers Fade (2)

LIL BOW WOW   '00

Born Shad Moss on 3/9/87 in Columbus, Ohio. Male rapper.

DEBUT	PEAK	WKS	RIAA	CD	Album Title	$	Label & Number
10/14/00	8	51↑	▲²	©	Beware Of Dog	$10	So So Def 69981

Bounce With Me *20*
Bow Wow (That's My Name) *21*

Dog In Me
Future, The
Ghetto Girls *91*

Puppy Love *75*
This Playboy
You Already Know

You Know Me

LIL' CEASE   '99

Born James Lloyd in 1977 in Brooklyn, New York. Male rapper. Member of **Junior M.A.F.I.A.**.

DEBUT	PEAK	WKS		CD	Album Title	$	Label & Number
7/31/99	26	6		©	The Wonderful World Of Cease A Leo	$10	Queen Bee 92783

Chickenheads
Dolly Baby
Don't Stop

Everything
4 My Niggaz
Future Sport

Get Out Our Way
Girlfriend
Long Time Comin'

Looking For A Lady
More Dangerous
Mr. Nasty

Play Around
Work It Out

LIL ITALY   '99

Born Clifton Dickson on 12/15/73 in Vallejo, California. Male rapper.

DEBUT	PEAK	WKS		CD	Album Title	$	Label & Number
8/21/99	99	3		©	On Top Of Da World	$10	No Limit 50108

Bodicussy
Come And Get It
Doggs Ride

Down-N-Dirty
Fake A** Friends
Fo' The Love Of Money

Game Tight
Ghetto Fame
Hoez And Tramps

I Can't Believe
Killafornia
Oh! U Don't Know

On Top Of Da World
Power
7 Dayz A Week

We Ain't Hard 2 Find
We Riderz
What U Gone Do

LIL JON AND THE EAST SIDE BOYZ '01
R&B group led by Jonathan "Lil Jon" Smith. The East Side Boyz are: Lil Bo, Big Sam and Playa Poncho.

6/9/01 43 17↑ © **Put Yo Hood Up** .... $10 BME 2220

Bia' Bia'
Bounce Dat
Can't Stop Pimpin

DJ Hershey Live At The Blue
  Flamelude
Go Shawty Go
Heads Off (My Niggas)

I Like Dem Girlz
Let My Nuts Go
Move Bitch
Nasty Girl

Nothins Free
Outro Chynalude
Put Yo Hood Up
Uhh Ohh

Where Dem Girlz At
Who U Wit
Yall Ain't Ready

LIL' KEKE '98
Born Marcus Edwards in Houston. Male rapper.

4/11/98 176 1 © **The Commission** .... $10 Jam Down 481000

Baller In The Mix
Bounce & Turn
Comin' Down

Don't Mess Wit Texas
Don't You Know
Fo Sure

Gettin' Paid
In The Door
It's Goin' Down

Paper Money
Pimps, Players & Hustlas
Southside

Still Pimping Pens (Screwed)
Wise Guys

LIL' KIM '00
Born Kimberly Jones on 7/11/75 in Brooklyn, New York. Female rapper. Member of **Junior M.A.F.I.A.**

11/30/96 11 47 ▲² © 1 **Hard Core** .... $10 Undeas 92733

7/15/00 4 37 ▲ © 2 **The Notorious KIM** .... $10 Queen Bee 92840

Aunt Dot (2)
Big Momma Thang (1)
Crush On You (1)
Custom Made (Give It To You)
  (2)
Do What You Like (2)

Don't Mess With Me (2)
Dreams (1)
Drugs (1)
**** You (1)
Hold On (2)
How Many Licks? (2) 75

I'm Human (2)
Lil' Drummer Boy (2)
M.A.F.I.A. Land (1)
No Matter What They Say
  (2) 60
No Time (1) 18

Not Tonight (1) 6
Notorious KIM (2)
Off The Wall (2)
Queen B@#$h (1)
Queen Bitch Pt. 2 (2)
Revolution (2)

Right Now (2)
She Don't Love You (2)
Single Black Female (2)
Spend A Little Doe (1)
Suck My D**k (2)
We Don't Need It (1)

Who's Number One? (2)

LIL SOLDIERS '99
Male rap duo from New Jersey: brothers Ikeim and Freequon.

5/15/99 80 3 © **Boot Camp** .... $10 No Limit 50038

Best In The World
Bring It 2 You
Chipped Out Tank

Close 2 A Bomb
Close 2 You
For My Shorties

Get Up
I Ain't Livin' Right
Mama Need A New Blouse

Okey Dokey
School On Lock
School Yard Battlin'

Shout It Out
Soulja By Blood
Soulja Style

Tank In My Hand
Where The Little Souljas At?

LIL' TROY '99
Born Troy Carter in Philadelphia. Male rapper.

5/1/99 20 51 ▲ © **Sittin' Fat Down South** .... $10 Short Stop 53278

Ain't No Luv
Another Head Put To Rest
Chop, Chop, Chop

Diamond & Gold
Don't Fuck Wit Us
Fuck Them Niggas

Lock N Da Game
Loyal To The Sign
Rollin'

Scarface
Small Time
Still A Bitch

Thugs Niggas
Wanna Be A Baller 70
Where's The Love

LIL WAYNE '99
Born Wayne Carter in 1983 in New Orleans. Male rapper. Member of **Cash Money Millionaires** and **Hot Boy$**.

11/20/99 3 26 ▲ © 1 **Tha Block Is Hot** .... $10 Cash Money 153919

1/6/01 16 20 © ● 2 **Lights Out** .... $10 Cash Money 860911

Act A A** (2)
Beef (2)
Biznite (2)
Block Is Hot (1) 72
Blues, Tha (2)
Break Me Off (2)

Come On (1)
Drop It Like It's Hot (1)
Enemy Turf (1)
Everything (2)
F*** Tha World (1)
F**k Wit Me Now (2)

Get Off The Corner (2)
Grown Man (2)
High Beamin' (1)
Hit U Up (2)
Jump Jiggy (2)
Kisha (1)

Let's Go (2)
Lights Off (1)
Lil One (2)
Loud Pipes (1)
Not Like Me (1)
On The Grind (2)

Realized (2)
Remember Me (1)
Respect Us (1)
Shine (2)
Up To Me (1)
Watcha Wanna Do (1)

Wish You Would (2)
You Want War (1)
Young Playa (1)

LIL' ZANE '00
Born in 1982 in Yonkers, New York; raised in Atlanta. Male rapper.

9/9/00 25 20 © **Young World: The Future** .... $10 Priority 50145

All About The Fun
Beautiful Feelin'
Callin' Me 21

Die Famous
M.O.N.E.Y.
None Tonight

Partners Come Along Too
Ride On Em
Too Hot To Stop

Top Down
Ways Of The World
We Ain't The One

What Must I Do
What's Up
You Must Really Love Me

LIMAHL '85
Born Chris Hamill on 12/19/58 in England. Former lead singer of **Kajagoogoo**.

4/27/85 41 20 **Don't Suppose...** .... $10 EMI America 17142

Don't Suppose
I Was A Fool

Never Ending Story 17
Oh Girl

Only For Love 51
Tar Beach

That Special Something
Too Much Trouble

Waiting Game
Your Love

★351★ LIMELITERS, The '62
Folk trio formed in Hollywood: **Glenn Yarbrough**, Lou Gottlieb and Alex Hassilev. Yarbrough went solo in 1963; replaced by Ernie Sheldon. Gottlieb died of cancer on 7/11/96 (age 72).
  1)Tonight: In Person 2)The Slightly Fabulous Limeliters 3)Sing Out!

2/27/61 5 74 © 1 **Tonight: In Person** [L] $20 RCA Victor 2272
  recorded on 7/29/60 at the Ash Grove in Hollywood

9/4/61 40 18 © 2 **The Limeliters** .... $20 Elektra 7180

10/2/61+ 8 36 © 3 **The Slightly Fabulous Limeliters** [L] $20 RCA Victor 2393

2/3/62 14 31 © 4 **Sing Out!** .... $20 RCA Victor 2445

6/9/62 25 29 © 5 **Through Children's Eyes** .... $20 RCA Victor 2512
  recorded on 12/29/61 at the Berkeley Community Theater

9/29/62 21 12 6 **Folk Matinee** .... $20 RCA Victor 2547

2/2/63 37 25 © 7 **Our Men In San Francisco** [L] $20 RCA Victor 2609
  recorded at the Hungry i in San Francisco

5/25/63 83 6 8 **Makin' A Joyful Noise** .... $20 RCA Victor 2588

9/28/63 73 8 9 **Fourteen 14K Folk Songs** .... $20 RCA Victor 2671

5/9/64 118 5 10 **More Of Everything!** .... $20 RCA Victor 2844

Amazing Grace (8)
America The Beautiful (medley)
  (5)
Aravah, Aravah (3)
B-A Bay (5)
Battle At Gandessa (2)

Bear Chase (2)
Best Is Yet To Come (10)
Betty And Dupree (9)
Blow The Candles Out (9)
Blue Mountain Lake (6)

Bound For The Promised Land
  (8)
Bring Me A Rose (10)
Burro (2)
By The Risin' Of The Moon (7)

Casinha Pequenina (Little
  House) (10)
Charlie, The Midnight Marauder
  (2)
Charmin' Betsy (4)
Civil War Medley (7)

Come And Dine (8)
Corn Whiskey (7)
Curima (3)
Die Gedanken Sind Frei (6)
Down By The Riverside
  (medley) (8)

Drill Ye Tarriers (9)
Everywhere I Look This Mornin'
  (4)
Far Side Of The Hill (1)
Faretheewell (Dink's Song) (9)
Funk (6)

LIMELITERS, The — Cont'd

Gambler's Blues (9)
Gari Gari (2)
Gilgarry Mountain (Darlin' Sportin' Jenny) (4)
God Save The People (8)
Golden Bell (4)
Goodnight Ladies (medley) (7)
Gotta Travel On (4)
Grace Darling (5)
Gunslinger (3)
Hammer Song (2)
Hangman, Hangman (9)
Hard Ain't It Hard (3)
Hard Travelin' (medley) (3)
Harry Pollitt (3)
Headin' For The Hills (1)
Hey Jimmy Joe John Jim Jack (5)
Hey Li Lee Li Lee (1)

Hold On (8)
How Bright Is The Day (8)
I Had A Mule (5)
I'm Goin' Away (9)
I'm Goin' Back (7)
Jam On Jerry's Rock (7)
Jehosephat (4)
John Henry, The Steel Driving Man (2)
John Riley (9)
Join Into The Game (5)
Joy Across The Land (4)
Just A Closer Walk With Thee (8)
La Llorona (10)
Lass From The Low Country (3)
Last Class Seaman (10)
Leaving A Song (medley) (10)
Lily Of The Valley (8)

Lion And The Lamb (4)
Little Land (4)
Lollipop Tree (5)
Lonesome Traveler (2)
Lute Player (7)
Madeira, M'Dear (1)
Malaguena Salerosa (2)
Mama Don't 'Low (3)
March On (medley) (8)
Marty (5)
Marvin (4)
Max Goolis (7)
Midnight Special (9)
Minneapolis - St. Paul (10)
Minstrel Boy (4)
Molly Malone (1)
Monks Of St. Bernard (1)
Morningtown Ride (5)
Mount Zion (medley) (3)

No Man Is An Island (10)
No More Cane (9)
Old Time Religion (medley) (8)
Pretty Far Out (4)
Proshchai (1)
Reedy River (6)
Remember Me (When The Candlesticks Are Gleaming) (10)
Revive Us Again (8)
Riddle Song (5)
Rumania, Rumania (1)
Run, Little Donkey (5)
Seven Daffodils (1)
Sing Hallelujah (6)
Sleep Soft (Lullaby) (7)
Spanish Is The Loving Tongue (9)
Stay On The Sunny Side (5)

Sweet Betsy From Pike (9)
Sweet Water Rolling (6)
Take My True Love By The Hand (2)
Tamborito (6)
There's A Meetin' Here Tonight (1)
There's Many A River (10)
This Land Is Your Land (medley) (10)
This Train (5)
Those Were The Days (6)
Time Of Man (3)
To Everything There Is A Season (Turn! Turn!) (6)
Uncle Benny's Celebration (6)
Vikki Dougan (3)
Wabash Cannonball (2)
Wake Up, Dunia (6)

Wayfaring Stranger (4)
We Will Overcome (8)
Western Wind (3)
Whale, The (5)
When I First Came To This Land (2)
Where Shall I Be? (8)
Whistling Gypsy (3)
Who Will Join? (8)
Whoopee Ti Yi Yo (4)
Why Don't You Come Home (10)
Wild Colonial Boy (10)
Willow Tree (10)
Wondrous Love (medley) (8)
Yerakina (7)
Youth Of The Heart (9)
Zhankoye (2)

LIMP BIZKIT   '99
Hard-rock/hip-hop group from Jacksonville, Florida: Fred Durst (vocals), Wes Borland (guitar), Sam Rivers (bass) and John Otto (drums). Borland formed **Bigdumbface**.

4/4/98+	22	77	▲²	©	1 **Three Dollar Bill, Y'all$**		C:❶³/50	$10	Flip 90124
7/10/99	❶⁴	103	▲⁷	©	2 **Significant Other**		C:#11/14	$10	Flip 90335
11/4/00	❶²	48↑	▲⁵	©	3 **Chocolate Starfish And The Hot Dog Flavored Water**			$10	Flip 490759

Boiler (3)
Break Stuff (2)
Clunk (1)
Counterfeit (1)
Don't Go Off Wandering (2)
Everything (1)
Faith (1)

Full Nelson (3)
Getcha Groove On (3)
Hold On (3)
Hot Dog (3)
I'm Broke (2)
Indigo Flow (1)
It'll Be OK (3)

Just Like This (2)
Leech (1)
Lesson Learned (2)
Livin' It Up (3)
My Generation (3)
My Way (3) 75
n 2 gether now (2) 73

9 Teen 90 Nine (2)
No Sex (2)
Nobody Like You (2)
Nobody Loves Me (1)
Nookie (2) 80
One, The (3)
Pollution (1)

Re-Arranged (2) 88
Rollin' (3) 65
Show Me What You Got (2)
Sour (1)
Stalemate (3)
Stinkfinger (1)
Stuck (1)

Take A Look Around (3)
Trust? (2)

LIND, Bob   '66
Born on 11/25/44 in Baltimore. Folk-rock singer/songwriter.

4/16/66	148	2		**Don't Be Concerned**		$25	World Pacific 1841

Cheryl's Goin' Home
Counting
Dale Anne

Drifter's Sunrise
Elusive Butterfly 5
I Can't Walk Roads Of Anger

It Wasn't Just The Morning
Mister Zero
Unlock The Door

Truly Julie's Blues (I'll Be There) 65

World Is Just A "B" Movie
You Should Have Seen It

LINDLEY, David   '81
Born in 1944 in San Marino, California. Rock session guitarist. Leader of **Kaleidoscope**. Worked with **James Taylor**, **Linda Ronstadt** and **Jackson Browne**. In 1980, formed El Rayo-X with Jorge Calderon, Walfredo Reyes, William Smith and Ray Woodbury.

5/16/81	83	18	©	1 **El Rayo-X**		$12	Asylum 524
9/24/88	174	6	©	2 **Very Greasy**		$10	Elektra 60768

DAVID LINDLEY & EL RAYO X
produced by **Linda Ronstadt**

Ain't No Way (1)
Bye Bye, Love (1)
Do Ya' Wanna Dance? (2)
Don't Look Back (1)

El Rayo-X (1)
Gimme Da' Ting (2)
I Just Can't Work No Longer (2)
Mercury Blues (1)

Never Knew Her (1)
Papa Was A Rolling Stone (2)
Pay The Man (1)
Petit Fleur (1)

Quarter Of A Man (1)
She Took Off My Romeos (1)
Talk About You (2)
Talkin' To The Wino Too (2)

Texas Tango (2)
Tiki Torches At Twilight (2)
Tu-ber-cu-lucas And The Sinus Blues (1)

Twist And Shout (1)
Werewolves Of London (2)
Your Old Lady (1)

LINDSAY, Mark   '70
Born on 3/9/42 in Cambridge, Idaho. Pop singer/songwriter. Lead singer of **Paul Revere & The Raiders**.

3/7/70	36	19		1 **Arizona**		$15	Columbia 9986
9/5/70	82	10		2 **Silverbird**		$15	Columbia 30111
10/9/71	180	2		3 **You've Got A Friend**		$15	Columbia 30735

All I Really See Is You (3)
And The Grass Won't Pay No Mind (2) 44
Arizona (1) 10
Been Too Long On The Road (3) 98
Bookends (2)

Come Saturday Morning (2)
Feel The Warm (2)
First Hymn From Grand Terrace (1) 81
Funny How Little Men Care (2)
Help Me Make It Through The Night (3)
I'll Never Fall In Love Again (1)

If You Could Read My Mind (3)
It's Too Late (3)
Leaving On A Jet Plane (1)
Long And Winding Road (medley) (2)
Love's Been Good To Me (1)
Man From Houston (1)
Miss America (1) 44

Name Of My Sorrow (1)
Need A Little Time (3)
Never Can Say Goodbye (2)
Old Man At The Fair (3)
Pretty, Pretty (3)
Silver Bird (2) 25
Small Town Woman (1)
So Hard To Leave You (2)

Something (1)
Sunday Mornin' Comin' Down (1)
We've Only Just Begun (2)
Windy Wakefield (2)
Yesterday (medley) (2)
You've Got A Friend (3)

LINEAR   '90
Pop trio: Charlie Pennachio (vocals), Wyatt Pauley (guitar) and Joey Restivo (percussion).

4/28/90	52	20	©	**Linear**		$10	Atlantic 82090

Don't You Come Cryin' 70
Dream About Me

Heartache
I Never Felt This Way

Lies
Sending All My Love 5

Something Going On
Still In Love

You're My Lady

LINK   '98
Born Lincoln Browder on 10/12/64 in Dallas. Male rapper.

7/18/98	187	1	©	**Sex Down**		$10	Relativity 1645

All Night Freakin'
D.A.N.C.E. With Me
Don't Runaway

Gimmie Some
I Don't Wanna See
I Really Wanna Sex Your Body

Link's Message
911-0024
One Of A Kind Love

Sex Down
Sex-Lude
Spill

Whatcha Gone Do? 23

LINKIN PARK   '01
Rap-rock group from Los Angeles: Chester Bennington (vocals), Mike Shinoda (rap vocals), Joseph Hahn (DJ), Brad Delson (guitar), Phoenix (bass) and Rob Bourdon (drums).

11/11/00+	7	47↑	▲³	©	**Hybrid Theory**	$10	Warner 47755

By Myself
Crawling

Cure For The Itch
Forgotten

In The End
One Step Closer 75

Papercut
Place For My Head

Points Of Authority
Pushing Me Away

Runaway
With You

LINKLETTER, Art '67
Born Arthur Kelly on 7/17/12 in Moose Jaw, Saskatchewan, Canada. Popular radio and TV personality.

12/31/66+ **143** 3   **For The Children Of The World, Art Linkletter narrates**
     "The Bible..In The Beginning" .... [S-T] **$20** 20th Century Fox 3187
       Art adds narration to music, dialogue and sound effects from the soundtrack

| Abraham | Adam And Eve | Cain And Abel | Creation, The | Noah And The Ark | Tower Of Babel |

LINX '81
Funk group from London: David Grant (vocals), Canute Edwards (guitar), Bob Carter (keyboards), Peter Martin (bass) and Andy Duncan (drums).

6/20/81 **175** 4   **Intuition** .... **$12** Chrysalis 1332

| Count On Me | I Won't Forget | Rise And Shine | Throw Away The Key | Wonder What You're Doing | You're Lying |
| Don't Get In My Way | Intuition | There's Love | Together We Can Shine | Now | |

LIONS & GHOSTS '87
Rock group from Hollywood: Rick Parker (vocals), Michael Lockwood (guitar), Todd Hoffman (bass) and Michael Murphy (drums).

10/24/87 **187** 3 ©   **Velvet Kiss, Lick of the Lime** .... **$10** EMI America 46959

| Contradiction | Love & Kisses From The Gutter | Mary Goes 'Round | Passion | Street Angel | Wilton House |
| Girl On A Swing | Man In A Car | One Theme | Stay | When The Moon Is Full | |

LIPPS, INC. '80
Funk project from Minneapolis formed by producer/songwriter/multi-instrumentalist Steven Greenberg. Vocals by Cynthia Johnson.

4/19/80 **5** 26 ●   1 **Mouth To Mouth** .... **$12** Casablanca 7197
10/11/80 **63** 9   2 **Pucker Up** .... **$12** Casablanca 7242

| All Night Dancing (1) | Funkytown (1) *1* | How Long (2) | Power (1) | There They Are (2) |
| Always Lookin' (2) | Gossip Song (2) | Jazzy (2) | **Rock It** (1) *64* | Tight Pair (2) |

LISA LISA AND CULT JAM '87
R&B trio from Harlem, New York: Lisa Velez (vocals; born on 1/15/67), Alex Moseley (guitar) and Mike Hughes (drums). Assembled and produced by **Full Force**.

8/31/85 **52** 66 ▲ © 1 **Lisa Lisa & Cult Jam with Full Force** .... **$10** Columbia 40135
5/9/87 **7** 48 ▲ © 2 **Spanish Fly** .... **$10** Columbia 40477
5/13/89 **77** 13 © 3 **Straight To The Sky** .... **$10** Columbia 44378
9/7/91 **133** 6 © 4 **Straight Outta Hell's Kitchen** .... **$10** Columbia 46035

All Cried Out (1) *8*	Face In The Crowd (2)	I Like It, I Like It (4)	**Let The Beat Hit 'Em** (4) *37*	Rainstorm Interlude (medley)	This Is Cult Jam (1)
Behind My Eyes (1)	Fool Is Born Everyday (2)	I Love What You Do To Me (3)	Let The Music Play (4)	(4)	U Never Nu How Good U Had It
Can You Feel The Beat (1) *69*	Forever (4)	I Promise You (2)	Little Jackie Wants To Be A	Sensuality (4)	(3)
Dance Forever (3)	Give Me Some Of Your Time	**I Wonder If I Take You Home**	Star (3) *29*	Someone To Love Me For Me	Where Were You When I
Do It Like That (4)	(1)	(1) *34*	Lost In Emotion (2) *1*	(2) *78*	Needed You (4)
Don't Say Goodbye (medley)	Gotta Find Somebody New (3)	Just Git It Together (3)	Love Will Get Us By (4)	Something 'Bout Love (4)	You + Me = Love (4)
(4)	**Head To Toe** (2) *1*	Kiss Your Tears Away (3)	Playing With Fire (2)	Straight To The Sky (3)	You'll Never Change (1)
Everything Will B-Fine (2)	I Can't Take No More (3)	Let It Go (4)	Private Property (1)	Take Me Home (Rap) (1)	

LIT '99
Rock group from Los Angeles: brothers A.J. (vocals) and Jeremy (bass) Popoff, Kevin Blades (bass) and Allen Shellenberger (drums).

3/13/99 **31** 72 ▲ ©   **A Place In The Sun** .... **$10** RCA 67775

| Best Is Yet To Come Undone | Four | Lovely Day | **My Own Worst Enemy** *51* | Perfect One | Quicksand |
| Down | Happy | Miserable | No Big Thing | Place In The Sun | Zip-Lock |

LITTER '69
Hard-rock group from Detroit: Mark Gallagher (vocals), Ray Melina and Dan Rinaldi (guitars), J. Worthington Kane (bass) and Tom Murray (drums).

8/16/69 **175** 5 ©   **Emerge** .... **$50** Probe 4504

| Blue Ice | Feeling | Future Of The Past | Little Red Book | |
| Breakfast At Gardenson's | For What It's Worth | Journeys | Silly People | |

LITTLE, Rich '82
Born on 11/26/38 in Ottawa, Ontario, Canada. Comedian/impressionist.

2/13/82 **29** 13   **The First Family Rides Again** .... [C] **$12** Boardwalk 33248
     with Melanie Chartoff, Michael Richards, Shelley Hack, Jenilee Harrison, Earle Doud (producer) and **Vaughn Meader**

Air Force One	Funeral, The	Happy Birthday	Lincoln Room	Press Conference	Wake Up
Big Game	God	Integration	Mr. Bill	Psychiatrist, The	Washington Portrait
Bugs	Happening, The	Late Night Phone Call	Preparing The President	Reaganomics	White House Tour

LITTLE AMERICA '87
Rock group formed in Los Angeles: Mike Magrisi (vocals, bass), Andy Logan and John Hussey (guitars), and Custer (drums).

4/25/87 **102** 14 ©   **Little America** .... **$10** Geffen 24113

| Conversations | Lies | Out Of Bounds | Standin' On Top | Underground | Walk The Land |
| Heroes | Lost Along The Way | Perfect World | That's The Way It Stays | Walk On Fire | You Were Right |

LITTLE ANTHONY AND THE IMPERIALS '65
R&B vocal group from Brooklyn, New York: Anthony Gourdine (born on 1/8/40), Ernest Wright, Tracy Lord, Glouster Rogers and Clarence Collins. Sammy Strain, who joined group in 1964, left in 1975 to join **The O'Jays**.

1/16/65 **135** 4 © 1 **I'm On The Outside (Looking In)** .... **$25** DCP 6801
2/20/65 **74** 13 © 2 **Goin' Out Of My Head** .... **$25** DCP 6808
3/5/66 **97** 23 © 3 **The Best Of Little Anthony & The Imperials** .... [G] **$25** DCP 6809
10/4/69 **172** 5 © 4 **Out Of Sight, Out Of Mind** .... **$20** United Artists 6720

Easy To Be Hard (4)	**Hurt So Bad** (2,3) *10*	Love That Dies (4)	Reputation (2,3)	Walk On By (1)	
Exodus (1)	I Look At You (4)	Make It Easy On Yourself (1)	Ride, The (4)	What A Difference A Day Made	
Funny (1)	**I Miss You So** (2,3) *34*	Never Again (2,3)	Shimmy Shimmy Ko-Ko Bop (3)	(2)	
Get Out Of My Life (2,3)	**I'm On The Outside (Looking**	Our Song (1)	Summer's Comin' In (4)	Where Are You (2)	
Girl From Ipanema (1)	**In)** (1,3) *15*	**Out Of Sight, Out Of Mind**	Take Me Back (2,3) *16*	Where Did Our Love Go? (1)	
Goin' Out Of My Head (2,3) *6*	It's Just A Matter Of Time (2)	(4) *52*	Tears On My Pillow (1,3)	Who's Sorry Now? (2)	
Goodbye Goodtimes (4)	Let The Sunshine In (4)	People (1)	**Ten Commandments Of Love**	You Bring Me Down (4)	
Hurt (2,3) *51*	Letter A Day (1)	Please Go (1)	(4) *82*		

LITTLE CAESAR '90

Hard-rock group formed in Los Angeles: Ron Young (vocals), Apache and Louren Molinare (guitars), Fidel Paniagua (bass), and Tom Morris (drums). Group named after a 1930 gangster movie.

6/30/90	**139**	8	©	**Little Caesar**	$10	DGC 24288

Cajun Panther / Down-N-Dirty / From The Start / I Wish It Would Rain / Little Queenie / Rock-N-Roll State Of Mind
Chain Of Fools 88 / Drive It Home / Hard Times / **In Your Arms 79** / Midtown / Wrong Side Of The Tracks

LITTLE EVA '62

Born Eva Narcissus Boyd on 6/29/43 in Belhaven, North Carolina. Discovered by songwriters **Carole King** and Gerry Goffin while babysitting their daughter **Louise Goffin**.

11/3/62	**97**	6		**Llllloco-Motion**	$200	Dimension 6000

Breaking Up Is Hard To Do / I Have A Love / Loco-Motion 1 / Some Kind-A Wonderful / Where Do I Go
Down Home / **Keep Your Hands Off My** / Run To Her / Up On The Roof / Will You Love Me Tomorrow
He Is The Boy / **Baby 12** / Sharing You / Uptown

★404★ LITTLE FEAT '78

Rock group formed in Los Angeles: Lowell George (vocals; **Frank Zappa**'s Mothers Of Invention), Paul Barrere (guitar), Bill Payne (keyboards), Kenny Gradney (bass), Sam Clayton (percussion) and Richie Hayward (drums). Zappa named group after George's shoe size. Disbanded in April 1979. George died of drug-related heart failure on 6/29/79 (age 34). Reunited briefly in 1985. Regrouped in 1988, adding Craig Fuller (vocals, guitar; **Pure Prairie League**) and Fred Tackett (guitar). Fuller left in 1994; replaced by Shaun Murphy.

1)Waiting For Columbus 2)Down On The Farm 3)Time Loves A Hero

9/7/74	**36**	16	●	©	1	**Feats Don't Fail Me Now**	$15	Warner 2784
11/15/75	**36**	15		©	2	**The Last Record Album**	$15	Warner 2884
5/14/77	**34**	18	●	©	3	**Time Loves A Hero**	$12	Warner 3015
3/11/78	**18**	25	▲	©	4	**Waiting For Columbus** [L]	$15	Warner 3140 [2]
12/8/79+	**29**	21		©	5	**Down On The Farm**	$12	Warner 3345
8/22/81	**39**	13		©	6	**Hoy-Hoy!** [K]	$15	Warner 3538 [2]
8/20/88	**36**	33	●	©	7	**Let It Roll**	$10	Warner 25750
4/28/90	**45**	16		©	8	**Representing The Mambo**	$10	Warner 26163
10/12/91	**126**	6		©	9	**Shake Me Up**	$10	Morgan Creek 20005
5/13/95	**154**	3			10	**Ain't Had Enough Fun**	$10	Zoo 11097

Ain't Had Enough Fun (10) / Day At The Dog Races (3) / Framed (6) / Long Distance Love (2) / Rock & Roll Everynight (10) / Teenage Warrior (8)
All That You Can Stand (10) / Day Or Night (2,4) / Front Page News (5,6) / Long Time Till I Get Over You (7) / Rocket In My Pocket (3,4,6) / Texas Twister (8)
All That You Dream (2,4,6) / Dixie Chicken (4) / Gringo (4) / Loved And Lied To (9) / Romance Dance (2) / That's A Pretty Good Love (10)
Apolitical Blues (4) / Don't Bogart That Joint (4) / Hangin' On To The Good Times (7) / Mercenary Territory (2,4) / Romance Without Finance (10) / That's Her, She's Mine (8)
Be One Now (5) / Don't Try So Hard (9) / Hate To Lose Your Lovin' (7) / Missin' You (3) / Sailin' Shoes (4) / Things Happen (9)
Big Bang Theory (10) / Down Below The Borderline (2) / Heaven's Where You Find It (10) / Mojo Haiku (9) / Shake Me Up (9) / Those Feat'll Steer Ya Wrong Sometimes (8)
Blue Jean Blues (10) / Down In Flames (9) / Hi Roller (3) / New Delhi Freight Train (3) / Shakeytown (10) / Time Loves A Hero (3,4)
Boom Box Car (9) / Down On The Farm (5) / Ingenue, The (8) / Oh Atlanta (1,4) / Silver Screen (8) / Tripe Face Boogie (1,4)
Borderline Blues (10) / Down The Road (1) / Join The Band (4) / Old Folks Boogie (3,4) / Six Feet Of Snow (5) / Two Trains (6)
Business As Usual (7) / Drivin' Blind (10) / Keepin' Up With The Joneses (3) / One Clear Moment (7) / Skin It Back (1,6) / Voices On The Wind (7)
Cadillac Hotel (10) / Easy To Slip (6) / Kokomo (5) / One Love Stand (2) / Somebody's Leavin' (2) / Wake Up Dreaming (5)
Cajun Girl (7) / Fan, The (1,6) / Let It Roll (7) / Over The Edge (6) / Spanish Moon (1,4) / Willin' (4)
Cajun Rage (10) / Fast & Furious (9) / Listen To Your Heart (7) / Perfect Imperfection (5) / Spider's Blues (Might Need It Sometime) (6) / Woman In Love (8)
Changin' Luck (7) / Fat Man In The Bathtub (1,4,6) / Livin' On Dreams (9) / Rad Gumbo (8) / Straight From The Heart (5)
China White (6) / Feats Don't Fail Me Now (1,4,6) / Lonesome Whistle (6) / Red Streamliner (3) / Strawberry Flats (6)
Clownin' (9) / Feel The Groove (5) / Representing The Mambo (8) / Teenage Nervous Breakdown (6)
Cold Cold Cold (medley) (1) / Feelin's All Gone (8) / Rock And Roll Doctor (1,6)
Daily Grind (8) / Forty-Four Blues (6)

LITTLE MILTON '65

Born Milton Campbell on 9/7/34 in Inverness, Mississippi. Blues singer/guitarist.

6/5/65	**101**	14		1	**We're Gonna Make It**	$100	Checker 2995
6/14/69	**159**	7	©	2	**Grits Ain't Groceries**	$25	Checker 3011
3/28/70	**197**	2	©	3	**If Walls Could Talk**	$25	Checker 3012

Ain't No Big Deal On You (1) / Country Style (1) / I Can't Quit You, Baby (2) / Just A Little Bit (2) 97 / Stand By Me (1) / You're Welcome To The Club (1)
Baby I Love You (3) 82 / Did You Ever Love A Woman (2) / I Don't Know (3) / Kansas City (3) / Steal Away (2) / Your Precious Love (3)
Believe In Me (1) / I Play Dirty (3) / Let's Get Together (3) / Things That I Used To Do (3)
Blind Man (1) 86 / Good To Me As I Am To You (3) / I'll Always Love You (2) / Life Is Like That (1) / Twenty-Three Hours (2)
Blues Get Off My Shoulder (3) / I'm Gonna Move To The Outskirts Of Town (1) / Poor Man (3) / **We're Gonna Make It** (1) 25
Blues In The Night (1) / **Grits Ain't Groceries (All Around The World)** (2) 73 / So Blue (Without You) (3) / Who's Cheating Who? (1) 43
Can't Hold Back The Tears (1) / **If Walls Could Talk** (3) 71 / Spring (2) / You're The One (2)

LITTLE RICHARD '57

Born Richard Wayne Penniman on 12/5/32 in Macon, Georgia. R&B-rock and roll singer/pianist. Nicknamed the "Georgia Peach." Appeared in the movies *Don't Knock The Rock, The Girl Can't Help It, Mister Rock 'n' Roll* and *Down And Out In Beverly Hills*. Earned theology degree in 1961 and was ordained a minister. Left R&B for gospel music, 1959-62, and again in the mid-1970s. One of the key figures in the transition from R&B to rock and roll. Inducted into the Rock and Roll Hall of Fame in 1986. Won Grammy's Lifetime Achievement Award in 1993.

8/5/57	**13**	5	©	1	**Here's Little Richard** [G]	$200	Specialty 2100
8/19/67	**184**	3	©	2	**Little Richard's Greatest Hits** [L]	$25	Okeh 14121
11/13/71	**193**	4		3	**King Of Rock And Roll**	$20	Reprise 6462

Anyway You Want Me (2) / Get Down With It (2) / Jenny, Jenny (1,2) 10 / Oh Why? (1) / Slippin' And Slidin' (Peepin' And Hidin') (1) 33 / Whole Lotta Shakin' Goin' On (2)
Baby (1) / Girl Can't Help It (2) / Joy To The World (3) / **Ready Teddy** (1) 44 / You Gotta Feel It (2)
Born On The Bayou (3) / Good Golly Miss Molly (2) / King Of Rock And Roll (3) / Rip It Up (1) 17 / **True, Fine Mama** (1,2) 68
Brown Sugar (3) / Green Power (3) / **Long Tall Sally** (1,2) 6 / Send Me Some Lovin' (2) / Tutti-Frutti (1,2) 17 / Way You Do The Things You Do (3)
Can't Believe You Wanna Leave (1) / I'm So Lonesome I Could Cry (3) / Lucille (2) / Settin' The Woods On Fire (3)
Dancing In The Street (3) / In The Name (3) / Midnight Special (3) / She's Got It (1)
Miss Ann (1) 56

★379★ LITTLE RIVER BAND '79

Pop-rock group formed in Australia: Glenn Shorrock (vocals), Rick Formosa, Beeb Birtles and Graham Goble (guitars), Roger McLachlan (bass) and Derek Pellicci (drums). George McArdle replaced McLachlan in 1977. David Biggs replaced Formosa in 1978. John Farnham and Steve Hudson replaced Shorrock and Briggs in 1983. Steven Prestwich replaced Pellicci in 1984.

10/2/76	**80**	24		©	1	**Little River Band**	$12	Harvest 11512
6/25/77	**49**	48	●	©	2	**Diamantina Cocktail**	$12	Harvest 11645
6/17/78	**16**	61	▲	©	3	**Sleeper Catcher**	$12	Harvest 11783

DEBUT	PEAK	WKS	RIAA	CD	ARTIST — Album Title	Catalog	Sym	$	Label & Number

LITTLE RIVER BAND — Cont'd

8/4/79	10	33	▲	©	4 First Under The Wire			$12	Capitol 11954
4/19/80	44	10		©	5 Backstage Pass		[L]	$15	Capitol 12061 [2]
9/19/81	21	50	●	©	6 Time Exposure			$10	Capitol 12163
12/4/82+	33	30	▲²	©	7 Greatest Hits	C:#29/1	[G]	$10	Capitol 12247
6/18/83	61	21		©	8 The Net			$10	Capitol 12273
2/9/85	75	14		©	9 Playing To Win			$10	Capitol 12365

LRB

Another Runway (2)
Ballerina (6)
Blind Eyes (9)
Broke Again (2)
By My Side (4)
Cool Change (4,7) *10*
Count Me In (9)
Curiosity (Killed The Cat) (1)
Danger Sign (8)
Days On The Road (2)
Don't Blame Me (9)
Don't Let The Needle Win (5)
Down On The Border (7,8)

Easy Money (8)
Emma (6)
Every Day Of My Life (9)
Fall From Paradise (3,5)
Falling (8)
Full Circle (6)
Guiding Light (6)
Happy Anniversary (2,7) *16*
Hard Life (4,5)
Help Is On Its Way (2,5,7) *14*
Home On Monday (2)
I Don't Worry No More (5)
I Know It (1)

I'll Always Call Your Name (1) *62*
Inner Light (2)
It's A Long Way There (1,5,7) *28*
It's Not A Wonder (4,5) *51*
Just Say That You Love Me (6)
Lady (3,7) *10*
Let's Dance (5)
Light Of Day (3,5)
Lonesome Loser (4,7) *6*
Love Will Survive (6)
Man In Black (1,5)

Man On The Run (4,5)
Man On Your Mind (6,7) *14*
Meanwhile (1)
Middle Man (4)
Mistress Of Mine (4,5)
Mr. Socialite (8)
My Lady And Me (1)
Net, The (8)
Night Owls (6,7) *6*
No More Tears (8)
One For The Road (3)
One Shot In The Dark (9)
Orbit Zero (6)

Other Guy (7) *11*
Piece Of The Dream (9)
Playing To Win (9) *60*
Reappear (9)
Red-Headed Wild Flower (3)
Red Shoes (5)
Relentless (9)
Reminiscing (3,5,7) *3*
Rumor, The (4,5)
Sanity's Side (3)
Shut Down Turn Off (3)
Sleepless Nights (8)
So Many Paths (3,5)

Statue Of Liberty (1,5)
Suicide Boulevard (6)
Sweet Old Fashioned Man (5)
Take It Easy On Me (6,7) *10*
Take Me Home (2)
Through Her Eyes (9)
Too Lonely Too Long (5)
We Two (8) *22*
When Cathedrals Were White (9)
You're Driving Me Out Of My Mind (8) *35*

LITTLE STEVEN AND THE DISCIPLES OF SOUL   '84

Born Steven Van Zandt on 11/22/50 in Boston; raised in New Jersey. Rock singer/guitarist/actor. Formed **Southside Johnny & The Jukes** with co-lead singer Johnny Lyon in 1974. Joined **Bruce Springsteen**'s E Street Band in 1975. Organized **Artists United Against Apartheid**. Plays "Silvio Dante" on TV's *The Sopranos*.

12/4/82+	118	18		©	1 Men Without Women			$12	EMI America 17086
6/9/84	55	17		©	2 Voice Of America			$12	EMI America 17120
6/13/87	80	12		©	3 Freedom No Compromise			$10	Manhattan 53048

LITTLE STEVEN

Among The Believers (2)
Angel Eyes (1)
Bitter Fruit (3)
Can't You Feel The Fire (3)
Checkpoint Charlie (2)
Fear (2)

Forever (1) *63*
Freedom (3)
I Am A Patriot (And The River Opens For The Righteous) (2)
I've Been Waiting (1)
Inside Of Me (1)

Justice (1)
Los Desaparecidos (The Disappeared Ones) (2)
Lyin' In A Bed Of Fire (1)
Men Without Women (1)
Native American (3)

No More Party's (3)
Out Of The Darkness (2)
Pretoria (3)
Princess Of Little Italy (1)
Sanctuary (3)
Save Me (1)

Solidarity (2)
Trail Of Broken Treaties (3)
Undefeated (Everybody Goes Home) (3)
Under The Gun (1)
Until The Good Is Gone (1)

Voice Of America (2)

LITTLE TEXAS   '94

Country group from Arlington, Texas: Tim Rushlow (vocals), Porter Howell and Dwayne O'Brien (guitars), Brady Seals (keyboards), Duane Propes (bass) and Del Gray (drums). Seals is the cousin of Jim Seals (of **Seals & Crofts**) and "England" **Dan Seals**. Jeff Huskins replaced Seals in 1995.

3/21/92	99	12	●	©	1 First Time For Everything			$10	Warner 26820
6/5/93+	55	71	▲²	©	2 Big Time			$10	Warner 45276
10/15/94	51	21	▲	©	3 Kick A Little			$10	Warner 45739
10/14/95	82	16	●	©	4 Greatest Hits		[G]	$10	Warner 46017

Amy's Back In Austin (3,4)
Better Way (1)
Country Crazy (4)
Cry On (1)
Cutoff Jeans (2)
Dance (1)

Down In The Valley (1)
First Time For Everything (1,4)
Forget About Forgetting You (3)
God Blessed Texas (2,4) *55*
Hit Country Song (3)
I'd Hold On To Her (3)

I'd Rather Miss You (1,4)
Inside (3)
Just One More Night (1)
Kick A Little (3,4)
Life Goes On (4)
Love And Learn (2)

My Love (2,4) *83*
My Town (2)
Night I'll Never Remember (3)
Only Thing I'm Sure Of (2)
Peaceful Easy Feeling (2)
Redneck Like Me (3)

She's Cool (3)
Some Guys Have All The Love (1,4)
Southern Grace (3)
Stop On A Dime (3)
This Time It's Real (2)

What Might Have Been (2,4) *74*
What Were You Thinkin' (1)
You And Forever And Me (1,4)
Your Days Are Numbered (3)

LITTLE VILLAGE   '92

All-star group: John Hiatt (vocals), Ry Cooder (guitar), Nick Lowe (bass) and Jim Keltner (drums).

| 3/7/92 | 66 | 12 | | © | Little Village .... | | | $10 | Reprise 26713 |

Action, The
Big Love
Do You Want My Job

Don't Bug Me When I'm Working
Don't Go Away Mad

Don't Think About Her When You're Trying To Drive
Fool Who Knows

Inside Job
She Runs Hot
Solar Sex Panel

Take Another Look

LIVE   '95

Rock group formed in York, Pennsylvania: Ed Kowalczyk (vocals), Chad Taylor (guitar), Pat Dahlheimer (bass) and Chad Gracey (drums).

1/18/92	73	24	●	©	1 Mental Jewelry	C:#8/30		$10	Radioactive 10346
5/14/94+	❶¹	121	▲⁸	©	2 Throwing Copper	C:#16/15		$10	Radioactive 10997
3/8/97	❶¹	46	▲	©	3 Secret Samadhi			$10	Radioactive 11590
10/23/99	4	26	▲	©	4 The Distance To Here			$10	Radioactive 11966

All Over You (2)
Beauty Of Gray (1)
Brothers Unaware (1)
Century (3)
Dam At Otter Creek (2)
Dance With You (4)
Distance, The (4)
Dolphin's Cry (4) *78*
Face And Ghost (4)
Feel The Quiet River Rage (4)

Freaks (3)
Gas Hed Goes West (3)
Ghost (3)
Good Pain (1)
Graze (3)
Heropsychodreamer (3)
I Alone (2)
Insomnia And The Hole In The Universe (3)
Iris (2)

Lakini's Juice (3)
Lightning Crashes (2)
Meltdown (4)
Merica (3)
Mirror Song (1)
Mother Earth Is A Vicious Crowd (1)
Operation Spirit (The Tyranny Of Tradition) (1)
Pain Lies On The Riverside (1)

Pillar Of Davidson (2)
Rattlesnake (3)
Run To The Water (4)
Selling The Drama (2) *43*
Shit Towne (2)
Sparkle (4)
Stage (2)
Stood Up For Love (4)
Sun (4)
T.B.D. (2)

Take My Anthem (1)
10,000 Years (Peace Is Now) (1)
Tired Of "Me" (1)
Top (2)
Turn My Head (3)
Unsheathed (3)
Voodoo Lady (4)
Waitress (2)
Waterboy (1)

We Walk In The Dream (4)
Where Fishes Go (4)
White, Discussion (2)
You Are The World (1)

LIVING COLOUR   '89

Black rock group from New York City: Corey Glover (vocals), Vernon Reid (guitar), Muzz Skillings (bass) and William Calhoun (drums). Doug Wimbish replaced Skillings in early 1992. Glover played "Francis" in the movie *Platoon*.

9/3/88+	6	76	▲²	©	1 Vivid			$10	Epic 44099
9/15/90	13	35	●	©	2 Time's Up			$10	Epic 46202
8/3/91	110	5		©	3 Biscuits		[M]	$10	Epic 47988
3/20/93	26	12		©	4 Stain			$10	Epic 52780

Auslander (4)
Bi (4)
Broken Hearts (1)
Burning Of The Midnight Lamp (3)

Cult Of Personality (1) *13*
Desperate People (1,3)
Elvis Is Dead (2)
Fight The Fight (2)
Funny Vibe (1)

Glamour Boys (1) *31*
Go Away (4)
Hemp (4)
History Lesson (2)
I Want To Know (1)

Ignorance Is Bliss (4)
Information Overload (2)
Leave It Alone (4)
Love And Happiness (3)
Love Rears Its Ugly Head (2)

Memories Can't Wait (1,3)
Middle Man (1)
Mind Your Own Business (4)

LIVING COLOUR — Cont'd

Money Talks (3)	Ology (2)	Pride (2)	Talkin' Loud And Sayin' Nothing	Time's Up (2)	Wall (4)
Never Satisfied (4)	**Open Letter (To A Landlord)**	Solace Of You (2)	(3)	Type (2)	What's Your Favorite Color?
New Jack Theme (2)	(1) *82*	Someone Like You (2)	This Is The Life (2)	Under Cover Of Darkness (2)	(Theme Song) (1)
Nothingness (4)	Postman (4)	Tag Team Partners (2)	This Little Pig (4)	WTFF (4)	Which Way To America? (1)

LIVING IN A BOX '87

Pop trio formed in Sheffield, England: Richard Darbyshire (vocals), Marcus Vere (keyboards) and Anthony Critchlow (drums).

8/8/87	89	13	©	Living In A Box	$10	Chrysalis 41547

Can't Stop The Wheel	Generate The Wave	Human Story	Love Is The Art	**So The Story Goes** *81*
From Beginning To End	Going For The Big One	**Living In A Box** *17*	Scales Of Justice	

LIVING STRINGS '61

Studio orchestra from Europe. Arranged and conducted by Hill Bowen.

2/27/61	26	6	©	1	Living Strings Play All The Music From Camelot	[I]	$15	RCA Camden 657
2/27/61	42	7	©	2	Living Strings Play Music Of The Sea	[I]	$15	RCA Camden 639
12/9/67	30ˣ	6		3	The Spirit of Christmas	[X-I]	$15	RCA Camden 783

Christmas charts: 30/'67, 33/'68

A-Roving (medley) (2)	Come Back To Sorrento (Torna	How To Handle A Woman (1)	La Mer (medley) (2)	Rio Grande (2)	We Wish You A Merry
Aloha Oe (Farewell To Thee)	A Surriento) (medley) (2)	I Loved You Once In Silence (1)	Little Drummer Boy (3)	Shenandoah (medley) (3)	Christmas (medley) (3)
(medley) (2)	Come To Capri (medley) (2)	I Wonder What The King Is	Lusty Month Of May (1)	Silent Night (medley) (3)	What Do Simple Folks Do (1)
Around The World (medley) (2)	Coventry Carol (medley) (3)	Doing Tonight (medley) (1)	Mary's Boy Child (Mary's Little	Silver Bells (3)	White Christmas (3)
Away In A Manger (medley) (3)	Ebb Tide (2)	I'll Be Home For Christmas (3)	Boy Chile) (3)	Simple Joys Of Maidenhood	
Banana Boat Song (medley) (2)	Far Away Places (medley) (2)	If Ever I Would Leave You (1)	O Come, All Ye Faithful	(medley) (1)	
C'est Moi (1)	Fie On Goodness (medley) (1)	Isle Of Capri (medley) (2)	(medley) (3)	Sleepy Lagoon (medley) (2)	
Camelot (1)	Follow Me (1)	It's Beginning To Look Like	O Holy Night (medley) (3)	(There's No Place Like) Home	
Christmas Song (Chestnuts	Guinevere (medley) (1)	Christmas (3)	Oh Little Town Of Bethlehem	For The Holidays (3)	
Roasting On An Open Fire)	Have Yourself A Merry Little	Jamaica Farewell (medley) (2)	(medley) (3)	We Three Kings (medley) (3)	
(3)	Christmas (3)	Quests, The (medley) (1)			

LIVING TRIO '67

Studio trio from Europe: an organ, a guitar and an accordion.

| 12/30/67 | 78ˣ | 1 | | | I'll Be Home For Christmas .... | [X-I] | $15 | RCA Camden 2159 |

Angels We Have Heard On	Home For The Holidays	Joy To The World (medley)	Oh! Little Town Of Bethlehem	We Need A Little Christmas
High (medley)	(medley)	Little Drummer Boy (medley)	(medley)	Now (medley)
Away In A Manger (medley)	I Saw Mommy Kissing Santa	Mary's Little Boy Child (medley)	One Bright Star (medley)	We Three Kings Of Orient Are
Carol, Sweetly Carol (medley)	Claus (medley)	Merry Christmas Merry Go	Patapan (medley)	(medley)
Deck The Halls (medley)	I'll Be Home For Christmas	Round (medley)	Rudolph The Red-Nosed	We Wish You A Merry
God Rest You Merry,	(medley)	O' Bambino (medley)	Reindeer (medley)	Christmas (medley)
Gentlemen (medley)	It Came Upon A Midnight Clear	O Christmas Tree (medley)	Silent Night (medley)	White Christmas (medley)
Hark! The Herald Angels Sing	(medley)	O Come, All Ye Faithful	That Christmas Feeling	
(medley)	Jingle Bells (medley)	(medley)	(medley)	
Here We Come A-Caroling	Jolly Old Saint Nicholas	O Holy Night (medley)	Up On The House Top (medley)	
(medley)	(medley)		Wassail Song (medley)	

LIVING VOICES '67

Arranged and conducted by **Anita Kerr**.

| 12/9/67 | 35ˣ | 4 | | | The Little Drummer Boy .... | [X] | $15 | RCA Camden 911 |

Be A Santa	I Heard The Bells On Christmas	Jingle Bells (medley)	Pine Cones And Holly Berries	We Wish You A Merry
Blue Christmas	Day	Little Christmas Tree Waltz	(medley)	Christmas (medley)
Do You Hear What I Hear	It's Beginning To Look Like	(medley)	Silver Bells (medley)	What Are You Doing New
Holly Jolly Christmas	Christmas (medley)	Little Drummer Boy	Sleigh Ride (medley)	Year's Eve

LIZZY BORDEN '87

Hard-rock group from Los Angeles: Lizzy Borden (vocals), Gene Allen (guitar), Mike Davis (bass) and Joey Scott (drums).

11/1/86	144	10	©	1	Menace To Society		$10	Enigma 73224
5/2/87	188	6	©	2	Terror Rising	[M]	$10	Enigma 73254
9/26/87	146	7	©	3	Visual Lies	[I]	$10	Enigma 73288
8/26/89	133	10	©	4	Master Of Disguise		$10	Enigma 73413

American Metal (2)	Eyes Of A Stranger (3)	Me Against The World (3)	Psychodrama (4)	Terror Rising (2)	Waiting In The Wings (4)
Be One Of Us (4)	Generation Aliens (1)	Menace To Society (1)	Rod Of Iron (2)	Ultra Violence (1)	We Got The Power (4)
Bloody Mary (1)	Give 'Em The Axe (2)	Never Too Young (4)	Roll Over And Play Dead (4)	Under The Rose (4)	White Rabbit (2)
Brass Tactics (1)	Lord Of The Flies (3)	Notorious (1)	Shock (3)	Ursa Minor (1)	
Catch Your Death (2)	Love Is A Crime (3)	One False Move (4)	Sins Of The Flesh (4)	Visions (4)	
Den Of Thieves (3)	Love Kills (1)	Outcast (3)	Stiletto (Voice Of Command) (1)	Visual Lies (3)	
Don't Touch Me There (2)	Master Of Disguise (4)	Phantoms (4)	Terror On The Town (1)	Voyeur (I'm Watching You) (3)	

★301★ LL COOL J '00

Born James Todd Smith on 8/16/68 in Queens, New York. Male rapper/actor. Stage name is abbreviation for Ladies Love Cool James. Appeared in several movies and TV shows.

1/11/86	46	38	▲	©	1	Radio		$10	Columbia 40239
6/20/87	3	53	▲²	©	2	Bigger And Deffer		$10	Def Jam 40793
7/1/89	6	21	▲	©	3	Walking With A Panther		$10	Def Jam 45172
10/6/90	16	76	▲²	©	4	Mama Said Knock You Out		$10	Def Jam 46888
4/17/93	5	24	●		5	14 Shots To The Dome		$10	Def Jam 53325
12/9/95+	20	62	▲²	©	6	Mr. Smith		$10	Def Jam 529583
11/23/96	29	28	▲	©	7	All World	[G]	$10	Def Jam 534125
11/1/97	7	23	▲	©	8	Phenomenon		$10	Def Jam 539186
9/30/00	❶¹	12	●		9	G.O.A.T. Featuring James T. Smith The Greatest Of All Time		$10	Def Jam 546819

Ahh, Let's Get Ill (3)	Buckin' Em Down (5)	**Doin It** (6,7) *9*	Funkadelic Relic (5)	Homicide (9)	**I'm That Type Of Guy** (3) *15*
Ain't No Stoppin' This (5)	Can't Think (9)	Don't Be Late, Don't Come Too	Get Da Drop On 'Em (6)	Hot, Hot, Hot (8)	Ill Bomb (9)
All We Got Left Is The Beat (5)	Candy (8)	Soon (8)	Get Down (2)	**How I'm Comin'** (5) *57*	Illegal Search (4)
Another Dollar (8)	Cheesy Rat Blues (4)	Droppin' Em (3)	Go Cut Creator Go (2)	I Can Give You More (1)	**Imagine That** (9) *98*
Around The Way Girl (4,7) *9*	Clap Your Hands (3)	Eat Em Up L Chill (4)	**G.O.A.T., The** (9)	I Can't Live Without My Radio	It Gets No Rougher (3)
Back Seat (5,7) *42*	Crossroads (5)	Farmers (9)	God Bless (9)	(1,7)	Jack The Ripper (7)
Back Where I Belong (9)	Dangerous (1)	Farmers Blvd. (Our Anthem) (4)	**Going Back To Cali** (7) *31*	I Need A Beat (1,7)	Jealous (1)
Big Ole Butt (3,7)	Dear Yvette (1)	Fast Peg (3)	Hello (9)	**I Need Love** (2,7) *14*	Jingling Baby (3,4,7)
Boomin' System (4,7) *48*	Def Jam In The Motherland (9)	**Father** *18*	**Hey Lover** (6,7) *3*	I Shot Ya (6)	Kanday (7)
Breakthrough, The (2)	Diggy Down (5)	**4,3,2,1** (8) *75*	Hip Hop (6)	I Want You (1)	LL Cool J (9)
Bristol Hotel (2)	Do Wop (2)	Fuhgidabowdit (9)	Hollis To Hollywood (6)	**I'm Bad** (2,7) *84*	Life As... (6)

LL COOL J — Cont'd

Little Somethin' (5)	Murdergram (4)	One Shot At Love (3)
Loungin (6,7) *3*	My Rhyme Ain't Done (2)	**Phenomenon** (8) *55*
Make It Hot (6)	(NFA) No Frontin' Allowed (5)	**Pink Cookies In A Plastic Bag**
Mama Said Knock You Out	Nitro (3)	**Getting Crushed By**
(4,7) *17*	No Airplay (6)	**Buildings** (5) *96*
Milky Cereal (4)	Nobody Can Freak You (8)	Power Of God (4)
Mr. Smith (6)	On The Ill Tip (2)	Queens Is (9)
Mr. Good Bar (4)	1-900 L.L. Cool J (3)	Rock The Bells (1,7)

6 Minutes Of Pleasure (4) *95* · This Is Us (9) · You And Me (9)
Smokin', Dopin' (3) · .357 - Break It On Down (2) · You Can't Dance (1)
Soul Survivor (5) · To Da Break Of Dawn (4) · You'll Rock (1)
Stand By Your Man (5) · Two Different Worlds (3) · You're My Heart (3)
Starsky And Hutch (8) · U Can't F**k With Me (9)
Straight From Queens (5) · Wanna Get Paid (8)
Take It Off (9) · Why Do You Think They Call It
That's A Lie (1) · Dope? (3)

LLOYD, Charles, Quartet   '67
Born on 3/15/38 in Memphis. Jazz tenor saxophonist.

DEBUT	PEAK	WKS	CD	#	Album	Sym	$	Label & Number
7/15/67	188	4	©	1	Forest Flower	[I-L]	$20	Atlantic 1473
					recorded on 9/18/66 at the Monterey Jazz Festival			
8/19/67	171	7		2	Love-In	[I-L]	$20	Atlantic 1481
					recorded at the Fillmore in San Francisco			

East Of The Sun (1) · Here There And Everywhere (2) · Love-In (2) · Song Of Her (1) · Temple Bells (2)
Forest Flower - Sunrise (1) · Is It Really The Same? (2) · Memphis Dues Again (medley) · Sorcery (1) · Tribal Dance (2)
Forest Flower - Sunset (1) · Island Blues (medley) (2) · (2) · Sunday Morning (2)

LOBO   '73
Born Roland Kent Lavoie on 7/31/43 in Tallahassee, Florida. Pop singer/songwriter/guitarist.

DEBUT	PEAK	WKS	#	Album	Sym	$	Label & Number
6/5/71	178	10	1	Introducing Lobo		$15	Big Tree 2003
10/14/72+	37	31	2	Of A Simple Man		$15	Big Tree 2013
5/5/73	163	5	3	Introducing Lobo	[R]	$15	Big Tree 2100
				new cover features a picture of Lobo			
6/30/73	128	14	4	Calumet		$15	Big Tree 2101
8/10/74	183	4	5	Just A Singer		$12	Big Tree 89501
4/5/75	151	7	6	A Cowboy Afraid Of Horses		$12	Big Tree 89505

Albatross, The (1,3) · I'd Love You To Want Me (2) *2* · Me And You And A Dog · Rock And Roll Days (4) · Thinking Of You (6)
All For The Love Of A Girl (5) · I'm Only Sleeping (5) · Named Boo (1,3) *5* · Running Deer (2) · Three Pick-Ups (6)
Am I True To Myself (2) · **Don't Tell Me Goodnight** · Morning Sun (5) · **She Didn't Do Magic** (1,3) *46* · Try (4)
Another Hill To Climb (medley) · (6) *27* · My Momma Had Soul (6) · Shelter Of Your Eyes (5) · Universal Soldier (5)
(1,3) · Everyday Is My Way (6) · One And The Same Thing (4) · **Simple Man** (2) *56* · War To End All Wars (6)
Armstrong (5) · Goodbye Is Just Another Word · Pee-ro Juan Valdez Sam · Something To See Me Through · We'll Be One By Two Today
Big Red Kite (2) · (4) · Quixote (2) · (6) · (1,3)
Country Feelings (1,3) · Gypsy And The Midnight Ghost · Reaching Out For Someone · **Standing At The End Of The** · We'll Make It...I Know We Will
Cowboy Afraid Of Horses (6) · (2) · (1,3) · **Line** (4) *37* · (1,3)
Daydream Believer (5) · Hope You're Proud Of Me Girl · Reason To Believe (5) · Stoney (4) · Would I Still Have You (6)
Don't Expect Me To Be Your · (4) · Recycle Sally (2) · Then I Met You (6)
Friend (2) *8* · How Can I Tell Her (4) *22* · Rings (5) *43* · **There Ain't No Way** (2) *68*
· However... (6) · **Love Me For What I Am** (4) *86*
· Little Joe (They're Out To Get
· Ya) (1,3)
· Lodi (5)
· Let Me Down Easy (2)
· Let's Get Together (5)
· Little Different (1,3)

LOCAL H   '98
Rock duo from Zion, Illinois: Scott Lucas (vocals, guitar, bass) and Joe Daniels (drums).

DEBUT	PEAK	WKS	CD	#	Album	$	Label & Number
1/11/97	147	7	©	1	As Good As Dead	$10	Island 524202
9/19/98	140	2	©	2	Pack Up The Cats	$10	Island 524549

All-Right (Oh, Yeah) (2) · Cool Magnet (2) · Fritz's Corner (1) · Laminate Man (2) · No Problem (1)
All The Kids Are Right (2) · Deep Cut (2) · High-Fiving MF (1) · Lead Pipe Cinch (2) · Nothing Special (1)
Back In The Day (1) · Eddie Vedder (1) · Hit The Skids Or: How I · Lovey Dovey (1) · O.K. (1)
Bound For The Floor (1) · Fine And Good (2) · Learned To Stop Worrying · Lucky (1) · She Hates My Job (2)
"Cha!" Said The Kitty (2) · 500,000 Scovilles (2) · And Love The Rock (2) · Lucky Time (2) · Stoney (2)
· Freeze-Dried (F)lies (1) · I Saw What You Did And I · Manifest Density Pt. 1 & 2 (1) · What Can I Tell You? (2)
· Know Who You Are (1)

LODGE, John   '75
Born on 7/20/45 in Birmingham, England. Bassist for **The Moody Blues**.

DEBUT	PEAK	WKS	CD	#	Album	$	Label & Number
3/29/75	16	23	©	1	Blue Jays	$20	Threshold 14
					JUSTIN HAYWARD/JOHN LODGE		
4/23/77	121	9	©	2	Natural Avenue	$15	London 683

Broken Dreams, Hard Road (2) · Maybe (1) · Piece Of My Heart (2) · Say You Love Me (2) · Who Are You Now (1)
Carry Me (2) · My Brother (1) · Rainbow (2) · Summer Breeze (2) · Who Could Change (2)
Children Of Rock 'N' Roll (2) · Natural Avenue (2) · Remember Me, My Friend (1) · This Morning (1) · You (1)
I Dreamed Last Night (1) *47* · Nights, Winters, Years (1) · Saved By The Music (1) · When You Wake Up (1)

LOEB, Lisa   '95
Born on 3/11/68 in Bethesda, Maryland; raised in Dallas. Female singer/songwriter/guitarist. Nine Stories consisted of Tim Bright (guitar), Joe Quigley (bass) and Jonathan Feinberg (drums).

DEBUT	PEAK	WKS	RIAA	CD	#	Album	$	Label & Number
10/14/95	30	23	●	©	1	Tails	$10	Geffen 24734
						LISA LOEB & NINE STORIES		
11/29/97+	88	19	●	©	2	Firecracker	$10	Geffen 25141

Alone (1) · Furious Rose (2) · It's Over (1) · Sandalwood (1) · This (2) · Wishing Heart (2)
Dance With The Angels (2) · Garden of Delights (1) · Jake (2) · Snow Day (1) · Truthfully (2)
Do You Sleep? (1) *18* · How (2) · **Let's Forget About It** (2) *71* · Split Second (2) · **Waiting for Wednesday** (1) *83*
Falling In Love (2) · Hurricane (1) · Lisa Listen (1) · **Stay (I Missed You)** (1) *1* · When All the Stars Were Falling
Firecracker (2) · **I Do** (2) *17* · Rose-Colored Times (1) · Taffy (1) · (1)

LOFGREN, Nils   '77
Born on 6/21/51 in Chicago; raised in Maryland. Pop-rock singer/guitarist/pianist. Leader of **Grin** (1969-1974). Member of **Bruce Springsteen**'s E Street Band from 1984-85.

DEBUT	PEAK	WKS	CD	#	Album	Sym	$	Label & Number
3/22/75	141	9	©	1	Nils Lofgren		$12	A&M 4509
4/17/76	32	16		2	Cry Tough		$12	A&M 4573
3/19/77	36	12		3	I Came To Dance		$12	A&M 4628
10/29/77	44	10		4	Night After Night	[L]	$15	A&M 3707 [2]
7/21/79	54	14		5	Nils		$12	A&M 4756
9/26/81	99	11		6	Night Fades Away		$12	Backstreet 5251
6/22/85	150	5	©	7	Flip		$10	Columbia 39982
3/30/91	153	8	©	8	Silver Lining		$10	Rykodisc 10170

Ancient History (6) · Be Good Tonight (1) · Can't Buy A Break (1) · Delivery Night (7) · Duty (8) · For Your Love (2)
Anytime At All (6) · Beggars Day (4) · Can't Get Closer (WCGC) (2) · Dirty Money (6) · Empty Heart (6) · From The Heart (7)
Back It Up (1,4) · Bein' Angry (8) · Code Of The Road (3,4) · Don't Touch Me (6) · Flip Ya Flip (7) · Girl In Motion (8)
Baltimore (5) · Big Tears Fall (7) · Cry Tough (2,4) · Dreams Die Hard (7) · Fool Like Me (5) · Goin' Back (1,4)

DEBUT	PEAK	WKS	RIAA	CD	ARTIST — Album Title	Catalog	Sym	$	Label & Number

LOFGREN, Nils — Cont'd

Goin' South (3,4)
Gun And Run (8)
Happy (3)
Happy Ending Kids (3)
Home Is Where The Hurt Is (3)
I Came To Dance (3,4)
I Don't Want To Know (1)
I Found Her (5)
I Go To Pieces (6)

I'll Cry Tomorrow (5)
If I Say It, It's So (1)
In Motion (6)
Incidentally...It's Over (2,4)
It's Not A Crime (2,4)
Jailbait (2)
Jealous Gun (3)
Keith Don't Go (Ode To The Glimmer Twin) (1,4)

King Of The Rock (7)
Kool Skool (5)
Like Rain (4)
Little Bit O' Time (8)
Live Each Day (8)
Moon Tears (4)
Mud In Your Eye (2)
New Holes In Old Shoes (7)
Night Fades Away (6)

No Mercy (5)
One More Saturday Night (1)
Rock And Roll Crook (1,4)
Rock Me At Home (3)
Sailor Boy (6)
Secrets In The Street (7)
Share A Little (2)
Shine Silently (1)
Silver Lining (8)

Steal Away (5)
Sticks And Stones (8)
Streets Again (6)
Sun Hasn't Set On This Boy Yet (1)
Sweet Midnight (7)
Take You To The Movies (4)
To Be A Dreamer (8)
Trouble's Back (8)

Two By Two (1)
Valentine (8)
Walkin' Nerve (8)
You Lit A Fire (2)
You're So Easy (5)
You're The Weight (4)

LO FIDELITY ALLSTARS '99

Rock group from Brighton, Sussex, England: Dave Randall (vocals), Martin Whiteman (keyboards), Andy Dickinson (bass) and Johnny Machin (drums).

| 5/8/99 | 115 | 19 | | © | **How To Operate With A Blown Mind** .... | | | $10 | Skint 69654 |

Battle Flag
Blisters On My Brain

How To Operate With A Blown Mind
I Used To Fall In Love

Kasparov's Revenge
Kool Roc Bass
Lazer Sheep Dip Funk

Nightime Story
Vision Incision
Warming Up The Brain Farm

Will I Get Out Of Jail?

LOGGINS, Dave '74

Born on 11/10/47 in Mountain City, Tennessee. Pop-country singer/songwriter. Cousin of **Kenny Loggins**.

| 11/2/74 | 54 | 16 | | | **Apprentice (In A Musical Workshop)** .... | | | $12 | Epic 32833 |

Girl From Knoxville
Let Me Go Now

My Father's Fiddle
My Lover's Keeper

Please Come To Boston **5**
Second Hand Lady

So You Couldn't Get To Me
Someday **57**

Sunset Woman
Wonder'n As The Days Go By

★232★ LOGGINS, Kenny '80

Born on 1/7/47 in Everett, Washington; raised in Alhambra, California. Pop-rock singer/songwriter/guitarist. Cousin of **Dave Loggins**. Half of **Loggins & Messina** duo.

1)Nightwatch 2)Kenny Loggins Alive 3)High Adventure

5/7/77	27	33	▲	©	1 **Celebrate Me Home** ....C:#18/60			$12	Columbia 34655
7/22/78	7	31	▲	©	2 **Nightwatch**			$12	Columbia 35387
10/20/79+	16	43	▲	©	3 **Keep The Fire**			$12	Columbia 36172
10/4/80	11	31	●	©	4 **Kenny Loggins Alive** .... [L]			$15	Columbia 36738 [2]
9/25/82	13	44	●	©	5 **High Adventure**			$10	Columbia 38127
4/20/85	41	31	●	©	6 **Vox Humana**			$10	Columbia 39174
					title is Latin for "Human Voice"				
8/20/88	69	14		©	7 **Back To Avalon**			$10	Columbia 40535
9/28/91	71	58	●	©	8 **Leap Of Faith**			$10	Columbia 46140
9/4/93	60	13		©	9 **Outside: From The Redwoods** .... [L]			$10	Columbia 57391
					recorded on 6/23/93 in Santa Cruz, California				
5/28/94	65	42	▲	©	10 **Return To Pooh Corner**			$10	Sony Wonder 57674
4/12/97	39	31	▲	©	11 **Yesterday, Today, Tomorrow - The Greatest Hits Of Kenny Loggins** ..... [G]			$10	Columbia 67986
7/26/97	107	7		©	12 **The Unimaginable Life**			$10	Columbia 67865
12/5/98	148	6		©	13 **December** ....C:#10/2	[X]		$10	Columbia 69351

Christmas charts: 7/'98, 15/'99

All Alone Tonight (4)
All I Ask (12)
All The Pretty Little Ponies (10)
Angelique (2,4)
Angels In The Snow (13)
Angry Eyes (9)
Art Of Letting Go (12)
At Last (4)
Back To Avalon (7)
Bells Of Christmas (13)
Birth Energy (12)
Blue On Blue (7)
Celebrate Me Home (1,4,9,11)
Christmas Song (Chestnuts Roasting On An Open Fire) (13)
Christmas Time Is Here (13)
Cody's Song (8,10)
Conviction Of The Heart (8,9,11) **65**
Coventry Carol (13)

Daddy's Back (1)
Danger Zone (11) **2**
December (13)
Don't Fight It (5,11) **17**
Down In The Boondocks (3)
Down 'N Dirty (2,4)
Easy Driver (2,4) **60**
Enter My Dream (1)
Footloose (9,11) **1**
For The First Time (11)
Forever (6,11) **40**
Give It Half A Chance (3)
Have Yourself A Merry Little Christmas (13)
Heart To Heart (5,11) **15**
Heartlight ..see: Welcome To Heartlight
Here There And Everywhere (4)
Hope For The Runaway (7)
Horses, The (10)
I Am Not Hiding (12)

I Believe In Love (1,4) **66**
I Gotta Try (5)
I Would Do Anything (8,9)
I'll Be There (6) **88**
I'm Alright (4,9,11) **7**
I'm Gonna Do It Right (6)
I'm Gonna Miss You (7) **82**
I've Got The Melody (Deep In My Heart) (1)
If It's Not What You're Looking For (5)
If You Be Wise (1)
If You Believe (8,9)
Isabella's Eyes (5)
It Must Be Imagination (5)
Junkanoo Holiday (Fallin'-Flyin') (3,4)
Just Breathe (12)
Keep The Fire (3,4) **36**
Lady Luck (1)
Last Unicorn (10)

Leap Of Faith (8,9)
Let The Pendulum Swing (12)
Let There Be Love (6)
Loraine (2)
Love (10)
Love Has Come Of Age (3,4)
Love Will Follow (6,9)
Love's Got Nothin' To Prove (12)
Meet Me Half Way (7,11) **11**
More We Try (5)
Mr. Night (3)
My Father's House (5)
Neverland Medley (10)
Nightwatch (2)
No Doubt About Love (12)
No Lookin' Back (5)
Nobody's Fool (7) **8**
Now And Then (3,4,9)
Now Or Never (8)
Now That I Know Love (12)

On Christmas Morning (13)
One Chance At A Time (12)
One Woman (7)
Only A Miracle (5)
Rainbow Connection (10)
Real Thing (8,11)
Rest Of Your Life (11,12)
Return To Pooh Corner (10,11)
Set It Free (1)
She's Dangerous (8)
Some Children See Him (13)
Somebody Knows (2)
St. Judy's Comet (10)
Swear Your Love (5)
Sweet Reunion (8)
Tell Her (7) **76**
This Is It (4,9,11) **11**
This Island Earth (12)
To-Ra-Loo-Ra (10)
Too Early For The Sun (8)
True Confessions (7)

Unimaginable Life (12)
Vox Humana (6) **29**
Wait A Little While (2,4)
Walking In The Air (13)
Welcome To Heartlight (5) **24**
What A Fool Believes (2,4,9)
Whenever I Call You "Friend" (2,4,11) **5**
White Christmas (13)
Who's Right, Who's Wrong (3)
Why Do People Lie (1,4)
Will It Last (3)
Will Of The Wind (8)
You Don't Know Me (1,4)
Your Mama Don't Dance (9)
Your Spirit And My Spirit (12)

★320★ LOGGINS & MESSINA '74

Pop-rock duo of **Kenny Loggins** (see above bio) and **Jim Messina** (born on 12/5/47 in Maywood, California. Messina was a member of **Buffalo Springfield** and **Poco**.

3/18/72+	70	113	▲	©	1 **Sittin' In**			$12	Columbia 31044
11/11/72+	16	61	▲	©	2 **Loggins And Messina**			$12	Columbia 31748
11/10/73+	10	49	▲	©	3 **Full Sail**			$12	Columbia 32540
5/11/74	5	37	▲	©	4 **On Stage** .... [L]			$15	Columbia 32848 [2]
11/9/74	8	29	●	©	5 **Mother Lode**			$12	Columbia 33175
9/13/75	21	13			6 **So Fine**			$12	Columbia 33810
					featuring popular '50s tunes				
1/31/76	16	17	●	©	7 **Native Sons**			$12	Columbia 33578
12/11/76+	61	12	▲²		8 **The Best Of Friends** ....C:#12/70	[G]		$12	Columbia 34388
11/12/77	83	8			9 **Finale** .... [L]			$15	Columbia 34167 [2]

Angry Eyes (2,4,8)
Another Road (4)
Back To Georgia (1,4)
Be Free (5,8,9)
Boogie Man (7,9)
Brighter Days (5,9)
Changes (5,9) **84**

Coming To You (3)
Danny's Song (4,8,9)
Didn't I Know You When (3)
Fever Dream (4)
Fox Fire (7)
Get A Hold (5)
Golden Ribbons (2,4)

Good Friend (2)
Growin' (5,9) **52**
Hello Mary Lou (6)
Hey, Good Lookin' (6)
Holiday Hotel (4)
Honky Tonk - Part II (6)
House At Pooh Corner (1,4,8,9)

I Like It Like That (6) **84**
I'm Movin' On (6,9)
It's Alright (7)
Just Before The News (2,4)
Keep Me In Mind (5,9)
Lady Of My Heart (2,4)
Lahaina (3)

Lately My Love (5,9)
Listen To A Country Song (1,4,9)
Long Tail Cat (4)
Love Song (3,9)
Lover's Question (6) **89**
Lovin' Me (medley) (1,4)

Motel Cowboy (9)
Move On (5)
My Baby Left Me (6)
My Lady, My Love (7)
My Music (3,8,9) **16**
Native Son (7)
Nobody But You (1,4) **86**

509

LOGGINS & MESSINA — Cont'd

Oh, Lonesome Me (6,9)
Oklahoma, Home Of Mine (9)
Pathway To Glory (3)
Peace Of Mind (1,4,8)
Peacemaker (7,9)

Pretty Princess (7,9)
Rock 'N Roll Mood (1)
Sailin' The Wind (3)
Same Old Wine (1)
So Fine (6)

Splish Splash (6,9)
Sweet Marie (1)
Thinking Of You (2,8,9) *18*
Till The Ends Meet (3)
Time To Space (5)

To Make A Woman Feel
  Wanted (medley) (1,4)
Travelin' Blues (3,9)
Wake Up Little Susie (6)

Wasting Our Time (7)
Watching The River Run
  (3,8) *71*
When I Was A Child (7)
Whiskey (2)

You Could Break My Heart (4)
You Need A Man (3,9)
You Never Can Tell (6)
Your Mama Don't Dance
  (2,4,8) *4*

LO-KEY?   '93
Funk group from Minneapolis: Prof T. and Dre (vocals), Lance Alexander (keyboards), T-Bone (bass) and "D" (drums).

| 11/14/92+ | **121** | 21 | | © | **Where Dey At?** | | | $10 | Perspective 1003 |

Attention: Shawanda's Soulful
  Mix
Attention: The Shawanda Story

Autumn Love
Don't You Know By Now
Hey There Pretty Lady

I Got A Thang 4 Ya! *27*
I Wanna Make U Mine
Lo-Key?...Where Dey At?!

Milkshake
More Ways Than One
Stay Awhile

Sweet On U *91*
Ya Gots 2 B True

LOMAX, Jackie   '69
Born on 5/10/44 in Wallasey, Merseyside, England. Male singer/songwriter.

| 6/21/69 | **145** | 9 | | | **Is This What You Want?** | | | $25 | Apple 3354 |

Baby You're A Lover
Eagle Laughs At You

Fall Inside Your Eyes
I Just Don't Know

Is This What You Want?
Little Yellow Pills

New Day
Sour Milk Sea

Speak To Me
Sunset

Take My Word
You've Got Me Thinking

LOMBARDO, Guy, And His Royal Canadians   '58
Born on 6/19/02 in London, Ontario, Canada. Died on 11/5/77 (age 75). Leader of the #1 dance band of the 1930s and 1940s. Known for his classic theme "Auld Lang Syne," which he traditionally played to climax his annual New Year's Eve broadcasts.

1/19/57	**18**	2			1 **Your Guy Lombardo Medley**		[I]	$20	Capitol 739
7/28/58	**12**	4			2 **Berlin By Lombardo**		[I]	$20	Capitol 1019
12/2/67	**24**[X]	5			3 **Sing The Songs Of Christmas**		[X]	$15	Capitol 1443

vocals by children from St. Patrick's Parish in Stoneham, Massachusetts

Adeste Fideles (O, Come All Ye
  Faithful) (3)
All Alone (medley) (2)
All By Myself (medley) (2)
Always (medley) (2)
April In Paris (medley) (1)
April Showers (medley) (1)
Auld Lang Syne (medley) (1)
Be Careful, It's My Heart
  (medley) (2)
Be My Love (medley) (1)
Best Thing For You (medley)
  (2)
Birth Of The Blues (medley) (1)
Blue Room (medley) (1)
Blue Skies (medley) (2)
Body And Soul (medley) (1)
Coquette (medley) (1)
Crinoline Days (medley) (2)
Dancing On The Ceiling
  (medley) (1)
Deck The Hall (3)

Deep Purple (medley) (1)
Did I Remember (medley) (1)
Dinner At Eight (medley) (1)
Easter Parade (medley) (2)
Ebb Tide (medley) (1)
First Noel (3)
Girl That I Marry (medley) (2)
God Bless America (medley) (2)
Good Night Sweetheart
  (medley) (1)
Hark, The Herald Angels Sing
  (3)
Here Comes Santa Claus (3)
Hold Me (medley) (1)
Honey (medley) (1)
How Deep Is The Ocean (How
  High Is The Sky) (medley) (2)
I Don't Know Why (medley) (1)
I Love A Piano (medley) (2)
I Want To Go Back To Michigan
  (Down On The Farm)
  (medley) (2)

I'll See You In My Dreams
  (medley) (1)
I'm In The Mood For Love
  (medley) (1)
I'm Putting All My Eggs In One
  Basket (medley) (2)
If You Were Only Mine (medley)
  (1)
Isn't This A Lovely Day
  (medley) (1)
It Came Upon The Midnight
  Clear (3)
It Had To Be You (medley) (1)
It's A Lovely Day Today
  (medley) (1)
It's Only A Paper Moon
  (medley) (1)
Jingle Bells (3)
Josephine (medley) (1)
Joy To The World (3)
Just A Cottage Small (medley)
  (1)

Just A Memory (medley) (1)
Lady Of The Evening (medley)
  (2)
Lazy (medley) (2)
Let's Face The Music And
  Dance (medley) (1)
Love Is The Sweetest Thing
  (medley) (1)
Love Nest (medley) (1)
Mandy (medley) (2)
Marie (medley) (1)
Maybe It's Because (I Love You
  Too Much) (medley) (2)
Night And Day (medley) (1)
Night Is Filled With Music
  (medley) (1)
Nobody Knows (And Nobody
  Seems To Care) (medley) (2)
O, Little Town Of Bethlehem (3)
Paradise (medley) (1)
Play A Simple Melody (medley)
  (2)

Pretty Girl Is Like A Melody
  (medley) (2)
Rain (medley) (1)
Reaching For The Moon
  (medley) (2)
Remember (medley) (2)
Rose Room (medley) (1)
Rudolph The Red-Nosed
  Reindeer (3)
Russian Lullaby (medley) (2)
Say It Isn't So (medley) (1)
Say It With Music (medley) (2)
September In The Rain
  (medley) (1)
Serenade (medley) (1)
Silent Night (3)
Sleepy Time Gal (medley) (1)
Snuggled On Your Shoulder
  (medley) (1)
Soft Lights And Sweet Music
  (medley) (2)
Some Sunny Day (medley) (2)

Song Is Ended (medley) (2)
They Say It's Wonderful
  (medley) (2)
Very Thought Of You (medley)
  (1)
We Wish You A Merry
  Christmas (3)
What Is This Thing Called
  Love? (medley) (1)
What'll I Do (medley) (2)
When Day Is Done (medley) (1)
When I Lost You (medley) (1)
White Christmas (medley) (2)
Winter Wonderland (3)
You Go To My Head (medley)
  (1)
You Keep Coming Back Like A
  Song (medley) (2)
You'd Be Surprised (medley) (2)
You're A Sweetheart (medley)
  (1)

LONDON, Julie   '56
Born Julie Peck on 9/26/26 in Santa Rosa, California. Died of a stroke on 10/18/2000 (age 74). Singer/actress. Played "Dixie McCall" on TV's *Emergency*. Married to **Jack Webb** from 1945-53.

1/28/56	**2**[2]	14		©	1 **Julie Is Her Name**			$60	Liberty 3006
8/11/56	**16**	8			2 **Lonely Girl**			$60	Liberty 3012
12/15/56+	**18**	6		©	3 **Calendar Girl**			$60	Liberty 9002
7/22/57	**15**	4			4 **About The Blues**			$50	Liberty 3043
6/1/63	**127**	3		©	5 **The End Of The World**			$40	Liberty 7300
11/23/63	**136**	4			6 **The Wonderful World Of Julie London**			$40	Liberty 7324

About The Blues (4)
All Alone (2)
Basin Street Blues (4)
Blues In The Night (4)
Blues Is All I Ever Had (4)
Bouquet Of Blues (4)
Bye, Bye Blues (4)
Call Me Irresponsible (5)
Can't Get Used To Losing You
  (6)
Can't Help Lovin' That Man (1)
Chances Are (5)
Cry Me A River (1) *9*
Days Of Wine And Roses (5)
Don't Take Your Love From Me
  (2)

Easy Street (1)
End Of The World (5)
February Brings The Rain (3)
Fly Me To The Moon (In Other
  Words) (5)
Fools Rush In (2)
Get Set For The Blues (4)
Gone With The Wind (1)
Good Life (5)
Guilty Heart (6)
How Can I Make Him Love Me
  (6)
How Deep Is The Ocean (2)
I Gotta Right To Sing The Blues
  (4)

I Left My Heart In San
  Francisco (5)
I Lost My Sugar In Salt Lake
  City (2)
I Love You (1)
I Love You And Don't You
  Forget It (6)
I Remember You (5)
I Should Care (1)
I Wanna Be Around (5)
I'll Remember April (3)
I'm Coming Back To You (4)
I'm Glad There Is You (1)
I'm In The Mood For Love (1)
In The Still Of The Night (4)
Invitation To The Blues (4)

It Never Entered My Mind (1)
It's The Talk Of The Town (2)
June In January (3)
Laura (1)
Little Things Mean A Lot (6)
Lonely Girl (2)
Love For Sale (6)
Mean To Me (2)
Meaning Of The Blues (4)
Melancholy March (3)
Memphis In June (3)
Moments Like This (2)
My Coloring Book (5)
Nightingale Can Sing The Blues
  (4)
No Moon At All (1)

November Twilight (3)
Our Day Will Come (5)
People Who Are Born In May
  (3)
Remember (2)
S'Wonderful (1)
Say It Isn't So (1)
Say Wonderful Things (6)
September In The Rain (3)
Sleigh Ride In July (3)
Slightly Out Of Tune
  (Desafinado) (5)
Soft Summer Breeze (6)
Sunday Blues (4)
Taste Of Honey (6)
Thirteenth Month (3)

This October (3)
Time For August (3)
Warm December (3)
What'll I Do (2)
When Snow Flakes Fall In The
  Summer (6)
When Your Lover Has Gone (2)
Where Or When (2)

LONDONBEAT   '91
R&B-pop group based in England. Vocal trio of Americans Jimmy Helms and George Chandler, with Trinidad native Jimmy Chambers. Backed by British producer/multi-instrumentalist Willy M.

| 3/2/91 | **21** | 25 | ● | © | **In The Blood** | | | $10 | Radioactive 10192 |

Better Love *18*
Crying In The Rain
Getcha Ya Ya

I've Been Thinking About
  You *1*
In An I Love You Mood

It's In The Blood
No Woman No Cry

She Broke My Heart (In 36
  Places)
She Said She Loves Me

Step Inside My Shoes
This Is Your Life
You Love And Learn

LONDON QUIREBOYS, The   '90
Hard-rock group formed in London: Spike (vocals), Guy Bailey and Guy Griffin (guitars), Chris Johnstone (keyboards), Nigel Mogg (bass) and Ian Wallace (drums).

| 5/5/90 | **111** | 21 | | © | **A Bit Of What You Fancy** | | | $10 | Capitol 93177 |

Hey You
I Don't Love You Anymore *76*

Long Time Comin'
Man On The Loose

Misled
Roses & Rings

7 O'Clock
Sex Party

Sweet Mary Ann
Take Me Home

There She Goes Again
Whippin' Boy

LONDON SYMPHONY ORCHESTRA '86
Studio orchestra from England. Performed on many of the top soundtrack scores.

DEBUT	PEAK	WKS	CD	#	Title	Sym	$	Label & Number
4/21/79	185	2	©	1	Classic Rock - Volume One	[I]	$12	RSO 3043
3/5/83	145	3	©	2	Hooked On Rock Classics	[I]	$12	RCA Victor 4608
1/11/86	93	13	©	3	A Classic Case - The London Symphony Orchestra Plays The Music Of Jethro Tull	[I]	$10	RCA Victor 7067
6/11/94	196	2	©	4	Symphonic Music Of The Rolling Stones	[I]	$10	RCA Victor 62526

Angie (4)
Aqualung (3)
As Tears Go By (4)
Baker Street (2)
Bohemian Rhapsody (1)
Bourree (3)
Bungle In The Jungle (medley) (3)
Dandelion (4)
Elegy (3)
Eye Of The Tiger (2)
First Time Ever I Saw Your Face (4)
Fly By Night (3)
Get Back (2)
Gimme Shelter (4
I'm Not In Love (1)
Jumpin' Jack Flash (4)
Layla (2)
Living In The Past (3)
Locomotive Breath (3)
Lucy In The Sky With Diamonds (1)
Nights In White Satin (1)
Paint It Black (1,2,4)
Rainbow Blues (medley) (3)
Reach Out I'll Be There (2)
Rhapsody In Black (2)
Rock Classics Medley (2)
Ruby Tuesday (2,4)
She's A Rainbow (4)
Standing In The Shadows Of Love (2)
Street Fighting Man (4)
Sympathy For The Devil (4)
Teacher (medley) (3)
Thick As A Brick (3)
Too Old To Rock 'N' Roll; Too Young To Die (3)
Under My Thumb (4)
War Child (3)
Whiter Shade Of Pale (1)
Whole Lotta Love (1)
Without You (1)

LONE JUSTICE '85
Country-rock group from Los Angeles: **Maria McKee** (vocals), Ryan Hedgecock (guitar), Marvin Etzioni (bass) and Don Heffington (drums). Etzioni and Heffington left in early 1986; Shane Fontayne (guitar), Bruce Brody (keyboards), Gregg Sutton (bass) and Rudy Richman (drums) joined.

DEBUT	PEAK	WKS	CD	#	Title	$	Label & Number
5/11/85	56	25	©	1	Lone Justice	$10	Geffen 24060
11/29/86+	65	30	©	2	Shelter	$10	Geffen 24122

After The Flood (1)
Beacon (2)
Belfry (2)
Dixie Storms (2)
Don't Toss Us Away (1)
Dreams Come True (Stand Up And Take It) (2)
East Of Eden (1)
Gift, The (2)
I Found Love (2)
Inspiration (2)
Pass It On (1)
Reflected (On My Side) (2)
Shelter (2) *47*
Soap, Soup And Salvation (1)
Sweet, Sweet Baby (I'm Falling) (1) *73*
Wait 'Til We Get Home (1)
Ways To Be Wicked (1) *71*
Wheels (2)
Working Late (1)
You Are The Light (1)

LONESTAR '99
Country group from Nashville: Richie McDonald (vocals, guitar), Michael Britt (guitar), Dean Sams (keyboards), John Rich (bass) and Keech Rainwater (drums). Rich left in January 1998.

DEBUT	PEAK	WKS	RIAA	CD	#	Title	Catalog	Sym	$	Label & Number
3/2/96	69	17	●	©	1	Lonestar			$10	BNA 66642
7/5/97	166	3		©	2	Crazy Nights			$10	BNA 67422
6/19/99	28	96	▲³	©	3	Lonely Grill	C:#21/9		$10	BNA 67762
12/2/00	95	8		©	4	This Christmas Time		[X]	$10	BNA 67975

Christmas chart: 6/'00

All The Way (3)
Amazed (3) *1*
Amie (2)
Cheater's Road (2)
Christmas Song (Chestnuts Roasting On An Open Fire) (4)
Come Cryin' To Me (2)
Crazy Nights (2)
Does Your Daddy Know About Me (1)
Don't Let's Talk About Lisa (3)
Everything's Changed (2,3) *95*
Have Yourself A Merry Little Christmas (4)
Heartbroke Every Day (1)
I Love The Way You Do That (1)
I've Gotta Find You (3)
If Every Day Could Be Christmas (4)
John Doe On A John Deere (2)
Keys To My Heart (2)
Little Drummer Boy (4)
Lonely Grill (3)
No News (1)
O Holy Night (4)
Paradise Knife And Gun Club (1)
Please Come Home For Christmas (4)
Ragtop Cadillac (1)
Reason For The Season (4)
Runnin' Away With My Heart (1)
Santa Claus Is Comin' To Town (4)
Saturday Night (3)
Say When (2)
Simple As That (3)
Smile (3) *39*
Tell Her (3) *39*
Tequila Talkin' (2)
This Christmas Time (4)
Week In Juarez (2)
What About Now (3) *30*
What Child Is This (4)
What Do We Do With The Rest Of The Night (2)
What Would It Take (1)
When Cowboys Didn't Dance (1)
Winter Wonderland (4)
You Don't Know What Love Is (3)
You Walked In (2) *93*

LONG BEACH DUB ALLSTARS '99
Rock-reggae group from Long Beach, California: Opie Ortiz (vocals), Ras-1 (guitar), Jack Maness (keyboards), Marshall Goodman (percussion), Tim Wu (sax), Eric Wilson (bass) and Bud Gaugh (drums). Wilson and Gaugh were members of **Sublime**.

DEBUT	PEAK	WKS	CD	Title	$	Label & Number
10/16/99	67	5	©	Right Back	$10	DreamWorks 50213

Fugazi
Kick Down
Like A Dog
My Own Life
New Sun
Pass It On
Righteous Dub
Rosarito
Saw Red
Sensi
Soldiers
Trailer Ras

LONGET, Claudine '67
Born on 1/29/42 in Paris. Singer/actress. Married to **Andy Williams** from 1962-67. Charged but later acquitted for fatally shooting her boyfriend, skier Spider Savich.

DEBUT	PEAK	WKS	RIAA	#	Title	$	Label & Number
4/15/67	11	54	●	1	Claudine	$12	A&M 4121
10/14/67	33	29		2	The Look Of Love	$12	A&M 4129
4/13/68	29	21		3	Love Is Blue	$12	A&M 4142
2/1/69	155	7		4	Colours	$12	A&M 4163

Am I Blue? (4)
Both Sides Now (4)
Catch The Wind (4)
Colours (4)
Creators Of Rain (2)
Dindi (Jin-Jee) (3)
End Of The World (2)
Falling In Love Again (Can't Help It) (3)
Felicidade, A (1)
For Bobbie (For Baby) (4)
Good Day Sunshine (2) *100*
Happy Talk (3)
Hello, Hello (1) *91*
Here, There And Everywhere (1)
Holiday (3)
How Insensitive (Insensatez) (2)
Hurry On Down (4)
I Believed It All (4)
I Love How You Love Me (2)
I Think It's Gonna Rain Today (4)
It's Hard To Say Goodbye (3)
Let It Be Me (Je T'Appartiens) (4)
Look Of Love (2)
Love Is Blue (L'Amour Est Bleu) (3) *71*
Man And A Woman (1)
Man In A Raincoat (2)
Manha De Carnaval (2)
Meditation (Meditacao) (1) *98*
My Guy (1)
Pussywillows, Cat-Tails (4)
Scarborough Fair/Canticle (4)
Small Talk (3)
Snow (3)
Sunrise, Sunset (1)
Think Of Rain (2)
Tu As Beau Sourire (1)
Until It's Time For You To Go (4)
Walk In The Park (3)
Wanderlove (1)
When I Look In Your Eyes (3)
When I'm Sixty-Four (2)
Who Needs You (1)

LOOKING GLASS '72
Pop-rock group formed in New Jersey: Elliot Lurie (vocals, guitar), Larry Gonsky (keyboards), Piet Sweval (bass) and Jeff Grob (drums). Sweval died on 1/23/90 (age 51).

DEBUT	PEAK	WKS	Title	$	Label & Number
7/1/72	113	18	Looking Glass	$15	Epic 31320

Brandy (You're A Fine Girl) *1*
Catherine Street
Dealin' With The Devil
Don't It Make You Feel Good
From Stanton Station
Golden Rainbow
Jenny-Lynne
One By One

LOOSE ENDS '85
R&B vocal trio from London: Carl McIntosh, Steve Nichol and Jane Eugene. Nichol and Eugene left in 1990; replaced by Sunay Suleyman and Linda Carriere.

DEBUT	PEAK	WKS	CD	#	Title	$	Label & Number
7/6/85	46	19	©	1	A Little Spice	$10	MCA 5588
4/4/87	59	14	©	2	Zagora	$10	MCA 5745
7/23/88	80	15	©	3	The Real Chuckeeboo	$10	MCA 42196
12/8/90+	124	16	©	4	Look How Long	$10	MCA 10044

Be Thankful (Mama's Song) (2)
Cheap Talk (4)
Choose Me (1)
Dial 999 (1)
Don't Be A Fool (4)
Don't You Ever (Try To Change Me) (4)
Easier Said Than Done (3)
Hangin' On A String (Contemplating) (1) *43*
Hold Tight (4)
Hungry (4)
I Can't Wait (Another Minute) (2)
I Don't Need To Love (4)
Is It Ever Too Late? (3)
Let's Get Back To Love (2)
Let's Rock (1)
Let's Wax A Fatty (4)
Life (3)
Little Spice (1)
Look How Long (4)
Love Controversy Pt. 1 (4)
Love's Got Me (4)
Music Takes Me Higher (1)
Nights Of Pleasure (2)
Ooh, You Make Me Feel (2)
Real Chuckeeboo Medley (3)
Remote Control (3)
Slow Down (2)
So Much Love (1)
Stay A Little While, Child (2)
Sweetest Pain (4)
Symptoms Of Love (4)
Tell Me What You Want (1)

LOOSE ENDS — Cont'd

(There's No) Gratitude (3) Try My Love (4) What Goes Around (3) You Can't Stop The Rain (2)
Time Is Ticking (4) Watching You (3) Who Are You? (2)

LOPEZ, Denise   '88
Born in Queens, New York. Female dance singer.

| 11/26/88 | 184 | 4 | | © | Truth In Disguise | | | $10 | A&M 5226 |

Causa' U If You Feel It 94 Sayin' Sorry (Don't Make It Stop The Fight Too Much Too Late
I Wanna Fall In Love With You Power Of Suggestion Right) 31 Tell Me What It Is Truth In Disguise

LOPEZ, Jennifer   '01
Born on 7/24/70 in the Bronx, New York. Latin singer/actress.

| 6/19/99 | 8 | 53 | ▲³ | © 1 | On The 6 | | | $10 | Work 69351 |
| 2/10/01 | ❶¹ | 34↑ | ▲² | © 2 | J.Lo | | | $10 | Epic 63786 |

Ain't It Funny (2) Dance With Me (2) It's Not That Serious (1) Play (2) 18 Talk About Us (1) Waiting For Tonight (1) 8
Cariño (2) Feelin' So Good (1) 51 Let's Get Loud (1) Promise Me You'll Try (1) That's Not Me (1) Walking On Sunshine (2)
Come Over (2) I'm Gonna Be Alright (2) Love Don't Cost A Thing (1) 3 Secretly (2) That's The Way (2) We Gotta Talk (2)
Could This Be Love (1) I'm Real (2) 1 No Me Ames (1) Should've Never (1) Too Late (1)
Dame (2) If You Had My Love (1) 1 Open Off My Love (1) Si Ya Se Acabó (2) Una Noche Mas (1)

★230★   LOPEZ, Trini   '63
Born Trinidad Lopez on 5/15/37 in Dallas. Pop-folk singer/guitarist. Played "Pedro Jiminez" in the movie *The Dirty Dozen*.
1)Trini Lopez At PJ'S 2)More Trini Lopez At PJ'S 3)The Latin Album

7/20/63	2⁶	101		● © 1	Trini Lopez At PJ'S	[L]		$15	Reprise 6093
12/7/63+	11	19		© 2	More Trini Lopez At PJ'S	[L]		$15	Reprise 6103
4/11/64	32	33		3	On The Move	[L]		$15	Reprise 6112
8/22/64	18	24		4	The Latin Album	[F]		$15	Reprise 6125
10/24/64	30	22		5	Live At Basin St. East	[L]		$15	Reprise 6134
1/30/65	18	23		6	The Folk Album			$15	Reprise 6147
6/12/65	32	19		7	The Love Album			$15	Reprise 6165
8/28/65	46	12		8	The Rhythm & Blues Album			$15	Reprise 6171
12/18/65+	101	10		9	The Sing-Along World Of Trini Lopez			$15	Reprise 6183
5/7/66	54	16		10	Trini			$15	Reprise 6196
8/27/66	110	8		11	The Second Latin Album	[F]		$15	Reprise 6215
11/26/66+	47	11		12	Greatest Hits!	[G]		$15	Reprise 6226
3/4/67	114	6		13	Trini Lopez In London			$15	Reprise 6238
9/2/67	162	7		14	Trini Lopez - Now!			$15	Reprise 6255

Adalita (4) Dixie Belle (9) I Wanna Be Around (13) Moon River (7) Side By Side (9) Watermelon Man (8)
Alla En El Rancho Grande Don't Let Go (8) I Wanna Be Free (14) My Love, Forgive Me (11) Sin Ti (Without You) (11) We'll Sing In The Sunshine (6)
(medley) (4) Don't Think Twice, It's All Right I Will Wait For You (10) My Melancholy Baby (9) Sinner Man (12) 54 Wee Wee Hours (8)
Alright, Okay, You Win (5) (6) I'm Comin' Home, Cindy Never On Sunday (2) Smile (9) What Have I Got Of My Own
A-me-ri-ca (1,12) Double Trouble (8) (10,12) 39 Oh, Lonesome Me (2) So Fine (8) (3,12) 43
Amor (Love) (11) Down By The Riverside I'm Gonna Be A Wheel Once I Wondered (14) Spanish Harlem (11) What'd I Say (1,5)
Angelito (4) (medley) (1) Someday (14) One Of Those Songs (10) Stagger Lee (5) When The Saints Go Marching
Are You Sincere (7,12) 85 El Reloj (4) If I Had A Hammer (1,5,12) 3 Ooh Poo Pah Doo (8) Story Of Love (11) In (medley) (1)
Around The World (9) Eyes Of Love (14) If You Wanna Be Happy (2) Our Day Will Come (7) Strangers In The Night (13) Where's The Love (14)
Ay! Jalisco, No Te Rajes Fever (13) If You Were Me (10) Pancho Lopez (11) Sunny (14) Wherever You Are (4)
(medley) (3) Fly Me To The Moon (10) In The Land Of Plenty (14) People (7) Sweet And Lovely (9) Ya Ya (3)
Baby, The Rain Must Fall (10) Go To The Mountains (2) Irresistible You (3) Perfidia (4) Sweet Georgia Brown (9) Yeah (2)
Be Careful, It's My Heart (5) Gonna Get Along Without Ya' It Had To Be You (13) Personality (5) Takin' The Back Roads (13) Yesterday (10)
Besame Mucho (4) Now (13) 93 Jailer, Bring Me Water (3) 94 Piel Canela (4) Tammy (7) You Are My Sunshine (4)
Bill Bailey, Won't You Please Goody Goody (2) Jezebel (5) Pretty Eyes (6) Taste Of Honey (4) You Belong To My Heart (11)
Come Home (4) Gotta Travel On (medley) (1) Kansas City (2,12) 23 Puff (The Magic Dragon) (6) Tengo Nada (11) You Can't Say Good-by (3)
Blowin' In The Wind (6) Granada (1,4) La Bamba - Part I (1,5,12) 86 Put Your Arms Around Me, That's What Makes The World You Know (9)
Blue Velvet (7) Green, Green (3) La Malaguena (4) Honey (9) Go Round (13) You Need Hands (5)
Born Free (14) Greenback Dollar (6) Lady Jane (13) Quizas, Quizas, Quizas (4) There's A Kind Of Hush (All You Talk Too Much (14)
Bye Bye Blackbird (1) Guantanamera (Lady Of Laura (7) Return To Me (7) Over The World) (14) You'll Be Sorry (1)
Bye Bye Love (3) Guantanamo) (14) Lemon Tree (6,12) 20 Sad Tomorrows (7,12) 94 32nd Of May (10) You'll Never Know (9)
Call Me (10) Hall Of Fame (12) Let The Four Winds Blow (14) Saints, The (9) This Land Is Your Land (1) Your Ever Changin' Mind (13)
Chamaka (3) Hallelujah, I Love Her So (5) Little Miss Happiness (8) San Francisco De Assisi (11) This Little Girl Of Mine (3) Yours (11)
Cielito Lindo (1) Happy (13) Lonesome Road (3) Sand Pebbles (And We Were This Train (5)
Corazon De Melon Heart Of My Heart (2) Lonesome Traveler (4) Lovers), Theme From The Trini Dice Te Amo (Trini Says
(Watermelon Heart) (2) Hello, Dolly! (5) Love Letters (13) (14) He Loves You) (11)
Cotton Fields (3) Hold Me Now And Forever (14) Love Me With All Your Heart Scarlet Ribbons (For Her Hair) Trini's Tune (10)
Crooked Little Man (6) Hurtin' Inside (8) ..see: Cuando Calienta El Sol (6) Unchain My Heart (1)
Cu Cu Rru Cu Cu, Paloma (4) I Got A Woman (8) Mame (13) Shadow Of Your Smile (10) Volare (medley) (1)
Cuando Calienta El Sol (4) I Love Your Beautiful Brown Marianne (medley) (1) She's About A Mover (8) Walk Right In (2)
Dear Heart (7) Eyes (5) Michael (6,12) 42 Shout (8) Watch What Happens (11)

LORBER, Jeff   '87
Born on 11/4/52 in Philadelphia. Jazz fusion keyboardist. His fusion group included **Kenny G** (flute), Danny Wilson (bass) and Dennis Bradford (drums).

THE JEFF LORBER FUSION:

9/8/79	119	14		© 1	Water Sign	[I]		$12	Arista 4234
5/31/80	123	12		© 2	Wizard Island	[I]		$12	Arista 9516
4/18/81	77	15		3	Galaxian			$12	Arista 9545

JEFF LORBER:

3/27/82	73	13		4	It's A Fact			$10	Arista 9583
5/5/84	106	7		5	In The Heat Of The Night			$10	Arista 8025
3/9/85	90	16		© 6	Step By Step			$10	Arista 8269
11/15/86+	68	26		© 7	Private Passion			$10	Warner 25492

Above The Clouds (4) Can't Get Enough (2) Every Woman Needs It (6) In The Heat Of The Night (5) Lava Lands (2) Night Love (3)
Always There (4) City (2) Facts Of Love (7) 27 It Takes A Woman (6) Lights Out (1) On The Wild Side (6)
Back In Love (7) Country (1) Full Moon (4) It's A Fact (4) Magic Lady (3) Pacific Coast Highway (6)
Best Part Of The Night (6) Delevans (4) Fusion Juice (2) Jamaica (7) Magician, The (4) Private Passion (7)
Blast Off (5) Don't Say Yes (5) Galaxian (3) Keep On Lovin' Her (7) Midnight Snack (7) Rain Dance (1)
Bright Sky (3) Double Bad (5) Groovacious (6) Kristen (7) Monster Man (3) Really Scarey (5)

DEBUT	PEAK	WKS	RIAA	CD	ARTIST — Album Title	Catalog	Sym	$	Label & Number

LORBER, Jeff — Cont'd

Reflections (2)
Right Here (1)
Rock II (5)
Rooftops (2)
Sand Castles (7)

Seventh Heaven (3)
Seventh Mountain (3)
Shadows (2)
Sparkle (1)
Spur Of The Moment (3)

Step By Step (6)
Sushi Monster (5)
Sweet (2)
Think Back And Remember (3)
This Is The Night (6)

Tierra Verde (4)
Toad's Place (1)
Tropical (5)
True Confessions (7)
Tune 88 (1)

Warm Springs (4)
Water Sign (1)
Waterfall (3)
When You Gonna Come Back Home (6)

Wizard Island (2)
Your Love Has Got Me (4)

LORDS OF ACID '97
Techno duo from Belgium: Oliver Adams and Praga Khan.

9/6/97	100	6		©	1 **Our Little Secret**			$10	Antler Subway 6036
8/14/99	194	1		©	2 **Expand Your Head**	[K]		$10	Antler Subway 6047
3/17/01	160	1		©	3 **Farstucker**			$10	Antler Subway 6969

Am I Sexy? (2)
As I Am (2)
Crablouse (2)
Cybersex (1)
Dark Lover Rising (3)
Deep Sexy Space (1)
Doggie Tom (1)
Feed My Hungry Soul (3)

Fingerlickin' Good (1)
Get Up And Jam (3)
Get Up. Get High (3)
Glad I'm Not God! (3)
I Like It (3)
I Must Increase My Bust (2)
I Sit On Acid (2)
Kiss Eternal (3)

LSD = Truth (1)
Let's Get High (2)
Lick My Chakra (3)
Lover (1,2)
Lover Boy/Lover Girl (3)
Lucy's F*ck*ng Sky (3)
Man's Best Friend (1)
Marijuana In Your Brain (2)

Me And Myself (1)
Pain & Pleasure Concerto (3)
Power Is Mine (1)
Pussy (1,2)
Ride With Satan's Little Helpers (3)
Rough Sex (2)
Rover Take Over (3)

Rubber Doll (1,2)
Scrood Bi U (3)
Sex Bomb (3)
Slave To Love (3)
Spank My Booty (1,2)
Stripper (3)
Surfin' Muncheez (3)
Take Off (3)

(Treatise On The Practical Methods Whereby One Can) Worship The Lords (3)
Who Do You Think You Are? (2)
You Belong To Me (1)

LORDS OF THE NEW CHURCH, The '85
Rock group formed in England: Cleveland native Stiv Bator (vocals), Brian James (guitar), Dave Tregunna (bass) and Nicky Turner (drums). Bator (former lead singer of the **Dead Boys**) died on 6/4/90 (age 40), after being hit by a car.

| 4/27/85 | 158 | 7 | | © | **The Method To Our Madness** | | | $10 | I.R.S. 70049 |

Do What Thou Wilt
I Never Believed

Kiss Of Death
Method To My Madness

Murder Style
My Kingdom Come

Pretty Baby Scream
S.F. & T.

Seducer, The
When Blood Runs Cold

LORDS OF THE UNDERGROUND '93
Rap trio from Raleigh, North Carolina: Mr. Funke, DoItAll and DJ Lord Jazz.

| 4/17/93 | 66 | 25 | | © | 1 **Here Come The Lords** | | | $10 | Pendulum 61415 |
| 11/19/94 | 57 | 3 | | © | 2 **Keepers Of The Funk** | | | $10 | Pendulum 30710 |

Check It (1)
Chief Rocka (1) *55*
Faith (2)
Flow On (New Symphony) (1)
From Da Bricks (1)

Frustrated (2)
Funky Child (1) *74*
Grave Digga (1)
Here Come The Lords (1) *93*
Keep It Underground (1)

Keepers Of The Funk (2)
L.O.T.U.G. (Lords Of The Underground) (1)
Lord Jazz Hit Me One Time (Make It Funky) (1)

Lords Prayer (1)
Madd Skillz (1)
Neva Faded (1)
No Pain (2)
Psycho (1)

Ready Or Not (2)
Sleep For Dinner (1)
Steam From Da Knot (2)
Tic Toc (2) *73*
What I'm After (2)

What U See (2)
What's Goin' On (1)
Yes Y'all (2)

LORD SUTCH AND HEAVY FRIENDS '70
Born David Sutch in 1941 in Harrow, Middlesex, England. Committed suicide on 6/16/99 (age 58). Rock singer. Heavy Friends: **Jimmy Page**, **Jeff Beck**, **Nicky Hopkins**, John Bonham (**Led Zeppelin**) and Noel Redding (**The Jimi Hendrix Experience**).

| 2/21/70 | 84 | 13 | | | **Lord Sutch And Heavy Friends** | | | $30 | Cotillion 9015 |

Baby, Come Back
Brightest Light

'Cause I Love You
Flashing Lights

Gutty Guitar
L-o-n-d-o-n

One For You, Baby
Smoke And Fire

Thumping Beat
Union Jack Car

Wailing Sounds
Would You Believe

LORD TARIQ & PETER GUNZ '98
Rap duo from New York City: Sean Hamilton ("Lord Tariq") and Peter Panky ("Peter Gunz").

| 6/20/98 | 38 | 10 | | © | **Make It Reign** | | | $10 | Columbia 69010 |

Cross Bronx Expressway
Deja Vu (Uptown Baby) *9*
Fiesta

Keep On
Make It Reign
Massive Heat

My Time To Go
Night In The Bronx With Lord & Gunz
One Life To Live
Startin' Somethin'
Streets To Da Stage

We Will Ball
Who Am I
Worldwide

LORENZ, Trey '92
Born on 1/19/69 in Florence, South Carolina. Male R&B singer.

| 10/24/92 | 111 | 8 | | © | **Trey Lorenz** | | | $10 | Epic 47840 |

Always In Love
Baby I'm In Heaven

Find A Way
How Can I Say Goodbye

It Only Hurts When It's Love
Just To Be Close To You

Photograph Of Mary
Run Back To Me

Someone To Hold *19*
When Troubles Come

Wipe All My Tears Away

LORING, Gloria '86
Born on 12/10/46 in New York City. Played "Liz Curtis" on TV's *Days Of Our Lives*. Married to Alan Thicke from 1970-83.

| 9/6/86 | 61 | 14 | | © | **Gloria Loring** | | | $10 | Atlantic 81679 |

Changes Of Heart
Close My Eyes

Don't Let Me Change The Way You Are

Friends And Lovers *2*
Goodbye, The

If You Remember Me
Since I Don't Have You

Smokin'
What's One More Time

You Always Knew

LOS ADMIRADORES '60
Percussion group produced by **Enoch Light**.

| 8/29/60 | 2[1] | 50 | | | 1 Bongos Bongos Bongos | [I] | | $20 | Command 809 |
| 10/24/60 | 3 | 34 | | | 2 Bongos/Flutes/Guitars | [I] | | $20 | Command 812 |

All Of Me (1)
Between The Devil & The Deep Blue Sea (1)
Bidin' My Time (1)
Birth Of The Blues (2)

Blue Moon (1)
By The River St. Marie (2)
C'est Si Bon (2)
Caravan (2)
Don't Blame Me (1)

East Of The Sun (2)
Friendly Persuasion (2)
Golden Earrings (2)
Greensleeves (1)
How High The Moon (2)

I Can Dream, Can't I (2)
Laura (2)
Londonderry Air (1)
Making Whoopie (2)
My Funny Valentine (2)

Sylvie (1)
Tenderly (1)
Unchained Melody (1)
Very Thought Of You (1)

You & The Night & The Music (1)

LOS BRAVOS '66
Rock group formed in Spain: Mike Kogel (vocals; born in Germany), Tony Martinez(guitar), Manuel Fernandez (organ), Miguel Danus (bass) and Pablo Gomez (drums).

| 11/12/66 | 93 | 7 | | © | **Black Is Black** | | | $50 | Press 83003 |

Baby, Baby
Baby, Believe Me

Black Is Black *4*
Don't Be Left Out In The Cold

I Don't Care
I Want A Name

I'm Cuttin' Out
Make It Easy For Me

She Believes In Me
Stop That Girl

Trapped
You Won't Get Far

LOS DEL RIO '96
Flamenco guitar duo from Seville, Spain: Antonio Romero Monge and Rafael Ruiz Perdigones. Formed duo in the 1960s. In 1993, they wrote and recorded "Macarena," which became a worldwide dance craze after it was remixed by the Miami production team of The Bayside Boys.

| 8/24/96 | 41 | 20 | | © | **Macarena - Non Stop** | [F] | | $10 | Ariola 37587 |

La Niña (Del Pañuelo Colorado)
Macarena (bayside boys mix) *1*

Macarena (non stop) *23*
Pure Carroceria

LOS HURACANES DEL NORTE   '00
Latin group from El Centro, Mexico: brothers Rocky (vocals), Jesus (accordian), Lupillo (sax) and Pancho (bass) Garcia, with Wico Lopez (drums). Group name is Spanish for "The Hurricanes of the North."

| 8/19/00 | 181 | 1 | | © | 1 En Que Trabaja El Muchacho .... | | [F] | $10 | Fonovisa 6088 |

title is Spanish for "In What The Boy Works"

| Aunque Te Duela | El Gringo | Herida De Amor | Pa'que Te Casabas Juan | Tierra De Jefes |
| Bonita | En Que Trabaja El Muchacho | La Gorda | Sangre De Gallo | Una Tumba Mas |

LOS INDIOS TABAJARAS   '64
Brazilian Indian brothers: Natalicio and Antenor Lima.

| 11/16/63+ | 7 | 31 | | © | 1 Maria Elena | | [E-I] | $20 | RCA Victor 2822 |

originally released in 1958 as Sweet And Savage on RCA 1788

| 5/16/64 | 85 | 10 | | © | 2 Always In My Heart .... | | [I] | $20 | RCA Victor 2912 |

A La Orilla Del Lago (1)	Baion Bon (1)	Magic Is The Moonlight (2)	Moonlight And Shadows (2)	Over The Rainbow (2)	Ternura (1)
Always In My Heart (2) *82*	Central Park (2)	Maran Cariua (1)	Moonlight Serenade (1)	Pajaro Campana (1)	Vals Criollo (2)
Amapola (2)	Jungle Dream (1)	**Maria Elena** (1) *6*	More Brandy - Please (2)	¿Por Que Eres Asi? (2)	Wide Horizon (2)
Ay Maria (1)	Los Indios Danzan (1)	Maria My Own (2)	New Orleans (2)	Star Dust (1)	You Belong To My Heart (2)

LOS LOBOS   '87
Latin rock group formed in East Los Angeles: David Hildago (vocals), Cesar Rosas (guitar), Steve Berlin (sax), Conrad Lozano (bass) and Louie Perez (drums).

12/15/84+	47	34		©	1 How Will The Wolf Survive?			$10	Slash 25177
2/14/87	47	32		©	2 By The Light Of The Moon			$10	Slash 25523
7/25/87	❶²	44	▲²	©	3 La Bamba		[S]	$10	Slash 25605

*includes "Crying, Waiting, Hoping" by **Marshall Crenshaw**, "Lonely Teardrops" by Howard Huntsberry, "Who Do You Love" by Bo Diddley and "Summertime Blues" by Brian Setzer*

| 11/5/88 | 179 | 4 | | © | 4 La Pistola Y El Corazon .... | | | $10 | Slash 25790 |

title is Spanish for "The Pistol and The Heart"

9/22/90	103	9		©	5 The Neighborhood			$10	Slash 26131
6/13/92	143	10		©	6 Kiko			$10	Slash 26786
9/18/93	196	1		©	7 Just Another Band From East L.A. - A Collection		[K]	$15	Slash 45367 [2]
4/6/96	81	6		©	8 Colossal Head			$10	Warner 46172
8/7/99	135	3		©	9 This Time			$10	Hollywood 62185

All I Wanted To Do Was Dance (2)	Corrida #1 (1)	High Places (9)	Life Is Good (8)	Que Nadie Sepa Mi Sufrir (4)	That Train Don't Stop Here (6)
Angel Dance (5,7)	Cumbia Raza (9)	I Can't Understand (5,7)	Lil' King Of Everything (1)	Reva's House (6)	This Bird's Gonna Fly (8)
Angels With Dirty Faces (6,7)	Deep Dark Hole (5)	I Got Loaded (1)	Little Japan (8)	Revolution (8)	This Time (9)
Anselma (7)	Don't Worry Baby (1,7)	I Got To Let You Know (1,7)	Little John Of God (5)	Rio De Tenampa (8)	Turn Around (7)
Arizona Skies (6)	Donna (1)	I Walk Alone (5)	Manny's Bones (8)	River Of Fools (2,7)	Two Janes (6)
Be Still (5,7)	Down On The Riverbed (5,7)	I Wan'na Be Like You (The Monkey Song) (2)	Maricela (8)	Run Away With You (9)	Viking (7)
Bella Maria De Mi Alma (7)	Dream In Blue (6)	Is This All There Is? (2)	Mas Y Mas (8)	Sabor A Mi (2)	Volver, Volver (7)
Bertha (7)	El Canelo (4)	Jenny's Got A Pony (5)	Matter Of Time (1,7)	Saint Behind The Glass (6,7)	Wake Up Dolores (6)
Blue Moonlight (7)	El Cuchipe (7)	Just A Man (6)	Mess We're In (2)	Serenata Nortena (1)	We Belong Together (3)
Breakdown, The (1)	El Gusto (2,7)	Kiko And The Lavender Moon (6,7)	My Baby's Gone (2)	Set Me Free (Rosa Lee) (2,7)	What's Going On (7)
Buddy Ebsen Loves The Night Time (8)	Emily (5)	La Bamba (3,7) *1*	Neighborhood, The (5,7)	Shakin' Shakin' Shakes (2,7)	When The Circus Comes (6,7)
Can't Stop The Rain (8)	Estoy Sentado Aqui (4,7)	La Feria De La Flores (7)	New Zandu (7)	Short Side Of Nothing (6)	Whiskey Trail (6)
Carabina .30-30 (1)	Evangeline (1)	La Guacamaya (4)	Oh Yeah (9)	Si You Quisiera (4)	Why We Wish (7)
Charlena (3)	Everybody Loves A Train (8)	La Pistola Y El Corazon (4,7)	One Time One Night (2,7)	Some Say, Some Do (9)	Wicked Rain (6,7)
Colossal Head (8)	Framed (3)	La Playa (9)	Ooh! My Head (3)	Someday (7)	Will The Wolf Survive? (1,7) *78*
Come On, Let's Go (3,7) *21*	Georgia Slop (5)	Las Amarillas (4)	Our Last Night (1)	(Sonajas) Mananitas Michoacanas (4)	Wrong Man Theme (7)
Corazón (9)	Giving Tree (5)	Let's Say Goodnight (7)	Peace (6,7)	Take My Hand (5)	
	Goodnight My Love (3)		Politician (9)	Tears Of God (2,7)	
	Hardest Time (2)		Prenda Del Alma (2)		

LOST BOYZ   '96
Rap group from Queens, New York: Spigg Nice, Mr. Cheeks, Freekie Tah and Pretty Lou. Freekie Tah (real name: Raymond Rogers) was shot to death on 3/29/99 (age 28).

6/22/96	6	23	●	©	1 Legal Drug Money			$10	Universal 53010
7/5/97	9	19	●	©	2 Love, Peace And Nappiness			$10	Universal 53080
10/16/99	32	6		©	3 LB IV Life			$10	Universal 153268

All Right (1)	Day 1 (2)	Ghetto Lifestyle (3)	**Lifestyles Of The Rich And Shameless** (1) *91*	Only Live Once (3)	Take A Hike (One) (3)
Beasts From The East (2)	5 A.M. (3)	Is This Da Part (1)	Jeeps, Lex Coups, Bimaz & Benz (1) *67*	Plug Me In (3)	Tight Situations (3)
Can't Hold Us Down (3)	From My Family To Yours (Dedication) (2)	Love & Nappiness (2)	Me & My Crazy World (2) *52*	Renee (1) *33*	We Got That Hot S... (3)
Certain Things We Do (2)	Games (2)	Keep It Real (1)	Music Makes Me High (1) *51*	Risin' To The Top (No Stoppin' Us) (3)	What's Wrong (2)
Channel Zero (1)	Get Up (1) *60*	LB Fam 4 Life (3)	My Crew (2)	So Love (2)	Why (2)
Cheese (3)	Get Your Hustle On (3)	Legal Drug Money (1)	New York City War Call (3)	Straight From Da Ghetto (1)	Yearn, The (1)
Colabo (3)	Ghetto Jiggy (3)	Let's Roll Dice (3)	1,2,3 (1)	Summer Time (2)	
Da Game (3)					

LOS TEMERARIOS   '00
Latin vocal group from Mexico: brothers Adolfo, Guztavo and Fernando Angel, with Karlos Vidal and Carlos Obrego. Group name is Spanish for "The Reckless."

| 2/21/98 | 175 | 1 | ▲ | © | 1 Como Te Recuerdo .... | | [F] | $10 | Fonovisa 0515 |

title is Spanish for "How I Remember You"

| 3/18/00 | 75 | 5 | ● | © | 2 En La Madrugada Se Fue .... | | [F] | $10 | Fonovisa 0519 |

title is Spanish for "In The Morning She Left"

Adiós Te Extrañaré (2)	Dicen Que La Distancia (2)	Es Ella La Causa (1)	Me Resisto (1)	Quise Olvidarme De Ti (2)
Bella Pero Mala (1)	Dijiste Adios (1)	Estaba Solo (1)	No Es Tan Fácil Olvidarme (1)	Sufriendo Penas (2)
Botella Envenenada (1)	En La Madrugada Se Fue (2)	He Intentado Tanto, Tanto (2)	Por Que Te Conoci (2)	Te Hice Mal (2)
Como Te Recuerdo (1)	Eras Todo Para Mi (2)	Me Extrañarás (2)	Que Te Vas (1)	Yo Quiero Ser Feliz (1)

LOS TIGRES DEL NORTE   '99
Latin group from Rosa Morada, Mexico: brothers Jorge (vocals, accordian), Eduardo, Hernan and Raul Hernandez (guitars), with cousin Oscar Lara (drums) and friend Guadalupe Olivio (sax). Group name is Spanish for "The Tigers of the North."

| 7/5/97 | 149 | 3 | ● | © | 1 Jefe De Jefes .... | | [F] | $15 | Fonovisa 80711 [2] |

title is Spanish for "Chief Of Chiefs"

| 7/10/99 | 92 | 5 | | © | 2 Herencia De Familia .... | | [F] | $15 | Fonovisa 80761 [2] |

title is Spanish for "Family Heritage"

| 10/14/00 | 92 | 4 | ● | © | 3 De Paisano A Paisano .... | | [F] | $10 | Fonovisa 6092 |

title is Spanish for "From Compatriot To Compatriot"

LOS TIGRES DEL NORTE — Cont'd

Adiós Amigo (2)
Al Mil Por Uno (3)
Al Sur Del Bravo (3)
Alla En El Rancho Grande (medley) (2)
Ando Amanecido (2)
Carne Quemada (1)
Con La Soga Al Cuello (2)
De Harina Y De Maiz (3)
De Paisano A Paisano (3)

El Aguilillo (3)
El Cura (2)
El Dolor De Un Padre (1)
El General (1)
El Mojado Acaudalado (1)
El No Te Dió Nada (2)
El Planton (1)
El Prisionero (1)
El Rengo Del Gallo Giro (1)
El Siete Leguas (2)

El Sucesor (2)
El Tarasco (1)
El Triunfo (2)
Jefe De Jefes (1)
Jesus Amado (1)
La Inflacion (3)
La Liebre (2)
La Loba (2)
La Paloma (1)
La Resortera (2)

La Valentina (medley) (2)
Lágrimas (Lágrimas Del Corazón) (1)
Las Novias Del Traficante (1)
Leña Del Arbol Caido (3)
Libros De Recuerdos (2)
Lo Que Sembre Alla En La Sierra (1)
Me Declaro Culpable (3)
Mis Dos Patrias (1)

My Promise/Mi Promesa (2)
Necesito Mi Libertad (3)
Ni Aqui Ni Alla (1)
No Quiero Tu Lástima (2)
Perdiendo El Tiempo (3)
Pokar Alto (3)
Por Debajo Del Agua (1)
Por Ser Sinaloense (2)
Prisión De Amor (1)
Quien Corresponda (3)

Tambien Las Mujeres Pueden (1)
Tu Con El Yo Con Ella (2)
Tu, Yo Y La Luna (3)
Un Hasta Aqui (3)
Vamos A Las Vegas (2)

LOS TRI-O   '99
Latin vocal trio: Andres, Esteban and Manuel.

| 3/13/99 | 120 | 13 | © | | **Nuestro Amor** .... | | [F] | $10 | Ariola 58436 |

title is Spanish for "Our Love"

Adoracion
Anhelo

Ausencia
Desengaño

Eternidad
Evocacion

Obsesion
Recuerdo

Resignacion
Soneando

Sufrimiento

LOS TUCANES DE TIJUANA   '97
Latin vocal group: Mario Quintero, Joel Higuera, David Servin and Mario Moreno. Group name is Spanish for "The Toucans of Tijuana."

| 5/24/97 | 199 | 1 | ● | © | **Tucanes De Oro, Secuestro De Amor** .... | | [F] | $10 | EMI Latin 56921 |

title is Spanish for "Toucans Of Gold, Prisoners Of Love"

Ando Bien Arreglado
El Arabe

El Tucanazo
Eres Mi Sueño

Es Tu Bronca
Es Verdad

Esa Locion Me Mata
Hacemos Bonita Pareja

La Fiesta De Los Panes
Pense Pegarme Un Tiro

Secuestro De Amor
Veneno

LOUDNESS   '86
Hard-rock group from Japan: Minoru Niihara (vocals), Akira Takasaki (guitar), Masayoshi Yamashita (bass) and Munetaka Higuchi (drums).

3/2/85	74	24		1	**Thunder In The East**			$10	Atco 90246
5/31/86	64	16	©	2	**Lightning Strikes**			$10	Atco 90512
8/15/87	190	4	©	3	**Hurricane Eyes**			$10	Atco 90619

Ashes In The Sky (2)
Black Star Oblivion (2)
Clockwork Toy (1)
Complication (2)
Crazy Nights (1)

Dark Desire (2)
Face To Face (2)
Heavy Chains (1)
Hungry Hunter (3)
In My Dreams (3)

In This World Beyond (3)
Let It Go (2)
Like Hell (1)
Lines Are Down (1)
Never Change Your Mind (1)

No Way Out (1)
1000 Eyes (2)
Rock 'N Roll Gypsy (3)
Rock This Way (3)
Run For Your Life (1)

S.D.I. (3)
So Lonely (3)
Street Life Dream (2)
Strike Of The Sword (3)
Take Me Home (3)

This Lonely Heart (3)
We Could Be Together (1)
Who Knows (2)

LOUIE LOUIE   '90
Born Louis Cordero in Los Angeles. Dance singer/songwriter.

| 6/2/90 | 136 | 10 | © | | **The State I'm In** .... | | | $10 | WTG 45285 |

Hurt Baby
I Wanna Get Back With You *69*

I'm Sorry That It Happened To You
Let Me Divorce You

Mata Hari
Penny Lady
Rodeo Clown

Sittin' In The Lap Of Luxury *19*
State I'm In

Stop Lookin' For Someone Else
Variety Is The Spice Of Life

LOUISIANA'S LE ROUX — see LE ROUX

LOVE   '66
Rock group from Los Angeles. Core members from 1966-68: Arthur Lee (vocals), John Echols and Bryan MacLean (guitars) and Ken Forssi (bass). In 1969, Lee assembled a new lineup featuring Jay Donnellan (guitar), Frank Fayad (bass) and George Suranovich (drums). Forssi died of cancer on 1/5/98 (age 63). MacLean died of a heart attack on 12/25/98 (age 52).

5/14/66	57	18	©	1	**Love**			$50	Elektra 74001
2/11/67	80	11	©	2	**Da Capo**			$40	Elektra 74005
1/6/68	154	15	©	3	**Forever Changes**			$40	Elektra 74013
9/6/69	102	12	©	4	**Four Sail**			$30	Elektra 74049
12/27/69+	176	5		5	**Out Here**			$30	Blue Thumb 9000 [2]
9/5/70	142	7		7	**Revisited**		[G]	$25	Elektra 74058
12/26/70	184	3	©	7	**False Start**			$25	Blue Thumb 8822

Abalony (5)
Alone Again Or (3,6) *99*
Always See Your Face (4)
And More (1)
Andmoreagain (3,6)
Anytime (7)
August (4)
Between Clark And Hilldale (3)
Bummer In The Summer (3)
Can't Explain (1)
Car Lights On In The Day Time Blues (5)

Castle, The (2)
Colored Balls Falling (1)
Daily Planet (3)
Discharged (5)
Doggone (5)
Dream (4)
Emotions (1)
Everlasting First (7)
Feel Daddy Feel Good (7)
Flying (1)
Gather Round (5)
Gazing (1)

Gimi A Little Break (7)
Good Humor Man (3)
Good Times (4,6)
Hey Joe (1,6)
House Is Not A Motel (3)
I Still Wonder (5)
I'll Pray For You (5)
I'm Down (5)
I'm With You (4)
Instra-Mental (5)
Keep On Shining (7)
Listen To My Song (5)

Live And Let Live (3)
Love Is Coming (7)
Love Is More Than Words Or Better Late Than Never (5)
Message To Pretty (1)
Mushroom Clouds (1)
My Flash On You (1)
Nice To Be (5)
No Matter What You Do (1)
Nothing (4)
Old Man (3)

Orange Skies (2,6)
Que Vida (2)
Red Telephone (3)
Revelation (2)
Ride That Vibration (7)
Robert Montgomery (4)
Run To The Top (5)
She Comes In Colors (2,6)
Signed D.C. (1,5,6)
Singing Cowboy (4)
Slick Dick (7)

Softly To Me (1,6)
Stand Out (5,7)
Stephanie Knows Who (2)
Talking In My Sleep (4)
Willow Willow (5)
You Are Something (5)
You'll Be Following (1)
You Set The Scene (3,6)
Your Friend And Mine - Neil's Song (4,6)
Your Mind And We Belong Together (6)

LOVE, G., & Special Sauce   '99
Born on 10/3/72 in Philadelphia. Blues singer/guitarist. Special Sauce is bassist Jim Prescott and drummer Jeff Clemens.

10/7/95	122	1	©	1	**Coast To Coast Motel**			$10	Okeh 67152
11/15/97	120	2	©	2	**Yeah, It's That Easy**			$10	Okeh 67784
8/21/99	113	7	©	3	**Philadelphonic**			$10	Okeh 69746
5/12/01	138	2	©	4	**Electric Mile**			$10	Okeh 61420

Around The World (Thank You) (3)
Bye Bye Baby (1)
Chains #3 (1)
Coming Home (1)
Do It For Free (3)
Dreamin' (3)
Electric Mile (4)
Everybody (1)
Free At Last (4)

Friday Night (Hundred Dollar Bill) (3)
Gimme Some Lovin' (3)
Honor And Harmony (3)
Hopeless Case (4)
100 Magic Rings (4)
I-76 (2)
Kick Drum (3)
Kiss And Tell (1)
Lay Down The Law (2)

Leaving The City (1)
Love (3)
Making Amends (2)
Nancy (1)
Night Of The Living Dead (4)
No Turning Back (3)
Numbers (1)
Parasite (4)
Poison (4)
Praise Up (4)

Pull The Wool (2)
Rain Jam (4)
Recipe (1)
Relax (3)
Roaches (3)
Rock & Roll (Shouts Out Back To The Rappers) (3)
Rodeo Clowns (3)
Sara's Song (4)
Shy Girl (4)

Slipped Away (The Ballad Of Lauretha Vaird) (2)
Small Fish (4)
Soda Pop (1)
Sometimes (1)
Stepping Stones (2)
Sweet Sugar Mama (1)
Take You There (4)
Tomorrow Night (1)
200 Years (2)

Unified (4)
When We Meet Again (2)
Willow Tree (2)
Yeah, It's That Easy (2)
You Shall See (2)

LOVE, Monie   '91
Born Simone Johnson on 7/2/70 in London. Female rapper.

| 11/24/90+ | 109 | 12 | © | **Down To Earth** | | | $10 | Warner 26358 |

R U Single / Down 2 Earth / It's A Shame (My Sister) 26 / Pups Lickin' Bone / Swiney Swiney
Dettrimentally Stable / Grandpa's Party / Just Don't Give A Damn / Read Between The Lines
Don't Funk Wid The Mo / I Do As I Please / Monie In The Middle / Ring My Bell

LOVE AND KISSES   '78
Disco studio group assembled by European producer **Alec R. Costandinos**. Singers included Don Daniels, Elaine Hill, Dianne Brooks and Jean Graham.

| 7/30/77 | 135 | 14 | | 1 **Love And Kisses** | | | $12 | Casablanca 7063 |
| 5/13/78 | 85 | 17 | | 2 **How Much, How Much I Love You** | | | $12 | Casablanca 7091 |

Accidental Lover (1) / Beauty And The Beast (2) / How Much, How Much I Love You (2) / I Found Love (Now That I've Found You) (1) / Maybe (2)

LOVE AND MONEY   '89
Pop trio from Scotland: James Grant (guitar, vocals), Bobby Paterson (bass) and Paul McGeechan (keyboards). Drummer Stuart Kerr of the group **Texas** was an early member.

| 3/25/89 | 175 | 7 | © | **Strange Kind Of Love** | | | $10 | Mercury 836498 |

Avalanche / **Hallelujah Man** 75 / Jocelyn Square / Shape Of Things To Come / Up Escalator
Axis Of Love / Inflammable / Razorsedge / Strange Kind Of Love / Walk The Last Mile

LOVE AND ROCKETS   '89
Pop-rock trio formed in England: **Daniel Ash** (guitar, vocals), David Jay (bass) and Kevin Haskins (drums).

11/1/86+	72	30	©	1 **Express**			$10	Big Time 6011
10/31/87+	64	28	©	2 **Earth.Sun.Moon**			$10	Big Time 6058
5/20/89	14	26	● ©	3 **Love And Rockets**			$10	Beggars Banquet 9715
4/6/96	172	1	©	4 **Sweet F.A.**			$10	American 43058

All In My Mind (1) / Here Come The Comedown (4) / Life In Laralay (1) / No Words No More (3) / Spiked (4) / Welcome Tomorrow (2)
American Dream (1) / Here On Earth (2) / Light, The (2) / Pearl (4) / Sun, The (2) / Words Of A Fool (1)
Ball Of Confusion (1) / I Feel Speed (3) / Love Me (1) / Purest Blue (3) / Sweet F.A. (4) / Yin And Yang The Flower Pot
Bound For Hell (3) / It Could Be Sunshine (1) / Mirror People (2) / Rain Bird (2) / Sweet Lover Hangover (4) / Man (1)
Clean (4) / Judgement Day (4) / Motorcycle (3) / Rock And Roll Babylon (3) / Teardrop Collector (3) / Youth (2)
Everybody Wants To Go To / ****(Jungle Law) (3) / Natacha (4) / Sad And Beautiful World (4) / Telephone Is Empty (2)
Heaven (2) / Kundalini Express (1) / **No Big Deal** (3) 82 / Shelf Life (4) / Use Me (4)
Fever (4) / Lazy (2) / No New Tale To Tell (2) / **So Alive** (3) 3 / Waiting For The Flood (2)

LOVE CHILDS AFRO CUBAN BLUES BAND   '75
Disco studio group assembled by **Michael Zager**.

| 7/12/75 | 168 | 5 | | **Out Among 'Em** | | [I] | $12 | Roulette 3016 |

Ask Me / Black Skin Blue Eyed Boys / Honeybee / **Life And Death In G&A** 90 / Where Do We Go From Here
Bang Bang / Get Dancin' / Jerry's Theme / Once You Get Started

LOVE/HATE   '90
Rock group from Los Angeles: Jizzy Pearl (vocals), Jon Love (guitar), Skid Rose (bass) and Joey Gold (drums).

| 7/14/90 | 154 | 5 | © | **Blackout In The Red Room** | | | $10 | Columbia 45263 |

Blackout In The Red Room / Mary Jane / She's An Angel / Straightjacket / Why Do You Think They Call It
Fuel To Run / One More Round / Slave Girl / Tumbleweed / Dope?
Hell, Ca., Pop. 4 / Rock Queen / Slutsy Tipsy

LOVELESS, Patty   '94
Born Patricia Ramey on 1/4/57 in Pikesville, Kentucky. Country singer/songwriter.

9/28/91	151	11	©	1 **Up Against My Heart**			$10	MCA 10336
5/8/93+	63	45	▲ ©	2 **Only What I Feel**			$10	Epic 53236
9/10/94	60	46	▲ ©	3 **When Fallen Angels Fly**			$10	Epic 64188
2/10/96	86	43	▲ ©	4 **The Trouble With The Truth**			$10	Epic 67269
10/18/97	68	16	● ©	5 **Long Stretch Of Lonesome**			$10	Epic 67997
4/10/99	99	8	©	6 **Classics**		[G]	$10	Epic 69809
9/16/00	126	2	©	7 **Strong Heart**			$10	Epic 69880

All I Need (Is Not To Need You) (2) / High On Love (5) / If You Don't Want Me (1) / Nothin' But The Wheel (2,6) / **That's The Kind Of Mood I'm** / You Don't Even Know Who I
Blame It On Your Heart (2,6) / How About You (2) / Jealous Bone (1) / Old Weakness (Coming On / **In** (7) 71 / Am (3,6)
Can't Get Enough (6) 96 / How Can I Help You Say / Key Of Love (7) / Strong) (3) / Thirsty (7) / You Don't Get No More (7)
Can't Stop Myself From Loving / Goodbye (2,6) / Last Thing On My Mind (7) / Over My Shoulder (3) / Thousand Times A Day (4) / You Don't Know How Lucky
You (1) / I Already Miss You (Like You're / Like Water Into Wine (5) / Party Ain't Over Yet (5) / To Feel That Way At All (4) / You Are (2)
Everybody's Equal In The Eyes / Already Gone) (1) / Lonely Too Long (4,6) / Pieces On The Ground (7) / To Have You Back Again (5) / You Don't Seem To Miss Me
Of Love (4) / I Came Straight To You (1) / Long Stretch Of Lonesome (5) / She Drew A Broken Heart (4) / Too Many Memories (5) / (5,6)
Feelin' Good About Feelin' Bad / I Don't Want To Feel Like That / Love Builds The Bridges (Pride / She Never Stopped Loving Him / Trouble With The Truth (4) / You Will (2)
(3) / (5) / Builds The Walls) (2) / (7) / Waitin' For The Phone To Ring / You're So Cool (7)
God Will (1) / I Just Wanna Be Loved By You / Mr. Man In The Moon (2) / Ships (3) / (1)
Halfway Down (3) / (6) / My Heart Will Never Break This / Someday I Will Lead The / What's A Broken Heart (2)
Handful Of Dust (3) / I Miss Who I Was (With You) / Way Again (7) / Parade (4) / When The Fallen Angels Fly (3)
He Hurt Me Bad (1) / (4) / My Kind Of Woman, My Kind Of / Strong Heart (7) / Where I'm Bound (5)
Here I Am (3,6) / I Try To Think About Elvis (3,6) / Man (6) / Tear-Stained Letter (4) / You Can Feel Bad (4,6)
If It's The Last Thing I Do (1) / Nobody Loves You Like I Do (1) / That's Exactly What I Mean (5)

LOVERBOY   '82
Rock group formed in Canada: Mike Reno (vocals), **Paul Dean** (guitar), Doug Johnson (keyboards), Scott Smith (bass) and Matt Frenette (drums). Smith drowned on 11/30/2000 (age 45).

1/31/81	13	105	▲² ©	1 **Loverboy**			$10	Columbia 36762
11/14/81+	7	122	▲⁴ ©	2 **Get Lucky**			$10	Columbia 37638
7/2/83	7	39	▲² ©	3 **Keep It Up**			$10	Columbia 38703
9/14/85	13	44	▲² ©	4 **Lovin' Every Minute Of It**			$10	Columbia 39953
9/12/87	42	21	● ©	5 **Wildside**			$10	Columbia 40893
12/23/89	189	2	©	6 **Big Ones**		[G]	$10	Columbia 45411

Ain't Looking For Love (2) / Chance Of A Lifetime (3) / Emotional (2) / **Hot Girls In Love** (3,6) 11 / **Kid Is Hot Tonite** (1,6) 55 / **Lovin' Every Minute Of It**
Always On My Mind (1) / D.O.A. (1) / For You (6) / It Don't Matter (1) / Lady Of The 80's (1) / (4,6) 9
Break It To Me Gently (5) / **Dangerous** (4) 65 / Friday Night (4) / It's Never Easy (3) / **Lead A Double Life** (4) 68 / Lucky Ones (2,6)
Bullet In The Chamber (4) / Destination Heartbreak (4) / Gangs In The Street (2) / It's Your Life (2) / Little Girl (1) / Meltdown (3)
Can't Get Much Better (5) / Don't Let Go (5) / Hometown Hero (5) / Jump (2) / Love Will Rise Again (5) / **Notorious** (5,6) 38

LOVERBOY — Cont'd

One-Sided Love Affair (3)
Passion Pit (3)
Prime Of Your Life (3)
Prissy Prissy (1)

Queen Of The Broken Hearts (3) *34*
Read My Lips (5)
Steal The Thunder (4)
Strike Zone (3)

Take Me To The Top (2)
Teenage Overdose (1)
That's Where My Money Goes (5)
This Could Be The Night (4) *10*

Too Hot (6) *84*
Too Much Too Soon (4)
Turn Me Loose (1,6) *35*
Walkin' On Fire (5)
Watch Out (2)

When It's Over (2) *26*
Wildside (5)
Working For The Weekend (2,6) *29*

LOVE SPIT LOVE   '94

Rock group featuring brothers/former **Psychedelic Furs** Richard (vocals) and Tim (bass) Butler, with Richard Fortus (guitar) and Frank Ferrer (drums).

| 10/8/94 | 195 | 1 | © | Love Spit Love | $10 | Imago 21030 |

Am I Wrong *83*
Change In The Weather

Codeine
Green

Half A Life
Jigsaw

More
Please

Seventeen
St. Mary's Gate

Superman
Wake Up

LOVETT, Lyle   '96

Born on 11/1/56 in Houston; raised in Klein, Texas. Country singer/songwriter/guitarist. Acted in several movies. Married to actress Julia Roberts from 1993-95.

2/20/88	117	14	●	©	1	Pontiac	$10	MCA/Curb 42028
2/18/89	62	21	●	©	2	Lyle Lovett and his Large Band	$10	MCA/Curb 42263
4/18/92	57	34	●	©	3	Joshua Judges Ruth	$10	Curb 10475
10/15/94	26	13	●	©	4	I Love Everybody	$10	Curb/MCA 10808
7/6/96	24	16	●	©	5	The Road To Ensenada	$10	Curb/MCA 11409
10/10/98	55	7	©	6	Step Inside This House	$15	Curb 11831 [2]
7/17/99	94	9	©	7	Live In Texas	[L]	$10	Curb 11964

Ain't It Somethin' (4)
All My Love Is Gone (3)
Babes In The Woods (6)
Ballad Of The Snow Leopard And The Tanqueray Cowboy (6)
Baltimore (3)
Bears (4)
Black And Blue (1)
Blues Walk (2)
Christmas Morning (5)
Church (3,7)
Closing Time (7)
Creeps Like Me (4)
Cryin' Shame (2)
Don't Touch My Hat (5)
Family Reserve (3)
Fat Babies (4)
Fat Girl (4)

Fiona (5)
Flyin' Shoes (6)
Flyswatter/Ice Water (Monty Trenckmann's Blues) (3)
Give Back My Heart (1)
Glory Of Love (medley) (6)
Good Intentions (2)
Good-bye To Carolina (4)
Hello Grandma (4)
Her First Mistake (5)
Here I Am (2,7)
Highway Kind (6)
I Can't Love You Anymore (5)
I Know You Know (2)
I Love Everybody (4)
I Loved You Yesterday (1)
I Married Her Just Because She Looks Like You (2)

I Think You Know What I Mean (4)
I'll Come Knockin' (6)
I've Been To Memphis (3,7)
I've Got The Blues (4)
I've Had Enough (6)
If I Had A Boat (1,7)
If I Needed You (6)
If You Were To Wake Up (2)
It Ought To Be Easier (5)
Just The Morning (4)
L.A. County (1)
La To The Left (4)
Lonely In Love (6)
Long Tall Texan (5)
Lungs (6)
Memphis Midnight/Memphis Morning (6)
M-o-n-e-y (1,7)

Moon On My Shoulder (4)
More Pretty Girls Than One (6)
Nobody Knows Me (2,7)
North Dakota (3,7)
Old Friend (4)
Once Is Enough (2)
Penguins (4,7)
Pontiac (1)
Private Conversation (5)
Promises (5)
Record Lady (4)
Road To Ensenada (5)
Rollin' By (6)
She Makes Me Feel Good (3)
She's Already Made Up Her Mind (3)
She's Hot To Go (1)
She's Leaving Me Because She Really Wants To (3)

She's No Lady (1,7)
Simple Song (1)
Since The Last Time (3)
Skinny Legs (4)
Sleepwalking (6)
Sonja (4)
Stand By Your Man (2)
Step Inside This House (6)
Teach Me About Love (6)
Texas River Song (6)
Texas Trilogy: Bosque County Romance (6)
Texas Trilogy: Daybreak (6)
Texas Trilogy: Train Ride (6)
That's Right (You're Not From Texas) (5,7)
They Don't Like Me (4)
Walk Through The Bottomland (1)

West Texas Highway (6)
What Do You Do (2,7)
Which Way Does That Old Pony Run (2)
Who Loves You Better (5)
Wild Women Don't Get The Blues (7)
You Can't Resist It (7)
You've Been So Good Up To Now (3)

LOVE UNLIMITED   '74

R&B vocal trio from San Pedro, California: sisters Glodean and Linda James, with Diane Taylor. Glodean was married to **Barry White** from 1974-88.

4/29/72	151	12		1	Love Unlimited	$15	Uni 73131
9/8/73+	3	44	●	2	Under The Influence Of...	$12	20th Century 414
10/12/74	85	27		3	In Heat	$12	20th Century 443
2/26/77	192	3	©	4	He's All I've Got	$12	Unlimited Gold 101

Another Chance (1)
Are You Sure (1)
Fragile - Handle With Care (4)
He's All I've Got (4)
He's Mine (No, You Can't Have Him) (4)
I Belong To You (3) *27*
I Can't Let Him Down (4)

I Did It For Love (4)
I Guess I'm Just Another Girl In Love (4)
I Needed Love - You Were There (3)
I Should Have Known (1)

I'll Be Yours Forever More (1)
If This Would Ever End (4)
Is It Really True Boy - Is It Really Me (1)
It May Be Winter Outside, **(But In My Heart It's Spring)** (2) *83*
Love's Theme (2,3) *1*

Lovin' You, That's All After (2)
Move Me No Mountain (3)
Never, Never Say Goodbye (4)
Oh I Should Say, It's Such A Beautiful Day (2)
Oh Love, Well We Finally Made It (2)

Say It Again (2)
Share A Little Love In Your Heart (3)
Someone Really Cares For You (2)
Together (1)
Under The Influence Of Love (2) *76*

Walkin' In The Rain With The One I Love (1) *14*
Whisper You Love Me (4)
Yes, We Finally Made It (2)

LOVE UNLIMITED ORCHESTRA   '74

Studio orchestra assembled by **Barry White**. Backing group for **Love Unlimited** and White's solo records. **Kenny G** was a member at age 17.

2/9/74	8	25	●	©	1	Rhapsody In White	[I]	$12	20th Century 433
7/6/74	96	10		2	Together Brothers	[I-S]	$12	20th Century 101
11/9/74+	28	27	●	©	3	White Gold	[I]	$12	20th Century 458
1/10/76	92	15		4	Music Maestro Please	[I]	$12	20th Century 480
10/30/76	123	8		5	My Sweet Summer Suite	[I]	$12	20th Century 517

Alive And Well (2)
Always Thinking Of You (3)
Are You Sure (5)
Baby Blues (1)
Barry's Love (Part I & II) (3)
Barry's Theme (1)
Blues Concerto (5)
Brazilian Love Song (5)
Bring It On Up (4)
Can't Seem To Find Him (2)

Do Drop In (2)
Don't Take It Away From Me (1)
Dream On (2)
Dreamin' (2,3)
Find The Man Bros. (2)
Forever In Love (4)
Get Away (4)
Give Up Your Love Girl (4)
Here Comes The Man (2)
Honey, Please Can't You See (2)

I Feel Love Coming On (1)
I Wanna Stay (4)
I'm Falling In Love With You (5)
It's Only What I Feel (4)
Just Like A Baby (3)
Just Living It Up (3)
Killer Don't Do It (2)
Killer's Back (2)
Killer's Lullaby (2)
Love's Theme (1) *1*

Makin' Believe That It's You (4)
Midnight And You (1)
Midnight Groove (4)
My Sweet Summer Suite (5) *48*
Only You Can Make Me Blue (3)
People Of Tomorrow Are The Children Of Today (1)
Power Of Love (3)

Rhapsody In White (1) *63*
Rip, The (2)
Satin Soul (3) *22*
So Nice To Hear (2)
Somebody's Gonna Off The Man (2)
Spanish Lei (3)
Stick Up (2)
Strange Games & Things (5)

Together Brothers, Theme From (2)
What A Groove (1)
You Gotta Case (2)
You I Adore (5)
You Make Me Feel Like This (When You Touch Me) (3)
You're All I Want (4)
You've Given Me Something (5)

LOVICH, Lene   '80

Born Lili Marlene Premilovich on 3/30/49 in Detroit; raised in England. Singer/actress. Acted in the movies *Cha-Cha* and *Mata Hari*.

8/4/79	137	10	©	1	Stateless	$12	Stiff 36102
3/8/80	94	8	©	2	Flex	$12	Stiff 36308
1/15/83	188	4		3	No-Man's-Land	$12	Stiff 38399

Angels (2)
Bird Song (2)
Blue Hotel (3)
Egg Head (2)
Faces (3)
Freeze, The (2)

Home (1)
I Think We're Alone Now (1)
It's You, Only You (Mein Schmerz) (3)
Joan (2)
Lucky Number (1)

Maria (3)
Momentary Breakdown (1)
Monkey Talk (2)
Night, The (2)
One In 1,000,000 (1)
Rocky Road (3)

Savages (3)
Say When (1)
Sister Video (3)
Sleeping Beauty (1)
Special Star (3)
Telepathy (1)

Tonight (1)
Too Tender (To Touch) (1)
Walking Low (3)
What Will I Do Without You (2)
Wonderful One (2)
Writing On The Wall (1)
You Can't Kill Me (2)

LOVIN' SPOONFUL, The '66

Pop-rock group formed in New York City: John Sebastian (vocals, guitar), Zal Yanovsky (guitar), Steve Boone (bass) and Joe Butler (drums). Sebastian had been with the Even Dozen Jug Band; did session work at Elektra. Yanovsky and Sebastian were members of the Mugwumps with Mama Cass Elliot and Denny Doherty (later with The Mamas & The Papas). Yanovsky replaced by Jerry Yester (keyboards) in 1967. Disbanded in 1968. Inducted into the Rock and Roll Hall of Fame in 2000.

DEBUT	PEAK	WKS	CD	#	Album Title	Sym	$	Label & Number
12/4/65+	32	35	©	1	Do You Believe In Magic		$30	Kama Sutra 8050
4/2/66	10	31	©	2	Daydream		$30	Kama Sutra 8051
9/24/66	126	9	©	3	What's Up, Tiger Lily?	[S]	$30	Kama Sutra 8053
12/17/66+	14	26	©	4	Hums Of The Lovin' Spoonful		$30	Kama Sutra 8054
3/18/67	3	52	●	5	The Best Of The Lovin' Spoonful	[G]	$25	Kama Sutra 8056
4/15/67	160	5	©	6	You're A Big Boy Now	[S]	$25	Kama Sutra 8058
1/20/68	118	7	©	7	Everything Playing		$25	Kama Sutra 8061
3/30/68	156	5		8	The Best Of The Lovin' Spoonful, Volume 2	[G]	$25	Kama Sutra 8064
4/24/76	183	3		9	The Best...Lovin' Spoonful	[G]	$20	Kama Sutra 2608 [2]

Bald Headed Lena (2)
Barbara's Theme (6)
Bes' Friends (4)
Big Noise From Speonk (2)
Blues In The Bottle (1,5)
Boredom (7,8)
Butchie's Tune (2,5)
Close Your Eyes (7)
Coconut Grove (4,9)
Cool Million (3)
Darlin' Companion (4,8)
Darling Be Home Soon (6,8,9) **15**
Day Blues (2)

Daydream (2,5,9) **2**
Did You Ever Have To Make Up Your Mind? (1,5,9) **2**
Didn't Want To Have To Do It (2,5,9)
Dixieland Big Boy (6)
Do You Believe In Magic (1,5,9) **9**
Fishin' Blues (1,3)
Forever (2)
4 Eyes (4,9)
Full Measure (4,8) **87**
Girl, Beautiful Girl (Barbara's Theme) (6)

Gray Prison Blues (2)
Henry Thomas (4)
It's Not Time Now (2)
Jug Band Music (2,5,9)
Kite Chase (6)
Let The Boy Rock And Roll (2)
Letter To Barbara (4)
Lonely (Amy's Theme) (6)
Lookin' To Spy (3)
Lovin' You (4,8,9)
March (6)
Miss Thing's Thang (6)
Money (7,8,9) **48**
My Gal (1)

Nashville Cats (4,8,9) **8**
Never Going Back (9) **73**
Night Owl Blues (1,5,9)
Old Folks (7,8)
On The Road Again (1)
Only Pretty, What A Pity (7)
Other Side Of This Life (1)
POW (3)
POW Revisited (3)
Peep Show Percussion (6)
Phil's Love Theme (3)
Priscilla Millionaira (7)
Rain On The Roof (4,8,9) **10**
Respoken (3)

She Is Still A Mystery (7,8,9) **27**
Six O'Clock (7,8,9) **18**
Speakin' Of Spoken (3)
Sportin' Life (1)
Summer In The City (4,5,9) **1**
There She Is (2)
Till I Run With You (9)
Try A Little Bit (7)
Try And Be Happy (6)
Unconscious Minuet (3)
Voodoo In My Basement (4)
Warm Baby (2,9)
Wash Her Away (6)

What's Up, Tiger Lily? (End Title) (3)
Wild About My Lovin' (1,5)
You Baby (1)
You Didn't Have To Be So Nice (2,5,9) **10**
You're A Big Boy Now (6)
Younger Generation (7,8,9)
Younger Girl (1,5,9)

LOWE, Nick '79

Born on 3/25/49 in Walton, Surrey, England. Pop-rock singer/songwriter/guitarist. Member of Rockpile. Married to Carlene Carter from 1979-90.

DEBUT	PEAK	WKS	CD	#	Album Title	Sym	$	Label & Number
4/29/78	127	10	©	1	Pure Pop For Now People		$12	Columbia 35329
7/14/79	31	22	©	2	Labour Of Lust	C:#44/8	$12	Columbia 36087
2/20/82	50	14	©	3	Nick The Knife		$10	Columbia 37932
4/2/83	129	7	©	4	The Abominable Showman		$10	Columbia 38589
6/23/84	113	12	©	5	Nick Lowe & His Cowboy Outfit		$10	Columbia 39371
9/21/85	119	12	©	6	The Rose Of England		$10	Columbia 39958
					NICK LOWE & HIS COWBOY OUTFIT (above 2)			
4/7/90	182	3	©	7	Party Of One		$10	Reprise 26132

All Men Are Liars (7)
American Squirm (2)
Awesome (4)
Ba Doom (3)
Big Kick, Plain Scrap (2)
Bobo Ska Diddle Daddle (6)
Born Fighter (2)
Break Away (5)
Burning (4)
Chicken And Feathers (4)
Cool Reaction (4)
Couldn't Love You (Any More Than I Do) (3)
Cracking Up (2)
Cruel To Be Kind (2) **12**
Darlin' Angel Eyes (6)

Dose Of You (2)
Everyone (6)
Gai-Gin Man (7)
Gee And The Rick And The Three Card Trick (5)
God's Gift To Women (5)
Half A Boy And Half A Man (5)
Heart (3)
Heart Of The City (1)
(Hey Big Mouth) Stand Up And Say That (5)
Honeygun (7)
(Hope To God) I'm Right (6)
How Do You Talk To An Angel (4)
I Can Be The One You Love (6)

I Don't Know Why You Keep Me On (7)
I Knew The Bride (When She Use To Rock And Roll) (6) **77**
(I Love The Sound Of) Breaking Glass (1)
(I Want To Build A) Jumbo Ark (7)
Indoor Fireworks (6)
L.A.F.S. (5)
Let Me Kiss Ya (3)
Little Hitler (1)
Live Fast, Love Hard, Die Young (5)
Long Walk Back (6)

Love Like A Glove (5)
Love So Fine (2)
Man Of A Fool (4)
Marie Provost (1)
Maureen (5)
Mess Around With Love (4)
Music For Money (1)
My Heart Hurts (4)
No Reason (1)
Nutted By Reality (1)
One's Too Many (And A Hundred Ain't Enough) (3)
Paid The Price (4)
Queen Of Sheba (3)
Raging Eyes (4)

Raining Raining (3)
Refrigerator White (7)
Rocky Road (7)
Rollers Show (1)
Rose Of England (6)
Saint Beneath The Paint (4)
7 Nights To Rock (6)
She Don't Love Nobody (4)
Shting-Shtang (7)
Skin Deep (2)
So It Goes (1)
Stick It Where The Sun Don't Shine (3)
Switch Board Susan (2)
Tanque-Rae (4)
They Called It Rock (1)

36 Inches High (1)
Time Wounds All Heels (4)
Tonight (1)
Too Many Teardrops (3)
We Want Action (4)
What's Shakin' On The Hill (7)
Who Was That Man? (7)
Wish You Were Here (4)
Without Love (2)
You Got The Look I Like (7)
You'll Never Get Me Up (In One Of Those) (5)
Zulu Kiss (3)

LOWRY, Mark '01

Born on 6/24/58 in Houston. Christian comedian.

DEBUT	PEAK	WKS	CD	#	Album Title	Sym	$	Label & Number
5/5/01	130	1	©		On Broadway	[C]	$10	Spring House 42270

Bein' Happy
Comedy - The Home Depot/An Atheists' Faith/Mary Raising Jesus
Comedy - Old Age Hair
Comedy - Singing at Independent Fundamental Baptist Churches
Comedy - Wal-Mart Commercial

Don't Rain On My Parade
I Cannot Dance Tonight (Because I'm Southern Baptist)
I Thirst

Just A Little While
Let Freedom Ring
Living For Deep Fried Okra
Mary, Did You Know?
Meeting In The Air

Mom
On Broadway
One (Singular Sensation)
Walk On The Water
Whole New World

LOX, The '98

Rap trio from New York City: David Styles, Sean Jacobs and Jason Phillips. Members of Ruff Ryders.

DEBUT	PEAK	WKS	CD	#	Album Title	Sym	$	Label & Number
1/31/98	3	22	▲	1	Money, Power & Respect		$10	Bad Boy 73015
2/12/00	5	16	●	2	We Are The Streets		$10	Ruff Ryders 490599
								Y'All Fucked Up Now (2)

All For The Love (1)
Bitches From Eastwick (1)
Blood Pressure (2)
Breathe Easy (2)
Bring It On (2)
Can I Live (2)

Can't Stop, Won't Stop (1)
Everybody Wanna Rat (1)
Felony Niggas (2)
Fuck You (2)
Get This $ (1)
Goin' Be Some Sh*t (1)

Heist (Part I) (1)
I Wanna Thank You (1)
If You Know (2)
If You Think I'm Jiggy (1)
Let's Start Rap Over (1)
Livin' The Life (1)

Money, Power & Respect (1) **17**
Not To Be F**ked With (1)
Recognize (2)
Ryde Or Die, Bitch (2) **73**
Scream L.O.X. (2)

So Right (1)
U Told Me (2)
We Are The Streets (2)
We'll Always Love Big Poppa (1)
Wild Out (2)

L7 '94

Female punk-rock group from Los Angeles: Suzi Gardner (guitar, vocals), Donita Sparks (guitar, vocals), Jennifer Finch (bass, vocals) and Dee Plakas (drums). Finch left in August 1996.

DEBUT	PEAK	WKS	CD	#	Album Title	Sym	$	Label & Number
8/8/92	160	7	©	1	Bricks Are Heavy		$10	Slash 26784
7/30/94	117	7	©	2	Hungry For Stink		$10	Slash 45624
3/15/97	172	1	©	3	The Beauty Process: Triple Platinum		$10	Slash 46327

Andres (2)
Bad Things (2)
Baggage (2)
Beauty Process (3)
Bitter Wine (3)
Bomb, The (2)

Can I Run (2)
Diet Pill (1)
Drama (3)
Everglade (1)
Freak Magnet (2)
Fuel My Fire (2)

I Need (3)
Lorenza, Giada, Alessandra (3)
Masses Are Asses (3)
Me, Myself & I (3)
Monster (1)
Moonshine (3)

Mr. Integrity (1)
Must Have More (3)
Non-Existent Patricia (3)
Off The Wagon (1)
One More Thing (1)
Pretend We're Dead (1)

Questioning My Sanity (2)
Riding With A Movie Star (3)
Scrap (1)
She Has Eyes (3)
Shirley (2)
Shitlist (1)

Slide (1)
Stuck Here Again (2)
Talk Box (2)
This Ain't Pleasure (1)
Wargasm (1)

DEBUT	PEAK	WKS	RIAA	CD	ARTIST — Album Title	Catalog	Sym	$	Label & Number

LSG '97

All-star R&B trio: **Gerald Levert**, **Keith Sweat** and **Johnny Gill**.

| 11/29/97 | 4 | 42 | ▲ | © | **Levert - Sweat - Gill** | | | $10 | EastWest 62125 |

All The Times · Door #1 · Let A Playa Get His Freak On · **My Body** *4* · Round & Round · Where Would We Go
Curious · Drove Me To Tears · Love Hurts · My Side Of The Bed · Where Did I Go Wrong · You Got Me

L.T.D. '78

R&B-funk group from Greensboro, North Carolina: brothers **Jeffrey Osborne** (vocals, drums) and Billy Osborne (keyboards), with John McGhee (guitar), Abraham Miller and Lorenzo Carnegie (saxophones), Jimmie Davis (keyboards), Carle Vickers (trumpet), Jake Riley (trombone), Henry Davis (bass) and Alvino Bennett (drums). The Osborne brothers left in 1980. Leslie Wilson and Andre Ray joined as vocalists. L.T.D.: Love, Togetherness and Devotion.

8/21/76	52	30		© 1	**Love To The World**			$12	A&M 4589
8/13/77+	21	34	●	© 2	**Something To Love**			$12	A&M 4646
6/17/78	18	26	▲	© 3	**Togetherness**			$12	A&M 4705
7/21/79	29	24	●	© 4	**Devotion**			$12	A&M 4771
9/6/80	28	28		© 5	**Shine On**			$12	A&M 4819
11/28/81+	83	12		© 6	**Love Magic**			$12	A&M 4881

Age Of The Showdown (2) · Feel It (4) · Lady Love (5) · Make Someone Smile, Today! (2) · **Shine On** (5) *40* · Where Did We Go Wrong (5)
April Love (6) · Get Your It Together (1) · Let The Music Keep Playing (1) · · Sometimes (4) · Will Love Grow (5)
Burnin' Hot (6) · Getaway (3) · Let's All Live And Give Together · Material Things (2) · Stand Up L.T.D. (4) · (Won't Cha) Stay With Me (2)
Concentrate On You (3) · **Holding On (When Love Is** · (3) · **Never Get Enough Of Your** · Stay On The One (6) · Word, The (1)
Cuttin' It Up (6) · **Gone)** (1) · **Love Ballad** (1) *20* · **Love** (2) *56* · Stranger (4) · You Come First At Last (2)
Dance 'N' Sing 'N' (4) · If You're In Need (2) · Love Is What You Need (5) · Now (6) · Time For Pleasure (1) · You Fooled Me (3)
Don't Stop Loving Me Now (1) · It Must End (6) · Love Magic (6) · One On One (4) · Together Forever (3) · You Save Me (5)
Don'tcha Know (5) · It's Time To Be Real (3) · **Love To The World** (1) *91* · Promise You'll Stay (4) · We Both Deserve Each Other's · You Must Have Known I
(Every Time I Turn Around) · Jam (3) · Love To The World Prayer (1) · Say That You'll Be Mine (4) · Love (3) · Needed Love (3)
Back In Love Again (2) *4* · Kickin' Back (6) · Lovers Everywhere (5) · Share My Love (4) · We Party Hearty (2)

L'TRIMM '88

Female rap duo: Tigra (from New York) and Bunny D. (from Chicago).

| 11/5/88 | 132 | 16 | | © | **Grab It!** | | | $10 | Atlantic 81925 |

Better Yet L'Trimm · Cuttie Pie · Grab It · Sexy
Cars With The Boom *54* · Don't Come To My House · He's A Mutt · We Can Rock The Beat

LUBOFF, Norman, Choir '55

Born on 5/14/17 in Chicago. Died of cancer on 9/22/87 (age 70). Composer/conductor.

| 10/15/55 | 14 | 3 | | 1 | **Songs Of The West** | | | $20 | Columbia 657 |

EP: Columbia B-2003 (#14); LP: Columbia CL-657 (#15).

7/14/56	19	2		© 2	**Songs Of The South**			$20	Columbia 860
5/27/57	19	4		© 3	**Calypso Holiday**			$20	Columbia 1000
1/13/58	22	1		© 4	**Songs Of Christmas**		[X]	$20	Columbia 926

Christmas charts: 57/65, 44/66.

| 12/19/64 | 28ˣ | 2 | | © 5 | **Christmas with the Norman Luboff Choir** | | [X] | $15 | RCA Victor 2941 |

A La Nanita Nana (4) · Dance De Limbo (3) · Here We Come A-Wassailing · Little Drummer Boy (5) · Red River Valley (1) · Un Deux Trois (2)
Balance (3) · Dansez Calenda (3) · (medley) (4,5) · My Old Kentucky Home (2) · Salangadou (3) · Wassail, Wassail All Over The
Ballad Of The Boll Weevil (2) · Deck The Hall With Boughs Of · Holly And The Ivy (medley) (4) · Night Herding Song (1) · Santa Claus Is Comin' To Town · Town ..see: Here We Come
Baloo Lammy (medley) (4,5) · Holly (medley) (4,5) · Home On The Range (1) · Nobody Knows The Trouble I've · (5) · A-Wassailing
Bamboo-Tamboo (3) · Deep River (2) · I Must Walk That Lonesome · Seen (2) · Silent Night (4,5) · Water (3)
Black Is The Color Of My True · Do You Hear What I Hear (3) · Valley (2) · O Come, All Ye Faithful (Adeste · Silver Bells (5) · We Three Kings Of Orient Are
Love's Hair (3) · Doney Gal (1) · I Ride An Old Paint (1) · Fideles) (4,5) · Sound De Fire Alarm (3) · (medley) (4)
Bury Me Not On The Lone · Down In The Valley (2) · I Saw Three Ships (medley) (4) · O Holy Night (4,5) · Streets Of Laredo (Cowboy's · What Child Is This? (medley)
Prairie (1) · First Noël (medley) (4,5) · Jingle Bells (5) · O Little Town Of Bethlehem · Lament) (1) · (4)
Calypso Carnival (3) · Fisherman's Song (3) · Joseph Dearest Joseph Mine · (medley) (4,5) · Sweet Lorena (2) · Whence Comes This Rush Of
Carry Me Back To Old Virginny · God Rest Ye Merry, Gentlemen · (medley) (4) · Oh Tannenbaum (medley) (4) · Swing Low Sweet Chariot (2) · Wings (medley) (4,5)
(2) · (medley) (4,5) · Joy To The World (medley) · Old Chisholm Trail (1) · Tender Love (2) · White Christmas (5)
Colorado Trail (1) · Hark! The Herald Angels Sing · (4,5) · Pig Knuckles And Rice (3) · Tumbling Tumbleweeds (1) · Whoopie Ti Yi Yo (1)
Cool Water (1) · (medley) (4,5) · Kemo Kimo (2) · Poor Lonesome Cowboy (1) · Twelve Days Of Christmas · Yellow Bird (3)
Coventry Carol (medley) (4) · Like My Heart (3) · Proposal, The (3) · (medley) (4)

LUCAS '94

Born in 1970 in Copenhagen, Denmark. Male rapper/producer.

| 10/22/94 | 183 | 4 | | © | **Lucacentric** | | | $10 | Big Beat 92467 |

Born · Inflatable People · Muted Trumpet · Spin The Globe · Wau Wau Wau
CityZen · Livin' In A Silicone Dream · Pendulum Swings · Statusphere, Part One & Part · Work In Progress
In It For The Lifelong · **Lucas With The Lid Off** *29* · Red White And Blues · Two

LUCAS, Carrie '79

Born in Los Angeles. R&B singer.

4/23/77	183	5		1	**Simply Carrie**			$12	Soul Train 2220
5/19/79	119	10		2	**Carrie Lucas In Danceland**			$12	Solar 3219
1/31/81	185	3		3	**Portrait Of Carrie**			$12	Solar 3579
9/11/82	180	3		4	**Still In Love**			$12	Solar 60008

Are You Dancing (2) · I Gotta Get Away From Your · I'm Gonna Make You Happy (2) · Just A Memory (4) · Play By Your Rule (1) · Southern Star (2)
Career Girl (3) · Love (1) · Is It A Dream (4) · Keep Smilin' (3) · Rockin' For Your Love (4) · Still In Love (4)
Dance With You (2) *70* · **I Gotta Keep Dancin'** (1) *64* · It's Not What You Got (It's How · Lovin' Is On My Mind (3) · Show Me Where You're Coming · Sweet Love (4)
Danceland (2) · I Just Can't Do Without Your · You Use It) (3) · Me For You (1) · From (4) · Tender (1)
Dreamer (2) · Love (4) · Jammin' Tenderly (Tender Part · Men (4) · Sometimes A Love Goes · Use It Or Lose It (3)
Fashion (3) · I'll Close Loves Door (1) · II) (1) · Men Kiss And Tell (1) · Wrong (2) · What's The Question (1)

LUCY PEARL '00

All-star R&B trio: Raphael Saadiq (of **Tony Toni Toné**), Dawn Robinson (of **En Vogue**) and Ali Shaheed Muhammad (of **A Tribe Called Quest**). Joi replaced Robinson in 2001.

| 6/10/00 | 26 | 21 | ● | © | **Lucy Pearl** | | | $10 | Pookie 78059 |

Can't Stand Your Mother · Don't Mess With My Man · Hollywood · Lucy Pearl's Way · Trippin'
Dance Tonight · Everyday · LaLa · Remember The Times · Without You
Do It For The People · Good Love · Lucy Pearl Tells · They Can't · You

LUDACRIS '00
Born Chris Bridges in 1977 in Atlanta. Male rapper.

| 10/7/00 | 179 | 2 | | © | 1 Ludacris Presents Incognegro .... | | | $10 | Disturbing Tha P. 911 |
| 11/4/00 | 4 | 48↑ ▲² | © | 2 | **Back For The First Time** | | | $10 | Def Jam South 548138 |

Catch Up (1,2)
1st & 10 (1,2)
Game Got Switched (1,2)

Get Off Me (1,2)
Ho (1,2)
Hood Stuck (1,2)

It Wasn't Us (1)
Midnight Train (1)
Mouthing Off (1,2)

Phat Rabbit (2)
Rock And A Hard Place (1)
Southern Hospitality (2)

Stick 'Em Up (2)
U Got A Problem? (1,2)
What's Your Fantasy (1,2)

LUHRMANN, Baz '99
Born in Australia. Directed such movies as *Romeo + Juliet* and *Strictly Ballroom*.

| 3/27/99 | 24 | 14 | ● | © | Something For Everybody .... | | | $10 | Capitol 57636 |

Angel
Aquarius/Let The Sunshine In
Bazmark Fanfare
Che Gelida Manina (Your Tiny Hand Is Frozen)

everybody's free (to wear Sunscreen) The Speech
Song 45
Happy Feet
I'm Losing You

Jupiter
Love Is In The Air
Lovefool
Now Until The Break Of Day
Nutbod

Os Quindos De Ya Ya
Perhaps Perhaps Perhaps
Time After Time
When Doves Cry
Young Hearts Run Free

LUKE '96
Born Luther Campbell in 1960 in Miami. Male rapper. Leader of **The 2 Live Crew** until 1996.

2/29/92	52	17		©	1 **I Got Shit On My Mind**			$10	Luke 91830
6/26/93	54	11		©	2 **In The Nude**			$10	Luke 200
7/30/94	174	3		©	3 **Freak For Life 6996**			$10	Luke 6996
6/1/96	51	11		©	4 **Uncle Luke**			$10	Luther Camp. 161000
4/1/00	140	2		©	5 **Luke's Freak Fest 2000**			$10	Luke 1876

includes "Creeping" by Jiggie, "Baby Be Mine" by **Quad City DJ's**, "Tear It Up" by No Good But So Good, "Loving You" by **Sylvia**; "Can I Holla" by Tightwork; "Lay Your Ass Down" by Underground, "Dirty Bottom" by **Goodie Mob** & No Good, "What We Like" by **95 South**, and "Slob On My Nob" by **Tear Da Club Up Thugs**

| 4/28/01 | 149 | 4 | | © | 6 **Something Nasty** .... | | | $10 | Luke 8250 |

UNCLE LUKE

Ain't Spending Nothing (5)
Ain't That A Bitch Part I & II (1)
All My Ex's (3)
Anal S- (3)
Asshole Naked (4)
B-otch (6)
Bad Land Boogie (2)
Beat Your Lover (3)
Bone (4)
Bounce To Da Beat (4)
Breakdown (1)
Bust A Nut (2,4)
Cisco (1)
Clip On Clicks (3)
Club Rats (5)
Come On (3)
Cool (Some Cool Sh-t) (3)

Could It Be (6)
Cowards In Compton (2)
Do-It Do-It (4)
Do You Hear The Lambs Calling (2)
Dre's Momma Needs A Haircut (2)
Eat The P*ssy (6)
Fakin' Like Gangsters (1)
Fat Girls (6)
Freak For Life (6)
Freak Shawty (5)
Freaky Bitches (4)
Freaky Business (5)
Freestyle Joint (2)
Get Rowdy (5)
Head Head And More Head (1)

Head, Head & More Head Pt. II (2)
Headbanger (2)
Hero, The (2)
H*e Stories (6)
Hoe Surprise (5)
H*es (4)
Holla (6)
Hop, The (2)
I Ain't Bullshittin' Part IV (1)
If It Wasn't 4 Us (6)
It's Your Birthday (3)
JC's Detailed Car Wash (3)
L.L.O.L.M. (2)
Lollipop (6)
Luke Mega Mix (4)

Megamix (1,3)
Menage A Tois Pt. II (2)
Menage A Trois (1)
Movin' Along (3)
Never Forget From Whence You Came (4)
No Rubber (4)
Off Da Hook (4)
Ol' G (4)
One Black And A Bunch Of Dirty White Boys (1)
$100 Bet (3)
Party Don't Start (6)
Pre-Masterbatorial (3)
Pussy Ass Kid And Hoe Ass Play (Payback Is A Mutha Fucker) (1)

R U Ready (4)
Represent (3)
Roll Wit Luke (6)
Save Me From The Devil (6)
Scarred (4) *64*
Shout Outs (4)
Show, The (5,6)
Slippery When Wet (5)
Some Ol Bullsh-t (3)
Sonia (1)
Straight Beef (4)
Strokin' (5)
Suck This D*ck (3)
Take It Off (2)
Talkin' 'Bout (5)
Talkin' Sh*t (6)
Tell Me What You Know (2)

That's How I Feel (3)
We Are The Weave (3)
We Want Big D*ck (6)
We Want Some Head (6)
Wear A Rubber (4)
Welcome To The Quiet Storm (3)
Whatever (2)
Where Them Ho's At (3)
Where's The Ti--ie (3)
Work It Baby (4)
Work It Out (2)
You And Me (1)
You Have Been Bad (3)

I Wanna Rock (1) *73*

LULU '67
Born Marie Lawrie on 11/3/48 in Glasgow, Scotland. Pop singer/actress. Married to Maurice Gibb (of the **Bee Gees**) from 1969-73. Appeared in the 1967 movie *To Sir With Love*.

11/11/67	24	20			1 **To Sir With Love**			$30	Epic 26339
2/21/70	88	14			2 **New Routes**			$15	Atco 310
9/26/81	126	10			3 **Lulu**			$12	Alfa 11006

After All (I Live My Life) (2)
Best Of Both Worlds (1) *32*
Boat That I Row (1)
Can't Hold Out On Love (3)
Day Tripper (1)
Dirty Old Man (2)

Don't Take Love For Granted (3)
Feelin' Alright (2)
I Could Never Miss You (More Than I Do) (3) *18*
If I Were You (3) *44*

If You're Right (3)
In The Morning (2)
Is That You Love (2)
Last Time (3)
Let's Pretend (1)
Love Loves To Love Love (1)
Loving You (3)

Marley Purt Drive (2)
Morning Dew (1) *52*
Mr. Bojangles (2)
Oh Me Oh My (I'm A Fool For You Baby) (2) *22*
People In Love (2)
Rattler (1)

Sweep Around Your Own Back Door (2)
Take Me In Your Arms (And Love Me) (1)
To Love Somebody (1)
To Sir With Love (1) *1*
Where's Eddie (2)

Who's Foolin' Who (3)
You And I (1)
You Are Still A Part Of Me (3)
You Win, I Lose (3

LUNIZ '95
Rap duo from Oakland: Jerold **"Yukmouth"** Ellis and Garrick **"Knumskull"** Husband.

| 7/22/95 | 20 | 31 | ▲ | © | 1 **Operation Stackola** .... | | | $10 | Noo Trybe 40523 |
| 11/29/97 | 34 | 11 | | © | 2 **Lunitik Muzik** .... | | | $10 | Noo Trybe 44966 |

Broke Hos (1)
Broke Niggaz (1)
5150 (1)
Funkin Over Nuthin' (2)
Game (2)

Handcuff Your Hoes (2)
Highest Niggaz In The Industry (2)
Hypnotize (2)
I Got 5 On It (1) *8*

In My Nature (2)
Is It Kool? (2)
Jus Mee & U (2)
Killaz On The Payroll (2)
Mobb Sh.. (2)

My Baby Mamma (2)
900 Blame A Nigga (1)
Operation Stackola (1)
Phillies (2)
Pimps, Playas & Hustlas (1)

Playa Hata (1)
Plead Guilty (1)
Put The Lead On Ya (1)
Sad Millionaire (2)
She's Just A Freak (1)

So Much Drama (1)
20 Bluntz A Day (2)
Y Do Thugz Die (2)
Yellow Brick Road (1)

LUSCIOUS JACKSON '97
Female pop-rock group from New York City: Jill Cunniff (vocals, bass), Gabrielle Glaser (vocals, guitar), Vivian Trimble (keyboards) and Kate Schellenbach (drums). Trimble left in 1998. Group named after the former pro basketball player.

9/10/94	114	4		©	1 **Natural Ingredients**			$10	Grand Royal 28356
11/16/96+	72	32		©	2 **Fever In Fever Out**			$10	Grand Royal 35534
7/17/99	102	6		©	3 **Electric Honey**			$10	Grand Royal 96084

Alien Lover (3)
Angel (1)
Beloved (3)
Christine (3)
Citysong (1)
Country's A Callin' (3)
Deep Shag (1)

Devotion (3)
Don't Look Back (2)
Door (2)
Electric (2)
Energy Sucker (1)
Faith (2)
Fantastic Fabulous (3)

Find Your Mind (1)
Fly (3)
Friends (3)
Gypsy (3)
Here (1)
LP Retreat (3)
Ladyfingers (3)

Lover's Moon (3)
Mood Swing (2)
Naked Eye (2) *36*
Nervous Breakthrough (3)
One Thing (2)
Parade (2)
Pele Merengue (1)

Rock Freak (1)
Rollin' (1)
Sexy Hypnotist (3)
Soothe Yourself (2)
Space Diva (3)
Stardust (2)
Strongman (1)

Summer Daze (3)
Surprise (1)
Take A Ride (2)
Under Your Skin (2)
Water Your Garden (2)
Why Do I Lie? (2)

LUSH '96
Rock group from London: Miki Berenyi (vocals, guitar), Emma Anderson (guitar), Philip King (bass) and Chris Acland (drums). Acland committed suicide on 10/17/96 (age 30).

| 7/2/94 | 195 | 1 | | © | 1 **Split** .... | | | $10 | 4 A D 45578 |
| 3/23/96 | 189 | 1 | | © | 2 **Lovelife** .... | | | $10 | 4 A D 46170 |

DEBUT	PEAK	WKS	RIAA	CD		ARTIST — Album Title	Catalog	Sym	$	Label & Number

LUSH — Cont'd

Blackout (1)	500 (2)	Invisible Man (1)	Light From A Dead Star (1)	Olympia (2)	Starlust (1)
Childcatcher, The (2)	Heavenly Nobodies (2)	Kiss Chase (1)	Lit Up (1)	Papasan (2)	Tralala (2)
Ciao! (2)	Hypocrite (1)	Ladykillers (2)	Lovelife (1)	Runaway (2)	Undertow (1)
Desire Lines (1)	I've Been Here Before (2)	Last Night (2)	Never-Never (1)	Single Girl (1)	When I Die (1)

LYMAN, Arthur '59
Born on 2/2/32 in Kauai, Hawaii. Plays vibraphone, guitar, piano and drums. Formerly with **Martin Denny**.

5/12/58+	6	62	©	1 Taboo	[I]	$30	HiFi 806
7/24/61	10	30	©	2 Yellow Bird	[I]	$25	HiFi 1004
3/30/63	36	6		3 I Wish You Love	[I]	$25	HiFi 1009

Adventures In Paradise (2)	Caravan (2)	It's So Right To Love (3)	Love Is A Many Splendored	Sea Breeze (1)	To You (My Love) (3)
Akaka Falls (1)	China Clipper (1)	John Henry (2)	Thing (3)	Secret Love (3)	When I Fall In Love (3)
Andalusia (2)	Dahil Sayo (1)	Kalua (1)	Misirlou (1)	Sentimental Journey (3)	**Yellow Bird** (2) *4*
Arrivederci Roma (2)	Granada (2)	Katsumi Love Theme (1)	Mutiny On The Bounty, Love	September Song (2)	
Autumn Leaves (2)	Havah Nagilah (2)	Love (3)	Song From (3)	Sim Sim (1)	
Bamboo Tamboo (2)	Hilo March (1)	Love Dance (3)	Pagan Love Song (3)	Sweet And Lovely (2)	
Bolero (2)	I Wish You Love (3)	**Love For Sale** (3) *43*	Ringo Oiwake (1)	**Taboo** (1) *55*	

LYMON, Frankie, and The Teenagers '57
R&B vocal group from the Bronx, New York. Lead singer Lymon was born on 9/30/42 in New York City. Died of a drug overdose on 2/28/68 (age 25). Other members included Herman Santiago, Jimmy Merchant, Joe Negroni (died on 9/5/78, age 37) and Sherman Garnes (died on 2/26/77, age 36). Group appeared in the movies *Rock, Rock, Rock* and *Mister Rock 'n' Roll*. Inducted into the Rock and Roll Hall of Fame in 1993.

1/19/57	19	1		The Teenagers featuring Frankie Lymon	$500	Gee 701

ABC's Of Love *77*	Baby, Baby	**I Want You To Be My Girl** *13*	I'm Not A Know It All	Please Be Mine	**Who Can Explain** *flip*
Am I Fooling Myself Again	**I Promise To Remember** *57*	I'm Not A Juvenile Delinquent	Love Is A Clown	Share	**Why Do Fools Fall In Love** *6*

LYNCH, George '93
Born on 9/28/54 in Spokane, Washington; raised in Sacramento, California. Hard-rock guitarist. Member of **Dokken** and **Lynch Mob**.

8/21/93	137	1		©	Sacred Groove	$10	Elektra 61422

Beast Part I & II	Flesh And Blood	Love Power From The Mama	Memory Jack	Tierra Del Fuego
Cry Of The Brave	I Will Remember	Head	Not Necessary Evil	We Don't Own This World

LYNCH, Ray '89
Born on 7/3/43 in Utah; raised in Texas. New Age pianist.

6/24/89	197	2		©	No Blue Thing	[I]	$10	Music West 103

Clouds Below Your Knees	Evenings, Yes	Homeward At Last	True Spirit Of Mom & Dad
Drifted In A Deeper Land	Here & Never Found	No Blue Thing	

LYNCH MOB '90
Hard-rock group formed in Los Angeles: **George Lynch** (guitars), Oni Logan (vocals), Anthony Esposito (bass) and Mick Brown (drums). Lynch and Brown were members of **Dokken**.

11/10/90	46	23	©	1 Wicked Sensation	$10	Elektra 60954
5/16/92	56	9	©	2 Lynch Mob	$10	Elektra 61322

All I Want (1)	For A Million Years (1)	Jungle Of Love (2)	River Of Love (1)	Sweet Sister Mercy (1)	When Darkness Calls (2)
Cold Is The Heart (2)	Heaven Is Waiting (2)	No Bed Of Roses (1)	Secret, The (2)	Tangled In The Web (2)	Wicked Sensation (1)
Dance Of The Dogs (1)	Hell Child (1)	No Good (2)	She's Evil But She's Mine (1)	Through These Eyes (1)	
Dream Until Tomorrow (2)	I Want It (2)	Rain (1)	Street Fightin' Man (1)	Tie Your Mother Down (2)	

LYNN, Cheryl '79
Born Cheryl Lynn Smith on 3/11/57 in Los Angeles. R&B singer.

11/18/78+	23	30	●	©	1 Cheryl Lynn	$12	Columbia 35486
1/19/80	167	4			2 In Love	$12	Columbia 36145
7/11/81	104	13			3 In The Night	$12	Columbia 37034
7/17/82	133	20			4 Instant Love	$12	Columbia 38057
4/28/84	161	5			5 Preppie	$12	Columbia 38961

All My Lovin' (1)	Don't Let It Fade Away (2)	Hurry Home (3)	In Love (2)	Nothing To Say (1)	With Love On Our Side (3)
Baby (3)	**Encore** (5) *69*	I Just Wanna Be Your Fantasy	In The Night (3)	Preppie (5)	You Saved My Day (1)
Believe In Me (4)	Feel It (2)	(4)	Instant Love (4)	Say You'll Be Mine (4)	You're The One (1)
Chances (2)	Fix It (5)	I'm On Fire (3)	Keep It Hot (2)	**Shake It Up Tonight** (3) *70*	
Change The Channel (4)	Fool A Fool (5)	I've Got Faith In You (2)	Life's Too Short (5)	Show You How (3)	
Come In From The Rain (2)	Free (5)	I've Got Just What You Need	Look Before You Leap (4)	Sleep Walkin' (4)	
Day After Day (4)	Give My Love To You (1)	(2)	Love Bomb (2)	**Star Love** (1) *62*	
Daybreak (Storybook Children)	**Got To Be Real** (1) *12*	If This World Were Mine (4)	Love Rush (5)	This Time (1)	
(1)	Hide It Away (2)	If You'll Be True To Me (3)	No One Else Will Do (5)	What's On Your Mind (3)	

★495★ LYNN, Loretta '71
Born Loretta Webb on 4/14/35 in Butcher Holler, Kentucky. Country singer/songwriter/guitarist. Sister of **Crystal Gayle**. The movie *Coal Miner's Daughter* of 1980 was based on Loretta's autobiography.
1)Honky Tonk Angels 2)We Only Make Believe 3)Don't Come Home A Drinkin'

3/4/67	140	9		©	1 You Ain't Woman Enough	$30	Decca 74783
4/8/67	80	20	●	©	2 Don't Come Home A Drinkin'	$30	Decca 74842
12/23/67	103ˣ	2			3 Country Christmas	[X]	$30	Decca 74817
4/5/69	168	5			4 Your Squaw Is On The Warpath	$25	Decca 75084
8/9/69	148	4			5 Woman Of The World/To Make A Man	$25	Decca 75113
2/28/70	146	11			6 Wings Upon Your Horns	$25	Decca 75163
2/13/71	81	17	●	©	7 Coal Miner's Daughter	$20	Decca 75253
3/13/71	78	14	●		8 We Only Make Believe	$20	Decca 75251
					CONWAY TWITTY & LORETTA LYNN		
6/26/71	110	7			9 I Wanna Be Free	$20	Decca 75282
3/4/72	106	13	●		10 Lead Me On	$20	Decca 75326
					CONWAY TWITTY & LORETTA LYNN		
4/8/72	109	9			11 One's On The Way	$20	Decca 75334
8/25/73	153	9			12 Louisiana Woman-Mississippi Man	$15	MCA 335
					CONWAY TWITTY-LORETTA LYNN		

521

LYNN, Loretta — Cont'd

9/22/73	183	2			13 Love Is The Foundation			$15	MCA 355
4/19/75	182	2	©	14	Back To The Country			$15	MCA 471
11/20/93	42	16	●	© 15	Honky Tonk Angels			$10	Columbia 53414

DOLLY PARTON, LORETTA LYNN, TAMMY WYNETTE

After The Fire Is Gone (8) *56*
Another Man Loved Me Last Night (7)
Another You (14)
Any One, Any Worse, Any Where (7)
As Good As A Lonely Girl Can Be (12)
Away In A Manger (3)
Back Street Affair (10)
Back To The Country (14)
Before Your Time (12)
Big Ole Hurt (6)
Big Sister, Little Sister (5)
Blue Christmas (3)
Blueberry Hill (11)
Bye Bye Love (12)
Christmas Without Daddy (3)
Coal Miner's Daughter (7) *83*
Country Christmas (3)
Darkest Day (1)
Devil Gets His Dues (2)
Don't Come Home A Drinkin' (With Lovin' On Your Mind) (2)
Don't Tell Me You're Sorry (8)
Drive You Out Of My Mind (9)
Easy Loving (10)
Five Fingers Left (13)
For Heavens Sake (12)
For The Good Times (7)
Frosty The Snow Man (3)
Get Some Loving Done (10)
Get What 'Cha Got And Go (2)
Gift Of The Blues (3)
God Gave Me A Heart To Forgive (1)
Hands Of Yesterday (14)
Hangin' On (8)

Harper Valley P.T.A. (4)
He's All I Got (11)
He's Somewhere Between You And Me (4)
Hello Darlin' (7)
Help Me Make It Through The Night (9)
Hey Loretta (13)
How Far Can We Go (10)
I Can Help (14)
I Can't Keep Away From You (2)
I Can't See Me Without You (11)
I Dreamed Of A Hillbilly Heaven (15)
I Forgot More Than You'll Ever Know (15)
I Gave Everything (That A Girl In Love Should Never Give) (13)
I Got Caught (2)
I Love You, I Love You (13)
I Only See The Things I Wanna See (6)
I Really Don't Want To Know (2)
I Started Loving You Again (5)
I Walk Alone (4)
I Won't Decorate Your Christmas Tree (3)
I Wonder If You Told Her About Me (10)
I'd Rather Be Gone (6)
I'll Still Be Missing You (6)
I'm Dynamite (6)
I'm Living In Two Worlds (2)
I'm Lonesome For Trouble Tonight (5)

I'm Losing My Mind (11)
I'm One Man's Woman (9)
I'm So Used To Loving You (8)
If I Never Love Again (It'll Be Too Soon) (9)
If You Handle The Merchandise (6)
If You Touch Me, (You've Got To Love Me) (12)
If You Were Mine To Lose (5)
Is It Wrong (For Loving You) (1)
It Wasn't God Who Made Honky Tonk Angels (15)
It Won't Seem Like Christmas (3)
It'll Be Open Season On You (7)
It'll Feel Good When It Quits Hurtin' (11)
It's Another World (1)
It's Not The Miles You Traveled (11)
It's Only Make-Believe (8) *1*
It's Time To Pay The Fiddler (14)
Jimmy On My Mind (14)
Johnny One Time (5)
Just To Satisfy (The Weakness In A Man) (13)
Kaw-Liga (4)
Keep Your Change (1)
Lead Me On (10)
Less Of Me (7)
Let Her Fly (15)
Let Me Go, You're Hurtin' Me (4)
Let's Get Back Down To Earth (6)
Living My Lifetime For You (4)
Living Together Alone (12)

Louisiana Woman, Mississippi Man (12)
L-o-v-e, Love (11)
Love's On The Loose (11)
Lovesick Blues (15)
Mad Mrs. Jesse Brown (14)
Making Plans (2)
Man I Hardly Know (1)
Man Of The House (7)
Me And Bobby McGee (9)
Morning After Baby Let Me Down (11)
(My Little Girl) ..see: This Stranger
Never Ending Song Of Love (10)
No One Will Ever Know (5)
One I Can't Live Without (8)
One Little Reason (5)
One's On The Way (11)
Only Time I Hurt (5)
Our Conscience You And Me (12)
Paper Roses (14)
Pickin' Wild Mountain Berries (8)
Pill, The (14) *70*
Playing House Away From Home (10)
Please Help Me I'm Falling (In Love With You) (15)
Put It Off Until Tomorrow (1,15)
Put Your Hand In The Hand (9)
Release Me (12)
Rose Garden (9)
Saint To A Sinner (2)
Santa Claus Is Comin' To Town (3)

Satin Sheets (13)
See That Mountain (9)
Shoe Goes On The Other Foot Tonight (2)
Silver Bells (3)
Silver Threads And Golden Needles (15)
Sittin' On The Front Porch Swing (15)
Sneakin' In (4)
Snowbird (7)
Someone Before Me (1)
Stand By Your Man (5)
Take Me (8)
Taking The Place Of My Man (4)
Talking To The Wall (1)
That's The Way It Should Have Been (5)
There Goes My Everything (2)
There's More To Leaving Than Just Saying Goodbye (13)
These Boots Are Made For Walkin' (1)
This Stranger (My Little Girl) (6)
Tippy Toeing (1)
To Heck With Ole Santa Claus (3)
To Make A Man (Feel Like A Man) (5)
Tomorrow Never Comes (2)
Too Far (7)
Too Wild To Be Tamed (11)
We've Closed Our Eyes To Shame (8)
What Are We Gonna Do About Us (12)
What Makes Me Tick (7)

What Sundown Does To You (13)
When I Reach The Bottom (You'd Better Be There) (6)
When I Turn Off My Lights (Your Memory Turns On) (10)
When You Leave My World (9)
When You're Poor (9)
White Christmas (3)
Why Me (13)
Will You Be There (14)
Will You Visit Me On Sunday (8)
Wings Of A Dove (15)
Wings Upon Your Horns (6)
Woman Of The World (Leave My World Alone) (5)
Working Girl (8)
Wouldn't It Be Great (15)
You Ain't Woman Enough (1)
You Blow My Mind (10)
You Lay So Easy On My Mind (12)
You Love Everybody But You (14)
You Wouldn't Know An Angel (If You Saw One) (6)
You're Still Lovin' Me (13)
You're The Reason (10)
You've Just Stepped In (From Stepping Out On Me) (4)
Your Squaw Is On The Warpath (4)

LYNNE, Gloria   '64
Born on 11/23/31 in New York City. Jazz-styled singer.

9/18/61	51	13	©	1	I'm Glad There Is You			$30	Everest 5126
10/16/61	101	7	©	2	He Needs Me			$30	Everest 5128
10/30/61	57	18	©	3	This Little Boy Of Mine			$30	Everest 5131
4/7/62	58	22	©	4	Gloria Lynne at Basin Street East		[L]	$30	Everest 5137
2/9/63	39	27	©	5	Gloria Lynne at the Las Vegas Thunderbird		[L]	$30	Everest 5208
					recorded on 12/1/62				
9/21/63+	27	22	©	6	Gloria, Marty & Strings			$30	Everest 5220
					arranged and conducted by Marty Paich (Emmy-winning songwriter and father of **Toto**'s David Paich)				
6/6/64	43	19	©	7	I Wish You Love			$30	Everest 5226
6/5/65	82	10		8	Soul Serenade			$25	Fontana 27541

All Alone (1)
All Night Long (1)
And This Is My Beloved (4,7)
Autumn Leaves (4)
Baby Won't You Please Come Home (8)
Be My Love (7)
Birth Of The Blues (1)
But Not For Me (3)
Condemned Without Trial (3)
Don't Go To Strangers (8)
Don't Take Your Love From Me (6) *76*
Don't Worry About Me (6)
Dreamy (3)
Drinking Again (4)

End Of A Love Affair (5,7)
Folks That Live On The Hill (6)
Getting To Know You (3)
Greensleeves (3)
He Needs Me (2)
Here Today, Gone Tomorrow (5)
Home (2)
Humming Blues (3)
I Believe In You (5)
I Can't Give You Anything But Love (7)
I Get A Kick Out Of You (4)
I Got Rhythm (4)
I Know Love (3,7)
I See Your Face Before Me (1)
I Should Care (6) *64*

I Thought About You (2)
I Wish You Love (6,7) *28*
I'll Be Around (8)
I'll Buy You A Star (9)
I'll Take Romance (2)
I'm Glad There Is You (1)
I've Got It Bad And That Ain't Good (2)
If I Loved You (8)
If You Love Me (2,7)
Impossible (3) *95*
In Love In Vain (5)
In Other Words (4)
Indian Love Call (7)
It Could Happen To You (8)
It Just Happened To Me (4)
It Never Entered My Mind (4)

Jazz In You (3)
Joey, Joey, Joey (8)
Just In Time (3)
Lamp Is Low (2)
Love, I've Found You (7)
Mack The Knife (4)
Make The Man Love Me (2)
My Devotion (6)
My Romance (3)
Night Has A Thousand Eyes (6)
Old Man River (1)
On Christmas Day (1)
Out Of This World (6)
People Will Say We're In Love (8)
Record Company Blues (5)
Second Time Around (4)

Serenade In Blue (6)
So This Is Love (5)
Something Wonderful (5)
Soul Serenade (8)
Stella By Starlight (1)
Sunday, Monday And Always (5)
Sweet Pumpkin' (1)
Tall Hope (4)
Teach Me Tonight (8)
That's My Desire (8)
That's No Joke (1)
There Is No Greater Love (3,7)
This Could Be The Start Of Something Big (5)
This Little Boy Of Mine (3)

Through A Long And Sleepless Night (2)
Trouble Is A Man (1)
Watermelon Man (8) *62*
What Is There To Say (6)
What Kind Of Fool Am I (5)
What'll I Do (1)
Whispering Grass (6)
Wild Is The Wind (7)
Wouldn't It Be Lovely (4,7)
You Don't Know What Love Is (2,7)
You're Mine You (2)
Young And Foolish (1)

LYNNE, Jeff   '90
Born on 12/30/47 in Birmingham, England. Leader of **Electric Light Orchestra** and **The Move**. Otis Wilbury of the **Traveling Wilburys**. Production work for **George Harrison**, **Roy Orbison**, **Tom Petty** and Del Shannon.

| 6/30/90 | 83 | 9 | © | | Armchair Theatre | | | $10 | Reprise 26184 |

Blown Away
Don't Let Go

Don't Say Goodbye
Every Little Thing

Lift Me Up
Nobody Home

Now You're Gone
Save Me Now

September Song
Stormy Weather

What Would It Take

LYNNE, Shelby   '01
Born Shelby Lynn Moorer on 10/22/68 in Quantico, Virginia; raised in Jackson, Alabama. Female singer. Won the 2000 Best New Artist Grammy Award.

| 3/10/01 | 165 | 1 | © | | I Am Shelby Lynne | | | $10 | Island 546177 |

Black Light Blue
Dreamsome

Gotta Get Back
Leavin'

Life Is Bad
Lookin' Up

Thought It Would Be Easier
Where I'm From

Why Can't You Be?
Your Lies

LYNYRD SKYNYRD ★118★   '77

Rock group formed in Jacksonville, Florida: Ronnie Van Zant (vocals), Gary Rossington, Allen Collins and Ed King (guitars), Billy Powell (keyboards), Leon Wilkeson (bass) and Robert Burns (drums). King was a member of **Strawberry Alarm Clock**. Steve Gaines replaced King in 1976. Group named after their gym teacher Leonard Skinner. Plane crash on 10/20/77 in Gillsburg, Mississippi, killed Ronnie Van Zant, Steve Gaines and his sister Cassie Gaines. Gary and Allen formed the **Rossington Collins Band** in 1980; split in 1982. Rossington and vocalist **Johnny Van Zant** (the younger brother of Ronnie and lead singer of **38 Special**, Donnie Van Zant) regrouped with old and new band members for the 1987 Lynyrd Skynyrd Tribute Tour. Collins (paralyzed in a car accident in 1986) died of pneumonia on 1/23/90 (age 37). Rossington, Van Zant, Pyle, Wilkeson, King, Powell regrouped in 1991 with Randall Hall (guitar) and Custer (drums). Pyle left by 1993; replaced by Mike Estes. Custer left by 1994 and Owen Hale joined. Original drummer Rickey Medlocke (of **Blackfoot**) joined as a guitarist in 1995. Guitarist Hughie Thomasson (of **The Outlaws**) joined in 1996. Wilkeson died on 7/27/2001 (age 49).

1)Street Survivors 2)One More From The Road 3)Nuthin' Fancy

9/22/73+	27	79	▲²	© 1	**Lynyrd Skynyrd (pronounced leh-nerd skin-nerd)**	C:#9/216	$15	MCA/Sounds 363
5/4/74	12	45	▲²	© 2	**Second Helping**	C:#38/18	$15	MCA/Sounds 413
4/12/75	9	20	▲	© 3	**Nuthin' Fancy**		$12	MCA 2137
2/21/76	20	16	●	© 4	**Gimme Back My Bullets**		$12	MCA 2170
10/2/76	9	43	▲³	© 5	**One More From The Road**	[L]	$15	MCA 6001 [2]

recorded July 1976 at the Fabulous Fox Theatre in Atlanta

11/5/77	5	34	▲²	© 6	**Street Survivors**	C:#34/28	$30	MCA 3029

album released 3 days before the plane crash; original cover pictured the group engulfed in flames; after the crash, MCA issued a new cover omitting the flames ($12)

9/23/78	15	18	▲	© 7	**Skynyrd's First And...Last**	[E]	$12	MCA 3047

recordings from 1970-72

12/15/79+	12	65	▲³	© 8	**Gold & Platinum**	[G]	$15	MCA 11008 [2]
11/20/82	171	7		© 9	**Best Of The Rest**	[K]	$12	MCA 5370
10/10/87	41	17	●	© 10	**Legend**	[L]	$12	MCA 42084

live concert versions of previously unreleased material featuring the vocals of the late Ronnie Van Zant

4/16/88	68	11		© 11	**Southern By The Grace Of God/Lynyrd Skynyrd Tribute Tour - 1987**	[L]	$15	MCA 8027 [2]
6/29/91	64	16		© 12	**Lynyrd Skynyrd 1991**		$10	Atlantic 82258
7/27/91+	11ᶜ	198	▲⁵	© 13	**Skynyrd's Innyrds/Their Greatest Hits**	[G]	$10	MCA 42293
3/6/93	64	7		© 14	**The Last Rebel**		$10	Atlantic 82447
8/27/94	115	4		© 15	**Endangered Species**		$10	Capricorn 42028
5/17/97	97	6		© 16	**Twenty**		$10	CMC Int'l. 86211
6/12/99+	146	27	●	© 17	**The Best Of Lynyrd Skynyrd - 20th Century Masters - The Millennium Collection**	[G]	$10	MCA 11941
8/28/99	96	2		© 18	**Edge Of Forever**		$10	CMC Int'l. 86272

Ain't No Good Life (6)
All I Can Do Is Write About It (4)
All I Have Is A Song (15)
Am I Losin' (3,15)
Backstreet Crawler (12)
Ballad Of Curtis Loew (2)
Berneice (16)
Best Things In Life (14)
Blame It On A Sad Song (16)
Born To Run (14)
Bring It On (16)
Call Me The Breeze (2,5,9,11,13)
Can't Take That Away (14)
Cheatin' Woman (3)
Comin' Home (7,8,11)
Crossroads (5)
Cry For The Bad Man (4)
Devil In The Bottle (15)
Dixie (medley) (11)
Don't Ask Me No Questions (2,13)

Double Trouble (4,9,13,17) *80*
Down South Jukin' (7,8,15)
Edge Of Forever (18)
End Of The Road (12)
Every Mother's Son (4)
FLA (18)
Four Walls Of Raiford (10)
Free Bird (1,13,17) *19*
Free Bird [live] (5,8,11) *38*
Full Moon Night (18)
G.W.T.G.G. (18)
Georgia Peaches (10)
Gimme Back My Bullets (4,8,11)
Gimme Three Steps (1,5,8,13,17)
Gone Fishin' (18)
Good Lovin's Hard To Find (14)
Good Luck, Bad Luck (15)
Good Thing (12)
Gotta Go (9)
Heartbreak Hotel (15)

Hillbilly Blues (15)
Home Is Where The Heart Is (16)
Honky Tonk Night Time Man (6)
How Soon We Forget (16)
I Ain't The One (1,5,8,13,15,17)
I Got The Same Old Blues (4)
I Know A Little (6,8,11)
I Need You (2)
I Never Dreamed (6,9)
I'm A Country Boy (3,9)
I've Been Your Fool (9)
I've Seen Enough (12)
It's A Killer (12)
Keeping The Faith (12)
Kiss Your Freedom Goodbye (14)
Last Rebel (14,15)
Lend A Helpin' Hand (7)
Love Don't Always Come Easy (14)
Made In The Shade (3)

Mama (Afraid To Say Goodbye) (12)
Mean Streets (18)
Mississippi Kid (1)
Money Back Guarantee (18)
Money Man (12)
Mr. Banker (10)
Needle And The Spoon (2,5)
Never Too Late (16)
None Of Us Are Free (16)
O.R.R. (16)
On The Hunt (3,8)
One In The Sun (16)
One More Time (6)
One Thing (14)
Outta Hell In My Dodge (14)
Poison Whiskey (1,15)
Preacher Man (3)
Preacher's Daughter (7)
Pure & Simple (12)
Railroad Song (3)
Roll Gypsy Roll (4)

Rough Around The Edges (18)
Saturday Night Special (3,5,8,13,15,17) *27*
Searching (16)
Seasons, The (7)
Simple Man (1,8,10)
Smokestack Lightning (12)
South Of Heaven (14)
Southern Women (12)
Swamp Music (2,11,13,17)
Sweet Home Alabama (2,5,8,11,13,15,17) *8*
Sweet Little Missy (10)
T For Texas (5,9)
Take Your Time (16)
Talked Myself Right Into It (16)
That Smell (6,8,11,13,17)
Things Goin' On (1,7,15)
Through It All (18)
Tomorrow's Goodbye (18)
Travelin' Man (5,16)
Truck Drivin' Man (10,13)

Trust (4)
Tuesday's Gone (1,5,8)
Voodoo Lake (16)
Was I Right Or Wrong (7)
We Ain't Much Different (16)
What's Your Name (6,8,11,13,17) *13*
When You Got Good Friends (10)
Whiskey Rock-A-Roller (3,5,8)
White Dove (7)
Wino (7)
Workin' (18)
Workin' For MCA (2,5,9,11,13)
You Got That Right (6,8,11,17) *69*

LYTLE, Johnny   '66

Born on 10/13/32 in Springfield, Ohio. Died of kidney failure on 12/15/95 (age 63). Jazz vibraphonist.

2/26/66	141	2	©		**The Village Caller!**	[I]	$25	Riverside 480

Can't Help Loving Dat Man
Kevin Devin

On Green Dolphin Street
Pedro Strodder

Solitude
Unhappy Happy Soul

Village Caller
You Don't Know What Love Is

M

M   '80

Born Robin Scott on 4/1/47 in England. Male new-wave singer.

12/22/79+	79	8	©		**New York-London-Paris-Munich**		$12	Sire 6084

Cowboys And Indians
Made In Munich

Moderne Man (medley)
Moonlight And Muzak

Pop Muzik 1
Satisfy Your Lust (medley)

That's The Way The Money Goes
Unite Your Nation
Woman Make Man

MA, Yo-Yo   '92

Born on 10/7/55 in Paris (Chinese parents). Classical cellist.

2/15/92	93	18	●	© 1	**Hush**		$10	Sony 48177

YO-YO MA & BOBBY McFERRIN

4/22/00	170	2	©	2	**Appalachian Journey**	[I]	$10	Sony Classical 66782

YO-YO MA/EDGAR MEYER/MARK O'CONNOR

Air For The G String (1)
Allegro Prestissimo (1)
Andante (1)
Ave Maria (1)
Benjamin (2)
Caprice For Three (2)

Cloverfoot Reel (2)
Coyote (2)
Duet For Cello And Bass (2)
Emily's Reel (2)
Fisher's Hornpipe (2)
Flight Of The Bumble Bee (1)

Good-Bye (1)
Grace (1)
Hard Times Come Again No More (2)
Hoedown! (1)
Hush Little Baby (1)

Indecision (2)
Limerock (2)
Misty Moonlight Waltz (2)
Musette (1)
1B (2)
Poem For Carlita (2)

Second Time Around (2)
Slumber My Darling (2)
Stars (1)
Vistas (2)
Vocalise (1)

★347★ MABLEY, Moms · '61

Born Loretta Mary Aiken on 3/19/1894 in Brevard, North Carolina. Died on 5/23/75 (age 81). Black comedienne/actress. Appeared in the movies *Boarding House Blues*, *Emperor Jones* and *Amazing Grace*.

1)Moms Mabley At The "UN" 2)Young Men, Si - Old Men, No 3)Moms Mabley Breaks It Up

DEBUT	PEAK	WKS						$	Label & Number
5/1/61	16	57		1	Moms Mabley At The "UN"		[C]	$25	Chess 1452
7/10/61	121	5		2	Moms Mabley Onstage		[C]	$25	Chess 1447
10/30/61	39	27		3	Moms Mabley at The Playboy Club		[C]	$25	Chess 1460
3/31/62	28	24		4	Moms Mabley At Geneva Conference		[C]	$25	Chess 1463
9/1/62	27	21		5	Moms Mabley Breaks It Up		[C]	$25	Chess 1472
1/12/63	19	18		6	Young Men, Si - Old Men, No		[C]	$25	Chess 1477
6/29/63	41	16		7	I Got Somethin' To Tell You!		[C]	$25	Chess 1479
1/4/64	134	5	©	8	The Funny Sides Of Moms Mabley		[C]	$25	Chess 1482
2/29/64	48	24		9	Out On A Limb		[C]	$25	Mercury 60889
7/18/64	118	10		10	Moms Wows		[C-E]	$25	Chess 1486

recorded 1961 at the Playboy Club, Chicago

9/19/64	128	4		11	Moms The Word		[C]	$20	Mercury 60907
11/13/65	133	3		12	Now Hear This		[C]	$20	Mercury 61012
9/6/69	173	3		13	The Youngest Teenager		[C]	$15	Mercury 61229

no track titles listed on albums #1-10 & 12-13

Help The Bear (11)   If I Had Money (11)   Lullaby Of The Leaves (11)   Pray, Little Children, Pray (11)   Skitty-Poo (11)   That Don't Pay My Rent (11)

MAC · '98

Born in New Orleans. Male rapper.

| 8/8/98 | 11 | 11 | © | 1 | Shell Shocked | | | $10 | No Limit 50727 |
| 10/16/99 | 44 | 5 | © | 2 | World War III | | | $10 | No Limit 50109 |

Assassin Nation (2)   Callin' Me (1)   Father's Day (2)   Meet Me At The Hotel (1)   Paranoid (1)   War Party (2)
Battle Cry (Tomorrow) (2)   Camouflage Love (1)   Game, The (1)   Memories (1)   Shell Shocked (1)   We Deadly (2)
Be All You Can Be (1)   Can I Ball (1)   Genocide (2)   Money Gets (1)   Slow Ya Roll (1)   We Don't Love 'Em (1)
Beef (1)   Can U Love Me? (Eyes Of A   If It's Cool (2)   Murda, Murda, Kill, Kill (2)   Soldier Party (1)   Wooo (1)
Best Friends (2)   Killer) (2)   Just Another Thug (2)   My Brother (1)   Still Callin' Me (2)   You Never Know (2)
Bloody (2)   Cops And Robbers (2)   Like Before (2)   Nobody Make A Sound (1)   Tank Dogs (1)
Boss Chick (1)   Empire (1)   Lockdown (2)   Paradise (2)   That's Hip Hop (2)

MacALPINE, Tony · '87

Born in Connecticut. Black hard-rock guitarist.

| 7/4/87 | 146 | 11 | © | | Maximum Security | | | $10 | Squawk 832249 |

Autumn Lords   Etude #4 Opus #10   Key To The City   Porcelain Doll   Tears Of Sahara   Vision, The
Dreamstate   Hundreds Of Thousands   King's Cup   Sacred Wonder   Time And The Test

MAC BAND · '88

R&B group from Flint, Michigan: brothers Charles, Derrick, Kelvin and Ray McCampbell (vocals), Mark Harper (guitar), Rodney Frazier (keyboards), Ray Flippin (bass) and Slye Fuller (drums).

| 7/23/88 | 109 | 14 | © | | Mac Band | | | $10 | MCA 42090 |

Girl Your Love's So Fine   Jealous   Roses Are Red   Stuck   You Plus Me
Got To Get Over You   Midnight Lady   Stalemate   That's The Way I Look At Love

MacDONALD, Jeanette, & Nelson Eddy · '59

Top movie duo of the 1930s. MacDonald was born on 6/18/03 in Philadelphia. Died of a heart attack on 1/14/65 (age 61). Eddy was born on 6/29/01 in Providence, Rhode Island. Died of a stroke on 3/6/67 (age 65).

| 5/25/59 | 40 | 3 | ● | | Favorites In Hi-Fi | | | $30 | RCA Victor 1738 |

Ah, Sweet Mystery Of Life   Giannina Mia   Rosalie   Wanting You   Will You Remember
Beyond The Blue Horizon   Indian Love Call   Rose-Marie   While My Lady Sleeps   (Sweetheart)
Breeze And I   Italian Street Song   Stouthearted Men

MacDONALD, Ralph · '78

Born in 1944 in Harlem, New York. Session percussionist/bandleader.

9/25/76	114	16		1	Sound Of A Drum		[I]	$12	Marlin 2202
3/4/78	57	17		2	The Path		[I]	$12	Marlin 2210
7/14/79	110	10		3	Counterpoint			$12	Marlin 2229
10/13/84	108	10	©	4	Universal Rhythm			$10	Polydor 823323

Always Something Missing (3)   If I'm Still Around Tomorrow (2)   Only Time You Say You Love   Path, The (2)   Where Is The Love (1)
Calypso Breakdown (1)   In The Name Of Love (4) 58   Me (Is When We're Making   Playpen (4)   You Are In Love (3)
Discolypso (3)   It Feels So Good (2)   Love) (1)   Smoke Rings And Wine (2)
East Dry River (3)   (It's) The Game (4)   Outcasts (Another Time,   Sound Of A Drum (1)
Game ..see: (It's) The   Jam On The Groove (1)   Another Place), Theme From   Tell The Truth (3)
I Cross My Heart (2)   Mister Magic (1)   The (4)   Tradewinds (4)
I Need Someone (3)   Park Plaza (4)   Universal Rhythm (4)

MacGREGOR, Mary · '77

Born on 5/6/48 in St. Paul, Minnesota. Pop singer.

| 1/15/77 | 17 | 19 | | | Torn Between Two Lovers | | | $12 | Ariola America 50015 |

For A While 90   It's Too Soon (To Let Our Love   Mama   This Girl (Has Turned Into A   Why Did You Wait (To Tell Me)
Good Together   End)   Take Your Love Away   Woman) 46
I Just Want To Love You   Lady I Am   Torn Between Two Lovers 1

MACHINE HEAD · '99

Rock group from Oakland: Robb Flynn (vocals), Logan Mader (guitar), Adam Duce (bass) and Dave McClain (drums). Ahrue Luster replaced Mader in 1998.

| 4/12/97 | 138 | 1 | © | 1 | The More Things Change... | | | $10 | Roadrunner 8860 |
| 8/28/99 | 88 | 2 | © | 2 | The Burning Red | | | $10 | Roadrunner 8651 |

Bay Of Pigs (1)   Burning Red (2)   Exhale The Vile (2)   Message In A Bottle (2)   Take My Scars (1)
Blistering (1)   Desire To Fire (2)   Five (2)   Nothing Left (2)   Ten Ton Hammer (1)
Blood Of The Zodiac (1)   Devil With The King's Card (2)   From This Day (2)   Silver (2)   Violate (1)
Blood, The Sweat, The Tears   Down To None (1)   Frontlines, The (1)   Spine (1)
(2)   Enter The Phoenix (2)   I Defy (2)   Struck A Nerve (1)

MACHO '78
Disco studio group assembled by producer Mauro Malavasi.

| 10/7/78 | 101 | 14 | | | I'm A Man | | | $12 | Prelude 12160 |

Because There Is Music In The Air   Hear Me Calling
Because There Is Music In The   I'm A Man

MACK, Craig '94
Born in Long Island, New York. Male rapper.

| 10/8/94 | 21 | 19 | ● | © | 1 Project: Funk Da World | | | $10 | Bad Boy 73001 |
| 7/12/97 | 46 | 6 | | © | 2 Operation: Get Down | | | $10 | Street Life 75521 |

Can You Still Love Me (2)   Funk Wit Da Style (1)   Mainline (1)   Put It On You (2)   Sit Back & Relax (2)   Welcome To 1994 (1)
Do You See (2)   Get Down (1) *38*   Making Moves with Puff (1)   Rap Hangover (2)   Style (2)   What I Need (2)
Drugs, Guns And Thugs (2)   Jockin' My Style (2)   Prime Time Live (2)   Real Raw (1)   That Y'all (1)   When God Comes (1)
Flava In Ya Ear (1) *9*   Judgement Day (1)   Project: Funk Da World (1)   Rock Da Party (2)   Today's Forecast (2)   You! (2)

MACK, Lonnie '63
Born Lonnie McIntosh on 7/18/41 in Aurora, Indiana. Rockabilly guitarist.

| 11/30/63 | 103 | 9 | | | 1 The Wham Of That Memphis Man! | | | $200 | Fraternity 1014 |
| 6/15/85 | 130 | 21 | | © | 2 Strike Like Lightning | | | $12 | Alligator 4739 |

Baby, What's Wrong (1) *93*   Down In The Dumps (1)   I'll Keep You Happy (1)   Oreo Cookie Blues (2)   Strike Like Lightning (2)   Why (1)
Bounce, The (1)   Falling Back In Love With You (2)   If You Have To Know (2)   Satisfied (1)   Suzie-Q (1)   You Ain't Got Me (2)
Double Whammy (2)   Long Way From Memphis (2)   Satisfy Susie (2)   **Wham!** (1) *24*
Down And Out (1)   Hound Dog Man (2)   **Memphis** (1) *5*   Stop (2)   Where There's A Will (1)

MACK 10 '97
Born David Rolison on 8/9/71 in Inglewood, California. Male rapper. Married T-Boz (of **TLC**) on 8/19/2000.

7/8/95	33	19	●	©	1 Mack 10			$10	Priority 53938
10/4/97	14	22	●	©	2 Based On A True Story			$10	Priority 50675
10/24/98	15	8	●	©	3 The Recipe			$10	Hoo Bangin' 53512
9/23/00	19	9		©	4 The Paper Route			$10	Hoo-Bangin' 50148

Armed & Dangerous (1)   For The Money (3)   Hustle Game (4)   Made Niggaz (3)   Pop X (4)   Wanted Dead (1)
Backyard Boogie (2) *37*   From Tha Streetz (4)   I'm Dope (4)   **Money's Just A Touch Away** (3) *54*   Recipe, The (3)   Weekend, Tha (4)
Based On A True Story (2)   Gangsta Shit's Like A Drug (3)   Inglewood Swangin' (2)   Mozi-Wozi (1)   Should I Stay Or Should I Go (3)   Westside Slaughterhouse (1)
Can't Stop (2)   Get A Lil Head (3)   Keep It Gangsta (4)   Nobody (4)   Spousal Abuse (4)   What You Need? (2)
Chicken Hawk (1)   Get Yo Ride On (3)   LBC And The ING (3)   #1 Crew In The Area (3)   10 Million Ways (1)   You Ain't Seen Nothin (3)
Chicken Hawk II (2)   Ghetto Horror Show (3)   Let The Games Begin (3)   On Them Thangs (1)   Tight To Def (4)
Dopeman (2)   Guppies, The (2)   Letter, The (3)   Only In California (2)   Tonight's The Night (2)
Foe Life (1) *71*   H-O-E-K (1)   Mack 10, Mack 10 (2)   Pimp Or Die (4)   W/S Foe Life (2)
For Sale (4)   Here Comes The G (1)   Mack 10's The Name (1)

MAC MALL '96
Born Jamal Darocker in Vallejo, California. Male rapper.

| 5/11/96 | 35 | 8 | | © | 1 Untouchable | | | $10 | Relativity 1505 |
| 4/10/99 | 185 | 1 | | © | 2 Illegal Business? 2000 | | | $10 | Don't Give Up 2034 |

Chicken Head & Hot Wings (2)   Free Reign (2)   Lets Get A Telly (1)   Pimp Or Die (1)   Servin Game (1)   Wide Open (2)
Clock Work (2)   Get Away (1)   Mac's Fashion (2)   Playa Tip (1)   Straight Lace (1)   With Me Or Against Me (2)
Crestside (1)   Get Right (1)   Mohave (2)   Playas Wit Da Choppas (1)   Untouchable (1)   Young Nigga (1)
Don't Move (2)   Ghetto Stardom (1)   Opening Doors (1)   Pussy Whipped (2)   What's Ya Name? (2)
Dopefiends Lullaby (1)   Keys 2 The City (2)   People Ever Ask You? (2)   Rude Boy (2)   When They Come For Me (2)

MADAME X '87
Female R&B vocal trio: Iris Parker, Valerie Victoria and Alisa Randolph.

| 10/10/87 | 162 | 5 | | © | Madame X | | | $10 | Atlantic 81774 |

Cherries In The Snow   I Want Your Body   I'm Weak For You   Madame X   Marry Me (If You Really Love Me)
Flirt   I Wonder   Just That Type Of Girl

MAD COBRA '92
Born Ewart Everton Brown on 3/31/68 in Kingston; raised in St. Mary's, Jamaica. Reggae rapper.

| 11/7/92 | 125 | 15 | | © | Hard To Wet, Easy To Dry | | | $10 | Columbia 52751 |

Dead End Street   Glue   If Looks Could Kill   Mi Sorry   Release
Elbow   Good Body Gal   Legacy   Minute To Pray   Run Him
Flex *13*   Hard To Wet, Easy To Dry   Mate A Talk   Really Do It   Wet Dream

MADD RAPPER, The '00
Born Deric Angelettie in New York City. Male rapper/producer.

| 2/5/00 | 76 | 3 | | © | Tell Em Why U Madd | | | $10 | Crazy Cat 69832 |

Bird Call   Dice Game   How We Do   Shysty Braods   They Just Don't Know   You're All Alone
Bongo Break   Esta Loca   I'm Dope   Stir Crazy   Too Many Ho's
Car Jack   Ghetto   Not The One   Surviving The Game   Whateva
DOT Vs. TMR   How To Rob   Roll With The Cat   That's What's Happenin'   Wildside

MADE MEN '99
Male rap trio: Benzino, Antonio Twice Thou and Mr. Gzus.

| 9/11/99 | 61 | 6 | | © | Classic Limited Edition | | | $10 | Restless 72981 |

Blowin' Circles In The Wind   Drama Still   Just You And I   Not The One (That B**ch Is Done)   3 Stripe Killaz
Classic Limited Edition   15 Years In   Keep It Movin'   Tommy's Theme
Clockin' C Notes   I Wanna Made Man   Must Be Love   Right Now   Wise Guys For Life
Cold Hearted   Is It You? (Déjà Vu)   No Matter What   Sticky Situation

MADHOUSE '87
Jazz-fusion group from Minneapolis. Led by saxophonist Eric Leeds.

| 2/21/87 | 107 | 11 | | © | 8 | | [I] | $10 | Paisley Park 25545 |

One   Three   Five   Seven
Two   Four   Six   Eight

MAD LADS, The   '69

R&B vocal group from Detroit: Julius Green, Sam Nelson, Quincy Billops and Robert Phillips.

| 8/9/69 | **180** | 2 | | | **The Mad, Mad, Mad, Mad, Mad Lads** ...... | | | $30 | Volt 6005 |

By The Time I Get To Phoenix *84*
Cry Baby

I Just Can't Forget
I've Never Found A Girl
It's Loving Time

Love Is Here Today And Gone
Tomorrow
Make Room (In Your Heart)

Make This Young Lady Mine
Monkey Time '69
No Strings Attached

So Nice
These Old Memories

MAD LION   '95

Born Oswald Preist in London; raised in Jamaica. Male reggae rapper.

| 5/27/95 | **114** | 4 | © | | **Real Ting** ...... | | | $10 | Weeded 2006 |

Baby Father
Bad Luck
Big Box Of Blunts

Body And Shape
Crazy
Double Trouble

Nine On My Mind
Own Destiny
Play De Selection

Real Lover
Real Ting
See A Man Face

Shoot To Kill
Stop Dat Shit
Take It Easy *69*

Teaser
That's All We Need

MADNESS   '83

Ska-rock group formed in London: Graham McPherson (vocals), Chris Foreman (guitar), Mike Barson (keyboards), Carl Smyth (trumpet), Lee Thompson (sax), Mark Bedford (bass) and Dan Woodgate (drums).

3/8/80	**128**	9			1 **One Step Beyond...**			$12	Sire 6085
11/22/80	**146**	4	©		2 **Absolutely**			$12	Sire 6094
4/30/83	**41**	29			3 **Madness**			$10	Geffen 4003
3/17/84	**109**	8	©		4 **Keep Moving**			$10	Geffen 4022

Baggy Trousers (2)
Bed & Breakfast Man (1)
Believe Me (1)
Blue Skinned Beast (3)
Brand New Beat (4)
Cardiac Arrest (3)
Chipmunks Are Go! (1)
Close Escape (2)
Disappear (2)

Embarrassment (2)
E.R.N.I.E. (2)
Give Me A Reason (4)
Grey Day (3)
House Of Fun (3)
In The Middle Of The Night (1)
In The Rain (3)
It Must Be Love (3) *33*
Keep Moving (4)

Land Of Hope & Glory (1)
Madness (1)
Madness (Is All In The Mind) (3)
March Of The Gherkins (4)
Michael Caine (4)
Mummy's Boy (1)
My Girl (1)
Night Boat To Cairo (1,3)
Not Home Today (2)

On The Beat Pete (2)
One Better Day (4)
One Step Beyond... (1)
Our House (3) *7*
Overdone (4)
Primrose Hill (3)
Prince, The (1)
Prospects (4)
Razor Blade Alley (1)

Return Of The Los Palmas 7 (2)
Rise And Fall (3)
Rockin' In A (1)
Samantha (4)
Shadow Of Fear (2)
Shut Up (3)
Solid Gone (2)
Sun And The Rain (4) *72*
Swan Lake (1)

Take It Or Leave It (2)
Tarzan's Nuts (1)
Tomorrow's Just Another Day (3)
Turning Blue (4)
Victoria Gardens (4)
Wings Of A Dove (A Celebratory Song) (4)
You Said (2)

MADONNA ★70★   '85

Born Madonna Louise Ciccone on 8/16/58 in Bay City, Michigan. To New York in the late '70s; performed with the Alvin Ailey dance troupe. Member of the **Breakfast Club** in 1979. Formed her own band, Emmy, in 1980. Married to actor Sean Penn from 1985-89. Acted in several movies. Appeared in Broadway's *Speed-The-Plow*. Released concert tour documentary movie *Truth Or Dare* in 1991. Married British movie director Guy Ritchie on 12/22/2000.

1)Like A Prayer 2)True Blue 3)Like A Virgin

9/3/83+	**8**	168	▲5	©	1 **Madonna**			$10	Sire 23867
12/1/84+	**❶3**	108	▲10	©	2 **Like A Virgin**			$10	Sire 25157
7/19/86	**❶5**	82	▲7	©	3 **True Blue**			$10	Sire 25442
8/15/87	**7**	28	▲	©	4 **Who's That Girl**		[S]	$10	Sire 25611

includes "Best Thing Ever" by **Scritti Politti**, "El Coco Loco (So So Bad)" by Coati Mundi, "Step By Step" by **Club Nouveau**, "Turn It Up" by Michael Davidson and "24 Hours" by Duncan Faure

12/5/87+	**14**	22	▲	©	5 **You Can Dance**		[K]	$10	Sire 25535
4/8/89	**❶6**	77	▲4	©	6 **Like A Prayer**			$10	Sire 25844
6/9/90	**2³**	25	▲2	©	7 **I'm Breathless**		[S]	$10	Sire 26209

songs from and songs inspired by the movie *Dick Tracy*

12/1/90+	**2²**	141	▲9	©	8 **The Immaculate Collection**	C:#8/201	[G]	$10	Sire 26440
11/7/92	**2¹**	53	▲2	©	9 **Erotica**			$10	Maverick 45154
11/12/94	**3**	48	▲2	©	10 **Bedtime Stories**			$10	Maverick 45767
11/25/95	**6**	34	▲3	©	11 **Something To Remember**		[G]	$10	Maverick 46100
11/30/96+	**2²**	30	▲4	©	12 **Evita**		[S]	$15	Warner 46346 [2]

includes "On This Night Of A Thousand Stars" by Jimmy Nail; "The Lady's Got Potential" and "And The Money Kept Rolling In (And Out)" by Antonio Banderas; "On The Balcony Of The Casa Rosada 1" and "She Is A Diamond" by Jonathan Pryce; and "A Cinema In Buenos Aires, 26 July 1952", "Requiem For Evita", "Santa Evita" and "Latin Chant" by **Andrew Lloyd Webber**

| 8/23/97 | **167** | 4 | | © | 13 **Evita** ...... | | [S] | $10 | Warner 46692 |

includes "On This Night Of A Thousand Stars" by Jimmy Nail; "And The Money Kept Rolling In (And Out)" by Antonio Banderas; "She Is A Diamond" by Jonathan Pryce; and "Requiem For Evita" by **Andrew Lloyd Webber**

| 3/21/98 | **2²** | 78 | ▲4 | © | 14 **Ray Of Light** ...... | C:#50/1 | | $10 | Maverick 46847 |
| 10/7/00 | **❶1**↑ | 52↑ | ▲2 | © | 15 **Music** ...... | | | $10 | Maverick 47598 |

Act Of Contrition (6)
Actress Hasn't Learned The Lines (You'd Like To Hear) (12)
Amazing (15)
Angel (2) *5*
Another Suitcase In Another Hall (12,13)
Art Of The Possible (medley) (12)
Back In Business (7)
Bad Girl (9) *36*
Bedtime Story (10) *42*
Borderline (1,8) *10*
Burning Up (1)
Bye Bye Baby (9)
Can't Stop (4)
Candy Perfume Girl (14)
Causing A Commotion (4) *2*
Charity Concert (medley) (12)

Cherish (6,8) *2*
Crazy For You (8,11) *1*
Cry Baby (7)
Dear Jessie (6)
Deeper And Deeper (9) *7*
Don't Cry For Me Argentina (12,13) *8*
Don't Tell Me (15) *4*
Dress You Up (2) *5*
Drowned World/Substitute For Love (14)
Erotica (9) *3*
Eva And Magaldi (medley) (12,13)
Eva Beware Of The City (medley) (12,13)
Eva's Final Broadcast (12,13)
Everybody (1,5)
Express Yourself (6,8) *2*
Fever (9)

Forbidden Love (10,11)
Frozen (14) *2*
Gone (15)
Goodnight And Thank You (12,13)
Hanky Panky (7) *10*
He's A Man (7)
Hello And Goodbye (12)
High Flying, Adored (12,13)
Holiday (1,5,8) *16*
Human Nature (10) *46*
I Deserve It (15)
I Know It (1)
I Want You (1)
I'd Be Surprisingly Good For You (12,13)
I'd Rather Be Your Lover (10)
I'll Remember (11) *2*
I'm Going Bananas (7)
Impressive Instant (15)
In This Life (9)

Inside Of Me (10)
Into The Groove (5,8)
Jimmy Jimmy (3)
Justify My Love (8) *1*
Keep It Together (6) *8*
La Isla Bonita (3,8) *4*
Lament (12,13)
Like A Prayer (6,8) *1*
Like A Virgin (2,8) *1*
Little Star (14)
Live To Tell (3,8,11) *1*
Look Of Love (8)
Love Don't Live Here Anymore (2,11) *78*
Love Makes The World Go Round (8)
Love Song (6)
Love Tried To Welcome Me (10)
Lucky Star (1,8) *4*
Material Girl (2,8) *2*

Mer Girl (14)
More (7)
Music (15) *1*
New Argentina (12,13)
Nobody's Perfect (15)
Nothing Really Matters (14) *93*
Now I'm Following You (Part I & II) (7)
Oh Father (6,11) *20*
Oh What A Circus (12,13)
On The Balcony Of The Casa Rosada 2 (12)
One More Chance (11)
Open Your Heart (3,8) *1*
Over And Over (2,5)
Papa Don't Preach (3,8) *1*
Paradise (Not For Me) (15)
Partido Feminista (7)
Peron's Latest Flame (12,13)
Physical Attraction (1,5)

Power Of Good-Bye (14) *11*
Pretender (2)
Promise To Try (6)
Rain (9,11) *14*
Rainbow High (12,13)
Rainbow Tour (12)
Ray Of Light (14) *5*
Rescue Me (8) *9*
Runaway Lover (15)
Sanctuary (15)
Secret (10) *3*
Secret Garden (9)
Shanti/Ashtangi (14)
Shoo-Bee-Doo (2)
Skin (14)
Sky Fits Heaven (14)
Something To Remember (7,11)
Sooner Or Later (7)
Spanish Eyes (6)
Spotlight (5)

MADONNA — Cont'd

Stay (2)
Survival (10)
Swim (14)
Take A Bow (10,11) *1*
Theme From "With Honors"
..see: I'll Remember

Thief Of Hearts (9)
Think Of Me (1)
**This Used To Be My
Playground** (11) *1*
Till Death Do Us Part (6)
To Have And Not To Hold (14)

True Blue (3) *3*
Vogue (7,8) *1*
Waiting (9)
Waltz For Eva And Che (12,13)
What Can You Lose (7)

What It Feels Like For A Girl
(15) *23*
Where Life Begins (9)
Where's The Party (3,5)
White Heat (3)
Who's That Girl (4) *1*

Why's It So Hard (9)
Words (9)
You Must Love Me (12,13) *18*
You'll See (11) *6*
Your Little Body's Slowly
Breaking Down (12)

MAD RIVER '69

Folk-rock group from Berkeley, California: David Robinson and Rick Bockner (guitars), Laurence Hammond (bass) and Greg Dewey (drums). All share vocals.

| 8/9/69 | 192 | 2 | | © | **Paradise Bar And Grill** .... | | | $50 | Capitol 185 |

Academy Cemetery
Cherokee Queen
Copper Plates

Equinox
Harfy Magnum
Leave Me (medley)

Love's Not The Way To Treat A
Friend
Paradise Bar And Grill

Revolution's In My Pockets
Stay (medley)
They Brought Sadness

MAD SEASON '95

All-star rock project: Layne Staley (vocals, guitar; **Alice In Chains**), Mike McCready (guitar; **Pearl Jam**), John Baker Saunders (bass) and Barrett Martin (drums; **Screaming Trees**). Band name is an English term for the time of year when psilocybin mushrooms are in full bloom.

| 4/1/95 | 24 | 27 | ● | © | **Above** .... | | | $10 | Columbia 67057 |

All Alone
Artificial Red

I Don't Know Anything
I'm Above

Lifeless Dead
Long Gone Day

November Hotel
River Of Deceit

Wake Up
X-Ray Mind

MAD SKILLZ '96

Born David Lewis in Richmond, Virgina. Male rapper.

| 3/2/96 | 154 | 1 | | © | **From Where???** .... | | | $10 | Big Beat 92623 |

All In It
Doin' Time In The Cypha
Extra Abstract Skillz

Get Your Groove On
Inherit The World
It's Goin' Down

Jam, The
Move Ya Body
Nod Factor

Street Rules
Tip Of The Tongue
Tongues Of The Next Shit

Unseen World
VA. In The House

MADURA '71

Folk-rock trio from Chicago: Alan DeCarlo (vocals, guitar), David "Hawk" Wolinski (keyboards) and Ross Solomone (drums). DeCarlo and Wolinski were members of **Bangor Flying Circus**. Wolinski was also a member of **Rufus**.

| 10/30/71 | 186 | 2 | | | **Madura** .... | | | $25 | Columbia 30794 [2] |

Damnation
Don't Be Afraid
Dreams
Drinking No Wine
Free From The Devil

Hawk Piano
I Think I'm Dreaming
It's A Good Time For Loving
Johnny B. Goode

Joy In Old Age By Way Of Self
Observation
Man's Rebirth Through
Childbirth - Part I & II
My Love Is Free

My My What A World
Plain As Day
Realization
See For Yourself
Stimulation

Talking To Myself
Trapped

MAGGARD, Cledus, And The Citizen's Band '76

Born Jay Huguely in Quick Sand, Kentucky. Recorded "The White Knight" while working at the Leslie Advertising agency in Greenville, South Carolina.

| 3/13/76 | 135 | 8 | | | **The White Knight** .... | [N] | | $12 | Mercury 1072 |

C.B. Rock
C.B. '76

Cledus's C.B. Lingo Dictionary
Dad I Gotta Go

Jaw Jackin'
Kentucky Moonrunner *85*

Mercy Day
White Knight *19*

Who We Got On That End?
(You're The Only Friend I Got)

MAGIC '98

Born Atwood Johnson in New Orleans. Male rapper.

| 10/3/98 | 15 | 6 | | © | 1 **Skys The Limit** .... | | | $10 | No Limit 50017 |
| 9/18/99 | 53 | 7 | | © | 2 **Thuggin'** .... | | | $10 | No Limit 50110 |

Ball 'Til We Fall (1)
Chastity (1)
Club Thang (2)
Depend On Me (1)
Did What I Had 2 (1)
Do You Really Want Peace (2)

Freaky (2)
Ghetto Godzilla (1)
Gimpin' (1)
Good Lookin Out (2)
Hard Times (1)
I Got Love 4 Ya (1)

I Never (1)
Ice On My Wrist (2)
Keep It Gangsta (2)
Life Is A Bitch (1)
Mobb 4 Ever (1)
Money Don't Make Me (1)

New Generation (1)
9th Ward (1,2)
No Hope (1)
No Limit (1)
Party Time (1)
Puff Puff (2)

Skys The Limit (1)
Soldier (2)
Special Forces (1)
Take It To Da Streets (1)
Thank You Lord For My Life (2)
That's Me (2)

Wanna Get Away (2)
We Gon Ride (1)
What I Gotta (1)
When Drama Came (1)
Wobble, Wobble (2)

MAGIC ORGAN, The '72

The Magic Organ is actually solo organist **Jerry Smith**.

| 5/6/72 | 135 | 7 | | | **Street Fair** .... | [I] | | $12 | Ranwood 8092 |

All In The Family ..see: Those
Were The Days
Beautiful Dishwasher

It's A Small World
Liechtensteiner Polka
Pennsylvania Polka

Ranger's Waltz
Street Fair
Sweet 'N Sassy

Those Were The Days
Truck Stop
Under The Double Eagle

Wheels
When In Rome

MAGNIFICENT MEN, The '67

White R&B-styled group from Harrisburg, Pennsylvania: David Bupp (vocals), Terry Crousore (guitar), Tommy Hoover (organ), Tom Pane (sax), Buddy King (trumpet), Jimmy Seville (bass) and Bob Angelucci (drums).

| 4/8/67 | 171 | 2 | | | 1 **The Magnificent Men** .... | | | $20 | Capitol 2678 |
| 7/29/67 | 89 | 9 | | | 2 **The Magnificent Men "Live!"** .... | [L] | | $20 | Capitol 2775 |

Cry With Me Baby (1)
Do A Justice To Your Heart (1)
Doin' The Philly Dog (2)
Function At The Junction (2)

I Got News (1)
I Wish You Love (1)
I'm Gonna Miss You (2)
I've Been Trying (2)

Just Be True (2)
Just Walk In My Shoes (1)
Keep On Climbing (1)
Maybe, Maybe Baby (1)

Misty (1,2)
Much, Much, More Of Your
Love (1)
Peace Of Mind (1,2)

Show Me (2)
Stormy Weather (1,2)
Sweet Soul Medley - Part 1
(2) *90*

Whispers (2)
You Don't Know Like I Know (2)

MAGOO — see TIMBALAND

MAHAL, Taj '69

Born Henry Fredericks on 5/17/40 in New York City. Blues singer/guitarist.

2/22/69	160	14		©	1 **The Natch'l Blues**			$15	Columbia 9698
10/11/69	85	9		©	2 **Giant Step/De Ole Folks At Home**			$20	Columbia 18 [2]
6/12/71	84	13		©	3 **The Real Thing**	[L]		$20	Columbia 30619 [2]

recorded at the Fillmore East in New York City

1/15/72	181	6		©	4 **Happy Just To Be Like I Am**			$15	Columbia 30767
11/4/72	177	4		©	5 **Recycling The Blues & Other Related Stuff**	[L]		$15	Columbia 31605
12/1/73	190	5			6 **Oooh So Good 'N Blues**			$15	Columbia 32600
10/12/74	165	6		©	7 **Mo' Roots**			$15	Columbia 33051
10/18/75	155	7			8 **Music Keeps Me Together**			$15	Columbia 33801

MAHAL, Taj — Cont'd

DEBUT	PEAK	WKS	CD	#	Album Title	$	Label & Number
1/29/77	134	8		9	Music Fuh Ya' (Musica Para Tu)	$12	Warner 2994

Ain't Gwine To Whistle Dixie (Anymo') (2,3)
Ain't That A Lot Of Love (1)
Annie's Lover (2)
Aristocracy (8)
Baby, You're My Destiny (9)
Bacon Fat (2)
Big Kneed Gal (3)
Big Mama (7)
Black Spirit Boogie (7)
Blackjack Davey (7)
Blind Boy Rag (2)
Bound To Love Me Some (5)
Brown-Eyed Handsome Man (8)
Buck Dancer's Choice (6)
Built For Comfort (6)
Cajun Tune (5)

Cajun Waltz (7)
Cakewalk Into Town (5)
Candy Man (2)
Chevrolet (4)
Clara (St. Kitts Woman) (7)
Cluck Old Hen (2)
Colored Aristocracy (2)
Corinna (1,5)
Country Blues #1 (2)
Cuckoo, The (1)
Curry (9)
Dear Ladies (8)
Desperate Lover (7)
Diving Duck Blues (3)
Done Changed My Way Of Living (1)
Dust My Broom (6)
Eighteen Hammers (4)

Farther On Down The Road (You Will Accompany Me) (2)
Fishing Blues (2,3)
Four Mills Brothers (9)
Frankie And Albert (6)
Free Song (Rise Up Children Shake The Devil Out Of Your Soul) (5)
Freight Train (7)
Further On Down The Road (8)
Gitano Negro (5)
Give Your Woman What She Wants (2)
Going Up To The Country, Paint My Mailbox Blue (1,3)
Good Morning Little School Girl (2)
Good Morning Miss Brown (1)

Happy Just To Be Like I Am (4)
Honey Babe (9)
I Ain't Gonna Let Nobody Steal My Jellyroll (1)
John, Ain't It Hard (3)
Johnny Too Bad (7)
Kalimba (1)
Keep Your Hands Off Her (2)
Light Rain Blues (2)
Linin' Track (2)
Little Red Hen (6)
Little Soulful Tune (4)
Music Keeps Me Together (8)
My Ancestors (8)
Oh Mama Don't You Know (6)
Oh Susanna (4)
Railroad Bill (6)
Ricochet (5)

Roll, Turn, Spin (8)
Sailin' Into Walker's Cay (9)
She Caught The Katy And Left Me A Mule To Ride (1)
Six Days On The Road (2)
Slave Driver (7)
Stagger Lee (2)
Stealin' (4)
Sweet Home Chicago (5)
Sweet Mama Janisse (3)
Take A Giant Step (2)
Teacup's Jazzy Blues Tune (6)
Texas Woman Blues (5)
Tom And Sally Drake (3)
Tomorrow May Not Be Your Day (4)
Truck Driver's Two-Step (2)
West Indian Revelation (4,8)

When I Feel The Sea Beneath My Soul (8)
Why?...And We Repeat
Why?...And We Repeat! (8)
Why Did You Have To Desert Me? (7)
Wild Ox Moan (2)
You Ain't No Street Walker Mama, Honey But I Do Love The Way You Strut Your Stuf (3)
You Don't Miss Your Water ('Til Your Well Runs Dry) (1)
You Got It (9)
You're Gonna Need Somebody On Your Bond (2,3)

MAHARIS, George '62

Born on 9/1/28 in New York City. Actor/singer. Played "Buz Murdock" on TV's *Route 66*.

DEBUT	PEAK	WKS	Sym	#	Album Title	$	Label & Number
6/2/62	10	30	©	1	George Maharis Sings!	$20	Epic 26001
9/8/62	32	24	©	2	Portrait In Music	$20	Epic 26021
3/30/63	129	10		3	Just Turn Me Loose!	$20	Epic 26037
9/14/63	77	7		4	Where Can You Go For A Broken Heart?	$20	Epic 26064

After The Lights Go Down Low (1)
All Of You (3)
Alright, Okay, You Win (3)
Baby Has Gone Bye Bye (3) *62*
Can't Help Falling In Love (1)
Don't Fence Me In (3) *62*
End Of A Love Affair (4)
Fool Such As I ..see: (Now And Then There's) A

Fools Rush In (Where Angels Fear To Tread) (2)
(Get Your Kicks On) Route 66! (1)
Good-Bye (4)
Here's That Rainy Day (2)
How Do You Keep From Cryin' (4)
Hurt (1)
I Can't Believe That You're In Love With Me (2)

I Can't Stop Loving You (2)
I Remember You (3)
I Wanna Be Loved (2)
I Want To Be Wanted (1)
I'll Be Around (4)
I'll Be Here Waiting For You (4)
I'll Never Smile Again (1)
I'll Walk Alone (4)
I'm Gonna Laugh You Out Of My Life (4)
If Love Were All (2)

It All Adds Up To Me (4)
It's All In The Game (1)
Laughing On The Outside (3)
Little Girl (4)
Little White Lies (3)
Lollipops And Roses (2)
Love Could Change My Mind (2)
Love Me As I Love You (2) *54*
Moon River (1)
More I See You (2)
My Kind Of Girl (1)

(Now And Then, There's) A Fool Such As I (4)
Oh Lonesome Me (4)
Route 66 ..see: (Get Your Kicks On)
Take Me In Your Arms (3)
Talk To Me (2)
Teach Me Tonight (2) *25*
They Knew About You (2)
What A Diff'rence A Day Made (2)

What Kind Of Fool Am I? (3)
Where Are You? (2)
Where Can You Go (For A Broken Heart) (4)
Witchcraft (2)
You Don't Know What Love Is (4)
You Must Have Been A Beautiful Baby (1)

MAHOGANY RUSH '74

Hard-rock trio formed in Montreal: **Frank Marino** (guitar, vocals), Paul Harwood (bass) and Jim Ayoub (drums). Frank's brother Vince (guitar) joined in 1980.

DEBUT	PEAK	WKS	CD	#	Album Title	Sym	$	Label & Number
8/24/74	74	15	©	1	Child Of The Novelty		$25	20th Century 451
3/1/75	159	4		2	Maxoom		$25	20th Century 463
6/21/75	84	13	©	3	Strange Universe		$20	20th Century 482
6/5/76	175	3		4	Mahogany Rush IV		$15	Columbia 34190

FRANK MARINO & MAHOGANY RUSH:

DEBUT	PEAK	WKS		#	Album Title	Sym	$	Label & Number
5/28/77	184	2		5	World Anthem		$15	Columbia 34677
3/11/78	129	11	©	6	Frank Marino & Mahogany Rush Live	[L]	$15	Columbia 35257
5/12/79	129	10	©	7	Tales Of The Unexpected	[L]	$15	Columbia 35753

side 1: studio; side 2: live

DEBUT	PEAK	WKS		#	Album Title	$	Label & Number
3/8/80	88	9		8	What's Next	$15	Columbia 36204
8/14/82	185	4		9	Juggernaut	$15	Columbia 38023

FRANK MARINO

All Along The Watchtower (7)
All In Your Mind (2)
Answer, The (4,6)
Back Door Man (medley) (6)
Back On Home (2)
Blues (2)
Boardwalk Lady (2)
Bottom Of The Barrel (7)
Broken Heart Blues (5)
Buddy (2)
Chains Of (S) Pace (1)
Changing (1)
Child Of The Novelty (1)
Dancing Lady (3)

Dear Music (9)
Ditch Queen (9)
Door Of Illusion (7)
Down, Down, Down (7)
Dragonfly (4,6)
Electric Reflections Of War (medley) (6)
Finish Line (8)
For Your Love (9)
IV...(The Emperor) (4)
Free (9)
Funky Woman (2)
Guit War (1)
Hey, Little Lover (5)

I'm A King Bee (medley) (6)
I'm Going Away (4)
In My Ways (5)
Introduction (6)
It's Begun To Rain (4)
Jive Baby (4)
Johnny B. Goode (6)
Juggernaut (9)
King Who Stole (...The Universe) (3)
Lady (5)
Land Of 1000 Nights (3)
Little Sexy Annie (3)
Look At Me (5)

Look Outside (1)
Loved By You (8)
Madness (2)
Magic Man (2)
Makin' My Wave (1)
Man At The Back Door (4)
Maxoom (2)
Maybe It's Time (9)
Midnight Highway (9)
Mona (8)
Moonlight Lady (3)
Moonwalk (4)
New Beginning (2)
New Rock And Roll (1,6)

Norwegian Wood (This Bird Has Flown) (7)
Once Again (3)
Plastic Man (1)
Purple Haze (6)
Requiem For A Sinner (5)
Roadhouse Blues (8)
Rock Me Baby (6)
Rock 'N' Roll Hall Of Fame (8)
Satisfy Your Soul (3)
Sister Change (7)
Something's Comin' Our Way (8)
Stories Of A Hero (9)

Strange Dreams (9)
Strange Universe (3)
Tales Of The Spanish Warrior (3)
Tales Of The Unexpected (7)
Talking 'Bout A Feelin' (1,6)
Thru The Milky Way (1)
Try For Freedom (5)
Tryin' Anyway (3)
Who Do Ya Love (medley) (6)
Woman (7)
World Anthem (5,6)
You Got Livin' (8)

MAIN INGREDIENT, The '74

R&B vocal trio from New York City: Donald McPherson, Luther Simmons and Tony Sylvester. McPherson died of leukemia on 7/4/71; replaced by Cuba Gooding. Gooding's son, Cuba Jr., is a prominent movie actor.

DEBUT	PEAK	WKS	CD	#	Album Title	$	Label & Number
8/22/70	200	1		1	The Main Ingredient L.T.D.	$15	RCA Victor 4253
3/13/71	146	9		2	Tasteful Soul	$15	RCA Victor 4412
10/2/71	176	5		3	Black Seeds	$15	RCA Victor 4483
6/24/72	79	27		4	Bitter Sweet	$15	RCA Victor 4677
5/5/73	132	13	©	5	Afrodisiac	$15	RCA Victor 4834
3/9/74	52	31		6	Euphrates River	$12	RCA Victor 0335
5/10/75	90	12		7	Rolling Down A Mountainside	$12	RCA Victor 0644
12/13/75+	158	8		8	Shame On The World	$12	RCA Victor 1003
3/5/77	177	3		9	Music Maximus	$12	RCA Victor 1558

Another Day Has Come (3)
Baby Change Your Mind (3)
Black Seeds Keep On Growing (3) *97*
Broken Heart Don't Really Break (7)
Brotherly Love (1)

By The Time I Get To Phoenix (medley) (1)
California My Way (6) *75*
Can't Get Ready (For Losing You) (9)
Car Of Love (9)
Comes The Night (9)
Don't Wonder Why (3)

Don't You Worry 'Bout A Thing (6)
Euphrates (6)
Everybody Plays The Fool (4) *3*
Family Man (7)
Fly Baby Fly (4)
Get Back (1)

Girl Blue (5)
Girl I Left Behind (1)
Good Old Days (7)
Goodbye My Love (9)
Half A Chance (9)
Happiness Is Just Around The Bend (6) *35*
Have You Ever Tried It (6)

I Am Yours (5)
I Can't See Me Without You (4)
I Can't Stand Your Love (1)
I Gotta Know You (9)
I Want To Make You Glad (7)
I Was Born To Lose (1)
I'm Better Off Without You (2) *91*

I'm Leaving This Time (3)
I'm So Proud (2) *49*
I've Fallen For You (3)
If I'm Gonna Be Sad (8)
Instant Love (9)
It's So Sweet (Loving You) (3)
Jamaica (Let Me Go Home) (8)

MAIN INGREDIENT, The — Cont'd

Just Don't Want To Be Lonely (6) *10*
Just Say It Again (3)
Laughing Song (9)
Let Me Prove My Love To You (8)
Life Won't Be The Same (Without You) (1)
Lillian (3)
Look At Me (2)

Looks Like Rain (6)
Love Of My Life (5)
Magic Shoes (1,2)
Make It With You (2)
Many Women In My Life (9)
Movin' On (3)
Need Her Love (Mr. Bugler) (9)
No Tears (In The End) (4)
Of This I'm Sure (7)
Old Greyhound (9)

Over You (8)
Prologue (9)
Put Your Love In My Hands (8)
Searching (2)
Shame On The World (8)
Somebody's Been Sleeping (2)
Something 'Bout Love (5)
Something Lovely (5)

Spinning Around (I Must Be Falling In Love) (2) *52*
Summer Breeze (6)
Superwoman (9)
Thanks For The Laughs (7)
That Ain't My Style (7)
That's What Fate Will Do (2)
Traveling (4)
Una Bella Melodia Brazilania (1)

Where Are You? (4)
Where Do Broken Hearted Lovers Go? (4)
Where Were You When I Needed You (5)
Whirl-Wind (4)
Who Can I Turn To (When Nobody Needs Me) (4)
Who You Really Are (9)
Why Can't We All Unite (3)

Wichita Lineman (medley) (1)
Work To Do (5)
You Ain't Got It No Way (3)
You And Me - Me And You (7)
You Can Call Me Rover (5)
You've Been My Inspiration (1) *64*
You've Got To Take It (If You Want It) (4) *46*

MAJOR FIGGAS   '00
Rap group from Philadelphia: female Bianca Jones with males Far'd Nasir, Maurice Brown, Michael Allen, Antonio Walker, Asa Burbage and Rennard East.

| 9/9/00 | 115 | 4 | © | | Figgas 4 Life | | | $10 | Ruffnation 47749 |

Crack, The
Don't Let A 'igga Stress U Girl
I Love Being A Gangsta

Is It My Style?
It Ain't Sh*t 2 Us
It's Our Life

Reese "Fu*kin'" Rolx
Smooth Thug
Thugs In The Clubs

What U Hatin' For?
What U Know 'Bout Ballin'?
Ya'll Can't *uck With Da Figgas

Yeah That's Us
You Didn't Feel Me Then

MAKAVELI — see 2 PAC

MAKEBA, Miriam   '68
Born Zensi Miriam Makeba on 3/4/32 in Johannesburg, South Africa. Folk singer. Married to **Hugh Masekela** from 1964-66.

11/16/63	86	10			1 The World Of Miriam Makeba			$20	RCA Victor 2750
5/30/64	122	4			2 The Voice Of Africa			$20	RCA Victor 2845
7/10/65	85	11			3 An Evening With Belafonte/Makeba			$20	RCA Victor 3420
					HARRY BELAFONTE/MIRIAM MAKEBA				
11/18/67	182	4			4 Miriam Makeba In Concert!		[L]	$15	Reprise 6253
					recorded at Lincoln Center in New York City				
12/9/67+	74	22			5 Pata Pata			$15	Reprise 6274

Amampondo (1)
Banoyi (4)
Beware, Verwoerd! (3)
Cannon (3)
Click Song #1 (5)
Click Song #2 (4)
Come To Glory (2)
Dubula (1)
Forbidden Games (1)

Ha Po Zamani (4)
Hurry, Mama, Hurry! (3)
Ibabalazie (4)
In The Land Of The Zulus (3)
Into Yam (1)
Jolinkomo (4,5)
Kwedini (1)
Langa More (2)
Le Fleuve (2)

Little Boy (1)
Lovely Lies (2)
Mamoriri (2)
Maria Fulo (5)
Mas Que Nada (4)
Mayibuye (2)
Mommy (4)
My Angel (3)
Nomthini (4)

Pata Pata (5) *12*
Piece Of Ground (4,5)
Pole Mze (1)
Qhude (2)
Reza (4)
Ring Bell, Ring Bell (5)
Saduva (5)
Shihibolet (2)
To Those We Love (3)

Tonados De Media Noche (Song At Midnight) (1)
Train Song (4)
Tuson (3)
Umhome (1)
Uyadela (2)
Vamos Chamar Ovento (1)
West Wind (5)
What Is Love (5)

When I've Passed On (4)
Where Can I Go? (1)
Willow Song (2)
Wonders And Things (1)
Yetentu Tizaleny (5)

MAKEM, Tommy — see CLANCY BROTHERS

MALICE   '87
Hard-rock group from Los Angeles: James Neal (vocals), Jay Reynolds and Mick Zane (guitars), Mark Behn (bass) and Cliff Carothers (drums).

| 4/11/87 | 177 | 6 | | | License To Kill | | | $10 | Atlantic 81714 |

Against The Empire
Breathin' Down Your Neck

Chain Gang Woman
Christine

Circle Of Fire
License To Kill

Murder
Sinister Double

Vigilante

MALKMUS, Stephen   '01
Born on 5/30/66 in Santa Monica, California. Rock singer/songwriter/guitarist. Former member of **Pavement**.

| 3/3/01 | 124 | 2 | © | | Stephen Malkmus | | | $10 | Matador 444 |

Black Book
Church On White

Deado
Discretion Grove

Hook, The
Jenny & The Ess-Dog

JoJo's Jacket
Phantasies

Pink India
Trojan Curfew

Troubbble
Vague Space

MALMSTEEN, Yngwie J.   '85
Born on 6/30/63 in Stockholm, Sweden. Rock guitarist. Formerly with **Alcatrazz**. Backed by band Rising Force: **Joe Lynn Turner** (vocals), Jens Johansson (keyboards) and Anders Johansson (drums).

5/4/85	60	43	©		1 Rising Force			$10	Polydor 825324
9/7/85	52	28	©		2 Marching Out			$10	Polydor 825733
					YNGWIE J, MALMSTEEN'S RISING FORCE (above 2)				
10/11/86	44	23	©		3 Trilogy			$10	Polydor 831073
4/23/88	40	18	©		4 Odyssey			$10	Polydor 835451
					YNGWIE J. MALMSTEEN'S RISING FORCE				
11/11/89	128	8	©		5 Trial By Fire: Live In Leningrad		[L]	$10	Polydor 839726
5/26/90	112	6	©		6 Eclipse			$10	Polydor 843361
2/29/92	121	5	©		7 Fire And Ice			$10	Elektra 61137

All I Want Is Everything (7)
Anguish And Fear (2)
As Above, So Below (1)
Bedroom Eyes (6)
Bite The Bullet (4)
Black Star (1,5)
C'est La Vie (7)
Caught In The Middle (2)
Cry No More (7)
Crying (1)
Crystal Ball (4)

Dark Ages (3)
Deja Vu (4,5)
Demon Driver (6)
Devil In Disguise (6)
Disciples Of Hell (2)
Don't Let It End (3)
Dragonfly (7)
Dreaming (Tell Me) (4,5)
Eclipse (6)
Evil Eye (1)
Far Beyond The Sun (1,5)
Farewell (1)

Faster Than The Speed Of Light (4)
Faultline (5)
Final Curtain (7)
Fire (3)
Fire And Ice (7)
Forever Is A Long Time (7)
Fury (3)
Golden Dawn (7)
Heaven Tonight (4,5)
Hold On (4)
How Many Miles To Babylon (7)

I Am A Viking (2)
I'll See The Light Tonight (2)
I'm My Own Enemy (7)
Icarus' Dream Suite Opus 4 (1)
Judas (4)
Krakatau (4)
Leviathan (7)
Liar (3,5)
Little Savage (1)
Magic Mirror (3)
Making Love (6)
Marching Out (2)

Memories (4)
Motherless Child (6)
No Mercy (7)
Now Is The Time (4)
Now Your Ships Are Burned (1)
On The Run Again (2)
Overture 1383 (2)
Perpetual (7)
Queen In Love (3,5)
Riot In The Dungeons (4)
Rising Force (4)
Save Our Love (6)

See You In Hell (Don't Be Late) (6)
Soldier Without Faith (2)
Spanish Castle Magic (5)
Spasebo Blues (7)
Teaser (7)
Trilogy Suite Op:5 (3)
What Do You Want (6)
You Don't Remember, I'll Never Forget (3,5)

MALO   '72
Latin rock group from San Francisco. Core members: Arcelio Garcia (vocals), Jorge Santana (guitar; brother of **Carlos Santana**), Richard Kermode (keyboards) and Pablo Tellez (bass). Malo is Spanish for "Bad." Also see **Santana Brothers**.

2/12/72	14	31	©		1 Malo			$15	Warner 2584
11/11/72	62	14			2 Dos			$15	Warner 2652
4/28/73	101	11			3 Evolution			$15	Warner 2702
3/23/74	188	3			4 Ascencion			$15	Warner 2769

A La Escuela (4)
All For You (3)

Cafe (1)
Chevere (4)

Close To Me (4)
Dance To My Mambo (3)

Entrance To Paradise (3)
Everlasting Night (4)

Hela (2)
I Don't Know (3)

I'm For Real (2)
Just Say Goodbye (1)

MALO — Cont'd

Latin Bugaloo (2)	Merengue (3)	Moving Away (3)	Offerings (4)	Peace (1)	Think About Love (4)
Latin Woman (4)	Midnight Thoughts (2)	Nena (1)	Oye Mama (2)	Street Man (3)	Tiempo De Recordar (4)
Love Will Survive (4)	Momotombo (2)	No Matter (4)	Pana (1)	**Suavecito** (1) 18	

MAMA CASS '71

Born Ellen Naomi Cohen on 9/19/41 in Baltimore. Died of a heart attack on 7/29/74 (age 32). Cass Elliot of **The Mamas & The Papas**.

10/19/68	87	10			1 **Dream A Little Dream**...			$20	Dunhill/ABC 50040
7/5/69	91	14			2 **Bubble Gum, Lemonade &....Something For Mama**.................................			$20	Dunhill/ABC 50055
12/6/69+	169	6			3 **Make Your Own Kind Of Music**.................................... [R]			$20	Dunhill/ABC 50071
					MAMA CASS ELLIOT				
					reissue of #2 above plus song "Make Your Own Kind Of Music"				
3/13/71	49	7	©		4 **Dave Mason & Cass Elliot**.................................			$20	Blue Thumb 25
3/13/71	194	1	©		5 **Mama's Big Ones** .... [G]			$20	Dunhill/ABC 50093
					includes "Words Of Love" by **The Mamas & The Papas**				

Ain't Nobody Else Like You (5)	Easy Come, Easy Go (2,3,5)	Long Time Loving You (1)	Pleasing You (4)	Sweet Believer (1)	When I Just Wear My Smile
Blow Me A Kiss (2,3)	Glittering Facade (4)	**Make Your Own Kind Of**	Room Nobody Lives In (1)	Talkin' To Your Toothbrush (1)	(2,3)
Blues For Breakfast (1)	Good Times Are Coming (5)	**Music** (3,5) 36	Rubber Band (1)	To Be Free (4)	Who's To Blame (2,3)
Burn Your Hatred (1)	He's A Runner (2,3)	Move In A Little Closer, Baby	Sit And Wonder (4)	Too Much Truth, Too Much	You Know Who I Am (1)
California Earthquake (1) 67	Here We Go Again (4)	(2,3,5)	Something To Make You Happy	Love (4)	
Don't Let The Good Life Pass	I Can Dream, Can't I (2,3)	**New World Coming** (5) 42	(4)	Walk To The Point (4)	
You By (5)	It's Getting Better (2,3,5) 30	Next To You (4)	**Song That Never Comes**	Welcome To The World (2,3)	
Dream A Little Dream Of Me	Jane, The Insane Dog Lady (1)	On And On (4)	(5) 99	What Was I Thinking Of (1)	
(1,5) 12	Lady Love (2,3)	One Way Ticket (5)	Sour Grapes (2,3)		

★316★ MAMAS & THE PAPAS, The '66

Folk-pop group formed in Los Angeles: **John Phillips**, Michelle Phillips, Denny Doherty and **Mama Cass** Elliot. Disbanded in 1968, reunited briefly in 1971. John and Michelle were married from 1962-70; their daughter is Chynna Phillips of the **Wilson Phillips** trio. John is also the father of actress MacKenzie Phillips. Michelle Phillips later became a successful actress; briefly married to actor Dennis Hopper in 1970. Mama Cass died of a heart attack on 7/29/74 (age 32). John Phillips died of heart failure on 3/18/2001 (age 65). Group inducted into the Rock and Roll Hall of Fame in 1998.

3/12/66	❶¹	105	●	©	1 **If You Can Believe Your Eyes And Ears**			$25	Dunhill 50006
10/1/66	4	76	●	©	2 **The Mamas & The Papas**			$25	Dunhill 50010
3/18/67	2⁷	55	●	©	3 **The Mamas & The Papas Deliver**			$25	Dunhill 50014
11/11/67	5	65	●		4 **Farewell To The First Golden Era**	C:#46/2 [G]		$20	Dunhill/ABC 50025
5/25/68	15	34		©	5 **The Papas & The Mamas**			$20	Dunhill/ABC 50031
9/28/68	53	13			6 **Golden Era, Vol. 2**.................................. [G]			$20	Dunhill/ABC 50038
9/27/69	61	26	©		7 **16 Of Their Greatest Hits** .... [G]			$20	Dunhill/ABC 50064
11/6/71	84	8	©		8 **People Like Us** .... [G]			$20	Dunhill/ABC 50106
3/3/73	186	4			9 **20 Golden Hits** .... [G]			$20	Dunhill/ABC 50145 [2]

Blueberries For Breakfast (8)	European Blueboy (8)	I Call Your Name (1,4,7,9)	Midnight Voyage (5)	Rooms (5)	Trip, Stumble & Fall (2,6,7,9)
Boys & Girls Together (3)	Even If I Could (2)	I Can't Wait (2)	**Monday, Monday** (1,4,7,9) 1	Safe In My Garden (5) 53	**Twelve Thirty** (Young Girls
California Dreamin' (1,4,7,9) 4	**For The Love Of Ivy**	I Saw Her Again (2,4,7,9) 5	My Girl (3,6,7,9)	Shooting Star (8)	**Are Coming To The Canyon)**
Creeque Alley (3,4,7,9) 5	(5,6,7,9) 81	I Wanna Be A Star (8)	My Heart Stood Still (2)	Sing For Your Supper (3,6)	(4,5,7,9) 20
Dancing Bear (2) 51	Free Advice (3)	In Crowd (1)	No Dough (8)	Snowqueen Of Texas (9)	Twist And Shout (3,6,7,9)
Dancing In The Street	Frustration (3)	John's Music Box (3)	No Salt On Her Tail (2,6)	Somebody Groovy (1)	**Words Of Love** (2,4,7,9) 5
(2,4,7,9) 73	Gemini Childe (5)	Lady Genevieve (8)	Nothing's Too Good For My	Spanish Harlem (1)	You Baby (1,6,9)
Dedicated To The One I Love	**Glad To Be Unhappy** (6) 26	**Look Through My Window**	Little Girl (5,6)	**Step Out** (8) 81	
(3,4,7,9) 2	Go Where You Wanna Go	(3,4,7,9) 24	Once Was A Time I Thought (2)	Straight Shooter (1,9)	
Did You Ever Want To Cry (3)	(1,4,7,9)	Mansions (5)	Pacific Coast Highway (8)	Strange Young Girls (2)	
Do You Wanna Dance (1,6) 76	Got A Feelin' (1,4,9)	Meditation Mama	Pearl (8)	String Man (3)	
Dream A Little Dream Of Me	Grasshopper (8)	(Transcendental Woman	People Like Us (8,9)	That Kind Of Girl (2)	
(5,6,7,9) 12	Hey Girl (1,6)	Travels) (5)	Right Somebody To Love (5)	Too Late (5)	

MAMA'S BOYS '85

Rock trio from Northern Ireland: brothers Pat (guitar), John (vocals, bass) and Tommy (drums) McManus.

8/11/84	172	8			1 **Mama's Boys**....................................			$10	Jive 8214
6/15/85	151	6			2 **Power And Passion**.............................			$10	Jive 8285

Crazy Daisy's House Of	Hard 'N' Loud (2)	Lonely Soul (1)	Needle In The Groove (2)	Run (2)
Dreams (1)	In The Heat Of The Night (1)	Mama We're All Crazee Now	Power And Passion (2)	Runaway Dreams (1)
Don't Tell Mama (2)	Let's Get High (2)	(1)	Professor, The (1)	Straight Forward (No Looking
Gentlemen Rogues (1)	Lettin' Go (2)	Midnight Promises (1)	Professor II, The (2)	Back) (1,2)

MANÁ '97

Latin rock group: Fher (vocals), Sergio Vallin (guitar), Juan Calleros (bass) and Alex Gonzalez (drums).

11/1/97	67	4	▲	©	1 **Sueños Liquidos** .... [F]			$10	WEA Latina 20430
					title is Spanish for "Liquid Dreams"				
7/10/99	83	15	●	©	2 **MTV Unplugged** .... [F-L]			$10	WEA Latina 27864

Amame Hasta Que Me Muera	Clavado En Un Bar (1)	En El Muelle De San Blas (1,2)	No Ha Parado De Llover (It	Rayando El Sol (Reaching For	Un Lobo Por Tu Amor (1)
(1)	Coladito (2)	Falta Amor (Lacking Love) (2)	Hasn't Stopped Raining) (2)	The Sun) (2)	Vivir Sin Aire (To Live Without
Ana (2)	Como Dueles En Los Labios (1)	Hechicera (1)	Oye Mi Amor (Listen My Love)	Robame El Alma (1)	Air) (2)
Cachito (A Piece Of Your Heart)	Como Te Extraño Corazon (1)	La Sirena (1)	(2)	Se Me Olvido Otra Vez (2)	
(2)	Cuando Los Angeles Lloran (2)	Me Voy A Convertir En Un Ave	Perdido En Un Barco (Lost On	Te Solte La Rienda (2)	
Chaman (1)	Desapariciones (2)	(1)	A Barque) (2)	Tu Tienes Lo Que Quiero (1)	

MANASSAS — see STILLS, Stephen

★327★ MANCHESTER, Melissa '75

Born on 2/15/51 in the Bronx, New York. Singer/songwriter/pianist. Former backup singer for **Bette Midler**.
1)Melissa 2)Hey Ricky 3)Better Days & Happy Endings

6/23/73	156	13			1 **Home To Myself**..................................			$15	Bell 1123
5/4/74	159	5			2 **Bright Eyes**......................................			$15	Bell 1303
3/1/75	12	41	●	©	3 **Melissa**..			$12	Arista 4031
2/21/76	24	17			4 **Better Days & Happy Endings**			$12	Arista 4067
11/20/76+	60	13			5 **Help Is On The Way**			$12	Arista 4095
7/23/77	60	11			6 **Singin'...**			$12	Arista 4136
12/9/78+	33	27		©	7 **Don't Cry Out Loud**			$12	Arista 4186

MANCHESTER, Melissa — Cont'd

DEBUT	PEAK	WKS	RIAA/CD	ARTIST — Album Title	Sym	$	Label & Number
11/3/79	63	21	© 8	Melissa Manchester		$12	Arista 9506
9/13/80	68	11	9	For The Working Girl		$12	Arista 9533
5/15/82	19	39	10	Hey Ricky		$12	Arista 9574
2/26/83	43	21	● © 11	Greatest Hits	[G]	$12	Arista 9611
12/3/83	135	9	12	Emergency		$12	Arista 8094
5/18/85	144	6	13	Mathematics		$10	MCA 5587

All Tied Up (13)
Almost Everything (7)
Alone (2)
Any Kind Of Fool (9)
Bad Weather (7)
Be Happy Now (1)
Be Somebody (5)
Better Days (4) *71*
Boys In The Back Room (9)
Bright Eyes (2)
Caravan (7)
City Nights (12)
Come In From The Rain (4,10,11)
Dirty Work (5)
Doing The Best (That He Can) (1)
Don't Cry Out Loud (7,11) *10*
Don't Want A Heartache (8)
Dream, The (13)
Easy (1)
Emergency (12)
End Of The Affair (12)
Energy (13)
Fire In The Morning (8) *32*

Fool In Love (5)
Fool's Affair (9)
Funny That Way (1)
Good News (4)
Happier Than I've Ever Been (9)
Happy Endings (4)
He Is The One (2)
Headlines (5)
Help Is On The Way (5)
Hey Ricky (You're A Low-Down Heel) (10)
Holdin' On To The Lovin' (8)
Home To Myself (1)
How Does It Feel Right Now (8)
I Can't Get Started (2)
I Don't Care What The People Say (12)
I Don't Want To Hear It Anymore (3)
I Got Eyes (3)
I Know Your Love Won't Let Me Down (3)
I Wanna Be Where You Are (6)
I'll Always Love You (10)

Ice Castles (Through The Eyes Of Love), Theme From (11) *76*
If It Feels Good (Let It Ride) (1)
If This Is Love (9)
Inclined (2)
It's All In The Sky Above (8)
It's Gonna Be Alright (3)
Jenny (1)
Johnny And Mary (12)
Just One Lifetime (13)
Just Too Many People (3,11) *30*
Just You And I (4,11) *27*
Knowin' My Love's Alive (7)
Let Me Serenade You (6)
Lights Of Dawn (8)
Looking For The Perfect Ahh (10)
Love Havin' You Around (3)
Love Of Your Own (6)
Lovers After All (9) *54*
Mathematics (13) *74*
Midnight Blue (3,11) *6*
Monkey See, Monkey Do (5)

My Boyfriend's Back (medley) (11)
My Love Is All I Know (6)
My Sweet Thing (4)
Nice Girls (11) *42*
Night Creatures (13)
No One Can Love You More Than Me (12) *78*
No One's Ever Seen This Side Of Me (6)
No. 1 (Ahwant Gimmeh) (2)
O Heaven (How You've Changed To Me) (2)
Ode To Paul (2)
One More Mountain To Climb (1)
Party Music (3)
Pick Up The Good Stuff (1)
Pretty Girls (8) *39*
Race To The End (10)
Rescue Me (4) *78*
Restless Love (13)
Ruby And The Dancer (2)
Runaway (medley) (11)
Sad Eyes (6)

Shine Like You Should (7)
Shocked (13)
Sing, Sing, Sing (4)
Singing From My Soul (5,7)
Slowly (10)
So's My Old Man (5)
Someone To Watch Over Me (10)
Something To Do With Loving You (1)
Stand (6)
Stand Up Woman (4)
Stevie's Wonder (3)
Stop Another Heart Breakin' (12)
Such A Morning (7)
Talk (9)
Talkin' To Myself (5)
Tears Of Joy (9)
That Boy (12)
There's More Where That Came From (5)
This Lady's Not Home Today (3)
Through The Eyes Of Grace (7)

(Through The Eyes Of Love) ..see: Ice Castles, Theme From
Thunder In The Night (13)
Time (6,12)
To Make You Smile Again (7)
Victims Of The Modern Heart (13)
Warmth Of The Sun (6)
We've Got Time (8)
When We Loved (8)
Whenever I Call Your Friend (8,11)
White Rose (12)
Wish We Were Heroes (10)
Without You (9)
Working Girl (For The) (9)
You And Me (9)
You Can Make It All Come True (4)
You Make It Easy (6)
You Should Hear How She Talks About You (10,11) *5*
Your Place Or Mine (10)

MANCHILD   '77

R&B group from Indianapolis: Flash Ferrell (vocals), Kenneth Edmonds (guitar), Reggie Griffin (reeds), Daryl Simmons (percussion), Chuckie Bush (keyboards), Anthony Johnson (bass) and Robert Parson (drums). Edmonds later formed **The Deele** and recorded solo as **Babyface**.

DEBUT	PEAK	WKS		ARTIST — Album Title	$	Label & Number
10/15/77	154	6		Power And Love	$12	Chi-Sound 765

Especially For You
Funky Situation

(I Want To Feel Your) Power And Love
Red Hot Daddy
Takin' It To The Streets

These Are The Things That Are Special To Me

We Need We
You Get What You Give

MANCINI, Henry ★19★   '62

Born on 4/16/24 in Cleveland; raised in Aliquippa, Pennsylvania. Died of cancer on 6/14/94 (age 70). Leading movie and TV composer/arranger/conductor. Staff composer for Universal Pictures from 1952-58. Winner of Grammy's Lifetime Achievement Award in 1995. Married Ginny O'Connor, an original member of **Mel Torme**'s Mel-Tones, in 1947.

1)Breakfast At Tiffany's 2)The Music From Peter Gunn 3)Music From Mr. Lucky 4)Hatari! 5)Uniquely Mancini

DEBUT	PEAK	WKS	RIAA/CD	ARTIST — Album Title	Sym	$	Label & Number
2/9/59	❶[10]	119	● © 1	The Music From Peter Gunn	[I-TV]	$30	RCA Victor 1956
				1958 Grammy winner: Album of the Year			
6/22/59	7	35	2	More Music From Peter Gunn	[I-TV]	$30	RCA Victor 2040
3/28/60	2[1]	70	3	Music From Mr. Lucky	[I-TV]	$30	RCA Victor 2198
5/8/61	28	26	© 4	Mr. Lucky Goes Latin	[I]	$30	RCA Victor 2360
10/9/61+	❶[12]	96	● 5	Breakfast At Tiffany's	[I-S]	$30	RCA Victor 2362
3/3/62	28	14	© 6	Combo!	[I]	$30	RCA Victor 2258
				released in 1960			
6/2/62	37	12	7	Experiment In Terror	[I-S]	$30	RCA Victor 2442
7/21/62	4	50	8	Hatari!	[I-S]	$25	RCA Victor 2559
2/16/63	12	40	9	Our Man In Hollywood		$25	RCA Victor 2604
6/29/63	5	22	10	Uniquely Mancini	[I]	$25	RCA Victor 2692
12/28/63+	6	42	© 11	Charade	[I-S]	$25	RCA Victor 2755
4/11/64	8	88	● 12	The Pink Panther	[I-S]	$25	RCA Victor 2795
8/1/64	15	19	13	The Concert Sound of Henry Mancini	[I]	$20	RCA Victor 2897
8/8/64	42	35	● 14	The Best Of Mancini	[G]	$20	RCA Victor 2693
1/30/65	11	25	15	Dear Heart And Other Songs About Love		$20	RCA Victor 2990
6/26/65	46	17	16	The Latin Sound Of Henry Mancini	[I]	$20	RCA Victor 3356
10/2/65	63	22	17	The Great Race	[I-S]	$20	RCA Victor 3402
3/12/66	74	13	18	The Academy Award Songs		$25	RCA Victor 6013 [2]
9/10/66	142	4	19	Arabesque	[I-S]	$20	RCA Victor 3623
9/10/66	148	2	20	What Did You Do In The War, Daddy?	[I-S]	$20	RCA Victor 3648
12/3/66+	12[X]	12	21	A Merry Mancini Christmas	[X]	$20	RCA Victor 3612
				Christmas charts: 20/'66, 33/'67, 12/'70			
12/17/66+	121	19	22	Music of Hawaii	[I]	$15	RCA Victor 3713
3/18/67	65	13	23	Mancini '67	[I]	$15	RCA Victor 3694
10/28/67	183	3	24	Two For The Road	[I-S]	$15	RCA Victor 3802
12/9/67+	126	12	25	Encore! More Of The Concert Sound Of Henry Mancini	[I]	$15	RCA Victor 3887
5/3/69	5	42	● © 26	A Warm Shade Of Ivory	[I]	$15	RCA Victor 4140
11/1/69	91	16	27	Six Hours Past Sunset	[I]	$15	RCA Victor 4239
4/25/70	111	17	28	Theme From "Z" and Other Film Music	[I]	$15	RCA Victor 4350

MANCINI, Henry — Cont'd

DEBUT	PEAK	WKS	CD		ARTIST — Album Title	Catalog	Sym	$	Label & Number
9/26/70	196	2		29	This Is Henry Mancini	[G]		$20	RCA Victor 6029 [2]
12/19/70+	91	17	©	30	Mancini Country	[I]		$15	RCA Victor 4307
1/23/71	26	22		31	Mancini plays the Theme From Love Story			$15	RCA Victor 4466
7/31/71	85	11		32	Mancini Concert	[I]		$15	RCA Victor 4542
1/29/72	109	15		33	Big Screen - Little Screen			$15	RCA Victor 4630
4/29/72	74	19	©	34	Brass On Ivory	[I]		$12	RCA Victor 4629
					HENRY MANCINI & DOC SEVERINSEN				
9/23/72	195	5		35	The Mancini Generation	[I]		$12	RCA Victor 4689
6/9/73	185	3	©	36	Brass, Ivory & Strings	[I]		$12	RCA Victor 0098
					HENRY MANCINI & DOC SEVERINSEN				
2/14/76	159	6		37	Symphonic Soul	[I]		$12	RCA Victor 1025
9/18/76	161	4	©	38	A Legendary Performer	[G]		$12	RCA Victor 1843
6/11/77	126	8		39	Mancini's Angels	[I]		$12	RCA Victor 2290
1/10/87	197	2		40	The Hollywood Musicals			$10	Columbia 40372
					JOHNNY MATHIS & HENRY MANCINI				

Adventurers, Love Theme From The (28)
Adventures In Paradise (22)
African Symphony (37)
Airport Love Theme (28)
All His Children (33)
All The Way (18)
Almost Persuaded (30)
Aloha Oe (Farewell To Thee) (22)
Amazing Grace (35)
Aquarium Scene (medley) (19)
Arabesque (19)
Artistry In Rhythm (medley) (32)
As Time Goes By (28)
Ascot (19)
Autumn Nocturne (21)
Away In A Manger (medley) (21)
Baby Elephant Walk (8,14,29,38)
Baby, It's Cold Outside (18)
Bachelor In Paradise (9)
Bagdad On Thames (19)
Baia (16)
Banzai Pipeline (10) *93*
Bateau Mouche (11)
Ben (36)
Beyond The Reef (22)
Big Band Bwana (8)
Big Blow Out (5)
Big Heist (5)
Bistro (11)
Blue Flame (medley) (32)
Blue Hawaii (22)
Blue Mantilla (4)
Blue Satin (3)
Blue Steel (2)
Blues For Mother's (2)
Bluish Bag (37)
Borsalino, Theme From (31)
Brass On Ivory (34)
Breakfast At Tiffany's (5)
Breeze And I (16)
Brian's Song (34)
Brief And Breezy (1)
Brothers Go To Mother's (1,29)
Buon Giorno (Good Morning) (20)
But Beautiful (medley) (40)
Butterfly (37)
Buttons And Bows (13,18)
By The Time I Get To Phoenix (26)
Bye Bye Charlie (11)
C Jam Blues (10)
Cade's County, Theme From (33)
Call Me Irresponsible (18)
Can't Buy Me Love (15)
Car Wash (39)
Carnavalito (16)
Carol For Another Christmas (21)
Castle Rock (6)
Cat, The (23)
Champagne And Quail (12)
Charade (11,14) *36*
Charade (Carousel) (11)
Charade (Main Title) (11,25,35,38)
Charleston Alley (6)
Charlie's Angels, Theme From (39) *45*
Chaser, The (24)
Cheers! (1)
Chelsea Bridge (10)
Cherokee (Indian Love Song) (23)

Chim Chim Cher-ee (18)
Chime Time (3)
Christmas Song (Chestnuts Roasting On An Open Fire) (21)
Cirifiribin (medley) (32)
Cold Finger (17)
Come To The Mardi Gras (16)
Congarocka (24)
Conquest (23)
Continental (You Kiss While You're Dancing) (18)
Cortina (12)
Cow Bells And Coffee Beans (4)
Crazy World (40)
Crocodile, Go Home! (8)
Cycles (26)
Dancing Cat (4)
Day In The Life Of A Fool (26)
Days Of Wine And Roses (9,14,18,25,29,38) *33*
Dear Heart (15,29,38) *77*
Deck The Halls (medley) (21)
Didn't We (27)
Doc, Theme From (33)
Domain St. Juste (Din-Din Music) (24)
Donk, The (24)
Down By The Wharf (7)
Dream (15)
Dream A Little Dream Of Me (26)
Dream Of You (6)
Dream Street (19)
Dreamsville (1,9,13,29,34)
Driftwood And Dreams (22)
Drink More Milk (9)
Drip-Dry Waltz (11)
Eager Beaver (35)
Echoes Of Sicily (20)
End Of The World (30)
Evergreen (39)
Everybody Blow! (16)
Experiment In Terror (7,14)
Experiment In Terror (Twist) (7)
Facade (19)
Fallout! (1,14)
Far East Blues (6)
Festa! (20)
Final Out At Candlestick Park (7)
First Noel (medley) (21)
Floater, The (1)
Floating Pad (3)
Fluters' Ball (7)
(Follow Me) ..see: Mutiny On The Bounty
Foreign Film Festival Medley (25)
Fox, Theme From The (27)
French Provincial (24)
Frosty The Snow Man (medley) (21)
Gigi (18)
Gina (20)
Girl From Ipanema (15)
Girl Talk (27)
Girls Up-A-Stairs (20)
God Rest Ye Merry, Gentlemen (medley) (21)
Golden Gate Twist (7)
Gonna Fly Now (Theme From Rocky) (34)
Good Old Days (7)
Goofin' At The Coffee House (2)
Great Race March (medley) (32)
Great Race March (A Patriotic Medley) (17)

Green Onions (10)
Guarare (Cumbieras) (16)
Happy Barefoot Boy (24)
Happy Carousel (11)
Hark! The Herald Angels Sing (medley) (21)
Harmonica Man (31)
Hatari!, Theme From (8,14,38) *95*
Hawaii (Main Title) (22)
Hawaiian War Chant (22)
Hawaiian Wedding Song (22)
Hawaiians, Theme From The (31)
He Shouldn't-A, Hadn't-A, Oughtn't-A Swang On Me! (17)
Help Me Make It Through The Night (36)
High Hopes (18)
High Noon (11)
Hills Of Yesterday (28)
Holly (5)
Hot Canary (10)
House Of The Rising Sun (23)
How Soon (11)
Hub Caps And Tail Lights (5)
I Can't Get Started (36)
I Can't Stop Loving You (30)
I Had The Craziest Dream (40)
(I Love You And) Don't You Forget It (15)
I'm Gettin' Sentimental Over You (medley) (32)
If (34)
In The Arms Of Love (20)
In The Cool, Cool, Cool Of The Evening (18)
In The Wee Small Hours Of The Morning (26)
Inspector Clouseau Theme (39) (also see: Pink Panther Theme)
Ironside Theme (33)
It Came Upon A Midnight Clear (medley) (21)
It Could Happen To You (medley) (40)
It Had Better Be Tonight (12)
It Might As Well Be Spring (18,40)
Jean (28)
Jesus Christ, Superstar Medley (32)
Jingle Bells (medley) (21)
Joanna (2,13)
Johnny's Theme (33)
Joy (35)
Joy To The World (medley) (21)
Just For Tonight (8)
Kelly's Tune (7)
Killer Joe (35)
La Raspa (16)
Last Date (30)
Last Time I Saw Paris (18)
Latin Golightly (5)
Latin Snowfall (11)
Laura, Love Theme For (36)
Leap Frog (medley) (32)
Let It Be Me (30)
Let's Dance (medley) (32)
Life Is What You Make It (33)
Lightly (2)
Lightly Latin (3,13,29)
Little Drummer Boy (21)
Little Man Theme (2)
Lonely Princess (12)
Lonesome (10)
Long Ago (And Far Away) (40)
Loose Caboose (9)

Loss Of Love (31)
Love Is A Many-Splendored Thing (13,18)
Love Story, Theme From (31) *13*
Lovely Wife (24)
Lover Man (Oh, Where Can You Be?) (36)
Lujon (4,14)
Lullaby Of Birdland (10)
Lullaby Of Broadway (18)
Make It With You (36)
Make The World Go Away (30)
Mambo Parisienne (11)
Man, A Horse, And A Gun (28)
Man's Favorite Sport (15)
Mancini Generation, Theme From The (35)
March Of The Cue Balls (3,13,14,29,32)
M*A*S*H, Song From (31)
Masterpiece, The (35)
Meditation (26)
Megeve (11)
Memphis Underground (35)
Midnight Cowboy (27,29)
Misty (29,34)
Moanin' (6)
Molly Maguires, Theme From The (28)
Moment To Moment (26,38)
Mona Lisa (18)
Moneychangers (39)
Moon Of Manakoora (22)
Moon River (5,13,14,18,25,29,38) *11*
Moon River Cha Cha (4)
Moonlight Becomes You (medley) (40)
Moonlight Serenade (10,32)
Moonlight Sonata (27) *87*
Mostly For Lovers (13)
Mr. Hobbs Theme (9)
Mr. Lucky (3,13,14,15,29,38) *21*
Mr. Lucky (Goes Latin) (4)
Mr. Yunioshi (1)
Music From Hollywood Medley (25)
Music Of David Rose Medley (13)
Music To Become King By (17)
Mutiny On The Bounty (Follow Me), Love Song From (4)
My Friend Andamo (3,13,29)
My Manne Shelly (2)
My One And Only Love (29)
Mystery Movie Theme (33)
Nancy (7)
Natalie (27)
Never My Love (34)
Never On Sunday (13,18)
New Frankie And Johnnie Song (15)
Nicholas And Alexandra, Theme From (33)
Night Flower (3)
Night, Night Sweet Prince (17)
Night Side (8)
Night Train (10)
Night Visitor, Theme From The (31)
Nightmare (medley) (32)
No-Cal Sugar Loaf (4)
Not From Dixie (14)
O Come, All Ye Faithful (Adeste Fideles) (medley) (21)
O Holy Night (medley) (21)
O Little Town Of Bethlehem (medley) (21)

Odd Ball (2)
On The Atchison, Topeka And The Santa Fe (18)
One Eyed Cat (3)
Orange Tamoure (11)
Over The Rainbow (13,18)
Overture (17)
Overture From Tommy (A Rock Opera) (32)
Patton Theme (28)
Pearly Shells (22)
Perhaps, Perhaps, Perhaps (16)
Peter Gunn (1,13,14,29,37,38)
Phaedra, Love Theme From (9)
Phone Call To The Past (30)
Piano And Strings (12)
Pick Up The Pieces (37)
Pie-In-The-Face Polka (17)
Pink Panther Theme (12,29,38) *31* (also see: Inspector Clouseau Theme)
Playboy's Theme (6)
Poor Butterfly (34)
Portrait Of Simon And Garfunkel Medley (32)
Portrait Of The Beatles Medley (25)
Powdered Wig (6)
Preciosa (15)
Profound Gass (1)
Punch And Judy (11)
Push The Botton, Max! (17)
Quentin's Theme (27)
Quiet Gass (3)
Quiet Nights Of Quiet Stars (Corcovado) (15)
Quiet Village (16)
Rain Drops In Rio (4)
Raindrops Keep Fallin' On My Head (28)
Release Me (30)
Rhapsody In Blue (10,38)
Robbin's Nest (29)
Romeo & Juliet, Love Theme From (26,29,38) *1*
Roots Medley (39)
'Round Midnight (23,36)
Royal Blue (12)
Royal Waltz (3)
Rudolph The Red-Nosed Reindeer (medley) (21)
Sally's Tomato (5)
Sandpiper, Theme From The ..see: Shadow Of Your Smile
Satin Doll (23)
Satin Soul (37)
Scandinavian Shuffle (6)
Secret Love (18)
"Senor" Peter Gunn (16)
Session At Pete's Pad (1)
Seventy Six Trombones (9)
Shades Of Sennett (12)
Shadow Of Your Smile (23)
Shaft, Theme From (33)
Shower Of Paradise (19)
Sicily Forever (20)
Sidewalks Of Cuba (6)
Siesta (11)
Silent Night (medley) (21)
Silver Bells (medley) (21)
Silver Streak (39)
Six Hours Past Sunset (27)
Sleigh Ride (medley) (21)
Slow And Easy (1)
Slow Hot Wind (37)
Snowfall (21)
Soft Sounds (1)

Soft Touch (4)
Softly (3)
Softly, As I Leave You (27,29)
Soldier In The Rain (15,34)
Something For Audrey (24)
Something For Cat (5)
Something For Sellers (12)
Something For Sophia (19)
Something Loose (2)
Sometimes (34)
Song About Love (15)
Sorta Blue (1)
Soul Saga (Song Of The Buffalo Soldier) (37)
Sound Of Silver (4)
Sounds Of Hatari (8)
Speedy Gonzales (4)
Spook! (2)
Stairway To The Stars (10)
Stand By Your Man (30)
Stockholm Sweetnin' (23)
Stolen Sweets (23)
Summer Knows (Theme From Summer Of '42) (33)
Sun Goddess (37)
Sweet Leilani (18)
Sweetheart Tree (17,29)
Swing Lightly (6)
Swing March (20,32)
Swingin' On A Star (18)
Swingin' Shepherd Blues (35)
Symphonic Soul (37)
Take Me To The World (30)
Take The "A" Train (medley) (32)
Taking A Chance On Love (40)
Tango Americano (4)
Tarantella Mozzarella (18)
Taras Bulba (The Wishing Star), Theme From (9)
Tavern In Valerno (20)
Teen-age Hostage (7)
Tender Thieves (20)
Tequila (6)
Thank You Very Much (31)
Thanks For The Memory (18)
That's It And That's All (3)
They're Off! (17)
Those Were The Days (33)
Three, Theme For (31)
Three Coins In The Fountain (18)
Tiber Twist (12)
Tico-Tico (Tico-Tico No Fuba) (16)
Tijuana Taxi (27)
Time After Time (40)
Timothy (2,13,14,32)
Tinpanola (4)
Tiny Bubbles (22)
Tipsy (7)
Tommy (A Rock Opera) ..see: Overture
Tomorrow Is My Friend (31)
Too Little Time (9)
Tooty Twist (7)
Traces (27)
Tribute To Victor Young Medley (13)
True Love (40)
Turtles (23)
Two For The Road (24,27,38)
Two For The Road (Main Title) (24)
Vereda Tropical (16)
Village Inn (12)
Walk On The Wild Side (9)
Walkin' Bass (2)
Watch What Happens (26)

MANCINI, Henry — Cont'd

Wave (36)
Way You Look Tonight (18)
We Three Kings Of Orient Are (medley) (21)
We've Loved Before (Yasmin's Theme) (19)
We've Only Just Begun (34)

What's Happening!! Theme (39)
Whatever Will Be, Will Be (Que Sera, Sera) (18)
When I Look In Your Eyes (26)
When You Wish Upon A Star (18,40)

Whistling Away The Dark (31,40)
White Christmas (18,21)
White On White (7)
Willow Weep For Me (34)
Windmills Of Your Mind (26)
Wine And Women (20)

Winter Wonderland (medley) (21)
Without You (36)
Wonderful World Of The Brothers Grimm, Theme From The (9)
You Don't Know Me (30)

You Stepped Out Of A Dream (40)
You'll Never Know (18)
Your Father's Feathers (8)
Z (Life Goes On), Theme From (28)
Zip-A-Dee Doo Dah (18)

MANCOW   '98

Born Erich Muller on 6/21/69 in Kansas City. Morning radio show host.

| 12/2/95 | **171** | 1 | © | **1** | **Box Of Sharpies**.. | | [C] | **$10** | Anon 7400 |
| 12/7/96 | **141** | 1 | © | **2** | **Fat Boy Pizza Breasts** .... | | [C] | **$10** | Anon 7500 |

no track titles listed

| 4/4/98 | **137** | 1 | © | **3** | **In The Kingdom Of The Blind The One Eyed Man Is King**........ | | [C] | **$10** | Anon 7700 |

Aerosmith With Cow (3)
Are You Ready For The Mancow? (1)
Bill The Dog Pimp (1)
Bitch Bang (1)
Bong World (1)
Booty Squirts (1)
Calling The Prez (1)
Cheap Trick Sings "The Mancow Song" (1)
Chocolate Thunder (1)
Clinton Sings "Gimme 3 Shakes Paula" (1)
Cock Ring (1)
Cow Is Eagle Man (3)
Cowboy Dick (1)
Crap On Shitzu (3)
Creepy Autopsy Call (1)
DJ Special Ed (3)

Dr. Dirty (3)
Donny Osmond Goes Grunge (1)
"Each It & I" (Say It Fast) Snothead Live (3)
FCC Rules For Mancow (3)
Friday (1)
Friday Night (1)
Hairclub President And Jack Nicholson (1)
Harry Carey Gets Hairy (1)
Here Are My Shades? (1)
Hey Howard Sperm (1)
Hey Now! (1)
Homeless Larry Gives Directions (3)
I Like The Cow (3)
"Insane Clown Posse" Parody "3 Little Piggies" (3)

Insane Clown Posse "We Down With The Cow!" (3)
Issac Hayes & Hyapatia Lee Duet (3)
James Brown Gets Pissy (1)
Leper Colony (3)
Liar Liar Clinton Liar (3)
Lil' Johnny Muller's Potty Mouth (3)
Mancow As A Kiddie (1)
Mancow Is An Idiot! (1)
Mancow Militia Margarita Phone (3)
Mancow Phone Scam: Born With No Tongue (3)
Mancow Phone Scam: Did His Brother! (3)
Mancow Phone Scam: Fast Food Reservations (3)

Mancow Phone Scam: Fun With 411 (3)
Mancow Phone Scam: He She (3)
Mancow Phone Scam: Mr. Dicksmack (3)
Mancow Phone Scam: Mr. Lipshitz (3)
Mancow Phone Scam: Starsky & Hutch (3)
Mancow Phone Scam: Tampon Hotline (3)
Mancow Phone Scam: Where's My Dot? (3)
Mancow's Official "Friday In Chicago" Song (1)
Mr. Bingo The Monkey That Impersonates Clinton (3)
Mr. Glackameatman (1)

Mr. Methane Farts The Hits (3)
911 (3)
Now You're In Cow's World! (3)
Pailhead (1)
Peter & Dick Share A Shave (1)
Phonegirl At The OB/GYN (3)
Pimps, The (1)
Possessed Boy And Psychic Nut (1)
Prison Diary Of OJ (1)
Puck It (1)
SLAM-O-RAMA! (3)
Sex With A Zoo Monkey (1)
Snap Crackle Phone (1)
Summer In Chicago (1)
Tards Battle (1)
Toy Story (3)
Tribute To Chris Farley (3)
2Pac Man (1)

Turd Goes To Hell (3)
Turd Montage (1)
Turd, Turd, Here Comes The Turd! (3)
Turddy (3)
Uck Yen! (1)
Voice Of A Nation (3)
We Are On The Air! (3)
Where's My Freakin' Teeth? (1)
Whisker Biscuit (1)
Whotta' Bitch (1)
Windows (1)
Womb Woman! (3)

MANDEL, Harvey   '69

Born on 3/11/45 in Detroit. Guitarist for **Canned Heat** from 1969-74.

5/10/69	**187**	3		**1**	**Righteous**..		[I]	**$20**	Philips 306
9/20/69	**169**	4	©	**2**	**Cristo Redentor**		[I]	**$20**	Philips 281
7/22/72	**198**	3	©	**3**	**The Snake**		[I]	**$15**	Janus 3037

Before Six (2)
Bite The Electric Eel (3)
Boo-Bee-Doo (1)
Bradley's Barn (2)
Campus Blues (1)

Cristo Redentor (2)
Divining Rod (3)
Jive Samba (1)
Just A Hair More (1)
Lark, The (2)

Levitation (3)
Lights Out (3)
Long Wait (2)
Love Of Life (1)
Lynda Love (1)

Nashville 1 A.M. (2)
Ode To The Owl (3)
Pegasus (3)
Peruvian Flake (3)
Poontang (3)

Righteous (1)
Short's Stuff (1)
Snake (2,3)
Summer Sequence (1)
Uno Ino (3)

Wade In The Water (2)
You Can't Tell Me (2)

MANDEL, Howie   '86

Born on 11/29/55 in Toronto. Comedian/actor. Played "Dr. Wayne Fiscus" on TV's *St. Elsewhere* (1982-88).

| 6/21/86 | **148** | 6 | © | | **Fits Like a Glove** .... | | [C] | **$10** | Warner 25427 |

Being From Canada
Bernadette

Bill
Bobby

Danny
Going To School

I Became A Dad
I Do The Watusi

Missy & Mom
My Name Is Ernest

Restaurant

MANDELL, Steve — see WEISSBERG, Eric

MANDRE   '77

Born Andre Lewis. R&B singer/songwriter/keyboardist/bassist.

| 9/17/77 | **64** | 13 | | | **Mandre** .... | | | **$12** | Motown 886 |

Dirty Love
Keep Tryin'

Masked Marauder
Masked Music Man

Money (That's What I Want)
Solar Flight (Opus I)

Third World Calling (Opus II)
Wonder What I'd Do

MANDRELL, Barbara   '81

Born on 12/25/48 in Houston; raised in Oceanside, California. Country singer. Host of own TV variety series from 1980-82.

2/24/79	**170**	4	●	©	**1**	**The Best Of Barbara Mandrell**		[G]	**$12**	ABC 1119
5/26/79	**132**	9			**2**	**Moods**			**$12**	ABC 1088
10/13/79	**166**	5			**3**	**Just For The Record**			**$12**	MCA 3165
9/27/80	**175**	6			**4**	**Love Is Fair**			**$12**	MCA 5136
9/5/81	**86**	24	●		**5**	**Barbara Mandrell Live**		[L]	**$12**	MCA 5243

recorded at the Roy Acuff Theater in Nashville

5/29/82	**153**	6			**6**	**...in Black & White**			**$10**	MCA 5295
9/3/83	**140**	4			**7**	**Spun Gold**			**$10**	MCA 5377
9/8/84	**89**	13	©		**8**	**Meant For Each Other**			**$10**	MCA 5477

BARBARA MANDRELL/LEE GREENWOOD

| 12/15/84 | **8**[X] | 2 | © | | **9** | Christmas At Our House | | [X] | **$10** | MCA 5519 |

After The Lovin' (1)
As Well As Can Be Expected (7)
Bad Boys (7)
Battle Hymn Of The Republic (5)
Best Of Strangers (4)
Black And White (6)
Born To Die (9)
Can't Get Too Much Of A Good Thing (8)
Christmas At Our House (9)
Christmas Story (9)
Coming On Strong (4)
Country Girl (5)
Crackers (4)
Cryin' All The Way To The Bank (4)
Darlin' (3)
Doin' It Right (5)

Don't Bother To Knock (2)
Dreams Don't Lie (6)
Early Fall (2)
Fireball Mail (medley) (5)
Fooled By A Feeling (3) **89**
From Our House To Yours (9)
Getting Over A Man (6)
He's Out Of My Life (4)
Held Over (8)
Hey Good Lookin' (5)
Hold Me (1)
I Believe You (2)
I Feel The Hurt Coming On (2)
I Was Country When Country Wasn't Cool (3)
I'll Be Home For Christmas (9)
I'll Never Stop Loving You (8)
I'm Afraid He'll Find You (Somewhere In My Heart) (4)

(If Loving You Is Wrong) I Don't Want To Be Right (2) **31**
In My Heart (5)
In Times Like These (7)
Is It Love Yet (3)
It Can Wait (3)
It Must Have Been The Mistletoe (Our First Christmas) (9)
It Should Have Been Love By Now (8)
It's A Crying Shame (2)
Just One More Of Your Goodbyes (2)
Long Time No Love (4)
Love Is Fair (4,5)
Love Is Thin Ice (1)
Love Takes A Long Time To Die (3)
Loveless (7)

Man's Not A Man ('Til He's Loved By A Woman) (7)
Married But Not To Each Other (1)
Midnight Angel (1)
Mountain Dew (medley) (5)
My Bonnie Lies Over And Over (4)
My Love Can Do No Wrong (3)
No Walls, No Ceilings, No Floors (2)
Not Tonight I've Got A Heartache (1)
Now You See Us, Now You Don't (8)
Old Joe Clark (medley) (5)
One Night A Year (9)
One Of A Kind Pair Of Fools (7)
One On One, Eye To Eye, Heart To Heart (8)

Only Now And Then (7)
Operator, Long Distance Please (6)
Overnight Sensation (7)
Pity Party (2)
Rolling Stone (6)
Santa, Bring My Baby Home (9)
Selfish (3)
She's Out There Dancin' Alone (3,5)
Sleeping Single In A Double Bed (1,2,5)
Soft Shoulder (8)
Some Things Never Change (6)
Sometime, Somewhere, Somehow (4)
Standing Room Only (1)
That's What Friends Are For (1)
This Time Of The Year (9)
Thrill Is Gone (6)

'Till You're Gone (6)
To Me (8)
Tonight (1)
Uncle Joe's Boogie (medley) (5)
Unsung Heros (5)
Using Him To Get To You (3)
We Were Meant For Each Other (8)
We're A Perfect Match (6)
Why Am I Still In Love (6)
Winter Wonderland (9)
Wish You Were Here (5)
Woman To Woman (1) **92**
Years (3,5)
You Are No Angel (7)
You're Not Supposed To Be Here (6)

MANDRILL '73

Latin jazz-rock group from Brooklyn, New York: brothers Louis (trumpet), Richard (sax) and Carlos (flute) Wilson, Omar Mesa (guitar), Claude Cave (keyboards), Fudgie Kae (bass) and Charlie Pardo (drums).

4/24/71	48	22	©	1 Mandrill	$15	Polydor 4050
4/29/72	56	24	©	2 Mandrill Is	$15	Polydor 5025
2/17/73	28	30	©	3 Composite Truth	$15	Polydor 5043
10/13/73	82	15	©	4 Just Outside Of Town	$15	Polydor 5059
4/26/75	92	14		5 Solid	$15	United Artists 408
7/26/75	194	2	©	6 The Best Of Mandrill	[G] $15	Polydor 6047
2/7/76	143	8		7 Beast From The East	$15	United Artists 577
11/12/77	124	10		8 We Are One	$12	Arista 4144
1/13/79	154	5		9 New Worlds	$12	Arista 4195

Afrikus Retrospectus (4)
Ape Is High (2,6)
Aqua-Magic (7)
Aspiration Flame (4)
Can You Get It (Suzie Caesar) (8)
Central Park (2)
Children Of The Sun (2,6)
Closer To You (8)
Cohelo (2,6)
Dirty Ole Man (7)
Disco Lypso (7)
Don't Mess With People (3)
Don't Stop (9)
Fat City Strut (4)
Fencewalk (3,6) 52
Funky Monkey (8)
Gilly Hines (8)
Git It All (2,6)
Golden Stone (3)
Hagalo (3)
Hang Loose (3,6) 83
Happy Beat (8)
Having A Love Attack (9)
Here Today Gone Tomorrow (2)
Holiday (8)
Honey-Butt (7)
House Of Wood (6)
I Refuse To Smile (2,6)
It's So Easy Lovin' You (9)
Kofijahm (2)
Livin' It Up (7)
Lord Of The Golden Baboon (2)
Love Is Happiness (7)
Love One Another (8)
Love Song (4)
Mandrill (1,6) 94
Mango Meat (4,6)
Mean Streets (9)
Moroccan Nights (3)
Never Die (4)
Out With The Boys (3)
Panama (7)
Peace And Love (Amani Na Mapenzi) Medley (2)
Peaceful Atmosphere (7)
Peck Ya Neck (5)
Polk Street Carnival (3)
Ratchet (Como Se Va La Cosa) (7)
Rollin' On (1)
She Ain't Lookin' Too Tough (4)
Silk (5)
Solid (5)
Stay Tonite (9)
Stop & Go (5)
Sun Must Go Down (2)
Symphonic Revolution (1,6)
Synthia Song (7)
Tee Vee (5)
Third World Girl (9)
Too Late (9)
Two Sisters Of Mystery (4)
Universal Rhythms (2)
Warning Blues (1)
When You Smile (9)
Wind On Horseback (5)
Yucca Jump (5)

★463★ MANFRED MANN '64

Born Michael Lubowitz on 10/21/40 in Johannesburg, South Africa. Formed pop-rock group in England: Mann (keyboards), Paul Jones (vocals), Michael Vickers (guitar), Tom McGuinness (bass) and Mike Hugg (drums). Mike D'Abo replaced Jones in 1967. McGuinness left to form McGuinness Flint in 1970. Manfred Mann formed his new Earth Band in 1971: Mann, Mick Rogers (vocals), Colin Pattenden (bass) and Chris Slade (drums). Rogers replaced by Chris Thompson (vocals, guitar) in 1976. Pattenden replaced by Pat King in June 1977. Thompson also recorded with own group Night in 1979. Lineup in 1979: Mann, Thompson, King, Steve Waller (guitar, vocals) and Geoff Britton (drums). King replaced by Matt Irving in 1981. Earth Band dissolved in 1986.
1)The Roaring Silence 2)the Manfred Mann album 3)Somewhere In Afrika

11/21/64+	35	18	©	1 the Manfred Mann album	$50	Ascot 16015
3/6/65	141	4	©	2 the five faces of Manfred Mann	$50	Ascot 16018
6/1/68	176	5		3 The Mighty Quinn	$25	Mercury 61168

MANFRED MANN'S EARTH BAND:

2/26/72	138	6	©	4 Manfred Mann's Earth Band	$20	Polydor 5015
6/23/73	196	2		5 Get Your Rocks Off	$20	Polydor 5050
3/2/74	96	15	©	6 Solar Fire	$20	Polydor 6019
11/30/74	157	3		7 The Good Earth	$15	Warner 2826
9/13/75	120	10	©	8 Nightingales & Bombers	$15	Warner 2877
9/25/76+	10	37	● ©	9 The Roaring Silence	$15	Warner 2965
3/11/78	83	6	©	10 Watch	$15	Warner 3157
5/12/79	144	13	©	11 Angel Station	$15	Warner 3302
1/24/81	87	16	©	12 Chance	$12	Warner 3498
1/28/84	40	21	©	13 Somewhere In Afrika	$12	Arista 8194

Adolescent Dream (12)
Angelz At My Gate (11)
As Above So Below (8)
Be Not Too Hard (7)
"Belle" (The Earth (11)
Big Betty (3)
Blinded By The Light (9) 1
Bring It To Jerome (1)
Brothers And Sisters Of Africa (medley) (13)
Brothers And Sisters Of Azania (medley) (13)
Buddah (5)
California (10)
California Coastline (4)
Can't Believe (4)
Captain Bobby Stout (4)
Chicago Institute (10)
Circles (10)
Cloudy Eyes (5)
Come Tomorrow (2) 50
Countdown (8)
Country Dancing (3)
Crossfade (8)
Cubist Town (3)
Dashing Away With The Smoothing Iron (2)
Davy's On The Road Again (10)
Demolition Man (13)
Did You Have To Do That (2)
Don't Ask Me What I Say (1)
Don't Kill It Carol (11)
Down The Road Apiece (1)
Drowning On Dry Land (10)
Each And Every Day (3)
Earth Hymn (Part 1 & 2) (7)
Earth, The Circle (6)
Everyday Another Hair Turns Grey (3)
Eyes Of Nostradamus (13)
Fat Nelly (8)
Father Of Day, Father Of Night (6)
For You (12)
Fritz The Blank (12)
Get Your Rocks Off (5)
Give Me The Good Earth (7)
Got My Mojo Working (1)
Groovin' (2)
Ha Ha Said The Clown (3)
Heart On The Street (12)
Hello, I Am Your Heart (12)
Hollywood Town (11)
Hubble Bubble (Toil And Trouble) (2)
I'll Be Gone (7)
I'm Up And I'm Leaving (4)
I'm Your Hoochie Coochie Man (1)
I'm Your Kingpin (2)
In The Beginning, Darkness (6)
It's Gonna Work Out Fine (1)
It's So Easy Falling (3)
John Hardy (2)
Joybringer (6)
Jump Sturdy (4)
Koze Kobenini (How Long Must We Wait?) (medley) (13)
Lalela (13)
Launching Place (7)
Lies (Through The 80's) (12)
Living Without You (4) 69
Mardi Gras Day (5)
Martha's Madman (10)
Messin' (5)
Mighty Quinn (Quinn The Eskimo) (3,10) 10
Nightingales And Bombers (8)
No Better, No Worse (3)
No Guarantee (12)
On The Run (12)
Part Time Man (4)
Please Mrs. Henry (4)
Pluto The Dog (6)
Prayer (4)
Pretty Good (5)
Questions (9)
Quinn The Eskimo ..see: Mighty Quinn
Quit Your Low Down Ways (8)
Rebel (13)
Redemption Song (No Kwazulu) (13)
Resurrection (11)
Road To Babylon (9)
Runner (13) 22
Sack O'Woe (1)
Sadjoy (5)
Saturn, Lord Of The Ring
Mercury, The Winged Messenger (6)
Semi-Detached Suburban Mr. James (3)
Sha La La (2) 12
She (2)
Singing The Dolphin Through (9)
Sky High (7)
Sloth (4)
Smokestack Lightning (1)
Solar Fire (6)
Somewhere In Africa (13)
Spirit In The Night (8) 97
Starbird (9)
Stranded (12)
Third World Service (13)
This Side Of Paradise (9)
Time Is Right (8)
To Bantustan? (medley) (13)
Tribal Statistics (13)
Tribute (4)
Untie Me (1)
Vicar's Daughter (3)
Visionary Mountains (8)
Waiter, There's A Yawn In My Ear (9)
Waiting For The Rain (11)
Watermelon Man (2)
What You Gonna Do? (1)
Without You (1)
You Angel You (11) 58
You Are - I Am (11)
You've Got To Take It (2)

★245★ MANGIONE, Chuck '78

Born on 11/29/40 in Rochester, New York. Flugelhorn player/bandleader/composer.
1)Feels So Good 2)Fun And Games 3)Children Of Sanchez

7/3/71	116	11		1 Friends & Love...A Chuck Mangione Concert	[I-L] $15	Mercury 800 [2]
11/20/71	194	4		2 Together: A New Chuck Mangione Concert	[I-L] $15	Mercury 7501 [2]
				above 2 with the Rochester Philharmonic Orchestra		
7/15/72	180	6		3 The Chuck Mangione Quartet	[I] $12	Mercury 631
12/8/73+	157	12	©	4 Land Of Make Believe	[L] $12	Mercury 684
				with the Hamilton Philharmonic Orchestra		
4/26/75	47	19	● ©	5 Chase The Clouds Away	C:#9/2 [I] $12	A&M 4518
11/29/75+	68	15	©	6 Bellavia	[I] $12	A&M 4557
12/6/75+	102	10		7 Encore/The Chuck Mangione Concerts	[K-L] $12	Mercury 1050
11/20/76+	86	24	©	8 Main Squeeze	[I] $12	A&M 4612

MANGIONE, Chuck — Cont'd

10/29/77+	2²	88	▲²	© 9	**Feels So Good**	[I]	$12	A&M 4658
9/16/78	105	6		10	The Best Of Chuck Mangione	[K-L]	$15	Mercury 8601 [2]
9/23/78	14	44	●	© 11	**Children Of Sanchez**	[I-S]	$15	A&M 6700 [2]
6/30/79	27	23		© 12	An Evening Of Magic - Chuck Mangione Live At The Hollywood Bowl	[I-L]	$15	A&M 6701 [2]
2/23/80	8	23	●	© 13	**Fun And Games**	[I]	$12	A&M 3715
5/16/81	55	15		14	Tarantella	[I-L]	$15	A&M 6513 [2]
7/17/82	83	10		© 15	Love Notes	[I]	$10	Columbia 38101
6/25/83	154	7		16	Journey To A Rainbow	[I]	$10	Columbia 38686
9/15/84	148	8		© 17	Disguise		$10	Columbia 39479

All Blues (14)
And In The Beginning (1,7,10)
As Long As We're Together (4,7,10)
B'bye (11,12)
Bellavia (6,11,14)
Buttercorn Lady (16)
Can't We Do This All Night (5)
Carousel (6)
Chaia's Theme (16)
Chase The Clouds Away (5,12) **96**
Children Of Sanchez Finale (11,12)
Children Of Sanchez (Main Theme) (12)
Children Of Sanchez Medley (11)
Children Of Sanchez Overture (11)

Come Take A Ride With Me (6)
Consuelo's Love Theme (11)
Dance Of The Windup Toy (6)
(Day After) Our First Night Together (8,12)
Death Scene (11)
Diana "D" (17)
Do I Dare To Fall In Love (16)
Doin' Everything With You (8,12)
Echano (5,11)
El Gato Triste (4)
XIth Commandment (9,12)
XIth Commandment Suite (14)
Fanfare (11)
Feel Of A Vision (1)
Feelin' (2)
Feels So Good (9,12) **4**

Firewatchers (2)
Floating (3)
Freddie's Walkin' (2,10)
Friends & Love (7)
Friends & Love Medley (1,10)
Fun And Games (13)
Give It All You Got (13) **18**
Give It All You Got, But Slowly (13)
Gloria From The Mass Of St. Bernard (4)
He Was A Friend Of Mine (5)
Hide And Seek (9,12)
Hill Where The Lord Hides (1,2,7,10,12,14) **76**
Hot Consuelo (11)
I Get Crazy (When Your Eyes Touch Mine) (8,12)
I Never Missed Someone Before (11)

If You Know Me Any Longer Than Tomorrow (8)
Josephine (17)
Journey To A Rainbow (16)
Lake Placid Fanfare (14)
Land Of Make Believe (3,4,7,10,12) **86**
Last Dance (9)
Legacy Medley (2)
Legend Of The One-Eyed Sailor (4,7,10,14)
Leonardo's Lady (17)
Listen To The Wind (6)
Little Sunflower (3)
London & Davis In New York, Love Theme From (17)
Look To The Children (2,7)
Love Bug Boogie (16)
Love Note (15)
Love The Feelin' (8,12)

Love Wears No Disguise (17)
Lullaby For Nancy Carol (2,4,10)
Lullabye (11)
Main Squeeze (8,12)
Manha De Carnival (3)
Manteca (7)
Market Place (11)
Maui-Waui (3)
Memories Of Scirocco (15)
My One And Only Love (14)
No Problem (15)
Pages From A Journal In America (2)
Pilgrimage (Part I & II) (11)
Pina Colada (13)
Places Warm (2)
Please Stay The Night (16)
'Round Midnight (14)
Self Portrait (3)

She's Not Mine To Love (No More) (17)
Shirley MacLaine (17)
Side Street, Theme From (9)
Sixty-Miles-Young (2)
Soft (5)
Song For A Latin Lady (16)
Song Of The New Moon (5)
Songs From The Valley Of The Nightingale (1)
Steppin' Out (15)
Sun Shower (2,7,10)
Tarantellas Medley (14)
Things To Come (14)
To The 80's (15)
Torreano (6)
You're The Best There Is (13)

MANHATTANS, The '76

R&B vocal group from Jersey City, New Jersey: Gerald Alston, Winfred Lovett, Edward Bivins, Kenneth Kelly and Richard Taylor. Taylor left in 1976; died on 12/7/87 (age 47).

1)The Manhattans 2)After Midnight 3)It Feels So Good

8/11/73	150	8		1	**There's No Me Without You**	$15	Columbia 32444
3/1/75	160	4		2	**That's How Much I Love You**	$15	Columbia 33064
5/1/76	16	27	●	3	**The Manhattans**	$12	Columbia 33820
2/26/77	68	20	●	4	**It Feels So Good**	$12	Columbia 34450
3/4/78	78	12		5	**There's No Good In Goodbye**	$12	Columbia 35252
4/14/79	141	7		6	**Love Talk**	$12	Columbia 35693
4/19/80	24	26	●	7	**After Midnight**	$12	Columbia 36411
12/13/80+	87	10		© 8	**Manhattans Greatest Hits**	[G]	$12	Columbia 36861
8/8/81	86	10		© 9	**Black Tie**	$12	Columbia 37156
8/6/83	104	8		10	**Forever By Your Side**	$12	Columbia 38600
4/13/85	171	6		11	**Too Hot To Stop It**	$12	Columbia 39277

After You (6)
Am I Losing You (5)
Angel Of The Night (11)
Blackbird (2)
C'est La Vie (1)
Change Is Gonna Come (2)
Closer You Are (7)
Cloudy, With A Chance Of Tears (7)
Crazy (10) **72**
Day The Robin Sang To Me (1)
Deep Water (9)
Devil In The Dark (6)
Do You Really Mean Goodbye? (8)
Don't Say No (11)
Don't Take Your Love (2,8) **37**
Dreamin' (11)
Everybody Has A Dream (5)
Falling Apart At The Seams (1)
Fever (2)

Forever By Your Side (10)
Girl Of My Dream (7)
Goodbye Is The Saddest Word (5)
Happiness (3)
Here Comes The Hurt Again (6)
Honey, Honey (9)
How Can Anything So Good Be So Bad For You? (3)
Hurt (3,8) **97**
I Don't Want To Pay The Price Of Losing You (2)
I Just Wanna Be The One In Your Life (6)
I Kinda Miss You (4,8) **46**
I Wanta Thank You (9)
I Was Made For You (9)
I'll Never Find Another (Find Another Like You) (8)
I'll Never Run Away From Love Again (7)

I'll See You Tomorrow (4)
I'm Not A Run Around (1)
I'm Ready To Love You Again (10)
If My Heart Could Speak (medley) (7)
If You're Ever Gonna Love Me (3)
It Couldn't Hurt (7)
It Feels So Good To Be Loved So Bad (4,8) **66**
It Just Can't Stay This Way (4)
It's Not The Same (7)
It's So Hard Loving You (1)
It's You (4)
Just As Long As I Have You (7)
Just Can't Seem To Get Next To You (9)
Just One Moment Away (9)
Just The Lonely Talking Again (10)

Kiss And Say Goodbye (3,8) **1**
La La La Wish Upon A Star (3)
Let Our Love Come Down (9)
Let's Start It All Over Again (4)
Locked Up In Your Love (10)
Love Is Gonna Find You (10)
Love Talk (6)
Lover's Paradise (10)
Memories (medley) (6)
Mind Your Business (4)
Movin' (5)
New York City (6)
Nursery Rhymes (2)
One Life To Live (medley) (7)
Other Side Of Me (1)
Reasons (3)
Right Feeling At The Wrong Time (6)
Save Our Goodbyes (2)
Searching For Love (3)
Share My Life (5)

Shining Star (7,8) **5**
Soul Train (1)
Start All Over Again (10)
Strange Old World (2)
Summertime In The City (2)
Take It Or Leave It (3)
That's How Much I Love You (2)
That's Not Part Of The Show (6)
Then You Can Tell Me Goodbye (9)
There's No Good In Goodbye (5)
There's No Me Without You (1,8) **43**
Tired Of The Single Life (7)
Tomorrow (5)
Too Hot To Stop It (11)
Too Much For Me To Bear (4)
Up On The Street (Where I Live) (4)
Way We Were (medley) (6)

We Made It (1)
We Never Danced To A Love Song (4,8) **93**
We Tried (6)
We'll Have Forever To Love (3)
When I Leave Tomorrow (9)
When We Are Made As One (11)
When You See Me Laughing (9)
Wish That You Were Mine (1)
Wonderful World Of Love (3)
You Send Me (11) **81**
You Stand Out (9)
You'd Better Believe It (1) **77**
You're Gonna Love Being Loved By Me (11)
You're My Life (5)

★314★ MANHATTAN TRANSFER, The '81

Vocal harmony group formed in New York City: Tim Hauser, Alan Paul, Janis Siegel and Laurel Masse. Cheryl Bentyne replaced Masse in 1979. Group hosted own TV variety show on CBS in 1975.

1)Mecca For Moderns 2)The Manhattan Transfer 3)Coming Out

5/3/75	33	38	●	© 1	**The Manhattan Transfer**	$12	Atlantic 18133
9/18/76	48	9		© 2	**Coming Out**	$12	Atlantic 18183
2/18/78	66	10		© 3	**Pastiche**	$12	Atlantic 19163
12/8/79+	55	37		© 4	**Extensions**	$12	Atlantic 19258
6/13/81	22	27		© 5	**Mecca For Moderns**	$12	Atlantic 16036
12/12/81+	103	11	▲	© 6	**The Best Of The Manhattan Transfer**	[G]	$12	Atlantic 19319
10/8/83	52	27		© 7	**Bodies And Souls**	$10	Atlantic 80104
1/5/85	127	11		© 8	**Bop doo-wopp**	[L]	$10	Atlantic 81233
8/10/85	74	40		© 9	**Vocalese**	$10	Atlantic 81266
5/30/87	187	3		© 10	**Live**	[L]	$10	Atlantic 81723
					recorded in Toyko			
12/5/87+	96	19		© 11	**Brasil**	$10	Atlantic 81803

MANHATTAN TRANSFER, The — Cont'd

DEBUT	PEAK	WKS	RIAA	CD	ARTIST — Album Title	Sym	$	Label & Number
9/21/91	179	2		© 12	The Offbeat Of Avenues		$10	Columbia 47079
12/12/92	120	4		© 13	The Christmas Album ....C:#35/4	[X]	$10	Columbia 52968
					Christmas charts: 25/'92, 30/'93			
3/4/95	123	6		© 14	Tonin'		$10	Atlantic 82661
9/2/95	157	1		© 15	The Very Best Of The Manhattan Transfer	[G]	$10	Rhino 71560

Agua (11)
Airegin (9,10)
Along Comes Mary (14)
American Pop (7)
Another Night In Tunisia (9)
Baby Come Back To Me (The Morse Code Of Love) (8,15) *83*
Birdland (4,6,15)
Blee Blop Blues (9)
Blue Champagne (1)
Blue Serenade (12)
Blues For Pablo (12)
Body And Soul (4,6)
Boy From New York City (5,6,15) *7*
Candy (1,6,15)
Capin (11)
Caroling, Caroling (13)
Chanson D'Amour (2)
Christmas Love Song (13)
Christmas Song (Chestnuts Roasting On An Open Fire) (13)
Clap Your Hands (1)
Code Of Ethics (7)
Confide In Me (12)

Coo Coo U (4)
Don't Let Go (2)
Down South Camp Meetin' (7)
Dream Lover (14)
Duke Of Dubuque (8,10)
Foreign Affair (4)
Four Brothers (3,6,10,15)
Gal In Calico (3)
Gentleman With A Family (12)
Gloria (1,6,10,15)
God Only Knows (14)
Goodbye Love (7)
Goodnight (13)
Groovin' (14)
Happy Holiday (medley) (13)
Have Yourself A Merry Little Christmas (13)
Hear The Voices (11)
Heart's Desire (1,8)
Helpless (2)
Holiday Season (medley) (13)
Hot Fun In The Summertime (14)
How High The Moon (8)
I Second That Emotion (14)
In A Mellow Tone (3)

It Came Upon The Midnight Clear (13)
It Wouldn't Have Made Any Difference (2)
It's Gonna Take A Miracle (14)
It's Not The Spotlight (3)
Java Jive (1,6,15)
Je Voulais (Te Dire Que Je T'Attends) (3)
Jeannine (8)
Jungle Pioneer (11)
Kafka (5)
La-La Means I Love You (14)
Let It Snow, Let It Snow, Let It Snow (13)
Let's Hang On (14)
Love For Sale (3)
Malaise In Malaisie (7)
Metropolis (11)
Move (9,10)
My Cat Fell In The Well (Well! Well! Well!) (8)
Mystery (7)
Night That Monk Returned To Heaven (7)
Nightingale Sang In Berkeley Square (5,6,15)

Notes From The Underground (11)
Nothin' You Can Do About It (4)
Occapella (1)
Offbeat Of Avenues (12)
Oh Yes, I Remember Clifford (9)
On A Little Street In Singapore (3)
On The Boulevard (5,10)
Operator (1,6,15) *22*
Pieces Of Dreams (3)
Poinciana (The Song Of The Tree) (2)
Popsicle Toes (2)
Quietude (Encuentro De Animales) (12)
Rambo (9)
Ray's Rockhouse (9,10,15)
Route 66 (8,15) *78*
S.O.S. (3)
Safronia B (8)
Santa Claus Is Coming To Town (medley) (13)
Santa Man (medley) (13)
Sassy (12)
Save The Last Dance For Me (14)

Scotch And Soda (2)
Shaker Song (4,10)
Silent Night, Holy Night (13)
Sing Joy Spring (9,10)
Smile Again (5)
Snowfall (13)
So You Say (4,10)
Soldier Of Fortune (7)
Soul Food To Go (11,15)
Speak Up Mambo (Cuentame) (2)
Spice Of Life (7,15) *40*
Spies In The Night (5)
Sweet Talking Guy (1)
10 Minutes Till The Savages Come (12)
That Cat Is High (1)
That's Killer Joe (9,10)
That's The Way It Goes (8)
This Independence (7)
Thought Of Loving You (2)
Thrill Is Gone (14)
To You (9,10)
Too Busy Thinking About My Baby (14)
Trickle Trickle (4,6,15) *73*
Tuxedo Junction (1,6,15)

Twilight Zone/Twilight Tone (4,6,15) *30*
Unchained Melody (8)
Until I Met You (Corner Pocket) (5)
Wacky Dust (4)
Walk In Love (3)
(Wanted) Dead Or Alive (5)
What Goes Around Comes Around (12)
Where Did Our Love Go (3)
Who, What, When, Where, Why (3)
Why Not! (7)
Women In Love (12)
(Word Of) Confirmation (5)
World Apart (12)
You Can Depend On Me (1)
(You Should) Meet Benny Bailey (9,10)
Zindy Lou (2)
Zoo Blues (11)

MANILOW, Barry ★66★   '77
Born Barry Alan Pincus on 6/17/46 in Brooklyn, New York. Singer/songwriter/pianist. Studied at New York's Juilliard School. Music director for the WCBS-TV series *Callback*. Worked at New York's Continental Baths bathhouse/nightclub in New York as Bette Midler's accompanist in 1972; later produced her first two albums. First recorded solo as Featherbed. Wrote numerous commercial jingles in the 1970s.

1)Barry Manilow/Live 2)Even Now 3)Tryin' To Get The Feeling 4)This One's For You 5)Greatest Hits

DEBUT	PEAK	WKS	RIAA	CD	ARTIST — Album Title	Sym	$	Label & Number
11/23/74+	9	58	▲	© 1	Barry Manilow II	[E]	$12	Arista 4016
					first released on Bell 1314 in 1974 ($20)			
8/2/75	28	51	●	© 2	Barry Manilow I	[E]	$12	Arista 4007
					first released on Bell 1129 in 1973 ($25)			
11/8/75+	5	87	▲2	© 3	Tryin' To Get The Feeling		$12	Arista 4060
8/21/76+	6	60	▲2	© 4	This One's For You		$12	Arista 4090
5/28/77	❶1	67	▲3	© 5	Barry Manilow/Live	[L]	$15	Arista 8500 [2]
2/25/78	3	58	▲3	© 6	Even Now		$12	Arista 4164
12/2/78+	7	75	▲3	7	Greatest Hits	[G]	$15	Arista 8601 [2]
10/20/79	9	25	▲	© 8	One Voice		$12	Arista 9505
12/13/80+	15	20	▲	9	Barry		$12	Arista 9537
10/17/81	14	25	●	© 10	If I Should Love Again		$12	Arista 9573
9/25/82	69	9		11	Oh, Julie!	[M]	$10	Arista 2500
12/18/82+	32	27	●	12	Here Comes The Night		$10	Arista 9610
12/3/83+	30	19	●	13	Barry Manilow/Greatest Hits, Vol. II	[G]	$10	Arista 8102
12/15/84+	28	20	●	© 14	2:00 AM Paradise Cafe		$10	Arista 8254
6/29/85	100	12	●	15	The Manilow Collection - Twenty Classic Hits	[G]	$10	Arista 8274
11/30/85	42	24		© 16	Manilow		$10	RCA Victor 7044
12/12/87+	70	21		© 17	Swing Street		$10	Arista 8527
5/20/89	64	16		© 18	Barry Manilow		$10	Arista 8570
6/30/90	196	1		© 19	Live On Broadway	[L]	$10	Arista 8638
					recorded on 12/3/89 at the Chicago Theatre			
12/1/90	40	8	●	© 20	Because It's Christmas ....C:#14/8	[X]	$10	Arista 8644
					Christmas charts: 1/'90, 8/'91, 28/'92			
10/12/91	68	8		© 21	Showstoppers		$10	Arista 18687
1/2/93	182	1		© 22	The Complete Collection And Then Some...	[K]	$40	Arista 18714 [4]
10/29/94	59	21	●	© 23	Singin' With The Big Bands		$10	Arista 18771
12/7/96	82	11		© 24	Summer Of '78		$10	Arista 18809
11/28/98	122	7		© 25	Manilow Sings Sinatra		$10	Arista 19033

Ain't It A Shame (22)
Ain't Nothing Like The Real Thing (16)
Air That I Breathe (24)
All I Need Is The Girl (21)
All Or Nothing At All (23)
All The Time (4,7,22)
All The Way (25)
And The Angels Sing (23)
Angel Eyes (25)
Another Life (22)
Anyone Can Do The Heartbreak (18)

As Sure As I'm Standing Here (3,22)
At The Dance (16)
Ave Maria (22)
Avenue C (1,5)
Baby, It's Cold Outside (20,22)
Bandstand Boogie (3,5,7)
Beautiful Music (3,5,7,22)
Because It's Christmas (For All The Children) (medley) (20)
Bells Of Christmas (medley) (20)
Bermuda Triangle (9)

Best Of Me (22)
Best Seat In The House (19)
Big City Blues (14,22)
Big Fun (17,22)
Black And Blue (17)
Blue (14)
Bluer Than Blue (24)
Bobbie Lee (What's The Difference, I Gotta Live) (8)
Brandy (22)
Break Down The Door (10)
Bring Him Home (21)
Brooklyn Blues (17,19,22)

But The World Goes 'Round (21)
Can't Smile Without You (6,7,15,22) *3*
Carol Of The Bells (medley) (20)
Chattanooga Choo Choo (23)
Christmas Song (20)
Cloudburst (2,5)
Come Dance With Me (medley) (25)
Come Fly With Me (medley) (25)

Copacabana (At The Copa) (6,7,15,22) *8*
Can't Smile Without You (6,7,15,22) *3*
Could It Be Magic (2,5,7,15,22) *6*
Dance Away (9)
Dancin' Fool (23)
Dancing In The Dark (21)
Daybreak (4,5,7,22) *23*
Do Like I Do (19)
Don't Fall In Love With Me (13)
Don't Get Around Much Anymore (23)

Don't Sit Under The Apple Tree (23)
Don't Talk To Me Of Love (22)
Early Morning Strangers (1)
Even Now (6,7,15,22) *19*
Excerpt From Handel's Messiah (medley) (20)
First Noel (medley) (20)
Flashy Lady (2)
Fools Get Lucky (10)
Friends (2)
Fugue For Tinhorns (21,22)
Getting Over Losing You (12)

MANILOW, Barry — Cont'd

Give My Regards To Broadway (21,22)
God Bless The Other 99 (19)
Gonzo Hits Medley (19)
Good-bye My Love (14)
Green Eyes (23)
Have Yourself A Merry Little Christmas (medley) (20)
He Doesn't Care (But I Do) (16)
Heart Of Steel (12)
Heaven (11)
Here Comes The Night (12)
Here's To The Man (25)
Hey Mambo (17,22) **90**
Home Again (1)
How Do I Stop Loving You? (22)
I Am Your Child (2,22)
I Can't Get Started (23)
I Can't Teach My Old Heart New Tricks (22)
I Don't Want To Walk Without You (8,22) **36**
I Go Crazy (24)
I Guess There Ain't No Santa Claus (medley) (20)
I Haven't Changed The Room (10)
I Just Want To Be The One In Your Life (6)
I Made It Through The Rain (9,13,15,22) **10**
I Should Care (23)
I Wanna Do It With You (12)
I Want To Be Somebody's Baby (1,22)
I Was A Fool (To Let You Go) (6)
I Write The Songs (3,5,7,15,22) **1**
I'd Really Love To See You Tonight (24)

I'll Be Seeing You (21)
(I'll Be With You) In Apple Blossom Time (23)
I'll Never Smile Again (23)
I'm Gettin' Sentimental Over You (23)
I'm Gonna Sit Right Down And Write Myself A Letter (11,12)
I'm Your Man (16,22) **86**
I've Got The World On A String (25)
I've Never Been So Low On Love (11)
If I Can Dream (19,22)
If I Should Love Again (10,22)
If Tomorrow Never Comes (22)
If We Only Have Love (Quand On N'a Que L'amour) (21)
If You Remember Me (11)
If You Were Here With Me Tonight (16)
In Another World (18)
In Search Of Love (16)
In The Wee Small Hours Of The Morning (25)
It's A Long Way Up (16,19)
It's A Miracle (1,5,7,15,19,22) **12**
It's All Behind Us Now (16)
It's Just Another New Year's Eve (5,20)
Jingle Bells (20)
Joey (22)
Joy To The World (medley) (20)
Jump Shout Boogie (4,5,7)
Jumpin' At The Woodside (medley) (5)
Just Remember (22)
Just Remember I Love You (24)
Keep Each Other Warm (18)
Kid Inside (21)
Last Duet (9,22)

Lay Me Down (3,5,22)
Leavin' In The Morning (6)
Let Freedom Ring (22)
Let Me Be Your Wings (22)
Let Me Go (4)
Let's Get On With It (12)
Let's Hang On (10,13) **32**
Let's Take All Night (To Say Goodbye) (10)
Life Will Go On (9,22)
Linda Song (6)
Little Travelling Music, Please (18,22)
London (9)
Lonely Together (9) **45**
Look To The Rainbow (21,22)
Looks Like We Made It (4,5,7,15,22) **1**
Losing Touch (6)
Love's Theme (24)
Luck Be A Lady (21)
Mandy (1,5,7,15,19,22) **1**
Memory (12,13,15,19,22) **39**
Moonlight Serenade (23)
My Baby Loves Me (22)
My Girl (medley) (22)
My Kind Of Town (Chicago Is) (25)
My Moonlight Memories Of You (18)
Never Met A Man I Didn't Like (21,22)
Never My Love (24)
New York City Rhythm (3,5,7,22)
Nice Boy Like Me (3)
Night Song (14)
No One In This World (medley) (22)
No Other Love (19)
Oh Julie (11) **38**
Oh My Lady (2)

Old Friends (21)
Old Songs (10,13,22) **15**
On The Sunny Side Of The Street (23)
Once And For All (18)
Once In Love With Amy (21)
Once When You Were Mine (17)
One Man In A Spotlight (25)
One More Time (17)
One Of These Days (2)
One That Got Away (18)
One Voice (8,13,15,22)
Only In Chicago (9)
Overture Of Overtures (21)
Paradise Cafe (14)
Please Don't Be Scared (18,22)
Put A Quarter In The Jukebox (13)
Put Your Dreams Away (25)
Rain (8)
Read 'Em And Weep (13,15,22) **18**
Ready To Take A Chance Again (7,15,22) **11**
Real Live Girl (21)
Reminiscing (24)
Riders To The Stars (4,5,22)
Run To Me (15)
Sandra (1,22)
Saturday Night (Is The Loneliest Night In The Week) (25)
Say No More (14)
Say The Words (4)
Second Time Around (25)
See The Show Again (4)
Send In The Clowns (medley) (22)
Sentimental Journey (23)
Seven More Years (2)
She's A Star (3)

Ships (8,13,22) **9**
Silent Night (medley) (20)
Sing It (2)
Singin' With The Big Bands (23)
Some Girls (12)
Some Good Things Never Last (18,19)
Some Kind Of Friend (11,12,13,15) **26**
Some Sweet Day (16)
Something's Comin' Up (1)
Sometimes When We Touch (24)
Somewhere Down The Road (10,13,22) **21**
Somewhere In The Night (6,7,15,22) **9**
Stardust (17)
Starting Again (6)
Stay (12)
Stompin' At The Savoy (17)
Strangers In The Night (25)
Studio Musician (5)
Summer Of '78 (24)
Summer Wind (24)
Summertime (17)
Sunday Father (8)
Sunrise (6)
Sweet Heaven (I'm In Love Again) (16)
Sweet Life (2,19,22)
Sweetwater Jones (2)
Swing Street (17)
This One's For You (4,5,7,15,22) **29**
Tryin' To Get The Feeling Again (3,7,15,22) **10**
Twenty Four Hours A Day (9)
Two Of Us (1)
Up Front (19)
Very Strange Medley (V.S.M.) (5)

We Still Have Time (Theme from Tribute) (9)
We Wish You A Merry Christmas (medley) (20)
We've Got Tonite (24)
Weekend In New England (4,5,7,15,22) **10**
What Am I Doin' Here (14)
When I Need You (24)
When I Wanted You (8) **20**
When Love Is Gone (14)
When October Goes (14,15,22)
When The Good Times Come Again (18)
When The Meadow Was Bloomin' (medley) (20)
Where Are They Now (8)
Where Do I Go From Here (6)
Where Does The Time Go? (23)
Where Have You Gone (14)
Where Or When (21)
White Christmas (20)
Who Needs To Dream (22)
Who's Been Sleeping In My Bed (8)
Why Don't We Live Together (3,5)
(Why Don't We Try) A Slow Dance (9)
Wild Places (22)
You Begin Again (18)
You Can Have The TV (21)
You Could Show Me (8,22)
You Make Me Feel So Young (25)
You Oughta Be Home With Me (4)
You're Leaving Too Soon (3)
You're Lookin' Hot Tonight (13)

MANN, Aimee
Born on 8/9/60 in Richmond, Virginia. Former lead singer of 'Til Tuesday. Married **Michael Penn** on 12/29/97.

'00

DEBUG	PEAK	WKS		CD	#	Title	Sym	$	Label & Number
5/29/93	127	4		©	1	Whatever		$10	Imago 21017
2/17/96	82	4		©	2	I'm With Stupid		$10	DGC 24951
1/22/00	58	17	●	©	3	Magnolia	[S]	$10	Reprise 47583

includes "Goodbye Stranger" and "Logical Song" by **Supertramp**, "Dreams" by **Gabrielle** and "Magnolia" by Jon Brion

| 5/20/00 | 134 | 4 | | © | 4 | Bachelor No. 2 Or, The Last Remains Of The Dodo | | $10 | SuperEgo 002 |

All Over Now (2)
Amateur (1)
Build That Wall (1)
Calling It Quits (4)
Choice In The Matter (4)
Could've Been Anyone (1)
Deathly (3,4)
Driving Sideways (3,4)

Fall Of The World's Own Optimist (4)
Fifty Years After The Fair (1)
4th Of July (1)
Frankenstein (2)
Ghost World (4)
How Am I Different (4)
I Could Hurt You Now (1)

I Know There's A Word (1)
I Should've Known (1)
I've Had It (1)
It Takes All Kinds (1)
It's Not Safe (2)
Jacob Marley's Chain (1)
Just Like Anyone (1)
Long Shot (2)

Momentum (3)
Mr. Harris (1)
Nothing Is Good Enough (3,4)
One (3)
Par For The Course (2)
Put Me On Top (1)
Ray (2)
Red Vines (4)

Satellite (4)
Save Me (3)
Say Anything (1)
Stupid Thing (1)
Sugarcoated (2)
Superball (2)
Susan (1)
That's Just What You Are (2)

Way Back When (1)
Wise Up (3)
You Could Make A Killing (2)
You Do (3,4)
You're With Stupid Now (2)

MANN, Herbie
★217★

'69

Born Herbert Jay Solomon on 4/16/30 in Brooklyn, New York. Jazz flutist. First recorded with Mat Mathews Quintet for Brunswick in 1953. First recorded as a solo for Bethlehem in 1954.

1)Memphis Underground 2)Discotheque 3)Herbie Mann at the Village Gate 4)Waterbed 5)Super Mann

DEBUG	PEAK	WKS		CD	#	Title	Sym	$	Label & Number
7/28/62	30	41		©	1	Herbie Mann at the Village Gate	[I-L]	$20	Atlantic 1380
11/24/62	100	4		©	2	Right Now	[I]	$20	Atlantic 1384
3/2/63	86	7		©	3	Do The Bossa Nova With Herbie Mann	[I]	$20	Atlantic 1397
12/21/63+	104	8		©	4	Herbie Mann Live At Newport	[I-L]	$20	Atlantic 1413
11/27/65	143	3		©	5	Standing Ovation At Newport	[I-L]	$20	Atlantic 1445
10/8/66	139	6		©	6	Our Mann Flute	[I]	$20	Atlantic 1464
2/3/68	151	12		©	7	Glory Of Love	[I]	$15	A&M 3003
5/24/69	20	44		©	8	Memphis Underground	[I]	$15	Atlantic 1522
11/22/69	139	10			9	Live At The Whisky A Go Go	[I-L]	$15	Atlantic 1536
3/7/70	184	3		©	10	Stone Flute	[I]	$15	Embryo 520
3/28/70	189	2		©	11	The Best Of Herbie Mann	[G-I]	$15	Atlantic 1544
4/17/71	137	3			12	Memphis Two-Step		$15	Embryo 531
10/30/71	119	23		©	13	Push Push	[I]	$15	Embryo 532
2/3/73	172	8			14	The Evolution of Mann	[I-K]	$20	Atlantic 300 [2]
6/16/73	163	6			15	Hold On, I'm Comin'	[I-L]	$15	Atlantic 1632
9/22/73	146	8		©	16	Turtle Bay	[I]	$15	Atlantic 1642
3/30/74	109	10		©	17	London Underground	[I]	$15	Atlantic 1648
8/17/74	141	11		©	18	Reggae	[I]	$15	Atlantic 1655
4/19/75	27	18		©	19	Discotheque	[I]	$15	Atlantic 1670
9/27/75	75	7		©	20	Waterbed	[I]	$15	Atlantic 1676
5/8/76	178	2		©	21	Surprises	[I]	$15	Atlantic 1682
2/12/77	132	7		©	22	Bird In A Silver Cage	[I]	$12	Atlantic 18209
10/1/77	122	7		©	23	Herbie Mann & Fire Island		$12	Atlantic 19112
5/27/78	165	5			24	Brazil-Once Again	[I]	$12	Atlantic 19169
2/24/79	77	13			25	Super Mann		$12	Atlantic 19221

MANN, Herbie — Cont'd

Acapulco Rain (12)
Amor Em Paz (Love In Peace) (3)
Anata (I Wish You Were Here With Me) (21)
Aria (22)
Asa Branca (21)
Bang! Bang! (20)
Battle Hymn Of The Republic (8)
Bird In A Silver Cage (22)
Bird Of Beauty (19)
Birdwalk (22)
Bitch (17)
Blues Walk (3)
Body Oil (20,25)
Bossa Velha (Old Bossa) (3)
Butterfly In A Stone Garden (21)
Cajun Moon (21)
Carnival (2)
Chain Of Fools (8)
Challil (2)
Comin' Home Baby (1,5,11,20)
Consolation (3,14)
Cool Man (12)
Creepin' (21)
Cricket Dance (21)
Cries And Whispers, Theme From (16)
Desafinado (2,4)
Deus Xango (20)
)

Deve Ser Amor (It Must Be Love) (3)
Dingue Li Bangue (24)
Django (25)
Do It Again (16)
Don't You Know (4)
Don't You Know The Way (How I Feel About You) (10)
Down By The Riverside (6)
Down On The Corner (12)
Draw Your Breaks (21)
Drown In My Own Tears (14)
Easter Rising (21)
Etagui (25)
Family Affair (16)
Feeling Good (14)
Fiddler On The Roof (14)
Flute Love (23)
Fly, Robin, Fly (22)
Flying (10)
Free For All (2)
Frere Jacques (8)
Garota De Ipanema (4)
Georgia On My Mind (10)
(Gimme Some Of That Good Old) Soul Beat Momma (15)
Glory Of Love (7)
Good Lovin' (6)
Guava Jelly (19)
Guinnevere (12)
Gymnopedie (14)
Happier Than The Morning Sun (16)

Happy Brass (6)
High Above The Andes (19)
Hijack (19) *14*
Hold On, I'm Comin' (7,8,15)
House Of The Risin' Sun (7)
I Can't Turn You Loose (19)
I Got A Woman (20)
I Won't Last A Day Without You (19)
If (13)
In And Out (7)
In Memory Of Elizabeth Reed (16)
In Tangier (medley) (10)
In The Summertime (23)
Incense (14)
It Ain't Necessarily So (1)
Jisco Dazz (25)
Jumpin' With Symphony Sid (2)
(Just An Old) Balalaika Love Song (16)
Kabuki Rock (12)
Lady Marmalade (19)
Layla (17)
Letter, The (7)
Love Is Stronger Far Than We (7)
Lugar Comum (Common Place) (24)
Malamondo (Funny World), Theme From (6)
Man And A Woman (11) *88*
Man's Hope (13)

Meditation (2)
Mediterranean (19)
Mellow Yellow (17)
Memphis Spoon Bread & Dover Sole (17)
Memphis Two-Step (12)
Memphis Underground (8,11,15) *44*
Menina Feia (Ugly Girl) (3)
Miss Free Spirit (10)
Monday Monday (6)
Motherless Child (14)
Mushi Mushi (5)
My Girl (18)
Never Can Say Goodbye (13,15)
Never Ending Song Of Love (16)
New Orleans (8,14)
Night They Drove Old Dixie Down (12)
Nirvana (14)
No Use Crying (7)
Not Now - Later On (14)
Now I've Found A Lady (Soul Rachanga) (16)
O Barquinho (2)
O Meu Amor Chorou (Cry Of Love) (24)
Ob-La-Di, Ob-La-Da (18)
Oh, How I Want To Love You (7,24)
Once I Had A Love (23)

One Note Samba (Samba De Uma Nota So) (3)
Ooh Baby (9)
Our Man Flint (6)
Paper Sun (17)
Paradise Beach (medley) (10)
Paradise Music (20)
Patato (5,14)
Pele (24)
Pendulum (10)
Philly Dog (6,9,11) *93*
Pick Up The Pieces (19)
Piper, The (22)
Please Send Me Someone To Love (14)
Push Push (13)
Rainy Night In Georgia (16)
Respect Yourself (15)
Reverend Lee (16)
Rhythmatism (23)
Right Now (2)
Rivers Of Babylon (18)
Rock Freak (25)
Samba De Orfeu (4)
Scratch (6,14)
Skip To My Lou (6)
Soft Winds (4)
Something In The Air (17)
Soul Man (12)
Sound Of Windwood (21)
Spin Ball (17)
Spirit In The Dark (13)
Stolen Moments (5)

Stomp Your Feet (25)
Summer Strut (23)
Summertime (1)
Superman (25) *26*
Swingin' Shepherd Blues (18)
This Is My Beloved, Theme From (6)
This Little Girl Of Mine (11)
Turkish Coffee (14)
Turtle Bay (16)
Unchain My Heart (7) *81*
Upa, Neguinho (7)
Violet Don't Be Blue (20)
Voce E Eu (You And I) (3)
Waltz For My Son (10)
Waterbed (7)
Welcome Sunrise (23)
What'd I Say (13)
What's Going On (13)
Whiter Shade Of Pale (17)
Why Don't You Do Right (14)
Years Of Love (22)
Yesterday's Kisses (14)
You Are The Song (23)
You Never Give Me Your Money (17)

MANN, Johnny, Singers   '67

Born on 8/30/28 in Baltimore. Musical director for Joey Bishop's TV talk show.

DEBUT	PEAK	WKS		ARTIST — Album Title	Sym	$	Label & Number
10/12/63	90	4	1	Golden Folk Song Hits, Volume Two		$20	Liberty 7296
10/3/64	77	15	2	Invisible Tears		$20	Liberty 7387
7/15/67	51	23	3	We Can Fly! Up-Up And Away		$20	Liberty 7523
12/9/67	68[X]	4	4	The Christmas Album	[X]	$25	Sunset 5186

4 BOBBY VEE with the JOHNNY MANN SINGERS
reissue of Vee's 1962 album *Merry Christmas From Bobby Vee* on Liberty 7267 (minus 2 tracks)

| 12/16/67 | 31[X] | 3 | 5 | We Wish You A Merry Christmas | [X] | $20 | Liberty 7522 |

Al-Di-La (2)
As Lately We Watched (5)
Blue Christmas (4)
Blue Velvet (2)
Deck The Halls (5)
Dedicated To The One I Love (3)
Everybody Loves Somebody (5)
First Noel (5)
Foggy Foggy Dew (1)
Girl From Ipanema (2)

Go Tell It On The Mountain (5)
Go Where You Wanna Go (3)
Gotta Travel On (1)
Green Leaves Of Summer (1)
Greenback Dollar (3)
Hello, Dolly! (4)
Honeycomb (1)
I Got Rhythm (3)
I'll Be Home For Christmas (4)
If I Had A Hammer (1)
Invisible Tears (2)

Jingle-Bell Rock (4)
Jingle Bells (5)
Joey Is The Name (3)
Johnny Bring The Pine Tree In (5)
Lo How A Rose (5)
Love Me With All Your Heart (2)
Monday, Monday (3)
My Christmas Love (4)
Not So Merry Christmas (4)
O Christmas Tree (5)

O Little Town Of Bethlehem (5)
People (2)
Portrait Of My Love (3)
Puff (The Magic Dragon) (1)
Release Me (3)
Shangri-La (2)
Silent Night (4)
Silver Bells (4)
Sleep, Sweet Jesus, Sleep (5)
Somethin' Stupid (3)
Susan Belle (3)

(There's No Place Like) Home For The Holidays (4)
Thievin' Stranger (1)
This Is My Song (3)
Today (2)
Two Brothers (1)
Up-Up And Away (3) *91*
Walk Right In (1)
Waltzing Matilda (1)
We Wish You A Merry Christmas (5)

White Christmas (4)
Wimoweh (1)
Winter Wonderland (4)
World I Used To Know (2)
World Without Love (2)
Yellow Balloon (3)

MANN, Manfred — see MANFRED MANN

MANNA, Charlie   '61

Born on 10/6/20 in New York City. Died on 11/9/71 (age 51). Comedian.

| 7/24/61 | 27 | 14 | | Manna Overboard!! | [C] | $25 | Decca 4159 |

Astronaut, The   Breakfast At The White House   Hey, Bud!   Inside You   Perfect Squelch   War At Sea

★367★ MANNHEIM STEAMROLLER   '95

Classical-rock group from Omaha, Nebraska. Under the direction of composer/producer/drummer **Chip Davis**, who founded American Gramaphone Records in 1974. Other members are Jackson Berkey, Amanda Berkey, Ron Cooley and Arnie Roth. Gained recognition through performance on a series of "Old Home Bread" TV commercials. Davis wrote **C.W. McCall's** "Convoy." Group named after a term from the 1700s meaning crescendo.

1)Christmas In The Aire 2)A Fresh Aire Christmas 3)Mannheim Steamroller Christmas

DEBUT	PEAK	WKS	RIAA	CD		ARTIST — Album Title	Catalog	Sym	$	Label & Number
12/22/84+	110	6	▲5	©	1	Mannheim Steamroller Christmas	C:❶4/83	[X-I]	$10	American Gram. 1984

Christmas charts: 3/84, 2/85, 2/87, 2/88, 3/89, 2/90, 1/91, 6/92, 3/93, 3/94, 3/95, 4/96, 10/97, 8/98, 13/99, 25/00

12/21/85	117	5		©	2	Mannheim Steamroller Christmas		[X-I-R]	$10	American Gram. 1984
12/13/86+	155	14	●	©	3	Fresh Aire VI		[I]	$10	American Gram. 386
12/20/86	126	5		©	4	Mannheim Steamroller Christmas		[X-I-R]	$10	American Gram. 1984
12/19/87+	118	19	●	©	5	Classical Gas		[I]	$10	American Gram. 800

5 MASON WILLIAMS & MANNHEIM STEAMROLLER

| 11/26/88 | 36 | 8 | ▲5 | © | 6 | A Fresh Aire Christmas | C:❶17/81 | [X-I] | $10 | American Gram. 1988 |

Christmas charts: 1/88, 2/89, 3/90, 1/91, 5/92, 2/93, 3/94, 4/95, 3/96, 10/97, 6/98, 28/99, 21/00

11/26/88+	50	8		©	7	Mannheim Steamroller Christmas		[X-I-R]	$10	American Gram. 1984
12/2/89+	43	8		©	8	A Fresh Aire Christmas		[X-I-R]	$10	American Gram. 1988
12/2/89+	54	8		©	9	Mannheim Steamroller Christmas		[X-I-R]	$10	American Gram. 1984
2/17/90	167	8	●	©	10	Yellowstone - The Music Of Nature		[I]	$10	American Gram. 3089
12/1/90+	47	8		©	11	A Fresh Aire Christmas		[X-I-R]	$10	American Gram. 1988
12/1/90+	59	7		©	12	Mannheim Steamroller Christmas		[X-I-R]	$10	American Gram. 1984
12/1/90	77	16	●	©	13	Fresh Aire 7		[I]	$10	American Gram. 777
9/30/95	3	18	▲4	©	14	Christmas In The Aire	C:#2 13/41	[X-I]	$10	American Gram. 1995

Christmas charts: 1/95, 2/96, 5/97, 5/98, 13/99, 20/00

| 11/15/97 | 24 | 9 | ▲ | © | 15 | Christmas Live | C:#6/15 | [X-I-L] | $10 | American Gram. 1997 |

recorded on 1/3/96 at the Orpheum Theater in Omaha, Nebraska; Christmas charts: 1/97, 14/98, 19/00

MANNHEIM STEAMROLLER — Cont'd

11/14/98	25	11	▲	© 16	The Christmas Angel - A Family Story	C:#11/7 [X-I]	$10	American Gram. 1998
					story narrated by Olivia Newton-John and Chip Davis; Christmas charts: 2/'98, 10/'99			
4/3/99	89	10		© 17	Mannheim Steamroller Meets The Mouse	[I]	$10	Walt Disney 60641
10/16/99	168	1		© 18	25 Year Celebration Of Mannheim Steamroller	[I-K]	$15	American Gram. 25 [2]

Above The Northern Lights (16)
Allegro 1 & 3 (10)
Angels We Have Heard on High (14,15,16)
Ballad Of Davy Crockett (17)
Ballade (10)
Baroque-A-Nova (5,18)
Bring A Torch, Jeannette, Isabella (1,2,4,7,9,12)
Cantique De Noel (O Holy Night) (6,8,11)
Carol Of The Bells (6,8,11,16)
Carol Of The Birds (1,2,4,7,9,12,15)
Chim Chim Cher-ee (17)
Chocolate Coffee (18)
Chocolate Fudge (18)
Christmas Lullaby (14,15,18)
Classical Gas (5)
Come Home To The Sea (3,10)
Conjuring The Number 7 (13)

Country Idyll (5)
Coventry Carol (1,2,4,7,9,12)
Crystal (6)
Dancin' In The Stars (18)
Deck The Halls (1,2,4,7,9,12,16)
Doot-Doot (5)
Dream, The (16)
Earthrise (10)
Eclectic Blue (18)
Four Rows Of Jacks (18)
Fourth Door (18)
Gagliarda (14,15)
Go The Distance (17)
God Rest Ye Merry, Gentlemen (1,2,4,7,9,12,15)
Going To Another Place (15)
Good King Wenceslas (1,2,4,7,9,12,16)
Grand Canyon Suite (10)
Greensleeves (5,6,8,11,16)

Hakuna Matata (17)
Hark! The Herald Angels Sing (6,8,11)
Hark! The Herald Trumpets Sing (6,8,11)
Harp Seals (18)
Heigh-Ho (17)
Herbei, oh mein Glaubigan (O Come All Ye Faithful) (14)
Holly And The Ivy (6,8,11,18)
I Saw Three Ships (1,2,4,7,9,12,15)
In Dulci Jubilo (6,8,11,15)
Jingle Bells (14)
Joseph Dear Oh Joseph Mine (14)
Joy To The World (14,15,16)
Kanbai (18)
Katydid's Ditty (5)
Kling, Glockchen (14)
La Chanson De Claudine (5)

Little Drummer Boy (6,8,11)
Lo How A Rose E'er Blooming (6,8,11)
Los Peces en el Rio (14,15)
McCall (5)
Messengers Of Christmas (14)
Mickey Mouse March (17)
Morning (10,18)
Morning Blend (18)
Nepenthe (3,10)
Night Festival At Rhodes (medley) (3)
O' Little Town of Bethlehem (14)
Olympics, The (3)
Orpheus Suite Medley (3)
Pat A Pan (14,15)
Pines Of Rome (18)
Pini Del Gianicolo (18)
Pini Di Villa Borghese (10)
Reflection (17)

Reggae Mañana Mon (18)
Return To The Earth (10)
Rudolph The Red Nosed Reindeer (14,15)
Ruslan And Ludmilla (18)
Samba Beach (5)
Saturday Night At The World (5)
7 C's (13)
7 Chakras Of The Body Medley (13)
7 Colours Of The Rainbow (13)
7 Metals Of Alchemy (13,18)
7 Stars Of The Big Dipper (13)
Shady Dell (5)
Sirens (3)
Sky, The (10)
Slo Dancin' In The Living Room (18)
Sonata Bach's Lunch (18)
Steamroller, The (18)
Still Still Still (6,8,11)

Stille Nacht (Silent Night) (1,2,4,7,9,12,15,16)
Sunday The 7th Day (13)
Sunflower (5)
Sunrise At Rhodes (3,10)
Supercalifragilisticexpialidocious (17)
Traditions Of Christmas (6,8,11)
Twilight At Rhodes (3,18)
Under The Sea (17)
Vancouver Island (5)
Veni Veni (O Come O Come Emanuel) (6,8,11)
Wassail, Wassail (1,2,4,7,9,12,15,18)
We Three Kings (1,2,4,7,9,12)
When You Wish Upon A Star (17)
Winter's Day (18)
You've Got A Friend In Me (17)
Zip-A-Dee-Doo-Dah (17,18)

MANSON, Marilyn   '98

Born Brian Warner on 1/5/69 in Canton, Ohio. Hard-rock singer/songwriter. Noted for his controversial stage performances. His band includes: Scott "Daisy Berkowitz" Putesky (guitar), Steve "Madonna Wayne Gacy" Bier (keyboards), Jeordi "Twiggy Ramirez" White (bass) and Ken "Ginger Fish" Wilson (drums).

11/11/95+	31	50	▲	© 1	Smells Like Children		$10	Nothing 92641
10/26/96	3	52	▲	© 2	Antichrist Superstar		$10	Nothing 90086
12/13/97	102	3		© 3	Remix & Repent	[K-M]	$10	Nothing 95017
10/3/98	❶[1]	33	▲	© 4	Mechanical Animals		$10	Nothing 90273
12/4/99	82	4		© 5	The Last Tour On Earth	[L]	$10	Nothing 490524
12/2/00	13	13		© 6	Holy Wood (In The Shadow Of The Valley Of Death)		$10	Nothing 490832

Angel With The Scabbed Wings (2)
Antichrist Superstar (2,3,5)
Astonishing Panorama Of The Endtimes (5)
Beautiful People (2,5)
Born Again (6)
Burning Flag (6)
Coma Black (6)
Coma White (4)
Count To 6 And Die (6)
Cruci-Fiction In Space (6)
Cryptorchid (2)
Dance Of The Dope Hats (1)

Dancing With The One-Legged... (1)
Death Song (6)
Deformography (2)
Diary Of A Dope Fiend (1)
Disassociative (4)
Disposable Teens (6)
Dope Show (4,5)
Dried Up, Tied And Dead To The World (2,3)
Everlasting C***sucker (1)
Fall Of Adam (6)
Fight Song (6)
F*** Frankie (1)

Fundamentally Loathsome (4)
Get Your Gunn (5)
Godeatgod (6)
Great Big White World (4,5)
Hands Of Small Children (1)
Horrible People (3)
I Don't Like The Drugs (But The Drugs Like Me) (4,5)
I Put A Spell On You (1)
I Want To Disappear (4)
In The Shadow Of The Valley Of Death (6)
Inauguration Of The Mechanical Christ (5)

Irresponsible Hate Anthem (2,5)
Kiddie Grinder (1)
Kinderfeld (2)
King Kill 33 (6)
Lamb Of God (6)
Last Day On Earth (4,5)
Little Horn (2)
Love Song (6)
Lunchbox (5)
Man That You Fear (2,3)
May Cause Discoloration Of The Urine Or Feces (1)
Mechanical Animals (4)
Minute Of Decay (2)

Mister Superstar (2)
New Model No. 15 (4)
1996 (2)
Nobodies, The (6)
Place In The Dirt (6)
Posthuman (4)
"President Dead" (6)
Reflecting God (2,5)
Rock Is Dead (4,5)
Rock 'n' Roll Nigger (1)
Scabs, Guns And Peanut Butter (1)
S****y Chicken Gang Bang (1)
Speed Of Pain (4)

Sweet Dreams (5)
Sweet Dreams (Are Made Of This) (1)
Sympathy For The Parents (1)
Target Audience (6)
Tourniquet (2)
Tourniquet Prosthetic Dance Mix (3)
User Friendly (4)
Valentine's Day (6)
White Trash (1)
Wormboy (2)

MANTOVANI ★10★   '58

Born Annunzio Paolo Mantovani on 11/15/05 in Venice, Italy. Died on 3/29/80 (age 74). Classical violinist/bandleader. Known for his 40-piece orchestra and distinctive "cascading strings" sound.

1)Film Encores 2)Mantovani plays music from Exodus and other great themes 3)Christmas Carols 4)Gems Forever 5)Mantovani Stereo Showcase

2/19/55	13	2			1	The Music Of Rudolf Friml	[I]	$25	London 1150
						sequel to his 1953 album The Music of Victor Herbert (#1) on London 746			
3/19/55	14	2			2	Waltz Time	[I]	$25	London 1094
7/9/55	8	8	●	© 3	Song Hits From Theatreland	[I]	$25	London 1219
5/26/56	12	7		4	Waltzes Of Irving Berlin	[I]	$25	London 1452
5/27/57+	❶[1]	231	●	5	Film Encores	[I]	$25	London 1700
12/9/57	4	6	●	© 6	Christmas Carols	[X-I]	$20	London 913
						first released in 1953 and charted in 1954 (#6)			
3/24/58	22	1		7	Mantovani Plays Tangos	[I-E]	$20	London 768
						first released in 1953			
5/19/58	5	104	●	© 8	Gems Forever...	[I]	$20	London 3032
11/24/58+	7	68	●	9	Strauss Waltzes	[I]	$20	London 685
						first released in 1953			
12/22/58	3	3		© 10	Christmas Carols	[X-I-R]	$20	London 913
2/16/59+	13	46		11	Continental Encores	[I]	$20	London 3095
6/1/59	6	11		12	Mantovani Stereo Showcase	[I-K]	$20	London SS1
6/15/59	14	26		13	Film Encores, Vol. 2	[I]	$20	London 3117
12/21/59	16	3	© 14		Christmas Carols	[X-I-R]	$20	London 913
1/4/60	8	18		15	All-American Showcase	[I-K]	$25	London 3122 [2]
3/28/60	11	30		16	The American Scene	[I]	$20	London 3136
7/25/60	21	53		17	Songs To Remember	[I]	$20	London 3149

DEBUT	PEAK	WKS	RIAA	CD	ARTIST — Album Title	Sym	$	Label & Number
					MANTOVANI — Cont'd			
12/5/60+	2[5]	71	●		18 **Mantovani plays music from Exodus and other great themes**	[I]	$20	London 3231
12/19/60	8	3		©	19 **Christmas Carols**	[X-I-R]	$20	London 913
2/20/61	22	12			20 **Operetta Memories**...............................	[I]	$20	London 3181
5/29/61	8	50			21 **Italia Mia**	[I]	$20	London 3239
8/14/61	29	10			22 **Themes From Broadway**	[I]	$20	London 3250
12/18/61+	36	6		©	23 **Christmas Carols**	[X-I-R]	$20	London 913
1/13/62	83	8			24 **Songs Of Praise**	[I]	$15	London 245
6/9/62	8	26			25 **American Waltzes**	[I]	$15	London 248
10/27/62	24	15			26 **Moon River and other great film themes**	[I]	$15	London 249
1/5/63	136	4			27 **Stop The World-I Want To Get Off/Oliver!**.....	[I]	$15	London 270
6/1/63	10	18			28 **Latin Rendezvous**	[I]	$15	London 295
6/8/63	41	12			29 **Classical Encores**	[I]	$15	London 269
11/9/63+	51	22		©	30 **Mantovani/Manhattan**	[I]	$15	London 328
12/14/63	7[X]	15			31 **Christmas Greetings From Mantovani And His Orchestra**	[X-I]	$15	London 338
					Christmas charts: 7/'63, 23/'65, 42/'66, 20/'67, 10/'68			
3/14/64	134	3		©	32 **Kismet**		$15	London 44043
					vocals by opera stars Robert Merrill and Regina Resnik and chorus			
4/18/64	135	6			33 **Folk Songs Around The World**	[I]	$15	London 360
11/7/64	37	43		©	34 **The Incomparable Mantovani**	[I]	$15	London 392
3/20/65	26	31			35 **The Mantovani Sound - Big Hits From Broadway And Hollywood**..........	[I]	$15	London 419
10/23/65	41	21			36 **Mantovani Ole**	[I]	$15	London 422
3/5/66	23	26			37 **Mantovani Magic**	[I]	$15	London 448
10/8/66	27	35			38 **Mr. Music...Mantovani**	[I]	$15	London 474
3/11/67	53	33	●	©	39 **Mantovani's Golden Hits**	[G-I]	$15	London 483
9/23/67	49	22			40 **Mantovani/Hollywood**	[I]	$15	London 516
3/2/68	64	25		©	41 **The Mantovani Touch**	[I]	$15	London 526
6/15/68	148	7			42 **Mantovani/Tango**	[I]	$15	London 532
11/9/68	143	7		©	43 **Mantovani...Memories**	[I]	$15	London 542
4/5/69	73	17			44 **The Mantovani Scene**	[I]	$15	London 548
11/1/69	92	17			45 **The World Of Mantovani**	[I]	$15	London 565
4/4/70	77	24			46 **Mantovani Today**	[I]	$15	London 572
11/7/70	167	3			47 **Mantovani In Concert**	[I-L]	$15	London 578
					recorded at the Royal Festival Hall in London			
3/27/71	105	15			48 **From Monty, With Love**	[I-K]	$20	London 585 [2]
10/30/71	150	9			49 **To Lovers Everywhere U.S.A.**	[I]	$15	London 598
5/27/72	156	12			50 **Annunzio Paolo Mantovani**	[I]	$15	London 610

A Media Luz (7)
Abide With Me (24)
Accelerations (9)
Adeste Fideles (6,10,14,19,23)
Adios (36)
Adios Muchachos (7,42)
Advise And Consent (26)
Affair To Remember ..see: Our Love Affair
Ah! Sweet Mystery Of Life (15)
Air For The G String (29,48)
Alfie (41)
Alice Blue Gown (25)
All Alone (4)
All Of A Sudden (49)
All The Things You Are (8)
All Through The Night (medley) (33)
Almost Like Being In Love (3)
Almost There (41)
Always (4,15)
Amapola (28)
And This Is My Beloved (32)
Andalucia (The Breeze And I) (28)
Anema E Core (With All My Heart And Soul) (11)
Annie Laurie (medley) (33)
Anniversary Waltz (43)
Answer Me (11)
Apartment, The (26)
April In Portugal (11)
April Love (13)
Aquarius (45,47)
Arana De La Noche (7)
Around The World (13,39) 12
Arrivederci Roma (11)
As Long As He Needs Me (27,35)
As Time Goes By (34)
Ascot Gavotte (22)
Auf Wiederseh'n Sweetheart (37)
Aura Lee (medley) (33,48)
Autumn In New York (30)
Autumn Leaves (11,47)
Ave Maria (29)
Ay-Ay-Ay (36)
Babette (2)
Barabbas (26)

Barcarolle (29)
Baubles, Bangles And Beads (32)
Be Mine Tonight (28)
Be My Love (13)
Beautiful Dreamer (16)
Beautiful Isle Of Somewhere (24)
Beautiful Ohio (25)
Because I Love You (4)
Belle Of New York (30)
Ben Hur (40)
Besame Mucho (7,42)
Bewitched (8)
Beyond The Sea (11)
Bible, The (40)
Big Country (26)
Blaue Himmel (Blue Sky) (7,42)
Blowin' In The Wind (46)
Blue Danube (9,48)
Blue Star (17)
Blue-Tail Fly (medley) (33)
Blue Tango (42)
Born Free (40)
Both Sides Now (44)
Bowery, The (30)
By The Time I Get To Phoenix (44)
C'est Magnifique (3)
Camptown Races (16)
Capriccio Italien, Op. 45, Theme From (21,47)
Cara Mia (37)
Carmen Fantasy (36)
Carnival, Theme From (22)
Carnival Of Venice (21)
Carousel Waltz (18)
Catari, Catari (21)
Catch A Falling Star (34)
Certain Smile (13)
Charade (35)
Charmaine (2,39,47)
Chim Chim Cher-ee (37)
Chiquita Mia (7)
Chitty Chitty Bang Bang (44)
Christmas Bells (31)
Cielito Lindo (28)
Clementine (25)
Climb Ev'ry Mountain (35)
Come Back To Sorrento (21)

Come Prima (For The First Time) (11,12)
Come September (I'll Remember) (44)
Consider Yourself (27)
Count Of Luxembourg - Waltz (20)
Cradle Song (29)
Day In The Life Of A Fool (41)
Days Of Wine And Roses (41)
Dear Heart (35)
Dear Love, My Love (1)
Deck The Halls With Boughs Of Holly (31)
Delilah (44)
Desert Song (15)
Deserted Shore (46)
Diane (2,39)
Die Fledermaus - Overture (20,47)
Do-Re-Mi (22)
Dr. Zhivago ..see: Lara's Theme
Donkey Serenade (1,15)
Door Of Her Dreams (1)
E Bersaglieri (21)
Early One Morning (medley) (33)
Ebb Tide (38)
Edelweiss (41)
El Choclo (Kiss Of Fire) (15)
El Relicario (36)
Elvira Madigan, Theme From (45,48)
Embraceable You (43)
Emperor Waltz (9)
Espana (28,48)
Estrellita (28)
Eternal Father Strong To Save (24)
Etude No. 3 (29)
Everybody's Talkin' (46)
Exodus (Ari's Theme), Main Theme From (18,39) **31**
Fanny (26)
Fantasy On Italian Melodies (47)
Faraway Places (17)
Fascination (18)
Fate (32)
Fiddler On The Roof (35,50)
First Nowell (6,10,14,19,23)

Fledermaus Waltz (Du Und Du) (9)
Fly Me To The Moon (34)
Folk Songs From European Countries Medley (33)
For Once In My Life (44)
For The Very First Time (4,15)
For You (2)
Four Horsemen Of The Apocalypse (26)
Friendly Persuasion (Thee I Love) (13)
From Russia With Love (38)
Games That Lovers Play (39)
Gesticulate (32)
Giannina Mia (1)
Gigi (17)
Girl That I Marry (4,15)
Give My Regards To Broadway (30)
God Rest Ye Merry, Gentlemen (6,10,14,19,23)
Goldfinger (40)
Gone With The Wind ..see: Tara's Theme
Gonna Build A Mountain (27)
Good Morning Starshine (46)
Goodbye Again (26)
Goodnight Irene (16)
Goodnight, Sweetheart (27)
Granada (28)
Grandfather's Clock (16)
Green Cockatoo (36)
Green Leaves Of Summer (18)
Greensleeves (12,33,39,47)
Gwendolyn (48)
Gypsy Baron - Waltz (Your Eyes Shine In My Own) (20)
Gypsy Carnival (47)
Gypsy Flower Girl (48)
Gypsy Love - Waltz (20)
Gypsy Princess - Waltz (20)
Hark! The Herald Angels Sing (6,10,14,19,23)
Harlem Nocturne (30)
Hava Nagila (35)
He Who Loves And Runs Away (1)
He's In Love (32)

Hello Dolly (35)
Hello Young Lovers (3)
Hernando's Hideaway (42)
Hey There (8)
Hi-Lili, Hi-Lo (5)
High And The Mighty (13)
High Noon (5)
Holly And The Ivy (31)
Holy City (24)
Home On The Range (16)
Honey (44)
Hora Staccato (47)
How Are Things In Glocca Morra (43)
How Soon (38)
Hungarian Dance No. 5 (29)
I Can't Remember (4)
I Can't Stop Loving You (49)
I Could Have Danced All Night (8,12)
I Dream Of Jeannie (16,48)
I Feel Pretty (22)
I Have Dreamed (35)
I Know About Love (22)
I Live For You (2)
I Love Paris (18)
I Only Know I Love You (11)
I Saw Three Ships (31)
I Talk To The Trees (3)
I Wanna Be Rich (27)
I Will Wait For You (49)
I Wish You Love (37)
I Wonder Who's Kissing Her Now (34)
I'd Do Anything (27)
I'll Be Seeing You (34)
I'll Get By (34)
I'll Never Fall In Love Again (46)
I'm A Better Man (45)
I'm Falling In Love With Someone (15)
I've Grown Accustomed To Her Face (35)
I've Never Been In Love Before (3)
If Ever I Would Leave You (22)
If I Loved You (3)
If I Only Had Time (48)

If I Were A Rich Man (44,50)
Impossible Dream (41)
In The Still Of The Night (43)
Indian Love Call (1,15)
Indian Summer (15)
Intermezzo (5)
Irma La Douce (18)
It Came Upon The Midnight Clear (31)
It's Impossible (48)
Italia Mia (21)
Italian Fantasia Medley (21)
Jamaica Farewell (17)
Jealousy (7,36)
Jesu Joy Of Man's Desiring (24)
Jesu Lover Of My Soul (24)
Jingle Bells (31)
Joy To The World (6,10,14,19,23)
Judgment At Nuremberg (26)
Just A Wearyin' For You (16)
Just For A While (2)
Karen (18)
Kiss In The Dark (15)
Kiss Me Again (15)
Kisses In The Dark (7)
La Cumparsita (7)
La Paloma (28)
La Vie En Rose (11,39)
Lara's Theme (40)
Largo (29)
Last Summer (48)
Laura (5)
Lawrence Of Arabia (40)
Leaving On A Jet Plane (46)
Lemon Tree (46)
Les Bicyclettes De Belsize (44)
Let Me Call You Sweetheart (25)
Limelight, Theme From (5,12)
Little Brown Church In The Vale (24)
Little Green Apples (48)
Little Swiss Waltz (2)
Long Ago (4)
Lord's My Shepherd (24)
Loss Of Love (48)
Love And Marriage (38)
Love Everlasting (1,15)

540

MANTOVANI — Cont'd

Love Is A Many Splendored Thing (5)
Love Is All (46)
Love Is Blue (44)
Love Is Like A Firefly (1)
Love Letters (8)
Love Me Tonight (45)
Love Me With All Your Heart (37)
Love Story, Theme From (48)
Lover (37)
Lover, Come Back To Me (15)
Lumbered (27)
Magnificent Seven (40)
Malaguena (27)
Man And A Woman (41)
Man Without Love (44)
Manhattan Lullaby (30)
Manhattan Serenade (30)
Marcheta (25)
Maria Elena (28)
Marie (4,15)
Mary's Boy Child (31)
Mattinata (21)
May Each Day (48)
Me And My Shadow (49)
Meet Me In St. Louis, Louis (25)
Meilinki Meilchick (27)
Melba Waltz (2)
Merry Widow - Waltz (20)
Mexican Hat Dance (36,48)
Midnight Cowboy (46)
Midnight Waltz (6,10,14,19,23)
Mighty Fortress Is Our God (24)
Minstrel Boy (medley) (33)
Missouri Waltz (25)
Misty (37)
Mona Lisa (37)
Mondo Cane ..see: More
Moon On The Ruined Castle (33)
Moon River (26,39,47)
More (34)
Morgen Blatter (9)
Most Beautiful Girl In The World (37)
Moulin Rouge Theme (39)
Mr. Wonderful (18)
My Cherie Amour (45)
My Cup Runneth Over (41)
My Foolish Heart (5)

My Heart Is So Full Of You (22)
My Hero (20)
My Old Kentucky Home (16)
My Prayer (48)
My Way (45)
Nadia's Theme (26)
Nazareth (6,10,14,19,23)
Nearer My God To Thee (24)
Nearness Of You (8)
Nessun Dorma (21)
Never On Sunday (26)
New Fangled Tango (42)
Night Of My Nights (32)
No Other Love (17)
None But The Lonely Heart (29)
Not Since Ninevah (32)
O Holy Night (6,10,14,19,23)
O Little Town Of Bethlehem (6,10,14,19,23)
O Maiden, My Maiden (20)
O Mein Papa (Oh My Papa) (11)
O Tannenbaum (6,10,14,19,23)
O Thou That Tellest Good Tidings (31)
Oh! Susanna (medley) (33)
Old Folks At Home (16)
Olive Tree (32)
Oliver (27)
On A Clear Day (41)
On Wings Of Song (29)
Once In A Lifetime (27)
Once In Royal David's City (31)
Once Upon A Time (43)
Onedin Line Theme (50)
Only A Rose (1,15)
Onward Christian Soldiers (24)
Oom-Pah-Pah (27)
Orange Vendor (42)
Oscar, Theme From The (38)
Our Dream Waltz (2)
Our Love Affair (8)
Out Of My Dreams (3)
Over The Rainbow (5)
People (35)
Perfidia (Tonight) (28)
Perhaps, Perhaps, Perhaps (36)
Piccolo Bolero (36)
Play Gypsies, Dance Gypsies (20)

Poppa Piccolino (11)
Puppet On A String (41)
Quando, Quando, Quando (49)
Queen Elizabeth Waltz (2)
Quentin's Theme (45)
Rahadlakum (32)
Rain In Spain (42)
Reaching For The Moon (4)
Red Petticoats (7,42)
Red River Valley (medley) (33)
Red Roses For A Blue Lady (37)
Release Me (41)
Return To Me (21)
Return To Peyton Place (26)
Reviewing The Situation (27)
Rhymes Have I (medley) (32)
Ring De Banjo (16)
Rock Of Ages (24)
Romeo And Juliet, Theme From (45)
Rose Marie (1,15)
Roses From The South (9)
Rosy's Theme (48)
Russian Lullaby (4)
Samaris Dance (32)
Sands Of Time (medley) (32)
Schon Rosmarin (12)
Scottish Rhapsody (50)
Secret Love (13)
Separate Tables (34)
September In The Rain (34)
September Song (5,49)
Serenade (15)
Serenade (20)
76 Trombones (18,47)
Shadow Of Your Smile (38)
Shall We Dance (22)
Shenandoah (medley) (33)
Siboney (28)
Sidewalks Of New York (25)
Silent Night, Holy Night (6,10,14,19,23)
Skaters Waltz (6,10,14,19,23)
Skip To My Lou (medley) (33,48)
Slaughter On Tenth Avenue (30)
Slavonic Dance No. 2 (29)
Smile (28)
Smoke Gets In Your Eyes (43)

Snow Frolic (50)
So In Love (22)
Softly As I Leave You (38)
Softly, As In A Morning Sunrise (15)
Solveig's Song (29)
Some Enchanted Evening (3,12,39)
Someday (1)
Someone Nice Like You (27)
Something To Remember You By (8)
Song Is Ended (4)
Song Of The Vagabonds (1)
Song Without End (18)
Sound Of Music (18)
Spanish Eyes (50)
Spanish Flea (38)
Spanish Gypsy Dance (36)
Stardust (37)
Stranger In Paradise (3,32)
Strangers In The Night (38)
Streets Of Laredo (medley) (33)
Summer Place, Theme From A (18)
Summertime (8)
Summertime In Venice (5,39)
Sundowners, Theme From The (18) **93**
Sunrise, Sunset (43,50)
Swan Lake, Theme From (48)
Swedish Rhapsody (39)
Sweet Leilani (43)
Sweetest Sounds (35)
Sweetheart Of Sigma Chi (25)
Sweethearts (15)
Sympathy (1,15)
Take The "A" Train (30)
Takes Two To Tango (42)
Tales From The Vienna Woods (9)
Tammy (12,13)
Tango De La Luna (7)
Tango Delle Rose (7,42)
Tango In D (29)
Tara's Theme (40)
Taste Of Honey (40)
Tea For Two (49)
Tenderly (17)
Tenement Symphony (30)
Theme For A Western (50)

They Say It's Wonderful (3)
This Is My Song (40)
This Nearly Was Mine (8)
This Way Mary (50)
Those Were The Days (44)
Thousand And One Nights (9)
Three Coins In The Fountain (5)
Three O'Clock In The Morning (38)
Thunder And Lightning Polka (48)
Tico-Tico (36)
Till (50)
Till There Was You (22)
Till Tomorrow (22)
Tonight (17)
Totem Tom Tom (1)
Toy Waltz (31)
Treasure Waltz (9)
Trees (50)
Trolley Song (43)
True Love (8)
Try To Remember (43,48)
Turkey In The Straw (16)
Twelve Days Of Christmas (31)
Two Different Worlds (17)
Two Guitars (33)
Unchained Melody (5)
Under Paris Skies (11)
Under The Roofs Of Paris (2)
Up, Up And Away (46)
Valencia (36)
Vaya Con Dios (17)
Very Precious Love (17)
Village Swallows (9,12)
Virginian, Theme From The (45,47)
Vissi D'Arte (21)
Voices Of Spring (9)
Waltz You Saved For Me (25)
Wand'ring Star (46)
Was I Wazir? (32)
Way You Look Tonight (49)
West Side Story Medley (30)
What A Wonderful World (43)
What Kind Of Fool Am I (27,35)
What Now My Love (41)
What'll I Do (4,15)
Whatever Lola Wants (42)
Whatever Will Be, Will Be (Que Sera, Sera) (13)

When I Fall In Love (17)
When I Grow Too Old To Dream (15)
When Love Is Kind (medley) (33)
When The Moon Comes Over The Mountain (25)
When You Wish Upon A Star (13)
Where Are You (34)
Where Did Our Summers Go (45)
Where Have All The Flowers Gone (48)
Where Is Love? (27,45)
Whiffenpoof Song (25)
While Shepherds Watched (31)
Whispering (49)
Whispering Hope (24)
White Christmas (6,10,14,19,23)
Who Can I Turn To (35)
Who Will Buy? (27)
Wi' A Hundred Pipers (medley) (33)
Will You Remember? (2,15)
Windmills Of Your Mind (45)
Wine, Women And Song (9)
Winter World Of Love (49)
With ..also see: Wi'
With These Hands (17)
Without Love (There Is Nothing) (46)
Woman In Love (8)
Wunderbar (3)
Wyoming (2)
Yellow Bird (49)
Yellow Rose Of Texas (16)
Yesterday (38)
Yesterdays (34)
You Are Beautiful (22)
(You Forgot To) Remember (4,15)
You Keep Coming Back Like A Song (8)
You Only Live Twice (40)
You'll Never Walk Alone (43)
You've Got To Pick A Pocket Or Two (27)
Zorba, The Greek (40)
Zubbediya (32)

MANTRONIX '88
Rap duo from New York City: Curtis "Mantronik" Kahleel and Bryce Wilson. Wilson later formed **Groove Theory**.

DEBUT	PEAK	WKS		CD	Title			$	Label & Number
4/9/88	108	8		© 1	In Full Effect			$10	Capitol 48336
3/17/90	161	7		© 2	This Should Move Ya			$10	Capitol 91119

Do You Like...Mantronik (?) (1)
Don't You Want More (2)
Gangster Boogie (Walk Like Sex...Talk Like Sex) (1)
Get Stupid (Part III) (1)
Get Stupid Part IV (Get On Up '90) (2)
Got To Have Your Love (2) **82**
I Get Lifted (2)
I Like The Way (You Do It!) (2)
(I'm) Just Adjustin My Mic (2)
In Full Effect (1)
Join Me Please...(Home Boys - Make Some Noise) (1)
King Of The Beats Lesson #1 (2)
Love Letter (Dear Tracy) (1)
Mega-Mix ('88) (1)
Sex-N-Drugs And Rock-N-Roll (2)
Simple Simon (You Gotta Regard) (1)
Sing A Song (Break It Down) (1)
Stone Cold Roach (2)
This Should Move Ya (2)
Tonight Is Right (2)

MANUELLE, Victor '99
Born in New York City; raised in Puerto Rico. Latin singer.

DEBUT	PEAK	WKS		CD	Title			$	Label & Number
10/16/99	96	3		© 1	Inconfundible	[F]		$10	Sony Discos 83310
					title is Spanish for "Distinct"				
2/17/01	197	1		© 2	Instinto Y Deseo	[F]		$10	Sony Discos 83768
					title is Spanish for "Urge & Desire"				

Al Igual Que Ayer (1)
Así Fue (2)
Bella Sin Alma (1)
Como Duele (1)
Como Quisiera Decirte (1)
Cómo Se No Explico Al Corazón (2)
Cuando Tu Amor Se Acabe (1)
Instinto Y Deseo (2)
Lejos (2)
Me Da Lo Mismo (2)
Ni Un Día Más (2)
No Eres La Mujer (2)
Pero Dile (1)
Por Ella (1)
Por Tí (1)
Quisiera Inventar (2)
Si La Ves (1)
Si Por Tí Fuera (1)
Te Voy A Encontrar (2)

MANZANERA, Phil '79
Born on 1/31/51 in London. Lead guitarist of **Roxy Music** from 1972-83.

DEBUT	PEAK	WKS		CD	Title		$	Label & Number
2/10/79	176	3		©	K-Scope		$12	Polydor 6178

Cuban Crisis
Gone Flying
Hot Spot
K-Scope
N-Shift
Numbers
Remote Control
Slow Motion TV
Walking Through Heaven's Door
You Are Here

MANZAREK, Ray '75
Born on 2/12/35 in Chicago. Keyboardist of **The Doors**.

DEBUT	PEAK	WKS		CD	Title		$	Label & Number
2/8/75	150	6			The Whole Thing Started With Rock & Roll Now It's Out Of Control		$12	Mercury 1014

Art Deco Fandango
Begin The World Again
Bicentennial Blues (Love It Or Leave It)
Gambler, The
I Wake Up Screaming
Perfumed Garden
Whirling Dervish
Whole Thing Started With Rock & Roll Now It's Out Of Control

MARCH, Little Peggy '63
Born Margaret Battavio on 3/7/48 in Lansdale, Pennsylvania. Pop singer.

DEBUT	PEAK	WKS		CD	Title		$	Label & Number
8/17/63	139	3			I Will Follow Him		$75	RCA Victor 2732

As Young As We Are
Dream World
I Will Follow Him *1*
I Wish I Were A Princess *32*
I'll Never Forget Last Night
John, John
Johnny Cool
My Teenage Castle (Is Tumblin' Down)
Oh-Oh, I'm Falling In Love Again
Teasin'
Wind-Up Doll
You Make Me Laugh

MARCY PLAYGROUND '98
Rock trio from New York City: John Wozniak (vocals, guitar), Dylan Keefe (bass) and Dan Reiser (drums).

12/6/97+ **21** 41 ▲ © **Marcy Playground** .... **$10** Capitol 53569

Ancient Walls Of Flowers | Dog And His Master | One More Suicide | Poppies | Sex And Candy *8* | Sherry Fraser
Cloak Of Elvenkind | Gone Crazy | Opium | Saint Joe On The School Bus | Shadow Of Seattle | Vampires Of New York

MARDONES, Benny '80
Born on 11/9/48 in Cleveland. Pop singer/songwriter.

6/7/80 **65** 24 © **Never Run Never Hide** .... **$12** Polydor 6263

American Bandstand | Hey Baby | Hometown Girls | Mighta Been Love | Too Young
Crazy Boy | Hold Me Down | Into The Night *11* | She's So French

MARIACHI BRASS Featuring Chet Baker '66
Chet Baker was born on 12/23/29 in Yale, Oklahoma. Died on 5/13/88 (age 58). Trumpeter/bandleader.

2/26/66 **120** 4 **A Taste Of Tequila** .... [I] **$15** World Pacific 21839

Come A Little Bit Closer | El Paso | Hot Toddy | Mexico | Tequila
Cuando Calienta El Sol | Flowers On The Wall | La Bamba | Speedy Gonzales | Twenty Four Hours From Tulsa

★489★ MARIE, Teena '81
Born Mary Christine Brockert on 3/5/56 in Santa Monica; raised in Venice, California. White funk singer/songwriter.

5/5/79	**94**	20	©	1	**Wild and Peaceful**			**$12**	Gordy 986
3/15/80	**45**	23	©	2	**Lady T**			**$12**	Gordy 992
9/13/80	**38**	29	©	3	**Irons In The Fire**			**$12**	Gordy 997
6/13/81	**23**	25	● ©	4	**It Must Be Magic**			**$12**	Gordy 1004
11/26/83+	**119**	24	©	5	**Robbery**			**$10**	Epic 38882
12/15/84+	**31**	35	● ©	6	**Starchild**			**$10**	Epic 39528
7/5/86	**81**	11	©	7	**Emerald City**			**$10**	Epic 40318
4/16/88	**65**	13	©	8	**Naked To The World**			**$10**	Epic 40872
10/13/90	**132**	10	©	9	**Ivory**			**$10**	Epic 45101

Aladdin's Lamp (2) | De Ja Vu (I've Been Here | Irons In The Fire (3) | Once Is Not Enough (7) | Starchild (6) | Yes Indeed (4)
Alibi (6) | Before) (1) | It Must Be Magic (4) | Ooo La La La (8) *85* | Stop The World (5) | You Make Love Like Springtime
Ask Your Momma (5) | Dear Lover (5) | Ivory (A Tone Poem) (9) | Opus III (Does Anybody Care) | Sugar Shack (9) | (3)
Ball, The (8) | Don't Look Back (1) | Jammin (6) *81* | (4) | Sunny Skies (7) | You So Heavy (7)
Ballad Of Cradle Rob And Me | Emerald City (7) | Just Us Two (9) | Opus III - The Second | Surrealistic Pillow (8) | You're All The Boogie I Need
(4) | First Class Love (3) | Light (6) | Movement (8) | 365 (4) | (2)
Batucada Suite (7) | Fix It (5) | Lips To Find You (7) | Out On A Limb (9) | Too Many Colors (Tee's | Young Girl In Love (2)
Behind The Groove (2) | Help Youngblood Get To The | Lonely Desire (2) | Playboy (5) | Interlude) (2) | Young Love (3)
Call Me (I Got Yo Number) (8) | Freaky Party (6) | Love Me Down Easy (7) | Portuguese Love (4) | Trick Bag (8)
Can It Be Love (2) | Here's Looking At You (9) | Lovergirl (6) *4* | Red Zone (9) | Tune In Tomorrow (3)
Cassanova Brown (5) | How Can You Resist It (9) | Midnight Magnet (5) | Revolution (4) | Turnin' Me On (1)
Chains (3) | I Can't Love Anymore (1) | Miracles Need Wings To Fly (9) | Robbery (5) | We've Got To Stop (Meeting
Cradle Rob And Me ..see: | **I Need Your Lovin'** (2) *37* | Mr. Icecream (9) | Shadow Boxing (5) | Like This) (6)
Ballad Of | I'm A Sucker For Your Love (1) | My Dear Mr. Gaye (6) | Shangri-La (7) | Where's California (4)
Crocodile Tears (8) | I'm Gonna Have My Cake (And | Naked To The World (8) | Since Day One (9) | Why Did I Fall In Love With You
Cupid Is A Real Straight | Eat It Too) (1) | Now That I Have You (2) | Snap Your Fingers (9) | (2)
Shooter (9) | If I Were A Bell (9) | Once And Future Dream (8) | **Square Biz** (4) *50* | Work It (8)

MARILLION '85
Rock group from Aylesbury, England: Derek "Fish" Dick (vocals), Steve Rothery (guitar), Mark Kelly (keyboards), Pete Trewavas (bass) and Mick Pointer (drums). Ian Mosley replaced Pointer in 1984.

6/25/83	**175**	7	©	1	**Script For A Jester's Tear**			**$10**	Capitol 12269
8/24/85	**47**	35	©	2	**Misplaced Childhood**			**$10**	Capitol 12431
3/22/86	**67**	10	©	3	**Brief Encounter**		[L-M]	**$10**	Capitol 15023
7/11/87	**103**	11	©	4	**Clutching At Straws**			**$10**	Capitol 12539

Bitter Suite Medley (2) | Freaks (3) | Hotel Hobbies (4) | Lavender (2) | That Time Of The Night (The | Web, The (1)
Blind Curve (2) | Fugazi (3) | Incommunicado (4) | Lords Of The Backstage (2) | Short Straw) (4) | White Feather (2)
Chelsea Monday (1) | Garden Party (1) | Just For The Record (4) | Pseudo Silk Kimono (2) | Torch Song (4) | White Russian (4)
Childhoods End? (2) | He Knows, You Know (1) | Kayleigh (2,3) *74* | Script For A Jester's Tear (1,3) | Warm Wet Circles (4)
Forgotten Sons (1) | Heart Of Lothian Medley (2) | Lady Nina (3) | Slainte Mhath (4) | Waterhole (Expresso Bongo)
| | Last Straw (4) | Sugar Mice (4) | (2)

MARILYN MANSON — see MANSON, Marilyn

MARINO, Frank — see MAHOGANY RUSH

MARK-ALMOND '73
Pop-rock duo from England: Jon Mark and Johnny Almond.

6/5/71	**154**	15	©	1	**Mark-Almond**			**$15**	Blue Thumb 27
1/15/72	**87**	16		2	**Mark-Almond II**			**$15**	Blue Thumb 32
10/21/72	**103**	14		3	**Rising**			**$15**	Columbia 31917
5/26/73	**177**	7	©	4	**The Best of Mark-Almond**		[G]	**$15**	Blue Thumb 50
8/25/73	**73**	14		5	**Mark-Almond 73**		[L]	**$15**	Columbia 32486

side 1: live; side 2: studio

| 7/31/76 | **112** | 14 | © | 6 | **To The Heart** .... | | | **$12** | ABC 945 |

Ballad Of A Man (medley) (2) | Everybody Needs A Friend (6) | Little Prince (3) | One Way Sunday (2,4) *94* | Sunset (medley) (2)
Bay, The (medley) (2) | Friends (2,4) | Lonely Girl (5) | Organ Grinder (3) | Trade Winds (6)
Bridge, The (medley) (2) | Get Yourself Together (5) | Love Medley (1) | Phoenix, The (3) | Tramp And The Young Girl
Busy On The Line (6) | Ghetto, The (1,4) | Monday Bluesong (3) | Return To The City (medley) (6) | (1,4)
City Medley (1,4) | Here Comes The Rain (Part | Neighborhood Man (5) | Riding Free (3) | What Am I Living For (3,5)
Clowns (The Demise Of The | One & Two) (6) | New York State Of Mind | Solitude (2,4)
European Circus With No | Home To You (5) | (medley) (6) | Song For A Sad Musician (3)
Thanks To Fellini) (5) | I'll Be Leaving Soon (3) | One More For The Road (6) | Song For You (1,4)

MARK AND BRIAN '97
Nationally syndicated radio DJ duo of Mark Thompson and Brian Phelps. Based in Los Angeles.

| 11/29/97 | **48** | 5 | © | 1 | **You Had To Be There!** .... | | [C] | **$15** | Oglio 957 [2] |
| 11/25/00 | **62** | 2 | © | 2 | **Little Drummer Boys** .... | | [X-C] | **$15** | Oglio 86958 [2] |

DEBUT	PEAK	WKS	RIAA	CD	ARTIST — Album Title	Catalog	Sym	$	Label & Number

MARK AND BRIAN — Cont'd

All I Want (1)
Amazing Walter Sneath (Out Of Work) Stage Hypnotist (1)
Baby It's Cold Outside (2)
Barking Seals (2)
Battle Of Jenny Ledge (1)
Blue Christmas (2)
Blue Moon (1)
Christmas Medley (2)
Christmas Song (2)
Dip Doodle (2)
Down South Jukin' (1)

Dustin's Special Talent (1)
Elan At The Republican Convention (1)
Electronic Football Guy (1)
Elfis (2)
Feliz Navidad (2)
Frankenstein (1)
Gary Miller (2)
Girlfriend's Got A Wiener (1)
Good Day For The Blues (1)
Great White Hunter (1)
Greensleeves (1)

Help Yourself (1)
House At Pooh Corner (1)
I've Got Some Presents For Santa (1)
Innovative Embalmers (2)
James Woods Advance Man (2)
Jerry & Dick Van Dyke (1)
Kids Name Expert (2)
King Moonraiser (Misfit Toys) (2)
King Of New Orleans (1)
Little Drummer Boy (2)

Little White Lie (1)
Low Down (1)
Matchbox (1)
Miniature Theatre (1,2)
Need You Tonight (1)
Nixon-Ford Presidential Pardon (1)
Nut Rocker (2)
Old Yeller, The Sequel (1)
Pay Phone At The Olympics (1)
Pick Up The Pieces (1)
Right Hand Man (1)

Roid Be Gone (2)
Rudolph The Red Nosed Reindeer (2)
Run, Run Rudolph (1)
Sick Of Myself (1)
Silver Bells (2)
Suicide Night (1)
Tom Cruise Meets Gene Wilder? (1)
Tribute By Paul Anka (1)
'Twas The Night Before Christmas (2)

Two Princes (1)
Wipe Out (1)
Wonderful Life (1)
You're A Mean One, Mr. Grinch (2)
Zit Be Gone (2)

MARKETTS, The '64

Instrumental group formed in Hollywood: Ben Benay (guitar), Mike henderson (sax), Richard Hobriaco (keyboards), Ray Pohlman (bass) and Gene Pello (drums).

DEBUT	PEAK	WKS	RIAA	CD	#	Album Title	Sym	$	Label & Number
2/8/64	37	14		©	1	Out Of Limits!	[I]	$50	Warner 1537
3/12/66	82	12			2	The Batman Theme	[I]	$50	Warner 1642

Bat Cape (2)
Bat Cave (2)
Bat (Dance) (2)
Bat Signal (2)

Batman Theme (2) *17*
Batmobile (2)
Bell Star (1)
Bella Dalena (1)

Borealis (1)
Cat Woman (2)
Collision Course (1)
Dr. Death (2)

Hyper-Space (1)
Joker, The (2)
Limits Beyond (1)
Love 1985 (1)

Other Limits (1)
Out Of Limits (1) *3*
Penguin, The (2)
Re-Entry (1)

Riddler, The (2)
Robin, The Boy Wonder (2)
Saturn (1)
Twilight City (1)

MAR-KEYS — see BOOKER T. & THE MG's

MARKHAM, Pigmeat '68

Born Dewey Markham on 4/18/06 in Durham, North Carolina. Died of a stroke on 12/13/81 (age 75). Black comedian. Regular on TV's *Laugh-In* (1968-69).

DEBUT	PEAK	WKS			Album Title	Sym	$	Label & Number
7/20/68	109	9			Here Come The Judge	[C]	$20	Chess 1523

Fast News
Frisco Kate

Here Come The Judge
Here Comes The Judge *19*

I Got The Number
My Wife, I Ain't Seen Her

News Reporter
Trial, The

MARKY MARK And The Funky Bunch '92

Born Mark Wahlberg on 6/5/71 in Boston. Singer/actor. Starred in several movies. Younger brother of Donnie Wahlberg of **New Kids On The Block**. The Funky Bunch is DJ Terry Yancey and three male and two female dancers.

DEBUT	PEAK	WKS	RIAA	CD	#	Album Title	$	Label & Number
8/10/91+	21	45	▲	©	1	Music For The People	$10	Interscope 91737
10/3/92	67	14		©	2	You Gotta Believe	$10	Interscope 92203

Ain't No Stoppin' The Funky Bunch (2)
American Dream (2)
Bout Time I Funk You (1)
Don't Ya Sleep (2)

Get Up (2)
Go On (2)
Gonna Have A Good Time (2)
Good Vibrations (1) *1*
I Need Money (1) *61*

I Run Rhymes (2)
I Want You (2)
Last Song On Side B (1)
Loungin' (2)
M, The (2)

Make Me Say Ooh! (1)
Marky Mark Is Here (1)
Music For The People (1)
On The House Tip (1)
Peace (1)

So What Chu Sayin (1)
Super Cool Mack Daddy (2)
Wildside (1) *10*
You Gotta Believe (2) *49*

MARLEY, Bob, & The Wailers ★119★ '76

Born on 2/6/45 in Rhoden Hall, Jamaica. Died of cancer on 5/11/81 (age 36). Legendary reggae singer/guitarist. The Wailers included **Peter Tosh** and Bunny Wailer; both left in 1974. Wrote **Eric Clapton**'s hit "I Shot The Sheriff." Father of **Ziggy Marley** and Rohan Marley (former football player for the University of Miami Hurricanes). In 1990, Marley's birthday proclaimed a national holiday in Jamaica. Inducted into the Rock and Roll Hall of Fame in 1994.

1)Rastaman Vibration 2)Exodus 3)Uprising 4)Kaya 5)Legend

DEBUT	PEAK	WKS	RIAA	CD	#	Album Title	Sym	$	Label & Number
5/10/75	92	28		©	1	Natty Dread		$20	Island 9281
10/11/75	151	6	●	©	2	Burnin'		$20	Island 9256
						THE WAILERS			
11/8/75	171	5		©	3	Catch A Fire		$20	Island 9241
5/15/76	8	22	●	©	4	Rastaman Vibration		$15	Island 9383
10/23/76	90	9	●	©	5	Live!	[L]	$15	Island 9376
						recorded on 7/18/75 at the Lyceum in London			
6/11/77	20	24	●	©	6	Exodus		$15	Island 9498
4/22/78	50	17	●	©	7	Kaya		$15	Island 9517
12/16/78+	102	16		©	8	Babylon By Bus	[L]	$20	Island 11 [2]
11/17/79	70	14		©	9	Survival		$15	Island 9542
8/9/80	45	23	●	©	10	Uprising		$15	Island 9596
10/31/81	117	6		©	11	Chances Are	[E]	$12	Cotillion 5228
						BOB MARLEY			
						recorded 1968-72			
7/2/83	55	15	●	©	12	Confrontation		$12	Island 90085
8/18/84	54	113	▲10	©	13	Legend	C.❶73/525	[K] $10	Island 90169
9/6/86	140	9		©	14	Rebel Music	[K]	$10	Island 90520
2/23/91	103	13		©	15	Talkin' Blues	[L]	$10	Tuff Gong 848243
10/24/92	86	15	▲2	©	16	Songs Of Freedom	[K]	$40	Tuff Gong 512280 [4]
7/30/94	34^C	1		©	17	At His Best	[K]	$10	Special Music 4808
						BOB MARLEY (above 2)			
6/10/95	67	14	●	©	18	Natural Mystic	[K]	$10	Tuff Gong 524103
12/4/99+	60	24	●	©	19	Chant Down Babylon		$10	Tuff Gong 546404
						BOB MARLEY			
6/9/01	60	16		©	20	One Love: The Very Best Of Bob Marley & The Wailers	[G]	$10	UTV 542855

Acoustic Medley (16)
Africa Unite (9,16,18)
Am-A-Do (15)
Ambush In The Night (9)
Baby We've Got A Date (Rock It Baby) (3)

Babylon System (9,16)
Back Out (16)
Bad Card (10,16)
Bend Down Low (1,15,16)
Blackman Redemption (12)
Buffalo Soldier (12,13,20)

Burnin' And Lootin' (2,5,15,16,19)
Bus Dem Shut (16)
Caution (16)
Chances Are (11)
Chant Down Babylon (12)

Coming In From The Cold (10,16)
Concrete Jungle (3,8,16,19)
Could You Be Loved (10,13,16,20)
Craven Choke Puppy (16)

Crazy Baldhead (4,14,16,18)
Crisis (7)
Cry To Me (4)
Dance Do The Reggae (11)
Do It Twice (16)
Don't Rock The Boat (16)

Duppy Conqueror (2,16)
Easy Skanking (7,16,18)
Exodus (6,8,13,16,20)
Forever Loving Jah (10,16)
400 Years (1)

543

MARLEY, Bob, & The Wailers — Cont'd

Get Up, Stand Up (2,5,13,14,15,16,20)
Give Thanks (12)
Give Thanks And Praise (16)
Gonna Get You (11)
Guava Jelly (16)
Guiltiness (6,19)
Hallelujah Time (12)
Hammer (16)
Heathen, The (6,8)
High Tide Or Low Tide (16)
Hypocrites (16)
I Know (12)
I Know A Place (20)
I Shot The Sheriff (2,5,13,15,16,20)
(I'm) Hurting Inside (11,16)
I'm Still Waiting (16)
Iron Lion Zion (16,18,20)
Is This Love (7,8,13,16,20)

Jah Live (16)
Jamming (6,8,13,16,19,20)
Johnny Was (4,16,19)
Judge Not (16)
Jump Nyabinghi (12)
Kaya (9)
Keep On Moving (16,17,18)
Kinky Reggae (3,8,15,19)
Lick Samba (16)
Lively Up Yourself (1,5,8,16,17,20)
Mellow Mood (11,16,17)
Midnight Ravers (3)
Misty Morning (7)
Mix Up, Mix Up (12)
Mr Brown (16)
My Cup (17)
Natty Dread (1,16)
Natural Mystic (6,16,18)
Nice Time (16)

Night Shift (4)
No More Trouble (3,8,14,16,19)
No Woman, No Cry (1,5,13,16,20)
One Cup Of Coffee (16)
One Drop (9,16,18)
One Dub (16)
One Foundation (2)
One Love (medley) (6,13,16,20)
Pass It On (2)
People Get Ready (medley) (6,13,16,20)
Pimper's Paradise (10,18)
Positive Vibration (4,8)
Punky Reggae Party (8)
Put It On (2,16)
Rasta Man Chant (2,15,16,19)
Rastaman Live Up! (12,16)
Rat Race (4,8,14,16)
Real Situation (10,16)

Rebel Music (3 O'Clock Road Block) (1,8,14,19)
Rebel's Hop (17)
Redemption Song (10,13,16,20)
Reggae On Broadway (11)
Revolution (1)
Ride Natty Ride (9,14,16)
Riding High (17)
Roots (14)
Roots, Rock, Reggae (4,18,19,20) *51*
Running Away (7,16)
Satisfy My Soul (7,13)
Screw Face (16)
She's Gone (7)
Simmer Down (16)
Slave Driver (3,14,15,16)
Small Axe (2,16,17)
Smile Jamaica (16)
So Jah Seh (1)

So Much Things To Say (6)
So Much Trouble In The World (9,14,16,18,20)
Soul Rebel (11,16,17)
Soul Shake Down Party (16,17)
Stand Alone (11)
Stay With Me (11)
Stiff Necked Fools (12)
Stir It Up (3,8,13,16,20)
Stop That Train (3)
Sun Is Shining (7,16,17,18,20)
Survival (9,16,19)
Talkin' Blues (1,15)
Thank You Lord (16)
Them Belly Full (But We Hungry) (1,5,14)
Three Little Birds (6,13,16,20)
Time Will Tell (7,16,18)
Top Rankin' (9)
Trench Town (12)

Trenchtown Rock (5,16,18)
Try Me (17)
Turn Your Lights Down Low (6,19,20)
Waiting In Vain (6,13,16,20)
Wake Up And Live (9)
Walk The Proud Land (15)
Want More (4)
War (4,8,14,16,18)
We And Dem (10)
Who The Cap Fit (4,16,18)
Why Should I (16)
Work (10)
You Can't Blame The Youth (15)
Zimbabwe (9,16)
Zion Train (10)

MARLEY, Ziggy, And The Melody Makers '88
Family reggae group from Kingston, Jamaica. Children of **Bob Marley**: David "Ziggy" (vocals, guitar), Stephen, Sharon and Cedella Marley.

4/23/88	23	42	▲	©	1	Conscious Party	$10	Virgin 90878
8/12/89	26	18	●	©	2	One Bright Day	$10	Virgin 91256
6/15/91	63	19		©	3	Jahmekya	$10	Virgin 91626
7/17/93	178	2		©	4	Joy And Blues	$10	Virgin 87961
7/29/95	170	5		©	5	Free Like We Want 2 B	$10	Elektra 61702

African Herbsman (4)
All Love (2)
Beautiful Mother Nature (5)
Black My Story (Not History) (2)
Brothers And Sisters (4)
Bygones (5)
Conscious Party (1)
Don't Go Nowhere (5)
Drastic (3)
Dreams Of Home (1)
First Night (3)

Free Like We Want 2 B (5)
G7 (5)
Garden (4)
Generation (3)
Good Time (3) *85*
Hand To Mouth (5)
Have You Ever Been To Hell (1)
Head Top (4)
Herbs An' Spices (3)
In The Flow (5)

Jah Is True And Perfect (3)
Joy And Blues (5)
Justice (2)
Keep On (5)
Kozmik (3)
Lee And Molly (1)
Live It Up (5)
Look Who's Dancing (2)
Love Is The Only Law (5)
Mama (4)
Namibia (3)

New Love (1)
New Time & Age (3)
One Bright Day (2)
Pains Of Life (2)
Power To Move Ya (5)
Problem With My Woman (3)
Rainbow Country (3)
Raw Riddim (3)
Rebel In Disguise (4)
Small People (3)
So Good So Right (3)

Talk (4)
There She Goes (4)
This One (4)
Tipsy Blues (5)
Today (5)
Tomorrow People (1) *39*
Tumblin' Down (1)
Urb-an-Music (2)
Water And Oil (5)
We Propose (2)
What Conquers Defeat (3)

What's True (1)
When The Lights Gone Out (3)
Who A Say (1)
Who Will Be There (2)
World So Corrupt (4)
Wrong Right Wrong (3)
X Marks The Spot (4)

MARLEY MARL '91
Born Marlon Williams on 9/30/62 in Queens, New York. Rapper/producer. Member of **QB Finest**.

| 10/8/88 | 163 | 5 | | © | 1 | In Control Volume I | $10 | Cold Chillin' 25783 |
| 10/19/94 | 152 | 2 | | © | 2 | In Control Volume II - For Your Steering Pleasure | $10 | Cold Chillin' 26257 |

America Eats The Young (2)
Another Hooker (2)
At The Drop Of A Dime (2)
Buffalo Soldier (2)
Cheatin' Days Are Over (2)
Check The Mirror (2)

Droppin' Science (1)
Duck Alert (1)
Fools In Love (2)
Freedom (1)
Girl, I Was Wrong (2)
I Be Gettin' Busy (2)

Keep Control (2)
Keep Your Eye On The Prize (1)
Level Check (2)
Live Motivator (1)
Mobil Phone (2)

No Bullshit (2)
Out For The Count (2)
Reach Out (2)
Rebel, The (1)
Scanning The Dial (2)
Simon Says (1)

Something Funky To Listen To (2)
Sweet Tooth (2)
Symphony, The (1)
Symphony, Pt. II (2)
Wack Itt (1)

We Write The Songs (1)

MARMALADE, The '70
Pop group from Scotland: Thomas "Dean Ford" McAleese (vocals), Junior Campbell (guitar), Patrick Fairley (piano), Graham Knight (bass) and Alan Whitehead (drums).

| 6/20/70 | 71 | 13 | | | | Reflections Of My Life | $20 | London 575 |

And Yours Is Piece Of Mine
Carolina In My Mind

Dear John
Fight Say The Mighty

I'll Be Home (In A Day Or So)
Kaleidoscope

Life Is
Reflections Of My Life *10*

Some Other Guy
Super Clean Jean

MARRINER, Neville '85
Born on 4/15/24 in Lincoln, England. Conductor/arranger.

| 11/24/84+ | 56 | 78 | ▲ | © | | Amadeus | [S] | $15 | Fantasy 1791 [2] |

Abduction From The Seraglio, Turkish Finale
Ah Tutti Contenti
Commendatore Scene
Concerto For Two Pianos, K. 365 (III)

Early 18th Century Gypsy Music
Ecco La Marcia
Mass In C Minor, K. 427, Kyrie
Piano Concerto In D Minor, K. 466 (III)

Piano Concerto In E Flat, K. 482 (III)
Quando Corpus Morietur And Amen
Requiem, K. 626 Medley
Ruhe Sanft

Serenade For Winds, K. 361 (III)
Symphonie Concertante, K. 364 (I)
Symphony No. 29 in A.K. 201 (I)

Symphony No. 25 In G Minor, K. 183 (I)

MARSALIS, Branford '90
Born on 8/26/60 in New Orleans. Jazz saxophonist. Brother of **Wynton Marsalis**. Leader of the *Tonight Show with Jay Leno* band from 1992-95. Appeared in the movies *Bring On The Night*, *Throw Mama From The Train* and *School Daze*.

| 5/19/84 | 164 | 7 | | © | 1 | Scenes in the City | [I] | $10 | Columbia 38951 |
| 8/25/90 | 63 | 14 | | © | 2 | Mo' Better Blues | [S] | $10 | Columbia 46792 |

THE BRANFORD MARSALIS QUARTET FEATURING TERENCE BLANCHARD

Again Never (2)
Beneath The Underdog (2)
Harlem Blues (2)

Jazz Thing (2)
Knocked Out The Box (2)
Mo' Better Blues (2)

No Backstage Pass (1)
No Sidestepping (1)
Parable (1)

Pop Top 40 (2)
Say Hey (2)
Scenes In The City (1)

Solstice (1)
Waiting For Tain (1)

MARSALIS, Wynton '84
Born on 10/18/61 in New Orleans. Jazz trumpeter. Brother of saxophonist **Branford Marsalis**. Member of **Fuse One**.

3/6/82	165	5		©	1	Wynton Marsalis	[I]	$10	Columbia 37574
7/9/83+	102	27		©	2	Think Of One	[I]	$10	Columbia 38641
10/13/84	90	39	●	©	3	Hot House Flowers	[I]	$10	Columbia 39530
10/19/85	118	10		©	4	Black Codes (From The Underground)	[I]	$10	Columbia 40009
11/1/86	185	4		©	5	J Mood	[I]	$10	Columbia 40308
9/26/87	153	5	●	©	6	Marsalis Standard Time - Volume 1	[I]	$10	Columbia 40461
12/23/89	26[X]	3		©	7	Crescent City Christmas Card	[X-I]	$10	Columbia 45287
7/7/90	101	16		©	8	Standard Time Vol. 3 - The Resolution Of Romance	[I]	$10	Columbia 46143
4/13/91	112	6		©	9	Standard Time Vol. 2 - Intimacy Calling	[I]	$10	Columbia 47346

MARSALIS, Wynton — Cont'd

After (5)
April In Paris (6)
Aural Oasis (4)
Autumn Leaves (6)
Bell Ringer (2)
Big Butter And Egg Man (8)
Black Codes (4)
Blues (4)
Bona And Paul (8)
Bourbon Street Parade (9)
Caravan (6)
Carol Of The Bells (7)
Chambers Of Tain (4)
Cherokee (6)
Crepuscule With Nellie (9)
Delfeayo's Dilemma (4)
Django (3)
East Of The Sun (West Of The Moon) (9)

Embraceable You (9)
End Of A Love Affair (9)
Everything Happens To Me (8)
Father Time (1)
Flamingo (8)
Foggy Day (6)
For All We Know (3)
For Wee Folks (4)
Fuchsia (2)
God Rest Ye Merry Gentlemen (7)
Goodbye (6)
Hark! The Herald Angels Sing (7)
Hesitation (1)
Hot House Flowers (3)
How Are Things In Glocca Morra (7)
I Cover The Waterfront (8)

I Gotta Right To Sing The Blues (8)
I'll Be There When The Time Is Right (1)
I'll Remember April (9)
I'm Confessin' (That I Love You) (3)
In The Afterglow (9)
In The Court Of King Oliver (8)
In The Wee Small Hours Of The Morning (8)
Indelible And Nocturnal (5)
Insane Asylum (5)
It's Easy To Remember (8)
It's Too Late Now (8)
J Mood (5)
Jingle Bells (7)
Knozz-Moe-King (2)
Later (2)

Lazy Afternoon (3)
Let It Snow! Let It Snow! Let It Snow! (7)
Little Drummer Boy (7)
Lover (9)
Melancholia (2,3)
Melodique (5)
Memories Of You (6)
Much Later (5)
My Ideal (2)
My Romance (4)
Never Let Me Go (8)
New Orleans (6)
O Come All Ye Faithful (7)
Oh Tannenbaum (7)
Phryzzinian Man (4)
Presence That Lament Brings (5)
RJ (1)

Seductress, The (8)
Silent Night (7)
Sister Cheryl (1)
Skain's Domain (5)
Skylark (8)
Sleepin' Bee (8)
Sleigh Ride (7)
Song Is You (6)
Soon All Will Know (6)
Stardust (3)
Street Of Dreams (8)
Taking A Chance On Love (8)
Think Of One (2)
Twas The Night Before Christmas (7)
Twilight (1)
Very Thought Of You (8)
We Three Kings (7)

What Is Happening Here (Now)? (2)
What Is This Thing Called Love? (9)
When It's Sleepytime Down South (9)
When You Wish Upon A Star (3)
Where Or When (8)
Who Can I Turn To (When Nobody Needs Me) (1)
Winter Wonderland (7)
Yesterdays (9)
You Don't Know What Love Is (9)
You're My Everything (7)

MARSHALL, Amanda '96
Born in 1972 in Toronto. Female singer/songwriter.

11/2/96	156	7	©		**Amanda Marshall**			$10	Epic 67562

Beautiful Goodbye
Birmingham 43
Dark Horse
Fall From Grace
Last Exit To Eden
Let It Rain
Let's Get Lost
Promises
Sitting On Top Of The World
Trust Me (This Is Love)

★280★ MARSHALL TUCKER BAND, The '75
Rock group from South Carolina: Doug Gray (vocals), brothers Toy (guitar) and Tommy (bass) Caldwell, George McCorkle (guitar), Jerry Eubanks (sax, flute) and Paul Riddle (drums). Tommy died in a car crash on 4/28/80 (age 30); replaced by Franklin Wilkie. Toy left band in 1984; died of respiratory failure on 2/25/93 (age 45). Marshall Tucker was the owner of the band's rehearsal hall.

1)Searchin' For A Rainbow 2)Together Forever 3)Carolina Dreams

7/7/73	29	40	●	©	1	The Marshall Tucker Band		$15	Capricorn 0112
3/9/74	37	28	●	©	2	A New Life		$15	Capricorn 0124
12/21/74+	54	14	●	©	3	Where We All Belong	[L]	$20	Capricorn 0145 [2]
						record 1: studio; record 2: live			
9/13/75	15	34	●	©	4	Searchin' For A Rainbow		$15	Capricorn 0161
6/26/76	32	20		©	5	Long Hard Ride		$15	Capricorn 0170
2/26/77	23	36	▲	©	6	Carolina Dreams		$15	Capricorn 0180
5/13/78	22	16		©	7	Together Forever		$15	Capricorn 0205
10/21/78	67	32	▲	©	8	Greatest Hits	[G]	$15	Capricorn 0214
5/5/79	30	22		©	9	Running Like The Wind		$12	Warner 3317
3/22/80	32	15		©	10	Tenth		$12	Warner 3410
5/23/81	53	12		©	11	Dedicated		$12	Warner 3525
						in memory of bassist Tommy Caldwell			
6/12/82	95	7		©	12	Tuckerized		$12	Warner 3684

AB's Song (1)
Ace High Love (12)
Am I The Kind Of Man (5)
Another Cruel Love (2)
Answer To Love (9)
Anyway The Wind Blows Rider (12)
Asking Too Much Of You (7)
Blue Ridge Mountain Sky (2)
Bob Away My Blues (4)
Bound And Determined (4)
Can't You See (1,4,8) **75**
Cattle Drive (10)
Change Is Gonna Come (7)
Desert Skies (6)
Disillusion (10)
Dream Lover (7) **75**
Even A Fool Would Let Go (12)

Everybody Needs Somebody (7)
Everyday (I Have The Blues) (3)
Fire On The Mountain (4,8) **38**
Fly Eagle Fly (2)
Fly Like An Eagle (6)
Foolish Dreaming (10)
Gospel Singin' Man (10)
Heard It In A Love Song (6,8) **14**
Heartbroke (12)
Hillbilly Band (1)
Holding On To You (5)
How Can I Slow Down (3)
I Should Have Never Started Lovin' You (6)
I'll Be Loving You (7)

If You Think You're Hurtin' Me (Girl You're Crazy) (12)
In My Own Way (3)
It Takes Time (10) **79**
Jimi (10)
Keeps Me From All Wrong (4)
Last Of The Singing Cowboys (9) **42**
Life In A Song (6)
Long Hard Ride (5,8)
Losing You (1)
Love Is A Mystery (2)
Love Some (11)
Low Down Ways (3)
Melody Ann (9)
Mr. President (12)
My Best Friend (1)
My Jesus Told Me So (1)

Never Trust A Stranger (6)
New Life (2)
Now She's Gone (3)
Pass It On (9)
Property Line (5)
Ramblin' (1,3,8)
Reachin' For A Little Bit More (12)
Ride In Peace (11)
Rumors Are Raging (11)
Running Like The Wind (9)
Save My Soul (10)
Sea, Dreams & Fairy Tales (12)
Searchin' For A Rainbow (4,8)
See You Later, I'm Gone (1)
See You One More Time (10)
Silverado (2)
Sing My Blues (10)

Singing Rhymes (7)
Something's Missing In My Life (11)
Southern Woman (2)
Special Someone (11)
Sweet Elaine (12)
Take The Highway (1,3)
Tell It To The Devil (6)
Tell The Blues To Take Off The Night (11)
This Ol' Cowboy (3,8) **78**
This Time I Believe (11)
Time Has Come (11)
Tonight's The Night (For Making Love) (11)
Too Stubborn (2)
Try One More Time (3)
24 Hours At A Time (2,3,8)

Unforgiven (12)
Unto These Hills (9)
Virginia (4)
Walkin' And Talkin' (4)
Walkin' The Streets Alone (5)
Where A Country Boy Belongs (3)
Windy City Blues (5)
Without You (10)
You Ain't Foolin' Me (2)
You Don't Live Forever (5)
You Say You Love Me (5)

MARTHA & THE MUFFINS '84
New-wave group from Toronto: Martha Johnson (vocals), Mark Gane (guitar), Andy Haas (sax), Carl Finkle (bass) and Tim Gane (drums). By 1984, reduced to duo of Johnson and Gane (recorded as **M+M**).

9/13/80	186	3			1	Metro Music		$12	Virgin 13145
5/21/83	184	4		©	2	Danseparc		$12	RCA Victor 4664
7/28/84	163	4		©	3	Mystery Walk		$12	Current 3
						M+M			

Alibi Room (3)
Big Trees (3)
Black Stations/White Stations (3) **63**
Boys In The Bushes (2)
Cheesies And Gum (1)

Come Out And Dance (3)
Cooling The Medium (3)
Danseparc (Every Day It's Tomorrow) (2)
Echo Beach (1)
Garden In The Sky (3)

Hide And Seek (1)
I Start To Stop (3)
In Between Sleep And Reason (3)
Indecision (1)
Monotone (1)

Nation Of Followers (3)
Obedience (2)
Paint By Number Heart (1)
Revenge (Against The World) (1)
Rhythm Of Life (3)

Saigon (1)
Several Styles Of Blonde Girls Dancing (2)
Sinking Land (1)
Sins Of Children (2)
Terminal Twilight (1)

Walking Into Walls (3)
What People Do For Fun (2)
Whatever Happened To Radio Valve Road? (2)
World Without Borders (2)

MARTHA & THE VANDELLAS '66
Female R&B vocal trio from Detroit: Martha Reeves (born on 7/18/41), Annette Beard and Rosalind Ashford. Betty Kelly replaced Beard in 1964. Group disbanded from 1969-71, re-formed with Martha and sister Lois Reeves, and Sandra Tilley in 1971. Martha Reeves went solo in late 1972. Group inducted into the Rock and Roll Hall of Fame in 1995.

11/23/63	125	5	©		1	Heat Wave		$150	Gordy 907
5/29/65	139	3	©		2	Dance Party		$75	Gordy 915
6/11/66	50	15	©		3	Greatest Hits	[G]	$50	Gordy 917
1/21/67	116	8	©		4	Watchout!		$50	Gordy 920
10/7/67	140	5			5	Martha & The Vandellas Live!	[L]	$50	Gordy 925
						recorded at the 20-Grand in Detroit			

545

MARTHA REEVES & THE VANDELLAS:

6/1/68	**167**	8			6 **Ridin' High**			$30	Gordy 926
4/1/72	**146**	7		©	7 **Black Magic**			$30	Gordy 958

Anyone Who Had A Heart (7)
Benjamin (7)
Bless You (7) *53*
Come And Get These Memories (3) *29*
Dance Party (2)
Dancing In The Street (2,3,5) *2*
Dancing Slow (2)
Danke Schoen (1)
Do Right Woman (medley) (5)
For Once In My Life (5)
Forget Me Not (6) *93*
Go Ahead And Laugh (4)
Happiness Is Guaranteed (4)
He Doesn't Love Her Anymore (4)

Heat Wave (1) *4*
Hello Stranger (1)
Hey There Lonely Boy (1)
Hitch Hike (2)
Honey Chile (6) *11*
Hope I Don't Get My Heart Broke (7)
I Can't Help Myself (Sugar Pie, Honey Bunch) (medley) (5)
I Found A Love (5)
I Promise To Wait My Love (6) *62*
I Say A Little Prayer (6)
I Want You Back (7)
I'll Follow You (4)
I'm In Love (And I Know It) (6)
I'm Ready For Love (4,5) *9*

(I've Given You) The Best Years Of My Life (7)
If I Had A Hammer (1)
In And Out Of My Life (7)
In My Lonely Room (3) *44*
Introduction (5)
Jerk, The (2)
Jimmy Mack (4,5) *10*
Just One Look (1)
Keep It Up (4)
Leave It In The Hands Of Love (6)
Let This Day Be (4)
Live Wire (3) *42*
Love Bug Leave My Heart Alone (5,6) *25*
Love Is Like A Heat Wave (3,5)

Love Like Yours (Don't Come Knocking Everyday) (3)
Love (Makes Me Do Foolish Things) (3,5) *70*
Mickey's Monkey (2)
Mobile Lil The Dancing Witch (2)
Mocking Bird (1)
More (1)
Motoring (2)
My Baby Loves Me (3,5) *22*
My Boyfriend's Back (1)
No More Tearstained Make Up (4)
No One There (7)
Nobody'll Care (7)
Nowhere To Run (2,3,5) *8*

One Way Out (4)
Quicksand (3) *8*
Respect (medley) (5)
Show Me The Way (6)
Something (7)
Sweet Soul Music (medley) (5)
Tear It On Down (7)
Then He Kissed Me (1)
There He Is - At My Door (2)
(There's) Always Something There To Remind Me (6)
To Sir, With Love (6)
Uptight (Everything's Alright) (medley) (5)
Wait Till My Bobby Gets Home (1)

(We've Got) Honey Love (6) *56*
What Am I Going To Do Without Your Love (4) *71*
Wild One (2,3) *34*
Without You (6)
You've Been In Love Too Long (3,5) *36*
Your Love Makes It All Worthwhile (7)

MARTIKA

Born Marta Marrera on 5/18/69 in Los Angeles. Latin singer/actress. Starred in the TV program *Kids, Incorporated*. Appeared in the 1982 movie musical *Annie*.

										'89
2/4/89	**15**	39	●	©	1 **Martika**			$10	Columbia 44290	
9/14/91	**111**	9		©	2 **Martika's Kitchen**			$10	Columbia 46827	

Alibis (1)
Broken Heart (2)
Coloured Kisses (2)
Cross My Heart (1)

Don't Say U Love Me (2)
I Feel The Earth Move (1) *25*
If You're Tarzan, I'm Jane (1)
It's Not What You're Doing (1)

Love...Thy Will Be Done (2)
Magical Place (2)
Martika's Kitchen (2) *93*
Mi Tierra (2)

10 More Than You Know (1) *18*
Pride & Prejudice (2)
Safe In The Arms Of Love (2)
See If I Care (1)

Spirit (2)
Take Me To Forever (2)
Temptation (2)
Toy Soldiers (1) *1*

Water (1)
You Got Me Into This (1)

MARTIN, Bobbi

Born Barbara Martin on 11/29/38 in Brooklyn, New York; raised in Baltimore. Died of cancer on 5/2/2000 (age 61). Female pop singer.

										'65
3/6/65	**127**	5			1 **Don't Forget I Still Love You**			$20	Coral 57472	
5/30/70	**176**	5			2 **For The Love Of Him**			$15	United Artists 6700	

Anytime (1)
Crazy Arms (2)
Dear Heart (1)
Don't Forget I Still Love You (1) *19*
Don't Touch Me, Jimmy Brown (2)

Everybody Loves Somebody (1)
For The Love Of Him (2) *13*
Here Comes My Baby Back Again (2)
I Can't Stop Loving You (1)
I Fall To Pieces (2)
I Walk The Line (2)

I'm A Fool (To Go On Loving You) (1)
I'm So Lonesome I Could Cry (2)
Kiss Me Goodnight (1)
Livin' In A House Full Of Love (2)

Long Line Of Fools (2)
Lovesick Blues (2)
Loving You (1)
Million Thanks To You (Kung Di Lang Sa Lyo) (1)
Someday (You'll Want Me To Want You) (1)

Tennessee Waltz (2)
This Love Of Mine (1)
We'll Sing In The Sunshine (1)
Your Cheatin' Heart (2)

MARTIN, Dean ★76★

Born Dino Crocetti on 6/7/17 in Steubenville, Ohio. Died on 12/25/95 (age 78). Pop singer/actor. Teamed with comedian **Jerry Lewis** in 1946. Starred in numerous movies. Hosted own TV series from 1965-74. His son Dino was in **Dino, Desi & Billy**.

1)*Everybody Loves Somebody* 2)*The Door Is Still Open To My Heart* 3)*Dean Martin* 4)*Houston* 5)*(Remember Me) I'm The One Who Loves You*

									'64
1/8/55	**10**	6		1 Dean Martin	[EP]		$50	Capitol 9123	
5/12/62	**73**	16		2 **Dino - Italian love songs**			$30	Capitol 1659	
1/26/63	**99**	5		3 **Dino Latino**			$20	Reprise 6054	
3/30/63	**109**	4		4 **Country Style**			$20	Reprise 6061	
8/15/64	**2**⁴	49	●	5 Everybody Loves Somebody			$15	Reprise 6130	
8/29/64	**15**	31	●	6 **Dream With Dean**			$15	Reprise 6123	
11/14/64	**9**	30	●	7 The Door Is Still Open To My Heart			$15	Reprise 6140	
2/13/65	**13**	29	●	8 **Dean Martin Hits Again**			$15	Reprise 6146	
8/28/65	**12**	39	●	9 **(Remember Me) I'm The One Who Loves You**			$15	Reprise 6170	
11/20/65+	**11**	34	●	10 **Houston**			$15	Reprise 6181	
12/18/65+	**12**ˣ	12		11 **Holiday Cheer**	[X]		$15	Capitol 2343	
				originally issued in 1959 as *A Winter Romance* on Capitol 1285; Christmas charts: 27/'65, 17/'66, 35/'67, 12/'68					
3/12/66	**40**	27	●	12 **Somewhere There's A Someone**			$15	Reprise 6201	
7/2/66	**108**	3		13 **The Silencers**	[S]		$15	Reprise 6211	
				includes 4 instrumentals by the Ernie Freeman and **Gene Page** Orchestras: "Anniversary Song," "Lord, You Made The Night Too Long," "Lovey Kravezit" and "The Silencers"					
8/27/66	**50**	25		14 **The Hit Sound Of Dean Martin**			$15	Reprise 6213	
12/3/66	**❶**¹ˣ	19	●	15 The Dean Martin Christmas Album	[X]		$15	Reprise 6222	
				Christmas charts: 1/'66, 2/'67, 4/'68, 10/'69, 14/'70					
12/3/66+	**34**	31		16 **The Dean Martin TV Show**			$15	Reprise 6233	
12/17/66+	**95**	13	©	17 **The Best Of Dean Martin**	[G]		$15	Capitol 2601	
5/13/67	**46**	25		18 **Happiness Is Dean Martin**			$15	Reprise 6242	
9/2/67	**20**	48	●	19 **Welcome To My World**			$15	Reprise 6250	
6/1/68	**26**	39	●	20 **Dean Martin's Greatest Hits! Vol. 1**	[G]		$15	Reprise 6301	
9/7/68	**83**	21	●	21 **Dean Martin's Greatest Hits! Vol. 2**	[G]		$15	Reprise 6320	
1/4/69	**14**	25	●	22 **Gentle On My Mind**			$15	Reprise 6330	
2/22/69	**145**	7		23 **The Best Of Dean Martin, Vol. 2**	[G]		$15	Capitol 140	
10/4/69	**90**	17		24 **I Take A Lot Of Pride In What I Am**			$15	Reprise 6338	
9/12/70	**97**	12		25 **My Woman, My Woman, My Wife**			$15	Reprise 6403	
2/27/71	**113**	15		26 **For The Good Times**			$15	Reprise 6428	
2/5/72	**117**	4		27 **Dino**			$15	Reprise 2053	

MARTIN, Dean — Cont'd

Ain't Gonna Try Anymore (4,14)
(Alla En) El Rancho Grande (3)
Always In My Heart (3)
Always Together (7)
Any Time (4,12,14)
April Again (22)
Arrivederci, Roma (2,23)
Baby, It's Cold Outside (11)
Baby-O (5)
Baby Won't You Please Come Home (6,16)
Besame Mucho (3)
Birds And The Bees (9,20)
Blue, Blue Day (4,12)
Blue Christmas (15)
Blue Memories (27)
Blue Moon (6)
Born To Lose (9)
Bouquet Of Roses (12)
Bumming Around (9,20)
By The Time I Get To Phoenix (22)
Canadian Sunset (11,23)
Candy Kisses (12)
Cha Cha Cha D'Amour (Melodie D'Amour) (23)
Clinging Vine (7)
Come Back To Sorrento (17)
Come Running Back (14,20) **35**
Corrine Corrina (5)
Crying Time (24)
Detour (10)
Detroit City (25)
Do You Believe This Town (24)
Don't Let The Blues Make You Bad (14)
Door Is Still Open To My Heart (7,21) **6**
Down Home (10)
Drowning In My Tears (22)
Empty Saddles In The Old Corral (13)
Every Minute, Every Hour (7,20)
Everybody But Me (10)
Everybody Loves Somebody (5,6,20) **1**
Face In A Crowd (4,5)
First Thing Ev'ry Morning (And The Last Thing Ev'ry Night) (10)

Fools Rush In (6)
For Once In My Life (26)
For The Good Times (26)
From Lover To Loser (5)
Gentle On My Mind (22)
Georgia Sunshine (26)
Gimme A Little Kiss Will Ya Huh? (6)
Glory Of Love (13,21)
Green, Green Grass Of Home (19)
Guess Who (27)
Hammer And Nails (10)
Hands Across The Table (6)
Have A Heart (8)
He's Got You (18)
Heart Over Mind (25)
Here Comes My Baby (9)
Here We Go Again (25)
Hey Brother Pour The Wine (17)
Hey, Good Lookin' (4)
Home (16)
Honey (22)
Houston (10,20) **21**
I Can Give You What You Want Now (27)
I Can't Help It (12)
I Can't Help Remembering You (19,20)
I Don't Know What I'm Doing (27)
I Don't Know Why (I Just Do) (6)
I Don't Think You Love Me Anymore (9)
I Have But One Heart (2)
I Take A Lot Of Pride In What I Am (24) **75**
I Walk The Line (4,12)
I Will (10,21) **10**
I'll Be Home For Christmas (15)
I'll Be Seeing You (8)
I'll Buy That Dream (6)
I'll Hold You In My Heart ('Till I Can Hold You In My Arms) (8)
I'm Confessin' (That I Love You) (6)
I'm Gonna Change Everything (7)
I'm Living In Two Worlds (14)
I'm Not The Marrying Kind (18)

I'm So Lonesome I Could Cry (4,12)
I'm Yours (17)
I'm Yours (17)
I've Got My Love To Keep Me Warm (11)
I've Grown Accustomed To Her Face (16,23)
If I Ever Get Back To Georgia (18)
If I Had You (16)
If Love Is Good To Me (23)
If You Ever Get Around To Loving Me (24)
If You Knew Susie (13)
If You Were The Only Girl (9)
In A Little Spanish Town (3)
In The Chapel In The Moonlight (8,19,20) **25**
In The Misty Moonlight (7,21) **46**
Invisible Tears (26)
It Just Happened That Way (18)
It Keeps Right On-A-Hurtin' (25)
It Won't Cool Off (11)
It's The Talk Of The Town (16)
Jingle Bells (15)
June In January (11)
Just A Little Lovin' (12)
Just Close Your Eyes (5)
Just Friends (6)
Just In Time (17)
Just Say I Love Her (2,23)
Just The Other Side Of Nowhere (27)
King Of The Road (9,21)
Kiss The World Goodbye (27)
La Paloma (3)
Last Round-Up (13)
Lay Some Happiness On Me (18,21) **55**
Let It Snow! Let It Snow! Let It Snow! (11,15)
Let Me Go, Lover (1)
Little Green Apples (24)
Little Lovely One (10)
Little Ole Wine Drinker, Me (19,21) **38**
Little Voice (6)
Love, Love, Love (10)
Magic Is The Moonlight (3)
Make It Rain (24)
Make The World Go Away (25)

Mambo Italiano (1)
Manana (26)
Marry Me (26)
Marshmallow World (15)
Memories Are Made Of This (17) **1**
Middle Of The Night Is My Cryin' Time (7)
Million And One (41)
My Heart Cries For You (4,5)
My Heart Is An Open Book (8)
My Heart Reminds Me (2)
My Melancholy Baby (6)
My One And Only Love (23)
My Shoes Keep Walking Back To You (9)
My Sugar's Gone (7)
My Woman, My Woman, My Wife (25)
Naughty Lady Of Shady Lane (1)
Nobody But A Fool (Would Love You) (14)
Nobody's Baby Again (18,20) **60**
Non Dimenticar (2)
Not Enough Indians (22) **43**
Old Yellow Line (10,21)
On An Evening In Roma (2) **59**
On The Sunny Side Of The Street (3)
Once A Day (25)
One Cup Of Happiness (And One Peace Of Mind) (24)
One I Love (Belongs To Somebody Else) (16)
One Lonely Boy (14)
(Open Up The Door) Let The Good Times In (18,21) **55**
Out In The Cold Again (11)
Pardon (2)
Party Dolls And Wine (27)
Perfect Mountain (26)
Place In The Shade (19)
Pretty Baby (23)
Pride (19)
Rainbows Are Back In Style (22)
Raindrops Keep Fallin' On My Head (26)
Raining In My Heart (26)

Red Roses For A Blue Lady (9)
Red Sails In The Sunset (13)
Release Me (And Let Me Love Again) (19)
(Remember Me) I'm The One Who Loves You (9,20) **32**
Return To Me (2,17) **4**
Right Kind Of Woman (27)
Room Full Of Roses (4,12)
Rudolph, The Red-Nosed Reindeer (11)
S'posin' (16)
Second Hand Rose (Second Hand Heart) (12)
Send Me Some Lovin' (8)
Send Me The Pillow You Dream On (8,21) **22**
Shades (14)
She's A Little Bit Country (26)
Shutters And Boards (4,5)
Side By Side (13)
Siesta Fiesta (7)
Silent Night (15)
Silver Bells (15)
Singing The Blues (1)
Small Exception Of Me (27)
Smile (6)
Snap Your Fingers (10)
Sneaky Little Side Of Me (24)
So Long Baby (7)
Somewhere There's A Someone (12,21) **32**
South Of The Border (3,13)
Standing On The Corner (22)
Sun Is Shinin' (On Everybody But Me) (24)
Supposin' ..see: S'posin'
Sway (17)
Sweet, Sweet Lovable You (18)
Sweetheart (26)
Take Me (7)
Take Me In Your Arms (2)
Take These Chains From My Heart (9)
Tangerine (3)
Terrible, Tangled Web (14)
That Old Clock On The Wall (12)
That Old Time Feelin' (22)
That's All I Want From You (1)
That's Amore (1)

That's When I See The Blues (In Your Pretty Brown Eyes) (22)
There's No Tomorrow (O Sole Mio) (2)
Things (4,5)
Things We Did Last Summer (11,15,16)
Think About Me (18)
Thirty More Miles To San Diego (18)
Tips Of My Fingers (25)
Today Is Not The Day (14)
Together Again (25)
Turn The World Around (25)
Turn To Me (19)
Vieni Su (2,23)
Volare (Nel Blu Dipinto Di Blu) (17) **12**
Walk On By (9)
Wallpaper Roses (19)
We'll Sing In The Sunshine (7)
Wedding Bells (9)
Welcome To My Heart (22)
Welcome To My World (9,19)
What A Diff'rence A Day Made (3)
What Can I Say After I Say I'm Sorry? (16)
What's Yesterday (27)
Where The Blue And Lonely Go (24)
White Christmas (11,15)
Winter Wonderland (11,15)
You'll Always Be The One I Love (8,20) **64**
You're Breaking My Heart (2)
You're Nobody Till Somebody Loves You (7,8,17,20) **25**
You're The Reason I'm In Love (10)
You've Still Got A Place In My Heart (18,21) **60**
Your Other Love (5)

MARTIN, Eric, Band   '83
Born on 10/10/60 in San Francisco. His band included John Nyman and Mark Ross (guitars), David Jacobson (keyboards), Tom Duke (bass) and Troy Luccketta (drums); **Tesla**. Martin formed **Mr. Big** in 1988.

9/24/83	191	2			Sucker For A Pretty Face			$10	Elektra 60238

Catch Me If You Can
Don't Stop
Just Another Pretty Boy
Letting It Out
Love Me
One More Time
Private Life
Sucker For A Pretty Face
Ten Feet Tall
Young At Heart

MARTIN, George   '64
Born on 1/3/26 in London. Prolific producer for **The Beatles**, **Billy J. Kramer**, **Gerry And The Pacemakers**, **America**, **Jeff Beck** and others. Knighted by Queen Elizabeth II in 1996.

9/5/64	111	10	©	1	Off The Beatle Track	[I]		$80	United Artists 3377
11/7/98	158	1	©	2	In My Life			$10	Echo 11841

All I've Got To Do (1)
All My Loving (1)
Because (1)
Being For The Benefit Of Mr. Kite (2)
Can't Buy Me Love (1)
Carry That Weight (medley) (2)
Come Together (2)
Day In The Life (2)
Don't Bother Me (1)
End, The (medley) (2)
Friends And Lovers (2)
From Me To You (1)
Golden Slumbers (medley) (2)
Hard Day's Night (1)
Here Comes The Sun (2)
Here There & Everywhere (2)
I Am The Walrus (2)
I Saw Her Standing There (1)
I Want To Hold Your Hand (1)
In My Life (2)
Little Child (1)
Pepperland Suite (2)
Please Please Me (1)
Ringo's Theme (This Boy) (1) **53**
She Loves You (1)
There's A Place (1)

MARTIN, Marilyn   '86
Born in Louisville, Kentucky. Former session singer.

2/22/86	72	11			Marilyn Martin			$10	Atlantic 81292

Beauty Or The Beast
Body And The Beat
Dream Is Always The Same
Here Is The News
Move Closer
Night Moves 28
One Step Closer
Too Much Too Soon
Turn It On
Wildest Dreams

MARTIN, Moon   '79
Born John Martin in 1950 in Oklahoma. Pop-rock singer/songwriter/guitarist.

9/8/79	80	11	©	1	Escape From Domination			$12	Capitol 11933
11/15/80	138	15	©	2	Street Fever			$12	Capitol 12099

Bad News (2)
Bootleg Woman (1)
Breakout Tonight (2)
Cross Your Fingers (2)
Dangerous (1)
Dreamer (1)
Feeling's Right (1)
Five Days Of Fever (2)
Gun Shy (1)
Hot House Baby (1)
I've Got A Reason (1)
Love Gone Bad (1)
No Chance (1) **50**
No Dice (2)
Pushed Around (2)
Rolene (1) **30**
Rollin' In My Rolls (2)
She Made A Fool Of You (1)
Signal For Help (1)
Stranded (2)
Whispers (2)

MARTIN, Ray, & His Orchestra   '61
Born on 10/11/18 in Vienna, Austria; later moved to England. Died in February 1988 (age 69). Conductor/arranger.

8/14/61	43	6			Dynamica	[I]		$20	RCA Victor 2287

Bye Bye Blues
Cry Me A River
Flight Of The Bumble Bee
Humoresque
Indian Summer
Lullaby Of The Leaves
Malaguena
Mood Indigo
Moon Was Yellow
Pagan Love Song
Shadrack
Stormy Weather

MARTIN, Ricky '99

Born Enrique Martin on 12/24/71 in San Juan, Puerto Rico. Singer/actor. Member of **Menudo** from 1984-88. Acted on the TV soap *General Hospital* and on Broadway in *Les Miserables*.

DEBUT	PEAK	WKS	RIAA	CD				$	Label & Number
2/28/98+	**40**	41	▲	©	1	Vuelve		[F] $10	Sony 82653
5/29/99	**❶**¹	67	▲⁷	©	2	Ricky Martin		$10	Columbia 69891
12/2/00	**4**	31	▲²	©	3	Sound Loaded		$10	Columbia 61394
3/17/01	**83**	8		©	4	La Historia		[F-K] $10	Sony Discos 84300

Amor (3)
Are You In It For Love (3)
Asi Es La Vida (1)
Be Careful (Cuidado Con Mi Corazón) (2)
Bella (She's All I Ever Had) (2,4)
Bombón De Azúcar (4)
Cambia La Piel (3)

Casi Un Bolero (1)
Come To Me (3)
Corazonado (1)
Cup Of Life (2) *45*
El Amor De Mi Vida (4)
Fuego Contra Fuego (4)
Fuego De Noche, Nieve De Día (4)
Gracias Por Pensar En Mi (1)

Hagamos El Amor (1)
I Am Made Of You (4)
I Count The Minutes (2)
If You Ever Saw Her (3)
Jezabel (3)
La Bomba (1,4)
La Copa De La Vida (1,4)
Livin' La Vida Loca (2,4) *1*
Loaded (3) *97*

Lola, Lola (1)
Love You For A Day (2)
Marcia Baila (1)
Maria (2,4) *88*
Medio Vivir (4)
No Importa La Distancia (1)
Nobody Wants To Be Lonely (3) *13*
One Night Man (3)

Perdido Sin Ti (1,4)
Por Arriba, Por Abajo (1,4)
Private Emotion (2) *67*
Saint Tropez (3)
Shake Your Bon-Bon (2) *22*
She Bangs (3,4) *12*
She's All I Ever Had (2) *2*
Sólo Quiero Amarte (Nobody Wants to be Lonely) (4)

Spanish Eyes (2)
Te Extraño, Te Olvido, Te Amo (4)
Touch, The (3)
Ven A Mí (Come To Me) (3)
Volveras (4)
Vuelve (1,4)
You Stay With Me (2)

MARTIN, Steve '78

Born on 6/8/45 in Waco, Texas; raised in California. Comedian/actor. Starred in several movies.

DEBUT	PEAK	WKS	RIAA	CD				$	Label & Number
10/8/77	**10**	68	▲	©	1	Let's Get Small		[C] $12	Warner 3090
11/4/78	**2**⁶	26	▲²	©	2	A Wild And Crazy Guy		[C] $12	Warner 3238
10/6/79	**25**	22	●	©	3	Comedy Is Not Pretty!		[C] $12	Warner 3392
11/14/81	**135**	4			4	The Steve Martin Brothers.................		[C-I] $12	Warner 3477

side 1: comedy; side 2: banjo music by Martin

All Being (3)
American Photography (4)
Banana Banjo (4)
Born To Be Wild (3)
Cat Handcuffs (2)
Charitable Kind Of Guy (2)
College (2)
Comedy Is Not Pretty (3)
Creativity In Action (2)
Cruel Shoes (3) *91*

Drop Thumb Medley (3)
Excuse Me (1)
Exposé, An (2)
Freddie's Lift, Parts I And II (4)
Funny Comedy Gags (4)
Googlephonics (3)
Gospel Maniacs (4)
Grandmother's Song (1) *72*
Hoedown At Alice's (4)
Hostages (3)

How To Meet A Girl (3)
I'm Feelin' It (2)
I'm In The Mood For Love (4)
Jackie O. And Farrah F. (3)
John Henry (4)
King Tut (2) *17*
Language (2)
Let's Get Small (1)
Love God (4)
Mad At My Mother (1)

Make The Rent (4)
McDonald's (3)
Men's Underwear (3)
My Real Name (2)
One Way To Leave Your Lover (1)
Philosophy (2)
Pitkin County Turn Around (4)
Ramblin' Man (1)
Real Me (4)

Religion (2)
Rubberhead (3)
Saga Of The Old West (4)
Sally Goodin' (4)
Scientific Question (4)
Show Biz Moment (4)
Smoking (1)
Song Of Perfect Spaces (4)
Vegas (1)
Waterbound (4)

What I Believe (4)
Wild And Crazy Guy (2)
You Can Be A Millionaire (3)
You Naive Americans (2)

MARTINEZ, Angie '01

Born in New York City (Puerto Rican parents). Female rapper. Radio personality at Hot 97 in New York City.

DEBUT	PEAK	WKS	RIAA	CD				$	Label & Number
5/5/01	**32**	11		©		Up Close And Personal		$10	Elektra 62366

Breathe
Coast 2 Coast (Suavemente)
Dem Thangz (Dem Thangz)

Every Little Girl
Go!! (M********a)
Gutter 2 The Fancy Ish

Ladies & Gents
Live At Jimmy's
Live From The Streets

Mi Amor
New York, New York
No Playaz

Thug Love

MARTINEZ, Nancy '87

Born in Quebec. Dance singer/actress.

DEBUT	PEAK	WKS	RIAA	CD				$	Label & Number
2/21/87	**178**	3		©		Not Just The Girl Next Door		$10	Atlantic 81720

Crazy Love
For Tonight *32*

Hurt Me Twice (Shame On You)
I'll Be There

In The Heat Of The Night
It Happens All The Time

Move Out
Rhythm Of Your Heart

Without Love

MARTINO, Al ★116★ '63

Born Alfred Cini on 10/7/27 in Philadelphia. Pop singer. Played singer "Johnny Fontane" in the 1972 movie *The Godfather*. Boyhood friend of **Mario Lanza**. Winner on *Arthur Godfrey's Talent Scouts* in 1952.

1)I Love You Because 2)Spanish Eyes 3)Painted, Tainted Rose 4)Living A Lie 5)My Cherie

DEBUT	PEAK	WKS	RIAA	CD				$	Label & Number
12/1/62	**109**	6		©	1	The Exciting Voice Of Al Martino.................		$20	Capitol 1774
6/15/63	**7**	60			2	I Love You Because		$20	Capitol 1914
10/12/63	**9**	44			3	Painted, Tainted Rose		$20	Capitol 1975
2/8/64	**13**	28			4	Living A Lie.................		$20	Capitol 2040
4/18/64	**57**	15			5	The Italian Voice Of Al Martino		$20	Capitol 1907
6/27/64	**31**	25			6	I Love You More And More Every Day/Tears And Roses		$20	Capitol 2107
12/5/64	**8**ˣ	11		©	7	A Merry Christmas		[X] $15	Capitol 2165
						Christmas charts: 8/'64, 19/'65, 59/'66, 23/'67			
2/6/65	**41**	15			8	We Could.................		$15	Capitol 2200
6/19/65	**42**	12			9	Somebody Else Is Taking My Place		$15	Capitol 2312
9/11/65+	**19**	47			10	My Cherie.................		$15	Capitol 2362
2/19/66	**8**	73	●	©	11	Spanish Eyes		$15	Capitol 2435
6/18/66	**116**	6			12	Think I'll Go Somewhere And Cry Myself To Sleep		$15	Capitol 2528
10/29/66+	**57**	13			13	This Is Love		$15	Capitol 2592
3/25/67	**99**	12			14	This Love For You		$15	Capitol 2654
6/24/67	**23**	21			15	Daddy's Little Girl		$15	Capitol 2733
10/14/67+	**63**	21			16	Mary In The Morning		$15	Capitol 2780
3/30/68	**129**	4			17	This Is Al Martino		$15	Capitol 2843
4/20/68	**56**	17			18	Love Is Blue		$15	Capitol 2908
8/31/68	**108**	16		©	19	The Best Of Al Martino.................		[G] $15	Capitol 2946
7/19/69	**189**	4			20	Sausalito		$15	Capitol 180
12/20/69	**196**	2			21	Jean		$15	Capitol 379
4/11/70	**184**	5			22	Can't Help Falling In Love		$15	Capitol 405
11/28/70	**172**	6			23	My Heart Sings		$15	Capitol 497

DEBUT	PEAK	WKS	RIAA	CD	ARTIST — Album Title	Catalog	Sym	$	Label & Number

MARTINO, Al — Cont'd

| 6/3/72 | 138 | 10 | | | 24 Love Theme From "The Godfather" | | | $15 | Capitol 11071 |
| 2/8/75 | 129 | 8 | | | 25 To The Door Of The Sun | | | $12 | Capitol 11366 |

Adios Mexico (12)
Affair To Remember (14)
Al Di La (5)
All (14)
All My Dreams (6)
(All Of A Sudden) My Heart Sings (23)
Always Together (8) *33*
Am I Losing You? (6)
And That Reminds Me (17)
Anita, You're Dreaming (12)
Are You Lonesome Tonight? (4)
Autumn Leaves (14)
Because You're Mine (1)
Born Free (15)
Bouquet Of Roses (2)
By The River Of The Roses (11)
Call, The (23)
Call Me (18)
Can't Help Falling In Love (22) *51*
Can't Take My Eyes Off You (16)
Careless (4)
Careless Hands (6)
Chitarra Romana (5)
Close To You (14)
Come Into My Life (25)
Crying In The Chapel (10)
Crying Time (12)
Cuore Di Mamma (5)
Daddy's Little Girl (15,19) *42*
Dear Heart (8)
Devotion (14)
Dicitencello Vuie ..see: Just Say I Love Her
Don't Cry Joe (Let Her Go, Let Her Go, Let Her Go) (4)
Don't Leave Me Now (5)
Don't Take Your Love From Me (13)
End Of The World (11)
Every Day Of My Life (24)
Everybody's Talkin' (21)
Exodus Song (1)
Fascination (10)
Fenesta Che Lucive (The Window) (1)
For All We Know (13)
Forgive Me (11) *61*
Georgia On My Mind (18)
Glad She's A Woman (20)
Glory Of Love (17)
Godfather, Love Theme From The ..see: Speak Softly Love

Godfather Waltz (Come Live Your Life With Me) (24)
Goin' Out Of My Head (18)
Got To Live It Up To Live You Down (12)
Granada (1)
Gypsy In You (24)
Happy Time (17)
Harbor Lights (3)
Have I Told You Lately That I Love You? (3)
Here In My Heart (1) *86*
Hold Back The Dawn (14)
Honey Come Back (22)
Husbands and Wives (12)
Hush...Hush, Sweet Charlotte (9,19)
I Can't Stop My Lovin' You (12)
I Don't See Me In Your Eyes Any More (3)
I Don't Want To See Tomorrow (8)
I Dream Of You (More Than You Dream I Do) (16)
I Have But One Heart (24)
I Love You And You Love Me (15)
I Love You Because (2,19) *3*
I Love You More And More Every Day (6,19) *9*
I Love You Truly (3)
I Really Don't Want To Know (2)
I Will Wait For You (14)
I Wish You Love (10)
I Won't Forget You (8)
I'll Always Be In Love With You (6)
I'll Be Home For Christmas (9)
I'll Hold You In My Heart (Till I Can Hold You In My Arms) (11)
I'll Never Find Another You (10)
I'm A Better Man (21)
I'm Carryin' The World On My Shoulders (18)
I'm In The Mood For Love (4)
I'm Living My Heaven With You (6)
I'm Saving All My Love For You (12)
I'm Still Not Thru Missin' You (24,25)
If Ever I Would Leave You (17)
If I Loved You (9)
If I Never Get To Heaven (2)
If I Were A Carpenter (22)

If Tears Were Roses (21)
If You Go Away (14)
In The Arms Of Love (14)
It Only Hurts For A Little While (10)
It's A Sin (2)
Jealous Heart (8)
Jean (21)
Joanne (23)
Just As Much As Ever (18)
Just Call Me Lonesome (2)
Just Loving You (18)
Just Say I Love Her (1,24)
Just Yesterday (13) *77*
La Strada Del Bosco (5)
Less Than Tomorrow (8)
Let It Be Me (18)
Let Me Stay Awhile With You (21)
Letter, The (20)
Lies (4)
Lili Marlene (18) *87*
Little Drummer Boy (7)
Living A Lie (4,19) *22*
Lonely Drifter (2)
Long Long Time (23)
Losing You (2)
Love Is A Many-Splendored Thing (17)
Love Is Blue (18,19) *57*
Love Letters (4)
Love Letters In The Sand (16)
Love Me Tender (16)
Love, Where Are You Now (1)
Love Will Conquer All (25)
Loveliest Night Of The Year (1)
Lovely Lady Of Arcadia (25)
Loving You (23)
Make Me Believe (1)
Make The World Go Away (11)
Making Memories (16)
Man Without Love (24)
Many Tears Ago (6)
Maria Mari (Ah! Marie) (5)
Mary Go Lightly (25)
Mary In The Morning (15,16,19) *27*
Mattinata (1)
Melody Of Love (15)
Memories (20)
Merry-go-round (2)
Mexicali Rose (4)
Minute You're Gone (12)
Moon Over Naples (Spanish Eyes) (10) *15*
More (3)

More I See You (4)
More Than The Eye Can See (17) *54*
My Cherie (10) *88*
My Cherie Amour (21)
My Cup Runneth Over (15)
My Darling, I Love You (8)
My Foolish Heart (11)
My Heart Sings ..see: (All Of A Sudden)
My Heart Would Know (9) *52*
My Love, Forgive Me (10)
My Love Is Stronger Than My Pride (11)
My Way (22)
Nessun Dorma (1)
Never My Love (17)
New World In The Morning (23)
No More (1)
No One Will Ever Know (6)
No Other Arms, No Other Lips (9)
Non Ti Scordar Di Me (1)
Now (Before Another Day Goes By) (16)
O Come All Ye Faithful (7)
O Holy Night (7)
Once Upon A Time (15)
One Has My Name...The Other Has My Heart (11)
One More Mile (And Darlin', I'll Be Home) (22)
One Pair Of Hands (23)
Oscurita (20)
Painted, Tainted Rose (3,19) *15*
Pardon Me (9)
Raindrops Keep Fallin' On My Head (22)
Ramona (22)
Red Is Red (16)
Red Roses For A Blue Lady (9,19)
Release Me (16)
Rise And Fall Of A Fool (24)
Rondine Al Nido (5)
Room Full Of Roses (4)
Rudolph The Red-Nosed Reindeer (7)
Sandy When She's Sleepin' (20)
Sausalito (20) *99*
Senza Nisciuno (5)
Shadow Of Your Smile (17)
Shadows (20)
She'll Always Love You (15)
Silent Night (7)

Silver Bells (medley) (7)
Snowbird (23)
Somebody Else Is Taking My Place (9) *53*
Something In Our Hearts (14)
Somewhere (13)
Somewhere In This World (15)
Somewhere In Your Heart (9)
Somewhere, My Love (13)
Song Of Joy (25)
Spanish Eyes (11,19) *15*
Speak Softly Love (24) *80*
Stay (21)
Still (2)
Strangers In The Night (13)
Sunrise To Sunrise (8)
Sweet Caroline (Good Times Never Seemed So Good) (22)
Take My Hand For A While (20)
Take These Chains From My Heart (2)
Tears And Roses (6) *20*
That's My Desire (4)
That's The Way It's Got To Be (3)
Then I'll Be Over You (20)
Then You Can Tell Me Goodbye (8)
There Are Such Things (17)
There Must Be A Way (1)
There's No Such Thing As Love (21)
These Things I Offer You (13)
They'll Never Take Her Love From Me (1)
Think I'll Go Somewhere And Cry Myself To Sleep (11,12) *30*
This Guy's In Love With You (21)
This Is My Song (15)
This Love Of Mine (13)
Three Coins In The Fountain (10)
Till (10)
Till Then (3)
Till Then, My Love (11)
To Each His Own (3)
To The Door Of The Sun (Alle Porte Del Sole) (25) *17*
Today I Found You (25)
Together Again (12)
Torna (5)
Torna A Sorriento (Come Back To Sorrento) (5)
Traces (20)
True Love (14)

True Love Is Greater Than Friendship (23)
Two Different Worlds (13)
Unchained Melody (16)
Until It's Time For You To Go (20)
Vaya Con Dios (4)
Vurria (I Would Like) (5)
Walk Away (17)
Walkin' In The Sand (And The Seasons Come And Go) (25)
Watch What Happens (18)
Way It Used To Be (20)
We Could (8) *41*
We Wish You A Merry Christmas (medley) (7)
What Child Is This? (7)
What Kind Of Girl Are You (18)
What Now, My Love (10)
Whatever Happened (Baby) To You And I (22)
Wheel Of Hurt (15) *59*
Where Do You Go (23)
White Christmas (7)
White Rose Of Athens (11)
Who Can I Turn To (When Nobody Needs Me) (13)
Wiederseh'n (12) *57*
With All My Heart (9)
Woman In Love (15)
Words (22)
Year Ago Tonight (6)
Yesterday (1)
Yesterday, When I Was Young (21)
You Always Hurt The One You Love (3)
You Can't Hide The Truth (From Your Eyes) (4)
You Don't Know Me (8)
You Hurt Me (12)
You Win Again (2)
You'll Never Know (9)
You're All I Want For Christmas (7)
You're All The Woman That I Need (22)
You're Breaking My Heart (24)

MARVELETTES, The   '66

Female R&B vocal group from Inkster, Michigan: Gladys Horton, Georgeanna Marie Tillman Gordon (married Billy Gordon of The Contours), Wanda Young (married Bobby Rogers of **The Miracles**), Katherine Anderson and Juanita Cowart. Young and Horton both sang lead. Cowart left in 1962. Gordon left in 1965; died of lupus on 1/6/80 (age 35). Horton left in 1967, replaced by Anne Bogan (later a member of Love, Peace & Happiness and **The New Birth**). Disbanded in 1969. Also recorded as The Darnells.

| 3/19/66 | 84 | 16 | | | 1 Greatest Hits | | [G] | $30 | Tamla 253 |
| 4/8/67 | 129 | 8 | © | | 2 The Marvelettes | | | $30 | Tamla 274 |

As Long As I Know He's Mine (1) *47*
Barefootin' (2)
Beechwood 4-5789 (1) *17*
Danger Heartbreak Dead Ahead (1) *61*
Day You Take One (You Have To Take The Other) (2)
Don't Mess With Bill (1) *7*
Forever (1) *78*
He Was Really Sayin' Somethin' (2)
Hunter Gets Captured By The Game (2) *13*
I Can't Turn Around (2)
I Know Better (2)
I Need Someone (2)
Keep Off, No Trespassing (2)
Locking Up My Heart (1) *44*
Message To Michael (2)
Playboy (1) *7*
Please Mr. Postman (1) *1*
Strange I Know (1) *49*
This Night Was Made For Love (2)
Too Many Fish In The Sea (1) *25*
Twistin' Postman (1) *34*
When I Need You (2)
When You're Young And In Love (2) *23*
You're My Remedy (1) *48*

MARVELOUS 3   '00

Rock trio from Atlanta: Butch Walker (vocals, guitar), Jayce Fincher (bass) and Slug (drums).

| 9/30/00 | 196 | 1 | © | | Readysexgo | | | $10 | Elektra 62536 |

Beautiful
Better Off Alone
Cigarette Lighter Love Song
Cold As Hell
Get Over
Grant Park
I Could Change
I'm Losing You
Little Head
Radio Tokyo
Sugarbuzz
Supernatural Blonde
This Time

MARX, Groucho   '73

Born Julius Henry Marx on 10/2/1890 in New York City. Died of pneumonia on 8/19/77 (age 86). Legendary TV/movie comedian. Member of **The Marx Brothers** with Chico, Harpo and Zeppo Marx.

| 10/11/69 | 155 | 3 | | | 1 The Marx Bros. (The Original Voice Tracks From Their Greatest Movies) | | [C] | $15 | Decca 79168 |

THE MARX BROTHERS
narration by Gary Owens

| 11/25/72+ | 160 | 15 | © | | 2 An Evening With Groucho | | [C] | $20 | A&M 3515 [2] |

transcription of his one-man concert tour; no track titles listed on this album

Chico In Recital (1)
Collected Speeches Of Groucho (1)
Groucho Marx Does His Thing (1)
Implausible Chico (1)
Inimitable Groucho (1)
Meet The Brothers Marx (1)
Sounds Of Harpo (1)
Zaniness Of The Marx Brothers (1)

MARX, Richard '89
Born on 9/16/63 in Chicago. Pop-rock singer/songwriter. Married Cynthia Rhodes (of **Animotion**) on 1/8/89.

DEBUT	PEAK	WKS	RIAA	CD	#	Album Title	$	Label & Number
6/20/87+	8	86	▲³	©	1	Richard Marx	$10	EMI-Manhattan 53049
5/20/89	❶¹	66	▲⁴	©	2	Repeat Offender	$10	EMI 90380
11/23/91+	35	58	▲	©	3	Rush Street	$10	Capitol 95874
2/26/94	37	23	▲	©	4	Paid Vacation	$10	Capitol 81232
4/26/97	70	6		©	5	Flesh And Bone	$10	Capitol 31528
11/22/97	140	11		©	6	Greatest Hits	[G] $10	Capitol 21914

Angel's Lullaby (6)
Angelia (2,6) **4**
Big Boy Now (3)
Breathless (5)
Calling You (3)
Can't Lie To My Heart (5)
Chains Around My Heart (3) **44**
Children Of The Night (2,6) **13**
Don't Mean Nothing (1,6) **3**

Endless Summer Nights (1,6) **2**
Eternity (5)
Flame Of Love (1)
Fool's Game (5)
Goodbye Hollywood (4)
Hands In Your Pocket (3)
Have Mercy (1)
Hazard (3,6) **9**
Heart On The Line (1)
Heaven Only Knows (1)

Heaven's Waiting (4)
Hold On To The Nights (1,6) **1**
I Get No Sleep (3)
If You Don't Want My Love (2)
Image, The (5)
Keep Coming Back (3,6) **12**
Lonely Heart (1)
Love Unemotional (3)
Miracle (5)
My Confession (5)
Nothin' You Can Do About It (2)

Nothing Left Behind Us (4)
Nothing To Hide (4)
Now And Forever (4,6) **7**
One Man (4)
One More Try (4)
Playing With Fire (3)
Real World (2)
Remember Manhattan (1)
Rhythm Of Life (1)
Right Here Waiting (2,6) **1**
Satisfied (2,6) **1**

Should've Known Better (1,6) **3**
Silent Scream (4)
Soul Motion (4)
Streets Of Pain (3)
Superstar (3)
Take This Heart (3,6) **20**
Too Late To Say Goodbye (2) **12**
Touch Of Heaven (5,6)
Until I Find You Again (5,6) **42**

Wait For The Sunrise (2)
Way She Loves Me (4,6) **20**
What You Want (4)
What's The Story (5)
What's Wrong With That (5)
You Never Take Me Dancing (5)
Your World (3)

MARY JANE GIRLS '85
Female R&B vocal group: Joanne McDuffie, Candice Ghant, Kim Wuletich and Yvette Marina.

DEBUT	PEAK	WKS	RIAA	CD	#	Album Title	$	Label & Number
5/14/83	56	41	●	©	1	Mary Jane Girls	$12	Gordy 6040
3/16/85	18	38	●	©	2	Only Four You	$12	Gordy 6092

All Night Long (1)
Boys (1)
Break It Up (2)

Candy Man (1)
Girlfriend (2)
I Betcha (1)

In My House (2) **7**
Jealousy (1)
Leather Queen (2)

Lonely For You (2)
Musical Love (1)
On The Inside (1)

Prove It (1)
Shadow Lover (2)
Wild And Crazy Love (2) **42**

You Are My Heaven (1)

MARY MARY '00
Female gospel vocal duo from Inglewood, California: sisters Erica and Tina Atkins.

DEBUT	PEAK	WKS	RIAA	CD	Album Title	$	Label & Number
5/20/00	59	54↑	●	©	Thankful	$10	Columbia 63740

Be Happy
Can't Give Up Now
Good To Me

I Got It
I Sings
Joy

One Minute
Shackles (Praise You) **28**
Somebody

Still My Child
Thankful
Wade In The Water

What A Friend

MAS, Carolyne '79
Born in the Bronx, New York. Rock singer/guitarist.

DEBUT	PEAK	WKS	RIAA	CD	Album Title	$	Label & Number
9/22/79	172	3			Carolyne Mas	$12	Mercury 3783

Baby Please
Call Me (Crazy To)

Do You Believe I Love You
It's No Secret

Never Two Without Three
Quote Goodbye Quote

Sadie Says
Sittin' In The Dark

Snow
Stillsane **71**

MA$E '97
Born Mason Betha on 3/24/70 in Jacksonville, Florida; raised in Harlem, New York. Male rapper.

DEBUT	PEAK	WKS	RIAA	CD	#	Album Title	$	Label & Number
11/15/97	❶²	54	▲⁴	©	1	Harlem World	$10	Bad Boy 73017
7/3/99	11	11		©	2	Double Up	$10	Bad Boy 73029

All I Ever Wanted (2)
Another Story To Tell (2)
Blood Is Thicker (2)
Cheat On You (1)
Do It Again (2)

Do You Wanna Get $? (1)
Feel So Good (1) **5**
From Scratch (2)
F#!* Me, F#!* You (2)
Get Ready (2)

Gettin' It (2)
I Need To Be (1)
If You Want To Party (2)
Jealous Guy (1)
Lookin' At Me (1) **8**

Love U So (1)
Make Me Cry (2)
Niggaz Wanna Act (1)
No Matter What (2)
Player Way (1)

Same Niggas (2)
Stay Out Of My Way (2)
Take What's Yours (1)
24 Hrs. To Live (1)
Wanna Hurt Mase? (1)

What You Want (1) **6**
Will They Die 4 You? (1)
You Ain't Smart (2)

MASEKELA, Hugh '68
Born on 4/4/39 in Wilbank, South Africa. Trumpeter/bandleader/arranger. Married to **Miriam Makeba** from 1964-66.

DEBUT	PEAK	WKS	RIAA	CD	#	Album Title	$	Label & Number
8/5/67	151	10			1	Hugh Masekela's Latest	$15	Uni 73010
1/6/68	90	10			2	Hugh Masekela Is Alive And Well At The Whisky	[L] $15	Uni 73015
6/8/68	17	22		©	3	The Promise Of A Future	$15	Uni 73028
3/29/69	195	2			4	Masekela	$15	Uni 73041
9/28/74	149	4			5	I Am Not Afraid	$15	Blue Thumb 6015
8/9/75	132	9			6	The Boy's Doin' It	$15	Casablanca 7017
2/11/78	65	19		©	7	Herb Alpert/Hugh Masekela	[I] $12	Horizon 728

African Secret Society (5)
African Summer (7)
Ain't No Mountain High Enough (3)
Almost Seedless (3)
Arrastao (1)
Ashiko (6)
Baby, Baby, Baby (1)
Bajabula Bonke (The Healing Song) (3)
Been Such A Long Time Gone (5)

Blues For Huey (4)
Boeremusiek (4)
Boy's Doin' It (6)
Coincidence (4)
Excuse Me Please (6)
Extra Added Attraction (4)
Fuzz (4)
Gafsa (4)
Gold (4)
Grazing In The Grass (3) **1**
Groove Me (1)
Ha Lese Le Di Khanna (2)

Happy Hanna (7)
Head Peepin' (4)
Here, There And Everywhere (1)
I Just Wasn't Meant For These Times (1)
I'll Be There For You (7)
If There's Anybody Out There (4)
In The Jungle (6)
In The Market Place (5)
Jungle Jim (5)

Lily The Fox (1)
Little Miss Sweetness (2)
Lobo (7)
MRA (Christopher Columbus) (2)
Mace And Grenades (4)
Madonna (3)
Mago (1)
Mama (6)
Mazeze (1)
Moonza (7)
Night In Tunisia (5)

Nina (5)
No Face, No Name And No Number (3)
Otis (4)
Person Is A Sometime Thing (6)
Reza (Laia Ladaia) (1)
Ring Bell (7)
Riot (4) **55**
Senor Coraza (2)
Skokiaan (7)
Sobukwe (4)

Society's Child (Baby I've Been Thinking) (1)
Son Of Ice Bag (2)
Stimela (Coaltrain) (5)
Stop (3)
There Are Seeds To Sow (3)
Thula (1)
Up-Up And Away (2) **71**
Vuca (Wake Up) (3)
Whiter Shade Of Pale (2)

MASKED MARAUDERS, The '70
Canadian group masquerading as **Bob Dylan**, **Mick Jagger**, **John Lennon** and **Paul McCartney**. Group based on a fictional *Rolling Stone* article on 12/13/69.

DEBUT	PEAK	WKS	RIAA	CD	Album Title	$	Label & Number
1/3/70	114	12			The Masked Marauders	$25	Deity 6378

Book Of Love
Cow Pie
Duke Of Earl

I Am The Japanese Sandman (Rang Tang Ding Dong)
I Can't Get No Nookie

Later
More Or Less Hudson's Bay Again

Saturday Night At The Cow Palace
Season Of The Witch

MASON, Barbara '73
Born on 8/9/47 in Philadelphia. R&B singer/songwriter.

DEBUT	PEAK	WKS	RIAA	CD	#	Album Title	$	Label & Number
10/2/65	129	8			1	Yes, I'm Ready	$50	Arctic 1000
2/3/73	95	12			2	Give Me Your Love	$15	Buddah 5117
2/22/75	187	2			3	Love's The Thing	$15	Buddah 5628

MASON, Barbara — Cont'd

Bed And Board (2) **70**
Come See About Me (1)
Come To Me (1)
Everything I Own (2)
From His Woman To You
(3) **28**

Girls Have Feelings Too (1)
Give Me Your Love (2) **31**
Got To Get You Off My Mind (1)
(He Wants) The Two Of Us (3)
I Call Out Your Name (3)
Keep Him (1)

Let Me In Your Life (2)
Misty (1)
Moon River (1)
One-Two-Three (You Her Or Me) (3)
Out Of This World (2)

Sad, Sad Girl (1) **27**
Shackin' Up (3) **91**
So He's Yours Now (3)
Something You Got (1)
(There's) One Man Between Us (3)

Trouble Child (1)
What Am I Gonna Do (3)
What Do You Say (3)
When I Fall In Love (2)
Who Will You Hurt Next (2)
Yes, I'm Ready (1,2) **5**

You Can Be With The One You Don't Love (2)
You Got What It Takes (1)
Your Sweet Love (3)

★299★ MASON, Dave '70

Born on 5/10/46 in Worcester, England. Singer/songwriter/guitarist. Original member of **Traffic**. Joined **Delaney & Bonnie** for a short time in 1970. Joined **Fleetwood Mac** in 1993.

1)Alone Together 2)Dave Mason 3)Split Coconut

DEBUT	PEAK	WKS	RIAA	CD	#	Album Title	Sym	$	Label & Number
7/4/70	22	25	●	©	1	**Alone Together**		$20	Blue Thumb 19
3/13/71	49	7		©	2	**Dave Mason & Cass Elliot**		$20	Blue Thumb 25
2/26/72	51	14		©	3	**Headkeeper**	[L]	$15	Blue Thumb 34
						side 1: studio; side 2: live			
4/21/73	116	11			4	**Dave Mason Is Alive!**	[L]	$15	Blue Thumb 54
11/10/73	50	28		©	5	**It's Like You Never Left**		$12	Columbia 31721
6/29/74	183	9			6	**The Best Of Dave Mason**	[G]	$12	Blue Thumb 6013
11/2/74	25	25	●	©	7	**Dave Mason**		$12	Columbia 33096
3/22/75	133	3			8	**Dave Mason At His Best**	[K]	$12	Blue Thumb 880
10/18/75	27	17		©	9	**Split Coconut**		$12	Columbia 33698
11/27/76+	78	17		©	10	**Certified Live**	[L]	$15	Columbia 34174 [2]
4/30/77	37	49	▲	©	11	**Let It Flow**		$12	Columbia 34680
7/1/78	41	19	●	©	12	**Mariposa De Oro**		$12	Columbia 35285
						title is Spanish for "Gold Butterfly"			
10/28/78	179	4		©	13	**Very Best Of Dave Mason**	[K]	$12	Blue Thumb 6032
6/14/80	74	10		©	14	**Old Crest On A New Wave**		$12	Columbia 36144

All Along The Watchtower (7,10)
All Gotta Go Sometime (12)
Baby...Please (5)
Bird On The Wind (12)
Bring It On Home To Me (7,10)
Can't Stop Worrying, Can't Stop Loving (1,3,6,8,13)
Crying, Waiting, Hoping (9)
Don't It Make You Wonder (12)
Every Woman (5,7,10)
Feelin' Alright? (3,4,10,13)
Get Ahold On Love (7)
Get It Right (14)
Gimme Some Lovin' (12)
Give Me A Reason Why (9,10)
Glittering Facade (2)
Goin' Down Slow (10)
Gotta Be On My Way (14)

Harmony & Melody (7)
Headkeeper (3,5,8,13)
Heartache, A Shadow, A Lifetime (3,6,8)
Here We Go Again (2,3,6,8)
I'm Missing You (14)
If You've Got Love (5)
In My Mind (3,6,8)
It Can't Make Any Difference To Me (7)
It's Like You Never Left (5)
Just A Song (1,3,4,13)
Let It Go, Let It Flow (11) **45**
Life Is A Ladder (14)
Lonely One (5)
Long Lost Friend (9)
Look At You Look At Me (1,4,6,8,10)
Maybe (5)

Misty Morning Stranger (5)
Mystic Traveler (11)
Next To You (3)
No Doubt About It (12)
Old Crest On A New Wave (14)
On And On (2)
Only You Know And I Know (1,4,6,8,10,13) **42**
Paralyzed (14)
Pearly Queen (3,10,13)
Pleasing You (2)
Relation Ships (7)
Sad And Deep As You (1,4,10,13)
Save Me (14) **71**
Save Your Love (9)
Searchin' (For A Feeling) (12)
Seasons (11)
Share Your Love (12)

She's A Friend (9)
Shouldn't Have Took More Than You Gave (1,4,6,8,13)
Show Me Some Affection (7,10)
Side Tracked (5)
Silent Partner (5)
Sit And Wonder (2)
So Good To Be Home (12)
So High (Rock Me Baby And Roll Me Away) (11) **89**
Something To Make You Happy (2)
Spend Your Life With Me (11)
Split Coconut (9)
Sweet Music (9)
Take It To The Limit (10)
Takin' The Time To Find (11)
Talk To Me (14)
Then It's Alright (11)

To Be Free (2,3,6,8)
Too Much Truth, Too Much Love (2)
Tryin' To Get Back To You (14)
Two Guitar Lovers (9)
Waitin' On You (1,13)
Walk To The Point (2,4,6)
Warm And Tender Love (12)
Warm Desire (12)
We Just Disagree (11) **12**
What Do We Got Here? (11)
Will You Still Love Me Tomorrow (12) **39**
Words, The (12)
World In Changes (1,3,10,13)
You Can Lose It (9)
You Can't Take It When You Go (7)

You Just Have To Wait Now (11)
You're A Friend Of Mine (14)

MASON, Harvey '79

Born on 2/22/47 in Atlantic City, New Jersey. Session drummer. Joined **Fourplay** in 1991.

DEBUT	PEAK	WKS			#	Album Title	Sym	$	Label & Number
4/28/79	149	8			1	**Groovin' You**		$12	Arista 4227
5/30/81	186	3			2	**M.V.P.**		$12	Arista 4283

Don't Doubt My Lovin' (2)
Going Through The Motions (2)
Groovin' You (1)

Here Today, Gone Tomorrow (1)
How Does It Feel (2)
I'd Still Be There (1)

Kauai (1)
Never Give You Up (1)
On And On (2)
Race, The (1)

Say It Again (1)
Spell (2)
Universal Rhyme (2)
Wave (1)

We Can (1)
We Can Start Tonight (2)
You And Me (2)

MASON, Jackie '62

Born Yacov Maza on 6/9/31 in Sheboygan, Wisconsin. Comedian/actor. Appeared in several movies and TV shows.

DEBUT	PEAK	WKS			#	Album Title	Sym	$	Label & Number
7/14/62	77	7			1	**I'm The Greatest Comedian In The World Only Nobody Knows It Yet**	[C]	$25	Verve 15033
						no track titles listed on this album			
1/9/88	146	9			2	**The World According To Me!**	[C]	$10	Warner 25603

Beverly Hills: Producers/Mercedes (2)
Jews And Gentiles (2)

One Man Show: Sex/Hookers/Psychiatry (2)
Soliloquy (2)

World And Politics: Armies/Nationalities/Reagan And Other Great Men (2)

MASON, Nick '85

Born on 1/27/45 in Birmingham, England. Drummer of **Pink Floyd**.

DEBUT	PEAK	WKS			#	Album Title	Sym	$	Label & Number
7/4/81	170	3		©	1	**Nick Mason's Fictitious Sports**		$10	Columbia 37307
8/31/85	154	5		©	2	**Profiles**	[I]	$10	Columbia 40142
						NICK MASON & RICK FENN			

And The Address (2)
At The End Of The Day (2)
Black Ice (2)

Boo To You Too (1)
Can't Get My Motor To Start (1)
Do Ya? (1)

Hot River (1)
I Was Wrong (1)
I'm A Mineralist (1)

Israel (2)
Lie For A Lie (2)
Malta (2)

Mumbo Jumbo (2)
Profiles Parts 1-3 (2)
Rhoda (2)

Siam (1)
Wervin' (1)
Zip Code (2)

MASON PROFFIT '71

Country-rock group from Chicago: brothers Terry (vocals, guitar) and John (guitar, vocals) Talbot, Bruce "Creeper" Kurnow (piano), Tim Ayres (bass) and Art Nash (drums).

DEBUT	PEAK	WKS			#	Album Title	Sym	$	Label & Number
4/17/71	177	8			1	**Movin' Toward Happiness**		$15	Happy Tiger 1019
11/6/71+	186	14			2	**Last Night I Had The Strangest Dream**		$15	Ampex 10138
5/19/73	198	5		©	3	**Bareback Rider**		$12	Warner 2704

Belfast (medley) (3)
Black September (medley) (3)
Children (1)
Cottonwood (3)
Dance Hall Girl (3)
Eugene Pratt (2)

Everybody Was Wrong (1)
Five Generations (3)
500 Men (2)
Flying Arrow (1)
Freedom (1)
Good Friend Of Mary's (1)

Hard Luck Woman (1)
He Loves Them (1)
Hokey Joe Pony (1)
Hope (2)
I Saw The Light (3)
In The Country (medley) (2)

Jewel (2)
Last Night I Had The Strangest Dream (2)
Let Me Know Where You're Goin' (1)
Lilly (3)

Melinda (1)
Michael Dodge (1)
Mother (2)
My Country (2)
Old Joe Clark (1)
Sail Away (3)

Setting The Woods On Fire (3)
Sparrow (medley) (3)
Stoney River (3)
To Be A Friend (3)
24 Hour Sweetheart (2)

MASSIVE ATTACK '98
Techno group from Bristol, England: Robert Delnaja, Gary Marshall and Andy Vowles.

| 5/30/98 | 60 | 7 | © | | Mezzanine | | | $10 | Virgin 45599 |

| Angel | Dissolved Girl | Group Four | Man Next Door | Risingson |
| Black Milk | Exchange | Inertia Creeps | Mezzanine | Teardrop |

MASS PRODUCTION '79
Disco-funk group from Richmond, Virginia: Agnes "Tiny" Kelly (female vocals), Larry Marshall (male vocals), LeCoy Bryant (guitar), James Drumgole (trumpet), Gregory McCoy (sax), Tyrone Williams (keyboards), Emanual Redding (percussion), Kevin Douglas (bass) and Ricardo Williams (drums).

1/8/77	142	10		1	Welcome To Our World			$12	Cotillion 9910
8/27/77	83	9		2	Believe			$12	Cotillion 9918
7/21/79	43	17		3	In The Purest Form			$12	Cotillion 5211
3/29/80	133	9		4	Massterpiece			$12	Cotillion 5218
5/16/81	166	6		5	Turn Up The Music			$12	Cotillion 5226

Angel	Eknuf (4)	I Believe In Music (2)	Magic (1)	Saucey (5)	Welcome To Our World (Of
Being Here (2)	Eyeballin' (3)	I Can't Believe You're Going	Nature Lover (4)	Shante (4)	Merry Music) (1) 68
Bopp (5)	Firecracker (medley) (3) 43	Away (5)	Next Year (3)	Strollin' (3)	Wine-Flow Disco (1)
Can't You See I'm Fired Up (3)	Forever (4)	I Got To Have Your Love (3)	Our Thought (Purity) (3)	Sunshine (3)	With Pleasure (3)
Clinch Quencher (5)	Free And Happy (2)	I Like To Dance (1)	Our Thought (To The World) (1)	Superlative (2)	Your Love (4)
Come Back Hot (4)	Fun In The Sun (1)	Just A Song (1)	Our Thought (Tomorrow) (5)	Turn Up The Music (5)	
Cosmic Lust (2)	Galaxy (1)	Keep My Heart Together (2)	People Get Up (2)	We Love You (2)	
Diamond Chips (5)	Gonna Make You Love Me (4)	Love You (medley) (3)	Please Don't Leave Me (4)		

MASTA ACE INCORPORATED '95
Born Duvall Clear in Brownsville, New York. Male rapper.

| 5/22/93 | 134 | 3 | © | 1 | SlaughtaHouse | | | $10 | Delicious Vinyl 92249 |
| 5/20/95 | 69 | 10 | | 2 | Sittin' On Chrome | | | $10 | Delicious Vinyl 32873 |

Ain't No Game (2)	Born To Roll (2) 23	4 Da Mind (2)	Late Model Sedan (1)	Saturday Nite Live (1)	Turn It Up (2)
Ain't U Da Masta (1)	Crazy Drunken Style (1)	Freestyle ? (2)	Mad Wunz (1)	Sittin' On Chrome (2) 84	U Can't Find Me (2)
B-Side, The (2)	Da Answer (2)	I.N.C. Ride (2) 69	People In My Hood (2)	Slaughtahouse (1)	Walk Thru The Valley (1)
Big East (1)	Don't F*** Around (1)	Jack B. Nimble (1)	Phat Kat Ride (2)	Style Wars (1)	What's Going On! (2)
Boom Bashin' (1)	Eastbound (2)	Jeep Ass Niguh (1)	Rollin' Wit Umdada (1)	Terror (2)	Who U Jackin'? (1)

MASTER P '98
Born Percy Miller on 4/29/70 in New Orleans. Male rapper/producer. Member of 504 Boyz and Tru. Founder of the No Limit record label. Played professional basketball for the CBA's Fort Wayne Fury in 1998. Brother of Silkk The Shocker. Father of Lil' Romeo.

5/4/96	26	57	●	©	1	Ice Cream Man	C:#30/12		$10	No Limit 53978
9/13/97	❶¹	80	▲²	©	2	Ghetto D	C:#49/1		$10	No Limit 50659
11/22/97	❶²ᶜ	11		©	3	The Ghettos Tryin To Kill Me!			$10	No Limit 50696
6/13/98	❶²	42	▲⁴	©	4	MP Da Last Don			$15	No Limit 53538 [2]
11/13/99	2¹	15		●	©	5	Only God Can Judge Me			$10	No Limit 50092
12/16/00	26	17		●	©	6	Ghetto Postage			$10	No Limit 26008

After Dollars, No Cents (2)	Dear Mr. President (4)	1/2 On A Bag Of Dank (1)	My Babooski (6)	Roll How We Roll (6)	Time For A 187 (1)
Ain't Nothing Changed (5)	Don Is Back (6)	Hands Of A Dead Man (3)	My Ghetto Heroes (1)	Say Brah (5)	Time To Check My Crackhouse
Always Come Back To You (6)	Doo Rags (6)	Hot Boys And Girls (4)	My Three Uncles (6)	Sellin' Ice Cream (1)	(1)
Always Look A Man In The	Eternity (4)	How G's Ride (1)	Never Ending Game (1)	Snitches (4)	Tryin 2 Do Something (2)
Eyes (3)	Eyes On Your Enemies (2)	Hush (6)	No Limit Party (3)	So Many Souls Deceased (4)	Twerk That Thang (6)
Anything Goes (3)	Gangsta B... (4)	I Don't Give Ah What (6)	No More Tears (1)	Soldiers, Riders, And G's (4)	211 (3)
"B" I Like (6)	Gangstas Need Love (2)	I Got The Dank (3)	Nobody Moves (5)	Some Jack (3)	War Wounds (4)
Back Up Off Me (1)	Get Yo Mind Right (5)	Ice On My Wrist (1)	Oh Na Nae (5)	Somethin For The Street (3)	Watch Dees Hoes (1)
Bastard Child (3)	Get Your Paper (4)	It Don't Get No Better (6)	Only God Can Judge Me (5)	Soulja Boo (6)	We Riders (2)
Black And White (4)	Ghetto D (2)	Just An Everyday Thang (3)	Only Time Will Tell (2)	Soulja (6) 98	Weed & Money (2)
Boonapalist (5)	Ghetto Honeys (5)	Killer Pussy (1)	Pass Me Da Green (2)	Step To Dis (5) 88	Welcome To My City (4)
Bout Dat (6)	Ghetto In The Sky (5)	Late Night Creepin' (3)	Plan B (3)	Still Ballin (2)	Where Do We Go From Here
Bout It, Bout It II (1)	Ghetto Life (4)	Let My 9 Get Em' (4)	Playa From Around The Way	Stop Hatin (2)	(5)
Bout That Drama (1)	Ghetto Love (4)	Let's Get 'Em (2,4)	(1)	Stop Playing Wit Me (5)	Who Down To Ride (5)
Break 'Em Off Somethin' (1)	Ghetto Prayer (5)	Life Ain't Easy (5)	Playa Haterz (3)	These Streets Keep Me Rollin'	Would You (6)
Burbons And Lacs (2)	Ghetto Won't Change (1)	Life I Live (6)	Pockets Gone' Stay Fat (6)	(4)	Y'all Don't Know (5)
Captain Kirk (2)	Ghetto's Got Me Trapped (4)	Make Em Say Uhh! (2) 16	Poppin' Them Collars (6)	Things Ain't What They Used	Y'all Don't Want None (5)
Come And Get Some (2)	Ghettos Tryin To Kill Me! (3)	Make Em Say Uhh #2 (4)	Problems (6)	To Be (1)	
Commercial (5)	Going Through Somethangs (2)	Mama Raised Me (4)	Real, The (6)	Thinkin' Bout U (4)	
Crazy Bout Ya (5)	Golds In They Mouth (6)	More 2 Life (4)	Return Of Da Don (5)	Throw 'Em Up (2)	
Da Ballers (5)	Goodbye To My Homies	Mr. Ice Cream Man (1) 90	Ride (4)	Thug Girl (4)	
Da Last Don (4)	(4) 27		Robbery (3)	Till We Dead And Gone (4)	

MATCHBOX TWENTY '00
Pop-rock group from Orlando, Florida: Rob Thomas (vocals), Kyle Cook and Adam Gaynor (guitars), Brian Yale (bass) and Paul Doucette (drums).

3/22/97	5	118	▲¹¹	©	1	Yourself Or Someone Like You	C:❶¹/110		$10	Lava 92721
						MATCHBOX 20				
6/10/00	3	69↑	▲³	©	2	Mad Season			$10	Lava 83339

Angry (2)	Black & White People (2)	Girl Like That (1)	Leave (2)	Rest Stop (2)
Argue (1)	Burn, The (2)	Hang (1)	Long Day (1)	Shame (1)
Back 2 Good (1) 24	Busted (2)	If You're Gone (2) 5	Mad Season (2) 48	Stop (2)
Bed Of Lies (2)	Crutch (1)	Kody (1)	Push (1)	3 am (1)
Bent (2) 1	Damn (1)	Last Beautiful Girl (2)	Real World (1) 38	You Won't Be Mine (2)

MATERIAL ISSUE '91
Pop trio from Chicago: Jim Ellison (vocals, guitar), Ted Ansani (bass) and Mike Zelenko (drums). Ellison committed suicide on 6/20/96 (age 31).

| 3/16/91 | 86 | 11 | © | | International Pop Overthrow | | | $10 | Mercury 848155 |

Chance Of A Lifetime	International Pop Overthrow	Renee Remains The Same	This Letter	Very First Lie
Crazy	Li'l Christine	There Was A Few	Trouble	Very Good Idea
Diane	Out Right Now	This Far Before	Valerie Loves Me	

MATHIESON, Muir   '61
Born on 1/24/11 in Stirling, Scotland. Died on 8/2/75 (age 64). Conductor/arranger.

| 5/29/61 | 50 | 21 | | | **Gone With The Wind** .... [I] | $25 | Warner 1322 |

newly recorded version of the Max Steiner original score

Ashley (medley)
Ashley And Melanie (Love Theme) (medley)
Belle Watling (medley)

Bonnie Blue Flag (medley)
Bonnie's Death (medley)
Bonnie's Theme (medley)

Invitation To The Dance (medley)
Melanie's Theme (medley)
Oath, The (medley)

Prayer, The (medley)
Return To Tara (medley)
Rhett Butler (medley)
Scarlet O'Hara (medley)

Scarlet's Agony (medley)
Tara's Theme (medley)
War (medley)

MATHIEU, Mireille   '69
Born on 7/24/46 in Avignon, France. Female singer.

| 10/4/69 | 118 | 8 | | | **Mireille Mathieu** .... [F] | $15 | Capitol 306 |

Celui Que J'Aime (The One I Love)
Ensemble (Sometimes)

Et Merci Quand Meme (And Thanks Just The Same)
Je Ne Suis Rien Sans Toi (I'm Coming Home)

Les Bicyclettes De Belsize (The Bicycles Of Belsize)
Quand Tu T'en Iras (Non Pensare A Me) (Don't Think Of Me)

Tous Les Amoureux (All The Loves)
Un Homme Et Une Femme (A Man And A Woman)

Une Rose Au Coeur De L'Hiver (If You Change Your Mind)
Viens Dans Ma Rue (Come To My Street)

MATHIS, Johnny ★4★   '58
Born on 9/30/35 in San Francisco. Studied opera from age 13. Track scholarship at the San Francisco State College. Invited to Olympic tryouts; chose singing career instead. Discovered by George Avakian of Columbia Records. To New York City in 1956. Initially recorded as jazz-styled singer. Columbia A&R executive **Mitch Miller** switched him to singing pop ballads, subsequently became young America's favorite smooth ballad singer.

1)Heavenly 2)Johnny's Greatest Hits 3)Portrait Of Johnny 4)Warm 5)More Johnny's Greatest Hits

9/9/57	4	26			1	**Wonderful Wonderful**		$30	Columbia 1028
12/23/57+	2⁴	113	●		2	**Warm**		$30	Columbia 1078
4/7/58	10	12		©	3	**Good Night, Dear Lord**		$30	Columbia 1119
4/14/58	❶³	490	▲	©	4	**Johnny's Greatest Hits**	[G]	$25	Columbia 1133
9/8/58	6	16	●		5	**Swing Softly**		$25	Columbia 1165
12/15/58+	3	4	▲²	©	6	**Merry Christmas**	C:#10/30 [X]	$25	Columbia 1195

Christmas charts: 2/'63, 2/'64, 7/'65, 2/'66, 2/'67, 5/'68, 15/'69, 3/'73, 18/'88, 20/'89, 16/'90, 17/'91, 12/'92, 21/'93, 35/'94, 39/'96

2/9/59	4	96	●	©	7	**Open Fire, Two Guitars**		$25	Columbia 1270
7/27/59	2²	93	●	©	8	**More Johnny's Greatest Hits**	[G]	$25	Columbia 1344
9/21/59	❶⁵	295	▲	©	9	**Heavenly**		$25	Columbia 1351
12/21/59+	10	3		©	10	**Merry Christmas**	[X-R]	$25	Columbia 1195
1/18/60	2¹	75	●		11	**Faithfully**		$20	Columbia 1422 / 8219
8/29/60	4	65			12	**Johnny's Mood**		$20	Columbia 1526 / 8326
10/3/60	6	27			13	**The Rhythms And Ballads Of Broadway**		$20	Columbia 17 / 803 [2]
12/26/60	10	2		©	14	**Merry Christmas**	[X-R]	$25	Columbia 1195
5/15/61	38	23		©	15	**I'll Buy You A Star**		$20	Columbia 1623 / 8423
8/28/61	2⁷	63			16	**Portrait Of Johnny**	[G]	$20	Columbia 1644 / 8444
12/18/61+	31	7		©	17	**Merry Christmas**	[X-R]	$25	Columbia 1195
2/24/62	14	39			18	**Live It Up!**		$20	Columbia 1711 / 8511
10/27/62	12	37			19	**Rapture**		$20	Columbia 1915 / 8715
12/8/62	12	4		©	20	**Merry Christmas**	[X-R]	$25	Columbia 1195
4/20/63	6	45			21	**Johnny's Newest Hits**	[G]	$20	Columbia 2016 / 8816
8/24/63	20	27		©	22	**Johnny**		$20	Columbia 2044 / 8844
11/30/63	2²ˣ	20			23	**Sounds Of Christmas**	[X]	$20	Mercury 60837

Christmas charts: 2/'63, 7/'64, 13/'65, 45/'66, 18/'67, 11/'68

12/28/63+	23	27			24	**Romantically**		$20	Columbia 2098 / 8898
2/15/64	13	28			25	**Tender Is The Night**		$20	Mercury 60890
5/9/64	35	16			26	**I'll Search My Heart and Other Great Hits**	[K]	$20	Columbia 2143 / 8943
7/25/64	75	10			27	**The Wonderful World Of Make Believe**		$20	Mercury 60913
8/1/64	88	10			28	**The Great Years**	[G]	$25	Columbia 34 / 834 [2]
10/17/64	40	20			29	**This Is Love**		$15	Mercury 60942
3/20/65	52	11			30	**Love Is Everything**		$15	Mercury 60991
10/16/65	71	26			31	**The Sweetheart Tree**		$15	Mercury 61041
4/2/66	9	45			32	**The Shadow Of Your Smile**		$15	Mercury 61073
10/8/66+	50	18			33	**So Nice**		$15	Mercury 61091
4/1/67	103	11			34	**Johnny Mathis Sings**		$15	Mercury 61107
12/23/67	60	20			35	**Up, Up And Away**		$15	Columbia 2726 / 9526
4/13/68	26	40			36	**Love Is Blue**		$15	Columbia 9637
12/14/68+	60	21			37	**Those Were The Days**		$15	Columbia 9705
8/16/69	163	4			38	**The Impossible Dream**		$15	Columbia 9872
9/13/69	192	2			39	**People**		$15	Columbia 9871
9/20/69	52	24			40	**Love Theme From "Romeo And Juliet"**		$15	Columbia 9909
12/6/69	❶¹ˣ	20	●	©	41	**Give Me Your Love For Christmas**	[X]	$15	Columbia 9923

Christmas charts: 1/'69, 3/'70, 5/'71, 3/'72, 19/'73, 19/'87, 18/'88

4/4/70	38	26			42	**Raindrops Keep Fallin' On My Head**		$15	Columbia 1005
10/10/70	61	9			43	**Close To You**		$15	Columbia 30210
1/23/71	169	7			44	**Johnny Mathis sings the music of Bacharach & Kaempfert**		$20	Columbia 30350 [2]
3/13/71	47	18			45	**Love Story**		$15	Columbia 30499

DEBUT	PEAK	WKS	RIAA	CD	ARTIST — Album Title	Catalog	Sym	$	Label & Number
					MATHIS, Johnny — Cont'd				
9/4/71	80	10			46 You've Got A Friend			$15	Columbia 30740
2/5/72	128	7			47 Johnny Mathis In Person		[L]	$20	Columbia 30979 [2]
					recorded at Caesar's Palace in Las Vegas				
6/10/72	71	15		©	48 The First Time Ever (I Saw Your Face)			$15	Columbia 31342
6/24/72	141	15	▲		49 Johnny Mathis' All-Time Greatest Hits		[G]	$20	Columbia 31345 [2]
10/21/72	83	18			50 Song Sung Blue			$15	Columbia 31626
2/17/73	83	14			51 Me And Mrs. Jones			$12	Columbia 32114
6/30/73	120	7			52 Killing Me Softly With Her Song			$12	Columbia 32258
11/17/73+	115	22			53 I'm Coming Home			$12	Columbia 32435
12/28/74+	139	7			54 The Heart Of A Woman			$12	Columbia 33251
4/19/75	99	13			55 When Will I See You Again			$12	Columbia 33420
11/8/75+	97	21	●		56 Feelings			$12	Columbia 33887
6/26/76	79	15			57 I Only Have Eyes For You			$12	Columbia 34117
3/19/77	139	5			58 Mathis Is			$12	Columbia 34441
4/1/78	9	24	▲	©	59 You Light Up My Life			$12	Columbia 35259
7/29/78	19	16	●	©	60 That's What Friends Are For			$12	Columbia 35435
					JOHNNY MATHIS & DENIECE WILLIAMS				
2/24/79	122	7		©	61 The Best Days Of My Life			$12	Columbia 35649
8/9/80	164	5			62 Different Kinda Different			$12	Columbia 36505
12/27/80+	140	7	●	©	63 The Best Of Johnny Mathis 1975-1980		[G]	$12	Columbia 36871
7/25/81	173	4			64 The First 25 Years - The Silver Anniversary Album		[G]	$15	Columbia 37440 [2]
5/8/82	147	9		©	65 Friends In Love			$10	Columbia 37748
3/10/84	157	19		©	66 A Special Part Of Me			$10	Columbia 38718
1/10/87	197	2		©	67 The Hollywood Musicals			$10	Columbia 40372
					JOHNNY MATHIS & HENRY MANCINI				
1/11/92	189	1		©	68 Better Together - The Duet Album			$10	Columbia 47982
12/12/92	29 X	1		©	69 Christmas Eve With Johnny Mathis	C:#44/2	[X]	$10	Columbia 40447
					first released in 1986				
12/18/93	162	3		©	70 The Christmas Music Of Johnny Mathis - A Personal Collection		[X-K]	$10	Legacy 57194
5/25/96	119	1		©	71 All About Love			$10	Columbia 67509
5/10/97	150	1		©	72 The Global Masters		[K]	$15	Columbia 64894 [2]
					all songs recorded from 1963-66				

MATHIS, Johnny — Cont'd

It's Gone (54)
It's Impossible (45)
It's Not For Me To Say (4,28,47,49,64) **5**
It's Only A Paper Moon (24)
It's The Most Wonderful Time Of The Year (69,70)
It's Too Late (46)
Jean (42)
Jenny (16)
Jingle Bell Rock (41)
Jingle Bells (69)
Joey, Joey, Joey (22)
Johnny One Note (18)
Joy Of Loving You (26)
Jump For Joy (22)
Just Friends (18)
Just Move Along, Meadow Lark (29)
Just Once In My Life (medley) (51)
Just The Way You Are (60,63)
Killing Me Softly With Her Song (52)
Kol Nidre (3)
Lady (44)
Lady Sings The Blues ..see: Happy
Lady Smiles (44)
Lament (Love, I Found You Gone) (19)
(Last Night) I Didn't Get To Sleep At All (48)
Last Time I Felt Like This (61,63,68)
Lately (65)
Laughter In The Rain (55)
Laura (25,39,72)
Lead Me To Your Love (66)
Lean On Me (50)
Let It Rain (8)
Let It Snow, Let It Snow, Let It Snow (23,70)
Let Me Be The One (55,71)
Let Me Love You (1)
Let The Sunshine In (medley) (40)
Let Your Heart Remember (71)
Let's Do It (13)
Let's Love (8) **44**
Let's Misbehave (13)
Life Is A Song Worth Singing (53) **54**
Life And Breath (48)
Life Is What You Make It (48)
Light My Fire (37)
Lights Of Rio (62)
Like No One In The World (71)
Like Someone In Love (5)
Limehouse Blues (29,72)
Little Drummer Boy (23,41,70)
Little Green Apples (37)
Live For Life (40)
Live It Up (18)
Long Ago (And Far Away) (30,46,67)
Long And Winding Road (43)
Look Of Love (36,44)
Looking At You (1)
Lord's Prayer (41)
Loss Of Love (45)
Lost In Loveliness (19)
Love (18,44)
Love Eyes (13)
Love Is A Gamble (13)
Love Is Blue (36)
Love Is Everything (30)
Love Look Away (15,28)
Love Me As Though There Were No Tomorrow (19)
Love Me Tonight (40)
Love Nest (19)
Love Never Felt So Good (66)
Love Story ..see: (Where Do I Begin)
Love Walked In (5)
Love Without Words (62)
Love Won't Let Me Wait (66,68)
Lovely Things You Do (2)

Lovely Way To Spend An Evening (9)
Lovers In New York (34,72)
Loving You - Losing You (58)
Lullaby Of Love (58)
Magic Garden (15)
Make It Easy On Yourself (50)
Man And A Woman (42)
Man Of La Mancha (I, Don Quixote) (33)
Mandy (55)
Manhattan (72)
Maria (11,28,47,49) **78**
Marianna (21) **86**
Marshmallow World (23,70)
May The Good Lord Bless And Keep You (3)
Me And Mrs. Jones (51)
Me For You, You For Me (60)
Melinda (32)
Memories Don't Leave Like People Do (54)
Memory (65)
Michelle (32)
Midnight Blue (56)
Midnight Cowboy (42)
Miracles (22)
Mirage (31)
Misty (9,28,47,49,64) **12**
Misty Roses (35,49)
Moanin' Low (14)
Moment To Moment (32,38)
Moments Like This (19)
Mondo Cane ..see: More
Moon River (14)
Moonlight Becomes You (9,67)
Moonlight In Vermont (24)
More (29,39,72)
More I See You (35)
More Than You Know (9)
Morningside Of The Mountain (35)
Most Beautiful Girl In The World (22)
Music That Makes Me Dance (33,72)
My Darling, My Darling (19)
My Favorite Dream (26)
My Favorite Things (41)
My Funny Valentine (7,49)
My Heart And I (15)
My Love For You (16) **47**
My One And Only Love (2)
My Romance (13)
My Sweet Lord (45)
Neither One Of Us (Wants To Be The First To Say Goodbye) (52)
Never Can Say Goodbye (46)
Never Givin' Up On You (62)
Never Let Me Go (30)
Never My Love (36)
Never Never Land (22)
Nice To Be Around (55)
99 Miles From L.A. (56,63)
No Love (But Your Love) (4) **21**
No Man Can Stand Alone (22)
No Strings (25)
Nobody Knows (How Much I Love You) (11)
Nothing Between Us But Love (64)
O Holy Night (6,10,14,17,20)
Odds And Ends (42,44)
Oh How I Try (15)
Oh That Feeling (16)
On A Clear Day You Can See Forever (32,38,72) **98**
On A Cold And Rainy Day (18)
On A Wonderful Day Like Today (72)
On The Sunny Side Of The Street (13)
Once (12)
One Day In Your Life (56)
One God (3)
One Look (21)
One Love (66)

One More Mountain (30)
One More Night (71)
One Starry Night (11)
Only You (And You Alone) (55)
Ooh What We Do (57)
Open Fire (7)
Over The Weekend (29)
Paradise (62)
Party's Over (13)
People (30,39)
Pieces Of Dreams (43)
Play Me (50)
Please Be Kind (7)
Poinciana (Song Of The Tree) (29)
Poor Butterfly (22)
Priceless (66)
Put On A Happy Face (29)
(Quest, The) ..see: Impossible Dream
Quiet Girl (21)
Quiet Nights Of Quiet Stars (32,39)
Raindrops Keep Fallin' On My Head (42)
Rapture (19)
Ready Or Not (60,64)
Remember (51)
Remember When (We Made These Memories) (44)
Ride On A Rainbow (9)
Right Here And Now (66)
Ring The Bell (15)
Riviera, The (18)
Romeo And Juliet (A Time For Us), Love Theme From (40,47,49,64) **96**
Rosary, The (3)
Rose Garden (45)
Rudolph The Red-Nosed Reindeer (23)
Run To Me (50)
Sail On White Moon (54)
Sandpiper, Love Theme From The ..see: Shadow Of Your Smile
Sands Of Time (27)
Santa Claus Is Comin' To Town (41,70)
Saturday Sunshine (34)
Second Time Around (34)
Secret Love (11)
Secret Of Christmas (23)
Send In The Clowns (44)
September Song (24,28)
Shadow Of Your Smile (32,39)
Shangri-La (27,72)
Ship Without A Sail (25)
Should I Wait (Or Should I Run To Her) (16)
Show And Tell (52)
Silent Night (6,10,14,17,20,70)
Silver Bells (6,10,14,17,20,70)
Simple (66) **81**
Since I Fell For You (48)
Sing (52)
Sky Full Of Rainbows (27)
Skye Boat Song (Scotch Folk Song) (31)
Sleigh Ride (6,10,14,17,20,70)
Small World (8,28,49) **20**
Smile (15)
So Nice (Summer Samba) (33,38,72)
Solitaire (56)
Someone (8) **35**
Somethin's Goin' On (65)
Something (9)
Something I Dreamed Last Night (9)
Something's Coming (32,72)
Sometimes Love's Not Enough (71)
Somewhere (25)
Somewhere, My Love (34,38)
Somewhere My Love (Lara's Theme) (72)
Song Of Joy (43)
Song Sung Blue (50)

Sooner Or Later (26) **84**
Soul And Inspiration (medley) (51)
Sound Of Music (24)
Sounds Of Christmas (23)
Spanish Eyes (44)
(Speak Softly Love) ..see: Godfather
Spring Is Here (13)
Stairway To The Sea (Scalinatella) (8)
Stairway To The Stars (15,28)
Starbright (16,26) **25**
Stardust (56,64)
Stars Fell On Alabama (19)
Stay Warm (12)
Stella By Starlight (19,28)
Stop Look And Listen To Your Heart (53)
Story Of Our Love (16) **93**
Stranger In Paradise (9)
Strangers In Dark Corners (54)
Strangers In The Night (34,38,44)
Street Of Dreams (28)
Sudden Love (15)
Summer Breeze (51)
Summer Me, Winter Me (medley) (51)
Summer Of '42 (The Summer Knows), Theme From (48)
(Summer Samba) ..see: So Nice
Sunny (34,39)
Sweet Child (53)
Sweet Lorraine (5)
Sweet Love Of Mine (58)
Sweet Surrender (51)
Sweet Thursday (21,28) **99**
Sweetheart Tree (31,72)
Swing Low, Sweet Chariot (3)
Symphony (31)
Taking A Chance On Love (13,67)
Taste Of Honey (32)
Teacher, Teacher (8) **21**
Temptation (62)
Ten Times Forever More (45)
Tender Is The Night (25)
Tenderly (7)
That Old Black Magic (1)
That's All (9)
That's All She Wrote (56)
That's The Way It Is (21)
That's What Friends Are For (60)
Then I'll Be Tired Of You (2)
There Goes My Heart (2)
There! I've Said It Again (64)
There You Are (21,61)
(There's) Always Something There To Remind Me (34)
There's No You (12)
They Long To Be Close To You (43,47)
They Say It's Wonderful (9)
Things I Might Have Been (55)
This Guy's In Love With You (37,44)
This Heart Of Mine (5)
This Is All I Ask (30)
This Is Love (31)
Those Were The Days (37)
1000 Blue Bubbles (30)
Three Times A Lady (64)
Till Love Touches Your Life (59)
Time After Time (67)
(Time For Us) ..see: Romeo And Juliet
Times Will Change (44)
To Be In Love (A Fantastical Love Song) (52)
Tomorrow Song (25)
Tonight (11,28,47)
Too Close For Comfort (7)
Too Much, Too Little, Too Late (59,63,64,68) **1**
Too Much Too Soon (18)
Too Young (26)

Too Young To Go Steady (24)
Touch Of Your Lips (29,72)
Touching Me With Love (60)
Toyland (69)
Traces (45)
True Love (67)
Turn Around Look At Me (37)
Twelfth Of Never (4,28,47,49) **9**
Unaccustomed As I Am (21,28)
Under A Blanket Of Blue (29)
Until It's Time For You To Go (43)
Until You Come Back To Me (That's What I'm Gonna Do) (60)
Up, Up And Away (35)
Venus (36,49)
Very Much In Love (8)
Very Thought Of You (31,38)
Wake The Town And Tell The People (34)
Walk On By (36,44)
Warm (2,65)
Warm And Tender (4)
Warm And Willing (15)
Wasn't The Summer Short? (21) **89**
Watch What Happens (42)
Wave (43)
Way We Planned It (54)
Way We Were (55)
Way You Look Tonight (64)
We (40)
We Can Work It Out (46)
We Need A Little Christmas (69,70)
We're In Love (61)
We've Only Just Begun (45,47)
Weaver Of Dreams (22)
Welcome Home (71)
Wendy (54)
What Are You Doing New Year's Eve (41)
What Are You Doing The Rest Of Your Life (45)
What Child Is This (6,10,14,17,20)
What Do You Do With The Love (65)
What Do You Feel In Your Heart (29)
What I Did For Love (56,63)
What Now My Love (33)
What The World Needs Now Is Love (33,39)
What To Do About Love (26)
What Will Mary Say (21,28,49) **9**
What'll I Do (2)
What's Forever For (65)
When A Child Is Born (57,63)
When I Am With You (4)
When I Fall In Love (7,28)
When I Look In Your Eyes (35)
When My Sugar Walks Down The Street (15)
When Sunny Gets Blue (4,47,49,64)
When The Lovin' Goes Out Of The Lovin' (65)
When The World Was Young (22)
When Will I See You Again (55)
When You Wish Upon A Star (27,67,72)
Where Are The Words (35)
Where Are You? (11)
Where Can I Find Christmas? (medley) (69)
Where Can I Go? (3)
(Where Do I Begin) Love Story (45,47,49)
Where Do You Think You're Going (11)
Where Is Love? (25)
Where Is The Love (50)
Where Or When (59)
Wherever You Are It's Spring (26)

While We're Young (2)
While You're Young (16)
Whistling Away The Dark (67)
White Christmas (6,10,14,17,20,70)
Who Can I Turn To? (34)
Who Can Say (34)
Who's Counting Heartaches (68)
Why Goodbye (71)
Why Not (18)
Wild Is The Wind (4,47,49) **22**
Wildflower (52)
Will I Find My Love Today (1)
Windmills Of Your Mind (40)
Winter Wonderland (6,10,14,17,20,70)
With You I'm Born Again (62,63)
Without Her (40)
Without You (48)
Woman, Woman (54)
Wonderful Day Like Today (31,39)
Wonderful! Wonderful! (4,28,47,49,64) **14**
Wonderful World Of Make-Believe (27)
Wonderland By Night (44)
World I Threw Away (40)
World I Used To Know (37)
World Of Laughter (58)
Would You Like To Spend The Night With Me (61)
Year After Year (1)
Yellow Days (43)
Yellow Roses On Her Gown (57)
Yesterday (32)
Yesterday When I Was Young (40)
You And Me Against The World (55)
You Are Beautiful (8) **60**
You Are Everything To Me (8)
You Are The Sunshine Of My Life (52)
You Better Go Now (11)
You Brought Me Love (68)
You Do Something To Me (13)
You Hit The Spot (5)
You Light Up My Life (59,63)
You Love Me (29)
You Make Me Think About You (37)
You Set My Heart To Music (16)
You Stepped Out Of A Dream (1,67)
You'd Be So Nice To Come Home To (5)
You'll Never Know (7)
You're A Lady (51)
You're A Special Part Of Me (66,68)
You're A Special Part Of My Life (60)
You're All I Need To Get By (60,68) **47**
You're As Right As Rain (55)
You've Come Home (19)
You've Got A Friend (46)
Young And Foolish (30)

MATLOCK, Matty — see HEINDORF, Ray

MATTEA, Kathy
'90

Born on 6/21/59 in Cross Lanes, West Virginia. Country singer/guitarist.

DEBUT	PEAK	WKS	RIAA	CD			ARTIST — Album Title	$	Label & Number
3/3/90	82	19	●	©	1	**Willow In The Wind**		$10	Mercury 836950
9/22/90	80	34	▲	©	2	**A Collection Of Hits**	[G]	$10	Mercury 842330
4/13/91	72	25	●	©	3	**Time Passes By**		$10	Mercury 846975

DEBUT	PEAK	WKS	RIAA	CD	ARTIST — Album Title	Catalog	Sym	$	Label & Number

MATTEA, Kathy — Cont'd

DEBUT	PEAK	WKS		CD	Album Title			$	Label & Number
10/24/92	182	7	● ©	4	Lonesome Standard Time			$10	Mercury 512567
6/4/94	87	8	● ©	5	Walking Away A Winner			$10	Mercury 518852
2/22/97	121	14	©	6	Love Travels			$10	Mercury 532899

All Roads To The River (6)
Amarillo (4)
Another Man (5)
Asking Us To Dance (3)
Battle Hymn Of Love (2)
Beautiful Fool (6)
Bridge, The (6)
Burnin' Old Memories (1)
Cape, The (5)
Clown In Your Rodeo (5)
Come From The Heart (1)

Eighteen Wheels And A Dozen Roses (2)
End Of The Line (6)
Few Good Things Remain (2,3)
Forgive And Forget (4)
455 Rocket (6)
From A Distance (3)
Further And Further Away (6)
Goin' Gone (2)
Grand Canyon (5)
Harley (5)

Here's Hopin' (1)
Hills Of Alabam' (1)
I Wear Your Love (3)
I'll Take Care Of You (1)
I'm On Your Side (6)
If That's What You Call Love (6)
Last Night I Dreamed Of Loving You (4)
Life As We Knew It (2)
Listen To The Radio (4)
Lonely At The Bottom (5)

Lonesome Standard Time (4)
Love At The Five & Dime (2)
Love Chooses You (1)
Love Travels (6)
Maybe She's Human (5)
Nobody's Gonna Rain On Our Parade (5)
Patiently Waiting (6)
Quarter Moon (3)
Ready For The Storm (3)
Seeds (4)

Sending Me Angels (6)
She Came From Fort Worth (1)
Slow Boat (4)
Standing Knee Deep In A River (Dying Of Thirst) (4)
Streets Of Your Town (5)
Summer Of My Dreams (3)
33, 45, 78 (Record Time) (4)
Time Passes By (3)
Train Of Memories (2)
True North (1)

Untold Stories (2)
Walk The Way The Wind Blows (2)
Walking Away A Winner (5)
What Could Have Been (3)
Where've You Been (1,2)
Who Turned Out The Light (5)
Who's Gonna Know (3)
Whole Lotta Holes (3)
Willow In The Wind (1)

★250★ **MATTHEWS, Dave, Band** '01

Born on 1/9/67 in Johannesburg, South Africa; raised in New York City. Rock singer/guitarist. His band: Leroi Moore (sax), Boyd Tinsley (violin), Stefan Lessard (bass) and Carter Beauford (drums).

DEBUT	PEAK	WKS	RIAA	CD	Album Title	Catalog	Sym	$	Label & Number
10/15/94+	11	116	▲6 ©	1	Under The Table And Dreaming	C:#8/108		$10	RCA 66449
5/18/96	2¹	104	▲7 ©	2	Crash	C:#4/163		$10	RCA 66904
7/19/97	163	9	©	3	Recently	[E-M]		$10	Bama Rags 67548
11/15/97	3	36	▲2 ©	4	Live At Red Rocks 8.15.95	[L]		$15	Bama Rags 67587 [2]
					recorded on 8/15/95 at Red Rocks in Denver				
5/16/98	❶¹	89	▲3 ©	5	Before These Crowded Streets	C:#13/20		$10	RCA 67660
2/6/99	2¹	51	▲3 ©	6	Live At Luther College	C:#23/2	[L]	$15	Bama Rags 67755 [2]
					DAVE MATTHEWS/TIM REYNOLDS				
					recorded on 2/6/96 in Decorah, Iowa				
12/11/99	15	22	▲2 ©	7	Listener Supported		[L]	$15	RCA 67898 [2]
					recorded on 9/11/99 at Continental Airlines Arena in East Rutherford, New Jersey				
3/17/01	❶²	29↑	▲2 ©	8	Everyday			$10	RCA 67988

All Along The Watchtower (3,4,7)
Angel (8)
Ants Marching (1,4,6)
Best Of What's Around (1,4)
Christmas Song (6)
Crash Into Me (2,6,7)
Crush (5) 75
Cry Freedom (2,6)
Dancing Nancies (1,3,4,6)
Deed Is Done (6)

Don't Drink The Water (5,7)
Dreaming Tree (5)
Dreams Of Our Fathers (8)
Drive In Drive Out (2,4)
Everyday (8)
Fool To Think (8)
Granny (6,7)
Halloween (3,5,6)
I Did It (8) 71
If I Had It All (8)
Jimi Thing (1,6,7)

Last Stop (5)
Let You Down (2)
Lie In Our Graves (2,4)
Little Thing (6)
Long Black Veil (7)
Lover Lay Down (1,4,6)
Minarets (6)
Mother Father (8)
#34 (1)
#41 (2,4,7)
#40 (7)

#41 (6,7)
One Sweet World (6)
Pantala Naga Pampa (7)
Patala Naga Pampa (5)
Pay For What You Get (1)
Pig (5)
Proudest Monkey (2,4)
Rapunzel (8)
Recently (3,4)
Rhyme & Reason (1,4,7)
Satellite (1,4,6)

Say Goodbye (2,6)
Seek Up (4,6)
Sleep To Dream Her (8)
So Much To Say (2)
So Right (8)
Space Between (8) 22
Spoon (5)
Stay (Wasting Time) (5,7)
Stone, The (5,7)
Stream (6)
Too Much (2,7)

Tripping Billies (2,4,6)
True Reflections (7)
Two Step (2,4,6,7)
Typical Situation (1,4,6)
Warehouse (1,3,4,6,7)
What Would You Say (1,6)
What You Are (8)
When The World Ends (8)

MATTHEWS, David '77

Born on 4/3/42 in Sonora, Kentucky. Jazz pianist.

DEBUT	PEAK	WKS			Album Title		Sym	$	Label & Number
9/3/77	169	7			Dune		[I]	$12	CTI 5005

Dune Medley

Princess Leia's Theme | Silent Running | Space Oddity | Star Wars, Main Theme From

---

MATTHEWS, Ian '71

Born Ian Matthews MacDonald on 6/16/46 in Scunthorpe, Lincolnshire, England. Founder of Fairport Convention and Matthews' Southern Comfort. Also see Southern Comfort.

DEBUT	PEAK	WKS			Album Title			$	Label & Number
4/17/71	72	15		1	Later That Same Year			$15	Decca 75264
					MATTHEWS' SOUTHERN COMFORT				
2/12/72	196	3		2	Tigers Will Survive			$15	Vertigo 1010
9/22/73	181	7		3	Valley Hi			$15	Elektra 75061
11/11/78+	80	24		4	Stealin' Home			$12	Mushroom 5012

And Me (1)
And When She Smiles (She Makes The Sun Shine) (1)
Blue Blue Day (3)
Brand New Tennessee Waltz (1)
Carefully Taught (4)
Close The Door Lightly (2)
Da Doo Ron Ron (When He Walked Me Home) (2) 96

Don't Hang Up Your Dancing Shoes (4)
For Melanie (1)
Gimme An Inch (4)
Hope You Know (2)
House Of Unamerican Blues Activity Dream (2)
Keep On Sailing (3)
King Of The Night (4)
Leaving Alone (3)

Let There Be Blues (4)
Man In The Station (4)
Mare, Take Me Home (1) 96
Midnight On The Water (2)
Morning Song (2)
My Lady (1)
Never Again (2)
Old Man At The Mill (3)
Only Dancer (2)
Please Be My Friend (2)

Propinquity (3)
Right Before My Eyes (2)
Road To Ronderlin (1)
Sail My Soul (4)
Save Your Sorrows (3)
7 Bridges Road (4)
Shady Lies (1)
Shake It (4) 13
Slip Away (4)
Smile (medley) (4)

Stealin' Home (4)
Sylvie (1)
Tell Me Why (1) 98
These Days (3)
Tigers Will Survive (2)
To Love (1)
What Are You Waiting For (3)
Woodstock (1) 23
Yank & Mary (medley) (4)

MAURIAT, Paul '68

Born on 3/4/25 in Marseilles, France. Orchestra leader.

DEBUT	PEAK	WKS			Album Title		Sym	$	Label & Number
12/16/67+	❶⁵	50	●	1	Blooming Hits		[I]	$15	Philips 600248
12/23/67+	25ˣ	6		2	The Christmas Album		[X-I]	$15	Philips 600255
					Christmas charts: 49/'67, 30/'68, 25/'70				
3/30/68	122	22		3	More Mauriat		[I]	$15	Philips 600226
6/8/68	71	18	©	4	Mauriat Magic		[I]	$15	Philips 600270
10/12/68	142	7		5	Prevailing Airs		[I]	$15	Philips 600280
3/1/69	77	18		6	Doing My Thing		[I]	$15	Philips 600292
5/3/69	157	8		7	The Soul Of Paul Mauriat		[I]	$15	Philips 600299
11/1/69	186	3		8	L.O.V.E.		[I]	$15	Philips 600320
9/19/70	184	3		9	Gone Is Love		[I]	$15	Philips 600345
5/29/71	180	3		10	El Condor Pasa		[I]	$15	Philips 600352
					title is Spanish for "The Condor Passes By"				

A Banda (Parade) (4)
Abraham, Martin & John (6)
Adeste Fideles (2)
Adieu A La Nuit (Adieu To The Night) (1)
Angelica (4)

Aquarius (8)
Bang Bang (My Baby Shot Me Down) (3)
Black Harlem (10)
Black Is Black (3)
Bridge Over Troubled Water (9)

Burning Bridges (10)
Catherine (8)
Cent Mille Chansons (100,000 Songs) (3)
Chitty Chitty Bang Bang (6) 76

Classical Gas (9)
Comme Un Garcon (What A Guy) (5)
Could This Be Me (9)
Delilah (5)
Dr. Zhivago ...see: Lara's Theme

El Condor Pasa (10)
Eleanor Rigby (5)
Elenore (6)
En Bandouliere (3)
Entre Le Boeuf Et L'Ane Gris (2)

Etude In The Form Of Rhythm & Blues (10)
Gentle On My Mind (10)
Get Back (8)
Gloria In Excelsis Deo (2)
Go Away (Un Adieu) (4)

MAURIAT, Paul — Cont'd

Gone Is Love (9)
Goodbye (8)
Guantanamera (3)
Hey Jude (6)
Home Again (9)
Honey (5)
I Gotta Get Back To Lovin' You (9)
I Heard It Through The Grapevine (7)
I Never Loved A Man (7)
I Say A Little Prayer (6)
I Waited For You (4)
I'm Coming Home (5)
I'm Gonna Make You Love Me (7)

I've Been Loving You Too Long (7)
Il Est Ne Le Divin Enfant (2)
In The Midnight Hour (7)
Inch Allah (1)
Irresistiblement (Irresistibly) (6)
Is Paris Burning, Theme From (3)
Isadora's Theme From The Loves Of Isadora (8)
It's A Man's World (7)
Jingle Bells (2)
L'Amour Te Ressemble (Love Is The Image Of You) (5)
La Source (The Spring) (5)
Lady Madonna (5)
Lara's Theme (4)

Last Waltz (4)
Let It Be (9)
Live For Life (4)
Lonely Days (10)
Love Child (7)
Love In Every Room (4) *60*
Love Is Blue (1) *1*
Love Me, Please Love Me (3)
Love Story (10)
Ma Maison Et La Riviere ..see: My House And The River
Mama (1)
Melancholy Man (10)
Merci Cherie (4)
Michelle (4)
Mrs. Robinson (5)
My Girl (7)

My House And The River (6,9)
My Sweet Lord (10)
Ne Sois Pas Triste (Don't Be Sad) (6)
O' Holy Night (2)
O' Tannenbaum (O' Christmas Tree) (2)
Oh Happy Day (8)
Penny Lane (1)
Petit Papa Noel (2)
Ponteio (2)
Puppet On A String (1)
Rain And Tears (5)
Raindrops Keep Fallin' On My Head (9)
Reach Out I'll Be There (3)
Respect (7)

Rin Rin (2)
San Francisco (Wear Some Flowers In Your Hair) (4)
Serenade To Summertime (8)
Seuls Au Monde (Alone In The World) (1)
She Is A Little Bit Sweeter (9)
Siffler Sur La Colline (Whistle On The Hill) (6)
Silent Night, Holy Night (2)
Silver Fingertips (8)
Somethin' Stupid (1)
Somewhere, My Love ..see: Lara's Theme
Sunny (3)
There's A Kind Of Hush (All Over The World) (1)

This Guy's In Love With You (5)
This Is My Song (1)
Those Were The Days (6)
To Be The One You Love (10)
Tonta Gafay Boba (1)
Trois Anges Sont Venus (2)
Un Jour Un Enfant (Through The Eyes Of A Child) (8)
When A Man Loves A Woman (7)
White Christmas (2)
Winchester Cathedral (3)
Windmills Of Your Mind (8)
World We Knew (4)
You Keep Me Hangin' On (7)
You, Love, And Me (8)

MAVERICKS, The   '94
Country group from Miami: Raul Malo (vocals, guitar), David Lee Holt (guitar), Robert Reynolds (bass) and Paul Deakin (drums). Nick Kane replaced Holt in early 1995. Reynolds was married to **Trisha Yearwood** from 1994-99.

DEBUT	PEAK	WKS	RIAA	CD		ARTIST — Album Title	$	Label & Number
3/26/94	54	74	▲	©	1	What A Crying Shame	$10	MCA 10961
10/14/95	58	39	●	©	2	Music For All Occasions	$10	MCA 11257
3/28/98	96	6		©	3	Trampoline	$10	MCA 70018

Ain't Found Nobody (1)
All That Heaven Will Allow (1)
All You Ever Do Is Bring Me Down (2)
Dance The Night Away (3)
Dolores (3)
Dream River (3)

Fool #1 (3)
Foolish Heart (2)
Here Comes The Rain (2)
I Don't Even Know Your Name (3)
I Hope You Want Me Too (3)
I Should Have Been True (1)

I Should Know (3)
I'm Not Gonna Cry For You (2)
I've Got This Feeling (3)
If You Only Knew (2)
Just A Memory (1)
Losing Side Of Me (1)
Loving You (2)

Melbourne Mambo (3)
Missing You (2)
My Secret Flame (2)
Neon Blue (1)
O What A Thrill (1)
One Step Away (2)
Pretend (1)

Save A Prayer (3)
Someone Should Tell Her (3)
Something (2)
Tell Me Why (3)
There Goes My Heart (1)
Things You Said To Me (1)
To Be With You (3)

What A Crying Shame (1)
Writing On The Wall (2)

MAX DEMIAN BAND, The   '79
Rock group from Florida: Paul Rose (vocals), Jim LeFevre (guitar), Dan Howe (keyboards), Kirt Pennebaker (bass) and Pete Siegel (drums).

DEBUT	PEAK	WKS		ARTIST — Album Title	$	Label & Number
3/3/79	159	5		Take It To The Max	$12	RCA Victor 3273

Burnin' Up Inside
Havin' Such A Good Day

Hear My Song
High School Star

Lizard Song
Paradise

See Me Comin' Down
Still Hosed

Through The Eye Of A Storm

MAX Q   '89
Rock duo formed in Melbourne, Australia: **Michael Hutchence** (of **INXS**) and Ian Olsen. Max Q is the name of Olsen's dog. Hutchence committed suicide on 11/22/97 (age 37).

DEBUT	PEAK	WKS	CD		ARTIST — Album Title	$	Label & Number
10/7/89	182	8	©		Max Q	$10	Atlantic 82014 Zero-2-0

Buckethead
Concrete

Everything
Ghost Of The Year

Monday Night By Satellite
Ot-ven-rot

Sometimes
Soul Engine

Tight
Way Of The World

MAXWELL   '98
Born on 5/23/73 in Brooklyn, New York. R&B singer/songwriter/producer.

DEBUT	PEAK	WKS	RIAA	CD		ARTIST — Album Title	Sym	$	Label & Number
5/18/96+	37	78	▲	©	1	Maxwell's Urban Hang Suite		$10	Columbia 66434
8/2/97	53	15	●	©	2	MTV Unplugged	C:#32/10 [L-M]	$10	Columbia 68515
7/18/98	3	18	▲	©	3	Embrya		$10	Columbia 68968

Arroz Con Pollo (3)
Ascension (Don't Ever Wonder) (1,2) *36*
Dancewitme (3)
Drowndeep:Hula (3)
EachHourEachSecondEachMinuteEachDay:Of My Life (3)
Embrya (3)

Everwanting:To Want You To Want (3)
Gestation:Mythos (3)
Gotta Get: Closer (2)
Gravity:Pushing To Pull (3)
I'm You:You Are Me And We Are You (pt me & you) (3)

Know These Things:Shouldn't You (3)
Lady Suite (2)
Lonely's The Only Company (I&II) (3)
Luxury:Cococure (3)
Matrimony:Maybe You (3)
Mello: Sumthin (The Hush) (2)

Reunion (1)
Submerge:Til We Become The Sun (3)
Suite Theme (1)
Suite Urban Theme (The Hush) (2)
Suitelady (The Proposal Jam) (1)

Sumthin' Sumthin' (1)
This Woman's Work (2)
...Til The Cops Come Knockin' (1)
Urban Theme (1)
Welcome (1)
Whenever Wherever Whatever (1,2)

MAXWELL, Robert, His Harp And Orchestra   '64
Born on 4/19/21 in New York City. Jazz harpist/composer. With NBC Symphony under Toscanini at age 17. Also recorded as Mickey Mozart.

DEBUT	PEAK	WKS		ARTIST — Album Title	Sym	$	Label & Number
4/18/64	17	24		Shangri-La	[I]	$20	Decca 74421

Bewitched
Breeze And I
It's Magic

Magic Is The Moonlight (Te Quiero Dijiste)
Nature Boy

Old Devil Moon
Poinciana (Song Of The Tree)
Strange Music

Sounds Of Summer
Tears

That Old Black Magic
Shangri-La *15*

MAY, Billy, And His Orchestra   '55
Born on 11/10/16 in Pittsburgh. Conductor/arranger.

DEBUT	PEAK	WKS	CD		ARTIST — Album Title	Sym	$	Label & Number
3/5/55	7	6	©		Sorta-May	[I]	$20	Capitol 562

All You Want To Do Is Dance
Blues In The Night

Chicago
Deep Purple

Donkey Serenade
In A Persian Market

Just One Of Those Things
Soon

They Didn't Believe Me
Thou Swell

You Go To My Head
You're The Top

MAY, Brian   '83
Born on 7/19/47 in Twickenham, Middlesex, England. Lead guitarist of **Queen**.

DEBUT	PEAK	WKS	CD		ARTIST — Album Title	Sym	$	Label & Number
11/19/83	125	9		1	Star Fleet Project	[M]	$10	Capitol 15014
					BRIAN MAY & FRIENDS			
2/20/93	159	2	©	2	Back To The Light		$10	Hollywood 61404

Back To The Light (2)
Blues Breaker (1)
Dark, The (2)
Driven By You (2)

I'm Scared (2)
Just One Life (2)
Last Horizon (2)
Let Me Out (1)

Let Your Heart Rule Your Head (2)
Love Token (2)
Nothin' But Blue (2)

Resurrection (2)
Rollin' Over (2)
Star Fleet (1)
Too Much Love Will Kill You (2)

MAYALL, John   ★265★   '70
Born on 11/29/33 in Macclesfield, Cheshire, England. Blues-rock singer. His band spawned many of Britain's leading rock musicians.
1)USA Union 2)The Turning Point 3)Empty Rooms

DEBUT	PEAK	WKS	CD		ARTIST — Album Title	$	Label & Number
2/17/68	136	14	©	1	John Mayall's Blues Breakers Crusade	$25	London 529
6/15/68	128	5	©	2	The Blues Alone	$20	London 534

DEBUT	PEAK	WKS	RIAA	CD	ARTIST — Album Title	Catalog Sym	$	Label & Number
					MAYALL, John — Cont'd			
9/14/68	59	19	©	3	**Bare Wires**		$20	London 537
					JOHN MAYALL'S BLUES BREAKERS			
2/22/69	68	17	©	4	**Blues From Laurel Canyon**		$20	London 545
9/13/69	79	12	©	5	**Looking Back**	[K]	$20	London 562
9/20/69	32	55	● ©	6	**The Turning Point**	[L]	$15	Polydor 4004
2/28/70	93	11	©	7	**The Diary Of A Band**	[E-L]	$15	London 570
					recorded in 1967			
3/14/70	33	19	©	8	**Empty Rooms**		$15	Polydor 4010
10/24/70	22	22	©	9	**USA Union**		$15	Polydor 4022
4/17/71	52	15	©	10	**Back To The Roots**		$20	Polydor 3002 [2]
5/1/71	146	8		11	**John Mayall-Live In Europe**	[E-L]	$15	London 589
					recorded in 1967			
11/13/71	164	7	©	12	**Thru The Years**	[K]	$20	London 600 [2]
11/13/71	179	5	©	13	**Memories**		$15	Polydor 5012
6/17/72	64	18	©	14	**Jazz Blues Fusion**	[L]	$15	Polydor 5027
10/28/72	116	11		15	**Moving On**	[L]	$15	Polydor 5036
2/10/73	158	7		16	**Down The Line**	[K-L]	$20	London 618 [2]
					record 1: studio cuts 1965-68; record 2: 1964 live concert			
10/6/73	157	7		17	**Ten Years Are Gone**		$20	Polydor 3005 [2]
3/15/75	140	4	©	18	**New Year, New Band, New Company**		$15	Blue Thumb 6019
8/25/90	170	8	©	19	**A Sense Of Place**		$15	Island 842795

Accidental Suicide (10)
Alabama March (12)
All My Life (19)
Anzio Ann (medley) (7)
Back From Korea (13)
Bare Wires (3)
Bear, The (4,12)
Better Pass You By (17)
Black Cat Moan (19)
Blood On The Night (7)
Blue City Shakedown (5)
Blue Fox (10)
Blues In B (11)
Boogie Albert (10)
Brand New Start (2)
Broken Wings (2,16)
Brown Sugar (2)
Burning Sun (17)
California (6)
California Campground (17)
Can't Get Home (18)
Cancelling Out (2)
Catch That Train (2)
Change Your Ways (14)
Checking On My Baby (1)
Chicago Line (16)
Christmas 71 (15)
City, The (13)
Congo Square (19)
Counting The Days (8)
Country Road (14)
Crawling Up A Hill (16)
Crocodile Walk (16)
Crying (9)
Crying Shame (11)
Curly (12)

Dark Of The Night (17)
Death Of J.B. Lenoir (1)
Deep Blue Sea (9)
Devil's Tricks (17)
Do It (15)
Don't Hang Me Up (17)
Don't Kick Me (2,12)
Don't Pick A Flower (8)
Doreen (16)
Double Trouble (5)
Down The Line (2)
Dream With Me (10)
Drifting (17)
Driving On (18)
Driving Sideways (1)
Driving Till The Break Of Day (17)
Dry Throat (14)
Edmonton-Cooks Ferry Inn (7)
Exercise In C Major (14)
Fighting Line (13)
Fire (3,16)
First Time Alone (4,16)
Fly Tomorrow (4,16)
Force Of Nature (10)
Full Speed Ahead (10)
God Save The Queen (7)
Good Looking Stranger (17)
Good Times Boogie (14)
Goodbye December (10)
Got To Be This Way (14)
Grandad (13)
Greeny (12)
Groupie Girl (10)
Harmonica Free Form (17)

Harp Man (2)
Hartley Quits (3)
Have You Heard (12)
Heartache (16)
Help Me (11)
Hide And Seek (12)
Hideaway (16)
High Pressure Living (15)
Home Again (10)
Home In A Tree (13)
Hoot Owl (16)
I Can't Complain (19)
I Can't Quit You Baby (1,7)
I Know Now (3)
I Need Your Love (16)
I Started Walking (3,16)
I Still Care (17)
I Wanna Teach You Everything (16)
I Want To Go (19)
I'm A Stranger (3,12)
I'm Gonna Fight For You J.B. (6)
Introduction (17)
It Hurts Me Too (5)
Jacksboro Highway (19)
Jenny (5)
Keep Our Country Green (15)
Key To Love (12)
Killing Time (3)
Knockers Step Forward (12)
Laurel Canyon Home (4)
Laws Must Change (6)
Lesson, The (medley) (7)
Let's Work Together (19)
Local Boy Makes Good (11)

Long Gone Midnight (4)
Look In The Mirror (3)
Looking At Tomorrow (10)
Looking Back (5)
Lying In My Bed (8)
Mama, Talk To Your Daughter (12)
Man Of Stone (1,16)
Many Miles Apart (8)
Marriage Madness (10)
Marsha's Mood (2)
Me And My Woman (1,12)
Medicine Man (4)
Memories (13)
Messin' Around (14)
Miss James (4)
Missing You (12)
Moving On (15)
Mr Censor Man (10)
Mr. James (5)
My Children (10)
My Own Fault (7)
My Pretty Girl (9)
My Time After A While (1)
My Train Time (18)
Nature's Disappearing (9)
Night Flyer (9)
No More Tears (2)
No Reply (3,12)
Nobody Cares (14)
Off The Road (9)
Oh, Pretty Woman (1,16)
Open Up A New Door (3)
Out Of Reach (12)
People Cling Together (8)
Picture On The Wall (5)

Plan Your Revolution (8)
Play The Harp (13)
Please Don't Tell (2,12)
Possessive Emotions (9)
Prisons On The Road (10)
R And B Time Medley (16)
Ready To Ride (4)
Reasons (15)
Red Sky (9)
Respectfully Yours (18)
Room To Move (6)
Runaway (16)
Sandy (3)
Saw Mill Gulch Road (6)
Send Me Down To Vicksburg (19)
Sensitive Kind (19)
Separate Ways (13)
She's Too Young (3)
Sitting Here Thinking (17)
Sitting In The Rain (5)
Sitting On The Outside (18)
Snowy Wood (1,7)
So Hard To Share (6)
So Many Roads (5)
So Much To Do (18)
Somebody Acting Like A Child (4)
Someday After A While (You'll Be Sorry) (16)
Something New (8)
Sonny Boy Blow (2,12)
Soul Of Short, Fat Man (11)
Stand Back Baby (1,12)
Step In The Sun (18)
Stormy Monday Blues (5,16)

Streamline (1)
Sugarcane (19)
Supernatural, The (12)
Suspicions - Part 1 (9)
Suspicions - Part 2 (5)
Sweet Scorpio (18)
Taxman Blues (18)
Tears In My Eyes (1)
Television Eye (7)
Ten Years Are Gone (17)
Things Go Wrong (15)
Thinking Of My Woman (8)
Thoughts About Roxanne (6)
To A Princess (9)
To Match The Wind (18)
Took The Car (9)
Train, The (11)
Travelling (10)
2401 (4)
Unanswered Questions (10)
Undecided (17)
Vacation (4)
Waiting For The Right Time (8)
Walking On Sunset (4)
What's The Matter With You (16)
When I Go (8)
When I'm Gone (16)
Where Did I Belong? (3)
Where Did My Legs Go (9)
Wish I Knew A Woman (13)
Without Her (19)
Worried Mind (15)
You Must Be Crazy (9)
Your Funeral And My Trial (12)

Don't Waste My Time (8) 81

					★272★			

MAYFIELD, Curtis   '72

Born on 6/3/42 in Chicago. Died on 12/26/99 (age 57). R&B singer/songwriter/producer. Leader of **The Impressions** from 1957-70. Started own Curtom record label in 1968. Played "Pappy" in the movie *Short Eyes*. Paralyzed from the chest down when a stage lighting tower fell on him before a concert on 8/13/90. Won Grammy's Lifetime Achievement Award in 1995. Inducted into the Rock and Roll Hall of Fame in 1999.

1)Superfly 2)Back To The World 3)Curtis

DEBUT	PEAK	WKS	RIAA	CD	ARTIST — Album Title	Catalog Sym	$	Label & Number
10/3/70	19	49	● ©	1	**Curtis**		$15	Curtom 8005
5/29/71	21	38	©	2	**Curtis/Live!**	[L]	$20	Curtom 8008 [2]
					recorded at the Bitter End in New York City			
11/6/71	40	19	©	3	**Roots**		$15	Curtom 8009
8/26/72	❶⁴	46	● ©	4	**Superfly**	[S]	$15	Curtom 8014
3/3/73	180	6		5	**Curtis Mayfield/His Early Years With The Impressions**	[G]	$25	ABC 780 [2]
6/9/73	16	26	● ©	6	**Back To The World**		$15	Curtom 8015
11/17/73	135	10	©	7	**Curtis In Chicago**	[L]	$15	Curtom 8018
					includes "Once In My Life" and "Preacher Man" by **The Impressions**, "Duke Of Earl" by **Gene Chandler** and "Love Oh Love" by **Leroy Hutson**			
5/25/74	39	22	©	8	**Sweet Exorcist**		$15	Curtom 8601
11/16/74	76	7	©	9	**Got To Find A Way**		$15	Curtom 8604
6/7/75	120	11	©	10	**There's no place like America Today**		$15	Curtom 5001
7/4/76	171	8		11	**Give, Get, Take And Have**		$15	Curtom 5007
3/26/77	173	3	©	12	**Never Say You Can't Survive**		$15	Curtom 5013
8/11/79	42	16	©	13	**Heartbeat**		$12	RSO 3053
7/19/80	180	4	©	14	**The Right Combination**		$12	RSO 3084
					LINDA CLIFFORD/CURTIS MAYFIELD			
7/26/80	128	10	©	15	**Something To Believe In**		$12	RSO 3077
10/19/96	137	18	©	16	**New World Order**		$10	Warner 46348

MAYFIELD, Curtis — Cont'd

Ain't Got Time (8)
Ain't No Love Lost (9,14)
All Night Long (12)
Amen (5,7)
Back To Living Again (16)
Back To The World (6)
Beautiful Brother Of Mine (3)
Between You Baby And Me (13,14)
Billy Jack (10)
Blue Monday People (10)
Can't Say Nothin' (6) **88**
Can't Work No Longer (5)
Cannot Find A Way (9)
Check Out Your Mind (2)
(Don't Worry) If There's A Hell Below We're All Going To Go (1,2) **29**
Eddie You Should Know Better (4)
Emotions (1)
For Your Precious Love (7)
Freddie's Dead (Theme From "Superfly") (4) **4**
(also see: Superfly)
Future Shock (6) **39**

Future Song (Love A Good Woman, Love A Good Man) (6)
Get A Little Bit (Give, Get, Take And Have) (11)
Get Down (3) **69**
Get Up And Move (5)
Girl I Find Stays On My Mind (16)
Give It Up (1)
Give Me Your Love (Love Song) (4)
Got Dang Song (16)
Grow Closer Together (5)
Gypsy Woman (2,5)
Hard Times (10)
Heartbeat (13)
Here But I'm Gone (16)
I Believe In You (2)
I Plan To Stay A Believer (2)
I'm Gonna Win Your Love (12)
I'm So Proud (5,7,14)
I'm The One Who Loves You (5)
If I Were Only A Child Again (6,7)

In Your Arms Again (Shake It) (11)
It Was Love That We Needed (16)
It's All Right (5,15)
It's Lovin' Time (Your Baby's Home) (11)
Jesus (10)
Junkie Chase (4)
Just A Little Bit Of Love (16)
Just Want To Be With You (12)
Keep On Keeping On (3)
Keep On Pushing (5)
Keep On Trippin' (6)
Kung Fu (8) **40**
Let's Not Forget (16)
Little Child Runnin' Wild (4)
Love Me, Love Me Now (15)
Love Me (Right In The Pocket) (9)
Love To Keep You In My Mind (3)
Love To The People (10)
Love's Sweet Sensation (14)
Make Me Believe In You (8)
Makings Of You (1,2)

Mighty Mighty (Spade And Whitey) (2)
Miss Black America (1)
Mothers' Son (9)
Move On Up (1)
Mr. Welfare Man (11)
Ms. Martha (16)
Never Let Me Go (5,15)
Never Say You Can't Survive (12)
Never Stop Loving Me (15)
New World Order (16)
No One Knows About A Good Thing (You Don't Have To Cry) (16)
No Thing On Me (Cocaine Song) (4)
Now You're Gone (3)
Oh So Beautiful (16)
Only You Babe (11)
Other Side Of Town (1)
Over The Hump (13)
P.S. I Love You (11)
Party Night (11)
People Get Ready (2,5)
People Never Give Up (15)

Power To The People (8)
Prayer, A (9)
Pusherman (4)
Ridin' High (5)
Right Combination (14)
Right On For The Darkness (6)
Rock You To Your Socks (14)
Sad, Sad Girl And Boy (5)
Show Me Love (12)
So In Love (10) **67**
So You Don't Love Me (9)
Something To Believe In (15)
Sometimes I Wonder (5)
Soul Music (11)
Sparkle (12)
Stare And Stare (2)
Stone Junkie (2)
Suffer (8)
Superfly (4,7) **8**
(also see: Freddie's Dead)
Sweet Exorcist (8)
Talking About My Baby (5)
Tell Me, Tell Me (How Ya Like To Be Loved) (13)
Think (4)

This Love Is Sweet (11)
To Be Invisible (8)
Tripping Out (15)
Underground (3)
Victory (13)
We Got To Have Peace (3)
We The People Who Are Darker Than Blue (1,2,16)
We're A Winner (2,5)
We're Rolling On (5)
We've Only Just Begun (2)
What Is My Woman For? (13)
When Seasons Change (10)
When We're Alone (12)
When You Used To Be Mine (12)
Wild And Free (1)
Woman's Got Soul (5)
You Better Stop! (13)
You Must Believe Me (5)
You're So Good To Me (13)

MAZARATI   '86
Funk-rock group from Minneapolis: Sir Casey Terry (vocals), Craig Powell and Tony Christian (guitars), Aaron Paul Keith and Marr Starr (keyboards), Romeo (bass) and Kevin Patricks (drums).

4/19/86	133	8			**Mazarati**			$10	Paisley Park 25368

I Guess It's All Over
Lonely Girl On Bourbon Street

100 MPH
Players' Ball

She's Just That Kind of Lady
Strawberry Lover

Stroke
Suzy

★352★   MAZE Featuring Frankie Beverly   '83
R&B group formed in Philadelphia: Frankie Beverly (vocals), Wayne Thomas (guitar), Sam Porter (keyboards), Ronald Lowry (percussion), Robin Duhe (bass) and McKinley Williams (drums).
1)We Are One 2)Golden Time Of Day 3)Joy And Pain

DEBUT	PEAK	WKS	RIAA	CD	#	Album Title	$	Label & Number
2/26/77	52	45	●	©	1	Maze Featuring Frankie Beverly	$12	Capitol 11607
2/4/78	27	22	●	©	2	Golden Time Of Day	$12	Capitol 11710
4/7/79	33	22	●	©	3	Inspiration	$12	Capitol 11912
8/2/80	31	23	●	©	4	Joy And Pain	$12	Capitol 12087
7/4/81	34	27	●	©	5	Live In New Orleans .... [L]	$15	Capitol 12156 [2]
5/28/83	25	26		©	6	We Are One	$10	Capitol 12262
3/30/85	45	30	●	©	7	Can't Stop The Love	$10	Capitol 12377
9/20/86	92	11		©	8	Live In Los Angeles .... [L]	$15	Capitol 12479 [2]
9/23/89	37	22	●	©	9	Silky Soul	$10	Warner 25802
9/11/93	37	26	●	©	10	Back To Basics	$10	Warner 45297

Ain't It Strange (3)
All Night Long (10)
Back In Stride (7,8) **88**
Before I Let Go (5,8)
Call On Me (3)
Can't Get Over You (9)
Can't Stop The Love (7)
Change Our Ways (9)
Changing Times (4,5)
Color Blind (1)
Dee's Song (8)
Don't Wanna Lose Your Love (10)

Family (4)
Feel That You're Feelin' (3,5,8) **67**
Freedom (South Africa) (8)
Golden Time Of Day (2)
Happiness (4)
Happy Feelin's (1,5,8)
I Love You Too Much (6)
I Need You (2)
I Wanna Be With You (8)
I Wanna Thank You (6,8)
I Want To Feel I'm Wanted (7,8)
I Wish You Well (2)

In Time (10)
Introduction (5)
Joy And Pain (4,5,8)
Just Us (9)
Lady Of Magic (1)
Laid-Back Girl (10)
Look At California (1,5)
Look In Your Eyes (4,5)
Love Is (10)
Love Is The Key (6) **80**
Love's On The Run (9)
Lovely Inspiration (3)
Magic (7)

Mandela (9)
Metropolis (6)
Morning After (10)
Never Let You Down (6)
Nobody Knows What You Feel Inside (10)
Place In My Heart (7)
Reaching Down Inside (7)
Reason (5)
Right On Time (6)
Roots (4)
Running Away (5,8)
Silky Soul (9)

Somebody Else's Arms (9)
Song For My Mother (2)
Songs Of Love (3)
Southern Girl (4,5)
Time Is On My Side (1)
Timin' (3)
Too Many Games (7,8)
Travelin' Man (2)
Twilight (10)
We Are One (6,8)
We Need Love To Live (5)
Welcome Home (3)
What Goes Up (10)

When You Love Someone (8)
While I'm Alone (1) **89**
Woman Is A Wonder (4)
Workin' Together (2)
You (3,5)
You're Not The Same (2)
Your Own Kind Of Way (6)

MAZZY STAR   '94
Pop-rock duo from California: songwriter/guitarist David Roback and vocalist Hope Sandoval.

7/23/94	36	31	▲	©	1	So Tonight That I Might See	$10	Capitol 98253
11/16/96	68	5		©	2	Among My Swan	$10	Capitol 27224

All Your Sisters (2)
Bells Ring (1)
Blue Light (1)
Cry, Cry (2)

Disappear (2)
Fade Into You (1) **44**
Five String Serenade (1)
Flowers In December (2)
Happy (2)

I've Been Let Down (2)
Into Dust (1)
Look On Down From The Bridge (2)
Mary Of Silence (1)

Rhymes Of An Hour (2)
Roseblood (2)
She's My Baby (1)
So Tonight That I Might See (1)
Still Cold (2)

Take Everything (2)
Umbilical (2)
Unreflected (1)
Wasted (1)

MBULU, Letta   '77
Born on 8/23/42 in Johannesburg, South Africa. Female singer.

3/19/77	192	3			There's Music In The Air	$12	A&M 4609

produced by **Herb Alpert**

Ain't No Way To Treat A Lady
Feelings
Let's Go Dancing (medley)

Maru A Pula (Clouds Of Rain)
Music Man
Rainy Day Music

Sacred Drum
There's Music In The Air
Tristeza (Reuniao De Tristeza)

You've Lost That Lovin' Feeling (medley)

MC/M.C.:

M.C. BRAINS   '92
Born James Davis in 1975 in Cleveland. Male rapper.

4/4/92	47	17		©	Lovers Lane	$10	Motown 6342

"B" Is Dumb
Boyz II Men (The Sequel)
Brains Goin' Cra-ze

Brainstorming 69
Don't Let Me Get Loose

Everybody's Talking About M.C. Brains
G-String

Oochie Coochie 21
Strawberry Lane

559

MC BREED　'94
Born Eric Breed in Flint, Michigan. Male rapper.

DEBUT	PEAK	WKS	CD	#	Album Title	$	Label & Number
8/31/91	142	10	©	1	M.C. Breed & DFC	$10	S.D.E.G. 4103
5/30/92	155	4	©	2	20 Below	$10	Wrap 8109
5/15/93	156	15	©	3	The New Breed	$10	Wrap 8120
6/25/94	106	6	©	4	Funkafied	$10	Wrap 8133
7/8/95	143	2	©	5	Big Baller	$10	Wrap 8148
4/10/99	180	1	©	6	It's All Good	$10	Power 5290

Ain't No Future In Yo' Frontin' (1) 66
Ain't To Be F...ed With (2)
Ain't 2 Good (3)
Ain't Too Much Worried (2)
B.R. Double E.D. (4)
Back Up In Ya! (4)
Be Myself (2)
Been Round For Years (5)
Better Terms (1)
Black For Black (1)
Boom Boom (6)
Break Yourself (4)
Business Never Personal (6)
Comin' Real Again (3)
Conversations (3)
Deal Is Da Funk (4)
Dis Mode (2)
Everyday Ho (3)
Flash's Groove (2)
Flashbacks (3)
Flava Uv Phony (4)
Game For Life (5)
Gangsta Shit (6)
Get Loose (1)
Gotta Get Mine (3,6) 96
Great Depression (2)
Guanja (1)
I Will Excell (1)
It's All Good (6)
Jealous Pimp (2)
Job Corp (1)
Just Another Clip (3)
Just Kickin' It (1)
Late Nite Creep (Booty Call) (4)
Let's Go To Da Club (6)
Life Of A Flintstone (2)
Little Child Running Wild (2)
More Power (1)
Nightlife (5)
No Frontin' Allowed (2)
Ol' School (4)
One Time (4)
Real MC (5)
Rule No.1 (6)
SFNU (5)
Say What (5)
Sea Of Bud (5)
Seven Years (4)
Shootin' From The Hip (4)
Smoke Wit A Nigga (6)
Smokin' (4)
Some Otha (5)
Something 2 Smoke 2 (3)
Teach My Kids (4)
That's Life (1)
Tight (3)
Tricks (6)
20 Below (2)
Underground Address (4)
Underground Slang (1)
Watch Your Own Back (3)
What Do You Get (5)
What You Want (4)
Whenever You Want Me (2)
Work It From The Bottom (6)
You Slippin' (5)

MC EIHT　'94
Born Aaron Tyler in Los Angeles. Male rapper. Leader of **Compton's Most Wanted** (CMW). Played "A-Wax" in the movie *Menace II Society*.

DEBUT	PEAK	WKS		CD	#	Album Title	$	Label & Number
8/6/94	5	14	●	©	1	We Come Strapped	$10	Epic Street 57696
4/27/96	16	8		©	2	Death Threatz	$10	Epic Street 67139
						MC EIHT FEATURING CMW (above 2)		
11/29/97	64	2		©	3	Last Man Standing	$10	Epic Street 68041
6/26/99	54	7		©	4	Section 8	$10	Hoo Bangin' 50021
7/8/00	95	6		©	5	N' My Neighborhood	$10	Hoo-Bangin' 50103

Ain't Nuthin 2 It (2)
All Around The Hood (5)
All For The Money (1)
Any Meanz (3)
Anything U Want (3)
Automatic (4)
Business, Tha (3)
Can I Get Mine (3)
Can I Still Kill It (1)
Caution (4)
Collect My Stripez (2)
Compton Bomb (1)
Compton Cyco (1)
Compton 4 Death (3)
Dayz Of 89' (4)
Def Wish III (1)
Def Wish IV (Tap That Azz) (2)
Drugs & Killin (2)
Endoness (2)
Flatline (1)
From Yo Hood 2 My Hood (5)
Fuc Em All (2)
Fuc Your Hood (5)
Git Money (5)
Goin' Out Like Geez (1)
Got Cha Humpin' (3)
Hangin' (3)
Hard Times (1)
Hit The Floor (3)
Hold Up (5)
Hood Is Mine (5)
Hood Ratz (5)
Hood Still Got Me Under (4)
Hubtouchablez (3)
Killin Nigguz (2)
Killin Season (2)
Kind Of Pimpish (3)
Late Nite Hype Part 2 (2)
Living N' Tha Streetz (4)
Love 4 Tha Hood (2)
Lunatic (5)
Me & My Bitch (3,4)
Murder At Night (1)
Must Be Murder (5)
My Life (4)
Niggaz Make The Hood Go Round (1)
Niggaz That Kill (1)
Nuthin' But High (1)
Nuthin' But Tha Gangsta (1)
On Top Of All That (3)
Once Upon A Time N' The Ghetto (1)
Return Fire (3)
Run 4 Your Life (2)
Set Trippin (2)
So Ruff (5)
Strawberriez-N-Cream (4)
Take 2 With Me (1)
Thicker Than Water (4)
Ill Tha Hood Way (4)
Thuggin It Up (2)
Till I Die (5)
2 Tha Westside (1)
Tough Guyz (3)
Under Attack (3)
Way We Run It (3)
We Come Strapped (1)
When All Hell Breaks Loose (3)
Who's Tha Man (3)
You Can't See Me (2)

MC5　'69
Hard-rock group from Detroit: Rob Tyner (vocals), Wayne Kramer and Fred "Sonic" Smith (guitars), Michael Davis (bass) and Dennis Thompson (drums). Tyner died of a heart attack on 9/17/91 (age 46). Smith married **Patti Smith** in 1980; died of a heart attack on 11/4/94 (age 45). MC5 is short for Motor City Five.

DEBUT	PEAK	WKS	CD	#	Album Title	Sym	$	Label & Number
3/8/69	30	23	©	1	Kick Out The Jams	[L]	$50	Elektra 74042
					recorded on 10/31/68 at the Grande Ballroom in Detroit			
2/21/70	137	7	©	2	Back In The USA		$50	Atlantic 8247

American Ruse (2)
Back In The USA (2)
Borderline (1)
Call Me Animal (2)
Come Together (1)
High School (2)
Human Being Lawnmower (2)
I Want You Right Now (1)
Kick Out The Jams (1) 82
Let Me Try (2)
Looking At You (2)
Motor City Is Burning (1)
Ramblin' Rose (1)
Rocket Reducer No. 62 (Rama Lama Fa Fa Fa) (1)
Shakin' Street (2)
Starship (1)
Teenage Lust (2)
Tonight (2)
Tutti-Frutti (2)

★396★　M.C. HAMMER　'90
Born Stanley Kirk Burrell on 3/30/63 in Oakland. Male rapper. Billed as **Hammer** from 1991-94.

DEBUT	PEAK	WKS	RIAA	CD	#	Album Title	$	Label & Number
12/3/88+	30	80	▲²	©	1	Let's Get It Started	$10	Capitol 90924
3/10/90	❶²¹	108	▲¹⁰	©	2	Please Hammer Don't Hurt 'Em	$10	Capitol 92857
11/16/91	2²	54	▲³	©	3	Too Legit To Quit	$10	Capitol 98151
3/19/94	12	25	▲	©	4	The Funky Headhunter	$10	Giant 24545
						HAMMER (above 2)		
9/30/95	119	3		©	5	V Inside Out	$10	Giant 24637

Anything Goes On The Dance Floor (5)
Black Is Black (2)
Break 'Em Off Somethin' Proper (4)
Brighter Day (5)
Brothers Hang On (3)
Bustin' Loose (5)
Clap Yo' Hands (4)
Cold Go M.C. Hammer (1)
Count It Off (3)
Crime Story (2)
Dancin' Machine (2)
Do Not Pass Me By (3) 62
Don't Fight The Feelin' (4)
Don't Stop (4)
Everything Is Alright (5)
Feel My Power (1)
Find Yourself A Friend (3)
Funky Headhunter (4)
Gaining Momentum (3)
Goin' Up Yonder (5)
Good To Go (3)
Have You Seen Her (2) 4
He Keeps Doing Great Things For Me (3)
Help Lord (Won't You Come) (4)
Help The Children (2)
Here Comes The Hammer (2) 54
I Hope Things Change (5)
I Need That Number (5)
It's All Good (4) 46
It's All That (4)
It's Gone (1)
Keep On (5)
Let's Get It Started (1)
Lets Go Deeper (2)
Living In A World Like This (3)
Lovehold (3)
Luv-N-Happiness (5)
Nothing But Love (A Song For Eazy) (5)
Oaktown (2)
On Your Face (2)
One Mo' Time (4)
Pray (2) 2
Pump It Up (Here's The News) (1)
Pumps And A Bump (4) 26
Releasing Some Pressure (3)
Ring 'Em (1)
She's Soft And Wet (2)
Sleepin' On A Master Plan (4)
Somethin' 'Bout The Goldie In Me (4)
Somethin' For The O.G.'s (4)
Son Of The King (1)
Street Soldiers (3)
Sultry Funk (5)
Tell Me (Why Can't We Live Together) (4)
That's What I Said (1)
They Put Me In The Mix (1)
This Is The Way We Roll (3) 86
2 Legit 2 Quit (3) 5
Turn This Mutha Out (1)
U Can't Touch This (2) 8
Work This (2)
Yo!! Sweetness (2)
You're Being Served (1)

MC LYTE　'96
Born Lana Moorer on 10/11/71 in Queens, New York. Female rapper.

DEBUT	PEAK	WKS	CD	#	Album Title	$	Label & Number
10/21/89	86	20	©	1	Eyes On This	$10	First Priority 91304
10/5/91	102	16	©	2	Act Like You Know	$10	First Priority 91731
7/10/93	90	16	©	3	Ain't No Other	$10	First Priority 92230
9/14/96	59	6	©	4	Bad As I Wanna B	$10	EastWest 61781

Absolutely Positively.....Practical Jokes (2)
Act Like You Know (2)
Ain't No Other (3)
All That (2)
Beyond The Hype (2)
Big Bad Sister (2)
Brooklyn (3)
Can I Get Some Dap (3)
Can You Dig It (2)
Cappucino (1)
Cha Cha Cha (1)
Cold Rock A Party (4) 11
Druglord Superstar (4)
Everyday (4)
Eyes Are The Soul (2)
F--k That M-----f--king Bulls--t (3)
Funky Song (1)
Hard Copy (3)
Have U Ever (4)
I Am The Lyte (1)
I Cram To Understand U - 1990 (3)
I Go On (3)
K-Rock's The Man (2)
K-Rocks Housin' (1)
Kamikaze (2)
Keep On, Keepin' On (4) 10
Let Me Ride (3)
Like A Virgin (4)
Lil Paul (1)
Lola From The Copa (2)

MC LYTE — Cont'd

Never Heard Nothin' Like This (3)
Not Wit' A Dealer (1)
One Nine Nine Three (3)
One On One (4)

Please Understand (1)
Poor Georgie (2) *83*
Rhyme Hangover (1)
Ruffneck (3) *35*
Search 4 The Lyte (2)

Shut The Eff Up! (Hoe) (1)
Slave 2 The Rhythm (1)
Steady F--king (3)
Stop, Look, Listen (1)
Survival Of The Fittest (1)

TRG (The Rap Game) (4)
Take It Off (2)
Throwin' Words At U (1)
2 Young 4 What (2)
Two Seater (4)

What's My Name Yo (3)
When In Love (2)
Who's House (3)
Zodiac (4)

M.C. MADNESS — see D.J. MAGIC MIKE

MC POOH '92
Born Lawrence Thomas in Los Angeles. Male rapper.

| 3/28/92 | 158 | 6 | | © | Funky As I Wanna Be .... | | | $10 | Jive 41476 |

POOH-MAN (MC POOH)

Big Gangster
Don't Cost A Dime

Eatin' Pussy
Fuckin' Wit Dank

Funky As I Wanna Be
Mellow Man

Niggas Ain't Playin'
Player Haters

Projects, The
Racia

Sex, Money And Murder
Your Dick

MC REN '92
Born Lorenzo Patterson in Los Angeles. Male rapper. Former member of **N.W.A.**

7/18/92	12	13	▲	©	1	Kizz My Black Azz			$10	Ruthless 53802
12/4/93	22	14		©	2	Shock Of The Hour			$10	Ruthless 5505
4/27/96	31	6		©	3	The Villain In Black			$10	Ruthless 5544
7/18/98	100	3		©	4	Ruthless For Life			$10	Ruthless 69313

All Bullshit Aside (2)
All The Same (4)
Attack On Babylon (2)
Behind The Scenes (1)
Bitch Made Nigga Killa (3)
Bring It On (3)
CPT All Day (4)

Check It Out Y'all (1)
Comin' After You (2)
Do You Believe (2)
11:55 (2)
Final Frontier (1)
Fuck What Ya Heard (2)
Great Elephant (3)

Hound Dogz (1)
I Don't Give A Damn (3)
It's Like That (3)
Keep It Real (3)
Kizz My Black Azz (1)
Live From Compton 'Saturday Night' (3)

Mad Scientist (3)
Mayday On The Front Line (3)
Mind Blown (3)
Mr. Fuck Up (2)
Muhammad Speaks (3)
Must Be High (4)
Nigga Called Ren (4)

One False Move (2)
Pimpin' Is Free (4)
Right Up My Alley (1)
Ruthless For Life (4)
Same Old Shit (2) *90*
Shock Of The Hour (2)
Shot Caller (4)

So Whatcha Want (4)
Still The Same Nigga (3)
Voyage To Compton (4)
Who Got That Street Shit (4)
Who In The Fuck (4)
You Wanna Fuck Her (2)

MC SERCH '92
Born Michael Berrin in Queens, New York. White rapper. Member of **3rd Bass**.

| 9/12/92 | 103 | 11 | | © | | Return Of The Product .... | | | $10 | Def Jam 52964 |

Back To The Grill
Can You Dig It

Daze In A Weak
Don't Have To Be

Hard But True
Here It Comes *71*

Hits The Head
Return Of The Product

Scenes From The Mind
Social Narcotics

MC SHY-D '87
Born Peter Jones in the Bronx, New York. Male rapper.

| 6/27/87 | 197 | 1 | | | | Got To Be Tough .... | | | $10 | Luke Skyywalker 1004 |

Bust This
DJ Man Cuts It Up (Part II)

Don't Take Me Seriously
I Will Go Off

I'm Not A Star
I've Got To Be Tough

Paula's On Crack
Rap Will Never Die (Part II)

Shy-D's Theme
So Take That

We Don't Play (live)
Yes Yes Y'All

MC SKAT KAT And The Stray Mob '91
MC Skat Kat is an animated character featured in **Paula Abdul**'s "Opposites Attract" video. Created by Michael Patterson and Candace Reckinger. The Stray Mob are Fatz, Taboo, Leo, Micetro, Katleen and Silk.

| 9/28/91 | 197 | 2 | | © | | The Adventures Of MC Skat Kat And The Stray Mob .... | | | $10 | Captive 91396 |

Big Time
Gotta Get Up

I Ain't No Kitty
I Go Crazy

Kat In The Casino
Kat Stories

New Kat Swing
No Dogs Allowed

On The Prowl
Skat Kat's Theme

Skat Strut *80*
So Sweet So Young

Mc:

McAULEY SCHENKER GROUP — see SCHENKER, Michael, Group

McBRIDE, Martina '99
Born Martina Schiff on 7/29/66 in Sharon, Kansas. Country singer.

7/2/94	106	30	▲	©	1	The Way That I Am			$10	RCA 66288
10/14/95	77	25	▲	©	2	Wild Angels			$10	RCA 66509
9/13/97+	24	93	▲³	©	3	Evolution	C:#11/17		$10	RCA 67516
11/28/98	68	7	●	©	4	White Christmas	C:#3/16	[X]	$10	RCA 67654

Christmas charts: 6/98, 8/99, 14/00

| 10/2/99 | 19 | 37 | ▲ | © | 5 | Emotion .... | | | $10 | RCA 67824 |

All The Things We've Never Done (4)
Anything And Everything (5)
Anything's Better Than Feelin' The Blues (5)
Ashes (4)
Away In A Manger (4)
Be That Way (3)
Beyond The Blue (2)
Born To Give My Love To You (2)
Broken Wing (3) *61*

Christmas Song (Chestnuts Roasting On An Open Fire) (4)
Cry On The Shoulder Of The Road (2)
Do What You Do (5)
From The Ashes (5)
Goin' To Work (1)
Good Bye (5)
Great Disguise (2)
Happy Girl (3)

Have Yourself A Merry Little Christmas (4)
Heart Trouble (1)
Here In My Heart (3)
I Ain't Goin' Nowhere (5)
I Don't Want To See You Again (3)
I Love You (5) *24*
I Won't Close My Eyes (3)
I'll Be Home For Christmas (4)
I'm Little But I'm Loud (3)
Independence Day (1)

It's My Time (5)
Keeping My Distance (3)
Let It Snow, Let It Snow, Let It Snow (4)
Life #9 (1)
Love's The Only House (5) *42*
Make Believe (5)
My Baby Loves Me (5)
O Holy Night (4)
One Day You Will (3)
Phones Are Ringin' All Over Town (2)

Safe In The Arms Of Love (2)
She Ain't Seen Nothing Yet (1)
Silent Night (4)
Silver Bells (4)
Some Say I'm Running (3)
Still Holding On (3)
Strangers (1)
Swingin' Doors (2)
That Wasn't Me (1)
There You Are (5) *60*
This Uncivil War (5)
Two More Bottles Of Wine (2)

Valentine (3) *50*
What Child Is This (4)
Whatever You Say (3) *37*
Where I Used To Have A Heart (1)
White Christmas (4)
Wild Angels (2)
Wrong Again (3) *36*
You've Been Driving All The Time (2)

McBRIDE & THE RIDE '92
Country trio formed in Nashville: Terry McBride (vocals, bass), Ray Herndon (guitar) and Billy Thomas (drums).

| 6/29/91 | 180 | 8 | | © | 1 | Burnin' Up The Road .... | | | $10 | MCA 42343 |
| 5/16/92 | 144 | 10 | ● | © | 2 | Sacred Ground .... | | | $10 | MCA 10540 |

Ain't No Big Deal (1)
All I Have To Offer You Is Me (2)
Baby I'm Loving You Now (2)

Burnin' Up The Road (1)
Can I Count On You (1)
Chains Of Memory (1)
Every Step Of The Way (1)

Felicia (1)
Going Out Of My Mind (2)
I'm The One (2)
Just One Night (2)

Love's On The Line (2)
Makin' Real Good Time (2)
Nobody's Fool (1)
Sacred Ground (2)

Same Old Star (1)
Stone Country (1)
Trick Rider (2)
Turn To Blue (1)

Your One And Only (2)

McCAIN, Edwin '99

Born on 1/20/70 in Greenville, South Carolina. Singer/songwriter/guitarist.

DEBUT	PEAK	WKS			Album		$	Label & Number
9/2/95	107	12		© 1	Honor Among Thieves		$10	Lava 92597
4/18/98	73	42	▲	© 2	Misguided Roses		$10	Lava 82995
7/3/99	59	22	●	© 3	Messenger		$10	Lava 83197

Alive (1)
America Street (1)
Anything Good About Me (3)
Beautiful Life (3)
Bitter Chill (1)
Cleveland Park (2)
Darwin's Children (2)
Do Your Thing (3)
Don't Bring Me Down (1)
Ghosts Of Jackson Square (3)
Go Be Young (3)
Grind Me In The Gears (2)
Guinevere (1)
Holy City (2)
How Strange It Seems (2)
I Could Not Ask For More (3) 37
I'll Be (2,3) 5
(I've Got To) Stop Thinkin' 'Bout That (2)
Jesters, Dreamers & Thieves (1)
Kitchen Song (1)
Prayer To St. Peter (3)
Promise Of You (3)
Punish Me (2)
Rhythm Of Life (2)
Russian Roulette (1)
See Off This Mountain (3)
See The Sky Again (2)
Sign On The Door (3)
Solitude (1) 72
Sorry To A Friend (1)
Take Me (2)
Thirty Pieces (1)
3 AM (1)
What Matters (2)
Wish In This World (3)

McCALL, C.W. '76

Born William Fries on 11/15/28 in Audubon, Iowa. The character "C.W. McCall" was created for the Mertz Bread Company. Fries was its advertising man. Elected mayor of Ouray, Colorado in the early 1980s.

DEBUT	PEAK	WKS		Album		$	Label & Number
4/12/75	143	9	1	Wolf Creek Pass		$12	MGM 4989
11/29/75+	12	19	● 2	Black Bear Road		$12	MGM 5008
5/8/76	143	4	3	Wilderness		$12	Polydor 6069

Aurora Borealis (3)
Black Bear Road (2)
Classified (1)
Columbine (3)
Convoy (2) 1
Crispy Critters (3)
Four Wheel Cowboy (3)
Four Wheel Drive (1)
Ghost Town (2)
Glenwood Canyon (1)
Green River (2)
I've Trucked All Over This Land (1)
Jackson Hole (3)
Lewis And Clark (2)
Little Brown Sparrow And Me (3)
Long Lonesome Road (2)
Mountains On My Mind (2)
Night Rider (1)
Old Home Filler-Up An' Keep On-A-Truckin' Cafe (1) 54
Old 30 (1)
Oregon Trail (2)
Riverside Slide (3)
Rocky Mountain September (1)
Roy (3)
Silver Iodide Blues (3)
Silverton, The (2)
Sloan (1)
Telluride Breakdown (3)
There Won't Be No Country Music (There Won't Be No Rock 'N' Roll) (3) 73
Wilderness (3)
Wolf Creek Pass (1) 40
Write Me A Song (2)

McCALLUM, David '66

Born on 9/19/33 in Glasgow, Scotland. Studio orchestra conductor/actor. Played "Illya Kuryakin" on TV's *The Man From U.N.C.L.E.*

DEBUT	PEAK	WKS		Album		Sym	$	Label & Number
2/26/66	27	24	1	Music - A Part Of Me		[I]	$20	Capitol 2432
6/11/66	79	12	2	Music: A Bit More Of Me		[I]	$20	Capitol 2498

Batman Theme (2)
Call Me (2)
Downtown (1)
Edge, The (2)
Far Away Blue (2)
Far Side Of The Moon (1)
Final (2)
5 O'Clock World (2)
I Can't Get No Satisfaction (1)
"In" Crowd (1)
Insomnia (1)
Isn't It Wonderful (2)
It Won't Be Wrong (2)
Louise (1)
Michelle (2)
My World Is Empty Without You (2)
1-2-3 (1)
Shadow Of Your Smile (Love Theme From The Sandpiper) (1)
Sugar Cane (1)
Taste Of Honey (1)
Turn, Turn, Turn (1)
Uptight (Everything's Alright) (2)
We Gotta Get Out Of This Place (1)
Yesterday (1)

McCAMPBELL BROTHERS — see MAC BAND

McCANN, Les '70

Born on 9/23/35 in Lexington, Kentucky. Jazz keyboardist.

DEBUT	PEAK	WKS			Album		Sym	$	Label & Number
3/29/69	169	10	©	1	Much Les		[I]	$20	Atlantic 1516
12/13/69+	29	38	©	2	Swiss Movement		[I-L]	$20	Atlantic 1537

LES McCANN & EDDIE HARRIS
recorded June 1969 at the Montreaux Jazz Festival in Switzerland

5/29/71	41	27	©	3	Second Movement		[I]	$20	Atlantic 1583

EDDIE HARRIS & LES McCANN

4/8/72	141	6	©	4	Invitation To Openness		[I]	$15	Atlantic 1603
10/7/72	181	6	©	5	Talk To The People			$15	Atlantic 1619
1/18/75	166	4	©	6	Another Beginning			$15	Atlantic 1666
11/22/75	161	4	©	7	Hustle To Survive			$15	Atlantic 1679

Beaux J. Poo Boo (4)
Benjamin (1)
Burnin' Coal (1)
Butterflies (medley) (7)
Carry On Brother (3)
Changing Seasons (7)
Cold Duck Time (2)
Compared To What (2) 85
Doin' That Thing (1)
Everytime I See A Butterfly (medley) (7)
Generation Gap (2)
Go On And Cry (6)
Got To Hustle To Survive (7)
Kathleen's Theme (4)
Let It Lay (5)
Let Your Learning Be Your Eyes (7)
Love For Sale (1)
Lovers, The (4)
Maybe You'll Come Back (6)
Morning Song (6)
My Soul Lies Deep (6)
North Carolina (5)
Poo Pye McGoochie (And His Friends) (4)
Roberta (1)
Samia (3)
Says Who Says What? (7)
Seems So Long (5)
Set Us Free (3)
Shamading (5)
She's Here (5)
Shorty Rides Again (3)
Somebody's Been Lying 'Bout Me (6)
Someday We'll Meet Again (6)
Song Of Love (6)
Talk To The People (5)
Universal Prisoner (3)
Us (7)
Well, Cuss My Daddy (7)
What's Going On (5)
When It's Over (6)
Why Is Now (7)
Will We Ever Find Our Fathers (7)
With These Hands (1)
You Got It In Your Soulness (2)

McCANN, Lila '99

Born in 12/4/81 in Steilacoom, Washington. Country singer.

DEBUT	PEAK	WKS			Album		$	Label & Number
7/19/97	86	43	▲	© 1	Lila		$10	Asylum 62042
4/10/99	85	18		© 2	Something In The Air		$10	Asylum 62355

Almost Over You (1)
Already Somebody's Lover (1)
Can You Hear Me (2)
Changing Faces (1)
Crush (2)
Down Came A Blackbird (1)
Go Girl (1)
Hit By Love (2)
I Feel For You (1)
I Reckon I Will (2)
I Wanna Fall In Love (1)
I Will Be (2)
Just One Little Kiss (1)
Kiss Me Now (2)
Rain Of Angels (1)
Rhymes With (2)
Saddle My Dreams (1)
Something In The Air (2)
When You Walked Into My Life (2)
With You (2) 41
Yippy Ky Yay (1)
You're Gone (2)

McCANN, Peter '77

Born in Connecticut. Pop singer/songwriter.

DEBUT	PEAK	WKS		Album		$	Label & Number
7/30/77	82	12		Peter McCann		$12	20th Century 544

Broken White Line (1)
Do You Wanna Make Love 5
Everybody's Got To Hold On To Something
I Can't Live Without You
If You Can't Find Love
It's Easy
Right Time Of The Night
Save Me Your Love
Suicide And Vine
Things You Left Behind

McCARTNEY, Paul/Wings ★24★   '74

Born James Paul McCartney on 6/18/42 in Allerton, Liverpool, England. Founding member/bass guitarist of **The Beatles**. Married Linda Eastman on 3/12/69. First solo album in 1970. Formed group **Wings** in 1971 with Linda (keyboards, backing vocals), Denny Laine (guitar; **Moody Blues**) and Denny Seiwell (drums). Henry McCullough (guitar; **Grease Band**) joined in 1972. Seiwell and McCullough left in 1973. In 1975, Joe English (drums) and **Thunderclap Newman** guitarist Jimmy McCulloch (died on 9/27/79, age 26) joined; both left in 1977. Wings officially disbanded in April 1981. Backing band since 1989 included Linda, Hamish Stuart (guitar; **AWB**), Robbie McIntosh (guitar; **Night, The Pretenders**), Paul Wickens (piano) and Chris Whitten (drums). Blair Cunningham (**Haircut One Hundred**) replaced Whitten by 1993. McCartney starred in own movie *Give My Regards To Broad Street* (1984). Won Grammy's Lifetime Achievement Award in 1990. Knighted by Queen Elizabeth II in 1997. Inducted into the Rock and Roll Hall of Fame in 1999. Linda died of cancer on 4/17/98 (age 55).

1)Wings At The Speed Of Sound 2)Band On The Run 3)McCartney 4)Red Rose Speedway 5)Tug Of War

DEBUT	PEAK	WKS	RIAA	CD	#	Album Title	Sym	$	Label & Number
5/9/70	❶³	47	▲²	©	1	McCartney		$30	Apple 3363
						PAUL AND LINDA McCARTNEY:			
6/5/71	2²	37	▲	©	2	Ram		$30	Apple 3375
						WINGS:			
12/25/71+	10	18	●	©	3	Wild Life		$20	Apple 3386
5/12/73	❶³	31	●	©	4	Red Rose Speedway		$20	Apple 3409
12/22/73+	❶⁴	116	▲³	©	5	Band On The Run	C:❶¹/44	$20	Apple 3415
						PAUL McCARTNEY & WINGS (above 2)			
6/14/75	❶¹	77	▲	©	6	Venus And Mars		$15	Capitol 11419
4/10/76	❶⁷	51	▲	©	7	Wings At The Speed Of Sound		$15	Capitol 11525
12/25/76+	❶¹	86	▲	©	8	Wings Over America	[L]	$25	Capitol 11593 [3]
4/15/78	2⁶	28	▲	©	9	London Town		$15	Capitol 11777
12/9/78+	29	18	▲	©	10	Wings Greatest	[G]	$15	Capitol 11905
6/30/79	8	24	▲	©	11	Back To The Egg		$15	Columbia 36057
						PAUL McCARTNEY:			
6/14/80	3	19	●	©	12	McCartney II		$12	Columbia 36511
1/31/81	158	3			13	The McCartney Interview	[T]	$12	Columbia 36987
						no track titles listed on this album			
5/15/82	❶³	29	▲	©	14	Tug Of War		$12	Columbia 37462
11/19/83	15	24	▲	©	15	Pipes Of Peace		$12	Columbia 39149
11/10/84	21	18	●	©	16	Give my regards to Broad Street	[S]	$12	Columbia 39613
9/13/86	30	22		©	17	Press To Play		$10	Capitol 12475
12/19/87+	62	17	▲²	©	18	All The Best!	C:#36/1 [G]	$15	Capitol 48287 [2]
6/24/89	21	49	●	©	19	Flowers In The Dirt		$10	Capitol 91653
11/24/90	26	16		©	20	Tripping The Live Fantastic	[L]	$15	Capitol 94778 [2]
12/15/90+	141	9	▲	©	21	Tripping The Live Fantastic - highlights!	[L]	$10	Capitol 95379
6/22/91	14	8		©	22	Unplugged (The Official Bootleg)	[L]	$10	Capitol 96413
11/16/91	109	3		©	23	CHOBA B CCCP - The Russian Album		$10	Capitol 97615
						title is Russian for "Back In The USSR"			
11/16/91	177	6		©	24	Paul McCartney's Liverpool Oratorio		$15	EMI 54371 [2]
2/27/93	17	20	●	©	25	Off The Ground		$10	Capitol 80362
12/4/93	78	4		©	26	Paul Is Live	[L]	$10	Capitol 27704
6/14/97	2¹	20	●	©	27	Flaming Pie		$10	Capitol 56500
11/1/97	194	1		©	28	Paul McCartney's Standing Stone		$10	EMI Classics 56484
10/23/99	27	6		©	29	Run Devil Run		$10	Capitol 22351
5/26/01	2¹	14	▲²	©	30	Wingspan: Hits and History	[K]	$15	MPL 32946 [2]

After Heavy Light Years (28)
After The Ball (medley) (11)
Again And Again And Again (11)
Ain't No Sunshine (22)
Ain't That A Shame (20,23)
All My Loving (26)
And I Love Her (22)
All Shook Up (29)
Angry (17)
Another Day (10,18,20,30) *5*
Arrow Through Me (11) *29*
Average Person (15)
Baby's Request (17)
Back In The U.S.S.R. (20,21)
Back Seat Of My Car (2,30)
Backwards Traveller (medley) (9)
Ballroom Dancing (14,16)
Band On The Run (5,8,10,18,20,30) *1*
Be-Bop-A-Lula (22)
Be What You See (14)
Beautiful Night (27)
Beware My Love (7,8)
Big Barn Bed (4)
Biker Like An Icon (25,26)
Bip Bop (3,30)
Birthday (20,21)
Blackbird (8,22)
Blue Jean Bop (29)
Blue Moon Of Kentucky (22)
Bluebird (5,8,30)
Bogey Music (12)
Bring It On Home To Me (23)
Broadcast, The (11)

Brown Eyed Handsome Man (29)
C Moon (18,30)
Cafe On The Left Bank (9)
Calico Skies (27)
Call Me Back Again (6,8,30)
Can't Buy Me Love (20,21)
Carry That Weight (medley) (20,21)
Children Children (9)
C'mon People (25,26)
Cook Of The House (7)
Coquette (29)
Corridor Music (16)
Crackin' Up (20,23)
Crises (24)
Crossroads Theme (6)
Crypt (24)
Cuff Link (medley) (9)
Darkroom (12)
Daytime Nightime Suffering (30)
Dear Boy (2)
Dear Friend (3)
Deliver Your Children (9)
Distractions (19)
Don't Be Careless Love (19)
Don't Get Around Much Anymore (23)
Don't Let It Bring You Down (9)
Don't Let The Sun Catch You Crying (20)
Dress Me Up As A Robber (14)
Drive My Car (26)
Eat At Home (2)

Ebony And Ivory (14,18,20) *1*
Eleanor Rigby (16,20,21)
Eleanor's Dream (medley) (16)
End, The (medley) (20,21)
Every Night (1,22,30)
Famous Groupies (9)
Father (24)
Feel The Sun (medley) (17)
Figure Of Eight (19,20) *92*
Fine Day (26)
Flaming Pie (27)
Fool On The Hill (20)
Footprints (17)
For No One (16)
Front Parlour (12)
Frozen Jap (12)
Get Back (20,21)
Get It (14)
Get On The Right Thing (4)
Get Out Of The Way (25)
Getting Closer (11) *20*
Girlfriend (9,30)
Glasses (medley) (1)
Go Now (8)
Golden Earth Girl (25)
Golden Slumbers (medley) (20,21)
Good Day Sunshine (16)
Good Rockin' Tonight (22,26)
Good Times Coming (medley) (17)
Goodnight Tonight (18,30) *5*
Got To Get You Into My Life (20,21)
Great Day (27)
Hands Of Love (medley) (4)

He Awoke Startled (28)
Heart Of The Country (2,30)
Heaven On A Sunday (27)
Helen Wheels (5,30) *10*
Here, There And Everywhere (16,22,26)
Here Today (14)
Hey Diddle (medley) (30)
Hey Hey (15)
Hey Jude (20,21)
Hi-Heel Sneakers (22)
Hi, Hi, Hi (8,10,30) *10*
Hold Me Tight (medley) (4)
Honey Hush (29)
Hope Of Deliverance (25,26) *83*
Hot As Hot (medley) (1)
Hotel In Benidorm (16)
How Many People (19)
However Absurd (17)
I Am Your Singer (3)
I Got Stung (29)
I Lost My Little Girl (22)
I Owe It All To You (25)
I Saw Her Standing There (20,21)
I Wanna Be Your Man (26)
I'm Carrying (9)
I'm Gonna Be A Wheel Someday (23)
I'm In Love Again (23)
I've Had Enough (9) *25*
I've Just Seen A Face (8,22)
If I Were Not Upon The Stage (20)
If You Wanna (27)

Inner City Madness (20)
Jet (5,8,10,18,20,30) *7*
Junior's Farm (10,18,30) *3*
Junk (1,22,30)
Just Because (23)
Kansas City (23,26)
Keep Under Cover (15)
Kreen-Akrore (1)
Lady Madonna (8,26)
Lawdy Miss Clawdy (23)
Lazy Dynamite (medley) (4)
Let 'Em In (7,8) *3*
Let It Be (20,21)
Let Me Roll It (5,8,26,30)
Letting Go (6,8) *39*
Listen To What The Man Said (6,8,18,30) *1*
Little Lamb Dragonfly (4)
Little Willow (30)
Live And Let Die (8,10,18,20,26,30) *2*
London Town (9) *39*
Lonesome Town (29)
Long And Winding Road (8,16,20,21)
Long Haired Lady (2)
Looking For Changes (25,26)
Loup (1st Indian On The Moon) (4)
Love Awake (medley) (11)
Love In Song (6)
Love Is Strange (3)
Lovely Linda (1,30)
Lovers That Never Were (25)
Lucille (23)
Magical Mystery Tour (26)

Magneto And Titanium Man (6,8)
Mamunia (5)
Man, The (15)
Man We Was Lonely (1,30)
Matchbox (20)
Maybe I'm Amazed (1,8,20,30) *10*
Medicine Jar (6,8)
Michelle (26)
Midnight Special (23)
Million Miles (medley) (11)
Mistress And Maid (25)
Momma Miss America (1)
Monkberry Moon Delight (2)
Morse Moose And The Grey Goose (9)
Motor Of Love (19)
Move Over Busker (17)
Movie Magg (29)
Mrs. Vandebilt (5)
Mull Of Kintyre (10,30)
Mumbo (3)
Must Do Something About It (7)
My Brave Face (19,20,21) *25*
My Love (4,8,10,18,26,30) *1*
Name And Address (9)
Nineteen Hundred And Eighty Five (5)
No More Lonely Nights (16,18,30) *6*
No Other Baby (29)
No Values (16)
No Words (5)
Nobody Knows (12)
Not Such A Bad Boy (16)

McCARTNEY, Paul/Wings — Cont'd

Note You Never Wrote (7)
Off The Ground (25)
Old Siam, Sir (11)
On The Way (12)
One More Kiss (4)
One Of These Days (12)
Only Love Remains (17)
Oo You (1)
Other Me (15)
Paperback Writer (26)
Party (29)
Peace (24)
Peace In The Neighbourhood (25,26)
Penny Lane (26)
Picasso's Last Words (Drink To Me) (5,8)
Pipes Of Peace (15,30)
Pound Is Sinking (14)
Power Cut (medley) (4)

Press (17) *21*
Pretty Little Head (17)
Put It There (19,20,21)
Ram On (2)
Really Love You (27)
Reception (11)
Richard Cory (8)
Robbie's Bit (Thanks Chet) (26)
Rockestra Theme (11,30)
Rough Ride (19,20)
Run Devil Run (29)
Sally (2)
San Ferry Anne (7)
San Francisco Bay Blues (22)
Say Say Say (15,18) *1*
School (24)
Sgt. Pepper's Lonely Hearts Club Band (20,21)
Shake A Hand (29)
She Said Yeah (29)

She's A Woman (22)
She's My Baby (7)
Showtime (20)
Silly Love Songs (7,8,10,16,18,30) *1*
Singalong Junk (1)
Singing The Blues (22)
Single Pigeon (4)
Smile Away (2)
So Bad (15) *23*
So Glad To See You Here (11)
Soily (8)
Some People Never Know (3)
Somebody Who Cares (14)
Somedays (27)
Song We Were Singing (27)
Souvenir (27)
Spin It On (11)
Spirits Of Ancient Egypt (6,8)
Stranglehold (17) *81*

Strings Pluck, Horns Blow, Drums Beat (28)
Subtle Colours Merged Soft Contours (28)
Summer's Day Song (12)
Summertime (23)
Sweetest Little Show (15)
Take It Away (14,30) *10*
Talk More Talk (17)
Teddy Boy (1)
Temporary Secretary (12)
That Day Is Done (19)
That Would Be Something (1,22)
That's All Right Mama (23)
Things We Said Today (20,21)
This One (19,20) *94*
3 Legs (2)
Through Our Love (15)
Time To Hide (7,8)

To You (11)
Together (20)
Tomorrow (3,30)
Too Many People (2,30)
Treat Her Gently - Lonely Old People (6)
Try Not To Cry (29)
Tug Of Peace (15)
Tug Of War (14,30) *53*
Twenty Flight Rock (20,23)
Uncle Albert/Admiral Halsey (2,10,18,30) *1*
Used To Be Bad (27)
Valentine Day (1)
Venus And Mars Rock Show (6,8,30) *12*
Wanderlust (14,16)
War (24)
Warm And Beautiful (7)
Waterfalls (12,30)

We Can Work It Out (22,26)
We Got Married (19,20,21)
We're Open Tonight (11)
Wedding (24)
What It Is (29)
What's That You're Doing? (14)
When The Night (4)
Wild Life (3)
Winedark Open Sea (25)
Wino Junko (7)
Winter Rose (medley) (11)
With A Little Luck (9,10,18,30) *1*
Work (24)
World Tonight (27) *64*
Yesterday (8,16,20)
You Gave Me The Answer (6,8)
You Want Her Too (19)
Young Boy (27)

McCLAIN, Alton, & Destiny   '79

Female R&B vocal trio: Alton McClain, Delores Warren and Robyrda Stiger. Warren died in a car crash on 2/22/85 (age 32).

| 3/31/79 | 88 | 16 | | | **Alton McClain & Destiny** | | | $12 | Polydor 6163 |

Crazy Love

God Said, "Love Ye One Another"
It Must Be Love *32*
My Empty Room

Power Of Love
Push And Pull

Sweet Temptation
Taking My Love For Granted

McCLINTON, Delbert   '81

Born on 11/4/40 in Lubbock, Texas. Played harmonica on **Bruce Channel**'s hit "Hey Baby." Leader of The Ron-Dels.

6/30/79	146	6	©	1	**Keeper Of The Flame**			$12	Capricorn 0223
11/22/80+	34	28	©	2	**The Jealous Kind**			$12	Capitol 12115
12/5/81+	181	9	©	3	**Plain' From The Heart**			$12	Capitol 12188
5/30/92	118	13	©	4	**Never Been Rocked Enough**			$10	Curb 77521
10/25/97	116	5	©	5	**One Of The Fortunate Few**			$10	Rising Tide 53042
3/24/01	103	3	©	6	**Nothing Personal**			$10	New West 6024

All Night Long (6)
All There Is Of Me (6)
Baby Ruth (2)
Baggage Claim (6)
Be Good To Yourself (3)
Best Of Me (5)
Better Off With The Blues (5)
Birmingham Tonight (6)
Blues As Blues Can Get (4)
Bright Side Of The Road (2)
Can I Change My Mind (6)
Cease And Desist (4)

Desperation (6)
Don't Leave Home Without It (6)
Everytime I Roll The Dice (4)
Fool In Love (3)
Giving It Up For Your Love (2) *8*
Going Back To Louisiana (2)
Good Man, Good Woman (4)
Gotta Get It Worked On (6)
Have A Little Faith In Me (4)
Have Mercy (1)
Heartbreak Radio (3)

I Can't Quit You (2)
I Don't Want To Hear It Anymore (1)
I Feel So Bad (3)
I Received A Letter (1)
I Used To Worry (4)
I Wanna Thank You Baby (3)
I'm Talking About You (1)
I've Got Dreams To Remember (3)
In The Midnight Hour (3)
Jealous Kind (2)

Just A Little Bit (1)
Leap Of Faith (5)
Lie No Better (5)
Lipstick Traces (On A Cigarette) (3)
Livin' It Down (6)
Mess Of Blues (1)
Miss You Fever (4)
Monkey Around (5)
My Sweet Baby (2)
Never Been Rocked Enough (4)
Nothin' Lasts Forever (6)

Old Weakness (Coming On Strong) (5)
Plain Old Makin' Love (1)
Read Me My Rights (6)
Rooster Blues (3)
Sandy Beaches (3)
Seesaw (1)
Sending Me Angels (5)
Shaky Ground (2)
Shot From The Saddle (1)
Shotgun Rider (2) *70*
Somebody To Love You (5)

Squeeze Me In (6)
Stir It Up (4)
Take Me To The River (2)
Too Much Stuff (5)
Two More Bottles Of Wine (1)
Watchin' The Rain (6)
When Rita Leaves (6)
Why Me? (4)
You Were Never Mine (5)

McCLURKIN, Donnie   '01

Born in 1961 in Los Angeles. Gospel singer.

| 9/9/00+ | 69 | 50↑● | © | | **Live In London And More...** | | | [L] $10 | Verity 43150 |

recorded at Fairfield Hall in London

Caribbean Medley
Didn't You Know

Great Is Your Mercy
I Do I Do

I'll Trust You, Lord
Just For Me

Lord I Lift Your Name On High
Psalm 27

That's What I Believe
Victory Chant (Hail Jesus)

We Fall Down
Who Would've Thought

McCOO, Marilyn, & Billy Davis, Jr.   '77

Husband-and-wife vocal duo. McCoo was born on 9/30/43 in Jersey City, New Jersey. Davis was born on 6/26/39 in St. Louis. Both were members of **The 5th Dimension**. Married in 1969. Duo hosted own summer variety TV series in 1977. McCoo co-hosted TV's *Solid Gold* from 1981-84.

9/18/76+	30	38	●	©	1	**I Hope We Get To Love In Time**			$12	ABC 952
8/20/77	57	8			2	**The Two Of Us**			$12	ABC 1026
10/7/78	146	6			3	**Marilyn & Billy**			$12	Columbia 35603

Carry Me (3)
Easy Way Out (1)
Hard Road Down (2)
I Got Love For You (3)
I Got The Words, You Got The Music (3)

I Hope We Get To Love In Time (1) *91*
I Still Will Be With You (1)
I Thank You (3)
I Thought It Took A Little Time (But Today I Fell In Love) (3)

In My Lifetime (2)
Look What You've Done To My Heart (2) *51*
My Love For You (Will Always Be The Same) (1)
My Reason To Be Is You (2)

My Very Special Darling (2)
Never Gonna Let You Go (1)
Nightsong (2)
Nothing Can Stop Me (1)
Saving All My Love For You (3)
Shine On Silver Moon (3)

So Many Things For Free (3)
Stay With Me (3)
Times, The (2)
Two Of Us (2)
We've Got To Get It On Again (1)

Wonderful (3)
You Can't Change My Heart (1)
You Don't Have To Be A Star (To Be In My Show) (1) *1*
You Got The Love (3)
Your Love (1) *15*

McCORMICK, Gayle   '71

Born in 1949 in St. Louis. Former lead singer of **Smith**.

| 10/16/71 | 198 | 3 | | | **Gayle McCormick** | | | $15 | Dunhill/ABC 50109 |

C'est La Vie
Everything Has Got To Be Free
Gonna Be Alright Now *84*

If Only You Believe
It's A Cryin' Shame *44*
Natural Woman

Rescue Me
Save Me
Superstar

You Really Got A Hold On Me *98*

McCOY, Charlie   '72

Born on 3/28/41 in Oak Hill, West Virginia. Country harmonica player.

5/6/72	98	25	©	1	**The Real McCoy**			[I] $12	Monument 31359
11/25/72	120	13		2	**Charlie McCoy**			[I] $12	Monument 31910
7/21/73	155	6		3	**Good Time Charlie**			[I] $12	Monument 32215

Danny Boy (2)
Delta Dawn (2)
Don't Touch Me (3)
Easy Lovin' (1)
First Time Ever (I Saw Your Face) (2)
Good Time Charlie's Got The Blues (3)
Grade A (2)

Hangin' On (1)
Help Me Make It Through The Night (1)
How Can I Unlove You (1)
I Can't Stop Loving You (2)
I Really Don't Want To Know (2)
I'm So Lonesome I Could Cry (2)

Is Anybody Goin' To San Antone (1)
Jackson (1)
John Henry (3)
Louisiana Man (3)
Loving Her Was Easier (Than Anything I'll Ever Do Again) (1)
Me And Bobby McGee (2)

Minor Miner (3)
Only Daddy That'll Walk The Line (1)
Orange Blossom Special (1,3)
Real McCoy (1)
Rocky Top (2)
Shenandoah (3)
Something (3)
Soul Song (3)

Take Me Home Country Roads (1)
'Till I Get It Right (3)
To Get To You (2)
Today I Started Loving You Again (1)
Woman (Sensuous Woman) (2)

DEBUT	PEAK	WKS	RIAA	CD	ARTIST — Album Title	Catalog	Sym	$	Label & Number

McCOY, Neal '97
Born Hubert Neal McGauhey on 7/30/58 in Jacksonville, Texas. Country singer.

2/26/94	84	34	▲	©	1 No Doubt About It			$10	Atlantic 82568
2/11/95	68	24	▲	©	2 You Gotta Love That!			$10	Atlantic 82727
6/22/96	61	17	●	©	3 Neal McCoy			$10	Atlantic 82907
6/28/97	55	29	●	©	4 Greatest Hits		[G]	$10	Atlantic 83011
11/15/97	135	9		©	5 Be Good At It			$10	Atlantic 83057

Back (5)
Basic Goodbye (5)
Betcha Can't Do That Again (3)
Broken Record (5)
City Put The Country Back In Me (1,4)
For A Change (2,4)
Going, Going, Gone (3)

Heaven (5)
Hillbilly Rap (3)
I Ain't Complainin' (3)
I Apologize (1)
I Know You (5)
If I Was A Drinkin' Man (2,4)
If It Hadn't Been So Good (3)
If You Can't Be Good, Be Good At It (5)

It Should've Happened That Way (3)
Love Happens Like That (5)
Me Too (3)
Mudslide (3)
No Doubt About It (1,4) 75
Now I Pray For Rain (4)
Party On (5)
Plain Jane (2)

Please Don't Leave Me Now (2)
Same Boots (5)
Shake, The (4,5)
She Can (3)
Small Up And Simple Down (1)
Something Moving In Me (1)
Spending Every Minute In Love (2)
That Woman Of Mine (3)

Then You Can Tell Me Goodbye (3,4)
They're Playin' Our Song (2,4)
Twang (2)
21 To 17 (5)
Why Not Tonight (1)
Why Now (1)
Wink (1,4) 91
Y-O-U (2)

You Gotta Love That (2,4)
You'll Always Be In My Life (5)
You're Backin' Up (2)

McCOY, Van '75
Born on 1/6/40 in Washington DC. Died of a heart attack on 7/6/79 (age 39). Disco songwriter/producer.

| 4/26/75 | 12 | 23 | | | 1 Disco Baby | | | $12 | Avco 69006 |

VAN McCOY & The Soul City Symphony

| 8/16/75 | 181 | 4 | | | 2 From Disco To Love | | [E] | $12 | Buddah 5648 |

originally released in 1972

10/18/75	80	7			3 The Disco Kid			$12	Avco 69009
5/8/76	106	17			4 The Real McCoy			$12	H&L 69012
1/8/77	193	2			5 The Hustle And Best Of Van McCoy		[G]	$12	H&L 69016

African Symphony (4)
Change With The Times (3,5) 46
Disco Baby (1,5)
Disco Kid (3,5)
Doctor's Orders (1)
Don't Hang Me Up (2)

Don't Rock The Boat (2)
Earthquake (3)
Fire (1)
Get Dancin' (3)
Good Night, Baby (3)
Hey Girl, Come And Get It (1,5)
Hustle, The (1,5) 1

I Would Love To Love You (1)
I'm Gonna Love You (3)
I'm In Love With You Baby (2)
Jet Setting (4)
Just In Case (2)
Keep On Hustlin' (3)
Let Me Down Easy (2)

Love At First Sight (4)
Love Child (3)
Love Is The Answer (5)
Night Walk (4) 96
Now That You're Gone (2)
Party (4,5) 69
Pick Up The Pieces (1)

Roll With The Punches (3)
Shakey Ground (1)
So Many Mountains (2)
Soul Cha Cha (5)
Soul Improvisations (2)
Spanish Boogie (1)
Star Trek, Theme From (4,5)

Sweet, Sweet Rhythm (4)
(To Each His Own) That's My Philosophy (4)
Turn This Mother Out (1)
Walk, The (3)
Words Spoken Softly At Midnight (3)

McCOYS, The '66
Pop-rock group from Union City, Indiana: brothers Rick (vocals, guitar) and Randy (drums) Zehringer, Randy Hobbs (bass) and Ronnie Brandon (keyboards). Rick later recorded as **Rick Derringer**. Hobbs died on 8/5/93 (age 45).

| 11/20/65+ | 44 | 19 | | | Hang On Sloopy | | | $50 | Bang 212 |

All I Really Want To Do
Fever 7
Hang On Sloopy 1

High Heel Sneakers
I Can't Explain It
I Can't Help Fallin In Love

I Don't Mind
If You Tell A Lie
Meet The McCoys

Papa's Got A Brand New Bag
Sorrow
Stormy Monday Blues

Stubborn Kind Of Fellow

McCRAE, George '74
Born on 10/19/44 in West Palm Beach, Florida. Disco singer. Married to **Gwen McCrae** from 1967-77.

| 8/3/74 | 38 | 15 | | | 1 Rock Your Baby | | | $12 | TK 501 |
| 7/5/75 | 152 | 5 | | | 2 George McCrae | | | $12 | TK 602 |

Baby Baby Sweet Baby (2)
Honey I (2) 65
I Ain't Lyin' (2)

I Can't Leave You Alone (1) 50
I Get Lifted (1) 37
I Need Somebody Like You (1)

It's Been So Long (2)
Look At You (1) 95
Make It Right (1)

Rock Your Baby (1) 1
Sing A Happy Song (2)
Take This Love Of Mine (2)

When I First Saw You (2)
You Can Have It All (1)
You Got My Heart (1)

You Got To Know (2)
You Treat Me Good (2)

McCRAE, Gwen '75
Born on 12/21/43 in Pensacola, Florida. Disco singer. Married to **George McCrae** from 1967-77.

| 6/28/75 | 121 | 10 | | © | Rockin' Chair | | | $12 | Cat 2605 |

For Your Love
He Don't Ever Lose His Groove

He Keeps Something Groovy
Goin' On

It Keeps On Raining
It's Worth The Hurt

Let Them Talk
Move Me Baby

90% Of Me Is You
Rockin' Chair 9

McCRARYS, The '78
R&B vocal group: siblings Linda, Charity, Alfred and Sam McCrary.

| 9/9/78 | 138 | 9 | | | Loving Is Living | | | $12 | Portrait 34764 |

Don't Wear Yourself Out
Givin' It Up

Here's That Feeling
Looking Ahead

Loving Is Living
Take Me To Your Leader

Thinking About You
Wonderful Feeling

You 45
You Are The Key

McCREADY, Mindy '96
Born on 11/30/75 in Fort Myers, Florida. Country singer.

5/18/96	40	58	▲	©	1 Ten Thousand Angels			$10	BNA 66806
11/22/97	83	9	●	©	2 If I Don't Stay The Night			$10	BNA 67504
10/2/99	155	1		©	3 I'm Not So Tough			$10	BNA 67765

All I Want Is Everything (3)
All That I Am (1)
Breakin' It (1)
Cross Against The Moon (2)
Dream On (3)

Fine Art Of Holding A Woman (2)
For A Good Time Call (2)
Girl's Gotta Do (What A Girl's Gotta Do) (1)
Guys Do It All The Time (1) 72

Have A Nice Day (1)
Hold Me (3)
I'm Not So Tough (3)
I've Got A Feeling (3)
If I Don't Stay The Night (2)
It Ain't A Party (1)

Long, Long Time (2)
Lucky Me (3)
Maybe He'll Notice Her Now (1)
Oh Romeo (2)
Only A Whisper (2)
Other Side Of This Kiss (2)

Over And Over (3)
Take Me Apart (3)
Tell Me Something I Don't Know (1)
Ten Thousand Angels (1)
This Is Me (2)

Thunder And Roses (3)
Tumble And Roll (3)
Two Different Things (3)
What If I Do (2)
Without Love (1)
You'll Never Know (2)

McCULLOCH, Ian '89
Born on 5/5/59 in Liverpool, England. Lead singer of **Echo & The Bunnymen**.

| 11/25/89 | 179 | 1 | | © | Candleland | | | $10 | Sire 26012 |

Candleland
Cape, The

Faith And Healing
Flickering Wall

Horse's Head
I Know You Well

In Bloom
Proud To Fall

Start Again
White Hotel

McDONALD, Audra '00
Born on 7/3/70 in Berlin, Germany; raised in Fresno, California. Classically-trained soprano singer/actress. Starred in several Broadway shows.

| 3/18/00 | 197 | 2 | | © | How Glory Goes | | | $10 | Nonesuch 79580 |

Any Place I Hang My Hat Is Home
Bill

Come Down From The Tree
How Glory Goes
I Had Myself A True Love

I Hid My Love
I Never Has Seen Snow
I Won't Mind

Lay Down Your Head
Man That Got Away
Sleepin' Bee

Somewhere
Was That You?
When Did I Fall In Love?

McDONALD, Country Joe — see COUNTRY JOE

McDONALD, Kathi '74
Born on 9/25/48 in Anacortes, Washington. Former session singer.

4/6/74	156	11			Insane Asylum			$30	Capitol 11224

All I Want To Be   Down To The Wire   Heartbreak Hotel   Insane Asylum   Somethin' Else   To Love Somebody
Bogart To Bowie   Freak Lover   If You Need Me   (Love Is Like A) Heat Wave   Threw My Love Away

McDONALD, Michael '82
Born on 2/12/52 in St. Louis. Pop-rock singer/songwriter/keyboardist. Former lead singer of **The Doobie Brothers**. Married to singer **Amy Holland**.

8/28/82	6	32	●	© 1	If That's What It Takes			$10	Warner 23703
9/7/85	45	15		© 2	No Lookin' Back			$10	Warner 25291
6/2/90	110	14		3	Take It To Heart			$10	Reprise 25979

All We Got (3)   Get The Word Started (3)   I Keep Forgettin' (Every Time You're Near) (1) 4   Lost In The Parade (3)   One Step Away (3)   That's Why (1)
Any Foolish Thing (2)   Homeboy (3)   Love Can Break Your Heart (3)   Our Love (2)   You Show Me (3)
Bad Times (2)   I Can Let Go Now (1)   (I'll Be Your) Angel (2)   Love Lies (1)   Playin' By The Rules (1)
Believe In It (1)   I Gotta Try (1) 44   If That's What It Takes (1)   No Amount Of Reason (3)   Searchin' For Understanding (3)
By Heart (2)   (I Hang) On Your Every Word (2)   Lonely Talk (3)   No Lookin' Back (2) 34   Take It To Heart (3) 98
Don't Let Me Down (2)   Losin' End (1)   No Such Luck (1)   Tear It Up (3)

McDUFF, Brother Jack '63
Born Eugene McDuffy on 9/17/26 in Champaign, Illinois. Died of a heart attack on 1/23/2001 (age 74). Jazz organist.

6/15/63	101	4		© 1	Screamin'	[I]		$40	Prestige 7259
11/9/63	81	14		© 2	Live!	[I-L]		$40	Prestige 7274
7/23/66	137	4		3	Together Again!	[I]		$25	Prestige 7364
					WILLIS JACKSON with JACK McDUFF				
12/13/69+	192	6		© 4	Down Home Style	[I]		$20	Blue Note 84322

After Hours (1)   Electric Surfboard, Theme From (4) 95   I Cover The Waterfront (1)   One O'Clock Jump (1)   Soulful Drums (1)   Vibrator, The (4)
As She Walked Away (4)   It Ain't Necessarily So (2)   Real Good'un (2)   This'll Get To Ya' (3)   Whistle While You Work (2)
Butter (For Yo Popcorn) (4)   Glad 'A See Ya' (3)   It Might As Well Be Spring (3)   Rock Candy (2)   Three Little Words (3)
Down Home Style (4)   Groovin' (4)   It's All A Joke (3)   Sanctified Samba (2)   Tu'Gether (3)
He's A Real Gone Guy (1)   Memphis In June (4)   Screamin' (1)   Undecided (2)

McENTIRE, Reba ★152★ '94
Born on 3/28/54 in Chockie, Oklahoma. Country singer/actress. Appeared in several movies and TV shows. Played "Heather Gummer" in the movie *Tremors*. Starred in own TV sitcom in 2001. Also acted in several other movies and TV shows.

1)Read My Mind 2)Greatest Hits Volume Two 3)Starting Over

6/6/87	139	23	▲³ ©	1	Reba McEntire's Greatest Hits	C:#20/25 [G]		$10	MCA 5979
10/10/87	102	20	▲ ©	2	The Last One To Know			$10	MCA 42030
12/19/87+	19ˣ	15	▲² ©	3	Merry Christmas To You	C:#15/16 [X]		$10	MCA 42031
					Christmas charts: 30/'87, 27/'92, 25/'93, 19/'94, 36/'95, 30/'96, 38/'97, 38/'99				
5/21/88	118	10	▲ ©	4	Reba	C:#50/1		$10	MCA 42134
6/3/89	78	18	▲ ©	5	Sweet Sixteen	C:#40/1		$10	MCA 6294
10/14/89	124	8	▲ ©	6	Live	[L]		$10	MCA 8034
					recorded on 4/3/89 at the McCallum Theatre in Palm Desert, California				
9/22/90+	39	89	▲³ ©	7	Rumor Has It			$10	MCA 10016
10/19/91	13	80	▲³ ©	8	For My Broken Heart			$10	MCA 10400
1/2/93	8	56	▲³ ©	9	It's Your Call			$10	MCA 10673
10/16/93	5	94	▲⁵ ©	10	Greatest Hits Volume Two	[G]		$10	MCA 10906
5/14/94	2¹	83	▲³ ©	11	Read My Mind			$10	MCA 10994
10/21/95	5	38	▲ ©	12	Starting Over			$10	MCA 11264
11/23/96	15	42	▲ ©	13	What If It's You			$10	MCA 11500
6/20/98	8	30	▲ ©	14	If You See Him			$10	MCA 70019
11/20/99	85	9	©	15	Secret Of Giving - A Christmas Collection	[X]		$10	MCA 170092
					Christmas charts: 8/'99, 32/'00				
12/11/99	28	40	▲ ©	16	So Good Together			$10	MCA 170119

All Dressed Up (With Nowhere To Go) (8)   Do Right By Me (4)   Heart Hush (14)   I'll Give You Something To Miss (14)   Lonely Alone (14)   Read My Mind (11)
All This Time (14)   Does He Love You (10)   Heart Is A Lonely Hunter (11)   I'm Not Your Girl (16)   Love Will Find Its Way To You (2,10)   Respect (4,6)
Am I The Only One Who Cares (5)   Everything That You Want (11)   Heart Won't Lie (9)   I've Still Got The Love We Made (2)   Mama Tried (6)   Ring On Her Finger, Time On Her Hands (12)
And Still (11)   Everytime You Touch Her (4)   How Blue (1)   If I Had Only Known (8)   Mary, Did You Know? (15)   Roses (16)
Angels Sang (15)   Face To Face (14)   How Was I To Know (13)   If You See Him, If You See Her (14)   Never Had A Reason To (13)   Rumor Has It (7,10)
Away In A Manger (3)   Fallin' Out Of Love (9)   I Don't Want To Be Alone (2)   Invisible (14)   New Fool At An Old Game (4,6)   San Antonio Rose (6)
Baby's Gone Blues (9)   Fancy (7,10)   I Don't Want To Mention Any Names (2)   Is There Life Out There (8,10)   New Love (5)   Santa Claus Is Coming Back To Town (15)
Back Before The War (16)   Fear Of Being Alone (13)   I Know How He Feels (4,6)   It Always Rains On Saturday (5)   Night Life (9)   Say The Word (5)
Bobby (8)   Five Hundred Miles Away From Home (12)   I Saw Mama Kissing Santa Claus (15)   It Don't Matter (13)   Night The Lights Went Out In Georgia (8)   Secret Of Giving (15)
Buying Her Roses (8)   For Herself (9)   I Wish That I Could Tell You (11)   It's Your Call (9)   Nobody Dies From A Broken Heart (16)   She Thinks His Name Was John (11)
By The Time I Get To Phoenix (12)   For My Broken Heart (8,10)   I Won't Mention It Again (12)   Jolene (6)   Now You Tell Me (7)   She Wasn't Good Enough For Him (16)
Can't Stop Now (6)   Forever Love (14)   I Won't Stand In Line (11)   Just A Little Love (1)   O Holy Night (3)   She's Callin' It Love (13)
Cathy's Clown (5,6)   Girl Who Has Everything (2)   I Wouldn't Go That Far (8)   Just Across The Rio Grande (2)   On My Own (12)   Silent Night (3)
Christmas Guest (3)   Greatest Man I Never Knew (8,10)   I Wouldn't Know (14)   Just Looking For Him (13)   On This Day (3)   Silly Me (4)
Christmas Letter (3)   Happy Birthday Jesus (I'll Open This One Just For You) (3)   I Wouldn't Wanna Be You (11)   Keep Hangin' On (12)   One Child, One Day (15)   So, So, So Long (4,6)
Christmas Song (Chestnuts Roasting On An Open Fire) (3)   He Broke Your Memory Last Night (8)   I'd Rather Ride Around With You (13)   Last One To Know (2)   One Honest Heart (14) 54   Somebody Should Leave (1)
Climb That Mountain High (7)   He Wants To Get Married (9)   I'll Be (16) 51   Let The Music Lift You Up (6)   One Last Good Hand (9)   Somebody Up There Likes Me (5,6)
Close To Crazy (13)   He's In Dallas (8)   I'll Be Home For Christmas (3)   Lighter Shade Of Blue (9)   One Promise Too Late (1,6)   Someone Else (2)
         Little Girl (5,6)   Only In My Mind (1)
         Little Rock (1,6)   Please Come To Boston (12)

DEBUG	PEAK	WKS	RIAA	CD	ARTIST — Album Title	Catalog	Sym	$	Label & Number

McENTIRE, Reba — Cont'd

Stairs, The (2)
Starting Over Again (12)
State Of Grace (13)
Straight From You (9)
Sunday Kind Of Love (4,6)
Sweet Dreams (6)
Take It Back (9)

Talking In Your Sleep (12)
That's All She Wrote (7)
They Asked About You (10)
This Christmas (15)
This Is My Prayer For You (15)
This Picture (7)
'Til I Said It To You (16)
'Til Love Comes Again (5)

'Til The Season Comes 'Round
  Again (15)
Till You Love Me (11) *78*
Up And Flying (14)
Up On The Housetop (15)
Waitin' For The Deal To Go
  Down (7)
Walk On (5,10)

We're All Alone (16)
We're So Good Together (16)
What Am I Gonna Do About
  You (1)
What Do You Say (16) *31*
What If It's You (13)
What You Gonna Do About Me
  (2)

When You're Not Trying To (16)
Where You End And I Begin
  (16)
White Christmas (3)
Whoever's In New England (1,6)
Why Haven't I Heard From You
  (11)
Will He Ever Go Away (9)

Wish I Were Only Lonely (4)
Wrong Night (14) *52*
You Lie (7,10)
You Must Really Love Me (5,6)
You Remember Me (7)
You're No Good (12)
You're The One I Dream About
  (4)

McFADDEN & WHITEHEAD '79
R&B duo from Philadelphia: Gene McFadden and John Whitehead. Wrote numerous hit songs.

| 6/2/79 | 23 | 17 | ● | © | 1 McFadden & Whitehead | | | $12 | Philadelphia Int'l. 35800 |
| 10/4/80 | 153 | 6 | | | 2 I Heard It In A Love Song | | | $12 | TSOP 36773 |

Ain't No Stoppin' Us Now
  (1) *13*
Always Room For One More (2)
Do You Want To Dance (1)
Don't Feel Bad (2)

Got To Change (1)
I Got The Love (1)
I Heard It In A Love Song (2)
I Know What I'm Gonna Do (2)
I've Been Pushed Aside (1)

Just Wanna Love You Baby (1)
Love Song Number 690 (Life's
  No Good Without You) (1)
Mr. Music (1)

That Lets Me Know I'm In Love
  (2)
This Is My Song (2)
Why Oh Why (2)

You're My Someone To Love
  (1)

McFARLAND, Gary '69
Born on 10/23/33 in Los Angeles. Died of a heart attack on 11/1/71 (age 38). Jazz vibraphonist.

| 4/19/69 | 189 | 3 | | © | America The Beautiful | [I] | | $15 | Skye 8 |

Due To A Lack Of Interest,
  Tomorrow Has Been
  Cancelled

80 Miles An Hour Through
  Beer-Can Country
If I'm Elected

Last Rites For The Promised
  Land
On This Site Shall Be Erected...

Suburbia - Two Poodles And A
  Plastic Jesus

McFERRIN, Bobby '88
Born on 3/11/50 in New York City. Unaccompanied, jazz-styled improvisation vocalist.

3/21/87	103	19		©	1 Spontaneous Inventions			$10	Blue Note 85110
4/23/88	5	55	▲	©	2 Simple Pleasures			$10	EMI-Manhattan 48059
11/24/90	146	22		©	3 Medicine Music			$10	EMI 92048
2/15/92	93	18	●	©	4 Hush			$10	Sony 48177

YO-YO MA & BOBBY McFERRIN

Air For The G String (4)
All I Want (2)
Allegro Prestissimo (4)
Andante (4)
Angry (3)
Another Night In Tunisia (1)
Ave Maria (4)
Baby (3)

Beverly Hills Blues (1)
Cara Mia (1)
Come To Me (2)
Common Threads (3)
Coyote (3)
Discipline (3)
Don't Worry Be Happy (2) *1*
Drive (2)

Drive My Car (2)
Flight Of The Bumble Bee (4)
From Me To You (1)
Garden, The (3)
Good-Bye (4)
Good Lovin' (2)
Grace (4)
He Ran All The Way (3)

Hoedown! (4)
Hush Little Baby (4)
I Hear Music (1)
Manana Iguana (1)
Medicine Man (3)
Musette (4)
Opportunity (1)
Simple Pleasures (2)

Soma So De La De Sase (3)
Stars (4)
Sunshine Of Your Love (2)
Susie Q (2)
Sweet In The Mornin' (3)
Them Changes (2)
There Ya Go (1)
Thinkin' About Your Body (1)

Train, The (3)
Turtle Shoes (1)
23rd Psalm (3)
Vocalise (4)
Walkin' (1)
Yes, You (3)

McGEE, Pat, Band '00
Born in Richmond, Virginia. Male rock singer/guitarist. His band: Al Walsh (guitar), Chardy McEwan (percussion), Jon Williams (keyboards),
John Small (bass) and Chris Williams (drums).

| 4/29/00 | 181 | 1 | | © | Shine | | | $10 | Giant 24734 |

Anybody
Drivin'
Fine

Gibby
Haven't Seen For A While
Hero

I Know
Lost
Minute

Rebecca
Runaway
Shine

What Ya Got

McGOVERN, Maureen '73
Born on 7/27/49 in Youngstown, Ohio. Pop singer. Acted in the Broadway show *Pirates Of Penzance*.

| 7/28/73 | 77 | 16 | | | 1 The Morning After | | | $15 | 20th Century 419 |
| 9/8/79 | 162 | 10 | | | 2 Maureen McGovern | | | $12 | Warner/Curb 3327 |

And This I Find Is Beautiful (2)
Can You Read My Mind (2) *52*
Can't Take My Eyes Off You (2)
Can't You Hear The Song (1)
Carolina Moon (2)

Darlene (1)
Different Worlds (2) *18*
Don't Try To Close A Rose (1)
He's A Rebel (2)

**I Won't Last A Day Without
  You** (1) *89*
I'm Happy Just To Dance With
  You (2)
If I Wrote You A Song (1)

In Too Deep (2)
It Might As Well Stay Monday
  (From Now On) (1)
Life's A Long Way To Run (2)
Midnight Storm (2)

Morning After (1) *1*
Until It's Time For You To Go
  (1)
Very Special Love (2)
Yes, I'm Ready (2)

McGRATH, Bob '70
Born on 7/11/33 in Beaumont, Texas. Joined TV's *Sesame Street* in 1969.

| 8/15/70 | 126 | 11 | | | Bob McGrath From Sesame Street | | | $15 | Affinity 1001 |

Best Friend
Good Good Morning Day
Groovin' On The Sunshine

Hold On To Your Dream
I Can Do It!!
Me

So It Doesn't Whistle
Sunshine Guitar
Why Choose To Be Afraid

Why Does It Have To Rain On
  Sunday??

★339★ McGRAW, Tim '94
Born on 5/1/67 in Delhi, Louisiana. Country singer. Son of ex-professional baseball player Tug McGraw. Married **Faith Hill** on 10/6/96.

4/9/94	❶²	115	▲⁵	©	1 Not A Moment Too Soon	C:#43/1		$10	Curb 77659
10/7/95	4	71	▲²	©	2 All I Want			$10	Curb 77800
6/21/97	2¹	104	▲⁴	©	3 Everywhere	C:#5/75		$10	Curb 77886
5/22/99	❶¹	86	▲³	©	4 A Place In The Sun			$10	Curb 77942
12/9/00	4	43↑	▲²	©	5 Greatest Hits	[G]		$10	Curb 77978
5/12/01	2¹	21↑	▲	©	6 Set This Circus Down			$10	Curb 78711

Ain't That Just Like A Dream (1)
Ain't That The Way It Always
  Ends (3)
All I Want Is A Life (2)
Angel Boy (6)
Angry All The Time (6)
Can't Be Really Gone (2) *87*
Carry On (4)
Cowboy In Me (6)
Don't Mention Memphis (2)
Don't Take The Girl (1,5) *17*
Down On The Farm (1,5)
Everywhere (3)

Eyes Of A Woman (4)
For A Little While (3,5) *37*
Forget About Us (6)
40 Days And 40 Nights (3)
Give It To Me Strait (4)
Great Divide (2)
Grown Men Don't Cry (6) *25*
Hard On The Ticker (3)
I Didn't Ask And She Didn't Say
  (2)
I Do But I Don't (3)
I Like It, I Love It (2,5) *25*
Indian Outlaw (1,5) *15*

It Doesn't Get Any Countrier
  Than This (1)
It's Your Love (3,5) *7*
Just To See You Smile (3,5)
Let Love You (6)
Let's Make Love (5) *54*
Maybe We Should Just Sleep
  On It (2,5)
My Best Friend (4,5) *29*
My Next Thirty Years (4,5) *27*
Not A Moment Too Soon (1)
One Of These Days (3) *74*
Place In The Sun (4)

Please Remember Me (4,5) *10*
Refried Dreams (1)
Renegade (2)
Señorita Margarita (4)
Set This Circus Down (6)
Seventeen (4)
She Never Lets It Go To Her
  Heart (2,5)
She'll Have You Back (4)
Smilin' (6)
Some Things Never Change
  (4) *58*
**Where The Green Grass
  Grows** (3,5) *79*

Somebody Must Be Prayin' For
  Me (4)
Something Like That (4,5) *28*
Take Me Away From Here (6)
Telluride (6)
That's Just Me (2)
Things Change (6)
Trouble With Never (4)
Unbroken (2)
When She Wakes Up (And
  Finds Me Gone) (2)

Why We Said Goodbye (6)
Wouldn't Want It Any Other
  Way (1)
You Don't Love Me Anymore (4)
You Get Used To Somebody
  (6)
You Got The Wrong Man (2)
You Just Get Better All The
  Time (3)
You Turn Me On (3)

McGRIFF, Jimmy '63
Born on 4/3/36 in Philadelphia. Jazz organist.

12/1/62+	22	27	©	1 I've Got A Woman	[I]	$40	Sue 1012
11/21/64	146	2	©	2 Topkapi	[I]	$40	Sue 1033
12/5/64	15ˣ	4	©	3 Christmas With McGriff	[X-I]	$40	Sue 1018
5/29/65	130	6	©	4 Blues For Mister Jimmy	[I]	$40	Sue 1039
12/28/68+	161	19		5 The Worm	[I]	$30	Solid State 18045

After Hours (1)   Discotheque U.S.A. (4)   I've Got A Woman Part I (1) 20   Party's Over (4)   Sermon (1)   Woman Of Straw (2)
All About My Girl (1) 50   Dog (You Dog) (4)   Jingle Bells (3)   People (2)   Sho' Nuff (4)   World Of Suzie Wong, Love
Blue Juice (5)   Exodus Song (2)   Keep Loose (5)   Pink Panther (2)   Take The "A" Train (3)   Theme From The (2)
Blue Star (2)   Flying Home (1)   Lock It Up (5)   Rawhide (4)   Taste Of Honey (2)   Worm, The (5) 97
Blues For Joe (4)   From Russia With Love (2)   M.G. Blues (1) 95   'Round Midnight (1)   That's The Way I Feel (1)
Blues For Mr. Jimmy (4)   Girl Talk (5)   Man With The Golden Arm,   Rudolph The Red Nosed   Think (5)
Bump De Bump (4)   Heavyweight (5)   Theme From The (2)   Reindeer (3)   Topkapi (2)
Cash Box (4)   Hip Santa (3)   Mr. Lucky (4)   Santa Claus Is Coming To   Turn Blue (4)
Christmas With McGriff (3)   I Saw Mommy Kissing Santa   On The Street Where You Live   Town (3)   White Christmas (3)
   Claus (3)   (1)   Satin Doll (1)   Winter Wonderland (3)

McGRUFF '98
Born in New York City. Male rapper.

| 7/4/98 | 169 | 1 | © | Destined To Be | | $10 | Uptown 53126 |

Before We Start   Exquisite   Harlem Kidz Get Biz   Stop It   What Part Of The Game
Dangerzone   Freestyle   Many Know   This Is How We Do   What You Want
Destined To Be   Gruff Express   Reppin' Uptown   What Cha Doin' To Me   Who Holds His Own

McGUFFEY LANE '82
Country-rock group from Columbus, Ohio: Bob McNelley (vocals), Terry Efaw and John Schwab (guitars), Stephen Douglass (keyboards), Stephen Reis (bass) and Dave Rangeler (drums). Group name taken from a street in Athens, Ohio. Douglass died in a car crash on 1/12/84 (age 33). McNelley died from a self-inflicted gunshot wound on 1/7/87 (age 36).

| 1/23/82 | 193 | 6 | | Aqua Dream | | $12 | Atco 144 |

Bag Of Rags Medley   Dream About You   It Comes From The Heart   Start It All Over 97
Don't You Think About Me   Fair Weather Friends   New Beginning   Tennessee
(When I'm Gone)   Fallin' Timber   Outlaw Rider

McGUINN, Mark '01
Born in 1969 in Greensboro, North Carolina. Country singer/songwriter/guitarist.

| 5/26/01 | 117 | 4 | © | Mark McGuinn | | $10 | VFR 734757 |

All About The Ride   Done It Right   If The World Was Mine   Mrs. Steven Rudy 44   One Of Their Own   Silver Platter
Busy Signal   Heaven Must Be Missin' You   Love Don't Float   No Way   She Doesn't Dance   That's A Plan

McGUINN, Roger '91
Born James McGuinn on 7/13/42 in Chicago. Lead singer/guitarist of The Byrds. Changed name to Roger in 1968. With Bobby Darin's band and The Chad Mitchell Trio, prior to forming The Byrds.

7/14/73	137	9	©	1 Roger McGuinn	[I]	$12	Columbia 31946
9/28/74	92	6		2 Peace On You		$12	Columbia 32956
7/5/75	165	5		3 Roger McGuinn & Band		$12	Columbia 33541
1/26/91	44	17	©	4 Back From Rio		$10	Arista 8648

Bag Full Of Money (1)   Draggin' (1)   If We Never Meet Again (4)   M' Linda (1)   So Long (1)   Together (2)
Better Change (2)   Easy Does It (3)   King Of The Hill (4)   My New Woman (1)   Somebody Loves You (3)   Trees Are All Gone (4)
Born To Rock And Roll (3)   Gate Of Horn (2)   Knockin' On Heaven's Door (3)   Painted Lady (3)   Someone To Love (4)   Water Is Wide (1)
Bull Dog (3)   Going To The Country (2)   Lady, The (2)   Peace On You (2)   Stone (1)   Without You (2)
Car Phone (4)   Hanoi Hannah (1)   Lisa (3)   (Please Not) One More Time   Suddenly Blue (4)   Without Your Love (4)
Circle Song (3)   Heave Away (1)   Lost My Drivin' Wheel (1)   (2)   Time Cube (1)   You Bowed Down (4)
Do What You Want To (2)   I'm So Restless (1)   Lover Of The Bayou (3)   Same Old Sound (2)   Time Has Come (4)   Your Love Is A Gold Mine (4)

McGUINN, CLARK & HILLMAN '79
Pop-rock trio: Roger McGuinn, Gene Clark and Chris Hillman. All were founding members of The Byrds. Clark died on 5/24/91 (age 46).

| 2/24/79 | 39 | 19 | © | 1 McGuinn, Clark & Hillman | | $12 | Capitol 11910 |
| 2/16/80 | 136 | 7 | | 2 City | | $12 | Capitol 12043 |

ROGER McGUINN AND CHRIS HILLMAN FEATURING GENE CLARK

Backstage Pass (1)   Don't You Write Her Off (1) 33   Little Mama (1)   Release Me Girl (1)   Street Talk (1)
Bye Bye, Baby (1)   Feelin' Higher (1)   Long Long Time (1)   Sad Boy (1)   Surrender To Me (1)
City (2)   Givin' Herself Away (2)   One More Chance (2)   Skate Date (2)   Who Taught The Night (2)
Deeper In (2)   Let Me Down Easy (2)   Painted Fire (2)   Stopping Traffic (1)   Won't Let You Down (2)

McGUINNESS FLINT '71
Rock group formed in England: Tom McGuinness (guitar; Manfred Mann), Hughie Flint (drums), Dennis Coulson (vocals), Graham Lyle (guitar) and Benny Gallagher (bass).

| 1/30/71 | 155 | 8 | | 1 McGuinness Flint | | $15 | Capitol 625 |
| 9/11/71 | 198 | 2 | | 2 Happy Birthday, Ruthy Baby | | $15 | Capitol 794 |

Bodang Buck (1)   Dream Darling Dream (1)   Happy Birthday, Ruthy Baby (2)   Jimmy's Song (2)   Mister, Mister (1)   When I'm Alone With You (2)
Brother Pysche (1)   Faith And Gravy (2)   Heritage (1)   Klondike (2)   Piper Of Dreams (2)   When I'm Dead And Gone
Changes (2)   Fixer (2)   I'm Letting You Know (1)   Lazy Afternoon (1)   Reader To Writer (2)   (1) 47
Conversation (2)   Friends Of Mine (2)   International (1)   Let It Ride (1)   Sparrow (2)   Who You Got To Love (1)

McGUIRE, Barry '65
Born on 10/15/37 in Oklahoma City. Folk-rock singer. Member of The New Christy Minstrels from 1962-65.

| 9/25/65 | 37 | 21 | | Eve Of Destruction | | $40 | Dunhill 50003 |

Ain't No Way I'm Gonna   Eve Of Destruction 1   She Belongs To Me   Try To Remember   Why Not Stop And Dig It While   You Were On My Mind
   Change My Mind   Mr. Man On The Street - Act   Sins Of A Family   What Exactly's The Matter With   You Can
Baby Blue   One   Sloop John B.   Me   You Never Had It So Good

DEBUT	PEAK	WKS	RIAA	CD	ARTIST — Album Title	Catalog	Sym	$	Label & Number

McGUIRE SISTERS, The '55
Vocal trio from Middletown, Ohio: sisters Phyllis (born on 2/14/31), Christine (born on 7/30/29) and Dorothy (born on 2/13/30) McGuire.

| 2/5/55 | 2² | 16 | | | **By Request...** | | [M] | $50 | Coral 56123 |

EP: Coral EC-81098 (#2); LP: Coral CRL-56123 (#11)

Goodnight, Sweetheart, Goodnight · Melody Of Love · Muskrat Ramble · Naughty Lady Of Shady Lane · **No More 17** · Open Up Your Heart (And Let The Sunshine In) · Seems Like Old Times · **Sincerely 1**

McINTYRE, Joey '99
Born on 12/3/72 in Needham, Massachusetts. Former member of **New Kids On The Block**.

| 4/3/99 | 49 | 18 | ● | © | **Stay The Same**............ | | | $10 | Columbia 69856 |

All I Wanna Do · Because Of You · Couldn't Stay Away From Your Love · Give It Up · I Can't Do It Without You · I Cried · **I Love You Came Too Late 54** · Let Me Take You For A Ride · One Night · **Stay The Same 10** · Way That I Loved You · We Can Get Down · Without Your Love

McKAGAN, Duff '93
Born Michael McKagan on 2/5/64 in Seattle. Bassist of **Guns N' Roses**.

| 10/16/93 | 137 | 2 | | © | **Believe In Me**............ | | | $10 | Geffen 24605 |

Believe In Me · Could It Be U · Fuck You · (Fucked Up) Beyond Belief · I Love You · Just Not There · Lonely Tonite · Majority, The · Man In The Meadow · Punk Rock Song · Swamp Song · 10 Years · Trouble

McKEE, Maria '89
Born on 8/17/64 in Los Angeles. Former lead singer of **Lone Justice**.

| 7/1/89 | 120 | 15 | | | **Maria McKee**............ | | | $10 | Geffen 24229 |

Am I The Only One (Who's Ever Felt This Way?) · Breathe · Can't Pull The Wool Down (Over The Little Lamb's Eyes) · Has He Got A Friend For Me? · I've Forgotten What It Was In You (That Put The Need In Me) · More Than A Heart Can Hold · Nobody's Child · Panic Beach · This Property Is Condemned · To Miss Someone

McKENDREE SPRING '75
Folk-pop group: Fran McKendree (vocals, guitar), Martin Slutsky (guitar), Michael Dreyfuss (violin) and Larry Tucker (bass). By 1974, Tucker had been replaced by Christopher Bishop and drummer Carson Michaels had joined.

11/28/70	192	2			1 **Second Thoughts**............			$15	Decca 75230
5/20/72	163	7			2 **McKendree Spring 3**............			$15	Decca 75332
5/3/75	118	8			3 **Get Me To The Country**............			$12	Pye 12108
3/27/76	193	3			4 **Too Young To Feel This Old**............			$12	Pye 12124

Because It's Time (1) · Cairo Hotel (1) · Clown (4) · Divide & Concord (4) · Down By The River (2) · Easier Things Have Been Done (3) · Fading Lady (2) · Feeling Bad Ain't Good Enough (2) · Fire And Rain (1) · Flying Dutchman (2) · For What Was Gained (1) · Friends Die Easy (1) · Get Me To The Country (3) · Give All You've Got To Give (3) · Give It Some Time (3) · God Bless The Conspiracy (4) · Got No Place To Fall (1) · Heart Is Like A Wheel (4) · Hobo Lady (2) · Hold On (3) · Hustler, The (3) · I'm Gonna Lose That Game Again (1) · I'm In Love (4) · I've Been On The Mountain (3) · 'Lani (1) · Meeting In Paris (3) · My Kind Of Life (4) · Oh In The Morning (4) · Oh Now My Friend (1) · Oh, What A Feeling (4) · Run Like The Wind (4) · She'd Never Leave Chicago (3) · (She's A Housewife) No More Rock 'N' Roll (4) · So Long Daddy-O (3) · Susie, Susie (1) · Take It From The Heart (4) · Too Young To Feel This Old (4)

McKENNITT, Loreena '98
Born in 1957 in Morden, Manitoba, Canada. Female singer/harpist.

| 4/9/94 | 143 | 11 | ● | © | 1 **The Mask And Mirror**............ | | | $10 | Warner 45420 |
| 10/18/97+ | 17 | 61 | ▲ | © | 2 **The Book Of Secrets**............ | | | $10 | Warner 46719 |

Bonny Swans (1) · Ce He Mise Le Ulaingt? The Two Trees (1) · Dante's Prayer (2) · Dark Night Of The Soul (1) · Full Circle (1) · Highwayman, The (2) · La Serenissima (2) · Marco Polo (2) · Marrakesh Night Market (1) · **Mummers' Dance (2) 18** · Mystic's Dream (1) · Night Ride Across The Caucasus (2) · Prospero's Speech (1) · Santiago (1) · Skellig (2)

McKENZIE, Bob & Doug '82
Canadian comedians Rick Moranis ("Bob") and Dave Thomas ("Doug") of *SCTV*. Both featured in the movie *Strange Brew*. Moranis later starred in *Ghostbusters*, *Spaceballs*, *Honey, I Shrunk The Kids* and many others. Thomas, the brother of singer Ian Thomas, hosted own CBS-TV series in 1990 and was a cast member of TV's *Grace Under Fire*.

| 1/9/82 | 8 | 21 | ● | © | **Great White North** | | [C] | $12 | Mercury 4034 |

Beerhunter, The · Black Holes · Coffee Sandwich · Doug's Mouth · Elron McKenzie · Ernie's Mom · Gimme A Smoke · Miracle Of Music · O.K., This Is The End, Eh? · Peter's Donuts · Ralph The Dog · School Announcements · **Take Off 16** · This Is Our Album, Eh? · Twelve Days Of Christmas · Welcome To Side Two · You Are Our Guest (See Page 11 Of Daily Hoser)

McKENZIE, Scott '68
Born Philip Blondheim on 1/10/39 in Jacksonville, Florida; raised in Virginia. Folk singer.

| 12/9/67+ | 127 | 7 | | | **The Voice Of Scott McKenzie**............ | | | $30 | Ode 44002 |

Celeste · Don't Make Promises · It's Not Time Now · **Like An Old Time Movie 24** · No, No, No, No, No · Reason To Believe · Rooms · **San Francisco (Be Sure To Wear Flowers In Your Hair) 4** · Twelve-Thirty · What's The Difference (Chapter I & II)

McKNIGHT, Brian '99
Born on 6/5/69 in Buffalo, New York. R&B singer/songwriter. His older brother is Claude McKnight of **Take 6**.

9/12/92+	58	37	▲	©	1 **Brian McKnight**............			$10	Mercury 848605
8/26/95	22	27	●	©	2 **I Remember You**............			$10	Mercury 528280
10/11/97+	13	62	▲²	©	3 **Anytime**............			$10	Mercury 536215
12/12/98+	95	6		©	4 **Bethlehem**............		C:#15/1	[X]	$10	Motown 530944

Christmas charts: 8/'98, 32/'99

| 10/9/99 | 7 | 52 | ▲² | © | 5 **Back At One** | | | $10 | Motown 153708 |

After The Love (1) · Anytime (3) · Anyway (2) · **Back At One (5) 2** · Bethlehem Tonight (4) · Can You Read My Mind (5) · Cherish (5) · Christmas Eve With You (4) · Christmas Time Is Here (4) · Could (3) · Crazy Love (2) · Day The Earth Stood Still (2) · Don't Let Me Go (4) · Every Beat Of My Heart (2) · Everytime We Say Goodbye (3) · First Noel (4) · Goodbye My Love (1) · Hail Mary (4) · Have Yourself A Merry Little Christmas (4) · **Hold Me (3) 35** · Home (5) · Home For The Holidays (4) · I Belong To You (3) · I Can't Go For That (1) · I Couldn't Say (1) · I Remember You (2) · Is The Feeling Gone (1) · It's All About Love (1) · Jam Knock (3) · Kiss Your Love Goodbye (2) · Last Dance (5) · Let It Snow (4) · Lonely (5) · Love Me, Hold Me (1) · Marilie (2) · Must Be Love (2) · My Prayer (1) · Never Felt This Way (1) · Niko's Lullaby (2) · Oh Lord (1) · **On The Down Low (2) 73** · On The Floor (2) · **One Last Cry (1) 13** · Only One For Me (3) · Played Yourself (5) · Shall We Begin (5) · Show Me The Way Back To Your Heart (3) · Silent Night (4) · 6, 8, 12 (5) · Stay (5) · **Stay Or Let It Go (5) 76** · Stay The Night (1) · Still In Love (2) · Til I Get Over You (4) · Up Around My Way (2) · Way Love Goes (1) · When The Chariot Comes (3) · You (2) · You Could Be The One (5) · You Got The Bomb (3) · **You Should Be Mine (Don't Waste Your Time) (3) 17** · Your Love Is Ooh (2) · Yours (1)

McKUEN, Rod   '69

Born on 4/29/33 in Oakland. Poet/singer/songwriter/producer/actor. Also see **San Sebastian Strings** and **Glenn Yarbrough**.

DEBUT	PEAK	WKS		CD	#	Title		$	Label & Number
1/27/68	178	6		©	1	Listen To The Warm		$20	RCA Victor 3863
11/16/68	175	5		©	2	Lonesome Cities		$20	Warner 1758
3/1/69	149	10			3	Greatest Hits Of Rod McKuen	[K]	$20	Warner 1772
8/16/69	175	4			4	The Best Of Rod McKuen	[K]	$20	RCA Victor 4127
10/11/69	96	16		©	5	Rod McKuen At Carnegie Hall	[L]	$25	Warner 1794 [2]
						recorded on 4/29/69			
3/14/70	126	13			6	New Ballads		$15	Warner 1837
9/19/70	148	8			7	Rod McKuen's Greatest Hits-2	[K]	$15	Warner 2560
3/20/71	182	4			8	Pastorale		$20	Warner 1894 [2]
11/6/71	177	3			9	Rod McKuen Grand Tour	[L]	$20	Warner 1947 [2]

Ain't You Glad You're Livin', Joe (4)
All I Need (6)
Ally, Ally Oxen Free (3,5)
Along The Coasts Of France - Cannes (2)
Amsterdam (5)
And To Each Season (9)
And Tonight (6)
April People (9)
Art Of Catching Trains (2,5)
As I Love My Own (6,7)
Atlantic Crossing (2)
Beautiful Strangers (7,9)
Before I Loved No One (6)
Before The Monkeys Came (8,9)
Bend Down And Touch Me (5)
Blessings In Shades Of Green (3)
Boat Ride - Los Angeles (2)
Boy Named Charlie Brown (7)
Brown October (1)
Cat Named Sloopy (1,5)
Celebrations - Gstaad (2)
Champion Charlie Brown (5)
Channing Way (4)
Children One And All (9)
Church Windows - San Francisco (2)
Concerto For Four Hands - Gstaad (2)
Cowboys - Cheyenne (2,9)
Dandelion Days (1)
Do It Yourself Protest Songs & Don't Ban The Bomb (5)
Do You Like The Rain? (4)
Doesn't Anybody Know My Name (3)
Ducks On The Millpond (1)
Each Of Us Alone (9)
Earth, Song From The (9)
El Monte (medley) (9)
Ever Constant Sea (7)
Everybody's Rich But Us (5)
Fields Of Wonder (8)
Find Another Rainbow (8)
First Encounter (medley) (9)
Fly Me To The North (8)
Friendly Sounds (9)
Gee, It's Nice To Be Alone (5)
Gifts From The Sea (4)
Gone With The Cowboys (6,9)
Green Hills Of England (8)
Happy Birthday (medley) (5)
He Ain't Heavy, He's My Brother (8)
Hit 'Em In The Head With Love (6,9)
I Live Alone (1,4)
I Looked At You A Long Time (6)
I Think Of You (8,9)
I'll Catch The Sun (3,5)
I'll Fly Northward (medley) (8)
I'll Never Be Alone (1)
I'm Not Afraid (6)
I've Been To Town (5)
I've Saved The Summer (8)
If You Go Away (3,5,9)
Importance Of The Rose (4,5)
In Someone's Shadow (6)
Inside Of Me (7)
It's Raining (1)
Ivy That Clings To The Wall (3,5)
Jean (5,7)
Jef (medley) (9)
Joanna (5,7)
Kaleidoscope (3,5)
Kelly And Me (medley) (9)
Kill The Wind (8)
Language Of Hello - Paris (2)
Listen To The Warm (1,4,5,7)
Lonesome Cities (2,3)
Long, Long Time (9)
Love, Let Me Not Hunger (8)
Love's Been Good To Me (5,7)
Lovers, The (3)
Make It With You (8)
Man Alone (7)
Manhattan Beach (2)
Marvelous Clouds (3)
Merci Beaucoup (5)
Midnight Walk (1)
Mister Kelly (7,9)
Morning - San Francisco (2)
Moving Day (8)
Natalie (7)
Not So Greatest Hits Medley (9)
Nothin's Going To Change My World (Across The Universe) (8)
Of Monarchs And Pretenders (9)
One By One (3)
One Day I'll Follow The Birds (1)
One Day Soon (9)
Pastorale: Part 1 (8)
Pastures Green (medley) (8,9)
Pavements Gray (medley) (8)
People On Their Birthdays (5)
Philadelphia (6)
Railroad Song (8)
Rock Gently (6)
Round, Round, Round (1,9)
Royal Albert Hall Overture Medley (9)
Scandalous John, Themes From (9)
Seasons In The Sun (3,5)
She (7)
Silver Apples Of The Moon (3)
Singing Of The Wind (1)
Single Man (4,8)
So Long San Francisco (2)
So Long, Stay Well (5)
So Many Others (9)
Soldiers Who Want To Be Heroes (9)
Some (8)
Some Of Them Fall (medley) (9)
Some Trust In Chariots (4,7)
Something (8)
Stanyan Street (3,5)
Summer Come Down Easy (9)
Summer In My Eye (9)
Sun Is A Moveable Target - Venice (2)
Thank You For Christmas (6)
Things Men Do (5)
Three (8)
Three Poems From Sea Cycle (Numbers 1, 4, And 14) (9)
To Share The Summer Sun (1)
To Watch The Trains (2,5)
Tomorrow And Today (6)
Trashy (5)
Up (9)
Vienna (medley) (9)
Waiting For What? - London (2)
We (5)
Weekend (1)
When Am I Ever Going Home? (8)
Where Are We Now? (1)
While More With You (6)
Wind Of Change (8)
Without A Worry In The World (9)
World I Used To Know (3,5)
Yet Another Sunset (8)
Zangra (medley) (9)

McLACHLAN, Sarah   '97

Born on 1/28/68 in Halifax, Nova Scotia, Canada. Singer/songwriter/guitarist.

DEBUT	PEAK	WKS	RIAA	CD	#	Title	Catalog	$	Label & Number
4/29/89	132	12	●	©	1	Touch	C:#50/1	$10	Arista 8594
4/25/92	167	4	●	©	2	Solace		$10	Arista 18631
3/5/94	50	100	▲³	©	3	Fumbling Towards Ecstasy	C:#2¹/138	$10	Arista 18725
4/15/95	78	5	●	©	4	The Freedom Sessions	[M]	$10	Nettwerk 18784
8/2/97	2¹	108	▲⁶	©	5	Surfacing	C:#2¹/43	$10	Arista 18970
7/3/99	3	68	▲³	©	6	Mirrorball	[L]	$10	Arista 19049

Adia (5,6) **4**
Angel (5,6) **4**
Back Door Man (2)
Ben's Song (1)
Black (2)
Black & White (5)
Building A Mystery (5,6) **13**
Circle (3)
Do What You Have To Do (5,6)
Drawn To The Rhythm (2)
Elsewhere (3,4)
Fear (3,6)
Full Of Grace (5)
Fumbling Towards Ecstasy (3,6)
Good Enough (3,4,6) **77**
Hold On (3,4,6)
Home (2)
I Love You (5,6)
I Will Not Forget You (2)
I Will Remember You (6) **14**
Ice (3,4)
Ice Cream (3,4,6)
Into The Fire (2)
Last Dance (5)
Lost (2)
Mary (3,4)
Mercy (2)
Ol'55 (4)
Out Of The Shadows (1)
Path Of Thorns (2)
Path Of Thorns (Terms) (6)
Plenty (3,4)
Possession (3,6) **73**
Sad Clown (1)
Shelter (2)
Steaming (1)
Strange World (1)
Sweet Surrender (5,6) **28**
Touch (1)
Trust (1)
Uphill Battle (1)
Vox (1)
Wait (3)
Wear Your Love Like Heaven (2)
Witness (5)

McLAGAN, Ian   '80

Born on 5/12/45 in London. Keyboardist of **Small Faces** and **Faces**.

DEBUT	PEAK	WKS			#	Title		$	Label & Number
1/19/80	125	9				Troublemaker		$12	Mercury 3786

Headlines
Hold On
If It's Alright
La De La
Little Troublemaker
Movin' Out
Mystifies Me
Sign
Somebody
Truly

McLAREN, Malcolm   '84

Born on 1/22/46 in London. British entrepeneur. Former manager of the **New York Dolls** and the **Sex Pistols**.

DEBUT	PEAK	WKS		CD	#	Title		$	Label & Number
2/18/84	173	6			1	D'ya Like Scratchin'	[M]	$10	Island 90124
2/2/85	190	6		©	2	Fans		$10	Island 90242

Boys' Chorus (2)
Buffalo Gals (1)
Carmen (2)
D'ya Like Scratchin' (1)
Death Of Butterfly (2)
Fans (2)
Hobo (1)
Lauretta (2)
Madam Butterfly (2)
She's Looking Like A Hobo (1)
World's Famous (1)

★373★   McLAUGHLIN, John   '73

Born on 1/4/42 in Yorkshire, England. Jazz-fusion guitarist. Formed his Mahavishnu Orchestra in 1971 with **Billy Cobham**, **Jan Hammer**, Rick Laird, and **Jerry Goodman**. Original group disbanded in 1973.

1)Love Devotion Surrender 2)Birds Of Fire 3)Between Nothingness & Eternity

DEBUT	PEAK	WKS		CD	#	Title		$	Label & Number
1/29/72	89	26		©	1	The Inner Mounting Flame	[I]	$15	Columbia 31067
						MAHAVISHNU ORCHESTRA WITH JOHN McLAUGHLIN			
7/1/72	194	4		©	2	My Goal's Beyond	[I]	$15	Douglas 30766
						MAHAVISHNU JOHN McLAUGHLIN			
10/21/72	152	6		©	3	Extrapolation	[E-I]	$15	Polydor 5510
						recorded in 1969			
2/10/73	15	37	●	©	4	Birds Of Fire	[I]	$15	Columbia 31996
						MAHAVISHNU ORCHESTRA			
7/7/73	14	24	●	©	5	Love Devotion Surrender	[I]	$15	Columbia 32034
						CARLOS SANTANA/MAHAVISHNU JOHN McLAUGHLIN			
12/22/73+	41	14		©	6	Between Nothingness & Eternity	[I-L]	$12	Columbia 32766
						recorded August 1973 in Central Park			

DEBUT	PEAK	WKS	RIAA	CD	ARTIST — Album Title	Catalog	Sym	$	Label & Number

McLAUGHLIN, John — Cont'd

6/1/74	43	14	©	7	**Apocalypse**	[I]		$12	Columbia 32957
					with the **London Symphony Orchestra** conducted by Michael Tilson Thomas				
3/22/75	68	11	©	8	**Visions Of The Emerald Beyond**	[I]		$12	Columbia 33411
					MAHAVISHNU ORCHESTRA (above 3)				
2/21/76	118	7	©	9	**Inner Worlds**			$12	Columbia 33908
					MAHAVISHNU ORCHESTRA JOHN McLAUGHLIN				
6/12/76	194	2		10	**Shakti with John McLaughlin**	[I]		$12	Columbia 34162
4/2/77	168	4		11	**A Handful Of Beauty**	[I]		$12	Columbia 34372
					SHAKTI WITH JOHN McLAUGHLIN (above 2)				
5/27/78	105	14	©	12	**Electric Guitarist**	[I]		$12	Columbia 35326
					JOHNNY McLAUGHLIN				
4/28/79	147	5	©	13	**Electric Dreams**	[I]		$12	Columbia 35785
					JOHN McLAUGHLIN WITH THE ONE TRUTH BAND				
5/30/81	97	13	©	14	**Friday Night In San Francisco**	[I-L]		$12	Columbia 37152
					JOHN McLAUGHLIN/AL DI MEOLA/PACO DE LUCIA				
					recorded on 12/5/80 at the Warfield Theatre				
12/12/81	172	4		15	**Belo Horizonte**	[I]		$12	Warner 3619
8/20/83	171	5	©	16	**Passion, Grace & Fire**	[I]		$12	Columbia 38645
					JOHN McLAUGHLIN/AL DI MEOLA/PACO DE LUCIA				

All Bliss-All Bliss (medley) (10)
All In The Family (9)
Are You The One? Are You The One? (12)
Argen's Bag (3)
Aspan (16)
Awakening (1)
Be Happy (8)
Belo Horizonte (15)
Binky's Beam (3)
Birds Of Fire (4)
Blue In Green (2)
Can't Stand Your Funk (8)
Celestial Terrestrial Commuters (4)
Chiquito (16)
Cosmic Strut (8)
Dance Of Maya (1)
Dark Prince (13)
David (16)
Dawn (1)
Desire And The Comforter (13)

Do You Hear The Voices That You Left Behind? (12)
Dream (6)
Earth Ship (8)
Electric Dreams, Electric Sighs (13)
Eternity's Breath Part 1 & 2 (8)
Every Tear From Every Eye (12)
Extrapolation (3)
Faith (8)
Fantasia Suite (14)
Follow Your Heart (2)
Frevo Rasgado (14)
Friendship (12)
Gita (9)
Goodbye Pork-Pie Hat (2)
Guardian Angels (13,14)
Hearts And Flowers (2)
Hope (4)
Hymn To Him (7)
I Am Dancing At The Feet Of The Lord (medley) (10)

If I Could See (8)
In My Life (9)
India (11)
Inner Worlds Part 1 & 2 (9)
Isis (11)
It's Funny (3)
Joy (10)
Kriti (11)
La Baleine (15)
La Danse Du Bonheur (11)
La Mere De La Mer (medley) (6)
Lady L (11)
Let Us Go Into The House Of The Lord (medley)
Life Divine (1)
Lila's Dance (8)
Lotus Feet (9,10)
Lotus On Irish Streams (1)
Love And Understanding (13)
Love Supreme (1)
Manitas D'oro (For Paco De Lucia) (15)

Meditation (5)
Miami (14)
Mediterranean Sundance (medley) (14)
Meeting Of The Spirits (1)
Miles Beyond (Miles Davis) (4,13)
Miles Out (9)
Morning Calls (9)
My Foolish Heart (12)
Naima (5)
New York On My Mind (12)
Noonward Race (1)
On The Way Home To Earth (9)
One Melody (15)
One Word (4)
Open Country Joy (4)
Opus 1 (8)
Orient Blue Suite (Part I, II, III) (16)
Passion, Grace & Fire (16)
Pastoral (8)
Peace One (2)
Peace Two (2)

Peace Piece (3)
Pegasus (8)
Pete The Poet (3)
Phenomenon: Compulsion (12)
Phillip Lane (2)
Planetary Citizen (9)
Power Of Love (7)
Really You Know (3)
Resolution (4)
Rio Ancho (medley) (14)
River Of My Heart (9)
Sanctuary (4)
Sapphire Bullets Of Pure Love (4)
Short Tales Of The Black Forest (14)
Sichia (16)
Singing Earth (13)
Sister Andrea (4)
Smile Of The Beyond (7)
Something Spiritual (2)
Song For My Mother (2)
Spectrum (3)

Stardust On Your Sleeve (15)
Sunlit Path (medley) (6)
This Is For Us To Share (3)
Thousand Island Park (4)
Tomorrow's Story Not The Same (medley) (6)
Two For Two (3)
Two Sisters (11)
Unknown Dissident (13)
Very Early (Homage To Bill Evans) (15)
Vision Is A Naked Sword (7)
Vital Transformation (1)
Waltz For Bill Evans (2)
Waltz For Katia (15)
Way Of The Pilgrim (9)
What Need Have I For This-What Need Have I For That (medley) (10)
Wings Of Karma (7)
You Know You Know (1)
Zamfir (15)

McLAUGHLIN, Pat   **'88**
Born in Waterloo, Iowa. Male singer/songwriter/mandolin player.

4/16/88	195	1	©		**Pat McLaughlin**			$10	Capitol 48033

Heartbeat From Havin' Fun
In The Mood

Is That My Heart Breakin'
Lynda

Moment Of Weakness
No Problem

Prisoner Of Your Love
Real Thing

Without A Melody
Wrong Number

You Done Me Wrong

McLEAN, Don   **'72**
Born on 10/2/45 in New Rochelle, New York. Singer/songwriter/guitarist.

11/13/71+	**❶**⁷	48	●	©	1 **American Pie**	C:#3/266		$15	United Artists 5535
2/12/72	111	10		©	2 **Tapestry**	[E]		$15	United Artists 5522
					released in 1971				
12/23/72+	23	19		©	3 **Don McLean**			$15	United Artists 5651
11/23/74	120	8		©	4 **Homeless Brother**			$15	United Artists 315
2/14/81	28	21		©	5 **Chain Lightning**			$12	Millennium 7756
11/28/81+	156	11		©	6 **Believers**			$12	Millennium 7762

American Pie - Parts I & II (1) **1**
And I Love You So (2)
Babylon (1)
Bad Girl (2)
Believers (6)
Birthday Song (3)
Bronco Bill's Lament (3)
Castles In The Air (2) **flip**
Castles In The Air (6) **36**
Chain Lightning (2)
Circus Song (2)

Crazy Eyes (6)
Crossroads (1)
Crying (5) **5**
Crying In The Chapel (4)
Did You Know (4)
Empty Chairs (1)
Everybody Loves Me, Baby (1)
Falling Through Time (3)
General Store (2)
Genesis (In The Beginning) (5)
Grave, The (1)

Great Big Man (4)
Homeless Brother (4)
I Tune The World Out (6)
If We Try (3) **58**
Isn't It Strange (6)
It Doesn't Matter Anymore (5)
It's A Beautiful Life (5)
It's Just The Sun (5) **83**
Jerusalem (6)
La La Love (6)
Left For Dead On The Road Of Love (6)

Legend Of Andrew McGrew (4)
Lotta Lovin' (5)
Love Hurts (6)
Love Letters (6)
Magdalene Lane (2)
More You Pay (The More It's Worth) (3)
Narcisissma (3)
No Reason For Your Dreams (2)
Oh My What A Shame (3)
On The Amazon (3)

Orphans Of Wealth (2)
Pride Parade (3)
Respectable (2)
Sea Cruise (3)
Sea Man (6)
Since I Don't Have You (5) **23**
Sister Fatima (1)
Sunshine Life For Me (Sail Away Raymond) (4)
Tangled (Like A Spider In Her Hair) (4)
Tapestry (2)

Three Flights Up (1)
Till Tomorrow (1)
Vincent (1) **12**
Winter Has Me In Its Grip (4)
Winterwood (1)
Wonderful Baby (4) **93**
Wonderful Night (5)
Words And Music (5)
You Have Lived (4)
Your Cheating Heart (5)

McMURTRY, James   **'89**
Born on 3/18/62 in Fort Worth, Texas. Folk-rock guitarist. Son of novelist Larry McMurtry.

10/14/89	125	9	©		**Too Long In The Wasteland**			$10	Columbia 45229

Angeline
Crazy Wind
I'm Not From Here

Outskirts
Painting By Numbers
Poor Lost Soul

Shining Eyes
Song For A Deck Hand's Daughter

Talkin' At The Texaco
Terry
Too Long In The Wasteland

McNICHOL, Kristy & Jimmy   **'78**
Duo of acting siblings. Kristy was born on 9/11/62. Jimmy was born on 7/2/61. Each starred in several movies.

8/19/78	116	4			**Kristy & Jimmy McNichol**			$12	RCA Victor 2875

Box On Wheels
Girl You Really Got Me Goin'

Go For It
He's A Dancer

He's So Fine **70**
Hot Tunes

My Boyfriend's Back
Page By Page

Rock & Roll Is Here To Stay
Slow Dance

McRAE, Carmen   **'67**
Born on 4/8/20 in New York City. Died on 11/10/94 (age 74). Jazz singer/pianist.

1/14/67	150	2			**Alfie**			$20	Mainstream 56084

Alfie
And I Love Him

Don't Ever Leave Me
He Loves Me

Music That Makes Me Dance
Night Has A Thousand Eyes

Once Upon A Summertime
Shadow Of Your Smile

Sweetest Sounds
Who Can I Turn To?

McVIE, Christine '84

Born Christine Perfect on 7/12/43 in Birmingham, England. Singer/keyboardist with **Fleetwood Mac** since 1970. Married to Fleetwood Mac bassist John McVie (1968-77).

8/14/76	104	10			1 The Legendary Christine Perfect Album		[E]	$15	Sire 7522

recorded in 1969

2/18/84	26	23		©	2 Christine McVie			$10	Warner 25059

And That's Saying A Lot (1)
Ask Anybody (2)
Challenge, The (2)
Close To Me (1)
Crazy 'Bout You (1)
For You (1)

Got A Hold On Me (2) *10*
I Want You (1)
I'd Rather Go Blind (1)
I'm On My Way (1)
I'm The One (1)

I'm Too Far Gone (To Turn Around) (1)
Keeping Secrets (2)
Let Me Go (Leave Me Alone) (1)
Love Will Show Us How (2) *30*

No Road Is The Right Road (1)
One In A Million (2)
Smile I Live For (2)
So Excited (2)
Wait And See (1)
When You Say (1)

Who's Dreaming This Dream (2)

MDFMK '00

Rock trio from Chicago: Lucia Cifarelli (vocals), Tim Skold (guitar) and Sascha Konietzko (bass). Konietzko was a member of **KMFDM**.

4/15/00	182	1		©	MDFMK			$10	Republic 157522

Be.Like.Me
©ontrol¿

Gasoline
Get.Out.Of.My.Head

Hydro-Electric
Now

Rabblerouser
Stare.At.The.Sun

Torpedoes
Transmutation

Witch.Hunt

MEADER, Vaughn '62

Born on 3/20/36 in Boston. President **John F. Kennedy** impersonator.

12/8/62	❶12	49	●	©	1 The First Family		[C]	$30	Cadence 3060

1962 Grammy winner: Album of the Year

5/25/63	4	17		©	2 The First Family, volume two		[C]	$30	Cadence 3065

above albums feature Naomi Brossart as Jackie Kennedy

After Dinner Conversation (1)
Announcement, The (2)
Astronauts (1)
Auld Lang Syne (1)
Bedtime Story (1)
Biography (2)

Brothers Three (2)
But Vote !! (1)
Caroline's First Date (2)
Concert, The (2)
Crisis, The (2)
Decision, The (1)

Dress, The (1)
Economy Lunch (2)
Equal Time (2)
Evening With JFK (2)
Experiment, The (1)
First Daughter, The (2)

First Family March (2)
Law, The (2)
Malayan Ambassador (1)
Motorcade (1)
Movie, The (2)
1958 (2)

1996 (2)
Party, The (1)
Press Conference (1)
Relatively Speaking (1)
Saturday Night, Sunday Morning (1)

Stop The World (2)
Taxes (2)
Tour, The (1)
Trail, The (2)
White House Visitor (1)

★426★ MEAT LOAF '93

Born Marvin Lee Aday on 9/27/47 in Dallas. Pop-rock singer. Sang lead vocals on **Ted Nugent's** 1976 *Free-For-All* album. Played "Eddie" in the Los Angeles production and movie of *The Rocky Horror Picture Show*. Appeared in several other movies.

10/29/77+	14	82	▲14	©	1 Bat Out Of Hell	C:❶22/369		$12	Cleveland Int'l. 34974
9/19/81	45	11		©	2 Dead Ringer			$12	Cleveland Int'l. 36007
5/18/85	74	10		©	3 Bad Attitude			$12	RCA Victor 5451
10/2/93	❶1	55	▲5	©	4 Bat Out Of Hell II: Back Into Hell			$10	MCA 10699
12/2/95	17	14	▲	©	5 Welcome To The Neighborhood			$10	MCA 11341
10/2/99	129	5		©	6 VH1 Storytellers		[L]	$10	Beyond 78065

recorded on 10/5/98 in New York City

All Revved Up With No Place To Go (1,6)
Amnesty Is Granted (5)
Back Into Hell (4)
Bad Attitude (3)
Bat Out Of Hell (1,6)
Cheatin' In Your Dreams (3)
Dead Ringer For Love (2)
Don't Leave Your Mark On Me (3)
Everything Is Permitted (2)
Everything Louder Than Everything Else (4)
Fiesta De Las Almas Perdidas (5)

For Crying Out Loud (1)
45 Seconds Of Ecstasy (5)
Good Girls Go To Heaven (Bad Girls Go Everywhere) (4)
Heaven Can Wait (1,6)
I'd Do Anything For Love (But I Won't Do That) (4,6) *1*
I'd Lie For You (And That's The Truth) (5) *13*
I'll Kill You If You Don't Come Back (2)
I'm Gonna Love Her For Both Of Us (2) *84*
If This Is The Last Kiss (Let's Make It Last All Night) (5)

Is Nothing Sacred (6)
It Just Won't Quit (4)
Jumpin' The Gun (3)
Lawyers, Guns And Money (6)
Left In The Dark (5)
Life Is A Lemon And I Want My Money Back (4,6)
Lost Boys And Golden Girls (4)
Martha (3)
Modern Girl (4)
More Than You Deserve (2,6)
Nocturnal Pleasure (2)
Not A Dry Eye In The House (5) *82*
Nowhere Fast (3)

Objects In The Rear View Mirror May Appear Closer Than They Are (4) *38*
Original Sin (5)
Out Of The Frying Pan (And Into The Fire) (4)
Paradise By The Dashboard Light (1,6) *39*
Peel Out (2)
Piece Of The Action (3)
Read 'Em And Weep (2)
Rock And Roll Dreams Come Through (4) *13*
Runnin' For The Red Light (I Gotta Life) (5)

Sailor To A Siren (3)
Surf's Up (3)
Two Out Of Three Ain't Bad (1,6) *11*
Wasted Youth (4)
Where Angels Sing (5)
Where The Rubber Meets The Road (3)
You Took The Words Right Out Of My Mouth (1,6) *39*

MEAT PUPPETS '94

Rock trio from Phoenix: brothers Curt (guitar) and Cris (bass) Kirkwood with Derrick Bostrom (drums).

4/2/94	62	27	●	©	1 Too High To Die			$10	London 828484
10/21/95	183	1		©	2 No Joke!			$10	London 828665

Backwater (1) *47*
Chemical Garden (2)
Cobbler (2)
Comin' Down (1)
Evil Love (1)

Eyeball (2)
Flaming Heart (1)
For Free (2)
Head (2)
Inflatable (1)

Never To Be Found (1)
Nothing (2)
Poison Arrow (2)
Predator (2)
Roof With A Hole (1)

Scum (2)
Severed Goddess Hand (1)
Shine (1)
Station (1)
Sweet Ammonia (2)

Taste Of The Sun (2)
Things (1)
Vampires (2)
Violet Eyes (1)
We Don't Exist (1)

Why? (1)

MECO '77

Born Domenico Monardo on 11/29/39 in Johnsonburg, Pennsylvania. Disco producer.

8/6/77	13	28	▲	©	1 Star Wars And Other Galactic Funk		[I]	$12	Millennium 8001
1/14/78	62	13			2 Encounters Of Every Kind		[I]	$12	Millennium 8004
9/23/78	68	12			3 The Wizard Of Oz		[I]	$12	Millennium 8009

the single "Themes From The Wizard Of Oz" hit #35 on the *Hot 100*

8/2/80	140	8			4 Meco Plays Music From The Empire Strikes Back		[I-M]	$12	RSO 3086
12/13/80	61	6		©	5 Christmas In The Stars/Star Wars Christmas Album		[X]	$12	RSO 3093
4/3/82	68	9			6 Pop Goes The Movies		[I]	$10	Arista 9598

the single "Pop Goes The Movies" hit #35 on the *Hot 100*

Apartment, Theme From The (6)
As Time Goes By (medley) (6)
Asteroid Field (medley) (4)
Atchison, Topeka And The Santa Fe (medley) (6)
Battle In The Snow (4)
Bells, Bells, Bells (5)
Chariots Of Fire, Theme From (6)
Christmas In The Stars (5)

Christmas Sighting ('Twas The Night Before Christmas) (5)
Close Encounters, Theme From (2) *25*
Crazy Rhythm (2)
Cyclone (3)
Days Of Wine And Roses, Theme From (6)
Delirious Escape (medley) (3)
Desert And The Robot Auction (1)

Ding-Dong! The Witch Is Dead (3)
Dorothy's Rescue (3)
Empire Strikes Back Medley (4) *18*
Force Theme (4)
Funk (1)
Galactic (1)
Godfather, Theme From The (6)
Goldfinger (medley) (6)

Good, The Bad And The Ugly (medley) (6)
Hatari (medley) (6)
Haunted Forest (3)
High And The Mighty, The (6)
Hooray For Hollywood (medley) (6)
Hot In The Saddle (2)
Icebound (2)
If I Were King Of The Forest (3)

Imperial Attack (1)
In The Beginning (2)
James Bond Theme (medley) (6)
Lady Marion (2)
Land Of The Sand People (1)
Last Battle (1)
Laura (medley) (6)
Love Is A Many Splendored Thing (medley) (6)
Love Story, Theme From (6)

Magnificent Seven (medley) (6)
March Of The Winkies (3)
M.A.S.H., Theme From (6)
Meaning Of Christmas (5)
Meco's Theme (medley) (2)
Merry-Go-Round Broke Down (medley) (6)
Merry, Merry Christmas (5)
Merry Old Land Of Oz (3)
Munchkinland (3)
Never On Sunday (medley) (6)

MECO — Cont'd

Odds Against Christmas (5)
Optimistic Voices (2)
Other (1)
Over The Rainbow (3)
Pink Panther (medley) (6)
Poppies (3)
Princess Appears (1)

Princess Leia's Theme (1)
R2-D2 We Wish You A Merry Christmas (5)
Roman Nights (2)
Secret Love (medley) (6)
Shadow Of Your Smile (medley) (6)

Sleigh Ride (5)
Spell, The (3)
Star Wars Theme/Cantina Band (1) *1*
Strike Up The Band (medley) (6)
Tara's Theme (medley) (6)

Three Coins In The Fountain (medley) (6)
3 W. 57 (medley) (2)
Throne Room And End Title (1)
Time Machine (2)
Tom Jones (medley) (6)
Topsy (2)

20th Century Fox Trademark (medley) (6)
We're Off To See The Wizard (The Wonderful Wizard Of Oz) (3)
What Can You Get A Wookie For Christmas (When He

Already Owns A Comb?) (5) *69*
Windmills Of Your Mind (medley) (6)
Zorba The Greek (medley) (6)

MEDEIROS, Glenn   '90
Born on 6/24/70 in Hawaii. Pop singer.

| 6/13/87 | 83 | 17 | | © | 1 Glenn Medeiros .... | | | $10 | Amherst 3313 |
| 6/23/90 | 82 | 18 | | © | 2 Glenn Medeiros .... | | | $10 | MCA 6399 |

All I'm Missing Is You (2) *32*
Best Man (2)
Boyfriend (2)
Cracked Up (2)

Doesn't Matter Anymore (2)
Fool's Affair (1)
Just Like Rain (2)
Knocking At Your Door (1)

Lonely Won't Leave Me Alone (1) *67*
Lovelylittlelady (2)
Me - U = Blue (2) *78*

Niki (2)
Nothing's Gonna Change My Love For You (1) *12*
She Ain't Worth It (2) *1*

Stranger Tonight (1)
Watching Over You (1) *80*
What's It Gonna Take (1)
Wings Of My Heart (1)

You Left The Loneliest Heart (1)

MEDESKI, MARTIN & WOOD   '98
Jazz trio from New York City: John Medeski (organ), Bill Martin (percussion) and Chris Wood (bass).

| 8/29/98 | 174 | 1 | | © | Combustication .... | | [I] | $10 | Blue Note 93011 |

Church Of Logic
Coconut Boogaloo

Everyday People
Hey-Hee-Hi-Ho

Hypnotized
Just Like I Pictured It

Latin Shuffle
No Ke Ano Ahiahi

Nocturne
Start-Stop

Sugar Craft
Whatever Happened To Gus

MEDLEY, Bill   '69
Born on 9/19/40 in Santa Ana, California. Half of **The Righteous Brothers** duo.

| 10/12/68 | 188 | 4 | | | 1 Bill Medley 100% .... | | | $20 | MGM 4583 |
| 4/5/69 | 152 | 4 | | | 2 Soft And Soulful .... | | | $20 | MGM 4603 |

Any Day Now (2)
Brown Eyed Woman (1) *43*
For Your Precious Love (2)
Goin' Out Of My Head (1)
I Can't Make It Alone (1) *95*
I'm Gonna Die Me (2)
Let The Good Times Roll (1)

One Day Girl (1)
100 Years (2)
Peace Brother Peace (2) *48*
Quest (The Impossible Dream) (1)
Reaching Back (2)
Run To My Loving Arms (1)

Show Me (1)
Softly, As I Leave You (2)
Something's So Wrong (2)
Street Of Dirt (1)
That's Life (1)
Then You Can Tell Me Goodbye (2)

When Something Is Wrong With My Baby (2)
Who Can I Turn To (When Nobody Needs Me) (1)
Winter Won't Come This Year (2)

You Don't Have To Say You Love Me (1)
You're Nobody 'Till Somebody Loves You (1)

★324★   MEGADETH   '92
Hard-rock group formed in Los Angeles: Dave Mustaine (vocals, guitar), Marty Friedman (guitar), Dave Ellefson (bass) and Nick Menza (drums). Jimmy DeGrasso replaced Menza in 1998. Al Pitrelli replaced Friedman in 2000. Mustaine was an early guitarist with **Metallica**.

1)Countdown To Extinction 2)Youthanasia 3)Cryptic Writings

10/25/86	76	47	▲	©	1 Peace Sells...But Who's Buying?			$10	Capitol 12526
2/6/88	28	23	▲	©	2 so far, so good...so what!			$10	Capitol 48148
10/20/90	23	30	▲	©	3 Rust In Peace			$10	Capitol 91935
8/1/92	2¹	58	▲²	©	4 Countdown To Extinction			$10	Capitol 98531
11/19/94	4	23	▲	©	5 Youthanasia			$10	Capitol 29004
8/5/95	90	7		©	6 Hidden Treasures		[K-M]	$10	Capitol 33670
7/5/97	10	29	●	©	7 Cryptic Writings			$10	Capitol 38262
9/18/99	16	8		©	8 Risk			$10	Capitol 99134
11/11/00	66	3		©	9 Capitol Punishment: The Megadeth Years		[G]	$10	Capitol 25916
6/2/01	16	6		©	10 The World Needs A Hero			$10	Sanctuary 84503

Addicted To Chaos (5)
Almost Honest (7,9)
Anarchy In The U.K. (2)
Angry Again (6)
Architecture Of Aggression (4)
Ashes In Your Mouth (4)
Bad Omen (1)
Black Curtains (5)
Black Friday (medley) (1)
Blood Of Heroes (5)
Breadline (8)
Breakpoint (6)
Burning Bridges (10)
Captive Honour (4)
Conjuring, The (1)
Countdown To Extinction (4)
Crush 'Em (8,9)
Dawn Patrol (3)

Devils Island (1)
Diadems (6)
Disconnect (10)
Disintegrators, The (7)
Doctor Is Calling (8)
Dread & The Fugitive Mind (9,10)
Ecstasy (8)
Elysian Fields (5)
Enter The Arena (8)
FFF (7)
Family Tree (5)
Five Magics (3)
502 (2)
Foreclosure Of A Dream (4)
Go To Hell (6)
Good Mourning (medley) (1)
Hangar 18 (3,9)

Have Cool, Will Travel (7)
High Speed Dirt (4)
Holy Wars...The Punishment Due (3,9)
Hook In Mouth (2)
I Ain't Superstitious (1)
I Thought I Knew It All (5)
I'll Be There (8)
I'll Get Even (7)
In My Darkest Hour (2,9)
Insomnia (7)
Into The Lungs Of Hell (2)
Kill The King (9)
Killing Road (5)
Liar (2)
Losing My Senses (10)
Lucretia (3)
Mary Jane (2)

Mastermind (7)
Moto Psycho (10)
My Last Words (1)
99 Ways To Die (6)
No More Mr. Nice Guy (6)
1000 Times Goodbye (10)
Paranoid (6)
Peace Sells (1,9)
Poison Was The Cure (3)
Prince Of Darkness (8)
Problems (10)
Promises (10)
Psychotron (4)
Recipe For Hate...Warhorse (10)
Reckoning Day (5)
Return To Hangar (10)
Rust In Peace...Polaris (3)

Secret Place (7)
Set The World Afire (2)
Seven (8)
She-Wolf (7)
Silent Scorn (10)
Sin (7)
Skin O' My Teeth (4)
Sweating Bullets (4,9)
Symphony Of Destruction (4,9) *71*
Take No Prisoners (3)
This Was My Life (4)
Time: The Beginning (8)
Time: The End (8)
Tornado Of Souls (3)
Tout Le Monde (5,9)
Train Of Consequences (5,9)
Trust (7,9)

Use The Man (7,9)
Victory (5)
Vortex (7)
Wake Up Dead (1)
Wanderlust (8)
When (10)
World Needs A Hero (10)
Youthanasia (5)

MEHTA, Zubin   '94
Born on 4/29/36 in Bombay, India. Conductor of the Los Angeles Philharmonic Orchestra.

| 6/10/72 | 175 | 10 | | | 1 Gustav Holst: The Planets .... | | [I] | $15 | London 6734 |
| 3/4/78 | 130 | 8 | | | 2 Star Wars and Close Encounters Of The Third Kind .... | | [I] | $12 | London 1001 |

Battle, The (2)
Cantina Band (2)
Jupiter, The Bringer Of Jollity (1)

Little People (2)
Mars, The Bringer Of War (1)
Mercury, The Winged Messenger (1)

Neptune, The Mystic (1)
Princess Leia's Theme (2)
Saturn, The Bringer Of Old Age (1)

Star Wars, End Title From (2)
Star Wars, Main Title From (2)
Suite From "Close Encounters Of The Third Kind" (2)

Throne Room (2)
Uranus, The Magician (1)
Venus, The Bringer Of Peace (1)

MEISNER, Randy   '81
Born on 3/8/46 in Scottsbluff, Nebraska. Pop-rock singer/bassist. Member of **Poco** (1968-69), **Rick Nelson**'s Stone Canyon Band (1969-71) and the **Eagles** (1971-77).

| 11/1/80+ | 50 | 33 | | © | 1 One More Song .... | | | $12 | Epic 36748 |
| 8/21/82 | 94 | 11 | | | 2 Randy Meisner .... | | | $12 | Epic 38121 |

Anyway Bye Bye (1)
Come On Back To Me (1)
Darkness Of The Heart (2)
Deep Inside My Heart (1) *22*

Doin' It For Delilah (2)
Gotta Get Away (1)
Hearts On Fire (1) *19*
I Need You Bad (1)

Jealousy (2)
Never Been In Love (2) *28*
Nothing Is Said ('Til The Artist Is Dead) (2)

One More Song (1)
Playin' In The Deep End (2)
Still Runnin' (2)
Strangers (2)

Tonight (2)
Trouble Ahead (1)
White Shoes (1)

DEBUT	PEAK	WKS	RIAA	CD	ARTIST — Album Title	Catalog	Sym	$	Label & Number

MELACHRINO, George, And His Orchestra '55

Born George Militiades on 5/1/09 in London (Greek parents). Died on 6/18/65 (age 56). Conductor/arranger.

1/8/55	10	2		©	1 **Christmas In High Fidelity**	[X-I]	$25	RCA Victor 1045
5/25/59	30	1		©	2 **Under Western Skies**	[I]	$25	RCA Victor 1676

Adeste Fideles (1)
Colorado River (2)
Cool Water (2)
Empty Saddles (2)
Fairy On The Christmas Tree (1)
First Noel (1)

Good King Wenceslas (1)
Hark! The Herald Angels Sing (1)
Home On The Range (1)
I Saw Mommy Kissing Santa Claus (1)
Jingle Bells (1)

Last Round-Up (2)
Little Brown Jug (1)
Mrs. Santa Claus (1)
Northwest Trail (2)
Once More It's Christmas (1)
One-Armed Bandit (Nevada) (2)
Red River Valley (2)

Riders In The Sky (2)
Rudolph The Red Nosed Reindeer (1)
San Francisco (2)
Silent Night (1)
Skater's Waltz (1)
Sleigh Ride (1)

Tumbling Tumbleweeds (2)
Wagon Wheels (2)
White Christmas (1)
Winter Wonderland (1)

MEL AND TIM '73

R&B vocal duo from Holly Springs, Mississippi: cousins Mel Hardin and Tim McPherson.

1/6/73	175	7		©	**Starting All Over Again**		$20	Stax 3007

Carry Me
Don't Mess With My Money, My Honey Or My Woman

Free For All
Heaven Knows
I May Not Be What You Want

I'm Your Puppet
Starting All Over Again *19*
Too Much Wheelin' And Dealin'

What's Your Name
Wrap It Up

MELANIE '70

Born Melanie Safka on 2/3/47 in Queens, New York. Folk-pop singer/songwriter. Formed Neighborhood record label.

1)Gather Me 2)Candles In The Rain 3)Leftover Wine

11/15/69	196	2			1 **Melanie**		$20	Buddah 5041
5/9/70	17	37	●	©	2 **Candles In The Rain**		$20	Buddah 5060
9/26/70	33	19		©	3 **Leftover Wine**	[L]	$20	Buddah 5066
2/27/71	80	10			4 **The Good Book**		$20	Buddah 95000
11/13/71+	15	27	●		5 **Gather Me**		$15	Neighborhood 47001
12/4/71+	115	12			6 **Garden In The City**		$15	Buddah 5095
4/1/72	103	9			7 **Four Sides Of Melanie**	[K]	$20	Buddah 95005 [2]
11/11/72	70	20			8 **Stoneground Words**		$15	Neighborhood 47005
5/12/73	109	11			9 **Melanie At Carnegie Hall**	[L]	$20	Neighborhood 49001 [2]
5/11/74	192	4			10 **Madrugada**		$15	Neighborhood 48001

Actress (9,10)
Again (1)
Alexander Beetle (2)
Animal Crackers (3,7)
Any Guy (1,7,9)
Babe Rainbow (4,7,9)
Baby Day (5)
Baby Guitar (1,9)
Beautiful People (1,3,7,9)
Between The Road Signs (8)
Birthday Of The Rain (4)
Bitter Bad (9) *36*
Brand New Key (5,9) *1*
Carolina In My Mind (2)
Center Of The Circle (5)
Chords Of Fame (4)
Christopher Robin (7)

Citiest People (2)
Close To It All (3)
Deep Down Low (1)
Do You Believe (8)
Don't You Wait By The Water (6)
For My Father (1)
Garden In The City (6)
Good Book (4,7)
Good Guys (2)
Happy Birthday (3)
Hearing The News (medley) (9)
Here I Am (8)
Holding Out (10)
I Am Being Guided (10)
I Am Not A Poet (Night Song) (8)
I Don't Eat Animals (3,7)

I Really Loved Harold (7)
I Think It's Going To Rain Today (10)
I'm Back In Town (1,7)
In The Hour (7)
Introduction (1)
Isn't It A Pity (4)
It's Me Again (9)
Jigsaw Puzzle (6)
Johnny Boy (1,7)
Kansas (5)
Lay Down (Candles In The Rain) (2,7) *6*
Lay Lady Lay (6,7)
Lay Your Hands Across The Six Strings (9)
Leftover Wine (2,3,7)
Little Bit Of Me (5)

Love In My Mind (6)
Love To Lose Again (10)
Lover's Cross (10)
Lovin Baby Girl (2)
Maybe I Was (A Golf Ball) (8)
Maybe Not For A Lifetime (10)
Momma Momma (3)
Mr. Tambourine Man (7)
My Father (4)
My Rainbow Race (8,9)
Nickel Song (4,7) *35*
Peace Will Come (According To Plan) (3,7,9) *32*
People In The Front Row (6)
Pine And Feather (10)
Poet (9)
Pretty Boy Floyd (9,10)
Prize, The (4)

Psychotherapy (3,7,9)
Railroad (5)
Ring Around The Moon (5)
Ring The Living Bell Medley (5,9) *31*
Ruby Tuesday (2,7) *52*
Saddest Thing (3,4)
Seasons To Change (medley) (9)
Sign In The Window (4,7)
Some Day I'll Be A Farmer (5,9)
Some Say (I Got Devil) (5,9)
Somebody Loves Me (6,7)
Song Of The South (7)
Soul Sister Annie (1)
Steppin' (5)
Stoneground Words (8)

Stop I Don't Want To Hear It Anymore (6)
Summer Weaving (8)
Take Me Home (1)
Tell Me Why (5)
Together Alone (8,9) *86*
Tuning My Guitar (1,3)
Uptown Down (1,3)
We Don't Know Where We're Going (6)
What Have They Done To My Song Ma (2,7)
What Wondrous Love (5)
Wild Horses (10)
You Can Go Fishin' (4)

MELLENCAMP, John Cougar ★128★ '82

Born on 10/7/51 in Seymour, Indiana. Rock singer/songwriter/producer. Given name Johnny Cougar by David Bowie's manager, Tony DeFries. First recorded for MCA in 1976. Directed and starred in the 1992 movie *Falling From Grace*. Married model Elaine Irwin on 9/5/92. Recipient of *Billboard*'s Century Award in 2001.

1)American Fool 2)Scarecrow 3)The Lonesome Jubilee

JOHN COUGAR:

8/18/79+	64	29	●	©	1 **John Cougar**		$12	Riva 7401
10/4/80+	37	55	▲	©	2 **Nothin' Matters And What If It Did**		$12	Riva 7403
5/8/82	❶⁹	106	▲⁵	©	3 **American Fool**	C:#27/11	$12	Riva 7501

JOHN COUGAR MELLENCAMP:

11/5/83+	9	66	▲³	©	4 **Uh-Huh**		$10	Riva 7504
9/14/85	2³	75	▲⁴	©	5 **Scarecrow**	C:#30/7	$10	Riva 824865
9/19/87	6	53	▲³	©	6 **The Lonesome Jubilee**		$10	Mercury 832465
5/27/89	7	23	▲	©	7 **Big Daddy**		$10	Mercury 838220

JOHN MELLENCAMP:

10/26/91	17	46	▲	©	8 **Whenever We Wanted**		$10	Mercury 510151
9/25/93	7	24	▲	©	9 **Human Wheels**		$10	Mercury 518088
7/9/94	13	30	▲	©	10 **Dance Naked**		$10	Mercury 522428
9/28/96	9	30	▲	©	11 **Mr. Happy Go Lucky**		$10	Mercury 532896
12/6/97	33	63	▲	©	12 **The Best That I Could Do 1978-1988**	C:#24/35 [G]	$10	Mercury 536738
10/24/98	41	20	●	©	13 **John Mellencamp**		$10	Columbia 69602
9/4/99	99	4		©	14 **Rough Harvest**		$10	Mercury 558355

contains new acoustic versions of previous hits

Again Tonight (8) *36*
Ain't Even Done With The Night (2,12) *17*
Another Sunny Day 12/25 (10)
Authority Song (4,12) *15*

Beige To Beige (9)
Between A Laugh And A Tear (5,14)
Big Daddy Of Them All (7)
Big Jack (10)

Break Me Off Some (13)
Breakout, The (10)
Brothers (10)
Can You Take It (3)
Case 795 (The Family) (9)

Chance Meeting At The Tarantula (13)
Cheap Shot (2)
Check It Out (6,12) *14*
Cherry Bomb (6,12) *8*

China Girl (3)
Circling Around The Moon (11)
Close Enough (3)
Country Gentleman (7)
Crazy Ones (8)

Crumblin' Down (4,12) *9*
Cry Baby (2)
Dance Naked (10) *41*
Danger List (3)
Days Of Farewell (13)

MELLENCAMP, John Cougar — Cont'd

Do You Think That's Fair (1)
Don't Misunderstand Me (2)
Down And Out In Paradise (6)
Eden Is Burning (6)
Emotional Love (11)
Empty Hands (6)
Face Of The Nation (5)
Farewell Angelina (14)
French Shoes (9)
Fruit Trader (13)
Full Catastrophe (11,14)
Get A Leg Up (8) *14*
Golden Gates (4)
Grandma's Theme (5)
Great Mid-West (1)
Hand To Hold On To (3) *19*
Hard Times For An Honest Man (6)
Hot Night In A Cold Town (2)

Hotdogs And Hamburgers (6)
Human Wheels (9,14) *48*
Hurts So Good (3,12) *2*
I Ain't Ever Satisfied (8)
I Need A Lover (1,12) *28*
I'm Not Running Anymore (13)
In My Time Of Dying (14)
It All Comes True (13)
J.M.'s Question (3)
Jack & Diane (3,12) *1*
Jackamo Road (11)
Jackie Brown (7,14) *48*
Jackie O (4)
Jerry (11)
Junior (9)
Just Another Day (11) *46*
Justice And Independence '85 (5)

Key West Intermezzo (I Saw You First) (11,14) *14*
Large World Turning (11)
Last Chance (8)
Life Is Hard (1)
Little Night Dancin' (1)
Lonely Ol' Night (5,12) *6*
Love And Happiness (8,14)
Lovin' Mother Fo Ya (4)
L.U.V. (10)
Make Me Feel (4)
Mansions In Heaven (7)
Martha Say (7)
Melting Pot (8)
Miami (4)
Minutes To Memories (5,14)
Miss Missy (13)
Mr. Bellows (11)
Now More Than Ever (8)

Paper In Fire (6,12) *9*
Peppermint Twist (2)
Pink Houses (4,12) *8*
Play Guitar (4)
Pop Singer (7) *15*
Positively Crazy (13)
Pray For Me (1)
Rain On The Scarecrow (5,14) *21*
Real Life (6)
R.O.C.K. In The U.S.A. (5,12) *2*
Rooty Toot Toot (6) *61*
Rumbleseat (7) *28*
Serious Business (4)
Small Paradise (1) *87*
Small Town (5,12) *6*
Sometimes A Great Notion (7)
Sugar Marie (1)
Summer Of Love (13)

Suzanne And The Jewels (9)
Sweet Evening Breeze (9)
Taxi Dancer (1)
Theo And Weird Henry (7)
They're So Tough (8)
This May Not Be The End Of The World (11)
This Time (2) *27*
Thundering Hearts (3)
To Live (7)
To M.G. (Wherever She May Be) (2)
To The River (9)
Tonight (2)
Too Much To Think About (10)
Under The Boardwalk (14)
Void In My Heart (7)
Warmer Place To Sleep (4)
We Are The People (6)

Weakest Moments (3)
Welcome To Chinatown (1)
What If I Came Knocking (9)
When Jesus Left Birmingham (9,14)
When Margaret Comes To Town (10)
Whenever We Wanted (8)
Where The World Began (13)
Wild Angel (2)
Wild Night (10,14) *3*
Without Expression (12)
You've Got To Stand For Somethin' (5)
Your Life Is Now (13)

MELLOW MAN ACE '90

Born Ulpiano Sergio Reyez on 4/12/67 in Cuba; raised in Southgate, California. Male rapper. His brother Senen is a member of **Cypress Hill.**

6/2/90	69	16		©	Escape From Havana..........			$10	Capitol 91295

B-Boy In Love
En La Casa

Enquentren Amor
Gettin' Stupid

Hip Hop Creature
If You Were Mine

Mas Pingon
Mentirosa *14*

Rap Guanco
Rhyme Fighter

River Cubano
Talkapella

MELVIN, Harold, And The Blue Notes '76

Born on 6/25/39 in Philadelphia. Died of a stroke on 3/24/97 (age 57). R&B singer. The Blue Notes: **Teddy Pendergrass**, Lawrence Brown, Jerry Cummings and Bernard Wilson.

DEBUT	PEAK	WKS	RIAA	CD	#	Album Title	$	Label & Number
9/2/72	53	31			1	Harold Melvin & The Blue Notes............	$15	Philadelphia Int'l. 31648
11/10/73+	57	20			2	Black & Blue............	$15	Philadelphia Int'l. 32407
3/1/75	26	32	●		3	To Be True............	$15	Philadelphia Int'l. 33148
12/13/75+	9	24	▲	©	4	Wake Up Everybody	$15	Philadelphia Int'l. 33808
7/4/76	51	14			5	All Their Greatest Hits!............ [G]	$15	Philadelphia Int'l. 34232
2/5/77	56	10			6	Reaching For The World............	$12	ABC 969
3/22/80	95	20			7	The Blue Album............	$12	Source 3197

After You Love Me, Why Do You Leave Me (6)
Baby I'm Back (7)
Bad Luck (Part 1) (3,5) *15*
Be For Real (1,5)
Big Singing Star (6)
Cabaret (2)
Concentrate On Me (2)
Don't Leave Me This Way (4)
Ebony Woman (1)
He Loves You And I Do Too (6)

Hope That We Can Be Together Soon (3,5) *42*
Hostage Part 1 & 2 (6)
I Miss You (Part 1) (1,5) *58*
I Should Be Your Lover (7)
I'm Comin' Home Tomorrow (2)
I'm Searching For A Love (4)
I'm Weak For You (2)
If You Don't Know Me By Now (1,5) *3*
If You're Looking For Somebody To Love (7)

Is There A Place For Me (2)
It All Depends On You (3)
It's All Because Of A Woman (3)
Keep On Lovin' You (4)
Let It Be You (1)
Let Me Into Your World (1)
Love I Lost (Part 1) (2,5) *7*
Nobody Could Take Your Place (3)
Prayin' (7)
Pretty Flower (3)

Reaching For The World (6) *74*
Sandman (6)
Satisfaction Guaranteed (Or Take Your Love Back) (3,5) *58*
Somewhere Down The Line (3)
Stay Together (6)
Tell The World How I Feel About 'Cha Baby (4) *94*
To Be Free To Be Who We Are (4)
To Be True (3)

Tonight's The Night (7)
Wake Up Everybody (Part 1) (4,5) *12*
Where Are All My Friends (3,5) *80*
Where There's A Will - There's A Way (6)
Yesterday I Had The Blues (1) *63*
You Know How To Make Me Feel So Good (4)
Your Love Is Taking Me On A Journey (7)

MEMPHIS BLEEK '99

Born Malik Cox in Brooklyn, New York. Male rapper.

8/21/99	7	9	●	©	1	Coming Of Age	$10	Roc-A-Fella 538991
12/23/00	16	20	●	©	2	The Understanding............	$10	Roc-A-Fella 542587

All Types Of S*** (2)
Bounce B**** (2)
Change Up (2)
Do My... (2)
Everybody (1)

Everyday (2)
Hustlers (2)
I Get High (2)
I Won't Stop (1)
In My Life (2)

Is That Your Chick (2) *68*
Memphis Bleek Is... (1)
Murda 4 Life (1)
My Hood To Your Hood (1)
My Mind Right (1)

N.O.W. (1)
PYT (2)
Regular Cat (1)
Stay Alive In NYC (1)
They'll Never Play Me (2)

We Get Low (2)
What You Think Of That (1)
Who's Sleeping (1)
Why You Wanna Hate For (1)
You A Thug Nigga (1)

MEMPHIS HORNS, The '78

Studio group from Memphis: Wayne Jackson (trumpet), Andrew Love (tenor sax), James Mitchell (baritone sax), Lewis Collins (soprano sax) and Jack Hale (trombone).

6/10/78	163	9			1	The Memphis Horns Band II............	$12	RCA Victor 2643
10/6/90	51	32	●	©	2	Midnight Stroll............	$10	Mercury 846652

THE ROBERT CRAY BAND FEATURING THE MEMPHIS HORNS

Bouncin' Back (2)
Consequences (2)
Don't Change It (1)
Forecast (Calls For Pain) (2)

Give It To Me (1)
Hold On (1)
Holdin' Court (2)
Labor Of Love (2)

(Let's Go) All The Way (1)
Livin' For The Music (1)
Midnight Stroll (2)
Minute By Minute (1)

Move A Mountain (2)
My Problem (2)
New Beginning (1)
Our Love Will Survive (1)

Party Line (1)
These Things (2)
Things You Do To Me (2)
Walk Around Time (2)

You (1)

MEN AT LARGE '93

R&B vocal duo from Cleveland: David Tolliver and Jason Champion.

2/20/93	122	13		©	1	Men At Large............	$10	EastWest 92159
11/5/94	151	1		©	2	One Size Fits All............	$10	EastWest 92459

Ain't It Grand (1)
Better Off By Myself (2)
Da Ya (2)
Don't Cry (2)

Feet Wet (2)
First Day (2)
Funny Feeling (2)
Good Things Don't Last (2)

Heartbeat (2)
Holiday (2)
I Wanna Roll (2)
In A Freaky Mood (2)

Let's Talk About It (2)
Salty Dog (2)
So Alone (1) *31*
Stay The Night (1)

Um Um Good (1)
Use Me (Version #1 & 2) (1)
Will You Marry Me (2)

Would You Like To Dance (With Me) (1)
You Me (1)

MEN AT WORK '82

Pop-rock group from Melbourne, Australia: **Colin James Hay** (vocals, guitar), Ron Strykert (guitar), Greg Ham (sax, keyboards), John Rees (bass) and Jerry Speiser (drums). Won the 1982 Best New Artist Grammy Award. Speiser and Rees left in 1984.

7/3/82	❶ *15*	90	▲⁶	©	1	Business As Usual	$10	Columbia 37978
5/7/83	3	49	▲³	©	2	Cargo	$10	Columbia 38660
6/22/85	50	13	●	©	3	Two Hearts............	$10	Columbia 40078

Be Good Johnny (1)
Blue For You (2)
Catch A Star (1)

Children On Parade (3)
Dr. Heckyll & Mr. Jive (2) *28*
Down By The Sea (1)

Down Under (1) *1*
Everything I Need (3) *47*
Giving Up (3)

Hard Luck Story (3)
Helpless Automation (1)
High Wire (2)

I Can See It In Your Eyes (1)
I Like To (2)
It's A Mistake (2) *6*

Man With Two Hearts (3)
Maria (3)
No Restrictions (2)

MEN AT WORK — Cont'd

No Sign Of Yesterday (2)
Overkill (2) *3*

People Just Love To Play With Words (1)
Sail To You (3)

Settle Down My Boy (2)
Snakes And Ladders (3)
Stay At Home (3)

Still Life (3)
Touching The Untouchables (1)
Underground (1)

Upstairs In My House (2)
Who Can It Be Now? (1) *1*

★212★

MENDES, Sergio, & Brasil '66   '69

Born on 2/11/41 in Niteroi, Brazil. Pianist/bandleader. Brasil '66 consisted of Lani Hall and Janis Hansen (vocals), Joses Soares (percussion), Bob Matthews (bass) and Jao Palma (drums). Hall married **Herb Alpert**.

1)Fool On The Hill 2)Look Around 3)Sergio Mendes & Brasil '66

9/10/66	7	126	●	©	1 Sergio Mendes & Brasil '66	$20	A&M 4116
4/29/67	24	46	●		2 Equinox	$20	A&M 4122
3/9/68	5	51	●	©	3 Look Around	$20	A&M 4137
6/8/68	197	4			4 Sergio Mendes' Favorite Things .... [E-I]	$20	Atlantic 8177
12/7/68+	3	30	●	©	5 Fool On The Hill	$20	A&M 4160
8/16/69	33	17			6 Crystal Illusions	$20	A&M 4197
12/13/69+	71	16			7 Ye-Me-Le	$20	A&M 4236
7/4/70	101	20	©		8 Greatest Hits .... [G]	$20	A&M 4252
1/9/71	130	9			9 Stillness	$20	A&M 4284

SERGIO MENDES & BRASIL '77:

10/16/71	166	6	10 Pais Tropical	$15	A&M 4315
7/15/72	164	5	11 Primal Roots	$15	A&M 4353
6/2/73	116	15	12 Love Music	$15	Bell 1119
5/18/74	176	5	13 Vintage 74	$15	Bell 1305
2/15/75	105	10	14 Sergio Mendes	$12	Elektra 1027
3/27/76	180	2	15 Homecooking	$12	Elektra 1055
8/20/77	81	12	16 Sergio Mendes And The New Brasil '77	$12	Elektra 1102

SERGIO MENDES:

5/7/83	27	27	©	17 Sergio Mendes	$10	A&M 4937
5/19/84	70	22	©	18 Confetti	$10	A&M 4984

A Banda (Parade) (4)
After Midnight (10)
After Sunrise (11)
Agua De Beber (1)
Alibis (18) *29*
All In Love Is Fair (14)
Asa Branca (10)
Batucada (The Beat) (3)
Berimbau (1)
Bim-Bom (2)
Boa Palavra (The Good Word) (4)
Cancao Do Nosso Amor (Far Away Today) (9)
Canto De Ubiratan (11)
Canto Triste (5)
Carnaval (17)
Casa Forte (5)
Celebration Of The Sunrise (9)
Chelsea Morning (9)
Cinnamon And Clove (2)
Circle Game (11)
Comin' Home Baby (14)
Constant Rain (Chove Chuva) (2) *71*
Crystal Illusions (6)
Cut That Out (15)
Dance Attack (18)
Davy (14)
Daytripper (1,8)

Dois Dias (6)
Don't Let Me Be Lonely Tonight (12)
Don't You Worry 'Bout A Thing (13)
Double Rainbow (13)
Dream Hunter (17)
Easy To Be Hard (7)
Emorio (15)
Empty Faces (6)
Festa (8)
Fool On The Hill (5,8) *6*
For Me (2) *98*
For What It's Worth (9)
Frog, The (3)
Funny You Should Say That (13)
Gente (2)
Going Out Of My Head (1,8)
Gone Forever (10)
Here Comes The Sun (14)
Hey Look At The Sun (12)
Hey People Hey (15)
Homecooking (15)
I Believe (When I Fall In Love It Will Be Forever) (14)
I Can See Clearly Now (12)
I Know You (10)
I Say A Little Prayer (4)
I Won't Last A Day Without You (12)

Iemanja (11)
If I Ever Lose This Heaven (14)
If You Leave Me Now (16)
If You Really Love Me (13)
It's So Obvious That I Love You (15)
It's Up To You (15)
Joker, The (1)
Killing Me Softly With His Song (12)
Kisses (18)
Laia Ladaia (Reza) (5)
Lapinha (5)
Let Them Work It Out (14)
Let's Give A Little More This Time (18)
Life (16)
Life In The Movies (17)
Like A Lover (3,8)
Lonely Sailor (13)
Look Around (3,8)
Look Of Love (3,8) *4*
Look Who's Mine (7)
Lookin' For Another Pure Love (14)
Lost In Paradise (9)
Love City (16)
Love Is Waiting (17)
Love Me Tomorrow (16)
Love Music (4)
Mas Que Nada (1,8) *47*

Masquerade (7)
Moanin' (7)
Morrer De Amor (To Die Of Love) (18)
Morro Velho (13)
Mozambique (16)
My Favorite Things (4)
My Summer Love (17)
Never Gonna Let You Go (17) *4*
Night And Day (2,8) *82*
Norwegian Wood (7)
O Mar E Meu Chao (The Sea Is My Soil) (4)
O Pato (1)
One Note Samba (medley) (7)
P-Ka-Boo (16)
Pais Tropical (Tropical Land) (10)
Peninsula (14)
Pomba Gira (11)
Ponteio (4)
Pradizer Adeua (To Say Goodbye) (3)
Promise Of A Fisherman (11)
Put A Little Love Away (12)
Real Life (18)
Real Thing (16)

Righteous Life (9)
Roda (3)
Salt Sea (6)
Say It With Your Body (18)
Scarborough Fair (5,8) *16*
Shakara (15)
Si Senor (17)
(Sittin' On) The Dock Of The Bay (6) *66*
Slow Hot Wind (1)
So Danco Samba (Jazz 'N' Samba) (2)
So Many People (10)
So Many Stars (3,8)
So What's New (4)
Some Time Ago (7)
Someday We'll All Be Free (14)
Sometimes In Winter (9)
Song Of No Regrets (6)
Sound Of One Song (18)
Spanish Flea (medley) (1)
Stillness (9)
Sunny Day (15)
Superstition (13)
Tell Me In A Whisper (15)
Tempo Feliz (Happy Times) (4)
This Masquerade (13)
Tim Dom Dom (1)
Tonga (7)
Triste (2)
Tristeza (Goodbye Sadness) (2)

Trouble With Hello Is Goodbye (14)
Upa, Neguinho (5)
Veleiro (The Sailboat) (4)
Viola (8)
Viramundo (9)
Voce Abusou (13)
Voo Doo (17)
Waiting For Love (13)
Walk The Way You Talk (12)
Watch What Happens (2)
Waters Of March (13)
Wave (2)
What The World Needs Now (7)
When Summer Turns To Snow (5)
Where Are You Coming From? (7)
Where Is The Love (12)
Where To Now St. Peter (15)
Why (16)
Wichita Lineman (7) *95*
With A Little Help From My Friends (3,8)
Ye-Me-Le (7)
You Been Away Too Long (14)
You Can't Dress Up A Broken Heart (12)
You Stepped Out Of A Dream (6)
Zanzibar (10)

MEN OF VIZION   '96

R&B vocal group from Brooklyn, New York: George Spencer, Corley Randolph, Spanky Williams, Brian Deramus and Desmond Greggs.

7/6/96	186	4	©	Personal	$10	MJJ Music 66947

Do Thangz
Forgive Me

House Keeper *67*
Instant Love

It's Only Just A Dream
Joyride

Night And Day
Personal

Show You The Way To Go
That's Alright

When You Need Someone
You Told Me You Loved Me

MENUDO   '85

Teen vocal group from Puerto Rico. Many personnel changes due to rule that members must retire at age 16. Ricky Martin was a member from 1984-88.

3/10/84	108	12	©	1 Reaching Out	$10	RCA Victor 4993
5/25/85	100	19	©	2 Menudo	$10	RCA Victor 5420

Because Of Love (1)
Chocolate Candy (1)
Come Home (2)
Don't Hold Back (2)

Explosion (2)
Fly Away (1)
Gimme Rock (1)
Gotta Get On Movin' (1)

Heavenly Angel (1)
Hold Me (2) *62*
Indianapolis (1)
If You're Not Here (By My Side) (2)

Like A Cannonball (1)
Motorcycle Dreamer (1)
Oh, My Love (2)

Please Be Good To Me (2)
That's What You Do (1)
Transformation (2)
When I Dance With You (2)

You And Me All The Way (2)

MEN WITHOUT HATS   '83

Techno-rock group from Montreal: brothers Ivan (vocals), Stefan (guitar) and Colin (keyboards) Doroschuk, with Allan McCarthy (drums).

8/6/83	13	26	●	1 Rhythm Of Youth	$10	Backstreet 39002
10/6/84	127	4		2 Folk Of The '80s (Part III)	$10	MCA 5487
11/14/87+	73	25	©	3 Pop Goes The World	$10	Mercury 832730

Antarctica (1)
Ban The Game (1)
Bright Side Of The Sun (3)
Cocoricci (Le Tango Des Voleurs) (1)

End (Of The World) (3)
Eurotheme (2)
Folk Of The '80s (Part III) (2)
Great Ones Remember (1)
I Got The Message (1)

I Know Their Name (2)
I Like (1) *84*
I Sing Last (medley) (2)
Ideas For Walls (1)
In The Name Of Angels (3)

Jenny Wore Black (3)
La Valese D'Eugenie (3)
Lose My Way (3)
Messiahs Die Young (2)
Moonbeam (3)

Mother's Opinion (1)
No Dancing (2)
Not For Tears (medley) (2)

MEN WITHOUT HATS

O Sole Mio (3)	**Pop Goes The World** (3) *20*	**Safety Dance** (1) *3*	Unsatisfaction (2)	Where Do The Boys Go? (2)
On Tuesday (3)	Real World (3)	Things In My Life (1)	Walk On Water (medley) (3)	

MERCEDES '99
Born Raquel Miller in 1978 in Detroit. Female rapper.

7/17/99	72	5	©	**Rear End**		$10	No Limit 50085

Bonnie & Clyde	Crazy Bout Ya	Kiss Da Cat	Pu**y
Camouflage	Do You Wanna Ride	My Love	Talk 2 Me
Candlelight & Champagne	Free Game	N's Ain't S**t	What You Need
Chillin	Hit 'Em	Pony Ride	You're The Only One
	I Can Tell		
	I Need A Thug		
	It's Your Thing *96*		

MERCER, Roy D. '99
Roy D. Mercer is a fictional character invented by DJ's Phil Stone and Brent Douglas of KMOD in Tulsa, Oklahoma. Albums contain crank phone calls.

5/9/98	160	5	©	1	**How Big'a Boy Are Ya? Volume 4**	[C]	$10	Capitol 94301
2/13/99	138	4	©	2	**How Big'a Boy Are Ya? Volume 5**	[C]	$10	Virgin 46854
11/6/99	164	3	©	3	**How Big'a Boy Are Ya? Volume 6**	[C]	$10	Virgin 48214

Answering Machine Message (3)	Bowlin' Ball Fungus (3)	Dead Goat (1)	How Big'a Boy Are Ya? (3)	Septic Tank (2)	Vet Bill (3)
Arts & Craps (1)	Bury'd Cat (3)	Fingernails (1)	Love Birds (1)	Sharon Gene's Birthday (2)	X-ray-ologist (3)
Baby Sittin' (1)	Bus Driver (3)	Friday The 13th (2)	Modelin' Job (2)	Sissy Dog (2)	
Bad Popcorn (3)	Calf Fries (2)	Gas Meter (3)	Movers (3)	Spoilt Seed (3)	
Berth-A-Baby Down'ere (1)	Coffee Shop (2)	Good Fortune (2)	Orn'ry Mare (2)	Spring Fever (2)	
Boat Prop (3)	Corn Dog (1)	Horse Feed (3)	Pawn Shop (1)	Stuper Glue (3)	
	Cotton Candy Wigs (1)	Hot Tape Deck (2)	Safety Goggles (1)	Varnished Frogs (1)	

MERCHANT, Natalie '95
Born on 10/26/63 in Jamestown, New York. Lead singer of **10,000 Maniacs** from 1981-93.

7/8/95	13	92	▲[4]	©	1	**Tigerlily**		$10	Elektra 61745
6/6/98	8	51	▲	©	2	**Ophelia**		$10	Elektra 62196
11/27/99	82	7		©	3	**Live In Concert**	[L]	$10	Elektra 62444

recorded on 6/13/99 at the Neil Simon Theater in New York City

After The Gold Rush (3)	Dust Bowl (3)	I May Know The Word (1)	Life Is Sweet (2)	San Andreas Fault (1,3)	When They Ring The Golden Bells (2)
Beloved Wife (3)	Effigy (2)	**Jealousy** (1) *23*	Living, The (2)	Seven Years (1,3)	Where I Go (1)
Break Your Heart (2)	Frozen Charlotte (2)	Kind & Generous (2)	My Skin (3)	Space Oddity (3)	**Wonder** (1,3) *20*
Carnival (1,3) *10*	Gulf Of Araby (3)	King Of May (2)	Ophelia (2,3)	Thick As Thieves (2)	
Cowboy Romance (1)	Gun Shy (3)	Letter, The (1)	River (1)		

MERCURY, Freddie '85
Born Frederick Bulsara on 9/5/46 in Zanzibar, Tanzania. Died of AIDS on 11/24/91 (age 45). Lead singer of **Queen**.

5/18/85	159	6	©	**Mr. Bad Guy**		$10	Columbia 40071

Foolin' Around	Living On My Own	Made In Heaven	My Love Is Dangerous	Your Kind Of Lover
I Was Born To Love You *76*	Love Me Like There's No	Man Made Paradise	There Must Be More To Life	
Let's Turn It On	Tomorrow	Mr. Bad Guy	Than This	

MERCY '69
Pop group from Florida: James Marvell, Ronnie Caudill, Roger Fuentes, Buddy Good, Debbie Lewis and Brenda McNish.

6/21/69	38	15		**The Mercy & Love (Can Make You Happy)**		$20	Sundi 803

Back In My Arms Again	Hooked On A Feeling	**Love (Can Make You**	Our Winter Love
Daydream	I've Been Lonely Too Long	**Happy)** *2*	Tracks Of My Tears
Hey Jude		My Girl	Worst That Could Happen

MERRITT, Bishop Andrew '00
Born in 1950 in Detroit. Founded the Straight Gate Church in 1978 in Detroit. Elevated to Bishop in 1990.

10/21/00	68	1	©	**Faith In The House**	[L]	$10	Integrity 14482

BISHOP ANDREW MERRITT & THE STRAIGHT GATE MASS CHOIR

Call Of Faith (Spoken Word)	Faith To Believe	I Live By Faith	Mustard Seed Faith	There Is None Like You	Victory Chant
Come Into His Presence	Faith To Believe (Spoken Word)	I Was Created To Worship	Only Believe	Thy Word	We Sing Praises
Cover Me Lord	Hallowed Be Your Name	Lord Thy Word	Only Believe (Spoken Word)	Thy Word (Spoken Word)	We'll Be Faithful

MERRY-GO-ROUND, The '67
Pop group from Los Angeles: **Emitt Rhodes** (vocals), Gary Kato (guitar), Bill Rinehart (bass; **The Leaves**) and Joel Larson (drums: **The Grass Roots**).

11/18/67	190	2		**The Merry-Go-Round**		$40	A&M 4132

Clown's No Good	Gonna Leave You Alone	Low Down	We're In Love	**You're A Very Lovely**
Early In The Morning	Had To Run Around	On Your Way Out	Where Have You Been All Of	**Woman** *94*
Gonna Fight The War	**Live** *63*	Time Will Show The Wiser	My Life	

MERRYWEATHER & FRIENDS '69
Born Neil Merryweather in San Francisco. Rock guitarist. Friends: **Steve Miller**, **Dave Mason** and Barry Goldberg.

10/4/69	199	2		**Word Of Mouth**		$20	Capitol 278 [2]

Dr. Mason	Hooker Blues	Licked The Spoon	Rough Dried Woman	We Can Make It
Hard Times	I Found Love	Mrs. Roberts' Son	Sun Down Lady	Where I Am
Hello Little Girl	Just A Little Bit	News	Teach You How To Fly	

MESSINA, Jim '79
Born on 12/5/47 in Maywood, California; raised in Harlingen, Texas. Member of **Buffalo Springfield** (1967-68) and **Poco** (1968-70). Formed **Loggins & Messina** duo with **Kenny Loggins**. Joined the re-formed Poco in 1989.

10/20/79	58	14	©	1	**Oasis**		$12	Columbia 36140

JIMMY MESSINA

6/20/81	95	11	©	2	**Messina**		$12	Warner 3559

Break The Chain (2)	(Is This) Lovin' You Lady (1)	Magic Of Love (1)	Seeing You (For The First	Talk To Me (1)
Child Of My Dreams (2)	It's All Right Here (2)	Money Alone (2)	Time) (1)	Waitin' On You (1)
Do You Want To Dance (1)	Love Is Here (1)	Move Into Your Heart (2)	Stay The Night (2)	Whispering Waters (2)
Free To Be Me (1)	Lovin' You Every Minute (2)	New And Different Way (1)	Sweet Love (2)	

MESSINA, Jo Dee '00
Born on 8/25/70 in Holliston, Massachusetts. Country singer.

5/4/96	146	5		© 1	Jo Dee Messina			$10	Curb 77820
4/4/98	61	104	▲²	© 2	I'm Alright	C:#2²/19		$10	Curb 77904
8/19/00	19	39	●	© 3	Burn..			$10	Curb 77977

Angelene (3)
Another Shoulder At The Wheel (1)
Because You Love Me (2) 53
Bring On The Rain (3)
Burn (3) 42
Bye Bye (2) 43
Closer (3)
Cover Me (2)
Dare To Dream (3)
Do You Wanna Make Something Of It (1)
Downtime (3) 59
Even God Must Get The Blues (2)
Every Little Girl's Dream (1)
He'd Never Seen Julie Cry (1)
Heads Carolina, Tails California (1)
I Didn't Have To Leave You (1)
I Know A Heartache (1)
I'm Alright (2) 43
If Not You (3)
Lesson In Leavin' (2) 28
Let It Go (1)
No Time For Tears (1)
Nothing I Can Do (3)
On A Wing And A Prayer (1)
Saturday Night (3)
Silver Thunderbird (2)
Stand Beside Me (2) 34
That's The Way (3) 25
These Are The Days (3)
Walk To The Light (1)
You're Not In Kansas Anymore (1)

METAL CHURCH '89
Hard-rock group from Kent, Washington: David Wayne (vocals), Craig Wells and Kurdt Vanderhoof (guitars), Duke Erikson (bass) and Kirk Arrington (drums). By 1989, Mike Howe had replaced Wayne and John Marshall had replaced Vanderhoof.

| 11/8/86+ | 92 | 23 | | © 1 | The Dark.. | | | $10 | Elektra 60493 |
| 3/11/89 | 75 | 15 | | © 2 | Blessing In Disguise .... | | | $10 | Elektra 60817 |

Anthem To The Estranged (2)
Badlands (2)
Burial At Sea (1)
Cannot Tell A Lie (2)
Dark, The (1)
Fake Healer (2)
It's A Secret (2)
Line Of Death (1)
Method To Your Madness (1)
Of Unsound Mind (2)
Over My Dead Body (1)
Powers That Be (2)
Psycho (1)
Rest In Pieces (April 15, 1912) (2)
Spell Can't Be Broken (2)
Start The Fire (1)
Ton Of Bricks (1)
Watch The Children Pray (1)
Western Alliance (1)

METALLICA ★56★ '91
Hard-rock group formed in Los Angeles: James Hetfield (vocals, guitar), Kirk Hammett (guitar), Cliff Burton (bass) and Lars Ulrich (drums). Original guitarist Dave Mustaine left in 1982 to form **Megadeth**. Burton was killed in a bus crash on 9/27/86 (age 24); replaced by Jason Newsted.

1)Metallica 2)Load 3)Reload

9/29/84+	100	50	▲⁴	© 1	Ride The Lightning	C:#5/396		$15	Megaforce 769
					also issued on Elektra 60396 in November 1984				
3/29/86	29	72	▲⁵	© 2	Master Of Puppets	C:#6/416		$10	Elektra 60439
4/5/86	155	10		© 3	Kill 'Em All		[E]	$15	Megaforce 069
					reissue of their 1983 debut album				
9/12/87	28	30	▲	© 4	The $5.98 E.P.: Garage Days Re-Revisited	C:#11/25	[M]	$10	Elektra 60757
2/13/88	120	8	▲³	© 5	Kill 'Em All	C:#20/84	[E-R]	$10	Elektra 60766
					features 2 bonus tracks not included on original release				
9/24/88	6	83	▲⁷	© 6	...And Justice For All	C:#3/473		$15	Elektra 60812 [2]
8/31/91	❶⁴	281	▲¹²	© 7	Metallica	C:❶³³/246		$10	Elektra 61113
					due to the all black cover, also known among fans as *The Black Album*				
12/11/93	26	7		© 8	Live Shit: Binge & Purge		[L]	$50	Elektra 61594 [3]
					recorded at Mexico City's Sports Palace; includes 3 videocassettes of concerts in San Diego (1992) and Seattle (1989) plus a 72-page booklet and a "scary guy" stencil; packaged in a cardboard touring trunk replica				
6/22/96	❶⁴	98	▲⁴	© 9	Load	C:#31/12		$10	Elektra 61923
12/6/97	❶¹	75	▲³	© 10	Reload	C:#41/3		$10	Elektra 62126
12/12/98	2¹	44	▲⁵	© 11	Garage Inc.		[K]	$15	Elektra 62299 [2]
					disc 1: new recordings; disc 2: songs released from 1984-1995				
12/11/99	2¹	49	▲⁴	© 12	S&M		[L]	$12	Elektra 62504 [2]
					with the **San Francisco Symphony Orchestra**; recorded on 4/21/99 at the Berkeley Community Theater				

Ain't My Bitch (9)
Am I Evil? (5,8,11)
...And Justice For All (6)
(Anesthesia)-Pulling Teeth (3,5)
Astronomy (11)
Attitude (10)
Bad Seed (10)
Battery (2,8,12)
Better Than You (10)
Blackened (6)
Bleeding Me (9,12)
Blitzkrieg (5,11)
Breadfan (11)
Call Of Ktulu (11)
Call Of The Ktulu (12)
Carpe Diem Baby (10)
Crash Course In Brain Surgery (4,11)
Creeping Death (1,8)
Cure (9)
Damage Case (11)
Damage, Inc. (2)
Devil's Dance (10,12)
Die, Die My Darling (11)
Disposable Heroes (2)
Don't Tread On Me (7)
Dyers Eve (6)
Ecstacy Of Gold (12)
Enter Sandman (7,8,12) 16
Escape (11)
Eye Of The Beholder (6)
Fade To Black (1,8)
Fight Fire With Fire (1)
Fixxxer (10)
For Whom The Bell Tolls (1,8,12)
Four Horsemen (3,5,8)
Frayed Ends Of Sanity (6)
Free Speech For The Dumb (11)
Fuel (10,12)
God That Failed (7)
Green Hell (medley) (4,11)
Harvester Of Sorrow (6,8)
Helpless (4,11)
Hero Of The Day (9,12) 60
Hit The Lights (3,5)
Holier Than Thou (7)
House Jack Built (9)
- Human (12)
It's Electric (11)
Jump In The Fire (3,5)
Justice Medley (8)
Killing Time (11)
King Nothing (9) 90
Last Caress (4,8,11)
Leper Messiah (2)
Loverman (11)
Low Man's Lyric (10)
Mama Said (9)
Master Of Puppets (2,8,12)
Memory Remains (10,12) 28
Mercyful Fate (11)
Metal Militia (3,5)
More I See (11)
Motorbreath (3,5,8)
My Friend Of Misery (7)
No Leaf Clover (12) 74
No Remorse (3,5)
Nothing Else Matters (7,8,12) 34
Of Wolf And Man (7,8,12)
One (6,8,12) 35
Orion (2)
Outlaw Torn (9,12)
Overkill (11)
Phantom Lord (3,5)
Poor Twisted Me (9)
Prince, The (11)
Prince Charming (10)
Ride The Lightning (1)
Ronnie (9)
Sabbra Cadabra (11)
Sad But True (7,8,12) 98
Seek & Destroy (3,5,8)
Shortest Straw (7)
Slither (10)
Small Hours (4,11)
So What (11)
Solos (Bass/Guitar) (8)
Stone Cold Crazy (8,11)
Stone Dead Forever (11)
Struggle Within (7)
Thing That Should Not Be (2,12)
Thorn Within (9)
Through The Never (7,8)
To Live Is To Die (6)
Too Late Too Late (11)
Trapped Under Ice (1)
Tuesday's Gone (11)
Turn The Page (11)
2 X 4 (9)
Unforgiven, The (7,8) 35
Unforgiven II (10) 59
Until It Sleeps (9,12) 10
Wait, The (4,11)
Wasting My Hate (9)
Welcome Home (Sanitarium) (2,8)
Where The Wild Things Are (10)
Wherever I May Roam (7,8,12) 82
Whiplash (3,5,8)
Whiskey In The Jar (11)

METERS, The '69
R&B instrumental group formed in New Orleans: Arthur Neville (keyboards; brother of **Aaron Neville**), Leo Nocentelli (guitar), George Porter (bass) and Joseph Modeliste (drums). Group disbanded in 1977, when Art, Aaron, and brothers Charles and Cyril formed **The Neville Brothers**.

6/21/69	108	15		© 1	The Meters		[I]	$75	Josie 4010
1/24/70	198	2		© 2	Look-Ka Py Py		[I]	$75	Josie 4011
7/18/70	200	2		© 3	Struttin'			$75	Josie 4012
9/6/75	179	3		© 4	Fire On The Bayou			$50	Reprise 2228

Ann (1)
Art (1)
Britches (3)
Can You Do Without? (4)
Cardova (1)
Chicken Strut (3) 50
Cissy Strut (1) 23
Darlin' Darlin' (3)
Dry Spell (2)
Ease Back (1) 61
Fire On The Bayou (4)
Funky Miracle (2)
Go For Yourself (3)
Hand Clapping Song (3) 89
Here Comes The Meter Man (1)
Hey! Last Minute (3)
Joog (3)
Liar (4)
Little Old Money Maker (2)
Live Wire (1)
Liver Splash (3)
Look-Ka Py Py (2) 56
Love Slip Upon Ya (4)
Mardi Gras Mambo (4)
Middle Of The Road (4)
Mob, The (2)
9 'Til 5 (2)
Oh, Calcutta! (2)
Out In The Country (4)
Pungee (2)

METERS, The — Cont'd

Ride Your Pony (3)
Rigor Mortis (2)
Running Fast (4)
Same Old Thing (3)
Sehorns Farm (1)
Simple Song (1)
6V6 LA (1)
Sophisticated Cissy (1) *34*
Stormy (1)
Talkin' 'Bout New Orleans (4)
They All Ask'd For You (4)
Thinking (2)
This Is My Last Affair (2)
Tippi-Toes (3)
Wichita Lineman (3)
Yeah, You're Right (2)
You're A Friend Of Mine (4)

★240★ **METHENY, Pat, Group** '79

Born on 8/12/55 in Kansas City, Missouri. Jazz guitarist. Revolving lineup of group has included Lyle Mays (piano), Mark Egan (bass), Dan Gottlieb (drums), Nana Vasconcelos (vocals), Steve Rodby (bass), Pedro Aznar (percussion), Paul Wertico (drums), Armando Marcal (percussion), David Blamires (vocals) and Mark Ledford (vocals, trumpet).

1)New Chautauqua 2)Offramp 3)As Falls Wichita, So Falls Wichita Falls

DEBUT	PEAK	WKS	CD	#	Album Title	Sym	$	Label & Number
8/26/78	123	12	©	1	**Pat Metheny Group**	[I]	$12	ECM 1114
5/5/79	44	22	©	2	**New Chautauqua**	[I]	$12	ECM 1131

PAT METHENY

| 11/24/79+ | 53 | 24 | © | 3 | **American Garage** | [I] | $12 | ECM 1155 |
| 11/1/80 | 89 | 14 | © | 4 | **80/81** | [I] | $15 | ECM 1180 [2] |

PAT METHENY

| 6/20/81 | 50 | 21 | © | 5 | **As Falls Wichita, So Falls Wichita Falls** | [I] | $12 | ECM 1190 |

PAT METHENY & LYLE MAYS

5/22/82	50	28	©	6	**Offramp**	[I]	$12	ECM 1216
6/25/83	62	17	©	7	**Travels**	[I-L]	$15	ECM 23791 [2]
5/12/84	116	9	©	8	**Rejoicing**	[I]	$12	ECM 25006

PAT METHENY

10/13/84	91	35	©	9	**First Circle**	[I]	$12	ECM 25008
3/9/85	54	10	©	10	**The Falcon And The Snowman**	[I-S]	$12	EMI America 17150
8/22/87	86	15	● ©	11	**Still Life (Talking)**	[I]	$10	Geffen 24145
7/22/89	66	18	● ©	12	**Letter From Home**	[I]	$10	Geffen 24245
7/7/90	154	6	©	13	**Question and Answer**	[I]	$10	Geffen 24293

PAT METHENY/DAVE HOLLAND/ROY HAYNES

| 8/1/92 | 110 | 17 | ● © | 14 | **Secret Story** | [I] | $10 | Geffen 24468 |

PAT METHENY

| 8/7/93 | 170 | 2 | © | 15 | **The Road To You** | [I-L] | $10 | Geffen 24601 |
| 4/23/94 | 181 | 2 | © | 16 | **I Can See Your House From Here** | [I] | $10 | Blue Note 27765 |

JOHN SCOFIELD & PAT METHENY

2/4/95	83	10	©	17	**We Live Here**	[I]	$10	Geffen 24729
12/7/96	187	1	©	18	**"Quartet"**	[I]	$10	Geffen 24978
10/25/97	124	4	©	19	**Imaginary Day**	[I]	$10	Warner 46791

Above The Treetops (14)
Across The Sky (19)
Airstream (3)
All The Things You Are (13)
Always And Forever (14)
American Garage (3)
And Then I Knew (17)
Antonia (14)
April Joy (1)
Aprilwind (1)
Are We There Yet (12)
Are You Going With Me? (6,7)
As A Flower Blossoms (I Am Running To You) (14)
As Falls Wichita, So Falls Wichita Falls (5,7)
As I Am (18)
Au Lait (17)
Awakening, The (19)
Badland (18)
Barcarole (6)
Bat, The (4)
Bat Part II (6)
Beat 70 (12,15)
Better Days Ahead (12,15)
Blues For Pat (8)
Calling, The (8)
Capture (10)

Cathedral In A Suitcase (14)
Change Of Heart (13)
Chris (10)
Country Poem (2)
(Cross The) Heartland (3)
Daulton Lee (10)
Daybreak (2)
Dismantling Utopia (18)
Distance (18)
Double Blind (18)
Dream Of The Return (12)
Eighteen (6)
80/81 (4)
End Of The Game (9)
Epic, The (3)
Episode d'Azur (17)
Estupenda Graca (5)
Every Day (I Thank You) (4)
Every Summer Night (12)
Everybody's Party (16)
Extent Of The Lie (10)
Extradition (7)
Facing West (14)
Falcon, The (10)
Fallen Star (medley) (2)
Farmer's Trust (7)
Fields, The Sky (7)
Finding And Believing (14)

First Circle (9,15)
5-5-7 (12)
Flight Of The Falcon (medley) (10)
Follow Me (19)
45/8 (12)
Forward March (9)
Girls Next Door (17)
Glacier (18)
Goin' Ahead (4,7)
Goodbye (7)
H & H (13)
Half Life Of Absolution (15)
Have You Heard (12,15)
Heat Of The Day (19)
Here To Stay (17)
Hermitage (2)
Humpty Dumpty (8)
I Can See Your House From Here (16)
If I Could (9)
Imaginary Day (19)
In Her Family (11)
Into The Dream (19)
It's For You (5)
(It's Just) Talk (11)
Jaco (1)
James (6)

Language Of Time (18)
Last Train Home (11,15)
Law Years (13)
Letter From Home (12,15)
Level Of Deception (19)
Lone Jack (1)
Lonely Woman (8)
Long-Ago Child (medley) (2)
Longest Summer (14)
Mas Alla (Beyond) (9)
Message To My Friend (16)
Minuano (Six Eight) (11)
Mojave (18)
Montevideo (18)
Naked Moon (15)
Never Too Far Away (13)
New Chautauqua (2)
No Matter What (16)
No Way Jose (16)
Not To Be Forgotten (Our Final Hour) (14)
Oceania (18)
Offramp (6)
Old Folks (13)
One Way To Be (16)
Open (4)
Ozark (5)
Phase Dance (1,7)

Praise (9)
Pretty Scattered (4)
Psalm 121 (10)
Question And Answer (13)
Quiet Rising (16)
Rain River (14)
Red One (16)
Red Sky (17)
Rejoicing (8)
Road To You (15)
Roots Of Coincidence (19)
S.C.O. (16)
San Lorenzo (1,7)
Say The Brother's Name (16)
Search, The (3)
Second Thought (18)
See The World (14)
September Fifteenth (5)
Seven Days (18)
Slip Away (12)
So May It Secretly Begin (11)
Solar (13)
Solo from 'More Travels' (15)
Something To Remind You (17)
Sometimes I See (18)
Song For Bilbao (7)
Spring Ain't Here (12)
Story From A Stranger (8)

Story Within The Story (19)
Straight On Red (7)
Stranger In Town (17)
Sueno Con Mexico (2)
Sunlight (14)
Take Me There (18)
Tears Inside (8)
Tell Her You Saw Me (14)
Tell It All (9)
Third Wind (11,15)
This Is Not America (10) *32*
Three Flights Up (13)
To The End Of The World (17)
Too Soon Tomorrow (19)
Travels (7)
Truth Will Always Be (14)
Turnaround (4)
Two Folk Songs (4)
Vidala (12)
Waiting For An Answer (8)
We Live Here (17)
When We Were Free (18)
Yolanda, You Learn (9)
You Speak My Language (16)

METHOD MAN '98

Born Clifford Smith on 4/1/71 in Staten Island, New York. Male rapper. Member of **Wu-Tang Clan**.

DEBUT	PEAK	WKS	RIAA	CD	#	Album Title	$	Label & Number
12/3/94	4	43	▲	©	1	**Tical**	$10	Def Jam 523839

produced by Prince Rakeem (**Wu-Tang Clan**)

| 12/5/98 | 2[1] | 24 | ▲ | © | 2 | **Tical 2000: Judgement Day** | $10 | Def Jam 558920 |
| 10/16/99 | 3 | 33 | ▲ | © | 3 | **Blackout!** | $10 | Def Jam 546609 |

METHOD MAN/REDMAN

All I Need (1)
Big Dogs (2,3)
Biscuits (1)
Blackout (3)
Break Ups 2 Make Ups (2) *98*
Bring The Pain (1) *45*
Cereal Killer (3)
Cheka (3)

Cradle Rock (2)
Da Rockwilder (3)
Dangerous Grounds (2)
Dat's Dat S**t (1)
Elements (2)
Fire Ina Hole (3)
4 Seasons (3)
Grid Iron Rap (2)

How High (3)
I Get My Thang In Action (1)
Judgement Day (2)
Killin' Fields (2)
Maaad Crew (3)
Meth Vs. Chef (1)
Method Man (1)
Mi Casa (3)

Mr. Sandman (1)
1, 2, 1, 2 (3)
P.L.O. Style (1)
Party Crasher (2)
Perfect World (2)
Play IV Keeps (2)
?, The (3)
Release Yo' Delf (1) *98*

Retro Godfather (2)
Run 4 Cover (3)
Spazzola (2)
Step By Step (2)
Stimulation (1)
Sub Crazy (1)
Suspect Chin Music (2)
Sweet Love (2)

Tear It Off (3)
Tical (1)
Torture (2)
Well All Rite Cha (3)
What The Blood Clot (1)
Y.O.U. (1)
You Play Too Much (2)

METHODS OF MAYHEM '99

Group consists of former **Mötley Crüe** member Tommy Lee (vocals, guitar, drums) and male rapper Ti-Lo.

DEBUT	PEAK	WKS	RIAA	CD	#	Album Title	$	Label & Number
12/25/99	71	19	●	©	1	**Methods Of Mayhem**	$10	MCA 112020

Anger Management
Crash
Get Naked
Hypocritical
Metamorphosis
Mr. Onsomeothershits
Narcotic
New Skin
Proposition Fuck You
Spun
Who The Hell Cares

METHRONE '00

Born Carlos Methrone Reynolds on 11/6/75 in Plant City, Florida. R&B singer.

| 7/22/00 | 129 | 10 | | © | My Life | | | $10 | Clatown 27567 |

Got 2 Go — Hold Me — I Wanna Get Freaky — Last Time — Loving Each Other 4 Life — Methrone's Dance — My Life — Slow & Steady — You Don't Have 2 Worry — Your Body

MEYER, Edgar — see MA, Yo-Yo

MFSB '74

Group of studio musicians based at Philadelphia Sigma Sound Studios. Produced by Kenny Gamble and Leon Huff for their own label, Philadelphia International. Also recorded as The James Boys and Family. Name means "Mother, Father, Sister, Brother."

4/21/73	131	10		1	MFSB		[I]	$12	Philadelphia Int'l. 32046
1/19/74	4	35	●	2	Love Is The Message		[I]	$12	Philadelphia Int'l. 32707
6/14/75	44	13		3	Universal Love		[I]	$12	Philadelphia Int'l. 33158
12/6/75+	39	12		4	Philadelphia Freedom		[I]	$12	Philadelphia Int'l. 33845
7/10/76	106	9		5	Summertime			$12	Philadelphia Int'l. 34238

Back Stabbers (1) — Bitter Sweet (2) — Brothers And Sisters (4) — Cheaper To Keep Her (2) — Family Affair (1) — Ferry Avenue (4) — Freddie's Dead (1) — Get Down With The Philly Sound (4) — Hot Summer Nights (5) — Human Machine (3) — I Hear Music (medley) (2) — I'm On Your Side (5) — K-Jee (3) — Lay In Low (1) — Let's Go Disco (3) — Love Has No Time Or Place (3) — Love Is The Message (medley) (2) 85 — MFSB (3) — Morning Tears (4) — My Mood (3) — My One And Only Love (2) — Philadelphia Freedom (4) — Picnic In The Park (5) — Plenty Good Livin' (5) — Poinciana (1) — Sexy (3) 42 — Smile Happy (4) — Something For Nothing (1) — South Philly (4) — Summertime (5) — Summertime And I'm Feelin' Mellow (5) — Sunnin' And Funnin' (5) — T.L.C. (Tender Lovin' Care) (3) — TSOP (The Sound Of Philadelphia) (2) 1 — Touch Me In The Morning (medley) (2) — We Got The Time (5) — When Your Love Is Gone (4) — Zip, The (4) 91

MIAMI SOUND MACHINE — see ESTEFAN, Gloria

MIA X '98

Born Mia Young in Mississippi. Female rapper. Member of Tru.

| 7/12/97 | 21 | 17 | ● | © 1 | Unlady Like | | | $10 | No Limit 50705 |
| 11/21/98 | 7 | 10 | | © 2 | Mama Drama | | | $10 | No Limit 53502 |

Ain't 2 Be Played Wit (1) — All N's (1) — Bring Da Drama (1) — Bring It On (2) — Daddy (1) — Don't Blame Me (1) — Don't Start No Shit (2) — Fallen Angels (Dear Jill) (2) — Flip 2 Rip (2) — 4ever Tru (1) — Ghetto Livin' (2) — Hoodlum Poetry (1) — I Don't Know Why (1) — I Pitty U (1) — I Think Somebody (2) — I'll Take Ya Man '97 (1) — Imma Shine (2) — Let's Get It Straight (1) — Like Dat (2) — Mama Drama (2) — Mama's Family (1) — Mama's Tribute (2) — Mommie's Angels (1) — Party Don't Stop (1) — Play Wit Pussy (2) — Puttin' It Down (2) — Rainy Dayz (1) — Ride Or Run (2) — Rip Jill (2) — Sex Ed. (2) — TRU Bitches (2) — Thank You (1) — Thugs Like Me (2) — Unladylike (1) — What's Ya Point (2) — Whatcha Wanna Do? (2) 41 — Who Got Tha Clout (1) — You & Me (1) — You Don't Wanna Go 2 War (1)

MICHAEL, George/Wham! ★271★ '88

Born Georgios Kyriacos Panayiotou on 6/25/63 in Bushey, England. Wham!, formed in early '80s, centered around Michael's vocals and songwriting, and included Andrew Ridgeley (born on 1/26/63, Bushey, England) on guitar. Their association ended in 1986.

WHAM! U.K.:

| 8/20/83 | 83 | 44 | ● | © 1 | Fantastic | | | $10 | Columbia 38911 |

WHAM!:

| 11/10/84+ | ❶3 | 80 | ▲6 | © 2 | Make It Big | | | $10 | Columbia 39595 |
| 7/19/86 | 10 | 28 | ▲ | © 3 | Music From The Edge Of Heaven | | | $10 | Columbia 40285 |

GEORGE MICHAEL:

| 11/21/87+ | ❶12 | 87 | ▲10 | © 4 | Faith | | | $10 | Columbia 40867 |

1988 Grammy winner: Album of the Year

| 9/29/90 | 2¹ | 42 | ▲2 | © 5 | Listen Without Prejudice | | | $10 | Columbia 46898 |
| 5/8/93 | 46 | 15 | | © 6 | Five Live | | [L-M] | $10 | Hollywood 61479 |

GEORGE MICHAEL AND QUEEN with Lisa Stansfield — includes the studio track "Dear Friends" by Queen

6/1/96	6	24	▲	© 7	Older			$10	DreamWorks 50000
11/28/98	24	23	▲2	© 8	Ladies & Gentlemen - The Best Of George Michael		[G]	$15	Epic 69635 [2]
1/1/00	157	7		9	Songs From The Last Century			$10	Virgin 48740

Bad Boys (1) 60 — Battlestations (3) — Blue (3) — Brother Can You Spare A Dime (9) — Calling You (6) — Careless Whisper (2,8) 1 — Club Tropicana (1) — Come On (1) — Cowboys And Angels (5,8) — Credit Card Baby (2) — Desafinado (8) — Different Corner (3,8) 7 — Don't Let The Sun Go Down On Me (8) 1 — Edge Of Heaven (3) 10 — Everything She Wants (2) 1 — Faith (4,8) 1 — Fastlove (7,8) 8 — Father Figure (4,8) 1 — First Time Ever I Saw Your Face (9) — Free (7) — Freedom (2) 3 — Freedom (5,8) 8 — Hand To Mouth (4) — Hard Day (4,8) — Heal The Pain (5,8) — Heartbeat (2) — I Can't Make You Love Me (8) — I Knew You Were Waiting (For Me) (8) 1 — I Remember You (9) — I Want Your Sex (4,8) 2 — I'm Your Man (3) 3 — If You Were There (2) — It Doesn't Really Matter (7) — Jesus To A Child (7,8) 7 — Killer/Papa Was A Rollin' Stone (6,8) 69 — Kissing A Fool (4,8) 5 — Last Christmas (3) — Like A Baby (2) — Look At Your Hands (4) — Love Machine (1) — Miss Sarajevo (9) — Moment With You (8) — Monkey (4,8) 1 — Mother's Pride (5) 46 — Move On (7) — My Baby Just Cares For Me (9) — Nothing Looks The Same In The Light (1) — Older (7) — One More Try (4,8) 1 — Outside (8) — Praying For Time (5,8) 1 — Ray Of Sunshine (1) — Roxanne (9) — Secret Love (9) — Somebody To Love (6,8) 30 — Something To Save (5) — Soul Free (5) — Spinning The Wheel (7,8) — Star People (7) — Star People 97 (8) — Strangest Thing (7) — These Are The Days Of Our Lives (6) — They Won't Go When I Go (5) — To Be Forgiven (7) — Too Funky (8) 10 — Waiting For That Day (5,8) 27 — Wake Me Up Before You Go-Go (2) 1 — Wham! Rap '86 (3) — Wham Rap (Enjoy What You Do) (1) — Where Did Your Heart Go? (3) 50 — Where Or When (9) — Wild Is The Wind (9) — You Can't Always Get What You Want (medley) (8) — You Have Been Loved (7,8) — You've Changed (9) — Young Guns (Go For It!) (1)

MICHAELS, Lee '71

Born on 11/24/45 in Los Angeles. Rock singer/organist.

8/30/69	53	26		© 1	Lee Michaels			$15	A&M 4199
8/1/70	51	19		© 2	Barrel			$15	A&M 4249
6/5/71	16	36		© 3	"5th"			$15	A&M 4302
3/25/72	78	13		© 4	Space & First Takes			$15	A&M 4336
4/7/73	135	8		© 5	Lee Michaels Live		[L]	$20	A&M 3518 [2]
6/2/73	172	5		6	Nice Day For Something			$12	Columbia 32275

As Long As I Can (2) — Bell (6) — Call It Stormy Monday (5) — Can I Get A Witness (3) 39 — Day Of Change (2,5) — Didn't Have To Happen (3) — Didn't Know What I Had (2) — Do You Know What I Mean (3) 6 — (Don't Want No) Woman (medley) (1) — Drum Solo (5) — First Names (4) — Forty Reasons (5) — Frosty's (medley) (1) — Games (2) — Heighty Hi (1,5) — High Wind (6) — Hold On To Freedom (4,5) — I Don't Want Her (3) — Keep The Circle Turning (3) — Mad Dog (2,5)

580

MICHAELS, Lee

Murder In My Heart (For The Judge) (2)
My Friends (medley) (1)
My Lady (5)
Nothing Matters (But It Doesn't Matter) (6)
Oak Fire (3,5)
Olson Arrives At Two Fifty-Five (6)
Other Day (The Other Way) (6)
Own Special Way (As Long As) (4)
Rock & Roll Community (6)
Rock Me Baby (3,5)
Same Old Song (6)
So Hard (6)
Space And First Takes (4)
Stormy Monday (1)
Tell Me How Do You Feel (medley) (1)
Think I'll Cry (2)
Think I'll Go Back (medley) (1)
Thumbs (2,5)
Uummmm My Lady (2)
Want My Baby (1)
War (5)
Went Saw Mama (6)
What Now America (2)
When Johnny Comes Marching Home (2)
Who Could Want More (1)
Willie & The Hand Jive (3)
Ya Ya (3)
You Are What You Do (3)
Your Breath Is Bleeding (6)

MICHEL, Pras '98

Born Prakazrel Michael in 1972 in New York City. Member of **The Fugees**.

| 11/14/98 | 55 | 5 | | © | Ghetto Supastar .... | | | $10 | Ruffhouse 69516 |

PRAS

Amazing Grace
Blue Angels
Can't Stop The Shining (Rip Rock Pt. 2)
Dirty Cash
For The Love Of This Frowsey (Pt. 2)
Get Your Groove On
Ghetto Supastar (That Is What You Are) *15*
Hallelujah
Lowriders
Murder Dem
Wha' What Wha' What
What'cha Wanna Do
Yeah 'Eh Yeah 'Eh

MICHEL'LE '90

Born Michel'le Toussant in Los Angeles. R&B singer.

| 1/13/90 | 35 | 43 | ● | © | Michel'le .... | | | $10 | Ruthless 91282 |

produced by **Dr. Dre**

Close To Me
If?
Keep Watchin
Never Been In Love
Nicety *29*
No More Lies *7*
100% Woman
Silly Love Song
Something In My Heart *31*
Special Thanks

MIDLER, Bette ★126★ '89

Born on 12/1/45 in Paterson, New Jersey; raised in Hawaii. Singer/actress. In the Broadway show *Fiddler On The Roof* from 1967-70. Won the 1973 Best New Artist Grammy Award. **Barry Manilow** was her arranger/accompanist in early years. Starred in several movies.

1)Beaches 2)Some People's Lives 3)Bette Midler

| 12/9/72+ | 9 | 76 | ▲ | © 1 | The Divine Miss M | | | $15 | Atlantic 7238 |
| 12/8/73+ | 6 | 27 | ● | © 2 | Bette Midler | | | $15 | Atlantic 7270 |

above 2 co-produced by **Barry Manilow**

| 1/31/76 | 27 | 15 | | © 3 | Songs For The New Depression .... | | | $15 | Atlantic 18155 |
| 5/28/77 | 49 | 11 | | © 4 | Live At Last | | [L] | $20 | Atlantic 9000 [2] |

recorded at the Cleveland Music Hall

12/17/77+	51	14		© 5	Broken Blossom			$12	Atlantic 19151
9/22/79	65	17		© 6	Thighs And Whispers			$12	Atlantic 16004
12/22/79+	12	45	▲²	© 7	The Rose	C:#42/6	[L-S]	$12	Atlantic 16010
11/29/80	34	14		© 8	Divine Madness		[L-S]	$12	Atlantic 16022

recorded at the Pasadena Civic Auditorium

8/27/83	60	13		© 9	No Frills			$10	Atlantic 80070
12/21/85+	183	6		© 10	Mud Will Be Flung Tonight!		[C]	$10	Atlantic 81291
1/21/89	2³	176	▲³	© 11	Beaches		[S]	$10	Atlantic 81933
10/13/90+	6	73	▲²	© 12	Some People's Lives			$10	Atlantic 82129
11/30/91	22	21	●	© 13	For The Boys		[S]	$10	Atlantic 82329
7/10/93	50	37	▲	© 14	Experience The Divine - Greatest Hits	C:#26/18	[G]	$10	Atlantic 82497
12/25/93+	183	2		© 15	Gypsy		[TV]	$10	Atlantic 82551

aired on 12/12/93; includes the following tracks by members of the cast: "Overture," "May We Entertain You," "Baby June And Her Newsboys," "Little Lamb," "Dainty June And Her Farmboys," "If Momma Was Married," "All I Need Is The Girl," "You Gotta Get A Gimmick" and "Let Me Entertain You"

8/5/95	45	35	▲	© 16	Bette Of Roses			$10	Atlantic 82823
10/3/98	32	16	●	© 17	Bathhouse Betty			$10	Warner 47078
10/28/00	69	11		© 18	Bette			$10	Warner 47843

Alabama Song (medley) (4)
All I Need To Know (9) *77*
All Of A Sudden (12)
Am I Blue (1)
Around The World (medley) (4)
As Dreams Go By (16)
Baby It's Cold Outside (13)
Baby Mine (11)
Backstage (4)
Bang, You're Dead (4)
Beast Of Burden (9) *71*
Bed Of Roses (16)
Big Noise From Winnetka (6,8)
Big Socks (17)
Billy-A-Dick (13)
Birds (4)
Bless You Child (18)
Boogie Woogie Bugle Boy (1,4,8,14) *8*
Bottomless (16)
Boxing (17)
Breaking Up Somebody's Home (2)
Buckets Of Rain (3)
Camellia (1)
Chapel Of Love (1,8,14) *flip*
Color Of Roses (18)
Come Back Jimmy Dean (9)
Come Rain Or Come Shine (13)
Coping (1)
Cradle Days (6)
Da Doo Run Run (medley) (2)
Daytime Hustler (1)
Delta Dawn (1,4)
Dixie's Dream (medley) (13)
Do You Want To Dance? (1,4,14) *17*
Don't Say Nothin' Bad (About My Baby) (medley) (2)
Dream Is A Wish Your Heart Makes (5)
Dreamland (13)
Drinking Again (2,4)
E Street Shuffle (medley) (8)
Empty Bed Blues (5)
Every Road Leads Back To You (13) *78*
Everything's Coming Up Roses (15)
Favorite Waste Of Time (9) *78*
Fiesta In Rio (medley) (4)
Fire Down Below (8)
Fit Or Fat - Fat As I Am (10)
Fried Eggs (4)
Friends (1,4,14) *40*
Friendship (medley) (1)
From A Distance (12,14) *2*
Gift Of Love (12)
Girl Friend Of The Whirling Dervish (13)
Girl Is On To You (12)
Glory Of Love (11)
God Give Me Strength (18)
Hang On In There Baby (6)
South Seas Scene/Hawaiian War Chant (medley) (4)
He Was Too Good To Me (medley) (12)
Heart Over Head (9)
Hello In There (1,4,14)
Higher & Higher (Your Love Keeps Lifting Me) (2)
Hurricane (6)
Hurry On Down (4)
I Believe In You (16)
I Don't Want The Night To End (3)
I Know This Town (16)
I Know You By Heart (11)
I Never Talk To Strangers (5)
I Remember You (1)
I Shall Be Released (2,8)
I Sold My Heart To The Junkman (17)
I Think It's Going To Rain Today (11)
I'm Beautiful (17)
I'm Hip (17)
I've Still Got My Health (11)
In My Life (13,14)
In The Mood (2,4) *51*
In These Shoes (18)
In This Life (16)
Is It Love (9)
Istanbul (medley) (4)
It's Too Late (16)
Just My Imagination (Running Away With Me) (18)
Keep On Rockin' (7)
La Vie En Rose (5)
Last Time (16)
Laughing Matters (17)
Leader Of The Pack (1,8)
Let Me Call You Sweetheart (7)
Let Me Drive (9)
Let Me Just Follow Behind (3)
Long John Blues (4)
Love Me With A Feeling (7)
Love Says It's Waiting (3)
Love TKO (18)
Lullaby In Blue (17)
Lullaby Of Broadway (medley) (2,4)
Make Yourself Comfortable (5)
Marahuana (3)
Marriage, Movies, Madonna And Mick (10)
Married Men (4) *40*
Midnight In Memphis (7)
Millworker (6)
Miss Otis Regrets (12,14)
Moonlight Dancing (12)
Moses (18)
Mr. Goldstone (15)
Mr. Rockefeller (3,4)
My Eye On You (9)
My Knight In Black Leather (6)
My Mother's Eyes (8) *39*
My One True Friend (17)
Nanette (medley) (4)
Night And Day (12) *62*
No Jestering (3)
Nobody Else But You (18)
Oh Industry (11)
Oh My My (medley) (4)
Old Cape Cod (3)
One For My Baby (And One More For The Road) (14)
One Monkey Don't Stop No Show (17)
One More Round (12)
Only In Miami (9,14)
Optimistic Voices (medley) (2)
Otto Titzling (10,11)
P.S. I Love You (13)
Paradise (5,8)
Perfect Kiss (16)
Rain (6)
Ready To Begin Again (medley) (4)
Red (5)
Rose, The (7,14) *3*
Rose's Turn (15)
Samedi Et Vendredi (medley) (3)
Say Goodbye To Hollywood (5)
Shining Star (18)
Shiver Me Timbers (3,4,8,14)
Since You Stayed Here (medley) (12)
Skylark (2)
Small World (15)
Soda And A Souvenir (9)
Sold My Soul To Rock 'N' Roll (7)
Some People (15)
Some People's Lives (12)
Song Of Bernadette (17)
Soph (10)
Spring Can Really Hang You Up The Most (12)
Stay With Me (7,8)
Storybook Children (Daybreak) (5) *57*
Strangers In The Night (3)
Stuff Like That There (13)
Summer (The First Time) (medley) (8)
Superstar (1)
Surabaya Johnny (2)
Taking Aim (10)
That's How Heartaches Are Made (18)
That's How Love Moves (17)

MIDLER, Bette — Cont'd

To Comfort You (16)
To Deserve You (16)
Together, Wherever We Go (15)
Tragedy (3)
Twisted (2)

Ukulele Lady (17)
Under The Boardwalk (11)
Unfettered Boob (10)
Up The Ladder To The Roof (medley) (4)
Uptown (medley) (4)

Vickie And Mr. Valves (13)
Vickie Eydie - I'm Singing Broadway (10)
When A Man Loves A Woman (7,14) **35**
When Your Life Was Low (18)

Whose Side Are You On (7)
Why Bother? (10)
Wind Beneath My Wings (11,14) **1**
Yellow Beach Umbrella (5)

You Can't Always Get What You Want (medley) (8)
You Don't Know Me (5)
You'll Never Get Away From Me (15)

You're Movin' Out Today (4) **42**

MIDNIGHT OIL   '88

Rock group formed in Sydney, Australia: Peter Garrett (vocals), Martin Rotsey (guitar), James Moginie (keyboards), Peter Gifford (bass) and Rob Hirst (drums). Dwayne Hillman replaced Gifford in 1987.

DEBUT	PEAK	WKS	RIAA	CD	#	Album Title	Catalog	Sym	$	Label & Number
2/4/84	178	5		©	1	10,9,8,7,6,5,4,3,2,1	C:#34/1		$10	Columbia 38996
8/3/85	177	6		©	2	Red Sails In The Sunset			$10	Columbia 39987
2/13/88	21	55	▲	©	3	Diesel And Dust			$10	Columbia 40967
3/17/90	20	29	●	©	4	Blue Sky Mining			$10	Columbia 45398
5/30/92	141	3		©	5	Scream In Blue Live		[L]	$10	Columbia 52731
5/8/93	49	15		©	6	Earth And Sun And Moon			$10	Columbia 53793
11/2/96	155	1		©	7	Breathe			$10	Work 67822

Antarctica (4)
Arctic World (3)
Bakerman (2)
Barest Degree (7)
Bedlam Bridge (4)
Beds Are Burning (3,5) **17**
Bells And Horns In The Back Of Beyond (2)
Best Of Both Worlds (2)
Blue Sky Mine (4) **47**
Brave Faces (5)
Bring On The Change (7)
Bullroarer (3)
Bushfire (6)
Common Ground (7)

Dead Heart (3) **53**
Dreamworld (3,5)
Drums Of Heaven (6)
E-Beat (7)
Earth And Sun And Moon (6)
Feeding Frenzy (6)
Forgotten Years (4)
Gravelrash (7)
Harrisburg (2)
Helps Me Helps You (2)
Hercules (5)
Home (7)
In The Rain (7)
In The Valley (6)
Jimmy Sharman's Boxers (2)

King Of The Mountain (4)
Kosciusko (2)
Maralinga (1)
Minutes To Midnight (3)
Mountains Of Burma (4)
My Country (6)
Now Or Never Land (6)
One Country (4)
One Too Many Times (7)
Only The Strong (1,5)
Outbreak Of Love (6)
Outside World (1)
Powderworks (5)
Power And The Passion (1)
Progress (5)

Put Down That Weapon (3)
Read About It (1,5)
Renaissance Man (6)
River Runs Red (4)
Scream In Blue (1,5)
Sell My Soul (3,5)
Shakers And Movers (4)
Shipyards Of New Zealand (2)
Short Memory (1)
Sins Of Omission (7)
Sleep (2)
Somebody's Trying To Tell Me Something (1)
Sometimes (3,5)
Star Of Hope (7)

Stars Of Warburton (4,5)
Surf's Up Tonight (7)
Tell Me The Truth (6)
Time To Heal (7)
Tin Legs And Tin Mines (1)
Truganini (6)
US Forces (1)
Underwater (5)
Warakurna (3)
When The Generals Talk (2)
Who Can Stand In The Way (2)
Whoah (3)

MIDNIGHT STAR   '84

Funk group from Louisville, Kentucky: Belinda Lipscomb (vocals), brothers Reggie and Vince Calloway (horns), Jeff Cooper (guitar), Ken Gant (keyboards), Melvin Gentry (bass) and Bill Simmons (drums). The Calloway brothers later formed **Calloway**.

DEBUT	PEAK	WKS	RIAA	CD	#	Album Title	Sym	$	Label & Number
7/30/83+	27	96	▲²	©	1	No Parking On The Dance Floor		$10	Solar 60241
12/8/84+	32	32	●	©	2	Planetary Invasion		$10	Solar 60384
6/14/86	56	27	●	©	3	Headlines		$10	Solar 60454
11/5/88	96	15		©	4	Midnight Star		$10	Solar 72564

Body Snatchers (2)
Can You Stay With Me (2)
Close Encounter (3)
Close To Midnight (3)
Curious (2)
Dead End (3)

Don't Rock The Boat (4)
Electricity (3)
Engine No. 9 (3)
Feels So Good (1)
Freak-A-Zoid (1) **66**
Get Dressed (3)

Headlines (3) **69**
Heartbeat (4)
I Don't Wanna Be Lonely (4)
Let's Celebrate (2)
Love Song (4)
Midas Touch (3) **42**

Night Rider (1)
90 Days (Same As Cash) (4)
No Parking (On The Dance Floor) (1) **81**
Operator (2) **18**
Pamper Me (4)

Planetary Invasion (2)
Playmates (1)
Request Line (4)
Scientific Love (2) **80**
Searching For Love (3)
Slow Jam (1)

Snake In The Grass (4)
Stay Here By My Side (3)
Today My Love (2)
Wet My Whistle (1) **61**

MIDNIGHT STRING QUARTET   '67

Studio group assembled by producer **Tommy Garrett**.

DEBUT	PEAK	WKS	CD	#	Album Title	Sym	$	Label & Number
11/19/66+	17	59		1	Rhapsodies For Young Lovers	[I]	$15	Viva 6001
4/8/67	76	12		2	Spanish Rhapsodies For Young Lovers	[I]	$15	Viva 36004
7/29/67	67	15		3	Rhapsodies For Young Lovers, Volume Two	[I]	$15	Viva 36008
12/9/67	18ˣ	4	©	4	Christmas Rhapsodies For Young Lovers	[X-I]	$15	Viva 36010
3/30/68	129	17		5	Love Rhapsodies	[I]	$15	Viva 36013
8/17/68	194	3		6	The Look Of Love And Other Rhapsodies For Young Lovers	[I]	$15	Viva 36015

Alfie (3)
Apologize (6)
Blue Christmas (4)
Blue Star (The Medic Theme) (1)
Born Free (3)
By The Time I Get To Phoenix (6)
Can't Take My Eyes Off You (5)
Christmas Rhapsody (4)
Christmas Song (Chestnuts Roasting On An Open Fire) (4)
Clair De Lune (3)
Classical Gas (6)

Cuando Calienta El Sol (Love Me With All Your Heart) (2)
Dr. Zhivago ..see: Lara's Theme
El Relicario (2)
Fascination (5)
First Noel (4)
Girl From Ipanema (2)
Goin' Out Of My Head (5)
Gone With The Wind ..see: Tara's Theme
Good, The Bad And The Ugly (3)
Guantanamera (2)
Have Yourself A Merry Little Christmas (4)

I Hear A Symphony (3)
Impossible Dream (5)
It Came Upon A Midnight Clear (4)
Kiss Me Goodbye (6)
La Paloma (2)
Lara's Theme (1)
Little Drummer Boy (4)
Lonely Bull (2)
Look Of Her (6)
Look Of Love (6)
Love Is Blue (4)
Love Sonata (6)
Lover's Concerto (1)
MacArthur Park (6)

Maria Elena (2)
Meditation (2)
Michelle (2)
Midnight Memories (6)
Misty Night (5)
Moonlight Sonata (1)
My Cup Runneth Over (3)
My Heart's Symphony (1)
My Prayer (5)
Never My Love (5)
Oh, Holy Night (4)
Our Day Will Come (2)
Please Love Me Forever (5)
Portrait Of My Love (3)
Prelude To Love (3)

Prophesy Of Love (3)
Quiet Nights Of Quiet Stars (2)
Shadow Of Your Smile (Love Theme From The Sandpiper) (1)
Silent Night (4)
Sleigh Ride (4)
Softly (5)
Somewhere, My Love ..see: Lara's Theme
Spanish Eyes (2)
Strangers In The Night (1)
Strangers No More (3)
Summer Samba (2)
Tara's Theme (5)

This Is My Song (3)
Till (3)
Tonight's Dream (1)
Twilight Sonata (5)
Valley Of The Dolls, Theme From (6)
What Now My Love (1)
White Christmas (4)
Winter Wonderland (4)
Yesterday (1)
You Don't Have To Say You Love Me (1)
Young Girl (6)
Young Lovers' Rhapsody (1)

MIGHTY CLOUDS OF JOY   '74

Gospel group from Los Angeles: Willie Joe Ligon, Johnny Martin, Elmo Franklin, Richard Wallace, Leon Polk and David Walker. Martin died in 1987.

DEBUT	PEAK	WKS	#	Album Title	$	Label & Number
10/26/74	165	5	1	It's Time	$12	Dunhill/ABC 50177
1/24/76	168	6	2	Kickin'	$12	ABC 899

Everything Is Going Up (1)
Everything Is Love (2)
Heart Full Of Love (1)

I've Got The Music In Me (medley) (1)
Laugh (1)
Leanin' (2)

Master Plan (1)
Mighty Cloud Of Joy (1)
Mighty High (2) **69**
Millionaire (2)

Standing On The Real Side (2)
Stoned World (1)
Superstition (medley) (2)
Time (1)

Touch My Soul (2)
You Are So Beautiful (2)
(You Think You're Doin' It On Your Own (1)

MIGHTY LEMON DROPS, The   '90

Pop group from Wolverhampton, England: Paul Marsh (vocals), David Newton (guitar), Marcus Williams (bass) and Keith Rowley (drums).

DEBUT	PEAK	WKS	#	Album Title	$	Label & Number
3/10/90	195	2		Laughter	$10	Sire 26017

All That I Can Do (1)
At Midnight

Beautiful Shame
Heartbreak Thing

Into The Heart Of Love
One In A Million

Real World
Rumbletrain?

Second Time Around
Where Do We Go From Heaven

This Is My Song (3)
Written In Fiction

DEBUG	PEAK	WKS	RIAA	CD	ARTIST — Album Title	Catalog	Sym	$	Label & Number

MIGHTY MIGHTY BOSSTONES, The   '97

Ska-rock group from Boston: Dicky Barrett (vocals), Nate Albert (guitar), Ben Carr (dancer), Kevin Lenear, Tim Burton and Dennis Brockenborough (horns), Joe Gittleman (bass) and Joe Sirois (drums). Lawrence Katz replaced Albert and Roman Fleysher replaced Lenear in 1999.

6/5/93	187	1		©	1 **Don't Know How To Party**			$10	Mercury 514836
10/22/94	138	1		©	2 **Question The Answers**			$10	Mercury 522845
3/29/97	27	50	▲	©	3 **Let's Face It**			$10	Mercury 534472
11/7/98	144	1		©	4 **Live From The Middle East**		[L]	$10	Mercury 538247

recorded in December 1997 at the Middle East club in Cambridge, Massachusetts

| 5/20/00 | 74 | 4 | | © | 5 **Pay Attention** | | | $10 | Big Rig 542451 |

All Things Considered (5)
Allow Them (5)
Almost Anything Goes (1)
Another Drinkin' Song (3)
Bad News And Bad Breaks (5)
Break So Easily (3)
Bronzing The Garbage (2)
Cowboy Coffee (4)
Day He Didn't Die (4)
Desensitized (3)
Devil's Night Out (4)
Do Somethin' Crazy (4)
Dr. D (4)
Dogs And Chaplains (2)
Dollar And A Dream (2)
Don't Know How To Party (1)
Doves And Civilians (4)
Finally (5)
He's Back (4)
Hell Of A Hat (2,4)
High School Dance (5)
Holy Smoke (1,4)
Hope I Never Lose My Wallet (4)
Howwhywuz, Howwhyam (4)
I Know More (5)
I'll Drink To That (4)
Illegal Left (1)
Impression That I Get (3,4)
Issachar (1)
Jump Through The Hoops (2)
Kinder Words (2,4)
Last Dead Mouse (1)
Let Me Be (5)
Let's Face It (3,4)
Lights Out (4)
Man Without (1)
Nevermind Me (3)
Noise Brigade (3,4)
Numbered Days (3)
One Million Reasons (5)
Our Only Weapon (1)
Over The Eggshells (5)
Pictures To Prove It (2)
Rascal King (3,4)
Riot On Broad Street (5)
Royal Oil (3,4)
Sad Silence (2)
Seven Thirty Seven (medley) (1,4)
She Just Happened (5)
Shoe Glue (medley) (1,4)
Skeleton Song (5)
So Sad To Say (5)
Someday I Suppose (1,4)
Stand Off (2)
Temporary Trip (5)
That Bug Bit Me (3)
365 Days (2)
Tin Soldiers (1)
Toxic Toast (2)
We Should Talk (2)
What Was Was Over (1)
Where You Come From (5)
Where'd You Go? (4)

MIGUEL, Luis   '97

Born on 4/19/70 in Veracruz, Mexico. Latin singer/actor.

| 7/10/93 | 182 | 3 | | © | 1 **Aries** | | [F] | $10 | WEA Latina 92993 |
| 9/17/94 | 29 | 12 | ▲ | © | 2 **Segundo Romance** | | [F] | $10 | WEA Latina 97234 |

title is Spanish for "Second Romance"

| 11/4/95 | 45 | 6 | ● | © | 3 **El Concierto** | | [F-L] | $15 | WEA Latina 11212 [2] |

title is Spanish for "The Concert"

| 9/7/96 | 43 | 8 | ● | © | 4 **Nada Es Igual...** | | [F] | $10 | WEA Latina 15947 |

title is Spanish for "Nothing Is Equal"

| 8/30/97 | 14 | 19 | ▲ | © | 5 **Romances** | | [F] | $10 | WEA Latina 19798 |
| 10/2/99 | 36 | 8 | | © | 6 **Amarte Es Un Placer** | | [F] | $10 | WEA Latina 29288 |

title is Spanish for "Loving You Is A Pleasure"

| 10/21/00 | 93 | 4 | | © | 7 **Vivo** | | [F] | $10 | WEA Latina 84573 |

title is Spanish for "I Live"

Abrázame (4)
Alguien Como Tu (Somebody In Your Life) (5)
Amanecer (5)
Amaneci En Tus Brazos (3)
Amarte Es Un Placer (6)
Ayer (1)
Besame Mucho (3)
Cómo Es Posible Que A Mi Lado (4,7)
Como Yo Te Ame (2)
Contigo Aprendi (medley) (5)
Contigo (Estar Contigo) (5)
Culpable O No (medley) (3)
Dame (4)
Dame Tu Amor (1,3)
De Quererte Asi (De T'Avoir Aimee) (5)
Delirio (2)
Dimelo En Un Beso (6)
Dormir Contigo (5)
El Dia Que Me Quieras (2,3)
El Reloj (5)
El Rey (3)
Encadenados (5)
Entregate (medley) (3)
Ese Momento (6)
Fria Como El Viento (medley) (3)
Hasta El Fin (1)
Hasta Que Me Olvides (1,3)
Historia De Un Amor (2,3)
Jurame (5)
La Bikina (7)
La Gloria Eres Tu (5)
La Incondicional (medley) (3)
La Media Vuelta (2,3)
Luz Verde (3)
Mañana De Carnaval (Manha Do Carnival) (5)
Mas Alla (medley) (3)
Me Niego A Estar Solo (1)
Nada Es Igual (4)
No Me Fio (6)
No Se Tu (3)
Noche De Ronda (5)
Nosotros (2,3)
O Tu O Ninguna (6,7)
Pensar En Ti (1,3)
Por Debajo De La Mesa (5)
Que Nivel De Mujer (1,3)
Que Tú Te Vas (4)
Quiero (6,7)
Romance Medley (7)
Romances Medley (7)
Sabor A Mi (5)
Segundo Romance Medley (7)
Sera Que No Me Amas (3)
Si Nos Dejan (3)
Si Te Vas (4)
Sin Ti (2,3)
Sintiéndote Lejos (4)
Sol, Arena Y Mar (6,7)
Solamente Una Vez (2)
Somos Novios (2,3)
Soy Yo (6)
Suave (1,3,7)
Sueña (4)
Te Propongo Esta Noche (6,7)
Tengo Todo Excepto A Ti (medley) (3)
Todo Por Su Amor (4)
Todo Y Nada (2)
Tu Mirada (6)
Tu Solo Tu (6,7)
Tu Y Yo (1)
Un Día Más (4)
Uno (3)
Voy A Apagar La Luz (medley) (5)
Y (7)
Yo Que No Vivo Sin Ti (medley) (3)
Yo Se Que Volveras (2)

MIKE + THE MECHANICS   '89

Pop-rock group formed in England: **Mike** Rutherford (bass; **Genesis**), Paul Carrack and Paul Young (vocals; **Sad Cafe**), Adrian Lee (keyboards) and Peter Van Hooke (drums). Young, not to be confused with the same-named solo singer, died of a heart attack on 7/17/2000 (age 53).

11/23/85+	26	53	●	©	1 **Mike + The Mechanics**			$10	Atlantic 81287
11/19/88+	13	37	●	©	2 **Living Years**			$10	Atlantic 81923
4/20/91	107	5		©	3 **Word Of Mouth**			$10	Atlantic 82233

All I Need Is A Miracle (1) 5
Beautiful Day (2)
Before (The Next Heartache Falls) (3)
Black & Blue (2)
Blame (2)
Call To Arms (1)
Don't (2)
Everybody Gets A Second Chance (3)
Get Up (3)
Hanging By A Thread (1)
I Get The Feeling (1)
Let's Pretend It Didn't Happen (3)
My Crime Of Passion (3)
Nobody Knows (2)
Nobody's Perfect (2) 63
Par Avion (1)
Poor Boy Down (2)
Seeing Is Believing (2) 62
Silent Running (On Dangerous Ground) (1) 6
Stop Baby (3)
Take The Reins (1)
Taken In (1) 32
Time And Place (3)
Way You Look At Me (3)
Why Me? (2)
Word Of Mouth (3) 78
Yesterday, Today, Tomorrow (3)
You Are The One (1)
Living Years (2) 1

MILES, Buddy   '72

Born George Miles on 9/5/46 in Omaha. R&B singer/drummer. Member of **Jimi Hendrix**'s Band of Gypsies (1969-70). Was the voice of **The California Raisins**.

| 6/7/69 | 145 | 4 | | | 1 **Electric Church** | | | $15 | Mercury 61222 |

BUDDY MILES EXPRESS
co-produced by **Jimi Hendrix**

7/4/70	35	74			2 **Them Changes**			$15	Mercury 61280
11/14/70	53	26			3 **We Got To Live Together**			$15	Mercury 61313
4/10/71	60	24			4 **A Message To The People**			$15	Mercury 608
10/2/71	50	24			5 **Buddy Miles Live**		[L]	$20	Mercury 7500 [2]
7/8/72	8	33	▲	©	6 **Carlos Santana & Buddy Miles! Live!**		[L]	$15	Columbia 31308

recorded in Hawaii's Diamond Head volcano crater

| 3/10/73 | 123 | 9 | | | 7 **Chapter VII** | | | $15 | Columbia 32048 |

THE BUDDY MILES BAND

| 1/19/74 | 194 | 3 | | | 8 **Booger Bear** | | | $15 | Columbia 32694 |

BUDDY MILES EXPRESS

| 8/23/75 | 68 | 11 | | | 9 **More Miles Per Gallon** | | | $12 | Casablanca 7019 |

Blues City (9)
Booger Bear (8)
Cigarettes & Coffee (1)
Crazy Love (8)
Crossfire (7)
Destructive Love (1)
Do It To Me (9)
Don't Keep Me Wondering (4)
Down By The River (2,5) 68
Dreams (2) 86
Easy Greasy (3)
Elvira (7)
Evil Ways (6) 84
Free Form Funkafide Filth (6)
Hear No Evil (7)
Heart's Delight (9)
I Still Love You, Anyway (2)
Joe Tex (4,5)

MILES, Buddy — Cont'd

L.A. Resurrection (7)
Lava (6)
Life Is What You Make It Part 1 & 2 (7)
Livin' In The Right Space (9)
Louie's Blues (8)
Love (8)
Love Affair (7)

Marbles (6)
Memphis Train (2) 100
Midnight Rider (4)
Miss Lady (1)
My Chant (1)
My Last Words Of Love (9)
Nasty Disposition (9)
Nichols Canyon Fuunk (9)
No Time For Sorrow (9)

Paul B. Allen, Omaha, Nebraska (2)
Place Over There (4,5)
Rockin' And Rollin' On The Streets Of Hollywood (9) 91
Runaway Child (Little Miss Nothin') (3)
Segment, The (4,5)
69 Freedom Special (1)

Sudden Stop (4)
Take It Off Him And Put It On Me (3,5)
Texas (1)
That's The Way Life Is (4)
Them Changes (2,5) 81
Them Changes (6) flip
There Was A Time (7)
Thinking Of You (8)

United Nations Stomp (8)
Visions (7)
Walkin' Down The Highway (3)
Way I Feel Tonight (4)
We Got To Live Together - Part 1 (3,5) 86
Wholesale Love (4) 71
Why (8)
Wrap It Up (1,5)

You Are Everything (8)
You Don't Have A Kind Word To Say (9)
You Really Got Me (8)
Your Feeling Is Mine (2)

MILES, John

'77

Born on 4/23/49 in Jarrow, England. Rock singer/guitarist/keyboardist. Guest vocalist with the **Alan Parsons Project**.

DEBUT	PEAK	WKS			ARTIST — Album Title			$	Label & Number
5/22/76	171	4	©		1 Rebel			$12	London 669
3/19/77	93	15			2 Stranger In The City			$12	London 682

Do It Anyway (2)
Everybody Wants Some More (1)
Glamour Boy (2)

Highfly (1) 68
Lady Of My Life (1)
Manhattan Skyline (2)
Music (1) 88

Music Man (2)
Pull The Damn Thing Down (1)
Rebel (1)
Remember Yesterday (2)

Slowdown (2) 34
Stand Up (And Give Me A Reason) (1)
Stranger In The City (2)

Time (2)
When You Lose Someone So Young (1)
You Have It All (1)

MILES, Robert

'96

Born Roberto Concina on 11/3/69 in Venice, Italy. DJ/musician.

DEBUT	PEAK	WKS			ARTIST — Album Title			$	Label & Number
8/17/96	54	23	● ©		Dreamland		[I]	$10	Arista 18930

Children 21
Fable

Fantasya
In My Dreams

In The Dawn
Landscape

One And One 54
Princess Of Light

Red Zone

MILLER, Frankie

'77

Born in 1950 in Glasgow, Scotland. Rock singer.

DEBUT	PEAK	WKS			ARTIST — Album Title			$	Label & Number
6/18/77	124	12			1 Full House			$15	Chrysalis 1128
5/13/78	177	10			2 Double Trouble			$15	Chrysalis 1174
6/26/82	135	9			3 Standing On The Edge			$15	Capitol 12206

Angels With Dirty Faces (3)
Be Good To Yourself (1)
Danger Danger (3)
Don't Stop (3)
Doodle Song (1) 71
Double Heart Trouble (2)

Down The Honkytonk (1)
Firin' Line (3)
Good Time Love (2)
Goodnight Sweetheart (2)
Have You Seen Me Lately Joan (2)

(I Can't) Breakaway (2)
(I'll Never) Live In Vain (1)
It's All Coming Down Tonight (3)
Jealous Guy (1)
Jealousy (3)

Let The Candlelight Shine (1)
Love Is All Around (2)
Love Letters (1)
Love Waves (2)
On My Way (3)
Searching (1)

Standing On The Edge (3)
Stubborn Kind Of Fellow (2)
Take Good Care Of Yourself (1)
This Love Of Mine (1)
To Dream The Dream (3) 62
Train, The (2)

You'll Be In My Mind (2)
Zap Zap (3)

MILLER, Glenn, Orchestra

'57

Born Alton Glenn Miller on 3/1/04 in Clarinda, Iowa. Disappeared on a plane flight from England to France on 12/15/44 (age 40). Leader of most popular big band of all time. Played trombone for Ben Pollack, Red Nichols, **Benny Goodman** and **Jimmy & Tommy Dorsey**. Started own band in 1937.

DEBUT	PEAK	WKS			ARTIST — Album Title	Catalog	Sym	$	Label & Number
9/16/57	16	6			1 Marvelous Miller Moods		[E]	$40	RCA Victor 1494

GLENN MILLER ARMY AIR FORCE BAND
with Johnny Desmond (vocals); from radio broadcasts during 1943-44

DEBUT	PEAK	WKS			ARTIST — Album Title	Catalog	Sym	$	Label & Number
12/9/57	17	4			2 The New Glenn Miller Orchestra In Hi Fi			$40	RCA Victor 1522

directed by Ray McKinley (leader of the orchestra after Miller's death)

| 2/24/58 | 19 | 3 | © | | 3 The Glenn Miller Carnegie Hall Concert | | [E-L] | $40 | RCA Victor 1506 |

recorded on 10/6/39

| 1/25/75 | 115 | 9 | © | | 4 A Legendary Performer | | [E] | $20 | RCA Victor 0693 [2] |

previously unreleased performances from 1939-42

| 12/7/91 | 27 X | 7 | © | | 5 In The Christmas Mood | C:#38/10 | [X] | $10 | LaserLight 15418 |

recorded in 1988 by alumni of the Glenn Miller Orchestra; Christmas charts: 27/'91, 29/'92, 38/'94

| 12/25/93 | 199 | 1 | © | | 6 In The Christmas Mood II | C:#38/2 | [X-I] | $10 | LaserLight 12200 |

Accentuate The Positive (2)
Angels We Have Heard On High (medley) (6)
Anything Goes (2)
At Last (4)
Auld Lang Syne (6)
Ave Maria (medley) (6)
Away In A Manger (medley) (6)
Blue Is The Night (1)
Bugle Call Rag (medley) (4)
Chattanooga Choo Choo (4)
Christmas Song (5,6)
Danny Boy (3,4)
Deck The Halls (medley) (5)
Don't Be That Way (2)
Elmer's Tune (4)
Everything I Love (4)
FDR Jones (medley) (3)
Farewell Blues (1)

First Noel (medley) (6)
Frosty The Snowman (5)
God Rest Ye Merry Gentlemen (medley) (6)
Good King Wenceslas (6)
Hallelujah, I Just Love Her So (2)
Hark The Herald, Angels Sing (medley) (6)
Have Yourself A Merry Little Christmas (5)
Hold Tight (medley) (3)
Holiday For Strings (1)
Home For The Holidays (5,6)
I Almost Lost My Mind (2)
I Love You (1)
I'll Be Home For Christmas (5)
I'm Thrilled (2)
I've Got A Gal In Kalamazoo (4)

In The Christmas Mood (5)
In The Mood (3,4)
It Came Upon A Midnight Clear (medley) (5)
Jack And Jill (4)
Jim Jam Jump (medley) (3)
Jingle Bells (4,5)
Joy To The World (medley) (5)
Juke Box Saturday Night (4)
Let It Snow, Let It Snow, Let It Snow (5,6)
Little Brown Jug (3,4)
Londonderry Air ..see: Danny Boy
Long Ago And Far Away (1)
Lovely Way To Spend An Evening (1)
Lullaby Of Birdland (1)
Mine (2)

Moonlight Cocktail (4)
Moonlight Serenade (3,4)
My Ideal (1)
My Melancholy Baby (4)
My Prayer (1)
O Come All Ye Faithful (medley) (5)
O Holy Night (medley) (5)
Oh, Christmas Tree (medley) (5)
Oh, Little Town Of Bethlehem (medley) (5)
On The Street Where You Live (2)
One O'Clock Jump (3)
Pearls On Velvet (1)
Pennsylvania 6-5000 (4)
People Will Say We're In Love (1)

Piano Concerto No. 1 (4)
Rudolph, The Red-Nosed Reindeer (5)
Running Wild (medley) (3)
Santa Claus Is Coming To Town (5,6)
Sentimental Me (4)
Silent Night (5)
Silver Bells (5)
Sleigh Ride (5)
Slumber Song (2)
So You're The One (4)
Song Of The Volga Boatmen (4)
Stairway To The Stars (medley) (3)
Star Dust (1,4)
String Of Pearls (4)
Suddenly It's Spring (1)

Sunrise Serenade (3,4)
Take The "A" Train (4)
To You (medley) (3)
Tuxedo Junction (4)
Twelve Days Of Christmas (6)
We Three Kings (medley) (5)
We Wish You A Merry Christmas (6)
What Child Is This? (medley) (5)
Whistle Stop (2)
White Christmas (5,6)
Winter Wonderland (5,6)

MILLER, Jody

'71

Born Myrna Joy Brooks on 11/29/41 in Phoenix; raised in Blanchard, Oklahoma. Country singer.

DEBUT	PEAK	WKS			ARTIST — Album Title			$	Label & Number
6/26/65	124	6			1 Queen Of The House			$20	Capitol 2349
8/28/71	117	8			2 He's So Fine			$15	Epic 30659

Baby, I'm Yours (2) 91
Don't Be Cruel (2)
Don't Throw Your Love To The Wind (2)
Everybody's Somebody's Fool (1)

Good Lovin' (Makes It Right) (2)
Greatest Actor (1)
He Walks Like A Man (1) 66
He's So Fine (2) 53
I Walk The Line (1)
I'm Gonna Write A Song (2)

If I (1)
Let Him Have It (2)
Make Me Your Kind Of Woman (2)
Odds And Ends (1)
Queen Of The House (1) 12

Race Is On (1)
Sea Of Heartbreak (1)
Silver Threads And Golden Needles (1) 54
Soft And Gentle Ways (1)
These Are The Years (1)

We Had Love All The Way (2)
Woman Left Lonely (2)
You've Got A Friend (2)

MILLER, Mitch, & The Gang ★54★   '60

Born on 7/4/11 in Rochester, New York. Producer/conductor/arranger. Oboe soloist with the CBS Symphony from 1936-47. A&R executive for both Columbia and Mercury Records. Best known for his sing-along albums and TV show (1961-64).

1)Sing Along With Mitch 2)Christmas Sing-Along With Mitch 3)Holiday Sing Along With Mitch
4)TV Sing Along With Mitch 5)Still More! Sing Along With Mitch

DEBUT	PEAK	WKS		CD	#	Album Title	Sym	$	Label & Number
7/14/58	❶⁸	204	●	©	1	**Sing Along With Mitch**		$20	Columbia 1160
11/10/58+	4	171	●	©	2	**More Sing Along With Mitch**		$20	Columbia 1243
12/8/58	❶²	5	●	©	3	**Christmas Sing-Along With Mitch**	[X]	$20	Columbia 1205
3/23/59	4	130	●	©	4	**Still More! Sing Along With Mitch**		$20	Columbia 1283
6/1/59+	11	89	●		5	**Folk Songs Sing Along With Mitch**		$20	Columbia 1316
8/31/59+	7	100	●		6	**Party Sing Along With Mitch**		$20	Columbia 1331
12/14/59	8	4		©	7	**Christmas Sing-Along With Mitch**	[X-R]	$20	Columbia 1205
12/28/59+	10	91			8	**Fireside Sing Along With Mitch**		$20	Columbia 1389
4/4/60+	8	89	●		9	**Saturday Night Sing Along With Mitch**		$20	Columbia 1414
6/27/60	5	107	●		10	**Sentimental Sing Along With Mitch**		$20	Columbia 1457
10/10/60	40	16			11	**March Along With Mitch**	[I]	$20	Columbia 1475
10/31/60	5	78	●		12	**Memories Sing Along With Mitch**		$15	Columbia 1542 / 8342
12/19/60	6	3		©	13	**Christmas Sing-Along With Mitch**	[X-R]	$20	Columbia 1205
3/13/61	5	73	●		14	**Happy Times! Sing Along With Mitch**		$15	Columbia 1568 / 8368
3/13/61	9	27		©	15	**Mitch's Greatest Hits**	[G]	$15	Columbia 1544 / 8344
5/29/61	3	46			16	**TV Sing Along With Mitch**		$15	Columbia 1628 / 8428
9/18/61	6	44			17	**Your Request Sing Along With Mitch**		$15	Columbia 1671 / 8471
11/6/61+	❶¹	18	●	©	18	**Holiday Sing Along With Mitch**	[X]	$15	Columbia 1701 / 8501

Christmas charts: 9/'63, 15/'64, 22/'65, 14/'66, 17/'67, 37/'68

DEBUT	PEAK	WKS		CD	#	Album Title	Sym	$	Label & Number
12/4/61+	9	8		©	19	**Christmas Sing-Along With Mitch**	[X-R]	$20	Columbia 1205
3/10/62	21	23			20	**Rhythm Sing Along With Mitch**		$15	Columbia 1727 / 8527
6/9/62	27	15			21	**Family Sing Along With Mitch**		$15	Columbia 1773 / 8573
12/8/62	33	4			22	**Holiday Sing Along With Mitch**	[X-R]	$15	Columbia 1701 / 8501
12/22/62	37	2		©	23	**Christmas Sing-Along With Mitch**	[X-R]	$20	Columbia 1205

After The Ball (medley) (9)
Ain't She Sweet (medley) (9)
Ain't We Got Fun (20)
Alabamy Bound (medley) (14)
All I Do Is Dream Of You (medley) (10)
All Through The Night (medley) (8)
Alouette March (11)
Annie Laurie (medley) (8)
Anniversary Song (14)
At Sundown (medley) (12)
Auf Wiedersehen, My Dear (16)
Auld Lang Syne (medley) (8)
Aunt Rhody (The Old Gray Goose) (5)
Aura Lee (17)
Avalon (medley) (16)
Away In A Manger (Luther's Carol) (3,7,13,19,23)
Baby Face (9)
Back In Your Own Back Yard (17)
Bandit, The (11)
Barney Google (20)
Battle Hymn Of The Republic (12)
Be Kind To Your Web-Footed Friends (medley) (1)
Be My Little Baby Bumble Bee (medley) (2)
Bear Went Over The Mountain (medley) (5)
Beautiful Ohio (14)
Beer Barrel Polka (4)
Believe Me If All Those Endearing Young Charms (medley) (8)
Bell Bottom Trousers (medley) (1)
Bicycle Built For Two (medley) (4)
Bidin' My Time (20)
Bill Bailey, Won't You Please Come Home (medley) (12)
Billy Boy (medley) (5)
Bird In A Gilded Cage (medley) (6)
Black Bottom (20)
Blue Tail Fly (5)
Bonnie Eloise (15)

Bowery, The (medley) (12)
Bowery Grenadiers (15)
Breezin' Along With The Breeze (16)
By The Beautiful Sea (17)
By The Light Of The Silvery Moon (1)
Bye Bye Blackbird (9)
California (medley) (16)
Camptown Races (medley) (5)
Carolina In The Morning (2)
Cecilia (17)
Children's Marching Song (15) *16*
Chinatown, My Chinatown (20)
Christmas Song (Merry Christmas To You) (18,22)
Collegiate (medley) (14)
Comin' Through The Rye March (11)
Coventry Carol (3,7,13,19,23)
Cuddle Up A Little Closer (medley) (6)
Dancing With Tears In My Eyes (9)
Deck The Hall With Boughs Of Holly (3,7,13,19,23)
Deep Purple (21)
Diane (21)
Did You Ever See A Dream Walking? (17)
Dixie (11,12)
Do-Re-Mi (11,15) *70*
Do You Ever Think Of Me (21)
Don't Fence Me In (1)
Don't Sit Under The Apple Tree (With Anyone Else But Me) (21)
Down By The Old Mill Stream (1)
Down In The Valley (5)
Drifting And Dreaming (17)
Drink To Me Only With Thine Eyes (medley) (8)
Drunk Last Night (8)
First Noel (3,7,13,19,23)
Five Foot Two, Eyes Of Blue (medley) (12)
For Me And My Gal (medley) (2)
Forty-Second Street (20)
Frere Jacques March (11)

Frosty The Snowman (18,22)
Funiculi, Funicula (8)
Gang That Sang Heart Of My Heart (10)
Girl I Left Behind Me (medley) (11)
Give My Regards To Broadway (medley) (10)
God Rest Ye Merry, Gentlemen (3,7,13,19,23)
Good Night Sweetheart (4)
Goodnight, Irene (5)
Goodnight, Ladies (medley) (6)
Happy Days Are Here Again (16)
Harbor Lights (17)
Hark! The Herald Angels Sing (3,7,13,19,23)
Harrigan (medley) (6)
Has Anybody Here Seen Kelly (medley) (16)
Hello! My Baby (medley) (10)
Hey, Betty Martin (15)
Hey Little Baby (15)
Hinky Dinky Parlezvous (medley) (4)
Home On The Range (12)
Home, Sweet Home (medley) (6)
Honey (medley) (12)
I Found A Million Dollar Baby (In A Five And Ten Cent Store) (16)
I Love A Lassie (medley) (20)
I Love My Baby - My Baby Loves Me (medley) (14)
I Love You (12)
I Love You Truly (6)
I Saw Mommy Kissing Santa Claus (18,22)
(I Wanna Go Where You Go, Do What You Do) Then I'll Be Happy (17)
I Want To Be Happy (20)
I Wonder What's Become Of Sally? (medley) (9)
I Wonder Who's Kissing Her Now (6)
I'll Be With You In Apple Blossom Time (4)
I'll See You In My Dreams (10)
I'll Take You Home Again, Kathleen (6)

I'm Forever Blowing Bubbles (20)
I'm Going Back To Dixie (11,12)
I'm Just Wild About Mary (I'm Just Wild About Harry) (medley) (4)
I'm Looking Over A Four Leaf Clover (9)
I'm Nobody's Baby (medley) (12)
I'm Sitting On Top Of The World (21)
I've Been Working On The Railroad (medley) (1)
I've Got Rings On My Fingers (medley) (16)
I've Got Sixpence (medley) (1)
Ida (medley) (10)
If I Could Be With You (One Hour Tonight) (medley) (14)
If You Knew Susie (Like I Know Susie) (medley) (14)
If You Were The Only Girl (2)
In A Shanty In Old Shanty Town (4)
In The Evening By The Moonlight (2)
In The Gloaming (medley) (8)
In The Good Old Summertime (medley) (6)
In The Shade Of The Old Apple Tree (medley) (6)
Indiana (11)
Irish Medley (2)
It Came Upon The Midnight Clear (3,7,13,19,23)
It Happened In Monterey (21)
It's Been A Long, Long Time (17)
It's Only A Paper Moon (16)
Ja-Da (21)
Jeanie With The Light Brown Hair (10)
Jeannine (I Dream Of Lilac Time) (10)
Jeepers Creepers (20)
Jingle Bells (18,22)
Joy To The World (3,7,13,19,23)
Juanita (medley) (8)
June Night (Just Give Me A June Night, The Moonlight And You) (21)

Just A-Wearyin' For You (10)
K-K-K-Katy (21)
Kerry Dancer March (11)
Last Night On The Back Porch (I Loved Her Best Of All) (medley) (14)
Let It Snow! Let It Snow! Let It Snow! (18,22)
Let Me Call You Sweetheart (medley) (2)
Let The Rest Of The World Go By (1)
Let's Put Out The Lights And Go To Sleep (20)
Linger Awhile (21)
Listen To The Mocking Bird (5)
Little Annie Rooney (medley) (10)
Little Brown Jug (medley) (9)
Little Shepherd's March (11)
Loch Lomond March (11)
Love Nest (16)
Love's Old Sweet Song (8)
Man On The Flying Trapeze (medley) (9)
Mairzy Doats (21)
March From The River Kwai and Colonel Bogey (15) *20*
Meet Me In St. Louis, Louis (12)
Meet Me Tonight In Dreamland (6)
Memories (4)
Moonlight And Roses (2)
Moonlight Bay (medley) (16)
Mother Machree (9)
Must Be Santa (18,22)
My Blue Heaven (12)
My Bonnie Lies Over The Ocean (8)
My Buddy (2)
My Darling Clementine (5)
My Gal Sal (medley) (9)
My Melancholy Baby (14)
(Nel Blu Dipinto Di Blu) ..see: Volare
Now Is The Hour (9)
O Come, All Ye Faithful (Adeste Fideles) (3,7,13,19,23)
O, Katharina! (21)
O Little Town Of Bethlehem (3,7,13,19,23)

Oh Dear, What Can The Matter Be (medley) (8)
Oh Marie (21)
Oh Susanna! (medley) (5)
Oh! What A Pal Was Mary (medley) (6)
Oh, Where, Oh Where Has My Little Dog Gone (medley) (8)
Oh! You Beautiful Doll (medley) (4)
Old Friends (1)
Old Grey Mare (medley) (8)
On Top Of Old Smoky (5)
Our Boys Will Shine Tonight (medley) (1)
Paddlin' Madelin' Home (17)
Peg O' My Heart (medley) (12)
Peggy O'Neil (medley) (12)
Polly Wolly Doodle (medley) (8)
Poor Butterfly (19)
Pop! Goes The Weasel (medley) (5)
Pretty Baby (medley) (2)
Prisoner's Song (14)
Put On Your Old Grey Bonnet (medley) (4)
Ramblin' Wreck From Georgia Tech (6)
Ramona (12)
Red River Valley (5)
Roamin' In The Gloamin' (medley) (2)
Rudolph, The Red-Nosed Reindeer (18,22)
San Francisco (21)
Santa Claus Is Comin' To Town (18,22)
School Days (medley) (6)
She Wore A Yellow Ribbon (1)
She'll Be Coming 'Round The Mountain (medley) (5)
Shine On Harvest Moon (medley) (2)
Show Me The Way To Go Home (medley) (1)
Shuffle Off To Buffalo (16)
Side By Side (14)
Sidewalks Of New York (medley) (6)
Silent Night, Holy Night (3,7,13,19,23)
Silly Little Tune (15)

MILLER, Mitch, & The Gang — Cont'd

Silver Bells (18,22)
Silver Moon (9)
Silver Threads Among The Gold (medley) (4)
Sing Along (9,15)
Singin' In The Rain (medley) (10)
Skip To My Lou (medley) (5)
Sleepy Time Gal (medley) (12)
Sleigh Ride (18,22)
Smiles (4)
Somebody Stole My Gal (21)
Song For A Summer Night, Theme Song From (15) 8
Sunny Side Up (17)
Swanee (20)
Sweet Adeline (medley) (2)
Sweet And Low (medley) (8)
Sweet Genevieve (medley) (1)
Sweet Rosie O'Grady (medley) (6)

Sweet Violets (1)
Sweetest Story Ever Told (6)
Sweetheart Of Sigma Chi (17)
Ta-Ra-Ra-Boom-De-E (medley) (9)
Tea For Two (20)
That Old Gang Of Mine (1)
That's My Weakness Now (medley) (14)
That's Where My Money Goes (1)
There Is A Tavern In The Town (medley) (1)
There's A Long, Long Trail (2)
There's Yes! Yes! In Your Eyes (medley) (16)
Three O'Clock In The Morning (10)
Till We Meet Again (1)
Tip-Toe Thru The Tulips With Me (1)

Too-Ra-Loo-Ra-Loo-Ral (That's An Irish Lullaby) (medley) (9)
Toot, Toot, Tootsie! (Goodbye) (medley) (10)
Trail Of The Lonesome Pine (14)
Twelve Days Of Christmas (18,22)
Under The Bamboo Tree (17)
Vive L'Amour (medley) (8)
Volare (Nel Blu Dipinto Di Blu) (21)
Wagon Wheels (14)
Wait For The Wagon (medley) (8)
Wait Till The Sun Shines Nellie (medley) (6)
Walkin' Down To Washington (15)
We Three Kings Of Orient Are (3,7,13,19,23)

We're In The Money (20)
What Child Is This (3,7,13,19,23)
When Day Is Done (4)
When I Grow Too Old To Dream (10)
When It's Springtime In The Rockies (21)
When Johnny Comes Marching Home (5)
When The Red, Red Robin Comes Bob, Bob Bobbin' Along (17)
When The Saints Come Marching In (10)
When You And I Were Young, Maggie (8)
When You Were Sweet Sixteen (medley) (4)
When You Wore A Tulip (And I Wore A Big Red Rose) (21)

Where Do You Work-A, John (medley) (14)
Whiffenpoof Song (Baa! Baa! Baa!) (2)
While Strolling Through The Park One Day (medley) (10)
Whistler And His Dog (11)
White Christmas (18,22)
Winter Wonderland (18,22)
Would You Like To Take A Walk? (16)
Yankee Doodle (medley) (11)
Yankee Doodle Boy (medley) (12)
Yellow Rose Of Texas (15) 1
Yes! We Have No Bananas (medley) (14)
You Are My Sunshine (1)
You Must Have Been A Beautiful Baby (medley) (16)

You Tell Me Your Dream, I'll Tell You Mine (2)
You Were Meant For Me (medley) (12)
You're An Old Smoothie (20)
You're The Cream In My Coffee (17)

MILLER, Mrs.   '66

Born Elva Miller on 10/5/07 in Dodge City, Kansas. Died on 6/28/97 (age 89). Tone-deaf singer.

| 5/7/66 | 15 | 17 | | | Mrs. Miller's Greatest Hits | | [N] | $30 | Capitol 2494 |

Catch A Falling Star
Chim Chim Cher-ee

Dear Heart
Downtown 82

Gonna Be Like That
Hard Day's Night

Let's Hang On
Lover's Concerto 95

My Love
Shadow Of Your Smile

These Boots Are Made For Walkin'

MILLER, Ned   '63

Born Henry Ned Miller on 4/12/25 in Rains, Utah. Country singer/songwriter.

| 3/30/63 | 50 | 13 | | | From A Jack To A King | | | $50 | Fabor 1001 |

Billy Carino
Cry Of The Wild Goose

From A Jack To A King 6
Just Before Dawn

Lights In The Street
Long Shadow

Man Behind The Gun
Mona Lisa

One Among The Many
Stagecoach

Sunday Morning Tears
You Belong To My Heart

MILLER, Roger   '65

Born on 1/2/36 in Fort Worth, Texas; raised in Erick, Oklahoma. Died of cancer on 10/25/92 (age 56). Country singer/songwriter/guitarist. Hosted own TV show in 1966. Songwriter of 1985's Broadway musical *Big River*.

6/27/64	37	46	●	1	**Roger And Out**		[N]	$20	Smash 67049
					album also released as *Dang Me/Chug-A-Lug*				
2/6/65	4	47	●	2	**The Return Of Roger Miller**			$20	Smash 67061
7/24/65	13	24		3	**The 3rd Time Around**			$20	Smash 67068
11/13/65+	6	57	● ©	4	**Golden Hits**		[G]	$20	Smash 67073
11/19/66+	108	13		5	**Words And Music**			$20	Smash 67075
7/1/67	118	8		6	**Walkin' In The Sunshine**			$20	Smash 67092
8/24/68	173	8		7	**A Tender Look At Love**			$20	Smash 67103
8/30/69	163	7		8	**Roger Miller**			$20	Smash 67123
2/14/70	200	2		9	**Roger Miller 1970**			$20	Smash 67129

Absence (6)
Ain't That Fine (2)
All Fall Down (9)
As Long As There's A Shadow (2)
Atta Boy Girl (2,4)
Best Of All Possible Worlds (8)
Big Harlan Taylor (3)
Billy Bayou (5)
Boeing Boeing 707 (8)
By The Time I Get To Phoenix (7)
Chug-A-Lug (1,4) 9
Colonel Maggie (8)
Crystal Day (9)
Dad Blame Anything A Man Can't Quit (5)
Dang Me (1,4) 7
Darby's Castle (8)
Dear Heart (7)
Do-Wacka-Do (2,4) 31

Engine Engine #9 (3,4) 7
England Swings (4) 8
Every Which-A-Way (5)
Everybody's Talkin' (9)
Feel Of Me (1)
Fool, The (9)
Gentle On My Mind (9)
Good Old Days (3)
Got 2 Again (1)
Green Green Grass Of Home (6)
Hard Headed Me (2)
Heartbreak Hotel (5) 84
Hey Good Lookin' (6)
Home (5)
Honey (7)
Husbands And Wives (5) 26
I Ain't Comin' Home Tonight (1)
I Know Who It Is (And I'm Gonna Tell On 'Em) (9)
I'd Come Back To Me (6)

I'll Pick Up My Heart (And Go Home) (3)
I'm Gonna Teach My Heart To Bend (Instead Of Breaking) (8)
I've Been A Long Time Leavin' (But I'll Be A Long Time Gone) (5)
If You Want Me To (1)
In The Summertime (You Don't Want My Love) (2,4)
It Happened Just That Way (3,4)
It Takes All Kinds To Make A World (1)
Jody And The Kid (9)
Kansas City Star (3,4) 31
King Of The Road (2,4) 4
Last Word In Lonesome Is Me (3)
Less And Less (5)

Less Of Me (7)
Little Green Apples (7) 39
Lou's Got The Flu (1)
Love Is Not For Me (2)
Man Who Stayed In Monterey (9)
Me And Bobby McGee (8)
Million Years Or So (6)
Moon Is High (1)
My Elusive Dreams (7)
My Uncle Used To Love Me But She Died (5) 58
Mystery Train (9)
One Dyin' And A Buryin' (3,4) 34
Our Hearts Will Play The Music (2)
Our Little Love (6)
Pardon This Coffin' (6)
Precious Baby (9)

Private John Q (1)
Reincarnation (2)
Riddle, The (6)
Ruby (Don't Take Your Love To Town) (1)
Shame Bird (8)
Squares Make The World Go Round (1)
Swing Low Swingin' Chariot (3)
Swiss Cottage Place (4)
Swiss Maid (3)
T.J.'s Last Ride (9)
That's The Way It's Always Been (2)
That's Why I Love You Like I Do (1)
There I Go Dreamin' (2)
This Town (3)
Tolivar (7)
Tom Green County Fair (9)
Train Of Life (5)

Twelfth Of Never (7)
Vance (8) 80
Walkin' In The Sunshine (6) 37
Water Dog (3)
What I'd Give (To Be The Wind) (7)
Where Have All The Average People Gone (8)
With Pen In Hand (7)
Workin' Girl (5)
You Can't Roller Skate In A Buffalo Herd (2,4) 40
You Didn't Have To Be So Nice (6)
You're My Kingdom (5)

MILLER, Steve, Band ★89★   '76

Born on 10/5/43 in Milwaukee; raised in Dallas. Pop-rock singer/songwriter/guitarist. Formed band in high school, The Marksmen, which included **Boz Scaggs**. Moved to San Francisco in 1966; formed the Steve Miller Band, which featured a fluctuating lineup.

1)Book Of Dreams 2)The Joker 3)Abracadabra

6/15/68	134	18	©	1	**Children Of The Future**			$25	Capitol 2920
11/2/68	24	17	©	2	**Sailor**			$25	Capitol 2984
6/28/69	22	26	©	3	**Brave New World**			$20	Capitol 184
11/29/69+	38	14	©	4	**Your Saving Grace**			$15	Capitol 331
7/25/70	23	26	©	5	**Number 5**			$15	Capitol 436
10/9/71	82	9		6	**Rock Love**			$15	Capitol 748
4/1/72	109	10		7	**Recall The Beginning...A Journey From Eden**			$15	Capitol 11022
11/18/72+	56	39	● ©	8	**Anthology**		[K]	$20	Capitol 11114 [2]

DEBUT	PEAK	WKS	RIAA	CD	ARTIST — Album Title	Catalog	Sym	$	Label & Number

MILLER, Steve, Band — Cont'd

DEBUT	PEAK	WKS	RIAA	CD	Album			$	Label & Number
10/20/73	2[1]	38	▲	© 9	**The Joker**			$12	Capitol 11235
5/29/76	3	97	▲[4]	© 10	**Fly Like An Eagle**			$12	Capitol 11497
5/21/77	2[2]	68	▲[3]	© 11	**Book Of Dreams**			$12	Capitol 11630
12/9/78+	18	18	▲[8]	© 12	**Greatest Hits 1974-78**	C:●[3]/533	[G]	$12	Capitol 11872
11/14/81	26	17	●	© 13	**Circle Of Love**			$12	Capitol 12121
6/26/82	3	33	▲	© 14	**Abracadabra**			$12	Capitol 12216
4/30/83	125	7		© 15	**Steve Miller Band - Live!**		[L]	$10	Capitol 12263
11/10/84	101	10		© 16	**Italian X Rays**			$10	Capitol 12339
11/15/86+	65	23		© 17	**Living In The 20th Century**			$10	Capitol 12445
10/8/88	108	10		© 18	**Born 2B Blue**			$10	Capitol 48303

STEVE MILLER

DEBUT	PEAK	WKS	RIAA	CD	Album			$	Label & Number
6/26/93	85	15		© 19	**Wide River**			$10	Polydor 519441

Abracadabra (14,15) 1
Ain't That Lovin' You Baby (17)
All Your Love (I Miss Loving) (19)
Babes In The Wood (11)
Baby Wanna Dance (13)
Baby's Callin' Me Home (1)
Baby's House (4,8)
Beauty Of Time Is That It's Snowing (Psychedelic B.B.) (1)
Behind The Barn (17)
Big Boss Man (17)
Blue Eyes (19)
Blue Odyssey (10)
Blues With Out Blame (6)
Bongo Bongo (16) 84
Born To Be Blue (18)
Brave New World (3)
Can't You Hear Your Daddy's Heartbeat (1)
Caress Me Baby (17)
Celebration Song (3,8)
Children Of The Future (1)
Circle Of Fire (19)
Circle Of Love (13) 55
Come On In My Kitchen (9)
Conversation (16)
Cool Magic (14) 57

Cry Cry Cry (19)
Dance, Dance, Dance (10,12)
Daybreak (16)
Dear Mary (2)
Deliverance (6)
Dime-A-Dance Romance (2)
Don't Let Nobody Turn You Around (4,8)
Electro Lux Imbroglio (11)
Enter Maurice (7)
Evil (9)
Fandango (7)
Fanny Mae (1)
Feel So Glad (4)
Filthy McNasty (18)
Fly Like An Eagle (10,12,15) 2
Gangster Is Back (6)
Gangster Of Love (2,15)
Get On Home (13)
Give It Up (14) 60
God Bless The Child (18)
Going To Mexico (5,8)
Going To The Country (5,8) 69
Golden Opportunity (16)
Good Morning (1)
Goodbye Love (14)
Got Love 'Cause You Need It (3)

Harbor Lights (6)
Harmony Of The Spheres 1 & 2 (16)
Heal Your Heart (7)
Heart Like A Wheel (13) 24
High On You Mama (7)
Hollywood Dream (16)
Horse And Rider (19)
Hot Chili (5)
I Love You (5,8)
I Wanna Be Loved (But By Only You) (17)
I Want To Make The World Turn Around (17) 97
In My First Mind (1)
Industrial Military Complex Hex (5)
Italian X Rays (16)
Jackson-Kent Blues (5)
Jet Airliner (11,12,15) 8
Joker, The (9,12,15) 1
Jungle Love (11,12,15) 23
Junior Saw It Happen (1)
Just A Little Bit (18)
Just A Passin' Fancy In A Midnite Dream (4)
Keeps Me Wondering Why (14)
Key To The Highway (1)

Kow Kow (3,8)
LT's Midnight Dream (3)
Last Wombat In Mecca (4)
Let Me Serve You (6)
Little Girl (4,8)
Living In The 20th Century (17)
Living In The U.S.A. (2,8,15) 49
Lost In Your Eyes (19)
Love Shock (1)
Love's Riddle (7)
Lovin' Cup (3)
Lucky Man (2)
Macho City (13)
Maelstrom (17)
Mary Ann (18)
Mary Lou (9)
Mercury Blues (10,15)
Midnight Train (19)
Motherless Children (4,8)
My Babe (17)
My Dark Hour (3,8)
My Friend (2)
My Own Space (11)
Never Kill Another Man (5,8)
Never Say No (14)
Nobody But You Baby (17)
Nothing Lasts (2)
One In A Million (16)

Out Of The Night (16)
Overdrive (2)
Perfect World (19)
Pushed Me To It (1)
Quicksilver Girl (2)
Radio 1 & 2 (16)
Red Top (18)
Rock Love (6)
Rock'n Me (10,12,15) 1
Roll With It (1)
Sacrifice (11)
Seasons (3,8)
Serenade (10,15)
Shangri-La (16) 57
Shu Ba Da Du Ma Ma Ma Ma (9)
Slinky (17)
Somebody Somewhere Help Me (7)
Something Special (14)
Something To Believe In (9)
Song For Our Ancestors (2)
Space Cowboy (3,8)
Stake, The (11,12)
Steppin' Stone (1)
Steve Miller's Midnight Tango (5)
Stranger Blues (19)
Sugar Babe (9)

Sun Is Going Down (7)
Sweet Maree (10)
Swingtown (11,12) 17
Take The Money And Run (10,12,15) 11
Things I Told You (14)
Threshold (11,12)
Tokin's (5)
True Fine Love (11,12)
Walks Like A Lady (19)
Welcome (7)
When Sunny Gets Blue (18)
While I'm Waiting (14)
Who Do You Love (16)
Wide River (19) 64
Wild Mountain Honey (10,12)
Willow Weep For Me (18)
Window, The (10)
Winter Time (11,12)
Wish Upon A Star (11)
Ya Ya (18)
You Send Me (10)
You're So Fine (2)
You've Got The Power (1)
Young Girl's Heart (14)
Your Cash Ain't Nothin' But Trash (9) 51
Your Saving Grace (4,8)
Zip-A-Dee-Doo-Dah (18)

MILLIONS LIKE US '88
Pop-rock duo from England: John O'Kane (vocals) and Jeep MacNichol (guitar, keyboards).

DEBUT	PEAK	WKS	RIAA	CD	Album	$	Label & Number
12/19/87+	171	12		©	**...Millions Like Us**	$10	Virgin 90602

Beautiful Enemy
Chain
Guaranteed For Life 69
Heart To Heart
Heaven And The Sky
Ideal World
In Love With Yourself
Million Voices
Waiting For The Right Time
What You Want Is What You Get

MILLI VANILLI '89
Europop act formed in Germany by producer Frank Farian (creator of **Boney M**). Originally thought to be Rob Pilatus (from Germany) and Fabrice Morvan (from France). Duo was stripped of its 1989 Best New Artist Grammy Award when it was revealed that they didn't sing on their debut album. Actual vocalists were Charles Shaw, John Davis and Brad Howe. Pilatus died of a drug overdose on 4/2/98 (age 32).

DEBUT	PEAK	WKS	RIAA	CD	Album		$	Label & Number
3/25/89	●[8]	78	▲[6]	©	**1 Girl You Know It's True**		$10	Arista 8592
6/16/90	32	20	●	©	**2 The Remix Album**	[K]	$10	Arista 8622

All Or Nothing (1,2)
Baby Don't Forget My Number (1,2) 1
Blame It On The Rain (1,2) 1
Boy In The Tree (2)
Can't You Feel My Love (2)
Dreams To Remember (1)
Girl I'm Gonna Miss You (1,2) 1
Girl You Know It's True (1,2) 2
Hush (2)
It's Your Thing (1)
Money (2)
More Than You'll Ever Know (1)
Take It As It Comes (1)

MILLS, Frank '79
Born in 1943 in Toronto. Pianist/composer/producer/arranger.

DEBUT	PEAK	WKS	RIAA	CD	Album		$	Label & Number
3/17/79	21	16	●		**1 Music Box Dancer**	[I]	$12	Polydor 6192
11/24/79+	149	9			**2 Sunday Morning Suite**	[I]	$12	Polydor 6225

After You Mister Trumpet Man (2)
Ballet Russe (2)
Blackfoot Country (1)
From A Sidewalk Cafe (1)
Hennessey's Island (1)
Love's Like That (1)
Mama, Won't You Boogie With Me? (2)
Mary, Queen Of Scots (2)
Most People Are Nice (2)
Music Box Dancer (1) 3
Peter Piper (2) 48
Piano Lesson (2)
Poet And I (1)
Silver Broom, Theme From The (1)
Ski Fever (2)
Spanish Coffee (1)
Sunday Morning Suite (2)
Valse Classique (1)
When You Smile (1)
Wherever You Go (2)
You Don't Love No More (1)

★400★ MILLS, Stephanie '80
Born on 3/26/56 in Brooklyn, New York. R&B singer/actress. Played "Dorothy" in Broadway's *The Wiz*. Briefly married to Jeffrey Daniels of **Shalamar** in 1980.

DEBUT	PEAK	WKS	RIAA	CD	Album	$	Label & Number
5/19/79	22	34	●		**1 Whatcha Gonna Do...With My Lovin'?**	$12	20th Century 583
5/3/80	16	44	●		**2 Sweet Sensation**	$12	20th Century 603
5/16/81	30	23	●		**3 Stephanie**	$12	20th Century 700
8/7/82	48	19			**4 Tantalizingly Hot**	$10	Casablanca 7265
9/17/83	104	19			**5 Merciless**	$10	Casablanca 811364
10/13/84	73	15		©	**6 I've Got The Cure**	$10	Casablanca 822421
3/29/86	47	22		©	**7 Stephanie Mills**	$10	MCA 5669
6/27/87	30	36	●	©	**8 If I Were Your Woman**	$10	MCA 5996
7/22/89	82	38	●	©	**9 Home**	$10	MCA 6312

Ain't No Cookin' (9)
Automatic Passion (7)
Can't Change My Ways (8)
Comfort Of A Man (9)
D-A-N-C-I-N' (2)
Deeper Inside Your Love (1)
Do You Love Him? (1)
Don't Dancin' (1)
Don't Stop Doin' What 'Cha Do (3)
Edge Of The Razor (6)
Eternal Love (5)
Everlasting Love (6)
Fast Talk (9)
Feel The Fire (1)
Give It Half A Chance (6)
Good Girl Gone Bad (9)
Here I Am (5)
His Name Is Michael (5)
Hold On To Might (7)
Home (9)
How Come U Don't Call Me Anymore? (9)
I Believe In Love Songs (1)
I Can't Give Back The Love I Feel For You (4)
I Come To You (9)
I Feel Good All Over (8)

MILLS, Stephanie — Cont'd

I Have Learned To Respect The Power Of Love (7)
I Just Wanna Say (2)
If I Were Your Woman (8)
In My Life (6)
Jesse (8)
Just You (7)
Keep Away Girls (3)
Last Night (4)
Magic (3)

Medicine Song (6) *65*
Mixture Of Love (2)
My Body (5)
My Love's Been Good To You (3)
Never Get Enough Of You (5)
Never Knew Love Like This Before (2) *6*
Night Games (3)
'Ole Love (4)

Outrageous (1)
Pilot Error (5)
Put Your Body In It (1)
Real Love (2)
Rising Desire (7)
Rough Trade (6)
Running For Your Love (8)
Secret Lady (9)
Since We've Been Together (5)
So Good, So Right (9)

Something In The Way (You Make Me Feel) (9)
Stand Back (7)
Starlight (1)
Still Lovin' You (4)
Still Mine (2)
Sweet Sensation (2) *52*
Time Of Your Life (7)
Top Of My List (3)
Touch Me Now (8)

True Love Don't Come Easy (4)
Try My Love (2)
Two Hearts (3) *40*
Under Pressure (7)
Undercover (4)
What Cha Gonna Do With My Lovin' (1) *22*
Winner (3)
Wish That You Were Mine (2)
You And I (1)

You Can Get Over (1)
You Can't Run From My Love (4)
You Just Might Need A Friend (6)
(You're Puttin') A Rush On Me (8) *85*
Your Love Is Always New (4)

MILLS BROTHERS, The '68

Legendary family vocal group from Piqua, Ohio: father John Mills (died on 12/8/67, age 78), with sons Herbert (died on 4/12/89, age 67), Harry (died on 6/28/82, age 68) and Donald (died on 11/13/99, age 84) Mills.

DEBUT	PEAK	WKS	RIAA	CD	#	Album Title	Sym	$	Label & Number
3/16/68	21	26			1	Fortuosity		$15	Dot 25809
4/6/68	145	6			2	The Board Of Directors		$15	Dot 25838
						COUNT BASIE & THE MILLS BROTHERS			
8/10/68	190	3			3	My Shy Violet		$15	Dot 25872
12/21/68	36[X]	2	©		4	Merry Christmas	[X]	$15	Dot 25232
						first released in 1959			
5/24/69	184	5			5	Dream		$15	Dot 25927

Adeste Fideles (4)
Am I That Easy To Forget (3)
April In Paris (2)
Baby Dream Your Dream (5)
Bramble Bush (1)
Bring Me Sunshine (3)
But For Love (5)
By The Time I Get To Phoenix (3)
Cab Driver (1) *23*
Christmas Song (1)

December (2)
Didn't We (5)
Down - Down - Down (2)
Dream (5)
Everybody's Friend (1)
Flit Around (5)
Flower Road (3)
Fortuosity (1)
God Rest Ye Merry, Gentlemen (4)
Guy On The Go (5)

Hallelujah Baby! (1)
Happy Go Lucky Me (5)
Happy Together (1)
Here Comes Santa Claus (4)
I Dig Rock And Roll Music (4)
I Found A Love (1)
I May Be Wrong But I Think You're Wonderful (2)
I Want To Be Happy (2)
I'll Be Home For Christmas (4)
Jimtown Road (5)

Jingle Bells (4)
Joy To The World (4)
Lazy River (2)
Let Me Dream (2)
Long Long Ago (1)
More And More (1)
My Shy Violet (3) *73*
O Holy Night (4)
O Little Town Of Bethlehem (5)
Ol' Race Track (3) *83*
Release Me (2)

Rose (A Ring To The Name Of Rose) (3)
Santa Claus Is Comin' To Town (4)
Sherry (1)
Silent Night (4)
Straight Down The Middle (3)
Straight Life (5)
Sugar Boat (3)
This Is The Last Time (I'll Cry Over You) (3)

Tiny Bubbles (3)
What Have I Done For Her Lately (5)
When, When, When (5)
Whiffenpoof Song (2)
White Christmas (4)

★346★ MILSAP, Ronnie '81

Born on 1/16/43 in Robbinsville, North Carolina. Country singer/songwriter/pianist. Blind since birth.

1)There's No Gettin' Over Me 2)Greatest Hits 3)Keyed Up

DEBUT	PEAK	WKS	RIAA	CD	#	Album Title	Sym	$	Label & Number
2/15/75	138	7			1	A Legend In My Time		$15	RCA Victor 0846
11/29/75	191	2		©	2	Night Things		$15	RCA Victor 1223
9/10/77	97	15	●	©	3	It Was Almost Like A Song		$12	RCA Victor 2439
6/24/78	109	12	●		4	Only One Love In My Life		$12	RCA Victor 2780
6/16/79	98	15			5	Images		$12	RCA Victor 3346
4/5/80	137	13			6	Milsap Magic		$12	RCA Victor 3563
10/25/80+	36	41	▲²	©	7	Greatest Hits	[G]	$12	RCA Victor 3772
4/18/81	89	29			8	Out Where The Bright Lights Are Glowing		$12	RCA Victor 3932
9/5/81	31	31	●	©	9	There's No Gettin' Over Me		$12	RCA Victor 4060
7/3/82	66	14		©	10	Inside Ronnie Milsap		$12	RCA Victor 4311
4/30/83	36	19			11	Keyed Up		$12	RCA Victor 4670
6/2/84	180	3		©	12	One More Try For Love		$12	RCA Victor 5016
8/31/85	102	20	▲	©	13	Greatest Hits, Vol. 2	[G]	$10	RCA Victor 5425
5/3/86	121	12	●	©	14	Lost In The Fifties Tonight		$10	RCA Victor 7194
5/25/91	172	2			15	Back To The Grindstone		$10	RCA 2375
1/27/01	178	2		©	16	40 #1 Hits	[G]	$15	Virgin 48871 [2]

(After Sweet Memories) Play Born To Lose Again (2)
All Good Things Don't Have To End (5)
All Is Fair In Love And War (15)
Am I Losing You (8,13,16)
Any Day Now (10,13,16) *14*
Are You Lovin' Me Like I'm Lovin' You (15)
Back On My Mind Again (4,7,16)
Back To The Grindstone (15)
Biggest Lie (1)
Borrowed Angel (2)
Busiest Memory In Town (1)
Carolina Dreams (10)
Clap Your Hands (1)
Country Cookin' (1)
Cowboys And Clowns (16)
Crystal Fallin' Rain (5)
Daydreams About Night Things (2,7,16)
Dear Friend (8)
Delta Queen (5)
Don't Take It Tonight (14)
Don't You Ever Get Tired (Of Hurting Me) (16)
Don't You Know How Much I Love You (11,13,16) *58*
Don't Your Mem'ry Ever Sleep At Night (11)
Everywhere I Turn (There's Your Memory) (9)
Feelings Change (11)
Four Walls (8)
Future Is Not What It Used To Be (3)
Get It Up (5) *43*

Happy, Happy Birthday Baby (14,16)
Hate The Lies - Love The Liar (10)
He Got You (10,16) *59*
He'll Have To Go (8)
Here In Love (3)
Hi-Heel Sneakers (5)
How Do I Turn My Love On (14,16)
I Ain't Gonna Cry No More (15)
I Guess I Just Missed You (12)
I Guess I'm Crazy (8)
I Hate You (7)
I Heard It Through The Grapevine (14)
I Honestly Love You (1)
I Let Myself Believe (4)
I Live My Whole Life At Night (9)
I Love New Orleans Music (1)
I Might Have Said (12)
I Only Remember The Good Times (14)
I Really Don't Want To Know (5)
I Won't Forget You (8)
I Wouldn't Have Missed It For The World (9,13,16) *20*
(I'd Be) A Legend In My Time (1,7,16)
I'll Be There (If You Ever Want Me) (2)
I'll Leave This World Loving You (1)
I'll Take Care Of You (12)
(I'm A) Stand By My Woman Man (7,16)
I'm Beginning To Forget You (8)
I'm Getting Better (8)

I'm Just A Redneck At Heart (11)
I'm No Good At Goodbyes (2)
I'm Not Trying To Forget (4)
I'm Still Not Over You (1)
I've Got The Music In Me (4)
If You Don't Want Me To (6)
In Love (14,16)
In No Time At All (5)
Inside (10,13,16)
Is It Over (11)
It Don't Hurt To Dream (3)
It Happens Every Time (I Think Of You) (9)
It Was Almost Like A Song (3,7,16) *16*
It's A Beautiful Thing (6)
It's All I Can Do (9)
It's Already Taken (13)
It's Just A Room (10)
It's Written All Over Your Face (9)
Jesus Is Your Ticket To Heaven (9)
Just Because It Feels Good (5)
Just In Case (2,16)
Keep The Night Away (5)
Let My Love Be Your Pillow (7,16)
Let's Take The Long Way Around The World (4,7,16)
Like Children I Have Known (11)
Livin' On Love (16)
Long Distance Memory (3)
Lost In The Fifties Tonight (In The Still Of The Night) (13,14,16)

Love Certified (15)
Love Takes A Long Time To Die (2)
Lovin' Kind (3)
(Lying Here With) Linda On My Mind (2)
Make No Mistake She's Mine (16)
Misery Loves Company (6)
Missing You (8)
Money (That's What I Want) (14)
My Heart (6,16)
Nashville Moon (14)
Night By Night (12)
No One Will Ever Know (3)
No Relief In Sight (4)
Nobody Likes Sad Songs (5,16)
Old Fashioned Girl Like You (14)
Old Habits Are Hard To Break (15)
Once I Get Over You (4)
One More Try For Love (12)
Only One Love In My Life (4,16) *63*
Out Where The Bright Lights Are Glowing (8)
Please Don't Tell Me How The Story Ends (7,16) *95*
Pride Goes Before A Fall (8)
Prisoner Of The Highway (12)
Pure Love (7,16)
Remember To Remind Me (I'm Leaving) (2)
Santa Barbara (4)
Selfish (3)

She Came Here For The Change (1)
She Keeps The Home Fires Burning (13,16)
She Loves My Car (12) *84*
She Thinks I Still Care (6)
She's Always In Love (12)
Show Her (11,16)
Silent Night (After The Fight) (6)
Since I Don't Have You (15,16)
Smoky Mountain Rain (7,16) *24*
Snap Your Fingers (16)
Spare The Rod (Love The Child) (15)
Still In Love With You (6)
Still Losing You (12,16)
Stranger In My House (11,13,16) *23*
Stranger Things Have Happened (16)
Suburbia (12)
(There's) No Gettin' Over Me (9,13,16) *5*
Time, Love & Money (16)
Too Big For Words (9)
Too Late To Worry, Too Blue To Cry (1,16)
Too Soon To Know (4)
Turn That Radio On (15)
Two Hearts Don't Always Make A Pair (9)
Watch Out For The Other Guy (11)
We're Here To Love (16)
What A Difference You've Made In My Life (3,7,16) *80*

What Goes On When The Sun Goes Down (16)
What's One More Time (6)
When The Hurt Comes Down (15)
When Two Worlds Collide (8)
Where Do The Nights Go (16)
Who'll Turn Out The Lights (In Your World Tonight) (15)
Who's Counting (10)
Why Don't You Spend The Night (6,16)
Woman In Love (16)
Wrong End Of The Rainbow (10)
Yesterday's Lovers Never Make Good Friends (4)
You Don't Look For Love (5)
You Took Her Off My Hands (Now Take Her Off My Mind) (10)

MIMMS, Garnet, & The Enchanters '63

Born Garrett Mimms on 11/16/33 in Ashland, West Virginia. R&B singer. The Enchanters: Zola Pearnell, Sam Bell and Charles Boyer.

11/23/63	91	5	©	**Cry Baby And 11 Other Hits**			**$100** United Artists 3305

Anytime You Need Me · Cry Baby *4* · Don't Change Your Heart · I Keep Wanting You · Quiet Place *78* · So Close
Baby Don't You Weep *30* · Cry To Me · **For Your Precious Love** *26* · Nobody But You · Runaway Lover · Until You Were Gone

MINDBENDERS, The '65

Pop-rock group from Manchester, England: Wayne Fontana (vocals), Eric Stewart (guitar, vocals), Bob Lang (bass) and Ric Rothwell (drums). Stewart later formed **10cc**.

5/1/65	58	9	1 **The Game Of Love**	$30 Fontana 27542

WAYNE FONTANA & THE MINDBENDERS

7/16/66	92	9	2 **A Groovy Kind Of Love**	$30 Fontana 27554

All Night Worker (2) · Game Of Love (1) *1* · Jaguar And Thunderbird (1) · One Fine Day (2) · Way You Do The Things You
Can't Live With You, Can't Live · Girl Can't Help It (2) · Just A Little Bit (2) · One More Time (1) · Do (2)
  Without You (2) · Git It! (1) · Keep Your Hands Off My Baby · Seventh Son (2) · You Don't Know About Love (2)
Certain Girl (1) · **Groovy Kind Of Love** (2) *2* · (1) · She's Got The Power (1) · You Don't Know Me (1)
Cops & Robbers (1) · I'm Gonna Be A Wheel · Little Nightingale (2) · Too Many Tears (1)
Don't Cry No More (2) · Someday (1) · Love Is Good (2) · Trickie Dickie (2)

MINISTRY '96

An assemblage of musicians spearheaded by Chicago-based producers/performers Alain Jourgensen and Paul Barker. Formed by Jourgensen in 1981. Barker joined Ministry in 1986. Varying personnel are members of The Tribe, an affiliation of musicians from various groups.

6/25/83	96	14		©	1 **With Sympathy**	$12 Arista 6608
4/5/86	194	3		©	2 **Twitch**	$10 Sire 25309
11/5/88	164	4	●	©	3 **The Land Of Rape And Honey**	$10 Sire 25799
12/9/89	163	10	●	©	4 **The Mind Is A Terrible Thing To Taste**	$10 Sire 26004
8/1/92	27	36	▲	©	5 **Psalm 69**	$10 Sire 26727
2/17/96	19	10		©	6 **Filth Pig**	$10 Warner 45838
6/26/99	92	2		©	7 **Dark Side Of The Spoon**	$10 Warner 47311

Abortive (3) · Dead Guy (6) · Grace (5) · Missing, The (3) · She's Got A Cause (1) · Useless (6)
All Day Remix (2) · Deity (3) · Here We Go (1) · My Possession (2) · Should Have Known Better (1) · Vex & Violence (7)
Angel, The (2) · Destruction (3) · Hero (5) · N.W.O. (5) · So What (4) · We Believe (2)
Bad Blood (7) · Effigy (1) · I Wanted To Tell Her (1) · Never Believe (4) · Step (7) · What He Say (1)
Breathe (4) · Eureka Pile (7) · Jesus Built My Hotrod (5) · Nursing Home (7) · Stigmata (3) · Where You At Now? (medley)
Brick Windows (6) · Faith Collapsing (4) · Just Like You (2) · Over The Shoulder (2) · Supermanic Soul (7) · (2)
Burning Inside (4) · Fall, The (6) · Just One Fix (5) · Psalm 69 (5) · TV (5) · Whip And Chain (7)
Cannibal Song (4) · Filth Pig (6) · Kaif (7) · Reload (6) · 10/10 (7) · Work For Love (1)
Corrosion (5) · Flashback (3) · Land Of Rape And Honey (3) · Revenge (2) · Test (4) · You Know What You Are (3)
Crash And Burn (medley) (2) · Game Show (6) · Lava (6) · Say You're Sorry (1) · Thieves (4)
Crumbs (6) · Golden Dawn (3) · Lay Lady Lay (6) · Scare Crow (5) · Twitch (Version II) (medley) (2)

MINK DeVILLE '78

Rock trio formed in London: Willy DeVille (vocals, guitar), Ruben Siguenza (bass) and Thomas Allen (drums).

8/13/77	186	2	©	1 **Mink DeVille**	$12 Capitol 11631
6/10/78	126	5	©	2 **Return To Magenta**	$12 Capitol 11780
9/13/80	163	3	©	3 **Le Chat Bleu**	$12 Capitol 11955
10/24/81	161	5	©	4 **Coup De Grace**	$12 Atlantic 19311

"A" Train Lady (2) · Guardian Angel (2) · Just To Walk That Little Girl · Maybe Tomorrow (4) · Slow Drain (3) · Turn You Every Way But Loose
Bad Boy (3) · Gunslinger (1) · Home (3) · Mixed Up, Shook Up Girl (1) · So In Love Are We (4) · (3)
Cadillac Walk (1) · Heaven Stood Still (3) · Just Your Friends (2) · One Way Street (1) · Soul Twist (2) · Venus Of Avenue D (1)
Can't Do Without It (1) · Help Me To Make It (Power Of · Lipstick Traces (3) · Party Girls (1) · Spanish Stroll (1) · You Better Move On (4)
Confidence To Kill (2) · A Woman's Love) (4) · Little Girl (1) · Rolene (2) · Steady Drivin' Man (2) · You Just Keep Holding On (3)
Desperate Days (4) · I Broke That Promise (2) · Love & Emotion (4) · Savoir Faire (3) · Teardrops Must Fall (4)
Easy Slider (2) · Just Give Me One Good · Love Me Like You Did Before · She Was Made In Heaven (4) · That World Outside (4)
End Of The Line (4) · Reason (4) · (4) · She's So Tough (1) · This Must Be The Night (3)

MINNELLI, Liza '72

Born on 3/12/46 in Los Angeles. Singer/actress. Daughter of **Judy Garland** and movie director Vincente Minnelli. Starred in several movies and Broadway shows. Married to **Peter Allen** from 1967-73. Married to movie producer Jack Haley, Jr. from 1974-79. Won Grammy's Living Legends Award in 1989.

1)Liza With A "Z" 2)Liza Minnelli The Singer 3)"Live" At The London Palladium

11/21/64	115	8	1 **Liza! Liza!**	$25 Capitol 2174
9/4/65	41	14	2 **"Live" At The London Palladium**	[L] $30 Capitol 2295 [2]

JUDY GARLAND & LIZA MINNELLI
also see #6 below

11/28/70	158	3	3 **New Feelin'**	$20 A&M 4272
9/30/72	19	23	● ©	4 **Liza With A "Z"**	[TV] $15 Columbia 31762

recorded at the Lyceum Theater in New York City

3/24/73	38	20	5 **Liza Minnelli The Singer**	$15 Columbia 32149
6/9/73	164	8	6 **"Live" At The London Palladium**	[L] $20 Capitol 11191

JUDY GARLAND & LIZA MINNELLI
condensation of album #2 above

5/18/74	150	4	7 **Live At The Winter Garden**	[L] $15 Columbia 32854
11/14/87	156	8	©	8 **Liza Minnelli At Carnegie Hall**	[L] $15 Telarc 15502 [2]
11/11/89	128	10	9 **Results**	$10 Epic 45098

features backing and co-production by the **Pet Shop Boys**

7/6/96	156	1	©	10 **Gently**	$10 Angel 35470

Alexander's Ragtime Band (8) · Bob White (Whatcha Gonna · Can't Help Lovin' That Man Of · Does He Love You? (10) · He's Got The Whole World In · How Long Has This Been Goin'
All I Need Is One Good Break · Swing Tonight?) (medley) (2) · Mine (3) · Don't Drop Bombs (9) · His Hands (2,6) · On? (3)
  (medley) (8) · Brotherhood Of Man (medley) · Chances Are (10) · Don't Ever Leave Me (1) · Hello, Dolly! (2,6) · I Believe In Music (5)
And I In My Chair (Et Moi Dans · (6) · Chicago (medley) (2) · Don't Let Me Be Lonely Tonight · Here I'll Stay (medley) (8) · I Can See Clearly Now (7,8)
  Mon Coin) (8) · Buckle Down Winsocki (8) · Circle, The (10) · (5) · Hooray For Love (medley) (2,6) · I Can See It (medley)
Anywhere You Are (medley) (7) · But, The World Goes 'Round · City Lights (medley) (8) · Embraceable You (10) · How About You (medley) (2,6) · I Can't Say Goodnight (9)
Baby Don't Get Hooked On Me · (medley) (8) · Close Your Eyes (10) · Exactly Like Me (7) · How Could You Believe Me · I Don't Want To Know (8)
  (5) · By Myself (medley) (2,6) · Come Back To Me (medley) (7) · God Bless The Child (3,4) · When I Said I Love You... (2) · I Got Lost In His Arms (10)
Blue Moon (1) · Bye Bye Blackbird (3) · Come Rain Or Come Shine (3) · Gypsy In My Soul (2,6) · How Deep Is The Ocean (8)
· Cabaret (4,7,8) · Dancing In The Moonlight (5)

MINNELLI, Liza — Cont'd

I Gotcha (4)
I Happen To Like New York (8)
I Knew Him When (1)
I Never Has Seen Snow (8)
I Want You Now (9)
(I Wonder Where My) Easy
  Rider's Gone (3)
I'd Love You To Want Me (5)
I'm All I've Got (1)
I'm One Of The Smart Ones
  (7,8)
If I Were In Your Shoes (1)
If There Was Love (9)
If You Could Read My Mind
  (medley) (7)
If You Hadn't, But You Did (8)

In The Wee Small Hours Of
  Morning (10)
It All Depends On You (medley)
  (2,6)
It Had To Be You (10)
It Was A Good Time (4)
It's Just A Matter Of Time (1)
Lazy Bones (3)
Liza (medley) (4)
Liza With A "Z" (4,7,8)
Liza's Medley (2)
Lonely Feet (8)
Losing My Mind (9)
Lost In You (10)
Love For Sale (3)
Love Pains (9)

Lover, Come Back To Me
  (medley) (2,6)
Man I Love (3)
Married (medley) (4,8)
Maybe Soon (1)
Maybe This Time (1,3,4,7,8)
Meantime (1)
Mein Herr (medley) (8)
Money, Money (medley) (4,8)
More Than You Know (7)
My Mammy (2)
Natural Man (7)
Never Let Me Go (10)
New York, New York (8)
Oh, Babe, What Would You
  Say? (5)

Old Friends (8)
Our Love Is Here To Stay
  (medley) (8)
Pass That Peace Pipe (2)
Quiet Thing (7,8)
Rent (9)
Ring Them Bells (4,7,8)
San Francisco (medley) (2)
Shine On Harvest Moon (7)
Sing Happy (medley) (8)
Singer, The (5)
So Sorry, I Said (9)
Some Cats Know (10)
Some People (8)
Somewhere Out There (8)
Son Of A Preacher Man (4)

Stormy Weather (3)
Swanee (2,6)
Sweetest Sounds (8)
There Is A Time (Le Temps) (7)
Time Heals Everything (medley)
  (8)
Together Wherever We Go
  (1,2,6)
Tonight Is Forever (9)
Toot Toot Tootsie (8)
Travelin' Life (1,2)
Try To Remember (1)
Twist In My Sobriety (9)
Use Me (5)
We Could Make Such Beautiful
  Music (medley) (2)

When The Saints Go Marching
  In (medley) (2,6)
Where Is The Love (5)
Who's Sorry Now? (5)
Willkommen (medley) (4)
Yes (4,8)
You Are The Sunshine Of My
  Life (5)
You Better Sit Down, Kids
  (medley) (8)
You Can Have Him (medley) (8)
You Stepped Out Of A Dream
  (10)
You're So Vain (5)
You've Let Yourself Go (4)

MINOGUE, Kylie   '89

Born on 5/28/68 in Melbourne, Australia. Singer/actress. Regular on the Australian soap opera *Neighbours*.

| 9/10/88+ | 53 | 28 | ● | © | Kylie.................... | $10 | Geffen 24195 |

Got To Be Certain
I Miss You

I Should Be So Lucky *28*
I'll Still Be Loving You

It's No Secret *37*
Je Ne Sais Pas Pourquoi

Loco-Motion *3*
Look My Way

Love At First Sight
Turn It Into Love

MINOR DETAIL   '83

Duo from Ireland: brothers John and Willie Hughes.

| 10/1/83 | 187 | 2 | | | Minor Detail............ | $12 | Polydor 815004 |

Ask The Kids
Canvas Of Life *92*

Columbia
Hold On

I'll Always Love You
I've Got A Friend

Others Need You
20th Century

We Are Winners (Once We Try)
Why Take It Again

MINT CONDITION   '92

R&B group from Minneapolis: Stokley Williams (vocals, drums), Homer O'Dell (guitar), Larry Waddell and Keri Lewis (keyboards), Jeff Allen (sax) and Ricky Kinchen (bass). Lewis married **Toni Braxton** on 4/21/2001.

2/8/92	63	22		©	1 **Meant To Be Mint**	$10	Perspective 1001
1/29/94	104	13		©	2 **From The Mint Factory**	$10	Perspective 9005
10/12/96	76	25	●	©	3 **Definition Of A Band**	$10	Perspective 9028
12/4/99	64	9		©	4 **Life's Aquarium**	$10	Elektra 62353

Ain't Hookin' Me Up Enough (3)
Always (2)
Are You Free (1)
Back To Your Lovin' (2)
Be Like That Sometimes (4)
**Breakin' My Heart (Pretty
  Brown Eyes)** (1) *6*
Call Me (4)
Change Your Mind (3)

Definition Of A Band (3)
Do U Wanna (1)
Fidelity (2)
Forever In Your Eyes (1) *81*
Funky Weekend (3)
Gettin' It On (3)
Good For Your Heart (2)
Harmony (2)
Here We Go Again (3)
I Want It Again (3)

I Wonder If She Likes Me (1)
If It Wasn't For Your Love (3)
If The Feeling's Right (2)
If You Love Me (4) *30*
Is This Pain Our Pleasure (4)
Just The Man For You (4)
Leave Me Alone (4)
Let Me Be The One (3)
Missing (3)
My High (2)

Never That You'll Never Know
  (3)
Nobody Does It Betta (2)
On & On (3)
Outta Time, Outta Mind (1)
Pretty Lady (4)
Raise Up (3)
Sensuous Appeal (1)
She's A Honey (1)
Single To Mingle (1)

So Fine (2)
Someone To Love (2)
Sometimes (3)
Spanish Eyes (4)
10 Million Strong (2)
This Day, This Minute, Right
  Now (4)
Tonight (4)
Touch That Body (4)
True To Thee (1)

Try My Love (1)
U Send Me Swingin' (2) *33*
What Kind Of Man Would I Be
  (3) *17*
Who Can You Trust (4)
**You Don't Have To Hurt No
  More** (3) *32*

MIRABAI   '75

Female folk singer.

| 8/30/75 | 128 | 6 | | | **Mirabai**............ | $12 | Atlantic 18144 |

Cosmic Overload
Dedication, A

Determination
Exactly What You Are

Magical Time
Mirabai

Schumann's Song
Stairway To Heaven

Strength Of My Soul
To Be Young

You Are My Reason

MIRACLE   '00

Born Peter Evans in Augusta, Georgia. Male rapper.

| 5/27/00 | 56 | 9 | | © | **Miracle**............ | $10 | Sound Of Atl. 153283 |

Beat 'Em Down To The Floor
Bounce
Bounce Bass

Huntin' Season
I Gives A F*** (If The Sun Don't
  Shine)

I Love You So F*****! Much (I
  Hate U)
Life In The Dirty South

Momma
P&D
Smoka'

U Don't Want To Know The
  Truth
We Ain't Scared

We Fittin To Do This

MIRACLES, The   ★103★   '66

R&B vocal group from Detroit: **Smokey Robinson**, Claudette Rogers, Bobby Rogers, Ronnie White and Warren Moore. Claudette Rogers retired in 1964; married to Robinson from 1958-86. Bobby Rogers married Wanda Young of **The Marvelettes**. Robinson went solo in 1972, replaced by Billy Griffin. White died of leukemia on 8/26/95 (age 57).

1)*Greatest Hits, Vol. 2* 2)*Going To A Go-Go* 3)*Greatest Hits From The Beginning*
  4)*Time Out For Smokey Robinson & The Miracles* 5)*Make It Happen*

6/8/63	118	8			1 **The Fabulous Miracles**		$300	Tamla 238
10/5/63	139	5			2 **The Miracles On Stage**......	[L]	$200	Tamla 241
1/4/64	113	4		©	3 **doin' Mickey's Monkey**		$200	Tamla 245
12/19/64+	15ˣ	8		©	4 **Christmas With The Miracles**	[X]	$300	Tamla 236
					first released in 1963; Christmas charts: 29/64, 15/65, 59/67			
4/17/65	21	25			5 **Greatest Hits From The Beginning**	[G]	$75	Tamla 254 [2]
					SMOKEY ROBINSON & THE MIRACLES:			
11/27/65+	8	40		©	6 **Going To A Go-Go**		$50	Tamla 267
12/17/66+	41	27		©	7 **Away We A Go-Go**......		$30	Tamla 271
9/30/67	28	23		©	8 **Make It Happen**......		$30	Tamla 276
					also see #17 below			
2/24/68	7	44		©	9 **Greatest Hits, Vol. 2**	[G]	$25	Tamla 280
10/5/68+	42	23		©	10 **Special Occasion**		$25	Tamla 290
2/15/69	71	14		©	11 **Live!**	[L]	$25	Tamla 289
8/9/69	25	19		©	12 **Time Out For Smokey Robinson & The Miracles**......		$25	Tamla 295

MIRACLES, The — Cont'd

DEBUT	PEAK	WKS	CD	# Album Title	Sym	$	Label & Number
12/6/69+	78	12		13 Four In Blue		$25	Tamla 297
5/30/70	97	11	©	14 What Love Has...Joined Together		$20	Tamla 301
10/24/70	56	11		15 A Pocket Full Of Miracles		$20	Tamla 306
12/19/70	13ˣ	2	©	16 The Season For Miracles	[X]	$20	Tamla 307
12/26/70+	143	12	©	17 The Tears Of A Clown	[R]	$15	Tamla 276
				reissue (new title) of album #8 above			
9/25/71	92	10		18 One Dozen Roses		$15	Tamla 312
8/19/72	46	22		19 Flying High Together		$15	Tamla 318
1/6/73	75	16		20 1957-1972	[L]	$20	Tamla 320 [2]
				recorded on 7/14/72 at the Carter Barron Ampitheatre in Washington DC			

THE MIRACLES:

DEBUT	PEAK	WKS	CD	# Album Title	Sym	$	Label & Number
6/2/73	174	4		21 Renaissance		$15	Tamla 325
2/16/74	97	17	©	22 Smokey Robinson & The Miracles' Anthology	[G]	$25	Motown 793 [3]
9/14/74	41	21		23 Do It Baby		$15	Tamla 334
2/8/75	96	9		24 Don't Cha Love It		$15	Tamla 336
10/25/75+	33	30		25 City Of Angels		$15	Tamla 339
10/16/76	178	3		26 The Power Of Music		$15	Tamla 344
3/19/77	117	5		27 Love Crazy		$12	Columbia 34460

Abraham, Martin And John (12,20,22) *33*
After You Put Back The Pieces (I'll Still Have A Broken Heart) (8,17)
Ain't Nobody Straight In L.A. (25)
All I Want Is You (5)
All That's Good (6)
And I Love Her (14)
Away In A Manger (medley) (16)
Baby, Baby (7)
Baby, Baby Don't Cry (12,22) *8*
Backfire (15)
Bad Girl (5,20,22) *93*
Beauty Is Only Skin Deep (7)
Better Way To Live (27)
Bird Must Fly Away (27)
Bridge Over Troubled Water (15)
Bring A Torch, Jeannette, Isabella (medley) (16)
Brokenhearted Girl-Brokenhearted Boy (24)
California Soul (13)
Calling Out Your Name (23)
Can I Pretend (26)
Can You Love A Poor Boy (7)
Can't Get Ready For Losing You (23)
Cecilia (13)
Child Is Waiting (16)
Choosey Beggar (6,9,22)
Christmas Everyday (4)
Christmas Song (4,16)
City Of Angels (25)
Come On Do The Jerk (9,22) *50*
(Come 'Round Here) I'm The One You Need (7,9,22) *17*
Composer, The (12)
Coventry Carol (medley) (16)
Crazy About The La La La (18) *56*
Dance What You Wanna (3)
Dancin' Holiday (3)
Dancing's Alright (8,17)
Darling Dear (15,22) *100*

Day That Love Began (16)
Deck The Halls (medley) (16)
Do It Baby (23) *13*
Do You Love Me (3)
Doggone Right (12,22) *32*
Don't Cha Love It (24) *78*
Don't Let It End ('Til You Let It Begin) (21) *56*
Don't Say You Love Me (13)
Don't Take It So Hard (15)
Don't Think It's Me (8,17)
Dreams, Dreams (13)
Everybody Needs Love (10)
Faces (18)
Flower Girl (15)
Flying High Together (19)
Foolish Thing To Say (23)
For Once In My Life (12)
Fork In The Road (6)
Free Press (25)
From Head To Toe (6)
Gemini (24)
Get Ready (15)
Give Her Up (10)
Give Me Just Another Day (23)
Go Tell It On The Mountain (16)
God Rest Ye Merry Gentlemen (16)
Going To A Go-Go (6,9,11,20,22) *11*
Gonna Tell The World (Wedding Song) (24)
Gossip (26)
Got A Job (5,22)
Got Me Goin' (Again) (24)
Got To Be There (19,20)
Groovey Thing (3)
Happy Landing (1,2)
Heartbreak Road (11)
Here I Go Again (12,20,22) *37*
Hey Jude (13)
Hunter Gets Captured By The Game (18)
Hurt Is Over (12)
I Believe In Christmas Eve (16)
I Can Take A Hint (1)
I Can Tell When Christmas Is Near (16)
I Can Touch The Sky (27)
I Can't Stand To See You Cry (19,22) *45*

I Cry (5)
I Didn't Realize The Show Was Over (21)
I Don't Blame You At All (18,20,22) *18*
I Don't Need No Reason (21)
I Gotta Dance To Keep From Crying (3,5,22) *35*
I Heard It Through The Grapevine (14)
I Just Don't Know What To Do With Myself (7)
I Like It Like That (5,22) *27*
I Love You Dear (18)
I Love You Secretly (21)
I Love Your Baby (5)
I Need A Change (5)
(I Need Some) Money (5)
I Second That Emotion (9,11,22) *4*
I Wanna Be With You (21)
I'll Be Home For Christmas (4)
I'll Take You Any Way That You Come (12)
I'll Try Something New (5,22) *39*
I'm On The Outside (Looking In) (8,17)
I've Been Good To You (1,2,5,22)
If This World Were Mine (14)
If You Can Want (10,11,22) *11*
If You're Ever In The Neighborhood (21)
In Case You Need Love (6)
It Will Be Alright (19)
It's A Good Feeling (8,17)
It's Christmas Time (16)
Jingle Bells (16)
Just Losing You (10)
Keep On Keepin' On (Doin' What You Do) (24)
Land Of 1000 Dances (8)
Legend In Its Own Time (13)
Let It Snow (4)
Let Me Have Some (6)
Let The Children Play (26)
Little Piece Of Heaven (24)
Love Crazy (27)
Love I Saw In You Was Just A Mirage (8,9,17,22) *20*
Love Machine (Part 1) (25) *1*

Love She Can Count On (1,2,5,22) *31*
Love Story, Theme From (19)
Love To Make Love (26)
Mama Done Told Me (5)
Mickey's Monkey (3,5,11,20,22) *8*
Mighty Good Lovin' (2)
Monkey Time (3)
More Love (8,9,17,20,22) *23*
More, More, More Of Your Love (7)
Much Better Off (10)
My Baby Changes Like The Weather (6)
My Cherie Amour (14)
My Girl (12)
My Girl Has Gone (6,9,22) *14*
My Love For You (8,17)
My Love Is Your Love (Forever) (8,17)
My Name Is Michael (25)
My World Is Empty Without You (13)
Night Life (25)
No Wonder Love's A Wonder (18)
Noel (4)
Nowhere To Go (21)
O Holy Night (4)
Oh Baby Baby I Love You (18)
Oh Be My Love (7)
Oh Girl (19)
Once I Got To Know You (Couldn't Help But Love You) (12)
Once In A Lifetime (medley) (11)
Ooo Baby Baby (6,9,11,20,22) *16*
Peace On Earth (Goodwill Toward Men) (16)
Poinciana (11)
Point It Out (15,22) *37*
Poor Charlotte (25)
Power Of Music (26)
Reel Of Time (15)
Santa Claus Is Coming To Town (4)
Satisfaction (18,20,22) *49*
Save Me (7,9,22)
Shop Around (5,20,22) *2*

Silver Bells (4)
Since You Won My Heart (6)
Smog (25)
Something (medley) (15)
Something You Got (medley) (15)
Soulful Shack (8,17)
Special Occasion (10,22) *26*
Spy For Brotherhood (27)
Street Of Love (26)
Such Is Love, Such Is Life (1)
Sweet Sweet Lovin' (24)
Swept For You Baby (7)
Tears Of A Clown (8,17,18,20,22) *1*
That Girl (18)
That's What Love Is Made Of (5,22) *35*
This Guy's In Love With You (14)
Tomorrow Is Another Day (13)
Too Young (27)
Tracks Of My Tears (6,9,11,20,22) *16*
Twist, The (3)
Twist And Shout (3)
Up Again (23)
Up, Up And Away (11)
Valley Of The Dolls, Theme From (11)
Wah-Watusi (3)
Waldo Roderick DeHammersmith (25)
Walk By (7,11)
Way Over There (2,5,22) *94*
We Can Make It We Can (13)
We Feel The Same (23)
We Had A Love So Strong (19)
We've Come Too Far To End It Now (19,20,22) *46*
What Is A Heart Good For (21,23)
What Love Has Joined Together (14)
What's So Good About Good-By (2,5,22) *35*
Whatever Makes You Happy (1)
When Nobody Cares (13)
When Sundown Comes (18)
Where Are You Going To My Love (23)

White Christmas (4)
Who's Gonna Take The Blame (15,22) *46*
Who's Lovin' You (5,22)
Whole Lot Of Shakin' In My Heart (Since I Met You) (7,9) *46*
Wichita Lineman (12)
Wigs And Lashes (21)
Winter Wonderland (4)
Wish I Knew (13)
Wishful Thinking (15)
With Your Love Came (19)
Women (Make The World Go 'Round) (27)
Won't You Take Me Back (1)
Would I Love You (5)
Yester Love (10,11,22) *31*
Yesterday (10,11)
You Ain't Livin' Till You're Lovin' (19)
You And The Night And The Music (medley) (11)
You Are Love (23,24)
(You Can) Depend On Me (5,22)
You Don't Have To Say You Love Me (7)
You Must Be Love (8,17)
You Need A Miracle (26)
You Neglect Me (12)
You Only Build Me Up To Tear Me Down (13)
You Send Me (With Your Good Lovin') (13)
You've Got The Love I Need (15)
You've Lost That Lovin' Feelin' (13)
You've Made Me So Very Happy (14)
You've Really Got A Hold On Me (1,2,5,22) *8*
Your Love (1)
Your Mother's Only Daughter (10)

MISFITS '97

Hard-rock group from Lodi, New Jersey: Michale Graves (vocals), Doyle Wolfgang Von Frankenstein (guitar), Jerry Only (bass) and Dr. Chud (drums).

DEBUT	PEAK	WKS	CD	# Album Title	$	Label & Number
5/31/97	117	2	©	1 American Psycho	$10	Geffen 25126
10/23/99	138	1	©	2 Famous Monsters	$10	Roadrunner 8658

Abominable Dr. Phibes (1)
American Psycho (1)
Blacklight (1)
Crawling Eye (2)
Crimson Ghost (1)
Day Of The Dead (1)

Descending Angel (2)
Die Monster Die (2)
Dig Up Her Bones (1)
Don't Open 'Til Doomsday (1)
Dust To Dust (2)
Fiend Club (1)

Forbidden Zone (2)
From Hell They Came (1)
Hate The Living, Love The Dead (1)
Haunting, The (1)
Helena (1)

Hunger, The (1)
Hunting Humans (2)
Kong At The Gates (2)
Kong Unleashed (2)
Living Hell (2)
Lost In Space (2)

Mars Attacks (1)
Pumpkin Head (2)
Resurrection (1)
Saturday Night (2)
Scarecrow Man (2)
Scream! (2)

Shining (1)
Speak Of The Devil (1)
Them (2)
This Island Earth (1)
Walk Among Us (1)
Witch Hunt (2)

MISSETT, Judi Sheppard '81

Born in 1946 in Iowa. Created the Jazzercise fitness routine.

DEBUT	PEAK	WKS	CD	Album Title	$	Label & Number
12/5/81	117	20	●	Jazzercise	$10	MCA 5272
				music by studio musicians		

Animal House
Baretta's Theme
Boogie Woogie Bugle Boy

Car Wash
Don't Pull Your Love
Girl From Ipanema

Rockford Files
Squeeze Me
Sweet Nothin's

T'Ain't Nobody's Biz-Ness If I Do
Teach Me Tonight

Which Way Is Up

MISSING PERSONS '83

Pop-rock group formed in Los Angeles: Dale Bozzio (vocals), her then-husband Terry Bozzio (drums), Warren Cuccurullo (guitar), Patrick O'Hearn (bass, synthesizer) and Chuck Wild (keyboards). All but Wild were with **Frank Zappa**'s band. Disbanded in 1986. Terry Bozzio worked with **Jeff Beck** in 1989. Cuccurullo joined **Duran Duran** in 1990.

5/15/82	46	47			1 Missing Persons .... [M]			$10	Capitol 15001
10/30/82+	17	40	●	©	2 Spring Session M			$10	Capitol 12228
					title is an anagram of group's name				
3/31/84	43	16		©	3 Rhyme & Reason			$10	Capitol 12315
8/9/86	86	11		©	4 Color In Your Life			$10	Capitol 12465

All Fall Down (3)
Bad Streets (2)
Boy I Say To You (4)
Clandestine People (3)
Closer That You Get (3)
Color In Your Life (4)

Come Back For More (4)
Destination Unknown (1,2) 42
Face To Face (4)
Flash Of Love (4)
Give (3) 67
Go Against The Flow (4)

Here And Now (2)
I Can't Think About Dancin' (4)
I Like Boys (1)
If Only For The Moment (3)
It Ain't None Of Your Business (2)

Mental Hopscotch (1)
No Secrets (4)
No Way Out (2)
Noticeable One (2)
Now Is The Time (For Love) (3)
Racing Against Time (3)

Right Now (3)
Rock And Roll Suspension (2)
Surrender Your Heart (3)
Tears (2)
U.S. Drag (2)
Waiting For A Million Years (3)

Walking In L.A. (2) 70
We Don't Know Love At All (4)
Windows (2) 63
Words (1,2) 42

MISSION U.K., The '90

Rock group formed in Leeds, England: Wayne Hussey (vocals, guitar), Simon Hinkler (guitar), Craig Adams (bass) and Mick Brown (drums). Hussey and Adams were members of **The Sisters Of Mercy**.

3/7/87	108	18		©	1 Gods Own Medicine			$10	Mercury 830603
4/30/88	126	10		©	2 Children			$10	Mercury 834263
3/17/90	101	16		©	3 Carved In Sand			$10	Mercury 842251

Amelia (3)
And The Dance Goes On (1)
Belief (3)
Beyond The Pale (2)
Black Mountain Mist (2)
Breathe (2)

Bridges Burning (1)
Butterfly On A Wheel (3)
Child's Play (2)
Dance On Glass (1)
Deliverance (3)
Garden Of Delight (1)

Grapes Of Wrath (3)
Heat (2)
Heaven On Earth (2)
Hungry As The Hunter (3)
Hymn (For America) (2)
Into The Blue (3)

Kingdom Come (3)
Let Sleeping Dogs Die (1)
Love Me To Death (1)
Lovely (3)
Paradise (Will Shine Like The Moon) (3)

Sacrilege (1)
Sea Of Love (3)
Severina (1)
Shamera Kye (2)
Stay With Me (1)
Tower Of Strength (2)

Wasteland (1)
Wing And A Prayer (2)

MISSOURI '79

Rock group from St. Louis: Ron West (vocals, guitar), Web Waterman (guitar), Randall Platt (keyboards), Alan Cohen (bass) and Dan Billings (drums).

| 6/23/79 | 174 | 4 | | | Welcome Two Missouri .... | | | $12 | Polydor 6206 |

Can't Stop
Got Me Goin'

Gotta Be Me
Hangin' On

I Really Love You
Love On The Run

Movin' On
So Far Away

Sunshine Girl
Walk Like A Man

MISTA '96

R&B vocal group: Darryl Allen, Bobby Wilson, Brandon Brown and Byron Reeder.

| 8/17/96 | 183 | 3 | | © | Mista .... | | | $10 | EastWest 61912 |

Blackberry Molasses 53
Crossroads

Everything Must Change
Fresh Groove

I Think That I Should Be
I'll Sweat You

If My Baby
Lady 90

Tears, Scars & Lies
Things You Do

What About Us
? ♥ Is

MR. BIG '92

Rock group from San Francisco: **Eric Martin** (vocals), Paul Gilbert (guitar), Billy Sheehan (bass) and Pat Torpey (drums; **Impellitteri**).

7/22/89	46	18		©	1 Mr. Big			$10	Atlantic 81990
4/20/91+	15	38	▲	©	2 Lean Into It		C:#25/1	$10	Atlantic 82209
10/9/93	82	6		©	3 Bump Ahead			$10	Atlantic 82495

Addicted To That Rush (1)
Ain't Seen Love Like That (3) 83
Alive And Kickin' (2)
Anything For You (1)
Big Love (1)
Blame It On My Youth (1)

CDFF-Lucky This Time (2)
Colorado Bulldog (3)
Daddy, Brother, Lover, Little Boy (The Electric Drill Song) (2)
Green-Tinted Sixties Mind (2)
Had Enough (1)

How Can You Do What You Do (1)
Just Take My Heart (2) 16
Little Too Loose (2)
Merciless (1)
Mr. Big (3)
Mr. Gone (3)

My Kinda Woman (2)
Never Say Never (2)
Nothing But Love (3)
Price You Gotta Pay (3)
Promise Her The Moon (3)
Road To Ruin (3)
Rock & Roll Over (1)

Take A Walk (1)
Temperamental (3)
To Be With You (2) 1
Voodoo Kiss (2)
What's It Gonna Be (3)
Whole World's Gonna Know (3)
Wild World (3) 27

Wind Me Up (1)

MR. BUNGLE '95

Rock group from Eureka, California: Mike Patton (vocals; **Faith No More**), Trey Spruance (guitar), Trevor Dunn (bass) and Danny Heifetz (drums).

| 10/28/95 | 113 | 1 | | © | 1 Disco Volante .... | | | $10 | Warner 45963 |
| 7/31/99 | 144 | 1 | | © | 2 California .... | | | $10 | Warner 47447 |

After School Special (1)
Air-Conditioned Nightmare (2)
Ars Moriendi (1)
Backstrokin' (1)
Bends, The (1)
Carry Stress In The Jaw (1)

Chemical Marriage (1)
Desert Search For Techno Allah (1)
Everyone I Went To High School With Is Dead (1)

Golem II: The Bionic Vapour Boy (2)
Goodbye Sober Day (2)
Holy Filament (2)
Ma Meeshka Mow Skwoz (1)
Merry Go Bye Bye (1)

None Of Them Knew They Were Robots (2)
Phlegmatics (1)
Pink Cigarette (2)
Platypus (1)
Retrovertigo (2)

Sweet Charity (2)
Vanity Fair (2)
Violenza Domestica (1)

MR. C THE SLIDE MAN '01

Born William Perry in New York City. R&B singer/rapper.

| 1/13/01 | 64 | 19 | | © | Cha-Cha Slide .... | | | $10 | M.O.B. 159807 |

Bus Stop/Electric Slide
Casper Cha-Cha Slide

Cha-Cha Slide 83
DJ Eric-B Slide

R-U-Here
Step To This

Unworthy

MR. MARCELLO (FROM THE GHETTO) '00

Born in New Orleans. Male rapper.

| 8/12/00 | 172 | 1 | | © | Brick Livin .... | | | $10 | Priority 26159 |

Brick Livin
GTO
Ha Brah

Hold Up
Hot Sh--
How U Like It

Let's Do It
Live By It
Live It Up

Me & My Girl
187
Soldiers For Life

Somet'in
Sound Da Alarm
Southern Funk

U Never Know
Wildin
Y'all N's

MR. MIKE '96

Born Michael Walls in Corpus Christi, Texas. Male rapper. Member of **South Circle**.

| 8/17/96 | 29 | 8 | | © | 1 Wicked Wayz .... | | | $10 | Suave House 1519 |
| 9/25/99 | 172 | 2 | | © | 2 Rhapsody .... | | | $10 | Priority 50031 |

Can You Feel Me (1)
Come On Everybody (2)
Da Boogie Man (1)
Don't Nobody Really Care (2)
Dope Fiction (1)

Everytime I Close My Eyes (2)
G's Perspective (1)
Game Affiliation (2)
Ghetto Strain (2)
How Tha South Was Won (2)

In The Midst Of Smoke (1)
It's A Shame (2)
Killing Fields (2)
Know One Knows (2)
Life On Tha Line (1)

Partners In Crime (2)
Play The Cards I Was Given (2)
Rhapsody (2)
Southwest (1)
Stop Lying (1)

Texas 2000 (2)
Total Shock (1)
Untouchable (1)
What Da Deal Iz (2)
Where Ya Love At (1)

Why Fall In Love With The Struggle (2)
Wicked Wayz (1)

MR. MISTER '86

Pop-rock group formed in Los Angeles: Richard Page (vocals, bass), Steve Farris (guitar), Steve George (keyboards) and Pat Mastelotto (drums).

4/14/84	170	7		©	1 I Wear The Face			$10	RCA Victor 4864
8/31/85+	**❶**[1]	58	▲	©	2 Welcome To The Real World			$10	RCA Victor 8045
9/26/87	55	17		©	3 Go On...			$10	RCA Victor 6276

Black/White (2)
Border, The (3)
Broken Wings (2) *1*
Code Of Love (1)
Control (3)
Don't Slow Down (2)

Dust (3)
Healing Waters (3)
Hunters Of The Night (1) *57*
I Get Lost Sometimes (1)
I Wear The Face (1)
I'll Let You Drive (1)

Into My Own Hands (2)
Is It Love (2) *8*
Kyrie (2) *1*
Life Goes On (1)
Man Of A Thousand Dances (3)
Partners In Crime (1)

Power Over Me (3)
Run To Her (2)
Runaway (1)
Something Real (Inside Me/Inside You) (3) *29*
Stand And Deliver (3)

Talk The Talk (1)
Tangent Tears (2)
32 (1)
Tube, The (3)
Uniform Of Youth (2)
Watching The World (2)

Welcome To The Real World (2)

MR. SERV-ON '99

Born Edward Smith in Washington DC. Male rapper.

| 8/23/97 | 23 | 12 | | © | 1 Life Insurance | | | $10 | No Limit 50717 |
| 3/6/99 | 14 | 5 | | © | 2 Da Next Level | | | $10 | No Limit 50045 |

Affiliated (1)
Best Friend II (2)
Boot 'Em Up (2)
Cemetery Made (1)
Die Rich (1)
F.U. Serv (2)
5 Hollow Points (1)

Freaky Dreams (2)
From N.Y. To N.O. (2)
Head & Shoulders (1)
Heaven Is So Close (1)
Hit The Block (2)
Hustlin (1)
I Hate The Way I Live (2)

I Luv It (2)
I'll Be There (2)
It's Real (1)
Last Song (2)
Last Wordz (1)
Let's Get It Started (1)
Make 'Em Bleed (2)

Murder (2)
My Best Friend (1)
My Homies (2)
My Story (2)
1, 2, 3 (1)
P Dreams (1)
Snatch Them Hoez Up (2)

Straight Outta N.O. (2)
Strap Up (2)
Tank Nigga (2)
This Is For My Niggaz (2)
Throw Ya City Up (1)
Time To Check My Fetty (1)

Tryin' To Make It Out Da Ghetto (1)
We Ain't The Same (1)
Who Raised Me (1)
You Know I Would (1)

MR. SHORT KHOP '01

Born in Los Angeles. Male rapper.

| 4/7/01 | 154 | 6 | | © | Da Khop Shop | | | $10 | Heavyweight 2150 |

Braveheart
Da Ready Rock
Dey Trippin'

Dollaz, Drank & Dank
Es Mi Casa
Flashbacks

Kingpin And Da Kockhound (Pass The Pussy)
M.V.P.'s

My Loved One
One Way To Win
Short Khop & The Brain

2 Of 'Em and The Door Locked
Ya Baby Daddy

MISTRESS '79

Rock group from Georgia: Charlie Williams (vocals), Kenny Hopkins and Danny Chauncey (guitars), David Brown (bass) and Chris Paulsen (drums).

| 9/15/79 | 100 | 14 | | | Mistress | | | $12 | RSO 3059 |

China Lake
Cinnamon Girl

Dixie Flyer
High On The Ride

Letter To California
Mistrusted Love *49*

Situations
Tellin' Me Lies

Whose Side Are You On?
You Got The Love

MITCHELL, Chad, Trio '63

Born in 1939 in Spokane, Washington. Folk singer. His trio included Mike Koluk and Joe Frazier. Mitchell left in 1964. **John Denver** joined and group was renamed **The Mitchell Trio**.

3/24/62	39	21		©	1 Mighty Day On Campus		[L]	$25	Kapp 3262
					recorded at Brooklyn College				
9/1/62	81	9		©	2 The Chad Mitchell Trio At The Bitter End		[L]	$25	Kapp 3281
					recorded on 3/19/62 in New York City				
4/13/63	87	30		©	3 Blowin' In The Wind			$25	Kapp 3313
9/28/63	63	28			4 The Best Of Chad Mitchell Trio		[G]	$25	Kapp 3334
11/9/63	39	22			5 Singin' Our Mind			$20	Mercury 60838
3/7/64	29	30			6 Reflecting			$20	Mercury 60891

THE MITCHELL TRIO:

| 11/14/64+ | 128 | 11 | | | 7 The Slightly Irreverent Mitchell Trio | | | $20 | Mercury 60944 |
| 5/1/65 | 130 | 3 | | | 8 Typical American Boys | | | $20 | Mercury 60992 |

Adios Mi Corazon (3)
African Song (On That Great Civilized Morning) (7)
Ain't No More Cane On This Brazos (7)
Alabama Song (7)
Alberta (2)
Alice Revisited (3)
Alice: Sequel (3)
Alma Mater (5)
Ballad Of The Greenland Whalers (5)
Banks Of Sicily (6)
Barry's Boys (6)
Blowin' In The Wind (3)
Blues Around My Head (2)
Bonny Streets Of Fyve-io (5)
Cherry Tree Carol (8)

Come Along Home (Tom's Song) (2)
Don't Fence Me In (medley) (3,4)
Dona Dona Dona (1)
Draft Dodger Rag (7)
Dubarry Done About It (5)
Dying Business (7)
First Time Ever (6)
Four Strong Winds (5)
Golden Vanity (2)
Gorpus Morpus (8)
Great Historical Bum (The Bragging Song) (2,4)
Green Grow The Lilacs (3,4)
Greenland Whalers ..see:
Ballad Of
Hang On The Bell, Nellie (1,4)

Hello Susan Brown (2,4)
Hip Song (It Does Not Pay To Be Hip) (6)
I Can't Help But Wonder (7)
I Feel So Good About It (5)
If I Gave You (7)
In The Summer Of His Years (medley) (4)
Irish Song (5)
James James Morrison Morrison (2,4)
Jesse James (8)
John Birch Society (2,4) *44*
Johnnie (1)
Last Night I Had The Strangest Dream (2)
Last Thing On My Mind (8)

Leave Me If You Want To (3)
Lizzie Borden (1,4) *44*
Maladiozhenaya (The Young Ones) (5)
Mandy Lane (7)
Marvelous Toy (5) *43*
Me Voy Pa Bete (3)
Mighty Day (1)
Moscow Nights (2)
My Guitar (3)
My Name Is Morgan (8)
Natural Girl For Me (8)
Nobody Knows You (5)
On My Journey (1)
One Day When I Was Lost (Easter Morn) (3)
One Man's Hands (8)
Pride Of Petrovar (7)

Puttin' On The Style (1)
Queen Elinor's Confession (6)
Rally Round The Flag (medley) (6)
Rhymes For The Irreverent Medley (7)
Rum By Gum (1)
Run Run Run (3)
Sinking Of Reuben James (6)
Stewball (6)
Stewball And Griselda (7)
Story Of Alice - Part 1 (3)
Super Skier (1,4)
Tail Toddle (1)
Tarriers Song (6)
Tell Old Bill (6)
Twelve Days (5)
Unfortunate Man (2,4)

Virgin Mary (6)
Waves On The Sea (8)
What Did You Learn In School Today (6)
When I Was A Young Man (7)
Which Hat Shall I Wear (8)
Whistling Gypsy (1)
Whup Jamboree (1)
Willie Seton (5)
With God On Our Side (2,4)
You Can Tell The World (8)
You Were On My Mind (8)
Yowzah (1)

MITCHELL, Joni ★113★ '74

Born Roberta Joan Anderson on 11/7/43 in Fort McLeod, Alberta, Canada; raised in Saskatoon, Saskatchewan. Singer/songwriter/guitarist/pianist. Married to her producer/bassist, Larry Klein, from 1982-94. Recipient of *Billboard's* Century Award in 1995. Inducted into the Rock and Roll Hall of Fame in 1997.

1)Court And Spark 2)Miles Of Aisles 3)The Hissing Of Summer Lawns 4)For The Roses 5)Hejira

5/18/68	189	9		©	1 Joni Mitchell			$20	Reprise 6293
6/14/69	31	36	●	©	2 Clouds			$20	Reprise 6341
4/11/70	27	33	▲	©	3 Ladies Of The Canyon			$15	Reprise 6376
7/3/71	15	28	▲	©	4 Blue			$15	Reprise 2038
12/2/72+	11	28	●	©	5 For The Roses			$12	Asylum 5057

DEBUT	PEAK	WKS	RIAA	CD	ARTIST — Album Title	Catalog	Sym	$	Label & Number
					MITCHELL, Joni — Cont'd				
2/9/74	2⁴	64	▲²	© 6	Court And Spark			$12	Asylum 1001
12/14/74+	2¹	22	●	© 7	Miles Of Aisles		[L]	$12	Asylum 202
12/6/75+	4	17	●	© 8	The Hissing Of Summer Lawns			$12	Asylum 1051
12/11/76+	13	18	●	© 9	Hejira			$12	Asylum 1087
1/7/78	25	13	●	© 10	Don Juan's Reckless Daughter			$15	Asylum 701 [2]
7/7/79	17	18		© 11	Mingus			$12	Asylum 505
10/4/80	38	16		© 12	Shadows And Light		[L]	$15	Asylum 704 [2]
11/20/82	25	21		© 13	Wild Things Run Fast			$10	Geffen 2019
11/23/85	63	19		© 14	Dog Eat Dog			$10	Geffen 24074
4/9/88	45	16		© 15	Chalk Mark In A Rain Storm			$10	Geffen 24172
3/23/91	41	14		© 16	Night Ride Home			$10	Geffen 24302
11/12/94	47	9		© 17	Turbulent Indigo			$10	Reprise 45786
11/16/96	161	2		© 18	Hits		[G]	$10	Reprise 46326
10/17/98	75	4		© 19	Taming The Tiger			$10	Reprise 46451
4/8/00	66	11		© 20	Both Sides Now			$10	Reprise 47620

All I Want (4,7) — Amelia (9,12) — Answer Me, My Love (20) — Arrangement, The (3) — At Last (20) — Banquet (5) — Barangrill (5) — Be Cool (13) — Beat Of Black Wings (15) — **Big Yellow Taxi** (3,18) **67** — **Big Yellow Taxi** [live] (7) **24** — Bird That Whistles (15) — Black Crow (9,12) — Blonde In The Bleachers (5) — Blue (4,7) — Blue Boy (3) — Blue Motel Room (9) — Boho Dance (8) — Borderline (17) — Both Sides Now (2,7,18,20) — Cactus Tree (1,7) — California (4,18) — Car On A Hill (6) — **Carey** (4,7,18) **93** — Case Of You (4,7,20) — Centerpiece (medley) (8) — Chair In The Sky (11) — Chelsea Morning (2,18) — Cherokee Louise (16) — Chinese Café (medley) (13,18) — Circle Game (3,7,18) — Coin In The Pocket (Rap) (11) — Cold Blue Steel And Sweet Fire (5,7)

Come In From The Cold (16,18) — Comes Love (20) — Conversation (3) — Cool Water (15) — Cotton Avenue (10) — Court And Spark (6) — Coyote (9,12) — Crazy Cries Of Love (19) — Dancin' Clown (15) — Dawntreader, The (1) — Dog Eat Dog (14) — Don Juan's Reckless Daughter (10) — Don't Go To Strangers (20) — Don't Interrupt The Sorrow (8) — Don't Worry 'Bout Me (20) — Down To You (6) — Dreamland (10,12) — Dry Cleaner From Des Moines (11,12) — Edith And The Kingpin (8,12) — Electricity (3) — Ethiopia (14) — Face Lift (19) — Fiction (14) — Fiddle And The Drum (2) — For Free (3) — For The Roses (5) — **Free Man In Paris** (6,12,18) **22** — Funeral (Rap) (11) — Furry Sings The Blues (9,12) — Gallery, The (2) — God Must Be A Boogie Man (11,12)

Goodbye Pork Pie Hat (11,12) — **Good Friends** (14) **85** — Happy Birthday 1975 (Rap) (11) — Harlem In Havana (19) — Harry's House (medley) (8) — Hejira (9,12) — **Help Me** (6,18) **7** — Hissing Of Summer Lawns (8) — How Do You Stop (17) — I Don't Know Where I Stand (2) — I Had A King (1) — I Think I Understand (2) — I Wish I Were In Love Again (20) — I's A Muggin' (Rap) (11) — Impossible Dreamer (14) — **In France They Kiss On Main Street** (8,12) **66** — Introduction (12) — Jericho (7,10) — Judgement Of The Moon And Stars (Ludwig's Tune) (5) — Jungle Line (8) — Just Like This Train (6) — Ladies' Man (13) — Ladies Of The Canyon (3) — Lakota (15) — Last Chance Lost (17) — Last Time I Saw Richard (4,7) — Lead Balloon (19) — Lesson In Survival (5) — Let The Wind Carry Me (5) — Little Green (4) — Love (1)

Love Or Money (7) — Love Puts On A New Face (19) — Lucky Girl (14) — Lucky (Rap) (11) — Magdalene Laundries (17) — Man From Mars (19) — Man To Man (13) — Marcie (1) — Michael From Mountains (1) — Moon At The Window (13) — Morning Morgantown (3) — My Best To You (19) — My Old Man (4) — My Secret Place (15) — Nathan La Franeer (1) — Night In The City (1) — Night Ride Home (16) — No Apologies (19) — Not To Blame (17) — Nothing Can Be Done (16) — Number One (15) — Off Night Backstreet (10) — Only Joy In Town (16) — Otis And Marlena (10) — Paprika Plains (10) — Passion Play (When All The Slaves Are Free) (16) — People's Parties (6,7) — Pirate Of Penance (1) — Priest, The (3) — Rainy Night House (3,7) — **Raised On Robbery** (6,18) **65** — Ray's Dad's Cadillac (16) — Real Good For Free (7)

Refuge Of The Roads (9) — Reoccurring Dream (15) — River (4,18) — Roses Blue (2) — Same Situation (6) — See You Sometime (5) — Sex Kills (17) — Shades Of Scarlet Conquering (8) — Shadows And Light (8,12) — Shiny Toys (14) — Silky Veils Of Ardor (10) — Sire Of Sorrow (Job's Sad Song) (17) — Sisotowbell Lane (1) — Slouching Towards Bethlehem (16) — Smokin' (Empty, Try Another) (14) — Snakes And Ladders (15) — Solid Love (13) — Sometimes I'm Happy (20) — Song For Sharon (9) — Song To A Seagull (1) — Songs To Aging Children Come (2) — Stay In Touch (19) — Stormy Weather (20) — Strange Boy (9) — Sunny Sunday (17) — Sweet Bird (8) — Sweet Sucker Dance (11) — Talk To Me (10) — Taming The Tiger (19)

Tax Free (14) — Tea Leaf Prophecy (Lay Down Your Arms) (15) — Tenth World (10) — That Song About The Midway (2) — This Flight Tonight (4) — Three Great Stimulants (14) — Tiger Bones (19) — Tin Angel (2) — Trouble Child (6) — Turbulent Indigo (17) — Twisted (6) — Two Grey Rooms (16) — Unchained Melody (medley) (13,18) — Underneath The Streetlight (13) — Urge For Going (18) — Why Do Fools Fall In Love (12) — Wild Things Run Fast (13) — Willie (3) — Windfall (Everything For Nothing) (16) — Wolf That Lives In Lindsey (11) — Woman Of Heart And Mind (5,7) — Woodstock (3,7,12,18) — You Dream Flat Tires (13) — **You Turn Me On, I'm A Radio** (5,7,18) **25** — You're My Thrill (20) — **(You're So Square) Baby, I Don't Care** (13) **47** — You've Changed (20) — Yvette In English (17)

MITCHELL, Kim '85
Born on 7/10/52 in Sarnia, Ontario, Canada. Male rock singer/guitarist.

5/18/85	106	15		©	Akimbo Alogo			$10	Bronze 90257

All We Are — Called Off — Caroline — Diary For Rock 'N Roll Men — Feel It Burn — **Go For Soda** **86** — Lager & Ale — Love Ties — Rumour Has It — That's A Man

---

MITCHELL, Rubin '67
Jazz pianist.

4/15/67	164	2			Presenting Rubin Mitchell		[I]	$20	Capitol 2658

Cherish — Flamingo — Jitterbug Waltz — Mas Que Nada — My Liza Jane — My Love Forgive Me — Slaughter On 10th Avenue — Somewhere — Spanish Eyes — Summer Wind — That's All — What Now, My Love

---

MITCHELL, Willie '68
Born on 1/3/28 in Ashland, Mississippi; raised in Memphis. R&B keyboardist/arranger/producer. Led house band and later became president of Hi Records.

3/16/68	172	5		1	Willie Mitchell Live		[I-L]	$25	Hi 32042
					recorded at the Manhattan Club in Memphis				
5/11/68	151	7		2	Soul Serenade		[I]	$25	Hi 32039
11/7/70	188	2		3	Robbin's Nest		[I]	$25	Hi 32058

Boot-Leg (1) — Bum Daddy (1) — Chilly Chilly (3) — Cleo's Mood (2) — Greasy Spoon (3) — Have You Ever Had The Blues (2) — Honky Tonk (1) — I'll Be In Trouble (1) — Last Date (1) — Late Date (1) — Mercy Mercy Mercy (1) — Mustang Sally (1) — My Girl (1) — On The Other Side (3) — Ooh Baby, You Turn Me On (2) — Papa's Got A Brand New Bag (2) — Pearl Time (2) — Pin Head (1) — Raindrops Keep Fallin' On My Head (2) — Respect (2) — Robbin's Nest (3) — Sing A Simple Song (3) — Sleepy Lagoon (3) — **Slippin' & Slidin'** (2) **96** — Smokie (1) — Soul Finger (2) — **Soul Serenade** (2) **23** — Sunny (2) — Tails Out (3) — Tequila (1) — This Guys In Love With You (3) — Toddlin' (2) — Turn Back The Hands Of Time (3) — 20-75 (1) — Wade In The Water (1) — Willie's Mood (2)

MJG — see EIGHTBALL

MOBB DEEP '99
Rap duo from New York City: Havoc and Prodigy. Both are members of **QB Finest**. Also see **Prodigy Of Mobb Deep**.

5/13/95	18	18	●	© 1	The Infamous...			$10	Loud 66480
12/7/96	6	16	●	© 2	Hell On Earth			$10	Loud 66992
9/4/99	3	17	▲	© 3	Murda Muzik			$10	Loud 63715

Adrenaline (3) — Allustrious (3) — Animal Instinct (2) — Apostle's Warning (2) — Bloodsport (2) — Can't Fuck Wit (3) — Can't Get Enough Of It (2) — Cradle To The Grave (1) — Drink Away The Pain (Situations) (1) — Drop A Gem On 'Em (2) — Extortion (2)

594

DEBUT	PEAK	WKS	RIAA	CD	ARTIST — Album Title	Catalog	Sym	$	Label & Number

MOBB DEEP — Cont'd

Eye For A Eye (Your Beef Is Mines) (1)
Get Dealt With (2)
Give It Up Fast (2)
Give Up The Goods (Just Step) (1)
G.O.D. Pt. III (2)
Hell On Earth (Front Lines) (2)
I'm Going Out (3)
It's Mine (3)
Let A Ho Be A Ho (3)
Man Down (3)
More Trife Life (2)
Murda Muzik (3)
Nightime Vultures (2)
Party Over (1)
Q.U. - Hectic (1)
Quiet Storm (3)
Realest, The (3)
Right Back At You (1)
Shook Ones Pt. II (1) *59*
Spread Love (1)
Start Of Your Ending (41st Side) (1)
Still Shinin' (2)
Streets Raised Me (3)
Survival Of The Fittest (1) *69*
Temperature's Rising (1)
Thug Muzik (3)
Trife Life (1)
U.S.A. (Aiight Then) (3)
Up North Trip (1)
What's Ya Poison (1)
Where Ya From (3)
Where Ya Heart At (3)

MO B. DICK   '99
Born in Morgan City, Louisiana. Male rapper. Cousin of **Master P**. Member of **Tru**.

| 5/1/99 | 66 | 2 | | © | Gangsta Harmony .... | | | $10 | No Limit 50721 |

As The Ghetto Turns
Could It B?
Got 2 Git Mine
I'd B A Fool
Intercourse
It's Alright
Leave Her Alone
Mo B's Theme
Part 3
Picture U & Me
Shoot'm Up Movies
Smoke My Life Away
Station Identification
Twerk Some'm
U Fell N Love W/A Gangster
U Got That Fire
Want/Need
What's On Your Mind?

MOBY   '00
Born Richard Hall on 9/11/65 in Darien, Connecticut. Techno artist.

6/19/99+	38	94	▲²	©	1 Play ....C:#2²/16			$10	V2 27049
8/5/00	137	8		©	2 Mobysongs (1993-1998) .... [K]			$10	Elektra 62554
11/25/00	165	2		©	3 Play: The B-Sides			$10	V2 27085

Alone (2)
Anthem (2)
Bodyrock (1,3)
Down Slow (1,3)
Everloving (1,3)
Feeling So Real (2)
Find My Baby (1,3)
First Cool Hive (2)
Flower (3)
Flying Foxes (3)
Flying Over The Dateline (3)
Go (2)
God Moving Over The Face Of The Waters (2)
Grace (2)
Guitar Flute & String (1,3)
Honey (1,3)
Hymn (3)
I Like To Score (2)
If Things Were Perfect (1,3)
Inside (1,3)
Into The Blue (2)
Living (2)
Machete (1,3)
Memory Gospel (3)
Move [You Make Me Feel So Good] (2)
My Weakness (1,3)
Natural Blues (1,3)
Novio (2)
Now I Let It Go (2)
Porcelain (1,3)
Rain Falls And The Sky Shudders (2)
Run On (1,3)
Running (3)
Rushing (1,3)
7 (1,3)
Sky Is Broken (1,3)
South Side (1,3) *14*
Spirit (3)
Summer (3)
Sun Never Stops Setting (3)
Sunday (3)
Sunspot (3)
When It's Cold I'd Like To Die (2)
Whispering Wind (3)
Why Does My Heart Feel So Bad? (1,3)

MOBY GRAPE   '68
Rock group from San Francisco: Alexander "Skip" Spence (vocals, guitar), Jerry Miller and Peter Lewis (guitars), Bob Mosley (bass) and Don Stevenson (drums). Spence, former drummer with **Jefferson Airplane**, left in 1968. Lewis is the son of actress Loretta Young.

7/1/67	24	27		©	1 Moby Grape			$50	Columbia 2698 / 9498
5/4/68	20	28		©	2 Wow			$30	Columbia 9613 [2]
3/1/69	113	10			3 Moby Grape '69			$25	Columbia 9696
9/20/69	157	6			4 Truly Fine Citizen			$25	Columbia 9912
9/18/71	177	5		©	5 20 Granite Creek			$20	Reprise 6460

About Time (5)
Ain't No Use (1)
Ain't That A Shame (3)
Apocalypse (5)
Beautiful Is Beautiful (4)
Bitter Wind (2)
Black Currant Jam (2)
Boysenberry Jam (5)
Can't Be So Bad (2)
Captain Nemo (3)
Changes (1)
Changes, Circles Spinning (4)
Chinese Song (5)
Come In The Morning (1)
8:05 (1)
Fall On You (1)
Funky-Tunk (2)
Goin' Down To Texas (5)
Going Nowhere (3)
Gypsy Wedding (5)
He (2)
Hey Grandma (1)
Hoochie (3)
Horse Out In The Rain (5)
I Am Not Willing (4)
I'm The Kind Of Man That Baby You Can Trust (5)
If You Can't Learn From My Mistakes (3)
Indifference (1)
It's A Beautiful Day Today (3)
Just Like Gene Autry; A Foxtrot (2)
Lake (2)
Lazy Me (1)
Looper (4)
Love Song, Part One & Two (4)
Marmalade (2)
Miller's Blues (2)
Motorcycle Irene (4)
Mr. Blues (1)
Murder In My Heart For The Judge (2)
Naked, If I Want To (1,2)
Never (2)
Now I Know High (4)
Ode To The Man At The End Of The Bar (5)
Omaha (1) *88*
Ooh Mama Ooh (3)
Open Up Your Heart (4)
Place And The Time (4)
Right Before My Eyes (4)
Road To The Sun (5)
Rose Colored Eyes (2)
Roundhouse Blues (5)
Seeing (3)
Sitting By The Window (1)
Someday (1)
Three-Four (2)
Tongue-Tied (4)
Treat Me Bad (4)
Trucking Man (2)
Truly Fine Citizen (4)
What's To Choose (3)
Wild Oats Moan (5)

MOCEDADES   '74
Vocal group from Bilbao, Spain: siblings Amaya, Izaskun and Roberto Amezaga, with Jose Urien, Carlos Uribarri and Javier Barrenechea.

| 3/16/74 | 152 | 7 | | | Eres Tu "Touch The Wind" .... | | | $12 | Tara 53000 |

Adios Amor
Dime Senor
Eres Tu (Touch The Wind) *9*
Himno
I Ask The Lord
If You Miss Me From The Back Of The Bus
Mary Ann
Recuerdos De Mocedad
Rin Ron
Yesterday (It Was A Happy Day)

M.O.D.   '89
Hard-rock group from Los Angeles: Billy Milano (vocals), Tim McMurtrie (guitar), Ken Ballone (bass) and Keith Davis (drums). All but Milano left in 1988; replaced by Louie Svitek, Tim Mallare and John Monte. M.O.D.: Method Of Destruction.

11/7/87	153	5		©	1 U.S.A. For M.O.D.			$10	Megaforce 1344
9/17/88	186	6		©	2 Surfin' With M.O.D.			$10	Megaforce 1359
3/11/89	151	8		©	3 Gross Misconduct			$10	Megaforce 1360

Accident Scene (3)
A.I.D.S. (1)
Aren't You Hungry (1)
Ballad Of Dio (1)
Bubble Butt (1)
Bushwackateas (1)
Captain Crunch (medley) (1)
Color My World (2)
Come As You Are (3)
Confusion (1)
Dead Men (medley) (1)
Don't Feed The Bears (1)
E Factor (3)
Get A Real Job (1)
Godzula (1)
Goldfish From Hell (2)
Gross Misconduct (3)
Hate Tank (1)
I Executioner (1)
Imported Society (1)
In The City (3)
Jim Gordon (1)
Let Me Out (1)
Man Of Your Dreams (1)
Most (medley) (1)
Mr. Oofus (2)
No Glove No Love (3)
No Hope (3)
Ode To Harry (1)
P.B.M. (3)
Parents (1)
Party Animal (2)
Ride, The (3)
Ruptured Nuptuals (1)
Sargent Drexell Theme (2)
Satan's Cronies (3)
Short But Sweet (1)
Shout (2)
Spandex Enormity (1)
Surf's Up (2)
Surfin' U.S.A. (2)
That Noise (1)
Theme (3)
Thrash Or Be Thrashed (1)
True Colors (3)
Vents (1)
You're Beat (1)
You're X'ed (1)

MODELS   '86
Pop-rock group formed in Melbourne, Australia: Sean Kelly (vocals, guitar), Roger Mason (keyboards), James Valentine (sax), James Freud (bass) and Barton Price (drums).

| 5/3/86 | 84 | 18 | | | Out Of Mind Out Of Sight .... | | | $10 | Geffen 24100 |

Barbados
Big On Love
Cold Fever
I Hear Motion
King Of Kings
Out Of Mind Out Of Sight *37*
Ringing Like A Bell
Sooner In Heaven
Stormy Tonight
These Blues

MODERN ENGLISH   '83
New-wave group formed in Colchester, England: Robbie Grey (vocals), Gary McDowell (guitar), Stephen Walker (keyboards), Michael Conroy (bass) and Richard Brown (drums).

3/19/83	70	28	●	©	1 After The Snow			$10	Sire 23821
3/24/84	93	12			2 Ricochet Days			$10	Sire 25066
4/5/86	154	7			3 Stop Start			$10	Sire 25343
6/30/90	135	12		©	4 Pillow Lips			$10	TVT 2810

After The Snow (1)
Beautiful People (4)
Beauty (4)
Blue Waves (2)
Border, The (2)
Breaking Away (3)
Care About You (4)
Carry Me Down (1)
Chapter 12 (2)
Coming Up For Air (4)
Dawn Chorus (1)
Face Of Wood (1)
Greatest Show (3)
Hands Across The Sea (2) *91*
Heart (2)
I Don't Know The Answer (3)
I Melt With You (1) *78*
I Melt With You (4) *76*

595

MODERN ENGLISH — Cont'd

Ink And Paper (3)	Life's Rich Tapestry (4)	Machines (2)	Rainbow's End (2)	Spinning Me Round (2)	Take Me Away (4)
Let's All Dream (4)	Love Breaks Down (3)	Night Train (3)	Ricochet Days (2)	Start Stop/Stop Start (3)	You're Too Much (4)
Life In The Gladhouse (1)	Love Forever (3)	Pillow Lips (4)	Someone's Calling (1)	Tables Turning (1)	

MODEST MOUSE '00

Rock trio from Isaaquah, Washington: Isaac Brock (vocals, guitar), Eric Judy (bass) and Jeremiah Green (drums).

| 7/1/00 | 120 | 2 | © | The Moon & Antarctica | | | $10 | Epic 63871 |

Alone Down There	Different City	Life Like Weeds	Perfect Disguise	Tiny Cities Made Of Ashes
Cold Part	Gravity Rides Everything	Lives	Stars Are Projectors	What People Are Made Of
Dark Center Of The Universe	I Came As A Rat	Paper Thin Walls	3rd Planet	Wild Packs Of Family Dogs

MODUGNO, Domenico '58

Born on 1/9/28 in Polignano a Mare, Italy. Died of a heart attack on 8/6/94 (age 66). Singer/actor.

| 9/15/58 | 8 | 6 | | Nel Blu Dipinto Di Blu (Volare) and other Italian favorites | [F] | $50 | Decca 8808 |

Don Fifi	Nel Blu Dipinto Di Blu	O Specchio	Resta Cu Mme	Ventu D'Estati
La Cicoria	(Volare) 1	Pasqualino Maragia	Strade 'Nfosa	
Mariti In Citta	O Ccafe	Pizza C' 'A Pummarola	Vecchio Frak	

MOEN, Don '00

Born in Minneapolis. Christian singer/songwriter/choral director.

| 11/4/00 | 104 | 3 | © | I Will Sing | | | $10 | Hosanna! 17822 |

As We Worship You	Here We Are	Like Eagles	Our Father	Two Hands, One Heart
Glory To The Lord	I Will Sing	Lord We've Come To Worship	River Of Love	We Wait
Have Your Way	Lift Up Your Heads	Lord You Are Good	Sing For Joy	

MOFFATTS, The '99

Family vocal group from Canada: Scott (b: 3/30/84) with his triplet brothers, Dave, Bob and Clint (b: 3/8/85) Moffatt.

| 6/26/99 | 124 | 2 | © | Chapter I: A New Beginning | | | $10 | Capitol 97939 |

Crazy	I'll Be There For You	Love	Miss You Like Crazy	Say'n I Love U	Wild At Heart
Girl Of My Dreams	If Life Is So Short	Misery	Raining In My Mind	Until You Loved Me	Written All Over My Heart

MOFFO, Anna — see FRANCHI, Sergio

MOKENSTEF '95

Female R&B vocal trio from Los Angeles: Monifa, Kenya and Stephanie.

| 7/22/95 | 117 | 12 | © | Azz Izz | | | $10 | OutBurst 527364 |

Azz Izz	Don't Go There	It Goes On	Just Be Gentle	Let Them Know	Stop Callin' Me
Baby Come Close	He's Mine 7	It Happens	Laid Back	Sex In The Rain	

MOLLY HATCHET '79

Rock group formed in Jacksonville, Florida: **Danny Joe Brown** (vocals), Dave Hlubek, Duane Roland and Steve Holland (guitars), Banner Thomas (bass) and Bruce Crump (drums). Jimmy Farrar replaced Brown in 1980; Brown returned and replaced Farrar in 1983. Holland and Thomas left in 1983; John Galvin (keyboards) and Riff West (bass) joined.

11/11/78+	64	42	▲	©	1 Molly Hatchet	C:#49/4		$12	Epic 35347
9/29/79	19	48	▲²	©	2 Flirtin' With Disaster			$12	Epic 36110
9/20/80	25	21	▲	©	3 Beatin' The Odds			$12	Epic 36572
12/5/81+	36	14		©	4 Take No Prisoners			$12	Epic 37480
3/26/83	59	20		©	5 No Guts...No Glory			$12	Epic 38429
11/24/84	117	13		©	6 The Deed Is Done			$12	Epic 39621
12/7/85	130	9		©	7 Double Trouble Live	[L]		$15	Epic 40137 [2]

Ain't Even Close (5)	Dead And Gone (3)	Gator Country (1,7)	Lady Luck (4)	Price You Pay (1)	Under The Gun (5)
All Mine (4)	Dead Giveaway (4)	Get Her Back (3)	Let The Good Times Roll (2)	Rambler, The (3) 91	Walk On The Side Of The
Backstabber (6)	Don't Leave Me Lonely (4)	Good Rockin' (2)	Long Tall Sally (2)	Respect Me In The Morning (4)	Angels (7)
Beatin' The Odds (3,7)	Don't Mess Around (4)	Good Smoke And Whiskey (6)	Long Time (2)	Sailor (3)	Walk With You (7)
Big Apple (1)	Double Talker (3)	Gunsmoke (3)	Loss Of Control (4)	Satisfied Man (6,7) 81	What Does It Matter? (5)
Bloody Reunion (4,7)	Dreams I'll Never See (1,7)	Heartbreak Radio (6)	Man On The Run (6)	She Does She Does (6)	What's It Gonna Take? (5)
Boogie No More (2,7)	Edge Of Sundown (7)	I Ain't Got You (6)	On The Prowl (5)	Song For The Children (6)	Whiskey Man (2,7)
Both Sides (5)	Fall Of The Peacemakers (5,7)	I'll Be Running (1)	One Man's Pleasure (2)	Stone In Your Heart (6,7)	
Bounty Hunter (1,7)	Few And Far Between (3)	It's All Over Now (2)	Penthouse Pauper (3)	Straight Shooter (6)	
Cheatin' Woman (1)	Flirtin' With Disaster (2,7) 42	Jukin' City (2)	Poison Pen (3)	Sweet Dixie (5)	
Creeper, The (1)	Freebird (7)	Kinda Like Love (5)	Power Play (4) 96	Trust Your Old Friend (1)	

MOM & DADS, The '72

Polka group from Spokane, Washington: Quentin Ratliff (sax), Harold Hendren (drums), Les Welch (accordian) and Doris Crow (piano).

| 11/13/71+ | 85 | 23 | | 1 The Rangers Waltz | [I] | | $15 | GNP Crescendo 2061 |
| 5/6/72 | 165 | 6 | | 2 In The Blue Canadian Rockies | [I] | | $15 | GNP Crescendo 2063 |

Across The Alley From The	Cab Driver (2)	Judy (1)	Moon Wink (2)	Roses Of Picardy (2)	Till We Meet Again (2)
Alamo (1)	Ever True Evermore (2)	Just A Closer Walk With Thee	Oh Lonesome Me (2)	Silver Moon (1)	White Silver Sands (2)
Alabama Jubilee (1)	Georgianna Moon (1)	(1)	Quentin's B Flat Boogie (1)	Skirts (2)	
Anytime (1)	In The Blue Canadian Rockies	Marie (1)	Ragtime Annie (2)	Somewhere My Love (1)	
Blue Skirt Waltz (2)	(2)	Mom And Dads Schottische (2)	Rangers Waltz (1)	St. Louis Blues (2)	

MOMENTS, The/RAY, GOODMAN & BROWN '80

R&B vocal trio from Hackensack, New Jersey: Harry Ray, Al Goodman and Billy Brown. Changed group name to **Ray, Goodman & Brown** in 1978. Ray died of a stroke on 10/1/92 (age 45).

3/27/71	184	7	©	1 Moments Greatest Hits	[G]		$30	Stang 1004
5/15/71	147	8	©	2 The Moments Live at the New York State Womans Prison	[L]		$20	Stang 1006
7/12/75	132	8	©	3 Look At Me			$20	Stang 1026

RAY, GOODMAN & BROWN:

1/26/80	17	23	●	4 Ray, Goodman & Brown			$12	Polydor 6240
10/4/80	84	12		5 Ray, Goodman & Brown II			$12	Polydor 6299
1/9/82	151	7		6 Stay			$12	Polydor 6341

Another Day (4)	Friends (medley) (4)	Here I Go Again (medley) (2)	I'll Remember You With Love	Letter (2)	Me (5)
Beautiful Woman (3)	Girls (4)	How Can Love So Right (Be So	(5)	Look At Me (I'm In Love)	Midnight Lady (6)
Come Away With Me (3)	Going In Circles (2)	Wrong) (6)	I'm So Lost (1)	(3) 39	More Today Than Yesterday (2)
Deja Vu (4)	Good Ole' Days (6)	I Do (1,2) 62	I've Got The Need (3)	Love On A Two-Way Street	My Prayer (5) 47
Dolly My Love (3)	Got To Get To Know You (3)	I Feel So Good Again (3)	If I Didn't Care (1) 44	(1) 3	Not On The Outside (1,2) 57
Each Time Is Like The First	Happy Anniversary (5)	I Won't Do Anything (6)	Inside Of You (4) 76	Lovely Way She Loves (1)	Only You (And You Alone) (6)
Time (5)	Heaven In The Rain (6)		Just Having Your Love (3)	Lovers Night (Rain In May) (6)	Oo Baby, Baby (medley) (2)

MOMENTS, The/RAY, GOODMAN & BROWN — Cont'd

Overture (2)	Somebody Loves You Baby (1)	Thrill (medley) (4)	When The Lovin' Goes Out Of
Part Of You (5)	**Special Lady** (4) 5	Till The Right One Comes	The Lovin' (6)
Pool Of Love (6)	Stay (6)	Along (4)	When The Morning Comes (3)
Shoestrings (5)	**Sunday** (1,2) 90	Treat Her Right (4)	Where (1)
Slipped Away (4)	Sweet Sexy Woman (5)	Way It Should Be (4)	Wichita Lineman (2)

Yesterday (2)
You (5)

★393★ MONEY, Eddie '79
Born Edward Mahoney on 3/2/49 in Brooklyn, New York. Pop-rock singer.

1/7/78	37	49	▲²	©	1 **Eddie Money**	C:#44/24		$12	Columbia 34909
1/27/79	17	26	▲	©	2 **Life For The Taking**			$12	Columbia 35598
8/9/80	35	17		©	3 **Playing For Keeps**			$12	Columbia 36514
7/10/82	20	44	▲	©	4 **No Control**			$12	Columbia 37960
11/5/83	67	19		©	5 **Where's The Party?**			$12	Columbia 38862
8/30/86	20	58	▲	©	6 **Can't Hold Back**			$10	Columbia 40096
10/22/88	49	29		©	7 **Nothing To Lose**			$10	Columbia 44302
12/2/89+	53	18	●	©	8 **Greatest Hits Sound Of Money**		[G]	$10	Columbia 45381
2/1/92	160	10		©	9 **Right Here**			$10	Columbia 46756

Another Nice Day In L.A. (9)	Don't Worry (1)	I'll Get By (9) 21	Million Dollar Girl (3)	Running Back (3) 78	Trinidad (3)
Baby Hold On (1,8) 11	Drivin' Me Crazy (4)	It Could Happen To You (4)	My Friends, My Friends (4)	Satin Angel (3)	**Two Tickets To Paradise**
Back On The Road (5)	**Endless Nights** (6) 21	Jealousy's (1)	Nightmare (2)	Save A Little Room In Your	(1,8) 22
Backtrack (5)	**Fall In Love Again** (9) 54	Keep My Motor Runnin' (4)	No Control (4,8)	Heart For Me (1)	**Walk On Water** (7,8) 9
Bad Boy (7)	Far Cry From A Heartache (7)	Leave It To Me (5)	Nobody (2)	**Shakin'** (4,8) 63	Wanna Be A Rock 'N' Roll Star
Bad Girls (5)	Fire And Water (9)	**Let Me In** (7) 60	Nobody Knows (3)	She Takes My Breath Away (1)	(1)
Big Crash (5) 54	Forget About Love (7)	**Let's Be Lovers Again** (3,8) 65	One Chance (6)	So Good To Be In Love Again	**We Should Be Sleeping**
Boardwalk Baby (7)	Gamblin' Man (7)	Life For The Taking (8)	One Love (6)	(1)	(6,8) 90
Bring On The Rain (6)	**Get A Move On** (3) 46	Looking Through The Eyes Of	Passing By The Graveyard	Stop Steppin' On My Heart (8)	When You Took My Heart (3)
Call On Me (2)	Gimme Some Water (2)	A Child (8)	(Song For John B.) (4)	Stranger In A Strange Land (6)	Where's The Party? (5,8)
Calm Before The Storm (6)	Got To Get Another Girl (1)	**Love In Your Eyes** (7) 24	**Peace In Our Time** (8) 11	Take A Little Bit (4)	Wish, The (3)
Can't Keep A Good Man	Hard Life (4)	Love The Way You Love Me (2)	Prove It Every Night (9)	**Take Me Home Tonight** (6,8) 4	**You've Really Got A Hold On**
Down (2) 63	**Heaven In The Back Seat**	Magic (7)	Pull Together (7)	Things Are Much Better Today	**Me** (1) 72
Club Michelle (5) 66	(9) 58	Maureen (2)	Rock And Roll The Place (2)	(9)	
Dancing With Mr. Jitters (7)	I Can't Hold Back (6)	**Maybe I'm A Fool** (2) 22	Run Right Back (9)	**Think I'm In Love** (4,8) 16	
Don't Let Go (5)	**I Wanna Go Back** (6,8) 14	Maybe Tomorrow (5)	Runnin' Away (4)	Think Twice (9)	

MONEY, JT '99
Born Jeff Tompkins in Florida. Male rapper.

| 6/12/99 | 28 | 13 | | © | 1 **Pimpin On Wax** | | | $10 | Freeworld 50060 |
| 5/19/01 | 48 | 8 | | © | 2 **Blood Sweat And Years** | | | $10 | Freeworld 27069 |

Alright (1)	Hi-Lo (2)	Lil' Charlie (2)	Rap Ass Nigga (2)	Too Real (1)	Where My Thugs At (2)
Bustas And Haters (2)	Ho Problems (1)	Ni**az Better Run (2)	Something 'Bout Pimpin' (1)	War (2)	**Who Dat** (1) 5
Dank (1)	I Like The Way (2)	On Da Grind (1)	Sosa On That Chocha (2)	Watcha Want (1)	
Father To Son (2)	Kite 2 Da Boys (1)	Playa Ass Shit (1)	Superb**ch (2)	What Y'all Ni**az Want? (2)	

MONHEIT, Jane '01
Born in 1978 in New York City. Jazz singer.

| 6/30/01 | 153 | 2 | | © | **Come Dream With Me** | | | $10 | N-Coded 4219 |

Blame It On My Youth	I'll Be Seeing You	Over The Rainbow	Spring Can Really Hang You
Case Of You	I'm Through With Love	So Many Stars	Up The Most
Hit The Road To Dreamland	If	Something To Live For	Waters Of March

MONICA '98
Born Monica Arnold on 10/24/80 in Atlanta. R&B singer.

| 8/5/95 | 36 | 61 | ▲³ | © | 1 **Miss Thang** | | | $10 | Rowdy 37006 |
| 8/1/98 | 8 | 58 | ▲³ | © | 2 **The Boy Is Mine** | | | $10 | Arista 19011 |

Angel (1)	Don't Take It Personal (just	Gone Be Fine (2)	Miss Thang (1)	Skate (1)	Woman In Me (1)
Angel Of Mine (2) 1	one of dem days) (1) 2	I Keep It To Myself (2)	Misty Blue (2)	Street Symphony (2)	
Before You Walk Out Of My	**First Night** (2) 1	Inside (2)	Never Can Say Goodbye (1)	Take Him Back (2)	
Life (1) 7	**For You I Will** (2) 4	Let's Straighten It Out (1)	Now I'm Gone (1)	Tell Me If You Still Care (1)	
Boy Is Mine (2) 1	Forever Always (1)	**Like This And Like That**	Right Here Waiting (2)	**Why I Love You So Much** (1) 9	
'Cross The Room (2)	Get Down (1)	(1) flip	Ring Da Bell (2)	With You (1)	

MONIFAH '96
Born Monifah Carter in New York City. Female R&B singer.

6/8/96	42	15		©	1 **Moods...Moments**			$10	Uptown 53004
9/12/98+	96	32	●	©	2 **Mo'Hogany**			$10	Uptown 53155
11/18/00	151	2		©	3 **Home**			$10	Universal 157999

All I Want (1)	Fallin' In Love (2)	Hurry Up (3)	Lay With You (1)	Too Late (3)	**You Don't Have To Love Me**
Bad Girl (medley) (2)	Feva (3)	I Can Tell (3)	Monifah's Anthem (medley) (2)	**Touch It** (2) 9	(1) 82
Better Half Of Me (2)	Free Again (3)	I Miss You (Come Back Home)	Nana (3)	What's The Deal (2)	You Should Have Told Me (1)
Brown Eyes (3)	Hard To Say Goodbye (3)	(1)	Nobody's Body (1)	Whatcha Gonna Do (2)	You've Got My Heart (1)
Don't Waste My Time (1)	Have You Ever Been Loved (2)	I'm Loving You (2)	Peaches & Cream (3)	Why (2)	
Everything You Do (1)	Home (3)	It's Alright (1)	Rescue Me (3)	Would You (2)	
Fairytales (3)	(How) Ya Gonna Love Me (3)	Jesus Is Love (1)	Suga Suga (2)	**You** (1) 32	

MONK, Thelonious '63
Born on 10/10/17 in Rocky Mount, North Carolina. Died on 2/17/82 (age 68). Legendary jazz pianist. Father of **T.S. Monk**. Won Grammy's Lifetime Achievement Award in 1993.

| 11/30/63 | 127 | 3 | | © | **Criss-Cross** | | [I] | $30 | Columbia 2038 / 8838 |

Crepuscule With Nellie	Don't Blame Me	Hackensack	Tea For Two
Criss-Cross	Eronel	Rhythm-a-ning	Think Of One

MONK, T.S. '81
Born Thelonious Sphere Monk on 12/27/49 in New York City. R&B singer/drummer. Son of **Thelonious Monk**.

| 1/31/81 | 64 | 22 | | | 1 **House Of Music** | | | $12 | Mirage 19291 |
| 1/9/82 | 176 | 8 | | | 2 **More Of The Good Life** | | | $12 | Mirage 19324 |

Bon Bon Vie (Gimme The	Candidate For Love (1)	First Lady Of Love (2)	Last Of The Wicked Romancers	Stay Free Of His Life (1)
Good Life) (1) 63	Everybody Get On Up And	Hot Night In The City (1)	(1)	Too Much Too Soon (2)
Can't Keep My Hands To	Dance (2)	House Of Music (1)	More To Love (2)	You're Askin' Me, I'm Askin'
Myself (1)	Falling In Love With You (2)	Oh! Oh! Speedo (2)		You (Buggin' Me Out) (2)

MONKEES, The ★81★ '67

Pop group formed in Los Angeles in 1965. Members chosen from over 400 applicants for new Columbia TV series. Consisted of **Davy Jones** (vocals), **Michael Nesmith** (guitar, vocals), Peter Tork (bass, vocals) and Micky Dolenz (drums, vocals). Jones had been a racehorse jockey, and appeared in London musicals *Oliver* and *Pickwick*. Nesmith had done session work for Stax/Volt. Tork had been in the Phoenix Singers. Dolenz had appeared in TV series *Circus Boy*, using the name Mickey Braddock in 1956. Group starred in the movie *Head* (1968) and 58 episodes of *The Monkees* TV show, 1966-68. Tork left in 1968. Group disbanded in 1969. Re-formed (minus Nesmith) in 1986 and again (with Nesmith) in 1996.

1)More Of The Monkees 2)The Monkees 3)Pisces, Aquarius, Capricorn & Jones Ltd.

DEBUT	PEAK	WKS	RIAA	CD		ARTIST — Album Title	$	Label & Number
10/8/66	❶13	78	▲5	©	1	The Monkees	$40	Colgems 101
2/4/67	❶18	70	▲5	©	2	More Of The Monkees	$30	Colgems 102
6/10/67	❶1	51	▲2	©	3	Headquarters	$30	Colgems 103
11/25/67	❶5	47	▲2	©	4	Pisces, Aquarius, Capricorn & Jones Ltd.	$30	Colgems 104
5/11/68	3	39	▲	©	5	The Birds, The Bees & The Monkees	$30	Colgems 109
12/21/68+	45	15			6	Head .... [S]	$50	Colgems 5008
3/1/69	32	15		©	7	Instant Replay	$40	Colgems 113
6/28/69	89	12			8	The Monkees Greatest Hits .... [G]	$40	Colgems 115
11/1/69	100	14		©	9	The Monkees Present	$50	Colgems 117
8/7/76	58	30	▲	©	10	The Monkees Greatest Hits ....C:#4/259 [G]	$12	Arista 4089
						later released on Arista 8313		
7/26/86	21	34	▲	©	11	Then & Now...The Best Of The Monkees .... [G]	$12	Arista 8432
						includes 3 new songs by Micky Dolenz and Peter Tork		
8/16/86	92	24		©	12	The Monkees .... [R]	$10	Rhino 70140
8/16/86	96	26		©	13	More Of The Monkees .... [R]	$10	Rhino 70142
8/16/86	121	17		©	14	Headquarters .... [R]	$10	Rhino 70143
8/16/86	124	17		©	15	Pisces, Aquarius, Capricorn & Jones Ltd. .... [R]	$10	Rhino 70141
9/13/86	145	11		©	16	The Birds, The Bees & The Monkees ...... [R]	$10	Rhino 70144
11/8/86	152	4		©	17	Changes .... [E]	$10	Rhino 70148
						group reduced to duo of Micky Dolenz and **Davy Jones**; originally released in 1970 on Colgems 119 ($75)		
9/19/87	72	9		©	18	Pool It!	$10	Rhino 70706
7/15/00	21C	2		©	19	The Monkees Greatest Hits .... [G]	$10	Rhino 72190

Acapulco Sun (17)
All Alone In The Dark (17)
Anytime, Anyplace, Anywhere (11)
As We Go Along (6)
Auntie's Municipal Court (5,16)
Band 6 (3,14)
Bye Bye Baby Bye Bye (9)
Can You Dig It (6)
Circle Sky (6)
Counting On You (18)
Cuddly Toy (4,8,15)
D.W. Washburn (19) *19*
Daddy's Song (6)
Daily Nightly (4,15)
Day We Fall In Love (2,13)
Daydream Believer (5,8,10,11,16,19) *1*
Ditty Diego - War Chant (6)
Do You Feel It Too? (17)
Don't Bring Me Down (18)
Don't Call On Me (4,15)
Don't Listen To Linda (7)
Don't Wait For Me (7)
Door Into Summer (4,15)
Dream World (5,16)
Early Morning Blues And Greens (3,14)

Every Step Of The Way (18)
For Pete's Sake (3,14)
Forget That Girl (3,14)
French Song (9)
Gettin' In (18)
Girl I Knew Somewhere (11,19) *39*
Girl I Left Behind Me (7)
Goin' Down (19)
Gonna Buy Me A Dog (1,12)
Good Clean Fun (9) *82*
Hard To Believe (4,15)
Heart And Soul (18,19) *87*
Hold On Girl (2,13)
I Can't Get Her Off My Mind (3,14)
I Love You Better (17)
I Never Thought It Peculiar (17)
I Wanna Be Free (1,8,10,12,19)
I Won't Be The Same Without Her (7)
(I'd Go The) Whole Wide World (18)
I'll Be Back Up On My Feet (5,16)
I'll Be True To You (1,12)
(I'll) Love You Forever (18)

I'll Spend My Life With You (3,14)
I'm A Believer (2,8,10,11,13,19) *1*
(I'm Not Your) Steppin' Stone (2,8,10,11,13,19) *20*
If I Knew (9)
It's Got To Be Love (17)
It's Nice To Be With You (19) *51*
Just A Game (7)
Kicks (11)
Kind Of Girl I Could Love (2,13)
Ladies Aid Society (9)
Last Train To Clarksville (1,8,10,11,12,19) *1*
Laugh (2,13)
Let's Dance On (1,12)
Listen To The Band (9,10,19) *63*
Little Bit Me, A Little Bit You (8,10,11,19) *2*
Little Girl (9)
Long Title: Do I Have To Do This All Over Again (6)
Long Way Home (18)
Look Out (Here Comes Tomorrow) (2,13)

Looking For The Good Times (9)
Love Is Only Sleeping (4,15)
Magnolia Simms (5,16)
Man Without A Dream (7)
Mary, Mary (2,8,13,19)
Me Without You (7)
Midnight (18)
Midnight Train (17)
Mommy And Daddy (9)
Monkees, (Theme From) The (1,10,11,12,19)
Mr. Webster (3,14)
Never Tell A Woman Yes (9)
99 Pounds (17)
No Time (3,14)
Oh My My (17) *98*
Oklahoma Backroom Dancer (9)
P.O. Box 9847 (5,16)
Papa Gene's Blues (1,12)
Peter Percival Patterson's Pet Pig Porky (medley) (4,15)
Pillow Time (9)
Pleasant Valley Sunday (4,8,10,11,15,19) *3*
Porpoise Song (6,19) *62*
Poster, The (5,16)
Randy Scouse Git (3,8,14,19)
Salesman (17)

Saturday's Child (1,12)
Secret Heart (18)
Shades Of Gray (3,8,10,14)
She (2,8,10,13)
She Hangs Out (4,15)
She's Movin' In With Rico (18)
Shorty Blackwell (7)
Since You Went Away (18)
Sometime In The Morning (2,13)
Star Collector (4,15)
Sunny Girlfriend (3,14)
Sweet Young Thing (1,12)
Tapioca Tundra (5,16) *34*
Tear Drop City (7) *56*
Tell Me Love (17)
That Was Then, This Is Now (11,19) *20*
This Just Doesn't Seem To Be My Day (1,12)
Through The Looking Glass (7)
Ticket On A Ferry Ride (17)
Tomorrow's Gonna Be Another Day (1,12)
Valleri (5,8,11,16,19) *3*
We Were Made For Each Other (5,16)

What Am I Doing Hangin' 'Round? (4,11,15)
When Love Comes Knockin' (At Your Door) (2,13)
While I Cry (7)
Words (4,15,19) *11*
Writing Wrongs (5,16)
You And I (7)
You Just May Be The One (3,14)
You Told Me (3,14)
You're So Good To Me (17)
Your Auntie Grizelda (2,13)
Zilch (3,14)
Zor And Zam (5,8,16)

MONO '98

Dance duo from England: Siobahn DeMare (female vocals) and Martin Virgo (instruments).

| 3/7/98 | 137 | 7 | | © | Formica Blues .... | $10 | Echo 536676 |

Blind Man
Disney Town

Hello Cleveland!
High Life

Life In Mono *70*
Outsider, The

Penguin Freud
Playboys

Silicone
Slimcea Girl

MONRO, Matt '67

Born Terrence Parsons on 12/1/32 in London. Died of cancer on 2/7/85 (age 52). Pop singer.

10/2/61	87	14		©	1	My Kind Of Girl	$40	Warwick 2045
3/13/65	126	3		©	2	Walk Away	$25	Liberty 7402
5/13/67	86	22		©	3	Invitation To The Movies/Born Free	$20	Capitol 2730

Alfie (3)
April Fool (1)
Born Free (3)
Cheek To Cheek (1)
Come Sta (1)
Georgia On My Mind (2)
Georgy Girl (3)
Going Places (2)

Gonna Build A Mountain (2)
Here And Now (2)
How Soon (2)
I Get Along Without You Very Well (2)
I Will Wait For You (3)
I'll Dream Of You (1)
I've Got Love (2)

In The Arms Of Love (3)
It's A Breeze (2)
Let's Face The Music And Dance (1)
Love Is The Same Anywhere (1)
Man And A Woman (3)
Mirage (2)

Moment To Moment (3)
My Friend, My Friend (2)
My Kind Of Girl (1) *18*
No One Will Ever Know (1)
Portrait Of My Love (1)
Sand Pebbles (And We Were Lovers), Theme From The (3)
Softly As I Leave You (2)

Strangers In The Night (3)
There Are No Words For Love (1)
Thing About Love (1)
Time For Love (3)
Walk Away (2) *23*
Wednesday's Child (3)
Who Can I Turn To (2)

MONROE, Marilyn '62

Born Norma Jean Baker on 6/1/26 in Los Angeles. Died of a drug overdose on 8/5/62 (age 36). Legendary Hollywood actress/sex symbol. Married to baseball player Joe DiMaggio (1954) and playwright Arthur Miller (1956-61).

| 10/20/62 | 111 | 10 | | | | Marilyn .... | $150 | 20th Century Fox 5000 |

After You Get What You Want You Don't Want It
Bye Bye Baby

Diamonds Are A Girl's Best Friend
Heat Wave

I'm Going To File My Claim
Lazy
Little Girl From Little Rock

One Silver Dollar
River Of No Return
When Love Goes Wrong

MONROE, Michael '89
Born Matt Fagerholm on 6/17/60 in Helsinki, Finland. Hard-rock singer.

| 10/7/89 | 161 | 8 | | © | Not Fakin' It | | | $10 | Mercury 838627 |

All Night With The Lights On
Dead, Jail Or Rock 'N' Roll
Love Is Thicker Than Blood
Man With No Eyes
Not Fakin' It
Shakedown
She's No Angel
Smoke Screen
Thrill Me
While You Were Looking At Me

MONROES, The '82
Pop-rock group from San Diego: Jesus Ortiz (vocals), Rusty Jones (guitar), Eric Denton (keyboards), Bob Monroe (bass) and Jonnie Gilstrap (drums).

| 6/19/82 | 109 | 9 | | | The Monroes | | [M] | $15 | Alfa 15015 |

Blind Faith
Hungry Stranger
Pay Pay Pay
Somewhere In The Night
What Do All The People
Know 59

MONSTER MAGNET '98
Hard-rock group from Red Bank, New Jersey: David Wyndorf (vocals), Ed Mundell (guitar), Joe Calandra (bass) and Joe Kleiman (drums). Phil Caivano (guitar) joined in 2000.

| 7/4/98 | 97 | 23 | ● | © | 1 Powertrip | | | $10 | A&M 540908 |
| 4/28/01 | 153 | 1 | | © | 2 God Says No | | | $10 | A&M 490749 |

All Shook Out (2)
Atomic Clock (1)
Baby Götterdämerung (1)
Bummer (1)
Crop Circle (1)
Cry (2)
Doomsday (2)
God Says No (2)
Goliath And The Vampires (1)
Gravity Well (2)
Heads Explode (2)
Kiss Of The Scorpion (2)
Medicine (2)
Melt (2)
My Little Friend (2)
19 Witches (1)
Powertrip (1)
Queen Of You (2)
See You In Hell (1)
Silver Future (2)
Space Lord (1)
Take It (2)
Temple Of Your Dreams (1)
3rd Eye Landslide (1)
Tractor (1)
Your Lies Become You (1)

MONTANA ORCHESTRA '82
Studio group assembled by producer Vincent Montana. Also see **Salsoul Orchestra**.

| 12/19/81+ | 195 | 4 | | | Merry Christmas/Happy New Year's | | [X] | $12 | MJS 3302 |

side 1: Christmas medley; side 2: New Year's eve party medley

Get Down New Years Eve Medley
Montana Christmas Medley

MONTE, Lou '63
Born on 4/2/17 in Lyndhurst, New Jersey. Italian-styled novelty singer/guitarist.

| 12/22/62+ | 9 | 25 | | | Pepino The Italian Mouse & Other Italian Fun Songs | | [N] | $25 | Reprise 6058 |

Calypso Italiano
Eh Marie, Eh Marie
Good Man Is Hard To Find
Mala Femmena
Oh, Tessie
Pepino The Italian Mouse 5
Please Mr. Columbus (Turn The Ship Around)
Show Me The Way To Go Home
Sixteen Tons
Tici Ti-Tica To-Tici Ta
Twist Italiano
What Did Washington Say (When He Crossed The Delaware)

MONTENEGRO, Hugo '68
Born on 9/2/25 in New York City. Died of emphysema on 2/6/81 (age 55). Conductor/composer/arranger. Also see **Movie Soundtracks** (Hurry Sundown).

1/29/66	52	20			1 Original Music From The Man From U.N.C.L.E.		[I]	$40	RCA Victor 3475
2/17/68	9	39	●		2 Music From "A Fistful Of Dollars" & "For A Few Dollars More" & "The Good, The Bad And The Ugly"		[I]	$20	RCA Victor 3927
9/21/68	166	5			3 Hang 'Em High		[I]	$20	RCA Victor 4022
8/30/69	182	4			4 Moog Power		[I]	$20	RCA Victor 4170

Aces High (2)
Aquarius (medley) (4)
Bandolero! (3)
Bitter Love (3)
Bye, Bye Jill (1)
Dizzy (4)
Don't Leave Me (4)
Ecstasy Of Gold (2)
Fiddlesticks (1)
Fistful Of Dollars, Theme From A (2)
For A Few Dollars More (2)
For Love Of Ivy (3)
Fox, Theme From The (3)
Good, The Bad And The Ugly (2) 2
Greatest Love (4)
Hair (medley) (4)
Hang 'Em High (3) 82
Illya (1)
In The Heat Of The Night (3)
Invaders, The (1)
Keystone Kop (3)
MacArthur Park (Allegro Part III) (4)
Man From Thrush (1)
Man From U.N.C.L.E., Theme From The (1)
March With Hope (2)
Martini Built For Two (1)
Meet Mr. Solo (1)
Moog Power (4)
More Today Than Yesterday (4)
My Love (3)
My Way (4)
Sixty Seconds To What? (2)
Solo On A Raft (1)
Solo's Samba (1)
Square Dance (2)
Story Of A Soldier (2)
Theme For Three (3)
Titoli (2)
Tomorrow's Love (3)
Touch Me (4)
Traces (4)
Valley Of The Dolls, Theme From (3)
Vice Of Killing (2)
Watch Out! (1)
Wild Bike (1)
Wish I Knew (3)
You Showed Me (4)

MONTEZ, Chris '66
Born Ezekiel Christopher Montanez on 1/17/43 in Los Angeles. Pop-rock singer.

| 7/2/66 | 33 | 24 | | | 1 The More I See You/Call Me | | | $20 | A&M 4115 |
| 1/14/67 | 106 | 11 | | | 2 Time After Time | | | $20 | A&M 4120 |

Call Me (1) 22
Day By Day (1)
Elena (2)
Fly Me To The Moon (1)
Girl From Ipanema (1)
Going Out Of My Head (2)
Hey Baby (1)
How High The Moon (1)
I Wish You Love (2)
Just Friends (2)
Keep Talkin' (2)
Lil' Red Riding Hood (2)
Little White Lies (1)
More I See You (1) 16
One Note Samba (1)
Our Day Will Come (2)
Shadow Of Your Smile (1)
Sunny (2)
There Will Never Be Another You (1) 33
Very Thought Of You (1)
What A Diff'rence A Day Made (2)
Yesterday (2)
You, I Love You (1)

★398★ MONTGOMERY, John Michael '94
Born on 1/20/65 in Danville, Kentucky. Country singer/guitarist. Brother of Eddie Montgomery of **Montgomery Gentry**.

1/23/93	27	77	▲³	©	1 Life's A Dance			$10	Atlantic 82420
2/12/94	❶¹	82	▲⁴	©	2 Kickin' It Up			$10	Atlantic 82559
4/15/95	5	65	▲⁴	©	3 John Michael Montgomery			$10	Atlantic 82728
10/12/96	39	40	▲	©	4 What I Do The Best			$10	Atlantic 82947
11/1/97	33	29	▲	©	5 Greatest Hits		[G]	$10	Atlantic 83060
5/23/98	95	5		©	6 Leave A Mark			$10	Atlantic 83104
6/12/99	135	4		©	7 Home To You			$10	Atlantic 83185
10/14/00	15	19	●	©	8 Brand New Me			$10	Atlantic 83378

Ain't Got Nothin' On Us (4)
All In My Heart (2)
Angel In My Eyes (5)
Be My Baby Tonight (2,5) 73
Beer And Bones (1,5)
Brand New Me (8)
Bus To Birmingham (8)
Cloud 8 (4)
Cover You In Kisses (6) 91
Cowboy Love (3,5)
Dream On Texas Ladies (1)
Even Then (8)
Everytime I Fall (It Breaks Her Heart) (1)
Few Cents Short (4)
Friday At Five (2)
Friends (4,5) 69
Full-Time Love (2)
Great Memory (1)
Heaven Sent Me You (3)
Hello L.O.V.E. (7) 71
High School Heart (3)
Hold On To Me (6) 33
Holdin' On To Something (3)
Holding An Amazing Love (7)
Home To You (7) 45
How Was I To Know (4)
I Can Love You Like That (3,5)
I Can Prove You Wrong (4)
I Couldn't Dream (6)
I Don't Want This Song To End (6)
I Love It All (8)
I Love The Way You Love Me (1,5) 60
I Miss You A Little (4,5)
I Never Stopped Lovin' You (6)
If You've Got Love (2,5)
It Gets Me Every Time (5)
It's What I Am (3)
Just Like A Rodeo (3)
Kick It Up (2)
Life's A Dance (1,5)
Line On Love (1)
Little Cowboy's Cry (6)
Little Girl (8) 35
Long As I Live (3)
Love Is Our Business (7)
Love Made Me Do It (7)
Love Working On You (6)
Lucky Arms (4)
Nickels And Dimes And Love (1)
No Man's Land (3,5)
Nothing Catches Jesus By Surprise (7)
Oh How She Shines (2)
Paint The Town Redneck (4)
Real Love (8)
Rope The Moon (2,5)
She Don't Need A Band To Dance (2)
Sinkin' In (7)
Sold (The Grundy County Auction Incident) (3,5)

MONTGOMERY, John Michael — Cont'd

Taking Off The Edge (1)
Thanks For The G Chord (8)
That's Not Her Picture (8)
That's What I Like About You (8)
This One's Gonna 'Leave A Mark' (6)
Weekend Superstar (8)
What I Do The Best (4)
When Your Arms Were Around (7)
When Your Baby Ain't Around (1)
You Are (7)
You're The Ticket (6)
Your Love Lingers On (7)

★480★ MONTGOMERY, Wes   '67

Born John Leslie Montgomery on 3/6/25 in Indianapolis. Died on 6/15/68 (age 43). Jazz guitarist.
1)A Day In The Life 2)Down Here On The Ground 3)Tequila

DEBUT	PEAK	WKS	RIAA	CD		Catalog	$	Label & Number
12/11/65+	116	13		© 1	Bumpin'	[I]	$20	Verve 8625
9/3/66	51	32		© 2	Tequila	[I]	$20	Verve 8653
3/25/67	65	32		© 3	California Dreaming	[I]	$20	Verve 8672
5/20/67	129	23		© 4	Jimmy & Wes The Dynamic Duo	[I]	$20	Verve 8678
					JIMMY SMITH AND WES MONTGOMERY			
10/7/67	13	67	●	© 5	A Day In The Life	[I]	$15	A&M 3001
12/9/67+	56	38		© 6	The Best Of Wes Montgomery	[I-K]	$15	Verve 8714
5/4/68	38	30		© 7	Down Here On The Ground	[I]	$15	A&M 3006
9/7/68	187	8		8	The Best Of Wes Montgomery, Vol. 2	[I-K]	$15	Verve 8757
11/16/68	94	16		© 9	Road Song	[I]	$15	A&M 3012
4/4/70	175	9		© 10	Greatest Hits	[G-I]	$15	A&M 4247

Angel (5)
Baby, It's Cold Outside (4)
Big Hurt (2,8)
Bumpin' (1,8)
Bumpin' On Sunset (2,6)
California Dreaming (3,8)
California Nights (5)
Caravan (6)
Con Alma (1,6)
Day In The Life (5,10)
Down By The Riverside (4)
Down Here On The Ground (7,10)
Eleanor Rigby (5,10)
End Of A Love Affair (6)
Fly Me To The Moon (8)
Fox, Theme From The (7)
Georgia On My Mind (7,10) 91
Goin' On To Detroit (7)
Goin' Out Of My Head (8)
Green Leaves Of Summer (9)
Green Peppers (3)
Greensleeves (9)
Here's That Rainy Day (1)
How Insensitive (Insensatez) (2,6)
I Say A Little Prayer (7,10)
I'll Be Back (9)
James And Wes (4)
Joker, The (5)
Know It All (7)
Little Child (Daddy Dear) (2)
Mi Cosa (1)
Midnight Mood (2,8)
More, More, Amor (3)
Movin' Wes (Part 1) (6)
Mr. Walker (3)
Musty (1)
Naptown Blues (6)
Night Train (4)
O Morro (8)
Oh You Crazy Moon (3)
Other Man's Grass Is Always Greener (7)
Quiet Thing (1)
Road Song (9,10)
Sandpiper, Love Theme From The ..see: Shadow Of Your Smile
Scarborough Fair (Canticle) (9,10)
Serene (9)
Shadow Of Your Smile (1,6)
South Of The Border (Down Mexico Way) (3)
Sun Down (3)
Sunny (3)
Tear It Down (1)
Tequila (2,6)
13 (Death March) (4)
Thumb, The (2)
Trust In Me (5)
Twisted Blues (8)
Up And At It (7)
Watch What Happens (5)
What The World Needs Now Is Love (2,8)
When A Man Loves A Woman (5,10)
When I Look In Your Eyes (7)
Where Have All The Flowers Gone? (9)
Willow Weep For Me (5)
Wind Song (7)
Winds Of Barcelona (3,8)
Windy (5,10) 44
Without You (3)
Yesterday (9,10)

MONTGOMERY GENTRY   '01

Country vocal duo from Kentucky: Eddie Montgomery and Troy Gentry. Montgomery is the brother of **John Michael Montgomery**.

DEBUT	PEAK	WKS	RIAA	CD			$	Label & Number
4/24/99	131	8	●	© 1	Tattoos & Scars		$10	Columbia 69156
5/19/01	49	19		© 2	Carrying On		$10	Columbia 62167

All Night Long (1)
Black Jack Fletcher And Mississippi Sam (2)
Carrying On (2)
Cold One Comin' On (2)
Daddy Won't Sell The Farm (1) 79
Didn't Your Mama Tell Ya' (1)
Fine Line (2)
Hellbent On Saving Me (2)
I've Loved A Lot More Than I've Hurt (1)
If A Broken Heart Could Kill (1)
Lonely And Gone (1) 46
Lucky To Be Here (2)
My Father's Son (2)
Ramblin' Man (2)
Self Made Man (1)
She Couldn't Change Me (2) 37
Tattoos & Scars (1)
Too Hard To Handle...Too Free To Hold (2)
Tried And True (2)
Trouble Is (1)
Trying To Survive (1)
While The World Goes Down The Drain (2)

MONTROSE   '74

Hard-rock group from San Francisco: Ronnie Montrose (guitar, **Edgar Winter Group**, **Gamma**), **Sammy Hagar** (vocals), Bill Church (bass) and Denny Carmassi (drums; Gamma, **Heart**). Church left after first album, replaced by Alan Fitzgerald (**Night Ranger**). Hagar left after second album, replaced by Bob James. Fitzgerald left after third album, replaced by Jim Alcivar. Group disbanded in 1977. Montrose formed new group in 1987 with Johnny Edwards (vocals; **Foreigner**), Glenn Letsch (bass) and James Kottak (drums).

DEBUT	PEAK	WKS	RIAA	CD			$	Label & Number
5/11/74	133	12	▲	© 1	Montrose		$15	Warner 2740
11/16/74	65	14		© 2	Paper Money		$15	Warner 2823
10/18/75	79	7		3	Warner Bros. presents Montrose!		$15	Warner 2892
9/25/76	118	7		4	Jump On It		$15	Warner 2963
2/11/78	98	10		5	Open Fire		$12	Warner 3134
					RONNIE MONTROSE			
					produced by Edgar Winter			
5/30/87	165	7		6	Mean		$10	Enigma 73264

All I Need (3)
Bad Motor Scooter (1)
Black Train (3)
Clown Woman (3)
Connection (2)
Crazy For You (4)
Dancin' Feet (3)
Don't Damage The Rock (6)
Dreamer, The (2)
Flesh And Blood (2)
Game Of Love (6)
Good Rockin' Tonight (1)
Hard Headed Woman (6)
Heads Up (5)
I Don't Want It (1)
I Got The Fire (2)
Jump On It (4)
Leo Rising (3)
Let's Go (4)
M For Machine (6)
Make It Last (1)
Man Of The Hour (5)
Mandolinia (5)
Matriarch (3)
Merry-Go-Round (4)
Music Man (4)
My Little Mystery (5)
No Beginning/No End (5)
O Lucky Man (3)
One And A Half (3)
One Thing On My Mind (1)
Open Fire (5)
Openers (Overture) (5)
Paper Money (6)
Pass It On (6)
Ready Willing And Able (6)
Rich Man (4)
Rock Candy (1)
Rock The Nation (1)
Rocky Road (5)
Space Station #5 (1)
Spaceage Sacrifice (2)
Stand (6)
Starliner (2)
Town Without Pity (5)
Tuft-Sedge (4)
Twenty Flight Rock (3)
Underground (2)
We're Going Home (2)
Whaler (3)
What Are You Waitin' For? (4)

MONTY PYTHON   '75

Comedy troupe from England: Eric Idle, John Cleese, Terry Jones, Graham Chapman, Michael Palin and Terry Gilliam. Chapman died of cancer on 10/4/89 (age 48). Also see **The Rutles**.

DEBUT	PEAK	WKS	RIAA	CD			$	Label & Number
5/24/75	48	13		1	Matching Tie & Handkerchief	[C]	$20	Arista 4039
8/2/75	83	15		2	Monty Python's Flying Circus	[C]	$20	Pye 12116
8/23/75	87	11		3	The Album Of The Soundtrack Of The Trailer Of The Film Of "Monty Python And The Holy Grail"	[C-S]	$20	Arista 4050
6/5/76	186	3		4	Monty Python Live! At City Center	[C]	$20	Arista 4073
11/10/79	155	2		5	Life Of Brian	[C-S]	$20	Warner 3396
					individual skit names not shown on above 2 albums			
11/15/80	164	9		6	Monty Python's Contractual Obligation Album	[C]	$20	Arista 9536

Adventures Of Ralph Melish (1)
All Things Dull And Ugly (6)
Announcement (6)
Background To History (1)
Barber, The (2)
Bells (6)
Bishop (6)
Bishop On The Landing (1)
Bookshop (6)
Bring Me The Head Of Alfredo Garcia (1)
Bruces (1)
Buying A Bed (2)
Cheese Shop (1)
Children's Stories (2)
Cinema, The (2)
Crocodile (6)
Decomposing Composers (6)
Do Wot John (6)
Elephantoplasty (1)
Farewell To John Denver (6)
Fight Of The Century (1)
Finland (6)
Flying Sheep (2)
Great Actor (1)
Greater London Re-Development Plan For Haringey (3)
Henry Kissinger (6)
Herbie Rides Again (3)
Here Comes Another One (6)
Hot Dogs And Knickers (1)
I Bet You They Won't Play This Song On The Radio (6)
I Like Chinese (6)
I'm So Worried (6)
Interesting People (2)
Interviews (2)
King Arthur (3)
Martyrdom Of St. Victor (6)
Me, Doctor (1)
Medical Love Song (6)
Minister For Overseas Development (1)
More Television Interviews (2)
Mouse Problem (2)

DEBUT	PEAK	WKS	RIAA	CD	ARTIST — Album Title	Catalog	Sym	$	Label & Number

MONTY PYTHON — Cont'd

Muddy Knees (6)	Oscar Wilde And Friends (1)	Self Defense (2)	Television Interviews (2)	Visitors, The (2)
Never Be Rude To An Arab (6)	Pet Shop (2)	Sir Kenneth Clash (3)	Tiger Talk (1)	Wide World Of Novel Writing (1)
North Minehead Bye-Election (2)	Phone-in, The (1)	Sit On My Face (6)	Towering Inferno (3)	Word Association (1)
Nudge Nudge (2)	Rock Notes (6)	String (6)	Trade Description Act (2)	World War Noises In 4 (1)
	Scottish Farewell (6)	Taking In The Terrier (1)	Traffic Lights (6)	

MOODY BLUES, The ★82★   '72

Pop-rock group formed in Birmingham, England: Denny Laine (guitar, vocals), **Ray Thomas** (flute, vocals), **Michael Pinder** (keyboards, vocals), Clint Warwick (bass) and **Graeme Edge** (drums). Laine and Warwick left in the summer of 1966, replaced by **Justin Hayward** (vocals, guitar) and **John Lodge** (vocals, bass). Laine joined **Wings** in 1971. Switzerland-born **Patrick Moraz** (former keyboardist of **Yes**) replaced Pinder in 1978; left group in early 1992.

1)Seventh Sojourn 2)Long Distance Voyager 3)Every Good Boy Deserves Favour
4)Days Of Future Passed 5)A Question Of Balance

DEBUT	PEAK	WKS	RIAA	CD	#	Album Title	Catalog	Sym	$	Label & Number
5/4/68+	3	106	▲	©	1	Days Of Future Passed	C:#29/24		$20	Deram 18012
						with The London Festival Orchestra				
9/14/68	23	29	●	©	2	In Search Of The Lost Chord	C:#27/30		$20	Deram 18017
5/31/69	20	136	▲	©	3	On The Threshold Of A Dream	C:#23/38		$20	Deram 18025
1/10/70	14	44	●	©	4	To Our Children's Children's Children	C:#36/14		$15	Threshold 1
9/12/70	3	74	▲	©	5	A Question Of Balance	C:#26/18		$15	Threshold 3
8/21/71	2³	43	●	©	6	Every Good Boy Deserves Favour			$15	Threshold 5
11/18/72	❶⁵	44	●	©	7	Seventh Sojourn			$15	Threshold 7
11/23/74+	11	25	●	©	8	This Is The Moody Blues		[G]	$20	Threshold 12/13 [2]
6/4/77	26	15		©	9	Caught Live +5		[L]	$20	London 690/1 [2]
						first 3 sides recorded live at the Royal Albert Hall in 1969; side 4: previously unreleased studio recordings				
7/1/78	13	30	▲	©	10	Octave			$12	London 708
6/13/81	❶³	39	▲	©	11	Long Distance Voyager			$12	Threshold 2901
9/10/83	26	22		©	12	The Present			$12	Threshold 2902
3/23/85	132	9		©	13	Voices In The Sky/The Best Of The Moody Blues		[G]	$12	Threshold 820155
5/17/86	9	42	▲	©	14	The Other Side Of Life			$12	Threshold 829179
6/25/88	38	19		©	15	Sur la mer			$10	Polydor 835756
						title is French for "On The Sea"				
12/9/89+	113	16	●	©	16	Greatest Hits		[G]	$10	Threshold 840659
7/13/91	94	11		©	17	Keys Of The Kingdom			$10	Polydor 849433
3/27/93	93	5	●	©	18	A Night At Red Rocks With The Colorado Symphony Orchestra		[L]	$10	Polydor 517977
						recorded on 9/9/92 at Red Rocks Amphitheater in Colorado				
9/4/99	93	5		©	19	Strange Times			$10	Threshold 153565
8/26/00	185	1		©	20	Hall Of Fame: Recorded Live At The Royal Albert Hall		[L]	$10	Ark 21 810059
						recorded on 5/1/00				

Actor, The (2,8)	Eyes Of A Child - Part I (4,8)	I'm Just A Singer (In A Rock And Roll Band) (7,8,13,16,18,20) **12**	Morning - Another Morning (1)	Rock 'N' Roll Over You (14)	Tuesday Afternoon (Forever Afternoon) (1,8,9,16,18,20) **24**
After You Came (6)	Eyes Of A Child - Part II (4)		My Little Lovely (19)	Running Out Of Love (14)	
All That Is Real Is You (19)	Floating (4)		My Song (6)	Running Water (12)	22,000 Days (11)
And The Tide Rushes In (5,8)	Foolish Love (19)	I'm Your Man (10)	Nervous (11)	Say It With Love (17)	Under Moonshine (10)
Are You Sitting Comfortably (3,9)	For My Lady (7,8,18)	In My World (11)	Never Blame The Rainbows For The Rain (17)	Say What You Mean (Parts I & II) (17)	Under My Feet (12)
Balance, The (5)	Forever Now (19)	In The Beginning (3,8)		Send Me No Wine (3)	Veteran Cosmic Rocker (11,13)
Best Way To Travel (2)	Gemini Dream (11,13,16) **12**	Is This Heaven? (17)	**Never Comes The Day** (3,8,9) **91**	Shadows On The Wall (17)	Vintage Wine (11)
Beyond (4)	Gimme' A Little Somethin' (9)	**Isn't Life Strange** (7,8,13,16,18,20) **29**	New Horizons (7,8)	Simple Game (8)	Visions Of Paradise (2)
Bless The Wings (That Bring You Back) (17)	Going Nowhere (12)		Nice To Be Here (6)	**Sitting At The Wheel** (12,13) **27**	**Voice, The** (11,13,16,18) **15**
Blue World (12) **62**	Gypsy (Of A Strange And Distant Time) (4,9)	It May Be A Fire (14)	**Nights In White Satin** (1,8,9,13,16,18,20) **2**	Slings And Arrows (14)	Voices In The Sky (9)
Breaking Point (15)	Had To Fall In Love (10)	It's Cold Outside Of Your Heart (12)		So Deep Within You (3)	Voyage, The (3,8,9)
Candle Of Life (4)	Haunted (19,20)	It's Up To You (5)	No More Lies (15)	Sooner Or Later (Walkin' On Air) (19)	Want To Be With You (15)
Celtic Sonant (17)	Have You Heard - Part 1 & 2 (3,8,9)	King And Queen (9)	Nothing Changes (19)	Sorry (12)	Watching And Waiting (4,8)
Dawn - Dawn Is A Feeling (1)	Here Comes The Weekend (15)	Land Of Make-Believe (7)	OM (2)	Spirit, The (14)	What Am I Doing Here? (19)
Dawning Is The Day (5)	Higher And Higher (4)	Late Lament (8,18)	Once Is Enough (17)	**Steppin' In A Slide Zone** (10) **39**	When You're A Free Man (7)
Day Begins (1)	Hole In The World (12)	Lazy Day (3)	One, The (19)		Wherever You Are (19)
Day We Meet Again (10)	Hope And Pray (17)	Lean On Me (Tonight) (17,18)	One More Time To Live (6)	**Story In Your Eyes** (6,8,16,20) **23**	Word, The (2,8)
Dear Diary (3,8)	House Of Four Doors (Part 1 & 2) (2)	Legend Of A Mind (2,8,9,20)	One Step Into The Light (10)		Words You Say (19,20)
Deep (15)	How Is It (We Are Here) (5)	Long Summer Days (9)	**Other Side Of Life** (14,18) **58**	Strange Times (19)	You And Me (7)
Departure (2)	I Am (12)	Lost In A Lost World (7)	Our Guessing Game (6)	Sun Is Still Shining (4)	You Can Never Go Home (6)
Dr. Livingstone, I Presume (2,9)	I Just Don't Care (14)	Love Don't Come Easy (19)	Out And In (4)	Sunset, The (9)	**Your Wildest Dreams** (14,16,18,20) **9**
Don't You Feel Small (5)	**I Know You're Out There Somewhere** (15,16,18,20) **30**	Love Is On The Run (15)	Painted Smile (11)	Survival (10)	
Dream, The (3,8,9)		Lovely To See You (3,8,18)	Peak Hour (9)	Swallow, The (19)	
Driftwood (10,13) **59**	I Never Thought I'd Live To Be A Hundred (4)	Lunch Break - Peak Hour (1)	Please Think About It (9)	Talkin' Talkin' (14)	
Emily's Song (9)		Magic (17)	Procession (4)	**Talking Out Of Turn** (11) **65**	
English Sunset (19,20)	I Never Thought I'd Live To Be A Million (4)	Meanwhile (11)	**Question** (5,8,13,16,18,20) **21**	To Share Our Love (3)	
Eternity Road (4)		Meet Me Halfway (12)	Reflective Smile (11)	Top Rank Suite (10)	
Evening - The Sun Set: Twilight Time (1)	I'll Be Level With You (10)	Melancholy Man (5,8)	**Ride My See-Saw** (2,8,9,13,16,18,20) **61**	Tortoise And The Hare (5)	
		Minstrel's Song (5)	River Of Endless Love (15)		
		Miracle (15)			

MOOG MACHINE, The   '69

Group is actually synthesizer player Kenny Ascher (born on 10/26/44 in Washington DC).

9/27/69	170	8				Switched-On Rock		[I]	$20	Columbia 9921

Aquarius (medley)	Get Back	Let The Sunshine In (medley)	Weight, The	
59th Street Bridge Song (Feelin' Groovy)	Hey Jude	Spinning Wheel	You Keep Me Hangin' On	
	Jumpin' Jack Flash	Time Of The Season	Yummy Yummy Yummy	

MOON, Keith   '75

Born on 8/23/46 in London. Died of a drug overdose on 9/7/78 (age 32). Drummer of **The Who**.

4/5/75	155	3		©		Two Sides Of The Moon			$50	Track/MCA 2136

Back Door Sally	Don't Worry Baby	Kids Are Alright	One Night Stand	Teenage Idol
Crazy Like A Fox	In My Life	Move Over Ms. L	Solid Gold	Together

MOONGLOWS, The '72

R&B vocal group from Louisville, Kentucky: Harvey Fuqua, Bobby Lester, Alexander Graves and Prentiss Barnes, with Billy Johnson (guitar). Lester died on 10/15/80 (age 50). Johnson died on 4/29/87 (age 63). Inducted into the Rock and Roll Hall of Fame in 2000.

| 8/5/72 | 193 | 4 | | | **The Return Of The Moonglows** .... | | | $20 | RCA Victor 4722 |

Beat Of My Heart
I Was Wrong
I'll Stop Wanting You
Love Is A River
Most Of All
Penny Arcade
Sincerely
Ten Commandments
When I'm With You
You've Chosen Me

MOORE, Bob, and His Orch. '61

Born on 11/30/32 in Nashville. Top session bass player.

| 11/13/61 | 33 | 18 | © | | **Mexico and Other Great Hits!** .... | | [I] | $25 | Monument 4005 |

Blue Tango
Cielito Lindo
Corazon D'Oro
El Picador
La Paloma
Mexicali Rose
Mexico *7*
My Adobe Hacienda
Neuvo Laredo
Ninita Linda
South Of The Border
Vaya Con Dios

MOORE, Chanté '99

Born on 2/17/67 in San Francisco. Female R&B singer.

1/30/93	101	27	●	© 1	**Precious**			$10	Silas 10605
12/3/94	64	12		© 2	**A Love Supreme**			$10	Silas 11157
6/12/99	31	10		© 3	**This Moment Is Mine**			$10	Silas 11674
12/2/00	50	11		© 4	**Exposed**			$10	Silas 112377

Am I Losing You? (2)
As If We Never Met (1)
Because You're Mine (1)
Better Than Making Love (4)
Bitter (4)
Blooming Flower (3)
Candlelight & You (1)
Chanté's Got A Man (3) *10*
Easy (3)
Everything We Want (4)
Finding My Way Back To You (1)
Free/Sail On (2)
Go Ahead With All That (4)
Heartbeat (3)
I Cry To Myself (3)
I See You In A Different Light (3)
I Started Crying (3)
I Wanna Love (Like That Again) (1)
I Want To Thank You (2)
I'm Keeping You (4)
I'm What You Need (4)
I've Got The Love (3)
If I Gave Love (3)
In My Life (3)
It's Alright (1)
Listen To My Song (1)
Love And The Woman (3)
Love's Still Alright (4)
Love's Taken Over (1) *86*
Man (4)
Mood (2)
My Special Perfect One (2)
Old School Lovin' (3)
Precious (1)
Searchin' (2)
Sexy Thang (1)
Soul Dance (3)
Straight Up (4) *83*
Take Care Of Me (4)
Thank You For Loving Me (2)
This Moment Is Mine (3)
This Time (2)
Thou Shalt Not (2)
Train Of Thought (4)
When It Comes To Me (4)
Who Do I Turn To (4)
You Can't Leave Me (4)
Your Love's Supreme (2)

MOORE, Dorothy '76

Born on 10/13/47 in Jackson, Mississippi. R&B singer.

| 5/29/76 | 29 | 23 | © 1 | **Misty Blue** .... | | | $15 | Malaco 6351 |
| 8/6/77 | 120 | 13 | 2 | **Dorothy Moore** .... | | | $15 | Malaco 6353 |

Ain't That A Mother's Luck (1)
Daddy's Eyes (1)
Dark End Of The Street (1)
Enough Woman Left (To Be Your Lady) (1)
For Old Time's Sake (1)
Funny How Time Slips Away (1) *58*
I Believe You (2) *27*
I Don't Want To Be With Nobody But You (1)
It's So Good (1)
Laugh It Off (1)
Let The Music Play (2)
Love Me (2)
Loving You Is Just An Old Habit (2)
Make It Soon (2)
Misty Blue (1) *3*
1-2-3 (You And Me) (2)
Only Time You Ever Say You Love Me (1)
Too Blind To See (2)
Too Much Love (1)
With Pen In Hand (2)

MOORE, Gary '91

Born on 4/4/52 in Belfast, Ireland. Guitarist with **Thin Lizzy**.

4/23/83	149	13	© 1	**Corridors Of Power**			$12	Mirage 90077
6/9/84	172	5	© 2	**Victims Of The Future**			$12	Mirage 90154
3/15/86	146	7	© 3	**Run For Cover**			$12	Mirage 90482
5/16/87	139	15	© 4	**Wild Frontier**			$10	Virgin 90588
3/25/89	114	9	© 5	**After The War**			$10	Virgin 91066
7/14/90+	83	42	●	© 6	**Still Got The Blues**			$10	Charisma 91369
3/28/92	145	8	© 7	**After Hours**			$10	Charisma 91825

After The War (5)
All Messed Up (3)
All Your Love (6)
Always Gonna' Love You (1)
As The Years Go Passing By (6)
Blood Of Emeralds (5)
Blues Is Alright (7)
Cold Day In Hell (7)
Cold Hearted (1)
Devil In Her Heart (2)
Don't Take Me For A Loser (1)
Don't You Lie To Me (I Get Evil) (7)
Empty Rooms (2,3)
End Of The World (1)
Falling In Love With You (1)
Friday On My Mind (4)
Gonna' Break My Heart Again (1)
Hold On To Love (2)
Hurt Inside (7)
I Can't Wait Until Tomorrow (1)
Johnny Boy (4)
Jumpin' At Shadows (7)
Key To Love (7)
King Of The Blues (6)
Law Of The Jungle (2)
Led Clones (5)
Listen To Your Heartbeat (3)
Livin' On Dreams (5)
Loner, The (4)
Midnight Blues (6)
Military Man (3)
Moving On (6)
Murder In The Skies (2)
Nothing To Lose (3)
Nothing's The Same (7)
Oh Pretty Woman (6)
Once In A Lifetime (3)
Only Fool In Town (7)
Out In The Fields (3)
Over The Hills And Far Away (4)
Reach For The Sky (3)
Ready For Love (5)
Rockin' Every Night (7)
Run For Cover (3)
Running From The Storm (5)
Separate Ways (7)
Shapes Of Things (2)
Since I Met You Baby (7)
Speak For Yourself (5)
Still Got The Blues (6) *97*
Stop Messin' Around (7)
Story Of The Blues (7)
Strangers In The Darkness (4)
Take A Little Time (4)
Teenage Idol (2)
Texas Strut (7)
That Kind Of Woman (6)
This Thing Called Love (5)
Thunder Rising (4)
Too Tired (7)
Victims Of The Future (2)
Walking By Myself (6)
Wild Frontier (4)
Wishing Well (1)

MOORE, Mandy '00

Born Amanda Moore on 4/10/84 in Nashua, New Hampshire. Pop singer.

| 12/25/99+ | 31 | 23 | ▲ | © 1 | **So Real** .... | | | $10 | 550 Music 69917 |
| 5/27/00 | 21 | 28 | ● | © 2 | **I Wanna Be With You** .... | | | $10 | 550 Music 62195 |

Candy (1,2) *41*
Everything My Heart Desires (2)
I Like It (1,2)
I Wanna Be With You (2) *24*
Let Me Be The One (1)
Lock Me In Your Heart (1,2)
Love Shot (1)
Love You For Always (1)
Not Too Young (1)
Quit Breaking My Heart (1)
So Real (1,2)
Walk Me Home (1,2)
Want You Back (2)
Way To My Heart (2)
What You Want (1)
Your Face (2)

MOORE, Melba '86

Born Melba Hill on 10/29/45 in New York City. R&B singer/actress. Appeared in several movies and Broadway shows.

2/20/71	157	5	1	**Look What You're Doing To The Man**			$15	Mercury 61321
7/5/75	176	4	2	**Peach Melba**			$12	Buddah 5629
5/8/76	145	5	© 3	**This Is It**			$12	Buddah 5657
12/25/76+	177	7	4	**Melba**			$12	Buddah 5677
11/18/78+	114	18	5	**Melba**			$12	Epic 35507
11/13/82+	152	19	6	**The Other Side Of The Rainbow**			$10	Capitol 12243
12/24/83+	147	14	7	**Never Say Never**			$10	Capitol 12305
4/27/85	130	10	8	**Read My Lips**			$10	Capitol 12382
8/23/86+	91	29	9	**A Lot Of Love**			$10	Capitol 12471

Ain't No Love Lost (4)
Blood Red Roses (3)
Brand New (3)
Don't Go Away (6,9)
Dreams (8)
Falling (9)
Free (3)
Get Into My Mind (2)
Good Love Makes Everything Alright (4)
Got To Have Your Love (7)
Greatest Feeling (4)
Green Birds Fly (2)
Happy (5)
He Ain't Heavy He's My Brother (1)
Heaven Help Us All (1)
How's Love Been Treatin' You (6)
(I Need) Someone (4)
I Promise To Love You (5)
I'm His Lady (2)
I Can't Believe It (It's Over) (4)
I Can't Help Myself (Sugar Pie-Honey Bunch) (6)
If I Had A Million (1)
If I Lose (2)
If You Can Believe (2)
It's Been So Long (9)
It's Hard Not To Like You (5)
It's Really Love (7)
Keepin' My Lover Satisfied (7)
King Of My Heart (8)
Knack For Me (6)

DEBUT	PEAK	WKS	RIAA	CD	ARTIST — Album Title	Catalog	Sym	$	Label & Number

MOORE, Melba — Cont'd

Lean On Me (3,7)
Little Bit More (9)
Livin' For Your Love (7)
Long And Winding Road (4)
Look What You're Doing To The Man (1)
Love Can Be Good To You (2)
Love Me Right (7)
Love Of A Lifetime (8)
Love The One I'm With (A Lot Of Love) (9)

Love's Comin' At Ya (6)
Lovin' Touch (7)
Loving You Comes So Easy (1)
Make Me Believe In You (3)
Mighty Clouds Of Joy (4)
Million Years Before This Time (2)
Mind Over Matter (8)
Mind Up Tonight (6)
Must Be Dues (2)
My Soul Is Satisfied (2)

Natural Part Of Everything (2)
Never Say Never (7)
One Less Morning (3)
Other Side Of The Rainbow (6)
Patience Is Rewarded (1)
Pick Me Up, I'll Dance (5)
Play Boy Scout (3)
Read My Lips (8)
Searchin' For A Dream (1)
So Many Mountains (4)
Stay (1)

Stay Awhile (3)
Sunshine Superman (2)
There I Go Falling In Love Again (9)
There's No Other Like You (5)
This Is It (3) 91
Thrill Is Gone (From Yesterday's Kiss) (1)
To Those Who Wait (8)
Together Forever (5)
Twenty Five Miles (medley) (1)

Underlove (6)
Walk A Mile In My Shoes (medley) (1)
Way You Make Me Feel (4)
When We Touch (It's Like Fire) (9)
When You Love Me Like This (8)
Where Did You Ever Go (5)
Winner (8)

You Got The Power (To Make Me Happy) (1)
You Stepped Into My Life (5) 47
You Trip Me Out (9)

MOORE, Tim '74
Born in New York City. Pop singer/songwriter/guitarist/keyboardist.

| 10/12/74 | 119 | 9 | © | 1 | **Tim Moore** .... | | | $12 | Asylum 1019 |
| 8/2/75 | 181 | 3 | | 2 | **Behind The Eyes** .... | | | $12 | Asylum 1042 |

Aviation Man (1)
Bye Bye Man (2)
Charmer (1) 91

Fool Like You (1) 93
For The Minute (2)
High Feeling (1)
I Can Almost See The Light (1)

(I Think I Wanna) Possess You (2)
I'll Be Your Time (1)
If Somebody Needs It (2)

Kaptain Kidd (2)
Lay Down A Line To Me (2)
Love Enough (1)
Night We First Sailed Away (2)

Now I See (2)
Rock And Roll Love Letter (2)
Second Avenue (1) 58
Sister Lilac (1)

Sweet Navel Lightning (2)
When You Close Your Eyes (1)

MOORE, Vinnie '88
Born in 1965 in Newcastle, Delaware. Hard-rock guitarist.

| 6/18/88 | 147 | 7 | © | | **Time Odyssey** .... | | [I] | $10 | Squawk 834634 |

April Sky
As Time Slips By

Beyond The Door
Into The Future

Message In A Dream
Morning Star

Pieces Of A Picture
Race With Destiny

Tempest, The
While My Guitar Gently Weeps

M.O.P. '00
Rap duo from Brooklyn, New York: Lil' Fame and Billy Danzenie. M.O.P.: Mashed Out Posse.

11/9/96	94	2	©	1	**Firing Squad**			$10	Relativity 1555
8/29/98	80	4	©	2	**First Family 4 Life**			$10	Relativity 1618
10/28/00	25	5	©	3	**Warriorz**			$10	Loud 1778

Ante Up (Robbing-Hoodz Theory) (3)
Anticipation (1)
Background Niggaz (3)
Blood Sweat And Tears (2)
Born 2 Kill (1)
Breakin' The Rules (2)
Brooklyn/Jersey Get Wild (2)
Brownsville (1)

Calm Down (3)
Cold As Ice (3)
Dead & Gone (1)
Down 4 Whateva (2)
Downtown Swinga ('96) (1)
Downtown Swinga '98 (2)
Everyday (3)
Face Off (3)

Facing Off (2)
Firing Squad (1)
Fly Nigga Hill Figga (2)
Follow Instructions (3)
Foundation (3)
4 Alarm Blaze (2)
G-Building (3)
Handle Ur Bizness (2)

Home Sweet Home (3)
I Luv (2)
Illside Of Town (1)
Lifestyles Of A Ghetto Child (1)
My Kinda Nigga Part II (2)
New Jack City (1)
New York Salute (2)
Nig-Gotiate (3)

Nothin 2 Lose (1)
Old Timerz (1)
On The Front Line (3)
Operation Lockdown (3)
Power (3)
Revolution (1)
Ride With Us (2)
Roll Call (3)

Salute (1)
Salute Part II (2)
Stick To Ya Gunz (1)
Warriorz (3)
Welcome To Brownsville (3)
What The Future Holds (2)
World Famous (1)

MORALES, Michael '89
Born on 4/25/63 in San Antonio, Texas. Pop singer.

| 6/17/89 | 113 | 20 | © | | **Michael Morales** .... | | | $10 | Wing 835810 |

Cry, Cry, Cry
Eighteen
Hey Lori!

I Don't Know 81
I Don't Want You No More

I Only Want To Look In Your Eyes
Romeo

Way To Go Baby
What I Like About You 28

Who Do You Give Your Love To? 15

MORAZ, Patrick '76
Born on 6/24/48 in Morges, Switzerland. Keyboardist for **Yes** (1974-78) and **The Moody Blues** (1978-92).

| 6/5/76 | 132 | 5 | | | **i** .... | | | $12 | Atlantic 18175 |

Best Years Of Our Lives
Cachaca (Baiao)
Dancing Now

Descent
Impact
Impressions (The Dream)

Incantation-Procession
Indoors
Intermezzo

Like A Child In Disguise
Rise And Fall
Storm, The

Symphony In The Space
Warmer Hands

MORCHEEBA '00
Trip-hop trio from Hythe, Kent, England: brothers Ross and Paul Godfrey, with Skye Edwards.

| 8/19/00 | 113 | 5 | © | | **Fragments Of Freedom** .... | | | $10 | Sire 31137 |

Be Yourself
Coming Down Gently

Fragments Of Freedom
Good Girl Down

In The Hands Of The Gods
Let It Go

Love Is Rare
Love Sweet Love

Rome Wasn't Built In A Day
Shallow End

Well Deserved Break
World Looking In

MORGAN, Jane '57
Born Jane Currier in 1920 in Boston; raised in Florida. Pop singer.

| 12/9/57 | 13 | 3 | | 1 | **Fascination** .... | | | $30 | Kapp 1066 |

JANE MORGAN and THE TROUBADORS

| 11/26/66 | 134 | 4 | © | 2 | **Fresh Flavor** .... | | | $20 | Epic 26211 |

Affair To Remember (1)
Around The World (1)
Daydream (2)
Elusive Butterfly (2)
Fascination (1) 7

Good Lovin' (2)
Intermezzo (1)
It's Not For Me To Say (1)
Message To Michael (2)
Midnight In Athens (1)

Monday, Monday (2)
My Heart Reminds Me (And That Reminds Me) (1)
River Seine (1)
Sounds Of Silence (2)

Speak Low (1)
Stars In My Eyes (1)
Strangers In The Night (2)
These Boots Are Made For Walkin' (2)

Two Different Worlds (1) 41
When A Woman Loves A Man (2)
(You're My) Soul And Inspiration (2)

Yours Is My Heart Alone (1)

MORGAN, Lee '65
Born on 7/10/38 in Philadelphia. Fatally shot on 2/19/72 (age 33). Jazz trumpeter.

10/10/64+	25	30	©	1	**The Sidewinder**		[I]	$25	Blue Note 84157
11/26/66	143	3	©	2	**Search For The New Land**		[I]	$25	Blue Note 84169
3/1/69	190	3	©	3	**Caramba!**		[I]	$25	Blue Note 84289

Boy, What A Night (1)
Caramba (3)
Cunning Lee (3)

Gary's Notebook (1)
Helen's Ritual (3)
Hocus-Pocus (1)

Joker, The (2)
Melancholee (2)
Morgan The Pirate (2)

Mr. Kenyatta (2)
Search For The New Land (2)
Sidewinder, Part 1 (1) 81

Soulita (3)
Suicide City (3)
Totem Pole (1)

★410★ **MORGAN, Lorrie** '95

Born Loretta Lynn Morgan on 6/27/59 in Nashville. Country singer. Daughter of country singer George Morgan. Married to **Keith Whitley** from 1986-89 (his death). Married to singer Jon Randall from 1996-99.

1)Greatest Hits 2)War Paint 3)Something In Red

1/27/90	117	33	▲	©	1 Leave The Light On..			$10	RCA 9594
5/25/91+	53	95	▲	©	2 Something In Red...			$10	RCA 3021
10/31/92	65	65	▲	©	3 Watch Me..			$10	BNA 66047
12/11/93	115	5		©	4 Merry Christmas From London		[X]	$10	BNA 66282
					Christmas chart: 22/'93				
5/28/94	48	21	●	©	5 War Paint..			$10	BNA 66379
7/15/95	46	37	▲²	©	6 Greatest Hits		[G]	$10	BNA 66508
6/22/96	62	20	●	©	7 Greater Need...			$10	BNA 66847
8/30/97	98	11	●	©	8 Shakin' Things Up..			$10	BNA 67499
5/1/99	116	5		©	9 My Heart			$10	BNA 67763
5/5/01	114	3		©	10 I Finally Found Someone...			$10	RCA 67004

LORRIE MORGAN & SAMMY KERSHAW

Autumn's Not That Cold (2)
Ave Maria (4)
Back Among The Living (7)
Back In Your Arms Again (6)
Be My Reason (10)
Behind His Last Goodbye (4)
Best Woman Wins (2)
Between Midnight And Tomorrow (9)
Big Time (10)
Blue Snowfall (4)
By My Side (7)
Christmas Festival (Medley) (4)
Crazy From The Heat (8)
Dear Me (1,6)
Don't Stop In My World (7)
Don't Touch Me (5)
Eight Days A Week (1)
Evening Up The Odds (5)
Except For Monday (2,6)
Exit 99 (5)

Faithfully (4)
Far Side Of The Bed (1)
Finishing Touch (8)
Five Minutes (1,6)
From Our House To Yours (3)
Go Away (8) *85*
Gonna Leave The Light On (1)
Good As I Was To You (7)
Good Year For The Roses (5)
Greater Need (7)
Half Enough (3)
Hand Over Your Heart (2)
Hard Part Was Easy (5)
He Drinks Tequila (10)
He Talks To Me (1)
Heart Over Mind (5)
Here I Go Again (9)
I Can Buy My Own Roses (7)
I Can't Think Of Anything But You (10)
I Did (9)

I Didn't Know My Own Strength (6)
I Finally Found Someone (10)
I Guess You Had To Be There (3)
I Just Might Be (7)
I Must Be Gettin' Older (10)
I'll Take The Memories (1)
I'm Not That Easy To Forget (8)
I've Enjoyed As Much Of This As I Can Stand (8)
If I Didn't Love You (1)
If You Came Back From Heaven (5)
In A Perfect World (8)
In Tears (2)
It's A Heartache (3)
It's Too Late (To Love Me Now) (1)
Let It Snow! Let It Snow! (4)
Little Snow Girl (4)

Maybe Not Tonight (9) *86*
My Favorite Things (4)
My Heart (9)
My Night To Howl (5)
Never Been Good At Letting Go (9)
O Holy Night (4)
On This Bed (9)
1-800 Use To Be (5)
One Of Those Nights Tonight (8)
Only Thing That Looks Good On Me Is You (9)
Out Of Your Shoes (1)
Picture Of Me (Without You) (2,6)
Reading My Heart (7)
Sad City (10)
Shakin' Things Up (8)
She Walked Beside The Wagon (7)

She's Takin' Him Back Again (3)
Sleigh Ride (4)
Soldier Of Love (7)
Someone To Call Me Darling (3)
Something In Red (2,6)
Standing Tall (4)
Steppin' Stones (7)
Strong Enough To Cry (9)
Sugar (10)
Tears On My Pillow (2)
That's Where I'll Be (10)
Things We Do (9)
3 Seconds (10)
'Til A Tear Becomes A Rose (6)
Toyland (4)
Trainwreck Of Emotion (1)
29 Again (10)
Up On Santa Claus Mountain (4)

War Paint (5)
Watch Me (3,6)
We Both Walk (2)
What A Wonderful World (10)
What Part Of No (3,6)
Where Does That Leave Me (9)
Will You Love Me Tomorrow (8)
You Can't Take That (8)
You Leave Me Like This (3)
You'd Think He'd Know Me Better (8)

MORGAN, Meli'sa '86

Born in Queens, New York. Female R&B singer.

2/8/86	41	36		©	1 Do Me Baby..			$10	Capitol 12434
12/19/87+	108	19		©	2 Good Love...			$10	Capitol 46943

Do Me Baby (1) *46*
Do You Still Love Me? (1)
Fool's Paradise (1)

Getting To Know You Better (1)
Good Love (2)
Heart Breaking Decision (1)

Here Comes The Night (2)
I Still Think About You (2)
I'll Give It When I Want It (1)

I'll Love No More (2)
If You Can Do It: I Can Too!! (2)
Just For Your Touch (2)

Lies (1)
Love Changes (2)
Now Or Never (1)

Think It Over (2)
You're All I Got (2)

MORISSETTE, Alanis '95

Born on 6/1/74 in Ottawa, Canada. Female pop-rock singer/songwriter. At age 12, acted on the Nickelodeon cable-TV kids series *You Can't Do That On Television*.

7/1/95	❶¹²	113	▲¹⁶	©	1 Jagged Little Pill	C:#2¹/101		$10	Maverick 45901
					1995 Grammy winner: Album of the Year				
11/21/98	❶²	28	▲³	©	2 Supposed Former Infatuation Junkie.............................			$10	Maverick 47094
12/11/99	63	14	●	©	3 MTV Unplugged		[L]	$10	Maverick 47589

All I Really Want (1)
Are You Still Mad (2)
Baba (2)
Can't Not (2)
Couch, The (2)
Forgiven (1)

Front Row (2)
Hand In My Pocket (1)
Head Over Feet (1,3)
Heart Of The House (2)
I Was Hoping (2,3)
Ironic (1,3) *4*

Joining You (2,3)
King Of Pain (3)
Mary Jane (1)
No Pressure Over Cappuccino (3)
Not The Doctor (1)

One (2)
Perfect (1)
Princes Familiar (3)
Right Through You (1)
So Pure (2)
Sympathetic Character (2)

Thank U (2) *17*
That I Would Be Good (2,3)
These R The Thoughts (3)
UR (2)
Uninvited (3)
Unsent (2) *58*

Wake Up (1)
Would Not Come (2)
You Learn (1,3) *6*
You Oughta Know (1,3) *flip*
Your Congratulations (2)

MORMON TABERNACLE CHOIR, The '59

Popular 375-voice choir directed by Richard Condie (died on 12/22/85). Jerold Ottley took over after Condie's death.

1)The Lord's Prayer 2)The Spirit Of Christmas 3)Songs Of The North & South 1861-1865

10/19/59+	❶¹	80	●	©	1 The Lord's Prayer			$20	Columbia 6068
12/28/59+	5	2			2 The Spirit Of Christmas..		[X]	$20	Columbia 6100
					Christmas charts: 26/'63, 26/'65, 60/'67				
10/30/61	47	1			3 Songs Of The North & South 1861-1865			$20	Columbia 6259
12/25/61+	118	3			4 The Spirit Of Christmas..		[X-R]	$20	Columbia 6100
1/5/63	49	8		©	5 The Lord's Prayer, Volume II...			$20	Columbia 6367
11/30/63	6ˣ	7	●		6 The Mormon Tabernacle Choir sings Christmas Carols		[X]	$20	Columbia 5222
					first released in 1957; Christmas charts: 6/'63, 48/'67				
12/21/63+	8ˣ	12	●		7 The Joy of Christmas		[X]	$25	Columbia 5899 / 6499
					LEONARD BERNSTEIN/NEW YORK PHILHARMONIC/THE MORMON TABERNACLE CHOIR				
					Christmas charts: 12/'63, 32/'64, 8/'65, 62/'66, 106/'67, 28/'68, 20/'70				
12/12/64	22ˣ	3			8 Christmas with the Mormon Tabernacle Organ And Chimes		[X-I]	$20	Columbia 6037 / 6637
					Alexander Schreiner (organist)				
12/18/65+	3ˣ	11			9 Handel: Messiah		[X]	$25	Columbia 263 / 607 [2]
					THE PHILADELPHIA ORCHESTRA/EUGENE ORMANDY/THE MORMON TABERNACLE CHOIR				
					soloists: Eileen Farrell, Martha Lipton, Davis Cunningham, and William Warfield; first released in 1959; Christmas charts: 21/'65, 3/'69, 8/'70, 12/'71, 5/'72				
12/18/65	30ˣ	4			10 Christmas Carols Around The World...............................		[X]	$20	Columbia 5684 / 6284
					first released in 1961; Christmas charts: 30/'65, 48/'66				
12/21/91	29ˣ	1		©	11 Silent Night/The Greatest Hits of Christmas		[X]	$10	CBS Master. 37206
					with the Columbia Brass and Percussion Ensemble; first released in 1981				

MORMON TABERNACLE CHOIR, The — Cont'd

| 12/11/93 | 171 | 3 | © 12 | **Christmas With The Mormon Tabernacle Choir** | ....C:#14/17 | [X] | $10 | LaserLight 12198 |

Christmas charts: 19/'94, 25/'95, 21/'96

Adeste Fideles (8)
(also see: O Come, All Ye Faithful)
Angel's Song (10)
Angels We Have Heard On High (12)
Animal Carol (7)
Arise, Shine, For Thy Light Is Come (4)
As Lately We Watched (10)
Aura Lee (3)
Away In A Manger (6,7,8)
Battle Cry Of Freedom (3)
Battle Hymn Of The Republic (1,3) **13**
Beautiful Saviour (6)
Bethlehem Night (2,4)
Blessed Are They That Mourn (1)
Bonnie Blue Flag (3)
Boy Is Born (6)
Break Forth, O Beauteous Heavenly Light (2,4)
Brother John's Noel (10)
Carol Of The Bells (2,4,7,8,11)

Carol Of The Birds (12)
Carol Of The Drum (Little Drummer Boy) (11)
Christians, Awake (8)
Christmas Day (2,4,10)
Come, Come Ye Saints (1)
Come Sweet Death (5)
Coventry Carol (2,4)
David's Lamentation (1)
Deck The Hall With Boughs Of Holly (7,8)
Dixie (3)
Far, Far Away On Judea's Plains (6)
First Nowell (8,12)
For Christ Is Born (2,4)
For Unto Us A Child Is Born (1,11)
Give Unto The Meek (5)
Glory To God In The Highest (2,4)
God Rest Ye Merry, Gentlemen (7,8)
Good King Wenceslas (8)
Hallelujah Amen (5)

Hallelujah Chorus (11)
Hark! The Herald Angels Sing (2,4,8,12)
He's Gone Away (3)
Heavenly Father! (Ave Maria) (5)
Here We Come A-Caroling (10)
Holy City (6)
Holy, Holy, Holy (1)
How Great The Wisdom And The Love (1)
I Heard The Bells (6,8)
It Came Upon The Midnight Clear (8,10)
Jingle Bells (12)
Joseph Dearest, Joseph Mine (7)
Joy To The World (6,7,8,11,12)
Kathleen Mavourneen (3)
La Virgen Lava Panales (7)
Lippai (medley) (12)
Little Drummer Boy ..see: Carol Of The Drum
Lo, How A Rose E'er Blooming (2,4)

Londonderry Air (1)
Lord, Hear Our Prayer (5)
Lord's Prayer (1,5)
Lorena (3)
Lullay My Liking (7)
Messiah (9)
Mighty Fortress Is Our God (5)
My Shepherd Will Supply My Need (5)
O Be Joyful (5)
O Come, All Ye Faithful (2,4,7,11,12)
(also see: Adeste Fideles)
O Come, O Come, Emmanuel (6,10)
O Holy Night (6,8,12)
O Little One Sweet (8)
O Little Town Of Bethlehem (2,4,7,8,11,12)
O, My Father (1)
O Rejoice, Ye Christians, Loudly (10)
O Tannenbaum (11,12)
O Thou Joyful Day (8)
Old Things Are Done Away (5)

Once In Royal David's City (7)
148th Psalm (1)
Patapan (7)
Prayer from "Hansel And Gretel" (10)
See The Radiant Sky Above (10)
Shepherds' Story (2,4)
Silent Night, Holy Night (2,4,6,7,8,11,12)
Silver Bells (11)
Snow Lay On The Ground (2,4)
Sometimes I Feel Like A Motherless Child (3)
Song Of The Bagpipers (10)
Sweet Evelina (3)
Tell Us, Shepherd Maids (2,4,6)
Tenting On The Old Camp Ground (3)
There Shall A Star From Jacob (6)
This Little Babe (10)
Three Kings (2,4)
Tramp, Tramp, Tramp (3)
Twelfth Night Song (7)

Twelve Days Of Christmas (7)
Unfold, Ye Portals (5)
Up And Awake Thee, Peter Lad! (10)
Upon The Mountain (medley) (7)
Watts Nativity Carol (6)
We Three Kings Of Orient Are (8,10)
What Child Is This? (6)
What Child Is This (Greensleeves) (8)
What Perfume This? O Shepherds, Say! (2,4,8,10)
When Jesus Was A Little Child (6)
When Johnny Comes Marching Home (3)
While Shepherds Watched Their Flocks (2,4)
White Christmas (11)
Winter Wonderland (11)

MORODER, Giorgio '77

Born on 4/26/40 in Ortisel, Italy. Electronic composer/conductor/producer.

| 10/29/77 | 130 | 7 | © | **From Here To Eternity** | .... | | $12 | Casablanca 7065 |

GIORGIO

Faster Than The Speed Of Love

First Hand Experience In Second Hand Love
From Here To Eternity

I'm Left, You're Right, She's Gone
Lost Angeles

Too Hot To Handle
Utopia - Me Giorgio

MORPHINE '97

Rock trio from Boston: Mark Sandman (vocals, bass), Dana Colley (sax) and Billy Conway (drums). Both Sandman and Conway were members of **Treat Her Right**. Sandman died of a heart attack on 7/4/99 (age 46).

4/8/95	101	4	© 1	**Yes**	....		$10	Rykodisc 10320
3/29/97	67	6	© 2	**Like Swimming**	....		$10	DreamWorks 50009
2/19/00	137	4	© 3	**The Night**	....		$10	DreamWorks 50056

All Your Way (1)
Early To Bed (2)
Eleven O'Clock (2)
Empty Box (2)
Free Love (1)
French Fries w/Pepper (2)

Gone For Good (1)
Good Woman Is Hard To Find (3)
Hanging On A Curtain (2)
Honey White (1)
I Had My Chance (1)
I Know You (Pt. III) (2)

I'm Yours, You're Mine (3)
Jury, The (1)
Like A Mirror (3)
Like Swimming (2)
Lilah (2)
Murder For The Money (2)
Night, The (3)

Potion (3)
Radar (1)
Rope On Fire (3)
Scratch (1)
Sharks (1)
Slow Numbers (3)
So Many Ways (3)

Souvenir (3)
Super Sex (1)
Swing It Low (2)
Take Me With You (3)
Top Floor, Bottom Buzzer (3)
Way We Met (3)
Whisper (1)

Wishing Well (2)
Yes (1)

MORRIS, Gary '83

Born on 12/7/48 in Ft. Worth, Texas. Country singer/songwriter/guitarist.

| 10/15/83 | 174 | 8 | ● © | **Why Lady Why** | .... | | $10 | Warner 23738 |

Again
I Can Feel The Fire Going Out

I'd Be The First To Fall In Love Again
Love She Found In Me

Mama You Can't Give Me No Whippin'
Runaway Hearts

Velvet Chains
Way I Love You Tonight
Why Lady Why

Wind Beneath My Wings

MORRISON, Mark '97

Born in 1973 in Hanover, Germany; raised in Leicester, England. R&B singer.

| 3/29/97 | 76 | 24 | © | **Return Of The Mack** | .... | | $10 | Atlantic 82963 |

Candy
Crazy

Get High With Me
Horny

I Like
Let's Get Down

Moan And Groan 76
Return Of The Mack 2

Tears For You
Trippin'

MORRISON, Van ★50★ '72

Born George Ivan Morrison on 8/31/45 in Belfast, Ireland. Pop-rock singer/songwriter. Leader of **Them**. Inducted into the Rock and Roll Hall of Fame in 1993.

1)Saint Dominic's Preview 2)Tupelo Honey 3)Hard Nose The Highway 4)Wavelength 5)Back On Top

10/7/67	182	7	© 1	**Blowin' Your Mind!**	....		$50	Bang 218
3/14/70	29	22	▲³ © 2	**Moondance**	....		$20	Warner 1835
12/26/70+	32	17	© 3	**His Band And The Street Choir**	....		$20	Warner 1884
10/30/71	27	24	● © 4	**Tupelo Honey**	....		$20	Warner 1950
8/5/72	15	28	© 5	**Saint Dominic's Preview**	....		$20	Warner 2633
8/11/73	27	19	© 6	**Hard Nose The Highway**	....		$20	Warner 2712
1/26/74	181	4	© 7	**T.B. Sheets**	....	[E]	$20	Bang 400
3/16/74	53	17	© 8	**It's Too Late To Stop Now**	....	[L]	$20	Warner 2760 [2]
11/9/74	53	10	© 9	**Veedon Fleece**	....		$15	Warner 2805
5/7/77	43	11	© 10	**A Period Of Transition**	....		$15	Warner 2987
10/14/78	28	23	© 11	**Wavelength**	....		$15	Warner 3212
9/8/79	43	13	© 12	**Into The Music**	....		$15	Warner 3390
9/20/80	73	10	© 13	**Common One**	....		$15	Warner 3462
3/6/82	44	11	© 14	**Beautiful Vision**	....		$15	Warner 3652

DEBUT	PEAK	WKS	RIAA	CD	ARTIST — Album Title	Catalog	Sym	$	Label & Number
					MORRISON, Van — Cont'd				
4/9/83	116	8		© 15	Inarticulate Speech Of The Heart			$15	Warner 23802
3/9/85	61	17		© 16	A Sense Of Wonder			$12	Mercury 822895
8/16/86	70	13		© 17	No Guru, no Method, no Teacher			$12	Mercury 830077
10/10/87	90	22		© 18	Poetic Champions Compose			$12	Mercury 832585
7/23/88	102	13		© 19	Irish Heartbeat			$10	Mercury 834496
					VAN MORRISON & THE CHIEFTAINS				
7/1/89	91	39	●	© 20	Avalon Sunset			$10	Mercury 839262
5/26/90	41	242	▲³	© 21	The Best Of Van Morrison	C:#3/255	[G]	$10	Mercury 841970
11/24/90+	62	25		© 22	Enlightenment			$10	Mercury 847100
10/12/91	99	17	●	© 23	Hymns To The Silence			$15	Polydor 849026 [2]
3/27/93	176	3		© 24	The Best Of Van Morrison Volume Two		[G]	$10	Polydor 517760
6/26/93	29	16		© 25	Too Long In Exile			$10	Polydor 519219
6/4/94	125	4		© 26	A Night In San Francisco		[L]	$15	Polydor 521290 [2]
					recorded on 12/18/93 at The Masonic Auditorium in San Francisco				
7/8/95	33	16		© 27	Days Like This			$10	Polydor 527307
1/27/96	55	11		© 28	How Long Has This Been Going On		[L]	$10	Verve 529136
					VAN MORRISON with Georgie Fame & Friends				
					recorded on 5/3/95 at Ronnie Scott's Club in London				
3/22/97	32	16		© 29	The Healing Game			$10	Polydor 537101
7/4/98	87	4		© 30	The Philosopher's Stone		[E]	$15	Polydor 531789 [2]
					previously unreleased tracks recorded from 1971-1988				
3/27/99	28	20	●	© 31	Back On Top			$10	Pointblank 47148
10/21/00	161	2		© 32	You Win Again			$10	Pointblank 50258
					VAN MORRISON & LINDA GAIL LEWIS				

Across The Bridge Where Angels Dwell (14)
Ain't Nothin' You Can Do (8)
Ain't That Loving You Baby (26)
Alan Watts Blues (18)
All Saint's Day (23, 28)
Allegheny (medley) (26)
Allow Me (18)
Almost Independence Day (5)
Ancient Highway (27)
Ancient Of Days (16)
And It Stoned Me (2,21)
And The Healing Has Begun (12)
Angeliou (12)
Aryan Mist (14)
Autumn Song (6)
Avalon Of The Heart (22)
Baby Please Don't Go (21)
Baby (You Got What It Takes) (32)
Back On Top (31)
Ball & Chain (25)
Be-Bop-A-Lula (medley) (26)
Be Thou My Vision (23)
Beautiful Obsession (medley) (11)
Beautiful Vision (14,26)
Before The World Was Made (25)
Beside You (7)
Big Time Operators (25)
Blue Money (3) **23**
Blues In The Night (28)
Boffyflow And Spike (16)
Boogie Chillen (32)
Brand New Day (2)
Bright Side Of The Road (12,21,30)
Bring It On Home To Me (8)
Brown Eyed Girl (1,7,21) **10**
Bulbs (9)
Burning Ground (29)
By His Grace (23)
Cadillac (32)
Call Me Up In Dreamland (3) **95**
Caravan (2,8)
Carrickfergus (19)
Carrying A Torch (23)
Celtic Excavation (18)
Celtic Ray (14,19)
Celtic Swing (15)
Centerpiece (28)
Checkin' It Out (11)
Cleaning Windows (14,21)
Close Enough For Jazz (25)
Cold Wind In August (10)
Come Here My Love (9)
Come Running (2) **39**
Comfort You (9)
Coney Island (20,24)
Connswater (15)
Contacting My Angel (20)
Contemplation Rose (30)
Country Fair (9)
Crazy Arms (32)

Crazy Face (3)
Crazy Jane On God (30)
Crazy Love (2)
Cry For Home (15)
Cul De Sac (9)
Cypress Avenue (8)
Daring Night (20)
Days Like This (27)
Did Ye Get Healed? (18,21,26)
Domino (3,8,21) **9**
Don't Look Back (24)
Don't Worry About A Thing (28)
Don't Worry About Tomorrow (30)
Down The Line (medley) (26)
Drumshanbo Hustle (30)
Dweller On The Threshold (14,21)
Early In The Morning (medley) (26)
Eternal Kansas City (19)
Evening Meditation (16,24)
Everyone (2)
Fair Play (9)
Family Affair (medley) (26)
Fire In The Belly (29)
Flamingos Fly (10,30)
Foggy Mountain Top (30)
Fool For You (medley) (26)
For Mr. Thomas (30)
Foreign Window (17)
Four O'Clock In The Morning (medley) (26)
Full Force Gale (12,21)
Give Me A Kiss (3)
Give Me My Rapture (18)
Glad Tidings (2)
Gloria (8,21,25,26)
Goin' Down Geneva (31)
Golden Autumn Day (31)
Good Morning Little Schoolgirl (25,26)
Goodbye Baby (Baby Goodbye) (1)
Got To Go Back (17)
Great Deception (6)
Green (6)
Green Mansions (23)
Gypsy (5)
Gypsy Queen (3)
Hard Nose The Highway (6)
Haunts Of Ancient Peace (13)
Have I Told You Lately (20,21,26)
Have You Ever Loved A Woman? (medley) (26)
He Ain't Give You None (1,7)
Healing Game (29)
Heathrow Shuffle (28)
Heavy Connection (10)
Help Me (8,26)
Here Comes The Night (8,17,21)
High Spirits (30)
High Summer (31)
Higher Than The World (15)
How Long Has This Been Going On? (28)

Hungry For Your Love (11)
Hymns To The Silence (23,24)
I Believe To My Soul (8)
I Can't Stop Loving You (23)
I Forgot That Love Existed (18,26)
I Have Finally Come To Realise (30)
I Just Want To Make Love To You (8)
I Need Your Kind Of Loving (23)
I Wanna Roo You (Scottish Derivative) (4)
I Will Be There (5,28)
I'd Love To Write Another Song (20)
I'll Be Your Lover, Too (3)
I'll Never Be Free (27)
I'll Take Care Of You (25,26)
I'll Tell Me Ma (19,24)
I'm Not Feeling It Anymore (23)
I'm Tired Joey Boy (20)
I've Been Working (3,8,26)
If I Ever Needed Someone (3)
If You Love Me (29)
If You Only Knew (16)
In The Afternoon (27)
In The Days Before Rock 'N' Roll (22)
In The Forest (25)
In The Garden (17,24,26)
In The Midnight (31)
Inarticulate Speech Of The Heart No. 1 & 2 (15)
Into The Mystic (2,8)
Irish Heartbeat (15,19)
It Fills You Up (10,26)
It Must Be You (23)
It Once Was My Life (29)
It's A Man's Man's Man's World (medley) (26)
It's All In The Game (12,26)
It's All Over Now Baby Blue (14)
It's All Right (7)
Ivory Tower (17)
Jackie Wilson Said (I'm In Heaven When You Smile) (5,21) **61**
Jambalaya (32)
John Henry (30)
Joyous Sound (10,30)
Jumpin' With Symphony Sid (26)
Just A Closer Walk With Thee ...see: See Me Through
Kingdom Hall (11)
Laughing In The Wind (30)
Let The Slave (16)
Let's Talk About Us (32)
Lifetimes (14)
Linden Arden Stole The Highlights (9)
Listen To The Lion (5,8)
Lonely Avenue (25,26)
Lonesome Road (25)
Lover's Prayer (30)
Madame George (7)
Madame Joy (30)

Make It Real One More Time (medley) (26)
Marie's Wedding (19)
Master's Eyes (16)
Melancholia (27)
Memories (22)
Midnight Special (1)
Moondance (2,21,26,28) **92**
Moonshine Whiskey (4)
Moody's Mood For Love (25)
My Funny Valentine (medley) (26)
My Lagan Love (19)
Mystery, The (5,28)
Naked In The Jungle (30)
Natalia (11)
New Biography (31)
New Kind Of Man (16)
New Symphony Sid (28)
No Religion (27)
No Rollin' Blues (medley) (26)
No Way Pedro (32)
Northern Muse (Solid Ground) (14)
Not Supposed To Break Down (30)
Oh The Warm Feeling (17)
Old Black Joe (32)
Old Old Woodstock (4)
On Hyndford Street (23)
One Irish Rover (23)
Orangefield (20)
Ordinary Life (29)
Ordinary People (30)
Pagan Streams (23)
Perfect Fit (27)
Philosophers Stone (31)
Piper At The Gates Of Dawn (29)
Precious Time (31)
Professional Jealousy (23)
Purple Heather (6)
Quality Street (23)
Queen Of The Slipstream (18,21)
Raglan Road (19)
Rainecheck (27)
Rave On, John Donne (15,24)
Real Gone Lover (32)
Real Real Gone (22,24,30)
Really Don't Know (30)
Redwood Tree (5) **98**
Reminds Me Of You (31)
River Of Time (15)
Ro Ro Rosey (1,7)
Rolling Hills (12)
Rough God Goes Riding (29)
Russian Roulette (27)
Sack O' Woe (28)
Saint Dominic's Preview (5,8)
Santa Fe (11)
Satisfied (13)
Scandinavia (14)
See Me Through (22,26)
See Me Through Part II (Just A Closer Walk With Thee) (26)
Sense Of Wonder (16,24)

September Night (15)
Shakin' All Over (medley) (26)
She Gives Me Religion (14)
She Moved Through The Fair (19)
She's My Baby (22)
Shot Of Rhythm & Blues (32)
Showbusiness (30)
Snow In San Anselmo (6)
So Complicated (23)
So Quiet In Here (22,26)
Soldier Of Fortune (medley) (26)
Some Peace Of Mind (23)
Someone Like You (18)
Sometimes I Feel Like A Motherless Child (18,24)
Sometimes We Cry (29)
Song Of Being A Child (30)
Songwriter (27)
Sooner Or Later (medley) (26)
Spanish Rose (1)
Spanish Steps (18)
Spirit (13)
Star Of The County Down (19)
Start All Over Again (22)
Starting A New Life (4)
Stepping Out Queen (12)
Stepping Out Queen Part 2 (30)
(Straight To Your Heart) Like A Cannonball (23)
Stormy Monday (medley) (26)
Street Choir (3)
Street Only Knew Your Name (15,30)
Street Theory (30)
Streets Of Arklow (9)
Summertime In England (13)
Sweet Jannie (3)
Sweet Thing (21)
T.B. Sheets (1,7)
Ta Mo Chleamhnas Deanta (19)
Take It Where You Find It (11)
Take Me Back (23)
Take Your Hand Out Of My Pocket (8)
Tell Me What You Want (25)
Thank You Falettinme Be Mice Elf Agin (medley) (26)
Thanks For The Information (17)
That's Life (28)
That's Where It's At (medley) (26)
There There Child (30)
These Are The Days (20)
These Dreams Of You (2,8)
Think Twice Before You Go (32)
This Weight (29)
Till We Get The Healing Done (25)
Tir Na Nog (17)
Too Long In Exile (25)
Tore Down A La Rimbaud (16)
Town Called Paradise (17)
Trans-Euro Train (medley) (26)

Troubadours (12)
Try For Sleep (30)
Tupelo Honey (4,26) **47**
Twilight Zone (9)
Underlying Depression (27)
Vanlose Stairway (14,26)
Venice U.S.A. (11)
Village Idiot (23)
Virgo Clowns (3)
Waiting Game (29)
Warm Love (6,8,21)
Wasted Years (25)
Wavelength (11) **42**
Western Plain (30)
What Would I Do Without You (16)
When Heart Is Open (13)
When That Evening Sun Goes Down (4)
When The Leaves Come Falling Down (31)
When Will I Become A Man? (medley) (26)
When Will I Ever Learn To Live In God (20,24)
Whenever God Shines His Light (20,21)
Who Can I Turn To? (28)
Who Drove The Red Sports Car (1,7)
Who Was That Masked Man (9)
Why Don't You Love Me (32)
Why Must I Always Explain (23)
Wild Children (6,8)
Wild Honey (13)
Wild Night (4,21) **28**
Wonderful Remark (21,30)
You Don't Know Me (27)
You Don't Pull No Punches, But You Don't Push The River (9)
You Give Me Nothing But The Blues (medley) (26)
You Gotta Make It Through The World (10)
You Know What They're Writing About (12)
You Make Me Feel So Free (12,26)
You Send Me (medley) (26)
You Win Again (32)
You're My Woman (4)
Your Mind Is On Vacation (28)
Youth Of 1,000 Summers (22)

MORRISSEY '94

Born Stephen Morrissey on 5/22/59 in Davyhulme, Lancashire, England. Former lead singer/songwriter of **The Smiths**.

DEBUT	PEAK	WKS	RIAA	CD		Album		$	Label & Number
4/9/88	48	20	●	©	1	**Viva Hate**		$10	Sire 25699
11/24/90	59	16	●	©	2	**Bona Drag**		$10	Sire 26221
3/23/91	52	10		©	3	**Kill Uncle**		$10	Sire 26514
8/15/92	21	14		©	4	**Your Arsenal**		$10	Sire 26994
4/9/94	18	10		©	5	**Vauxhall And I**		$10	Sire 45451
3/11/95	134	1		©	6	**World Of Morrissey**	[K]	$10	Sire 45879
9/30/95	66	2		©	7	**Southpaw Grammar**		$10	Reprise 45939
8/30/97	61	3		©	8	**Maladjusted**		$10	Mercury 536036

Alma Matters (8)
Alsatian Cousin (1)
Ambitious Outsiders (8)
Ammunition (8)
Angel, Angel, Down We Go Together (1)
Asian Rut (3)
Bengali In Platforms (1)
Best Friend On The Payroll (7)
Billy Budd (5,6)
Boxers (6)
Boy Racer (7)
Break Up The Family (1)
Certain People I Know (4,6)
Dagenham Dave (7)
Dial-A-Cliche (1)
Disappointed (2)

Do Your Best And Don't Worry (7)
Driving Your Girlfriend Home (3)
Everyday Is Like Sunday (1,2)
Found Found Found (3)
Glamorous Glue (4)
Hairdresser On Fire (2)
Harsh Truth Of The Camera Eye (3)
Have-A-Go Merchant (6)
He Cried (8)
He Knows I'd Love To See Him (2)
Hold On To Your Friends (5)
I Am Hated For Loving (5)
I Don't Mind If You Forget Me (1)

I Know It's Gonna Happen Someday (4)
(I'm) The End Of The Family Line (3)
Interesting Drug (2)
Jack The Ripper (6)
King Leer (3)
Last Of The Famous International Playboys (2,6)
Late Night, Maudlin Street (1)
Lazy Sunbathers (5)
Lifeguard Sleeping, Girl Drowning (5)
Little Man, What Now? (1)
Loop, The (6)
Lucky Lisp (2)
Maladjusted (8)
Margaret On The Guillotine (1)

Moon River (6)
More You Ignore Me, The Closer I Get (5) *46*
Mute Witness (3)
My Love Life (6)
National Front Disco (4)
November Spawned A Monster (2)
Now My Heart Is Full (5)
Operation, The (7)
Ordinary Boys (1)
Ouija Board, Ouija Board (2)
Our Frank (3)
Papa Jack (8)
Piccadilly Palare (2)
Reader Meet Author (7)
Roy's Keen (8)
Satan Rejected My Soul (8)

Seasick, Yet Still Docked (4)
Sing Your Life (3)
Sister I'm A Poet (5)
Sorrow Will Come In The End (8)
Southpaw (7)
Speedway (5)
Spring-Heeled Jim (5,6)
Such A Little Thing Makes Such A Big Difference (2)
Suedehead (1,2)
Teachers Are Afraid Of The Pupils (7)
There's A Place In Hell For Me And My Friends (5)
Tomorrow (4)
Tony The Pony (3)
Trouble Loves Me (8)

Used To Be A Sweet Boy (5)
We Hate It When Our Friends Become Successful (4)
We'll Let You Know (4,6)
Whatever Happens, I Love You (6)
Why Don't You Find Out For Yourself (5)
Wide To Receive (8)
Will Never Marry (1)
Yes, I Am Blind (5)
You're Gonna Need Someone On Your Side (4)
You're The One For Me, Fatty (4,6)

MORSE, Steve, Band '84

Born on 7/28/54 in Hamilton, Ohio. Lead guitarist of the **Dixie Dregs**. Also a backing guitarist with **Kansas**.

DEBUT	PEAK	WKS	CD		Album		$	Label & Number
9/1/84	101	12	©	1	**The Introduction**	[I]	$12	Musician 60369
6/24/89	182	3	©	2	**High Tension Wires**	[I]	$10	MCA 6275

STEVE MORSE

Country Colors (2)
Cruise Missile (1)
Endless Waves (2)

General Lee (1)
Ghostwind (2)
Highland Wedding (2)

Huron River Blues Medley (1)
Introduction, The (1)
Leprechaun Promenade (2)

Looking Back (2)
Modoc (2)
Mountain Waltz (1)

On The Pipe (1)
Road Home (2)
Third Power (2)

Tumeni Notes (2)
V.H.F. (Vertical Hair Factor) (1)
Whistle, The (1)

MOSBY, Johnny and Jonie '69

Country vocal duo: Johnny (born on 4/26/33 in Fort Smith, Arkansas) and wife Jonie (born on 8/10/40 in Van Nuys, California) Mosby.

DEBUT	PEAK	WKS		Album	$	Label & Number
10/11/69	197	1		**Hold Me**	$20	Capitol 286

Gentle On My Mind
Hold Me, Thrill Me, Kiss Me
I Can Tell

Jackson
Johnny One Time

Let The World Keep On A Turnin'

One Has My Name (The Other Has My Heart)
Souvenirs Of Love

Sweet Thang
Walkin' Papers

MOS DEF '99

Born in New York City. Male rapper. Member of **Black Star**.

DEBUT	PEAK	WKS	RIAA	CD		Album	$	Label & Number
10/30/99	25	16	●	©		**Black On Both Sides**	$10	Rawkus 50141

Brooklyn
Climb
Do It Now

Fear Not Of Man
Got
Habitat

Hip Hop
Know That
Love

Mathematics
May-December
Mr. Nigga

Ms. Fat Booty
New World Water
Rock N Roll

Speed Law
Umi Says

MOTELS, The '82

Pop-rock group formed in Los Angeles in 1978. **Martha Davis** (vocals), Guy Perry (guitar), Marty Jourard (keyboards), Michael Goodroe (bass) and Brian Glascock (drums). Scott Thurston (guitar) joined in 1983. Group disbanded in 1987.

DEBUT	PEAK	WKS	RIAA	CD		Album	$	Label & Number
12/1/79	175	2		©	1	**Motels**	$12	Capitol 11996
7/12/80	45	20		©	2	**Careful**	$12	Capitol 12070
4/24/82	16	41	●	©	3	**All Four One**	$10	Capitol 12177
10/15/83	22	24	●	©	4	**Little Robbers**	$10	Capitol 12288
8/17/85	36	16		©	5	**Shock**	$10	Capitol 12378

Annie Told Me (5)
Anticipating (1)
Apocalypso (3)
Art Fails (3)
Atomic Cafe (1)
Bonjour Baby (2)
Careful (2)
Celia (1)
Change My Mind (3)

Closets & Bullets (1)
Counting (1)
Cries And Whispers (5)
Cry Baby (2)
Danger (2)
Days Are O.K. (But The Nights Were Made For Love) (2)
Dressing Up (1)
Envy (2)

Footsteps (4)
Forever Mine (3) *60*
He Hit Me (And It Felt Like A Kiss) (3)
Hungry (5)
Icy Red (5)
Into The Heartland (4)
Isle Of You (4)
Kix (1)

Little Robbers (4)
Love Don't Help (1)
Mission Of Mercy (3)
Monday Shut Down (4)
My Love Stops Here (5)
New York Times (5)
Night By Night (1)
Only The Lonely (3) *9*
Party Professionals (2)

People, Places And Things (2)
Porn Reggae (1)
Remember The Nights (4) *36*
Shame (5) *21*
Shock (5) *84*
Slow Town (4)
So L.A. (3)
State Of The Heart (5)
Suddenly Last Summer (4) *9*

Tables Turned (4)
Take The L. (3) *52*
Total Control (1)
Tragic Surf (3)
Trust Me (4)
Where Do We Go From Here (Nothing Sacred) (4)
Whose Problem? (2)

MOTHER EARTH '69

Country-rock group from Nashville: Tracy Nelson (vocals), Robert Cardwell and John Andrews (guitars), Andrew McMahon (keyboards), Tim Drummond (bass) and Karl Himmel (drums).

DEBUT	PEAK	WKS		Album	$	Label & Number
2/22/69	144	8	1	**Living With The Animals**	$25	Mercury 61194
8/23/69	95	9	2	**Make A Joyful Noise**	$25	Mercury 61226
5/15/71	199	2	3	**Bring Me Home**	$20	Reprise 6431

Blues For The Road (2)
Bring Me Home (3)
Come On And See (2)
Cry On (1)
Deliver Me (3)
Down So Low (1)

Goodnight Nelda Grebe, The Telephone Company Has Cut Us Off (1)
I Did My Part (1)
I Need Your Love So Bad (2)
I, The Fly (2)

I Wanna Be Your Mama Again (2)
I'll Be Long Gone (3)
It Won't Be Long (1)
Kingdom Of Heaven (Is Within You) (1)

Living With The Animals (1)
Lo And Behold (3)
Marvel Group (1)
Mother Earth (1)
My Love Will Never Die (1)
Seven Bridges Road (3)

Soul Of Sadness (3)
Soul Of The Man (2)
Stop The Train (3)
Temptation Took Control Of Me And I Fell (3)
Then I'll Be Moving On (2)

There Is No End (3)
Tonight The Sky's About To Cry (3)
Wait, Wait, Wait (2)
What Are You Trying To Do (2)
You Win Again (2)

DEBUT	PEAK	WKS	RIAA	CD	ARTIST — Album Title	Catalog	Sym	$	Label & Number

MOTHERLODE '69

Pop group from Canada: William Smith (vocals, keyboards), Ken Marco (guitar), Steve Kennedy (sax) and Wayne Stone (drums). Smith died of a heart attack on 12/1/97 (age 53).

| 10/4/69 | 93 | 12 | | © | When I Die .... | | | $20 | Buddah 5046 |

Can't You Find Love   Hard Life   Memories Of A Broken Promise   What Does It Take (To Win   You Ain't Lookin' In The Right
Child Without Mother   Help Me Find Peace Of Mind   Oh! See The White Light   Your Love)   Place Baby
Dear Old Daddy Bill   Living Life   Soft Shell   **When I Die** 18

MOTHER LOVE BONE '92

Rock group from Seattle: Andrew Wood (vocals), Bruce Fairweather and Stone Gossard (guitars), Jeff Ament (bass), and Greg Gilmore (drums). Wood died of a drug overdose on in March 1990. Gossard and Ament recorded with other Seattle notables as **Temple Of The Dog**, in tribute to Wood, then formed **Pearl Jam**.

| 10/10/92 | 77 | 12 | | © | Mother Love Bone .... | | | $15 | Stardog 512884 [2] |

Bone China   Chloe Dancer (medley)   Gentle Groove   Holy Roller   Mindshaker Meltdown   Stargazer
Capricorn Sister   Come Bite The Apple   Half Ass Monkey Boy   Lady Godiva Blues   Mr. Danny Boy   This Is Shangrila
Captain Hi-Top   Crown Of Thorns   Heartshine   Man Of Golden Words   Stardog Champion   Thru Fade Away

MOTHER'S FINEST '78

R&B group from Dayton, Ohio: husband-and-wife Glenn Murdoch and **Joyce Kennedy** (vocals), Gary Moore (guitar), Michael Keck (keyboards), Jerry Seay (bass) and Barry Borden (drums).

9/11/76	148	8			1 Mother's Finest			$12	Epic 34179
9/17/77	134	8		©	2 Another Mother Further			$12	Epic 34699
9/30/78	123	21		©	3 Mother Factor			$12	Epic 35546
5/23/81	168	8			4 Iron Age			$12	Atlantic 19302

All The Way (4)   Earthling (4)   Hard Rock Lover (2)   Movin' On (4)   Tell Me (3)
Baby Love (2) 58   Evolution (4)   I Can't Believe (4)   Mr. Goodbar (3)   Thank You For The Love (2)
Burning Love (2)   **Fire** (1) 93   Illusion (C'mon Over To My   My Baby (1)   Time (4)
Can't Fight The Feeling (4)   Fly With Me (Feel The Love) (1)   House) (1)   Niggizz Can't Sang Rock & Roll   Truth'll Set You Free (2)
Dis Go Dis Way, Dis Go Dat   Give It Up (3)   Love Changes (4)   (1)   U Turn Me On (4)
Way (2)   Give You All The Love (Inside   Luv Drug (4)   Piece Of The Rock (2)   Watch My Stylin' (3)
Don't Wanna Come Back (3)   Of Me) (1)   Mickey's Monkey (2)   Rain (1)
Dontcha Wanna Love Me (1)   Gone With Th' Rain (4)   More And More (3)   Rock N' Roll 2 Nite (4)

MOTHERS OF INVENTION, The — see ZAPPA, Frank

MO THUGS FAMILY '96

Gathering of rap acts from Cleveland. Assembled by **Bone Thugs-N-Harmony**. Acts include Tre, Graveyard Shift, Souljah Boy, Ken Dawg and II Tru.

11/23/96	2¹	23	▲	©	1 Family Scriptures			$10	Mo Thugs 1561
6/13/98	25	28	●	©	2 Family Scriptures Chapter II: Family Reunion			$10	Mo Thugs 1632
7/15/00	45	8		©	3 Layzie Bone Presents Mo Thugs III: The Mothership			$10	Mo Thugs 8111

Ain't No Reason (1)   Family Scriptures (1)   Killing Fields (1)   Otherside (2)   Seldom Seen (3)   U Don't Own Me (2)
Ain't Said No Names (2)   Ghetto Bluez (1)   Last Laugh (3)   Pimpin' Ain't Easy (2)   **Take Your Time** (1) 77   U Don't Want None (1)
All Good (2)   **Ghetto Cowboy** (2) 15   Low Down (1)   Playa In Me (1)   This Ain't Livin' (3)   Urban Souljah (2)
Backyard, The (3)   Gunline (3)   Mighty Mighty Warrior (2)   Queen, The (2)   Thug Devotion (1)   Wanna Be Ballers (3)
Believe (2)   Heart Of It (1)   Mighty Mo Thug (2)   Ride With A Playa (2)   Tighten Up Your Operation (3)   Welcome To My World (1)
Did He Really Wanna? (3)   Here With Me (1)   Mo' Murder (1)   Riot (1)   2 The Playaz (3)   Who Forgot About It (3)
Down From The Start (3)   If I Can Go Back (3)   Mo Thuggin' (2)   Rumors & War (1)   II Tru (1)
Everything Green (3)   It Don't Stop (3)   No Pretender (1)   Searchin' 4 Peace (1)   Total Kaos (3)

★222★ MÖTLEY CRÜE '89

Hard-rock group from Los Angeles: **Vince Neil** (vocals), Mick Mars (guitar), Nikki Sixx (bass) and Tommy Lee (drums). John Corabi replaced Neil from 1992-96. Sixx married actress Donna D'Errico on 12/23/96. Lee was married to actress Heather Locklear from 1986-93; married actress Pamela Anderson on 2/19/95. Lee left group in April 1999; formed **Methods Of Mayhem**. Drummer Randy Castillo joined in early 2000.

1)Dr. Feelgood 2)Girls, Girls, Girls 3)Decade Of Decadence - '81-'91

10/15/83+	17	111	▲⁴	©	1 Shout At The Devil			$10	Elektra 60289
12/17/83+	77	62	▲		2 Too Fast For Love		[E]	$10	Elektra 60174
					their first album				
7/13/85	6	72	▲⁴	©	3 Theatre Of Pain			$10	Elektra 60418
6/13/87	2¹	46	▲⁴	©	4 Girls, Girls, Girls			$10	Elektra 60725
9/23/89	❶²	109	▲⁶	©	5 Dr. Feelgood	C:#43/1		$10	Elektra 60829
10/19/91	2¹	37	▲²	©	6 Decade Of Decadence - '81-'91		[G]	$10	Elektra 61204
4/2/94	7	10	●	©	7 Mötley Crüe			$10	Elektra 61534
7/12/97	4	9	●	©	8 Generation Swine			$10	Elektra 61901
11/14/98	20	20	●	©	9 Greatest Hits		[G]	$10	Beyond 78002
12/11/99	133	2			10 Live: Entertainment Or Death		[L]	$15	Mötley 78034 [2]
7/29/00	41	6			11 New Tattoo			$10	Mötley 78120

Afraid (8,9)   Driftaway (7)   Home Sweet Home '91 (6) 37   Piece Of Your Action (2,6,10)   Shout At The Devil (1,6,10)   Treat Me Like The Dog I Am
All In The Name Of... (4)   Droppin Like Flies (7)   Hooligan's Holiday (7)   Poison Apples (7)   Shout At The Devil '97 (8,9)   (11)
Anarchy In The U.K. (6)   Enslaved (9)   In The Beginning (1)   Porno Star (11)   Slice Of Your Pie (5)   Uncle Jack (7)
Angela (6)   Fake (11)   Jailhouse Rock (3)   Power To The Music (7)   Smoke The Sky (7)   Use It Or Lose It (3)
Anybody Out There? (8)   Fight For Your Rights (3)   Keep Your Eye On The Money   **Primal Scream** (6,9,10) 63   **Smokin' In The Boys Room**   Welcome To The Numb (7)
Bad Boy Boogie (4)   Find Myself (8)   (3)   Public Enemy #1 (2,10)   (3,6,9,10) 16   White Punks On Dope (11)
Bastard (1)   1st Band On The Moon (11)   **Kickstart My Heart**   Punched In The Teeth By Love   Starry Eyes (2,10)   **Without You** (5,9,10) 8
Beauty (8)   Five Years Dead (4)   (5,6,9,10) 27   (11)   Sticky Sweet (5)   **You're All I Need** (4) 83
Bitter Pill (9)   Flush (8)   Knock 'Em Dead, Kid (1,10)   Raise Your Hands To Rock (3)   Sumthin' For Nuthin' (4)
Brandon (8)   Generation Swine (8)   Let Us Prey (8)   Rat Like Me (9)   T.N.T. (Terror 'N Tinseltown) (5)
City Boy Blues (3)   **Girls, Girls, Girls** (4,6,9,10) 12   Live Wire (2,6,10)   Rattlesnake Shake (5)   Take Me To The Top (2)
Come On And Dance (2)   Glitter (8,9)   **Looks That Kill** (1,6,9,10) 54   Red Hot (1)   Teaser (6)
Confessions (7)   God Bless The Children Of The   Louder Than Hell (3)   Rock N' Roll Junkie (6)   Ten Seconds To Love (1,10)
Dancing On Glass (4)   Beast (1)   Loveshine (7)   Rocketship (8)   Til Death Do Us Part (7)
Danger (1)   Hammered (7)   Merry-Go-Round (2,10)   **Same Ol' Situation (S.O.S.)**   Time For Change (7)
Dr. Feelgood (5,6,9,10) 6   Hell On High Heels (11)   Misunderstood (7)   (5,9,10) 78   Tonight (We Need A Lover) (3)
Don't Go Away Mad (Just Go   Helter Skelter (1,10)   New Tattoo (11)   Save Our Souls (3)   Too Fast For Love (2,9)
Away) (5,9,10) 19   Hollywood Ending (11)   Nona (4)   She Goes Down (5)   **Too Young To Fall In Love**
Dragstrip Superstar (11)   **Home Sweet Home** (3,9,10) 89   On With The Show (2)   She Needs Rock N Roll (11)   (1,10) 90

MOTÖRHEAD '91

Hard-rock group formed in London: Ian "Lemmy" Kilminster (vocals, bass; **Hawkwind**), "Fast Eddie" Clarke (guitar) and Phil Taylor (drums). Clarke left in May 1982 (later formed **Fastway**), replaced by Brian Robertson (**Thin Lizzy**). Taylor and Robertson left in August 1983. Kilminster then organized new foursome with guitarists Phil Campbell and Michael Burston, and drummer Pete Gill (**Saxon**). Taylor replaced Gill in 1991.

5/22/82	174	6	©	1	Iron Fist			$10	Mercury 4042
7/23/83	153	7	©	2	Another Perfect Day			$10	Mercury 811365
11/29/86	157	11	©	3	Orgasmatron			$10	GWR/Profile 1223
10/24/87	150	6	©	4	Rock 'N' Roll			$10	GWR/Profile 1240
3/23/91	142	9	©	5	1916			$10	WTG 46858

Ain't My Crime (3)
All For You (4)
America (1)
Angel City (5)
Another Perfect Day (2)
Back At The Funny Farm (2)
Bang To Rights (1)
Blackheart (4)
Boogeyman (4)

Built For Speed (3)
Claw (3)
Dancing On Your Grave (2)
Deaf Forever (3)
Die You Bastard (2)
Doctor Rock (3)
Dogs (3)
(Don't Let 'Em) Grind Ya Down (1)

(Don't Need) Religion (1)
Eat The Rich (4)
Go To Hell (1)
Going To Brazil (5)
Heart Of Stone (1)
I Got Mine (4)
I'm So Bad (Baby I Don't Care) (5)
I'm The Doctor (1)

Iron Fist (1)
Loser (1)
Love Me Forever (5)
Make My Day (5)
Marching Off To War (2)
Mean Machine (3)
Nightmare/The Dreamtime (5)
1916 (5)
No Voices In The Sky (5)

Nothing Up My Sleeve (3)
One To Sing The Blues (5)
One Track Mind (5)
Orgasmatron (3)
Ramones (5)
Riding With The Driver (3)
Rock It (2)
Rock 'N' Roll (4)
Sex And Outrage (1)

Shine (2)
Shut It Down (1)
Shut You Down (5)
Speedfreak (1)
Stone Deaf In The USA (4)
Tales Of Glory (2)
Traitor (4)
Wolf, The (4)

MOTORS, The '80

Pop-rock duo from England: Andy McMaster and Nick Garvey.

4/12/80	174	8			Tenement Steps			$12	Virgin 13139

Here Comes The Hustler
Love And Loneliness 78

Metropolis
Modern Man

Nightmare Zero
Slum People

Tenement Steps
That's What John Said

MOTTOLA, Tony '62

Born on 4/18/18 in Kearney, New Jersey. Latin-style guitarist. Produced by **Enoch Light**.

4/7/62	26	26		1	Roman Guitar	[I]		$20	Command 816
7/21/62	41	6		2	Roman Guitar, Volume Two	[I]		$20	Command 836
12/11/65+	85	13		3	Love Songs - Mexico/S.A.	[I]		$20	Command 889
12/2/67	198	3		4	A Latin Love-In	[I]		$15	Project 3 5010
5/16/70	189	3		5	Tony Mottola's Guitar Factory	[I]		$15	Project 3 5044

All (4)
Anema E Core (2)
Anna (1)
Arrivederci, Roma (1)
Autumn In Rome (2)
Besame Mucho (3)
Bewitched (5)
Black Orpheus (Manha De Carnaval), Theme From (3)
Bluesette (5)
Brasilia (3)

Call Me (4)
Carnival Of Venice (2)
Chewy-Chewy Gum-Gum (5)
Come Together (5)
Curacao (3)
Dream Theme From Act I (4)
Funiculi Funicula (2)
Girl From Ipanema (3)
Guadalajara (3)
Guaglione (2)
Guitar Thing (4)

I Love, I Live, I Love (4)
I Love You (4)
Italian Serenade (1)
La Bamba (3)
La Montana (4)
La Strada (1)
Lay, Lady, Lay (5)
Maria Elena (3)
Mexican Hat Dance (3)
Mexican Medley (3)
Na Voce (1)

Neopolitan Tarantella (1)
Nina (2)
Noche De Ronda (4)
Non Dimenticar (1)
Piel Canela (3)
Roman Guitar (1)
Sabor A Mi (Be True To Me) (3)
Samba De Orfeu (4)
Scalinatella (2)
Scapricciatiello (2)
So Nice (Summer Samba) (4)

Something (5)
Sorrento (1)
Souvenir D'Italie (2)
Spanish Harlem (4)
Spinning Wheel (5)
Sugar, Sugar (5)
Summertime In Venice (2)
Te Voio Ben (2)
Tequila (3)
Tra Veglia E Sono (2)
Violetta (1)

Volare (1)
What Now My Love (4)
Windy (5)
Woodpecker Song (1)
World Of Your Embrace (4)
Yester-Me, Yester-You, Yesterday (5)

MOTT THE HOOPLE '73

Glitter-rock group formed in England: **Ian Hunter** (vocals), Mick Ralphs (guitar), Pete Watts (bass) and Dale Griffin (drums). Group name taken from a Willard Manus novel. Ralphs left in 1973 to join **Bad Company**; guitarists Morgan Fisher and Ariel Bender joined. Hunter left in 1976; Fisher, Watts and Griffin formed the **British Lions**.

7/4/70	185	2	©	1	Mott The Hoople			$20	Atlantic 8258
11/11/72+	89	19	©	2	All The Young Dudes			$20	Columbia 31750
					produced by **David Bowie**				
8/25/73	35	29	©	3	Mott			$20	Columbia 32425
4/27/74	28	23	©	4	The Hoople			$20	Columbia 32871
6/15/74	112	11	©	5	Rock And Roll Queen	[E]		$20	Atlantic 7297
11/30/74+	23	13	©	6	Mott The Hoople Live	[L]		$15	Columbia 33282
					recorded on 5/9/74 at the Uris Theatre in New York City				
11/1/75	160	5		7	Drive On			$15	Columbia 33705

MOTT

After Lights (medley) (2)
Alice (4)
All The Way From Memphis (3,6)
All The Young Dudes (2,6) 37
Apologies (7)
At The Crossroads (1)
Backsliding Fearlessly (1)
Ballad Of Mott The Hoople (March 26, 1972 - Zurich) (3)
Born Late '58 (4)

By Tonight (7)
Crash Street Kidds (4)
Death May Be Your Santa Claus (5)
Drivin' Sister (3)
El Camino Dolo Roso (medley) (3)
Get Back (medley) (6)
Golden Age Of Rock 'N' Roll (4) 96
Great White Wail (7)

Half Moon Bay (1)
Here We Are (7)
Honaloochie Boogie (3)
Hymn For The Dudes (3)
I Can Show You How It Is (7)
I Wish I Was Your Mother (3)
I'll Tell You Something (7)
I'm A Cadillac (medley) (3)
It Takes One To Know One (3)
Jerkin' Crocus (2,6)
Keep A Knockin' (5)

Laugh At Me (1)
Love Now (7)
Marionette (4)
Midnight Lady (5)
Momma's Little Jewel (2)
Monte Carlo (7)
One Of The Boys (2,6) 96
Pearl 'N' Roy (England) (4)
Rabbit Foot And Toby Time (1)
Ready For Love (medley) (2)
Rest In Peace (6)

Rock And Roll Queen (1,5,6)
Roll Away The Stone (4)
Rose (4)
Sea Diver (2)
She Does It (3)
Soft Ground (2)
Stiff Upper Lip (7)
Sucker (4)
Sweet Angeline (6)
Sweet Jane (2)
Through The Looking Glass (4)

Thunderbuck Ram (5)
Trudi's Song (4)
Violence (3,6)
Walkin' With A Mountain (5,6)
Wheel Of The Quivering Meat Conception (5)
Whizz Kid (3)
Whole Lotta Shakin' Goin' Up (medley) (6)
Wrath And Wroll (1)
You Really Got Me (1,5)

MOULD, Bob '96

Born on 10/12/60 in Malone, New York. Rock singer/guitarist. Member of **Hüsker Dü** and **Sugar**.

5/27/89	127	14	©	1	Workbook			$10	Virgin 91240
9/15/90	123	10	©	2	Black Sheets Of Rain			$10	Virgin 91395
5/18/96	101	1	©	3	Bob Mould			$10	Rykodisc 10342
9/12/98	164	1	©	4	The Last Dog And Pony Show			$15	Rykodisc 10443 [2]

Along The Way (4)
Anymore Time Between (3)
Art Crisis (3)
Black Sheets Of Rain (2)
Brasilia Crossed With Trenton (1)
Classifieds (4)
Compositions For The Young And Old (1)

Deep Karma Canyon (3)
Disappointed (2)
Dreaming, I Am (1)
Egoverride (3)
First Drag Of The Day (4)
Fort Knox, King Solomon (3)
Hair Stew (3)
Hanging Tree (2)
Hear Me Calling (2)

Heartbreak A Stranger (4)
I Hate Alternative Rock (3)
It's Too Late (2)
Last Night (2)
Let There Be Peace (medley) (2)
Lonely Afternoon (1)
Megamanic (4)
Moving Trucks (4)

New #1 (4)
Next Time That You Leave (3)
One Good Reason (2)
Out Of Your Life (2)
Poison Years (1)
Reflecting Pool (4)
Roll Over And Die (3)
Sacrifice (medley) (2)
See A Little Light (1)

Sinners And Their Repentances (1)
Skintrade (4)
Stand Guard (2)
Stop Your Crying (2)
Sunspots (1)
Sweet Serene (4)
Taking Everything (4)
Thumbtack (3)

Vaporub (2)
Whichever Way The Wind Blows (1)
Who Was Around? (4)
Wishing Well (1)

MOUNTAIN '71

Male hard-rock group formed in New York City: **Leslie West** (vocals, bass), Felix Pappalardi (guitar), Steve Knight (keyboards) and Corky Laing (drums). Pappalardi was shot to death on 4/17/83 (age 44). Also see **West, Bruce & Laing**.

3/14/70	17	39	●	©	1 Mountain Climbing!			$20	Windfall 4501
2/6/71	16	29	●	©	2 Nantucket Sleighride			$20	Windfall 5500
12/18/71+	35	16		©	3 Flowers Of Evil			$20	Windfall 5501
5/13/72	63	18		©	4 Mountain Live (the road goes ever on)	[L]		$20	Windfall 5502
2/24/73	72	16		©	5 The Best Of Mountain	[G]		$15	Columbia 32079
3/9/74	142	8		©	6 Twin Peaks	[L]		$20	Columbia 32818 [2]
					recorded on 8/30/73 in Osaka, Japan				
8/10/74	102	9		©	7 Avalanche			$12	Columbia 33088
4/27/85	166	6			8 Go For Your Life			$10	Scotti Brothers 40006

Alisan (7)
Animal Trainer And The Toad (2,5) **76**
Babe In The Woods (8)
Back Where I Belong (7)
Bardot Damage (8)
Blood Of The Sun (6)
Boys In The Band (1,5)
Crossroader (3,4,5,6)
Don't Look Around (2,5)

Dreams Of Milk And Honey (medley) (3)
Flowers Of Evil (3)
For Yasgur's Farm (1,5)
Great Train Robbery (2)
Guitar Solo (3,6)
Hard Times (8)
I Love To See You Fly (7)
I Love Young Girls (4)

Imaginary Western, Theme For An (1,5,6)
King's Chorale (3,5)
Laird, The (1)
Last Of The Sunshine Days (7)
Little Bit Of Insanity (8)
Long Red (4)
Makin' It In Your Car (8)
Mississippi Queen (1,3,5,6) **21**
My Lady (2)

Nantucket Sleighride (2,4,5,6)
Never In My Life (1,5,6)
One Last Cold Kiss (3)
Pride And Passion (3)
Roll Over Beethoven (3,5,6)
Satisfaction (7)
She Loves Her Rock (And She Loves It Hard) (8)
Shimmy On The Footlights (8)
Silver Paper (1,6)

Sister Justice (7)
Sittin' On A Rainbow (1)
Spark (8)
Swamp Boy (7)
Swan Theme (medley) (3)
Taunta (Sammy's Tune) (2,5)
Thumbsucker (7)
Tired Angels (2)
To My Friend (1)
Travelin' In The Dark (2)

Variations (medley) (3)
Waiting To Take You Away (4)
Whole Lotta Shakin' Goin' On (7)
You Better Believe It (7)
You Can't Get Away (2)

MOUSKOURI, Nana '66

Born on 10/15/36 in Athens, Greece. Female singer.

4/9/66	124	8			1 An Evening With Belafonte/Mouskouri			$20	RCA Victor 3415
					HARRY BELAFONTE/NANA MOUSKOURI				
10/5/91	141	6		©	2 Only Love - The Very Best Of Nana Mouskouri	[K]		$10	Philips 510229

And I Love You So (2)
Baby Snake (1)
Both Sides Now (2)
Dream (1)

Even Now (2)
Every Time We Say Goodbye (2)

First Time Ever I Saw Your Face (2)
I Have A Dream (2)
If You Are Thirsty (1)

If You Love Me (2)
Irene (1)
Love Changes Everything (2)
Love Me Tender (2)

Only Love (2)
Power Of Love (2)
Time After Time (2)
Town Crier (1)

Train, The (1)
Why Worry (2)
Your Love, My Love (2)

MOUTH & MACNEAL '72

Pop vocal duo from Holland: Willem "Mouth" Duyn and Maggie MacNeal (real name: Sjoukje Van't Spijker).

| 7/1/72 | 77 | 16 | | | 1 How Do You Do? | | | $15 | Philips 700000 |

A.B.C.
Hey, You Love 87
How Do You Do? **8**

I Almost Lost My Mind
I Heard It Through The Grapevine

Isolation
It Happened Long Ago
Land Of Milk And Honey

Remember (Walking In The Sand)
Rosianna

Tell Me World
Why Did You, Why?

MOUZON, Alphonse '83

Born on 11/21/48 in Charleston, South Carolina. R&B singer/pianist/drummer.

| 12/4/82+ | 146 | 11 | | © | Distant Lover | | | $12 | Highrise 100 |

Everybody Party
Get Up And Dance

I Don't Want To Lose This Feeling

Lady In Red
Saving My Love For You

Step Into The Funk
That's Right

When We Were Young

MOVE, The — see ELECTRIC LIGHT ORCHESTRA

MOVING PICTURES '83

Pop group from Sydney, Australia: Alex Smith (vocals), Garry Frost (guitar), Andrew Thompson (sax), Charlie Cole (keyboards), Ian Lees (bass) and Paul Freeland (drums).

| 12/4/82+ | 101 | 16 | | | Days Of Innocence | | | $12 | Network 60202 |

Angel And The Madman
Bustin' Loose

Joni And The Romeo
Nothing To Do

Round Again
So Tired
Sweet Cherie

Streetheart
What About Me 29
Wings

MOYET, Alison '85

Born Genevieve Alison-Jane Moyet on 6/18/61 in Basildon, Essex, England. Female singer. Member of **Yaz**.

4/6/85	45	25		©	1 Alf			$10	Columbia 39956
6/20/87	94	17		©	2 Raindancing			$10	Columbia 40653
4/9/94	194	1		©	3 Essex			$10	Columbia 57448

All Cried Out (1)
And I Know (3)
Another Living Day (3)
Blow Wind Blow (2)
Boys Own (3)
Dorothy (3)

Falling (3)
For You Only (1)
Getting Into Something (3)
Glorious Love (2)
Honey For The Bees (1)
Invisible (1) **31**

Is This Love? (2)
Love Resurrection (1) **82**
Money Mile (1)
Ode To Boy (3)
Ordinary Girl (2)
Satellite (3)

Sleep Like Breathing (2)
So Am I (3)
Stay (2)
Steal Me Blind (1)
Take Of Me (3)
Twisting The Knife (1)

Weak In The Presence Of Beauty (2)
When I Say (No Giveaway) (2)
Where Hides Sleep (1)
Whispering Your Name (3)
Without You (2)

You Got Me Wrong (2)

MTUME '83

Funk group formed in Philadelphia: James Mtume (male vocals, drums), Tawatha Agee (female vocals), Reggie Lucas (guitar), Phil Fields (keyboards) and Ray Johnson (bass).

10/18/80	119	4			1 In Search Of The Rainbow Seekers			$10	Epic 36017
5/28/83	26	22	●	©	2 Juicy Fruit			$10	Epic 38588
9/15/84	77	19		©	3 You, Me And He			$10	Epic 39473
7/5/86	135	8		©	4 Theater Of The Mind			$10	Epic 40262

Anticipatin' (1)
Body & Soul (Take Me) (4)
Breathless (4)
C.O.D. (I'll Deliver) (3)
Dance Around My Navel (Doesn't Have To Make Sense, Just Cents) (1)
Deep Freeze (Rap-A-Song) Part I (4)

Deep Freeze (Tree's Tune) Part II (4)
Everything Good To Me (1)
Give It On Up (If You Want To) (1)
Green Light (2)
Hip Dip Skippedabeat (2)
Hips (2)

I Don't Believe You Heard Me (A Tribute To James Brown) (4)
I Simply Like (3)
I'd Rather Be With You (4)
Juicy Fruit (2) **45**
Juicy Fruit Part II (2)
Mrs. Sippi (1)
New Face Deli (4)

P.O.P. Generation (4)
Prime Time (3)
Ready For Your Love (2)
She's A Rainbow Dancer (1)
So You Wanna Be A Star (1)
Spirit Of The Dance (1)
Sweet For You And Me (Monogamy Mix) (3)

Theater Of The Mind, Theme For (4)
To Be Or Not To Bop That Is The Question (Whether We Funk Or Not) (4)
We're Gonna Make It This Time (1)

Would You Like To (Fool Around) (2)
You Are My Sunshine (3)
You Can't Wait For Love (1)
You, Me And He (3) **83**
Your Love's Too Good (To Spread Around) (2)

DEBUT	PEAK	WKS	RIAA	CD	ARTIST — Album Title	Catalog	Sym	$	Label & Number

M2M '00
Female pop vocal duo from Lorenskog, Norway: Marion Ravn and Marit Larsen.

| 4/22/00 | 89 | 14 | | © | Shades Of Purple | | | $10 | Atlantic 83258 |

Day You Went Away • Don't Mess With My Love • Girl In Your Dreams • Our Song • Why
Dear Diary • Don't Say You Love Me 21 • Give A Little Love • Pretty Boy
Do You Know What You Want • Everything You Do • Mirror Mirror 62 • Smiling Face

MUDHONEY '92
Rock group formed in Seattle: Mark Arm (vocals), Steve Turner (guitar), Matt Lukin (bass) and Dan Peters (drums).

| 10/31/92 | 189 | 1 | | © | Piece Of Cake | | | $10 | Reprise 45090 |

Acetone • Let Me Let You Down • No End In Sight • Take Me There • Youth Body Expression
Blinding Sun • Living Wreck • Ritzville • Thirteenth Floor Opening • Explosion
I'm Spun • Make It Now • Suck You Dry • When In Rome

MUDVAYNE '01
Hard-rock group from Peoria, Illinois: Chad Gray (vocals), Greg Tribbett (guitar), Ryan Martinie (bass) and Matt McDonough (drums).

| 9/16/00+ | 85 | 34↑ | © | | L.D. 50 | | | $10 | No Name 63821 |

Cradle • Everything And Nothing • (K)now F(orever) • Monolith • Pharmaecopia • Severed
Death Blooms • Golden Ratio • Lethal Dosage • Mutatis Mutandis • Prod • Under My Skin
Dig • Internal Primates Forever • -1 • Nothing To Gein • Recombinant Resurgence

MUHAMMAD, Idris '77
Born Leo Morris on 11/13/39 in New Orleans. R&B drummer.

| 6/18/77+ | 127 | 19 | | | Turn This Mutha Out | | [I] | $12 | Kudu 34 |

Camby Bolongo • Could Heaven Ever Be Like This (Part 1) 76 • Crab Apple • Moon Hymn • Say What • Tasty Cakes • Turn This Mutha Out

MULDAUR, Maria '74
Born Maria D'Amato on 9/12/43 in New York City. Female jazz-styled singer.

9/22/73+	3	56	●	©	1 Maria Muldaur			$15	Reprise 2148
11/9/74+	23	26		©	2 Waitress In The Donut Shop			$15	Reprise 2194
3/13/76	53	12			3 Sweet Harmony			$15	Reprise 2235
4/8/78	143	5			4 Southern Winds			$12	Warner 3162

Any Old Time (1) • Here Is Where Your Love Belongs (4) • I'll Keep My Light In My Window (4) • Lying Song (3) • Sad Eyes (3) • Walkin' One & Only (1)
As An Eagle Stirreth In Her Nest (3) • Honey Babe Blues (2) • I'm A Woman (2) 12 • Mad Mad Me (1) • Say You Will (4) • We Just Couldn't Say Goodbye (3)
Back By Fall (3) • I Can't Say No (4) • If You Haven't Any Hay (2) • Make Love To The Music (4) • Sweet Harmony (3) • Wild Bird (3)
Brickyard Blues (2) • I Can't Stand It (3) • It Ain't The Meat It's The Motion (2) • Midnight At The Oasis (1) 6 • Sweetheart (2) • Work Song (1)
Cajun Moon (4) • I Got A Man (4) • Jon The Generator (3) • My Sisters And Brothers (4) • That's The Way Love Is (4)
Cool River (2) • I Never Did Sing You A Love Song (1) • Joyful Noise (4) • My Tennessee Mountain Home (1) • Three Dollar Bill (1)
Don't You Make Me High (1) • Long Hard Climb (1) • Oh Papa (2) • Travelin' Shoes (1)
Gringo En Mexico (2) • Rockin' Chair (3) • Vaudeville Man (1)

MULL, Martin '78
Born on 8/18/43 in Chicago. Comedian/actor. Acted in several movies and TV shows.

| 3/26/77 | 184 | 2 | | | 1 I'm Everyone I've Ever Loved | | [C] | $12 | ABC 997 |
| 6/17/78 | 157 | 3 | | | 2 Sex & Violins | | [C] | $12 | ABC 1064 |

Artist Relations (Or Don't Write Me At Home) (1) • Buy Me A Drink (1) • Humming (2) • Men (1) • Trailer Waltz (2)
Best Of You (2) • Cleveland (Revisited) (2) • I Haven't Got The Vegas Idea (2) • It's Meantime, Folks (1) • Michelle (1) • Truth, The (1)
Birds Gotta Swim (Vinyl World, Pt. I) (1) • Dogs (2) • I'll Do The Samba (2) • It's Showtime, Folks (1) • Mother-In-Law Song (2) • Vinyl World, Pt. II (2)
Bombed Anyway (1) • Get Up, Get Down (1) • I'm Everyone I've Ever Loved (1) • Martin Goes And Does Where It's At (1) • Now Martin Suggests Where He's At (1) • Westward Ho! (2)
Boogie Man (1) • Goodnight (2) • It's Downtime, Folks (1) • Martin Reveals Where He's At (1) • Playtentype Shows Martin Where It's At (1)
Half Hour Of Heaven (And Eight Hours Of Sleep) (2) • It's Folktime, Folks (1) • Martin Touches The President's Very Desk (1) • They Never Met (1)
Honor Roll (1)

MULLIGAN('S), Gerry, Jazz Combo '59
Born on 4/6/27 in New York City. Died on 1/20/96 (age 68). Jazz saxophonist. Combo included Shelly Manne (drums), Art Farmer (trumpet), Bud Shank (sax), Frank Rosolino (trombone), Pete Jolly (piano) and Red Mitchell (bass).

| 5/25/59 | 39 | 10 | | © | I Want To Live! | | [I-S] | $50 | United Artists 5006 |

Barbara's Theme • Black Nightgown • Frisco Club • I Want To Live, Theme From • Life's A Funny Thing • Night Watch

MULLINS, Rich '98
Born on 10/21/55 in Richmond, Indiana. Died in a car crash on 9/19/97 (age 41). Christian singer/songwriter.

| 10/11/97 | 143 | 1 | | © | 1 Songs | | | $10 | Reunion 16205 |
| 7/18/98 | 113 | 14 | | © | 2 The Jesus Record | | | $15 | Word 69309 [2] |

All The Way To Kingdom Come (2) • Creed (1) • Jesus... (2) • Screen Door (1) • Verge Of A Miracle (1)
Alrightokuhhuhamen (1) • Elijah (1) • Let Mercy Lead (1) • Sing Your Praise To The Lord (1) • We Are Not As Strong As We Think We Are (1)
Awesome God (1) • Hard To Get (1) • Man Of No Reputation (2) • Sometimes By Step (1) • While The Nations Rage (1)
Boy Like Me/Man Like You (1) • Heaven In His Eyes (2) • My Deliverer (2) • Surely God Is With Us (2) • You Did Not Have A Home (2)
Calling Out Your Name (1) • Hold Me Jesus (1) • My One Thing (1) • That Were I Am There You (2)
• If I Stand (1) • Nothing Is Beyond You (2)

MULLINS, Shawn '98
Born on 3/8/68 in Atlanta. Male singer/songwriter/guitarist.

| 10/3/98 | 54 | 35 | ● | © | Soul's Core | | | $10 | Columbia 69637 |

Anchored In You • Ballad Of Billy Jo McKay • Patrick's Song • Soul Child • Twin Rocks, Oregon
And On A Rainy Night • Gulf Of Mexico • September In Seattle • Sunday Mornin' Comin' Down • You Mean Everything To Me
• Lullaby 7 • Shimmer • Tannin Bed Song

MUMBA, Samantha '01
Born in 1/18/83 in Dublin, Ireland. Female R&B singer.

| 11/18/00+ | 67 | 22 | | © | Gotta Tell You | | | $10 | Wild Card 549799 |

Always Come Back To Your Love • Baby, Come Over (This Is Our Night) 49 • Boy, The • Feelin' Is Right • Lately
• Body II Body • Don't Need You To Tell Me I'm Pretty • Gotta Tell You 4 • Never Meant To Be
• Isnt' It Strange • What's It Gonna Be

Jackie Lee
The Duck ('66)

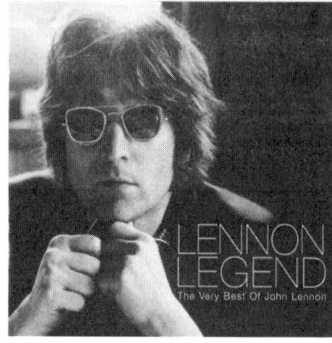

John Lennon...*Lennon Legend -
The Very Best Of John Lennon ('98)*

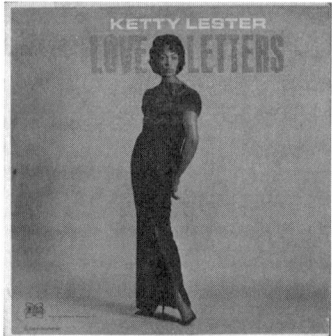

Ketty Lester
Love Letters ('62)

Jerry Lee Lewis
The Return Of Rock ('65)

Kenny Loggins
Outside: From The Redwoods ('93)

Lord Sutch
Lord Sutch and Heavy Friends ('70)

Arthur Lyman
I Wish You Love ('63)

Lynyrd Skynyrd
Twenty ('97)

Lonnie Mack
The Wham Of That Memphis Man! ('63)

Taj Mahal
Music Fuh Ya' ('77)

Mandrill
Mandrill ('71)

Martha & The Vandellas
Heat Wave ('63)

George Martin
Off The Beatle Track ('64)

Barbara Mason
Yes, I'm Ready ('65)

Jackie Mason... *I'm The Greatest
Comedian In The World ('62)*

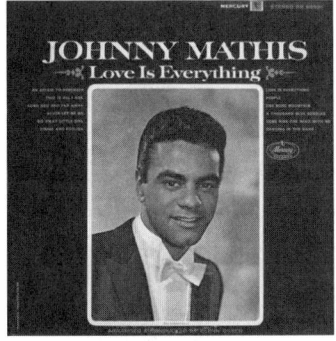

Johnny Mathis
Love Is Everything ('65)

John Mayall
The Blues Alone ('68)

Paul McCartney
Paul Is Live ('93)

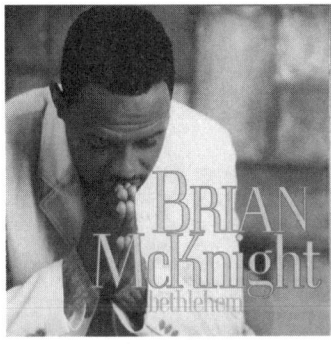

Brian McKnight
Bethlehem ('98)

Bill Medley
Bill Medley 100% ('68)

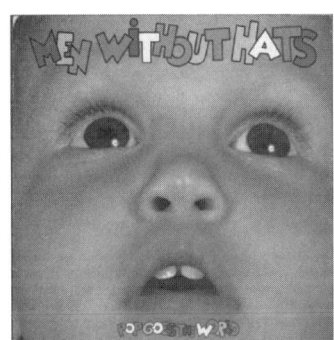

Men Without Hats
Pop Goes The World ('87)

Willie Mitchell
Robbin's Nest ('70)

Montana Orchestra
Merry Christmas ('81)

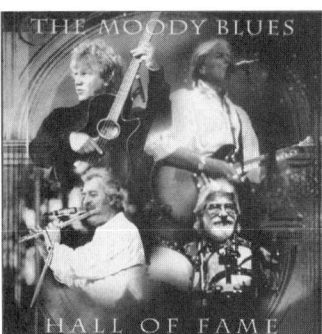

The Moody Blues
Hall Of Fame ('00)

MUNGO JERRY '70
Skiffle group formed in England: Ray Dorset (vocals, guitar), Colin Earl (piano), Paul King (banjo) and Mike Cole (bass).

| 9/12/70 | **64** | 11 | | | **Mungo Jerry** | | | **$20** | Janus 7000 |

Baby Let's Play House
In The Summertime 3

Johnny B. Badde
Maggie

Mother *!*!*! Boogie
Movin' On

My Friend
Peace In The Country

Sad Eyed Joe
San Francisco Bay Blues

See Me
Tramp

MUNICH MACHINE '78
Disco studio group formed by producers **Giorgio Moroder** and Pete Bellotte. Vocals by Chris Bennett.

| 7/1/78 | **190** | 3 | | | **A Whiter Shade Of Pale** | | | **$12** | Casablanca 7090 |

In Love With Love

It's All Wrong (But It's Alright)   It's For You

La Nuit Blanche

Love Fever

Whiter Shade Of Pale

MURAD, Jerry — see HARMONICATS

MURDERERS, The '00
Rap group from New York City: Ja Rule, Vita, Black Child and Tah Murdah.

| 4/8/00 | **15** | 10 | | © | **Irv Gotti Presents...The Murderers** | | | **$10** | Murder Inc. 542258 |

Black Or White
Crime Scene
Dem N****z

Get It Right
Holla Holla
How Many Wanna Die

If You Were My B***h
Murderers
96R-0709

Rebels Symphony
S**t Gets Ugly
Somebody's Gonna Die Tonight

Tales From The Darkside
Vita, Vita, Vita
We Different

We Don't Give A F**k
We Getting High Tonight
We Murderers Baby

MURDER SQUAD '95
Project of rapper/producer Prodeje (**South Central Cartel**).

| 3/4/95 | **106** | 5 | | © | **S.C.C. Presents Murder Squad Nationwide** | | | **$10** | DJ West 124040 |

"G" Slide
Ghetto Got Me Shadey

Gun Smoke
It's An S.C.C. Thang

Knock On Wood
No Peace

On Dat Ass
"187" Squad

Pass Da Dank
Straight Honey Made

Who's Da Star
Why Must G'z

MURDOCK, Shirley '87
Born in Toledo, Ohio. Female R&B singer.

| 2/14/87 | **44** | 26 | ● | © | 1 | **Shirley Murdock!** | | | **$10** | Elektra 60443 |
| 7/23/88 | **137** | 15 | | © | 2 | **A Woman's Point Of View** | | | **$10** | Elektra 60791 |

And I Am Telling You I'm Not
   Going (2)
As We Lay (1) 23
Be Free (1)

Danger Zone (1)
(Everybody Wants) Somethin'
   For Nothin' (2)
Found My Way (2)

Go On Without You (1)
Husband (2)
I Still Love You (2)
If I Know (2)

Instrument Of Praise (2)
Modern Girl (2)
No More (1)
Oh What A Feeling (2)

One I Need (1)
Spend My Whole Life (2)
Teaser (1)
Tribute (1)

Truth Or Dare (1)
Woman's Point Of View (2)

MURPHEY, Michael '75
Born on 3/14/45 in Oak Cliff, Texas. Country singer/songwriter. Appeared in the movie *Hard Country*.

9/23/72	**160**	9			1	**Geronimo's Cadillac**			**$15**	A&M 4358
6/16/73	**196**	2			2	**Cosmic Cowboy Souvenir**			**$15**	A&M 4388
2/22/75	**18**	38	●	©	3	**Blue Sky-Night Thunder**			**$12**	Epic 33290
12/6/75+	**44**	13		©	4	**Swans Against The Sun**			**$12**	Epic 33851
11/20/76	**130**	5			5	**Flowing Free Forever**			**$12**	Epic 34220
4/1/78	**99**	6			6	**Lonewolf**			**$12**	Epic 35013

MICHAEL MARTIN MURPHEY:

| 9/4/82 | **69** | 16 | | | 7 | **Michael Martin Murphey** | | | **$10** | Liberty 51120 |
| 10/29/83 | **187** | 3 | | | 8 | **The Heart Never Lies** | | | **$10** | Liberty 51150 |

Alleys Of Austin (2)
Arrows In The Darkness (6)
Backslider's Wine (1)
Blessing In Disguise (2)
Blue Sky Riding Song (3)
Boy From The Country (1)
Buffalo Gun (4)
Calico Silver (2)
Carolina In The Pines (3) 21
Changing Woman (5)
Cherokee Fiddle (5)
Cosmic Cowboy (Part One) (2)
Crack Up In Las Cruces (1)
Crazy Blue (8)

Crystal (7)
Dancing In The Meadow (4)
Desert Rat (3)
Disenchanted (8)
Don't Count The Rainy Days (8)
Drunken Lady Of The Morning
   (2)
First Taste Of Freedom (7)
Flowing Free Forever (5)
Geronimo's Cadillac (1) 37
Goodbye Money Mountain (8)
Harbor For My Soul (1)
Hard To Live Together (6)
Heart Never Lies (8)
Hearts In The Right Place (7)

High Country Caravan (aka
   Song For Stephen Stills) (5)
Honolulu (3)
Lights Of The City (1)
Loners (8)
Lost River (7)
Love Affairs (7)
Loving Time (6)
Mansion On The Hill (4)
Maybe This Time (8)
Medicine Man (3)
Michael Angelo's Blues (Song
   For Hogman) (1)
Natchez Trace (1)
Natural Bridges (4)

Night Patrol (6)
Night Thunder (3)
No Man's Land (6)
North Wind And A New Moon
   (5)
Nothing Is Your Own (6)
Our Lady Of Santa Fe (5)
Paradise Tonight (5)
Pink Lady (4)
Prometheus Busted (4)
Radio Land (8)
Rainbow Man (1)
Renegade (4) 39
Rhythm Of The Road (4)
Ring Of Truth (7)

Rings Of Life (3)
Rolling Hills (2)
Running Wide Open (5)
Sacred Heart (8)
Seasons Change (4)
Secret Mountain Hideout (3)
See How All The Horses Come
   Dancing (5)
Showdown (4)
Song Dog (6)
South Canadian River Song (2)
Still Taking Chances (7) 76
Swans Against The Sun (4)
Take It Like A Man (7)
Temperature Train (4)

Temple Of The Sun (4)
Two-Step Is Easy (7)
Waking Up (1)
Wandering Minstrel (5)
What Am I Doin' Hangin'
   Around? (1)
What's Forever For (7) 19
Wild Bird (3)
Wild West Show (4)
Wildfire (3) 3
Will It Be Love By Morning (8)
Without My Lady There (3)
Yellow House (5)

MURPHY, David Lee '95
Born on 1/7/59 in Herrin, Illinois. Country singer/songwriter/guitarist.

| 7/29/95 | **52** | 36 | ● | © | 1 | **Out With A Bang** | | | **$10** | MCA 11044 |
| 6/8/96 | **104** | 6 | | © | 2 | **Gettin' Out The Good Stuff** | | | **$10** | MCA 11423 |

Born That Way (2)
Breakfast In Birmingham (2)
Can't Turn It Off (1)
Dust On The Bottle (1)

Every Time I Get Around You
   (2)
Fish Ain't Bitin' (1)
Genuine Rednecks (1)

Gettin' Out The Good Stuff (2)
Greatest Show On Earth (1)
High Weeds And Rust (1)
100 Years Too Late (2)

I've Been A Rebel (And It Don't
   Pay) (2)
Just Once (1)
Mama 'N Them (1)

Out With A Bang (1)
Party Crowd (1)
Pirates Cove (2)
Road You Leave Behind (2)

She's Really Something To See
   (2)
Why Can't People Just Get
   Along (1)

MURPHY, Eddie '84
Born on 4/3/61 in Hempstead, New York. Comedian/actor. Former cast member of TV's *Saturday Night Live*. Starred in several movies. Married model Nicole Mitchell on 3/18/93.

8/14/82	**52**	53	▲	©	1	**Eddie Murphy**		[C]	**$10**	Columbia 38180
11/19/83+	**35**	44	▲²	©	2	**Eddie Murphy: Comedian**		[C]	**$10**	Columbia 39005
10/12/85+	**26**	26		©	3	**How Could It Be**			**$10**	Columbia 39952
8/26/89	**70**	9		©	4	**So Happy**			**$10**	Columbia 40970

Barbecue (2)
Black Movie Theaters (1)
Boogie In Your Butt (1)
Bubble Hill (4)
Buckwheat (1)
C-o-n Confused (3)
Christmas Gifts (1)
Do I (3)

Doo-Doo (1)
Drinking Fathers (1)
Effrom (1)
Enough Is Enough (1)
Everything's Coming Up Roses
   (3)
Faggots (1)
Faggots Revisited (2)

Fart Game (2)
Hit By A Car (1)
How Could It Be (3)
I Got It (4)
I, Me, Us, We (3)
I Wish (I Could Tell You When)
   (3)
Ice Cream Man (2)

Languages (2)
Let's Get With It (4)
Little Chinese (1)
Love Moans (4)
Modern Women (2)
My God Is Color Blind (3)
Myths (1)
Party All The Time (3) 2

Politics (2)
Pope And Ronald Reagan (1)
Pretty Please (4)
Put Your Mouth On Me (4) 27
Racism (2)
Sexual Crime (2)
Shoe Throwin' Mothers (2)
Singers (2)

So Happy (4)
TV (2)
Talking Cars (1)
Till The Money's Gone (4)
Tonight (4)
With All I Know (4)

MURPHY, Peter '90

Born on 7/11/57 in Northampton, England. Singer/songwriter. Member of **Bauhaus**.

5/14/88	135	19		©	1 **Love Hysteria**			$10	Beggars Banquet 7634
2/3/90	44	22		©	2 **Deep**			$10	Beggars Banquet 9877
5/2/92	108	3		©	3 **Holy Smoke**			$10	Beggars Banquet 66007

All Night Long (1)
Blind Sublime (1)
Crystal Wrists (2)
Cuts You Up (2) *55*
Deep Ocean Vast Sea (2)

Dragnet Drag (1)
Dream Gone By (3)
Funtime (1)
His Circle And Hers Meet (1)
Hit Song (3)
Indigo Eyes (1)

Keep Me From Harm (3)
Kill The Hate (3)
Let Me Love You (3)
Line Between The Devil's Teeth (And That Which Cannot Be Repeat) (2)

Low Room (3)
Marlene Dietrich's Favorite Poem (2)
My Last Two Weeks (1)
Our Secret Garden (3)
Roll Call (2)

Seven Veils (2)
Shy (3)
Socrates The Python (1)
Strange Kind Of Love (2)
Sweetest Drop (3)

Time Has Got Nothing To Do With It (1)
You're So Close (3)

MURPHY, Walter '76

Born in 1952 in New York City. Studied classical and jazz piano at Manhattan School of Music. Former arranger for **Doc Severinsen** and *The Tonight Show* orchestra.

| 9/4/76 | 15 | 29 | ● | © | 1 **A Fifth Of Beethoven** .... | | | $12 | Private Stock 2015 |

THE WALTER MURPHY BAND

| 7/16/77 | 175 | 3 | | | 2 **Rhapsody In Blue** .... | | | $12 | Private Stock 2028 |

California Strut (1)
Could It Be The Music (2)
Fifth Of Beethoven (1) *1*

Flight '76 (1) *44*
Get A Little Lovin' (1)
It Ain't Necessarily So (2)
Just A Love Song (1)

Love Eyes (2)
Midnight Express (1)
New York City Suite Medley (2)
Night Fall (1)

Only Two People In The World (2)
Rhapsody In Blue (2)
Russian Dressing (1)

Suite Love Symphony (1)
Sunflower (2)
You Are On My Mind (2)

(You've Got To) Be Your Own Best Friend (1)

MURRAY, Anne ★98★ '78

Born Morna Anne Murray on 6/20/45 in Springhill, Nova Scotia, Canada. Country-pop singer. Regular on **Glen Campbell**'s *Goodtime Hour* TV series.

1)Let's Keep It That Way 2)Anne Murray's Greatest Hits 3)New Kind Of Feeling 4)Love Song 5)I'll Always Love You

10/3/70	41	31	●		1 **Snowbird**			$15	Capitol 579
4/3/71	121	9			2 **Anne Murray**			$15	Capitol 667
10/9/71	179	4			3 **Talk It Over In The Morning**			$15	Capitol 821
12/11/71+	128	8		©	4 **Anne Murray/Glen Campbell**			$15	Capitol 869
5/20/72	143	8			5 **Annie**			$12	Capitol 11024
4/28/73	39	24		©	6 **Danny's Song**			$12	Capitol 11172
3/9/74	24	33			7 **Love Song**			$12	Capitol 11266
8/31/74	32	16	●	©	8 **Country**		[K]	$12	Capitol 11324
12/14/74+	70	13			9 **Highly Prized Possession**			$12	Capitol 11354
12/6/75+	142	11			10 **Together**			$12	Capitol 11433
10/2/76	96	6			11 **Keeping In Touch**			$12	Capitol 11559
3/4/78	12	52	▲	©	12 **Let's Keep It That Way**			$12	Capitol 11743
2/17/79	23	29	▲	©	13 **New Kind Of Feeling**			$12	Capitol 11849
11/3/79+	24	23	●	©	14 **I'll Always Love You**			$12	Capitol 12012
2/9/80	73	9			15 **A Country Collection**		[K]	$12	Capitol 12039
5/3/80	88	15		©	16 **Somebody's Waiting**			$12	Capitol 12064
10/4/80	16	64	▲⁴	©	17 **Anne Murray's Greatest Hits**	C:#15/23	[G]	$10	Capitol 12110
5/2/81	55	15	●		18 **Where Do You Go When You Dream**			$10	Capitol 12144
11/28/81+	54	8	▲²	©	19 **Christmas Wishes**	C:#25/11	[X]	$10	Capitol 16232

Christmas charts: 4/'83, 6/'84, 21/'88, 20/'91, 19/'92, 30/'93

8/28/82	90	12			20 **The Hottest Night Of The Year**			$10	Capitol 12225
10/15/83+	72	24	●	©	21 **A Little Good News**			$10	Capitol 12301
10/27/84	92	25	●		22 **Heart Over Mind**			$10	Capitol 12363
2/15/86	68	23	●	©	23 **Something To Talk About**			$10	Capitol 12466
6/20/87	149	6		©	24 **Harmony**			$10	Capitol 12562
12/24/88+	25ˣ	3			25 **Anne Murray Christmas**		[X]	$10	Capitol 90886
11/27/99+	38	38	●	©	26 **What A Wonderful World**			$15	Straight Way 20231 [2]

Ain't No Way To Rise Above (Fallin' In Love) (20)
Amazing Grace (26)
Another Pot O' Tea (7)
Another Sleepless Night (18) *44*
Anyone Can Do The Heartbreak (24)
Are You Still In Love With Me (24)
Away In A Manger (19)
Backstreet Lovin' (7)
Beautiful (5)
Beginning To Feel Like Home (16)
Bitter They Are, Harder They Fall (18)
Blessed Are The Believers (18) *34*
Blue-Finger Lou (10)
Born In Bethlehem (25)
Break My Mind (1,8)
Bridge Over Troubled Water (26)
Bring Back The Love (3,4)
Broken Hearted Me (14,17) *12*

Call, The (10) *91*
Call Me With The News (18)
Call Us Fools (23)
Canadian Sunset (4)
Caress Me Pretty Music (11)
Carolina Sun (11)
Child Of Mine (2)
Christmas In Killarney (25)
Christmas Song (25)
Christmas Wishes (21)
Come On Love (21)
Come To Me (21)
Cotton Jenny (3,8) *71*
Could I Have This Dance (17) *33*
Coventry Carol (25)
Dancin' All Night Long (11)
Danny's Song (6,8,17) *7*
Day Tripper (9) *59*
Daydream Believer (14,17) *12*
Days Of The Looking Glass (2)
Destiny (3)
Do You Hear What I Hear? (25)
Do You Think Of Me? (15,16)

Dream Lover (9)
Drown Me (5)
Ease Your Pain (4,6)
Easy Does It (20)
Easy Love (14)
Elijah (2)
Everything Has Got To Be Free (5)
Everything Old Is New Again (10)
Everything's Been Changed (5)
Fallin' In Love (Fallin' Apart) (20)
Falling Into Rhyme (5)
Fire And Rain (1)
For No Reason At All (13,15)
French Waltz (16)
Get Together (1)
Give Me Your Love (24)
Go Tell It On The Mountain (19)
Golden Oldie (11)
Good Old Days (14)
Gotcha (23)
Great Divide (24)
Harmony (24)

(He Can't Help It If) He's Not You (13,15)
He Thinks I Still Care (6,8)
Heart On The Line (20)
Heart Stealer (21)
Heartaches (23)
Heaven Is Here (13,15)
Hey! Baby! (20)
Highly Prized Possession (9)
Hold Me Tight (12)
Hottest Night Of The Year (20)
How Great Thou Art (26)
I Believe In You (26)
I Can See Clearly Now (26)
I Don't Think I'm Ready For You (22)
I Just Fall In Love Again (13,17) *12*
I Know (3,6)
I Like Your Music (5)
I Say A Little Prayer/By The Time I Get To Phoenix (4) *81*
I Should Know By Now (22)
I Still Wish The Very Best For You (12)

I'll Always Love You (14)
I'll Be Home (6)
I'll Be Home For Christmas (19)
I'll Be Your Baby Tonight (1)
I'll Never Fall In Love Again (2)
I'm Happy Just To Dance With You (16) *64*
I'm Not Afraid Anymore (21)
If A Heart Must Be Broken (18)
If It's Alright With You (10)
If You See My Savior (26)
In The Garden (26)
It Came Upon A Midnight Clear (25)
It Happens All The Time (24)
It Is No Secret (26)
It Should Have Been Easy (18)
It Takes Time (2)
It's All I Can Do (18) *53*
Jacob's Ladder (26)
Joy To The World (19)
Just A Closer Walk With Thee (medley) (26)
Just Another Woman In Love (21)

Just Bidin' My Time (1,8)
Just One Look (7) *86*
Just To Feel This Love From You (12,15)
Killing Me Softly With His Song (6)
Lady Bug (10)
Lay Me Down (Roll Me Out To Sea) (1)
Lean On Me (26)
Let It Be (26)
Let Me Be The One (3,4)
Let Sunshine Her's Day (6)
Let There Be Love (26)
Let Your Heart Do The Talking (22)
Let's Keep It That Way (12,15)
Lift Your Hearts To The Sun (9)
Little Drummer Boy (19)
Little Good News (21) *74*
Lord I Hope This Day Is Good (26)
Lord's Prayer (26)
Love Song (7,17) *12*
Love Story (You & Me) (4)

MURRAY, Anne — Cont'd

Love You Out Of Your Mind (22)
Lover's Knot (14)
Lucky Me (16) *42*
Lullaby (9)
Mary's Little Boy Child (25)
Million More (11)
Moon Over Brooklyn (16)
More We Try (21)
Most Of All (3)
Musical Friends (1)
My Ecstasy (4)
My Life's A Dance (23)
Natural Love (24)
Nearer My God To Thee (26)
Nevertheless (I'm In Love With You) (16)
Night Owl (3)
No Room At The Inn (25)
Nobody Loves Me Like You Do (22)
Now And Forever (You And Me) (23) *92*
O Come All Ye Faithful (25)
O Holy Night (19)

Old Rugged Cross (26)
On And On (23)
Once You've Had It (22)
One Day I Walk (2,6)
Only Love (18)
Other Side (26)
Our Love (22)
Out On The Road Again (10)
Part-Time Love (10)
Peace In The Valley (26)
People's Park (2)
Perfect Strangers (24)
Player In The Band (10)
Please Don't Sell Nova Scotia (9)
Please Smile (3)
Put A Little Love In Your Heart (26)
Put Your Hand In The Hand (1,6,8)
Rain (1)
Rainin' In My Heart (13)
Reach For Me (23)
Real Emotion (7)
Robbie's Song For Jesus (5)

Running (1)
Saved By The Grace Of Your Love (9)
Send A Little Love My Way (7) *72*
Sentimental Favorite (21)
Shadows In The Moonlight (13,17) *25*
Shine (11)
Silent Night (19)
Silver Bells (19)
Sing High - Sing Low (2) *83*
Slow Fall (9)
Snowbird (1,8,17) *8*
Softly And Tenderly (26)
Somebody's Always Saying Goodbye (20)
Somebody's Waiting (16)
Son Of A Rotten Gambler (7,8)
Song For The Mira (20)
Song Of Bernadette (26)
Stranger At My Door (14)
Stranger In My Place (2,8)
Sunday School To Broadway (11)

Sunday Sunrise (10) *98*
Sweet Little Jesus Boy (25)
Sweet Music Man (11)
Sycamore Slick (2)
Take Good Care Of My Heart (22)
Take My Hand Lord Jesus (medley) (26)
Take This Heart (13)
Talk It Over In The Morning (3) *57*
Tennessee Waltz (12,15)
That'll Keep You Dreamin' (20)
That's Not The Way (It's S'posed To Be) (21)
That's Why I Love You (13)
There's Always A Goodbye (12)
They Don't Call It Magic For Nothing (20)
Things (11) *89*
Time Don't Run Out On Me (22)
Together (10)
Tonight (I Want To Be In Love) (24)
United We Stand (4)

Uproar (9)
Walk Right Back (12,15)
Watching The River Run (7)
We All Pull The Load (4)
We Don't Have To Hold Out (18)
We Don't Make Love Anymore (12,15)
We Three Kings (25)
What A Wonderful World (26)
What About Me (6,8) *64*
What's Forever For (16)
When I Can't Have You (21)
When We Both Had The Time To Love (9)
When You're Gone (23)
Where Do You Go When You Dream (18)
Whispering Hope (26)
White Christmas (25)
Who's Leaving Who (23)
Why Don't You Stick Around (14)
Winter Wonderland (19)
Wintery Feeling (14,15)

Wishing Smiles Made It All True (2)
Without You (24)
You Can't Go Back (5)
You Can't Have A Hand On Me (5)
You Haven't Heard The Last Of Me (22)
You Made My Life A Song (5)
You Needed Me (12,17) *1*
You Never Know (23)
You Set My Dreams To Music (16)
You Won't See Me (7,17) *8*
You're A Part Of Me (12)
You're Easy To Love (4)
You've Got A Friend (3,26)
You've Got Me To Hold On To (14)
You've Got What It Takes (13)
Yucatan Cafe (13)

MURRAY, Keith   '94
Born in 1972 in Long Island, New York. R&B singer/rapper.

11/26/94	34	19	●	©	1	The Most Beautifullest Thing In This World	$10	Jive 41555
12/14/96	39	11		©	2	Enigma	$10	Jive 41595
1/30/99	39	6		©	3	It's A Beautiful Thing	$10	Jive 41646

Bad Day (3)
Bom Bom Zee (1)
Call My Name (2)
Danger (1)
Dangerous Ground (2)
Dip Dip Di (1)
Escapism (1)

Get Lifted (1) *71*
Herb Is Pumpin' (3)
High As Hell (3)
Hot To Def (3)
How's That (1)
Incredible (3)
Life On The Street (3)

Live From New York (1)
Love L.O.D. (2)
Manifique (Original Rules) (2)
Media (3)
Message From Keith (3)
Most Beautifullest Thing In This World (1) *50*

My Life (3)
Radio (3)
Rhyme, The (2)
Rhymin' Wit Kel (2)
Ride Wit Us (3)
Secret Indictment (3)
Shut The Fuck Up (3)

Slap Somebody (3)
Some Shit (3)
Straight Loonie (1)
Sychosymatic (1)
Take It To The Streetz (1)
To My Mans (2)
What A Feelin' (2)

When I Rap (3)
Whut's Happnin' (2)
World Be Free (2)
Yeah (2)

MURRAY THE "K" — see VARIOUS ARTIST COMPILATIONS

MUSCLE SHOALS HORNS   '76
Studio group from Muscle Shoals, Alabama: Harrison Calloway (vocals, trumpet), Ronnie Eades (sax), Charles Rose (trombone) and Harvey Thompson (flute).

| 7/4/76 | 154 | 8 | | | | Born To Get Down | $15 | Bang 403 |

Born To Get Down (Born To Mess Around)
Break Down
Bump De Bump Yo Boodie

Get It Up
Give It To Me

Hustle To The Music
Open Up Your Heart

Where I'm Coming From
Who's Gonna Love You

MUSICAL YOUTH   '83
Pop-reggae group from Birmingham, England: Dennis Seaton (vocals), with brothers Kelvin (guitar) and Michael (keyboards) Grant, and Patrick (bass) and Junior Waite (drums). Patrick Waite died on 2/18/93 (age 24).

| 1/8/83 | 23 | 22 | | | 1 | The Youth Of Today | $10 | MCA 5389 |
| 12/17/83+ | 144 | 12 | | | 2 | Different Style! | $10 | MCA 5454 |

Air Taxi (2)
Blind Boy (1)
Children Of Zion (1)
Heartbreaker (1)

Incommunicado (2)
Mash It The Youth Man, Mash It (2)
Mirror Mirror (1)

Never Gonna Give You Up (1)
No Strings (2)
Pass The Dutchie (1) *10*
Rockers (1)

Schoolgirl (1)
Shanty Town (007) (2)
She's Trouble (2) *65*
Sixteen (2)

Tell Me Why (2)
Whatcha Talking 'Bout (2)
Yard Stylee (2)
Young Generation (1)

Youth Of Today (1)

MUSIC EXPLOSION, The   '67
Pop-rock group from Mansfield, Ohio: James Lyons (vocals), Don Atkins and Richard Nesta (guitars), Burton Sahl (bass) and Bob Avery (drums).

| 8/26/67 | 178 | 2 | | | | Little Bit O' Soul | $30 | Laurie 2040 |

Everybody
Good Time Feeling
(Hey) La, La, La

I Can't Stop Now
I See The Light
Let Yourself Go

Little Bit O'Soul *2*
Love, Love, Love, Love, Love
96 Tears

One Potato Two
Patches Dawn

What Did I Do To Deserve Such A Fate

MUSIC MACHINE, The   '67
Rock group from Los Angeles: Sean Bonniwell (vocals, guitar), Mark Landon (guitar), Doug Rhodes (organ), Keith Olsen (bass) and Ron Edgar (drums). Olsen became a top record producer in the 1980s.

| 1/21/67 | 76 | 16 | | © | | (Turn On) The Music Machine | $50 | Original Sound 5015 |

Cherry Cherry
Come On In

Hey Joe
Masculine Intuition

96 Tears
People In Me *66*

See See Rider
Some Other Drum

Talk Talk *15*
Taxman

Trouble
Wrong

MUSIQ SOULCHILD   '01
Born Taalib Johnson in Philadelphia. Male R&B singer.

| 12/2/00+ | 24 | 41 | ● | © | | AIJUSWANASEING (I Just Want To Sing) | $10 | Def Soul 548289 |

Girl Next Door
Just Friends (Sunny) *31*
L' Is Gone

Love *24*
Mary Go Round
My Girl

143
Poparazzi
Settle For My Love

Seventeen
Speechless
You And Me

You Be Alright

MUSIQUE   '78
Disco trio: Christine Wiltshire, Gina Tharps and Mary Seymour.

| 9/30/78 | 62 | 17 | | | | Keep On Jumpin' | $12 | Prelude 12158 |

In The Bush *58*

Keep On Jumpin'

Summer Love

Summer Love Theme

MXPX '00
Christian punk-rock trio from Bremerton, Washington: Mike Herrera (vocals, bass), Tom Wisniewski (guitar) and Yuri Ruley (drums).

7/4/98	99	7	● ©	1	**Slowly Going The Way Of The Buffalo**			$10	A&M 540910
12/5/98	161	1	©	2	**Let It Happen**		[K]	$10	Tooth & Nail 1122
8/14/99	189	1	©	3	**Live At The Show**		[L]	$10	Tooth & Nail 1147
6/3/00	56	13	©	4	**The Ever Passing Moment**			$10	A&M 490656
6/9/01	128	1	©	5	**The Renaissance EP**			$10	Fat Wreck Chords 631

Andrea (3)
Begin To Start (2)
Biased Bigotry (2)
Buildings Tumble (4)
Can't See Not Saying (2)
Chick Magnet (2,3)
Christalena (2)
Circumstance (2)
Cold And All Alone (1,3)
Creation (2)
Do Your Feet Hurt (2)
Dolores (3)
Don't Look Back (5)

Downfall Of Western Civilization (1,3)
Easier Said Than Done (2)
Educated Guess (4)
Elvis Is Dead (2)
Final Slowdance (1)
First Class Mail (2)
Fist Vs. Tact (1,3)
Foolish (4)
For Always (1)
GSF (2,3)
Get With It! (1)
Here With Me (4)
Honest Answers (2)
Hot And Cold (2)

I'm OK, You're OK (1,3)
Important Enough To Mention (2)
Inches From Life (2)
Invitation To Understanding (1,3)
Is The Answer In The Question? (1)
It's Undeniable (2)
KKK Took My Baby Away (3)
Late Last Night (2)
Let It Happen (2)
Letting Go (5)
Life In General (2)
Lifetime Enlightenment (2,3)

Lonesome Town (5)
Middlename (3)
Misplaced Memories (4)
Move To Bremerton (2)
My Life Story (4)
Never Learn (2)
Next Big Thing (4)
Oh Donna (2)
One Step Closer To Life (4)
Opposite, The (5)
Party, My House, Be There (1,3)
Party II (Time To Go) (5)
Prove It To The World (4)
Punk Rawk Show (3)

Responsibility (4)
Rock And Roll Girl (2)
Self Serving With A Purpose (1)
Set The Record Straight (1)
Sick Boy (2)
Small Town Minds (2,3)
So Kill Me (2)
Sometimes You Have To Ask Yourself (3)
Sorry So Sorry (2)
South Bound (2)
Struggle, The (5)
Suggestion Box (2)
Swing Set Girl (2)
Talk Of The Town (2)

Theme Fiasco (1,3)
Thoughts And Ideas (2)
Time Brings Change (3)
Time Will Tell (5)
Tomorrow's Another Day (1,3)
Two Whole Years (4)
Under Lock And Key (1,3)
Unsaid (4)
Walking Bye (3)
Want Ad (2,3)
What's Mine Is Yours (1)
Without You (4)
Yuri Wakes Up Screaming (5)

MYA '00
Born Mya Harrison on 10/10/79 in Washington DC. Female R&B singer.

| 5/9/98 | 29 | 53 | ▲ © | 1 | **Mya** .... | | | $10 | University 90166 |
| 5/13/00 | 15 | 52 | © | 2 | **Fear Of Flying** .... | | | $10 | University 490853 |

Again & Again (2)
Anytime You Want Me (1)
Baby It's Yours (1)
Best Of Me (2) *50*
Bye Bye (1)

Can't Believe (2)
Case Of The Ex (2) *2*
Don't Be Afraid (1)
Fear Of Flying (2)
Free (2) *42*

How You Gonna Tell Me (2)
If You Died I Wouldn't Cry (2)
Cause You Never Loved Me Anyway (1)
If You Were Mine (1)

It's All About Me (1) *6*
Keep On Lovin' Me (1)
Lie Detector (2)
Man In My Life (2)
Movin' On (1) *34*

My First Night With You (1) *28*
Now Or Never (2)
Pussycats (2)
Ride & Shake (2)
Takin' Me Over (2)

That's Why I Wanna Fight (2)
We're Gonna Make Ya Dance (1)
What Cha Say (1)

MYERS, Alicia '84
Born in Detroit. R&B singer. Former lead singer of **One Way**.

| 12/8/84 | 186 | 5 | | | **I Appreciate** .... | | | $10 | MCA 5485 |

Appreciation
Don't Do Me This Way

Just Can't Stay Away
Just Praying

My Guy
Say That

You Get The Best From Me (Say, Say, Say)

MYERS, Billie '98
Born on 6/14/70 in Coventry, England. Female singer.

| 1/31/98 | 91 | 21 | © | | **Growing, Pains** .... | | | $10 | Universal 53100 |

Few Words Too Many
First Time

Having Trouble With The Language
Kiss The Rain *15*

Mother, Daughter, Sister, Lover
Much Change Too Soon
Opposites Attract

Please Don't Shout
Shark And The Mermaid
Tell Me

You Send Me Flying

MYLES, Alannah '90
Born on 12/25/55 in Toronto; raised in Buckhorn, Ontario, Canada. Female singer.

| 1/13/90 | 5 | 36 | ▲ © | | **Alannah Myles** .... | | | $10 | Atlantic 81956 |

Black Velvet *1*
Hurry Make Love

If You Want To
Just One Kiss

Kick Start My Heart
Love Is *36*

Lover Of Mine
Rock This Joint

Still Got This Thing
Who Loves You

MY LIFE WITH THE THRILL KILL KULT '93
Rock group from Chicago. Assembled by Mr. Groovie Mann (vocals) and Mr. Buzz McCoy (keyboards).

| 9/25/93 | 194 | 1 | | | **13 Above The Night** .... | | | $10 | Interscope 92258 |

Badlife
Blue Buddha
China de Sade

Delicate Terror
Dimentia 66
Dirty Little Secrets

Disko Fleshpot
Electrical Soul Wish
Final Blindness

Savage Sexteen
Starmartyr
13 Above The Night

Velvet Edge

MYRICK, Gary '83
Born in Texas. Rock guitarist. Joined British group **Havana 3 A.M.** in 1991.

| 8/6/83 | 186 | 3 | | | **Language** .... | | [M] | $10 | Epic 38637 |

Glamorous

Guitar, Talk, Love & Drums

Lost In Clubland

Message Is You

Time To Win

MYRON '98
Born Myron Davis in Cleveland. R&B singer.

| 8/15/98 | 156 | 2 | © | | **Destiny** .... | | | $10 | Island 524479 |

Angel
Come Around

Destiny *47*
Eastside Girl

Give My All To You
Heavenly Girl

Hit It
See You Cry

So Damn Much
So Fly

We Can Get Down *75*
You're My Everything

MYSTIC MOODS, The '66
Instrumental studio group assembled by producer Brad Miller.
1)One Stormy Night 2)Nighttide 3)Extensions

4/30/66	63	14	©	1	**One Stormy Night**		[I]	$15	Philips 600205
10/8/66	110	10	©	2	**Nighttide**		[I]	$15	Philips 600213
3/25/67	157	4		3	**More Than Music**		[I]	$15	Philips 600231
11/25/67	164	3		4	**Mexican Trip**		[I]	$15	Philips 600250
2/24/68	182	4		5	**The Mystic Moods Of Love**		[I]	$15	Philips 600260
11/9/68	194	3	©	6	**Emotions**		[I]	$15	Philips 600277
5/3/69	155	9		7	**Extensions**		[I]	$15	Philips 600301
11/22/69+	165	8		8	**Love Token**		[I]	$15	Philips 600321
5/23/70	165	15	©	9	**Stormy Weekend**		[I]	$15	Philips 600342
11/28/70+	174	9		10	**English Muffins**		[I]	$15	Philips 600349
4/29/72	184	3		11	**Love The One You're With**		[I]	$12	Warner 2577
5/5/73	190	4		12	**Awakening**		[I]	$12	Warner 2690

MYSTIC MOODS, The —Cont'd

Aja Toro (1)
And The Sun Will Shine (8)
Another Dawn (With You) (11)
Autumn Leaves (7)
Awakening, The (12)
Born Free (3)
Both Sides Now (8)
California Dreamin' (7)
Can't Take My Eyes Off You (5)
Carry That Weight (medley) (10)
Cielito Lindo (4)
Cloudy (6)
Colour Of My Love (10)
Come Saturday Morning (9)
Cosmic Sea (12) **83**
Daphne's Theme (2)
Days Of Wine And Roses (2)
Do You Know The Way To San Jose (6)
Don't Remind Me Now Of Time (8)
Dream (1)
Early In The Morning (10)
Early Mornin' Rain (6)

Eleanor Rigby (6)
England Swings (10)
Far From The Madding Crowd (5)
Fire Island (1)
First Day Of Forever (12)
First Of May (10)
Four Square City Medley (12)
4:22 A.M. (9)
Friendly Persuasion (Thee I Love) (5)
Gay Ranchero (4)
Glory Of Love (5)
Golden Slumbers (medley) (10)
Good Feelings (11)
Grand Prix, Theme From (3)
Here There And Everywhere (10)
Holly On My Mind (4)
Homeward Bound (6)
Hot Bagel (1)
How Do I Love You (11)
Hurt So Bad (8)
I Am, It Is (12)
I Can't Get Away From You (9)

If You Go Away (9)
If You Must Leave My Life (7)
In Your Arms (1)
Invitation (2)
Jim Webb Collage Medley (8)
Just 'Round The River Bend (3)
La Golondrina (2)
La Virgena De La Macarena (4)
Lalena (7)
Lara's Theme (Somewhere My Love) (2)
Las Chiapanecas (4)
Last Thing On My Mind (7)
Lay Lady Lay (11)
Listen To The Warm (6)
Live For Life (5)
Living Is Giving (11)
Local Freight (7)
Look Of Love (5)
Love (11)
Love Grows (Where My Rosemary Goes) (10)
Love Is Blue (9)
Love The One You're With (11)
Love Token (8)

Lovers Lullaby (9)
Malaguena Salerosa (4)
Maman (6)
Man And A Woman (3)
Maria Elena (4)
Massachusetts (10)
Mexican Hat Dance And Soliloquy (4)
Minstrel Boy (1)
Moments Ago (medley) (7)
Monday, Monday (9)
Moon River (2)
Moonlight (5)
My Own True Love (2)
Ne Dis Rien (Say No More) (9)
Nevada Smith (2)
New Testament, Theme From (3)
Norwegian Wood (7)
Nothing On My Mind (medley) (7)
One Stormy Night (1)
Paris Smiles (3)
Paul Simon Montage Medley (7)

Puerte De Manzanillo (4)
Queretaro-Tula Fast Freight (4)
Rhapsody, Love Theme From A (5)
Romeo & Juliet (8)
Sand Pebbles, Theme From The (3)
Sayonara (1)
Scarborough Fair/Canticle (medley) (6)
Sensuous Woman (11)
Seventh Plane (12)
Shane (2)
Shoes Of The Fisherman, Theme From (7)
Singin' In The Rain (2)
Soldier In The Rain (6)
Something (1)
Somewhere, My Love ..see: Lara's Theme
Sound Of Silence (medley) (6)
Stormy Weekend, Theme From (9)
Stragglers & Newcomers (12)
Strangers In The Night (2)

Summer Place, Theme From A (2)
Summertime (2)
Sunny Googe Street (6)
Sunshower (8)
Sweet Rollin' (11)
Symphony (3)
There's A Good Earth Out Tonight (7)
Ti-Pi-Tin (4)
Ticket To Ride (10)
Traces (8)
Trains, Boats & Planes (6)
Tristan And Isolde, Love Theme From (5)
Universal Mind (12)
Very Precious Love (5)
Visions (1)
Waltz For Tricia (9)
Warm Lovin' (1)
Webb Of Jim Collage Medley (7)
Wednesdays' Child (3)
When You Are There (3)
Words (10)

MYSTIKAL   '00
Born Michael Tyler in New Orleans. Male rapper. Member of **504 Boyz**.

DEBUT	PEAK	WKS	RIAA	CD	#	Album Title	$	Label & Number
10/28/95	103	11	●	©	1	**Mind Of Mystikal**	$10	Big Boy 41581
11/29/97	3	44	▲	©	2	**Unpredictable**	$10	No Limit 41620
1/2/99	5	24	▲	©	3	**Ghetto Fabulous**	$10	No Limit 41655
10/14/00	❶¹	37	▲²	©	4	**Let's Get Ready**	$10	Jive 41696

Ain't Gonna See Tomorrow (4)
Ain't No Limit (2)
Beware (1)
Big Truck Boys (4)
Born 2 Be A Soldier (2)
Braids, The (4)
Come See About Me (4)
Danger (Been So Long) (4) **14**
Dick On The Track (2)
Did I Do It (2)
Dirty South, Dirty Jerz (3)

Family (4)
Gangstas (2)
Ghetto Child (4)
Ghetto Fabulous (3)
Here I Go (1)
Here We Go (2)
I Rock, I Roll (4)
I Smell Smoke (3)
I'm (1)
I'm On Fire (3)
It Yearns (2)

Jump (4)
Keep It Hype (3)
Let's Go Do It (3)
Life Ain't Cool (3)
Man Right Chea (2)
Mind of Mystikal (1)
Mr. Hood Critic (1)
Murder 2 (2)
Murderer (1)
Murderer III (4)
Mystikal Fever (4)

Neck Uv Da Woods (4)
Never Gonna Bounce (The Dream) (4)
Not That Nigga (1)
Out That Boot Camp Clicc (1)
Ready To Rumble (4)
Respect My Mind (3)
Round Out The Tank (3)
Shake Ya Ass (4) **13**
Shine (2)
Sleepin' With Me (2)

Smoke Something (1)
Smoked Out (4)
Stack Yo Chips (3)
Stick Up (3)
Still Smokin' (2)
That Nigga Ain't Shit! (1)
That's The Nigga (3)
There He Go (3)
13 Years (2)
U Can't Handle This (2)
U Would If U Could (4)

Unpredictable (2)
We Got The Clout (2)
Whacha Want, Whacha Need (3)
What's Your Alias? (3)
Y'all Ain't Ready Yet (1)
Yaah! (3)

N

★459★   NABORS, Jim   '66
Born on 6/12/30 in Sylacauga, Alabama. Singer/actor. Appeared in several movies and TV shows.
1)Jim Nabors Sings Love Me With All Your Heart 2)The Jim Nabors Hour 3)Jim Nabors By Request

DEBUT	PEAK	WKS	CD	#	Album Title		$	Label & Number
10/15/66	24	56	●	1	**Jim Nabors Sings Love Me With All Your Heart**		$15	Columbia 2558 / 9358
5/20/67	50	40		2	**Jim Nabors By Request**		$15	Columbia 2665 / 9465
9/16/67	147	6		3	**The Things I Love**		$15	Columbia 2703 / 9503
12/2/67+	❶¹ˣ	25	©	4	**Jim Nabors' Christmas Album**	[X]	$15	Columbia 2731 / 9531
					Christmas charts: 7/'67, 7/'68, 1/'69, 3/'70, 6/'71, 5/'72, 20/'73			
7/13/68	153	26		5	**Kiss Me Goodbye**		$15	Columbia 9620
11/16/68	173	12	●	6	**The Lord's Prayer And Other Sacred Songs**		$15	Columbia 9716
6/14/69+	145	19		7	**Galveston**		$15	Columbia 9817
6/27/70	34	23		8	**The Jim Nabors Hour**		$15	Columbia 1020
9/5/70	124	26		9	**Everything Is Beautiful**		$15	Columbia 30129
3/27/71	75	13		10	**For The Good Times/The Jim Nabors Hour**	[L]	$15	Columbia 30449
7/24/71	122	10		11	**Help Me Make It Through The Night**		$15	Columbia 30810
10/23/71	166	4		12	**How Great Thou Art**		$15	Columbia 30671
6/17/72	157	8		13	**The Way Of Love**		$15	Columbia 31336

Abide With Me (12)
Almost Persuaded (11)
Amazing Grace (6)
And This Is My Beloved (3)
Anytime (10)
(At) The End (Of A Rainbow) (13)
Ave Maria (6,12)
Battle Hymn Of The Republic (6)
Blessed Assurance (12)
Born Free (5)
Bridge Over Troubled Water (9)
By The Time I Get To Phoenix (5)
Cabaret (2)
Christmas Eve In My Home Town (4)
(Cuando Calienta El Sol) ..see: Love Me With All Your Heart
Cycles (7)
Day In The Life Of A Fool (8)
Detroit City (10)
Didn't We (7)

Do You Hear What I Hear? (4)
Dr. Zhivago ..see: Somewhere, My Love
Don't You Know (3)
Everything Is Beautiful (9)
First Time Ever (I Saw Your Face) (13)
For Once In My Life (7)
For The Good Times (10)
Full Moon And Empty Arms (3)
Galveston (7)
Games People Play (8)
Go Tell It On The Mountain (4)
God Be With You (12)
God Is Love (12)
Godfather (Speak Softly Love), Love Theme From The (13)
Green Green Grass Of Home (7)
Hasta Luego (2)
Have A Little Faith (11)
Have I Stayed Away Too Long (11)

Help Me Make It Through The Night (11)
Hi-Lili, Hi-Lo (9)
Holy City (6)
Holy, Holy, Holy (6)
Honey (I Miss You) (5)
How Great Thou Art (12)
I Can't Help It (If I'm Still In Love With You) (4)
I Can't Stop Loving You (9)
I Love Paris (5)
I Must Have Been Out Of My Mind (5)
I Really Don't Want To Know (8)
I Will Wait For You (5)
I Won't Mention It Again (11)
I'd Like To Teach The World To Sing (In Perfect Harmony) (13)
I'll Be Home For Christmas (4)
I'll Begin Again (10)
I'm Yours (7)
I've Gotta Be Me (7)

If I Never Laugh Again (9)
Impossible Dream (1)
In A Humble Place (4)
In The Garden (6)
In The Sweet Bye And Bye (12)
It Hurts To Say Goodbye (2)
It's Impossible (13)
It's My Life (8)
Jean (8)
Jingle Bells (4)
Just A Closer Walk With Thee (6)
Kiss Me Goodbye (5)
Lamp Is Low (3)
Lara's Theme ..see: Somewhere, My Love
Les Bicyclettes De Belsize (7)
Little Green Apples (7)
Living In A House Divided (13)
Lord's Prayer (6)
Louisiana Lady (10)
Love Is Blue (5)
Love Me With All Your Heart (Cuando Calienta El Sol) (1)
Rock Of Ages (6)

Love Story, Theme From ..see: Romeo & Juliet, Love Theme From ..see: Time For Us (Where Do I Begin)
Make The World Go Away (11)
Mama, A Rainbow (9)
Mame (2)
More (2)
My Cup Runneth Over (2)
My Elusive Dreams (11)
My Reverie (3)
My Rosary (12)
My Woman, My Woman, My Wife (11)
O Come, All Ye Faithful (4)
O Holy Night (4)
Old Rugged Cross (6)
On A Clear Day You Can See Forever (1)
Our Love (3)
Panis Angelicus (O Lord Most Holy) (6)
Release Me (10)
Rock-A-Bye Your Baby With A Dixie Melody (1)

Romeo & Juliet, Love Theme From ..see: Time For Us
Rose Garden (11)
San Francisco (8)
Silent Night, Holy Night (4)
Sleigh Ride (4)
Softly And Tenderly (12)
Something (10)
Somewhere, My Love (3)
Story Of A Starry Night (3)
Stranger In Paradise (3)
Strangers In The Night (1)
Summer Of '42 (The Summer Knows), Theme From (13)
Sunrise, Sunset (2)
Swanee (1)
Sweetheart Tree (9)
Take My Hand, Precious Lord (8)
Tennessee Waltz (11)
There Goes My Everything (11)
There's A Kind Of Hush (All Over The World) (5)
Things I Love (3)

NABORS, Jim — Cont'd

This Is My Song (2)
Thomas Crown Affair, Theme From ..see: Windmills Of Your Mind
Three Wise Men, Wise Men Three (2)
Till The End Of Time (3)

Time After Time (2)
Time For Us (Love Theme From Romeo And Juliet) (9)
To Give (5)
Tomorrow Never Comes (5,8)
Try To Remember (5)
Turn Around Look At Me (7)

Until It's Time For You To Go (10)
Way Of Love (13)
What A Friend We Have In Jesus (6)
What Now My Love (1)
When The Roll Is Called Up Yonder (12)

(Where Do I Begin) Love Story (13)
White Christmas (4)
Wichita Lineman (7)
Windmills Of Your Mind (9)
With Pen In Hand (10)
With These Hands (10)
Without You (13)

World I Used To Know (9)
Yesterday When I Was Young (9)
You Don't Have To Say You Love Me (2)
You Don't Know Me (1)
You Gave Me A Mountain (7)

You Know You Don't Want Me (2)
You Must Have Faith (8)
You'll Never Walk Alone (8)
You're Gonna Hear From Me (1)
You've Got A Friend (13)

NADA SURF   '96
Rock trio from Los Angeles: Matthew Caws (vocals, guitar), Daniel Lorca (bass) and Ira Elliot (drums).

| 7/13/96 | 63 | 12 | | © | High/Low | | | $10 | Elektra 61913 |

produced by **Ric Ocasek**

Deeper Well
Hollywood

Icebox
Plan, The

Popular
Psychic Caramel

Sleep
Stalemate

Treehouse
Zen Brain

NAILS, The   '86
Rock group from New York City: Marc Campbell (vocals), Steve O'Rourke (guitar), David Kaufman (keyboards), Doug Guthrie (sax), George Kaufman (bass) and Mike Ratti (drums).

| 8/23/86 | 194 | 2 | | | Dangerous Dreams | | | $10 | RCA Victor 5831 |

Dangerous Dream
Darkness Grows Uncivilized

Dig Myself A Hole
First Time

Hello Janine
Ocean

Save Me
Things You Left Behind

Veil, The
Voices

NAJEE   '87
Born in New York City. Jazz saxophonist.

2/28/87	56	45	●	©	1 Najee's Theme	[I]		$10	EMI America 17241
7/9/88	76	21		©	2 Day By Day	[I]		$10	EMI-Manhattan 90096
4/28/90	63	17		©	3 Tokyo Blue	[I]		$10	EMI 92248
7/18/92	107	13	●	©	4 Just An Illusion	[I]		$10	EMI 99400
10/22/94	163	2		©	5 Share My World	[I]		$10	EMI 30789

All I Ever Ask (4)
Betcha Don't Know (1)
Breezy (4)
Broken Promises (5)
Buenos Aires (3)
Burn It Up (4)
Can't Hide Love (1)
Cruise Control (3)
Day By Day (2)
Deep Inside Your Love (4)

Feel So Good To Me (1)
For The Love Of You (1)
(G) Street (5)
Gina (2)
(He's) Armed 'N Dangerous (2)
Heart Like Mine (5)
Here We Go (4)
I Adore Mi Amor (4)
I Didn't Know (5)
I'll Be Good To You (3)

Joy (5)
Just An Illusion (4)
Laid Back (5)
Loving Every Moment (4)
My Angel (5)
My Old Friend (3)
Mysterious (5)
Najee's Nasty Groove (2)
Nation's Call (3)

Noah's Ark (4)
Now That I've Found You (5)
Only At Night (3)
Personality (2)
Saleemah's Dream (5)
Secret Admirer (5)
Share My World (5)
Skyline (4)
So Hard To Let Go (2)
Stand Up (2)

Stay (3)
(Superwoman) Where Were You When I Needed You (3)
Sweet Love (1)
Sweet Sensation (2)
Talkin' (3)
That's The Way Of The World (2)
Tokyo Blue (3)
Tonight I'm Yours (5)

Touch Of Heaven (4)
Until We Meet Again (4)
We're Still Family (1)
What You Do To Me (1)
Whenever We're Together (4)

NAKED EYES   '83
Pop duo from England: Pete Byrne (vocals) and Rob Fisher (keyboards, synthesizer). Fisher later formed **Climie Fisher**. Fisher died on 8/25/99 (age 39).

| 4/16/83 | 32 | 42 | | © | 1 Naked Eyes | | | $10 | EMI America 17089 |
| 9/8/84 | 83 | 10 | | | 2 Fuel For The Fire | | | $10 | EMI America 17116 |

Always Something There To Remind Me (1) **8**
Answering Service (2)
Burning Bridges (1)
Could Be (1)

Emotion In Motion (1)
Eyes Of A Child (2)
Flag Of Convenience (2)
Flying Solo (1)
Fortune And Fame (1)

I Could Show You How (1)
Low Life (1)
Me I See In You (2)
New Hearts (2)
No Flowers Please (2)

Once Is Enough (2)
Promises, Promises (1) **11**
Sacrifice (2)
Voices In My Head (2)

(What) In The Name Of Love (2) **39**
When The Lights Go Out (1) **37**

NAS   '96
Born Nasir Jones on 9/14/73 in Long Island, New York. Male rapper. Member of **The Firm** and **QB Finest**.

5/7/94	12	19	●	©	1 Illmatic			$10	Columbia 57684
7/20/96	❶⁴	34	▲²	©	2 It Was Written	C:#39/1		$10	Columbia 67015
4/24/99	❶²	25	▲²	©	3 I Am...			$10	Columbia 68773
12/11/99	7	26		©	4 Nastradamus			$10	Columbia 63930

Affirmative Action (2)
Big Girl (4)
Big Things (3)
Black Girl Lost (2)
Come Get Me (4)
Dr. Knockboot (3)
Family (4)
Favor For A Favor (3)
Genesis, The (1)

Ghetto Prisoners (3)
God Love Us (4)
Halftime (1)
Hate Me Now (2) **62**
I Gave You Power (2)
I Want To Talk To You (3)
If I Ruled The World (2) **53**
It Ain't Hard To Tell (1) **91**
K-I-SS-I-N-G (3)

Last Words (4)
Life Is What You Make It (3)
Life We Chose (4)
Life's A Bitch (1)
Live Nigga Rap (3)
Memory Lane (Sittin' In Da Park) (1)
Message, The (2)
Money Is My Bitch (3)

N.Y. State Of Mind (1,3)
Nas Is Coming (2)
Nas Is Like (3) **86**
Nastradamus (4) **92**
New World (4)
One Love (1)
One Time 4 Your Mind (1)
Outcome, The (4)
Prediction, The (4)

Project Windows (4)
Quiet Niggas (4)
Represent (1)
Set Up (2)
Shoot 'Em Up (4)
Shootouts (2)
Small World (3)
Some Of Us Have Angels (4)
Street Dreams (2) **22**

Suspect (2)
Take It In Blood (2)
Undying Love (3)
Watch Dem Niggas (2)
We Will Survive (1)
World Is Yours (1)
You Owe Me (4) **59**
You Won't See Me Tonight (3)

★492★ NASH, Graham   '72
Born on 2/2/42 in Blackpool, Lancashire, England. Pop-rock singer/songwriter/guitarist. Former member of **The Hollies**. Formed **Crosby, Stills & Nash** in 1968.

6/19/71	15	24	●	©	1 Songs For Beginners			$15	Atlantic 7204
4/22/72	4	26	●		2 Graham Nash/David Crosby			$15	Atlantic 7220
1/26/74	34	14		©	3 Wild Tales			$15	Atlantic 7288

DAVID CROSBY/GRAHAM NASH:

10/11/75	6	31	●	©	4 Wind On The Water			$12	ABC 902
7/24/76	26	15	●	©	5 Whistling Down The Wire			$12	ABC 956
11/19/77	52	8		©	6 Crosby/Nash - Live	[L]		$12	ABC 1042
10/28/78	150	4			7 The Best Of Crosby/Nash	[G]		$12	ABC 1102

GRAHAM NASH:

| 3/8/80 | 117 | 5 | | | 8 Earth & Sky | | | $12 | Capitol 12014 |
| 4/26/86 | 136 | 7 | | © | 9 Innocent Eyes | | | $10 | Atlantic 81633 |

And So It Goes (3)
Another Sleep Song (3)
Barrel Of Pain (Half-Life) (8)

Be Yourself (1)
Better Days (1)
Bittersweet (4,7)

Blacknotes (2)
Broken Bird (5)
Carry Me (4,7) **52**

Chicago (1,7) **35**
Chippin' Away (9)
Cowboy Of Dreams (4)

Dancer (5)
Deja Vu (6)

Don't Listen To The Rumours (9)
Earth & Sky (8)

NASH, Graham — Cont'd

Fieldworker (4,6)
Foolish Man (5,6)
Frozen Smiles (2)
Games (2)
Girl To Be On My Mind (2)
Glass And Steel (9)
Grave Concern (3)
Helicopter Song (3)
Hey You (Looking At The Moon) (3)
Homeward Through The Haze (4)

I Got A Rock (9)
I Miss You (3)
I Used To Be A King (1,6)
In The 80's (8)
Innocent Eyes (9) *84*
It's All Right (8)
J.B.'s Blues (5)
Keep Away From Me (9)
Laughing (7)
Leeshore, The (6)
Love Has Come (8)

Love Work Out (4,7)
Low Down Payment (4)
Magical Child (8)
Mama Lion (4,6)
Man In The Mirror (1)
Marguerita (9)
Military Madness (1) *73*
Mutiny (5)
Naked In The Rain (4)
Newday (9)
Oh! Camil (The Winter Soldier) (3)

On The Line (3)
Out Of The Darkness (5,7) *89*
Out On The Island (8)
Over The Wall (9)
Page 43 (2,6)
Prison Song (3)
Sad Eyes (9)
See You In Prague (9)
Simple Man (1,6)
Skychild (8)
Sleep Song (1)
Southbound Train (2,7) *99*

Spotlight (5)
Strangers Room (2)
T.V. Guide (8)
Take The Money And Run (4)
Taken At All (5)
There's Only One (1)
Time After Time (5)
To The Last Whale Medley (4,7)
Wall Song (2,7)
We Can Change The World (1)
Where Will I Be? (2)

Whole Cloth (2)
Wild Tales (3,7)
Wounded Bird (1)
You'll Never Be The Same (3)

NASH, Johnny — '72

Born on 8/19/40 in Houston. Singer/guitarist/actor. Appeared on local TV from age 13. With **Arthur Godfrey**'s TV and radio shows from 1956-63. In the movie *Take A Giant Step* in 1959. Own JoDa label in 1965.

11/23/68+	109	12			1 Hold Me Tight	$30	JAD 1207
10/7/72	23	31		©	2 I Can See Clearly Now	$15	Epic 31607
7/14/73	169	6			3 My Merry-Go-Round	$15	Epic 32158

Comma Comma (2)
Cream Puff (2)
Cupid (1) *39*
Don't Cry (1)
Don't Look Back (1)
Gonna Open Up My Heart Again (3)

Groovin' (1)
Guava Jelly (2)
Hold Me Tight (1) *5*
How Good It Is (2)
I Can See Clearly Now (2) *1*
(It Was) So Nice While It Lasted (2)
Love (1)

Love Is Not A Game (3)
Lovey Dovey (1)
Loving You (3) *91*
My Merry-Go-Round (3) *77*
Nice Time (3)
(Oh Jesus) We're Trying To Get Back To You (3)

Ooh Baby You've Been Good To Me (2)
Ooh What A Feeling (3)
People In Love (1)
Salt Annie Ginger Tree (3)
Stir It Up (2) *12*
That's The Way We Get By (2)

There Are More Questions Than Answers (2)
We're All Alike (3)
Yellow House (3)
You Better Stop (Messing Around) (3)
You Got Soul (1) *58*

You Got To Change Your Ways (1)
You Poured Sugar On Me (2)

NASHVILLE BRASS — see DAVIS, Danny

NATE DOGG — '98

Born Nathan Hale in Los Angeles. Male rapper. Former partner of **Warren G.** Cousin of **Snoop Dogg**.

| 8/8/98 | 58 | 5 | | © | G-Funk Classics Vol. 1 & 2 | $15 | Breakaway 3000 [2] |

Almost In Love
Bag O'Weed
Because I Got A Girl
Crazy, Dangerous
Dirty Hoe's Draws

Dogg Pound Gangstaville
First We Pray
Friends
G-Funk
Hardest Man In Town

I Don't Wanna Hurt No More
It's Goin' Down Tonight
Just Another Day
Me & My Homies
My Money

My World
Never Leave Me Alone *33*
Never Too Late
No Matter Where I Go
Nobody Does It Better *18*

Puppy Love
Scared Of Love
Sexy Girl
She's Strange
Stone Cold

These Days
Where Are You Going
Who's Playin' Games

NATIONAL LAMPOON — '73

Comedy troupe spawned from the magazine of the same name. Featured performers included Chevy Chase, John Belushi (**Blues Brothers**) and Christopher Guest (**Spinal Tap**).

9/2/72	132	12			1 Radio Dinner	[C]	$20	Banana 38
6/23/73	107	13			2 Lemmings	[C]	$20	Banana 6006
3/16/74	118	8			3 Missing White House Tapes	[C]	$20	Banana 6008

Admission Speech (3)
All Kidding Aside (1)
All Star Dead Band (2)
Calendar (3)
Catch It And You Keep It (1)
Checkers (3)
Colorado (2)
Concert In Bangla Desh (3)
Constitution Game (3)

Crowd Rain Chant (2)
Deteriorata (1) *91*
Energy Crisis (2)
FBI, The (3)
Farmer Yassir (2)
Gerry Ford Show (3)
Hearings (2)
Hell's Angel (2)
Highway Toes (2)

Impeachment Parade (3)
Impeachment, Swearing Out (3)
Inspiration (3)
It's Obvious (1)
Lemmings Lament (2)
Lonely At The Bottom (3)
Magical Misery Tour (1)
Megadeath (2)
Megagroupie (2)

Mission: Impeachable (3)
New VP (3)
News (3)
Ng Asi (1)
Oval Office (3)
Papa Was A Running Dog Lackey Of The Bourgeoisie (2)
Pennsylvania Avenue (3)

Phono Funnies (1)
Pigeons (1)
Pizza Man (2)
Plumber Commercial (3)
Positively Wall Street (2)
President's Qualities (3)
Profiles In Chrome (1)
Pull The Tregros (1)
'Quinas 'N' Rasmus (1)

Richie Havens (3)
Senate Hearings (3)
Send Money (3)
Support Your Local Police (1)
Teenyrap (1)
Those Fabulous Sixties (1)
Tooth Commercial (3)
Weather Person (2)
Wrap Up (3)

NATURAL FOUR — '75

R&B vocal group from San Francisco: Chris James, Darryl Canady, Steve Striplin and Delmos Whitley.

| 7/5/75 | 182 | 3 | | © | Heaven Right Here On Earth | $20 | Curtom 5004 |

Baby Come On
Count On Me

Give This Love A Try
Heaven Right Here On Earth

Love's So Wonderful
What Do You Do

What's Happening Here
While You're Away

NATURE — '00

Born Jermaine Baxter in New York City. Male rapper. Member of **The Firm** and **QB Finest**.

| 10/7/00 | 50 | 4 | | © | For All Seasons | $10 | Track Masters 68926 |

Don't Stop
Go Ahead

I Don't Give A Fuck
Man's World

Natures Shine
Remember

Shit Like This
Smoke

Talking That Shit
Ultimate High

We Ain't Friends
Young Love

NATURE'S DIVINE — '79

R&B group from Detroit: Lynn Smith (female vocals), Robert Carter (male vocals), Duane Mitchell (guitar), Charles Woods and Marvin Jones (keyboards), Charles Green and Opelton Parker (horns), Robert Johnson (percussion), Keith Fondren (bass) and Mark Mitchell (drums).

| 11/10/79 | 91 | 8 | | | In The Beginning | $12 | Infinity 9013 |

I Just Can't Control Myself *65*
I Never Felt This Way Before

Love Is You
Nature Divine

Questions
Success

Summer Nights

NAUGHTY BY NATURE — '93

Rap trio from East Orange, New Jersey: Anthony "Treach" Criss, Vincent Brown and Kier Gist. Appeared in the movies *The Meteor Man* and *Who's The Man?* Treach married Sandra "Pepa" Denton (of **Salt-N-Pepa**) on 7/24/99.

9/21/91	16	54	▲	©	1 Naughty By Nature	$10	Tommy Boy 1044
3/13/93	3	31	▲	©	2 19 Naughty III	$10	Tommy Boy 1069
6/17/95	3	18	●	©	3 Poverty's Paradise	$10	Tommy Boy 1111
5/15/99	22	17	●	©	4 Nineteen Naughty Nine - Nature's Fury	$10	Arista 19047

Blues, The (4)
Chain Remains (3)
City Of Ci-Lo (3)
Clap Yo Hands (3)
Connections (3)
Craziest (3) *51*
Cruddy Clique (2)

Daddy Was A Street Corner (2)
Dirt All By My Lonely (4)
Everyday All Day (1)
Feel Me Flow (3) *17*
Ghetto Bastard (1)
Guard Your Grill (1)
Hang Out And Hustle (2)

Hip Hop Hooray (2) *8*
Holdin' Fort (3)
Holiday (4)
Hood Comes First (2)
Hot Potato (3)
It's On (2) *74*
It's Workin' (3)

Jamboree (4) *10*
Klickow-Klickow (3)
Knock Em Out Da Box (2)
Let The Ho's Go (1)
Live Or Die (4)
Live Then Lay (4)
19 Naughty III (2)

O.P.P. (1) *6*
On The Run (1)
1,2,3 (1)
Only Ones (2)
Pin The Tail On The Donkey (1)
Poverty's Paradise (3)
Radio (4)

Ready For Dem (2)
Respect Due (3)
Rhyme'll Shine On (1)
Ring The Alarm (4)
Shivers, The (4)
Slang Bang (3)
Sleepin' On Jersey (2)

NAUGHTY BY NATURE — Cont'd

Sleepwalkin' II (2)
Strike A Nerve (1)
Sunshine (3)
Take It To Ya Face (2)

Thankx For Sleepwalking (1)
Thugs & Hustlers (4)
We Could Do It (4)
Wicked Bounce (4)

Wickedest Man Alive (1)
Work (4)
World Go Round (3)

Would've Done The Same For Me (4)
Written On Ya Kitten (2) 93
Yoke The Joker (1)

★376★ NAZARETH '76

Hard-rock group formed in Dunfermline, Fife, Scotland: Dan McCafferty (vocals), Manny Charlton (guitar), Pete Agnew (bass) and Darrell Sweet (drums). **Billy Rankin** (guitar) and John Locke (keyboards) added in 1981.

1)Hair Of The Dog 2)Close Enough For Rock 'N' Roll 3)Malice In Wonderland

8/18/73	157	13		©	1 Razamanaz			$15	A&M 4396
3/9/74	150	8		©	2 Loud 'N' Proud			$15	A&M 3609
7/13/74	157	9		©	3 Rampant			$15	A&M 3641
4/26/75+	17	40	▲	©	4 Hair Of The Dog			$12	A&M 4511
5/8/76	24	14		©	5 Close Enough For Rock 'N' Roll			$12	A&M 4562
12/4/76	75	9		©	6 Play 'N' The Game			$12	A&M 4610
7/2/77	120	6		©	7 Hot Tracks		[G]	$12	A&M 4643
11/19/77+	82	16		©	8 Expect No Mercy			$12	A&M 4666
2/3/79	88	14		©	9 No Mean City			$12	A&M 4741
2/16/80	41	19		©	10 Malice In Wonderland			$12	A&M 4799
2/14/81	70	13		©	11 The Fool Circle			$12	A&M 4844
10/10/81	83	9		©	12 'Snaz		[L]	$15	A&M 6703 [2]
7/10/82	122	10		©	13 2XS			$12	A&M 4901

Alcatraz (1)
All The King's Horses (8)
Another Year (11)
Back To The Trenches (13)
Bad, Bad Boy (1)
Ballad Of Hollis Brown (2)
Beggars Day (4,12)
Big Boy (10,12)
Born To Love (6,7)
Born Under The Wrong Sign (5)
Boys In The Band (13)
Broken Down Angel (1,7)
Busted (2)
Carry Out Feelings (5,7)
Changin' Times (4)
Child In The Sun (2)
Claim To Fame (9)
Cocaine (11,12)
Down Home Girl (6)

Dream On (13)
Dressed To Kill (11,12)
Every Young Man's Dream (11,12)
Expect No Mercy (8,12)
Fallen Angel (10)
Fast Cars (10)
Flying (6)
Freewheeler (2)
Games (13)
Gatecrash (13)
Gimme What's Mine (8)
Glad When You're Gone (3)
Go Down Fighting (2,7)
Gone Dead Train (4)
Hair Of The Dog (4,7,12)
Heart's Grown Cold (10,12)
Holiday (10,12) 87
Homesick Again (5)

I Don't Want To Go On Without You (6)
I Want To (Do Everything For You) (6,7,12)
Java Blues (12)
Jet Lag (3)
Juicy Lucy (12)
Just To Get Into It (9)
Kentucky Fried Blues (8)
L.A. Girls (6)
Let Me Be Your Leader (11,12)
Lift The Lid (5)
Light My Way (3)
Little Part Of You (11)
Lonely In The Night (13)
Loretta (5)
Love Hurts (4,7,12) 8
Love Leads To Madness (13)
Loved And Lost (3)

May The Sunshine (9)
Mexico (13)
Miss Misery (4)
Moonlight Eyes (11)
Morning Dew (12)
My White Bicycle (7)
New York Broken Toy (8)
Night Woman (4)
No Mean City (Parts 1 & 2) (9)
Not Faking It (3)
Place In Your Heart (8)
Please Don't Judas Me (4)
Pop The Silo (11)
Preservation (13)
Razamanaz (1,7,12)
Revenge Is Sweet (8)
Rose In The Heather (4)
Shanghai'd In Shanghai (3,7)
Shapes Of Things (3,12)

Ship Of Dreams (10)
Shot Me Down (7)
Showdown At The Border (10)
Silver Dollar Forger (Parts 1 And 2) (3)
Simple Solution (Parts 1 & 2) (9)
Sold My Soul (1)
Somebody To Roll (6)
Space Safari (medley) (6)
Star (9)
Sunshine (3)
Take The Rap (13)
Talkin' 'Bout Love (10)
Talkin' To One Of The Boys (10)
Teenage Nervous Breakdown (2)
Telegram Medley (5,12)

This Flight Tonight (2,7,12)
Too Bad, Too Sad (1)
Turn On Your Receiver (2)
Turning A New Leaf (10)
Tush (12)
Vancouver Shakedown (5,7)
Vicki (5)
Victoria (11)
Vigilante Man (1)
Waiting For The Man (6)
We Are The People (11)
What's In It For Me (9)
Whatever You Want Babe (9)
Whiskey Drinkin' Woman (4)
Wild Honey (6)
Woke Up This Morning (1)
You Love Another (13)
You're The Violin (5)

NAZZ '69

Rock group from Philadelphia: **Todd Rundgren** (guitar), Robert "Stewkey" Antoni (vocals), Carson Van Osten (bass) and Thom Mooney (drums).

10/19/68+	118	26		©	1 Nazz			$50	SGC 5001
5/10/69	80	15		©	2 Nazz Nazz			$50	SGC 5002

Back Of Your Mind (1)
Beautiful Song (1)
Crowded (1)
Featherbedding Lover (2)

Forget All About It (2)
Gonna Cry Today (2)
Hang On Paul (2)
Hello It's Me (1) 66

If That's The Way You Feel (1)
Kiddie Boy (2)
Lemming Song (1)
Letters Don't Count (2)

Meridian Leeward (2)
Not Wrong Long (2)
Open My Eyes (1)
Rain Rider (2)

See What You Can Be (1)
She's Goin' Down (1)
Under The Ice (2)
When I Get My Plane (1)

Wildwood Blues (1)

NDEGÉOCELLO, Me'Shell '96

Born on 8/29/69 in Berlin; raised in Oxon Hill, Maryland. Female singer/bassist.

3/12/94	166	9		©	1 Plantation Lullabies			$10	Maverick 45333
7/13/96	63	10		©	2 Peace Beyond Passion			$10	Maverick 46033
9/11/99	105	4		©	3 Bitter			$10	Maverick 47439

Adam (3)
Beautiful (3)
Bitter (3)
Bittersweet (2)
Call Me (1)
Deuteronomy: Niggerman (2)
Dred Loc (1)

Ecclesiastes: Free My Heart (3)
Eve (3)
Faithful (3)
Fool Of Me (3)
God Shiva (2)
Grace (3)
I'm Diggin' You (Like An Old Soul Record) (1)

If That's Your Boyfriend (He Wasn't Last Night) (1) 73
Leviticus: Faggot (2)
Loyalty (3)
Makes Me Wanna Holler (2)
Mary Magdalene (2)
May This Be Love (3)
Outside Your Door (1)

Picture Show (1)
Plantation Lullabies (1)
Satisfy (3)
Shoot'n Up And Gett'n High (1)
Sincerity (3)
Soul On Ice (1)
Stay (2)
Step Into The Projects (1)

Sweet Love (1)
Tear And A Smile (2)
Two Lonely Hearts (On The Subway) (1)
Untitled (1)
Wasted Time (1)
Way, The (1)

Who Is He And What Is He To You (2)
Womb, The (2)

NED'S ATOMIC DUSTBIN '92

Rock group from England: Jonathan Penney (vocals), Garath Pring (guitar), Alexander Griffin (bass), Matthew Cheslin (bass) and Daniel Worton (drums).

1/11/92	91	14		©	1 God Fodder			$10	Columbia 47929
11/28/92	183	1		©	2 Are You Normal?			$10	Columbia 53154

Capital Letters (1)
Cut Up (1)
Fracture (2)
Grey Cell Green (1)
Happy (1)

Intact (2)
Kill Your Television (1)
Leg End In His Own Boots (2)
Legoland (2)
Less Than Useful (1)

Not Sleeping Around (2)
Nothing Like (1)
Selfish (1)
Spring (2)
Suave And Suffocated (2)

Swallowing Air (2)
Tantrum (2)
Throwing Things (1)
Two And Two Made Five (2)
Until You Find Out (1)

Walking Through Syrup (2)
What Gives My Son? (1)
Who Goes First? (2)
You (1)
You Don't Want To Do That (2)

Your Complex (1)

NEELY, Sam '72

Born on 8/22/48 in Cuero, Texas. Pop-country singer/songwriter/guitarist.

9/16/72	147	11			1 Loving You Just Crossed My Mind			$15	Capitol 11097
2/10/73	175	6			2 Sam Neely-2			$15	Capitol 11143

Ain't It Good To Be Home (2)
Before Your Eyes (1)
Bless Me Miss America (2)
Blue Time (1)

Can't Help Wondering (1)
Cry Me A Song (1)
Every Day Is The Same As Today (1)

Gentle People (2)
It's Another Day (2)
Jesse California (1)
Kiss The Morning Sunshine (2)

Long Road To Texas (1)
Loving You Just Crossed My Mind (1) 29
Molly Bee (1)

Neither Do I (1)
Pray (1)
Rosalie (2) 43
Sweet Country Child (2)

Take Me Back Wife (2)
Young And Free (2)

DEBUT	PEAK	WKS	RIAA	CD	ARTIST — Album Title	Catalog	Sym	$	Label & Number

NEIL, Vince '93
Born Vincent Neil Wharton on 2/8/61 in Hollywood. Lead singer of **Motley Crue**.

| 5/15/93 | 13 | 13 | | © | 1 **Exposed** | | | $10 | Warner 45260 |
| 9/30/95 | 139 | 1 | | © | 2 **Carved In Stone** | | | $10 | Warner 45877 |

Black Promises (2) · Breakin' In The Gun (2) · Can't Change Me (1) · Can't Have Your Cake (1) · Crawl, The (2) · Edge, The (1) · Find A Dream (2) · Fine, Fine Wine (1) · Forever (1) · Gettin' Hard (1) · Living Is A Luxury (1) · Look In Her Eyes (1) · Make U Feel (2) · One Less Mouth To Feed (2) · One Way (2) · Rift, The (2) · Set Me Free (1) · Sister Of Pain (1) · Skylar's Song (2) · Writing On The Wall (2) · You're Invited (But Your Friend Can't Come) (1)

NEKTAR '74
Art-rock group formed in England: Roye Albrighton (vocals, guitar), Allan Freeman (keyboards), Derek Moore (bass) and Ron Howden (drums). Dave Nelson replaced Albrighton by 1977.

7/20/74	19	28			1 **Remember The Future**			$15	Passport 98002
2/15/75	32	20			2 **Down To Earth**			$15	Passport 98005
4/3/76	89	14			3 **Recycled**			$15	Passport 98011
9/18/76	141	4			4 **A Tab In The Ocean**		[I]	$15	Passport 98017
11/5/77	172	3			5 **Magic Is A Child**			$12	Polydor 6115

Astral Man (2) 91 · Automaton Horrorscope (3) · Away From Asgard (5) · Confusion (1) · Costa Del Sol (3) · Cryin' In The Dark (4) · Cybernetic Consumption (3) · Desolation Valley (4) · Early Morning Clown (2) · Eerie Lackawanna (5) · Fidgety Queen (2) · Finale (2) · Flight To Reality (3) · Images Of The Past (1) · It's All Over (3) · King Of The Twilight (4) · Let It Grow (1) · Listen (1) · Little Boy (2) · Love To Share (Keep Your Worries Behind You) (5) · Magic Is A Child (5) · Marvellous Moses (3) · Midnite Lite (2) · Nelly The Elephant (2) · Oh Willy (2) · On The Run (The Trucker) (5) · Path Of Light (1) · Questions And Answers (1) · Recognition (1) · Recycle (3) · Recycle Countdown (3) · Recycling (3) · Remember The Future (5) · Returning Light (1) · Sao Paulo Sunrise (3) · Show Me The Way (2) · Spread Your Wings (5) · Tab In The Ocean (4) · That's Life (2) · Tomorrow Never Comes (1) · Train From Nowhere (5) · Unendless Imaginations? (3) · Waves (4) · Wheel Of Time (1)

NELLY '00
Born Cornell Haynes on 11/2/74 in Travis, Texas; raised in St. Louis. Male rapper. Former member of **St. Lunatics**.

| 7/15/00 | ❶5 | 64↑▲7 | © | | **Country Grammar** | | | $10 | Fo' Reel 57743 |

Batter Up · E.I. · For My · Greed, Hate, Envy · **(Hot S**t) Country Grammar** 15 · Luven Me · Never Let 'Em C U Sweat · **Ride Wit Me** 3 · St. Louie · Steal The Show · Thicky Thick Girl · Tho Dem Wrappas · Utha Side · Wrap Sumden

NELSON '90
Pop-rock duo from Los Angeles: Gunnar (vocals, bass) and Matthew (vocals, guitar) Nelson. The identical twin sons (born on 9/20/67) of **Ricky Nelson**.

| 7/21/90 | 17 | 64 | ▲2 | © | **After The Rain** | | | $10 | DGC 24290 |

After The Rain 6 · Bits And Pieces · **(Can't Live Without Your) Love And Affection** 1 · Everywhere I Go · Fill You Up · I Can Hardly Wait · (It's Just) Desire · **More Than Ever** 14 · **Only Time Will Tell** 28 · Tracy's Song (medley) · Will You Love Me?

★214★ NELSON, Ricky '58
Born Eric Hilliard Nelson on 5/8/40 in Teaneck, New Jersey. Died in a plane crash on 12/31/85 (age 45) in DeKalb, Texas. Son of bandleader Ozzie Nelson and vocalist Harriet Hilliard. Rick and brother David appeared on Nelson's radio show from March 1949, later on TV, 1952-66. Formed own Stone Canyon Band in 1969. In movies *Rio Bravo*, *The Wackiest Ship In The Army* and *Love And Kisses*. Married to Kristin Harmon (sister of actor Mark Harmon) from 1963-82. Their daughter Tracy is a movie/TV actress. Their twin sons began recording as **Nelson** in 1990. Ricky was one of the first teen idols of the rock era. Inducted into the Rock and Roll Hall of Fame in 1987.
1)Ricky 2)Ricky Nelson 3)Rick Is 21

11/11/57+	❶2	33		©	1 **Ricky**			$100	Imperial 9048
7/28/58	7	9		©	2 **Ricky Nelson**			$100	Imperial 9050
2/2/59	14	19		©	3 **Ricky Sings Again**			$100	Imperial 9061
9/28/59+	22	26		©	4 **Songs By Ricky**			$100	Imperial 9082
8/29/60	18	22		©	5 **More Songs By Ricky**			$100	Imperial 9122

RICK NELSON:
5/29/61	8	49		©	6 **Rick Is 21**			$50	Imperial 9152
4/14/62	27	20		©	7 **Album Seven By Rick**			$50	Imperial 9167
3/2/63	112	4			8 **Best Sellers By Rick Nelson**		[G]	$50	Imperial 9218
5/4/63	128	5			9 **It's Up To You**		[K]	$50	Imperial 9223
6/8/63	20	19		©	10 **For Your Sweet Love**			$50	Decca 74419
1/4/64	14	22		©	11 **Rick Nelson sings "For You"**			$50	Decca 74479
2/21/70	54	19		©	12 **Rick Nelson In Concert**		[L]	$40	Decca 75162
					recorded at The Troubadour Club in Los Angeles				
11/7/70	196	2		©	13 **Rick Sings Nelson**			$40	Decca 75236
12/9/72+	32	18		©	14 **Garden Party**			$40	Decca 75391
2/23/74	190	4		©	15 **Windfall**			$20	MCA 383

RICK NELSON & THE STONE CANYON BAND (above 2)
| 2/21/81 | 153 | 6 | | © | 16 **Playing To Win** | | | $15 | Capitol 12109 |

Again (5,9) · Ain't Nothin' But Love (5) · Almost Saturday Night (16) · Am I Blue (1) · Anytime (13) · Are You Really Real? (14) · Baby I'm Sorry (5) · Baby Won't You Please Come Home (5,9) · Baby You Don't Know (7) · Back To Schooldays (16) · **Be-Bop Baby** (1,8) 3 · Be True To Me (3) · **Believe What You Say** (3,8,12,16) 4 · Blood From A Stone (4) · Boppin' The Blues (1,9) · Break My Chain (6,9) · California (13) · Call It What You Want (16) · Come On In (12) · **Congratulations** (7) 63 · Do The Best You Can (16) · Do You Know What It Means To Miss New Orleans (6) · Don't Leave Me (4) · Don't Leave Me Here (15) · Don't Leave Me This Way (2) · Don't Let Your Goodbye Stand (14) · Don't Look At Me (16) · Down Along The Bayou Country (13) · Down Home (11) · Down The Line (2) · **Easy To Be Free** (12) 48 · Everybody But Me (6) · Everytime I See You Smiling (10) · Everytime I Think About You (10) · Evil Woman Child (15) · Excuse Me Baby (7) · Flower Opens Gently By (14) · **Fools Rush In** (11) 12 · **For You** (11) 6 · For Your Sweet Love (10) · **Garden Party** (14) 6 · **Gypsy Woman** (10) 62 · Half Breed (4) · **Have I Told You Lately That I Love You?** (1,8) 29 · **Hello Mary Lou** (6,12) 9 · Hello Mister Happiness (11) · Here I Go Again (13) · Hey Pretty Baby (5) · Hey There, Little Miss Tease (11) · History Of Love (7) · Honeycomb (1) · How Long (13) · How Many Times (15) · I Can't Help It (3) · I Can't Stop Loving You (7) · I Can't Take It No More (16) · I Don't Want To Be Lonely Tonight (15) · **I Got A Woman** (10) 49 · **I Need You** (9) 83 · I Rise, I Fall (11) · I Shall Be Released (12) · I Wanna Be With You (14) · I Will Follow You (10) · I'd Climb The Highest Mountain (5,9) · I'll Make Believe (6) · I'll Walk Alone (2) · I'm All Through With You (5) · I'm Confessin' (1) · I'm Feelin' Sorry (2) · **I'm In Love Again** (2,8) 67 · I'm Talking About You (14) · I'm Walkin' (12) · I've Been Thinkin' (4) · **If You Can't Rock Me** (1,9) 100 · If You Gotta Go, Go Now (12) · It Hasn't Happened Yet (16) · It's All In The Game (3) · **It's Late** (3) 9 · **It's Up To You** (9) 6 · **Just A Little Too Much** (4,8) 9 · Just Take A Moment (11) · Legacy (15) · Legend In My Time (11) · I'll Bring You Along (14) · Let's Talk The Whole Thing Over (10) · Lifestream (15) · Little Miss American Dream (16) · **Lonesome Town** (3,8) 7 · Long Vacation (4) · Look At Mary (13) · Loser Babe Is You (16) · Louisiana Man (12) · Lucky Star (4) · Mad Mad World (7) · Make Believe (5) · Mr. Dolphin (13) · My Babe (2) · My One Desire (6) · My Woman (13)

622

DEBUT	PEAK	WKS	RIAA	CD	ARTIST — Album Title	Catalog	Sym	$	Label & Number

NELSON, Ricky — Cont'd

Nearness Of You (11)
Never Be Anyone Else But You (3) *6*
Nightime Lady (14)
Oh Yeah, I'm In Love (6)
Old Enough To Love (3) *94*
One Boy Too Late (10)
One Minute To One (4)
One Night Stand (15)
One Of These Mornings (3)
Palace Guard (14) *65*
Pick Up The Pieces (10)

Poor Little Fool (2,8) *1*
Poor Loser (7)
Proving My Love (5)
Reason Why (13)
Red Balloon (12)
Restless Kid (3)
She Belongs To Me (12) *33*
Shirley Lee (2,9)
So Long (4)
So Long Mama (14)
Someday (2)
Someone To Love (15)

Stars Fell On Alabama (6,9)
Stood Up (8) *2*
Stop Sneakin' 'Round (7)
String Along (10) *25*
Summertime (7) *89*
Sure Fire Bet (6)
Sweet Mary (13)
Sweeter Than You (4) *9*
Teenage Doll (1,8)
Thank You Darling (7)
That Same Old Feeling (11)
That Warm Summer Night (6)

That's All (4,8) *48*
That's All She Wrote (11)
There Goes My Baby (2)
There's Good Rockin' Tonight (2)
There's Not A Minute (7)
Time After Time (5)
Today's Teardrops (7) *54*
Travelin' Man (6) *1*
True Love (1)
Tryin' To Get To You (3,9)
Unchained Melody (2)

Violets Of Dawn (12)
Waitin' In School (8) *18*
We've Got A Long Way To Go (13)
What Comes Next? (10)
When Your Lover Has Gone (5)
Who Cares About Tomorrow - Promises (12)
Whole Lotta Shakin' Goin' On (1)
Wild Nights In Tulsa (15)
Windfall (15)

You Don't Love Me Anymore (And I Can Tell) (10) *47*
You Tear Me Up (3)
You'll Never Know What You're Missin' (4)
You're Free To Go (11)
You're So Fine (4)
Your True Love (1)

NELSON, Sandy   '62

Born Sander Nelson on 12/1/38 in Santa Monica, California. Male session drummer.

1)Let There Be Drums 2)Drums Are My Beat! 3)Drummin' Up A Storm

DEBUT	PEAK	WKS	CD	#	Album Title	Sym	$	Label & Number
1/20/62	6	48	©	1	**Let There Be Drums**	[I]	$30	Imperial 9159
4/14/62	29	24	©	2	**Drums Are My Beat!**	[I]	$30	Imperial 9168
7/14/62	55	11	©	3	**Drummin' Up A Storm**	[I]	$30	Imperial 9189
11/3/62	141	3	©	4	**Compelling Percussion**	[I]	$30	Imperial 9204
12/1/62	106	3		5	**Golden Hits**	[I]	$30	Imperial 9202
11/21/64+	122	11		6	**Live! In Las Vegas**	[I-L]	$25	Imperial 12272
3/6/65	135	5		7	**Teen Beat '65**	[I]	$25	Imperial 12278
7/10/65	120	8		8	**Drum Discotheque**	[I]	$25	Imperial 12283
10/2/65	118	11		9	**Drums A Go-Go**	[I]	$25	Imperial 12287
1/8/66	126	7		10	**Boss Beat**	[I]	$25	Imperial 12298
4/23/66	148	2		11	**"In" Beat**	[I]	$25	Imperial 12305

Alexes (4)
All Around The World With Drums (3)
All Night Long (3) *75*
And Then There Were Drums (4) *65*
Batman (11)
Be Bop Baby (5)
Beat From Another World (7)
Big Noise From Winnetka (1)
Birth Of The Beat (1) *75*
Bongo Rock (7)
Bony Moronie (5)
Boot-Leg (9)
Boss Beat (10)
Bouncy (1)
C Jam Blues (3)
Caravan (2)
Casbah (9)
Castle Rock (3)
Chicka Boom (4)

City, The (2)
Civilization (4)
Clapping Song (9)
Come On, Do The Jerk (7)
Day Drumming (2)
Day Tripper (11)
Do The Boomerang (9)
Down In The Boondocks (10)
Drum Bay (6)
Drum Dance (8)
Drum Discotheque (8)
Drum Roll (2)
Drum Stomp (2) *86*
Drum Stuff (6)
Drummin' Up A Storm (3) *67*
Drums A Go-Go (9)
Drums Are My Beat (2) *29*
Drums - For Drummers Only (4)
Drums - For Strippers Only (4)
Drums In A Sea Cave (10)
Duck, The (11)

Early In The Morning (5)
El Bandido (6)
El Pussycat (8)
Get With It (1)
Go-Go A Go-Go (8)
Hang On Sloopy (My Girl Sloopy) (11)
Hard Day's Night (11)
Hawaiian War Chant (2)
Here We Go Again (3)
Honky Tonk (5)
Honky Tonk '65 (7)
Hum Drum (2)
(I Can't Get No) Satisfaction (9)
I Like It Like That (9)
I Want To Walk You Home (5)
I'm Gonna Be A Wheel Someday (1)
I'm In Love Again (3)
"In" Beat (11)
"In" Crowd (10)

Jenny Take A Ride (11)
Jerk, The (7)
Johnny B. Goode (6)
Jolly Green Giant (8)
Jump Time (5)
Just Like Me (11)
Kansas City (3)
Kitty's Theme (9)
Land Of A Thousand Dances (8)
Let There Be Drums (1,6,8) *7*
Live It Up (5,6)
Louie, Louie (9)
Lover's Concerto (10)
Memphis (6)
Mr. John Lee (Part I & II) (6)
My Blue Heaven (2)
My Girl Josephine (1)
My Love (11)
My World Is Empty Without You (11)

No Matter What Shape (Your Stomach's In) (11)
Papa's Got A Brand New Bag (10)
Quite A Beat (1)
Raunchy '65 (7)
Rock House (5)
Sandy (3)
Scratchy (7)
Secret Agent Man (11)
Shotgun (8)
Sidewinder (8)
Skokiaan (8)
Slippin' And Slidin' (1)
Slow Down (10)
Soul Drums (9)
Splish Splash (5)
Taste Of Honey (10)
Teen Beach (8)
Teen Beat '65 (6,7) *44*
Tequila (1)

3rd Man Theme (10)
Tim Tom Drum (8)
Topsy (2)
Treat Her Right (10)
Tub-Thumpin' (3)
20 - 75 (7)
Twine Time (8)
Twisted (2)
Uptight (Everything's Alright) (11)
Walking To New Orleans (5)
What'd I Say (5)
Whittier Blvd. (9)
Wipe-Out (1)
Wooly Bully (9)
You Turn Me On (9)

NELSON, Tracy   '74

Born on 12/27/44 in French Camp, California. Lead singer of **Mother Earth**. Not to be confused with Ricky Nelson's actress daughter.

DEBUT	PEAK	WKS	Album Title				$	Label & Number
10/19/74	145	5	**Tracy Nelson**				$15	Atlantic 7310

After The Fire Is Gone
Down So Low

Hold An Old Friend's Hand
I Wish Someone Would Care

It Takes A Lot To Laugh, It Takes A Train To Cry

Lay Me Down Easy
Lean On Me

Love Has No Pride
Rock Me In Your Cradle

Slow Fall

NELSON, Willie   ★20★   '82

Born on 4/30/33 in Ft. Worth, Texas; raised in Abbott, Texas. Legendary country singer/songwriter. Played bass for **Ray Price**. Moved to Nashville in 1960. Moved back to Texas in 1970. Pioneered the "outlaw" country movement. Appeared in several movies including *The Electric Horseman* (1979), *Honeysuckle Rose* (1980) and *Barbarosa* (1982). Won Grammy's Living Legends Award in 1989.

1)Always On My Mind 2)The Outlaws 3)Honeysuckle Rose 4)Waylon & Willie 5)One For The Road

DEBUT	PEAK	WKS	RIAA	CD	#	Album Title	Sym	$	Label & Number
7/26/75	28	43	▲²	©	1	**Red Headed Stranger**		$15	Columbia 33482
11/8/75	196	3			2	**What Can You Do To Me Now**	[E]	$15	RCA Victor 1234
2/7/76	10	51	▲²	©	3	**The Outlaws**		$15	RCA Victor 1321
						WAYLON JENNINGS/WILLIE NELSON/JESSI COLTER/TOMPALL GLASER			
3/20/76	48	15	●	©	4	**The Sound In Your Mind**		$15	Columbia 34092
5/8/76	149	7			5	**Willie Nelson Live**	[L]	$12	RCA Victor 1487
						originally released in 1966 as *Live Country Music Concert*			
6/5/76	187	3		©	6	**Phases And Stages**	[E]	$12	Atlantic 7291
						recorded in 1964			
10/16/76	60	7	●	©	7	**The Troublemaker**		$12	Columbia 34112
5/21/77	78	15			8	**Before His Time**	[E]	$12	RCA Victor 2210
7/9/77	91	12		©	9	**To Lefty From Willie**		$12	Columbia 34695
						tribute to Lefty Frizzell			
2/4/78	12	29	▲²	©	10	**Waylon & Willie**		$12	RCA Victor 2686
						WAYLON JENNINGS & WILLIE NELSON			
5/13/78	30	117	▲⁴		11	**Stardust**		$12	Columbia 35305
12/2/78+	32	55	▲⁴	©	12	**Willie and Family Live**	[L]	$15	Columbia 35642 [2]
						recorded at Harrah's in Lake Tahoe			
3/3/79	154	5		©	13	**Sweet Memories**	[E]	$12	RCA Victor 3243

NELSON, Willie — Cont'd

DEBUT	PEAK	WKS	RIAA	CD	ARTIST — Album Title	Sym	$	Label & Number
6/30/79	25	18	●	© 14	One For The Road		$15	Columbia 36064 [2]
					WILLIE NELSON AND LEON RUSSELL			
11/17/79+	42	25	▲	© 15	Willie Nelson sings Kristofferson		$12	Columbia 36188
					songs written by Kris Kristofferson			
12/1/79+	73	8	▲	© 16	Pretty Paper	[X]	$12	Columbia 36189
					Christmas chart: 9/'83			
1/12/80	52	25	●	17	The Electric Horseman	[S]	$12	Columbia 36327
					side 1: songs performed by Nelson; side 2: instrumental score by Dave Grusin			
3/15/80	150	5		18	Danny Davis & Willie Nelson with The Nashville Brass		$12	RCA Victor 3549
					new instrumental backing for earlier recordings by Nelson			
6/14/80	70	25	●	© 19	San Antonio Rose		$12	Columbia 36476
					WILLIE NELSON and RAY PRICE			
9/6/80	11	36	▲²	© 20	Honeysuckle Rose	[L-S]	$15	Columbia 36752 [2]
					WILLIE NELSON & FAMILY			

includes "Fiddlin' Around" and "Jumpin' Cotton Eyed Joe" by Johnny Gimble; "Working Man Blues" by Jody Payne; "I Don't Do Windows" by Hank Cochran; "Coming Back To Texas" by Kenneth Threadgill; "If You Want Me To Love You I Will" by Amy Irving; "So You Think You're A Cowboy" by Emmylou Harris; "Two Sides To Every Story" by Dyan Cannon; and "Make The World Go Away" by Hank Cochran/Jeannie Seely

DEBUT	PEAK	WKS	RIAA	CD	ARTIST — Album Title	Sym	$	Label & Number
3/21/81	31	23	▲	© 21	Somewhere Over The Rainbow		$12	Columbia 36883
8/1/81	148	7		22	The Minstrel Man	[E]	$12	RCA Victor 4045
9/19/81	27	93	▲³	© 23	Willie Nelson's Greatest Hits (& Some That Will Be)	[G]	$15	Columbia 37542 [2]
3/20/82	2⁴	99	▲⁴	© 24	Always On My Mind		$12	Columbia 37951
10/30/82	57	22	●	© 25	WWII		$12	RCA Victor 4455
					WAYLON & WILLIE			
1/15/83	109	14		© 26	Kris, Willie, Dolly & Brenda...the winning hand		$15	Monument 38389 [2]
					KRIS KRISTOFFERSON, WILLIE NELSON, DOLLY PARTON & BRENDA LEE			
2/12/83	37	53	▲	© 27	Pancho & Lefty		$12	Epic 37958
					MERLE HAGGARD/WILLIE NELSON			
3/19/83	39	20		© 28	Tougher Than Leather		$10	Columbia 38248
5/21/83	60	16	●	© 29	Take It To The Limit		$10	Columbia 38562
					WILLIE NELSON with WAYLON JENNINGS			
11/26/83+	54	34	▲	© 30	Without A Song		$10	Columbia 39110
12/3/83	182	5		31	My Own Way	[E]	$10	RCA Victor 4819
6/16/84	116	7		32	Angel Eyes		$10	Columbia 39363
8/4/84	69	26	▲	© 33	City Of New Orleans		$10	Columbia 39145
11/10/84	152	5		34	Music from SongWriter	[S]	$12	Columbia 39531
					WILLIE NELSON & KRIS KRISTOFFERSON			
3/30/85	152	7		© 35	Me & Paul		$10	Columbia 40008
					title refers to Nelson and his drummer Paul English			
6/1/85	92	35	▲	© 36	Highwayman		$10	Columbia 40056
					WILLIE NELSON/JOHNNY CASH/WAYLON JENNINGS/KRIS KRISTOFFERSON			
10/12/85	178	3	●	© 37	Half Nelson		$10	Columbia 39990
3/17/90	79	13		© 38	Highwayman 2		$10	Columbia 45240
					WILLIE NELSON/JOHNNY CASH/WAYLON JENNINGS/KRIS KRISTOFFERSON			
8/3/91	193	3		© 39	Clean Shirt		$10	Epic 47462
					WAYLON & WILLIE			
4/10/93	75	16		© 40	Across The Borderline		$10	Columbia 52752
3/26/94	188	1		© 41	Moonlight Becomes You		$10	Justice 1601
11/19/94	103	11		© 42	Healing Hands Of Time		$10	Liberty 30420
1/21/95	193	2	▲	© 43	Super Hits	C:#25/9 [G]	$10	Columbia 64184
6/29/96	132	2		© 44	Spirit		$10	Island 524242
6/27/98	150	2		© 45	VH1 Storytellers	[L]	$10	American 69416
					JOHNNY CASH/WILLIE NELSON			
9/19/98	104	6		© 46	Teatro		$10	Island 524548
10/7/00	83	7		© 47	Milk Cow Blues		$10	Island 542517

NELSON, Willie — Cont'd

I Want To Be With You Always (9)
I'd Have To Be Crazy (4,23)
I'd Trade All Of My Tomorrows (For Just One Yesterday) (8)
I'll Be Seeing You (42)
I'll Be There (If You Ever Want Me) (19)
I'll Keep On Loving You (41)
I'm A Memory (2,8,12,31,35)
I'm Confessin' (That I Love You) (21)
I'm Gonna Sit Right Down And Write Myself A Letter (21)
I'm Not Trying To Forget You Anymore (44)
I'm Waiting Forever (44)
I've Just Destroyed The World (46)
I've Loved You All Over The World (46)
I've Seen That Look On Me (A Thousand Times) (2)
If I Can Find A Clean Shirt (39)
If I Had My Way (42)
If I Were The Man You Wanted (40)
If You Could Touch Her At All (10,12,20,23)
If You've Got The Money I've Got The Time (4,12,23)
In God's Eyes (41)
In The Garden (7)
It Should Be Easier Now (8,22)
It Turns Me Inside Out (33)
It Wouldn't Be The Same (Without You) (21)
It's A Dream Come True (44)
It's My Lazy Day (27)
It's Not Supposed To Be That Way (6,10,20)
Jim, I Wore A Tie Today (36)
Jingle Bells (16)
Just As I Am (1,12)
Just Out Of Reach (33)
Kansas City (47)
King Of A Lonely Castle (26)
Last Cowboy Song (36)
Last Letter (medley) (5)
Last Thing I Needed First Thing This Morning (24)
Laying My Burdens Down (22)
Let It Be Me (24) **40**
Let The Rest Of The World Go By (14)
Little Old Fashioned Karma (28)
Little Things (8,13,26)
Little Unfair (9)

Living In The Promiseland (43)
Living Legend (38)
Local Memory (18)
Lonely Street (47)
Look What Thoughts Will Do (9,23)
Loving Her Was Easier (Than Anything I'll Ever Do Again) (15,20)
Maker, The (46)
Makin's Of A Song (39)
Mammas Don't Let Your Babies Grow Up To Be Cowboys (10,12,17,23) **42**
Mariachi (44)
Matador (44)
Me And Bobby McGee (medley)
Me And Paul (3,35,45)
Midnight Ride (17)
Milk Cow Blues (47)
Minstrel Man (22)
Mom And Dad's Waltz (9)
Mona Lisa (21)
Moonlight Becomes You (41)
Moonlight In Vermont (11)
Most Unoriginal Sin (40)
Mountain Dew (22)
Mr. Record Man (5,12)
Mr. Shuck And Jive (25)
My Heroes Have Always Been Cowboys (17,23,43) **44**
My Life's Been A Pleasure (I Still Love You As I Did In Yesterday) (27)
My Love For The Rose (28)
My Mary (27)
My Mother's Eyes (21)
My Own Peculiar Way (2,5,18,31,46)
My Window Faces The South (32)
Night Life (4,12,18,19,42,45,47)
No Love Around (medley) (16)
No Love At All (29)
No Reason To Quit (27)
Nobody Said It Was Going To Be Easy (34)
Nobody Slides, My Friend (28)
Nothing I Can Do About It Now (43)
O Little Town Of Bethlehem (16)
O'er The Waves (1)
Oh, What It Seemed To Be (42)
Old Age And Treachery (39)
Old Five & Dimers Like Me (35)
Old Fords And A Natural Stone (24)

Old Friends (29)
On The Road Again (20,23,43,45) **20**
On The Sunny Side Of The Street (11)
Once In A While (30)
Once More With Feeling (2)
One Day At A Time (5,12,35)
One For My Baby And One More For The Road (14)
One In A Row (8,31)
Only Daddy That'll Walk The Line (12)
Opportunity To Cry (5,27)
Ou Es-Tu, Mon Amour? (Where Are You, My Love?) (46)
Outskirts Of Town (47)
Over The Rainbow (21)
Pancho And Lefty (27,37,43)
Party's Over (24)
Penny For Your Thoughts (4)
Permanently Lonely (2,5,24)
Phases And Stages (medley) (6)
Pick Up The Tempo (6,10,20)
Pilgrim: Chapter 33 (15)
Ping Pong (26)
Pins And Needles (In My Heart) (31)
Please Come To Boston (33)
Please Don't Talk About Me When I'm Gone (41)
Please Don't Tell Me How The Story Ends (15)
Precious Memories (7)
Pretend I Never Happened (6,35)
Pretty Paper (16)
Put It Off Until Tomorrow (26)
Put Me On A Train Back To Texas (39)
Railroad Lady (9,23)
Rainy Day Blues (18,31,47)
Reasons To Quit (27)
Red Headed Stranger (1,12)
Release Me (19)
Remember Me (1) **67**
Ridin' Down The Canyon (14)
Rocks From Rolling Stones (39)
Roll In My Sweet Baby's Arms (12)
Rudolph The Red-Nosed Reindeer (16)
Samba For Charlie (32)
San Antonio Rose (19)
Santa Claus Is Coming To Town (16)
Senses (22)

Sentimental Journey (41)
September Song (11)
Seven Spanish Angels (37)
Shall We Gather (7)
She Is Gone (44)
She's Gone (35)
She's Gone, Gone, Gone (9)
She's Not For You (8,40)
She's Out Of My Life (33)
Silent Night, Holy Night (16)
Silver Stallion (38)
Sioux City Sue (14)
Sister's Coming Home (medley) (6)
(Sittin' On) The Dock Of The Bay (25)
Sittin' On Top Of The World (47)
Slow Movin' Outlaw (37)
So You Think You're A Cowboy (17)
Somebody Pick Up My Pieces (46)
Someday (You'll Want Me To Want You) (41)
Someone Loves You Honey (26)
Someone To Watch Over Me (26)
Something To Think About (5)
Somewhere In Texas (Part I & II) (28)
Song For You (12,20)
Songs That Make A Difference (38)
Songwriter (34)
Sound In Your Mind (4)
Spirit Of E⁹ (44)
Stardust (11)
Staring Each Other Down (24)
Stay A Little Longer (12,23)
Stay Away From Lonely Places (8,31)
Still Is Still Moving To Me (40)
Still Water Runs The Deepest (27)
Stormy Weather (14)
Summer Of Roses (28)
Summertime (14)
Sunday Mornin' Comin' Down (15)
Sweet Bye & Bye (7)
Sweet Memories (13)
Take It To The Limit (29)
Take This Job And Shove It (12)
Tenderly (14)
Texas (38)

Texas Flood (47)
Texas On A Saturday Night (37)
Thank You (32)
Thanks Again (4)
That Lucky Old Sun (4,14)
That's The Way Love Goes (9)
There Are Worse Things Than Being Alone (42)
There Is A Fountain (7)
There Will Never Be Another You (32)
These Lonely Nights (46)
They All Went To Mexico (37)
This Cold War With You (19)
Three Days (46)
Thrill Is Gone (47)
Till I Gain Control Again (12,23,29)
Time Of The Preacher (1,12)
To All The Girls I've Loved Before (37) **5**
To Each His Own (30)
To Make A Long Story Short (She's Gone) (8,26)
Too Sick To Pray (44)
Touch Me (5)
Tougher Than Leather (28)
Trouble In Mind (14)
Troublemaker, The (7)
Tryin' To Outrun The Wind (39)
Tumbling Tumbleweed (32)
Twentieth Century Is Almost Over (36)
Twinkle, Twinkle Little Star (21)
Two Old Sidewinders (39)
Two Stories Wide (38)
Unchained (45)
Unchained Melody (11)
Uncloudy Day (7,12,20,23)
Under The Double Eagle (12)
Until It's Time For You To Go (33)
Valentine (40)
Wake Me When It's Over (2,13,47)
Walkin' (medley) (6)
Washing The Dishes (medley) (6)
We Don't Run (44)
We Had It All (29)
We're All In Your Corner (38)
Welfare Line (36)
What Can You Do To Me Now? (2)
What Do You Think About Lovin' (26)
What Was It You Wanted (40)

When The Roll Is Called Up Yonder (7)
Where Do You Stand? (22)
Where The Soul Never Dies (7)
Whiskey River (12,20,23)
Whispering Hope (7)
White Christmas (16)
Whiter Shade Of Pale (24)
Who'll Buy My Memories (34)
Who's Sorry Now? (21)
Why Are You Pickin' On Me (33)
Why Baby Why (29)
Why Do I Have To Choose (29)
Why Me (15)
Wild Side Of Life (14)
Will The Circle Be Unbroken (7,12)
Will You Remember? (13,22)
Wind Beneath My Wings (33)
Winter Wonderland (16)
Without A Song (30)
Won't You Ride In My Little Red Wagon (21)
Wonderful Future (13)
World Is Waiting For The Sunrise (41)
Worried Man (45)
Would You Lay With Me (In A Field Of Stone) (29)
Write Your Own Songs (25,34)
Year That Clayton Delaney Died (25)
Year 2003 Minus 25 (10)
Yesterday (5)
Yesterday's Wine (3,18)
You Always Hurt The One You Love (41)
You Are My Sunshine (14)
You Just Can't Play A Sad Song On A Banjo (41)
You Left A Long, Long Time Ago (2,22,26)
You Ought To Hear Me Cry (8)
You Show Me Yours (And I'll Show You Mine) (15,20)
You Wouldn't Cross The Street (To Say Goodbye) (35)
You'll Always Have Someone (26)
You'll Never Know (30,41)
You're Gonna Love Yourself (In The Morning) (26)
Your Memory Won't Die In My Grave (44)

NEMESIS '93

Rap group from Dallas: The Snake, M.C. Azim and Big Al. By 1993, group consisted of Big Al, **Ron "C"**, Devo X and M.C. Joe Macc.

DEBUT	PEAK	WKS		CD		Catalog		$	Label & Number
7/13/91	183	2		© 1	Munchies For Your Bass			$10	Profile 1411
7/24/93	159	2		© 2	Temple Of Boom			$10	Profile 1441

Ali English And The 40 Oz. Thieves (1)
Big, The Bad, The Bass (2)
Bitches And Money (1)
Brand New Team (2)

Cantfiguritout (2)
Cloud 7 (2)
Dallas We Come From (1)
Deep Up In It (2)
Dis-N-Dat (1)

Droppin' The Bass (1)
Get Ya Flow On (2)
Go Ron C (2)
Grind (1)
Hard From Birth (2)

I Want Your Sex (1)
Let's Have A Good Time (1)
Life In The 90's (1)
Munchies For Your Bass (1)
Nemesis On The Premises (2)

Nemesis To The Future (1)
On The One (1)
Parkin' Lot On Dixon (2)
Settin' The Record Straight (1)
S.O.U.L. (1)

Str8 Jackin' (2)
Temple Of Boom (2)

NENA '84

Rock group formed in Berlin, Germany: Gabriele "Nena" Kerner (vocals), Carlo Karges (guitar), Uwe Fahrenkrog-Petersen (keyboards), Jurgen Demel (bass) and Rolf Brendel (drums).

DEBUT	PEAK	WKS		CD		Catalog		$	Label & Number
3/24/84	27	14		©	99 Luftballons			$10	Epic 39294

Das Land Der Elefanten
Hangin' On You

Just A Dream
Kino

Let Me Be Your Pirate
Leuchtturm

99 Luftballons *2*
99 Red Balloons

?
Rette Mich

Uner Kannt Durch's Marchenland

★205★ NERO, Peter '63

Born on 5/22/34 in Brooklyn, New York. Pop-jazz-classical pianist. Won the 1961 Best New Artist Grammy Award.

1)Hail The Conquering Nero 2)For The Nero-Minded 3)Young And Warm And Wonderful 4)Summer of '42 5)Peter Nero In Person

DEBUT	PEAK	WKS			ARTIST — Album Title	Catalog	Sym	$	Label & Number
7/10/61	34	22		1	Piano Forte		[I]	$20	RCA Victor 2334
9/18/61	32	62		2	New Piano In Town		[I]	$20	RCA Victor 2383
3/17/62	22	23		3	Young And Warm And Wonderful		[I]	$20	RCA Victor 2484
7/7/62	16	38		4	For The Nero-Minded		[I]	$20	RCA Victor 2536
2/2/63	40	9		5	The Colorful Peter Nero		[I]	$20	RCA Victor 2618
3/30/63	5	28		6	Hail The Conquering Nero		[I]	$20	RCA Victor 2638
9/7/63	31	23		7	Peter Nero In Person		[I-L]	$20	RCA Victor 2710
					recorded at Webster Hall in New York City				
2/29/64	133	4		8	Sunday In New York		[I-S]	$20	RCA Victor 2827
6/6/64	38	26		9	Reflections		[I]	$20	RCA Victor 2853
10/10/64	42	21		10	Songs You Won't Forget		[I]	$20	RCA Victor 2935

DEBUT	PEAK	WKS	RIAA	CD	ARTIST — Album Title	Catalog	Sym	$	Label & Number

NERO, Peter — Cont'd

DEBUT	PEAK	WKS			Title		Sym	$	Label & Number
2/20/65	123	4			11 The Best Of Peter Nero .... [G-I]			$20	RCA Victor 2978
5/29/65	147	3			12 Career Girls .... [I]			$20	RCA Victor 3313
10/23/65	86	16			13 Nero Goes "Pops" .... [I]			$25	RCA Victor 2821

PETER NERO/BOSTON POPS/ARTHUR FIEDLER

2/19/66	114	6			14 The Screen Scene .... [I]			$15	RCA Victor 3496
7/16/66	141	3			15 Peter Nero-Up Close .... [I]			$15	RCA Victor 3550
5/13/67	193	2			16 Peter Nero plays Born Free and others .... [I]			$15	RCA Camden 2139
4/20/68	180	4			17 Peter Nero plays Love Is Blue and ten other great songs .... [I]			$15	RCA Victor 3936
5/10/69	193	3			18 I've Gotta Be Me .... [I]			$15	Columbia 9800
11/27/71+	23	27	● ©		19 Summer of '42 .... [I]			$15	Columbia 31105
7/8/72	172	9			20 The First Time Ever (I Saw Your Face) .... [I]			$15	Columbia 31335

All The Things You Are (7)
America (medley) (7)
And I Love Her (15)
Anna (1)
Are My Dreams Real? (7)
As Long As He Needs Me (9)
Autumn (10)
Baby I'm A Want You (20)
Bess, You Is My Woman (2)
Best Is Yet To Come (9)
Best Thing For You (15)
Bidin' My Time (13)
Black Is The Color Of My True Love's Hair (5)
Bluesette (9)
Body And Soul (2)
Born Free (16)
Boy Like That (medley) (7)
Brian's Song (20)
Button Up Your Overcoat (7)
Call Me Irresponsible (10)
Career Girl (12)
Certain Smile (12)
Cherokee (1)
Chim Chim Cheree (14)
Continental Holiday (6)
Cookie Crumbles (8)
Cute (7)
Dancing On The Ceiling (4)
Days Of Wine And Roses (9)
Deep Purple (5)
Don't Blame Me (3)
Don't Get Around Much Anymore (4)
Don't Speak Of Love (8,16)
Easy To Love (12)
Eileen's Theme (8)
Embraceable You (13)
England Swings (15)
Ev'rything I've Got (4)
Everything I Own (20)

First Time Ever (I Saw Your Face) (20)
Flick, The (14)
For All We Know (19)
For Once In My Life (18)
Forget Domani (Forget Tomorrow) (14)
Fox, Theme From The (17)
Free Again (17)
Get Me To The Church On Time (1)
Girl From Ipanema (10)
Gloomy Sunday (6)
Glory Of Love (17)
Go Away Little Girl (19)
Godfather, Love Theme From (20)
Golden Earrings (5)
Gone With The Wind (16)
Got To Be There (20)
Granada (6)
Green Leaves Of Summer (7)
Happy Time (17)
Harlow (Lovely Girl), Theme From (14)
Hello (8)
Hello, Dolly! (10)
Hello Hop (8)
Help! (14)
Here's That Rainy Day (15)
Hey Jude (5)
How Can You Mend A Broken Heart? (7)
Hurting Each Other (20)
I Can't Get Started (1)
I Could Have Danced All Night (12)
I Feel Pretty (medley)_ (7)
I Got Plenty O' Nuttin' (7,16)
I Got Rhythm (13)

I Love How You Love Me (18)
I Say A Little Prayer (17)
I Want To Hold Your Hand (10)
I Wish You Love (19)
I'm Gonna Make You Love Me (18)
I'm Gonna Sit Right Down And Write Myself A Letter (12)
I've Gotta Be Me (18)
I've Grown Accustomed To Her Face (1,11)
In Other Words (Fly Me To The Moon) (1)
Isn't It Romantic (4)
It's A Darn Good Thing (16)
It's All Right With Me (7,11)
Journey To Red Rocks (5)
Just One Of Those Things (2)
Just Squeeze Me (3)
Let's Not Waste A Moment (4)
Little Girl Blue (4)
Lo Mucho Que Te Quiero (All I Need Is Time) (18)
Londonderry Air (6)
Long Ago And Far Away (2)
Look For The Silver Lining (5)
Lot Of Livin' To Do (15)
Love (19)
Love Is A Many-Splendored Thing (7)
Love Is A Simple Thing (4)
Love Is Blue (17)
Love Is Here To Stay (13)
Love Story, Theme From (19)
Love That Never Ends (20)
Mack The Knife (6)
Made For Each Other, Theme From (20)
Make It With You (19)
Man I Love (13)
Maria (2,7,11)
Midnight In Moscow (6,11)

Moment Of Truth (9)
Mood Indigo (5,11)
Moon River (4,11)
More (9)
More In Love (8,11)
Most Beautiful Girl In The World (12)
Mountain Greenery (1)
My Bonnie Lies Over The Ocean (6)
My Coloring Book (9)
My Favorite Things (14)
My Funny Valentine (1)
My Man's Gone Now (4)
My Ship (17)
Never Can Say Goodbye (20)
Never My Love (19)
Never On Sunday (6)
Night And Day (1,11)
No Moon At All (15)
Ob-La-Di Ob-La-Da, Variations On The Theme (18)
On Frantic Fifth (8)
On Green Dolphin Street (5,11)
On The Street Where You Live (2)
Orange Colored Sky (5)
Out Of This World (12)
Over The Rainbow (1)
People (10)
Personality (12)
Philosopher, The (8)
Pick Yourself Up (15)
Pink Panther Theme (10)
Rain In My Heart (18)
Reflections (9)
Rhapsody In Blue (13)
Room Without Windows (10)
Sandpiper, Love Theme From The ..see: Shadow Of Your Smile
Scarborough Fair/Canticle (18)

Scarlet Ribbons (5)
Scratch My Bach (1)
Secret Love (3,11)
Serenade In Blue (5)
Shadow Of Your Smile (14)
Shangri-La (10)
She Loves Me (9)
Shelter Of Your Arms (10)
Ship Of Fools (1)
Show Me (12)
Silencers, Theme From The (14)
Slow Boat To China (2)
Someone To Watch Over Me (12)
Something's Coming (4,7)
Somewhere (medley) (7)
Soulful Strut (18)
Speak Low (12)
Spring Concerto (15)
Spring Is Here (1)
Spy Who Came In From The Cold, Theme From The (14)
St. Louis Blues (2)
Star Eyes (13)
Stella By Starlight (16)
Stormy Weather (2)
Strange Music (6)
Summer Of '42, Theme From (19) *21*
Sunday In New York (8,16)
Sunny (17)
Surrey With The Fringe On Top (1)
Sweetest Sounds (16)
Take The "A" Train (15)
Tangerine (1)
Taxi! (8)
Tea For Two (2)
Tender Is The Night (10)
That's All (1)
Then I'll Be Tired Of You (15)

They Can't Take That Away From Me (13)
(They Long To Be) Close To You (19)
This Is All I Ask (9)
Thou Swell (3)
Three Coins In The Fountain (2)
Thunderball (14)
Tonight (medley) (7)
Too Late Now (4)
Try To Remember (17)
Variations ..see: Ob-La-Di Ob-La-Da
Walk Right In (9)
Warm (3)
Wasn't The Summer Short (3)
Way You Look Tonight (3)
We've Only Just Begun (19)
What Kind Of Fool Am I? (6)
What's New Pussycat? (14)
When I Fall In Love (3)
When My Dream Boat Comes Home (15)
When The World Was Young (6,11)
Who Will Answer? (17)
Who's Afraid Of Virginia Woolf? (16)
Wichita Lineman (18)
Windy (17)
Without You (20)
Wives And Lovers (9)
Wonderful You (3,8,16)
Yellow Rose Of Texas (5)
Yesterday (15)
Yesterdays (4)
You Are Too Beautiful (3)
You've Got A Friend (19)
Young And Warm And Wonderful (3)

NESBY, Ann   **'96**

Born in Joliet, Illinois. Lead singer of **Sounds Of Blackness**.

| 10/19/96 | 157 | 13 | © | | I'm Here For You .... | | | $10 | Perspective 9022 |

Can I Get A Witness
Hold On
I'll Be Your Everything

I'll Do Anything For You
I'm Here For You
I'm Still Wearing Your Name

If You Love Me
In The Spirit
Let Old Memories Be

Let The Rain Fall
Lord How I Need You
This Weekend

Thrill Me
(What A) Lovely Evening

NESMITH, Michael, & The First National Band   **'70**

Born on 12/30/42 in Houston. Pop-rock singer/songwriter/guitarist. Member of **The Monkees**. Also see **The Wichita Train Whistle**.

10/17/70	143	3	©		1 Magnetic South			$30	RCA Victor 4371
1/2/71	159	4	©		2 Loose Salute			$30	RCA Victor 4415
8/4/79	151	9			3 Infinite Rider On The Big Dogma			$20	Pacific Arts 130

MICHAEL NESMITH

Beyond The Blue Horizon (1)
Bye, Bye, Bye (2)
Calico Girlfriend (1)
Capsule (Hello People A Hundred Years From Now) (3)
Carioca (Blue Carioca) (3)

Conversations (2)
Crippled Lion (1)
Cruisin' (Lucy And Ramona And Sunset Sam) (3)
Dance (Dance & Have A Good Time) (3)

Dedicated Friend (2)
Factions (The Daughter Of Rock N' Roll) (3)
First National Rag (1)
Flying (Silks & Satins) (3)
Hello Lady (1)
Hollywood (1)

Horserace (Beauty And The Magnum Force) (3)
I Fall To Pieces (2)
Joanne (1) *21*
Keys To The City (1)
Lady Of The Valley (2)
Light (The Eclectic Light) (3)

Listen To The Band (2)
Little Red Rider (1)
Magic (This Night Is Magic) (3)
Mama Nantucket (1)
Nine Times Blue (1)
One Rose (1)
Silver Moon (2) *42*

Tengo Amor (2)
Thanx For The Ride (2)
Tonite (The Television Song) (3)

NESS, Mike   **'99**

Born on 4/3/62 in Stoneham, Massachusetts. Lead singer of **Social Distortion**.

| 5/1/99 | 80 | 5 | © | | 1 Cheating At Solitaire .... | | | $10 | Time Bomb 43524 |
| 11/27/99 | 174 | 1 | © | | 2 Under The Influences .... | | | $10 | Time Bomb 43536 |

All I Can Do Is Cry (2)
Ball And Chain (Honky Tonk) (2)
Ballad Of A Lonely Man (1)
Big Iron (2)

Charmed Life (1)
Cheating At Solitaire (1)
Crime Don't Pay (1)
Devil In Miss Jones (1)
Don't Think Twice (1)

Dope Fiend Blues (1)
Funnel Of Love (2)
Gamblin' Man (2)
House Of Gold (2)
I Fought The Law (2)

I'm In Love w/ My Car (1)
If You Leave Before Me (1)
Let The Jukebox Keep On Playing (2)
Long Black Veil (1)

Misery Loves Company (1)
No Man's Friend (1)
Once A Day (2)
One More Time (2)
Rest Of Our Lives (1)

Send Her Back (1)
Six More Miles (2)
Thief In The Night (2)
Wildwood Flower (2)
You Win Again (1)

NETHERLANDS PHILHARMONIC ORCHESTRA, The   **'98**

Studio orchestra from Holland.

| 11/21/98 | 8[C] | 5 | © | | Brahms Symphony No. 4/Tragic Overture | | | $10 | LaserLight 14001 |

Allegro Energico E Passionato   Allegro Giocoso   Allegro Non Troppo   Andante Moderato   Tragic Overture Op, 81

NEVIL, Robbie '87
Born on 10/2/60 in Los Angeles. Pop singer/songwriter/guitarist.

| 11/29/86+ | 37 | 46 | | © | 1 Robbie Nevil | | | $10 | Manhattan 53006 |
| 11/26/88+ | 118 | 21 | | © | 2 A Place Like This | | | $10 | EMI 48359 |

Back On Holiday (2) 34 · Can I Count On You (2) · Holding On (2) · Love And Money (2) · Simple Life (Mambo Luv Thang) · Walk Your Talk (1)
Back To You (1) · Dominoes (1) 14 · Just A Little Closer (1) · Love Is Only Love (2) · (1) · Wot's It To Ya (1) 10
C'est La Vie (1) 2 · Getting Better (1) · Limousines (1) · Mary Lou (1) · Somebody Like You (2) 63
Here I Go Again (2) · Look Who's Alone Tonight (1) · Neighbors (1) · Too Soon (2)

NEVILLE, Aaron '90
Born on 1/24/41 in New Orleans. R&B singer. Member of The Neville Brothers. Father of Ivan Neville.

| 10/21/89+ | 7 | 58 | ▲² | © | 1 Cry Like A Rainstorm - Howl Like The Wind .... C:#37/6 | | | $10 | Elektra 60872 |

LINDA RONSTADT Featuring Aaron Neville

| 6/29/91 | 44 | 41 | ▲ | © | 2 Warm Your Heart .... | | | $10 | A&M 5354 |

co-produced by Linda Ronstadt

| 5/8/93 | 37 | 58 | ▲ | © | 3 The Grand Tour .... | | | $10 | A&M 540086 |
| 11/27/93 | 36 | 8 | ▲ | © | 4 Aaron Neville's Soulful Christmas .... C:#11/19 [X] | | | $10 | A&M 540127 |

Christmas charts: 8/93, 16/94, 16/95, 29/96, 28/97

| 5/6/95 | 64 | 20 | ● | © | 5 The Tattooed Heart .... | | | $10 | A&M 540349 |
| 11/1/97 | 188 | 1 | | © | 6 ...To Make Me Who I Am .... | | | $10 | A&M 540784 |

Ain't No Way (3) · Close Your Eyes (2) · For The Good Times (5) · Lord's Prayer (3) · Silent Night (4) · What Did I Do (To Deserve
All My Life (1) 11 · Crying In The Chapel (5) · God Made You For Me (4) · Louisiana Christmas Day (4) · Some Days Are Made For Rain · You) (4)
Angola Bound (2) · Don't Fall Apart On Me Tonight · Grand Tour (3) 90 · Louisiana 1927 (2) · (5) · When Something Is Wrong
Ave Maria (2) · (3) · I Bid You Goodnight (2) · Lovely Lady Dressed In Blue (6) · Somewhere, Somebody (2) · With My Baby (1) 78
Beautiful Night (5) · Don't Go Please Stay (2) · I Can't Change The Way You · My Brother, My Brother (3) · Song Of Bernadette (3) · White Christmas (4)
Bells, The (3) · Don't Know Much (1) 2 · Don't Feel (6) · My Precious Star (5) · Star Carol (4) · Why Should I Fall In Love (5)
Bells Of St. Mary's (4) · Don't Take Away My Heaven · I Need You (1) · O Holy Night (4) · Such A Night (4) · With You In Mind (2)
Betcha By Golly, Wow (3) · (3) 56 · I Owe You One (3) · O Little Town Of Bethlehem (4) · Sweet Amelia (6) · Yes, I Love You (6)
Can't Stop My Heart From · Down Into Muddy Water (5) · In Your Eyes (5) · Please Come Home For · That's The Way She Loves (3) · You Never Can Tell (3)
Loving You (The Rain Song) · Everybody Plays The Fool · It Feels Like Rain (2) · Christmas (4) · These Foolish Things (3) · Your Sweet And Smiling Eyes
(5) 99 · (2) 8 · Just To Be With You (6) · Please Remember Me (3) · To Make Me Who I Am (6) · (6)
Christmas Song (Chestnuts · Everyday of My Life (5) · La Vie Dansante (2) · Roadie Song (3) · Try (A Little Harder) (5)
Roasting On An Open Fire) · First Time Ever I Saw Your · Let It Snow, Let It Snow, Let It · Say What's In My Heart (6) · Use Me (5)
(4) · Face (5) · Snow (4) · Show Some Emotion (5) · Warm Your Heart (2)

NEVILLE, Ivan '89
Born in New Orleans. Rock singer/bassist. Son of Aaron Neville.

| 11/12/88+ | 107 | 23 | | © | If My Ancestors Could See Me Now .... | | | $10 | Polydor 834896 |

After All This Time · Falling Out Of Love 91 · Never Should Have Told Me · Out In The Streets · Sun
Another Day's Gone By · Money Talks · Not Just Another Girl 26 · Primitive Man · Up To You

NEVILLE BROTHERS, The '90
Family group from New Orleans: brothers Art, Charles, Cyril and Aaron Neville. Art was a member of The Meters (1966-77). Cyril was with The Meters (1975-77). Charles and Aaron also contributed to The Meters (1976-77).

8/29/81	166	3		©	1 Fiyo On The Bayou			$15	A&M 4866
4/11/87	178	3		©	2 Treacherous: A History Of The Neville Brothers 1955-1985 .... [K]			$15	Rhino 71494 [2]
5/2/87	155	9		©	3 Uptown			$10	EMI America 17249
4/8/89	66	24	●	©	4 Yellow Moon			$10	A&M 5240
8/25/90	60	15		©	5 Brother's Keeper			$10	A&M 5312
5/23/92	103	9		©	6 Family Groove			$10	A&M 5384
5/7/94	126	5		©	7 Live On Planet Earth .... [L]			$10	A&M 540225

All These Things (2) · Drift Away (3) · I Love Her Too (3) · Money Back Guarantee (My · Shake Your Tambourine (7) · Whatever It Takes (3)
Amazing Grace (2,7) · Fallin' Rain (5) · I Never Needed No One (3) · Love Is Guaranteed) (3) · Shek-A-Na-Na (3) · Where Is My Baby (2)
Amen (medley) (2) · Family Groove (6) · Iko Iko (medley) (1) · My Blood (5) · Sister Rosa (4,7) · Wild Injuns (4)
Arianne (2) · Fear, Hate, Envy, Jealousy (2) · It Takes More (6) · My Brother's Keeper (5) · Sitting In Limbo (1,2) · Will The Circle Be Unbroken (4)
Ballad Of Hollis Brown (4) · Fearless (5) · Jah Love (5) · Mystery Train (5) · Sons And Daughters (5) · With God On Our Side (4)
Bird On A Wire (5) · Fever (3) · Junk Man (7) · Old Habits Die Hard (3) · Spirits Of The World (3) · Witness (3)
Brother Blood (5) · Fire And Brimstone (4) · Let My People Go (6,7) · On The Other Side Of Paradise · Steer Me Right (5) · Wrong Number (I Am Sorry,
Brother Jake (5,7) · Fire On The Bayou (1,2) · Let's Live (2) · (6) · Sweet Honey Dripper (1) · Goodbye) (4)
Brother John (1,2) · Fly Like An Eagle (6) · Line Of Fire (6) · One Love (medley) (7) · Take Me To Heart (6) · Yellow Moon (4,7)
Cha Dooky-Do (2) · Forever...For Tonight (3) · Love The One You're With · One More Day (6) · Tell It Like It Is (2) · You Can't Always Get What
Change Is Gonna Come (4) · Get Up Stand Up (medley) (7) · (medley) (7) · Over You (7) · Ten Commandments Of Love · You Want (medley) (7)
Congo Square (4) · Greatest Love (2) · Maori Chant (3) · People Get Ready (medley) (7) · (1) · You're The One (3)
Dancing Jones (2) · Healing Chant (4) · Mardi Gras Mambo (2) · River Of Life (5) · True Love (6) · Zing, Zing (2)
Day To Day Thing (6) · Her African Eyes (7) · Meet De Boys On The · Run Joe (1) · Voodoo (4)
Dealer, The (7) · Hercules (2) · Battlefront (7) · Sands Of Time (7) · Waiting At The Station (2)
Down By The Riverside · Hey Pocky Way (1,2) · Midnight Key (3) · Saxafunk (6) · Wake Up (4)
(medley) (2) · I Can See It In Your Eyes (6) · Mona Lisa (1) · Sermon (medley) (7) · Washable Ink (2)

NEWBEATS, The '64
Pop vocal trio: Larry Henley, with brothers Dean and Marc Mathis.

| 10/3/64 | 56 | 19 | | | 1 Bread & Butter .... | | | $100 | Hickory 120 |
| 1/22/66 | 131 | 4 | | | 2 Run Baby Run .... | | | $75 | Hickory 128 |

Ain't That Lovin' You, Baby (1) · Hang On Sloopy (2) · It's Really Goodbye (2) · Oh, Pretty Woman (2) · Shoop Shoop Song (It's In His · This Old Heart (2)
Bread And Butter (1) 2 · Help (2) · Little Child (2) · Patent On Love (1) · Kiss) (1) · Thou Shalt Not Steal (1)
Bye, Bye, Love (1) · (I Can't Get No) Satisfaction (2) · Looking For Love (2) · Pink Dally Rue (1) · So Fine (1) · Tough Little Buggy (1)
Come See About Me (2) · I'm Blue (The Gong-Gong · Mean Wooly Willie (2) · Run, Baby Run (Back Into My · There Oughta Be A Law (Bout
Everything's Alright (1) 16 · Song) (1) · Oh, Girls, Girls (2) · Arms) (2) 12 · The Stuff I Saw) (1)

NEW BIRTH, The '73
R&B group from Louisville, Kentucky. Consisted of 17 members with two vocal groups (The New Birth and Love, Peace & Happiness) and band (The Nite-Liters). Band consisted of Tony Churchill, Austin Lander, James Baker, Robert Jackson, Leroy Taylor and Robin Russell. Vocal groups consisted of Ann Bogan, Melvin Wilson, Leslie Wilson, Bobby Downs, Londee Loren and Alan Frye. Bogan was a former member of The Marvelettes.

1)Birth Day 2)It's Been A Long Time 3)Comin' From All Ends

| 7/24/71 | 167 | 13 | | | 1 Morning, Noon & The Nite-Liters .... [I] | | | $15 | RCA Victor 4493 |

THE NITE-LITERS

| 10/30/71 | 189 | 2 | | | 2 Ain't No Big Thing, But It's Growing .... | | | $15 | RCA Victor 4526 |

DEBUT	PEAK	WKS	RIAA	CD	ARTIST — Album Title	Catalog	Sym	$	Label & Number

NEW BIRTH, The — Cont'd

| 5/20/72 | 198 | 2 | | | 3 Instrumental Directions .... | [I] | | $15 | RCA Victor 4580 |

THE NITE-LITERS

3/10/73	31	29		©	4 Birth Day			$12	RCA Victor 4797
11/17/73+	50	31	●	©	5 It's Been A Long Time			$12	RCA Victor 0285
8/17/74	56	15		©	6 Comin' From All Ends			$12	RCA Victor 0494
5/24/75	57	17		©	7 Blind Baby			$12	Buddah 5636
7/19/75	175	2			8 The Best Of The New Birth		[G]	$12	RCA Victor 1021
8/28/76	168	4			9 Love Potion			$12	Warner 2953
12/10/77+	164	6			10 Behold The Mighty Army			$12	Warner 3071

Afro-Strut (3) *49*
Ain't It Something (3)
Ain't No Change (5)
Bakers Instant (3)
Blind Baby (7)
Blind Man (7)
Brand X (3)
Buck & The Preacher, Theme From (4)
Cherish Every Precious Moment (3)
Come On And Dream Some Paradise (5)
Comin' From All Ends (6)
Deeper (10)
Do It Again (6,8)
Dream Merchant (7) *36*
Easy, Evil (7)
Echoes Of My Mind (6)

End To End (6)
Epilogue (6,7)
Fallin' In Love (9)
Fire & Rain (2)
Forever (3)
Funky-Doo (5)
Fuqua's Theme (medley) (3)
Got To Get A Knutt (4,8)
Granddaddy (Part 1) (7) *95*
Hang-Up (1)
Heaven Says (5)
Honeybee (2,8)
How Good It Feels (2)
How Will I Live (10)
Hurry Hurry (9)
I Can Understand It (4,8) *35*
I Never Felt This Way Before (9)

I Remember Well (7)
I Want To Make It With You (2)
I Wash My Hands Of The Whole Damn Deal, Part I (6) *88*
I'd Spend My Whole Life Loving You (5)
I've Got Dreams To Remember (3)
If I Were Your Woman (1)
It's Been A Long Time (5,8) *66*
It's Impossible (2,8) *52*
K-Jee (1) *39*
Keep On Doin' It (5)
Kool-Pick (1)
Lady Love (6)
Let It Be Me (2)
Listen Here (medley) (1)
Long And Winding Road (9)

MacArthur Park (medley) (3)
Mighty Army (10)
Never Can Say Goodbye (2,8)
Oh What A Feeling (9)
O-o-h Child (2)
Pains Of Love (5)
Patiently (6)
Pretty Music (9)
Respect To The Other Man (3)
Shaft, Theme From (3)
Slow Driving (9)
Squeezing Too Much Living (10)
Stinkin' Charlie (1)
Stop, Look, Listen (To Your Heart) (4)
Sure Thing (9)
Take This Train To Freedom (6)
Tanga Boo Gonk (1)

(Them) Changes (3)
Traveling (medley) (1)
Until It's Time For You To Go (4) *97*
Up Against The Wall (10)
We Are All God's Children (9)
(We've Got To) Pull Together (1)
We've Only Just Begun (1)
What's Going On (medley) (3)
Why Did I (7)
Wichita Lineman (3)
Wildflower (5,8) *45*
You Are What I'm All About (4)
Your Love Is (10)
Your Love Is In My Veins (10)

NEWBURY, Mickey   '72

Born Milton Newbury on 5/19/40 in Houston. Pop-country singer/songwriter/guitarist.

11/13/71+	58	15		©	1 'Frisco Mabel Joy			$15	Elektra 74107
3/10/73	173	5			2 Heaven Help The Child			$15	Elektra 75055
4/5/75	172	3			3 Lovers			$15	Elektra 1030

American Trilogy (1) *26*
Apples Dipped In Candy (3)
Cortelia Clark (2)
Frisco Depot (1)
Future's Not What It Used To Be (1)
Good Morning Dear (2)

Good Night (3)
Heaven Help The Child (2)
How I Love Them Old Songs (1)
How Many Times (Must The Piper Be Paid For His Song) (1)

How's The Weather (3)
If You Ever Get To Houston (3)
Lead On (3)
Let Me Sleep (3)
Lovers (3)
Mobile Blue (1)
Remember The Good (1)

Sail Away (3)
San Francisco Mabel Joy (2)
Song For Susan (1)
Sunshine (2) *87*
Sweet Memories (2)
Swiss Cottage Place (1)

When Do We Stop Starting Over (3)
Why You Been Gone So Long (2)
You're Not My Same Sweet Baby (1)

You've Always Got The Blues (3)

NEW CACTUS BAND — see CACTUS

   ★312★   **NEW CHRISTY MINSTRELS, The**   '63

Folk group named after the Christy Minstrels (formed in 1842 by Edwin "Pop" Christy). Group founded and led by Randy Sparks, and featured **Barry McGuire** (1963), **Kenny Rogers** (1966) and **Kim Carnes** (1968).

1)Today 2)Ramblin' Featuring Green, Green 3)The New Christy Minstrels

10/20/62	19	92			1 The New Christy Minstrels			$20	Columbia 1872 / 8672
2/23/63	30	20			2 The New Christy Minstrels In Person		[L]	$20	Columbia 1941 / 8741
5/25/63	20	22			3 Tall Tales! Legends & Nonsense			$20	Columbia 2017 / 8817
8/24/63	15	77	●	©	4 Ramblin' featuring Green, Green			$20	Columbia 2055 / 8855
12/21/63	5ˣ	8		©	5 Merry Christmas!		[X]	$20	Columbia 2096 / 8896

Christmas charts: 5/'63, 17/'64, 53/'65, 65/'66, 116/'67

| 4/18/64 | 9 | 34 | | © | 6 Today | | [S] | $20 | Columbia 2159 / 8959 |

featuring songs from the movie *Advance To The Rear*

8/29/64	48	23			7 Land Of Giants			$20	Columbia 2187 / 8987
2/13/65	62	11			8 Cowboys And Indians			$20	Columbia 2303 / 9103
6/26/65	22	22			9 Chim Chim Cher-ee			$20	Columbia 2369 / 9169
10/16/65	125	9			10 The Wandering Minstrels			$20	Columbia 2384 / 9184
6/18/66	76	16		©	11 Greatest Hits		[G]	$20	Columbia 2479 / 9279
11/28/70	195	2			12 You Need Someone To Love			$20	Gregar 102

Ambush At Teton Pass (8)
Anything Love Can Buy (6)
Appleseed John (7)
Beaucatcher Mountain (3)
Beautiful City (5)
Because (12)
Betsy From Pike (8)
Billy's Mule (3)
Bits And Pieces Medley (2)
Blacksmith Of Brandywine (7)
Brackenby's Music Box (6)
Brother (12)
Californio (1)
Can You Do The Can-Can? (10)
Casey Jones (7)
Cat, The (3)
Charleston Town (6)
Chim, Chim, Cheree (9,11) *81*
Christmas Trees (5)
Christmas Wishes (5)
Christmas World (5)
Company Of Cowards (6)
Corn Whiskey (8)
Cotton Fields (9,11)
Cotton Pickers' Song (1)

Deep Blue Sea (1)
Denver (2)
Don't Cry, Suzanne (1)
Down The Ohio (4)
Down To Darby (3)
Downtown (9,11)
Drinkin' Gourd (The Muddy Road To Freedom) (4,11)
Dying Convict (2)
East & West (12)
El Camino Real (7)
Everybody Loves Saturday Night (10,11)
Fire (2)
Freedom (9)
Girl From Ipanema (10)
Go, Lassie, Go (10)
Go Tell It On The Mountain ..see: Tell It On The Mountain
Golden Bells (2)
Green, Green (4,11) *14*
Guadalajara (10)
Hard To Be Without You (12)
He's A Loser (9)
Hi Jolly (4)
I Know Where I'm Goin' (1)
Ida Red (8,11)

In The Hills Of Shiloh (3)
In The Pines (1)
Invalids, The (2)
It'll Be A Merry Christmas (5)
It's Gonna Be Fine (5)
Jimmy Grove And Barbara Ellen (3)
Joe Magarac (7)
John Henry And The Steam Drill (7)
Julianne (3)
Kisses Sweeter Than Wine (9)
Ladies (3)
Land Of Giants (Theme) (7)
Lark Day (9)
Last Farewell (8)
Lily Langtry (8)
Little Bit Of Happiness (9,11)
Live! Live! Live! (Havah Nagilah) (10)
Liza Lee (3)
Louisiana Sue (2)
Lovely Greensleeves (10)
Make It With You (12)
Massacre (8)
Mighty Big Ways (7)
Mighty Mississippi (4,11)

Mount Rushmore (7)
My Dear Mary Anne (4)
My Last Gold Dollar Is Gone (8)
My Name Is Liberty (7)
Natural Man (7)
Navajo (8)
Nine Hundred Miles (1)
Oh! Shenando (3)
Old-Timer (3)
One Star (5)
Parson Brown (Our Christmas Dinner) (5)
Paul Bunyan (7)
Railroad Bill (1)
Ramblin' (4)
Red Clay Country (8)
Red River Shore (8)
Ride, Ride, Ride (4)
Rounder, The (8)
Rovin' Gambler (4)
Saints' Train (2)
Shepherd Boy (5)
Sing Along With Santa (5)
Sing Hosanna, Hallelujah (5)
Song Of The Pious Itinerant (Hallelujah, I'm A Bum) (3)

Song Of The Wandering Minstrels (10)
South American Get Away (12)
Springfield Fair (1)
Springtime (9)
Stormy (7)
(Story Of) The Preacher And The Bear (2)
Susianna (3)
Sweet Sorrento (10)
Tell It On The Mountain (5)
Tell Me (5)
That Big Rock Candy Mountain (1)
They Gotta Quit Kickin' My Dog Around (8)
(They Long To Be) Close To You (12)
This Land Is Your Land (1) *93*
This Ol' Riverboat (5)
Three Wheels On My Wagon (8)
Tie Me Kangaroo Down, Sport (10)
Today (6,11) *17*
Travelin' Man (4)

Treasury Of Nonsense Medley (3)
Turtles And Trees (12)
Wagoner's Song (Land Of The Sacramento) (4)
Way Down In Arkansas (6)
We'll Sing In The Sunshine (9,11)
Wellinbrook Well (1)
Whistle (1)
Whistlin' Dixie (6)
Wigwam (12)
Wimoweh (The Lion Sleeps Tonight) (1)
Yamao Toko No Uta (10)
You Know My Name (2)
You Need Someone To Love (12)

NEWCLEUS   '84

Rap group from Brooklyn, New York: brother-and-sister Ben and Yvette Cenad, with brother-and-sister Bob and Monique Crafton.

| 9/8/84 | 74 | 28 | | | **Jam On Revenge** | | | $12 | Sunnyview 4901 |

Auto-Man

Computer Age (Push The Button) · Destination Earth (1999) · I'm Not A Robot · Jam On It 56 · Jam On Revenge · No More Runnin' · Where's The Beat

NEW COLONY SIX, The   '68

Soft-rock group from Chicago: Ray Graffia (vocals), Gerald Van Kollenburg (guitar), Patrick McBride (harmonica), Ronnie Rice (organ), Les Kummel (bass) and Chic James (drums). Kummel died in a car crash on 12/18/78 (age 33).

9/2/67	172	7		© 1	**Colonization**			$75	Sentar 3001
7/20/68	157	6		2	**Revelations**			$30	Mercury 61165
11/1/69	179	4		3	**Attacking A Straw Man**			$30	Mercury 61228

Accept My Ring (1) · **Barbara, I Love You** (3) 78 · Blue Eyes (3) · **Can't You See Me Cry** (2) 52 · Come And Give Your Love To Me (3) · Come Away With You (3) · Dandy Handy Man (2) · Elf Song (Ballad Of The Wingbat Marmaduke) (1) · Free (3) · Girl Unsigned (2) · Hello Lonely (1) · Hold Me With Your Eyes (1) · **I Could Never Lie To You** (3) 50 · **I Want You To Know** (3) 65 · **I Will Always Think About You** (2) 22 · I'm Here Now (1) · I'm Just Waitin' (Anticipatin' For Her To Show Up) (1) · Just Feel Worse (1) · Let Me Love You (1) · Love, That's The Best I Can Do (3) · **Love You So Much** (1) 61 · Mister You're A Better Man Than I (1) · My Dreams Depend On You (1) · Power Of Love (1) · Prairie Grey (3) · Ride The Wicked Wind (3) · Summertime's Another Name For Love (1) · Sun Within You (3) · **Things I'd Like To Say** (2) 16 · Treat Her Groovy (2) · Warm Baby (1) · We Will Love Again (2) · Woman (1) · You Know Better (2) · You're Gonna Be Mine (1)

★469★ NEW EDITION   '96

R&B vocal group from Boston: **Ralph Tresvant**, Ronnie DeVoe, Michael Bivins, Ricky Bell and **Bobby Brown**. **Johnny Gill** replaced Brown in 1986. Bell, Bivins and DeVoe recorded as **Bell Biv DeVoe** in 1990. All six members reunited in 1996.

9/3/83	90	33		© 1	Candy Girl			$12	Streetwise 3301
10/13/84+	6	54	▲²	© 2	**New Edition**			$10	MCA 5515
12/7/85+	32	48	▲	© 3	**All For Love**			$10	MCA 5679
12/21/85	9ˣ	2		© 4	**Christmas All Over the World**		[X]	$10	MCA 39040
12/20/86+	43	23	●	© 5	**Under The Blue Moon**			$10	MCA 5912
7/9/88	12	50	▲²	© 6	**Heart Break**			$10	MCA 42207
10/19/91	99	6		© 7	**New Edition's Greatest Hits, Volume One**		[G]	$10	MCA 10434
9/28/96	❶¹	32	▲²	© 8	**Home Again**			$10	MCA 11480

All For Love (3) · All I Want For Christmas (Is My Girl) (4) · Baby Love (2) · Blue Moon (5) · Boys To Men (6,7) · Bring Back The Memories (5) · **Can You Stand The Rain** (6,7) 44 · Candy Girl (1,7) 46 · Competition (6) · **Cool It Now** (2,7) 4 · **Count Me Out** (3,7) 51 · Crucial (6) · Delicious (2) · Duke Of Earl (5) · **Earth Angel** (5) 21 · Gimme Your Love (1) · Give Love On Christmas Day (4) · Gotta Have Your Lovin' (1) · Happy Holidays To You (4) · Hear Me Out (8) · Hey There Lonely Girl (5) · Hide And Seek (2) · **Hit Me Off** (8) 3 · Home Again (8) · How Do You Like Your Love Served (8) · I'm Comin' Home (6) · I'm Leaving You Again (8) · **I'm Still In Love With You** (8) 7 · **If It Isn't Love** (6,7) 7 · **Is This The End** (1,7) 85 · It's Christmas (All Over The World) (4) · Jealous Girl (1) · Joy Of Christmas (4) · Kickback (3) · Kinda Girls We Like (2) · Let's Be Friends (3) · **Little Bit Of Love (Is All It Takes)** (3,7) 38 · **Lost In Love** (2,7) 35 · Maryann (2) · Million To One (5) · **Mr. Telephone Man** (2,7) 12 · My Secret (Didja Gitit Yet?) (2) · N.E. Heart Break (6) · Oh Yeah, It Feels So Good (8) · **One More Day** (8) 61 · Ooh Baby (1) · Pass The Beat (1) · Popcorn Love (1,7) · School (3) · She Gives Me A Bang (1) · Shop Around (8) · Should Have (1) · Since I Don't Have You (5) · Singing Merry Christmas (4) · Something About You (8) · Sweet Thing (3) · Tears On My Pillow (5) · Thank You (8) · That's The Way We're Livin' (6) · Thousand Miles Away (5) · Tighten It Up (8) · Tonight's Your Night (3) · Try Again (8) · What's Your Name (5) · Where It All Started (6) · Whispers In Bed (3) · Who Do You Trust (3) · **With You All The Way** (3) 51 · You Don't Have To Worry (8) · **You're Not My Kind Of Girl** (6) 95

NEW ENGLAND   '79

Rock group formed in New York City: John Fannon (vocals, guitar), Jimmy Waldo (keyboards), Gary Shea (bass) and Hirsh Gardner (drums). Waldo and Shea later joined **Alcatrazz**.

| 5/19/79 | 50 | 17 | | © 1 | **New England** | | | $12 | Infinity 9007 |

produced by **Paul Stanley**

| 7/18/81 | 176 | 4 | | 2 | **Walking Wild** | | | $12 | Elektra 346 |

produced by **Todd Rundgren**

Alone Tonight (1) · DDT (2) · Don't Ever Let Me Go (2) · **Don't Ever Wanna Lose Ya** (1) 40 · Elevator (2) · Encore (1) · Get It Up (2) · **Hello, Hello, Hello** (1) 69 · Holdin' Out On Me (2) · L-5 (2) · Last Show (1) · Love's Up In The Air (2) · Nothing To Fear (1) · P.U.N.K. (Puny Undernourished Kid) (1) · Shall I Run Away (1) · She's Gonna Tear You Apart (2) · Shoot (1) · Turn Out The Light (1) · Walking Wild (2) · You're There (1)

NEW ENGLAND CONSERVATORY RAGTIME ENSEMBLE   '74

Conducted by Gunther Schuller.

| 5/19/73+ | 65 | 36 | | | **Scott Joplin: The Red Back Book** | | [I] | $15 | Angel 36060 |

Cascades, The · Chrysanthemum, The · Easy Winners · Entertainer, The · Maple Leaf Rag · Rag Time Dance · Sugar Cane · Sun Flower Slow Drag

NEW FOUND GLORY   '01

Rock group from Coral Springs, Florida: Jordan Pundik (vocals), Chad Gilbert and Steve Klein (guitars), Ian Grushka (bass) and Cyrus Bolooki (drums).

| 10/14/00+ | 107 | 21 | | © | **New Found Glory** | | | $10 | Drive-Thru 112338 |

All About Her · Ballad For The Lost Romantics · Better Off Dead · Black & Blue · Boy Crazy · Dressed To Kill · Eyesore · Hit Or Miss · Second To Last · Sincerely Me · Sucker · Vegas

★428★ NEWHART, Bob   '60

Born on 9/5/29 in Oak Park, Illinois. Comedian/TV actor. Starred in three TV situation comedies: The Bob Newhart Show (1972-78), Newhart (1982-90) and Bob (1992-93). Won 1960 Best New Artist Grammy Award.

| 5/16/60 | ❶¹⁴ | 108 | ● | © 1 | **The Button-Down Mind Of Bob Newhart** | | [C] | $30 | Warner 1379 |

1960 Grammy winner: Album of the Year

11/14/60+	❶¹	70	●	© 2	**The Button-Down Mind Strikes Back!**		[C]	$30	Warner 1393
10/30/61	10	30		© 3	**Behind The Button-Down Mind Of Bob Newhart**		[C]	$30	Warner 1417
9/8/62	28	26		4	**The Button-Down Mind On TV**		[C]	$30	Warner 1467
2/29/64	113	11		5	**Bob Newhart Faces Bob Newhart (faces Bob Newhart)**		[C]	$30	Warner 1517
4/24/65	126	5		6	**The Windmills Are Weakening**		[C]	$30	Warner 1588

Abe Lincoln Vs. Madison Avenue (1) · African Movie (3) · Amateur Show Contestants (5) · Automation and A Private In Washington's Army (2) · Ben Franklin In Analysis (6) · Bus Drivers School (2) · Buying A House (6) · Cruise Of The U.S.S. Codfish (1) · Defusing A Bomb (4) · Driving Instructor (1) · Edison's Most Famous Invention (6) · Expectant Father (5) · Friend With A Dog (4) · General Chariot Corp. (4) · Grace L. Ferguson Airline (And Storm Door Co.) (2) · Herb Philbrick - Counter Spy (3) · Hold Out Huns (4) · Infinite Number Of Monkeys (2) · Introducing Tobacco To Civilization (4) · King Kong (6) · Krushchev Landing Rehearsal (1)

NEWHART, Bob — Cont'd

Ledge Psychology (2)
Man Who Looked Like Hitler (5)
Merchandising The Wright Brothers (1)
Nobody Will Ever Play Baseball (1)
Nudist Camp Expose (5)
On Poodles And Planes (5)
Reflections On TV Commercials (5)
Retirement Party (2)
Returning A Gift (6)
Rocket Scientist (3)
Seven Lost Cities Of The Incas (3)
Siamese Cat (4)
Superman And The Dry Cleaner (6)
TV Commercials (3)
Tourist Meets Khrushchev (3)
Uncle Freddie Show (3)
Upset Stomach Commercial (6)

★447★ NEW KIDS ON THE BLOCK '89

Pop vocal group from Boston: **Joey McIntyre**, Donnie Wahlberg, Danny Wood, and brothers Jon and **Jordan Knight**. Wahlberg is the brother of **Marky Mark** (actor Mark Wahlberg). Shortened group name to **NKOTB** in 1992.

DEBUT	PEAK	WKS	RIAA	CD	ARTIST — Album Title		Sym	$	Label & Number
8/27/88+	❶[2]	132	▲[8]	©	1 Hangin' Tough			$10	Columbia 40985
8/5/89+	25	80	▲[3]	©	2 New Kids On The Block		[E]	$10	Columbia 40475
					released in 1987				
10/14/89	9	18	▲[2]	©	3 Merry, Merry Christmas		[X]	$10	Columbia 45280
					Christmas charts: 1/'89, 4/'90				
6/23/90	❶[1]	49	▲[3]	©	4 Step By Step			$10	Columbia 45129
11/17/90+	48	10		©	5 Merry, Merry Christmas		[X-R]	$10	Columbia 45280
12/8/90+	19	32	●	©	6 No More Games/The Remix Album		[K]	$10	Columbia 46959
2/12/94	37	6		©	7 Face The Music			$10	Columbia 52969

NKOTB

Angel (2)
Are You Down? (2)
Baby, I Believe In You (4,6)
Be My Girl (2)
Call It What You Want (4,6)
Christmas Song (Chestnuts Roasting On An Open Fire) (3,5)
Cover Girl (1,6) *2*
Didn't I (Blow Your Mind) (2) *8*
Dirty Dawg (7) *66*
Don't Give Up On Me (2)
Face The Music (7)
Funky, Funky, Xmas (3,5)
Funny Feeling (4)
Games (4,6)
Girls (7)
Hangin' Tough (1,6) *1*
Happy Birthday (4)
Hold On (1)
I Can't Believe It's Over (7)
I Need You (1)
I Remember When (1)
I Still Believe In Santa Claus (3,5)
I Wanna Be Loved By You (2)
I'll Be Loving You (Forever) (1) *1*
I'll Be Missin You Come Christmas (A Letter To Santa) (3,5)
I'll Be Waitin' (7)
I'll Still Be Loving You (7)
If You Go Away (7)
Keep On Smilin' (7)
Keepin' My Fingers Crossed (7)
Last Night I Saw Santa Claus (3,5)
Let's Play House (7)
Let's Try It Again (4) *53*
Little Drummer Boy (3,5)
Merry, Merry Christmas (7)
Mrs. Right (7)
My Favorite Girl (1,6)
Never Gonna Fall In Love Again (4,6)
Never Let You Go (7)
New Kids On The Block (2)
Please Don't Go Girl (1,6) *10*
Popsicle (2)
Right Stuff ...see: You Got It
Since You Walked Into My Life (7)
Stay With Me Baby (4)
Step By Step (4,6) *1*
Stop It Girl (2)
This One's For The Children (3,5) *7*
Time Is On Our Side (4)
Tonight (4) *7*
Treat Me Right (2)
Valentine Girl (6)
What'cha Gonna Do (About It) (1,6)
Where Do I Go From Here? (4)
White Christmas (3,5)
You Got It (The Right Stuff) (1,6) *3*
You Got The Flavor (7)

NEW LIFE COMMUNITY CHOIR FEAT. JOHN P. KEE '00

Choir formed by John P. Kee in Charlotte, North Carolina.

DEBUT	PEAK	WKS	RIAA	CD	ARTIST — Album Title		Sym	$	Label & Number
2/11/95	147	2	●	©	1 Show Up!			$10	New Life 43010
11/15/97	107	3		©	2 Strength			$10	New Life 43108
11/11/00	102	4	●	©	3 Not Guilty...The Experience			$15	New Life 43139 [2]

Be Encouraged (1)
Best Friend (3)
Break Out (3)
Changed Me (3)
Clap Your Hands (2)
Come In (2)
Comfort Me (1)
Dance (3)
Eastside/Westside (2)
God Has Been So Good (1)
Going Home (2)
Grateful (3)
Greater (3)
He'll Welcome Me (1)
I Believe (3)
I Bow Out (2)
I Do Worship (2,3)
I Shall Do (1)
I Shall See Him (1)
I Surrender (1)
I'll Be Your Everything (2)
I'll Bless Your Name (3)
It's Possible (3)
Jesus (3)
Lord Help Me To Hold Out (2)
Lord Is Able (1)
Made Up Mind (1)
Mighty God (2)
My Healing (3)
No Christmas Without You (1)
Not Guilty (3)
One Phone Call (3)
Peace (3)
Rain On Us (3)
Rhema Word (3)
Right Here (3)
Show Up! (1)
Simple Song (3)
Sovereign (3)
Stop Hiding (3)
Strength (2)
Survive (1)
Sweeter (1)
Thank You Lord (He Did It All) (2)
Thou Art Worthy (3)
Thursday Love (2)
Turn Around (2)
We Made It (2)
Wedding Song (3)
What's The Verdict? (3)
You Blessed Me (3)

NEWMAN, Randy '78

Born on 11/28/43 in New Orleans. Singer/songwriter/pianist. Nephew of composers Alfred, Emil and Lionel Newman. Scored several movies. Recipient of *Billboard*'s Century Award in 2000.

DEBUT	PEAK	WKS	RIAA	CD	ARTIST — Album Title		Sym	$	Label & Number
10/2/71	191	3		©	1 Randy Newman/Live		[L]	$15	Reprise 6459
					recorded on 9/18/70 at the Bitter End in New York City				
6/17/72	163	18		©	2 Sail Away			$15	Reprise 2064
10/5/74	36	23		©	3 Good Old Boys			$15	Reprise 2193
10/22/77+	9	29	●	©	4 Little Criminals			$12	Warner 3079
9/1/79	41	11		©	5 Born Again			$12	Warner 3346
2/12/83	64	13		©	6 Trouble In Paradise			$12	Warner 23755
10/15/88	80	19		©	7 Land Of Dreams			$10	Reprise 25773
6/19/99	194	1		©	8 Bad Love			$10	DreamWorks 50115

Back On My Feet Again (3)
Bad News From Home (7)
Baltimore (4)
Better Off Dead (8)
Big Hat, No Cattle (4)
Birmingham (3)
Blues, The (6) *51*
Burn On (2)
Christmas In Capetown (6)
Cowboy (1)
Davy The Fat Boy (1)
Dayton, Ohio - 1903 (2)
Dixie Flyer (7)
Every Man A King (3)
Every Time It Rains (8)
Falling In Love (7)
Follow The Flag (7)
Four Eyes (7)
Ghosts (5)
Girls In My Life (Part 1) (5)
God's Song (That's Why I Love Mankind) (2)
Going Home (8)
Great Nations Of Europe (8)
Guilty (3)
Half A Man (3)
He Gives Us All His Love (2)
I Love L.A. (6)
I Miss You (8)
I Think It's Going To Rain Today (1)
I Want Everyone To Like Me (8)
I Want You To Hurt Like I Do (7)
I'll Be Home (1,4)
I'm Dead (But I Don't Know It) (8)
I'm Different (6)
In Germany Before The War (4)
It's Money That I Love (5)
It's Money That Matters (7) *60*
Jolly Coppers On Parade (4)
Kathleen (Catholicism Made Easier) (4)
Kingfish (3)
Last Night I Had A Dream (1,2)
Little Criminals (4)
Living Without You (1)
Lonely At The Top (1,2)
Louisiana 1927 (3)
Lover's Prayer (1)
Mama Told Me Not To Come (1)
Marie (3)
Masterman And Baby J (7)
Maybe I'm Doing It Wrong (1)
Memo To My Son (2)
Miami (4)
Mikey's (6)
Mr. President (Have Pity On The Working Man) (3)
Mr. Sheep (5)
My Country (8)
My Life Is Good (6)
Naked Man (3)
New Orleans Wins The War (7)
Old Kentucky Home (1)
Old Man (2)
Old Man On The Farm (4)
One You Love (8)
Pants (5)
Political Science (2)
Pretty Boy (5)
Real Emotional Girl (6)
Red Bandana (3)
Rednecks (3)
Rider In The Rain (4)
Roll With The Punches (7)
Rollin' (3)
Sail Away (2)
Same Girl (6)
Shame (8)
Short People (4) *2*
Sigmund Freud's Impersonation Of Albert Einstein In America (4)
Simon Smith And The Amazing Dancing Bear (2)
So Long Dad (1)
Something Special (7)
Song For The Dead (6)
Spies (5)
Story Of A Rock And Roll Band (5)
Take Me Back (6)
Texas Girl At The Funeral Of Her Father (4)
There's A Party At My House (6)
They Just Got Married (5)
Tickle Me (1)
Wedding In Cherokee County (3)
William Brown (5)
World Isn't Fair (8)
Yellow Man (1)
You Can Leave Your Hat On (2)
You Can't Fool The Fat Man (4)

NEW ORDER '93

Techno-dance group formed in Manchester, England. Formerly known as **Joy Division**. After suicide of lead singer Ian Curtis (May 1980), name changed to New Order and members Bernard Sumner (guitar, vocals), Peter Hook (bass) and Stephen Morris (drums) continued as trio. Female keyboardist Gillian Gilbert joined in October 1980. Sumner was also a member of **Electronic**. Hook also with **Revenge**.

DEBUT	PEAK	WKS	RIAA	CD	ARTIST — Album Title		Sym	$	Label & Number
6/8/85	94	22		©	1 Low-Life			$10	Qwest 25289
10/25/86	117	21		©	2 Brotherhood			$10	Qwest 25511
9/5/87+	36	60	▲	©	3 Substance		[G]	$15	Qwest 25621 [2]
2/11/89	32	28	●	©	4 Technique			$10	Qwest 25845

DEBUG	PEAK	WKS	RIAA	CD	ARTIST — Album Title	Catalog	Sym	$	Label & Number

NEW ORDER — Cont'd

5/29/93	11	16	●	© 5	**Republic**			$10	Qwest 45250
4/1/95	78	5		© 6	(the best of) NewOrder .... [G]			$10	Qwest 45794

Age Of Consent (6)	Ceremony (3)	Fine Time (4,6)	**Regret** (5,6) **28**	Subculture (1,3)	Vanishing Point (4,6)
All Day Long (2)	Chemical (5)	Guilty Partner (4)	**Round & Round** (4) **64**	Sunrise (1)	Way Of Life (2)
All The Way (4)	Confusion (3)	Let's Go (Nothing For Me) (6)	Round & Round-94 (6)	Temptation (3)	Weirdo (2)
Angel Dust (2)	Dream Attack (4)	Liar (5)	Ruined In A Day (5,6)	Thieves Like Us (3)	**World** (5,6) **92**
As It Is When It Was (2)	Dreams Never End (6)	Love Less (4)	Run (4,6)	This Time Of Night (1)	World In Motion (6)
Avalanche (5)	Elegia (1)	Love Vigilantes (1,6)	Shellshock (3)	Times Change (5)	Young Offender (5)
Bizarre Love Triangle (2,3,6) **98**	Every Little Counts (2)	Mr. Disco (4)	Sooner Than You Think (1)	Touched By The Hand Of God (6)	
Blue Monday 1988 (3,6) **68**	Everyone Everywhere (5)	1963-95 (4)	Special (3)	**True Faith** (3) **32**	
Broken Promise (2)	Everything's Gone Green (3)	Paradise (2)	Spooky (5)	True Faith-94 (6)	
	Face Up (1)	Perfect Kiss (1,3)	State Of The Nation (3)		

NEW RADICALS '99

Group is actually solo rock singer/musician Gregg Alexander.

11/28/98+	41	40	▲	©	**Maybe You've Been Brainwashed Too**			$10	MCA 11858

Crying Like A Church On Monday	I Don't Wanna Die Anymore	Jehovah Made This Whole Joint For You	Mother We Just Can't Get Enough	**You Get What You Give** **36**
Flowers	I Hope I Didn't Just Give Away The Ending	Maybe You've Been Brainwashed Too	Someday We'll Know	
Gotta Stay High	In Need Of A Miracle		Technicolor Lover	

NEW RIDERS OF THE PURPLE SAGE '72

Country-rock group formed in San Francisco: John Dawson (vocals, guitar), David Nelson (guitar), Dave Torbert (bass) and Spencer Dryden (drums; **Jefferson Airplane**). Guitarist Buddy Cage joined after first album. Torbert left in 1974 to join **Kingfish**; replaced by Skip Battin.

9/11/71	39	15		© 1	**New Riders Of The Purple Sage**			$15	Columbia 30888
5/6/72	33	18		© 2	**Powerglide**			$15	Columbia 31284
12/9/72+	85	13		© 3	**Gypsy Cowboy**			$15	Columbia 31930
10/20/73	55	18	●	© 4	**The Adventures of Panama Red**			$15	Columbia 32450
4/27/74	68	12		5	**Home, Home on the Road** .... [L]			$15	Columbia 32870
11/2/74	68	9		6	**Brujo**			$15	Columbia 33145
					title is Spanish for "Sorcerer"				
11/8/75	144	4		7	**Oh, What A Mighty Time**			$15	Columbia 33688
6/12/76	145	8	©	8	**New Riders**			$12	MCA 2196

All I Ever Wanted (1)	Duncan And Brady (2)	I Don't Know You (1)	Long Black Veil (3)	Sailin' (3)	Truck Drivin' Man (5)
Annie May (8)	Farewell Angelina (7)	**I Don't Need No Doctor** (2) **81**	Louisiana Lady (1)	School Days (5)	Up Against The Wall, Redneck (7)
Ashes Of Love (6)	Fifteen Days Under The Hood (8)	I Heard You Been Layin' My Old Lady (7)	Mighty Time (7)	She's Looking Better Every Beer (8)	Whatcha Gonna Do (1)
Big Wheels (6)	Garden Of Eden (1)	Important Exportin Man (4)	Neon Rose (6)	She's No Angel (3,5)	Whiskey (3)
California Day (2)	Glendale Train (1)	Instant Armadillo Blues (6)	Old Man Noll (6)	Singing Cowboy (6)	Willie And The Hand Jive (2)
Can't Get Over You (8)	Going Round The Horn (7)	It's Alright With Me (6)	On My Way Back Home (3)	Strangers On A Train (7)	Workingman's Woman (6)
Cement, Clay And Glass (4)	Groupie (3)	Kick In The Head (4,5)	On The Amazon (6)	Sunday Susie (5)	You Angel You (6)
Contract (2)	Gypsy Cowboy (3)	L.A. Lady (7)	On Top Of Old Smoky (7)	Superman (3)	You Never Can Tell (8)
Crooked Judge (6)	Hard To Handle (8)	La Bamba (7)	One Too Many Stories (4)	Sutter's Mill (3,5)	You Should Have Seen Me Runnin (4)
Dead Flowers (5,8)	Hello Mary Lou (2,5)	Last Lonely Eagle (1)	Over & Over (7)	Sweet Lovin' One (2)	
Death And Destruction (4)	Henry (1,5)	Linda (3)	Panama Red (4)	Swimming Song (8)	
Dim Lights, Thick Smoke (And Loud, Loud Music) (2)	Hi, Hello, How Are You (5)	Little Old Lady (7)	Parson Brown (6)	Take A Letter, Maria (7)	
Dirty Business (1)	Honky Tonkin' (I Guess I Done Me Some) (8)	Lochinvar (7)	Portland Woman (1)	Teardrops In My Eyes (4)	
Don't Put Her Down (8)		Lonesome L.A. Cowboy (4)	Rainbow (2)	Thank The Day (4)	
			Runnin' Back To You (2)		

NEWSBOYS '96

Christian rock group from Australia: John James (vocals), Jody Davis (guitar), Duncan Phillips (percussion), Jeff Frankenstein (keyboards), Philip Urry (bass) and Peter Furler (drums). James left the group in late 1997, Furler moved to vocals and Phillips moved to drums. By 1999, Phil Joel had replaced Philip Urry.

3/9/96	35	20	●	© 1	**Take Me To Your Leader**			$10	Star Song 20075
7/18/98	61	20	●	© 2	**Step Up To The Microphone**			$10	Virgin 45917
12/4/99	80	6		© 3	**Love Liberty Disco**			$10	Sparrow 51720
11/11/00	122	10		© 4	**Shine The Hits** .... [G]			$10	Sparrow 51787

Always (2)	Entertaining Angels (2,4)	I Surrender All (3)	Mega-Mix (4)	Step Up To The Microphone (2,4)	Turn Your Eyes Upon Jesus (medley) (4)
Beautiful Sound (3)	Everyone's Someone (3)	I Would Give Everything (3)	Miracle Child (1)	Take Me To Your Leader (1,4)	Where You Belong (medley) (4)
Believe (2,4)	Fall On You (3)	I'm Not Ashamed (4)	Praises (4)	Tide, The (2)	Who? (4)
Break (3)	Forever Man (4)	It's All Who You Know (1)	Reality (1,4)	Truth Be Known - Everybody Gets A Shot (2)	WooHoo (2)
Breakfast (1,4)	God Is Not A Secret (1,4)	Joy (4)	Say You Need Love (3)	Tuning In (2)	Woohoo (4)
Breathe (1)	Good Stuff (3)	Let It Go (1)	Shine (4)		
Cup O' Tea (1)	Hallelujah (4)	Lost The Plot (1)	Spirit Thing (4)		
Deep End (2)	I Got Your Number (4)	Love Liberty Disco (3)			

NEW SEEKERS, The '72

British-Australian group formed by former Seekers' member Keith Potger after disbandment of **The Seekers** in 1969. Consisted of Eve Graham, Lyn Paul, Peter Doyle, Marty Kristian and Paul Layton. Doyle died of cancer on 10/13/2001 (age 52).

4/3/71	136	6		1	**Beautiful People**			$15	Elektra 74088
12/25/71+	37	14		2	**We'd Like To Teach The World To Sing**			$15	Elektra 74115
7/15/72	166	10		3	**Circles**			$15	Elektra 75034
5/19/73	190	4		4	**Pinball Wizards**			$15	MGM/Verve 5098

Ain't Love Easy (1)	**Dance, Dance, Dance** (3) **84**	I'll Be Home (1)	No Man's Land (2)	Time Limit (4)
Allright My Love (1)	Eighteen Carat Friend (1)	Jean's Little Street Cafe (3)	One (1)	Tonight (2)
Beautiful People (1) **67**	Evergreen (2)	Just An Old Fashioned Love Song (3)	Out On The Edge Of Beyond (3)	Too Many Trips To Nowhere (2)
Beg, Steal Or Borrow (3) **81**	Feelin' (2)	Lay Me Down (2)	Perfect Love (3)	Utah (4)
Blackberry Way (1)	Further We Reach Out (4)	Look Look (4)	**Pinball Wizard/See Me, Feel Me** (4) **29**	Wanderer's Song (2)
Boom Town (2)	Good Old Fashioned Music (2)	**Look What They've Done To My Song Ma** (1) **14**	Reaching Out For Someone (4)	When There's No Love Left (1)
Brand New Song (4)	Holy Rollin' (3)	Mystic Queen (3)	Somebody Somewhere (4)	With Everything Changing (4)
Changes IV (3)	I Can Say You're Beautiful (3)	Never Ending Song Of Love (1)	Sweet Louise (2)	World I Wish For You (3)
Child Of Mine (2)	**I'd Like To Teach The World To Sing (In Perfect Harmony)** (2) **7**	**Nickel Song** (2) **81**	That's My Guy (4)	Your Song (1)
Cincinnati (1)				
Circles (3) **87**				

NEWSONG   '01

Christian pop group formed in Kennesaw, Georgia: Eddie Carswell (vocals), Billy Goodwin and Leonard Ahlstrom (guitars), Scotty Wilbanks (sax, keyboards), Mark Clay (bass) and Jack Pumphrey (drums).

| 12/30/00+ | 130 | 2 | | © | Sheltering Tree | | | $10 | Benson 83327 |

Anything But You
Christmas Shoes *42*
Defining Moment

Don't It Make You Want To Go Home
God & Time

God Made Man
Hope Changes Everything
Nothing Without Christ

Red Letter Day
Sheltering Tree
Wide Open

Wonderful One

NEWTON, Juice   '82

Born Judy Kay Cohen on 2/18/52 in Lakehurst, New Jersey. Pop-country singer/guitarist.

3/7/81+	22	86	▲	©	1 Juice			$10	Capitol 12136
5/29/82	20	46	●		2 Quiet Lies			$10	Capitol 12210
9/10/83	52	15			3 Dirty Looks			$10	Capitol 12294
7/14/84	128	10		©	4 Can't Wait All Night			$10	RCA Victor 4995
7/21/84	178	5	●	©	5 Greatest Hits		[G]	$10	Capitol 12353

Adios Mi Corazon (2)
All I Have To Do Is Dream (1)
Angel Of The Morning (1,5) *4*
Break It To Me Gently (2,5) *11*
Can't Wait All Night (4) *66*
Country Comfort (1)
Dirty Looks (3) *90*

Don't Bother Me (3)
Easy Way Out (4)
Ever True (2)
Eye Of A Hurricane (4)
Falling In Love (2)
For Believers (3)
He's Gone (4)
Headin' For A Heartache (1)

Heart Of The Night (2,5) *25*
I'm Dancing As Fast As I Can (2)
I'm Gonna Be Strong (2,5)
Keeping Me On My Toes (3)
Let's Dance (4)
Little Love (4) *44*
Love Sail Away (2)

Love's Been A Little Bit Hard On Me (2,5) *7*
Queen Of Hearts (1,5) *2*
Restless Heart (4)
Ride 'Em Cowboy (4)
River Of Love (1)
Runaway Hearts (3)
Shot Full Of Love (1,5)

Slipping Away (3)
Stranger At My Door (3)
Sweetest Thing (I've Ever Known) (1,5) *7*
Tell Her No (3,5) *27*
Texas Heartache (1)
Til I Loved You (3)
Trail Of Tears (2)

Twenty Years Ago (3)
Waiting For The Sun (4)
(You Don't Hear) The One That Gets You (4)
You Don't Know Me (4)

NEWTON, Wayne   '65

Born on 4/3/42 in Roanoke, Virginia. Singer/multi-instrumentalist. Top Las Vegas entertainer. Began singing career with regular appearances on Jackie Gleason's variety TV show in 1962. Appeared in the 1989 James Bond movie *License To Kill* and the 1990 movie *The Adventures Of Ford Fairlane*.

1)Red Roses For A Blue Lady 2)Daddy Don't You Walk So Fast 3)Danke Schoen

10/12/63	55	9			1 Danke Schoen			$20	Capitol 1973
5/1/65	17	20			2 Red Roses For A Blue Lady			$20	Capitol 2335
10/23/65	114	6			3 Summer Wind			$20	Capitol 2389
6/4/66	80	21			4 Wayne Newton - Now!			$20	Capitol 2445
12/3/66	10ˣ	10			5 Songs For A Merry Christmas		[X]	$20	Capitol 2588

Christmas charts: 10/'66, 29/'67, 40/'68

2/4/67	131	13			6 It's Only The Good Times			$20	Capitol 2635
10/7/67	194	4			7 The Best Of Wayne Newton		[G]	$20	Capitol 2797
6/1/68	186	5			8 One More Time			$15	MGM 4549
8/31/68	196	3			9 Walking On New Grass			$15	MGM 4523
6/17/72	34	21			10 Daddy Don't You Walk So Fast			$15	Chelsea 1001
11/18/72+	164	11			11 Can't You Hear The Song?			$15	Chelsea 1003

After The Laughter (4,7)
All Alone Am I (11)
All The Time (9)
All This World And Seven Seas (8)
Alone Again, Naturally (11)
Anthem (11) *65*
Baby I'm-a Want You (10)
Believe In Me (11)
Bill Bailey (7)
But Not For Me (1)
Bye Bye Blackbird (1)
Can't You Hear The Song? (11) *48*
Christmas In Washington Square (5)
Christmas Journey (5)
Christmas Song (Chestnuts Roasting On An Open Fire) (5)
Crazy Arms (9)
Daddy Don't You Walk So Fast (10) *4*
Danke Schoen (1,4,7) *13*

Days Of Wine And Roses (1,7)
Don't Talk To Me (2,4)
Don't Touch Me (9)
Everybody Loves Somebody (3)
Fool (11)
For Once In My Life (8)
Fraulein (2)
Games That Lovers Play (6,7) *86*
Half A World Away (6)
Have Yourself A Merry Little Christmas (7)
Heart! (I Hear You Beating) (2) *82*
Hello Ma Baby (8)
How Did It Get So Late So Early (3)
I Believe In Music (10)
I Cried For You (1)
I'll Be Standing By (3)
I'll Be With You In Apple Blossom Time (2,7) *52*
I'll Meet You Halfway (10)

I'll Remember April (1)
I'm Looking Over A Four Leaf Clover (2)
I've Got The World On A String (1)
In The Name Of Love (6)
It's Only The Good Times (6)
It's Such A Pretty World Today (9)
Jingle-Bell Rock (5)
Lady (8)
Last Waltz (9)
Laughing On The Outside (Crying On The Inside) (2)
Laura Lee (2,7)
Let It Snow! Let It Snow! Let It Snow! (5)
Like Everything Else (9)
Little Bit Of Heaven (3)
Little Drummer Boy (5)
Looking Through A Tear (9)
L-o-v-e (4)
Love Doesn't Live Here Anymore (10)

Minute You're Gone (4)
Moon Over Naples (4)
My Prayer (3)
My Shoes Keep Walking Back To You (9)
My Special Angel (6)
Nothing Matters But You (6)
Ol' Man Mose (1)
One Kiss For Old Times' Sake (3)
One More Memory (2)
One More Time (8)
Red Roses For A Blue Lady (2) *23*
Release Me (9)
Remember Me, I'm The One Who Loves You (3)
Remember When (4) *69*
Rock-A-Bye Your Baby With A Dixie Melody (8)
Rudolph The Red-Nosed Reindeer (5)
Silent Night, Holy Night (5)
Silver Bells (5)

Smile Is Just A Frown (Turned Upside-Down) (6)
So Long Lucy (4)
Some Sunday Morning (3)
Somebody To Love (6)
Somewhere (8)
Song Sung Blue (11)
Summer Wind (3,7) *78*
Superstar (10)
Take Good Care Of Yourself (10)
Talking In Your Sleep (11)
That Funny Feeling (6)
That's Life (8)
They Can't Take That Away From Me (1)
They'll Never Know (2)
Those Lazy-Hazy-Crazy Days Of Summer (3)
Tip Of My Fingers (9)
To Each His Own (6)
Together (11)
Toot, Toot, Tootsie! (1)
Volare (1)

Walkin' In The Sand (And The Seasons Come And Go) (10)
Walking On New Grass (9)
We'll Sing In The Sunshine (10)
What's He Doing In My World (3)
When I Lost You (8)
White Christmas (5)
Wiedersehn'n (4,7)
Winter Wonderland (5)
Wolverton Mountain (8)
Wonderland By Night (4)
Yo-Yo Puppet Song (5)
You Don't Have To Ask (11)
You Just Don't Know (4)
You Made Me Love You (1)
You're Nobody 'Til Somebody Loves You (7)
You've Got Your Troubles (11)
You've Let Yourself Go (6)
Your Cheatin' Heart (8)

NEWTON-JOHN, Olivia   ★122★   '74

Born on 9/26/48 in Cambridge, England; raised in Melbourne, Australia. Pop-rock-country singer. Granddaughter of Nobel Prize-winning German physicist Max Born. Starred in the movies *Grease*, *Xanadu* and *Two Of A Kind*. Married to actor Matt Lattanzi from 1985-95.

1)If You Love Me, Let Me Know 2)Have You Never Been Mellow 3)Xanadu

11/27/71	158	4			1 If Not For You			$100	Uni 73117
12/29/73+	54	20	●	©	2 Let Me Be There			$15	MCA 389
6/8/74	❶¹	61	●	©	3 If You Love Me, Let Me Know			$15	MCA 411
2/22/75	❶¹	31	●	©	4 Have You Never Been Mellow			$12	MCA 2133
10/11/75	12	22	●	©	5 Clearly Love			$12	MCA 2148
3/20/76	13	24	●	©	6 Come On Over			$12	MCA 2186
11/6/76	30	28	●	©	7 Don't Stop Believin'			$12	MCA 2223
7/9/77	34	16		©	8 Making A Good Thing Better			$12	MCA 2280
11/12/77+	13	19	▲²	©	9 Olivia Newton-John's Greatest Hits		[G]	$12	MCA 3028

NEWTON-JOHN, Olivia — Cont'd

DEBUT	PEAK	WKS	RIAA	CD	ARTIST — Album Title	$	Label & Number
12/9/78+	7	39	▲	© 10	**Totally Hot**	$12	MCA 3067
7/12/80	4	36	▲²	© 11	**Xanadu** [S]	$12	MCA 6100
					side 1: Newton-John; side 2: **Electric Light Orchestra**		
10/31/81	6	57	▲²	© 12	**Physical**	$12	MCA 5229
10/9/82	16	86	▲²	© 13	**Olivia's Greatest Hits, Vol. 2** [G]	$12	MCA 5347
11/2/85	29	16	●	© 14	**Soul Kiss**	$12	MCA 6151
9/3/88	67	9		© 15	**The Rumour**	$12	MCA 6245
12/2/89+	124	13		© 16	**Warm And Tender**	$10	Geffen 24257
6/27/92	121	8	●	© 17	**Back To Basics - The Essential Collection 1971-1992** [G]	$10	Geffen 24470
5/30/98	59	6		© 18	**Back With A Heart**	$10	MCA 70030

Air That I Breathe (4)
All The Pretty Little Horses (16)
And In The Morning (4)
Angel Of The Morning (2)
Attention (3)
Back With A Heart (18)
Banks Of The Ohio (1,2) **94**
Big And Strong (15)
Blue Eyes Crying In The Rain (6)
Boats Against The Current (10)
Borrowed Time (10)
Can't We Talk It Over In Bed (15)
Car Games (15)
Carried Away (12)
Changes (3,9)
Clearly Love (5)
Closer To Me (18)
Come On Over (6,9) **23**
Compassionate Man (7)
Coolin' Down (5)
Country Girl (3)
Crying, Laughing, Loving, Lying (5)
Culture Shock (14)
Dancin' (11)
Dancin' 'Round And 'Round (10) **82**
Deeper Than A River (17)
Deeper Than The Night (10,17) **11**
Don't Ask A Friend (8)

Don't Cry For Me Argentina (8)
Don't Say That (18)
Don't Stop Believin' (7,9) **33**
Don't Throw It All Away (6)
Driving Music (14)
Emotional Tangle (14)
Every Face Tells A Story (7) **55**
Falling (12)
Fight For Our Love (18)
Flower That Shattered The Stone (16)
Follow Me (4)
Free The People (3)
Get Out (15)
Gimme Some Lovin' (10)
God Only Knows (3)
Goodbye Again (4)
Greensleeves (6)
Have You Never Been Mellow (4,9,17) **1**
He Ain't Heavy...He's My Brother (5) **flip**
He's My Rock (5)
Heart Attack (13) **3**
Help Me Make It Through The Night (1,2)
Hey Mr. Dreammaker (7)
Home Ain't Home Anymore (3)
Hopelessly Devoted To You (13,17) **3**
I Don't Wanna Say Goodnight (18)

I Honestly Love You (3,9,17) **1**
I Honestly Love You (18) **67**
I Need Love (17) **96**
I Never Did Sing You A Love Song (2)
I Think I'll Say Goodbye (8)
I Want To Be Wanted (17)
I'll Bet You A Kangaroo (7)
If (1)
If I Could Read Your Mind (1,2)
If I Gotta Leave (1)
If Love Is Real (8)
If Not For You (1,2,9) **25**
If You Love Me (Let Me Know) (3,9,17) **5**
In A Station (1)
It'll Be Me (6)
It's Not Heaven (15)
It's So Easy (4)
Jenny Rebecca (16)
Jolene (6)
Just A Little Too Much (2)
Just A Lot Of Folk (The Marshmallow Song) (5)
Landslide (12) **52**
Last Time You Loved (7)
Let It Shine (5,9) **30**
Let Me Be There (2,9) **6**
Let's Talk About Tomorrow (1)
Lifestream (4)
Little More Love (10,13,17) **3**
Long And Winding Road (6)
Love And Let Live (15)

Love Is A Gift (18)
Love Make Me Strong (12)
Love Song (1,2)
Love You Hold The Key (7)
Lovers (5)
Loving Arms (4)
Lullaby (2)
Lullaby Lullaby My Lovely One (16)
Magic (11,13,17) **1**
Make A Move On Me (12,13) **5**
Making A Good Thing Better (8) **87**
Mary Skeffington (3)
Me And Bobby McGee (1,2)
Moth To A Flame (14)
Never Enough (10)
New-Born Babe (7)
No Regrets (1)
Not Gonna Be The One (17)
Over The Rainbow (16)
Overnight Observation (14)
Physical (12,13,17) **1**
Please Don't Keep Me Waiting (10)
Please Mr. Please (4,9,17) **3**
Pony Ride (6)
Precious Love (18)
Promise (The Dolphin Song) (12)
Queen Of The Publication (14)
Reach Out For Me (16)
Recovery (12)

Right Moment (14)
Ring Of Fire (8)
River's Too Wide (3)
Rock A Bye Baby (16)
Rocking (15)
Rumour, The (15) **62**
Sad Songs (8)
Sail Into Tomorrow (5)
Sam (7,9,17) **20**
Silvery Rain (2)
Sleep My Princess (16)
Slow Dancing (8)
Slow Down Jackson (5)
Small Talk And Pride (6)
Smile For Me (6)
So Easy To Begin (8)
Something Better To Do (5,9) **13**
Soul Kiss (14) **20**
Spinning His Wheels (18)
Stranger's Touch (12)
Suddenly (11,13) **20**
Summer Nights (17)
Summertime Blues (5)
Suspended In Time (11)
Take Me Home, Country Roads (2)
Talk To Me (10)
Thousand Conversations (7)
Tied Up (13) **38**
Totally Hot (10) **52**
Toughen Up (14)
Tutta La Vita (2)

Twelfth Of Never (16)
Twinkle Twinkle Little Star (16)
Twist Of Fate (17) **5**
Under My Skin (18)
Walk Through Fire (15)
Warm And Tender (16)
Water Under The Bridge (4)
Way You Look Tonight (16)
When You Wish Upon A Star (16)
Whenever You're Far Away From Me (11)
Where Are You Going To My Love? (17)
Who Are You Now? (6)
Wrap Me In Your Arms (6)
Xanadu (11,13) **8**
You Ain't Got The Right (3)
You Were Great, How Was I? (14)
You Won't See Me Cry (8)
You'll Never Walk Alone (16)
You're The One That I Want (13,17) **1**

NEW VAUDEVILLE BAND, The '67

Studio creation of songwriter/record producer Geoff Stephens (born on 10/1/34 in London). Arrangements similar to Rudy Vallee's hits during the 1930s.

DEBUT	PEAK	WKS	RIAA	CD	ARTIST — Album Title	$	Label & Number
12/10/66+	5	31	●	©	**Winchester Cathedral**	$20	Fontana 27560

Diana Goodbye
I Can't Go Wrong
Lilli Marlene

Nightingale Sang In Berkeley Square
Tap Your Feet (And Go Bo-De-De-Doo)

That's All For Now, Sugar Baby
There's A Kind Of Hush
Whatever Happened To Phyllis Puke?

Whispering
Winchester Cathedral 1
Your Love Ain't What It Used To Be

NEW YORK CITY '73

R&B vocal group from New York City: Tim McQueen, John Brown, Ed Shell and Claude Johnston.

DEBUT	PEAK	WKS	RIAA	CD	ARTIST — Album Title	$	Label & Number
6/16/73	122	10		©	**I'm Doin' Fine Now**	$15	Chelsea 0198

Ain't It So
By The Time I Get To Phoenix

Hang On Sloopy
Hang Your Head In Shame

I'm Doin' Fine Now 17
Make Me Twice The Man 93

Quick, Fast, In A Hurry 79
Reach Out

Sanity
Set The Record Straight

Uncle James

NEW YORK DOLLS '73

Glitter-rock group from New York City: **David Johansen** (vocals), Johnny "Thunders" Genzale (vocals, guitar), **Sylvain Sylvain** (guitar), Arthur Harold Kane (bass) and Jerry Nolan (drums). Managed by British entrepeneur **Malcolm McLaren** who later formed the **Sex Pistols**. Genzale died of a drug overdose on 4/23/91 (age 38).

DEBUT	PEAK	WKS	RIAA	CD	ARTIST — Album Title	$	Label & Number
9/1/73	116	12		© 1	**New York Dolls**	$50	Mercury 675
					produced by **Todd Rundgren**		
6/1/74	167	5		© 2	**In Too Much Too Soon**	$50	Mercury 1001

Babylon (2)
Bad Detective (2)
Bad Girl (1)
Chatterbox (2)

Don't Start Me Talkin' (2)
Frankenstein (Orig.) (1)
Human Being (2)
It's Too Late (2)

Jet Boy (1)
Lonely Planet Boy (1)
Looking For A Kiss (1)
Personality Crisis (1)

Pills (1)
Private World (1)
Puss 'N' Boots (2)
Stranded In The Jungle (2)

Subway Train (1)
(There's Gonna Be A) Showdown (2)
Trash (1)

Vietnamese Baby (1)
Who Are The Mystery Girls? (2)

NEXT '00

R&B vocal trio from Minneapolis: R.L., Tweety and T-Low.

DEBUT	PEAK	WKS	RIAA	CD	ARTIST — Album Title	$	Label & Number
10/18/97+	37	60	▲²	© 1	**Rated Next**	$10	Arista 18973
7/8/00	12	21	●	© 2	**Welcome II Nextasy**	$10	Arista 14643

Banned From TV (2)
Beauty Queen (2)
Butta Love (1) **16**
Call On Me (2)
Cozy (1)

Cybersex (2)
Do You Think About Me (1)
I Still Love You (1) **14**
Jerk (2)
Let's Make A Movie (2)

My Everything (2)
Next Experience (1)
Oh No No (2)
Penetration (1)
Phone Sex (1)

Problems (1)
Represent Me (1)
Rock On (1)
Sexitude (1)
Shorty (2)

Splash (1)
Stop, Drop & Roll (1)
Taste So Good (1)
Too Close (1) **1**
What U Want (2)

When We Kiss (2)
Wifey (2) **7**

NICE, The '72

Classical-rock trio from England: **Keith Emerson** (organ; **Emerson, Lake & Palmer**), Lee Jackson (vocals, bass) and Brian Davison (drums).

DEBUT	PEAK	WKS	RIAA	CD	ARTIST — Album Title	$	Label & Number
8/29/70	197	5		1	**Five Bridges** [I-L]	$15	Mercury 61295
2/26/72	152	8		© 2	**Keith Emerson with The Nice** [R]	$20	Mercury 6500 [2]
					reissue of *Five Bridges* and *Elegy* albums		

America (2)
Brandenburg Concerto No. 6 (medley) (1,2)

Bridge (1st-5th) (1,2)
Country Pie (medley) (1,2)
Hang On To A Dream (2)

Intermezzo Karelia Suite (1,2)
My Back Pages (2)
One Of Those People (1,2)

Symphony No. 6, "Pathetique," 3rd Movement (1,2)

633

NICE & SMOOTH   '94

Rap duo from New York City: Greg "Nice" Mays and Daryl "Smooth" Barnes.

| 10/5/91 | 141 | 19 | | © | 1 **Ain't A Damn Thing Changed** .... | | | $10 | RAL 47373 |
| 7/16/94 | 66 | 4 | | © | 2 **Jewel Of The Nile** .... | | | $10 | RAL 523336 |

Billy-Gene (1) — Do Whatcha Gotta (2) — Harmonize (1) — **Old To The New** (2) *59* — Return Of The Hip Hop Freaks (2) — **Sometimes I Rhyme Slow** (1) *44*
Blunts (2) — Doin' Our Own Thang (2) — Hip Hop Junkies (1) — One, Two And One More — Save The Children (2) — Step By Step (1)
Cake & Eat It Too (1) — Down The Line (1) — How To Flow (1) — Makes Three (1) — Sex, Sex, Sex (1)
Cheri (2) — Get Fucked Up (2) — Let's All Get Down (2) — Paranoia (1) — Sky's The Limit (1)
No Bones Remix (1) — Pump It Up (1)

NICHOLS, Mike, & Elaine May   '61

Improvisational comedy team. Nichols was born Michael Peschkowsky on 11/6/31 in Berlin. Prolific movie director. Married to network newscaster Diane Sawyer. May was born on 4/21/32 in Pennsylvania. Movie writer/director/actress.

6/1/59	39	7		©	1 **Improvisations To Music**		[C]	$30	Mercury 20376
1/23/61	10	32		©	2 **An evening with Mike Nichols and Elaine May**		[C]	$30	Mercury 2200
2/24/62	17	29		©	3 **Mike Nichols & Elaine May Examine Doctors**		[C]	$30	Mercury 20680

Adultery (2) — Cocktail Piano (1) — Merry Christmas, Doctor (3) — Out Of Africa (3) — Tango (1)
Bach To Bach (1) — Disc Jockey (2) — Morning Rounds (3) — Physical (3) — Telephone (2)
Bedside Manner (3) — Everybody's Doing It (1) — Mother And Son (2) — Second Piano Concerto (1) — Thank You Very Much (3)
Calling Dr. Marx (3) — Interrupted Hour (3) — Mysterioso (1) — Sonata For Piano And Celeste (1) — Transference (3)
Chopin (1) — Little More Gauze (3) — Nichols And May At Work (3) — Von Brauns At Home (3)

NICKELBACK   '00

Rock group from Vancouver: brothers Chad (vocals) and Mike (bass) Kroeger, Ryan Peake (guitar) and Ryan Vikedal (drums).

| 8/26/00 | 130 | 15↑ | | © | **The State** .... | | | $10 | Roadrunner 8586 |

Breathe — Deep — Hold Out Your Hand — Not Leavin' Yet — One Last Run
Cowboy Hat — Diggin' This — Leader Of Men — Old Enough — Worthy To Say

NICKEL CREEK   '01

Bluegrass group from Los Angeles: brother-and-sister Sean (guitar) and Sara (fiddle) Watkins, with Chris Thile (mandolin).

| 4/28/01 | 142 | 22↑ | | © | **Nickel Creek** .... | | | $10 | Sugar Hill 3909 |

Cuckoo's Nest — Hand Song — Lighthouse's Tale — Out Of The Woods — Reasons Why — Sweet Afton
Fox, The — House Of Tom Bombadil — Ode To A Butterfly — Pastures New — Robin And Marian — When You Come Back Down

★358★   NICKS, Stevie   '81

Born Stephanie Nicks on 5/26/48 in Phoenix; raised in San Francisco. Pop-rock singer/songwriter. Teamed up with **Lindsey Buckingham** in 1973. Both joined **Fleetwood Mac** in 1975.

8/15/81	❶[1]	143	▲[4]	©	1 **Bella Donna**			$10	Modern 139
1/29/83+	28[C]	22			2 **Buckingham Nicks**			$10	Polydor 5058
7/2/83	5	52	▲[2]	©	3 **The Wild Heart**			$10	Modern 90084
12/14/85+	12	35	▲	©	4 **Rock A Little**			$10	Modern 90479
6/10/89	10	21	▲	©	5 **The Other Side Of The Mirror**			$10	Modern 91245
9/21/91	30	24	▲	©	6 **TimeSpace - The Best Of Stevie Nicks**		[G]	$10	Modern 91711
6/25/94	45	10	●	©	7 **Street Angel**			$10	Modern 92246
5/16/98	85	2	●	©	8 **Enchanted**		[K]	$30	Atlantic 83093 [3]
5/19/01	5	20↑	●	©	9 **Trouble In Shangri-La**			$10	Reprise 47372

After The Glitter Fades (1,8) *32* — Don't Let Me Down Again (2) — How Still My Love (1) — Lola (My Love) (2) — Races Are Run (2) — Sweet Girl (8)
Alice (5) — Edge Of Seventeen (Just Like — **I Can't Wait** (4,6,8) *16* — Long Distance Winner (2,8) — Reconsider Me (8) — **Talk To Me** (4,6,8) *4*
Battle Of The Dragon (8) — The White Winged Dove) — I Miss You (9) — Long Way To Go (5) — Rhiannon (8) — That Made Me Stronger (9)
Beauty And The Beast (3,6,8) — (1,6,8) *11* — I Sing For The Things (4,8) — Love Changes (9) — Rock A Little (Go Ahead Lily) — Think About It (1)
Bella Donna (1,8) — Enchanted (3,8) — I Still Miss Someone (Blue — Love Is (9) — (4,8) — Thousand Days (8)
Blue Denim (7,8) — Every Day (9) — Eyes) (5) — Love Is Like A River (7) — **Rooms On Fire** (5,6,8) *16* — Too Far From Texas (9)
Blue Lamp (8) — Fall From Grace (9) — I Will Run To You (3) — Love's A Hard Game To Play — Rose Garden (7,8) — Trouble In Shangri-La (9)
Bombay Sapphires (9) — Fire Burning (5) — If Anyone Falls (3,6,8) *14* — (6) — Sable On Blond (3) — Twisted (8)
Candlebright (9) — Free Fallin' (8) — If I Were You (4) — **Maybe Love Will Change** — Sister Honey (4) — Two Kinds Of Love (5,8)
Cry Wolf (5) — Frozen Love (2) — Imperial Hotel (4) — **Your Mind** (7) *57* — Sleeping Angel (8) — Unconditional Love (8)
Crying In The Night (2) — Garbo (3) — It's Late (8) — **Nightbird** (3,8) *33* — Some Become Strangers (4) — Violet And Blue (8)
Crystal (2) — Gate And Garden (3) — It's Only Love (9) — Nightmare, The (4) — Somebody Stand By Me (4) — Whenever I Call You Friend (8)
Desert Angel (6,8) — Ghosts (5) — Jane (7) — No Spoken Word (4) — **Sometimes It's A Bitch** (6) *56* — Whole Lotta Trouble (5,6,8)
Destiny (7,8) — Gold (8) — Juliet (5) — Nothing Ever Changes (3) — Sorcerer (9) — Wild Heart (3,8)
Django (2) — Gold And Braid (8) — Just Like A Woman (7) — One More Big Time Rock And — **Stand Back** (3,6,8) *5* — Without A Leg To Stand On (2)
Docklands (7) — Greta (7) — Kick It (7) — Roll Star (8) — Stephanie (2)
Doing The Best That I Can — **Has Anyone Ever Written** — Kind Of Woman (1,8) — Ooh My Love (5,8) — **Stop Draggin' My Heart**
(Escape From Berlin) (5) — **Anything For You** (4,6,8) *60* — **Leather And Lace** (1,6,8) *6* — Outside The Rain (1,8) — **Around** (1,6,8) *3*
Highwayman (7) — Listen To The Rain (7) — Planets Of The Universe (9) — Street Angel (7,8)

NICOLE   '98

Born Nicole Wray in Salinas, California; raised in Portsmouth, Virginia. Female R&B singer.

| 9/12/98 | 42 | 9 | | © | **Make It Hot** .... | | | $10 | EastWest 62209 |

Borrowed Time — Eyes Better Not Wander — **Make It Hot** *5* — Radio DJ — Silly Love Song — Traffic Jam
Boy You Should Listen — I Can't See — Nervous — Raise Your Frown — Testing Our Love (Suga)
Curiosity — In Da Street — Pressure — Seventeen — Time Is Now

NIGHT   '79

Pop-rock group: Stevie Lange (female vocals), Chris Thompson (male vocals; **Manfred Mann's Earth Band**), Robbie McIntosh (guitar), **Nicky Hopkins** (piano), Billy Kristian (bass) and Rick Marotta (drums). McIntosh later joined **The Pretenders** and **Paul McCartney**'s backing band.

| 8/11/79 | 113 | 10 | | | **Night** .... | | | $12 | Planet 2 |

second pressings of album (on Planet 3) include Thompson's "If You Remember Me"

Ain't That Peculiar — Come Around (If You Want Me) — If You Gotta Make A Fool Of — **If You Remember Me** *17* — Party Shuffle — You Ain't Pretty Enough
Cold Wind Across My Heart — **Hot Summer Nights** *18* — Somebody — Love Message — Shocked

NIGHTHAWKS, The   '80

Blues-rock group from Washington DC: Mark Wenner (vocals), Jim Thackery (guitar), Jan Zukowski (bass) and Pete Ragusa (drums).

| 7/26/80 | 166 | 4 | | | **The Nighthawks** .... | | | $12 | Mercury 3833 |

Back To The City — Don't Go No Further — I Wouldn't Treat A Dog (The — Little Sister — One Nite Stand — Teen-Age Letter
Brand New Man — Everynight And Everyday — Way You Treated Me) — Mainline — Pretty Girls And Cadillacs — Upside Your Head

NIGHTINGALE, Maxine　'79

Born on 11/2/52 in Wembly, England. Acted in productions of *Hair*, *Jesus Christ Superstar*, *Godspell* and *Savages*.

DEBUT	PEAK	WKS				$	Label & Number
5/29/76	65	9			1 Right Back Where We Started From	$12	United Artists 626
7/21/79	45	18			2 Lead Me On	$12	Windsong 3404
1/8/83	176	4			3 It's A Beautiful Thing	$12	Highrise 101

Anyone Who Had A Heart (3)　Everytime I See A Butterfly (1)　(I Think I Wanna) Possess You (1)　Love Enough (1)　Reasons (1)　Turn To Me (3)
Ask Billy (They Tell Me) (2)　Give A Little Love (To Me) (3)　If I Ever Lose This Heaven (1)　Love Me Like You Mean It (2)　**Right Back Where We Started From** (1) *2*　You Are The Most Important Person In Your Life (2)
Bless You (1)　Good-Bye Again (1)　In Love We Grow (1)　Never Gonna Be Another One (3)　Shakin' Me Up (3)　You Got The Love (1)
(Bringing Out) The Girl In Me (2) *73*　**Gotta Be The One** (1) *53*　Life Has Just Begun (1)　No One Like My Baby (2)　So Right (3)　You Got To Me (2)
Darlin' Dear (2)　Hideaway (2)　**Lead Me On** (2) *5*　One Last Ride (1)　Stand Up For Your Heart (3)
I Don't Miss You At All (3)

NIGHT RANGER　'85

Rock group formed in San Francisco: Jack Blades (vocals, bass), Kelly Keagy (vocals, drums), Jeff Watson and Brad Gillis (guitars), and Alan Fitzgerald (keyboards). Blades and Gillis were members of **Rubicon**. Blades later joined **Damn Yankees** and formed duo with **Tommy Shaw**.

DEBUT	PEAK	WKS	RIAA	CD		$	Label & Number
12/25/82+	38	69		©	1 Dawn Patrol	$12	Boardwalk 33259
11/19/83+	15	69	▲	©	2 Midnight Madness	$10	MCA/Camel 5456
6/8/85	10	45	▲	©	3 7 Wishes	$10	MCA/Camel 5593
4/11/87	28	18	●	©	4 Big Life	$10	MCA/Camel 5839
10/22/88	81	8		©	5 Man In Motion	$10	MCA/Camel 6238

At Night She Sleeps (1)　**Don't Tell Me You Love Me** (1) *40*　**I Did It For Love** (5) *75*　Night Machine (3)　**Secret Of My Success** (4) *64*　Why Does Love Have To Change (2)
Better Let It Go (4)　Eddie's Comin' Out Tonight (1)　I Know Tonight (4)　Night Ranger (1)　**Sentimental Street** (3) *8*　Woman In Love (5)
Big Life (4)　Faces (3)　I Need A Woman (3)　Passion Play (2)　Seven Wishes (3)　**(You Can Still) Rock In America** (2) *51*
Call My Name (1)　**Four In The Morning (I Can't Take Any More)** (3) *19*　I Will Follow You (3)　Penny (1)　**Sing Me Away** (1) *54*
Can't Find Me A Thrill (1)　Interstate Love Affair (3)　Play Rough (1)　**Sister Christian** (2) *5*　Young Girl In Love (1)
Carry On (4)　**Goodbye** (3) *17*　Kiss Me Where It Hurts (5)　Rain Comes Crashing Down (4)　This Boy Needs To Rock (3)
Chippin' Away (2)　Halfway To The Sun (5)　Let Him Run (1)　Reason To Be (5)　Touch Of Madness (2)
Color Of Your Smile (4)　**Hearts Away** (4) *90*　Love Is Standing Near (4)　Restless Kind (5)　**When You Close Your Eyes** (2) *14*
Don't Start Thinking (I'm Alone Tonight) (5)　Here She Comes Again (5)　Love Shot Me Down (5)　Right On You (5)
　Man In Motion (5)　Rumours In The Air (2)

NILE, Willie　'80

Born Robert Noonan in 1949 in Buffalo, New York. Rock singer/songwriter.

DEBUT	PEAK	WKS	RIAA	CD		$	Label & Number
4/12/80	145	6		©	1 Willie Nile	$12	Arista 4260
5/2/81	158	8		©	2 Golden Down	$12	Arista 4284

Across The River (1)　Grenade (2)　I Like The Way (2)　Old Men Sleeping On The Bowery (1)　Shine Your Light (2)　They'll Build A Statue Of You (1)
Behind The Cathedral (1)　Hide Your Love (2)　I'm Not Waiting (1)　Poor Boy (1)　Shoulders (2)
Dear Lord (1)　I Can't Get You Off Of My Mind (2)　It's All Over (1)　She's So Cold (1)　Sing Me A Song (1)　Vagabond Moon (1)
Golden Down (2)　Les Champs Elysees (2)　That's The Reason (1)

★361★　NILSSON　'72

Born Harry Nelson on 6/15/41 in Brooklyn, New York. Died of a heart attack on 1/15/94 (age 52). Pop singer/songwriter.

1)Nilsson Schmilsson　2)Son Of Schmilsson　3)The Point!

DEBUT	PEAK	WKS	RIAA	CD		Sym	$	Label & Number
8/23/69	120	15		©	1 Harry		$15	RCA Victor 4197
3/6/71	25	32		©	2 The Point!	[TV]	$15	RCA Victor 1003
					songs and narration from his animated TV special			
7/17/71	149	3		©	3 Aerial Pandemonium Ballet	[K]	$15	RCA Victor 4543
					selections from *Pandemonium Shadow Show* and *Aerial Ballet* albums			
12/4/71+	3	46	●	©	4 Nilsson Schmilsson		$15	RCA Victor 4515
7/22/72	12	31	●	©	5 Son Of Schmilsson		$15	RCA Victor 4717
6/23/73	46	17		©	6 A Little Touch Of Schmilsson In The Night		$15	RCA Victor 0097
5/4/74	106	9			7 Son Of Dracula	[S]	$15	Rapple 0220
9/7/74	60	12		©	8 Pussy Cats		$20	RCA Victor 0570
					produced by **John Lennon**			
4/5/75	141	7			9 Duit On Mon Dei		$15	RCA Victor 0817
2/7/76	111	7			10 Sandman		$15	RCA Victor 1031
7/10/76	158	6			11 ...That's The Way It Is		$15	RCA Victor 1119
8/6/77	108	10		©	12 Knnillssonn		$15	RCA Victor 2276
6/17/78	140	5			13 Greatest Hits	[G]	$15	RCA Victor 2798

Abdication Of Count Down (7)　Driving Along (4)　Introduction (3)　Mother Nature's Son (1)　**Remember (Christmas)** (5,7,13) *53*　Turn On Your Radio (5)
All I Think About Is You (12)　Early In The Morning (4)　It Had To Be You (6)　Mt. Elga (medley) (8)　River Deep-Mountain High (3)　Turn Out The Light (9)
All My Life (8)　Easier For Me (9)　It Is He Who Will Be King (9)　Mournin' Glory Story (6)　Rock Around The Clock (8)　What'll I Do (6)
Always (6)　**Everybody's Talkin'** (3,13) *6*　It's A Jungle Out There (9)　Mr. Bojangles (1)　Sail Away (11)　What's Your Sign (9)
Ambush (5)　Everything's Got 'Em (2)　Ivy Covered Walls (1)　Mr. Richland's Favorite Song (3)　Salmon Falls (9)　Who Done It? (12)
Are You Sleeping? (2)　Fairfax Rag (1)　Jesus Christ You're Tall (9,10)　Save The Last Dance For Me (8)　Will She Miss Me (10)
As Time Goes By (6,13) *86*　Flying Saucer Song (10)　Joy (5)　Mucho Mungo (medley) (8)　She Sits Down On Me (11)　Without Her (3,13)
At My Front Door (5,7)　For Me And My Gal (6)　**Jump Into The Fire** (4,7,13) *27*　Nevertheless (I'm In Love With You) (6)　Simon Smith And The Amazing Dancing Bear (1)　**Without You** (4,7,13) *1*
Baby I'm Yours (medley) (11)　Frankenstein, Merlin And The Operation (7)　Just One Look (medley) (11)　1941 (3)　Sleep Late, My Lady Friend (3)　You Made Me Love You (I Didn't Want To Do It) (6)
Bath (3)　Game, The (2)　Kojak Columbo (7)　Nobody Cares About The Railroad Anymore (1)　Something True (10)　You're Breakin' My Heart (5)
Birds, The (2)　Goin' Down (12)　Laughin' Man (12)　Oblio's Return (2)　Spaceman (5,13) *23*　Zombie Jamboree (Back To Back) (11)
Black Sails (8)　Good For God (9)　Lazy Moon (6)　Old Bones (7)　Subterranean Homesick Blues (8)
Blanket For A Sail (12)　Good Old Desk (3)　Lean On Me (12)　Old Forgotten Soldier (8)　Sweet Surrender (12)
City Life (7)　Gotta Get Up (4)　Let The Good Times Roll (4)　One (3,13)　Take 54 (5)
Clearing In The Woods (2)　Home (9)　Life Line (2)　Open Your Window (1)　That Is All (11)
Closing (3)　How To Write A Song (10)　Loop De Loop (8)　P.O.V. Waltz (2)　This Is All I Ask (6)
Coconut (4,13) *8*　**I Guess The Lord Must Be In New York City** (1,13) *34*　Lottery Song (5)　Perfect Day (12)　Thousand Miles Away (11)
Count Down Meets Merlin And Amber (7)　I Need You (11)　Lullaby In Ragtime (6)　Perhaps This Is All A Dream (7)　Thursday Or, Here's Why I Did Not Go To Work Today (10)
Counts Vulnerability (7)　I Never Thought I'd Get This Lonely (12)　Makin' Whoopee! (6)　Pointed Man (2)　Together (2)
Daddy's Song (3)　I Wonder Who's Kissing Her Now (6)　Many Rivers To Cross (8)　Poli High (2)　Town, The (2)
Daybreak (7,13) *39*　I'd Rather Be Dead (5)　Marchin' Down Broadway (1)　Pretty Soon There'll Be Nothing Left For Everybody (10)　Trial & Banishment (2)
Daylight Has Caught Me (11)　I'll Never Leave You (4)　Maybe (1)　Puget Sound (9)
Don't Forget Me (3)　I'll Take A Tango (10)　**Me And My Arrow** (2,13) *34*　Puppy Song (1)
Don't Leave Me (3)　Moonbeam (4,7)　Rainmaker (1)
Down (4,7)　Moonshine Bandit (11)
Down By The Sea (9)　Most Beautiful World In The World (1)

NIMOY, Leonard   '67
Born on 3/26/31 in Boston. Actor/director. Played "Mr. Spock" on *Star Trek*.

| 6/10/67 | 83 | 25 | | © | **1 Mr. Spock's Music From Outer Space** | | | $100 | Dot 25794 |

Nimoy sings 3 songs and narrates 3 others; also includes 5 instrumentals by **Charles Grean**: "Beyond Antares," "Mission Impossible," "Music To Watch Space Girls By," "Theme From Star Trek" and "Where No Man Has Gone Before"

| 2/24/68 | 97 | 13 | | | **2 Two Sides Of Leonard Nimoy** | | | $100 | Dot 25835 |

side 1: performs as Mr. Spock; side 2: performs as Leonard Nimoy

Alien (1)	Cotton Candy (On A Summer	Gentle On My Mind (2)	Love Of The Common People	Spock Thoughts (2)	You Are Not Alone (1)
Amphibious Assault (2)	Day) (2)	Highly Illogical (2)	(2)	Twinkle, Twinkle Little Earth (1)	
Ballad Of Bilbo Baggins (2)	Difference Between Us (2)	If I Were A Carpenter (2)	Miranda (2)	Visit To A Sad Planet (1)	
By Myself (2)	Follow Your Star (2)	Lost In The Stars (1)	Once I Smiled (2)	Where Is Love (1)	

NINE   '95
Born on 9/19/69 in New York City. Male rapper.

| 3/25/95 | 90 | 8 | | © | **Nine Livez** | | | $10 | Profile 1460 |

Ahh Shit	Da Fundamentalz	Hit Em Like Dis	Redrum	Who U Won Test
Any Emcee	Everybody Won Heaven	Ova Confident	Retaliate	**Whutcha Want?** *50*
Cypha, Tha	Fo' Eva Blunted	Peel	Ta Rasss	

NINEDAYS   '00
Rock group from New York City: John Hampson (vocals, guitar), Brian Desveaux (vocals, guitar), Jeremy Dean (keyboards), Nick Dimichino (bass) and Vincent Tattanelli (drums).

| 6/3/00 | 67 | 19 | ● | © | **The Madding Crowd** | | | $10 | 550 Music 63634 |

Absolutely (Story Of A Girl) *6*	Bitter	Crazy	**If I Am** *68*	So Far Away	257 Weeks
Back To Me	Bob Dylan	End Up Alone	Revolve	Sometimes	Wanna Be

★403★   NINE INCH NAILS   '99
Group is actually industrial rock musician Trent Reznor (born on 5/17/65 in Mercer, Pennsylvania).

2/10/90+	75	113	▲²	©	**1 Pretty Hate Machine**	C:❶¹⁴/172		$10	TVT 2610
10/10/92	7	30	▲	©	**2 Broken**	C:#35/12		$10	Nothing 92213
3/26/94	2¹	115	▲⁴	©	**3 The Downward Spiral**	C:#46/1		$10	Nothing 92346
6/17/95	23	20	●	©	**4 Further Down The Spiral**	[M]		$10	Nothing 95811
10/9/99	❶¹	19	▲²	©	**5 The Fragile**			$15	Nothing 490473 [2]
12/9/00	67	5		©	**6 Things Falling Apart**			$10	Nothing 490744

Art Of Self Destruction, Part	Downward Spiral (3,4)	Head Like A Hole (1)	**March Of The Pigs** (3) *59*	Ripe (With Decay) (5)	Terrible Lie (1)
One (4)	Erased, Over, Out (4)	Help Me I Am In Hell (3)	Mark Has Been Made (5)	Ruiner (3)	That's What I Get (1)
At The Heart Of It All (4)	Eraser (3)	Heresy (3)	Metal (6)	Sanctified (1)	Underneath It All (5)
Beauty Of Being Numb (4)	Eraser (Denial; Realization) (4)	Hurt (3,4)	Mr Self Destruct (3)	Self Destruction, Part Two (4)	Warm Place (3)
Becoming, The (3)	Eraser (Polite) (4)	I Do Not Want This (3)	No, You Don't (5)	Self Destruction, Final (4)	Way Out Is Through (5)
Big Come Down (5)	Even Deeper (5)	I'm Looking Forward To Joining	Only Time (1)	Sin (1)	We're In This Together (5)
Big Man With A Gun (3)	Fragile, The (5)	You, Finally (5)	Piggy (3,4)	Slipping Away (6)	Where Is Everybody? (5,6)
Closer (3) *41*	Frail, The (5,6)	Into The Void (5)	Pilgrimage (5)	Something I Can Never Have	Wish (2)
Complication (5)	Gave Up (2)	Just Like You Imagined (5)	Pinion (2)	(1)	Wretched, The (5,6)
Day The World Went Away	Great Below (5)	Kinda I Want To (1)	Please (5)	Somewhat Damaged (5)	
(5) *17*	Great Collapse (6)	La Mer (5)	Reptile (3)	Starfuckers, Inc. (5,6)	
Down In It (1)	Happiness In Slavery (2)	Last (2)	Ringfinger (1)	10 Miles High (6)	

999   '80
New-wave group from London: Nick Cash (vocals), Guy Davis (guitar), John Watson (bass) and Pablo Labritain (drums). 999 is the emergency telephone number in England.

| 2/23/80 | 177 | 3 | | © | **1 The Biggest Prize In Sport** | | | $12 | Polydor 6256 |
| 6/27/81 | 192 | 2 | | © | **2 Concrete** | | | $12 | Polydor 6323 |

Biggest Prize In Sport (1)	Break It Up (2)	Found Out Too Late (1)	Lil' Red Riding Hood (2)	Silent Anger (1)	Stranger (1)
Boiler (1)	Don't You Know I Need You (2)	Fun Thing (1)	Mercy Mercy (2)	So Greedy (2)	Taboo (2)
Bongos On The Nile (2)	English Wipe-Out (1)	Hollywood (1)	Obsessed (2)	So Long (1)	That's The Way It Goes (2)
Boys In The Gang (1)	Fortune Teller (2)	Inside Out (1)	Public Enemy No. 1 (2)	Stop Stop (1)	Trouble (1)

9.9   '85
R&B vocal trio from Boston: Margo Thunder, Leslie Jones and Wanda Perry.

| 9/14/85 | 79 | 22 | | | **9.9** | | | $10 | RCA Victor 8049 |

All Of Me For All Of You *51*	Hooked On You	I Like The Way You Dance	Little Bitty Woman	
Feel The Fire	Hypnotized	I'll Help You Forget About Him	(Owch!) Hot Blood Pressure	

1910 FRUITGUM CO.   '68
Bubblegum group from New Jersey: Mark Gutkowski (vocals), Floyd Marcus, Pat Karwan, Steve Mortkowitz and Frank Jeckell.

4/20/68	162	8		©	**1 Simon Says**			$25	Buddah 5010
10/5/68	163	12			**2 1,2,3 Red Light**			$25	Buddah 5022
4/5/69	147	8			**3 Indian Giver**			$25	Buddah 5036

Blue Eyes And Orange Skies	Groovy Groovy (3)	Lookin' Back (2)	No Good Annie (3)	Song Song (2)	Yummy Yummy Yummy (2)
(2)	Happy Little Teardrops (1)	Magic Windmill (1)	**1, 2, 3, Red Light** (2) *5*	Soul Struttin' (1)	
Book, The (2)	I've Got To Have Your Love (3)	May I Take A Giant Step (Into	(Poor Old) Mr. Jensen (1)	**Special Delivery** (3) *38*	
Bubble Gum World (1)	**Indian Giver** (3) *5*	**Your Heart)** (1) *63*	Pop Goes The Weasel (1)	Story Of Flipper (1)	
Candy (2)	Keep Your Thoughts On The	Mighty Quinn (2)	Shirley Applegate (2)	Sweet Lovin' (2)	
Game Of Love (3)	Bright Side (1)	9,10, Let's Do It Again (2)	**Simon Says** (1) *4*	Take Away (2)	
Good Good Lovin' (3)	Let's Make Love (3)	1910 Cotton Candy Castle (3)	Sister John (2)	Year 2001 (1)	

98°   '00
White vocal group from Cincinnati: brothers Nick and Drew Lachey, with Jeff Timmons and Justin Jeffre.

8/23/97	145	9	●	©	**1 98°**	C:#24/2		$10	Motown 530796
11/14/98+	14	78	▲⁴	©	**2 98° And Rising**			$10	Motown 530956
11/6/99	27	12		©	**3 This Christmas**	C:#7/9	[X]	$10	Universal 153918

Christmas charts: 2/99, 2/00

| 10/14/00 | 2¹ | 24 | ▲² | © | **4 Revelation** | | | $10 | Universal 159354 |

Always You And I (4)	Christmas Song (Chestnuts	Completely (1)	Fly With Me (4)	Hand In Hand (1)	Heaven's Missing An Angel (1)
Ave Maria (3)	Roasting On An Open Fire)	Dizzy (4)	**Give Me Just One Night (Una**	**Hardest Thing** (2) *5*	**I Do (Cherish You)** (2) *13*
Because Of You (2) *3*	(3)	Do You Wanna Dance (2)	**Noche)** (4) *2*	He'll Never Be...(What I Used	I Wanna Love You (1)
	Christmas Wish (3)	Don't Stop The Love (1)	God Rest Ye Merry Gentlemen	To Be To You) (4)	I Wasn't Over You (1)
	Come And Get It (1)	Dreaming (1)	(3)	Heat It Up (2)	I'll Be Home For Christmas (3)

DEBUG	PEAK	WKS	RIAA	CD		ARTIST — Album Title	Catalog	Sym	$	Label & Number

98° — Cont'd

If Every Day Could Be Christmas (3)	Little Drummer Boy (3)	She's Out Of My Life (2)	Take My Breath Away (1)	Way You Do (4)	You Don't Know (4)
If She Only Knew (2)	**My Everything** (4) *34*	Silent Night (3)	**This Gift** (3) *49*	Way You Want Me To (4)	You Should Be Mine (4)
Invisible Man (1) *12*	Never Giving Up (4)	Stay The Night (4)	To Me You're Everything (2)	Yesterday's Letter (4)	
	Oh Holy Night (3)	Still (2)	True To Your Heart (2)	You Are Everything (1)	

95 SOUTH '93

Rap group from Miami: Nathaniel Orange, Church's, Black, Bootyman and K-Knock. Orange was also with Quad City DJ's.

5/15/93	71	26		©	1	Quad City Knock			$10	Toy 8117
2/18/95	158	2			2	One Mo' 'Gen			$10	Rip-It 9501

All The Way Down (2)	Da Kinda Bass (1)	Heiny Heiny (2)	One Mo' Gen (2)	Shake Rattle n' Roll (1)	**Whoot, There It Is** (1) *11*
Booty Hop (1)	Do It Baby (1)	Hump Wit' It (1)	One Time (1)	60 Seconds (1)	Wine & Dine (2)
Break It On Down (2)	Down South (2)	I Tell U What (2)	Quad City Funk (2)	So Clear (1)	
Bring Out da Ho's (1)	Freak Ya Down (2)	Let's Go to My Room (1)	Ride Out (1)	Trip 2 The Geto (2)	
Cowboy Mix (2)	Ghetto Style (1)	95 South in da House (1)	**Rodeo** (2) *77*	We Got da Bass (1)	

★334★ NIRVANA '92

Grunge-rock trio from Aberdeen, Washington: Kurt Cobain (vocals, guitar), Krist Novoselic (bass) and Dave Grohl (drums). Cobain married Courtney Love (lead singer of **Hole**) on 2/24/92. Cobain died of a self-inflicted gunshot wound on 4/8/94 (age 27). Grohl formed **Foo Fighters** in 1995.

10/12/91+	**①**²	252	▲¹⁰	©	1	**Nevermind**	C:#15/46		$10	DGC 24425
1/4/92	89	20	▲	©	2	Bleach	C:**①**²/71	[E]	$15	Sub Pop 34

debut album released in June 1989 by band's early lineup which included Chad Channing instead of Dave Grohl on drums; Jason Everman credited as guitarist but did not play on album

1/2/93	39	25	▲	©	3	Incesticide	C:#43/2	[K]	$10	DGC 24504

early recordings on independent labels, unreleased demos and performances on British radio broadcasts

10/9/93	**①**¹	87	▲⁵	©	4	**In Utero**	C:#48/1		$10	DGC 24607
11/19/94	**①**¹	81	▲⁵	©	5	**MTV Unplugged In New York**	C:#23/3	[L]	$10	DGC 24727

recorded on 11/18/93

10/19/96	**①**¹	21	▲	©	6	From The Muddy Banks Of The Wishkah		[L]	$10	DGC 25105

recorded from various performances between December 1989 and January 1994

About A Girl (2,5)	Dive (3)	Jesus Doesn't Want Me For A	Negative Creep (2,6)	School (2,6)	Swap Meet (2)
Aero Zeppelin (3)	Downer (2,3)	Sunbeam (5)	(New Wave) Polly (3)	Scoff (2)	Territorial Pissings (1)
All Apologies (4,5)	Drain You (1,6)	Lake Of Fire (5)	Oh Me (5)	Serve The Servants (4)	Tourette's (4,6)
Aneurysm (3,6)	Dumb (4,5)	Lithium (1,6)	On A Plain (1,5)	Sifting (2)	Turnaround (3)
Been A Son (3,6)	Endless Nameless (1)	Lounge Act (1)	Paper Cuts (2)	Sliver (3,6)	Very Ape (4)
Beeswax (3)	Floyd The Barber (2)	Love Buzz (2)	Pennyroyal Tea (4,5)	**Smells Like Teen Spirit** (1,6) *6*	Where Did You Sleep Last
Big Cheese (2)	Frances Farmer Will Have Her	Man Who Sold The World (5)	Plateau (5)	Something In The Way (1,5)	Night (5)
Big Long Now (3)	Revenge On Seattle (4)	Mexican Seafood (3)	Polly (1,5,6)	Son Of A Gun (3)	
Blew (2,6)	Hairspray Queen (3)	Milk It (4,6)	Radio Friendly Unit Shifter (4)	Spank Thru (6)	
Breed (1,6)	Heart-Shaped Box (4,6)	Molly's Lips (3)	Rape Me (4)	Stain (3)	
Come As You Are (1,5) *32*	In Bloom (1)	Mr. Moustache (2)	Scentless Apprentice (4,6)	Stay Away (1)	

NITRO '89

Hard-rock group: Jim Gillette (vocals), Michael Angelo (guitar), T.J. Racer (bass) and Bobby Rock (drums).

8/12/89	140	9		©		O.F.R.			$10	Rhino 70894

Bring It Down	Fighting Mad	Long Way From Home	Nasty Reputation	Shot Heard 'Round The World
Double Trouble	Freight Train	Machine Gunn Eddie	O.F.R.	

★416★ NITTY GRITTY DIRT BAND '74

Country-folk-rock group from Long Beach, California. Led by Jeff Hanna (vocals, guitar) and John McEuen (banjo, mandolin). Changed name to **Dirt Band** in 1976. Resumed using Nitty Gritty Dirt Band name in 1982. Various members included Jimmie Fadden (harmonica), Jim Ibbotson (guitar), Al Garth (violin) and **Bernie Leadon**, who replaced McEuen briefly in early 1987. In the movies *For Singles Only* and *Paint Your Wagon*. Hanna married country singer/songwriter Matraca Berg.

1)Stars & Stripes Forever 2)Make A Little Magic 3)Uncle Charlie & His Dog Teddy

4/8/67	151	8			1	The Nitty Gritty Dirt Band			$25	Liberty 7501
12/5/70+	66	32		©	2	Uncle Charlie & His Dog Teddy			$25	Liberty 7642
2/5/72	162	10		©	3	All The Good Times			$20	United Artists 5553
12/30/72+	68	32	▲	©	4	Will The Circle Be Unbroken			$30	United Artists 9801 [3]
7/13/74	28	21		©	5	Stars & Stripes Forever		[L]	$20	United Artists 184 [2]
10/4/75	66	9		©	6	Dream			$15	United Artists 469
12/18/76+	77	13		©	7	Dirt, Silver & Gold		[K]	$25	United Artists 670 [3]

THE DIRT BAND:

7/8/78	163	6		©	8	The Dirt Band..			$12	United Artists 854
1/26/80	76	14		©	9	An American Dream			$12	United Artists 974
7/19/80	62	16			10	Make A Little Magic			$12	United Artists 1042
9/5/81	102	9			11	Jealousy			$12	Liberty 1106
5/27/89	95	12		©	12	Will The Circle Be Unbroken, Volume Two			$10	Universal 12500 [2]

THE NITTY GRITTY DIRT BAND

(All I Have To Do Is) Dream (6,7) *66*	Buy For Me The Rain (1,5,7) *45*	Cure, The (2,7)	End, The (medley) (2)	Harmony (10)	It Came From The 50's (Blast From The Past) (5)
Amazing Grace (12)	Candy Man (1)	Daddy Was A Sailor (6)	End Of The World (4)	Hey Good Lookin' (6)	Jamaica Lady (7)
American Dream (9) *13*	Cannonball Rag (4)	Daisy (4)	Escaping Reality (8)	High School Yearbook (10)	Jamaica, Say You Will (3)
And So It Goes (12)	Catch The Next Dream (11)	Dance The Night Away (9)	Euphoria (1)	Holding (1)	**Jambalaya (On The Bayou)** (3,5) *84*
Angel (8)	Chicken Reel (medley) (2)	Dark As A Dungeon (4)	Falling Down Slow (7)	Honky Tonk Blues (4)	Jas'Moon (9)
Anxious Heart (10)	Circular Man (11)	Diggy Liggy Lo (3,5)	**Fire In The Sky** (11) *76*	Honky Tonkin' (4,5,7)	Jealousy (11)
Avalanche (4)	Civil War Trilogy (3)	Dismal Swamp (1)	Fish Song (3,5,7)	Hoping To Say (3)	Jesse James (medley) (2)
Badlands (10)	Classical Banjo I & II (medley) (6)	Dixie Hoedown (5)	Flint Hill Special (4)	**House At Pooh Corner** (2,5,7) *53*	Joshua Come Home (medley) (6)
Baltimore (3)	Clinch Mountain Backstep (medley) (2)	Do It! (Party Lights) (10)	Foggy Mountain Breakdown (7)	I Am A Pilgrim (4)	Keep On The Sunny Side (4)
Battle Of New Orleans (5,6,7) *72*	Collegiana (7)	Do You Feel It Too (3)	For A Little While (8)	I Saw The Light (4)	Leigh Anne (10)
Bayou Jubilee (6,7,12)	Cosmic Cowboy (Part 1) (5,7)	Do You Feel The Way That I Do (9)	Forget It! (11)	I Wish I Could Shimmy Like My Sister Kate (1)	Life's Railway To Heaven (12)
Billy In The Low Ground (2)	Crazy Words, Crazy Tune (1)	Doc's Guitar (7)	Gavotte No. 2 (5)	I'm Sittin' On Top Of The World (4)	Lights (8)
Black Mountain Rag (4)	Creepin' Round Your Back Door (3,7)	Don't You Hear Jerusalem Moan (12)	Glocoat-Blues (5)	I'm Thinking Tonight Of My Blue Eyes (4)	Listen To The Mockingbird (5)
Blues Berry Hill (12)	Cripple Creek (5)	Down In Texas (3)	Gotta Travel On (6)	**In For The Night** (8) *86*	Little Mountain Church House (12)
Both Sides Now (4)	Crossfire (11)	Down Yonder (4)	Grand Ole Opry Song (4)	In Her Eyes (9)	Livin' Without You (2,7)
Bowleg's (7)		Earl's Breakdown (4)	Grandpa Was A Carpenter (12)		
		Easy Slow (11)	Happy Feet (9)		
			Hard Hearted Hannah (The Vamp Of Savannah) (1)		

DEBUT	PEAK	WKS	RIAA	CD	ARTIST — Album Title	Catalog	Sym	$	Label & Number

NITTY GRITTY DIRT BAND — Cont'd

Lonesome Fiddle Blues (4)
Losin' You (Might Be The Best Thing Yet) (4)
Lost Highway (medley) (4)
Lost River (12)
Love Is The Last Thing (11)
Lovin' On The Side (12)
Make A Little Magic (10) *25*
Malaguena (medley) (6)
Mary Danced With Soldiers (12)
Melissa (1,7)
Moon Just Turned Blue (6)
Mother Earth (Provides For Me) (7)
Mother Of Love (6)
Mountain Whippoorwill (Or How Hillbilly Jim Won The Great Fiddler's Prize) (5)

Mournin' Blues (7)
Mr. Bojangles (2,5,7) *9*
Mullen's Farewell To America (10)
My True Story (5)
My Walkin' Shoes (4)
Nashville Blues (4)
New Orleans (9)
Nine-Pound Hammer (4)
Oh Boy (5)
On The Loose (8)
One Step Over The Line (12)
Opus 36, Clementi (John) (2,7)
Orange Blossom Special (4)
Pins And Needles (In My Heart) (4)
Precious Jewel (4)
Prodigal's Return (2)

Propinquity (2)
Raleigh-Durham Reel (medley) (6)
Randy Lynn Rag (2,7)
Rave On (2)
Resign Yourself To Me (5)
Riding Alone (10,12)
Ripplin' Waters (6,7)
Rocky Top (7)
Sailin' On To Hawaii (4)
Sally Was A Goodun (6,7)
Santa Monica Pier (6)
Santa Rosa (2)
Sheik Of Araby (5)
Sixteen Tracks (3,7)
Sleeping On The Beach (6)
Slim Carter (3)
So You Run (11)

Soldier's Joy (4,7)
Solstice (medley) (6)
Some Of Shelly's Blues (2,7) *64*
Song To Jutta (1)
Spanish Fandango (medley) (2)
Stars And Stripes Forever (5)
Sunny Side Of The Mountain (4)
Swanee River (medley) (2)
Symphonion Montage (medley) (6)
Take Me Back (9)
Teardrops In My Eyes (5)
Tennessee Stud (4)
Togary Mountain (4,7)
Too Close For Comfort (11)
Too Good To Be True (10)

Travelin' Mood (medley) (2)
Turn Of The Century (12)
Uncle Charlie (medley) (2)
Valley Road (12)
Visiting An Old Friend (7)
Wabash Cannonball (4)
Way Downtown (4)
What's On Your Mind (9)
When I Get My Rewards (12)
When It's Gone (12)
White Russia (8)
Whoa Babe (8)
Wild Nights (8)
Wildwood Flower (4)
Will The Circle Be Unbroken (4,7,12)
Willie The Weeper (7)
Win Or Lose (7)

Winterwhite (medley) (6)
Wolverton Mountain (9)
Woody Woodpecker (7)
Wreck On The Highway (4)
You Ain't Going Nowhere (12)
You Are My Flower (4,7)
You Can't Stop Loving Me Now (8)
You Don't Know My Mind (4)
You Took The Happiness (Out Of My Head) (1)
You're Gonna Get It In The End (1)
Yukon Railroad (2)

NITZER EBB   '91
Industrial-rock duo from Chelmford, Essex, England: Douglas McCarthy and Bon Harris.

11/16/91	146	2		©	**Ebbhead**			$10	Geffen 24456

Ascend
DJVD

Family Man
Godhead

I Give To You
Lakeside Drive

Reasons
Sugar Sweet

Time
Trigger Happy

NITZINGER   '72
Rock trio from Texas: John Nitzinger (vocals, guitar), Linda Waring (vocals, drums) and Curly Benton (bass).

9/2/72	170	8			**Nitzinger**			$15	Capitol 11091

Boogie Queen
Enigma

Hero Of The War
L.A. Texas Boy

Louisiana Cock Fight
My Last Goodbye

Nature Of Your Taste
No Sun

Ticklelick
Witness To The Truth

NIX, Don   '71
Born on 9/27/41 in Memphis. Singer/guitarist/saxophonist.

9/11/71	197	3			**Living By The Days**			$15	Elektra 74101

Going Back To Iuka
I Saw The Light

Living By The Days
Mary Louise

My Train's Done Come And Gone
Shape I'm In

Olena *94*

She Don't Want A Lover (She Just Needs A Friend)

Three Angels

NIXON, Mojo, & Skid Roper   '89
Novelty-rock duo. Nixon (vocals, guitar) was born Neill Kirby McMillan on 8/2/57 in Chapel Hill, North Carolina. Roper (washboard, bass) was born Richard Banke on 10/19/54 in National City, California. Split in early 1990. Nixon appeared in the 1989 movie *Great Balls Of Fire*.

10/10/87	189	2		© 1	**Bo-Day-Shus!!!**		[N]	$10	Enigma 73272
5/6/89	151	7		© 2	**Root Hog Or Die**		[N]	$10	Enigma 73335

B.B.Q. U.S.A. (1)
Burn Your Money (2)
Chicken Drop (2)
Circus Mystery (2)

Debbie Gibson Is Pregnant With My Two Headed Love Child (2)
Elvis Is Everywhere (1)
Gin Guzzlin' Frenzy (1)
I Ain't Gonna Piss In No Jar (1)

I'm A Wreck (2)
I'm Gonna Dig Up Howlin' Wolf (1)
Legalize It (2)
Lincoln Logs (1)
Louisiana Liplock (2)

Pirate Radio (2)
Polka Polka (1)
Positively Bodies Parking Lot (1)
She's Vibrator Dependent (2)
(619) 239-K.I.N.G. (2)

This Land Is Your Land (2)
Wash No Dishes No More (1)
We Gotta Have More Soul! (1)
Wide Open (1)

NIXONS, The   '96
Rock group from Dallas: Zac Maloy (vocals, guitar), Jesse Davis (guitar), Ricky Brooks (bass) and John Humphrey (drums).

3/30/96	77	23		© 1	**Foma**			$10	MCA 11209
7/12/97	188	1		© 2	**The Nixons**			$10	MCA 11644

...At The Sun (2)
Baton Rouge (2)
Blind (1)
Butterfly (2)
December (2)

Drink The Fear (1)
Fall, The (2)
Fellowship (1)
Foma (1)
Happy Song (1)

Head (1)
In Spite Of Herself... (2)
jIm (1)
Leave (2)
Miss USA (2)

Passion (1)
Sad, Sad Me (2)
Saving Grace (2)
Screaming Yellow (2)
Shine (2)

Sister (1)
Smile (1)
Sweet Beyond (1)
Trampoline (1)
Wire (1)

NKOTB — see NEW KIDS ON THE BLOCK

NOBLES, Cliff, & Co.   '68
Born in 1944 in Mobile, Alabama. R&B bandleader.

9/21/68	159	3			**The Horse**			$75	Phil-L.A. of Soul 4001

Boogaloo Down Broadway Theme
Burning Desire

Camel, The
Dry Your Eyes
Heartaches, I Can't Take

Horse, The *2*
Judge Baby, I'm Back
Let's Have A Good Time

Love Is All Right
More I Do For You Baby
Mule, The

Yes, I'm Ready

NOBODY'S ANGEL   '00
Female vocal group from Los Angeles: Amy Harding, Sarah Smith, Stacey Harper and Ali Navarro.

4/1/00	184	3		©	**Nobody's Angel**			$10	Hollywood 62184

Absolutely Maybe
Boom Boom
Cherry Crush

I Can't Help Myself
If You Wanna Dance
Keep Me Away

Next Stop Heaven
Nobody
Ooh La La La

Right There Waiting
Sugardaddy
We Are Family (Angel's Style)

Wishing On You

NO DOUBT   '96
Ska-rock group from Orange County, California: Gwen Stefani (vocals), Tom Dumont (guitar), Tony Kanal (bass) and Adrian Young (drums).

1/20/96	❶[9]	90	▲[10]	© 1	**Tragic Kingdom**	C:#4/30		$10	Trauma 92580
4/29/00	2[1]	46	▲	© 2	**Return Of Saturn**			$10	Trauma 490441

Artificial Sweetener (2)
Bathwater (2)
Climb, The (1)
Comforting Lie (2)
Dark Blue (2)

Different People (1)
Don't Speak (1)
End It On This (1)
Ex-Girlfriend (2)
Excuse Me Mr. (1)

Happy Now? (1)
Hey You (1)
Home Now (2)
Just A Girl (1) *23*
Magic's In The Makeup (2)

Marry Me (2)
New (2)
Simple Kind Of Life (2) *38*
Six Feet Under (2)
Sixteen (1)

Spiderwebs (1)
Staring Problem (2)
Sunday Morning (1)
Suspension Without Suspense (2)

Too Late (2)
Tragic Kingdom (1)
World Go 'Round (1)
You Can Do It (1)

NOEL   '88
Born Noel Pagan in the Bronx, New York. Latin singer.

10/22/88	126	13		©	**Noel**			$10	4th & B'way 4009

Change
City Streets

Fallen Angel
Fire To Ice

Like A Child *67*
Out Of Time

Silent Morning *47*
To Be With You

What I Feel For You

NOFX '00
Punk-rock group from Los Angeles: Fat Mike (vocals, bass), Eric Melvin and El Hefe (guitars), and Erik Sandin (drums).

DEBUT	PEAK	WKS						$	Label & Number
9/9/95	198	1	©	1	I Heard They Suck Live!!		[L]	$10	Fat Wreck Chords 528
2/17/96	63	4	©	2	Heavy Petting Zoo			$10	Epitaph 86457
11/29/97	79	2	©	3	So Long And Thanks For All The Shoes			$10	Epitaph 86518
12/11/99	200	1	©	4	The Decline		[M]	$10	Fat Wreck Chords 605
7/1/00	61	6	©	5	Pump Up The Valuum			$10	Epitaph 86584

All His Suits Are Torn (3)
All Outta Angst (3)
And Now For Something Completely Similar (5)
August 8th (2)
Beer Bong (1)
Black And White (2)
Bleeding Heart Disease (2)
Bob (1)
Bottles To The Ground (5)
Brews, The (1)
Buggley Eyes (1)

Champs Elysées (3)
Clams Have Feelings Too (Actually They Don't) (5)
Dad's Bad News (3)
Decline, The (4)
Desperation's Gone (3)
Dinosaurs Will Die (5)
Drop The World (3)
East Bay (1)
Eat The Meek (3)
Falling In Love (3)
Flossing A Dead Horse (3)

Freedom Lika Shopping Cart (2)
Herojuana (5)
Hot Dog In A Hallway (2)
I'm Telling Tim (3)
It's My Job To Keep Punk Rock Elite (3)
Kids Of The K-Hole (3)
Kill All The White Man (1)
Kill Rock Stars (3)
Life O' Riley (1)
Linoleum (1)

Liza (2)
Louise (5)
Love Story (2)
Monosyllabic Girl (3)
Moron Brothers (1)
Murder The Government (3)
My Vagina (5)
Nothing But A Nightmare (Sorta) (1)
Nowhere (1)
180 Degrees (3)
Pharmacist's Daughter (5)

Philthy Phil Philanthropist (2)
Punk Guy (1)
Quart In Session (3)
Release The Hostages (2)
Six Pack Girls (1)
Soul Doubt (1)
Stranger Than Fishin (5)
Take Two Placebos And Call Me Lame (5)
Thank God It's Monday (5)
Theme From A NOFX Album (5)

Together On The Sand (1)
Total Bummer (5)
What's The Matter With Kids Today? (2)
What's The Matter With Parents Today? (5)
Whatever Didi Wants (2)
You Drink, You Drive, You Spill (1)
You're Bleeding (1)

NOLAN, Kenny '77
Born in Los Angeles. Pop singer/songwriter.

DEBUT	PEAK	WKS						$	Label & Number
3/26/77	78	16			Kenny Nolan			$12	20th Century 532

I Like Dreamin' *3*
If You Ever Stopped Callin' Me Baby

Love's Grown Deep *20*
Monette
My Eyes Get Blurry *97*

My Jole
My World Will Wait For You
Time Ain't Time Enough

Today I Met The Girl I'm Gonna Marry
Wakin' Up To Love

NO MERCY '97
Male vocal trio: brothers Ariel and Gabriel Hernandez (from Miami), with Marty Cintron (from New York City).

DEBUT	PEAK	WKS						$	Label & Number
11/30/96+	104	22	●	©	No Mercy			$10	Arista 18941

Bonita
Do You Want Me

Don't Make Me Live Without You
How Much I Love You

Kiss You All Over *80*
Message Of Love
My Promise To You

Part Of Me
Please Don't Go *21*
When I Die *41*

Where Do You Go *5*

NONCHALANT '96
Born Tanya Pointer in Washington DC. Female singer/rapper.

DEBUT	PEAK	WKS						$	Label & Number
5/11/96	94	6		©	Until The Day			$10	MCA 11265

Crab Rappers
5 O'Clock *24*

Have A Good Time
It's All Love

Lights N' Sirens
Lookin' Good To Me

Mr. Good Stuff
Thank You

Until The Day

NONPOINT '01
Rock group from New York City: Elias Soriano (vocals), Andrew Goldman (guitar), KB (bass) and Robb Rivera (drums).

DEBUT	PEAK	WKS						$	Label & Number
6/2/01	166	1		©	Statement			$10	MCA 112364

Back Up
DoubleStakked

Endure
Hive

Levels
Mindtrip

Misled
Orgullo

Tribute
Victim

What A Day
Years

NO QUESTION '00
R&B vocal group from Philadelphia: Damon Core, Nicholas Johnson, Thomas Blackwell and Dante Massey.

DEBUT	PEAK	WKS						$	Label & Number
10/7/00	178	1		©	No Question			$10	RuffNation 47750

Come Back Home
Cover Me
Do What You Gotta Do
He Say, She Say

How You Like It (Lights On/Lights Off)
I Don't Care
I Know

If You Really Wanna Go
Just Can't Go On
New Love
Private Dancer

Remember Us
This Weekend
To Be Without You
Whose Is This

You Can Get That
You Make Me Feel Brand New

NOREAGA '98
Born Victor Santiago in New York City. Male rapper. Half of **Capone-N-Noreaga** duo.

DEBUT	PEAK	WKS						$	Label & Number
7/25/98	3	19	●	©	1	N.O.R.E.		$10	Penalty 3077
9/11/99	9	11	●	©	2	Melvin Flynt - Da Hustler		$10	Penalty 3097

Assignment, The (1)
Banned From TV (1)
Blood Money, Pt. 3 (2)
Body In The Trunk (1)
Change, The (1)
Cocaine Business (Hysteria) (2)

Da Hustla (2)
Da Story (1)
Fiesta (1)
First Day Home (2)
Flagrant Cops (2)
40 Island (1)

Gangsta's Watch (2)
Going Legit (2)
Hed (1)
Hold Me Down (2)
I Love My Life (1)
If U Want It (2)

It's Not A Game (1)
Mathematics (Esta Loca) (1)
N.O.R.E. (1)
Oh No (2)
Play That Shit (We Don't Play That) (2)

Real Or Fake Niggas (2)
Sometimes (2)
SuperThug (What What) (1) *36*
Way We Live (1)
Wethuggedout (2)

What The Fuck Is Up (2)

NORMA JEAN '78
Born Norma Jean Wright in Elyria, Ohio. R&B singer. Former member of **Chic**.

DEBUT	PEAK	WKS						$	Label & Number
8/26/78	134	11		©	Norma Jean			$12	Bearsville 6983

Having A Party
I Believe In You

I Like Love
Saturday

So I Get Hurt Again
Sorcerer

This Is The Love

NORMAN, Bebo '01
Born in 1973 in Atlanta. Male Christian singer/songwriter/guitarist.

DEBUT	PEAK	WKS						$	Label & Number
6/2/01	141	1		©	Big Blue Sky			$10	Watershed 10550

All That I Have Sown
Big Blue Sky

Break Me Through
Cover Me

I Am
Perhaps She'll Wait

Sons And Daughters
Tip Of My Heart

Underneath
Where You Are

You Surround Me

NORMAN, Jessye — see BATTLE, Kathleen

NORTH, Freddie '72
Born on 5/28/39 in Nashville. R&B singer/songwriter/guitarist.

DEBUT	PEAK	WKS						$	Label & Number
1/1/72	179	5			Friend			$15	Mankind 204

Ain't Nothing In The News (But The Blues)

Did I Come Back Too Soon (Or Stay Away Too Long)

I Did The Woman Wrong
Laid Back And Easy

Raining On A Sunny Day
She's All I Got *39*

Sidewalks Fences And Walls
Sweeter Than Sweetness

You And Me Together Forever
Yours Love

NOTORIOUS B.I.G., The   '97
Born Christopher Wallace on 5/21/72 in Brooklyn, New York. Shot to death on 3/9/97 (age 24). Male rapper. Also known as Biggy Smallz. Married singer **Faith Evans** in 1995.

10/1/94	15	59	▲4	©	1 Ready To Die..	C:#3/28		$10	Bad Boy 73000
4/5/97	❶4	79	▲10	©	2 Life After Death	C:#47/2		$15	Bad Boy 73011 [2]
12/25/99	❶1	22	▲2	©	3 Born Again			$10	Bad Boy 73023

Another (2) Big Booty Hoes (3) Big Poppa (1) 6 Biggie (3) Can I Get Witcha (3) Come On (3) Dangerous MC's (3) Dead Wrong (3) Everyday Struggle (1) Friend Of Mine (1)

#1* @ You Tonight (2) Gimme The Loot (1) Going Back To Cali (2) 26 Hope You Niggas Sleep (2) **Hypnotize** (2) 1 I Got A Story To Tell (2) I Love The Dough (2) I Really Want To Show You (3) If I Should Die Before I Wake (3)

Juicy (1) 27 Kick In The Door (2) Last Day (2) Let Me Get Down (3) Long Kiss Goodnight (2) Machine Gun Funk (1) Me & My Bitch (1) Miss U (2) **Mo Money Mo Problems** (2) 1 My Downfall (2)

Nasty Boy (2) Niggas (3) Niggas Bleed (2) **Notorious B.I.G.** (3) 82 Notorious Thugs (2) **One More Chance** (1) 2 Playa Hater (2) Rap Phenomenon (2) Ready To Die (1) Respect (1)

Sky's The Limit (2) 60 Somebody's Gotta Die (2) Suicidal Thoughts (1) Ten Crack Commandments (2) Things Done Changed (1) Tonight (3) **Unbelievable** (1) flip **Warning** (1) flip **What, The** (1) flip What's Beef? (2)

Who Shot Ya (3) World Is Filled... (2) Would You Die For Me (3) You're Nobody (Til Somebody Kills You) (2)

NOTTING HILLBILLIES, The   '90
Group of rock guitarists: **Mark Knopfler** and Guy Fletcher (both of **Dire Straits**), with Brendan Croker and Steve Phillips. Recorded at Knopfler's studio in London's Notting Hill Gate.

| 3/31/90 | 52 | 13 | | © | Missing...Presumed Having A Good Time.. | | | $10 | Warner 26147 |

Bewildered Blues Stay Away From Me

Feel Like Going Home One Way Gal

Please Baby Railroad Worksong

Run Me Down That's Where I Belong

Weapon Of Prayer Will You Miss Me

Your Own Sweet Way

NOVA, Aldo   '82
Born Aldo Scarporuscio in Montreal. Rock singer/songwriter/guitarist.

2/20/82	8	37	▲2	©	1 Aldo Nova			$12	Portrait 37498
10/15/83	56	20	●	©	2 Subject: Aldo Nova			$12	Portrait 38721
6/8/91	124	7		©	3 Blood On The Bricks..			$10	Jambco 848513

Africa (Primal Love) (2) All Night Long (2) Always Be Mine (2) Armageddon (2) Ball And Chain (1) Bang Bang (3)

Blood On The Bricks (3) Bright Lights (3) Can't Stop Lovin' You (1) Cry Baby Cry (2) **Fantasy** (1) 23 **Foolin' Yourself** (1) 65

Heart To Heart (1) Hey Operator (1) Hey Ronnie (Veronica's Song) (3) Hold Back The Night (2) Hot Love (1)

It's Too Late (1) Medicine Man (3) Modern World (3) Monkey On Your Back (2) Paradise (2) See The Light (1)

Someday (3) Subject's Theme (2) This Ain't Love (3) Touch Of Madness (3) Under The Gun (1) Victim Of A Broken Heart (2)

War Suite (2) You're My Love (1) Young Love (3)

NOVA, Heather   '98
Born in 1968 on an island in the Bermuda Sound. Raised on a 40-foot sailboat in the Caribbean. Later settled in London. Singer/songwriter.

| 11/4/95 | 179 | 4 | | © | 1 Oyster.. | | | $10 | Big Cat 67113 |
| 10/24/98 | 176 | 1 | | © | 2 Siren... | | | $10 | Big Cat 67953 |

Avalanche (2) Blood Of Me (2) Blue Black (1) Doubled Up (2) Heal (1)

Heart And Shoulder (2) I'm Alive (2) I'm The Girl (2) Island (1) Light Years (2)

London Rain (Nothing Heals Me) (2) Like You Do) (2) Make You Mine (2) Maybe An Angel (1) Not Only Human (2)

Paper Cup (2) Ruby Red (2) Sugar (1) Throwing Fire At The Sun (1) Truth And Bone (1)

Valley Of Sound (2) Verona (1) Walk This World (1) Walking Higher (1) What A Feeling (2)

Widescreen (2) Winterblue (1)

NOVO COMBO   '81
Rock group formed in New York City: Pete Hewlett (vocals), Jack Griffith (guitar), Stephen Dees (bass) and Michael Shrieve (drums; **Santana**).

| 10/10/81 | 167 | 6 | | | Novo Combo... | | | $12 | Polydor 6331 |

Axis Will Turn City Bound ("E" Train)

Do You Wanna Shake? Don't Do That

Hard To Say Goodbye Light Of The World

Long Road Sorry (For The Delay)

Tattoo Up Periscope

We Need Love

NRBQ   '69
Blues-rock group formed in Miami: Frank Gadler (vocals), Steve Ferguson (guitar), Terry Adams (keyboards), Joey Spampinato (bass) and Tom Staley (drums). Lineup in 1990: Al Anderson (vocals, guitar), Terry Adams (keyboards), Joey Spampinato (bass) and Tom Ardolino (drums). NRBQ: New Rhythm and Blues Quintet/Quartet. Spampinato was married to **Skeeter Davis** from 1983-96.

| 7/19/69 | 162 | 4 | | | 1 NRBQ .... | | | $25 | Columbia 9858 |
| 1/6/90 | 198 | 2 | | © | 2 Wild Weekend .... | | | $10 | Virgin 91291 |

Boozoo, That's Who! (2) Boy's Life (2) C'mon Everybody (1) C'mon If You're Comin' (1) Fergie's Prayer (1)

Fireworks (2) Fraction Of Action (2) Hey! Baby (1) Hymn Number 5 (1) I Didn't Know Myself (1)

Ida (1) If I Don't Have You (2) Immortal For A While (2) It's A Wild Week (2) Kentucky Slop Song (1)

Like A Locomotive (2) Little Floater (2) Liza Jane (1) Mama Get Down Those Rock And Roll Shoes (1)

One And Only (2) Poppin' Circumstance (2) Rocket Number 9 (1) Stay With Me (1) Stomp (1)

This Love Is True (2) You Can't Hide (1)

*NSYNC   '00
Male vocal group formed in Orlando, Florida: Chris Kirkpatrick, Josh Chasez, Joey Fatone, Justin Timberlake and Lance Bass. Timberlake was a regular on TV's *The Mickey Mouse Club* (1992-93).

4/11/98	2³	109	▲10	©	1 *NSync	C:#3/52		$10	RCA 67613
11/28/98	7	10	▲2	©	2 Home For Christmas	C:❶3/22	[X]	$10	RCA 67726
					Christmas charts: 2/98, 6/99, 3/00				
4/8/00	❶8	77	▲11	©	3 No Strings Attached			$10	Jive 41702

All I Want Is You This Christmas (2) Bringin' Da Noise (3) **Bye Bye Bye** (3) 4 Christmas Song (Chestnuts Roasting On An Open Fire) (2) Crazy For You (1) Digital Get Down (3) Everything I Own (1)

First Noel (2) For The Girl Who Has Everything (1) Giddy Up (1) **(God Must Have Spent) A Little More Time On You** (1) 8 Here We Go (1) Home For Christmas (2) **I Drive Myself Crazy** (1) 67

I Guess It's Christmas Time (2) I Just Wanna Be With You (1) I Need Love (1) I Never Knew The Meaning Of Christmas (2) I Thought She Knew (3) **I Want You Back** (1) 13 I'll Be Good For You (3) In Love On Christmas (2) It Makes Me III (3)

It's Christmas (2) **It's Gonna Be Me** (3) 1 Just Got Paid (3) Kiss Me At Midnight (2) Love's In Our Hearts On Christmas Day (2) Merry Christmas, Happy Holidays (2) No Strings Attached (2) O Holy Night (2)

Only Gift (2) Sailing (1) Space Cowboy (Yippie-Yi-Yay) (3) **Tearin' Up My Heart** (1) 59 That's When I'll Stop Loving You (3) **This I Promise You** (3) 5 Under My Tree (2) You Got It (1)

N2DEEP   '92
White rap duo from Vallejo, California: Jay Trujilo and T.L. Lyon.

| 7/11/92 | 55 | 37 | ● | © | Back To The Hotel.. | | | $10 | Profile 1427 |

Back To The Hotel 14 Comin' Legit Do Tha Crew

Get Mine Mack Daddyz N2deep (We're Who?)

Revenge Of Starchild Shakedown **Toss-Up** 92

V-Town Weekend, The What The F**k Is Goin' On?

Ya Gotta Go

NUCLEAR ASSAULT '90
Hard-rock group formed in New York City: John Connelly (vocals, guitar), Anthony Bramante (guitar), Danny Lilker (bass; **Anthrax**) and Glenn Evans (drums).

8/13/88	145	11		© 1	**Survive**			$10	I.R.S. 42195
11/18/89+	126	24		© 2	**Handle With Care**			$10	In-Effect 3010

Brainwashed (1)	F sharp (1)	Good Times Bad Times (1)	Mothers' Day (2)	Search & Seizure (2)	Torture Tactics (2)
Critical Mass (2)	F sharp (Wake Up) (2)	Got Another Quarter (1)	New Song (2)	Surgery (2)	Trail Of Tears (2)
Emergency (2)	Fight To Be Free (1)	Great Depression (1)	PSA (1)	Survive (1)	When Freedom Dies (2)
Equal Rights (1)	Funky Noise (2)	Inherited Hell (2)	Rise From The Ashes (1)	Technology (1)	Wired (1)

NUCLEAR VALDEZ '90
Rock group from Miami: Froilan Sosa (vocals), Jorge Barcala (guitar), Juan Diaz (bass) and Robert LeMont (drums).

2/24/90	175	5		© 1	**I Am I**			$10	Epic 45354

Apache	If I Knew Then	Strength	Unsung Hero (Song For Lenny	
Eve	Rising Sun	Summer	Bruce)	
Hope	Run Through The Fields	Trace The Thunder	Where Do We Go From Here	

★241★ NUGENT, Ted '76
Born on 12/13/48 in Detroit. Hard-rock singer/guitarist. Leader of **The Amboy Dukes**. Later joined **Damn Yankees**. An avid game hunter and an active supporter of the National Rifle Association.

1)Scream Dream 2)Double Live Gonzo! 3)Cat Scratch Fever

11/22/75+	28	62	▲²	© 1	**Ted Nugent**			$12	Epic 33692
10/2/76	24	32	▲²	© 2	**Free-For-All**			$12	Epic 34121
6/25/77	17	39	▲³	© 3	**Cat Scratch Fever**			$12	Epic 34700
2/11/78	13	22	▲³	© 4	**Double Live Gonzo!**		[L]	$15	Epic 35069 [2]
11/11/78	24	20	▲	© 5	**Weekend Warriors**			$12	Epic 35551
6/2/79	18	18	●	© 6	**State Of Shock**			$12	Epic 36000
5/31/80	13	18	●	© 7	**Scream Dream**			$12	Epic 36404
3/21/81	51	10		© 8	**Intensities In 10 Cities**		[L]	$12	Epic 37084
11/28/81	140	8	▲²	© 9	**Great Gonzos! The Best Of Ted Nugent** .... C:#47/1		[G]	$12	Epic 37667
7/17/82	51	14		© 10	**Nugent**			$10	Atlantic 19365
2/18/84	56	15		© 11	**Penetrator**			$10	Atlantic 80125
3/22/86	76	14		© 12	**Little Miss Dangerous**			$10	Atlantic 81632
3/5/88	112	7		© 13	**If You Can't Lick 'Em...Lick 'Em**			$10	Atlantic 81812
5/20/95	86	4		© 14	**Spirit Of The Wild**			$10	Atlantic 82611

Alone (6)	Flying Lip Lock (8)	I Got The Feelin' (5)	Loverjacker (14)	Snake Charmer (6)	Tight Spots (5)
Angry Young Man (12)	Fred Bear (14)	I Gotta Move (7)	Motor City Madhouse (1,4,9)	Snakeskin Cowboys (1)	Together (5)
Baby, Please Don't Go (4,9)	Free-For-All (2,9)	I Love You So I Told You A Lie	My Love Is Like A Tire Iron (8)	Spirit Of The Wild (14)	Tooth, Fang & Claw (14)
Bite Down Hard (6)	Funlover (3)	(2)	Name Your Poison (5)	Spit It Out (7)	Turn It Up (2)
Bite The Hand (13)	Go Down Fighting (11)	I Shoot Back (14)	**Need You Bad** (5) *84*	Spontaneous Combustion (8)	Venom Soup (5)
Blame It On The Night (11)	Gonzo (4)	I Take No Prisoners (8)	No Man's Land (11)	Spread Your Wings (13)	Violent Love (7)
Bound And Gagged (10)	Good And Ready (10)	I Want To Tell You (6)	No, No, No (10)	State Of Shock (6)	Wang Dang Sweet Poontang
Can't Live With 'Em (13)	Good Friends And A Bottle Of	If You Can't Lick 'Em...Lick 'Em	One Woman (5)	Stormtroopin' (1,4)	(3,4,9)
Can't Stop Me Now (10)	Wine (4)	(13)	Out Of Control (3)	Strangers (12)	**Wango Tango** (7,9) *86*
Cat Scratch Fever (3,4,9) *30*	Great White Buffalo (4)	It Don't Matter (6)	Painkiller (12)	Strangehold (1,4,9)	We're Gonna Rock Tonight (10)
Come And Get It (7)	Habitual Offender (10)	Jailbait (8)	Paralyzed (6,9)	Street Rats (2)	Weekend Warriors (5)
Crazy Ladies (12)	Hammerdown (2)	Just Do It Like This (14)	Primitive Man (14)	Sweet Sally (3)	When Your Body Talks (12)
Cruisin' (5)	Hard As Nails (7)	Just What The Doctor Ordered	Put Up Or Shut Up (8)	TNT Overture (8)	(Where Do You) Draw The Line
Death By Misadventure (3)	Harder They Come (The Harder	(1,4,9)	Queen Of The Forest (1)	Tailgunner (10)	(11)
Dog Eat Dog (2,9) *91*	I Get) (13)	Kiss My Ass (14)	Saddle Sore (6)	Take It Or Leave It (9)	Where Have You Been All My
Don't Cry (I'll Be Back Before	Heads Will Roll (8)	Knockin' At Your Door (11)	Satisfied (6)	Take Me Away (12)	Life (1)
You Know It Baby) (7)	Heart & Soul (13)	Land Of A Thousand Dances	Savage Dancer (12)	Take Me Home (11)	Workin' Hard, Playin' Hard (3)
Don't Push Me (10)	**Hey Baby** (1) *72*	(8)	Scream Dream (7)	Terminus Eldorado (7)	Writing On The Wall (9)
Don't You Want My Love (11)	Hibernation (4)	Lean Mean R&R Machine (11)	Separate The Men From The	That's The Story Of Love (13)	Wrong Side Of Town (14)
Ebony (3)	High Heels In Motion (12)	Light My Way (2)	Boys, Please (13)	Thighraceous (14)	**Yank Me, Crank Me** (4) *58*
Fightin' Words (10)	**Home Bound** (3) *70*	Little Miss Dangerous (12)	She Drives Me Crazy (13)	Thousand Knives (14)	You Make Me Feel Right At
Fist Fightin' Son Of A Gun (3)	Hot Or Cold (14)	Little Red Book (12)	Skintight (13)	Thunder Thighs (11)	Home (1)
Flesh & Blood (7)	I Am A Predator (8)	Live It Up (3)	Smokescreen (5)	Tied Up In Love (11)	

NUMAN, Gary '80
Born Gary Webb on 3/8/58 in Hammersmith, England. Synthesized techno-rock artist.

9/15/79	124	10		© 1	**Replicas**			$12	Atco 117

GARY NUMAN & TUBEWAY ARMY

2/2/80	16	30		© 2	**The Pleasure Principle**			$12	Atco 120
10/4/80	64	10		© 3	**Telekon**			$12	Atco 103
10/24/81	167	4		© 4	**Dance**			$12	Atco 143

Aircrash Bureau (3)	Crash (4)	I Nearly Married A Human (1)	Metal (2)	Remember I Was Vapour (3)	Telekon (3)
Airlane (2)	Cry The Clock Said (4)	I'm An Agent (3)	Moral (4)	Remind Me To Smile (3)	This Wreckage (3)
Are 'Friends' Electric? (1)	Down In The Park (1)	It Must Have Been Years (1)	My Brother's Time (4)	Replicas (1)	Tracks (2)
Boys Like Me (4)	Engineers (2)	Joy Circuit (3)	Night Talk (4)	She's Got Claws (4)	When The Machines Rock (1)
Cars (2) *9*	Films (2)	Machman, The (1)	Observer (2)	Slowcar To China (4)	You Are In My Vision (1)
Complex (2)	I Die: You Die (3)	M.E. (2)	Please Push No More (3)	Stories (4)	You Are You Are (4)
Conversation (2)	I Dream Of Wires (3)	Me! I Disconnect From You (1)	Praying To The Aliens (1)	Subway Called You (4)	

NUNN, Bobby '82
Born in Buffalo, New York. R&B singer/songwriter/keyboardist.

10/23/82	148	8			**Second To Nunn**			$12	Motown 6022

Get It While You Can	Never Seen Anything Like You	Sexy Sassy	You Need Non-Stop Lovin'
Got To Get Up On It	Party's Over	She's Just A Groupie	

NU SHOOZ '86
Husband-and-wife duo from Portland, Oregon: John Smith and Valerie Day.

5/31/86	27	32	●	© 1	**Poolside**			$10	Atlantic 81647
4/23/88	93	14		© 2	**Told U So**			$10	Atlantic 81804

Are You Lookin' For Somebody	Don't You Be Afraid (1)	If That's The Way You Want It	**Point Of No Return** (1) *28*	Told U So (2)
Nu (2)	Driftin' (2)	(2)	Savin' All My Time (2)	Wonder (2)
Doin' Alright (2)	Goin' Thru The Motions (1)	Lost Your Number (1)	Secret Message (1)	You Put Me In A Trance (1)
Don't Let Me Be The One (1)	**I Can't Wait** (1) *3*	Montecarlo Nite (2)	**Should I Say Yes?** (2) *41*	

N.W.A.   '91

Rap group from Los Angeles: Eric "**Eazy-E**" Wright, Lorenzo "**M.C. Ren**" Patterson, Andre "**Dr. Dre**" Young, O'Shea "**Ice Cube**" Jackson (left by 1990) and DJ Antoine "**Yella**" Carraby. N.W.A.: Niggaz With Attitude.

3/4/89	37	81	▲² ©	1 **Straight Outta Compton** ....C:#39/6	$10	Ruthless 57102
9/1/90	27	25	▲ ©	2 **100 Miles And Runnin'** .... [M]	$10	Ruthless 7224
6/15/91	❶¹	44	▲ ©	3 **EFIL4ZAGGIN**	$10	Ruthless 57126

title actually appears on album as an inverse image of NIGGAZ4LIFE

7/20/96	48	12	©	4 **Greatest Hits** .... [G]	$10	Ruthless 50561

Alwayz Into Somethin' (3,4)
Appetite For Destruction (3)
Approach To Danger (3)
Automobile (3)
Bitch Iz A Bitch (4)
Compton's N The House (1,4)
Dayz Of Wayback (3)
Don't Drink That Wine (3,4)
Dopeman (1)
Express Yourself (1,4)
Findum, Fuckum & Flee (3)
Fuck Tha Police (1,4)
Gangsta Gangsta (1,4)
I Ain't Tha 1 (1,4)
I'd Rather Fuck You (3)
If It Ain't Ruff (1,4)
Just Don't Bite It (2,4)
Kamurshol (2)
Message To B.A. (3)
Niggaz 4 Life (3)
100 Miles And Runnin' (2,4)
One Less Bitch (3)
1-900-2-COMPTON (3)
Parental Discretion Iz Advised (1)
Prelude (3)
Protest (3)
Quiet On Tha Set (1)
Real Niggaz (2,3,4)
Real Niggaz Don't Die (3,4)
Sa Prize (Part 2) (2)
She Swallowed It (3)
Straight Outta Compton (1,4)
To Kill A Hooker (3)

NYLONS, The   '87

Acapella group formed in Toronto: Marc Connors, Paul Cooper, Claude Morrison and Arnold Robinson. Connors died on 3/25/91 (age 41).

3/29/86	133	16	©	1 **Seamless**	$10	Open Air 0304
5/23/87	43	24	©	2 **Happy Together**	$10	Open Air 0306
6/10/89	136	10	©	3 **Rockapella**	$10	Windham Hill 1085

(All I Have To Do Is) Dream (3)
Another Night Like This (3)
Busy Tonight (3)
Chain Gang (2)
Combat Zone (1)
Count My Blessings (3)
Crazy In Love (Morning Comes Early) (2)
Dance Of Love (2)
Drift Away (3)
Face In The Crowd (2)
Grown Man Cry (2)
Happy Together (2) *75*
It's What They Call Magic (2)
Kiss Him Goodbye (2) *12*
Lion Sleeps Tonight (1)
Love This Is Love (3)
No Stone Unturned (3)
Oo-Wee, Oh Me, Oh My (1)
Perpetual Emotion (1)
Poison Ivy (3)
Remember (Walking In The Sand) (1)
Rise Up (3)
Stars Are Ours (1)
Stepping Stone (1)
Take Me To Your Heart (1)
This Boy (1)
This Island Earth (2)
Touch Of Your Hand (2)
Up On The Roof (1)
Wildfire (3)

NYMAN, Michael   '94

Born on 3/23/44 in London. Pianist/composer.

1/22/94	41	34	● ©	**The Piano** .... [I-S]	$10	Virgin 88274

All Imperfect Things
Bed Of Ferns
Big My Secret
Deep Into The Forest
Dreams Of A Journey
Embrace, The
Fling, The
Heart Asks Pleasure First
Here To There
I Clipped Your Wing
Little Impulse
Lost And Found
Mood That Passes Through You
Promise, The
Sacrifice, The
Scent Of Love
To The Edge Of The Earth
Wild And Distant Shore
Wounded, The

NYRO, Laura   '69

Born Laura Nigro on 10/18/47 in the Bronx, New York. Died of cancer on 4/8/97 (age 49). Singer/prolific songwriter.

8/10/68	181	7	©	1 **Eli And The Thirteenth Confession**	$40	Columbia 9626
11/1/69	32	17	©	2 **New York Tendaberry**	$25	Columbia 9737
12/26/70+	51	14	©	3 **Christmas And The Beads Of Sweat**	$25	Columbia 30259
12/25/71+	46	17	©	4 **Gonna Take A Miracle**	$25	Columbia 30987
2/3/73	97	11	©	5 **The First Songs** .... [E]	$20	Columbia 31410
3/13/76	60	14	©	6 **Smile**	$15	Columbia 33912
7/2/77	137	5		7 **Season of Lights...Laura Nyro in Concert** .... [L]	$15	Columbia 34786
3/10/84	182	3		8 **Mother's Spiritual**	$12	Columbia 39215

And When I Die (5,7)
Beads Of Sweat (3)
Been On A Train (3)
Bells, The (4)
Billy's Blues (5)
Blackpatch (3)
Blowing Away (5)
Brighter Song (8)
Brown Earth (3)
Buy And Sell (5)
California Shoeshine Boys (5)
Captain For Dark Mornings (5)
Captain Saint Lucifer (2,7)
Cat-Song (6,7)
Children Of The Junks (6)
Christmas In My Soul (3)
Confession, The (1,7)
Dancing In The Street (medley) (4)
December's Boudoir (3)
Desiree (4)
Eli's Comin (1)
Emmie (1,7)
Flim Flam Man (5)
Free Thinker (8)
Gibson Street (2)
Good By Joe (3)
He's A Runner (5)
I Am The Blues (6)
I Met Him On A Sunday (4)
I Never Meant To Hurt You (5)
It's Gonna Take A Miracle (4)
Jimmy Mack (4)
Late For Love (8)
Lazy Susan (5)
Lonely Women (1)
Lu (1)
Luckie (1)
Man In The Moon (8)
Man Who Sends Me Home (1)
Map To The Treasure (3)
Melody In The Sky (8)
Mercy On Broadway (8)
Midnite Blue (6)
Money (6,7)
Monkey Time (medley) (4)
Mother's Spiritual (8)
New York Tendaberry (2)
Nowhere To Run (4)
Once It Was Alright Now (Farmer Joe) (1)
Poverty Train (1)
Refrain (8)
Right To Vote (8)
Roadnotes (8)
Save The Country (2)
Sexy Mama (6)
Smile (6)
Sophia (8)
Spanish Harlem (4)
Stoned Soul Picnic (1)
Stoney End (5)
Stormy Love (6)
Sweet Blindness (1,7)
Sweet Lovin' Baby (2)
Talk To A Green Tree (8)
Time And Love (2)
Timer (1,7)
To A Child (8)
Tom Cat Goodbye (2)
Trees Of The Ages (8)
Up On The Roof (3,7) *92*
Upstairs By A Chinese Lamp (3,7)
Wedding Bell Blues (5)
When I Was A Freeport And You Were The Main Drag (3,7)
Wilderness (8)
Wind, The (4)
Woman's Blues (1)
You Don't Love Me When I Cry (2)
You've Really Got A Hold On Me (4)

O

OAKENFOLD, Paul   '01

Born on 8/30/63 in London. Dance DJ/producer.

10/21/00	114	5	©	1 **Perfecto Presents Another World**	$10	Sire 31035 [2]

includes "Sacrifice" by Lisa Gerrard

6/23/01	102	6	©	2 **Swordfish (The Album)** .... [I-S]	$10	Warner Sunset 31169

includes "The Word" by Dope Smugglaz, "Unafraid" by Jan Johnston, "New Born" by Muse, "Kneel Before Your God" by Lemon Jelly, "Lapdance" by Nerd, and "On Your Mind" by Patient Saints

Airtight (1)
Animal (1)
Babe I'm Gonna Leave You (1)
Back & Front (1)
Bar None (1)
Bullet In A Gun (1)
Chase (2)
Dark Machine (2)
Darker (1)
Eugina 2000 (1)
Flesh (1)
Get Out Of My Life Now (2)
Host Of The Seraphim (1)
Into Deep (1)
Majestic (1)
Music (1)
No Way Out (1)
Northsky (1)
Password (2)
Piledriver (1)
Planet Rock (2)
Rachel's Song (1)
Sanvean (1)
Silence 2000 (1)
Song To The Siren (Did I Dream) (1)
Speed (2)
Stanley's Theme (2)
Take Me Away (1)
Tears In Rain (1)
Ubik (1)

★474★ OAK RIDGE BOYS   '81

Country vocal group formed in Oak Ridge, Tennessee: Duane Allen, Joe Bonsall, Richard Sterban and William Golden.

1)Fancy Free 2)Bobbie Sue 3)American Made

2/18/78	120	9	● ©	1 **Y'all Come Back Saloon**	$12	ABC/Dot 2093
6/17/78	164	11	● ©	2 **Room Service**	$12	ABC 1065
3/29/80	154	6	● ©	3 **Together**	$10	MCA 3220
11/22/80	99	21	▲ ©	4 **Greatest Hits** .... [G]	$10	MCA 5150

OAK RIDGE BOYS — Cont'd

DEBUT	PEAK	WKS	RIAA	CD	ARTIST — Album Title	Sym	$	Label & Number
6/13/81	14	48	▲²	© 5	Fancy Free		$10	MCA 5209
2/20/82	20	21	●	© 6	Bobbie Sue		$10	MCA 5294
12/4/82+	73	7	●	© 7	Christmas	[X]	$10	MCA 5365
2/26/83	51	23	●	© 8	American Made		$10	MCA 5390
11/19/83	121	14	●	© 9	Deliver		$10	MCA 5455
9/8/84	71	24	▲	© 10	Greatest Hits 2	[G]	$10	MCA 5496
4/20/85	156	5		© 11	Step On Out		$10	MCA 5555

Ain't No Cure For The Rock And Roll (9)
Alice Is In Wonderland (9)
American Made (8,10) *72*
Amity (8)
Another Dream Just Came True (5)
Any Old Time You Choose (8)
Back In Your Arms Again (6)
Beautiful You (3,10)
Bobbie Sue (6) *12*
Break My Mind (9)
But I Do (2)
Callin' Baton Rouge (2)
Christmas Carol (7)
Christmas Is Paintin' The Town (7)
Class Reunion (9)
Come On In (2,4,11)
Cryin' Again (2,4)

Didn't She Really Thrill Them (Back In 1924) (1)
Doctor's Orders (6)
Down Deep Inside (9)
Down The Hall (8)
Dream Of Me (5)
Dream On (4)
Easy (1)
Elvira (5,10) *5*
Emmylou (1)
Everyday (10)
Fancy Free (5,10)
Freckles (1)
Happy Christmas Eve (7)
Heart Of Mine (3,4)
Heart On The Line (Operator, Operator) (8)
Holdin' On To You (3)
How Long Has It Been (5)
I Can Love You (2)

I Can't Imagine Laying Down (With Anyone But You) (3)
I Guess It Never Hurts To Hurt Sometimes (8)
I Wish You Could Have Turned My Head (And Left My Heart Alone) (6)
I Wish You Were Here (Oh My Darlin') (5)
I Would Crawl All The Way (To The River) (5)
I'll Be True To You (1,2,4)
I'm So Glad I'm Standing Here Today (8)
If There Were Only Time For Love (2)
If You Can't Find Love (2)
In The Pines (9)
It Could Have Been Ten Years Ago (2)
Jesus Is Born Today (It Is His Birthday) (7)

Lay Down Your Sword And Shield (2)
Leaving Louisiana In The Broad Daylight (4)
Let Me Be The One (1)
Little More Like Me (The Crucifixion) (3)
Little One (7)
Little Things (7)
Lots Of Matchbooks (2)
Love Is Everywhere (11)
Love Song (8,10)
Love Takes Two (4)
Make My Life With You (10)
Mary Christmas (7)
Oh Holy Night (7)
Old Kentucky Song (6)
Old Time Family Bluegrass Band (1)
Old Time Lovin' (2)
Only One I Love (11)

Ophelia (11)
Ozark Mountain Jubilee (9,10)
Ready To Take My Chances (3)
Roll Tennessee River (11)
Sail Away (4)
Santa's Song (7)
She's Gone To L.A. Again (5)
She's Not Just Another Pretty Face (8)
Silent Night (7)
Silver Bells (7)
So Fine (6) *76*
Somewhere In The Night (5)
Staying Afloat (11)
Step On Out (11)
Still Holding On (9)
Take This Heart (3)
Thank God For Kids (7,10)
Through My Eyes (9)
Touch A Hand, Make A Friend (11)

Trying To Love Two Women (3,4)
Until You (6)
Up On Cripple Creek (6)
When I'm With You (5)
When Love Calls You (5)
When You Get To The Heart (9)
Whiskey Lady (3)
White Christmas (7)
Would They Love Him Down In Shreveport (6)
Y'all Come Back Saloon (1,4)
You Made It Beautiful (8)
You're The One (1,4,8)

OAKTOWN'S 3.5.7   '89

Female rap group from Oakland: Djuana Johnican, Tabatha King, Vicious C and Sweet Pea.

DEBUT	PEAK	WKS	CD	ARTIST — Album Title	$	Label & Number
5/13/89	126	16	©	Wild & Loose	$10	Capitol 90926

I Betcha Wanna Take It
It's A Shame

Juicy Gotcha Krazy
Rock 'N' Soul

Say That Then
Stupid Def Ya'll

3.5.7 Straight At You
We Like It

Yeah, Yeah, Yeah

OASIS   '97

Rock group from Manchester, England: brothers Liam (vocals) and Noel (guitar) Gallagher, Paul Arthurs (guitar), Paul McGuigan (bass) and Tony McCarroll (drums). Alan White replaced McCarroll in 1995.

DEBUT	PEAK	WKS	RIAA	CD	ARTIST — Album Title	Sym	$	Label & Number
2/11/95	58	20	▲	© 1	Definitely Maybe		$10	Epic 66431
10/21/95+	4	76	▲⁴	© 2	(What's The Story) Morning Glory?		$10	Epic 67351
9/13/97	2¹	26	▲	© 3	Be Here Now		$10	Epic 68530
11/21/98	51	2		© 4	The Masterplan		$10	Epic 69647
3/18/00	24	8		© 5	Standing On The Shoulder Of Giants		$10	Epic 63586
12/9/00	182	1		© 6	Familiar To Millions	[L]	$15	Epic 85267 [2]

recorded on 7/21/00 at Wembley Stadium

Acquiesce (4,6)
All Around The World (3)
Be Here Now (3)
Bring It On Down (1)
Cast No Shadow (2)
Champagne Supernova (2,6)
Cigarettes & Alcohol (1,6)
Columbia (1)
D'You Know What I Mean? (3)
Digsy's Diner (1)
Don't Go Away (3)

Don't Look Back In Anger (2,6) *55*
Fade Away (4)
Fade In-Out (3)
Fuckin' In The Bushes (5,6)
Gas Panic! (5,6)
Girl In The Dirty Shirt (3)
Go Let It Out (5,6)
Going Nowhere (4)
Half The World Away (4)
Headshrinker (4)

Hello (2)
Helter Skelter (6)
Hey Hey, My My (Into The Black) (6)
Hey Now! (2)
I Am The Walrus (4)
I Can See A Liar (5)
I Hope, I Think, I Know (3)
It's Gettin' Better (Man!!) (3)
(It's Good) To Be Free (4)
Listen Up (4)

Little James (5)
Live Forever (1,6)
Magic Pie (3)
Married With Children (1)
Masterplan, The (4)
Morning Glory (2)
My Big Mouth (3)
Put Yer Money Where Yer Mouth Is (5)
Rock 'n' Roll Star (1,6)
Rockin' Chair (4)

Roll It Over (5)
Roll With It (2,6)
Shakermaker (1,6)
She's Electric (2)
Slide Away (1)
Some Might Say (2)
Stand By Me (3,6)
Stay Young (4)
Step Out (6)
Sunday Morning Call (5)
Supersonic (1,6)

Swamp Song (4)
Talk Tonight (4)
Underneath The Sky (4)
Up In The Sky (1)
Where Did It All Go Wrong? (5)
Who Feels Love? (5,6)
Wonderwall (2,6) *8*

O'BANION, John   '81

Born in Kokomo, Indiana. Pop singer.

DEBUT	PEAK	WKS	CD	ARTIST — Album Title	$	Label & Number
5/16/81	164	4		John O'Banion	$12	Elektra 342

Come To My Love
If You Love Me

Love Is Blind
Love Is In Your Eyes

Love You Like I Never Loved Before *24*

Our Love Can Make It
She's Not For You

Take A Chance On Love
Walk Away Renee

You're In My Life Again

OBERNKIRCHEN CHILDREN'S CHOIR, The   '65

Choir of children from Obernkirchen, Germany. Founded and conducted by Edith Moeller in 1950.

DEBUT	PEAK	WKS	CD	ARTIST — Album Title	Sym	$	Label & Number
12/25/65	50ˣ	1		Christmas Songs	[X-F]	$15	Angel 35914

Alle Jahre Wieder
Away In A Manger
Cherry Tree Carol
Der Heiland Ist Geboren

Es Hat Sich Halt Eröffnet
First Noel
Fum, Fum, Fum
Go, Tell It On The Mountain

Here, 'Mid The Ass And Oxen Mild
Ihr Kinderlein Kommet
Jingle Bells

Kling Clockchen
Maria Durch Ein Dornwald Ging
O Jesulein Zart
O Little Town Of Bethlehem

Petersburger Schlittenfahrt
Sleigh, The
Stille Nacht, Heilige Nacht

Un Flambeau, Jeanette, Isabelle
Vom Himmel Hoch

O'BRYAN   '84

Born O'Bryan Burnett in 1961 in Sneads Ferry, North Carolina. Male R&B singer.

DEBUT	PEAK	WKS	CD	ARTIST — Album Title	$	Label & Number
4/10/82	80	12		1 Doin' Alright	$10	Capitol 12192
3/12/83	87	27		2 You And I	$10	Capitol 12256
5/26/84	64	21		3 Be My Lover	$10	Capitol 12332

Be My Lover (3)
Breakin' Together (3)
Can't Live Without Your Love (1)
Dazzlin' Lady (2)

Doin' Alright (1)
Gigolo, The (1) *57*
Go On And Cry (3)
I'm Freaky (2)
I'm In Love Again (2)

It's Over (1)
Lady I Love You (3)
Love Has Found It's Way (1)
Lovelite (3)
Mother Nature's Callin' (1)

Right From The Start (1)
Shake (2)
Soft Touch (2)
Soul Train's A'Comin' (2)
Still Water (Love) (1)

Together Always (2)
Too Hot (3)
You And I (2)
You Gotta Use It (3)
You're Always On My Mind (3)

O.C.   '97

Born Omar Credle in 1973 in Brooklyn, New York. Male rapper.

DEBUT	PEAK	WKS	CD	ARTIST — Album Title	$	Label & Number
9/6/97	90	4	©	Jewelz	$10	Payday 524399

Can't Go Wrong
Chosen One
Crow, The

Dangerous
Far From Yours *81*
Hypocrite

It's Only Right
Jewelz
M.U.G.

My World
Stronjay
War Games

Win The G
You And Yours

OCASEK, Ric '83
Born Richard Otcasek on 3/23/49 in Baltimore. Lead singer/guitarist/songwriter of **The Cars**. Appeared in the 1987 movie *Made In Heaven*. Married supermodel/actress Paulina Porizkova on 8/23/89.

| 1/29/83 | 28 | 16 | | © | 1 Beatitude | | | $10 | Geffen 2022 |
| 10/11/86 | 31 | 23 | | © | 2 This Side Of Paradise | | | $10 | Geffen 24098 |

Coming For You (2) | I Can't Wait (1) | Mystery (2) | Quick One (1) | This Side Of Paradise (2)
Connect Up To Me (1) | Jimmy Jimmy (1) | Out Of Control (1) | Sneak Attack (1) | Time Bomb (1)
Emotion In Motion (2) *15* | Keep On Laughin' (2) | P.F.J. (1) | **Something To Grab For** (1) *47* | True Love (2)
Hello Darkness (2) | Look In Your Eyes (2) | Prove (1) | Take A Walk (1) | **True To You** (2) *75*

OCEAN '71
Pop group from London, Ontario, Canada: Janice Morgan (vocals), David Tamblyn (guitar), Greg Brown (keyboards), Jeff Jones (bass) and Charles Slater (drums).

| 5/29/71 | 60 | 13 | | | Put Your Hand In The Hand | | | $15 | Kama Sutra 2033 |

Deep Enough For Me *73* | One Who's Left | **Put Your Hand In The Hand** *2* | We Got A Dream *82*
No Other Woman | Pleasure Of Your Company | Stones I Throw | Will The Circle Be Unbroken

OCEAN, Billy '86
Born Leslie Sebastian Charles on 1/21/50 in Trinidad, West Indies; raised in England. R&B-pop singer.

7/25/81	152	3		©	1 Nights (Feel Like Getting Down)			$12	Epic 37406
8/25/84	9	86	▲²	©	2 Suddenly			$10	Jive 8213
5/17/86	6	48	▲²	©	3 Love Zone			$10	Jive 8409
3/19/88	18	31	▲	©	4 Tear Down These Walls			$10	Jive 8495
11/4/89	77	16	▲	©	5 Greatest Hits		[G]	$10	Jive 1271

Another Day Won't Matter (1) | Dancefloor (2) | I Sleep Much Better (In | **Loverboy** (2,5) *2* | Soon As You're Ready (4) | **There'll Be Sad Songs (To**
Are You Ready (1) | Don't Say Stop (1) | Someone Else's Bed) (5) | Lucky Man (2) | Stand And Deliver (4) | **Make You Cry)** (3,5) *1*
Because Of You (4) | Everlasting Love (1) | If I Should Lose You (2) | **Mystery Lady** (2) *24* | Stay The Night (1) | Whatever Turns You On (1)
Bitter Sweet (3) | **Get Outta My Dreams, Get** | It's Never Too Late To Try (3) | Nights (Feel Like Getting Down) | Suddenly (2,5) *4* | **When The Going Gets Tough,**
Calypso Crazy (4) | **Into My Car** (4,5) *1* | **Licence To Chill** (5) *32* | (1) | Syncopation (2) | **The Tough Get Going** (3,5) *2*
Caribbean Queen (No More | Gun For Hire (4) | Long And Winding Road (2) | Pleasure (4) | Taking Chances (1) | Who's Gonna Rock You (1)
Love On The Run) (2,5) *1* | Here's To You (4,5) | **Love Is Forever** (3) *16* | Promise Me (3) | Tear Down These Walls (4) | Without You (3)
Colour Of Love (4,5) *17* | | Love Zone (3,5) *10* | Showdown (3) | |

OCEAN BLUE, The '90
Pop-rock group formed in Hershey, Pennsylvania: Dave Schelzel (vocals, guitar), Steve Lau (keyboards), Bobby Mittan (bass) and Rob Minnig (drums).

| 2/3/90 | 155 | 8 | | © | The Ocean Blue | | | $10 | Sire 25906 |

Ask Me Jon | Between Something And | Drifting, Falling | Just Let Me Know | Office Of A Busy Man
Awaking To A Dream | Nothing | Familiar Face | Love Song | Vanity Fair
| Circus Animals | Frigid Winter Days | Myron |

OCHS, Phil '66
Born on 12/19/40 in El Paso, Texas. Committed suicide on 4/9/76 (age 25). Folk singer/songwriter.

7/9/66	149	2		©	1 Phil Ochs In Concert		[L]	$25	Elektra 7310
12/9/67	168	5		©	2 Pleasures Of The Harbor			$20	A&M 4133
6/14/69	167	7		©	3 Rehearsals For Retirement			$20	A&M 4181
3/14/70	194	2		©	4 Phil Ochs Greatest Hits			$20	A&M 4253

album contains all new recordings

Another Age (3) | Chords Of Fame (4) | Gas Station Women (4) | My Kingdom For A Car (4) | Pretty Smart On My Part (3) | When I'm Gone (1)
Bach, Beethoven, Mozart & Me | Cops Of The World (1) | I Kill Therefore I Am (3) | My Life (3) | Rehearsals For Retirement (3) | William Butler Yeats Visits
(4) | Cross My Heart (2) | I'm Going To Say It Now (1) | No More Songs (4) | Ringing Of Revolution (1) | Lincoln Park And Escapes
Basket In The Pool (4) | Crucifixion, The (2) | I've Had Her (2) | One Way Ticket Home (4) | Santo Domingo (1) | Unscathed (3)
Boy In Ohio (4) | Doesn't Lenny Live Here | Is There Anybody Here? (1) | Outside Of A Small Circle Of | Scorpion Departs, But Never | World Began In Eden And
Bracero (1) | Anymore (3) | Jim Dean Of Indiana (4) | Friends (2) | Returns (3) | Ended In Los Angeles (3)
Canons Of Christianity (1) | Doll House (3) | Love Me, I'm A Liberal (2) | Party, The (2) | Ten Cents A Coup (4) |
Changes (1) | Flower Lady (2) | Miranda (2) | Pleasures Of The Harbor (2) | There But For Fortune (1) |

O'CONNOR, Carroll '72
Born on 8/2/24 in New York City. Died of a heart attack on 6/21/01 (age 76). TV/movie actor. Acted in several movies. Played "Archie Bunker" on TV's *All In The Family* and "Chief Bill Gillespie" on *In The Heat Of The Night*.

| 6/17/72 | 118 | 13 | | | Remembering You | | | $15 | A&M 4340 |

About A Quarter To Nine | I Get Along Without You Very | Just A Memory | Love Is Here To Stay | Sweet And Lovely | Would You Like To Take A
Can't We Talk It Over | Well | Last Night When We Were | Remembering You | What Is There To Say | Walk
| I'll Never Be The Same | Young | So Rare |

O'CONNOR, Mark — see MA, Yo-Yo

O'CONNOR, Sinéad '90
Born on 12/12/66 in Glenageary, Ireland. Female singer/songwriter.

2/6/88	36	38	●	©	1 The Lion And The Cobra			$10	Chrysalis 41612
4/7/90	❶⁶	52	▲²	©	2 I Do Not Want What I Haven't Got			$10	Ensign 21759
10/10/92	27	9		©	3 Am I Not Your Girl?			$10	Ensign 21952
10/1/94	36	8		©	4 Universal Mother			$10	Ensign 30549
6/21/97	128	3		©	5 Gospel Oak EP		[M]	$10	Chrysalis 58651
7/1/00	55	11		©	6 Faith And Courage			$10	Atlantic 83337

All Apologies (4) | Famine (4) | I Do Not Want What I Haven't | Just Like U Said It Would B (1) | Petit Poulet (5) | 'Til I Whisper U Something (6)
All Babies (4) | Feel So Different (2) | Got (2) | Kyrié Eléison (5) | Red Football (4) | Tiny Grief Song (4)
Bewitched, Bothered And | Fire On Babylon (4) | I Want To Be Loved By You (3) | Lamb's Book Of Life (6) | Scarlet Ribbons (3) | Troy (1)
Bewildered (3) | 4 My Love (3) | I Want Your (Hands On Me) (1) | Last Day Of Our Acquaintance | Scorn Not His Simplicity (3) | What Doesn't Belong To Me (6)
Black Boys On Mopeds (2) | Gloomy Sunday (3) | If U Ever (6) | (2) | Secret Love (3) | Why Don't You Do Right? (3)
Black Coffee (3) | He Moved Through The Fair (5) | In This Heart (4) | Love Letters (3) | State I'm In (6) | You Cause As Much Sorrow (2)
Daddy I'm Fine (6) | Healing Room (4) | Jackie (1) | Mandinka (1) | Success Has Made A Failure Of |
Dancing Lessons (6) | Hold Back The Night (6) | Jealous (6) | My Darling Child (4) | Our Home (4) |
Don't Cry For Me Argentina (3) | How Insensitive (4) | Jerusalem (1) | Never Get Old (1) | Thank You For Hearing Me (4) |
Drink Before The War (1) | I Am Enough For Myself (5) | John I Love You (4) | No Man's Woman (6) | This Is A Rebel Song (5) |
Emma's Song (6) | I Am Stretched On Your Grave | Jump In The River (2) | **Nothing Compares 2 U** (2) *1* | This Is To Mother You (5) |
Emperor's New Clothes (2) *60* | (2) | Just Call Me Joe (1) | Perfect Indian (4) | Three Babies (2) |

OC SUPERTONES '99

Christian ska-rock group from Orange County, California: Matt Morginsky (vocals), Brian Johnson (guitar), Dan Spencer, Dave Chevalier and Darrin Mettler (horns), Tony Terusa (bass) and Jason Carson (drums). OC: Orange County.

6/21/97	117	6	©	1	Supertones Strike Back			$10	BEC 17401
3/13/99	95	5	©	2	Chase The Sun			$10	BEC 17415
10/28/00	168	1	©	3	Loud And Clear			$10	BEC 7440

Another Show (3)
Away From You (2)
Caught Inside (1)
Chase The Sun (2)
Dedication (2)
Escape From Reason (3)
Fade Away (2)

Father's World (3)
Forward To The Future (3)
Grace Flood (1)
Grounded (2)
Hallelujah (2)
Hanani (2)
Health And Wealth (2)

In Between (2)
Jury Duty (3)
Lift Me Up (3)
Like No One Else (1)
Little Man (1)
Louder Than The Mob (1)
Old Friend (2)

One Voice (2)
Pandora's Box (3)
Perseverance Of The Saints (1)
Refuge (In Conclusion) (2)
Resolution (1)
Return Of The Revolution (3)
Revolution (2)

Shut Up And Play (1)
So Great A Salvation (1)
Spend It With You (3)
Supertones Strike Back (1)
Sure Shot (2)
Tonight (1)
20/20 (3)

Unite (1)
What It Comes To (3)
Who Could It Be (3)
Wilderness (3)

OCTOBER PROJECT '95

Group from New Jersey: Mary Fahl (vocals), Marina Belica (vocals, keyboards), David Sabatino (guitar), Emil Adler (piano) and Julie Flanders (lyricist).

| 10/7/95 | 184 | 1 | © | | Falling Farther In | | | $10 | Epic 67019 |

Adam & Eve
After The Fall

Dark Time
Deep As You Go

Falling Farther In
Funeral In His Heart

If I Could
Johnny

One Dream
Something More Than This

Sunday Morning Yellow Sky

O'DAY, Alan '77

Born on 10/3/40 in Hollywood. Singer/songwriter/pianist.

| 9/3/77 | 109 | 9 | | | Appetizers | | | $12 | Pacific 4300 |

Angie Baby
Caress Me Pretty Music

Catch My Breath
Do Me Wrong, But Do Me

Gifts
Satisfied

Slot Machine
Soldier Of Fortune

Started Out Dancing, Ended
Up Making Love *73*

Undercover Angel *1*

ODETTA '63

Born Odetta Holmes on 12/31/30 in Birmingham, Alabama. Folk singer.

| 9/28/63 | 75 | 8 | | | Odetta sings Folk Songs | | | $25 | RCA Victor 2643 |

All My Trials
Anthem Of The Rainbow

Blowing In The Wind
Golden Vanity

I Never Will Marry
Maybe She Go

900 Miles
Roberta

Shenandoah
This Little Light Of Mine

Why Oh Why
Yes I See

O'DONNELL, Rosie '99

Born on 3/21/62 in Commack, New York. Acted in several movies; host of own TV talk show.

| 11/20/99 | 20 | 9 | ▲ © | 1 | A Rosie Christmas | C:#14/8 | [X] | $10 | Columbia 63685 |

includes "Last Christmas" by Darren Hayes and "O Holy Night" by Billy Porter; Christmas charts: 1/99, 9/00

| 11/11/00 | 45 | 11 | ● © | 2 | Another Rosie Christmas | | [X] | $10 | Columbia 85102 |

Christmas chart: 3/00

Ay, Ay, Ay It's Christmas (2)
Because It's Christmas (For All The Children) (2)
Christmas (Baby Please Come Home) (1)
Do You Hear What I Hear (1)

Gonna Eat For Christmas (1)
Have Yourself A Merry Little Christmas (1)
I Say Mommy Kissing Santa Claus (1)
I'm Gonna E-Mail Santa (1)

Little Drummer Boy (1)
Love's In Our Hearts On Christmas Day (1)
Magic Of Christmas Day (God Bless Us Everyone) (1)

Merry Christmas From The Family (2)
Nuttin' For Christmas (2)
Rockin' Around The Christmas Tree (2)

Santa Claus Is Comin' To Town (1)
Santa On The Rooftop (1)
Silver Bells (2)
White Christmas (1)
Winter Wonderland (1,2)

ODYSSEY '77

Disco vocal trio from New York City: Tony Reynolds, with sisters Lillian and Louise Lopez.

10/8/77	36	38		1	Odyssey			$12	RCA Victor 2204
11/11/78	123	5		2	Hollywood Party Tonight			$12	RCA Victor 3031
6/14/80	181	4		3	Hang Together			$12	RCA Victor 3526
7/18/81	175	5		4	I Got The Melody			$12	RCA Victor 3910

Baby That's All I Want (4)
Comin' Back For More (2)
Don't Tell Me, Tell Her (3)
Down Boy (3)
Easy Come, Easy Go (medley) (1)
Ever Lovin' Sam (1)
Follow Me (Play Follow The Leader) (3)

Golden Hands (1)
Hang Together (3)
Hey Bill (Last Night Was Really A Thrill) (2)
Hold De Mota Down (medley)
Hold On To Love (4)
I Can't Keep Holding Back My Love (4)

I Dare Ya (4)
I Got The Melody (4)
If You're Lookin' For A Way Out (3)
It Will Be Alright (4)
Lilly And Harvey, Late To The Party Again (2)
Lucky Star (2)

Never Had It All (3)
Oh No Not My Baby (4)
Pride (2)
Rooster Loose In The Barnyard (3)
Roots Suite Medley (4)
Single Again (medley) (2)
Thank You God For One More Day (1)

Use It Up And Wear It Out (3)
Weekend Lover (1) *57*
What Time Does The Balloon Go Up (medley) (2)
Woman Behind The Man (1)
You Keep Me Dancin' (1)
You Wouldn't Know A Real Live True Love If It Walked Right Up, Kissed You On The

Cheek And Said Hello Baby (2)

Native New Yorker (1) *21*

OFF BROADWAY USA '80

Rock group from Oak Park, Illinois: Cliff Johnson (vocals), Rob Harding and John Ivan (guitars), John Pazdan (bass) and Ken Harck (drums).

| 2/16/80 | 101 | 11 | © | | On | | | $15 | Atlantic 19263 |

Bad Indication
Bully Bully
Drop Me A Line

Full Moon Turn My Head Around
Hang On For Love

Money's No Good
New Little Girl
Oh, Boy!

Stay In Time *51*
You Belong To You

OFFSPRING, The '99

Punk-rock group from California: Brian "Dexter" Holland (lead singer), Kevin "Noodles" Wasserman (guitar), Greg Kriesel (bass) and Ron Welty (drums).

| 6/4/94 | 4 | 101 | ▲6 © | 1 | Smash | C:#12/45 | | $10 | Epitaph 86432 |
| 1/14/95 | 14C | 30 | ● © | 2 | Ignition | | [E] | $10 | Epitaph 86424 |

released in 1993

2/22/97	9	38	▲ ©	3	Ixnay On The Hombre			$10	Columbia 67810
12/5/98+	2²	67	▲4 ©	4	Americana			$10	Columbia 69661
12/2/00	9	24	▲ ©	5	Conspiracy Of One			$10	Columbia 61419

All Along (5)
All I Want (3)
Amazed (3)
Americana (4)
Bad Habit (1)
Burn It Up (2)
Change The World (3)
Come Out And Play (1)
Come Out Swinging (5)
Conspiracy Of One (5)
Cool To Hate (3)

Dammit, I Changed Again (5)
Denial, Revisited (5)
Dirty Magic (2)
Don't Pick It Up (3)
End Of The Line (4)
Feelings (4)
Forever And A Day (2)
Genocide (1)
Get It Right (2)
Gone Away (3)
Gotta Get Away (1)

Have Ever (4)
Hypodermic (2)
I Choose (3)
It'll Be A Long Time (1)
Kick Him When He's Down (4)
Kids Aren't Alright (4)
Killboy Powerhead (1)
Lapd (2)
Leave It Behind (3)
Living In Chaos (5)
Me & My Old Lady (3)

Meaning Of Life (3)
Million Miles Away (5)
Mota (3)
Nitro (Youth Energy) (1)
No Brakes (4)
No Hero (4)
Not The One (1)
Nothing From Something (2)
One Fine Day (5)
Original Prankster (5) *70*
Pay The Man (4)

Pretty Fly (For A White Guy) (4) *53*
Self Esteem (1)
Session (2)
She's Got Issues (4)
Smash (1)
So Alone (1)
Something To Believe In (1)
Special Delivery (5)
Staring At The Sun (4)
Take It Like A Man (2)

Time To Relax (1)
Vultures (5)
Walla Walla (4)
Want You Bad (5)
Way Down The Line (5)
We Are One (2)
Welcome (4)
What Happened To You? (1)
Why Don't You Get A Job? (4) *74*

DEBUT	PEAK	WKS	RIAA	CD	ARTIST — Album Title	Catalog	Sym	$	Label & Number

OHIO EXPRESS '68

Bubblegum group from Mansfield, Ohio: Joey Levine (vocals), Dale Powers and Doug Grassel (guitars), Jim Pflayer (keyboards), Dean Krastan (bass) and Tim Corwin (drums). Levine was lead singer with several studio groups.

| 7/6/68 | 126 | 11 | | | 1 **Ohio Express** .... | | | $25 | Buddah 5018 |
| 2/8/69 | 191 | 2 | | | 2 **Chewy, Chewy** .... | | | $25 | Buddah 5026 |

Chewy Chewy (2) *15*   Fun (2)   Little Girl (2)   She's Not Comin' Home (1)   Vacation (1)
Down At Lulu's (1) *33*   Into This Time (1)   Mary-Ann (1)   Simon Says (2)   Winter Skies (1)
Down In Tennessee (2)   It's A Sad Day (It's A Sad Time)   Nothing Sweeter Than My Baby   So Good, So Fine (2)   Yes Sir (2)
Firebird (2)   (1)   (2)   Time You Spent With Me (1)   **Yummy Yummy Yummy** (1) *4*
First Grade Reader (1)   Let It Take You (2)   1,2,3 Red Light (2)   Turn To Straw (1)

★210★ OHIO PLAYERS '75

Funk group from Dayton, Ohio: Clarence Satchell (vocals, sax), Leroy Bonner (vocals, guitar), Billy Beck (keyboards), Marvin Pierce and Ralph Middlebrook (trumpets), Marshall Jones (bass) and Jimmy Williams (drums). Satchell died of a brain aneurysm on 12/30/95 (age 55).

1)Fire 2)Honey 3)Skin Tight

3/4/72	177	7		©	1 **Pain**...			$15	Westbound 2015
2/24/73	63	22			2 **Pleasure**			$15	Westbound 2017
9/29/73	70	19			3 **Ecstasy**			$15	Westbound 2021
4/27/74	11	48	●	©	4 **Skin Tight**			$12	Mercury 705
11/2/74	102	8			5 **Climax**		[K]	$12	Westbound 1003
11/23/74+	❶¹	29		©	6 **Fire**			$12	Mercury 1013
2/22/75	92	7			7 **Ohio Players Greatest Hits**		[G]	$12	Westbound 1005
8/23/75	2¹	36	●	©	8 **Honey**			$12	Mercury 1038
12/20/75+	61	14			9 **Rattlesnake**...............................		[K]	$12	Westbound 211
6/12/76	12	20	●	©	10 **Contradiction**			$12	Mercury 1088
11/13/76	31	17	●	©	11 **Ohio Players Gold**		[G]	$12	Mercury 1122
4/9/77	41	27		©	12 **Angel**			$12	Mercury 3701
12/24/77+	68	10		©	13 **Mr. Mean**..................................			$12	Mercury 3707
9/9/78	69	9		©	14 **Jass-Ay-Lay-Dee**			$12	Mercury 3730
4/14/79	80	14			15 **Everybody Up**			$12	Arista 4226
4/11/81	165	3		©	16 **Tenderness**			$12	Boardwalk 37090

Ain't Givin' Up No Ground (8)   Far East Mississippi (10,11)   (I Wanna Know) Do You Feel It   My Ladies Run Me Crazy (10)   Reds, The (1)   Speak Easy (13)
Alone (8)   **Feel The Beat (Everybody**   (3)   My Life (10)   Rooster Poot (9)   Spinning (3,9)
Angel (12)   **Disco)** (11) *61*   **I Want To Be Free** (6,11) *44*   Never Had A Dream (1)   Ruffell Foot (5)   Streakin' Cheek To Cheek (4)
Bi-Centennial (10)   Feelings (medley) (6)   Introducing The Players (9)   Not So Sad And Lonely (3)   Runnin' From The Devil (6)   **Sweet Sticky Thing** (8,11) *33*
Big Score (13)   Fight Me, Chase Me (13)   Is Anybody Gonna Be Saved?   Nott Enuff (14)   Say It (15)   Take De Funk Off, Fly (15)
Black Cat (3)   **Fire** (6,11) *1*   (4)   **O-H-I-O** (12) *45*   She Locked It (9)   Tell The Truth (10)
Boardwalkin' (16)   Food Stamps Y'all (3,5)   It Takes A While (16)   Only A Child Can Love (11)   Shoot Yer Shot (medley) (14)   Time Slips Away (medley) (14)
Body Vibes (12)   **Fopp** (8,11) *30*   It's All Over (6)   Our Love Has Died (2)   Short Change (3)   Together (6)
Call Me (16)   Funk-O-Nots (14)   It's Your Night (medley) (4)   Pack It Up (5)   Silly Billy (3)   Try A Little Tenderness (16)
Can You Still Love Me (12)   **Funky Worm** (2,7) *15*   Jass-Ay-Lay-Dee (14)   Pain (Part II) (7)   Singing In The Morning (1)   Try To Be A Man (16)
Climax (5,7)   Glad To Know You're Mine (12)   **Jive Turkey (Part 1)** (4,11) *47*   **Pain (Part I)** (1,7) *64*   Sitting On The Dock Of The   Varee Is Love (2,7,9)
Contradiction (10)   Gone Forever (9)   Laid It (2,9)   Paint Me (2)   Bay (16)   Walked Away From You (2)
Controller's Mind (13)   Good Luck Charm (13)   Let's Love (8)   Players Balling (Players Doin'   **Skin Tight** (4,11) *13*   Walt's First Trip (2,7)
Dance (If Ya Wanta) (14)   Hard To Love Your Brother (14)   Little Lady Maria (10)   Their Own Thing) (1,5)   Skinny (16)   What It Is (9)
Don't Fight My Love (12)   Heaven Must Be Like This (4)   **Love Rollercoaster** (8,11) *1*   Pleasure (2,7)   Sleep Talk (3,5,7)   What The Hell (6)
Don't Say Goodbye (15)   Hollywood Hump (9)   Magic Trick (10)   Precious Love (10)   Sleepwalkin' (14)   What's Going On (5)
Ecstasy (3,7) *31*   Honey (8)   Make Me Feel (15)   Pride And Vanity (2)   Smoke (6)   **Who'd She Coo?** (10,11) *18*
Everybody Up (15)   Hustle Bird (9)   Merry Go Round (12)   Proud Mary (5)   Something Special (15)   Words Of Love (medley) (4)
Faith (12)   I Wanna Hear From You (1,7)   Mr. Mean (13)   **Rattlesnake** (9) *90*   Sometimes I Cry (16)   You And Me (3)

OINGO BOINGO '90

Rock group formed in Los Angeles: **Danny Elfman** (vocals), Steve Bartek (guitar), John Avila (bass) and Johnny Hernandez (drums). Group appeared in the 1986 movie *Back To School*. Elfman also scored several movies.

1)Boingo 2)Dark At The End Of The Tunnel 3)Boi-ngo

10/25/80	163	5			1 **Oingo Boingo**		[M]	$12	I.R.S. 70400
8/15/81	172	5		©	2 **Only A Lad**			$12	A&M 4863
9/4/82	148	9		©	3 **Nothing To Fear**			$12	A&M 4930
9/10/83	144	7		©	4 **Good For Your Soul**			$12	A&M 4959
11/16/85	98	16	●	©	5 **Dead Man's Party**			$10	MCA 5665
3/21/87	77	16		©	6 **Boi-ngo**			$10	MCA 5811
10/22/88	90	11		©	7 **Boingo Alive**		[L]	$15	MCA 8030 [2]
2/11/89	150	6		©	8 **Skeletons In The Closet: The Best Of Oingo Boingo**................		[G]	$10	A&M 5217
3/10/90	72	14		©	9 **Dark At The End Of The Tunnel**			$10	MCA 6365
6/4/94	71	3		©	10 **Boingo**			$10	Giant 24555
5/4/96	188	1		©	11 **Farewell: Live From The Universal Amphitheatre, Halloween 1995**.........		[L]	$15	A&M 540504 [2]

Ain't This The Life (1,11)   Fool's Paradise (5)   Insects (3,8,11)   Not My Slave (6,7)   Private Life (3,7,8)   Water (11)
Burn Me Up (11)   Glory Be (9)   Is This (9)   Nothing Bad Ever Happens   Reptiles And Samurai (3,11)   We Close Our Eyes (6,11)
Can't See (Useless) (10,11)   Good For Your Soul (4)   Islands (3)   (4,8)   Right To Know (9)   **Weird Science** (5) *45*
Capitalism (2)   Goodbye - Goodbye (7)   **Just Another Day** (5,7) *85*   Nothing To Fear (But Fear   Run Away (The Escape Song)   What You See (2)
Change (10,11)   Gratitude (7)   Little Girls (2,8,11)   Itself) (3,7,8)   (9)   When The Lights Go Out (9)
Cinderella Undercover (7,11)   Grey Matter (3,7,8,11)   Little Guns (4)   On The Outside (2,7,8,11)   Running On A Treadmill (9)   Where Do All My Friends Go (6)
Clowns of Death (11)   Heard Somebody Cry (5)   Long Breakdown (9)   Only A Lad (1,2,7,8,11)   Same Man I Was Before (5)   Who Do You Want To Be
Controller (2,11)   Help Me (5)   Lost Like This (10)   Only Makes Me Laugh (7)   Skin (9)   (4,7,8,11)
Cry Of The Vatos (4)   Helpless (11)   Mary (10,11)   Out Of Control (9)   Spider (10)   Whole Day Off (3,8,11)
Dead Man's Party (5,7,11)   Hey! (10,11)   My Life (6,7)   Outrageous (6)   Stay (5,7,11)   Why'd We Come (1)
Dead Or Alive (4,7)   Home Again (6)   Nasty Habits (2,8,11)   Pain (6)   Sweat (4,7)   Wild Sex (In The Working
Dream Somehow (9)   I Am The Walrus (10,11)   New Generation (6)   Pedestrian Wolves (10)   Try To Believe (9)   Class) (3,7,11)
Elevator Man (6)   I'm So Bad (1,11)   No One Lives Forever (5)   Perfect System (2)   Violent Love (1,7)   Winning Side (7)
Fill The Void (4)   Imposter (2)   No One Loves Forever (11)   Pictures Of You (4)   Wake Up (It's 1984) (4,8)   You Really Got Me (2)
Flesh 'N Blood (9)   Insanity (10,11)   No Spill Blood (4,7,11)   Piggies (11)   War Again (10)

O'JAYS, The ★137★   '76

R&B vocal trio from Canton, Ohio: **Eddie Levert**, Walter Williams and William Powell. Named after Cleveland DJ, Eddie O'Jay (died on 4/10/98). Sammy Strain (of **Little Anthony & The Imperials**) replaced Powell in 1975. Powell died on 5/26/77 (age 35). Eric Grant replaced Strain in 1996. Levert's sons **Gerald Levert** and **Sean Levert** are members of **Levert**.

1)So Full Of Love 2)Family Reunion 3)Back Stabbers 4)Ship Ahoy 5)Survival

DEBUT	PEAK	WKS	RIAA	CD	#	Album Title	Sym	$	Label & Number
9/9/72	10	44	●		1	**Back Stabbers**		$15	Philadelphia Int'l. 31712
4/28/73	156	8			2	The O'Jays In Philadelphia	[E]	$15	Philadelphia Int'l. 32120
						recordings from 1969			
11/10/73+	11	48	▲	©	3	Ship Ahoy		$12	Philadelphia Int'l. 32408
6/29/74	17	24	●	©	4	The O'Jays Live In London	[L]	$12	Philadelphia Int'l. 32953
						recorded December 1973 at the Hammersmith Odeon in London			
4/26/75	11	24	●	©	5	Survival		$12	Philadelphia Int'l. 33150
11/29/75+	7	34	▲	©	6	**Family Reunion**		$12	Philadelphia Int'l. 33807
10/2/76	20	22	●	©	7	Message In The Music		$12	Philadelphia Int'l. 34245
6/4/77	27	16	●		8	Travelin' At The Speed Of Thought		$12	Philadelphia Int'l. 34684
1/7/78	132	6		©	9	The O'Jays' Collectors' Items	[G]	$15	Philadelphia I. 35024 [2]
4/29/78	6	28	▲	©	10	**So Full Of Love**		$12	Philadelphia Int'l. 35355
9/15/79	16	30	▲		11	Identify Yourself		$12	Philadelphia Int'l. 36027
8/30/80	36	12		©	12	The Year 2000		$12	TSOP 36416
5/15/82	49	13		©	13	My Favorite Person		$12	Philadelphia Int'l. 37999
8/13/83	142	5			14	When Will I See You Again		$12	Epic 38518
10/19/85	121	12		©	15	Love Fever		$12	Philadelphia Int'l. 53015
10/10/87	66	25		©	16	Let Me Touch You		$10	EMI-Manhattan 53036
5/27/89	114	17		©	17	Serious		$10	EMI 90921
2/16/91	73	20	●	©	18	Emotionally Yours		$10	EMI 93390
8/14/93	75	11		©	19	Heartbreaker		$10	EMI 89740
8/2/97	75	10		©	20	Love You To Tears		$10	Global Soul 31149

Ain't Nothin' Wrong With Good Lovin' (14)
All Eyes On Africa (15)
Another Lonely Night (Did You Forget About Me) (20)
Answer's In You (12)
Baby You Know (20) *76*
Back Stabbers (1,4,9) *3*
Betcha Don't Know (What Comes After That) (14)
Branded Bad (2)
Brandy (10) *79*
Can't Let You Go (19)
Can't Slow Down (15)
Cause I Want You Back Again (16)
Closer To You (18)
Cry Together (10)
Cryin' The Blues (19)
Darlin' Darlin' Baby (Sweet, Tender, Love) (7,9) *72*
Decisions (17)
Deeper (In Love With You) (2) *64*
Desire Me (7)
Dollar Bill (15)
Don't Call Me Brother (3)
Don't Let Me Down (18)
Don't Let The Dream Get Away (16)
Don't Take Your Love Away (16)
Don't Walk Away Mad (13)
Don't You Know True Love (18)
Emotionally Yours (18)

Fading (17)
Family Reunion (6,9)
Feelings (8)
For The Love Of Money (3,9) *9*
Forever Mine (11) *28*
Friend Of A Friend (17)
Get On Out And Party (11)
Getting Along Much Better (20)
Girl, Don't Let It Get You Down (12) *55*
Give The People What They Want (5,9) *45*
Have You Had Your Love Today (17)
He Loves You (19)
Heartbreaker (19)
Help (Somebody Please) (10)
House Of Fire (14)
How Time Flies (5)
Hurry Up & Come Back (11)
I Can't Stand The Pain (14)
I Just Want Somebody To Love Me (16)
I Just Want To Satisfy You (13)
I Like To See Us Get Down (13)
I Love America (15)
I Love Music (Part 1) (6,9) *5*
I Should Be Your Lover (2)
I Swear, I Love No One But You (7)
I Wanna Be With You Tonight (15)
I Want My Cake (20)
I Want You Here With Me (11)

I've Got The Groove (2)
Identify (11)
If I Find Love Again (18)
It's Too Strong (2)
Just Another Lonely Night (15)
Just Can't Get Enough (2)
Keep On Lovin' Me (18)
Keep On Pleasin' Me (18)
Leave It Alone (17)
Let Life Flow (7)
Let Me In Your World (2)
Let Me Make Love To You (5,9) *75*
Let Me Touch You (16)
Let's Spend Some Time Together (8)
Letter To My Friends (14)
Lies (18)
Listen To The Clock On The Wall (1)
Little Green Apples (medley) (2)
Livin' For The Weekend (6,9) *20*
Looky Looky (Look At Me Girl) (2) *98*
Love & Trust (18)
Love Fever (15)
Love Train (1,4,9) *1*
Love You To Tears (20)
Lovin' You (16)
Make A Joyful Noise (7)
Make It Feel Good (18)
Message In Our Music (7) *49*
My Favorite Person (13)
Never Been Better (17)

Never Break Us Up (5)
Nice And Easy (14)
992 Arguments (1) *57*
No Can Do (19)
No Lies To Cloud My Eyes (16)
Now That We Found Love (3)
Once Is Not Enough (12)
One In A Million (Girl) (11)
One On One (13)
One Wonderful Girl (19)
Out In The Real World (13)
Out Of My Mind (17)
Paradise (11)
Pay The Bills (20)
People Keep Tellin' Me (3)
Pot Can't Call The Kettle Black (17)
Prayer, A (7)
Put Our Heads Together (14)
Put Your Hands Together (3,4) *10*
Rainbow (17)
Respect (18)
Rich Get Richer (5)
Serious Affair (20)
Serious Hold On Me (17)
She's Only A Woman (6)
Shiftless, Shady, Jealous Kind Of People (1)
Ship Ahoy (3)
Show Me The Right Way (19)
Sing A Happy Song (11)
Sing My Heart Out (10)

So Glad I Got You, Girl (8)
So Nice I Tried It Twice (11)
Somebody Else Will (19)
Something (medley) (2)
Something For Nothing (18)
Stairway To Heaven (6,9)
Stand Up (8)
Still Missing (16)
Strokety Stroke (10)
Sunshine Part II (1,4,9) *48*
Survival (5,9)
Take Me To The Stars (10)
That's How Love Is (18)
(They Call Me) Mr. Lucky (1)
This Air I Breathe (3)
This Time Baby (10)
Those Lies (Done Caught Up With You This Time) (8)
Time To Get Down (1) *33*
To Prove I Love You (12)
Travelin' At The Speed Of Thought (8)
Trouble (19)
True Love Never Dies (16)
Turned Out (20)
Undercover Lover (16)
Unity (8)
Use Ta Be My Girl (10) *4*
We're All In This Thing Together (8)
We're Still Together (15)
What A Woman (15)
What Am I Waiting For (5)

What Good Are These Arms Of Mine (15)
What's Stopping You (20) *73*
When The World's At Peace (1,4)
When Will I See You Again (14)
Where Did We Go Wrong (5)
Who Am I (1)
Wildflower (4,9)
Work On Me (8)
Year 2000 (12)
You And Me (6)
You Can Make Me Fall In Love Again (20)
You Got Your Hooks In Me (3,9)
You Won't Fail (12)
You'll Never Know (All There Is To Know 'Bout My Love) (12)
You're The Best Thing Since Candy (2)
You're The Girl Of My Dreams (Sho Nuff Real) (12)
Your Body's Here With Me (But Your Mind's On The Other Side Of Town) (13)
Your True Heart (And Shining Star) (13)

O'KAYSIONS, The   '68

White pop/rock group from Wilson, North Carolina: Donny Weaver (vocals, organ), Wayne Pittman (guitar), Ron Turner (trumpet), Jim Spidel (sax), Jimmy Hennant (bass) and Bruce Joyner (drums).

DEBUT	PEAK	WKS	#	Album Title	$	Label & Number
11/9/68	153	4		Girl Watcher	$40	ABC 664

Deal Me In
Dedicated To The One I Love
Girl Watcher *5*

How Are You Fixed For Love?
Little Miss Flirt
Love Machine *76*

My Baby's Love
My Song (Poor Man's Son)
Soul Clap

Sunday Will Never Be The Same

O'KEEFE, Danny   '72

Born in 1943 in Wenatchee, Washington. Pop singer/songwriter.

DEBUT	PEAK	WKS	CD	#	Album Title	$	Label & Number
9/2/72	87	16		1	O'Keefe	$15	Signpost 8404
8/11/73	172	9	©	2	Breezy Stories	$15	Atlantic 7264

American Dream (1)
Angel Spread Your Wings (2)
Babe, The (medley) (2)
Catfish (2)
Edge, The (2)

Farewell To Storyville (Good Time Flat Blues) (2)
Good Time Charlie's Got The Blues (1) *9*
Grease It (1)
Honky Tonkin' (1)

I Know You Really Love Me (1)
I'm Sober Now (1)
If Ya Can't Boogie, Woogie (You Sure Can't Rock & Roll) (2)
Junkman (2)

Louie The Hook Vs. The Preacher (1)
Mad Ruth (medley) (2)
Magdalena (1)
Portrait In Black Velvet (2)
Question (Obviously) (1)

Road, The (1)
Roseland Taxi Dancer (1)
She Said "Drive On, Driver" (2)
Shooting Star (1)
Steppin' Out Tonight (2)
Valentine Pieces (1)

OLD & IN THE WAY '75
Bluegrass group formed in San Francisco: **Jerry Garcia** (vocals, banjo; **Grateful Dead**), **David Grisman** (vocals, mandolin), Peter Rowan (vocals, guitar), John Kahn (bass) and Vassar Clements (fiddle).

| 3/29/75 | 99 | 8 | | © | Old & In The Way .... | | [L] | $25 | Round 103 |

recorded on 10/8/73 at the Boarding House in San Francisco

| Hobo Song | | Knockin' On Your Door | Midnight Moonlight | Panama Red | White Dove |
| Kissimmee Kid | | Land Of The Navajo | Old And In The Way | Pigs In The Pen | Wild Horses |

OLDFIELD, Mike '74
Born on 5/15/53 in Reading, England. Classical-rock, multi-instrumentalist/composer.

11/10/73+	3	45	●	©	1 **Tubular Bells**	C:#15/40	[I]	$15	Virgin 105
9/21/74	87	10		©	2 **Hergest Ridge**		[I]	$15	Virgin 109
12/20/75+	146	7		©	3 **Ommadawn**		[I]	$15	Virgin 33913
7/4/81	174	3		©	4 **QE2**		[I]	$12	Epic 37358
5/8/82	164	5		©	5 **Five Miles Out**		[I]	$12	Epic 37983
2/27/88	138	8		©	6 **Islands**			$10	Virgin 90645

Arrival (4)	Flying Start (6)	Molly (4)	Orabidoo (5)	Time Has Come (6)
Celt (4)	Hergest Ridge (2)	Mount Teidi (5)	QE2 (4)	**Tubular Bells** (1) 7
Conflict (4)	Islands (6)	North Point (4)	Sheba (4)	Wind Chimes Part One & Two
Family Man (5)	Magic Touch (6)	Ommadown - Part One & Two	Taurus I (4)	(6)
Five Miles Out (5)	Mirage (4)	(3)	Taurus II (5)	Wonderful Land (4)

OLD FRIENDS QUARTET '01
Gospel group: Ernie Haase, Jake Hess, Wesley Pritchard and George Younce.

| 6/9/01 | 159 | 1 | | © | Encore .... | | | $10 | Spring House 42321 |

Faith Unlocks The Door	He Knows Just What I Need	Move That Mountain	Practice What You Preach	Up Above My Head
Glory, Glory Clear The Road	How Long Has It Been	O What A Savior	Taller Than Trees	
Glory To God In The Highest	Light Of Love	Old Friends	Thanks To Calvary	

OL DIRTY BASTARD '95
Born Russell Jones on 11/15/68 in Brooklyn, New York. Male rapper. Member of **Wu-Tang Clan**.

| 4/15/95 | 7 | 21 | ● | © | 1 **Return To The 36 Chambers: The Dirty Version** | | | $10 | Elektra 61659 |
| 10/2/99 | 10 | 27 | ● | © | 2 **N***a Please** | | | $10 | Elektra 62414 |

All In Together Now (2)	Cold Blooded (2)	Drunk Game (Sweet Sugar Pie)	Harlem World (1)	Raw Hide (1)	You Don't Want To Fuck With
Baby C'mon (1)	Cuttin' Headz (1)	(1)	Hippa To Da Hoppa (1)	Recognize (2)	Me (2)
Brooklyn Zoo (1) 54	Damage (1)	Gettin' High (2)	I Can't Wait (2)	Rollin' Wit You (2)	
Brooklyn Zoo II (Tiger Crane)	Dirt Dog (2)	Goin' Down (1)	I Want Pussy (2)	Shimmy Shimmy Ya (1) 62	
(1)	Dirty Dancin' (1)	Good Morning Heartache (2)	Nigga Please (2)	Snakes (1)	
	Don't U Know (1)	**Got Your Money** (2) 33	Proteck Ya Neck II The Zoo (1)	Stomp, The (1)	

OLD 97's '01
Rock group from Dallas: Rhett Miller (vocals, guitar), Ken Bethea (guitar), Murry Hammond (bass) and Philip Peeples (drums).

| 4/7/01 | 121 | 1 | | © | Satellite Rides .... | | | $10 | Elektra 62531 |

Am I Too Late	Buick City Complex	King Of All The World	Rollerskate Skinny	What I Wouldn't Do
Bird In A Cage	Can't Get A Line	Nervous Guy	Up The Devil's Pay	
Book Of Poems	Designs On You	Question	Weightless	

OLEANDER '01
Rock group from Sacramento, California: Thomas Flowers (vocals), Ric Ivanisevich (guitar), Doug Eldridge (bass) and Fred Nelson (drums).

| 6/12/99 | 115 | 19 | ● | © | 1 February Son .... | | | $10 | Republic 53242 |
| 3/24/01 | 94 | 4 | | © | 2 Unwind .... | | | $10 | Republic 013377 |

Are You There? (2)	Champion (2)	Halo (2)	Lost Cause (1)	Stupid (1)	Why I'm Here (1)
Back Home Years Ago (2)	Come To Stay (2)	How Could I? (1)	Never Again (1)	Tightrope (2)	You'll Find Out (1)
Benign (2)	Down When I'm Loaded (1)	I Walk Alone (1)	She's Up, She's Down (2)	Unwind (2)	Yours If You Like (2)
Boys Don't Cry (1)	Goodbye (2)	Jimmy Shaker Day (2)	Shrinking The Blob (1)	Where Were You Then? (1)	

OLIVER '69
Born William Oliver Swofford on 2/22/45 in North Wilkesboro, North Carolina. Died of cancer on 2/12/2000 (age 54).

| 8/2/69 | 19 | 38 | | | 1 Good Morning Starshine .... | | | $20 | Crewe 1333 |
| 5/16/70 | 71 | 13 | | | 2 Oliver Again .... | | | $20 | Crewe 1344 |

Angelica (2) 97	Can't You See (1)	If You Go Away (2)	Letmekissyouwithadream (1)	Until It's Time For You To Go	Young Birds Fly (2)
Arrangement, The (1)	Comfort Me (2)	In My Life (1)	Picture Of Kathleen Dunne (2)	(2)	
Both Sides Now (Clouds) (1)	**Good Morning Starshine** (1) 3	**Jean** (1) 2	Ruby Tuesday (1)	Where Is Love (1)	
Buddy (2)	I Can Remember (2)	Leaving On A Jet Plane (2)	Twelfth Of Never (2)	Who Will Buy (1)	

OLIVER, David '78
Born in Florida. Died in 1981. R&B singer/songwriter.

| 5/27/78 | 128 | 8 | | | David Oliver .... | | | $10 | Mercury 1183 |

| Friends & Strangers | Love So Strong | Munchies | What Kinda Woman |
| Let's Make Happiness | Ms. | Playin' At Bein' A Winner | You And I |

OLIVIA '01
Born Olivia Longe in 1980 in Brooklyn; raised in Queens, New York. R&B singer.

| 6/2/01 | 55 | 6 | | | Olivia .... | | | $10 | J Records 20008 |

| Are U Capable | Bring Da Roof Down | Look Around | Silly Chick In Love | When 2 Souls Touch | Woop-T-Woo |
| **Bizounce** 15 | It's On Again | Lower 2 My Heart | 'Til He Comes Home | Whordie | You Got The Damn Thing |

OLIVOR, Jane '80
Born in 1947 in New York City. Jazz-styled singer.

10/22/77	86	8		©	1 Chasing Rainbows			$12	Columbia 34917
7/8/78	108	12		©	2 Stay The Night			$12	Columbia 35437
2/23/80	58	12		©	3 The Best Side Of Goodbye			$12	Columbia 36355
5/29/82	144	6		©	4 In Concert		[L]	$12	Columbia 37938

recorded on 12/21/81 at the Berkley School of Music in Boston

Annie's Song (4)	Better Days (Looks As Though	Can't Leave You 'Cause I Love	Carousel Of Love (4)	French Waltz (1)	Honesty (2)
Beautiful Sadness (1)	We're Doing Somethin' Right)	You (2)	Come In From The Rain (1)	Golden Pony (3)	
Best Side Of Goodbye (3)	(4)	Can't We Make It Right Again	Daydreams (4)	Greatest Love Of All (3)	
	Big Parade (1)	(2)	Don't Let Go Of Me (3)	**He's So Fine** (2) 77	

OLIVOR, Jane — Cont'd

I'm Always Chasing Rainbows (1)   Long And Lasting Love (3)   Pretty Girl (4)   Solitaire (2)   Weeping Willows, Cattails (3,4)
It's Over Goodbye (1)   Love This Time (3)   Race To The End (4)   Song For My Father (2)   Where There Is Love (4)
Lalena (1)   Manchild Lullaby (3)   Right Garden (2)   Stay The Night (2,4)   You (1)
Let's Make Some Memories (2)   Marigold Wings (Earthbound) (4)   Run For The Roses (4)   To Love Again (3)   You Wanna Be Loved (1)
   Seasons (4)   Vagabond (1)   You're The One I Love (2)

OLSEN, Mary-Kate & Ashley   '93

Fraternal twin sisters who shared the role of "Michelle Tanner " on the TV show *Full House*. Born on 6/13/86 (Ashley is two minutes older) in Sherman Oaks, California. Starred in series of movies.

12/11/93	149	5		©	I Am The Cute One	$10	Zoom Express 35038

MARY-KATE + ASHLEY OLSEN AND FRIENDS

Broccoli And Chocolate   Double Up   Ida Know   My Horse And Me   One Buffalo, Two Buffali
Don't Let Your Mom Go Shopping   I Am A Kid   Mom's Song (We Think We'll Keep You)   No One Tells The President   We Love To Scream
   I Am The Cute One   What To Do   Yakety Yak

OL SKOOL   '98

R&B group from St. Louis: Pookie (vocals), Tony Love (guitar), Curtis Jefferson (bass) and Bobby Crawford (drums).

3/14/98	49	9		©	Ol Skool	$10	Universal 53104

Am I Dreaming *31*   Don't Be Afraid   Just Between You And Me   Slip Away   Touch You
Come With Me   It Won't Let Go   Set You Free   Still Here 4 U   Without You

OLSSON, Nigel   '79

Born on 2/10/49 in Merseyside, England. Drummer for **Elton John**'s band from 1971-76.

3/24/79	140	5		©	Nigel	$12	Bang 35792

All It Takes   Cassey Blue (medley)   **Little Bit Of Soap** *34*   Part Of The Chosen Few   Thinking Of You
Au Revoir (medley)   **Dancin' Shoes** *18*   Living In A Fantasy   Say Goodbye To Hollywood   You Know I'll Always Love You

OMAR & THE HOWLERS   '87

Rock trio from Austin, Texas: Kent "Omar" Dykes (vocals, guitar), Bruce Jones (bass) and Gene Brandon (drums).

6/27/87	81	19		©	Hard Times In The Land Of Plenty	$10	Columbia 40815

Border Girl   Don't Rock Me The Wrong Way   Hard Times In The Land Of Plenty   Lee Anne   Same Old Grind   You Ain't Foolin' Nobody
Dancing In The Canebrake   Don't You Know   Mississippi Hoo Doo Man   Shadow Man

OMC   '97

Born Pauly Fuemana in Otara, New Zealand. Singer/songwriter. OMC: Otara Millionaires Club.

5/31/97	40	25	●	©	How Bizarre	$10	Mercury 533435

Angel In Disguise   How Bizarre   Lingo With The Gringo   On The Run   Right On
Breaking My Heart   Land Of Plenty   Never Coming Back   Pours Out Your Eyes   She Loves Italian

ONASIS, Erick   '00

Born in New York City. Male rapper.

7/15/00	53	7		©	Def Squad Presents Erick Onasis	$10	DreamWorks 450114

Ain't Shhh To Discuss   Don't Get Gassed   Feel Me Baby   Get Da Money   I Do 'Em   Vangundy
Can't Stop   Fat Gold Chain   Focus   Hostility   So Sweet   Why Not

O'NEAL, Alexander   '87

Born on 11/15/53 in Natchez, Mississippi. R&B singer.

4/27/85	92	18		©	1	Alexander O'Neal	$10	Tabu 39331
8/22/87	29	40	●	©	2	Hearsay	$10	Tabu 40320
12/17/88+	149	5		©	3	My Gift To You	[X] $10	Tabu 45016

     Christmas chart: 9/'88

2/25/89	185	5		©	4	All Mixed Up	[K] $10	Tabu 44492
2/16/91	49	15	●	©	5	All True Man	$10	Tabu 45349
2/27/93	89	8		©	6	Love Makes No Sense	$10	Tabu 9501

Alex 9000 (medley) (1)   Crying Overtime (2)   In The Middle (6)   My Gift To You (3)   Somebody (Changed Your Mind) (5)   What Is This Thing Called Love? (5)
All That Matters To Me (6)   Do You Wanna Like I Do (1)   Innocent (1,4)   **Never Knew Love Like This** (2,4) *28*   Sunshine (2)   What's Missing (1)
All True Man (5) *43*   Every Time I Get Up (5)   Innocent II (medley) (1)   Our First Christmas (3)   Thank You For A Good Year (3)   When The Party's Over (2)
Aphrodisia (6)   **Fake** (2) *25*   Lady (6)   Remember Why (It's Christmas) (3)   This Christmas (3)   Winter Wonderland (3)
Broken Heart Can Mend (1)   Fake 89 (4)   Little Drummer Boy (3)   Sentimental (5)   Time Is Running Out (5)   Yoke (G.U.O.T.R.) (5)
Change Of Heart (6)   Hang On (5)   Look At Us Now (1)   Shame On Me (5)   Used (5)   You Were Meant To Be My Lady (Not My Girl) (1,4)
Christmas Song (Chestnuts Roasting On An Open Fire) (3)   Hearsay (2)   Love Makes No Sense (6)   Since I've Been Lovin' You (6)   (What Can I Say) To Make You Love Me (2,4)   Your Precious Love (6)
   Home Is Where The Heart Is (4)   Lovers, The (2,4)   Sleigh Ride (3)
Criticize (2,4) *70*   If U Let It (6)   Midnight Run (5)
   If You Were Here Tonight (1)   Morning After (5)

O'NEAL, Jamie   '01

Born Jamie Murphy on 6/3/68 in Sydney, Australia; raised in Hawaii and Nevada. Female country singer.

11/18/00+	125	24	●	©	Shiver	$10	Mercury 170132

Frantic   No More Protecting My Heart   Shiver   **When I Think About Angels** *35*   Way It's Goin' Down (T.W.IsM. For Life) (4)
I'm Not Gonna Do Anything Without You   Only Thing Wrong   **There Is No Arizona** *40*   Where We Belong
I'm Still Waiting   Sanctuary   To Be With You   You Rescued Me
   She Hasn't Heard It Yet

O'NEAL, Shaquille   '93

Born on 3/6/72 in Newark, New Jersey. Male rapper/actor. Professional basketball player with the NBA's Orlando Magic and Los Angeles Lakers. Starred in the movies *Blue Chips*, *Kazaam* and *Steel*.

11/13/93	25	30	▲	©	1	Shaq Diesel	$10	Jive 41529
11/26/94	67	10	●	©	2	Shaq-Fu: da Return	$10	Jive 41550
12/7/96	82	6		©	3	You Can't Stop The Reign	$10	T.W.IsM. 90087

     includes "Player" by S.H.E. and "Don't Wanna Be Alone" by One Accord

10/3/98	58	5		©	4	Respect	$10	T.W.IsM. 540947

Are You A Roughneck (1)   Deeper (4)   I Hate 2 Brag (1)   Make This A Night To Remember (4)   Nobody (2)   Way It's Goin' Down (T.W.IsM. For Life) (4)
Best To Worst (3)   Edge Of Night (3)   **(I Know I Got) Skillz** (1) *35*   Mic Check 1-2 (2)   Pool Jam (4)   What's Up Doc? (Can We Rock) (1)
Big Dog Stomp (3)   Fiend '98 (4)   **I'm Outstanding** (1) *47*   More To Life (3)   Shaq's Got It Made (2)   Where Ya At? (1)
Biological Didn't Bother (2) *78*   Fly Like An Eagle (4)   It Was All A Dream (3)   My Dear (2)   Shoot Pass Slam (1)
Blaq Supaman (4)   Freaky Flow (2)   Just Be Good To Me (3)   My Style, My Stelo (2)   (So U Wanna Be) Hardcore (2)
Bomb Baby (4)   Game Of Death (3)   Legal Money (3)   Newark To C.I. (2)   Still Can't Stop The Reign (3)
Boom! (1)   Giggin' On Em (1)   Let Me In, Let Me In (1)   No Hook (2)   Strait Playin' (3)
Buzzer, The (4)   Got To Let Me Know (4)   Let's Wait A While (4)   No Love Lost (3)   3 X's Dope (3)
Can I Play (3)   Heat It Up (4)   Like What (4)   No Love Lost (3)   Voices (4)

101 STRINGS
European studio orchestra assembled by D.L. Miller.   '59

DEBUT	PEAK	WKS		CD	#	Album Title		Sym	$	Label & Number
5/25/59+	9	58		©	1	The Soul of Spain		[I]	$20	Somerset 6600
1/9/61	21	19			2	The Soul of Spain, Volume II		[I]	$20	Somerset 9900
1/9/61	46	15			3	101 Strings Play The Blues		[I]	$20	Somerset 5800
1/9/61	104	13		©	4	Concerto Under The Stars		[I]	$20	Somerset 6700

Basin Street Blues (3)
Birth Of The Blues (3)
Blues In The Night (3)
Blues Pizzacato (3)
Breeze And I (2)
Cantina Toreros (2)
Claire De Lune (4)
Cornish Rhapsody, Theme From (4)
Domingo En Seville (Sunday In Seville) (1)
El Relicario (2)
Espana (1)
Espana Cani (1)
Frankie And Johnny (3)
Granada (2)
La Violetera (1)
Le Cid (2)
Liebestraum (4)
Macarenas (Patron Saint Of The Matadors) (1)
Malaguena (1)
Matador (2)
Meditation From Thais (4)
Nocturne (4)
Shades Of Blues (3)
St. Louis Blues (3)
Study In E Major (4)
Swedish Rhapsody, Theme From (4)
Symphony For Blues (3)
Valencia (2)

100 PROOF AGED IN SOUL
R&B vocal trio from Detroit: Steve Mancha, Joe Stubbs and Eddie Anderson. Stubbs is the brother of Levi Stubbs (of the **Four Tops**).   '71

DEBUT	PEAK	WKS			Album Title			$	Label & Number
12/12/70+	151	7			Somebody's Been Sleeping In My Bed			$20	Hot Wax 704

Age Ain't Nothing But A Number Backtrack
Ain't That Lovin' You (For More Reasons Than One)
I Can't Sit And Wait (Til Johnny Comes Marching Home)
I've Come To Save You
Love Is Sweeter (The Second Time Around)
Not Enough Love To Satisfy
One Man's Leftovers (Is Another Man's Feast) 96
She's Not Just Another Woman
Somebody's Been Sleeping 8
Too Many Cooks (Spoil The Soup) 94

1NC
Gospel group from Dallas: Markita Knight, Jana Bell, Ashley Guilbert, Sheila Ingram, Brandon Kizer, Nate Larson, Frank Lawson, Nate Young and Myron Butler. 1NC: One Nation Crew.   '00

DEBUT	PEAK	WKS		CD	Album Title			$	Label & Number
9/2/00	58	10		©	Kirk Franklin Presents 1NC			$10	B-Rite 90325

Be Like Him
Breath Away
Could've Been Me
Donna
Free
Hands Up
I Can't Live Without You
In Your Grace
Lost Hearts
Movin' On
Nobody
Unconditional
When You Fall

112
R&B group from Atlanta: Daron Jones (keyboards), Marvin Scandrick (strings), Mike Keith (keyboards) and Quinnes Parker (drums). All share lead vocals. Group name pronounced: One Twelve.   '01

DEBUT	PEAK	WKS	RIAA	CD	#	Album Title		$	Label & Number
9/14/96	37	55	▲²	©	1	112		$10	Bad Boy 73009
11/28/98	20	53	▲²	©	2	Room 112		$10	Bad Boy 73021
4/7/01	2¹	26↑	▲	©	3	Part III		$10	Bad Boy 73039

All I Want Is You (3)
All My Love (2)
Anywhere (2) 15
Be With You (2)
Call My Name (1)
Can I Touch You (1)
Caught Up (3)
Come See Me (1) 33
Crazy Over You (2)
Cupid (1) 13
Dance With Me (3)
Do What You Gotta Do (3)
Don't Hate Me (3)
For Awhile (2)
Funny Feelings (2)
I Can't Believe (1)
I Think (3)
I Will Be There (1)
In Love With You (1)
It's Over Now (3)
Just A Little While (1)
Keep It Real (1)
Love Me (2) 17
Love You Like I Did (2)
Missing You (3)
Never Mind (2)
Now That We're Done (1)
Only One (2)
Only You (1) 13
Peaches & Cream (3)
Player (3)
Pleasure & Pain (1)
Sexy You (1)
Smile (3)
Someone To Hold (2)
Stay With Me (2)
Still In Love (3)
Sweet Love (3)
This Is Your Day (1)
Throw It All Away (1)
Whatcha Gonna Do (3)
Why (1)
Why Does (1)
Your Letter (2)

ONE WAY
R&B group from Detroit: Al Hudson (vocals), Dave Roberson (guitar), Kevin McCord (bass) and Greg Green (drums).   '82

DEBUT	PEAK	WKS			#	Album Title		$	Label & Number
11/17/79	181	5			1	One Way Featuring Al Hudson		$12	MCA 3178
8/2/80	128	12			2	One Way Featuring Al Hudson		$12	MCA 5127
3/7/81	157	8			3	Love Is...One Way		$12	MCA 5163
9/26/81	79	19			4	Fancy Dancer		$12	MCA 5247
4/3/82	51	23			5	Who's Foolin' Who		$12	MCA 5279
8/20/83	164	6			6	Shine On Me		$12	MCA 5428
5/26/84	58	20			7	Lady		$12	MCA 5470
8/10/85	156	9			8	Wrap Your Body		$12	MCA 5552

Age Ain't Nothing But A Number (5)
All Over Again (3)
Be Serious (3)
Believe In Me (8)
Bring It Down (6)
Burn It (4)
Can't Get Enough Of Your Love (7)
Come Dance With Me (1)
Come Give Me Your Love (4)
Condemned (8)
Copy This (2)
Cutie Pie (5) 61
Didn't You Know It (6)
Do Your Thang (2)
Don't Give Up On Love (8)
Don't Stop (7)
Dynomite (7)
Get It Over (3)
Get Up (4)
Give Me One More Chance (5)
Guess You Didn't Know (1)
He Is My Friend (4)
Hold It (4)
I Am Under Your Spell (1)
I Didn't Mean To Break Your Heart (3)
I Wanna Be With You (2)
I'll Make It Up To You (7)
I'm In Love With Lovin' You (2)
If I Knew (8)
If Only You Knew (7)
Lady Iou (4)
Let's Get Together (6)
Let's Go Out Tonite (2)
Let's Talk (8)
Love Is (3)
More Than Friends, Less Than Lovers (8)
Mr. Groove (7)
Music (1)
My Lady (3)
Now That I Found You (1)
Pop It (2)
Pull Fancy Dancer/Pull (4)
Push (3)
Runnin' Away (5)
Serving It (8)
Shake It Till It's Tight (6)
Shine On Me (6)
Show Me (4)
Smile (7)
So Afraid It's Over (6)
Something In The Past (2)
Sugar Rock (6)
Sweet Lady (5)
Together Forever (6)
Wait Until Tomorrow (3)
Who's Foolin' Who (5)
Wrap Your Body (8)
You (5)
You Can Do It (1)
You're So Very Special (5)
You're The One (2)
Your Love Is All I Need (4)

ONO, Yoko
Born on 2/18/33 in Tokyo. Moved to New York at age 14. Avant-garde artist/poet in the late 1960s. Married **John Lennon** in Gibraltar on 3/20/69.   '80

DEBUT	PEAK	WKS	RIAA	CD	#	Album Title		$	Label & Number
2/6/71	182	3		©	1	Yoko Ono/Plastic Ono Band		$25	Apple 3373
11/13/71	199	2		©	2	Fly		$30	Apple 3380 [2]
2/24/73	193	4		©	3	Approximately Infinite Universe		$30	Apple 3399 [2]
12/6/80	❶⁸	74	▲³	©	4	Double Fantasy		$15	Geffen 2001

JOHN LENNON & YOKO ONO
7 songs by Lennon, 7 by Ono; 1981 Grammy winner: Album of the Year

DEBUT	PEAK	WKS		CD	#	Album Title		$	Label & Number
6/27/81	49	9		©	5	Season Of Glass		$12	Geffen 2004
12/25/82+	98	13		©	6	It's Alright (I See Rainbows)		$10	Polydor 6364
2/11/84	11	19	●	©	7	Milk and Honey		$12	Polydor 817160

JOHN LENNON & YOKO ONO
6 songs by Lennon, 6 by Ono; recorded in 1980

Air Male (Tone Deaf Jam) (2)
Air Talk (3)
Aos (1)
Approximately Infinite Universe (3)
Beautiful Boys (4)
Catman (The Rosies Are Coming) (3)
Death Of Samantha (3)
Dogtown (3)
Don't Be Scared (7)
Don't Count The Waves (3)
Don't Worry Kyoko (3)
Dream Love (6)
Even When You're Far Away (5)
Every Man Has A Woman Who Loves Him (4)
Extension 33 (5)
Fly (2)
Give Me Something (4)
Goodbye Sadness (5)
Greenfield Morning I Pushed An Empty Baby Carriage All Over The City (1)
Hard Times Are Over (4)
Have You Seen A Horizon Lately (3)
Hirake (2)
I Don't Know Why (5)
I Felt Like Smashing My Face In A Clear Glass Window (3)
I Have A Woman Inside My Soul (3)
I See Rainbows (6)
I Want My Love To Rest Tonight (3)
I'm Moving On (4)
I'm Your Angel (4)
Is Winter Here To Stay? (3)
It's Alright (3)
Kiss Kiss Kiss (4)
Kite Song (3)
Let Me Count The Ways (7)
Let The Tears Dry (6)
Loneliness (6)
Looking Over From My Hotel Window (3)
Midsummer New York (2)
Mind Holes (3)
Mindtrain (2)

DEBUT	PEAK	WKS	RIAA	CD	ARTIST — Album Title	Catalog	Sym	$	Label & Number

ONO, Yoko — Cont'd

Mindweaver (5)
Mother Of The Universe (5)
Move On Fast (3)
Mrs. Lennon (2)
My Man (6)
Never Say Goodbye (6)
No, No, No (5)
Nobody Sees Me Like You Do (5)

Now Or Never (3)
O'Sanity (7)
O'Wind (Body Is The Scar Of Your Mind) (2)
Paper Shoes (1)
Peter The Dealer (5)
She Gets Down On Her Knees (5)
Shiranakatta (I Didn't Know) (3)

Silver Horse (5)
Sleepless Night (7)
Song For John (3)
Spec Of Dust (1)
Telephone Piece (2)
Toilet Piece (medley) (2)
Tomorrow May Never Come (6)
Touch Me (1)
Toyboat (5)

Turn Of The Wheel (5)
Unknown (medley) (2)
Waiting For The Sunrise (3)
Wake Up (6)
What A Bastard The World Is (3)
What A Mess (3)
What Did I Do! (3)
Why (1)

Why Not (1)
Will You Touch Me (5)
Winter Song (3)
Yang Yang (3)
You (2)
You're The One (7)
Your Hands (7)

ONYX   '98

Rap group from Jamaica, New York: **Fredro Starr**, Kirk "**Sticky Fingaz**" Jones, Chylow Parker and Tyrone Taylor. Starr acted in several movies.

DEBUT	PEAK	WKS		CD				$	Label & Number
4/17/93	17	37	▲ ©	1	Bacdafucup			$10	Def Jam 53302
11/11/95	22	6	©	2	All We Got Iz Us			$10	Def Jam 529265
6/20/98	10	10	©	3	Shut 'Em Down			$10	Def Jam 536988

All We Got Iz Us (Evil Streets) (2)
Atak Of Da Bal-Hedz (1)
Betta Off Dead (2)
Bichasniguz (1)
Blac Vagina Finda (1)
Black Dust (3)

Broke Willies (3)
Conspiracy (3)
Da Nex Niguz (2)
Face Down (3)
Fuck Dat (3)
Getto Mentalitee (3)
Ghetto Starz (3)

Here 'N' Now (1)
Last Dayz (2) *89*
Live Niguz (2)
Most Def (2)
Nigga Bridges (1)
Onyx Is Here (1)
Overshine (3)

Phat ('N' All Dat) (1)
Punkmotherfukaz (2)
Purse Snatchaz (2)
Raze It Up (3)
React (3)
Rob & Vic (3)
Shifftee (1) *92*

Shout (2)
Shut 'Em Down (3)
Slam (1) *4*
Stik 'N' Muve (1)
Street Nigguz (3)
Take That (3)
Throw Ya Gunz (1) *81*

2 Wrongs (2)
Veronica (3)
Walk In New York (2)
Worst, The (3)

OPUS   '86

Pop-rock group from Austria: Herwig Rudisser (vocals), Ewald Pfleger (guitar), Kurt Rene Plisnier (keyboards), Niki Gruber (bass) and Gunter Grasmuck (drums).

DEBUT	PEAK	WKS		CD				$	Label & Number
3/1/86	64	16	©		Up And Down			$10	Polydor 827952

Again And Again
End Of The Show

Flyin' High
Live Is Life *32*

No Job
Opuspocus

Positive
She Loves You

Up And Down
Vivian

ORB   '97

Electronic trio: LX Paterson, Andy Hughes and Thomas Fehlmann.

DEBUT	PEAK	WKS		CD				$	Label & Number
3/29/97	174	1	©		Orblivion		[I]	$10	Island 524347

Asylum
Bedouin

Delta MK II
Log Of Deadwood

Molten Love
Passing Of Time

Pi
S.A.L.T.

Secrets
72

Toxygene
Ubiquity

★254★ ORBISON, Roy   '89

Born on 4/23/36 in Vernon, Texas. Died of a heart attack on 12/6/88 (age 52). Pop-rock singer/songwriter/guitarist. Wife Claudette killed in a motorcycle accident on 6/7/66; two sons died in a fire in 1968. Inducted into the Rock and Roll Hall of Fame in 1987. Member of the **Traveling Wilburys**.

1)Mystery Girl 2)Roy Orbison's Greatest Hits 3)More Of Roy Orbison's Greatest Hits

DEBUT	PEAK	WKS		CD		ARTIST — Album Title	Sym	$	Label & Number
4/7/62	21	31	©	1	Crying		$150	Monument 4007
9/1/62	13	140	● ©	2	Roy Orbison's Greatest Hits	[G]	$50	Monument 4009
8/17/63	35	23	©	3	In Dreams	[G]	$50	Monument 18003
8/22/64	19	30		4	More Of Roy Orbison's Greatest Hits	[G]	$50	Monument 18024
10/17/64	101	11		5	Early Orbison	[K]	$50	Monument 18023
9/4/65	55	17		6	There Is Only One Roy Orbison		$40	MGM 4308
11/6/65+	136	11		7	Orbisongs	[K]	$40	Monument 18035
3/5/66	128	3		8	The Orbison Way		$40	MGM 4322
8/13/66	94	9		9	The Very Best Of Roy Orbison	[G]	$40	Monument 18045
6/21/86	87	12	©	10	Class Of '55 (Memphis Rock & Roll Homecoming)....C:#13/2		$10	America Smash 830002

CARL PERKINS/JERRY LEE LEWIS/ROY ORBISON/JOHNNY CASH

1/7/89	95	15	● ©	11	In Dreams: The Greatest Hits	[K]	$15	Virgin 90604 [2]

contains re-recorded versions of his early hits

1/7/89	110	13	©	12	For The Lonely: A Roy Orbison Anthology, 1956-1965	[G]	$15	Rhino 71493 [2]
2/18/89	5	27	▲ ©	13	Mystery Girl		$10	Virgin 91058
12/2/89	123	12	©	14	A Black And White Night Live	[L-S]	$10	Virgin 91295

ROY ORBISON AND FRIENDS

12/19/92	179	2	©	15	King Of Hearts	[K]	$10	Virgin 86520

unissued and posthumously completed tracks

1/30/93	48^C	1	▲ ©	16	The All-Time Greatest Hits Of Roy Orbison, Volume One	[G]	$10	Monument 44348
4/26/97	186	1	©	17	The Very Best Of Roy Orbison	[G]	$10	Virgin 42350

contains re-recorded versions of his early hits

Afraid To Sleep (6)
After The Love Has Gone (15,17)
(All I Can Do Is) Dream You (13,14)
All I Have To Do Is Dream (3)
Beautiful Dreamer (6)
Big As I Can Dream (6)
Big Train (From Memphis) (10)
Birth Of Rock And Roll (10)
Blue Angel (2,9,11,12,16,17) *9*
Blue Avenue (5)
Blue Bayou (3,4,11,12,14,17) *29*
Borne On The Wind (4)
Breakin' Up Is Breakin' My Heart (8) *31*
Bye Bye Love (5)
California Blue (13,17)
Candy Man (2,9,11,12,14,16) *25*
Careless Heart (13,15)
Class Of '55 (10)
Claudette (6,11,17)

Come Back To Me (My Love) (5)
Comedians, The (13,14)
Coming Home (10,15)
Crawling Back (8) *46*
Crowd, The (2,12) *26*
Cry (5)
Crying (1,2,9,11,12,14,15,16,17) *2*
Dance (1,7)
Devil Doll (12)
Dream (3)
Dream Baby (How Long Must I Dream) (2,9,11,12,14,16,17) *4*
Evergreen (2)
Falling (4,11,12,17) *22*
Go Away (8)
Go! Go! Go! (12)
Goodnight (7,12) *21*
Great Pretender (1,5)
Heartbreak Radio (15)
House Without Windows (3)
I Can't Stop Loving You (5)

I Drove All Night (15,17)
(I Get So) Sentimental (7)
I Will Rock And Roll With You (10)
I'd Be A Legend In My Time (7)
I'll Say It's My Fault (5)
I'm Hurtin' (2,11,12) *27*
I'm In A Blue, Blue Mood (6)
If You Can't Say Something Nice (6)
In Dreams (3,4,9,11,12,14,16,17) *7*
In The Real World (13)
Indian Wedding (4)
It Ain't No Big Thing (8)
It Wasn't Very Long Ago (8)
It's Over (4,9,11,12,14,16,17) *9*
Keep My Motor Running (10)
Lana (1,4,11)
Leah (4,11,12,14,16) *25*
Let The Good Times Roll (7) *81*
Let's Make A Memory (1)
Loneliness (1)

Lonely Wine (3)
Loner, The (8)
Love Hurts (1,5)
Love In Time (15)
Love So Beautiful (13)
Love Star (2)
Mama (8)
Maybe (8)
Mean Woman Blues (4,9,11,12,14,17) *5*
Move On Down The Line (14)
My Prayer (8)
Never (8)
New Star (8)
Nightlife (1,7)
No One Will Ever Know (3)
Oh, Pretty Woman (7,9,11,12,14,17) *1*
Only One (13)
Only The Lonely (Know How I Feel) (2,9,11,12,14,16,17) *2*
Ooby Dooby (11,12,14,17) *59*
Pretty One (5)
Pretty Paper (4,12,17) *15*

Raindrops (5)
Ride Away (6) *25*
Rock And Roll (Fais-Do-Do) (10)
Rockhouse (12)
Running Scared (1,2,9,11,12,14,17) *1*
(Say) You're My Girl (7,12) *39*
Shahdaroba (3)
She Wears My Ring (1,5)
She's A Mystery To Me (13)
Sixteen Candles (10)
Sleepy Hollow (7)
Sugar And Honey (6)
Summer Love (6)
Summer Song (1,5)
Sunset (3)
(They Call You) Gigolette (3)
This Is My Land (8)
This Is Your Song (6)
Time Changed Everything (8)
22 Days (7)
Two Of A Kind (8)
Up Town (2,11,12,14) *72*

Uptown (16)
Waymore's Blues (10)
We Remember The King (10)
We'll Take The Night (15)
Wedding Day (1,7)
What'd I Say (4)
Why Hurt The One Who Loves You (8)
Wild Hearts Run Out Of Time (15)
Windsurfer (5)
Wondering (6)
Workin' For The Man (4,11,12,16) *33*
Yo Te Amo Maria (7)
You Fool You (6)
You Got It (13,17) *9*
You're The One (15)

ORBIT, William '00
Born William Wainwright in England. Techno artist.

| 3/18/00 | 198 | 1 | | © | Pieces In A Modern Style | [I] | | $15 | Maverick 47596 [2] |

Adagio For Strings · Cavalleria Rusticana · In A Landscape · L'Inverno · Ogive Number 1 · Opus 132 · Pavane Pour Une Infante Défunte · Piece In The Old Style 1 · Piece In The Old Style 3 · Triple Concerto · Xerxes

ORBITAL '99
Electronic-dance duo from London: brothers Phil and Paul Hartnoll.

| 6/26/99 | 191 | 1 | | © | The Middle Of Nowhere | | | $10 | London 31065 |

I Don't Know You People · Know Where To Run · Nothing Left 1 & 2 · Otoño · Style · Spare Parts Express · Way Out

ORCHESTRAL MANOEUVRES IN THE DARK '85
Electro-pop group formed in England: keyboardists/vocalists Andrew McCluskey and Paul Humphreys, multi-instrumentalist Martin Cooper and drummer Malcolm Holmes. Humphreys left in 1989.

2/6/82	144	12		©	1 Architecture & Morality			$12	Epic 37721
4/23/83	162	6		©	2 Dazzle Ships			$12	Epic 38543
11/24/84	182	6		©	3 Junk Culture			$10	A&M 5027
7/27/85	38	53		©	4 Crush			$10	A&M 5077
10/18/86	47	23		©	5 The Pacific Age			$10	A&M 5144
3/26/88	46	29	●	©	6 in the dark/the best of OMD	[G]		$10	A&M 5186
7/17/93	169	1		©	7 Liberator			$10	Virgin 88225

ABC (Auto Industry) (2) · Agnus Dei (7) · All Wrapped Up (3) · Apollo (3) · Architecture & Morality (1) · Beginning And The End (1) · Best Years Of Our Lives (7) · Bloc Bloc Bloc (4) · Christine (7) · Crush (4) · Dazzle Ships (2) · Dead Girls (5) · Dollar Girl (7) · Dream Of Me (7) · **Dreaming** (6) *16* · 88 Seconds In Greensboro (4) · Electricity (1) · Enola Gay (6) · Everyday (7) · Flame Of Hope (5) · **(Forever) Live And Die** (5,6) *19* · Genetic Engineering (2) · Georgia (1) · Goddess Of Love (5) · Hard Day (3) · Heaven Is (7) · Hold You (4) · **If You Leave** (6) *4* · International (2) · Joan Of Arc (1,6) · Joan Of Arc (Maid Of Orleans) (1,6) · Junk Culture (3) · King Of Stone (7) · La Femme Accident (4) · Lights Are Going Out (4) · Locomotion (3,6) · Love And Hate You (7) · Love And Violence (3) · Maid Of Orleans ..see: Joan Of Arc · Messages (6) · Native Daughters Of The Golden West (4) · Never Turn Away (3) · New Stone Age (1) · Of All The Things We've Made (2) · Only Tears (7) · Pacific Age (5) · Radio Prague (3) · Radio Waves (2) · Romance Of The Telescope (2) · Sealand (1) · **Secret** (4,6) *63* · Shame (5) · She's Leaving (1) · Silent Running (2) · **So In Love** (4,6) *26* · Southern (1) · Souvenir (1,6) · Stand Above Me (7) · Stay (The Black Rose And The Universal Wheel) (5) · Sunday Morning (7) · Talking Loud And Clear (3,6) · Telegraph (1) · Tesla Girls (3,6) · This Is Helena (2) · Time Zones (2) · Watch Us Fall (5) · We Love You (5) · White Trash (3) · Women III (4)

ORGANIZED KONFUSION '97
Male rap duo from Queens, New York: Troy "**Pharoahe Monch**" Jamerson and Larry "Prince Poetry" Baskerville.

| 9/3/94 | 187 | 1 | | © | 1 Stress: The Extinction Agenda | | | $10 | Hollywood Basic 61406 |
| 10/11/97 | 141 | 1 | | © | 2 The Equinox | | | $10 | Priority 50560 |

Black Sunday (1) · Bring It On (1) · Chuck Chesse (2) · Confrontations (2) · Drop Bombs (1) · Extinction Agenda (1) · Hate (2) · Invetro (2) · Keep It Koming (1) · Let's Organize (1) · Maintain (1) · Move (2) · 9Xs Out Of 10 (2) · Numbers (2) · Questions (2) · Shugah Shorty (2) · Sin (2) · Somehow, Someway (2) · Soundman (2) · Stray Bullet (1) · Stress (1) · They Don't Want It! (2) · Thirteen (2) · 3-2-1 (1) · Why (2)

ORGY '00
Rock group from Los Angeles: Jay Gordon (vocals), Ryan Shuck (guitar), Amir Derakh (keyboards), Paige Haley (bass) and Bobby Hewitt (drums).

| 1/16/99 | 32 | 41 | ▲ | © | 1 Candyass | | | $10 | Elementree 46923 |
| 10/28/00 | 16 | 9 | ● | © | 2 Vapor Transmission | | | $10 | Elementree 47832 |

All The Same (1) · **Blue Monday** (1) *56* · Chasing Sirens (2) · Dissention (1) · Dizzy (1) · Dramatica (2) · Eva (2) · Eyes-Radio-Lies (2) · Fetisha (1) · Fiction (Dreams In Digital) (1) · Fiend (1) · Gender (1) · Odyssey, The (2) · 107 (2) · Opticon (2) · Pantomime (1) · Platinum (1) · Re-Creation (1) · Revival (2) · Saving Faces (2) · Social Enemies (1) · Spectrum (2) · Stitches (1) · Suckerface (2) · Where's Gerrold (2)

ORIGINAL LAST POETS — see LAST POETS, The

ORIGINALS, The '70
R&B vocal group from Detroit: Fred Gorman, Crathman Spencer, Henry Dixon and Walter Gaines.

| 1/17/70 | 174 | 4 | | © | 1 Baby, I'm For Real | | | $40 | Soul 716 |
| 7/11/70 | 198 | 2 | | © | 2 Portrait Of The Originals | | | $30 | Soul 724 |

Aquarius (medley) (2) · **Baby, I'm For Real** (1) *14* · **Bells, The** (2) *12* · Don't Stop Now (2) · Green Grow The Lilacs (1) · I Like Your Style (2) · I'll Wait For You (2) · I've Never Begged Before (1) · Just Another Morning (2) · Let The Sunshine In (The Flesh Failures) (medley) (2) · Love Is A Wonder (1) · Moment Of Truth (1) · My Way (2) · One Life We Live (1) · Red Sails In The Sunset (1) · Since I Fell For You (2) · There's A Place We'd Like To Know (2) · We've Got A Way Out Love (1) · When Will We Learn (1) · Why When Love Is Gone (1) · Wichita Lineman (2) · You May Not Like The Change (2) · You, Mysterious You (1) · You Want Hearts And Flowers (2) · You're The One (1)

ORIGINOO GUNN CLAPPAZ '96
Male rap trio: Starang Wondah, Louieville Sluggah and Top Dog. Members of **Boot Camp Clik**.

| 11/16/96 | 47 | 4 | | © | 1 Da Storm | | | $10 | Duck Down 50577 |
| 9/18/99 | 170 | 1 | | © | 2 The M-Pire Shrikez Back | | | $10 | Duck Down 50116 |

Big Ohh (2) · Boot Camp MFC Eastern Conference (2) · Bounce To The Ounce (2) · Calm Before Da Storm (1) · Da Storm (1) · Danjer (1) · Dirtiest Players In The Game (2) · Elements Of Da Storm (1) · Elite Fleet (1) · Flappin (1) · Girlz Ninety Now (2) · God Don't Like Ugly (1) · Gunn Clapp (1) · Hurricane Starang (1) · If You Feel Like I Feel (2) · M-Pire Shrikez Back (2) · No Fear (1) · Set Sail (2) · Shit Happens (2) · Shoot To Kill (2) · Slo Mo (2) · Sometimey (2) · Suspect Niggaz (2) · Wild Cowboys In Bucktown (1) · X-unknown (1) · You're Not Sure To See Tomorrow (2)

ORION THE HUNTER '84
Rock group formed in Boston: Fran Cosmo (vocals), **Barry Goudreau** (guitar), Bruce Smith (bass) and Michael DeRosier (drums). Goudreau was a member of **Boston** and **RTZ**. Cosmo joined **Boston** in 1994.

| 5/19/84 | 57 | 14 | | © | Orion The Hunter | | | $15 | Portrait 39239 |

All Those Years · Dark And Stormy · Dreamin' · Fast Talk · I Call It Love · Joanne · **So You Ran** *58* · Stand Up · Too Much In Love

ORLANDO, Tony — see DAWN

ORLEANS '75

Rock group founded in New York City by **John Hall** with the Hoppen brothers (Lawrence and Lance), Wells Kelly and Jerry Marotta. Hall and Marotta left in 1977, replaced by Bob Leinbach and R.A. Martin. Kelly died on 10/29/84 (age 35).

3/29/75	33	32			1 Let There Be Music			$15	Asylum 1029
8/28/76	30	16			2 Waking And Dreaming			$15	Asylum 1070
5/5/79	76	13			3 Forever			$12	Infinity 9006

Bum, The (2)
Business As Usual (1)
Cold Spell (1)
Dance With Me (1) *6*
Don't Throw Our Love Away (3)
Ending Of A Song (1)

Everybody Needs Some Music (3)
Flame And The Moth (3)
Forever (3)
Fresh Wind (1)
Give One Heart (1)

Golden State (2)
I Never Wanted To Love You (3)
If I Don't Have You (2)
Isn't It Easy (1)
Keep On Rollin' (3)

Let There Be Music (1) *55*
Love Takes Time (3) *11*
Path, The (2)
Reach (2) *51*
Sails (1)
Slippin' Away (3)

Spring Fever (2)
Still The One (2) *5*
Time Passes On (1)
Waking And Dreaming (2)
What I Need (2)
You've Given Me Something (1)

Your Life My Friend (1)

ORLONS, The '62

R&B vocal group from Philadelphia: Rosetta Hightower, Marlena Davis, Steve Caldwell and Shirley Brickley. Brickley was shot to death on 10/13/77 (age 32).

| 9/1/62 | 80 | 10 | | | 1 The Wah-Watusi | | | $75 | Cameo 1020 |
| 7/6/63 | 123 | 5 | | | 2 South Street | | | $75 | Cameo 1041 |

Between 18th & 19th On
  Chestnut Street (2)
Big Daddy (2)
Cement Mixer (2)
Charlie Brown (2)

Dedicated To The One I Love
  (1)
Don't Let Go (2)
Gather 'Round (2)
Gravy (For My Mashed
  Potatoes) (1)

(Happy Birthday) Mr.
  Twenty-One (1)
He's Gone (1)
I Met Him On A Sunday (Ronde
  Ronde) (2)
I'll Be True (1)

Let Me In (1)
Mashed Potato Time (1)
Mister Sandman (2)
Muskrat Ramble (2)
Over The Mountain, Across The
  Sea (1)

Plea, The (1)
Pokey Lou (2)
South Street (2) *3*
Tonight (1)
Wah Watusi (1) *2*
Walk Right In (2)

We Got Love (2)

ORMANDY, Eugene — see PHILADELPHIA ORCHESTRA

ORPHEUS '68

Soft-rock group from Boston: Bruce Arnold (vocals, guitar), Jack McKenes (guitar), John Eric Gulliksen (bass) and Harry Sandler (drums).

3/9/68	119	14			1 Orpheus			$25	MGM 4524
9/28/68	159	12			2 Ascending			$25	MGM 4569
10/11/69	198	1			3 Joyful			$25	MGM 4599

As They All Fall (3)
Borneo (2)
Brown Arms In Houston
  (3) *91*
By The Size Of My Shoes (1)
Can't Find The Time (1) *80*

Congress Alley (1)
Don't Be So Serious (2)
Door Knob Song (1)
Dream, The (1)
I Can Make The Sun Rise (3)
I'll Fly (2)

I'll Stay With You (1)
I've Never Seen Love Like This
  (1)
Joyful (3)
Just A Little Bit (2)
Just Got Back (2)

Lesley's World (1)
Love Over There (2)
Lovin' You (3)
Magic Air (2)
May I Look At You (3)
Me About You (3)

Mine's Yours (2)
Music Machine (1)
Never In My Life (1)
Of Enlightenment (3)
Roses (2)
She's Not There (2)

So Far Away In Love (2)
To Touch Our Love Again (3)
Walk Away Renee (2)

ORR, Benjamin '87

Born Benjamin Orzechowski on 8/9/47 in Cleveland. Died of cancer on 10/3/2000 (age 53). Bassist/vocalist of **The Cars**.

| 11/8/86+ | 86 | 22 | © | | The Lace | | | $10 | Elektra 60460 |

Hold On
In Circles

Lace, The
Skyline

Spinning
Stay The Night *24*

That's The Way
This Time Around

Too Hot To Stop
When You're Gone

ORRALL, Robert Ellis '83

Born on 5/4/55 in Winthrop, Massachusetts. Singer/songwriter/pianist.

| 4/16/83 | 146 | 9 | | | Special Pain | | [M] | $10 | RCA Victor 8502 |

Facts And Figures
I Couldn't Say No *32*

Senseless
Tell Me If It Hurts

(You've Had) Too Much To
  Think

ORRICO, Stacie '00

Born in 1987 in Seattle. Christian singer.

| 9/16/00 | 103 | 5 | © | | Genuine | | | $10 | Forefront 25253 |

Confidant
Dear Friend
Don't Look At Me

Everything
Genuine
Holdin' On

O.O. Baby
Restore My Soul
Ride

So Pray
Stay True
With A Little Faith

Without Love

ORTON, Beth '99

Born in 1970 in Norwich, Norfolk, England. Female singer/songwriter.

| 3/27/99 | 110 | 11 | © | | Central Reservation | | | $10 | Heavenly 19038 |

Blood Red River
Central Reservation

Couldn't Cause Me Harm
Devil Song

Feel To Believe
Love Like Laughter

Pass In Time
So Much More

Stars All Seem To Weep
Stolen Car

Sweetest Decline

OSBORNE, Jeffrey '84

Born on 3/9/48 in Providence, Rhode Island. R&B singer/songwriter/drummer. Lead singer of **L.T.D.** until 1980.

6/19/82	49	43	©		1 Jeffrey Osborne			$10	A&M 4896
8/6/83+	25	89	● ©		2 Stay With Me Tonight			$10	A&M 4940
10/20/84	39	37	● ©		3 Don't Stop			$10	A&M 5017
6/28/86	26	26	● ©		4 Emotional			$10	A&M 5103
8/27/88	18	16	©		5 One Love-One Dream			$10	A&M 5205
12/15/90+	95	23	©		6 Only Human			$10	Arista 8620
3/4/00	191	1	©		7 That's For Sure			$10	Private Music 82170

Ain't Nothin' Missin' (1)
All Because Of You (5)
All My Money (7)
Baby (1)
Baby Wait A Minute (6)
Back In Your Arms (4)
Borderlines, The (3) *38*
Call My Name (7)
Can't Find An Easy Way (7)
Can't Go Back On A Promise
  (5)
Cindy (5)
Come Midnight (4)
Come With Me (7)

Congratulations (1)
Crazy 'Bout Cha (5)
Don't Stop (3) *44*
Don't You Get So Mad (2) *25*
Eenie Meenie (1) *76*
Emotional (4)
Family, The (5)
Feel Like Making Love (6)
Forever Mine (2)
Getting Better All The Time (6)
Good Things Come To Those
  Who Wait (6)
Greatest Love Affair (2)
Hot Coals (3)

I Really Don't Need No Light
  (1) *39*
I'll Do It All For Love (7)
I'll Make Believe (2)
If My Brother's In Trouble (6)
In Your Eyes (4)
Is It Right (3)
Keepin' (7)
La Cuenta, Por Favor (5)
Lay Your Head (6)
Let Me Know (3)
Live For Today (3)
Love Ballad (7)
Love's Not Ready (4)

Morning After I Made Love To
  You (6)
My Heart Can Wait Forever (5)
New Love (1)
Nitetime (6)
On The Wings Of Love (1) *29*
One Love - One Dream (5)
Only Human (6)
Other Side Of The Coin (2)
Plane Love (2)
Power, The (3)
Ready For Your Love (1)
Room With A View (5)
Second Chance (4)

2nd Time Around (7)
Sending You A Love Song (6)
She's On The Left (5) *48*
Soft And Slow (7)
Soweto (4)
Stay With Me Tonight (2) *30*
That's For Sure (7)
True Believers (5)
Two Wrongs Don't Make A
  Right (2)
Was It Something I Said (7)
We Belong To Love (4)
We're Going All The Way
  (2) *48*

When Are You Comin' Back?
  (2)
Who Would Have Guessed (4)
Who You Talkin' To? (1)
Work That Body (7)
You Can't Be Serious (3)
(You Can't Get) Love From A
  Stone (5)
**You Should Be Mine (The
  Woo Woo Song)** (4) *13*
You Were Made To Love (1)

OSBORNE, Joan '96

Born on 7/8/62 in Anchorage, Kentucky. Singer/songwriter/guitarist.

| 9/9/95+ | 9 | 56 | ▲³ | © | 1 **Relish** .... | | | $10 | Blue Gorilla 526699 |
| 9/30/00 | 90 | 4 | | © | 2 **Righteous Love** .... | | | $10 | Interscope 490737 |

Angel Face (2)　Baby Love (2)　Crazy Baby (1)　Dracula Moon (1)
Grand Illusion (2)　Help Me (1)　Hurricane (2)　If I Was Your Man (2)
Ladder (1)　Let's Just Get Naked (1)　Love Is Alive (2)　Lumina (1)
Make You Feel My Love (2)　Man In The Long Black Coat (1)　One Of Us (1) *4*　Pensacola (1)
Poison Apples (Hallelujah) (2)　Right Hand Man (1)　Righteous Love (2)　Running Out Of Time (2)
Safety In Numbers (2)　Spider Web (1)　St. Teresa (1)

OSBORNE BROTHERS '70

Bluegrass duo of brothers from Hyden, Kentucky: Bobby (born on 12/7/31; mandolin) and Sonny (born on 10/29/37; banjo) Osborne.

| 7/4/70 | 193 | 1 | | | **Ru-beeeee** .... | | | $20 | Decca 75204 |

Fightin' Side Of Me　Let Me Be The First To Know
Listening To The Rain　Mid Night Angel
Put It Off Until Tomorrow　Ruby, Are You Mad
Siempre　Somebody's Back In Town
Tennessee Hound Dog　Thanks For All The Yesterdays
World Of Forgotten People

OSBOURNE, Ozzy ★180★ '95

Born John Osbourne on 12/3/48 in Birmingham, England. Former lead singer of **Black Sabbath**. Controversial in his concert antics. Married his manager Sharon Arden in 1982. Appeared in the 1986 movie *Trick Or Treat*.

1)Ozzmosis 2)The Ultimate Sin 3)Tribute

4/18/81	21	104	▲⁴	©	1 **Blizzard Of Ozz**			$12	Jet 36812
11/21/81	16	73	▲³	©	2 **Diary Of A Madman**			$12	Jet 37492
5/8/82	120	18			3 **Mr. Crowley**	[L-M]		$12	Jet 37640
12/11/82+	14	20	▲	©	4 **Speak Of The Devil**	[L]		$15	Jet 38350 [2]

recorded on 9/26/82 at The Ritz in New York City

12/10/83+	19	29	▲³	©	5 **Bark At The Moon**			$12	CBS Associated 38987
2/15/86	6	39	▲²	©	6 **The Ultimate Sin**			$12	CBS Associated 40026
5/9/87	6	23	▲²	©	7 **Tribute**	[L]		$15	CBS Assoc. 40714 [2]

OZZY OSBOURNE/RANDY RHOADS
live recordings from 1981 featuring Ozzy's guitarist, Randy Rhoads, who was killed in an airplane crash on 3/19/82 (age 25)

10/22/88	13	27	▲²	©	8 **No Rest For The Wicked**			$10	CBS Associated 44245
3/3/90	58	13	●		9 **Just Say Ozzy**	[M]		$10	CBS Associated 45451
8/18/90	163	2		©	10 **Ten Commandments**	[K]		$10	Priority 57129
10/5/91	7	86	▲⁴	©	11 **No More Tears**			$10	Epic/Associated 46795
7/3/93	22	14	▲	©	12 **Live & Loud**	[L]		$15	Epic/Assoc. 48973 [2]
11/11/95	4	44	▲²	©	13 **Ozzmosis**			$10	Epic 67091
11/29/97	13	42	▲²	©	14 **The Ozzman Cometh**	[G]		$15	Epic 67980 [2]

A.V.H. (11)　Back On Earth (14)　Bark At The Moon (5,10,12,14)　Behind The Wall Of Sleep (14)　Believer (4)　Black Sabbath (4,12,14)　Bloodbath In Paradise (8,9)　Breaking All The Rules (8)　Centre Of Eternity (5)　Changes (12)　Children Of The Grave (4,7)　Crazy Babies (8,14)　Crazy Train (1,7,10,12,14)　Dee (1,7)　Demon Alcohol (8)
Denial (13)　Desire (11,12)　Devil's Daughter (8)　Diary Of A Madman (2,10)　Drum Solo (12)　Fairies Wear Boots (4,14)　Fire In The Sky (8)　Flying High Again (2,7,10,12)　Fool Like You (6)　Ghost Behind My Eyes (13)　Goodbye To Romance (1,7,12,14)　Guitar Solo (12)　Hellraiser (11)　I Don't Know (1,7,12)
I Don't Want To Change The World (11,12,14)　I Just Want You (13,14)　Interview with Ozzy 1988 (14)　Iron Man (4,7)　Killer Of Giants (6)　Lightning Strikes (6)　Little Dolls (2,10)　**Mama, I'm Coming Home** (11,12,14) *28*　Miracle Man (8,9,12)　Mr. Crowley (1,3,7,12,14)　Mr. Tinkertrain (11)　My Jekyll Doesn't Hide (13)　My Little Man (13)
N.I.B. (4)　Never (6)　Never Know Why (6)　Never Say Die (4)　No Bone Movies (1,7)　No More Tears (11,12,14) *71*　Now You See It (Now You Don't) (5)　Old L.A. Tonight (13)　Over The Mountain (2,14)　Paranoid (4,7,12,14)　Perry Mason (13)　Revelation (Mother Earth) (1,7)　Road To Nowhere (11,12)　Rock 'N' Roll Rebel (5)
S.A.T.O. (2)　Sabbath, Bloody Sabbath (4)　Secret Loser (6)　See You On The Other Side (13)　**Shot In The Dark** (6,9,10,12,14) *68*　S.I.N. (11)　Slow Down (5)　Snowblind (4)　So Tired (5,10)　Steal Away (The Night) (1,7,10)　Suicide Solution (1,3,7,12)　Sweet Leaf (4,9)　Symptom Of The Universe (4)
Tattooed Dancer (8,9)　Thank God For The Bomb (6,10)　Thunder Underground (13)　Time After Time (11)　Tomorrow (13)　Tonight (2,10)　Ultimate Sin (6)　Waiting For Darkness (5)　War Pigs (4,9,12,14)　Wizard, The (4)　You Can't Kill Rock And Roll (2)　You Said It All (3)　You're No Different (5)　Zombie Stomp (11)

OSIBISA '71

Group formed in London. Core members : Ghana natives Teddy Osei (reeds), Nee Daku "Poatato" Adams (percussion), Mac Tontoh (bass) and Sol Amarfio (drums), with West Indian Wendell Richardson (guitar). Adams died of a heart attack on 1/1/95 (age 59).

7/3/71	55	19		©	1 **Osibisa**			$15	Decca 75285
2/12/72	66	17		©	2 **Wcyaya**			$15	Decca 75327
10/28/72	125	8		©	3 **Heads**			$15	Decca 75368
7/21/73	159	7			4 **Super Fly T.N.T.**	[S]		$12	Buddah 5136
9/28/74	175	4		©	5 **Osibirock**			$12	Warner 2802
4/24/76	200	2		©	6 **Welcome Home**			$12	Island 9355

African Jive (5)　Akwaaba (1)　Atinga Bells (5)　Ayiko Bia (1)　Beautiful 7 (2)　Brotherhood (4)　Che Che Kule (3)　Chooboi (Heave Ho!) (6)
Come Closer (If You're A Man) (4)　Dawn, The (1)　Densu (6)　Do It (Like It Is) (6)　Do You Know (3)　Home Affairs (5)　Kangaroo (5)　Kelele (4,5)
Kokorokoo (3)　Kolomashie (6)　Komfo (High Priest) (5)　La Ila I La La (4)　Mentumi (3)　Move On (2)　Music For Gong Gong (1)　Oranges (1)　Osibirock (5)
Oye Mama (4)　Phallus C (1)　Prophets (4)　Rabiato (2)　Right Now (6)　Seaside - Meditation (6)　So So Mi La So (3)　Spirits Up Above (2)　Sunshine Day (6)
Superfly Man (4)　Survival (2)　Sweet America (3)　Sweet Sounds (3)　T.N.T. (4)　Think About The People (1)　Uhuru (6)　Vicarage, The (4)　Wango Wango (3)
Wcyaya (2)　We Belong (5)　Welcome Home (6)　Who's Got The Paper (5)　Why (5)　Y Sharp (2)　Ye Tie Wo (3)

OSKAR, Lee '76

Born on 3/24/48 in Copenhagen, Denmark. Harmonica player. Member of **War**.

4/3/76	29	24		©	1 **Lee Oskar**	[I]		$12	United Artists 594
9/16/78	86	12		©	2 **Before The Rain**			$12	Elektra 150
8/1/81	162	6		©	3 **My Road Our Road**			$12	Elektra 526

BLT (1) *59*　Before The Rain (2)　Blisters (1)
Children's Song (You Can Find Your Way) (3)　Down The Nile (1)　Feelin' Happy (2)
Haunted House (2)　I Remember Home (A Peasant's Symphony) Medley (1)
More Than Words Can Say (2)　My Road (3)　Our Road Medley (3)　San Francisco Bay (2)
Sing Song (2)　Song For My Son (3)　Starkite (1)　Steppin' (2)
Sunshine Keri (1)　Up All Night (3)　Yes, I'm Singing (3)

OSLIN, K.T.   '88
Born Kay Toinette Oslin on 5/15/41 in Crossett, Arkansas; raised in Mobile, Alabama. Country singer/songwriter.

12/12/87+	68	32 ▲	©	1	80's Ladies	$10	RCA Victor 5924
9/24/88	75	52 ▲	©	2	This Woman	$10	RCA 8369
11/24/90+	76	26 ●	©	3	Love In A Small Town	$10	RCA 2365
5/22/93	126	7	©	4	Greatest Hits: Songs From An Aging Sex Bomb	[G] $10	RCA 66227

Come Next Monday (3,4)
Cornell Crawford (3)
Didn't Expect It To Go Down This Way (2)
Do Ya' (1,4)
Dr., Dr. (1)

80's Ladies (1,4)
Feeding A Hungry Heart (4)
Get Back In The Saddle (4)
Hey Bobby (2,4)
Hold Me (2,4)
I'll Always Come Back (1,4)

Jealous (1,4)
Lonely But Only For You (1)
Love Is Strange (3)
Mary And Willi (3)
Momma Was A Dancer (3)
Money (2)

New Way Home (3,4)
Old Pictures (1)
Oo-Wee (3)
Round The Clock Lovin' (4)
Still On My Mind (3)
This Woman (2,4)

Truly Blue (2)
Two Hearts (1,3)
Wall Of Tears (1)
Where Is A Woman To Go (2)
You Call Everybody Darling (3)
You Can't Do That (4)

Younger Men (1)

★292★   OSMOND, Donny   '72
Born on 12/9/57 in Ogden, Utah. Lead singer of **The Osmonds**. Brother of **Marie Osmond** and **Little Jimmy Osmond**. Starred in the stage musical *Joseph and The Amazing Technicolor Dreamcoat*.
  1)*Portrait Of Donny* 2)*Too Young* 3)*To You With Love, Donny*

7/10/71	13	37 ●		1	The Donny Osmond Album	$15	MGM 4782
11/6/71	12	33 ●		2	To You With Love, Donny	$15	MGM 4797
5/27/72	6	36 ●		3	Portrait Of Donny	$15	MGM 4820
7/22/72	11	30 ●		4	Too Young	$15	MGM 4854
12/16/72+	29	20 ●		5	My Best To You	[G] $15	MGM 4872
3/24/73	26	29		6	Alone Together	$15	MGM 4886
12/8/73+	58	13		7	A Time For Us	$15	MGM 4930
12/7/74+	57	17		8	Donny	$15	MGM 4978
8/21/76	145	8		9	Disco Train	$12	Polydor 6067
9/3/77	169	5		10	Donald Clark Osmond	$12	Polydor 6109
5/13/89	54	23	©	11	Donny Osmond	$10	Capitol 92354
11/17/90	177	2	©	12	Eyes Don't Lie	$10	Capitol 94051
11/21/98+	20ˣ	4	©	13	Christmas At Home	C:#50/1 [X] $10	Epic/Legacy 65780
					Christmas charts: 37/'98, 20/'99		
2/24/01	64	6	©	14	This Is The Moment	$10	Decca 013052
					collection of songs from Broadway musicals		

After December Slips Away (13)
All I Have To Do Is Dream (3)
Angels We Have Heard On High (13)
Are You Lonesome Tonight (7) *14*
At The Edge Of The World (14)
Baby, What You Goin' To Be? (13)
Before It's Too Late (12)
Big Man (3)
Boy Is Waiting (7)
Burning Bridges (1)
Bye Bye Love (2)
C'mon Marianne (9) *38*
Come To The Manger (13)
Deck The Halls (medley) (13)
Disco Dancin' (9)
Disco Train (9)
Divine (medley) (13)
Do You Want Me (6)
  (*also see: We Can Make It Together*)
Don't Need No Money (9)
Don't Say No (1)
Donna (4)
Eyes Don't Lie (12)
Faces In The Mirror (11)
Flirtin' (1)
Fly Into The Wind (10)

Give My Regards To Broadway (14)
Go Away Little Girl (2,5) *1*
God Rest Ye Merry Gentlemen (13)
Going Going Gone (To Somebody Else) (3)
Groove (11)
Guess Who (7)
Hark The Herald Angels Sing (medley) (13)
Hawaiian Wedding Song (Ke Kali Nei Au) (7)
Hey Girl (3,5) *9*
Hey Little Girl (1)
Hey Little Johnny (2)
Hey There, Lonely Girl (3)
Hold On (11) *73*
I Believe (7)
I Can't Put My Finger On It (9)
I Can't Stand It (10)
I Discovered You, You Discovered Me (7)
I Follow The Music (Disco Donny) (9)
I Got Your Lovin' (9)
I Have A Dream (8) *50*
I Haven't Had A Heartache All Day (10)
I Knew You When (2,5) *flip*

I Know The Truth (14)
I'll Be Good To You (11)
I'll Be Home For Christmas (13)
I'm Dyin' (8)
I'm Into Something Good (2)
I'm So Lonesome I Could Cry (8)
I'm Sorry (10)
I'm Your Puppet (1,5)
I've Been Looking For Christmas (13)
I've Got Plans For You (3)
If It's Love That You Want (11)
If Someone Ever Breaks Your Heart (8)
Immortality (14)
Inner Rhythm (11)
It Takes A Lot Of Love (6)
It's Hard To Say Goodbye (6)
It's Possible (14)
It's The Most Wonderful Time Of The Year (13)
Just Between You And Me (12)
Kid In Me (13)
Last Of The Red Hot Lovers (4)
Let My People Go (13)
Life Is Just What You Make It (6)
Little Bit (2)
Little Bit Me, A Little Bit You (2)

Lollipops, Lace And Lipstick (1)
Lonely Boy (4,5) *flip*
Love Me (3)
Love Will Survive (12)
Make It Last Forever (12)
Mary, Did You Know? (13)
Million To One (7) *23*
Mona Lisa (8)
More I Live (More I Love) (10)
My Grown-Up Christmas List (13)
My Love Is A Fire (12) *21*
My Secret Touch (11)
Never Gonna Let You Go (9)
Never Too Late For Love (12)
No Matter What (14)
Not While I'm Around (14)
O Holy Night (medley) (13)
Oh, It Must Be Love (10)
Old Man Auctioneer (9)
Only Heaven Knows (11)
Other Side Of Me (6)
Our Kind Of Love (14)
Ours (8)
Pretty Blue Eyes (4)
Private Affair (12)
Promise Me (3)
Puppy Love (3,5) *3*
Reachin' For The Feeling (9)

Run To Him (4)
Sacred Emotion (11) *13*
Seasons Of Love (14)
Sit Down, I Think I Love You (2)
Sixteen Candles (8)
So Shy (1)
Soldier Of Love (11) *2*
Soldier's King (13)
Solla Sollew (14)
Standin' In The Need Of Love (2)
Sunshine Rose (6)
Sure Lookin' (12) *54*
Sweet And Innocent (1,5) *7*
Swingin' City Gal (9)
Take Another Try (At Love) (12)
Take Good Care Of My Baby (4)
Tears On My Pillow (6)
Teenager In Love (4)
This Guy's In Love With You (3)
This Is The Moment (14)
This Time (8)
Time For Us (7)
To Run Away (4)
Too Young (4,5) *13*
Twelfth Of Never (6) *8*
Unchained Melody (7)
Wake Up, Little Susie (1)

We Can Make It Together (Do You Want Me?) (2,5)
  (*also see: Do You Want Me*)
What's He Doing In My World (8)
When I Fall In Love (7) *55*
Where Did All The Good Times Go (8)
Who Can I Turn To (When Nobody Needs Me) (6)
Who Took The Merry Out Of Christmas? (13)
Why (4,5) *13*
Wild Rover (Time To Ride) (1)
You Are The Music In My Life (10)
You'll Be Glad (10)
You've Got A Friend In Me (14)
You've Got Me Dangling On A String (10)
Young And In Love (7)
Young Love (6) *25*

OSMOND, Donny And Marie   '74
Brother-and-sister co-hosts of own musical/variety TV series and later of own daytime talk show. Starred in the movie *Goin' Coconuts*.

9/7/74	35	30 ●		1	I'm Leaving It All Up To You	$15	MGM 4968
6/28/75	133	6		2	Make The World Go Away	$15	MGM 4996
4/3/76	60	38 ●		3	Donny & Marie - Featuring Songs From Their Television Show	$12	Polydor 6068
11/27/76+	85	14 ●		4	Donny & Marie - New Season	$12	Polydor 6083
1/7/77	99	12		5	Winning Combination	$12	Polydor 6127
11/11/78	98	8 ●		6	Goin' Coconuts	[S] $12	Polydor 6169
					4 of 12 songs are from the movie (starring Donny and Marie)		

"A" My Name Is Alice (3)
Ain't Nothing Like The Real Thing (2) *21*
Angel Love (Heaven Is Where You Are) (5)
Anytime Sunshine (4)
Baby, I'm Sold On You (5)
Baby, Now That I've Found You (6)
Best Of Me (5)
Butterfly (3)
C'mon Marianne (3) *38*
Dandelion (3)

Day Late And A Dollar Short (1)
Deep Purple (3) *14*
Doctor Dancin' (4)
Don't Play With The One Who Loves You (6)
Everything Good Reminds Me Of You (1)
Fallin' In Love Again (6)
Gimme Some Time (6)
Gone (3)
Hold Me, Thrill Me, Kiss Me (4)
I Can't Do Without You (5)
I Want To Be In Your World (5)

I Want To Give You My Everything (5)
I Will (2)
I'm Leaving It (All) Up To You (1) *4*
It Takes Two (1,3)
It's All Been Said Before (4)
It's All In The Game (2)
Jigsaw (3)
Let It Be Me (1)
Let's Fall In Love (6)
Little Bit Country, A Little Bit Rock 'N Roll (3)

Living On My Suspicion (2)
Make The World Go Away (2) *44*
Mama Didn't Lie (2)
May Tomorrow Be A Perfect Day (3,6)
Morning Side Of The Mountain (1) *8*
Now We're Together (4)
Oh, Sweet Lovin' (5)
On The Shelf (6) *38*
One Of These Days (2)
Show Me (4)

Sing (4)
Sunshine Lady (3)
Sure Would Be Nice (5)
Take Me Back Again (1,3)
Together (2)
True Love (1)
Umbrella Song (1)
We Got Love (4)
Weeping Willow (3)
When Somebody Cares For You (2)
(When You're) Young And In Love (2)

Which Way You Goin' Billy (4)
Winning Combination (5)
You Bring Me Sunshine (6)
You Broke My Heart (4)
You Don't Have To Say You Love Me (6)
You Never Can Tell (6)
You Remind Me (5)
(You're My) Soul And Inspiration (5) *38*

OSMOND, Little Jimmy '73
Born on 4/16/63 in Canoga Park, California. Youngest of **The Osmonds**.

| 12/2/72+ | 105 | 14 | | | Killer Joe .... | | | $15 | MGM 4855 |

| If My Dad Were President | Let Me Be Your Teddy Bear | **Long Haired Lover From** | Mama'd Know What To Do | My Girl | **Tweedlee Dee** 59 |
| Killer Joe | Little Girls Are Fun | **Liverpool** 38 | Mother Of Mine | Rubber Ball | |

OSMOND, Marie '73
Born Olive Marie Osmond on 10/13/59 in Ogden, Utah. Sister of **The Osmonds**. Co-hosted the TV series *Ripley's Believe It Or Not* (1985-86). Played "Julia Wallace" on the TV series *Maybe This Time* (1995).

9/22/73	59	23			1 Paper Roses			$15	MGM 4910
7/20/74	164	9			2 In My Little Corner Of The World			$15	MGM 4944
3/8/75	152	6			3 Who's Sorry Now			$15	MGM 4979
4/30/77	152	6			4 This Is The Way That I Feel			$12	MGM 4910

All He Did Was Tell Me Lies (To Try To Woo Me) (4)
Among My Souvenirs (3)
Anytime (3)
Big Hurts Can Come (From Little White Lies) (2)
Clinging Vine (3)
Crazy Arms (2)
Cry, Baby, Cry (4)

Didn't I Love You, Boy? (4)
Everybody's Somebody's Fool (2)
Everything Is Beautiful (1)
Fool No. 1 (1)
I Love You Because (2)
I Love You So Much It Hurts (2)
In My Little Corner Of The World (2)

Invisible Tears (2)
It's Just The Other Way Around (2)
It's Such A Pretty World Today (1)
It's The Little Things (3)
Jealous Heart (3)
Least Of All You (1)
Louisiana Bayou (1)

Love Letters In The Sand (3)
Making Believe (3)
Miss You Nights (4)
Paper Roses (1) 5
Play The Music Loud (4)
Please Tell Him That I Said Hello (4)
Run To Me (4)
Singing The Blues (3)

Sweet Dreams (1)
Things I Tell My Pillow (3)
This I Promise You (3)
This Is The Way That I Feel (4) 39
Too Many Rivers (1)
True Love Lasts Forever (4)
True Love's A Blessing (4)
Where Did Our Love Go (4)

Who's Sorry Now (3) 40
You're My Superman (You're My Everything) (4)
You're The Only World I Know (1)

★380★ OSMONDS, The '72
Family group from Ogden, Utah. Alan (born on 6/22/49), Wayne (born on 8/28/51), Merrill (born on 4/30/53), Jay (born on 3/2/55) and **Donny Osmond**. Regulars on **Andy Williams**'s TV show from 1962-67.
1)Phase-III 2)The Osmonds "Live" 3)Osmonds

1/30/71	14	43	●		1 Osmonds			$15	MGM 4724
6/26/71	22	34	●		2 Homemade			$15	MGM 4770
1/29/72	10	35	●		3 Phase-III			$15	MGM 4796
6/17/72	13	29	●		4 The Osmonds "Live"		[L]	$20	MGM 4826 [2]
10/14/72	14	22	●		5 Crazy Horses			$15	MGM 4851
7/7/73	58	20			6 The Plan			$15	MGM 4902
11/2/74	47	14			7 Love Me For A Reason			$15	MGM 4939
8/30/75	160	5			8 The Proud One			$15	MGM 4993
12/20/75+	148	8			9 Around The World - Live In Concert		[L]	$20	MGM 5012 [2]
10/23/76	145	6			10 Brainstorm			$12	Polydor 6077
12/18/76+	127	5			11 The Osmond Christmas Album		[X]	$15	Polydor 8001 [2]
1/14/78	192	3			12 The Osmonds Greatest Hits		[G]	$15	Polydor 9005 [2]

Ain't Nothing Like The Real Thing (12) 21
And You Love Me (5)
Are You Lonesome Tonight? (9,12) 14
Are You Up There? (7)
At The Rainbows End (10)
Back On The Road Again (10,12)
Ballin' The Jack (7)
Before The Beginning (medley) (6)
Big Finish (5)
Blue Christmas (11)
Boogie Down (10)
Business (3)
Caroling Medley (11)
Carrie (2)
Catch Me Baby (1)
Check It Out (10)
Chilly Winds (2)
Christmas Medley (11)
Christmas Waltz (11)
C'mon Marianne (12) 38
Crazy Horses (5,9,12) 14
Darlin' (6)
Don't Panic (3)
Don't Take It Too Easy (6)
Double Lovin' (2,4) 14
Down By The Lazy River (3,4,9,12) 4

Everytime I Feel The Spirit (medley) (4)
Feelin' All Right (9)
Fever (7)
50's Medley (9)
Find 'Em, Fool 'Em And Forget 'Em (1)
Flirtin' (1)
Free (medley) (4)
Frightened Eyes (8)
Gabrielle (7)
Girl (5)
Girl I Love (7,9)
Go Away Little Girl (4,9,12) 1
Goin' Home (6,12) 36
Gotta Get Love (10)
Having A Party (7)
He Ain't Heavy...He's My Brother (1)
He's The Light Of The World (3)
Hey Girl (4)
Hey Love Me Over (medley) (9)
Hey, Mr. Taxi (5)
Hold Her Tight (5,9,12) 14
Honey Bee Song (2)
I Can See Love In You And Me (7)
I Can't Get Next To You, Babe (4,7,9)
I Can't Live A Dream (10) 46
I Got A Woman (medley) (4)

I'll Be Home For Christmas (11)
I'm Gonna Make You Love Me (medley) (4)
I'm Leaving It (All) Up To You (9,12) 4
I'm Sorry (6)
I'm Still Gonna Need You (8)
If Santa Were My Daddy (11)
If You're Gonna Leave Me (2)
In The Rest Of My Life (3)
It Never Snows In L.A. (11)
It Takes Two (medley) (9)
It'll Be Me (10)
It's All Up To You (6)
It's Alright (6)
It's Beginning To Look A Lot Like Christmas (medley) (11)
It's Your Babe (3)
Julie (5)
Kay Thompson's Jingle Bells (11)
Kind Of A Woman That A Man Wants (8)
Last Day Is Coming (8)
Last Days (6)
Learnin' How To Love Again (10)
Let It Snow! Let It Snow! Let It Snow! (11)
Let Me In (6,12) 36
Life Is Hard Enough Without Goodbyes (2)

Lonesome They Call Me, Lonesome I Am (1)
Long Haired Lover From Liverpool (9,12) 38
Love Is (3)
Love Me For A Reason (7,9,12) 10
Make The World Go Away (9)
Medicine Man (10)
Merrill's Banjo Medley (9)
Mirror, Mirror (9)
Mona Lisa (9)
Morning Side Of The Mountain (9,12) 8
Most Of All (1)
Motown Special (1,4)
Movie Man (medley) (6)
Music Makin' (medley) (9)
My Drum (3)
My World Is Empty Without You (medley) (4)
Never Can Say Goodbye (medley) (9)
Old Fashioned Christmas (11)
One Bad Apple (1,4,12) 1
One Way Ticket To Anywhere (6)
Paper Roses (9,12) 5
Peace (7)
Pine Cones And Holly Berries (medley) (11)
Promised Land (2)

Proud Mary (medley) (4)
Proud One (8,9) 22
Puppy Love (9,12) 3
Send A Little Love (7)
She Makes Me Warm (2)
Sho Would Be Nice (2)
Shuckin' And Jivin' (2)
Silent Night (11)
Silver Bells (11)
Sleigh Ride (11)
Some Kind Of Wonderful (9)
Someone To Go Home To (8)
Sometimes I Feel Like A Motherless Child (medley) (4)
Stevie Wonder Medley (9)
Sun, Sun, Sun (7)
Sweet And Innocent (1,4,12)
Take Love If Ever You Find Love (8)
Taste Of Rhythm And Blues (9)
Thank You (8)
That's My Girl (5)
Think (1)
This Christmas Eve (11)
This Is The Way That I Feel (12) 39
Too Young (12) 13
Traffic In My Mind (medley) (6)
Trouble (medley) (9)
Twelfth Of Never (12) 8
Utah (5)

Very Merry Christmas (11)
Walkin' In The Jungle (10)
War In Heaven (6)
We All Fall Down (5)
We Gotta Live Together (4)
We Never Said Forever (2)
What Are You Doing On New Year's Eve (11)
What Could It Be (5)
When He Comes Again (11)
Where Are You Going To My Love (8)
Where Could I Go But To The Lord (medley) (9)
Where Would I Be Without You (8)
White Christmas (11)
Who's Sorry Now (medley) (9)
Winter Wonderland (11)
Yo-Yo (3,4,12) 3
You Are So Beautiful (medley) (9)
You've Lost That Lovin' Feelin' (4)
Your Mama Don't Dance (9)
Your Song (4)

O'SULLIVAN, Gilbert '72
Born Raymond O'Sullivan on 12/1/46 in Waterford, Ireland. Pop singer.

8/12/72	9	29			1 Gilbert O'Sullivan-Himself			$15	MAM 4
1/6/73	48	19			2 Back To Front			$15	MAM 5
10/13/73	101	10			3 I'm A Writer, Not A Fighter			$15	MAM 7

Alone Again (Naturally) (1) 1
But I'm Not (2)
Bye Bye (1)
Can I Go With You (2)
Clair (2) 2
Friend Of Mine (3)
Get Down (3) 7
Golden Rule (2)
Houdini Said (1)

I Have Never Loved You As Much As I Love You Today (1)
I Hope You'll Stay (1)
I'm A Writer, Not A Fighter (3)
I'm In Love With You (2)
I'm Leaving (2)
If I Don't Get You (Back Again) (1)

If You Love Me Like You Love Me (3)
In My Hole (2)
Independent Air (1)
January Git (1)
Matrimony (1)
Not In A Million Years (3)
Nothing Rhymed (1)
Ooh Baby (3) 25

Out Of The Question (2) 17
Permissive Twit (1)
That's Love (2)
They've Only Themselves To Blame (3)
Thunder And Lightning (1)
Too Much Attention (1)
We Will (1)

What Could Be Nicer (Mum The Kettle's Boiling) (2)
Where Peaceful Waters Flow (3)
Who Knows, Perhaps Maybe (3)
Who Was It (2)

OTHER ONES, The '87

Pop-rock group consisting of Australian siblings Jayney (vocals), Alf (vocals) and Johnny (bass) Klimek, and Germans Andreas Schwarz-Ruszczynski (guitar), Stephen Gottwald (keyboards) and Uwe Hoffmann (drums).

| 5/16/87 | 139 | 6 | | © | The Other Ones .... | | | $10 | Virgin 90576 |

All Day, All Night   He's A Man   It Makes Me Higher   Moments   Stranger
All The Love   **Holiday 29**   Losing It   Stay With Me (It's Not Forever)   **We Are What We Are 53**

OTHER ONES, The '99

Rock group consisting of former **Grateful Dead** members **Bob Weir** (vocals, guitar), Phil Lesh (bass) and **Mickey Hart** (drums), with **Bruce Hornsby** (vocals, keyboards), Mark Karan and Steve Kimock (guitars), Dave Ellis (sax) and John Molo (drums).

| 2/27/99 | 112 | 2 | | © | The Strange Remain .... | | | $15 | Grateful Dead 14062 [2] |

Baba Jingo   Corrina   Friend Of The Devil   Mountains Of The Moon   Playing In The Band   Sugaree
Banyan Tree   Eleven, The (medley)   I Know You Rider (medley)   Only The Strange Remain   Rainbow's Cadillac   White-Wheeled Limousine
China Cat Sunflower (medley)   Estimated Prophet   Jack Straw   Other One   St. Stephen (medley)

OTIS, Shuggie '70

Born Johnny Alexander Veliotes on 11/30/53 in Los Angeles. Multi-instrumentalist. Son of R&B legend Johnny Otis.

1/24/70	182	5		1	Kooper Session			$15	Columbia 9951
					AL KOOPER Introduces SHUGGIE OTIS				
3/7/70	199	2		2	Here Comes Shuggie Otis			$15	Epic 26511
3/22/75	181	3	©	3	Inspiration Information			$15	Epic 33059

Aht Uh Mi Hed (3)   Funky Thithee (2)   Inspiration Information (3)   Lookin' For A Home (1)   Rainy Day (3)   Shuggie's Shuffle (1)
Baby, I Needed You (2)   Gospel Groove (3)   Island Letter (3)   Not Available (3)   Shuggie's Boogie (2)   Sparkle City (3)
Bootie Cooler (2)   Happy House (3)   Jennie Lee (3)   One Room Country Shack (1)   Shuggie's Old Time   12:15 Slow Goonbash Blues (1)
Bury My Body (1)   Hawks, The (2)   Knowing (That You Want Him)   Oxford Gray (2)   Dee-Di-Lee-Di-Leet-Deet   XL-30 (3)
Double Or Nothing (1)   Hurricane (2)   (2)   Pling! (3)   Slide Boogie (3)

O-TOWN '01

Pop vocal group from Orlando, Florida: Trevor Penick, Jacob Underwood, Ashley Parker Angel, Erik-Michael Estrada and Dan Miller. Group was put together while auditioning for the TV series *Making The Band*.

| 2/10/01 | 5 | 34↑▲ | | © | O-Town .... | | | $10 | J 20000 |

All For Love   Baby I Would   Girl   Love Should Be A Crime   Sensitive   Shy Girl
All Or Nothing 3   Every Six Seconds   **Liquid Dreams 10**   Painter, The   Sexiest Woman Alive   Take Me Under

OUR LADY PEACE '99

Rock group from Toronto: Raine Maida (vocals), Mike Turner (guitar), Duncan Coutts (bass) and Jeremy Taggart (drums).

9/6/97+	76	39	●	1	Clumsy			$10	Columbia 67940
10/16/99	69	4	©	2	Happiness...Is Not A Fish That You Can Catch			$10	Columbia 63707
3/31/01	81	4	©	3	Spiritual Machines			$10	Columbia 85368

All My Friends (3)   Car Crash (1)   Happiness & The Fish (2)   Life (3)   R.K. 2029 (3)   Story Of 100 Aisles (1)
Annie (2)   Carnival (1)   Hello Oskar (1)   Lying Awake (2)   R.K. 2029-97 (3)   Superman's Dead (1)
Are You Sad? (3)   Clumsy (1)   If You Believe (3)   Made To Heal (3)   R.K. On Death (3)   Thief (2)
Automatic Flowers (1)   Consequence Of Laughing (2)   In Repair (3)   Middle Of Yesterday (3)   Right Behind You (Mafia) (3)   Waited (2)
Big Dumb Rocket (1)   Everyone's A Junkie (3)   Is Anybody Home? (2)   One Man Army (2)   Shaking (1)   Wonderful Future (3)
Blister (2)   4 AM (1)   Let You Down (1)   Potato Girl (2)   Stealing Babies (1)

OUTFIELD, The '86

Pop-rock trio formed in London: Tony Lewis (vocals, bass), John Spinks (guitar) and Alan Jackman (drums). Jackman left by 1990; Lewis and Spinks continued as a duo.

11/2/85+	9	66	▲² ©	1	Play Deep			$10	Columbia 40027
7/4/87	18	21	● ©	2	Bangin'			$10	Columbia 40619
4/15/89	53	23	©	3	Voices Of Babylon			$10	Columbia 44449
11/24/90+	90	16	©	4	Diamond Days			$10	MCA 10111

After The Storm (4)   **Everytime You Cry** (1) 66   Magic Seed (4)   Night Ain't Over (3)   Reach Out (3)   Take It All (4)
All The Love In The World   Eye To Eye (4)   Main Attraction (2)   No Point (3)   Say It Isn't So (1)   Taken By Surprise (4)
(1) **19**   **For You** (4) **21**   Makin' Up (3)   No Surrender (2)   Shelter Me (3)   Taking My Chances (1)
Alone With You (2)   I Don't Need Her (1)   Moving Target (2)   One Night In Heaven (4)   **Since You've Been Gone**   Talk To Me (1)
Bangin' On My Heart (2)   Inside Your Skin (3)   **My Paradise** (3) **72**   Part Of Your Life (3)   (2) **31**   Unrespectable (4)
Better Than Nothing (2)   John Lennon (4)   Mystery Man (1)   Playground (2)   61 Seconds (1)   **Voices Of Babylon** (3) **25**
Burning Blue (4)   Long Way Home (2)   Nervous Alibi (1)   Raintown Boys (4)   Somewhere In America (2)   **Your Love** (1) **6**

OUTKAST '00

Male rap duo from Atlanta: Andre Benjamin and Antoine Patton.

5/14/94	20	26	▲ ©	1	Southernplayalisticadillacmuzik			$10	LaFace 26010
9/14/96	2¹	33	▲ ©	2	ATLiens			$10	LaFace 26029
10/17/98	2¹	43	▲ ©	3	Aquemini			$10	LaFace 26053
11/18/00	2²	46↑▲³	©	4	Stankonia			$10	LaFace 26072

ATLiens (2) **35**   Da Art Of Storytellin' (Part 1 &   Hold On, Be Strong (3)   Myintrotoletuknow (1)   Slump (3)   Toilet Tisha (4)
Ain't No Thang (1)   2) (3)   Hootie Hoo (1)   Nathaniel (3)   **Snappin' & Trappin'** (4)   Two Dope Boyz (In A Cadillac)
Aquemini (3)   Decatur Psalm (2)   Humble Mumble (4)   Ova Da Wudz (2)   **So Fresh, So Clean** (4) **30**   (2)
B.O.B. (4)   D.E.E.P. (1)   I'll Call Before I Come (4)   **Player's Ball** (1) **37**   Southernplayalisticadillac-   Wailin' (2)
Babylon (2)   E.T. (Extraterrestrial) (2)   **Jazzy Belle** (2) **52**   ? (4)   muzik (1) **74**   We Luv Deez Hoez (4)
Call Of Da Wild (1)   **Elevators (me & you)** (2) **12**   Liberation (3)   Red Velvet (4)   Spaghetti Junction (4)   West Savannah (3)
Chonkyfire (3)   Funky Ride (1)   Mainstream (3)   Return Of The "G" (3)   SpottieOttieDopaliscious (3)   Wheelz Of Steel (2)
Claimin' True (1)   Gangsta Shit (4)   Mamacita (3)   **Rosa Parks** (3) **55**   Stankonia (Stanklove) (4)   Xplosion (4)
Crumblin' Erb (1)   Gasoline Dreams (4)   Millennium (3)   Skew It On The Bar-B (3)   Synthesizer (3)   Y'All Scared (3)
   Git Up, Git Out (1)   **Ms. Jackson** (4) **1**   Slum Beautiful (4)   13th Floor/Growing Old (2)

★430★ OUTLAWS '75

Rock group formed in Tampa, Florida: Henry Paul (vocals, guitar), Hughie Thomasson and Billy Jones (guitars), Frank O'Keefe (bass) and Monte Yoho (drums). By 1981, Freddie Salem, Rick Cua and David Dix had replaced Paul, O'Keefe and Yoho. Paul was a member of **BlackHawk** by 1993. Thomasson joined **Lynyrd Skynyrd** in 1996. Jones died on 2/7/95 (age 45). O'Keefe died of a drug overdose on 2/26/95 (age 44).

1)Outlaws   2)Ghost Riders   3)Bring It Back Alive

| 8/9/75 | 13 | 16 | ● © | 1 | Outlaws .... | | | $12 | Arista 4042 |
| 4/10/76 | 36 | 12 | © | 2 | Lady In Waiting .... | | | $12 | Arista 4070 |

DEBUT	PEAK	WKS	RIAA	CD	ARTIST — Album Title	Catalog	Sym	$	Label & Number

OUTLAWS — Cont'd

DEBUT	PEAK	WKS			Album		Sym	$	Label & Number
5/28/77	51	27		© 3	Hurry Sundown			$12	Arista 4135
3/25/78	29	21	● © 4	Bring It Back Alive		[L]		$15	Arista 8300 [2]
					recorded on 9/9/77 in Chicago				
11/25/78	60	18		5	Playin' To Win....................			$12	Arista 4205
11/3/79	55	18		6	In The Eye Of The Storm			$12	Arista 9507
12/13/80+	25	26	● © 7	Ghost Riders			$12	Arista 9542
5/1/82	77	9		8	Los Hombres Malo			$12	Arista 9584
					title is Spanish for "The Bad Men"				
11/27/82+	136	9		© 9	Greatest Hits Of The Outlaws/High Tides Forever		[G]	$12	Arista 9614
11/8/86	160	10		10	Soldiers Of Fortune....................			$10	Pasha 40512

Ain't So Bad (2)
All Roads (8)
Angels Hide (7)
Back From Eternity (8)
Blueswater (6)
Breaker - Breaker (2) *94*
Cold And Lonesome (3,4)
Cold Harbor (10)
(Come On) Dance With Me (6)
Comin' Home (6)
Cry No More (1)
Cry Some More (5)
Devil's Road (7)
Dirty City (5)

Don't Stop (8)
Easy Does It (8)
Falling Rain (5)
Foxtail Lilly (8)
Freeborn Man (2,4)
Freedom Walk (7)
(Ghost) Riders In The Sky (7,9) *31*
Girl From Ohio (2)
Goodbye (8)
Green Grass & High Tides (1,4,9)
Gunsmoke (3)
Hearin' My Heart Talkin' (3)

Heavenly Blues (3)
Holiday (3,4,9)
Hurry Sundown (3,4,9) *60*
I Can't Stop Loving You (7)
I Hope You Don't Mind (4)
I'll Be Leaving Soon (6)
If Dreams Came True (8)
Introduction (4)
It Follows From Your Heart (1)
It's All Right (6)
Just For You (2)
Just The Way I Like It (10)
Keep Prayin' (1)
Knoxville Girl (1)

Lady Luck (10)
Lights Are On (But Nobody's Home) (6)
Long Gone (6)
Love At First Sight (5)
Lover Boy (2,4)
Man Of The Hour (5)
Miracle Man (6)
Night Cries (10)
Night Wines (3)
One Last Ride (10)
Outlaw, The (10)
Prisoner (2,4)
Racin' For The Red Light (10)

Real Good Feelin' (5)
Rebel Girl (8)
Running (8)
Saved By The Bell (10)
So Afraid (3)
Soldiers Of Fortune (10)
Song For You (1,4)
Song In The Breeze (1)
South Carolina (2)
Stay With Me (1)
Stick Around For Rock & Roll (2,4,9)
Sunshine (7)

Take It Anyway You Want It (5,9)
There Goes Another Love Song (1,4,9) *34*
Too Long Without Her (6)
Waterhole (1)
Whatcha Don't Do (10)
White Horses (7)
Wishing Wells (7)
Won't Come Out Of The Rain (8)
You Are The Show (5,9)
You Can Have It (5)

OUTLAWZ   '00
Rap group from Los Angeles: Edi, Kastro, Napoleon and Young Noble.

DEBUT	PEAK	WKS			Album			$	Label & Number
1/8/00	6	20	▲ © 1	Still I Rise			$10	Interscope 490413
					2PAC + OUTLAWZ				
11/25/00	95	3		© 2	Ride Wit Us Or Collide Wit Us....................			$10	Outlaw 2000

As The World Turns (1)
Baby Don't Cry (Keep Ya Head Up II) (1) *72*
Black Jesuz (1)
Black Rain (2)
Fuck With Me (2)

Get Paid (2)
Good Bye (2)
Good Die Young (1)
Hang On (2)
Hell 4 A Hustler (1)
High Speed (1)

Homeboyz (1)
Killuminati (2)
Letter To The President (1)
Life Is What You Make It (2)
Maintain (2)
Mask Down (2)

Murder Made Easy (2)
Nobody Cares (1)
Outlaw 2000 (1)
Secretz Of War (1)
Smash (2)
Soldier To A General (2)

Still I Rise (1)
Tattoo Tears (1)
Teardrops And Closed Caskets (1)
U Can Be Touched (1)
When I Go (2)

Who? (2)
Y'All Don't Know Us (1)

OUTSIDERS, The   '66
Rock group from Cleveland: Sonny Geraci (vocals), Tom King and Bill Bruno (guitars), Mert Madsen (bass) and Rick Baker (drums). Geraci later formed **Climax**.

DEBUT	PEAK	WKS			Album			$	Label & Number
5/28/66	37	16		1	Time Won't Let Me			$40	Capitol 2501
9/17/66	90	10		2	The Outsiders Album #2....................			$40	Capitol 2568
8/26/67	103	10		3	Happening 'Live!'		[L]	$40	Capitol 2745

Ain't Too Proud To Beg (3)
Backwards, Upside Down (2)
Chase Away The Tears (1)
Come On Up (3)
Cool Jerk (1)
Girl In Love (1,3) *21*

Gloria (3)
Good Lovin' (3)
Hanky Panky (2)
Help Me Girl (3) *37*
I Will Love You (2)
(Just Like) Romeo & Juliet (2)

Keep On Running (1)
Listen People (1)
Lonely Man (2)
Lost In My World (2)
Love Makes The World Go 'Round (3)

Maybe Baby (1)
Michelle (3)
My Girl (3)
Oh How It Hurts (3)
Respectable (2,3) *15*
Rockin' Robin (1)

She Cried (1)
Show Me (3)
Since I Lost My Baby (2)
Time Won't Let Me (1,3) *5*
Was It Really Real (1)

What Makes You So Bad You Weren't Brought Up That Way (1)
Wine Wine Wine (2)

OVERKILL   '88
Hard-rock group from New York City: Bobby Ellsworth (vocals), Bobby Gustafson (guitar), D.D. Verni (bass) and Rat Skates (drums). By 1988, Sid Falck had replaced Skates. Gustafson and Falck left by 1993; guitarists Rob Cannavino and Merritt Gant, and drummer Tim Mallare were members then.

DEBUT	PEAK	WKS			Album			$	Label & Number
4/11/87	191	1		© 1	Taking Over			$12	Megaforce 81735
7/30/88	142	13		© 2	Under The Influence			$12	Megaforce 81865
11/18/89+	155	8		© 3	The Years Of Decay			$12	Megaforce 82045
3/27/93	122	2		© 4	I Hear Black....................			$10	Atlantic 82476

Birth Of Tension (3)
Brainfade (2)
Deny The Cross (1)
Dreaming In Columbian (4)
Drunken Wisdom (2)
Electro-Violence (1)
Elimination (3)

End Of The Line (1)
E.vil N.ever D.ies (3)
Fatal If Swallowed (1)
Fear His Name (1)
Feed My Head (4)
Ghost Dance (4)
Head First (2)
Hello From The Gutter (2)

I Hate (3)
I Hear Black (4)
Ignorance & Innocence (4)
In Union We Stand (1)
Just Like You (4)
Mad Gone World (4)
Never Say Never (2)
Nothing To Die For (3)

Overkill II (The Nightmare Continues) (1)
Overkill III (Under The Influence) (2)
Playing With Spiders (medley) (3)
Powersurge (1)
Shades Of Grey (4)
Shred (3)

Skullrusher (medley) (3)
Spiritual Void (4)
Time To Kill (3)
Undying (4)
Use Your Head (1)
Weight Of The World (4)
Who Tends The Fire (3)
World Of Hurt (4)

Wrecking Crew (1)
Years Of Decay (3)

OVERSTREET, Paul   '91
Born on 3/17/55 in Antioch, Mississippi. Country singer/songwriter/guitarist.

DEBUT	PEAK	WKS			Album			$	Label & Number
2/23/91	163	6		©	Heroes			$10	RCA 2459

Ball & Chain
Billy Can't Read

Calm At The Center Of My Storm
Daddy's Come Around

Heroes
I'm So Glad I Was Dreaming
If I Could Bottle This Up

Love Lives On
She Supports Her Man
Straight And Narrow

'Til The Mountains Disappear

OWENS, Buck, And His Buckaroos   '64
Born Alvis Edgar Owens on 8/12/29 in Sherman, Texas; raised in Mesa, Arizona. Country singer/songwriter/guitarist. Co-host of TV's *Hee Haw* (1969-86). Backing group: The Buckaroos.

1)I've Got A Tiger By The Tail 2)The Best Of Buck Owens 3)Together Again/My Heart Skips A Beat

DEBUT	PEAK	WKS			Album			$	Label & Number
7/18/64	46	31	●	1	The Best Of Buck Owens....................		[G]	$25	Capitol 2105
9/5/64	88	18		© 2	Together Again/My Heart Skips A Beat....................			$25	Capitol 2135
					also see #12 below				
12/12/64	135	5		© 3	I Don't Care			$25	Capitol 2186
4/3/65	43	22		© 4	I've Got A Tiger By The Tail			$25	Capitol 2283
12/18/65	12^X	10		© 5	Christmas with Buck Owens and his buckaroos....................		[X]	$25	Capitol 2396
					Christmas charts: 12/'65, 23/'66, 23/'67; also see #19 below				

OWENS, Buck, And His Buckaroos — Cont'd

DEBUT	PEAK	WKS		CD	ARTIST — Album Title		Sym	$	Label & Number
3/12/66	106	10		© 6	Roll out the red carpet for Buck Owens and his Buckaroos			$25	Capitol 2443
9/24/66	114	10		© 7	Carnegie Hall Concert		[L]	$25	Capitol 2556
					recorded on 3/25/66				
9/30/67	177	7		© 8	Your Tender Loving Care			$25	Capitol 2760
12/21/68	31[X]	2		© 9	Christmas Shopping		[X]	$20	Capitol 2977
					also see #19 below				
2/15/69	199	2		10	I've Got You On My Mind Again			$20	Capitol 131
7/5/69	113	5		11	Buck Owens In London		[L]	$20	Capitol 232
					recorded at the London Palladium				
8/16/69	185	5		12	Close-Up		[R]	$25	Capitol 257 [2]
					reissue of *Together Again* and *No One But You* albums				
11/8/69	122	10		13	Tall Dark Stranger			$20	Capitol 212
2/7/70	141	6		14	Big In Vegas		[L]	$20	Capitol 413
					includes "Lodi" by Buddy Alan; "Let Me Get My Message Thru" by The Sanland Brothers; "Maybe If I Close My Eyes (It'll Go Away)" by Susan Raye; "Goin' Home To Your Mother" and "With Lonely" by The Hagers; "I'm A Natural Loser" by Doyle Holly; "Catfish Capers" by Don Rich; and "Cold Cold Wind" by Ira Allen				
4/25/70	198	2		15	Your Mother's Prayer			$20	Capitol 439
5/16/70	154	6		16	We're Gonna Get Together			$20	Capitol 448
					BUCK OWENS & SUSAN RAYE				
9/19/70	196	2		17	The Kansas City Song			$20	Capitol 476
11/28/70	190	2		18	I Wouldn't Live In New York City			$20	Capitol 628
12/26/70	34[X]	1		19	A Merry "Hee Haw" Christmas		[X-R]	$25	Capitol 486 [2]
					reissue of albums #5 and #9 above				

A-11 (2,12)
Abilene (3)
Above And Beyond (1,7)
Across This Town And Gone (13)
Act Naturally (1,7,11)
After You Leave Me (6)
Ain't It Amazin' Gracie (2)
Alabama, Louisiana, Or Maybe Tennessee (10)
All I Want For Christmas Is My Daddy (5)
All I Want For Christmas Is You (5)
Along Came Jones (14)
Amsterdam (17)
Band Keeps Playin' On (4)
Because It's Christmas Time (5,19)
Before You Go (12) *83*
Big In Vegas (14,18) *100*
Black Texas Dirt (17)
Blue Christmas Lights (5,19)
Blue Christmas Tree (5,19)
Bring Back My Peace Of Mind (17)
Buck's Polka (3)
Buckaroo (7) *60*
Bud's Bounce (3)
But You Know I Love You (13)
Cajun Fiddle (6,11)
Charlie Brown (12)
Christmas Ain't Christmas (5,19)
Christmas Morning (5,19)
Christmas Schottische (9,19)
Christmas Shopping (9,19)
Christmas Time Is Near (9,19)
Christmas Time's A Comin' (5,19)
Cinderella (6)

Close Up The Honky Tonks (2,12)
Cryin' Time (4,7,11,16)
Dang Me (3)
Darlin', You Can Depend On Me (13)
Diggy Liggy Lo (medley) (11)
Don't Ever Tell Me Goodbye (8)
Don't Let Her Know (3,7)
Don't Let True Love Slip Away (10)
Down In New Orleans (11)
Dust On Mother's Bible (11)
Everybody Needs Somebody (16)
Excuse Me (I Think I've Got A Heartache) (1,7)
Fallin' For You (4,16)
Foolin' Around (1,7,16)
Full Time Daddy (9)
Getting Used To Losing You (2,12)
Getting Used To Loving You (12)
Gonna Have Love (7,12)
Gonna Roll Out The Red Carpet (6)
Good Old Fashioned Country Christmas (9,19)
Great Judgment Day (15)
Hangin' On To What I Got (4)
Happening In London Town (11)
Happy Times Are Here Again (11)
He Don't Deserve You Anymore (6)
Hello Trouble (2,7,12)
Here Comes Santa Claus Again (5,19)
High As The Mountains (1)
Home On Christmas Day (9,19)
House Of Memories (8)

Houston-Town (18)
Hurry, Come Running Back To Me (10)
Hurtin' Like I've Never Hurt Before (13)
I Ain't A Gonna Be Treated This A Way (10)
I Betcha Didn't Know (12)
I Can't Stop (My Lovin' You) (1)
I Don't Care (Just As Long As You Love Me) (3,7) *92*
I Don't Hear You (12)
I Wanna Be Wild And Free (10)
(I Want) No One But You (12)
I Would Do Anything For You (13)
I Wouldn't Live In New York City (If They Gave Me The Whole Dang Town) (18)
I'd Love To Be Your Man (17)
(I'll Love You) Forever And Ever (6,10)
I'm Layin' It On The Line (6)
I've Got A Tiger By The Tail (4,7,11) *25*
I've Got You On My Mind Again (10)
If I Had You Back Again (3)
If You Fall Out Of Love With Me (4)
If You Want A Love (12)
In God I Trust (15)
In The Middle Of A Teardrop (13)
In The Palm Of Your Hand (medley) (7)
It Takes People Like You (To Make People Like Me) (11)
(It's A Long Way To) Londontown (17,18)
It's Christmas Time For Everyone But Me (5)
It's Not What You Give (9)

Jesus, Jesus, Hold To Me (15)
Jingle Bells (5,19)
Johnny B. Goode (11)
Jolly Christmas Polka (9,19)
Just A Few More Days (15)
Kansas City Song (17,18)
Kickin' Our Hearts Around (1)
Las Vegas Lament (14)
Let The Sad Times Roll On (4)
Let The World Keep On A Turnin' (10)
Lonesome Valley (15)
Loose Talk (1)
Louisiana Man (3,11)
Love Is Me (10)
Love Is Strange (16)
Love's Gonna Live Here (1,7,11)
Maiden's Prayer (4)
Maybe If I Close My Eyes (It'll Go Away) (13)
Memphis (4)
Merry Christmas From Our House To Yours (9,19)
My Heart Skips A Beat (2,7,12) *94*
My Savior Leads The Way (15)
No Fool Like An Old Fool (12)
No Milk And Honey In Baltimore (18)
Nobody's Fool But Yours (1)
Number One Heel (12)
One Of Everything You Got (9)
One Of Everything You Got (12)
Only You And You Alone (8)
Only You (Can Break My Heart) (7,8)
Open Up Your Heart (medley) (11)
Over And Over Again (2,12)
Playboy (3)
Reno Lament (18)

Rocks In My Head (8)
Rovin' Gambler (14)
Sam's Place (8,11) *92*
Santa Looked A Lot Like Daddy (Daddy Looked A Lot Like Him) (5,19)
Santa's Gonna Come In A Stagecoach (5,19)
Santo Domingo (18)
Save The Last Dance For Me (2)
Scandinavian Polka (17)
Second Fiddle (1)
Sing A Happy Song (10)
Sing Me Back Home (11)
Sing That Kind Of Song (13)
Someone With No One To Love (8)
Somewhere Between (16)
Song And Dance (8)
Storm Of Love (2,12)
Streets Of Laredo (4,7)
Sweet Rosie Jones (11)
Tall Dark Stranger (13)
That Old Time Religion (15)
That Sunday Feeling (15)
That's All Right With Me (If It's All Right With You) (10)
That's What I'm Like Without You (6)
There Never Was A Fool (6)
There's Gonna Come A Day (12)
There's Gotta Be Some Changes Made (13)
This Ol' Heart (3)
Together Again (2,7,11,12,14,16)
Togetherness (16)
Tom Cattin' (6)
Tomorrow Is Christmas Day (9,19)
Trouble And Me (4)

Truck Drivin' Man (2,7,12)
Under The Influence Of Love (1)
Under Your Spell Again (1,7)
Understand Your Man (3)
Very Merry Christmas (9,19)
Wait A Little Longer Please, Jesus (15)
Waitin' In Your Welfare Line (7) *57*
We Split The Blanket (6)
We Were Made For Each Other (16)
We're Gonna Get Together (16)
We're Gonna Let The Good Times Roll (4,14)
Wham Bam (4)
What A Liar I Am (8)
When The Roll Is Called Up Yonder (15)
Where Has Our Love Gone? (10)
White Satin Bed (13)
Who's Gonna Mow Your Grass (11)
Wind Blows Every Day In Chicago (18)
Wind Blows Every Day In Oklahoma (17)
You Can't Make Nothin' Out Of That But Love (17)
You Made A Monkey Out Of Me (8)
You're Welcome Anytime (3)
Your Mother's Prayer (15)
Your Tender Loving Care (8)

OXO   '83

Pop-rock group from Miami: Ish "Angel" Ledesma (vocals, **Foxy**), Orlando (guitar), Frank Garcia (bass) and Freddy Alwag (drums).

DEBUT	PEAK	WKS		CD	ARTIST — Album Title		Sym	$	Label & Number
4/30/83	117	7			Oxo			$10	Geffen 4001

Back In Town
Dance All Night

I'll Take You Back
In The Stars

Love I Need Her
My Ride

Runnin' Low
Waiting For You

Wanna Be Your Love
Whirly Girl *28*

You Make It Sound So Easy

OZARK MOUNTAIN DAREDEVILS   '75

Country-rock group from Springfield, Missouri: Larry Lee (vocals, drums), John Dillon (guitar), Steve Cash (harmonica) and Michael Granda (bass).

DEBUT	PEAK	WKS	RIAA	CD	ARTIST — Album Title		Sym	$	Label & Number
2/16/74	26	28	●	© 1	The Ozark Mountain Daredevils			$12	A&M 4411
12/14/74+	19	31		2	It'll Shine When It Shines			$12	A&M 3654
11/8/75	57	15		3	The Car Over The Lake Album			$12	A&M 4549
10/2/76	74	9		4	Men From Earth			$12	A&M 4601
11/19/77+	132	10		5	Don't Look Down			$12	A&M 4662
9/30/78	176	3		6	It's Alive		[L]	$15	A&M 6006 [2]
5/24/80	170	4		7	Ozark Mountain Daredevils			$12	Columbia 36375

Arroyo (4)
Backroads (5)
Beauty In The River (1)
Black Sky (1,6)
Breakaway (From Those Chains) (4)
Chicken Train (1,6)

Cobblestone Mountain (3)
Colorado Song (1)
Commercial Success (6)
Country Girl (1)
Crazy Lovin' (5)
E.E. Lawson (2)
Empty Cup (7)

Fly Away Home (4,6)
Following The Way That I Feel (5,6)
Fool's Gold (7)
Fox, The (5)
From Time To Time (3)
Giving It All To The Wind (5)

Gypsy Forest (3)
Homemade Wine (4,6)
Horse Trader (6)
If I Only Knew (3) *65*
If You Wanna Get To Heaven (1,6) *25*
It Couldn't Be Better (2)

It Probably Always Will (2)
It'll Shine When It Shines (2)
It's All Over Now (6)
It's How You Think (4)
Jackie Blue (2,6) *3*
Jump At The Chance (4)
Kansas You Fooler (2)

Keep On Churnin' (3)
Leatherwood (3)
Look Away (3)
Love Makes The Lover (5)
Lovin' You (7)
Lowlands (4)
Moon On The Rise (5)

OZARK MOUNTAIN DAREDEVILS — Cont'd

Mountain Range (4)
Mr. Powell (3)
Noah (4,6)
Oh, Darlin' (7)
Ooh Boys (It's Hot) (6)
Out On The Sea (3)

Red Plum (4)
River To The Sun (5,6)
Road To Glory (1)
Rosalie (7)
Runnin' Out (7)
Sailin' Around The World (7)

Satisfied Mind (6)
Snowbound (5)
Southern Cross (3)
Spaceship Orion (1)
Standin' On The Rock (1)
Stinghead (5)

Take You Tonight (7) 67
Thin Ice (3)
Tidal Wave (2)
True Believer (5)
Tuff Luck (7)
Walkin' Down The Road (2,6)

Watermill (4)
What's Happened Along In My Life (2)
Whippoorwill (3)
Within Without (1)

You Know Like I Know (4,6) 74
You Made It Right (2)

OZONE '82

R&B group from Nashville: Benny Wallace and Herman Brown (guitars), James Stewart (keyboards), Thomas Bumpass (trumpet), William White and Ray Woodard (saxophones), Charles Glenn (bass) and Paul Hines (drums).

9/4/82	152	6			Li'l Suzy			$10	Motown 6011

Aerobic Jamercise
Ain't Got Far To Go
Comin' After Your Love

Funkin' On The One (Make Your Body Move)
I'm Not Easy

Let The Ozone Take Your Mind
Li'l Suzy
Shake It Down

She's A Ten
You'll Never Know How Much (I Love You)

P

PABLO CRUISE '78

Pop-rock group from San Francisco: Dave Jenkins (vocals, guitar), Cory Lerios (keyboards), Bud Cockrell (bass; **It's A Beautiful Day**) and Stephen Price (drums). Bruce Day replaced Cockrell in 1977. John Pierce replaced Day, and Angelo Rossi (guitar) joined in 1980.

8/16/75	174	4		©	1 Pablo Cruise			$12	A&M 4528
4/17/76+	139	13			2 Lifeline			$12	A&M 4575
3/5/77	19	46	▲	©	3 A Place In The Sun			$12	A&M 4625
6/17/78	6	43	▲	©	4 Worlds Away			$12	A&M 4697
11/17/79	39	17			5 Part Of The Game			$12	A&M 3712
7/18/81	34	18			6 Reflector			$12	A&M 3726

Always Be Together (4)
Atlanta June (3)
Can't You Hear The Music? (3)
Cool Love (6) 13
Crystal (2)
Denny (1)
Don't Believe It (2)
Don't Let The Magic Disappear (6)
Don't Want To Live Without It (4) 21

Drums In The Night (6)
El Verano (3)
Family Man (4)
For Another Town (5)
Givin' It Away (5)
Good Ship Pablo Cruise (2)
How Many Tears? (5)
I Go To Rio (4) 46
I Just Wanna Believe (3)
(I Think) It's Finally Over (1)
I Want You Tonight (5) 19

In My Own Quiet Way (1)
Inside/Outside (6)
Island Woman (1)
Jenny (6)
Lifeline (4)
Lonely Nights (5)
Look To The Sky (2)
Love Will Find A Way (4) 6
Never Had A Love (3) 87
Never See That Girl Enough (2)
Not Tonight (1)

Ocean Breeze (1)
One More Night (6)
Paradise (Let Me Take You Into) (6)
Part Of The Game (5)
Raging Fire (3)
Rock N' Roller (1)
Runnin' (4)
Sailing To Paradise (4)
Sleeping Dogs (1)

Slip Away (6) 75
Tearin' Down My Mind (2)
Tell Me That You Love Me (5)
That's When (6)
This Time (6)
Tonight My Love (3)
What Does It Take (1)
Whatcha Gonna Do? (3) 6
When Love Is At Your Door (5)
Who Knows (2)
Worlds Away (4)

You're Out To Lose (4)
Zero To Sixty In Five (2)

PACIFIC GAS & ELECTRIC '70

Blues-rock group from California: Charles Allen (vocals), Glenn Schwartz and Tom Marshall (guitars), Brent Block (bass) and Frank Cook (drums). Allen spearheaded a new lineup in 1971; group name shortened to PG&E. Allen died on 5/7/90 (age 48).

2/1/69	159	12			1 Get It On			$25	Power 701
9/13/69	91	8		©	2 Pacific Gas And Electric			$15	Columbia 9900
7/4/70	101	11		©	3 Are You Ready			$15	Columbia 1017
8/28/71+	182	8			4 PG&E			$15	Columbia 30362

Are You Ready? (3) 14
Blackberry (3)
Bluesbuster (2)
Cry, Cry, Cry (1)
Death Row #172 (2,4)
Elvira (3)
Hawg For You (3)

Hunter (1)
Jelly, Jelly (1)
Live Love (1)
Long Handled Shovel (1)
Love, Love, Love, Love, Love (3)
Miss Lucy (2)

Mother, Why Do You Cry? (3)
Motor City's Burning (1)
My Women (3)
One More River To Cross (4)
PG&E Suite Medley (2)
Recall (4)
Redneck (2)

Rock And Roller's Lament (4)
Screamin' (3)
See The Monkey Run (4)
She's Long And She's Tall (2)
Short Dogs And Englishmen (4)
Staggolee (3)
Stormy Times (1)

Thank God For You Baby (4) 97
Time Has Come (To Make Your Peace) (4)
Wade In The Water (1)
When A Man Loves A Woman (3)
When The Sun Shines (4)

PAGE, Gene '75

Born on 9/13/38 in Los Angeles. Died on 8/24/98 (age 59). R&B keyboardist/arranger.

2/1/75	156	4			Hot City		[I]	$12	Atlantic 18111

produced by **Barry White**

All Our Dreams Are Coming True

Cream Corner (Get What You Want)

Don't Play That Song Gene's Theme

I Am Living In A World Of Gloom

Jungle Eyes
Satin Soul

She's My Main Squeeze
To The Bone

PAGE, Jimmy '94

Born on 1/9/44 in Heston, Middlesex, England. Rock guitarist. Member of **The Yardbirds** (1966-68). In October 1968, formed The New Yardbirds, which evolved into **Led Zeppelin**. Page produced all of the group's music. Joined **The Honeydrippers** in 1984, also co-founded **The Firm** with vocalist **Paul Rodgers**. Also see **Coverdale/Page**.

4/3/82	50	10			1 Death Wish II		[I-S]	$12	Swan Song 8511
7/9/88	26	20	●	©	2 Outrider			$10	Geffen 24188
11/26/94	4	23	▲	©	3 No Quarter			$10	Atlantic 82706
5/9/98	8	13	●	©	4 Walking Into Clarksdale			$10	Atlantic 83092

JIMMY PAGE & ROBERT PLANT (above 2)

7/22/00	64	9	●	©	5 Live At The Greek		[L]	$15	TVT 2140 [2]

JIMMY PAGE & THE BLACK CROWES

Battle Of Evermore (3)
Big Band, Sax, And Violence (1)
Blue Train (4)
Blues Anthem (2)
Burning Up (4)
Carole's Theme (1)
Celebration Day (5)
Chase, The (1)
City Don't Cry (3)
City Sirens (1)
Custard Pie (5)
Emerald Eyes (2)
Four Sticks (3)

Friends (3)
Gallow's Pole (4)
Heart In Your Hand (4)
Heartbreaker (5)
Hey Hey What Can I Do (5)
Hotel Rats And Photostats (1)
House Of Love (4)
Hummingbird (4)
Hypnotizing Ways (Oh Mamma) (1)
In My Time Of Dying (5)
Jam Sandwich (1)
Jill's Theme (1)
Kashmir (3)

Lemon Song (5)
Liquid Mercury (2)
Mellow Down Easy (5)
Most High (4)
No Quarter (3)
Nobody's Fault But Mine (3,5)
Oh Well (4)
Only One (2)
Out On The Tiles (5)
Please Read The Letter (4)
Prelude (1)
Prison Blues (2)
Release, The (1)
Shadow In The City (1)

Shake Your Money Maker (5)
Shapes Of Things To Come (5)
Shining In The Light (4)
Sick Again (5)
Since I've Been Loving You (3)
Sloppy Drunk (5)
Sons Of Freedom (4)
Ten Years Gone (5)
Thank You (1)
That's The Way (3)
Upon A Golden Horse (4)
Walking Into Clarksdale (4)
Wanna Make Love (2)
Wasting My Time (2)

What Is And What Should Never Be (5)
When I Was A Child (4)
When The World Was Young (4)
Who's To Blame (1)
Whole Lotta Love (5)
Woke Up This Morning (5)
Wonderful One (3)
Writes Of Winter (2)
Yallah (3)
You Shook Me (5)
Your Time Is Gonna Come (5)

DEBUT	PEAK	WKS	RIAA	CD	ARTIST — Album Title	Catalog	Sym	$	Label & Number

PAGE, Martin '95
Born on 9/23/59 in Southampton, Hampshire, England. Singer/songwriter.

| 4/1/95 | 161 | 11 | | © | **In The House Of Stone And Light** | | | $10 | Mercury 522104 |

Broken Stairway | I Was Made For You | **In The House Of Stone And** | Keeper Of The Flame *83* | Monkey In My Dreams | Shape The Invisible
Door, The | In My Room | Light *14* | Light In Your Heart | Put On Your Red Dress

PAGE, Patti '65
Born Clara Ann Fowler on 11/8/27 in Muskogee, Oklahoma; raised in Tulsa, Oklahoma. Pop singer. Used multi-voice effect on her recordings. Own TV series *The Patti Page Show* (1955-58) and *The Big Record* (1957-58). Acted in the 1960 movie *Elmer Gantry*.

11/24/56	18	2			1 Manhattan Tower			$30	Mercury 20226
9/1/62	115	5			2 Golden Hits Of The Boys			$25	Mercury 20712
9/21/63	83	6			3 Say Wonderful Things			$20	Columbia 2049 / 8849
5/22/65	27	26		©	4 Hush, Hush, Sweet Charlotte			$20	Columbia 2353 / 9153
12/25/65+	51ˣ	4		©	5 Christmas with Patti Page		[X]	$20	Columbia 2414 / 9214

Christmas charts: 60/'65, 51/'67

| 7/27/68 | 168 | 6 | | © | 6 Gentle On My Mind | | | $15 | Columbia 9666 |

Am I That Easy To Forget (6) | Don't Worry (2) | Honey (I Miss You) (6) | Love Letters (3) | **Repeat After Me** (1) *53* | 'Twas The Night Before
Big Bad John (2) | End Of The World (3) | **Hush, Hush, Sweet Charlotte** | Mack The Knife (2) | Rudolph, The Red-Nosed | Christmas (5)
Black Is The Color Of My True | Fly Me To The Moon (In Other | (4) *8* | March Marches On (1) | Reindeer (5) | We Wish You A Merry
Love's Hair (4) | Words) (3) | I Almost Lost My Mind (3) | Married I Can Always Get (1) | Santa Claus Is Comin' To Town | Christmas (5)
Call Me Irresponsible (3) | Four Walls (6) | I Wanna Be Around (3) | Moon River (3) | (5) | Who's Gonna Shoe My Pretty
Can't Get Used To Losing You | **Gentle On My Mind** (6) *66* | I'm Walkin' (3) | Never Leave Me (1) | Santo Natale (5) | Little Feet (4)
(3) | Georgia On My Mind (4) | If And When (3) | New York's My Home (1) | **Say Wonderful Things** (3) *81* | (You've Got) Personality (2)
Can't Help Falling In Love (4) | Good Life (3) | Indian Giver (1) | Once Upon A Dream (1) | Scarlet Ribbons (For Her Hair)
Christmas Bells (5) | Green Green Grass Of Home | It's Just A Matter Of Time (2) | Our Day Will Come (3) | (4)
Croce Di Oro (Cross Of Gold) | (6) | Jamaica Farewell (4) | Party (Noah) (1) | Silver Bells (5)
(4) *16* | Green Leaves Of Summer (4) | Jingle Bells (5) | Poor Little Fool (2) | Skip A Rope (6)
Danny Boy (4) | Happiness Cocktail (1) | Learnin' My Latin (1) | Pretty Snow Flakes (5) | Take Me To Your World (6)
Days Of Wine And Roses (3) | Happy Birthday, Jesus (A | Little Drummer Boy (5) | Put Your Head On My Shoulder | This Close To The Dawn (1)
Don't Be Cruel (To A Heart | Child's Prayer) (5) | **Little Green Apples** (6) *96* | (2) | This House (6)
That's True) (2) | Have A Little Faith (6) | Longing To Hold You Again (4) | Release Me (6) | Try To Remember (4)

PAGE, Tommy '90
Born on 5/24/69 in West Caldwell, New Jersey. Pop singer.

5/6/89	166	5		©	1 Tommy Page			$10	Sire 25740
3/24/90	38	23		©	2 Paintings In My Mind			$10	Sire 26148
6/15/91	192	2		©	3 From The Heart			$10	Sire 26583

African Sunset (1) | I Break Down (2) | Just Before (I Was Gonna Say I | My Shining Star (3) | Turn On The Radio (2) | Written All Over My Heart (3)
Can't Get You Outta My Mind | I Love London (1) | Love You) (2) | Never Gonna Fall In Love Again | Turning Me On (1) | You Are My Heaven (3)
(3) | I Still Believe In You And Me (3) | Love Takes Over (1) | (3) | Under The Rainbow (3) | You're The Best Thing (That
Don't Give Up On Love (2) | I Think I'm In Love (1) | Madly In Love (3) | Paintings In My Mind (2) | **When I Dream Of You** (2) *42* | Ever Happened To Me) (2)
Don't Walk Away (1) | **I'll Be Your Everything** (2) *1* | Making My Move (1) | **Shoulder To Cry On** (1) *29* | Whenever You Close Your | Zillion Kisses (1)
Hard To Be Normal (1) | I'll Never Forget You (3) | Minetta Lane (1) | Till The End Of Time (2) | Eyes (3)

PAIGE, Jennifer '98
Born on 9/3/75 in Marietta, Georgia. Pop singer.

| 8/29/98 | 139 | 14 | | © | Jennifer Paige | | | $10 | Edel America 62171 |

Always You | Busted | Get To Me | Let It Rain | Sober
Between You And Me | **Crush** *3* | Just To Have You | Questions | Somewhere, Someday

PAIGE, Kevin '89
Born in Memphis. Pop singer.

| 9/23/89 | 107 | 31 | | © | Kevin Paige | | | $10 | Chrysalis 21683 |

Anything I Want *29* | Black And White | Hypnotize | Love Of The World | Touch Of Paradise
Believe In Yourself | **Don't Shut Me Out** *18* | I Realize | Stop Messin' With Me | (You Put Me In) Another World

PAISLEY, Brad '01
Born on 10/28/72 in Glen Dale, West Virginia. Country singer/songwriter/guitarist.

| 10/9/99+ | 102 | 34 | ▲ | © | 1 Who Needs Pictures | | | $10 | Arista 18871 |
| 6/16/01 | 31 | 9 | | © | 2 Part II | | | $10 | Arista 67008 |

All You Really Need Is Love (2) | Holdin' On To You (1) | It Never Woulda Worked Out | Nervous Breakdown (1) | **Two People Fell In Love** (2) *51* | You Have That Effect On Me
Cloud Of Dust (1) | I Wish You'd Stay (2) | Anyway (1) | Old Rugged Cross (2) | **We Danced** (1) *29* | (2)
Come On Over Tonight (2) | I'm Gonna Miss Her (2) | Long Sermon (1) | Sleepin' On The Foldout (1) | Who Needs Pictures (1) *65* | You'll Never Leave Harlan Alive
Don't Breathe (1) | I've Been Better (1) | **Me Neither** (1,2) *85* | Too Country (2) | Wrapped Around (2) | (2)
He Didn't Have To Be (1) *30* | In The Garden (1) | Munster Rag (2) | Two Feet Of Topsoil (2)

PALM BEACH BAND BOYS, The '67
Vocal trio led by Roger Rigney and arranged by guitarist Billy Mure (**Leo Addeo & His Orchestra**).

| 1/28/67 | 149 | 1 | | | Winchester Cathedral | | | $15 | RCA Victor 3734 |

Bend It | I Don't Want To Set The World | I'm Gonna Sit Right Down And | It Looks Like Rain In Cherry | Little Bit Independent
Boo-Hoo | On Fire | Write Myself A Letter | Blossom Lane | Winchester Cathedral
Gypsy Caravan | | Ida, Sweet As Apple Cider | Let A Smile Be Your Umbrella

PALMER, Robert '86
★311★
Born Alan Palmer on 1/19/49 in Batley, Yorkshire, England; raised on the Mediterranean island of Malta. Pop-rock singer. Lead singer of **The Power Station**.

1)Riptide 2)Heavy Nova 3)Secrets

6/14/75	107	15		©	1 Sneakin' Sally Through The Alley			$15	Island 9294
11/22/75	136	8		©	2 Pressure Drop			$15	Island 9372
10/23/76	68	16		©	3 Some People Can Do What They Like			$12	Island 9420
4/1/78	45	25		©	4 Double Fun			$12	Island 9476
7/21/79	19	24		©	5 Secrets			$12	Island 9544
10/11/80	59	17		©	6 Clues			$12	Island 9595
5/15/82	148	5		©	7 Maybe It's Live		[L]	$12	Island 9665

recorded on 11/10/80 at the Dominion Theatre in London

| 4/30/83 | 112 | 19 | | © | 8 Pride | | | $12 | Island 90065 |

PALMER, Robert — Cont'd

DEBUT	PEAK	WKS	RIAA	CD	Title	$	Label & Number
11/23/85+	8	90	▲²	© 9	**Riptide**	$10	Island 90471
7/16/88	13	44	▲	© 10	Heavy Nova	$10	EMI-Manhattan 48057
11/25/89+	79	17	▲	© 11	"Addictions" Volume I	[G] $10	Island 91318
12/1/90	88	28		© 12	Don't Explain	$10	EMI 93955
11/14/92	173	1		© 13	Ridin' High	$10	EMI 98923

Addicted To Love (9,11) *1*
Aeroplane (12,13)
Baby It's Cold Outside (13)
Back In My Arms (2)
Bad Case Of Loving You (Doctor, Doctor) (5,7,11) *14*
Best Of Both Worlds (4,7)
Between Us (10)
Blackmail (1)
Can We Still Be Friends (5) *52*
Casting A Spell (10)
Chance (13)
Change His Ways (10)
Come Over (4)
Dance For Me (8)
Deadline (8)
Discipline Of Love (Why Did You Do It) (9) *82*
Disturbing Behaviour (10)
Do Nothin' Till You Hear From Me (13)
Don't Explain (12,13)
Dreams To Remember (12)
Early In The Morning (10) *19*

Every Kinda People (4,7,11) *16*
Fine Time (2)
Flesh Wound (9)
Found You Now (6)
From A Whisper To A Scream (1)
Get It Through Your Heart (9)
Get Outside (1)
Give Me An Inch Girl (2)
Goody Goody (13)
Gotta Get A Grip On You (Part II) (3)
Happiness (12)
Hard Head (3,13)
Have Mercy (3)
Here With You Tonight (2)
Hey Julia (1)
History (12)
Honeysuckle Rose (13)
Housework (12)
How Much Fun (1)
Hyperactive (9) *33*

I Didn't Mean To Turn You On (9) *2*
I Dream Of Wires (6)
I'll Be Your Baby Tonight (12)
In Walks Love Again (5)
It Could Happen To You (10)
It's Not Difficult (8)
Jealous (3)
Johnny And Mary (6,11)
Keep In Touch (3)
Light-Years (12)
Looking For Clues (6,11)
Love Can Run Faster (4)
(Love Is) The Tender Trap (13)
Love Me Or Leave Me (13)
Love Stop (5)
Man Smart, Woman Smarter (3) *63*
Maybe It's You (7)
Mean Old World (5)
Mercy Mercy Me (The Ecology)/I Want You (12) *16*
Mess Around (3)
More Than Ever (10)

Night People (4)
No Not Much (13)
Not A Second Time (6)
Not A Word (12)
Off The Bone (3)
One Last Look (3)
People Will Say We're In Love (12)
Pressure Drop (2)
Pride (8,11)
Remember To Remember (5)
Ridin' High (13)
Riptide (9)
Riverboat (2)
Sailing Shoes (11)
Say You Will (8)
She Makes My Day (10)
Si Chatouillieux (7)
Silver Gun (8)
Simply Irresistible (10,11) *2*
Sneakin' Sally Through The Alley (1,7)
Some Guys Have All The Luck (7,11)

Some Like It Hot (Power Station) (11) *6*
Some People Can Do What They Like (3)
Spanish Moon (3)
Style Kills (7,11)
Sulky Girl (6)
Sweet Lies (11) *94*
Tell Me I'm Not Dreaming (10) *60*
Through It All There's You (1)
Too Good To Be True (5)
Top 40 (12)
Trick Bag (9)
Trouble (2)
Under Suspicion (5)
Want You More (8,13)
What A Little Moonlight Can Do (13)
What Can You Bring Me (3)
What Do You Care (6,7)
What You Waiting For (8)
What's It Take? (5,7,11)
Where Can It Go? (4)

Which Of Us Is The Fool (2)
Witchcraft (13)
Woke Up Laughing (6,11)
Woman You're Wonderful (5)
Work To Make It Work (2)
You Are In My System (8) *78*
You Can Have It (Take My Heart) (8)
You Can't Get Enough Of A Good Thing (12)
You Overwhelm Me (4)
You Really Got Me (4)
You're Amazing (12) *28*
You're Gonna Get What's Coming (4)
You're My Thrill (12,13)
You're So Desirable (12)
Your Mother Should Have Told You (12)

PANTERA   '94

Hard-rock group formed in Texas: Philip Anselmo (vocals), Diamond Darrell (guitar), Rex Brown (bass) and Vinnie Paul (drums). Darrell and Paul are brothers. Diamond changed his first name to Dimebag in 1994. Group name is Spanish for Panther. Anselmo also with **Down** in 1995.

DEBUT	PEAK	WKS	RIAA	CD	Title	$	Label & Number
3/14/92	44	77	▲	© 1	Vulgar Display Of Power	C:#41/2 $10	Atco 91758
4/9/94	❶¹	29	▲	© 2	**Far Beyond Driven**	$10	EastWest 92302
3/18/95	43ᶜ	2	▲	© 3	Cowboys From Hell	[E] $10	Atco 91372
					released in 1990		
5/25/96	4	16	●	© 4	**The Great Southern Trendkill**	$10	EastWest 61908
8/16/97	15	12	●	© 5	Official Live: 101 Proof	[L] $10	EastWest 62068
4/8/00	4	12	●	© 6	**Reinventing The Steel**	$10	EastWest 62451

Art Of Shredding (3)
Becoming (2,5)
By Demons Be Driven (1)
Cemetery Gates (3,5)
Clash With Reality (3)
Cowboys From Hell (3,5)
Death Rattle (6)
Dom/Hollow (6)
Domination (3)
Drag The Waters (4)
5 Minutes Alone (2,5)

Floods (4)
Fucking Hostile (1)
Goddamn Electric (6)
Good Friends And A Bottle Of Pills (4)
Great Southern Trendkill (4)
Hard Lines, Sunken Cheeks (2)
Hellbound (3)
Heresy (3)
Hollow (1)
Hostile (5)

I Can't Hide (5)
I'll Cast A Shadow (4)
I'm Broken (2,5)
It Makes Them Disappear (6)
Live In A Hole (1)
Living Through Me (Hell's Wrath) (4)
Medicine Man (3)
Message In Blood (3)
Mouth For War (2)
New Level (1,5)

No Good (Attack The Radical) (1)
Planet Caravan (2)
Primal Concrete Sledge (3)
Psycho Holiday (3)
Regular People (Conceit) (1)
Revolution Is My Name (6)
Rise (1)
Sandblasted Skin (4,5)
Shattered (2)
Shedding Skin (2)

Slaughtered (2)
Sleep, The (3)
Strength Beyond Strength (2,5)
Suicide Note Pt. I & II (4,5)
10's (4)
13 Steps To Nowhere (4)
This Love (1,5)
Throes Of Rejection (2)
25 Years (2)
Underground In America (4)
Uplift (6)

Use My Third Arm (2)
Walk (1,5)
War Nerve (4,5)
We'll Grind That Axe For A Long Time (6)
Where You Come From (5)
Yesterday Don't Mean Shit (6)
You've Got To Belong To It (6)

PAPA ROACH   '00

Rock group from Vacaville, California: Coby Dick (vocals), Jerry Horton (guitar), Tobin Esperance (bass) and Dave Buckner (drums).

DEBUT	PEAK	WKS	RIAA	CD	Title	$	Label & Number
5/13/00	5	65	▲³	©	**Infest**	$10	DreamWorks 50223

Between Angels And Insects
Binge

Blood Brothers
Broken Home

Dead Cell
Infest

Last Resort *57*
Never Enough

Revenge
Snakes

Thrown Away

PAPERBOY   '93

Born in Los Angeles. Male rapper.

DEBUT	PEAK	WKS	RIAA	CD	Title	$	Label & Number
2/13/93	48	33	●	©	The Nine Yards	$10	Next Plateau 1012

Bumpin' (Adaptation Of Humpin')
Ditty *10*

Goin' On
Jack Move

Little Somethin' For The Summer
Nine Yards

Studs
Zooted

PAPER LACE   '74

Pop group formed in England: Phil Wright (vocals, drums), Michael Vaughan and Chris Morris (guitars), and Cliff Fish (bass).

DEBUT	PEAK	WKS	RIAA	CD	Title	$	Label & Number
9/7/74	124	8			Paper Lace	$15	Mercury 1008

Billy-Don't Be A Hero *96*
Black-Eyed Boys *41*
Cheek To Cheek

Dreams Are Ten A Penny
Happy Birthday Sweet Sixteen
Hitchin' A Ride

I Did What I Did For Maria
Love Song

Love - You're A Long Time Coming
Mary In The Morning

Night Chicago Died *1*
Sealed With A Kiss

PARAMOR, Norrie, His Strings and Orchestra   '56

Born in 1914 in England. Died on 9/9/79 (age 65). Conductor/composer/arranger.

DEBUT	PEAK	WKS	RIAA	CD	Title	$	Label & Number
9/8/56	18	3		©	In London, In Love...	[I] $25	Capitol Int'l. 10025

All The Things You Are
Dearly Beloved

Deep Purple
Embraceable You

I'll Get By
Nearness Of You

Someone To Watch Over Me
Stairway To The Stars

Stardust
Stars Fell On Alabama

Touch Of Your Lips
Very Thought Of You

PARIS   '76

Rock trio: **Bob Welch** (guitar; **Fleetwood Mac**), Glenn Cornick (bass; **Jethro Tull**) and Thom Mooney (drums; **Nazz**). Hunt Sales (later with **Tin Machine**) replaced Mooney in 1976.

DEBUT	PEAK	WKS	RIAA	CD	Title	$	Label & Number
2/7/76	103	9		1	Paris	$15	Capitol 11464
9/11/76	152	6		2	Big Towne, 2061	$15	Capitol 11560

Beautiful Youth (1)
Big Towne, 2061 (2)
Black Book (1)
Blue Robin (2)

Breathless (1)
Heart Of Stone (2)
Janie (2)
Money Love (2)

Narrow Gate (1)
Nazarene (1)
New Orleans (2)
1 In 10 (2)

Outlaw Game (2)
Pale Horse, Pale Rider (2)
Red Rain (1)
Religion (1)

Rock Of Ages (1)
Slave Trader (2)
Solitaire (1)
Starcage (1)

PARIS '94
Born Oscar Jackson on 10/29/67 in San Francisco. Male rapper.

DEBUT	PEAK	WKS		CD	Album Title			$	Label & Number
12/22/90+	158	8		© 1	The Devil Made Me Do It			$10	Tommy Boy 1030
12/12/92	182	3		© 2	Sleeping With The Enemy			$10	Scarface 100
10/22/94	128	4		© 3	Guerrilla Funk			$10	Priority 53882

Assata's Song (2)
Back In The Days (3)
Break The Grip Of Shame (1)
Bring It To Ya (3)
Brutal (1)
Bush Killa (2)
Check It Out Ch'All (2)
Coffee, Donuts & Death (2)
Conspiracy Of Silence (2)
Days Of Old (2)
Devil Made Me Do It (1)
Ebony (1)
Enema, The (2)
Escape From Babylon (1)
40 Ounces And A Fool (3)
Funky Lil' Party (2)
Guerrilla Funk (3)
Guerrillas In The Mist (2)
Hate That Hate Made (1)
House Niggas Bleed Too (2)
I Call Him Mad (1)
It's Real (3)
Long Hot Summer (2)
Make Way For A Panther (2)
Mellow Madness (1)
On The Prowl (1)
One Time Fo' Ya Mind (3)
Outta My Life (3)
Panther Power (1)
Rise (2)
Scarface Groove (1)
Shots Out (3)
Sleeping With The Enemy (2)
Thinka 'Bout It (2)
This Is A Test (1)
Warning (1)
Whatcha See? (3)
Wretched (1)

PARIS, Mica '89
Born Michelle Wallen on 4/27/69 in London. R&B singer.

DEBUT	PEAK	WKS		CD	Album Title			$	Label & Number
5/13/89	86	23		©	So Good			$10	Island 90970

Breathe Life Into Me
Don't Give Me Up
Great Impersonation
I'd Hate To Love You
Like Dreamers Do
My One Temptation 97
Nothing Hits Your Heart Like
Soul Music
So Good
Sway (Dance The Blues Away)
Where Is The Love

PARIS, Sarina '01
Born in Canada. Female singer.

DEBUT	PEAK	WKS		CD	Album Title			$	Label & Number
6/23/01	167	1		©	Sarina Paris			$10	Playland 50175

All In The Way
Angel
Dreamin' Of You
I Love You
Just About Enough
Look At Us 59
Love In Return
Romeo's Dead
Single Life
So I Wait
True Colors
True Love
You

PARIS, Twila '96
Born in 1959 in Forth Worth, Texas; raised in Fayetteville, Arkansas. Christian singer.

DEBUT	PEAK	WKS		CD	Album Title			$	Label & Number
4/20/96	87	9		© 1	Where I Stand			$10	Sparrow 51518
5/2/98	129	4		© 2	Perennial - Songs For The Seasons Of Life			$10	Sparrow 51627
10/9/99	112	5		© 3	True North			$10	Sparrow 51690

Amazing Grace (2)
Band Of Survivors (1)
Be Thou My Vision (2)
Come, Thou Fount Of Every
  Blessing (2)
Could You Believe (3)
Daughter Of Grace (3)
Delight My Heart (3)
Faithful Friend (1)
Faithful Men (2)
Father, We Are Here (2)
Fountain Of Grace (2)
Hold On (1)
Honor And Praise (1)
House Of Cards (1)
(I Am) Not Afraid Anymore (1)
I Choose Grace (3)
I Never Get Used To What You
  Do (1)
I Will Listen (1)
Jesus In You (1)
Love's Been Following You (1)
My Lips Will Praise You (2)
No Confidence (3)
Once In A Life (3)
Perennial (2)
Run To You (3)
True North (3)
We Seek His Face (2)
What Did He Die For? (1)
When The Roll Is Called Up
  Yonder (3)
When You Speak To Me (3)
Wisdom (3)
Wondering Out Loud (3)

PARISH, John '96
Singer/songwriter/guitarist/producer.

DEBUT	PEAK	WKS		CD	Album Title			$	Label & Number
10/12/96	178	1		©	Dance Hall At Louse Point			$10	Island 524278
					JOHN PARISH & POLLY JEAN HARVEY				

City Of No Sun
Civil War Correspondent
Dance Hall At Louse Point
Girl
Heela
Is That All There Is?
Lost Fun Zone
Rope Bridge Crossing
Taut
That Was My Veil
Un Cercle Autour Du Soleil
Urn With Dead Flowers In A
  Drained Pool

PARKER, Graham '79
Born on 11/18/50 in London. Pop-rock singer/songwriter/guitarist.
1)Squeezing Out Sparks 2)The Up Escalator 3)Another Grey Area

DEBUT	PEAK	WKS		CD	Album Title			$	Label & Number
1/29/77	169	7		© 1	Heat Treatment			$15	Mercury 1117
					GRAHAM PARKER AND THE RUMOUR:				
11/5/77	125	5		© 2	Stick To Me			$15	Mercury 3706
7/1/78	149	3		© 3	The Parkerilla	[L]		$20	Mercury 100 [2]
4/14/79	40	24		© 4	Squeezing Out Sparks			$15	Arista 4223
5/31/80	40	15		© 5	The Up Escalator			$15	Arista 9517
					GRAHAM PARKER:				
4/10/82	51	16		© 6	Another Grey Area			$12	Arista 9589
8/20/83	59	14		© 7	The Real Macaw			$12	Arista 8023
4/20/85	57	21		© 8	Steady Nerves			$12	Elektra 60388
					GRAHAM PARKER AND THE SHOT				
5/28/88	77	19		© 9	The Mona Lisa's Sister			$10	RCA 8316
2/24/90	165	9		© 10	Human Soul			$10	RCA 9876
3/23/91	131	8		© 11	Struck By Lightning			$10	BMG 3013

And It Shook Me (11)
Anniversary (7)
Another Grey Area (6)
Back Door Love (1)
Back In Time (9)
Back To Schooldays (3)
Beating Of Another Heart (5)
Beyond A Joke (7)
Big Fat Zero (6)
Big Man On Paper (10)
Black Honey (1)
Black Lincoln Continental (8)
Blue Highways (9)
Brand New Book (11)
Break Them Down (8)
Call Me Your Doctor (10)
Can't Waste A Minute (6)
Canned Laughter (8)
Children And Dogs (11)
Clear Head (2)
Crying For Attention (6)
Cupid (9)
Daddy's Postman (10)
Dancing For Money (10)
Dark Side Of The Bright Lights
  (6)
Devil's Sidewalk (5)
Discovering Japan (4)
Don't Ask Me Questions (3)
Don't Get Excited (4)
Don't Let It Break You Down (9)
Empty Lives (5)
Endless Night (5)
Everyone's Hand Is On The
  Switch (8)
Everything Goes (10)
Fear Not (6)
Fools' Gold (1,3)
Get Started, Start A Fire (9)
Girl Isn't Ready (9)
Glass Jaw (7)
Green Monkeys (10)
Guardian Angels (11)
Gypsy Blood (3)
Heat In Harlem (2,3)
Heat Treatment (1,3)
Help Me Shake It (1)
Hotel Chambermaid (1)
I Don't Know (9)
I Was Wrong (10)
I'm Gonna Tear Your Playhouse
  Down (2,3)
I'm Just Your Man (9)
It's All Worth Nothing Alone (6)
Jolie Jolie (5)
Just Like A Man (7)
Kid With The Butterfly Net (11)
Lady Doctor (3)
Last Couple On The Dance
  Floor (7)
Life Gets Better (7) 94
Little Miss Understanding (10)
Local Girls (4)
Locked Into Green (8)
Love Gets You Twisted (4)
Love Without Greed (5)
Lunatic Fringe (8)
Maneuvers (5)
Mighty Rivers (8)
Miracle A Minute (7)
My Love's Strong (10)
New York Shuffle (2,3)
No Holding Back (5)
No More Excuses (6)
Nobody Hurts You (4)
OK Hieronymus (9)
Over The Border (To America)
  (11)
Paralyzed (5)
Passion Is No Ordinary Word
  (4)
Passive Resistance (7)
Pourin' It All Out (1)
Problem Child (1)
Protection (4)
Raid, The (2)
Saturday Nite Is Dead (4)
She Wants So Many Things
  (11)
Silly Thing (3)
Slash And Burn (10)
Something You're Going
  Through (11)
Soul On Ice (2)
Soul Shoes (3)
Soultime (10)
Sounds Like Chains (7)
Stick To Me (2)
Strong Winds (11)
Stupefaction (5)
Success (9)
Sugar Gives You Energy (10)
Sun Is Gonna Shine Again (11)
Take Everything (8)
Temporary Beauty (6)
Ten Girls Ago (11)
Thankless Task (6)
That's What They All Say (1)
That's Where She Ends Up (11)
They Murdered The Clown (11)
Thunder And Rain (2)
(Too Late) The Smart Bomb (7)
Turned Up Too Late (1)
Under The Mask Of Happiness
  (9)
Waiting For The UFO's (4)
Wake Up (Next To You) (8) 39
Watch The Moon Come Down
  (2,3)
Weekend's Too Short (8)
Weeping Statues (11)
When I Was King (11)
When You Do That To Me (8)
Wrapping Paper (11)
You Can't Be Too Strong (4)
You Can't Take Love For
  Granted (7)
You Got The World (Right
  Where You Want It) (10)
You Hit The Spot (6)

★362★ PARKER, Ray Jr./Raydio '82

Born on 5/1/54 in Detroit. R&B singer/songwriter/guitarist. Prominent session guitarist in California; worked with **Stevie Wonder**, **Barry White** and others. Formed group Raydio in 1977 with Arnell Carmichael, **Jerry Knight**, Larry Tolbert, Darren Carmichael and Charles Fearing. Parker went solo in 1982. Knight later recorded in duo **Ollie & Jerry**.

1)The Other Woman 2)A Woman Needs Love 3)Raydio

RAYDIO:

2/11/78	27	23	●		1 Raydio			$12	Arista 4163
4/14/79	45	30	●		2 Rock On			$12	Arista 4212

RAY PARKER JR. & RAYDIO:

4/12/80	33	21	●		3 Two Places At The Same Time			$12	Arista 9515
4/18/81	13	26	●		4 A Woman Needs Love			$12	Arista 9543

RAY PARKER JR.:

4/24/82	11	27	●		5 The Other Woman			$10	Arista 9590
12/18/82+	51	22			6 Greatest Hits		[G]	$10	Arista 9612
11/26/83+	45	23			7 Woman Out Of Control			$10	Arista 8087
12/15/84+	60	15	●		8 Chartbusters		[G]	$10	Arista 8266
10/26/85	65	13			9 Sex And The Single Man			$10	Arista 8280
10/10/87	86	9	©		10 After Dark			$10	Geffen 24124

After Dark (10)
After Midnite (10)
All In The Way You Get Down (4)
Bad Boy (6) 35
Betcha You Can't Love Me Just Once (1)
Can't Keep From Cryin' (3)
Christmas Time Is Here (8)
Electronic Lover (7)
Everybody Makes Mistakes (3)
Everybody Wants Someone (9)
For Those Who Like To Groove (3,6)

Get Down (1)
Ghostbusters (8) 1
Girls Are More Fun (9) 34
Goin' Thru School And Love (2)
Good Time Baby (9)
Honey I'm A Star (2)
Honey I'm Rich (1)
I Don't Think That Man Should Sleep Alone (10) 68
I Don't Wanna Know (7)
I Love Your Daughter (10)
I Still Can't Get Over Loving You (7,8) 12

I'm A Dog (9)
I've Been Diggin You (8)
In The Heat Of The Night (7)
Invasion (7,8)
Is This A Love Thing (1)
It's Our Own Affair (5)
It's Time To Party Now (3)
It's Your Night (4)
Jack And Jill (1,6) 8
Jamie (8) 14
Just Havin' Fun (5)
Let Me Go (5,6) 38
Let's Get Off (5)

Let's Go All The Way (1)
Little Bit Of You (3)
Lovin' You (10)
Me (1)
Men Have Feelings Too (9)
More Than One Way To Love A Woman (2)
N2U2 (7)
Old Pro (4)
One Sided Love Affair (9)
Other Woman (5,6,8)
Over You (1)
Past, The (10)
People Next Door (6)

Perfect Lovers (10)
Rock On (2)
Sex And The Single Man (9)
She Still Feels The Need (7)
So Into You (4)
Stay The Night (5)
Still In The Groove (4)
Stop, Look Before You Love (5)
Streetlove (5)
That Old Song (4,6) 21
Tonight's The Night (3)
Two Places At The Same Time (3,6) 30
Until The Morning Comes (3)

What You Waitin' For (2)
When You're In Need Of Love (2)
Woman Needs Love (Just Like You Do) (4,6,8) 4
Woman Out Of Control (7,8)
You Can't Change That (2,6) 9
You Can't Fight What You Feel (4)
You Make My Nature Dance (10)
You Need This (To Satisfy That) (1)
You Shoulda Kept A Spare (10)

PARKS, Michael '70

Born on 4/4/38 in Corona, California. Singer/actor. Appeared in several movies. Played "Jim Bronson" in the 1969 TV series *Then Came Bronson*.

11/8/69+	35	46			1 Closing The Gap			$15	MGM 4646
5/23/70	24	21			2 Long Lonesome Highway			$15	MGM 4662
10/10/70	71	8			3 Blue			$15	MGM 4717
3/13/71	195	1			4 Lost And Found			$15	Verve 5079

Beautiful Means You (3)
Big "T" Water (2)
Born To Lose (3)
California's Fine (2)
Cold, Cold Heart (3)
Farther Along (medley) (4)
I Can't Help It (If I'm Still In Love With You) (3)
I Come To The Garden (3)
I Let You Take Advantage (4)

I Think Of You (2)
I Was Born In Kentucky (4)
I'm Lonely And Blue (3)
I'm So Lonesome I Could Cry (medley) (4)
It's You (medley) (4)
Long Lonesome Highway (2) 20
Look Down That Lonesome Road (4)

Lost And Found (4)
Midnight Wind (1)
Mountain High (2)
My Little Buckaroo (1)
My Melancholy Baby (2)
No One To Cry To (3)
Oklahoma Hills (1)
Pretty Piece Of Paper (1)
Re-Enlistment Blues (2)
Ride 'Em Cowboy (1)

Sally (Was A Gentle Woman) (3)
San Antonio Rose (1)
Save A Little, Spend A Little (Give A Little Away) (3)
Sneakin' In The Back Door Of Love (1)
Softly And Tenderly (4)
Soldier's Last Letter (1)
Statue Of A Fool (4)

Summer Days (2)
Sunshine Showers (2)
Sweet Misery (4)
There's Been A Change In Me (3)
Tie Me To Your Apron Strings Again (1)
Treasure Untold (1)
Turn Around Little Mama (4)
Wayfarin' Stranger (1)

When I've Learned (medley) (4)
Won't You Ride In My Little Red Wagon (1)
Yonder Comes The Blues (2)

★467★ PARLIAMENT '76

Highly influential and prolific funk aggregation of nearly 40 musicians spearheaded by **George Clinton** (producer/songwriter/lead singer). Clinton founded doo-wop group The Parliaments in 1955 in Newark, New Jersey. By 1967, evolved into a Detroit-based soul group with lineup of vocalists Clinton, Raymond Davis, Calvin Simon, Clarence "Fuzzy" Haskins and Grady Thomas. In 1968, Clinton formed **Funkadelic** with rhythm section of The Parliaments and changed The Parliaments name to Parliament. Although on different labels, Parliament and Funkadelic shared the same personnel which included several members of **The JB's**: brothers Phelps "Catfish" (guitar) and William "Bootsy" Collins (bass), Frank "Kash" Waddy (drums) and horn players Maceo Parker and **Fred Wesley**. Known as "A Parliafunkadelicament Thang," this funk corporation hosted various offshoots, including **The Brides Of Funkenstein**, among others. Concert tours featured elaborate staging and characters. Simon, Haskins and Thomas split from Parliament in 1977 and recorded as Funkadelic in 1981. The corporation disassembled in the early '80s. Clinton signed his first solo recording contract in 1982. Clinton regrouped with **The P-Funk Allstars** in 1996. Parliament/Funkadelic were inducted into the Rock and Roll Hall of Fame in 1997.

5/3/75	91	18	©		1 Chocolate City			$40	Casablanca 7014
2/21/76	13	37	▲	©	2 Mothership Connection			$30	Casablanca 7022
10/16/76	20	22	●	©	3 The Clones Of Dr. Funkenstein			$30	Casablanca 7034
5/21/77	29	19	●	©	4 Parliament Live/P. Funk Earth Tour		[L]	$40	Casablanca 7053 [2]
12/24/77	13	34	▲	©	5 Funkentelechy Vs. The Placebo Syndrome			$30	Casablanca 7084
12/16/78+	23	18	●	©	6 Motor-Booty Affair			$30	Casablanca 7125
12/22/79+	44	19	●	©	7 Gloryhallastoopid (Or Pin The Tale On The Funky)			$30	Casablanca 7195
1/10/81	61	7		©	8 Trombipulation			$25	Casablanca 7249

Agony Of Defeet (8)
Aqua Boogie (A Psychoalphadiscobetabioaquadoloop) (6) 89
Big Bang Theory (7)
Big Footin' (1)
Black Hole, Theme From (7)
Body Language (8)
Bop Gun (Endangered Species) (5)
Children Of Production (3,4)
Chocolate City (1) 94
Colour Me Funky (7)
Crush It (8)
Deep (6)

Do That Stuff (3,4)
Dr. Funkenstein (3,4)
Dr. Funkenstein's Supergroovalisticprosifunkstication Medley (3)
Everything Is On The One (3)
Fantasy Is Reality (4)
Flash Light (5) 16
Freeze (Sizzaleenmean) (7)
Funkentelechy (5)
Funkin' For Fun (3)
Gamin' On Ya (3,4)
Get Off Your Ass And Jam (medley) (4)
Getten' To Know You (3)

(Give Up The Funk) ..see: Tear The Roof Off The Sucker
(Gloryhallastoopid) Pin The Tale On The Funky (7)
Handcuffs (3)
I Misjudged You (1)
I've Been Watching You (Move Your Sexy Body) (3)
If It Don't Fit (Don't Force It) (1)
Landing (Of The Holy Mothership) (4)
Let Me Be (1)
Let's Play House (8)
Liquid Sunshine (6)
Long Way Around (8)

May We Bang You? (7)
Mothership Connection (Star Child) (2,4)
Motor-Booty Affair (6)
Mr. Wiggles (6)
New Doo Review (8)
Night Of The Thumpasorus Peoples (2,4)
One Of Those Funky Things (6)
P. Funk (Wants To Get Funked Up) (2,4)
Party People (7)
Peek-A-Groove (8)
Placebo Syndrome (5)
Prelude (3)

Ride On (1)
Rumpofsteelskin (6)
Side Effects (1)
Sir Nose D'Voidoffunk (Pay Attention - B3M) (5)
Supergroovalisticprosifunkstication (The Thumps Bump) (2)
Swing Down, Sweet Chariot (4)
Tear The Roof Off The Sucker (Give Up The Funk) (2,4) 15
This Is The Way We Funk With You (4)
Together (1)
Trombipulation (8)

Undisco Kidd (The Girl Is Bad!) (4)
Unfunky UFO (2)
What Comes Funky (1)
Wizard Of Finance (5)
(You're A Fish And I'm A) Water Sign (6)

PARNELL, Lee Roy '96

Born on 12/21/56 in Abilene, Texas. Country singer/songwriter/guitarist. Cousin of **Robert Earl Keen**.

| 4/27/96 | 173 | 3 | | © | We All Get Lucky Sometimes | | | $10 | Career 18790 |

Cat Walk / Givin' Water To A Drowning Man / Heart's Desire / I Had To Let It Go / If The House Is Rockin' / Knock Yourself Out / Little Bit Of You / Saved By The Grace Of Your Love / Squeeze Me In / We All Get Lucky Sometimes / When A Woman Loves A Man

PARR, John '85

Born on 11/18/54 in Nottingham, England. Pop-rock singer/songwriter.

| 12/15/84+ | 48 | 26 | | © | John Parr | | | $10 | Atlantic 80180 |

Don't Leave Your Mark On Me / Heartbreaker / Love Grammar 89 / Magical 73 / Naughty Naughty 23 / Revenge / She's Gonna Love You To Death / Somebody Stole My Thunder / Treat Me Like An Animal

★238★ PARSONS, Alan, Project '77

Born on 12/20/49 in London. Guitarist/keyboardist/producer. Engineered *Abbey Road* by **The Beatles** and *Dark Side Of The Moon* by **Pink Floyd**. Project features various musicians and vocalists. Eric Woolfson (vocals, keyboards) contributes most of the lyrics.

1)Eye In The Sky 2)I Robot 3)The Turn Of A Friendly Card

5/15/76	38	46		©	1	Tales Of Mystery And Imagination - Edgar Allan Poe			$15	20th Century 508
7/16/77	9	54	▲	©	2	I Robot			$12	Arista 7002
7/1/78	26	25		©	3	Pyramid			$12	Arista 4180
9/15/79	13	27	●	©	4	Eve	C:#12/89		$12	Arista 9504
11/15/80+	13	58	▲	©	5	The Turn Of A Friendly Card			$12	Arista 9518
6/19/82	7	41	▲	©	6	Eye In The Sky			$12	Arista 9599
11/19/83	53	29	●	©	7	The Best Of The Alan Parsons Project	[G]		$10	Arista 8193
3/17/84	15	26	●	©	8	Ammonia Avenue			$10	Arista 8204
3/9/85	46	19		©	9	Vulture Culture			$10	Arista 8263
2/1/86	43	18		©	10	Stereotomy			$10	Arista 8384
2/7/87	57	14		©	11	Gaudi			$10	Arista 8448
11/13/93	122	4		©	12	Try Anything Once			$10	Arista 18741

ALAN PARSONS

Ace Of Swords (medley) (5) / Ammonia Avenue (8) / Back Against The Wall (12) / Beaujolais (10) / Breakaway (12) / Breakdown (2) / Can't Take It With You (3,7) / Children Of The Moon (6) / Chinese Whispers (10) / Closer To Heaven (11) / Dancing On A High Wire (8) / Day After Day (The Show Must Go On) (2) / **Days Are Numbers (The Traveller) (9) 71** / **Don't Answer Me (8) 15** / Don't Hold Back (4) / **Don't Let It Show (2,7) 92** / Dream Within A Dream (1) / Dreamscape (12) / Eagle Will Rise Again (3) / Fall Of The House Of Usher Medley (1) / Games People Play (5,7) 16 / Gemini (8) / Genesis Ch.1. V.32 (2) / Gold Bug (5) / Hawkeye (9) / Hyper-Gamma-Spaces (3) / I Don't Wanna Go Home (5) / I Robot (2) / **I Wouldn't Want To Be Like You (2,7) 36** / I'd Rather Be A Man (4) / I'm Talkin' To You (12) / If I Could Change Your Mind (4) / In The Lap Of The Gods (3) / In The Real World (10) / Inside Looking Out (11) / Jigue (12) / La Sagrada Familia (11) / Let Me Go Home (8) / **Let's Talk About Me (9) 56** / Light Of The World (10) / Limelight (10) / Lucifer (4,7) / Mammagamma (6) / May Be A Price To Pay (5) / Money Talks (11) / Mr Time (12) / Nothing Left To Lose (medley) (5) / Nucleus (2) / Oh Life (There Must Be More) (12) / Old And Wise (6,7) / One Good Reason (8) / One More River (3) / Paseo De Gracia (11) / Pipeline (8) / **Prime Time (8) 34** / **Psychobabble (6,7) 57** / Pyramania (3,7) / **Raven, The (1) 80** / Re-Jigue (12) / Same Old Sun (9) / Secret Garden (4) / Separate Lives (9) / Shadow Of A Lonely Man (3) / Silence And I (6) / Since The Last Goodbye (8) / Siren Song (12) / Sirius (6) / **Snake Eyes (medley) (5) 67** / Some Other Time (2) / Somebody Out There (9) / Sooner Or Later (9) / Standing On Higher Ground (11) / Step By Step (6) / **Stereotomy (10) 82** / Stereotomy Two (10) / **(System Of) Doctor Tarr And Professor Fether (1) 37** / Tell-Tale Heart (1) / Three Of Me (12) / **Time (5,7) 15** / To One In Paradise (1) / Too Late (11) / Total Eclipse (2) / Turn It Up (12) / Turn Of A Friendly Card (Part One) (medley) (5) / Urbania (10) / Voice (2) / Voyager (3) / Vulture Culture (9) / **What Goes Up (3) 87** / Where's The Walrus? (10) / Winding Me Up (4) / Wine From The Water (12) / **You Don't Believe (7,8) 54** / You Lie Down With Dogs (4) / You Won't Be There (4) / You're Gonna Get Your Fingers Burned (6)

PARSONS, Gram '74

Born Cecil Connor on 11/5/46 in Winter Haven, Florida. Died of a drug overdose on 9/19/73 (age 26). Country-rock singer/guitarist. Member of **The Byrds** (1968) and the **Flying Burrito Brothers** (1968-70).

| 2/16/74 | 195 | 3 | | © | Grievous Angel | | | $20 | Reprise 2171 |

Brass Buttons / Cash On The Barrelhead (medley) / Hearts On Fire / Hickory Wind (medley) / I Can't Dance / In My Hour Of Darkness / Las Vegas / Love Hurts / $1000 Wedding / Return Of The Grievous Angel

PARTLAND BROTHERS '87

Duo from Colgan, Ontario, Canada: Chris (vocals, guitars) and G.P. (vocals, percussion) Partland.

| 6/27/87 | 146 | 5 | | | Electric Honey | | | $10 | Manhattan 53050 |

Best Love / Electric Honey / Heat Up The Feel / One Chance / Outside The City / Reason, The / **Soul City 27** / That's The Way It Will Be / This One's For You / Walk With Me

PARTON, Dolly ★87★ '78

Born on 1/19/46 in Sevier County, Tennessee. Country singer/songwriter/actress. Regular on **Porter Wagoner**'s TV show (1967-74). Starred in the movies *9 to 5*, *The Best Little Whorehouse In Texas*, *Steel Magnolias* and *Straight Talk*. In 1986, opened Dollywood theme park in the Smoky Mountains. Hosted own TV variety show in 1987.

*1)Trio 2)9 To 5 And Odd Jobs 3)Slow Dancing With The Moon 4)Here You Come Again
5)Eagle When She Flies*

| 3/22/69 | 184 | 4 | | | 1 | Just The Two Of Us | | | $20 | RCA Victor 4039 |
| 8/16/69 | 162 | 5 | | | 2 | Always, Always | | | $20 | RCA Victor 4186 |

PORTER WAGONER & DOLLY PARTON (above 2)

| 11/22/69 | 194 | 2 | | | 3 | My Blue Ridge Mountain Boy | | | $20 | RCA Victor 4188 |
| 4/4/70 | 137 | 7 | | | 4 | Porter Wayne And Dolly Rebecca | | | $20 | RCA Victor 4305 |

PORTER WAGONER & DOLLY PARTON

| 8/15/70 | 154 | 2 | | | 5 | A Real Live Dolly | [L] | | $20 | RCA Victor 4387 |

recorded on 4/25/70 at Sevier County High School in Tennessee

| 10/10/70 | 191 | 2 | | | 6 | Once More | | | $20 | RCA Victor 4388 |
| 3/13/71 | 142 | 3 | | © | 7 | Two Of A Kind | | | $20 | RCA Victor 4490 |

PORTER WAGONER & DOLLY PARTON (above 2)

DEBUT	PEAK	WKS	RIAA	CD	ARTIST — Album Title	Catalog	Sym	$	Label & Number
					PARTON, Dolly — Cont'd				
6/12/71	198	1			8 Joshua			$20	RCA Victor 4507
4/2/77	71	21			9 New Harvest...First Gathering			$12	RCA Victor 2188
10/29/77+	20	47	▲	©	10 Here You Come Again			$12	RCA Victor 2544
8/12/78	27	34	●	©	11 Heartbreaker			$12	RCA Victor 2797
6/23/79	40	17	●		12 Great Balls Of Fire			$12	RCA Victor 3361
5/3/80	71	13			13 Dolly Dolly Dolly			$12	RCA Victor 3546
12/6/80+	11	34	●	©	14 9 To 5 And Odd Jobs			$12	RCA Victor 3852
4/24/82	106	12			15 Heartbreak Express			$12	RCA Victor 4289
10/16/82	77	23	▲	©	16 Greatest Hits		[G]	$12	RCA Victor 4422
1/15/83	109	14		©	17 Kris, Willie, Dolly & Brenda...the winning hand			$15	Monument 38389 [2]
					KRIS KRISTOFFERSON, WILLIE NELSON, DOLLY PARTON & BRENDA LEE				
6/4/83	127	11			18 Burlap & Satin			$12	RCA Victor 4691
2/18/84	73	14			19 The Great Pretender			$12	RCA Victor 4940
7/21/84	135	7		©	20 Rhinestone		[S]	$10	RCA Victor 5032
					includes "Too Much Water" by Randy Parton; "The Day My Baby Died" by Rusty Buchanan; "Goin' Back To Heaven" by Stella Parton & Kin Vassy; "Drinkin' Stein" by Sylvester Stallone; and "Waltz Me To Heaven" by Floyd Parton				
12/8/84+	31	8	▲²	©	21 Once Upon A Christmas	C:#15/13	[X]	$10	RCA Victor 5307
					KENNY ROGERS & DOLLY PARTON				
					Christmas charts: 1/'84, 4/'85, 10/'87, 16/'88, 15/'89, 14/'90, 14/'91, 19/'92, 25/'93				
3/28/87	6	48	▲	©	22 Trio			$10	Warner 25491
					DOLLY PARTON, LINDA RONSTADT, EMMYLOU HARRIS				
12/19/87+	153	8			23 Rainbow			$10	Columbia 40968
4/6/91	24	47	▲	©	24 Eagle When She Flies			$10	Columbia 46882
4/25/92	138	3		©	25 Straight Talk		[S]	$10	Hollywood 61303
3/13/93	16	25	▲	©	26 Slow Dancing With The Moon			$10	Columbia 53199
11/20/93	42	16	●	©	27 Honky Tonk Angels			$10	Columbia 53414
					DOLLY PARTON, LORETTA LYNN, TAMMY WYNETTE				
10/15/94	87	10		©	28 Heartsongs - Live From Home		[L]	$10	Columbia 66123
					recorded on 4/23/94 at the Dollywood Celebrity Theater in Tennessee				
11/26/94	37ˣ	1	●	©	29 Home For Christmas	C:#37/4	[X]	$10	Columbia 46796
					first released in 1990				
9/16/95	54	14		©	30 Something Special			$10	Columbia 67140
10/12/96	122	10			31 Treasures			$10	Rising Tide 53041
9/12/98	167	2		©	32 Hungry Again			$10	Decca 70041
2/27/99	62	14		©	33 Trio II			$10	Asylum 62275
					EMMYLOU HARRIS, LINDA RONSTADT, DOLLY PARTON				
11/20/99	198	1		©	34 The Grass Is Blue			$10	Blue Eye 3900
2/10/01	97	9		©	35 Little Sparrow			$10	Sugar Hill 3927

DEBUT	PEAK	WKS	RIAA	CD	ARTIST — Album Title	Catalog	Sym	$	Label & Number

PARTON, Dolly — Cont'd

Rockin' Years (24)
Romeo (26) *50*
Rosewood Casket (22)
Rudolph The Red-Nosed Reindeer (29)
Run That By Me One More Time (4,5)
Runaway Feelin' (24)
Salt In My Tears (32)
Same Old Fool (13)
Sandy's Song (12)
Santa Claus Is Coming To Town (29)
Satin Sheets (31)
Save The Last Dance For Me (19) *45*
Savin' It For You (23)
Say Goodnight (13)
Seeker, The (30)
Send Me The Pillow You Dream On (18)
Seven Bridges Road (35)
She Don't Love You (Like I Love You) (19)
Shine (35)
Shine On (32)
Silent Night (21)

Silver And Gold (24)
Silver Dagger (34)
Silver Sandals (4)
Silver Threads And Golden Needles (27)
Sing For The Common Man (14)
Single Women (15)
Sittin' On The Front Porch Swing (27)
Sleigh Ride (medley) (21)
Slip Away Today (11)
Slow Dancing With The Moon (26)
Smoky Mountain Memories (28)
Someone Loves You Honey (17)
Something Fishy (medley) (5)
Something Special (30)
Something's Burning (31)
Somewhere Between (1)
Speakin' Of The Devil (30)
Star Of The Show (12)
Starting Over Again (13) *36*
Stay Out Of My Bedroom (20)
Steady As The Rain (34)

Straight Talk (25)
Sure Thing (11)
Sweet Agony (13)
Sweet Lovin' Friends (20)
Sweet Music Man (10)
Sweet Summer Lovin' (12) *77*
Tall Man (5)
Teach Me To Trust (19)
Telling Me Lies (22)
Tender Lie (35)
Tennessee Homesick Blues (20)
That's The Way It Should Have Been (27)
There (9)
There Never Was A Time (2)
There'll Be Love (7)
Those Memories Of You (22)
Thought I Couldn't Dance (25)
Thoughtfulness (6)
'Til Death Do Us Part (3)
Time And Tears (32)
To Daddy (28)
To Know Him Is To Love Him (22)
To Make A Long Story Short, She's Gone (17)

Today I Started Loving You Again (31)
Today, Tomorrow And Forever (7)
Tomorrow Is Forever (4,5)
Train, Train (34)
Travelin' Prayer (34)
True Blue (28)
Turn! Turn! Turn! (To Everything There Is A Season) (19)
Two Doors Down (10,16) *19*
Two Lovers (23)
Two Of A Kind (7)
Two Sides To Every Story (5)
Wabash Cannon Ball (5)
Walking On Sunshine (31)
Walls Of My Mind (8)
Walter Henry Hagan (28)
Wayfaring Stranger (28)
We Can't Let This Happen To Us (4)
We Had All The Good Things Going (3)
We Had It All (19)
We Three Kings (29)
We'll Get Ahead Someday (1)

We'll Sing In The Sunshine (19)
We're Through Forever ('Til Tomorrow) (11)
What A Friend We Have In Jesus (28)
What A Heartache (20,24)
What Do You Think About Lovin' (17)
What Will Baby Be (26)
When Jesus Comes Calling For Me (32)
When We're Gone, Long Gone (33)
Whenever Forever Comes (26)
Where Beauty Lives In Memory (9)
White Christmas (21)
Why Can't We (26)
Why Don't You Haul Off & Love Me (2)
Wildest Dreams (24)
Wildflowers (22)
Will He Be Waiting For Me (34)
Wings Of A Dove (27)
Winter Wonderland (medley) (21)
With Bells On (21)

With You Gone (11)
Woke Up In Love (20)
Working Girl (14)
Wouldn't It Be Great (27)
You All Come (Y'all Come) (5)
You Are (9)
You Can't Reach Me Anymore (8)
(You Got Me Over) A Heartache Tonight (26)
You Gotta Be My Baby (5)
You Left Me A Long, Long Time Ago (17)
You'll Always Have Someone (17)
You'll Never Be The Sun (33)
You're Gonna Love Yourself (In The Morning) (17)
You're The Only One (12) *59*
You're The Only One I Ever Needed (13)
(Your Love Has Lifted Me) Higher And Higher (9)
Yours Love (2)

★479★ PARTRIDGE FAMILY, The '71

Popularized through *The Partridge Family* TV series, broadcast from 1970-74. Recordings by series stars **David Cassidy** (lead singer) and real-time stepmother, Shirley Jones (backing vocals). David, son of actor Jack Cassidy, was born on 4/12/50 in New York City; raised in California. Shirley, born on 3/31/34 in Smithton, Pennsylvania, starred in the movie musicals *Oklahoma* and *The Music Man*; married David's father in 1956.

THE PARTRIDGE FAMILY Starring Shirley Jones Featuring David Cassidy:

DEBUT	PEAK	WKS		CD				$	
10/31/70+	4	68	●	©	1	The Partridge Family Album		$25	Bell 6050
4/3/71	3	53	●	©	2	Up To Date		$25	Bell 6059
8/28/71	9	35	●	©	3	The Partridge Family Sound Magazine		$25	Bell 6064
12/4/71	❶⁴ˣ	7	●	©	4	A Partridge Family Christmas Card	[X]	$25	Bell 6066
						Christmas charts: 1/'71, 9/'72			
3/25/72	18	17		©	5	The Partridge Family Shopping Bag		$25	Bell 6072
9/16/72	21	23	●		6	The Partridge Family at home with their Greatest Hits	[G]	$25	Bell 1107
12/16/72+	41	16		©	7	The Partridge Family Notebook		$25	Bell 1111
7/7/73	167	5			8	Crossword Puzzle		$25	Bell 1122

Am I Losing You (5,6) *59*
As Long As There's You (8)
As Long As You're There (7)
Bandala (1)
Blue Christmas (4)
Brand New Me (1)
Breaking Up Is Hard To Do (6) *28*
Brown Eyes (3,6)
Christmas Song (4)
Come On Love (8)
Doesn't Somebody Want To Be Wanted (2,6) *6*
Echo (Bell 2-6809 (3,6)
Every Little Bit O' You (5)
Every Song Is You (5)

Friend And A Lover (7) *99*
Frosty The Snowman (4)
Girl, You Make My Day (5)
Have Yourself A Merry Little Christmas (4)
Hello, Hello (5)
I Can Feel Your Heartbeat (1,6)
I Got Your Love All Over Me (2)
I Really Want To Know You (1)
I Think I Love You (1,6) *1*
I Woke Up In Love This Morning (3,6) *13*
I Would Have Loved You Anyway (3)
I'll Leave Myself A Little Time (2)

I'll Meet You Halfway (2,6) *9*
I'm Here, You're Here (2)
I'm On My Way Back Home (3)
I'm On The Road (1)
If You Ever Go (5)
It Means I'm In Love With You (8)
It Sounds Like You're Saying Hello (4)
It's A Long Way To Heaven (8)
It's All In Your Mind (5)
It's One Of Those Nights (Yes Love) (5,6) *20*
It's You (8)
Jingle Bells (4)
Last Night (5)
Lay It On The Line (2)

Let Your Love Go (8)
Looking Through The Eyes Of Love (7) *39*
Love Is All That I Ever Needed (3)
Love Must Be The Answer (7)
Maybe Someday (7)
Morning Rider On The Road (2)
My Christmas Card To You (4)
Now That You Got Me Where You Want Me (8)
One Day At A Time (8)
One Night Stand (3)
Only A Moment Ago (1)
Point Me In The Direction Of Albuquerque (1)
Rainmaker (3)

Rockin' Around The Christmas Tree (4)
Santa Claus Is Coming To Town (4)
She'd Rather Have The Rain (2,6)
Singing My Song (1)
Sleigh Ride (4)
Somebody Wants To Love You (1)
Something New Got Old (5)
Something's Wrong (7)
Storybook Love (7)
Summer Days (3)
Sunshine (8)
Take Good Care Of Her (7)
That'll Be The Day (7)

There'll Come A Time (5)
There's No Doubt In My Mind (2)
To Be Lovers (1)
Together We're Better (7)
Twenty-Four Hours A Day (3)
Umbrella Man (2)
Walking In The Rain (7)
We Gotta Get Out Of This Place (7)
White Christmas (4)
Winter Wonderland (4)
You Are Always On My Mind (3)
You Don't Have To Tell Me (3)

PARTY, The '91

Dance group from Florida: Tiffini Hale, Albert Fields, Chase Hampton, Damon Pampolina and Deedee Magno. All were cast members of TV's *The Mickey Mouse Club* in 1988.

DEBUT	PEAK	WKS		CD				$	
10/6/90	116	20		©	1	The Party		$10	Hollywood 60980
10/5/91	77	12		©	2	In The Meantime, In Between Time		$10	Hollywood 61225
9/12/92	163	4		©	3	Free		$10	Hollywood 61358

Adult Decision (2)
All About Love (3)
At All Times (3)
Cappuccino And Bacon (3)
Change On Me (3)
Coulda Shoulda Woulda (1)
Dancing In The City (1)

Free (3)
Frontin' (3)
I Found Love (1) *79*
I Gotcha (3)
I Know What Boys Like (2)
I Wanna Be Your Boyfriend (1)
I Want You (3)

I'm Just Wishin' (1)
In My Dreams (2) *34*
In My Life (3)
Independent Woman (3)
It's Out Of My Heart (3)
Let's Get Right Down To It (3)
Life Ain't Nothin' But A Party (3)

My Generation (2)
Needin' Someone (3)
Peace, Love And Understanding (2)
Private Affair (2)
Quien Es Mi Romeo (3)
Rodeo (1)

Spiders And Snakes (2)
Storm Me (1)
Sugar Is Sweet (1,2)
Summer Vacation (1) *72*
That's Why (1,2) *55*
Ton Of Bricks (1)
Walking In The Rain (1)

Where Is My Romeo (3)

PASADENAS, The '89

R&B vocal group from England: brothers Aaron, David and Michael Milliner, with John Banfield and Hammish Seelochan.

DEBUT	PEAK	WKS		CD				$	
3/18/89	89	12		©		To Whom It May Concern		$10	Columbia 45065

Enchanted Lady
Funny Feeling
Give A Little Peace

I Really Miss You
Justice For The World

Living In The Footsteps Of Another Man
New Love

Riding On A Train
Something Else
Tribute (Right On) *52*

PASSENGERS '95

Collaboration between **U2** and producer **Brian Eno**.

DEBUT	PEAK	WKS		CD				$	
11/25/95	76	4		©		Original Soundtracks 1		$10	Island 524166

Always Forever Now
Beach Sequence
Corpse (These Chains Are Way Too Long)

Different Kind Of Blue
Elvis Ate America
Ito Okashi
Let's Go Native, Theme From

Miss Sarajevo
One Minute Warning
Plot 180
Slug

Swan, Theme From The
United Colours
Your Blue Room

PASSION WORSHIP BAND   '00

Christian group which brings together various speakers and musicians from around the world. Spearheaded by Matt Redman (from England), Chris Tomlin (from Texas) and Charlie Hall (from Oklahoma).

| 4/1/00 | 139 | 1 | © | 1 | Passion: The Road To Oneday .... | | | $10 | Sparrow 51740 |
| 11/11/00 | 158 | 2 | © | 2 | Passion: Oneday Live.. | | [L] | $10 | Sparrow 51768 |

America (2)   Did You Feel The Mountains   Holy Roar (1)   Let My Words Be Few (2)   Salvation (1,2)   You Are My King (2)
Better Is One Day (2)   Tremble? (1)   Holy Visitation (1)   Make A Joyful Noise (medley)   Shout To The North (1)
Break Our Hearts (1)   Give Us Clean Hands (medley)   I Will Not Be Silent (medley) (1)   (1)   This Field (2)
Breathe (2)   (2)   Jesus, Lover Of My Soul (1)   Noise We Make (1,2)   We Are Hungry (1)
  Grace Flows Down (2)   Kindness (1,2)   One Pure And Holy Passion (2)   We Fall Down (1)

PASSPORT   '78

Jazz-fusion group from Germany. Led by Klaus Doldinger (sax, keyboards). Numerous personnel changes with Doldinger the only constant.

3/15/75	137	7		1	Cross-Collateral		[I]	$12	Atco 107
4/23/77	191	3	©	2	Iguacu..		[I]	$12	Atco 149
6/3/78	140	7		3	Sky Blue		[I]	$12	Atlantic 19177
4/5/80	163	4	©	4	Oceanliner		[I]	$12	Atlantic 19265
8/29/81	175	3	©	5	Blue Tattoo		[I]	$12	Atlantic 19304

Aguamarinha (2)   Bassride (4)   Guna Guna (2)   Louisiana (3)   Rambling (5)   Secret, The (3)
Albatros Song (1)   Bird Of Paradise (2)   Heavy Weight (2)   Mandrake (3)   Reng Ding Dang Dong (3)   Sky Blue (3)
Alegria (3)   Blue Tattoo (5)   Homunculus (1)   Oceanliner (4)   Riding On A Cloud (5)   Uptown Rendezvous (4)
Allegory (4)   Cross-Collateral (1)   Iguacu (2)   Piece For Rock Orchestra (5)   Rub-A-Dub (4)   Will-O' The-Wisp (1)
Ancient Saga (4)   Damals (1)   In A Melancholy Way (5)   Praia Leme (2)   Sambukada (2)
Ataraxia Part 1 & 2 (3)   Daybreak Delight (5)   Jadoo (1)   Radiation (5)   Scope (4)
Bahia Do Sol (2)   Departure (4)   Loco-Motive (3)   Ragtag And Bobtail (5)   Seaside (4)

PASTORIUS, Jaco   '81

Born on 12/1/51 in Norristown, Pennsylvania. Died of injuries suffered in a beating on 9/22/87 (age 35). Jazz-rock bassist. Member of **Weather Report**.

| 8/15/81 | 161 | 3 | © | | Word Of Mouth .... | | [I] | $12 | Warner 3535 |

Blackbird   Crisis   Liberty City   Word Of Mouth
Chromatic Fantasy   John And Mary   3 Views Of A Secret

PASTOR TROY   '01

Born in Augusta, Georgia. Male rapper.

| 8/12/00 | 102 | 3 | © | 1 | Book I.. | | | $10 | Hendu 00007 |

PASTOR TROY AND THE CONGREGATION

| 6/9/01 | 83 | 11 | © | 2 | Face Off .... | | | $10 | Madd Society 014173 |

Can You Stand The Game (2)   Down South Nigga Fa Life (1)   Ghetto Raised (1)   Move To Mars (2)   Rhonda (2)   Vica Versa (2)
Congregation, The (1)   Eternal Yard Dash (2)   Havin' A Bad Day (1)   My N***az Is The Grind (2)   This Tha City (2)   Walk Like Y'all Talk It (1)
Dirty South Affilliates (1)   Frame Me (2)   I'm Made (2)   No Mo Play In Ga (2)   Throw Dem Bows (1)
Do What We Do (1)   Get 'Em Up (1)   Look What I'm Going Thru (1)   Oh Father (2)   Throw Your Flags Up (2)

PATINKIN, Mandy   '95

Born Mandel Patinkin on 11/30/52 in Chicago. Actor/singer. Appeared in several movies, Broadway and TV shows.

| 11/11/95 | 136 | 5 | | | Oscar & Steve .... | | | $10 | Nonesuch 79392 |

Patinkin performs songs written by Oscar Hammerstein II and Stephen Sondheim.

Bali Ha'i   I Have The Room Above   Not A Day Goes By   Remember (medley)   When The Children Are Asleep
Beat Out Dat Rhythm On A   I Wish I Could Forget You   Ordinary Couple (medley)   There Won't Be Trumpets   (medley)
Drum   If I Loved You   Pleasant Little Kingdom   Too Many Mornings (medley)   You Are Beautiful
Children Will Listen (medley)   Kiss To Build A Dream On   (medley)   When I Grow Too Old To   You've Got To Be Carefully
Honey Bun   Loving You   Poems   Dream (medley)   Taught (medley)

PATRA   '94

Born Dorothy Smith on 11/22/72 in Kingston, Jamaica. Female dance-reggae singer.

| 4/23/94 | 103 | 25 | ● © | 1 | Queen Of The Pack .... | | | $10 | Epic 53763 |
| 9/2/95 | 151 | 4 | © | 2 | Scent Of Attraction .... | | | $10 | 550 Music 67094 |

Banana (2)   Either Or Either (2)   In The Mood (1)   **Pull Up To The Bumper** (2) *60*   Sexual Feeling (1)   Whining Skill (1)
Be Protected (1)   Goin' 2 The Chapel (1)   Knock Knock (1)   Queen Of The Pack (1)   Think (About It) (1)   Wok The Money (1)
Deep Inside (2)   Hardcore (1)   Mek Me Hot (2)   **Romantic Call** (1) *55*   Time Fi Wine (2)   **Worker Man** (1) *53*
Dip & Fall Back (2)   Hot Stuff (2)   Poor People's Song (1)   **Scent Of Attraction** (2) *82*   Undercover Lover (2)   You Want It (2)

PATTERSON, Don   '67

Born on 7/22/36 in Columbus, Ohio. Died on 2/10/88 (age 51). Jazz organist.

| 12/16/67 | 85ˣ | 3 | | | Holiday Soul .... | | [X-I] | $25 | Prestige 7415 |

Jingle Bells   Rudolph The Red Nosed   Santa Claus Is Coming To   What Are You Doing New
Merry Christmas Baby   Reindeer   Town   Years Eve
O Holy Night   Silent Night   You're All I Want For Christmas

PATTON, Robbie   '81

Born in England. Pop-rock singer/songwriter.

| 8/15/81 | 162 | 6 | | | Distant Shores.. | | | $12 | Liberty 1107 |

co-produced by **Christine McVie**

Alright   Distant Shores   Heartache   Last Night   She
Boulevard   **Don't Give It Up** *26*   How I Feel   One On One   When Love Disappears

PATTY, Sandi   '96

Born in 1956 in Oklahoma City; raised in Anderson, Indiana. Christian singer.

| 11/30/96 | 143 | 5 | © | 1 | O Holy Night! .... | | [X] | $10 | Word 67313 |

Christmas chart: 13/'96

| 11/29/97 | 155 | 3 | © | 2 | Artist Of My Soul... | | | $10 | Word 68583 |

Always (2)   Breathe On Me (2)   Doxology (2)   I'll Be Home For Christmas   Speechless (2)   Winter Wonderland (medley) (1)
Angels We Have Heard On   Carol Of The Bells (1)   I Heard The Bells On Christmas   (medley) (1)   Star Of Bethlehem (1)   You Alone (2)
High (1)   Child Of Peace (1)   Day (1)   My Favorite Things (1)   (There's No Place Like) Home   You Love Me (2)
Artist Of My Soul (2)   Christmas Song (1)   I Will Sing The Wondrous Story   O Holy Night! (1)   For The Holidays (medley) (1)   You Set Me Free (2)
Birds Still Dance (2)   Come To Me (2)   (2)   Silver Bells (1)   White Christmas (medley) (1)

PAUL, Billy '73

Born Paul Williams on 12/1/34 in Philadelphia. R&B singer.

1)360 Degrees Of Billy Paul 2)Let 'Em In 3)War Of The Gods

DEBUT	PEAK	WKS			ARTIST — Album Title			$	Label & Number
8/22/70	183	5			1 Ebony Woman			$20	Neptune 201
					also see #4 below				
10/16/71	197	2			2 Going East			$15	Philadelphia Int'l. 30580
11/25/72+	17	27	●		3 360 Degrees Of Billy Paul			$15	Philadelphia Int'l. 31793
4/28/73	186	3			4 Ebony Woman...........................		[R]	$15	Philadelphia Int'l. 32118
11/17/73+	110	26			5 War Of The Gods.....................			$12	Philadelphia Int'l. 32409
7/6/74	187	4			6 Live In Europe.....................		[L]	$12	Philadelphia Int'l. 32952
3/15/75	140	9			7 Got My Head On Straight...........			$10	Philadelphia Int'l. 33157
12/27/75+	139	20			8 When Love Is New...................			$12	Philadelphia Int'l. 33843
1/22/77	88	18		©	9 Let 'Em In...........................			$12	Philadelphia Int'l. 34389
1/28/78	152	4		©	10 Only The Strong Survive...........			$12	Philadelphia Int'l. 34923

Am I Black Enough For You (3) *79* — America (We Need The Light) (8) — Be Truthful To Me (7) — Billy's Back Home (7) — Black Wonders Of The World (7) — Brown Baby (3,6) — Compared To What (2) — Don't Give Up On Us (10) — East (2) — Ebony Woman (1,4) — Enlightenment (7) — Everybody's Breakin' Up (10) — Everyday People (1,4) — Everything Must Change (7) — How Good Is Your Game (9) — I See The Light (5) — I Think I'll Stay Home Today (9) — I Trust You (9) — I Want 'Cha Baby (8) — I Was Married (5) — I Wish It Were Yesterday (2) — I'm Gonna Make It This Time (3) — I'm Just A Prisoner (3) — I've Got So Much To Live For (7) — (If You Let Me Make Love To You Then) Why Can't I Touch You? (2) — It's Too Late (3) — Jesus Boy (You Only Look Like A Man) (2) — July, July, July, July (3) — Let 'Em In (9) — Let The Dollar Circulate (8) — Let's Fall In Love All Over (1,4) — **Let's Make A Baby** (8) *83* — Let's Stay Together (3) — Love Buddies (2) — Love Won't Come Easy (9) — Magic Carpet Ride (2) — Malorie (8) — **Me And Mrs. Jones** (3,6) *1* — Mrs. Robinson (1,4) — My Head's On Straight (7) — One Man's Junk (10) — Only The Strong Survive (10) — Peace Holy Peace (5) — People Power (8) — Proud Mary (1,4) — Psychedelic Sally (1,4) — Sooner Or Later (10) — Takin' It To The Streets (10) — **Thanks For Saving My Life** (5,6) *37* — There's A Small Hotel (2) — This Is Your Life (2) — Times Of Our Lives (10) — Traces (1,4) — War Of The Gods (5,6) — We All Got A Mission (9) — When It's Your Time To Go (7) — When Love Is New (8) — Where I Belong (10) — Whole Town's Talking (5) — Windmills Of Your Mind (1,4) — Windy (1,4) — Without You (9) — Word Sure Gets Around (9) — Your Song (3,6)

PAUL, Henry, Band '79

Born on 8/25/49 in Kingston, New York. Rock singer/guitarist. Member of the **Outlaws** and **BlackHawk**. His band: Dave Fiester and Billy Crain (guitars), Wally Dentz (bass) and Bill Hoffman (drums).

DEBUT	PEAK	WKS			ARTIST — Album Title			$	Label & Number
6/2/79	107	12			1 Grey Ghost			$12	Atlantic 19232
8/2/80	120	8			2 Feel The Heat.........................			$12	Atlantic 19273
12/26/81+	158	8			3 Anytime			$12	Atlantic 19325

All I Need (1) — Anytime (3) — Brown Eyed Girl (3) — Crazy Eyes (3) — Crossfire (1) — Distant Riders (3) — Feel The Heat (2) — Foolin' (1) — Go Down Rockin' (2) — Grey Ghost (1) — Hollywood Paradise (3) — I Can See It (2) — I Don't Need You No More (1) — **Keeping Our Love Alive** (3) *50* — Living Without Your Love (3) — Lonely Dreamer (1) — Longshot (2) — Night City (2) — One-Night Stands (1) — Outa My Mind (1) — Rising Star (In The Southern Sky) (3) — Running Away (2) — 766-2623 (Rom-ance) (3) — Shot To Hell (2) — So Long (1) — Turn It Up (2) — Whiskey Talkin' (2) — Wood Wind (1) — You Really Know (What I Mean) (1)

PAUL, Les, and Mary Ford '55

Pop duo. Paul was born Lester Polsfuss on 6/9/15 in Waukesha, Wisconsin. Ford was born Colleen Summers on 7/7/24 in Pasadena, California; died on 9/30/77 (age 53). Les Paul was an innovator in electric guitar and multi-track recordings. Married to vocalist Mary Ford from 1949-63. Les Paul won the Grammy's Trustees Award in 1983 and he was inducted into the Rock and Roll Hall of Fame in 1988. Also see **Chet Atkins**.

DEBUT	PEAK	WKS			ARTIST — Album Title			$	Label & Number
12/25/54+	7	16			1 Les Paul and Mary Ford		[EP]	$50	Capitol 9121
5/14/55	10	6			2 Les and Mary			$50	Capitol 577
					EP: Capitol EBF-577 (#10); LP: Capitol W-577 (#15)				

Baby, Won't You Please Come Home (2) — Best Things In Life Are Free (2) — Dangerous Curves (2) — Falling In Love With Love (2) — Farewell For Just Awhile (2) — I Need You Now (1) — I'm Movin' On (2) — Just One Of Those Things (2) — Lies (2) — Mister Sandman (1) — **Moritat (Theme from "Three Penny Opera")** (2) *49* — **Nuevo Laredo** (2) *91* — On The Sunny Side Of The Street (2) — Some Of These Days (2) — Swing Low, Sweet Chariot (2) — That's What I Like (1) — Things I Didn't Do (1) — Tico Tico (2) — Turista (2) — Twelfth Street Rag (2)

PAUL & PAULA '63

Pop vocal duo. Ray "Paul" Hildebrand was born on 12/21/40 in Joshua, Texas. Jill "Paula" Jackson was born on 5/20/42 in McCaney, Texas.

DEBUT	PEAK	WKS			ARTIST — Album Title			$	Label & Number
2/23/63	9	25			1 Paul & Paula Sing For Young Lovers			$40	Philips 600078
8/10/63	99	5			2 We Go Together........................			$40	Philips 600089
12/7/63	13ˣ	3			3 Holiday For Teens		[X]	$40	Philips 600101

All The Love (1) — Average Boy And Average Girl (2) — Ba-Hey-Be (1) — Beginning Of Love (2) — Blue Christmas (3) — Blue Roller Rink (1) — Christmas Song (3) — Come Softly To Me (1) — Don't Let It End (1) — Flipped Over You (2) — Gee Baby (1) — Happy Holiday (3) — Hey Baby (1) — **Hey Paula** (1) *1* — Holiday For Teens (3) — Holiday Hootenanny (3) — I'll Be Home For Christmas (3) — Jingle Bell Rock (3) — Love Comes Once (3) — My Happiness (1) — New Year, A New Ring (3) — Oh What A Love (2) — Pledging My Love (2) — Silver Bells (3) — So Fine (2) — **Something Old, Something New** (2) *77* — Stepping Stone (2) — Sweet Baby (1) — (There's No Place Like) Home For The Holidays (3) — Two People In The World (1) — We Go Together (2) — We Two Forever Shall Be One (2) — White Christmas (3) — Winter Wonderland (3) — You Send Me (2) — **Young Lovers** (1) *6*

PAULSEN, Pat '68

Born on 7/6/27 in South Bend, Washington. Died of kidney failure on 4/24/97 (age 69). Comedian.

DEBUT	PEAK	WKS			ARTIST — Album Title			$	Label & Number
10/19/68	71	10			Pat Paulsen For President		[C]	$20	Mercury 61179
					with commentary by Ralph Story				

Age Of Reason — Bandwagon, The — Big Shot — Counter-Attack — Critics Attack — Formal Announcement — Freedom To Censor — Humble Beginning — I Will Not Run — I Will Not Serve — In Your Gourd, You Know He's Good — Meet The Candidate — Meet The Prez — Messing Around — Questions And Evasions — Ruthless Denial — Simple Savior — Slip Of The Tongue — Soldiers' Lament — Two Cows — Victory Rally

PAUPERS, The '67

Folk-rock group from Toronto: Skip Prokop (vocals, drums; **Lighthouse**), Adam Mitchell (guitar), Chuck Beal (mandolin) and Dennis Gerrard (bass).

DEBUT	PEAK	WKS			ARTIST — Album Title			$	Label & Number
11/11/67	178	2			Magic People			$20	Verve Forecast 3026

Black Thank You Package — It's Your Mind — Let Me Be — Magic People — My Love Hides Your View — One Rainy Day — Simple Deed — Think I Care — Tudor Impressions — You And Me

DEBUT	PEAK	WKS	RIAA	CD	ARTIST — Album Title	Catalog	Sym	$	Label & Number

PAVAROTTI, Luciano   '80
Born on 10/12/35 in Modena, Italy. Operatic tenor. Starred in the movie *Yes, Giorgio*. Member of **The Three Tenors**.

11/24/79+	77	21	●		1 **O Sole Mio - Favorite Neapolitan Songs**		[F]	$10	London 26560
6/7/80	94	18			2 **Pavarotti's Greatest Hits**		[F-G]	$15	London 2003 [2]
4/24/82	141	7			3 **Luciano**		[F-K]	$10	London 2013
11/6/82	158	3			4 **Yes, Giorgio**		[S]	$10	London 9001
12/17/83+	6[X]	17	▲		5 **O Holy Night**	C:#25/9	[X-F]	$10	London 26473
					first released in 1976; Christmas charts: 7/'83, 6/'84, 21/'88, 19/'89, 20/'90, 14/'91, 22/'92				
9/8/84	103	14			6 **Mamma**		[F]	$10	London 411959
1/4/92	173	1		©	7 **Pavarotti Songbook**		[F]	$10	London 433513
7/1/95	185	1		©	8 **Pavarotti & Friends 2**		[L]	$10	London 444460

recorded at the Parco Novi Sad in Modena, Italy; with solos by special guests **Bryan Adams** ("Please Forgive Me"), **Andreas Vollenweider** ("Night Fire Dance"), Andrea Bocelli ("Mattinata"), Giorgio ("Who Wants To Live Forever") and Nancy Gustafson ("All I Ask Of You" and "O Silver Moon")

A Te O Cara (2)	Che Gelida Manina (2,3)	(I Left My Heart) In San	Mamma (6,7)	'O Sole Mio (1,4,7,8)	Santa Lucia Luntana (8)
A Vucchella (1,3,7)	Chitarra Romana (6,8)	Francisco (medley) (4)	Manon Lescaut (4)	'O Surdato 'Nnammurato (1)	Spirto Gentil (2)
Addio, Sogni Di Gloria (6)	Cielo E Mar (2,4)	If We Were In Love (4)	Marechiare (1,3,7)	Panis Angelicus (2,3,5)	Tarantella (4)
Adeste Fideles (5)	Di Qual Tetra...Ah, Si Ben	In Un Palco Della Scala (6)	Maria Mari! (1,3)	Parlami D'Amore, Mariu (8)	This Heart Of Mine (medley) (4)
Agnus Dei (5)	Mio (2)	Ingemisco (5)	Mattinata (2,4,7)	Pecche? (1)	Torna A Surriento (1,2,3,7)
All For Love (8)	Di Quella Pira (2,3)	L'Ultima Canzone (7)	Mille Cherubini In Coro (5)	Pieta Signore (5)	Tu, Ca Nun Chiagne! (1)
Aprile (3,7)	Di Rigori Armato (2)	La Campana Di San Giusto (6)	Moon River (8)	Piscatore 'E Pusilleco (1)	Una Furtiva Lagrima (2,4)
Ave Maria (2,4,5,8)	Did I Remember (medley) (4)	La Danza (2)	Musica Proibita (6,7)	Qual Ciglio Candido (Quinta	Vanne, O Rosa Fortunata (2,3)
Ballet Music From Aida (4)	E Lucevan Le Stelle (2,3)	La Donna E Mobile (2,4)	Nessun Dorma (2,4)	Parola) (5)	Verranno A Te (8)
Brindisi (4)	Fenesta Vascia (1)	La Ghirlandeina (6)	Non Ti Scordar Di Me (6,7)	Questa O Quella (2)	Vesti La Giubba (2,3)
Cantate Con Me (7)	Firenze Sogna (6)	La Mia Canzone Al Vento (6,7)	Notte 'E Piscatore (8)	Recondita Armonia (2)	Vieni Sul Mar (6)
Cantique Noel (O Holy	Flower Song (4)	La Serenata (7)	'O Marenariello (1)	Rondine Al Nido (6)	Vivere (6)
Night) (5)	Funiculi-Funicula (1,2)	Lolita (6,7)	O Mes Amis...Pour Mon	Salut! Demeure (2)	Voglio Vivere Cosi (6)
Celeste Aida (2,3)	Gesu Bambino (5)	Luna D'Estate (3)	Ame (2,3)	Sanctus (5)	Volare (7)
Chanson De L'Adieu (7)	Giorgio's Bedroom (medley) (4)	Malinconia D'Amore (7)	'O Paese D' 'O Sole (1)	Santa Lucia (4)	

PAVEMENT   '97
Rock group formed in Stockton, California: **Stephen Malkmus** (vocals, guitar), Scott Kannberg (guitar), Bob Nastanovich (percussion), Mark Ibold (bass) and Steve West (drums).

3/5/94	121	4	©	1 **Crooked Rain, Crooked Rain**		$10	Matador 92343
4/29/95	117	1	©	2 **Wowee Zowee**		$10	Matador 45898
3/1/97	70	4	©	3 **Brighten The Corners**		$10	Matador 55226
6/26/99	95	2	©	4 **Terror Twilight**		$10	Matador 260

AT & T (2)	Cut Your Hair (1)	Fin (3)	Hit The Plane Down (1)	Rattled By The Rush (2)	Type Slowly (3)
Ann Don't Cry (4)	Date With IKEA (3)	5 - 4 = Unity (1)	Kennel District (2)	Serpentine Pad (2)	Unfair (1)
Best Friends Arm (2)	Ell Esstwo (1)	Flux = Rad (2)	Major Leagues (4)	Shady Lane (3)	We Are Underused (3)
Billie (4)	Embassy Row (3)	Folk Jam (4)	Motion Suggests (2)	Silence Kid (1)	We Dance (2)
Black Out (2)	Extradition (2)	Gold Soundz (1)	Newark Wilder (1)	Speak, See, Remember (4)	Western Homes (2)
Blue Hawaiian (3)	Father To A Sister Of Thought	Grave Architecture (2)	Old To Begin (3)	Spit On A Stranger (4)	You Are A Light (4)
Brinx Job (2)	(2)	Grounded (2)	Passat Dream (3)	Starlings Of The Slipstream (3)	
Carrot Rope (4)	Fight This Generation (2)	Half A Canyon (2)	Platform Blues (4)	Stereo (3)	
Cream Of Gold (4)	Fillmore Jive (1)	Heaven Is A Truck (1)	Pueblo (2)	Stop Breathin (1)	
		Hexx, The (4)	Range Life (1)	Transport Is Arranged (3)	

PAVLOV'S DOG   '75
Rock group from St. Louis: David Surkamp (vocals), Steve Scorfina (guitar), David Hamilton (keyboards), Doug Rayburn (flute), Siegfried Carver (violin), Rick Stockton (bass) and Mike Safron (drums).

4/5/75	181	6	©	**Pampered Menial**		$25	ABC 866

Episode	Julia	Natchez Trace	Preludin	Subway Sue, Theme From
Fast Gun	Late November	Of Once And Future Kings	Song Dance	

PAVONE, Rita   '64
Born on 8/23/45 in Turin, Italy. Pop singer.

6/20/64	60	14		**Rita Pavone**		$20	RCA Victor 2900

Big Deal	Don't Tell Me Not To Love You	Just Once More	Like I Did	Remember Me *26*	Too Many
Boy Most Likely To Succeed	I Can't Hold Back The Tears	Kissin' Time	Little By Little	Say Goodbye To Bobby	Wait And See

PAXTON, Tom   '71
Born on 10/31/37 in Chicago. Folk singer/songwriter.

8/16/69	155	4		1 **The Things I Notice Now**		$15	Elektra 74043
6/6/70	184	4		2 **Tom Paxton 6**		$15	Elektra 74066
8/14/71	120	3		3 **How Come The Sun**		$15	Reprise 6443
8/26/72	191	4		4 **Peace Will Come**		$15	Reprise 2096

About The Children (1)	Cindy's Cryin' (2)	How Come The Sun (3)	Jesus Christ S.R.O. (Standing	Peace Will Come (4)	Uncle Jack (2)
All Night Long (1)	Crazy John (2)	I Give You The Morning (1)	Room Only) (4)	Prayin' For Snow (4)	What A Friend You Are (4)
Angeline Is Always Friday (2)	Dance In The Shadows (4)	I Had To Shoot That Rabbit (3)	Jimmy Newman (2)	Retrospective (4)	Whose Garden Was This (2)
Annie's Going To Sing Her	Dogs At Midnight (2)	I Lost My Heart On A 747 (4)	Little Lost Child (3)	Sailor's Life (3)	Wish I Had A Troubadour (1)
Song (2)	Forest Lawn (2)	I've Got Nothing But Time (2)	Louise (3)	Saturday Night (2)	You Came Throwing Colors (4)
Bishop Cody's Last Request (1)	General Custer (3)	Icarus (3)	Molly Bloom (2)	She's Far Away (3)	You Should Have Seen Me
California (4)	Hostage, The (4)	Iron Man (1)	Out Behind The Gypsy's (4)	Things I Notice Now (1)	Throw That Ball (4)

PAYCHECK, Johnny   '78
Born Donald Eugene Lytle on 5/31/38 in Greenfield, Ohio. Country singer/songwriter/guitarist.

2/18/78	72	14	▲ ©	**Take This Job And Shove It**		$12	Epic 35045

Barstool Mountain	Fool Strikes Again	From Cotton To Satin (From	Georgia In A Jug	Spirits Of St. Louis	When I Had A Home To Go To
Colorado Cool-Aid	4 "F" Blues	Birmingham To Manhattan)	Man From Bowling Green	Take This Job And Shove It	

PAYNE, Freda   '70
Born on 9/19/45 in Detroit. R&B singer. Sister of Scherrie Payne (of **The Supremes**).

8/22/70	60	13		1 **Band Of Gold**		$20	Invictus 7301
6/12/71	76	18		2 **Contact**		$20	Invictus 7307
4/15/72	152	8		3 **The Best Of Freda Payne**		[G]	$20	Invictus 9804

PAYNE, Freda — Cont'd

Band Of Gold (1,3) *3*
Bring The Boys Home (2,3) *12*
Cherish What Is Dear To You
 (While It's Near To You)
 (2,3) *44*
Come Back (3)
Deeper & Deeper (1,3) *24*

Easiest Way To Fall (1)
Happy Heart (1)
He's In My Life (3)
How Can I Live Without My Life
 (3)
I Left Some Dreams Back
 There (1)

I Shall Not Be Moved (2)
I'm Not Getting Any Better (2)
Just A Woman (3)
Love On Borrowed Time (1)
Mama's Gone (2)
Now Is The Time To Say
 Goodbye (1,3)

Odds And Ends (2)
Prelude (2)
Road We Didn't Take (2,3) *100*
Rock Me In The Cradle (1)
Suddenly It's Yesterday (2)
This Girl Is A Woman Now (1)

Through The Memory Of My
 Mind (1,3)
Unhooked Generation (1)
World Don't Owe You A Thing
 (1)
You Brought The Joy (2) *52*

You're The Only Bargain I've
 Got (3)
You've Got To Love Somebody
 (Let It Be Me) (2)

PEACHES & HERB   '79

R&B vocal duo from Washington DC: Francine "Peaches" Barker and Herb Fame. Re-formed with Fame and Linda "Peaches" Green in 1977.

3/25/67	30	25			1 Let's Fall In Love			$25	Date 4004
9/2/67	135	12			2 For Your Love			$25	Date 4005
9/21/68	187	3			3 Peaches & Herb's Greatest Hits		[G]	$25	Date 4012
11/25/78+	2[6]	46	▲		4 2 Hot!			$12	Polydor 6172
11/10/79	31	30	●		5 Twice The Fire			$12	Polydor 6239
10/11/80	120	6			6 Worth The Wait			$12	Polydor 6298
9/12/81	168	3			7 Sayin' Something!			$12	Polydor 6332

All-Night Celebration (6)
All Your Love (Give It Here) (4)
Answer Me My Love (2)
Because Of You (1)
Bluer Than Blue (7)
Close Your Eyes (1,3) *8*
Count On Me (2)
Discover You (6)
Door Is Still Open To My Heart
 (2)
Dream Come True (7)
Easy As Pie (4)

Embraceable You (2)
Everybody Loves A Lover (2)
For Your Love (2,3) *20*
Four's A Traffic Jam (4)
Freeway (7)
Funtime (6)
Gettin' Down, Gettin' Down (5)
Go With The Flow (7)
Gypsy Lady (5)
Hearsay (6)
Howzabout Some Love (5)
I Love How You Love Me (2)

I Need Your Love So
 Desperately (2,3)
I Pledge My Love (5) *19*
(I Want Us) Back Together (5)
I Will Watch Over You (1)
I Wish I Could Be A Kid Again
 (7)
I'm In The Mood For Love (1)
It's True I Love You (2,3)
Let's Fall In Love (1,3) *21*
Love Is Strange (3) *13*

Love It Up Tonight (5)
Love Lift (5)
Love Stealers (6)
Lovey Dovey (Girl & Guy) (6)
My Life (2)
One Child Of Love (6)
Picking Up The Pieces (7)
Put It There (5)
Red Hot Lover (7)
Reunited (4) *1*
Roller-Skatin' Mate (Part I)
 (5) *66*

Shake Your Groove Thing
 (4) *5*
Star Of My Life (4)
Star Steppin' (4)
Surrender (4)
Ten Commandments Of Love
 (3) *55*
Things I Want To Hear (Pretty
 Words) (2)
Time After Time (1)
True Love (1)
Two Little Kids (3) *31*

United (3) *46*
We Belong Together (1)
We've Got Love (4) *44*
We've Got To Love One
 Another (3)
Wear You Out (7)
What A Lovely Way (To Say
 Goodnight) (3)
When I Fall In Love (1)
Will You Love Me Tomorrow (1)

PEANUT BUTTER CONSPIRACY, The   '67

Psychedelic-rock group from Los Angeles: Sandi Robinson (vocals), Lance Fent and John Merrill (guitars), Al Brackett (bass) and Jim Voight (drums). Robinson died on 4/22/88 (age 43).

5/20/67	196	3	©		The Peanut Butter Conspiracy Is Spreading			$30	Columbia 2654

Dark On You Now
It's A Happening Thing *93*

Market Place
Most Up Till Now

Second Hand Man
Then Came Love

Twice Is Life
Why Did I Get So High

You Can't Be Found
You Should Know

You Took Too Much

PEARL HARBOR AND THE EXPLOSIONS   '80

Rock group from San Francisco: Pearl E. Gates (vocals), Peter Bilt (guitar), Hilary Stench (bass) and John Stench (drums).

1/26/80	107	11			1 Pearl Harbor And The Explosions			$12	Warner 3404
2/21/81	170	3			2 Don't Follow Me, I'm Lost Too			$12	Warner 3515

PEARL HARBOUR

Alone In The Dark (2)
At The Dentist (2)
Big One (1)
Cowboys & Indians (2)
Do Your Homework (2)

Don't Come Back (1)
Drivin' (1)
Everybody's Boring But My
 Baby (2)
Filipino Baby (2)

Fujiyama Mama (2)
Get A Grip On Yourself (1)
Heaven Is Gonna Be Empty (2)
Keep Going (1)
Let's Go Upstairs (1)

Losing To You (2)
Out With The Girls (2)
Rough Kids (2)
Shut Up And Dance (1)
So Much For Love (1)

Up And Over (1)
You Got It (Release It) (1)
You're In Trouble Again (2)

PEARL JAM   ★161★   '93

Rock group formed in Seattle: Eddie Vedder (vocals), Stone Gossard and Mike McCready (guitars), Jeff Ament (bass) and Dave Krusen (drums). Dave Abbruzzese replaced Krusen in 1993. Gossard and Ament were members of Mother Love Bone. All except Krusen recorded with Temple Of The Dog. Band acted in the movie *Singles* as Matt Dillon's band, Citizen Dick. Abbruzzese left band in August 1994. Drummer Jack Irons (of the Red Hot Chili Peppers) joined in late 1994. McCready also put together Mad Season in 1994. Matt Cameron replaced Irons in 1999.

1)*Vs.* 2)*No Code* 3)*Vitalogy* 4)*Ten* 5)*Yield*

1/4/92	2[4]	250	▲[11]	©	1 Ten	C:#8/21		$10	Epic/Associated 47857
11/6/93	❶[5]	67	▲[7]	©	2 Vs.			$10	Epic/Associated 53136
12/10/94	❶[1]	55	▲[5]	©	3 Vitalogy			$10	Epic 66900
9/14/96	❶[2]	24	▲	©	4 No Code			$10	Epic 67500
2/21/98	2[1]	36	▲	©	5 Yield			$10	Epic 68164
12/12/98	15	15	●	©	6 Live On Two Legs		[L]	$10	Epic 69752
6/3/00	2[1]	17	●	©	7 Binaural			$10	Epic 63665
10/14/00	103	1		©	8 16/6/00: Spodek, Katowice, Poland		[L]	$15	Epic 85052 [2]
10/14/00	125	1		©	9 22/6/00: Fila Forum Arena, Milan, Italy		[L]	$15	Epic 85064 [2]
10/14/00	134	1		©	10 20/6/00: Arena Di Verona, Verona, Italy		[L]	$15	Epic 85061 [2]
10/14/00	137	1		©	11 30/5/00: Wembley Arena, London, England		[L]	$15	Epic 85012 [2]
10/14/00	175	1		©	12 26/6/00: Sporthalle, Hamburg, Germany		[L]	$15	Epic 85073 [2]
3/17/01	159	1		©	13 Jones Beach, New York - August 25, 2000		[L]	$15	Epic 85545 [2]
3/17/01	163	1		©	14 Boston, Massachusetts - August 29, 2000		[L]	$15	Epic 85551 [2]
3/17/01	174	1		©	15 Indianapolis, Indiana - August 18, 2000		[L]	$15	Epic 85530 [2]
3/17/01	176	1		©	16 Pittsburgh, Pennsylvania - September 5, 2000		[L]	$15	Epic 85566 [2]
3/17/01	179	1		©	17 Philadelphia, Pennsylvania - September 1, 2000		[L]	$15	Epic 85557 [2]
3/17/01	181	1		©	18 Tampa, Florida - August 12, 2000		[L]	$15	Epic 85518 [2]
3/17/01	191	1		©	19 Memphis, Tennessee - August 15, 2000		[L]	$15	Epic 85524 [2]
4/14/01	98	1		©	20 Seattle, Washington - November 6, 2000		[L]	$15	Epic 85641 [3]
4/14/01	152	1		©	21 Las Vegas, Nevada - October 22, 2000		[L]	$15	Epic 85611 [2]

Alive (1,8,10,11,20)
All Those Yesterdays (5)
Animal (2,8,9,10,11,13,15,
 16,17,18,19,21)
Around The Bend (4)
Aye Davanita (3)

Baba O'Riley (12)
Baba O'Riley (13,16,19,20,21)
Better Man (3,6,9,10,12,13,
 14,15,16,17,18,19,20,21)
Black (1,6,8,9,10,11,12,
 13,15,16,17,19,21)
Bugs (3)

Blood (2)
Brain Of J. (5,15)
Breakerfall (7,10,12,14,16,19,21)
Breath (17)

Can't Help Falling In Love (19,21)
Corduroy (3,6,8,9,10,11,12,
 13,14,15,16,17,18,19,20,21)
Crazy Mary (12,14,15,16,17,20)
Crown Of Thorns (21)

Daughter (2,6,8,9,10,11,
 12,16,17,18,20) *97*
Deep (1)
Dissident (2,8,11,15,17,20,21)
Do The Evolution (5,6,9,10,11,
 12,13,14,15,17,18,19,20,21)

Elderly Woman Behind The
 Counter In A Small Town (2,6)
Encore Break
 (13,14,15,16,17,18,19,20)

671

PEARL JAM — Cont'd

Evacuation (7,8,12,13,18,20)
Even Flow (1,6,9,10,11,12, 13,14,15,16,17,18,19,20,21)
Faithfull (5,12)
Footsteps (19)
F*ckin' Up (6,14)
Garden (1,9,18)
Given To Fly (5,6,9,10,12,13, 14,15,16,17,19,21) *21*
Glorified G (2)
Go (2,6,9,12,13,14,15,16, 17,19,20)
God's Dice (9)
Gods' Dice (7,14,18)
Grievance (7,8,9,10,11,12, 13,14,15,16,17,18,19,20,21)
Habit (4,8,10,11,14)

Hail, Hail (4,6,8,10,11,16,18,20)
I Got Shit (8,16,19)
I Got You (10,16)
I'm Open (4)
Immortality (3,8,10,11,13,18,20)
In Hiding (5,8,11,13,20)
In My Tree (4,13,16,19)
In The Coliseum (10)
Indifference (2,15,18)
Insignificance (7,8,9,10,12,13, 14,15,16,17,18,19,21)
Interstellar Overdrive (15,18,21)
Jeremy (1,8,9,13,14,17, 18,20,21) *79*
Kids Are Alright (20)
Last Exit (3,8,11,16,17,18,19,21)
Last Kiss (10,15,21) *2*

Leash (5,13)
Leatherman (8,15,16,20)
Leaving Here (8)
Light Years (7,8,9,11,12,15,16,17,18,20)
Long Road (10)
Low Light (5)
Lukin (4,10,15,18,20,21)
MFC (5,6,8,9,10,11,12,13, 14,21)
Mankind (4,13,14,16,21)
No Way (5)
Not For You (3,9,11,15,20)
Nothing As It Seems (7,10,11, 14,15,16,18,19,20,21) *49*
Nothingman (3,6,9,19,20)
Oceans (1)

Of The Girl (7,8,9,14,19)
Off He Goes (4,6,8,11,13,20)
Once (1,10,12,14,16,17,20,21)
Parting Ways (7,20)
Patriot (14)
Pilate (5,10,15)
Porch (1,10,12,14,16,17,18,21)
Present Tense (4,9,12,13,17)
Pry, To (3)
Push Me, Pull Me (5)
RITFW (15,18)
RVM (9,10,12,13,14,15,16, 18,19,20,21)
Rats (2)
Rear View Mirror (2,11)
Red Mosquito (4,6,13,17)
Release (1,8,20)

Ritfw (9)
Rival (7,9,12,14)
Sleight Of Hand (7,8,9,14,18)
Small Town (9,10,11,12,13,15, 16,17,18,19,21)
Smile (4,8,9,12,13)
Soldier Of Love (8,12,14,18)
Sometimes (4,11,13,17)
Soon Forget (7,8,10,18,20)
Spin The Black Circle (3,15,17) *58*
State Of Love And Trust (8,9,10,11,15,18,19)
Stupid Mop (3)
Thin Air (7,8,9,11,13,19)

Throw Your Arms Around Me (15)
Tremor Christ (3,17,18,19) *18*
Untitled (6,11,13,14,21)
W.M.A. (2)
Wash (16)
Whipping (3,13,17)
Who You Are (4) *31*
Why Go (1)
Wishlist (5,9,10,14,17,19,21) *47*
Yellow Ledbetter (8,10,12,13,14,17,20,21) *flip*

PEARLS BEFORE SWINE
'69

Folk-rock group from New York City: Tom Rapp (vocals, guitar), Elizabeth (vocals), Wayne Harley (banjo) and Jim Fairs (guitar).

| 9/27/69 | 200 | 2 | | These Things Too | $30 | Reprise 6364 |

Footnote
Frog In The Window
Green And Blue

I Shall Be Released
I'm Going To City

If You Don't Want To (I Don't Mind)
Look Into Her Eyes

Man In The Tree
Mon Amour
Sail Away

These Things Too
When I Was A Child
Wizard Of Is

PEARSON, Duke
'69

Born Columbus Pearson on 8/17/32 in Atlanta. Died of multiple sclerosis on 8/4/80 (age 47). Jazz trumpeter/pianist.

| 4/5/69 | 193 | 2 | | The Phantom | $25 | Blue Note 84293 |

Blues For Alvina

Bunda Amerela (Little Yellow Streetcar)

Los Ojos Alegres (The Happy Eyes)

Moana Surf
Phantom, The

Say You're Mine

PEASTON, David
'89

Born in St. Louis. R&B singer/songwriter. Nephew of **Fontella Bass**.

| 8/5/89 | 113 | 18 | © | Introducing...David Peaston | $10 | Geffen 24228 |

Can I?
Don't Say No
Eyes Of Love

God Bless The Child
Take Me Now
Thank You For The Moment

Tonight
Two Wrongs (Don't Make It Right)

We're All In This Together

PEBBLES
'88

Born Perri McKissack on 8/29/65 in Oakland. Nicknamed "Pebbles" by her family for her resemblance to cartoon character Pebbles Flintstone. Formerly married to singer/songwriter/producer L.A. Reid (of **The Deele**). Cousin of **Cherrelle**. Assembled/managed **TLC**.

| 2/13/88 | 14 | 38 | ▲ © | 1 Pebbles | $10 | MCA 42094 |
| 9/29/90 | 37 | 36 | ● © | 2 Always | $10 | MCA 10025 |

Always (2)
Baby Love (1)
Backyard (2) *73*
Do Me Right (1)

First Step (In The Right Direction) (1)
Girlfriend (1) *5*
Give It To Me (2)

Give Me Your Love (1)
Giving You The Benefit (2) *4*
Good Thang (2)
Love/Hate (1)

Love Makes Things Happen (2) *13*
Mercedes Boy (1) *2*
Say A Prayer For Me (2)

Slip Away (1)
Stay With Me (2)
Take Your Time (1)
Two Hearts (1)

Why Do I Believe (2)

PEEBLES, Ann
'74

Born on 4/27/47 in St. Louis. R&B singer.

| 4/22/72 | 188 | 3 | © | 1 Straight From The Heart | $20 | Hi 32065 |
| 3/9/74 | 155 | 7 | © | 2 I Can't Stand The Rain | $20 | Hi 32079 |

Breaking Up Somebody's Home (1)
Do I Need You (2)
How Strong Is A Woman (1)

I Can't Stand The Rain (2) *38*
I Pity The Fool (1) *85*
I Take What I Want (1)
I'm Gonna Tear Your Playhouse Down (2)

I've Been There Before (1)
If We Can't Trust Each Other (2)
Love Vibration (1)
99 Pounds (1)

One Way Street (2)
Run, Run, Run (2)
Slipped, Tripped, Fell In Love (1)
Somebody's On Your Case (1)

Trouble, Heartaches & Sadness (You Keep Me) Hangin' On (1)
Until You Came Into My Life (2)
What You Laid On Me (1)
You Got To Feed The Fire (2)

PEEL, David, & The Lower East Side
'69

Group of street musicians from New York City: David Peel (vocals, harmonica), Larry Adam and Billy Joe White (guitars), George Cori (bass) and Harold Black (percussion).

| 5/24/69 | 186 | 3 | © | 1 Have A Marijuana | [L] | $50 | Elektra 74032 |

recorded on the streets of New York City

| 5/27/72 | 191 | 3 | | 2 The Pope Smokes Dope | $75 | Apple 3391 |

produced by **John Lennon** and **Yoko Ono**

Alphabet Song (1)
Ballad Of Bob Dylan (2)
Ballad Of New York City/John Lennon - Yoko Ono (2)
Birth Control Blues (2)

Chicago Conspiracy (2)
Everybody's Smoking Marijuana (2)
F Is Not A Dirty Word (2)
Happy Mother's Day (1)

Here Comes A Cop (1)
Hip Generation (2)
Hippie From New York City (2)
I Do My Bawling In The Bathroom (1)

I Like Marijuana (1)
I'm A Runaway (2)
I'm Gonna Start Another Riot (2)
I've Got Some Grass (1)

McDonalds Farm (2)
Mother Where Is My Father? (1)
Pope Smokes Dope (2)
Show Me The Way To Get Stoned (1)

Up Against The Wall (1)
We Love You (1)

PEEPLES, Nia
'88

Born on 12/10/61 in Los Angeles. Singer/actress. Played "Nicole Chapman" on TV's *Fame*. Hosted *Top Of The Pops* TV show and own syndicated music video dance TV program, *Party Machine*. Married to **Howard Hewett** from 1989-93.

| 5/14/88 | 97 | 21 | © | Nothin' But Trouble | $10 | Mercury 834303 |

Be My Lover
For The Sake Of Loving
High Time

I Know How (To Make You Love Me)
Is This Really Love

Never Gonna Get It
Poetry In Motion
Star Crossed Lovers

This Time I'll Be Sweeter
Trouble *35*

PENDERGRASS, Teddy
★236★ **'79**

Born on 3/26/50 in Philadelphia. R&B singer. Lead singer of **Harold Melvin & The Blue Notes** from 1970-76. Acted in the 1982 movie *Soup For One*. Auto accident on 3/18/82 left him partially paralyzed.

1)Teddy 2)Life Is A Song Worth Singing 3)TP

3/19/77	17	35	▲ ©	1 Teddy Pendergrass	$12	Philadelphia Int'l. 34390
7/1/78	11	35	▲ ©	2 Life Is A Song Worth Singing	$12	Philadelphia Int'l. 35095
6/23/79	5	31	▲ ©	3 Teddy	$12	Philadelphia Int'l. 36003
12/22/79+	33	15	● ©	4 Teddy Live! Coast To Coast	[L]	$15	Philadelphia I. 36294 [2]

side 4: interviews and new studio recordings

| 8/23/80 | 14 | 34 | ▲ © | 5 TP | $12 | Philadelphia Int'l. 36745 |

PENDERGRASS, Teddy — Cont'd

DEBUT	PEAK	WKS	CD	#	Title	$	Label & Number
10/3/81	19	27	● ©	6	It's Time For Love	$12	Philadelphia Int'l. 37491
8/21/82	59	15	©	7	This One's For You	$12	Philadelphia Int'l. 38118
1/7/84	123	9	©	8	Heaven Only Knows	$12	Philadelphia Int'l. 38646
6/16/84	38	35	● ©	9	Love Language	$10	Asylum 60317
12/7/85+	96	23	©	10	Workin' It Back	$10	Asylum 60447
5/28/88	54	24	● ©	11	Joy	$10	Elektra 60775
3/23/91	49	16	©	12	Truly Blessed	$10	Elektra 60891
10/23/93	92	8	©	13	A Little More Magic	$10	Elektra 61497
5/3/97	137	5	©	14	You And I	$10	Surefire 13045

All I Need Is You (3)
And If I Had (1)
Bad Luck (medley) (4)
Be Sure (1)
Believe In Love (13)
Can We Be Lovers (11)
Can We Try (14)
Can't Help Nobody (13)
Can't We Try (5) *52*
Close The Door (2,4) *25*
Cold, Cold World (2)
Come Go With Me (3,4)
Crazy About Your Love (8)
Do Me (3,4)
Don't Ever Stop (Giving Your Love To Me) (8)
Don't Keep Wastin' My Time (14) *90*
Don't Leave Me Out Along The Road (7)
Don't You Ever Stop (12)
Easy, Easy, Got To Take It Easy (1)
Feel The Fire (5)

Get Up, Get Down, Get Funky, Get Loose (2,4)
Girl You Know (5)
Give It To Me (14)
Glad To Be Alive (12)
Good To You (11)
Heaven Only Knows (8)
Hold Me (9) *46*
Hot Love (9)
How Can You Mend A Broken Heart (12)
Hurry Up (4)
I Can't Leave Your Love Alone (6)
I Can't Live Without Your Love (6)
I Can't Win For Losing (7)
I Choose You (13)
I Don't Love You Anymore (1) *41*
I Find Everything In You (12)
I Just Called To Say (5)
I Want My Baby Back (8)

I'll Never See Heaven Again (3)
I'm Always Thinking About You (13)
I'm Ready (11)
If You Don't Know Me By Now (medley) (4)
If You Know Like I Know (3)
In My Time (9)
Is It Still Good To Ya (5)
It Don't Hurt Now (2)
It Should've Been You (12)
It's Over (12)
It's Time For Love (6)
It's Up To You (What You Do With Your Life) (7)
It's You I Love (4)
Joy (11) *77*
Judge For Yourself (8)
Just Because You're Mine (8)
Keep On Lovin' Me (6)
Let Me Be Closer (10)
Let Me Love You (5)
Let's Talk About It (14)
Life Is A Circle (3)

Life Is A Song Worth Singing (2,4)
Life Is For Living (8)
Little More Magic (13)
Lonely Color Blue (10)
Love (9)
Love Emergency (10)
Love 4/2 (10)
Love I Lost (medley) (4)
Love Is The Power (11)
Love T.K.O. (5) *44*
Loving You Was Good (7)
More I Get, The More I Want (1)
My Father's Child (13)
Never Felt Like Dancin' (13)
Nine Times Out Of Ten (6)
No One Like You (13)
Now Tell Me That You Love Me (7)
One In A Million You (14)
One Of Us Fell In Love (10)
Only To You (7)
Only You (2,4)
Say It (13)

Set Me Free (3)
She Knocks Me Off My Feet (12)
She's Over Me (6)
Shout And Scream (4)
Slip Away (9)
Slow Ride To Heaven (14)
So Sad The Song (9)
Somebody Told Me (12)
Spend The Night (12)
Stay With Me (9)
Take Me In Your Arms Tonight (5)
Tender (13)
This Gift Of Life (7)
This Is The Last Time (11)
This One's For You (7)
This Time Is Ours (9)
Through The Falling Rain (Love Story) (11)
Truly Blessed (12)
Turn Off The Lights (3,4) *48*
2 A.M. (11)
Voodoo (13)

Wake Up Everybody (medley) (4)
Want You Back In My Life (10)
We Can't Keep Going On (Like This) (12)
When Somebody Loves You Back (2,4)
Where Did All The Lovin' Go (4)
Whole Town's Laughing At Me (1)
With You (12)
Without You (14)
Workin' It Back (10)
You And I (1)
You And Me For Right Now (8)
You Can't Hide From Yourself (1)
You Must Live On (6)
You're My Choice Tonight (Choose Me) (9)
You're My Latest, My Greatest Inspiration (6) *43*

PENISTON, Ce Ce   '92

Born on 9/6/69 in Dayton, Ohio; raised in Phoenix. Female R&B singer.

DEBUT	PEAK	WKS	CD	#	Title	$	Label & Number
2/15/92	70	36	● ©	1	Finally	$10	A&M 5381
2/12/94	96	19	©	2	Thought 'Ya Knew	$10	A&M 540138

Any Way You Wanna Go (2)
Crazy Love (1) *97*
Finally (1) *5*
Forever In My Heart (2)
Give What I'm Givin' (2)

Hit By Love (2) *90*
I See Love (1)
I Will Be Received (2)
I'm In The Mood (2) *32*
I'm Not Over You (2) *41*

If You Love Me, I Will Love You (2)
Inside That I Cried (1) *94*
It Should Have Been You (1)
Keep Givin' Me Your Love (2)

Keep On Walkin' (1)
Let My Love Surround You (2)
Lifeline (1)
Maybe It's The Way (1)
Searchin' (2)

Through Those Doors (2)
Virtue (1)
We Got A Love Thang (1) *20*
Whatever It Is (2)
You Win, I Win, We Lose (1)

PENN, Michael   '90

Born on 8/1/58 in New York City. Pop-rock singer/songwriter. Brother of actors Sean and Christopher Penn. Son of actor/director Leo Penn and actress Eileen Ryan. Married Aimee Mann on 12/29/97.

DEBUT	PEAK	WKS	CD	#	Title	$	Label & Number
11/25/89+	31	34	©	1	March	$10	RCA 9692
10/3/92	160	2	©	2	Free-For-All	$10	RCA 61113

Battle Room (1)
Bedlam Boys (medley) (1)
Big House (1)
Brave New World (1)
Bunker Hill (2)
By The Book (2)

Coal (2)
Cupid's Got A Brand New Gun (1)
Disney's A Snow Cone (medley) (1)
Drained (1)

Evenfall (1)
Free Time (2)
Half Harvest (1)
Innocent One (1)
Invisible (1)

Long Way Down (Look What The Cat Drug In) (2)
No Myth (1) *13*
Now We're Even (2)
Seen The Doctor (2)
Slipping My Mind (1)

Strange Season (2)
This & That (1) *53*

PENNARIO, Leonard   '59

Born on 7/9/24 in Buffalo, New York; raised in Los Angeles. Classical pianist.

DEBUT	PEAK	WKS	#	Title	Sym	$	Label & Number
6/8/59	29	13		Concertos under the Stars	[I]	$25	Capitol 8326

Adagio From Moonlight Sonata
Cornish Rhapsody

Liebestraum
Prelude In C Sharp Minor

Scherzo From Concerto
Symphonique

Swedish Rhapsody
Warsaw Concerto

PENNYWISE   '99

Hard-rock group from Hermosa Beach, California: Jim Lindberg (vocals), Fletcher Dragge (guitar), Randy Bradbury (bass) and Byron McMackin (drums).

DEBUT	PEAK	WKS	CD	#	Title	Sym	$	Label & Number
7/1/95	96	6	©	1	About Time		$10	Epitaph 86437
5/10/97	79	4	©	2	Full Circle		$10	Epitaph 86489
6/26/99	62	7	©	3	Straight Ahead		$10	Epitaph 86553
11/11/00	198	1	©	4	Live @ The Key Club	[L]	$10	Epitaph 86598

Alien (3,4)
American Dream (3)
Badge Of Pride (3)
Bro Hymn (4)
Bro Hymn Tribute (2)
Broken (2)
Can't Believe It (3,4)
Can't Take Anymore (3)
Date With Destiny (2)

Did You Really (2)
Every Single Day (1)
Every Time (2)
Fight Till You Die (2,4)
Final Chapters (4)
Final Day (2)
Freebase (1)
Get A Life (2)
Go Away (3)

Greed (3)
Homesick (4)
I Won't Have It (1)
It's What You Do With It (1)
Just For You (3)
Killing Time (1)
Living For Today (4)
Might Be A Dream (3)
Minor Threat (4)

My Own Country (3)
My Own Way (3)
Need More (3)
Never Know (3)
No Reason Why (4)
Not Far Away (1)
Nowhere Fast (2)
One Voice (3)
Peaceful Day (1,4)

Pennywise (4)
Perfect People (1,4)
Running Out Of Time (2)
Same Old Story (1,4)
Searching (1)
Society (1)
Still Can Be Great (3)
Straight Ahead (3,4)
Try (1)

Unknown Road (4)
Victim Of Reality (3)
Waste Of Time (1)
Watch Me As I Fall (3)
What If I (2)
Wouldn't It Be Nice (4)
You'll Never Make It (2)

PENTANGLE   '71

Folk group formed in England: Jacqui McShee (vocals), Bert Jansch and John Renbourn (guitars), Danny Thompson (bass) and Terry Cox (drums).

DEBUT	PEAK	WKS	CD	#	Title	$	Label & Number
12/21/68	192	3	©	1	The Pentangle	$20	Reprise 6315
1/31/70	200	2	©	2	Basket Of Light	$15	Reprise 6372
3/13/71	193	1	©	3	Cruel Sister	$15	Reprise 6430
12/4/71	183	3		4	Reflection	$15	Reprise 6463
10/28/72	184	4		5	Solomon's Seal	$15	Reprise 2100

Bells (1)
Bruton Town (1)

Cherry Tree Carol (5)
Cruel Sister (3)

Cuckoo, The (2)
Hear My Call (1)

Helping Hand (4)
High Germany (5)

House Carpenter (2)
Hunting Song (2)

Jack Orion (3)
Jump Baby Jump (5)

PENTANGLE — Cont'd

Lady Of Carlisle (5)
Let No Man Steal Your Thyme (1)
Light Flight (2)
Lord Franklin (3)

Lyke-Wake Dirge (2)
Maid That's Deep In Love (3)
Mirage (1)
No Love Is Sorrow (5)
Omie Wise (4)

Once I Had A Sweetheart (2)
Pentangling (1)
People On The Highway (5)
Rain And Snow (4)
Reflection (4)

Sally Free And Easy (5)
Sally Go Round The Roses (2)
Snows, The (5)
So Clear (3)
Springtime Promises (2)

Train Song (2)
Waltz (1)
Way Behind The Sun (1)
Wedding Dress (4)
When I Get Home (4)

When I Was In My Prime (3)
Will The Circle Be Unbroken? (4)
Willy Of Winsbury (5)

PENTHOUSE PLAYERS CLIQUE '92

Male rap duo: Playa Hamm and Tweed Cadillac.

| 5/16/92 | 76 | 10 | © | **Paid The Cost** | $10 | Ruthless 57181 |

Blak Iz A Poet
Chekmate
Explanation Of A Playa

Handle Yo Bizness
Jealous Knukle Heads
Jus 2 Kep Yo Attenchun

N-Trance
Nathen's Changed
P.L.F.

P.S. Phuk U 2
Pimp Lane
Smooth

They Don't Know
Trust No Bitch
U Cain't Check Me

Undaground Boss
X-It

PEOPLE '68

Pop-rock group from San Jose, California: Gene Mason and Larry Norman (vocals), Jeff Levin (guitar), Albert Ribisi (keyboards), Robb Levin (bass) and Denny Friedkin (drums).

| 7/27/68 | 128 | 8 | © | **I Love You** | $40 | Capitol 2924 |

Ashes Of Me
Crying Shoes
Epic, The

I Love You **14**
Nothing Can Stop The
Elephants

1,000 Years B.C.

We Need A Whole Lot More
Jesus (And A Lot Less Rock
'N' Roll)

PEOPLE'S CHOICE '75

R&B group from Philadelphia: Frankie Brunson (vocals), Guy Fiske and Darnell Jordan (guitars), Donald Ford (keyboards), Roger Andrews (bass) and David Thompson (drums).

| 9/6/75 | 56 | 15 | 1 | **Boogie Down U.S.A.** | $12 | TSOP 33154 |
| 6/26/76 | 174 | 3 | 2 | **We Got The Rhythm** | $12 | TSOP 34124 |

Are You Sure (1)
Boogie Down U.S.A. (1)
Cold Blooded &
Down-Right-Funky (2)

Do It Any Way You Wanna (1) **11**
Don't Send Me Away (1)
Here We Go Again (2)
I'm Leaving You (1)

If You Want Me Back (1)
Jam, Jam, Jam (All Night Long) (2)
Mellow Mood (2)
Mickey D's (1)

Movin' In All Directions (2)
Nursery Rhymes (Part I) (1) **93**
Opus-De-Funk (2)
Party Is A Groovy Thing (1)

Sooner You Get Here (1)
We Got The Rhythm (2)

PEPPERMINT RAINBOW, The '69

Pop group from Baltimore: sisters Bonnie and Pat Lamdin (vocals), Doug Lewis (guitar), Skip Harris (bass) and Tony Corey (drums).

| 8/2/69 | 106 | 9 | | **Will You Be Staying After Sunday** | $20 | Decca 75129 |

And I'll Be There
**Don't Wake Me Up In The
Morning, Michael 54**

Green Tambourine
I Found Out I Was A Woman
Jamais

Pink Lemonade
Rosemary
Run Like The Devil

Sierra (Chasin' Dream)
Walking In Different Circles

Will You Be Staying After
Sunday **32**

PEPSI AND SHIRLIE '88

Female vocal duo from England: Lawrie "Pepsi" DeMacque and Shirlie Holliman.

| 2/27/88 | 133 | 9 | © | **All Right Now** | $10 | Polydor 833724 |

All Right Now 66
Can't Give Me Love

Crime Of Passion
Goodbye Stranger

Heartache 78
High Time

Lovers' Revolution
Surrender

What's Going On Inside Your
Head

PERFECT CIRCLE, A '00

Rock duo from Hollywood: Maynard James Keenan (vocals) and Billy Howerdel (guitar). Keenan is also lead singer of **Tool**.

| 6/10/00 | 4 | 51 | ▲ © | **Mer De Noms** | $10 | Virgin 49253 |

Breña
Hollow, The

Judith
Magdalena

Orestes
Over

Renholdër
Rose

Sleeping Beauty
Thinking Of You

Thomas
3 Libras

PERFECT GENTLEMEN '90

R&B vocal trio from Boston: Corey Blakely, Maurice Starr Jr. and Tyrone Sutton. Starr's father managed and produced **New Edition** and **New Kids On The Block**.

| 5/26/90 | 72 | 14 | © | **Rated PG** | $10 | Columbia 46070 |

Birthday Girl
Girl In My Dreams
Mama

Move Me Groove Me
One More Chance

Ooh La La (I Can't Get Over
You) **10**
Rated PG

Rings Around The Moon
Tell Me Again

PERFECT STRANGER '95

Country group from Carthage, Texas: Steve Murray (vocals), Richard Raines (guitar), Shayne Morrison (bass) and Andy Ginn (drums).

| 7/29/95 | 68 | 14 | © | **You Have The Right To Remain Silent** | $10 | Curb 77799 |

Cut Me Off
Even The Jukebox Can't Forget
I Ain't Never

I Am A Stranger Here Myself
It's Up To You
One More Repossession

Remember The Ride
Ridin' The Rodeo
Who Are You

**You Have The Right To
Remain Silent 61**

PERKINS, Carl '86

Born on 4/9/32 in Tiptonville, Tennessee. Died of a stroke on 1/19/98 (age 65). Rockabilly singer/songwriter/guitarist. Member of **Johnny Cash**'s touring troupe from 1965-75. Appeared in the 1985 movie *Into The Night*. Inducted into the Rock and Roll Hall of Fame in 1987.

| 6/21/86 | 87 | 12 | © | **Class Of '55 (Memphis Rock & Roll Homecoming)** | C:#13/2 | $10 | America Smash 830002 |

CARL PERKINS/JERRY LEE LEWIS/ROY ORBISON/JOHNNY CASH

Big Train (From Memphis)
Birth Of Rock And Roll

Class Of '55
Coming Home

I Will Rock And Roll With You
Keep My Motor Running

Rock And Roll (Fais-Do-Do)
Sixteen Candles

Waymore's Blues
We Remember The King

PERRY, Joe, Project '80

Born on 9/10/50 in Lawrence, Massachusetts. Lead guitarist of **Aerosmith**. The Project included Charlie Farren (guitar), David Hull (bass) and Ronnie Stewart (drums).

| 4/12/80 | 47 | 13 | © 1 | **Let The Music Do The Talking** | $12 | Columbia 36388 |
| 7/4/81 | 100 | 10 | © 2 | **I've Got The Rock 'N' Rolls Again** | $12 | Columbia 37364 |

Break Song (1)
Buzz Buzz (2)
Conflict Of Interest (1)
Dirty Little Things (2)

Discount Dogs (1)
East Coast, West Coast (2)
I've Got The Rock 'N' Rolls
Again (2)

Let The Music Do The Talking (1)
Life At A Glance (1)
Listen To The Rock (2)

Mist Is Rising (1)
No Substitute For Arrogance (2)
Play The Game (2)
Ready On The Firing Line (1)

Rockin' Train (1)
Shooting Star (1)
Soldier Of Fortune (2)
South Station Blues (2)

TV Police (2)

PERRY, Phil '91

Born on 1/1/52 in Springfield, Illinois. R&B singer.

| 5/18/91 | 191 | 1 | © | **The Heart Of The Man** | $10 | Capitol 92115 |

Amazing Love
Best Of Me

Call Me
Forever

(Forever In The) Arms Of Love
God's Gift To The World

Good-bye
More Nights

Say Anything
Who Do You Love

Woman

PERRY, Steve   '84
Born on 1/22/49 in Hanford, California. Lead singer of **Journey**.

| 4/28/84 | 12 | 60 | ▲² | © | 1 **Street Talk** | | | $10 | Columbia 39334 |
| 8/6/94 | 15 | 14 | ● | © | 2 **For The Love Of Strange Medicine** | | | $10 | Columbia 44287 |

Anyway (2)
Captured By The Moment (1)
Donna Please (2)
Foolish Heart (1) *18*

For The Love Of Strange Medicine (2)
Go Away (1)
I Am (2)

I Believe (1)
It'c Only Love (1)
Listen To Your Heart (2)
Missing You (2) *74*

Oh Sherrie (1) *3*
Running Alone (1)
She's Mine (1) *21*
Somewhere There's Hope (2)

Stand Up (Before It's Too Late) (2)
Strung Out (1) *40*
Tuesday Heartache (2)

You Better Wait (2) *29*
You Should Be Happy (1)
Young Hearts Forever (2)

PERSUADERS, The   '72
R&B vocal group formed in New York City: Doug Scott, Willie Holland, James Barnes and Charles Stodghill.

| 3/11/72 | 141 | 7 | | © | 1 **Thin Line Between Love And Hate** | | | $25 | Win Or Lose 387 |
| 4/7/73 | 178 | 4 | | | 2 **The Persuaders** | | | $20 | Atco 7021 |

Bad Bold And Beautiful Girl (2)
Blood Brothers (1)
Can't Go No Further And Do No Better (1)
I Want To Make It With You (2)

If This Is What You Call Love (I Don't Want Any Part Of It) (1)
If You Feel Like I Do (2)
Is It Too Heavy For You (2)
Let's Get Down Together (1)

Love Goes Good When Things Go Bad (2)
Love Gonna Pack Up (And Walk Out) (1) *64*
Mr. Sunshine (1)
Peace In The Valley Of Love (2)
Please Stay (2)
Thanks For Loving Me (1)
Thigh Spy (1)

Thin Line Between Love & Hate (1) *15*
Trying Girls Out (2)
What Is The Definition Of Love (2)

You Musta Put Something In Your Love (1)
You Still Love Me (After All You've Been Through) (2)

PERSUASIONS   '72
Acappella group formed in New York City: Jerry Lawson, Jesse Russell, Jayotis Washington, Herb Rhoad and Jimmy Hayes. Rhoad died on 12/8/88 (age 44).

9/18/71	189	3		©	1 **We Came To Play**			$25	Capitol 791
2/12/72	88	12		©	2 **Street Corner Symphony**			$25	Capitol 872
11/18/72	195	3		©	3 **Spread The Word**			$25	Capitol 11101
6/9/73	178	3			4 **We Still Ain't Got No Band**			$20	Capitol 326

Another Night With The Boys (1)
Any More (4)
Baby What You Want Me To Do (You Got Me Running) (medley) (4)
Be Good To Me Baby (2)
Bright Lights, Big City (medley) (4)

Buffalo Soldier (2)
Chain Gang (1)
Chapel Of Love (4)
Christian's Automobile (2)
Dance With Me (4)
Don't It Make You Want To Go Home (1)
Don't Know Why I Love You (1)
Good Old Acappella (4)

Good Times (2)
Gypsy Woman (1)
He Ain't Heavy, He's My Brother (medley) (2)
Heaven Help Us All (3)
Hymn #9 (3)
I Could Never Love Another (After Loving You) (1)
Idol With The Golden Head (4)

It's You That I Need (1)
Lean On Me (3)
Let It Be (1)
Lord's Prayer (3)
Love You Most Of All (2)
Man In Me (2)
Man, Oh Man (1)
People Get Ready (2)
Send Me Some Lovin' (4)

So Much In Love (2)
Steal Away (4)
Sun, The (1)
T.A. Thompson (3)
Tempts Jam Medley (2)
Ten Commandments Of Love (3)
Three Angels (3)
Walk On The Wild Side (1)

When I Leave These Prison Walls (3)
When Jesus Comes (3)
Without A Song (3)
You Must Believe Me (4)
You've Got A Friend (medley) (2)

PETER AND GORDON   '64
Pop vocal duo formed in London: Peter Asher (born on 6/22/44 in London) and Gordon Waller (born on 6/4/45 in Braemar, Scotland). Asher later went into production and management, including work with **Linda Ronstadt**, **James Taylor** and **10,000 Maniacs**.

7/4/64	21	14			1 **A World Without Love**			$25	Capitol 2115
1/2/65	95	11			2 **I Don't Want To See You Again**			$25	Capitol 2220
5/22/65	51	15			3 **I Go To Pieces**			$25	Capitol 2324
8/14/65	49	13			4 **True Love Ways**			$25	Capitol 2368
4/16/66	60	14			5 **Woman**			$25	Capitol 2477
7/30/66	72	12			6 **The Best Of Peter And Gordon**		[G]	$25	Capitol 2549
2/4/67	80	13			7 **Lady Godiva**			$25	Capitol 2664

All My Trials (1)
All Shook Up (1)
Any Day Now (My Wild Beautiful Bird) (4)
As Long As I Have You (5)
Baby I'm Yours (7)
Broken Promises (4)
Brown, Black And Gold (5)
Cry To Me (4)
Crying In The Rain (4)
Don't Pity Me (4,6) *83*
Exodus Song (7)
Five Hundred Miles (1)

Freight Train (2)
Good Morning Blues (3)
Green Leaves Of Summer (5)
High Noon (5)
Hurtin' Is Lovin' (4)
I Don't Want To See You Again (2,6) *16*
I Go To Pieces (3,6) *9*
I Know A Man (5)
I Still Love You (3)
I Told You So (4)
If I Fell (7)

If I Were You (1,6)
If You Wish (3,6)
Lady Godiva (7) *6*
Land Of Oden (2)
Last Night I Woke (1)
Leave Me Alone (2)
Leave My Woman Alone (1)
Let It Be Me (2)
Lonely Avenue (2)
Love Is A Many-Splendored Thing (7)
Love Me, Baby (2,6)
Lucille (1)

Mess Of Blues (3)
Morning's Calling (7)
My Babe (2)
3:10 To Yuma (5)
Till There Was You (7)
To Know You Is To Love You (4,6) *24*
Trouble In Mind (1)
True Love Ways (4,6) *14*
Two Little Love Birds (2)
Whatcha Gonna Do 'Bout It (3)
When I Fall In Love (7)
When The Black Of Your Eyes Turns To Grey (4)

There's No Living Without Your Loving (5) *50*
Who's Lovin' You (4)
Willow Garden (1)
Woman (5,6) *14*
World Without Love (1,6) *1*
Wrong From The Start (5)
You Don't Have To Tell Me (1)
Young And Beautiful (7)

PETER, PAUL & MARY   ★130★   '63
Folk trio formed in New York City: Peter Yarrow (born on 5/31/38 in New York City), Paul Stookey (born on 12/30/37 in Baltimore) and **Mary Travers** (born on 11/7/37 in Louisville).

1)Peter, Paul and Mary 2)In The Wind 3)(Moving)

4/28/62	❶⁷	185	▲²	©	1 **Peter, Paul and Mary**			$25	Warner 1449
1/19/63	2⁸	99	●	©	2 **(Moving)**			$25	Warner 1473
10/26/63	❶⁵	80	●	©	3 **In The Wind**			$25	Warner 1507
8/15/64	4	54	●	©	4 **Peter, Paul and Mary In Concert**		[L]	$30	Warner 1555 [2]
4/10/65	8	38		©	5 **A Song Will Rise**			$25	Warner 1589
10/30/65	11	39	●	©	6 **See What Tomorrow Brings**			$25	Warner 1615
8/27/66	22	53		©	7 **Peter, Paul and Mary Album**			$20	Warner 1648
9/2/67	15	82	▲	©	8 **Album 1700**			$15	Warner 1700
9/14/68	14	22		©	9 **Late Again**			$15	Warner 1751
6/14/69	12	25	●	©	10 **Peter, Paul and Mommy**			$15	Warner 1785
6/20/70	15	40	▲²		11 **10 Years Together/The Best Of Peter, Paul and Mary**		[G]	$15	Warner 2552
10/21/78	106	7			12 **Reunion**			$12	Warner 3231
3/14/87	173	5		©	13 **No Easy Walk To Freedom**			$10	Gold Castle 171001

PETER, PAUL & MARY — Cont'd

All My Trials (3)
All Through The Night (10)
And When I Die (7)
Apologize (9)
Autumn To May (1)
Ballad Of Spring Hill (Spring Hill Disaster) (5)
Bamboo (1)
Because All Men Are Brothers (6)
Best Of Friends (12)
Betty & Dupree (6)
Big Boat (2) *93*
Blowin' In The Wind (3,4,11) *2*
Blue (4)
Boa Constrictor (10)
Bob Dylan's Dream (8)
Brother, (Buddy) Can You Spare A Dime? (6)
By Surprise (12)
Car, Car (4)
Christmas Dinner (10)
Come And Go With Me (5)
Cruel War (1) *52*
Cuckoo, The (5)
Day Is Done (10,11) *21*

Don't Think Twice, It's All Right (3,11) *9*
Early In The Morning (1)
Early Morning Rain (6,11) *91*
El Salvador (13)
First Time Ever I Saw Your Face (6)
500 Miles (1,4,11)
Flora (2)
For Baby (For Bobbie) (7)
For Lovin' Me (5,11) *30*
Forever Young (12)
Freight Train (3)
Gilgarry Mountain (5)
Going To The Zoo (9)
Gone The Rainbow (2)
Good Times We Had (7)
Great Mandella (The Wheel Of Life) (8)
Greenland Whale Fisheries (13)
Greenwood (13)
Hangman (6)
House Song (8)
Hurry Sundown (7)
Hush-A-Bye (3)
Hymn (9)

I Dig Rock And Roll Music (8,11) *9*
I Have A Song To Sing, O! (10)
I Need Me To Be For Me (12)
I Shall Be Released (9)
I'd Rather Be In Love (13)
I'm In Love With A Big Blue Frog (8)
If I Had A Hammer (The Hammer Song) (1,4,11) *10*
If I Had My Way (1,4)
If I Had Wings (8)
If I Were Free (7)
It's Raining (1,4,10)
Jane, Jane (6)
Jesus Met The Woman (4)
Jimmy Whalen (5)
King Of Names (7)
Kisses Sweeter Than Wine (7)
Last Thing On My Mind (6)
Le Deserteur (4)
Leatherwing Bat (10)
Leaving On A Jet Plane (8,11) *1*
Lemon Tree (1,11) *35*
Light One Candle (13)

Like The First Time (12)
Long Chain On (3)
Love City (Postcards To Duluth) (9)
Make-Believe Town (10)
Man Come Into Egypt (2)
Marvelous Toy (10)
Mockingbird (10)
Moments Of Soft Persuasion (9)
Mon Vrai Destin (7)
Monday Morning (5)
Morning Train (2)
Motherless Child (5)
Ms. Rheingold (13)
No Easy Walk To Freedom (13)
No Other Name (8)
Norman Normal (7)
Oh, Rock My Soul (Part I) (4) *93*
Old Coat (2)
On A Desert Island (With You In My Dreams) (6)
One Kind Favor (4)
Other Side Of This Life (7) *100*

Pack Up Your Sorrows (7)
Polly Von (3)
Pretty Mary (2)
Puff The Magic Dragon (2,4,10,11) *2*
Quit Your Low Down Ways (3)
Reason To Believe (9)
Rich Man Poor Man (9)
Right Field (13)
Rising Of The Moon (6)
Rocky Road (3)
Rolling Home (8)
San Francisco Bay Blues (5)
Settle Down (Goin' Down That Highway) (2) *56*
She Dreams (9)
Single Girl (4)
'Soalin', A (2,4)
Sometime Lovin' (7)
Song Is Love (8)
Sorrow (1)
State Of The Heart (13)
Stewball (3,11) *35*
Summer Highland Falls (12)
Sweet Survivor (12)
Talkin' Candy Bar Blues (5)

Tell It On The Mountain (3) *33*
There Is A Ship (4)
There's Anger In The Land (9)
This Land Is Your Land (2)
This Train (1)
Three Ravens (4)
Times They Are A Changin' (4)
Tiny Sparrow (2)
Too Much Of Nothing (9,11) *35*
Tramp On The Street (9)
Tryin' To Win (6)
Unicorn Song (12)
Very Last Day (3)
Wasn't That A Time (5)
Weave Me The Sunshine (13)
Weep For Jamie (8)
Well, Well, Well (7)
Whatshername (8)
When The Ship Comes In (5) *91*
Where Have All The Flowers Gone (1)
Whispered Words (13)
Yesterday's Tomorrow (9)

PETERS, Bernadette '80

Born Bernadette Lazzara on 2/28/44 in Queens, New York. Actress/singer. Appeared in several movies and Broadway shows.

5/3/80	114	14		1	**Bernadette Peters**	$12	MCA 3230
10/3/81	151	9		2	**Now Playing**	$12	MCA 5244

Broadway Baby (2)
Carrying A Torch (2)
Chico's Girl (1)
Dedicated To The One I Love (2) *65*

Don't (2)
Gee Whiz (1) *31*
Heartquake (1)
I Don't Know Why (I Just Do) (medley) (2)

I Never Thought I'd Break (1)
If You Were The Only Boy (1)
Maybe My Baby Will (2)
Mean To Me (medley) (2)
Only Wounded (1)

Other Lady (1)
Pearl's A Singer (2)
Should've Never Let Him Go (1)
Sweet Alibis (2)
Tears On My Pillow (2)

Weekend Of A Private Secretary (2)
You'll Never Know (1)

PETERSEN, Paul — see DARREN, James

PETERSON, Michael '97

Born on 8/7/59 in Tucson, Arizona. Country singer/songwriter/guitarist.

8/2/97	115	31	●	©	1 **Michael Peterson**	$10	Reprise 46618

By The Book
Drink, Swear, Steal & Lie *86*

For A Song
From Here To Eternity

I Finally Passed The Bar
Lost In The Shuffle

Love's Great
Since I Thought I Knew It All

That's What They Said About The Buffalo

Too Good To Be True
When The Bartender Cries

PETERSON, Oscar, Trio '63

Born on 8/15/25 in Montreal. Jazz pianist. His trio included Ray Brown (bass) and Ed Thigpen (drums).

2/9/63	145	2	©	1	**Bursting Out With The All Star Big Band!**	[I] $30	Verve 8476
6/8/63	127	2		2	**Affinity**	[I] $30	Verve 8516
10/31/64	81	12	©	3	**Oscar Peterson Trio + One**	[I] $30	Mercury 60975

with Clark Terry (trumpet)

Baubles, Bangles And Beads (2)
Blues For Big Scotia (1)
Blues For Smedley (3)
Brotherhood Of Man (3)

Daahoud (1)
Gravy Waltz (2)
Here's That Rainy Day (1)
I Love You (1)
I Want A Little Girl (3)

I'm A Fool To Want You (2)
I'm Old Fashioned (1)
Incoherent Blues (3)
Jim (1)
Mack The Knife (3)

Manteca (1)
Mumbles (3)
Roundalay (3)
Six And Four (2)
Squeaky's Blues (3)

Tangerine (2)
They Didn't Believe Me (3)
This Could Be The Start Of Something (2)
Tricrotism (1)

Waltz For Debbie (1)
West Coast Blues (1)
Young And Foolish (1)
Yours Is My Heart Alone (2)

PETRA '95

Christian rock group from Fort Wayne, Indiana: John Schlitt (vocals), Bob Harman (guitar), John Lawry (keyboards), Ronny Cates (bass) and Louie Weaver (drums).

9/9/95	91	8	©	1	**No Doubt**	$10	Word 62460
3/22/97	155	8	©	2	**Petra Praise 2 - We Need Jesus**	$10	Word 67933

Ancient Of Days (2)
Be Of Good Cheer (2)
Enter In (1)
For All You're Worth (1)
Heart Of A Hero (1)
Holiest Name (2)

I Love You Lord (2)
I Waited For The Lord (2)
Let Our Voices Rise Like Incense (2)
Lord, I Lift Your Name On High (2)
Lovely Lord (2)

More Than A Thousand Words (1)
No Doubt (1)
Only By Grace (medley) (2)
Right Place (1)
Show Your Power (2)
Sincerely Yours (1)

Song Of Moses Rev. 15:3-4 (2)
Think On These Things (1)
Think Twice (1)
To Him Who Sits On The Throne (medley) (2)
Two Are Better Than One (1)

We Hold Our Hearts Out To You (1)
We Need Jesus (1)
You Are Holy (medley) (2)

★359★ PET SHOP BOYS '86

Pop duo formed in England: Neil Tennant (vocals) and Chris Lowe (keyboards).
1)Please 2)Very 3)Actually

4/19/86	7	31	▲	©	1 **Please**	$10	EMI America 17193
12/27/86+	95	12		©	2 **Disco**	[K] $10	EMI America 17246
10/3/87	25	45	●	©	3 **Actually**	$10	EMI-Manhattan 46972
11/5/88	34	22	●	©	4 **Introspective**	$10	EMI-Manhattan 90868
11/17/90	45	25		©	5 **Behavior**	$10	EMI 94310
11/23/91	111	14	●	©	6 **Discography - The Complete Singles Collection**	[G] $10	EMI 97097
10/23/93	20	17	●	©	7 **Very**	$10	EMI 89721
10/8/94	75	3		©	8 **Disco 2**	[K] $10	EMI 28105
9/16/95	103	2		©	9 **Alternative**	$15	EMI 34023 [2]
9/28/96	39	6		©	10 **Bilingual**	$10	Atlantic 82915
11/20/99	84	3		©	11 **Nightlife**	$10	Parlophone 31086

Absolutely Fabulous (8)
Always On My Mind (4,6) *4*
Before (10)
Being Boring (5,6)

Bet She's Not Your Girlfriend (9)
Boy Strange (11)
Can You Forgive Her? (7,8)
Closer To Heaven (11)

DJ Culture (6)
Decadence (9)
Different Point Of View (7)
Discoteca (10)
Do I Have To? (9)

Domino Dancing (4,6) *18*
Don Juan (7)
Dreaming Of The Queen (7)
Electricity (10)
End Of The World (5)

Euroboy (6)
Footsteps (11)
For Your Own Good (11)
Go West (7,8)
Happiness Is An Option (11)

Heart (3,6)
Hey, Headmaster (9)
Hit Music (3)
How Can You Expect To Be Taken Seriously? (5) *93*

PET SHOP BOYS — Cont'd

I Don't Know What You Want But I Can't Give It Any More (11)
I Get Excited (You Get Excited Too) (9)
I Want A Dog (4,9)
I Want A Lover (1)
I Want To Wake Up (3)
I Wouldn't Normally Do This Kind Of Thing (7,8)
I'm Not Scared (4)
If You Were All (9)
In Denial (11)
In My House (medley) (4)
In The Night (2)
It Always Comes As A Surprise (10)

It Couldn't Happen Here (3)
It Must Be Obvious (9)
It's A Sin (3,6) *9*
It's Alright (4,6)
Jack The Lad (9)
Jealousy (5,6)
King's Cross (3)
Later Tonight (1)
Left To My Own Devices (4,6) *84*
Liberation (7,8)
Losing My Mind (9)
Love Comes Quickly (1,2,6) *62*
Man Could Get Arrested (9)
Metamorphosis (10)
Miserablism (9)

Music For Boys (9)
My October Symphony (5)
Nervously (5)
New Life (9)
New York City Boy (11)
One And One Make Five (7)
One In A Million (7)
One More Chance (3)
One Of The Crowd (9)
Only One (11)
Only The Wind (5)
Opportunities (Let's Make Lots Of Money) (1,2,6) *10*
Paninaro (2,9)
Radiophonic (11)
Red Letter Day (10)
Rent (3,6)

Saturday Night Forever (10)
Se A Vida É (That's The Way Life Is) (10)
Shameless (9)
Shopping (3)
Single (10)
So Hard (5,6,8) *62*
Some Speculation (9)
Sound Of The Atom Splitting (9)
Suburbia (1,2,6) *70*
Survivors, The (10)
That's My Impression (9)
Theatre, The (7)
This Must Be The Place I Waited Years To Leave (5)
To Face The Truth (5)
To Speak Is A Sin (7)

To Step Aside (10)
Tonight Is Forever (1)
Too Many People (9)
Two Divided By Zero (1)
Up Against It (10)
Vampires (11)
Violence (1,9)
Was It Worth It? (6)
Was That What It Was? (9)
We All Feel Better In The Dark (8,9)
West End Girls (1,2,6) *1*
What Have I Done To Deserve This? (3,6) *2*
What Keeps Mankind Alive? (9)

Where The Streets Have No Name (I Can't Take My Eyes Off You) (6) *72*
Why Don't We Live Together? (1)
Yesterday, When I Was Mad (7,8)
You Know Where You Went Wrong (9)
You Only Tell Me You Love Me When You're Drunk (11)
Young Offender (7)
Your Funny Uncle (9)

PETTY, Tom, And The Heartbreakers ★92★ '80

Born on 10/20/53 in Gainesville, Florida. Pop-rock singer/songwriter/guitarist. Formed The Heartbreakers in Los Angeles: Mike Campbell (guitar), Benmont Tench (keyboards), Ron Blair (bass) and Stan Lynch (drums). Howie Epstein replaced Blair in 1982. Lynch left in 1995. Petty appeared in the movies *FM* and *Made In Heaven*. Member of the **Traveling Wilburys**.

1)Damn The Torpedoes 2)Full Moon Fever 3)Greatest Hits

DEBUT	PEAK	WKS	RIAA	CD	#	ARTIST — Album Title	Catalog	Sym	$	Label & Number
9/24/77+	55	42	●	©	1	Tom Petty & The Heartbreakers	C:#10/81		$15	Shelter 52006
6/10/78	23	24	●	©	2	You're Gonna Get It!	C:#13/53		$15	Shelter 52029
11/10/79+	2[7]	66	▲2	©	3	**Damn The Torpedoes**	C:#8/120		$12	Backstreet 5105
5/23/81	5	31	▲	©	4	**Hard Promises**	C:#36/32		$12	Backstreet 5160
11/20/82+	9	32	●	©	5	**Long After Dark**			$12	Backstreet 5360
4/13/85	7	32	▲	©	6	**Southern Accents**			$12	MCA 5486
12/14/85+	22	26		©	7	**Pack Up The Plantation - Live!**		[L]	$15	MCA 8021 [2]
5/9/87	20	20	●	©	8	**Let Me Up (I've Had Enough)**			$10	MCA 5836
5/13/89	3	71	▲5	©	9	**Full Moon Fever**	C:#32/18		$10	MCA 6253
						TOM PETTY				
7/20/91	13	41	▲2	©	10	**Into The Great Wide Open**			$10	MCA 10317
12/4/93+	5	154	▲9	©	11	**Greatest Hits**	C:#3/228	[G]	$10	MCA 10813
11/19/94	8	53	▲3	©	12	**Wildflowers**			$10	Warner 45759
						TOM PETTY				
8/24/96	15	14	●	©	13	**She's The One**		[S]	$10	Warner 46285
5/1/99	10	23	●	©	14	**Echo**			$10	Warner 47294
11/18/00	132	2		©	15	Anthology: Through The Years		[G]	$15	MCA 170177 [2]

About To Give Out (14)
Accused Of Love (14)
Ain't Love Strange (8)
Airport (13)
All Mixed Up (8)
All Or Nothin' (10)
All The Wrong Reasons (10)
Alright For Now (9)
American Girl (1,7,11,15)
Angel Dream (13)
Anything That's Rock 'N' Roll (1)
Apartment Song (9)
Asshole (13)
Baby's A Rock 'N' Roller (2)
Best Of Everything (6,15)
Between Two Worlds (9)
Billy The Kid (14)
Breakdown (1,7,11,15) *40*
Built To Last (10)
Cabin Down Below (12)
California (13)
Century City (3)
Change Of Heart (5,15) *21*
Change The Locks (13)
Climb That Hill (13)
Counting On You (14)
Crawling Back To You (12)

Criminal Kind (4)
Damage You've Done (8)
Dark Of The Sun (10)
Deliver Me (5)
Depending On You (9)
Dogs On The Run (9)
Don't Bring Me Down (7)
Don't Come Around Here No More (6,11,15) *13*
Don't Do Me Like That (3,11,15) *10*
Don't Fade On Me (12)
Echo (14)
Even The Losers (3,11,15)
Face In The Crowd (9) *46*
Feel A Whole Lot Better (9)
Finding Out (5)
Fooled Again (I Don't Like It) (1)
Free Fallin' (9,11,15) *7*
Free Girl Now (14)
Grew Up Fast (13)
Hard On Me (12)
Here Comes My Girl (3,11,15) *59*
Higher Place (12)
Hometown Blues (1,15)
Honey Bee (12)

Hope On Board (13)
Hope You Never (13)
House In The Woods (12)
How Many More Days (8)
Hung Up And Overdue (13)
Hurt (2)
I Don't Wanna Fight (14)
I Need To Know (2,7,11,15) *41*
I Won't Back Down (9,11,15) *12*
Insider (4,7)
Into The Great Wide Open (10,11,15) *92*
It Ain't Nothin' To Me (6,7)
It'll All Work Out (8,15)
It's Good To Be King (12) *68*
Jammin' Me (8,15) *18*
Kings Highway (10)
Kings Road (4)
Learning To Fly (10,11,15) *28*
Let Me Up (I've Had Enough) (8)
Letting You Go (4)
Listen To Her Love (2,11,15) *59*
Lonesome Sundown (14)
Louisiana Rain (3)
Love Is A Long Road (9,15)

Luna (1)
Magnolia (2)
Make It Better (Forget About Me) (6) *54*
Makin' Some Noise (10)
Mary Jane's Last Dance (11,15) *14*
Mary's New Car (6)
Mind With A Heart Of Its Own (9)
My Life/Your World (8)
Mystery Man (1)
Needles And Pins (7) *37*
Nightwatchman (4)
No More (14)
No Second Thoughts (2)
One More Day, One More Night (14)
One Story Town (5)
Only A Broken Heart (12)
Out In The Cold (10)
Rebels (6,7,15) *74*
Refugee (3,7,11,15) *15*
Restless (13)
Rhino Skin (14)
Rockin' Around (With You) (1,7)
Room At The Top (14)
Runaway Trains (8)

Runnin' Down A Dream (9,11,15) *23*
Same Old You (5)
Self-Made Man (8)
Shadow Of A Doubt (A Complex Kid) (3)
Shout (7)
So You Want To Be A Rock & Roll Star (7)
Something Big (4)
Something In The Air (11)
Southern Accents (6,7)
Spike (6)
Stop Draggin' My Heart Around (15) *3*
Stories We Could Tell (7)
Straight Into Darkness (5,15)
Strangered In The Night (1)
Supernatural Radio (13)
Surrender (15)
Swingin' (14)
Thing About You (4)
Think About Me (8)
This One's For Me (14)
To Find A Friend (12)
Time To Move On (12)
Too Good To Be True (10)
Too Much Ain't Enough (2,15)

Two Gunslingers (10,15)
Waiting, The (4,7,11,15) *19*
Waiting For Tonight (15)
Wake Up Time (12)
Walls (13) *69*
Wasted Life (5)
We Stand A Chance (5)
What Are You Doin' In My Life? (3)
When The Time Comes (2)
Wild One, Forever (1,15)
Wildflowers (12)
Woman In Love (It's Not Me) (4,15) *79*
Won't Last Long (14)
Yer So Bad (9,15)
You And I Will Meet Again (10)
You Can Still Change Your Mind (4)
You Don't Know How It Feels (12) *13*
You Tell Me (13)
You Got Lucky (5,7,11,15) *20*
You Wreck Me (12)
You're Gonna Get It (2)
Zero From Outer Space (13)
Zombie Zoo (9)

P.F.M. '75

Progressive-rock group from Italy: Franco Mussida (vocals, guitar), Flavio Premoli (keyboards), Mauro Pagani (violin), Giorgio Piazza (bass) and Franz DiCioccio (drums). P.F.M.: Premiata Forneria Marconi.

DEBUT	PEAK	WKS	CD	#	ARTIST — Album Title	Sym	$	Label & Number
10/20/73	180	6		1	Photos Of Ghosts		$15	Manticore 66668
					PREMIATA FORNERIA MARCONI			
12/28/74+	151	8		2	P.F.M. 'Cook'	[I-L]	$15	Manticore 502

Alta Loma Nine Till Five (2)
Celebration (1,2)

Dove...Quando.... (2)
Four Holes In The Ground (2)

Il Banchetto (1)
Just Look Away (2)

Mr. Nine Till Five (1,2)
Old Rain (1)

Photos Of Ghosts (1)
Promenade The Puzzle (1)

River Of Life (1)

PFR   '96

Christian rock trio from Minnesota: Joel Hanson (guitar), Patrick Andrew (bass) and Mark Nash (drums). All share vocals. Nash is married to Leigh Nash of **Sixpence None The Richer**. PFR: Pray For Rain.

| 8/10/96 | 167 | 4 | | © | **Them**.. | | | **$10** | Vireo 51550 |

Anything   Face To Face   Garden   Line Of Love   Pour Me Out   Them
Daddy Never Cried   Fight   Kingdom Smile   Ordinary Day   Say   Tried To Tell Her

PHAIR, Liz   '94

Born on 4/17/67 in New Haven, Connecticut. Rock singer/songwriter.

2/5/94	196	1	●	©	1 **Exile In Guyville**....................................			**$10**	Matador 051
10/8/94	27	17	●	©	2 **Whip-Smart**...			**$10**	Matador 92429
8/29/98	35	9		©	3 **Whitechocolatespaceegg**......................			**$10**	Matador 53554

Alice Springs (2)   Divorce Song (1)   Glory (1)   Johnny Sunshine (1)   Polyester Bride (3)   Stratford-On-Guy (1)
Baby Got Going (3)   Dogs Of L.A. (2)   Go On Ahead (3)   Love Is Nothing (3)   Ride (3)   **Supernova** (2) *78*
Big Tall Man (3)   Explain It To Me (1)   Go West (2)   May Queen (2)   Shane (2)   Support System (2)
Canary (1)   Fantasize (3)   Gunshy (1)   Mesmerizing (1)   Shatter (1)   Uncle Alvarez (3)
Chopsticks (2)   Flower (1)   Headache (3)   Nashville (2)   Shitloads Of Money (3)   What Makes You Happy (3)
Cince De Mayo (2)   Fuck And Run (1)   Help Me Mary (1)   Never Said (1)   6'1" (1)   Whip-Smart (2)
Crater Lake (2)   Girls! Girls! Girls! (1)   Jealousy (2)   Only Son (3)   Soap Star Joe (1)   White Chocolate Space Egg (3)
Dance Of The Seven Veils (1)   Girls' Room (3)   Johnny Feelgood (3)   Perfect World (3)   Strange Loop (1)   X-Ray Man (2)

PHANTOM, ROCKER & SLICK   '85

Rock trio formed in New York City: Slim Jim Phantom (drums) and Lee Rocker (vocals, bass), and Earl Slick (guitar). Phantom and Rocker were members of the **Stray Cats** and Slick was a member of **Silver Condor**.

| 10/26/85 | 61 | 23 | | 1 | **Phantom, Rocker & Slick**...................... | | | **$10** | EMI America 17172 |
| 10/18/86 | 181 | 2 | | 2 | **Cover Girl**.. | | | **$10** | EMI America 17229 |

Can't Get It Right (2)   Going South (2)   It's Good To Be Alive (2)   Men Without Shame (1)   Runnin' From The Hounds (1)   Time Is On My Hands (1)
Cover Girl (2)   Hollywood Distractions (1)   Lonely Actions (1)   My Mistake (1)   Sidewalk Princess (2)   Well Kept Secret (1)
Dressed In Dirt (2)   I Found Someone Who Loves   Long Cool Woman (In A Black   No Regrets (1)   Sing For Your Supper (1)   What You Want (1)
Enough Is Enough (2)   Me (2)   Dress) (2)   Only Way To Fly (2)   Still Got Time (2)

PHARCYDE, The   '95

Male rap group from Los Angeles: Tre Hardson, Imani Wilcox, Romye Robinson and Derrick Stewart.

4/17/93	75	19	●	©	1 **Bizarre Ride II The Pharcyde**...............			**$10**	Delicious Vinyl 92222
12/2/95	37	12		©	2 **Labcabincalifornia**................................			**$10**	Delicious Vinyl 35102
11/25/00	157	1		©	3 **Plain Rap**...			**$10**	Delicious Vinyl 182232

All Live (2)   4 Better Or 4 Worse (1)   It's All Good! (2)   On The DL (2)   Rush (3)   Trust (1)
Blaze (3)   Frontline (3)   Little D (2)   Otha Fish (1)   She Said (2)   World (3)
Bullshit (2)   Groupie Therapy (2)   Misery (3)   Pack The Pipe (1)   Somethin' (3)   Y? (2)
Devil Music (2)   Guestlist (3)   Moment In Time (2)   **Passing Me By** (1) *52*   Somethin' That Means   Ya Mama (1)
Drop (2) *93*   Hey You (2)   Network (3)   Pharcyde (2)   Somethin' (2)
E.N.D., The (2)   Hustle, The (2)   Officer (1)   Return Of The B-Boy (1)   Soul Flower (1)
Evolution (3)   I'm That Type Of Nigga (1)   Oh Shit (1)   **Runnin'** (2) *55*   Splattitorium (2)

PHAROAHE MONCH   '99

Born Troy Jamerson in Queens, New York. Male rapper. Member of **Organized Konfusion**.

| 11/6/99 | 41 | 5 | | © | **Internal Affairs**..................................... | | | **$10** | Rawkus 50137 |

Ass, The   God Send - Organized   Light, The   Official   Right Here
Behind Closed Doors   Konfusion   Next Shit   Queens   **Simon Says** *97*
   Hell   No Mercy   Rape   Truth, The

PHIFE DAWG   '00

Born Malik Taylor on 4/10/70 in Brooklyn, New York. Male rapper. Member of **A Tribe Called Quest**.

| 10/14/00 | 175 | 4 | | © | **Ventilation: Da LP**................................. | | | **$10** | Groove Attack 068 |

Alphabet Soup   Ben Dova   D.R.U.G.S.   4 Horsemen (192 N' It)   Melody Adonis   Ventilation
Beats, Rhymes & Phife   Club Hoppa   Flawless   Lemme Find Out   Miscellaneous

PHILADELPHIA BRASS ENSEMBLE   '68

First-chair brass virtuosos of **The Philadelphia Orchestra**.

| 12/30/67+ | 58[X] | 2 | | | **A Festival Of Carols In Brass**................ | [X-I] | | **$15** | Columbia 6433 / 7033 |

Christmas charts: 113/'67, 58/'68

Angels We Have Heard On   God Rest Ye Merry, Gentlemen   Joy To The World (medley)   O Sanctissima (medley)   We Wish You A Merry
High (1980)   (medley)   Lo, How A Rose E'er Blooming   O Tannenbaum   Christmas (medley)
Away In A Manger (medley)   Good Christian Men Rejoice   (medley)   Silent Night, Holy Night   What Child Is This? (medley)
Bring A Torch, Jeanette Isabella   (medley)   O Come All Ye Faithful   (medley)
(medley)   Good King Wenceslas (medley)   (medley)   Twelve Days Of Christmas
Coventry Carol (medley)   Hark! The Herald Angels Sing   O Come, O Come, Emmanuel   Wassail Song (medley)
Deck The Hall With Boughs Of   (medley)   (medley)   We Three Kings Of Orient Are
Holly (medley)   It Came Upon The Midnight   O Holy Night (medley)   (medley)
First Noël (medley)   Clear (medley)   O Little Town Of Bethlehem

PHILADELPHIA ORCHESTRA, The   '62

Conductor Eugene Ormandy was born on 11/18/1899 in Budapest, Hungary; died on 3/12/85 (age 85). Conducted orchestra from 1938-1980. Also see **The Mormon Tabernacle Choir**.

| 5/19/62 | 17 | 13 | | 1 | **The Magnificent Sound Of The Philadelphia Orchestra** .... | [I-K] | | **$25** | Columbia 1 [2] |
| 12/22/62 | 109 | 2 | ● | 2 | **The Glorious Sound Of Christmas**.................................... | C:#15/13 | [X] | **$20** | Columbia 6369 |

with The Temple University Concert Choir; Christmas charts: 17/63, 22/'64, 45/'66, 19/'67, 26/'97, 15/'98, 11/'99, 13/'00

| 12/18/65+ | 3[X] | 11 | | 3 | **Handel: Messiah** | [X] | | **$25** | Columbia 263 / 607 [2] |

THE PHILADELPHIA ORCHESTRA/EUGENE ORMANDY/THE MORMON TABERNACLE CHOIR
first released in 1959; Christmas charts: 21/'65, 3/'69, 8/'70, 12/'71, 5/'72

| 5/6/78 | 136 | 8 | | © | 4 **David Bowie narrates Prokofiev's "Peter and The Wolf"** .... | | | **$15** | RCA Victor 2743 |

Air For The G String (1)   God Rest Ye Merry, Gentlemen   O Come, All Ye Faithful (Adeste   Peter And The Wolf, Op. 67 (4)   Toccata And Fugue In D Minor
Air From Water Music Suite (1)   (2)   Fideles) (2)   Polovtsian Dance No. 2 (1)   (1)
Alborada Del Gracioso (1)   Hark! The Herald Angels Sing   O Come, Little Children (2)   Prelude To The Afternoon Of A   Voices Of Spring (1)
Anitra's Dance (1)   (2)   O Come, O Come, Emanuel (2)   Faun (1)   Waltz From Sleeping Beauty (1)
Ave Maria (1)   Hungarian Rhapsody No. 2 (1)   O Holy Night (Cantique De   Russlan And Ludmilla Overture   Waltz From Swan Lake (1)
Danse Macabre (1)   Joy To The World (2)   Noel) (2)   (1)   Worship Of God (2)
Deck The Hall With Boughs Of   Les Toreadors (1)   O Little Town Of Bethlehem (2)   Silent Night, Holy Night (2)   Young Person's Guide To The
Holly (2)   March To The Scaffold (1)   O Sanctissima (O Du Frohliche)   Swan Of Tuonela (1)   Orchestra, Op. 34 (4)
First Noel (2)   Messiah (3)   (2)

PHILLIPS, Anthony '77

Born on 12/23/51 in Putney, England. Guitarist of **Genesis** from 1967-70.

3/26/77 **191** 3 © **The Geese & The Ghost**... $15 Passport 98020

Chinese Mushroom Cloud | Geese And The Ghost (Parts I | Henry, Portraits From Tudor | Which Way The Wind Blows
Collections | & II) | Times Medley | Wind-Tales
 | God If I Saw Her Now | Sleepfall: The Geese Fly West |

PHILLIPS, Esther '75

Born Esther Mae Jones on 12/23/35 in Galveston, Texas. Died of liver failure on 8/7/84 (age 48). R&B singer. Recorded with Johnny Otis as "Little Esther."

1/5/63 **46** 14 **1 Release Me!**... $150 Lenox 227
 "LITTLE ESTHER" PHILLIPS

1/2/71 **115** 15 © **2 Burnin'**.. [L] $25 Atlantic 1565
 recorded at Freddie Jett's Pied Piper Club in Los Angeles

3/18/72 **137** 15 © **3 From A Whisper To A Scream** .... $15 Kudu 05
12/30/72+ **177** 8 **4 Alone Again, Naturally** .... $15 Kudu 09
8/2/75 **32** 17 © **5 What A Diff'rence A Day Makes** $15 Kudu 23

1/31/76 **170** 4 © **6 Confessin' The Blues**... [L] $15 Atlantic 1680
 recorded at Freddie Jett's Pied Piper Club in Los Angeles

1/8/77 **150** 4 **7 Capricorn Princess** .... $15 Kudu 31

After Loving You (1) | Confessin' The Blues (6) | I Can't Help It (1) | If It's The Last Thing I Do (2) | Please Send Me Someone To | What A Diff'rence A Day
All The Way Down (7) | Cry Me A River Blues (2) | I Don't Want To Do Wrong (4) | In The Evenin' (6) | Love (2) | Makes (5) 20
Alone Again (Naturally) (4) | Do Right Woman, Do Right | I Haven't Got Anything Better | It Could Happen To You (6) | Release Me (1,2) 8 | Why Should We Try Anymore
Am I That Easy To Forget (1) | Man (4) | To Do (7) | Jelly Jelly Blues (medley) (6) | Romance In The Dark (6) | (1)
And I Love Him (2) 54 | Don't Let Me Lose This Dream | **I Love Paris** (6) | Just Out Of Reach (1) | Scarred Knees (3) | You And Me Together Forever
Baby, I'm For Real (3) | (2) | **I Really Don't Want To Know** | Let Me In Your Life (4) | Shangri-La (3) | (4)
Be Honest With Me (1) | Dream (7) | (1) 61 | Let's Move & Groove (4) | Sweet Touch Of Love (3) | You're Coming Home (5)
Beautiful Friendship (4) | From A Whisper To A Scream | I Wonder (6) | Long John Blues (medley) (6) | 'Til My Back Ain't Got No Bone | (Your Love Has Lifted Me)
Blow Top Blues (medley) (6) | (3) | I'd Fight The World (1) | Magic's In The Air (7) | (3) | Higher & Higher (7)
Boy, I Really Tied One On (7) | Georgia Rose (4) | I'm Gettin' 'Long Alright (2,6) | Makin' Whoopee (2) | To Lay Down Beside You (3) | Your Love Is So Doggone Good
Bye Bye Blackbird (6) | Home Is Where The Hatred Is | I've Forgotten More Than You'll | Mister Magic (5) | Turn Around, Look At Me (5) | (3)
C.C. Rider (6) | (3) | Ever Know About Him (1) | No Headstone On My Grave (1) | Use Me (4) |
Candy (7) | Hurtin' House (5) | I've Never Found A Man (To | Oh Papa (5) | |
Cherry Red (4,6) | I Can Stand A Little Rain (5) | Love Me Like You Do) (4) | One Night Affair (5) | |

PHILLIPS, John '70

Born on 8/30/35 in Paris Island, South Carolina. Died of heart failure on 3/18/2001 (age 65). Singer/songwriter/guitarist. Co-founder of The Mamas & The Papas. Father of actress MacKenzie Phillips and singer Chynna Phillips (of **Wilson Phillips**).

5/2/70 **181** 9 © **John Phillips (John The Wolfking of L.A.)** .... $20 Dunhill/ABC 50077

April Anne | Down The Beach | Holland Tunnel | Malibu People | Someone's Sleeping
Captain | Drum | Let It Bleed, Genevieve | **Mississippi** 32 | Topanga Canyon

PHILLIPS, Sam '94

Born Leslie Phillips on 1/28/62 in Glendale, California. Female pop-rock singer/songwriter/actress. Married **T-Bone Burnett** in 1989. Played "Katya" in the movie *Die Hard With A Vengeance*.

3/26/94 **182** 1 © **Martinis & Bikinis** .... $10 Virgin 39438

Baby I Can't Please You | Fighting With Fire | Love And Kisses | Signposts | When I Fall
Black Sky | Gimme Some Truth | Same Changes | Strawberry Road |
Circle Of Fire | I Need Love | Same Rain | Wheel Of The Broken Voice |

PHILLIPS, Shawn '75

Born on 2/3/43 in Fort Worth, Texas. Male singer/songwriter/guitarist.

12/2/72+ **57** 20 © **1 Faces** .... $15 A&M 4363
12/15/73+ **72** 13 © **2 Bright White** .... $15 A&M 4402
11/30/74+ **50** 12 © **3 Furthermore...** .... $15 A&M 3662
9/13/75 **101** 9 © **4 Do You Wonder** .... $15 A&M 4539

All The Kings And Castles (2) | Cape Barras (3) | Hey Miss Lonely (1) | Lasting Peace Of Mind (1) | Salty Tears (1) | Troof (3)
Anello (Where Are You) (1) | Chorale (1) | (I Took) A Walk (1) | Looking At The Angel (4) | See You (3) | Victoria Emmanuele (2)
As All Is Played (4) | City To City (4) | It's A Beautiful Morning (2) | Mr. President (3) | Song For Northern Ireland (3) | **We** (1) 89
Believe In Life (4) | Do You Wonder (4) | January First (3) | Ninety Two Years (3) | Starbright (3) | Xasper (4)
Blunt And Frank (4) | Dream Queen (2) | 'L' Ballade (1) | Parisian Plight II (1) | Summer Vignette (4) |
Breakthrough (3) | Furthermore (4) | Lady Of The Blue Rose (2) | Planned "O" (2) | Talking In The Garden (3) |
Bright White (2) | Golden Flower (4) | Landscape (3) | Planscape (3) | Technotronic Lad (2) |

PHILLIPS, CRAIG & DEAN '96

Christian vocal trio from Austin, Texas: Randy Phillips, Shawn Craig and Dan Dean.

11/23/96 **34**[X] 1 © **Repeat The Sounding Joy** .... [X] $10 Star Song 20100

All The Earth Bows Down | Be It Unto Me | Go Tell It On The Mountain | Joyful, Joyful, We Adore Thee | O Sanctissima (medley)
(medley) | Bow Down (medley) | (medley) | (medley) | Sleigh Ride
Amen (medley) | Call His Name Jesus | How Great Our Joy (medley) | Kid In Me |
Angels We Have Heard On | Chipmunk Song | I'll Be Home For Christmas | O Come, O Come, Emmanuel |
High (medley) | Glorify The Lord (medley) | Joy To The World! (medley) | O Holy Night (medley) |

PHISH '96

Rock group from Burlington, Vermont: Trey Anastasio (guitar), Page McConnell (keyboards), Mike Gordon (bass) and Jon Fishman (drums). All share vocals.

2/20/93 **51** 5 ● © **1 Rift** .... $10 Elektra 61433
4/16/94 **34** 13 ● © **2 (Hoist)** .... $10 Elektra 61628
7/15/95 **18** 14 ▲ © **3 A Live One** .... [L] $15 Elektra 61777 [2]
11/2/96 **7** 15 ● © **4 Billy Breathes** $10 Elektra 61971
11/15/97 **17** 8 © **5 Slip Stitch And Pass** .... [L] $10 Elektra 62121
 recorded on 3/1/97 at the Markthalle in Hamburg, Germany
11/14/98 **8** 5 © **6 The Story Of The Ghost** $10 Elektra 62297
12/11/99 **120** 2 ● © **7 Hampton Comes Alive** .... [L] $40 Elektra 62495 [6]
 recorded on 11/20/98 at the Coliseum in Hampton, Virginia
6/3/00 **12** 18 © **8 Farmhouse**... $10 Elektra 62521

PHISH — Cont'd

All Things Reconsidered (1)
Axilla I (7)
Axilla (Part II) (2)
Back On The Train (8)
Bathtub Gin (7)
Big Black Furry Creature From Mars (1)
Billy Breathes (4)
Birds Of A Feather (6)
Bliss (4)
Bold As Love (7)
Boogie On Reggae Woman (2)
Bouncing Around The Room (3)
Brian And Robert (6)
Bug (8)
Cars Trucks Buses (4)
Cavern (7)
Chalkdust Torture (3)

Character Zero (4,7)
Cities (5)
Cry Baby Cry (7)
Demand (1)
Dirt (8)
Divided Sky (7)
Dog Faced Boy (2)
Dogs Stole Things (7)
Down With Disease (2)
Driver (7)
End Of Session (6)
Farmhouse (7,8)
Fast Enough For You (1)
Fikus (6)
First Tube (8)
Foam (7)
Frankie Says (6)
Free (7)

Funky Bitch (7)
Gettin' Jiggy Wit It (7)
Ghost (6)
Gotta Jibboo (8)
Guelah Papyrus (7)
Gumbo (3)
Guyute (6,7)
Ha Ha Ha (7)
Harry Hood (3,7)
Heavy Things (8)
Hello My Baby (5)
Horn (1)
Horse, The (1)
If I Could (2)
Inlaw Josie Wales (8)
It's Ice (1)
Jesus Just Left Chicago (5)
Julius (2)

Lawn Boy (5,7)
Lengthwise (1)
Lifeboy (2)
Limb By Limb (6)
Mango Song (7)
Maze (1)
Meat (6,7)
Mike's Song (5,7)
Moma Dance (6)
Montana (3)
Mound (1)
My Friend, My Friend (1)
NICU (7)
Nellie Kane (7)
Piper (7,8)
Possum (7)
Prince Caspian (4)
Quinn The Eskimo (7)

Rift (1,7)
Rock And Roll Part 2 (7)
Roggae (6,7)
Roses Are Free (7)
Sabotage (7)
Sample In A Jar (2)
Sand (8)
Scent Of A Mule (2)
Shafty (6)
Silent In The Morning (1)
Simple (3,7)
Slave To The Traffic Light (3)
Sleep (8)
Sparkle (1)
Split Open And Melt (7)
Squirming Coil (3)
Stash (3,7)
Steep (4)

Swept Away (4)
Talk (4)
Taste (4,5)
Theme From The Bottom (4)
Train Song (4,7)
Tube (7)
Tubthumping (7)
Tweezer (3)
Twist (8)
Wading In The Velvet Sea (6,7)
Waste (4)
Water In The Sky (6)
Wedge, The (1,7)
Weekapaug Groove (5,7)
Weigh (1,5)
Wilson (3,7)
Wolfman's Brother (2,5)
You Enjoy Myself (3)

PHOTOGLO, Jim   '81
Born in Los Angeles. Pop singer/songwriter.

DEBUT	PEAK	WKS			ARTIST — Album Title	$	Label & Number
5/24/80	194	3		1	Photoglo	$12	20th Century 604
6/6/81	119	11		2	Fool In Love With You	$12	20th Century 621

Angelina (2)
Beg, Borrow Or Steal (1)
Best That I Can Be (1)
Don't Be Afraid To Love Somebody (1)

Faded Blue (1)
Fool In Love With You (2) 25
I Can't Let Go Of You (1)
I Don't Want To Be In This Movie (1)

More To Love (2)
Ruled By My Heart (2)
Run To Me (2)
Steal Away (1)

There's Always Another Chance Left For Love (2)
Tonight Will Last Forever (2)
Try It Again (2)
20th Century Fool (1)

We Were Meant To Be Lovers (1) 31
When Love Is Gone (1)
Won't Let You Do It To Me (2)
Young Girl (1)

PICKETT, Bobby "Boris", And The Crypt-Kickers   '62
Born on 2/11/40 in Somerville, Massachusetts. Novelty singer. The Crypt-Kickers: Leon Russell, Johnny MacCrae, Rickie Page and Gary Paxton.

DEBUT	PEAK	WKS		CD	ARTIST — Album Title	Sym	$	Label & Number
11/3/62	19	13		©	1 The Original Monster Mash	[N]	$200	Garpax 57001
9/29/73	173	4		©	2 The Original Monster Mash	[N-R]	$25	Parrot 71063

Bella's Bash (1,2)
Blood Bank Blues (1,2)
Graveyard Shift (1,2)

Irresistible Igor (1)
Let's Fly Away (1,2)
Me & My Mummy (1,2)

Monster Mash (1,2) 1
Monster Mash Party (1,2)
Monster Minuet (1,2)

Monster Motion (1)
Monsters' Holiday (2) 30
Rabian-The Fiendage Idol (1,2)

Sinister Stomp (1)
Skully Gully (1)
Transylvania Twist (1,2)

Wolfbane (1)

★354★ PICKETT, Wilson   '66
Born on 3/18/41 in Prattville, Alabama. R&B singer/songwriter. Nicknamed the "Wicked Pickett." Member of The Falcons from 1961-63. Inducted into the Rock and Roll Hall of Fame in 1991.

1)The Exciting Wilson Pickett 2)The Best Of Wilson Pickett 3)The Wicked Pickett

DEBUT	PEAK	WKS	CD		ARTIST — Album Title	Sym	$	Label & Number
10/30/65	107	6	©	1	In The Midnight Hour		$50	Atlantic 8114
8/27/66	21	29	©	2	The Exciting Wilson Pickett		$40	Atlantic 8129
1/21/67	42	31		3	The Wicked Pickett		$40	Atlantic 8138
8/12/67	54	11		4	The Sound Of Wilson Pickett		$40	Atlantic 8145
11/11/67+	35	54		5	The Best Of Wilson Pickett	[G]	$30	Atlantic 8151
2/24/68	70	15	©	6	I'm In Love		$25	Atlantic 8175
7/13/68	91	13		7	The Midnight Mover		$25	Atlantic 8183
3/1/69	97	14		8	Hey Jude		$20	Atlantic 8215
4/4/70	197	3		9	Right On		$20	Atlantic 8250
10/3/70	64	19	©	10	Wilson Pickett In Philadelphia		$20	Atlantic 8270
5/22/71	73	13		11	The Best Of Wilson Pickett, Vol. II	[G]	$20	Atlantic 8290
12/25/71+	132	14		12	Don't Knock My Love		$20	Atlantic 8300
2/10/73	178	8	©	13	Wilson Pickett's Greatest Hits	[G]	$25	Atlantic 501 [2]
4/28/73	187	3		14	Mr. Magic Man		$20	RCA Victor 4858

Ain't No Doubt About It (10)
Baby Man (14)
Back In Your Arms (8)
Barefootin' (2)
Born To Be Wild (8,11) 64
Bring It On Home To Me (6)
Bumble Bee (Sting Me) (10)
Call My Name, I'll Be There (12) 52
Cole, Cooke & Redding (11) 91
Come Home Baby (1)
Come Right Here (10)
Covering The Same Old Ground (1)
Danger Zone (2)
Days Go By (10)
Deborah (7)
Don't Cry No More (6)
Don't Fight It (1,5,13) 53
Don't Knock My Love - Pt. 1 (12,13) 13
Don't Knock My Love - Pt. 2 (12)
Don't Let The Green Grass Fool You (10,11,13) 17

Down By The Sea (7)
Engine Number 9 (10,11,13) 14
Everybody Needs Somebody To Love (3,5,13) 29
Fire And Water (12) 14
For Better Or Worse (1,7)
Funky Broadway (4,5,13) 8
Funky Way (1)
Get Me Back On Time, Engine Number 9 ..see: Engine Number 9
Groovy Little Woman (9)
Hello Sunshine (6)
Help The Needy (10)
Hey Joe (9,11) 59
Hey Jude (8,11,13) 23
Hot Love (12)
I Can't Let My True Love Slip Away (14)
I Found A Love - Part 1 (1,4,5,13) 32
I Found A Love, Part 2 (14)
I Found A True Love (7,11,13) 42
I Found The One (4)

I Keep Walking Straight Ahead (14)
I Need A Lot Of Loving Every Day (4)
I Sho' Love You (14)
I'm A Midnight Mover (7,11,13) 24
I'm Drifting (2)
I'm Gonna Cry (1,7)
I'm In Love (6,11,13) 45
I'm Not Tired (1)
I'm Sorry About That (4)
I've Come A Long Way (6)
If You Need Me (5,13,14) 64
In The Midnight Hour (1,2,5,13) 21
International Playboy (10)
It's A Groove (1)
It's All Over (2)
It's Still Good (9)
It's Too Late (5,13) 49
Jealous Love (6) 50
Knock On Wood (3)
Land Of 1000 Dances (2,5,13) 6
Let's Get An Understanding (7)

Let's Kiss And Make Up (1)
Lord Pity Us All (9)
Love Is A Beautiful Thing (4)
Love Is Beautiful (14)
Mama Told Me Not To Come (12,13) 99
Man And A Half (8,11,13) 42
Mercy, Mercy (2)
Mojo Mamma (4)
Mr. Magic Man (14) 98
Mustang Sally (3,5,13) 23
My Own Style Of Loving (8)
New Orleans (13)
Night Owl (8)
Ninety-Nine And A Half (Won't Do) (2,5,13) 53
Not Enough Love To Satisfy (12)
Nothing You Can Do (3)
Only I Can Sing This Song (14)
Ooh Poo Pah Doo (3)
People Make The World (8)
Pledging My Love (12)
Remember, I Been Good To You (7)
Run Joey Run (10)

Save Me (8)
Search Your Heart (8)
She Ain't Gonna Do Right (3)
She Said Yes (9) 68
She's Lookin' Good (6,11,13) 15
She's So Good To Me (2)
Sin Was The Blame (14)
Sit Down And Talk This Over (8)
634-5789 (Soulsville, U.S.A.) (2,5,13) 13
Something Within Me (4)
Something You Got (3)
Soul Dance Number Three (4,5,13) 55
Stag-O-Lee (6) 22
Steal Away (4)
Sugar Sugar (9,11,13) 25
Sunny (3)
Sweet Inspiration (9)
Take A Little Love (1)
Take This Love I've Got (1)
Teardrops Will Fall (1)
That Kind Of Love (6)
That's A Man's Way (1)

This Old Town (9)
Three Time Loser (3)
Time Is On My Side (3)
Toe Hold (8)
Trust Me (7)
Up Tight Good Woman (3)
We've Got To Have Love (6)
What It Is (14)
Woman Let Me Be Down Home (12)
Woman Likes To Hear That (9)
You Can't Judge A Book By Its Cover (12)
You Can't Stand Alone (4) 70
You Keep Me Hanging On (9,11,13) 92
You Left The Water Running (3)
You're So Fine (2)
(Your Love Has Brought Me) A Mighty Long Way (12)

PIECES OF A DREAM   '84
Jazz trio from Philadelphia: James Lloyd (keyboards), Cedric Napoleon (bass) and Curtis Harmon (drums).

DEBUT	PEAK	WKS	CD		ARTIST — Album Title	$	Label & Number
10/31/81	170	6	©	1	Pieces Of A Dream	$12	Elektra 350
8/28/82	114	15	©	2	We Are One	$12	Elektra 60142
2/25/84	90	15		3	Imagine This	$12	Elektra 60270
8/2/86	102	12	©	4	Joyride	$10	Manhattan 53023

PIECES OF A DREAM — Cont'd

All About Love (1)
Body Magic (1)
Careless Whisper (4)
Don't Be Sad (2)
Easy Road Home (1)
Fo-Fi-Fo (3)
For Ramsey (2)

For The Fun Of It (3)
Foreverlasting Love (3)
I Can Give You What You Want (4)
Imagine This (3)
It's Getting Hot In Here (3)
It's Time For Love (3)

Joyride (4)
Love Of My Life (4)
Lovers (1)
Mt. Airy Groove (2)
Outside In (4)
Pieces Of A Dream (1)
Please Don't Do This To Me (2)

Pop Rock (2)
Save Some Time For Me (4)
Say La La (4)
Shadow Of Your Smile (3)
Steady Glide (1)
Sunshine (4)
Tell Me A Bedtime Story (3)

Touch Me In The Spring (1)
Warm Weather (1)
We Are One (2)
When You Are Here With Me (2)
Winning Streak (4)
Yo Frat (2)

You Know I Want You (2)

PILOT   '75

Pop-rock trio from Edinburgh, Scotland: David Paton (vocals, guitar), Bill Lyall (keyboards) and Stuart Tosh (drums). Lyall died of AIDS in December 1989 (age 36).

| 5/31/75 | 82 | 14 | | | Pilot | | | $15 | EMI 11368 |
| | | | | | produced by **Alan Parsons** | | | | |

Auntie Iris
Don't Speak Loudly

Girl Next Door
High Into The Sky

Just A Smile *90*
Lovely Lady Smile

Lucky For Some
Magic *5*

Never Give Up
Over The Moon

Sky Blue
Sooner Or Later

PINDER, Michael   '76

Born on 12/27/41 in Birmingham, England. Keyboardist of **The Moody Blues**.

| 5/1/76 | 133 | 8 | | | The Promise | | | $15 | Threshold 18 |

Air
Carry On

Free As A Dove
I Only Want To Love You

Message
Promise, The

Seed, The
Someone To Believe In

You'll Make It Through

P!NK   '00

Born Alecia Moore on 9/6/79 in Philadelphia. Female R&B singer. Noted for her pink hair.

| 4/22/00 | 26 | 59 | ▲² © | | Can't Take Me Home | | | $10 | LaFace 26062 |

Can't Take Me Home
Do What U Do
Hell Wit Ya

Hiccup
Is It Love
Let Me Let You Know

Love Is Such A Crazy Thing
Most Girls *4*
Private Show

Split Personality
Stop Falling
There You Go *7*

You Make Me Sick *33*

PINK FLOYD ★25★   '80

Progressive-rock group formed in England: **David Gilmour** (guitar; replaced **Syd Barrett** in 1968), **Roger Waters** (bass), Rick Wright (keyboards) and **Nick Mason** (drums). Wright left in early 1982. Waters went solo in 1984. Band inactive from 1984-86. Gilmour, Mason and Wright regrouped in 1987. Inducted into the Rock and Roll Hall of Fame in 1996. Group name taken from Georgia bluesmen Pink Anderson and Floyd Council.

1)The Wall 2)The Division Bell 3)Wish You Were Here 4)The Dark Side Of The Moon 5)Pulse

DEBUT	PEAK	WKS	RIAA	CD	#	ARTIST — Album Title	Catalog	Sym	$	Label & Number
12/2/67+	131	11			1	Pink Floyd			$150	Tower 5093
1/3/70	74	27	▲ ©		2	Ummagumma		[L]	$40	Harvest 388 [2]
						record 1: live; record 2: studio				
11/7/70	55	13	● ©		3	Atom Heart Mother			$20	Harvest 382
7/31/71	152	7			4	Relics		[K]	$20	Harvest 759
						recordings from 1967-69				
11/6/71	70	73	▲² ©		5	Meddle			$20	Harvest 832
6/24/72	46	25	● ©		6	Obscured By Clouds		[S]	$20	Harvest 11078
						music from movie *The Valley*				
3/17/73	❶¹	741	▲¹⁵ ©		7	The Dark Side Of The Moon	C:❶¹⁸/535		$20	Harvest 11163
9/1/73	153	7	©		8	More		[E-S]	$20	Harvest 11198
						originally released in 1969				
12/22/73+	36	17	●		9	A Nice Pair		[E]	$25	Harvest 11257 [2]
						reissue of their early albums *The Piper At The Gates Of Dawn* and *A Saucerful Of Secrets*				
9/27/75	❶²	39	▲⁶ ©		10	Wish You Were Here	C:#11/36		$12	Columbia 33453
2/19/77	3	28	▲⁴ ©		11	Animals	C:#34/1		$12	Columbia 34474
12/15/79+	❶¹⁵	123	▲²³ ©		12	The Wall	C:❶¹/452		$15	Columbia 36183 [2]
12/12/81+	31	16	▲² ©		13	A Collection Of Great Dance Songs	C:#6/53	[G]	$12	Columbia 37680
4/9/83	6	23	▲² ©		14	The Final Cut			$12	Columbia 38243
6/18/83	68	9	©		15	Works		[K]	$12	Capitol 12276
						Harvest label recordings (1968-73)				
9/26/87	3	56	▲⁴ ©		16	A Momentary Lapse Of Reason	C:#12/18		$10	Columbia 40599
12/10/88+	11	21	▲³ ©		17	Delicate Sound Of Thunder	C:#40/9	[L]	$15	Columbia 44484 [2]
4/23/94	❶⁴	51	▲³ ©		18	The Division Bell			$10	Columbia 64200
6/24/95	❶¹	22	▲² ©		19	Pulse		[L]	$15	Columbia 67065 [2]
5/6/00	19	9	▲		20	Is There Anybody Out There? - The Wall Live 1980-1981		[L]	$15	Columbia 62055 [2]

Absolutely Curtains (6)
Alan's Psychedelic Breakfast Medley (3)
Another Brick In The Wall (Part I) (12,20)
Another Brick In The Wall (Part II) (12,13,17,19,20) *1*
Another Brick In The Wall (Part III) (12,20)
Any Colour You Like (7,19)
Arnold Layne (4,15)
Astronomy Domine (2,9,19)
Atom Heart Mother Suite Medley (3)
Biding My Time (4)
Bike (4)
Brain Damage (7,15,19)
Breathe (7,19)
Bring The Boys Back Home (12,20)

Burning Bridges (6)
Careful With That Axe, Eugene (2,4)
Chapter 24 (1,9)
Childhood's End (6)
Cirrus Minor (4,8)
Cluster One (18)
Comfortably Numb (12,17,19,20)
Coming Back To Life (18,19)
Corporal Clegg (2)
Crying Song (8)
Cymbaline (8)
Dogs (11)
Dogs Of War (16,17)
Don't Leave Me Now (12,20)
Dramatic Theme (4)
Echoes (5)
Eclipse (7,15,19)
Embryo (15)

Empty Spaces (12,20)
Fat Old Sun (3)
Fearless (5,15)
Final Cut (14)
Flaming (9)
Fletcher Memorial Home (14)
Free Four (6,15)
Get Your Filthy Hands Off My Desert (14)
Gnome, The (1,9)
Gold It's In The... (6)
Goodbye Blue Sky (12,20)
Goodbye Cruel World (12,20)
Grand Vizier's Garden Party: Pts. 1 - 3 (2)
Grantchester Meadows (2)
Great Day For Freedom (18,19)
Great Gig In The Sky (7,19)
Green Is The Colour (8)
Gunners Dream (14)

Happiest Days Of Our Lives (12,20)
Have A Cigar (10)
Hero's Return (14)
Hey You (12,19,20)
High Hopes (18,19)
Ibizar Bar (8)
If (3)
In The Flesh? (12,20)
Interstellar Overdrive (1,4,9)
Is There Anybody Out There? (12,20)
Jugband Blues (9)
Julia Dream (4)
Keep Talking (18,19)
Last Few Bricks (20)
Learning To Fly (16,17,19) *70*
Let There Be More Light (9)
Lost For Words (18)
Lucifer Sam (1,9)

Marooned (18)
Matilda Mother (1,9)
Money (7,13,17,19) *13*
More, Main Theme From (8)
More Blues (8)
Mother (12,20)
Mudmen (6)
Narrow Way - Parts 1, 2 & 3 (2)
New Machine Part 1 & 2 (16)
Nile Song (4,8)
Nobody Home (12,20)
Not Now John (14)
Obscured By Clouds (6)
On The Run (7,19)
On The Turning Away (16,17)
One Of My Turns (12,20)
One Of The Few (14)
One Of These Days (5,13,15,17)
One Slip (16)

Outside The Wall (12,20)
Paint Box (4)
Paranoid Eyes (14)
Party Sequence (8)
Pigs On The Wing (Part One & Two) (11)
Pigs (Three Different Ones) (11)
Pillow Of Winds (5)
Poles Apart (18)
Post War Dream (14)
Pow R Toc H (1,9)
Quicksilver (8)
Remember A Day (4,9)
Round And Around (16,17)
Run Like Hell (12,17,19,20) *53*
San Tropez (5)
Saucerful Of Secrets (8)
Saucerful Of Secrets Medley (2)
Scarecrow, The (1,9)

PINK FLOYD — Cont'd

Seamus (5)
See Emily Play (1,4,15)
See-Saw (9)
Set The Controls For The Heart Of The Sun (2,9,15)
Several Species of Small Furry Animals Gathered Together In

A Cave And Grooving With A Pict (2,15)
Sheep (11,13)
Shine On You Crazy Diamond (10,13,17,19)
Show Must Go On (12,20)
Signs Of Life (16)
Sorrow (16,17,19)

Southampton Dock (14)
Spanish Piece (8)
Speak To Me (7,19)
Stay (6)
Stop (12,20)
Summer '68 (3)
Sysyphus - Parts 1, 2, 3 & 4 (2)
Take It Back (18) *73*

Take Up Thy Stethoscope And Walk (1,9)
Terminal Frost (16)
Thin Ice (12,20)
Time (7,17,19)
Trial, The (12,20)
Two Suns In The Sunset (20)
Up The Khyber (8)

Us And Them (7,19)
Vera (12,20)
Waiting For The Worms (12,20)
Wearing The Inside Out (18)
Welcome To The Machine (10)
What Do You Want From Me (18,19)
What Shall We Do Now? (20)

When You're In (6)
Wish You Were Here (10,13,17,19)
Wots...Uh The Deal (6)
Yet Another Movie (16,17)
Young Lust (12,20)
Your Possible Pasts (14)

PIPKINS, The   '70
Vocal duo formed in England: Roger Greenaway and Tony Burrows (low voice). Worked together in studio group **White Plains**.

8/8/70	**132**	4			Gimme Dat Ding!		[N]	$25	Capitol 483

All You'll Ever Get From Me
Are You Cookin' Goose?

Busy Line
Gimme Dat Ding *9*

Here Come De Kins
My Baby Loves Lovin'

People Dat You Wanna Phone Ya!

Sunny Honey Girl
Yakety Yak

You Can't Go Wrong

PIRATES OF THE MISSISSIPPI   '91
Country group from Montgomery, Alabama: Bill McCorvey (vocals), Rich Alves and Pat Severs (guitars), Dean Townson (bass) and Jimmy Lowe (drums).

5/18/91	**80**	23		©	Pirates Of The Mississippi			$10	Capitol 94389

Anything Goes
Down And Out In Birmingham
Feed Jake

Honky Tonk Blues
I Take My Comfort In You
Jolly Roger (medley)

Pirates Of The Mississippi (medley)
Redneck Rock N' Roll

Rollin' Home
Speak Of The Devil
Talkin' 'Bout Love

PISCOPO, Joe   '85
Born on 6/17/51 in Passaic, New Jersey. Actor/comedian. Cast member of TV's *Saturday Night Live* (1980-84).

7/27/85	**168**	3		©	New Jersey		[C]	$10	Columbia 40046

Biography
Candid Radio
Fat Boy

Good Morning America
Honeymooners Rap

I Wanna Sound Like A Black Man
Late Night

MTV
Music Minus One
My Oh My

New Jersey
Nightclub, The
Witchcraft

★407★   PITNEY, Gene   '63
Born on 2/17/41 in Hartford, Connecticut; raised in Rockville, Connecticut. Pop singer/songwriter.
1)World-Wide Winners 2)It Hurts To Be In Love 3)Looking Through The Eyes Of Love

12/1/62	**48**	15		©	1	Only Love Can Break A Heart		$50	Musicor 3003
5/18/63	**85**	7		©	2	Gene Pitney Sings Just For You..		$50	Musicor 3004
8/3/63	**41**	31		©	3	World-Wide Winners	[G]	$50	Musicor 3005
11/23/63	**105**	6			4	Blue Gene		$50	Musicor 3006
4/4/64	**87**	9			5	Gene Pitney's Big Sixteen	[G]	$50	Musicor 3008
11/14/64	**42**	17			6	It Hurts To Be In Love		$40	Musicor 3019
3/20/65	**141**	4		©	7	George Jones & Gene Pitney		$40	Musicor 3044
7/17/65	**112**	9			8	I Must Be Seeing Things		$40	Musicor 3056
9/18/65	**43**	24			9	Looking Through The Eyes Of Love		$40	Musicor 3069
3/19/66	**123**	8			10	Big Sixteen, Vol. 3		$40	Musicor 3085
12/17/66+	**61**	51			11	Greatest Hits Of All Times	[G]	$40	Musicor 3102
9/14/68	**193**	3			12	She's A Heartbreaker		$30	Musicor 3164

Aladdin's Lamp (2,5)
All The Way (9,10)
Amor Mio (10)
Angels Got Together (2)
Answer Me, My Love (4)
Anywhere I Wander (9)
As Long As She Needs Me (9)
Autumn Leaves (4)
Backstage (11) *25*
Blue Gene (4)
Born To Lose (7,10)
Close To My Heart (10)
Cornflower Blue (2)
Cry Your Eyes Out (1,5)
Don't Let The Neighbors Know (2)
Don't Rob Another Man's Castle (7)
Don't Take Candy From A Stranger (8)
Donna Means Heartbreak (1,5)
Down In The Subway (8)

E Se Domani (If Tomorrow) (6)
Every Breath I Take (3,11) *42*
Follow The Sun (6)
Garden Of Love (3)
Going To Church On Sunday (1)
Half Heaven - Half Heartache (1,3,5,11) *12*
Half The Laughter, Twice The Tears (4)
Hate (12)
Hawaii (6)
Heaven Held (12)
Hello Mary Lou (3)
House Without Windows (2,4)
I Can't Run Away (4)
I Can't Stop Loving You (10)
I Lost Tomorrow (Yesterday) (8)
I Love You More Today (6)
I Must Be Seeing Things (8,11) *31*
I Really Don't Want To Know (7,10)

I Should Try To Forget (1)
(I Wanna) Love My Life Away (3) *39*
I'll Be Seeing You (4)
I'm A Fool To Care (7)
I'm Afraid To Go Home (10)
I'm Gonna Be Strong (6,11) *9*
I'm Gonna Find Myself A Girl (6)
I've Got A New Heartache (7)
I've Got Five Dollars And It's Saturday Night (7) *99*
If I Didn't Have A Dime (To Play The Jukebox) (1,3) *58*
If I Only Had Time (12)
If Mary's There (8)
It Hurts To Be In Love (6,11) *7*
Just One Smile (8) *64*
Keep Tellin' Yourself (4,5)
Last Chance To Turn Around (10,11) *13*
Last Two People On Earth (6)
Lips Are Redder On You (6)
Little Betty Falling Star (1)

Lonely Night Dreams (Of Far Away Arms) (4)
Looking Through The Eyes Of Love (8,9,10,11) *28*
Louisiana Mama (3)
Love Grows (12)
(Man Who Shot) Liberty Valance (1,3,5,11) *4*
Maria (9)
Marianne (8)
Maybe You'll Be There (4)
Mecca (2,5) *12*
Misty (9)
More (9)
Mr. Moon, Mr. Cupid And I (3)
My Heart, Your Heart (1)
My Shoes Keep Walking Back To You (7)
Not Responsible (2,5)
On The Street Where You Live (9,10)
One Day (9)
One Has My Name (7)

(1-2-3-4-5-6-7) Count The Days (12)
Only Love Can Break A Heart (1,3,5,11) *2*
Peanuts, Popcorn And Crackerjacks (4)
Princess In Rags (10) *37*
Rags To Riches (9,10)
Remind My Baby Of Me (10)
Run, Run, Roadrunner (12)
Save Your Love (9)
She's A Heartbreaker (12) *16*
She's Still There (8)
Ship True Love Goodbye (2,5)
Small Town, Bring Down (12)
Somewhere In The Country (12)
Stay (10)
Sweeter Than The Flowers (7)
Take Me Tonight (5)
Teardrop By Teardrop (2,5)
Tell The Moon To Go To Sleep (2)

That Girl Belongs To Yesterday (6) *49*
There's No Livin' Without Your Lovin' (8,10)
Time And The River (2)
Tonight (9)
Tower Tall (1,3,5)
Town Without Pity (3,5,11) *13*
True Love Never Runs Smooth (1,5) *21*
Twenty Four Hours From Tulsa (4,5,11) *17*
Unchained Melody (9,10)
Walk (6)
Who Needs It (6)
Wreck On The Highway (7)
Yesterday's Hero (4) *64*
Yours Until Tomorrow (12)

PIXIES   '90
Pop-rock group formed in Boston: **Frank Black** (vocals), Joey Santiago (guitar), Kim Deal (bass) and David Lovering (drums). Deal was also a member of **The Breeders**.

5/6/89	**98**	27	●	©	1	Doolittle		$10	Elektra 60856
9/1/90	**70**	12		©	2	Bossanova		$10	Elektra 60963
10/26/91	**92**	8		©	3	Trompe Le Monde		$10	Elektra 61118
						title is French for "Fooling The World"			
10/25/97	**180**	1		©	4	Death To The Pixies	[K-L]	$15	Elektra 62118 [2]
						contains previous recordings and a 1990 concert recorded in Holland			

Alec Eiffel (3)
All Over The World (2)
Allison (2,4)
Ana (2)
Bird Dream Of The Olympus Mons (3)
Blown Away (2)
Bone Machine (4)
Broken Face (4)
Caribou (4)

Cecilia Ann (2,4)
Crackity Jones (1,4)
Dead (1,4)
Debaser (1,4)
Dig For Fire (2,4)
Distance Equals Rate Times Time (3,4)
Down To The Well (2)
Ed Is Dead (4)
Gigantic (4)

Gouge Away (1,4)
Hang Wire (2)
Hangwire (4)
Happening, The (2)
Havalina (2)
Head On (3)
Here Comes Your Man (1,4)
Hey (1,4)
Holiday Song (4)
I Bleed (1)

Into The White (4)
Is She Weird (2)
Isla De Encanta (4)
La La Love You (1)
Letter To Memphis (3)
Lovely Day (3)
Monkey Gone To Heaven (1,4)
Motorway To Roswell (3)
Mr. Grieves (1)
Navajo Know (3)

Nimrod's Son (4)
No. 13 Baby (1)
Palace Of The Brine (3)
Planet Of Sound (3,4)
Rock Music (2,4)
Sad Punk (3)
Silver (1)
Something Against You (4)
Space (I Believe In) (3)
Stormy Weather (2)

Subbacultcha (3)
Tame (1,4)
There Goes My Gun (1)
Tony's Theme (4)
Trompe Le Monde (3)
U-Mass (3,4)
Vamos (4)
Velouria (2,3)
Wave Of Mutilation (1,4)
Where Is My Mind? (4)

682

PLANET P '83
Studio group assembled by German producer Peter Hauke. **Tony Carey** was lead singer.

| 3/26/83 | 42 | 23 | | © | 1 Planet P | | | $10 | Geffen 4000 |
| 12/1/84+ | 121 | 14 | | | 2 Pink World | | | $15 | MCA 8019 [2] |

PLANET P PROJECT

Adam And Eve (1)   Armageddon (1)   Baby's At The Door (2)   Behind The Barrier (Part 1 & 2) (2)   Boy Who Can't Talk (Part 1 & 2) (2)   Breath (2)   I Won't Wake Up (1)   In The Forest (2)   In The Woods (2)   In The Zone (2)   King For A Day (1)   Letter From The Shelter (1)   March Of The Artemites (2)   One Star Falling (2)   Only You And Me (1)   Pink World (2)   Pink World Coming Down (2)   Power (2)   Power Tools (1)   Requiem (2)   Send It In A Letter (1)   Shepherd, The (2)   Static (1)   Stranger, The (2)   This Perfect Place (Part 1 & 2) (2)   To Live Forever (Part 1 & 2) (2)   Top Of The World (1)   What Artie Knows (Part 1 & 2) (2)   What I See (Part 1 & 2) (2)   Why Me? (1) *64*

PLANET SOUL '96
Dance duo from Miami: producer George Costa and singer Nadine Renee.

| 5/11/96 | 165 | 3 | | © | Energy And Harmony | | | $10 | Strictly Rhythm 325 |

Believe In Yo Self   Cosmic Orgazim   **Feel The Music** *73*   Look Into My Eyes   See Da Light   **Set U Free** *26*   Something On My Mind   Track Me Down   What Ever U Got

★383★ PLANT, Robert '82
Born on 8/20/48 in West Bromwich, England. Lead singer of **Led Zeppelin** and **The Honeydrippers**.

7/17/82	5	53	▲	©	1 Pictures At Eleven			$10	Swan Song 8512
7/30/83	8	40	▲	©	2 The Principle Of Moments			$10	Es Paranza 90101
6/15/85	20	19	●	©	3 Shaken 'N' Stirred			$10	Es Paranza 90265
3/12/88	6	48	▲³	©	4 Now And Zen			$10	Es Paranza 90863
4/7/90	13	25	●	©	5 Manic Nirvana			$10	Es Paranza 91336
6/12/93	34	24	●	©	6 Fate Of Nations			$10	Es Paranza 92264
11/26/94	4	23	▲	©	7 No Quarter			$10	Atlantic 82706
5/9/98	8	13	●	©	8 Walking Into Clarksdale			$10	Atlantic 83092

JIMMY PAGE & ROBERT PLANT (above 2)

Anniversary (5)   Battle Of Evermore (7)   **Big Log** (2) *20*   Big Love (5)   Billy's Revenge (4)   Blue Train (8)   **Burning Down One Side** (1) *64*   Burning Up (8)   Calling To You (6)   City Don't Cry (7)   Come Into My Life (6)   Dance On My Own (4)   Doo Doo A Do Do (3)   Down To The Sea (6)   Easily Lead (3)   Fat Lip (1)   Four Sticks (7)   Friends (7)   Gallow's Pole (7)   Great Spirit (6)   Greatest Gift (6)   Heart In Your Hand (8)   Heaven Knows (4)   Helen Of Troy (4)   Hip To Hoo (3)   Horizontal Departure (2)   House Of Love (8)   **Hurting Kind (I've Got My Eyes On You)** (5) *46*   I Believe (6)   I Cried (5)   If I Were A Carpenter (6)   **In The Mood** (2) *39*   Kallalou Kallalou (3)   Kashmir (7)   Liars Dance (5)   Like I've Never Been Gone (1)   **Little By Little** (3) *36*   Memory Song (Hello Hello) (8)   Messin' With The Mekon (2)   Moonlight In Samosa (1)   Most High (8)   Mystery Title (1)   Network News (6)   Nirvana (5)   No Quarter (7)   Nobody's Fault But Mine (7)   Other Arms (2)   Pink And Black (3)   Please Read The Letter (8)   **Pledge Pin** (1) *74*   Promised Land (6)   S S S & Q (5)   She Said (1)   Shining In The Light (8)   **Ship Of Fools** (4) *84*   Since I've Been Loving You (7)   Sixes And Sevens (3)   Slow Dancer (1)   Sons Of Freedom (8)   Stranger Here...Than Over There (2)   **Tall Cool One** (4) *25*   Thank You (7)   That's The Way (7)   Thru' With The Two Step (2)   Tie Dye On The Highway (5)   Too Loud (3)   Trouble Your Money (3)   29 Palms (6)   Upon A Golden Horse (8)   Walking Into Clarksdale (8)   Watching You (5)   Way I Feel (4)   When I Was A Child (8)   When The World Was Young (8)   White, Clean And Neat (4)   Why (4)   Wonderful One (7)   Worse Than Detroit (1)   Wreckless Love (2)   Yallah (7)   Your Ma Said You Cried In Your Sleep Last Night (5)

PLASMATICS '81
Punk-rock group from New York City: Wendy O. Williams (vocals), Richie Stotts and Wes Beech (guitars), **Jean Beauvoir** (bass) and Stu Deutsch (drums). Williams died of a self-inflicted gunshot wound on 4/6/98 (age 48).

2/21/81	134	10		©	1 New Hope For The Wretched			$12	Stiff 9
6/6/81	142	9		©	2 Beyond The Valley Of 1984			$12	Stiff 11
12/5/81	177	3		©	3 Metal Priestess		[M]	$12	Stiff 666

Black Leather Monster (3)   Butcher Baby (1)   Concrete Shoes (1)   Corruption (1)   Doom Song (3)   Dream Lover (1)   Fast Food Service (1)   Headbanger (2)   Hitman (2)   Incantation (2)   Living Dead (1,2)   Lunacy (3)   Masterplan (2,3)   Monkey Suit (1)   Nothing (2)   Pig Is A Pig (2)   Plasma Jam (2)   Sex Junkie (2,3)   Sometimes I (1)   Squirm (1)   Summer Nite (2)   Test Tube Babies (1)   Tight Black Pants (1)   12 Noon (3)   Want You Baby (1)   Won't You (1)

PLASTIC COW, The '69
Born Michael Melvoin on 5/10/37 in Oshkosh, Wisconsin. Jazz keyboardist. His son Jonathan Melvoin, a touring keyboardist with **The Smashing Pumpkins**, died of a drug overdose on 7/12/96 (age 34). Wendy Melvoin (**Prince**'s Revolution, **Wendy & Lisa**) and Susannah Melvoin (**The Family**) are his twin daughters.

| 11/8/69 | 184 | 2 | | | The Plastic Cow Goes Mooooooog | | [I] | $20 | Dot 25961 |

Ballad Of John And Yoko   Born To Be Wild   Brown Arms In Houston   Lady Jane   Lay Lady Lay   Medicine Man   One   One Man, One Volt   Plastic Cow   Spinning Wheel   Sunshine Of Your Love   Tomorrow Tomorrow

PLATTERS, The '60
R&B vocal group from Los Angeles: Tony Williams, David Lynch, Paul Robi, Herb Reed and Zola Taylor. Sonny Turner replaced Williams in 1961. Sandra Dawn and Nate Nelson (of The Flamingos) replaced Taylor and Robi in 1965. Lynch died of cancer on 1/2/81 (age 61). Nelson died of a heart attack on 6/1/84 (age 52). Robi died of cancer on 2/1/89 (age 57). Williams died of emphysema on 8/14/92 (age 64). Group inducted into the Rock and Roll Hall of Fame in 1990.

7/14/56	7	26			1 The Platters			$100	Mercury 20146
1/19/57	12	8			2 The Platters, Volume Two			$100	Mercury 20216
3/30/59	15	8			3 Remember When?			$50	Mercury 20410
3/14/60	6	174	●		4 Encore Of Golden Hits		[G]	$50	Mercury 20472
11/14/60+	20	18	●		5 More Encore Of Golden Hits		[G]	$50	Mercury 20591
7/9/66	100	6			6 I Love You 1,000 Times			$25	Musicor 3091
4/10/93	49ᶜ	1		©	7 20 Greatest Hits		[G]	$10	Federal 4415

contains re-recordings of their classic hits

A-Tisket A-Tasket (3)   Alone In The Night (7)   At Your Beck And Call (1)   Bewitched, Bothered And Bewildered (1)   Doesn't It Ring A Bell (3)   Don't Blame Me (5)   **Enchanted** (4) *12*   Glory Of Love (1)   **Great Pretender** (4,7) *1*   **Harbor Lights** (5,6,7) *8*   Have Mercy (1)   Heart Of Stone (2)   **Heaven On Earth** (1,4,6,7) *39*   I Can't Get Started With You (3)   I Don't Know Why (2)   I Give You My Word (3)   I Love You 1000 Times (6,7) *31*   I Love You Because (6,7)   **I Wanna** (1) *flip*   **I Wish** (5) *42*   I'd Climb The Highest Mountain (2)   **I'll Be Home** (6) *97*   I'll Get By (2)   I'll Never Smile Again (3) *25*   **I'm Sorry** (1,4,7) *11*   **If I Didn't Care** (3) *30*   If I Had A Love (6,7)   If I Had You (6)   In The Still Of The Night (2)   **It's Raining Outside** (5) *93*   Love In Bloom (3)   Lovely (6)   Magic Touch ..see: (You've Got) The   My Blue Heaven (3)   **My Dream** (4) *24*   **My Prayer** (1,4,7) *1*   My Secret (1)   My Way (7)   **On My Word Of Honor** (1) *20*   One In A Million (4) *20*   **Only You (And You Alone)** (4,6,7) *5*   Prisoner Of Love (3)   Red Sails In The Sunset (7)   **Remember When** (1,3,4) *47*   September In The Rain (2)   **Sleepy Lagoon** (4) *65*   Smoke Gets In Your Eyes (3,4,6,7) *1*

PLATTERS, The — Cont'd

Somebody Loves Me (3)
Someone To Watch Over Me (1)
Sound And The Fury (5)
Sweet, Sweet Lovin' (7)

Take Me In Your Arms (2)
Temptation (2)
Thanks For The Memory (3)
That Old Feeling (5)
To Each His Own (5) *21*

Twilight Time (4,7) *1*
Unchained Melody (7)
Until The Real Thing Comes Along (3)
Wagon Wheels (2)

What Does It Matter (5)
Where (5) *44*
Why (7)
Why Should I? (1)
Wish It Were Me (5) *61*

With This Ring (7)
You Can Depend On Me (2)
You've Changed (2)
(You've Got) The Magic Touch (4,6,7) *4*

PLAYA '98

R&B vocal trio from Louisville, Kentucky: Ben Bush, John Peacock and Stephen Garrett.

| 4/11/98 | 86 | 8 | © | Cheers 2 U | ...... | $10 | Def Jam 536386 |

All The Way
Buggin' Over You
Cheers 2 U *38*

Derby City-Interlude
Don't Stop The Music *73*

Everybody Wanna Luv Somebody
Gospel Interlude

I-65
I Gotta Know
I'll B 2 C U

Ms. Parker
One Man Woman
Push

Together
Top Of The World

PLAYAZ '94

Rap group from Chicago: Masta Will, Carverman, Tavo, Oby G, Beaner and Zupee Wags.

| 1/1/94 | 187 | 1 | © | Bulletproof | ...... | $10 | SPS 252 |

Better Not F*** Wid Me
Boom Boom

Compton Craze
Gangsta Nation

Illegal Street S***
Just Another Brotha Down

Mi Cheebas
911

Ridin' High, Drivin' By
Santa'z Phat Gatz

Thuggin' For A Mug
Wheat Fields

PLAYER '78

Pop-rock group formed in Los Angeles: Peter Beckett (vocals, guitar), John Crowley (vocals, guitar), Wayne Cooke (keyboards), Ronn Moss (bass) and John Friesen (drums). Moss played "Ridge Forrester" on the TV soap *The Bold & The Beautiful*.

11/5/77+	26	34	●	©	1 Player	......	$12	RSO 3026
9/9/78	37	23	●	©	2 Danger Zone	......	$12	RSO 3036
2/6/82	152	7			3 Spies Of Life	......	$10	RCA Victor 4186

Baby Come Back (1) *1*
Born To Be With You (3)
Cancellation (1)
Come On Out (1)
Every Which Way (1)
Forever (2)

Goodbye (That's All I've Ever Heard) (1)
I Just Wanna Be With You (2)
I'd Rather Be Gone (3)
I've Been Thinkin' (2)
If Looks Could Kill (3) *48*

In Like Flynn (3)
It Only Hurts When I Breathe (3)
Join In The Dance (2)
Let Me Down Easy (2)
Love In The Danger Zone (2)

Love Is Where You Find It (1)
Melanie (1)
Movin' Up (1)
My Mind's Made Up (3)
My Survival (1)
Prisoner Of Your Love (2) *27*

Silver Lining (2) *62*
Some Things Are Better Left Unsaid (3)
Take Me Back (3)
Thank You For The Use Of Your Love (3)

This Time I'm In It For Love (1) *10*
Tryin' To Write A Hit Song (1)
Wait Until Tomorrow (1)

PLEASURE '79

R&B group from Portland, Oregon: Sherman Davis (vocals), Marlon McClain (guitar), brothers Donald and Michael Hepburn (keyboards), Bruce Smith (percussion), Dennis Springer (sax), Nathaniel Phillips (bass) and Bruce Carter (drums).

8/28/76	162	5		1 Accept No Substitutes	......	$12	Fantasy 9506
4/23/77	113	11		2 Joyous	......	$12	Fantasy 9526
5/13/78	119	13		3 Get To The Feeling	......	$12	Fantasy 9550
8/11/79	67	29		4 Future Now	......	$12	Fantasy 9578
7/12/80	97	14		5 Special Things	......	$12	Fantasy 9600
5/15/82	164	6		6 Give It Up	......	$10	RCA Victor 4209

All The Way (6)
Beginnings (6)
Can't Turn You Loose (2)
Carolyn (6)
Celebrate The Good Things (3)
Dance To The Music (2)
Dedication To The Past (4)
Departure (4)

Foxy Lady (3)
Future Now (4)
Get To The Feeling (3)
Ghettos Of The Mind (1)
Give It Up (6)
Happiness (3)
I'm Mad (1)
It's So Hard (6)

Jammin' With Pleasure (1)
Joyous (2)
Ladies Night Out (3)
Law Of The Raw (5)
Let Me Be The One (2)
Let's Dance (1)
Living Without You (5)
Love Of My Life (1)
Moonchild, Theme For The (1)

No Matter What (3)
Nothin' To It (4)
Now You Choose Me (5)
Only You (2)
Pleasure For Your Pleasure (1)
Real Thing (4)
Sassafras Girl (2)
Sassy Baby (6)
Selim (3)
Sending My Love (6)

Space Is The Place (4)
Special Things (5)
Spread That Feelin' (All Around) (5)
Stone Love (6)
Strong Love (4)
Take A Chance (5)
Take It To The Streets (6)
Thanks For Everything (3)
Thoughts Of Old Flames (4)

Tune In (2)
2 For 1 (1)
We Have So Much (1)
What's It Gonna Be (6)
Yearnin' Burnin' (5)
You Are My Star (5)
Your Love Means Life (Memories) (3)

Farewell, Goodbye (3)
Glide (4) *55*

PLIMSOULS, The '81

Rock group from Los Angeles: Peter Case (vocals), Eddie Munoz (guitar), Dave Pahoa (bass) and Lou Ramirez (drums). Group name is British slang for gym shoes.

| 4/4/81 | 153 | 4 | | 1 The Plimsouls | ...... | $12 | Planet 13 |
| 7/23/83 | 186 | 4 | © | 2 Everywhere At Once | ...... | $10 | Geffen 4002 |

Everyday Things (1)
Everywhere At Once (2)
How Long Will It Take? (2)
Hush, Hush (1)

I Want What You Got (1)
I Want You Back (1)
I'll Get Lucky (1)
In This Town (1)

Inch By Inch (2)
Lie, Beg, Borrow And Steal (2)
Lost Time (1)
Magic Touch (2)

Million Miles Away (2) *82*
Mini-Skirt Minnie (1)
My Life Ain't Easy (2)
Nickels And Dimes (1)

Now (1)
Oldest Story In The World (2)
Play The Breaks (2)
Shaky City (2)

Women (1)
Zero Hour (1)

PLUS ONE '00

Christian vocal group: Gabe Combs, Jeremy Mhire, Nathan Walters, Nate Cole aned Jason Perry.

| 6/10/00 | 76 | 51 | ● | © | The Promise | ...... | $10 | 143 83329 |

Be
God Is In This Place

Here In My Heart
I Will Rescue You

Last Flight Out
My Friend

My Life
Promise, The

Run To You
Soul Tattoo

When Your Spirit Gets Weak
Written On My Heart

PMD — see EPMD

PM DAWN '93

Rap duo from Jersey City: brothers Attrell "Prince Be" and Jarrett Cordes.

10/19/91+	48	28	●	©	1 Of The Heart, Of The Soul And Of The Cross: The Utopian Experience	......	$10	Gee Street 510276
4/10/93	30	25	●	©	2 The Bliss Album...?	......	$10	Gee Street 514517
10/21/95	119	3	©	3 Jesus Wept	......	$10	Gee Street 524147

About Nothing (For The Love Of Destiny) (2)
Apathy...Superstar!? (3)
Beautiful, The (1)
Beyond Infinite Affections (2)
Coconut (medley) (3)
Comatose (3)
Downtown Venus (3) *48*
Even After I Die (1)

Filthy Rich (I Don't Wanna Be) (2)
Forever Damaged (The 96th) (3)
I'd Die Without You (2)
I'll Be Waiting For You (3)
If I Wuz U (1)
In The Presence Of Mirrors (1)

Lifetime, A (3)
Looking Through Patient Eyes (2) *6*
Miles From Anything (3)
More Than Likely (2)
My Own Personal Gravity (3)
9:45 Wake-Up Dream (3)
1999 (medley) (3)
Nocturnal Is In The House (2)

Norwegian Wood (This Bird Has Flown) (2)
On A Clear Day (1)
Once In A Lifetime (medley) (3)
Paper Doll (1) *28*
Plastic (3)
Puppet Show (3)
Reality Used To Be A Friend Of Mine (1)

Set Adrift On Memory Bliss (1) *1*
Shake (1)
So On And So On (2)
Sometimes I Miss You So Much (3) *95*
Sonchyenne (3)
To Love Me More (2)
To Serenade A Rainbow (1)

Watcher's Point Of View (Don't 'Cha Think) (1)
Ways Of The Wind (2) *54*
When It's Raining Cats And Dogs (2)
When Midnight Sighs (2)
Why God Loves You (3)

POCKETS '77

R&B group from Baltimore: Larry Jacobs (vocals), Jacob Sheffer (guitar), Albert McKinney (keyboards), Charles Williams (trumpet), Irving Madison (sax), Kevin Barnes (trombone), Gary Grainger (bass) and George Gray (drums).

| 10/22/77 | 57 | 24 | | | 1 Come Go With Us | | | $12 | Columbia 34879 |
| 10/28/78 | 85 | 6 | | | 2 Take It On Up | | | $12 | Columbia 35384 |

Come Go With Me (1) *84*
Doin' The Do (1)
Elusive Lady (1)

Funk It Over (2)
Got To Find My Way (2)
Happy For Love (2)
Heaven Only Knows (2)

In The Pocket (1)
In Your Eyes (2)
Lay Your Head (On My Shoulder) (2)

Nothing Is Stronger (1)
One Day At A Time (1)
Pasado (1)
Sphinx (2)

Take It On Up (2)
Tell Me Why (2)
Wizzard Wuzzit (1)
You And Only You (2)

POCO ★172★ '79

Country-rock group formed in Los Angeles by Rusty Young and **Buffalo Springfield** members **Richie Furay** and **Jim Messina**. **Randy Meisner** (later of the **Eagles**) left in 1969, replaced by **Timothy B. Schmit**. As of second album, group consisted of Furay, Messina, Young, Schmit and George Grantham. Messina left in 1970, replaced by Paul Cotton, and Furay left in 1973. Grantham and Schmit (joined Eagles) left in 1977; replacements: Charlie Harrison, Kim Bullard and Steve Chapman. Disbanded in 1984. In 1989, Young, Furay, Messina, Grantham and Meisner reunited.

1)Legend 2)Deliverin' 3)Crazy Eyes 4)Legacy 5)Head Over Heels

6/28/69	63	21		©	1 Pickin' Up The Pieces			$15	Epic 26460
6/6/70	58	19		©	2 Poco			$15	Epic 26522
2/6/71	26	21		©	3 Deliverin'		[L]	$15	Epic 30209

recorded at the Boston Music Hall and the Felt Forum in New York City

9/25/71	52	11		©	4 From The Inside			$15	Epic 30753
11/25/72+	69	20		©	5 A Good Feelin' To Know			$15	Epic 31601
9/15/73	38	23		©	6 Crazy Eyes			$15	Epic 32354
5/11/74	68	13		©	7 Seven			$15	Epic 32895
11/30/74+	76	11		©	8 Cantamos			$15	Epic 33192

title is Spanish for "We Sing"

7/19/75	43	18		©	9 Head Over Heels			$12	ABC 890
8/2/75	90	8		©	10 The Very Best Of Poco		[G]	$15	Epic 33537 [2]
4/3/76	169	4		©	11 Live		[L]	$12	Epic 33336

recorded November 1974 at Yale University

5/29/76	89	15		©	12 Rose Of Cimarron			$12	ABC 946
5/14/77	57	18		©	13 Indian Summer			$12	ABC 989
11/25/78+	14	52	●	©	14 Legend	C:#46/5		$12	ABC 1099
7/26/80	46	16		©	15 Under The Gun			$12	MCA 5132
7/25/81	76	10		©	16 Blue And Gray			$12	MCA 5227
2/20/82	131	8		©	17 Cowboys & Englishmen			$12	MCA 5288
12/4/82	195	3		©	18 Ghost Town			$12	Atlantic 80008
5/19/84	167	6		©	19 Inamorata			$12	Atlantic 80148

title is Italian for "In Love"

| 9/23/89 | 40 | 28 | ● | © | 20 Legacy | | | $10 | RCA 9694 |

All Alone Together (12)
All The Ways (8)
And Settlin' Down (5,10)
Angel (7,11)
Another Time Around (8,10)
Anyway Bye Bye (2)
Ashes (medley) (17)
Bad Weather (4,10,11)
Barbados (14)
Bitter Blue (8)
Blue And Gray (16)
Blue Water (6,11)
Boomerang (14)
Brass Buttons (6)
Break Of Hearts (18)
Brenda X (19)
Cajun Moon (17)
Calico Lady (1)
Call It Love (20) *18*
Child's Claim To Fame (medley) (3)
C'mon (3,10) *69*
Company's Comin' (12)
Consequently So Long (1,3,10)
Cowboy's Desire (14)
Crazy Eyes (6)
Crazy Love (14) *17*
Cry No More (18)
Dallas (9)
Dance Medley (13)
Daylight (19)

Days Gone By (19) *80*
Do You Feel It Too (4)
Don't Let It Pass By (2)
Down In The Quarter (9)
Down On The River Again (16)
Down To The Wire (15)
Downfall (13)
Drivin' Wheel (7)
Early Times (5)
El Tonto De Nadie, Regresa (medley) (2)
Everlasting Kind (15)
Faith In The Families (7,10)
Feudin' (medley) (17)
Find Out In Time (13)
First Love (1)
Flyin' Solo (9)
Follow Your Dreams (20)
Fool's Paradise (15)
Fools Gold (6,10,11)
Footsteps Of A Fool (Shaky Ground) (15)
Foreword (medley) (1)
Friends In Distance (15)
From The Inside (4)
Georgia, Bind My Ties (9)
Ghost Town (18)
Glorybound (16)
Go And Say Goodbye (5)
Good Feelin' To Know (5,10,11)
Grand Junction (1,3,10)

Hard Luck (medley) (3)
Hear That Music (3)
Heart Of The Night (14) *20*
Here Comes That Girl Again (16)
Here We Go Again (6,10)
High And Dry (8,11)
High Sierra (18)
Hoe Down (4)
Honky Tonk Downstairs (2)
How Many Moons (19)
How Will You Feel Tonight (18)
Hurry Up (2)
I Can See Everything (5)
I Guess You Made It (3)
I'll Be Back Again (9)
If It Wasn't For You (20)
If You Could Read My Mind (17)
Indian Summer (13) *50*
Just Call My Name (7)
Just For Me And You (4,10)
Just In Case It Happens, Yes Indeed (1,3,10)
Just Like Me (12)
Keep On Believin' (2)
Keep On Tryin' (9) *50*
Keeper Of The Fire (5)
Kind Woman (3)
Krikkit's Song (Passing Through) (7)

Land Of Glory (16)
Last Goodbye (14)
Legend (14)
Let Me Turn Back To You (9)
Let's Dance Tonight (6)
Little Darlin' (14)
Living In The Band (13)
Love Comes Love Goes (14)
Love's So Cruel (18)
Lovin' Arms (9)
Lovin' You Every Minute (20)
Made Of Stone (15)
Magnolia (6)
Make Me A Smile (medley) (1)
Makin' Love (9)
Man Like Me (3,10)
Me And You (13)
Midnight Rain (15) *74*
Midnight Rodeo (In The Lead Tonight) (18)
Nature Of Love (20)
No Relief In Sight (17)
Nobody's Fool (1,2)
Nothin' To Hide (20) *39*
Odd Man Out (19)
Oh Yeah (1)
Ol' Forgiver (4)
One Horse Blue (8)
P.N.S. (When You Come Around) (12)
Pickin' Up The Pieces (1,3,10)

Please Wait For Me (16)
Price Of Love (17)
Railroad Days (4,10)
Reputation (15)
Restrain (5,11)
Ribbon Of Darkness (17)
Ride The Country (5,11)
Right Along (6,10)
Rocky Mountain Breakdown (7,10,11)
Rose Of Cimarron (12) *94*
Rough Edges (20)
Sagebrush Serenade (8)
Save A Corner Of Your Heart (19)
Sea Of Heartbreak (17)
Shoot For The Moon (18) *50*
Short Changed (medley) (1)
Sittin' On A Fence (9)
Skatin' (7,10)
Slow Poke (12)
Sometimes (We Are All We Got) (16)
Special Care (18)
Spellbound (14)
Standing In The Fire (19)
Starin' At The Sky (12)
Stay (Night Until Noon) (13)
Stealaway (12)
Storm, The (19)
Streets Of Paradise (16)

Susannah (8)
Sweet Lovin' (5,10)
There Goes My Heart (17)
This Old Flame (19)
Tomorrow (1)
Too Many Nights Too Long (12)
Tulsa Turnaround (12)
Twenty Years (13)
Under The Gun (15) *48*
Us (9)
Western Waterloo (8)
What A Day (medley) (1)
What Am I Gonna Do (4)
What Do People Know (20)
What If I Should Say I Love You (4)
Whatever Happened To Your Smile (8)
When Hearts Collide (18)
When It All Began (20)
When You Love Someone (19)
While We're Still Young (15)
While You're On Your Way (17)
Who Else (20)
Widowmaker (16)
Win Or Lose (13)
Writing On The Wall (14)
You Are The One (4)
You Better Think Twice (2,3,10) *72*
You've Got Your Reasons (7)

P.O.D. '00

Christian hard-rock group from San Diego: Sonny (vocals), Marcos (guitar), Traa (bass) and Wuv (drums). P.O.D.: Payable On Death.

| 9/11/99+ | 51 | 47 | ▲ | © | The Fundamental Elements Of Southtown | | | $10 | Atlantic 83216 |

Bullet The Blue Sky
Follow Me

Freestyle
Hollywood

Image
Lie Down

Outkast
Rock The Party (Off The Hook)

Set Your Eyes To Zion
Southtown

Tribal

POE '96

Born Annie Danielewski in New York City. Female singer/songwriter.

| 8/3/96 | 71 | 30 | ● | © | 1 Hello | | | $10 | Modern 92605 |
| 11/18/00 | 115 | 14 | | © | 2 Haunted | | | $10 | FEI 83362 |

POE — Cont'd

Amazed (2)	Choking The Cherry (1)	Fingertips (1)	Hey Pretty (2)	Not A Virgin (2)	Trigger Happy Jack (Drive by A
Angry Johnny (1)	Control (2)	5&1/2 Minute Hallway (2)	House Of Leaves (2)	Spanish Doll (2)	Go-Go) (1)
Another World (1)	Could've Gone Mad (2)	Fly Away (1)	If You Were Here (2)	Terrible Thought (2)	Walk The Walk (2)
Beautiful Girl (1)	Dolphin (1)	Haunted (2)	Junkie (1)	That Day (1)	Wild (2)
		Hello (1)	Lemon Meringue (2)		

POGUES, The '88

Punk-folk group formed in London: Shane MacGowan (vocals), Philip Chevron (guitar), Terry Woods (mandolin), Spider Stacy (tin whistle), James Fearnley (accordion), Jem Finer (banjo), Darryl Hunt (bass) and Andrew Ranken (drums). Original bassist Cait O'Riordan married **Elvis Costello** on 5/16/86.

DEBUT	PEAK	WKS		CD						$	Label & Number
2/27/88	88	16		©	1 **If I Should Fall From Grace With God**					$10	Island 90872
8/12/89	118	9		©	2 **Peace & Love**					$10	Island 91225
12/15/90	187	3		©	3 **Hell's Ditch**					$10	Island 422846

Birmingham Six (medley) (1)	Fiesta (1)	House Of The Gods (3)	Metropolis (3)	Sayonara (3)	Turkish Song Of The Damned
Blue Heaven (2)	Five Green Queens And Jean	If I Should Fall From Grace	Misty Morning, Albert Bridge (2)	Sit Down By The Fire (1)	(1)
Boat Train (2)	(3)	With God (1)	Night Train To Lorca (2)	Six To Go (3)	USA (2)
Bottle Of Smoke (1)	Galway Races (medley) (1)	London You're A Lady (2)	Rain Street (3)	Streets Of Sorrow (medley) (1)	Wake Of The Medusa (3)
Broad Majestic Shannon (1)	Gartloney Rats (2)	Lorca's Novena (3)	Rainbow Man (3)	Summer In Siam (3)	White City (2)
Cotton Fields (2)	Ghost Of A Smile (3)	Lorelei (2)	Recruiting Sergeant (medley)	Sunnyside Of The Street (3)	Worms (1)
Down All The Days (2)	Gridlock (2)	Lullaby Of London (1)	(1)	Thousands Are Sailing (1)	Young Ned Of The Hill (2)
Fairytale Of New York (1)	Hell's Ditch (3)	Maidrin Rua (3)	Rocky Road (medley) (1)	Tombstone (2)	

POINDEXTER, Buster — see JOHANSEN, David

POINT BLANK '81

Rock band from Texas. Core members: John O'Daniel (vocals), Rusty Burns and Kim Davis (guitars), Bill Randolph (bass) and Peter "Buzzy" Gruen (drums). Bubba Keith replaced O'Daniel in late 1980.

								$	Label & Number
9/11/76	175	3	1 **Point Blank**					$12	Arista 4087
8/18/79	175	9	2 **Airplay**					$12	MCA 3160
5/31/80	110	13	3 **The Hard Way**					$12	MCA 5114
4/25/81	80	24	4 **American Exce$$**					$12	MCA 5189
4/17/82	119	17	5 **On A Roll**					$12	MCA 5312

Bad Bees (1)	Free Man (1)	Highway Star (3)	Love On Fire (5)	Rock 'N Roll Soldier (3)	Two Time Loser (2)
Cadillac Dragon (4)	Getaway, The (4)	I Just Want To Know (5)	Mean To Your Queenie (2)	Shine On (2)	Walk Across The Fire (4)
Changed My Mind (2)	Go On Home (4)	In This World (1)	Moving (1)	Take Me Up (5)	Wandering (1)
Danger Zone (2)	Gone Hollywood (5)	Let Her Go (5)	Nicole (4) *39*	Takin' It Easy (2)	Way You Broke My Heart (4)
Distance (1)	Great White Line (5)	Let Me Stay With You Tonight	On A Roll (5)	Thank You Mama (3)	Wrong To Cry (3)
Do It All Night (4)	Guessing Game (3)	(4)	On The Run (3)	That's The Law (1)	
Don't Look Down (5)	Hard Way (3)	Lone Star Fool (1)	Penthouse Pauper (4)	Thunder And Lightning (2)	
		Louisiana Leg (2)	Restless (3)	Turning Back (3)	

POINTER, Bonnie '80

Born on 7/11/50 in Oakland. Member of the **Pointer Sisters** from 1971-78.

								$	Label & Number
12/16/78+	96	15	1 **Bonnie Pointer**					$12	Motown 911
12/22/79+	63	14	2 **Bonnie Pointer**					$12	Motown 929

Ah Shoot (1)	**Free Me From My**	**I Can't Help Myself (Sugar**	Jimmy Mack (2)	When I'm Gone (1)	
Come See About Me (2)	**Freedom/Tie Me To A Tree**	**Pie, Honey Bunch) (2)** *40*	More And More (1)	When The Lovelight Starts	
Deep Inside My Soul (2)	**(Handcuff Me) (1)** *58*	I Love To Sing To You (1)	My Everything (1)	Shining Through His Eyes (2)	
	Heaven Must Have Sent You	I Wanna Make It (In Your	Nowhere To Run (Nowhere To		
	(1) *11*	World) (1)	Hide) (2)		

POINTER, Noel '78

Born in Brooklyn, New York. Died of a stroke on 12/19/94 (age 39). Jazz-fusion violinist.

				CD						$	Label & Number
6/18/77	144	8		©	1 **Phantazia**				[I]	$12	Blue Note 736
3/18/78	95	13		©	2 **Hold-On**					$12	United Artists 848
9/1/79	138	7			3 **Feel It**					$12	United Artists 973
8/16/80	167	4			4 **Calling**				[I]	$12	United Artists 1050

As Long As I Know (4)	For You (A Disco Concerto) (3)	Mirabella (1)	Phantazia (1)	Staying With You (2)	'Tween The Lines (4)
Calling (4)	Higher Than Heaven (4)	Morning Song (4)	Precious Pearl (4)	Superwoman (Where Were You	Wayfaring Stranger (1)
Cappriccio Stravagante (2)	Hold On (2)	Movin' In (2)	Prelude (4)	When I Needed You) (4)	
Captain Jarvis (3)	I Don't Care (4)	Night Song (1)	Rainstorm (1)	Take A Look (4)	
Feel It (3)	Living For The City (1)	Niteroi (3)	Roots Suite Medley (2)	There's A Feeling (When You	
Fiddler On The Roof (1)	Love Is (4)	Peace On Earth (4)	Stardust Lady (2)	Touch Me) (4)	

★225★ POINTER SISTERS '84

R&B vocal group from Oakland: sisters Ruth, Anita, June and **Bonnie Pointer**. Sang in nostalgic 1940s style from 1973-77. Appeared in the 1976 movie *Car Wash*. Bonnie went solo in 1978, group continued as trio in a more contemporary style.

1)Break Out 2)Black & White 3)Energy

DEBUT	PEAK	WKS	RIAA	CD						$	Label & Number
6/23/73	13	37	●	©	1 **The Pointer Sisters**					$15	Blue Thumb 48
3/9/74	82	10	●		2 **That's A Plenty**					$15	Blue Thumb 6009
9/14/74	96	15			3 **Live At The Opera House**				[L]	$20	Blue Thumb 8002 [2]
					recorded on 4/21/74 in San Francisco; includes "Prelude To Islandia" by Tom Salisbury						
6/14/75	22	22			4 **Steppin**					$15	Blue Thumb 6021
12/4/76	164	6			5 **The Best Of The Pointer Sisters**				[G]	$20	Blue Thumb 6026 [2]
12/24/77+	176	3			6 **Having A Party**					$15	Blue Thumb 6023
12/2/78+	13	32	●		7 **Energy**					$12	Planet 1
9/22/79	72	8			8 **Priority**					$12	Planet 9003
8/30/80	34	24			9 **Special Things**					$12	Planet 9
7/11/81	12	22	●	©	10 **Black & White**					$12	Planet 18
7/17/82	59	28			11 **So Excited!**					$12	Planet 4355
11/13/82	178	3		©	12 **Pointer Sisters' Greatest Hits**				[G]	$12	Planet 60203
11/26/83+	8	105	▲²	©	13 **Break Out**					$12	Planet 4705
					second pressings of album substitute "I'm So Excited" for "Nightline"						
8/10/85	24	34	▲	©	14 **Contact**					$10	RCA Victor 5487
11/29/86	48	18		©	15 **Hot Together**					$10	RCA Victor 5609
3/19/88	152	6		©	16 **Serious Slammin'**					$10	RCA 6562

POINTER SISTERS — Cont'd

All I Know Is The Way I Feel (15) *93*
All Of You (11)
All Your Love (8)
American Music (11) *16*
Angry Eyes (7)
As I Come Of Age (7)
Automatic (13) *5*
Baby Come And Get It (13) *44*
Back In My Arms (14)
Bangin' On The Pipes (medley) (2)
Bei Mir Bist Du Schoen (medley) (3)
Black Coffee (2,3,5)
Blind Faith (8)
Bodies And Souls (14)
Bring Your Sweet Stuff Home To Me (6)
Burn Down The Night (14)
Chainey Do (4)
Cloudburst (1,3,5)
Come And Get Your Love (7)

Contact (14)
Could I Be Dreaming (9,12) *52*
Dance Electric (13)
Dare Me (14) *11*
Dirty Work (7)
Don't It Drive You Crazy (14)
Don't Let A Thief Steal Into Your Heart (8)
Dreaming As One (8)
Easy Days (4,5)
Easy Persuasion (13)
Echoes Of Love (7)
Everybody Is A Star (7)
Evil (9)
Eyes Don't Lie (15)
Fairytale (2,3,5) *13*
Fall In Love Again (10)
Fire (7,12) *2*
Flirtatious (16)
Freedom (14) *59*
Going Down Slowly (4,5) *61*
Goldmine (15) *33*
Got To Find Love (10)

Grinning In Your Face (2)
Hands Up (medley) (3)
Happiness (7,12) *30*
Happy (8)
Having A Party (6)
He's So Shy (9,12) *3*
He Turned Me Out (16)
Heart Beat (11)
Heart To Heart (11)
Here Is Where Your Love Belongs (9)
Hey You (14)
Hot Together (15)
How Long (Betcha' Got A Chick On The Side) (4,5) *20*
Hypnotized (7)
I Ain't Got Nothin' But The Blues Medley (4)
I Feel For You (11)
I Need A Man (6)
I Need You (13) *48*
I Will Be There (16)
I'll Get By Without You (6)

I'm In Love (16)
I'm So Excited (11) *30*
I'm So Excited [remix] (13) *9*
If You Wanna Get Back Your Lady (11) *67*
Jada (1,3,5)
Jump (For My Love) (13) *3*
Lay It On The Line (7)
Let It Be Me (3)
Little Pony (2,5)
Lonely Gal (6)
Love In Them There Hills (2,3)
Love Too Good To Last (9,12)
Mercury Rising (15)
Moonlight Dancing (16)
My Life (15,16)
Naked Foot (1)
Neutron Dance (13) *6*
Nightline (13)
Old Songs (1,3)
Operator (13)
Pains And Tears (1)
Pound, Pound, Pound (14)

Pride (16)
River Boulevard (1)
Salt Peanuts (2,3,5)
Save The Bones For Henry Jones (4)
Save This Night For Love (9)
Say The Word (15)
See How The Love Goes (11)
Serious Slammin' (16)
Set Me Free (15)
Sexual Power (13)
Shaky Flat Blues (2,3,5)
Shape I'm In (8)
(She's Got) The Fever (8)
Should I Do It (10,12) *13*
Shut Up And Dance (16)
Sleeping Alone (4,5)
Slow Hand (10,12) *2*
Someday We'll Be Together (10,12)
Special Things (9,12)
Steam Heat (2,3,5)
Sugar (1,5)

Surfeit, U.S.A. (medley) (2,5)
Sweet Lover Man (10)
Take My Heart, Take My Soul (10,12)
Taste (15)
Telegraph Your Love (13)
That's A Plenty (medley) (2,3,5)
That's How I Feel (1)
Turned Up Too Late (8)
Twist My Arm (14) *83*
Uh Uh (15)
Waiting On You (6)
Wang Dang Doodle (1,3,5) *61*
Wanting Things (4)
We're Gonna Make It (10)
We've Got The Power (9)
What A Surprise (10)
Where Did The Time Go (9)
Who Do You Love (8)
Yes We Can Can (1,3,5) *11*
You Gotta Believe (5)

POINT OF GRACE   '01

Female Christian vocal group formed in Arkadelphia, Arkansas: Shelley Phillips, Terry Jones, Denise Jones and Heather Floyd.

DEBUT	PEAK	WKS	RIAA	CD	#	Album Title	Catalog	Sym	$	Label & Number
12/9/95	132	2	●	©	1	The Whole Truth			$10	Word 5608
9/28/96	46	39	▲	©	2	Life Love & Other Mysteries			$10	Word 69460
8/22/98	24	27	●	©	3	Steady On...			$10	Word 69456
10/23/99	35	13	●	©	4	A Christmas Story	C:#35/4	[X]	$10	Word 63609
						Christmas charts: 4/'99, 30/'00				
5/27/00	106	5		©	5	Rarities & Remixes		[K]	$10	Word 63804
5/19/01	20	17		©	6	Free To Fly			$10	Word 86112

All That I Need (6)
Amazing (3)
Angels We Have Heard On High (4)
Any Road, Any Cost (2)
Begin With Me (6)
Better Days (3)
Blue Skies (6)
By Heart (6)
Carol Of The Bells (medley) (4)
Circle Of Friends (2,5)
Coventry Carol (4)
Drawing Me Closer (3)
Dying To Reach You (1)

Emmanuel, God With Us (medley) (4)
Fairest Lord Jesus (5)
Faith, Hope & Love (5)
Forever On And On (5)
Free Indeed (6)
Gather At The River (1,5)
God Forbid (2)
God Is With Us (1,5)
Gone Are The Dark Days (2)
Great Divide (1,5)
He Sends His Love (6)
He's The Best Thing (5)

House That Mercy Built (1)
How Great Our Joy (4)
Jesus Doesn't Care (2)
Jesus Is (3)
Jesus Will Still Be There (5)
Jingle Bell Rock (4)
Joy To The World (4)
Keep The Candle Burning (2)
La La La (4)
Let It Snow, Let It Snow, Let It Snow (medley) (4)
Life Love & Other Mysteries (2)
Light Of The World (4)
Love He Has For You (1)

Love Like No Other (1)
More Than Anything (1,5)
My God (3)
No More Pain (5)
Not That Far From Bethlehem (4)
Nothing But The Blood (5)
O Come, O Come Emmanuel (medley) (4)
O Holy Night (4)
One King (4)
One More Broken Heart (5)
Praise Forevermore (4)
Rain Down On Me (3)

Santa Claus Is Comin' To Town (4)
Saving Grace (3)
Say So (5)
Sing A Song (2)
Sleigh Ride (medley) (4)
Something So Good (6)
Song Is Alive (3)
Steady On (3)
Take Me Back (1)
That's The Way It's Meant To Be (2)
Washed In The Blood Of The Lamb (5)

What Child Is This? (medley) (4)
What's He Gonna Say About Me (1)
When Love Came Down (4)
When The Wind Blows (3)
Who Am I? (3)
Without The Love Of Jesus (1)
Wonder Of It All (3)
Yes, I Believe (6)
You Are The Answer (2)
You Will Never Walk Alone (6)

★454★   POISON   '88

Hard-rock group formed in Harrisburg, Pennsylvania: Bret Michaels (vocals), C.C. DeVille (guitar), Bobby Dall (bass) and Rikki Rockett (drums). Richie Kotzen replaced DeVille from 1992-97.

DEBUT	PEAK	WKS	RIAA	CD	#	Album Title	Sym	$	Label & Number
8/2/86+	3	101	▲³	©	1	Look What The Cat Dragged In		$10	Capitol 12523
5/21/88	2¹	70	▲⁵	©	2	Open Up And Say...Ahh!		$10	Enigma 48493
7/28/90	2¹	63	▲³	©	3	Flesh & Blood		$10	Capitol 91813
11/30/91	51	13	●	©	4	Swallow This Live	[L]	$15	Capitol 98046 [2]
3/6/93	16	13	●	©	5	Native Tongue		$10	Capitol 98961
2/6/99	2¹ᶜ	56	▲	©	6	Poison's Greatest Hits 1986-1996	[G]	$10	Capitol 53375
4/1/00	131	1		©	7	Crack A Smile...And More!	[K]	$10	Capitol 24781
7/1/00	166	1		©	8	Power To The People	[L]	$10	Cyanide 6969

Ain't That The Truth (5)
Baby Gets Around A Bit (7)
Back To The Rocking Horse (2)
Bad To Be Good (2)
Ball And Chain (3)
Bastard Son Of A Thousand Blues (7)
Be The One (7)
Best Thing You Ever Had (7)
Blame It On You (1)
Blind Faith (5)
Body Talk (5)
Bring It Home (5)
C.C. Solo (8)
Can't Bring Me Down (8)

Come Hell Or High Water (3)
Cover Of The Rolling Stone (7)
Crack A Smile Unfinished Demo (7)
Cry Tough (1,6)
Doin' As I Seen On My TV (7)
Don't Give An Inch (3)
Every Rose Has Its Thorn (2,4,6,7,8) *1*
Face The Hangman (7)
Fallen Angel (2,4,6,8) *12*
(Flesh & Blood) Sacrifice (3,6)
Good Love (2,4)
I Hate Every Bone In Your Body But Mine (8)

I Want Action (1,4,6,8) *50*
I Won't Forget You (1,6) *13*
Last Song (8)
Lay Your Body Down (6,7)
Let It Play (3,4,8)
Let Me Go To The Show (1)
Life Goes On (3,4,6) *35*
Life Loves A Tragedy (3)
Look But You Can't Touch (2,4)
Look What The Cat Dragged In (1,4,6,8)
Love On The Rocks (2,4,8)
Mr. Smiley (7)
Native Tongue (5)
No More Lookin' Back (4)

No Ring, No Gets (7)
Nothin' But A Good Time (2,4,8) *6*
#1 Bad Boy (1)
One More For The Bone (7)
Only Time Will Tell (4)
Play Dirty (1)
Poor Boy Blues (3,4)
Power To The People (8)
Richie's Acoustic Thang (5)
Ride Child Ride (5)
Ride The Wind (3,4,6) *38*
Riki Solo (8)
Scream, The (5)
Set You Free (7)

7 Days Over You (5)
Sexual Thing (6,7)
Shut Up, Make Love (7)
So Tell Me Why (4,6)
Something To Believe In (3,4,6,8) *4*
Souls On Fire (4)
Stand (5,6) *50*
Stay Alive (5)
Strange (8)
Strange Days Of Uncle Jack (3)
Strike Up The Band (5)
Swampjuice (Soul-O) (3)
Talk Dirty To Me (1,4,6,7,8) *9*
Tearin' Down The Walls (2)

That's The Way I Like It (7)
Theatre Of The Soul (5)
Tragically Unhip (7)
Unskinny Bop (3,4,6,7,8) *3*
Until You Suffer Some (Fire And Ice) (5)
Valley Of Lost Souls (3)
Want Some, Need Some (1)
Your Mama Don't Dance (2,4,6,7) *10*

POISON CLAN   '93

Rap duo from Florida: Jeff "JT Money" Tompkins and Debonaire.

DEBUT	PEAK	WKS	RIAA	CD	#	Album Title	$	Label & Number
9/18/93	97	4		©		Ruff Town Behavior	$10	Luke 202

Afraid Of The Flavor (5)
Check Out The Ave Pt I & II
City Boy

Comin Strap
Game Recognize Game
Goin' All Out

Ho Stories Pt II
Let's Get Serious
Listen

MC Sundance
Peepin
Put Shit Pass No Ho

Ruff Town Behavior
Some More Shit
Sugarhill Style

Word From A Player

POLICE, The ★194★ '83

Pop-rock trio formed in England: Gordon "Sting" Sumner (vocals, bass), **Andy Summers** (guitar) and **Stewart Copeland** (drums). Sting went on to a highly successful solo career. Copeland formed **Animal Logic** in 1989.

1)Synchronicity 2)Ghost In The Machine 3)Zenyatta Mondatta

DEBUT	PEAK	WKS	RIAA	CD	#	Album Title	Catalog	$	Label & Number
3/3/79	23	63	▲	©	1	Outlandos d'Amour		$15	A&M 4753
11/3/79	25	100	●	©	2	Reggatta de Blanc		$15	A&M 4792
10/25/80+	5	153	▲	©	3	Zenyatta Mondatta		$12	A&M 4831
10/24/81	2[6]	109	▲[2]	©	4	Ghost In The Machine		$12	A&M 3730
7/2/83	❶[17]	75	▲[4]	©	5	Synchronicity		$10	A&M 3735
11/22/86	7	26	▲[3]	©	6	Every Breath You Take - The Singles	C:#23/110	[G] $10	A&M 3902
10/16/93	79	5	●	©	7	Message In A Box: The Complete Recordings		[K] $40	A&M 540150 [4]
7/1/95	86	5	▲	©	8	Live!		[L] $15	A&M 540222 [2]
						Disc 1: recorded November 1979 at The Orpheum in Boston; Disc 2: recorded November 1983 at The Omni in Atlanta			
12/13/97	100	13		©	9	The Very Best Of Sting & The Police		[G] $10	A&M 540834
5/13/00	33[C]	1		©	10	Every Breath You Take: The Classics		[G] $10	A&M 540380

Be My Girl (medley) (1,7,8)
Bed's Too Big Without You (2,7,8)
Behind My Camel (3,7)
Bombs Away (3,7)
Born In The 50's (1,7,8)
Bring On The Night (2,7,8)
Can't Stand Losing You (1,6,7,8,9,10)
Canary In A Coalmine (3,7)
Contact (2,7)
Darkness (4,7)
De Do Do Do, De Da Da Da (3,6,7,8,10) *10*
Dead End Job (7)
Deathwish (2,7)
Demolition Man (4,7)

Does Everyone Stare (2,7)
Don't Stand So Close To Me (3,7,8,9,10) *10*
Don't Stand So Close To Me '86 (6,7,10) *46*
Driven To Tears (3,7)
Englishman In New York (9)
Every Breath You Take (5,6,7,8,9,10) *1*
Every Little Thing She Does Is Magic (4,6,7,9,10) *3*
Fallout (7,8)
Fields Of Gold (9)
Flexible Strategies (7)
Friends (7)
Hole In My Life (1,7,8)

How Stupid Mr Bates (7)
Hungry For You (J'Aurais Toujours Faim De Toi) (4,7)
I Burn For You (7)
If I Ever Lose My Faith In You (9)
If You Love Somebody Set Them Free (9)
Invisible Sun (4,6,7,10)
It's Alright For You (2,7)
Kind Of Loving (7)
King Of Pain (5,6,7,8,10) *3*
Landlord (7,8)
Let Your Soul Be Your Pilot (9)
Low Life (7)
Man In A Suitcase (3,7)
Masoko Tanga (1,7)

Message In A Bottle (2,6,7,8,9,10) *74*
Miss Gradenko (5,7)
Mother (5,7)
Murder By Numbers (7)
Next To You (1,7,8)
No Time This Time (2,7)
Nothing Achieving (7)
O My God (5,7,8)
Omegaman (4,7)
On Any Other Day (2,7)
Once Upon A Daydream (7)
One World (Not Three) (4,7)
Other Way Of Stopping (3,7)
Peanuts (1,7,8)
Reggatta De Blanc (2,7)
Rehumanize Yourself (4,7)

Roxanne (1,6,7,8,9,10) *32*
Roxanne '97 - Puff Daddy Remix (9) *59*
Russians (9)
Sally (medley) (1,7,8)
Secret Journey (4,7) *46*
Sermon, A (7)
Shadows In The Rain (3,7)
Shambelle (7)
So Lonely (1,7,8)
Someone To Talk To (7)
Spirits In The Material World (4,6,7,8,10) *11*
Synchronicity I (5,7,8)
Synchronicity II (5,7,8) *16*
Tea In The Sahara (5,7,8)
Too Much Information (4,7)

Truth Hits Everybody (1,7,8)
Visions Of The Night (7)
Voices Inside My Head (3,7)
Walking In Your Footsteps (5,7,8)
Walking On The Moon (2,6,7,8,9,10)
When The World Is Running Down, You Make The Best Of What's Still Around (3,7)
When We Dance (9)
Wrapped Around Your Finger (5,6,7,8,10) *8*

POLNAREFF, Michel '76

Born in France. Pop singer/guitarist/keyboardist.

DEBUT	PEAK	WKS				Album Title		$	Label & Number
2/21/76	117	13				Michel Polnareff		$12	Atlantic 18153

Come On Lady Blue
Fame A La Mode
Holding On To Smoke

If You Only Believe (Jesus For Tonite) *48*
No No No No No Not Now

Rainy Day Song
Since I Saw You
So Long Beauty

Wandering Man

★414★ PONTY, Jean-Luc '77

Born on 9/29/42 in Normandy, France. Jazz-rock violinist. Worked with **Frank Zappa** and **Elton John**. Member of **Mahavishnu Orchestra** from 1973-75.

1)Enigmatic Ocean 2)Cosmic Messenger 3)Mystical Adventures

DEBUT	PEAK	WKS		CD	#	Album Title	Catalog	$	Label & Number
7/26/75	158	5		©	1	Upon The Wings Of Music	[I]	$12	Atlantic 18138
4/10/76	123	13		©	2	Aurora	[I]	$12	Atlantic 18165
12/4/76+	67	23		©	3	Imaginary Voyage	[I]	$12	Atlantic 18195
10/1/77	35	16		©	4	Enigmatic Ocean	[I]	$12	Atlantic 19110
9/2/78	36	28		©	5	Cosmic Messenger	[I]	$12	Atlantic 19189
5/19/79	68	10			6	Jean-Luc Ponty: Live	[I-L]	$12	Atlantic 19229
10/27/79	54	21		©	7	A Taste For Passion	[I]	$12	Atlantic 19253
10/18/80	73	18		©	8	Civilized Evil	[I]	$12	Atlantic 16020
2/13/82	44	14		©	9	Mystical Adventures	[I]	$12	Atlantic 19333
8/27/83	85	15		©	10	Individual Choice	[I]	$10	Atlantic 80098
12/8/84	171	13		©	11	Open Mind	[I]	$10	Atlantic 80185
11/2/85	166	4		©	12	Fables	[I]	$10	Atlantic 81276

Art Of Happiness (5)
As (9)
Aurora - Part I, II (2,6)
Beach Girl (7)
Between You And Me (2)
Bowing - Bowing (1)
Cats Tales (12)
Computer Incantations For World Peace (10)
Cosmic Messenger (5)
Demagomania (8)
Don't Let The World Pass You By (5)
Dreamy Eyes (7)
Echoes Of The Future (1)

Egocentric Molecules (5,6)
Elephants In Love (12)
Enigmatic Ocean - Part I, II, III, IV (4)
Ethereal Mood (5)
Eulogy To Oscar Romero (10)
Fake Paradise (5)
Far From The Beaten Paths (10)
Farewell (7)
Fight For Life (9)
Final Truth - Part I, II (9)
Forms Of Life (8)
Gardens Of Babylon (3)
Give Us A Chance (7)

Good Guys, Bad Guys (8)
Happy Robots (8)
I Only Feel Good With You (5)
Imaginary Voyage - Part I, II, III, IV (3)
Imaginary Voyage - Part III, IV (6)
In Case We Survive (8)
In Spiritual Love (10)
In Spite Of All (10)
In The Kingdom Of Peace (12)
Infinite Pursuit (10)
Intuition (11)
Is Once Enough? (2)

Jig (9)
Life Cycles (7)
Lost Forest (2)
Mirage (4,6)
Modern Times Blues (11)
Mystical Adventures (Suite) - Part I, II, III, IV, V (9)
New Country (3)
No Strings Attached (6)
Nostalgia (10)
Nostalgic Lady (4)
Now I Know (1)
Obsession (7)
Once A Blue Planet (8)
Once Upon A Dream (3)

Open Mind (11)
Orbital Encounters (11)
Overture (4)
Passenger Of The Dark (2)
Peace Crusaders (8)
Perpetual Rondo (12)
Plastic Idols (12)
Polyfolk Dance (1)
Puppets' Dance (5)
Question With No Answer (1)
Radioactive Legacy (12)
Reminiscence (7)
Renaissance (2)
Rhythms Of Hope (9)
Shape Up Your Mind (8)

Solitude (11)
Stay With Me (7)
Struggle Of The Turtle To The Sea - Part I, II, III (4)
Sunset Drive (7)
Tarantula (3)
Taste For Passion (7)
Trans-Love Express (4)
Upon The Wings Of Music (1)
Waking Dream (2)
Wandering On The Milky Way (3)
Watching Birds (11)
Waving Memories (1)

POOH-MAN — see M.C. POOH

POOR RIGHTEOUS TEACHERS '90

Rap trio from Trenton, New Jersey: Wise Intelligent, Culture Freedom and Father Shaheed.

DEBUT	PEAK	WKS		CD	#	Album Title		$	Label & Number
6/16/90	142	22		©	1	Holy Intellect		$10	Profile 1289
9/21/91	155	3		©	2	Pure Poverty		$10	Profile 1415
10/2/93	167	2		©	3	Black Business		$10	Profile 1443

POOR RIGHTEOUS TEACHERS— Cont'd

Black Business (3)
Butt Naked Booty Bless (1)
Can I Start This? (1)
Da Rill Shit (3)
Each One Teach One (2)
Easy Star (2)
Freedom Or Death (2)
Get Off The Crack (3)

Ghetto We Love (3)
Here We Go Again (3)
Holy Intellect (1)
Hot Damn I'm Great (2)
I'm Comin' Again (2)
Just Scrvin' Justice (2)
Lessons Taught (medley) (1)

Lick Shots (3)
Methods Of Droppin' Mental (2)
Mi Fresh (3)
Nation's Anthem (2)
Nobody Move (3)
None Can Test (3)
144K (3)
Poor Righteous Teachers (1)

Pure Poverty (2)
Rappin' Black (2)
Rich Mon Time (3)
Rock Dis Funky Joint (1)
Selah (3)
Self-Styled Wisdom (2)
Shakiyla (1,2)
So Many Teachers (1)

Speaking Upon A Blackman (1)
Strictly Ghetto (1)
Strictly Mash'ion (2)
Style Dropped (medley) (1)
Time To Say Peace (1)
Word From The Wise (1)

POP, Iggy '77

Born James Jewel Osterberg on 4/21/47 in Muskegon, Michigan. Punk-rock pioneer. Leader of **The Stooges** from 1969-74. Acted in the movies *Cry Baby*, *Hardware* and *The Crow: City Of Angels*. Adopted nickname "Iggy" from his first band, The Iguanas.

1)*The Idiot* 2)*Blah-Blah-Blah* 3)*Brick By Brick*

DEBUT	PEAK	WKS	CD	#	Album	$	Label & Number
8/23/69	106	11	©	1	The Stooges	$50	Elektra 74051
4/28/73	182	3	©	2	Raw Power	$50	Columbia 32111

IGGY AND THE STOOGES

4/9/77	72	13	©	3	The Idiot	$15	RCA Victor 2275
9/17/77	120	6	©	4	Lust For Life	$15	RCA Victor 2488
10/6/79	180	4	©	5	New Values	$12	Arista 4237
3/8/80	125	7	©	6	Soldier	$12	Arista 4259
9/19/81	166	5	©	7	Party	$12	Arista 9572
10/18/86	75	27	©	8	Blah-Blah-Blah	$10	A&M 5145
7/23/88	110	12	©	9	Instinct	$10	A&M 5198
7/28/90	90	37	©	10	Brick By Brick	$10	Virgin 91381

African Man (5)
Ambition (6)
Angel (5)
Ann (1)
Baby (3)
Baby, It Can't Fall (8)
Bang Bang (7)
Billy Is A Runaway (9)
Blah-Blah-Blah (8)
Brick By Brick (10)
Butt Town (10)
Candy (10) **28**
China Girl (3)
Cold Metal (9)
Cry For Love (8)
Curiosity (5)
Death Trip (2)
Dog Food (6)
Don't Look Down (5)

Dum Dum Boys (3)
Easy Rider (9)
Eggs On Plate (7)
Endless Sea (5)
Fall In Love With Me (4)
Fire Girl (8)
Five Foot One (5)
Funtime (3)
Get Up And Get Out (6)
Gimme Danger (2)
Girls (5)
Happy Man (7)
Hideaway (8)
High On You (9)
Home (10)
Houston Is Hot Tonight (7)

How Do Ya Fix A Broken
  Part (5)

I Need More (6)
I Need Somebody (2)
I Snub You (6)
I Wanna Be Your Dog (1)
I Won't Crap Out (10)
I'm A Conservative (6)
I'm Bored (5)
Instinct (9)
Isolation (8)
Knocking 'Em Down (In The
  City) (6)
Little Doll (1)
Loco Mosquito (6)
Lowdown (9)
Lust For Life (4)
Main Street Eyes (10)
Mass Production (3)
Moonlight Lady (10)
Mr. Dynamite (6)

My Baby Wants To Rock & Roll
  (10)
Neighborhood Threat (4)
Neon Forest (10)
New Values (5)
Nightclubbing (3)
1969 (1)
No Fun (1)
Not Right (1)
Passenger, The (4)
Penetration (2)
Play It Safe (6)
Pleasure (7)
Power & Freedom (9)
Pumpin' For Jill (7)
Pussy Power (10)
Raw Power (2)
Real Cool Time (1)
Real Wild Child (Wild One) (8)

Rock And Roll Party (7)
Sea Of Love (7)
Search And Destroy (2)
Shades (8)
Shake Appeal (2)
Sincerity (7)
Sister Midnight (3)
Sixteen (4)
Some Weird Sin (4)
Something Wild (10)
Squarehead (9)
Starry Night (10)
Strong Girl (9)
Success (4)
Take Care Of Me (6)
Tell Me A Story (5)
Time Won't Let Me (7)
Tiny Girls (3)
Tom Tom (9)

Tonight (4)
Tuff Baby (9)
Turn Blue (4)
Undefeated, The (10)
We Will Fall (1)
Winners & Losers (8)
Your Pretty Face Is Going To
  Hell (2)

POPE JOHN XXIII '63

Born Angelo Guiseppe Roncalli on 11/25/1881 in Sotto il Monte, Italy. Died on 6/3/63 (age 81). Served as Pope from 1958-63.

DEBUT	PEAK	WKS			$	Label & Number
8/3/63	126	3		Pope John XXIII .... [T]	$20	Mercury 200

excerpts of the Pope's voice and events during his reign

Canonization
Closing Ceremonies, 2nd Vatican
  Ecumenical Council

Coronation, His Holiness
Pope John XXIII

Election, His Holiness Pope
John XXIII
Papal Audience

Papal Blessing, St. Peter's
  Square

POPE JOHN PAUL II '79

Born Karol Jozef Wojtyla on 5/18/20 in Wadowice, Poland. Has served as Pope since 1978.

DEBUT	PEAK	WKS	CD	#	Album	$	Label & Number
11/3/79	126	4		1	Pope John Paul II Sings At The Festival Of Sacrosong	$12	Infinity 9899
4/10/99	175	2	©	2	Abbà Pater .... [F]	$10	Sony Classical 61705

Abbà Pater (2)
Brown Madonna (1)
Cercate Il Suo Volto (2)
Cristo È Liberazione (2)
Do Not Be Afraid, Mary, You Lily (1)
Dove C'è Amore, C'è Dio (2)

Fanfare For The Pope (1)
Huzulen Song (1)
La Legge Delle Beatitudini
  (2)
Little Cantata (1)
Madre Di Tutte Le Genti (2)

Moment Of The Entire Life (1)
Oh, God, I Place My Trust In
  You (1)
On A December Night (1)
Our Father; Blessing (1)
Padre Della Luce (2)

Padre, Ti Chiediamo Perdono
  (2)
Peter's Song (1)
Prayer To The Mother Of God
  (1)
Queen, Black Madonna (1)

Raftsmen, The (1)
Temple Is Our House (1)
Un Comandamento Nuovo (2)
Verbum Caro Factum Est (2)
Vieni, Santo Spirito (2)

We Are Never Alone Like
Skipping Stones (1)

POPPER, John '99

Born in 1967 in Cleveland. Lead singer/harmonica player of **Blues Traveler**.

DEBUT	PEAK	WKS	CD		Album	$	Label & Number
9/25/99	185	1	©		Zygote	$10	A&M 490408

Evil In My Chair
Fledgling
Growing In Dirt

His Own Ideas
Home
How About Now

Love For Free
Lunatic
Miserable Bastard

Once You Wake Up
Open Letter
Tip The Domino

POPPY FAMILY, The '70

Pop group from Canada: Susan Jacks (vocals), her husband **Terry Jacks** (guitar), Craig MacCaw (guitar) and Satwan Singh (percussion). Group and marriage broke up in 1973; Susan and Terry began solo careers.

DEBUT	PEAK	WKS			Album	$	Label & Number
6/20/70	76	11			Which Way You Goin' Billy?	$20	London 574

Beyond The Clouds
For Running Wild
Free From The City

Good Thing Lost
Happy Island
Of Cities And Escapes

Shadows On My Wall
That's Where I Went
Wrong 29

There's No Blood In Bone
What Can The Matter Be?
Which Way You Goin' Billy? 2

You Took My Moonlight Away

POP WILL EAT ITSELF '89

Psychedelic-rap-rock group from Stourbridge, England: Clint Mansell and Graham Crabb (vocals), Adam Mole (guitar) and Richard March (bass).

DEBUT	PEAK	WKS	CD		Album	$	Label & Number
8/26/89	169	6	©		This Is The Day...This Is The Hour...This Is This!	$10	RCA 9742

Can U Dig It?
Def Con One
Fuses Have Been Lit
Inject Me

Not Now James, We're
  Busy
PWEI Is A Four Letter Word
Poison To The Mind

Preaching To The Perverted
Radio P.W.E.I.
Satellite Ecstatica

Shortwave Transmission On
  "Up To The Minuteman Nine"
Sixteen Different Flavours Of
  Hell

Wake Up, Time To Die
Wise Up Sucker

PORNO FOR PYROS '93

Rock group formed by former **Jane's Addiction** members Perry Farrell (vocals) and Stephen Perkins (drums). Includes Peter DiStefano (guitar) and Martyn LeNoble (bass). **Mike Watt** replaced LeNoble in 1995.

DEBUT	PEAK	WKS	CD	#	Album	$	Label
5/15/93	3	21	● ©	1	Porno For Pyros	$10	Warner 45228
6/15/96	20	11	©	2	Good God's Urge	$10	Warner 46126

Bad Shit (1)
Bali Eyes (2)
Black Girlfriend (1)
Blood Rag (1)

Cursed Female (1)
Cursed Male (1)
Dogs Rule The Night (2)
Freeway (2)

Good God's://Urge! (2)
Kimberly Austin (2)
Meija (1)
100 Ways (2)

Orgasm (1)
Packin' .25 (1)
Pets (1) *67*
Porno For Pyros (1)

Porpoise Head (2)
Sadness (1)
Tahitian Moon (2)
Thick Of It All (2)

Wishing Well (2)

PORTER, David '71

Born on 11/21/41 in Memphis. R&B singer/songwriter. Songwriting partnership with **Isaac Hayes**.

| 3/28/70 | 163 | 10 | | 1 | Gritty, Groovy, & Gettin' It | $15 | Enterprise 1009 |
| 1/30/71 | 104 | 9 | | 2 | David Porter...Into A Real Thing | $15 | Enterprise 1012 |

Can't See You When I Want To (1)
Grocery Man (2)
Guess Who (1)

Hang On Sloopy (2)
I Don't Know Why I Love You
I Don't Want To Cry (2)

I Only Have Eyes For You (1)
I'm A-Tellin' You (1)
Just Be True (1)
One Part - Two Parts (1)

Ooo-Wee Girl (2)
Thirty Days (2)
Too Real To Live A Lie (2)

Way You Do The Things You
Do (1)

PORTISHEAD '97

Duo from Bristol, England: multi-instrumentalist Geoff Barrow and vocalist Beth Gibbons. Duo named after a coastal shipping town near Bristol.

1/28/95	79	17	● ©	1	Dummy	$10	London 828553
10/18/97	21	16	©	2	Portishead	$10	London 539189
11/28/98	155	1	©	3	Roseland NYC Live	[L]	$10	London 559424

recorded on 7/24/97 at the Roseland Ballroom in New York City

All Mine (2,3)
Biscuit (1)
Cowboys (2,3)
Elysium (2)

Glory Box (1,3)
Half Day Closing (2,3)
Humming (2,3)
It Could Be Sweet (1)

It's A Fire (1)
Mourning Air (2)
Mysterons (1,3)
Numb (1)

Only You (2,3)
Over (2,3)
Pedestal (1)
Roads (1,3)

Seven Months (2)
Sour Times (1,3) *53*
Strangers (1,3)
Undenied (2)

Wandering Star (1)
Western Eyes (2)

PORTRAIT '93

Male R&B vocal group: Eric Kirkland and Michael Saulsberry (from Los Angeles), Irving Washington (from Providence, Rhode Island) and Phillip Johnson (from Tulsa, Oklahoma). In 1995, Johnson was replaced by Kurt Jackson (from Aurora, Colorado).

| 1/9/93 | 70 | 21 | © | 1 | Portrait | $10 | Capitol 93496 |
| 3/25/95 | 131 | 5 | © | 2 | All That Matters | $10 | Capitol 28709 |

All Natural Girl (2)
All That Matters (2)
Commitment (1)
Day By Day (1)

Down Wit Dat (1)
Feelings (1)
Friday Night (2)
Heartache (1)

Heartstrings (2)
Here We Go Again! (1) *11*
Here's A Kiss (2)
Hold Me Close (2)

Honey Dip (1)
How Deep Is Your Love (2) *93*
I Can Call You (2)
Lay You Down (2)

Lovin' U Is Ah-ight (1)
Me Oh My (2)
Much Too Much (2)
On And On (1)

Precious Moments (1)
Problems (1)
You (1)
Yours Forever (1)

POSEY, Sandy '67

Born on 6/18/44 in Jasper, Alabama; raised in West Memphis, Arkansas. Pop singer.

| 12/17/66+ | 129 | 7 | | 1 | Born A Woman | $20 | MGM 4418 |
| 9/30/67 | 182 | 4 | | 2 | I Take It Back | $20 | MGM 4480 |

Arms Full Of Sin (1)
Big Hurt (2)
Blue Is My Best Color (1)
Born A Woman (1) *12*

Boy I Love (2)
Bread And Butter (2)
Caution To The Wind (1)
Come Softly To Me (2)

Halfway To Paradise (2)
I Can Show You How To Live
(2)
If Tears Had Color In Them (1)

It's All In The Game (1)
It's Wonderful To Be In Love (2)
Just Out Of Reach (2)
Love Of The Common People
(2)

Miss Lonely (1)
Satin Pillows (1)
Standing In The Rain (2)
Strangers In The Night (1)
Sunglasses (2)

This Time (1)
You Got To Have Love To Be
Happy (1)

POSITIVE K '93

Born Darryl Gibson in the Bronx, New York. Male rapper.

| 2/20/93 | 168 | 10 | © | | The Skills Dat Pay Da Bills | $10 | Island 514057 |

Ain't No Crime
Carhoppers
Flower Grows In Brooklyn

Friends
How The F*?#! Would You
Know

I Got A Man *14*
It's All Over
Minnie The Moocher

Nightshift
One 2 The Head
Pass The Mic

Shakin'
Shout Out

POST, Mike '82

Born on 9/29/44 in Los Angeles. Composer/producer.

| 11/8/75 | 195 | 3 | | 1 | Railhead Overture | [I] | $15 | MGM 5005 |
| 2/27/82 | 70 | 17 | | 2 | Television Theme Songs | [G-I] | $12 | Elektra 60028 |

Blade (1)
Georgia On My Mind (1)
Greatest American Hero
(Believe It Or Not), Theme
From (2) *2*

Hill Street Blues, Theme From
(2) *10*
Lay Back Lafayette (1)
Magnum P.I., Theme From
(2) *25*

Manhattan Spiritual (1) *56*
Pictures At An Exhibition (1)
Railhead Overture (1)
Rockford Files (1,2) *10*

School's Out (2)
Viking (1)
White Shadow, Theme From (2)
Will The Circle Be Unbroken (1)

Wouldn't It Be Nice (1)

POTLIQUOR '72

Rock group from Baton Rouge, Louisiana: George Ratzlaff (vocals), Les Wallace (guitar), Guy Schaeffer (bass) and Jerry Amoroso (drums).

| 2/19/72 | 168 | 7 | | | Levee Blues | $20 | Janus 3033 |

Beyond The River Jordan
Chattanooga
Cheer *65*

Lady Madonna
Levee Blues
Rooster Blues

Train, The
When God Dips His Love In My
Heart

You're No Good

POUSETTE-DART BAND '77

Pop group from Canada: Jon Pousette-Dart (vocals), John Curtis (guitar), John Troy (bass) and Michael Dawe (drums).

| 3/19/77 | 143 | 7 | © | 1 | Amnesia | $12 | Capitol 11608 |
| 6/10/78 | 161 | 5 | | 2 | Pousette-Dart Band 3 | $12 | Capitol 11781 |

Amnesia (1)
County Line (1)
Fall On Me (1)
I Don't Know Why (1)

I Stayed Away Too Long (2)
I Think I Know (1)
Listen To The Spirit (1)
Lord's Song (2)

Louisiana (2)
Love Is My Belief (2)
May You Dance (1)
Mr. Saturday Night (2)

Next To You (2)
Stand By Me (2)
Too Blue To Be True (2)
Where Are You Going (2)

Who's That Knockin' (1)
Winterness (1)
Yaicha (1)

POWELL, Adam Clayton '67

Born on 11/29/08 in New Haven, Connecticut. Died on 4/4/72 (age 63). Congressman from Harlem, New York (1944-70).

| 2/25/67 | 112 | 9 | | | Keep The Faith, Baby! | [T] | $25 | Jubilee 2062 |

Burn, Baby, Burn

Death Of Anyman

Handwriting On The Wall

Keep The Faith, Baby!

My Dear Colleagues

One Day

POWELL, Jesse '99
Born in Gary, Indiana. Male R&B singer/songwriter.

| 2/6/99 | 63 | 21 | ● | © | 1 'Bout It | | | $10 | Silas 11789 |
| 4/14/01 | 71 | 7 | | © | 2 JP | | | $10 | Silas 112401 |

After We Make Love (2) • Are You Missin' My Love? (1) • 'Bout It, 'Bout It (1) • Can't Take It (2) • Go Upstairs (2) • I Can Tell (1) • I Didn't Realize (2) • **I Wasn't With It** (1) *85* • I'd Rather Be Alone (2) • I'm Leaving (2) • If I (2) • Invisible Man (2) • It'll Take The World (2) • On Your Mind (2) • She Wasn't Last Night (1) • Something In The Past (2) • Take My Breath Away (2) • Up And Down (1) • **You** (1) *10* • You Should Know (1) • You're The One I Love (1)

POWERMAN 5000 '99
Hard-rock group from Boston: Spider One (vocals), Adam 12 and M.33 (guitars), Dorian 27 (bass) and Al 3 (drums).

| 8/7/99 | 29 | 44 | ▲ | © | Tonight The Stars Revolt! | | | $10 | DreamWorks 50107 |

Automatic • Blast Off To Nowhere • Eye Is Upon You • Good Times Roll • Nobody's Real • Operate, Annihilate • Son Of X-51 • Supernova Goes Pop • System 11:11 • They Know Who You Are • Tonight The Stars Revolt! • Watch The Sky For Me • When Worlds Collide

POWER STATION, The '85
All-star rock group: **Robert Palmer** (vocals), **Andy Taylor** (guitar), John Taylor (bass) and Tony Thompson (drums). The Taylors were members of **Duran Duran**. Thompson was a member of **Chic**.

| 4/13/85 | 6 | 44 | ▲ | © | The Power Station | | | $10 | Capitol 12380 |

Communication *34* • **Get It On** *9* • Go To Zero • Harvest For The World • Lonely Tonight • Murderess • Some Like It Hot *6* • Still In Your Heart

POZO-SECO SINGERS '67
Folk-rock trio from Texas: **Don Williams**, Susan Taylor and Lofton Kline. Williams later became a major country star.

| 7/30/66 | 127 | 6 | | © | 1 Time | | | $20 | Columbia 9315 |
| 2/4/67 | 81 | 10 | | © | 2 I Can Make It With You | | | $20 | Columbia 9400 |

Almost Persuaded (2) • Blue Eyes (2) • Changes (2) • Come A Little Bit Closer (1) • Diet (2) • Forget His Name (2) • Guantanamera (1) • House Of The Rising Sun (1) • **I Can Make It With You** (2) *32* • I'll Be Gone (1) *92* • If I Fell (1) • If I Were A Carpenter (2) • It Ain't Worth The Lonely Road Back (1) • Johnny (2) • **Look What You've Done** (2) *32* • Mary Jenkins (2) • Ribbon Of Darkness (2) • She Understands Me (1) • Silver Threads And Golden Needles (1) • **Time** (1) *47* • Tomorrow Is A Long Time (1) • You've Lost That Lovin' Feelin' (1)

PRADO, Perez '59
Born Damaso Perez Prado on 12/11/16 in Mantanzas, Cuba. Died of a stroke on 9/14/89 (age 72). Bandleader/organist. Known as "The King of The Mambo." Appeared in the movie *Underwater!*

| 5/25/59 | 22 | 3 | | | "Prez" | | [I] | $40 | RCA Victor 1556 |

Adios Mi Chaparrita (Goodbye My Little Angel) • Come Back To Sorrento (Torna A Sorrento) • Cu-Cu-Rru-Cu-Cu Paloma • Fireworks • Flight Of The Bumblebee • La Borrachita (I'll Never Love Again) • Leo's Special • Lullaby Of Birdland • Machaca • Maria Bonita • Marta

PRAGUE MADRIGAL SINGERS, The '66
Choral group from Czechoslovakia. Conducted by Miroslav Venhoda.

| 12/10/66 | 29[X] | 3 | | | The Christmas Carols Of Europe | | [X-F] | $30 | Crossroads 0054 |

Bulgarskaja Koledna Pesen (medley) • Byla Cesta, Byla Uslapaná (medley) • Chtíc Aby Spal (medley) • Dej Buh Stestí (medley) • Der Heiland Ist Geboren (medley) • Detátko Se Narodilo (medley) • Dormi, Dormi, Bel Bambin (medley) • Entre Le Boeuf Et L'âne Gris (medley) • Es Ist Ein' Ros' Entsprungen (medley) • Gloria, Gloria (medley) • Good King Wenceslas (medley) • Já Bych Rád K Betlému (medley) • Jak Jsi Krásné Jezulátko (medley) • Jeg Er Sa Glad Hver Julekveld (medley) • Jezus Malusienki (medley) • Kerstlied (medley) • Kristus Pán Se Narodil (medley) • Los Animales Ante El Nacimiento (medley) • Narodil Se Kristus Pán (medley) • Nous Étions Trois Bergerettes (medley) • Nu Ár Det Jul Igen (medley) • Pásli Ovce Valasi (medley) • Poslechnete Me Málo (medley) • Pujdem Spolu Do Betléma (medley) • Rajsko Strune Zadonite (medley) • Slyste, Slyste, Pastuskové (medley) • Syn Bozí Se Nám Narodil (medley) • Ta Kalimera Tón Christoygennon (medley) • Vondrási, Matósi (medley)

PRAS — see MICHEL, Pras

PRATT, Andy '77
Born on 1/25/47 in Boston. Soft-rock singer/songwriter/ keyboardist/guitarist.

5/12/73	192	4			1 Andy Pratt			$15	Columbia 31722
7/10/76	104	10			2 Resolution			$12	Nemperor 438
8/27/77	90	9			3 Shiver In The Night			$12	Nemperor 443

All I Want Is You (3) • All The King's Weight (1) • **Avenging Annie** (1) *78* • Born To Learn (3) • Call Up That Old Friend (1) • Can't Stop My Love (2) • Constant Heat (2) • Deer Song (1) • Dreams (3) • Everything Falls Into Place (Lillian's Song) (2) • Give It All To Music (1) • I Want To See You Dance (3) • If You Could See Yourself (Through My Eyes) (2) • Inside Me Wants Out (1) • It's All Behind You (1) • Karen's Song (2) • Keep Your Dream Alive (3) • Landscape (3) • Love Song (2) • Mama's Getting Love (3) • My Love Is So Tender (3) • Rainbow (3) • Resolution (2) • Set Your Sights (2) • Sittin' Down In The Twilight (1) • So Faint (3) • So Fine (It's Frightening) (1) • Some Things Go On Forever (2) • Summer, Summer (1) • That's When Miracles Occur (2) • Treasure That Canary (2) • What's Important To You (3) • Who Am I Talking To (1)

PRATT & McCLAIN '76
Pop vocal duo: Truett Pratt (from San Antonio, Texas) and Jerry McClain (from Pasadena, California).

| 7/10/76 | 190 | 2 | | | Pratt & McClain Featuring "Happy Days" | | | $12 | Reprise 2250 |

California Cowboy • **Devil With A Blue Dress** *71* • Happy Days *5* • Midnight Ride • One Way Or The Other • Our Last Song Together • Raised On Rock • Summertime In The City • Tonight We're Gonna Fall In Love • Whachersign • Who Needs It

PREFAB SPROUT '85
Pop group from England: brothers Paddy (vocals, guitar) and Martin (bass) McAloon, with Wendy Smith (vocals) and Neil Conti (drums).

| 11/2/85 | 178 | 5 | | © | Two Wheels Good | | | $12 | Epic 40100 |

Appetite • Blueberry Pies • Bonny • Desire As • Faron • Goodbye Lucille #1 • Hallelujah • Horsin' Around • Moving The River • When Love Breaks Down • When The Angels

PRELUDE '74
Folk trio formed in England: husband-and-wife Irene (vocals) and Brian (vocals, guitar) Hume, with Ian Vardy (guitar).

| 12/7/74 | 94 | 7 | | © | 1 After The Gold Rush | | | $15 | Island 9282 |
| 11/22/75+ | 111 | 14 | | | 2 Owlcreek Incident | | | $15 | Pye 12120 |

Adventures On The Way (1) • **After The Goldrush** (1) *22* • Amsterdam (2) • Best Of A Bad Time (2) • Dear Jesus (1) • Faites Vos Jeux (2) • Fly (1) • Follow Me Down (1) • **For A Dancer** (2) *63* • Hotel Room (1) • Lady From A Small Town (1) • Love Song (2) • Me And The Boy (2) • Meet On The Ledge (1) • Old Sam (2) • Open Book (1) • Owlcreek Incident (2) • Rock Dreams (1) • Rufus (1) • Shalle (2) • To Hell With The War (1)

PREMIATA FORNERIA MARCONI — see P.F.M.

PRESIDENTS, The '71
R&B vocal trio from Washington DC: Archie Powell, Bill Shorter and Tony Boyd.

| 1/30/71 | 158 | 6 | | | **5-10-15-20-25-30 years of love** .... | | | $25 | Sussex 7005 |

Fiddle De De
5-10-15-20 (25-30 Years Of Love) 11

For You	How Can You Say You're	It's All Over	Triangle Of Love (Hey Diddle
Girl You Cheated On Me	Leavin'	Sweet Magic	Diddle) 68
Gotta Keep Movin'	I'm Still Dancing	This Is My Dream World	Why Are You So Good To Me

PRESIDENTS OF THE UNITED STATES OF AMERICA '96
Rock trio from Seattle: Chris Ballew (vocals), Dave Dederer (guitar) and Jason Finn (drums).

| 9/2/95+ | 6 | 55 | ▲3 | © 1 | The Presidents Of The United States Of America | | | $10 | Columbia 67291 |
| 11/23/96 | 31 | 13 | ● | © 2 | II .... | | | $10 | Columbia 67577 |

Back Porch (1)	Candy (1)	Kitty (1)	Lunatic To Love (2)	Stranger (1)	Volcano (2)
Bath Of Fire (2)	Dune Buggy (1)	Ladies And Gentlemen Part I &	Mach 5 (2)	Supermodel (2)	We Are Not Going To Make It
Body (1)	Feather Pluckn (1)	II (2)	Naked And Famous (1)	Tiki God (2)	(1)
Boll Weevil (1)	Froggie (2)	L.I.P. (2)	Peaches (1) 29	Toob Amplifier (2)	
Bug City (2)	Kick Out The Jams (1)	Lump (1)	Puffy Little Shoes (2)	Twig (2)	

PRESLEY, Elvis ★1★ '61
Born on 1/8/35 in Tupelo, Mississippi. Died of heart failure on 8/16/77 (age 42). Known as "The King of Rock & Roll." Moved to Memphis in 1948. First recorded for Sun in 1954. Signed to RCA Records on 11/22/55. His backing group included The Jordanaires (vocals), Scotty Moore (guitar), **Bill Black** (bass) and D.J. Fontana (drums). Starred in 31 feature movies (beginning with *Love Me Tender* in 1956). In U.S. Army from 3/24/58 to 3/5/60. Married Priscilla Beaulieu on 5/1/67; divorced on 10/11/73. Priscilla pursued acting in the 1980s beginning with a role on TV's *Dallas*. Their only child, Lisa Marie, (born on 2/1/68) was married to **Michael Jackson** from 1994-96. Elvis' last "live" performance was in Indianapolis on 6/26/77. Won Grammy's Lifetime Achievement Award in 1971. Inducted into the Rock and Roll Hall of Fame in 1986.

1)Blue Hawaii 2)G.I. Blues 3)Elvis Presley 4)Loving You 5)Elvis

3/31/56	❶10	48	●	© 1	Elvis Presley			$300	RCA Victor LPM-1254
11/10/56	❶5	32	●	© 2	Elvis			$300	RCA Victor LPM-1382
5/13/57	3	9	▲	3	Peace In The Valley		[EP]	$150	RCA Victor EPA-4054
7/22/57	❶10	29	●	© 4	Loving You		[S]	$300	RCA Victor LPM-1515
9/2/57	18	1	▲	5	Loving You, Vol. II		[EP-S]	$150	RCA EPA 2-1515
9/2/57	22	1	▲	6	Love Me Tender		[EP-S]	$150	RCA Victor EPA-4006
9/30/57	16	1		7	Just For You		[EP]	$150	RCA Victor EPA-4041
12/2/57	❶4	7	▲3	© 8	Elvis' Christmas Album	C:#10/28 [X]		$500	RCA Victor LOC-1035

gatefold cover with 10 pages of bound-in color photos of Elvis; Christmas charts: 5/'63, 3/'64, 2/'65, 2/'66, 3/'67, 3/'68, 2/'69, 2/'70, 9/'72, 6/'85, 11/'87, 10/'88, 22/'89, 22/'90, 29/'92, 27/'94, 19/'95, 12/'96, 31/'97, 30/'99

4/21/58	3	74	▲6	© 9	Elvis' Golden Records	C:#14/32 [G]		$250	RCA Victor LPM-1707
9/15/58	2¹	15	●	© 10	King Creole		[S]	$250	RCA Victor LPM-1884
3/23/59	19	8		© 11	For LP Fans Only		[E]	$250	RCA Victor LPM-1990

recordings from 1956

| 9/21/59 | 32 | 8 | | © 12 | A Date With Elvis .... | | [E] | $400 | RCA Victor LPM-2011 |

recordings from 1956-57

2/15/60	31	6	▲	© 13	50,000,000 Elvis Fans Can't Be Wrong - Elvis' Gold Records-Volume 2	[G]		$200	RCA Victor LPM-2075
5/9/60	2³	56	●	© 14	Elvis Is Back!			$200	RCA Victor LSP-2231
10/31/60	❶10	111	▲	© 15	G.I. Blues		[S]	$150	RCA Victor LSP-2256
12/31/60	33	1		© 16	Elvis' Christmas Album		[X-R]	$150	RCA Victor LPM-1951

repackage of LOC-1035 album (no gatefold or photos)

1/9/61	13	20	▲	© 17	His Hand in Mine			$150	RCA Victor LSP-2328
7/10/61	❶3	25	●	© 18	Something for Everybody			$150	RCA Victor LSP-2370
10/23/61	❶20	79	▲²	© 19	Blue Hawaii		[S]	$100	RCA Victor LSP-2426
1/6/62	120	2		© 20	Elvis' Christmas Album		[X-R]	$150	RCA Victor LPM-1951
7/14/62	4	31		© 21	Pot Luck			$100	RCA Victor LSP-2523
12/8/62+	3	32	●	© 22	Girls! Girls! Girls!		[S]	$100	RCA Victor LSP-2621
12/8/62	59	4		© 23	Elvis' Christmas Album		[X-R]	$150	RCA Victor LPM-1951
4/20/63	4	26		© 24	It Happened At The World's Fair		[S]	$100	RCA Victor LSP-2697
9/14/63	3	63	▲	© 25	Elvis' Golden Records, Volume 3		[G]	$100	RCA Victor LSP-2765
12/21/63+	3	24		© 26	Fun in Acapulco		[S]	$100	RCA Victor LSP-2756
4/11/64	6	30		© 27	Kissin' Cousins		[S]	$100	RCA Victor LSP-2894
11/14/64+	❶1	27	●	© 28	Roustabout		[S]	$100	RCA Victor LSP-2999
4/17/65	8	31	●	© 29	Girl Happy		[S]	$75	RCA Victor LSP-3338
8/14/65	10	27		© 30	Elvis For Everyone!		[K]	$75	RCA Victor LSP-3450
11/13/65+	8	23		© 31	Harum Scarum		[S]	$75	RCA Victor LSP-3468
4/23/66	20	19		© 32	Frankie And Johnny		[S]	$75	RCA Victor LSP-3553
7/16/66	15	19		© 33	Paradise, Hawaiian Style......................................		[S]	$75	RCA Victor LSP-3643
10/29/66	18	32		© 34	Spinout		[S]	$75	RCA Victor LSP-3702
3/25/67	18	29	▲²	© 35	How Great Thou Art		[S]	$75	RCA Victor LSP-3758
6/24/67	47	20		© 36	Double Trouble		[S]	$75	RCA Victor LSP-3787
12/2/67+	40	14		© 37	Clambake...		[S]	$75	RCA Victor LSP-3893
3/2/68	33	22	●	© 38	Elvis' Gold Records, Volume 4		[G]	$75	RCA Victor LSP-3921
7/6/68	82	13		© 39	Speedway		[S]	$75	RCA Victor LSP-3989

includes "Your Groovy Self" by **Nancy Sinatra**

| 12/21/68+ | 8 | 32 | ▲ | © 40 | Elvis | | [TV] | $50 | RCA Victor LPM-4088 |

aired on NBC-TV (better known as "The '68 Comeback Special")

DEBUT	PEAK	WKS	RIAA	CD	ARTIST — Album Title	Catalog	Sym	$	Label & Number
					PRESLEY, Elvis — Cont'd				
4/19/69	96	16	●		41 **Elvis sings Flaming Star**		[K]	$30	RCA Camden 2304
					only the title song is from the movie; others recorded from 1963-68				
6/14/69	13	34	●	©	42 **From Elvis In Memphis**			$50	RCA Victor LSP-4155
11/29/69	12	24	●		43 **From Vegas To Memphis/From Memphis To Vegas**		[L]	$50	RCA Vic. LSP-6020 [2]
					record 1: Elvis in Person at the International Hotel in Las Vegas; record 2: Elvis Back In Memphis (studio)				
5/9/70	105	11	●		44 **Let's Be Friends**		[K]	$30	RCA Camden 2408
					recordings from 1962-69				
6/20/70	13	20	▲	©	45 **On Stage-February, 1970**		[L]	$40	RCA Victor LSP-4362
					recorded at the International Hotel in Las Vegas				
8/22/70	45	36	▲²	©	46 **Worldwide 50 Gold Award Hits, Vol. 1**		[G]	$100	RCA Vic. LPM-6401 [4]
11/21/70	65	18			47 **Almost In Love**		[K]	$30	RCA Camden 2440
					recordings from 1966-69				
11/21/70	183	3		©	48 **Elvis Back In Memphis**		[R]	$40	RCA Victor LSP-4429
					previously issued as record 2 of #43 above				
12/12/70+	21	23	●		49 **Elvis-That's The Way It Is**		[L-S]	$40	RCA Victor LSP-4445
1/23/71	12	21	●	©	50 **Elvis Country ("I'm 10,000 Years Old")**			$40	RCA Vic. LSP-4460
3/20/71	69	12	▲	©	51 **You'll Never Walk Alone**		[K]	$30	RCA Camden 2472
6/26/71	33	15		©	52 **Love Letters from Elvis**			$40	RCA Victor LSP-4530
					all songs recorded in Nashville during June 1970				
7/24/71	70	11			53 **C'mon Everybody**		[K]	$30	RCA Camden 2518
					songs from his movies				
8/28/71	120	7		©	54 **The Other Sides - Worldwide Gold Award Hits, Vol. 2**		[G]	$100	RCA Vic. LPM-6402 [4]
					22 of 50 songs are from 6 E.P.s released 1956-58				
11/27/71	104	8			55 **I Got Lucky**		[K]	$30	RCA Camden 2533
					songs from his movies				
12/4/71+	❶³ˣ	12	▲³		56 **Elvis sings The Wonderful World of Christmas**		[X]	$25	RCA Victor LSP-4579
					Christmas charts: 2/'71, 1/'72, 1/'73				
2/12/72	43	19	●	©	57 **Elvis Now**			$25	RCA Victor LSP-4671
4/22/72	79	10	▲		58 **He Touched Me**			$25	RCA Victor LSP-4690
7/8/72	11	34	▲³	©	59 **Elvis As Recorded At Madison Square Garden**		[L]	$25	RCA Victor LSP-4776
					recorded on 6/10/72				
7/8/72	87	15			60 **Elvis sings hits from his movies, volume 1**		[K]	$25	RCA Camden 2567
11/11/72+	22	25	▲		61 **Burning Love and hits from his movies, volume 2**		[K]	$25	RCA Camden 2595
1/27/73	46	18	●		62 **Separate Ways**		[K]	$25	RCA Camden 2611
2/24/73	❶¹	52	▲³	©	63 **Aloha from Hawaii via Satellite**		[TV]	$50	RCA VPSX-6089 [2]
					recorded on 1/14/73				
7/21/73	52	13		©	64 **Elvis**			$50	RCA Victor APL-0283
11/24/73+	50	13		©	65 **Raised On Rock/For Ol' Times Sake**			$25	RCA Victor APL-0388
2/2/74	43	28	▲²	©	66 **Elvis-A Legendary Performer, Volume 1**		[K]	$25	RCA Victor CPL-0341
4/6/74	90	8		©	67 **Good Times**			$25	RCA Victor CPL-0475
7/27/74	33	13	●	©	68 **Elvis Recorded Live On Stage In Memphis**		[L]	$25	RCA Victor CPL-0606
11/2/74	130	7			69 **Having Fun with Elvis On Stage**		[T]	$25	RCA Victor CPM-0818
2/1/75	47	12		©	70 **Promised Land**			$25	RCA Victor APL-0873
6/7/75	57	13		©	71 **Today**			$25	RCA Victor APL-1039
2/7/76	46	17	▲²	©	72 **Elvis-A Legendary Performer, Volume 2**		[K]	$25	RCA Victor CPL-1349
4/17/76	76	11		©	73 **The Sun Sessions**		[E]	$20	RCA Victor APM-1675
					recorded from 1954-55				
6/5/76	41	17	●	©	74 **From Elvis Presley Boulevard, Memphis, Tennessee**			$20	RCA Victor APL-1506
4/16/77	44	25	▲		75 **Welcome To My World**		[K-L]	$20	RCA Victor APL-2274
					recordings from 1969-73				
7/23/77	3	31	▲²	©	76 **Moody Blue**			$15	RCA Victor AFL-2428
10/29/77	5	18	▲	©	77 **Elvis In Concert**		[TV]	$20	RCA Vic. APL-2587 [2]
					record 1: from the CBS-TV Special; record 2: from his final tour in June 1977				
5/13/78	113	8	●		78 **He Walks Beside Me**		[K]	$15	RCA Victor AFL-2772
					inspirational recordings from 1966-72				
8/5/78	130	11		©	79 **Elvis sings for Children and Grownups Too!**		[K]	$15	RCA Victor CPL-2901
					songs from his movies				
11/4/78	86	7			80 **Elvis-A Canadian Tribute**		[K]	$15	RCA Victor KKL-7065
1/6/79	113	11	●		81 **Elvis-A Legendary Performer, Volume 3**		[K]	$15	RCA Victor CPL-3082
3/10/79	132	7	●		82 **Our Memories of Elvis**		[K]	$15	RCA Victor AQL-3279
8/25/79	157	5			83 **Our Memories of Elvis, Volume 2**		[K]	$15	RCA Victor AQL-3448
8/23/80	27	14	▲	©	84 **Elvis Aron Presley**		[K]	$100	RCA Vic. CPL-3699 [8]
2/14/81	49	12			85 **Guitar Man**		[K]	$15	RCA Victor AAL-3917
					remixed versions of previously released recordings				
4/25/81	115	10			86 **This Is Elvis**		[K-S]	$20	RCA Vic. CPL-4031 [2]
12/19/81+	142	7			87 **Elvis-Greatest Hits, Volume One**		[K-L]	$15	RCA Victor AHL-2347
8/7/82+	32ᶜ	14	▲²	©	88 **Pure Gold**		[K]	$15	RCA Victor ANL-0971
11/27/82	133	9			89 **The Elvis Medley**		[K]	$15	RCA Victor AHL-4530
5/21/83	103	6			90 **I Was The One**		[K]	$15	RCA Victor AHL-4678
					recordings from 1956-60				
3/17/84	163	4			91 **Elvis: The First Live Recordings**		[E-L]	$15	Music Works 3601
					performances from the *Louisiana Hayride* (1955-56)				
11/17/84+	80	19		©	92 **Elvis - A Golden Celebration**		[K-L]	$50	RCA Vic. CPM-5172 [6]
					contains performances from various TV shows and other concert appearances from 1954-68				
12/8/84+	154	13		©	93 **Rocker**		[K]	$15	RCA Victor AFM-5182
					recordings from 1956-57				
3/2/85	154	3		©	94 **A Valentine Gift For You**		[K]	$15	RCA Victor AFL1-5353
					recordings from 1956-66				

Adam And Evil (34)
After Loving You (42,85,101,102)
Ain't That Loving You Baby (38,46,98) 16
All I Needed Was The Rain (41)
All Shook Up (9,40,43,46,59, 84,88,96,97,98,101,102) 1
All That I Am (34) 41
Almost (44)
Almost Always True (19)
Almost In Love (47) 95
Aloha Oe (19)
Always On My Mind (62,86,89,101,102)
Am I Ready (34,61)
Amazing Grace (84)
Amen (medley) (77,84)
America The Beautiful (84)
American Trilogy (59,63,68, 84,86,101,102) 66
And I Love You So (1,77,101)
And The Grass Won't Pay No Mind (43,48)
Angel (53,79)
Animal Instinct (31)
Any Day Now (42,54)
Anyone (Could Fall In Love With You) (27)
Anyplace Is Paradise (2,98,102)
Anything That's Part Of You (25,46,102) 31
Anyway You Want Me (That's How I Will Be) (9,46,98,102) 20
Are You Lonesome To-night? (25,43,46,66,77,84,86,92,94, 96,97,101,102) 1
Are You Sincere (65,82,101,104)
As Long As I Have You (10,54,98)
Ask Me (38,54) 12
Baby, I'll Give Me All Of Your Love (36)
Baby Let's Play House (12,73, 90,91,92,98,101,102)
Baby What You Want Me To Do (40,72,84,92,101)
Bad Nauheim Medley (101)
Barefoot Ballad (27)
Beach Boy Blues (19)
Beach Shack (34)
Because Of Love (22)
Beginner's Luck (32)
Beyond The Bend (24)
Beyond The Reef (84)
Big Boots (15,79)
Big Boss Man (37,40,60,102) 38
Big Hunk O' Love (13,46,63, 87,96,97,98,101,102) 1
Big Love Big Heartache (28)
Bitter They Are, Harder They Fall (74)
Blowin' In The Wind (101)
Blue Christmas (8,16,20,23,40, 72,84,92,95,98,99,100,103)
Blue Eyes Crying In The Rain (74,104)
Blue Hawaii (19,72)
Blue Moon (1,73,98,101) 55
Blue Moon Of Kentucky (12,73,92,98,104)
Blue River (36) 95
Blue Suede Shoes (1,15,43, 63,72,84,86,92,93,98,102) 20
Blueberry Hill (4,7,68,98,101)
Bosom Of Abraham (58,101)
Bossa Nova Baby (26,46,97,101) 8
Boy Like Me, A Girl Like You (22)

Bridge Over Troubled Water (49,101)
Bringing It Back (71) 65
Britches (81)
Bullfighter Was A Lady (26)
Burning Love (61,63,84, 87,89,97,101,102) 2
By And By (35)
Can't Help Falling In Love (19,40,43,46,59,63,66,68,77, 84,94,97,101,102) 2
Cane And A High Starched Collar (72)
Carny Town (28)
Catchin' On Fast (27)
Cattle Call (101)
Change Of Habit (44)
Charro (47)
Chesay (32)
Cindy, Cindy (52)
City By Night (36)
Clambake (37)
Clean Up Your Own Back Yard (47,85) 35
Come Along (32)
C'mon Everybody (53)
Confidence (37,60)
Cotton Candy Land (24,79)
Could I Fall In Love (36)
Crawfish (10,54,98)
Cross My Heart And Hope To Die (29)
Crying In The Chapel (35,46,81,97) 3
Danny (81,98)
Danny Boy (74,92,101)
Dark Moon (92)
Datin' (33,84)
Didja' Ever (15)
Dirty, Dirty Feeling (14)
Dixieland Rock (10,54,98)
Do Not Disturb (29)
Do The Clam (29) 21
Do The Vega (41)
Do You Know Who I Am? (43,48)
Dog's Life (33,84)
Doin' The Best I Can (15)
Don't (13,46,90,96,97,98, 101,102) 1
Don't Ask Me Why (10,54,98) 25
Don't Be Cruel (9,46,59,66, 77,84,86,88,89,92,96,97,98, 101,102) 1
Don't Cry Daddy (46,87,97,102) 6
Don't Leave Me Now (4,98)
Don't Think Twice, It's All Right (64,83)
Doncha' Think It's Time (13,54,98) 15
Double Trouble (36)
Down By The Riverside (medley) (32,60)
Down In The Alley (34,102)
Drums Of The Islands (33)
Early Morning Rain (57,77,80,104)
Earth Angel (Will You Be Mine) (92)
Earth Boy (22)
Easy Come, Easy Go (53)
Echoes Of Love (27)
Edge Of Reality (47)
El Toro (26)
Elvis Medley (89) 71
Evening Prayer (58,78)
Everybody Come Aboard (32)
Eyes Of Texas (medley) (41)
Faded Love (50,85)
Fair's Moving On (43,48)
Fairytale (71,77)

Fame And Fortune (25,54,81,94,101) 17
Farther Along (35)
Fever (14,63,88,94)
Find Out What's Happening (65,83)
Finders Keepers, Losers Weepers (20)
First In Line (2,98)
First Noel (56,99,100)
First Time Ever I Saw Your Face (84)
Five Sleepyheads (39,79)
Flaming Star (41) 14
Flip, Flop And Fly (medley) (68,86,92,101)
Follow That Dream (53,84) 15
Fool (64,84) flip
Fool, The (50,92)
Fool, Fool, Fool (98)
Fool Such As I ..see: (Now And Then There's) A
Fools Fall In Love (55)
Fools Rush In (Where Angels Fear To Tread) (57)
For Ol' Times Sake (65) flip
For The Good Times (59,75,101)
For The Heart (74,83,101,104) flip
For The Millionth And The Last Time (30)
Forget Me Never (30,62)
Fort Lauderdale Chamber Of Commerce (29)
Fountain Of Love (21)
Frankfort Special (15,81)
Frankie And Johnny (32,60) 25
From A Jack To A King (43,48,104)
Fun In Acapulco (26)
Funny How Time Slips Away (50,59,84,101,104)
G.I. Blues (15,86)
Gentle On My Mind (42,75,104)
Gently (18)
Get Back (medley) (84)
Girl Happy (29)
Girl I Never Loved (37)
Girl Next Door Went A'Walking (14)
Girl Of Mine (65,82)
Girl Of My Best Friend (14,102)
Girls! Girls! Girls! (22)
Give Me The Right (18,94)
Go East Young Man (31)
Goin' Home (39)
Golden Coins (31)
Gonna Get Back Home Somehow (21)
Good Luck Charm (25,46,96,97,102) 1
Good Rockin' Tonight (12,73,98,101,102)
Good Time Charlie's Got The Blues (67,104)
Got A Lot O' Livin' To Do! (4,5,54,98,102)
Got My Mojo Working (52)
Green Green Grass Of Home (71,83,104)
Greensleeves ..see: Stay Away
Guadalajara (26,61,81)
Guitar Man (37,40,60,101,102) 43
Guitar Man [re-mix] (85) 28
Happy Ending (24)
Harbor Lights (72,92,98)
Hard Headed Woman (10,46,89,96,97,98,102) 1
Hard Knocks (28)
Hard Luck (32)

Harem Holiday (31)
Have A Happy (44,79)
Have I Told You Lately That I Love You? (4,7,98,104)
Hawaiian Sunset (19)
Hawaiian Sweetheart) ..see: Ku-u-i-po
Hawaiian Wedding Song (19,77)
He Is My Everything (58,78)
He Touched Me (58,101)
He'll Have To Go (76,104)
He's Only A Prayer Away (92)
He's Your Uncle Not Your Dad (39)
Heart Of Rome (52)
Heartbreak Hotel (9,40,46,59, 66,84,86,89,92,96,97,98,101, 102) 1
Help Me (68,70)
Help Me Make It Through The Night (57,75)
Here Comes Santa Claus (Right Down Santa Claus Lane) (8,16,20,23,95, 98,100,103)
Hey, Hey, Hey (37)
Hey Jude (57)
Hey Little Girl (31)
Hi-Heel Sneakers (84)
His Hand In Mine (17,101)
Holly Leaves And Christmas Trees (56,100)
Home Is Where The Heart Is (55)
Hot Dog (4,5,54,98)
Hound Dog (9,40,43,46,59, 63,68,77,81,84,86,89,91,92, 93,96,97,98,101,102) 1
House Of Sand (19)
House That Has Everything (37)
How Can You Lose What You Never Had (37)
How Do You Think I Feel (2,98)
How Great Thou Art (35,68,72,77,78,84,101)
How The Web Was Woven (49)
How Would You Like To Be (24,60,79)
How's The World Treating You (2,98)
Hurt (74,77,101) 28
I Beg Of You (13,46,97,98) 8
I Believe (3,8,16,20,23,51,95,98)
I Believe In The Man In The Sky (17,54)
I Can Help (71,83)
I Can't Help It (If I'm Still In Love With You) (101)
I Can't Stop Loving You (43,59,63,68,75)
I Don't Care If The Sun Don't Shine (73,92,98) 74
I Don't Wanna Be Tied (22)
I Don't Want To (22)
I Feel So Bad (25,46,97,101) 5
I Feel That I've Known You Forever (21)
I Forgot To Remember To Forget (12,73,98,104)
I Got A Feelin' In My Body (67,83)
I Got A Woman (1,68,77, 84,88,92,93,98,101)
I Got Lucky (55)
I Got Stung (13,46,97,98) 8
I Gotta Know (25,46) 20
I, John (58)
I Just Can't Help Believin' (49,102)
I Love Only One Girl (36,61)

I Love You Because (1,66,73,98)
I Met Her Today (30,62)
I Miss You (65)
I Need Somebody To Lean On (55,94)
I Need You So (4,7,98)
I Need Your Love Tonight (13,54,84,86,97,98,101) 4
I Really Don't Want To Know (50,54,75,77,104) 21
I Slipped, I Stumbled, I Fell (18,62)
I Think I'm Gonna Like It Here (26)
I Wanna Play House With You ..see: Baby Let's Play House
I Want To Be Free (12,54,98)
I Want You, I Need You, I Love You (9,46,72,92,96, 97,98,101) 1
I Want You With Me (18)
I Was Born About Ten Thousand Years Ago (50,57)
I Was The One (11,46,90, 92,94,98,101) 19
I Washed My Hands In Muddy Water (50,101)
I Will Be Home Again (14)
I Will Be True (64,84)
I'll Be Back (34)
I'll Be Home For Christmas (8,16,20,23,95,98,99,100,103)
I'll Be Home On Christmas Day (56,100,101)
I'll Be There (If You Ever Want Me) (44)
I'll Hold You In My Heart (Till I Can Hold You In My Arms) (42,102)
I'll Never Fall In Love Again (74,82)
I'll Never Know (52)
I'll Never Let You Go (Little Darlin') (1,73,92,98)
I'll Never Stand In Your Way (101)
I'll Remember You (34,63,84)
I'll Take Love (53)
I'll Take You Home Again Kathleen (64,84)
I'm Beginning To Forget You (101)
I'm Comin' Home (18,101)
I'm Counting On You (1,98,101)
I'm Falling In Love Tonight (24,84)
I'm Gonna Sit Right Down And Cry (Over You) (1,98)
I'm Gonna Walk Dem Golden Stairs (17)
I'm Leavin' (84,102) 36
I'm Left, You're Right, She's Gone (11,73,92,98)
I'm Movin' On (42,80,85,104)
I'm Not The Marrying Kind (53)
I'm So Lonesome I Could Cry (63,75,104)
I'm Yours (21) 11
I've Got A Thing About You Baby (67,86,101,104) 39
I've Got Confidence (58)
I've Got To Find My Baby (59)
I've Lost You (49,54,102) 32
If Every Day Was Like Christmas (100,103)
If I Can Dream (40,46,72,78,101,102) 12
If I Get Home On Christmas Day (56,100)
If I Were You (52)
If I'm A Fool (For Loving You) (44)
If That Isn't Love (67)

If The Lord Wasn't Walking By My Side (35)
If We Never Meet Again (17)
If You Don't Come Back (65)
If You Love Me (Let Me Know) (76,77,84)
If You Talk In Your Sleep (70) 17
If You Think I Don't Need You (55)
Impossible Dream (The Quest) (59,78)
In My Father's House (17)
In My Way (30,62)
In The Garden (58)
In The Ghetto (42,43,46,81, 84,88,97,101,102) 3
In Your Arms (18)
Indescribably Blue (38) 33
Inherit The Wind (43,48)
Is It So Strange (7,12,62,98)
Island Of Love (19)
It Ain't No Big Thing (But It's Growing) (52)
It Feels So Right (14,94,101) 55
It Hurts Me (38,54,81,102) 29
It Is No Secret (What God Can Do) (3,8,16,20,23,51,95,98)
It Keeps Right On A-Hurtin' (42,104)
It Won't Be Long (36)
It Won't Seem Like Christmas (Without You) (56,100)
(It's A) Long Lonely Highway (27)
It's A Matter Of Time (61)
It's A Sin (18)
It's A Wonderful World (28)
It's Carnival Time (28)
It's Easy For You (76)
It's Impossible (64,88)
It's Midnight (70,82,101)
It's Now Or Never (25,46,72, 77,84,96,97,101,102) 1
It's Only Love (84) 51
It's Over (63)
It's Still Here (64,84)
It's Your Baby, You Rock It (50)
Ito Eats (19)
Jailhouse Rock (9,40,46,68, 72,77,80,84,86,88,89,93,96, 97,98,101,102) 1
Jesus Knows What I Need (17)
Johnny B. Goode (43,63,77,84,101)
Joshua Fit The Battle (17)
Judy (18) 78
Just A Little Bit (65)
Just Because (1,73,98)
Just Call Me Lonesome (37,85,104)
Just For Old Time Sake (21)
Just Pretend (49)
Just Tell Her Jim Said Hello (38,54) 55
Kentucky Rain (46,84,88,104) 16
King Creole (10,54,98)
King Of The Whole Wide World (53) 30
Kismet (81)
Kiss Me Quick (21) 34
Kissin' Cousins (27,46) 12
Kissin' Cousins (Number 2) (27)
Known Only To Him (17,78)
Ku-u-i-po (Hawaiian Sweetheart) (19)
Last Farewell (84)
Lawdy Miss Clawdy (11,40,68, 84,92,93,98,102)
Lead Me, Guide Me (58)
Let It Be Me (45,81)

PRESLEY, Elvis — Cont'd

Let Me (6,54,98)
Let Me Be There (68,76,84)
(Let Me Be Your) Teddy Bear
(4,9,46,59,77,79,80,84,86,
89,96,97,98,101,102) **1**
Let Us Pray (51)
Let Yourself Go (39,81) **71**
Let's Be Friends (44)
Let's Forget About The Stars
(44)
Life (52) **53**
Like A Baby (14,102)
Little Bit Of Green (43,48)
Little Cabin On The Hill (50)
Little Darlin' (76,80,84)
Little Egypt (28,40)
Little Less Conversation
(47) **69**
Little Sister (25,46,77,84,90,
97,102) **5**
Lonely Man (38,54) **32**
Lonesome Cowboy (4,5,54,98)
Long Black Limousine (42)
**Long Legged Girl (With The
Short Dress On)**
(36,47,60) **63**
Long Live Rock And Roll (84)
Long Tall Sally
(2,63,68,84,92,93,98)
Look Out, Broadway (32)
Love Coming Down (74)
Love Letters (38,52,94) **19**
Love Machine (51)
Love Me (2,9,54,59,63,66,
68,77,84,92,97,98,102) **2**
Love Me, Love The Life I Lead
(64)
Love Me Tender
(6,9,40,46,59,66,84,86,88,
92,96,97,98,101,102) **1**
Love Me Tonight (26)
Love Song Of The Year (70)
Lover Doll (10,54,98)
Lovin' Arms (67,85)
Loving You
(4,9,46,80,88,98) **20**
Make Me Know It (14)
Make The World Go Away
(50,75,104)
Mama (44)
Mama Don't Dance (medley)
(68)
Mama Liked The Roses (103)
Mansion Over The Hilltop (17)
Marguerita (26)
**(Marie's the Name) His Latest
Flame** (25,54,86,97,102) **4**
Mary In The Morning (49)
Maybellene (91,98)
Mean Woman Blues
(4,5,54,86,98)
Meanest Girl In Town (29)
Memories (40,86) **35**
Memphis, Tennessee (30,102)
Merry Christmas Baby
(56,86,100,102)
Mess Of Blues
(38,46,101,102) **32**
Mexico (26)
Milkcow Blues Boogie
(12,73,98)
Milky White Way (17,101)
Mine (39)
Miracle Of The Rosary
(57,78,101)
Mirage (31)
Money Honey
(1,84,92,93,98,101) **76**

Moody Blue
(76,86,101,104) **31**
Moonlight Swim (19)
Mr. Songman (70)
My Babe (43,84)
My Baby Left Me
(11,54,68,86,90,98,102) **31**
My Boy (67,82) **20**
My Desert Serenade (31)
My Happiness (98)
My Heart Cries For You (92)
My Little Friend (47)
My Way (63,77,80,84,86,
101) **22**
My Wish Came True
(13,54,98) **12**
Mystery Train (11,43,73,84,
98,101,102)
Never Again (74,82)
Never Been To Spain (59)
Never Ending (36)
Never Say Yes (34)
New Orleans (10,54,98,101)
Next Step Is Love (49,54) **flip**
Night Life (41)
Night Rider (21)
No More (19,61)
Nothingville (medley) (40)
**(Now And Then There's) A
Fool Such As I** (13,46,66,
84,97,98,102,104) **2**
O Come, All Ye Faithful
(56,99,100)
Oh How I Love Jesus (101)
In Little Town Of Bethlehem
(8,16,20,23,95,98,100,103)
Old MacDonald (36,60,79)
Old Shep (2,62,79,98,104) **47**
On A Snowy Christmas Night
(56,100)
Once Is Enough (27)
One Boy Two Little Girls (27)
One Broken Heart For Sale
(24,46) **11**
One Night (13,40,54,84,92,97,
98,102) **4**
One Night Of Sin (98)
One-Sided Love Affair (1,98)
One Track Heart (28)
Only Believe (52) **flip**
Only The Strong Survive
(42,102)
Padre (64,78)
Paradise, Hawaiian Style (33)
Paralyzed (2,54,90,98) **59**
Party (4,98)
Patch It Up (49,54) **flip**
Peace In The Valley ..see:
(There'll Be)
Petunia, The Gardener's
Daughter (32)
Pieces Of My Life (71)
Playing For Keeps
(11,46,94,98) **21**
Please Don't Drag That String
Around (38,54)
Please Don't Stop Loving Me
(32) **45**
Pledging My Love (76,101)
Pocketful Of Rainbows (15)
Poison Ivy League (28)
Polk Salad Annie
(45,59,84,102)
Poor Boy (6,11,54,98) **24**
Power Of My Love (42,101)
Promised Land
(70,86,101,102) **14**
Proud Mary (45,59)

Puppet On A String
(29,54,79) **14**
Put The Blame On Me (18)
Put Your Hand In The Hand
(57,80)
Queenie Wahine's Papaya (33)
Rags To Riches (84) **flip**
Raised On Rock (65) **41**
Reach Out To Jesus (58)
Ready Teddy (2,90,92,93,98)
Reconsider Baby
(14,84,98,101,102)
Relax (24)
Release Me (And Let Me Love
Again) (45,75,101)
Return To Sender
(22,46,97,101,102) **2**
Riding The Rainbow (55)
Rip It Up (2,54,90,93,98,101)
Rock-A-Hula Baby (19,46) **23**
Roustabout (28)
Rubberneckin' (47) **flip**
Run On (35,102)
Runaway (45)
Sand Castles (33)
Santa Bring My Baby Back
(To Me) (8,16,20,23,95,98,
100,103)
Santa Claus Is Back In Town
(8,16,20,23,95,98,100,102,
103)
Santa Lucia (30,61)
Saved (medley) (40)
Scratch My Back (Then I'll
Scratch Yours) (33)
See See Rider
(45,63,68,77,84,101)
Seeing Is Believing (58)
Sentimental Me (18,62)
Separate Ways (62,101) **20**
Shake A Hand (71)
Shake, Rattle And Roll
(11,86,92,93,98,101)
Shake That Tambourine (31)
She Thinks I Still Care
(76,82,85,104) **flip**
She Wears My Ring (67,83)
She's A Machine (41)
She's Not You
(25,46,97,102) **5**
Shoppin' Around (15,84)
Shout It Out (32)
Silent Night (8,16,20,23,95,
98,99,100,103)
Silver Bells (56,99,100)
Sing You Children (41)
Singing Tree (37)
Slicin' Sand (19)
Slowly But Surely (26)
Smokey Mountain Boy (27)
Smorgasbord (34)
Snowbird (30,84)
So Close, Yet So Far (From
Paradise) (31)
So Glad You're Mine (2,98)
So High (35)
Softly, As I Leave You (84)
Soldier Boy (14,92)
Solitaire (74,82)
Somebody Bigger Than You
And I (35,78)
Something (63)
Something Blue (21,101)
Song Of The Shrimp (22)
Sound Advice (30)
Sound Of Your Cry (87,101)
Spanish Eyes (67,82)
Speedway (39)

Spinout (34) **40**
Spring Fever (29)
Stand By Me (35)
Startin' Tonight (29)
Starting Today (18)
Stay Away, Joe (44,47)
Steadfast, Loyal And True
(10,98)
Steamroller Blues
(63,87,101) **17**
Steppin' Out Of Line (21)
Stop, Look And Listen (24)
Stop Where You Are (33)
Stranger In My Own Home
Town (43,48,102)
Stranger In The Crowd (49)
Stuck On You
(25,46,96,97,101,102) **1**
Such A Night
(14,72,84,102) **16**
(Such An) Easy Question
(21) **11**
Summer Kisses, Winter Tears
(30)
Suppose (39,92)
Surrender
(25,46,81,96,97,102) **1**
Susan When She Tried (71)
Suspicion (21)
Suspicious Minds
(43,46,59,63,84,86,87,89,
96,97,101,102) **1**
Sweet Angeline (65)
Sweet Caroline (45,84)
Swing Down Sweet Chariot
(17,84)
Sylvia (37)
Take Good Care Of Her
(67,82,101,104) **flip**
Take Me To The Fair (24)
Take My Hand, Precious Lord
(3,8,16,20,23,51,95,98)
Talk About The Good Times
(67)
Teddy Bear ..see: (Let Me Be
Your)
Tell Me Why (54,94,98) **33**
Tender Feeling (27,61)
Tennessee Waltz (101)
Thanks To The Rolling Sea
(22,84)
That's All Right (11,59,66,73,
77,84,86,91,92,98,101,102)
**That's Someone You Never
Forget** (21,102) **92**
(That's What You Get) For
Lovin' Me (64,80)
**That's When Your Heartaches
Begin** (9,46,98) **58**
There Ain't Nothing Like A Song
(39)
There Goes My Everything
(50,54,87,104) **flip**
There Is No God But God (58)
There Is So Much World To
See (36)
**(There'll Be) Peace In The
Valley (For Me)** (3,8,16,20,
23,51,66,92,95,98,101) **25**
There's A Brand New Day On
The Horizon (28)
There's A Honky Tonk Angel
(Who Will Take Me Back In)
(70,83)
There's Always Me (18) **56**
There's Gold In The Mountains
(27)
(There's) No Room To Rhumba
In A Sports Car (26)

They Remind Me Too Much
Of You (24,54,60,84) **53**
Thing Called Love (58)
Thinking About You (70,83)
This Is Living (53)
This Is My Heaven (33)
This Is Our Dance (52)
This Is The Story (43,48)
Thrill Of Your Love (14)
Tiger Man (41,43,84,92,
101,102)
Today, Tomorrow And Forever
(53)
Tomorrow Is A Long Time
(34,94,102)
Tomorrow Never Comes (50)
Tomorrow Night (30,98)
Tonight Is So Right For Love
(15,61,66,84,101)
Too Much (9,46,92,96,97,98) **1**
Too Much Monkey Business
(41,85,86)
Treat Me Nice (9,46,98,102) **18**
T-R-O-U-B-L-E
(71,84,101,102) **35**
Trouble (10,40,54,98)
True Love (4,98)
True Love Travels On A Gravel
Road (42)
Tryin' To Get To You (1,66,68,
73,77,84,92,98,101,102)
Tutti Frutti (1,92,93,98)
Tweedle Dee (91,98)
Twenty Days And Twenty
Nights (49)
U.S. Male (47) **28**
Unchained Melody (76,84)
Until It's Time For You To Go
(57,80) **40**
Up Above My Head (medley)
(40)
Vino, Dinero Y Amor (26)
Viva Las Vegas (46,86) **29**
Walk A Mile In My Shoes (45)
Walls Have Ears (22)
Way Down (76,83,101) **18**
We Call On Him (51)
We Can Make The Morning
(57)
We'll Be Together (22,61)
We're Coming In Loaded (22)
We're Gonna Move (6,12,54,98)
**Wear My Ring Around Your
Neck** (13,46,90,97,98,102) **2**
Wearin' That Loved On Look
(42)
Welcome To My World
(63,75,84,104)
Western Union (39)
What A Wonderful Life (55)
What Every Woman Lives For
(32)
What Now My Love (63)
What Now, What Next, Where
To (36,62)
What'd I Say (38,77,87,101) **21**
What's She Really Like (15)
Wheels On My Heels (28)
When I'm Over You (52)
When It Rains, It Really Pours
(30,92,98)
**When My Blue Moon Turns
To Gold Again**
(2,54,92,98,101,104) **19**
When The Saints Go Marching
In (32,60,101)

Where Could I Go But To The
Lord (35,40)
Where Did They Go, Lord
(78) **33**
Where Do I Go From Here (64)
Where Do You Come From
(22,46) **99**
Where No One Stands Alone
(35)
Whistling Tune (53)
White Christmas (8,16,20,23,
95,98,99,100,103)
Who Am I? (51,78)
Who Are You? (Who Am I?)
(39)
Who Needs Money (37)
Whole Lot-ta Shakin' Goin' On
(50,63,68)
Why Me Lord (68,84)
Wild In The Country
(54,84) **26**
Winter Wonderland (56,99,100)
Wisdom Of The Ages (31)
Witchcraft (38,54) **32**
Without Him (35)
Without Love (There Is Nothing)
(43,48)
Wolf Call (29)
Woman Without Love (71)
Wonder Of You
(45,54,84,87,97,101,102) **9**
Wonderful World (41)
Wonderful World Of Christmas
(56,100)
Wooden Heart (15,46,79)
Words (43,101)
Working On The Building (17)
World Of Our Own (24)
Write To Me From Naples (92)
Yellow Rose Of Texas (medley)
(41)
Yesterday (45,84)
Yoga Is As Yoga Does (55)
You Asked Me To (70,85)
You Can't Say No In Acapulco
(26)
**You Don't Have To Say
You Love Me**
(49,54,59,101,102) **11**
You Don't Know Me
(37,60,104) **44**
You Gave Me A Mountain
(63,77,84)
You Gotta Stop (55)
You'll Be Gone (29)
You'll Never Walk Alone
(51,87,101) **90**
You'll Think Of Me (43,48,54)
You're A Heartbreaker
(11,73,98)
**(You're So Square) Baby I Don't
Care** (12,54,90,93,98,102)
(You're the) Devil In Disguise
(38,46,97,102) **3**
You've Lost That Lovin' Feelin'
(49,59,84)
Young And Beautiful
(12,54,90,94,98)
Young Dreams (10,54,98)
Your Cheatin' Heart
(30,75,98,104)
Your Love's Been A Long Time
Coming (70,82)
**Your Time Hasn't Come Yet,
Baby** (39) **72**

★462★

PRESTON, Billy '73
Born on 9/9/46 in Houston. R&B singer/keyboardist. Prolific session musician. Regular on *Shindig* TV show. Appeared in the 1978 movie *Sgt. Pepper's Lonely Hearts Club Band*.
1)The Kids & Me 2)I Wrote A Simple Song 3)Music Is My Life

DEBUT	PEAK	WKS	CD		ARTIST — Album Title	Sym	$	Label & Number
6/12/65	143	3		1	The Most Exciting Organ Ever	[I]	$40	Vee-Jay 1123
7/9/66	118	6		2	Wildest Organ In Town!	[I]	$40	Vee-Jay 2532
1/22/72	32	38	©	3	I Wrote A Simple Song		$15	A&M 3507
6/10/72	127	12	©	4	That's The Way God Planned It	[E]	$20	Apple 3359
					originally released in 1969; produced by **George Harrison**			
12/23/72+	32	35		5	Music Is My Life		$12	A&M 3516
10/27/73	52	18		6	Everybody Likes Some Kind Of Music		$12	A&M 3526
9/21/74	17	14		7	The Kids & Me		$12	A&M 3645
7/19/75	43	14		8	It's My Pleasure		$12	A&M 4532
3/8/80	49	18		9	Late At Night		$12	Motown 925
8/8/81	127	9		10	Billy Preston & Syreeta		$12	Motown 958

PRESTON, Billy — Cont'd

Advice (2)
Ain't Got No Time To Play (2)
Ain't That Nothin' (5)
All I Wanted Was You (9)
All Of My Life (8)
Billy's Bag (1)
Blackbird (5)
Bus, The (3)
Creature Feature (7)
Do It While You Can (8)
Do What You Want (4)
Do You Love Me? (6)
Don't Let The Sun Catch You Crying (4)
Drown In My Tears (1)
Duck, The (2)
Everybody Likes Some Kind Of Music (6)
Everything's All Right (4)
Fancy Lady (8) *71*

Found The Love (8)
Free Funk (2)
Give It Up, Hot (9)
God Is Great (3)
God Loves You (5)
Hard Day's Night (2)
Heart Full Of Sorrow (5)
Hey Brother (4)
Hey You (10)
How Long Has The Train Been Gone (6)
I Am Coming Through (1)
(I Can't Get No) Satisfaction (2)
I Can't Stand It (8)
I Come To Rest In You (9)
I Got You (I Feel Good) (8)
I Want To Thank You (4)
I Wonder Why (5)
I Wrote A Simple Song (3) *77*
I'm So Tired (9)

If I Had A Hammer (1)
"In" Crowd (2)
In The Midnight Hour (2)
It Doesn't Matter (4)
It Will Come In Time (9)
It's Alright Ma (I'm Only Bleeding) (6)
It's Got To Happen (2)
It's My Pleasure (8)
It's So Easy (10)
John Henry (3)
John The Baptist (7)
Just For You (10)
Keep It To Yourself (4)
Late At Night (9)
Let Me Know (1)
Let Us All Get Together Right Now (4)
Listen To The Wind (6)
Little Black Boys And Girls (7)

Long And Lasting Love (10)
Looner Tune (3)
Love (10)
Love Makes Me Do Foolish Things (2)
Lovely Lady (9)
Low Down (1)
Make The Devil Mad (Turn On To Jesus) (5)
Masquerade Is Over (1)
Minuet For Me (6)
Morning Star (4)
Music's My Life (5)
My Country 'Tis Of Thee (3)
My Soul Is A Witness (6)
New Way To Say I Love You (10)
Nigger Charlie (5)
Nothing From Nothing (7) *1*
Octopus, The (1)

One More Try (10)
One Time Or Another (5)
Outa-Space (3) *2*
Sad Sad Song (9)
Searchin' (10)
She Belongs To Me (4)
Should've Known Better (3)
Sister Sugar (7)
Slippin' And Slidin' (1)
Sock-It, Rocket (9)
Someone Special (10)
Sometimes I Love You (7)
Song Of Joy (8)
Soul Meetin' (1)
Space Race (6) *4*
St. Elmo (7)
Steady Gettin' It (1)
Struttin' (7) *22*
Sunday Morning (6)
Swing Down Chariot (3)

Tell Me You Need My Loving (7)
That's Life (8)
That's The Way God Planned It (4) *62*
This Is It (4)
Uptight (Everything's Alright) (2)
We're Gonna Make It (5)
What About You (4)
What We Did For Love (10)
Will It Go Round In Circles (5) *1*
With You I'm Born Again (9) *4*
Without A Song (3)
You (9)
You Are So Beautiful (7)
You Done Got Older (3)
You're So Unique (6) *48*
You've Got Me For Company (6)

★313★   PRETENDERS, The   '84

Pop-rock group formed in England: Chrissie Hynde (vocals, guitar; born on 9/7/51 in Akron, Ohio), James Honeyman-Scott (guitar), Pete Farndon (bass) and Martin Chambers (drums). Honeyman-Scott died of a drug overdose on 6/16/82 (age 25); replaced by Robbie McIntosh (of **Night**). Fardon died of a drug overdose on 4/14/83 (age 30); replaced by Malcolm Foster. Hynde was married to Jim Kerr of **Simple Minds** from 1984-90. Lineup in 1994: Hynde, Chambers, Adam Seymour (guitar) and Andy Hobson (bass). Tom Kelly replaced Hobson in 1998.

1)Learning To Crawl 2)Pretenders 3)Pretenders II

DEBUT	PEAK	WKS	RIAA	CD	ALBUM	Catalog	Sym	$	Label & Number
1/26/80	9	78	▲	© 1	Pretenders	C:#10/8		$12	Sire 6083
4/18/81	27	29		2	Extended Play	C:#4/137	[M]	$12	Sire 3563
8/29/81	10	19	●	© 3	Pretenders II			$12	Sire 3572
2/4/84	5	42	▲	© 4	Learning To Crawl			$10	Sire 23980
11/15/86	25	29		© 5	Get Close			$10	Sire 25488
12/5/87	69	15	●	© 6	The Singles		[G]	$10	Sire 25664
6/9/90	48	17		© 7	packed!			$10	Sire 26219
5/28/94	41	22	●	© 8	Last Of The Independents			$10	Warner 45572
11/11/95	100	5		© 9	The Isle Of View		[L]	$10	Warner 46085
7/10/99	158	2		© 10	¡Viva El Amor!			$10	Warner 47342

Adultress, The (3)
All My Dreams (8)
Baby's Breath (10)
Back On The Chain Gang (4,6,9) *5*
Bad Boys Get Spanked (3)
Biker (10)
Birds Of Paradise (3)
Brass In Pocket (I'm Special) (1,6,9) *14*
Chill Factor (5,9)
Criminal (7,9)
Cuban Slide (2)
Dance! (1)
Day After Day (3,6)

Don't Get Me Wrong (5,6) *10*
Downtown (Akron) (7)
Dragway 42 (1)
English Roses (3)
Every Mothers' Son (8)
Forever Young (8)
From The Heart Down (10)
Hold A Candle To This (7)
Hollywood Perfume (8)
How Do I Miss You (7)
How Much Did You Get For Your Soul? (5)
Human (7)
Hymn To Her (5,6,9)
I Go To Sleep (3,6,9)

I Got You Babe [UB40 w/Chrissie Hynde]* (6) *28*
I Hurt You (4,9)
I Remember You (5)
I'll Stand By You (8) *16*
I'm A Mother (8)
Jealous Dogs (3)
Kid (1,6,9)
Legalise Me (10)
Let's Make A Pact (7)
Light Of The Moon (5)
Louie Louie (3)
Love Colours (8)
Lovers Of Today (1,9)
May This Be Love (7)

Message Of Love (2,3,6)
Middle Of The Road (4,6) *19*
Millionaires (8)
Money Talk (8)
My Baby (5,6) *64*
My City Was Gone (4)
Mystery Achievement (1)
Nails In The Road (10)
Never Do That (7)
Night In My Veins (8) *71*
977 (8)
No Guarantee (7)
One More Time (10)
Pack It Up (3)
Phone Call (1,9)

Popstar (10)
Porcelain (3)
Precious (1,2)
Private Life (1,9)
Rabo De Nube (8)
Rebel Rock Me (8)
Revolution (8,9)
Room Full Of Mirrors (5)
Samurai (10)
Sense Of Purpose (7,9)
Show Me (4,6) *28*
Space Invader (1)
Stop Your Sobbing (1,6) *65*
Talk Of The Town (2,3,6)
Tattooed Love Boys (1)

Tequila (8)
Thin Line Between Love And Hate (4,6) *83*
Thumbelina (4)
Time The Avenger (4)
Tradition Of Love (5)
2000 Miles (4,6,9)
Up The Neck (1)
Wait, The (1)
Waste Not Want Not (3)
Watching The Clothes (4)
When I Change My Life (5)
When Will I See You (7)
Who's Who (10)

PRETTY BOY FLOYD   '90

Male hard-rock group: Steve Summers (vocals), Kristy Majors (guitar), Vinnie Chas (bass) and Kari Kane (drums).

DEBUT	PEAK	WKS		CD	ALBUM			$	Label & Number
3/24/90	130	9		©	Leather Boyz With Electric Toyz			$10	MCA 6341

48 Hours
I Wanna Be With You
Last Kiss

Leather Boyz With Electric Toyz
Only The Young

Rock & Roll (Is Gonna Set The Night On Fire)
Rock And Roll Outlaws

Toast Of The Town
Wild Angels
Your Mama Won't Know

PRETTY MAIDS   '87

Hard-rock group formed in Denmark: Ronnie Atkins (vocals), Ken Hammer (guitar), Alan Owen (keyboards), Allan Delong (bass) and Phil Moorhead (drums).

DEBUT	PEAK	WKS		CD	ALBUM			$	Label & Number
6/20/87	165	8		©	Future World			$10	Epic 40713

Eye Of The Storm
Future World

Long Way To Go
Loud 'N' Proud

Love Games
Needles In The Dark

Rodeo
We Came To Rock

Yellow Rain

PRETTY POISON   '88

Dance group from Philadelphia: Jade Starling (vocals), Whey Cooler (keyboards), Louie Franco (guitar) and Bobby Corea (drums).

DEBUT	PEAK	WKS		CD	ALBUM			$	Label & Number
4/30/88	104	8		©	Catch Me I'm Falling			$10	Virgin 90885

Catch Me (I'm Falling) *8*
Closer

Don't Cry Baby
Heaven

Hold Me
Let Freedom Ring

Look, The
Nightime *36*

Shine
When I Look Into Your Eyes

PRETTY THINGS   '75

Rock group from England: Jack Green (vocals), Pete Tolson (guitar; **T. Rex**), Phil May (percussion), John Povey (keyboards), Gordon Edwards (bass) and Skip Alan (drums).

DEBUT	PEAK	WKS		CD	ALBUM			$	Label & Number
3/1/75	104	9		© 1	Silk Torpedo			$15	Swan Song 8411
2/21/76	163	6		© 2	Savage Eye			$15	Swan Song 8414

Atlanta (1)
Belfast Cowboys (1)
Bridge Of God (1)
Bruise In The Sky (1)

Come Home Momma (1)
Dream (1)
Drowned Man (2)
I'm Keeping (2)

Is It Only Love (1)
It Isn't Rock 'N' Roll (2)
It's Been So Long (2)
Joey (1)

L.A.N.T.A. (1)
Maybe You Tried (1)
Michelle, Theme For (2)
My Song (2)

Remember That Boy (2)
Sad Eye (2)
Singapore Silk Torpedo (1)
Under The Volcano (2)

PREVIN, Andre '59

Born on 4/6/29 in Berlin. Pianist/conductor/arranger/composer. Musical director for several MGM movies. In the 1970s, served as resident conductor of the **London Symphony Orchestra**. Married to actress Mia Farrow from 1970-79.

6/29/59	16	21			1 **Secret Songs For Young Lovers**	[I]	$25	MGM 3716
7/4/60+	25	28		©	2 **Like Love**..........	[I]	$20	Columbia 1437
10/16/61	118	9			3 **A Touch Of Elegance**..........	[I]	$20	Columbia 8449
11/30/63	130	4			4 **Andre Previn in Hollywood**..........	[I]	$20	Columbia 8834
12/19/64	147	4			5 **My Fair Lady**..........	[I]	$20	Columbia 8995
3/14/81	149	9			6 **A Different Kind Of Blues**..........	[I]	$12	Angel 37780

ITZHAK PERLMAN/ANDRE PREVIN

At Long Last Love (2)
Best Years Of Our Lives, Theme From (4)
Blame It On My Youth (1)
Chocolate Apricot (6)
Different Kind Of Blues (6)
Falling In Love Again (2)
Fascination (4)
Five Of Us (6)
Get Me To The Church On Time (5)
Gigi (4)
Hi-Lili, Hi-Lo (4)

I Could Have Danced All Night (5)
I Got It Bad (And That Ain't Good) (3)
I Let A Song Go Out Of My Heart (3)
I Love A Piano (2)
I Wish I Were In Love Again (3)
I'm A Dreamer, Aren't We All? (4)
I'm An Ordinary Man (5)
I've Grown Accustomed To Her Face (5)
In Love In Vain (2)

Irma La Douce (Look Again), Theme From (4)
It Don't Mean A Thing (If It Ain't Got That Swing) (3)
It Might As Well Be Spring (4)
Last Night When We Were Young (1)
Last Time I Saw Paris (4)
Laura (4)
Le Sucrier Velours (3)
Like Love (2)
Like Someone In Love (2)
Like Young (1) *46*
Little Face (6)

Look At Him Go (6)
Looking For Love (2)
Love Is For The Very Young (1)
Love Is Here To Stay (2)
Love Me Or Leave Me (2)
Make Up Your Mind (6)
Night Thoughts (6)
Nothin' To Do With Love (2)
On The Street Where You Live (5)
Perdido (5)
Portrait Of Bert Williams (3)
Prelude To A Kiss (3)
Rain In Spain (5)

Satin Doll (3)
Second Time Around (4)
Solitude (5)
Sophisticated Lady (3)
Too Young To Be True (1)
Too Young To Go Steady (1)
Touch Of Elegance (3)
Two For The Seesaw (A Second Chance), Song From (4)
We Kiss In A Shadow (4)
What Am I Here For (3)
When I Fall In Love (2)
While We're Young (1)

Who Reads Reviews (6)
With A Little Bit Of Luck (5)
Without You (5)
Wouldn't It Be Loverly (5)
Year Of Youth (1)
You Did It (5)
You Make Me Feel So Young (1)
Young And Tender (1)
Young Man's Lament (1)
Younger Than Springtime (1)

PRICE, Alan '73

Born on 4/19/42 in Fairfield, Durham, England. Organist with **The Animals**; left in 1965; rejoined group in 1983.

| 8/11/73 | 117 | 14 | | © | 1 **O Lucky Man!**.......... | [S] | $15 | Warner 2710 |
| 11/19/77 | 187 | 3 | | © | 2 **Alan Price**.......... | | $12 | Jet 809 |

Arrival (1)
Changes (1)
I Wanna Dance (2)

I'm A Gambler (2)
I've Been Hurt (2)
Is It Right (2)

Just For You (2)
Justice (1)
Let Yourself Go (2)
Life Is Good (2)

Look Over Your Shoulder (1)
My Home Town (1)
O Lucky Man! (1)
Pastoral (1)

Poor Boy (2)
Poor People (1)
Rainbow's End (2)
Same Love (2)

Sell Sell (1)
Thrill, The (2)

PRICE, Kelly '00

Born in New York City. Female R&B singer.

| 8/29/98 | 15 | 35 | ▲ | © | 1 **Soul Of A Woman**.......... | | $10 | Island 524516 |
| 7/15/00 | 5 | 30 | ▲ | © | 2 **Mirror Mirror**.......... | | $10 | Def Soul 542472 |

All I Want Is You (2)
As We Lay (2) *65*
At Least (The Little Things) (2)
Can't Run Away (2)
Don't Say Goodbye (1)

Friend Of Mine (1) *12*
Good Love (2)
Her (1)
I Know Who Holds Tomorrow (2)

Kiss Test (1)
Like You Do (2)
Lord Of All (1)
Love Sets You Free (2) *91*

Lullaby, The (2)
Married Man (2)
Mirror Mirror (2)
Secret Love (1)

She Wants You (2)
Soul Of A Woman (1)
Take Me To A Dream (1)
3 Strikes (2)

You Complete Me (1)
You Should've Told Me (2) *64*
Your Love (1)

PRICE, Leontyne '63

Born on 2/10/27 in Laurel, Mississippi. Legendary opera soprano. Won Grammy's Lifetime Achievement Award in 1989.

12/18/61+	55	5			1 **A Christmas Offering**..........	[X]	$25	London 25280
					Christmas chart: 23/'63			
12/29/62	128	1			2 **A Christmas Offering**..........	[X-R]	$25	London 25280
4/27/63	29	12			3 **Giacomo Puccini: Madama Butterfly**	[F]	$40	RCA Victor 6160 [3]
9/7/63	79	6			4 **Giacomo Puccini: Tosca**	[F]	$30	RCA Victor 7022 [2]
10/5/63	66	16			5 **Great Scenes from Gershwin's "Porgy And Bess"**		$25	RCA Victor 2679
10/31/64	147	3			6 **Georges Bizet: Carmen**	[F]	$40	RCA Victor 6164 [3]

Alleluja (1,2)
Angels We Have Heard On High (1,2)
Ave Maria (1,2)
Bess, You Is My Woman (5)
Carmen (Acts I thru IV) (6)

God Rest Ye Merry, Gentlemen (1,2)
Gone, Gone, Gone (5)
Hark! The Herald Angels Sing (1,2)
I Got Plenty O' Nuttin' (5)

I Loves You, Porgy (5)
It Ain't Necessarily So (5)
It Came Upon The Midnight Clear (1,2)
Madama Butterfly (Acts I thru III) (3)

O Holy Night (1,2)
O Tannenbaum (1,2)
Oh Bess, Oh Where's My Bess (5)
Oh Lawd, I'm On My Way (5)
Silent Night (1,2)

Summertime (medley) (5)
Sweet Little Jesus Boy (1,2)
There's A Boat Dat's Leavin Soon For New York (5)
Tosca (Acts I thru III) (4)
Vom Himmel Hoch (1,2)

We Three Kings Of Orient Are (1,2)
What You Want Wid Bess? (5)
Woman Is A Sometime Thing (medley) (5)

PRICE, Ray '71

Born on 1/12/26 in Perryville, Texas; raised in Dallas. Country singer. Known as "The Cherokee Cowboy."

3/4/67	129	12			1 **Touch My Heart**..........		$20	Columbia 2606 / 9406
6/10/67	106	17			2 **Danny Boy**..........		$20	Columbia 2677 / 9477
9/12/70+	28	59	●		3 **For The Good Times**..........		$15	Columbia 30106
6/12/71	49	24			4 **I Won't Mention It Again**..........		$15	Columbia 30510
12/4/71	146	5			5 **Welcome To My World**..........	[K]	$20	Columbia 30878 [2]
7/29/72	145	12			6 **The Lonesomest Lonesome**..........		$15	Columbia 31546
9/9/72	165	10	●		7 **Ray Price's All-Time Greatest Hits**..........	[G]	$20	Columbia 31364 [2]
4/21/73	161	7			8 **She's Got To Be A Saint**..........		$15	Columbia 32033
6/14/80	70	25	●	©	9 **San Antonio Rose**..........		$12	Columbia 36476

WILLIE NELSON and RAY PRICE

Across The Wide Missouri (2)
Am I That Easy To Forget (1)
April's Fool (7)
Black And White Lies (3)
Born To Lose (2)
Bridge Over Troubled Water (4,7)
Burden Of Freedom (4)
Burning Memories (5)
But I Was Lying (6)
By The Time I Get To Phoenix (5,7)
City Lights (5) *71*
Cold, Cold Heart (4)
Cold Day In July (3)

Crazy (2)
Crazy Arms (3,5,7,9) *67*
Danny Boy (2,7) *60*
Deep Water (9)
Don't You Ever Get Tired (Of Hurting Me) (9)
Empty Chairs (6)
Enough For You (8)
Enough To Lie (1)
Everything That's Beautiful (Reminds Me Of You) (8)
Faded Love (9)
For The Good Times (3,7) *11*
Forgive Her (4)

Funny How Time Slips Away (5,9)
Goin' Away (8)
Gonna Burn Some Bridges (3)
Grazin' In Greener Pastures (3)
Greensleeves (3)
Heartaches By The Number (3,5,7)
Help Me (8)
Help Me Make It Through The Night (3,5)
I Can't Help It (If I'm Still In Love With You) (5)
I Fall To Pieces (9)
I Keep Looking Back (8)

I Lie A Lot (1)
I Won't Mention It Again (4,7) *42*
(I'd Be) A Legend In My Time (5)
I'd Rather Be Sorry (4,7) *70*
I'll Be There (If You Ever Want Me) (5)
I'll Go To A Stranger (3)
It's Only Love (1)
Jesse Younger (4)
Just For The Record (1)
Just The Other Side Of Nowhere (6)
Kiss The World Goodbye (4)

Last Letter (5)
Little Green Apples (5,7)
Lonely World (3,7)
Lonesomest Lonesome (6)
Loving Her Was Easier (4,7)
Make The World Go Away (5) *100*
My Baby's Gone (8)
Night Life (5,9)
Nobody Wins (8)
Oh, Lonesome Me (6)
One Night To Remember (6)
Over (6)
Pretend (2)
Pride (5)

Release Me (1)
Same Two Lips (1)
San Antonio Rose (9)
She Wears My Ring (7)
She's Got To Be A Saint (8) *93*
Soft Rain (2)
Spanish Eyes (2)
Sunday (9)
Sunday Morning Comin' Down (4,7)
Sweet Memories (4,7)
Sweetest Tie (8)
Sweetheart Of The Year (7)

PRICE, Ray — Cont'd

Swinging Doors (Swang In Doors) (1)
Take Me As I Am (Or Let Me Go) (7)
Take These Chains From My Heart (5)
That's What Leaving's About (6)
There Goes My Everything (1)
This Cold War With You (9)
This House (6)
Time (Old Faithful Friend Of Mine) (6)
Touch My Heart (1)
Turn Around, Look At Me (8)
Unloved, Unwanted (5)
Vaya Con Dios (2,5)
Wake Up Yesterday (6)
Way To Survive (1)
Welcome To My World (5)
What's Come Over My Baby (2)
When I Loved Her (4,7)
Yesterday (5,7)
You Can't Take It With You (3)
You Took My Happy Away (1)
You Wouldn't Know Love (7)

★263★ PRIDE, Charley '69

Born on 3/18/38 in Sledge, Mississippi. Black country singer.

1)Just Plain Charley 2)The Best Of Charley Pride 3)Charley Pride's 10th Album

DEBUT	PEAK	WKS	CD	#	ARTIST — Album Title	Sym	$	Label & Number
3/30/68	199	2	●	1	The Country Way		$25	RCA Victor 3895
2/15/69	62	43	● ©	2	Charley Pride-In Person	[L]	$20	RCA Victor 4094
					recorded at Panther Hall in Fort Worth, Texas			
6/28/69	44	39	● ©	3	The Sensational Charley Pride		$20	RCA Victor 4153
11/1/69	24	65	● ©	4	The Best Of Charley Pride	[G]	$20	RCA Victor 4223
2/28/70	22	27	●	5	Just Plain Charley		$20	RCA Victor 4290
7/18/70	30	38	●	6	Charley Pride's 10th Album		$20	RCA Victor 4367
12/12/70+	5ˣ	9		7	Christmas in My Home Town	[X]	$20	RCA Victor 4406
					Christmas charts: 8/'70, 5/'71, 8/'72, 15/'73			
2/6/71	42	26	●	8	From Me To You		$20	RCA Victor 4468
4/17/71	76	15	●	9	Did You Think To Pray		$20	RCA Victor 4513
7/24/71	50	19		10	I'm Just Me		$20	RCA Victor 4560
12/4/71+	38	26	●	11	Charley Pride Sings Heart Songs		$20	RCA Victor 4617
3/18/72	50	15	● ©	12	The Best Of Charley Pride, Volume 2	[G]	$20	RCA Victor 4682
8/19/72	115	15		13	A Sunshiny Day with Charley Pride		$20	RCA Victor 4742
1/6/73	189	8		14	The Incomparable Charley Pride	[K]	$15	RCA Camden 2584
2/17/73	149	8		15	Songs of Love by Charley Pride		$15	RCA Victor 4837
7/28/73	166	6		16	Sweet Country		$15	RCA Victor 0217
1/22/77	188	2		17	The Best Of Charley Pride, Vol. III	[G]	$12	RCA Victor 2023
11/21/81	185	7		18	Greatest Hits	[G]	$12	RCA Victor 4151

Able Bodied Man (6)
Act Naturally (1)
All I Have To Offer You (Is Me) (4) 91
Along The Mississippi (16)
Amazing Love (17)
Angel Band (9)
Anywhere (Just Inside Your Arms) (11,14)
Back To The Country Roads (13)
Before I Met You (4)
Billy Bayou (3)
Brand New Bed Of Roses (5)
Burgers And Fries (18)
Christmas And Love (7)
Christmas In My Home Town (7)
Church In The Wildwood (9)
Come On Home And Sing The Blues To Daddy (3)
Cotton Fields (2)
Crystal Chandelier (1,2)
(Darlin' Think Of Me) Every Now And Then (15)
Day The World Stood Still (1,4)
Deck The Halls (With Boughs Of Holly) (7)
Did You Think To Pray (9)
Does My Ring Hurt Your Finger (1,4)
Don't Fight The Feelings Of Love (16,17)
Easy Part's Over (4)
Even After Everything She's Done (3)
Fifteen Years Ago (8)

First Christmas Morn (7)
Give A Lonely Heart A Home (15)
Gone, Gone, Gone (5)
Gone, On The Other Hand (1,4)
Good Chance Of Tear-Fall Tonight (5)
Good Hearted Woman (15)
Got Leavin' On Her Mind (2)
Happiest Song On The Jukebox (16)
Happiness Of Having You (17)
Happy Christmas Day (7)
Happy Street (5)
Hello Darlin' (10)
Honky Tonk Blues (18)
Hope You're Feelin' Me (Like I'm Feelin' You) (17)
I Ain't All Bad (17)
I Can't Believe That You've Stopped Loving Me (8) *71*
I Don't Deserve A Mansion (17)
I Know One (2,4)
I Love You More In Memory (15)
I Think I'll Take A Walk (6)
I Threw Away The Rose (1)
I'd Rather Love You (10,12,14) *79*
I'll Fly Away (9)
I'll Wander Back To You (1)
I'm A Lonesome Fugitive (5)
I'm Beginning To Believe My Own Lies (11)
I'm Building Bridges (15)

I'm Just Me (10,12) *94*
I'm Learning To Love Her (16)
(I'm So) Afraid Of Losing You Again (5,12) *74*
If You Had Only Taken The Time (5)
Image Of Me (4)
(In My World) You Don't Belong (10,12)
Instant Loneliness (10,14)
Is Anybody Goin' To San Antone (6,12) *70*
It's All Right (3)
It's Gonna Take A Little Bit Longer (13)
(It's Just A Matter Of) Making Up My Mind (3)
It's The Little Things (3)
Jeanie Norman (11,14)
Jesus, Don't Give Up On Me (9)
Just Between You And Me (2,4)
Just To Be Loved By You (16)
Kaw-Liga (2,4)
Kiss An Angel Good Mornin' (11,12) *21*
Last Thing On My Mind (2)
Let Me Live (9,12)
Let Me Live Again (3)
Let The Chips Fall (3,4)
Life Turned Her That Way (1)
Little Drummer Boy (7)
Little Folks (1)
Lord, Build Me A Cabin In Glory (9)
Louisiana Man (3)
Love Unending (16)
Lovesick Blues (2)

Mama Don't Cry For Me (1)
Me And Bobby McGee (5)
Miracles, Music And My Wife (11)
Missin' You (18)
Mississippi Cotton Picking Delta Town (17) *70*
My Eyes Can Only See As Far As You (17)
My Love Is Deep, My Love Is Wide (11)
Never Been So Loved (In All My Life) (18)
Never More Than I (3)
No One Could Ever Take Me From You (11)
Nothin' Left But Leavin' (13)
O Holy Night (7)
Oklahoma Morning (17)
On The Southbound (10)
Once Again (11)
One More Year (13)
One Time (5)
Pass Me By (16)
Pirogue Joe (8,14)
Place For The Lonesome (10,12)
Poor Boy Like Me (6)
Pretty House For Sale (11)
Put Back My Ring On Your Hand (13)
Roll On Mississippi (18)
Santa And The Kids (7)
Searching For The Morning Sun (17)
Sentimental 'Ol Me (5)
Seven Years With A Wonderful Woman (13)

She's Helping Me Get Over You (13)
She's Just An Old Love Turned Memory (18)
She's Still Got A Hold On You (3)
She's That Kind (15)
She's Too Good To Be True (15)
Shelter Of Your Eyes (16)
Shoulder To Cry On (16)
Shutters And Boards (2)
Silent Night (7)
Six Days On The Road (2)
Snakes Crawl At Night (4)
Someone Loves You Honey (18)
Special (5)
Streets Of Baltimore (2)
Sunshiny Day (13)
Sweet Promises (8)
Take Care Of The Little Things (3)
Tennessee Girl (16)
That's My Way (10)
That's The Only Way Life's Good To Me (8)
That's Why I Love You So Much (5)
Then Who Am I (17)
(There's) Nobody Home To Go Home To (6)
(There's Still) Someone I Can't Forget (8,12)
They Stood In Silent Prayer (7)
Things Are Looking Up (6)
This Highway Leads To Glory (9,14)

This Is My Year For Mexico (6)
Thought Of Losing You (6)
Through The Years (5)
Time Out For Jesus (9,14)
Time (You're Not A Friend Of Mine) (8,14)
Today Is That Tomorrow (8)
Too Hard To Say I'm Sorry (1,4)
Too Weak To Let You Go (15)
Was It All Worth Losing You (8,14)
We Had All The Good Things Going (3)
What Money Can't Buy (11)
When I Stop Leaving (I'll Be Gone) (18)
When The Trains Come In (13,14)
Where Do I Put Her Memory (18)
Whispering Hope (9)
Whole Lotta Things To Sing About (18)
Wonder Could I Live There Anymore (8) *87*
You Can Tell The World (1)
You Never Gave Up On Me (10)
You Were All The Good In Me (15)
You'll Still Be The One (11,12)
You're My Jamaica (10)
You're Still The Only One I'll Ever Love (10)
You're Wanting Me To Stop Loving You (13)

PRIDE & GLORY '94

Rock trio formed in New York City: Zakk Wylde (vocals, guitar), James LoMenzo (bass) and Brian Tichy (drums). Wylde formerly with **Ozzy Osbourne**'s band.

DEBUT	PEAK	WKS	CD	#	ARTIST — Album Title	$	Label & Number
6/25/94	173	1	©		Pride & Glory	$10	Geffen 24703

Chosen One
Cry Me A River
Fadin' Away
Found A Friend
Harvester Of Pain
Hate Your Guts
Horse Called War
Losin' Your Mind
Lovin' Woman
Machine Gun Man
Shine On
Sweet Jesus
Toe'n The Line
Troubled Wine

PRIEST, Maxi '90

Born Max Elliott on 6/10/60 in London (Jamaican parents). Dancehall reggae singer.

DEBUT	PEAK	WKS	CD	#	ARTIST — Album Title	Sym	$	Label & Number
12/3/88+	108	17	©	1	Maxi Priest		$10	Virgin 90957
8/4/90	47	37	● ©	2	Bonafide		$10	Charisma 91384
12/7/91	189	2	©	3	Best Of Me		$10	Charisma 91804
12/12/92	191	1	©	4	Fe Real	[G]	$10	Charisma 86500
7/27/96	108	10	©	5	Man With The Fun		$10	Virgin 41612

Ain't It Enough (5)
All Kinds Of People (5)
Amazed Are We (4)
Are You Ready For Me (5)
Best Of Me (2,3)
Can't Turn Away (4)
Caution (3)
Close To You (2,3) *1*
Crazy Love (3)
Frienenemy (5)
Golden Teardrops (3)
Goodbye To Love Again (1)
Groovin' In The Midnight (4) *63*
Happy Days (5)
Hard To Get (4)
Heartbreak Lover (5)
Housecall (Your Body Can't Lie To Me) (3) *37*
How Can We Ease The Pain? (1,3)
Human Cry (5)
Human Work Of Art (2)
I Know Love (3)
In The Springtime (3)
It Ain't Easy (1)
Just A Little Bit Longer (2,3) *62*
Just Wanna Know (4)
Let Me Know (1)
Life (2)
Love Will Cross Over (5)
Make My Day (4)
Man With The Fun (5)
Marcus (1)

PRIEST, Maxi — Cont'd

Message In A Bottle (5)
Never Did Say Goodbye (2)
One More Chance (4)
Peace Throughout The World (2,3)

Prayer For The World (2)
Problems (1)
Promises (2)
Same Old Story (1)

Should I (3)
Some Guys Have All The Luck (1,3)
Space In My Heart (2)

Strollin' On (3)
Sublime (4)
Sure Fire Love (3)
Suzie - You Are (1)

Temptress (2)
Ten To Midnight (4)
That Girl (5) *20*
Watching The World Go By (5)

Wild World (1,3) *25*
Woman In You (3)
Won't Let It Slip Away (5)
You (2)

PRIMA, Louis, & Keely Smith   '58

Prima was born on 12/7/11 in New Orleans. Died on 8/24/78 (age 66). Jazz trumpeter/singer/bandleader. Smith was born on 3/9/32 in Norfolk, Virginia. Female singer. They were married from 1952-61.

DEBUT	PEAK	WKS	CD		ARTIST — Album Title	Sym	$	Label & Number
6/23/58	12	4		1	Las Vegas Prima Style	[L]	$50	Capitol 1010
					recorded at the Sahara Hotel			
10/20/58	14	8	©	2	Politely!		$50	Capitol 1073
5/25/59	23	9	©	3	Swingin' Pretty		$50	Capitol 1145
					KEELY SMITH (above 2)			
5/25/59	37	2		4	Hey Boy! Hey Girl!	[S]	$50	Capitol 1160
11/2/59	43	4		5	Louis and Keely!		$30	Dot 3210
1/4/60	40	1	©	6	Be My Love		$30	Dot 3241
					KEELY SMITH			
1/16/61	9	11		7	Wonderland By Night	[I]	$30	Dot 25352

LOUIS PRIMA

All I Do Is Dream Of You (5)
All The Way (2)
And The Angels Sing (5)
Autumn Leaves (4)
Banana Split For My Baby (4)
Be My Love (6)
Bei Mir Bist Du Schon (5) *69*
By The Light Of The Silvery Moon (7)
Cheek To Cheek (5)
Cocktails For Two (2)
Don't Let The Stars Get In Your Eyes (5)
East Of The Sun (And West Of The Moon) (2)
Embraceable You (medley) (1)
Fascination (6)
Fever (4)

Goodnight My Love (7)
Greenback Dollar Bill (1)
Hey, Boy! Hey, Girl! (4)
Holiday For Strings (1)
Honeysuckle Rose (medley) (1)
How Deep Is The Ocean (6)
I Can't Believe That You're In Love With Me (medley) (1)
I Can't Get Started (7)
I Could Have Danced All Night (7)
I Don't Know Why (5)
I Got It Bad And That Ain't Good (medley) (1)
I Never Knew (I Could Love Anybody Like I'm Loving You) (2)
I Want Some Lovin' (7)

I'd Climb The Highest Mountain (6)
I'll Get By (As Long As I Have You) (2)
I'll Never Smile Again (2)
I'm Confessin' (That I Love You) (5)
I'm Gonna Sit Right Down And Write Myself A Letter (6)
I've Grown Accustomed To Her Face (5)
Indian Love Call (3)
It's All In The Game (6)
It's Been A Long, Long Time (3)
It's Magic (3)
Lazy River (4)
Love Of My Life (O Sole Mio) (1)

Lovely Way To Spend An Evening (7)
Lullaby Of The Leaves (3)
Make Love To Me (5)
Man I Love (3)
Moonlight Becomes You (7)
Moonlight In Vermont (7)
My Reverie (6)
Nearness Of You (3)
Night And Day (5)
Night Is Young (And You're So Beautiful) (7)
Nitey-Nite (4)
Oh, Marie (4)
On The Sunny Side Of The Street (7)
Polka Dots And Moonbeams (7)
Pretend (3)

S'posin' (4)
Should I (medley) (1)
Smoke Gets In Your Eyes (4)
Someone To Watch Over Me (3)
Song Is You (2)
Stardust (3)
Stormy Weather (3)
Sweet And Lovely (2)
Tea For Two (5)
Them There Eyes (medley) (1)
There Will Never Be Another You (3)
Tiger Rag (1)
Too Marvelous For Words (1)
Twilight Time (7)
What Can I Say After I Say I'm Sorry (3)

What Is This Thing Called Love? (3)
When The Saints Go Marching In (4)
White Cliffs Of Dover (1)
Why Do I Love You (5)
Wonderland By Night (7) *15*
You And The Night And The Music (7)
You Are My Love (4)
You Made Me Love You (6)
You're Driving Me Crazy (4)
You're My Everything (5)
You're Nobody 'Til Somebody Loves You (6)

PRIME MINISTER PETE NICE & DADDY RICH   '93

Rap duo. Former members of **3rd Bass**. Nice was born Peter Nash on 2/5/67 in New York City. Daddy Rich was born Richard Lawson in New York City.

DEBUT	PEAK	WKS	CD	ARTIST — Album Title	$	Label & Number
7/31/93	171	1	©	Dust To Dust	$10	Def Jam 53454

Blowin' Smoke
Double Duty Got Dicked
Dust To Dust

Ho
Kick The Bobo
Lumberjack, The

Outta My Way Baby
Rapsody (In J Minor)
Rat Bastard

Rich Bring 'Em Back
Sleeper, The
3 Blind Mice

Verbal Massage

PRIME SUSPECTS   '98

Male rap trio from New Orleans: E, Gangsta T and Skinow.

DEBUT	PEAK	WKS	CD	ARTIST — Album Title	$	Label & Number
10/24/98	36	4	©	Guilty Til Proven Innocent	$10	No Limit 50728

All 4 One
Bust Back
Children Of The Corn
Consequences Of The Streets

Daily Routine
Fear
Guilty Til Proven Innocent
Here I Go Again

Last Days
Liquidation Of The Ghetto
Mac's And Choppers
Money Makes...

My Old Lady
Of All Da Hustlers
Ride Wit My Heat
Soldier 4 Life

Someone Shoulda Told Me
Tweekin'
We Gots To Do 'Em
Young Niggas

PRIMITIVE RADIO GODS   '96

Group is actually solo artist Chris O'Connor. Touring group includes Luke McAuliffe (guitar), Jeff Sparks (bass) and Tim Lauteiro (drums).

DEBUT	PEAK	WKS		CD	ARTIST — Album Title	$	Label & Number
7/6/96	36	17	●	©	Rocket	$10	Ergo 67600

Are You Happy
Chain Reaction
Motherfucker

Rise And Fall Of Ooo Man
Rocket
Skin Turns Blue

Standing Outside A Broken Phone Booth With Money In My Hand

Where The Monkey Meets The Man
Who Say

Women

PRIMITIVES, The   '88

Pop-rock group from Coventry, England: Tracy Tracey (vocals), Paul Court (guitar), Steve Dullaghan (bass) and Tig Williams (drums).

DEBUT	PEAK	WKS	CD		ARTIST — Album Title	$	Label & Number
9/10/88	106	9	©	1	Lovely	$10	RCA 8443
12/23/89+	113	15	©	2	Pure	$10	RCA 9934

All The Way Down (2)
Buzz Buzz Buzz (1)
Can't Bring Me Down (2)
Carry Me Home (1)
Crash (1)

Dizzy Heights (2)
Don't Want Anything To Change (1)
Dreamwalk Baby (1)
I'll Stick With You (1)

Keep Me In Mind (2)
Lonely Streets (2)
Never Tell (2)
Nothing Left (1)
Ocean Blue (1)

Out Of Reach (1)
Outside (2)
Run Baby Run (1)
Secrets (2)
Shadow (1)

Shine (2)
Sick Of It (2)
Spacehead (1)
Stop Killing Me (1)
Summer Rain (2)

Thru' The Flowers (1)
Way Behind Me (1,2)

PRIMUS   '93

Rock trio from San Francisco: **Les Claypool** (vocals, bass), Larry LaLonde (guitar) and Tim Alexander (drums). Brian Mantia replaced Alexander in 1996.

DEBUT	PEAK	WKS			CD		ARTIST — Album Title	$	Label & Number
6/1/91	116	36	●		©	1	Sailing The Seas Of Cheese	$10	Interscope 91659
5/8/93	7	34	▲		©	2	Pork Soda	$10	Interscope 92257
6/24/95	8	19	●		©	3	Tales From The Punchbowl	$10	Interscope 92553
7/26/97	21	8			©	4	Brown Album	$10	Interscope 90126
8/29/98	106	2			©	5	Rhinoplasty	$10	Interscope 90214
11/6/99	44	4			©	6	Antipop	$10	Interscope 90414

Air Is Getting Slippery (2)
American Life (1)
Amos Moses (5)
Antipop, The (6)
Arnie (4)
Ballad Of Bodacious (6)
Behind My Camel (5)
Bob (2)

Bob's Party Time Lounge (4,5)
Camelback Cinema (4)
Captain Shiner (3)
Chastising Of Renegade (4)
Coattails Of A Dead Man (6)
Coddingtown (4)
DMV (2)
De Anza Jig (3)

Del Davis Tree Farm (3)
Dirty Drowning Man (6)
Duchess And The Proverbial Mind Spread (4)
Eclectic Electric (6)
Electric Uncle Sam (6)
Eleven (1)
Family And The Fishing Net (5)

Final Voyage Of The Liquid Sky (6)
Fish On (1)
Fisticuffs (6)
Glass Sandwich (3)
Golden Boy (4)
Greet The Sacred Cow (6)
Hail Santa (2)

Hamburger Train (2)
Hats Off (4)
Hellbound 17 1/2 (Theme From) (3)
Here Come The Bastards (1)
Is It Luck? (1)
Jerry Was A Race Car Driver (1)

Kalamazoo (4)
Laquer Head (6)
Los Bastardos (1)
Mama Didn't Raise No Fool (6)
Mr. Krinkle (2)
Mrs. Blaileen (3)
My Name Is Mud (2)
Natural Joe (6)

PRIMUS — Cont'd

Nature Boy (2)	Over The Falls (4)	Puddin' Taine (4)	Sgt. Baker (1)	Those Damned Blue-Collar	Wynona's Big Brown Beaver (3)

Nature Boy (2)
Ol' Diamondback Sturgeon (Fisherman's Chronicles, Part 3) (2)
On The Tweek Again (3)
Over The Electric Grapevine (3)

Over The Falls (4)
Pork Soda (2)
Power Mad (6)
Pressman, The (2)
Professor Nutbutter's House Of Treats (3)

Puddin' Taine (4)
Restin' Bones (4)
Return Of Sathington Willoughby (4)
Sathington Waltz (1)
Scissor Man (5)

Sgt. Baker (1)
Shake Hands With Beef (4)
Silly Putty (5)
Southbound Pachyderm (3)
Space Farm (3)
Thing That Should Not Be (5)

Those Damned Blue-Collar Tweekers (1)
Tommy The Cat (1,5)
Too Many Puppies (5)
Welcome To This World (2)
Wounded Knee (2)

Wynona's Big Brown Beaver (3)
Year Of The Parrot (3)

PRINCE ★27★ '84

Born Prince Roger Nelson on 6/7/58 in Minneapolis. R&B singer/songwriter/multi-instrumentalist. Starred in the movies *Purple Rain*, *Under The Cherry Moon*, *Sign 'O' The Times* and *Graffiti Bridge*. Founded the Paisley Park record label. The Revolution: Wendy Melvoin (guitar), Lisa Coleman and Matt Fink (keyboards), Eric Leeds (sax; **Madhouse**), Brownmark (bass) and Bobby Z (drums). Melvoin and Coleman formed duo **Wendy & Lisa** in 1987. The New Power Generation: Rosie Gaines (vocals), Levi Seacer (guitar), Tommy Barbarella (keyboards), Sonny T (bass) and Michael Bland (drums). Prince changed his name on 6/7/93 to a combination male/female symbol. By 1994 referred to as "The Artist Formerly Known As Prince" or "The Artist." Announced in May 2000 that he would once again be known as "Prince."

1)Purple Rain 2)Batman 3)Around The World In A Day 4)Parade 5)Diamonds And Pearls

DEBUT	PEAK	WKS	RIAA	CD	ARTIST — Album Title	Catalog	Sym	$	Label & Number
10/28/78	163	5		© 1	**For You**			$20	Warner 3150
11/17/79+	22	28	▲	© 2	**Prince**			$15	Warner 3366
11/8/80	45	52	●	© 3	**Dirty Mind**			$15	Warner 3478
11/7/81	21	64	▲	© 4	**Controversy**			$15	Warner 3601
11/20/82+	9	153	▲⁴	© 5	**1999**	C:#6/2		$15	Warner 23720 [2]
					also see #27 below				

PRINCE & THE REVOLUTION:

DEBUT	PEAK	WKS	RIAA	CD	ARTIST — Album Title	Catalog	Sym	$	Label & Number
7/14/84	❶²⁴	72	▲¹³	© 6	**Purple Rain**	C:#35/11	[S]	$10	Warner 25110
5/11/85	❶³	40	▲²	© 7	**Around The World In A Day**			$10	Paisley Park 25286
4/19/86	3	28	▲	© 8	**Parade**		[S]	$10	Paisley Park 25395
					music from the movie Under The Cherry Moon				

PRINCE:

DEBUT	PEAK	WKS	RIAA	CD	ARTIST — Album Title	Catalog	Sym	$	Label & Number
4/18/87	6	54	▲	© 9	**Sign "O" The Times**			$15	Paisley Park 25577 [2]
5/28/88	11	21	●	© 10	**Lovesexy**			$10	Paisley Park 25720
7/8/89	❶⁶	34	▲²	© 11	**Batman**		[S]	$10	Warner 25936
9/8/90	6	24	●	© 12	**Graffiti Bridge**		[S]	$10	Paisley Park 27493
					*includes "Round And Round" by **Tevin Campbell**; "Melody Cool" by **Mavis Staples**; "We Can Funk" by **George Clinton** and "Release It," "Latest Fashion," "Love Machine" and "Shake!" by **The Time***				

PRINCE & THE NEW POWER GENERATION:

DEBUT	PEAK	WKS	RIAA	CD	ARTIST — Album Title	Catalog	Sym	$	Label & Number
10/19/91	3	45	▲²	© 13	**Diamonds And Pearls**			$10	Paisley Park 25379
10/31/92	5	34	▲	© 14	⚥			$10	Paisley Park 45037

PRINCE:

DEBUT	PEAK	WKS	RIAA	CD	ARTIST — Album Title	Catalog	Sym	$	Label & Number
10/2/93	19	12	▲	© 15	**The Hits/The B-Sides**		[G]	$25	Paisley Park 45440 [3]
					of the 56 tracks, 6 are previously unreleased, 18 are rare B-sides				
10/2/93	46	20	▲	© 16	**The Hits 1**	C:#3/2	[G]	$10	Paisley Park 45431
					disc one of The Hits/The B-Sides				
10/2/93	54	19	▲	© 17	**The Hits 2**		[G]	$10	Paisley Park 45435
					disc two of The Hits/The B-Sides				

⚥:

DEBUT	PEAK	WKS	RIAA	CD	ARTIST — Album Title	Catalog	Sym	$	Label & Number
6/4/94	92	12		© 18	**The Beautiful Experience**		[M]	$10	NPG 71003
					7 mixes of "The Most Beautiful Girl In The World"				
9/3/94	15	10	●	© 19	**Come**			$10	Warner 45700

PRINCE (1958-1993)

DEBUT	PEAK	WKS	RIAA	CD	ARTIST — Album Title	Catalog	Sym	$	Label & Number
12/10/94	47	11		© 20	**The Black Album**		[E]	$10	Warner 45793

PRINCE

recorded in 1987

DEBUT	PEAK	WKS	RIAA	CD	ARTIST — Album Title	Catalog	Sym	$	Label & Number
10/14/95	6	8	●	© 21	**The Gold Experience**			$10	Warner 45999
4/6/96	75	4		© 22	**Girl 6**		[S]	$10	Warner 46239

PRINCE

*includes "Nasty Girl" by **Vanity 6** and "The Screams Of Passion" by **The Family***

DEBUT	PEAK	WKS	RIAA	CD	ARTIST — Album Title	Catalog	Sym	$	Label & Number
7/27/96	26	4		© 23	**Chaos And Disorder**			$10	Warner 46317
12/7/96	11	21	▲²	© 24	**Emancipation**			$25	NPG 54982 [3]
3/14/98	62	5		© 25	**Crystal Ball**		[K]	$30	NPG 9871 [4]
7/18/98	22	8		© 26	**Newpower Soul**			$10	NPG 9872

⚥ **& NEW POWER GENERATION**

DEBUT	PEAK	WKS	RIAA	CD	ARTIST — Album Title	Catalog	Sym	$	Label & Number
2/20/99	150	1		© 27	**1999: The New Master**		[M-R]	$10	NPG 1999

PRINCE AND THE REVOLUTION

7 mixes of "1999"

DEBUT	PEAK	WKS	RIAA	CD	ARTIST — Album Title	Catalog	Sym	$	Label & Number
9/11/99	85	5		© 28	**The Vault...Old Friends 4 Sale**		[E]	$10	Warner 47522

PRINCE

songs recorded from 1985-94

DEBUT	PEAK	WKS	RIAA	CD	ARTIST — Album Title	Catalog	Sym	$	Label & Number
11/27/99	18	15	●	© 29	**Rave Un2 The Joy Fantastic**			$10	NPG 14624

Acknowledge Me (25)
Adore (9,15,16,22)
All The Critics Love U In New York (5)
Alphabet St. (10,15,16) *8*
America (7) *46*
And God Created Woman (14)
Anna Stesia (10)
Annie Christian (4)
Another Lonely Christmas (15)

Anotherloverholenyohead (8) *63*
Arms Of Orion (11) *36*
Around The World In A Day (7)
Arrogance (14)
Automatic (5)
Baby (1)
Baby I'm A Star (6)
Baby Knows (29)
Ballad Of Dorothy Parker (9)
Bambi (2)

Batdance (11) *1*
Beautiful Ones (6)
Betcha By Golly Wow! (24)
Billy Jack Bitch (21)
Blue Light (14)
Bob George (20)
Calhoun Square (25)
Can't Stop This Feeling I Got (12)
Chaos And Disorder (23)
Christopher Tracy's Parade (8)

Cindy C. (20)
Cloreen Bacon Skin (25)
Come (19)
Come On (26)
Computer Blue (6)
Condition Of The Heart (7)
Continental, The (14)
Controversy (4,15,17) *70*
Count The Days (25)
Courtin' Time (24)
Crazy You (1)

Cream (13,15,17) *1*
Cross, The (9,22)
Crucial (25)
Crystal Ball (25)
Curious Child (24)
D.M.S.R. (5)
Da Bang (25)
Da, Da, Da (24)
Daddy Pop (13)
Damn U (14)
Damned If I Do (24)

Dance On (10)
Dark (19)
Darling Nikki (6)
Days Of Wild (25)
Dead On It (20)
Delirious (5,15,17) *8*
Diamonds And Pearls (13,15,16) *3*
Dig U Better Dead (23)
Dinner With Delores (23)
Dirty Mind (3,15,17)

DEBUT	PEAK	WKS	RIAA	CD	ARTIST — Album Title	Catalog	Sym	$	Label & Number

PRINCE — Cont'd

Do It All Night (3)
Do Me, Baby (4,15,17)
Do U Lie? (8)
Dolphin (21)
Don't Talk 2 Strangers (22)
Dream Factory (25)
Dreamin' About U (24)
18 & Over (25)
Electric Chair (11)
Elephants & Flowers (12)
Emale (24)
Emancipation (24)
Endorphinmachine (21)
Erotic City (15,22)
Escape (15)
Everyday Is A Winding Road (29)
Extraordinary (28)
Face Down (24)
Feel U Up (15)
5 Women (28)
Flow, The (14)
4 The Tears In Your Eyes (15)
For You (1)
Forever In My Life (9)
Freaks On This Side (26)
Free (5)
Friend, Lover, Sister, Mother/Wife (24)
Future, The (11)
Get Loose (25)
Get Yo Groove On (24)
Gett Off (13,15,17) *21*
Girl (15)
Girl 6 (22)
Girls & Boys (8,22)
Glam Slam (10)
God (19)
Gold (21) *88*
Good Love (25)
Goodbye (25)
Gotta Broken Heart Again (3)
Gotta Stop (Messin' About) (15)
Graffiti Bridge (12)
Greatest Romance Ever Sold (29) *63*
Had U (23)
Head (3,15,17)

Hello (15)
Hide The Bone (25)
Holy River (24)
Honest Man (25)
Horny Toad (15)
Hot Thing (9,22) *63*
Hot Wit U (29)
Housequake (9)
How Come U Don't Call Me Anymore (15,22)
Human Body (24)
I Can't Make U Love Me (24)
I Could Never Take The Place Of Your Man (9,15,16) *10*
I Feel For You (2,15,16)
I Hate U (21) *12*
I No (10)
(I Like) Funky Music (26)
I Like It There (23)
I Love U, But I Don't Trust U Anymore (29)
I Love U In Me (15)
I Rock, Therefore I Am (23)
I Wanna Be Your Lover (2,15,17) *11*
I Wanna Melt With U (14)
I Will (23)
I Wish U Heaven (10)
I Wonder U (8)
I Would Die 4 U (6,15,17) *8*
I'm Yours (1)
If I Was Your Girlfriend (9,15,17) *67*
In Love (1)
In This Bed I Scream (24)
Insatiable (13) *77*
Interactive (25)
International Lover (5)
Into The Light (23)
Irresistible Bitch (15)
It (9)
It's About That Walk (28)
It's Gonna Be A Beautiful Night (9)
It's Gonna Be Lonely (2)
Jack U Off (4)
Jam Of The Year (24)
Joint 2 Joint (24)

Joy In Repetition (12)
Jughead (13)
Just As Long As We're Together (1)
Kiss (8,15,17) *1*
La, La, La, He, He, Hee (15)
La, La, La Means I Love You (24)
Ladder, The (7)
Lady Cab Driver (5)
Last Heart (20)
Le Grind (20)
Lemon Crush (11)
Let's Go Crazy (6,15,17) *1*
Let's Have A Baby (24)
Let's Pretend We're Married (5) *52*
Let's Work (4)
Letitgo (19) *31*
Life Can Be So Nice (8)
Little Red Corvette (5,15,17) *6*
Live 4 Love (13)
Loose! (19)
Love 2 The 9's (14)
Love We Make (24)
Lovesexy (10)
Lovesign (10)
Mad Sex (26)
Make Your Mama Happy (25)
Man'O'War (29)
Max, The (14)
Money Don't Matter 2 Night (13) *23*
Morning Papers (14) *44*
Most Beautiful Girl In The World (18,21) *3*
Mountains (8) *23*
Movie Star (25)
Mr. Happy (24)
My Computer (24)
My Little Pill (28)
My Love Is Forever (1)
My Name Is Prince (14) *36*
New Position (8)
New Power Generation (12) *64*
New Power Generation (Pt. II)

New World (24)
Newpower Soul (26)
1999 (5,15,16,27) *12*
Nothing Compares 2 U (15,16)
Now (21)
Old Friends 4 Sale (28)
One, The (26)
One Kiss At A Time (24)
One Of Us (24)
Orgasm (19)
P Control (21)
P. Control (25)
Paisley Park (7)
Papa (19)
Partyman (11) *18*
Partyup (3)
Peach (15,17)
Pheromone (19)
Pink Cashmere (15,16,22) *50*
Plan, The (24)
Play In The Sunshine (9)
PoomPoom (25)
Pop Life (7,15,16) *7*
Pope (15,17)
Positivity (10)
Power Fantastic (15)
Private Joy (4)
Purple Rain (6,15,17) *2*
Push (13)
Push It Up! (26)
Question Of U (12)
Race (19)
Raspberry Beret (7,15,17) *2*
Rave Un2 The Joy Fantastic (29)
Rest Of My Life (28)
Ride, The (25)
Right Back Here In My Arms (24)
Right The Wrong (23)
Ripopgodazippa (25)
Rockhard In A Funky Place (20)
Ronnie, Talk To Russia (4)
Sacrifice Of Victor (14)
Same December (23)
Sarah (28)
Saviour (24)
Scandalous (11)

Scarlet Pussy (15)
7 (14,15,16) *7*
17 Days (15)
Sex In The Summer (24)
Sexual Suicide (25)
Sexuality (2)
Sexy Dancer (2)
Sexy M.F. (14,15,17) *66*
She Gave Her Angels (25)
She Spoke 2 Me (22,28)
She's Always In My Hair (15)
Shhh (21)
Shockadelica (15)
Shoo-Bed-Ooh (26)
Shy (21)
Sign 'O' The Times (9,15,16) *3*
Silly Game (29)
Sister (24)
Slave (24)
Sleep Around (24)
Slow Love (9)
So Blue (1)
So Dark (25)
So Far, So Pleased (29)
Soft And Wet (1,15,16) *92*
Solo (19)
Somebody's Somebody (24)
Something In The Water (Does Not Compute) (5)
Sometimes It Snows In April (8)
Soul Sanctuary (24)
Space (19)
Starfish And Coffee (9)
Still Waiting (2)
Still Would Stand All Time (12)
Strange But True (29)
Strange Relationship (9)
Strays Of The World (25)
Strollin' (13)
Style (24)
Sun, The Moon And Stars (29)
Superfunkycalifragisexy (20)
Sweet Baby (14)
Take Me With U (6) *25*
Tamborine (9)
Tangerine (29)
Tell Me How U Wanna B Done (25)

Temptation (7)
There Is Lonely (28)
Thieves In The Temple (12,15,16) *6*
3 Chains O' Gold (14)
319 (21)
Thunder (13)
Tick, Tick, Bang (12)
2morrow (21)
Trust (11)
200 Balloons (15)
2 Nigs United 4 West Compton (20)
U Got The Look (9,15,17) *2*
Under The Cherry Moon (8)
Until U're In My Arms Again (26)
Uptown (3,15,16)
Venus De Milo (8)
Vicki Waiting (11)
Walk Don't Walk (13)
We Gets Up (24)
We March (21)
What's My Name (25)
When Doves Cry (6,15,16) *1*
When The Lights Go Down (28)
When 2 R In Love (10,20)
When U Love Somebody (26)
When We're Dancing Close And Slow (2)
When You Were Mine (3,15,16)
Wherever U Go, Whatever U Do (29)
White Mansion (24)
Why You Wanna Treat Me So Bad? (2,15,16)
Willing And Able (13)
With You (2)
Zannalee (23)

PRINCE PAUL   '99
Born Paul Huston on 4/2/67 in Long Island, New York. Male rapper. Member of **Gravediggaz**.

3/13/99	**138**	2		©	**A Prince Among Thieves**			$10	Tommy Boy 1210

Central Booking
Crazy Lou's Hideout
Every Beginning Must Have An Ending
Handle Your Time

How It All Started
Hustles On
Just Another Day
MC Hustler
Macula's Theory

Men In Blue
Mood For Love
More Than U Know
Mr. Large
My Big Chance

My First Day
Other Line
Pain
Put The Next Man On
Room 69

Sermon
Showdown
Steady Slobbin'
War Party
Weapon World

What U Got
You Got Shot

PRINE, John   '75
Born on 10/10/46 in Maywood, Illinois. Singer/songwriter.
1)Common Sense 2)Bruised Orange 3)Sweet Revenge

2/26/72	**154**	3		© 1	**John Prine**			$12	Atlantic 8296
10/28/72	**148**	10		© 2	**Diamonds In The Rough**			$12	Atlantic 7240
11/24/73	**135**	11		© 3	**Sweet Revenge**			$12	Atlantic 7274
4/26/75	**66**	10		© 4	**Common Sense**			$12	Atlantic 18127
1/15/77	**196**	2	●	© 5	**Prime Prine-The Best Of John Prine**		[G]	$12	Atlantic 18202
7/8/78	**116**	13		© 6	**Bruised Orange**			$12	Asylum 139
9/8/79	**152**	7		© 7	**Pink Cadillac**			$12	Asylum 222
8/30/80	**144**	7		© 8	**Storm Windows**			$12	Asylum 286
4/22/95	**159**	9		© 9	**Lost Dogs And Mixed Blessings**			$10	Oh Boy 013
10/2/99	**197**	1		© 10	**In Spite Of Ourselves**			$10	Oh Boy 019

Accident (Things Could Be Worse) (3)
Ain't Hurtin' Nobody (9)
All Night Blue (8)
All The Way With You (9)
Angel From Montgomery (1)
Automobile (7)
Aw Heck (6)
Baby Let's Play House (7)
Baby Ruth (8)
Back Street Affair (10)
Big Fat Love (9)
Billy The Bum (2)
Blue Umbrella (3)
Bruised Orange (Chain Of Sorrow) (6)
Chinatown (7)
Christmas In Prison (3)
Clocks And Spoons (2)
Cold War (This Cold War With You) (7)

Come Back To Us Barbara Lewis Hare Krishna Beauregard (4,5)
Common Sense (4)
Crooked Piece Of Time (6)
Day Is Done (9)
Dear Abby (3,5)
Dear John (I Sent Your Saddle Home) (10)
Diamonds In The Rough (2)
Donald And Lydia (1,5)
Down By The Side Of The Road (7)
Everybody (2)
Far From Me (1)
Fish And Whistle (6)
Flashback Blues (1)
Forbidden Jimmy (4)
Frying Pan (2)
Good Time (3)
Grandpa Was A Carpenter (3,5)
Great Compromise (2,5)

He Forgot That It Was Sunday (9)
He Was In Heaven Before He Died (4)
Hello In There (1,5)
Hobo Song (4)
How Lucky (7)
Humidity Built The Snowman (9)
I Had A Dream (8)
I Know One (10)
I Love You So Much It Hurts (9)
If You Don't Want My Love (6)
Illegal Smile (1,5)
In A Town This Size (10)
In Spite Of Ourselves (10)
Iron One Betty (6)
It's A Cheating Situation (10)
It's Happening To You (8)
Just Wanna Be With You (8)
Killing The Blues (7)
Lake Marie (9)

Late John Garfield Blues (2)
Leave The Lights On (9)
Let's Invite Them Over (10)
Let's Turn Back The Years (medley) (10)
Living In The Future (8)
Loose Talk (10)
Mexican Home (3)
Middle Man (4)
Milwaukee Here I Come (10)
My Own Best Friend (4)
New Train (9)
Nine Pound Hammer (9)
No Name Girl (7)
Often Is A Word I Seldom Use (3)
One Red Rose (8)
Onomatopoeia (3)
Paradise (1)
Please Don't Bury Me (3,5)
Pretty Good (1)
Quiet Man (1)

Quit Hollerin' At Me (9)
Rocky Mountain Time (2)
Sabu Visits The Twin Cities Alone (6)
Saddle In The Rain (4,5)
Saigon (7)
Sam Stone (1,5)
Same Thing Happened To Me (9)
Shop Talk (8)
Six O'Clock News (1)
Sleepy Eyed Boy (8)
So Sad (To Watch Good Love Go Bad) (10)
Sour Grapes (2)
Souvenirs (2,5)
Spanish Pipedream (1)
Storm Windows (8)
Sweet Revenge (3)
Take The Star Out Of The Window (2)
That Close To You (4)

That's The Way That The World Goes 'Round (6)
There She Goes (6)
This Love Is Real (8)
'Til A Tear Becomes A Rose (10)
Torch Singer (2)
Ubangi Stomp (7)
Way Down (4)
We Are The Lonely (9)
We Could (10)
We Must Have Been Out Of Our Minds (10)
(We're Not) The Jet Set (10)
Wedding Bells (medley) (10)
Wedding Day In Funeralville (4)
When Two Worlds Collide (10)
Yes I Guess They Oughta Name A Drink After You (2)
You Never Can Tell (4)
Your Flag Decal Won't Get You Into Heaven Anymore (1)

PRISM '82

Rock group from Canada: Ron Tabak (vocals), Lindsay Mitchell and Tom Lavin (guitars), John Hall (keyboards), Ab Bryant (bass; **Chilliwack**, **Headpins**), Rodney Higgs (drums). Bryant and Higgs left after first album, replaced by Allen Harlow and Rocket Norton. Tabak left after second album, replaced by Henry Small. Tabak died in a car crash in 1984.

DEBUT	PEAK	WKS						$	Label & Number
10/1/77	137	10			1 **Prism**			$15	Ariola 50020
7/29/78	158	8			2 **See Forever Eyes**			$15	Ariola 50034
2/6/82	53	20			3 **Small Change**			$12	Capitol 12184

Amelia (1)
Crime Wave (2)
Don't Let Him Know (3) *39*
Flyin' (2) *53*
Freewill (1)
Heart And Soul (3)

Hello (1)
Hole In Paradise (3)
I Ain't Lookin' Anymore (1)
In The Jailhouse Now (1)
It's Over (1)
Julie (1)

Just Like Me (1)
N-N-N-No! (2)
Nickles And Dimes (2)
Open Soul Surgery (1)
Rain (3)
See Forever Eyes (2)

Spaceship Superstar (1) *82*
Stay (3)
Take Me Away (2)
Take Me To The Kaptin (1) *59*
Turn On Your Radar (3) *64*
Vladivostok (1)

When Love Goes Wrong
 (You're Not Alone) (3)
When Will I See You Again (3)
Wings Of Your Love (3)
You're Like The Wind (2)
You're My Reason (2)

PRITCHARD, Peter '95

Born in Wellington, New Zealand. New Age pianist.

DEBUT	PEAK	WKS						$	Label & Number
9/2/95	149	1		©	**Studies For The New Zealand Harmonic Piano** [I]			$10	White Cloud 11001

Arthur's Pass
Autumn In Otago

Clouds Over Mount Aspiring
High Blue Sky

Homecoming
Morning In The Bush

Rotoiti Dawn
Seascape

Valley Of The Deer

PROCLAIMERS, The '93

Pop duo from Edinburgh, Scotland: identical twin brothers Craig and Charlie Reid (born on 3/5/62).

DEBUT	PEAK	WKS						$	Label & Number
4/8/89+	31	37	●	©	**Sunshine On Leith**			$10	Chrysalis 41668

originally charted for 11 weeks, peaking at position 125 on 5/6/89 for 2 weeks; re-entered on 6/5/93 on Chrysalis 21668

Cap In Hand
Come On Nature

I'm Gonna Be (500 Miles) *3*
I'm On My Way

It's Saturday Night
My Old Friend The Blues

Oh Jean
Sean

Sunshine On Leith
Teardrops

Then I Met You
What Do You Do

★365★ PROCOL HARUM '72

Pop-rock group formed in England: Gary Brooker (vocals, piano), Keith Reid (lyrics), Ray Royer (guitar), Matthew Fisher (organ), Dave Knights (bass) and Bobby Harrison (drums). Royer and Harrison left after first album, replaced by **Robin Trower** and Barrie Wilson. Knights and Fisher left in early 1969; bassist Chris Copping added. Trower left in mid-1971, replaced by Dave Ball; bassist Alan Cartright added while Copping switched to keyboards. Ball left in mid-1972, replaced by Mick Grabham. Cartright left in mid-1976; Copping moved to bass and keyboardist Pete Solley joined. Wilson died of pneumonia in October 1990 (age 43).

1)*Procol Harum Live In Concert with the Edmonton Symphony Orchestra* 2)*Grand Hotel*
3)*Shine On Brightly*

DEBUT	PEAK	WKS						$	Label & Number
9/23/67	47	16		©	1 **Procol Harum**			$50	Deram 18008
10/12/68	24	20		©	2 **Shine On Brightly**			$20	A&M 4151
5/10/69	32	20		©	3 **A Salty Dog**			$20	A&M 4179
7/11/70	34	15		©	4 **Home**			$15	A&M 4261
5/8/71	32	20		©	5 **Broken Barricades**			$15	A&M 4294
5/13/72	5	28	●	©	6 **Procol Harum Live In Concert with the Edmonton Symphony Orchestra** [L]			$15	A&M 4335

recorded on 11/18/71 at the Jubilee Auditorium

DEBUT	PEAK	WKS						$	Label & Number
3/31/73	21	22		©	7 **Grand Hotel**			$15	Chrysalis 1037
10/20/73	131	10		©	8 **The Best Of Procol Harum** [G]			$15	A&M 4401
4/20/74	86	9		©	9 **Exotic Birds And Fruit**			$12	Chrysalis 1058
8/23/75	52	8		©	10 **Procol's Ninth**			$12	Chrysalis 1080
3/26/77	147	6		©	11 **Something Magic**			$12	Chrysalis 1130

About To Die (4)
All This And More (3,6)
As Strong As Samson (9)
Barnyard Story (4)
Beyond The Pale (9)
Boredom (3)
Bringing Home The Bacon (7)
Broken Barricades (5)
Butterfly Boys (9)
Cerdes (Outside The Gates Of)
 (1)
Christmas Camel (1)
Conquistador (1,6,8) *16*
Crucifiction Lane (3)
Dead Man's Dream (4)
Devil Came From Kansas (3)

Eight Days A Week (10)
Final Thrust (10)
Fires (Which Burnt Brightly) (7)
Fools Gold (10)
For Liquorice John (7)
Fresh Fruit (9)
Grand Hotel (7)
Homburg (8) *34*
I Keep Forgetting (10)
Idol, The (9)
In Held Twas In I (2,6)
(In The Wee Small Hours Of)
 Sixpence (8)
Juicy John Pink (3)
Kaleidoscope (1)
Lime Street Blues (8)

Long Gone Geek (8)
Luskus Delph (5)
Mabel (1)
Magdalene (My Regal
 Zonophone) (2)
Mark Of The Claw (11)
Memorial Drive (4)
Milk Of Human Kindness (3)
Monsieur R. Monde (9)
New Lamps For Old (9)
Nothing But The Truth (9)
Nothing That I Didn't Know (4)
Pandora's Box (10)
Piggy Pig Pig (4)
Pilgrims Progress (3)
Piper's Tune (10)

Playmate Of The Mouth (5)
Poor Mohammed (5)
Power Failure (5)
Quite Rightly So (2,8)
Rambling On (2)
Repent Walpurgis (1)
Robert's Box (7)
Rum Tale (7)
Salad Days (Are Here Again)
 (1)
Salty Dog (3,6,8)
She Wandered Through The
 Garden Fence (1)
Shine On Brightly (2,8)
Simple Sister (5,8)
Skating On Thin Ice (11)

Skip Softly (My Moonbeams)
 (2)
Something Following Me (1)
Something Magic (11)
Song For A Dreamer (5)
Souvenir Of London (7)
Still There'll Be More (4)
Strangers In Space (11)
T.V. Ceasar (7)
Taking The Time (10)
Thin End Of The Wedge (9)
Too Much Between Us (3)
Toujours L'Amour (7)
Typewriter Torment (10)
Unquiet Zone (10)
Whaling Stories (4,6)

Whisky Train (4,8)
Whiter Shade Of Pale (1,8) *5*
Wish Me Well (2)
Without A Doubt (10)
Wizard Man (11)
Worm & The Tree Medley (11)
Wreck Of The Hesperus (11)
Your Own Choice (4)

PRODIGY '97

Techno-dance group from England: Maxim Reality and Keith Flint (vocals), Liam Howlett (instruments) and Leeroy Thornhill (dancer).

DEBUT	PEAK	WKS						$	Label & Number
2/22/97	198	2		©	1 **Music For The Jilted Generation** C:#31/5 [I]			$10	Mute 9003
7/19/97	❶¹	57	▲²	©	2 **The Fat Of The Land**			$10	Maverick 46606

Break & Enter (1)
Breathe (2)
Claustrophobic Sting (1)
Climbatize (2)

Diesel Power (2)
Firestarter (2) *30*
Fuel My Fire (2)
Full Throttle (1)

Funky Shit (2)
Heat (The Energy) (1)
Mindfields (2)
Narayan (2)

No Good (Start The Dance) (1)
One Love - The Narcotic Suite
 (1)
Poison (1)
Serial Thrilla (2)

Skylined (1)
Smack My Bitch Up (2) *89*
Speedway (Theme From
 Fastlane) (1)
Their Law (1)

3 Kilos (2)
Voodoo People (1)

PRODIGY OF MOBB DEEP '00

Born in 1975 in Queens, New York. Male rapper. Member of **Mobb Deep**.

DEBUT	PEAK	WKS						$	Label & Number
12/2/00	18	15	●	©	**H-N-I-C**			$10	Loud 1873

Can't Complain
Delt With The Bullshit
Diamond

Do It
Genesis
Gun Play

H.N.I.C.
Infamous Minded
Keep It Thoro

Rock Dat Shit
Three
Trials Of Love

Veteran's Memorial
Wanna Be Thugs
Whut U Rep

Y.B.E.
You Can Never Feel My Pain

PRODUCERS, The '81

Pop-rock group from Atlanta: Van Temple (vocals, guitar), Wayne Famous (keyboards), Kyle Henderson (bass) and Bryan Holmes (drums).

DEBUT	PEAK	WKS						$	Label & Number
6/6/81	163	2		©	**The Producers**			$12	Portrait 37097

Body Language
Boys Say When/Girls Say Why
Certain Kinda Girl

End, The
Here's To You
I Love Lucy

Life Of Crime
Sensations

**What She Does To Me (The
 Diana Song)** *61*
What's He Got?

Who Do You Think You Are?
You Go Your Way

PROFESSOR GRIFF '90

Born Richard Griffin in Long Island, New York. Male rapper. Former member of **Public Enemy**.

| 4/14/90 | 127 | 8 | © | **Pawns In The Game** .... | | | $10 | Skyywalker 111 |

Vth Amendment / L.A.D. / Pass The Ammo / Real African People Pt. 1 & 2 / Word Of God
Interview, The / Love Thy Enemy / Pawns In The Game / Suzi Wants To Be A Rock Star
It's A Blax Thanx / 1-900 Stereotype / Rap Terrorist / Verdict, The

PROFYLE '00

Male R&B vocal group from Shreveport, Louisiana: Baby Boy, Face, Hershey and L Jai.

| 11/4/00 | 50 | 10 | © | **Nothin' But Drama**.. | | | $10 | Motown 159744 |

Addicted / Can We Talk (About Us) / Every Little Thing / Nasty / You Bring The Freak
Can We Make Love / Changes / I Do / No Trickin'
(Can We) M.A.K.E. L.U.V. / Damn / Liar *14* / One Night

PROJECT PAT '01

Born in 1974 in Memphis. Male rapper. Member of **Hypnotize Camp Posse**.

10/2/99	52	7	©	1 **Ghetty Green**			$10	Hypnotize Minds 1743
8/12/00	176	1	©	2 **Murderers & Robbers Underground**...			$10	Project 9996
3/17/01	4	26	©	3 **Mista Don't Play - Everythangs Workin**			$10	Hypnotize Minds 1950

Aggravated Robbery (3) / Don't Save Her (3) / I Get Da Chewin (2) / Out There (1) / Run A Train (1) / Up There (1)
Ballers (1) / Easily Executed (2) / If You Ain't From My Hood (3) / Puttin Hoez On Da House (2) / Shake That Ass (1) / We Ain't Scared Hoe (3)
Bitch Smackin Killa (2) / 528-CASH (1) / Life We Live (3) / Red Rum (2) / Ski Mask (1) / We Can Get Gangsta (3)
Break Da Law 2001 (3) / Fuck A Bitch (2) / Murderers & Robbers (2) / Represent It (1) / Slangin' Rocks (1) / Whole Lotta Weed (3)
Cheese And Dope (3) / F*ckin' With The Best (3) / Niggas Got Me Fucked Up (1) / Ridin On Chrome (2) / So Hi (3) / Y'all Niggaz Ain't No Killaz,
Chickenhead (3) *87* / Ghetty Green (1) / North Memphis (1) / Rinky Dink II/We're Gonna / Stabbers (1) /   Y'all Niggaz Some Hoes (3)
Choices (1) / Gold Shine (1) / North, North (2,3) /   Rumble (1) / Sucks On Dick (1) / You Know The Biss (1)
Choppers (1) / Gorilla Pimp (3) / Ooh Nuthin' (3) / Rinky Dink/Whatever Ho (1) / This Ain't No Game (2)

PRONG '96

Rock trio from New York City: Tommy Victor (guitar, vocals), Troy Gregory (bass, vocals) and Ted Parsons (drums). Paul Raven replaced Gregory in 1995.

| 2/12/94 | 126 | 2 | © | 1 **Cleansing** .... | | | $10 | Epic 53019 |
| 6/1/96 | 107 | 4 | © | 2 **Rude Awakening** .... | | | $10 | Epic 66945 |

Another Worldly Device (1) / Controller (2) / Home Rule (1) / Not Of This Earth (1) / Rude Awakening (2) / Test (1)
Avenue Of The Finest (2) / Cut-Rate (1) / Innocence Gone (2) / One Outnumbered (1) / Slicing (2) / Unfortunately (2)
Broken Peace (1) / Dark Signs (2) / Mansruin (2) / Out Of This Misery (1) / Snap Your Fingers, Snap Your / Whose Fist Is This Anyway? (1)
Caprice (2) / Face Value (2) / No Question (1) / Proud Division (2) /   Neck (1) / Without Hope (1)
Close The Door (2) / / / / Sublime (1)

PROPELLERHEADS '98

Duo from Bath, England: Alex Gifford and Will White.

| 4/11/98 | 100 | 10 | © | **Decksandrumsandrockandroll** .... | | | $10 | DreamWorks 50031 |

Bang On! / Cominagetcha / On Her Majesty's Secret / Take California / Winning Style
Better? / History Repeating /   Service / 360° (Oh Yeah?) / You Want It Back
Bigger? / Number Of Microphones / Spybreak! / Velvet Pants

PROPHET '88

Hard-rock group: Russell Arcara (vocals), Ken Dubman (guitar), Joe Zujkowski (keyboards), Scott Metaxas (bass) and Michael Sterlacci (drums).

| 3/12/88 | 137 | 7 | © | **Cycle Of The Moon** .... | | | $10 | Megaforce 81822 |

As One / Can't Hide Love / Frontline / Hyperspace / Sound Of A Breaking Heart
Asylum / Cycle Of The Moon / Hands Of Time / Red Line Rider / Tomorrow Never Comes

PROPHET POSSE '98

Rap group: **Indo G**, **Gangsta Boo**, Paul, Juicy J, M-Child, Scarecrow, Crunchy Black, The Kaze and Droopy Drew Dog.

| 3/7/98 | 168 | 2 | © | **Body Parts** .... | | | $10 | Prophet 4406 |

After Dark / Bullet With Yo Name On It / Judgement Night / Notha Nigga Car/Clothes / Talkin' Sh*t
All For One / Catch A Blast / Left'em Dead / Nothin' But Pimp Sh*t / Triple Six Club House
Bitches On My Jock / Drinkin' N Thinkin' / Life In Bondage / Orange Mound / Turn Into Killaz
Bout The South / Favorite Scary Movie / Murderer, Robber / Smoked Out, Loced Out / Wha's Next

PROVINE, Dorothy '61

Born in Deadwood, South Dakota. Singer/actress. Played "Pinky Pinkham" in the TV series *The Roaring 20's* (1960-62).

| 5/15/61 | 34 | 66 | | **The Roaring 20's** .... | | | $25 | Warner 1394 |

Am I Blue? (medley) / Crazy Words-Crazy Tune / I Wanna Be Loved By You / Laugh! Clown! Laugh! (medley) / Poor Butterfly (medley) / Whisper Song (When The
Avalon (medley) /   (medley) /   (medley) / Let's Do It (medley) / Roaring Twenties (medley) /   Pussywillow Whispers To The
Barney Google (medley) / Cup Of Coffee, A Sandwich / I'm Forever Blowing Bubbles / Let's Misbehave (medley) / Someone To Watch Over Me /   Catnip)
Black Bottom (medley) /   And You (medley) /   (medley) / Limehouse Blues (medley) /   (medley)
Bye Bye Blackbird (medley) / Do-Do-Do (medley) / I'm Looking Over A Four Leaf / Mountain Greenery (medley) / Sweet Georgia Brown (medley)
Charleston (medley) / Doin' The Racoon (medley) /   Clover (medley) / Nagasaki (medley) / Tea For Two (medley)
Clap Hands! Here Comes / Don't Bring Lulu (medley) / It Had To Be You (medley) / O-oo Ernest (Are You Earnest
  Charley! (medley) / Girl Friend (medley) / Just A Memory (medley) /   With Me) (medley)

PRU '01

Born Pru Renfro in Houston. Female R&B singer/songwriter.

| 2/3/01 | 176 | 2 | | **Pru** .... | | | $10 | Capitol 23120 |

Aaroma / Candles / Hazy Shades / Prophecy Of A Flower / Sketches Of Pain / Until The End
Can't Compare Your Love / Got Me High / 183 Miles / Reason Why / Smooth Operator / What They Gone Do?

PRUETT, Jeanne '73

Born Norma Jean Bowman on 1/30/37 in Pell City, Alabama. Country singer/songwriter.

| 7/7/73 | 122 | 9 | | **Satin Sheets** .... | | | $15 | MCA 338 |

Baby's Gone / Is Her Love Any Better Than / **Satin Sheets** *28* / What My Thoughts Do All The
Hold On Woman /   Mine / Sweet Sweetheart /   Time
I've Been So Wrong, For So / Lonely Women Cryin' / Walking Piece Of Heaven / Your Memory's Comin' On
  Long / Only Way To Hold Your Man

★420★ PRYOR, Richard '75

Born on 12/1/40 in Peoria, Illinois. Black comedian/actor. Starred in several movies.

1)Is It Something I Said? 2)Richard Pryor Live On The Sunset Strip 3)Bicentennial Nigger

DEBUT	PEAK	WKS	RIAA	CD	#	Album Title	Sym	$	Label & Number
6/15/74	29	53	●		1	That Nigger's Crazy	[C]	$15	Partee 2404
8/23/75	12	25	▲	©	2	Is It Something I Said?	[C]	$12	Reprise 2227
10/9/76	22	19	●		3	Bicentennial Nigger	[C]	$12	Warner 2960
5/28/77	58	9		©	4	Are You Serious???	[C-E]	$12	Laff 196
6/4/77	114	5			5	L.A. Jail	[C-E]	$12	Tiger Lily 14023
6/25/77	68	12	▲		6	Richard Pryor's Greatest Hits	[C-K]	$12	Warner 3057
12/16/78+	32	20	●		7	Wanted	[C]	$15	Warner 3364 [2]
9/8/79	176	4			8	Outrageous	[C-E]	$12	Laff 206
4/17/82	21	17			9	Richard Pryor Live On The Sunset Strip	[C-S]	$10	Warner 3660
						filmed live at the Hollywood Palladium			
11/12/83	71	13			10	Richard Pryor: Here And Now	[C-S]	$10	Warner 23981
						filmed live at the Saenger Theater in New Orleans			

Acid (3)
Africa (9)
Ali (6,7)
Arrested (5)
Back Down (1)
Bad Breath (4)
Bathroom (8)
Bathrooms (5)
Being Born (4)
Being Famous (10)
Being Sensitive (7)
Bicentennial Nigger (3)
Bicentennial Prayer (3)
Big Daddy (5)
Black & White Life Styles (1)
Black & White Women (3)
Black Funerals (7)
Black Hollywood (3)
Black Jack (5)

Black Man/White Woman (1)
Brick Eight (3)
Chain Gang (5)
Chinese Food (7)
Chinese Restaurant (3)
Chow Line (5)
Cocaine (2,6)
Country Singer (5)
Craps (6)
Deer Hunter (7)
Deodorant (4)
Discipline (5)
Dogs And Horses (7)
Eulogy (2)
Exorcist (1,6)
Farting Smells (5)
Fighting (8)
Fire Exit (10)
Flying Saucers (1)

Freebase (9)
Funky People (5)
G - D (4)
Good Night Kiss (2)
Grandmothers (4)
Groovy Feelings (5)
Hair (5)
Have Your Ass Home By 11:00 (1,6)
Heart Attacks (7)
Here And Now (10)
Hi Way 16 (8)
Hillbilly (3,4)
Hospital (9)
I Feel (8)
I Hope I'm Funny (1)
I Like Women (10)
I Met The President (10)
I Remember (10)
Improvisation (8)

Inebriated (10)
Jail (8)
Jesse (4)
Jim Brown (7)
Judgement Day (5)
Just Us (2)
Keeping In Shape (7)
Kids (7)
Leon Spinks (7)
Leroy (4)
Looters (8)
Mafia (4)
Mafia Club (5)
Mankind (4)
Monkeys (7)
Moses (5)
Motherland (10)
Mudbone (9,10)
Mudbone - Little Feets (2,6)

Mudbone Goes To Hollywood (3)
My Father (6)
My Neighborhood (6)
Nature (7)
New Niggers (2)
New Year's Eve (7)
Nigger Babys' (4)
Nigger With A Seizure (1,6)
Niggers Vs. Police (1)
9 Pound Pill (4)
One Day At A Time (10)
One Night Stands (10)
Operation, The (8)
Our Gang (3)
Our Text For Today (2)
Pimples (5)
Prison (9)
Processed Hair (4)
Shortage Of White People (2)

Slavery (10)
Southern Hospitality (10)
State Park (5)
Things In The Woods (7)
Throw Up (8)
True Story Of J.C. (8)
2001 (5)
Virgins (4)
War Movies (4)
When Your Woman Leaves You (2,6)
White And Black People (7)
White Chicks (8)
Wino & Junkie (1)
Wino Dealing With Dracula (1,6)
Women (9)
Women Are Beautiful (2)

PRYSOCK, Arthur '64

Born on 1/2/29 in Spartanburg, South Carolina. Died on 6/14/97 (age 68). R&B singer.

DEBUT	PEAK	WKS	#	Album Title	$	Label & Number
7/13/63	138	7	1	Coast To Coast	$25	Old Town 2005
12/28/63+	97	7	2	A Portrait Of Arthur Prysock	$25	Old Town 2006
8/15/64	131	8	3	Everlasting Songs For Everlasting Lovers	$25	Old Town 2007
7/17/65	116	7	4	A Double Header with Arthur Prysock	$25	Old Town 2009
3/26/66	107	13	5	Arthur Prysock/Count Basie	$20	Verve 8646
1/29/77	153	4	6	All My Life	$12	Old Town 12-004

Ain't No Use (5)
All I Need Is You Tonight (6)
All My Life (6)
All Or Nothing At All (4)
Am I Asking Too Much (2)
April Showers (1)
Are You Ready For A Laugh (2)
Autumn Leaves (2)
Baby I'm The One (6)
Because (2)
Blue Velvet (1)
Close Your Eyes (3)
Come Home (5)
Come Rain Or Come Shine (5)

Don't Go To Strangers (5)
Ebb Tide (2)
Fly Me To The Moon (1)
For Your Love (3)
Gone Again (5)
Goodnight My Love (Pleasant Dreams) (1)
Hard Day's Night (4)
I Could Have Told You (5)
I Could Write A Book (5)
I Left My Heart In San Francisco (1)
I Live My Love (4)
I Love Makin' Love To You (6)

I Wantcha Baby (6)
I Wonder Where Our Love Has Gone (2)
I Worry 'Bout You (5)
I'll Be Around (2)
I'll Follow You (1)
I'm A Fool To Want You (3)
I'm Gonna Sit Right Down And Write Myself A Letter (5)
I'm Lost (5)
Jet (2)
Let It Be Me (4)
Let Me Call You Sweetheart (4)
Let There Be Love (3)

Let's Start All Over Again (3)
Love Look Away (1)
Make Someone Love You (1)
My Everlasting Love (3)
My Wish (2)
One Broken Heart (6)
Open Up Your Heart (4)
Stella By Starlight (2)
Stranger In Town (4)
Sun, The Sand And The Sea (4)
There Goes My Heart (4)
There Will Never Be Another You (2)

They All Say I'm The Biggest Fool (1)
They Say You're Laughing At Me (4)
This Is What You Mean To Me (6)
What Kind Of Fool Am I (1)
What Will I Tell My Heart (5)
What's New (1)
When Love Is New (6) 64
Where Can I Go (2)
Where Or When (3)
Who Can I Turn To (When Nobody Needs Me) (4)

Without The One You Love (3)
You Are Too Beautiful (1)
You Don't Know What Love Is (3)
You'll Never Know (1)
You're Nothing But A Girl (4)
You've Changed (3)

PSEUDO ECHO '87

Pop-rock group formed in Melbourne, Australia: Brian Canham (vocals, guitar), James Leigh (keyboards), Pierre Gigliotti (bass) and Vince Leigh (drums).

DEBUT	PEAK	WKS	Album Title	$	Label & Number
3/21/87	54	27	Love An Adventure	$10	RCA Victor 5730
			second pressings of album substitute "Funky Town" for "Don't Go"		

Beat For You
Destination Unknown

Don't Go
Funky Town 6

I Will Be You
Lies Are Nothing

Listening
Living In A Dream 57

Lonely Without You
Love An Adventure

Try

PSYCHEDELIC FURS '87

Techno-rock group formed in England: brothers Richard (vocals) and Tim (bass) Butler, John Ashton (guitar), and Vince Ely (drums). Philip Calvert replaced Ely in 1983. The Butler brothers formed Love Spit Love in 1994.

DEBUT	PEAK	WKS	RIAA	CD	#	Album Title	Sym	$	Label & Number
11/22/80	140	7		©	1	The Psychedelic Furs	C:#32/10	$12	Columbia 36791
6/27/81	89	14		©	2	Talk Talk Talk	C:#15/72	$12	Columbia 37339
11/13/82+	61	32	●	©	3	Forever Now		$12	Columbia 38261
						produced by Todd Rundgren			
5/26/84	43	27	●	©	4	Mirror Moves	C:#29/8	$12	Columbia 39278
3/7/87	29	27		©	5	Midnight To Midnight		$10	Columbia 40466
9/24/88	102	8		©	6	All Of This And Nothing	[G]	$10	Columbia 44377
11/25/89	138	4			7	Book Of Days		$10	Columbia 45412

Alice's House (4)
All Of The Law (5)
All Of This & Nothing (2,6)
All That Money Wants (6)
Angels Don't Cry (5)
Book Of Days (7)
Danger (4)
Dumb Waiters (2,6)
Entertain Me (7)
Fall (1)

Flowers (1)
Forever Now (3)
Ghost In You (4,6) 59
Goodbye (3)
Heartbeat (4)
Heartbreak Beat (5,6) 26
Heaven (4,6)
Here Come Cowboys (4)
Highwire Days (4,6)
House (7)

I Don't Mine (7)
I Wanna Sleep With You (2)
Imitation Of Christ (1,6)
India (1)
Into You Like A Train (2)
It Goes On (2)
Like A Stranger (4)
Love My Way (3,6) 44
Midnight To Midnight (5)
Mother - Son (7)

Mr. Jones (2)
My Time (4)
No Easy Street (3)
No Release (5)
No Tears (2)
One More Word (5)
Only A Game (4)
Only You And I (3)
Parade (7)
President Gas (3,6)

Pretty In Pink (2,6) 41
Pulse (1)
Run And Run (3)
Shadow In My Heart (6)
She Is Mine (2)
Shine (5)
Shock (5)
Should God Forget (7)
Sister Europe (1,6)
Sleep Comes Down (3)

So Run Down (2)
Soap Commercial (1)
Susan's Strange (4)
Torch (7)
Torture (5)
We Love You (1)
Wedding (2)
Wedding Song (1)
Yes I Do (3)

PSYCHO REALM, The   '97

Rap trio: brothers Jacken and Mr. Duke, with **Cypress Hill** member Louis Freeze.

| 11/15/97 | 183 | 1 | © | 1 | The Psycho Realm | | | $10 | Ruffhouse 68153 |

Big Payback
Bullets
Confessions Of A Drug Addict
La Conecta (Pt. 1 & 2)
Lost Cities
Love From The Sick Side
Premonitions
Psycho City Blocks
Psyclones
R.U. Experienced
Showdown
Stone Garden
Temporary Insanity

PUBLIC ANNOUNCEMENT   '98

R&B vocal group from Chicago: Earl Robinson, Felony Davis, Euclid Gray and Glen Wright. Former backing group for **R. Kelly**.

| 4/11/98 | 81 | 24 | © | 1 | All Work, No Play | | | $10 | A&M 540882 |
| 2/24/01 | 89 | 7 | | 2 | Don't Hold Back | | | $10 | RCA 69310 |

All Work, No Play (1)
Alone (1)
Body Bumpin' (Yippie-Yi-Yo) (1) *5*
Children Hold On (To Your Dreams) (1)
D.O.G. In Me (1)
Don't Hold Back (2)
Homey (1)
It's About Time (1)
John Doe (2)
Lonely (1)
Long Long Summer (We Can) (2)
Lose A Love (2)
Mamacita (2)
Man Ain't Supposed To Cry (2)
Papi (2)
Rithickulous (2)
Slow Dance (2)
Spilt Milk (2)
Step On Pt. II (2)
Straight From The Heart (1)
Turn The Hands (1)
U Tryin' To Ride (2)
When I See You (2)
Why You Not Trustin' Me (1)
Y To The Yippie (Step On) (1)

PUBLIC ENEMY   '91

Rap group from Long Island, New York: Carlton Ridenhour ("**Chuck D**"), William Drayton ("Flavor Flav"), Norman Rogers ("**Terminator X**") and William Griffin ("**Professor Griff**"). Griffin left in 1989.

1/23/88	125	12	●	©	1	Yo! Bum Rush The Show			$10	Def Jam 40658
7/23/88	42	51	▲	©	2	It Takes A Nation Of Millions To Hold Us Back			$10	Def Jam 44303
4/28/90	10	27	▲	©	3	Fear Of A Black Planet	C:#32/5		$10	Def Jam 45413
10/19/91	4	37	▲	©	4	Apocalypse 91...The Enemy Strikes Black			$10	Def Jam 47374
10/3/92	13	14	●	©	5	Greatest Misses		[K]	$10	Def Jam 53014
9/10/94	14	8	●	©	6	Muse Sick-N-Hour Mess Age			$10	Def Jam 523362
5/16/98	26	10		©	7	He Got Game		[S]	$10	Def Jam 558130

Aintnuttin Buttersong (6)
Air Hoodlum (5)
Anti-Nigger Machine (3)
B. Side Wins Again (3)
Bedlam 13:13 (6)
Black Steel In The Hour Of Chaos (2)
Bring The Noise (2,4)
Brothers Gonna Work It Out (3)
Burn Hollywood Burn (3)
By The Time I Get To Arizona (4)
Can't Do Nuttin' For Ya Man (3)
Can't Truss It (4) *50*
Caught, Can We Get A Witness? (1)
Cold Lampin' With Flavor (2)
Contract On The World Love Jam (3)
Countdown To Armageddon (2)
Death Of A Carjacka (6)
Don't Believe The Hype (2)
Fear Of A Black Planet (3)
Fight The Power (3)
Final Count Of The Collision Between Us And The Damned
Game Face (7)
Get The F___ Outta Dodge (4)
Gett Off My Back (5)
Give It Up (6) *33*
Go Cat Go (7)
Godd Complexx (6)
Gotta Do What I Gotta Do (5)
Harry Allen's Interactive Superhighway Phone Call To Chuck D (6)
Hazy Shade Of Criminal (5)
He Got Game (7)
Hit Da Road Jack (5)
Hitler Day (6)
House Of The Rising Sun (6)
How To Kill A Radio Consultant (4,5)
I Ain't Mad At All (6)
I Don't Wanna Be Called Yo Niga (4)
I Stand Accused (6)
Is Your God A Dog (7)
Leave This Off Your Fu*kin Charts (3)
Letter To The NY Post (4)
Live And Undrugged Pt. 1 & 2 (6)
Living In A Zoo (6)
Lost At Birth (4)
Louder Than A Bomb (2,5)
M.P.E. (1)
Meet The G That Killed Me (3)
Megablast (1,5)
Mind Terrorist (2)
Miuzi Weighs A Ton (1)
More News At 11 (4)
Move! (4)
Night Of The Living Baseheads (2)
Nighttrain (4)
911 Is A Joke (3)
1 Million Bottlebags (4)
Party For Your Right To Fight (2,5)
Politics Of The Sneaker Pimps (7)
Pollywanacraka (3)
Power To The People (3)
Prophets Of Rage (2)
Public Enemy No. 1 (1)
Race Against Time (1)
Raise The Roof (1)
Rebel Without A Pause (2)
Rebirth (4)
Reggie Jax (3)
Resurrection (7)
Revelation 33 1/3 Revolutions (7)
Revolutionary Generation (3)
Rightstarter (Message To A Black Man) (1)
Security Of The First World (2)
Shake Your Booty (7)
She Watch Channel Zero?! (2)
Show 'Em Whatcha Got (2)
Shut Em Down (4,5)
So Whatcha Gone Do Now? (6)
Sophisticated Bitch (1)
Stop In The Name... (6)
Sudden Death (7)
Super Agent (7)
Terminator X Speaks With His Hands (1)
Terminator X To The Edge Of Panic (2)
Thin Line Between Law & Rape (6)
Tie Goes To The Runner (5)
Timebomb (1)
Too Much Posse (1)
Unstoppable (7)
War At 33 1/3 (3)
Welcome To The Terrordome (3)
What Kind Of Power We Got? (6)
What Side You On? (6)
What You Need Is Jesus (7)
Who Stole The Soul? (3,5)
Whole Lotta Love Goin On In The Middle Of Hell (4)
Yo! Bum Rush The Show (1)
You're Gonna Get Yours (1,5)

PUBLIC IMAGE LTD.   '89

Punk-rock group formed by lead singer Johnny "Rotten" Lydon (of the **Sex Pistols**). Featured an ever-changing lineup with Lydon the only constant.

5/10/80	171	3	©	1	Second Edition			$15	Island 3288 [2]
5/30/81	114	4	©	2	The Flowers Of Romance			$10	Warner 3536
3/8/86	115	16	©	3	Album			$10	Elektra 60438
10/24/87	169	10	©	4	Happy?			$10	Virgin 90642
6/3/89	106	23	©	5	9			$10	Virgin 91062

Albatross (1)
Angry (4)
Armada (5)
Bad Baby (1)
Bags (3)
Banging The Door (2)
Body, The (4)
Brave New World (5)
Careering (1)
Chant (1)
Disappointed (5)
Ease (3)
FFF (3)
Fat Chance Hotel (4)
Fishing (3)
Flowers Of Romance (2)
Four Enclosed Walls (2)
Francis Massacre (2)
Go Back (2)
Graveyard (1)
Happy (5)
Hard Times (4)
Home (3)
Hymie's Him (2)
Like That (5)
Memories (1)
No Birds (1)
Open And Revolving (4)
Phenagen (2)
Poptones (1)
Radio 4 (1)
Rise (3)
Round (3)
Rules And Regulations (4)
Same Old Story (3)
Sand Castles In The Snow (5)
Save Me (4)
Seattle (4)
Socialist (1)
Suit, The (1)
Swan Lake (1)
Track 8 (2)
U.S.L.S. 1 (5)
Under The House (2)
Warrior (5)
Worry (5)

PUCKETT, Gary, And The Union Gap   '68

Born on 10/17/42 in Hibbing, Minnesota. Pop singer/guitarist. The Union Gap: Gary Withem (keyboards), Dwight Bement (sax), Kerry Chater (bass) and Paul Wheatbread (drums).

| 2/17/68 | 22 | 45 | © | 1 | Woman, Woman | | | $20 | Columbia 9612 |

THE UNION GAP Featuring Gary Puckett

| 5/18/68 | 21 | 39 | ● | © | 2 | Young Girl | | | $20 | Columbia 9664 |
| 11/2/68+ | 20 | 20 | | 3 | Incredible | | | $20 | Columbia 9715 |

12/6/69+	50	14		4	The New Gary Puckett And The Union Gap Album			$20	Columbia 9935
7/11/70	50	33	▲	©	5	Gary Puckett & The Union Gap's Greatest Hits		[G]	$20	Columbia 1042
10/16/71	196	2		6	The Gary Puckett Album			$15	Columbia 30862

GARY PUCKETT

All That Matters (6)
Angelica (6)
Beggar, The (5)
Believe Me (1)
By The Time I Get To Phoenix (1)
Can You Tell (3)
Common Cold (3)
Delta Lady (6)
Do You Really Have A Heart (4)
Don't Give In To Him (4,5) *15*
Don't Make Promises (1,5)
Dreams Of The Everyday Housewife (2)
Feeling Bad (6)
Gentle Woman (6)
Give In (3)
Hard Tomorrow (4)
Hello Morning (6)
His Other Woman (4)
Home (4,5)
Honey (I Miss You) (2)
I Just Don't Know What To Do With Myself (6) *61*
I Want A New Day (1)
I'm Just A Man (3)
I'm Losing You (2)
I've Done All I Can (3)
If The Day Would Come (3)
If We Only Have Love (6)
Keep The Customer Satisfied (6) *71*
Kentucky Woman (1)
Kiss Me Goodbye (2)
Lady Madonna (3)
Lady Willpower (3,5) *2*
Let's Give Adam And Eve Another Chance (5) *41*
Lullaby (4)
M'Lady (1)
Mighty Quinn (3)
My Son (1,4)
Now And Then (3)
Out In The Cold Again (4)
Over You (3,5) *7*
Paindrops (1)
Pleasure Of You (2)
Reverend Posey (3,5)
Say You Don't Need Me (2)
Shimmering Eyes (6)
Simple Man (4)
Stay Out My World (4)
(Sweet, Sweet Baby) Since You've Been Gone (2)
Take Your Pleasure (3)
This Girl Is A Woman Now (4,5) *9*
To Love Somebody (1)
Wait Till The Sun Shines On You (2)
Woman, Woman (1,5) *4*
You Better Sit Down Kids (1)
Young Girl (2,5) *2*

PUFF DADDY '97

Born Sean Combs on 11/4/70 in Harlem, New York. Songwriter/producer/rapper. Founded the Bad Boy record label. Changed performing name briefly to P. Diddy in 2001.

| 8/9/97 | ❶ 4 | 66 | ▲ 7 | © | 1 **No Way Out** | | | $10 | Bad Boy 73012 |

PUFF DADDY & THE FAMILY

| 9/11/99 | 2 1 | 27 | ▲ | © | 2 **Forever** | | | $10 | Bad Boy 73033 |

Angels With Dirty Faces (2) | Do You Like It...Do You Want It... (2) | Gangsta Sh*t (2) | Is This The End? (1,2) | Real Niggas (2) | What You Want (2)
Been Around The World (1) *4* | Don't Stop What You're Doing (1) | I Got The Power (1) | **It's All About The Benjamins** (1) *2* | Reverse (2) | Young G's (1)
Best Friend (2) *59* | Fake Thugs Dedication (2) | I Hear Voices (2) | Journey Through The Life (2) | **Satisfy You** (2) *2* |
Can't Nobody Hold Me Down (1) *1* | Friend (1) | I Love You Baby (1) | P.E. 2000 (2) | Senorita (1) |
Do You Know? (1) | | **I'll Be Missing You** (1) *1* | Pain (1,2) | **Victory** (1) *19* |
| | I'll Do This For You (2) | | What You Gonna Do? (1) |

PULP '98

Rock group from Sheffield, England: Jarvis Cocker (vocals), Russell Senior and Mark Webber (guitars), Steve Mackey (bass) and Nick Banks (drums).

| 4/18/98 | 114 | 2 | | © | **This Is Hardcore** | | | $10 | Island 524492 |

Day After The Revolution | Glory Days | Like A Friend | Seductive Barry | This Is Hardcore
Dishes | Help The Aged | Little Soul | Sylvia |
Fear, The | I'm A Man | Party Hard | TV Movie |

PURE LOVE & PLEASURE '70

Pop-rock group: David McAnally and Pegge Ann May (vocals), Bob Bohanna (guitar), John Allair (keyboards) and Dick Rogers (drums).

| 4/25/70 | 195 | 2 | | | **A Record Of Pure Love & Pleasure** | | | $20 | Dunhill/ABC 50076 |

All In My Mind | Joyce | Love, Love, Love You | My Lies | Too Scared To Go
Hard Times | Lord's Prayer | Mama Said | Relax | What'cha Gonna Do

★487★ PURE PRAIRIE LEAGUE '75

Country-rock group formed in Cincinnati. Core members: Craig Fuller (vocals, guitar), George Ed Powell and Larry Goshorn (guitars), Michael Connor (keyboards), Mike Reilly (bass) and Billy Hinds (drums). Fuller left after their first album, Powell and Reilly took over lead vocals. **Vince Gill** joined as lead singer in 1979. Group disbanded in 1983. Fuller joined **Little Feat** by 1988.

2/8/75	34	24	●	©	1 **Bustin' Out**	C:#36/8		$15	RCA Victor 4769
6/7/75	24	14		©	2 **Two Lane Highway**			$15	RCA Victor 0933
2/7/76	33	16		©	3 **If The Shoe Fits**			$15	RCA Victor 1247
11/20/76	99	14			4 **Dance**			$15	RCA Victor 1924
9/10/77	68	11		©	5 **Live!! Takin' The Stage**		[L]	$20	RCA Victor 2404 [2]
5/13/78	79	11			6 **Just Fly**			$15	RCA Victor 2590
6/23/79	124	6		©	7 **Can't Hold Back**			$15	RCA Victor 3335
5/17/80	37	24		©	8 **Firin' Up**			$12	Casablanca 7212
5/2/81	72	15		©	9 **Something In The Night**			$12	Casablanca 7255

All The Lonesome Cowboys (4,5) | Don't Keep Me Hangin' (9) | I Can Only Think Of You (3) | Kansas City Southern (2,5) | Misery Train (7) | Tell Me One More Time (5)
All The Way (4) | Early Morning Riser (1) | I Can't Believe (7) | Kentucky Moonshine (2,5) | My Young Girl (6) | That'll Be The Day (3,5)
Amie (1,5) *27* | Fade Away (4,5) | I Can't Hold Back (7) | Leave My Heart Alone (1) | Out In The Street (3,5) | Too Many Heartaches In
Angel (1) | Falling In And Out Of Love (1) | **I Can't Stop The Feelin'** (8) *77* | **Let Me Love You Tonight** | Pickin' To Beat The Devil (2,5) | Paradise (8)
Angel #9 (1) | Feel The Fire (9) | I Wanna Know Your Name (9) | (8) *10* | Place In The Middle (6) | Tornado Warning (4)
Aren't You Mine (3) | Feelin' Of Love (5) | I'll Be Damned (8) | Lifetime (6) | Restless Woman (7) | **Two Lane Highway** (2,5) *97*
Bad Dream (6) | Fool Fool (7) | I'll Change Your Flat Tire, Merle | Lifetime Of Nighttime (8) | Rude Rude Awakening (7) | White Line (7)
Boulder Skies (1) | Gimme Another Chance (3) | (2,5) | Livin' Each Day At A Time (4) | Runner (2) | Working In The Coal Mine (6)
Call Me, Tell Me (1) | Give It Up (8) | **I'm Almost Ready** (8) *34* | Livin' It Alone (7) | San Antonio (4) | You Are So Near To Me (3)
Came Through (5) | Give Us A Rise (2) | I'm Goin' Away (7) | Long Cold Winter (3) | She's All Mine (8) | You Don't Have To Be Alone (6)
Catfishin' (4) | Goin' Home (1) | In The Morning (4) | Louise (What I Did) (5) | Sister's Keeper (2) | **You're Mine Tonight** (9) *68*
Country Song (5) | Goodbye So Long (7) | Janny Lou (8) | Love Is Falling (6) | Slim Pickin's (6) | You're My True Love (8)
Dance (4,5) | Harvest (2,5) | Jazzman (1) | Love Me Again (8) | Slim Pickin's (6) |
Dark Colours (5) | Heart Of Her Own (5) | Jerene (7) | Love Will Grow (6) | Something In The Night (9) |
Do You Love Me Truly, Julie (9) | Help Yourself (4) | Just Can't Believe It (2) | Lucille Crawfield (3,5) | **Still Right Here In My Heart** |
| Hold On To Our Hearts (9) | Just Fly (6) | Memories (2) | (9) *28* |
| | | | Sun Shone Lightly (3,5) |

PURE SOUL '95

Female R&B vocal group from Washington DC: Shawn Allen, Heather Perkins, Keitha Shepherd and Kirstin Hall.

| 10/21/95 | 173 | 3 | | © | **Pure Soul** | | | $10 | Step Sun 92638 |

Baby I'm Leaving | Something About The Way That | Turns Me On | What Did We Do? | You Stay On My Mind
I Feel Like Running | You Do | Wait For You | Wish You Were Here |
I Want You Back | **Stairway To Heaven** *79* | **We Must Be In Love** *65* | Woman That I Am |

PURIM, Flora '76

Born on 3/6/42 in Rio de Janeiro. Female singer. Married to **Airto**.

2/15/75	172	5		©	1 **Stories To Tell**			$12	Milestone 9058
3/13/76	59	15		©	2 **Open Your Eyes You Can Fly**			$12	Milestone 9065
10/16/76	146	5		©	3 **500 Miles High**		[L]	$12	Milestone 9070

recorded on 7/6/74 at the Montreaux Jazz Festival

3/26/77	163	4			4 **Nothing Will Be As It Was...Tomorrow**			$12	Warner 2985
8/13/77	194	3		©	5 **Encounter**			$12	Milestone 9077
6/3/78	174	4			6 **Everyday, Everynight**			$12	Warner 3168

Above The Rainbow (5) | Corre Nina (4) | I Just Don't Know (6) | Latinas (5) | Search For Peace (1) | Walking Away (6)
Andei (I Walked) (2) | Cravo E Canela (Cinnamon | I Just Want To Be Here | Mountain Train (1) | Silver Sword (1) | White Wing/Black Wing (2)
Angels (4) | And Cloves) (3) | (medley) | Nothing Will Be As It Was - | Sometime Ago (2) | Why I'm Alone (6)
Baia (3) | Dedicated To Bruce (3) | I'm Coming For Your Love (4) | Nada Sera Como Antes (4) | Stories To Tell (1) | Windows (5)
Black Narcissus (5) | Encounter (5) | In Brasil (6) | O Cantador (1,3) | Time's Lie (2) | You Love Me Only (4)
Blues Ballad (6) | Everyday, Everynight (6) | Ina's Song (Trip To Bahia) | Open Your Eyes You Can Fly | To Say Goodbye (1) |
Bridge (3) | Fairy Tale Song (4) | (medley) | (2) | Tomara (I Wish) (5) |
Bridges (4) | Five-Four (6) | Insensatez (1) | Overture (6) | Transition (medley) (2) |
Casa Forte (1) | 500 Miles High (3) | Jive Talk (3) | Samba Michel (6) | Uri (The Wind) (3,5) |
Conversation (2) | Hope, The (6) | Las Olas (6) | San Francisco River (2) | Vera Cruz (Empty Faces) (1) |

PURSELL, Bill '63

Born on 6/9/26 in Oakland; raised in Tulare, California. Session pianist.

| 4/6/63 | 28 | 14 | | © | **Our Winter Love** | | [I] | $20 | Columbia 1992 |

Born To Lose | Four Walls | I Walk The Line | Stranger | There'll Be No Teardrops
Bye Bye Love | I Can't Help It (If I'm Still In Love | Love Can't Wait | That Which Is Loved | Tonight
Dark Alley | With You) | **Our Winter Love** *9* | | Wound Time Can't Erase

DEBUT	PEAK	WKS	RIAA	CD	ARTIST — Album Title	Catalog	Sym	$	Label & Number

PURSUIT OF HAPPINESS, The '89

Rock group from Toronto: Moe Berg (male vocals, guitar), Leslie Stanwyck (female vocals), Kris Abbott (guitar), Johnny Sinclair (bass) and Dave Gilby (drums).

| 12/17/88+ | 93 | 21 | | © | **Love Junk** .... | | | **$10** | Chrysalis 41675 |

Beautiful White
Consciousness Raising As A
 Social Tool

Hard To Laugh
I'm An Adult Now
Killed By Love

Looking For Girls
Man's Best Friend
She's So Young

Ten Fingers
Tree Of Knowledge
Walking In The Woods

When The Sky Comes Falling
 Down

PYRAMIDS, The '64

Surf group from Long Beach, California: Skip Mercer and Willie Glover (guitars), Tom Pittman (sax), Steve Leonard (bass) and Ron McMullen (drums). Performed with shaved heads. Appeared in the movie *Bikini Beach*.

| 3/14/64 | 119 | 6 | | | **The Original Penetration! and other favorites** .... | | | **$200** | Best 16501 |

Do The Slauson
Everybody

Here Comes Marsha
Koko Joe

Long Tall Texan
Louie Louie

Out Of Limits
Paul

Penetration 18
Pyramid Stomp

Road Runnah
Sticks And Skins

PYTHON LEE JACKSON '72

Rock group from Australia: David Bently (keyboards), Mick Liber and Gary Boyle (guitars), Tony Cahill (bass) and David Montgomery (drums).

| 10/7/72 | 182 | 6 | | | **In A Broken Dream** .... | | | **$15** | GNP Crescendo 2066 |

Blues, The
Boogie Woogie Joe
Doin' Fine

If It's Meant To Be A Party
If The World Stopped Still
 Tonight

In A Broken Dream 56
Second Time Around The
 Wheel

Sweet Consolation
Turn The Music Down
Your Wily Ways

Q

Q '77

Pop group from Beaver Falls, Pennsylvania: Don Garvin (guitar), Robert Peckman (bass), Bill Thomas (keyboards) and Bill Vogel (drums). All share vocals.

| 6/18/77 | 140 | 2 | | | **Dancin' Man** .... | | | **$12** | Epic 34691 |

Dancin' Man 23
Do I Love You?

Feel It In Your Backbone, Got It
In Your Feet

Feelin' That Rhythm To The
 Bone

Have I Sinned
If It Ain't One Thing, It's Another

Jump For Joy
Knee Deep In Love

Make Us One Again
Sweet Summertime

QB FINEST '01

All-star rap group: **Nas**, **Capone**, **Mobb Deep**, Tragedy, MC Shan, **Marley Marl**, **Nature**, Cormega and Millennium Thug. QB: Queen's Bridge.

| 1/6/01 | 53 | 23 | ● | © | **Nas & Ill Will Records Presents Queensbridge The Album** .... | | | **$10** | Ill Will 63807 |

Da Bridge 2001
Die 4
Find Ya Wealth

Fire
Kids In Da PJ's
Money

Oochie Wally 26
Our Way
Power Rap

Real Niggas
Self Conscience
Straight Outta Q.B.

Street Glory
Teenage Thug
We Break Bread

We Live This

Q-TIP '99

Born Jonathan Davis on 11/20/70 in New York City. Male rapper. Member of **A Tribe Called Quest**.

| 12/18/99 | 28 | 18 | ● | © | **Amplified** .... | | | **$10** | Arista 14619 |

All In
Breathe And Stop 71
Do It

Do It, Be It, See It
End Of Time
Go Hard

Higher
Let's Ride
Moving With U

N.T.
Things U Do
Vivrant Thing 26

Wait Up

QUAD CITY DJ'S '96

Dance trio from Orlando, Florida: Nathaniel Orange, Johnny McGowan and Lana LeFleur. Orange was a member of **95 South**.

| 7/13/96 | 31 | 42 | ▲ | © | **Get On Up And Dance** .... | | | **$10** | Atlantic 82905 |

Bass, The
C'mon N' Ride It (The Train) 3

Get On Up And Dance
Hey DJ

Let's Do It
Move To This

Party Over Here
Quad City Funk

Ride That Bass
Stomp-N-Grind

Summer Jam
Work Baby Work (The Prep)

QUARTERFLASH '82

Pop-rock group from Portland, Oregon: husband-and-wife Marv (guitar) and Rindy (vocals, saxophone) Ross, with Jack Charles (guitar), Rick DiGiallonardo (keyboards), Rich Gooch (bass) and Brian David Willis (drums). Group originally known as Seafood Mama.

10/31/81+	8	52	▲	©	1 **Quarterflash**			**$10**	Geffen 2003
7/9/83	34	21		©	2 **Take Another Picture**			**$10**	Geffen 4011
10/5/85	150	5		©	3 **Back Into Blue**			**$10**	Geffen 24078

Back Into Blue (3)
Caught In The Rain (3)
Come To Me (3)
Critical Times (1)
Cruisin' With The Deuce (1)
Eye To Eye (2)

Find Another Fool (1) *16*
Grace Under Fire (3)
Harden My Heart (1) *3*
I Want To Believe It's You (3)
It All Becomes Clear (2)
It Don't Move Me (2)

Just For You (3)
Love Should Be So Kind (1)
Love Without A Net (You Keep
 Falling) (3)
Make It Shine (2)
Nowhere Left To Hide (2)

One More Round To Go (2)
Right Kind Of Love (1) *56*
Shakin' The Jinx (2)
Shane (2)
Take Another Picture (2) *58*
Take Me To Heart (2) *14*

Talk To Me (3) *83*
Try To Make It True (1)
Valerie (1)
Walking On Ice (3)
Welcome To The City (3)
Williams Avenue (1)

QUATEMAN, Bill '77

Born in 1951 in Chicago. Singer/songwriter/guitarist.

| 2/12/77 | 129 | 8 | | | **Night After Night** .... | | | **$12** | RCA Victor 2027 |

Au Claire
Back By The River

Carolina
Dance Baby Dance

Doncha Wonder
Down To The Bone

Mama Won't You Roll Me
Night After Night

You're The One
Your Money Or Your Life

QUATRO, Suzi '79

Born on 6/3/50 in Detroit. Rock singer/songwriter/guitarist. Played "Leather Tuscadero" on TV's *Happy Days* in 1977. Her sister Patti was a member of **Fanny**.

3/30/74	142	13		©	1 **Suzi Quatro**			**$15**	Bell 1302
10/5/74	126	10		©	2 **Quatro**			**$15**	Bell 1313
5/10/75	146	6		©	3 **Your Mama Won't Like Me**			**$12**	Arista 4035
3/24/79	37	20			4 **If You Knew Suzi...**			**$12**	RSO 3044
10/6/79	117	14			5 **Suzi...And Other Four Letter Words**			**$12**	RSO 3064
11/1/80	165	5			6 **Rock Hard**			**$12**	Dreamland 5006

QUATRO, Suzi — Cont'd

All Shook Up (1) **85**	Glad All Over (6)	Klondyke Kate (2)	Official Suburban Superman (1)	Shine My Machine (1)	Trouble (2)
Breakdown (4)	Glycerine Queen (1)	Lay Me Down (6)		Shot Of Rhythm And Blues (2)	Wild One (2)
Can The Can (1) **56**	Hard Headed (6)	**Lipstick** (6) **51**	Paralysed (3)	Skin Tight Skin (1)	Wiser Than You (4)
Can't Trust Love (3)	Hit The Road Jack (2)	Lonely Is The Hardest (6)	Primitive Love (1)	Space Cadets (5)	Wish Upon Me (6)
Cat Size (2)	Hollywood (5)	Love Hurts (5)	Prisoner Of Your Imagination (3)	Starlight Lady (5)	Woman Cry (6)
Devil Gate Drive (2)	I Bit Off More Than I Could Chew (3)	Love Is Ready (6)	Race Is On (4)	State Of Mind (6)	You Are My Lover (5)
Don't Change My Luck (4)	I Wanna Be Your Man (1)	Mama's Boy (5)	Rock And Roll Hoochie Koo (4)	Sticks And Stones (1)	You Can Make Me Want You (3)
Ego In The Night (6)	**I've Never Been In Love** (5) **44**	Michael (3)	Rock Hard (6)	Strip Me (3)	Your Mama Won't Like Me (3)
Fever (3)	**If You Can't Give Me Love** (4) **45**	Mind Demons (5)	Savage Silk (2)	**Stumblin' In** (4) **4**	
48 Crash (1)		Move It (2)	Shakin' All Over (1)	Suicide (4)	
Four Letter Words (5)	Keep A Knockin' (2)	New Day Woman (3)	**She's In Love With You** (5) **41**	Tired Of Waiting (4)	
		Non-Citizen (4)		Too Big (2)	

QUAZAR '78

Funk group from New Jersey: Peachena (female vocals), Kevin Goins (male vocals, guitar), Harvey Banks (guitar), Monica Peters (trumpet), Darryl Dixon (sax), Greg Fitz and Richard Banks (keyboards), Darryl Deliberto (percussion), Eugene Jackson (bass) and Jeff Adams (drums).

11/11/78	**121**	5			Quazar			$12	Arista 4187

Funk 'N' Roll (Dancin' In The "Funkshine")	Funk With A Capital "G"	Savin' My Love For A Rainy Day	Starlight Circus
Funk With A Big Foot	Love Me Baby	Shades Of Quaze	Workin' On The Buildin'
			Your Lovin' Is Easy

QUEEN ★63★ '80

Pop-rock group formed in England: **Freddie Mercury** (vocals), **Brian May** (guitar), John Deacon (bass) and **Roger Taylor** (drums). Mercury died of AIDS on 11/24/91 (age 45). Group inducted into the Rock and Roll Hall of Fame in 2001.

1)The Game 2)News Of The World 3)A Night At The Opera 4)Classic Queen 5)A Day At The Races

DEBUT	PEAK	WKS	RIAA	CD		ARTIST — Album Title	Sym	$	Label & Number
11/3/73+	**83**	22	●	©	1	Queen		$25	Elektra 75064
5/11/74	**49**	13		©	2	Queen II		$15	Elektra 75082
12/14/74+	**12**	32	●	©	3	Sheer Heart Attack		$15	Elektra 1026
12/27/75+	**4**	56	●	©	4	**A Night At The Opera**	C:#3/35	$15	Elektra 1053
1/15/77	**5**	19	●	©	5	**A Day At The Races**		$15	Elektra 101
11/26/77+	**3**	37	●	©	6	**News Of The World**	C:#6/26	$15	Elektra 112
12/9/78+	**6**	18	▲		7	**Jazz**		$15	Elektra 166
7/7/79	**16**	14	●		8	Queen Live Killers ....C:#10/16	[L]	$20	Elektra 702 [2]
7/19/80	**❶**[5]	43	▲		9	**The Game**		$12	Elektra 513
12/27/80+	**23**	15		©	10	Flash Gordon	[S]	$12	Elektra 518
11/14/81	**14**	26	▲		11	Greatest Hits	[G]	$12	Elektra 564
5/29/82	**22**	21	●	©	12	Hot Space		$12	Elektra 60128
3/17/84	**23**	20	●	©	13	The Works		$10	Capitol 12322
7/19/86	**46**	13		©	14	A Kind of Magic		$10	Capitol 12476
6/24/89	**24**	14		©	15	The Miracle		$10	Capitol 92357
2/23/91	**30**	17	●	©	16	Innuendo		$10	Hollywood 61020
3/28/92	**4**	68	▲[2]	©	17	Classic Queen	C:#48/2 [G]	$10	Hollywood 61311
6/20/92	**53**	15	▲		18	Live At Wembley '86	[L]	$15	Hollywood 61104 [2]
						recorded on 7/11/86			
10/3/92	**11**	207	▲	©	19	Greatest Hits ....C:#13/214	[G]	$10	Hollywood 61265
5/8/93	**46**	15		©	20	Five Live	[L-M]	$10	Hollywood 61479
						GEORGE MICHAEL AND QUEEN with Lisa Stansfield			
11/25/95	**58**	11	●	©	21	Made In Heaven		$10	Hollywood 62017

Action This Day (12)	Don't Lose Your Head (14)	Headlong (16,17)	Keep Yourself Alive (1,8,11,17)	Modern Times Rock 'N' Roll (1)	Scandal (15)
All Dead, All Dead (6)	**Don't Stop Me Now** (7,8,19) **86**	Heaven For Everyone (21)	Khashoggi's Ship (15)	More Of That Jazz (7)	Seaside Rendezvous (4)
All God's People (16)	Don't Try So Hard (16)	Hello Mary Lou (Goodbye Heart) (18)	**Killer Queen** (3,8,11,19) **12**	Mother Love (21)	Seven Seas Of Rhye (1,2,18,19)
Another One Bites The Dust (9,11,18,19) **1**	Don't Try Suicide (9)	Hero (10)	**Kind Of Magic** (14,17,18) **42**	Mustapha (7)	She Makes Me (Stormtrooper In Stilettoes) (3)
Arboria (Planet Of The Tree Man) (10)	Dragon Attack (9)	Hitman (16)	Kiss (Aura Resurrects Flash) (10)	My Baby Does Me (15)	Sheer Heart Attack (6,8)
Back Chat (12)	Dreamer's Ball (7,8)	I Can't Live With You (16)	Las Palabras De Amor (The Words Of Love) (12)	My Fairy King (1)	Show Must Go On (16,17)
Battle Theme (10)	Drowse (5)	**I Want It All** (15,17) **50**		My Life Has Been Saved (21)	Sleeping On The Sidewalk (6)
Bicycle Race (7,8,11,19) **24**	Escape From The Swamp (10)	**I Want To Break Free** (13,18,19) **45**	Lazing On A Sunday Afternoon (4)	My Melancholy Blues (6)	Some Day One Day (2)
Big Spender (18)	Execution Of Flash (10)	I Was Born To Love You (21)	Leaving Home Ain't Easy (7)	**Need Your Loving Tonight** (9) **44**	**Somebody To Love** (5,11,19,20) **30**
Bijou (16)	Fairy Feller's Master-Stroke (2)	I'm Going Slightly Mad (16,17)	Let Me Entertain You (7,8)	Nevermore (2)	Son And Daughter (1)
Body Language (12,19) **11**	**Fat Bottomed Girls** (7,11,19) **flip**	I'm In Love With My Car (4,8)	Let Me Live (21)	Night Comes Down (1)	Spread Your Wings (6,8)
Bohemian Rhapsody (4,8,11,17,18) **2**	Father To Son (2)	If You Can't Beat Them (7)	Liar (1)	Now I'm Here (3,8,18,19)	Staying Power (12)
Breakthru (15)	Fight From The Inside (6)	Impromptu (18)	Life Is Real (Song For Lennon) (12)	Ogre Battle (2)	Stone Cold Crazy (3,17)
Brighton Rock (3,8,18)	**Flash's Theme aka Flash** (10,11) **42**	In Only Seven Days (7)	Lily Of The Valley (3)	**One Vision** (14,17,18) **61**	Sweet Lady (4)
Bring Back That Leroy Brown (3)	Flash To The Rescue (10)	In The Death Cell (Love Theme Reprise) (10)	Loser In The End (2)	One Year Of Love (14,17)	Tear It Up (13,18)
Calling All Girls (12) **60**	Flick Of The Wrist (3)	In The Lap Of The Gods (3,18)	Love Of My Life (4,8,18)	Pain Is So Close To Pleasure (14)	Tenement Funster (3)
Coming Soon (9)	Football Fight (10)	In The Space Capsule (The Love Theme) (10)	Machines (or Back To Humans) (13)	Party (15)	Teo Torriatte (Let Us Cling Together) (5)
Cool Cat (12)	Friends Will Be Friends (14,18)	Innuendo (16)	Made In Heaven (21)	**Play The Game** (9,11,19) **42**	These Are The Days Of Our Lives (16,17,20)
Crash Dive On Ming City (10)	Fun It (7)	Invisible Man (15)	Man On The Prowl (13)	Princes Of The Universe (14)	'39 (4,8)
Crazy Little Thing Called Love (9,11,18,19) **1**	Funny How Love Is (2)	Is This The World We Created...? (14,18)	March Of The Black Queen (2)	Procession (2)	**Tie Your Mother Down** (5,8,17,18) **49**
Dancer (12)	Get Down, Make Love (6,8)	It's A Beautiful Day (21)	Marriage Of Dale And Ming (And Flash Approaching) (10)	Prophet's Song (2)	Too Much Love Will Kill You (21)
Dead On Time (7)	Gimme Some Lovin' (18)	**It's A Hard Life** (13) **72**	Millionaire Waltz (5)	Put Out The Fire (12)	Tutti Frutti (18)
Dear Friends (3,20)	Gimme The Prize (Kurgan's Theme) (14)	**It's Late** (6) **74**	Ming's Theme (In The Court Of Ming The Merciless) (10)	**Radio Ga-Ga** (13,17,18) **16**	**Under Pressure** (11,12,17,18) **29**
Death On Two Legs (Dedicated To...) (4,8)	God Save The Queen (4,8,18)	Jealousy (7)	Miracle, The (15,17)	Rain Must Fall (9)	
Delilah (16)	Good Company (4)	Jesus (1)	Misfire (3)	Ride The Wild Wind (16)	
Doing All Right (1)	Good Old-Fashioned Lover Boy (5,19)	Keep Passing The Open Windows (13)		Ring (Hypnotic Seduction Of Dale) (10)	
	Great King Rat (1)			Rock It (Prime Jive) (9)	
	Hammer To Fall (13,17,18)			Sail Away Sweet Sister (9)	
				Save Me (9,19)	

QUEEN — Cont'd

Vultan's Theme (Attack Of The Hawk Men) (10)	**We Will Rock You** (6,8,11,18,19) *52*	Wedding March (10)	Who Wants To Live Forever (14,17,18)	You Take My Breath Away (5)
Was It All Worth It (15)	charted at POS 52 as "We Will Rock You/We Are The Champions" in 1992	White Man (5)	Winter's Tale (21)	**You're My Best Friend** (4,8,11,19) *16*
We Are The Champions (6,8,11,18,19) *4*		White Queen (As It Began) (2)	You And I (5)	(You're So Square) Baby I Don't Care (18)
		Who Needs You (6)	You Don't Fool Me (21)	

QUEEN LATIFAH '94

Born Dana Owens on 3/18/70 in Newark, New Jersey. Female rapper/actress. Appeared in several movies. Played "Khadijah James" on TV's *Living Single*. Latifah is Arabic for delicate and sensitive.

DEBUT	PEAK	WKS		CD	#	Title	$	Label & Number
12/16/89+	124	17		©	1	All Hail The Queen	$10	Tommy Boy 1022
9/21/91	117	23		©	2	Nature Of A Sista'	$10	Tommy Boy 1035
12/4/93+	60	31	●	©	3	Black Reign	$10	Motown 6370
7/4/98	95	4		©	4	Order In The Court	$10	Motown 530895

Bad As A Mutha (2)	Court Is In Session (4)	Inside Out (1)	Love Again (2)	**Paper** (4) *50*	Turn You On (4)
Bananas [Who You Gonna Call?] (4)	Dance For Me (1)	It's Alright (4)	Mama Gave Birth To The Soul Children (1)	Parlay (4)	**U.N.I.T.Y.** (3) *23*
Black Hand Side (3)	Evil That Men Do (1)	**Just Another Day...** (3) *54*	Mood Is Right (3)	Princess Of The Posse (1)	**Weekend Love** (3) *70*
Black On Black Love (4)	Fly Girl (4)	King And Queen Creation (1)	Nature Of A Sista' (2)	Pros, The (1)	What Ya Gonna Do (4)
Bring The Flavor (3)	Give Me Your Love (2)	Ladies First (1)	No Work (3)	Queen Of Royal Badness (1)	Winki's Theme (2)
Brownsville (4)	How Do I Love Thee (2)	Latifah's Had It Up 2 Here (2)	No/Yes (4)	Rough... (3)	Wrath Of My Madness (1)
Come Into My House (1)	I Can't Understand (3)	Latifah's Law (1)	Nuff' Of The Ruff' Stuff' (1)	Sexy Fancy (4)	
Coochie Bang... (3)	I Don't Know (4)	Life (4)	One Mo' Time (2)	Superstar (3)	
	If You Don't Know (2)	Listen 2 Me (3)		That's The Way We Flow (2)	

QUEEN PEN '98

Born Lynise Walters in New York City. Female rapper.

DEBUT	PEAK	WKS		CD	#	Title	$	Label & Number
1/17/98	78	20		©	1	My Melody	$10	Lil' Man 90151
6/9/01	134	2		©	2	Conversations With Queen	$10	Motown 013785

All My Love (2) *28*	Ghetto Divorce (2)	It's True (1)	P***y Ain't For Free (2)	So Many Ways (1)
Baby Daddy (2)	Girlfriend (1)	**Man Behind The Music** (1) *84*	QP Walks (2)	True (2)
Cold Cold World (2)	I Got Cha (2)	My Melody (1)	Queen Of The Click (1)	Warn U (2)
For You (1)	I Reps (2)	No Hooks (1)	Revolution (2)	What Yall Wanna Hear (2)
Get Away (1)	I'm Gon Blow Up (1)	**Party Ain't A Party** (1) *74*	Set Up (1)	Who's The (2)

★340★ QUEENSRŸCHE '90

Hard-rock group from Bellevue, Washington: Geoff Tate (vocals), Chris DeGarmo and Michael Wilton (guitars), Eddie Jackson (bass), and Scott Rockenfield (drums).

1)Promised Land 2)Empire 3)Hear In The Now Frontier

DEBUT	PEAK	WKS		CD	#	Title	Sym	$	Label & Number
9/17/83	81	22		©	1	Queensrÿche	[M]	$10	EMI America 19006
10/13/84	61	23	●	©	2	The Warning		$10	EMI America 17134
7/26/86	47	21	●	©	3	Rage For Order		$10	EMI America 17197
5/21/88	50	52	▲	©	4	Operation:mindcrime	C:#30/8	$10	EMI-Manhattan 48640
9/22/90	7	129	▲³	©	5	Empire	C:#23/15	$10	EMI 92806
11/23/91	38	11		©	6	Operation:livecrime	[L]	$10	EMI 97048
11/5/94	3	19	▲	©	7	Promised Land		$10	EMI 30711
4/12/97	19	12		©	8	Hear In The Now Frontier		$10	EMI 56141
10/2/99	46	5		©	9	Q2K		$10	Atlantic 83225
7/15/00	149	3		©	10	Greatest Hits	[G]	$10	Virgin 49422

All I Want (8)	Chemical Youth (We Are Rebellion) (3)	Hand On Heart (5)	Miles Away (8)	Promised Land (7)	Spool (8)
Anarchy-X (4,6)	Child Of Fire (2)	Hero (8)	Mission, The (4,6)	Queen Of The Reich (1,10)	Spreading The Disease (4,6)
Another Rainy Night (Without You) (5)	Cuckoo's Nest (8)	Hit The Black (8)	My Empty Room (4,6)	Reach (8)	Suite Sister Mary (4,6)
Anybody Listening? (5)	Damaged (7)	How Could I? (9)	My Global Mind (7)	Resistance (5)	Surgical Strike (3)
Anytime/Anywhere (8)	Deliverance (8)	I Am I (7,10)	NM 156 (2)	Revolution Calling (4)	Take Hold Of The Flame (2,10)
Before The Storm (2)	Della Brown (5)	I Don't Believe In Love (4,6,10)	Needle Lies (4,6)	Right Side Of My Mind (9)	Thin Line (7)
Beside You (9)	Disconnected (7)	I Dream In Infrared (3,10)	Neue Regel (3)	Roads To Madness (2)	Voice Inside (8)
Best I Can (5)	Electric Requiem (4,6)	I Remember Now (4,6)	Nightrider (1)	Sacred Ground (9)	Waiting For 22 (4,6)
Blinded (1)	Empire (5,10)	I Will Remember (3)	9:28 a.m. (7)	Saved (8)	Walk In The Shadows (3,10)
Breakdown (9)	En Force (3)	Jet City Woman (5,10)	No Sanctuary (2)	Screaming In Digital (3)	Warning (2,10)
Breaking The Silence (4,6)	Eyes Of A Stranger (4,6,10)	Killing Words (3)	One And Only (5)	Sign Of The Times (8,10)	When The Rain Comes... (4)
Bridge (7)	Falling Down (8)	Lady Jane (7)	One Life (9)	**Silent Lucidity** (5,10) *9*	Whisper, The (3)
Burning Man (9)	Get A Life (8)	Lady Wore Black (1,10)	One More Time (7)	Some People Fly (8)	Wot Kinda Man (9)
Chasing Blue Sky (10)	Gonna Get Close To You (1)	Liquid Sky (9)	Operation: Mindcrime (4,6)	Someone Else? (7,10)	You (8)
		London (3)	Out Of Mind (7)	Speak (4,6)	

? (QUESTION MARK) & THE MYSTERIANS '66

Rock group formed in Texas: Rudy "?" Martinez (vocals), Bobby Balderrama (guitar), Frank Rodriguez (organ), Frank Lugo (bass) and Eddie Serrato (drums).

DEBUT	PEAK	WKS			#	Title	$	Label & Number
11/19/66	66	15				96 Tears	$100	Cameo 2004

Don't Break This Heart Of Mine	"8" Teen	Midnight Hour	Set Aside	Ten O'Clock	Why Me
Don't Tease Me	**I Need Somebody** *22*	**96 Tears** *1*	Stormy Monday	nd Side	You're Telling Me Lies

QUICKSAND '95

Hard-rock group from New York City: Walter Schreifels (vocals, guitar), Tom Capone (guitar), Sergio Vega (bass) and Alan Cage (drums).

DEBUT	PEAK	WKS		CD	#	Title	$	Label & Number
3/18/95	134	1		©		Manic Compression	$10	Island 526564

Backward	Brown Gargantuan	Divorce	It Would Be Cooler If You Did	Simpleton	Supergenius
Blister	Delusional	East 3rd St.	Landmine Spring	Skinny (It's Overflowing)	Thorn In My Side

★497★ QUICKSILVER MESSENGER SERVICE '70

Rock group from San Francisco: Gary Duncan (vocals, guitar), John Cipollina (guitar), David Freiberg (bass) and Greg Elmore (drums). Dino Valenti joined as lead singer in 1970. Freiberg left in 1973 to join **Jefferson Starship**. Cipollina died on 5/29/89 (age 45). Valenti died on 11/16/94 (age 57).

DEBUT	PEAK	WKS		CD	#	Title	Sym	$	Label & Number
6/22/68	63	25		©	1	Quicksilver Messenger Service		$40	Capitol 2904
3/29/69	27	30	●	©	2	Happy Trails	[L]	$30	Capitol 120
1/24/70	25	24		©	3	Shady Grove		$25	Capitol 391
8/22/70	27	24		©	4	Just For Love		$25	Capitol 498
1/23/71	26	20		©	5	What About Me		$25	Capitol 630
12/4/71+	114	9		©	6	Quicksilver		$25	Capitol 819

QUICKSILVER MESSENGER SERVICE — Cont'd

DEBUT	PEAK	WKS		CD	Title			$	Label & Number
5/6/72	134	10	©	7	Comin' Thru			$15	Capitol 11002
5/19/73	108	10	©	8	Anthology		[K]	$20	Capitol 11165 [2]
11/15/75	89	12	©	9	Solid Silver			$15	Capitol 11462

All In My Mind (5)
Baby Baby (5)
Bears (8)
Bittersweet Love (9)
California State Correctional Facility Blues (7)
Call On Me (5)
Calvary (2)
Changes (7)
Chicken (7)
Cobra (4)
Cowboy On The Run (9)
Dino's Song (1,8)

Doin' Time In The U.S.A. (7)
Don't Cry My Lady Love (6,8)
Don't Lose It (7)
Edward, The Mad Shirt Grinder (3,8)
Fire Brothers (6,8)
Flames (9)
Flashing Lonesome (3)
Flute Song (3)
Fool, The (1,8)
Forty Days (7)
Freeway Flyer (4)

Fresh Air (4,8) 49
Gold And Silver (1)
Gone Again (4)
Good Old Rock And Roll (5)
Gypsy Lights (9)
Happy Trails (2)
Hat, The (4)
Heebie Jeebies (9)
Holy Moly (3)
Hope (6,8)
How You Love (2)
I Found Love (6,8)
I Heard You Singing (9)

It's Been Too Long (1)
Joseph's Coat (3)
Just For Love (Part 1 & 2) (4,8)
Letter, The (9)
Light Your Windows (1)
Local Color (5,8)
Long Haired Lady (5)
Maiden Of The Cancer Moon (2)
Mojo (7)
Mona (2,8)
Out Of My Mind (6)
Play My Guitar (6)

Pride Of Man (1,8)
Rebel (6)
Shady Grove (3)
Song For Frisco (5)
Spindrifter (5,8)
Subway (5)
They Don't Know (9)
Three Or Four Feet From Home (3,8)
Too Far (3)
Truth, The (6)
What About Me (5,8) 100
When You Love (2)

Where You Love (2)
Which Do You Love (2)
Who Do You Love (2) 91
Witch's Moon (9)
Wolf Run (Part 1 & 2) (4)
Won't Kill Me (5)
Words Can't Say (3)
Worryin' Shoes (9)

QUIET RIOT '83

Hard-rock group formed in Los Angeles: Kevin DuBrow (vocals), Carlos Cavazo (guitar), Rudy Sarzo (bass) and Frankie Banali (drums). Chuck Wright replaced Sarzo in 1985. DuBrow and Wright left group in 1987; replaced by Paul Shortino (vocals) and Sean McNabb (bass).

DEBUT	PEAK	WKS	RIAA	CD	Title			$	Label & Number
4/23/83	❶¹	81	▲⁶	©	1 Metal Health			$10	Pasha 38443
8/4/84	15	28	▲	©	2 Condition Critical			$10	Pasha 39516
8/2/86	31	27		©	3 QR III			$10	Pasha 40321
11/19/88	119	11		©	4 Quiet Riot			$10	Pasha 40981

Bad Boy (2)
Bang Your Head (Metal Health) (1) 31
Bass Case (3)
Battle Axe (1)
Breathless (4)
Callin' The Shots (4)
Condition Critical (2)
Coppin' A Feel (4)

Cum On Feel The Noize (1) 5
Don't Wanna Be Your Fool (4)
Don't Wanna Let You Go (1)
Down And Dirty (3)
Empty Promises (4)
Helping Hands (3)
I'm Fallin' (4)
In A Rush (4)
Joker, The (4)

King Of The Hill (4)
Let's Get Crazy (1)
Love's A Bitch (1)
Lunar Obsession (4)
Main Attraction (3)
Mama Weer All Crazee Now (2) 51
Metal Health ..see: Bang Your Head

Party All Night (2)
Pump, The (3)
Put Up Or Shut Up (3)
Red Alert (2)
Rise Or Fall (3)
Run For Cover (1)
Run To You (4)
Scream And Shout (2)
Sign Of The Times (2)

Slave To Love (3)
Slick Black Cadillac (1)
Stay With Me Tonight (4)
Still Of The Night (3)
Stomp Your Hands, Clap Your Feet (2)
Thunderbird (1)
Twilight Hotel (3)
(We Were) Born To Rock (2)

Wild And The Young (3)
Winners Take All (2)

QUINN, Carmel '55

Born in 1931 in Dublin, Ireland. Female singer.

DEBUT	PEAK	WKS			Title			$	Label & Number
4/2/55	3	10			Arthur Godfrey presents Carmel Quinn			$25	Columbia 629

EP: Columbia B-491 (#3); LP: Columbia CL-629 (#4)

Ballymaquilty Band
Cuttin' The Corn In Creeshla
Doonaree

Galway Bay
Green Glens Of Antrim
Humour Is On Me Now

If I Were A Blackbird
Isle Of Innisfree
Mick McGilligan's Ball

Spinning Wheel
Whistling Gypsy

With My Shillelagh Under My Arm

R

RABBITT, Eddie '81

Born on 11/27/41 in Brooklyn, New York; raised in East Orange, New Jersey. Died of cancer on 5/7/98 (age 56). Country singer/songwriter/guitarist.

DEBUT	PEAK	WKS		CD	Title			$	Label & Number
6/24/78	143	7			1 Variations			$12	Elektra 127
6/9/79	91	20			2 Loveline			$12	Elektra 181
11/24/79+	151	12	●		3 The Best of Eddie Rabbitt		[G]	$12	Elektra 235
7/12/80+	19	54	▲		4 Horizon			$12	Elektra 276
8/22/81	23	34	●	©	5 Step By Step			$12	Elektra 532
11/6/82+	31	25		©	6 Radio Romance			$12	Elektra 60160
10/1/83	131	11		©	7 Greatest Hits, Volume II		[G]	$10	Warner 23925

All My Life, All My Love (6)
Amazing Love (2)
Bedroom Eyes (6)
Bring Back The Sunshine (5)
Caroline (1)
Crossin' The Mississippi (1)
Dim Dim The Lights (5)
Do You Right Tonight (3)
Drinkin' My Baby (Off My Mind) (3)
Drivin' My Life Away (4,7) 5
Early In The Mornin' (5)

Every Which Way But Loose (3) 30
Gone Too Far (2,7) 82
Good Night For Falling In Love (6)
Hearts On Fire (1,3)
Hurtin' For You (1)
I Can't Help Myself (3) 77
I Don't Know Where To Start (5) 35
I Don't Wanna Make Love (With Anyone Else But You) (2)
I Just Want To Love You (1,3)

I Love A Rainy Night (4,7) 1
I Need To Fall In Love Again (4)
I Will Never Let You Go Again (2)
It's Always Like The First Time (2)
Just The Way It Is (4)
Kentucky Rain (1)
Laughing On The Outside (6)
Loveline (2)
My Only Wish (5)
Nobody Loves Me Like My Baby (5)

Nothing Like Falling In Love (7)
One And Only One (2)
Our Love Will Survive (6)
Plain As The Pain On My Face (1)
Pour Me Another Tequila (2)
Pretty Lady (4)
Rivers (1)
Rockin' With My Baby (4)
Rocky Mountain Music (3) 76
Room At The Top Of The Stairs (1)
747 (4)

Short Road To Love (4)
Skip-A-Beat (5)
So Deep In Your Love (4)
So Fine (2)
Someone Could Lose A Heart Tonight (5,7) 15
Song Of Ireland (4)
Step By Step (5,7) 5
Stranger In Your Eyes (6)
Suspicions (2,7) 13
Two Dollars In The Jukebox (3)
We Can't Go On Living Like This (3)

What Will I Write (4)
Years After You (6)
You And I (6,7) 7
You Can't Run From Love (6,7) 55
You Don't Love Me Anymore (1,3) 53
You Got Me Now (6)
You Put The Beat In My Heart (7) 81

RABIN, Trevor '89

Born on 1/13/54 in Johannesburg, South Africa. Rock singer/songwriter/guitarist. Joined Yes in 1982.

DEBUT	PEAK	WKS		CD	Title			$	Label & Number
12/9/78	192	4		©	1 Trevor Rabin			$12	Chrysalis 1196
8/19/89	111	10		©	2 Can't Look Away			$10	Elektra 60781

All I Want Is Your Love (1)
Cape, The (2)
Cover Up (2)
Etoile Noir (2)

Eyes Of Love (2)
Fantasy (1)
Finding Me A Way Back Home (1)

Getting To Know You Better (1)
Hold On To Me (2)
I Can't Look Away (2)
I Didn't Think It Would Last (2)

I Miss You Now (2)
Live A Bit (1)
Love Life (1)
Painted Picture (1)

Promises (2)
Red Desert (2)
Sludge (2)
Something To Hold On To (2)

Sorrow (Your Heart) (2)
Stay With Me (1)

RACING CARS '77

Rock group from Manchester, England: Gareth Mortimer (vocals), Ray Ennis (vocals, banjo), Graham Williams (guitar), David Land (bass) and Robert Wilding (drums).

DEBUT	PEAK	WKS			Title			$	Label & Number
4/2/77	198	3			Downtown Tonight			$12	Chrysalis 1099

Calling The Tune
Downtown Tonight

Four Wheel Drive
Get Out And Get It

Hard Working Woman
Ladee-Lo

Moonshine Fandango
Pass The Bottle

They Shoot Horses Don't They

RADIATORS, The '89
Rock group from New Orleans: Dave Malone (vocals), Camile Baudoin (guitar), Ed Volker (keyboards), Glenn Sears (percussion), Reggie Scanlan (bass) and Frank Bua (drums).

| 12/19/87+ | 139 | 16 | | © | 1 Law Of The Fish | | | $10 | Epic 40888 |
| 4/1/89 | 122 | 11 | | © | 2 Zigzagging Through Ghostland | | | $10 | Epic 44343 |

Boomerang (1)
But It's Alright (2)
Confidential (2)
Dedicated To You (2)
Doctor Doctor (1)
Fall Of Dark (2)
Hard Time Train (1)
Hardcore (2)
Holiday (1)
I Want To Live (2)
Law Of The Fish... (1)
Like Dreamers Do (1)
Love Grows On Ya (2)
Love Is A Tangle (1)
Memories Of Venus (2)
Mood To Move (1)
Oh Beautiful Loser (1)
Raw Nerve (2)
Red Dress (2)
Sparkplug (1)
Squeeze Me (2)
Suck The Head (1)
This Wagon's Gonna Roll (1)
Zigzagging Through Ghostland (2)

RADIOHEAD '00
Rock group from Oxford, England: Thom Yorke (vocals), brothers Jon (guitar) and Colin (bass) Greenwood, Ed O'Brien (guitar), and Phil Selway (drums).

5/29/93	32	26	▲	©	1 Pablo Honey			$10	Capitol 81409
5/13/95+	88	24	▲	©	2 The Bends			$10	Capitol 29626
7/19/97	21	55	▲	©	3 OK Computer	C:#20/7		$10	Capitol 55229
5/9/98	56	3		©	4 Airbag / How Am I Driving?	[M]		$10	Capitol 58701
10/21/00	❶¹	27	▲	©	5 Kid A			$10	Capitol 27753
6/23/01	2¹	15↑	●	©	6 Amnesiac			$10	Capitol 32764

Airbag (3,4)
Anyone Can Play Guitar (1)
Bends, The (2)
Black Star (2)
Blow Out (1)
Bones (2)
Bullet Proof..I Wish I Was (2)
Climbing Up The Walls (3)
Creep (1) 34
Dollars & Cents (6)
Electioneering (3)
Everything In Its Right Place (5)
Exit Music (For A Film) (3)
Fake Plastic Trees (2)
Fitter Happier (3)
High And Dry (2) 78
How Do You? (1)
How To Disappear Completely (5)
Hunting Bears (6)
I Can't (1)
I Might Be Wrong (6)
Idioteque (5)
In Limbo (5)
Just (2)
Karma Police (3)
Kid A (5)
Knives Out (6)
Let Down (3)
Life In A Glasshouse (6)
Like Spinning Plates (6)
Lucky (3)
Lurgee (1)
Meeting In The Aisle (4)
Melatonin (4)
Morning Bell (5)
Morning Bell/Amnesiac (6)
Motion Picture Soundtrack (5)
My Iron Lung (2)
National Anthem (5)
(Nice Dream) (2)
No Surprises (3)
Optimistic (5)
Packt Like Sardines In A Crushd Tin Box (6)
Palo Alto (4)
Paranoid Android (3)
Pearly (4)
Planet Telex (2)
Polyethylene (Parts 1 & 2) (4)
Prove Yourself (1)
Pulk/Pull Revolving Doors (6)
Pyramid Song (6)
Reminder, A (4)
Ripcord (1)
Stop Whispering (1)
Street Spirit (Fade Out) (2)
Subterranean Homesick Alien (3)
Sulk (2)
Thinking About You (1)
Tourist, The (3)
Treefingers (5)
Vegetable (1)
You (1)
You And Whose Army? (6)

RADNER, Gilda '80
Born on 6/28/46 in Detroit. Died of cancer on 5/20/89 (age 42). Actress/comedienne. Appeared in several movies. Cast member of TV's *Saturday Night Live* (1975-80). Married actor Gene Wilder in 1984.

| 12/1/79+ | 69 | 12 | | © | Live From New York | [C] | | $12 | Warner 3320 |

Emily Litella
Gimme Mick
Goodbye Saccharine
Honey (Touch Me With My Clothes On)
I Love To Be Unhappy
If You Look Close
Let's Talk Dirty To The Animals
Roseanne Roseannadanna
Way We Were

RAEKWON '95
Born Corey Woods in New York City. Male rapper. Member of **Wu-Tang Clan**. Also recorded as **Chef Raekwon**.

| 8/19/95 | 4 | 21 | ● | © | 1 Only Built 4 Cuban Linx... | | | $10 | Loud 66663 |
| 12/4/99 | 9 | 9 | ● | © | 2 Immobilarity | | | $10 | Loud 63844 |

CHEF RAEKWON

All I Got Is You Pt. II (2)
Can It Be All So Simple (1)
Casablanca (2)
Criminology (1) *flip*
Forecast (2)
Friday (2)
F**k Them (2)
Glaciers Of Ice (1) *43*
Guillotine (Swordz) (1)
Heart To Heart (2)
Heaven & Hell (1)
Ice Cream (1) *37*
Ice Water (1)
Incarcerated Scarfaces (1) *71*
Jury (2)
Knowledge God (1)
Knuckleheadz (1)
Live From New York (2)
My Favorite Dred (2)
North Star (Jewels) (1)
100 Rounds (2)
Pop S**t (2)
Power (2)
Rainy Dayz (1)
Raw (2)
Real Life (2)
Shark Niggas (Biters) (1)
Sneakers (2)
Spot Rusherz (1)
Striving For Perfection (1)
Table, The (2)
Verbal Intercourse (1)
Wisdom Body (1)
Wu-Gambinos (1)
Yae Yo (2)

RAES, The '79
Husband-and-wife disco duo: Robbie (born in Resloven, Wales) and Cherrill (born in Carlisle, Wales) Rae.

| 3/24/79 | 161 | 5 | | | Dancing Up A Storm | | | $12 | A&M 4754 |

Don't Make Waves
Don't Turn Around
Gonna Burn My Boogie Shoes
Honest I Do
I Only Wanna Get Up And Dance
Little Lovin' (Keeps The Doctor Away) *61*
School

RAFFERTY, Gerry '78
Born on 4/16/47 in Paisley, Scotland. Singer/songwriter/guitarist. Co-leader of **Stealers Wheel**.

5/6/78	❶¹	49	▲	©	1 City to City			$12	United Artists 840
6/16/79	29	21	●		2 Night Owl			$12	United Artists 958
6/14/80	61	9			3 Snakes And Ladders			$12	United Artists 1039

Already Gone (2)
Ark, The (1)
Baker Street (1) *2*
Bring It All Home (3)
Cafe In Cabotin (3)
City To City (1)
Days Gone Down (Still Got The Light In Your Eyes) (2) *17*
Didn't I (3)
Don't Close The Door (3)
Family Tree (3)
Garden Of England (3)
Get It Right Next Time (2) *21*
Home And Dry (1) *28*
I Was A Boy Scout (3)
Island (1)
It's Gonna Be A Long Night (2)
Johnny's Song (3)
Look At The Moon (3)
Mattie's Rag (1)
Night Owl (2)
Right Down The Line (1) *12*
Royal Mile (Sweet Darlin') (3) *54*
Stealin' Time (1)
Syncopatin Sandy (3)
Take The Money And Run (2)
Tourist, The (2)
Waiting For The Day (1)
Wastin' Away (3)
Way That You Do It (2)
Welcome To Hollywood (3)
Whatever's Written In Your Heart (1)
Why Won't You Talk To Me? (2)

RAFFI '87
Born Raffi Cavoukian on 7/8/48 in Cairo, Egypt; raised in Toronto. Singer/songwriter/guitarist specializing in children's songs.

| 12/19/87 | 22ˣ | 8 | | © | Raffi's Christmas Album | [X] | | $10 | Shoreline 0226 |

first released in 1983; Christmas charts: 22/'87, 24/'88, 27/'89

Away In A Manger (medley)
Christmas Time's A Coming
Deck The Halls (medley)
Douglas Mountain
Every Little Wish
First Noel (medley)
Frosty The Snowman
Jingle Bells
Must Be Santa
Old Toy Trains
On Christmas Morning
Petit Papa Noël
Rudolph The Red-Nosed Reindeer
Silent Night (medley)
There Was A Little Baby
Up On The House-Top
We Wish You A Merry Christmas

RAGE AGAINST THE MACHINE '96
Hard-rock group formed in Los Angeles: Zack DeLa Rocha (vocals), Tom Morello (guitar), Timmy C (bass) and Brad Wilk (drums).

5/1/93+	45	89	▲³	©	1 Rage Against The Machine	C:#2²/124		$10	Epic/Associated 52959
5/4/96	❶¹	74	▲³	©	2 Evil Empire	C:#21/15		$10	Epic 57523
11/20/99	❶¹	51	▲²	©	3 The Battle Of Los Angeles			$10	Epic 69630
12/23/00	14	22	▲	©	4 Renegades			$10	Epic 85289

RAGE AGAINST THE MACHINE — Cont'd

Ashes In The Fall (3)
Beautiful World (4)
Bombtrack (1)
Born As Ghosts (3)
Born Of A Broken Man (3)
Bullet In The Head (1)
Bulls On Parade (2)
Calm Like A Bomb (3)

Down On The Street (4)
Down Rodeo (2)
Fistful Of Steel (1)
Freedom (1)
Ghost Of Tom Joad (4)
How I Could Just Kill A Man (4)
I'm Housin' (4)

In My Eyes (4)
Kick Out The Jams (4)
Killing In The Name (1)
Know Your Enemy (1)
Maggie's Farm (4)
Maria (3)
Mic Check (3)
Microphone Fiend (4)

New Millennium Homes (3)
People Of The Sun (2)
Pistol Grip Pump (4)
Renegades Of Funk (4)
Revolver (2)
Roll Right (2)
Settle For Nothing (1)
Sleep Now In The Fire (3)

Snakecharmer (2)
Street Fighting Man (4)
Take The Power Back (1)
Testify (3)
Tire Me (2)
Township Rebellion (1)
Vietnow (2)
Voice Of The Voiceless (3)

Wake Up (1)
War Within A Breath (3)
Wind Below (2)
Without A Face (3)
Year Of Tha Boomerang (2)

RAGING SLAB   '89

Hard-rock group from New York City: Greg Strempka (vocals), Mark Middleton and Elyse Steinman (guitars), Alec Morton (bass) and Bob Pantella (drums).

| 10/28/89 | 113 | 15 | | © | Raging Slab .... | | | $10 | RCA 9680 |

Bent For Silver
Dig A Hole

Don't Dog Me
Geronimo

Get Off My Jollies
Joy Ride

Love Comes Loose
San Loco

Shiny Mama
Sorry's All I Got

Waiting For The Potion

RAH DIGGA   '00

Born Rashia Fisher in 1975 in Newark, New Jersey. Female rapper. Member of **Flipmode Squad**.

| 4/22/00 | 18 | 12 | | © | Dirty Harriet .... | | | $10 | Flipmode 62386 |

Break Fool
Curtains
Do The Ladies Run This...

F**k Ya'll N*gg*s
Harriet Thugman
Imperial

Just For You
Last Word
Lessons Of Today

Showdown
So Cool
Straight Spittin', Part II

Tight
What They Call Me
What's Up Wit' That

RAHZEL   '99

Born Rahzel Brown in New York City. Male singer/rapper.

| 8/28/99 | 51 | 5 | | © | Make The Music 2000 .... | | | $10 | MCA 11938 |

All I Know
Bubblin, Bubblin (Pina Colada)

Carbon Copy (I Can't Stop)
Make The Music 2000

Night Riders
Southern Girl

Steal My Soul
Suga Sista

Super Dee Jay
To The Beat

RAIDERS — see REVERE, Paul

RAIL   '84

Hard-rock group: Terry Young (vocals, bass), Richard Knotts and Andrew Baldwin (guitars) and Kelly Nobles (drums).

| 8/25/84 | 143 | 10 | | | Rail .... | [M] | | $10 | EMI America 19010 |

Fantasy

Hard Girl To Love

1-2-3-4 Rock And Roll

You've Got To Give

★431★   RAINBOW   '82

Hard-rock group led by British guitarist Ritchie Blackmore and bassist **Roger Glover**, both members of **Deep Purple**. Fluctuating lineup included vocalists Ronnie James Dio, Graham Bonnet (**Michael Schenker Group**, **Alcatrazz**) and **Joe Lynn Turner**, keyboardist **Tony Carey** and drummer Cozy Powell (**Emerson, Lake & Powell**). Group split up upon re-formation of Deep Purple in 1984. In 1990, Turner joined Deep Purple and Powell joined **Black Sabbath**. Powell died in a car crash on 4/5/98 (age 50).

1)Straight Between The Eyes 2)Ritchie Blackmore's R-A-I-N-B-O-W 3)Bent Out Of Shape

9/6/75	30	15		©	1	Ritchie Blackmore's R-A-I-N-B-O-W			$15	Oyster 6049
6/5/76	48	17		©	2	Rainbow Rising			$15	Oyster 1601
						BLACKMORE'S RAINBOW (above 2)				
7/16/77	65	9		©	3	On Stage	[L]		$20	Oyster 1801 [2]
5/6/78	89	11		©	4	Long Live Rock 'N' Roll			$12	Polydor 6143
8/25/79	66	15		©	5	Down To Earth			$12	Polydor 6221
3/7/81	50	16		©	6	Difficult To Cure			$12	Polydor 6316
11/14/81	147	4			7	Jealous Lover	[M]		$12	Polydor 502
5/8/82	30	23		©	8	Straight Between The Eyes _____			$12	Mercury 4041
10/1/83	34	21		©	9	Bent Out Of Shape			$12	Mercury 815305
3/15/86	87	10		©	10	Finyl Vinyl	[L]		$15	Mercury 827987 [2]

recordings from 1978-84

All Night Long (5)
Anybody There (9)
Bad Girl (10)
Black Sheep Of The Family (1)
Blues (medley) (3)
Bring On The Night (Dream Chaser) (8)
Can't Happen Here (6,7,10)
Can't Let You Go (9)
Catch The Rainbow (1,3)
Danger Zone (5)
Death Alley Driver (8)

Desperate Heart (9)
Difficult To Cure (6,10)
Do You Close Your Eyes (2)
Drinking With The Devil (9)
Eyes Of Fire (8)
Eyes Of The World (5)
Fire Dance (9)
Fool For The Night (9)
Freedom Fighter (6)
Gates Of Babylon (4)
I Surrender (6,7,10)
If You Don't Like Rock 'N' Roll (1)

Jealous Lover (7,10)
Kill The King (3,4)
L.A. Connection (4)
Lady Of The Lake (4)
Light In The Black (2)
Long Live Rock 'N' Roll (4,10)
Lost In Hollywood (5)
Love's No Friend (5)
Magic (6)
Make Your Move (9)
Makin' Love (5)
Man On The Silver Mountain (1,3,10)

Midtown Tunnel Vision (6)
Miss Mistreated (8,10)
Mistreated (3)
No Release (6)
No Time To Lose (5)
Intro: Over The Rainbow (medley) (4)
Power (8,10)
Rainbow Eyes (4)
Rock Fever (8)
Run With The Wolf (2)
Self Portrait (1)
Sensitive To Light (4)

Shed (Subtle) (4)
Since You Been Gone (5,10) *57*
Sixteenth Century Greensleeves (1,3)
Snake Charmer (1)
Snowman (3)
Spotlight Kid (6,10)
Stargazer (3)
Starstruck (2,3)
Still I'm Sad (1,3)
Stone Cold (8,10) *40*
Stranded (9)

Street Of Dreams (9) *60*
Tarot Woman (2)
Tearin' Out My Heart (8,10)
Temple Of The King (1)
Tite Squeeze (8)
Vielleicht Das Nachster Zeit (Maybe Next Time) (6)
Weiss Heim (7,10)

RAINMAKERS, The   '86

Rock group from Kansas City: Bob Walkenhorst (vocals), Steve Phillips (guitar), Rich Ruth (bass) and Pat Tomek (drums).

| 9/13/86 | 85 | 22 | | © | 1 | The Rainmakers .... | | | $10 | Mercury 830214 |
| 11/28/87 | 116 | 19 | | © | 2 | Tornado .... | | | $10 | Mercury 832795 |

Big Fat Blonde (1)
Doomsville (1)
Downstream (1)
Drinkin' On The Job (1)

Government Cheese (1)
I Talk With My Hands (2)
Information (1)
Lakeview Man (2)

Let My People Go-Go (1)
Long Gone Long (1)
No Romance (2)
Nobody Knows (1)

One More Summer (2)
One That Got Away (1)
Other Side Of The World (2)
Rainmaker (2)

Rockin' At The T-Dance (1)
Small Circles (2)
Snakedance (2)
Tornado Of Love (2)

Wages Of Sin (2)

RAITT, Bonnie ★167★   '90

Born on 11/8/49 in Burbank, California. Blues-rock singer/guitarist. Daughter of Broadway actor/singer John Raitt. Married to actor Michael O'Keefe from 1991-99. Inducted into the Rock and Roll Hall of Fame in 2000.

1)Nick Of Time 2)Longing In Their Hearts 3)Luck Of The Draw

10/21/72	138	15		©	1 Give It Up			$12	Warner 2643
10/27/73	87	20		©	2 Takin My Time			$12	Warner 2729
11/2/74	80	8		©	3 Streetlights			$12	Warner 2818
10/11/75	43	12		©	4 Home Plate			$12	Warner 2864
4/23/77	25	22	●	©	5 Sweet Forgiveness			$12	Warner 2990
10/13/79	30	21		©	6 The Glow			$12	Warner 3369
3/6/82	38	18		©	7 Green Light			$12	Warner 3630
8/30/86	115	11		©	8 Nine Lives			$10	Warner 25486
4/15/89+	❶³	185	▲⁵	©	9 Nick Of Time		C:#32/8	$10	Capitol 91268
					1989 Grammy winner: Album of the Year				
7/28/90	61	15	●		10 The Bonnie Raitt Collection		[K]	$10	Warner 26242
7/13/91	2²	120	▲⁷	©	11 Luck Of The Draw		C:#15/47	$10	Capitol 96111
4/9/94	❶¹	47	▲²	©	12 Longing In Their Hearts			$10	Capitol 81427
11/25/95	44	21	●	©	13 Road Tested		[L]	$15	Capitol 33705 [2]
4/25/98	17	20	●	©	14 Fundamental			$10	Capitol 56397

About To Make Me Leave Home (5,10)
Ain't Nobody Home (3)
All At Once (11)
All Day, All Night (8)
Angel (8)
Angel From Montgomery (3,10,13)
Baby Come Back (7)
Blue For No Reason (14)
Boy Can't Help It (6)
Burning Down The House (13)
Bye Bye Baby (6)
Can't Get Enough (7)
Circle Dance (12)
Come To Me (11,13)
Cool, Clear Water (12)
Crime Of Passion (8)
Cry Like A Rainstorm (2)
Cry On My Shoulder (9)
Cure For Love (14)
Dimming Of The Day (12,13)
Everybody's Cryin' Mercy (2)
Everything That Touches You (3)
Excited (8)
Fearless Love (14)
Feeling Of Falling (12,13)

Finest Lovin' Man (10)
Fool Yourself (4)
Freezin' (For A Little Human Love) (8)
Fundamental Things (14)
Gamblin' Man (5)
Give It Up Or Let Me Go (1,10)
Glow, The (6,10)
(Goin') Wild For You Baby (6,10)
Good Enough (4)
Good Man, Good Woman (11)
Got You On My Mind (3)
Green Lights (7)
Guilty (2,10)
Have A Heart (9,13) 49
Hell To Pay (12)
Home (1)
I Ain't Gonna Let You Break My Heart Again (9)
I Believe I'm In Love With You (13)
I Can't Help Myself (7)
I Can't Make You Love Me (11,13) **18**
(I Could Have Been Your) Best Old Friend (6)
I Feel The Same (2,10)

I Gave My Love A Candle (2)
I Got Plenty (3)
I Know (1)
I Need Love (14)
I Sho Do (12)
I Thank You (6)
I Thought I Was A Child (2)
I Will Not Be Denied (9)
I'm Blowin' Away (4)
I'm On Your Side (14)
If You Gotta Make A Fool Of Somebody (1)
Keep This Heart In Mind (7)
Kokomo Blues (medley) (2)
Kokomo Medley (13)
Let Me In (2)
Let's Keep It Between Us (7)
Longing In Their Hearts (12,13)
Louise (5,10,13)
Love Has No Pride (1,10)
Love Letter (9,13)
Love Me Like A Man (1,10,13)
Love Sneakin' Up On You (12,13) **19**
Lover's Will (14)
Luck Of The Draw (11)
Matters Of The Heart (13)
Me And The Boys (7)

Meet Me Half Way (14)
My First Night Alone Without You (4,10)
My Opening Farewell (5,13)
Never Make Your Move Too Soon (13)
Nick Of Time (9) **92**
No Business (11)
No Way To Treat A Lady (8,10)
Nobody's Girl (9)
Not The Only One (11) **34**
Nothing Seems To Matter (1)
One Belief Away (14)
One Part Be My Lover (11)
Papa Come Quick (Jody And Chico) (11)
Pleasin' Each Other (4)
Rainy Day Man (3)
Real Man (9)
River Of Tears (7)
Road's My Middle Name (9)
Rock Steady (13) **73**
Round & Round (14)
Run Like A Thief (4)
Runnin' Back To Me (8)
Shadow Of Doubt (12)
Shake A Little (13)

Sleep's Dark And Silent Gate (6)
Slow Ride (4)
Something To Talk About (11,13) **5**
Spit Of Love (14)
Stand Up To The Night (8)
Standin' By The Same Old Love (6)
Steal Your Heart Away (12)
Storm Warning (12)
Streetlights (3)
Sugar Mama (4,10)
Sweet Forgiveness (5)
Takin' My Time (5)
Talk To Me (7)
Tangled And Dark (11)
That Song About The Midway (3)
Thing Called Love (9,13)
Three Time Loser (5,13)
Too Long At The Fair (1)
Too Soon To Tell (9)
True Love Is Hard To Find (8,10)
Two Lives (5)
Under The Falling Sky (1,10)
Wah She Go Do (2)

Walk Out The Front Door (4)
What Do You Want The Boy To Do (4)
What Is Success (3,10)
Who But A Fool (Thief Into Paradise) (8)
Willya Wontcha (7,10)
Women Be Wise (10)
Write Me A Few Of Your Lines (medley) (2)
You (12) **92**
You Got To Be Ready For Love (If You Wanna Be Mine) (3)
You Got To Know How (1)
You Told Me Baby (1)
You're Gonna Get What's Coming (6) **73**
You've Been In Love Too Long (2)
Your Good Thing (Is About To End) (6)
Your Sweet And Shiny Eyes (4)

RALSTON, Bob   '67

Born in 1937 in Los Angeles. Pianist/organist/arranger. Joined **Lawrence Welk**'s TV show in 1963.

12/30/67	77ˣ	1			Christmas Hymns & Carols		[X]	$15	RCA Camden 994

Angels We Have Heard On High (medley)
Away In A Manger (medley)
Bring A Torch, Jeanette Isabella (medley)
Coventry Carol (medley)
Deck The Halls (medley)
Ding-A-Ling, Ding-A-Ling (medley)
First Noël (medley)

God Rest You Merry, Gentlemen (medley)
Hark! The Herald Angels Sing (medley)
Here Comes Santa Claus (Right Down Santa Claus Lane) (medley)
Here We Come A-Caroling (medley)

It Came Upon A Midnight Clear (medley)
Jingle Bells (medley)
Joy To The World (medley)
Little Stranger In A Manger (medley)
Night Before Christmas (medley)
O Come, All Ye Faithful (medley)

O Holy Night (medley)
Oh! Little Town Of Bethlehem (medley)
Rejoice! (medley)
Rudolph The Red-Nosed Reindeer (medley)
Santa Claus Is Coming To Town (medley)
Silent Night (medley)
Snow Bells (medley)

Star Of The North (medley)
Twelve Days Of Christmas (medley)
We Three Kings Of Orient Are (medley)
We Wish You A Merry Christmas (medley)
White Christmas (medley)
Winter Wonderland (medley)

RAMATAM   '72

Rock group formed in San Francisco: Mike Pinera (vocals, guitar; **Iron Butterfly**, **Blues Image**, **Cactus**), April Lawton (guitar), Tommy Sullivan (keyboards), Russ Smith (bass) and Mitch Mitchell (drums; **Jimi Hendrix** Experience).

9/2/72	182	7			Ramatam			$15	Atlantic 7236

Ask Brother Ask
Can't Sit Still

Changing Days
Heart Song

Strange Place
Wayso

What I Dream I Am
Whiskey Place

Wild Like Wine

RAMBEAU, Eddie   '65

Born Edward Flurie on 6/30/43 in Hazleton, Pennsylvania. Pop singer/songwriter.

7/24/65	148	2		©	Concrete And Clay			$25	DynoVoice 9001

Baby, Baby Me
Concrete And Clay 35
Don't Believe Him

Girl Don't Come
I Fell In Love So Easily
I Just Need Your Love

It's Not A Game Anymore
It's Not Unusual
King Of The Road

(Look For The) Rainbow
My Name Is Mud
Same Old Room

Save The Last Dance For Me
Yesterday's Newspapers

RAMIN, Sid, and Orchestra   '63

Born on 1/22/24 in Boston. Conductor/composer/arranger.

5/25/63	34	6			New Thresholds In Sound		[I]	$20	RCA Victor 2658

April In Paris
Bewitched

Embraceable You
Granada

Hernando's Hideaway
I Believe In You

Life Is Just A Bowl Of Cherries
Spring Is Here

Strike Up The Band
Swanee

Sweetest Sounds
Varsity Drag

RAM JAM '77

Rock group formed in New York City: Myke Scavone (vocals), Bill Bartlett (guitar), Howie Blauvelt (bass) and Peter Charles (drums). Bartlett was a member of **The Lemon Pipers**. Blauvelt died of a heart attack on 10/25/93 (age 44).

| 9/10/77 | **34** | 12 | | | **Ram Jam** | | | $12 | Epic 34885 |

All For The Love Of Rock N' Roll   **Black Betty 18** 404   Hey Boogie Woman   High Steppin'   Keep Your Hands On The Wheel   Let It All Out   Overloaded   Right On The Money   Too Bad On Your Birthday

RAMMSTEIN '98

Hard-rock group from Berlin, Germany: Till Lindemann (vocals), Richard Kruspe and Paul Landers (guitars), Flake Lorenz (keyboards), Oliver Riedel (bass) and Christoph Schneider (drums).

| 6/27/98 | **45** | 31 | ▲ | © 1 | **Sehnsucht** | [F] | $10 | Motor 539901 |
| 9/18/99 | **179** | 1 | | © 2 | **Live Aus Berlin** | [F-L] | $10 | Motor 547590 |

recorded on 8/22/98 at Parkbuhne Wuhlheide in Berlin

| 4/21/01 | **77** | 6 | | © 3 | **Mutter** | [F] | $10 | Motor 549639 |

Adios (3)   Alter Mann (1)   Asche Zu Asche (2)   Bestrafe Mich (1,2)   Bück Dich (1,2)   Du Hast (1,2)   Du Riechst So Gut (2)   Eifersucht (1)   Engel (1,2)   Feuer Frei! (3)   Heirate Mich (2)   Ich Will (3)   Klavier (1)   Küss Mich (Fellfrosch) (1)   Laichzeit (2)   Links 2 3 4 (3)   Mein Herz Brennt (3)   Mutter (3)   Nebel (3)   Rammstein (2)   Rein Raus (3)   Seemann (2)   Sehnsucht (1,2)   Sonne (3)   Spiel Mit Mir (1,2)   Spieluhr (3)   Tier (1)   Weisses Fleisch (2)   Wilder Wein (3)   Wollt Ihr Das Bett In Flammen Sehen? (2)   Zwitter (3)

★499★ RAMONES '78

Punk-rock group formed in New York City. All members have taken Ramone as their last name: Joey (Jeffrey Hyman; vocals), Johnny (John Cummings; guitar), Dee Dee (Douglas Colvin; bass) and Tommy (Tom Erdelyi; drums). Tommy became the band's co-producer in 1978, replaced by Marky (Marc Bell). Ritchie (Richard Beau) replaced Marky in 1983. Marky returned in 1988. Dee Dee left band in 1989 and C.J. (Chris Ward) was added. Group appeared in the 1979 movie *Rock 'n' Roll High School*. Joey Ramone died of cancer on 4/15/2001 (age 49).

1)End Of The Century 2)Rocket To Russia 3)Pleasant Dreams

6/5/76	**111**	18		© 1	**Ramones**		$25	Sire 7520
2/12/77	**148**	10		© 2	**Leave Home**		$25	Sire 7528
11/26/77+	**49**	25		© 3	**Rocket To Russia**		$15	Sire 6042
10/21/78	**103**	11		© 4	**Road To Ruin**		$15	Sire 6063
2/23/80	**44**	14		© 5	**End Of The Century**		$15	Sire 6077
8/8/81	**58**	11		© 6	**Pleasant Dreams**		$15	Sire 3571
3/26/83	**83**	9		© 7	**Subterranean Jungle**		$12	Sire 23800
11/3/84	**171**	6		© 8	**Too Tough To Die**		$12	Sire 25187
6/21/86	**143**	6		© 9	**Animal Boy**		$12	Sire 25433
10/10/87	**172**	3		© 10	**Halfway To Sanity**		$12	Sire 25641
6/25/88	**168**	5	●	© 11	**Ramones Mania**	[G]	$15	Sire 25709 [2]
6/17/89	**122**	6		© 12	**Brain Drain**		$12	Sire 25905
9/26/92	**190**	1		© 13	**Mondo Bizarro**		$10	Radioactive 10615
1/29/94	**179**	1		© 14	**Acid Eaters**		$10	Radioactive 10913
7/22/95	**148**	2		© 15	**Adios Amigos**		$10	Radioactive 11273

All Screwed Up (12)   All The Way (5)   All's Quiet On The Eastern Front (6)   Animal Boy (9,11)   Anxiety (13)   Apeman Hop (9)   Baby, I Love You (5)   Bad Brain (4)   Beat On The Brat (1,11)   Blitzkrieg Bop (1,11)   Bop 'Til You Drop (10,11)   Born To Die In Berlin (15)   Bye Bye Baby (10)   Cabbies On Crack (13)   California Sun (1)   Can't Get You Outta My Mind (12)   Can't Seem To Make You Mine (14)   Censorshit (13)   Chain Saw (1)   Chasing The Night (8)   Chinese Rock (5,11)   Come Back, Baby (12)   Come On Now (6)   Commando (2,11)   Cretin Family (15)   Cretin Hop (3,11)   Crummy Stuff (9)   Crusher, The (15)   Danger Zone (8)   Danny Says (5)   Daytime Dilemma (Dangers Of Love) (8)

Death Of Me (10)   Do You Remember Rock 'N' Roll Radio? (5,11)   **Do You Wanna Dance** (3) **86**   Don't Bust My Chops (12)   Don't Come Close (4)   Don't Go (6)   Durango 95 (8)   Eat That Rat (9)   Endless Vacation (8)   Everytime I Eat Vegetables It Makes Me Think Of You (7)   53rd & 3rd (1)   Freak Of Nature (9)   Garden Of Serenity (10)   Gimme Gimme Shock Treatment (2,11)   Glad To See You Go (2)   Go Lil' Camaro Go (10)   Go Mental (4)   Got Alot To Say (15)   Hair Of The Dog (9)   Havana Affair (1)   Have A Nice Day (15)   Have You Ever Seen The Rain (14)   Heidi Is A Headcase (13)   Here Today, Gone Tomorrow (3)   High Risk Insurance (5)   Highest Trails Above (7)   Howling At The Moon (Sha-La-La) (8,11)   Human Kind (8)

I Believe In Miracles (12)   I Can't Control Myself (14)   I Can't Give You Anything (3)   I Can't Make It On Time (5)   I Don't Care (3)   I Don't Wanna Go Down To The Basement (1)   I Don't Wanna Walk Around With You (1)   I Don't Want To Grow Up (15)   I Don't Want You (4)   I Just Want To Have Something To Do (4,11)   I Know Better Now (10)   I Lost My Mind (13)   I Love You (15)   I Need Your Love (7)   I Remember You (2)   I Wanna Be Sedated (4,11)   I Wanna Be Well (3)   I Wanna Be Your Boyfriend (1,11)   I Wanna Live (10,11)   I Wanted Everything (4)   I Won't Let It Happen (13)   I'm Affected (5)   I'm Against It (4)   I'm Not Afraid Of Life (8)   I'm Not Jesus (10)   Ignorance Is Bliss (12)   In The Park (7)   Indian Giver (11)   It's A Long Way Back (4)   It's Gonna Be Alright (13)   It's Not For Me To Know (15)

It's Not My Place (In The 9 To 5 World) (6)   Job That Ate My Brain (13)   Journey To The Center Of The Mind (14)   Judy Is A Punk (1)   KKK Took My Baby Away (6,11)   Learn To Listen (12)   Let's Dance (1)   Let's Go (5)   Life's A Gas (15)   Listen To My Heart (1)   Little Bit O' Soul (3)   Locket Love (3)   Loudmouth (1)   Love Kills (9)   Main Man (13)   Makin Monsters For My Friends (15)   Mama's Boy (8,11)   Mental Hell (9)   Merry Christmas (I Don't Want To Fight Tonight) (12)   My Back Pages (14)   My Brain Is Hanging Upside Down (Bonzo Goes To Bitburg) (9,11)   My-My Kind Of A Girl (7)   Needles & Pins (4,11)   No Go (8)   Now I Wanna Be A Good Boy (2)   Now I Wanna Sniff Some Glue (1)

Oh Oh I Love Her So (2)   Out Of Time (14)   Outsider (7,11)   Palisades Park (12)   Pet Sematary (12)   Pinhead (2)   Planet Earth 1988 (8)   Poison Heart (13)   Psycho Therapy (7,11)   Punishment Fits The Crime (12)   Questioningly (4)   Ramona (4)   Real Cool Time (10)   Return Of Jackie And Judy (5)   Rock 'N' Roll High School (5,11)   **Rockaway Beach** (3,11) **66**   Scattergun (15)   7 And 7 Is (14)   7-11 (6)   Shape Of Things To Come (14)   She Belongs To Me (9)   She Talks To Rainbows (15)   She's A Sensation (6)   She's The One (4)   **Sheena Is A Punk Rocker** (2,3,11) **81**   Sitting In My Room (6)   Somebody Like Me (7)   Somebody Put Something In My Drink (9,11)   Somebody To Love (14)   Something To Believe In (9)   Strength To Endure (13)   Substitute (14)   Surf City (14)

Surfin' Bird (3)   Suzy Is A Headbanger (2)   Swallow My Pride (2)   Take It As It Comes (13)   Take The Pain Away (15)   Teenage Lobotomy (3,11)   This Ain't Havana (5)   This Business Is Killing Me (6)   Time Bomb (7)   Time Has Come Today (7)   Today Your Love, Tomorrow The World (1)   Tomorrow She Goes Away (13)   Too Tough To Die (8)   Touring (13)   Wart Hog (8,11)   We Want The Airwaves (6,11)   We're A Happy Family (3,11)   Weasel Face (10)   What'd Ya Do? (7)   What's Your Game (2)   When I Was Young (14)   Why Is It Always This Way (3)   Worm Man (10)   You Didn't Mean Anything To Me (6)   You Should Have Never Opened That Door (2)   You Sound Like You're Sick (6)   You're Gonna Kill That Girl (2)   Zero Zero UFO (12)

RAMPAGE '97

Born in New York City. Male rapper.

| 8/16/97 | **65** | 4 | | © | **Scouts Honor...By Way Of Blood** | | $10 | Violator 62022 |

Conquer Da World   Da Night B4 My Shit Drop   Flipmode Enemy #1   Flipmode Iz Da Squad   Get The Money And Dip   Hall Of Fame   Niggaz Iz Bad   Set Up   **Take It To The Streets 34**   Talk Of The Town   We Getz Down   Wild For Da Night

RAMPAL, Jean-Pierre, & Claude Bolling　'76

Rampal was born on 1/7/22 in Marseilles, France. Died of heart failure on 5/20/2000 (age 78). Flute player. Bolling was born on 4/10/30 in Cannes, France. Pianist.

1/31/76	173	4	●		Suite for Flute and Jazz Piano	[I]		$12	Columbia 33233

Baroque And Blue　Irlandaise　Sentimentale　Versatile
Fugace　Javanaise　Veloce

RANCID　'98

Punk-rock group from Berkeley, California: Tim Armstrong (vocals, guitar), Lars Frederiksen (guitar), Matt Freeman (bass) and Brett Reed (drums).

2/18/95	97	11	●	©	1 Let's Go			$10	Epitaph 86434
9/9/95	45	34	●	©	2 ...And Out Come The Wolves			$10	Epitaph 86444
7/18/98	35	5		©	3 Life Won't Wait			$10	Epitaph 86497
8/19/00	68	4		©	4 Rancid			$10	Hellcat 80427

Antennas (4)　Coppers (4)　Harry Bridges (1)　Listed M.I.A. (2)　Radio (1)　St. Mary (1)
As One (1)　Corazon De Oro (3)　Hooligans (3)　Lock, Step & Gone (2)　Radio Havana (4)　Tenderloin (1)
As Wicked (2)　Corruption (4)　Hoover Street (3)　Loki (4)　Rattlesnake (4)　Time Bomb (2)
Avenues & Alleyways (2)　Crane Fist (3)　I Am Forever (4)　Maxwell Murder (2)　Reconciliation (4)　Turntable (2)
Axiom (4)　Daly City Train (2)　I Am The One (1)　Meteor Of War (4)　Rigged On A Fix (4)　Wars End (2)
Backslide (1)　Dead Bodies (4)　International Cover-Up (1)　Midnight (1)　Roots Radicals (2)　Warsaw (3)
Ballad Of Jimmy & Johnny (1)　Disgruntled (4)　It's Quite Alright (4)　Motorcycle Ride (1)　Ruby Soho (2)　Way I Feel (2)
Black & Blue (1)　Disorder And Disarray (2)　Journey To The End Of The　Name (1)　Rwanda (4)　Who Would've Thought (3)
Black Derby Jacket (4)　Don Giovanni (4)　　East Bay (2)　New Dress (3)　Salvation (1)　You Don't Care Nothin' (2)
Black Lung (3)　Dope Sick, Girl (1)　Junkie Man (2)　Nihilism (1)　7 Years Down (1)　Young Al Capone (4)
Blackhawk Down (4)　11th Hour (2)　Lady Liberty (3)　1998 (3)　She's Automatic (2)
Bloodclot (3)　GGF (4)　Leicester Square (3)　Not To Regret (4)　Side Kick (1)
Burn (1)　Gave It Away (1)　Let Me Go (4)　Old Friend (2)　Solidarity (1)
Cash, Culture And Violence (3)　Ghetto Box (1)　Let's Go (1)　Olympia Wa. (2)　Something In The World Today
Cocktails (3)　Gunshot (1)　Life Won't Wait (3)　Poison (4)　　(3)

★482★　RANDOLPH, Boots　'67

Born Homer Randolph on 6/3/27 in Paducah, Kentucky. Session saxophonist.

1)Boots With Strings 2)The Sound Of Boots 3)Sunday Sax

6/15/63+	79	49	●		1 Boots Randolph's Yakety Sax	[I]		$25	Monument 18002
11/13/65	118	5			2 Boots Randolph plays More Yakety Sax!	[I]		$20	Monument 18037
1/14/67	36	47	●		3 Boots with Strings	[I]		$20	Monument 18066
2/3/68	189	5			4 Boots Randolph with the Knightsbridge Strings & Voices	[I]		$20	Monument 18082
3/23/68	76	12		©	5 Sunday Sax	[I]		$20	Monument 18092
8/31/68	60	24			6 The Sound Of Boots	[I]		$20	Monument 18099
5/10/69	82	17			7 ...with love/The Seductive Sax of Boots Randolph	[I]		$20	Monument 18111
12/27/69	16[X]	1			8 Boots And Stockings	[X-I]		$20	Monument 18127
1/10/70	113	18			9 Yakety Revisited	[I]		$20	Monument 18128
10/10/70	157	9			10 Hit Boots 1970	[I]		$20	Monument 18144
1/9/71	168	3			11 Boots With Brass	[I]		$20	Monument 18147
6/12/71	141	11			12 Homer Louis Randolph, III	[I]		$15	Monument 30678
11/27/71	144	8			13 The World Of Boots Randolph	[I-K]		$20	Monument 30963 [2]
12/2/72	192	3			14 Boots Randolph Plays The Great Hits Of Today	[I]		$15	Monument 31908

All The Time (6)　Do You Know The Way To San　I Fall To Pieces (1)　Lonely Street (1)　Release Me (9,13)　Unchained Melody (3)
Am I That Easy To Forget? (9)　　Jose? (10)　I Left My Heart In San　Look Of Love (7,13)　Rocky Top (14)　Viva Tirado (11)
Amazing Grace (12)　Don't Touch Me (6)　　Francisco (13)　Lookin' (14)　Rose Garden (12)　Walk Right In (1)
Amen (5)　Down Yonder (9)　I Really Don't Want To Know (1)　Lord's Prayer (5)　Rudolph The Red-Nosed　Walking On New Grass (9)
Aquarius (medley) (10)　Drowning In A Sea Of Love (14)　I'll Be Home For Christmas (8)　Love Is Blue (7,13)　　Reindeer (9)　Waterloo (2)
Ave Maria (5)　Elusive Butterfly (6,13)　I'll Be There (11)　Love Is On (2)　Santa Claus Is Comin' To Town　We've Only Just Begun (11)
Baby, I'm A Want You (14)　Ev'ry Day Of My Life (14)　I'll Just Walk Away (6)　Love Letters (4)　　(medley) (9)　What A Diff'rence A Day Made
Battle Of New Orleans (9)　Fire And Rain (11)　I'm Glad There Is You (7)　Love Story, Theme From (12)　Shadow Of Your Smile (3) 93　　(7)
Because Of You (7)　Flowers On The Wall (6)　I'm Gonna Be A Wheel　Love's Been Good To Me (10)　Silver Bells (8)　What Kind Of Fool Am I? (3)
Big Daddy (9)　For The Good Times (12)　　Someday (7)　Make The World Go Away (6)　Sleigh Ride (8)　What Now My Love (3)
Black Orpheus (Manha De　Frosty The Snow Man (8)　I'm In The Mood For Love (7)　May The Good Lord Bless And　Smoke Gets In Your Eyes (1)　When The Saints Go Marching
　Carnaval), Theme From (4,13)　Games People Play (9)　I'm Walking The Floor (Over　　Keep You (5)　Snowbird (14)　　In (5)
Born To Lose (9)　Gentle On My Mind (6,13)　　You) (2)　Me And Bobby McGee (12)　Somewhere My Love (Lara's　White Christmas (8)
Both Sides Now (10)　Godfather, Love Theme From　If You've Got The Money (I've　Me And Julio Down By The　　Theme from Dr. Zhivago) (4)　Who Can I Turn To (4,13)
Bridge Over Troubled Water　　The (14)　　Got The Time) (1)　　Schoolyard (14)　Spinning Wheel (11)　Wichita Lineman (9,13)
　(10,13)　Gotta Travel On (2)　It Keeps Right On A Hurtin' (1)　Meditation (7)　Stranger On The Shore (3)　Will The Circle Be Unbroken (5)
By The Time I Get To Phoenix　Green Green Grass Of Home　It's Impossible (12)　Michelle (3)　Strangers In The Night (7)　Without Love (There Is Nothing)
　(6,13)　　(6)　It's Not Unusual (4,13)　Mickey's Tune (6)　Summer Of '42, Theme From　　(10)
C.C. Rider (11)　Greensleeves (8)　Jackson (3)　Misty (4,13)　　(3)　Without You (14)
Cacklin' Sax (1)　Have Yourself A Merry Little　Jingle Bells (8)　Moon River (3)　Sunday Mornin' Comin' Down　Y'all Come (2)
Cast Your Fate To The Wind (4)　　Christmas (8)　Jolly Old St. Nick (medley) (8)　More (4,13)　　(10)　Yesterday (3)
Charade (4)　He'll Have To Go (3)　Just A Closer Walk With Thee　My Sweet Lord (12)　Sunshine (14)　Yesterday, When I Was Young
Charlie Brown (1)　Help Me Make It Through The　　(5)　Nearness Of You (7,13)　Sweet Caroline (12)　　(9)
Christmas Song (Chestnuts　　Night (12)　King Of The Road (13)　(Now And Then There's) A Fool　Take A Letter Maria (11)　You Don't Have To Say You
　Roasting On An Open Fire)　Here Comes My Baby (2)　Last Date (2)　　Such As I (2)　Temptation (4) 93　　Love Me (12)
　(8)　Here Comes Santa Claus　Let It Be Me (7)　Peace In The Valley (5)　Tenderly (7,13)　You Don't Know Me (2,13)
Cotton Fields (1)　　(medley) (8)　Let The Sunshine In (medley)　People (4,13)　(They Long To Be) Close To　You'll Never Walk Alone (5)
Crackety Jacks (6)　Hi Heel Sneakers (11)　　(10)　Proud Mary (10)　　You (11)　You've Lost That Lovin' Feelin'
Days Of Wine And Roses (3)　I Believe (8)　Letter, The (11)　Race Is On (2)　Those Were The Days (10)　　(3)
Dear Heart (3)　I Can't Stop Loving You (1)　Light My Fire (11)　Raindrops Keep Fallin' On My　Tragedy (9)
Desafinado (13)　　Little Band Of Gold (9)　　Head (10,13)　25 Or 6 To 4 (11)
　　Rainy Night In Georgia (10)　Yakety Sax (1) 35

RANK & FILE　'83

Country-rock group from Los Angeles: brothers Chip (vocals) and Tony (bass) Kinman, Alejandro Escovedo (guitar) and Slim Evans (drums).

5/7/83	165	5			Sundown			$10	Slash 23833

Amanda Ruth　Coyote　I Don't Go Out Much Anymore　Lucky Day　Sundown
Conductor Wore Black　(Glad I'm) Not In Love　I Went Walking　Rank And File

RANKIN, Billy　'84

Born on 4/25/59 in Glasgow, Scotland. Rock singer/guitarist. Member of **Nazareth** from 1981-82.

3/24/84	119	11			Growin' Up Too Fast			$10	A&M 4977

Baby Come Back *52*　Burning Down　Day In The Life　Never In A Million Years　Think I'm In Love
Baby's Got A Gun　Call Me Automatic　I Wanna Be Alone Tonight　Rip It Up　Where Are You Now

RANKIN, Kenny — '75

Born in 1945 in New York City. Singer/songwriter/guitarist.

DEBUT	PEAK	WKS	CD	#	Album Title	$	Label & Number
9/9/72	184	8	©	1	Like A Seed	$12	Little David 1003
11/16/74+	63	25	©	2	Silver Morning	$12	Little David 3000
12/13/75+	81	15	©	3	Inside	$12	Little David 1009
3/12/77	99	23	©	4	The Kenny Rankin Album	$12	Little David 1013
6/28/80	171	6	©	5	After The Roses	$10	Atlantic 19271

After The Roses (5) / Bad Times Make You Strong (1) / Birembau (2) / Blackbird (2) / Catfish (2) / Comin' Down (1) / Creepin' (3) / Cue #1 & #2 (5) / Down The Backstairs Of My Life (5) / Eartheart (1) / Feeling, The (3) / Groovin' (4) / Haven't We Met (2) / Here's That Rainy Day (4) / House Of Gold (4) / I Love You (4) / I Was Born (1) / If I Should Go To Pray (1) / In The Name Of Love (2) / Inside (3) / Killed A Cat (2) / Like A Seed (1) / Lost Up In Loving You (3) / Lyin' Eyes (5) / Make Believe (4) / Marie (3) / On And On (4) / One More Goodbye, One More Hello (5) / Peaceful (1) / Penny Lane (2) / People Get Ready (2) / Pussywillows, Cat-Tails (2) / Regrets (5) / Roll-A-Round (A Warmup Lick) (3) / She's A Lady (3) / Silver Morning (2) / Sometimes (1) / Stringman (1) / Strings (5) / Sunday Kind Of Love (3) / Through The Eye Of The Eagle (4) / To A Wild Rose (5) / Up From The Skies (3) / What Matters Most (5) / When Sunny Gets Blue (4) / While My Guitar Gently Weeps (4) / With A Little Help From My Friends (5) / Woman, Woman (5) / Yesterday's Lies (1) / You (3) / You Are My Woman (1) / You Are So Beautiful (4)

RANKING ROGER — '88

Born Roger Charley on 2/21/61 in Birmingham, England. Lead singer of **English Beat** and **General Public**.

DEBUT	PEAK	WKS	CD	Album Title	$	Label & Number
8/13/88	151	7	©	Radical Departure	$10	I.R.S. 42197

Falling Down / I Told You / I'll Be There / In Love With You / Mono Gone To Stereo / One Minute Closer (To Death) / Point Of View / Smashing Down Another Door / So Excited / Time To Mek A Dime / Your Problems

RANKS, Shabba — '92

Born Rawlston Fernando Gordon on 1/17/66 in Sturgetown, Jamaica. Male reggae singer.

DEBUT	PEAK	WKS	RIAA	CD	#	Album Title	$	Label & Number
6/22/91	89	51	●		1	As Raw As Ever	$10	Epic 47310
8/1/92	78	11		©	2	Rough & Ready - Vol. 1	$10	Epic 52443
10/17/92	64	28	●	©	3	X-tra Naked	$10	Epic 52464
7/1/95	133	4		©	4	A Mi Shabba	$10	Epic 57801

Ambi Get Scarce (1) / Another One Program (1) / Bad & Wicked (2) / Bedroom Bully (3) / Ca'an Dun (2) / Cocky Rim (3) / Fattie Fattie (4) / Fist-A-Ris (1) / 5-F Man (3) / Flesh Axe (1) / Gal Nuh Ready (4) / Gal Yuh' Good (2) / Gone Up (1) / Gun Pon Me (1) / Hard And Stiff (2) / High Seat (4) / **Housecall (Your Body Can't Lie To Me)** (1) *37* / Ice Cream Love (4) / Jam, The (1) / Just Reality (2) / **Let's Get It On** (4) *81* / Medal And Certificate (4) / Mi Di Girls Dem Love (1) / **Mr. Loverman** (2) *40* / Muscle Grip (3) / Original Woman (4) / Park Yu Benz (1) / Pirates Anthem (1) / Raggamuffin (2) / Ram Dancehall (4) / Ready-Ready, Goody-Goody (3) / Rough Life (4) / Rude Boy (1) / Shine Eye Gal (4) / **Slow And Sexy** (3) *33* / Spoil Mi Appetite (4) / Ting-A-Ling (3) / Trailor Load A Girls (1) / Two Breddrens (3) / Well Done (2) / What 'Cha Gonna Do? (3) / Where Does Slackness Come From (1) / Wicked In Bed (2) / Will Power (1) / Woman Tangle (1) / Woodtop (2)

RAPPIN' 4-TAY — '96

Born Anthony Forte in 1969 in San Francisco. Male rapper.

DEBUT	PEAK	WKS	CD	#	Album Title	$	Label & Number
9/24/94	174	7	©	1	Don't Fight The Feelin' - She's A Sell Out	$10	Rag Top 30889
4/6/96	38	7	©	2	Off Parole	$10	Rag Top 35509
11/8/97	169	1	©	3	4 Tha Hard Way	$10	Noo Trybe 57117

Ain't No Playa (2) *73* / Ain't Nobody Coachin' (1) / Back Again (1) / Back At Cha (3) / Biggie, The (3) / Boogie Bang Bang (2) / Brin' The Beat Back (3) / Call It What You Want Too (1) / Can U Buckem' (1) / Check Ya Self (2) / Cold Blooded (3) / Comin' Back (2) / Dank Season (3) / Element Of Surprize (3) / 4-Tha Hardway (3) / Game On The Shelf (2) / Gift, The (1) / Hala At A Playa (2) / I Got Cha Back (1) / I Paid My Dues (2) / **I'll Be Around** (1) *39* / Just Cause I Called You A Bitch (1) / Keep One In The Chamba (1) / Lay Ya Gunz Down (3) / Lil Some'em Some'em (2) / Money Makes The Man (2) / Never Talk Down (2) / New Trump (2) / Off Parole (2) / One Nite (3) / Out 4000 (1) / Phat Like That (2) / Playa 4 Life (3) / **Playaz Club** (1) *36* / Playaz Dedication (3) / Shake It (3) / She's A Sell Out (1) / Still Ph#@*in' Wit My Folk$ (2) / Sucka Free (1) / Tear The Roof Off (1) / Thinking About You (3) / This Is What I Know (1) / 25-2-Life (2) / What Fo' (3) / What's Wrong Wit The Game (2) / Where You Playin' At (3) / Where's The Party (2)

RARE BIRD — '70

Rock group formed in England: Steve Gould (vocals, bass, **Runner**), David Kaffinetti (keyboards), Graham Field (organ) and Mark Ashton (drums). By 1972, Field and Ashton were replaced by Fred Kelly, Ced Curtis, Paul Holland and Paul Karas.

DEBUT	PEAK	WKS	#	Album Title	$	Label & Number
3/7/70	117	13	1	Rare Bird	$25	Probe 4514
8/18/73	194	2	2	Epic Forest	$15	Polydor 5530

Baby Listen (2) / Beautiful Scarlet (1) / Bird On A Wing (1) / Epic Forest (2) / Fears Of The Night (2) / God Of War (1) / Her Darkest Hour (2) / Hey Man (2) / House In The City (2) / Iceberg (1) / Melanie (1) / Natures Fruit (1) / Sympathy (1) / Times (1) / Title No. 1 Again (Birdman) (2) / Turn It All Around (2) / Turning The Lights Out (2) / You Went Away (1)

★481★ RARE EARTH — '70

Rock group from Detroit: Gil Bridges (vocals, sax), Rod Richards (guitar), Mark Olson (keyboards), Ed Guzman (percussion), John Persh (bass) and Pete Rivera (drums). Numerous personnel changes through the years. Persh of a staph virus in January 1981 (age 38). Olson died of alcohol-related complications in 1982. Guzman died on 7/29/93 (age 49).

DEBUT	PEAK	WKS	RIAA	CD	#	Album Title	Sym	$	Label & Number
12/6/69+	12	77		©	1	Get Ready		$15	Rare Earth 507
7/11/70	15	49	●	©	2	Ecology		$15	Rare Earth 514
7/17/71	28	25			3	One World		$15	Rare Earth 520
1/1/72	29	21	●	©	4	Rare Earth In Concert	[L]	$20	Rare Earth 534 [2]
11/25/72+	90	20			5	Willie Remembers..		$15	Rare Earth 543
6/16/73	65	23		©	6	Ma		$15	Rare Earth 546
7/12/75	59	11			7	Back To Earth		$15	Rare Earth 548
10/1/77	187	6			8	Rare Earth		$12	Prodigal 10019
6/3/78	156	6			9	Band Together		$12	Prodigal 10025

Ah Dunno (8) / Any Man Can Be A Fool (3) / Big John Is My Name (6) / Boogie With Me Children (7) / **Born To Wander** (2,4) *17* / City Life (1) / Come With Me (6) / Come With Your Lady (5) / Crazy Love (8) / Delta Melody (7) / Dreamer (9) / Eleanor Rigby (2) / Every Now And Then We Get To Go On Down To Miami (5) / Feeling Alright (1) / Foot Loose And Fancy Free (8) / **Get Ready** (1,4) *4* / **Good Time Sally** (5) *67* / Got To Get Myself Back Home (5) / Happy Song (9) / **Hey Big Brother** (4) *19* / Hum Along And Dance (4) / I Couldn't Believe What Happened Last Night (5) / **I Just Want To Celebrate** (3,4) *7* / **(I Know) I'm Losing You** (2,4) *7* / I Really Love You (8) / If I Die (3) / In Bed (1) / Is Your Teacher Cool? (8) / It Makes You Happy (But It Ain't Gonna Last Too Long) (7) / Keeping Me Out Of The Storm (7) / Let Me Be Your Sunshine (7) / Long Time Leavin' (2) / Love Do Me Right (9) / Love Has Lifted Me (8) / Love Is What You Get (If Love Is What You Give Me) (9) / Love Music (9) / Ma (6) / Magic Key (1) / Maybe The Magic (9) / Mota Molata (9) / Nice Place To Visit (2) / Nice To Be With You (4) / No. 1 Man (2) / Road, The (3) / Rock 'N' Roll Man (9) / Satisfaction Guaranteed (2) / Seed, The (3) / Share My Love (8)

DEBUT	PEAK	WKS	RIAA	CD	ARTIST — Album Title	Catalog	Sym	$	Label & Number

RARE EARTH — Cont'd

Smiling Faces Sometimes (6)
Someone To Love (3)
Think Of The Children (5)
Thoughts (4)

Tin Can People (8)
Tobacco Road (1)
Train To Nowhere (1)
Under God's Light (3)

Wallking Schtick (7)
Warm Ride (9) *39*
We're Gonna Have A Good Time (5) *93*

What'd I Say (3,4) *61*
When I Write (8)
Would You Like To Come Along (5)

You (9)

RASCAL FLATTS   '00

Country vocal trio formed in Columbus, Ohio: Jay DeMarcus, Gary LeVox and Joe Don Rooney.

| 6/24/00 | 122 | 41 | ● | © | Rascal Flatts ...... | | | $10 | Lyric Street 65011 |

From Time To Time
I'm Movin' On

It's Not Just Me
Long Slow Beautiful Dance

One Good Love
Prayin' For Daylight *38*

See Me Through
Some Say

This Everyday Love *56*
Waiting All My Life

While You Loved Me *60*

★357★   RASCALS, The   '68

Pop-rock group formed in New York City: Felix Cavaliere (vocals, organ), Gene Cornish (vocals, guitar), Eddie Brigati (vocals, bass) and Dino Danelli (drums). All except Danelli had been in **Joey Dee & the Starliters**. Brigati and Cornish left in 1971, replaced by Robert Popwell (bass), **Buzzy Feiten** (guitar; **Larsen-Feiten Band**) and Ann Sutton (vocals). Group disbanded in 1972. Cavaliere, Cornish and Danelli reunited in June 1988. Group inducted into the Rock and Roll Hall of Fame in 1997. Also see **Bulldog** and **Fotomaker**.

1)Time Peace/The Rascal's Greatest Hits 2)Groovin' 3)Once Upon A Dream

THE YOUNG RASCALS:

5/7/66	15	84	●	©	1	The Young Rascals			$25	Atlantic 8123
1/21/67	14	74	●	©	2	Collections			$25	Atlantic 8134
8/12/67	5	59	●	©	3	Groovin'			$25	Atlantic 8148

THE RASCALS:

3/2/68	9	30			4	Once Upon A Dream			$20	Atlantic 8169
7/13/68	❶[1]	58	●	©	5	Time Peace/The Rascals' Greatest Hits	[G]		$20	Atlantic 8190
3/29/69	17	16	●		6	Freedom Suite			$20	Atlantic 901 [2]
1/10/70	45	16			7	See			$15	Atlantic 8246
3/20/71	198	1			8	Search And Nearness			$15	Atlantic 8276
6/5/71	122	12		©	9	Peaceful World			$15	Columbia 30462 [2]
5/13/72	180	3			10	The Island Of Real			$15	Columbia 31103

Adrian's Birthday (6)
Almost Home (8)
America The Beautiful (6)
Any Dance'll Do (6)
Away Away (7)
Baby I'm Blue (6)
Baby Let's Wait (6)
Be On The Real Side (10)
Beautiful Morning (5) *3*
Bells (4)
Bit Of Heaven (9)
Boom (6)
Brother Tree (10)
Buttercup (10)
Carry Me Back (7) *26*
Come On Up (2,5) *43*
Cute (6)
Death's Reply (7)

Do You Feel It (1)
Easy Rollin' (4,5)
Echoes (10)
Find Somebody (3)
Fortunes (8)
Getting Nearer (9)
Girl Like You (3,5) *10*
Glory Glory (8) *58*
Good Lovin' (1,5) *1*
Groovin' (3,5) *1*
Happy Song (9)
Heaven (8) *9*
Hold On (7) *51*
How Can I Be Sure (3,5) *4*
Hummin' Song (10)
I Ain't Gonna Eat Out My Heart Anymore (1,5) *52*
I Believe (1,8)

I Don't Love You Anymore (3)
I'd Like To Take You Home (7)
I'm Blue (7)
I'm Gonna Love You (4)
I'm So Happy Now (3)
I've Been Lonely Too Long (2,5) *16*
Icy Water (9)
If You Knew (3)
In And Out Of Love (9)
In The Midnight Hour (1,5)
Island Of Love (6)
Island Of Real (10)
It's Love (3)
It's Wonderful (4,5) *20*
Jungle Walk (10)
Just A Little (1)
Lament (10)

Land Of 1000 Dances (5)
Letter, The (8)
Like A Rolling Stone (1)
Little Dove (9)
Look Around (6)
Love Is A Beautiful Thing (2,5)
Love Letter (9)
Love Lights (medley) (2)
Love Me (9) *95*
Love Was So Easy To Give (6)
Lucky Day (10)
Me & My Friends (6)
Mickey's Monkey (medley) (2)
More (2)
Mother Nature Land (9)
Mustang Sally (1,5)
My Hawaii (6)
My World (4)

Nama (8)
Nineteen Fifty-Six (2)
No Love To Give (2)
Nubia (7)
Of Course (6)
Once Upon A Dream (4)
Peaceful World (9)
People Got To Be Free (6) *1*
Place In The Sun (3)
Please Love Me (4)
Rainy Day (4)
Ray Of Hope (6) *24*
Ready For Love (8)
Real Thing (7)
Remember Me (7)
Right On (8)
Saga Of New York (10)
Sattva (4)

See (7) *27*
Silly Girl (4)
Since I Fell For You (2)
Singin' The Blues Too Long (4)
Sky Trane (9)
Slow Down (1)
Sound Effect (4)
Stop And Think (7)
Sueno (3)
Temptation's 'Bout To Get Me (7)
Thank You Baby (8)
Time Will Tell (10)
Too Many Fish In The Sea (2)
Visit To Mother Nature Land (9)
What Is The Reason (2)
You Better Run (3,5) *20*
You Don't Know (8)

RAS KASS   '98

Born John Austin in Carson, California. Male rapper.

| 10/19/96 | 169 | 1 | | © | 1 | Soul On Ice ...... | | | $10 | Priority 50529 |
| 10/10/98 | 63 | 3 | | © | 2 | Rasassination ...... | | | $10 | Priority 50739 |

All Or Nuthin' (2)
Anything Goes (1)
Conceited Bastard (2)
Drama (1)
End, The (2)

Etc. (1)
Evil That Men Do (1)
Get At Me (2)
Ghetto Fabulous (2)
Grindin' (2)

H2OProof (2)
I Ain't Fuckin' With You (2)
Ice Age (2)
If/Then (1)
Interview With A Vampire (2)

It Is What It Is (2)
Lapdance (2)
Marinatin' (1)
Miami Life (1)
Nature Of The Threat (1)

On Earth As It Is... (1)
OohWee! (2)
Ordo Abchao (Order Out Of Chaos) (1)
Rasassination (2)

Reelishymn (1)
Sonset (1)
Soul On Ice (1)
Wild Pitch (2)

RASPBERRIES   '72

Pop-rock group formed in Mentor, Ohio: Eric Carmen (vocals, guitar), Wally Bryson (guitar; **Fotomaker**), David Smalley (bass) and Jim Bonfanti (drums). Smalley and Bonfanti replaced by Scott McCarl and Michael McBride in 1974. Carmen went solo in 1975.

5/20/72	51	30			1	Raspberries			$30	Capitol 11036
12/9/72+	36	16			2	Fresh			$30	Capitol 11123
10/6/73	128	7			3	Side 3			$25	Capitol 11220
10/19/74	143	6			4	Starting Over			$20	Capitol 11329
6/12/76	138	4		©	5	Raspberries' Best Featuring Eric Carmen	[G]		$15	Capitol 11524

All Through The Night (4)
Come Around And See Me (1)
Cruisin' Music (4)
Cry (4)
Don't Want To Say Goodbye (1,5) *86*
Drivin' Around (2,5)
Ecstacy (3,5)
Every Way I Can (2)

Get It Moving (1)
Go All The Way (1,5) *5*
Goin' Nowhere Tonight (2)
Hands On You (4)
Hard To Get Over A Heartbreak (3)
I Can Hardly Believe You're Mine (4)
I Can Remember (1,5)

I Don't Know What I Want (4)
I Reach For The Light (2)
I Saw The Light (1)
I Wanna Be With You (2,5) *16*
I'm A Rocker (3) *94*
If You Change Your Mind (2)
It Seemed So Easy (2)
Last Dance (4)
Let's Pretend (2,5) *35*

Making It Easy (3)
Might As Well (2)
Money Down (3)
Nobody Knows (2)
On The Beach (3)
Overnight Sensation (Hit Record) (4,5) *18*
Party's Over (1)
Play On (4)

Rock & Roll Mama (1)
Rose Coloured Glasses (4)
Should I Wait (3)
Starting Over (4,5)
Tonight (3,5) *69*
Waiting (1)
With You In My Life (1)

RATCHELL   '72

Rock group: brothers Pat (vocals) and Chris (drums) Couchois, Larry Byrom (guitar) and Howard Messer (bass). Also see **Couchois**.

| 4/15/72 | 176 | 3 | | | | Ratchell ...... | | | $15 | Decca 75330 |

And If I Will
Here On My Face

Home
How Many Times

Julie My Woman
Lazy Lady

My My
Out Of Hand

Peace Of Mind
Problems

Saycus
Warm And Tender Love

RATT '84

Hard-rock group formed in Los Angeles: Stephen Pearcy (vocals), Warren DeMartini and Robbin Crosby (guitars), Juan Croucier (bass) and Bobby Blotzer (drums). Pearcy joined **Arcade**. Blotzer joined **Contraband**. Pearcy, Blotzer and Blotzer reunited in 1998 with Robbie Crane (bass).

DEBUT	PEAK	WKS	RIAA	CD	#	Album Title	Sym	$	Label & Number
3/24/84	7	56	▲³	©	1	Out Of The Cellar		$10	Atlantic 80143
6/30/84	133	19		©	2	Ratt	[E-M]	$10	Time Coast 2203
						first released in 1983			
6/29/85	7	42	▲²	©	3	Invasion Of Your Privacy		$10	Atlantic 81257
10/25/86	26	40	▲	©	4	Dancing Undercover		$10	Atlantic 81683
11/19/88	17	27	▲	©	5	Reach For The Sky		$10	Atlantic 81929
9/8/90	23	17	●	©	6	Detonator		$10	Atlantic 82127
9/21/91	57	18	●	©	7	Ratt & Roll 81-91	[G]	$10	Atlantic 82260
7/24/99	169	1		©	8	Ratt		$10	Portrait 69586

All Or Nothing (6)
All The Way (8)
Back For More (1,2,7)
Between The Eyes (3)
Body Talk (4,7)
Bottom Line (5)
Breakout (8)
Can't Wait On Love (6)
Chain Reaction (5)
City To City (5)
Closer To My Heart (3)
Dance (4,7) 59
Dangerous But Worth The Risk (3)
Dead Reckoning (8)
Don't Bite The Hand That Feeds (5)
Drive Me Crazy (4)
Enough Is Enough (4)
Gave Up Givin' Up (8)
Give It All (3)
Givin' Yourself Away (6,7)
Got Me On The Line (3)
Hard Time (6)
Heads I Win, Tails You Lose (6,7)
I Want A Woman (5,7)
I Want To Love You Tonight (5)
I'm Insane (1)
In Your Direction (1)
It Ain't Easy (8)
It Doesn't Matter (4)
Lack Of Communication (1,7)
Lay It Down (3,7) 40
Live For Today (8)
Looking For Love (4)
Lovin' You's A Dirty Job (6,7)
Luv Sick (8)
Morning After (1)
Never Use Love (3)
No Surprise (5)
Nobody Rides For Free (7)
One Good Lover (4)
One Step Away (6,7)
Over The Edge (8)
Round And Round (1,7) 12
Scene Of The Crime (1)
Scratch That Itch (6)
7th Avenue (4)
Shame Shame Shame (6,7)
She Wants Money (1)
Slip Of The Lip (4,7)
So Good, So Fine (8)
Sweet Cheater (2)
Take A Chance (4)
Tell The World (2,7)
Top Secret (6)
Tug Of War (8)
U Got It (2)
Walkin' The Dog (2)
Wanted Man (1,7) 87
Way Cool Jr. (5,7) 75
We Don't Belong (8)
What I'm After (5)
What You Give Is What You Get (3)
What's It Gonna Be (5)
You Should Know By Now (3)
You Think You're Tough (2,7)
You're In Love (3,7) 89
You're In Trouble (1)

RAVAN, Genya '79

Born Goldie Zelkowitz in 1942 in Lodz, Poland; raised in New York City. Lead singer of **Ten Wheel Drive**.

DEBUT	PEAK	WKS	#	Album Title	$	Label & Number
9/2/78	147	6	1	Urban Desire	$12	20th Century 562
9/29/79	106	6	2	...And I Mean It!	$12	20th Century 595

Aye Co'lorado (1)
Back In My Arms Again (1) 92
Cornered (1)
Darling, I Need You (1)
Do It Just For Me (1)
I Won't Sleep On The Wet Spot (1)
No More (2)
I'm Wired, Wired, Wired (2)
It's Me (2)
Jerry's Pigeons (1)
Junkman (1)
Knight Ain't Long Enough (1)
Love Isn't Love (2)
Messin Around (1)
Night Owl (1)
Pedal To The Metal (2)
Roto Root Her (2)
Shadowboxing (1)
Shot In The Heart (1)
Steve... (2)
Stubborn Kinda Girl (1)
Sweetest One (1)

RAVEN '85

Hard-rock trio from Newcastle, England: brother John (vocals, bass) and Mark (guitar) Gallagher, with Rob Hunter (drums).

DEBUT	PEAK	WKS	CD	#	Album Title	$	Label & Number
3/23/85	81	15	©	1	Stay Hard	$10	Atlantic 81241
3/8/86	121	10	©	2	The Pack Is Back	$10	Atlantic 81629

All I Want (2)
Bottom Line (1)
Don't Let It Die (2)
Extract The Action (1)
Get Into Your Car (2)
Get It Right (1)
Gimme Some Lovin' (2)
Hard Ride (1)
Hyperactive (2)
Nightmare Ride (2)
On And On (1)
Pack Is Back (2)
Power And The Glory (1)
Pray For The Sun (1)
Restless Child (1)
Rock Dogs (2)
Screamin' Down The House (2)
Stay Hard (1)
When The Going Gets Tough (1)
Young Blood (2)

RAWLS, Lou ★141★ '66

Born on 12/1/35 in Chicago. R&B singer known for his very deep voice. Hosted own TV variety show with **The Golddiggers** in 1969. Appeared in the movies *Angel Angel, Down We Go* and *Believe In Me*. Voice of many Budweiser beer ads and featured singer in the *Garfield* TV specials.

1)Lou Rawls Live! 2)All Things In Time 3)Lou Rawls Soulin' 4)Too Much! 5)Lou Rawls Carryin' On!

DEBUT	PEAK	WKS	RIAA	CD	#	Album Title	Sym	$	Label & Number
4/6/63	130	3			1	Black And Blue		$25	Capitol 1824
						also see #12 below			
5/7/66	4	74	●	©	2	Lou Rawls Live!	[L]	$20	Capitol 2459
9/10/66	7	51	●		3	Lou Rawls Soulin'		$20	Capitol 2566
1/21/67	20	31			4	Lou Rawls Carryin' On!		$20	Capitol 2632
5/6/67	18	22			5	Too Much!		$20	Capitol 2713
8/26/67	29	20			6	That's Lou		$20	Capitol 2756
12/2/67	2¹ˣ	11		©	7	Merry Christmas Ho! Ho! Ho!	[X]	$20	Capitol 2790
						Christmas charts: 2/'67, 22/'68, 18/'69, 26/'70			
3/9/68	103	22			8	Feelin' Good		$20	Capitol 2864
7/20/68	165	6			9	You're Good For Me		$20	Capitol 2927
8/31/68	103	16			10	The Best Of Lou Rawls	[G]	$20	Capitol 2948
6/14/69	71	23			11	The way it was - The way it is		$20	Capitol 215
8/23/69	191	3			12	Close-Up	[R]	$20	Capitol 261 [2]
						reissue of *Black And Blue* and *Tobacco Road* albums			
12/20/69	200	2			13	Your Good Thing		$20	Capitol 325
4/18/70	172	3			14	You've Made Me So Very Happy		$20	Capitol 427
9/4/71+	68	24			15	Natural Man		$15	MGM 4771
2/26/72	186	4			16	Silk & Soul		$20	MGM 4809 [2]
6/5/76	7	35	▲	©	17	All Things In Time		$12	Philadelphia Int'l. 33957
4/16/77	41	29	▲	©	18	Unmistakably Lou		$12	Philadelphia Int'l. 34488
12/10/77+	41	34	●	©	19	When You Hear Lou, You've Heard It All		$12	Philadelphia Int'l. 35036
11/11/78	108	8		©	20	Lou Rawls Live	[L]	$15	Phil. Int'l 35517 [2]
						recorded at the Mack Hellinger Theater in New York City			
6/2/79	49	15		©	21	Let Me Be Good To You		$12	Philadelphia Int'l. 36006
1/12/80	81	18		©	22	Sit Down And Talk To Me		$12	Philadelphia Int'l. 36304
1/10/81	110	6			23	Shades Of Blue		$12	Philadelphia Int'l. 36774
5/14/83	163	4			24	When The Night Comes		$10	Epic 38553

RAWLS, Lou — Cont'd

Ain't That Loving You (22)
All God's Children (14)
All The Way (18)
Autumn Leaves (3)
Baby I Could Be So Good At Lovin' You (9)
Baby What You Want Me To Do (23)
Bark, Bite (Fight All Night) (21)
Be Anything (But Be Mine) (23)
Beautiful Friendship (9)
Believe In Me (16)
Blues For A Four String Guitar (12)
Breaking My Back (Instead Of Using My Mind) (3)
Bye Bye Blackbird (medley) (20)
Chained And Bound (13)
Child With A Toy (14)
Christmas Is (7)
Christmas Song (7)
Christmas Will Really Be Christmas (7)
Cottage For Sale (23)
Cotton Fields (12)
Couple More Years (24)
Dead End Street (5,10,20) **29**
Devil In Your Eyes (4)
Did You Ever Love A Woman (23)
Dixieland Joe (medley) (20)
Dollar Green (19)
Don't Explain (3)
Down Here On The Ground (9) **69**
Early Morning Love (18,20)
Encore (8)
Even When You Cry (8)
Everyday I Have The Blues (1,12)
Everywhere I Go (15)
Evil Woman (8)
Fa Fa Fa Fa Fa (Sad Song) (11)
Feelin' Alright (14)
Feelin' Good (8)
Find Out What's Happening (4)
For What It's Worth (8)
From Now On (17)

Gentle On My Mind (11)
Georgia On My Mind (12)
Girl From Ipanema (2)
Give Me Your Love (13)
Goin' To Chicago Blues (1,2,12)
Golden Slumbers (16)
Good Time Christmas (7)
Got A Lotta Love (15)
Got To Get You Into My Life (15)
Gotta Find A Way (8)
Groovy People (17,20) **64**
Hallelujah For A Friend (16)
Hang-Ups (8)
Hard To Get Thing Called Love (6)
Have Yourself A Merry Little Christmas (7)
Heartaches (Just When You Think You're Loved) (22)
Hello Dolly (medley) (20)
Here's That Rainy Day (16)
His Song Shall Be Sung (16)
Hoochie Coochie Man (23)
How Can That Be (14)
(How Do You Say) I Don't Love You Anymore (6)
How Long, How Long Blues (1,12)
How Thoughtless I've Become (15)
Hurtin' (14)
I Been Him (24)
I Can't Make It Alone (13) **63**
I Go Crazy (23)
I Got It Bad And That Ain't Good (2)
I Just Want To Make Love To You (5)
I Love You Yes I Do (11)
I Wanna Little Girl (5)
I Want To Be Loved (But Only By You) (11)
I Want To Hear It From You (9)
I Wish It Were Yesterday (4)
I Wonder (11)
I Wonder Where Our Love Has Gone (13)
I'd Rather Drink Muddy Water (1,2,12)

I'll Take Time (5)
I'm A King Bee (15)
I'm Gonna Use What I Got (To Get What I Need) (8)
I'm Satisfied (9)
I'm Waiting (16)
If I Coulda, Woulda, Shoulda (19)
If You're Gonna Love Me (24)
In The Evening When The Sun Goes Down (2,20)
It Was A Very Good Year (3,10)
It's An Uphill Climb To The Bottom (5)
It's Our Anniversary Today (18)
It's You (11)
Just Squeeze Me (But Don't Tease Me) (13)
Kansas City (1,12)
Lady Love (19,20) **24**
Let Me Be Good To You (21)
Let's Burn Down The Cornfield (14)
Let's Fall In Love All Over Again (17)
Letter, The (8)
Life That I Lead (4)
Life Time (9)
Little Boy Dear (5)
Little Drummer Boy (7)
Love Is A Hurtin' Thing (3,10,20) **13**
Love That I Give (6)
Lovely Way To Spend An Evening (20)
Lover's Holiday (21)
Mack The Knife (medley) (20)
Make The World Go Away (13)
Mama Told Me Not To Come (14)
Mean Black Snake (4)
Memory Lane (3)
Merry Christmas, Baby (7)
Midnight Sunshine (24)
Mona Lisa (medley) (20)
My Ancestors (8,10)
My Son (8)
Natural Man (15,20) **17**
Need You Forever (17)
No More (16)

Not The Staying Kind (19)
Oh, What A Beautiful Mornin' (15)
Ol' Man River (9,12)
Old Folks (3)
Old Times (22)
On A Clear Day (You Can See Forever) (3)
On Broadway (4)
One Day Soon You'll Need Me (22)
One For My Baby (And One More For The Road) (9)
One I Sing My Love Songs To (24)
One Life To Live (19)
Please Give Me Someone To Love (6)
Problems (6)
Pure Imagination (17,20)
Red Top (13)
Rockin' Chair (12)
Roll 'Em Pete (1)
Sandpiper, Love Theme From ...see: Shadow Of Your Smile
Santa Claus Is Comin' To Town (7)
Season Of The Witch (11)
Secret Tears (18)
See You When I Git There (18,20) **66**
Send In The Clowns (20)
Sentimental Journey (12)
Shadow Of Your Smile (2)
Show Business (6) **45**
Sir Duke (medley) (20)
Sit Down And Talk To Me (22)
Six Cold Feet Of Ground (1,12)
So Hard To Laugh, So Easy To Cry (3)
Some Day You'll Be Old (18)
Some Folks Never Learn (18)
Something (16)
Something Stirring In My Soul (4)
Sophisticated Lady (16,20)
Soul Serenade (9)
Spring Again (18)
St. James Infirmary (1,2)
St. Louis Blues (12)

Stay Awhile With Me (20)
Stormy Monday (2,20)
Stormy Weather (12)
Strange Fruit (1,12)
Street Of Dreams (6)
Summertime (12)
Sweet Tender Nights (21)
Take The "A" Train (medley) (20)
That Would Do It For Me (19)
That's When The Magic Begins (24)
Then You Can Tell Me Goodbye (5)
There Will Be Love (19)
They Don't Give Medals (To Yesterday's Heroes) (6)
Think (23)
This One's For You (20)
This Song Will Last Forever (17,20)
Three O'Clock In The Morning (10) **83**
Till Love Touches Your Life (15)
Time (17)
Time Will Take Care Of Everything (21)
Tobacco Road (2,10,12,20)
Tomorrow (3)
Trade Winds (19)
Trouble Down Here Below (4,10) **92**
Trouble In Mind (1,12)
Trying Just As Hard As I Can (11)
Twelfth Of Never (5)
Unforgettable (19,20)
Upside Down (24)
Walking Proud (4)
Watch What Happens (16)
We Keep Getting Closer (To Being Further Apart) (23)
We Understand Each Other (18,20)
Wee Baby Blues (13)
What Are You Doing About Today (6)
What Are You Doing New Year's Eve (7)

(What Did I Do To Be So) Black And Blue (1,12)
What Now My Love (3)
What's The Matter With The World (21)
When A Man Loves A Woman (11)
When I Fall In Love (15)
When Love Goes Wrong (6)
When She Speaks (13)
When Someone Comes Along (14)
When The Night Comes (24)
When You Get Home (22)
When You Say Budweiser, You've Said It All (20)
Whole Lotta Sunlight (14)
Whole Lotta Woman (3)
Why (Do I Love You So) (5)
Will Someone Carry The Ball (14)
Wind Beneath My Wings (24) **65**
Woman Who's A Woman (11)
World Of Trouble (1,2,10,12)
Yes It Hurts (Doesn't It?) (5)
Yesterday (4)
Yesterday's Dreams (14)
You Are (22)
You Can Bring Me All Your Heartaches (4) **55**
You Can't Hold On (15)
You Can't Take It With You (24)
You'll Never Find Another Love Like Mine (17,20) **2**
You're Always On My Mind (5)
You're Gonna Hear From Me (4)
You're Good For Me (9)
You're My Blessing (22) **77**
You're Takin' My Bag (5)
You're The One (3,17)
You've Lost That Lovin' Feelin' (23)
You've Made Me So Very Happy (14) **95**
Your Good Thing (Is About To End) (11,13) **18**

RAY, Don   '78

Born in Germany. Disco producer/arranger/composer.

| 9/23/78 | 113 | 11 | | © | The Garden Of Love | | | $12 | Polydor 6150 |

Body And Soul — Garden Of Love — Got To Have Loving **44** — Midnight Madness — My Desire — Standing In The Rain

RAY, Jimmy   '98

Born on 10/3/75 in Walthamstow, East London, England. Pop-rock singer.

| 3/28/98 | 112 | 6 | | © | Jimmy Ray | | | $10 | Epic 69104 |

Are You Jimmy Ray? **13** — Free At Last — I Got Rolled — Look Inside For Love — Trippin' On Baby Blue — Daddy's Got A Gun — Goin' To Vegas — Let It Go Go — Sex For Beginners — Way Low

RAY, Johnnie   '57

Born on 1/10/27 in Dallas, Oregon. Died of liver failure on 2/25/90 (age 63). Pop singer best known for his pleading vocals.

| 3/2/57 | 19 | 2 | | | The Big Beat | | | $50 | Columbia 961 |

Everyday (Everyday I Have The Blues) — I Miss You So — I'll Never Be Free — Lotus Blossom — Shake A Hand — How Long, How Long Blues — I Want To Be Loved (But Only By You) — I'm Gonna Move To The Outskirts Of Town — Pretty-Eyed Baby — So Long — Sent For You Yesterday — Trouble In Mind

RAYDIO — see PARKER, Ray Jr.

★476★   RAYE, Collin   '92

Born on 8/22/59 in DeQueen, Arkansas. Country singer.

11/30/91+	54	43	▲	©	1	All I Can Be			$10	Epic 47468
9/12/92	42	50	▲	©	2	In This Life			$10	Epic 48983
2/12/94	73	45	▲	©	3	Extremes			$10	Epic 53952
9/9/95	40	95	▲	©	4	I Think About You			$10	Epic 67033
12/14/96	126	4		©	5	Christmas: The Gift	[X]		$10	Epic 67751
						Christmas chart: 20/'96				
9/13/97	33	37	▲	©	6	The Best Of Collin Raye - Direct Hits	[G]		$10	Epic 67893
8/1/98	55	11		©	7	The Walls Came Down			$10	Epic 68876
5/20/00	81	7		©	8	Tracks			$10	Epic 69995

All I Can Be (Is A Sweet Memory) (1)
All My Roads (7)
Angel Of No Mercy (3)
Angels We Have Heard On High (5)
Any Old Stretch Of Blacktop (1)
Anyone Else (7) **37**
April Fool (7)
Away In A Manger (5)

Bible And A Bus Ticket Home (3)
Big River (2)
Blue Magic (1)
Christmas Song (5)
Completely (8)
Corner Of The Heart (7)
Couldn't Last A Moment (8) **43**
Dark Secrets (7)

Dreaming My Dreams With You (3)
Eleventh Commandment (7)
Every Second (1)
Faithful Old Flame (7)
First Noel (5)
Gift, The (6)
Harder Cards (8)
Heart Full Of Rain (4)
I Can Still Feel You (7)
I Love Being Wrong (4)

I Think About You (4,6)
I Volunteer (4)
I Want To Be There (8)
I Want You Bad (And That Ain't Good) (2)
I Wish I Could (7)
I'll Be Home For Christmas (5)
If I Were You (1,3,6)
In This Life (2,6)
It Could Happen Again (5)
It Could've Been So Good (1)

Landing In Love (8)
Latter Day Cowboy (2)
Let It Be Me (2)
Little Drummer Boy (5)
Little Red Rodeo (3)
Little Rock (3,6)
Long Way To Go (8)
Love, Me (1,6)
Love Remains (4)
Loving This Way (4)
Make Sure You've Got It All (7)

Man Of My Word (3)
Many A Mile (2)
My Kind Of Girl (3,6)
Not That Different (4,6)
Nothin' A Little Love Won't Cure (3)
O Holy Night (5)
On The Verge (4)
One Boy, One Girl (4,6) **87**
Open Arms (4)
Sadly Ever After (1)

RAYE, Collin — Cont'd

'Scuse Moi, My Heart (1)
She's All That (8)
She's Gonna Fly (8)
Silent Night (5)
Somebody Else's Moon (2)

Someone You Used To Know (7) *37*
Start Over Georgia (7)
Survivors (7)
Sweet Miss Behavin' (4)

Walls Came Down (7)
Water And Bridges (8)
What If Jesus Comes Back Like That (4)
What The Heart Wants (6)

That Was A River (2,6)
That's My Story (3,6)
Time Machine (4)
To The Border And Beyond (3)

What They Don't Know (2)
White Christmas (5)
Winter Wonderland (5)
You Can't Take It With You (2)
You Still Take Me There (8)

You Will Always Be Mine (8)

RAYE, Susan   '70

Born on 10/18/44 in Eugene, Oregon. Country singer. Regular on TV's *Hee-Haw*.

5/16/70	154	6			1 We're Gonna Get Together			$20	Capitol 448
					BUCK OWENS & SUSAN RAYE				
9/26/70	190	2			2 One Night Stand			$15	Capitol 543

Cryin' Time (1)
Everybody Needs Somebody (1)
Fallin' For You (1)
Foolin' Around (1,2)

Heartaches Have Just Started (2)
I Ain't A Gonna Be Treated This Way (2)
I've Carried This Torch Much Too Long (2)

Living Tornado (2)
Love Is Strange (1)
Maybe If I Close My Eyes (It'll Go Away) (2)
One Night Stand (2)

Put A Little Love In Your Heart (2)
Rocks In My Head (2)
She Don't Deserve You Anymore (2)
Somewhere Between (1)

Together Again (1)
Togetherness (1)
We Were Made For Each Other (1)
We're Gonna Get Together (1)

RAY, GOODMAN & BROWN — see MOMENTS, The

R.B.L. POSSE   '97

Rap duo from San Francisco: Christian Mathews and Kyle Church. Church was shot to death on 12/31/95. R.B.L: Ruthless By Law.

| 12/3/94 | 197 | 1 | | © | 1 Ruthless By Law .... | | | $10 | In-A-Minute 8700 |
| 10/18/97 | 70 | 3 | | © | 2 An Eye For An Eye .... | | | $10 | Big Beat 92771 |

Blue Bird (1)
Bounce To This (1)
Concrete Jungle (2)
Dedication (Bitch Or A Hoe) (1)
Eye For An Eye (2)

Feels Good To Be A Gangsta (1)
FunkDaFied (1)
Gone Away (2)
Gotta Git Mine (2)

How We Comin' (2)
I Got My Nine (1)
Individual, The (2)
Listen To My Creep (1)
Livin That Life (1)

M.N.O.H.P. (1)
More Game (2)
Niggas On The Jock (1)
1 Time 4 The Homies (1)
Pass The ZigZags (1)

Smoke A Blunt (1)
So Tuff (2)
Sound, The (1)
Still Aint Learned (1)
Straight Lacin' (2)

Strictly This Game (2)
Til' The End (2)
You Can't Hang (2)

RBX   '95

Born in Long Beach, California. Male rapper. RBX: Reality Born Unknown.

| 10/14/95 | 62 | 3 | | © | The RBX Files .... | | | $10 | Premeditated 45866 |

A.W.O.L.
Akebulan
BMS On The Attack

Burn
Edge, The
Feathers In The Wind

Fightin' The Devil
Mom's Are Cryin'
No Time

Our Time Is Now
Rough Is The Texture
Slip Into Long Beach

Sounds Of Reality
Tundra

REA, Chris   '78

Born on 3/4/51 in Middlesborough, Cleveland, England. Pop-rock singer/songwriter.

8/12/78	49	12	●		1 Whatever Happened To Benny Santini?			$12	United Artists 879
3/4/89	92	13		©	2 New Light Through Old Windows			$10	Geffen 24232
3/17/90	107	19		©	3 The Road To Hell			$10	Geffen 24276
5/18/91	176	1		©	4 Auberge			$10	Atco 91662

Ace Of Hearts (2)
And You My Love (4)
Auberge (4)
Because Of You (1)
Bows And Bangles (1)
Candles (1)
Closer You Get (1)
Dancing With Charlie (1)

Daytona (3)
Every Second Counts (4)
Fires Of Spring (4)
Fool (If You Think It's Over) (1) *12*
Gone Fishing (4)
Heaven (4)
I Can Hear Your Heartbeat (2)

I Just Wanna Be With You (3)
Josephine (4)
Just One Of Those Days (1)
Let's Dance (2,3) *81*
Looking For A Rainbow (3)
Looking For The Summer (4)
Mention Of Your Name (4)
On The Beach (2)

Red Shoes (4)
Road To Hell (Part I & II) (3)
Set Me Free (4)
Sing A Song Of Love To Me (4)
Stainsby Girls (2)
Standing In Your Doorway (1)
Steel River (2)
Tell Me There's A Heaven (3)

Texas (3)
That's What They Always Say (3)
Three Angels (3)
Whatever Happened To Benny Santini? (1) *71*
Windy Town (2)
Working On It (2) *73*

You Must Be Evil (3)
You're Not A Number (4)
Your Warm And Tender Love (3)

READY FOR THE WORLD   '85

R&B group from Flint, Michigan: **Melvin Riley** (vocals), Gordon Strozier (guitar), Gregory Potts (keyboards), Willie Triplett (percussion), John Eaton (bass) and Gerald Valentine (drums).

6/22/85	17	48	▲	©	1 Ready For The World			$10	MCA 5594
12/6/86+	32	26	●	©	2 Long Time Coming			$10	MCA 5829
10/15/88	65	10		©	3 Ruff 'N' Ready			$10	MCA 42198

Baby (Let Me Love You) (2)
Ceramic Girl (1)
Cowboy (3)
Darlin', Darlin' (3)
Deep Inside Your Love (1)

Digital Display (1) *21*
Do You Get Enough (2)
Don't You Wanna (With Me) (3)
Gently (3)
Here I Am (2)

Human Toy (1)
I'm The One Who Loves You (1)
In My Room (2)
It's All A Game (2)

It's Funny (3)
Late Saturday Night (3)
Long Time Coming (2)
Love You Down (2) *9*
Mary Goes 'Round (2)

Money (3)
My Girly (3)
Oh Sheila (1) *1*
Out Of Town Lover (1)
Shame (3)

Slide Over (1)
So In Love (2)
Some People Don't Care (2)
Tonight (1)

REAL LIFE   '84

Pop-rock group from Melbourne, Australia: David Sterry (vocals, guitar), Richard Zatorski (keyboards), Allan Johnson (bass) and Danny Simcic (drums).

| 1/7/84 | 58 | 24 | | © | 1 Heart Land .... | | | $10 | Curb 5459 |
| 7/1/89 | 191 | 3 | | © | 2 Send Me An Angel '89 .... | [K] | | $10 | Curb 10614 |

Always (1,2)
Babies (2)
Breaking Point (1)

Broken Again (1)
Burning Blue (1)
Catch Me I'm Falling (1,2) *40*

Exploding Bullets (1)
Face To Face (2)
Hammer Of Love (2)

Heartland (1)
Let's Fall In Love (2)
No Shame (2)

One Blind Love (2)
Openhearted (1)
Send Me An Angel (1) *29*

Send Me An Angel '89 (2) *26*
Under The Hammer (1)

REAL McCOY   '95

Dance trio: German rapper/songwriter Olaf "O-Jay" Jeglitza with American singers Vanessa Mason and Lisa Cork.

| 4/15/95 | 13 | 46 | ▲² | © | 1 Another Night .... | | | $10 | Arista 18778 |
| 4/12/97 | 79 | 6 | | © | 2 One More Time .... | | | $10 | Arista 18965 |

Another Night (1) *3*
Automatic Lover (Call For Love) (1) *52*
Come And Get Your Love (1) *19*

Give A Little Love (2)
I Wanna Come (With You) (2)
I Want You (1)
If You Should Ever Be Lonely (Deep In The Night) (1)

(If You're Not In It For Love) I'm Outta Here (2)
Look At Me (2)
Love Almost Faded (2)
Love & Devotion (1)

Love Is A Stranger (2)
Love Save Me (2)
One More Time (2) *27*
Ooh Boy (1)
Operator (2)

Run Away (1) *3*
Sky Is The Limit (2)
Sleeping With An Angel (1)
Take A Look At Your Life (2)
Tomorrow (2)

Tonight (2)

REBELS, The — see ROCKIN' REBELS

DEBUT	PEAK	WKS	RIAA	CD	ARTIST — Album Title	Catalog	Sym	$	Label & Number

RECORDS, The '79

Rock group from England: Huw Gower (vocals), John Wicks (guitar), Phil Brown (bass) and Will Birch (drums). **Jude Cole** replaced Gower in late 1979, left in 1981.

| 8/25/79 | **41** | 14 | | | The Records .... | | | $15 | Virgin 13130 |

includes a 4-track EP record

Affection Rejected	Another Star	Insomnia	Teenarama
All Messed Up And Ready To Go	Girl	Phone, The	Up All Night
	Girls That Don't Exist	**Starry Eyes** 56	

REDBONE '74

Pop-rock group formed in Los Angeles: brothers Lolly (vocals, guitar) and Pat (vocals, bass) Vegas, Anthony Bellamy (guitar) and Peter De Poe (drums).

11/7/70+	**99**	17			1 Potlatch			$15	Epic 30109
2/5/72	**75**	9			2 Message From A Drum			$15	Epic 30815
3/16/74	**66**	16	©		3 Wovoka			$15	Epic 32462
10/26/74	**174**	3			4 Beaded Dreams Through Turquoise Eyes........			$15	Epic 33053

Alcatraz (1)	Come And Get Your Love	Interstate Highway 101 (4)	Moon When Four Eclipse (4)	Someday (A Good Song) (3)	Who Can Say? (1)
Bad News Ain't No News At All (1)	(3) 5	Jerico (2)	New Blue Sermonette (1)	Sun Never Shines On The Lonely (2)	**Witch Queen Of New Orleans** (2) 21
(Beaded Dreams Through) Turquoise Eyes (4)	Cookin' With D'Redbone (4)	Judgment Day (1)	Niji Trance (2)	Suzi Girl (4)	Without Reservation (1)
Beautiful Illusion (4)	Day To Day Life (medley) (3)	Light As A Feather (1)	One Monkey (2)	Sweet Lady Of Love (3)	Wovoka (3)
Blood Sweat And Tears (4)	Drinkin' And Blo (1)	Liquid Truth (3)	One More Time (4)	13th Hour (1)	
Clouds In My Sunshine (3)	Emotions (2)	**Maggie** (1) 45	Only You And Rock And Roll (4)	23rd And Mad (3)	
	Fate (2)	Maxsplivitz (2)	Perico (2)	When You Got Trouble (2)	
	I'll Never Stop Loving You (4)	Message From A Drum (2)			

REDBONE, Leon '77

Born on 10/29/29 in New York City. Blues singer. Rose to fame in the mid-1970s with appearances on TV's *Saturday Night Live*. Baritone voice of several TV commercials.

7/31/76	**87**	15	●	©	1 On The Track			$15	Warner 2888
1/22/77	**38**	13		©	2 Double Time			$15	Warner 2971
9/16/78	**163**	4		©	3 Champagne Charlie			$15	Warner 3165
4/11/81	**152**	11		©	4 From Branch To Branch			$12	Emerald City 136

Ain't Misbehavin' (I'm Savin' My Love For You) (1)	Diddy Wa Diddie (2)	Lazybones (1)	My Melancholy Baby (2)	Sheik Of Araby (2)	When You Wish Upon A Star (4)
Alabama Jubilee (3)	Extra Blues (4)	Lulu's Back In Town (1)	My Walking Stick (1)	Shine On Harvest Moon (2)	Why (4)
Big Bad Bill (Is Sweet William Now) (3)	Haunted House (1)	(Mama's Got A Baby Named) Te Na Na (4)	Nobody's Sweetheart (2)	Some Of These Days (1)	Winin' Boy Blues (2)
Big Time Woman (1)	Hot Time In The Old Town Tonight (4)	Marie (1)	One Rose (That's Left In My Heart) (3)	Step It Up And Go (4)	Yearning (Just For You) (3)
Champagne Charlie (3)	I Hate A Man Like You (3)	Mississippi Delta Blues (2)	Please Don't Talk About Me When I'm Gone (3)	Sweet Mama Hurry Home Or I'll Be Gone (1)	Your Cheatin' Heart (4)
Crazy Blues (2)	If Someone Would Only Love Me (3)	Mississippi River Blues (2)	Polly Wolly Doodle (1)	Sweet Mama Papa's Getting Mad (4)	
Desert Blues (Big Chief Buffalo Nickel) (1)	If We Never Meet Again This Side Of Heaven (2)	Mr. Jelly Roll Baker (1)	Prairie Lullaby (4)	Sweet Sue (Just You) (4)	
		My Blue Heaven (4)	**Seduced** (4) 72	T.B. Blues (3)	

★234★ REDDING, Otis '68

Born on 9/9/41 in Dawson, Georgia. Killed in a plane crash on 12/10/67 (age 26) in Lake Monona in Madison, Wisconsin. R&B singer/songwriter/producer/pianist. Own record label, Jotis. Plane crash also killed four members of the **Bar-Kays**. Otis's sons formed **The Reddings**. Inducted into the Rock and Roll Hall of Fame in 1989.

1)The Dock Of The Bay 2)History Of Otis Redding 3)Monterey International Pop Festival

5/2/64	**103**	8		©	1 Pain In My Heart			$250	Atco 161
4/10/65	**147**	3		©	2 The Great Otis Redding Sings Soul Ballads........			$100	Volt 411
10/16/65+	**75**	34		©	3 Otis Blue/Otis Redding Sings Soul			$50	Volt 412
4/30/66	**54**	29		©	4 The Soul Album			$50	Volt 413
11/26/66+	**73**	15		©	5 Complete & Unbelievable....The Otis Redding Dictionary Of Soul			$50	Volt 415
4/22/67	**36**	31		©	6 King & Queen			$50	Stax 716

OTIS REDDING & CARLA THOMAS

8/19/67	**32**	42	©	7 Otis Redding Live In Europe		[L]	$50	Volt 416
12/2/67+	**9**	50		8 History Of Otis Redding		[G]	$50	Volt 418
3/23/68	**4**	42		9 The Dock Of The Bay			$30	Volt 419
7/20/68	**58**	21	©	10 The Immortal Otis Redding			$20	Atco 252
11/30/68+	**82**	17	©	11 Otis Redding In Person At The Whisky A Go Go		[L]	$20	Atco 265

recorded April 1966

7/19/69	**46**	14	©	12 Love Man		[K]	$20	Atco 289
8/29/70	**200**	2	©	13 Tell The Truth		[K]	$20	Atco 333
9/19/70	**16**	20	●	14 Monterey International Pop Festival........		[L-S]	$40	Reprise 2029

OTIS REDDING/THE JIMI HENDRIX EXPERIENCE

recorded June 1967 and featured in the movie *Monterey Pop*; side 1: songs performed by The **Jimi Hendrix** Experience; side 2: songs performed by Otis Redding

| 9/16/72 | **76** | 15 | © | 15 The Best Of Otis Redding .... | | [G] | $25 | Atco 801 [2] |

Amen (10) 36	Down In The Valley (3,15)	Huckle-Buck (9)	It Takes Two (6)	My Girl (3,7,15)	**Security** (1,8) 97
Any Ole Way (4,11)	Everybody Makes A Mistake (4)	(I Can't Get No) Satisfaction ..see: Satisfaction	It's Growing (4)	**My Lover's Prayer** (5,8,15) 61	**Shake** (3,7,8,14,15) 47
Are You Lonely For Me Baby (6)	**Fa-Fa-Fa-Fa-Fa (Sad Song)** (5,7,8,15) 29	I Can't Turn You Loose (7,8,11,15)	It's Too Late (2)	New Year's Resolution (6)	She Put The Hurt On Me (5)
Bring It On Home To Me (6)	Fool For You (10)	I Got The Will (13)	Johnny's Heartbreak (13)	Nobody Knows You (When You're Down And Out) (4,9)	**(Sittin' On) The Dock Of The Bay** (9,15) 1
Can't Turn You Loose ..see: I Can't Turn You Loose	For Your Precious Love (2)	I Love You More Than Words Can Say (9) 78	**Just One More Day** (4,11,15) 85	Nobody's Fault But Mine (10)	634-5789 (4)
Chain Gang (4,15)	Free Me (12)	I Need Your Lovin' (1)	Keep Your Arms Around Me (2)	Nothing Can Change This Love (2)	Slippin' And Slidin' (13)
Chained And Bound (2) 70	Give Away None Of My Love	I Want To Thank You (2)	**Knock On Wood** (6) 30	Ole Man Trouble (3,9,15)	Snatch A Little Piece (13)
Champagne And Wine (10)	**Glory Of Love** (9) 60	I'll Let Nothing Separate Us (12)	Let Me Be Good To You (6)	Ooh Carla, Ooh Otis (6)	Something Is Worrying Me (1)
Change Is Gonna Come (3,15)	Good To Me (4)	I'm A Changed Man (12)	Let Me Come On Home (9)	Open The Door (9)	Stand By Me (1)
Cigarettes And Coffee (4,15)	Got To Get Myself Together (12)	I'm Coming Home (9)	Look At That Girl (12)	Out Of Sight (13)	Sweet Lorene (5)
Come To Me (2) 69	Groovin' Time (12)	I'm Depending On You (11)	Louie Louie (1)	**Pain In My Heart** (1,8,11,15) 61	Swingin' On A String (13)
Day Tripper (5,7)	**Happy Song (Dum-Dum)** (10) 25	I'm Sick Y'all (5)	Love Have Mercy (5)	**Papa's Got A Brand New Bag** (11) 21	Tell It Like It Is (6)
Demonstration (13)	**Hard To Handle** (10) 51	I've Been Loving You Too Long (To Stop Now) (3,7,8,14,15)	**Love Man** (12,15) 72	**Respect** (3,7,8,11,14,15) 35	Tell The Truth (13,15)
Direct Me (12)	Hawg For You (13)	I've Got Dreams To Remember (10) 41	**Lover's Question** (12) 48	Rock Me Baby (3,15)	Tennessee Waltz (5)
Dock Of The Bay ..see: (Sittin' On)	Hey Hey Baby (1)		Lovey Dovey (6) 60	**Satisfaction** (3,7,8,11,14,15) 31	That's A Good Idea (12)
Dog, The (1)	Home In Your Heart (2)		Lucille (1)	Scratch My Back (4)	**That's How Strong My Love Is** (2,15) 74
Don't Mess With Cupid (9)			Match Game (13)		That's What My Heart Needs (1)
			Mr. Pitiful (2,8,11) 41		

721

REDDING, Otis — Cont'd

These Arms Of Mine (1,7,8,11,15) **85**	Tramp (6,9,15) **26**
Think About It (10)	Treat Her Right (4)
Thousand Miles Away (10)	Try A Little Tenderness (5,7,8,14,15) **25**
Ton Of Joy (5)	Waste Of Time (10)

When Something Is Wrong With My Baby (6)
Wholesale Love (13)
Woman, Lover, A Friend (2)
Wonderful World (3)

You Don't Miss Your Water (3,15)
You Made A Man Out Of Me (10)
You Send Me (1)

You're Still My Baby (5)
Your Feeling Is Mine (12)
(Your Love Has Lifted Me) Higher And Higher (12)
Your One And Only Man (2)

REDDINGS, The '81

R&B group formed in Atlanta: **Otis Redding**'s sons Dexter (vocals, bass) and Otis III (guitar), with cousin Mark Locket (vocals, drums, keyboards).

DEBUT	PEAK	WKS					$	Label & Number
12/20/80	174	12			1 The Awakening		$10	Believe 36875
8/1/81	106	5			2 Class		$10	Believe 37175
5/29/82	153	12			3 Steamin' Hot		$10	Believe 37974

Awakening Pt. 1 & 2 (1)
Class (Is What You Got) (2)
Come On In Out The Rain (1)
Doin' It (1)
Follow Me (3)
For You (3)

Funkin' On The One (1)
Hurts So Bad (2)
I Know You Got Another (Don't Matter) (1)
I Want It (1)
If You Feel It (2)

It's Friday Night (1)
Lady Be My Lovesong (1)
Love Dance (2)
Love Is Over (2)
Main Nerve (2)
Remote Control (1) **89**

Seriously (2)
(Sittin' On) The Dock Of The Bay (3) **55**
Steamin' Hot (3)
Time Won't Wait (3)
You Bring Me Joy (3)

You Can Be A Star (3)
You're The Only One (2)

★325★ REDDY, Helen '73

Born on 10/25/41 in Melbourne, Australia. Pop singer. Acted in the movies *Airport 1975*, *Pete's Dragon* and *Sgt. Pepper's Lonely Hearts Club Band*.

1)Helen Reddy's Greatest Hits 2)Long Hard Climb 3)Free And Easy

DEBUT	PEAK	WKS	RIAA	CD	ARTIST — Album Title	$	Label & Number
6/5/71+	100	37	●		1 I Don't Know How To Love Him	$15	Capitol 762
12/4/71+	167	7			2 Helen Reddy	$15	Capitol 857
12/9/72+	14	62	▲		3 I Am Woman	$12	Capitol 11068
8/11/73	8	43	●		4 Long Hard Climb	$12	Capitol 11213
4/20/74	11	35	●		5 Love Song For Jeffrey	$12	Capitol 11284
11/2/74+	8	28	●		6 Free And Easy	$12	Capitol 11348
7/12/75	11	34	●	©	7 No Way To Treat A Lady	$12	Capitol 11418
12/6/75+	5	51	▲²		8 Helen Reddy's Greatest Hits [G]	$12	Capitol 11467
8/14/76	16	13	●		9 Music, Music	$12	Capitol 11547
5/21/77	75	19			10 Ear Candy	$12	Capitol 11640

Ah, My Sister (5)
Ain't No Way To Treat A Lady (7,8) **8**
And I Love You So (3)
Angie Baby (6,8) **1**
Aquarius Miracle (4)
Baby, I'm A Star (10)
Best Friend (1)
Birthday Song (7)
Bit O.K. (4)
Bluebird (7) **35**
Come On John (2)
Crazy Love (1) **51**
Delta Dawn (4,8) **1**
Don't Let It Mess Your Mind (7)
Don't Make Promises (1)
Don't Mess With A Woman (4)

Emotion (6,8) **22**
Free And Easy (6)
Get Off Me Baby (9)
Gladiola (9)
Happy Girls (10) **57**
Hit The Road, Jack (3)
Hold Me In Your Dreams Tonight (9)
How? (2)
How Can I Be Sure (1)
I Believe In Music (1)
I Can't Hear You No More (9) **29**
I Didn't Mean To Love You (3)
I Don't Know How To Love Him (1,8) **13**

I Don't Remember My Childhood (2)
I Got A Name (5)
I Think I'll Write A Song (6)
I Think It's Going To Rain Today (2)
I'll Be Your Audience (6)
I've Been Wanting You So Long (6)
If It's Magic (10)
If We Could Still Be Friends (4)
Keep On Singing (5,8) **15**
L.A. Breakdown (1)
Ladychain (9)
Laissez Les Bontemps Rouler (10)
Last Blues Song (3)

Leave Me Alone (Ruby Red Dress) (4,8) **3**
Loneliness (6)
Long Distance Love (10)
Long Hard Climb (4)
Long Time Looking (7)
Love Song For Jeffrey (5)
Lovin' You (4)
Mama (9)
Midnight Skies (10)
More Than You Could Take (2)
Music Is My Life (9) *flip*
Music, Music (9)
New Year's Resovolution (2)
Nice To Be Around (9)
No Sad Song (2) **62**
Nothing Good Comes Easy (7)

Old Fashioned Way (4)
One More Night (10)
Our House (1)
Peaceful (3,8) **12**
Pretty, Pretty (5)
Raised On Rock (6)
Showbiz (9)
Somewhere In The Night (7) **19**
Song For You (1)
Songs (5)
Stella By Starlight (9)
Summer Of '71 (2)
Ten To Eight (7)
Thank You (10)
That Old American Dream (5)
This Masquerade (3)

Time (2)
Tulsa Turnaround (2)
Until It's Time For You To Go (4)
West Wind Circus (4)
What Would They Say (3)
Where Is My Friend (3)
Where Is The Love (3)
You And Me Against The World (5,8) **9**
You Don't Need A Reason (7)
You Have Lived (6)
You Know Me (7)
You Make It So Easy (9)
You're My Home (5)
You're My World (10) **18**

REDEYE '71

Rock group formed in Los Angeles: Douglas "Red" Mark (vocals), Dave Hodgkins (guitar), Bill Kirkham (bass) and Bob Bereman (drums). Mark was a member of **The Sunshine Company**.

DEBUT	PEAK	WKS				$	Label & Number
12/12/70+	113	12			Redeye	$15	Pentagram 10003

Collections Of Yesterday And Now
Dadaeleus' Unfinished Dream
Down Home Run

Empty White Houses
Games **27**

Green Grass
Mississippi Stateline

199 Thoughts Too Late
Oregon Bound

Your Train Is Leaving

RED FLAG '89

Duo from Liverpool, England: brothers Mark (vocals) and Chris (piano) Reynolds.

DEBUT	PEAK	WKS		CD		$	Label & Number
9/23/89	178	4		©	Naive Art	$10	Enigma 73523

All Roads Lead To You
Broken Heart

Count To Three
Fur Michelle

Give Me Your Hand
I Don't Know Why

If I Ever
Pretty In Pity

Rain
Russian Radio

Save Me Tonight

REDHEAD KINGPIN AND THE FBI '91

Born David Guppy in Englewood, New Jersey. Male rapper. The FBI: Wildstyle, Bo Roc, Lt. Squeak, Buzz and Poochie.

DEBUT	PEAK	WKS		CD		$	Label & Number
4/27/91	182	1		©	The Album With No Name	$10	Virgin 91608

All About Red
Dave & Kwame (Gimme Dat Girl)

Get It Together
Got 2 Go
Harlem Brown

It's A Love Thang (Word)
Nice & Slow
No Reason

Soap
Song With No Name
3-2-1-Pump **52**

We Don't Have A Plan B
What Do U Hate

★433★ RED HOT CHILI PEPPERS '99

Rock group formed in Los Angeles: Anthony Kiedis (vocals), Hillel Slovak (guitar), Michael "Flea" Balzary (bass) and Jack Irons (drums). Slovak died of a drug overdose on 6/25/88 (age 26); replaced by John Frusciante. Irons left in 1988 and later joined **Eleven**, then **Pearl Jam**; replaced by Chad Smith. Frusciante left in May 1992; replaced by Zander Schloss (**Thelonious Monster**, **The Magnificent Bastards**), then by Arik Marshall, then by Jesse Tobias and finally by Dave Navarro (**Jane's Addiction**) in September 1993. Frusciante returned in 1998, replacing Navarro. Kiedis appeared in the movie *Point Break*. Flea and Kiedis appeared in the movie *The Chase*.

DEBUT	PEAK	WKS	RIAA	CD	ARTIST — Album Title	Catalog	$	Label & Number
11/21/87+	148	18		©	1 The Uplift Mofo Party Plan		$10	EMI-Manhattan 48036
9/16/89	52	42	●	©	2 Mother's Milk	C:#32/24	$10	EMI 92152
10/12/91+	3	97	▲⁷	©	3 Blood Sugar Sex Magik		$10	Warner 26681
10/17/92	22	30	▲	©	4 What Hits!?		$10	EMI 94762
11/19/94	82	2		©	5 Out In L.A.	[K]	$10	EMI 29665
9/30/95	4	46	▲²	©	6 One Hot Minute		$10	Warner 45733
6/26/99	3	101	▲⁴	©	7 Californication	C:#23/12	$10	Warner 47386

RED HOT CHILI PEPPERS — Cont'd

- Aeroplane (6)
- Apache Rose Peacock (3)
- Around The World (7)
- Backwoods (1,4)
- Behind The Sun (1,4,5)
- Blood Sugar Sex Magik (3)
- Blues For Meister (5)
- Breaking The Girl (3)
- Brothers Cup (4)
- **Californication** (7) *69*
- Castles Made Of Sand (5)
- Catholic School Girls Rule (4)
- Coffee Shop (6)
- Deck The Halls (5)
- Deep Kick (6)
- Easily (7)
- Emit Remmus (7)
- F.U. (5)
- Falling Into Grace (6)
- Fight Like A Brave (1,4)
- Fire (2,4)
- Flea Fly (5)
- Funky Crime (1)
- Funky Monks (3)
- Get On Top (7)
- Get Up And Jump (4,5)
- **Give It Away** (3) *73*
- Good Time Boys (2)
- Green Heaven (5)
- Greeting Song (3)
- Higher Ground (2,4,5)
- Hollywood (7)
- I Could Have Lied (3)
- I Like Dirt (7)
- If You Have To Ask (3)
- If You Want Me To Stay (4,5)
- Johnny Kick A Hole In The Sky (2,4)
- Jungle Man (4)
- Knock Me Down (2,4)
- Love Trilogy (1)
- Magic Johnson (2)
- Me And My Friends (1,4)
- Mellowship Slinky In B Major (3)
- My Friends (6)
- My Lovely Man (3)
- Naked In The Rain (3)
- Nevermind (5)
- No Chump Love Sucker (1)
- Nobody Weird Like Me (2)
- One Big Mob (6)
- One Hot Minute (6)
- Organic Anti-Beat Box Band (1)
- **Otherside** (7) *14*
- Out In L.A. (5)
- Parallel Universe (4)
- Pea (6)
- Police Helicopter (5)
- Porcelain (7)
- Power Of Equality (3)
- Pretty Little Ditty (2)
- Punk Rock Classic (2)
- Purple Stain (7)
- Right On Time (7)
- Righteous & The Wicked (3)
- Road Trippin' (7)
- Savior (7)
- **Scar Tissue** (7) *9*
- Sex Rap (5)
- Sexy Mexican Maid (2)
- Shallow Be Thy Game (6)
- Show Me Your Soul (4)
- Sir Psycho Sexy (3)
- Skinny Sweaty Man (1)
- Special Secret Song Inside (1,5)
- Stone Cold Bush (2)
- Stranded (5)
- Subterranean Homesick Blues (1)
- Subway To Venus (2)
- Suck My Kiss (3)
- Taste The Pain (2,4)
- Tearjerker (6)
- They're Red Hot (3)
- This Velvet Glove (7)
- Transcending (6)
- True Men Don't Kill Coyotes (4)
- **Under The Bridge** (3,4) *2*
- Walkabout (6)
- Walkin' On Down The Road (1)
- Warped (6)
- What It Is (5)

REDMAN '99

Born Reggie Noble in Newark, New Jersey. Male rapper.

DEBUT	PEAK	WKS	RIAA	CD	ARTIST — Album Title	$	Label & Number
10/24/92	49	24	●	©	1 Whut? Thee Album	$10	RAL 52967
12/10/94	13	16	●	©	2 Dare Iz A Darkside	$10	RAL 523846
12/28/96	12	17	●	©	3 Muddy Waters	$10	Def Jam 533470
12/26/98	11	24	▲	©	4 Doc's Da Name 2000	$10	Def Jam 558945
10/16/99	3	33	▲	©	5 Blackout!	$10	Def Jam 546609

METHOD MAN/REDMAN

DEBUT	PEAK	WKS	RIAA	CD	ARTIST — Album Title	$	Label & Number
6/9/01	4	16	●	©	6 Malpractice	$10	Def Jam 548381

- Basically (2)
- Beet Drop (4)
- Big Dogs (5)
- Blackout (5)
- Blow Your Mind (1)
- Bobyahed2dis (2)
- Boodah Break (4)
- Brick City Mashin'! (4)
- Bricks Two (6)
- **Can't Wait** (2) *94*
- Case Closed (3)
- Cereal Killer (5)
- Cheka (5)
- Close Ya Doorz (4)
- Cosmic Slop (2)
- Creepin' (3)
- D.O.G.S. (4)
- Da Bulls**t (6)
- Da Bump (3)
- Da Da DaHHH (4)
- Da Funk (1)
- Da Goodness (4)
- Da Ill Out (3)
- Da Rockwilder (5)
- Dat B***h (6)
- Dat's Dat S**t (5)
- Day Of Sooperman Lover (1)
- Diggy Doc (6)
- Do What Ya Feel (3)
- Doggz II (6)
- Down South Funk (4)
- Encore (1)
- Enjoy Da Ride (6)
- Fire Ina Hole (5)
- 4 Seasons (5)
- Funky Uncles (1)
- Get It Live (4)
- Green Island (2)
- Hardcore (1)
- How High (5)
- How To Roll A Blunt (1)
- I Don't Kare (4)
- I Got A Seecret (4)
- I'll Bee Dat! (4)
- I'm A Bad (1)
- **It's Like That (My Big Brother)** (3) *95*
- Iz He 4 Real (3)
- Jam 4 U (1)
- Jersey Yo! (4)
- Journey Throo Da Darkside (2)
- J.U.M.P. (6)
- Keep On '99 (4)
- Let Da Monkey Out (4)
- **Let's Get Dirty (I Can't Get In Da Club)** (6) *97*
- Lick A Shot (6)
- Maaad Crew (5)
- Mi Casa (3)
- Million And 1 Buddah Spots (3)
- Muh-F***a (6)
- My Zone! (4)
- Noorotic (2)
- On Fire (3)
- 1, 2, 1, 2 (5)
- Pick It Up (3)
- Psycho Ward (1)
- ?, The (5)
- Rated "R" (1)
- Real N***z (6)
- Redman Meets Reggie Noble (1)
- Rock Da Spot (3)
- Rockafella (2)
- Rockafella (R.I.P.) (2)
- Rollin' (3)
- Run 4 Cover (5)
- Slide And Rock On (2)
- Smash Sumthin' (6)
- Smoke Buddah (3)
- So Ruff (1)
- Soopaman Luva (Part I & II) (6)
- Soopaman Luva II (2)
- Soopaman Luva III (3)
- Soopaman Luva IV (4)
- Tear It Off (5)
- Time 4 Sum Aksion (1)
- Tonight's Da Night (1)
- Tonight's Da Nite (2)
- Uh-Huh (6)
- Watch Yo Nuggets (1)
- We Run N.Y. (2)
- Welcome 2 Da Bricks (4)
- Well All Rite Cha (4,5)
- What U Lookin' 4 (3)
- **Whateva Man** (3) *42*
- Whut I'ma Do Now (6)
- Winicumuhround (2)
- Wrong 4 Dat (6)
- Wudittooklike (2)
- Y.O.U. (1)
- Yesh Yesh Ya'll (3)

REDNEX '95

Studio group from Sweden. Core members: Goran Danielsson, Annika Ljungberg, Cool James and Pat Reiniz (vocals), Bosse Nilsson (fiddle), General Custer (banjo) and Animal (drums).

DEBUT	PEAK	WKS	RIAA	CD	ARTIST — Album Title	$	Label & Number
5/13/95	68	12		©	Sex & Violins	$10	Battery 46000

- **Cotton-Eye Joe** *25*
- Fat Sally Lee
- Hittin' The Hay
- Mary Lou
- McKenzie Brothers
- Nowhere In Idaho
- Old Pop In An Oak
- Riding Alone
- Rolling Home
- Sad But True Story Of Ray Mingus, The Lumberjack Of Bulk Rock City, And ...
- Shooter
- Wild And Free
- Wish You Were Here

RED RIDER — see COCHRANE, Tom

RED ROCKERS '83

Rock group from Algiers, Louisiana: John Griffith (vocals), James Singletary (guitar), Darren Hill (bass) and Jim Reilly (drums).

DEBUT	PEAK	WKS	RIAA	CD	ARTIST — Album Title	$	Label & Number
5/14/83	71	16		©	Good As Gold	$12	Columbia 38629

- Answers To The Questions
- Change The World Around
- **China** *53*
- (Come On Into) My House
- Dreams Fade Away
- Fanfare For Metropolis
- Good As Gold
- Home Is Where The War Is
- Running Away From You
- 'Til It All Falls Down

RED 7 '85

Rock trio: Gene Stashuk (vocals), Michael Becker (keyboards) and Paul Revelli (drums).

DEBUT	PEAK	WKS	RIAA	CD	ARTIST — Album Title	$	Label & Number
5/25/85	105	10			1 Red 7	$10	MCA 5508
5/30/87	175	3		©	2 When The Sun Goes Down...	$10	MCA 5792

- Big Boys (Talk Tuff) (2)
- Can't Much Anymore (1)
- Condition Red (2)
- Heartbeat (1)
- Hearts In Flames (2)
- I'm On Your Side (2)
- Inspiration (2)
- Less Than Perfect (1)
- Let Me Use You (1)
- No Sorry (1)
- Questions And Answers (1)
- Relentless (1)
- Rise And The Fall (2)
- Say You Will (2)
- Shades Of Grey (1)
- This Dark Hour (1)
- True Confessions (2)
- Under The Water (2)
- Way, The (1)
- When The Sun Goes Down (2)

RED SIREN '89

Rock group: Kristin Massey (vocals), Robert Haas (guitar), Jon Brant (bass) and Gregg Potter (drums).

DEBUT	PEAK	WKS	RIAA	CD	ARTIST — Album Title	$	Label & Number
4/8/89	124	12		©	All Is Forgiven	$10	Mercury 836776

- All Is Forgiven
- Don't Let Go
- Good Kid
- How Dare A Woman
- Love Shut Down
- Master Of The Land
- One Good Lover
- Rock-A-Bye
- So Far Away
- Stand Up

REED, Dan, Network '88

Funk-rock group from Portland, Oregon: Dan Reed (vocals), Brion James (guitar), Blake Sakomoto (keyboards), Melvin Brannon (bass) and Daniel Pred (drums).

DEBUT	PEAK	WKS	RIAA	CD	ARTIST — Album Title	$	Label & Number
4/2/88	95	19		©	1 Dan Reed Network	$10	Mercury 834309
10/21/89	160	6		©	2 Slam	$10	Mercury 838868

- All My Lovin' (2)
- Baby Don't Fade (1)
- Come Back Baby (2)
- Cruise Together (2)
- Doin' The Love Thing (2)
- Forgot To Make Her Mine (1)
- Get To You (1)
- Halfway Around The World (1)
- Human (1)
- I'm Lonely, Please Stay (2)
- I'm So Sorry (1)
- Lover (2)
- Make It Easy (2)
- Rainbow Child (2)
- Resurrect (1)
- **Ritual** (1) *38*
- Rock You All Night Long (1)
- Seven Sisters Road (2)
- Slam (2)
- Stronger Than Steel (2)
- Tamin' The Wild Nights (1)
- Tiger In A Dress (2)
- Under My Skin (2)
- World Has A Heart Too (1)

REED, Jerry　　'71

Born Jerry Reed Hubbard on 3/20/37 in Atlanta. Country singer/songwriter/guitarist/actor. Acted in several movies. Regular on TV's *Concrete Cowboys*.

5/16/70	194	2	©	1 Cookin'	$15	RCA Victor 4293
3/6/71	102	11	©	2 Georgia Sunshine	$15	RCA Victor 4391
5/1/71	45	20		3 When You're Hot, You're Hot	$15	RCA Victor 4506
9/18/71	153	5		4 Ko-Ko Joe	$15	RCA Victor 4596
4/1/72	196	2	©	5 Smell The Flowers	$15	RCA Victor 4660
7/15/72	116	12		6 The Best Of Jerry Reed	[G] $15	RCA Victor 4729
8/11/73	183	4	©	7 Lord, Mr. Ford	$15	RCA Victor 0238

Alabama Jubilee (1)
Amos Moses (2,3,6) *8*
Another Puff (4) *65*
Aunt Maudie's Fun Garden (1)
Big Daddy (3)
Brand New Day (4)
Claw, The (6)
Country Boy's Dream (4)
Don't Get Heavy (5)
Don't Let The Good Life Pass You By (5)
Don't Think Twice It's All Right (3)
Dream Sweet Dreams About Me (2)

Early Morning Rain (4)
Eight More Miles To Louisville (2)
Endless Miles Of Highway (5)
Folsom Prison Blues (7)
Framed (4)
Georgia On My Mind (6)
Georgia Sunshine (2,6)
Gomyeyonyo (1)
Good Friends And Neighbors (2)
Guitar Man (6)
How Many Tomorrows (1)
I Shoulda Stayed Home (1)

I'll Be Around (In All The Old Places) (3)
I'm Gonna Write A Song (7)
If I Ever (Love Again) (5)
It Ain't Home, But It Ain't Bad (5)
It Don't Work That Way (5)
Just To Satisfy You (1)
Ko-Ko Joe (4,6) *51*
Lady Is A Woman (7)
(Love Is) A Stranger To Me (4)
Mule Skinner Blues (Blue Yodel No. 8) (2)
My Guitar And My Song (5)

My Kinda Love (3)
My Next Impersonation (1)
Not As A Sweetheart (But Just As A Friend) (4)
One Sweet Reason (7)
Pave Your Way Into Tomorrow (5)
Pickie, Pickie, Pickie (7)
Plastic Saddle (1)
Preacher And The Bear (5)
Rainbow Ride (7)
Ruby, Don't Take Your Love To Town (3)
Seasons Of My Mind (4)
Semi-Great Predictor (1)

She Understands Me (3)
Smell The Flowers (5)
Sometimes Feelin' (1)
Take It Easy (In Your Mind) (5)
Talk About The Good Times (2)
Thank You Girl (3)
That Lucky Old Sun (Just Rolls Around Heaven All Day) (7)
That's All Part Of Losing (2)
Thing Called Love (6)
Today Is Mine (6)
Tupelo Mississippi Flash (6)
Turn It Around In Your Mind (7)
Turned On (3)
Two-Timin' (7)

U.S. Male (6)
Ugly Woman (2)
When You're Hot, You're Hot (3,6) *9*
With You (Missing You) (3)
You Can't Keep Me Here In Tennessee (7)
You'll Never Walk Alone (4)

REED, Jimmy　　'61

Born Mathis James Reed on 9/6/25 in Dunleith, Mississippi. Died from an epileptic seizure on 8/29/76 (age 50). Blues singer/guitarist. Inducted into the Rock and Roll Hall of Fame in 1991.

| 10/16/61 | 46 | 31 | © | 1 Jimmy Reed at Carnegie Hall | [G] $75 | Vee-Jay 1035 [2] |

record 1: studio re-creation of his Carnegie Hall program; record 2: The Best of Jimmy Reed

| 10/20/62 | 103 | 6 | © | 2 Just Jimmy Reed | $50 | Vee-Jay 1050 |

Ain't That Lovin' Baby (1)
Aw Shucks, Hush Your Mouth (1) *93*
Baby What You Want Me To Do (1) *37*
Back Home At Noon (2)

Big Boss Man (1) *78*
Blue Blue Water (1)
Blue Carnegie (1)
Boogie In The Dark (1)
Bright Lights Big City (1) *58*
Found Joy (1)

Found Love (1) *88*
Going To New York (1)
Good Lover (2) *77*
Hold Me Close (1)
Honest I Do (1) *32*
Hush-Hush (1) *75*

I'll Change That Too (2)
I'm A Love You (1)
I'm Mr. Luck (1)
In The Morning (2)
Kansas City Baby (2)
Kind Of Lonesome (2)

Let's Get Together (2)
Oh John (2)
Sun Is Shining (1) *65*
Take It Slow (2)
Take Out Some Insurance (1)
Tell Me You Love Me (1)

Too Much (2)
What's Wrong Baby? (1)
You Can't Hide (2)
You Don't Have To Go (1)
You Got Me Dizzy (1)

REED, Lou　★199★　　'74

Born on 3/2/42 in Freeport, Long Island, New York. Lead singer/songwriter of the New York seminal rock band **Velvet Underground**. Regarded as the godfather of punk rock. Appeared in the movie *One Trick Pony*.

1)Sally Can't Dance　2)Transformer　3)New York　4)Coney Island Baby　5)Rock N Roll Animal

| 6/24/72 | 189 | 2 | | 1 Lou Reed | $15 | RCA Victor 4701 |
| 12/16/72+ | 29 | 31 | © | 2 Transformer | $15 | RCA Victor 4807 |

produced by David Bowie

| 10/20/73 | 98 | 11 | © | 3 Berlin | $15 | RCA Victor 0207 |
| 3/2/74 | 45 | 27 | ● © | 4 Rock N Roll Animal | C:#24/2 [L] $15 | RCA Victor 0472 |

recorded at the Academy of Music in New York City

| 10/5/74 | 10 | 14 | © | 5 Sally Can't Dance | $15 | RCA Victor 0611 |
| 4/5/75 | 62 | 10 | © | 6 Lou Reed Live | [L] $15 | RCA Victor 0959 |

from same live sessions as album #4

2/7/76	41	14	©	7 Coney Island Baby	$15	RCA Victor 0915
11/13/76	64	8	©	8 Rock And Roll Heart	$12	Arista 4100
4/16/77	156	6	©	9 Walk On The Wild Side-The best of Lou Reed	C:#48/4 [G] $12	RCA Victor 2001
4/8/78	89	9	©	10 Street Hassle	$12	Arista 4169
6/2/79	130	4	©	11 The Bells	$12	Arista 4229
5/10/80	158	5	©	12 Growing Up In Public	$12	Arista 9522
12/20/80	178	4	©	13 Rock And Roll Diary 1967-1980	[K] $15	Arista 8603 [2]
2/27/82	169	4	©	14 The Blue Mask	$10	RCA Victor 4221
4/9/83	159	7	©	15 Legendary Hearts	$10	RCA Victor 4568
6/16/84	56	32		16 New Sensations	$10	RCA Victor 4998
5/24/86	47	21	©	17 Mistrial	$10	RCA Victor 7190
1/28/89	40	22	● ©	18 New York	$10	Sire 25829
5/12/90	103	8	©	19 Songs For Drella	$10	Sire 26140

LOU REED/JOHN CALE
fictitious account of the life of Andy Warhol

2/1/92	80	7	©	20 Magic And Loss	$10	Sire 26662
3/9/96	110	3	©	21 Set The Twilight Reeling	$10	Warner 46159
4/22/00	183	1	©	22 Ecstasy	$10	Reprise 47425

Adventurer (21)
All Through The Night (11,13)
Andy's Chest (2)
Animal Language (5)
Average Guy (14)
Baby Face (5)
Banging On My Drum (8)
Baton Rouge (22)

Bed, The (3)
Beginning Of A Great Adventure (18)
Beginning To See The Light (13)
Bells, The (11)
Berlin (1,3,13)
Betrayed (15)

Big Sky (22)
Billy (5)
Blue Mask (14)
Bottoming Out (15)
Busload Of Faith (18)
Caroline Says I & II (3)
Charley's Girl (7)
Chooser And The Chosen (8)

City Lights (11)
Claim To Fame (8)
Coney Island Baby (7,9,13)
Crazy Feeling (7)
Cremation (20)
Day John Kennedy Died (17)
Dime Store Mystery (18)
Dirt (10)

Dirty Blvd. (18)
Disco Mystic (11)
Doin' The Things That We Want To (16)
Don't Hurt A Woman (17)
Don't Talk To Me About Work (15)
Dorita (20)

Dream, A (19)
Dreamin' (20)
Ecstasy (22)
Egg Cream (21)
Endless Cycle (18)
Endlessly Jealous (16)
Ennui (5)
Faces And Names (19)

REED, Lou — Cont'd

Families (11)
Femme Fatale (13)
Finish Line (21)
Fly Into The Sun (16)
Follow The Leader (8)
Forever Changed (19)
Future Farmers Of America (22)
Gassed And Stoked (20)
Gift, A (7)
Gimmie Some Good Times (10)
Going Down (1)
Good Evening Mr. Waldheim (18)
Goodby Mass (20)
Goodnight Ladies (2)
Great Defender (Down At The Arcade) (14)
Growing Up In Public (12)
Gun, The (14)
Halloween Parade (18)
Hang On To Your Emotions (21)
Hangin' 'Round (2)
Harry's Circumcision (20)
Heavenly Arms (14)
Hello It's Me (19)
Heroin (4,13,14)
High In The City (16)
Hold On (18)

Home Of The Brave (15)
Hooky Wooky (21)
How Do You Speak To An Angel (12,13)
How Do You Think It Feels (3,9)
I Believe (19)
I Believe In Love (8)
I Can't Stand It (1)
I Heard Her Call My Name (13)
I Love You (1,9)
I Love You, Suzanne (16)
I Remember (17)
I Wanna Be Black (10)
I Want To Boogie With You (11)
I'm So Free (2)
I'm Waiting For The Man (8)
Images (11)
It Wasn't Me (19)
Keep Away (12,13)
Kicks (7)
Kids, The (3,13)
Kill Your Sons (5)
Ladies Pay (8)
Lady Day (3,4)
Last Great American Whale (18)
Last Shot (15)
Leave Me Alone (10)
Legendary Hearts (15)

Like A Possum (22)
Lisa Says (1)
Looking For Love (11)
Love Is Here To Stay (12)
Love Makes You Feel (1)
Mad (22)
Magic And Loss (20)
Magician (20)
Make Up (2)
Make Up Mind (15)
Mama's Got A Lover (17)
Martial Law (15)
Men Of Good Fortune (3,13)
Mistrial (17)
Modern Dance (22)
My Friend George (16)
My House (14)
My Old Man (12)
My Red Joystick (16)
Mystic Child (22)
N.Y. Stars (5)
NYC Man (21)
New Sensations (16)
New York Telephone Conversation (2,9)
No Chance (20)
No Money Down (17)
Nobody But You (19)
Nobody's Business (7)

Nowhere At All (9)
Ocean (1)
Oh Jim (3,6)
Ooohhh Baby (7)
Open House (19)
Original Wrapper (17)
Outside (17)
Pale Blue Eyes (13)
Paranoia Key Of E (22)
Perfect Day (2)
Pow Wow (15)
Power And Glory (Parts I & II) (20)
Power Of Positive Drinking (12)
Proposition, The (21)
Real Good Time Together (10)
Ride Into The Sun (1)
Ride Sally Ride (5)
Riptide (21)
Rock And Roll Heart (8)
Rock Minuet (22)
Rock 'N' Roll (4,13)
Romeo Had Juliette (18)
Rooftop Garden (15)
Rouge (22)
Sad Song (3,6)
Sally Can't Dance (5,9)
Satellite Of Love (2,6,9)
Senselessly Cruel (8)

Set The Twilight Reeling (21)
Sex With Your Parents (Motherfucker) Part II (21)
She's My Best Friend (7)
Sheltered Life (8)
Shooting Star (10)
Sick Of You (18)
Slip Away (A Warning) (10,19)
Smalltown (19)
Smiles (15)
So Alone (12,13)
Spit It Out (17)
Standing On Ceremony (12)
Starlight (19)
Strawman (18)
Street Hassle (10,13)
Stupid Man (11)
Style It Takes (19)
Sweet Jane (4,13)
Sword Of Damocles (20)
Tatters (22)
Teach The Gifted Children (12)
Tell It To Your Heart (17)
Temporary Thing (8,13)
There Is No Time (18)
Think It Over (12)
Trade In (21)
Trouble With Classicists (19)
Turn Out The Light (15)

Turn To Me (16)
Turning Time Around (22)
Underneath The Bottle (14)
Vicious (2,6)
Vicious Circle (8)
Video Violence (17)
Wagon Wheel (2)
Wait (10)
Waiting For The Man (13)
Walk And Talk It (1)
Walk On The Wild Side (2,6,9,13) *16*
Waltzing Matilda (medley) (10)
Warrior King (2)
Waves Of Fear (14)
What Becomes A Legend Most (16)
What's Good (20)
White Light/White Heat (4,9,13)
White Prism (1,9)
Wild Child (14)
With You (11)
Women (14)
Work (19)
Xmas In February (18)
You Wear It So Well (8)

REEL BIG FISH   '97

Ska-punk group from Huntington Beach, California: Aaron Barrett (vocals, guitar), Scott Klopfenstein (vocals, trumpet), Tavis Werts (trumpet), Grant Barry and Dan Regan (trombones), Matt Wong (bass) and Andrew Gonzales (drums).

| 5/31/97 | 57 | 32 | ● | © | 1 Turn The Radio Off | | | $10 | Mojo 53013 |
| 11/7/98 | 67 | 3 | | © | 2 Why Do They Rock So Hard? | | | $10 | Mojo 53159 |

All I Want Is More (1)
Alternative, Baby (1)
Beer (1)
Big Star (2)
Brand New Song (2)
Down In Flames (2)

Everything Is Cool (2)
Everything Sucks (1)
I Want Your Girlfriend To Be My Girlfriend Too (2)
I'll Never Be (1)
I'm Cool (2)

Join The Club (1)
Kids Don't Like It (2)
Nothin' (1)
S.R. (1)
Say "Ten" (1)
Scott's A Dork (2)

Sell Out (1)
Set Up (You Need This) (2)
She Has A Girlfriend Now (1)
She's Famous Now (2)
Skatanic (1)
Snoop Dog, Baby (1)

Somebody Hates Me (2)
Song #3 (2)
Thank You For Not Moshing (2)
Trendy (1)
241 (1)
Victory Over Peter Bones (2)

We Care (2)
You Don't Know (2)

REEL TIGHT   '99

R&B vocal group from Chattanooga, Tennessee: Reggie Long, Danny Johnson, Bobby Rice and Bobby Torrence.

| 6/5/99 | 197 | 1 | | © | Back To The Real | | | $10 | G-Funk 72966 |

(Do You) Wanna Ride *80*
Don't Be Afraid

Don't Wake Me
How Can I See

I Lied
I Want U

I'm So Sorry
Lady

No More Pain
Reasons

Sittin In The Club
Thank You Lord'

REESE, Della   '60

Born Delloreese Patricia Early on 7/6/31 in Detroit. R&B singer/actress. Appeared in several movies and TV shows.

3/7/60	35	2			1 Della			$25	RCA Victor 2157
10/23/61	113	6			2 Special Delivery			$25	RCA Victor 2391
4/7/62	94	6			3 The Classic Della			$25	RCA Victor 2419
10/22/66	149	2			4 Della Reese Live		[L]	$20	ABC 569

And The Angels Sing (1)
Baby, Won't You Please Come Home (1)
Blue Skies (1)
But Beautiful (4)
Detour Ahead (4)
Don't Know (3) *2*
Driftin' Blues (4)
Girl Talk (4)
Gone (3)
Good Morning Blues (4)
Goody Goody (1)

Gotta Travel On (4)
Have You Ever Been Lonely? (2)
I Got It Bad And That Ain't Good (4)
I Used To Love You (But It's All Over Now) (2)
I'll Get By (1)
I'm Always Chasing Rainbows (2)
I'm Beginning To See The Light (1)

I'm Just A Lucky So And So (2)
If I Could Be With You One Hour Tonight (1)
If You Are But A Dream (3)
Ill Wind (4)
Lady Is A Tramp (1)
Let's Get Away From It All (1)
Moon Love (3)
My Reverie (3)
Please Don't Talk About Me When I'm Gone (2)
Serenade (3)

Softly My Love (3)
Someday Sweetheart (2)
Someday (You'll Want Me To Want You) (1) *56*
Story Of A Starry Night (3)
Stranger In Paradise (3)
Take My Heart (3)
There Will Never Be Another You (4)
These Are The Things I Love (3)
Thou Swell (1)

Three O'Clock In The Morning (3)
Till The End Of Time (3)
Until The Real Thing Comes Along (2)
What's The Reason I'm Not Pleasin' You (2)
Who Can I Turn To? (When Nobody Needs Me) (4)
Won'cha Come Home, Bill Bailey (2) *98*

You Made Me Love You (I Didn't Want To Do It) (2)
You're Driving Me Crazy (1)
You're Nobody 'Til Somebody Loves You (2)

REEVES, Dianne   '90

Born in 1956 in Detroit; raised in Denver. Jazz singer.

| 4/23/88 | 172 | 12 | | © | 1 Dianne Reeves | | | $10 | Blue Note 46906 |
| 3/10/90 | 81 | 14 | | © | 2 Never Too Far | | | $10 | EMI 92401 |

Better Days (1)
Bring Me Joy (2)
Chan's Song (Never Said) (1)
Come In (2)

Company (2)
Eyes On The Prize (2)
Fumilayo (2)
Harvest Time (1)

Hello (Haven't I Seen You Before) (2)
How Long (2)
I'm O.K. (1)

I've Got It Bad And That Ain't Good (1)
More To Love (2)
Never Too Far (2)

Sky Islands (1)
That's All (1)
We Belong Together (2)
Yesterdays (1)

REEVES, Jim   '64

Born on 8/20/24 in Panola County, Texas. Killed in a plane crash on 7/31/64 (age 39). Country singer. Appeared in the 1963 movie *Kimberly Jim*.

5/23/60	18	26			1 He'll Have To Go			$40	RCA Victor 2223
6/16/62	97	11			2 A Touch Of Velvet			$25	RCA Victor 2487
12/14/63	15^X	11			3 Twelve Songs Of Christmas		[X]	$25	RCA Victor 2758
					Christmas charts: 15/'63, 34/'64, 49/'66, 32/'67				
6/13/64	30	30			4 Moonlight and Roses			$25	RCA Victor 2854
8/8/64	9	43	●	©	5 The Best Of Jim Reeves		[G]	$25	RCA Victor 2890
3/6/65	45	13			6 The Jim Reeves Way			$25	RCA Victor 2968
2/12/66	100	6			7 The Best Of Jim Reeves, Vol. II		[G]	$25	RCA Victor 3482
6/4/66	21	29	●		8 Distant Drums		[K]	$25	RCA Victor 3542
7/15/67	185	5			9 Blue Side Of Lonesome		[K]	$25	RCA Victor 3793

REEVES, Jim — Cont'd

According To My Heart (7)
Adios Amigo (5) *90*
After Awhile (1)
All Dressed Up And Lonely (2)
Am I Losing You (5) *31*
Am I That Easy To Forget (2)
Anna Marie (5) *93*
Be Honest With Me (2)
Billy Bayou (1,5) *95*
Blizzard, The (5) *62*
Blue Boy (5) *45*
Blue Christmas (3)
Blue Side Of Lonesome (9) *59*
Blue Skies (2)
Blue Without My Baby (9)
Bolandse Nooientjie (6)
Carolina Moon (4)
C-H-R-I-S-T-M-A-S (3)
Crying Is My Favorite Mood (9)

Danny Boy (5)
Deep Dark Water (9)
Distant Drums (8) *45*
Drinking Tequila (7)
Ek Verlang Na Jou (6)
Four Walls (5) *11*
Gods Were Angry With Me (8)
Good Morning Self (8)
Guilty (5) *91*
Have You Ever Been Lonely
(Have You Ever Been Blue)
(2)
He'll Have To Go (1,5) *2*
Home (1,7)
Honey, Won't You Please
Come Home (1)
I Can't Stop Loving You (6)
I Catch Myself Crying (9)
I Fall To Pieces (2)

I Guess I'm Crazy (7) *82*
I Know One (9) *82*
I Love You More (1)
I Missed Me (8) *44*
I Won't Come In While He's
There (9)
I Won't Forget You (7) *93*
I'd Like To Be (1)
I'm A Fool To Care (2)
I'm Beginning To Forget You (1)
I'm Gettin' Better (5) *37*
If Heartache Is The Fashion (1)
In The Misty Moonlight (6)
Is It Really Over? (8) *79*
Is This Me? (7)
It Hurts So Much (To See You
Go) (6)
(It's No) Sin (2)
It's Only A Paper Moon (5)

Jingle Bells (3)
Just Walking In The Rain (2)
Letter To My Heart (8)
Losing Your Love (8) *89*
Love (I Love To Say, "I Love
You"), Theme Of (1)
Make The World Go Away (6)
Mary's Little Boy Child (3)
Maureen (6)
Merry Christmas Polka (3)
Mexicali Rose (4)
Mexican Joe (3)
Moon River (4)
Moonlight And Roses (Bring
Mem'ries Of You) (4)
My Lips Are Sealed (7)
Nickel Piece Of Candy (6)
Not Until The Next Time (8)
O Little Town Of Bethlehem (3)

Oh Come, All Ye Faithful
(Adeste Fideles) (3)
Oh What It Seemed To Be (4)
Old Christmas Card (3)
One Dozen Roses (4)
Overnight (8)
Partners (1)
Penny Candy (7)
Rosa Rio (4)
Roses (4)
Seabreeze (9)
Señor Santa Claus (3)
Silent Night (3)
Silver Bells (3)
Snow Flake (8) *66*
Somewhere Along The Line (6)
Stand At Your Window (5)
Teardrops On The Rocks (9)
Then I'll Stop Loving You (7)

There's A New Moon Over My
Shoulder (4)
There's Always Me (2)
There's That Smile Again (6)
This Is It (8) *88*
Trying To Forget (9)
Welcome To My World (2,7)
What's In It For Me (4)
When I Lost You (4)
Where Do I Go To Throw A
Picture Away (6)
Where Does A Broken Heart
Go? (8)
White Christmas (3)
Wild Rose (2)
Wishful Thinking (1)
Yonder Comes A Sucker (7)
You'll Never Know (6)

REEVES, Martha — see MARTHA & THE VANDELLAS

RE-FLEX '84

Techno-rock group formed in London: Baxter (vocals, guitar), Paul Fishman (keyboards), Nigel Ross-Scott (bass) and Roland Kerridge (drums).

DEBUT	PEAK	WKS			Title			$	Label & Number
12/24/83+	53	28	©		The Politics Of Dancing			$10	Capitol 12314

Couldn't Stand A Day
Hit Line

Hurt *82*
Jungle

Keep In Touch
Pointless

Politics Of Dancing *24*
Praying To The Beat

Sensitive
Something About You

REFRESHMENTS, The '96

Rock group from Tempe, Arizona: Roger Clyne (vocals, guitar), Brian Blush (guitar), Buddy Edwards (bass) and P.H. Naffah (drums).

| 6/8/96 | 97 | 19 | © | 1 | Fizzy Fuzzy Big & Buzzy | | | $10 | Mercury 528999 |
| 10/4/97 | 150 | 1 | © | 2 | The Bottle & Fresh Horses | | | $10 | Mercury 536203 |

Banditos (1)
Birds Sing (2)
Blue Collar Suicide (1)
Broken Record (2)
Buy American (2)

Carefree (1)
Dolly (2)
Don't Wanna Know (1)
Down Together (1)
European Swallow (1)

Fonder And Blonder (2)
Girly (1)
Good Year (2)
Heaven Or The Highway Out Of
Town (2)

Horses (2)
Interstate (1)
Mekong (1)
Mexico (1)
Nada (1)

Preacher's Daughter (2)
Sin Nombre (2)
Suckerpunch (1)
Tributary Otis (2)
Una Soda (1)

Wanted (2)

REGINA '86

Born Regina Richards in New York City. Female dance singer.

| 10/4/86 | 102 | 8 | © | | Curiosity | | | $10 | Atlantic 81671 |

Baby Love *10*
Beat Of Love

Bring Me All Your Love
Curiosity

Head On
Just Like You

Love Time
Say Goodbye

Sentimental Love

REICHEL, Keali'i '97

Born in Hawaii. Male singer.

| 11/8/97 | 189 | 1 | © | | E O Mai | | | $10 | Punahele 005 |

'Auhea Wale Ana 'Oe
Ballad Of The Broken Word
E O Mai
Hawaiian Lullaby (medley)

He Lei No Kamaile
If I Had Words (Theme from
Babe)
Ka 'Ano'i Pua

Ka 'Opihi O Kanapou
Malie's Song (medley)
My Love Is A Natural Thing
Nematoda

Patchwork Quilt
Pua Hinano
Sovereignty Song

REID, Terry '69

Born on 11/13/49 in Huntingdon, England. Male rock singer/guitarist.

12/21/68+	153	8	©	1	bang, bang you're Terry Reid			$20	Epic 26427
10/18/69	147	5	©	2	Terry Reid			$20	Epic 26477
4/7/73	172	8		3	River			$15	Atlantic 7259

Avenue (3)
Bang, Bang (My Baby Shot Me
Down) (1)
Dean (3)
Dream (3)
Erica (1)

Friends (medley) (2)
Highway 61 Revisited (medley)
(2)
July (2)
Live Life (3)
Loving Time (1)

Marking Time (2)
May Fly (2)
Milestones (3)
Rich Kid Blues (2)
River (3)
Season Of The Witch (1)

Silver White Light (2)
Something's Gotten Hold Of My
Heart (1)
Speak Now Or Forever Hold
Your Peace (2)
Stay With Me Baby (2)

Summertime Blues (medley) (1)
Super Lungs (Supergirl) (2)
Sweater (1)
Things To Try (3)
Tinker Taylor (3)
When You Get Home (1)

Without Expression (1)
Writing On The Wall (medley)
(1)

REINER, Carl, & Mel Brooks '74

Reiner was born on 3/20/22 in the Bronx, New York. Actor/writer/director. Appeared in many TV shows and movies. Father of actor/director Rob Reiner. Brooks was born Melvin Kaminsky on 6/28/26 in Brooklyn, New York. Actor/writer/director. Directed and starred in several movies. Married actress Anne Bancroft on 8/5/64.

| 11/24/73+ | 150 | 12 | © | | 2000 and Thirteen | | [C] | $15 | Warner 2741 |

revival of the 1961 *2000 Year Old Man* act

America's Economic Plight
Ancient Poetry
Asparagus
Dolly Madison

Fig Leaf
Generals
Great Inventions
Greatest Invention

Hope For Mankind
Jesus And The Apostles
Jolson
Lord Byron

Ma And Pa
Miracle Fruits
Natural Foods
Origin Of Words

Paul Revere
Phil
Slow Growth
Strawberries

21,000 Doctors
War Of The Roses
Will To Live
Winston Churchill

R.E.M. ★136★ '91

Rock group formed in Athens, Georgia: Michael Stipe (vocals), Peter Buck (guitar), Mike Mills (bass) and Bill Berry (drums). Developed huge following with college audiences in the early 1980s as one of the first "alternative rock" bands. Buck, Mills and Berry also recorded with **Warren Zevon** as the **Hindu Love Gods**. Berry retired from the group in 1997.

1)Out Of Time 2)Monster 3)Automatic For The People

5/14/83	36	30	●	©	1	Murmur			$12	I.R.S. 70604
5/5/84	27	53	●	©	2	Reckoning			$12	I.R.S. 70044
6/29/85	28	42	●	©	3	Fables Of The Reconstruction			$12	I.R.S. 5592
8/23/86	21	32	●	©	4	Lifes Rich Pageant			$12	I.R.S. 5783

R.E.M. — Cont'd

DEBUT	PEAK	WKS	RIAA	CD	ARTIST — Album Title	Catalog	Sym	$	Label & Number
5/16/87	52	14		© 5	Dead Letter Office	[K]		$12	I.R.S. 70054
9/26/87	10	33	▲	© 6	R.E.M. No. 5: Document		C:#19/4	$12	I.R.S. 42059
10/22/88	44	19		© 7	Eponymous	[K]		$12	I.R.S. 6262
11/26/88+	12	40	▲2	© 8	Green			$10	Warner 25795
3/30/91	❶2	109	▲4	© 9	Out Of Time		C:#36/6	$10	Warner 26496
10/24/92	22	75	▲4	© 10	Automatic For The People			$10	Warner 45138
10/15/94	❶2	54	▲4	© 11	Monster			$10	Warner 45740
9/28/96	21	22	▲	© 12	New Adventures In Hi-Fi			$10	Warner 46320
10/25/97	185	1		© 13	R.E.M. In The Attic	[K]		$10	Capitol 21321
					contains recordings from 1985-89				
11/14/98	3	16	●	© 14	Up			$10	Warner 47112
6/2/01	6	10	●	© 15	Reveal			$10	Warner 47946

Ages Of You (5)
Airportman (14)
All The Way To Reno (You're Gonna Be A Star) (15)
Apologist, The (14)
At My Most Beautiful (14)
Auctioneer (Another Engine) (3)
Bandwagon (5)
Bang And Blame (11) 19
Be Mine (12)
Beachball (15)
Beat A Drum (15)
Begin The Begin (4)
Belong (9)
Binky The Doormat (12)
Bittersweet Me (12) 46
Burning Down (5)
Burning Hell (5)
Camera (2)
Can't Get There From Here (3,7,13)
Catapult (1)
Chorus And The Ring (15)
Circus Envy (11)
Country Feedback (9)
Crazy (5,13)
Crush With Eyeliner (11)
Cuyahoga (4)
Daysleeper (14) 57

Departure (12)
Diminished (14)
Disappear (15)
Disturbance At The Heron House (1)
(Don't Go Back To) Rockville (2,7)
Dream (All I Have To Do) (13)
Drive (10) 28
Driver 8 (3,7,13)
E-Bow The Letter (12) 49
Electrolite (12) 96
Endgame (9)
Everybody Hurts (10) 29
Exhuming McCarthy (6)
Fall On Me (4,7) 94
Falls To Climb (14)
Feeling Gravitys Pull (3)
Femme Fatale (5)
Find The River (10)
Finest Worksong (6,7,13)
Fireplace (6)
Flowers Of Guatemala (4)
Gardening At Night (7,13)
Get Up (8)
Good Advices (3)
Green Grow The Rushes (3)
Hairshirt (8)
Half A World Away (9)
Harborcoat (2)

Hope (14)
How The West Was Won And Where It Got Us (12)
Hyena (4)
I Believe (4)
I Don't Sleep, I Dream (11)
I Remember California (8)
I Took Your Name (11)
I'll Take The Rain (15)
I've Been High (15)
Ignoreland (10)
Imitation Of Life (15) 83
Its The End Of The World As We Know It (And I Feel Fine) (6,7) 69
Just A Touch (4,13)
King Of Comedy (11)
King Of The Birds (6)
King Of The Road (5)
Kohoutek (3)
Last Date (13)
Laughing (1)
Leave (12)
Let Me In (11)
Letter Never Sent (2)
Life And How To Live It (3)
Lifting, The (15)
Lightnin' Hopkins (6)
Little America (2)
Losing My Religion (9) 4

Lotus (14)
Low (9)
Low Desert (12)
Man On The Moon (10) 30
Maps And Legends (3,13)
Me In Honey (9)
Monty Got A Raw Deal (10)
Moral Kiosk (1)
Near Wild Heaven (9)
New Orleans Instrumental No. 1 (10)
New Test Leper (12)
Nightswimming (10)
Oddfellows Local 151 (6)
Old Man Kensey (3)
One I Love (6,7,13) 9
Orange Crush (8)
Pale Blue Eyes (5)
Parakeet (14)
Perfect Circle (1)
Pilgrimage (1)
Pop Song 89 (8) 86
Pretty Persuasion (3)
Radio Free Europe (1,7) 78
Radio Song (9)
Red Rain (medley) (13)
Romance (7)
Rotary Ten (5)
Sad Professor (14)

Saturn Return (15)
Second Guessing (2)
7 Chinese Bros. (2)
Shaking Through (1)
She Just Wants To Be (15)
Shiny Happy People (9) 10
Sidewinder Sleeps Tonite (10)
Sitting Still (1)
So Fast, So Numb (12)
so. Central Rain (I'm Sorry) (2,7,13) 85
Stand (8) 6
Star Me Kitten (10)
Star 69 (11)
Strange (6)
Strange Currencies (11) 47
Summer Turns To High (15)
Superman (4)
Suspicion (14)
Swan Swan H (4,13)
Sweetness Follows (10)
Talk About The Passion (1,7)
Texarkana (9)
There She Goes Again (5)
These Days (4)
Time After Time (Annelise) (2,13)
Tired Of Singing Trouble (13)
Tongue (11)
Toys In The Attic (5,13)

Try Not To Breathe (10)
Turn You Inside - Out (8)
Underneath The Bunker (4)
Undertow (12)
Voice Of Harold (5)
Wake-Up Bomb (12)
Walk Unafraid (14)
Walters Theme (5)
We Walk (1)
Welcome To The Occupation (6)
Wendell Gee (3)
West Of The Fields (1)
What If We Give It Away? (4)
What's The Frequency, Kenneth? (11) 21
White Tornado (5)
Why Not Smile (14)
Windout (5)
World Leader Pretend (8)
Wrong Child (8)
You (11)
You Are The Everything (8)
You're In The Air (14)
Zither (12)

REMBRANDTS, The   '95

Pop-rock duo from Los Angeles: **Danny Wilde** and Phil Solem.

DEBUT	PEAK	WKS	RIAA	CD	ARTIST — Album Title		$	Label & Number
1/19/91	88	24		© 1	The Rembrandts		$10	Atco 91412
6/10/95	23	21	▲	© 2	L.P.		$10	EastWest 61752

April 29 (2)
As Long As I Am Breathing (2)
Burning Timber (1)
Call Me (2)
Comin' Home (2)
Confidential Information (1)

Don't Hide Your Love (2)
Drowning In Your Tears (2)
Easy To Forget (2)
End Of The Beginning (2)
Every Secret Thing (1)
Everyday People (1)

Follow You Down (1)
Friends, Theme from ..see: I'll Be There For You
Goodnight (1)
I'll Be There For You (2) 17
If Not For Misery (1)

Just The Way It Is, Baby (1) 14
Lovin' Me Insane (2)
Moonlight On Mt. Hood (1)
My Own Way (1)
New King (1)

Other Side Of Night (2)
Save Me (1)
Show Me Your Love (1)
Someone (1) 78
There Goes Lucy (2)

This House Is Not A Home (2) flip
What Will It Take (2)

REMEDY   '01

Born in New York City. White male rapper.

DEBUT	PEAK	WKS	RIAA	CD	ARTIST — Album Title		$	Label & Number
5/19/01	130	7		©	The Genuine Article		$10	Fifth Angel 7001

Ambush, The
Calm But Deadly
Can Can

Education
Fallen Angels
Girlfriend

Hip Hop Music
Never Again
Reuven Ben Menachem

U Don't Care
Warning
Whiteboy

Words To Live By

RENAISSANCE   '77

Classical-rock trio from Surrey, England: **Annie Haslam** (vocals), Michael Dunford (guitar) and Jon Camp (bass).

DEBUT	PEAK	WKS	RIAA	CD	ARTIST — Album Title		$	Label & Number
9/22/73	171	4		© 1	Ashes Are Burning		$15	Sovereign 11216
8/3/74	94	21		© 2	Turn Of The Cards		$12	Sire 7502
8/30/75	48	13		3	Scheherazade and other stories		$12	Sire 7510
6/5/76	55	20		4	Live At Carnegie Hall	[L]	$15	Sire 3902 [2]
2/5/77	46	16		© 5	Novella		$12	Sire 7526
3/25/78	58	14		© 6	A Song For All Seasons		$12	Sire 6049
6/16/79	125	9		© 7	Azure d'or		$12	Sire 6068
					title is French for "Blue Gold"			
12/12/81	196	4		© 8	Camera Camera		$12	I.R.S. 70019

Ashes Are Burning (1,4)
At The Harbour (1)
Back Home Once Again (6)
Black Flame (2)
Bonjour Swansong (8)
Camera Camera (8)
Can You Hear Me? (5)
Can You Understand? (1,4)
Captive Heart (5)

Carpet Of The Sun (1,4)
Closer Than Yesterday (6)
Cold Is Being (2)
Day Of The Dreamer (6)
Discovery, The (7)
Faeries (Living At The Bottom Of The Garden) (8)
Flood At Lyons (7)
Forever Changing (7)

Friends (7)
Golden Key (7)
I Think Of You (2)
Jekyll And Hyde (7)
Jigsaw (8)
Kalynda (A Magical Isle) (7)
Kindness (At The End) (6)
Let It Grow (1)
Midas Man (5)

Mother Russia (2,4)
Northern Lights (6)
Ocean Gypsy (3,4)
Okichi-San (8)
On The Frontier (1)
Only Angels Have Wings (7)
Opening Out (7)
Prologue (4)
Remember (8)

Running Away From You (8)
Running Hard (2,4)
Scheherazade (4)
Secret Mission (7)
She Is Love (6)
Sisters, The (5)
Song For All Seasons (6)
Song Of Scheherazade Medley (3)

Things I Don't Understand (2)
Touching Once (Is So Hard To Keep) (5)
Trip To The Fair (3)
Tyrant-Tula (8)
Ukraine Ways (8)
Vultures Fly High (3)
Winter Tree (7)

RENAISSANCE, The   '71

Studio group assembled by producer **Tommy Garrett**.

DEBUT	PEAK	WKS	RIAA	CD	ARTIST — Album Title		$	Label & Number
1/9/71	198	2			Bacharach Baroque	[I]	$15	Ranwood 8084

Alfie
Blue On Blue
Do You Know The Way To San Jose?

I Say A Little Prayer
I'll Never Fall In Love Again
Look Of Love

Raindrops Keep Fallin' On My Head
(There's) Always Something There To Remind Me

(They Long To Be) Close To You
Walk On By

What The World Needs Now Is Love

RENAY, Diane
Born Renee Diane Kushner in Philadelphia.   '64

| 4/4/64 | 54 | 11 | © | | Navy Blue | | | $100 | 20th Century Fox 4133 |

Bell Bottom Trousers   Hello Heartaches   Man Of Mystery   Please Forget Me   Soft-Spoken Guy   Sooner Or Later
He Promised Me Forevermore   **Kiss Me Sailor** 29   **Navy Blue** 6   Present From Eddie   Soldier Boy   Unbelievable Guy

RENÉ AND ANGELA
R&B vocal duo from Los Angeles: René Moore and **Angela Winbush**.   '86

| 8/22/81 | 100 | 8 | | 1 | Wall To Wall | | | $12 | Capitol 12161 |
| 7/6/85+ | 64 | 70 | ● | 2 | Street Called Desire | | | $10 | Mercury 824607 |

Come My Way (1)   **I'll Be Good** (2) 47   Love's Alright (1)   Secret Rendezvous (1)   Wanna Be Close To You (1)   **Your Smile** (2) 62
Drive My Love (2)   Imaginary Playmates (1)   No How - No Way (2)   Street Called Desire (2)   Who's Foolin' Who (2)
I Love You More (1)   Just Friends (1)   Save Your Love (For #1) (2)   Wall To Wall (1)   **You Don't Have To Cry** (2) 75

RENE & RENE
Vocal duo from Laredo, Texas: Rene Ornelas (born on 8/26/36) and Rene Herrera (born on 10/2/35).   '69

| 1/11/69 | 129 | 9 | | | Lo Mucho Que Te Quiero | | | $15 | White Whale 7119 |

title is Spanish for "The More That I Love You"

Cuando Llegue A Phoenix (By   Enchilada Jose   Hand Me Down   Lloraras   Mornin'
The Time I Get To Phoenix)   Far Away   Hidin' In The Shadows   **Lo Mucho Que Te Quiero**   Relampago
Day Tripper   Las Cosas   **(The More I Love You)** 14

REO SPEEDWAGON ★183★   '81
Rock group from Champaign, Illinois: Mike Murphy (vocals), Gary Richrath (guitar), Neal Doughty (keyboards), Gregg Philbin (bass) and Alan Gratzer (drums). Kevin Cronin replaced Murphy in 1976. Bruce Hall replaced Philbin in 1978. Graham Lear replaced Gratzer in 1988. Lineup in 1990: Cronin, Doughty and Hall, joined by new members Dave Amato (guitar), Jesse Harms (keyboards) and Bryan Hitt (drums). Group appeared in the movie *FM*.

1)*Hi Infidelity*   2)*Good Trouble*   3)*Wheels Are Turnin'*

1/12/74+	171	8	▲	© 1	Ridin' The Storm Out	C:#49/2	$12	Epic 32378
11/16/74+	98	14		© 2	Lost In A Dream		$12	Epic 32948
8/2/75	74	10		© 3	This Time We Mean It		$12	Epic 33338
6/19/76	159	5		© 4	R.E.O.		$12	Epic 34143
3/19/77	72	50	▲	© 5	REO Speedwagon Live/You Get What You Play For	[L]	$15	Epic 34494 [2]
4/22/78	29	48	▲²	© 6	You can Tune a piano, but uou can't Tuna fish		$12	Epic 35082
8/11/79	33	23	●	© 7	Nine Lives		$12	Epic 35988
4/19/80	55	34	▲	© 8	A Decade Of Rock And Roll 1970 To 1980	[K]	$15	Epic 36444 [2]
12/13/80+	❶¹⁵	101	▲⁹	© 9	Hi Infidelity		$10	Epic 36844
7/10/82	7	24	▲	© 10	Good Trouble		$10	Epic 38100
11/24/84+	7	49	▲²	© 11	Wheels Are Turnin'		$10	Epic 39593
2/28/87	28	48	●	© 12	Life As We Know It		$10	Epic 40444
6/25/88	56	22	▲³	© 13	The Hits	C:#40/34 [G]	$10	Epic 44202
8/18/90	129	8		© 14	The Earth, A Small Man, His Dog And A Chicken		$10	Epic 45246

Accidents Can Happen (12)   Down By The Dam (2)   Here With Me (13) 20   Little Queenie (5)   Out Of Season (9)   **Sweet Time** (10) 26
All Heaven Broke Loose (14)   Dream Weaver (3)   (I Believe) Our Time Is Gonna   **Live Every Moment** (11) 34   Over The Edge (12)   **Take It On The Run** (9,13) 5
Any Kind Of Love (4,5)   Drop It (An Old Disguise) (7)   Come (4,5,8)   Live It Up (14)   Reelin' (3,8)   Take Me (7)
Back In My Heart Again (10)   Easy Money (7)   **I Do'wanna Know** (11) 29   Lost In A Dream (2,8)   **Ridin' The Storm Out**   **That Ain't Love** (12,13) 16
Back On The Road Again (7,8)   Every Now And Then (10)   I Don't Want To Lose You (13)   Love In The Future (14)   (1,5,8,13) 94   They're On The Road (2)
Being Kind (Can Hurt Someone   Find My Fortune (11)   I Need You Tonight (7)   Love To Hate (14)   River Of Life (3)   Throw The Chains Away (2)
   Sometimes) (1)   Flying Turkey Trot (4,5,8)   I Wish You Were There (9)   **Love Is A Rock** (14) 65   Rock & Roll Music (7)   Thru The Window (11)
Blazin' Your Own Trail Again (6)   Follow My Heart (9)   I'll Follow You (10)   Lucky For You (6)   Rock 'N Roll Star (11)   **Time For Me To Fly** (6,8,13) 56
Break His Spell (11)   Gambler (3)   I'm Feeling Good (2)   Meet Me On The Mountain (7)   **Roll With The Changes**   Tired Of Gettin' Nowhere (12)
Breakaway (4,8)   Girl With The Heart Of Gold   **In My Dreams** (12,13) 19   Movin' (1)   (6,8,13) 58   Tonight (4)
Can't Fight This Feeling   (10)   **In Your Letter** (9) 20   Music Man (5)   Runnin' Blind (6)   Tough Guys (9)
   (11,13) 1   Give Me A Ride (Roller   It's Everywhere (1)   New Way To Love (12)   Say You Love Me Or Say   Unidentified Flying Tuna Trot
Can't Get You Out Of My Heart   Coaster) (2)   **Keep On Loving You** (9,13) 1   Like You Do (5,8)   Goodnight (6,8)   (6)
   (12)   Go For Broke (14)   Keep Pushin' (4,5,8,13)   Oh Woman (1)   Screams And Whispers (12)   **Variety Tonight** (12) 60
Can't Live To My Heart (14)   Golden Country (5,8)   **Keep The Fire Burnin'** (10) 7   157 Riverside Avenue (5,8)   Shakin' It Loose (9)   Wheels Are Turnin' (11)
Candalera (3)   Good Trouble (10)   Key, The (10)   **One Lonely Night** (11) 19   Sing To Me (6)   Whiskey Night (1)
Dance (3)   Gotta Feel More (11)   Lay Me Down (5)   One Too Many Girlfriends (12)   Sky Blues (2)   Wild As The Western Wind (2)
Do You Know Where Your   Half Way (14)   Let's Be-Bop (10)   (Only A) Summer Love (4,5)   Someone Tonight (9)   Without Expression (Don't Be
   Woman Is Tonight (6)   Headed For A Fall (3)   L.I.A.R. (14)   Only The Strong Survive (7,8)   Son Of A Poor Man (1,5,8)   The Man) (1)
Do Your Best (2)   Heart Survives (14)   Lies (3)   Open Up (1)   Sophisticated Lady (8)   You Better Realize (3)
Don't Let Him Go (9,13) 24   Heavy On Your Love (7)   Lightning (4,8)   Out Of Control (3)   Start A New Life (1)   You Can Fly (2)
   Stillness Of The Night (10)   You Won't See Me (14)

REPLACEMENTS, The   '89
Rock group from Minneapolis: **Paul Westerberg** (vocals, guitar, piano), Slim Dunlap (guitar), Tommy Stinson (bass) and Chris Mars (drums). Steve Foley replaced Mars in early 1990.

2/1/86	183	7	© 1	Tim		$10	Sire 25330
5/30/87	131	19	© 2	Pleased To Meet Me		$10	Sire 25557
2/18/89	57	19	© 3	Don't Tell A Soul		$10	Sire 25831
10/13/90	69	14	© 4	All Shook Down		$10	Sire 26298
11/15/97	143	1	© 5	All For Nothing - Nothing For All	[K]	$15	Reprise 46807 [2]

Achin' To Be (3,5)   Attitude (4)   Darlin' One (3)   I Won't (3)   Ledge, The (2,5)   Nobody (4,5)
Alex Chilton (2,5)   Back To Back (3)   Date To Church (5)   I'll Be You (3,5) 51   Left Of The Dial (1,5)   One Wink At A Time (4)
All He Wants To Do Is Fish (5)   Bastards Of Young (1,5)   Dose Of Thunder (1)   I'll Buy (1)   Like A Rolling Pin (5)   Portland (5)
All Shook Down (4,5)   Beer For Breakfast (3)   Election Day (5)   I.O.U. (2)   Little Mascara (1)   Red Red Wine (2)
Another Girl, Another Planet (5)   Bent Out Of Shape (4)   Happy Town (4)   Jungle Rock (5)   Merry Go Round (4,5)   Rock 'N' Roll Ghost (3)
Anywhere's Better Than Here   Birthday Gal (5)   Here Comes A Regular (1,5)   Kiss Me On The Bus (1,5)   My Little Problem (4)   Sadly Beautiful (4,5)
   (3,5)   Can't Hardly Wait (2,5)   Hold My Life (1)   Last, The (4)   Never Mind (2)   Satellite (5)
Asking Me Lies (3)   Cruella DeVille (5)   I Don't Know (2)   Lay It Down Clown (1)   Nightclub Jitters (2)   Shooting Dirty Pool (2)

REPLACEMENTS, The — Cont'd

Skyway (2,5)	Talent Show (3,5)	Torture (4)
Someone Take The Wheel (4,5)	They're Blind (3)	Valentine (2)
Swingin Party (1)	Till We're Nude (5)	Waitress In The Sky (1)

Wake Up (5)
We Know The Night (5)
We'll Inherit The Earth (3)

When It Began (4)
Who Knows (5)

REPUBLICA   '96

Rock group from London: Saffron (female vocals), Johnny Male (guitar), Tim Dorney and Andy Todd (keyboards) and Dave Barbarossa (drums).

9/28/96	153	16	©		Republica			$10	Deconstruction 66899

Bitch
Bloke

Don't You Ever
Drop Dead Gorgeous *93*

Get Off
Holly

Out Of The Darkness
Picture Me

Ready To Go *56*
Wrapp

RESTLESS HEART   '87

Country group formed in Nashville: Larry Stewart (vocals), Greg Jennings (guitar), Dave Innis (keyboards), Paul Gregg (bass) and John Dittrich (drums). Stewart left in early 1992.

4/11/87	73	25	●	©	1	Wheels			$10	RCA Victor 5648
8/27/88	114	11	●	©	2	Big Dreams In A Small Town			$10	RCA 8317
2/24/90	78	17	●	©	3	Fast Movin' Train			$10	RCA 9961
11/16/91+	144	12		©	4	The Best Of Restless Heart		[G]	$10	RCA 61041
11/7/92+	116	34		©	5	Big Iron Horses			$10	RCA 66049

As Far As I Can Tell (5)	Calm Before The Storm (2)	I've Never Been So Sure (3)	New York (Hold Her Tight) (1)	Til I Loved You (4)
Big Dreams In A Small Town (2)	Dancy's Dream (3)	Jenny Come Back (2)	No Way Out (2)	Truth Hurts (3)
Big Iron Horses (5)	Eldorado (2)	Just In Time (5)	River Of Stone (3)	Victim Of The Game (1)
Blame It On Love (5)	Familiar Pain (5)	Lady Luck (3)	Say What's In Your Heart (2)	We Got The Love (5)
Bluest Eyes In Texas (2,4)	Fast Movin' Train (3,4)	Little More Coal On The Fire (3)	Sweet Auburn (3)	We Owned This Town (1)
Born In A High Wind (5)	Hard Time (1)	Long Lost Friend (3)	Tender Lie (2,4)	We're Gonna Be OK (5)
Boy's On A Roll (1)	Hummingbird (3)	Meet Me On The Other Side (5)	That Rock Won't Roll (1,4)	Wheels (1,4)
	I'll Still Be Loving You (1,4) *33*	Mending Fences (5)	This Time (2)	**When She Cries** (5) *11*

When Somebody Loves You (3)
Why Does It Have To Be
(Wrong Or Right) (1,4)
You Can Depend On Me (4)

RETURN TO FOREVER   '74

Jazz-rock group: **Al Di Meola** (guitar), **Chick Corea** (keyboards), **Stanley Clarke** (bass) and **Lenny White** (drums).

12/8/73	124	15			1	Hymn Of The Seventh Galaxy		[I]	$15	Polydor 5536
9/28/74	32	23			2	Where Have I Known You Before		[I]	$15	Polydor 6509
3/15/75	39	13			3	No Mystery		[I]	$15	Polydor 6512
4/3/76	35	15	●		4	Romantic Warrior		[I]	$12	Columbia 34076
4/2/77	38	17			5	Musicmagic			$12	Columbia 34682
3/3/79	155	4			6	Return To Forever Live		[L]	$12	Columbia 35281

recorded on 5/20/77 at the Palladium Theatre in New York City

After The Cosmic Rain (1)	Earth Juice (2)	Interplay (3)	Musicmagic (5,6)	Space Circus Part I (medley) (1)
Beyond The Seventh Galaxy (2)	Endless Night (Part 1 & 2) (5,6)	Jungle Waterfall (3)	No Mystery (3)	Vulcan Worlds (2)
Captain Senor Mouse (1)	First Movement Of Heavy	Magician, The (3)	Romantic Warrior (4)	Where Have I Danced With You
Celebration Suite Part I & II (3)	Metal, Excerpt From The (3)	Majestic Dance (4)	Shadow Of Lo (2)	Before (2)
Come Rain Or Come Shine (6)	Flight Of The Newborn (3)	Medieval Overture (4)	So Long Mickey Mouse (5,6)	Where Have I Known You
Dayride (3)	Game Maker (1)	Moorish Warrior And Spanish	Sofistifunk (5)	Before (2)
Do You Ever (5)	Hello Again (5)	Princess (6)	Song To The Pharaoh Kings (2)	Where Have I Loved You
Duel Of The Jester And The	Hymn Of The Seventh Galaxy	Mothership, Theme To The (1)	Sorceress (4)	Before (2)
Tyrant (Part I & Part II) (4)	(1)	Musician, The (5,6)		

REVENGE   '90

Rock trio from Manchester, England: Peter Hook (vocals, bass; **New Order**), Dave Hicks (guitar) and Chris Jones (keyboards).

9/1/90	190	2		©		One True Passion			$10	Capitol 94053

Big Bang
Bleachman

Fag Hag
It's Quiet

Kiss The Chrome
Pineapple Face

7 Reasons
Slave

Surf Nazi

REVERBERI   '76

Born Gianpiero Reverberi in Italy. Classical pianist.

2/21/76	169	7				Reverberi & Schumann, Chopin, Liszt		[I]	$12	Pausa 7003

Carnaval Op. 9/1-3

Preludio Op. 28 No. 4 & 20

Studio Da Concerto No. 6

Studio Op. 10 No. 3 & N.12

★257★   REVERE, Paul, And The Raiders   '66

Born on 1/7/42 in Boise, Idaho. Pop-rock keyboardist. The Raiders had numerous personnel changes through the years. Core members: **Mark Lindsay** (vocals), **Freddy Weller** (guitar), Keith Allison (bass) and Michael Smith (drums). On ABC-TV show *Where The Action Is* in 1965. Own TV show *Happening* in 1968. Smith died on 3/6/2001 (age 58).

1)*Just Like Us!* 2)*The Spirit Of '67* 3)*Greatest Hits*

7/3/65+	71	45		©	1	Here They Come!			$40	Columbia 2307 / 9107
2/5/66	5	43	●	©	2	Just Like Us!			$40	Columbia 2451 / 9251
6/11/66	9	43	●	©	3	Midnight Ride			$40	Columbia 2508 / 9308
12/31/66+	9	33	●	©	4	The Spirit Of '67			$40	Columbia 2595 / 9395
						also see #12 below				
5/13/67	9	47	●	©	5	Greatest Hits		[G]	$40	Columbia 2662 / 9462
9/2/67	25	21		©	6	Revolution!			$40	Columbia 2721 / 9521
						also see #12 below				
12/2/67	10[X]	5		©	7	A Christmas Present...And Past		[X]	$40	Columbia 2755 / 9555
						PAUL REVERE AND THE RAIDERS Featuring Mark Lindsay				
3/2/68	61	23		©	8	Goin' To Memphis			$25	Columbia 2805 / 9605
9/14/68	122	14		©	9	Something Happening			$20	Columbia 9665
4/5/69	51	19		©	10	Hard 'N' Heavy (With Marshmallow)			$20	Columbia 9753
8/23/69	48	12		©	11	Alias Pink Puzz			$20	Columbia 9905
11/8/69	166	4			12	Two All-Time Great Selling LP's		[R]	$25	Columbia 12 [2]
						reissue of albums #4 and #6 above				
4/11/70	154	9			13	Collage			$20	Columbia 9964
6/19/71	19	20			14	Indian Reservation			$15	Columbia 30768
						RAIDERS (above 2)				
7/8/72	143	8			15	All-Time Greatest Hits		[G]	$20	Columbia 31464 [2]

REVERE, Paul, And The Raiders — Cont'd

Action (2)
Ain't Nobody Who Can Do It Like Leslie Can (6,12)
All About Her (4,12)
All I Really Need Is You (3)
Baby, Please Don't Go (2)
Ballad Of A Useless Man (3)
Big Boy Pete (1)
Birds Of A Feather (14) **23**
Boogaloo Down Broadway (8)
Boys In The Band (13)
Brotherly Love (7)
Burn Like A Candle (9)
Call On Me (10)
Catch The Wind (2)
Christmas Spirit (7)
Cinderella Sunshine (10,15) **58**
Come In, You'll Get Pneumonia (14)
Communication (Part 1 & 2) (9)
Cry On My Shoulder (8)
Dear Mr. Claus (7)
Do Unto Others (15)
Do You Love Me (1)
Dr. Fine (13)

Doggone (2)
Don't Take It So Hard (9,15) **27**
Down In Amsterdam (11)
Eve Of Destruction (14)
Every Man Needs A Woman (8)
Fever (1)
Frankfort Side Street (11)
Free (9)
Freedom Man (11)
Get It On (3)
Get Out Of My Mind (9)
Goin' To Memphis (8)
Gone (1)
Gone - Movin' On (6,12,13)
Good Thing (4,5,12,15) **4**
Good Times (9)
Great Airplane Strike (4,5,12,15) **20**
Happening '68 (9)
Happens Every Day (9)
Hard And Heavy 5 String Soul Banjo (10)
Heaven Help Us All (14)
Heavy Christmas Message (7)
Here Comes The Pain (11)

Hey Babro (11)
Him Or Me - What's It Gonna Be? (6,12,15) **5**
Hungry (4,5,12,15) **6**
I Can't Get No Satisfaction (2)
I Don't Know (11)
I Don't Want Nobody (To Lead Me On) (8)
I Had A Dream (6,12,15) **17**
I Hear A Voice (6,12)
I Know (2)
I Need You (11)
I'm Crying (2)
I'm A Loser Too (8)
I'm Not Your Stepping Stone (2)
In My Community (4,12)
Indian Reservation (The Lament Of The Cherokee Reservation Indian) (14) **1**
Interlude (To Be Forgotten) (13)
Jingle Bells (7)
Just Like Me (2,5,15) **11**
Just Remember You're My Sunshine (14)
Just Seventeen (13,15) **82**
Kicks (3,5,15) **2**

Kiss To Remember You By (1)
Legend Of Paul Revere (5,15)
Let (11,15) **20**
Little Girl In The 4th Row (3)
Louie, Go Home (3,5)
Louie, Louie (1,5,15)
Louise (4,12)
Louisiana Redbone (11)
Love Makes The World Go Round (Don't You Let It Stop) (9)
Love You So (8)
Macy's Window (7)
Make It With Me (6,12)
Melody For An Unknown Girl (3,5)
Mo'reen (6,12)
Money Can't Buy Me (10)
Money (That's What I Want) (1)
Mr. Sun, Mr. Moon (10,15) **18**
My Way (8)
New Orleans (2)
Night Train (2)
No Sad Songs (8)
Observation From Flight 285 (In 3/4 Time) (9)

Oh! To Be A Man (4,12)
One Night Stand (8)
1001 Arabian Nights (4,12)
Oo Poo Pah Doo (1)
Original Handy Man (11)
Our Candidate (4,12)
Out Of Sight (2)
Out On That Road (10)
Peace (7)
Peace Of Mind (8,15) **42**
Prince Of Peace (14)
Rain, Sleet, Snow (7)
Reno (6,12)
Ride On My Shoulder (10)
Save The Country (13)
Shape Of Things To Come (14)
Sometimes (1)
Sorceress With Blues Eyes (13)
Soul Man (8)
Steppin' Out (2,5,15) **46**
Take A Look At Yourself (3)
Take Me Home (14)
Thank You (11)
There She Goes (3)
There's Always Tomorrow (3)

These Are Bad Times (For Me And My Baby) (1)
Think Twice (13)
Tighter (6,12,13)
Time After Time (10)
Time Is On My Side (1)
Too Much Talk (9,15) **19**
Trishalana (10)
Turkey, The (14)
Undecided Man (4,12)
Upon Your Leaving (6,12)
Ups And Downs (5,15) **22**
Valley Forge (7)
Wanting You (6,12)
We Gotta All Get Together (13,15) **50**
Wear A Smile At Christmas (7)
Wednesday's Child (13)
Where You Goin' Girl (10)
Why? Why? Why? (Is It So Hard) (4,12)
Without You (10)
You Can't Sit Down (1)

REVEREND HORTON HEAT '96

Rock trio from Corpus Christi, Texas: Jim "Reverend" Horton Heath (vocals, guitar), Jimbo Wallace (bass) and Scott Churilla (drums).

7/20/96	**165**	1	©	1 **It's Martini Time**		**$10**	Interscope 90065
4/11/98	**187**	1	©	2 **Space Heater**		**$10**	Interscope 90168

Baby I'm Drunk (2)
Big Red Rocket Of Love (1)
Cinco De Mayo (2)
Couch Surfin' (2)
Cowboy Love (1)

Crooked Cigarette (1)
For Never More (2)
Forbidden Jungle (1)
Generation Why (1)
Goin' Manic (2)

Hello Mrs. Darkness (2)
It's Martini Time (1)
Jimbo Song (2)
Lie Detector (2)
Mi Amor (2)

Native Tongue Of Love (2)
Now, Right Now (1)
Or Is It Just Me (1)
Pride Of San Jacinto (2)
Prophet Stomp (2)

Revolution Under Foot (2)
Rock The Joint (1)
Slingshot (1)
Slow (1)
Space Heater (2)

Spell On Me (1)
Starlight Lounge (2)
Texas Rock-A-Billy Rebel (2)
That's Showbiz (1)
Time To Pray (1)

REYNOLDS, Debbie '66

Born Mary Reynolds on 4/1/32 in El Paso, Texas. Actress/singer. Starred in several movies. Married to **Eddie Fisher** from 1955-59. Mother of actress Carrie Fisher.

4/30/66	**23**	25	1 **The Singing Nun**		[S] **$25**	MGM 7
5/26/84	**182**	3	2 **Do It Debbie's Way**		**$10**	K-Tel 9190

music by a "switched on swing" big band; no track titles listed

Alleluia (medley) (1)
Avec Toi (With You I Shall Walk) (medley) (1)

Beyond The Stars (Entre Les Etoiles) (1)
Brother John (1)

Dibwe Diambula Kabanda (medley) (1)
Dominique (1)
I'd Like To Be (Je Voudrais) (1)

It's A Miracle (Une Fleur) (1)
Kyrie (medley) (1)
Lovely (1)
Pied Piper (Petit Pierrot) (1)

Put On Your Pretty Skirt (Mets Ton Joli Jupon) (1)
Raindrops (1)
Sister Adele (Soeur Adele) (1)

REYNOLDS, Tim — see MATTHEWS, Dave, Band

RHEIMS, Robert '59

Born in Los Angeles. Arranger/conductor.

1/5/59	**25**	1	1 **Merry Christmas in Carols**		[X-I] **$20**	Rheims 6006

Christmas charts: 16/'63, 67/'66, 23/'67

1/4/60	**39**	1	2 **We Wish You A Merry Christmas**		[X] **$20**	Rheims 6008

ROBERT RHEIMS CHORALIERS

12/21/63+	**17**[X]	11	3 **For The Whole Family At Christmas**		[X-I] **$20**	Rheims 6010

Christmas charts: 26/'63, 22/'64, 17/'65, 117/'67, 21/'68

Angels We Have Heard On High (medley) (1,2)
Away In A Manger (medley) (1,2)
Bells Of Christmas (medley) (2)
Bring A Torch, Jeannette Isabella (medley) (2)
Carol Of The Drum (medley) (3)
Christmas Chimes Are Pealing (medley) (1)
Christmas Song (3)
Coventry Carol (medley) (2)
Deck The Halls (medley) (1,2)

Firl Noel (medley) (1,2)
From Every Spire On Christmas Eve (medley) (1)
Frosty The Snowman (medley) (1,2)
God Rest Ye Merry, Gentlemen (medley) (3)
Good King Wenceslas (medley) (3)
Hark! The Herald Angels Sing (1,2)
Here We Come A Caroling (medley) (2)

I Heard The Bells On Christmas Day (medley) (1,2,3)
I Saw Three Ships (medley) (1,2)
I'll Be Home For Christmas (medley) (3)
It Came Upon A Midnight Clear (medley) (1,2)
Jingle Bells (medley) (3)
Jolly Old St. Nicholas (medley) (3)
Joy To The World (medley) (1,2)

Night Before Christmas Song (medley) (3)
O Christmas Tree (medley) (1)
O Come All Ye Faithful (1,2)
O Holy Night (1,2)
O Little Town Of Bethlehem (1,2)
Rudolph The Red-Nosed Reindeer (medley) (3)
Santa Claus Is Coming To Town (medley) (3)
Shepherd Shake Off Your Drowsy Sleep (medley) (2)

Silent Night (1,2)
Silver Bells (medley) (3)
(There's No Place Like) Home For The Holidays (medley) (3)
Too Fat For The Chimney (medley) (3)
Up On The House Top (medley) (3)
We Three Kings Of Orient Are (medley) (1,2)
We Wish You A Merry Christmas (2,3)
What Child Is This (medley) (2)

When Santa Claus Gets Your Letter (medley) (3)
While Shepherds Watched Their Flocks By Night (medley) (2)
White Christmas (3)
Winter Wonderland (3)

RHINOCEROS '69

Rock group from Los Angeles: John Finley (vocals), Danny Weis and Doug Hastings (guitars), Michael Fonfara and Alan Gerber (keyboards), Jerry Penrod (bass) and Billy Mundi (drums). By 1969, Peter Hodgson had replaced Penrod. By 1970, Larry Leishman had replaced Hastings and Duke Edwards had replaced Mundi.

12/28/68+	**115**	22	1 **Rhinoceros**		**$25**	Elektra 74030
9/27/69	**105**	9	2 **Satin Chickens**		**$20**	Elektra 74056
7/11/70	**178**	6	3 **Better Times Are Coming**		**$20**	Elektra 74075

Along Comes Tomorrow (1)
Apricot Brandy (1) **46**
Back Door (2)
Belbuekus (1)
Better Times (1)
Chicken (2)

Don't Come Crying (2)
Find My Hand (2)
Funk Butt (2)
Happiness (3)
I Need Love (2)
I Will Serenade You (1)

I've Been There (2)
In A Little Room (2)
Insanity (3)
It's A Groovy World (3)
It's The Same Thing (2)
Just Me (3)

Lady Of Fortune (3)
Let's Party (3)
Monkee Man (2)
Old Age (3)
Rain Child (3)
Same Old Way (1)

Satin Doll (2)
Somewhere (3)
Sugar Foot Rag (2)
Sweet, Nice 'N' High (3)
That Time Of The Year (1)
Top Of The Ladder (2)

When You Say You're Sorry (1)
You're My Girl (I Don't Want To Discuss It) (1)

RHODES, Emitt '71

Born in 1949 in Hawthorne, California. Lead singer of **The Merry-Go-Round**.

12/12/70+	**29**	20	©	1 **Emitt Rhodes**		**$15**	Dunhill/ABC 50089
4/17/71	**194**	1		2 **The American Dream**		[E] **$15**	A&M 4254

recordings from 1967-68

11/27/71	**182**	4	3 **Mirror**		**$15**	Dunhill/ABC 50111

DEBUT	PEAK	WKS	RIAA	CD	ARTIST — Album Title	Catalog	Sym	$	Label & Number

RHODES, Emitt — Cont'd

Better Side Of Life (3)
Birthday Lady (3)
Bubblegum The Blues (medley) (3)
Come Ride, Come Ride (2)
Ever Find Yourself Running? (1)

Fresh As A Daisy (1) *54*
Golden Child Of God (3)
Holly Park (2)
I'm A Cruiser (medley) (3)
In Days Of Old (2)
Let's All Sing (2)
Live Till You Die (1)

Long Time No See (1)
Love Will Stone You (3)
Lullabye (1)
Man He Was (2)
Mary Will You Take My Hand (2)
Mirror (3)

Mother Earth (2)
My Love Is Strong (3)
Pardon Me (2)
Promises I've Made (1)
Really Wanted You (3)
She's Such A Beauty (1)
Side We Seldom Show (3)

Somebody Made For Me (1)
Someone Died (2)
Take You Far Away (3)
Textile Factory (2)
'Til The Day After (2)
With My Face On The Floor (1)
You Must Have (1)

You Should Be Ashamed (1)
You Take The Dark Out Of The Night (1)
You're A Very Lovely Woman (2)

RHYTHM CORPS   '88

Rock group from Detroit: Michael Persh (vocals), Greg Apro (guitar), Davey Holmbo (bass) and Richie Lovsin (drums).

| 8/13/88 | 104 | 14 | | © | Common Ground .... | | | $10 | Pasha 44159 |

Cold Wire
Common Ground

Faith & Muscle
Father's Footsteps

Giants
I Surrender

Perfect Treason
Revolution Man

Solidarity
Streets On Fire

RHYTHM HERITAGE   '76

Studio group assembled by producers Steve Barri and Michael Omartian. Vocals by Oren and Luther Waters.

| 3/6/76 | 40 | 17 | | 1 | Disco-Fied .... | [I] | | $12 | ABC 934 |
| 2/19/77 | 138 | 6 | | 2 | Last Night On Earth .... | [I] | | $12 | ABC 987 |

Baretta's Theme ("Keep Your Eye On The Sparrow") (1) *20*
Blockbuster (1)

Caravan (2)
Cisco Kid (medley) (2)
Dance The Night Away (2)

Disco-Fied (1)
Disco Queen (1)
Do It Again (medley) (2)

(It's Time To) Boogie Down (1)
Last Night On Earth Medley (2)
Lipstick, Theme From (2)

My Cherie Amour (1)
Rocky, Theme From (2) *94*
S.W.A.T., Theme From (1) *1*

Three Days Of The Condor (1)

RICE, Chris   '98

Born in Clinton, Maryland. Male Christian singer/songwriter.

| 10/3/98 | 167 | 2 | | © | Past The Edges .... | | | $10 | Word 69613 |

And Your Praise Goes On
Big Enough

Live By Faith
Missin' You

Naive
One Of Those Days

Power Of A Moment
Smellin' Coffee

Thirsty
Wind And Spirit

RICH, Buddy   '67

Born Bernard Rich on 6/30/17 in New York City. Died of a brain tumor on 4/2/87 (age 69). Legendary jazz drummer. With **Tommy Dorsey** from 1939-46.

12/31/66+	91	27		© 1	Swingin' New Big Band	[I-L]		$20	Pacific Jazz 20113
					recorded at The Chez in Hollywood				
7/15/67	97	21		© 2	Big Swing Face	[I-L]		$20	Pacific Jazz 20117
11/30/68	186	6		© 3	Mercy, Mercy	[I-L]		$15	World Pacific 20133
					recorded at Caesars Palace in Las Vegas				
9/13/69	186	3		© 4	Buddy & Soul	[I-L]		$15	World Pacific 20158
					recorded at the Whiskey A-Go-Go in Hollywood				
5/20/72	180	5		5	Rich In London	[I-L]		$15	RCA Victor 4666
					recorded at Ronnie Scott's				

Acid Truth (3)
Alfie (3)
Basically Blues (1)
Beat Goes On (2)
Big Mama Cass (3)
Big Swing Face (2)
Bugle Call Rag (2)
Channel 1 Suite (3)

Comin' Home Baby (4)
Critic's Choice (1)
Dancing Men (5)
Goodbye Yesterday (3)
Greensleeves (4)
Hello I Love You (4)
Little Train (5)
Love And Peace (4)

Love For Sale (4)
Love Story, Theme From (5)
Meaning Of The Blues (4)
Mercy, Mercy, Mercy (3)
Mexicali Nose (2)
Monitor Theme (2)
More Soul (1)
My Man's Gone Now (1)

Norwegian Wood (This Bird Has Flown) (2)
Ode To Billy Joe (3)
Preach And Teach (3)
Readymix (1)
Ruth (4)
Sister Sadie (1)
Soul Kitchen (1)

Soul Lady (4)
St. Marks Square (A Special Day) (1)
St. Petersberg Race (4)
That's Enough (5)
Time Being (5)
Two Bass Hit (4)
Uptight (Everything's Alright) (1)

Wack Wack (2)
West Side Story Medley (1)
Willowcrest (2)
Wonderbag (4)
Word, The (5)

★408★   RICH, Charlie   '74

Born on 12/14/32 in Colt, Arkansas. Died of a blood clot on 7/25/95 (age 62). Country singer/songwriter/pianist. Known as "The Silver Fox."
1)Behind Closed Doors 2)Very Special Love Songs 3)The Silver Fox

5/19/73+	8	105	▲	© 1	**Behind Closed Doors**			$15	Epic 32247
2/23/74	36	27	●	2	There Won't Be Anymore	[E]		$15	RCA Victor 0433
3/23/74	24	31	●	3	Very Special Love Songs			$15	Epic 32531
4/27/74	89	19		4	The Best Of Charlie Rich			$15	Epic 31933
					new recordings of early non-Epic hits				
10/19/74	177	4		5	Charlie Rich Sings the Songs of Hank Williams & Others	[E]		$15	Hi 32084
10/26/74	84	15		6	She Called Me Baby	[E]		$15	RCA Victor 0686
12/7/74+	25	17		7	The Silver Fox			$15	Epic 33250
6/21/75	54	20		8	Every Time You Touch Me (I Get High)			$15	Epic 33455
6/21/75	162	4		9	Greatest Hits	[G]		$15	RCA Victor 0857
4/3/76	160	6		© 10	Silver Linings			$12	Epic 33545
7/4/76	148	6		© 11	Greatest Hits	[G]		$12	Epic 34240
10/29/74	180	3		12	Rollin' With The Flow			$15	Epic 34891

All Over Me (8,11)
Almost Persuaded (3)
Amazing Grace (10)
America, The Beautiful (1976) (11)
Are You Still My Baby (6)
Beautiful Woman (12)
Behind Closed Doors (1,7,11) *15*
Big Boss Man (4,9)
Big Build Up (2)
Big Jack (6)
Break-Up (medley) (7)
Caught In The Middle (9)
Charlie's Swing (medley) (7)
Cold Cold Heart (5)
Daddy Don't You Walk So Fast (4)
Don't Put No Headstone On My Grave (medley) (7)
Down By The Riverside (10)
Every Time You Touch Me (I Get High) (8,11) *19*

Field Of Yellow Daisies (3)
Half As Much (5)
He Follows My Footsteps (3)
Hey Good Lookin' (5)
I Can't Help It (5)
I Do My Swingin' At Home (4)
I Don't See Me In Your Eyes Anymore (2,9) *47*
I Feel Like Going Home (medley) (7)
I Love My Friend (7,11) *24*
I Need A Thing Called Love (6)
I Take It On Home (1,4)
I'm Not Going Hungry Anymore (1)
I'm Right Behind You (6)
I'm So Lonesome I Could Cry (5)
If I Knew Then What I Know Now (2)
If You Wouldn't Be My Lady (1)
It Just Goes To Show (You Never Know About Love) (2)

It's All Over Now (2)
July 12, 1939 (4) *85*
Just A Closer Walk With Thee (10)
Let Me Go My Merry Way (4)
Life Has Its Little Ups And Downs (4,11)
Little Bit Here (A Little Bit There) (8)
Lonely Weekends (9) *22*
Love Survived (12)
Mellow Melody (8)
Midnight Blues (8)
Milky White Way (10)
Most Beautiful Girl (1,11) *1*
My Elusive Dreams (7,11) *49*
My Heart Would Know (8)
My Mountain Dew (9)
Nice 'N' Easy (2,4)
Night Talk (12)
No Room To Dance (2)
Nobody's Lonesome For Me (5)

Nothing In The World (To Do With Me) (1)
Ol' Man River (6)
Old Time Religion (10)
Part Of Your Life (4)
Pass On By (8)
Peace On You (1,1)
Pieces Of My Life (7)
Pretty People (3)
Rendezvous (8)
Rollin' With The Flow (12)
Rondo A La Charlie (medley) (7)
Satisfied Man (3)
Set Me Free (4)
Share Your Love With Me (6)
She (8)
She Called Me Baby (6,9) *47*
Since I Fell For You (8,11) *71*
Sittin' And Thinkin' (4,9)
Somebody Wrote That Song For Me (12)

Sometimes I Feel Like A Motherless Child (10)
Somewhere In My Lifetime (3,11) *11*
Stay (3)
Sunday Kind Of Woman (1)
Swing Low, Sweet Chariot (10)
Take These Chains From My Heart (9)
Take Time To Love (3)
Ten Dollars And A Clean White Shirt (9)
That's The Way A Cowboy Rocks And Rolls (12)
That's What Love Is (12)
There Won't Be Anymore (2,3,9) *18*
They'll Never Take Her Love From Me (9)
'Til I Can't Take It Anymore (1)
To Sing A Love Song (12)
Tomorrow Night (9)
Too Many Teardrops (9)
Tragedy (6)

Turn Around And Face Me (2)
Very Special Love Song (3,11) *11*
We Love Each Other (1)
Wedding Bells (5)
Were You There? (10)
Whatever Happened (7)
Who Will The Next Fool Be (9)
Why Don't We Go Somewhere And Love (3)
Why Me (10)
Why, Oh Why (3)
Will The Circle Be Unbroken? (10)
Windsong (12)
Woman Left Lonely (4)
You And I (8)
You Never Really Wanted Me (1)
You Win Again (5)
Your Cheatin' Heart (4)
Your Place Is Here With Me (7)

RICH, Tony, Project '96
Born in Detroit. R&B singer/songwriter/keyboardist.

| 2/3/96 | 31 | 47 | ▲ | © | Words | | | $10 | LaFace 26022 |

Billy Goat · Grass Is Green · Leavin' 88 · Little Ones · Nobody Knows 2
Ghost · Hey Blue · Like A Woman 41 · Missin' You · Under Her Spell

RICHARD, Cliff '80
Born Harry Rodger Webb on 10/14/40 in Lucknow, India (British parents); raised in England. Pop singer/songwriter/guitarist/actor. Appeared in the movies *Expresso Bongo, The Young Ones, Summer Holiday* and *Wonderful Life*. Knighted by Queen Elizabeth II in 1995.

4/18/64	115	7			1 It's All In The Game			$25	Epic 26089
8/7/76	76	15			2 I'm Nearly Famous			$12	Rocket 2210
12/8/79+	93	15			3 We Don't Talk Anymore			$12	EMI America 17018
10/11/80	80	34			4 I'm No Hero			$12	EMI America 17039
10/17/81	132	4			5 Wired For Sound			$12	EMI America 17059

Anything I Can Do (4) · Fly Me To The Moon (In Other · I Only Know I Love You (1) · Kiss (1) · Secret Love (1) · Young Love (5)
Better Than I Know Myself (5) · Words) (1) · I Wish You'd Change Your Mind · Language Of Love (3) · Since I Lost You (1)
Broken Doll (5) · Give A Little Bit More (4) 41 · (2) · Little In Love (4) 17 · Such Is The Mystery (2)
Carrie (3) 34 · Heart Will Break Tonight (4) · I'm In The Mood For Love (1) · Lost In A Lonely World (5) · Summer Rain (5)
'Cos I Love That Rock 'N' Roll · Here (4) · I'm Nearly Famous (2) · Lovers (2) · Take Another Look (4)
(5) · Hot Shot (3) · I'm No Hero (4) · Magic Is The Moonlight (1) · We Don't Talk Anymore (3) 7
Daddy's Home (5) 23 · I Can't Ask For Anymore · If You Walked Away (2) · Miss You Nights (2) · Where The Four Winds Blow
Devil Woman (2) 6 · Than You (2) 80 · In The Night (4) · Monday Thru Friday (3) · (1)
Doing Fine (3) · I Found A Rose (1) · It's All In The Game (1) 25 · Oh No, Don't Let Go (5) · Wired For Sound (5) 71
Dreaming (4) 10 · I Only Came To Say Goodbye · It's Alright Now (2) · Once In A While (5) · You Know That I Love You (3)
Everyman (4) · (1) · It's No Use Pretending (5) · Rock N Roll Juvenile (3) · You've Got To Give Me All Your
Fallin' In Luv (3) · I Only Have Eyes For You (1) · Junior Cowboy (2) · Sci-Fi (3) · Lovin' (2)

RICHARDS, Keith '88
Born on 12/18/43 in Dartford, Kent, England. Lead guitarist of **The Rolling Stones**. Married model Patti Hansen on 12/18/83.

| 10/22/88 | 24 | 23 | ● | © | 1 Talk Is Cheap | | | $10 | Virgin 90973 |
| 11/7/92 | 99 | 10 | | © | 2 Main Offender | | | $10 | Virgin 86499 |

Big Enough (1) · Hate It When You Leave (2) · Locked Away (1) · Runnin' Too Deep (2) · Wicked As It Seems (2) · You Don't Move Me (1)
Bodytalks (2) · How I Wish (1) · Make No Mistake (1) · Struggle (1) · Will But You Won't (2)
Demon (2) · I Could Have Stood You Up (1) · 999 (2) · Take It So Hard (1) · Words Of Wonder (2)
Eileen (2) · It Means A Lot (1) · Rockawhile (1) · Whip It Up (1) · Yap Yap (2)

★368★ RICHIE, Lionel '83
Born on 6/20/49 in Tuskegee, Alabama. R&B singer/songwriter/pianist. Former lead singer of the **Commodores**. Appeared in the movie *Thank God It's Friday*.

10/23/82	3	140	▲⁴	©	1 Lionel Richie			$10	Motown 6007
11/12/83	❶³	160	▲¹⁰	©	2 Can't Slow Down			$10	Motown 6059
					1984 Grammy winner: Album of the Year				
8/30/86	❶²	58	▲⁴	©	3 Dancing On The Ceiling			$10	Motown 6158
5/23/92	19	29	▲	©	4 Back To Front		[G]	$10	Motown 6338
5/4/96	28	14	●	©	5 Louder Than Words			$10	Mercury 532240
7/11/98	152	3		©	6 Time			$10	Mercury 558518
4/7/01	62	15		©	7 Renaissance			$10	Island 548225

All Night Long (All Night) · Deep River Woman (3) 71 · How Long (7) · My Love (1) 5 · Say I Do (5) · Three Times A Lady (4) 1
(2,4) 1 · Do It To Me (4) 21 · I Hear Your Voice (6) · Nothing Else Matters (5) · Say You, Say Me (3,4) 1 · Time (6)
Angel (7) 70 · Don't Stop (3) · I Wanna Take You Down (5) · Only One (2) · Se La (3) 20 · To The Rhythm (6)
Ballerina Girl (3) 7 · Don't Stop The Music (7) · It May Be The Water (7) · Ordinary Girl (5) · Serves You Right (1) · Tonight (7)
Can't Get Over You (5) · Don't Wanna Lose You (5) 39 · Just Put Some Love In Your · Paradise (5) · Someday (6) · Tonight Will Be Alright (3)
Can't Slow Down (2) · Don't You Ever Go Away (7) · Heart (1) · Penny Lover (2,4) 8 · Stay (6) · Touch (6)
Change (5) · Easy (4) 4 · Lady (6) · Piece Of Love (5) · Still (1) 1 · Truly (1,4) 1
Cinderella (7) · Endless Love (4) 1 · Love, Oh Love (4) · Piece Of My Heart (7) · Still In Love (5) · Wandering Stranger (1)
Climbing (5) · Everytime (6) · Love Will Conquer All (3) 9 · Round And Round (1) · Stuck On You (2) 3 · Wasted Time (7)
Closest Thing To Heaven (6) · Forever (6) · Love Will Find A Way (2) · Running With The Night · Tell Me (1) · You Are (1) 4
Dance The Night Away (7) · Hello (2,4) 1 · Lovers At First Sight (5) · (2,4) 7 · Tender Heart (7) · You Mean More To Me (1)
Dancing On The Ceiling (3) 2 · Here Is My Heart (7) · My Destiny (4) · Sail On (4) 4 · That's The Way I Feel (6) · Zoomin' (6)

RICHIE RICH '96
Born Richard Serrell on 6/25/67 in Oakland. Male rapper.

| 11/23/96 | 35 | 17 | | © | Seasoned Veteran | | | $10 | Def Jam 533471 |

Check Em · Fresh Out · It's Not About You · Niggas Done Changed · Real Pimp
Do G's Get To Go To · Funk · It's On · Pillow · Real Sh*t
Heaven? 57 · Guess Who's Back · Let's Ride 67 · Questions · Touch Myself

RICHTER, Sviatoslav '61
Born on 3/20/15 in Zhitomir, Ukraine, Russia. Died on 8/1/97 (age 82). Classical pianist.

| 12/12/60+ | 5 | 26 | | | Brahms: Piano Concerto No. 2 | | [I] | $25 | RCA Victor 2466 |

Concerto No. 2, In B-Flat, Op.
83

RICKLES, Don '68
Born on 5/8/26 in New York City. Insult comic/actor. Appeared in several movies and TV shows.

6/15/68	54	29		©	1 Hello Dummy!		[C]	$20	Warner 1745
					no track titles listed on this album				
4/12/69	180	4			2 Don Rickles Speaks!		[C]	$20	Warner 1779

Capsule Comments (2) · Famous Men And Women (2) · Night Clubs (2) · Sinatra (2) · Some Good Friends (2) · Television (2)
Current Events (2) · Names In The News (2) · Show Biz And Travel (2) · Some Big Stars (2) · Sports (2) · Thoughts (2)

RICOCHET '96
Country group from Texas: Heath Wright (vocals, guitar), Teddy Carr (guitar), Junior Bryant (fiddle), Eddie Kilgallon (keyboards), Greg Cook (bass) and Jeff Bryant (drums).

| 6/15/96 | 101 | 17 | ● | © | Ricochet | | | $10 | Columbia 67223 |

Daddy's Money · From Good To Bad To Worse · I Can't Dance · Little Bit Of Love (Is A · Love Is Stronger Than Pride · Truth Is I Lied
Ease My Troubled Mind · To Gone · I Wasn't Ready For You · Dangerous Thing) · Rowdy · What Do I Know

RIDDLE, Nelson '58
Born on 6/1/21 in Oradell, New Jersey. Died on 10/6/85 (age 64). Trombonist/prolific arranger/conductor.

5/27/57	20	1	©	1	Hey...Let Yourself Go!	[I]	$25	Capitol 814
2/17/58	20	1	©	2	C'mon...Get Happy!	[I]	$25	Capitol 893
10/20/62	48	9	©	3	Route 66 Theme and Other Great TV Themes	[I]	$25	Capitol 1771

Alvin Show Theme (3) | Get Happy (2) | Jeannine (I Dream Of Lilac | S'posin' (2) | Time Was (2)
Am I Blue? (2) | Have You Got Any Castles, | Time) (1) | Sam Benedict, Theme From (3) | Untouchables, The (3)
Andy Griffith Theme (3) | Baby? (1) | Let Yourself Go (1) | September In The Rain (2) | Without A Song (2)
Ben Casey Theme (3) | I Can't Escape From You (1) | Let's Face The Music And | Sing Along (3) | You And The Night And The
Darn That Dream (1) | I Get Along Without You Very | Dance (1) | Something To Remember You | Music (1)
Defenders Theme (3) | Well (1) | My Three Sons (2) | By (2) | You Are My Lucky Star (1)
Diga Diga Doo (2) | I'll Get By (As Long As I Have | Naked City Theme (3) | Then I'll Be Happy (1) | You Leave Me Breathless (1)
Dr. Kildare, Theme From (3) | You) (2) | Rain (2) | This Could Be The Start Of | You're An Old Smoothie (1)
For All We Know (2) | | **Route 66 Theme** (3) *30* | Something (3) | Younger Than Springtime (1)

RIDGELEY, Andrew '90
Born on 1/26/63 in Bushey, England. Former guitarist of **Wham!**.

6/16/90	130	3	©		Son Of Albert		$10	Columbia 46188

Baby Jane | Flame | Kiss Me | Price Of Love | **Shake** *77*
Big Machine | Hangin' | Mexico | Red Dress |

RIDGWAY, Stan '86
Born in 1954 in Los Angeles. Lead singer of **Wall Of Voodoo** from 1977-83.

4/12/86	131	9	©		The Big Heat		$10	I.R.S. 5637

Big Heat | Can't Stop The Show | Pick It Up (And Put It In Your | Pile Driver | Twisted
Camouflage | Drive She Said | Pocket) | Salesman | Walkin' Home Alone

RIFF '91
R&B vocal group from Paterson, New Jersey: Ken Kelly, Steven Capers, Anthony Fuller, Dwayne Jones and Michael Best.

5/25/91	177	3	©		Riff		$10	SBK 95828

All Or Nothing | Baby It's Wonderful | I Can't Believe We Just Met | Little Girls | Read My Eyes
April's Fool | Everytime My Heart Beats | **If You're Serious** *88* | **My Heart Is Failing Me** *25* | Temporary Insanity

RIFKIN, Joshua '74
Born on 4/22/44 in New York City. Classical/jazz/ragtime pianist.

12/11/65+	83	17		1	The Baroque Beatles Book	[I]	$25	Elektra 7306
6/22/74	75	15		2	Piano Rags By Scott Joplin, Volumes I & II	[I]	$20	Nonesuch 73026 [2]
12/14/74	126	5		3	Piano Rags By Scott Joplin, Volume III	[I]	$15	Nonesuch 71305

Bethena (2) | Eugenia (2) | I Want To Hold Your Hand (1) | Original Rags (2) | She Loves You (medley) (1) | Weeping Willow (3)
Cascades, The (3) | Euphonic Sounds (2) | I'll Be Back (1) | Paragon Rag (2) | Solace (2) | You've Got To Hide Your Love
Chrysanthemum, The (3) | Fig Leaf Rag (2) | I'll Cry Instead (1) | Pine Apple Rag (2) | Stoptime Rag (3) | Away (1)
Country Club (3) | Gladiolus Rag (2) | Leola (1) | Please Please Me (1) | Sugar Cane (3)
Eight Days A Week (1) | Hard Day's Night (medley) (1) | Magnetic Rag (2) | Ragtime Dance (2) | Thank You Girl (medley) (1)
Elite Syncopations (2) | Help! (1) | Maple Leaf Rag (2) | Rose Leaf Rag (2) | Things We Said Today (1)
Entertainer (2) | Hold Me Tight (1) | Nonpareil, The (3) | Scott Joplin's New Rag (2) | Ticket To Ride (1)

RIGHTEOUS BROTHERS, The ★163★ '65
White vocal duo: **Bill Medley** (born on 9/19/40 in Santa Anna, California) and Bobby Hatfield (born on 8/10/40 in Beaver Dam, Wisconsin). Formed duo in 1962. First recorded as the Paramours for Smash in 1962. On *Hullabaloo* and *Shindig* TV shows. Split up from 1968-74. Medley went solo, replaced by Jimmy Walker (**The Knickerbockers**); rejoined Hatfield in 1974.

1)*You've Lost That Lovin' Feelin'* 2)*Soul & Inspiration* 3)*Just Once In My Life...*
4)*Right Now!* 5)*Some Blue-Eyed Soul*

1/2/65	11	21		1	Right Now!	[E]	$40	Moonglow 1001
1/16/65	14	20		2	Some Blue-Eyed Soul	[E]	$40	Moonglow 1002
1/23/65	4	67		3	You've Lost That Lovin' Feelin'		$40	Philles 4007
5/29/65	9	41		4	Just Once In My Life...		$40	Philles 4008
6/19/65	39	20		5	This Is New!	[E]	$40	Moonglow 1003
12/25/65+	16	26		6	Back To Back		$40	Philles 4009
4/30/66	7	32	●	7	Soul & Inspiration		$25	Verve 5001
5/21/66	130	11		8	The Best Of The Righteous Brothers	C:❶¹⁹/127 [G]	$30	Moonglow 1004
9/3/66	32	20		9	Go Ahead And Cry	[G]	$25	Verve 5004
4/8/67	155	15		10	Sayin' Somethin'	[G]	$25	Verve 5010
9/16/67	21	50	● ©	11	Greatest Hits	C:#16/70 [G]	$25	Verve 5020
10/28/67	198	2		12	Souled Out	[G]	$25	Verve 5031
12/14/68	187	2		13	One For The Road	[L]	$25	Verve 5058
4/5/69	126	5		14	Greatest Hits, Vol. 2	[G]	$25	Verve 5071
8/31/74	27	18		15	Give It To The People		$15	Haven 9201
8/25/90	31	81	©	16	Greatest Hits	[G]	$10	Verve 823119
10/27/90	178	3	●	17	Anthology (1962-1974)	[K]	$15	Rhino 71488 [2]
11/24/90	161	3	▲ ©	18	Best Of The Righteous Brothers	[G]	$10	Curb 77381
8/8/92	35ᶜ	8	©	19	Unchained Melody	[G]	$10	Polygram 511078
11/21/92	14ᶜ	1		20	The Very Best Of The Righteous Brothers/Unchained Melody	[G]	$10	Verve 847248

All The Way (16) | Baby, What You Want Me To | **Brown Eyed Woman** (17) *43* | Dream On (15,17) *32* | Georgia On My Mind | Great Pretender (4,11,16)
Along Came Jones (10) | Do (2) | Burn On Love (5) | Drown In My Own Tears (9) | (1,8,11,16,17,18) *62* | Guess Who (4,11,16)
American Rock And Roll (18) | Been So Nice (12) | Bye Bye Love (1,8,14) | **Ebb Tide** | **Give It To The People** | Hallelujah I Love Her So (6)
And I Thought You Loved Me | Big Boy Pete (4) | Change Is Gonna Come (7) | (6,11,16,17,18,19,20) *5* | (15,17) *20* | Hang Ups (17)
(15) | Big Time Ben (9) | Come Rain Or Come Shine (16) | Fannie Mae (2,8) | **Go Ahead And Cry** | Harlem Shuffle (10)
Angels Listened In (3) | Blues, The (4) | Country Boy (16) | Fee-Fi-Fidily-I-Oh (1) | (9,14,17,20) *30* | **He** (7,17,20) *18*
At My Front Door (5,8) | Bring It Home To Me (7) | Cryin' Blues (5) | For Sentimental Reasons (6) | God Bless The Child (6) | **He Will Break Your Heart**
B-Flat Blues (1) | **Bring Your Love To Me** | Dr. Rock And Roll (15) | For Your Love (2,8) | Gospel Medley (13) | (7) *91*
Baby She's Mine (6) | (2,17) *83* | Don't Fight It (10) | | Gotta Tell You How I Feel (5) | Here I Am (12)

RIGHTEOUS BROTHERS, The — Cont'd

Hey Girl (7,19)
Hold On I'm Comin' (10)
Hot Tamales (6)
Hung On You
(6,11,16,17,19,20) **47**
I Believe (9)
I Can't Make It Alone (17) **95**
I Don't Believe In Losing (12)
I Just Wanna Be Me (15)
I Just Want To Make Love To You (2,8,14,17)
(I Love You) For Sentimental Reasons (11,16)
I Need A Girl (5)
(I Need) Someone Like You (12)
I Still Love You (5)
I Who Have Nothing (10)
I'm Leaving It Up To You (7)
I'm So Lonely (1)
I've Got The Beat (9)
If I Ruled The World (16)

If Loving You Is Wrong (I'm Sorry) (12)
If You're Lying, You'll Be Crying (5)
In That Great Gettin' Up Mornin' (1)
In The Midnight Hour (7)
Island In The Sun (9)
It's Up To You (12)
Jimmy's Blues (10)
Just Once In My Life (4,11,16,17,18,19,20) **9**
Justine (5,8,14,17) **85**
Ko Ko Mo (3)
Koko Joe (1,17)
Late Late Night (6)
Let It Be Me (9)
Let The Good Times Roll (1,8,13,14)
Lines (15)
Little Latin Lupe Lu (1,8,13,14,17,18,20) **49**

Look At Me (3)
Love Is Not A Dirty Word (15)
Love Keeps Callin' My Name (12)
Love Or Magic (1)
Loving You (6,14)
Man Without A Dream (10,17,19)
Melancholy Music Man (17) **43**
Mine All Mine (7)
My Babe (1,13,17,18) **75**
My Darling Clementine (16)
My Girl (10)
My Prayer (1,8,14)
My Tears Will Go Away (2)
Night Owl (2)
Old Man River (3)
Oldies But Goodies Medley (13)
On This Side Of Goodbye (10,17,19,20) **47**
Ooh Poo Pah Doo (4,13)

Over And Over (3)
Rat Race (7)
Rock And Roll Heaven (15,17) **3**
Save The Last Dance For Me (9)
Secret Love (16)
See That Girl (4,11,16,17,19,20)
Sick And Tired (3)
Since I Fell For You (16)
So Many Lonely Nights Ahead (12)
Something You Got (9)
Something's Got A Hold On Me (2,8)
Somewhere (16)
Soul City (3)
Soulville (19)
Stagger Lee (9)
Stand By (7,17)
Sticks And Stones (4)

Stranded In The Middle Of Noplace (12,17) **72**
Summertime (3)
That Lucky Old Sun (Just Rolls Around Heaven All Day) (13)
That's All (16)
There She Goes (5,17)
There's A Woman (3)
Things Didn't Go Your Way (9)
This Little Girl Of Mine (2,8,14,17)
Together Again (15)
Try To Find Another Man (Woman) (2,8,17,18)
Turn On Your Love Lights (7)
Unchained Melody (4,11,13,16,17,19,20) **4**
Unchained Melody (18) **19**
What Now My Love (9,14)
What'd I Say (13)
White Cliffs Of Dover (6,11,16,17,19,20)

Will You Love Me Tomorrow (10,19)
Without A Doubt (6)
Without A Song (16)
Without You I'd Be Lost (12)
Yes Indeed (10)
You Are My Sunshine (4)
You Bent My Mind (12)
You Can Have Her (5,8,17,18) **67**
You Turn Me Around (15)
You'll Never Walk Alone (4,11,13,16)
(You're My) Soul And Inspiration (7,13,14,17,18,19,20) **1**
You've Lost That Lovin' Feelin' (3,11,13,16,17,18) **1**
You've Lost That Lovin' Feeling (19,20)

RIGHT SAID FRED '92
Pop vocal trio from England: brothers Richard (vocals) and Fred (guitar) Fairbrass, with Rob Manzoli (guitar).

3/21/92	46	20	●	©	**Up**			$10	Charisma 92107

Deeply Dippy
Do Ya Feel
Don't Talk Just Kiss 76
I'm Too Sexy 1
Is It True About Love
Love For All Seasons
No-One On Earth
Swan
Those Simple Things
Upon My Heart

RILEY, Cheryl Pepsii '88
Born in Brooklyn, New York. R&B singer.

11/12/88	128	11		©	**Me, Myself And I**			$10	Columbia 44409

Every Little Thing About You
Falling From The Floor
He Said - She Said
Life Goes On
Me, Myself And I
Seein' Is Believin'
Sister Knows What She Wants
Sisters
Thanks For My Child 32

RILEY, Jeannie C. '68
Born Jeannie Carolyn Stephenson on 10/19/45 in Anson, Texas. Country singer.

10/12/68	12	27	●	©	1 **Harper Valley P.T.A.**			$20	Plantation 1
3/15/69	187	5			2 **Yearbooks and Yesterdays**			$15	Plantation 2
9/13/69	142	7			3 **Things Go Better With Love**			$15	Plantation 3

Artist, The (3)
Back Side Of Dallas (3)
Back To School (2)
Ballad Of Louise (1)
Box Of Memories (2)
Cotton Patch (1)
Edna Burgoo (1)
Girl Most Likely (2) **55**

Harper Valley P.T.A. (1) **1**
I'm Only A Woman (3)
I'm The Woman (3)
Little Town Square (1)
Mr. Harper (1)
My Scrapbook (2)
No Brass Band (1)
Our Minnie (3)

Part Of Honey (2)
Real Woman (3)
Rib, The (3)
Run Jeannie Run (1)
Satan Place (1)
Shed Me No Tears (1)
Sippin' Shirley Thompson (1)
Sunday After Church (3)

Taste Of Tears (2)
Teardrops On Page Forty-Three (2)
That's How It Is With Him And Me (2)
There Never Was A Time (3) **77**
Thin Ribbon Of Smoke (3)

Things Go Better With Love (3)
Wedding Cake (3)
What Ever Happened To Charlie Brown (2)
What Was Her Name (2)
Widow Jones (1)
Yearbooks And Yesterdays (2)

RILEY, Melvin '94
Born in Flint, Michigan. Former lead singer of **Ready For The World**.

8/13/94	155	3		©	**Ghetto Love**			$10	MCA 11016

Bone In The Bag
Cutta Me Loose
Ghetto Love
Goin' Thru A Thang
I'm All In
If You Don't Tell I Won't Tell
Little Somethin' Somethin'
Love's Gonna Get Cha
#1 Nigga From The Hood
Servin' It
Spoil You
Tabs On Ya
What Makes A Man (Wanna Cheat On His Woman)
Whose Is It?

★405★ RIMES, LeAnn '97
Born Margaret LeAnn Rimes on 8/28/82 in Jackson, Mississippi; raised in Garland, Texas. Country singer. Won the 1996 Best New Artist Grammy Award.

7/27/96	3	97	▲6	©	1 **Blue**	C:#27/7		$10	Curb 77821
3/1/97	❶1	54	▲2	©	2 **Unchained Melody/The Early Years**	[E]		$10	Curb 77856
9/27/97	❶3	55	▲4	©	3 **You Light Up My Life - Inspirational Songs**			$10	Curb 77885
5/23/98	3	37	▲	©	4 **Sittin' On Top Of The World**			$10	Curb 77901
11/13/99	8	23	▲	©	5 **LeAnn Rimes**			$10	Curb 77947
2/17/01	10	26	●	©	6 **I Need You**			$10	Curb 77979

All The Lovin' And Hurtin' (4)
Amazing Grace (3)
Big Deal (5) **23**
Blue (1) **26**
Blue Moon Of Kentucky (2)
Born To Lose (5)
Bridge Over Troubled Waters (3)
Broken Wing (2)
But I Do Love You (6)
Can't Fight The Moonlight (6) **71**
Cattle Call (1)
Clinging To A Saving Hand (3)

Commitment (4)
Cowboy's Sweetheart (2)
Crazy (5)
Cryin' Time (5)
Don't Worry (5)
Fade To Blue (5)
Faded Love (5)
Feels Like Home (4)
God Bless America (3)
Good Lookin' Man (1)
Heart Never Forgets (4)
Honestly (1)
How Do I Live (2) **2**

Hurt Me (1)
I Believe (3)
I Believe In You (6)
I Fall To Pieces (5)
I Know Who Holds Tomorrow (3)
I Need You (6) **11**
I Will Always Love You (2)
I'll Get Even With You (1)
Insensitive (4)
Leavin' On My Mind (5)
Light In Your Eyes (1)
Looking Through Your Eyes (4) **18**

Love Must Be Telling Me Something (4)
Lovesick Blues (5)
Me And Bobby McGee (5)
More Than Anyone Deserves (4)
My Baby (1)
National Anthem (3)
Nothin' New Under The Moon (4)
On The Side Of Angels (3)
One Of These Days (6)
One Way Ticket (Because I Can) (1)

Purple Rain (4)
Rest Is History (2)
River Of Love (2)
Rock Me (4)
Rose, The (3)
Share My Love (2)
She's Got You (5)
Sittin' On Top Of The World (4)
Soon (6)
Sure Thing (2)
Surrender (4)
Talk To Me (1)
Ten Thousand Angels Cried (3)
These Arms Of Mine (4)

Together, Forever, Always (6)
Unchained Melody (2)
Undeniable (4)
When Am I Gonna Get Over You (4)
Written In The Stars (6) **29**
You Are (6)
You Light Up My Life (3) **34**
Your Cheatin' Heart (5)

RINGS, The '81
Rock group from Boston: Mark Sutton (vocals, guitar), Mike Baker (keyboards), Bob Gifford (bass) and Matt Thurber (drums).

2/21/81	164	6			**The Rings**			$12	MCA 5165

Got My Wish
I Need Strange
Let Me Go 75
My Kinda Girl
Opposites Attract
Third Generation
This One's For The Girls
Too Much Of Nothin'
Watch You Break
Who's She Dancin' With

RIOS, Miguel '70
Born on 6/7/44 in Granada, Spain. Pop singer.

8/22/70	140	4			**A Song Of Joy**			$15	A&M 4267

Himno A La Alegria   Like An Old Time Movie (El   Look To Your Soul (Mira Hacia   Second Glance (Despiera)   **Song Of Joy (Himno A La**
Life I Knew (Mi Vida Fue)   Viaje)   Ti)   She's Gone (Ella Se Fue)   **Alegria) 14**
   River, The   Soledad   Vuelvo A Granada

RIOS, Waldo De Los '71
Born in 1934 in Buenos Aires, Argentina. Committed suicide on 3/28/77 (age 42). Composer/conductor.

6/5/71	53	16			**Sinfonias**		[I]	$15	United Artists 6802

Eighth Symphony In C Minor   Symphony No. 5, E Minor, 2nd   Symphony No. 9, Opus 95,   Symphony Of The Toys In C
Fourth Symphony In A Major,   Movement   New World, 4th Movement,   Major, 2nd Movement
"Italian", 1st Movement   **Symphony No. 40 In G Minor**   2nd Movement (Largo)   Third Symphony In F Major, 3rd
Ode To Joy   **K. 550, 1st Movement 67**   Movement

RIOT '81
Hard-rock group formed in New York City: Rhett Forrester (vocals), Mark Reale and Rick Ventura (guitars), Kip Leming (bass) and Sandy Slavin (drums). Forrester was shot to death in Atlanta on 1/22/94 (age 37).

9/12/81	99	11	©	1	**Fire Down Under**			$12	Elektra 546
1/14/84	175	6	©	2	**Born In America**			$12	Quality 1008
5/14/88	150	10	©	3	**Thundersteel**			$10	CBS Associated 44232

Altar Of The King (1)   Devil Woman (2)   Fire Down Under (1)   Johnny's Back (3)   Run For Your Life (1)   Vigilante Killer (2)
Bloodstreets (3)   Don't Bring Me Down (1)   Flashbacks (1)   No Lies (1)   Running From The Law (2)   Where Soldiers Rule (2)
Born In America (2)   Don't Hold Back (1)   Flight Of The Warrior (3)   On Wings Of Eagles (3)   Sign Of The Crimson Storm (3)   Wings Of Fire (2)
Buried Alive (Tell Tale Heart)   Feel The Same (1)   Gunfighter (2)   Outlaw (1)   Swords And Tequila (1)   You Burn In Me (2)
(3)   Fight Or Fall (3)   Heavy Metal Machine (2)   Promised Land (2)   Thundersteel (3)

RIP CHORDS, The '64
Rock group formed in California: Terry Melcher, Bruce Johnston, Phil Stewart, Richard Rotkin, Arnie Marcus and Ernie Bringas. Melcher is the son of **Doris Day**. Johnston went on to join **The Beach Boys**.

2/22/64	56	17			**Hey Little Cobra and other Hot Rod Hits**			$50	Columbia 8951

Ding Dong   '40 Ford Time   **Gone 88**   **Hey Little Cobra 4**   Queen, The   Shut Down
Drag City   409   **Here I Stand 51**   Little Deuce Coupe   She Thinks I Still Care   Trophy Machine

RIPERTON, Minnie '75
Born on 11/8/47 in Chicago. Died of cancer on 7/12/79 (age 31). R&B singer. Member of **Rotary Connection** from 1967-70. Her daughter Maya Rudolph is a cast member of TV's *Saturday Night Live*.

8/17/74+	4	47	● ©	1	**Perfect Angel**			$15	Epic 32561
11/16/74	160	4	©	2	**Come To My Garden**	[E]		$15	Janus 7011
					recorded in 1969				
5/31/75	18	23	©	3	**Adventures In Paradise**			$15	Epic 33454
3/19/77	71	10	©	4	**Stay In Love**			$15	Epic 34191
5/19/79	29	27		5	**Minnie**			$12	Capitol 11936
9/6/80	35	15		6	**Love Lives Forever**			$12	Capitol 12097

Adventures In Paradise (3)   Dancin' & Actin' Crazy (5)   Give Me Time (6)   Light My Fire (5)   Oh Darlin'...Life Goes On (4)   Stay In Love (4)
Alone In Brewster Bay (3)   Don't Let Anyone Bring You   Here We Go (4)   Love And Its Glory (3)   Only When I'm Dreaming (2)   Stick Together (4)
Baby, This Love I Have (3)   Down (3)   How Could I Love You More (4)   Love Hurts (5)   Our Lives (1)   Strange Affair (6)
Can You Feel What I'm Saying?   Edge Of A Dream (1)   I'm A Woman (5)   Lover And Friend (5)   Perfect Angel (1)   Take A Little Trip (4)
(4)   Every Time He Comes Around   I'm In Love Again (6)   **Lovin' You** (1) 1   Rainy Day In Centerville (4)   When It Comes Down To It (3)
Close Your Eyes And   (1)   **Inside My Love** (3) 76   Memory Band (2)   Reasons (1)   Whenever-Wherever (2)
Remember (2)   Expecting (2)   Island In The Sun (6)   Memory Lane (4)   Return To Forever (5)   Wouldn't Matter Where You Are
Come To My Garden (2)   Feelin' That Your Feelin's Right   It's So Nice (To See Old   Minnie's Lament (3)   Seeing You This Way (1)   (4)
Completeness (2)   (3)   Friends) (1)   Never Existed Before (5)   Simple Things (3)   You Take My Breath Away (6)
Could It Be I'm In Love (4)   Gettin' Ready For Your Love (4)   Les Fleur (2)   Oh, By The Way (2)   Song Of Life (La-La-La) (6)   Young, Willing And Able (4)

RIPPINGTONS Featuring Russ Freeman '89
Russ Freeman was born on 2/11/60 in Nashville. Jazz guitarist/keyboardist. The Rippingtons: Jeff Kashiwa (sax), Steve Reid (percussion), Kim Stone (bass) and Tony Morales (drums).

5/7/88	110	15	©	1	**Kilimanjaro**		[I]	$10	Passport Jazz 88042
6/10/89	85	12	©	2	**Tourist In Paradise**		[I]	$10	GRP 9588
8/31/91	148	7	©	3	**Curves Ahead**		[I]	$10	GRP 9651
9/5/92	147	3	©	4	**Weekend In Monaco**		[I]	$10	GRP 9681
3/12/94	118	7	©	5	**The Benoit/Freeman Project**		[I]	$10	GRP 9739
					THE BENOIT/FREEMAN PROJECT				
9/17/94	192	2	©	6	**Sahara**		[I]	$10	GRP 9781
					RUSS FREEMAN & THE RIPPINGTONS				
10/4/97	147	5	©	7	**Black Diamond**		[I]	$10	Windham Hill 11271

After The Love Has Gone (5)   Dreams Of The Sirens (1)   Journey's End (6)   Morocco (1)   Princess, The (2)   That's All I Could Say (5)
Angelfire (7)   Earthbound (2)   Jupiter's Child (2)   Native Sons Of A Distant Land   Principles Of Desire (6)   'Til We're Together Again (6)
Aruba! (7)   End Of Our Season (5)   Katrina's Dance (1)   (6)   Reunion (5)   Tourist In Paradise (2)
Aspen (3)   Girl With The Indigo Eyes (6)   Kilimanjaro (1)   Nature Of The Beast (3)   Sahara (4)   True Companion (6)
Backstabbers (1)   Highroller (4)   Let's Stay Together (2)   North Peak (7)   Santa Fe Trail (3)   Vienna (4)
Best Is Yet To Come (6)   I'll Be Around (6)   Los Cabos (1)   North Star (3)   Seven Nights In Rome (7)   Weekend In Monaco (4)
Big Sky (7)   If I Owned The World (7)   Love Notes (1)   Northern Lights (1)   Smartypants (5)   When She Believed In Me (5)
Black Diamond (7)   In Another Life (7)   Mediterranean Nights (5)   Oceansong (1)   Snowbound (3)   Where The Road Will Lead Us
Carnival! (7)   Indian Summer (4)   Miles Away (3)   One Ocean Way (2)   Soul Seeker (7)   (4)
Curves Ahead (3)   It's The Thought That Counts   Mirage (5)   One Summer Night In Brazil (2)   St. Tropez (4)
Deep Powder (7)   (5)   Moka Java (4)   Place For Lovers (4)   Swept Away (5)
Destiny (2)   Jewel Thieves (7)   Morning Song (4)   Porscha (6)   Take Me With You (3)

RITCHARD, Cyril '61
Born on 12/1/1897 in Sydney, Australia. Died on 12/18/77 (age 80). Acted in several movies and Broadway shows.

1/9/61	19	8			**Alice In Wonderland: The Mad Tea Party/The Lobster Quadrille**	[T]		$25	Riverside 1406

Lobster Quadrille   Mad Tea Party

New Edition
Candy Girl ('83)

New Riders Of The Purple Sage
The Adventures of Panama Red ('73)

Carroll O'Connor
Remembering You ('72)

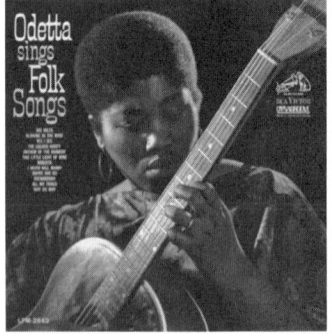

Odetta
Odetta sings Folk Songs ('63)

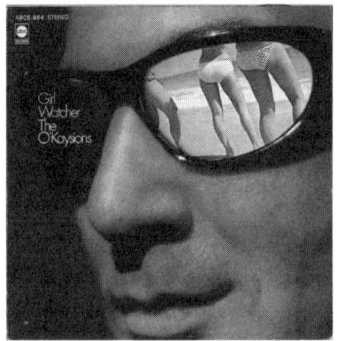

The O'Kaysions
Girl Watcher ('68)

Shaquille O'Neal
Respect ('98)

Roy Orbison
The Orbison Way ('66)

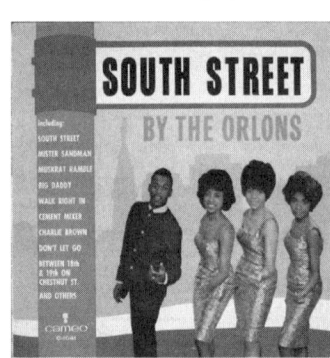

The Orlons
South Street ('63)

Dolly Parton
Burlap & Satin ('83)

Rita Pavone
Rita Pavone ('64)

Bobby (Boris) Pickett
The Original Monster Mash ('62)

Wilson Pickett
The Sound Of Wilson Pickett ('67)

P.M. Dawn
Jesus Wept ('95)

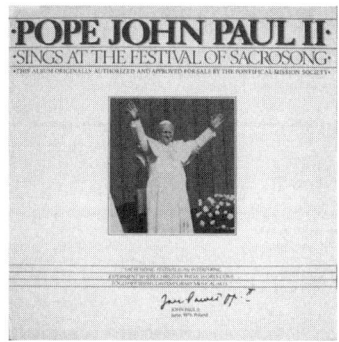

Pope John Paul II
Sings At The Festival Of Sacrosong ('79)

Adam Clayton Powell
Keep The Faith, Baby! ('67)

Perez Prado
"Prez" ('59)

Louis Prima & Keely Smith
Louis and Keely! ('59)

Primus
Rhinoplasty ('98)

Public Enemy
He Got Game ('98)

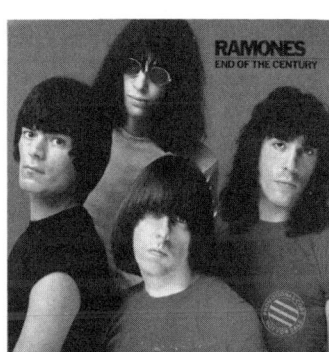

Ramones
End Of The Century ('80)

Raspberries
Side 3 ('72)

Jim Reeves
He'll Have To Go ('60)

The Refreshments
Fizzy Fuzzy Big & Buzzy ('96)

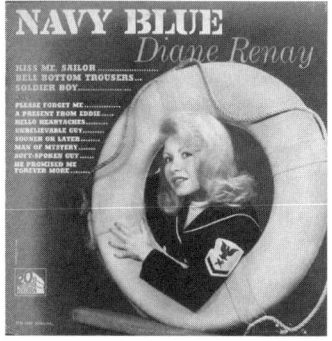

Diane Renay
Navy Blue ('64)

RITCHIE FAMILY, The '76

Female disco trio from Philadelphia: Cheryl Jackson, Cassandra Wooten and Gwen Oliver. Named for producer Ritchie Rome.

DEBUT	PEAK	WKS			Album Title			$	Label & Number
10/4/75	53	12			1 **Brazil**			$12	20th Century 498
7/24/76	30	25			2 **Arabian Nights**			$12	Marlin 2201
2/12/77	100	10			3 **Life Is Music**			$12	Marlin 2203
7/30/77	164	12			4 **African Queens**			$12	Marlin 2206
9/2/78	148	6			5 **American Generation**			$12	Marlin 2215

African Queens (4)   Big Spender (medley) (5)   I Feel Disco Good (medley) (5)   Liberty (3)   Peanut Vendor (1)   Summer Dance (4)
American Generation (medley) (5)   **Brazil** (1) *11*   **I Want To Dance With You**   Life Is Fascination (1)   Pinball (1)   Super Lover (3)
Arabian Nights Medley (2)   Cleopatra, Theme Of (4)   **(Dance With Me)** (1) *84*   Life Is Music (3)   Queen Of Sheba, Theme Of   Voodoo (4)
Baby I'm On Fire (2)   Disco Blues (3)   Lady Champagne (1)   Long Distance Romance (3)   The (4)
Best Disco In Town (2) *17*   Frenesi (1)   Lady Luck (3)   Music Man (5)   Quiet Village (4)
  Good In Love (medley) (5)   Let's Pool (1)   Nefertiti, Theme Of (4)   Romantic Love (2)

RITENOUR, Lee '81

Born on 1/11/52 in Los Angeles. Guitarist/composer/arranger. Nicknamed "Captain Fingers." Member of **Fourplay**.

DEBUT	PEAK	WKS		CD	Album Title			$	Label & Number
6/4/77	178	5		©	1 **Captain Fingers**		[I]	$12	Epic 34426
6/24/78	121	7		©	2 **The Captain's Journey**		[I]	$12	Elektra 136
6/16/79	136	6		©	3 **Feel The Night**		[I]	$12	Elektra 192
5/9/81	26	23		©	4 **Rit**			$12	Elektra 331
4/17/82	163	6		©	5 **Rio**		[I]	$10	Musician 60024
12/4/82	99	14		©	6 **Rit/2**			$10	Elektra 60186
6/23/84	145	8		©	7 **Banded Together**			$10	Elektra 60358
10/5/85	192	2		©	8 **Harlequin**		[I]	$10	GRP 1015

DAVE GRUSIN/LEE RITENOUR
includes "Before It's Too Late (Antes Que Seja Tarde)" and "Harlequin (Arlequim Desconhecido)" by Ivan Lins

DEBUT	PEAK	WKS		CD	Album Title			$	Label & Number
1/21/89	156	8		©	9 **Festival**		[I]	$10	GRP 9570

Amaretto (7)   Fantasy, A (6)   Isn't She Lovely (1)   Midnight Lady (3)   Rainbow (5)   Sunset Drivers (7)
Be Good To Me (7)   Feel The Night (3)   It Happens Everyday (5)   Morning Glory (2)   Rio Funk (5)   That's Enough For Me (2)
Bird, The (8)   Fly By Night (1)   (Just) Tell Me Pretty Lies (4)   Mr. Briefcase (4)   Rio Sol (9)   Tied Up (6)
Captain Fingers (1,4)   French Roast (3)   Keep It Alive (6)   New York/Brazil (9)   Rit Variations II (7)   Uh Oh! (3)
Captain's Journey Medley (2)   Good Question (4)   Latin Lovers (9)   Night Rhythms (9)   Road Runner (6)   Voices (6)
Cats Of Rio (8)   Grid-Lock (8)   Linda (Voce E Linda) (9)   No Sympathy (4)   San Juan Sunset (5)   What Do You Want? (2)
Cross My Heart (6) *69*   Heavenly Bodies (7)   Little Bit Of This And A Little Bit   Odile, Odila (9)   San Ysidro (5)   Wicked Wine (3)
Dolphin Dreams (1)   Humana (9)   Of That (5)   On The Boardwalk (6)   Shadow Dancing (7)   (You Caught Me) Smilin' (4)
Dreamwalk (4)   I'm Not Responsible (7)   Malibu (6)   On The Slow Glide (4)   Silent Message (8)   You Make Me Feel Like
Dreamwalkin' (Along With Me)   Inner Look (9)   Mandela (7)   Operator (Thief On The Line)   Simplicidad (5)   Dancing (3)
(6)   Ipanema Sol (5)   Margarita (1)   (7)   Space Glide (1)
Early A.M. Attitude (8)   **Is It You** (4) *15*   Market Place (3)   Other Love (7)   Sugarloaf Express (2)
Etude (2)   Matchmakers (2)   Promises, Promises (6)   Sun Song (1)

RIVERA, Lupillo '01

Born Guadalupe Rivera on 1/30/72 in La Barca, Jalisco, Mexico; raised in Long Beach, California. Latin singer.

DEBUT	PEAK	WKS			Album Title			$	Label & Number
3/3/01	163	3	● ©		**Despreciado**		[F]	$10	Sony Discos 84276

Copa Tras Copa   El Barzon   Que Te Ha Dado Esa Mujer   Tomando Y Tomando   Tu Recuerdo Y Yo
Despreciado   Mi Gusto Es   Se Les Pelo El Moreño   Tragos Amargos   Yo No Fui

RIVERS, Bob '94

Born in North Branford, Connecticut. Hosted own *Twisted Radio* show in Seattle. Specializes in song parodies.

DEBUT	PEAK	WKS		CD	Album Title			$	Label & Number
12/24/88+	19ˣ	7	● ©		1 **Twisted Christmas**	C:#35/6	[X-N]	$10	Critique 90671

BOB RIVERS COMEDY CORP
Christmas charts: 19/'88, 23/'90, 30/'91, 33/'94

DEBUT	PEAK	WKS		CD	Album Title			$	Label & Number
12/18/93+	106	4		©	2 **I Am Santa Claus**	C:#42/2	[X-N]	$10	Atlantic 82548

BOB RIVERS & TWISTED RADIO
Christmas charts: 23/'93, 34/'94

Chimney Song (1)   I'm Dressin' Up Like Santa   Message From The King (1)   Teddy The Red-Nosed Senator   Walkin 'Round In Women's
Didn't I Get This Last Year? (2)   (When I Get Out On Parole)   O Christmas Tree (2)   (2)   Underwear (2)
Foreigners (1)   (1)   O Come All Ye Grateful   There's Another Santa Claus   We Wish You Weren't Living
Grahbe Yahbalz (2)   Jingle Hells Bells (2)   Dead-Heads (1)   (2)   With Us (1)
I Am Santa Claus (2)   Joy To The World (1)   O Little Town Of Bethlehem (2)   Twelve Pains Of Christmas (1)   "What's It To Ya" Chorus (2)
I Came Upon A Roadkill Deer   Kids, The (2)   Restroom Door Said,   Under Tree World Of Jacques   Wreck The Malls (1)
(2)   Letter To Santa (2)   "Gentlemen" (1)   Cousteau (2)
  Magical Kingdom Of Claus (2)   Visit From St. Nicholson (1)

RIVERS, Joan '83

Born Joan Molinsky on 6/8/33 in Brooklyn, New York. Popular comedienne. Hosted own TV talk show in 1989. Directed the 1978 movie *Rabbit Test*.

DEBUT	PEAK	WKS			Album Title			$	Label & Number
4/23/83	22	21		©	**What Becomes A Semi-Legend Most?**		[C]	$10	Geffen 4007

Anchors Aweigh   Being Married   Great Movie Star   Men She Dated   Nurses And Stewardesses
Battle Hymn Of The Republic   Childbirth   Heidi Abromowitz   Men Vs. Women   Rock Stars
Before And After Marriage   Drugs   How God Divides   National Enquirer And U.F.O.   Royal Family
Being A Bridesmaid   Going To The Gynecologist   Living In New York   Sightings

RIVERS, Johnny '68

★203★

Born John Ramistella on 11/7/42 in New York City; raised in Baton Rouge, Louisiana. Pop-rock singer/songwriter/guitarist. Recorded with the Spades for Suede in 1957. Named Johnny Rivers by DJ Alan Freed in 1958. To Los Angeles in 1961. Recorded for 12 different labels (1958-64) before his smash debut on Imperial. Began own Soul City label in 1966. Recorded Christian music in the early 1980s.

1)Realization 2)Johnny Rivers At The Whisky a Go Go 3)Rewind

DEBUT	PEAK	WKS		CD	Album Title			$	Label & Number
6/20/64	12	45			1 **Johnny Rivers At The Whisky a Go Go**		[L]	$25	Imperial 12264
10/17/64	38	23			2 **Here We a Go Go Again!**		[L]	$25	Imperial 12274
2/20/65	42	14			3 **Johnny Rivers In Action!**		[L]	$25	Imperial 12280
6/26/65	21	19		©	4 **Meanwhile Back At The Whisky a Go Go**		[L]	$25	Imperial 12284
9/25/65	91	18		©	5 **Johnny Rivers Rocks The Folk**			$25	Imperial 12293
4/16/66	52	21			6 **"...and I know you wanna dance"**		[L]	$25	Imperial 12307
9/24/66	29	36	●		7 **Johnny Rivers' Golden Hits**		[G]	$20	Imperial 12324
12/17/66+	33	46		©	8 **Changes**			$20	Imperial 12334
6/24/67	14	21		©	9 **Rewind**			$20	Imperial 12341

RIVERS, Johnny — Cont'd

DEBUT	PEAK	WKS	RIAA	CD	ARTIST — Album Title		$	Label & Number
6/29/68	5	41	●	© 10	**Realization**		$20	Imperial 12372
6/14/69	26	25	●		11 A Touch Of Gold	[G]	$20	Imperial 12427
8/8/70	100	9			12 Slim Slo Slider		$20	Imperial 16001
9/11/71	148	4			13 Home Grown		$15	United Artists 5532
11/4/72+	78	20			14 L.A. Reggae		$15	United Artists 5650
9/20/75	147	6			15 New Lovers and Old Friends		$12	Epic 33681
1/14/78	142	8			16 Outside Help		$12	Big Tree 76004

Apple Tree (12)
Ashes And Sand (16) 96
Baby I Need Your Lovin' (9,11) 3
Baby What You Want Me To Do (2)
Better Life (11)
Blowin' In The Wind (5)
Brass Buttons (12)
Break Up (4)
Brother Where Are You (10)
Brown-Eyed Girl (14)
Brown Eyed Handsome Man (1)
By The Time I Get To Phoenix (8,11)
California Dreamin' (8)
Can I Change My Mind (15)
Can't Buy Me Love (2)
Carpet Man (9)
Cast Your Fate To The Wind (8)
Catch The Wind (5)
City Ways (11)
Come Home America (14)
Crazy Mama (14)
Cupid (3) 76
Curious Mind (Um, Um, Um, Um, Um, Um) (16) 41
Dancin' In The Moonlight (15)
Dang Me (2)
Days Of Wine And Roses (8)
Do What You Gotta' Do (9,11)
Do You Wanna Dance? (8)

Eleventh Song (9)
Enemies And Friends (12)
Every Day I Have To Cry (6)
500 Miles (8)
Fire And Rain (13) 94
Flying Away With You (16)
Foolkiller (6)
For Emily, Whenever I May Find Her (9)
For You (16)
Gettin' Ready For Tomorrow (8)
Glory Train (12)
Going Back To Big Sur (10,11)
Green, Green (5)
Greenback Dollar (4)
He Don't Love You, Like I Love You (3)
Help Me Rhonda (15) 22
Hey Joe (10)
High Heel Sneakers (2)
I Can't Help Myself (Sugar Pie Honey Bunch) (6)
I Should Have Known Better (3)
(I Washed My Hands In) Muddy Water (7) 19
I'll Cry Instead (4)
I'm In Love Again (3)
I've Got A Woman (2)
If I Had A Hammer (5)
If I Were A Carpenter (8)
In The Midnight Hour (6)
Into The Mystic (12) 51

It Wouldn't Happen With Me (1,7)
It'll Never Happen Again (9)
It's All Over Now (3)
It's The Same Old Song (15)
Jailer Bring Me Water (5)
Jesus Is A Soul Man (12)
John Lee Hooker (7)
Johnny B. Goode (2)
Josephine (3)
Keep A-Knockin' (3)
Knock On Wood (14)
La Bamba (medley) (1,7)
Land Of A Thousand Dances (4)
Lawdy Miss Clawdy (1)
Life Is A Game (14)
Long Time Man (5)
Look At The Sun (13)
Look To Your Soul (10,11) 49
Maybelline (2,7) 12
Memphis (1,7,14) 2
Michael (Row The Boat Ashore) (5)
Midnight Special (2,7) 20
Monkey Time (16)
Moody River (3)
Mother And Child Reunion (14)
Mountain Of Love (3,7) 9
Moving To The Country (13)
Mr. Tambourine Man (5)
Muddy River (12) 41

Muddy Water ..see: (I Washed My Hands In)
Multiplication (1)
My New Life (13)
New Lovers and Old Friends (15)
New York City Dues (1)
Ode To John Lee (11)
Oh Lonesome Me (1)
Oh, Pretty Woman (3)
On The Borderline (14)
One Last Dance (For The Melody) (16)
Our Lady Of The Well (13)
Outside Help (16)
Parchman Farm (2)
People Get Ready (13)
Permanent Change (13)
Positively 4th Street (10)
Postcards From Hollywood (15)
Promised Land (3)
Rainy Night In Georgia (12)
Respect (6)
Resurrection (12)
Rhythm Of The Rain (3)
Rock Me On The Water (13)
Rockin' Pneumonia - Boogie Woogie Flu (14) 6
Roll Over Beethoven (2)
Rosecrans Boulevard (9)
Rotation (16)

Run For Your Life (6)
Secret Agent Man (6,7) 3
Seventh Son (4,7) 7
Shadow Of Your Smile (8)
Sidewalk Song (medley) (9)
Silver Threads And Golden Needles (4)
Slim Slo Slider (12)
Snake, The (6)
So Far Away (13)
Softly As I Leave You (8)
Something Strange (10)
Song For Michael (13)
Spare Me A Little (15)
Stagger Lee (4)
Stop! In The Name Of Love (4)
Stories To A Child (14)
Strangers In The Night (8)
Summer Rain (10,11) 14
Susie Q (4)
Swayin' To The Music (Slow Dancin') (16) 10
Sweet Smiling Children (9)
Tall Oak Tree (8)
Taste Of Honey (8)
Think His Name (13) 65
Tom Dooley (5)
Tracks Of My Tears (9,11) 10
Tunesmith (9)
27th Street (medley) (9)
Twist And Shout (medley) (1,7)
U.F.O. (15)

Un-Square Dance (4)
Uptight (Everything's Alright) (6)
Use The Power (14)
Walk Myself On Home (2)
Walkin' The Dog (1)
Way We Live (10)
What Am I Doin' Here With You (3)
What's The Difference (10)
Where Have All The Flowers Gone (5,7) 26
Whisky-A-Go-Go (5)
Whiter Shade Of Pale (10)
Whole Lotta Shakin' Goin' On (2)
Work Song (4)
Wrote A Song For Everyone (12)
You Better Move On (11,15)
You Can Get It If You Really Want (15)
You Can Have Her (I Don't Want Her) (1)
You Dig (6)
You Must Believe (4)
You've Lost That Lovin' Feelin' (6)

RIVIERAS, The '64

Rock group from South Bend, Indiana: Marty Fortson (vocals), Jim Boal and Willie Gout (guitars), Otto Nuss (organ), Doug Gean (bass) and Paul Dennert (drums).

DEBUT	PEAK	WKS			ARTIST — Album Title		$	Label & Number
6/13/64	115	5			Let's Have A Party		$150	U.S.A. 102

California Sun 5
Church Key

Danny Boy
H.B. Goose Step

Keep A Knockin
Killer Joe

Let's Have A Party 99
Little Donna 93

Oh, Boy
Rockin' Robin 96

Twist & Shout
When The Saints

ROACHFORD '89

R&B-rock group formed in England: Andrew Roachford (vocals, keyboards), Hawi Gondwe (guitar), Derrick Taylor (bass) and Chris Taylor (drums).

DEBUT	PEAK	WKS			ARTIST — Album Title		$	Label & Number
5/20/89	109	12		©	Roachford		$10	Epic 45097

Cuddly Toy (Feel For Me) 25
Family Man

Find Me Another Love
Give It Up

Kathleen
Lying Again

No Way
Nobody But You

Shotgun (Crazy World We Live In)
Since

ROAD, The '70

Pop-rock group: brothers Jerry and Phil Hudson (vocals), Ralph Parker (guitar), brothers Jim (organ) and Joe (bass) Hess, and Nick Distefano (drums).

DEBUT	PEAK	WKS			ARTIST — Album Title		$	Label & Number
1/31/70	199	2			The Road		$15	Kama Sutra 2012

Dance To The Music
Grass Looks Greener On The Other Side

I Can Only Give You Everything
In Love
Love Is All

Love-it-is
Mr. Soul
Never Gonna Give You Up

Rock & Roll Woman
See You There
She's Not There

Taste Of Honey

ROB BASE & D.J. E-Z ROCK '88

Rap duo from Harlem, New York: Robert "Rob Base" Ginyard with Rodney "D.J. E-Z Rock" Bryce.

DEBUT	PEAK	WKS	RIAA	CD	ARTIST — Album Title		$	Label & Number
10/8/88	31	81	▲	©	1 It Takes Two		$10	Profile 1267
12/9/89+	50	26	●	©	2 The Incredible Base		$10	Profile 1285

ROB BASE

Ain't Nothing Like The Real Thing (1)
Check This Out (1)
Creativity (1)

Crush (1)
Don't Sleep On It (1)
Dope Mix (2)
Get On The Dance Floor (1)

Get Up And Have A Good Time (2)
Hype It Up (2)
If You Really Want To Party (2)

Incredible Base (2)
It Takes Two (1) 36
Joy And Pain (1) 58
Keep It Going Now (1)

Make It Hot (1)
Outstanding (2)
Rumors (2)
Times Are Gettin' Ill (1)

Turn It Out (Go Base) (2)
War (2)

ROBBINS, Marty '60

Born Martin Robinson on 9/26/25 in Glendale, Arizona. Died of a heart attack on 12/8/82 (age 57). Country singer/songwriter/guitarist. Appeared in the movies *Road To Nashville* and *Guns Of A Stranger*.

1)*Gunfighter Ballads And Trail Songs* 2)*More Gunfighter Ballads And Trail Songs* 3)*Devil Woman*

DEBUT	PEAK	WKS	RIAA	CD	ARTIST — Album Title		$	Label & Number
12/28/59+	6	57	▲	©	1 **Gunfighter Ballads and Trail Songs**		$30	Columbia 1349 / 8158
1/9/61	21	12			2 More Gunfighter Ballads and Trail Songs		$30	Columbia 1481 / 8272
11/3/62+	35	22			3 Devil Woman		$30	Columbia 1918 / 8718
12/2/67	21ˣ	5		©	4 Christmas with Marty Robbins	[X]	$30	Columbia 2735 / 9535
12/14/68	160	7			5 I Walk Alone		$20	Columbia 9725
7/19/69	194	4			6 It's A Sin		$20	Columbia 9811
5/23/70	117	16			7 My Woman, My Woman, My Wife		$15	Columbia 9978
5/8/71	143	10	●		8 Marty Robbins' Greatest Hits, Vol. III	[G]	$15	Columbia 30571
9/18/71	175	6			9 Today		$15	Columbia 30816
1/22/83	170	9	●	©	10 Biggest Hits	[G]	$12	Columbia 38309

ROBBINS, Marty — Cont'd

Ain't Life A Crying Shame (3)
Another Day Has Gone By (9)
Begging To You (5) *74*
Big Iron (1) *26*
Billy The Kid (1)
Can't Help Falling In Love (7)
Chair, The (9)
Christmas Is For Kids (4)
Christmas Kisses (4)
Christmas Prayer (4)
Christmas Time Is Here Again (4)
Completely Out Of Love (10)
Cool Water (1)
Devil Woman (3,8) *16*
Early Morning Sunshine (9)
El Paso (1,10) *1*
Five Brothers (2) *74*
Fresh Out Of Tears (6)

Girl With Gardenias In Her Hair (8)
Hands You're Holding Now (3)
Hark! The Herald Angels Sing (4)
Hello Daily News (6)
Hundred And Sixty Acres (1)
I Can't Help It (If I'm Still In Love With You) (5)
I Can't Say Goodbye (6)
I Feel Another Heartbreak Coming On (5)
I Started Loving You Again (5)
I Walk Alone (5,8) *65*
I'm Beginning To Forget (3)
I'm Not Blaming You (9)
I've Got A Woman's Love (7)
I've Got No Use For The Women (2)
If I Want To (6)

In The Ashes Of An Old Love Affair (3)
In The Valley (1)
It's A Sin (6,8)
Jenny (10)
Jolie Girl (8)
Joy Of Christmas (4)
Kinda Halfway Feel (3)
Last Letter (5)
Late Great Lover (9)
Let Me Live In Your World (5)
Lily Of The Valley (5)
Little Green Valley (1)
Little Joe The Wrangler (2)
Little Rich Girl (3)
Little Stranger (In A Manger) (4)
Love Is A Hurting Thing (3)
Love Is Blue (8)
Love Me Tender (7)
Many Christmases Ago (4)

Maria (If I Could) (7)
Martha Ellen Jenkins (7)
Master's Call (1)
Master's Touch (7)
Merry Christmas To You From Me (4)
My Greatest Memory (10)
My Happy Heart Sings (7)
My Love (2)
My Woman My Woman, My Wife (7,8) *42*
O Little Town Of Bethlehem (4)
Occasional Rose (10)
One Of You (In Every Size) (4)
Padre (8,10)
Prairie Fire (2)
Progressive Love (3)
Put A Little Rainbow In Your Pocket (9)
Quiet Shadows (9)

Rainbows (6)
Ribbon Of Darkness (8,10)
Ride, Cowboy Ride (2)
Running Gun (1)
San Angelo (2)
Seventeen Years (9)
She Thinks I Still Care (5)
She Was Young And She Was Pretty (2)
She's Just A Drifter (10)
Song Of The Bandit (4)
Strawberry Roan (1)
Streets Of Laredo (3)
Teardrops In My Heart (10)
Thanks, But No Thanks, Thanks To You (9)
They'll Never Take Her Love From Me (5)
They're Hanging Me Tonight (1)
This Peaceful Sod (7)

This Song (6)
Three Little Words (7)
Time Can't Make Me Forget (3)
Times Have Changed (6)
Tonight Carmen (8)
Too Many Places (9)
Utah Carol (1)
Very Special Way (7)
We're Getting Mighty Close (6)
When My Turn Comes Around (6)
Windows Have Pains (5)
Wine Flowed Freely (3)
Without You To Love (7)
Worried (3)
You Gave Me A Mountain (6,8,10)
You Say It's Over (9)

ROBBINS, Rockie '80

Born Edward Robbins in Minneapolis. R&B singer.

DEBUT	PEAK	WKS				$	Label & Number
6/7/80	71	16		1	You And Me	$12	A&M 4805
9/12/81	147	6		2	I Believe In Love	$12	A&M 4869

Act Of Love (2)
After Loving You (1)
For The Sake Of A Memory (1)
For You, For Love (2)

Girl I'm Gonna Get Ya (1)
Give Our Love A Chance (2)
Hang Tough (1)
I Believe In Love (2)

I Never Knew (1)
I'll Turn To You (2)
Look Before You Leap (2)
Lost In Love Again (1)

My Old Friend (2)
Nothing Like Love (2)
Point Of View (1)
Talk To Me (2)

Time To Think (2)
Together (1)
You And Me (1) *80*

ROBBS, The '68

Rock group from Oconomowoc, Wisconsin: brothers Dee, Craig, Joe and Bruce Donaldson.

DEBUT	PEAK	WKS				$	Label & Number
1/13/68	200	1			The Robbs	$50	Mercury 61130

Bittersweet
Cynthia Loves

Girls, Girls
In A Funny Sort Of Way

Jolly Miller
Next Time You See Me

Race With The Wind
Rapid Transit

See Jane Run
Violets Of Dawn

ROBERTINO '62

Born Robertino Loreti in 1947 in Italy. Pop singer.

DEBUT	PEAK	WKS				Sym	$	Label & Number
12/1/62	96	6			The Young Italian Singing Sensation	[F]	$25	Kapp 3293

Anema E Core
Buon Anno-Buona Fortuna
Francesina

La Paloma
Lullaby
Luna Rossa

Oh! My Papa (O Mein Papa)

Parlami D'Amore Mariu (Tell Me That You Love Me)
Serenade

Signora Fortuna
Silenzio Cantatore
Torna\

ROBERTSON, Robbie '87

Born Jaime Robbie Robertson on 7/5/44 in Toronto. Rock singer/songwriter/guitarist. Member of **The Band**.

DEBUT	PEAK	WKS	CD			Sym	$	Label & Number
11/14/87	38	34	● ©	1	Robbie Robertson		$10	Geffen 24160
10/19/91	69	10	©	2	Storyville		$10	Geffen 24303
10/22/94	149	5	©	3	Music For The Native Americans	[TV]	$10	Capitol 28295

ROBBIE ROBERTSON & THE RED ROAD ENSEMBLE
from the TNT-TV special *The Native Americans*

| 3/28/98 | 119 | 3 | © | 4 | Contact From The Underworld Of Redboy | | $10 | Capitol 54243 |

Akua Tuta (3)
American Roulette (1)
Ancestor Song (3)
Breakin The Rules (2)
Broken Arrow (1)
Cherokee Morning Song (3)
Code Of Handsome Lake (4)
Coyote Dance (3)

Day Of Reckoning (Burnin For You) (2)
Fallen Angel (1)
Ghost Dance (3)
Go Back To Your Woods (2)
Golden Feather (3)
Hell's Half Acre (1)
Hold Back The Dawn (2)

In The Blood (4)
It Is A Good Day To Die (3)
Lights, The (4)
Mahk Jchi (Heartbeat Drum Song) (3)
Making A Noise (4)
Night Parade (2)
Peyote Healing (4)

Rattlebone (4)
Resurrection (2)
Sacrifice (4)
Shake This Town (2)
Showdown At Big Sky (1)
Sign Of The Rainbow (2)
Skinwalker (3)
Soap Box Preacher (2)

Somewhere Down The Crazy River (1)
Sonny Got Caught In The Moonlight (1)
Sound Is Fading (4)
Stomp Dance (Unity) (4)
Sweet Fire Of Love (1)
Take Your Partner By The Hand (4)

Testimony (1)
Twisted Hair (3)
Unbound (4)
Vanishing Breed (3)
What About Now (2)
Words Of Fire, Deeds Of Blood (3)

ROBIN S '93

Born Robin Stone in Queens, New York. Female dance singer.

DEBUT	PEAK	WKS	CD				$	Label & Number
7/24/93	110	15	©		Show Me Love		$10	Big Beat 82509

Back And Forth
Back It Up
Brighter Day

I Want To Thank You
I'm Gonna Love You Right [Tonight]
My Kind Of Man

If We Could Just Be Friends
Love For Love *53*
Show Me Love *5*
What I Do Best

Once In A Lifetime Love
Show Me Love *5*
Who's Gonna Raise The Child

When You Find Love

ROBINSON, Freddy '70

Born on 2/24/39 in Memphis. Blues guitarist.

DEBUT	PEAK	WKS				Sym	$	Label & Number
9/19/70	133	7			The Coming Atlantis	[I]	$20	Pacific Jazz 20162

Before Six
Black Fox *56*

Coming Atlantis
Freddy's Sermon

(I'm A) Fool For You
Monkin' Around

Oogum Boogum Song
Rita

ROBINSON, Smokey ★184★ '80

Born William Robinson on 2/19/40 in Detroit. R&B singer/prolific songwriter. Lead singer of **The Miracles**. Married to Claudette Rogers (also with The Miracles) from 1958-86. Vice president of Motown Records (1985-88). Inducted into the Rock and Roll Hall of Fame in 1987. Won Grammy's Living Legends Award in 1989.

1)Being With You 2)Warm Thoughts 3)Where There's Smoke..

DEBUT	PEAK	WKS	CD				$	Label & Number
7/14/73	70	19	©	1	Smokey		$12	Tamla 328
4/13/74	99	17	©	2	Pure Smokey		$12	Tamla 331
4/19/75	36	42	©	3	A Quiet Storm		$12	Tamla 337
3/6/76	57	15		4	Smokey's Family Robinson		$12	Tamla 341
2/19/77	47	14		5	Deep In My Soul		$12	Tamla 350
4/15/78	75	19		6	Love Breeze		$12	Tamla 359

ROBINSON, Smokey — Cont'd

DEBUT	PEAK	WKS	CD	#	Album Title	Sym	$	Label & Number
1/20/79	165	6		7	Smokin'	[L]	$15	Tamla 363 [2]
6/30/79+	17	47	©	8	Where There's Smoke..		$12	Tamla 366
3/15/80	14	21		9	Warm Thoughts		$12	Tamla 367
3/14/81	10	28	● ©	10	Being With You		$12	Tamla 375
2/20/82	33	17		11	Yes It's You Lady		$10	Tamla 6001
1/29/83	50	17		12	Touch The Sky		$10	Tamla 6030
9/3/83	124	7	©	13	Blame It On Love & All The Great Hits	[G]	$10	Tamla 6064
6/30/84	141	11		14	Essar		$10	Tamla 6098
2/15/86	104	13	©	15	Smoke Signals		$10	Tamla 6156
3/28/87	26	58	● ©	16	One Heartbeat		$10	Motown 6226
3/17/90	112	11	©	17	Love, Smokey		$10	Motown 6268
10/16/99	134	3	©	18	Intimate		$10	Motown 153741

Agony And The Ecstasy (3,7) **36**
All My Life's A Lie (12)
All Of Mine (18)
And I Don't Love You (14)
Are You Still Here (11)
As You Do (10)
Asleep On My Love (2)
Baby Come Close (1,7,13) **27**
Baby That's Backatcha (3,7) **26**
Bad Girl (medley) (7)
Be Kind To The Growing Mind (15)
Because Of You (It's The Best It's Ever Been) (15)
Being With You (10,13) **2**
Blame It On Love (13) **48**
Bottom Line (18)
Can't Fight Love (10)
Castles Made Of Sand (4)
Close Encounters Of The First Kind (14)
Coincidentally (3)
Come To Me Soon (17)
Cruisin' (8,13) **4**
Daylight And Darkness (6,7) **75**
Destiny (11)
Do Like I Do (4)
Don't Play Another Love Song (13)

Don't Wanna Be Just Physical (17)
Driving Thru Life In The Fast Lane (14)
Dynamite (12)
Easy (17)
Easy To Love (18)
Even Tho' (12)
Ever Had A Dream (8)
Everything You Touch (17)
Family Song (1)
Feeling You, Feeling Me (6)
Feelings Flowing (18)
Food For Thought (10)
Fulfill Your Need (2)
Get Out Of Town (4)
Get Ready (8)
Gimme What You Want (12)
Girl I'm Standing There (14)
Gone Again (12)
Gone Forever (12)
Hanging On By A Thread (15)
Happy (Love Theme From Lady Sings The Blues) (3)
Heavy On Pride (Light On Love) (9)
Here I Go Again (7)
Hold On To Your Love (15)
Holly (1)
Humming Song (Lost For Words) (5)
Hurt's On You (8)

I Am I Am (2) **56**
I Can't Find (14,17)
I Hear The Children Singing (10)
I Love The Nearness Of You (8)
I Second That Emotion (7)
I Want To Be Your Love (10)
I'll Try Something New (11)
I'm Loving You Softly (4)
I'm The One (18)
I've Made Love To You A Thousand Times (12)
If You Wanna Make Love (Come 'Round Here) (10,13)
If You Want My Love (5)
In My Corner (5)
International Baby (11)
Intimate (18)
Into Each Rain Some Life Must Fall (9)
It's A Good Night (8)
It's Been A Long Time (Since I Been In Love) (5)
It's Her Turn To Live (2) **82**
It's The Same Old Love (17)
It's Time To Stop Shoppin' Around (16)
Jasmin (17)
Just A Touch Away (13)
Just Another Kiss (17)
Just Let Me Love You (18)
Just Like You (13)

Just My Soul Responding (1)
Just Passing Through (2)
Just To See Her (16) **8**
Keep Me (16)
Let Me Be The Clock (9,13) **31**
Let's Do The Dance Of Life Together (5)
Like Nobody Can (4)
Little Girl Little Girl (14)
Love Between Me And My Kids (2)
Love Brought Us Here Tonight (16)
Love Don't Give No Reason (16)
Love Is The Light (17)
Love Letters (3)
Love Love Again (18)
Love 'N Life (17)
Love So Fine (6,7)
Madam X (6,7)
Melody Man (9)
Merry-Go-Ride (17)
Mickey's Monkey (7)
Never Can Say Goodbye (medley) (1)
Never My Love (medley) (1)
No Time To Stop Believing (15)
Old Fashioned Love (11) **60**
One Heartbeat (16) **10**
Only Game In Town (11)
Ooo Baby Baby (7)

Open (4) **81**
Photograph In My Mind (15)
Quiet Storm (3,7) **61**
Ready To Roll (18)
Sad Time (12)
Share It (8)
She's Only A Baby Herself (2)
Shoe Soul (6,7)
Silent Partner In A Three-Way Love Affair (1)
Sleepin' In (18)
Sleepless Nights (15)
So In Love (4)
Some People (Will Do Anything For Love) (15)
Sweet Harmony (1) **48**
Take Me Through The Night (17)
Tattoo, A (2)
Te Quiero Como Si No Hubiera Un Manana (I'm Gonna Love You Like There's No Tomorrow) (15)
Tears Of A Clown (7)
Tell Me Tomorrow - Part I (11,13) **33**
There Will Come A Day (I'm Gonna Happen To You) (5) **42**
Touch The Sky (12)
Tracks Of My Tears (7)
Train Of Thought (14)

Travelin' Through (9)
Trying It Again (6)
Tu Me Besas Muy Rico (18)
Unless You Do It Again (17)
Virgin Man (2) **56**
Vitamin U (5,7)
Wanna Know My Mind (1)
Wedding Song (3)
What's In Your Life For Me (9)
What's Too Much (16) **79**
When You Came (4)
Who's Sad (17)
Why Are You Running From My Love (14)
Why Do Happy Memories Hurt So Bad (16)
Why You Wanna See My Bad Side (6,7)
Will You Love Me Tomorrow? (1)
Wine, Women And Song (9)
Wishful Thinking (15)
Yes It's You Lady (11)
You Are Forever (10) **59**
(You Can) Depend On Me (medley) (1)
You Cannot Laugh Alone (5)
You Don't Know What It's Like (16)
You Made Me Feel Love (17)
You've Really Got A Hold On Me (7)

ROBINSON, Tom, Band   '78
Born on 6/1/50 in Cambridge, England. Rock singer/bassist. His band: Danny Kustow (guitar), Mark Ambler (organ) and Dolphin Taylor (drums).

DEBUT	PEAK	WKS	CD	#	Album Title	$	Label & Number
7/15/78	144	8	©	1	Power In The Darkness	$15	Harvest 11778 [2]
5/12/79	163	7	©	2	TRB Two	$12	Harvest 11930

produced by **Todd Rundgren**

Ain't Gonna Take It (1)
All Right All Night (2)
Better Decide Which Side You're On (1)
Black Angel (2)
Blue Murder (2)

Bully For You (2)
Crossing Over The Road (2)
Days Of Rage (2)
Don't Take No For An Answer (1)
Glad To Be Gay (1)

Grey Cortina (1)
Hold Out (2)
I Shall Be Released (1)
I'm Alright Jack (1)
Law & Order (2)
Let My People Be (2)

Long Hot Summer (1)
Man You Never Saw (1)
Martin (1)
Power In The Darkness (2)
Right On Sister (1)
Sorry Mr. Harris (2)

Too Good To Be True (1)
2-4-6-8 Motorway (1)
Up Against The Wall (2)
Why Should I Mind (2)
Winter Of '79 (1)
You Gotta Survive (1)

ROBINSON, Vicki Sue   '76
Born on 5/31/54 in Philadelphia. Died of cancer on 4/27/2000 (age 45). Disco singer. Appeared in the original Broadway productions of *Hair* and *Jesus Christ Superstar*.

DEBUT	PEAK	WKS	#	Album Title	$	Label & Number
4/10/76	49	39	1	Never Gonna Let You Go	$12	RCA Victor 1256
10/23/76	45	16	2	Vicki Sue Robinson	$12	RCA Victor 1829
2/11/78	110	9	3	Half And Half	$12	RCA Victor 2294

Act Of Mercy (1)
After All This Time (2)
Can't Find No Love (2)
Common Thief (1)
Daylight (2) **63**

Don't Try To Win Me Back Again (3)
Falling In Love (2)
Feels So Good It Must Be Wrong (3)

Freeway Song (3)
Half And Half (3)
How About Me (2)
I Won't Let You Go (medley) (2)

Jealousy (3)
Lack Of Respect (3)
Let Me Down Easy (2)
Never Gonna Let You Go (1)
Should I Stay (medley) (2)

Something Like A Dream (2)
Trust In Me (3)
Turn The Beat Around (1) **10**
We Can Do Almost Anything (1)
We Found Each Other (3)

When You're Lovin' Me (1)
Wonderland Of Love (1)

ROBINSON, Wanda   '71
Born on 11/18/49 in Baltimore. Black poetess.

DEBUT	PEAK	WKS	#	Album Title	Sym	$	Label & Number
10/16/71+	186	13		Black Ivory	[T]	$15	Perception 18

Black Oriented Love Poem
Celebration
Compromise

Final Hour
First Time I Saw Loneliness
Good Things Come

Great American Passtime
Grooving
Instant Replay

John Harvey's Blues
Meeting Place
Parting Is Such

Read St. Festival
Tragedy No. 456
Trouble With Dreams

Word To The Wise

ROBYN   '98
Born Robyn Carlsson on 6/12/79 in Stockholm, Sweden. Female dance singer.

DEBUT	PEAK	WKS	RIAA	CD	Album Title	$	Label & Number
7/12/97+	57	54	▲	©	Robyn Is Here	$10	RCA 67477

Bumpy Ride
Do You Know (What It Takes) **7**

Do You Really Want Me (Show Respect)
Don't Want You Back

Here We Go
How
I Wish

In My Heart
Just Another Girlfriend
Last Time

Robyn Is Here
Show Me Love **7**
You've Got That Somethin'

ROCHES, The   '79
Vocal trio from New York City: sisters Maggie, Suzzy and Terre Roche. Suzzy was briefly married to **Loudon Wainwright III** in the 1980s.

DEBUT	PEAK	WKS	CD	#	Album Title	$	Label & Number
6/16/79	58	11	©	1	The Roches	$12	Warner 3298
11/22/80	130	7	©	2	Nurds	$12	Warner 3475
11/13/82	183	3	©	3	Keep On Doing	$12	Warner 23735

ROCHES, The — Cont'd

Boat Family (2)	Hammond Song (1)	Largest Elizabeth In The World (3)	Nurds (2)	Scorpion Lament (3)	We (1)
Bobby's Song (2)	I Fell In Love (3)	Losing True (3)	On The Road To Fairfax County (3)	Sex Is For Children (3)	
Damned Old Dog (1)	It's Bad For Me (2)	Louis (2)	One Season (2)	Steady With The Maestro (3)	
Death Of Suzzy Roche (2)	Jerks On The Loose (medley) (3)	Married Men (1)	Pretty And High (1)	This Feminine Position (2)	
Factory Girl (2)	Keep On Doing What You Do (medley) (3)	Mr. Sellack (1)	Quitting Time (1)	Train, The (1)	
Hallelujah Chorus (3)		My Sick Mind (2)	Runs In The Family (1)	Troubles, The (1)	
				Want Not Want Not (3)	

ROCK, Chris   '99

Born on 2/7/66 in Andrews, South Carolina; raised in Brooklyn, New York. Actor/comedian. Regular on TV's *Saturday Night Live* from 1989-91. Acted in several movies.

| 4/26/97 | 93 | 7 | © | 1 Roll With The New | [C] | $10 | DreamWorks 50008 |
| 7/31/99 | 44 | 12 | © | 2 Bigger & Blacker | [C] | $10 | DreamWorks 50055 |

Another Face Song (1)	Crazy White Kids (2)	Luther Campbell (1)	NYPD (2)	Porno PSA (2)	Table Dance (2)
Bad Phone Sex (1)	Crickets (1)	Marion Barry (1)	Nerd & Fly Girl (2)	Press Conference (1)	Taxes (1)
Black Mall (2)	I Loved The Show (1)	Me & ODB (2)	Niggas Vs. Black People (1)	Race (2)	This Show Sucks #1-3 (1)
Champagne (1)	I'm Back (1)	Million Man March (1)	No Sex (2)	Roger & Zapp (2)	Tossed Salad (1)
Cheap Pete (1)	Insurance (2)	Monica Interview (2)	O.J. & O'Jays (1)	Savion Glover (2)	Two Women (2)
Commitment Dilemma (1)	Introducing Mary Wong (1)	My Favorite Joke (1)	O.J., I Understand (1)	Snow Flake (2)	Women (2)

ROCK, Pete, & C.L. Smooth   '98

Rap duo from Mt. Vernon, New York.

6/27/92	43	15	©	1 Mecca And The Soul Brother	$10	Elektra 60948
11/26/94	51	4	©	2 The Main Ingredient	$10	Elektra 61661
11/28/98	39	4	©	3 Soul Survivor	$10	Loud 67616

PETE ROCK

Act Like You Know (1)	For Pete's Sake (1)	In The House (2)	On And On (1)	Straighten It Out (1)	Truly Yours '98 (3)
All The Places (1)	Game, Tha (3)	It's About That Time (3)	One Life To Life (3)	Strange Fruit (3)	Verbal Murder 2 (3)
Anger In The Nation (1)	Get On The Mic (2)	It's Like That (1)	Respect Mine (3)	Sun Won't Come Out (2)	Wig Out (1)
Basement, The (1)	Ghettos Of The Mind (1)	It's On You (2)	Return Of The Mecca (1)	Take You There (3) 76	Worldwide (2)
Can't Front On Me (1)	Half Man Half Amazin' (3)	Lots Of Lovin (1)	Rock Steady Part II (3)	Take Your Time (3)	
Carmel City (2)	I Get Physical (2)	Main Ingredient (2)	Searching (2)	Tell Me (2)	
Check It Out (2)	I Got A Love (2)	Massive (Hold Tight) (2)	Skinz (1)	They Reminisce Over You (T.R.O.Y.) (1) 58	
Da Two (3)	If It Ain't Rough, It Ain't Right (1)	Mind Blowin' (3)	Soul Brother #1 (1)	Tru Master (3)	
Escape (2)	In The Flesh (2)	#1 Soul Brother (3)	Soul Survivor (3)		

ROCK AND HYDE   '87

Pop-rock duo from Vancouver: Paul Hyde (vocals) and Bob Rock (guitar, keyboards). Both formerly with **Paul Hyde & The Payolas**.

| 5/2/87 | 94 | 15 | © | Under The Volcano | $10 | Capitol 12569 |

Blind, The Deaf And The Lame (1)	I Will	Knocking On Closed Doors (1)	Oh Ruby	There's Always Someone	What Children Say
Dirty Water 61	It's Always Raining	Middle Of The Night	Talk To Me	Tougher	

ROCKETS   '79

Rock group from Detroit: David Gilbert (vocals), Jim McCarty and Dennis Robbins (guitars), Donnie Backus (keyboards), Bobby Neil Haralson (bass) and John Badanjek (drums). McCarty and Badanjek were members of **Mitch Ryder & The Detroit Wheels**. Gilbert died of cancer on 8/1/2001 (age 49).

4/14/79	56	26		1 Rockets	$12	RSO 3047
2/2/80	53	15		2 No Ballads	$12	RSO 3071
8/8/81	165	5		3 Back Talk	$12	Elektra 351

American Dreams (3)	I Can't Get Satisfied (3)	Lift You Up (3)	Lucille (1)	Something Ain't Right (1)
Back Talk (3)	I Want You To Love Me (2)	Long Long Gone (1)	Oh Well (1) 30	Takin' It Back (2)
Can't Sleep (1) 51	I'll Be Your Lover (3)	Lost Forever - Left For Dreaming (1)	Restless (2)	Time After Time (2)
Desire (2) 70	Is It True (2)	Love For Hire (3)	Sad Songs (2)	Tired Of Wearing Black (3)
Don't Hold On (2)	Jealous (3)	Love Me Once Again (1)	Sally Can't Dance (2)	Troublemaker (3)
Feel Alright (1)	Lie To Me (3)		Shanghaied (3)	Turn Up The Radio (1)

ROCKIN' REBELS   '63

Instrumental group from Buffalo, New York: Lee Carroll (guitar), Eddy Jay (saxophone), Kenny Mills (bass) and Tony DiMaria (drums).

| 3/23/63 | 53 | 19 | | Wild Weekend | [I] | $200 | Swan 509 |

Honky Tonk	Ram-Bunk-Shus	Rumble	Sweet Little Sixteen	Tequila	Wild Rebel
Hully Gully Rock	**Rockin' Crickets** 57	Stripper, The	Telstar	Whole Lotta Shakin' Goin On	**Wild Weekend** 8

ROCKIN' SIDNEY   '85

Born Sidney Semien on 4/9/38 in Lebeau, Louisiana. Died of cancer on 2/25/98 (age 59). Zydeco singer/musician.

| 8/24/85 | 166 | 4 | | My Toot-Toot | [M] | $10 | Epic 40153 |

Dance And Show Off	Joe Pete Is In The Bed	My Toot-Toot	My Zydeco Shoes

ROCKPILE   '80

Pop-rock group formed in London: **Dave Edmunds** (vocals, guitar), **Nick Lowe** (vocals, bass), Billy Bremner (guitar) and Terry Williams (drums).

| 11/15/80 | 27 | 19 | © | Seconds Of Pleasure | $15 | Columbia 36886 |

includes a 4 song EP record

Crying In The Rain	Knife And A Fork	Play That Fast Thing (One More Time)	**Teacher Teacher** 51	You Ain't Nothin' But Fine
Fool Too Long	Now And Always	Poor Jenny	When I Write The Book	
Heart	Oh What A Thrill	Take A Message To Mary	When Will I Be Loved	
If Sugar Was As Sweet As You	Pet You And Hold You		Wrong Again (Let's Face It)	

ROCKWELL   '84

Born Kennedy Gordy on 3/15/64 in Detroit. R&B singer. Son of Motown chairman Berry Gordy.

| 2/11/84 | 15 | 30 | ● | 1 Somebody's Watching Me | $10 | Motown 6052 |
| 2/23/85 | 120 | 9 | | 2 Captured | $10 | Motown 6122 |

Captured (By An Evil Mind) (1)	Don't Make You Cry (2)	Knife (1)	Runaway (1)	T.V. Psychology (2)	Wasting Away (1)
Change Your Ways (1)	Foreign Country (1)	**Obscene Phone Caller** (1) 35	**Somebody's Watching Me** (1) 2	Taxman (1)	We Live In A Jungle (2)
Costa Rica (2)	He's A Cobra (2)	Peeping Tom (2)		Tokyo (2)	

RODGERS, Jimmie — '57

Born on 9/18/33 in Camas, Washington. Pop singer/guitarist/pianist. Hosted own TV variety series in 1959. Career hampered following mysterious assault on the San Diego Freeway on 12/1/67, which left him with a fractured skull. Returned to performing a year later. Starred in movies *The Little Shepherd of Kingdom Come* and *Back Door To Hell*. Not to be confused with the country music pioneer of the same name.

DEBUT	PEAK	WKS				$	Label & Number
12/16/57	15	3			1 Jimmie Rodgers		$50	Roulette 25020
7/30/66	145	4			2 It's Over		$25	Dot 25717
1/6/68	162	4			3 Child Of Clay		$20	A&M 4130
8/30/69	183	4			4 Windmills Of Your Mind		$20	A&M 4187

Ballad Of Black Gold (1) · Better Loved You'll Never Be (1) · Both Sides Now (4) · **Child Of Clay** (3) *31* · Cycles (4) · Girl In The Wood (4) · Good Times Are Gone (4) · Grass Is Greener (2) · Hey Little Baby (1) · **Honeycomb** (1) *1* · How Do You Say Goodbye (4) · I Believed It All (3) · I Keep Thinking (You'll Come Back To Me) (2) · I Wanna Be Free (3) · I'll Never Fall In Love Again (3) · I'll Say Goodbye (3) · I'm Just A Country Boy (1) · If I Were The Man (3) · **It's Over** (2) *37* · **Kisses Sweeter Than Wine** (1) *3* · L.A. Breakdown (And Let Me In) (4) · La-De-Da (2) · Land Of Milk And Honey (2) · Let's Go Away (2) · Let's Stay Together (2) · Little Boy Born (2) · Lonely Tears (2) · Lovers, The (3) · Mating Call (1) · Me About You (4) · Morning Means Tomorrow (2) · My Love Is A Wanderer (3) · Preacher, The (1) · Scarlet Ribbons (For Her Hair) (1) · Sloop John B (2) · Suzanne (4) · Time (2) · Today (3) · Try To Remember (3) · Turnaround (3) · Water Boy (1) · Windmills Of Your Mind (4) · Windows Of The World (4) · Woman From Liberia (1) · You Pass Me By (3)

RODGERS, Paul — '93

Born on 12/17/49 in Middlesbrough, Cleveland, England. Lead singer of **Free** (1969-73), **Bad Company** (1974-82), **The Firm** (1984-86) and **The Law** (1991).

DEBUT	PEAK	WKS		CD		$	Label & Number
11/26/83+	135	10		©	1 Cut Loose		$10	Atlantic 80121
5/8/93	91	7		©	2 Muddy Water Blues - A Tribute To Muddy Waters		$10	Victory 480013

Boogie Mama (1) · Born Under A Bad Sign (2) · Cut Loose (1) · Fragile (1) · Good Morning Little School Girl (Part 1 & 2) (2) · Hunter, The (2) · I Can't Be Satisfied (2) · I Just Want To Make Love To You (2) · I'm Ready (2) · I'm Your Hoochie Coochie Man (2) · Live In Peace (1) · Louisiana Blues (2) · Morning After The Night Before (1) · Muddy Water Blues (2) · Northwinds (1) · Rising Sun (1) · Rollin' Stone (1) · She Moves Me (2) · She's Alright (2) · Standing Around Crying (2) · Superstar Woman (1) · Sweet Sensation (1) · Talking Guitar Blues (1)

RODNEY O & JOE COOLEY — '90

Rap trio from Los Angeles: Rodney Oliver, Joe Cooley and Jeff Page.

DEBUT	PEAK	WKS		CD		$	Label & Number
3/4/89	187	2		©	1 Me And Joe		$10	Egyptian Empire 00777
3/31/90	128	9		©	2 Three The Hard Way		$10	Atlantic 82082

Beat Blaster (2) · Can U Back It Up (2) · Cooley High (1) · DJ's & MC's Part II (2) · Down Goes Another (2) · Everlasting Bass (1) · Fun, Fun, Fun (2) · Give Me The Mic (1) · Hocus Pocus (2) · It's My Rope (1) · Let's Have Some Fun (1) · Me And Joe (1) · Nobody Disses Me (1) · Once Again (2) · Party (1) · Say It Loud (1) · See Ya... (2) · Supercuts (1) · This Is For The Homies (1) · Three The Hard Way (2) · We're Gonna Kick It Once (2) · We've Arrived (Oh! But Yes) (1) · When He Plays (2) · When The Beats Come In (2)

RODRIGUEZ, Johnny — '73

Born on 12/10/51 in Sabinal, Texas. Country singer/songwriter/guitarist.

DEBUT	PEAK	WKS				$	Label & Number
4/7/73	156	14			1 Introducing Johnny Rodriguez		$15	Mercury 61378
10/27/73	174	4			2 All I Ever Meant To Do Was Sing		$15	Mercury 686

All I Ever Meant To Do Was Love You (2) · Answer To Your Letter (1) · Easy Come Easy Go (1) · Good Lord Knows I Tried (2) · I Really Don't Want To Know (2) · I Wonder Where You Are Tonight (1) · I'll Just Have To Learn To Stay Away From You (2) · Jealous Darlin' (1) · Jealous Heart (1) · Jimmy Was A Drinkin' Kind Of Man (2) · Leavin' Somethin' Left To Do (1) · Love Ain't Such An Easy Thing To Find (2) · Love And Honor (2) · Music City Band (2) · One More Chance To Be With You (1) · Pass Me By (If You're Only Passing Through) (1) · Release Me (2) · **Ridin' My Thumb To Mexico** (2) *70* · That's The Way Love Goes (2) · We Had A Good Time Trying (1) · **You Always Come Back (To Hurting Me)** (1) *86* · You Go Around (1)

RODRIGUEZ, Jose Luis — '98

Born in Mexico. Latin singer/songwriter.

DEBUT	PEAK	WKS		CD		Sym	$	Label & Number
2/28/98	175	1	●	©	Inolvidable	[F]	$10	Sony 82635

title is Spanish for "Unforgettable"

Amorcito Corazon · Caminemos · Camino Verde · Contigo · Esta Cobardia · La Hiedra · Mar Y Cielo · No Me Quieras Tanto · Perdon · Poquita Fe · Rayito De Luna · Si Tu Me Dices Ven · Sin Un Amor · Toda Una Vida · Un Siglo De Ausencia

ROE, Tommy — '69

Born on 5/9/42 in Atlanta. Pop-rock singer/songwriter/guitarist.

DEBUT	PEAK	WKS				Sym	$	Label & Number
11/10/62	110	3			1 Sheila			$50	ABC-Paramount 432
11/5/66+	94	13			2 Sweet Pea	[K]		$40	ABC-Paramount 575
4/22/67	159	3			3 It's Now Winters Day			$25	ABC 594
4/12/69	25	18			4 Dizzy			$25	ABC 683
12/27/69+	21	29			5 12 In A Roe/A Collection Of Tommy Roe's Greatest Hits	[G]		$25	ABC 700
10/31/70	134	6			6 We Can Make Music			$20	ABC 714

Aggravation (3) · Blue Ghost (1) · Brush A Little Sunshine And Love (6) · **Carol** (5) *61* · Cinnamon (4) · Cry On Crying Eyes (3) · **Dizzy** (4,5) *1* · Dollar's Worth Of Pennies (4) · Evergreen (6) · **Everybody** (2,5) *3* · Firefly (6) · **Folk Singer** (2,5) *84* · Golden Girl (3) · Gotta Keep Rolling Along (4) · Greatest Love (6) · Have Pity On Me (3) · Heart Beat (1) · **Heather Honey** (4,5) *29* · **Hooray For Hazel** (2,5) *6* · I Found A Love (4) · **It's Now Winters Day** (3,5) *23* · **Jack And Jill** (5) *53* · **Jam Up Jelly Tight** (5) *8* · Kick Me Charlie (2) · King Of Fools (6) · Leave Her (3) · Little Hollywood Girl (1) · Long Live Love (3) · Look At Me (1) · Look Out Girl (4) · Makin' Music (4) · Maybellene (1) · Misty Eyes (3) · Money Is My Pay (4) · Moon Talk (3) · Nightime (3) · No Sad Songs (6) · **Party Girl** (2,5) *85* · Pearl (6) *50* · Piddle De Pat (1) · Pleasing You Pleases Me (2) · Pretty Flamingo (2) · Proud Mary (4) · Raining In My Heart (4) · **Sheila** (1,2,5) *1* · **Sing Along With Me** (3) *91* · **Stir It Up And Serve It** (6) *50* · Stormy (4) · **Susie Darlin'** (1) *35* · **Sweet Pea** (2,5) *8* · Sweet Sounds (3) · There Will Be Better Years (1) · There's A Great Day A Coming (1) · (They Long To Be) Close To You (6) · Think About The Good Things (1) · Traffic Jam (6) · Under My Thumb (2) · **We Can Make Music** (6) *49* · Where Were You When I Needed You (2) · Wild Thing (2)

ROGER — '81

Born Roger Troutman on 11/29/51 in Hamilton, Ohio. Shot to death by his brother Larry in a murder-suicide on 4/25/99 (age 47). R&B singer/songwriter/guitarist. Leader of the family funk group **Zapp**.

DEBUT	PEAK	WKS	RIAA	CD		Catalog	Sym	$	Label & Number
10/3/81	26	25	●		1 The Many Facets Of Roger			$12	Warner 3594
6/2/84	64	14			2 The Saga Continues...			$12	Warner 23975
11/28/87+	35	24	●	©	3 Unlimited!			$10	Reprise 25496
11/13/93	39	29	▲	©	4 All The Greatest Hits	C:#26/1	[G]	$10	Reprise 45143

ZAPP & ROGER

Be Alright (4) · Been This Way Before (3) · Blue (A Tribute To The Blues) (1) · Break Song (2) · Bucket Of Blood (2) · Chunk Of Sugar (1) · Composition To Commemorate (May 30, 1918) (3) · Computer Love (4) · Curiosity '93 (4)

ROGER — Cont'd

Dance Floor (4)
Do It Roger (1,4)
Doo Wa Ditty (Blow That Thing) (4)
Girl, Cut It Out (2)

Heartbreaker (Part I, Part II) (4)
I Can Make You Dance (4)
I Heard It Through The Grapevine (Part 1) (1,4) **79**
I Keep Trying (2)

I Really Want To Be Your Man (3)
I Want To Be Your Man (3,4) **3**
If You're Serious (3)
In The Mix (2,4)

Maxx Axe (1)
Mega Medley (4) **54**
Midnight Hour (2,4)
More Bounce To The Ounce - Part I (4) **86**
Night And Day (3,4)

Papa's Got A Brand New Bag (3)
Play Your Guitar, Brother Roger (2)
Private Lover (3)
Slow And Easy (4) **43**

So Ruff, So Tuff (1,4)
TC Song (2)
Tender Moments (3)
Thrill Seekers (3)

ROGERS, D.J.   '76

Born DeWayne Julius Rogers in Los Angeles. R&B singer/songwriter/keyboardist.

| 9/18/76 | 175 | 5 | | | On The Road Again | | | $12 | RCA Victor 1697 |

Girl I Love You
Holding On To Love

Let My Life Shine (Part I & II)
Love Can Be Found

On The Road Again
One More Day

Only While It Lasts
Say You Love Me **98**

Secret Lady

ROGERS, Eric, & His Orchestra   '61

Born on 9/25/21 in Halifax, Yorkshire, England. Died in 1978 (age 57). Conductor/arranger.

| 12/4/61 | 37 | 8 | | | 1 The Percussive Twenties | | [I] | $20 | London Phase 4 44006 |
| 11/12/66 | 114 | 3 | | | 2 Vaudeville! | | | $20 | London Phase 4 44083 |

Ain't She Sweet (1)
Birth Of The Blues (1,2)
Black Bottom (1)
Charleston (1)

Chicago (1)
Coast-To-Coast Medley (2)
Fascinating Rhythm (1)
Finale Medley (2)

Hearts And Flowers (2)
Light Cavalry (1)
Me And My Shadow (1)
Minstrels Medley (2)

Mooners Medley (2)
She's Funny That Way (1)
Sing Along Medley (2)
Swan, The (2)

Tea For Two (1)
Tiger Rag (1)
Tillies From Tucson Medley (2)
Whispering (1)

Who? (1)
Ziegfield Medley (2)

ROGERS, Kenny/First Edition   ★33★   '80

Born on 8/21/38 in Houston. Country singer/songwriter/guitarist/actor. Member of **The New Christy Minstrels**. Formed and fronted **The First Edition** in 1967. Original lineup included Thelma Camacho, Mike Settle, Terry Williams and Mickey Jones. All but Jones were members of The New Christy Minstrels. Group hosted own syndicated TV variety show *Rollin* in 1972. Rogers split from group in 1973. Starred in movie *Six Pack* and several TV movies. Married to actress Marianne Gordon from 1977-93. Later started the Kenny Rogers Roasters restaurant chain.

1)Kenny Rogers' Greatest Hits 2)Kenny 3)Eyes That See In The Dark 4)Share Your Love 5)The Gambler

THE FIRST EDITION:

| 1/13/68 | 118 | 15 | | | 1 The First Edition | | | $25 | Reprise 6276 |
| 3/22/69 | 164 | 4 | | | 2 The First Edition 69 | | | $25 | Reprise 6328 |

KENNY ROGERS & THE FIRST EDITION:

10/11/69	48	18			3 Ruby, Don't Take Your Love To Town			$20	Reprise 6352
4/18/70	26	24			4 Something's Burning			$20	Reprise 6385
10/31/70	61	16			5 Tell It All Brother			$20	Reprise 6412
2/20/71	57	16	▲		6 Greatest Hits		[G]	$20	Reprise 6437
9/25/71	155	3			7 Transition			$20	Reprise 2039
2/5/72	118	14			8 The Ballad Of Calico			$25	Reprise 6476 [2]

KENNY ROGERS:

5/7/77	30	25	▲	©	9 Kenny Rogers			$12	United Artists 689
8/20/77	39	21	▲	©	10 Daytime Friends			$12	United Artists 754
2/4/78	33	103	▲⁴	©	11 Ten Years Of Gold		[G]	$12	United Artists 835
7/29/78	53	12	●		12 Love Or Something Like It			$12	United Artists 903
12/16/78+	12	112	▲⁵	©	13 The Gambler			$12	United Artists 934
4/14/79	82	23	▲		14 Classics			$12	United Artists 946

KENNY ROGERS & DOTTIE WEST

| 9/29/79+ | 5 | 53 | ▲³ | © | 15 Kenny | | | $12 | United Artists 979 |
| 1/5/80 | 186 | 3 | ● | | 16 Every Time Two Fools Collide | | | $12 | United Artists 864 |

KENNY ROGERS & DOTTIE WEST

4/12/80	12	34	▲	©	17 Gideon			$12	United Artists 1035
10/18/80	❶²	181	▲¹²	©	18 Kenny Rogers' Greatest Hits		[G]	$10	Liberty 1072
7/11/81	6	50	▲	©	19 Share Your Love			$10	Liberty 1108

produced by **Lionel Richie**

| 11/21/81+ | 34 | 9 | ▲² | © | 20 Christmas | | [X] | $10 | Liberty 51115 |

Christmas charts: 1/'83, 3/'84, 27/'88

7/24/82	34	24	▲	©	21 Love Will Turn You Around			$10	Liberty 51124
12/25/82+	149	4		©	22 Christmas		[X-R]	$10	Liberty 51115
3/12/83	18	27	▲	©	23 We've Got Tonight			$10	Liberty 51143
9/24/83	6	38	▲²	©	24 Eyes That See In The Dark			$10	RCA Victor 4697

produced by **Barry Gibb**

11/12/83+	22	30	▲⁴	©	25 Twenty Greatest Hits	C:#31/2	[G]	$10	Liberty 51152
5/5/84	85	11	▲		26 Duets		[K]	$10	Liberty 51154
9/22/84	31	31	▲	©	27 What About Me?			$10	RCA Victor 5043
12/8/84+	31	8	▲²	©	28 Once Upon A Christmas	C:#15/13	[X]	$10	RCA Victor 5307

KENNY ROGERS & DOLLY PARTON
Christmas charts: 1/'84, 4/'85, 10/'87, 16/'88, 15/'89, 14/'90, 14/'91, 19/'92, 25/'93

| 4/20/85 | 145 | 7 | ● | | 29 Love Is What We Make It | | [E] | $10 | Liberty 51157 |

contains previously unreleased recordings

10/19/85	51	28		©	30 The Heart Of The Matter			$10	RCA Victor 7023
12/13/86+	137	15		©	31 They Don't Make Them Like They Used To			$10	RCA Victor 5633
9/26/87	163	4		©	32 I Prefer The Moonlight			$10	RCA Victor 6484
5/27/89	141	8	●	©	33 Something Inside So Strong			$10	Reprise 25792
12/16/89+	119	6	●	©	34 Christmas In America		[X]	$10	Reprise 25973

Christmas charts: 12/'89, 28/'91

| 12/14/96 | 63 | 5 | ● | © | 35 The Gift | C:#14/6 | [X] | $10 | Magnatone 108 |

Christmas charts: 9/'96, 17/'97

| 8/9/97 | 193 | 1 | | © | 36 Across My Heart | | | $10 | Magnatone 116 |

DEBUT	PEAK	WKS	RIAA	CD	ARTIST — Album Title	Catalog	Sym	$	Label & Number
					ROGERS, Kenny/First Edition — Cont'd				
12/19/98	**164**	3		©	37 **Christmas From The Heart** Christmas charts: 28/'98, 16/'99, 31/'00	C:#30/1	[X]	**$10**	Dreamcatcher 001
2/6/99+	**171**	3		©	38 **With Love**	C:#15/6		**$10**	Madacy 0371
5/29/99	**60**	56	▲	©	39 **She Rides Wild Horses**			**$10**	Dreamcatcher 004
10/21/00	**121**	3		©	40 **There You Go Again**			**$10**	Dreamcatcher 006

After All (I Live My Life) (5)
After All This Time (31)
All God's Lonely Children (7)
All I Ever Need Is You (14,26)
All My Life (23) *37*
All That I Am (2)
All That You Could Be (40)
Always Leaving, Always Gone (3)
Am I Too Late (10)
Anyone Who Isn't Me Tonight (16,26)
Anything At All (31)
As God Is My Witness (36)
Away In A Manger (34,35)
Baby I'm-A Want You (16,26)
Bad Enough (23)
Ballerina Song (37)
Beautiful Lies (16)
Best Of Me (30)
Blaze Of Glory (19) *66*
Blue Train (40)
Born To Love Me (29)
Buckeroos, The (17)
Buried Treasure (24)
Buried Treasures (12)
But You Know I Love You (2,6,11) *19*
Buy Me A Rose (39) *40*
Calico Saturday Night (8)
Calico Silver (8)
Call Me Up (The Phone Is In The Cradle) (17)
Camptown Ladies (5)
Carol Of The Bells (20,22)
Chosen One (medley) (35)
Christmas Everyday (20,22)
Christmas In America (34)
Christmas Is My Favorite Time Of The Year (20,22)
Christmas Song (28,37)
Christmas To Remember (28)
Christmas Without You (28)
Church Without A Name (1)
Coward Of The County (15,18,25) *3*
Crazy (27) *79*
Crazy Me (40)
Daytime Friends (10,11,25) *28*
Desperado (10)
Didn't We? (27)
Don't Fall In Love With A Dreamer (17,18,25,26) *4*
Don't Look In My Eyes (30)
Dorsey, The Mail-Carrying Dog (8)
Dream Dancin' (27)
Dream On (1)
Elvira (4)
Empty Handed Compadres (8)
Endless Love (38)
Even A Fool Would Let Go (12)
Evening Star (24)
Every Time Two Fools Collide (16,18,26)
Eyes That See In The Dark (24) *79*
Factory, The (32)
Farther I Go (23)
Fightin' Fire With Fire (21)
Find A Little Grace (36)
First Noel (34,35)
Fool In Me (21)
For The Good Times (7)
Gambler, The (13,18,25) *16*
Ghost Of Another Man (10)
Gideon Tanner (17)
Girl, Get A Hold Of Yourself (3)
God Rest Ye Merry Gentlemen (34)
Goin' Back To Alabama (19)
Good Lady of Toronto (7)
Good Life (19)
Good Time Liberator (3)
Goodbye Marie (15)
Greatest, The (39)
Greatest Gift Of All (28) *81*
Green Green Grass Of Home (9)
Grey Beard (19)
Harbor For My Soul (8)
Have A Little Faith In Me (36)
Have I Told You Lately That I Love You (38)
Have Yourself A Merry Little Christmas (34)
He Will, She Knows (40)
Heart Of The Matter (30)
Heart To Heart (27)
Heed The Call (5,6) *33*
Help Somebody Find Their Way (37)
Heroes (37)
Hey, Little Christmas Tree (37)
(Hey Won't You Play) Another Somebody Done Somebody Wrong Song (14,26)
Highway Flyer (12)
Hold Me (24)
Homeland (40)
Homemade Lies (1)
Hoodooin' Of Miss Fannie Deberry (13)
How Long (23)
Hurry Up Love (1)
I Believe In Music (6)
I Believe In Santa Claus (28)
I Can't Believe Your Eyes (30)
I Can't Help Falling In Love (38)
I Can't Make You Love Me (39)
I Could Be So Good For You (12)
I Do It For Your Love (40)
I Don't Call Him Daddy (32)
I Don't Need You (19,25) *3*
I Don't Wanna Have To Worry (30)
I Don't Want To Know Why (27)
I Found A Reason (1)
I Get A Funny Feeling (1)
I Just Wanna Give My Love To You (2)
I Prefer The Moonlight (32)
I Promise You (37)
I Trust You (35)
I Wanna Be A Christmas Present (37)
I Want A Son (21)
I Want To Make You Smile (15)
I Was The Loser (1)
I Wasn't Man Enough (9)
I Will Always Love You (24,38)
I Will Remember You (39)
I Wish I Could Say That (40)
I Wish That I Could Hurt That Way Again (13)
I Won't Forget (40)
I'll Be Home For Christmas (34)
I'll Just Write My Music And Sing My Songs (10)
I'll Take Care Of You (21)
I'm Gonna Sing You A Sad Song Susie (5)
If I Could Hold On To Love (31)
If I Ever Fall In Love Again (33)
If I Knew Then What I Know Now (33)
If I Only Had Your Heart (37)
If Wishes Were Horses (1)
If You Can Lie A Little Bit (21)
In And Out Of Your Heart (15)
Islands In The Stream (24) *1*
It Happened In The Best Of Dreams (29)
It Turns Me Inside Out (29)
It's A Crazy Afternoon (4)
It's Gonna Be Better (2)
It's Just Not Christmas (37)
It's Raining In My Mind (2)
It's The Messiah (35)
Joy To The World (34,35)
Just Dropped In (To See What Condition My Condition Was In) (1,6,11) *5*
Just Remember You're My Sunshine (4)
Just The Thought Of Losing You (31)
Just The Way You Are (14)
Kentucky Homemade Christmas (20,22)
Kids (20,22)
Kind Of Fool Love Makes (39)
King Of Oak Street (5,13)
Lady (18,25,38) *1*
Last Few Threads Of Love (2)
Laura (What's He Got That I Ain't Got) (9)
Lay Down Beside Me (9)
Lay It Down (7)
Let It Be Me (14,39)
Let It Snow, Let It Snow, Let It Snow (37)
Let Me Sing For You (10)
Let's Take The Long Way Around The World (14)
Life Is Good, Love Is Better (31)
Listen To The Music (3)
Little More Like Me (The Crucifixion) (13)
Living With You (24)
Long Arm Of The Law (18)
Love Don't Live Here Anymore (39)
Love Is What We Make It (29)
Love Lifted Me (11,25) *97*
Love, Love, Love (23)
Love Or Something Like It (12,25) *32*
Love Song (21) *47*
Love The Way You Do (33)
Love The World Away (18) *14*
Love Will Turn You Around (21,25) *13*
Love Woman (5,6)
Loving Arms (39)
Loving Gift (16)
Lucille (9,11,18,25) *5*
Lying Again (10)
Madame De Lil And Diabolical Bill (8)
Make No Mistake, She's Mine (32)
Makes Me Wonder If I Ever Said Goodbye (19)
Making Music For Money (13)
Man Came Up From Town (8)
Marcia: 2 A.M. (1)
Mary, Did You Know (35)
Maybe (33)
Maybe In The End (29)
Maybe You Should Know (21)
Me And Bobby McGee (3)
Merry Christmas (37)
Midnight Flyer (14)
Midsummer Nights (24)
Mister Perfect (37)
Molly (5)
Momma's Waiting (4,6,12)
Money Isn't What Really Matters (37)
Morgana Jones (13)
Morning Desire (30) *72*
Mother Country Music (9)
My Favorite Things (20,22,37)
My Washington Woman (4)
My World Begins And Ends With You (10)
New Design (3)
Night Goes On (27)
No Dreams (23)
No Good Texas Rounder (17)
Now And Forever (32)
O' Come All Ye Faithful (37)
O' Holy Night (20,22,35)
O Little Town Of Bethlehem (34)
Old Folks (15)
Old Mojave Highway (8)
Once Again She's All Alone (3)
Once Upon A Christmas (28)
One Lonely Room (8)
One Man's Woman (15)
One More Day (32)
One Night (33)
One Place In The Night (17)
Only Once In A Lifetime (36)
Only Way I Know (36)
Our Perfect Song (30)
People In Love (30)
Planet Texas (33)
Poem For My Little Lady (7)
Pretty Little Baby Child (35)
Puttin' In Overtime At Home (9)
Road Agent (8)
Rock And Roll Man (10)
Rockin' Chair Theme (8)
Ruben James (3,6,11,18,25) *26*
Ruby, Don't Take Your Love To Town (2,3,6,11,18,25) *6*
Run Through Your Mind (2)
Sail Away (12)
Sally Grey's Epitaph (8)
San Francisco Mabel Joy (13)
Santiago Midnight Moonlight (15)
Sayin' Goodbye (17)
Scarlet Fever (23,25) *94*
School Teacher (8) *91*
See Me Through (36)
Shadow In The Corner Of Your Mind (1)
Share Your Love With Me (19) *14*
She Believes In Me (13,18,25,38) *5*
She Even Woke Me Up To Say Goodbye (4)
She Rides Wild Horses (39)
She's A Mystery (15)
She's Ready For Someone To Love Her (32)
Shine On Ruby Mountain (5)
Silent Night (28,34,35)
Silver Bells (34)
Sing Me Your Love Song (36)
Sleep Comes Easy (2)
Sleep Tight, Goodnight Man (13)
Sleigh Ride (medley) (28)
Slow Dance More (39)
So In Love With You (19)
Soldier's King (35)
Somebody Help Me (17)
Somebody Took My Love (27)
Something About Your Song (12)
(Something Inside) So Strong (33)
Something's Burning (4,6,11,25) *11*
Somewhere Between Lovers And Friends (21)
Son Of Hickory Holler's Tramp (9)
Starting Again (12)
Starting Today, Starting Over (29)
Still Hold On (29)
Stranger, The (27)
Stranger In My Place (4,29)
Sunshine (3)
Sunshine Joe (4)
Sweet Little Jesus Boy (20,22,35)
Sweet Music Man (10) *44*
Take My Hand (7) *91*
Take This Heart (21)
Tell It All Brother (5,6) *17*
Tennessee Bottle (13)
That's The Way It Could Have Been (16,26)
Then I Miss You (4)
There Lies The Difference (33)
There You Go Again (40)
There's A Lot Of That Going Around (12)
These Chains (17)
They Don't Make Them Like They Used To (31)
This Love We Share (31)
This Woman (24) *23*
Through The Years (19,25) *13*
Ticket To Nowhere (1)
Tie Me To Your Heart Again (29)
'Til I Can Make It On My Own (14,25,26)
'Til The Season Comes 'Round Again (35,37)
Till I Get It Right (9)
Time For Love (31)
To Me (36)
Today I Started Loving You Again (11)
Together Again (14,26)
Tomb Of The Unknown Love (30)
Toy Shoppe (37)
Trigger Happy Kid (8)
Trying Just As Hard As I Can (2)
Tulsa Turnaround (7,15)
Twentieth Century Fool (29)
Twenty Years Ago (31)
Two Hearts One Love (27)
Two Little Boys (7)
Unforgettable (38)
Until Forever's Gone (40)
Vachel Carling's Rubilator (8)
Vows Go Unbroken (Always True To You) (33)
Way It Used To Be (8)
We All Got To Help Each Other (5)
We Could Have Been The Closest Of Friends (12)
We Don't Make Love Anymore (10)
We Fell In Love Anyway (32)
We Love Each Other (16)
We Three Kings (medley) (35)
We're Doin' Alright (32)
We've Got Tonight (23,25,26) *6*
What A Wonderful Beginning (35)
What About Me? (27) *15*
What Am I Gonna Do (7)
What Child Is This (34)
What I Learned From Loving You (23)
What That Means (40)
What's Wrong With Us Today (16)
When A Child Is Born (20,22)
When A Man Loves A Woman (38)
When I Fall In Love (38)
When We Made Love (40)
When You Put Your Heart In It (33)
Where Does Rosie Go (7)
While I Play The Fiddle (9)
While The Feeling's Good (11)
White Christmas (20,22,28,37)
Why Don't We Go Somewhere And Love (9,16)
Wind Beneath My Wings (38)
Winter Wonderland (28,34)
With Bells On (28)
Without You In My Life (19)
Write Me Down (Don't Forget My Name) (8)
Write Your Name (Across My Heart) (36)
You And I (24)
You And Me (16)
You Are So Beautiful (23,38)
You Can't Say (You Don't Love Me Anymore) (32)
You Decorated My Life (15,18,25) *7*
You Light Up My Life (38)
You Made Me Feel Love (30)
You Needed Me (14)
You Turn The Light On (15)
You Were A Good Friend (17,25)
You're My Love (31)
You're Not Asking Much (36)
You've Lost That Lovin' Feelin' (14)

ROGERS, Roy — '91

Born Leonard Franklin Slye on 11/5/11 in Cincinnati. Died on 7/6/98 (age 86). Popular "singing cowboy" who starred in several movies. Original member of the famous western group Sons Of The Pioneers. Starred in close to 100 movie Westerns, then in a popular radio and TV series with his wife, Dale Evans.

DEBUT	PEAK	WKS	RIAA	CD	ARTIST — Album Title	Catalog	Sym	$	Label & Number
12/23/67	**92**^{X}	2			1 **Christmas Is Always** ROY ROGERS & DALE EVANS		[X]	**$30**	Capitol 2818
11/9/91	**113**	9		©	2 **Roy Rogers Tribute** includes "King Of The Cowboys" by Dusty Rogers			**$10**	RCA 3024

Alive And Kickin' (2)
Christmas Is Always (1)
Christmas Prayer (1)
December Time (1)
Don't Fence Me In (2)
Final Frontier (2)
Happy Birthday, Gentle Saviour (medley) (1)
Happy Trails (2)
Here's Hopin' (2)
Hold On Partner (2)
I'll Be Home For Christmas (1)
It's The Most Wonderful Time Of The Year (1)
Jingle Bells (medley) (1)
Let There Be Peace On Earth (1)
Little Joe The Wrangler (2)
Merry Christmas, My Darling (1)
Remember Whose Birthday It Is (medley) (1)
Rodeo Road (2)
Sleigh Ride (medley) (1)
Star Of Hope (1)
Sweet Little Jesus Boy (medley) (1)
That's How The West Was Swung (2)
Tumbling Tumbleweeds (2)
What Child Is This? (medley) (1)
What Color Is Love? (1)
When Pay Day Rolls Around (2)

ROLLING STONES, The ★6★ '66

Rock group formed in London: **Mick Jagger** (vocals), **Keith Richards** and Brian Jones (guitars), **Bill Wyman** (bass) and Charlie Watts (drums). Group took name from a **Muddy Waters** song. Promoted as the bad boys in contrast to **The Beatles**. Jones drowned on 7/3/69 (age 27); replaced by Mick Taylor. **Ronnie Wood** replaced Taylor in 1975. Movie *Gimme Shelter* is a documentary of the group's performance at the 1969 Altamont concert. Won Grammy's Lifetime Achievement Award in 1986. Inducted into the Rock and Roll Hall of Fame in 1989. Wyman left group in late 1992. Bassist Darryl Jones (billed as a "side musician") played on the 1994 *Voodoo Lounge* album and tour. Considered by many as the world's all-time greatest rock and roll band.

1)Tattoo You 2)Emotional Rescue 3)Sticky Fingers 4)Exile On Main St. 5)Goats Head Soup

DEBUT	PEAK	WKS	RIAA	CD	#	Album Title	Catalog	Sym	$	Label & Number
6/27/64	11	35	●	©	1	England's Newest Hit Makers/The Rolling Stones			$50	London 375
11/14/64	3	38	●	©	2	12 x 5			$40	London 402
3/20/65	5	53	●	©	3	The Rolling Stones, Now!			$40	London 420
8/7/65	❶³	66	▲	©	4	Out Of Our Heads			$40	London 429
12/11/65+	4	33	●	©	5	December's Children (and everybody's)			$40	London 451
4/16/66	3	99	▲²	©	6	Big Hits (High Tide And Green Grass)		[G]	$30	London 1
7/9/66	2²	50	▲	©	7	Aftermath			$30	London 476
12/17/66+	6	48	●	©	8	got Live if you want it!		[L]	$30	London 493
						recorded at the Royal Albert Hall in London				
2/18/67	2⁴	47	●	©	9	Between The Buttons			$30	London 499
7/22/67	3	35	●	©	10	Flowers		[G]	$30	London 509
12/23/67+	2⁶	30	●	©	11	Their Satanic Majesties Request			$30	London 2
12/14/68+	5	32	▲	©	12	Beggars Banquet			$20	London 33
9/13/69	2²	32	▲	©	13	Through The Past, Darkly (Big Hits Vol. 2)		[G]	$20	London 3
12/6/69	3	44	▲²	©	14	Let It Bleed			$20	London 4
10/17/70	6	23	▲	©	15	'Get Yer Ya-Ya's Out!'		[L]	$20	London 5
						recorded in November 1969 at Madison Square Garden				
5/15/71	❶⁴	62	▲³	©	16	Sticky Fingers	C:#14/11		$15	Rolling Stones 59100
1/8/72	4	243	▲⁶	©	17	Hot Rocks 1964-1971	C:#16/27	[G]	$20	London 606/7 [2]
6/10/72	❶⁴	43	▲	©	18	Exile On Main St.	C:#16/9		$20	Rolling Stones 2900 [2]
12/30/72+	9	29	●	©	19	More Hot Rocks (big hits & fazed cookies)		[G]	$20	London 626/7 [2]
9/29/73	❶⁴	37	▲³	©	20	Goats Head Soup			$15	Rolling Stones 59101
11/2/74	❶¹	20	▲	©	21	It's Only Rock 'N Roll			$15	Rolling Stones 79101
6/21/75	6	17	▲	©	22	Made In The Shade		[G]	$15	Rolling Stones 79102
6/21/75	8	13			23	Metamorphosis		[K]	$15	Abkco 1
5/8/76	❶⁴	24	▲	©	24	Black And Blue			$15	Rolling Stones 79104
10/8/77	5	17	●	©	25	Love You Live		[L]	$20	Rolling Stones 9001 [2]
6/24/78	❶²	82	▲⁶	©	26	Some Girls	C:#29/11		$12	Rolling Stones 39108
7/19/80	❶⁷	51	▲²	©	27	Emotional Rescue			$12	Rolling Stones 16015
4/4/81	15	12	●	©	28	Sucking In The Seventies		[G]	$12	Rolling Stones 16028
9/12/81	❶⁹	58	▲⁴	©	29	Tattoo You			$12	Rolling Stones 16052
6/26/82	5	23	▲	©	30	"Still Life" (American Concert 1981)		[L]	$12	Rolling Stones 39113
11/26/83	4	23	▲	©	31	Undercover			$12	Rolling Stones 90120
7/28/84	86	11	●	©	32	Rewind (1971-1984)		[G]	$12	Rolling Stones 90176
4/12/86	4	25	▲	©	33	Dirty Work			$12	Rolling Stones 40250
9/9/89	91	22	▲	©	34	Singles Collection* The London Years		[K]	$30	Abkco 1218 [4]
9/16/89	3	36	▲²	©	35	Steel Wheels			$10	Rolling Stones 45333
4/20/91	16	17	●	©	36	Flashpoint		[L]	$10	Rolling Stones 47456
7/30/94	2¹	38	▲²	©	37	Voodoo Lounge			$10	Virgin 39782
12/2/95	9	19	▲	©	38	Stripped		[L]	$10	Virgin 41040
11/2/96	92	3		©	39	Rock And Roll Circus		[L]	$10	Abkco 1268
						recorded in a North London TV studio on 12/10/68 for a BBC-TV special that never aired; includes "Song For Jeffrey" by **Jethro Tull**, "A Quick One While He's Away" by **The Who**, "Ain't That A Lot Of Love" by **Taj Mahal** "Something Better" by **Marianne Faithfull**, "Yer Blues" by **John Lennon** and "Whole Lotta Yoko" by **Yoko Ono**				
10/18/97	3	27	▲	©	40	Bridges To Babylon			$10	Virgin 44712
11/21/98	34	8		©	41	No Security		[L]	$10	Virgin 46740

ROLLING STONES, The — Cont'd

How Can I Stop (40)
I Am Waiting (7)
I Can't Be Satisfied (19)
(I Can't Get No) Satisfaction (4,6,8,17,30,34,36) *1*
I Don't Know Why (23,34) *42*
I Go Wild (37)
I Got The Blues (16)
I Just Want To Make Love To You (1,34)
I Just Want To See His Face (18)
I Wanna Be Your Man (34)
I Want To Be Loved (34)
I'd Much Rather Be With The Boys (23)
I'm A King Bee (1)
I'm All Right (4,8)
I'm Free (5,19,34,38)
I'm Going Down (23)
I'm Moving On (5)
I've Been Loving You Too Long (8)
If I Was A Dancer (Dance Pt. 2) (28)
(also see: Dance)
If You Can't Rock Me (21,25)
If You Let Me (23)
If You Need Me (2)
If You Really Want To Be My Friend (21)
In Another Land (11,34)
Indian Girl (27)
It Must Be Hell (31)
It's All Over Now (2,6,19,34) *26*
It's Not Easy (7)
It's Only Rock 'N Roll (But I Like It) (21,22,25) *16*
Jig-Saw Puzzle (12)
Jiving Sister Fanny (23,34)
Jumpin' Jack Flash (13,15,17,25,34,36) *3*

Jumping Jack Flash (39)
Just My Imagination (Running Away With Me) (26,30)
Lady Jane (7,8,10,19,34) *24*
Lantern, The (11,34)
Last Time (4,6,8,19,34,41) *9*
Let It Bleed (14,19,38)
Let It Loose (18)
Let Me Go (27,30)
Let's Spend The Night Together (9,10,13,17,30,34) *55*
Lies (26)
Like A Rolling Stone (38)
Little Baby (38)
Little By Little (1,34)
Little Queenie (15)
Little Red Rooster (3,25,34,36)
Little T & A (29)
Live With Me (14,15,41)
Long Long While (19,34)
Look What You've Done (5)
Love In Vain (14,15,38)
Love Is Strong (37) *91*
Loving Cup (18)
Low Down (40)
Luxury (21)
Mannish Boy (25,28)
Mean Disposition (37)
Melody (24)
Memo From Turner (23,34)
Memory Motel (24,41)
Mercy Mercy (3)
Midnight Rambler (14,15,17)
Might As Well Get Juiced (40)
Miss Amanda Jones (9)
Miss You (26,32,36) *1*
Mixed Emotions (35) *5*
Mona (I Need You Baby) (3)
Money (19)
Monkey Man (14)
Moon Is Up (37)

Moonlight Mile (16)
Mothers Little Helper (10,13,17,34) *8*
My Girl (10)
My Obsession (9)
Neighbors (29)
New Faces (37)
19th Nervous Breakdown (6,8,17,34) *2*
No Expectations (12,19,34,39)
No Use In Crying (29)
Not Fade Away (1,6,8,19,34,38) *48*
Now I've Got A Witness (1)
Off The Hook (3,34)
Oh Baby (We Got A Good Thing Goin') (3)
On With The Show (11)
One Hit (To The Body) (33) *28*
100 Years Ago (20)
One More Try (4)
Out Of Control (40,41)
Out Of Tears (37) *60*
Out Of Time (10,19,23,34) *81*
Pain In My Heart (3)
Paint It, Black (7,13,17,34,36) *1*
Parachute Woman (12,39)
Play With Fire (4,6,17,34) *96*
Please Go Home (10)
Poison Ivy (19)
Pretty Beat Up (31)
Prodigal Son (12)
Respectable (26,41)
Ride On Baby (10)
Rip This Joint (18,22)
Rock And A Hard Place (35,36) *23*
Rocks Off (18)
Route 66 (1,5)
Ruby Tuesday (9,10,13,17,34,36) *1*

Sad Day (34)
Sad Sad Sad (35,36)
Saint Of Me (40,41) *94*
Salt Of The Earth (12,39)
Satisfaction ..see: (I Can't Get No)
Send It To Me (27)
Sex Drive (36)
Shake Your Hips (18)
Shattered (26,28,30) *31*
She Said Yeah (5)
She Smiled Sweetly (9)
She Was Hot (31) *44*
She's A Rainbow (11,13,19,34) *25*
She's So Cold (27) *26*
Shine A Light (18,38)
Short And Curlies (21)
Silver Train (20)
Sing This All Together (11)
Sing This All Together (See What Happens) (11)
Singer Not The Song (5,34)
Sister Morphine (16,41)
Sittin' On A Fence (10,19)
Slave (29)
Sleep Tonight (33)
Slipping Away (35,38)
Some Girls (29)
Something Happened To Me Yesterday (9)
Soul Survivor (18)
Sparks Will Fly (37)
Spider And The Fly (4,34,38)
Star Star (20,25)
Start Me Up (29,30,32,36) *2*
Stoned (34)
Stop Breaking Down (18)
Stray Cat Blues (12,15)
Street Fighting Man (12,13,15,17,34,38) *48*
Stupid Girl (7,34)

Suck On The Jugular (37)
Summer Romance (27)
Surprise, Surprise (3,34)
Susie Q (2)
Sway (16)
Sweet Black Angel (18)
Sweet Virginia (18,38)
Sweethearts Together (37)
Sympathy For The Devil (12,15,17,25,34,36,39)
Take It Or Leave It (10)
Talkin' About You (5)
Tell Me (You're Coming Back) (1,6,19,34) *24*
Terrifying (35)
That's How Strong My Love Is (4)
Thief In The Night (40,41)
Think (7)
Thru And Thru (37)
Tie You Up (The Pain Of Love) (31)
Till The Next Goodbye (21)
Time Is On My Side (2,6,8,17,30,34) *6*
Time Waits For No One (21,28)
Too Much Blood (31)
Too Rude (33)
Too Tight (40)
Too Tough (31)
Tops (29)
Torn And Frayed (18)
Try A Little Harder (23,34)
Tumbling Dice (18,22,25,32) *7*
Turd On The Run (18)
Twenty Flight Rock (30)
2120 South Michigan Avenue (2)
2,000 Light Years From Home (11,13,19,34)
2,000 Man (11)

Under Assistant West Coast Promotion Man (4,34)
Under My Thumb (7,8,17,30)
Under The Boardwalk (2)
Undercover Of The Night (31,32) *9*
Ventilator Blues (18)
Waiting On A Friend (29,32,41) *13*
(Walkin' Thru The) Sleepy City (23)
Walking The Dog (1)
Wanna Hold You (31)
We Love You (19,34) *50*
What A Shame (3,34)
What To Do (19)
When The Whip Comes Down (26,28)
Where The Boys Go (27)
Who's Been Sleeping Here (9)
Who's Driving Your Plane? (34)
Wild Horses (16,17,22,34,38) *28*
Winning Ugly (33)
Winter (19)
Worried About You (29)
Worst, The (37)
Yesterday's Papers (9)
You Better Move On (5)
You Can Make It If You Try (1)
You Can't Always Get What You Want (14,17,25,34,36,39) *42*
You Can't Catch Me (3)
You Don't Have To Mean It (40)
You Got Me Rocking (37,41)
You Got The Silver (14)
You Gotta Move (16,25)

ROLLINS BAND '94
Born Henry Garfield on 2/13/61 in Washington DC. Hard-rock singer/poet/actor. Acted in several movies. His band: Chris Haskett (guitar), Andrew Weiss (bass) and Sim Cain (drums). Melvin Gibbs replaced Weiss in 1993. New band in 1999: Jim Wilson (guitar), Marcus Blake (bass) and Jason MacKenroth (drums).

DEBUT	PEAK	WKS	RIAA	CD				$	Label & Number
4/25/92	160	4		©	1	**The End Of Silence**		$10	Imago 21006
4/30/94	33	23		©	2	**Weight**		$10	Imago 21034
4/12/97	89	5		©	3	**Come In And Burn**		$10	DreamWorks 50007
3/18/00	180	1		©	4	**Get Some - Go Again**		$10	DreamWorks 50216

Alien Blueprint (2)
All I Want (1)
Almost Real (1)
Another Life (1)
Are You Ready? (4)
Blues Jam (1)
Brother Interior (4)
Change It Up (4)
Civilized (2)
Disconnect (2)
Divine Object Of Hatred (2)
During A City (3)
End Of Something (3)
Fool (2)
Get Some Go Again (4)
Grip (1)
Hotter And Hotter (4)
I Go Day Glo (4)
Icon (2)
Illumination (4)
Illuminator (4)
Inhale Exhale (4)
Just Like You (1)
Liar (2)
Love's So Heavy (4)
Low Self Opinion (1)
Monster (4)
Neon (3)
Obscene (1)
On My Way To The Cage (3)
On The Day (4)
Rejection (3)
Saying Goodbye Again (3)
Shame (3)
Shine (2)
Spilling Over The Side (3)
Starve (4)
Step Back (2)
Tearing (1)
Thinking Cap (4)
Thursday Afternoon (3)
Tired (2)
Volume 4 (2)
What Do You Do (1)
Wrong Man (1)
You Didn't Need (1)
You Let Yourself Down (1)

ROMAN HOLLIDAY '83
Pop-rock group from London: Steve Lambert (vocals), Brian Bonhomme (guitar), Adrian York (keyboards), John Eacott (trumpet), Rob Lambert (sax), Jon Durno (bass) and Simon Cohen (drums). Group named after the 1953 movie starring Audrey Hepburn.

DEBUT	PEAK	WKS	RIAA	CD				$	Label & Number
9/3/83	142	11			1	**Roman Holliday**		[M] $12	Jive 8086
10/22/83	116	6			2	**Cookin' On The Roof**		$12	Jive 8101

Beat My Time (1)
Don't Try To Stop It (1,2) *68*
Furs And High Heels (2)
I.O.U. (1,2)
Jive Dive (2)
Midnight Bus (2)
Motor Mania (1,2)
No Ball Games (2)
One More Jilt (2)
Serious Situation (2)
Stand By (1,2) *54*

ROMANTICS, The '84
Pop-rock group from Detroit: Wally Palmar (vocals, guitar), Coz Canler (guitar), Mike Skill (bass) and Jimmy Marinos (drums). David Petratos replaced Marinos in early 1985.

DEBUT	PEAK	WKS	RIAA	CD				$	Label & Number
2/2/80	61	15		©	1	**The Romantics**		$12	Nemperor 36273
12/6/80	176	7		©	2	**National Breakout**		$12	Nemperor 36881
11/14/81	182	2		©	3	**Strictly Personal**		$12	Nemperor 37435
10/22/83+	14	36	●	©	4	**In Heat**		$12	Nemperor 38880
9/21/85	72	11		©	5	**Rhythm Romance**		$12	Nemperor 40106

All That I Want (1)
Be My Everything (5)
Better Make A Move (5)
Bop (3)
Can't Get Over You (3)
C'mon Girl (Work Out With Me) (3)
Diggin' On You (4)
Do Me Anyway You Wanna (4)
Don't You Put Me On Hold (3)
First In Line (1)
Forever Yours (4)
Friday At The Hideout (1)
Gimme One More Chance (1)
Girl Next Door (1)
Got Me Where You Want Me (4)
Hung On You (1)
I Can't Tell You Anything (2)
I Got It If You Want It (5)
I'm Hip (4)
In The Nighttime (3)
Keep In Touch (1)
Let's Get Started (5)
Little White Lies (1)
Look At Her (3)
Love Me To The Max (4)
Make It Last (5)
Mystified (5)
National Breakout (2)
Never Thought It Would Be Like This (5)
New Cover Story (2)
Night Like This (2)
No One Like You (3)
One In A Million (4) *37*
Open Up Your Door (4)
Poison Ivy (5)
Poor Little Rich Girl (2)
Rhythm Romance (5)
Rock You Up (4)
Shake A Tail Feather (4)
She's Got Everything (1)
She's Hot (3)
Spend A Little Love On Me (4)
Stone Pony (2)
Take Me Out Of The Rain (2)
Talking In Your Sleep (4) *3*
Tell It To Carrie (1)
Test Of Time (5) *71*
Till I See You Again (1)
Tomboy (3)
21 And Over (2)
What I Like About You (1) *49*
When I Look In Your Eyes (1)
Why'd You Leave Me (3)

ROME '97
Born Jerome Woods in Benton Harbor, Michigan. Male R&B singer.

DEBUT	PEAK	WKS	RIAA	CD				$	Label & Number
5/3/97	30	30	●	©		**Rome**		$10	RCA 67441

Crazy Love
Do Me Right
Do You Like This *31*
Feelin' Kinda Good
Heaven
I Belong To You (Every Time I See Your Face) *6*
I Gotta Be Down
Just Once, Once More, Three Times
Let Me Come Home
Never Find Another Love Like Mine
Real Joy
Real Love
That's The Way I Feel About 'Cha

ROMEO'S DAUGHTER '88
Rock trio from England: Leigh Matty (vocals), Craig Joiner (guitars, vocals) and Tony Mitman (keyboards).

| 11/19/88 | 191 | 2 | © | 1 **Romeo's Daughter** | $10 | Jive 1135 |

Colour You A Smile
Don't Break My Heart *73*
Heaven In The Back Seat

Hymn (Look Through Golden Eyes)
I Cry Myself To Sleep At Night

I Like What I See
Inside Out
Stay With Me Tonight

Velvet Tongue
Wild Child

ROMEO VOID '84
Pop-rock group from San Francisco: Debora Iyall (vocals), Peter Woods (guitar), Ben Bossi (sax), Frank Zincavage (bass) and Aaron Smith (drums).

3/6/82	147	6		1 **Never Say Never**	[M]	$12	415 Records 0007
9/4/82	119	13		2 **Benefactor**		$10	Columbia 38182
8/25/84	68	19		3 **Instincts**		$10	Columbia 39155

Billy's Birthday (3)
Chinatown (2)
Flashflood (2)

Girl In Trouble (Is A Temporary Thing) (3) *35*
Going To Neon (3)
In The Dark (1)

Instincts (3)
Just Too Easy (3)
Never Say Never (1,2)
Not Safe (1)

Orange (2)
Out On My Own (3)
Present Tense (1)
S.O.S. (2)

Say No (3)
Shake The Hands Of Time (2)
Six Days And One (3)
Undercover Kept (2)

Ventilation (3)
Wrap It Up (2)
Your Life Is A Lie (3)

RON "C" '90
Born Ron Carey in Oakland. Male rapper. Member of **Nemesis**.

| 5/19/90 | 170 | 7 | © | 1 **"C" Ya** | $10 | Profile 1284 |
| 7/25/92 | 183 | 3 | © | 2 **Back On The Street** | $10 | Profile 1431 |

And I'm Ron C (2)
Anotha Trick (2)
Back On The Street (2)
Capping (1)
Do Dat Danz (1)

Dookie Booty (2)
Funky Lyrics (1)
Funky Lyrics II (2)
Good To Go (1)
It's On (2)

Lock Down Tight (2)
MMM There It Is (1)
Mad Man (2)
Make It Funky (1)
Mary Had A Pimp (2)

On And On (2)
Pimpin' Lyrics (2)
Ron "C" (1)
Smooth Attack (2)
South Dallas Drop (1)

They Can't Handle It (2)
Trendsetter (1)
Trendsetter Jam (2)
We Outta Here (2)
What's Tha Tip? (1)

RONETTES, The '65
Female vocal trio from New York City: sisters Veronica "Ronnie Spector" Bennett and Estelle Bennett Vann, with cousin Nedra Talley Ross. Veronica was married to Phil Spector from 1968-74.

| 12/26/64+ | 96 | 8 | | **...presenting the fabulous Ronettes featuring Veronica** | $400 | Philles 4006 |

Baby, I Love You *24*
Be My Baby *2*

(Best Part Of) Breakin' Up *39*
Chapel Of Love

Do I Love You? *34*
How Does It Feel?

I Wonder
So Young

Walking In The Rain *23*
What'd I Say

When I Saw You
You Baby

RONNY & THE DAYTONAS '64
Pop-rock group formed in Tulsa, Oklahoma: Ronny Dayton (vocals), Jimmy Johnson (guitar), Van Evans (bass) and Lynn Williams (drums).

| 12/5/64 | 122 | 6 | © | **G.T.O.** | $150 | Mala 4001 |

Antique '32 Studebaker Dictator Coupe
Back In The U.S.A.

Bucket "T" *54*
California Bound *72*
G.T.O. *4*

Hey Little Girl
Hot Rod Baby
Hot Rod City

Little Rail Job
Little Scrambler
Little Sting Ray That Could

Surfin' In The Summertime

RONSON, Mick '75
Born on 5/26/45 in Hull, Yorkshire, England. Died of cancer on 4/30/93 (age 46). Guitarist with **David Bowie** from 1969-73 and **Mott The Hoople** in late 1974.

4/6/74	156	5	©	1 **Slaughter On 10th Avenue**	$12	RCA Victor 0353
2/8/75	103	9	©	2 **Play Don't Worry**	$12	RCA Victor 0681
10/28/89+	157	20	©	3 **Y U I ORTA**	$10	Mercury 838973

IAN HUNTER/MICK RONSON

American Music (3)
Angel No. 9 (2)
Beg A Little Love (3)
Big Time (3)
Billy Porter (2)

Cool (3)
Empty Bed (Io Me Ne Andrei) (2)
Girl Can't Help It (2)
Growing Up And I'm Fine (1)

Hazy Days (2)
Hey Ma Get Papa (medley) (1)
I'm The One (1)
Livin' In A Heart (3)
Loner, The (3)

Love Me Tender (1)
Music Is Lethal (1)
Only After Dark (1)
Play Don't Worry (2)
Pleasure Man (medley) (1)

Slaughter On Tenth Avenue (1)
Sons 'N' Lovers (3)
Sweet Dreamer (3)
Tell It Like It Is (3)
This Is For You (2)

White Light/White Heat (2)
Woman (2)
Womens Intuition (3)

RONSTADT, Linda ★38★ '77
Born on 7/15/46 in Tucson, Arizona. Pop-rock singer. Formed **The Stone Poneys** with Bobby Kimmel (guitar) and Ken Edwards (keyboards). Went solo in 1968. In 1971 formed backing band with **Glenn Frey**, **Don Henley**, **Randy Meisner** and **Bernie Leadon** (later became the **Eagles**). Appeared in the 1978 movie *FM*. Acted in the Broadway and movie versions of *The Pirates of Penzance*.

1)Simple Dreams 2)Heart Like A Wheel 3)Living In The USA 4)What's New 5)Mad Love

| 12/2/67+ | 100 | 15 | | © | 1 **Evergreen, Vol. 2** | | $25 | Capitol 2763 |

THE STONE PONEYS

10/24/70	103	10		©	2 **Silk Purse**		$20	Capitol 407
2/12/72	163	10		©	3 **Linda Ronstadt**		$20	Capitol 635
10/20/73+	45	56	●	©	4 **Don't Cry Now**		$15	Asylum 5064
2/2/74	92	15		©	5 **Different Drum**	[K]	$15	Capitol 11269
12/7/74+	❶[1]	51	▲[2]	©	6 **Heart Like A Wheel**		$15	Capitol 11358
6/14/75	172	4		©	7 **The Stone Poneys Featuring Linda Ronstadt**	[E]	$15	Capitol 11383

first released in 1967 as *The Stone Poneys* on Capitol 2666 ($30)

10/4/75	4	28	▲	©	8 **Prisoner In Disguise**		$12	Asylum 1045
8/28/76	3	36	▲	©	9 **Hasten Down The Wind**		$12	Asylum 1072
12/18/76+	6	80	▲[5]	©	10 **Greatest Hits**	C:#17/20 [G]	$12	Asylum 1092
5/21/77	46	9	●	11 **A Retrospective**	[K]	$15	Capitol 11629 [2]
9/24/77	❶[5]	47	▲[3]	©	12 **Simple Dreams**		$12	Asylum 104
10/7/78	❶[1]	32	▲[2]	©	13 **Living In The USA**		$12	Asylum 155
3/15/80	3	36	▲	©	14 **Mad Love**		$12	Asylum 510
11/8/80	26	21	▲	©	15 **Greatest Hits, Volume Two**	[G]	$12	Asylum 516
10/16/82	31	28	●	©	16 **Get Closer**		$10	Asylum 60185

DEBUT	PEAK	WKS	RIAA	CD	ARTIST — Album Title	Catalog	Sym	$	Label & Number
					RONSTADT, Linda — Cont'd				
10/1/83	3	81	▲³	© 17	What's New			$10	Asylum 60260
12/8/84+	13	26	▲	© 18	Lush Life			$10	Asylum 60387
10/11/86	46	27	●	© 19	For Sentimental Reasons			$10	Asylum 60474
10/11/86	124	17		© 20	'Round Midnight			$25	Asylum 60489 [3]
					deluxe set of albums #17-19; above 4 arranged and conducted by **Nelson Riddle**				
3/28/87	6	48	▲	© 21	Trio			$10	Warner 25491
					DOLLY PARTON, LINDA RONSTADT, EMMYLOU HARRIS				
12/12/87+	42	35	▲	© 22	Canciones de mi Padre		[F]	$10	Elektra 60765
					title is Spanish for "My Father's Songs"				
10/21/89+	7	58	▲²	© 23	Cry Like A Rainstorm - Howl Like The Wind	C:#37/6		$10	Elektra 60872
					LINDA RONSTADT Featuring Aaron Neville				
12/7/91+	88	13		© 24	Mas Canciones		[F]	$10	Elektra 61239
					title is Spanish for "More Songs"				
10/3/92	193	1		© 25	Frenesi		[F]	$10	Elektra 61383
					title is Spanish for "Frenzy"				
12/11/93	92	12		© 26	Winter Light			$10	Elektra 61545
4/1/95	75	12		© 27	Feels Like Home			$10	Elektra 61703
6/29/96	78	11		© 28	Dedicated To The One I Love			$10	Elektra 61916
7/11/98	160	2		© 29	We Ran			$10	Elektra 62206
2/27/99	62	14		© 30	Trio II			$10	Asylum 62275
					EMMYLOU HARRIS, LINDA RONSTADT, DOLLY PARTON				
9/11/99	73	7		© 31	Western Wall - The Tucson Sessions			$10	Asylum 62408
					LINDA RONSTADT & EMMYLOU HARRIS				
12/23/00	179	2		© 32	A Merry Little Christmas		[X]	$10	Elektra 62572

Across The Border (31)
Adios (23)
Adonde Voy (26)
After The Gold Rush (27,30)
Alison (13)
All I Left Behind (31)
All My Life (23) *11*
All That You Dream (13)
All The Beautiful Things (7)
Alma Adentro (25)
Am I Blue (19,20)
Angel Baby (28)
Anyone Who Had A Heart (26)
Are My Thoughts With You? (2)
Autumn Afternoon (1)
Away In A Manger (32)
Baby I Love You (28)
Back Home (7)
Back In The U.S.A. (13,15) *16*
Back On The Street Again (1)
Be My Baby (28)
Bewitched Bothered &
   Bewildered (19,20)
Bicycle Song (Soon Now) (7)
Birds (3,11)
Blowing Away (13)
Blue Bayou (12,15) *3*
Blue Train (27,30)
Brahms' Lullaby (28)
But Not For Me (19,20)
Can't We Be Friends (18,20)
Carmelita (12)
Christmas Song (32)
Colorado (1)
Corrido De Cananea (22)
Cost Of Love (14)
Crazy (9)
Crazy Arms (3,11)
Crazy He Calls Me (17,20)
Cry Like A Rainstorm (23)
Cry 'Til My Tears Run Dry (29)
Cuando Me Querias Tu (25)
Damage (29)
Dark End Of The Street (6)
December Dream (1)
Dedicated To The One I Love
   (28)
Desperado (4,10)
Despojos (25)
Devoted To You (28)
Different Drum (1,5,10,11) *13*
Do I Ever Cross Your Mind (30)
Do What You Gotta Do (26)
Don't Cry Now (4)
Don't Know Much (23) *2*
Don't Talk (Put Your Head On
   My Shoulder) (26)
Dos Arbolitos (22)

Down So Low (9)
Dreams Of The San Joaquin
   (29)
Driftin' (1)
Easy For You To Say (16) *54*
El Camino (24)
El Crucifijo De Piedra (24)
El Gustito (24)
El Sol Que Tu Eres (22)
El Sueno (24)
El Toro Relajo (24)
En Mi Soledad (25)
Entre Abismos (25)
Evergreen Part One & Two (1)
Everybody Loves A Winner (4)
Faithless Love (6,11)
Falling Down (31)
Falling In Love Again (18,20)
Farther Along (21)
Fast One (4)
Feels Like Home (27,30)
For A Dancer (31)
Frenesi (25)
Get Closer (16) *29*
Girls Talk (14)
Give Me A Reason (29)
Give One Heart (9)
Good Night (28)
Good-bye (17,20)
Goodbye My Friend (23)
Gritenme Piedras Del Campo
   (24)
Guess I'll Hang My Tears Out
   To Dry (17,20)
Hasten Down The Wind (9)
Have Yourself A Merry Little
   Christmas (32)
Hay Unos Ojos (22)
He Dark The Sun (1)
He Rode All The Way To Texas
   (30)
He Was Mine (31)
Heart Like A Wheel (6)
Heartbeats Accelerating (26)
Heartbreak Kind (29)
Heat Wave (8,10) *5*
Hey Mister, That's Me Up On
   The Jukebox (6)
High Sierra (27,30)
Hobo (5,11)
Hobo's Meditation (21)
How Do I Make You (14,15) *10*
Hurt So Bad (14,15) *8*
I Ain't Always Been Faithful (3)
I Believe In You (4)
I Can Almost See It (4)
I Can't Help It (If I'm Still In Love
   With You) (6,11)
I Can't Let Go (14,15) *17*

I Don't Stand A Ghost Of A
   Chance With You (17,20)
I Fall To Pieces (3,11)
I Feel The Blues Movin In (30)
I Get Along Without You Very
   Well (19,20)
I Go To Pieces (29)
I Just Don't Know What To Do
   With Myself (26)
I Keep It Hid (23)
I Knew You When (16) *37*
I Love You For Sentimental
   Reasons (19,20)
I Need You (23)
I Never Will Marry (12)
I Still Miss Someone (3)
I Think It's Gonna Work Out
   Fine (16)
I Will Always Love You (8)
I Won't Be Hangin' Round (1)
I Wonder As I Wander (32)
I'll Be Home For Christmas (32)
I'll Be Your Baby Tonight (5,11)
I'm A Fool To Want You (18,20)
I'm Leavin' It All Up To You (2)
I've Got A Crush On You
   (17,20)
I've Got To Know (1)
I've Had Enough (21)
Icy Blue Heart (29)
If He's Ever Near (9)
If I Should Fall Behind (29)
If I Were You (1)
In My Reply (3,5)
In My Room (28)
It Doesn't Matter Anymore
   (6,10,11) *47*
It Never Entered My Mind
   (18,20)
It's So Easy (12,15) *5*
It's Too Soon To Know (26)
Just A Little Bit Of Rain (7,11)
Just Like Tom Thumb's Blues
   (29)
Just One Look (13,15) *44*
Justine (14)
Keep Me From Blowing Away
   (6)
La Barca De Guaymas (22)
La Calandria (22)
La Charreada (22)
La Cigarra (22)
La Mariquita (24)
Lies (16)
Life Is Like A Mountain Railway
   (2)
Little Girl Blue (19,20)
Lo, How A Rose E're Blooming
   (32)

Lo Siento Mi Vida (9)
Long Long Time
   (2,5,10,11) *25*
Long Way Around (11) *flip*
Look Out For My Love (14)
Los Laureles (22)
Lose Again (9) *76*
Louise (2,11)
Love Has No Pride (4,10) *51*
Love Is A Rose (8,10) *63*
Love Me Tender (13)
Lover Man (Oh Where Can You
   Be) (17,20)
Lover's Return (27,30)
Lovesick Blues (2,11)
Loving The Highway Man (31)
Lush Life (18,20)
Mad Love (14)
Making Plans (21)
Many Rivers To Cross (8)
Maybe I'm Right (12)
Mean To Me (18,20)
Mental Revenge (2)
Mentira Salome (25)
Meredith (On My Mind) (7)
Mi Ranchito (24)
Mohammed's Radio (13)
Moon Is A Harsh Mistress (16)
Morning Blues (27)
Mr. Radio (16)
My Blue Tears (16)
My Dear Companion (21)
My Funny Valentine (19,20)
My Old Flame (18,20)
New Hard Times (1)
1917 (31)
Nobody's (2)
O Come, O Come, Emmanuel
   (32)
O Magnum Mysterium (32)
Oh No, Not My Baby (26)
Old Paint (12)
One For One (1)
Ooh Baby Baby (13,15) *7*
Orion (7)
Pain Of Loving You (21)
Palomita De Ojos Negros (24)
Party Girl (17)
Past Three O'clock (32)
Pena De Los Amores (24)
People Gonna Talk (16)
Perfidia (25)
Piel Canela (25)
Piensa En Mi (25)
Poor Poor Pitiful Me
   (12,15) *31*
Por Un Amor (22)
Prisoner In Disguise (8)

Quiereme Mucho (25)
Raise The Dead (31)
Ramblin' 'Round (3,11)
Rescue Me (3,11)
River (32)
River For Him (26)
Rivers Of Babylon (9)
Rock Me On The Water
   (3,5,11) *85*
Rogaciano El Huapanguero
   (22)
Roll Um Easy (8)
Rosewood Casket (31)
'Round Midnight (19,20)
Ruler Of My Heart (29)
Sail Away (4)
Shattered (23)
Siempre Hace Frio (24)
Silent Night (32)
Silver Blue (8)
**Silver Threads And Golden
   Needles** (4,10,11) *67*
Simple Man, Simple Dream (12)
Sisters Of Mercy (31)
Skylark (18,20)
So Right, So Wrong (23)
Some Of Shelly's Blues (5,11)
**Someone To Lay Down
   Beside Me** (9,15) *42*
Someone To Watch Over Me
   (17,20)
Sometimes You Just Can't Win
   (16)
Song About The Rain (1)
Sophisticated Lady (18,20)
Sorrow Lives Here (12)
Still Within The Sound Of My
   Voice (23)
Stoney End (5)
Straighten Up And Fly Right
   (19,20)
Sweet Spot (31)
Sweet Summer Blue And Gold
   (7)
Sweetest Gift (8)
Talk To Me Of Mendocino (16)
Talking In The Dark (14)
Tata Dios (24)
Tattler, The (7)
Te Quiero Dijiste (25)
Teardrops Will Fall (27)
Tell Him (16)
Telling Me Lies (21)
That'll Be The Day (9,10) *11*
This Is To Mother You (31)
Those Memories Of You (21)
To Know Him Is To Love Him
   (21)
Toys In Time (1)

Tracks Of My Tears (8,10) *25*
Train And The River (7)
Trouble Again (23)
Try Me Again (9)
Tu Solo Tu (22)
Tumbling Dice (12,15) *32*
2:10 Train (7)
Up To My Neck In High
   Muddy Water (5) *93*
Valerie (31)
Verdad Amarga (25)
Waiting, The (27)
Walk On (27)
We Will Rock You (28)
Welsh Carol (32)
Western Wall (31)
What'll I Do (17,20)
What's New (17,20) *53*
When I Fall In Love (18,20)
When I Grow Too Old To
   Dream (13)
**When Something Is Wrong
   With My Baby** (23) *78*
When We Ran (29)
When We're Gone, Long Gone
   (30)
When Will I Be Loved
   (6,10,11) *2*
When You Wish Upon A Star
   (19,20)
When Your Lover Has Gone
   (18,20)
White Christmas (32)
White Rhythm & Blues (13)
Wild About My Lovin' (7)
Wildflowers (21)
Will You Love Me Tomorrow?
   (2,5,11)
Willing (6)
Winter Light (26,28)
Women 'Cross The River (27)
Xicochi, Xicochi (32)
Y Andale (22)
You Can Close Your Eyes (6)
You Can't Treat The Wrong
   Man Right (26)
You Go To My Head (19,20)
You Tell Me That I'm Falling
   Down (8)
You Took Advantage Of Me
   (18,20)
You'll Never Be The Sun (30)
You're No Good (6,10,11) *1*

ROOFTOP SINGERS, The '63

Folk trio from New York City: Erik Darling, Lynne Taylor and Willard Svanoe. Taylor died in 1982 (age 54).

2/16/63	15	20			Walk Right In!			$25	Vanguard 9123

Brandy Leave Me Alone
Cool Water
Ha Ha Thisaway

Ham And Eggs
Hey, Boys
Houston Special

Rained Five Days
Shoes
Somebody Came Home

Stagolee
Tom Cat *20*
Walk Right In *1*

You Don't Know

ROOTS, The '99

Hip-hop group from Philadelphia: Tariq Trotter, Ahmir-Khalib Thompson, Malik Abdul-Basit and Leonard Hubbard.

2/4/95	104	10		©	1 **Do You Want More?!!!??!**			$10	DGC 24708
10/12/96	21	16		©	2 **Illadelph Halflife**			$10	DGC 24972
3/13/99	4	18	●	©	3 **Things Fall Apart**			$10	MCA 11948
11/20/99	50	3		©	4 **The Roots Come Alive**		[L]	$10	MCA 112059

Act Too (Love Of My Life) (3)
Act Won (Things Fall Apart) (3)
Adrenaline! (3,4)
Adventures In Wonderland (2)
Ain't Sayin' Nothin' New (3)
Clones (3)
Concerto Of The Desperado (2)
Datskat (1)
Dave vs. US (2)
Diedre Vs. Dice (3)
Distortion To Static (1)

Do You Want More?!!!??! (1)
Don't See Us (3,4)
Double Trouble (3)
Dynamite (3)
Episodes (2)
Essaywhuman?!!!??! (1,4)
Hypnotic, The (2)
I Remain Calm (1)
It Just Don't Stop (2)
Ital (The Universal Side) (4)
Lazy Afternoon (1)

Lesson Pt. 1 (1)
Lesson - Part III (It's Over Now) (4)
Love Of My Life (4)
Mellow My Man (1)
Mellow My Man/Jusufckwithis (4)
Next Movement (3,4)
No Alibi (2)
No Great Pretender (2)
Notic, The (4)

100% Dundee (3,4)
One Shine (2)
Panic!!!!! (2)
Proceed (1,4)
Push Up Ya Lighter (2)
? vs. Rahzel (1)
? vs. Scratch (2)
Respond/React (2)
Return To Innocence Lost (3)
Section (2)
Silent Treatment (1,4)

Spark, The (3)
Step Into The Realm (3,4)
Swept Away (1)
Table Of Contents (Parts 1 & 2) (3)
There's Something Goin' On (1)
3rd Acts: ? Vs. Scratch 2...Electric Boogaloo (3)
Ultimate, The (4)
UNIverse at War (2)
Unlocking, The (1)

We Got You (4)
What Goes On Pt. 7 (1)
What They Do (2) *34*
What You Want (4)
Without A Doubt (3)
You Ain't Fly (1)
You Got Me (3,4) *39*

ROPER, Skid — see NIXON, Mojo

ROS, Edmundo '59

Born on 12/7/10 in Trinidad. Bandleader/drummer based in London.

5/25/59	28	2			1 **Hollywood Cha Cha Cha**		[I]	$25	London 152
12/4/61	41	4			2 **Bongos From The South**		[I]	$20	London Phase 4 44003
9/22/62	31	6			3 **Dance Again**		[I]	$20	London Phase 4 44015

Around The World (1)
As Time Goes By (1)
Blue Tango (3)
Brazil (2)
Carnival Procession (La Comparsa) (2)
Cherry Pink And Apple Blossom White (3)

Cocktails For Two (3)
Colonel Bogey (2) *75*
Deep In The Heart Of Texas (2)
Dixie (medley) (2)
El Cumbanchero (2)
Fascination (1)
High Noon (1)
I Came, I Saw, I Conga'd (3)

In A Little Spanish Town (2)
It's Magic (1)
Lady Of Spain (2)
Lisbon Antigua (2)
Love Is A Many-Splendored Thing (1)
Mambo Number Five (3)
Miami Beach Rumba (3)

Moon Over Miami (2)
Moonglow and Theme From "Picnic" (1)
Moulin Rouge Theme (1)
My Old Kentucky Home (2)
Patricia (3)
Roses From The South (2)
Taboo (2)

Tammy (1)
Tea For Two (3)
3rd Man Theme (1)
Three Coins In The Fountain (1)
Tropical Merengue (3)
True Love (1)
Wedding Samba (3)

When The Moon Comes Over The Mountain (3)
When The Saints Go Marching In (medley) (2)

ROSE, Biff '69

Born in New Orleans. Singer/songwriter/pianist.

| 2/8/69 | 75 | 14 | | | 1 **The Thorn In Mrs. Rose's Side** | | | $15 | Tetragrammaton 103 |
| 7/12/69 | 181 | 7 | | | 2 **Children Of Light** | | | $15 | Tetragrammaton 116 |

Ain't No Great Day (2)
American Waltz (1)
Angel Tension (1)
Ballad Of Cliches (2)
Buzz The Fuzz (1)

Children Of Light (2)
Color Blind Blues (2)
Communist Sympathizer (2)
Evolution (2)
Fill Your Heart (1)

Gentle People (1)
I've Got You Covered (medley) (2)
It's Happening (1)
Just Like A Man (2)

Mama's Boy (1)
Man, The (1)
Molly (1)
Paradise Almost Lost (poem) (1)

Son In Moon (2)
Spaced Out (medley) (2)
Stars, The (1)
To Baby (2)
What's Gnawing At Me (1)

ROSE, David, and His Orchestra '62

Born on 6/15/10 in London; raised in Chicago. Died of heart failure on 8/23/90 (age 80). Conductor/composer/arranger. Married to Martha Raye (1938-41) and Judy Garland (1941-45).

| 6/30/62 | 3 | 50 | ● | | **The Stripper and other fun Songs for the family** | | [I] | $25 | MGM 4062 |

Banned In Boston
Black And Tan Fantasy
Blue Prelude

Harlem Nocturne
Mood Indigo
My Heart Belongs To Daddy

Night Train
Soft Lights And Sweet Music
Sophisticated Lady

St. James Infirmary
Stripper, The *1*

What Is This Thing Called Love?

ROSE GARDEN, The '68

Pop group formed in Parkensburg, West Virginia: Diana Di Rose (vocals), Johnny Noreen and James Groshong (guitars), William Fleming (bass, piano) and Bruce Boudin (drums).

| 3/16/68 | 176 | 2 | | | **The Rose Garden** | | | $25 | Atco 225 |

Coins Of Fun
February Sunshine

Flower Town
I'm Only Second

Long Time
Look What You've Done

Next Plane To London *17*
Rider

She Belongs To Me
Till Today

ROSELLI, Jimmy '65

Born in 1926 in Hoboken, New Jersey.

6/26/65	96	11			1 **Life & Love Italian Style**		[F]	$15	United Artists 6429
9/11/65	145	5			2 **The Great Ones!**			$15	United Artists 6438
12/24/66	66 [X]	4		©	3 **The Christmas Album**		[X]	$15	United Artists 6538
					Christmas charts: 66/'66, 83/'67				
11/18/67	191	3		©	4 **There Must Be A Way**			$15	United Artists 6611
6/21/69	184	3		©	5 **Core Spezzato**		[F]	$15	United Artists 6698

'A Tazza 'E Cafe (1)
All The Time (4)
Anema E Core (1)
Anema Nera (1)
Because You're Mine (1)
Buon Natale (Means Merry Christmas To You) (3)
Chapel In The Moonlight (2)
Christmas (3)
Christmas Song (Chestnuts Roasting On An Open Fire) (3)

Core Spezzato (5)
Cry (2)
Dooje Stelle So' Cadute (1)
'E Rrose Parlano (5)
Famme Sunna (Parlami D'Amore, Mariu) (5)
Get Out Of My Heart (4)
Guaglione (1)
I Apologize (2)
I Don't Want To Walk Without You (4)
I Surrender Dear (2)

I'll Be Home For Christmas (3)
I'te Vurria Vasa! (5)
Ida (1)
Just Say I Love Her (Dicitencello Vuie) (1)
Little Pal (2)
Maria, Mari (Oh Marie) (1)
Moments To Remember (4)
My Mother's Eyes (2)
Na Sera 'E Maggio (1)
Night Before Christmas (3)
Oh What It Seemed To Be (4)

Piscatore 'E Pusilleco (1)
Prisoner Of Love (2)
Purtatele'sti Rrose (5)
Rock-A-Bye Your Baby (2)
Rudolph The Red-Nosed Reindeer (3)
Santa Claus Is Comin' To Town (3)
Senza Mamma E Nnamurata! (5)
Silent Night! (3)
Silenzio Cantatore (5)

Somewhere Along The Way (2)
Sweet Lorraine (2)
Te Purtavo'na Rosa (5)
That's My Desire (2)
There Goes My Everything (4)
There Must Be A Way (4) *93*
There's No Tomorrow (O Sole Mio) (1)
Torna (1)
Vurria (1)
Walkin' My Baby Back Home (4)

White Christmas (3)
Winter Wonderland (3)
You Make Me Feel So Young (2)
You Wanted Someone To Play With, I Wanted Someone To Love (4)

ROSE ROYCE '77

R&B group from Los Angeles: Gwen Dickey (vocals), Kenji Brown (guitar), Victor Nix (keyboards), Ken Copeland, Fred Dunn and Mike Moore (horns), Terral Santiel (percussion), Lequient Jobe (bass) and Henry Garner (drums).

10/9/76+	14	40	●	©	1 **Car Wash**		[S]	$15	MCA 6000 [2]
8/27/77	9	33	▲	©	2 **Rose Royce II/In Full Bloom**			$12	Whitfield 3074
9/9/78	28	24	●		3 **Rose Royce III/Strikes Again!**			$12	Whitfield 3227
9/8/79	74	8			4 **Rose Royce IV/Rainbow Connection**			$12	Whitfield 3387
1/24/81	160	7			5 **Golden Touch**			$12	Whitfield 3512

DEBUT	PEAK	WKS	RIAA	CD	ARTIST — Album Title	Catalog	Sym	$	Label & Number

ROSE ROYCE — Cont'd

And You Wish For Yesterday (5)
Angel In The Sky (3)
Bad Mother Funker (4)
Born To Love You (1)
Car Wash (1) *1*
Crying (1)
Daddy Rich (1)
Do It, Do It (3)
Do Your Dance - Part 1 (2) *39*

Doin' What Comes Naturally (1)
First Come, First Serve (3)
Funk Factory (2)
Funkin' Around (5)
Get Up Off Your Fat (3)
Golden Touch (5)
Help (3)
Help Yourself (5)
I Wanna Get Next To You (1) *10*
I Wanna Make It With You (5)

I Wonder Where You Are
Tonight (4)
I'm Going Down (1) *70*
I'm In Love (And I Love The Feeling) (3)
Is It Love You're After (4)
It Makes You Feel Like Dancin' (2)
Keep On Keepin' On (1)
Let Me Be The First To Know (1)

Lock It Down (4)
Love Don't Live Here Anymore (3) *32*
Love Is In The Air (5)
Love, More Love (2)
Mid Day DJ Theme (1)
Ooh Boy (2) *72*
Pazazz (4)
Put Your Money Where Your Mouth Is (1)
Righteous Rhythm (1)

Shine Your Light (4)
6 O'Clock DJ (Let's Rock) (1)
Sunrise (1)
That's What's Wrong With Me (3)
Water (1)
What You Waitin' For (4)
Wishing On A Star (2)
Would You Please Be Mine (5)
Yo Yo (1)
You Can't Please Everybody (2)

You Can't Run From Yourself (4)
You Gotta Believe (1)
You're A Winner (5)
You're My World Girl (2)
You're On My Mind (1)
Zig Zag (1)

ROSE TATTOO   '80
Hard-rock group from Australia: Angry Anderson (vocals), Peter Wells and Michael Cocks (guitars), Geordie Leech (bass) and Dallas Royall (drums).

| 11/29/80 | 197 | 3 | | | **Rock 'N' Roll Outlaw** .... | | | **$12** | Mirage 19280 |

Astra Wally
Bad Boy For Love

Butcher And Fast Eddy
Nice Boys

One Of The Boys
Remedy

Rock 'N' Roll Outlaw
Stuck On You

T.V.
Tramp

ROSS, Diana ★44★   '73
Born on 3/26/44 in Detroit. R&B singer/actress. Lead singer of **The Supremes** from 1961-69. Starred in the movies *Lady Sings The Blues*, *Mahogany* and *The Wiz*. Own Broadway show *An Evening With Diana Ross* in 1976. Married to Norwegian shipping magnate Arne Naess from 1986-2000.

1)*Lady Sings The Blues* 2)*Diana* 3)*Touch Me In The Morning* 4)*Diana Ross* 5)*Diana Ross' Greatest Hits*

7/11/70	19	28		©	1 **Diana Ross**..			$20	Motown 711
11/21/70	42	16			2 **Everything Is Everything**			$20	Motown 724
4/24/71	46	15		©	3 **Diana!**	[TV]		$20	Motown 719

includes medleys of "Mama's Pearl/Walk On By/The Love You Save" and "I'll Be There/Feeling Alright" by the **Jackson 5**

| 8/7/71 | 56 | 17 | | © | 4 **Surrender** .... | | | $20 | Motown 723 |
| 11/25/72+ | ❶² | 54 | | © | 5 **Lady Sings The Blues** .... | [S] | | $25 | Motown 758 [2] |

includes "Love Theme" and "Closing Theme" by **Michel LeGrand**; "Had You Been Around" by Michele Aller and "T'Ain't Nobody's Bizness If I Do" by Blinky Williams

| 7/14/73 | 5 | 28 | | © | 6 **Touch Me In The Morning** .... | | | $20 | Motown 772 |
| 11/17/73 | 26 | 47 | | © | 7 **Diana & Marvin** .... | | | $20 | Motown 803 |

DIANA ROSS & MARVIN GAYE

12/29/73+	52	17			8 **Last Time I Saw Him**			$15	Motown 812
6/15/74	64	17			9 **Diana Ross Live At Caesars Palace**	[L]		$15	Motown 801
3/6/76	5	32		©	10 **Diana Ross**			$15	Motown 861
8/7/76	13	23			11 **Diana Ross' Greatest Hits**	[G]		$15	Motown 869
2/12/77	29	14			12 **An Evening With Diana Ross**	[L]		$20	Motown 877 [2]

recorded at the Ahmanson Theatre in Los Angeles

10/8/77	18	19			13 **Baby It's Me**			$15	Motown 890
10/21/78	49	17			14 **Ross**			$15	Motown 907
6/16/79	14	37	●	©	15 **The Boss**			$12	Motown 923
6/14/80	2²	52	▲	©	16 **Diana**			$12	Motown 936
3/14/81	32	14			17 **To Love Again**	[K]		$12	Motown 951
10/24/81	37	32	●		18 **All The Great Hits**	[G]		$15	Motown 960 [2]
11/7/81	15	33	▲		19 **Why Do Fools Fall In Love**			$12	RCA Victor 4153
10/23/82	27	24	●	©	20 **Silk Electric**			$12	RCA Victor 4384
6/11/83	63	12		©	21 **Diana Ross Anthology**	[G]		$15	Motown 6049 [2]
7/16/83	32	17		©	22 **Ross**			$10	RCA Victor 4677
9/29/84	26	45	●	©	23 **Swept Away**			$10	RCA Victor 5009
10/12/85	45	20		©	24 **Eaten Alive**			$10	RCA Victor 5422
5/30/87	73	14		©	25 **Red Hot Rhythm & Blues**			$10	RCA Victor 6388
6/24/89	116	6		©	26 **Workin' Overtime**			$10	Motown 6274
9/28/91	102	3		©	27 **The Force Behind The Power**			$10	Motown 6316
12/18/93	154	3		©	28 **Christmas In Vienna**	[X-L]		$10	Sony Classical 53358

PLACIDO DOMINGO-DIANA ROSS-JOSE CARRERAS
recorded on 12/23/92 at the Rathaus in Vienna

| 10/14/95 | 114 | 2 | | © | 29 **Take Me Higher** .... | | | $10 | Motown 0586 |
| 5/22/99 | 108 | 4 | | © | 30 **Every Day Is A New Day** .... | | | $10 | Motown 549522 |

After You (10)
Ain't No Mountain High Enough (1,3,9,11,12,18,21) *1*
Ain't No Sad Song (2)
Ain't Nothin' But A Maybe (10)
All For One (15)
All Night Lover (13)
All Of Me (5)
All Of My Life (6)
All Of You (23) *19*
All The Befores (4)
Amazing Grace (28)
And If You See Him (4)
Anywhere You Run To (20)
Aux Iles Hawaii (12)
Baby, I Love Your Way (21)
Baby It's Love (2)
Baby It's Me (13)

Baby Love (9,12)
Battlefield (27)
Behind Closed Doors (8)
Being Green (9)
Big Mable Murphy (9)
Blame It On The Sun (27)
Bottom Line (26)
Brown Baby (medley) (6,21)
Can't It Wait Until Tomorrow (1)
Carol Of The Drum (28)
Carry On (30)
Chain Reaction (24) *95*
Change Of Heart (27)
Come In From The Rain (13)
Come Together (21)
Confide In Me (13)
Corner Of The Sky (9)

Crime Of Passion (24)
Cross My Heart (25)
Cryin' My Heart Out For You (17)
Dance: Ten, Looks: Three (12)
Dark Side Of The World (1)
Did You Read The Morning Paper? (4)
Didn't You Know (You'd Have To Cry Sometime) (4)
Dirty Looks (25)
Don't Explain (5)
Don't Give Up On Each Other (24)
Don't Knock My Love (7) *46*
Don't Rain On My Parade (3,9)
Don't Stop (29)

Doobedood'ndoobe, Doobedood'ndoobe, Doobedood'ndoo (2)
Eaten Alive (24) *77*
Endless Love (18,19,21) *1*
Every Day Is A New Day (30)
Everybody's Got 'Em (12)
Everything Is Everything (2)
Experience (24)
Fine And Mellow (5)
Fingertips (27)
Fool For Your Love (20)
Force Behind The Power (27)
Forever Young (23)
Friend To Friend (16)
Gettin' Ready For Love (13,21) *27*

Gimme A Pigfoot And A Bottle Of Beer (5)
Girls (12,22)
Give Up (16)
God Bless The Child (5,9)
Goin' Through The Motions (26)
Gone (29)
Got To Be Free (30)
Have Fun (Again) (16)
He Lives In You (30)
Heart (Don't Change My Mind) (27)
Heavy Weather (27)
Here I Am (12)
Hope Is An Open Window (30)
How About You (2)

I Ain't Been Licked (15)
I Am Me (20)
I Can't Give Back The Love I Feel For You (4)
I Cried For You (5,12)
I Hear A Symphony (9,12,18)
I Heard A Love Song (But You Never Made A Sound) (8)
(I Love) Being In Love With You (24)
I Love You (Call Me) (2,3)
I Loves Ya Porgy (9)
I Need A Little Sugar In My Bowl (12)
I Never Loved A Man Before (29)

751

ROSS, Diana — Cont'd

I Thought It Took A Little Time (But Today I Fell In Love) (10,11,17) 47
I Thought That We Were Still In Love (29)
I Want You Back (12)
I Will Survive (29)
I Won't Last A Day Without You (6)
I Wouldn't Change A Thing (12)
I Wouldn't Change The Man He Is (1)
I'll Settle For You (4)
I'm A Winner (4)
I'm Coming Out (16,18,21) 5
I'm Falling In Love With You (7)
I'm In The World (15)
I'm Still Waiting (2,21) 63
I'm Watching You (24)
If We Hold On Together (27,28)
If You're Not Gonna Love Me Right (29)
Imagine (6,21)
Improvisations (12)
In Your Arms (20)
Include Me In Your Life (7)
It's Hard For Me To Say (25)
It's My House (15,18)
It's My Turn (17,18,21) 9
It's Never Too Late (19)
It's The Most Wonderful Time Of The Year (28)
It's Your Move (23)
Jingle Bells (28)
Joy To The World (medley) (28)
Jump In The Pot (And Let's Get Hot) (12)
Just Say, Just Say (7)
Keep An Eye (1)
Keep It Right There (29)
Keep On (Dancin') (26)

Kiss Me Now (10)
La Virgen Lava Panales (medley) (28)
Lady Is A Tramp (9,12)
Lady Sings The Blues (5,9,12)
Last Time I Saw Him (8,11,21) 14
Leave A Little Room (6)
Let Somebody Know (29)
Let's Go Up (22) 77
Lifeline (12)
Little Girl Blue (6)
Long And Winding Road (2)
Love Child (medley) (18)
Love Hangover (10,11,12,18,21) 1
Love Is All That Matters (30)
Love Is Here And Now You're Gone (medley) (18)
Love Is Here To Stay (7)
Love Lies (20)
Love Me (8)
Love On The Line (24)
Love Or Loneliness (22)
Love Story (3)
Love Theme (5)
Love Twins (7)
Love Will Make It Right (22)
Lover Man (Oh Where Can You Be?) (5)
Lovin', Livin' & Givin' (14)
Mahogany (Do You Know Where You're Going To), Theme From (10,11,12,17,18,21) 1
Man I Love (5)
Me And My Arrow (12)
Mean To Me (5)
Minuit, Chretien (medley) (28)
Mirror, Mirror (19) 8
Missing You (23) 10

Money (That's What I Want) (12)
More And More (24)
Muscles (20) 10
Music In The Mirror (12)
My Baby (My Baby My Own) (6)
My Man (5,9,12)
My Mistake (Was To Love You) (7) 19
My Old Piano (16,18)
My Place (2)
My World Is Empty Without You (9,12,18)
Never Say I Don't Love You (14)
No One Gets The Prize (15)
No One's Gonna Be A Fool Forever (8,17)
Nobody Makes Me Crazy Like You Do (23)
Not Over You Yet (30)
Now That There's You (1)
Now That You're Gone (16)
O Little Town Of Bethlehem (medley) (28)
O Tannenbaum (medley) (28)
Oh Teacher (24)
Once In The Morning (15)
One Love In My Lifetime (10,11) 25
One More Chance (17) 79
One Shining Moment (27)
Only Love Can Conquer All (29)
Overture (9,12)
Paradise (26)
Pieces Of Ice (22) 31
Please Mr. Postman (12)
Pledging My Love (7)
Reach Out And Touch (Somebody's Hand) (1,9,11,12,18,21) 20

Reach Out I'll Be There (4,14,21) 29
Reflections (12,18)
Remember Me (3,4,11,18,21) 16
Rescue Me (23)
Same Love That Made Me Laugh (13)
Save The Children (medley) (6,21)
Say We Can (26)
Selfish One (25)
Send In The Clowns (medley) (12)
Shine (25)
Shockwaves (25)
Silent Night ..see: Stille Nacht
Simple Thing Like Cry (4)
Sleepin' (8) 70
Smile (10,12)
So Close (20) 40
So They Say (30)
Someday We'll Be Together (12,18)
Someone That You Loved Before (30)
Something On My Mind (1)
Sorry Doesn't Always Make It Right (14)
Sparkle (15)
Stay With Me (17)
Still In Love (20)
Stille Nacht (28)
Stone Liberty (8)
Stop! In The Name Of Love (9,12)
Stop, Look, Listen (To Your Heart) (7)
Stormy Weather (12)
Strange Fruit (5)
Stranger In Paradise (25)

Sugarfree (30)
Summertime (25)
Surrender (4,21) 38
Sweet Nothings (19)
Sweet Surrender (19)
Swept Away (23) 19
T'Ain't Nobody's Bizness If I Do (5,9,12)
Take Me Higher (29)
Take The Bitter With The Sweet (26)
Telephone (23)
Tell Me Again (25)
Tenderness (16,18)
That's How You Start Over (22)
Them There Eyes (5)
There Goes My Baby (25)
These Things Will Keep Me Loving You (1)
(They Long To Be) Close To You (2,3)
Think I'm In Love (99)
This House (26)
To Love Again (14,17)
Together (14)
Too Shy To Say (13,21)
Top Of The World (13)
Touch By Touch (23)
Touch Me In The Morning (6,11,12,17,18,21) 1
Tu Scendi Dalle Stelle (medley) (28)
Turn Around (8)
Turn Me Over (20)
Two Can Make It (19)
Until We Meet Again (30)
Up Front (22)
Upside Down (16,18,21) 1
Voice Of The Heart (29)
Waiting In The Wings (27)

We Are The Children Of The World (23)
We Need You (6)
We Stand Together (26)
What A Little Moonlight Can Do (5)
What Can One Person Do (26)
What I Did For Love (12)
What You Gave Me (14)
When Will I Come Home To You (8)
When You Tell Me That You Love Me (27)
Where Did We Go Wrong (14)
Where There Was Darkness (1)
White Christmas (28)
Why Do Fools Fall In Love (19) 7
Work That Body (19) 44
Workin' Overtime (26)
You (8)
You Are Everything (7)
You Can't Hurry Love (12,18)
You Do It (22)
You Got It (13) 49
You Keep Me Hangin' On (12,18)
You Were The One (14)
You're A Special Part Of Me (7) 12
You're All I Need To Get By (1)
You're Gonna Love It (27)
You're Good My Child (10)
You've Changed (5)
Young Mothers (21)
Your Love Is So Good For Me (13) 49

ROSSINGTON COLLINS BAND   '80

Rock group formed in Jacksonville, Florida: Dale Krantz (vocals), Gary Rossington, Allen Collins and Barry Harwood (guitars), Billy Powell (keyboards), Leon Wilkeson (bass) and Derek Hess (drums). Rossington, Collins, Powell and Wilkeson were members of **Lynyrd Skynyrd**. Disbanded in 1982. Rossington and wife Dale, Jay Johnson (guitar), Ronnie Eades (sax), Tim Sharpton (keyboards), Tim Lindsey (bass) and Mitch Rigel (drums) recorded as **The Rossington Band** in 1988. Collins died of pneumonia on 1/23/90 (age 37). Wilkeson died on 7/27/2001 (age 49).

7/12/80	13	29	● ©	1 Anytime, Anyplace, Anywhere	$12	MCA 5130
10/10/81	24	16		2 This Is The Way	$12	MCA 5207
7/16/88	140	4	©	3 Love Your Man	$10	MCA 42166

THE ROSSINGTON BAND

Call It Love (3)
Don't Misunderstand Me (1) 55
Don't Stop Me Now (2)
Fancy Ideas (2)
Getaway (1)

Gonna Miss It When It's Gone (2)
Gotta Get It Straight (2)
Holdin' My Own (3)
I Don't Want To Leave You (3)
I'm Free Today (2)

Losin' Control (3)
Love Your Man (3)
Means Nothing To You (2)
Misery Loves Company (1)
Next Phone Call (2)
Nowhere To Run (3)

One Good Man (1)
Opportunity (1)
Pine Box (2)
Prime Time (1)
Rock On (3)
Say It From The Heart (3)

Seems Like Every Day (2)
Sometimes You Can Put It Out (3)
Stay With Me (3)
Tashauna (2)
Three Times As Bad (1)

Welcome Me Home (2)
Winners And Losers (1)

ROTARY CONNECTION   '68

R&B group from Chicago: **Minnie Riperton**, Judy Hauff and Sid Barnes (vocals), Bobby Simms (guitar), Charles Stepney (keyboards), Mitch Aliotta (bass) and Kenny Venegas (drums).

3/16/68	37	31	©	1 Rotary Connection	$25	Cadet Concept 312
10/19/68	176	5	©	2 Aladdin	$25	Cadet Concept 317
12/28/68+	24ˣ	2	©	3 Peace	[X] $25	Cadet Concept 318

Christmas charts: 34/'68, 24/'69

Aladdin (2)
Amen (1)
Black Noise (1)
Christmas Child (3)
Christmas Love (3)
Didn't Want To Have To Do It (1)

I Feel Sorry (2)
I Must Be There (2)
I Took A Ride (Caravan) (2)
If Peace Was All We Had (3)
Lady Jane (1)
Last Call For Peace (3)

Let Them Talk (3)
Life Could (2)
Like A Rolling Stone (1)
Magical World (2)
Memory Band (1)
Opening Round (3)

Paper Castle (2)
Peace At Least (3)
Pink Noise (1)
Rapid Transit (1)
Rotary Connection (1)
Ruby Tuesday (1)

Santa's Little Helpers (3)
Shopping Bag Menagerie (3)
Sidewalk Santa (3)
Silence (3)
Silent Night (3)
Silent Night Chant (3)

Soul Man (1)
Sursum Mentes (1)
Teach Me How To Fly (2)
Turn Me On (1)
V.I.P. (2)

ROTH, David Lee   '86

Born on 10/10/55 in Bloomington, Indiana. Lead singer of **Van Halen** from 1973-1985.

2/23/85	15	33	▲ ©	1 Crazy From The Heat	[M] $10	Warner 25222
7/26/86	4	36	▲ ©	2 Eat 'Em And Smile	$10	Warner 25470
2/13/88	6	27	▲ ©	3 Skyscraper	$10	Warner 25671
2/2/91	18	19	● ©	4 A Little Ain't Enough	$10	Warner 26477
3/26/94	78	2	©	5 Your Filthy Little Mouth	$10	Reprise 45391
11/15/97	199	1	©	6 The Best	[G] $10	Rhino 72941
6/27/98	172	1	©	7 DLR Band	$10	Wawazat 1217

Baby's On Fire (4)
Big Train (5,6)
Big Trouble (2,6)
Black Sand (7)
Blacklight (7)
Bottom Line (3)
Bump And Grind (2)
California Girls (1,6) 3
Cheatin' Heart Cafe (5)
Coconut Grove (1)
Counter-Blast (4)

Damn Good (3)
Dogtown Shuffle (4)
Don't Piss Me Off (4)
Drop In The Bucket (4)
Easy Street (1)
Elephant Gun (4)
Everybody's Got The Monkey (5)
Experience (4)
40 Below (4)
Goin' Crazy! (2,6) 66
Going Places... (7)

Hammerhead Shark (4)
Hey, You Never Know (5)
Hina (3)
Hot Dog And A Shake (3,6)
I'm Easy (2)
Indeedido (7)
It's Showtime! (4,6)
Just A Gigolo/I Ain't Got Nobody (1,6) 12
Just Like Paradise (3,6) 6
King Of The Hill (7)

Knucklebones (3)
Ladies' Nite In Buffalo? (2,6)
Lady Luck (4)
Land's Edge (5,6)
Last Call (4)
Lil' Ain't Enough (4,6)
Little Luck (5)
Little Texas (7)
Lose The Dress (Keep The Shoes) (7)
Night Life (5)

No Big 'Ting (5)
Perfect Timing (3)
Relentless (7)
Right Tool For The Job (7)
Sensible Shoes (4,6)
She's My Machine (5,6)
Shoot It (4)
Shyboy (2,6)
Skyscraper (3,6)
Slam Dunk! (4)
Stand Up (3,6) 64

Sunburn (5)
Tell The Truth (4)
That's Life (2) 85
Tight (7)
Tobacco Road (2,6)
Two Fools A Minute (3)
Wa Wa Zat!! (7)
Weekend With The Babysitter (7)
Yankee Rose (2,6) 16
You're Breathin' It (5)
Your Filthy Little Mouth (5)

ROTTIN RAZKALS '95
Rap trio from East Orange, New Jersey: Jeff Ray, Chap and FAM.

| 4/8/95 | 190 | 1 | | © | **Rottin Ta Da Core** | | | $10 | Illtown 0461 |

A-yo · Come On Ya'll · Get Up, Stand Up · Homiez Niggaz · Lik A Shot · One Time For Ya Mind · Batter Up · Frustration · Hey Alright · Life Of A Bastard · Oh Yeah

ROUGH DIAMOND '77
Rock group from England: David Byron (vocals, **Uriah Heep**), Clem Clempson (guitar; **Humble Pie**), Damon Butcher (keyboards), Willie Bath (bass) and Geoff Britton (drums). Byron died on 2/28/85 (age 38).

| 5/7/77 | 103 | 8 | | | **Rough Diamond** | | | $12 | Island 9490 |

By The Horn · Hobo · Lock & Key · Rock 'N' Roll · Seasong · End Of The Line · Link, The · Lookin' For You · Scared

ROUSSOS, Demis '78
Born on 6/15/47 in Alexandria, Egypt (Greek parents). Male rock singer.

| 6/17/78 | 184 | 6 | | © | **Demis Roussos** | | | $12 | Mercury 3724 |

Feel Like I'll Never Feel This Way Again · I Just Don't Know What To Do With Myself · Life In The City · Other Woman · That Once In A Lifetime *47* · Hey Friend · I Just Live · L.O.V.E. Got A Hold Of Me · This Song · Loving Arms

ROUTERS, The '63
Instrumental group formed in Los Angeles: Mike Gordon, Al Kait, Bill Moody and Lynn Frazier.

| 3/2/63 | 104 | 4 | | | **Let's Go! with The Routers** | | [I] | $50 | Warner 1490 |

Bucket Seats · Half Time · **Let's Go** *19* · Make It Snappy · Mating Call · Snap Happy · Grandstand Stomp · Let's Dance · Limbo Rock · Mashy · Pep Rally · **Sting Ray** *50*

ROVERS, The — see IRISH ROVERS, The

ROWLES, John '71
Born on 3/26/47 in Whakatane, New Zealand. Pop singer.

| 3/20/71 | 197 | 1 | | | **Cheryl Moana Marie** | | | $15 | Kapp 3637 |

Another Tear Falls · Come On Back And Get It · House Is Not A Home · Love I Had With You · Salty Tears · What Greater Love · **Cheryl Moana Marie** *64* · Heaven Here On Earth · In The Name Of Heaven · One Room World · Time For Love

ROXETTE '91
Pop-rock duo from Sweden: Marie Fredriksson (born on 5/30/58) and Per Gessle (born on 6/12/59).

4/22/89+	23	71	▲	©	1 **Look Sharp!**			$10	EMI 91098
4/20/91	12	56	▲	©	2 **Joyride**			$10	EMI 94435
10/24/92	117	8		©	3 **Tourism**		[K]	$10	EMI 99929

old and new tracks recorded live on stage or in studio or hotel rooms during their *Join The Joyride* world tour

Big L. (2) · Dangerous (1) *2* · Heart Shaped Sea (3) · **Listen To Your Heart** (1) *1* · Shadow Of A Doubt (1) · Things Will Never Be The Same (2,3)
Chances (1) · (Do You Get) Excited? (2) · Here Comes The Weekend (3) · **Look, The** (1,3) *1* · Silver Blue (3) · View From A Hill (1)
Church Of Your Heart (2) *36* · **Dressed For Success** (1) *14* · Never Is A Long Time (3) · Sleeping Single (1) · Watercolours In The Rain (2)
Cinnamon Street (3) · **Fading Like A Flower (Every Time You Leave)** (2) *2* · **How Do You Do!** (3) *58* · Paint (1) · Small Talk (2)
Come Back (Before You Leave) (3) · Fingertips (3) · It Must Have Been Love (3) · Perfect Day (2) · So Far Away (3)
Cry (1) · Half A Woman, Half A Shadow (1) · **Joyride** (2,3) *1* · Physical Fascination (2) · Soul Deep (2)
Dance Away (1) · Keep Me Waiting (3) · Queen Of Rain (3) · **Spending My Time** (2) *32*
Knockin' On Every Door (2) · Rain, The (3)

ROXY MUSIC '79
Art-rock group from England: Bryan Ferry (vocals, keyboards), **Phil Manzanera** (guitar), Andy MacKay (horns) and Paul Thompson (drums).

1)Manifesto 2)Flesh + Blood 3)Country Life

7/28/73	193	2		©	1 **For Your Pleasure**			$30	Warner 2696
5/18/74	186	4		©	2 **Stranded**			$20	Atco 7045
1/25/75	37	15		©	3 **Country Life**			$20	Atco 106
11/29/75+	50	20		©	4 **Siren**			$20	Atco 127
8/7/76	81	7		©	5 **Viva! Roxy Music**		[L]	$12	Atco 139
3/31/79	23	16		©	6 **Manifesto**			$12	Atco 114
6/28/80	35	19		©	7 **Flesh + Blood**			$12	Atco 102
6/19/82	53	27	▲	©	8 **Avalon**			$10	Warner 23686
4/9/83	67	22			9 **Musique/The High Road**		[L-M]	$10	Warner 23808

recorded at the Apollo Theatre in Glasgow, Scotland

| 1/21/84 | 183 | 6 | | © | 10 **The Atlantic Years 1973-1980** | | [K] | $10 | Atco 90122 |
| 8/26/89 | 100 | 11 | | | 11 **Street Life-20 Great Hits** | | [G] | $15 | Reprise 25857 [2] |

BRYAN FERRY/ROXY MUSIC
6 **Bryan Ferry** solos (see Ferry for tracks) and 14 **Roxy Music** hits from 1972-85

Ain't That So (6,10) · Dance Away (6,10,11) *44* · Jealous Guy (9,11) · Out Of The Blue (3,5) · Spin Me Round (6) · Virginia Plain (11)
All I Want Is You (3) · Do The Strand (1,5,10,11) · Just Another High (4) · **Over You** (7,10,11) *80* · Still Falls The Rain (6,10) · While My Heart Is Still Beating (8)
Amazona (2) · Editions Of You (1) · Just Like You (2) · Prairie Rose (3) · Street Life (2,11)
Angel Eyes (6,10,11) · Eight Miles High (7) · Like A Hurricane (9) · Psalm (2) · Strictly Confidential (1) · Whirlwind (4)
Avalon (8,11) · End Of The Line (4) · **Love Is The Drug** (4,10,11) *30* · Rain Rain Rain (7) · Stronger Through The Years (6)
Beauty Queen (1) · Flesh And Blood (7) · Main Thing (8) · Really Good Time (3) · Sunset (2)
Bitter-Sweet (3) · For Your Pleasure (1) · Manifesto (6) · Running Wild (7) · Take A Chance With Me (8)
Bogus Man (1,5) · Grey Lagoons (1) · More Than This (8,11) · Same Old Scene (7,11) · Tara (8)
Both Ends Burning (4,5) · If It Takes All Night (5) · Mother Of Pearl (2) · Sentimental Fool (4) · Three And Nine (3)
Can't Let Go (9) · If There Is Something (5) · My Little Girl (6) · Serenade (2) · Thrill Of It All (3)
Casanova (3) · In Every Dream Home A Heartache (1,5) · My Only Love (7,9,10) · She Sells (4) · To Turn You On (8)
Chance Meeting (5) · In The Midnight Hour (7,10,11) · Nightingale (4) · Song For Europe (2) · Trash (2)
Could It Happen To Me? (4) · India (8) · No Strange Delight (7) · Space Between (8) · Triptych (3)
Cry, Cry, Cry (6) · Oh Yeah (7,10,11) · True To Life (8)

ROYAL, Billy Joe '65
Born on 4/3/42 in Valdosta, Georgia; raised in Marietta, Georgia. Country-rock singer/guitarist.

| 9/18/65 | 96 | 7 | | © | 1 **Down In The Boondocks** | | | $25 | Columbia 9203 |
| 1/3/70 | 100 | 9 | | © | 2 **Cherry Hill Park** | | | $25 | Columbia 9974 |

Ain't It The Truth (2)
Burning A Hole (2)
Cherry Hill Park (2) *15*
Children (2)
Down Home Lovin' (2)

Down In The Boondocks (1)
Funny How Time Slips Away (1)
Heartaches And Teardrops (1)
Helping Hand (2)
I Knew You When (1) *14*

9 I've Got To Be Somebody
(1) *38*
If I Had It To Do Again (2)
King Of Fools (1)
Leaning On You (1)

Mama' Song (2)
My Fondest Memories (1)
Oh, What A Night (1)
Pick Up The Pieces (2)
Pollyanna (1)

Steal Away (1)
Those Railroad Tracks In
Between (1)
You Can Make Me Feel Good
(2)

You Can't Manufacture Love (2)

ROYAL CROWN REVUE '98
Swing group: Eddie Nichols (vocals), James Anchor (guitar), Mando Dorame, Bill Ungerman, Scott Steen (horns), Veikko Lepisto (bass) and Daniel Glass (drums).

| 9/12/98 | 172 | 2 | | © | **The Contender** | | | $10 | Warner 47020 |

Big Boss Lee
Contender, The
Deadly Nightcall

Everyone Knows You're Crazy
Friday The 13th
Morning Light

Port-Au-Prince (Travels With
Bettie Page)
Salt Peanuts

Stormy Weather
Walkin' Like Brando
Work Baby Work

Zip Gun Bop (Reloaded)

ROYAL GUARDSMEN, The '67
Novelty-pop group from Ocala, Florida: Barry Winslow (vocals, guitar), Chris Nunley (vocals), Tom Richards (guitar), Bill Balough (bass) and Billy Taylor (organ). "Snoopy" songs inspired by Snoopy the Beagle in the "Peanuts" comic strip.

| 2/11/67 | 44 | 22 | | © | 1 **Snoopy vs. The Red Baron** | | [N] | $30 | Laurie 2038 |
| 12/23/67+ | 46 | 11 | | © | 2 **Snoopy And His Friends** | | [X-N] | $30 | Laurie 2042 |

Christmas charts: 6/'67, 19/'68

| 8/31/68 | 189 | 2 | | © | 3 **Snoopy For President** | | [N] | $30 | Laurie 2046 |

Airplane Song (My Airplane)
(2) *6*
Alley-Oop (1)
Baby Let's Wait (1) *35*
Battle Of New Orleans (1)
Bears (1)
Biplane Evermore (3)

Bo Diddley (1)
Bonnie & Clyde (3)
Bottle Of Wine (3)
By The Time I Get To Phoenix
(3)
Come On Down To My Boat (3)
Cry Like A Baby (medley) (3)

Down Behind The Lines (2)
Honey (3)
I Say Love (2) *72*
It Kinda Looks Like Christmas
(2)
It's Sopwith Camel Time (2)
Jolly Green Giant (1)

Letter, The (medley) (3)
Li'l Red Riding Hood (1)
Liberty Valance (1)
Peanut Butter (1)
Return Of The Red Baron
(2) *15*
Road Runner (1)

Simon Says (3)
Snoopy For President (3) *85*
Snoopy Vs. The Red Baron
(1,2) *2*
So Right (To Be In Love) (2)
Story Of Snoopy's Christmas
(2)

Sweetmeats Slide (1)
Yummy, Yummy, Yummy (3)

ROYAL PHILHARMONIC ORCHESTRA '82
Orchestra from England. Conducted by Louis Clark.

11/14/81+	4	68	▲		1 **Hooked On Classics**		[I]	$10	RCA Victor 4194
8/28/82	33	41	●		2 **Hooked On Classics II (Can't Stop the Classics)**		[I]	$10	RCA Victor 4373
4/23/83	89	14			3 **Hooked On Classics III (Journey Through the Classics)**		[I]	$10	RCA Victor 4588

Also Sprach Zarathustra (3)
Can't Stop The Classics (Part 1
& 2) (2)
Dance Of The Furies (3)
Hooked On A Can Can (1)
Hooked On A Song (1)

Hooked On America (2)
Hooked On Bach (1)
Hooked On Baroque (2)
Hooked On Classics (1) *10*
Hooked On Classics Part 3 (1)
Hooked On Haydn (3)

Hooked On Marching (3)
Hooked On Mendelssohn (1)
Hooked On Mozart (1)
Hooked On Rodgers &
Hammerstein (3)
Hooked On Romance (1)

Hooked On Romance (Opus 3)
(3)
Hooked On Romance (Part 2)
(2)
Hooked On Tchaikovsky (1)
If You Knew Sousa (2)

If You Knew Sousa (And
Friends) (2)
Journey Through America (3)
Journey Through The Classics
(Part 1 & 2) (3)
Night At The Opera (2)

Scotland The Brave (Hookery
Jiggery Jock) (3)
Symphony Of The Seas (3)
Tales Of The Vienna Waltz (2)
Viva Vivaldi (3)

ROYAL SCOTS DRAGOON GUARDS '72
The military band of Scotland's armored regiment. Led by bagpipe soloist Major Tony Crease.

| 6/24/72 | 34 | 15 | | © | **Amazing Grace** | | [I] | $15 | RCA Victor 4744 |

Abide With Me
Amazing Grace *11*

Cornet Carillon
Going Home
Jubilant

March, Strathspeys, Reels &
March Medley
Marches Medley

Quick Marches Medley
Reveille
Russian Imperial Anthem

Scotland The Brave
Slow Air & Jigs Medley
Slow March & Walk Medley

Trot & Canter Medley

RTZ '92
Rock group formed in Boston: Brad Delp (vocals), **Barry Goudreau** (guitar), Brian Maes (keyboards), Tim Archibald (bass) and David Stefanelli (drums). Delp and Goudreau were members of **Boston**. Goudreau was also with **Orion The Hunter**. RTZ: Return To Zero.

| 3/7/92 | 169 | 5 | | © | **Return To Zero** | | | $10 | Giant 24422 |

All You've Got *56*
Devil To Pay

Every Door Is Open
Face The Music *49*

Hard Time (In The Big House)
Livin' For The Rock 'N' Roll

Rain Down On Me
Return To Zero

There's Another Side
This Is My Life

**Until Your Love Comes Back
Around** *26*

RUBBER BAND, The '69
Studio group assembled by producer Michael Lloyd.

| 8/2/69 | 135 | 6 | | | 1 **Cream Songbook** | | [I] | $25 | GRT 10000 |
| 9/6/69 | 116 | 8 | | | 2 **Hendrix Songbook** | | [I] | $25 | GRT 10007 |

All Along The Watch Tower (2)
Dance The Night Away (1)
Deserted Cities Of The Heart
(1)

Fire (2)
Foxey Lady (2)
Little Miss Lover (2)
Manic Depression (2)

Purple Haze (2)
Rubber Jam (2)
Strange Brew (1)
Sunshine Of Your Love (1)

Sweet Wine (1)
Those Were The Days (1)
Toad (1)
We're Going Wrong (1)

White Room (1)
Wind Cries Mary (2)

RUBICON '78
Pop-rock group from San Francisco: Greg Eckler (vocals, drums), Brad Gillis (guitar), Jerry Martini, Max Haskett and Dennis Marcellino (horns), Jim Pugh (keyboards), and Jack Blades (bass). Martini was a member of **Sly & The Family Stone**. Gillis and Blades later formed **Night Ranger**.

| 3/25/78 | 147 | 7 | | | **Rubicon** | | | $12 | 20th Century 552 |

And The Moon's Out Tonight
Cheatin'
Closely

Far Away
I Want To Love You

I'm Gonna Take Care Of
Everything *28*
It's All For The Show

That's The Way Things Are
Vanilla Gorilla

RUBINSTEIN, Arthur '61
Born on 1/28/1887 in Lodz, Poland. Died on 12/20/82 (age 95). Classical pianist. Father of Broadway/TV actor John Rubinstein. Won Grammy's Lifetime Achievement Award in 1994.

| 1/9/61 | 117 | 15 | | | 1 **Rachmaninoff: Piano Concerto No. 2/ Liszt: Piano Concerto No. 1** | | [I] | $25 | RCA Victor 2068 |
| 2/13/61 | 30 | 12 | | | 2 **Heart of the Piano Concerto** | | [I] | $20 | RCA Victor 2495 |

Concerto For Piano In A-Minor,
Op. 16 (2)

Concerto No. 1, In E-Flat For
Piano (1,2)

Concerto No. 3 For Piano, In C
Minor, Op. 37 (2)

Concerto No. 2, In C Minor, Op.
18 (1,2)
Concerto No. 2 In F Minor (2)

Concerto No. 2, In G Minor, Op.
22 (2)

RUBIO, Paulina   '01
Born on 6/17/71 in Mexico City. Latin singer.

| 2/17/01 | **156** | 15 | © | **Paulina** .... [F] | **$10** | Universal Latino 543319 |

Baby Paulina   El Ultimo Adios   Mirame A Los Ojos   Sin Aire   Tan Sola   Y Yo Sigo Aqui
Cancun Y Yo   Lo Hare Por Ti   Sexi Dance   Tal Vez, Quiza   Vive El Verano   Yo No Soy Esa Mujer

RUBY AND THE ROMANTICS   '63
R&B vocal group from Akron, Ohio: Ruby Nash Curtis (born on 11/12/39), Leroy Fann, Ed Roberts, George Lee and Ronald Mosley. Fann died in November 1973 (age 37). Roberts died of cancer on 8/10/93 (age 57).

| 5/11/63 | **120** | 6 | | **Our Day Will Come** .... | **$50** | Kapp 3323 |

By The Way   Heartaches   (I'm Afraid) The Masquerade Is   Lonely People Do Foolish   My Prayer
Day Dreaming   I Don't Know Why (I Just Do)   Over   Things   **Our Day Will Come 1**
End Of The World   I'm Sorry   Moonlight And Music   Stranger On The Shore

RUDE BOYS   '91
R&B vocal group from Cleveland: brothers Ed Banks and J. Little, with Larry Marcus and Melvin Sephus.

| 2/23/91 | **68** | 16 | © | **Rude Awakenings** .... | **$10** | Atlantic 82121 |

Are You Lonely For Me   Fool For You   I Feel For You   I'm Going Thru   Pressure
Come On Let's Do This   Heaven   I Need You   Never Get Enough Of It   **Written All Over Your Face 16**

RUFF ENDZ   '00
R&B vocal duo from Baltimore: David Chance and Dante Jordan.

| 9/9/00 | **52** | 11 | © | **Love Crimes** .... | **$10** | Epic 69719 |

Are U F***in' Around   I'm Not Just Sayin' That, I'm   Love Crimes   Phone Sex   Shout Out   World To Me
Cuban Linx 2000   Feeling That   Missing You   Please Don't Forget About Me   Where Does Love Go From
I Apologize   If I Was The One   **No More 5**   Saying I Love You   Here

RUFFIN, David   '76
Born on 1/18/41 in Meridian, Mississippi. Died of a drug overdose on 6/1/91 (age 50). R&B singer. Brother of **Jimmy Ruffin**. Co-lead singer of **The Temptations** from 1963-68. Also see **Daryl Hall & John Oates**.

6/21/69	**31**	17		1 **My Whole World Ended**	**$20**	Motown 685
12/13/69+	**148**	7		2 **Feelin' Good**	**$20**	Motown 696
11/7/70	**178**	3		3 **I Am My Brother's Keeper**	**$20**	Soul 728
				THE RUFFIN BROTHERS (Jimmy & David)		
3/17/73	**160**	7		4 **David Ruffin**	**$15**	Motown 762
11/15/75+	**31**	27		5 **Who I Am** _____	**$15**	Motown 849
6/12/76	**51**	12		6 **Everything's Coming Up Love**	**$15**	Motown 866

Blood Donors Needed (Give All   Flower Child (1)   I Pray Everyday You Won't   Letter, The (2)   Put A Little Love In Your Heart   Turn Back The Hands Of Time
You Can) (4)   Forgotten Man (2)   Regret Loving Me (2)   Little More Trust (4)   (2)   (3)
Common Man (4)   Go On With Your Bad Self (4)   I'm Just A Mortal Man (4)   Lo And Behold (3)   Ready, Willing And Able (6)   Until We Said Goodbye (3)
Day In The Life, Of A Working   Good Good Times (6)   **I'm So Glad I Fell For You**   Love Can Be Hazardous To   Rovin' Kind (4)   Walk Away From Love (5) 9
Man (4)   Got To See If I Can't Get   (2) 53   Your Health (5)   Set 'Em Up (Move In For The   We'll Have A Good Thing Going
Didn't I (Blow Your Mind This   Mommy (To Come Back   I've Got Nothing But Time (5)   Loving You (Is Hurting Me) (2)   Thrill) (3)   On (1)
Time) (3)   Home) (3)   I've Got To Find Myself A Brand   Message From Maria (1)   Somebody Stole My Dream (1)   What You Gave Me (2)
Discover Me (6)   He Ain't Heavy, He's My   New Baby (1)   My Love Is Growing Stronger   **Stand By Me** (3) 61   When My Love Hand Comes
Double Cross (1)   Brother (3)   **I've Lost Everything I've Ever**   (1)   Statue Of A Fool (5)   Down (3)
Everlasting Love (1)   Heavy Love (5) 47   **Loved** (5) 58   **My Whole World Ended (The**   There Will Always Be Another   Who I Am (5)
Everything's Coming Up Love   I Could Never Be President (2)   (If Loving You Is Wrong) I Don't   **Moment You Left Me)** (1) 9   Song To Sing (4)   Wild Honey (5)
(6) 49   I Don't Know Why I Love You   Want To Be Right (4)   On And Off (6)   Things We Have To Do (3)   World Of Darkness (1)
Feeling Alright (2)   (2)   It Takes All Kinds Of People To   One More Hurt (3)   True Love Can Be Beautiful (3)   Your Love Was Worth Waiting
Finger Pointers (5)   I Let Love Slip Away (2)   Make A World (5)   Pieces Of A Man (1)   For (3)
First Round Knock-Out (6)   I Miss You (4)   Let's Get Into Something (6)

RUFFIN, Jimmy   '67
Born on 5/7/39 in Collinsville, Mississippi. R&B singer. Brother of **David Ruffin**.

5/13/67	**133**	11	©	1 **Top Ten**	**$30**	Soul 704
4/19/69	**196**	2	©	2 **Ruff'N Ready**	**$30**	Soul 708
11/7/70	**178**	3		3 **I Am My Brother's Keeper**	**$20**	Soul 728
				THE RUFFIN BROTHERS (Jimmy & David)		
5/31/80	**152**	6		4 **Sunrise**	**$12**	RSO 3078

As Long As There Is L-O-V-E   Everybody Needs Love (2)   He Ain't Heavy, He's My   Lo And Behold (3)   Songbird (4)   When My Love Hand Comes
Love (1)   Farewell Is A Lonely Sound (2)   Brother (3)   Lonely Lonely Man Am I (2)   **Stand By Me** (3) 61   Down (3)
Black Is Black (1)   Forever (4)   **Hold On To My Love** (4) 10   Love Gives, Love Takes Away   Steppin' On A Dream (3)   Where Do I Go (4)
Bless You (1)   **Gonna Give Her All The Love**   How Can I Say I'm Sorry (1)   (2)   Things We Have To Do (3)   World So Wide, Nowhere To
Changin' Me (1)   **I've Got** (1) 29   I Want Her Love (1)   Night Of Love (4)   Tomorrow's Tears (1)   Hide (From Your Heart) (1)
Didn't I (Blow Your Mind This   Gonna Keep On Tryin' Till I Win   **I'll Say Forever My Love** (2) 77   96 Tears (2)   True Love Can Be Beautiful (3)   You Got What It Takes (2)
Time) (3)   Your Love (2)   **I've Passed This Way Before**   Sad And Lonesome Feeling (2)   Turn Back The Hands Of Time   Your Love Was Worth Waiting
Don't Let Him Take Your Love   Got To See If I Can't Get   (1) 17   Searchin' (4)   (3)   For (3)
From Me (2)   Mommy (To Come Back   It's Wonderful (To Be Loved By   Set 'Em Up (Move In For The   Two People (4)
Don't You Miss Me A Little Bit   Home) (3)   You) (2)   Thrill) (3)   **What Becomes Of The**
Baby (2) 68   Halfway To Paradise (1)   Jealousy (4)   Since I've Lost You (1)   **Brokenhearted** (1) 7

RUFFNER, Mason   '87
Born in Fort Worth, Texas. Rock singer/songwriter/guitarist.

| 6/13/87 | **80** | 16 | © | **Gypsy Blood** .... | **$10** | CBS Associated 40601 |
| | | | | produced by **Dave Edmunds** | | |

Ain't Gonna Get It   Courage   Distant Thunder   Gypsy Blood   Runnin'
Baby, I Don't Care No More   Dancin' On Top Of The World   Fightin' Back   Red Hot Lover   Under Your Spell

RUFF RYDERS   '99
All-star rap group from New York City: **DMX**, **Drag-On**, **Eve**, **The Lox** and **Swizz Beatz**.

| 5/15/99 | **❶**[1] | 37 | ▲ © | 1 **Ruff Ryders - Ryde Or Die Vol. I** | **$10** | Ruff Ryders 90315 |
| 7/22/00 | **2**[1] | 17 | ▲ © | 2 **Ruff Ryders - Ryde Or Die Vol. II** | **$10** | Ruff Ryders 90625 |

Bugout (1)   Go Head (2)   I'm A Ruff Ryder (1)   Piña Colada (1)   Stomp (2)   **What Ya Want** (1) 29
Do That Shit (1)   Got It All (2)   It's Going Down (2)   Platinum Plus (1)   Twisted Heat (2)
Dope Money (1)   Great, The (2)   **Jigga My Nigga** (1) 28   Ryde Or Die (1)   2 Tears In A Bucket (2)
Down Bottom (1)   Holiday (2)   Kiss Of Death (1)   Ryde Or Die Boyz (2)   WW III (2)
Fright Night (2)   Hood, The (1)   My Name Is Kiss (2)   Some X Shit (1)   Weed, Hoes, Dough (2)

★326★ RUFUS Featuring Chaka Khan '74

R&B group from Chicago: **Chaka Khan** (vocals), Tony Maiden (guitar), Nate Morgan and Kevin Murphy (keyboards), Bobby Watson (bass), and Andre Fischer (drums; **American Breed**). Khan has been recording solo and with Rufus since 1978. After 1978, Malden and David Wolinski also sang lead.

1)Rags To Rufus 2)Rufus Featuring Chaka Khan 3)Rufusized

8/4/73	175	6		©	1	Rufus			$12	ABC 783
6/29/74	4	30	●	©	2	Rags To Rufus			$12	ABC 809
						RUFUS (above 2)				
1/4/75	7	24	●	©	3	Rufusized			$12	ABC 837
12/6/75+	7	32	●	©	4	Rufus Featuring Chaka Khan			$12	ABC 909
2/5/77	12	25	▲	©	5	Ask Rufus			$12	ABC 975
2/11/78	14	26	●	©	6	Street Player			$12	ABC 1049
2/10/79	81	9			7	Numbers			$12	ABC 1098
						RUFUS				
11/17/79	14	26	●	©	8	Masterjam			$12	MCA 5103
3/28/81	73	11			9	Party 'Til You're Broke			$12	MCA 5159
						RUFUS				
10/31/81	98	14			10	Camouflage			$12	MCA 5270
9/3/83	50	33			11	Live-Stompin' At The Savoy		[L]	$15	Warner 23679 [2]

recorded in February 1982 at the Savoy Theatre in New York City

A-Flat Fry (medley) (5)
Afterwards (9)
Ain't Nobody (11) **22**
Ain't Nobody Like You (7)
Ain't Nothin' But A Maybe (2)
Ain't That Peculiar (11)
Any Love (8)
Are We? (7)
At Midnight (My Love Will Lift You Up) (5,11) **30**
Best Of Your Heart (6)
Bet My Dreams (7)
Better Days (5)
Better Together (10)
Blue Love (6)
Body Heat (8)
Can I Show You (9)
Change Your Ways (6)
Circles (4)
Close The Door (5)

Dance Wit Me (4,11) **39**
Dancin' Mood (7)
Destiny (6)
Do You Love What You Feel (8,11) **30**
Don't Go To Strangers (11)
Don't You Sit Alone (7)
Earth Song (5)
Egyptian Song (5)
Everlasting Love (5)
Everybody Has An Aura (4)
Feel Good (1)
Finale (6)
Fool's Paradise (4)
Half Moon (3)
Haulin' Coal (1)
Have A Good Time (4)
Heaven Bound (8)
Highlight (10)
Hold On To A Friend (9)

Hollywood (5) **32**
I Finally Found You (1)
I Got The Right Street (But The Wrong Direction) (2)
I'm A Woman (I'm A Backbone) (3,11)
I'm Dancing For Your Love (8)
In Love We Grow (2)
Jigsaw (10)
Jive Talkin' (4)
Keep It Coming (1)
Keep It Together (Declaration Of Love) (7)
Life In The City (7)
Lilah (10)
Little Boy Blue (4)
Live In Me (8)
Look Through My Eyes (2)
Loser In Love (10)
Love Is Taking Over (9)

Love The One You're With (medley) (1)
Magic In Your Eyes (5)
Masterjam (8)
Maybe Your Baby (1)
Music Man (The D.J. Song) (10)
On Time (4)
Once You Get Started (3,11) **10**
One Million Kisses (11)
Ooh I Like Your Loving (4)
Pack'd My Bags (3,11)
Party 'Til You're Broke (9)
Please Pardon Me (You Remind Me Of A Friend) (3) **48**
Pleasure Dome (7)
Quandary (10)
Rags To Rufus (2)
Red Hot Poker (7)

Right Is Right (3)
Rufusized (3)
Satisfied (1)
Secret Friend (10)
Secret Love (9)
Sharing The Love (10) **91**
Sideways (2)
Sit Yourself Down (medley) (1)
Slip 'N Slide (7)
Slow Screw Against The Wall (medley) (5)
Smokin' Room (2)
Somebody's Watching You (3)
Stay (6,11) **38**
Stop On By (1)
Stranger To Love (6)
Street Player (6)
Sweet Thing (4,11) **5**
Swing Down Chariot (2)
Take Time (6)

Tell Me Something Good (2,11) **3**
There's No Tellin' (1)
Tonight We Love (9)
True Love (10)
Try A Little Understanding (11)
Turn (6)
Walk The Rockway (8)
Walkin' In The Sun (7)
We Got The Way (9)
What Am I Missing? (8)
What Cha' Gonna Do For Me (11)
What Is It (9)
Whoever's Thrilling You (Is Killing Me) (1)
You Got The Love (2,11) **11**
You're Made For Me (9)
You're To Blame (3)
Your Smile (3)

RUMOUR, The '77

Backing group for **Graham Parker**: Brinsley Schwarz (vocals, guitar), Martin Belmont (guitar), Bob Andrews (keyboards), Andrew Bodnar (bass) and Stephen Goulding (drums).

8/13/77	124	10			1	Max			$12	Mercury 1174
8/4/79	160	3		©	2	Frogs Sprouts Clogs And Krauts			$12	Arista 4235

Airplane Tonight (1)
All Fall Down (2)
Do Nothing 'Till You Hear From Me (1)

Emotional Traffic (2)
Euro (2)
Face To Face (1)
Frozen Years (2)

Hard Enough To Show (1)
I Can't Help Myself (2)
I Wanna Make Her Love Me (1)
I'm So Glad (1)

Leaders (2)
Looking After No. 1 (1)
Loving You (Is Far Too Easy) (2)

Mess With Love (1)
New Age (medley) (2)
One Good Night (2)
Somethin's Goin' On (1)

This Town (1)
Tired Of Waiting (2)
We Believe In You (medley) (2)

RUNAWAYS, The '77

Hard-rock group formed in Los Angeles: Cherie Currie (vocals), **Joan Jett** and **Lita Ford** (guitars), Micki Steele (bass), and Sandy West (drums). Steele later joined the **Bangles**.

8/21/76	194	2		©	1	The Runaways			$25	Mercury 1090
2/5/77	172	4		©	2	Queens Of Noise			$25	Mercury 1126

American Nights (1)
Blackmail (1)
Born To Be Bad (1)
California Paradise (2)

Cherry Bomb (1)
Dead End Justice (1)
Heartbeat (2)
Hollywood (2)

I Love Playin' With Fire (2)
Is It Day Or Night? (1)
Johnny Guitar (2)
Lovers (1)

Midnight Music (2)
Neon Angels On The Road To Ruin (1)
Queens Of Noise (2)

Rock And Roll (1)
Secrets (1)
Take It Or Leave It (2)
Thunder (1)

You Drive Me Wild (1)

★344★ RUNDGREN, Todd '73

Born on 6/22/48 in Upper Darby, Pennsylvania. Pop-rock singer/songwriter/multi-instrumentalist. Leader of **Nazz** and **Utopia**.

1)Something/Anything? 2)Hermit Of Mink Hollow 3)Healing

1/9/71	185	6		©	1	Runt			$50	Ampex 10105
3/25/72+	29	48	●	©	2	Something/Anything?			$20	Bearsville 2066 [2]
3/31/73	86	15		©	3	A Wizard/A True Star			$15	Bearsville 2133
3/16/74	54	17		©	4	Todd			$20	Bearsville 6952 [2]
6/14/75	86	7		©	5	Initiation			$12	Bearsville 6957
5/15/76	54	15		©	6	Faithful			$12	Bearsville 6963
5/6/78	36	26		©	7	Hermit Of Mink Hollow			$12	Bearsville 6981
12/2/78+	75	15		©	8	Back To The Bars		[L]	$15	Bearsville 6986 [2]
2/21/81	48	13		©	9	Healing			$12	Bearsville 3522
1/22/83	66	13		©	10	The Ever Popular Tortured Artist Effect			$12	Bearsville 23732
10/12/85	128	8		©	11	A Cappella			$10	Warner 25128
6/17/89	102	11		©	12	Nearly Human			$10	Warner 25881
2/16/91	118	8		©	13	2nd Wind			$10	Warner 26478

All The Children Sing (7)
Baby, Let's Swing (medley) (1)
Bag Lady (1)
Bang The Drum All Day (10) **63**
Believe In Me (1)
Birthday Carol (1)
Black And White (6,8)
Black Maria (2,8)

Blue Orpheus (11)
Boogies (Hamburger Hell) (6)
Born To Synthesize (5)
Bread (1)
Breathless (2)
Broke Down And Busted (1)
Can We Still Be Friends (7) **29**
Can't Stop Running (12)
Change Myself (13)

Chant (10)
Cliche (6,8)
Cold Morning Light (2)
Compassion (9)
Cool Jerk (medley) (3)
Couldn't I Just Tell You (2,8) **93**
Da Da Dali (medley) (3)
Death Of Rock And Roll (5)

Determination (7)
Devil's Bite (1)
Does Anybody Love You? (3)
Dogfight Giggle (3)
Don't Hurt Yourself (10)
Don't Tie My Hands (medley) (1)
Don't You Ever Learn? (4,8)
Drive (10)
Dream Goes On Forever (4,8) **69**

Drunken Blue Rooster (4)
Dust In The Wind (2)
Eastern Intrigue (5,8)
Elpee's Worth Of Toons (4)
Emperor Of The Highway (10)

Everybody's Going To Heaven (medley) (4)
Fade Away (7)
Fair Warning (5)Feel It (12)
Fidelity (12)
Fire Of Mind Or Solar Fire (5)
Fire Of Spirit Or Electric Fire (5)
Flamingo (3)

RUNDGREN, Todd — Cont'd

Flesh (9)
Gaya's Eyes (13)
Golden Goose (9)
Good Vibrations (6) *34*
Happenings Ten Years Time Ago (6)
Hawking (12)
Healer (9)
Healing Part I, II & III (9)
Heavy Metal Kids (4)
Hello It's Me (2,8) *5*
Hideaway (10)
Hodja (11)
Honest Work (11)
How About A Little Fanfare? (4)
Hungry For Love (3)
Hurting For You (7)
I Don't Want To Tie You Down (3)
I Love My Life (12)
I Saw The Light (2,8) *16*
I Think You Know (4)

I Went To The Mirror (2)
I'm In The Clique (1)
I'm So Proud (medley) (3,8)
If I Have To Be Alone (13)
If Six Was Nine (4)
In And Out The Chakras We Go (formerly: Shaft Goes To Outer Space) (4)
Influenza (10)
Initiation (5,8)
Internal Fire Or Fire By Friction Medley (5)
International Feel (3)
Is It My Name? (3)
It Takes Two To Tango (2)
It Wouldn't Have Made Any Difference (2,8)
Izzat Love? (4)
Johnee Jingo (11)
Just Another Onionhead (medley) (11)
Just One Victory (3)
Kindness (13)

King Kong Reggae (medley) (4)
La La Means I Love You (medley) (3,8)
Last Ride (4,8)
Last Thing You Said (medley) (1)
Le Feel Internacionale (3)
Little Red Lights (2)
Lockjaw (11)
Lord Chancellor's Nightmare Song (4)
Lost Horizon (11)
Love In Action (8)
Love In Disguise (13)
Love Of The Common Man (6,8)
Love Science (13)
Lucky Guy (7)
Marlene (2)
Mighty Love (11)
Miracle In The Bazaar (11)
Most Likely You Go Your Way And I'll Go Mine (6)

Never Never Land (3,8)
Night The Carousel Burned Down (2)
Number 1 Lowest Common Denominator (4)
Once Burned (1)
One More Day (No Word) (2)
Onomatopoeia (7)
Ooh Baby Baby (medley) (3,8)
Out Of Control (7)
Parallel Lines (12)
Piss Aaron (2)
Prana (5)
Pretending To Care (11)
Public Servant (13)
Pulse (9)
Rain (6)
Range War (8)
Real Man (5,8) *83*
Rock And Roll Pussy (3)
Saving Grace (2)
Second Wind (13)

Shine (9)
Sidewalk Cafe (4)
Slut (2)
Smell Of Money (13)
Some Folks Is Even Whiter Than Me (2)
Something To Fall Back On (11)
Sometimes I Don't Know What To Feel (3,8)
Sons Of 1984 (4)
Spark Of Life (4)
Strawberry Fields Forever (6)
Sunset Blvd. (medley) (3)
Sweeter Memories (2)
There Are No Words (1)
There Goes Your Baybay (10)
Tic Tic Tic It Wears Off (3)
Tin Soldier (10)
Too Far Gone (7)
Torch Song (2)
Unloved Children (12)

Useless Begging (4)
Verb "To Love" (6,8)
Viking, Song Of The (2)
Waiting Game (12)
We Gotta Get You A Woman (1) *20*
When I Pray (6)
When The Shit Hits The Fan (medley) (3)
Who's Sorry Now (13)
Who's That Man (1)
Wolfman Jack (2)
You Cried Wolf (7)
You Don't Have To Camp Around (3)
You Left Me Sore (2)
You Need Your Head (3)
Zen Archer (3,8)

★468★ RUN-D.M.C. '86

Rap trio from Queens, New York: rappers Joseph Simmons (Run) and Darryl McDaniels (DMC) with DJ Jason Mizell (Jam Master Jay). Group appeared in the movies *Krush Groove* and *Tougher Than Leather*.

DEBUT	PEAK	WKS	RIAA	CD		ARTIST — Album Title		$	Label & Number
6/23/84	53	65	●	©	1	Run-D.M.C.		$10	Profile 1202
2/23/85	52	56	▲	©	2	King Of Rock		$10	Profile 1205
6/14/86	3	71	▲³	©	3	Raising Hell		$10	Profile 1217
6/4/88	9	28	▲	©	4	Tougher Than Leather		$10	Profile 1265
12/8/90+	81	15		©	5	Back From Hell		$10	Profile 1401
12/7/91	199	1		©	6	Greatest Hits 1983-1991	[G]	$10	Profile 1419
5/22/93	7	16	●	©	7	Down With The King		$10	Profile 1440
4/21/01	37	6		©	8	Crown Royal		$10	Arista 16400

Ahhh (8)
Ave., The (5,6)
Ay Papi (8)
Back From Hell (5)
Beats To The Rhyme (4,6)
Big Willie (7)
Bob Your Head (5)
Can I Get A Witness (7)
Can I Get It, Yo (7)
Can You Rock It Like This (2)
Christmas In Hollis (6)
Come On Everybody (7)
Crown Royal (8)
Daryll & Joe (Krush-Groove 3) (2)
Don't Stop (5)

Down With The King (7) *21*
Dumb Girl (3)
Faces (5)
Get Open (7)
Groove To The Sound (6)
Hard Times (1,6)
Here We Go (6)
Here We Go 2001 (8)
Hit 'Em Hard (7)
Hit It Run (3)
Hollis Crew (Krush-Groove 2) (1)
How'd Ya Do It Dee (4)
I'm Not Going Out Like That (4)
In The House (7)
Is It Live (3)

It's Like That (1,6)
It's Not Funny (7)
It's Over (8)
Jam-Master Jammin' (2)
Jam-Master Jay (1,6)
Jay's Game (1)
Kick The Frama Lama Lama (medley) (2,6)
King Of Rock (2)
Let's Stay Together (Together Forever) (8)
Livin' In The City (5)
Mary, Mary (4) *75*
Miss Elaine (4)
My Adidas (3,6)
Naughty (5)

Not Just Another Groove (5)
Ooh, Whatcha Gonna Do (7)
P Upon A Tree (3)
Papa Crazy (4)
Party Time (5)
Pause (5,6)
Perfection (3)
Peter Piper (3,6)
Proud To Be Black (3)
Queens Day (8)
Radio Station (4)
Ragtime (4)
Raising Hell (3)
Rock Box (1,6)
Rock Show (8)
Rock The House (2)

Roots, Rap, Reggae (2)
Run's House (4)
School Of Old (8)
Simmons Incorporated (8)
Son Of Byford (3)
Soul To Rock And Roll (4)
Sucker D.J.'s (5)
Sucker M.C.'s (Krush-Groove 1) (1,6)
Take The Money And Run (8)
Them Girls (8)
They Call Us Run-D.M.C. (4)
30 Days (1)
3 In The Head (7)
Three Little Indians (7)

Together Forever (Krush-Groove 4) (6)
Tougher Than Leather (4)
Wake Up (1)
Walk This Way (3,6) *4*
What's It All About (5)
What's Next (7)
Word Is Born (5)
Wreck Shop (7)
You Be Illin' (3,6) *29*
You Talk Too Much (2)
You're Blind (2)

RUNNER '79

Rock group from England: Steve Gould (vocals, guitar; **Rare Bird**), Allan Merrill (guitar), Mickie Feat (bass) and Dave Dowle (drums).

DEBUT	PEAK	WKS				ARTIST — Album Title		$	Label & Number
6/23/79	167	4				Runner		$12	Island 9536

Broken Hearted Me
Dynamite

Fooling Myself
Gone Too Long

Living Is Loving You
Restless Wind

Rock 'N' Roll Soldiers
Run For Your Life

Sooner Than Later
Truly From Within

RuPAUL '93

Born RuPaul Andre Charles on 11/17/60 in San Diego. Black male transvestite. Appeared in the movies *Crooklyn* and *The Brady Bunch Movie*. Hosted own talk show on VH-1.

DEBUT	PEAK	WKS		CD		ARTIST — Album Title		$	Label & Number
6/26/93	109	6		©		Supermodel Of The World		$10	Tommy Boy 1058

All Of A Sudden
Back To My Roots
Everybody Dance

Free Your Mind
House Of Love
Miss Lady DJ

Prisoner Of Love
Shade Shady (Now Prance)
Stinky Dinky

Supermodel (You Better Work) *45*
Supernatural

Thinkin' 'Bout You

RUSH ★74★ '81

Hard-rock trio formed in Toronto: **Geddy Lee** (vocals, bass), Alex Lifeson (guitar) and John Rutsey (drums). Neil Peart replaced Rutsey after first album. Also see **Victor**.

1)Counterparts 2)Moving Pictures 3)Roll The Bones 4)Permanent Waves 5)Test For Echo

DEBUT	PEAK	WKS	RIAA	CD		ARTIST — Album Title	Catalog	$	Label & Number
9/21/74	105	13	●	©	1	Rush	C:#12/91	$12	Mercury 1011
3/15/75	113	8	▲	©	2	Fly By Night	C:#16/121	$12	Mercury 1023
10/18/75	148	6	●	©	3	Caress Of Steel	C:#13/109	$12	Mercury 1046
4/10/76	61	34	▲³	©	4	2112		$12	Mercury 1079
10/2/76	40	23	▲	©	5	All The World's A Stage	[L]	$15	Mercury 7508 [2]
						recorded on 6/12/76 at Massey Hall in Toronto			
9/24/77	33	17	▲	©	6	A Farewell To Kings		$12	Mercury 1184
4/15/78	121	6	▲		7	Archives	[R]	$25	Mercury 9200 [3]
						reissue of albums #1-3 above			
11/18/78	47	21	▲	©	8	Hemispheres		$12	Mercury 3743
2/2/80	4	36	▲	©	9	Permanent Waves		$12	Mercury 4001

RUSH — Cont'd

DEBUT	PEAK	WKS	RIAA	CD	ARTIST — Album Title	Catalog	Sym	$	Label & Number
3/7/81	3	68	▲⁴	© 10	Moving Pictures	C:#18/8		$12	Mercury 4013
11/14/81	10	21	▲	© 11	Exit...Stage Left	[L]		$15	Mercury 7001 [2]
10/2/82	10	33	▲	© 12	Signals			$12	Mercury 4063
5/5/84	10	27	▲	© 13	Grace Under Pressure			$10	Mercury 818476
11/9/85	10	28	▲	© 14	Power Windows			$10	Mercury 826098
9/26/87	13	30	●	© 15	Hold Your Fire			$10	Mercury 832464
1/28/89	21	15	●	© 16	A Show Of Hands	[L]		$15	Mercury 836346 [2]
12/2/89	16	27	●	© 17	Presto			$10	Atlantic 82040
9/22/90	51	19	▲²	© 18	Chronicles	[K]		$15	Mercury 838936 [2]
9/21/91	3	43	▲	© 19	Roll The Bones			$10	Atlantic 82293
11/6/93	2¹	26		© 20	Counterparts			$10	Atlantic 82528
9/28/96	5	15	●	© 21	Test For Echo			$10	Atlantic 82925
11/28/98	35	6	●	© 22	Different Stages / Live	[L]		$25	Atlantic 83122 [3]

recorded from 1978-98

Afterimage (13)
Alien Shore (20)
Anagram (For Mongo) (17)
Analog Kid (12,22)
Animate (20,22)
Anthem (2,5,7,18,22)
Available Light (17)
Bastille Day (3,5,7,18,22)
Before And After (1,7)
Beneath, Between, & Behind (2,7,11)
Best I Can (2,7)
Between Sun & Moon (20)
Between The Wheels (13)
Big Money (14,16,18) 45
Big Wheel (19)
Body Electric (13)
Bravado (19,22)
Broon's Bane (11)
By-Tor & The Snow Dog Medley (2,5,7,22)
Camera Eye (10)
Carve Away The Stone (21)
Chain Lightning (17)

Chemistry (12)
Cinderella Man (6,22)
Circumstances (8)
Closer To The Heart (2,5,7,18,22) 76
Closer To The Heart [live] (11,16) 69
Cold Fire (20)
Color Of Right (21)
Countdown (12)
Cut To The Chase (20)
Cygnus X-1 (6,22)
Different Strings (9)
Digital Man (12)
Distant Early Warning (13,16,18)
Dog Years (21)
Double Agent (20)
Dreamline (19,22)
Driven (21,22)
Emotion Detector (14)
Enemy Within (13)
Entre Nous (9)
Everyday Glory (20)

Face Up (19)
Farewell To Kings (6,18,22)
Finding My Way (1,5,7,18)
Fly By Night (2,5,7,18,22) 88
hit "Hot 100" as a medley with "In The Mood"
Force Ten (15,16,18)
Fountain Of Lamneth Medley (3,7)
Freewill (9,11,18,22)
Ghost Of A Chance (19)
Grand Designs (14)
Half The World (21)
Hand Over Fist (17)
Hemispheres Medley (8)
Here Again (1,7)
Heresy (19)
High Water (15)
I Think I'm Going Bald (3,7)
In The End (2,5,7)
In The Mood (1,5,7,22) 88
hit "Hot 100" as a medley with "Fly By Night"
Jacob's Ladder (9,11)

Kid Gloves (13)
La Villa Strangiato (8,11,18)
Lakeside Park (3,5,7,18)
Leave That Thing Alone (20,22)
Lessons (4)
Limbo (21)
Limelight (10,18,22) 55
Lock And Key (15)
Losing It (12)
Madrigal (6)
Making Memories (2,7)
Manhattan Project (14,16,18)
Marathon (14,16)
Middletown Dreams (14)
Mission (15,16)
Mystic Rhythms (14,16,18)
Natural Science (9,22)
Necromancer Medley (3,7)
Need Some Love (1,7)
Neurotica (19)
New World Man (12,18) 21
Nobody's Hero (20,22)
Open Secrets (15)

Pass, The (17)
Passage To Bangkok (4,11,18)
Presto (17)
Prime Mover (15)
Red Barchetta (10,11,18)
Red Lenses (13)
Red Sector A (13,16,18)
Red Tide (17)
Resist (21,22)
Rhythm Method (16,22)
Rivendell (2,7)
Roll The Bones (19,22)
Scars (17)
Second Nature (15)
Show Don't Tell (17,18,22)
Something For Nothing (4,5,22)
Speed Of Love (20)
Spirit Of Radio (9,11,18,22) 51
Stick It Out (20,22)
Subdivisions (12,16,18)
Superconductor (17)
Tai Shan (15)
Take A Friend (1,7)

Tears (4)
Territories (14)
Test For Echo (21,22)
Time And Motion (21)
Time Stand Still (15,16,18)
Tom Sawyer (10,11,18,22) 44
Totem (21)
Trees, The (8,11,18,22)
Turn The Page (15,16)
2112 Medley (4,5,18,22)
Twilight Zone (4)
Virtuality (21)
Vital Signs (10)
War Paint (17)
Weapon, The (12)
What You're Doing (1,5,7,18)
Where's My Thing? (19)
Witch Hunt (10,16)
Working Man (1,5,7,18,22)
Xanadu (6,11,22)
YYZ (10,11,22)
You Bet Your Life (19)

RUSH, Jennifer   '87

Born Heidi Stern on 9/29/60 in Queens, New York. Pop singer.

DEBUT	PEAK	WKS	RIAA	CD	ARTIST — Album Title	Catalog	Sym	$	Label & Number
6/27/87	118	10		©	Heart Over Mind			$10	Epic 40825

Call My Name
Down To You

Flames Of Paradise 36
Heart Over Mind

Heart Wars
I Come Undone

Love Of A Stranger
Search The Sky

Sidekick
Stronghold

RUSH, Merrilee   '68

Born in Seattle. Female pop singer.

DEBUT	PEAK	WKS	RIAA	CD	ARTIST — Album Title	Catalog	Sym	$	Label & Number
10/19/68	196	4			Angel Of The Morning			$25	Bell 6020

Angel Of The Morning 7
Billy Sunshine
Do Unto Others
Handy

Hush
It's Worth It All
Observation From Flight 285 (In 3/4 Time)

San Francisco (Be Sure To Wear Some Flowers In Your Hair)
Sandcastles

Sunshine & Roses
That Kind Of Woman 76
Working Girl

RUSH, Tom   '68

Born on 2/8/41 in Portsmouth, New Hampshire. Singer/songwriter.

DEBUT	PEAK	WKS	RIAA	CD	ARTIST — Album Title	Catalog	Sym	$	Label & Number
6/11/66	122	7		1	Take A Little Walk With Me			$15	Elektra 7308
4/20/68	68	14		© 2	The Circle Game			$15	Elektra 74018
3/14/70	76	16		© 3	Tom Rush			$15	Columbia 9972
12/26/70+	110	9		4	Wrong End Of The Rainbow			$15	Columbia 30402
3/27/71	198	1		5	Classic Rush	[K]		$15	Elektra 74062
4/29/72	128	10		© 6	Merrimack County			$12	Columbia 31306
10/19/74	124	9		© 7	Ladies Love Outlaws			$12	Columbia 33054
2/7/76	184	3		8	The Best Of Tom Rush	[K]		$12	Columbia 33907

Biloxi (4)
Black Magic Gun (7)
Came To See Me Yesterday In The Merry Month Of (medley) (4)
Child's Song (3,8)
Circle Game (2,5)
Claim On Me (7)
Colors Of The Sun (3)
Cuckoo, The (5)
Desperados Waiting For The Train (7)

Drop Down Mama (3,8)
Galveston Flood (1,5)
Glory Of Love (7)
Gone Down River (6)
Gypsy Boy (6)
Hobo's Mandolin (7,8)
Indian Woman From Wichita (7)
Jamaica Say You Will (6)
Jazzman (3)
Jenny Lynn (7)
Joshua Gone Barbados (1,5)

Kids These Days (6,8)
Ladies Love Outlaws (7,8)
Livin' In The Country (3)
Lost My Drivin' Wheel (3,8)
Love's Made A Fool Of You (1,5)
Lullaby (3)
Maggie (7)
Merrimack County (6)
Merrimack County II (6)
Mink Julip (6,8)
Money Honey (1)

Mother Earth (6,8)
No Regrets (2,5,7,8)
Old Man's Song (5)
On The Road Again (1,5)
One Day I Walk (7)
Paddy West (medley) (4)
Rainy Day Man (3)
Riding On A Railroad (4)
Rockport Sunday (2,5)
Roll Away The Grey (6)
Rotunda (4,8)
Seems The Songs (6)

Shadow Dream Song (2,5)
So Long (2)
Something In The Way She Moves (2,5)
Starlight (4,8)
Statesboro Blues (1)
Sugar Babe (1)
Sunshine Sunshine (2)
Sweet Baby James (4)
These Days (3,8)
Tin Angel (2)
Too Much Monkey Business (1)

Turn Your Money Green (1)
Urge For Going (2,5)
Who Do You Love (1,5)
Wild Child (World Of Trouble) (3)
Wind On The Water (6)
Wrong End Of The Rainbow (4)
You Can't Tell A Book By The Cover (1)

RUSHEN, Patrice   '82

Born on 9/30/54 in Los Angeles. R&B singer/songwriter/pianist.

DEBUT	PEAK	WKS	RIAA	CD	ARTIST — Album Title	Catalog	Sym	$	Label & Number
4/16/77	164	4		1	Shout It Out			$15	Prestige 10101
2/17/79	98	6		2	Patrice			$12	Elektra 160
11/24/79+	39	22		3	Pizzazz			$12	Elektra 243
11/29/80+	71	18		4	Posh			$12	Elektra 302
5/1/82	14	28		© 5	Straight From The Heart			$12	Elektra 60015
6/16/84	40	25		6	Now			$12	Elektra 60360

DEBUT	PEAK	WKS	RIAA	CD	ARTIST — Album Title	Catalog	Sym	$	Label & Number

RUSHEN, Patrice — Cont'd

| 3/28/87 | 77 | 19 | | © 7 | **Watch Out!** | | | $10 | Arista 8401 |

All My Love (7)
All We Need (5)
Anything Can Happen (7)
Breakin' All The Rules (7)
Breakout! (5)
Burnin' (7)
Call On Me (3)
Cha-Cha (2)
Changes (In Your Life) (2)
Come Back To Me (7)
Didn't You Know? (2)
Don't Blame Me (4)

Dream, The (4)
Feels So Real (Won't Let Go) (6) **78**
Forget Me Nots (5) **23**
Funk Won't Let You Down (4)
Get Off (You Fascinate Me) (6)
Givin' It Up Is Givin' Up (3)
Gone With The Night (6)
Gotta Find It (6)
Hang It Up (2)
Haven't You Heard (3) **42**
Heartache Heartbreak (4)

High In Me (6)
Hump, The (1)
I Need Your Love (4)
I Was Tired Of Being Alone (5)
If Only (5)
It's Just A Natural Thing (2)
Keepin' Faith In Love (3)
Let The Music Take Me (3)
Let There Be Funk (1)
Let Your Heart Be Free (1)
Let's Sing A Song Of Love (2)
Long Time Coming (7)

Look Up (4)
Message In The Music (3)
Music Of The Earth (2)
My Love's Not Going Anywhere (6)
Never Gonna Give You Up (Won't Let You Be) (4)
Number One (5)
Perfect Love (6)
Play! (2)
Remind Me (5)
Roll With The Punches (1)

Settle For My Love (3)
(She Will) Take You Down To Love (5)
Shout It Out (1)
Sojourn (1)
Somewhere (7)
Stepping Stones (1)
Superstar (6)
Tender Lovin' (1)
This Is All I Really Know (4)
Till She's Out Of Your Mind (7)
Time Will Tell (4)

To Each His Own (6)
Watch Out (7)
When I Found You (2)
Where There Is Love (5)
Wishful Thinking (2)
Yolon (1)

RUSSELL, Bobby '71

Born on 4/19/41 in Nashville. Died of a heart attack on 11/19/92 (age 51). Singer/songwriter. Married to **Vicki Lawrence** from 1972-74.

| 10/16/71 | 183 | 3 | | | **Saturday Morning Confusion** .... | | | $15 | United Artists 5548 |

Confidential
Goodbye
It Hurts

Little Boy Tears
Little Ol' Song About Love

Saturday Morning Confusion 28
Song That I Can't Write

Then And Only Then
When You Find Out Where You're Goin'

Who Is She Now
You Babe

RUSSELL, Brenda '88

Born Brenda Gordon in Brooklyn, New York. R&B singer/songwriter/pianist.

9/22/79	65	20	©	1	**Brenda Russell**			$12	Horizon 739
4/11/81	107	8		2	**Love Life**			$12	A&M 4811
3/19/88	49	28	©	3	**Get Here**			$10	A&M 5178

Deep Dark And Mysterious (2)
Get Here (3)
God Bless You (1)
Gravity (3)

If Only For One Night (1)
If You Love (2)
In The Thick Of It (1)
Just A Believer (3)

Le Restaurant (3)
Little Bit Of Love (1)
Love Life (2)
Lucky (2)

Make My Day (3)
Midnight Eyes (3)
Piano In The Dark (3) **6**
Rainbow (2)

Sensitive Man (2)
So Good, So Right (1) **30**
Something I Like To Do (2)
Thank You (2)

Think It Over (1)
This Time I Need You (3)
Way Back When (1)
You're Free (1)

★246★ RUSSELL, Leon '72

Born on 4/2/41 in Lawton, Oklahoma. Rock singer/songwriter/multi-instrumentalist. Prolific session musician. Regular with Phil Spector's "Wall of Sound" session group. Formed Shelter Records in 1970. Recorded as **Hank Wilson** in 1973. Also see **Joe Cocker**.
1)Carney 2)Leon Live 3)Leon Russell & The Shelter People

4/11/70	60	19		© 1	**Leon Russell**			$20	Shelter 1001
5/29/71	17	29	●	© 2	**Leon Russell & The Shelter People**			$15	Shelter 8903
12/4/71+	70	20		© 3	**Asylum Choir II**		[E]	$15	Shelter 8910
					LEON RUSSELL & MARC BENNO recorded April 1969				
7/15/72	2[4]	35	●	© 4	**Carney**			$15	Shelter 8911
7/7/73	9	26	●	© 5	**Leon Live**		[L]	$20	Shelter 8917 [3]
					recorded at the Long Beach Arena in California				
9/22/73	28	15		© 6	**Hank Wilson's Back, Vol. I**			$15	Shelter 8923
					HANK WILSON				
6/22/74	34	16		© 7	**Stop All That Jazz**			$15	Shelter 2108
5/3/75	30	40	●	© 8	**Will O' The Wisp**			$15	Shelter 2138
5/1/76	34	28		9	**Wedding Album**			$12	Paradise 2943
					LEON & MARY RUSSELL				
10/23/76	40	16	●	10	**Best Of Leon**		[G]	$12	Shelter 52004
6/25/77	142	5		11	**Make Love To The Music**			$12	Paradise 3066
					LEON & MARY RUSSELL				
8/12/78	115	10		12	**Americana**			$12	Paradise 3172
6/30/79	25	18	●	© 13	**One For The Road**			$15	Columbia 36064 [2]
					WILLIE NELSON AND LEON RUSSELL				
4/4/81	187	2		14	**The Live Album**		[L]	$12	Paradise 3532
					LEON RUSSELL & NEW GRASS REVIVAL recorded on 5/15/80 at Perkins Palace in Pasadena, California				

Acid Annapolis (4)
Alcatraz (2,5)
Always (13)
Am I Blue (13)
Am I That Easy To Forget (6)
Back To The Island (8,10) **53**
Ballad For A Soldier (3)
Ballad Of Hollis Brown (7)
Ballad Of Mad Dogs And Englishmen (2)
Battle Of New Orleans (6)
Because Of You (13)
Beware Of Darkness (2)
Bluebird (8,10)
Cajun Love Song (4)
Can't Get Over Losing You (8)
Caribbean (14)
Carney (4)
Crystal Closet Queen (2,5)
Danny Boy (13)
Daylight (9)
Delta Lady (1,5,10)
Detour (13)
Dixie Lullaby (1,5)
Don't Fence Me In (13)
Down On Deep River (8)
Down On The Base (3)
Easy Love (11)
Elvis And Marilyn (12)

Fantasy (9)
Far Away Places (13)
From Maine To Mexico (12)
Georgia Blues (14)
Give Peace A Chance (1)
Goodnight Irene (6)
Great Day (5)
Hard Rain's A Gonna Fall (7)
Heartbreak Hotel (13)
Hello, Little Friend (3)
Hold On To This Feeling (11)
Home Sweet Oklahoma (2)
Housewife (12)
Hummingbird (1,10)
Hurtsome Body (7)
I Believe To My Soul (14)
I Put A Spell On You (14)
I Saw The Light (13)
I Want To Be At The Meeting (14)
I'll Sail My Ship Alone (6)
I'm So Lonesome I Could Cry (6) **flip**
I've Just Seen A Face (14)
If I Were A Carpenter (7) **73**
If The Shoe Fits (4)
Island In The Sun (11)
It Takes A Lot To Laugh, It Takes A Train To Cry (2)
It's All Over Now, Baby Blue (5)

It's Been A Long Time Baby (5)
It's Only Me (12)
Jambalaya (On The Bayou) (6,14)
Jesus On My Side (12)
Joyful Noise (11)
Jumping Jack Flash (5,14)
Ladies Of The Night (12)
Lady Blue (8,10) **14**
Lady In Waiting (3)
Lavender Blue (Dilly Dilly) (9)
Laying Right Here In Heaven (8)
Learn How To Boogie (3)
Leaving Whipporwhill (7)
Let The Rest Of The World Go By (13)
Let's Get Started (12)
Like A Dream Come True (9)
Little Hideaway (8)
Lost Highway (6)
Love Crazy (11)
Love Is In Your Eyes (11)
Love's Supposed To Be That Way (7)
Magic Mirror (4)
Make Love To The Music (11)
Make You Feel Good (8)
Manhattan Island Serenade (4)
Me And Baby Jane (4)
She Smiles Like A River (2)

Midnight Lover (12)
Mighty Quinn Medley (5)
Mona Lisa Please (7)
My Cricket (4)
My Father's Shoes (8)
Now Now Boogie (11)
Of Thee I Sing (2,5)
Old Masters (1)
One For My Baby And One More For The Road (13)
One More Love Song (14)
Out In The Woods (4,5,10)
Over The Rainbow (14)
Pilgrim Land (14)
Pisces Apple Lady (1)
Prince Of Peace (1,5,14)
Queen Of The Roller Derby (5) **89**
Quiet Nights (9)
Rainbow In Your Eyes (9) **52**
Ridin' Down The Canyon (13)
Roll Away The Stone (1,5,10)
Roll In My Sweet Baby's Arms (6,14) **78**
Roller Derby (4)
Salty Candy (3)
Satisfy You (9)
Say You Will (11)
Shadow And Me (12)
She Smiles Like A River (2)

She Thinks I Still Care (6)
Shoot Out On The Plantation (1,5,10)
Sioux City Sue (13)
Six Pack To Go (6)
Smashed (7)
Some Day (5)
Song For You (1,10)
Spanish Harlem (7)
Stay Away From Sad Songs (8)
Stop All That Jazz (7)
Stormy Weather (13)
Straight Brother (3)
Stranger In A Strange Land (2,5,10,14)
Streaker's Ball (7)
Summertime (13)
Sweeping Through The City (5)
Sweet Emily (2,5)
Sweet Home Chicago (5)
Tenderly (13)
That Lucky Old Sun (13)
This Masquerade (4,10)
Tight Rope (4,10) **11**
Time For Love (7)
Trouble In Mind (13)
Truck Drivin' Man (6)
Tryin' To Stay 'Live (3)
Uncle Pen (6)

When A Man Loves A Woman (12)
When You Wish Upon A Fag (3)
Wild Horses (14)
Wild Side Of Life (13)
Will O' The Wisp (8)
Window Up Above (6)
Windsong (9)
Working Girl (7)
Yes I Am (medley) (5)
You Are My Sunshine (13)
You Are On My Mind (9)
Youngblood (medley) (5)

RUSTED ROOT '96

Rock group from Pittsburgh: Mike Glabicki (vocals, guitar), John Buynak, Liz Berlin, Jenn Wertz and Jim DiSpirito (percussion), Patrick Norman (bass), and Jim Donovan (drums). Wertz left in 1995.

9/10/94+	**51**	46	▲ ©	1 **When I Woke**............	$10	Mercury 522713
11/9/96	**38**	13	● ©	2 **Remember**............	$10	Mercury 534050
11/21/98	**165**	2	©	3 **Rusted Root**............	$10	Mercury 538283

Agbadza (3) · Airplane (3) · Away From (3) · Baby Will Raam (3) · Back To The Earth (1) · Beautiful People (1) · Bullets In The Fire (2) · Cat Turned Blue (1) · Circle Of Remembrance (2) · Cruel Sun (1) · Dangle (2) · Drum Trip (1) · Ecstasy (1) · Faith I Do Believe (2) · Flower (3) · Food & Creative Love (1) · Heaven (2) · Infinite Space (2) · Infinite Tamboura (1) · Kill You Dead (3) · Laugh As The Sun (1) · Live A Long Time (3) · Lost In A Crowd (1) · Magenta Radio (3) · Martyr (1) · Moon (3) · My Love (3) · Rain (1) · Rising Sun (3) · River In A Cage (2) · Scattered (3) · **Send Me On My Way** (1) 72 · She Roll Me Up (3) · Silver-N-Gold (2) · Sister Contine (1) · Virtual Reality (2) · Voodoo (2) · Who Do You Tell It To (2) · You Can't Always Get What You Want (3)

RUSTIX, The '69

Rock group from Rochester, New York: Albe Galich and Chuck Brucato (vocals), Bob D'Andrea (guitar), Vinnie Strenk (keyboards), Ronny Colins (bass) and David Colon (drums).

11/15/69	**200**	2		**Bedlam**............	$25	Rare Earth 508

Can't You Hear The Music Play · Country · Feeling Alright · Free Again · I Can't Make It Without You · I Guess This Is Goodbye · I Heard It Through The Grapevine · Lady In My Dreams · That's What Poppa Told Me · Wednesday's Child

RUTHERFORD, Mike '82

Born on 10/2/50 in Guildford, Surrey, England. Bassist of **Genesis** and leader of **Mike + The Mechanics**.

4/5/80	**163**	11	©	1 **Smallcreep's Day**............	$12	Passport 9843
10/9/82	**145**	6	©	2 **Acting Very Strange**............	$10	Atlantic 80015

Acting Very Strange (2) · Couldn't Get Arrested (2) · Day To Remember (2) · Every Road (1) · Halfway There (1) · Hideaway (2) · I Don't Wanna Know (2) · Maxine (2) · Moonshine (1) · Overnight Job (1) · Romani (1) · Smallcreep's Day Medley (1) · Time And Time Again (1) · Who's Fooling Who (2)

RUTLES, The '78

Parody of **The Beatles**: Neil Innes ("Ron Nasty"), Eric Idle ("Dirk McQuickly"), Rikki Fataar ("Stig O'Hara") and John Halsey ("Barry Wom"). Innes was with the **Bonzo Dog Band** and Idle was a member of **Monty Python**. A pseudo-documentary of the group aired on NBC-TV on 3/22/78.

3/25/78	**63**	9	©	**The Rutles**............	$25	Warner 3151

Another Day · Cheese And Onions · Doubleback Alley · Good Times Roll · Hold My Hand · I Must Be In Love · Let's Be Natural · Living In Hope · Love Life · Nevertheless · Number One · Ouch! · Piggy In The Middle · With A Girl Like You

RYDELL, Bobby '61

Born Robert Ridarelli on 4/26/42 in Philadelphia. Pop singer. Appeared in the movies *Bye Bye Birdie* and *That Lady From Peking*.

2/27/61	**12**	34		1 **Bobby's Biggest Hits**............	[G] $60	Cameo 1009
10/23/61	**56**	9		2 **Rydell At The Copa**............ recorded on 7/4/61	[L] $60	Cameo 1011
12/18/61+	**7**	30		3 **Bobby Rydell/Chubby Checker**	$60	Cameo 1013
9/1/62	**88**	11		4 **All The Hits**............	$50	Cameo 1019
12/22/62+	**61**	12		5 **Bobby Rydell/Biggest Hits, Volume 2**............	[G] $50	Cameo 1028
1/18/64	**67**	9		6 **the Top Hits of 1963**............ includes a bonus 7" single	$50	Cameo 1070
3/7/64	**98**	4		7 **Forget Him**............	$50	Cameo 1080

Alley Cat Song (6) · Baby It's You (5) · Best Man Cried (5) · Bless 'Em All (2) · Blue On Blue (6) · Blue Velvet (6) · Break It To Me Gently (4) · Can't Get Used To Losing You (6) · **Cha-Cha-Cha** (5) 10 · Darling Jenny (7) · **Ding-A-Ling** (1) 18 · Don't Be Afraid (2,5) · Don't Break The Heart That Loves You (4) · Door To Paradise (5) 85 · Dream Baby (4) · **Fish, The** (5) 25 · **Forget Him** (7) 4 · Gee, It's Wonderful (5) · Go Away Little Girl (6) · **Good Time Baby** (5) 11 · **Groovy Tonight** (1) 70 · Hey Baby (4) · Hey Everybody (7) · Homesick Thats All (2) · **I Dig Girls** (1) 46 · I Know (4) · **I Wanna Thank You** (5) 21 · I Will Follow Her (6) · I'd Do It Again (1) · **I'll Never Dance Again** (4,5) 14 · **I've Got Bonnie** (4,5) 18 · If I Had A Hammer (6) · It's Time We Parted (7) · **Jingle Bell Rock** (3) 21 · Jingle Bells Imitations (3) · **Kissin' Time** (1) 11 · **Little Bitty Girl** (1) 19 · **Lose Her** (5) 69 · Lot Of Living To Do (2) · **Make Me Forget** (7) 43 · Mammy (3) · My Baby Just Cares For Me (3) · My Coloring Book (6) · New Love (7) · Old Man River (2) · One Who Really Loves You (4) · Our Day Will Come (6) · Our Faded Love (6) · Ruby Baby (6) · Side By Side (3) · Since We Fell In Love (7) · So Much In Love (6) · Soldier Boy (4) · **Sway** (1,2) 14 · **Swingin' School** (1) 5 · Swingin' Together (5) · Teach Me To Twist (3) · They Don't Write Them Like That Anymore (2) · Too Much Too Soon (7) · Twistin' The Night Away (4) · Until I Met You (7) · Voce De La Notte (Voice Of The Night) (7) · **Volare** (1) 4 · Voodoo (You Remind Me Of The Guy) (3) · Walkin' My Baby Back Home (3) · **We Got Love** (1) 6 · What Are You Doing New Year's Eve (3) · What's Your Name (4) · **Wild One** (1) 2 · Wish You Were Here (7) · Wonderful! Wonderful! (5) · Words Written On Water (7) · World Without Love (6) · You'll Never Tame Me (1) · Your Hits And Mine Medley (3)

RYDER, Mitch, And The Detroit Wheels '67

Born William Levise on 2/26/45 in Detroit. Rock singer. The Detroit Wheels: Jim McCarty and Joe Cubert (guitars), Earl Elliott (bass) and John Badanjek (drums). Ryder formed **Detroit**. McCarty and Badanjek formed the **Rockets**.

3/5/66	**78**	7	©	1 **Take A Ride**............	$30	New Voice 2000
8/6/66+	**23**	34	©	2 **Breakout...!!!**............	$30	New Voice 2002
4/8/67	**34**	16	©	3 **Sock It To Me!**............	$30	New Voice 2003
10/14/67+	**37**	26	©	4 **All Mitch Ryder Hits!**............	[G] $30	New Voice 2004
7/9/83	**120**	9		5 **Never Kick A Sleeping Dog**............ MITCH RYDER produced by **John Cougar**	$12	Riva 7503

Baby Jane (Mo-Mo Jane) (1) · B.I.G.T.I.M.E. (5) · **Break Out** (2,4) 62 · Bring It On Home To Me (1) · Code Dancing (5) · Come Again (5) · Come See About Me (1) · Cry To Me (5) · **Devil With A Blue Dress On &** **Good Golly Miss Molly** (2,4) 4 · Face In The Crowd (3) · I Can't Hide It (3) · I Got You (1) · I Had It Made (2) · I Hope (1) · I Like It Like That (2) · I Need Help! (2) · I Never Had It Better (3) · I'd Rather Go To Jail (3,4) · I'll Go Crazy (1) · In The Midnight Hour (2,4) · **Jenny Take A Ride!** (1,4) 10 · **Joy** (4) 41 · Just A Little Bit (1) · Let Your Lovelight Shine (1) · **Little Latin Lupe Lu** (2,4) 17 · Oo Papa Doo (7) · Please, Please, Please (1) · Rue De Trahir (5) · Shake A Tail Feather (1,4) · Shakedown (3) · Shakin' With Linda (2) · Slow Fizz (3) · **Sock It To Me-Baby!** (3,4) 6 · Stand (5) · Sticks And Stones (1) · Stubborn Kind Of Fellow (2) · **Takin' All I Can Get** (3,4) 100 · Thrill Of It All (5) · Thrill's A Thrill (5) · **Too Many Fish In The Sea &** **Three Little Fishes** (4) 24 · Walk On By (3) · Walking The Dog (2) · **When You Were Mine** (5) 87 · Wild Child (3) · You Get Your Kicks (2)

RZA '98

Born Robert Diggs in New York City. Rapper/producer. Member of **Wu-Tang Clan** and **Gravediggaz**.

12/12/98	**16**	12	● ©	**RZA As Bobby Digital In Stereo**............	$10	Gee Street 32521

Airwaves · B.O.B.B.Y. · Bobby Did It (Spanish Fly) · Daily Routine · Domestic Violence · Fuck What You Think · Handwriting On The Wall · Holocaust (Silkworm) · Kiss Of A Black Widow · Lab Drunk · Love Jones · Mantis · My Lovin' Is Digi · N.Y.C. Everything · Project Talk · Terrorist · Unspoken Word

S

SAAD, Sue, And The Next '80
Rock group: Sue Saad (vocals), Tony Riparetti and Billy Anstatt (guitars), Bobby Manzer (bass) and James Lance (drums).

3/1/80	131	12			Sue Saad And The Next			$12	Planet 4

Cold Night Rain · Danger Love · Gimme Love/Gimme Pain · I I Me Me · I Want Him · It's Gotcha · Prisoner · Won't Give It Up · Young Girl · Your Lips-Hands-Kiss-Love

SACRED REICH '90
Hard-rock group from Phoenix: Phil Rind (vocals, bass), Wiley Arnett and Jason Rainey (guitars) and Greg Hall (drums).

7/28/90	153	9		©	The American Way			$10	Enigma 73560

American Way · Crimes Against Humanity · I Don't Know · Love ... Hate · State Of Emergency · 31 Flavors · Way It Is · Who's To Blame

SADAT X '96
Born Derek Murphy on 12/29/68 in New York City. Male rapper. Former member of **Brand Nubian**.

8/3/96	83	3		©	Wild Cowboys			$10	Loud 66922

Do It Again · Escape From New York · Funkiest, The · Game's Sober · **Hang 'Em High** *98* · Hashout, The · Interview, The · Lump Lump · Move On · Open Bar · Petty People · Sauce For Birdheads · Smoking On The Low · Stages And Lights · Wild Cowboys

SAD CAFE '79
Pop-rock group formed in Manchester, England: Paul Young (vocals; **Mike + The Mechanics**), Ashley Mulford and Ian Wilson (guitars), Vic Emerson (keyboards), John Stimpson (bass) and Tony Cresswell (drums). By 1979, Dave Irving had replaced Cresswell. Young died of a heart attack on 7/17/2000 (age 53).

1/27/79	94	14	©	1	Misplaced Ideals	[K]		$12	A&M 4737
9/15/79	146	5	©	2	Facades			$12	A&M 4779
8/15/81	160	6		3	Sad Cafe			$12	Swan Song 16048

Angel (2) · Babylon (1) · Black Rose (1) · Crazy Oyster (2) · Digital Daydream Blues (3) · Dreamin' (3) · Emptiness (2) · Everyday (2) · Feel Like Dying (1) · Get Me Outta' Here (2) · Here Come The Clowns (1) · Hungry Eyes (1) · I Believe (Love Will Survive) (1) · I'm In Love Again (3) · Keeping It From The Troops (3) · **La-Di-Da** (3) *78* · Losin' You (3) · Love Today (3) · My Oh My (2) · No Favours - No Way (3) · Nothing Left To Lose (2) · On With The Show (1) · Restless (1) · **Run Home Girl** (1) *71* · Shellshock (1) · Strange Little Girl (1) · Take Me To The Future (2) · Time Is So Hard To Find (2) · What Am I Gonna Do (3)

★345★ SADE '86
Born Helen Folasade Adu on 1/16/59 in Ibadan, Nigeria; raised in London. Jazz-styled singer. Appeared in the 1986 movie *Absolute Beginners*. Won the 1985 Best New Artist Grammy Award. Also see **Sweetback**.

2/23/85	5	81	▲⁴	© 1	Diamond Life	C:#19/40		$10	Portrait 39581
12/21/85+	❶²	46	▲⁴	© 2	Promise	C:#43/4		$10	Portrait 40263
6/4/88	7	45	▲³	© 3	Stronger Than Pride	C:#32/19		$10	Epic 44210
11/21/92	3	103	▲⁴	© 4	Love Deluxe			$10	Epic 53178
11/26/94	9	80	▲⁴	© 5	Best Of Sade	C:#17/106	[G]	$10	Epic 66686
12/2/00	3	44↑	▲³	© 6	Lovers Rock			$10	Epic 85185

All About Our Love (6) · Bullet Proof Soul (4) · **By Your Side** (6) *75* · Cherish The Day (4,5) · Cherry Pie (1) · Clean Heart (3) · Every Word (6) · Fear (2) · Feel No Pain (4) · Flow (6) · Frankie's First Affair (1) · Give It Up (3) · Hang On To Your Love (1,5) · Haunt Me (3) · I Couldn't Love You More (4) · I Never Thought I'd See The Day (1) · I Will Be Your Friend (1) · Immigrant (6) · Is It A Crime (2,5) · It's Only Love That Gets You Through (6) · Jezebel (2,5) · Keep Looking (3) · King Of Sorrow (6) · Kiss Of Life (4,5) *78* · Like A Tattoo (4,5) · Love Is Stronger Than Pride (3,5) · Lovers Rock (6) · Maureen (2) · Mermaid (4) · Mr. Wrong (4) · **Never As Good As The First Time** (2,5) *20* · **No Ordinary Love** (4,5) *28* · Nothing Can Come Between Us (3,5) · **Paradise** (3,5) *16* · Pearls (4,5) · Please Send Me Someone To Love (5) · Sally (1) · Siempre Hay Esperanza (3) · Slave Song (6) · **Smooth Operator** (1,5) *5* · Somebody Already Broke My Heart (6) · Sweetest Gift (6) · **Sweetest Taboo** (2,5) *5* · Tar Baby (2) · Turn My Back On You (3) · War Of The Hearts (2) · When Am I Going To Make A Living (1) · Why Can't We Live Together (1) · **Your Love Is King** (1,5) *54*

SADLER, SSgt Barry '66
Born on 11/1/40 in Carlsbad, New Mexico. Died of heart failure on 11/5/89 (age 49). Staff Sergeant of U.S. Army Special Forces (Green Berets). Served in Vietnam.

2/26/66	❶⁵	32	●	© 1	Ballads of the Green Berets			$20	RCA Victor 3547
7/9/66	130	3		2	The "A" Team			$20	RCA Victor 3605

"A" Team (2) *28* · Autumn Of My Life (2) · Badge Of Courage (1) · **Ballad Of The Green Berets** (1) *1* · Bamiba (1) · Chains On A Man (2) · Dear Darlin' (2) · Drifting Years (2) · Empty Glass (2) · Forty Nine Broken Hearts (2) · Garet Trooper (1) · I'm A Lucky One (1) · I'm Watching The Raindrops Fall (1) · Letter From Vietnam (1) · Little Bird Of Vietnam (1) · Lullaby (1) · One Son-Of-A-Gun Of A Gun (2) · Saigon (1) · Salute To The Nurses (1) · Soldier Has Come Home (1) · Till The Time Comes (2) · Time (2) · Time Goes By (2) · Trooper's Lament (1)

SA-FIRE '89
Born Wilma Cosme in New York City. Female dance singer.

10/8/88+	79	46		©	Sa-Fire			$10	Cutting 834922

Better Be The Only One · **Boy, I've Been Told** *48* · **Gonna Make It** *71* · I Wanna Make You Mine · It's A Crime · Love At First Sight · Love Is On Her Mind · **Thinking Of You** *12* · Together · You Said You Loved Me

SAGA '83
Rock group formed in Toronto: Michael Sadler (vocals), brothers Ian (guitar) and Jim (bass) Crichton, Jim Gilmour (keyboards), and Steve Negus (drums).

10/23/82+	29	36	●	© 1	Worlds Apart			$12	Portrait 38246
10/22/83	92	9		© 2	Heads Or Tales			$12	Portrait 38999
9/21/85	87	10		© 3	Behaviour			$12	Portrait 40145

Amnesia (1) · Cat Walk (2) · Conversations (1) · Easy Way Out (3) · **Flyer, The** (2) *79* · Framed (1) · (Goodbye) Once Upon A Time (3) · Here I Am (3) · Intermission (2) · Interview (1) · Listen To Your Heart (3) · Misbehaviour (3) · Nine Lives Of Miss Midi (3) · No Regrets (Chapter V) (1) · No Stranger (Chapter VIII) (1) · **On The Loose** (1) *26* · Out Of The Shadows (3) · Pitchman, The (2) · Promises (3) · Scratching The Surface (2) · Social Orphan (2) · Sound Of Strangers (2) · Take A Chance (3) · Time's Up (1) · Vendetta (Still Helpless) (2) · What Do I Know? (3) · **Wind Him Up** (1) *64* · Writing, The (2) · You And The Night (3)

SAGER, Carole Bayer '81
Born on 3/8/46 in New York City. Singer/prolific songwriter. Married to **Burt Bacharach** from 1982-91.

| 5/16/81 | **60** | 22 | | | **Sometimes Late At Night**.. | | | $12 | Boardwalk 37069 |

Easy To Love Again — Just Friends — Somebody's Been Lying — **Stronger Than Before 30** — Wild Again — You Don't Know Me
I Won't Break — On The Way To The Sky — Sometimes Late At Night — Tell Her — You And Me (We Wanted It All)

SAHL, Mort '61
Born on 5/11/27 in Montreal. Topical satirist/actor.

| 10/24/60+ | **22** | 13 | | | 1 **Mort Sahl At The Hungry i** .... | | [C] | $25 | Verve 15012 |

no track titles listed on this album

| 6/30/73 | **149** | 7 | | | 2 **Sing A Song of Watergate...** .... | | [C] | $15 | GNP Crescendo 2070 |

California Politics (2) — Conventions, The (2) — Kennedy's Plane (2) — Nixon's Plane (2) — Prisoners Of War (2) — Watergate (2)
Candidates (2) — Foreign Policy (2) — Nixon's Odyssey (2) — Our Distinguished Leaders (2) — San Clemente (2)

SAHM, Doug, And Band '73
Born on 11/5/41 in San Antonio, Texas. Died of heart failure on 11/18/99 (age 58). Rock singer/songwriter/guitarist. Formed the **Sir Douglas Quintet** and the **Texas Tornados**.

| 2/17/73 | **125** | 10 | | | **Doug Sahm And Band** .... | | | $15 | Atlantic 7254 |

Blues Stay Away From Me — Faded Love — (Is Anybody Going To) San — Me And Paul — Wallflower
Dealer's Blues — I Get Off — Antone — Papa Ain't Salty — Your Friends
Don't Turn Around — It's Gonna Be Easy — Poison Love

SAIGON KICK '92
Hard-rock group formed in Miami: Matt Kramer (vocals), Jason Bieler (guitar), Tom DeFile (bass) and Phil Varone (drums).

| 6/20/92 | **80** | 26 | ● | © | **The Lizard** .... | | | $10 | Third Stone 92158 |

All Alright — Chanel — Freedom — Lizard, The — My Dog — World Goes Round
All I Want — Cruelty — God Of 42nd Street — **Love Is On The Way 12** — Peppermint Tribe
Body Bags — Feel The Same Way — Hostile Youth — Miss Jones — Sleep

SAILCAT '72
Pop duo from Alabama: Court Pickett (vocals) and John Wyker (vocals, guitar).

| 8/12/72 | **38** | 14 | | | **Motorcycle Mama** .... | | | $15 | Elektra 75029 |

Ambush — Dream, The — Highway Riff (medley) — It'll Be A Long Long Time — On The Brighter Side Of It All — Thief, The
B.B. Gunn — Highway Rider (medley) — If You've Got A Daughter — **Motorcycle Mama 12** — Rainbow Road — Walking Together Backwards

SAINTE-MARIE, Buffy '66
Born on 2/20/41 in Saskatchewan, Canada. Folk singer/songwriter.

5/21/66	**97**	10		©	1 **Little Wheel Spin And Spin**			$15	Vanguard 79211
7/8/67	**126**	6		©	2 **Fire & Fleet & Candlelight**			$15	Vanguard 79250
8/3/68	**171**	7		©	3 **I'm Gonna Be A Country Girl Again**			$15	Vanguard 79280
10/24/70	**142**	7		©	4 **The Best Of Buffy Sainte-Marie**..		[G]	$20	Vanguard 3/4 [2]
4/10/71	**182**	6		©	5 **She Used To Wanna Be A Ballerina**..			$15	Vanguard 79311
5/6/72	**134**	8		©	6 **Moonshot**..			$15	Vanguard 79312

Bells (5) — Guess Who I Saw In Paris (4) — Little Boy Dark Eyes (2) — 97 Men In This Here Town (medley) (2) — Sir Patrick Spens (1) — They Gotta Quit Kickin' My Dawg Around (3)
Better To Find Out For Yourself (4) — He's A Keeper Of The Fire (4) — Little Wheel Spin And Spin (1,4) — Not The Lovin' Kind (6) — Smack Water Jack (5) — Timeless Love (1)
Carousel, The (2) — He's A Pretty Good Man If You Ask Me (3) — Lord Randall (2) — Now That The Buffalo's Gone (3,4) — Soldier Blue (5) — Uncle Joe (3)
Circle Game (2,4) — **He's An Indian Cowboy In The Rodeo (6) 98** — Los Pescadores (4) — Now You've Been Gone For A Long Time (5) — Sometimes I Get To Thinkin' (1,3,4) — Universal Soldier (4)
Cod'ine (4) — Helpless (5) — Love Of A Good Man (3) — Piney Wood Hills (3,4) — Song Of The French Partisan (5) — Until It's Time For You To Go (4)
Doggett's Gap (2) — Hey, Little Bird (2) — Lyke Wake Dirge (2) — Poor Man's Daughter (1) — Song To A Seagull (2) — Vampire (4)
Don't Call Me Honey (medley) (2) — House Carpenter (1) — Many A Mile (4) — Reynardine - A Vampire Legend (2) — Soulful Shade Of Blue (3,4) — Waly Waly (1)
From The Bottom Of My Heart (3) — I Wanna Hold Your Hand Forever (6) — Men Of The Fields (1) — Rollin' Mill Man (5) — Summer Boy (2,4) — Wedding Song (2)
God Is Alive, Magic Is Afoot (4) — **I'm Gonna Be A Country Girl Again (4) 98** — **Mister Can't You See (6) 38** — Rolling Log Blues (1,4) — Surfer, The (5) — Winter Boy (1,4)
Gonna Feel Much Better When You're Gone (3) — Jeremiah (6) — Moonshot (6) — Seeds Of Brotherhood (2) — Sweet Memories (6) — You Know How To Turn On Those Lights (6)
Ground Hog (4) — Lady Margaret (1) — Moratorium - Bring Our Brothers Home (5) — She Used To Wanna Be A Ballerina (5) — Sweet September Morning (5)
— Lay It Down (6) — My Baby Left Me (6) — — T'es Pas Un Autre (2)
— — My Country 'Tis Of Thy People You're Dying (1,4) — — Take My Hand For Awhile (3,4)
— — Native North American Child (6) — — Tall Trees In Georgia (3)

ST. JAMES, Rebecca '00
Born in 1977 in Sydney, Australia. Christian singer.

7/13/96	**200**	1		©	1 **God**			$10	ForeFront 25141
11/29/97	**30**[X]	1		©	2 **Christmas**		[X]	$10	ForeFront 25176
11/7/98	**168**	1		©	3 **Pray**			$10	ForeFront 25189
11/11/00	**166**	1		©	4 **Transform**			$10	ForeFront 25251

Abba (Father) (1) — Give Myself Away (3) — Lean On (4) — O Come Emmanuel (2) — Reborn (4) — What Child Is This (2)
All Around Me (4) — Go And Sin No More (1) — Lord You're Beautiful (3) — O Holy Night (2) — Silent Night (2) — You Then Me (1)
Carry Me High (1) — God (1) — Love To Love You (3) — OK (3) — Speak To Me (1) — You're The Voice (1)
Cold Heart Turns (1) — Happy Christmas (2) — Me Without You (1) — Omega (4) — Stand (4)
Come Quickly Lord (1) — Hold Me Jesus (3) — Merciful (4) — One (4) — Sweet Little Jesus Boy (2)
Cradle Prayer (2) — I'll Carry You (3) — Mirror (3) — One Small Child (2) — That's What Matters (1)
Don't Worry (4) — In Me (4) — My Hope (4) — Peace (3) — Universe (4)
For The Love Of God (4) — Jesu Joy Of Man's Desiring (2) — O Come All Ye Faithful (2) — Pray (3) — Wait For Me (4)

ST. LUNATICS '01
Rap group from St. Louis: Ali, City Spud, Kyjuan and Murphy Lee. **Nelly** was a former member.

| 6/23/01 | **3** | 15↑▲ | | © | **Free City** | | | $10 | Fo' Reel 014119 |

Boom D Boom — Here We Come — Love You So — Real N****z — Show Em What They Won
Dis Iz Da Life — Jang A Lang — **Midwest Swing 88** — S.T.L. — Summer In The City
Groovin Tonight — Let Me In Now — Okay — Scandalous

SAINT TROPEZ '79
Female disco trio: Teresa Burton, Kathy Deckard and Phyllis Rhodes.

| 11/26/77 | **131** | 10 | | | 1 **Je T'aime**... | | [F] | $12 | Butterfly 002 |
| 5/5/79 | **65** | 11 | | | 2 **Belle de Jour**.. | | | $12 | Butterfly 3100 |

Belle De Jour (2) — Hold On To Love (2) — Most Of All (2) — Think I'm Gonna Fall In Love With Love (2) — When You Are Gone (2)
Coeur A Coeur (1) — Je T'aime (1) — On A Rien A Perdre (1) — Violation (1)
Fill My Life With Love (1) — La Symphonie Africaine (1) — **One More Minute (2) 49**

SAKAMOTO, Kyu '63
Born in 1941 in Kawasaki, Japan. Died in a plane crash on 8/12/85 (age 43) near Tokyo. Male singer.

| 6/15/63 | 14 | 17 | | | Sukiyaki and other Japanese hits .... [F] | | | $25 | Capitol 10349 |

Anoko No Namaewa — Nantenkana — Boku No Hoshi | Good Timing — Goodbye, Joe — Hige No Uta | Hitoribocchi No Futari — Kiminaka Kiminaka — Kyu-Chan No Zuntatatta | Kyu-Chan Ondo — Mo Hitori No Boku — **Sukiyaki** 1 | Tsun Tsun Bushi

SALES, Soupy '65
Born Milton Supman on 1/8/26 in Franklinton, North Carolina. Slapstick comedian. Hosted own TV show. His sons, Hunt and Tony, were members of the group **Tin Machine**.

| 4/24/65 | 102 | 7 | | | 1 Spy With A Pie .... [N] | | | $25 | ABC-Paramount 503 |
| 5/15/65 | 80 | 7 | | | 2 Soupy Sales Sez do The Mouse and other teen hits .... [N] | | | $25 | ABC-Paramount 517 |

Dressing Room Menagerie (1) — Forever Friends (2) — Hey, Pearl (2) — King Kong (2) — Leona (1) | Mighty Clem (2) — **Mouse, The** (2) 76 — Mouse Trap (2) — Mr. Cab Driver (2) — Name Game (2) | Nitty Gritty (2) — Pachalafaka (2) — Pie-Face (1) — Pie In The Sky (1) — Sad Sack (2) | Soupy Of The Secret Service (1) — Speedy Gonzales (2) — There's Nothing To Do Today (1) | Thirty Five Pounds, Nine Feet Tall (1) — Vy You Spyink On Me (1) — We're Going To The Circus (1) — What Did The Animals Say (1) | Your Brains'll Fall Out (2)

SALIVA '01
Rock group: Josey Scott (vocals), Wayne Swinny (guitar), Dave Novotny (bass) and Paul Crosby (drums).

| 4/14/01 | 56 | 25↑ | ● | © | Every Six Seconds .... | | | $10 | Island 542959 |

After Me — Beg | Click Click Boom — Doperide | Faultline — Greater Than/Less Than | Hollywood — Lackluster | Musta Been Wrong — My Goodbyes | Superstar — Your Disease

SALSOUL ORCHESTRA '76
Disco orchestra conducted by producer/arranger Vincent Montana. Vocalists included Phyllis Rhodes, Ronni Tyson, Carl Helm, Philip Hurt and **Jocelyn Brown**. Also see **Montana Orchestra**.

11/29/75+	14	45			1 The Salsoul Orchestra	[I]		$12	Salsoul 5501
10/23/76	61	14			2 Nice 'N' Naasty			$12	Salsoul 5502
12/11/76+	83	6	©		3 Christmas Jollies	[X]		$12	Salsoul 5507
6/25/77	61	20	©		4 Magic Journey			$12	Salsoul 5515
11/26/77+	100	15			5 Cuchi-Cuchi			$12	Salsoul 5519

CHARO & THE SALSOUL ORCHESTRA

12/24/77+	48	7	©		6 Christmas Jollies	[X-R]		$12	Salsoul 5507
3/25/78	117	8			7 Up The Yellow Brick Road			$12	Salsoul 8500
9/9/78	97	13			8 Greatest Disco Hits/Music For Non-Stop Dancing	[G]		$12	Salsoul 8508
12/19/81+	170	5			9 Christmas Jollies II	[X]		$12	Salsoul 8547

Alpha Centuri (4) — Borriquito (5) — Chicago Bus Stop (Ooh, I Love It) (1,8) — Christmas Song (medley) (3,6) — Christmas Time (3,6) — Cookie Jar (5) — Cuchi-Cuchi (5) — Dance A Little Bit Closer (5) — Deck The Halls (3,6,9) — Don't Beat Around The Bush (2,8) — Ease On Down The Road (4) — El Reloj (The Clock) (5) — Evergreen (7) | Feelings (medley) (2) — Fiddler On The Roof Medley (7) — First Noel (medley) (3,6) — Get Happy (1) — Getaway (4,8) — God Rest Ye Merry Gentlemen (9) — Guantanamera (4) — Hark! The Herald Angels Sing (medley) (3,6) — I'll Be Home For Christmas (medley) (3,6) — It Don't Have To Be Funky (2) — It's A New Day (4) — It's Good For The Soul (2,8) | Jack And Jill (2) — Jingle Bells (medley) (3,6) — Journey To Phoebus (4) — Joy To The World (3,6,9) — Joyful Spirit (9) — Let's Spend The Night Together (5) — Little Drummer Boy (3,6) — Love Letters (1) — Magic Bird Of Fire (4,8) — Merry Christmas All (3,6) — Montreal Olympics, 1976 Medley, Themes From (4) — More Of You (5) — New Year's Medley (3,6) | **Nice 'N' Naasty** (2,8) 30 — Nightcrawler (2) — O Come All Ye Faithful (medley) (3,6) — Only You (Can Make My Empty Life Worthwhile) (5) — **Ritzy Mambo** (2) 99 — Rudolph The Red-Nosed Reindeer (medley) (3,6) — Run Away (4) — **Salsoul Hustle** (1,8) 76 — Salsoul Rainbow (1,8) — Salsoul 3001 (2,8) | Santa Claus Is Coming To Town (medley) (3,6) — Sgt. Pepper's Lonely Hearts Club Band (7) — Short Shorts (4) — Silent Night (3,6) — Sleigh Ride (3,6) — Speedy Gonzalez (5) — Standing And Waiting On Love (2) — Tale Of Three Cities (1) — Tangerine (1,8) 18 — There's Someone Who's Knocking (3,6) | We Wish You A Merry Christmas (medley) (3,6) — We've Only Just Begun (medley) (2) — West Side Story Medley (7) — White Christmas (medley) (3,6) — Winter Wonderland (medley) (3,6) — You're All I Want For Christmas (9) — **You're Just The Right Size** (1,5,8) 88

SALTER, Sam '97
Born on 2/16/75 in Los Angeles. R&B singer.

| 10/18/97 | 199 | 1 | © | | It's On Tonight .... | | | $10 | LaFace 26040 |

After 12, Before 6 51 — Coulda' Been Me | Every Time A Car Drives By — Give Me My Baby | I Love You Both — It Took A Song | It's On Tonight — On My Heart | Show You That I Care — **There You Are** 57 | Thinkin' & Trippin' — Your Face

SALT-N-PEPA '94
Female rap trio from Queens, New York: Cheryl "Salt" James, Sandra "Pepa" Denton and Dee Dee "Spinderella" Roper. Appeared in the movie Who's The Man?. Pepa married Treach (of **Naughty By Nature**) on 7/24/99.

8/1/87+	26	53	▲	©	1 Hot, Cool & Vicious			$10	Next Plateau 1007
8/13/88	38	31	●	©	2 A Salt With A Deadly Pepa			$10	Next Plateau 1011
4/7/90	38	71	▲	©	3 Blacks' Magic			$10	Next Plateau 1019
10/5/91+	21 C	33		©	4 A Blitz of Salt-N-Pepa Hits: The Hits Remixed	[K]		$10	Next Plateau 1025
10/30/93+	4	89	▲5	©	5 Very Necessary			$10	Next Plateau 828392
11/8/97	37	12	●	©	6 Brand New			$10	London 828959

Beauty And The Beat (1) — Big Shot (5) — Blacks' Magic (3) — Boy Toy (5) — Brand New (6) — Break Of Dawn (5) — Chick On The Side (1) — Clock Is Tickin' (6) — Do Me Right (6) — **Do You Want Me** (3) 21 — Doper Than Dope (3) | Everybody Get Up (2) — **Expression** (3,4) 26 — Friends (6) — Get Up Everybody (Get Up) (4) — **Gitty Up** (6) 50 — Good Life (6) — Groove Me (5) — Heaven Or Hell (5) — Hold On (6) — Hyped On The Mic (2) — I Desire (1) | I Don't Know (3) — I Gotcha (2) — I Gotcha (Once Again) (4) — I Like It Like That (2) — I Like To Party (3) — I'll Take Your Man (1,4) — I've Got AIDS (5) — Imagine (6) — Independent (3,4) — It's All Right (1) — It's Alright (4) | Knock Knock (6) — Let The Rhythm Run (2) — **Let's Talk About Sex** (3) 13 — Live And Let Die (3) — My Mic Sounds Nice (1,4) — Negro Wit' An Ego (3) — No One Does It Better (5) — **None Of Your Business** (5) 32 — Push It (4) — R U Ready (6) — Salt With A Deadly Pepa (2) | Say Ooh (6) — Sexy Noises Turn Me On (5) — Shake Your Thang (2,4) — **Shoop** (5) 4 — Showstopper, The (1) — Silly Of You (6) — Solo Power (Let's Get Paid) (2) — Solo Power (Syncopated Soul) (2) — Somebody's Gettin' On My Nerves (5) | Somma Time Man (5) — Spinderella's Not A Fella (But A Girl DJ) (2) — Start The Party (3) — Step (5) — Swift (5) — Tramp (1,4) — Twist And Shout (2) — **Whatta Man** (5) 3 — **You Showed Me** (3) 47

SALTY DOG '90
Hard-rock group formed in Los Angeles: Jimmi Bleacher (vocals), Pete Reveen (guitar), Michael Hannon (bass) and Khurt Maier (drums).

| 4/7/90 | 176 | 3 | | © | Every Dog Has Its Day .... | | | $10 | Geffen 24270 |

Cat's Got Nine — Come Along — Heave Hard (She Comes Easy) | Just Like A Woman — Keep Me Down — Lonesome Fool | Nothin' But A Dream — Ring My Bell — Sacrifice Me | Sim Sala Bim — Slow Daze — Spoonful | Where The Sun Don't Shine

SAM & DAVE '66

R&B vocal duo: Sam Moore (born on 10/12/35 in Miami) and Dave Prater (born on 5/9/37 in Ocilla, Georgia). Prater was killed in a car crash on 4/9/88 (age 50). Duo inducted into the Rock and Roll Hall of Fame in 1992.

8/6/66	45	15		©	1 **Hold On, I'm Comin'**			$50	Stax 708
1/21/67	118	13		©	2 **Double Dynamite**			$50	Stax 712
11/18/67+	62	13		©	3 **Soul Men**			$50	Stax 725
2/15/69	87	17			4 **The Best Of Sam & Dave**		[G]	$25	Atlantic 8218

Blame Me (Don't Blame My Heart) (1) — Ease Me (1) — **I Thank You** (4) *9* — Just Me (1) — **Soul Man** (3,4) *2* — **You Don't Know What You Mean To Me** (4) *48*
Broke Down Piece Of Man (3) — Good Runs The Bad Away (3) — I'm With You (3) — Let It Be Me (3) — Sweet Pains (2) — You Got It Made (1)
Can't You Find Another Way (Of Doing It) (4) *54* — Hold It Baby (3) — I'm Your Puppet (2) — May I Baby (3,4) — That's The Way It's Gotta Be (2) — **You Got Me Hummin'** (2,4) *77*
Don't Help Me Out (1) — **Hold On! I'm A Comin'** (1,4) *21* — I've Seen What Loneliness Can Do (3) — Rich Kind Of Poverty (3) — Use Me (2)
Don't Knock It (3) — Home At Last (2) — It's A Wonder (1) — **Said I Wasn't Gonna Tell Nobody** (2,4) *64* — **When Something Is Wrong With My Baby** (2,4) *42*
Don't Make It So Hard On Me (1) — I Don't Need Nobody (To Tell Me 'Bout My Baby) (2) — If You Got The Loving (1) — Sleep Good Tonight (3) — Wrap It Up (1)
I Got Everything I Need (1) — Just Can't Get Enough (2) — Small Portion Of Your Love (1) — **You Don't Know Like I Know** (1,4) *90*
I Take What I Want (1,4) — Just Keep Holding On (3) — **Soothe Me** (2,4) *56*

SAMBORA, Richie '91

Born on 7/11/59 in Woodbridge, New Jersey. Guitarist of **Bon Jovi**. Married actress Heather Locklear on 12/17/94.

9/21/91	36	11		©	1 **Stranger In This Town**			$10	Mercury 848895
3/21/98	174	1		©	2 **Undiscovered Soul**			$10	Mercury 536972

All That Really Matters (2) — Church Of Desire (1) — Hard Times Come Easy (2) — Made In America (2) — River Of Love (1) — Who I Am (2)
Answer, The (1) — Downside Of Love (2) — Harlem Rain (2) — Mr. Bluesman (1) — Rosie (1) — You're Not Alone (2)
Ballad Of Youth (1) *63* — Fallen From Graceland (2) — If God Was A Woman (2) — One Light Burning (2) — Stranger In This Town (1)
Chained (2) — Father Time (1) — In It For Love (2) — Rest In Peace (1) — Undiscovered Soul (2)

SAMMIE '00

Born Sammie Bush on 3/1/87 in Boynton Beach, Florida. Male R&B singer.

4/1/00	46	31	●	©	**From The Bottom To The Top**			$10	Freeworld 23168

Bottom, The — Catching Feelings — Crazy Things I Do — Fell For Her — Hero — If I Can
Can't Let Go — Count — Do It For You — Friend Like You — **I Like It** *24* — Stuff Like This

SAMPLE, Joe '79

Born on 2/1/39 in Houston. Jazz keyboardist. Member of **The Crusaders**.

2/25/78	62	25		©	1 **Rainbow Seeker**		[I]	$12	ABC 1050
2/10/79	56	26		©	2 **Carmel**		[I]	$12	ABC 1126
1/31/81	65	20		©	3 **Voices In The Rain**		[I]	$12	MCA 5172
4/16/83	125	14		©	4 **The Hunter**		[I]	$12	MCA 5397
4/15/89	129	14		©	5 **Spellbound**			$10	Warner 25781
4/10/93	194	1		©	6 **Invitation**		[I]	$10	Warner 45209
5/29/99	196	1		©	7 **The Song Lives On**			$10	GRP 9956

JOE SAMPLE Featuring Lalah Hathaway

All God's Children (5) — Django (6) — Just A Little Higher (4) — Night Flight (4) — Spellbound (5) — Wings Of Fire (4)
As Long As It Lasts (1) — Dream Of Dreams (3) — Leading Me Back To You (5) — One Day I'll Fly Away (7) — Stormy Weather (6)
Beauty And The Beast (4) — Eye Of The Hurricane (3) — Living In Blue (7) — Paintings (2) — Street Life (7)
Bitter Sweet (7) — Fever (2) — Long Way From Home (7) — Rainbow Seeker (1) — Summertime (6)
Black Is The Color (6) — Fly With Wings Of Love (1) — Looking Glass (2) — Rainy Day In Monterey (4) — Sunrise (2)
Blue Ballet (4) — For All We Know (7) — Luna En New York (5) — Sermonized (5) — There Are Many Stops Along The Way (4)
Bones Jive (5) — Greener Grass (3) — Melodies Of Love (1) — Seven Years Of Good Luck (5) — Together We'll Find A Way (1)
Burnin' Up The Carnival (3) — House Is Not A Home (6) — Midnight And Mist (2) — Shadows (3) — U Turn (5)
Cannery Row (2) — Hunter, The (4) — Mood Indigo (6) — Somehow Our Love Survives (5) — Voices In The Rain (3)
Carmel (2) — In All My Wildest Dreams (1) — More Beautiful Each Day (2) — Sonata In Solitude (3) — When The World Turns Blue (7)
Come Along With Me (7) — Invitation (6) — My One And Only Love (6) — Song Lives On (7) — When Your Life Was Low (7)
Come Rain Or Come Shine (6) — Islands In The Rain (1) — Nica's Dream (6)

SAMPLES, The '94

Rock group from Boulder, Colorado: Sean Kelly (vocals, guitar), Al Laughlin (keyboards), Andy Sheldon (bass) and Jeep MacNichol (drums).

10/1/94	122	1		©	1 **Autopilot**			$10	W.A.R.? 60008
8/3/96	175	1		©	2 **Outpost**			$10	MCA 11435

All My Thoughts (Johnny Station Wagon) (2) — Birth Of Words (2) — Foreign Countries (2) — It's Curtains (2) — Only To You (1) — Who Am I? (1)
Anyone (2) — Buffalo Herds & Windmills (1) — Hunt, The (1) — Learjet (2) — Seasons In The City (1)
As Tears Fall (1) — Did You Ever Look So Nice (2) — I Remember Dying (2) — Lost Children (A Slow Motion Crash) (2) — Shine On (2)
Big Bird (2) — Dinosaur Bones (1) — Indiana (2) — Madmen (1) — Water Rush (1)
Finest Hour (1) — Information (2) — Weight Of The World (1)

SAM THE SHAM AND THE PHARAOHS '65

Born Domingo Samudio in 1940 in Dallas. The Pharaohs: Ray Stinnet (guitar), Butch Gibson (sax), David Martin (bass) and Jerry Patterson (drums). Martin died on 8/2/87 (age 50).

6/12/65	26	18			1 **Wooly Bully**			$40	MGM 4297
9/24/66	82	7			2 **Li'l Red Riding Hood**			$40	MGM 4407
3/11/67	98	17			3 **the best of Sam the Sham and the pharaohs**		[G]	$40	MGM 4422

Deputy Dog (2) — Go-Go Girls (1) — Haunted House (1) — **Lil' Red Riding Hood** (2,3) *2* — Mystery Train (3) — Ring Them Bells (2)
El Toro De Goro (The Peace Loving Bull) (2,3) — Grasshopper (2) — I Found Love (1) — Little Miss Muffet (2) — Phantom, The (2) — Shotgun (1)
Every Woman I Know (Crazy 'Bout An Auto) (1) — Green'ich Grendel (2) — I Wish It Were Me (3) — Long Tall Sally (1) — Pharaoh-A-Go Go (3) — Sorry 'Bout That (1)
Gangster Of Love (1) — **Hair On My Chinny Chin Chin** (3) *22* — (I'm In With) The Out Crowd (3) — Mary Is My Little Lamb (1) — Ready Or Not (3) — Standing Ovation (1)
— Hanky Panky (2) — **Ju Ju Hand** (3) *26* — Mary Lee (1) — **Red Hot** (3) *82* — Sweet Talk (2)
— — Juiminos (Let's Went) (1) — Memphis Beat (1) — Ring Dang Doo (3) *33* — **Wooly Bully** (1,3) *2*

★296★ SANBORN, David '81

Born on 7/30/45 in Tampa, Florida; raised in St. Louis. Saxophonist/flutist. Played with **Paul Butterfield** from 1967-71 and with **Stevie Wonder** from 1972-73. Formed own group in 1975.

1)Voyeur 2)Double Vision 3)Close-Up

8/28/76	125	8		©	1 **Sanborn**		[I]	$12	Warner 2957
6/3/78	151	6		©	2 **Heart To Heart**		[I]	$12	Warner 3189
3/8/80	63	19	●	©	3 **Hideaway**		[I]	$12	Warner 3379
4/18/81	45	22	●	©	4 **Voyeur**		[I]	$12	Warner 3546

SANBORN, David — Cont'd

DEBUT	PEAK	WKS	RIAA	CD	ARTIST — Album Title	Catalog	Sym	$	Label & Number
7/10/82	70	23		© 5	As We Speak		[I]	$10	Warner 23650
11/26/83+	81	33	●	© 6	Backstreet		[I]	$10	Warner 23906
2/9/85	64	32	●	© 7	Straight To The Heart		[I]	$10	Warner 25150
6/14/86	50	64	▲	© 8	Double Vision		[I]	$10	Warner 25393

BOB JAMES/DAVID SANBORN

DEBUT	PEAK	WKS	RIAA	CD	ARTIST — Album Title	Catalog	Sym	$	Label & Number
2/14/87	74	37	●	© 9	A Change Of Heart		[I]	$10	Warner 25479
7/16/88	59	28	●	© 10	Close-Up		[I]	$10	Reprise 25715
7/20/91	170	7		© 11	Another Hand		[I]	$10	Elektra 61088
5/16/92	107	31	●	© 12	Upfront		[I]	$10	Elektra 61272
6/25/94	116	8		© 13	Hearsay		[I]	$10	Elektra 61620
4/15/95	124	11		© 14	Pearls		[I]	$10	Elektra 61759
10/12/96	180	2		© 15	Songs From The Night Before		[I]	$10	Elektra 61950

Again An Again (3)
Alcazar (12)
All I Need Is You (4)
Another Hand (11)
Anything You Want (3)
Anywhere I Wander (2)
As We Speak (5)
Back Again (3)
Back To Memphis (13)
Backstreet (6)
Bang Bang (12) *53*
Believer (6)
Benny (12)
Better Believe It (5)
Big Foot (13)
Blue Beach (6)
Breaking Point (9)
Bums Cathedral (6)
CEE (11)
Carly's Song (3)
Change Of Heart (9)
Chicago Song (9)
Come Rain Or Come Shine (14)
Come To Me, Nina (11)
Concrete Boogie (1)
Creeper (3)
Crossfire (12)
D.S.P. (15)
Dream, The (9)
Dukes & Counts (11)
Everything Must Change (14)
First Song (11)
For All We Know (14)
Full House (12)
Goodbye (12)
Got To Give It Up (13)
Heba (2)
Herbs (1)
Hey (12)
Hideaway (3,7)
High Roller (9)
Hobbies (11)
I Do It For Your Love (1)
I Told U So (6)
If You Would Be Mine (3)
Imogene (9)
Indio (1)
Infant Eyes (15)
It's You (4,8)
J.T. (10)
Jaws (13)
Jesus (11)
Just For You (4)
Lesley Ann (10)
Let's Just Say Goodbye (4)
Lisa (3,7)
Listen Here (15)
Little Face (13)
Lonely From The Twilight Zone (medley) (11)
Long Goodbye (13)
Lotus Blossom (2,7)
Love & Happiness (7)
Love Is Not Enough, Theme From (2)
Love Will Come Someday (5)
Mamacita (1)
Maputo (8)
Mirage (13)
Missing You (15)
Monica Jane (11)
Moon Tune (8)
More Than Friends (8)
Neither One Of Us (6)
Never Enough (8)
Nobody Does It Better (14)
Ojiji (13)
One Hundred Ways (7)
One In A Million (4)
Over And Over (5)
Pearls (14)
Port Of Call (5)
Prayers For Charlie From The Devil At Four O'Clock (medley) (11)
Pyramid (10)
Rain On Christmas (5)
Ramblin' (12)
Relativity (15)
Rikke (15)
Rumpelstiltskin (15)
Run For Cover (4,7)
Rush Hour (5)
Same Girl (14)
Savanna (13)
7th Ave. (1)
Short Visit (2)
Since I Fell For You (8)
Slam (10)
Smile (1,7)
Smoke Gets In Your Eyes (14)
Snakes (12)
So Far Away (10)
Solo (2)
Sophisticated Squaw (1)
Soul Serenade (12)
Southern Exposure (15)
Spooky (15)
Straight To The Heart (5,7)
Summer (9)
Sunrise Gospel (2)
Superstar (14)
Tear For Crystal (8)
This Masquerade (14)
Tintin (3)
Tough (10)
Try A Little Tenderness (14)
Wake Me When It's Over (4)
Weird From One Step Beyond (11)
When You Smile At Me (6)
Willow Weep For Me (14)
You Are Everything (14)
You Don't Know Me (8)

SANDALS, The　'67

Instrumental rock group from Los Angeles: John Blakeley and Walter Georis (guitars), Gaston Georis (piano), John Gibson (bass) and Danny Brawner (drums).

DEBUT	PEAK	WKS	RIAA	CD	ARTIST — Album Title	Catalog	Sym	$	Label & Number
2/4/67	110	13		©	The Endless Summer		[I-S]	$30	World Pacific 1832

Decoy
Drifting
Endless Summer, Theme From
Good Greeves
Jet Black
Lonely Road
Out Front
Scrambler
6 Pac
TR-6
Trailing
Wild As The Sea

SANDERS, Pharoah　'78

Born Farrel Sanders on 10/13/40 in Little Rock, Arkansas. Jazz tenor saxophonist.

DEBUT	PEAK	WKS	RIAA	CD	ARTIST — Album Title	Catalog	Sym	$	Label & Number
8/16/69	188	4		© 1	Karma		[I]	$15	Impulse! 9181
7/31/71	175	3		© 2	Thembi		[I]	$15	Impulse! 9206
5/20/78	163	5		3	Love Will Find A Way			$12	Arista 4161

Answer Me My Love (3)
As You Are (3)
Astral Traveling (2)
Bailophone Dance (2)
Colors (1)
Creator Has A Master Plan (1)
Everything I Have Is Good (3)
Got To Give It Up (3)
Love (2)
Love Is Here (3)
Love Will Find A Way (3)
Morning Prayer (2)
Pharomba (3)
Red, Black & Green (2)
Thembi (2)

SANDLER, Adam　'99

Born on 9/9/66 in Brooklyn, New York. Actor/comedian. Cast member of TV's *Saturday Night Live* (1990-95). Starred in several movies.

DEBUT	PEAK	WKS	RIAA	CD	ARTIST — Album Title	Catalog	Sym	$	Label & Number
12/11/93+	129	55	▲	© 1	They're All Gonna Laugh At You!	C:#17/17	[C]	$10	Warner 45393
3/2/96	18	57	▲²	© 2	What The Hell Happened To Me?	C:#17/10	[C]	$10	Warner 46151
10/4/97	18	17	●	© 3	What's Your Name?		[N]	$10	Warner 46738
10/9/99	16	17	●	© 4	Stan And Judy's Kid		[C]	$10	Warner 47429

Adventures Of The Cow (2)
Assistant Principal's Big Day (1)
At A Medium Pace (1)
Bad Boyfriend (3)
Beating Of A High School Bus Driver (1)
Beating Of A High School Janitor (1)
Beating Of A High School Science Teacher (1)
Beating Of A High School Spanish Teacher (1)
Buddy (1)
Buffoon And The Dean Of Admissions (1)
Buffoon And The Valedictorian (1)
Champion, The (4)
Chanukah Song (2) *80*
Chanukah Song Part II (4)
Cheerleader, The (1)
Cool Guy 1-5 (4)
Corduroy Blues (3)
Crazy Love (2)
Dancin' And Pantsin' (3)
Dee Wee (My Friend The Massive Idiot) (4)
Dip Doodle (2)
Do It For Your Mama (2)
Excited Southerner At A Job Interview (2)
Excited Southerner Gets Pulled Over (2)
Excited Southerner Meets Mel Gibson (2)
Excited Southerner Orders A Meal (2)
Excited Southerner Proposes To A Woman (2)
Fatty Arbuckle (3)
Food Innuendo Guy (1)
Four Years Old (3)
Goat, The (2)
Goat Song (3)
Hot Water Burn Baby (4)
Hypnotist, The (2)
I'm So Wasted (1)
Inner Voice (4)
Joining The Cult (2)
Listenin' To The Radio (3)
Lonesome Kicker (3)
Longest Pee (1)
Lunchlady Land (1)
Memory Lane (2)
Moyda (3)
Mr. Bake-O (2)
Mr. Spindel's Phone Call (1)
My Little Chicken (1)
Ode To My Car (2)
Oh Mom... (1)
Peeper, The (4)
Pickin' Daisies (3)
Psychotic Legend Of Uncle Donnie (4)
Red Hooded Sweatshirt (3)
Respect (2)
Respect Chant (3)
Right Field (4)
7 Foot Man (4)
Sex Or Weight Lifting (2)
She Comes Home To Me (4)
Steve Polychronopolous (2)
Sweet Beatrice (3)
Teenage Love On The Phone (4)
Thanksgiving Song (1)
Toll Booth Willie (1)
Voodoo (3)
Welcome My Son (4)
What The Hell Happened To Me? (2)
Whitey (4)
Zittly Van Zittles (3)

SANDLER, Tony, & Ralph Young　'67

Vocal duo. Sandler was born in 1934 in Kortrjk, Belgium. Young was born in 1919 in New York City.

DEBUT	PEAK	WKS	RIAA	CD	ARTIST — Album Title	Catalog	Sym	$	Label & Number
12/17/66+	85	19		1	Side By Side			$15	Capitol 2598
4/15/67	166	3		2	On The Move			$15	Capitol 2686
7/5/69	188	4		3	Pretty Things Come In Twos			$15	Capitol 241
7/11/70	199	2		4	Honey Come Back			$15	Capitol 449

And When I Die (1)
Autumn Leaves (1)
Blackbird (4)
Blue And Broken Hearted (3)
Bon Soir Dame (3)
C'est Si Bon (2)
Can't Help Falling In Love (4)
Canadian Sunset (1)
Chanson D'Amour (Song Of Love) (2)
Chicago (4)
Coco (4)
Cu-Cu-Rru-Cu-Cu, Paloma (2)
Dominique (1)
El Soldado De Levita (3)
French Lullaby (1)
Gonna Build A Mountain (2)
Heather (3)
Honey Come Back (4)
I'll Never Fall In Love Again (4)
If We Only Have Love (Quand On N'A Que L'Amour) (3)
Impossible Dream (The Quest) (1)
Just Say I Love Her (Dicitencello Vuie) (2)
(Lo Mucho Que Te Quiero) The More I Love You (3)
Love Me With All Your Heart (Quando Caliente El Sol) (1)
Love Of The Common People (4)
Man And A Woman (2)
Midnight Cowboy (4)
Misty Morning Eyes (3)
Our Day Will Come (1)
Pretty Things Come In Twos (3)
Put On A Happy Face (2)
Raindrops Keep Fallin' On My Head (4)
Sand & Sea (Plein Soleil) (2)
Side By Side (1)
Sunrise, Sunset (2)
There Will Never Be Another You (2)
Traces (4)
Vaya Con Dios (May God Be With You) (1)
Very Thought Of You (3)
What Now, My Love? (1)
Yellow Bird (1)
Yesterday I Heard The Rain (3)
You And Only You (Un Bacio Alla Volta) (3)

SANDPIPERS, The   '67
Pop vocal trio from Los Angeles: Jim Brady, Michael Piano and Richard Shoff.

DEBUT	PEAK	WKS						$	Label & Number
10/29/66+	13	37	●	©	1 Guantanamera			$15	A&M 4117
5/27/67	53	28		©	2 The Sandpipers			$15	A&M 4125
1/13/68	135	5			3 Misty Roses			$15	A&M 4135
9/7/68	180	5			4 Softly			$15	A&M 4147
5/10/69	194	5			5 The Wonder Of You			$15	A&M 4180
4/18/70	160	10			6 Greatest Hits		[G]	$15	A&M 4246
8/15/70	96	11			7 Come Saturday Morning			$15	A&M 4262

All My Loving (4,6)
And I Love Her (3,6)
Angelica (1,6)
Autumn Afternoon (7)
Back On The Street Again (4)
Beyond The Valley Of The Dolls (7)
Bon Soir Dame (7)
Cancion De Amor (Wanderlove) (4,6)
Carmen (1)
Cast Your Fate To The Wind (1)
Come Saturday Morning (7) *17*
Cuando Sali De Cuba (The Wind Will Change Tomorrow) (3,6)
Daydream (3)
Drifter, The (7)
Enamorado (1,6)
Find A Reason To Believe (4)
Fly Me To The Moon (3)
For Baby (2)
Free To Carry On (7) *94*
French Song (2)
Glass (2)
Gloria Patri (Gregorian Psalm Tone III) (4)
Guantanamera (1,6) *9*
(He's Got The) Whole World In His Hands (7)
Honeywind Blows (3)
I Believed It All (3)
I'll Remember You (2)
If I Were The Man (5)
Inch Worm (2)
It's Over (2)
Jenifer Juniper (4)
Kumbaya (5)
La Bamba (1)
La Mer (Beyond The Sea) (1)
Let Go (5)
Lo Mucho Que Te Quiero (The More I Love You) (5)
Long And Winding Road (7)
Louie, Louie (1) *30*
Love Is Blue (4)
Michelle (2)
Misty Roses (3,6)
Ojos De Espana (Spanish Eyes) (4)
Pretty Flamingo (5)
Quando M'Innamoro (4,6)
Rain, Rain Go Away (2)
Santo Domingo (7)
Softly (4)
Softly As I Leave You (2)
Song Of Joy (7)
Sound Of Love (7)
Stasera Gli Angeli Non Volano (For The Last Time) (1)
Strange Song (3)
Strangers In The Night (5)
Suzanne (4)
Temptation (5)
That Night (5)
Things We Said Today (1)
To Put Up With You (4)
Today (3)
Try To Remember (2)
Wave (5)
What Makes You Dream, Pretty Girl? (1)
Where There's A Heartache (5)
Windmills Of Your Mind (5)
Wonder Of You (5,7)
Wooden Heart (5)
Yellow Days (5)
Yesterday (2,6)

SANDS, Tommy   '57
Born on 8/27/37 in Chicago. Pop singer/actor. Married to **Nancy Sinatra** from 1960-65. Acted in the movies *Sing Boy Sing*, *Mardi Gras*, *Babes In Toyland* and *The Longest Day*.

DEBUT	PEAK	WKS						$	Label & Number
5/6/57	4	18		©	1 Steady Date with Tommy Sands			$50	Capitol 848
2/24/58	17	4			2 Sing Boy Sing		[S]	$50	Capitol 929

"A" - You're Adorable (The Alphabet Song) (1)
Bundle Of Dreams (2)
Crazy 'Cause I Love You (1)
Goin' Steady (1) *16*
Gonna Get A Girl (1)
Graduation Day (1)
I Don't Care Who Knows It (1)
I Don't Know Why (I Just Do) (1)
I'm Gonna Walk And Talk With My Lord (2)
Just A Little Bit More (2)
People In Love (2)
Ring My Phone (1) *flip*
Rock Of Ages (2)
Sing Boy Sing (2) *24*
Soda-Pop Pop (2)
Somewhere Along The Way (1)
Teach Me Tonight (1)
That's All I Want From You (2)
Too Young (1)
Too Young To Go Steady (1)
Walkin' My Baby Back Home (1)
Who Baby (2)
Would I Love You (2)
Your Daddy Wants To Do Right (2)

SANFORD/TOWNSEND BAND, The   '77
Pop-rock duo from Los Angeles: Ed Sanford and John Townsend.

DEBUT	PEAK	WKS						$	Label & Number
8/13/77	57	15			1 The Sanford/Townsend Band			$12	Warner 2966
					album also released as *Smoke From A Distant Fire*				
2/11/78	92	8			2 Duo-Glide			$12	Warner 3081

Ain't It So, Love (2)
Cryin' Like A Child (2)
Does It Have To Be You (1)
Eights And Aces (2)
Eye Of My Storm (Oh Woman) (2)
In For The Night (1)
Livin' Easy (2)
Lou (1)
Mississippi Sunshine (2)
Moolah Moo Mazuma (Sin City Wahh-oo) (1)
Oriental Gate (No Chance Of Changin' My Mind) (1)
Paradise (2)
Rainbows Colored In Blue (1)
Shake It To The Right (1)
Smoke From A Distant Fire (1) *9*
Sometimes When The Wind Blows (2)
Squire James (1)
Starbrite (2)
Sunshine In My Heart Again (1)
Voodoo (2)

SAN FRANCISCO SYMPHONY ORCHESTRA   '73
Conducted by Seiji Ozawa (born on 9/1/35 in Japan).

DEBUT	PEAK	WKS						$	Label & Number
4/7/73	105	15			William Russo: Three Pieces for Blues Band and Orchestra/ Leonard Bernstein: Symphonic Dances from West Side Story		[I]	$15	DG 2530 309

Symphonic Dances From West Side Story (1961)
Three Pieces For Blues Band And Symphony Orchestra Op. 50 (1968)

SANG, Samantha   '78
Born Cheryl Gray on 8/5/53 in Melbourne, Australia. Pop singer.

DEBUT	PEAK	WKS						$	Label & Number
3/11/78	29	14	●		Emotion			$12	Private Stock 7009

But If She Moves You
Change Of Heart
Charade
Emotion *3*
I Don't Wanna Go
La La La - I Love You
Living Without Your Love
Love Of A Woman
When Love Is Gone
You Keep Me Dancing *56*

SAN SEBASTIAN STRINGS, The   '68
Music composed by **Anita Kerr** (with sound effects), featuring narration of the poetry of **Rod McKuen**.

DEBUT	PEAK	WKS						$	Label & Number
3/25/67+	52	143	●	©	1 The Sea		[I-T]	$15	Warner 1670
9/23/67	115	13			2 The Earth		[I-T]	$15	Warner 1705
2/17/68	68	25			3 The Sky		[I-T]	$15	Warner 1720
1/18/69	20	20			4 Home To The Sea		[I-T]	$15	Warner 1764
11/22/69	84	17			5 For Lovers		[I-T]	$15	Warner 1795
1/17/70	162	5			6 The Complete Sea		[I-T-R]	$25	Warner 1827 [3]
					deluxe set of albums #1, #4 and #7				
9/26/70	171	5			7 The Soft Sea		[I-T]	$15	Warner 1839

Afternoon Shadows (1,6)
Another Evening With The Gypsies (4,6)
Bathtub Surfing (4,6)
Beyond The Bend Ahead (1,6)
Body Surfing With The Jet Set (6,7)
Butterfly Is Drunk On Sunshine (3)
Buy For Me The Wind (1,6)
Capri In July (2)
Come On In, The Water's Fine (6,7)
Dancing In The Kitchen (5)
Day They Built The Road (2)
Days Of The Dancing (1,6)
Do You Like The Rain? (1,6)
Doorways I Haven't Found (2)
Dragonflies (4,6)
Earthquake (2)
Ever Constant Sea (1,6,7)
Floating Past The Fields (4,6)
Flower People (2)
For Lovers (5)
Forehead Of The Morning (3)
Foreign Movies (5)
Gifts From The Sea (1,6)
Growing Old Together (5)
Gypsy Camp (1,6)
Haunted Mansion On The Hill (5)
Home (2)
Home To The Sea (4,6)
How Many Colors Of Blue? (3)
I'll Carry Home An Orchard (5)
In Summing Up (3)
Looking Up Through Wednesday's Silence (5)
Love Hasn't Any Windows (5)
Love Me Slowly (5)
Lovers Too Have Lullabies (5)
Make A Bigger Circle, With A Softer Touch (5)
Monotony Of Games (6,7)
Moonlight Swim (5)
Mr. God's Trombones (3)
Mud Kids (2)
My Dog Likes Oranges (3)
My Friend The Sea (1,6)
My Mother Wanted Me To Play Mozart (2)
Naked In The Sunlight (6,7)
New Lullabye (For Suzie & Kelly) (3)
Night Talk (3)
Night Watch (4,6)
No Islands Left (6,7)
No Loving Without Losing (5)
November Resolution (4,6)
Oh Yes, The Wind (6,7)
One In The Same (4)
Overture To The Soft Sea (6,7)
Part Of Every Ocean (4,6)
Passage Home (4,6)
Patch Of Sky, Away From Everything (3)
Pushing The Clouds Away (1,6)
Running Out Of Strangers (4,6)
Sailing Through The Sun (4,6)
Saving Sea Shells (6,7)
Sea, The (1,6)
So Little Sun (3)
So Much For The Pipers (6,7)
Song From The Earth (2)
Storm, The (1,6)
Sunday (2)
Tender Earth (2)
There Are No Beaches In Magic City, Texas (4,6)
Time Of Noon (1,6)
Underground Train (2)
Wake Up (6,7)
Walk With The Angels (3)
Waltz, The (2)
We Two Are Drifting (6,7)
What About Tomorrow? (6,7)
When Winter Comes (3)
While Drifting (1,6)
Who Has Touched The Sky (3)
Why I Follow The Tigers (5)
You Even Taste Like The Sun (1,6)
You Wonder Why I Love You (5)

SANTA ESMERALDA '78

Disco studio group assembled by producers Nicolas Skorsky and Jean-Manuel de Scarano. Vocalists include Leroy Gomez and Jimmy Goings.

DEBUT	PEAK	WKS	RIAA	CD	#	Album	$	Label & Number
11/12/77+	25	23	●	©	1	Don't Let Me Be Misunderstood	$12	Casablanca 7080
2/25/78	41	14		©	2	The House Of The Rising Sun	$12	Casablanca 7088
9/2/78	141	6		©	3	Beauty	$12	Casablanca 7109

Black Pot (1)
Dance You Down Tonight (2)
Danse De La Beaute (Part 1 & 2) (3)
Don't Let Me Be Misunderstood (1) *15*
Esmeralda Suite (1)
Gloria (1)
Hey! Gip (2)
Hey Joe (3)
House Of The Rising Sun (2) *78*
Learning The Game (3)
Nothing Else Matters (2)
Only Beauty Survives (3)
Quasimodo Suite (2)
Wages Of Sin (Parts 1-3) (3)
You're My Everything (1)

SANTAMARIA, Mongo '63

Born Ramon Santamaria on 4/7/22 in Havana, Cuba. Conga player.

DEBUT	PEAK	WKS	RIAA	CD	#	Album	Sym	$	Label & Number
5/4/63	42	10		©	1	Watermelon Man!	[I]	$25	Battle 96120
3/27/65	112	10			2	El Pussy Cat	[I]	$20	Columbia 9098
8/28/65	79	15			3	La Bamba	[I]	$20	Columbia 9175
6/4/66	135	5			4	Hey! Let's Party	[I]	$20	Columbia 9273
8/10/68	171	18			5	Soul Bag	[I]	$20	Columbia 9653
3/1/69	62	24			6	Stone Soul	[I]	$20	Columbia 9780
11/29/69	193	2			7	Workin' On A Groovy Thing	[I]	$20	Columbia 9937
4/11/70	171	3			8	Feelin' Alright	[I]	$15	Atlantic 8252
10/3/70	195	2		©	9	Mongo '70	[I]	$15	Atlantic 1567

Adobo Criollo (9)
Afro Lypso (2)
Ah Ha (2)
Ain't That Peculiar (7)
Baby What You Want Me To Do (5)
Baila Dance (4)
Bayou Roots (1)
Black-Eyed Peas (2)
Boogie Cha Cha Blues (1)
By The Time I Get To Phoenix (8)
Call Me (4)
Chili Beans (5)
Cloud Nine (6) *32*
Coconut Milk (3)
Cold Sweat (5)
Cuidado (2)
Cut That Cane! (1)
Dedicated To Love (9)
Do It To It (3)
Don't Bother Me No More (1)
El Bikini (4)
El Pussy Cat (2) *97*
Fat Back (3)
Feeling Alright (8) *96*
Fever (8)
From Me To You All (3)
Funny Money (1)
Get Back (7)
Get The Money (1)
Getting It Out Of My System (7)
Go Git It! (1)
Grass Roots (9)
Green Onions (5)
Groovin' (5)
Hammer Head (2)
Heighty-Hi (8)
Hey! (4)
Hip-Hug-Her (8)
Hitchcock Railway (6)
Hold On, I'm Comin' (8)
Hot Dog (7)
I Can't Get Next To You (8)
(I Can't Get No) Satisfaction (4)
I Got You (I Feel Good) (4)
In-A-Gadda-Da-Vida (8)
In The Midnight Hour (5)
In The Mood (4)
It's Your Thing (7)
Jose Outside (3)
Just Say Goodbye (3)
La Bamba (3)
La Gitana (2)
Little Green Apples (6)
Look Away (9)
Louie, Louie (4)
Love Child (6)
Love, Oh Love (1)
Manha De Carnaval (Morning Of The Carnival) (3)
March Of The Panther (9)
Mo' Do' (9)
My Cherie Amour (7)
My Girl (5)
Night Crawler (9)
Now Generation (4)
On Broadway (8)
Peanut Vendor (1)
Proud Mary (7)
Respect (5)
Ricky Tick (3)
Ritmo Negro (2)
Sarai (2)
See-Saw (6)
Shotgun (4)
Sitting On The Dock Of The Bay (5)
Son-Of-A-Preacher Man (6)
Spinning Wheel (7)
Stoned Soul Picnic (6)
Streak O'Lean (3)
Suavito (1)
Summertime (3)
Sunshine Of Your Love (9)
Together (2)
Too Busy Thinking About My Baby (7)
Tracks Of My Tears (8)
Twenty-Five Miles (7)
Up, Up And Away (5)
Walk On By (4)
Watermelon Man (1,3) *10*
We Got Latin Soul (7)
Where We Are (6)
Whistler, The (9)
Who's Making Love (6)
Windjammer (7)
Workin' On A Groovy Thing (7)
Yeh-Yeh! (1) *92*
Yesterday's Tomorrow (9)

SANTANA ★60★ '99

Latin-rock group formed in San Francisco by **Carlos Santana**. Various members over the years include Alex Ligertwood (vocals), Gregg Rolie (keyboards, vocals), **Neal Schon** (guitar), David brown (bass) and **Michael Shrieve** (drums). Schon and Rolie formed **Journey**. Shrieve formed **Automatic Man**.

1)*Supernatural* 2)*Abraxas* 3)*Santana III* 4)*Santana* 5)*Caravanserai*

DEBUT	PEAK	WKS	RIAA	CD	#	Album	Catalog	Sym	$	Label & Number
9/13/69	4	108	▲2	©	1	Santana			$15	Columbia 9781
10/10/70	❶6	88	▲5	©	2	Abraxas			$15	Columbia 30130
10/16/71	❶5	39	▲2	©	3	Santana III			$15	Columbia 30595
11/4/72	8	32	▲	©	4	Caravanserai			$15	Columbia 31610
12/1/73	25	21	●		5	Welcome			$15	Columbia 32445
7/27/74	17	21	▲7	©	6	Santana's Greatest Hits	C:#12/71	[G]	$15	Columbia 33050
11/2/74	20	19	●	©	7	Borboletta			$15	Columbia 33135
4/10/76	10	26	●	©	8	Amigos			$15	Columbia 33576
1/22/77	27	19	●	©	9	Festival			$15	Columbia 34423
11/5/77	10	24	▲2	©	10	Moonflower		[L]	$20	Columbia 34914 [2]
11/4/78	27	33	●	©	11	Inner Secrets			$12	Columbia 35600
10/20/79	25	22	●	©	12	Marathon			$12	Columbia 36154
4/18/81	9	32	▲	©	13	Zebop!			$12	Columbia 37158
9/4/82	22	23	●	©	14	Shango			$12	Columbia 38122
						title is Spanish for "Monkey"				
3/23/85	50	21		©	15	Beyond Appearances			$10	Columbia 39527
3/7/87	95	11		©	16	Freedom			$10	Columbia 40272
10/29/88	142	6	●	©	17	Viva Santana		[L]	$20	Columbia 44344 [3]
						recordings from 1969-87				
7/21/90	85	11		©	18	Spirits Dancing In The Flesh			$10	Columbia 46065
5/23/92	102	13		©	19	Milagro			$10	Polydor 513197
						title is Spanish for "Miracle"				
11/20/93	181	1		©	20	Sacred Fire - Live In South America		[L]	$10	Polydor 521082
4/18/98+	82	20	▲	©	21	The Best Of Santana	C:#7/15	[G]	$10	Columbia 65561
7/3/99	❶12	102	▲14	©	22	Supernatural	C:#22/13		$10	Arista 19080

1999 Grammy winner: Album of the Year

A Dios (19)
Abi Cama (17)
Africa Bamba (22)
Agua Que Va Caer (19)
All I Ever Wanted (12,21)
All The Love Of The Universe (4)
American Gypsy (13)
Angel Negro (7)
Angels All Around Us (20)
Aqua Marine (12,17)
Aspirations (7)
Bahia (10)
Ballin' (17)
Bambara (17)
Bambele (17)
Batuka (3)
Before We Go (16)
Bella (21)
Black Magic Woman (2,6,10,17,20,21) *4*
Body Surfing (14)
Borboletta (7)
Breaking Out (15)
Brightest Star (13)
Brotherhood (15,17)
Calling, The (22)
Canto De Los Flores (7)
Caramba (8)
Carnaval (9,10)
Changes (13)
Choose (18)
Corazon Espinado (22)
(Da Le) Yaleo (22)

SANTANA — Cont'd

Dance Sister Dance (Baila Mi Hermana) (8,10,17,21)
Daughter Of The Night (17)
Dawn (medley) (10)
Dealer (medley) (11)
Deeper, Dig Deeper (16)
Do You Like The Way (22)
Don't Try This At Home (medley) (20)
E Papa Re (13)
El Farol (22)
El Morocco (10)
El Nicoya (2)
Esperando (20)
Eternal Caravan Of Reincarnation (4)
Europa (Earth's Cry Heaven's Smile) (8,10,17,20,21)
Every Step Of The Way (4)
Everybody's Everything (3,6,17,21) *12*
Everything's Coming Our Way (3,6)
Evil Ways (1,6,17,21) *9*
Facts Of Love (11)
Flame-Sky (5)
Flor D'Luna (Moonflower) (10)
Flor De Canela (7)
Free All The People (South Africa) (12)
Full Moon (18)
Future Primitive (4)
Gitano (8)
Give And Take (7)
Give Me Love (9)
Go Within (medley) (10)

Going Home (5)
Goodness And Mercy (18)
Guajira (3,17,20)
Gypsy/Grajonca (19)
Gypsy Queen (medley) (2,10,17,20,21)
Gypsy Woman (18)
Hannibal (13)
Hard Times (12)
Head, Hands & Feet (medley) (10)
Here And Now (7)
Hold On (14,21) *15*
Holiday (medley) (11)
Hong Kong Blues (medley) (17)
Hope You're Feeling Better (2,6)
How Long (15)
I Love You Much Too Much (13)
I'll Be Waiting (10)
I'm The One Who Loves You (15)
Incident At Neshabur (2,17)
It's A Jungle Out There (18)
Jingo (1,6,17,18,20,21) *56*
Jugando (9,10)
Jungle Strut (3,17)
Just In Time To See The Sun (4)
Just Let The Music Speak (17)
La Fuente Del Ritmo (4)
Let It Shine (8) *77*
Let Me (8)
Let Me Inside (14)
Let The Children Play (9,10)

Let The Music Set You Free (9)
Let There Be Light (medley) (18)
Life Is A Lady (medley) (11)
Life Is Anew (7)
Life Is For Living (19)
Light Of Life (5)
Lightning In The Sky (12)
Look Up (To See What's Coming Down) (4)
Love (12)
Love, Devotion & Surrender (5)
Love Is You (16)
Love Of My Life (22)
Make Somebody Happy (19,20)
Mandela (16)
Marathon (21)
Maria Caracoles (3)
Maria Maria (22) *1*
Migra (22)
Mirage (7)
(Moonflower) ..see: Flor D'Luna
Mother Africa (5)
Mother Earth (medley) (18)
Mother's Daughter (2)
Move On (11)
Night Hunting Time (14)
Nile, The (14)
No One To Depend On (3,20,21) *36*
Nowhere To Run (14) *66*
Nueva York (14)
Once It's Gotcha (16)
One Chain (Don't Make No Prison) (11) *59*
One With The Sun (7)

Open Invitation (11,17,21)
Over And Over (13)
Oxun (Oshun) (14)
Oye Como Va (2,6,17,20,21) *13*
Para Los Rumberos (3)
Paris Finale (17)
Peace On Earth (medley) (18)
Peraza I & II (17)
Persuasion (1,6,17)
Practice What You Preach (7)
Praise (16)
Primavera (22)
Primera Invasion (13)
Promise Of A Fisherman (7)
Put Your Lights On (22)
Reach Up (9)
Red Prophet (19)
Revelations (9)
Right Now (15)
Right On (medley) (19)
River, The (9)
Runnin (12)
Saja (medley) (19)
Samba De Sausalito (5)
Samba Pa Ti (2,6,20,21)
Savor (1,10)
Say It Again (15) *46*
Se A Cabo (2,6)
Searchin' (13)
Sensitive Kind (13) *56*
Shades Of Time (1)
Shango (14)
She Can't Let Go (16)
She's Not There (10,17,21) *27*

Singing Winds, Crying Beasts (2)
Smooth (22) *1*
Somewhere In Heaven (19)
Song Of The Wind (4,17)
Songs Of Freedom (16)
Soul Sacrifice (1,10,17,20,21)
Soweto (Africa Libre) (18)
Spanish Rose (medley) (11)
Spirit (15)
Spirits Dancing In The Flesh (medley) (18)
Spring Manifestations (7)
Stand Up (12)
Stay (Beside Me) (12)
Stone Flower (4)
Stormy (11) *32*
Summer Lady (12)
Super Boogie (medley) (17)
Taboo (17)
Take Me With You (8)
Tales Of Kilimanjaro (13)
Tell Me Are You Tired (8)
Third Stone From The Sun (medley) (18)
Touchdown Raiders (15)
Toussaint L'Overture (3,10,20)
Transcendance (10)
Treat (1)
Try A Little Harder (9)
Veracruz (15)
Verao Vermelho (9)
Victim Of Circumstance (16)
Vilato (17)
Vive La Vida (20)

Waiting (1)
Warrior (14)
Waves Within (4)
We Don't Have To Wait (19)
Welcome (5)
Well All Right (11) *69*
Wham! (11)
What Does It Take (To Win Your Love) (14)
When I Look Into Your Eyes (5)
Who Loves You (15)
Who's That Lady (18)
Winning (13,21) *17*
Wishing It Was (22)
Written In Sand (15)
You Just Don't Care (1)
You Know That I Love You (12) *35*
Your Touch (19)
Yours Is The Light (5)
Zulu (10)

SANTANA, Carlos '72

Born on 7/20/47 in Autlan de Navarro, Mexico. Latin-rock guitarist. Leader of **Santana**. Added "Devadip" to his name in 1973. Recipient of *Billboard*'s Century Award in 1996.

DEBUT	PEAK	WKS	RIAA	CD	#	ARTIST — Album Title	Sym	$	Label & Number
7/8/72	8	33	▲	©	1	Carlos Santana & Buddy Miles! Live!	[L]	$15	Columbia 31308
						recorded in Hawaii's Diamond Head volcano crater			
7/7/73	14	24	●	©	2	Love Devotion Surrender	[I]	$15	Columbia 32034
						CARLOS SANTANA/MAHAVISHNU JOHN McLAUGHLIN			
10/12/74	79	8			3	Illuminations	[I]	$12	Columbia 32900
						TURIYA ALICE COLTRANE/DEVADIP CARLOS SANTANA			
3/31/79	87	9			4	Oneness/Silver Dreams-Golden Reality	[I]	$12	Columbia 35686
						DEVADIP			
9/6/80	65	10		©	5	The Swing Of Delight	[I]	$15	Columbia 36590 [2]
						DEVADIP CARLOS SANTANA			
4/23/83	31	17		©	6	Havana Moon		$10	Columbia 38642
11/7/87	195	1		©	7	Blues for Salvador	[I]	$10	Columbia 40875

Angel Of Air (medley) (3)
Angel Of Sunlight (3)
Angel Of Water (medley) (3)
Aquatic Park (medley) (7)
Arise Awake (4)
Bailando (medley) (7)
Bella (7)
Bliss: The Eternal Now (3)
Blues For Salvador (7)
Chosen Hour (4)
Cry Of The Wilderness (4)

Daughter Of The Night (6)
Deeper, Dig Deeper (7)
Ecuador (6)
Evil Ways (1) *84*
Free As The Morning Sun (4)
Free Form Funkafide Filth (1)
Gardenia (5)
Golden Dawn (4)
Golden Hours (5)
Guru Sri Chinmoy Aphorism (3)
Guru's Song (3)

Hannibal (4)
Havana Moon (6)
I Am Free (4)
I'm Gone (7)
Illuminations (3)
Jharna Kala (3)
Jim Jeannie (4)
La Llave (5)
Lava (1)
Let Us Go Into The House Of The Lord (2)

Life Divine (3)
Life Is Just A Passing Parade (4)
Light Versus Darkness (4)
Lightnin' (6)
Love Supreme (2)
Marbles (1)
Meditation (2)
Mingus (7)
Mudbone (6)
Naima (2)

Now That You Know (7)
One With You (6)
Oneness (4)
Phuler Matan (5)
Shere Khan, The Tiger (5)
Silver Dreams Golden Smiles (4)
Song For Devadip (4)
Song For My Brother (5)
Spartacus, Love Theme From (5)

Swapan Tari (5)
Tales Of Kilimanjaro (6)
Them Changes (1) *flip*
They All Went To Mexico (6)
'Trane (4)
Transformation Day (4)
Vereda Tropical (6)
Victory (4)
Watch Your Step (6)
Who Do You Love (6)

SANTANA BROTHERS '94

Brothers Jorge and **Carlos Santana**, with nephew Carlos Hernandez. Jorge was guitarist for **Malo**.

DEBUT	PEAK	WKS	RIAA	CD	#	ARTIST — Album Title	Sym	$	Label & Number
10/15/94	191	1		©		Santana Brothers		$10	Island 523677

Blues Latino
Brujo
Contigo (With You)
En Aranjuez Con Tu Amor
Industrial (medley)
La Danza
Luz Amor Y Vida
Morning In Marin
Reflections
Thoughts
Transmutation (medley)
Trip, The

SANTO & JOHNNY '60

Guitar duo from Brooklyn, New York: brothers Santo (born on 10/24/37) and Johnny (born on 4/30/41) Farina.

DEBUT	PEAK	WKS	RIAA	CD	#	ARTIST — Album Title	Sym	$	Label & Number
1/18/60	20	29			1	Santo & Johnny	[I]	$75	Canadian-Am. 1001
9/26/60	11	36			2	Encore	[I]	$50	Canadian-Am. 1002
6/26/61	80	13			3	Hawaii	[I]	$50	Canadian-Am. 1004

Adventures In Paradise (3)
Alabamy Bound (2)
All Night Diner (1)
Aloha (3)
Annie (3)
Blue Hawaii (3)

Blue Moon (1)
Breeze And I (2)
Canadian Sunset (1)
Caravan (1) *48*
Deep Purple (2)
Dream (1)

Harbor Lights (1)
Hawaiian War Chant (3)
Hawaiian Wedding Song (3)
Isle Of Dreams (3)
Lazy Day (2)
Long Walk Home (2)

Now Is The Hour (3)
Old Man River (2)
Over The Rainbow (2)
Pineapple Princess (3)
Prisoner Of Love (2)
Raunchy (1)

Reflections (3)
School Day (1)
Sea Shells (3)
Slave Girl (1)
Sleep Walk (1) *1*
Song Of The Islands (3)

Summertime (1)
Sweet Lelani (3)
Tear Drop (2) *23*
Tenderly (1)
Venus (2)
You Belong To Me (2)

SANZ, Alejandro '00

Born on 12/18/68 in Madrid. Latin singer/guitarist.

DEBUT	PEAK	WKS	RIAA	CD	#	ARTIST — Album Title	Sym	$	Label & Number
10/14/00	148	2		©		El Alma Al Aire	[F]	$10	WEA Latina 84774

title is Spanish for "The Soul With The Air"

Cuando Nadie Me Ve
El Alma Al Aire
Hay Un Universo De Pequeñas Cosas
Hicimos Un Trato
Llega, Llego Soledad
Me Iré
Para Que Me Quieras
Quisiera Ser
Silencio
Tiene Que Ser Pecado

DEBUT	PEAK	WKS	RIAA	CD	ARTIST — Album Title	Catalog	Sym	$	Label & Number

SARAYA   '89
Rock group from New Jersey: Sandi Saraya (vocals), Tony Rey (guitar), Gregg Munier (keyboards), Gary Taylor (bass) and Chuck Bonfante (drums).

| 4/29/89 | 79 | 39 | | © | **Saraya** .... | | | $10 | Polydor 837764 |

Alsace Lorraine
Back To The Bullet *63*

Drop The Bomb
Fire To Burn

Get U Ready
Gypsy Child

Healing Touch
Love Has Taken Its Toll *64*

One Night Away
Runnin' Out Of Time

St. Christopher Medal

SARDUCCI, Father Guido   '80
Born Don Novello on 1/1/43 in Ashtabula, Ohio. Comedian/actor. Featured on TV's *Saturday Night Live.*

| 5/10/80 | 179 | 2 | | | **Live at St. Douglas Convent** .... | | [C] | $12 | Warner 3440 |

Alien Invaders
Cattle Mutilation Theories

Coming And Going Planet
Five Minute University

Guide To The Confessional
Mass Confession

People's Space Program
St. Ann Seton

What Happens To You After
You Die

Women Priests

SASHA & JOHN DIGWEED   '00
Duo of dance DJs. Sasha was born Alexander Coe on 9/4/69 in Bangor, Wales. Digweed was born in 1967 in Hastings, England.

| 7/8/00 | 149 | 2 | | © | **Communicate** .... | | [I] | $15 | Kinetic 54657 [2] |

Baguio Track
Barbarella
Blue Hour
ECI-PS

Enjoyed
Force 51
Fusion
Get Lost

Lifestyles
Like A Bitch
Musak
Narcotic

Once More
Pushing Too Hard
Put Your Earphones On
Roaches

Ruhe
Tyrantanic
Voices
WAAH!

West On 27th

★442★   SATRIANI, Joe   '92
Born on 7/15/57 in Carle Place, New York. Rock guitarist.

| 11/21/87+ | 29 | 75 | ▲ | © | 1 **Surfing With The Alien** .... | | [I] | $10 | Relativity 8193 |
| 11/26/88+ | 42 | 26 | ● | © | 2 **Dreaming #11** .... | | [I-L-M] | $10 | Relativity 8265 |

recorded on 6/11/88 at the California Theater in San Diego

11/18/89	23	39	●	©	3 **Flying In A Blue Dream**		[I]	$10	Relativity 1015
8/8/92	22	28	●	©	4 **The Extremist**		[I]	$10	Relativity 1053
11/13/93	95	8	●	©	5 **Time Machine**		[I-K-L]	$15	Relativity 1177 [2]

recordings from 1984

| 10/28/95 | 51 | 7 | | © | 6 **Joe Satriani** .... | | [I] | $10 | Relativity 1500 |
| 6/21/97 | 108 | 3 | | © | 7 **G3 - Live In Concert** .... | | [I-L] | $10 | Epic 67920 |

JOE SATRIANI/ERIC JOHNSON/STEVE VAI

| 3/21/98 | 50 | 8 | | © | 8 **Crystal Planet** .... | | [I] | $10 | Epic 68018 |
| 4/1/00 | 90 | 3 | | © | 9 **Engines Of Creation** .... | | [I] | $10 | Epic 67860 |

All Alone (5)
also known as "Left Alone"
Always With Me, Always With
  You (1,5)
Attack (9)
Back To Shalla-Bal (3)
Banana Mango (5)
Banana Mango II (5)
Baroque (5)
Bells Of Lal (Part One & Two)
  (3)
Big Bad Moon (3,5)
Borg Sex (9)
Can't Slow Down (3)
Ceremony (9)
Champagne? (9)
Circles (1,5)

Clouds Race Across The Sky
  (9)
Cool #9 (6,7)
Crazy (5)
Crush Of Love (2,5)
Crushing Day (1)
Cryin' (4,5)
Crystal Planet (8)
Day At The Beach (New Rays
  From An Ancient Sun) (3)
Devil's Slide (9)
Down, Down, Down (6)
Dreaming #11 (5)
Drum Solo (7)
Dweller On The Threshold (5)
Echo (5)
Engines Of Creation (9)

Extremist, The (4)
Feeling, The (3)
Flavor Crystal (9)
Flying In A Blue Dream (3,5,7)
Forgotten (Part One & Two) (3)
Friends (4)
Going Down (7)
Headless (4)
Hill Of The Skull (1)
Home (4)
Hordes Of Locusts (2)
House Full Of Bullets (8)
I Am Become Death (5)
I Believe (3)
Ice 9 (1,2)
If (6)
Into The Light (3)
Killer Bee Bop (6)

Lights Of Heaven (8)
Look My Way (6)
Lords Of Karma (1,5)
Love Thing (4)
Luminous Flesh Giants (6)
Memories (2)
Midnight (1)
Mighty Turtle Head (5)
Moroccan Sunset (6)
Motorcycle Driver (4)
My Guitar Wants To Kill Your
  Mama (7)
Mystical Potato Head Groove
  Thing (3)
New Blues (4)
One Big Rush (3)
Phone Call (5)
Piece Of Liquid (8)

Power Cosmic 2000-Part I & II
  (9)
Psycho Monkey (8)
Raspberry Jam Delta-V (8)
Red House (7)
Ride (3)
Rubina (5)
Rubina's Blue Sky Happiness
  (4)
S.M.F. (6)
Satch Boogie (1,5)
Saying Goodbye (5)
Secret Prayer (8)
Sittin' 'Round (6)
Slow And Easy (9)
Slow Down Blues (6)
Speed Of Light (5)
Strange (3)

Summer Song (4,5,7)
Surfing With The Alien (1,5)
Tears In The Rain (4,5)
Thinking Of You (5)
Time (8)
Time Machine (5)
Train Of Angels (8)
Until We Say Goodbye (9)
Up In The Sky (8)
War (4)
Why (4)
With Jupiter In Mind (8)
Woodstock Jam (5)
(You're) My World (6)
Z.Z.'s Song (8)

SATTERFIELD, Esther   '76
Born in 1946 in North Carolina. Jazz-styled vocalist.

| 7/24/76 | 180 | 4 | | | **The Need To Be** .... | | | $12 | A&M 3411 |

produced, arranged and orchestrated by **Chuck Mangione**

Bird Of Beauty
Chase The Clouds Away
He's Gone

If You Know Me Any Longer
  Than Tomorrow
Long Hard Climb

Need To Be
New World Comin'
Sarah

You Must Believe In Spring

SATURDAY NIGHT BAND   '78
Disco studio group assembled by producers Jesse Boyce and Moses Dillard.

| 5/27/78 | 125 | 17 | | | **Come On Dance, Dance** .... | | | $12 | Prelude 12155 |

Come On Dance, Dance

Don't (Take My Love Away)

Touch Me On My Hot Spot

SAUCE MONEY   '00
Born Todd Gaither in New York City. Male rapper.

| 6/10/00 | 72 | 3 | | © | **Middle Finger U.** .... | | | $10 | Priority 24031 |

C My 1's
Chart Climbing
Do You See

Face Off 2000
For My Hustlaz
Intruder Alert

Love & War
Middle Finger U.
Pregame

Say Unkle
Section 53, Row 78
We Gonna Rock

What We Do
What's My Name
What's That, F*** That

SAUNDERS, Merl   '73
Born on 2/14/34 in San Mateo, California. Jazz keyboardist.

| 6/2/73 | 197 | 5 | | © | **Fire Up** .... | | [I] | $20 | Fantasy 9421 |

After Midnight
Benedict Rides

Charisma (She's Got)
Chock-Lite Puddin'

Expressway (To Your Heart)
Lonely Avenue

Soul Roach
System, The

SAVAGE, Chantay   '96
Born in Chicago. Female R&B singer/songwriter.

| 3/30/96 | 106 | 8 | | © | **I Will Survive (Doin' It My Way)** .... | | | $10 | RCA 66775 |

All Night All Day
All Of My Love
Alright

Baby: Drive Me Crazy
Body
Brown Sugar

Callin'
Do You My Way
I Will Survive *24*

I'm Willing
Let's Do It Right
Love Need Want

90 In The Red
Pillow Talk
Turned Away

SAVAGE GARDEN '98
Pop duo from Brisbane, Australia: Darren Hayes and Daniel Jones.

| 5/3/97+ | 3 | 104 | ▲⁷ © | 1 Savage Garden | C:#10/63 | $10 | Columbia 67954 |
| 11/27/99 | 6 | 59 | ▲³ © | 2 Affirmation | | $10 | Columbia 63711 |

Affirmation (2)
Animal Song (2) *19*
Best Thing (2)
Break Me Shake Me (1)
Carry On Dancing (1)
Chained To You (2)
Crash And Burn (2) *24*
Gunning Down Romance (2)
Hold Me (2)
I Don't Know You Anymore (2)
I Knew I Loved You (2) *1*
I Want You (1) *4*
Lover After Me (2)
Promises (1)
Santa Monica (1)
Tears Of Pearls (1)
Thousand Words (1)
To The Moon & Back (1) *24*
Truly Madly Deeply (1) *1*
Two Beds And A Coffee Machine (2)
Universe (1)
Violet (1)
You Can Still Be Free (2)

SAVAGE GRACE '70
Rock group from Detroit: Ron Koss (vocals, guitar), John Seanor (keyboards), Al Jacquez (bass) and Larry Zack (drums).

| 6/6/70 | 182 | 8 | | Savage Grace | | $20 | Reprise 6399 |

All Along The Watchtower
Come On Down
Dear Lenore
Hymn To Freedom
Lady Rain
Night Of The Hunter
1984
Turn Your Head

SAVALAS, Telly '75
Born Aristotle Savalas on 1/21/24 in Garden City, Long Island, New York. Died of cancer on 1/22/94 (age 70). Popular TV/movie actor. Gained fame as the star of TV's *Kojak*.

| 1/4/75 | 117 | 8 | | Telly | | $15 | MCA 436 |

Help Me Make It Through The Night
How Insensitive
If
Rubber Bands And Bits Of String
Something
Song For You
Without Her
You And Me Against The World
You're A Lady
You've Lost That Lovin' Feelin'

SAVATAGE '88
Hard-rock group from Florida: Zachary Stevens (vocals), Criss Oliva (guitar), Johnny Lee Middleton (bass) and Steve Wacholz (drums). Oliva died in a car crash on 10/17/93 (age 30).

6/21/86	158	7	©	1 Fight For The Rock		$10	Atlantic 81634
10/10/87+	116	23	©	2 Hall Of The Mountain King		$10	Atlantic 81775
2/24/90	124	12	©	3 Gutter Ballet		$10	Atlantic 82008

Beyond The Doors Of The Dark (2)
Crying For Love (1)
Day After Day (1)
Devastation (2)
Edge Of Midnight (1)
Fight For The Rock (1)
Gutter Ballet (2)
Hall Of The Mountain King (2)
Hounds (3)
Hyde (1)
Lady In Disguise (1)
Last Dawn (2)
Legions (2)
Mentally Yours (3)
Of Rage And War (3)
Out On The Streets (1)
Prelude To Madness (2)
Price You Pay (2)
Red Light Paradise (1)
She's In Love (3)
She's Only Rock 'N Roll (1)
Silk And Steel (3)
Strange Wings (2)
Summer's Rain (3)
Temptation Revelation (3)
Thorazine Shuffle (3)
24 Hrs. Ago (2)
Unholy, The (3)
When The Crowds Are Gone (3)
White Witch (2)
Wishing Well (1)

SAVE FERRIS '97
Ska-rock group from California: Monique Powell (vocals), Brian Mashburn (vocals, guitar), Eric Zamora, T-Bone Willy and Jose Castellanos (horns), Bill Uechi (bass) and Marc Harismendy (drums). Evan Kilbourne replaced Harismendy in 1998.

| 9/27/97 | 75 | 17 | © | 1 It Means Everything | | $10 | Starpool 68183 |
| 11/6/99 | 136 | 2 | © | 2 Modified | | $10 | Starpool 69866 |

Angry Situation (2)
Come On Eileen (1)
Everything I Want To Be (1)
Goodbye (1)
Holding On (2)
I'm Not Cryin' For You (2)
Let Me In (2)
Lies (1)
Little Differences (1)
Mistaken (2)
No Love (2)
Nobody But Me (1)
One More Try (2)
Only Way To Be (2)
Sorry My Friend (1)
Spam (1)
Superspy (1)
Turn It Up (2)
Under 21 (1)
What You See Is What You Get (2)
World Is New (1)
Your Friend (2)

SAVOY BROWN '72
Blues-rock group formed in England: Chris Youlden (vocals), Lonesome Dave Peverett (vocals, guitar), Kim Simmonds (guitar), Tony Stevens (bass) and Roger Earl (drums). Youlden left in mid-1970. Peverett, Stevens and Earl left in 1971 to form **Foghat**. Many personnel changes thereafter, with Simmonds the only constant member. Peverett died of cancer on 2/7/2000 (age 57).

1)Hellbound Train 2)Looking In 3)A Step Further

| 4/12/69 | 182 | 2 | © | 1 Blue Matter | [L] | $25 | Parrot 71027 |

side 2: recorded live on 12/6/68 at Leicester College in England

| 9/13/69 | 71 | 14 | © | 2 A Step Further | [L] | $20 | Parrot 71029 |

side 2: recorded live on 5/12/69 at The Cooks Ferry Inn in London

4/25/70	121	18	©	3 Raw Sienna		$20	Parrot 71036
10/17/70	39	19	©	4 Looking In		$20	Parrot 71042
9/18/71	75	17	©	5 Street Corner Talking		$20	Parrot 71047
3/18/72	34	21	©	6 Hellbound Train		$20	Parrot 71052
11/4/72	151	10	©	7 Lion's Share		$20	Parrot 71057
6/30/73	84	14	©	8 Jack The Toad		$20	Parrot 71059
4/20/74	101	8		9 Boogie Brothers		$12	London 638
11/22/75	153	7		10 Wire Fire		$12	London 659
7/25/81	185	4	©	11 Rock 'n' Roll Warriors		$12	Town House 7002

All I Can Do (5)
Always The Same (9)
Bad Breaks (11)
Bad Girls (Make Me Feel Good) (11)
Boogie Brothers (9)
Born Into Pain (10)
Can't Get On (10)
Casting My Spell (8)
Cold Hearted Woman (11)
Coming Down Your Way (8)
Deep Water (10)
Denim Demon (7)
Doin' Fine (6)
Don't Tell Me I Told You (11)
Don't Turn Me From Your Door (1)
Endless Sleep (8)
Everybody Loves A Drinking Man (9)
Georgie (11)
Got Love If You Want It (11)
Gypsy (4)
Hard Way To Go (3)
Hate To See You Go (7)
Hellbound Train (6)
Here Comes The Music (10)
Hero To Zero (10)
Highway Blues (9)
Hold Your Fire (8)
Howling For My Darling (7)
I Can't Find You (7)
I Can't Get Next To You (5)
I'll Make Everything Alright (6)
I'm Crying (3)
I'm Tired (2) *74*
If I Could See An End (6)
If I Want To (8)
Is That So (3)
It Hurts Me Too (1)
It'll Make You Happy (6)
Jack The Toad (8)
Just Cos' You Got The Blues Don't Mean You Gotta Sing (8)
Lay Back In The Arms Of Someone (11)
Leavin' Again (4)
Life's One Act Play (2)
Little More Wine (3)
Looking In (4)
Lost And Lonely Child (6)
Louisiana Blues (1)
Love Me Please (7)
Made Up My Mind (2)
Master Hare (3)
May Be Wrong (1)
Me And The Preacher (9)
Money Can't Save Your Soul (4)
My Love's Lying Down (9)
Needle And Spoon (3)
Nobody's Perfect (11)
Ooh What A Feeling (10)
Poor Girl (4)
Put Your Hands Together (10)
Ride On Babe (8)
Rock And Roll On The Radio (Let It Rock) (5)
Rock 'N' Roll Star (9)
Romanoff (4)
Saddest Feeling (7)
Savoy Brown Boogie Medley (2)
Second Try (7)
She's Got A Ring In His Nose And A Ring On Her Hand (1)
Shot Down By Love (11)
Shot In The Head (7)
Sitting An' Thinking (4)
So Tired (7)
Some People (8)
Stay While The Night Is Young (3)
Stranger Blues (10)
Street Corner Talking (5)
Sunday Night (4)
Take It Easy (4)
Tell Mama (5) *83*
That Same Feelin' (3)
This Could Be The Night (11)
Threegy Blues (9)
Time Does Tell (5)
Tolling Bells (1)
Train To Nowhere (1)
Troubled By These Days And Times (6)
Vicksburg Blues (1)
Waiting In The Bamboo Grove (2)
Wang Dang Doodle (5)
When I Was A Young Boy (3)
Where Am I (2)
You Don't Love Me (9)

SAWYER BROWN — '95

Country group formed in Nashville: Mark Miller (vocals), Bobby Randall (guitar), Gregg Hubbard (keyboards), Jim Scholten (bass) and Joe Smyth (drums). Duncan Cameron replaced Randall in 1992.

DEBUT	PEAK	WKS	RIAA	CD	#	Album Title	Sym	$	Label & Number
2/23/85	140	11		©	1	Sawyer Brown		$10	Capitol/Curb 12391
8/31/91	140	11		©	2	Buick		$10	Curb 94260
2/1/92	68	30	●	©	3	The Dirt Road		$10	Curb 95624
9/19/92+	117	20		©	4	Cafe On The Corner		$10	Curb 77574
8/28/93	81	24	●	©	5	Outskirts Of Town		$10	Curb 77626
2/11/95	44	29	●	©	6	Greatest Hits 1990-1995	[G]	$10	Curb 77689
9/16/95	77	8		©	7	This Thing Called Wantin' And Havin' It All		$10	Curb 77785
5/3/97	73	24		©	8	Six Days On The Road		$10	Curb 77883
3/20/99	99	7		©	9	Drive Me Wild!		$10	Curb 77902

Ain't That Always The Way (3)
All These Years (4,6)
All Wound Up (9)
Another Mile (7)
Another Side (8)
Another Trip To The Well (3)
Between You And Paradise (8)
Big Picture (7)
Boys And Me (5,6)
Break My Heart Again (9)
Broken Candy (1)
Burnin' Bridges (On A Rocky Road) (3)
Cafe On The Corner (4,6)
Chain Of Love (4)
Different Tune (4)

Dirt Road (3,6)
Drive Away (5)
Drive Me Wild (9) 44
800 Pound Jesus (9)
Every Little Thing (9)
Every Twist And Turn (8)
Eyes Of Love (5)
Farmer Tan (5)
Feel Like Me (1)
Fire In The Rain (3)
48 Hours Till Monday (2)
Going Back To Indiana (1)
Half A Heart (8)
Hard To Say (5)
Heartbreak Highway (5)
Hold On (5)

Homestead In My Heart (4)
I Don't Believe In Goodbye (6)
I Kept My Motor Runnin' (4)
I Will Leave The Light On (7)
I'm In Love With Her (9)
It All Comes Down To Love (9)
It's Hard To Keep A Good Love Down (1)
Leona (1)
Less Than Love ..see: Nothin' Less Than Love
Lesson In Love (4)
Like A John Deere (7)
Listenin' For You (5)
Love Like This (8)
Love To Be Wanted (5)

Mama's Little Baby Loves Me (2)
Moon Over Miami (9)
My Baby Drives A Buick (2)
Nebraska Song (9)
Night And Day (8)
Nothin' Less Than Love (7)
One Less Pony (2)
Outskirts Of Town (5)
Playin' A Love Song (9)
'Round Here (7)
Ruby Red Shoes (3)
She's Gettin' There (7)
Sister's Got A New Tattoo (4)
Six Days On The Road (8)
Small Talk (8)

Small Town Hero (7)
Smokin' In The Rockies (1)
Some Girls Do (3,6)
Sometimes A Hero (3)
Soul Searchin' (9)
Stayin' Afloat (1)
Stealin' Home (2)
Step That Step (1)
Still Water (2)
Sun Don't Shine On The Same Folks All The Time (1)
Superman's Daughter (2)
Talkin' 'Bout You (8)
Thank God For You (5,6)
This Night Won't Last Forever (8)

(This Thing Called) Wantin' And Havin' It All (7)
This Time (6)
Thunder Bay (2)
Time And Love (3)
Transistor Rodeo (8)
Travelin' Shoes (4)
Treat Her Right (7)
Trouble On The Line (4,6)
Used To Blue (5)
Walk, The (2,3,6)
We're Everything To Me (9)
When Twist Comes To Shout (3)
When You Run From Love (2)
With This Ring (8)

SAXON — '85

Hard-rock group formed in England: Biff Byford (vocals), Graham Oliver and Paul Quinn (guitars), Steve Dawson (bass) and Nigel Glocker (drums). Paul Johnson replaced Dawson in 1986.

DEBUT	PEAK	WKS	RIAA	CD	#	Album Title	Sym	$	Label & Number
6/18/83	155	10			1	Power & The Glory		$10	Carrere 38719
4/14/84	174	5			2	Crusader		$10	Carrere 39284
11/2/85	130	8			3	Innocence Is No Excuse		$10	Capitol 12420
2/14/87	149	6		©	4	Rock The Nations		$10	Capitol 12519

Back On The Streets (3)
Bad Boys (Like To Rock 'N Roll) (2)
Battle Cry (4)
Broken Heroes (3)
Call Of The Wild (3)
Crusader (2)

Devil Rides Out (3)
Do It All For You (4)
Eagle Has Landed (1)
Empty Promises (4)
Everybody Up (3)
Give It Everything You've Got (3)

Gonna Shout (3)
Just Let Me Rock (2)
Little Bit Of What You Fancy (4)
Nightmare (1)
Northern Lady (4)
Party Til You Puke (4)
Power And The Glory (1)

Raise Some Hell (3)
Redline (1)
Rock City (2)
Rock N' Roll Gipsy (3)
Rock The Nations (4)
Rockin' Again (3)
Run For Your Lives (2)

Running Hot (4)
Sailing To America (2)
Set Me Free (2)
Suzi Hold On (1)
This Town Rocks (1)
Waiting For The Night (4)
Warrior (1)

Watching The Sky (1)
We Came Here To Rock (4)
You Ain't No Angel (4)

SAYER, Leo — '77

Born Gerard Sayer on 5/21/48 in Shoreham, Sussex, England. Pop singer/songwriter.

DEBUT	PEAK	WKS	RIAA	CD	#	Album Title	Sym	$	Label & Number
2/8/75	16	22			1	Just A Boy		$12	Warner 2836
10/11/75	125	7			2	Another Year		$12	Warner 2885
11/27/76+	10	51	▲	©	3	Endless Flight		$12	Warner 2962
10/22/77	37	15			4	Thunder In My Heart		$12	Warner 3089
8/19/78	101	14			5	Leo Sayer		$12	Warner 3200
10/18/80+	36	23			6	Living In A Fantasy		$12	Warner 3483

Another Time (1)
Another Year (2)
Bedsitterland (1)
Bells Of St. Marys (1)
Dancing The Night Away (5)
Don't Look Away (5)
Easy To Love (4) 36
Endless Flight (3)
Everything I've Got (4)
Fool For Your Love (4)
Frankie Lee (5)
Giving It All Away (1)

Hold On To My Love (3)
How Much Love (3) 17
I Can't Stop Loving You (Though I Try) (5)
I Hear The Laughter (3)
I Think We Fell In Love Too Fast (3)
I Want You Back (4)
I Will Not Stop Fighting (2)
In My Life (1)
It's Over (4)
Kid's Grown Up (3)

La Booga Rooga (5)
Last Gig Of Johnny B. Goode (2)
Leave Well Enough Alone (4)
Let Me Know (6)
Living In A Fantasy (6) 23
Long Tall Glasses (I Can Dance) (1) 9
Magdalena (3)
Millionaire (6)
Moonlighting (2)
More Than I Can Say (6) 2

No Business Like Love Business (3)
No Looking Back (5)
On The Old Dirt Road (2)
Once In A While (6)
One Man Band (1) 96
Only Dreaming (2)
Only Foolin' (6)
Raining In My Heart (5) 47
Reflections (3)
Running To My Freedom (5)
She's Not Coming Back (6)

Solo (1)
Something Fine (5)
Stormy Weather (2)
Streets Of Your Town (2)
Telepath (1)
There Isn't Anything (4)
Thunder In My Heart (4) 38
Time Ran Out On You (6)
Train (1)
Unlucky In Love (2)
We Can Start All Over Again (4)

When I Came Home This Morning (1)
When I Need You (3) 1
Where Did We Go Wrong (6)
World Keeps On Turning (4)
You Make Me Feel Like Dancing (3) 1
You Win - I Lose (6)

★300★ SCAGGS, Boz — '76

Born William Royce Scaggs on 6/8/44 in Ohio; raised in Texas. Pop-rock singer/songwriter.

1)Silk Degrees 2)Middle Man 3)Down Two Then Left

DEBUT	PEAK	WKS	RIAA	CD	#	Album Title	Sym	$	Label & Number
4/17/71	124	9		©	1	Moments		$15	Columbia 30454
12/11/71	198	2		©	2	Boz Scaggs & Band		$15	Columbia 30796
9/23/72	138	9		©	3	My Time		$12	Columbia 31384
3/23/74	81	20	●	©	4	Slow Dancer		$15	Columbia 32760
7/13/74+	171	5		©	5	Boz Scaggs	[E]	$12	Atlantic 8239
						first released in 1969			
3/20/76	2[5]	115	▲[5]	©	6	Silk Degrees		$12	Columbia 33920
12/10/77+	11	23	▲	©	7	Down Two Then Left		$12	Columbia 34729
4/19/80	8	33	▲	©	8	Middle Man		$12	Columbia 36106
11/29/80+	24	26	▲	©	9	Hits!	C:#3/156 [G]	$12	Columbia 36841
6/4/88	47	18		©	10	Other Roads		$10	Columbia 40463
4/23/94	91	14		©	11	Some Change		$10	Virgin 39489
4/26/97	94	10		©	12	Come On Home		$10	Virgin 42984

SCAGGS, Boz — Cont'd

After Hours (12)	Downright Women (1)	I Don't Hear You (10)	Love Letters (12)	Sail On White Moon (4)	We're Waiting (7)

After Hours (12)
Alone, Alone (1)
Angel Lady (Come Just In Time) (4)
Angel You (8)
Another Day (Another Letter) (5)
Ask Me 'Bout Nothin' (But The Blues) (12)
Breakdown Dead Ahead (8,9) *15*
Call Me (11)
Can I Make It Last (Or Will It Just Be Over) (1)
Claudia (10)
Clue, A (7)
Come On Home (12)
Cool Running (10)
Crimes Of Passion (10)
Dinah Flo (3,9) *86*
Do Like You Do In New York (8)
Don't Cry No More (12)

Downright Women (1)
Early In The Morning (12)
Finding Her (5)
Flames Of Love (2)
Fly Like A Bird (11)
Follow That Man (11)
Found Love (12)
Freedom For The Stallion (4)
Full-Lock Power Slide (3)
Funny (10)
Georgia (6)
Gimme The Goods (7)
Goodnight Louise (12)
Harbor Lights (6)
Hard Times (7) *58*
He's A Fool For You (3)
Heart Of Mine (10) *35*
Hello My Lover (3)
Hercules (4)
Here To Stay (2)
Hollywood (7) *49*
Hollywood Blues (1)

I Don't Hear You (10)
I Got Your Number (4)
I Will Forever Sing (The Blues) (1)
I'll Be Long Gone (5)
I'll Be The One (11)
I'm Easy (5)
I've Got Your Love (12)
Illusion (11)
Isn't It Time (8)
It All Went Down The Drain (12)
It's Over (6) *38*
JoJo (8,9) *17*
Jump Street (6)
Let It Happen (4)
Lido Shuffle (6,9) *11*
Loan Me A Dime (5)
Look What I Got (5)
Look What You've Done To Me (9) *14*
Lost It (11)
Love Anyway (2)

Love Letters (12)
Love Me Tomorrow (6)
Lowdown (6,9) *3*
Mental Shakedown (10)
Middle Man (8)
Might Have To Cry (3)
Miss Sun (9) *14*
Moments (1)
Monkey Time (2)
My Time (3)
Near You (1) *96*
Night Of Van Gogh (10)
1993 (7)
Nothing Will Take Your Place (2)
Now You're Gone (5)
Old Time Lovin' (3)
Pain Of Love (4)
Painted Bells (2)
Picture Of A Broken Heart (12)
Right Out Of My Head (10)
Runnin' Blue (2)

Sail On White Moon (4)
Sick And Tired (12)
Sierra (11)
Simone (8)
Slow Dancer (4)
Slowly In The West (3)
Some Change (11)
Still Falling For You (7)
Sweet Release (5)
T-Bone Shuffle (12)
Take It For Granted (4)
Then She Walked Away (7)
There Is Someone Else (4)
Time (11)
Tomorrow Never Came (7)
Up To You (2)
Waiting For A Train (5)
We Been Away (1)
We Were Always Sweethearts (1) *61*
We're All Alone (6,9)
We're Gonna Roll (3)

We're Waiting (7)
What Can I Say (6) *42*
What Do You Want The Girl To Do (6)
What's Number One? (10)
Whatcha Gonna Tell Your Man (7)
Why Why (2)
You Can Have Me Anytime (8,9)
You Got My Letter (11)
You Got Some Imagination (8)
You Make It So Hard (To Say No) (4,9)
You're So Good (2)
Your Good Thing (Is About To End) (12)

SCANDAL '84

Rock group from New York City: **Patty Smyth** (vocals), Zack Smith and Keith Mack (guitars), Ivan Elias (bass) and Thommy Price (drums).

DEBUT	PEAK	WKS	RIAA	CD		ARTIST — Album Title	Sym	$	Label & Number
1/29/83	39	32	●	©	1	Scandal	[M]	$10	Columbia 38194
8/4/84	17	41	▲	©	2	Warrior		$10	Columbia 39173

SCANDAL FEATURING PATTY SMYTH

All I Want (2)
Another Bad Love (1)
Beat Of A Heart (2) *41*

Goodbye To You (1) *65*
Hands Tied (2) *41*
Less Than Half (2)

Love's Got A Line On You (1) *59*
Maybe We Went Too Far (2)

Only The Young (2)
Say What You Will (2)
She Can't Say No (1)

Talk To Me (2)
Tonight (2)
Warrior, The (2) *7*

Win Some, Lose Some (1)

SCARBURY, Joey '81

Born on 6/7/55 in Ontario, California. Pop singer.

DEBUT	PEAK	WKS			ARTIST — Album Title	$	Label & Number
8/22/81	104	9			America's Greatest Hero	$12	Elektra 537

Down The Backstairs (Of My Life)
Everything But Love

"Greatest American Hero" (Believe It Or Not), Theme From *2*

Love Me Like The Last Time
Some Of My Old Friends

Stolen Night
Take This Heart Of Mine

That Little Bit Of Us
There Is A River

When She Dances *49*

SCARFACE '97

Born Brad Jordan on 11/9/69 in Houston. Male rapper. Member of **The Geto Boys**.

DEBUT	PEAK	WKS	RIAA	CD		ARTIST — Album Title	$	Label & Number
10/26/91	51	27	●	©	1	Mr. Scarface Is Back	$10	Rap-A-Lot 57167
9/4/93	7	16	●	©	2	The World Is Yours	$10	Rap-A-Lot 53861
11/5/94	2[1]	32	▲	©	3	The Diary	$10	Rap-A-Lot 39946
3/29/97	❶[1]	25	▲	©	4	The Untouchable	$10	Rap-A-Lot 42799
3/21/98	4	17	▲	©	5	My Homies	$15	Rap-A-Lot 45471 [2]
10/21/00	7	19	●	©	6	The Last Of A Dying Breed	$10	Rap-A-Lot 49867

All Night Long (5)
And Yo (6)
Body Snatchers (1)
Boo Boo'n (5)
Born Killer (1)
City Under Siege (5)
Cocaine (5)
Comin' Agg (2)
Conspiracy Theory (6)
Diary, The (3)
Diary Of A Madman (1)
Do What You Do (5)
Do What You Want (5)
Dog These Ho's (5)
Don't Testify (5)
Dying With Your Boots On (2)

Faith (4)
For Real (4)
Fuck Faces (5)
Funky Lil Aggin (2)
G's (3)
Game Over (4)
Gangsta Sh*t (6)
Get Out (6)
Geto, The (5)
Goin' Down (3)
Good Girl Gone Bad (1)
Greed (5)
Hand Of The Dead Body (3) *74*
He's Dead (2)
Homies & Thuggs (5)

Hustler (5)
I Need A Favor (2)
I Seen A Man Die (3) *37*
I'm Black (2)
I'm Dead (1)
In & Out (6)
In My Blood (5)
In My Time (6)
It Ain't Part II (6)
Jesse James (3)
Krunch Time (5)
Last Of A Dying Breed (6)
Let Me Roll (2)
Lettin' Em Know (2)
Look Me In My Eyes (6)
Ma Homiez (5)

Mary Jane (4)
Menace Niggas Never Die (4)
Mind Playin' Tricks 94 (3)
Minute To Pray And A Second To Die (1)
Money And The Power (1)
Money Makes The World Go Round (4)
Mr. Scarface (1)
Mr Scarface: Part III The Final Chapter (2)
Murder By Reason Of Insanity (1)
No Tears (3)
No Warning (4)
Now I Feel Ya (2)

O.G. To Me (6)
One (3)
One Time (2,3)
Overnight (5)
P D Roll 'Em (1)
Pimp, The (1)
Rules 4 Real Niggas (5)
Sleepin In My Nikes (5)
Small Time (5)
Smartz (6)
Smile (4) *12*
Sorry For What? (6)
Southside (4)
Southside: Houston, Texas (5)
Still That Aggin (2)
Strictly For The Funk Lovers (2)

Sunshine (4)
They Down With Us (6)
2 Real (5)
Untouchable (4)
Use Them Ho's (5)
Wall, The (2)
Warriors (5)
Watch Ya Step (6)
What's Goin On (5)
White Sheet (3)
Who Run This (5)
Win Lose Or Draw (5)
Ya Money Or Ya Life (4)
You Don't Hear Me Doe (4)
You Owe Me (1)
Your Ass Got Took (1)

SCARLETT & BLACK '88

Pop duo from England: Robin Hild and Sue West.

DEBUT	PEAK	WKS		CD		ARTIST — Album Title	$	Label & Number
3/19/88	107	11		©		Scarlett & Black	$10	Virgin 90647

City Of Dreams (The Last Frontier)

Dream Out Loud
If It's All The Same To You

Let Yourself Go-Go
Miracle Or Mirage

Real Love
Someday

What Is Love
Yesterday's Gone

You Don't Know *20*

SCATTERBRAIN '90

Hard-rock group from New York City: Tommy Christ (vocals), Glen Cummings and Paul Nieder (guitars), Guy Brogna (bass) and Mike Boyko (drums).

DEBUT	PEAK	WKS		CD		ARTIST — Album Title	$	Label & Number
6/16/90	138	16		©		Here Comes Trouble	$10	In-Effect 3012

Don't Call Me Dude
Down With The Ship (Slight Return)

Drunken Milkman
Earache My Eye
Goodbye Freedom, Hello Mom

Here Comes Trouble
I'm With Stupid

Mr. Johnson And The Juice Crew
Outta Time

Sonata #3
That's That

SCHAFER, Kermit '58

Born on 3/24/23 in New York City. Died on 3/8/79 (age 55). Compiled several albums made up of radio and TV bloopers.

DEBUT	PEAK	WKS				ARTIST — Album Title	Sym	$	Label & Number
1/27/58	17	1				Pardon My Blooper! Volume 6	[C]	$25	Jubilee 6

no track titles listed on this album; Volume 1 charted in 1954 (#9) and Volume 2 charted in 1954 (#12)

SCHENKER, Michael, Group '81

Born on 1/10/55 in Savstedt, Germany. Hard-rock guitarist. Former member of **Scorpions** and **UFO**. Lead singer Robin McAuley joined in 1987; changed name to **McAuley Schenker Group**.

DEBUT	PEAK	WKS		CD		ARTIST — Album Title	$	Label & Number
9/20/80	100	14		©	1	The Michael Schenker Group	$12	Chrysalis 1302
10/24/81	81	8		©	2	MSG	$12	Chrysalis 1336
4/9/83	151	7		©	3	Assault Attack	$12	Chrysalis 1393

DEBUT	PEAK	WKS	RIAA	CD	ARTIST — Album Title	Catalog	Sym	$	Label & Number

McAULEY SCHENKER GROUP:

10/24/87	95	24	©	4	Perfect Timing			$10	Capitol 46985
2/3/90	92	14	©	5	Save Yourself			$10	Capitol 92752
3/7/92	180	4	©	6	MSG			$10	Impact 10385

SCHENKER/McAULEY

Anytime (5) *69*
Are You Ready To Rock (2)
Armed And Ready (1)
Assault Attack (3)
Attack Of The Mad Axeman (2)
Bad Boys (5)
Bijou Pleasurette (1)
Broken Promises (3)
But I Want More (2)
Crazy (6)

Cry For The Nations (1)
Dancer (3)
Desert Song (3)
Destiny (5)
Don't Stop Me Now (4)
Eve (6)
Feels Like A Good Thing (1)
Follow The Night (4)
Get Down To Bizness (5)
Get Out (4)

Gimme Your Love (4)
Here Today - Gone Tomorrow (4)
I Am Your Radio (5)
I Don't Wanna Lose (4)
Into The Arena (1)
Invincible (6)
Let Sleeping Dogs Lie (2)
Lonely Nights (6)
Looking For Love (2)
Looking Out From Nowhere (1)

Lost Horizons (1)
Love Is Not A Game (4)
Never Ending Nightmare (6)
Never Trust A Stranger (2)
No Time For Losers (4)
On And On (2)
Paradise (6)
Rock 'Til You're Crazy (4)
Rock You To The Ground (3)
Samurai (3)
Save Yourself (5)

Searching For A Reason (3)
Secondary Motion (2)
Shadow Of The Night (5)
Take Me Back (5)
Tales Of Mystery (1)
There Has To Be Another Way (5)
This Broken Heart (6)
This Is My Heart (5)
This Night Is Gonna Last Forever (6)

Time (4)
Ulcer (3)
Victim Of Illusion (1)
We Believe In Love (6)
What Happens To Me (6)
What We Need (5)
When I'm Gone (6)

SCHIFRIN, Lalo '63
Born Boris Schifrin on 6/21/32 in Buenos Aires, Argentina. Pianist/conductor/composer. Scored several movies.

| 12/22/62+ | 35 | 3 | | | 1 Bossa Nova - New Brazilian Jazz .... | [I] | | $25 | Audio Fidelity 1981 |
| 12/30/67+ | 47 | 31 | | | 2 music from Mission: Impossible .... | [I] | | $20 | Dot 25831 |

Barney Does It All (2)
Boato (Bistro) (1)
Bossa Em Nova York (1)
Chega De Saudade (1)
Chora Tua Tristeza (1)

Cinnamon (The Lady Was Made To Be Loved) (2)
Danger (2)
Jim On The Move (2)

Menina Feia (1)
Mission: Accomplished (2)
Mission-Impossible (2) *41*
O Amor E A Rosa (1)
O Apito No Samba (1)

O Menino Desce O Morro (Little Brown Boy) (1)
Operation Charm (2)
Ouca (1)
Patinho Feio (1)

Plot, The (2)
Poema De Adeus (1)
Rollin Hand (1)
Samba De Uma Nota So (1)
Sniper, The (2)

Wide Willy (2)

SCHILLING, Peter '84
Born on 1/28/56 in Stuttgart, Germany. Pop singer/songwriter.

| 10/8/83+ | 61 | 23 | | | Error In The System .... | | | $10 | Elektra 60265 |

Error In The System
I Have No Desire

(Let's Play) U.S.A.
Lifetime Guarantee

Major Tom (Coming Home) *14*
Major Tom, Part II

Noah Plan
Only Dreams

Stille Nacht, Heilige Nacht (Silent Night, Holy Night)

SCHMIT, Timothy B. '87
Born on 10/30/47 in Sacramento, California. Member of **Poco** and the **Eagles**.

| 11/10/84 | 160 | 5 | | | 1 Playin' It Cool .... | | | $12 | Asylum 60359 |
| 10/3/87 | 106 | 11 | © | | 2 Timothy B. .... | | | $10 | MCA 42049 |

Better Day Is Coming (2)
Boys Night Out (2) *25*
Don't Give Up (2)

Down Here People Dance Forever (2)
Everybody Needs A Lover (2)
Gimme The Money (1)

Hold Me In Your Heart (2)
I Guess We'll Go On Living (2)
Into The Night (2)
Jazz Street (2)

Lonely Girl (1)
Playin' It Cool (1)
So Much In Love (1) *59*
Something's Wrong (1)

Take A Good Look Around You (1)
Tell Me What You Dream (1)
Voices (1)

Wrong Number (1)

SCHNEIDER, John '81
Born on 4/8/60 in Mount Kisco, New York. Country singer/actor. Played "Bo Duke" on TV's *The Dukes Of Hazzard*. Appeared in many TV movies.

6/27/81	37	22			1 Now Or Never			$12	Scotti Brothers 37400
12/5/81+	155	7	©		2 White Christmas	[X]		$12	Scotti Brothers 37617
11/17/84	111	12	©		3 Too Good To Stop Now			$10	MCA 5495

(Am I) Fallin' In Love With Love (1)
Christmas Song (Chestnuts Roasting On An Open Fire) (2)
Country Girls (3)

Have Yourself A Merry Little Christmas (2)
Hollywood Heroes (3)
I'm Your Man (3)
I've Been Around Enough To Know (3)
It's Christmas (2)

It's Now Or Never (1) *14*
Katey's Christmas Card (2)
Let Me Love You (1)
Low Class Reunion (3)
Next Time Around (1)
No. 34 In Atlanta (1)
O Little Town Of Bethlehem (2)

Party Of The First Part (3)
Rudolph, The Red Nosed Reindeer (2)
Silent Night, Holy Night (2)
Silver Bells (2)
Stay (1)
Stay With Me (1)

Still (1) *69*
Them Good Ol' Boys Are Bad (1)
Time Of My Life (3)
Too Good To Stop Now (3)
Trouble (3)
What'll You Do About Me (3)

White Christmas (2)
Winter Wonderland (2)
You Could Be The One Woman (1)

SCHON, Neal, & Jan Hammer '81
Schon was born on 2/27/54 in San Mateo, California. Rock singer/guitarist. Member of **Santana**, **Azteca**, **Journey** and **Bad English**. Also see **Hagar, Schon, Aaronson, Shrieve**.

| 10/17/81 | 115 | 8 | | | 1 Untold Passion .... | | | $10 | Columbia 37600 |
| 2/5/83 | 122 | 12 | | | 2 Here To Stay .... | | | $10 | Columbia 38428 |

Arc (1)
Covered By Midnight (2)
Don't Stay Away (2)
Hooked On Love (1)

I'm Down (1)
I'm Talking To You (1)
It's Alright (1)
Long Time (2)

No More Lies (2)
On The Beach (2)
Peace Of Mind (1)
Ride, The (1)

Self Defense (2)
Sticks And Stones (2)
Time Again (2)
Turnaround (2)

Untold Passion (1)
Wasting Time (1)
(You Think You're) So Hot (2)

SCHOOLLY D '88
Born Jesse Weaver on 6/22/66 in Philadelphia. Male rapper.

| 8/6/88 | 180 | 3 | © | | Smoke Some Kill .... | | | $10 | Jive 1101 |

Another Poem
Black Man
Coqui 900
Fat Gold Chain

Gangster Boogie II
Here We Go Again
Mr. Big Dick
No More Rock N' Roll

Same White Bitch (Got You Strung Out On Cane)
Signifying Rapper
Smoke Some Kill

This Is It (Ain't Gonna Rain)
Treacherous
We Don't Rock, We Rap

SCHOOL OF FISH '91
Pop-rock group from Los Angeles: Josh Clayton-Felt (vocals, guitar), Michael Ward (guitar, vocals), Dominic Nardini (bass) and M.P. (drums). Clayton-Felt died of cancer on 1/19/2000 (age 32).

| 9/14/91 | 142 | 7 | © | | School Of Fish .... | | | $10 | Capitol 94557 |

Deep End
Euphoria

Fell
King Of The Dollar

Rose Colored Glasses
Speechless

Talk Like Strangers
3 Strange Days

Under The Microscope
Wrong

SCHORY, Dick '60
Born on 12/13/31 in Chicago; raised in Ames, Iowa. Percussionist/bandleader.

| 6/29/59+ | 11 | 26 | | | 1 Music For Bang, Baa-room and Harp .... | [I] | | $25 | RCA Victor 1866 |

DICK SCHORY'S New Percussion Ensemble

| 4/20/63 | 13 | 13 | | | 2 Supercussion .... | [I] | | $20 | RCA Victor 2613 |

DICK SCHORY'S Percussion Pops Orchestra

April In Paris (1)
Autumn Leaves (2)
Baia (1)
Bijou (2)
Brush Off (2)

Buck Dance (1)
Ding Dong Polka (1)
Duel On The Skins (1)
Hindustan (1)
Holiday In A Hurry (1)

Krazy Kwilt (2)
National Emblem March (1)
Nomad (1)
On Green Dolphin Street (2)
Perdido (2)

September In The Rain (1)
Sheik Of Araby (1)
Shimboo (2)
Stompin' At The Savoy (1)
String Of Pearls (2)

Take The "A" Train (2)
Tiddly Winks (1)
Typee (1)
Way Down Yonder In New Orleans (1)

SCHUUR, Diane '91
Born in 1953 in Auburn, Washington. Jazz singer/pianist. Blind since birth.

| 11/12/88 | 170 | 10 | | © 1 | Talkin' 'Bout You .... | | | $10 | GRP 9567 |
| 2/16/91 | 148 | 10 | | © 2 | Pure Schuur .... | | | $10 | GRP 9628 |

Ain't That Love (1)
All Caught Up In Love (2)
Baby You Got What It Takes (2)
Cry Me A River (1)
Deed I Do (2)

For Your Love (1)
Funny (But I Still Love You) (1)
Hard Drivin' Mama II (1)
Hearts Take Time (1)
Hold Out (1)
I Could Get Used To This (2)

Louisiana Sunday Afternoon (1)
Nobody Does Me (2)
Nothing In The World (Can Make Me Love You More Than I Do) (1)
Somethin' Real (1)

Talkin' 'Bout You (1)
Touch (2)
Unforgettable (2)
We Can Only Try (2)

What A Difference A Day Makes (2)
You Don't Remember Me (2)

SCHWARTZ, Eddie '82
Born in 1949 in Toronto. Pop singer/songwriter.

| 2/6/82 | 195 | 6 | | | No Refuge .... | | | $12 | Atco 141 |

All Our Tomorrows 28
Auction Block

Good With Your Love
Heart On Fire

No Refuge
Over The Line 91

Spirit Of The Night
Tonight

S CLUB 7 '01
Pop vocal group formed in England: Tina Barrett, Paul Cattermole, Jon Lee, Bradley McIntosh, Jo O'Meara, Hannah Spearritt and Rachel Stevens. Group stars in it's own TV series on the Fox Family Channel.

| 4/29/00 | 112 | 18 | | © 1 | S Club .... | | | $10 | Polydor 543103 |
| 12/2/00+ | 69 | 30 | ● © 2 | 7 .... | | | $10 | Polydor 549628 |

All In Love Is Fair (2)
Best Friend (2)
Bring It All Back (1)
Bring The House Down (2)

Colour Of Blue (2)
Cross My Heart (2)
Everybody Wants Ya (1)
Friday Night (1)

Gonna Change The World (1)
Hope For The Future (1)
I Really Miss You (1)
I'll Be There (2)

I'll Keep Waiting (2)
It's A Feel Good Thing (1)
Lately (2)
Love Train (2)

Natural (2)
Never Had A Dream Come True (2) 10
Reach (2)

S Club Party (1)
Two In A Million (1,2)
Viva La Fiesta (1)
You're My Number One (1)

SCOFIELD, John '94
Born on 12/26/51 in Dayton, Ohio. Jazz guitarist.

| 4/23/94 | 181 | 2 | | © | I Can See Your House From Here .... | | [I] | $10 | Blue Note 27765 |

JOHN SCOFIELD & PAT METHENY

Everybody's Party
I Can See Your House From Here

Message To My Friend
No Matter What
No Way Jose

One Way To Be
Quiet Rising
Red One

S.C.O.
Say The Brother's Name
You Speak My Language

★278★ SCORPIONS '88
Hard-rock group from Germany: Klaus Meine (vocals), Rudolf Schenker and Matthias Jabs (guitars), Francis Buchholz (bass) and Herman Rarebell (drums). Ralph Rieckermann replaced Buchholz in 1992. Curt Cress replaced Rarebell in 1995. Schenker is the brother of **Michael Schenker**.

1)Savage Amusement 2)Love At First Sting 3)Blackout

7/28/79	55	23	● © 1	Lovedrive			$12	Mercury 3795
11/17/79	180	4	© 2	Best Of Scorpions		[E-K]	$12	RCA Victor 3516
5/17/80	52	21	▲ © 3	Animal Magnetism			$12	Mercury 3825
3/27/82	10	74	▲ © 4	**Blackout**			$12	Mercury 4039
5/7/83+	37 C	24	© 5	Virgin Killer		[E]	$12	RCA Victor 3659
					released in 1977				
3/17/84	6	63	▲3 © 6	**Love At First Sting**			$12	Mercury 814981
8/4/84	175	4	© 7	Best Of Scorpions, Vol. 2		[E-K]	$12	RCA Victor 5085
7/13/85	14	43	▲ © 8	World Wide Live		[L]	$15	Mercury 824344 [2]
5/7/88	5	43	▲ © 9	**Savage Amusement**			$10	Mercury 832963
12/2/89+	43	23	© 10	Best Of Rockers 'N' Ballads	C:#24/16	[G]	$10	Mercury 842002
11/24/90+	21	73	▲2 © 11	Crazy World			$10	Mercury 846908
10/9/93	24	9	© 12	Face The Heat			$10	Mercury 518258
6/8/96	99	3	© 13	Pure Instinct			$10	Atlantic 82913

Alien Nation (12)
All Night Long (7)
Always Somewhere (1)
Animal Magnetism (3)
Another Piece Of Meat (1,8)
Are You The One? (13)
Arizona (4)
As Soon As The Good Times Roll (6)
Backstage Queen (2,5)
Bad Boys Running Wild (6,8)
Believe In Love (9)
Big City Nights (6,8,10)
Blackout (4,8,10)
But The Best For You (13)
Can't Get Enough (1,8)
Can't Live Without You (4,8)
Catch Your Train (5,7)
China White (4)

Coast To Coast (1,8)
Coming Home (6,8)
Countdown (8)
Crazy World (11)
Crossfire (6)
Crying Days (5,7)
Dark Lady (2)
Does Anyone Know (13)
Don't Believe Her (11)
Don't Make No Promises (Your Body Can't Keep) (3)
Don't Stop At The Top (9)
Dynamite (4,8)
Every Minute Every Day (9)
Falling In Love (3)
Hate To Be Nice (12)
He's A Woman - She's A Man (2)
Hell Cat (2,5)

Hey You (10)
Hit Between The Eyes (11)
Hold Me Tight (3)
Holiday (1,8,10)
I Can't Explain (10)
I'm Leaving You (6)
In Trance (2)
In Your Park (5)
Is There Anybody There? (1)
Kicks After Six (11)
Lady Starlight (3)
Lonely Nights (12)
Longing For Fire (7)
Love On The Run (9)
Lovedrive (1,10)
Loving You Sunday Morning (1,8)
Lust Or Love (11)
Make It Real (3,8)

Media Overkill (9)
Money And Fame (11)
Nightmare Avenue (12)
No One Like You (4,8,10) 65
No Pain No Gain (12)
Now! (4)
Oh Girl (I Wanna Be With You) (13)
Only A Man (3)
Passion Rules The Game (9)
Pictured Life (2,5)
Polar Nights (5)
Restless Nights (11)
Rhythm Of Love (9,10) 75
Robot Man (2)
Rock You Like A Hurricane (6,8,10) 25
Sails Of Chardon (2)
Same Thrill (6)

Send Me An Angel (11) 44
Ship Of Fools (12)
Six String Sting (8)
Someone To Touch (12)
Soul Behind The Face (13)
Speedy's Coming (2,7)
Steamrock Fever (5)
Still Loving You (6,8,10) 64
Stone In My Shoe (13)
Sun In My Hand (7)
Taxman Woman (12)
Tease Me Please Me (11)
They Need A Million (7)
This Is My Song (7)
Time Will Call Your Name (13)
To Be With You In Heaven (11)
Top Of The Bill (7)
Twentieth Century Man (3)
Under The Same Sun (12)

Unholy Alliance (12)
Virgin Killer (2,5)
Walking On The Edge (9)
We Let It Rock...You Let It Roll (9)
We'll Burn The Sky (7)
When The Smoke Is Going Down (7)
When You Came Into My Life (13)
Where The River Flows (13)
Wild Child (13)
Wind Of Change (11) 4
Woman (12)
Yellow Raven (5)
You And I (13)
You Give Me All I Need (4,10)
Zoo, The (3,8,10)

SCOTT, Christopher '69
Born Dave Mullaney in New York City. Moog synthesizer player.

| 10/4/69 | 175 | 3 | | | Switched-On Bacharach .... | | [I] | $15 | Decca 75141 |

Alfie
April Fools

Do You Know The Way To San Jose
Look Of Love

I Say A Little Prayer
Walk On By

This Guy's In Love With You
What The World Needs Now Is Love

What's New Pussycat?
Wives And Lovers

SCOTT, Jill '01
Born in 1972 in Philadelphia. R&B singer/songwriter.

| 8/5/00+ | 17 | 61↑ | ▲ © | Who Is Jill Scott? Words And Sounds Vol. 1 .... | | | $10 | Hidden Beach 62137 |

Brotha
Do You Remember
Exclusively

Gettin' In The Way
He Loves Me (Lyzel In E Flat)
Honey Molasses

I Think It's Better
It's Love
Long Walk 43

Love Rain
One Is The Magic #
Show Me

Slowly Surely
Try
Watching Me

Way, The 60

SCOTT, Marilyn '79
Born on 12/21/49 in Alta Dena, California. Jazz-styled singer.

| 4/21/79 | 189 | 4 | | | **Dreams Of Tomorrow** .... | | | $12 | Atco 109 |

Beach, The | Highways Of My Life | Let's Not Talk About Love | Yes I Can (I Can Get Along | You Are All I Need
Dreams Of Tomorrow | Let's Be Friends | Why-Oh-You (Y-O-U) | Without Them) | You Made Me Believe

SCOTT, Tom '75
Born on 5/19/48 in Los Angeles. Pop-jazz-fusion saxophonist. Session work for **Joni Mitchell**, **Steely Dan**, **Carole King** and others. Composer of movie and TV scores. Led the house band for TV's *Pat Sajak Show*. Son of Nathan Scott, a composer of TV scores for *Dragnet, Wagon Train, My Three Sons* and others.

| 4/27/74 | 141 | 16 | © | 1 | **Tom Scott & The L.A. Express** .... | [I] | | $15 | Ode 77021 |
| 3/15/75 | 18 | 27 | © | 2 | **Tom Cat** | [I] | | $15 | Ode 77029 |

TOM SCOTT & THE L.A. EXPRESS (above 2)

12/20/75+	42	25	©	3	**New York Connection**	[I]		$15	Ode 77033
9/10/77	87	14	©	4	**Blow It Out**	[I]		$15	Ode 34966
11/18/78+	123	13		5	**Intimate Strangers**	[I]		$12	Columbia 35557
12/15/79	162	6		6	**Street Beat**	[I]		$12	Columbia 36137
7/11/81	123	11		7	**Apple Juice**	[I-L]		$12	Columbia 37419

recorded on 1/15/81 at The Bottom Line in New York City

| 9/25/82 | 164 | 7 | © | 8 | **Desire** .... | [I] | | $12 | Musician 60162 |

Apple Juice (7) | Do You Feel Me Now (5) | Greed (6) | Love Poem (2) | Shakedown, The (6) | We Belong Together (7)
Appolonia (Foxtrata) (3) | Down To Your Soul (4) | Heading Home (6) | Maybe I'm Amazed (8) | Smoothin' On Down (4) | We Can Fly (6)
Backfence Cattin' (2) | Dream Lady (4) | Hi Steppers (5) | Meet Somebody (3) | Sneakin' In The Back (1) | You're Gonna Need Me (3)
Beautiful Music (5) | Easy Life (1) | I Wanna Be (4) | Midtown Rush (3) | So White And So Funky (7) | You're So Good To Me (5)
Bless My Soul (1) | Garden (3) | In My Dreams (7) | Mondo (2) | Spindrift (1) | You've Got The Feel'n (4)
Breezin' Easy (5) | Getaway Day (5) | Instant Relief (7) | New York Connection (3) | Street Beat (6) |
Car Wars (6) | Gettin' Up (7) | It Is So Beautiful To Be (4) | Nite Creatures (5) | Stride (8) |
Chunk O' Funk (8) | Give Me Your Love (6) | Johnny B. Badd (8) | Nunya (1) | Strut Your Stuff (1) |
Come Closer, Baby (6) | Gonna Do It Right (7) | Keep On Doin' It (2) | Only One (8) | Sure Enough (8) |
Dahomey Dance (1) | Good Evening Mr. & Mrs. | King Cobra (1) | Puttin' The Bite On You (5) | Time And Love (3) |
Day Way (2) | America & All The Ships At | L.A. Expression (1) | Refried (2) | Tom Cat (2) |
Desire (8) | Sea (2) | Looking Out For Number 7 (3) | Rock Island Rocket (2) | **Uptown & Country** (3) *80* |
Dirty Old Man (3) | Gotcha (4) | Lost Inside The Love Of You (5) | Shadows (4) | Vertigo (1) |

SCOTT-ADAMS, Peggy '97
Born Peggy Stoutmeyer on 6/25/48 in Opp, Alabama; raised in Pensacola, Florida. Recorded in the male-female duo **Peggy Scott & Jo Jo Benson**.

| 3/1/69 | 196 | 5 | | 1 | **Soulshake** .... | | | $20 | SSS Int'l. 1 |

PEGGY SCOTT & JO JO BENSON

| 2/1/97 | 72 | 13 | © | 2 | **Help Yourself** .... | | | $10 | Miss Butch 4003 |

Bill (2) *87* | Fine As Frog Hair (1) | I'm Getting What I Want (2) | Part Time Lover, Full Time Fool | **Soulshake** (1) *37* | You, Her And His (2)
Blow Your Mind (1) | Help Yourself (2) | If That's The Only Way (1) | (2) | 'Til The Morning Comes (1) |
Burning (2) | Here With Me (1) | Love Will Come Sneaking Up | **Pickin' Wild Mountain Berries** | We Got Our Bag (1) |
Cleaning House (2) | I Don't Wanna Steal It (2) | On You (1) | (1) *27* | We Were Made For Each Other |
Doin' Our Thing (1) | I'll Take Care Of You (2) | **Lover's Holiday** (1) *31* | Slow Drag (1) | (2) |

SCOTT-HERON, Gil, And Brian Jackson '75
Scott-Heron was born on 4/1/49 in Chicago; raised in Jackson, Tennessee. Keyboardist/singer/songwriter/author/poet. Met keyboardist/singer/songwriter Jackson while attending Lincoln University in Pennsylvania. Duo was together from 1974-78. Scott-Heron then recorded solo.

2/1/75	30	17	©	1	**The First Minute Of A New Day**			$12	Arista 4030
11/8/75	103	5	©	2	**From South Africa To South Carolina**			$12	Arista 4044
11/13/76	168	5	©	3	**It's Your World**	[L]		$15	Arista 5001 [2]

recorded on 7/1/76 at Paul's Mall in Boston

10/22/77	130	5		4	**Bridges**			$12	Arista 4147
9/9/78	61	21	©	5	**Secrets**			$12	Arista 4189
3/8/80	82	12		6	**1980**			$12	Arista 9514

GIL SCOTT-HERON:

12/20/80+	159	6		7	**Real Eyes**			$10	Arista 9540
9/26/81+	106	27	©	8	**Reflections**			$10	Arista 9566
10/2/82	123	9		9	**Moving Target**			$10	Arista 9606

Ain't No Such Thing As | Cane (5) | Inner City Blues (8) | 95 South (All Of The Places | Sharing (1) | Vildgolia (Deaf, Dumb & Blind)
Superman (1) | Combinations (7) | Is That Jazz? (8) | We've Been) (4) | Show Bizness (5) | (4)
Alien (Hold On To Your | Corners (6) | It's Your World (3) | No Exit (9) | Shut 'um Down (6) | Waiting For The Axe To Fall (7)
Dreams) (6) | Delta Man (Where I'm Comin' | Johannesburg (2) | Not Needed (7) | Song Of The Wind (4) | Washington, D.C. (9)
Alluswe (1) | From) (4) | Klan, The (7) | Offering (1) | South Carolina (Barnwell) (2) | We Almost Lost Detroit (4)
Angel Dust (5) | Essex (2) | Late Last Night (6) | Pardon Our Analysis (We Beg | Storm Music (4) | Western Sunrise (1)
Angola, Louisiana (5) | Explanations (9) | Legend In His Own Mind (7) | Your Pardon) (1) | Summer Of '42 (2) | Willing (6)
"B" Movie (8) | Fast Lane (9) | Liberation Song (Red, Black | Possum Slim (Ed Myers) (3) | Third World Revolution (5) | Winter In America (1)
Beginnings (The First Minute Of | Fell Together (2) | And Green) (1) | Prayer For Everybody (medley) | Three Miles Down (5) | World, The (medley) (9)
A New Day) (2) | Grandma's Hands (8) | Lovely Day (2) | (5) | To Be Free (medley) (5) | You Could Be My Brother (7)
Better Days Ahead (3) | Guerilla (1) | Madison Avenue (5) | Push Comes To Shove (6) | Toast To The People (2) | Your Daddy Loves You (For Gia
Bicentennial Blues (3) | Gun (8) | Morning Thoughts (8) | Racetrack In France (4) | Tomorrow's Trane (3) | Louise) (7)
Black History (medley) (3) | Hello Sunday! Hello Road! (4) | Must Be Something (1,3) | Ready Or Not (3) | Train From Washington (3) |
Blue Collar (9) | Home Is Where The Hatred Is | New York City (3) | 17th Street (3) | Tuskeegee #626 (4) |
Bottle, The (3) | (3) | 1980 (6) | Shah Mot Medley (6) | Under The Hammer (4) |

SCREAMING BLUE MESSIAHS, The '88
Punk-rock trio from London: Bill Carter (vocals, guitar), Chris Thompson (bass) and Kenny Harris (drums).

| 1/16/88 | 172 | 11 | © | | **Bikini Red** .... | | | $10 | Elektra 60755 |

All Shook Down | Bikini Red | I Can Speak American | Jesus Chrysler Drives A Dodge | Sweet Water Pools | Waltz
Big Brother Muscle | 55-The Law | I Wanna Be A Flintstone | Lie Detector | Too Much Love |

SCREAMING TREES '96

Hard-rock group from Ellensburg, Washington: brothers Van (bass) and Gary Lee (guitar) Conner with Mark Lanegan (vocals) and Barrett Martin (drums).

| 1/30/93 | 141 | 7 | | © | 1 **Sweet Oblivion** .... | | | $10 | Epic 48996 |
| 7/13/96 | 134 | 3 | | © | 2 **Dust** .... | | | $10 | Epic 64178 |

All I Know (2)
Butterfly (1)
Dime Western (2)
Dollar Bill (1)

Dying Days (2)
For Celebrations Past (1)
Gospel Plow (2)
Halo Of Ashes (2)

Julie Paradise (1)
Look At You (1)
Make My Mind (2)
More Or Less (1)

Nearly Lost You (1)
No One Knows (1)
Secret Kind (1)
Shadow Of The Season (1)

Sworn And Broken (2)
Traveler (2)
Troubled Times (1)
Winter Song (1)

Witness (2)

SCRITTI POLITTI '86

Pop trio formed in England: Green Gartside (vocals), David Gamson (keyboards) and Fred Maher (drums).

| 8/3/85+ | 50 | 28 | | © | 1 **Cupid & Psyche 85** .... | | | $10 | Warner 25302 |
| 7/16/88 | 113 | 8 | | © | 2 **Provision** .... | | | $10 | Warner 25686 |

Absolute (1)
All That We Are (2)
Bam Salute (2)
Best Thing Ever (2)
Boom! There She Was (2) 53

Don't Work That Hard (1)
First Boy In This Town
(Lovesick) (1)
Hypnotize (1)
Little Knowledge (1)

Lover To Fall (1)
Oh Patti (Don't Feel Sorry For
Loverboy) (1)
Overnite (2)
Perfect Way (1) 11

Philosophy Now (2)
Small Talk (1)
Sugar And Spice (2)
Wood Beez (Pray Like Aretha
Franklin) (1) 91

Word Girl (Flesh & Blood) (1)

SCRUFFY THE CAT '89

Rock group from Boston: Charlie Chesterman (vocals), Stephen Fredette (guitar), Burns Stanfield (keyboards), Mac Stanfield (bass) and Randall Gibson (drums).

| 12/17/88+ | 177 | 8 | | © | **Moons Of Jupiter** .... | | | $10 | Relativity 8237 |

Beg, Borrow And Steal
Betty Drops In
Bus Named Desire

Capital Moonlight
Everything
I Do

Just Like Cathy's Clown
Kissing Galaxy
Love So Amazing

Moons Of Jupiter
Nova SS 1968
Places

2Day 2Morrow 4Ever

SCRUGGS, Earl, Revue '75

Born on 1/6/24 in Flintville, North Carolina. Banjo player. Half of **Flatt & Scruggs** duo. His revue consisted of sons Gary (vocals, bass), Randy (guitar) and Steve (keyboards) Scruggs, with Jim Murphey (steel guitar) and Jody Maphis (drums). Steve Scruggs murdered his wife, then killed himself on 9/23/92.

9/22/73	169	5			1 **The Earl Scruggs Revue**			$12	Columbia 32426
6/21/75	104	10			2 **Anniversary Special, Volume One**			$12	Columbia 33416
4/17/76	161	4			3 **The Earl Scruggs Revue, Volume II**			$12	Columbia 34090

Back Slider's Wine (1)
Banjo Man (2)
Bleeker Street Rag (2)
Broad River (3)
Come On Train (1)
Down In The Flood (1)

Every Man Has Got His Own
Price (1)
Fairytale (3)
Gospel Ship (2)
Harbor For My Soul (3)
Harley (3)

Hey Porter (2)
Holiday Hotel (1)
I Still Miss Someone (3)
I've Got A Thing About You
Baby (3)
If I'd Only Come And Gone (1)

Instrumental In D Minor (3)
It Takes A Lot To Laugh, It
Takes A Train To Cry (1)
Love In My Time (1)
My Ship Will Sail (3)
Passing Through (2)

Rita Ballou (3)
Rollin' In My Dreams (2)
Royal Majesty (2)
Salty Dog Blues (1)
Some Of Shelley's Blues (1)
Song To Woody (2)

Station Break (1)
Step It Up And Go (1)
Swimming Song (2)
Tears (1)
Third Rate Romance (2)

SEA, Johnny '66

Born on 7/15/40 in Gulfport, Mississippi. Country singer/guitarist.

| 8/6/66 | 147 | 2 | | | **Day For Decision** .... | | | $25 | Warner 1659 |

America
Day For Decision 35
Generation

God Bless America
I Believe
Star Spangled Banner

This Land
Turning Point
What Is So Rare?

When Johnny Comes Marching
Home

SEA HAGS '89

Hard-rock group from San Francisco: Ron Yocom (vocals, guitar), Frank Wilsex (guitar), Chris Schlosshardt (bass) and Adam Maples (drums). Wilsex later joined **Arcade**. Schlosshardt died of a drug overdose on 2/1/91 (age 26).

| 6/24/89 | 163 | 7 | | © | **Sea Hags** .... | | | $10 | Chrysalis 41665 |

All The Time
Back To The Grind

Bunkbed Creek
Doghouse

Half The Way Valley
In The Mood For Love

Miss Fortune
Someday

Three's A Charm
Too Much T-Bone

Under The Night Stars

SEAL '95

Born Sealhenry Samuel on 2/19/63 in Paddington, England (Nigerian/Brazilian parents). Male singer.

7/20/91	24	63	▲	©	1 **Seal** ....C:#23/46			$10	Sire 26627
6/18/94+	15	118	▲⁴	©	2 **Seal**			$10	ZTT 45415
12/5/98	22	13	●	©	3 **Human Being**			$10	Warner 46828

Beginning, The (1)
Bring It On (2)
Colour (3)
Crazy (1) 7
Deep Water (1)

Don't Cry (2) 33
Dreaming In Metaphors (2)
Excerpt From (3)
Fast Changes (2)
Future Love Paradise (1)

Human Beings (3)
I'm Alive (2)
If I Could (3)
Just Like You Said (3)
Killer (1) 100

Kiss From A Rose (2) 1
Latest Craze (3)
Lost My Faith (3)
Newborn Friend (2)
No Easy Way (3)

People Asking Why (2)
Prayer For The Dying (2) 21
Princess (2)
Show Me (1)
State Of Grace (3)

Still Love Remains (3)
Violet (1)
When A Man Is Wrong (3)
Whirlpool (1)
Wild (1)

SEA LEVEL '78

Blues-rock group: Chuck Leavell (vocals, keyboards), Jimmy Nalls (guitar), Lamar Williams (bass) and Jai Johanny Johanson (drums). Leavell, Williams and Johanson were also members of **The Allman Brothers Band**. After first album, Randall Bramblett (piano), Davis Causey (guitar) and George Weaver (drums) joined. Johanson and Weaver left after the second album, replaced by Joe English. Matt Greeley (percussion) joined in 1979.

3/5/77	43	15		©	1 **Sea Level**			$12	Capricorn 0178
2/4/78	31	16		©	2 **Cats On The Coast**			$12	Capricorn 0198
10/28/78	137	16		©	3 **On The Edge**			$12	Capricorn 0212
8/23/80	152	6			4 **Ball Room**			$10	Arista 9531

Anxiously Awaiting (4)
Bandstand (4)
Cats On The Coast (2)
Comfort Range (4)
Country Fool (1)
Don't Want To Be Wrong (4)
Electron Cold (3)

Every Little Thing (2)
Fifty-Four (3)
Grand Larceny (1)
Had To Fall (2)
It Hurts To Want It So Bad (2)
Just A Good Feeling (1)
King Grand (3)

Living A Dream (3)
Lotta Colada (3)
Midnight Pass (2)
Nothing Matters But The Fever
(1)
On The Wing (3)
Rain In Spain (1)

Scarborough Fair (1)
School Teacher (4)
Shake A Leg (1)
Song For Amy (3)
Storm Warning (2)
Struttin' (1)
That's Your Secret (2) 50

This Could Be The Worst (3)
Tidal Wave (1)
Uptown Downtown (3)
We Will Wait (4)
Wild Side (4)
You Mean So Much To Me (4)

SEALS, Dan '86

Born on 2/8/45 in McCamey, Texas; raised in Rankin, Texas. Singer/songwriter/guitarist. Half of the duo **England Dan & John Ford Coley**. Brother of Jim Seals (of **Seals & Crofts**) and cousin of country singers Johnny Duncan, Troy Seals and Brady Seals (of **Little Texas**).

| 2/8/86 | 59 | 15 | ● | © | **Won't Be Blue Anymore** .... | | | $10 | EMI America 17166 |

Bop 42
City Kind Of Girl

Everything That Glitters (Is Not
Gold)

Headin' West
I Won't Be Blue Anymore

Meet Me In Montana
So Easy To Need

Still A Little Bit Of Love
Tobacco Road

You Plant Your Fields
Your Love

DEBUT	PEAK	WKS	RIAA	CD	ARTIST — Album Title	Catalog	Sym	$	Label & Number

★282★   SEALS & CROFTS   '73

Pop duo: Jim Seals (born on 10/17/41 in Sidney, Texas) and Dash Crofts (born on 8/14/40 in Cisco, Texas). With The Champs from 1958-65. Jim is the brother of **Dan Seals** and the cousin of country singers Troy Seals (Jo Ann & Troy), Brady Seals (of **Little Texas**) and Johnny Duncan.

1)Diamond Girl 2)Summer Breeze 3)Greatest Hits

DEBUT	PEAK	WKS	RIAA	CD	#	Album Title	$	Label & Number
10/31/70	122	10			1	**Down Home**	$25	TA 5004
12/4/71+	133	20			2	**Year Of Sunday**	$15	Warner 2568
9/2/72	7	109	▲2	©	3	**Summer Breeze**	$15	Warner 2629
4/21/73	4	77	●		4	**Diamond Girl**	$15	Warner 2699
3/2/74	14	34	●		5	**Unborn Child**	$15	Warner 2761
8/10/74	81	12			6	**Seals & Crofts I And II** [R]	$20	Warner 2809 [2]
						reissue of first 2 albums on TA label: Seals & Crofts *and* Down Home		
4/5/75	30	23	●		7	**I'll Play For You**	$12	Warner 2848
11/15/75+	11	54	▲2	©	8	**Greatest Hits** [G]	$12	Warner 2886
5/1/76	37	29	●		9	**Get Closer**	$12	Warner 2907
12/11/76+	73	10			10	**Sudan Village**	$12	Warner 2976
10/8/77	118	7			11	**One On One** [S]	$12	Warner 3076
5/13/78	78	13			12	**Takin' It Easy**	$12	Warner 3163

Advance Guards (3,10)
Ancient Of The Old (2)
Antoinette (2)
Arkansas Traveller (10)
Ashes In The Snow (6)
Baby Blue (9)
Baby, I'll Give It To You (10) *58*
Basketball Game (11)
Big Mac (5)
Birthday Of My Thoughts (6)
Blue Bonnet Nation (7)
Boy Down The Road (3)
Breaking In A Brand New Love (12)
Castles In The Sand (7,8)
'Cause You Love (2,10)
Cotton Mouth (1,6)
Cows Of Gladness (6)
Dance By The Light Of The Moon (1,6)

Desert People (5)
Diamond Girl (4,8) *6*
Don't Fail (9)
Dust On My Saddle (4)
Earth (6)
East Of Ginger Trees (3,8,10)
Eighth Of January (10)
Euphrates, The (3)
Fiddle In The Sky (3)
Fire And Vengeance (7)
Flyin' (11)
Follow Me (5)
Forever Like The Rose (12)
Freaks Fret (7)
Funny Little Man (3)
Gabriel Go On Home (1,6)
Get Closer (9) *6*
Golden Rainbow (7)
Goodbye Old Buddies (9)
Granny Will Your Dog Bite? (1,6)

Hand-Me-Down Shoe (1,6)
High On A Mountain (2)
Hollow Reed (1,6)
Hummingbird (3,8) *20*
Hustle (11)
I'll Play For You (7,8) *18*
In Tune (6)
Intone My Servant (4)
Irish Linen (2)
It'll Be All Right (11)
It's Gonna Come Down (On You) (4)
Janet's Theme (11)
Jekyll And Hyde (6)
Jessica (4)
John Wayne (11)
King Of Nothing (5,8) *60*
Leave (1,6)
Ledges (5)
Love Conquers All (11)
Magnolia Moon (12)

Midnight Blue (12)
Million Dollar Horse (9)
My Fair Share (11) *28*
Nine Houses (4)
Nobody Gets Over Lovin' You (12)
Not Be Found (6)
One More Time (12)
One On One ..see: My Fair Share
Paper Airplanes (2)
Party, The (11)
Passing Thing (9)
Picnic (11)
Purple Hand (1,6)
Put Your Love In My Hands (10)
Rachel (5)
Red Long Ago (9)
Reflections (11)
Ridin' Thumb (1,6)

Robin (1,6)
Ruby Jean And Billie Lee (4,8)
Say (3)
Sea Of Consciousness (6)
See My Life (6)
Seldom's Sister (6)
Seven Valleys (6)
Springfield Mill (2)
Standin' On A Mountain Top (4)
Story Of Her Love (5)
Sudan Village (2,10)
Summer Breeze (3,8) *6*
Sunrise (12)
Sweet Green Fields (9)
Takin' It Easy (12) *79*
This Day Belongs To Me (11)
Thunderfoot (10)
Time Out (11)
Tin Town (1,6)
Today (1,6)
Tribute To 'Abdu'l-Baha' (12)

Truth Is But A Woman (7)
29 Years From Texas (5)
Ugly City (7)
Unborn Child (5) *66*
Wayland The Rabbit (7)
We May Never Pass This Way (Again) (4,8) *21*
When I Meet Them (2,8)
Windflowers (5)
Wisdom (4)
Year Of Sunday (2)
Yellow Dirt (3)
You're The Love (12) *18*

SEARCHERS, The   '64

Pop-rock group from Liverpool, England: Mike Pender and John McNally (vocals, guitars), Tony Jackson (vocals, bass) and Chris Curtis (drums).

DEBUT	PEAK	WKS	RIAA	CD	#	Album Title	$	Label & Number
4/11/64	22	21		©	1	**Meet The Searchers/Needles & Pins**	$75	Kapp 3363
6/20/64	120	8			2	**Hear! Hear!** [E-L]	$75	Mercury 60914
						recorded at the Star Club in Hamburg, Germany		
8/29/64	97	14			3	**This Is Us**	$50	Kapp 3409
3/20/65	112	7			4	**The New Searchers LP**	$50	Kapp 3412
10/23/65	149	2			5	**The Searchers No. 4**	$50	Kapp 3449
3/15/80	191	2			6	**The Searchers**	$15	Sire 6082

Ain't Gonna Kiss Ya (1)
Ain't That Just Like Me (1,2) *61*
Alright (1)
Be My Baby (I Don't Mean Maybe) (5)
Bumble Bee (4) *21*
Can't Help Forgiving You (3)
Cherry Stones (1)
Coming From The Heart (6)
Does She Really Care For Me (5)
Don't Cha Know (1)
Don't Hang On (6)

Don't Throw Your Love Away (3) *16*
Don't You Know Why (5)
Each Time (5)
Everybody Come Clap Your Hands (4)
Everything You Do (4)
Farmer John (1)
Feeling Fine (6)
Four Strong Winds (5)
Goodbye My Lover Goodbye (5) *52*
Goodnight Baby (4)
He's Got No Love (5) *79*

Hearts In Her Eyes (6)
Hey Joe (4)
Hi-Heel Sneakers (3)
Hully Gully (2)
Hungry For Love (3)
I Can Tell (2)
I Count The Tears (3)
I Don't Want To Go On Without You (4)
I Pretend I'm With You (3)
I Sure Know A Lot About Love (2)
I'll Be Doggone (5)
I'm Your Loving Man (5)

If I Could Find Someone (4)
It's In Her Kiss (3)
It's Too Late (6)
Led In The Game (2)
Listen To Me (2)
Lost In Your Eyes (4)
Love Potion Number Nine (3) *3*
Love's Gonna Be Strong (6)
Magic Potion (4)
Mashed Potatoes (2)
Needles And Pins (1) *13*
No Dancing (6)
Oh My Lover (1)

Rosalie (2)
Saturday Night Out (1)
Sea Of Heartbreak (3)
Sick And Tired (4)
Since You Broke My Heart (1)
So Far Away (5)
Some Other Guy (1)
Something You Got (4)
Sweets For My Sweet (2)
Switchboard Susan (6)
Tear Fell (4)
This Empty Place (3)
This Kind Of Love Affair (6)
Till I Met You (5)

Till You Say You Are Mine (4)
Tricky Dicky (1)
Unhappy Girls (3)
What Have They Done To The Rain (4) *29*
What'd I Say (Parts 1 And 2) (2)
Where Have You Been (3)
You Can't Lie To A Liar (5)
You Wanna Make Her Happy (4)

SEASE, Marvin   '87

Born on 2/16/46 in Blackville, South Carolina. R&B singer/songwriter/producer.

DEBUT	PEAK	WKS	RIAA	CD	#	Album Title	$	Label & Number
7/18/87	114	17		©		**Marvin Sease**	$10	London 830794

Candy Licker
Double Crosser

Dreaming
Ghetto Man

Let's Get Married Today
Love Me Or Leave Me

You're Number One

SEATRAIN   '71

Fusion-rock band from Marin County, California: John Gregory (vocals, guitar), Jim Roberts (lyricist), Richard Greene (violin), Donald Kretmar (sax), Andy Kulberg (bass) and Roy Blumenfeld (drums). Greene, Kulberg and Blumenfeld were members of **The Blues Project**. Gregory, Kretmar and Blumenfeld left after first album, replaced by Lloyd Baskin (vocals), Peter Rowan (guitar) and Larry Atamanuik (drums).

DEBUT	PEAK	WKS	RIAA	CD	#	Album Title	$	Label & Number
5/17/69	168	4			1	**Sea Train**	$20	A&M 4171
1/30/71	48	23		©	2	**Seatrain**	$15	Capitol 659
10/9/71	91	9		©	3	**The Marblehead Messenger**	$15	Capitol 829
						above 2 produced by **George Martin**		

As I Lay Losing (1)
Broken Morning (2)
Creepin' Midnight (2)
Despair Tire (3)
Gramercy (3)

Home To You (2)
How Sweet Thy Song (3)
I'm Willin' (3)
Let The Duchess No (1)
London Song (3)

Lonely's Not The Only Way To Go (3)
Losing All The Years (3)
Marblehead Messenger (3)
Mississippi Moon (3)

Oh My Love (medley) (2)
Orange Blossom Special (2)
Out Where The Hills (2)
Portrait Of The Lady As A Young Artist (1)

Protestant Preacher (3)
Pudding Street (1)
Rondo (3)
Sally Goodin' (medley) (2)
Sea Train (1)

Song Of Job (2)
State Of Georgia's Mind (3)
Sweet Creek's Suite (1)
13 Questions (2) *49*
Waiting For Elijah (2)

SEAWIND '80

Jazz-pop group formed in Hawaii: husband-and-wife Pauline (vocals) and Bob (drums) Wilson, Bud Nuanez (guitar), Larry Williams (keyboards), Kim Hutchcroft (sax), Jerry Hey (trumpet) and Ken Wild (bass). Pauline is the only native Hawaiian in the group.

DEBUT	PEAK	WKS	CD	Album	$	Label & Number
5/7/77	188	2		1 Seawind	$12	CTI 5002
1/21/78	122	7		2 Window Of A Child	$12	CTI 5007
3/24/79	143	14		3 Light The Light	$12	Horizon 734
10/25/80	83	11		4 Seawind	$12	A&M 4824

Angel Of Mercy (2)
Campanas De Invierno (Bells Of Winter) (4)
Countin' The Days (2)
Devil Is A Liar (1)
Do Listen To (2)
Enchanted Dance (3)
Everything Needs Love (4)
Follow Your Road (3)
Free (3)
Hallelujah (2)
He Loves You (1)
Hold On To Love (3)
I Need Your Love (4)
Imagine (3)
Light The Light (3)
Long, Long Time (4)
Love Him, Love Her (4)
Love Song (medley) (1)
Lovin' You (2)
Make Up Your Mind (1)
Morning Star (3)
One Sweet Night (2)
Pra Vose (4)
Praise (Part I) (1)
Roadways (Parts I & II) (2)
Seawind (medley) (1)
Shout (4)
Sound Rainbow (3)
Still In Love (4)
Two Of Us (4)
We Got A Way (1)
What Cha Doin' (4)
Window Of A Child (2)
Wings Of Love (2)
You Gotta Be Willin' To Lose (Part II) (1)

SEBADOH '96

Rock trio from Boston: Lou Barlow (vocals, guitar), Jason Lowenstein (bass) and Bob Fay (drums). Russ Pollard replaced Fay in 1998.

DEBUT	PEAK	WKS	CD	Album	$	Label & Number
9/7/96	126	2	©	1 Harmacy	$10	Sub Pop 370
3/13/99	197	1	©	2 The Sebadoh	$10	Sup Pop 31044

Beauty Of The Ride (1)
Bird In The Hand (2)
Break Free (2)
Can't Give Up (1)
Colorblind (2)
Crystal Gypsy (1)
Cuban (2)
Decide (2)
Drag Down (2)
Flame (1)
Hillbilly II (1)
I Smell A Rat (1)
It's All You (2)
Love Is Stronger (2)
Love To Fight (1)
Mind Reader (1)
Nick Of Time (2)
Nothing Like You (1)
Ocean (1)
On Fire (1)
Open Ended (1)
Perfect Way (1)
Prince-S (1)
Sforzando! (1)
So Long (2)
Sorry (2)
Thrive (2)
Too Pure (1)
Tree (2)
Weed Against Speed (1)
Weird (1)
Willing To Wait (1)
Worst Thing (1)
Zone Doubt (1)

SEBASTIAN, John '70

Born on 3/17/44 in New York City. Pop-rock singer/songwriter. Formed **The Lovin' Spoonful** in 1965.

DEBUT	PEAK	WKS	Album	$	Label & Number
3/28/70	20	31	1 John B. Sebastian	$20	MGM 4654
10/10/70	129	3	2 John Sebastian Live [L]	$20	MGM 4720
4/24/71	75	13	3 cheapo-cheapo productions presents Real Live John Sebastian [L]	$15	Reprise 2036
9/18/71	93	9	4 The Four Of Us	$15	Reprise 2041
5/15/76	79	10	5 Welcome Back	$12	Reprise 2249

Amy's Theme (3)
Apple Hill (4)
Baby, Don't Ya Get Crazy (1)
Black Satin Kid (4)
Black Snake Blues (4)
Blue Suede Shoes (3)
Blues For Dad (medley) (3)
Coconut Grove (2)
Darlin' Be Home Soon (2,3)
Did You Ever Have To Make Up Your Mind (3)
Didn't Wanna Have To Do It (5)
Fa-Fana-Fa (1)
Fishin' Blues (2,3)
Four Of Us (4)
Goodnight Irene (3)
Hideaway (5) *95*
How Have You Been (1)
I Don't Want Nobody Else (4)
I Had A Dream (1,2)
I Needed Her Most When I Told Her To Go (5)
In The Still Of The Night (I Remember Parris) (3)
JB's Happy Harmonica (medley) (3)
Let This Be Our Time To Get Along (5)
Lovin' You (2,3)
Magical Connection (1,2)
Mobile Line (Gonna Carry Me Away From The Bull Frog Blues) (3)
My Gal (2,3)
Nashville Cats (3)
One Step Forward, Two Steps Back (5)
Rainbows All Over Your Blues (1)
Red-Eye Express (1,2)
Room Nobody Lives In (1)
Rooty-Toot (3)
She's A Lady (1,2) *84*
She's Funny (5)
Song A Day In Nashville (5)
Sweet Muse (4)
Waiting For A Train (3)
Warm Baby (4)
We'll See (4)
Welcome Back (5) *1*
Well, Well, Well (4)
What She Thinks About (1)
You Go Your Way And I'll Go Mine (5)
You're A Big Boy Now (1,2)
Younger Generation (2,3)
Younger Girl (3)

SECADA, Jon '93

Born Juan Secada on 10/4/63 in Havana, Cuba; raised in Hialeah, Florida. Singer/songwriter.

DEBUT	PEAK	WKS	RIAA	CD	Album	Catalog	$	Label & Number
6/6/92+	15	103	▲³	©	1 Jon Secada	C:#39/2	$10	SBK 98845
6/11/94	21	46	▲	©	2 Heart, Soul & A Voice		$10	SBK 29272
4/12/97	40	13		©	3 Secada		$10	SBK 55897
8/5/00	173	2		©	4 Better Part Of Me		$10	550 Music 69840

After All Is Said And Done (3)
Always Something (1)
Angel (1) *18*
Asi (4)
Believe (3)
Better Part Of Me (4)
Break The Walls (1)
Dentro De Ti (4)
Do You Believe In Us (1) *13*
Do You Really Want Me (1)
Don't Be Silly (2)
Dreams That I Carry (1)
Eyes Of A Fool (2)
Fat Chance (1)
Forever (Is As Long As It Lasts) (3)
Get Me Over You (3)
Good Feelings (2)
Heaven Is You (3)
I Live For You (3)
I'm Free (1) *27*
If You Go (1) *10*
It's Enough (3)
Just Another Day (1) *5*
La, La, La (2)
Lost Inside Of You (4)
Love's About To Change My Mind (1)
Mental Picture (2) *29*
Misunderstood (1)
One Of A Kind (4)
Otro Dia Mas Sin Verte (1)
Papi (2)
Ready For Love (3)
Si Te Vas (If You Go) (2)
Speak To The Wind (4)
Stay (2)
Stop (4)
Take Me (2)
There's No Sunshine Anymore (4)
Time Heals (1)
Too Late, Too Soon (3) *41*
Tuyo (Take Me) (1)
When You're Gone (4)
Where Do I Go From You (2)
Whipped (2) *65*
Who Will Take Care Of Me (3)
You Should Be Mine (1)

2ND II NONE '92

Male rap duo from Los Angeles: cousins Dee and KK.

DEBUT	PEAK	WKS	CD	Album	$	Label & Number
11/16/91+	83	34	©	1 2nd II None	$10	Profile 1416
10/30/99	162	1	©	2 Classic 220	$10	Arista 16401

Ain't Nothin' Wrong (1)
Back Up Off The Wall (1)
Be True To Yourself (1) *78*
Comin' Like This (1)
Don't Do Dat (2)
Don't U Hide It (2)
Got A Nu Woman (2)
If U Ain't F#!@in' (2)
If You Want It (1) *64*
Just Ain't Me (1)
Let The Rhythm Take You (1)
Life Of A Player (1)
Love U (2)
Make 'Em Understand (2)
More Than A Player (1)
Mystic (1)
Niggaz Trippin' (1)
Pawdy (1)
Princess (2)
Punk Mutha Fuckaz (1)
Stragglaz (2)
Underground Terror (1)
Up 'N Da Club (2)
What Goes Up (1)
Whateva U Want (2)
Y? (2)

SEDAKA, Neil '75

Born on 3/13/39 in Brooklyn, New York. Pop singer/songwriter/pianist. Prolific songwriting partnership with Howard Greenfield.

DEBUT	PEAK	WKS	CD	Album	$	Label & Number
1/5/63	55	9	©	1 Neil Sedaka Sings His Greatest Hits [G]	$50	RCA Victor 2627
12/7/74+	23	62	● ©	2 Sedaka's Back	$15	Rocket 463
3/1/75	161	4		3 Neil Sedaka Sings His Greatest Hits [G-R]	$15	RCA Victor 0928
10/11/75	16	32	● ©	4 The Hungry Years	$15	Rocket 2157
5/1/76	26	22	©	5 Steppin' Out	$15	Rocket 2195
9/18/76	159	4		6 Solitaire [E]	$15	RCA Victor 1790
				first released in 1972 on Kirshner 117		
5/28/77	59	7		7 A Song	$12	Elektra 102
10/22/77	143	5		8 Neil Sedaka's Greatest Hits [G]	$12	Elektra 2297
5/17/80	135	13		9 In The Pocket	$12	Elektra 259

Adventures Of A Boy Child Wonder (6)
Alone At Last (7)
Amarillo (1) *44*
Anywhere You're Gonna Be (Leba's Song) (6)
Baby Blue (4)
Bad And Beautiful (5)
Bad Blood (4,8) *1*
Beautiful You (6)
Better Days Are Coming (6)
Breaking Up Is Hard To Do (1,3) *1*
Breaking Up Is Hard To Do (4,8) *8*
Calendar Girl (1,3) *4*
Cardboard California (5)
Crossroads (4)
Diary, The (1,3) *14*
Dimbo Man (6)
Do It Like You Done It When You Meant It (9)
Don't Let It Mess Your Mind (6)
Express Yourself (6)
Good Times, Good Music, Good Friends (5)
Happy Birthday, Sweet Sixteen (1,3) *6*
Here We Are Falling In Love Again (5)
Hollywood Lady (7)
Home (6)
Hot And Sultry Nights (7)
Hungry Years (4,8)

SEDAKA, Neil — Cont'd

I Let You Walk Away (5)	Little Brother (2)	#1 With A Heartache (5)	Sing Me (5)
I've Never Really Been In Love Before (7)	**Little Devil** (1,3) *11*	**Oh! Carol** (1,3) *9*	Sleazy Love (7)
Immigrant, The (2,8) *22*	Little Lovin' (2)	One Night Stand (7)	Solitaire (2,6,8)
It's Good To Be Alive Again (4)	Lonely Night (Angel Face) (4,8)	Other Side Of Me (2)	Song, A (7)
Junkie For Your Love (9)	**Love In The Shadows** (5,8) *16*	Our Last Song Together (2)	**Stairway To Heaven** (1,3) *9*
King Of Clowns (1,3) *45*	Love Will Keep Us Together (2,8)	Perfect Strangers (5)	Standing On The Inside (2,8)
Laughter In The Rain (2,8) *1*	My Friend (9)	**Run Samson Run** (1,3) *28*	Stephen (4)
Leaving Game (7)	New York City Blues (4)	Sad Eyes (2)	**Steppin' Out** (5,8) *36*
Letting Go (9)	**Next Door To An Angel** (1,3) *5*	**Should've Never Let You Go** (9) *19*	Summer Nights (5)
			Sweet Little You (1,3) *59*

That's When The Music Takes Me (2,6,8) *27* — Tin Pan Alley (7) — Tit For Tat (4) — Trying To Say Goodbye (6) — Way I Am (2) — What A Difference A Day Makes (9) — When You Were Lovin' Me (4) — You (9) — You Better Leave That Girl Alone (9) — **You Gotta Make Your Own Sunshine** (5) *53* — **You Mean Everything To Me** (1,3) *17* — You Never Done It Like That (7) — You're So Good For Me (9) — Your Favorite Entertainer (4)

SEDUCTION '90

Female vocal trio from New York City: Idalis Leon, April Harris and Michelle Visage. Idalis was a VJ for MTV.

DEBUT	PEAK	WKS	RIAA	CD	ARTIST — Album Title	$	Label & Number
10/28/89+	**36**	47	●	©	**Nothing Matters Without Love**	$10	A&M 5280

Breakdown *82* — Could This Be Love *11* — Give My Love To You — Heartbeat *13* — (Nothing Matters) Without Love — One Mistake — Seduction's Theme — **Two To Make It Right** *2* — You're My One And Only (True Love) *23*

SEEDS, The '67

Los Angeles garage-rock quartet: Sky Saxon (b: Richard Marsh; lead singer, bass), Jan Savage (guitar), Rick Aldridge (drums) and Daryl Hooper (keyboards).

DEBUT	PEAK	WKS		CD	ARTIST — Album Title	$	Label & Number
1/14/67	**132**	7		© 1	**The Seeds**	$50	GNP Crescendo 2023
8/12/67	**87**	8		© 2	**Future**	$50	GNP Crescendo 2038

Can't Seem To Make You Mine (1) *41* — Evil Hoodoo (1) — Excuse, Excuse (1) — Fallin' (2) — Fallin' In Love (1) — Flower Lady & Her Assistant (2) — Girl I Want You (1) — It's A Hard Life (1) — Lose Your Mind (1) — March Of The Flower Children (2) — No Escape (1) — Nobody Spoil My Fun (1) — Now A Man (2) — Out Of The Question (2) — Painted Doll (2) — **Pushin' Too Hard** (1) *36* — Six Dreams (2) — **Thousand Shadows** (2) *72* — Travel With Your Mind (2) — Try To Understand (1) — Two Fingers Pointing On You (2) — Where Is The Entrance Way To Play (2) — You Can't Be Trusted (1)

SEEGER, Pete '64

Born on 5/3/19 in New York City. Legendary folk singer/songwriter. Formed **The Weavers** in 1948. Won Grammy's Lifetime Achievement Award in 1993. Inducted into the Rock and Roll Hall of Fame in 1996 as an early influence.

DEBUT	PEAK	WKS		CD	ARTIST — Album Title	Sym	$	Label & Number
12/14/63+	**42**	36		© 1	**We Shall Overcome**	[L]	$25	Columbia 8901
					recorded on 6/8/63 at Carnegie Hall			
5/17/75	**181**	4		2	**Together In Concert**	[L]	$20	Reprise 2214 [2]
					PETE SEEGER & ARLO GUTHRIE			

City Of New Orleans (2) — Declaration Of Independence (2) — Deportee (Plane Wreck At Los Gatos) (2) — Don't Think Twice, It's All Right (2) — Estadio Chile (2) — Get Up And Go (2) — Golden Vanity (2) — Guantanamera (1,2) — Hard Rain's A-Gonna Fall (1) — Henry My Son (2) — I Ain't Scared Of Your Jail (1) — If You Miss Me At The Back Of The Bus (1) — Joe Hill (2) — Keep Your Eyes On The Prize (1) — **Little Boxes** (1) *70* — Lonesome Valley (2) — Mail Myself To You (1) — May There Always Be Sunshine (2) — Mother, The Queen Of My Heart (2) — That's What I Learned In School (1) — Oh, Freedom! (1) — On A Monday (2) — Presidential Rag (2) — Quite Early Morning (2) — Roving Gambler (2) — Stealin' (2) — Sweet Rosyanne (2) — That's What I Learned In School (1) — Three Rules Of Discipline And The Eight Rules Of Attention (2) — Tshotsholosa (Road Song) (1) — Walkin' Down The Line (2) — Way Out There (2) — We Shall Overcome (1) — Well May The World Go (2) — Who Killed Davy Moore? (1) — Who Killed Norma Jean? (1) — Yodeling (2)

SEEKERS, The '67

Pop-folk group formed in Australia: Judith Durham (vocals), Keith Potger and Bruce Woodley (guitars), and Athol Guy (standup bass). Potger formed **The New Seekers** in 1970.

DEBUT	PEAK	WKS		CD	ARTIST — Album Title	Sym	$	Label & Number
6/5/65	**145**	3		1	**The Seekers**		$20	Marvel 2060
6/12/65	**62**	16		2	**The New Seekers**		$20	Capitol 2319
9/25/65	**123**	6		© 3	**A World Of Our Own**		$20	Capitol 2369
2/25/67	**10**	28		4	Georgy Girl		$20	Capitol 2431
8/19/67	**97**	10		© 5	**The Best Of The Seekers**	[G]	$20	Capitol 2746

All My Trials (1) — All Over The World (Dans Le Monde En Entier) (4) — Allentown Jail (3) — Blowin' In The Wind (2) — California Dreamin' (4) — Carnival Is Over (5) — Chilly Winds (1,2) — Come The Day (4) — Dese Bones G'wine Rise Again (1) — Don't Tell Me My Mind (3) — Don't Think Twice, It's All Right (3) — Four Strong Winds (3) — **Georgy Girl** (4) *2* — **I'll Never Find Another You** (5) *4* — If I Had A Hammer (The Hammer Song) (1) — Island Of Dreams (4) — Just A Closer Walk With Thee (3) — Katy Cline (1) — Kumbaya (1,2) — Lady Mary (2) — Last Thing On My Mind (4) — Leaving Of Liverpool (3) — Light From The Lighthouse (1) — Lonesome Traveller (1) — Louisiana Man (4) — **Morningtown Ride** (2,5) *44* — Ox Driving Song (2) — Red Rubber Ball (4) — Run Come See (1) — Sinner Man (5) — Someday, One Day (5) — This Land Is Your Land (3) — This Little Light Of Mine (2) — This Train (1) — Times They Are A Changin' (3,5) — Turn, Turn, Turn (To Everything There Is A Season) (4,5) — Two Summers (4) — Walk With Me (5) — Water Is Wide (2) — We're Moving On (2,5) — Well, Well, Well (2,4) — What Have They Done To The Rain (2) — When The Stars Begin To Fall (1,5) — Wild Rover (1) — **World Of Our Own** (3,5) *19* — Yesterday (4) — You Can Tell The World (3)

SEGAL, George '67

Born on 2/13/34 in Great Neck, Long Island, New York. Popular TV/movie actor.

DEBUT	PEAK	WKS		CD	ARTIST — Album Title	$	Label & Number
9/2/67	**199**	2			**The Yama Yama Man**	$20	Philips 242

Baby Won't You Please Come Home — Bennie Badoo — Bye Bye Blackbird (medley) — Gee But I Hate To Go Home Alone — Glory Of Love — I Always Think I'm Up In Heaven When I'm Down In Dixieland — Ja-Da (medley) — Moving Picture Ball — On The Old Dominion Line — Show Me The Way To Go Home (medley) — Yama, Yama Man — Yes Sir That's My Baby

SEGER, Bob ★107★ '80

Born on 5/6/45 in Dearborn, Michigan; raised in Detroit. Rock singer/songwriter/guitarist. Formed own backing group, The Silver Bullet Band, in 1976: Alto Reed (horns), Robyn Robbins (keyboards), Drew Abbott (guitar), Chris Campbell (bass) and Charlie Martin (drums). Various personnel changes since then.

1)Against The Wind 2)Nine Tonight 3)Like A Rock

BOB SEGER SYSTEM:

DEBUT	PEAK	WKS		CD	ARTIST — Album Title	$	Label & Number
2/8/69	**62**	10		© 1	**Ramblin' Gamblin' Man**	$30	Capitol 172
10/31/70	**171**	4		© 2	**Mongrel**	$30	Capitol 499

BOB SEGER:

DEBUT	PEAK	WKS	RIAA	CD	ARTIST — Album Title	$	Label & Number
7/22/72	**180**	11		© 3	**Smokin' O.P.'s**	$25	Palladium 1006
3/3/73	**188**	6		4	**Back In '72**	$25	Reprise 2126
4/12/75	**131**	18	▲ ©	5	**Beautiful Loser**	$12	Capitol 11378

BOB SEGER & THE SILVER BULLET BAND:

DEBUT	PEAK	WKS	RIAA	CD	ARTIST — Album Title	Catalog	Sym	$	Label & Number
5/1/76	34	167	▲4 ©	6	'Live' Bullet		[L]	$15	Capitol 11523 [2]
					recorded on 9/4/75 at Cobo Hall in Detroit				
11/13/76+	8	88	▲5 ©	7	**Night Moves**			$12	Capitol 11557
5/27/78	4	110	▲5 ©	8	**Stranger In Town**			$12	Capitol 11698
3/15/80	❶6	110	▲4 ©	9	**Against The Wind**			$12	Capitol 12041
9/26/81	3	70	▲3 ©	10	**Nine Tonight**	C:#24/77	[L]	$15	Capitol 12182 [2]
					recorded in Detroit and Boston				
1/15/83	5	39	▲ ©	11	**The Distance**			$10	Capitol 12254
4/19/86	3	62	▲ ©	12	**Like A Rock**			$10	Capitol 12398
9/14/91	7	29	▲ ©	13	**The Fire Inside**			$10	Capitol 91134
11/12/94	8	114	▲4 ©	14	**Greatest Hits**	C:#2¹/246	[G]	$10	Capitol 30334
11/11/95	27	24	● ©	15	**It's A Mystery**			$10	Capitol 99774

Aftermath, The (12)
Against The Wind (9,10,14) **3**
Ain't Got No Money (8)
Always In My Heart (13)
American Storm (12) **13**
Back In '72 (4)
Beautiful Loser (5,6)
Betty Lou's Gettin' Out Tonight (9,10)
Big River (2)
Black Eyed Girl (1)
Black Night (5)
Blind Love (13)
Bo Diddley (3,6)
Boomtown Blues (11)
Brave Strangers (8)
By The River (15)
C'est La Vie (14)
Come To Poppa (7)
Comin' Home (11)
Doctor Fine (1)
Down Home (1)
Even Now (11) **12**

Evil Edna (2)
Famous Final Scene (8)
Feel Like A Number (8,10) **48**
Fine Memory (5)
Fire Down Below (7,10)
Fire Inside (13,14)
Fire Lake (9,10) **6**
Get Out Of Denver (6) **80**
Golden Boy (15)
Gone (1)
Good For Me (9)
Hands In The Air (13)
Heavy Music (3,6)
Her Strut (9,10)
Highway Child (2)
Hollywood Nights (8,10,14) **12**
Horizontal Bop (9) **42**
House Behind A House (11)
Hummingbird (2)
I Can't Save You Angelene (15)
I Wonder (15)
I've Been Workin' (4,6)
I've Got Time (4)

If I Were A Carpenter (3) **76**
In Your Time (14)
It's A Mystery (15)
It's You (12) **52**
Ivory (1) **97**
Jesse James (3)
Jody Girl (5)
Katmandu (5,6) **43**
Last Song (Love Needs To Be Loved) (1)
Leanin' On My Dream (2)
Let It Rock (6,10)
Little Victories (11)
Like A Rock (12,14) **12**
Lock And Load (15)
Long Twin Silver Line (9)
Long Way Home (13)
Lookin' Back (6) **96**
Love The One You're With (3)
Love's The Last To Know (11)
Lucifer (2) **84**
Mainstreet (7,10,14) **24**
Makin' Thunderbirds (11)

Manhattan (15)
Mary Lou (7)
Miami (12) **70**
Midnight Rider (4)
Momma (2)
Mongrel (2)
Mongrel Too (2)
Mountain, The (13)
Neon Sky (4)
New Coat Of Paint (13)
Night Moves (7,10,14) **4**
Nine Tonight (10)
No Man's Land (9)
Nutbush City Limits (5,6) **69**
Old Time Rock & Roll (8,10,14) **28**
Ramblin' Gamblin' Man (1,6) **17**
Real At The Time (13)
Real Love (13) **24**
Revisionism Street (15)
Ring, The (12)
Rite Of Passage (15)

River Deep - Mountain High (2)
Rock And Roll Never Forgets (7,10) **41**
Roll Me Away (11,14) **27**
Rosalie (4)
Sailing Nights (5)
Shame On The Moon (11) **2**
She Can't Do Anything Wrong (13)
Shinin' Brightly (9)
Ship Of Fools (7)
Sightseeing (13)
16 Shells From A 30-6 (15)
So I Wrote You A Song (4)
Someday (3)
Sometimes (12)
Somewhere Tonight (12)
Song To Rufus (2)
Stealer (4)
Still The Same (8,14) **4**
Sunburst (7)
Sunspot Baby (7)
Take A Chance (13)

Tales Of Lucy Blue (1)
Teachin Blues (2)
Tightrope (12)
Till It Shines (8)
Travelin' Man (5,6)
Tryin' To Live My Life Without You (10) **5**
Turn On Your Lovelight (3)
Turn The Page (4,6,14)
2 + 2 = ? (1)
We've Got Tonite (8,10,14) **13**
West Of The Moon (15)
Which Way (13)
White Wall (1)
You'll Accomp'ny Me (9,10,14) **14**

SEINFELD, Jerry '98
Born on 4/29/54 in Brooklyn, New York. Comedian/actor. Starred in own popular sitcom form 1990-98.

DEBUT	PEAK	WKS	RIAA	CD	ARTIST — Album Title	Catalog	Sym	$	Label & Number
10/10/98	59	14	▲ ©	1	I'm Telling You For The Last Time		[C]	$10	Universal 53175
					recorded at the Broadhurst Theater in New York City				

Air Travel
Bathroom
Cab Drivers
Chinese People

Clothing
Crooks
Doctors
Drugstores

Florida
Halloween
Horses
Late TV

McDonalds
Men & Women
No. 1 Fear
Olympics

Phones
Q & A
Scuba Diving
Sky Diving/The Helmet

Supermarkets

SELECTER '80
Ska group from Coventry, England: Pauline Black and Arthur Hendrickson (vocals), Noel Davies and Compton Amanor (guitars), Desmond Brown (keyboards), Charley Anderson (bass) and Charley Bembridge (drums).

DEBUT	PEAK	WKS	RIAA	CD	ARTIST — Album Title	Catalog	Sym	$	Label & Number
5/3/80	175	4	©		Too Much Pressure			$12	Chrysalis 1274

Black And Blue
Carry Go Bring Come
Danger

James Bond
Missing Words
Murder

My Collie (Not A Dog)
On My Radio
Out On The Streets

Street Feeling
They Make Me Mad
Three Minute Hero

Time Hard
Too Much Pressure

★349★ **SELENA** '95
Born Selena Quintanilla on 4/16/71 in Corpus Christi, Texas. Shot to death by Yolanda Saldivar (founder of Selena's fan club) on 3/31/95 (age 23). Latin singer. Married her guitarist, Chris Perez. **Jennifer Lopez** starred in the 1997 biographical movie Selena. Sister of A.B. Quintanilla (of **Kumbia Kings**).

1)Dreaming Of You 2)Selena 3)Amor Prohibido

DEBUT	PEAK	WKS	RIAA	CD	ARTIST — Album Title	Catalog	Sym	$	Label & Number
6/18/94+	29	23	▲ ©	1	Amor Prohibido		[F]	$10	EMI Latin 28803
4/22/95	64	10	©	2	12 Super Exitos		[F]	$10	EMI Latin 30907
4/22/95	79	7	● ©	3	Live		[F-L]	$10	EMI Latin 42770
4/22/95	97	7	● ©	4	Entre A Mi Mundo		[F]	$10	EMI Latin 42635
4/22/95	147	4	©	5	Las Reinas Del Pueblo		[F]	$10	EMI Latin 32639
					SELENA Y GRACIELA BELTRAN				
					6 solo cuts by Selena and 6 solo cuts by Beltran: "Baraja De Oro," "Pilares De Cristal," "Tu Me Dijiste Adios," "Mi Triunfo," "Tu Recado" and "Morena Y Delgadita"				
5/6/95	❶2C	9	©	6	Mis Mejores Canciones-17 Super Exitos		[F]	$10	EMI Latin 27190
5/6/95	22C	2	©	7	Ven Conmigo		[F]	$10	EMI Latin 42359
8/5/95	❶1	49	▲3 ©	8	Dreaming Of You	C:#11/19		$10	EMI Latin 34123
11/23/96	82	5	©	9	Siempre Selena		[E-F]	$10	EMI Latin 53585
					previously unreleased tracks in Spanish and English				
3/29/97	7	64	▲ ©	10	Selena		[S]	$10	EMI Latin 55535
					includes "Blue Moon/We Belong Together" by The Vidal Brothers; "Vivirás Selena" by Pete Astudillo, Graciela Beltrán, Barrio Boyzz, Emilio, Jennifer Peña & Bobby Pulido; and "One More Time" by Lil' Ray				
4/25/98	131	6	©	11	Anthology		[F-K]	$20	EMI Latin 94110 [3]
3/27/99	54	19	● ©	12	All My Hits - Todos Mis Exitos		[F-G]	$10	EMI Latin 97886
3/18/00	149	6	©	13	All My Hits - Todos Mis Exitos Vol. 2		[F-G]	$10	EMI Latin 23332
4/14/01	176	2	©	14	Live - The Last Concert		[L]	$10	EMI Latin 32119

Always Mine (11)
Amame (4,11)
Amame, Quiereme (medley) (3)
Amor Prohibido (1,8,12,14)
Aunque No Salga El Sol (7,13)
Baila Esta Cumbia (3,6,7,10,11,12,14)

Besitos (3,6)
Bidi Bidi Bom Bom (1,2,5,8,10,12,13,14)
Boy Like That (10)
Captive Heart (8,11,13)
Cariño Mío (11)
Cien Años (9,13)

Cobarde (1,14)
Como La Flor (2,3,4,5,6,8,10,12,14)
Cómo Quisiera (9)
Corazoncito (1)
Costumbres (6,9)
Dáme Tu Amor (11)

Despues De Enero (6,7)
Diferentes (11)
Disco Medley (14)
Don't Throw Away My Love (11)
Dreaming Of You (8,10,12) **22**
El Chico Del Apartamento 512 (1,12,13,14)

El Ramalazo (11)
El Toro Relajo (8)
Enamorada De Ti (7,11,13)
Estoy Contigo (6)
Fotos y Recuerdos (13)
Fotos Y Recuerdos "Back In The Chain Gang" (1)

Funky Town (medley) (10,12)
God's Child (Baila Conmigo) (8)
Hustle, The (medley) (10,11,12)
I Could Fall In Love (8,10,12)
I Will Survive (medley) (10,12)
I'm Getting Used To You (8,11,12)

SELENA — Cont'd

Is It The Beat? (10)	Million To One (9,13)	Pa' Qué Me Sirve La Vida (11)	Si Una Vez (1,2,13,14)	Tu Robaste Mi Corazon	Ya No (1,9)

Is It The Beat? (10)
La Bamba (11)
La Carcacha (2,3,4,5,6,10,12,14)
La Llamada (2,3,5,11,12)
La Puerta Se Cerró (11)
La Tracalera (6,7)
Las Cadenas (2,3,4)
Last Dance (medley) (10,11,12)
Mentiras (6)

Million To One (9,13)
Missing My Baby (2,4,8,11,12)
Muñequito De Trapo (13)
No Debes Jugar (2,3,5,11,12)
No Me Queda Mas (1,12,13,14)
No Quiero Saber (2,6,7,11,13)
On The Radio (medley) (10,11,12)
Only Love (9,10)

Pa' Qué Me Sirve La Vida (11)
Perdoname (medley) (3)
Porque Le Gusta Bailar Cumbia (3)
Que Creias (2,3,4,5,6,11,12)
Quiero Estar Contigo (11)
Rama Caída (11)
Sabes (11)
Salta La Ranita (11)
Si La Quieres (3,4)

Si Una Vez (1,2,13,14)
Siempre Estoy Pensando En Ti (3,4)
Siempre Hace Frio (9,11,13)
Soy Amiga (9)
Sukiyaki (8)
Te Amo Solo A Ti (11)
Techno Cumbia (1,2,8,13,14)
Tengo Ganas De Llorar (6)
Tu Eres (6)

Tu Robaste Mi Corazon (2,3,9,13)
Tu Solo Tu (8,11,12)
Tus Desprecios (1,14)
Ven Conmigo (3,7)
Vuelve A Mi (4,6)
Where Did The Feeling Go? (10)
Wherever You Are (Dondequiera Que Estes) (8)

Ya No (1,9)
Ya No Quiero Saber (9)
Ya Ves (3,7,14)
Yo Fui Aquella (6,11,13)
Yo Me Voy (6,7)
Yo Te Amo (3,7)
Yo Te Daré (11)
Yo Te Sigo Queriendo (4)

SEMBELLO, Michael '83
Born on 4/17/54 in Philadelphia. Pop singer/guitarist. Prolific studio musician.

10/8/83	80	10			**Bossa Nova Hotel**			$12	Warner 23920

Automatic Man *34*
Cadillac

Cowboy
First Time

Godzilla
It's Over

Lay Back
Maniac *1*

Superman
Talk

SEMISONIC '98
Rock trio from Minneapolis: Dan Wilson (vocals, guitar), John Munson (bass) and Jacob Slichter (drums).

4/11/98	43	43	▲	©	1	**Feeling Strangely Fine**			$10	MCA 11733
3/31/01	103	2		©	2	**All About Chemistry**			$10	MCA 112355

Act Naturally (2)
All Worked Out (1)
Bed (2)
California (1)

Chemistry (2)
Closing Time (1)
Completely Pleased (1)
DND (1)

El Matador (2)
Follow (2)
Get A Grip (2)
Gone To The Movies (1)

I Wish (2)
Made To Last (1)
Never You Mind (1)
One True Love (2)

Secret Smile (1)
She Spreads Her Wings (1)
She's Got My Number (2)
Singing In My Sleep (1)

Sunshine & Chocolate (2)
Surprise (2)
This Will Be My Year (1)
Who's Stopping You? (2)

SEPULTURA '96
Speed-metal group from Belo Horizonte, Brazil: brothers Max (vocals, guitar) and Igor (drums) Cavalera with Andreas Kisser (guitar) and Paulo Jr. (bass). Max Cavalera left in early 1998 to form **Soulfly**; replaced by Derrick Green. Sepultura is Portuguese for grave.

5/4/91	119	4		©	1	**Arise**			$10	RC 9328
11/6/93	32	7	●	©	2	**Chaos A.D.**			$10	Roadrunner 57458
3/30/96	27	10		©	3	**Roots**			$10	Roadrunner 8900
6/21/97	162	2		©	4	**Blood-Rooted**	[K]		$10	Roadrunner 8821
10/24/98	82	3		©	5	**Against**			$10	Roadrunner 8700
4/7/01	134	1		©	6	**Nation**			$10	Roadrunner 8560

Against (5)
Altered State (1)
Ambush (3)
Amen (2)
Arise (1)
Attitude (3)
Beneath The Remains/Escape To The Void (4)
Biotech Is Godzilla (2,4)
Border Wars (6)
Born Stubborn (3)
Boycott (5)
Breed Apart (3)

Choke (5)
Clenched Fist (2,4)
Common Bonds (5)
Crucificados Pelo Sistema (4)
Cut-Throat (3)
Dead Embryonic Cells (1)
Desperate Cry (1)
Dictatorshit (3)
Drowned Out (5)
Drug Me (4)
Dusted (3,4)
Endangered Species (5)
Floaters In Mud (5)

F.O.E. (5)
Hatred Aside (5)
Human Cause (6)
Hunt, The (2)
Infected Voice (1)
Inhuman Nature (4)
Itsari (3)
Jasco (3)
Kaiowas (2,4)
Kamaitachi (5)
Lookaway (3,4)
Manifest (3)
Meaningless Movements (1)

Mine (4)
Murder (1)
Nomad (2)
Old Earth (5)
One Man Army (4)
Policia (1)
Politricks (6)
Procreation (Of The Wicked) (4)
Propaganda (2,4)
Ratamahatta (3)
Refuse/Resist (4)
Refuse/Resist (2)
Reject (5)

Revolt (6)
Reza (5)
Roots Bloody Roots (3,4)
Rumors (5)
Saga (6)
Sepulnation (6)
Slave New World (2,4)
Spit (5)
Straighthate (3)
Subtraction (1)
Symptom Of The Universe (4)
T3rcermillennium (5)
Territory (2)

Tribe To A Nation (6)
Tribus (5)
Uma Cura (6)
Unconscious (5)
Under Siege (Regnum Irae) (1)
Valtio (6)
Vox Populi (6)
War (4)
Water (6)
Ways Of Faith (6)
We Who Are Not As Others (2)
Who Must Die? (6)

SERENDIPITY SINGERS, The '64
Pop-folk group formed in Denver: Jon Arbenz, Mike Brovsky, Diane Decker, Brooks Hatch, John Madden, Bryan Sennett, Tom Tiemann, Lynne Weintraub and Bob Young.

3/7/64	11	29		©	1	**The Serendipity Singers**			$20	Philips 600115
6/27/64	68	15		©	2	**The Many Sides Of The Serendipity Singers**			$20	Philips 600134
1/16/65	149	2			3	**Take Your Shoes Off with the Serendipity Singers**			$20	Philips 600151

Autumn Wind (3)
Beans In My Ears (2) *30*
Boots And Stetsons (The Lilies Grow High) (1)
Cloudy Summer Afternoon (1)
Don't Let The Rain Come Down (Crooked Little Man) (1) *6*

Down Where The Winds Blow (2)
Fast Freight (2)
Foghorn (3)
Freedom's Star (1)
Goin' Home (1)
Hi-Lili-Hi-Lo (3)
High North Star (3)

Jimmy-O (3)
Lazy Afternoon (3)
Let Me Fly (2)
Little Brown Jug (3)
Look Away Over Yondro (2)
Mill Girls Don't Sing Or Dance (2)
Movin' In My Heart (2)

Mud (Hippopotamus Song) (1)
New Frankie And Johnny Song (2)
Rider (3)
Sailing Away (1)
Same Old Reason (3)
Sing Out (1)
Sinner Man (1)

Six Foot Six (2)
Six Wheel Driver (1)
Sobbin' Women (3)
Soon It's Gonna Rain (2)
Spring (3)
Take Your Shoes Off (3)
That's My Home (3)
Waggoner Lad (1)

Whale Of A Tale (3)
You Don't Know (3)

SERMON, Erick — see EPMD

SETZER, Brian '98
Born on 4/10/60 in Long Island, New York. Lead singer/guitarist of the **Stray Cats**. Played Eddie Cochran in the 1987 movie *La Bamba*. Formed own 16-piece swing orchestra in 1994. Formed trio **'68 Comeback Special** (named after **Elvis Presley**'s 1968 TV special) with Mark Winchester (bass) and Bernie Dresel (drums).

3/22/86	45	18		©	1	**The Knife Feels Like Justice**			$10	EMI America 17178
5/28/88	140	8		©	2	**Live Nude Guitars**			$10	EMI-Manhattan 46963

THE BRIAN SETZER ORCHESTRA:

4/9/94	158	4		©	3	**The Brian Setzer Orchestra**			$10	Hollywood 61565
7/11/98	9	43	▲²	©	4	**The Dirty Boogie**			$10	Interscope 90183
8/19/00	62	7		©	5	**Vavoom!**			$10	Interscope 490733
6/30/01	152	1		©	6	**Ignition!**			$10	Surfdog 167124

BRIAN SETZER '68 COMEBACK SPECIAL

Americano (5)
As Long As I'm Singin' (4)
Aztec (1)
Ball And Chain (3)
Barbwire Fence (1)
Blue Café (6)
Bobby's Back (1)
Boulevard Of Broken Dreams (1)
Brand New Cadillac (3)
Breath Of Life (1)

Caravan (5)
Chains Around Your Heart (1)
Dirty Boogie (4)
Dreamsville (6)
Drink That Bottle Down (4)
Drive Like Lightning (Crash Like Thunder) (5)
8-Track (3)
Every Tear That Falls (2)
'59 (6)
5 Years, 4 Months, 3 Days (6)

Footloose Doll (5)
'49 Mercury Blues (5)
From Here To Eternity (5)
Gettin' On The Ropes (6)
Gettin' In The Mood (5)
Gloria (5)
Good Rockin' Daddy (3)
Haunted River (1)
Hell Bent (4)
Hollywood Nocturne (4)
Hot Rod Girl (5)

If You Can't Rock Me (5)
Ignition (6)
Jukebox (5)
Jump Jive An' Wail (4) *94*
Jumpin' East Of Java (5)
Knife Feels Like Justice (1)
Lady Luck (3)
(Legend Of) Johnny Kool (Part 2) (6)
Let's Live It Up (4)

Love Is Repaid By Love Alone (2)
Mack The Knife (5)
Malagueña (6)
Maria (1)
Nervous Breakdown (2)
Nightingale Sang In Berkeley Square (4)
Nosey Joe (4)
Pennsylvania 6-5000 (5)
Radiation Ranch (1)

Rain Washed Everything Away (2)
Rebelene (2)
Red Lightning Blues (2)
Rock This Town (4)
Rockability (2)
Rooster Rock (3)
Rosie In The Middle (6)
Route 66 (3)
Santa Rosa Rita (6)
September Skies (3)

SETZER, Brian — Cont'd

She Thinks I'm Trash (2)
Since I Don't Have You (4)
Sittin' On It All The Time (3)
Sleepwalk (4)
So Young, So Bad, So What? (2)
Straight Up (3)
Switchblade 327 (4)
Temper Sure Is Risin' (2)
That's The Kind Of Sugar Papa Likes (5)
There's A Rainbow 'Round My Shoulder (3)
This Cat's On A Hot Tin Roof (4)
This Old House (4)
Three Guys (1)
When The Sky Comes Tumblin' Down (2)
Who Would Love This Car But Me? (6)
You're The Boss (4)
Your True Love (3)

SEVENDUST   '99

Rock group from Atlanta: Lajon (vocals), Clint Lowery and John Connelly (guitars), Vinnie Hornsby (bass), and Morgan Rose (drums).

| 3/28/98 | 165 | 16 | ● | © | 1 **Sevendust** .... | | | $10 | TVT 5730 |
| 9/11/99 | 19 | 14 | ● | © | 2 **Home** .... | | | $10 | TVT 5820 |

Bender (2)
Bitch (1)
Black (1)
Born To Die (1)
Crumbled (2)
Denial (2)
Face (1)
Feel So (2)
Grasp (2)
Grasshopper (2)
Headtrip (2)
Home (2)
Insecure (2)
Licking Cream (2)
My Ruin (2)
Prayer (1)
Reconnect (2)
Rumble Fish (2)
Speak (1)
Terminator (1)
Too Close To Hate (1)
Waffle (2)
Will It Bleed (1)
Wired (1)

SEVEN MARY THREE   '96

Rock group from Virginia: Jason Ross (vocals), Jason Pollock (guitar), Casey Daniel (bass) and Giti Khalsa (drums). Thomas Juliano replaced Pollock in 2000.

11/4/95+	24	52	▲	©	1 **American Standard**			$10	Mammoth 92633
6/21/97	75	7		©	2 **Rock Crown**			$10	Mammoth 83018
8/1/98	121	2		©	3 **Orange Ave.**			$10	Mammoth 83114
6/23/01	178	1		©	4 **The Economy Of Sound**			$10	Mammoth 165516

Anything (1)
Blessing In Disguise (3)
Breakdown (4)
Chasing You (3)
Cumbersome (1) *39*
Devil Boy (1)
Devil's Holy Joke (3)
Each Little Mystery (3)
Faster (4)
Favorite Dog (1)
First Time Believers (4)
Flagship Eleanor (3)
Gone Away (2)
Hang On (3)
Headstrong (1)
Home Stretch (2)
Honey (4)
Honey Of Generation (2)
Houdini's Angels (2)
I Could Be Wrong (2)
In-Between (3)
Joliet (3)
Lame (1)
Lucky (2)
Make Up Your Mind (1)
Man In Control? (4)
Margaret (1)
My My (1)
Needle Can't Burn (What The Needle Can't Find) (2)
Oven (2)
Over Your Shoulder (3)
Peel (3)
People Like New (2)
Player Piano (2)
Punch In Punch Out (1)
RockCrown (2)
Roderigo (1)
Sleepwalking (4)
Southwestern State (3)
Steal A Car (4)
Still I Find You (4)
Summer Is Over (4)
Super-Related (3)
This Evening's Great Excuse (2)
Times Like These (2)
Tug (4)
Wait (4)
Water's Edge (1)
What Angry Blue? (2)
Zeroes & Ones (4)

702   '99

Female R&B vocal trio from Las Vegas: Kameelah Williams, with sisters Irish and Lemisha Grinstead. Group named after the Las Vegas area code.

| 2/1/97 | 82 | 30 | ● | © | 1 **No Doubt** .... | | | $10 | Biv Ten 0738 |
| 7/3/99 | 34 | 21 | ● | © | 2 **702** .... | | | $10 | Motown 549526 |

All I Want (1) *35*
Don't Go Breaking My Heart (2)
Finally (2)
Finding My Way (1)
Get Down Like Dat (1)
Get It Together (1) *10*
Gotta Leave (2)
Make Time (2)
No Doubt (1)
Not Gonna (1)
Round & Round (1)
Seven (2)
Show You My Love (1)
Steelo (1) *32*
Tell Your Girl (2)
What More Can He Do (2)
Where My Girls At (2) *4*
Will You Be OK (2)
Word Iz Bond (2)
You Don't Know (2)
You'll Just Never Know (2)

707   '82

Rock group from Detroit: Kevin Russell (vocals, guitar), Phil Bryant (bass) and Jim McClarty (drums). Kevin Chalfant (vocals) and Tod Howarth (keyboards) added in 1982. Chalfant co-founded **The Storm** in 1991.

| 2/7/81 | 159 | 6 | | © | 1 **The Second Album** .... | | | $15 | Casablanca 7248 |
| 7/3/82 | 129 | 9 | | | 2 **Mega Force** .... | | | $12 | Boardwalk 33253 |

Can't Hold Back (2)
City Life (1)
Get To You (2)
Heartbeat (2)
Hell Or High Water (2)
Hello Girl (2)
Live With The Girl (1)
Live Without Her (1)
Love On The Run (1)
Mega Force (2) *62*
Millionaire (1)
No Better Feeling (2)
Out Of The Dark (2)
Party's Over (1)
Pressure Rise (1)
Rockin' Is Easy (1)
Strings Around My Heart (1)
Tonite's Your Nite (1)
We Will Last (2)
Write Again (2)

7 SECONDS   '90

Hard-rock trio from Los Angeles: Kevin Seconds (vocals, guitar), Steve Youth (bass) and Troy Mowat (drums).

| 11/4/89+ | 153 | 19 | | © | **Soulforce Revolution** .... | | | $10 | Restless 72344 |

Busy Little People
Copper Ledge
4 A.M. In Texas
I Can Sympathize
It All Makes A Lot Less Sense Now
Mother's Day
Satyagraha
Soul To Keep (For Phyllis)
Swansong
Tickets To A Better Place
Tribute Freedom Landscape

SEVERINSEN, Doc   '86

Born Carl Severinsen on 7/7/27 in Arlington, Oregon. Legendary trumpeter. Leader of the *Tonight Show* band (1967-92).

8/27/66	147	2			1 **Fever!**		[I]	$15	Command 893
11/26/66	133	6			2 **Command Performances**		[I]	$15	Command 904
10/16/71	185	2			3 **Brass Roots**		[I]	$12	RCA Victor 4522
4/29/72	74	19		©	4 **Brass On Ivory**		[I]	$12	RCA Victor 4629
6/9/73	185	3		©	5 **Brass, Ivory & Strings**		[I]	$12	RCA Victor 0098
					HENRY MANCINI & DOC SEVERINSEN (above 2)				
4/17/76	189	4			6 **Night Journey**		[I]	$10	Epic 34078
11/1/86	65	26		©	7 **The Tonight Show Band with Doc Severinsen**		[I]	$10	Amherst 3311
12/14/91	171	4		©	8 **Merry Christmas from Doc Severinsen and The Tonight Show Orchestra**		[X-I]	$10	Amherst 94406

Christmas chart: 16/'91

Baubles, Bangles And Beads (2)
Begin The Beguine (7)
Ben (2)
Bluesette (2)
Brass On Ivory (4)
Brass Roots (3)
Brian's Song (4)
Bye, Bye Blues (7)
Celebrate (3)
Christmas Song (Chestnuts Roasting On An Open Fire) (8)
Cleopatra's Asp (1)
Cotton Fields (2)
Dance Of The Sugar Plum Fairy (8)
Doc, Theme For (5)
Don't Worry 'Bout Me (2)
Dreamsville (4)
Fever (1)
Flying Home (7)
Good Medicine (3)
Hark! The Herald Angels Sing (8)
Have Yourself A Merry Little Christmas (8)
He's Got The Whole World In His Hands (1)
Help Me Make It Through The Night (5)
How Long Has This Been Going On (7)
I Can't Get Started (5)
I Wanna Be With You (6)
I'm Getting Sentimental Over You (7)
If (4)
In A Little Spanish Town (1,2)
It Ain't Necessarily So (2)
Ja-Da (1)
Jingle Bells (8)
Johnny's Theme (The Tonight Show Theme) (7)
Joy To The World (8)
King Porter Stomp (7)
Lady In Red (1)
Laura, Love Theme For (5)
Let It Snow, Let It Snow (8)
Little Drummer Boy (8)
Little Tiny Feets (6)
Lookin' Good (6)
Love For Sale (2)
Love Story, Theme From (3)
Lover Man (Oh, Where Can You Be?) (5)
Make It With You (5)
March Of The Toys (8)
Misty (2)
Move Over (3)
My Funny Valentine (2)
Never My Love (4)
Night Journey (6)
Now And Then (6)
O Come, All Ye Faithful (Adeste Fideles) (8)
Okefenokee (3)
On A Clear Day (You Can See Forever) (1,2)
One O'Clock Jump (7)
Open The Gates Of Love (6)
Poor Butterfly (4)
Psalm 150 (8)
Raggedy Jim (1)
'Round Midnight (5)
Rudolph The Red-Nosed Reindeer (8)
Santa Claus Is Coming To Town (8)
Sax Alley (7)
Shawnee (7)
Sidewinder, The (1)
Silent Night, Holy Night (8)
Skyliner (7)
Sleigh Ride (8)
Soldier In The Rain (4)
Sometimes (4)
Spanish Dreams (6)
Stardust (2)
Stormy Weather (7)
Summertime (2)
Tennessee Waltz (7)
Tippin' In (7)
Tonight Show Theme ..see: Johnny's Theme

SEVERINSEN, Doc — Cont'd

Walk Right In (1)
Wave (5)
We've Only Just Begun (4)
When The Saints Come Marching In (2)
White Christmas (8)
Willow Weep For Me (4)
Winter Wonderland (8)
Without You (5)
World's Gone Home (6)
You Put The Shine On Me (6)

SEX PISTOLS '78

Legendary punk-rock group formed in London: Johnny "Rotten" Lydon (vocals), Steve Jones (guitar), Sid Vicious (bass) and Paul Cook (drums). Disbanded in January 1978. Lydon formed **Public Image Ltd.** in 1978. Vicious died of a drug overdose on 2/2/79 (age 21), while out on bail for the fatal stabbing of girlfriend Nancy Spungen four months earlier. Jones later joined **Chequered Past**. Movies about group include *The Great Rock 'n' Roll Swindle*, *D.O.A.* and *Sid & Nancy*. Lydon, Jones, Matlock and Cook reunited in 1996.

| 12/10/77+ | 106 | 12 | ▲ | © | Never Mind The Bollocks, Here's The Sex Pistols | C:#14/36 | | $20 | Warner 3147 |

Anarchy In The U.K.
Bodies
EMI
God Save The Queen
Holidays In The Sun
Liar
New York
No Feelings
Pretty Vacant
Problems
Seventeen
Sub-Mission

SEXTON, Charlie '86

Born on 8/11/68 in San Antonio, Texas. Rock singer/guitarist. Lead guitarist for **Joe Ely**'s band. Co-founder of the **Arc Angels**. Appeared in the movie *Thelma & Louise*. His brother is the leader of **Will And The Kill**.

| 11/30/85+ | 15 | 34 | | © | 1 | Pictures For Pleasure | | | $10 | MCA 5629 |
| 2/18/89 | 104 | 9 | | © | 2 | Charlie Sexton | | | $10 | MCA 6280 |

Attractions (1)
Battle Hymn Of The Republic (2)
Beat's So Lonely (1) *17*
Blowing Up Detroit (2)
Cry Little Sister (2)
Don't Look Back (2)
For All We Know (2)
Hold Me (1)
I Can't Cry (2)
Impressed (1)
Pictures For Pleasure (1)
Question This (2)
Restless (1)
Save Yourself (2)
Seems So Wrong (2)
Space (1)
Tell Me (1)
While You Sleep (2)
You Don't Belong Here (1)

SEYMOUR, Phil '81

Born on 5/15/52 in Tulsa, Oklahoma. Died of cancer on 8/17/93 (age 41). Rock singer/drummer. Formerly with the **Dwight Twilley** Band and the **Textones**.

| 2/21/81 | 64 | 16 | | | | Phil Seymour | | | $12 | Boardwalk 36996 |

Baby It's You
Don't Blow Your Life Away
I Found A Love
I Really Love You
Let Her Dance
Love You So Much
Precious To Me *22*
Then We Go Up
Trying To Get To You
We Don't Get Along
Won't Finish Here

SHADOWFAX '84

Jazz-fusion group from Chicago. Core members: G.E. Stinson (guitar), Chuck Greenberg (sax), Phil Maggini (bass) and Stuart Nevitt (drums). Band name taken from J.R.R. Tolkien's novel, *Lord Of The Rings*. Greenberg died of a heart attack on 9/4/95 (age 45).

11/19/83+	145	19		©	1	Shadowdance		[I]	$10	Windham Hill 1029
11/17/84	126	20		©	2	The Dreams Of Children		[I]	$10	Windham Hill 1038
7/12/86	114	16		©	3	Too Far To Whisper		[I]	$10	Windham Hill 1051
5/14/88	168	5		©	4	Folksongs For A Nuclear Village		[I]	$10	Capitol 46924

Above The Wailing Wall (2)
Against The Grain (4)
Another Country (3)
Behind Green Eyes (4)
Big Song (2)
Brown Rice (medley) (1)
China Blue (3)
Distant Voices (1)
Dreams Of Children (2)
Elephant Ego (4)
Firewalker, The (4)
Folksong For A Nuclear Village (4)
Ghost Bird (1)
Karmapa Chenno (medley) (1)
Kindred Spirits (2)
Lucky Mud (4)
Maceo (3)
Madagascar Cafe (4)
New Electric India (1)
No Society (4)
Orangutan Gang (Strikes Back) (3)
Ritual (3)
Road To Hanna (3)
Shadowdance (1)
Shaman Song (2)
Slim Limbs Akimbo (3)
Snowline (2)
Solar Wind (4)
Song For My Brother (1)
Streetnoise (3)
Too Far To Whisper (3)
Tsunami (3)
Watercourse Way (1)
We Used To Laugh (4)
What Goes Around (3)
Word From The Village (2)

SHADOWS OF KNIGHT, The '66

Garage-rock group from Chicago: Jim Sohns (vocals), Joe Kelley and Jerry McGeorge (guitars), Warren Rogers (bass) and Tom Schiffour (drums).

| 5/14/66 | 46 | 18 | | © | | Gloria | | | $100 | Dunwich 666 |

Boom Boom
Dark Side
Gloria *10*
I Got My Mojo Working
I Just Want To Make Love To You
(I'm Your) Hoochie Coochie Man
It Always Happens That Way
Let It Rock
Light Bulb Blues
Oh Yeah *39*
You Can't Judge A Book (By The Cover)

SHAGGY '01

Born Orville Richard Burrell on 10/22/68 in Kingston, Jamaica. Reggae singer.

| 7/29/95 | 34 | 37 | ▲ | © | 1 | Boombastic | | | $10 | Virgin 40158 |
| 8/26/00+ | ❶ [6] | 58↑ | ▲[6] | © | 2 | Hotshot | | | $10 | MCA 112096 |

Angel (2) *1*
Boombastic (1) *3*
Chica Bonita (2)
Dance & Shout (2)
Day Oh (1)
Finger Smith (1)
Forgive Them Father (1)
Freaky Girl (1)
Gal Yu A Pepper (1)
Heartbreak Suzie (1)
Hey Love (2)
Hope (2)
Hot Shot (2)
How Much More (1)
In The Summertime (1) *flip*
Island Lover (1)
It Wasn't Me (2) *1*
Jenny (1)
Keep'n It Real (2)
Leave It To Me (2)
Lonely Lover (2)
Luv Me, Luv Me (2) *76*
Not Fair (2)
Something Different (1)
Train Is Coming (1)
Why Me Lord? (2)
Why You Treat Me So Bad (1)
Woman A Pressure Me (1)

SHAI '93

R&B vocal group formed in Washington DC: Garfield Bright, Marc Gay, Carl Martin and Darnell Van Rensalier.

1/9/93	6	52	▲[2]	©	1	...If I Ever Fall In Love			$10	Gasoline Alley 10762
1/1/94	127	8		©	2	Right Back At Cha		[K]	$10	Gasoline Alley 10945
11/4/95	42	11		©	3	Blackface			$10	Gasoline Alley 11176

Baby I'm Yours (1) *10*
Changes (1,2)
Come Home To My Love (2)
Come With Me (3) *43*
Comforter (1,2) *10*
Concert A (The Hidden One) (3)
Did You Know (3)
Don't Wanna Play (1)
During The Storm (3)
Falling (3)
Flava (1)
I Don't Wanna Be Alone (3) *89*
If I Ever Fall In Love (1,2) *2*
If I Gave (A Confession Of Hope) (3)
Let's Go Back (3)
Lord I've Come (1)
Mr. Turn U Out (3)
"95" (3)
Place Where You Belong (3) *34*
Planet Solitude (3)
Sexual (1)
Sexual (Tonight Is The Night) (2)
Show Me (2)
To Get To Know You (3)
Together Forever (1,2)
Waiting For The Day (1,2)
Will I Find Someone (3)
Yours (2) *63*

SHAKESPEAR'S SISTER '92

Female vocal duo: Siobhan Fahey and Marcella Detroit. Fahey was a member of **Bananarama**. Married David A. Stewart (of **Eurythmics**). Detroit was born Marcy Levy in Detroit.

| 7/18/92 | 56 | 29 | | © | | Hormonally Yours | | | $10 | London 828266 |

Are We In Love Yet
Black Sky
Catwoman
Emotional Thing
Goodbye Cruel World
Hello (Turn Your Radio On)
I Don't Care *55*
Let Me Entertain You
Moonchild
My 16th Apology
Stay *4*
Trouble With Andre

SHAKIRA '00

Born Shakira Isabel Mebarak Ripoll on 2/9/77 in Barranquilla, Columbia. Female singer.

| 10/17/98 | 131 | 22 | ● | © | 1 | Dónde Están Los Ladrones? | C:#30/2 | [F] | $10 | Sony Discos 82746 |

title is Spanish for "Where Are The Thieves?"

| 3/18/00 | 124 | 8 | | © | 2 | MTV Unplugged | | [F-L] | $10 | Sony Discos 83775 |

SHAKIRA — Cont'd

Ciega, Sordomuda (1,2)
Dónde Están Los Ladrones? (1,2)
Estoy Aquí (2)
Inevitable (1,2)
Moscas En La Casa (1,2)
No Creo (1,2)
Octavo Día (1,2)
Ojos Así (1,2)
Que Vuelvas (1)
Si Te Vas (1,2)
Sombra De Ti (1,2)
Tú (1,2)

SHAKTI — see McLAUGHLIN, John

SHALAMAR   '80

R&B vocal trio formed in Los Angeles: **Jody Watley**, Jeffrey Daniels and **Howard Hewett**.

DEBUT	PEAK	WKS		CD	#	Album Title	$	Label & Number
5/21/77	48	14		©	1	Uptown Festival	$12	Soul Train 2289
11/4/78	171	4			2	Disco Gardens	$12	Solar 2895
11/10/79+	23	36	●	©	3	Big Fun	$12	Solar 3479
1/10/81	40	36	●	©	4	Three For Love	$10	Solar 3577
10/24/81	115	15			5	Go For It	$10	Solar 3984
2/20/82	35	25	●	©	6	Friends	$10	Solar 28
8/6/83	38	23		©	7	The Look	$10	Solar 60239
12/8/84+	90	24		©	8	Heart Break	$10	Solar 60385

Amnesia (8) *73*
Appeal (5)
Attention To My Baby (4)
Beautiful Night (1)
Cindy, Cindy (2)
Closer (7)
Dancing In The Sheets (8) *17*
Dead Giveaway (7) *22*
Deceiver (8)
Disappearing Act (7)
Don't Get Stopped In Beverly Hills (1)
Don't Try To Change Me (6)
Final Analysis (5)
Forever Came Today (1)
Friends (6)
Full Of Fire (4) *55*
Girl (3)
Go For It (5)
Good Feelings (8)
Heart Break (8)
Help Me (6)
High On Life (1)
I Can Make You Feel Good (6)
I Don't Wanna Be The Last To Know (8)
I Just Stopped By Because I Had To (6)
I Owe You One (3)
Inky Dinky Wang Dang Doo (1)
Leave It All Up To Love (2)
Let's Find The Time For Love (3)
Look, The (7)
Lovely Lady (8)
Make That Move (4) *60*
Melody (An Erotic Affair) (8)
My Girl Loves Me (8)
Night To Remember (6) *44*
No Limits (The Now Club) (7)
On Top Of The World (6)
Ooh Baby, Baby (1)
Over And Over (7)
Playing To Win (6)
Pop Along Kid (4)
Right Here (7)
Right In The Socket (3)
Right Time For Us (3)
Rocker (5)
Second Time Around (3) *8*
Shalamar Disco Gardens (2)
Some Things Never Change (4)
Somewhere There's A Love (4)
Stay Close To Love (2)
Sweeter As The Days Go By (5)
Take Me To The River (3)
Take That To The Bank (2) *79*
Talk To Me (5)
There It Is (6)
This Is For The Lover In You (4)
Tossing, Turning And Swinging (2)
Uptown Festival (Part 1) (1) *25*
Whenever You Need Me (8)
Work It Out (4)
You Can Count On Me (7)
You Know (1)
You Won't Miss Love (Until It's Gone) (7)
You're The One For Me (7)
You've Got Me Running (5)

SHAMEN, The   '92

Techno-rave dance group from Aberdeen, Scotland: brothers Derek and Keith McKenzie, Richard West, Colin Angus, Will Sinnott and Peter Stephenson. Sinnott drowned on 5/23/90 (age 31).

DEBUT	PEAK	WKS		CD		Album Title	$	Label & Number
2/1/92	138	8		©		En-Tact	$10	Epic 48722

Evil Is Even
Hear Me
Human NRG
Hyperreal Orbit
Hyperreal Selector
Lightspan
Lightspan Soundwave
Make It Mine
Make It Minimal
Move Any Mountain (Progen 91) *38*
Omega Amigo
Oxygen Restriction
Possible Worlds
666 Edit

SHANA   '90

Born Shana Petrone on 5/8/72 in Parkridge, Illinois; raised in Ft. Lauderdale, Florida. Female dance singer.

DEBUT	PEAK	WKS		CD		Album Title	$	Label & Number
1/27/90	165	11		©		I Want You	$10	Vision 3316

All Of Me
Best Part Of Breaking Up
Falling Slowly
(Hey Boy) Tell Me Why
I Want You *40*
I'd Do Anything For Your Love
I'm In Love
Is This Love (An Illusion)
You Can't Get Away *82*
Zero To Sixty

SHA NA NA   '73

Rock and roll group specializing in 1950's-style music. Core members: John "Bowzer" Bauman, Scott Powell, Johnny Contardo, Fred Greene, Don York and Rich Joffe. Group hosted own TV show variety from 1977-81.

DEBUT	PEAK	WKS		CD	#	Album Title		$	Label & Number
12/13/69	183	7		©	1	Rock & Roll Is Here To Stay!		$15	Kama Sutra 2010
8/7/71	122	9			2	Sha Na Na	[L]	$15	Kama Sutra 2034
						side 1: recorded live on 3/1/71 at Columbia University in New York City; side 2: studio			
7/1/72	156	14			3	The Night Is Still Young		$15	Kama Sutra 2050
4/21/73	38	24	●		4	The Golden Age Of Rock 'N' Roll	[L]	$20	Kama Sutra 2073 [2]
12/1/73+	140	11			5	From The Streets Of New York	[L]	$15	Kama Sutra 2075
						recorded on 8/29/73 in Central Park			
6/1/74	165	6			6	Hot Sox		$15	Kama Sutra 2600
8/9/75	162	4			7	Sha Na Now		$15	Kama Sutra 2605
11/13/99	27 [C]	1		©	8	Halloween Oldies Party		$10	Madacy 0358

At The Hop (4)
Bad Boy (6)
Basement Party (7)
Bless My Soul (3)
Blue Moon (2,4)
Boney Maroney (8)
Book Of Love (1)
Bounce In Your Buggy (3)
Breaking Up Is Hard To Do (7)
Canadian Money (2)
Chances Are (6)
Chantilly Lace (1)
Charlie Brown (8)
Chills In My Spine (7)
Circles Of Love (7)
Come Go With Me (1,5)
Da Doo Ron Ron (8)
Depression (2)
Don't Want To Say Goodbye (7)
Don't You Just Know It (6)
Dreams Come True (6)
Duke Of Earl (2)
Earth Angel (5)
Easier Said Than Done (6)
Get A Job (4,5)
Glasses (3)
Goodnight Sweetheart (5)
Great Balls Of Fire (2,4)
Heartbreak Hotel (1,4)
High School Confidential (5)
His Latest Flame (4)
Hot Sox (6)
Hound Dog (4)
I Wonder Why (2,4)
In The Still Of The Night (3)
It Ain't Love (3)
It's What You Do With What You Got (3)
Itsy Bitsy Teeny Weeny Yellow Polka Dot Bikini (8)
Jailhouse Rock (2,4)
Just A Friend (2)
(Just Like) Romeo And Juliet (6,7) *55*
Little Darlin' (1,4)
Little Girl Of Mine (1)
Long Tall Sally (1)
Lover's Question (4)
Lovers Never Say Goodbye (1,4)
Maybe I'm Old Fashioned (6)
Monster Mash (8)
Oh! Lonesome Boy (3)
Only One Song (2)
Party Lights (7)
Pretty Little Angel Eyes (4)
Purple People Eater (8)
Rama Lama Ding Dong (4)
Remember Then (1)
Ring Around Your Neck (5)
Rock And Roll Is Here To Stay (1,2,4)
Rock Around The Clock (4)
Rockin' Robin (3)
Ruin Me Blues (2)
Runaround Sue (4)
Runaway (4)
Sea Cruise (3,4)
Sh-Boom (Life Could Be A Dream) (5,6)
Sha Bumpin' (7)
Shake, Rattle 'N' Roll (4)
Shanghied (7)
Shot Down In Denver (7)
Silhouettes (1)
Sixteen Candles (4)
Sleepin' On A Song (3)
So Fine - You're So Fine (3)
Splish Splash (5,8)
Stroll All Night (6)
Summertime Summertime (5)
Sunday Morning Radio (3)
Tears On My Pillow (4)
Teen Angel (1)
Teenager In Love (1,4)
Tell Laura I Love Her (2,4)
Too Chubby To Boogie (6)
Top Forty (Of The Lord) (2) *84*
Tossin' And Turnin' (5)
(Vote Song) (3)
Walk Don't Run (4)
Wanderer, The (5)
Whole Lotta Shakin' Goin' On (4)
Why Do Fools Fall In Love (4)
Wild Weekend (7)
Witch Doctor (8)
Wooly Bully (8)
Yakety Yak (2,4)
You Can Bet They Do (3)
You Talk Too Much (6)
You're The Only Light On My Horizon Now (7)
Young Love (1)

SHANGRI-LAS, The   '65

Vocal group from Queens, New York. Consisted of two sets of sisters: Mary and Betty Weiss, and twins Mary Ann and Marge Ganser. Mary Ann died of encephalitis in 1971 (age 27). Marge died of cancer on 7/28/96 (age 48).

DEBUT	PEAK	WKS		CD		Album Title	$	Label & Number
3/13/65	109	6		©		Leader Of The Pack	$150	Red Bird 101

side 2 has live sounds dubbed in

Bull Dog
Give Him A Great Big Kiss *18*
Good Night, My Love, Pleasant Dreams
It's Easier To Cry
Leader Of The Pack *1*
Maybe *91*
Remember (Walkin' In The Sand) *5*
Shout
So Much In Love
Twist And Shout
What Is Love
You Can't Sit Down

SHANICE '99

Born Shanice Wilson on 5/14/73 in Pittsburgh; raised in Los Angeles. Female R&B singer.

DEBUT	PEAK	WKS		CD	Album			$	Label & Number
11/28/87+	149	18		©	1 Discovery			$10	A&M 5128

SHANICE WILSON

1/18/92	83	26	●	©	2 Inner Child			$10	Motown 6319
7/9/94	184	3		©	3 21...Ways To Grow			$10	Motown 0302
3/27/99	56	14		©	4 Shanice			$10	LaFace 26058

Ace Boon Coon (3) · Ain't Got No Remedy (4) · **(Baby Tell Me) Can You Dance** (1) *50* · Do I Know You (1) · Doin' My Thang (4) · Don't Break My Heart (3) · Don't Fight It (4) · Fall For You (4) · Fly Away (4) · Forever In Your Love (2) · Give Me The Love I Need (3) · He's So Cute (1) · I Hate To Be Lonely (2) · I Like (3) · **I Love Your Smile** (2) *2* · I Think I Love You (1) · I Wanna Give It To You (3) · I Wish (3) · I'll Be There (3) · I'll Bet She's Got A Boyfriend (1) · I'm Cryin' (2) · Just A Game (1) · Lovin' You (2) · Never Changing Love (3) · No 1/2 Steppin' (1) · Peace In The World (2) · Reason, A (4) · **Silent Prayer** (2) *31* · Somebody Else (4) · Somewhere (3) · Spend Some Time With Me (1) · Stop Cheatin' On Me (2) · Turn Down The Lights (3) · Wanna Hear You Say (4) · Way You Love Me (1) · **When I Close My Eyes** (4) *12* · When I Say That I Love You (3) · Yesterday (4) · You Ain't All That (2) · You Can Bounce (4) · You Didn't Think I'd Come Back This Hard (2) · You Need A Man (4) · You Were The One (2)

SHANK, Bud '66

Born Clifford Shank on 5/27/26 in Dayton, Ohio. Jazz saxophonist.

| 2/12/66 | 56 | 21 | | | Michelle | | [I] | $20 | World Pacific 21840 |

As Tears Go By · Blue On Blue · Girl · **Michelle** *65* · Petite Fleur (Little Flower) · Sounds Of Silence · Turn! Turn! Turn! (To Everything There Is A Season) · Umbrellas Of Cherbourg (I Will Wait For You), Love Theme · Yesterday · You Didn't Have To Be So Nice

SHANKAR, Ravi '68

Born on 4/7/20 in Benares, India. Classical sitarist.

| 7/15/67 | 161 | 7 | | © | 1 West Meets East | | [I] | $20 | Angel 36418 |

YEHUDI MENUHIN & RAVI SHANKAR

7/29/67	148	7		©	2 Ravi Shankar In New York		[I]	$20	World Pacific 21441
11/18/67+	43	19		©	3 Ravi Shankar At The Monterey International Pop Festival		[I-L]	$20	World Pacific 21442
8/3/68	140	4		©	4 Ravi Shankar In San Francisco		[I-L]	$20	World Pacific 21449
1/11/75	176	3			5 Shankar Family & Friends			$12	Dark Horse 22002

produced by **George Harrison**

Dawn: Awakening (5) · Dawn: Peace & Hope (5) · Dhun (A Morning Raga In Sindhi Bhairavi) (5) · Dhun (Dadra And Fast Teental) (3) · Dream: Festivity & Joy (1,5) · Dream: Love-Dance Ecstasy (1,5) · I Am Missing You (5) · Jaya Jagadish Hare (5) · Kahan Gayelava Shyam Salone (5) · Nata Bhairavi (2) · Nightmare: Despair & Sorrow (5) · Nightmare: Disillusionment & Frustration (5) · Nightmare: Dispute & Violence (5) · Nightmare: Lust (5) · Overture (5) · Prabhati (Raga Gunkali) (1) · Raga Bariragi (2) · Raga Bhimpalasi (3) · Raga Bhupal Todi (4) · Raga Marwa (2) · Raga Puriya Kalyan (1) · Sonata No. 3 In A Minor, Op. 25 (1) · Supane Me Aye Preetam Sainya (5) · Swara-Kakali (Raga Tilang) (1) · Tabla Solo In Ektal (3) · Tabla Solo In Shikhar Tal (4)

SHANNON '84

Born Brenda Shannon Greene in 1958 in Washington DC. Female dance singer.

| 2/11/84 | 32 | 37 | ● | | 1 Let The Music Play | | | $12 | Mirage 90134 |
| 5/25/85 | 92 | 16 | | © | 2 Do You Wanna Get Away | | | $12 | Mirage 90267 |

Bedroom Eyes (2) · **Do You Wanna Get Away** (2) *49* · Doin' What You're Doin' (2) · **Give Me Tonight** (1) *46* · It's You (1) · Let Me See Your Body Move (2) · **Let The Music Play** (1) *8* · My Heart's Divided (1) · One Man (1) · Someone Waiting Home (1) · Stop The Noise (2) · Stronger Together (2) · Sweet Somebody (1) · Urgent (2) · Why Can't We Pretend (2)

SHANNON, Del '63

Born Charles Westover on 12/30/34 in Coopersville, Michigan. Died of a self-inflicted gunshot wound on 2/8/90 (age 55). Pop singer/songwriter. Inducted into the Rock and Roll Hall of Fame in 1999.

| 6/22/63 | 12 | 26 | | © | 1 Little Town Flirt | | | $200 | Big Top 1308 |
| 12/12/81+ | 123 | 14 | | © | 2 Drop Down And Get Me | | | $12 | Elektra 568 |

produced by **Tom Petty**

Dream Baby (1) · Drop Down And Get Me (2) · Go Away Little Girl (1) · Happiness (1) · Hats Off To Larry (1) *5* · Hey Baby (1) · **Hey! Little Girl** (1) *38* · Kelly (1) · Liar (1) · Life Without You (2) · **Little Town Flirt** (1) *12* · Maybe Tomorrow (2) · Midnight Train (2) · Never Stop Tryin' (2) · Out Of Time (2) · Runaround Sue (1) · **Runaway** (1) *1* · **Sea Of Love** (2) *33* · She Thinks I Still Care (1) · Sucker For Your Love (2) · To Love Someone (2) · **Two Kind Of Teardrops** (1) *50*

SHARKEY, Feargal '86

Born on 8/13/58 in Londonderry, Northern Ireland. Pop-rock singer. Former member of **The Undertones**.

| 3/8/86 | 75 | 11 | | | Feargal Sharkey | | | $10 | A&M 5108 |

Ashes And Diamonds · Bitter Man · Don't Leave It To Nature · Ghost Train · **Good Heart** *74* · It's All Over Now · Love And Hate · Made To Measure · Someone To Somebody · You Little Thief

SHARKS '73

Rock group formed in England: Snips (vocals), Chris Spedding (guitar), Andy Fraser (bass; **Free**) and Marty Simon (drums).

| 8/25/73 | 189 | 4 | | © | First Water | | | $15 | MCA 351 |

Broke A Feeling · Brown-Eyed Boy · Doctor Love · Driving Sideways · Follow Me · Ol' Jelly Roll · Snakes And Swallowtails · Steal Away · World Park Junkies

SHARP, Dee Dee '62

Born Dione LaRue on 9/9/45 in Philadelphia. R&B singer. Married record producer Kenny Gamble in 1967.

| 6/23/62 | 44 | 17 | | | 1 It's Mashed Potato Time | | | $60 | Cameo 1018 |
| 11/17/62 | 117 | 4 | | | 2 Down To Earth | | | $60 | Cameo 1029 |

CHUBBY CHECKER/DEE DEE SHARP

(Dee Dee) Be My Girl (1) · Do You Love Me (2) · Down To Earth (2) · Eddie, My Love (1) · Gee (1) · **Gravy (For My Mashed Potatoes)** (1) *9* · Hello, Baby, Goodbye (2) · Hurry On Down (1) · I Really Don't Want To Know (2) · I Sold My Heart To The Junkman (1) · Let The Good Times Roll (2) · Love Is Strange (medley) (2) · Loving You (2) · Make Love To Me (2) · **Mashed Potato Time** (1) *2* · One Hundred Pounds Of Clay (1) · One More Time (2) · Play It Fair (2) · Pledging My Love (2) · Remember You're Mine (1) · Rockin' Good Way (To Mess Around And Fall In Love) (medley) (1) · Slow Twistin' (1) · Splish-Splash (1) · Two Lovers (2) · You Came A Long Way From St. Louis (2)

SHARP, Kevin '97

Born on 12/10/70 in Weiser, Idaho. Country singer.

| 11/23/96+ | 40 | 36 | ● | © | Measure Of A Man | | | $10 | Asylum 61930 |

I'm Already Loving You Too Much · If You Love Somebody · Love At The End Of The Road · Love Bomb · Measure Of A Man · Nobody Knows · Population 4000 Minus 1 · She's Sure Taking It Well · Somebody's Baby · Strength To Love · There's Only You

SHARPLES, Bob, and His Music '61
Born in Bury, Lancashire, England. Bandleader/arranger.

DEBUT	PEAK	WKS						$	Label & Number
10/9/61	11	25			**Pass In Review**		[I]	$25	London Phase 4 44001

Anchors Aweigh (medley)
Bells Of St. Mary's (medley)
Buckle Down, Winsocki (medley)
Caissons Go Rolling Along (medley)
Dixie (medley)
Fanfare (medley)
Indian Drums (medley)
La Marseillaise (medley)
La Ritirata Italiana (medley)
Lili Marlene (medley)
Marines' Hymn (medley)
Matilda (medley)
Meadowland (medley)
Mexican Hat Dance (medley)
Onward Christian Soldiers
Rule Britannia (medley)
Scotland The Brave (medley)
She Wore A Yellow Ribbon (medley)
Stars And Stripes Forever (medley)
U.S. Air Force (medley)
Waltzing Matilda (medley)
Wearin' Of The Green (medley)
When The Saints Go Marching In (medley)
Yankee Doodle (medley)

SHAW, Marlena '77
Born Marlena Burgess on 9/22/42 in New Rochelle, New York. Jazz-styled singer. Band vocalist with **Count Basie** from 1967-72.

DEBUT	PEAK	WKS		CD				$	Label & Number
7/5/75	159	5		©	1 **Who Is This Bitch, Anyway?**			$15	Blue Note 397
4/2/77	62	14			2 **Sweet Beginnings**			$12	Columbia 34458
4/8/78	171	4			3 **Acting Up**			$12	Columbia 35073

Davy (1)
Dreamin' (3)
Feel Like Makin' Love (1)
Go Away Little Boy (2)
I Think I'll Tell Him (2)
I Wonder (3)
I'm Back For More (3)
Johnny (2)
Look At Me, Look At You (We're Flying) (2)
Looking For Mr. Goodbar (Don't Ask To Stay Until Tomorrow), Theme From (3)
Lord Giveth And The Lord Taketh Away (1)
Loving You Was Like A Party (1)
Mama Tried (3)
Moonrise (3)
More (3)
No Deposit, No Return (2)
Pictures And Memories (2)
Places (3)
Rhythm Of Love (3)
Rose Marie (Mon Cherie) (1)
Street Walkin' Woman (medley) (1)
Sweet Beginnings (2)
Walk Softly (2)
Writing's On The Wall (2)
You (1)
You Been Away Too Long (1)
You Bring Out The Best In Me (3)
You Taught Me How To Speak In Love (1)
Yu-Ma (2)

SHAW, Robert, Chorale '58
Born on 4/30/16 in Red Bluff, California. Died of a stroke on 1/25/99 (age 82). Conductor/arranger. Not to be confused with the actor of the same name.

DEBUT	PEAK	WKS	RIAA			Catalog	Sym	$	Label & Number
12/23/57+	5	4	●		1 **Christmas Hymns And Carols**		[X]	$20	RCA Victor 1711

first charted in 1949 (#5) on RCA Victor 1077; Christmas charts: 9/'63, 31/'64, 41/'66

DEBUT	PEAK	WKS					Sym	$	Label & Number
12/22/58	13	3			2 **Christmas Hymns And Carols**		[X-R]	$20	RCA Victor 1711
5/25/59	21	1			3 **Deep River and Other Spirituals**			$15	RCA Victor 2247
4/27/63	27	10			4 **America, The Beautiful**			$15	RCA Victor 2662
12/21/63	11[X]	9			5 **The Many Moods of Christmas**		[X]	$15	RCA Victor 2684

Christmas charts: 11/'63, 29/'65, 68/'66, 28/'67

DEBUT	PEAK	WKS					Sym	$	Label & Number
12/7/68	8[X]	6			6 **Handel: Messiah**		[X]	$40	RCA Victor 6175 [3]

George Frideric Handel composed this magnificent oratorio in 1741; soloists: Richard Lewis, Thomas Paul, Judith Raskin, Florence Kopleff; Christmas charts: 8/'68, 17/'69

Ain'-A That Good News (medley) (3)
America (4)
America, The Beautiful (4)
Angels We Have Heard On High (medley) (1,2,5)
Away In A Manger (medley) (1,2,5)
Battle Hymn Of The Republic (4)
Break Forth, O Beauteous (medley) (5)
Bring A Torch, Jeanette, Isabella (medley) (1,2,5)
Carol Of The Bells (medley) (1,2)
Christmas Hymn (medley) (1,2)
Civil War-North Medley (4)
Civil War-South Medley (4)
Columbia The Gem Of The Ocean (4)
Coventry Carol (medley) (1,2)
Deck The Halls With Boughs Of Holly (medley) (1,2,5)
Deep River (medley) (3)
Didn't My Lord Deliver Daniel (medley) (3)
Dry Bones (medley) (3)
Every Time I Feel The Spirit (medley) (3)
First Noel (medley) (1,2,5)
Fum Fum Fum (medley) (5)
Go Tell It On The Mountain (medley) (1,2)
God Bless America (4)
God Rest You Merry, Gentlemen (medley) (1,2)
Good Christian Men, Rejoice (medley) (5)
Hark! The Herald Angels Sing (medley) (1,2,5)
Heav'nly Light (medley) (5)
I Saw Three Ships (medley) (5)
I Wanna Be Ready (medley) (3)
I Wonder As I Wander (medley) (1,2)
It Came Upon The Midnight Clear (medley) (1,2)
Joy To The World (medley) (1,2,5)
Lord, If I Got My Ticket (medley) (3)
March Of The Kings (medley) (5)
Messiah (6)
My Dancing Day (medley) (1,2)
My Lord, What A Morning (medley) (3)
O Come, All Ye Faithful (medley) (1,2,5)
O Come, O Come, Emanuel (medley) (1,2)
O Little Town Of Bethlehem (medley) (1,2,5)
O Sanctissima (medley) (5)
Patapan (medley) (1,2,5)
Revolutionary War Medley (4)
Service Songs Medley (4)
Set Down, Servant (medley) (3)
Shepherd's Carol (medley) (1,2)
Silent Night (medley) (1,2,5)
Soon-A Will Be Done (medley) (3)
Soon One Mornin' (medley) (3)
Star Spangled Banner (4)
Swing Low, Sweet Chariot (medley) (3)
There Is A Balm In Gilead (medley) (3)
This Little Light O' Mine (medley) (3)
This Ol' Hammer (medley) (3)
Wassail Song (medley) (1,2)
We Three Kings (medley) (1,2)
What Child Is This? (medley) (5)
Who Is That Yonder (medley) (3)

SHAW, Roland '65
Born in London. Conductor/arranger.

DEBUT	PEAK	WKS					Sym	$	Label & Number
2/27/65	38	25			1 **Themes From The James Bond Thrillers**		[I]	$20	London 412
2/5/66	119	5			2 **More Themes From The James Bond Thrillers**		[I]	$20	London 445

Arrival Of The Bomb And Countdown (2)
Dawn Raid On Fort Knox (1)
Death Of Goldfinger (2)
Dr. No's Fantasy (1)
007 Theme (1)
From Russia With Love (1)
Girl Trouble (1)
Golden Horn (1)
Goldfinger (1)
Guitar Lament (2)
Gypsy Camp (2)
James Bond Theme (1)
Kingston Calypso (2)
Leila Dances (1)
Miami (2)
Pussy Galore's Flying Circus (2)
Spectre Island (2)
Tania Meets Klebb (2)
Thunderball (2)
Twisting With James (1)
Underneath The Mango Tree (2)

SHAW, Sandie '65
Born Sandra Goodrich on 2/26/47 in Dagenham, Essex, England. Pop singer.

DEBUT	PEAK	WKS		CD				$	Label & Number
6/12/65	100	4		©	**Sandie Shaw**			$50	Reprise 6166

Baby I Need Your Lovin'
Don't Be That Way
Downtown
Everybody Loves A Lover
Girl Don't Come 42
Gotta See My Baby Every Day
I'll Stop At Nothing
It's In His Kiss
Lemon Tree
Stop Feeling Sorry For Yourself
Talk About Love
(There's) Always Something There To Remind Me 52

SHAW, Tommy '84
Born on 9/11/53 in Montgomery, Alabama. Rock singer/guitarist. Member of **Styx** and **Damn Yankees**.

DEBUT	PEAK	WKS		CD				$	Label & Number
10/20/84	50	25		©	1 **Girls With Guns**			$10	A&M 5020
10/26/85	87	9		©	2 **What If**			$10	A&M 5097

Bad Times (2)
Come In And Explain (1)
Count On You (2)
Fading Away (1)
Free To Love You (1)
Friendly Advice (2)
Girls With Guns (1) 33
Heads Up (1)
Jealousy (2)
Kiss Me Hello (1)
Little Girl World (1)
Lonely School (1) 60
Nature Of The Beast (2)
Outside In The Rain (1)
Race Is On (1)
Reach For The Bottle (2)
Remo's Theme (What If) (2) 81
See Me Now (2)
This Is Not A Test (2)
True Confessions (2)

SHEARING, George, Quintet '60
Born on 8/13/19 in London. Jazz pianist. Blind since birth.

DEBUT	PEAK	WKS		CD				$	Label & Number
10/6/56	20	1		©	1 **Velvet Carpet**		[I]	$25	Capitol 720
10/7/57	13	3		©	2 **Black Satin**		[I]	$25	Capitol 858
8/25/58	17	2		©	3 **Burnished Brass**		[I]	$25	Capitol 1038
7/25/60	11	35		©	4 **White Satin**			$25	Capitol 1334
10/30/61	82	14			5 **Satin Affair**			$25	Capitol 1628
5/5/62	27	16		©	6 **Nat King Cole sings/George Shearing plays**			$30	Capitol 1675

Affair To Remember (4)
All Of You (1)
As Long As I Live (medley) (1)
Autumn Leaves (1)
Azure-Te (5)
Basie's Masement (3)
Baubles, Bangles And Beads (5)
Beautiful Friendship (6)
Beautiful Love (3)
Black Satin (2)
Blame It On My Youth (3)
Blue Malibu (4)
Bolero #3 (5)
Burnished Brass (3)
Cheek To Cheek (3)
Cuckoo In The Clock (3)
Dancing On The Ceiling (1)
Don't Go (6)
Dream (4)
Early Autumn (5)
Fly Me To The Moon (In Other Words) (6)
Foggy Day (1)

DEBUT	PEAK	WKS	RIAA	CD		ARTIST — Album Title	Catalog	Sym	$	Label & Number

SHEARING, George, Quintet — Cont'd

Folks Who Live On The Hill (2)
Have You Met Miss Jones? (1)
Here's What I'm Here For (5)
How Long Has This Been Going On (4)
I Got It Bad And That Ain't Good (6)
I Like To Recognize The Tune (5)

I'll Close My Eyes (1)
I'll Take Romance (4)
I'm Lost (6)
If I Should Lose You (2)
If You Were Mine (3)
It's Not You (5)
Laura (4)
Let There Be Love (6)
Let's Live Again (medley) (1)

Lost April (6)
Love's Melody (4)
Lulu's Back In Town (3)
Memories Of You (3)
Midnight Sun (5)
Mine (3)
Moon Song (2)
Moonlight Becomes You (4)
My Own (5)

My Romance (5)
No Moon At All (1)
Nothing Ever Changes My Love For You (2)
Old Folks (4)
One Morning In May (2)
Party's Over (5)
Pick Yourself Up (6)
'Round Midnight (1)

September Song (1,6)
Serenata (6)
Sometimes I Feel Like A Motherless Child (3)
Star Dust (5)
Starlight Souvenirs (2)
Starlit Hour (1)
There'll Be Another Spring (4)
There's A Lull In My Life (6)

There's A Small Hotel (4)
These Things You Left Me (3)
What Is There To Say (2)
You Don't Know What Love Is (2)
You Were Never Lovelier (5)
Your Name Is Love (4)

SHeDAISY '00
Country vocal trio from Magda, Utah: sisters Kristyn, Kelsi and Kassidy Osborn.

| 5/29/99+ | 70 | 102 | ▲ | © | 1 | The Whole SheBang | | | $10 | Lyric Street 65002 |
| 11/25/00 | 92 | 8 | | © | 2 | Brand New Year | | [X] | $10 | Lyric Street 65007 |

Christmas chart: 8/'00

Before Me And You (1)
Brand New Year (My Revolution) (2)
Carol Of The Bells (medley) (2)
'Cause I Like It That Way (1)

Christmas Children (2)
Dancing With Angels (1)
Deck The Halls (2) *61*
Hark The Herald Angels Sing (medley) (1)

I Will...But (1) *43*
Jingle Bells (2)
Little Good-Byes (1) *43*
Lucky 4 You (Tonight I'm Just Me) (1) *79*

Night To Remember (1)
Punishment (2)
Santa's Got A Brand New Bag (2)
Secret Of Christmas (2)

Sleigh Ride (2)
Still Holding Out For You (1)
That's What I Want For Christmas (2)
This Woman Needs (1) *57*

Tinseltown (2)
Twist Of The Magi (2)
What Child Is This (2)
Without Your Love (1)

SHEIK, Duncan '97
Born on 11/18/69 in Hilton Head, South Carolina. Singer/songwriter/guitarist.

| 2/1/97 | 83 | 36 | ● | © | 1 | Duncan Sheik | | | $10 | Atlantic 82879 |
| 10/24/98 | 163 | 2 | | © | 2 | Humming | | | $10 | Atlantic 83138 |

Alibi (2)
Barely Breathing (1) *16*
Bite Your Tongue (2)
Body Goes Down (2)

Days Go By (1)
End Of Outside (1)
Everyone, Everywhere (1)
Home (1)

House Full Of Riches (2)
In Between (2)
In The Absence Of Sun (1)
Little Hands (1)

Nichiren (2)
Nothing Special (2)
November (1)
Out Of Order (1)

Reasons For Living (1)
Rubbed Out (2)
Serena (1)
She Runs Away (1)

That Says It All (2)
Varying Degrees Of Con-Artistry (2)

SHEILA E. '84
Born Sheila Escovedo on 12/12/59 in San Francisco. Latin singer/percussionist. With father Pete Escovedo in the band **Azteca** in the mid-1970s. Her brother Peto was in **Con Funk Shun**. Her uncle **Coke Escovedo** was a noted percussionist.

7/7/84	28	46	●	©	1	The Glamorous Life			$10	Warner 25107
9/21/85+	50	33	●	©	2	Romance 1600			$10	Paisley Park 25317
3/21/87	56	12		©	3	Sheila E.			$10	Paisley Park 25498
4/20/91	146	5		©	4	Sex Cymbal			$10	Warner 26255

Bedtime Story (2)
Belle Of St. Mark (1) *34*
Boy's Club (4)
Cry Baby (4)
Dear Michaelangelo (2)
Droppin' Like Flies (4)
808 Kate (4)

Faded Photographs (4)
Family Affair (4)
Funky Attitude (4)
Glamorous Life (1) *7*
Heaven (4)
Hold Me (3) *68*
Hon E Man (3)

Koo Koo (3)
Lady Marmalade (4)
Love Bizarre (2) *11*
Love On A Blue Train (3)
Loverboy (4)
Merci For The Speed Of A Mad Clown In Summer (2)

Mother Mary (4)
Next Time Wipe The Lipstick Off Your Collar (4)
Noon Rendezvous (1)
Oliver's House (1)
One Day (I'm Gonna Make You Mine) (3)

Pride And The Passion (3)
Private Party (Tu Para Mi) (4)
Promise Me Love (4)
Romance 1600 (2)
Sex Cymbal (4)
Shortberry Strawcake (1)
Sister Fate (2)

Soul Salsa (3)
Toy Box (2)
Wednesday Like A River (3)
What'cha Gonna Do (4)
Yellow (2)

SHELLEY, Pete '82
Born Peter McNeish on 4/17/55 in Leigh, Lancashire, England. Lead singer/guitarist of the **Buzzcocks** (1976-81).

| 6/26/82 | 121 | 10 | | © | 1 | Homosapien | | | $10 | Arista 6602 |
| 7/23/83 | 151 | 5 | | | 2 | XL1 | | | $10 | Arista 8017 |

Guess I Must Have Been In Love With Myself (1)
Homosapien (1)
I Don't Know What It Is (1)
I Generate A Feeling (1)

I Just Wanna Touch (2)
If You Ask Me (I Won't Say No) (2)
In Love With Somebody Else (1)

Just One Of Those Affairs (1)
Love In Vain (1)
Many A Time (2)
(Millions Of People) No One Like You (2)

Qu'est-Ce Que C'est Que Ca (1)
Telephone Operator (2)
Twilight (2)
What Was Heaven? (2)

Witness The Change (1)
XL 1 (2)
Yesterday's Not Here (1)
You And I (2)

You Know Better Than I Know (2)

SHELTON, Ricky Van '91
Born on 1/12/52 in Danville, Virginia; raised in Grit, Virginia. Country singer.

12/26/87+	76	41	▲	©	1	Wild-Eyed Dream			$10	Columbia 40602
10/29/88	78	24	▲	©	2	Loving Proof			$10	Columbia 44221
12/23/89+	16 [X]	3	●	©	3	Ricky Van Shelton Sings Christmas		[X]	$10	Columbia 45269
2/3/90	53	61	▲	©	4	RVS III			$10	Columbia 45250
6/8/91	23	57	▲	©	5	Backroads			$10	Columbia 46855
5/23/92	122	24	●	©	6	Don't Overlook Salvation			$10	Columbia 46854
8/29/92	50	31	▲	©	7	Greatest Hits Plus		[G]	$10	Columbia 52753
9/11/93	91	8	●	©	8	A Bridge I Didn't Burn			$10	Columbia 48992

After The Lights Go Out (5)
Baby, I'm Ready (1)
Backroads (5)
Bridge I Didn't Burn (8)
Call Me Up (5)
Christmas (3)
Christmas Long Ago (3)
Country Christmas (3)
Crazy Over You (1)
Crime Of Passion (1)
Don't Overlook Salvation (6)
Don't Send Me No Angels (2)
Don't We All Have The Right (1,7)
Family Bible (6)
From A Jack To A King (2,7)

He's Got You (2)
Heartache Big As Texas (8)
Hole In My Pocket (2)
Holy (I Bowed On My Knees And Cried Holy) (6)
I Am A Simple Man (5,7)
I Don't Care (1)
I Know The Way By Broken Heart (8)
I Meant Every Word He Said (4)
I Saw A Man (6)
I Shall Not Be Moved (6)
I Still Love You (4)
I Wouldn't Take Nothin' For My Journey (6)
I'll Be Home For Christmas (3)

I'll Leave This World Loving You (2,7)
I'm Starting Over (4)
I've Cried My Last Tear For You (4,7)
If It Weren't For Me (8)
If They Turn Off Our Lights (8)
If You're Ever In My Arms (5)
Just As I Am (6,7)
Keep It Between The Lines (5,7)
Let Me Live With Love (And Die With You) (2)
Life Turned Her That Way (1,7)
Life's Little Ups And Downs (4)
Linda Lu (8)

Living Proof (2,7)
Love Is Burnin' (4)
Mansion Over The Hilltop (6)
My First Reaction (8)
Not That I Care (2)
Oh Heart Of Mine (5)
Oh Pretty Woman (4)
Old Rugged Cross (6)
Picture, The (2)
Please Come Home For Christmas (3)
Pretty Paper (3)
Rockin' Years (5,7)
Roses After The Rain (8)
Santa Claus Is Coming To Town (3)

Silent Night (3)
Silver Bells (3)
Some Things Are Better Left Alone (5)
Somebody Lied (1,7)
Somebody's Back In Town (2)
Statue Of A Fool (4,7)
Still Got A Couple Of Good Years Left (8)
Supper Time (6)
Sweet Memories (4)
Swimming Upstream (2)
Talking To God (8)
To My Mansion In The Sky (6)
Ultimately Fine (1)

Wear My Ring Around Your Neck (7)
What Child Is This (3)
Where Was I (8)
White Christmas (3)
Who'll Turn Out The Lights (5)
Wild-Eyed Dream (1)
Wild Man (7)
Working Man Blues (1)
You Would Do The Same For Me (4)

SHENANDOAH '95
Country group formed in Muscle Shoals, Alabama: Marty Raybon (vocals), Jim Seales (guitar), Stan Thorn (keyboards), Ralph Ezell (bass) and Mike McGuire (drums).

| 7/13/91 | 186 | 4 | ● | © | 1 | Extra Mile | | | $10 | Columbia 45490 |
| 2/25/95 | 182 | 4 | | © | 2 | In The Vicinity Of The Heart | | | $10 | Liberty 31109 |

Always Have, Always Will (2)
Cabin Fever (2)

Call It Love (2)
Daddy's Little Man (2)

Darned If I Don't (Danged If I Do) (2)

Every Fire (2)
Ghost In This House (2)

Goin' Down With My Pride (1)
Heaven Bound (I'm Ready) (2)

I Got You (1)
I Wouldn't Know (2)

787

DEBUT	PEAK	WKS	RIAA	CD		ARTIST — Album Title	Catalog Sym	$	Label & Number

SHENANDOAH — Cnt'd

Moon Over Georgia (1)
Next To You, Next To Me (1)
Puttin' New Roots Down (1)
She Could Care Less (2)
She Makes The Coming Home (Worth The Being Gone) (1)
She's A Natural (1)
Somewhere In The Vicinity Of The Heart (2)
When You Were Mine (1)
You Can Say That (2)

SHEPARD, Vonda '98
Born on 7/7/63 in New York City; raised in Los Angeles. Singer/songwriter/keyboardist. Has a recurring role as a singer on TV's *Ally McBeal*.

5/23/98	7	41	▲	©	1	Songs From Ally McBeal	[TV]	$10	550 Music 69365
5/8/99	79	9		©	2	By 7:30		$10	Jacket 2222
11/27/99	60	14	●	©	3	Heart And Soul - New Songs From Ally McBeal	[TV]	$10	550 Music 63915
12/2/00	59	6		©	4	Ally McBeal: A Very Ally Christmas	[X-TV]	$10	550 Music 85196

includes "Santa Claus Got Stuck In My Chimney" by Lisa Nicole Carson, "River" by Robert Downey, Jr., "Santa Baby" by Calista Flockhart, "Winter Wonderland" by Macy Gray, and "I Saw Mommy Kissing Santa Claus" and "Run, Rudolph, Run" by Jane Krakowski; Christmas chart: 9/00

5/12/01	34	11		©	5	Ally McBeal: For Once In My Life	[TV]	$10	Epic 85195

includes "Snakes" by Robert Downey, Jr., "Every Breath You Take" by Robert Downey, Jr. & Sting, "How Can You Mend A Broken Heart" by Al Green, "When The Heartache Is Over" by Tina Turner, and "You're The First, The Last, My Everything" by Barry White

Alone Again (Naturally) (5)
Ask The Lonely (1)
Baby, Don't You Break My Heart Slow (2,3)
By 7:30 (2)
Can We Still Be Friends (5)
Chances Are (5)
Clear (2)
Confetti (2,3)
Cross To Bear (2)
Crying (3)
Don't Think Twice, It's All Right (5)
End Of The World (1)
For Once In My Life (5)
Have Yourself A Merry Little Christmas (4)
Home Again (5)
Hooked On A Feeling (1)
100 Tears Away (3)
I Know Him By Heart (3)
I Only Want To Be With You (1)
It's In His Kiss (The Shoop Shoop Song) (1)
Let It Snow, Let It Snow, Let It Snow (4)
Love Is Alive (5)
Man With The Bag (4)
Maryland (1)
Mercy (2)
Neighborhood (1)
Newspaper Wife (2)
Please Come Home For Christmas (4)
Read Your Mind (3)
Reason To Believe (5)
Sail On By (2)
Searchin' My Soul (1)
Silver Bells (4)
Someday We'll Be Together (3)
Someone You Use (1)
Soothe Me (2)
Souvenir (2)
Sweet Inspiration (5)
Tell Him (1)
This Christmas (4)
This Is Crazy Now (2,3)
This Old Heart Of Mine (Is Weak For You) (5)
To Sir, With Love (3)
Venus Is Breaking (2)
Vincent (Starry Starry Night) (3)
Walk Away Renee (1)
What Are You Doing New Year's Eve (4)
What Becomes Of The Brokenhearted (3)
White Christmas (4)
Wildest Times Of The World (1)
Will You Marry Me? (1)
World Without Love (3)
You And Me (2,5)
You Belong To Me (1)

SHEPHERD, Kenny Wayne '99
Born on 6/12/77 in Shreveport, Louisiana. Blues-rock guitarist. His band: Noah Hunt (vocals), Robby Emerson (bass) and Sam Bryant (drums). Keith Christopher replaced Emerson in 1998.

1/27/96	108	33	●	©	1	Ledbetter Heights		$10	Giant 24621

KENNY WAYNE SHEPHERD BAND:

10/25/97	74	62	▲	©	2	Trouble Is...		$10	Giant 24689
10/30/99	52	6	●	©	3	Live On		$10	Giant 24729

Aberdeen (1)
Blue On Black (2) 78
Born With A Broken Heart (1)
Chase The Rainbow (2)
Deja Voodoo (3)
Electric Lullaby (3)
Every Time It Rains (3)
Everybody Gets The Blues (1)
Everything Is Broken (2)
I Don't Live Today (1)
I Found Love (When I Found You) (1)
I'm Leaving You (Commit A Crime) (1)
In 2 Deep (3)
King's Highway (2)
Last Goodbye (2)
Ledbetter Heights (1)
(Let Me Up) I've Had Enough (1)
Live On (3)
(Long) Gone (2)
Losing Kind (3)
Never Mind (3)
Nothing To Do With Love (2)
Oh Well (3)
One Foot On The Path (1)
Riverside (1)
Shame, Shame, Shame (1)
Shotgun Blues (3)
Slow Ride (2)
Somehow, Somewhere, Someway (2)
Them Changes (3)
Trouble Is... (2)
True Lies (2)
Was (3)
What's Goin' Down (1)
Where Was I? (3)
While We Cry (1)
Wild Love (3)
You Should Know Better (3)

SHEPPARD, T.G. '81
Born William Browder on 7/20/44 in Humbolt, Tennessee. Country singer.

4/25/81	119	12			1	I Love 'Em All		$10	Warner/Curb 3528
1/30/82	152	13			2	Finally!		$10	Warner/Curb 3600
6/11/83	189	3			3	T.G. Sheppard's Greatest Hits	[G]	$10	Warner/Curb 23841

All My Cloudy Days Are Gone (2)
Crazy In The Dark (2)
Do You Wanna Go To Heaven (3)
Face The Night Alone (1)
Finally (2,3) 58
I Loved 'Em Every One (1,3) 37
I Wish You Could Have Turned My Head (And Left My Heart Alone) (2)
I'll Be Coming Back For More (3)
In Another Minute (2)
Last Cheater's Waltz (3)
Only One You (2,3) 68
Party Time (1,3)
She's Got Everything It Takes (To Make Me Stay) (2)
Silence On The Line (1)
State Of Our Union (1)
Touch Me All Over Again (1)
Troubled Waters (1)
War Is Hell (On The Homefront Too) (3)
Wasn't It A Short Forever (2)
We Belong In Love Tonight (1)
We're Walking On Thin Ice (2)
What's Forever For (1)
Without You (3)
You Feel Good All Over (3)
You Waltzed Yourself Right Into My Life (1)
You're The First To Last (This Long) (2)

SHERBS '81
Pop-rock group from Australia: Daryl Braithwaite (vocals), Harvey James (guitar), Garth Porter (keyboards), Tony Mitchell (bass) and Alan Sandow (drums). Group originally known as Sherbet.

2/28/81	100	16		©		The Skill		$12	Atco 137

Back To Zero
Cindy Is Waiting
Crazy In The Night
I Have The Skill 61
I'll Be Faster
I'm O.K.
Into The Heat
Juliet And Me
Love You To Death
Never Surrender
No Turning Back
Parallel Bars

SHERIDAN, Tony — see BEATLES, The

SHERIFF '89
Pop-rock group from Toronto: Freddy Curci (vocals), Steve DeMarchi (guitar), Arnold Lanni (keyboards), Wolf Hassel (bass) and Rob Elliott (drums). Disbanded in 1983. Hassel and Lanni formed **Frozen Ghost**. Curci and DeMarchi formed **Alias**.

1/7/89	60	14		©		Sheriff		$10	Capitol 91216

originally "Bubbled Under" on 6/25/83 (#210) on Capitol 12227

California
Crazy Without You
Elisa
Give Me Rock 'N' Roll
Kept Me Coming
Living For A Dream
Makin' My Way
Mama's Baby
When I'm With You 1
You Remind Me

★391★ SHERMAN, Allan '63
Born Allan Copelon on 11/30/24 in Chicago. Died on 11/21/73 (age 48). Novelty singer/songwriter. Creator/producer of TV's *I've Got A Secret*.

11/3/62	❶²	51	●		1	My Son, The Folk Singer	[C]	$25	Warner 1475
1/19/63	❶¹	47			2	My Son, The Celebrity	[C]	$25	Warner 1487
8/17/63	❶⁸	32			3	My Son, The Nut	[C]	$25	Warner 1501
4/11/64	25	19			4	Allan In Wonderland	[C]	$25	Warner 1539
11/21/64+	53	14			5	Peter And The Commissar	[C]	$25	RCA Victor 2773

ALLAN SHERMAN/BOSTON POPS/ARTHUR FIEDLER

11/28/64+	32	17			6	For Swingin' Livers Only!	[C]	$25	Warner 1569

SHERMAN, Allan — Cont'd

12/18/65+	88	11			7 **My Name Is Allan**	[C]		$25	Warner 1604

Al 'N Yetta (2)
America's A Nice Italian Name (6)
Automation (3)
Average Song (7)
Ballad Of Harry Lewis (1)
Barry Is The Baby's Name (medley) (2)
Beautiful Teamsters (6)
Bronx Bird Watcher (2)
(Bye Bye Blackbird) Bye Bye Blumberg (6)
(C'est Si Bon) I See Bones (3)
Call Me Irresponsible (Call Me) (7)
Chim Chim Cheree (7)

Continental (The Painless Dentist Song) (7)
Drinking Man's Diet (7) 98
Drop-Outs March (4)
End Of A Symphony (5)
(Five Foot Two, Eyes Of Blue) Eight Foot Two, Solid Blue (3)
Get On The Garden Freeway (medley) (2)
Go To Sleep, Paul Revere! (7)
Good Advice (4)
(Green Eyes) Green Stamps (4)
Grow, Mrs. Goldfarb (6)
Hail To Thee, Fat Person (3)
Harvey And Sheila (6)
(Heart) Skin (4)

(Heartaches) Headaches (3)
Hello Mudduh, Hello Fadduh! (A Letter From Camp) (3) 2
Here's To The Crabgrass (3)
(Holiday For Strings) Holiday For States (4)
Horowitz (medley) (2)
Hungarian Goulash No. 5 (3)
I Can't Dance (4)
It's A Most Unusual Day (It's A Most Unusual Play) (7)
J.C. Cohen (6)
Jump Down, Spin Around (Pick A Dress O' Cotton) (1)
Kiss Of Myer (6)
Laarge Daark Aardvark Song (7)

Let's All Call Up A.T.&T. And Protest To The President March (2)
Little Butterball (4)
Lotsa Luck (4)
(Love Is Here to Stay) Your Mother's Here To Stay (6)
Me (2)
Mexican Hat Dance (2)
My Zelda (1)
Night And Day (With Punctuation Marks) (4)
No One's Perfect (2)
Oh Boy (1)
One Hippopotami (3)
Peter And The Commissar (5)
Peyton Place, U.S.A. (7)

Pop Hates The Beatles (6)
(Rag Mop) Rat Fink (3)
Sarah Jackman (3)
Secret Love (Secret Code) (7)
Seltzer Boy (1)
Shake Hands With Your Uncle Max (1)
(Shine On Harvest Moon) Shine On, Harvey Bloom (6)
Shticks And Stones (1)
Shticks Of One And Half A Dozen Of The Other (2)
Sir Greenbaum's Madrigal (1)
(Smiles) Pills (6)
Streets Of Miami (1)
That Old Black Magic (That Old Back Scratcher) (7)

Twelve Gifts Of Christmas (6)
Variations On "How Dry I Am" (5)
When I Was A Lad (2)
Won't You Come Home Disraeli? (2)
(You Came A Long Way From St. Louis) You Went The Wrong Way, Old King Louie (3)
You Need An Analyst (7)
(You're Getting To Be A Habit With Me) You're Getting To Be A Rabbit With Me (3)

SHERMAN, Bobby   '70

Born on 7/22/43 in Santa Monica, California. Pop singer/actor. Regular on TV's *Shindig*. Played "Jeremy Bolt" on TV's *Here Come The Brides*.

11/8/69+	11	35	●	©	1 **Bobby Sherman**			$15	Metromedia 1014
4/11/70	10	48	●	©	2 **Here Comes Bobby**			$15	Metromedia 1028
10/24/70	20	26	●	©	3 **With Love, Bobby**			$15	Metromedia 1032
4/24/71	48	14		©	4 **Portrait Of Bobby**			$15	Metromedia 1040
10/9/71	71	8		©	5 **Getting Together**			$15	Metromedia 1045
12/25/71+	2¹ˣ	5		©	6 **Bobby Sherman Christmas Album**		[X]	$15	Metromedia 1038
					Christmas charts: 2/'70, 11/'71				
3/25/72	83	9		©	7 **Bobby Sherman's Greatest Hits**		[G]	$15	Metromedia 1048

Amen (6)
August (4)
Blame It On The Pony Express (5)
Blue Christmas (6)
Bluechip (1)
Bubble Gum And Braces (4)
Christmas Is (Make It Sweet) (6)
Christmas On Her Mind (6)
Christmas Wish (6)
Come Close To Me (2)
Cried Like A Baby (4,7) 16

Drum, The (4,7) 29
Easy Come, Easy Go (2,7) 9
Fun And Games (2)
Getting Together (5,7)
Goin' Home (Sing A Song Of Christmas Cheer) (6)
Good For Each Other (3)
Goodtime Song (5)
Hey, Honey Bun (2)
Hey, Mister Sun (3,7) 24
I Think I'm Gonna Be Alright (4)
I Think I'm Gonna Rain (3)
I'll Never Let You Go (3)
I'm In A Tree (4)

I'm Still Looking For The Right Girl (4)
Is Anybody There (4)
It Boggles The Mind (5)
Jennifer (5,7) 60
Jingle Bell Rock (6)
Julie, Do Ya Love Me (3,7) 5
July Seventeen (2)
La La La (If I Had You) (2,7) 9
Lady Is Waiting (2)
Land Of Make Believe (1)
Little Woman (1,7) 3
Love (1)
Love's Been Good To Me (4)

Love's What You're Gettin' For Christmas (6)
Make Your Own Kind Of Music (2)
Marching To The Music (5)
Maybe You Know Something I Don't Know (4)
Message To My Brother (3)
Oh, It Must Be Love (5)
Oklahoma City Times (3)
One Too Many Mornings (1)
Rainy Day Thought (1)
Run Away (1)
Santa Claus Is Comin' To Town (6)

Seattle (1,7)
She's A Lady (2)
Show Me (3)
Song Of Joy (6)
Sounds Along The Way (1)
Spend Some Time Lovin' Me (3,7)
Step My Way (4)
Sweet Gingerbread Man (3)
Sweet Touch Of Life (4)
This Guy's In Love With You (1)
Time (1)
Time For Us (Love Theme from Romeo And Juliet) (1)

Tired Soul (5)
Turtles And Trees (2)
Two Blind Minds (2)
Waiting At The Bus Stop (5,7) 54
Where Did That Little Girl Go? (5)
Wherefore And Why (4)
Yesterday's Christmas (6)

SHINEHEAD   '90

Born Edmund Carl Aiken on 4/10/62 in London; raised in Jamaica and the Bronx, New York. Reggae rapper.

11/5/88	185	4		©	1 **Unity**			$10	Elektra 60802
7/28/90	155	5		©	2 **The Real Rock**			$10	Elektra 60890

Chain Gang-Rap (1)
Cigarette Breath (2)
Dance Down The Road (2)
Do It With Ease (1)

Family Affair (2)
Gimme No Crack (1)
Golden Touch (1)
Good Things (2)

Hello Y'all (1)
Know How Fe Chat (1)
Love And Marriage Rap (2)
Musical Madness (2)

Potential (2)
Raggamuffin (1)
Real Rock (2)
Strive (2)

Till I Kissed You (2)
Truth, The (1)
Unity, The (1)
Who The Cap Fits (1)

World Of The Video Game (2)

SHIRELLES, The   '63

Female R&B vocal group from Passaic, New Jersey: Shirley Owens Alston, Beverly Lee, Doris Kenner and Addie "Micki" Harris. Harris died on 6/10/82 (age 42). Kenner died of cancer on 2/4/2000 (age 58). Group inducted into the Rock and Roll Hall of Fame in 1996.

5/5/62	59	13		©	1 **Baby It's You**			$100	Scepter 504
1/26/63	19	49		©	2 **The Shirelles Greatest Hits**		[G]	$100	Scepter 505
6/29/63	68	9		©	3 **Foolish Little Girl**			$100	Scepter 511

Abra Ka Dabra (3)
Baby It's You (1,2) 8
Big John (1,2) 21
Blue Holiday (2)
Dedicated To The One I Love (2) 3
Don't Say Goodnight And Mean Goodbye (3) 26

Everybody Loves A Lover (2) 19
Foolish Little Girl (3) 4
Hard Times (3)
I Didn't Mean To Hurt You (1)
I Don't Think So (3)
Irresistible You (1)
It's Love That Really Counts (2)

Make The Night A Little Longer (1)
Mama Said (2) 4
Not For All The Money In The World (3) 100
Only When I Will Tell (3)
Ooh Poo Pah Doo (3)
Putty In Your Hands (1)

Same Old Story (1)
Soldier Boy (1,2) 1
Stop The Music (2) 36
Talk Is Cheap (3)
Thing Of The Past (1,2) 41
Things I Want To Hear (Pretty Words) (1)
Tonights The Night (2) 39

Twenty One (1)
Twistin' U.S.A. (1)
Twitch, The (3)
Voice Of Experience (1)
Welcome Home Baby (2) 22
What A Sweet Thing That Was (2) 54
What's The Matter Baby (3)

Will You Love Me Tomorrow (2) 1

SHIRLEY, Don   '55

Born on 1/27/27 in Kingston, Jamaica. Pianist/organist.

4/2/55	14	4		©	1 **Tonal Expressions**		[I]	$50	Cadence 1001

Answer Me My Love
Dancing On The Ceiling
I Cover The Waterfront

Love Is Here To Stay
Man I Love
My Funny Valentine

"New Faces" Medley
No Two People
Secret Love

They Can't Take That Away From Me

SHIRLEY (AND COMPANY)   '75

Disco group: Shirley Goodman (female vocals), Jesus Alvarez (male vocals), Walter Morris (guitar), Bernadette Randle (keyboards), Seldon Powell (sax), Jonathan Williams (bass) and Clarence Oliver (drums). Goodman was half of Shirley & Lee duo.

8/2/75	169	3		©	1 **Shame Shame Shame**			$12	Vibration 128

Another Tear Will Fall
Cry Cry Cry 91

Disco Shirley
I Gotta Get Next To You

I Guess Things Have To Change
Keep On Rolling On

Jim Doc Kay
Love Is

Shame, Shame, Shame 12

SHOCKED, Michelle   '89

Born Michelle Johnston on 2/24/62 in Dallas. Folk singer/songwriter.

9/17/88+	73	35		©	1 **Short Sharp Shocked**			$10	Mercury 834294
11/11/89	95	26		©	2 **Captain Swing**			$10	Mercury 838878

SHOCKED, Michelle — Cont'd

Anchorage (1) 66	God Is A Real Estate Developer (2)	L&N Don't Stop Here Anymore (1)	Memories Of East Texas (1)	Streetcorner Ambassador (2)

Anchorage (1) *66*
Black Widow (1)
Cement Lament (2)
(Don't You Mess Around With) My Little Sister (2)

God Is A Real Estate Developer (2)
Graffiti Limbo (1)
Hello Hopeville (1)
If Love Was A Train (1)

L&N Don't Stop Here Anymore (1)
Looks Like Mona Lisa (2)
(Making The Run To) Gladewater (1)

Memories Of East Texas (1)
Must Be Luff (2)
On The Greener Side (2)
Silent Ways (2)
Sleep Keeps Me Awake (2)

Streetcorner Ambassador (2)
Too Little Too Late (2)
V.F.D. (1)
When I Grow Up (1)

SHOCKING BLUE, The '70

Pop-rock group from Holland: Mariska Veres (vocals), Robbie Leeuwen (guitar), Klaasje Wal (bass) and Cor Beek (drums). Beek died on 4/2/98 (age 49).

| 2/14/70 | 31 | 17 | | | The Shocking Blue .... | | | $25 | Colossus 1000 |

Acka Ragh
Bool Weevil

Butterfly And I
California Here I Come

I'm A Woman
Long And Lonesome Road *75*

Love Buzz
Love Machine

Mighty Joe *43*
Poor Boy

Send Me A Postcard
Venus *1*

SHOES '79

Rock group from Zion, Illinois: Gary Klebe (vocals), brothers Jeff (guitar) and John (bass) Murphy, and Skip Meyer (drums).

| 10/13/79 | 50 | 12 | © | 1 | Present Tense .... | | | $12 | Elektra 244 |
| 2/7/81 | 140 | 7 | © | 2 | Tongue Twister .... | | | $12 | Elektra 303 |

Burned Out Love (2)
Cruel You (1)
Every Girl (1)
Found A Girl (2)

Girls Of Today (2)
Hangin' Around With You (1)
Hate To Run (2)
Hopin' She's The One (2)

I Don't Miss You (1)
I Don't Wanna Hear It (1)
In My Arms Again (1)
Karen (2)

Now And Then (1)
Only In My Sleep (2)
She Satisfies (2)
Somebody Has What I Had (1)

Things You Do (2)
Three Times Medley (1)
Tomorrow Night (1)
Too Late (1) *75*

When It Hits (2)
Yes Or No (2)
Your Imagination (2)
Your Very Eyes (1)

SHOOTING STAR '81

Rock group formed in Kansas City in 1977: Gary West (vocals), Van McLain (guitar, vocals), Bill Guffey (keyboards), Charles Waltz (violin), Ron Verlin (bass) and Steve Thomas (drums). Guffey left in mid-1982.

3/15/80	147	14	©	1	Shooting Star			$12	Virgin 13133
9/19/81	92	30	©	2	Hang On For Your Life			$10	Epic 37407
8/7/82	82	9	©	3	III Wishes			$10	Epic 38020
7/30/83	162	6	©	4	Burning			$10	Epic 38683
11/4/89	151	7	©	5	Touch Me Tonight-The Best Of Shooting Star .... [G]			$10	Enigma 73549

Are You On My Side (2)
Are You Ready (3)
Breakout (2,5)
Bring It On (1,5)
Burning (4)
Christmas Together (5)
Couldn't Get Enough (3)
Do You Feel Alright (3)

Don't Stop Now (1)
Dreams (4)
Flesh And Blood (2,5)
Go For It (4)
Hang On For Your Life (2,5)
Heartache (3,5)
Higher (1)
Hollywood (2,5) *70*

Just Friends (1)
Last Chance (1,5)
Let It Out (3)
Midnight Man (1)
Preview (4)
Rainfall (1)
Reach Out I'll Be There (4)
Reckless (4)

She's Got Money (2)
Standing In The Light (3)
Straight Ahead (4,5)
Stranger (1)
Sweet Elatia (2)
Taken Enough (4)
Teaser (2)
Theme (4)

Tonight (1,5)
Touch Me Tonight (5) *67*
Train Rolls On (4,5)
Turn It On (3)
Weary Eyes (3)
Where You Gonna Run (3)
Whole World's Watching (3)
Winner (4)

You're So Good (2)
You've Got Love (2)
You've Got What I Need (1,5) *76*

SHORT, Bobby '72

Born on 9/15/24 in Danville, Illinois. Jazz singer/pianist.

| 3/4/72 | 169 | 8 | © | | Bobby Short Loves Cole Porter .... | | | $25 | Atlantic 606 [2] |

At Long Last Love
By Candlelight
Do I Love You
Hot-House Rose

How Could We Be Wrong
How's Your Romance
I Hate You, Darling
I'm In Love Again

I've Got You On My Mind
Just One Of Those Things
Katie Went To Haiti
Let's Fly Away

Once Upon A Time
Pilot Me
Rap Tap On Wood
So Near And Yet So Far

Weren't We Fools
Where Have You Been
Why Don't We Try Staying Home

Why Shouldn't I
You Don't Know Paree
You've Got That Thing

SHORTER, Wayne '75

Born on 8/25/33 in Newark, New Jersey. Jazz saxophonist. Played with Art Blakey (1959-63) and **Miles Davis** (1964-70).

| 7/12/75 | 183 | 3 | © | | Native Dancer .... | | | $12 | Columbia 33418 |

Ana Maria
Beauty And The Beast

Diana
From The Lonely Afternoons

Joanna's Theme
Lilia

Miracle Of The Fishes
Ponta De Areia

Tarde

SHOTGUN '79

Funk group from Detroit: Ernest Lattimore (vocals, guitar), Tyrone Steels (vocals, drums), Billy Talbert (keyboards), Greg Ingram (sax), William Gentry (trumpet), Larry Austin (bass) and Robert Resch (drums).

| 4/29/78 | 172 | 5 | | 1 | Good, Bad & Funky .... | | | $12 | ABC 1060 |
| 5/5/79 | 163 | 4 | | 2 | Shotgun III .... | | | $12 | MCA 1118 |

All Spaced Out (All Funked Up) (1)
Big Legs (2)
Burnin' Passion (2)

Danger Of The Stranger (1)
Don't You Wanna Make Love? (2)
Fire It Up (1)

Good, Bad And Funky (1)
I Wish I Could See You Again (1)
I'm All Strung Out (1)

Love Attack (1)
Midnight Breakdown (2)
Sister Love (1)
Skate (2)

Space-N (1)
Special Lady (2)
Stone Women (2)

SHOTGUN MESSIAH '89

Hard-rock group from Sweden: Zinny J. San (vocals), Harry Cody (guitar), Tim Skold (bass) and Stixx Galore (drums). San left by 1992 and Skold became vocalist with Bobby Lycon joining on bass.

| 10/21/89 | 99 | 23 | © | 1 | Shotgun Messiah .... | | | $10 | Relativity 88561 |
| 5/2/92 | 199 | 1 | © | 2 | Second Coming .... | | | $10 | Relativity 1060 |

Babylon (2)
Bop City (1)
Can't Fool Me (2)
Dirt Talk (1)

Don't Care 'Bout Nothin' (1)
Explorer, The (1)
Free (2)
Heartbreak Blvd (2)

I Wanna Know (2)
I Want More (2)
I'm Your Love (1)
Living Without You (2)

Nervous (2)
Nobody's Home (2)
Nowhere Fast (1)
Red Hot (2)

Ride The Storm (2)
Sexdrugsrockn'roll (2)
Shout It Out (1)
Squeezin' Teazin' (1)

Trouble (2)
You & Me (2)

SHRIEKBACK '87

Pop-rock group formed in London. Barry Andrews (**XTC**) fronted fluctuating lineup. Dave Allen (**Gang Of Four**) was bassist from 1983-87. Allen, drummer Martyn Barker and guitarist Steve Halliwell formed **King Swamp** in 1988. Disbanded in 1989.

6/25/83	188	3		1	Care			$10	Warner 23874
2/21/87	145	6	©	2	Big Night Music			$10	Island 90552
7/23/88	169	12	©	3	Go Bang!			$10	Island 90949

Accretions (1)
Big Fun (3)
Black Light Trap (2)
Brink Of Collapse (1)
Clear Trails (1)

Cradle Song (2)
Dust And A Shadow (3)
Evaporation (1)
Exquisite (2)
Get Down Tonight (3)

Go Bang! (3)
Gunning For The Buddha (2)
Into Method (1)
Intoxication (3)
Lined Up (1)

Lines From The Library (1)
My Spine (Is The Bassline) (1)
New Man (3)
Nighttown (3)
Over The Wire (3)

Petulant (2)
Pretty Little Things (2)
Reptiles And I (2)
Running On The Rocks (2)
Shark Walk (3)

Shining Path (2)
Sticky Jazz (2)
Sway (1)
Underwaterboys (2)

SHRIEVE, Michael — see HAGAR, Sammy / YAMASHTA, Stomu

SHY '87
Rock group from Birmingham, England: Tony Mills (vocals), Steve Harris (guitar), Pat McKenna (keyboards), Roy Davis (bass) and Alan Kelly (drums).

6/27/87	193	2		©	**Excess All Areas**			$10	RCA Victor 6311

Break Down The Walls / Can't Fight The Nights — Devil Woman / Emergency — Just Love Me / Talk To Me — Telephone / Under Fire — When The Love Is Over / Young Heart

SHYHEIM '94
Born Shyheim Franklin in 1980 in New York City. Male rapper.

5/7/94	52	5		©	1	**AKA The Rugged Child**		$10	Virgin 39385
6/15/96	63	4		©	2	**The Lost Generation**		$10	Noo Trybe 41583

Buckwylyn (1) / Can You Feel It (2) / Dear God (2) / Don't Front/Let's Chill (2) / 5 Elements (2) — Here Come The Hits (1) / Here I Am (1) / Jiggy Comin' (2) / Life As A Shorty (2) / Little Rascals (1) — Move It Over Here (1) / Napsack (1) / **On And On** (1) *89* / One's 4 Da Money (1) / Party's Goin' On (1) — Pass It Off (1) / Real Bad Boys (2) / Rugged Onez (1) / See What I See (2) / Shaolin Style (2) — Shit Iz Real (2) / Still There (2) / Things Happen (2) / What Makes The World Go Round (2) — You The Man (1) / Young Gods (2)

SHYNE '00
Born Jamal Barrow in 1978 in New York City. Male rapper. Sentenced to ten years in prison on 6/1/01 for a shooting incident on 12/27/99 in New York City.

10/14/00	5	30	●	©	**Shyne**			$10	Bad Boy 73032

Bad Boyz *57* / Bang / Bonnie & Shyne — Commission / Get Out / Hit, The — It's OK / Let Me See Your Hands / Life, The — Niggas Gonna Die / Spend Some Cheese / That's Gangsta — Whatcha Gonna Do

SIBERRY, Jane '86
Born on 10/12/55 in Toronto. Folk singer/songwriter.

6/14/86	149	8		©	**The Speckless Sky**			$10	Open Air 0305

Empty City / Map Of The World (Part II) — Mein Bitte / One More Colour — Seven Steps To The Wall / Taxi Ride — Very Large Hat / Vladimir Vladimir

SIDE EFFECT '78
R&B vocal group from Los Angeles: Augie Johnson, Sylvia St. James, Louis Patton and Greg Matta. Their backing band is the **L.A. Boppers**.

3/19/77	115	13			1	**What You Need**		$12	Fantasy 9513
1/7/78	86	15			2	**Goin' Bananas**		$12	Fantasy 9537
1/20/79	135	8			3	**Rainbow Visions**		$12	Fantasy 9569

Always There (1) / Back In Time (2) / Changes (1) / Cloudburst (2) / Disco Junction (3) — Falling In Love Again (3) / Finally Found Someone (1) / Goin' Bananas (2) / Honky Tonk Scat (1) / I Know You Can (1) — I Like Dreaming (3) / I'm A Winner (3) / Illee, Illee, Oh I Know (3) / It's All In Your Mind (2) / Keep On Keepin' On (2) — Keep That Same Old Feeling (1) / Life Is What You Make It (1) / Mr. Monday (2) / Never Be The Same (2) — Open Up Your Heart (3) / Peace Of Mind (3) / Private World (2) / Rainbow Visions (3) / S.O.S. (1) — She's A Lady (3) / Time Has No Ending (1) / Watching Life (2)

SIDEWINDERS '89
Rock group from Arizona: Dave Slutes (vocals, guitar), Rich Hopkins (guitar), Mark Perrodin (bass) and Andrea Curtis (drums).

5/13/89	169	5		©	**Witchdoctor**			$10	Mammoth 9663

Bad, Crazy Sun / Before Our Time — Cigarette / Love '88 — Solitary Man / Tears Like Flesh — What Am I Supposed To Do? / What She Said — Witchdoctor

SIGEL, Beanie '00
Born Dwight Grant in 1974 in Philadelphia. Male rapper.

3/18/00	5	16	●	©	**The Truth**			$10	Roc-A-Fella 546621

includes "Anything" by **Jay-Z**

Die / Everybody Wanna Be A Star / Mac And Brad — Mac Man / Playa / Raw & Uncut — Remember Them Days / Ride 4 My / Stop, Chill — Truth, The / What A Thug About / What Your Life Like — Who Want What

SIGLER, Bunny '78
Born Walter Sigler on 3/27/41 in Philadelphia. R&B singer/songwriter.

2/25/78	77	13		©	1	**Let Me Party With You**		$12	Gold Mind 7502
4/7/79	119	9		©	2	**I've Always Wanted To Sing...Not Just Write Songs**		$12	Gold Mind 9503

By The Way You Dance (I Knew It Was You) (2) / Cry My Eyes Out (2) / Don't Even Try (Give It Up) (1) — Glad To Be Your Lover (2) / Half A Man (2) / I Got What You Need (1) / I'm A Fool (1) — I'm Funkin' You Tonight (With My Music) (2) / It's Time To Twist (1) — **Let Me Party With You (Part 1) (Party, Party, Party)** (1) *43* / Let's Get Freaky Now (2) / Simple Things You Do (2) — Your Love Is So Good (1)

SIGUE SIGUE SPUTNIK '86
Rock group formed in England: Martin Degville (vocals), Neal X (guitar), Tony James (bass; Generation X, **The Sisters Of Mercy**), Yana Ya Ya (effects) and Ray Mayhew and Chris Kavanagh (drums).

8/23/86	96	10		©	**Flaunt It**			$10	Manhattan 53033

Atari Baby / Love Missile F1-11 — Massive Retaliation / Rockit Miss USA — Sex Bomb Boogie / She's My Man — Teenage Thunder / 21st Century Boy

SILENCERS, The '87
Pop-rock group from Scotland: Jimme O'Neill (vocals, guitar), Cha Burns (guitar), Joe Donnelly (bass) and Martin Hanlin (drums).

8/22/87	147	11		©	1	**A Letter From St. Paul**		$10	RCA Victor 6442
2/24/90	168	5		©	2	**A Blues For Buddha**		$10	RCA 9960

Answer Me (2) / Blue Desire (1) / Blues For Buddha (2) / Bullets And Blue Eyes (1) — God's Gift (1) / I Can't Cry (1) / I Ought To Know (1) / I See Red (1) — Letter From St. Paul (1) / My Love Is Like A Wave (medley) (1) / **Painted Moon** (1) *82* — Possessed (1) / Razor Blades Of Love (2) / Real Mc Coy (2) / Sacred Child (2) — Sand And Stars (2) / Scottish Rain (2) / Skin Games (2) / Walk With The Night (2) — Wayfaring Stranger (2)

SILK '69
Folk-rock group from Cleveland: Michael Stanley Gee (vocals, bass), Randy Sabo (vocals, keyboards) and brothers Chris (guitar) and Courtney (drums) Johns. Gee dropped his last name and went on to form the **Michael Stanley Band**.

11/8/69	191	2			**Smooth As Raw Silk**			$25	ABC 694

Come On Down Girl / Custody — For All Time / Foreign Trip — Hours / Introduction — Long Haired Boy / Not A Whole Lot I Can Do — Scottish Thing / Skitzo Blues — Walk In My Mind

SILK '93
R&B vocal group from Atlanta: Tim Cameron, Jimmy Gates, John Rasboro, Gary Jenkins and Gary Glenn.

DEBUT	PEAK	WKS	RIAA	CD	Album Title	$	Label & Number
12/5/92+	7	47	▲²	© 1	Lose Control	$10	Elektra 61394
12/2/95	46	18	●	© 2	Silk	$10	Elektra 61849
4/10/99	21	40	▲	© 3	Tonight	$10	Elektra 62234
6/30/01	20	11		© 4	Love Session	$10	Elektra 62642

Afterplay (4)
Ahh (4)
Baby Check Your Friend (3)
Baby It's You (1)
Back In My Arms (3)
Because Of Your Love (2)
Don't Cry For Me (2)
Don't Go (4)
Don't Go To Bed Mad (2)
Don't Keep Me Waiting (1)
Don't Rush (2) *91*
Ebony Eyes (4)
Freak Me (1) *1*
Girl U For Me (1) *26*
Happy Days (1) *86*
Hooked On You (2) *54*
How Could You Say Love Me (2)
I Can Go Deep (2)
I Didn't Mean To (4)
I Gave To You (1)
I Wonder (3)
I'm Sorry (4)
If You (Lovin' Me) (3) *13*
It Had To Be You (1)
It's So Good (2)
Let's Make Love (3)
Lose Control (1) *flip*
Love Session (4)
Love You Down (2)
Meeting In My Bedroom (3) *62*
Now That I've Lost You (2)
Nursery Rhymes (4)
Playa Road (3)
Please Don't Go (3)
Remember Me (2)
Return, The (3)
Satisfied (3)
Sexcellent (3)
Superstar (4)
Tonight (3)
Treated Like A Lady (4)
Turn-U-Out (3)
Vaughn Harper Interview (3)
We're Callin' You (4)
What Kind Of Love Is This (2)
When I Think About You (1)

SILKK THE SHOCKER '99
Born Zyshonne Miller in New Orleans. Male rapper. Brother of **Master P**. Member of **504 Boyz** and **Tru**.

DEBUT	PEAK	WKS	RIAA	CD	Album Title	$	Label & Number
9/7/96	49	9		© 1	Silkk The Shocker	$10	No Limit 50591
3/7/98	3	40	▲	© 2	Charge It 2 Da Game	$10	No Limit 50716
2/6/99	❶¹	20	▲	© 3	Made Man	$10	No Limit 50003
3/17/01	12	11		© 4	My World, My Way	$10	No Limit 23221

Ain't Nothing (1)
All Because Of You (3)
All Night (2)
Beef (4)
D-Game (4)
Day After (4)
Day I Was Made (3)
End Of The Road (3)
Executive Thug (4)
Free Loaders (1)
Funny Guy (4)
Get It Up (3)
Ghetto Rain (3)
Ghetto Tears (1)
Ghetto 211 (1)
Give Me The World (2)
Go Down (4)
Got Em Fiending (1)
Haters (4)
He Did That (4)
How Many... (2)
How We Mobb (1)
I Ain't Takin No Shorts (1)
I Represent (3)
I Want To Be With You (3)
I Wish (4)
I'm A Soldier (2)
If I Don't Gotta (2)
If It Don't Make $ (3)
If My 9 Could Talk (1)
It Ain't My Fault (1)
It Ain't My Fault 2 (3) *18*
It Takes More (3)
It's Going Around Outside (3)
It's On (1)
It's Time To Ride (1)
Just Be Straight With Me (2) *57*
Let Me Hit It (2)
Mama Always Told Me (2)
Me And You (2)
MR. (1)
Mr. '99 (3)
Murder (1)
My Car (1)
My World, My Way (4)
Na Na Na (4)
No Limit (4)
No Limit Party (1)
1 Morning (1)
Pop Lockin' (4)
Put It On Something (1)
Run (1)
Seem Like A Thug (4)
Shocker, The (1)
Somebody Like Me (3)
Southside Niggas (3)
Tell Me (2)
That's Cool (4)
Them Boyz (4)
This Is 4 My (3)
Throw Yo Hood Up (2)
Thug 'N' Me (2)
Uh Ha (4)
We Can Dance (2)
We Won't Stop (3)
What Gangstas Do (2)
What I'm Looking For (4)
What You Know (4)
What's Heaven Like (4)
Who Can I Trust (2)
Who I Be (2)
Why My Homie (1)
You Ain't Gotta Lie To Kick It (2)
You Know What We Bout (3)

SILLS, Beverly '76
Born on 5/25/29 in Brooklyn, New York. Legendary opera singer.

DEBUT	PEAK	WKS	RIAA	CD	Album Title	$	Label & Number
1/3/76	113	6			Music of Victor Herbert	$15	Angel 37160

Ah! Sweet Mystery Of Life
Art Is Calling For Me
Italian Street Song
Kiss In The Dark
Kiss Me Again
Orchestral Medley 1
Orchestral Medley 2
Romany Life
Thine Alone
To The Land Of My Own Romance
When You're Away

SILOS, The '90
Rock group: Bob Rupe (vocals, bass), Walter Salas-Humara (vocals, guitar), Kenny Margolis (piano), J.D. Foster (bass) and Brian Doherty (drums).

DEBUT	PEAK	WKS	RIAA	CD	Album Title	$	Label & Number
4/21/90	141	9		©	The Silos	$10	RCA 2051

Anyway You Choose Me
Caroline
Commodore Peter
Don't Talk That Way
Here's To You
I'm Over You
Maybe Everything
Only Story I Tell
Picture Of Helen
Porque No
Take My Country Back
(We'll Go) Out Of Town

SILVER '76
Country-rock group: John Batdorf (vocals, guitar; **Batdorf & Rodney**), Greg Collier (guitar), Brent Mydland (keyboards), Tom Leadon (bass) and Harry Stinson (drums). Mydland later joined the **Grateful Dead**; died of a drug overdose on 7/26/90 (age 37).

DEBUT	PEAK	WKS	RIAA	CD	Album Title	$	Label & Number
9/25/76	142	6			Silver	$12	Arista 4076

All I Wanna Do
Climbing
Goodbye, So Long
It's Gonna Be Alright
Memory
Musician (It's Not An Easy Life)
No Wonder
Right On Time
Trust In Somebody
Wham Bam *16*

SILVER, Horace, Quintet '65
Born on 9/2/28 in Norwalk, Connecticut. Jazz pianist.

DEBUT	PEAK	WKS	RIAA	CD	Album Title	Sym	$	Label & Number
6/12/65	95	10		© 1	Song For My Father (Cantiga Para Meu Pai)	[I]	$20	Blue Note 84185
2/26/66	130	2		© 2	The Cape Verdean Blues	[I]	$20	Blue Note 84220

African Queen (2)
Bonita (2)
Calcutta Cutie (1)
Cape Verdean Blues (2)
Kicker, The (1)
Lonely Woman (2)
Mo' Joe (2)
Natives Are Restless Tonight (1)
Nutville (2)
Pretty Eyes (2)
Que Pasa (1)
Song For My Father (1)

SILVER APPLES '68
Electronic rock duo: Dan Taylor and Simeon.

DEBUT	PEAK	WKS	RIAA	CD	Album Title	$	Label & Number
8/3/68	193	3		©	Silver Apples	$30	Kapp 3562

Dancing Gods
Dust
Lovefingers
Misty Mountain
Oscillations
Program
Seagreen Serenades
Velvet Cave
Whirly-Bird

SILVERCHAIR '95
Rock trio from Newcastle, Australia: Daniel Johns (vocals, guitar), Chris Joannou (bass) and Ben Gillies (drums).

DEBUT	PEAK	WKS	RIAA	CD	Album Title	$	Label & Number
7/15/95	9	48	▲²	© 1	Frogstomp	$10	Epic 67247
2/22/97	12	20	●	© 2	Freak Show	$10	Epic 67905
4/3/99	50	30	●	© 3	Neon Ballroom	$10	Epic 69816

Abuse Me (2)
Ana's Song (Open Fire) (3)
Anthem For The Year 2000 (3)
Black Tangled Heart (3)
Cemetery (2)
Cicada (1)
Closing, The (2)
Dearest Helpless (3)
Do You Feel The Same (3)
Door, The (2)
Emotion Sickness (3)
Faultline (1)
Findaway (1)
Freak (2)
Israel's Son (1)
Learn To Hate (2)
Leave Me Out (1)
Lie To Me (2)
Madman (1)
Miss You Love (3)
No Association (2)
Nobody Came (2)
Paint Pastel Princess (3)
Petrol & Chlorine (2)
Point Of View (3)
Pop Song For Us Rejects (2)
Pure Massacre (1)
Roses (2)
Satin Sheets (3)
Shade (1)
Slave (2)
Spawn Again (3)
Steam Will Rise (3)
Suicidal Dream (1)
Tomorrow (1)
Undecided (1)

SILVER CONDOR '81
Rock group: Joe Cerisano (vocals), Earl Slick (guitar), John Corey (keyboards), Jay Davis (bass) and Claude Pepper (drums). Slick joined **Phantom, Rocker & Slick** in 1985.

DEBUT	PEAK	WKS	RIAA	CD	Album Title	$	Label & Number
7/4/81	141	12			Silver Condor	$12	Columbia 37163

Angel Eyes
Carolina (Nobody's Right, Nobody's Wrong)
For The Sake Of Survival
Goin' For Broke
It's Over
One You Left Behind
Sayin' Goodbye
Standin' In The Rain
We're In Love
You Could Take My Heart Away *32*

SILVER CONVENTION '75
Disco studio group from Germany. Vocals by Penny McLean, Ramona Wolf and Linda Thompson.

9/13/75	10	25	●		1 Save Me			$12	Midland Int'l. 1129
4/10/76	13	24			2 Silver Convention			$12	Midland Int'l. 1369
11/13/76	65	12			3 Madhouse			$12	Midland Int'l. 1824
7/16/77	71	10			4 Golden Girls			$12	Midsong Int'l. 2296

Another Girl (1)
Blame It On The Music (4)
Boy With The Ohh-La-La (2)
Chains Of Love (1)
Dancing In The Aisle (3)
Disco Ball (4)
Everybody's Talking 'Bout Love (3)
Fancy Party (3)
Fly, Robin, Fly (1) 1
Get Up And Boogie (That's Right) (2) 2
Heart Of Stone (1)
Hollywood Movie (4)
Hotshot (4)
I Like It (1)
I'm Not A Slot Machine (3)
Land Of Make Believe (3)
Madhouse (3)
Magic Mountain (3)
Midnight Lady (3)
No, No, Joe (2) 60
Old Wine In New Bottles (2)
Plastic People (3)
Play Me Like A Yo-Yo (2)
Please Don't Change (1)
San Francisco Hustle (2)
Save Me (1)
Save Me '77 (4)
Son Of A Gun (1)
Summer Nights (4)
Telegram (4)
Thank You Mr. D.J. (2)
Tiger Baby (1)
Voodoo Woman (4)
Wolfchild (4)
You Turned Me On, But You Can't Turn Me Off (2)
You've Got What It Takes (To Please Your Woman) (2)

SILVERSTEIN, Shel '73
Born on 9/25/30 in Chicago. Died of a heart attack on 5/9/99 (age 68). Satirical songwriter/poet/author/cartoonist.

1/20/73	155	8			Freakin' At The Freakers Ball		[N]	$20	Columbia 31119

All About You
Don't Give A Dose To The One You Love Most
Freakin' At The Freakers Ball
I Got Stoned And I Missed It
Liberated Lady 1999
Man Who Got No Sign
Masochistic Baby
Peace Proposal
Polly In A Porny
Sahra Cynthia Sylvia Stout Would Not Take The Garbage Out
Stacy Brown Got Two
Thumbsucker

SIMEONE, Harry, Chorale '62
Born on 5/9/11 in Newark, New Jersey. Conductor/arranger.

1/6/62	119	2	●		1 Sing We Now Of Christmas		[X]	$15	20th Century Fox 3002
12/22/62	44	2		©	2 Sing We Now Of Christmas		[X-R]	$15	20th Century Fox 3002
					album later repackaged as The Little Drummer Boy				
11/30/63+	❶4X	32			3 The Little Drummer Boy		[X-R]	$15	20th Century Fox 3100
					repackaged version of Sing We Now Of Christmas; Christmas charts: 2/'63, 1/'64, 1/'65, 1/'66, 5/'67, 8/'68, 5/'69, 13/'70				
12/11/65+	5X	11			4 O Bambino/The Little Drummer Boy		[X]	$15	Kapp 3450
					includes Simeone's new recording of "The Little Drummer Boy"; Christmas charts: 17/'65, 5/'66, 9/'72, 7/'73				

Adeste Fideles (medley) (1,2,3)
Angels We Have Heard On High (medley) (1,2,3)
Away In A Manger (medley) (1,2,3)
Bring A Torch, Isabella (medley) (1,2,3)
Carol Of The Bells (4)
Christian Men Rejoice (medley) (1,2,3)
Christmas Greeting (medley) (1,2,3)
Christmas Is A Birthday (4)
Christmas Tree (4)
Coventry Carol (medley) (1,2,3)
Deck The Halls (medley) (1,2,3)
Ding Dong (medley) (1,2,3)
First Christmas Carol (4)
First Noel (medley) (1,2,3)
Friendly Beasts (medley) (1,2,3)
Go Tell It On The Mountain (1,2,3)
God Rest Ye Merry Gentlemen (medley) (1,2,3)
Good King Wenceslas (medley) (1,2,3)
Hallelujah (4)
Hark, The Herald Angels Sing (medley) (1,2,3)
It Came Upon A Midnight Clear (medley) (1,2,3)
Joy To The World (medley) (1,2,3)
Little Drummer Boy (1,2,3,4) 13
Lo, How A Rose E'er Blooming (medley) (1,2,3)
Mary's Little Boy Chile (4)
Master's In The Hall (medley) (1,2,3)
O Bambino (One Cold And Blessed Winter) (4)
O' Come Little Children (medley) (1,2,3)
O' Holy Night (1,2,3)
O' Little Town Of Bethlehem (medley) (1,2,3)
O' Tannenbaum (medley) (1,2,3)
Rise Up Shepherds (medley) (1,2,3)
Silent Night (medley) (1,2,3)
Sing Of A Merry Christmas (4)
Sing We Now Of Christmas (medley) (1,2,3)
'Twas The Night Before Christmas (4)
Villancico (medley) (1,2,3)
We Three Kings (medley) (1,2,3)
What Child Is This? (1,2,3,4)
While Shepherds Watched Their Flocks By Night (medley) (1,2,3)

SIMMONS, Gene '64
Born in 1933 in Tupelo, Mississippi. Nicknamed "Jumpin' Gene."

11/14/64	132	5			jumpin' Gene Simmons			$75	Hi 32018

Bony Moronie
Don't Let Go
Green Door
Haunted House 11
Hotel Happiness
(I'm) Comin' Down With Love
Just A Little Bit
No Help Wanted
Rock Around The Clock
Slippin' And Sliddin'
Teen-Age Letter
You Can Have Her

SIMMONS, Gene '79
Born Chaim Witz on 8/25/49 in Haifa, Israel. Bass guitarist of Kiss. Appeared in the movies Runaway and Trick Or Treat.

10/14/78+	22	22	▲	©	Gene Simmons			$20	Casablanca 7120

Always Near You (medley)
Burning Up With Fever
Living In Sin
Man Of 1000 Faces
Mr. Make Believe
Nowhere To Hide (medley)
Radioactive 47
See You In Your Dreams
See You Tonite
True Confessions
Tunnel Of Love
When You Wish Upon A Star

SIMMONS, Patrick '83
Born on 1/23/50 in Aberdeen, Washington; raised in San Jose, California. Rock singer/songwriter/guitarist. Member of The Doobie Brothers.

5/7/83	52	11			Arcade			$10	Elektra 60225

Don't Make Me Do It 75
Dream About Me
Have You Seen Her
If You Want A Little Love
Knocking At Your Door
Out On The Streets
So Wrong 30
Sue Sad
Too Long
Why You Givin' Up

SIMMONS, Richard '82
Born Milton Simmons on 7/12/48 in New Orleans. Fitness and diet guru.

6/5/82	44	40	▲		Reach			$10	Elektra 60122
					songs sung by Simmons, backed by studio musicians				

Don't Tell Me
Laugh
Lift It Up
Live It
Reach
Stop And Start
This Time
Wake Up
What Are You Waiting For?
You Can Do It

SIMON, Carly ★100★ '73
Born on 6/25/45 in New York City. Pop singer/songwriter. Father co-founded Simon & Schuster publishing. Folk duo with sister Lucy (The Simon Sisters) in the mid-1960s. Won the 1971 Best New Artist Grammy Award. Married to James Taylor from 1972-83.

1)No Secrets 2)Hotcakes 3)Boys In The Trees 4)Playing Possum 5)The Best Of Carly Simon

4/24/71	30	25		©	1 Carly Simon			$15	Elektra 74082
11/27/71+	30	31	●	©	2 Anticipation			$15	Elektra 75016
12/9/72+	❶5	71	▲	©	3 No Secrets			$15	Elektra 75049
2/2/74	3	35	●	©	4 Hotcakes			$15	Elektra 1002
5/3/75	10	17		©	5 Playing Possum			$15	Elektra 1033

SIMON, Carly — Cont'd

DEBUT	PEAK	WKS	RIAA	CD	#	Album Title	Catalog	Sym	$	Label & Number
12/6/75+	17	19	▲³	©	6	The Best Of Carly Simon	C:#46/1	[G]	$15	Elektra 1048
6/26/76	29	13		©	7	Another Passenger			$15	Elektra 1064
4/22/78	10	29	▲	©	8	Boys In The Trees			$12	Elektra 128
6/30/79	45	13		©	9	Spy			$12	Elektra 506
7/12/80	36	32		©	10	Come Upstairs			$12	Warner 3443
10/17/81	50	24		©	11	Torch			$12	Warner 3592
10/8/83	69	17		©	12	Hello Big Man			$12	Warner 23886
7/20/85	88	11		©	13	Spoiled Girl			$12	Epic 39970
4/25/87	25	60	▲	©	14	Coming Around Again			$10	Arista 8443
8/27/88	87	13	▲	©	15	Greatest Hits Live	C:#48/1	[L]	$10	Arista 8526
3/31/90	46	17		©	16	My Romance			$10	Arista 8582
10/13/90	60	32		©	17	Have You Seen Me Lately?			$10	Arista 8650
11/19/94	129	8		©	18	Letters Never Sent			$10	Arista 18752
10/4/97	84	8		©	19	Film Noir			$10	Arista 18984
6/3/00	90	6		©	20	The Bedroom Tapes			$10	Arista 14627

Actress (20)
After The Storm (5)
All I Want Is You (14,15) **54**
Alone (1)
Another Door (1)
Anticipation (2,6,15) **13**
Anyone But Me (13)
Are You Ticklish (5)
As Time Goes By (14)
Attitude Dancing (5,6) **21**
Back Down To Earth (8)
Be With Me (7)
Best Thing (1)
Better Not Tell Her (17)
Bewitched (16)
Big Dumb Guy (20)
Blue Of Blue (11)
Body And Soul (1)
Born To Break My Heart (18)
Boys In The Trees (8)
By Myself (medley) (16)
Can't Give It Up (13)
Carter Family (3)
Come Back Home (13)
Come Upstairs (10)
Coming Around Again
  (14,15) **18**
Coming To Get You (9)
Cow Town (7)
Cross The River (20)
Damn You Get To Me (12)
Dan, My Fling (1)
Danny Boy (16)
Darkness 'Til Dawn (7)
Davy (18)
De Bat (Fly In Me Face) (8)

Desert, The (10)
Devoted To You (8) **36**
Didn't I? (17)
Dishonest Modesty (7)
Do The Walls Come Down
  (14,15)
Don't Smoke In Bed (19)
Don't Wrap It Up (17)
Embrace Me, You Child (3)
Ev'ry Time We Say Goodbye
  (19)
Fairweather Father (7)
Film Noir (19)
Fisherman's Song (17)
Floundering (12)
Fools Coda (19)
For Old Times Sake (8)
Forever My Love (4)
From The Heart (11)
Garden, The (2)
Girl You Think You See (2)
Give Me All Night (14) **61**
Grownup (4)
Half A Chance (7)
Halfway 'Round The World (18)
Happy Birthday (17)
Haunting (8)
Have You Seen Me Lately? (17)
**Haven't Got Time For The
  Pain** (4,6) **14**
He Likes To Roll (7)
He Was Too Good To Me (16)
Hello Big Man (12)
His Friends Are More Than
  Fond Of Robin (3)
Hold What You've Got (14)
Holding Me Tonight (17)

Hotcakes (4)
Hurt (11)
I Forget (20)
I Get Along Without You Very
  Well (11)
I Got It Bad And That Ain't
  Good (11)
I See Your Face Before Me
  (medley) (16)
I'd Rather It Was You (18)
I'm A Fool To Want You (19)
I'm Really The Kind (20)
I've Got To Have You (2)
In A Small Moment (8)
In Honor Of You (George) (20)
In Pain (10)
In The Wee Small Hours Of The
  Morning (16)
In Times When My Head (7)
Interview (13)
Is This Love (12)
It Happens Everyday (12,15)
It Keeps You Runnin' (7) **46**
It Should Have Been Me (14)
It Was So Easy (3)
It's Not Like Him (17)
Itsy Bitsy Spider (14,15)
James (10)
Jesse (10) **11**
Julie Through The Glass (2)
Just A Sinner (1)
Just Like You Do (9)
Just Not True (4)
Last Night When We Were
  Young (19)
Laura (19)

Legend In Your Own Time
  (2,6) **50**
Letters Never Sent (18)
Libby (7)
Life Is Eternal (17)
Like A River (18)
Lili Marlene (19)
Little Girl Blue (16)
Look Me In The Eyes (5)
Lost In Your Love (18)
Love Of The Loser (5)
Love You By Heart (9)
Love's Still Growing (1)
Make Me Feel Something (13)
Memorial Day (9)
Menemsha (16)
Mind On My Man (4)
Misfit (4)
Mockingbird (4,6) **5**
More And More (5) **94**
My Funny Valentine (16)
My New Boyfriend (13)
My Romance (16)
Never Been Gone (9,15)
Night Owl (3,6)
Nobody Does It Better (15)
Not A Day Goes By (11)
Older Sister (4)
One Love Stand (7)
One Man Woman (8)
One More Time (1)
Orpheus (12)
Our Affair (20)
Our First Day Together (2)
Playing Possum (5)
Pretty Strange (11)

Private (18)
Pure Sin (9)
Reason, The (18)
Reunions (1)
Right Thing To Do (3,6,15) **17**
Riverboat Gambler (7)
Rolling Down The Hills (1)
Safe And Sound (4)
Scar (20)
Share The End (2)
Slave (5)
So Many Stars (20)
Something Wonderful (16)
Somewhere In The Night (19)
Sons Of Summer (5)
Spoiled Girl (13)
Spring Is Here (11)
Spring Will Be A Little Late This
  Year (19)
Spy (9)
Stardust (10)
Stuff That Dreams Are Made Of
  (14)
Such A Good Boy (12)
Summer's Coming Around
  Again (2)
Take Me As I Am (10)
**That's The Way I've Always
  Heard It Should Be** (1,6) **10**
Them (1)
Think I'm Gonna Have A Baby
  (4)
Three Days (2)
Three Of Us In The Dark (10)
Time After Time (16)
Tired Of Being Blonde (13) **70**
Tonight And Forever (13)

Touched By The Sun (18)
Tranquillo (Melt My Heart) (8)
Two Hot Girls (On A Hot
  Summer Night) (14,15)
Two Sleepy People (19)
Vengeance (9) **48**
Waited So Long (3)
Waiting At The Gate (17)
Waterfall (5) **78**
We Have No Secrets (3,6)
We Just Got Here (17)
We Your Dearest Friends (20)
We're So Close (9)
What Has She Got (16)
What Shall We Do With The
  Child (11)
Whatever Became Of Her (20)
When You Close Your Eyes (3)
When Your Lover Has Gone
  (16)
Wives Are In Connecticut (13)
You Belong To Me (8,15) **6**
You Don't Feel The Same (12)
You Have To Hurt (14)
You Know What To Do (12) **83**
You Won't Forget Me (19)
You're So Vain (3,6,15) **1**
You're The One (8)

SIMON, Joe   '72

Born on 9/2/43 in Simmesport, Louisiana. R&B singer.

DEBUT	PEAK	WKS	CD	#	Album Title	Sym	$	Label & Number
6/21/69	81	17	©	1	The Chokin' Kind		$25	Sound Stage 7 15006
11/29/69	192	2	©	2	Joe Simon...better than ever		$25	Sound Stage 7 15008
4/3/71	153	12	©	3	The Sounds Of Simon		$20	Spring 4701
3/25/72	71	12	©	4	Drowning In The Sea Of Love		$20	Spring 5702
12/30/72+	147	8		5	The Best Of Joe Simon	[G]	$20	Sound Stage 7 15009
2/17/73	97	12	©	6	The Power Of Joe Simon		$15	Spring 5704
7/19/75	129	12	©	7	Get Down		$15	Spring 6706

After The Lights Go Down Low
  (2)
All My Hard Times (3) **93**
**Baby, Don't Be Looking In My
  Mind** (1,5) **72**
Chokin' Kind (1,5) **13**
Don't Let Me Lose The Feeling
  (1)
Drowning In The Sea Of Love
  (4,6) **11**
Farther On Down The Road
  (5) **56**
Fire Burning (3)
Georgia Blue (3,6)
**Get Down, Get Down (Get On
  The Floor)** (7) **8**

Glad To Be Your Lover (4)
Hangin' On ..see: (You Keep
  Me)
**Help Me Make It Through The
  Night** (3,6) **69**
Help Yourself (To All My Lovin')
  (3)
I Can't See Nobody (3)
I Found My Dad (4) **78**
I Got A Whole Lot Of Lovin' (2)
I Love You More (Than
  Anything) (3)
I'm Too Far Gone To Turn
  Around (1)
In My Baby's Arms (7)

In The Ghetto (2)
In The Still Of The Night (I'll
  Remember) (1)
It Be's That Way Sometimes (7)
It's Crying Time In Memphis (7)
Let Me Be The One (The One
  Who Loves You) (4)
Little Green Apples (1)
Lonely Man (1)
Message From Maria (5) **75**
Mirror Don't Lie (4)
Moon Walk Part 1 (5) **54**
Most Of All (3)
Music In My Bones (7) **92**
My Special Prayer (5) **87**

My Woman, My Woman, My
  Wife (3)
Nine Pound Steel (5) **70**
No More Me (3)
O'le Night Owl (4)
Pool Of Bad Luck (4) **42**
Power Of Love (6) **11**
Put Your Trust In Me (Depend
  On Me) (5)
Rainbow Road (2)
**San Francisco Is A Lonely
  Town** (2) **79**
Silver Spoons And Coffee Cups
  (2)
(Sittin' On The) Dock Of The
  Bay (1)

Something You Can Do Today
  (4)
Step By Step (6) **37**
Still At The Mercy Of Your Love
  (7)
Straight Down To Heaven (2)
Talk Don't Bother Me (6)
Teenager's Prayer (5) **66**
Time And Space (2)
To Lay Down Beside You (3,6)
Trouble In My Home (6) **50**
When (2)
Wichita Lineman (1)
Wounded Man (2)
You Are Everything (4)
You Are The One (6)

You Don't Want To Believe It
  (My Man) (7)
(You Keep Me) Hangin' On
  (5) **25**
Your Time To Cry (3,6) **40**
Yours Love (1,5) **78**

SIMON, Paul ★181★ '87

Born on 10/13/41 in Newark, New Jersey; raised in Queens, New York. Singer/songwriter/guitarist. Met **Art Garfunkel** in high school, recorded together as Tom & Jerry in 1957. Worked as Jerry Landis, Tico And The Triumphs, Paul Kane, Harrison Gregory and True Taylor in the early '60s. To England from 1963-64. Returned to the U.S. and recorded first album with Garfunkel in 1964. Went solo in 1971. Married to actress/author Carrie Fisher from 1983-85. Married singer **Edie Brickell** on 5/30/92. In the movies *Annie Hall* and *One-Trick Pony*. Inducted into the Rock and Roll Hall of Fame in 2001.

1)Still Crazy After All These Years 2)There Goes Rhymin' Simon 3)Graceland

DEBUT	PEAK	WKS	RIAA	CD	#	Album Title	Catalog	Sym	$	Label & Number
2/12/72	4	36	▲	©	1	Paul Simon			$12	Columbia 30750
5/26/73	2²	48	▲	©	2	There Goes Rhymin' Simon			$12	Columbia 32280
3/23/74	33	17	●	©	3	Paul Simon In Concert/Live Rhymin'		[L]	$12	Columbia 32855
10/25/75	❶¹	40	●	©	4	Still Crazy After All These Years			$12	Columbia 33540
						1975 Grammy winner: Album of the Year				
12/3/77+	18	23	▲	©	5	Greatest Hits, Etc.		[G]	$12	Columbia 35032
9/6/80	12	26	●	©	6	One-Trick Pony		[S]	$10	Warner 3472
11/19/83+	35	18		©	7	Hearts And Bones			$10	Warner 23942
9/13/86+	3	97	▲⁵	©	8	Graceland	C:#14/33		$10	Warner 25447
						1986 Grammy winner: Album of the Year				
11/12/88+	110	14	▲	©	9	Negotiations And Love Songs, 1971-1986		[G]	$15	Warner 25789 [2]
11/3/90	4	53	▲²	©	10	The Rhythm Of The Saints			$10	Warner 26098
11/23/91+	74	11		©	11	Paul Simon's Concert In The Park		[L]	$15	Warner 26737 [2]
						recorded on 8/15/91 in Central Park				
10/16/93	173	2	●	©	12	1964/1993		[K]	$25	Warner 45394 [3]
12/6/97	42	11		©	13	Songs From The Capeman			$10	Warner 46814
10/21/00	19	21	●	©	14	You're The One			$10	Warner 47844

Ace In The Hole (6)
Adios Hermanos (13)
All Around The World Or The Myth Of Fingerprints (8)
Allergies (7) *44*
America (3,11,12) *97*
American Tune (2,3,5,12) *35*
Armistice Day (1)
Bernadette (13)
Born At The Right Time (10,11,12)
Born In Puerto Rico (13)
Boxer, The (3,11,12) *7*
Boy In The Bubble (8,11,12) *86*
Breakup, The (12)
Bridge Over Troubled Water (3,11,12)
Can I Forgive Him (13)
Can't Run But (10,12)
Cars Are Cars (7)
Cecilia (11,12) *4*
Coast, The (10,11)
Congratulations (1,12)
Cool, Cool River (10,11,12)

Crazy Love, Vol. II (8)
Darling Lorraine (14)
Diamonds On The Soles Of Her Shoes (8,9,11,12)
Duncan (1,3,5,12) *52*
El Condor Pasa (3,12) *18*
Everything Put Together Falls Apart (1)
50 Ways To Leave Your Lover (4,5,9,12) *1*
Further To Fly (10,12)
God Bless The Absentee (6)
Gone At Last (4,12) *23*
Graceland (8,9,11,12) *81*
Gumboots (8)
Have A Good Time (4,5,9,12)
Hearts And Bones (7,9,11,12)
Hey, Schoolgirl (12) *49*
Hobo's Blues (1)
Homeless (8,12)
Homeward Bound (3)
How The Heart Approaches What It Yearns (6,12)
Hurricane Eye (14)
I Do It For Your Love (4,5)

I Know What I Know (8,11)
Jesus Is The Answer (3)
Jonah (6,12)
Kathy's Song (12)
Killer Wants To Go To College (11)
Kodachrome (2,5,9,11,12) *2*
Late Great Johnny Ace (7,12)
Late In The Evening (6,9,11,12) *6*
Learn How To Fall (2)
Leaves That Are Green (12)
Long, Long Day (6)
Look At That (14)
Love (14)
Loves Me Like A Rock (2,3,5,9,11,12) *2*
Me And Julio Down By The Schoolyard (1,3,5,9,11,12) *22*
Mother And Child Reunion (1,3,5,9,12) *4*
Mrs. Robinson (12) *1*
My Little Town (4,12) *9*
Night Game (4)

Nobody (6)
Obvious Child (10,11,12) *92*
Oh, Marion (6)
Old (14)
One Man's Ceiling Is Another Man's Floor (2)
One-Trick Pony (6) *40*
Papa Hobo (1)
Paranoia Blues (1)
Peace Like A River (1,12)
Pigs, Sheep And Wolves (14)
Proof (10,11)
Quality (13)
Quiet (14)
Rene And Georgette Magritte With Their Dog After The War (7,9,12)
Rhythm Of The Saints (10)
Run That Body Down (1)
Satin Summer Nights (13)
Señorita With A Necklace Of Tears (14)
She Moves On (10,11,12)
Silent Eyes (4)
Slip Slidin' Away (5,9,12) *5*

Some Folks Lives Roll Easy (4)
Something So Right (2,5,9,12)
Song About The Moon (7)
Sound Of Silence (3,11,12) *1*
Spirit Voices (10,12)
St. Judy's Comet (2,9,12)
Still Crazy After All These Years (4,5,9,11,12) *40*
Stranded In A Limousine (5)
Sunday Afternoon (13)
Take Me To The Mardi Gras (2,5,12)
Teacher, The (14)
Tenderness (2,12)
That Was Your Mother (8,12)
That's Where I Belong (14)
That's Why God Made The Movies (6)
Thelma (12)
Think Too Much (Part 1 & 2) (7)
Time Is An Ocean (13)
Trailways Bus (13)
Train In The Distance (7,9,11)
Under African Skies (8,12)
Vampires, The (13)

Virgil (13)
Was A Sunny Day (2)
When Numbers Get Serious (7)
You Can Call Me Al (8,9,11,12) *23*
You're Kind (4)
You're The One (14)

SIMON & GARFUNKEL ★147★ '68

Folk-rock duo from New York City: **Paul Simon** and **Art Garfunkel**. Recorded as Tom & Jerry in 1957. Duo split in 1964; Simon was working solo in England; Garfunkel was in graduate school. They re-formed in 1965 and stayed together until 1971. Reunited briefly in 1981 for national tour. Inducted into the Rock and Roll Hall of Fame in 1990.

DEBUT	PEAK	WKS	RIAA	CD	#	Album Title	Catalog	Sym	$	Label & Number
1/22/66	30	31	▲	©	1	Wednesday Morning, 3 AM			$25	Columbia 9049
2/19/66+	21	143	▲³	©	2	Sounds of Silence	C:#18/32		$25	Columbia 9269
11/12/66	4	145	▲³	©	3	Parsley, Sage, Rosemary and Thyme			$25	Columbia 9363
3/16/68	❶⁹	69	▲²	©	4	The Graduate		[S]	$20	Columbia 3180
						includes "The Folks," "A Great Effect," "On The Strip," "The Singleman Party Foxtrot," "Sunporch Cha-Cha-Cha" and "Whew" by **Dave Grusin**				
4/27/68	❶⁷	66	▲²	©	5	Bookends	C:#31/40		$20	Columbia 9529
2/14/70	❶¹⁰	85	▲⁸	©	6	Bridge Over Troubled Water	C:#22/101		$15	Columbia 9914
						1970 Grammy winner: Album of the Year				
7/1/72	5	127	▲¹³	©	7	Simon And Garfunkel's Greatest Hits	C:#12/50	[G]	$15	Columbia 31350
3/13/82	6	34	▲²	©	8	The Concert In Central Park		[L]	$15	Warner 3654 [2]
						recorded on 9/19/81				

America (5,7,8) *97*
American Tune (8)
Anji (2)
April Come She Will (2,4,8)
At The Zoo (5) *16*
Baby Driver (6)
Benedictus (1)
Big Bright Green Pleasure Machine (3,4)
Bleecker Street (1)

Blessed (2)
Bookends (5,7)
Boxer, The (6,7,8) *7*
Bridge Over Troubled Water (6,7,8) *1*
Bye Bye Love (6)
Cecilia (6,7) *4*
Cloudy (3)
Dangling Conversation (3) *25*
El Condor Pasa (6,7) *18*

Fakin' It (5) *23*
59th Street Bridge Song (Feelin' Groovy) (3,7,8)
Fifty Ways To Leave Your Lover (8)
Flowers Never Bend With The Rainfall (3)
For Emily, Whenever I May Find Her (3,7) *53*
Go Tell It On The Mountain (1)
Hazy Shade Of Winter (5) *13*

He Was My Brother (1)
Heart In New York (8)
Homeward Bound (3,7,8) *5*
I Am A Rock (2,7) *3*
Kathy's Song (2)
Keep The Customer Satisfied (6)
Kodachrome (medley) (8)
Last Night I Had The Strangest Dream (1)
Late In The Evening (8)

Leaves That Are Green (2)
Mabellene (medley) (8)
Me And Julio Down By The Schoolyard (8)
Most Peculiar Man (2)
Mrs. Robinson (4,5,7,8) *1*
Old Friends (5,8)
Only Living Boy In New York (6)
Overs (5)
Patterns (3)Peggy-O (1)

Poem On The Underground Wall (3)
Punky's Dilemma (5)
Richard Cory (2)
Save The Life Of My Child (5)
Scarborough Fair (/Canticle) (3,4,7,8)
7 O'Clock News (medley) (3)
Silent Night (medley) (3)

SIMON & GARFUNKEL — Cont'd

Simple Desultory Philippic (Or How I Was Robert McNamara'd Into Submission) (3)
Slip Slidin' Away (8)
So Long, Frank Lloyd Wright (6)
Somewhere They Can't Find Me (2)
Song For The Asking (6)
Sounds Of Silence (1,2,4,7,8) **1**
Sparrow (1)
Still Crazy After All These Years (8)
Sun Is Burning (1)
Times They Are A-Changin' (1)
Wake Up Little Susie (8) **27**
We've Got A Groovey Thing Goin' (2)
Wednesday Morning, 3 A.M. (1)
Why Don't You Write Me (6)
You Can Tell The World (1)

SIMONE, Nina   '61
Born Eunice Waymon on 2/21/33 in Tryon, South Carolina. Jazz-styled singer.
1)Nina At Newport 2)I Put A Spell On You 3)Nina Simone In Concert

DEBUT	PEAK	WKS		CD		ARTIST — Album Title	Sym	$	Label & Number
3/6/61	23	5		©	1	Nina At Newport	[L]	$30	Colpix 412
						recorded on 6/30/60			
9/19/64	102	11		©	2	Nina Simone In Concert	[L]	$20	Philips 600135
6/26/65	99	8		©	3	I Put A Spell On You		$20	Philips 600172
10/16/65	139	7		©	4	Pastel Blues		$20	Philips 600187
11/5/66	110	9		©	5	Wild Is The Wind		$20	Philips 600207
11/25/67	158	4			6	Silk & Soul		$15	RCA Victor 3837
4/19/69	187	3		©	7	The Best Of Nina Simone	[K]	$15	Philips 600298
3/14/70	149	12			8	Black Gold	[L]	$15	RCA Victor 4248
7/25/70	189	3		©	9	The Best Of Nina Simone	[K]	$15	RCA Victor 4374
8/21/71	190	4			10	Here Comes The Sun		$15	RCA Victor 4536

Ain't Got No; I Got Life (8) **94**
Ain't No Use (4)
Angel Of The Morning (10)
Assignment Sequence (8)
Be My Husband (4)
Beautiful Land (3)
Black Is The Color Of My True Love's Hair (5,8)
Blues On Purpose (3)
Break Down And Let It All Out (5,7)
Cherish (3)
Chilly Winds Don't Blow (4)
Compensation (9)
Consummation (6)
Day And Night (9)
Do What You Gotta Do (9) **83**
Don't Let Me Be Misunderstood (7)
Don't Smoke In Bed (2)
Either Way I Lose (5)
End Of The Line (4)
Feeling Good (3)
Flo Me La (1)
Four Women (5,7)
Gimme Some (3)
Go Limp (2)
Go To Hell (8,9)
Here Comes The Sun (10)
How Long Must I Wander (10)
I Love Your Lovin' Ways (5)
I Loves You, Porgy (2,7) **18**
I Put A Spell On You (3,7)
I Shall Be Released (9)
I Want A Little Sugar In My Bowl (9)
I Wish I Knew How It Would Feel To Be Free (6,9)
If I Should Lose You (5)
In The Evening By The Moonlight (1)
In The Morning (9)
Introduction (8)
It Be's That Way Sometime (6,9)
July Tree (3)
Just Like A Woman (10)
Lilac Wine (5)
Little Liza Jane (1)
Look Of Love (6)
Love O' Love (6)
Marriage Is For Old Folks (3)
Mississippi Goddam (2,7)
Mr. Bojangles (10)
My Man's Gone Now (9)
My Way (10)
Ne Me Quitte Pas (3)
New World Coming (10)
Nina's Blues (7)
Nobody Knows You When You're Down And Out (4) **93**
Old Jim Crow (2)
One September Day (3)
O-o-h Child (10)
Pirate Jenny (2,7)
Plain Gold Ring (2)
Porgy (1)
See-Line Woman (7)
Sinnerman (4,7)
Some Say (6)
Strange Fruit (4)
Suzanne (9)
Take Care Of Business (3)
Tell Me More And More And Then Some (4)
To Be Young, Gifted And Black (8) **76**
Tomorrow Is My Turn (3)
Trouble In Mind (1,4) **92**
Turn Me On (6)
Turning Point (6)
Westwind (6)
Who Knows Where The Time Goes (8)
Why Keep On Breaking My Heart (5)
Why? (The King Of Love Is Dead) (7)
Wild Is The Wind (5,7)
You'd Be So Nice To Come Home To (1)
You've Got To Learn (1)

SIMPLE MINDS   '86
Pop-rock group formed in Glasgow, Scotland: Jim Kerr (vocals), Charles Burchill (guitar, keyboards), Michael MacNeil (keyboards), John Giblin (bass) and Mel Gaynor (drums). MacNeil and Giblin left in 1989. Kerr was briefly married to Chrissie Hynde (of The Pretenders).

DEBUT	PEAK	WKS	RIAA	CD		ARTIST — Album Title	Sym	$	Label & Number
2/19/83	69	19		©	1	New Gold Dream (81-82-83-84)		$10	A&M 4928
2/18/84	64	24		©	2	Sparkle in the Rain		$10	A&M 4981
11/9/85+	10	42	●	©	3	Once Upon A Time		$10	A&M 5092
7/18/87	96	10		©	4	Simple Minds Live: In The City Of Light	[L]	$15	A&M 6850 [2]
5/20/89	70	12		©	5	Street Fighting Years		$10	A&M 3927
5/4/91	74	11		©	6	Real Life		$10	A&M 5352
2/25/95	87	7		©	7	Good News From The Next World		$10	Virgin 39922

African Skies (6)
Alive & Kicking (3,4) **3**
All The Things She Said (3) **28**
And The Band Played On (7)
Banging On The Door (6)
Belfast Child (5)
Big Sleep (1,4)
Biko (5)
Book Of Brilliant Things (2,4)
"C" Moon Cry Like A Baby (2)
Colours Fly And Catherine Wheel (1)
Come A Long Way (3)
Criminal World (7)
Dance To The Music (medley) (4)
Don't You Forget About Me (4)
East At Easter (2,4)
Ghost Dancing (3,4)
Ghostrider (6)
Glittering Prize (1)
Great Leap Forward (7)
Hunter And The Hunted (1)
Hypnotised (7)
I Wish You Were Here (3)
Kick Inside Of Me (2)
Kick It In (5)
King Is White And In The Crowd (1)
Let It All Come Down (5)
Let The Children Speak (6)
Let There Be Love (6)
Love Song (medley) (4)
Mandela Day (5)
My Life (7)
New Gold Dream (1,4)
Night Music (7)
Oh Jungleland (3,4)
Once Upon A Time (3,4)
Promised You A Miracle (1,4)
Real Life (6)
Rivers Of Ice (6)
Sanctify Yourself (3,4) **14**
See The Lights (6) **40**
7 Deadly Sins (7)
Shake Off The Ghosts (2)
She's A River (7) **52**
Somebody Up There Likes You (1)
Someone Somewhere In Summertime (1,4)
Soul Crying Out (5)
Speed Your Love To Me (2)
Stand By Love (6)
Street Fighting Years (5)
Street Hassle (2)
Sun City (medley) (4)
Take A Step Back (5)
This Is Your Land (5)
This Time (7)
Travelling Man (6)
Up On The Catwalk (2)
Wall Of Love (5)
Waterfront (2,4)
When Two Worlds Collide (6)
White Hot Day (2)
Woman (6)

SIMPLY RED   '86
Born Mick Hucknall on 6/8/60 in Denton, Manchester, England. Pop-soul singer. Nicknamed "Red" because of his red hair. His backing group included Fritz McIntyre and Tim Kellett (keyboards), Sylvan Richardson (guitar), Tony Bowers (bass) and Chris Joyce (drums). Group disbanded in 1990. Hucknall continued Simply Red as a solo vehicle with various backing musicians.

DEBUT	PEAK	WKS	RIAA	CD		ARTIST — Album Title	Sym	$	Label & Number
4/19/86	16	60	▲	©	1	Picture Book		$10	Elektra 60452
3/28/87	31	26		©	2	Men And Women		$10	Elektra 60727
3/11/89	22	39	●	©	3	A New Flame		$10	Elektra 60828
10/19/91+	76	43	●	©	4	Stars		$10	EastWest 91773
11/11/95	75	13		©	5	Life		$10	EastWest 61853
11/9/96	116	5		©	6	Greatest Hits	[G]	$10	EastWest 61993
6/6/98	145	3		©	7	Blue		$10	EastWest 62222

Air That I Breathe (7)
Angel (6)
Blue (7)
Broken Man (7)
Come Get Me Angel (7)
Come To My Aid (1)
Enough (3)
Ev'ry Time We Say Goodbye (2)
Fairground (5,6)
For Your Babies (4,6)
Freedom (4)
Heaven (1)
High Fives (7)
Hillside Avenue (5)
Holding Back The Years (1,6) **1**
How Could I Fall (4)
I Won't Feel Bad (2)
If You Don't Know Me By Now (3,6) **1**
Infidelity (2)
It's Only Love (3,6) **57**
Jericho (1)
Let Me Have It All (2)
Lives And Loves (5)
Look At You Now (1)
Love Fire (2)
Love Has Said Goodbye Again (7)
Love Lays Its Tune (3)
Maybe Someday... (2)
Mellow My Mind (7)
Model (4)
Money$ Too Tight (To Mention) (1,6) **28**
More (3)
Move On Out (2)
Never Never Love (6)
New Flame (3,6)
Night Nurse (7)
No Direction (1)
(Open Up The) Red Box (1)
Out On The Range (5)
Picture Book (1)
Remembering The First Time (5)
Right Thing (2,6) **27**
Sad Old Red (1)
Say You Love Me (7)
She'll Have To Go (3)
She's Got It Bad (4)
Shine (2)
So Beautiful (5,6)
So Many People (3)
Someday In My Life (7)
Something Got Me Started (4,6) **23**
Stars (4,6) **44**
Suffer (2)
Thrill Me (4,6)
To Be Free (7)
To Be With You (3)
Turn It Up (3)
We're In This Together (5)
Wonderland (4)
You Make Me Believe (5)
You've Got It (3,6)
Your Mirror (4,6)

SIMPSON, Jessica   '01
Born on 7/10/80 in Dallas. Pop singer.

| 12/11/99+ | 25 | 62 | ▲² | © | 1 Sweet Kisses .... | | | $10 | Columbia 69096 |
| 6/23/01 | 6 | 15↑ | ● | © | 2 **Irresistible** | | | $10 | Columbia 62136 |

Betcha She Don't Love You (1)
Final Heartbreak (1)
For Your Love (2)
Forever In Your Eyes (2)
Heart Of Innocence (1)

His Eye Is On The Sparrow (2)
Hot Like Fire (2)
I Never (2)
I Think I'm In Love With You (1) 21

I Wanna Love You Forever (1) 3
I've Got My Eyes On You (1)
Imagination (2)
Irresistible (2) 15

Little Bit (2)
My Wonderful (1)
Sweet Kisses (1)
There You Were (2)
To Fall In Love Again (2)

What's It Gonna Be (2)
When You Told Me You Loved Me (2)
Where You Are (1) 62
Woman In Me (1)

Your Faith In Me (1)

SIMPSON, Valerie   '71
Born on 8/26/46 in New York City. R&B singer/prolific songwriter. Half of husband-and-wife duo **Ashford & Simpson**.

| 7/31/71 | 159 | 6 | | | 1 Valerie Simpson Exposed .... | | | $15 | Tamla 311 |
| 8/26/72 | 162 | 6 | | | 2 Valerie Simpson | | | $15 | Tamla 317 |

Back To Nowhere (1)
Benjie (2)
Can't It Wait Until Tomorrow (1)
Could Have Been Sweeter (2)
Drink The Wine (2)

Fix It Alright (2)
Genius I & II (2)
I Believe I'm Gonna Take This Ride (2)
I Don't Need No Help (1)

I Just Wanna Be There (1)
Keep It Coming (2)
Love Woke Me Up This Morning (1)
Now That There's You (1)

One More Baby Child Born (2)
Silly Wasn't I (2) 63
Sinner Man (Don't Let Him Catch You) (1)
There Is A God (1)

We Can Work It Out (1)
World Without Sunshine (1)

SIMPSONS, The   '91
The voices of the Fox network's animated TV series. Nancy Cartwright is Bart; Dan Castellaneta is Homer; Julie Kavner is Marge; Yeardley Smith is Lisa; and the show's creator Matt Groening is Maggie.

12/22/90+	3	39	▲²	©	1 **The Simpsons Sing The Blues**		[N]	$10	Geffen 24308
4/5/97	103	12		©	2 **Songs In The Key Of Springfield**		[TV]	$10	Rhino 72723
11/20/99	197	1		©	3 **Go Simpsonic With The Simpsons**		[TV]	$10	Fox 75480

All Singing, All Dancing (Medley) (3)
Apu In "The Jolly Bengali" Theme (3)
Bagged Me A Homer (2)
Ballad Of Jebediah Springfield (3)
Bart Sells His Soul (Medley) (2)
Blessed Be The Guy That Bonds ("McBain" End Credits) (3)
Boozehound Named Barney (3)
Born Under A Bad Sign (1)
Boy Scoutz N The Hood (Medley) (2)
Can I Borrow A Feeling? (3)
Canyonero (3)
Cape Feare (Medley) (3)
Cash And Cary (3)
"Chief Wiggum, P.I." Main Title (3)
City Of New York Vs. Homer Simpson (Medley) (3)

Cletus The Slack-Jawed Yokel! (3)
Cool (2)
Cut Every Corner (3)
Dancin' Homer (Medley) (2)
Day The Violence Died (Medley) (3)
Deep, Deep Trouble (1) 69
Do The Bartman (1)
Everyone Loves Ned Flanders (3)
"Eye On Springfield" Theme (3)
Field Of Excellence (3)
Fish Called Selma (Medley) (3)
Flaming Moe's (2)
Garbageman, The (3)
God Bless The Child (1)
Happy Birthday, Lisa (2)
Happy Birthday, Mr. Burns (3)
Happy Birthday, Mr. Smithers (3)
Happy Just The Way We Are (3)

Homer & Apu (Medley) (3)
Homer's Barbershop Quartet (Medley) (3)
Honey Roasted Peanuts (2)
I Love To See You Smile (1)
In Marge We Trust (Medley) (3)
In Search Of An Out Of Body Vibe (2)
It Was A Very Good Year (2)
"Itchy & Scratchy & Poochie Show" Theme (3)
"Itchy & Scratchy" End Credits Theme (2)
"Itchy & Scratchy" Main Title Theme (2)
Jingle Bells (2)
Kamp Krusty (Medley) (2)
"Kamp Krusty" Theme Song (3)
"Krusty The Clown" Main Title (3)
Land Of Chocolate (3)
Like Father, Like Clown (Medley) (3)

Lisa's Sax (Medley) (3)
Lisa's Wedding (Medley) (2)
Look At All Those Idiots (1)
"Love-Matic Grampa" Main Title (3)
Meet The Flintstones (2)
Moanin' Lisa Blues (1)
Monorail Song (2)
Mr. Plow (2)
"Oh, Streetcar!" (The Musical) (2)
Plow King (3)
Poochie Rap Song (3)
Presidents' Song (3)
"Quimby" Campaign Commercial (3)
Rappin' Ronnie Reagan (3)
'Round Springfield (Medley) (2)
School Day (1)
"Scorpio" End Credits (3)
Send In The Clowns (2)
Señor Burns (2,3)
Sibling Rivalry (1)

"Simpsoncalifragilisticexpiala (Annoyed Grunt)cious" End Credits Suite (3)
Simpsoncalifragilisticexpiala (Annoyed Grunt)cious (Medley) (3)
Simpsons End Credits Theme (2,3)
Simpsons Halloween Special End Credits Theme ("The Addams Family" Homage) (2)
"Simpsons" Main Title (3)
Simpsons Main Title Theme (2)
Simpsons Spin-Off Showcase (Medley) (3)
"Skinner & The Superintendent"Theme (3)
$pringfield (Medley) (3)
Springfield Soul Stew (1)
Star Spangled Banner (3)
TV Sucks! (2)
Talkin' Softball (3)

Trash Of The Titans (Medley) (3)
Treehouse Of Horror V (Medley) (2)
Two Dozen And One Greyhounds (Medley) (3)
Underwater Wonderland (3)
Union Strike Folks Song (Parts 1 & 2) (3)
We Do (The Stonecutters' Song) (2)
We Love To Smoke (3)
We Put The Spring In Springfield (3)
Who Shot Mr. Burns? (Part One) (Medley) (2)
"Ya-Hoo" Main Title (3)
You're Gonna Like Me (The Gabbo Song) (3)
Your Wife Don't Understand You (2)

SINATRA, Frank ★2★   '61
Born on 12/12/15 in Hoboken, New Jersey. Died of a heart attack on 5/14/98 (age 82). With **Harry James** from 1939-40, first recorded for Brunswick in 1939; with **Tommy Dorsey**, 1940-42. Went solo in late 1942. Appeared in many movies from 1941. Won an Oscar for the movie *From Here To Eternity* in 1953. Own TV show in 1957. Own Reprise record company in 1961, sold to Warner Bros. in 1963. Won Grammy's Lifetime Achievement Award in 1965. Father of **Nancy Sinatra**. Married to actress Ava Gardner from 1951-57. Married to actress Mia Farrow from 1966-68. Regarded by many as the greatest popular singer of the 20th century.

1)*Nice 'N' Easy* 2)*Frank Sinatra sings for Only The Lonely* 3)*Come fly with me*
4)*in the Wee Small Hours* 5)*Strangers In The Night*

1/8/55	11	4			1 Frank Sinatra sings songs from his WARNER BROS. picture "Young At Heart"	[EP]		$50	Capitol 571
5/28/55	❶⁴	44		©	2 **in the Wee Small Hours**	C:#28/1		$50	Capitol 581
					EP: Capitol EBF-581 (#1); LP Capitol W-581 (#2)				
10/15/55	2³	7			3 **Our Town**	[EP-TV]		$50	Capitol 673
					from the NBC-TV production starring Sinatra and Eva Marie Saint				
3/31/56	2¹	50	●	©	4 **songs for Swingin' Lovers!**			$50	Capitol 653
					sequel to his 1954 album *Songs For Young Lovers* (#3)				
12/22/56+	8	17	●		5 **This Is Sinatra!**	[G]		$50	Capitol 768
					also see #56 below				
3/2/57	5	14		©	6 **Close To You**			$50	Capitol 789
5/27/57	2¹	36		©	7 **a Swingin' Affair!**			$50	Capitol 803
9/23/57	3	21		©	8 **Where are you?**			$50	Capitol 855
11/11/57	2¹	27			9 **Pal Joey**	[S]		$50	Capitol 912
					orchestra numbers conducted by Morris Stoloff: "Main Title," "Do It The Hard Way," "Great Big Town," "Plant You Now, Dig You Later," "You Mustn't Kick It Around" and "Strip Number"; includes "Bewitched" and "Zip" by Rita Hayworth; "My Funny Valentine" and "That Terrific Rainbow" by Kim Novak				
12/30/57+	18	2	▲	©	10 **a Jolly Christmas from Frank Sinatra**	C:#10/4 [X]		$50	Capitol 894
					Christmas charts: 27/'63, 15/'64, 20/'65, 29/'66, 53/'67, 10/'84, 28/'87, 23/'90, 19/'98				
2/3/58	❶⁵	71		©	11 **Come Fly with me**			$50	Capitol 920
4/28/58	8	7			12 **This Is Sinatra, Volume Two**	[G]		$50	Capitol 982
					also see #56 below				
6/2/58	12	1			13 **The Frank Sinatra Story**	[K]		$50	Columbia 6 [2]
9/29/58	❶⁵	120	●	©	14 **Frank Sinatra sings for Only The Lonely**	C:#21/1		$40	Capitol 1053

DEBUT	PEAK	WKS	RIAA	CD	ARTIST — Album Title	Catalog	Sym	$	Label & Number
					SINATRA, Frank — Cont'd				
2/9/59	2[5]	141	●	© 15	Come Dance With Me!			$40	Capitol 1069
					1959 Grammy winner: Album of the Year				
6/1/59	8	15		16	Look to Your Heart		[K]	$40	Capitol 1164
8/24/59	2[2]	74		© 17	No One Cares			$40	Capitol 1221
8/22/60	❶[9]	86	●	© 18	Nice 'n' Easy			$40	Capitol 1417
2/13/61	3	36		© 19	Sinatra's Swingin' Session!!!	C:#14/2		$40	Capitol 1491
4/10/61	4	60		© 20	All The Way		[G]	$40	Capitol 1538
5/1/61	4	35		© 21	Ring-A-Ding Ding!			$25	Reprise 1001
8/14/61	6	22		22	Sinatra Swings			$25	Reprise 1002
8/14/61	8	39		© 23	Come Swing With Me!			$25	Capitol 1594
11/6/61	3	42		© 24	I Remember Tommy...			$25	Reprise 1003
					tribute to **Tommy Dorsey**				
3/17/62	8	31		© 25	Sinatra & Strings			$25	Reprise 1004
4/21/62	19	29		© 26	Point Of No Return			$25	Capitol 1676
8/18/62	15	18		27	Sinatra Sings...of love and things		[K]	$25	Capitol 1729
9/1/62	18	16		© 28	Sinatra and Swingin' Brass			$25	Reprise 1005
11/10/62	25	17		© 29	All Alone			$25	Reprise 1007
12/22/62	120	2		© 30	a Jolly Christmas from Frank Sinatra		[X-R]	$50	Capitol 894
2/2/63	5	42		© 31	Sinatra-Basie			$25	Reprise 1008
					FRANK SINATRA/COUNT BASIE				
6/22/63	6	35		© 32	The Concert Sinatra			$20	Reprise 1009
9/28/63	129	4		33	Tell Her You Love Her		[K]	$20	Capitol 1919
10/5/63	8	43	●	© 34	Sinatra's Sinatra			$20	Reprise 1010
4/11/64	10	24		© 35	Days Of Wine And Roses, Moon River, and other academy award winners			$20	Reprise 1011
5/30/64	116	7		36	America, I Hear You Singing			$20	Reprise 2020
					FRANK SINATRA/BING CROSBY/FRED WARING				
8/22/64	13	31		© 37	It Might As Well Be Swing			$20	Reprise 1012
					FRANK SINATRA/COUNT BASIE				
12/12/64	9[X]	3		38	12 Songs Of Christmas		[X]	$20	Reprise 2022
					BING CROSBY/FRANK SINATRA/FRED WARING And The Pennsylvanians				
12/19/64+	19	28		© 39	Softly, As I Leave You			$20	Reprise 1013
7/3/65	9	44		40	Sinatra '65			$20	Reprise 6167
8/21/65+	5	69	●	© 41	September Of My Years			$20	Reprise 1014
					1965 Grammy winner: Album of the Year				
12/25/65+	9	32	▲	© 42	A Man And His Music		[K]	$25	Reprise 1016 [2]
					1966 Grammy winner: Album of the Year				
12/25/65+	30	16		© 43	My Kind Of Broadway			$20	Reprise 1015
4/23/66	34	14		© 44	Moonlight Sinatra			$20	Reprise 1018
6/18/66	❶[1]	73	▲	© 45	Strangers In The Night			$20	Reprise 1017
8/20/66	9	44	●	© 46	Sinatra At The Sands	C:#44/1	[L]	$25	Reprise 1019 [2]
					with **Count Basie**				
12/31/66+	6	61	●	© 47	That's Life			$20	Reprise 1020
4/15/67	19	28		© 48	Francis Albert Sinatra & Antonio Carlos Jobim			$20	Reprise 1021
7/29/67	195	2		49	The Movie Songs		[K]	$20	Capitol 2700
9/16/67	24	23		50	Frank Sinatra			$20	Reprise 1022
12/23/67+	42[X]	3		51	Have Yourself a Merry Little Christmas		[X]	$30	Harmony 7400 / 11200
					1944-47 recordings; originally released in 1948 as *Christmas Songs by Sinatra* on Columbia 167 ('78' package); reissued in 1957 as *Christmas Dreaming* on Columbia 1032; Christmas charts: 86/'67, 42/'68				
2/24/68	78	13		© 52	Francis A. & Edward K.			$20	Reprise 1024
					FRANK SINATRA & DUKE ELLINGTON				
9/7/68	55	25	▲[2]	© 53	Frank Sinatra's Greatest Hits!	C:#3/14	[G]	$20	Reprise 1025
12/28/68+	18	28	●	© 54	Cycles			$20	Reprise 1027
5/10/69	11	19	●	© 55	My Way			$20	Reprise 1029
8/23/69	186	3		56	Close-Up		[R]	$25	Capitol 254 [2]
					reissue of albums #5 & 12 above				
9/6/69	30	16		© 57	A Man Alone & Other Songs of Rod McKuen			$20	Reprise 1030
12/6/69	3[X]	4		© 58	The Sinatra Family Wish You A Merry Christmas		[X]	$20	Reprise 1026
					Frank with daughters Tina and **Nancy Sinatra**, and son Frank Jr.; first released in 1968				
4/11/70	101	10		© 59	Watertown			$15	Reprise 1031
4/24/71	73	15		© 60	Sinatra & Company			$15	Reprise 1033
6/10/72	88	17	▲	© 61	Frank Sinatra's Greatest Hits, Vol. 2	C:#16/1	[G]	$15	Reprise 1034
10/27/73	13	22	●	© 62	Ol' Blue Eyes Is Back			$15	Reprise 2155
8/3/74	48	12		© 63	Some Nice Things I've Missed			$15	Reprise 2195
12/7/74+	37	12		© 64	Sinatra - The Main Event Live		[L]	$15	Reprise 2207
					recorded at Madison Square Garden; with **Woody Herman** & The Young Thundering Herd				
1/4/75	170	3		65	Round #1		[K]	$20	Capitol 11357 [2]
4/12/80	17	24	●	© 66	Trilogy: Past, Present, Future			$25	Reprise 2300 [3]
12/5/81+	52	13		© 67	She Shot Me Down			$10	Reprise 2305
8/25/84	58	13		© 68	L.A. Is My Lady			$10	Qwest 25145
12/8/90+	126	11	●	© 69	The Capitol Years		[G]	$40	Capitol 94777 [3]
12/15/90+	98	10	●	© 70	The Reprise Collection		[K]	$40	Reprise 26340 [4]
4/27/91	138	27	▲[2]	© 71	Sinatra Reprise - The Very Good Years	C:#2[6]/33	[G]	$10	Reprise 26501

SINATRA, Frank — Cont'd

DEBUT	PEAK	WKS	RIAA	CD	ARTIST — Album Title	Catalog	Sym	$	Label & Number
12/5/92	8[X]	39		© 72	**It's Christmas Time**	C:#6/41 [X]		$10	LaserLight 15152
					BING CROSBY • FRANK SINATRA • NAT KING COLE				
					Christmas charts: 8/'92, 17/'93, 12/'94, 13/'95				
11/20/93	2[3]	38	▲[3]	© 73	**Duets**	C:#12/2		$10	Capitol 89611
12/3/94	9	18	▲	© 74	**Duets II**	C:#32/1		$10	Capitol 28103
12/2/95	61	9		© 75	Sinatra 80th - Live In Concert	C:#19/2 [L]		$10	Capitol 31723
12/9/95	66	5		© 76	Sinatra 80th - All The Best	[G]		$15	Capitol 35952 [2]
5/30/98	5[C]	4	●	© 77	**The Capitol Collectors Series**	[G]		$10	Capitol 92160
5/30/98	7[C]	10		© 78	**The Best Of The Capitol Years**	[G]		$10	Capitol 99225
6/6/98	124	2	●	© 79	**The Very Best Of Frank Sinatra**	[G]		$15	Reprise 46589 [2]
11/21/98	21[X]	7		© 80	**It's Christmas Time**	C:#13/5 [X]		$10	LaserLight 15152
					BING CROSBY • FRANK SINATRA • LOUIS ARMSTRONG				

#72 & 80 released with same title, same packaging and same label number; however, Louis Armstrong (2 songs) replaces Nat King Cole (6 songs), and only 6 of 33 tracks appear on both releases

DEBUT	PEAK	WKS	RIAA	CD	ARTIST — Album Title	Catalog	Sym	$	Label & Number
12/26/98	50[C]	1	▲	© 81	**The Sinatra Christmas Album**	[X]		$10	Reprise 45743

Adeste Fideles (10,30,51)
After You've Gone (68)
Ain't She Sweet (28)
All Alone (29,70)
All I Need Is The Girl (52,70)
All My Tomorrows (20,49,55,76)
All Of Me (46,69)
All Of You (66)
All Or Nothing At All (13,25,42,45,70,71,79)
All The Way (20,34,35,42,49,64,69,73,76,77,78,79) *2*
Almost Like Being In Love (23,69)
Always (19)
America The Beautiful (70)
American Beauty Rose (23)
Angel Eyes (14,46,64,65,69,75)
Anything Goes (4)
Anytime At All (40) *46*
Anytime-Anywhere (16)
April In Paris (11,13)
Are You Lonesome Tonight? (29)
Around The World (11)
As Time Goes By (26)
At Long Last Love (7,28)
Autumn In New York (11,64,65,69)
Autumn Leaves (8)
Available (39)
Baby Just Like You (81)
Baby Won't You Please Come Home (4)
Bad, Bad Leroy Brown (63,64) *83*
Bang Bang (My Baby Shot Me Down) (67)
Baubles, Bangles And Beads (15,48)
Be Careful, It's My Heart (21)
Beautiful Strangers (57)
Before The Music Ends (66)
Begin The Beguine (13)
Bein' Green (60,61)
Bells Of Christmas (Greensleeves) (58,81)
Best Is Yet To Come (37,70,71,74,79)
Best Of Everything (68)
Bewitched (9,32,74)
Birth Of The Blues (13)
Blame It On My Youth (6)
Blue Hawaii (11)
Blue Moon (19,65)
Blues In The Night (14,76)
Born Free (50)
Brazil (11)
But Not For Me (66)
By The Time I Get To Phoenix (54)
C'est Magnifique (49)
California (70)
Call Me (45)
Call Me Irresponsible (34,42) *78*
Can I Steal A Little Love (77)
Can't We Be Friends (33)
Cardinal ..see: Stay With Me
Castle Rock (13)
Change Partners (48)
Charmaine (29)
Cheek To Cheek (15)
Chicago (27,69,76,77) *84*
Christmas Dreaming (A Little Early This Year) (51)
Christmas Memories (81)
Christmas Song (10,30,72,76)

Christmas Waltz (10,30,58,72,81)
Ciribiribin (They're So In Love) (Theme Song) (13)
Close To You (6,60,69)
Coffee Song (21,70)
Come Back To Me (52)
Come Blow Your Horn (39)
Come Dance With Me (15,65,69)
Come Fly With Me (11,42,46,69,74,76,78,79)
Come Rain Or Come Shine (25,70,73,79)
Continental, The (35)
Cottage For Sale (17)
Crazy Love (12) *60*
Curse Of An Aching Heart (22)
Cycles (54,61) *23*
Dancing In The Dark (15)
Dancing On The Ceiling (2)
Day By Day (23)
Day In - Day Out (15)
Day In The Life Of A Fool (Manha De Carnaval) (55)
Daybreak (24)
Days Of Wine And Roses (35)
Dear Heart (39)
Deep In A Dream (2)
Didn't We (55)
Dindi (48,70)
Don'cha Go 'Way Mad (28,70,79)
Don't Be That Way (22)
Don't Cry Joe (22)
Don't Ever Go Away (60)
Don't Like Goodbyes (6,69)
Don't Sleep In The Subway (50)
Don't Take Your Love From Me (23,65,70)
Don't Wait Too Long (41)
Don't Worry 'Bout Me (5,46,56,77)
Downtown (45)
Dream (18,65)
Dream Away (62)
Dream Suspense Medley (9)
Drinking Again (50,70)
Drinking Water (60)
Early American (36)
East Of The Sun (And West Of The Moon) (24)
Ebb Tide (14,69)
Elizabeth (59)
Embraceable You (18,69,74)
Emily (39,70)
Empty Is (57)
Empty Tables (70)
End Of A Love Affair (6)
Ev'rybody Has The Right To Be Wrong! (At Least Once) (43)
Eventide (34)
Everybody Loves Somebody (12,56,69)
Everything Happens To Me (6)
Fairy Tale (16) *flip*
Falling In Love With Love (22)
Fine Romance (21)
First Noel (10,30)
Five Minutes More (23)
Fly Me To The Moon (37,42,46,70,71,74,79)
Foggy Day (21,74,79)
Follow Me (52)
Fools Rush In (18)
For A While (59)
For Once In My Life (55,74,75)
For The Good Times (66)
Forget Domani (53) *78*

Forget To Remember (70) *flip*
French Foreign Legion (20,69) *61*
From Both Sides, Now (54)
From Here To Eternity (5,42,56,69,76,77)
From Promise To Promise (57)
From This Moment On (7)
Future, The (66)
Gal That Got Away (5,56,67,70)
Garden In The Rain (70)
Gentle On My Mind (54)
Get Me To The Church On Time (46)
Girl From Ipanema (48)
Girl Next Door (29,79)
Give Her Love (47)
Glad To Be Unhappy (2)
Go Tell It On The Mountain (38,81)
Goin' Out Of My Head (61) *79*
Golden Moment (43)
Gone With The Wind (14)
Good-Bye (14)
Good Life (37)
Good Thing Going (67)
Goodbye (She Quietly Says) (59)
Goody Goody (28)
Granada (22) *64*
Guess I'll Hang My Tears Out To Dry (14,69,73,76)
Half As Lovely (Twice As True) (12,56)
Hallelujah, I Love Her So (55)
Hark! The Herald Angels Sing (10,30,72)
Have You Met Miss Jones? (22,43)
Have Yourself A Merry Little Christmas (10,30,51,72,81)
Hello, Dolly! (37,43)
Hello, Young Lovers (41)
Here Goes (69)
Here's That Rainy Day (17,69)
Here's To The Band (70)
Here's To The Losers (39,70)
Hey! Jealous Lover (12,56,69,76,77) *3*
Hey Look, No Crying (81)
Hidden Persuasion (27)
High Hopes (20,49,69,76,77,78) *30*
House I Live In (13,36,42,64,74)
How About You? (4)
How Are Ya' Fixed For Love? (76)
How Deep Is The Ocean (13,18)
How Do You Keep The Music Playing? (68,74)
How Insensitive (48,70)
(How Little It Matters) How Little We Know (12,34,42,56,69,76,77,78) *13*
How Old Am I? (41)
Hundred Years From Today (68)
I Believe (12,56)
I Believe In You (37)
I Can't Believe I'm Losing You (39) *60*
I Can't Believe That You're In Love With Me (19,69)
I Can't Get Started (17)
I Can't Stop Loving You (37)
I Concentrate On You (13,19,48,70)

I Could Have Danced All Night (15)
I Could Have Told You (16)
I Could Write A Book (9)
I Couldn't Care Less (69)
I Couldn't Sleep A Wink Last Night (6)
I Cover The Waterfront (32,70)
I Didn't Know What Time It Was (9)
I Don't Stand A Ghost Of A Chance With You (17)
I Get A Kick Out Of You (28,64,65,69,70,71,76,78,79)
I Get Along Without You Very Well (2)
I Got It Bad And That Ain't Good (33)
I Got Plenty O' Nuttin' (7,69)
I Gotta Right To Sing The Blues (27,69)
I Guess I'll Have To Change My Plan (33)
I Had The Craziest Dream (66)
I Hadn't Anyone Till You (25)
I Have Dreamed (32,70)
I Heard The Bells On Christmas Day (38,81)
I Like The Sunrise (52)
I Like To Lead When I Dance (40)
I Love My Wife (70)
I Love Paris (27,76)
I Love You (28,69)
I Loved Her (67)
I Never Knew (22)
I Only Have Eyes For You (31)
I See It Now (41)
I See Your Face Before Me (2)
I Think Of You (8)
I Thought About You (4,69)
I Wanna Be Around (37)
I Will Drink The Wine (60)
I Will Wait For You (47)
I Wish I Were In Love Again (7,69)
I Wish You Love (37)
I Wished On The Moon (44,70)
I Won't Dance (7,31)
I Would Be In Love (Anyway) (59) *88*
I Wouldn't Trade Christmas (58,81)
I'll Be Around (2)
I'll Be Home For Christmas (If Only In My Dreams) (10,30,72)
I'll Be Seeing You (24,26,42,69) *58*
I'll Never Be The Same (2)
I'll Never Smile Again (17,42,69)
I'll Only Miss Her When I Think Of Her (43,70)
I'll Remember April (26)
I'll See You Again (26)
I'm A Fool To Want You (8,69)
I'm Beginning To See The Light (28)
I'm Getting Sentimental Over You (24)
I'm Glad There Is You (13)
I'm Gonna Live Till I Die (16)
I'm Gonna Make It All The Way (63)
I'm Gonna Sit Right Down And Write Myself A Letter (31)
I'm Not Afraid (61)
I'm Walking Behind You (76,77)
I've Been There! (66)

I've Been To Town (57)
I've Got A Crush On You (13,18,46,65,69,73)
I've Got My Love To Keep Me Warm (21)
I've Got The World On A String (5,56,69,73,76,77,78)
I've Got You Under My Skin (4,34,42,44,64,65,69,70,71,73,76,78,79)
I've Had My Moments (6)
I've Heard That Song Before (23,69)
I've Never Been In Love Before (40)
If (63,75)
If I Had Three Wishes (16)
If I Had You (7,65,69)
If I Loved You (13)
If I Should Lose You (68)
If You Are But A Dream (12,13,56)
If You Go Away (55)
I'll Never Come To Me (48)
Ill Wind (33)
Imagination (43)
Impatient Years (3,16,76)
Impossible Dream (47)
In The Cool, Cool, Cool Of The Evening (35)
In The Still Of The Night (21,75)
In The Wee Small Hours Of The Morning (2,34,42,69,73,76,78,79)
Indian Summer (52,70)
Indiscreet (29)
Isle Of Capri (11)
It All Depends On You (19)
It Came Upon A Midnight Clear (10,30,51,80)
It Could Happen To You (6)
It Gets Lonely Early (41)
It Had To Be You (66)
It Happened In Monterey (4)
It Might As Well Be Spring (25,35)
It Never Entered My Mind (33,67,70)
It Started All Over Again (70)
It Was A Very Good Year (41,46,53,64,70,71,79) *28*
It's A Blue World (26)
It's A Wonderful World (22)
It's All Right With Me (49,68)
It's Always You (24)
It's Easy To Remember (6)
It's Nice To Go Trav'ling (11)
It's Only A Paper Moon (19,65)
It's Over, It's Over, It's Over (20)
It's Such A Lonely Time Of Year (58)
It's Sunday (70)
It's The Same Old Dream (12,56,69)
Jingle Bells (10,30,51,72,80)
Johnny Concho Theme (Wait For Me) (12) *75*
Just As Though You Were Here (70)
Just Friends (17)
Just In Time (15,69)
Just One Of Those Things (1)
Just The Way You Are (66)
Kids (63)
L.A. Is My Lady (68)
Lady Day (60)
Lady Is A Tramp (9,64,69,70,71,73,76,78,79)
Last Dance (15,70,71)

Last Night When We Were Young (2,41)
Laura (8,13)
Lean Baby (69,76)
Learnin' The Blues (5,31,42,56,69,76,77,78) *1*
Leaving On A Jet Plane (60)
Let Me Try Again (62,64) *63*
Let Us Break Bread Together (36)
Let's Face The Music And Dance (21,66,79)
Let's Fall In Love (21,70,79)
Let's Get Away From It All (11,65,69)
Little Drummer Boy (38,81)
Little Green Apples (54)
London By Night (11)
Lonely Town (8)
Lonesome Cities (57)
Lonesome Road (7,69)
Long Night (67,70)
Look Of Love (39)
Look To Your Heart (3,16)
Looking At The World Thru Rose Colored Glasses (31)
Lost In The Stars (32,43)
Love And Marriage (3,5,42,56,69,70,71,76,77,78,79) *5*
Love Is A Many-Splendored Thing (35)
Love Is Here To Stay (33)
Love Is Just Around The Corner (28)
(Love Is) The Tender Trap (5,31,49,56,69,76,77,78,79) *7*
Love Isn't Just For The Young (39)
Love Locked Out (6)
Love Looks So Well On You (27)
Love Me Tender (66)
Love Walked In (22,70)
Lover (23)
Loves Been Good To Me (57,61) *75*
Luck Be A Lady (40,42,43,70,71,74,79)
MacArthur Park (66)
Mack The Knife (68,70,74)
Makin' Whoopee (33,46)
Mam'selle (18)
Man Alone (57,61,70)
Man In The Looking Glass (41)
Maybe This Time (75)
Maybe You'll Be There (8)
Me And My Shadow (70) *64*
Meditation (48)
Melody Of Love (76,77)
Memories Of You (26,69)
Michael & Peter (59)
Million Dreams Ago (26)
Mistletoe And Holly (10,30)
Misty (32)
Monday Morning Quarterback (67)
Monique (27,49)
Mood Indigo (2)
Moody River (54)
Moon Got In My Eyes (44)
Moon Love (44)
Moon River (35)
Moon Song (44)
Moon Was Yellow (27,44,76) *99*
Moonlight Becomes You (44)
Moonlight In Vermont (11,44,70)
Moonlight Mood (44)

799

SINATRA, Frank — Cont'd

Moonlight On The Ganges (22)
Moonlight Serenade (44,70)
More (37)
More Than You Know (66,70)
Most Beautiful Girl In The World (45)
Mr. Success (27) **41**
Mrs. Robinson (55)
My Baby Just Cares For Me (45)
My Blue Heaven (19)
My Funny Valentine (medley) (74)
My Heart Stood Still (32,75)
My Kind Of Girl (31)
My Kind Of Town (40,42,46,64,70,71,74,79)
My One And Only Love (5,56)
My Shining Hour (66,70)
My Sweet Lady (60)
My Way (55,61,64,70,71,75,79) **27**
My Way Of Life (54) **64**
Nancy (13,34,42,70,71,79)
Nearness Of You (27)
Nevertheless (58)
New York, New York, Theme From (66,70,71,73,75,79) **32**
Nice 'N' Easy (18,65,69,76,77,78) **60**
Nice Work If You Can Get It (7,31,43,79)
Night (57)
Night And Day (25,33,42,65,69,70,71,76,78,79)
Night We Called It A Day (9)
Nightingale Sang In Berkeley Square (70)
No One Ever Tells You (7,76)
Noah (62)
Nobody Wins (62)
None But The Lonely Heart (17)
Not As A Stranger (16)
O Bambino (One Cold And Blessed Winter) (58)
O Come All Ye Faithful (30)
O Little Town Of Bethlehem (10,30,51,72,80)
Oh, How I Miss You Tonight (29)
Oh! Look At Me Now (7)
Oh, What It Seemed To Be (34,42)
Oh, You Crazy Moon (44,70)
Ol' MacDonald (20) **25**
Ol' Man River (13,32)
Old Devil Moon (4,79)
Old-Fashioned Christmas (38,81)
Oldest Established (Permanent Floating Crap Game In New York) (42)

On A Clear Day (You Can See Forever) (45)
On The Road To Mandalay (11)
On The Sunny Side Of The Street (23,69)
Once I Loved (48,70)
Once Upon A Time (41)
One For My Baby (13,14,46,69,73)
One I Love Belongs To Somebody Else (24,42,69)
One Note Samba (60)
One O'Clock Jump (46)
Only The Lonely (14,69)
Our Town (3,16,69)
Out Beyond The Window (57)
P.S. I Love You (6)
Paper Doll (23)
Pass Me By (39)
Pennies From Heaven (31,33,65,70)
Pick Yourself Up (28)
Please Be Kind (31,70,79)
Please Don't Talk About Me When I'm Gone (22)
Pocketful Of Miracles (34,79) **34**
Polka Dots And Moonbeams (24,42)
Poor Butterfly (52)
Pretty Colors (54)
Prisoner Of Love (25)
Put Your Dreams Away (For Another Day) (12,13,34,42,56,65,69,79)
Quiet Nights Of Quiet Stars (Corcovado) (48)
Rain (Falling From The Skies) (70)
Rain In My Heart (54) **62**
Reaching For The Moon (44)
Remember (29)
Ring-A-Ding Ding (21,42)
River, Stay 'Way From My Door (20) **82**
S'posin' (19)
Same Old Saturday Night (16,76,77) **81**
Sand And Sea (47)
Sandpiper, Love Theme From ...see: Shadow Of Your Smile
Santa Claus Is Comin' To Town (51,58)
Satisfy Me One More Time (63)
Saturday Night (Is The Loneliest Night Of The Week) (15,69)
Second Time Around (34,42,70,79) **50**
Secret Love (35)
Send In The Clowns (62,70,71)
Sentimental Baby (27)
Sentimental Journey (23)

September In The Rain (19,65)
September Of My Years (41,42,46,61)
September Song (26,41,70)
Serenade In Blue (28)
Shadow Of Your Smile (46,70)
She Says (59)
She's Funny That Way (18)
Should I (19)
Silent Night (10,30,51,80)
Single Man (57)
Sleep Warm (20)
So Long, My Love (12) **74**
Softly, As I Leave You (39,42,53,79) **27**
Soliloquy (13,32,42,70,75)
Some Children See Him (58)
Some Enchanted Evening (40)
Some Traveling Music (57)
Someone To Light Up My Life (60)
Someone To Watch Over Me (1,69,76)
Somethin' Stupid (50,53,70,79) **1**
Something (61,66,70)
Something Wonderful Happens In Summer (12,27,69)
Something's Gotta Give (15)
Somewhere Along The Way (26)
Somewhere In Your Heart (40,53) **32**
Somewhere My Love (Lara's Theme) (47)
Song Is Ended (29)
Song Is You (15,66,69,70)
Song Sung Blue (66)
Song Without Words (66)
South Of The Border (5,56,69,76,77,78)
South - To A Warmer Place (67)
Star! (61)
Stardust (25,79) **98**
Stars Fell On Alabama (7,69)
Stay With Me (40) **81**
Stormy Weather (13,17,68)
Strangers In The Night (45,53,70,71,75,79) **1**
Street Of Dreams (46,66,70)
Summer Knows (63)
Summer Me, Winter Me (66)
Summer Wind (45,53,70,71,73,79) **25**
Summit, The (42)
Sunny (52)
Sunrise In The Morning (60)
Sweet Caroline (63)
Sweet Lorraine (70)
Swingin' Down The Lane (4)
Swinging On A Star (35)
Take Me (24)

Taking A Chance On Love (69)
Talk To Me (20) **38**
Talk To Me Baby (39)
Tangerine (28)
Teach Me Tonight (68)
Tell Her You Love Her (33)
Tell Her (You Love Her Every Day) (40,47,53) **57**
Thanks For The Memory (67)
That Old Black Magic (23)
That Old Feeling (18)
That's All (25)
That's Life (47,53,70,71,79) **4**
That's What God Looks Like To Me (86)
Then Suddenly Love (39)
There Are Such Things (24,42)
There Used To Be A Ballpark (62,70)
There Will Never Be Another You (26)
There's A Small Hotel (9)
There's No You (8)
These Foolish Things (Remind Me Of You) (26)
They All Laughed (66)
They Came To Cordura (27,49)
They Can't Take That Away From Me (28,43,69,73,79)
This Happy Madness (60)
This Is All I Ask (41,70)
This Is My Love (50)
This Is My Song (50)
This Love Of Mine (2)
This Nearly Was Mine (32)
This Town (50,53) **53**
This Was My Love (20)
Three Coins In The Fountain (5,35,49,56,69,76,77,78)
Tie A Yellow Ribbon Round The Ole Oak Tree (63)
Time After Time (12,56,76)
Tina (70)
To Love And Be Loved (20,49,69)
Together (29)
Too Close For Comfort (15)
Too Marvelous For Words (4,69)
Train, The (59)
Triste (60)
Try A Little Tenderness (18)
Twelve Days Of Christmas (58,81)
Until The Real Thing Comes Along (68)
Wait For Me (76)
Wandering (54)
Watch What Happens (55)
Watertown (59)
Wave (60,70,79)
Way You Look Tonight (35,70,71,79)

We Wish You A Merry Christmas (81)
We Wish You The Merriest (38)
We'll Be Together Again (4)
Weep They Will (33,69)
Well Did You Evah? (76)
What A Funny Girl (You Used To Be) (59)
What Are You Doing The Rest Of Your Life? (63,70)
What Is This Thing Called Love? (2,69,76,78)
What Now My Love (47,73,75)
What Time Does The Next Miracle Leave? (66)
What'll I Do (29,70)
What's New (14,75)
What's Now Is Now (59,61)
Whatever Happened To Christmas (58,81)
When I Lost You (29)
When I Stop Loving You (16)
When I Take My Sugar To Tea (21)
When I'm Not Near The Girl I Love (40)
When No One Cares (17,69)
When Somebody Loves You (40,53)
When The Wind Was Green (41)
When The World Was Young (26)
When You're Smiling (The Whole World Smiles With You) (19,65)
When Your Lover Has Gone (33)
Where Are You? (8,69)
Where Do You Go? (17)
Where Or When (46,74,75)
White Christmas (70)
Why Try To Change Me Now? (17)
Why Was I Born (13)
Willow Weep For Me (14)
Winchester Cathedral (47)
Winners (62)
Witchcraft (20,34,42,69,73,76,77,78,79) **6**
With Every Breath I Take (6)
Without A Song (24,43,70)
Wives And Lovers (37)
World War None! (66)
World We Knew (Over And Over) (50,53) **30**
Yellow Days (52)
Yes Indeed! (23)
Yes Sir, That's My Baby (45)
Yesterday (55)
Yesterdays (25,43)

You And Me (We Wanted It All) (66)
You And The Night And The Music (21)
You Are The Sunshine Of My Life (63,64,75)
You Are There (50)
You Brought A New Kind Of Love To Me (4,40)
You Do Something To Me (19)
You Forgot All The Words (12)
You Go To My Head (13,18,65)
You Make Me Feel So Young (4,46,65,69,70,73,76,78)
You, My Love (1,16)
You Never Had It So Good (36)
You Turned My World Around (63) **83**
You Will Be My Music (62,75)
You'd Be So Easy To Love (21,70)
You'd Be So Nice To Come Home To (7)
You'll Always Be The One I Love (12)
You'll Never Know (13)
You'll Never Walk Alone (13,32)
You're A Lucky Fellow, Mr. Smith (36)
You're Cheatin' Yourself (If You're Cheatin' On Me) (12) **25**
You're Driving Me Crazy! (45)
You're Getting To Be A Habit With Me (4)
You're Gonna Hear From Me (47)
You're Nobody 'Til Somebody Loves You (22,70)
You're Sensational (69) **52**
You're So Right (For What's Wrong In My Life) (62)
Young-At-Heart (1,5,34,42,49,56,69,76,77,78,79)
Zing! Went The Strings Of My Heart (70)

★424★　　SINATRA, Nancy　　'66

Born on 6/8/40 in Jersey City, New Jersey; raised in Los Angeles. Daughter of **Frank Sinatra**. Married to **Tommy Sands** from 1960-65. Appeared in the movies *For Those Who Think Young, Get Yourself A College Girl, The Oscar* and *Speedway*.

DEBUT	PEAK	WKS	RIAA	CD	ARTIST — Album Title	Sym	$	Label & Number
3/12/66	5	42	●	©	1 **Boots**		$30	Reprise 6202
6/4/66	41	15		©	2 **How Does That Grab You?**		$25	Reprise 6207
9/3/66	122	7		©	3 **Nancy In London**		$25	Reprise 6221
2/18/67	18	24		©	4 **Sugar**		$25	Reprise 6239
9/2/67	43	26		©	5 **Country, My Way**		$25	Reprise 6251
1/13/68	37	32		©	6 **Movin' With Nancy**	[TV]	$25	Reprise 6277
4/13/68	13	44	●		7 **Nancy & Lee**		$20	Reprise 6273
					NANCY SINATRA & LEE HAZLEWOOD			
5/3/69	91	8		©	8 **Nancy**		$20	Reprise 6333
10/3/70	99	7			9 **Nancy's Greatest Hits**	[G]	$20	Reprise 6409

All By Myself (4)
As Tears Go By (1)
Bang, Bang (2)
Big Boss Man (8)
Button Up Your Overcoat (9)
By The Way (I Still Love You) (5)
Call Me (2)
Coastin' (4)
Crying Time (2)
Day Tripper (1)
Elusive Dreams (7)
End, The (3)
End Of The World (5)
Flowers On The Wall (1)
For Once In My Life (8)
Friday's Child (3,6,9) **36**
Get While The Gettin's Good (5)

God Knows I Love You (8) **97**
Greenwich Village Folk Song Salesman (7)
Hard Hearted Hannah (The Vamp Of Savannah) (4)
Help Stamp Out Loneliness (5)
Here We Go Again (8) **98**
How Does That Grab You, Darlin'? (2,9) **7**
Hutchinson Jail (3)
I Can't Grow Peaches On A Cherry Tree (3)
I Gotta Get Out Of This Town (6)
I Move Around (1)
I'm Just In Love (8)
I've Been Down So Long (It Looks Like Up To Me) (7)

If He'd Love Me (1)
In My Room (1)
It Ain't Me Babe (1)
It's Such A Pretty World Today (5)
Jackson (5,6,7,9) **14**
Just Bein' Plain Old Me (8)
Lady Bird (7) **20**
Lay Some Happiness On Me (5)
Let It Be Me (2)
Let's Fall In Love (4)
Lies (1)
Light My Fire (8)
Lightning's Girl (9) **24**
Limehouse Blues (4)
Lonely Again (5)
Long Time Woman (8)

Mama Goes Where Papa Goes (Or Papa Don't Go Out Tonight) (4)
Memories (8)
More I See You (3)
My Baby Cried All Night Long (2)
My Buddy (4)
My Dad (My Pa) (8)
My Mother's Eyes (8)
Not The Lovin' Kind (2)
Oh Lonesome Me (5)
Oh! You Beautiful Doll (4)
On Broadway (1)
Run For Your Life (1)
Sand (2,7)
See The Little Children (6)
Shades (3)

Shadow Of Your Smile (2)
So Long Babe (1) **86**
Some Velvet Morning (6,7,9) **26**
Somethin' Stupid (9) **1**
Son-Of-A-Preacher Man (8)
Sorry 'Bout That (2)
Step Aside (3)
Storybook Children (7)
Sugar Town (4,9) **5**
Summer Wine (3,7,9) **49**
Sundown, Sundown (1)
Sweet Georgia Brown (4)
These Boots Are Made For Walkin' (1,9) **1**
Things (6,9)
This Little Bird (3)
This Town (6)

Time (2)
Up, Up And Away (6)
Vagabond Shoes (4)
Wait Till You See Him (6)
Walk Through This World With Me (5)
What'd I Say (8)
What'll I Do (4)
When It's Over (5)
Who Will Buy (6)
Wishin' And Hopin' (3)
You Only Live Twice (9) **44**
You've Lost That Lovin' Feelin' (7)
Younger Than Springtime (6)

SINFIELD, Pete '73
Born in London. Rock singer/songwriter. Lyrical partner of **Robert Fripp** in **King Crimson**.

| 10/6/73 | 190 | 5 | | | **Still** | | | $15 | Manticore 66667 |

Envelopes Of Yesterday | Night People | Song Of The Sea Goat | Under The Sky | Will It Be You
House Of Hopes And Dreams | Piper, The | Still | Wholefood Boogie

SINGING NUN, The '63
Sister Luc-Gabrielle (real name: Jeanine Deckers) from the Fichermont, Belgium, convent. Recorded under the name Soeur Sourire ("Sister Smile"). **Debbie Reynolds** played Soeur Sourire in fictional 1966 movie about her life. Committed suicide on 3/31/85 (age 52).

| 11/9/63 | ❶ 10 | 39 | ● | © 1 | **The Singing Nun** | | [F] | $20 | Philips 203 |
| 4/11/64 | 90 | 14 | | 2 | **Her Joy, Her Songs** | | [F] | $20 | Philips 209 |

Alleluia (1) | Croix Du Sud (2) | Je Voudrais (1) | Midi (2) | Tous Les Chemins (1)
Avec Toi (2) | Dans Les Magasins (2) | Kabinda (Ma Petite Amie | Pauvre Devant Toi (2) | Une Fleur (2)
Chante Riviere (2) | **Dominique** (1) 1 | D'Afrique) (2) | Petit Pierrot (1)
Coeur De Dieu (2) | Entre Les Etoiles (1) | Les Mouettes (2) | Plume De Radis (1)
Complainte Pour | Fleur De Cactus (1) | Ma Petite Muse (2) | Resurrection (1)
Marie-Jacques (1) | J'ai Trouve Le Seineur (1) | Mets Ton Joli Jupon (1) | Soeur Adele (1)

SINGLETARY, Daryle '98
Born on 3/10/71 in Cairo, Georgia. Country singer/songwriter.

| 3/14/98 | 160 | 3 | | © | **Ain't It The Truth** | | | $10 | Giant 24696 |

Ain't It The Truth | Love Or The Lack Of | My Baby's Lovin' | Real Deal | Thing Called Love
I'd Live For You | Miracle In The Making | Note, The 90 | That's Where You're Wrong | You Ain't Heard Nothin' Yet

SIOUXSIE AND THE BANSHEES '91
Avant-punk group formed by singer Siouxsie Sioux (Susan Dallion) and bassist Steve Severin (Steve Havoc). Fluctuating personnel around nucleus of group: Sioux, Severin and Peter "Budgie" Clark (drums). Husband-and-wife, Sioux and Budgie, also recorded as **The Creatures**.

7/7/84	157	7		© 1	**Hyaena**			$10	Geffen 24030
5/24/86	88	15		© 2	**Tinderbox**			$10	Geffen 24092
4/11/87	188	3		© 3	**Through The Looking Glass**			$10	Geffen 24134
10/1/88	68	20		© 4	**Peepshow**			$10	Geffen 24205
6/29/91	65	21		© 5	**Superstition**			$10	Geffen 24387
3/4/95	127	2		© 6	**The Rapture**			$10	Geffen 24630

Belladonna (1) | Dear Prudence (1) | Killing Jar (4) | Ornaments Of Gold (4) | Shadowtime (5) | This Town Ain't Big Enough For
Blow The House Down (1) | Double Life (6) | **Kiss Them For Me** (5) 23 | Partys Fall (2) | Sick Child (6) | The Both Of Us (3)
Bring Me The Head Of The | Drifter (5) | Lands End (2) | Passenger, The (3) | Silly Thing (5) | This Unrest (2)
Preacher Man (1) | Fall From Grace (6) | Last Beat Of My Heart (4) | **Peek-A-Boo** (4) 53 | Silver Waterfalls (5) | This Wheel's On Fire (3)
Burn-Up (4) | Falling Down (6) | Little Johnny Jewel (3) | Pointing Bone (1) | Softly (5) | Trust In Me (3)
Candyman (2) | Fear (Of The Unknown) (5) | Little Sister (5) | Rapture, The (6) | Stargazer (6) | Turn To Stone (4)
Cannons (2) | Forever (6) | Lonely One (6) | Rawhead And Bloodybones (4) | Strange Fruit (3) | We Hunger (1)
Carousel (4) | Ghost In You (5) | Love Out Me (6) | Rhapsody (4) | Sweetest Chill (2) | You're Lost Little Girl (3)
Cities In Dust (2) | Got To Get Up (5) | 92 (2) | Running Town (1) | Swimming Horses (1)
Cry (5) | Gun (3) | Not Forgotten (6) | Scarecrow (4) | Take Me Back (1)
Dazzle (1) | Hall Of Mirrors (3) | O Baby (6) | Sea Breezes (3) | Tearing Apart (6)

SIR DOUGLAS QUINTET '69
Rock group formed in Houston: **Doug Sahm** (vocals, guitar), Augie Meyers (organ), Frank Morin (horns), Harvey Regan (bass) and John Perez (drums). Re-grouped in 1980 with Sahm, Meyers, Perez, Alvin Crow and Speedy Sparks. Sahm died of heart failure on 11/18/99 (age 58).

| 4/19/69 | 81 | 11 | | 1 | **Mendocino** | | | $25 | Smash 67115 |
| 2/14/81 | 184 | 4 | | 2 | **Border Wave** | | | $12 | Takoma 7088 |

And It Didn't Even Bring Me | I Don't Want (1) | It Was Fun While It Lasted (2) | Oh, Baby It Just Don't Matter | Sheila Tequila (2)
Down (1) | I Keep Wishing For You (2) | Lawd, I'm Just A Country Boy In | (1) | Texas Me (1)
At The Crossroads (1) | I Wanna Be Your Mama Again | This Great Big Freaky City (1) | Old Habits, Die Hard (2) | Tonite, Tonite (2)
Border Wave (2) | (1) | **Mendocino** (1) 27 | Revolutionary Ways (1) | Who'll Be The Next In Line (2)
Down On The Border (2) | If You Really Want Me To (1) | | **She's About A Mover** (1) 13 | You're Gonna Miss Me (2)

SIR LORD BALTIMORE '71
Rock trio from Brooklyn, New York: John Garner (vocals, drums), Louis Dambra (guitar) and Gary Justin (bass).

| 2/6/71 | 198 | 2 | | | **Kingdom Come** | | | $15 | Mercury 61328 |

Ain't Got Hung On You | Helium Head (I Got A Love) | I Got A Woman | Lady Of Fire | Master Heartache
Hard Rain Fallin' | Hell Hound | Kingdom Come | Lake Isle Of Innersfree | Pumped Up

SIR MIX-A-LOT '92
Born Anthony Ray on 8/12/63 in Seattle. Male rapper. Appeared as the host of the anthology TV series *The Watcher*.

10/22/88+	82	58	▲	© 1	**Swass**	C:#29/8		$10	Nastymix 70123
11/18/89	67	41	●	© 2	**Seminar**			$10	Nastymix 70150
2/22/92	9	61	▲	© 3	**Mack Daddy**			$10	Def American 26765
8/6/94	69	9		© 4	**Chief Boot Knocka**			$10	Rhyme Cartel 45540
9/14/96	123	4		© 5	**Return Of The Bumpasaurus**			$10	Rhyme Cartel 43081

Aintsta (5) | Buttermilk Biscuits (Keep On | I Got Game (2) | Mall Dropper (5) | (Peek-A-Boo) Game (2) | Slide (5)
Aunt Thomasina (5) | Square Dancin') (1) | I'll Roll You Up (2) | Man U Luv Ta Hate (5) | Playthang (5) | Something About My Benzo (2)
Baby Got Back (3) 1 | Chief Boot Knocka (4) | I'm Your New God (3) | Message To A Drag Artist (5) | **Posse' On Broadway** (1) 70 | Sprung On The Cat (4)
Bark Like You Want It (5) | Da Bomb (5) | Iron Man (1) | Mob Style (5) | Put 'Em On The Glass (4) | Square Dance Rap (1)
Beepers (2) | Denial (5) | Jack Back (3) | Monsta' Mack (4) | Rapper's Reputation (5) | Swap Meet Louie (3)
Boss Is Back (3) | Don't Call Me Da Da (4) | **Jump On It** (5) 97 | My Bad Side (2) | Ride (4) | Swass (5)
Bremelo (1) | Funk Fo Da Blvd. (5) | Just Da Pimpin' In Me (4) | My Hooptie (2) | Rippn' (1) | Testarossa (4)
Brown Shuga (4) | Gold (1) | Lead Yo Horse (5) | Nasty Dog (4) | Sag (1) | Top Ten List (5)
Buckin' My Horse (5) | Gortex (2) | Let It Beaounce (4) | National Anthem (2) | Seattle Ain't Bullshittin' (3) | What's Real (4)
Bumpasaurus (5) | Hip Hop Soldier (1) | Lockjaw (3) | No Holds Barred (3) | Seminar (2) | You Can Have Her (5)
Bumpasaurus Cometh (5) | I Checks My Bank (4) | Mack Daddy (4) | One Time's Got No Case (3) | Sleepin' Wit My Fonk (4)

SISQÓ '00
Born Mark Andrews in 1977 in Baltimore. Member of **Dru Hill**.

| 12/18/99+ | 2 1 | 60 | ▲4 | © | **Unleash The Dragon** | | | $10 | Dragon 546816 |

includes "Enchantment Passing Through" and "You Are Everything" by **Dru Hill**

Addicted | How Can I Love U 2Nite | Is Love Enough | Your Love Is Incredible
Got To Get It 40 | **Incomplete** 1 | So Sexual | **Thong Song** 3 | Unleash The Dragon

SISTER HAZEL · '97

Pop-rock group formed in Gainesville, Florida: Ken Block (vocals), Ryan Newell and Andrew Copeland (guitars), Jeff Beres (bass) and Mark Trojanowski (drums).

DEBUT	PEAK	WKS	RIAA	CD	#	Album	$	Label & Number
6/7/97	47	50	▲	©	1	...Somewhere More Familiar	$10	Universal 53030
7/15/00	63	12		©	2	Fortress	$10	Universal 157883

All for You (1) *11*
Back Porch (2)
Beautiful Thing (2)
Cerilene (2)
Champagne High (2)

Change Your Mind (2) *59*
Concede (1)
Elvis (2)
Fortress (2)
Give In (2)

Happy (1)
Just Remember (1)
Look to the Children (1)
Out There (1)
Save Me (2)

Shame On Me (2)
So Long (1)
Starfish (1)
Strange Cup Of Tea (2)
Superman (1)

Surreal (2)
Thank You (2)
Think About Me (1)
Wanted it to Be (1)
We'll Find It (1)

Your Winter (2)

SISTER SLEDGE · '79

R&B vocal group from Philadelphia: sisters Debra, Joni, Kim and Kathy Sledge.

DEBUT	PEAK	WKS	RIAA	CD	#	Album	$	Label & Number
2/24/79	3	33	▲	©	1	We Are Family	$12	Cotillion 5209
3/8/80	31	15		©	2	Love Somebody Today	$12	Cotillion 16012
2/28/81	42	29		©	3	All American Girls	$12	Cotillion 16027
2/13/82	69	14			4	The Sisters	$12	Cotillion 5231
6/4/83	169	8			5	Bet Cha Say That To All The Girls	$12	Cotillion 90069

All American Girls (3) *79*
All The Man I Need (4)
B.Y.O.B. (Bring Your Own Baby) (5)
Bet Cha Say That To All The Girls (5)
Don't You Let Me Lose It (3)
Dream On (5)
Easier To Love (1)
Easy Street (2)

Everybody's Friend (4)
Get You In Our Love (4)
Got To Love Somebody (2) *64*
Gotta Get Back To Love (5)
Grandma (4)
Happy Feeling (3)
He's Just A Runaway (3)
He's The Greatest Dancer (1) *9*
How To Love (2)

I Don't Want To Say Goodbye (3)
I'm A Good Girl (2)
If You Really Want Me (3)
Il Macquillage Lady (4)
Jacki's Theme: There's No Stopping Us (4)
Let Him Go (5)
Let's Go On Vacation (5)
Lifetime Lover (5)

Lightfootin' (4)
Lost In Music (1)
Make A Move (3)
Music Makes Me Feel Good (3)
My Guy (4) *23*
My Special Way (4)
Next Time You'll Know (3) *82*
Once In Your Life (5)
One More Time (1)
Ooh, You Caught My Heart (3)

Pretty Baby (2)
Reach Your Peak (2)
Shake Me Down (5)
Smile (5)
Somebody Loves Me (1)
Super Bad Sisters (4)
Thank You For The Party (5)
Thinking Of You (1)
We Are Family (1) *2*
You Fooled Around (2)

You're A Friend To Me (1)

SISTERS OF MERCY, The · '88

Rock duo formed in Leeds, England: Andrew Taylor (vocals) and Patricia Morrison (bass). Morrison left in early 1990; expanded to a quintet which included Tony James (bass; Generation X, Sigue Sigue Sputnik), Tim Bricheno and Andreas Bruhn (guitars), and Doktor Avalanche (drums).

DEBUT	PEAK	WKS	RIAA	CD	#	Album	$	Label & Number
2/6/88	101	16		©	1	Floodland	$10	Elektra 60762
12/1/90	136	23		©	2	Vision Thing	$10	Elektra 61017

Detonation Boulevard (2)
Doctor Jeep (2)
Dominion/Mother Russia (1)

Driven Like The Snow (1)
Flood I & II (1)
I Was Wrong (2)

Lucretia My Reflection (1)
More (2)
Never Land (A Fragment) (1)

1959 (1)
Ribbons (2)
Something Fast (2)

This Corrosion (1)
Vision Thing (2)
When You Don't See Me (2)

SIXPENCE NONE THE RICHER · '99

Pop group from Austin, Texas: Leigh Nash (vocals), Matt Slocum and Sean Kelly (guitars), Justin Cary (bass) and Dale Baker (drums). Nash is married to Mark Nash of PFR.

DEBUT	PEAK	WKS	RIAA	CD	Album	Catalog	Sym	$	Label & Number
3/6/99	89	39	▲	©	Sixpence None The Richer	C:#44/2		$10	Squint 7032

Anything
Easy To Ignore
I Can't Catch You

I Won't Stay Long
Kiss Me *2*
Lines Of My Earth

Love
Moving On
Puedo Escribir

Sister, Mother
There She Goes *32*
Waiting Room

We Have Forgotten

69 BOYZ · '95

Rap duo from Jacksonville, Florida: Albert Bryant and Mike Phillips.

DEBUT	PEAK	WKS	RIAA	CD	#	Album	$	Label & Number
7/16/94+	59	60	▲	©	1	Nineteen Ninety Quad	$10	Downlow 6901
8/1/98	114	4		©	2	The Wait Is Over	$10	QuadraSound 83031

All Men R Dawgs (1)
Backseat (2)
Beep-Beep (2)
Booty Drop (1)
Buddy-Buddy (1)
Catch 22 (2)
Da Mote (1)

Da Set (1)
Da Set, Part II (2)
Da Train (1)
Ding Dong Song (1)
Do You Want It, Baby? (2)
Ease On Down Da Road (1)
Freak You Down 2 Da Bass (1)

Get On Your Feet (2)
Get Together (1)
Girls Just Wanna (2)
Hennessy (1)
Hump N' Ya Back (1)
I Need You '98 (2)
ICU (1)

Kitty-Kitty (1) *51*
Land 69 (1)
Loose Booty (1)
One God, One Judge (2)
Puddin Tame (1)
Roll Call (2)
Roll Wit It (2)

Sticky (2)
Strip Club Luv (2)
Survival Of Da Fittest (1)
Teenie Weenie (1)
10 Chicken Wings & A Bottle Of Dom (1)
Tootsee Roll (1) *8*

2 A.M. (Whatcha Doin'?) (2)
Wasn't Me (2)
What's A Catch 22? (2)
Wilbert (2)
Woof Woof (2) *31*

SIZE, Roni/Reprazent · '00

Born in 1968 in St. Andrews, Bristol, England (Jamaican parents). Techno artist.

DEBUT	PEAK	WKS	RIAA	CD	Album	$	Label & Number
11/11/00	181	1		©	In The Mode	$10	Talkin' Loud 548201

Centre Of The Storm
Dirty Beats
Ghetto Celebrity

Heavy Rotation
Idi Banashapan
In + Out

In Tune With The Sound
Lucky Pressure
Mexican

Out Of The Game
Play The Game
Railing Pt. 2

Snapshot
Staircase
Switchblade

System Check
Who Told You?

SKAGGS, Ricky · '82

Born on 7/18/54 in Cordell, Kentucky. Country singer/songwriter/mandolin player.

DEBUT	PEAK	WKS	RIAA	CD	#	Album	$	Label & Number
6/12/82	77	30	●		1	Waitin' For The Sun To Shine	$10	Epic 37193
10/16/82	61	12	▲	©	2	Highways & Heartaches	$10	Epic 37996
11/10/84	180	5	●	©	3	Country Boy	$10	Epic 39410
3/9/85	181	4		©	4	Favorite Country Songs	[K] $10	Epic 39409

Baby, I'm In Love With You (3)
Brand New Me (3)
Can't You Hear Me Callin' (2,4)
Country Boy (3)
Crying My Heart Out Over You (1)
Don't Get Above Your Raising (1)

Don't Let Your Sweet Love Die (2)
Don't Think I'll Cry (1)
Heartbroke (2)
Highway 40 Blues (2)
I Don't Care (1)
I Wouldn't Change You If I Could (2)

I'll Take The Blame (4)
I'm Ready To Go (3)
If That's The Way You Feel (1,4)
Let's Love The Bad Times Away (2)
Lost To A Stranger (1,4)
Low And Lonely (1)

Nothing Can Hurt You (2,4)
One Way Rider (2)
Patiently Waiting (3)
Rendezvous (3)
So Round, So Firm, So Fully Packed (1)
Something In My Heart (3)
Sweet Temptation (4)

Two Highways (3)
Waitin' For The Sun To Shine (1,4)
Wheel Hoss (3)
Window Up Above (3)
Wound Time Can't Erase (4)
You May See Me Walkin' (1,4)
You've Got A Lover (2)

Your Old Love Letters (1,4)

SKEE-LO · '95

Born Anthony Roundtree on 3/5/75 in Riverside, California. Male rapper.

DEBUT	PEAK	WKS	RIAA	CD	Album	$	Label & Number
7/15/95	53	20	●	©	I Wish	$10	Sunshine 75486

Burger Song
Come Back To Me

Crenshaw
Holdin' On

I Wish *13*
Never Crossed My Mind

Superman
This Is How It Sounds

Top Of The Stairs
Waitin' For You

You Ain't Down

SKID ROW '91

Hard-rock group formed in New Jersey: Sebastian Bach (vocals), Dave Sabo and Scott Hill (guitars), Rachel Bolan (bass) and Rob Affuso (drums).

2/11/89	**6**	78	▲5	©	1 **Skid Row**	C:#34/9	$10	Atlantic 81936
6/29/91	**❶**1	46	▲2	©	2 **Slave To The Grind**		$10	Atlantic 82278
10/10/92	**58**	6	●	©	3 **B-Side Ourselves** .... [M]		$10	Atlantic 82431
4/15/95	**35**	9		©	4 **Subhuman Race**		$10	Atlantic 82730

Beat Yourself Blind (4)	Creepshow (2)	Here I Am (1)	Makin' A Mess (1)	Psycho Love (2)	Subhuman Race (4)
Beggar's Day (2)	Delivering The Goods (3)	**I Remember You** (1) *6*	Medicine Jar (4)	Psycho Therapy (3)	Sweet Little Sister (1)
Big Guns (1)	**18 And Life** (1) *4*	In A Darkened Room (2)	Midnight (medley) (1)	Quicksand Jesus (2)	Threat, The (2)
Bonehead (4)	Eileen (4)	Into Another (4)	Monkey Business (2)	Rattlesnake Shake (1)	Tornado (medley) (1)
Breakin' Down (4)	Face Against My Soul (4)	Ironwill (4)	Mudkicker (2)	Remains To Be Seen (4)	**Wasted Time** (2) *88*
Can't Stand The Heartache (1)	Firesign (4)	Little Wing (3)	My Enemy (4)	Riot Act (2)	What You're Doing (3)
C'mon And Love Me (3)	Frozen (4)	Livin' On A Chain Gang (2)	Piece Of Me (1)	Slave To The Grind (2)	**Youth Gone Wild** (1) *99*

SKINNY PUPPY '96

Industrial-rock trio from Vancouver: Kevin "Nivek Ogre " Oglivie (vocals), Cevin Key (various instruments) and Dwayne Goettel (keyboards). Goettel died of a drug overdose on 8/23/95 (age 31).

4/11/92	**193**	1		©	1 **Last Rights**....................		$10	Nettwerk 98037
3/16/96	**102**	1		©	2 **The Process**....................		$10	American 43057

Amnesia (2)	Circustance (1)	Download (1)	Killing Game (1)	Mirror Saw (1)	Scrapyard (1)
Blue Serge (2)	Cult (2)	Hardset Head (2)	Knowhere? (1)	Morter (2)	
Candle (2)	Curcible (2)	Inquisition (1)	Love In Vein (1)	Process (2)	
Cellar Heat (2)	Death (2)	Jahya (2)	Lust Chance (1)	Riverz End (1)	

SKRAPE '01

Hard-rock group from Orlando, Florida: Billy Keeton (vocals), Mike Lynchard (guitar), Brian Milner (keyboards), Pete Sison (bass) and Will Hunt (drums).

4/7/01	**157**	3		©	**New Killer America**....................		$10	RCA 67935

Blow Up	Goodbye	Isolated	Rake	Sleep	Waste
Broken Knees	I Know	Kill Control	Rise	Sunshine	What You Say

SKULL DUGGERY '98

Born Marcell Turner in New Orleans. Male rapper.

9/26/98	**21**	5		©	**These Wicked Streets**....................		$10	Penalty 3082

Drama	I'm Not A Victim	It's No Limit	My Regiment	Set Up	These Wicked Streets
For The Fans	If It Don't Make $$$...	Mistakes In The Game	Pain	Shakin In The Streets	What What
Ghetto N*ggas	If U Feel	Murder Crime	Satisfied	Testimony	Where You From

SKY '71

Rock trio from Detroit: Doug Fieger (vocals, bass), John Coury (guitar) and Rob Stawinski (drums). Fieger was later the leader of **The Knack**.

12/19/70+	**160**	6			**Sky**....................		$15	RCA Victor 4457

Feels Like 1,000 Years	How's That Treatin' Your	Make It In Time	Take Off And Fly
Goodie Two Shoes	Mouth, Babe?	One Love	There In The Greenbriar
Homin' Ground	I Still Do	Rockin' Me Yet	

SKY '81

Classical-rock group: John Williams and Kevin Peek (guitars), Francis Monkman (keyboards), Herb Flowers (bass) and Tristan Fly (drums).

11/1/80+	**125**	15			1 **Sky**.................... [I]		$15	Arista 8302 [2]
5/2/81	**181**	3			2 **Sky 3**.................... [I]		$12	Arista 4288

Adagio (1)	Dance Of The Little Fairies (1)	Hotta (1)	Sahara (1)	Tristan's Magic Garden (1)
Andante (1)	El Cielo (1)	Keep Me Safe And Keep Me	Sarabande (2)	Tuba Smarties (1)
Ballet-Volta (1)	Fifo (1)	Warm, Shelter Me From	Scherzo (1)	Vivaldi (1)
Chiropodie No. 1 (2)	Gavotte & Variations (1)	Darkness (2)	Scipio Parts I And II (1)	Watching The Aeroplanes (1)
Connecting Rooms (2)	Grace (2)	Meheeco (2)	Sister Rose (2)	Westwind (2)
Dance Of The Big Fairies (2)	Hello (2)	Moonroof (2)	**Toccata** (1) *83*	

SKYLARK '73

Pop group from Vancouver: Donny Gerrard and Bonnie Jean Cook (vocals), with **David Foster** (keyboards) and Duris Maxwell (drums). Foster was later a prolific producer/songwriter.

4/7/73	**102**	16			**Skylark**....................		$15	Capitol 11048

Brother Eddie	I'm In Love Again	Shall I Fail	Twenty-Six Years	**Wildflower** *9*
I'll Have To Go Away	Long Way To Go	Suites For My Lady	What Would I Do Without You	Writing's On The Wall

SKYY '82

Funk group from Brooklyn, New York: sisters Denise, Delores and Bonne Dunning (vocals), Solomon Roberts (vocals, guitar), Anibal Sierra (guitar), Larry Greenberg (keyboards), Gerald LaBon (bass) and Tommy McConnell (drums). Wayne Wilentz replaced Greenberg in 1982.

5/19/79	**117**	9			1 **Skyy**		$12	Salsoul 8517
3/15/80	**61**	23			2 **Skyway**		$12	Salsoul 8532
12/6/80+	**85**	20			3 **Skyyport**		$12	Salsoul 8537
11/21/81+	**18**	33	●	©	4 **Skyy Line**		$12	Salsoul 8548
11/20/82+	**81**	13			5 **Skyyjammer**		$12	Salsoul 8555
8/6/83	**183**	3			6 **Skyylight**		$12	Salsoul 8562
5/27/89	**155**	5		©	7 **Start Of A Romance**		$10	Atlantic 81853

Arrival (3)	Freak Outta (5)	Let Love Shine (5)	Music, Music (2)	Show Me The Way (6)	This Song Is For You (5)
Bad Boy (6)	Get Into The Beat (4)	Let's Celebrate (4)	My Sun Won't Shine (3)	Skyy Zoo (2)	Together (5)
Call Me (4) *26*	Girl In Blue (4)	Lets Get Up (S-K-Y-Y) (1)	No Music (3)	Skyyjammin (5)	When You Touch Me (4)
Dance, Dance, Dance (2)	Gonna Get It On (4)	Let's Touch (7)	Now That We've Found Love	Stand By Me (1)	Who's Gonna Love Me (2)
Disco Dancin' (1)	Groove Me (7)	Lets Turn It Out (1)	(6)	Start Of A Romance (7)	Won't You Be Mine (5)
Don't Stop (2)	Here's To You (3)	Love All The Way (7)	Questions No Answers (6)	Sunshine (7)	You Got Me Up (2)
Fallin' In Love Again (1)	Hey Girl (6)	Love Plane (2)	**Real Love** (7) *47*	Superlove (3)	
Feelin' It Now (7)	High (2)	Married Man (6)	Sendin' A Message (7)	Swing It (6)	
First Time Around (1)	I Can't Get Enough (3)	Miracle (5)	Sexy Minded (7)	Take It Easy (3)	
For The First Time (3)	Jam The Box (4)	Movin' Violation (5)	She's Gone (6)	This Groove Is Bad (1)	

SLADE '84

Hard-rock group formed in Wolverhampton, England: Noddy Holder (vocals), David Hill (guitar), Jim Lea (bass, keyboards) and Don Powell (drums). Group starred in the movie *Flame*.

DEBUT	PEAK	WKS	CD	#	Album Title	Sym	$	Label & Number
10/7/72	158	11		1	Slade Alive!	[L]	$15	Polydor 5508
2/17/73	69	26		2	Slayed?		$15	Polydor 5524
10/20/73	129	7		3	Sladest	[K]	$15	Reprise 2173
3/9/74	168	5		4	Stomp Your Hands, Clap Your Feet		$12	Warner 2770
7/5/75	93	14		5	Slade In Flame	[S]	$15	Warner 2865
5/5/84	33	23	©	6	Keep Your Hands Off My Power Supply		$10	CBS Associated 39336
5/4/85	132	6		7	Rogues Gallery		$10	CBS Associated 39976

(And Now - The Waltz) C'est La Vie (6)
Bangin' Man (5)
Born To Be Wild (1)
Can't Tame A Hurricane (6)
Cheap 'N' Nasty Luv (6)
Coz I Luv You (5)
Cum On Feel The Noize (3) 98
Darling Be Home Soon (1)
Do We Still Do It (4)
Don't Blame Me (4)
Everyday (4)
Far Far Away (5)
Find Yourself A Rainbow (4)
Get Down With It (1,3)
Good Time Gals (4)
Gudbuy Gudbuy (2)
Gudbuy T' Jane (2,3) 68
Harmony (7)
Hear Me Calling (1)
Hey Ho Wish You Well (7)
High And Dry (6)
How Can It Be (4)
How D' You Ride (2)
How Does It Feel? (5)
I Don' Mind (2)
I Win, You Lose (7)
I Won't Let It 'Appen Agen (2)
I'll Be There (7)
In Like A Shot From My Gun (1)
In The Doghouse (6)
Just Want A Little Bit (4)
Keep On Rocking (1)
Keep Your Hands Off My Power Supply (6)
Know Who You Are (1)
Lay It Down (5)
Let The Good Times Roll (2)
Little Sheila (7) 86
Lock Up Your Daughters (7)
Look At Last Night (2)
Look Wot You Dun (3)
Mama Weer All Crazee Now (2,3) 76
Miles Out To Sea (4)
My Friend Stan (3)
My Oh My (6) 37
My Town (3)
Myzsterious Mizster Jones (7)
O.K. Yesterday Was Yesterday (5)
Ready To Explode Medley (6)
Run Runaway (6) 20
7 Year Bitch (7)
Skweeze Me Pleeze Me (3)
Slam The Hammer Down (6)
So Far So Good (5)
Standin' On The Corner (5)
Take Me Back 'Ome (3) 97
Thanks For The Memories (5)
Them Kinda Monkeys Can't Swing (5)
This Girl (5)
Time To Rock (7)
Walking On Water, Running On Alcohol (7)
We're Really Gonna Raise The Roof (4)
When The Lights Are Out (4)
Whole World's Goin' Crazee (2)

SLASH'S SNAKEPIT '95

Born Saul Hudson on 7/23/65 in Staffordshire, England; raised in Los Angeles. Lead guitarist of **Guns N' Roses**. His group included **Gilby Clarke** (guitar; Guns N' Roses), Eric Dover (guitar), Mike Inez (bass; **Alice In Chains**) and Matt Sorum (drums; Guns N' Roses).

DEBUT	PEAK	WKS	CD	#	Album Title	Sym	$	Label & Number
3/4/95	70	6	©	1	It's Five O'Clock Somewhere		$10	Geffen 24730

Back And Forth Again
Be The Ball
Beggars & Hangers-On
Dime Store Rock
Doin' Fine
Good To Be Alive
I Hate Everybody (But You)
Jizz Da Pit
Lower
Monkey Chow
Neither Can I
Some City Ward
Take It Away
What Do You Want To Be

SLATKIN, Felix '63

Born in 1915 in St. Louis. Died on 2/9/63 (age 47). Conductor/composer/arranger.

DEBUT	PEAK	WKS	#	Album Title	Sym	$	Label & Number
4/6/63	20	12		Our Winter Love	[I]	$20	Liberty 7287

Days Of Wine And Roses
Fly Me To The Moon
Gina
I Left My Heart In San Francisco
Lawrence Of Arabia, Theme From
Lollipops And Roses
Love Letters
Meditation
Our Winter Love
Stranger On The Shore
Twelfth Of Never
What Kind Of Fool Am I

SLAUGHTER '92

Hard-rock group formed in Las Vegas: Mark Slaughter (vocals), Tim Kelly (guitar), Dana Strum (bass) and Blas Elias (drums). Slaughter and Strum were with the **Vinnie Vincent Invasion**. Kelly died in a car crash on 2/5/98 (age 35).

DEBUT	PEAK	WKS	RIAA	CD	#	Album Title	Sym	$	Label & Number
2/17/90	18	85	▲²	©	1	Stick It To Ya		$10	Chrysalis 21702
11/24/90+	123	20		©	2	Stick It Live	[L-M]	$10	Chrysalis 21816
5/9/92	8	23	●	©	3	The Wild Life		$10	Chrysalis 21911
5/20/95	182	1		©	4	Fear No Evil		$10	CMC 7403

Breakdown N' Cry (4)
Burnin' Bridges (1,2)
Dance For Me Baby (3)
Days Gone By (3)
Desperately (1)
Divine Order (4)
Do Ya Know (3)
Eye To Eye (1,2)
Fly To The Angels (1,2) 19
Gave Me Your Heart (1)
Get Used To It (4)
Hard Times (4)
Hold On (3)
It'll Be Alright (4)
Let The Good Times Roll (4)
Live Like There's No Tomorrow (4)
Loaded Gun (1,2)
Mad About You (1)
Move To The Music (3)
Old Man (3)
Out For Love (3)
Outta My Head (4)
Prelude (4)
Reach For The Sky (3)
Real Love (3)
Searchin' (4)
Shake This Place (3)
She Wants More (1)
Spend My Life (1) 39
Streets Of Broken Hearts (3)
That's Not Enough (1)
Thinking Of June (1)
Times They Change (3)
Unknown Destination (4)
Up All Night (1,2) 27
Wild Life (3)
Wingin' It (1)
Yesterday's Gone (4)
You Are The One (1)

SLAVE '77

Funk group from Dayton, Ohio, formed by Steve Washington (trumpet). Longtime members of group included Mark Adams (bass), Floyd Miller (vocals, horns) and Danny Webster (vocals, guitar). Washington and members Curt Jones and Starleana Young (vocals) and Tom Lockett (sax) left to form **Aurra** in 1979. Steve Arrington (drums, vocals) was a member from 1979-82. Young and Jones later formed **Déja**.

DEBUT	PEAK	WKS	RIAA	CD	#	Album Title	Sym	$	Label & Number
4/9/77	22	28	●	©	1	Slave		$12	Cotillion 9914
12/17/77+	67	15			2	The Hardness Of The World		$12	Cotillion 5201
8/19/78	78	10			3	The Concept		$12	Cotillion 5206
12/8/79+	92	15			4	Just A Touch Of Love		$12	Cotillion 5217
11/1/80+	53	34	●	©	5	Stone Jam		$12	Cotillion 5224
10/10/81	46	23			6	Show Time		$12	Cotillion 5227
1/15/83	177	6			7	Visions Of The Lite		$10	Cotillion 90024
10/22/83	168	5			8	Bad Enuff		$10	Cotillion 90118

Are You Ready For Love? (4)
Baby Sinister (2)
Bad Girl (8)
Be My Babe (7)
Can't Get Enough Of You (2)
Come To Blow Ya Mind (7)
Coming Soon (4)
Dance (4)
Do You Like It...(Girl) (7)
Drac Is Back (3)
Dreamin' (5)
Feel My Love (5)
For The Love Of U (6)
Friday Nites (7)
Funken Town (4)
Funky Lady (Foxy Lady) (2)
Great American Funk Song (2)
Happiest Days (1)
I'll Be Gone (7)
Just A Touch Of Love (4)
Just Freak (3)
Let's Spend Some Time (5)
Life Can Be Happy (2)
Love Me (1)
Never Get Away (5)
Painted Pictures (4)
Party Hardy (1)
Party Lites (6)
Party Song (6)
Rendezvous (8)
Roots (4)
Screw Your Wig On Tite (1)
Separated (1)
Shake It Up (8)
Shine (4)
Show Down (8)
Sizzlin' Hot (5)
Slide (1) 32
Smokin (6)
Snap Shot (6) 91
Son Of Slide (1)
Spice Of Life (Oh Yes, You're The Best) (6)
Starting Over (5)
Stay In My Life (7)
Steal Your Heart (6)
Stellar Fungk (3)
Steppin' Out (8)
Stone Jam (8)
Sweet Thang (7)
Thank You (4)
Thank You Lord (3)
Turn You Out (In & Out) (8)
Visions (7)
Volcano Rupture (4)
Wait For Me (6)
Warning (4)
Watching You (5) 78
Way You Love Is Heaven (3)
We Can Make Love (2)
We've Got Your Party (3)
World's On Hard (3)
You And Me (1)

SLAYER '94

Hard-rock group formed in Los Angeles: Tom Araya (vocals, bass), Jeff Hanneman and Kerry King (guitars), and Dave Lombardo (drums). Paul Bostaph replaced Lombardo in 1995.

DEBUT	PEAK	WKS	RIAA	CD	#	Album Title	Sym	$	Label & Number
11/15/86	94	18	●	©	1	Reign In Blood		$10	Def Jam 24131
8/6/88	57	19	●	©	2	South Of Heaven		$10	Def Jam 24203
10/27/90	40	23	●	©	3	Seasons In The Abyss		$10	Def American 24307
11/9/91	55	10		©	4	Live - Decade Of Aggression	[L]	$15	Def American 26748 [2]
10/15/94	8	9	●	©	5	Divine Intervention		$10	American 45522
6/15/96	34	5		©	6	Undisputed Attitude		$10	American 43072

SLAYER — Cont'd

| 6/27/98 | 31 | 6 | © | 7 | Diabolus In Musica | | | $10 | American 69192 |

Abolish Government/Superficial Love (6) · Altar Of Sacrifice (1,4) · Angel Of Death (1,4) · Anti-Christ (4) · Behind The Crooked Cross (2) · Bitter Peace (7) · Black Magic (4) · Blood Red (3,4) · Born Of Fire (1,4) · Can't Stand You (6) · Captor Of Sin (4) · Chemical Warfare (4) · Circle Of Beliefs (5) · Cleanse The Soul (2) · Criminally Insane (1) · Ddamm (6) · Dead Skin Mask (3,4) · Death's Head (7) · Desire (4) · Die By The Sword (4) · Disintegration/Free Money (6) · Dissident Aggressor (2) · Dittohead (2) · Divine Intervention (5) · Epidemic (1) · Expendable Youth (3,4) · Fictional Reality (5) · Filler/I Don't Want To Hear It (6) · Gemini (6) · Ghosts Of War (2) · Guilty Of Being White (6) · Hallowed Point (3,4) · Hell Awaits (4) · I Hate You (6) · I'm Gonna Be Your God (6) · In The Name Of God (7) · Jesus Saves (1,4) · Killing Fields (5) · Live Undead (2) · Love To Hate (7) · Mandatory Suicide (2,4) · Mind Control (5) · Mr. Freeze (6) · Necrophobic (1) · Overt Enemy (7) · Perversions Of Pain (7) · Piece By Piece (1) · Point (7) · Postmortem (1,4) · Raining Blood (1,4) · Read Between The Lies (2) · Reborn (1) · Richard Hung Himself (6) · SS-3 (5) · Screaming From The Sky (7) · Scrum (7) · Seasons In The Abyss (3,4) · Serenity In Murder (5) · Sex. Murder. Art. (5) · Silent Scream (2) · Skeletons Of Society (3) · South Of Heaven (2,4) · Spill The Blood (2) · Spirit In Black (3,4) · Spiritual Law (6) · Stain Of Mind (7) · Temptation (3) · 213 (5) · Verbal Abuse/Leeches (6) · Violent Pacification (6) · War Ensemble (3,4)

SLEATER-KINNEY '00

Female rock trio from Olympia, Washington: Corin Tucker (vocals, guitar), Carrie Brownstein (bass) and Janet Weiss (drums).

| 3/13/99 | 181 | 1 | © | 1 | The Hot Rock | | | $10 | Kill Rock Stars 321 |
| 5/20/00 | 177 | 1 | © | 2 | All Hands On The Bad One | | | $10 | Kill Rock Stars 360 |

All Hands On The Bad One (2) · Ballad Of A Ladyman (2) · Banned From The End Of The World (1) · Burn, Don't Freeze! (1) · Don't Talk Like (1) · End Of You (1) · Get Up (1) · God Is A Number (1) · Hot Rock (1) · Ironclad (2) · Leave You Behind (1) · Living In Exile (1) · Male Model (1) · Memorize Your Lines (1) · Milkshake n' Honey (2) · #1 Must Have (2) · One Song For You (1) · Pompeii (2) · Professional, The (2) · Quarter To Three (1) · Size Of Our Love (1) · Start Together (1) · Swimmer, The (2) · Was It A Lie? (2) · You're No Rock n' Roll Fun (2) · Youth Decay (2)

SLEDGE, Percy '66

Born on 11/25/40 in Leighton, Alabama. R&B singer.

6/4/66	37	21	©	1	When A Man Loves A Woman			$50	Atlantic 8125
11/26/66	136	3		2	Warm & Tender Soul			$50	Atlantic 8132
8/5/67	178	3		3	The Percy Sledge Way			$50	Atlantic 8146
5/25/68	148	6	©	4	Take Time To Know Her			$50	Atlantic 8180
3/1/69	133	11	©	5	The Best Of Percy Sledge		[G]	$25	Atlantic 8210

Baby, Help Me (4,5) 87 · Between These Arms (4) · Come Softly To Me (4) · **Cover Me** (4,5) 42 · Dark End Of The Street (3,5) · Drown In My Own Tears (3) · Feed The Flame (4) · Heart Of A Child (2) · High Cost Of Leaving (4) · I Had A Talk With My Woman (3) · I Love Everything About You (4) · I Stand Accused (2) · I'm Hanging Up My Heart For You (2) · I've Been Loving You Too Long (To Stop Now) (3) · **It Tears Me Up** (2,5) 20 · It's All Wrong But It's Alright (4) · **Just Out Of Reach (Of My Two Empty Arms)** (3,5) 66 · Love Makes The World Go Round (1) · Love Me All The Way (1) · Love Me Like You Mean It (1) · **Love Me Tender** (2) 40 · My Adorable One (1) · **My Special Prayer** (3,5) 93 · Oh How Happy (2) · Pledging My Love (3) · Put A Little Lovin' On Me (1) · So Much Love (2) · Spooky (4) · Success (1) · **Sudden Stop** (4,5) 63 · Sweet Woman Like You (2) · **Take Time To Know Her** (4,5) 11 · Tell It Like It Is (3) · That's How Strong My Love Is (2) · Thief In The Night (4) · Try A Little Tenderness (2) · **Warm And Tender Love** (2,5) 17 · **What Am I Living For** (3) 91 · **When A Man Loves A Woman** (1,5) 1 · When She Touches Me (Nothing Else Matters) (1) · You Don't Miss Your Water (3) · You Fooled Me (1) · You Send Me (1) · You're All Around Me (5) · You're Pouring Water On A Drowning Man (1) · You've Really Got A Hold On Me (2)

SLEEZE BEEZ '90

Hard-rock group formed in Holland: Andrew Elt (vocals), Chriz Van Jaarsveld and Don Van Spall (guitars), Ed Jongsma (bass) and Jan Koster (drums).

| 5/19/90 | 115 | 15 | © | | Screwed Blued & Tattooed | | | $10 | Atlantic 82069 |

Damned If We Do, Damned If We Don't · Don't Talk About Roses · Girls Girls, Nasty Nasty · Heroes Die Young · House Is On Fire · Rock In The Western World · Screwed Blued 'N Tattooed · Stranger Than Paradise · This Time · When The Brains Go To The Balls

SLICK, Grace '80

Born Grace Wing on 10/30/39 in Chicago. Female lead singer of **Jefferson Airplane/Starship**.

5/4/68	166	4		1	Conspicuous Only In Its Absence		[E-L]	$30	Columbia 9624
					THE GREAT SOCIETY with GRACE SLICK				
					recorded in 1965				
12/25/71+	89	9	©	2	Sunfighter			$15	Grunt 1002
					PAUL KANTNER/GRACE SLICK				
6/23/73	120	12	©	3	Baron von Tollbooth & The Chrome Nun			$15	Grunt 0148
					PAUL KANTNER, GRACE SLICK & DAVID FREIBERG				
2/9/74	127	7		4	Manhole			$15	Grunt 0347
4/5/80	32	16		5	Dreams			$12	RCA Victor 3544
2/14/81	48	14		6	Welcome To The Wrecking Ball!			$12	RCA Victor 3851

Across The Board (3) · Angel Of Night (5) · Arbitration (6) · Ballad Of The Chrome Nun (3) · Better Lying Down (4) · China (4) · ¿Come Again? Toucan (4) · Diana - Part 1 & 2 (2) · Didn't Think So (1) · Do It The Hard Way (5) · Dreams (5) · Earth Mother (2) · El Diablo (5) · Epic (#38) (4) · Face To The Wind (5) · Fat (3) · Father Bruce (1) · Fishman (3) · Flowers Of The Night (3) · Full Moon Man (3) · Garden Of Man (5) · Grimly Forming (1) · Harp Tree Lament (3) · Holding Together (2) · It's Only Music (4) · Jay (4) · Just A Little Love (6) · Let It Go (5) · Lines (6) · Look At The Wood (2) · Manhole, Theme From (4) · Million (2) · Mistreater (6) · No More Heroes (6) · Often As I May (1) · Outlaw Blues (1) · Right Kind (6) · Round & Round (6) · Sally Go 'Round The Roses (1) · Sea Of Love (6) · **Seasons** (5) 95 · Shooting Star (6) · Shot In The Dark (6) · Silver Spoon (2) · Sketches Of China (3) · Somebody To Love (1) · Sunfighter (2) · Titanic (2) · Universal Copernican Mumbles (2) · Walkin (3) · When I Was A Boy I Watched The Wolves (2) · White Boy (Transcaucasian Airmachine Blues) (3) · White Rabbit (1) · Wrecking Ball (6) · Your Mind Has Left Your Body (3)

SLICK RICK '99

Born Ricky Walters on 1/14/65 in London (Jamaican parents). Moved to New York City in 1979. Male rapper.

1/21/89	31	40	▲	©	1	The Great Adventures Of Slick Rick			$10	Def Jam 40513
7/20/91	29	13		©	2	The Ruler's Back			$10	Def Jam 47372
12/10/94	51	6		©	3	Behind Bars			$10	Def Jam 523847
6/12/99	8	17	●	©	4	The Art Of Storytelling			$10	Def Jam 558936

Adults Only (4) · All Alone (No One To Be With) (3) · **Behind Bars** (3) 87 · Bond (2) · Children's Story (1) · Cuz It's Wrong (3) · Frozen (4) · Get A Job (3) · Hey Young World (4) · I Own America Parts 1 & 2 (4) · I Run This (4) · I Shouldn't Have Done It (2) · I'm Captive (3) · Impress The Kid (4) · Indian Girl (An Adult Story) (1) · It's A Boy (2,3) · Kill Niggaz (4) · King (2) · King Piece In The Chess Game (4) · Kit (What's The Scoop) (1) · La Di Da Di Live (4) · Let's All Get Down (3) · Let's Get Crazy (1) · Lick The Balls (1) · Love That's True (Part I & II) (3) · Me & Nas Bring It To Your Hardest (4) · Memories (4) · Mistakes Of A Woman In Love With Other Men (2) · Moment I Feared (1) · Mona Lisa (4) · Moses (2) · Ruler's Back (1)

SLICK RICK — Cont'd

Runaway (2)	Sittin' In My Car (3)	Teacher, Teacher (1)	Top Cat (2)	2 Way Street (4)	We Turn It On (4)
Ship (2)	Slick Rick-The Ruler (4)	Teenage Love (1)	Trapped In Me (4)	Unify (4)	Who Rotten 'Em (4)
Show Live (4)	Street Talkin' (4)	Tonto (2)	Treat Her Like A Prostitute (1)	Venus (2)	Why, Why, Why (4)

SLIPKNOT '00

Hard-rock group from Des Moines, Iowa: Corey Taylor (vocals), Mick Thomson and Jim Root (guitars), Sid Wilson (DJ), Craig Jones (samples), Chris Fehn and Shawn Crahan (percussion), Paul Gray (bass) and Joey Jordison (drums).

| 7/17/99+ | 51 | 77 ▲ © | Slipknot | 742617000027 | $10 | I Am 8655 |

Diluted	Liberate	Prosthetics	Surfacing
Eyeless	No Life	Purity	(Sic)	Tattered & Torn
Frail Limb Nursery	Only One	Scissors	Spit It Out	Wait And Bleed

SLUM VILLAGE '00

Rap trio from Detroit: Baatin, T3 and Jay Dee.

| 8/26/00 | 180 | 1 © | Fantastic, Vol. 2 | $10 | GoodVibe 2025 |

CB4	Fall In Love	Hold Tight	Players	2U4U
Climax (Girl Sh**)	Forth And Back	I Don't Know	Raise It Up	Untitled/Fantastic
Conant Gardens	Get Dis Money	Jealousy	Tell Me	What It's All About
Eyes Up	Go Ladies	Once Upon A Time	Thelonious

★406★ SLY & THE FAMILY STONE '71

Born Sylvester Stewart on 3/15/44 in Dallas. R&B singer/keyboardist/producer. Formed The Family Stone in San Francisco: Sly's brother Freddie Stone (guitar), Cynthia Robinson (trumpet), Jerry Martini (saxophone), Sly's sister Rosie Stone (piano, vocals), Sly's cousin **Larry Graham** (bass) and Gregg Errico (drums). Graham formed **Graham Central Station** in 1973. Group inducted into the Rock and Roll Hall of Fame in 1993.

5/4/68	142	7	©	1	Dance To The Music	$20	Epic 26371
12/7/68	195	5	©	2	Life	$20	Epic 26397
4/26/69	13	102 ▲	©	3	Stand!	$20	Epic 26456
11/7/70	2¹	79 ▲⁵	©	4	Greatest Hits	[G]	$15	Epic 30325
11/13/71	❶²	31 ▲	©	5	There's A Riot Goin' On	$15	Epic 30986
6/30/73	7	33 ●	©	6	Fresh	$15	Epic 32134
7/27/74	15	15 ●		7	Small Talk	$15	Epic 32930
11/8/75	45	10		8	High On You	$15	Epic 33835

SLY STONE

| 11/10/79 | 152 | 3 | 9 | Back On The Right Track | $12 | Warner 3303 |

Africa Talks To You "The Asphalt Jungle" (5)	Dynamite! (2)	I Get High On You (8) 52	Livin' While I'm Livin' (7)	Runnin' Away (5) 23	Thank You For Talkin' To Me Africa (5)
Are You Ready (1)	Everybody Is A Star (4) flip	I Want To Take You Higher (3,4) 38	Loose Booty (7) 84	Same Thing (Makes You Laugh, Makes You Cry) (9)	Thankful N' Thoughtful (6)
Babies Makin' Babies (6)	Everyday People (3,4) 1		Love City (2)	Say You Will (7)	That's Lovin' You (8)
Back On The Right Track (9)	Family Affair (5) 1	I'm An Animal (2)	Luv N' Haight (5)	Sex Machine (3)	There's A Riot Goin' On (5)
Better Thee Than Me (7)	Frisky (6) 79	If It Were Left Up To Me (6)	M'Lady (2,4) 93	Sheer Energy (9)	This Is Love (7)
Brave & Strong (5)	Fun (2,4)	If It's Not Addin' Up.... (9)	Mother Beautiful (7)	Shine It On (9)	Time (5)
Can't Strain My Brain (7)	Green Eyed Monster Girl (8)	If You Want Me To Stay (6) 12	My World (8)	Sing A Simple Song (3,4) 89	Time For Livin' (7) 32
Chicken (2)	Greed (8)	In Time (6)	Never Will I Fall In Love Again (1)	Skin I'm In (6)	Who Do You Love? (8)
Color Me True (1)	Harmony (2)	Into My Own Thing (2)	Organize (8)	Small Talk (7)	Who's To Say? (9)
Crossword Puzzle (8)	Higher (1)	It Takes All Kinds (9)	Plastic Jim (2)	So Good To Me (8)	Wishful Thinkin' (7)
Dance To The Medley (1)	Holdin' On (7)	Jane Is A Groupee (2)	Poet (5)	Somebody's Watching You (3)	You Can Make It If You Try (3,4)
Dance To The Music (1,4) 8	Hot Fun In The Summertime (4) 2	Just Like A Baby (5)	Que Sera, Sera (Whatever Will Be, Will Be) (6)	Spaced Cowboy (5)	(You Caught Me) Smilin' (5)
Don't Burn Baby (1)	I Ain't Got Nobody (For Real) (1)	Keep On Dancin' (6)	Remember Who You Are (9)	Stand! (3,4) 22	
Don't Call Me Nigger, Whitey (3)	I Don't Know (Satisfaction) (6)	Le Lo Li (8)	Ride The Rhythm (1)	Thank You (Falettinme Be Mice Elf Agin) (4) 1	
		Let Me Have It All (6)			
		Life (2,4) 93			

SLY FOX '86

Duo of Gary "Mudbone" Cooper and Michael Camacho.

| 3/1/86 | 31 | 22 | Let's Go All The Way | $10 | Capitol 12367 |

Como Tu Te Llama? (What Is Your Name)	Don't Play With Fire	If Push Comes To A Shove	Merry-Go-Round	Won't Let You Go (A Wedding Song)
	I Still Remember	Let's Go All The Way 7	Stay True 94	

SMALL, Millie '64

Born Millicent Smith on 10/6/46 in Jamaica. Nicknamed "The Blue Beat Girl."

| 8/8/64 | 132 | 5 | My Boy Lollipop | $50 | Smash 67055 |

Bluey Louey	He's Mine	My Boy Lollipop 2	Since You've Been Gone	Sweet William 40	Until You're Mine
Don't You Know	I'm In Love Again	Oh, Henry	Sugar Dandy	Tom Hark	What Am I Living For

SMALL FACES '68

Rock group formed in England: Steve Marriott (vocals, guitar), **Ian McLagen** (organ), **Ronnie Laine** (bass) and Kenney Jones (drums). In 1968, Marriott formed **Humble Pie**. Remaining members evolved into **Faces** in 1969; disbanded in 1975. Jones joined **The Who** in 1978, formed **The Law** in 1991. Marriott died in a fire on 4/20/91 (age 44). Lane died of multiple sclerosis on 6/4/97 (age 51).

| 3/16/68 | 178 | 3 | © | 1 | There Are But Four Small Faces | $50 | Immediate 52002 |
| 9/21/68 | 159 | 9 | © | 2 | Ogdens' Nut Gone Flake | $50 | Immediate 52008 |

features a round album cover

| 8/5/72 | 176 | 10 | | 3 | Early Faces | [E] | $20 | Pride 0001 |
| 3/17/73 | 189 | 6 | | 4 | Ogdens' Nut Gone Flake | [R] | $15 | Abkco 4225 |

new cover is nearly identical to original, inside a square sleeve

Afterglow (2,4)	Here Come The Nice (1)	Journey, The (2,4)	Ogdens' Nut Gone Flake (2,4)	Song Of A Baker (2,4)	What's The Matter Baby (3)
Come Back And Take This Hurt Off Me (3)	Hey Girl (3)	Lazy Sunday (2,4)	Rene (2,4)	Sorry She's Mine (3)	Whatcha Gonna Do About It (3)
Get Yourself Together (1)	Hungry Intruder (2,4)	Long Agos And Worlds Apart (2,4)	Rollin' Over (2,4)	Talk To You (1)	
Green Circles (1)	I Feel Much Better (3)	Mad John (2,4)	Runaway (2,4)	(Tell Me) Have You Ever Seen Me (1)	
Happiness Stan (2,4)	I Got Mine (3)	My Mind's Eye (3)	Sha La La La Lee (3)	Tin Soldier (1) 73	
Happydaystoytown (2,4)	I'm Only Dreaming (1)	My Way Of Giving (1)	Shake (3)	Up The Wooden Hills (1)	
	Itchycoo Park (1) 16		Show Me The Way (1)		

★372★ SMASHING PUMPKINS, The '95

Rock group from Chicago: Billy Corgan (vocals, guitar), **James Iha** (guitar), D'Arcy Wretzky (bass) and Jimmy Chamberlin (drums). Touring keyboardist Jonathan Melvoin, son of Mike Melvoin (**The Plastic Cow**) and brother of Wendy (**Wendy & Lisa**) and Susannah (**The Family**) Melvoin, died of a drug overdose on 7/12/96 (age 34).

DEBUT	PEAK	WKS	RIAA	CD	ARTIST — Album Title	Catalog	Sym	$	Label & Number
9/7/91	195	1	▲	©	1 Gish	C:#20/32		$20	Caroline 1705
8/14/93	10	89	▲⁴	©	2 **Siamese Dream**	C:#4/69		$10	Virgin 88267
10/22/94	4	23	▲	©	3 **Pisces Iscariot**		[K]	$10	Virgin 39834
					contains B-sides and previously unavailable tracks				
11/11/95	❶¹	93	▲⁹	©	4 **Mellon Collie And The Infinite Sadness**			$15	Virgin 40861 [2]
5/11/96	46	12	●	©	5 **Zero**		[M]	$10	Virgin 38545
12/14/96	42	6	▲	©	6 **The Aeroplane Flies High**		[K]	$25	Virgin 38564 [5]
6/20/98	2¹	25	▲	©	7 **Adore**			$10	Virgin 45879
3/18/00	3	13		©	8 **Machina/The Machines Of God**			$10	Virgin 48936

Aeroplane Flies High (Turns Left, Looks Right) (6)
Age Of Innocence (8)
Annie-Dog (7)
Appels + Oranjes (7)
Ava Adore (7) *42*
Beautiful (4)
Behold! The Night Mare (7)
Believe (6)
Bells, The (6)
Blank (6)
Blank Page (7)
Blew Away (3)
Blue (3)
Blue Skies Bring Tears (8)
Bodies (4)
Boy, The (6)
Bullet With Butterfly Wings (4,6) *22*
Bury Me (1)
By Starlight (4)

Cherry (6)
Cherub Rock (2)
Clones (We're All) (6)
Crestfallen (7)
Crush (-)
Crying Tree Of Mercury (8)
Cupid De Locke (4)
Daphne Descends (7)
Daydream (1)
Destination Unknown (6)
Disarm (2)
Dreaming (6)
Everlasting Gaze (8)
Farewell And Goodnight (4)
For Martha (7)
Frail And Bedazzled (3)
Fristessa (1)
Fuck You (An Ode To No One) (4)
Galapogos (4)
Geek U.S.A. (2)
Girl Named Sandoz (3)

Glass And The Ghost Children (8)
God (5,6)
Heavy Metal Machine (8)
Hello Kitty Kat (3)
Here Is No Why (4)
Hummer (2)
I Am One (1)
I Of The Mourning (8)
Imploding Voice (4)
In The Arms Of Sleep (4)
Jellybelly (4)
Jupiter's Lament (6)
La Dolly Vita (3)
Landslide (3)
Last Song (6)
Lily (My One And Only) (4)
Love (4)
Luna (2)
Marquis In Spades (5,6)
Mayonaise (2)
Medellia Of The Gray Skies (6)

Meladori Magpie (6)
Mellon Collie And The Infinite Sadness (4)
Mouths Of Babes (5,6)
Muzzle (4)
My Blue Heaven (6)
Night Like This (6)
1979 (4,6) *12*
Obscured (3)
Once Upon A Time (7)
Pastichio Medley (5,6)
Pennies (5,6)
Perfect (7) *54*
Pissant (3)
Plume (3)
Porcelina Of The Vast Oceans (4)
Pug (7)
Quiet (2)
Raindrops + Sunshowers (8)
Rhinoceros (1)
Rocket (2)

Rotten Apples (6)
Sacred And Profane (8)
...Said Sadly (6)
Set The Ray To Jerry (6)
Shame (7)
Silverfuck (2)
Siva (1)
Snail (1)
Soma (2)
Soothe (3)
Spaceboy (7)
Spaced (3)
Stand Inside Your Love (8)
Starla (1)
Stumbleine (4)
Suffer (1)
Sweet Sweet (2)
Take Me Down (4)
Tale Of Dusty And Pistol Pete (7)
Tales Of A Scorched Earth (4)
Tear (7)

Thirty-Three (4,6) *39*
This Time (8)
Thru The Eyes Of Ruby (4)
To Forgive (4)
To Sheila (7)
Today (7)
Tonight, Tonight (4,6) *36*
Transformer (6)
Tribute To Johnny (5,6)
Try, Try, Try (8)
Ugly (6)
We Only Come Out At Night (4)
Where Boys Fear To Tread (4)
Whir (3)
Window Paine (1)
With Every Light (8)
Wound (8)
X.Y.U. (4)
You're All I've Got Tonight (6)
Zero (4,5,6)

SMASH MOUTH '99

Pop-rock group from San Jose: Steve Harwell (vocals), Greg Camp (guitar), Paul DeLisle (bass) and Kevin Coleman (drums).

DEBUT	PEAK	WKS	RIAA	CD	ARTIST — Album Title	Catalog	Sym	$	Label & Number
8/2/97+	19	60	▲²	©	1 **Fush Yu Mang**			$10	Interscope 90142
6/26/99	6	66	▲³	©	2 **Astro Lounge**			$10	Interscope 90316

All Star (2) *4*
Beer Goggles (1)
Can't Get Enough Of You Baby (2)
Come On Come On (2)

Defeat You (2)
Diggin' Your Scene (2)
Disconnect The Dots (1)
Fallen Horses (2)
Flo (1)

Fonz (1)
Heave-Ho (1)
Home (2)
I Just Wanna See (2)
Let's Rock (1)

Nervous In The Alley (2)
Padrino (1)
Pet Names (1)
Push (1)
Radio (2)

Road Man (2)
Satellite (2)
Stoned (2)
Then The Morning Comes (2) *11*

Walkin' On The Sun (1)
Waste (2)
Who's There (2)
Why Can't We Be Friends (1)

SMITH '69

Pop-rock group from Los Angeles: **Gayle McCormick** (vocals), Rick Cliburn and Alan Parker (guitars), Larry Moss (keyboards), Jerry Carter (bass) and Robert Evans (drums).

DEBUT	PEAK	WKS	RIAA	CD	ARTIST — Album Title	Catalog	Sym	$	Label & Number
8/23/69	17	28		©	1 **a group called Smith**			$20	Dunhill/ABC 50056
7/4/70	74	12			2 **Minus-Plus**			$20	Dunhill/ABC 50081

Baby It's You (1) *5*
Born In Boston (2)
Circle Man (2)
Comin' Back To Me (1)

Feel The Magic (2)
I Don't Believe (I Believe) (1)
I Just Wanna Make Love To You (1)

I'll Hold Out My Hand (1)
Jason (2)
Last Time (1)
Let's Get Together (1)

Let's Spend The Night Together (1)
Minus-Plus (2)
Mojaleskey Ridge (1)

Since You've Been Gone (2)
Take A Look Around (2) *43*
Tell Him No (1)
What Am I Gonna Do (2) *73*

Who Do You Love (1)
You Don't Love Me (Yes I Know) (2)

SMITH, Cal '69

Born Calvin Grant Shofner on 4/7/32 in Gans, Oklahoma; raised in Oakland. Country singer/guitarist.

DEBUT	PEAK	WKS	RIAA	CD	ARTIST — Album Title	Catalog	Sym	$	Label & Number
9/6/69	170	2			1 **Cal Smith Sings**			$20	Kapp 3608
4/14/73	191	3			2 **I've Found Someone Of My Own**			$15	Decca 75369

At The Sight Of You (1)
Ballad Of Forty Dollars (1,2)
Darling, You Know I Wouldn't Lie (1)
Empty Arms (2)

For My Baby (2)
Handful Of Stars (2)
I Come Home A Drinkin' (1)
I Don't Get No Better Without You (1)

I Love You More Today (2)
I've Found Someone Of My Own (2)
It Takes Me All Night Long (1)
Life Of The Party Charlie (1)

Lord Knows I'm Drinking (2) *64*
Margie's At The Lincoln Park Inn (1)
Old Faithful (1)

She's Lookin' Better By The Minute (1)
(Sittin' On) The Dock Of The Bay (2)
Song Sung Blue (2)

Sweet Things I Remember About You (2)
That's What It's Like To Be Lonesome (2)
When Two Worlds Collide (1)

SMITH, Connie '65

Born Constance June Meador on 8/14/41 in Elkhart, Indiana; raised in Hinton, West Virginia, and Warner, Ohio. Country singer.

DEBUT	PEAK	WKS	RIAA	CD	ARTIST — Album Title	Catalog	Sym	$	Label & Number
5/22/65	105	5		©	**Connie Smith**			$20	RCA Victor 3341

Darling, Are You Ever Coming Home
Don't Forget (I Still Love You)

Hinges On The Door
I Don't Love You Anymore
I'm Ashamed Of You

It's Just My Luck
Once A Day
Other Side Of You

Tell Another Lie
Then And Only Then
Threshold, The

Tiny Blue Transistor Radio

SMITH, Elliott '00

Born in Portland, Oregon. Rock singer/songwriter/guitarist.

DEBUT	PEAK	WKS	RIAA	CD	ARTIST — Album Title	Catalog	Sym	$	Label & Number
9/12/98	104	3		©	1 **XO**			$10	DreamWorks 50048
5/6/00	99	5		©	2 **Figure 8**			$10	DreamWorks 50225

Amity (1)
Baby Britain (1)
Bled White (1)
Bottle Up And Explode! (1)
Bye (2)

Can't Make A Sound (2)
Color Bars (2)
Easy Way Out (2)
Everybody Cares, Everybody Understands (1)

Everything Means Nothing To Me (2)
Everything Reminds Me Of Her (2)
Happiness (2)
I Better Be Quiet Now (2)

I Didn't Understand (1)
In The Lost And Found (Honky Bach) (2)
Independence Day (1)
Junk Bond Trader (2)
LA (2)

Oh Well, Okay (1)
Pitseleh (1)
Pretty Mary K (2)
Question Mark (1)
Somebody That I Used To Know (2)

Son Of Sam (2)
Stupidity Tries (2)
Sweet Adeline (1)
Tomorrow Tomorrow (1)
Waltz #1 & #2 (1)
Wouldn't Mama Be Proud? (2)

SMITH, Frankie '81

Born in Philadelphia. R&B singer/songwriter/producer.

DEBUT	PEAK	WKS	RIAA	CD	ARTIST — Album Title	Catalog	Sym	$	Label & Number
8/8/81	54	10		©	**Children Of Tomorrow**			$12	WMOT 37391

Auction, The
Children Of Tomorrow

Double Dutch
Double Dutch Bus *30*

Hand Bone
Slang Thang (Slizang Thizang)

Teeny-Bopper Lady
Triple Dutch

SMITH, Hurricane   '73
Born Norman Smith in 1923 in England. Pop singer/producer.

| 1/6/73 | 53 | 18 | | | Hurricane Smith | | | $15 | Capitol 1139 |

Auntie Vi's   Getting To Know You   **Oh, Babe, What Would You**   Theme From An Unmade Silent   Wonderful Lily
Back In The Country   Many Happy Returns   **Say?** *3*   Movie
Don't Let It Die   Take Suki Home   **Who Was It?** *49*

SMITH, Jerry, and His Pianos   '69
Session pianist.

| 7/26/69 | 200 | 2 | | | Truck Stop | | [I] | $15 | ABC 692 |

I'll Always Be In Love With You   Smokey Corners   Street Singers (Y Cantanti Della   Sweet 'N Sassy
My Happiness   Speakeasy (1929)   Strada)   Tokyo Butterfly
Pretend   Sunrise Serenade   **Truck Stop** *71*

SMITH, Jimmy ★133★   '63
Born on 12/8/25 in Norristown, Pennsylvania. Jazz organist. Won Major Bowes Amateur Show in 1934. With father (James Sr.) in song-and dance team in 1942. First recorded for Blue Note in 1956.

1)Bashin' 2)Hobo Flats 3)The Cat 4)Back At The Chicken Shack 5)Organ Grinder Swing

2/17/62	28	51		©	1 Midnight Special		[I]	$50	Blue Note 84078
6/2/62	10	34		©	2 Bashin'		[I]	$25	Verve 8474
3/9/63	14	22			3 Back At The Chicken Shack		[I]	$30	Blue Note 84117
5/18/63	11	30			4 Hobo Flats		[I]	$25	Verve 8544
11/9/63	25	33			5 Any Number Can Win		[I]	$25	Verve 8552
11/9/63	64	8			6 Rockin' The Boat		[E-I]	$30	Blue Note 84141
11/30/63	108	4		©	7 Blue Bash!		[I]	$25	Verve 8553
					KENNY BURRELL/JIMMY SMITH				
4/18/64	16	31		©	8 Who's Afraid Of Virginia Woolf?		[I]	$25	Verve 8583
8/1/64	86	20		©	9 Prayer Meetin'		[E-I]	$30	Blue Note 84164
9/19/64	12	32		©	10 The Cat		[I]	$25	Verve 8587
12/5/64	8[X]	4			11 Christmas '64		[X-I]	$25	Verve 8604
					also see #14 below				
5/8/65	35	24			12 Monster		[I]	$25	Verve 8618
9/18/65	15	31		©	13 Organ Grinder Swing		[I]	$25	Verve 8628
3/12/66	28	27		©	14 Got My Mojo Workin'		[I]	$25	Verve 8641
9/10/66	77	14		©	15 Hoochie Cooche Man		[I]	$25	Verve 8667
11/12/66	121	9		©	16 "Bucket"!		[E-I]	$25	Blue Note 84235
12/24/66	75[X]	3		©	17 Christmas Cookin'		[X-I-R]	$25	Verve 8666
					reissue (new title and cover) of #11 above; Christmas charts: 75/'66, 87/'67				
5/20/67	129	23		©	18 Jimmy & Wes The Dynamic Duo		[I]	$20	Verve 8678
					JIMMY SMITH & WES MONTGOMERY				
10/7/67	60	20			19 Respect		[I]	$20	Verve 8705
12/9/67	185	4			20 The Best Of Jimmy Smith		[G-I]	$20	Verve 8721
6/8/68	128	4			21 Jimmy Smith's Greatest Hits!		[G-I]	$25	Blue Note 89901 [2]
10/26/68	169	10			22 Livin' It Up!		[I]	$20	Verve 8750
7/26/69	144	3			23 The Boss		[I]	$20	Verve 8770
5/23/70	197	3			24 Groove Drops		[I]	$20	Verve 8794

Ain't That Just Like A Woman (15)
All Day Long (21)
Any Number Can Win, Theme From (5) *96*
Ape Women (5)
Baby, It's Cold Outside (18)
Back At The Chicken Shack, Part 1 (3) *63*
Bashin' (2)
Basin Street Blues (10)
Beggar For The Blues (2)
Bewitched, Theme From (12)
Big Boss Man (22)
Blue Bash (7)
Blueberry Hill (4)
Blues And The Abstract Truth (15)
Blues For C.A. (5)
Blues For Del (7)
Blues For J (13)
Blues In The Night (10)
Bluesette (8)
Boom Boom (15)
Boss, The (23)
Bucket (16)
Burning Spear (22)
By The Time I Get To Phoenix (24)

C Jam Blues (14)
Can Heat (6,21)
Careless Love (16)
Carpetbaggers, Main Title From The (10)
Cat, The (10,20) *67*
Champ, The (21)
Chicago Serenade (10)
Christmas Song (11,17)
Come Rain Or Come Shine (16)
Creeper, The (12)
Days Of Wine And Roses (24)
Delon's Blues (10)
Down By The Riverside (18)
Easy Living (7)
Fever (7)
Fingers (23)
Flamingo (21)
Funky Broadway (19)
G'won Train (5)
Gentle Rain (22)
Georgia On My Mind (5)
Get Out Of My Life (19)
Gloomy Sunday (12)
Go Away Little Girl (22)
God Rest Ye Merry Gentlemen (11,17)

Goldfinger (Part I & II) (12)
Got My Mojo Working (Part I) (14,20) *51*
Greensleeves (13)
Groove Drops (24)
High Heel Sneakers (14,20)
Hobo Flats - Part 1 (4,20) *69*
Hobson's Hop (14)
I Almost Lost My Mind (9)
(I Can't Get No) Satisfaction (14)
I Can't Stop Loving You (4)
I'll Close My Eyes (13)
I'm An Old Cowhand (From The Rio Grande) (2)
I'm Your Hoochie Coochie Man (Part I) (15,20) *94*
In A Mellow Tone (2)
James And Wes (18)
Jingle Bells (11,17)
John Brown's Body (8,16)
Johnny Come Lately (19)
Joy House, Theme From (10)
Jumpin' The Blues (1)
Just A Closer Walk With Thee (6)
Just Squeeze Me (16)
Kenny's Sound (7)
Livin' It Up (22)

Man With The Golden Arm, Theme From The (12)
Matilda, Matilda! (6)
Meditation (4)
Mercy, Mercy, Mercy (19)
Messy Bessie (3)
Midnight Special, Part 1 (1,21) *69*
Minor Chant (3)
Mission: Impossible (22)
Monlope (12)
Munsters, Theme From The (12)
Mustard Greens (14)
Night Train (18)
Ode To Billy Joe (24)
Oh, No, Babe (13)
Ol' Man River (2,20) *82*
One Mint Julep (15)
One O'Clock Jump (1)
1-2-3 (14)
Organ Grinder's Swing (13,20) *92*
Picknickin' (4)
Please Send Me Someone To Love (6)
Pork Chop (6)
Prayer Meetin' (9,21)
Preacher, The (4)

Red Top (9)
Refractions (22)
Respect (19)
Ruby (5)
Santa Claus Is Comin' To Town (11,17)
Sassy Mae (16)
Satin Doll (13)
Sermon, The (5,21)
Silent Night (11,17)
Slaughter On Tenth Avenue (8)
Soft Winds (7)
Some Of My Best Friends Are Blues (23)
St. James Infirmary (12)
St. Louis Blues (10)
Step Right Up (2)
Stone Cold Dead In The Market (9)
Subtle One (1)
Sunny (24)
T-Bone Steak (19)
TNT (15)
13 (Death March) (18)
This Guy's In Love With You (23)
This Nearly Was Mine (22)
3 For 4 (16)
Travelin' (7)

Trouble In Mind (4)
Trust In Me (6)
Tubs (5)
Tuxedo Junction (23)
Valley Of The Dolls (22)
Walk On The Wild Side - Part 1 (2,20) *21*
Walk Right In (4)
We Three Kings Of Orient Are (11,17)
What'd I Say? (5)
When I Grow Too Old To Dream (3)
When Johnny Comes Marching Home (21)
When My Dream Boat Comes Home (6)
When The Saints Go Marching In (9)
White Christmas (11,17)
Who Can I Turn To (When Nobody Needs Me) (24)
Who's Afraid Of Virginia Woolf? (8) *72*
Why Was I Born (1)
Wives And Lovers (8)
Women Of The World (8)
You Came A Long Way From St. Louis (5)

SMITH, Kate '66

Born on 5/1/07 in Greenville, Virginia. Died on 6/17/86 (age 79). Legendary soprano singer. Best known for her rendition of "God Bless America."

12/21/63+	83	18	©	1	Kate Smith at Carnegie Hall .... [L]	$20	RCA Victor 2819
					recorded on 11/2/63		
10/31/64	145	2	©	2	The Sweetest Sounds	$20	RCA Victor 2921
1/15/66	36	24	©	3	How Great Thou Art	$20	RCA Victor 3445
6/25/66	130	3		4	The Kate Smith Anniversary Album	$20	RCA Victor 3535
12/3/66	148	2		5	Kate Smith Today	$20	RCA Victor 3670
12/17/66	15ˣ	9		6	The Kate Smith Christmas Album ....[X]	$20	RCA Victor 3607

Christmas charts: 21/'66, 15/'67, 44/'68

All The Things You Are (medley) (4)
Along The Santa Fe Trail (medley) (4)
As Long As He Needs Me (1)
Ballad Of The Green Berets (5)
Beautiful Isle Of Somewhere (3)
Carolina Moon (medley) (1)
Christmas Eve in My Home Town (6)
Christmas Song (Chestnuts Roasting On An Open Fire) (6)
Daydream (5)
Days Of Wine And Roses (2)
Deck The Halls (medley) (6)
Deep Purple (medley) (4)
Do You Hear What I Hear (6)
Dr. Zhivago ..see: Lara's Theme
Don't Blame Me (medley) (4)
Don't Fence Me In (medley) (4)
Don't Sit Under The Apple Tree (With Anyone Else But Me) (medley) (4)

Don't Take Your Love From Me (medley) (4)
Fine And Dandy (medley) (1)
First Noël (medley) (6)
God Bless America (medley) (1)
Happy Birthday, Dear Christ Child (4)
He Loves Me (2)
How Are Things In Glocca Morra (medley) (4)
How Deep Is The Ocean (1)
How Great Thou Art (3)
I Didn't Know What Time It Was (medley) (4)
I Do, I Do (5)
I Heard The Bells On Christmas Day (6)
I Left My Heart In San Francisco (1)
I May Never Pass This Way Again (3)
I See God (3)
I Wanna Be Around (2)

I Wish You Love (2)
I'll Be Seeing You (1)
If Ever I Would Leave You (2)
If He Walked Into My Life (5)
Impossible Dream (The Quest) (5)
It Came Upon A Midnight Clear (medley) (6)
It Is No Secret (What God Can Do) (3)
It Took A Miracle (3)
It's Beginning To Look Like Christmas (6)
Joy To The World (medley) (6)
Just In Time (2)
Lara's Theme (5)
Lollipops And Roses (2)
Long Ago (And Far Away) (medley) (4)
Lord's Prayer (3)
Make Someone Happy (2)
Margie (medley) (1)
May The Good Lord Bless And Keep You (3)

Mondo Cane ..see: More
Moon River (4)
More (2)
My Best Beau (My Best Girl) (5)
My Coloring Book (2)
Nightingale Sang In Berkeley Square (medley) (4)
O Holy Night (medley) (6)
Old Lamplighter (medley) (4)
On A Clear Day (You Can See Forever) (1)
Once In A While (medley) (4)
Please (medley) (1)
Sandpiper, Love Theme From The ..see: Shadow Of Your Smile
Seems Like Old Times (medley) (4)
September In The Rain (medley) (4)
Shadow Of Your Smile (5)
Silent Night (medley) (6)
Silver Bells (6)

Some Sunday Morning (medley) (1)
Somebody Else Is Taking My Place (medley) (4)
Somewhere, My Love ..see: Lara's Theme
Strangers In The Night (5)
Sweetest Sounds (2)
Symphony (medley) (4)
That Old Feeling (medley) (4)
There Goes That Song Again (medley) (4)
(There'll Be Blue Birds Over) The White Cliffs Of Dover (medley) (4)
This Is All I Ask (1)
Touch Of His Hand On Mine (3)
Until Then (3)
Were You There? (3)
What Kind Of Fool Am I? (1)
What's New (4)
When The Moon Comes Over The Mountain (medley) (1,4)

When Your Lover Has Gone (medley) (1)
White Christmas (6)
Who Can I Turn To (When Nobody Needs Me) (5)
Who Cares (medley) (1)
Wrap Your Troubles In Dreams (And Dream Your Troubles Away) (medley) (4)
Yesterday (5)
You'd Be So Nice To Come Home To (medley) (4)

SMITH, Kathy '82

Born on 12/11/51 in New York City. Aerobics instructor.

| 3/13/82 | 144 | 13 | | | Kathy Smith's Aerobic Fitness .... | $10 | MuscleTone 72151 |
| | | | | | music by studio musicians | | |

Banana Boat Song   Cruisin'   Don't Stop 'Til You Get Enough   Give Me The Night   I Love A Rainy Night   Ride Like The Wind

SMITH, Keely — see PRIMA, Louis

SMITH, Lonnie '70

Born in Buffalo, New York. Jazz organist.

| 5/16/70 | 186 | 2 | © | | Move Your Hand .... [I-L] | $20 | Blue Note 84326 |
| | | | | | recorded on 8/9/69 at Club Harlem in Atlantic City | | |

Charlie Brown   Layin' In The Cut   Move Your Hand   Sunshine Superman

SMITH, Lonnie Liston '77

Born on 12/28/40 in Richmond, Virginia. Jazz keyboardist/trumpeter.

LONNIE LISTON SMITH & THE COSMIC ECHOES:

5/24/75	85	13	©	1	Expansions	$15	Flying Dutchman 0934
10/18/75	74	15	©	2	Visions Of A New World	$15	Flying Dutchman 1196
4/10/76	75	14		3	Reflections Of A Golden Dream.................	$15	Flying Dutchman 1460
12/11/76+	73	20		4	Renaissance	$12	RCA Victor 1822

LONNIE LISTON SMITH:

7/30/77	58	11		5	Live! .... [I-L]	$12	RCA Victor 2433
					recorded on 5/19/77 at Smucker's Cabaret in Brooklyn		
4/22/78	120	13		6	Loveland	$12	Columbia 35332
2/17/79	123	8		7	Exotic Mysteries	$12	Columbia 35654
7/30/83	193	2	©	8	Dreams Of Tomorrow	$10	Doctor Jazz 38447

Beautiful Woman (3)
Between Here And There (4)
Bright Moments (6)
Chance For Peace (7)
Colors Of The Rainbow (2)
Desert Nights (1)
Devika (Goddess) (2)
Divine Light (8)
Dreams Of Tomorrow (8)
Exotic Mysteries (7)
Expansions (1,5)

Explorations (6)
Floating Through Space (6)
Garden Of Peace (8)
Get Down Everybody (It's Time For World Peace) (3)
Goddess Of Love (3)
Golden Dreams (3)
Inner Beauty (3)
Journey Into Love (6)
Journey Into Space (3)
Lonely Way To Be (8)

Love Beams (2)
Love I See In Your Eyes (8)
Loveland (6)
Magical Journey (7)
Mardi Gras (Carnival) (4)
Meditations (6)
Mongotee (4)
My Love (1,5)
Mystic Woman (8)
Mystical Dreamer (A Tribute To Miles Davis) (7)

Never Too Late (8)
Night Flower (7)
Peace (1)
Peace & Love (3)
Prelude (5)
Quiet Dawn (3)
Quiet Moments (7)
Rainbows Of Love (8)
Renaissance (4)
Shadows (1)
Singing For Love (7)

Song Of Love (4)
Sorceress (5)
Space Lady (4)
Space Princess (7)
Springtime Magic (6)
Starlight And You (4)
Summer Days (1)
Summer Nights (2)
Sunbeams (3)
Sunburst (6)
Sunset (2,5)

Twilight (7)
Visions Of A New World (Phase I & II) (2,5)
Voodoo Woman (1)
Watercolors (5)
We Can Dream (6)

SMITH, Michael W. '95

Born in Kenova, West Virginia. Christian singer/songwriter/keyboardist.

6/8/91	74	19	● ©	1	Go West Young Man	$10	Reunion 24325
9/19/92+	86	29	▲ ©	2	Change Your World.............................	$10	Reunion 24491
9/9/95	16	39	● ©	3	I'll Lead You Home	$10	Reunion 83953
5/16/98	23	18	● ©	4	Live The Life	$10	Reunion 10007
11/14/98	90	9	©	5	Christmastime ....C:#2¹/5 [X]	$10	Reunion 10015
					Christmas charts: 4/'98, 7/'99		
12/11/99	21	13	● ©	6	This Is Your Time	$10	Reunion 0041
12/9/00	70	7	©	7	Freedom .... [I]	$10	Reunion 0002

SMITH, Michael W. — Cont'd

Agnus Dei (1)
Angels Unaware (3)
Anna (6)
As It Is In Heaven (3)
Away In A Manger (medley) (5)
Breakdown (3)
Breathe In Me (3)
Call, The (7)
Calling Heaven (3)
Carol Ann (7)
Carols Sing (5)
Child In The Manger (medley) (5)
Christmas Waltz (5)
Christmastime (5)
Color Blind (2)

Cross My Heart (1)
Cross Of Gold (2)
Crown Him With Many Crowns (3)
Cry For Love (3)
Cry Of The Heart (7)
Don't Give Up (4)
Emily (1)
Emmanuel (medley) (5)
Everybody Free (6)
For You (1) 60
Free Man (7)
Freedom (7)
Freedom Battle (7)
Friends (2)
Give It Away (2)

Giving, The (7)
Go West Young Man (1)
Happiest Christmas (5)
Hello, Good-Bye (4)
Hey You It's Me (6)
Hibernia (7)
Hope Of Israel (5)
How Long Will Be Too Long (1)
I Believe In You Now (4)
I Know Your Name (4)
I Saw Three Ships (medley) (5)
I Still Have The Dream (6)
I Wanna Tell The World (4)
I Will Be Here For You (2) 27
I Will Be Your Friend (6)
I Will Carry You (6)

I'll Be Around (7)
I'll Lead You Home (3)
I'm Gone (6)
I'm Waiting For You (3)
In My Arms Again (4)
Joy To The World (medley) (7)
Kay Thompson's Jingle Bells (5)
Let Me Show You The Way (4)
Letter To Sarah (7)
Little Stronger Everyday (3)
Live The Life (4)
Love Crusade (1)
Love Me Good (4) 61
Love One Another (2)
Matter Of Time (4)
Missing Person (4)

Never Been Unloved (4)
1990 (1)
O Christmas Tree (5)
O Come O Come Emmanuel (medley) (5)
Offering, The (7)
Other Side Of Me (3)
Out Of This World (2)
Picture Perfect (2)
Place In This World (1) 6
Prayer For Taylor (7)
Reach Out To Me (6)
Rince Dé (6)
Seed To Sow (1)
She Walks With Me (6)

Sing We Now Of Christmas (medley) (5)
Somebody Love Me (2) 71
Someday (3)
Somewhere Somehow (2)
Song For Rich (4)
Straight To The Heart (3)
This Is Your Time (6)
Thy Word (7)
We Three Kings (5)
Welcome To Our World (5)
Worth It All (6)

SMITH, O.C.   '68

Born Ocie Lee Smith on 6/21/36 in Mansfield, Louisiana. Male R&B singer.

DEBUT	PEAK	WKS			ARTIST — Album Title			$	Label & Number
6/15/68	19	42		1	Hickory Holler Revisited			$15	Columbia 9680
3/1/69	50	15		2	For Once In My Life			$15	Columbia 9756
10/18/69	58	16		3	O.C. Smith At Home			$15	Columbia 9908
9/19/70	177	5		4	O.C. Smith's Greatest Hits		[G]	$15	Columbia 30227
7/31/71	159	7		5	Help Me Make It Through The Night			$15	Columbia 30664

Best Man (1)
By The Time I Get To Phoenix (1)
Can't Take My Eyes Off You (3)
Clean Up Your Own Back Yard (3)
Color Him Father (3)
Cycles (2)
Daddy's Little Man (3,4) 34
Diamond In The Rough (5)

Didn't We (3)
Empty Arms (5)
For Once In My Life (2)
For The Good Times (5)
Friend, Lover, Woman, Wife (3,4) 47
Help Me Make It Through The Night (5) 91
Hey Jude (2)
Honey (I Miss You) (1,4) 44

House Next Door (1)
I Ain't The Worryin' Kind (2)
I Stop By Heaven (5)
If I Leave You Now (3)
Isn't It Lonely Together (2,4) 63
Keep On Keepin' On (2)
Learning Tree (3)
Little Green Apples (1,4) 2
Long Black Limousine (1)

Long Drive Home (5)
Main Street Mission (1,4)
Me And You (4)
Melodee (2)
Moody (4)
My Cherie Amour (3)
Primrose Lane (4) 86
Promises (2)
Really Big Shoe (5)
Remembering (5)

San Francisco Is A Lonely Town (3)
Seven Days (1)
Sitting On The Dock Of The Bay (1)
Son Of Hickory Holler's Tramp (1,4) 40
Sounds Of Goodbye (2)
Stormy (2)
Sweet Changes (3)

Take Time To Know Her (1)
Tall Oak Tree (5)
That's Life (1)
Watching Scotty Grow (5)
What You See (5)
Wichita Lineman (2)

SMITH, Patti, Group   '79

Born on 12/31/46 in Chicago; raised in New Jersey. Punk-rock singer. Married to Fred "Sonic" Smith of the MC5 from 1980-94. Her group: Lenny Kaye (guitar), Richard Sohl (keyboards), Ivan Kral (bass) and J.D. Daughtery (drums). Sohl died on 6/3/90 (age 37). Not to be confused with Patty Smyth of Scandal.

DEBUT	PEAK	WKS	CD		ARTIST — Album Title			$	Label & Number
12/13/75+	47	17	©	1	Horses			$12	Arista 4066
					PATTI SMITH				
11/27/76+	122	8	©	2	Radio Ethiopia			$12	Arista 4097
4/8/78	20	23	©	3	Easter			$12	Arista 4171
5/19/79	18	19	©	4	Wave			$12	Arista 4221
					PATTI SMITH:				
7/30/88	65	15	©	5	Dream Of Life			$10	Arista 8453
7/6/96	55	5	©	6	Gone Again			$10	Arista 18747
10/18/97	152	1	©	7	Peace And Noise			$10	Arista 18986
4/8/00	178	1	©	8	Gung Ho			$10	Arista 14618

About A Boy (6)
Ain't It Strange (2)
Ask The Angels (1)
Babelogue (medley) (3)
Because The Night (3) 13
Beneath The Southern Cross (6)
Birdland (1)
Blue Poles (7)
Boy Cried Wolf (8)
Break It Up (1)
Broken Flag (4)
China Bird (8)
Citizen Ship (4)
Dancing Barefoot (4)
Dead City (7)

Dead To The World (8)
Death Singing (7)
Distant Fingers (2)
Don't Say Nothing (7)
Dream Of Life (5)
Easter (3)
Elegie (1)
Farewell Reel (6)
Fireflies (6)
Frederick (4) 90
Free Money (1)
Ghost Dance (4)
Glitter In Their Eyes (8)
Gloria Medley (1)
Going Under (5)
Gone Again (6)

Gone Pie (8)
Grateful (8)
Gung Ho (8)
High On Rebellion (medley) (3)
Hymn (4)
Jackson Song (5)
Kimberly (1)
Land Medley (1)
Last Call (7)
Libbie's Song (8)
Lo And Beholden (8)
Looking For You (I Was) (5)
Memento Mori (7)
My Madrigal (6)
New Party (8)
1959 (7)

One Voice (8)
Paths That Cross (5)
People Have The Power (5)
Persuasion (8)
Pissing In A River (2)
Poppies (3)
Privilege (Set Me Free) (3)
Pumping (My Heart) (1)
Radio Ethiopia Medley (2)
Ravens (6)
Redondo Beach (1)
Revenge (4)
Rock N Roll Nigger (medley) (3)
Seven Ways Of Going (4)
So You Want To Be (A Rock 'N' Roll Star) (4)

Space Monkey (3)
Spell (7)
Strange Messengers (8)
Summer Cannibals (6)
Till Victory (3)
25th Floor (medley) (3)
Up There Down There (5)
Upright Come (8)
Waiting Underground (7)
Wave (4)
We Three (3)
Where Duty Calls (5)
Whirl Away (7)
Wicked Messenger (6)
Wing (6)

SMITH, Rex   '79

Born on 9/19/56 in Jacksonville, Florida. Actor/singer. Acted in several movies and Broadway shows. Brother of Michael Lee Smith of Starz.

DEBUT	PEAK	WKS	Sym		ARTIST — Album Title			$	Label & Number
4/28/79	19	19	●	1	Sooner Or Later			$10	Columbia 35813
1/12/80	165	3		2	Forever, Rex Smith			$10	Columbia 36275
8/22/81	167	4		3	Everlasting Love			$10	Columbia 37494

Ain't That Peculiar (1)
All Or Nothing (2)
Better Than It's Ever Been Before (1)
Don't Go Believin' (3)
Everlasting Love (3) 32

Everytime I See You (2)
Forever (2)
I Don't Want Your Love (Out Of My Life) (2)
If You Think You Know How To Love Me (1)

Let's Make A Memory (2)
Love Street (1)
Love Will Always Make You Cry (3)
Never Gonna Give You Up (1)
Oh Girl (3)

Oh What A Night For Romance (1)
Remember The Love Songs (3)
Rock Me Slowly (3)
Saturday Night (2)
Simply Jessie (1)

Sooner Or Later (1)
Still Thinking Of You (3)
Superhero (2)
Sway (1)
To You, To You! (Say Goodbye To You) (2)

Tonight (2)
What Becomes Of The Brokenhearted (3)
Without You (2)
You Take My Breath Away (1) 10

SMITH, Sammi   '71

Born Jewel Fay Smith on 8/5/43 in Orange, California; raised in Oklahoma. Female country singer.

DEBUT	PEAK	WKS			ARTIST — Album Title			$	Label & Number
2/13/71	33	21		1	Help Me Make It Through The Night			$15	Mega 1000
8/21/71	191	2		2	Lonesome			$15	Mega 1007

But You Know I Love You (1)
Don't Blow No Smoke On Me (1)
Fire And Rain (2)
For The Kids (2)
Haven't You Heard (2)

He Makes It Hard To Say Goodbye (2)
He's Everywhere (1)
Help Me Make It Through The Night (1) 8
Here's To Forever (2)

Jimmy's In Georgia (2)
Last Word In Lonesome Is Me (2)
Lonely Street (1)
Mr. Bojangles (2)
Saunders' Ferry Lane (1)

Sunday Mornin' Comin' Down (1)
Then You Walk In (2)
There He Goes (1)
This Room For Rent (1)
Weight, The (2)

When Michael Calls (1)
Willie (2)
With Pen In Hand (1)

SMITH, Will '99

Born on 9/25/68 in Philadelphia. Rapper/actor. One-half of **D.J. Jazzy Jeff and The Fresh Prince** from 1986-93. Starred on TV's *Fresh Prince of Bel Air* and in several movies. Married actress Jada Pinkett on 12/31/97.

| 12/13/97+ | 8 | 99 | ▲⁹ | © | 1 | Big Willie Style | C:#16/8 | $10 | Columbia 68683 |
| 12/4/99 | 5 | 26 | ▲² | © | 2 | Willennium | | $10 | Columbia 69985 |

Afro Angel (2)
Big Willie Style (1)
Can You Feel Me? (2)
Candy (1)
Chasing Forever (1)

Da Butta (2)
Don't Say Nothin' (1)
Freakin' It (2) *99*
Gettin' Jiggy Wit It (1) *1*
I Loved You (1)

I'm Comin' (2)
It's All Good (1)
Just The Two Of Us (1) *20*
La Fiesta (2)
Men In Black (1)

Miami (1) *17*
No More (2)
Potnas (2)
Pump Me Up (2)
Rain, The (2)

So Fresh (2)
Uuhhh (2)
Who Am I (2)
Wild Wild West (2) *1*
Will 2K (2) *25*

Y'All Know (1)
Yes Yes Y'All (1)

SMITHEREENS, The '90

Pop-rock group formed in New Jersey: Pat DiNizio (vocals, guitar), Jim Babjak (guitar), Mike Mesaros (bass) and Dennis Diken (drums).

8/16/86+	51	50		©	1	Especially For You		$10	Enigma 73208
4/9/88	60	31		©	2	Green Thoughts		$10	Capitol 48375
11/18/89+	41	38	●	©	3	11		$10	Enigma 91194
9/28/91	120	3		©	4	Blow Up...........................		$10	Capitol 94963
5/14/94	133	2		©	5	A Date With The Smithereens		$10	RCA 66391

Afternoon Tea (5)
Alone At Midnight (1)
Anywhere You Are (4)
Baby Be Good (1)
Behind The Wall Of Sleep (1)
Blood And Roses (1)
Blue Period (3)
Blues Before And After (3) *94*
Can't Go Home Anymore (5)
Cigarette (1)

Crazy Mixed-Up Kid (1)
Cut Flowers (3)
Deep Black (2)
Drown In My Own Tears (2)
Elaine (2)
Especially For You (2)
Evening Dress (4)
Everything I Have Is Blue (5)
Get A Hold Of My Heart (4)
Girl In Room 12 (4)

Girl Like You (3) *38*
Gotti (5)
Green Thoughts (2)
Groovy Tuesday (1)
Hand Of Glory (1)
House We Used To Live In (2)
I Don't Want To Lose You (1)
If The Sun Doesn't Shine (1)
If You Want The Sun To Shine (4)

In A Lonely Place (1)
Indigo Blues (4)
It's Alright (1)
Kiss Your Tears Away (3)
Life Is So Beautiful (5)
Listen To Me Girl (1)
Long Way Back Again (5)
Love Is Gone (1)
Maria Elena (3)
Miles From Nowhere (5)

Now And Then (4)
Only A Memory (2) *92*
Over And Over Again (4)
Point Of No Return (5)
Room Without A View (3)
Sick Of Seattle (4)
Sleep The Night Away (5)
Something New (2)
Spellbound (2)
Strangers When We Meet (1)

Tell Me When Did Things Go So Wrong (4)
Time And Time Again (1)
Too Much Passion (4) *37*
Top Of The Pops (4)
War For My Mind (5)
William Wilson (3)
World We Know (2)
Yesterday Girl (3)

SMITHS, The '87

Rock group formed in Manchester, England: **Morrissey** (vocals), Johnny Marr (guitar), Andy Rourke (bass) and Mike Joyce (drums). Marr later joined **The The** and **Electronic**.

5/5/84	150	11		©	1	The Smiths...........................	C:#29/16	$10	Sire 25065
3/2/85	110	32		©	2	Meat Is Murder...........................		$10	Sire 25269
7/19/86	70	37	●	©	3	The Queen Is Dead...........................		$10	Sire 25426
4/25/87	62	25	●	©	4	Louder Than Bombs...........................	[K]	$15	Sire 25569 [2]
10/10/87	55	27	●	©	5	Strangeways, Here We Come		$10	Sire 25649
10/1/88	77	8		©	6	Rank...........................	[L]	$10	Sire 25786
						recorded October 1986 at The National Ballroom in London			
10/17/92	139	3		©	7	Best...I...........................	[K]	$10	Sire 45042

Ask (4,6)
Asleep (4)
Back To The Old House (1)
Barbarism Begins At Home (1)
Bigmouth Strikes Again (3,6)
Boy With The Thorn In His Side (3,6)
Cemetry Gates (3,6)
Death At One's Elbow (5)
Death Of A Disco Dancer (5)
Draize Train (6)
Frankly, Mr. Shankly (3)
Girl Afraid (4)
Girlfriend In A Coma (5,7)
Golden Lights (4)
Half A Person (4,7)
Hand In Glove (1,4,7)

Hand That Rocks The Cradle (1)
Headmaster Ritual (2)
Heaven Knows I'm Miserable Now (4)
How Soon Is Now? (2,7)
I Don't Owe You Anything (1)
I Know It's Over (3,6)
I Started Something I Couldn't Finish (5)
I Want The One I Can't Have (2)
I Won't Share You (5)
Is It Really So Strange? (4,6)
Last Night I Dreamt That Somebody Loved Me (5)
London (4,6)

(Marie's The Name) His Latest Flame (medley) (6)
Meat Is Murder (2)
Miserable Lie (1)
Never Had No One Ever (3)
Nowhere Fast (2)
Oscillate Wildly (4)
Paint A Vulgar Picture (5)
Panic (4,6,7)
Please Please Please Let Me Get What I Want (4,7)
Pretty Girls Make Graves (1)
Queen Is Dead (3,6)
Reel Around The Fountain (1)
Rubber Ring (4,7)
Rush And A Push And The Land Is Ours (5)
Rusholme Ruffians (2,6)

Shakespeare's Sister (4)
Sheila Take A Bow (4,7)
Shoplifters Of The World Unite (4,7)
Some Girls Are Bigger Than Others (3,7)
Still Ill (1,6)
Stop Me If You Think You've Heard This One Before (5,7)
Stretch Out And Wait (4)
Suffer Little Children (1)
Sweet And Tender Hooligan (4)
Take Me Back To Dear Old Blighty (medley) (3)
That Joke Isn't Funny Anymore (2)
There Is A Light That Never Goes Out (3)

These Things Take Time (4)
This Charming Man (1,7)
This Night Has Opened My Eyes (4)
Unhappy Birthday (5)
Unloveable (5)
Vicar In A Tutu (3,6)
Well I Wonder (2)
What Difference Does It Make? (1,7)
What She Said (2,6)
William, It Was Really Nothing (4,7)
You Just Haven't Earned It Yet, Baby (4)
You've Got Everything Now (1)

SMOKESTACK LIGHTNIN' '69

White blues group: Ron Darling (vocals), Ric Eiserling (guitar), Kelly Green (bass) and Art Guy (drums).

| 4/12/69 | 200 | 2 | | | | Off The Wall........................... | | $20 | Bell 6026 |

I Idolize You
Light In My Window

Long Stemmed Eyes (John's Song)

Smokestack Lightnin'
Something's Got A Hold On Me

Three Hundred Pounds Of Heavenly Joy

Watch Your Step
Well Tuesday

Who's Been Talkin'

SMOKIE '77

Pop-rock group from Bradford, Yorkshire, England: Chris Norman (vocals), Alan Silson (guitar), Terry Utley (bass) and Pete Spencer (drums).

| 1/22/77 | 173 | 6 | | | | Midnight Cafe........................... | | $12 | RSO 3005 |

I'm Going Home
If You Think You Know How To Love Me *96*

Living Next Door To Alice *25*
Make Ya Boogie
Poor Lady

Something's Been Making Me Blue
Stranger

When My Back Was Against The Wall
Wild, Wild Angels

SMOOTHEDAHUSTLER '96

Born in Brooklyn, New York. Male rapper.

| 5/4/96 | 93 | 4 | | © | | Once Upon A Time In America........................... | | $10 | Profile 1467 |

Broken Language
Dedication
Dollar Bill

Family Conflicts
Food For Thoughts
Fuck Whatcha Heard

Glocks On Cock
Hustler's Theme
Hustlin'

Murdafest
My Brother My Ace
Neva Die Alone

Once Upon A Time...
Only Human

★366★ SMOTHERS BROTHERS, The '64

Comedy team from New York City: brothers Tom (born on 2/2/37) and Dick (born on 11/20/39) Smothers. Hosted their own TV variety series from 1967-69.

1)Curb Your Tongue, Knave! 2)It Must Have Been Something I Said! 3)The Two Sides Of The Smothers Brothers

10/20/62	26	66	●		1	The Two Sides Of The Smothers Brothers	[C]	$20	Mercury 20675
4/6/63+	27	63	●		2	(Think Ethnic!)	[C]	$20	Mercury 20777
7/13/63+	45	50	●		3	The Songs And Comedy Of The Smothers Brothers!	[C-E]	$20	Mercury 20611
						first released in 1962			
12/14/63+	13	33			4	Curb Your Tongue, Knave!	[C]	$20	Mercury 20862

SMOTHERS BROTHERS, The — Cont'd

5/23/64	23	28			5 It Must Have Been Something I Said!	[C]		$20	Mercury 20904
12/19/64+	58	20			6 Tour De Farce American History And Other Unrelated Subjects	[C]		$20	Mercury 20948
6/5/65	57	10			7 Aesop's Fables The Smothers Brothers Way	[C]		$20	Mercury 20989
10/16/65+	39	28			8 Mom Always Liked You Best!	[C]		$20	Mercury 21051
8/13/66	119	6			9 Golden Hits Of The Smothers Brothers, Vol. 2	[C]		$20	Mercury 21089
11/16/68	164	4			10 Smothers Comedy Brothers Hour	[C]		$20	Mercury 61193

Aesop Knew (7)
Aesop's Fables Our Way (7)
American History - 1A (4)
American History - 2A & 2B (6)
Anne Marie And Jean Pierre (5)
Apples, Peaches And Cherries (1)
Bird And The Jar (7)
Black Is The Color Of My True Love's Hair (2,5)
Boy Who Cried Wolf (7)
Cabbage (1,9)
Car (Maybe I'd Better Stay Me) (7)
Carnival (Manha De Carnival) (5)
Caught In The Draft (10)
Chocolate (1)
Church Bells (4,9)
Civil War Song (5)

Controversial Material (10)
Crabs Walk Sideways (5)
Dance, Boatman Dance (5)
Daniel Boone (2)
Dog And The Thief (7)
Down In The Valley (3)
Eskimo Dog (6)
Farmer And His Sons (7)
Flamenco (2)
Fly (Maybe I'd Better Stay Me) (7)
Four Winds And The Seven Seas (1)
Fox, The (2)
Fox And The Grapes (7)
Fox (Maybe I'd Better Stay Me) (7)
Gnus (2)
Greedy Dog (7)
Hangman (1,9)

Hiawatha (5)
I Don't Care (1)
I Never Will Marry (2,3)
I Talk To The Trees (4,9)
I Wish I Wuz In Peoria (3)
If It Fits Your Fancy (1)
Impersonation (8)
Impossible Dream (The Quest) (10)
Incredible Jazz Banjoist (4)
Intermission Bit (9)
Jellyfish (Maybe I'd Better Stay Me) (7)
Jenny Brown (5) *84*
Jezebel (3)
Laredo (1)
Last Great Waltz (8)
Life And The Song Of Life (6)
Little Known Song And Dance (8)

Lonesome Traveler (4)
Longtime Blues (8)
Map Of The World (1)
Mary Was Pretty (2)
Measles Song (6)
Mediocre Fred (6)
Michael, Row The Boat Ashore (5,9)
Military Lovers (6)
Mom Always Liked You Best (4)
Morons (10)
Mosquito (Maybe I'd Better Stay Me) (7)
My Old Man (2,9)
Population Explosion (5)
President Johnson (10)
Pretoria (3,9)
Put-On Song (6)
Reminiscences (8)
Saga Of John Henry (2)

Sailor's Lament (1)
Santa Claus (8)
Santa Claus Is Coming To Town (3)
She's Gone Forever (6)
Shrimp, The (5)
Siblings (6)
Since My Canary Died (6)
Slithery Dee (5)
Smart Juice (10)
Soap (2)
Spread Of Democracy (10)
Stella's Got A New Dress (1)
Swiss Christmas (4)
Tattoo Song (8)
That's My Song (6)
They Call The Wind Maria (3)
Three Song (8)
Time And Song Of Time (6)

Tom Dooley (3)
Tom's Party (10)
Tommy's Song (10)
Troubador Song (10)
Two Frogs (7)
Tzena, Tzena, Tzena, Tzena (3)
United Nations (10)
Venezuelan Rain Dance (2)
We Love Us (8)
Where The Lilac Grows (1)
Worm (Maybe I'd Better Stay Me) (7)
Wreck Of The Old 49 (2)
You Can Call Me Stupid (8)
You Didn't Come In (10)

SMUT PEDDLERS   '01

Male rap duo: Mr. Eon and Cage.

| 3/10/01 | 184 | 1 | | © | Porn Again | | | $10 | Eastern Con. 50164 |

Amazing Feats
Anti Hero's
Beats, Boxes, and Boobtube

Botton Feeders
Diseases
54

Josie
Medicated Minutes
My Rhyme Aint Done

One By One
Smut Council
Stank MCs

Talk Like Sex
That Smut

SMYTH, Patty   '92

Born on 6/26/57 in New York City. Lead singer of **Scandal**. Formerly married to Richard Hell (of **Television**); married tennis star John McEnroe in April 1997.

| 3/21/87 | 66 | 20 | | © | 1 Never Enough | | | $10 | Columbia 40182 |
| 9/5/92 | 47 | 34 | ● | © | 2 Patty Smyth | | | $10 | MCA 10633 |

Call To Heaven (1)
Downtown Train (1) *95*
Give It Time (1)
Heartache Heard Round The World (1)

I Should Be Laughing (2) *86*
Isn't It Enough (1)
Make Me A Believer (2)
My Town (2)
Never Enough (1) *61*

No Mistakes (2) *33*
One Moment To Another (2)
Out There (2)
River Cried (1)
River Of Love (2)

Shine (2)
Sometimes Love Just Ain't Enough (2) *2*
Sue Lee (1)
Too Much Love (2)

Tough Love (1)

SNAIL   '78

Pop-rock group from Santa Cruz, California: Bob O'Neill (vocals, guitar), Ken Kraft (guitar), Jack Register (bass) and Jim Norris (drums). Register and Norris left after first album, replaced by Brett Bloomfield (bass) and Don Baldwin (drums; **Jefferson Starship**).

| 7/8/78 | 135 | 12 | | | 1 Snail | | | $12 | Cream 1009 |
| 11/10/79 | 186 | 2 | | | 2 Flow | | | $12 | Cream 1012 |

And Your Bird Can Sing (2)
Broke Up, Broke Down (2)
Carry Me (1)
Catch Me (1)

Childhood Dreams (1)
Forever (2)
Freedom In The Country (1)
Here With You (2)

I've Got A Lady (2)
Joker, The (1) *93*
Keep On Livin' (1)
Lettin' Go (2)

Love Should Flow (2)
Music Is My Mistress (1)
Rollin' In Your Love (2)
Threw It Away (2)

Tonight (2)
Try And Wonder (1)
You Gotta Run (1)

SNAP!   '90

German studio project assembled by producers Michael Muenzing and Luca Anzilotti. Features a revolving lineup of lead singers including Durron Butler, Jackie Harris, Penny Ford, Thea Austin, Niki Harris and Paula Brown.

| 6/16/90 | 30 | 49 | ● | © | 1 World Power | | | $10 | Arista 8536 |
| 10/31/92 | 121 | 20 | | © | 2 The Madman's Return | | | $10 | Arista 18693 |

Believe In It (2)
Believe The Hype (1)
Blase, Blase (1)

Colour Of Love (Massive Version) (2)
Cult Of Snap (1)
Don't Be Shy (2)

EX-Terminator (2)
I'm Gonna Get You (To Whom It May Concern) (1)
Madman's Return (2)

Mary Had A Little Boy (1)
Money (2)
Ooops Up (1) *35*
Power, The (1) *2*

Rhythm Is A Dancer (2) *5*
See The Light (2)
Who Stole It? (2)
Witness The Strength (1)

SNEAKER   '82

Pop-rock group formed in Los Angeles: Mitch Crane (vocals, guitar), Michael Carey Schneider (vocals, keyboards), Tim Torrance (guitar), Jim King (keyboards), Michael Cottage (bass) and Mike Hughes (drums).

| 12/12/81+ | 149 | 17 | | | Sneaker | | | $12 | Handshake 37631 |

Don't Let Me In *63*
Get Up, Get Out

In Time
Jaymes

Looking For Someone Like You
Millionaire

More Than Just The Two Of Us *34*

No More Lonely Days
One By One

SNEAKER PIMPS   '97

Rock trio from Manchester, England: Kelli Drayton (vocals), Chris Comer (guitar) and Liam Howe (keyboards).

| 5/31/97 | 111 | 23 | | © | Becoming X | | | $10 | Virgin 42587 |

Becoming X
How Do

Low Place Like Home
Post-Modern Sleaze

Roll On
6 Underground *45*

Spin Spin Sugar *87*
Tesko Suicide

Walking Zero
Waterbaby
Wasted Early Sunday Morning

SNIFF 'N' THE TEARS   '79

Rock group formed in London: Paul Roberts (vocals), Loz Netto and Mick Dyche (guitars), Alan Fealdman (keyboards), Chris Birkin (bass) and Luigi Salvoni (drums). Disbanded after first album. Roberts led new lineup for second album: Les Davidson (guitar), Mike Taylor (keyboards), Nick South (bass) and Jamie Lane (drums). Roberts joined **The Stranglers** in 1991.

| 7/28/79 | 35 | 17 | | © | 1 Fickle Heart | | | $12 | Atlantic 19242 |
| 9/19/81 | 192 | 2 | | © | 2 Love Action | | | $12 | MCA 5242 |

Carve Your Name On My Door (1)
Don't Frighten Me (2)
Driver's Seat (1) *15*
Driving Beat (2)

Fight For Love (1)
For What They Promise (2)
Last Dance (1)
Looking For You (1)
Love Action (2)

New Lines On Love (1)
Put Your Money Where Your Mouth Is (2)
Rock 'N' Roll Music (1)
Shame (2)

Sing (1)
Slide Away (1)
Snow White (2)
Steal My Heart (2)
That Final Love (2)

This Side Of The Blue Horizon (1)
Thrill Of It All (1)
Without Love (2)

★423★ SNOOP DOGGY DOGG '93
Born Calvin Broadus on 10/20/72 in Long Beach, California. Male rapper. Member of **Tha Eastsidaz**.

| 12/11/93 | **❶**³ | 72 | ▲⁴ | © | 1 Doggy Style | C:#7/12 | | $10 | Death Row 92279 |
| 11/30/96 | **❶**¹ | 30 | ▲² | © | 2 Tha Doggfather | | | $10 | Death Row 90038 |

SNOOP DOGG:

8/22/98	**❶**²	33	▲²	©	3 Da Game Is To Be Sold, Not To Be Told			$10	No Limit 50000
5/29/99	**2**¹	40	▲	©	4 No Limit Top Dogg			$10	No Limit 50052
11/18/00	24	5		©	5 Dead Man Walkin	[K]		$10	D3 33349

contains new songs built around shelved vocal tracks from 1996

| 1/6/01 | 4 | 36 | ▲ | © | 6 Tha Last Meal | | | $10 | No Limit 23225 |

Ain't Nut'in Personal (3)
Aint No Fun (If The Homies Cant Have None) (1)
B-Please (4) *77*
Back Up Off Me (6)
Bathtub (1)
Betta Days (4)
Blueberry (2)
Brake Fluid (Biiittch Pump Yo Brakes) (6)
Bring It On (6)
Buck 'Em (4)
Buss'n Rocks (4)
C-Walkin (5)
Change Gone Come (5)
County Blues (5)
(D.J.) Wake Up (2)
DP Gangsta (3)

Doggfather (2)
Doggy Dogg World (1)
Doggyland (4)
Doggz Gonna Get Ya (3)
D.O.G.'s Get Lonely 2 (3)
Doin' Too Much (4)
Dolomite (3)
Don't Let Go (3)
Don't Tell (4)
Down 4 My N's (4)
Downtown Assassins (2)
For All My Niggaz & Bitches (1)
Freestyle Conversation (2)
Game Of Life (3)
Gangsta Ride (4)
Gangsta Walk (5)
Get Bout It & Rowdy (3)
Ghetto Symphony (4)

Gin And Juice (1) *8*
Gin & Juice II (3)
Go Away (6)
Gold Rush (2)
Groupie (2)
Gz And Hustlas (1)
Gz Up, Hoes Down (1)
Head Doctor (5)
Hennesey N Buddah (6)
Hit Rocks (5)
Hoes, Money & Clout (3)
Hustle & Ball (3)
I Can't Swim (6)
I Love My Momma (4)
I Will Survive (5)
In Love With A Thug (4)
Issues (6)
Just Dippin' (4)

Lay Low (6) *50*
Leave Me Alone (6)
Lodi Dodi (1)
Loosen' Control (6)
May I (5)
Me And My Doggs (5)
Murder Was The Case (1)
My Favorite Color (5)
My Heat Goes Boom (4)
Next Episode (1)
Party With A D.P.G. (4)
Pay For P... (3)
Picture This (3)
Ready 2 Ryde (6)
See Ya When I Get There (3)
Serial Killa (1)
Set It Off (6)
Shiznit, Tha (1)

Show Me Love (3)
6 Bedtime Stories (2)
Sixx Minutes (2)
Slow Down (3)
Snoop Bounce (2)
Snoop Dogg (6) *77*
Snoop World (3)
Snoop's Upside Ya Head (2)
Snoopafella (4)
Somethin Bout Yo Bidness (4)
Stacey Adams (6)
Still A G Thang (3) *19*
(Tear 'Em Off) Me & My Doggz (2)
Tommy Boy (5)
Too Black (5)
Tru Tank Dogs (3)
True Lies (6)

Trust Me (4)
20 Dollars To My Name (3)
20 Minutes (4)
2001 (2)
Up Jump Tha Boogie (2)
Vapors (2)
What's My Name? (1) *8*
Whatcha Gon Do? (3)
Who Am I ..see: What's My Name?
Woof! (3) *62*
Wrong Idea (6)
Y'all Gone Miss Me (6)
You Thought (2)

SNOW '93
Born Darrin O'Brien on 10/30/69 in Toronto. White male reggae singer.

| 2/6/93 | 5 | 38 | ▲ | © | 12 Inches Of Snow | | | $10 | EastWest 92207 |

Can't Get Enough
Champion Sound
Creative Child

Drunken Styles
Ease Up
50 Ways

Girl, I've Been Hurt *19*
Hey Pretty Love
Informer *1*

Lady With The Red Dress
Lonely Monday Morning
Runway

Uhh In You

SNOW, Hank '67
Born Clarence Eugene Snow on 5/9/14 in Brooklyn, Nova Scotia, Canada. Country singer/songwriter/guitarist. Known as "The Singing Ranger."

| 12/16/67 | 72ˣ | 3 | | | Christmas With Hank Snow .... | [X] | | $40 | RCA Victor 3826 |

Blue Christmas
C-H-R-I-S-T-M-A-S
Christmas Cannonball

Christmas Roses
Christmas Wants
Frosty The Snow Man

God Is My Santa Claus
Little Stranger (In A Manger)
Reindeer Boogie

Rudolph The Red-Nosed Reindeer
Silent Night

White Christmas

SNOW, Phoebe '75
Born Phoebe Laub on 7/17/52 in New York City; raised in New Jersey. Jazz-styled singer.

9/7/74+	4	58	●	©	1 Phoebe Snow			$12	Shelter 2109
2/14/76	13	22	●	©	2 Second Childhood			$12	Columbia 33952
11/6/76	29	21		©	3 It Looks Like Snow			$12	Columbia 34387
10/22/77	73	15		©	4 Never Letting Go			$12	Columbia 34875
10/28/78	100	7			5 Against The Grain			$12	Columbia 35456
4/4/81	51	18			6 Rock Away			$10	Mirage 19297
4/15/89	75	20		©	7 Something Real			$10	Elektra 60852

All Over (2)
Autobiography (Shine, Shine, Shine) (3)
Baby Please (6)
Best Of My Love (7)
Cardiac Arrest (7)
Cash In (2)
Cheap Thrills (6)
Do Right Woman, Do Right Man (5)
Don't Let Me Down (3)
Down In The Basement (6)
Drink Up The Melody (Bite The Dust, Blues) (3)

Either Or Both (1)
Electra (4)
Every Night (5)
Fat Chance (3)
Games (6) *46*
Garden Of Joy Blues (4)
Gasoline Alley (4)
Goin' Down For The Third Time (2)
Good Times (Let The Good Times Roll) (1)
Harpo's Blues (1)
He's Not Just Another Man (5)
I Believe In You (6)

I Don't Want The Night To End (1)
I'm Your Girl (7)
If I Can Just Get Through The Night (7)
In My Girlish Days (7)
In My Life (5)
Inspired Insanity (2)
Isn't It A Shame (2)
It Must Be Sunday (1)
Keep A Watch On The Shoreline (7)
Love Makes A Woman (4)
Majesty Of Life (4)

Mama Don't Break Down (5)
Married Men (5)
Mercy, Mercy, Mercy (6) *52*
Mercy On Those (3)
Middle Of The Night (4)
Mr. Wondering (7)
My Faith Is Blind (3)
Never Letting Go (4)
No Regrets (2)
No Show Tonight (1)
Oh L.A. (5)
Poetry Man (1) *5*
Pre-Dawn Imagination (2)
Random Time (5)

Ride The Elevator (4)
Rock Away (6)
San Francisco Bay Blues (1)
Shakey Ground (3) *70*
Shoo-Rah Shoo-Rah (6)
Something Good (6)
Something Real (7)
Something So Right (4)
Soothin' (7)
Stand Up On The Rock (3)
Stay Away (7)
Sweet Disposition (2)
Take Your Children Home (1)
Teach Me Tonight (3)

There's A Boat That's Leavin' Soon For New York (2)
Touch Your Soul (7)
Two Fisted Love (2)
We Might Never Feel This Way Again (7)
We're Children (4)
You Have Not Won (5)

SNYPAZ '01
Male rap duo from Chicago: Iren Moore and Charles Paxton.

| 6/23/01 | 174 | 3 | | © | Livin' In The Scope .... | | | $10 | Rap-A-Lot 10367 |

Comin' Wit It
Dollar Bill
Hot Onez

Juke It
Kamakazi
Kill-Steal-Will

Playa Like Me
Roll Wit Thugs
Searchin'

Tear Da Roof Off
That's On Everything
Thorough

U Don't Wanna Blaze
We Do

SO '88
Pop-rock duo from London: singer/guitarist Mark Long and multi-instrumentalist Marcus Bell.

| 3/19/88 | 124 | 9 | | © | Horseshoe In The Glove .... | | | $10 | EMI-Manhattan 46997 |

Are You Sure *41*
Burning Bush

Capitol Hill
Dreaming

Horseshoe In The Glove
Tips On Crime

Villians
Would You Die For Me

SOCCIO, Gino '79
Born in 1955 in Montreal. Disco singer/multi-instrumentalist.

| 4/21/79 | 79 | 13 | | | 1 Outline .... | | | $12 | RFC 3309 |
| 5/23/81 | 96 | 14 | | | 2 Closer .... | | | $10 | Atlantic 16042 |

Closer (2)
Dance To Dance (1)

Dancer (1) *48*
Hold Tight (2)

(It's Been) Too Long (2)
Love Is (2)

So Lonely (1)
Street Talk (2)

There's A Woman (1)
Try It Out (2)

Visitors, The (1)

SOCIAL DISTORTION '96

Rock group formed in Los Angeles: Mike Ness (vocals, guitar), Dennis Danell (guitar), John Maurer (bass) and Christopher Reece (drums). Danell died of a brain aneurysm on 2/29/2000 (age 38).

5/26/90	128	22	●	©	1 Social Distortion			$10	Epic 46055
2/29/92	76	16	●	©	2 Somewhere Between Heaven And Hell			$10	Epic 47978
10/5/96	27	10		©	3 White Light White Heat White Trash			$10	550 Music 64380
7/18/98	121	2		©	4 Live At The Roxy		[L]	$10	Time Bomb 43516

recorded in Hollywood

Another State Of Mind (4)
Bad Luck (2,4)
Ball And Chain (1,4)
Born To Lose (2)
Bye Bye Baby (2)
Cold Feelings (2,4)
Creeps, The (4)

Crown Of Thorns (3)
Dear Lover (3)
Don't Drag Me Down (3,4)
Down Here (W/The Rest Of Us) (3)
Down On The World Again (3)
Drug Train (1)

Ghost Town Blues (2)
Gotta Know The Rules (3)
I Was Wrong (3,4)
It Coulda Been Me (1)
King Of Fools (2)
Let It Be Me (1,4)
Making Believe (2)

Mass Hysteria (4)
Mommy's Little Monster (4)
1945 (4)
99 To Life (2)
No Pain, No Gain (4)
Place In My Heart (1)
Pleasure Seeker (3)

Prison Bound (4)
Ring Of Fire (1,4)
She's A Knockout (1)
Sick Boys (1)
So Far Away (1)
Sometimes I Do (2)
Story Of My Life (1,4)

Telling Them (4)
This Time Darlin' (2)
Through These Eyes (3)
Under My Thumb (3,4)
Untitled (3)
When She Begins (2)
When The Angels Sing (3)

SOFT CELL '82

Techno-pop group from London: **Marc Almond** (vocals) and David Ball (synthesizer).

1/30/82	22	41		©	1 Non-Stop Erotic Cabaret			$10	Sire 3647
8/14/82	57	14		©	2 Non-Stop Ecstatic Dancing		C:#14/6 [M]	$10	Sire 23694
2/26/83	84	8		©	3 The Art of Falling Apart			$12	Sire 23769 [2]

includes a bonus mini album

Art Of Falling Apart (3)
Baby Doll (3)
Bedsitter (1)
Chips On My Shoulder (1)
Entertain Me (1)

Forever The Same (3)
Frustration (1)
Heat (3)
Hendrix Medley (3)
Insecure...Me? (2)

Kitchen Sink Drama (3)
Loving You, Hating Me (3)
Man Could Get Lost (2)
Martin (3)
Memorabilia (2)

Numbers (3)
Say Hello, Wave Goodbye (1)
Secret Life (1)
Seedy Films (1)
Sex Dwarf (1,2)

Tainted Love (1) **8**
What (2)
Where Did Our Love Go (2)
Where The Heart Is (3)
Youth (1)

SOFT MACHINE, The '69

Experimental rock trio from England: Robert Wyatt (vocals, drums), Michael Ratledge (organ) and Kevin Ayers (guitar).

12/21/68+	160	9		©	The Soft Machine			$40	Probe 4500

Box 25/4 LID
Certain Kind

Hope For Happiness
Joy Of A Toy

Lullabye Letter
Plus Belle Qu'une Poubele

Priscilla
Save Yourself

So Boot If At All
We Did It Again

Why Am I So Short?
Why Are We Sleeping?

SOHO '90

Dance trio formed in London: identical twin sisters Jackie and Pauline Cuff (vocals), with Tim Brinkhurst (guitar).

11/24/90	134	10		©	Goddess			$10	Savage 91585

Another Year
Boy '90
Freaky

Girl On A Motorbike
God's Little Joke
Goddess

Hippychick 14
Love Generation
Nuthin' On My Mind

Out Of My Mind
Shake Your Thing

Zombies Walk The Cardboard
City

SOLÉ '99

Born in Kansas City. Female rapper.

10/16/99	127	13		©	Skin Deep			$10	DreamWorks 50118

Accurate Math
Ain't Nobody ****** Wit It
Da Story

4 The Love Of You
4,5,6 21
Get Up In It

I'm Coming
It Wasn't Me
Iy Yi Yi

Never Thought I
Our World
Pain

Spell My Name Right
We've Been Trying Too Long
Who Dat 5

Young

SOLEIL, Stella '01

Born Stella Katsoudas in New York City. Female dance singer.

6/9/01	106	2		©	Dirty Little Secret			$10	Cherry 013991

Angel Face
Dance With Me

Imperfect
Kiss Kiss

Let's Just Go To Bed
Look My Way

Love You To Death
Pretty Young Thing

Runaway Crush
Stand Up

Twilight
You

SOLIS, Marco Antonio '01

Born in Michoacan, Mexico. Latin singer.

2/13/99	157	4	▲	©	1 Trozos De Mi Alma		[F]	$10	Fonovisa 0516

title is Spanish for "Piece Of My Soul"

6/16/01	104	6	●	©	2 Mas De Mi Alma		[F]	$10	Fonovisa 0527

title is Spanish for "More Of My Soul"

Amor En Silencio (1)
Boca De Angel (2)
Cuando Te Acuerdes De Mi (2)
Donde Estara Mi Primavera (2)

El Peor De Mis Fracasos (1)
En Desventaja (2)
Fue Mejor Asi (2)
Inventame (1)

La Ultima Parte (1)
Mi Eterno Amor Secreto (1)
Mujeres Solitas (2)
O Me Voy O Te Vas (2)

Que Me Quedo Contigo (1)
Resignacion (2)
Se Que Me Va A Dejar (2)
Se Va Muriendo Mi Alma (1)

Si No Te Hubieras Ido (1)
Si Te Pudiera Mentir (1)
Sigue Sin Mi (1)
Tu Hombre Perfecto (2)

SOLO '96

R&B vocal group from New York City: Eunique Mack, Darnell Chavis, Dan Stokes and Robert Anderson.

9/30/95+	52	40	●	©	1 Solo			$10	Perspective 549017
10/10/98	123	2		©	2 4 Bruthas & A Bass			$10	Perspective 549040

Another Saturday Night
(medley) (1)
Back 2 Da Street (1)
Blowin' My Mind (1)
Change Is Gonna Come (1)
Crazy Bout U (2)

Everybody Loves To Cha Cha
Cha (medley) (1)
Forgive Me (2)
Get Off! (2)
He's Not Good Enough (1)
Heaven (1) **42**
Holdin' On (1)

I'm Sorry (1)
In Bed (1)
It's Such A Shame (1)
Keep It Right Here (1)
(Last Night I Made Love) Like
Never Before (1)
Let Me See The Sun (1)

Love You Down (2)
Luv-All-Day (2)
Make Me Know It (2)
Nights Like This (2)
Sumpthin Kinda Special (2)
Till Death Do Us Part (2)
Touch Me (2) **59**

Under The Boardwalk (1)
What A Wonderful World (1)
What Would This World Be (2)
**Where Do U Want Me To Put
It** (1) **50**
Xxtra (1)

SOMERVILLE, Jimmy '90

Born on 6/22/61 in Glasgow, Scotland. Former lead singer of **Bronski Beat** and **Communards**.

5/5/90	192	2		©	Read My Lips			$10	London 828166

Adieu!
And You Never Thought That
This Could Happen To You
Comment Te Dire Adieu

Control
Don't Know What To Do
(Without You)

Heaven Here On Earth (With
Your Love)
My Heart Is In Your Hands
Perfect Day

Rain
Read My Lips (Enough Is
Enough)

**You Make Me Feel (Mighty
Real) 87**

SOMETHIN' FOR THE PEOPLE — '00

R&B vocal trio from Oakland: Jeff Young, Curtis Wilson and Rochad Holiday.

| 10/11/97 | 154 | 15 | | © | 1 **This Time It's Personal** | | | $10 | Warner 46753 |
| 8/5/00 | 124 | 1 | | © | 2 **Issues** | | | $10 | Warner 47354 |

Act Like You Want It (1,2) • All I Do (1) 47 • Bitch With No Man (2) • Can We Make Love (2) • Come Clean (2) • Days Like This (1) • Feel So Good (1) • I Apologize (2) • I Don't Get Down Like That (1) • I Got Love (1) • Last Call (2) • **My Love Is The Shhh!** (1) 4 • Now U Wanna (2) • Ooh Wee (2) • Playin' The Field (1) • She's Always In My Hair (1) • Somebody's Always Talkin' (1) • Take It Off (2) • Take It Or Leave It (1) • Things Must Change (2) • Think Of You (1) • What In The World? (1) • Where U At (2) • You (2)

SOMMERS, Joanie — '62

Born on 2/24/41 in Buffalo, New York. Pop singer. Appeared in the movies *Everything's Duckie* and *The Lively Set*.

| 9/22/62 | 103 | 3 | | © | **Johnny Get Angry** | | | $50 | Warner 1470 |

I Don't Want To Walk Without You • I Need Your Love • **Johnny Get Angry** 7 • Little Girl Blue • Mean To Me • Nightingale Sang In Berkeley Square • **One Boy** 54 • Piano Boy • Seems Like Long, Long Ago • Shake Hands With A Fool • Since Randy Moved Away • Summer Place, Theme From A

SON BY FOUR — '00

Latin vocal group from Puerto Rico: brothers Javier and George Montes, with cousin Pedro Quiles and friend Angel Lopez.

| 4/29/00 | 94 | 28 | ● | © | **Son By Four** | [F] | | $10 | Sony Discos 83943 |

Como Decírselo • Donde Esta Tu Amor • Lo Que Yo Mas Quiero • Lo Que Yo No Tengo • Lunática • Mi Corazón Te Recuerda • Muévelo • Pero Eres Tú • Poca Mujer • **Purest Of Pain (A Puro Dolor)** 26 • Sofía • Que Esta Pasando

SONICFLOOD — '99

Christian rock group: Jeff Deyo (vocals), Dwayne Larring (guitar), Jason Halbert (keyboards), Rick Heil (bass) and Aaron Blanton (drums).

| 10/23/99 | 158 | 2 | | © | 1 **Sonicflood** | | | $10 | Gotee 2802 |
| 4/28/01 | 172 | 3 | | © | 2 **Sonicpraise** | [L] | | $10 | Gotee 2827 |

Before The Throne Of God Above (2) • Carried Away (1,2) • Did You Feel The Mountains Tremble (2) • Heart Of Worship (1) • Holiness (1) • Holy One (1,2) • I Could Sing Of Your Love Forever (1,2) • I Have Come To Worship (1,2) • I Need You (1) • I Want To Know You (1,2) • Invocation (1) • Lord, I Lift Your Name On High (2) • My Refuge (1) • Open The Eyes Of My Heart (1,2) • Something About That Name (1) • Spontaneous Worship (2) • You Are Worthy Of My Praise (2)

SONIC YOUTH — '94

Rock group formed in New York City: Thurston Moore and Lee Ranaldo (guiatrs), Kim Gordon (bass) and Steve Shelley (drums). All share vocals. Moore and Gordon married in 1983.

7/14/90	96	15		©	1 **Goo**			$10	DGC 24297
8/8/92	83	11		©	2 **Dirty**			$10	Geffen 24493
5/28/94	34	10		©	3 **Experimental Jet Set, Trash And No Star**			$10	DGC 24632
10/14/95	58	3		©	4 **Washing Machine**			$10	DGC 24825
5/30/98	85	2		©	5 **A Thousand Leaves**			$10	DGC 25203
6/3/00	172	1		©	6 **NYC Ghosts & Flowers**			$10	Geffen 490650

Androgynous Mind (3) • Becuz (4) • Bone (3) • Bull In The Heather (3) • Chapel Hill (3) • Cinderella's Big Score (1) • Contre Le Sexisme (5) • Creme Brulee (2) • Diamond Sea (4) • Dirty Boots (1) • Disappearer (1) • Doctor's Orders (3) • Drunken Butterfly (2) • Female Mechanic Now On Duty Karen Koltrane (5) • Free City Rhymes (6) • French Tickler (5) • Heather Angel (5) • Hits Of Sunshine (For Allen Ginsberg) (5) • Hoarfrost (5) • In The Mind Of The Bourgeois Reader (5) • Ineffable Me (5) • JC (2) • Junkie's Promise (4) • Karen Koltrane (5) • Kool Thing (1) • Lightnin' (6) • Little Trouble Girl (4) • Mary-Christ (1) • Mildred Pierce (1) • Mote (1) • My Friend Goo (4) • NYC Ghosts & Flowers (6) • Nevermind (What Was It Anyway) (6) • Nic Fit (3) • No Queen Blues (4) • On The Strip (2) • 100% (2) • Orange Rolls, Angel's Spit (2) • Panty Lies (4) • Purr (2) • Quest For The Cup (3) • Renegade Princess (6) • Saucer-Like (4) • Scooter + Jinx (1) • Screaming Skull (2) • Self-Obsessed And Sexxee (3) • Shoot (2) • Side2side (6) • Skink (3) • Skip Tracer (4) • Small Flowers Crack Concrete (6) • Snare, Girl (5) • Starfield Road (3) • StreamXsonik Subway (6) • Sugar Kane (2) • Sunday (5) • Sweet Shine (3) • Swimsuit Issue (2) • Theresa's Sound-world (2) • Titanium Expose (1) • Tokyo Eye (3) • Tunic (Song For Karen) (1) • Unwind (4) • Waist (3) • Washing Machine (4) • Wildflower Soul (5) • Winner's Blues (3) • Wish Fulfillment (2) • Youth Against Fascism (2)

SONIQUE — '00

Born in England. Female DJ.

| 3/4/00 | 67 | 26 | | © | **Hear My Cry** | | | $10 | Serious 157536 |

Are You Ready? • Can't Get Enough • Cold And Lonely • Drama • Empty (Hideaway) • Hear My Cry • I Put A Spell On You • **It Feels So Good** 8 • Learn To Forget • Love Is On Our Side • Move Closer • Sky

SONNY & CHER — ★310★ — '65

Husband-and-wife duo: Sonny Bono (born on 2/16/35 in Detroit) and Cher (born on 5/20/46). Began career as session singers for Phil Spector. First recorded as Caesar & Cleo for Vault in 1963. Married from 1969-75. In the movies *Good Times* (1967) and *Chastity* (1969). Own CBS-TV variety series from 1971-74. Brief TV reunion in 1975. Sonny was mayor of Palm Springs, California, from 1988-92; elected to Congress in 1994. Sonny died in a skiing accident on 1/5/98 (age 62).

1)*Look At Us* 2)*All I Ever Need Is You* 3)*The Best of Sonny & Cher*

| 8/21/65 | 2[8] | 44 | ● | © | 1 **Look At Us** | | | $25 | Atco 177 |

also see #9 below

| 10/23/65 | 69 | 16 | | | 2 **Baby Don't Go** | [E] | | $40 | Reprise 6177 |

includes "Their Hearts Were Full Of Spring," "Two Hearts," and "When" by **The Lettermen**; "I Surrender (To Your Touch)," "Leavin' Town," and "Wo Yeah!" by **Bill Medley**; and "La La La La La" by The Blendells

| 4/16/66 | 34 | 20 | | © | 3 **The Wondrous World Of Sonny & Cher** | | | $20 | Atco 183 |
| 3/25/67 | 45 | 29 | | © | 4 **In Case You're In Love** | | | $20 | Atco 203 |

also see #9 below

5/27/67	73	18		©	5 **Good Times**	[S]		$20	Atco 214
8/12/67	23	64			6 **The Best Of Sonny & Cher**	[G]		$20	Atco 219
10/2/71	35	40	●		7 **Sonny & Cher Live**	[L]		$15	Kapp 3654
2/26/72	14	29	●		8 **All I Ever Need Is You**			$15	Kapp 3660
9/9/72	122	12			9 **The Two Of Us**	[R]		$25	Atco 804 [2]

reissue of albums #1 & #4 above

6/30/73	132	6			10 **Mama Was A Rock And Roll Singer Papa Used To Write All Her Songs**			$15	MCA 2101
12/22/73+	175	7			11 **Sonny & Cher Live In Las Vegas, Vol. 2**	[L]		$20	MCA 8004 [2]
9/28/74	146	6			12 **Greatest Hits**	[G]		$15	MCA 2117

SONNY & CHER — Cont'd

All I Ever Need Is You (8,11,12) **7**
Baby Don't Go (2,9) **8**
Bang Bang (My Baby Shot Me Down) (11)
Beat Goes On (4,6,7,9,12) **6**
Beautiful Story (6) **53**
Bring It On Home To Me (3)
Brother Love's Traveling Salvation Show (10,11)
But You're Mine (3,6) **15**
By Love I Mean (10)
Cheryl's Goin Home (4,9)
Cowboys Work Is Never Done (8,11,12) **8**
Crystal Clear (medley) (8,12)
Danny Boy (7)
Do You Want To Dance (2)
Don't Talk To Strangers (5)
500 Miles (1)

Good Times (5)
Gotta Get You Into My Life (7)
Greatest Show On Earth (10)
Groovy Kind Of Love (4,9)
Gypsys, Tramps & Thieves (11)
Here Comes That Rainy Day Feeling (8)
Hey Jude (7)
I Believe In You (10)
I Can See Clearly Now (10,11)
I Got You Babe (1,5,6,7,9,11,12) **1**
I Look For You (3)
I Love What You Did With The I Love I Gave You (8)
I'm Gonna Love You (5)
I'm Leaving It All Up To You (3)
It Never Rains In Southern California (10)
It's Gonna Rain (1,9)

It's The Little Things (5,6) **50**
Just A Name (5)
Just You (1,6,9) **20**
Laugh At Me (3,6,7) **10**
Leave Me Be (3)
Let It Be Me (1,6,9)
Let The Good Times Roll (3)
Letter, The (1,9) **75**
Listen To The Music (10)
Little Man (4,6,9) **21**
Living For You (4,6,9) **87**
Love Don't Come (4,9)
Love Is Strange (2)
Mama Was A Rock And Roll Singer Papa Used To Write All Her Songs (10,12) **77**
Misty Roses (4,9)
Monday (4,9)
More Today Than Yesterday (7,8)

Muddy Waters (medley) (8,12)
Once In A Lifetime (7)
Podunk (4,9)
Rhythm Of Your Heart Beat (10)
Set Me Free (3)
Sing C'est La Vie (1,6,9)
So Fine (3)
Somebody (8)
Someday (You'll Want Me To Want You) (7)
Something (7)
Stand By Me (4,9)
Summertime (3)
Superstar (11)
Tell Him (3)
Then He Kissed Me (1,9)
Trust Me (5)
Turn Around (3)
Unchained Melody (1,9)

United We Stand (8,12)
Walkin' The Quetzal (2)
We'll Sing In The Sunshine (4,9)
We'll Watch The Sun Coming Up (Shining Down On Our Love) (8)
What Now My Love (3,6,7,12) **14**
When You Say Love (12) **32**
Where You Lead (medley) (11)
Why Don't They Let Us Fall In Love (1,9)
You And I (11)
You Baby (4,9)
You Better Sit Down Kids (8,11,12)
You Don't Love Me (1,9)
You Know Darn Well (10)

You've Got A Friend (medley) (11)
You've Really Got A Hold On Me (1,9)

SONS OF CHAMPLIN '76

Rock group from San Francisco: Bill Champlin (vocals, guitar), Terry Haggerty (guitar), Geoffrey Palmer (keyboards), David Schallock (bass) and James Preston (drums). Champlin joined **Chicago** in 1982.

6/14/69	**137**	9	©	1 **Loosen Up Naturally**			$40	Capitol 200 [2]
11/8/69	**171**	6		2 **The Sons**			$25	Capitol 332
6/9/73	**186**	5	©	3 **Welcome To The Dance**			$15	Columbia 32341
6/5/76	**117**	10		4 **A Circle Filled With Love**			$12	Ariola America 50007
5/28/77	**188**	4		5 **Loving Is Why**			$12	Ariola America 50017

Big Boss Man (5)
Black And Blue Rainbow (1)
Boomp Boomp Chop (2)
Circle Filled With Love (4)
Country Girl (2)
Doin' It For You (5)
Don't Fight It, Do It! (1)
Everywhere (1)
Follow Your Heart (4)
For A While (4)

For Joy (3)
Freedom (1)
Get High (1)
Heaven Only Knows (medley) (3)
Hello Sunlight (1)
Helping Hand (4)
Here Is Where Your Love Belongs (4) **80**
Hold On (4) **47**

Imagination's Sake (4)
It's Time (2)
Knickanick (4)
Let That Be A Lesson (5)
Lightnin' (3)
Love Can Take Me Now (5)
Love Of A Woman (2)
Loving Is Why (5)
Misery Isn't Free (1)
1982-A (1)

No Mo' (3)
Right On (3)
Rooftop (1)
Saved By The Grace Of Your Love (5)
Slippery When It's Wet (4)
Still In Love With You (4)
Swim, The (3)
Terry's Tune (2)
Thing To Do (1)

Things Are Gettin' Better (1)
Time Will Bring You Love (5)
To The Sea (4)
Welcome To The Dance Medley (3)
West End (5)
Whatcha Gonna Do (5)
Where I Belong (5)
Who (medley) (3)

Why Do People Run From The Rain (3)
You (4)
You Can Fly (2)

SONS OF FUNK '98

Rap group from Richmond, California: brothers G-Smooth and Dez with thier cousins Renzo and Rico.

| 5/9/98 | **44** | 6 | © | **The Game Of Funk** .... | | | $10 | No Limit 50725 |

Don't Wanna Let You Go
First Time
Hey Lady

I Got The Hook-Up! **16**
Make Love To A Thug
Makin' Luv To My B...

Pushin' Inside You **97**
Side To Side
Sons Reasons

Sons...I Got The Hook-Up (R&B)
Time Will Tell

Y'all I Want
You And Me

SON VOLT '97

Rock group formed in New Orleans: Jay Farrar (vocals), brothers Dave (guitar) and Jim (bass) Boquist, and Mike Heidorn (drums).

10/7/95	**166**	1	©	1 **Trace**			$10	Warner 46010
5/10/97	**44**	3	©	2 **Straightaways**			$10	Warner 46518
10/24/98	**93**	2	©	3 **Wide Swing Tremolo**			$10	Warner 47059

Back Into Your World (2)
Been Set Free (2)
Blind Hope (3)
Carry You Down (3)
Caryatid Easy (2)
Catching On (1)

Cemetery Savior (2)
Chanty (3)
Creosote (2)
Dead Man's Clothes (3)
Driving The View (3)
Drown (1)

Flow (3)
Hanging Blue Side (3)
Last Minute Shakedown (2)
Left A Slide (2)
Live Free (3)
Loose String (1)

Medicine Hat (3)
Mystifies Me (1)
No More Parades (2)
Out Of The Picture (1)
Picking Up The Signal (2)
Question (3)

Right On Through (3)
Route (1)
Straightface (3)
Strands (3)
Streets That Time Walks (3)
Tear Stained Eye (1)

Ten Second News (1)
Too Early (1)
Way Down Watson (2)
Windfall (1)

SOPWITH "CAMEL", The '67

Pop group from San Francisco: Peter Kraemer (vocals, sax), Terry MacNeil and William Sievers (guitars), Martin Beard (bass), and Norman Mayell (drums). Named after a type of airplane used in World War I.

| 10/28/67 | **191** | 2 | © | **Sopwith Camel** .... | | | $30 | Kama Sutra 8060 |

Cellophane Woman
Frantic Desolation
Great Morpheum

Hello Hello **26**
Little Orphan Annie
Maybe In A Dream

Postcard From Jamaica **88**
Saga Of The Low Down Let Down

Things That I Could Do With You
Walk In The Park

You Always Tell Me Baby

S.O.S. BAND, The '80

Funk group from Atlanta: Mary Davis (vocals, keyboards), Bruno Speight (guitar), Willie Killebrew (sax), Bill Ellis (flute), Jason Bryant (keyboards), John Simpson (bass) and James Earl Jones III (drums).

6/28/80	**12**	20	●		1 **S.O.S.**			$10	Tabu 36332
8/22/81	**117**	6			2 **Too**			$10	Tabu 37449
12/25/82+	**172**	8			3 **S.O.S. III**			$10	Tabu 38352
8/27/83	**47**	29	●	©	4 **On The Rise**			$10	Tabu 38697
9/1/84	**60**	27		©	5 **Just The Way You Like It**			$10	Tabu 39332
5/24/86	**44**	20	●	©	6 **Sands Of Time**			$10	Tabu 40279
11/4/89	**194**	2		©	7 **Diamonds In The Raw**			$10	Tabu 44147
11/4/95	**185**	1			8 **The Best Of The S.O.S. Band** .... [G]			$10	Tabu 0594

Are You Ready? (2)
Body Break (5)
Borrowed Love (6)
Break Up (5)
Can't Get Enough (3)
Crossfire (Part I & II) (2)
Do It Now (2)
Do You Know Where Your Children Are? (2)
Do You Love Me? (7)
Do You Still Want To? (6)
Even When You Sleep (6,8)

Feeling (5)
Finest, The (6,8) **44**
For The Brothers That Ain't Here (2)
For Your Love (4)
Get Out Of My Life (7)
Goldmine (3)
Good & Plenty (3)
Groovin' (That's What We're Doin') (3)
Have It Your Way (3)
High Hopes (3,8)

Hold Out (7)
I Don't Want Nobody Else (5)
I'm In Love (5)
I'm Not Runnin' (4)
I'm Still Missing Your Love (7)
If You Want My Love (4)
It's A Long Way To The Top (2)
Just Be Good To Me (4,8) **55**
Just The Way You Like It (5) **64**
Looking For You (3)
Love Won't Wait For Love (1)

Men Don't Cry (7)
No Lies (6)
No One's Gonna Love You (5,8)
Nothing But The Best (6)
On The Rise (4)
One Lover (7)
One Letter (1)
S.O.S. (Dit Dit Dit Dat Dat Dat Dit Dit) (1)
Sands Of Time (6,8)
Secret Wish (7)
Stay (2)

Steppin' The Stones (4)
Take Love Where You Find It (1)
Take Your Time (Do It Right) Part 1 (1,8) **3**
Tell Me If You Still Care (4,8) **65**
There Is No Limit (2)
These Are The Things (4)
Two Time Lover (2)
Unborn Child (2)
Weekend Girl (5,8)

What's Wrong With Our Love Affair? (1,8)
Who's Making Love (4)
You (2)
You Shake Me Up (3)
Your Love (It's The One For Me) (3)

SOUL, David '77
Born David Solberg on 8/28/43 in Chicago. Actor/singer. Played "Joshua Bolt" on TV's *Here Come The Brides* and "Ken Hutchinson" on TV's *Starsky & Hutch.*

| 1/22/77 | 40 | 22 | | | 1 **David Soul** | | | $12 | Private Stock 2019 |
| 9/10/77 | 86 | 7 | | | 2 **Playing To An Audience Of One** | | | $12 | Private Stock 7001 |

Bird On A Wire (1)
Black Bean Soup (1)
By The Devil I Was Tempted (2)
Can't We Just Sit Down And Talk It Over (2)

Don't Give Up On Us (1) *1*
Ex Lover (1)
Going In With My Eyes Open (2) *54*
Hooray For Hollywood (1)

I Wish I Was... (2)
Kristofer David (1)
Landlord (1)
Mary's Fancy (2)
1927 Kansas City (1)

Nobody But A Fool Or A Preacher (2)
Playing To An Audience Of One (2)
Rider (2)

Seem To Miss So Much (Coalminer's Song) (1)
Silver Lady (2) *52*
Tattler (2)
Tomorrow Child (2)

Topanga (1)
Wall, The (1)

SOUL ASSASSINS, The '00
Collective of revolving rappers assembled by producer DJ Muggs.

| 10/21/00 | 178 | 1 | | © | **Muggs Presents The Soul Assassins II** | | | $10 | RuffLife 60002 |

Don't Trip
Heart Of The Assassin

Millennium Thrust
Razor To Your Throat

Real Life
Suckers Are Hidin

This Some'n To
Victory Or Defeat

We Will Survive
When The Fat Lady Sings

When The Pain Inflict
You Better Believe It

SOUL ASYLUM '95
Rock group from Minneapolis: Dave Pirner (vocals, guitar), Dan Murphy (guitar), Karl Mueller (bass) and Grant Young (drums). Pirner appeared in the movie *Reality Bites.* Sterling Campbell (**Duran Duran**) replaced Young in 1995.

11/21/92+	11	76	▲²	©	1 **Grave Dancers Union**			$10	Columbia 48898
6/24/95	6	21	▲	©	2 **Let Your Dim Light Shine**			$10	Columbia 57616
5/30/98	121	2		©	3 **Candy From A Stranger**			$10	Columbia 67618

April Fool (1)
Bittersweetheart (2)
Black Gold (1)
Blood Into Wine (3)
Caged Rat (2)
Close (3)
Cradle Chain (3)

Crawl (2)
Creatures Of Habit (3)
Draggin' The Lake (3)
Eyes Of A Child (2)
Game, The (3)
Get On Out (1)
Growing Into You (1)

Homesick (3)
Hopes Up (2)
I Did My Best (3)
I Will Still Be Laughing (3)
Just Like Anyone (2)
Keep It Up (1)
Lies Of Hate (3)

Misery (2) *20*
New World (1)
New York Blackout (3)
99% (1)
No Time For Waiting (3)
Nothing To Write Home About (2)

Promises Broken (2) *63*
Runaway Train (1) *5*
See You Later (1)
Shut Down (2)
Somebody To Shove (1)
String Of Pearls (2)
Sun Maid (1)

Tell Me When (2)
To My Own Devices (2)
Without A Trace (1)

SOUL CHILDREN, The '69
R&B vocal group from Memphis: Anita Louis, Shelbra Bennett, John Colbert and Norman West.

| 9/6/69 | 154 | 6 | | | 1 **Soul Children** | | | $30 | Stax 2018 |
| 4/29/72 | 159 | 6 | | © | 2 **Genesis** | | | $30 | Stax 3003 |

All Day Preachin' (2)
All That Shines Ain't Gold (2)
Doin' Our Thang (1)
Don't Take My Sunshine (2)

Get Up About Yourself (2)
Give 'Em Love (1)
Hearsay (2) *44*
I Want To Be Loved (2)

I'll Understand (1)
I'm Loving You More Everyday (2)
It Hurts Me To My Heart (2)

Just The One (I've Been Looking For) (2)
Move Over (1)
My Baby Specializes (1)

Never Get Enough Of Your Love (2)
Super Soul (1)
Sweeter He Is - Part I (2) *52*

Sweeter He Is - Part II (1)
Take Up The Slack (1)
Tighten Up My Thang (1)
When Tomorrow Comes (1)

SOUL COUGHING '98
Rock group from New York City: Mike Doughty (vocals, guitar), Mark Antoni (keyboards), Sebastian Steinberg (bass) and Yuval Gabay (drums).

| 7/27/96 | 136 | 4 | | © | 1 **Irresistible Bliss** | | | $10 | Slash 46175 |
| 10/17/98 | 49 | 10 | | © | 2 **El Oso** | | | $10 | Slash 46800 |

Blame (2)
Circles (2)
Collapse (1)
Disseminated (1)

4 Out Of 5 (1)
Fully Retractable (2)
Houston (1)
How Many Cans? (1)
I Miss The Girl (2)

Idiot Kings (1)
Incumbent, The (2)
Lazybones (1)
Maybe I'll Come Down (2)
Misinformed (2)

Monster Man (2)
Paint (1)
Pensacola (2)
Rolling (2)
Sleepless (1)

So Far I Have Not Found The Science (2)
Soft Serve (1)
Soundtrack To Mary (1)
St. Louise Is Listening (2)

Super Bon Bon (1)
$300 (2)
White Girl (1)

SOULDECISION '00
Male vocal trio from Vancouver: David Bowman, Ken Lewko and Trevor Guthrie.

| 9/9/00 | 103 | 29 | | © | **No One Does It Better** | | | $10 | MCA 112361 |

Baby Come Back
Faded *22*

Feelin' You
Gravity

I Don't Need Anyone
Let's Do It Right

Next Time
No One Does It Better

Only In My Mind
Ooh It's Kinda Crazy

Stay

SOULFLY '00
Rock group: Max Cavalera (vocals; **Sepultura**), Jackson Bandeira (guitar), Marcello Rapp (bass) and Roy Mayorga (drums). Mickey Doling and Joe Nunez replaced Bandeira and Mayorga in 1999.

| 5/9/98 | 79 | 3 | | © | 1 **Soulfly** | | | $10 | Roadrunner 8748 |
| 10/14/00 | 32 | 5 | | © | 2 **Primitive** | | | $10 | Roadrunner 8565 |

Back To The Primitive (2)
Bleed (2)
Boom (2)
Bring It (2)
Bumba (1)

Bumbklaatt (1)
Eye For An Eye (1)
Fire (1)
First Commandment (1)
Flyhigh (2)

In Memory Of... (2)
Jumpdafuckup (2)
Karmageddon (1)
Mulambo (2)
No (1)

No Hope = No Fear (1)
Pain (2)
Prejudice (1)
Prophet, The (2)
Quilombo (2)

Son Song (2)
Song Remains Insane (1)
Soulfly (1)
Soulfly II (2)
Terrorist (2)

Tribe (1)
Umbabarauma (1)

SOUL FOR REAL '95
R&B vocal group from Long Island, New York: brothers Chris, Andre, Brian and Jason Dalyrimple.

| 4/15/95 | 23 | 30 | ▲ | © | 1 **Candy Rain** | | | $10 | Uptown 11125 |
| 10/12/96 | 119 | 2 | | © | 2 **For Life...** | | | $10 | Uptown 53012 |

Ain't No Sunshine (1)
All In My Mind (1)
Being With You (1)
Can't You Tell (2)

Candy Rain (1) *2*
Every Little Thing I Do (1) *17*
Good To You (2)
I Don't Know (1)

I Don't Wanna Say Goodbye (2)
I Wanna Be Your Friend (1)
I'm Coming Home (1)
If Only You Knew (1)

If You Want It (1)
Leavin' (2)
Let's Stay Together (2)
Love You So (2)

Never Felt This Way (2)
Spend The Night (1)
Stay (2)
Thinking Of You (1)

Where Do We Go (2)
You Just Don't Know (2)
Your Love Is Calling (2)

SOULFUL STRINGS, The '68
Instrumental studio group from Chicago: Lennie Druss (oboe, flute), Bobby Christian (vibes), Philip Upchurch and Ron Steel (guitars). Arranged and conducted by Richard Evans.

8/26/67	166	15			1 **Paint It Black**		[I]	$15	Cadet 776
11/11/67+	59	34			2 **Groovin' With The Soulful Strings**		[I]	$15	Cadet 796
8/3/68	189	4			3 **Another Exposure**		[I]	$15	Cadet 805
12/28/68	35ˣ	1		©	4 **The Magic Of Christmas**		[X-I]	$15	Cadet 814
5/3/69	125	6			5 **In Concert/Back By Demand**		[I-L]	$15	Cadet 820
					recorded on 11/6/68 at The London House in Chicago				
11/29/69+	183	4			6 **Spring Fever**		[I]	$15	Cadet 834

SOULFUL STRINGS, The — Cont'd

Alfie (2)
Alice Blue Gown (3)
All Blues (2)
Burning Spear (2) *64*
California Dreamin' (1)
Chocolate Candy (6)
Christmas Song (4)
Clair De Lune (5)
Comin' Home Baby (2)
Dance Of The Sugarplum Fairy (4)
Deck The Halls (4)

Eight Miles High (1)
Groovin' (3)
Hello, Goodbye (3)
High Rise Blues (6)
(I Know) I'm Losing You (2)
I Wish It Would Rain (5)
I'm A Girl Watcher (5)
Inner Light (3)
It Ain't Necessarily So (3)
It's Cold Duck Time (6)
Jericho (3)
Jingle Bells (4)

Lady Madonna (3)
Listen Here (5)
Little Drummer Boy (4)
Love Is A Hurtin' Thing (1)
Love Song (6)
Lover's Concerto (1)
MacArthur Park (5)
Merry Christmas, Baby (4)
Message To Michael (1)
Minor Adjustment (3)
1974 Blues (6)
Oboe Flats (5)

On The Dock Of The Bay (3)
Our Day Will Come (2)
Paint It Black (1)
Parade Of The Wooden Soldiers (4)
Pavanne (3)
Santa Claus Is Coming To Town (4)
Sidewinder, The (1)
Since You've Been Gone (3)
Sleigh Ride (4)
Snowfall (4)

Sometimes I Feel Like A Motherless Child (6)
Soul Message (3)
Soul Prelude (3)
Stepper, The (3)
Sunny (1)
Take Five (1)
There Was A Time (5)
Valdez In The Country (6)
Voices Inside (6)
Wade In The Water (1)
What Now My Love (2)

When A Man Loves A Woman (1)
Who Who Song (3)
Wildwood (6)
Within You Without You (2)
You're All I Need (5)
Zambezi (6)

SOULJA SLIM   '98
Born James Smith in New Orleans. Male rapper.

6/6/98	13	10		©	Give It 2 'Em Raw			$10	No Limit 53547

Anything
At The Same Time
From What I Was Told
Get High With Me

Getting Real
Head Buster
Hustlin' Is A Habit
Imagine

Law Brekaz
Me And My Cousin
N.L. Party
Only Real N...

Pray For Your Baby
Street Life
Takin' Hits
What's Up, What's Happening

Wootay
Wright Me
You Ain't Never Seen
You Got It (II)

SOULS OF MISCHIEF   '93
Rap group from Oakland: Tajai Massey, Opio Lindsey, Damani Thompson and Adam Carter.

10/16/93	85	8		©	1 93 'Til Infinity			$10	Jive 41514
10/28/95	111	2		©	2 No Man's Land			$10	Jive 41551

Anything Can Happen (1)
Batting Practice (1)
Bumpshit (2)
Come Anew (1)
Dirty D's Theme (Hoe Or Die) (2)

Disseshowedo (2)
Do You Want It? (2)
Fa Sho Fo Real (2)
Freshdopedope (2)
Hotel, Motel (2)
Let 'Em Know (1)

Limitations (1)
Live And Let Live (1)
Make Your Mind Up (1)
Name I Call Myself (1)
Never No More (1)
'94 Via Satellite (2)

93 'Til Infinity (1) *72*
No Man's Land (2)
Rock It Like That (2)
Secret Service (2)
So You Wanna Be A... (2)
Tell Me Who Profits (1)

That's When Ya Lost (1)
Times Ain't Fair (1)
What A Way To Go Out (1)
Where The Fuck You At? (2)
Ya Don't Stop (2)
Yeah It Was You (2)

SOUL SURVIVORS   '68
White group from New York City: brothers Charles and Richard Ingui (vocals), Ken Jeremiah (vocals), Ed Leonetti (guitar), Paul Venturini (organ) and Joe Forigone (drums).

11/18/67+	123	13			When The Whistle Blows Anything Goes			$50	Crimson 502

Change Is Gonna Come
Dathon's Theme

Do You Feel It
Expressway To Your Heart *4*

Hey Gyp
Please, Please, Please

Respect
Rydle, The

Shake (medley)
Taboo-India

Too Many Fish In The Sea (medley)

SOUL II SOUL   '89
Group from London led by the duo of Beresford Romeo and Nellee Hooper. Features female vocalists **Caron Wheeler**, Do'Reen Marcia Lewis and Rose Windross, and musical backing by the Reggae Philharmonic Orchestra. Wheeler left in 1990.

7/8/89	14	51	▲²	©	1 Keep On Movin'			$10	Virgin 91267
6/16/90	21	19	●	©	2 Vol II - 1990 - A New Decade			$10	Virgin 91367
5/16/92	88	8		©	3 Volume III Just Right			$10	Virgin 91771

African Dance (1)
Back To Life (However Do You Want Me) (1) *4*
Courtney Blows (2)
Dance (1)
Direction (3)

Dreams A Dream (2) *85*
Everywhere (3)
Fairplay (1)
Feel Free (1)
Feeling Free (1)
Future (3)

Get A Life (2) *54*
Happiness (1)
Holdin' On (1)
In The Heat Of The Night (2)
Intelligence (3)
Jazzie's Groove (1)

Joy (3)
Just Right (3)
Keep On Movin' (1) *11*
Love Come Through (2)
Missing You (2)
Mood (3)

Move Me No Mountain (3)
1990 - A New Decade (2)
Our Time Has Now Come (2)
People (2)
Storm (3)
Take Me Higher (3)

Time (Untitled)

SOUNDGARDEN   '94
Hard-rock group from Seattle: **Chris Cornell** (vocals), Kim Thayil (guitar), Hiro Yamamoto (bass) and Matt Cameron (drums). Ben Shepherd replaced Yamamoto in 1991. Cornell and Cameron also recorded with **Temple Of The Dog**. Group disbanded on 4/9/97.

1/27/90	108	16		©	1 Louder Than Love			$10	A&M 5252
10/26/91+	39	58	▲²	©	2 Badmotorfinger			$10	A&M 5374
3/26/94	❶¹	75	▲⁵	©	3 Superunknown	C:#50/1		$10	A&M 540198
6/8/96	2¹	43	▲	©	4 Down On The Upside			$10	A&M 540526
11/22/97	63	11		©	5 A-Sides		[G]	$10	A&M 540833

Applebite (4)
Big Dumb Sex (1)
Black Hole Sun (3,5)
Bleed Together (5)
Blow Up The Outside World (4,5)
Boot Camp (4)
Burden In My Hand (4,5)
Day I Tried To Live (3,5)
Drawing Flies (2)

Dusty (4)
Face Pollution (2)
Fell On Black Days (3,5)
Flower (1)
4th Of July (3)
Fresh Tendrils (3)
Full On Kevin's Mom (1)
Get On The Snake (1,5)
Gun (1)
Half (3)

Hands All Over (1,5)
Head Down (3)
Holy Water (2)
I Awake (1)
Jesus Christ Pose (2,5)
Kickstand (3)
Let Me Drown (3)
Like Suicide (3)
Limo Wreck (3)
Loud Love (1,5)

Mailman (3)
Mind Riot (2)
My Wave (3)
Never Named (4)
Never The Machine Forever (4)
New Damage (2)
No Attention (4)
No Wrong No Right (1)
Nothing To Say (5)
Outshined (2,5)

Overfloater (4)
Power Trip (1)
Pretty Noose (4,5)
Rhinosaur (4)
Room A Thousand Years Wide (2)
Rusty Cage (2,5)
Searching With My Good Eye Closed (2)
Slaves & Bulldozers (2)

Somewhere (2)
Spoonman (3,5)
Superunknown (3)
Switch Opens (4)
Tighter & Tighter (4)
Ty Cobb (4,5)
Ugly Truth (1)
Uncovered (1)
Unkind, An (4)
Zero Chance (4)

SOUNDS OF BLACKNESS   '94
Gospel group from Minneapolis. Directed by Gary Hines. Featured vocalist is **Ann Nesby**.

11/16/91	176	2	●	©	1 The Evolution Of Gospel			$10	Perspective 1000
12/19/92+	129	4		©	2 The Night Before Christmas - A Musical Fantasy		[X]	$10	Perspective 9000
					Christmas chart: 20/'92				
5/7/94	109	18	●	©	3 Africa To America: The Journey Of The Drum			$10	Perspective 9006
5/24/97	144	5		©	4 Time For Healing			$10	Perspective 9029

African Medley (3)
Africana (4)
Ah Been 'Buked (Pt. 1 & 2) (3)
Ah Been Workin' (1)
Away In A Manger (2)
Better Watch Your Behavior (1)
Black Butterfly (3)
Blackness Blues (4)
Born In A Manger (2)
Chains (1)
Children Go (1)
Crisis (4)
Dance, Chitlins, Dance (2)

Dash Away All (medley) (2)
Drum (Africa To America) (3)
Everything Is Gonna Be Alright (3)
Familiar Waters (4)
Give Us A Chance (2)
God Cares (4)
Gonna Be Free One Day (1)
Hallelujah Lord! (1)
Harambee (1)
Harder They Are The Bigger They Fall (3)
He Holds The Future (1)

He Took Away All My Pain (3)
Hold On (Change Is Comin') (4)
Hold On (Don't Let Go) (4)
Hold On (Pt. 1 & 2) (3)
Holiday Love (2)
I Believe (3) *99*
I'll Fly Away (1)
I'm Going All The Way (3)
It's Christmas Time (2)
Jolly One's Here (2)
Livin' The Blues (3)
Lord Will Make A Way (1)
Love Train (4)

Love Will Never Change (4)
Merry Christmas To The World (2)
O' Come All Ye Faithful (2)
O', Holy Night (2)
Optimistic (1)
Peace On Earth For Everyone (2)
Place In My Heart (3)
Please Take My Hand (1)
Pressure Pt. 1 & 2 (1)
Reindeer Revolt (medley) (2)
Santa Watch Yo' Step (2)

Santa Won't You Come By? (2)
Santa's Comin' To Town (2)
So Far Away (1)
Soul Holidays (2)
Spirit (4)
Spiritual Medley (4)
Stand (1)
Strange Fruit (3)
Sun Up To Sundown (3)
Testify (1)
Time For Healing (4)
Very Special Love (3)

We Are Gonna Make It Through (Parts 1-3) (4)
We Give You Thanks (1)
What Shall I Call Him? (1)
Why Don't You Believe In Me? (2)
You Can Make It If You Try (4)
You've Taken My Blues & Gone (3)
Your Wish Is My Command (1)

SOUNDS OF SUNSHINE   '71
Pop vocal trio from Los Angeles: brothers Walt, Warner and George Wilder.

| 8/14/71 | **187** | 8 | | | Love Means You Never Have To Say You're Sorry .... | | | $15 | Ranwood 8089 |

Anything Can Happen / I Do All My Crying In The Rain / Livin' It Day By Day / Make It With You / Yesterday Keeps Getting In The
El Condor Pasa / If / **Love Means (You Never Have** / Put Your Hand In The Hand / Way
For The Good Times / It's Impossible / **To Say You're Sorry)** 39 / Rainy Days And Mondays

SOUNDS ORCHESTRAL   '65
Studio trio from England: John Pearson (piano), Tony Reeves (bass) and Ken Clare (drums).

| 5/29/65 | **11** | 28 | | | Cast Your Fate To The Wind .... [I] | | | $20 | Parkway 7046 |

At The Mardi Gras (While We / **Cast Your Fate To The** / Have Faith In Your Love / Scarlatti Potion No. 5 / To Wendy With Love
Danced) / **Wind** 10 / Like The Lonely / Scarlatti Potion No. 9 / When Love Has Gone
Carnival (Manha De Carnaval) / Downtown / Love Letters / Something's Coming

SOUP DRAGONS, The   '90
Pop-rock group from Glasgow, Scotland: Sean Dickinson (vocals), Jim McCulloch (guitar), Sushil Dade (bass) and Paul Quinn (drums).

| 10/20/90 | **88** | 29 | © | 1 | Lovegod .... | | | $10 | Big Life 842985 |
| 6/27/92 | **97** | 22 | © | 2 | Hotwired .... | | | $10 | Big Life 13178 |

Absolute Heaven (2) / **Divine Thing** (2) 35 / Everlasting (2) / **I'm Free** (1) 79 / Mindless (2) / Running Wild (2)
Backwards Dog (1) / Dream-E-Forever (1) / Everything (2) / Kiss The Gun (1) / Mother Universe (1) / Softly (1)
Beauty Freak (1) / Dream-On (Solid Gone) (2) / Forever Yesterday (2) / Love You To Death (1) / No More Understanding (2) / Sweet Layabout (2)
Crotch Deep Trash (1) / Drive The Pain (1) / Getting Down (2) / Lovegod (1) / **Pleasure** (2) 69 / Sweetmeat (1)

SOUTH, Joe   '70
Born Joe Souter on 2/28/40 in Atlanta. Pop-country singer/guitarist.

2/8/69	**117**	14		1	Introspect			$20	Capitol 108
1/17/70	**60**	23		2	Don't It Make You Want To Go Home?			$15	Capitol 392
9/12/70	**125**	11		3	Joe South's Greatest Hits .... [G]			$15	Capitol 450

All My Hard Times (1) / Clock Up On The Wall (2) / Down In The Boondocks (3) / Million Miles Away (2) / **Walk A Mile In My Shoes**
Be A Believer (2) / **Don't It Make You Want To Go** / Gabriel (1) / Mirror Of Your Mind (1) / (2,3) 12
Before It's Too Late (2) / **Home** (2,3) 41 / Games People Play (1,3) 12 / Redneck (1) / What Makes Lovers Hurt One
Birds Of A Feather (1,3) 96 / Don't Throw Your Love To The / Greatest Love (1,3) / Rose Garden (1) / Another (2)
Bittersweet (2) / Wind (1) / Hush (3) / Shelter (2)
Children (2,3) 51 / Don't You Be Ashamed (1) / I Knew You When (3) / These Are Not My People (1,3)

SOUTH CENTRAL CARTEL   '94
Rap group from Los Angeles: Cary Calvin, Austin Patterson, Brian West, Larry Sanders, Greg Scott and Perry Rayson. By 1997, reduced to duo of Patterson and West.

| 5/28/94 | **32** | 15 | © | 1 | 'N Gatz We Truss .... | | | $10 | GWK 57294 |
| 6/21/97 | **178** | 1 | © | 2 | All Day Everyday .... | | | $10 | Def Jam 531159 |

All Day Everyday (2) / Drive Bye Homicide (1) / Gangsta Luv Pt. 2 (2) / I'm A Rider (2) / No Get Bacc (2) / U Couldn't Deal Wit Dis (1)
Bring It On (1) / Family Thang (2) / Gangsta Team (1) / It Don't Stop (2) / Rollin' Down Da Block (1) / W.C. Rocks (2)
Can I Roll Wit U (2) / 4 Yo Ear (2) / Get 'Em (1) / It's A S.C.C. Thang (1) / S.C.G.'z (2) / West Coast Gangstas (2)
Champagne Wishes (2) / Funk U Up (2) / Had To Be Loc'd (1) / Lil Knucklehead (1) / Servin' 'Em Heat (1)
Da Bomb (2) / G's Game (2) / Hit The Chaw (2) / Marinate (1) / Seventeen Switches (1)
Do It SC Style (1) / Gang Stories (2) / Hoo Riding' In Da Central (1) / Niggas Git Dealt Wit (2) / Stay Out Da Hood (1)

SOUTH CIRCLE   '95
Rap trio from Houston: Suave House, **Mr. Mike** Walls and Rex Robinson.

| 7/22/95 | **63** | 7 | © | | Anotha Day Anotha Balla .... | | | $10 | Suave 1518 |

Anotha Day Anotha Balla / Final Call / It's Going Down / New Day / Unsolved Mysteries
Attitudes / Geto Madness / Mental Murder / No Escape
Everyday Allday / Gotta Maintain / Neva Take Me Alive / Pimp Thang

SOUTHER, J.D.   '79
Born John David Souther on 11/2/45 in Detroit; raised in Amarillo, Texas. Pop-rock singer/songwriter/guitarist. Member of **The Souther, Hillman, Furay Band**.

| 5/8/76 | **85** | 11 | © | 1 | Black Rose .... | | | $12 | Asylum 1059 |

JOHN DAVID SOUTHER

| 9/22/79 | **41** | 22 | © | 2 | You're Only Lonely .... | | | $12 | Columbia 36093 |

Baby Come Home (1) / Doors Swing Open (1) / If You Have Crying Eyes (1) / Silver Blue (1) / Trouble In Paradise (1)
Banging My Head Against The / Faithless Love (1) / Last In Love (1) / Simple Man, Simple Dream (1) / White Rhythm And Blues (2)
Moon (1) / Fifteen Bucks (2) / Midnight Prowl (1) / Songs Of Love (1) / **You're Only Lonely** (2) 7
Black Rose (1) / If You Don't Want My Love (1) / Moon Just Turned Blue (2) / 'Til The Bars Burn Down (2) / Your Turn Now (1)

SOUTHER, HILLMAN, FURAY BAND, The   '74
Country-rock trio: **J.D. Souther**, **Chris Hillman** and **Richie Furay**.

| 7/20/74 | **11** | 22 | ● | 1 | The Souther, Hillman, Furay Band .... | | | $12 | Asylum 1006 |
| 6/21/75 | **39** | 11 | | 2 | Trouble In Paradise .... | | | $12 | Asylum 1036 |

Believe Me (1) / Flight Of The Dove (1) / Heavenly Fire (2) / On The Line (2) / Safe At Home (1)
Border Town (1) / Follow Me Through (1) / Love And Satisfy (2) / Pretty Goodbyes (1) / Somebody Must Be Wrong (2)
Deep, Dark And Dreamless (1) / For Someone I Love (2) / Mexico (2) / Prisoner In Disguise (2) / Trouble In Paradise (2)
Fallin' In Love (1) 27 / Heartbreaker, The (1) / Move Me Real Slow (2) / Rise And Fall (1)

SOUTHERN COMFORT   '71
Backing group for Ian Matthews: Mark Griffiths, Carl Barnwell and Gordon Huntley (guitars), Andy Leigh (bass) and Ray Duffy (drums).

| 8/14/71 | **196** | 2 | | | Frog City .... | | | $15 | Capitol 800 |

April Lady / Get Back Home / Leaving Song / Return To Frog City
(Dreadful Ballad Of) Willie / Good Lord D.C. / My Old Kentucky Home / Roses
Hurricane / I Sure Like Your Smile / Passing, The / Take A Message

SOUTHSIDE JOHNNY & THE JUKES   '79
Born John Lyon on 12/4/48 in Neptune, New Jersey. Rock singer/harmonica player. Core members of The Jukes: Billy Rush (guitar), Kevin Kavanaugh (keyboards) and Alan Berger (bass).
1)The Jukes 2)Love Is A Sacrifice 3)Reach Up And Touch The Sky

SOUTHSIDE JOHNNY & THE ASBURY JUKES:

7/10/76	**125**	9	©	1	I Don't Want To Go Home			$12	Epic 34180
5/7/77	**85**	9	©	2	This Time It's For Real			$12	Epic 34668
11/4/78+	**112**	20	©	3	Hearts Of Stone			$12	Epic 35488

SOUTHSIDE JOHNNY & THE JUKES — Cont'd

8/18/79	48	14		© 4	The Jukes			$12	Mercury 3793
6/14/80	67	15		© 5	Love Is A Sacrifice			$12	Mercury 3836
5/9/81	80	12		© 6	Reach Up And Touch The Sky		[L]	$15	Mercury 8602 [2]

SOUTHSIDE JOHNNY & THE JUKES:

10/1/83	154	6		7	Trash It Up!			$10	Mirage 90113
9/8/84	164	8		8	In The Heat			$10	Mirage 90186
6/21/86	189	4		9	At Least We Got Shoes			$10	Atlantic 81654
12/3/88	198	1		© 10	Slow Dance			$10	Cypress 0115

SOUTHSIDE JOHNNY

11/16/91	96	7		© 11	Better Days			$10	Impact 10445

Act Of Love (10)
Action Speaks Louder Than Words (8)
Ain't Gonna Eat Out My Heart Anymore (7)
Ain't That Peculiar (10)
All I Needed Was You (11)
All I Want Is Everything (4,6)
All Night Long (11)
All The Way Home (11)
Back In The U.S.A. (6)
Beast Within (7)
Bedtime (7)
Better Days (11)
Bring It On Home To Me (6)
Broke Down Piece Of Man (1)
Can't Stop Thinking Of You (7)
Captured (8)
Check Mr. Popeye (2)
Coming Back (11)

Don't Look Back (8)
Fannie Mae (1)
Fever, The (1,6)
First Night (2)
Get Your Body On The Job (7)
Goodbye Love (5)
Got To Be A Better Way Home (3)
Got To Get You Off My Mind (1)
Hard To Find (9)
Having A Party (Part 1 & 2) (6)
Hearts Of Stone (3,6)
How Come You Treat Me So Bad (1)
I Ain't Got The Fever No More (2)
I Can't Live Without Love (8)
I Can't Wait (9)
I Choose To Sing The Blues (1)

I Don't Want To Go Home (1,6)
I Only Want To Be With You (9)
I Played The Fool (3)
I Remember Last Night (4)
I've Been Working Too Hard (11)
I'm So Anxious (4,6) 71
It Ain't The Meat (It's The Motion) (1)
It Hurts (5)
It's Been A Long Time (11)
Keep Our Love Simple (5)
Light Don't Shine (3)
Little Calcutta (10)
Little Girl So Fine (2)
Living In The Real World (4)
Long Distance (9)
Lorraine (9)
Love Goes To War (8)
Love Is The Drug (8)

Love On The Wrong Side Of Town (2)
Love When It's Strong (5)
Ms. Park Avenue (7)
Murder (9)
My Baby's Touch (7)
New Coat Of Paint (8)
New Romeo (9)
Next To You (3)
No Secret (11)
On The Air (10)
On The Beach (5)
Over My Head (8)
Paris (4)
Restless Heart (5,6)
Ride The Night Away (11)
Right To Walk Away (11)
Roll Out The Barrel (medley) (6)
Sam Cooke Medley (6)
Security (4)

Shake 'Em Down (11)
She Got Me Where She Wants Me (2)
Sirens Of The Night (10)
Slow Burn (7)
Slow Dance (10)
Some Things Just Don't Change (2)
Soul's On Fire (11)
Stagger Lee (6)
Sweeter Than Honey (1)
Take It Inside (3)
Take My Love (9)
Talk To Me (3,6)
Tell Me Lies (8)
Tell Me (That Our Love's Still Strong) (9)
This Time Baby's Gone For Good (3)
This Time It's For Real (2)

Till The End Of The Night (9)
Time, The (4)
Trapped Again (3,6)
Trash It Up (7)
Under The Sun (9)
Vertigo (4,6)
Wait In Vain (4)
Walk Away Renee (9) 98
Walking Through Midnight (10)
When The Moment Is Right (10)
When You Dance (3)
Why (5)
Why Is Love Such A Sacrifice (5,6)
Without Love (2)
You Can Count On Me (9)
You Mean So Much To Me (1)
Your Precious Love (10)
Your Reply (4)

SOVINE, Red '76

Born Woodrow Wilson Sovine on 7/17/18 in Charleston, West Virginia. Died of a heart attack on 4/4/80 (age 61). Country singer/songwriter/guitarist.

9/11/76	119	6		©	Teddy Bear			$15	Starday 968

Bootlegger King
Daddy

Does Steppin' Out Mean Daddy
Took A Walk

18 Wheels Hummin' Home Sweet Home
1460 Elder Street

It Ain't No Big Thing
Last Mile Of The Way
Little Rosa

Love Is
Sad Violins
Teddy Bear 40

SPACE '97

Rock group from Liverpool, England: Tommy Scott (vocals), Jamie Murphy (guitar), Franny Griffith (keyboards) and Andy Parle (drums).

3/8/97	189	5		©	Spiders			$10	Universal 53028

Charlie M
Dark Clouds
Drop Dead

Female Of The Species
Growler
Kill Me

Lovechild Of The Queen
Major Pager
Me & You Vs. The World

Mister Psycho
Money
Neighbourhood

No-One Understands
Voodoo Roller

SPACEHOG '96

Rock group from Leeds, England: Royston Langdon (vocals, bass), Richard Steel and Antony Langdon (guitars), and Jonny Cragg (drums).

1/27/96	49	22	● ©		Resident Alien			$10	Sire 61834

Candyman
Cruel To Be Kind
In The Meantime 32

Last Dictator
Never Coming Down (Parts I & II)

Only A Few
Ship Wrecked
Space Is The Place

Spacehog
Starside
Zeroes

To Be A Millionaire...Was It Likely?

SPANDAU BALLET '83

Pop group formed in London: Tony Hadley (vocals), brothers Gary (guitar) and Martin (bass) Kemp, Steve Norman (sax) and John Keeble (drums). The Kemps starred in the 1990 movie The Krays. Gary Kemp was married to actress Sadie Frost from 1988-97.

5/14/83	19	37		© 1	True			$10	Chrysalis 41403
8/18/84	50	16		© 2	Parade			$10	Chrysalis 41473

Always In The Back Of My Mind (2)
Code Of Love (1)

Communication (1) 59
Foundation (1)
Gold (1) 29

Heaven Is A Secret (1)
Highly Strung (2)
I'll Fly For You (2)

Lifeline (1)
Nature Of The Beast (2)
Only When You Leave (2) 34

Pleasure (1)
Revenge For Love (2)
Round And Round (2)

True (1) 4
With The Pride (2)

SPANKY AND OUR GANG '68

Folk-pop group formed in Chicago: Elaine "Spanky" McFarlane (vocals; born on 6/19/42 in Peoria, Illinois), Malcolm Hale, Lefty Baker and Nigel Pickering (guitars), Kenny Hodges (bass), and John Seiter (drums). Spanky became lead singer of the new **Mamas & The Papas** in the early 1980s. Hale died of liver failure on 10/31/68 (age 27). Baker died of liver failure on 8/11/71 (age 29).

9/9/67	77	15		1	Spanky And Our Gang			$20	Mercury 61124
4/27/68	56	25		2	Like To Get To Know You			$20	Mercury 61161
2/15/69	101	7		3	Anything You Choose/Without Rhyme Or Reason			$20	Mercury 61183
11/1/69+	91	17		© 4	Spanky's Greatest Hit(s)		[G]	$20	Mercury 61227

And She's Mine (3,4) 97
Anything You Choose (3) 86
Brother Can You Spare A Dime (1)
But Back Then (3)
Byrd Avenue (1)
Chick-A-Ding-Ding (2)
Come And Open Your Eyes (1)

Commercial (1,4)
Distance (1)
Everybody's Talkin' (2,4)
5 Definitions Of Love (1)
Give A Damn (3,4) 43
Hong Kong Blues (3)
If You Could Only Be Me (1)

It Ain't Necessarily Bird Avenue (4)
Jane (3)
Jet Plane (1)
Lazy Day (1,4) 14
Leopard Skin Phones (3)
Like To Get To Know You (2,4) 17

Making Every Minute Count (1,4) 31
Mecca Flat Blues (3)
My Bill (2)
Nowhere To Go (3)
1-3-5-8 (Pedagogical Round #2) (3)
Prescription For The Blues (2)

Since You've Gone (3)
Stardust (2)
Stuperflabbergasted (2)
Sunday Mornin' (2,4) 30
Sunday Will Never Be The Same (1,4) 9
Suzanne (2)
Swingin' Gate (2)

Three Ways From Tomorrow (2,4)
Trouble (1)
Without Rhyme Or Reason (3)
Yesterday's Rain (3,4) 94

SPARKLE '98

Born in New York City. Female R&B singer.

6/6/98	3	17	● ©	1	Sparkle			$10	Rock Land 90149
11/10/00	121	2		© 2	Told You So			$10	Motown 159743

All I Want (2)
Be Careful (1)
Don't Know Why (2)
Everything (2)
Games (2)

Ghetto, The (2)
Good Life (1,2)
I'm Gone (1)
Into My Life (2)
It's A Fact (2)

Lean On Me (1)
Lovin A Man (2)
Lovin' You (1)
Never Can Say Goodbye (2)
Nothing Compare (1)

Play On (1)
Plenty Good Lovin' (1)
Somebody Else (2)
Straight Up (1)
Time To Move On (1)

Turn Away (1)
Vegas (1)
What About (1)
When A Woman's Heart Is Broken (2)

SPARKS '75
Rock duo from Los Angeles: brothers Ron (born on 8/12/50) and Russell (born on 10/5/55) Mael.

DEBUT	PEAK	WKS					$	Label & Number
8/24/74	101	14	©	1	Kimono My House		$12	Island 9272
2/8/75	63	13		2	Propaganda		$12	Island 9312
11/29/75+	169	6		3	Indiscreet		$12	Island 9345
8/15/81	182	2	©	4	Whomp That Sucker		$10	RCA Victor 4091
5/22/82	173	6	©	5	Angst In My Pants		$10	Atlantic 19347
4/30/83	88	17	©	6	Sparks In Outer Space		$10	Atlantic 80055

Achoo (2)
All You Ever Think About Is Sex (6)
Amateur Hour (1)
Angst In My Pants (5)
At Home At Work At Play (2)
B.C. (1)
Bon Voyage (2)
Complaints (1)
Cool Places (6) 49
Dance Godammit (6)
Decline And Fall Of Me (5)
Don't Leave Me Alone With Her (2)
Don't Shoot Me (4)
Eaten By The Monster Of Love (5)
Equator (1)
Falling In Love With Myself Again (1)
Fun Bunch Of Guys From Outer Space (6)
Funny Face (4)
Get In The Swing (3)
Happy Hunting Ground (3)
Hasta Manana Monsieur (1)
Here In Heaven (1)
Hospitality On Parade (3)
How Are You Getting Home? (3)
I Married A Martian (4)
I Predict (5) 60
I Wish I Looked A Little Better (6)
In My Family (1)
In The Future (3)
Instant Weight Loss (5)
It Ain't 1918 (3)
Lady Is Lingering (3)
Looks, Looks, Looks (3)
Lucky Me, Lucky You (6)
Mickey Mouse (5)
Miss The Start, Miss The End (3)
Moustache (5)
Never Turn Your Back On Mother Earth (2)
Nicotina (5)
Pineapple (3)
Please, Baby, Please (6)
Popularity (6)
Prayin' For A Party (6)
Propaganda (2)
Reinforcements (2)
Rockin' Girls (6)
Sextown U.S.A. (5)
Sherlock Holmes (5)
Something For The Girl With Everything (2)
Suzie Safety (4)
Talent Is An Asset (1)
Tarzan And Jane (5)
Thank God It's Not Christmas (1)
Thanks But No Thanks (2)
That's Not Nastassia (4)
This Town Ain't Big Enough For Both Of Us (1)
Tips For Teens (4)
Tits (3)
Under The Table With Her (3)
Upstairs (4)
Wacky Women (4)
Where's My Girl (4)
Who Don't Like Kids (2)
Willys, The (4)
Without Using Hands (3)

SPEARS, Britney '99
Born on 12/2/81 in Kentwood, Louisiana. Female singer/actress. Regular on TV's *The Mickey Mouse Club* (1992-93).

DEBUT	PEAK	WKS	RIAA	CD		Catalog	$	Label & Number
1/30/99	❶⁶	103	▲¹³	©	1 ...Baby One More Time	C:#9/17	$10	Jive 41651
6/3/00	❶¹	70↑	▲⁹	©	2 Oops!...I Did It Again		$10	Jive 41704

...Baby One More Time (1) 1
Beat Goes On (1)
Born To Make You Happy (1)
Can't Make You Love Me (2)
Dear Diary (2)
Don't Go Knockin' On My Door (2)
Don't Let Me Be The Last To Know (2)
E-Mail My Heart (1)
From The Bottom Of My Broken Heart (1) 14
(I Can't Get No) Satisfaction (2)
I Will Be There (1)
I Will Still Love You (1)
Lucky (2) 23
One Kiss From You (2)
Oops!...I Did It Again (2) 9
Soda Pop (1)
Sometimes (1) 21
Stronger (2) 11
Thinkin' About You (1)
What U See (Is What U Get) (2)
When Your Eyes Say It (2)
Where Are You Now (2)
(You Drive Me) Crazy (1) 10

SPECIAL ED '89
Born Edward Archer in Brooklyn, New York. Male rapper.

DEBUT	PEAK	WKS		CD		$	Label & Number
6/3/89	73	28		©	1 Youngest In Charge	$10	Profile 1280
8/18/90	84	13		©	2 Legal	$10	Profile 1297
7/15/95	107	4		©	3 Revelations	$10	Profile 1463

Ak-Shun (1)
Bush, The (1)
Club Scene (1)
Come On, Let's Move It (2)
Crazy (3)
Everyday Iza Gunshot (3)
5 Men And A Mic (2)
Fly M.C. (1)
Freaky Flow (3)
Heds And Dreds (1)
Here I Go Again (1)
Hoedown (1)
I Got It Made (1)
I'm Special Ed (2)
I'm The Magnificent (1,2)
It's Only Gettin' Worse (3)
Just A Killa (3)
Just Like Dat (3)
Livin' Like A Star (2)
Lyrics (3)
Mission, The (2)
Monster Jam (1)
Neva Go Back (3)
Ready 2 Attack (2)
Rough 2 The Endin' (3)
Rukus (3)
See It Ya (2)
Taxing (1)
Think About It (1)
Walk The Walk (3)
We Rule (3)
Won't Be Long (3)
Ya Not So Hot (2)
Ya Wish Ya Could (2)

SPECIALS '80
Ska-rock group from Coventry, England: Terry Hall and Neville Staples (vocals), Lynval Golding and Roddy Radiation (guitars), Jerry Dammers (keyboards), Horace Gentleman (bass) and John Bradbury (drums). Hall, Staples and Golding went on to form **Fun Buy Three**.

DEBUT	PEAK	WKS		CD		$	Label & Number
1/26/80	84	21		©	1 The Specials	$12	Chrysalis 1265
11/8/80	98	5		©	2 More Specials	$12	Chrysalis 1303

Blank Expression (1)
Concrete Jungle (1)
(Dawning Of A) New Era (1)
Do Nothing (2)
Do The Dog (1)
Doesn't Make It Alright (1)
Enjoy Yourself (2)
Gangsters (1)
Hey, Little Rich Girl (2)
Holiday Fortnight (2)
I Can't Stand It (2)
International Jet Set (2)
It's Up To You (1)
Little Bitch (1)
Man At C&A (2)
Message To You Rudy (1)
Monkey Man (1)
Nite Klub (1)
Pearl's Cafe (2)
Rat Race (2)
Sock It To 'Em J.B. (2)
Stereotypes Part 1 & 2 (2)
Stupid Marriage (1)
Too Hot (1)
Too Much Too Young (1)
You're Wondering Now (1)

SPEER, Paul — see LANZ, David

SPENCE, Judson '88
Born in Pascagoula, Mississippi. Singer/songwriter/multi-instrumentalist.

DEBUT	PEAK	WKS		CD		$	Label & Number
12/10/88	168	13		©	Judson Spence	$10	Atlantic 81902

Attitude
Dance With Me
Down In The Village
Everything She Do
Forever Me, Forever You
Higher
Hot & Sweaty
If You Don't Like It
Love Dies In Slow Motion
Yeah, Yeah, Yeah 32

SPENCER, Jon, Blues Explosion '96
Born in Hanover, New Hampshire. Blues-rock singer/guitarist. His group included Judah Bauer (guitar) and Russell Simins (drums).

DEBUT	PEAK	WKS		CD		$	Label & Number
11/2/96	121	1		©	1 Now I Got Worry	$10	Matador 53553
11/7/98	180	1		©	2 Acme	$10	Matador 95566

Attack (2)
B. L. Got Soul (1)
Bernie (2)
Blue Green Olga (2)
Calvin (2)
Can't Stop (1)
Chicken Dog (2)
Desperate (2)
Do You Wanna Get Heavy? (2)
Dynamite Lover (1)
Eyeballin (1)
Firefly Child (1)
Fuck Shit Up (1)
Get Over Here (1)
Give Me A Chance (2)
High Gear (2)
Hot Shot (1)
I Wanna Make It All Right (2)
Identify (1)
Love All Of Me (1)
Lovin' Machine (2)
Magical Colors (2)
Rocketship (1)
Skunk (1)
Sticky (1)
Talk About The Blues (2)
Torture (1)
2Kindsa Love (1)
Wail (1)

SPENCER, Tracie '91
Born on 7/12/76 in Waterloo, Iowa. R&B singer.

DEBUT	PEAK	WKS		CD		$	Label & Number
6/25/88	146	21		©	1 Tracie Spencer	$10	Capitol 48186
2/23/91	107	11		©	2 Make The Difference	$10	Capitol 92153
7/17/99	114	7		©	3 Tracie	$10	Capitol 34287

Because Of You (1)
Closer (3)
Cross My Heart (1)
Double O Rhythm (3)
Feelin' You (3)
Hide And Seek (1)
I Have A Song To Sing (2)
I Like That (1)
If U Wanna Get Down (3)
Imagine (1) 85
In My Dreams (3)
It's All About You (Not About Me) (3) 18
It's On Tonight (3)
Love Me (2) 48
Love To You (3)
Lullaby Child (1)
My First Broken Heart (1)
My Heart Beats Only 4 U (1)
No Matter (3)
Not Gonna Cry (3)
Nothing Broken But My Heart (3)
Save Your Love (3)
Still In My Heart (3) 88
Sweeter Love (2)
Symptoms Of True Love (1) 38
Tender Kisses (2) 42
This House (2) 3
This Time Make It Funky (2) 54
Too Much Of Nothing (2)
Tracie's Hideout (2)
Unbelievable (3)
Wanna Be (1)
You Make The Difference (2)

SPHEERIS, Jimmie '75
Born on 11/5/49 in Greece; raised in California. Died in a car crash on 7/4/84 (age 34). Singer/songwriter/guitarist.

| 9/20/75 | 135 | 6 | © | | **The Dragon Is Dancing** .... | | | $12 | Epic 33565 |

Blown Out · Dragon Is Dancing · In The Misty Woods · Love's In Vain · Snake Man · Sunken Skies
Blue Streets · Eternity Spin · Lost In The Midway · Sighs In A Shell · Summer Salt · Tequila Moonlite

SPICE GIRLS '97
Female vocal group from England: Victoria Addams (Posh Spice), Melanie Brown (Scary Spice), Emma Bunton (Baby Spice), Melanie Chisholm (Sporty Spice) and Geri Halliwell (Ginger Spice). Group starred in the movie *Spiceworld*. Halliwell left in May 1998.

2/22/97	❶[5]	105	▲[7]	©	1 **Spice**	C:#2^2/15		$10	Virgin 42174
11/22/97+	3	74	▲[4]	©	2 **Spiceworld**		[S]	$10	Virgin 45111
11/25/00	39	7		©	3 **Forever**			$10	Virgin 50467

Denying (2) · If You Wanna Have Some Fun (3) · Mama (1) · Right Back At Ya (3) · Tell Me Why (3) · Wasting My Time (3)
Do It (2) · Lady Is A Vamp (2) · Move Over (2) · Saturday Night Divas (2) · Time Goes By (3) · Weekend Love (3)
Get Down With Me (3) · Last Time Lover (1) · Naked (3) · **Say You'll Be There** (1) *3* · **Too Much** (2) *9* · Who Do You Think You Are (1)
Goodbye (3) *11* · Let Love Lead The Way (3) · Never Give Up On The Good · Something Kinda Funny (1) · **2 Become 1** (1) *4*
Holler (3) · Love Thing (1) · Times (2) · **Spice Up Your Life** (2) *18* · Viva Forever (2)
If U Can't Dance (1) · Oxygen (3) · **Stop** (2) *16* · **Wannabe** (1) *1*

SPICE 1 '93
Born Robert Green in Bryan, Texas; raised in Oakland. Male rapper.

| 5/2/92 | 82 | 31 | ● | © | 1 **Spice 1** .... | | | $10 | Jive 41481 |
| 10/16/93 | 10 | 18 | ● | © | 2 **187 He Wrote** | | | $10 | Jive 41513 |

187 is slang for murder

12/10/94	22	18	●	©	3 **AmeriKKKa's Nightmare**			$10	Jive 41547
12/23/95	30	10		©	4 **1990-Sick**			$10	Jive 41583
11/15/97	28	4		©	5 **The Black Bossalini (aka Dr. Bomb From Da Bay)**			$10	Jive 41596
10/30/99	111	2		©	6 **Immortalized**			$10	Jive 41690

Ain't No Love (4) · Drama (4) · In My Neighborhood (1) · 187 Proof (1,6) · Tales Of The Niggas Who Got · Young Nigga (1)
All He Wrote (2) · Dumpin' Em In Ditches (2) · Jealous Got Me Strapped (3) · 187 Pure (1) · Crept On (4)
Ballin' (5) · East Bay Gangster (1) · Kill Street Blues (5) · 1-900-Spice (1) · Tell Me What That Mail Like (3)
Boss Mobsta (5) · Face Of A Desperate Man (3) · Killerfornia (3) · Peace To My Nine (1) · 380 On That Ass (2)
Break Yourself (1) · Faces Of Death (4) · Make Sure They Bleed (6) · Playa Man (5) · Three Strikes (3)
Busta's Can't See Me (3) · Fetty Chico And The Mack (5) · Mind Of A Sick Nigga (4) · RIP (2) · Thug In Me (5)
Can I Hit It? (6) · 510,213 (5) · Mo' Mail (2) · Recognize Game (5) · Thug Poetry (6)
Can U Feel It (4) · Fuck The World (6) · Mobbin' (4) · Ride Fo' Mine (6) · Too Deep In The Game (6)
Caught Up In My Gunplay (5) · Fucked In The Game (1) · Money Gone (1) · Ride Wit Me (6) · Trigga Gots No Heart (2)
City Streets (1) · Funky Chickens (4) · Money Or Murder (1) · Runnin' Out Da Crackhouse (3) · Trigga Happy (2)
Clip & The Trigga (2) · Gas Chamber (2) · Murda Show (2) · Smoke 'Em Like A Blunt (2) · 2 Hands & A Razorblade (5)
D-Boyz Got Love For Me (3) · Give The "G" A Gat (3) · Murder Ain't Crazy (3) · Snitch Killas (2) · U Can't Fade Me (1)
Diamonds (5) · Gone With The Wind (6) · Nigga Sings The Blues (3) · Stickin' To The "G" Code (3) · Wanna Be A G (5)
Dirty Bay (4) · Hard To Kill (3) · 1990-Sick (Kill 'Em All) (4) · Strap On The Side (3) · Welcome To The Ghetto (1)
Don't Ring The Alarm (The · High Powered (6) · 1-800-Spice (1) · Sucka Ass Niggas (4) · What The Fuck (6)
Heist) (2) · I'm High (5) · 1-800 (Straight From The Pen) · Suckas Do What They Can · You Can Get The Gat For That
Doncha Runaway (3) · I'm The Fuckin' Murderer (2) · (4) · (Real Playaz) (6) · (3)
Down Payment On Heaven (5) · Immortalized (6) · 187 He Wrote (2) · Survival (4) · You Done Fucked Up (3)

SPIDER '80
Rock group formed in New York City: Amanda Blue (vocals), Keith Lentin (guitar), Holly Knight (keyboards), Jimmy Lowell (bass) and Anton Fig (drums). Knight, later joined *Device*. Fig joined house band of TV's *Late Night With David Letterman*.

| 5/17/80 | 130 | 10 | | © | 1 **Spider** .... | | | $12 | Dreamland 5000 |
| 7/11/81 | 185 | 2 | | © | 2 **Between The Lines** .... | | | $12 | Dreamland 5007 |

Better Be Good To Me (2) · Can't Live This Way Anymore · Don't Waste Your Time (1) · Going By (2) · Little Darlin' (1) · What's Going On (1)
Between The Lines (2) · (2) · **Everything Is Alright** (1) *86* · I Love (2) · **New Romance (It's A Mystery)** · Zero (1)
Brotherly Love (1) · Change (2) · Faces Are Changing (2) · I Think I Like It (2) · (1) *39*
Burning Love (1) · Crossfire (1) · Go And Run (2) · It Didn't Take Long (2) *43* · Shady Lady (1)

SPIDERS FROM MARS '76
Backing group for *David Bowie*: Pete McDonald (vocals), Dave Black (guitar), Trevor Bolder (bass) and Woody Woodmansey (drums).

| 4/3/76 | 197 | 2 | | © | **Spiders From Mars** .... | | | $15 | Pye 12125 |

Can It Be Far · Good Day America · Prisoner · Red Eyes · Stranger To My Door
Fallen Star · (I Don't Wanna Do No) Limbo · Rainbow · Shine A Light · White Man Black Man

SPINAL TAP '92
Parody heavy-metal trio introduced in the 1984 mock documentary movie *This Is Spinal Tap*. Actor Michael McKean portrays "David St. Hubbins," Christopher Guest is "Nigel Tufnel" and Harry Shearer is "Derek Smalls". Guest married actress Jamie Lee Curtis on 12/18/84. McKean played "Lenny" on TV's *Laverne & Shirley*. All three have been regular castmembers of *Saturday Night Live*.

| 4/28/84 | 121 | 10 | | © | 1 **This Is Spinal Tap** .... | | [S] | $10 | Polydor 817846 |
| 4/4/92 | 61 | 6 | | © | 2 **Break Like The Wind** .... | | | $10 | MCA 10514 |

All The Way Home (2) · Christmas With The Devil (2) · Hell Hole (1) · Rock And Roll Creation (1) · Sun Never Sweats (2)
America (1) · Clam Caravan (2) · Just Begin Again (2) · Sex Farm (1) · Tonight I'm Gonna Rock You
Big Bottom (1) · Cups And Cakes (1) · (Listen To The) Flower People · Springtime (2) · Tonight (1)
Bitch School (2) · Diva Fever (2) · (1) · Stinkin' Up The Great Outdoors
Break Like The Wind (2) · Gimme Some Money (1) · Majesty Of Rock (2) · (2)
Cash On Delivery (2) · Heavy Duty (1) · Rainy Day Sun (2) · Stonehenge (1)

SPIN DOCTORS '93
Rock group from New York City: Christopher Barron (vocals), Eric Schenkman (guitar), Mark White (bass) and Aaron Comess (drums). Anthony Krizan replaced Schenkman in 1993.

7/4/92+	3	115	▲[5]	©	1 **Pocket Full Of Kryptonite**			$10	Epic/Associated 47461
1/9/93	145	15		©	2 **Homebelly Groove...Live**		[L]	$10	Epic/Associated 53309
7/2/94	28	16	▲	©	3 **Turn It Upside Down**			$10	Epic 52907

At This Hour (3) · Forty Or Fifty (1) · Hungry Hamed's (3) · Mary Jane (3) · Shinbone Alley (1,2) · Yo Baby (3)
Bags Of Dirt (3) · Freeway Of The Plains · Indifference (3) · More Than Meets The Ear (3) · Someday All This Will Be Road · Yo Mamas A Pajama (2)
Beasts In The Woods (3) · (medley) (2) · **Jimmy Olsen's Blues** (1) *78* · More Than She Knows (1) · (3) · **You Let Your Heart Go Too**
Big Fat Funky Booty (3) · Hard To Exist (medley) (1) · Lady Kerosene (medley) (2) · Off My Line (1,2) · Stepped On A Crack (2) · **Fast** (3) *42*
Biscuit Head (3) · How Could You Want Him · Laraby's Gang (3) · Refrigerator Car (1,2) · Sweet Widow (2)
Cleopatra's Cat (3) *84* · (When You Know You Could · **Little Miss Can't Be Wrong** · Rosetta Stone (2) · **Two Princes** (1) *7*
· Have Me?) (1) · (1,2) *17* · · What Time Is It? (1,2)

DEBUT	PEAK	WKS	RIAA	CD	ARTIST — Album Title	Catalog	Sym	$	Label & Number

SPINESHANK '00

Hard-rock group from Los Angeles: Johnny Santos (vocals), Mike Sarkisyan (guitar), Robert Garcia (bass) and Tom Decker (drums).

| 10/28/00 | 183 | 1 | | © | **The Height Of Callousness** .... | | | $10 | Roadrunner 8563 |

Asthmatic — Cyanide 2600 — Malnutrition — New Disease — Seamless — Transparent
(Can't Be) Fixed — Height Of Callousness — Negative Space — Play God — Synthetic

★247★ SPINNERS '75

R&B vocal group formed in Detroit: G.C. Cameron, Henry Fambrough, Bobby Smith, Billy Henderson and Pervis Jackson. Philippe Wynne replaced Cameron in early 1972. John Edwards replaced Wynne in 1977. Wynne died on 7/14/84 (age 43).
1)Pick Of The Litter 2)New And Improved 3)Spinners

11/14/70	199	2			1	**2nd Time Around**..........			$40	V.I.P. 405
4/21/73	14	28	●	©	2	**Spinners**..........			$12	Atlantic 7256
5/12/73	124	10		©	3	**The Best Of The Spinners**..........		[K]	$15	Motown 769
3/16/74	16	35	●	©	4	**Mighty Love**..........			$12	Atlantic 7296
12/14/74+	9	26	●	©	5	**New And Improved**..........			$12	Atlantic 18118
8/9/75	8	26	●	©	6	**Pick Of The Litter**..........			$12	Atlantic 18141
12/13/75+	20	21		©	7	**Spinners Live!**..........		[L]	$15	Atlantic 910 [2]
7/31/76	25	30	●	©	8	**Happiness Is Being With The Detroit Spinners**..........			$12	Atlantic 18181
4/2/77	26	13		©	9	**Yesterday, Today & Tomorrow**..........			$12	Atlantic 19100
12/24/77+	57	13		©	10	**Spinners/8**..........			$12	Atlantic 19146
5/20/78	115	9		©	11	**The Best Of The Spinners**..........		[G]	$12	Atlantic 19179
5/26/79	165	4		©	12	**From Here To Eternally**..........			$12	Atlantic 19219
1/19/80	32	20		©	13	**Dancin' And Lovin'**..........			$10	Atlantic 19256
6/21/80	53	13		©	14	**Love Trippin'**..........			$10	Atlantic 19270
4/4/81	128	6		©	15	**Labor Of Love**..........			$10	Atlantic 16032
1/16/82	196	4			16	**Can't Shake This Feelin'**..........			$10	Atlantic 19318
1/8/83	167	6			17	**Grand Slam**..........			$10	Atlantic 80020

Ain't No Price On Happiness (4)
All That Glitters Ain't Gold (6)
Almost All The Way To Love (15)
Are You Ready For Love (12)
Baby I Need Your Love (You're The Only One) (10)
Back In The Arms Of Love (10)
Bad, Bad Weather (Till You Come Home) (1,3)
Be My Love (15)
Body Language (13)
Can Sing A Rainbow (medley) (1)
Can't Shake This Feelin' (16)
City Full Of Memories (17)
Clown, The (8)
Could It Be I'm Falling In Love (2,7,11) 4
Cupid/I've Loved You For A Long Time (14) 4
Deacon, The (15)
Didn't I Blow Your Mind (16)
Disco Ride (13)
Don't Let The Green Grass Fool You (2)
Don't Let The Man Get You (12)
Easy Come, Easy Go (10)
Fascinating Rhythm (7)
Forgive Me, Girl ..see: Working My Way Back To You

Four Hands In The Fire (8)
Funny How Time Slips Away (17) 67
Ghetto Child (2,11) 29
Give Your Lady What She Wants (15)
Got To Be Love (16)
He'll Never Love You Like I Do (4)
Heaven On Earth (So Fine) (10) 89
Heavy On The Sunshine (14)
Honest I Do (6)
Honey, I'm In Love With You (9)
How Could I Let You Get Away (2,7,11) 77
I Could Never (Repay Your Love) (2)
I Don't Want To Lose You (6)
I Found Love (When I Found You) (9)
I Just Want To Be With You (14)
I Just Want To Fall In Love (14)
I Love The Music (12)
I Must Be Living For A Broken Heart (9)
I'll Always Love You (3) 35
I'll Be Around (2,11) 3
I'm Calling You Now (17)

I'm Coming Home (4) 18
I'm Glad You Walked Into My Life (4)
I'm Gonna Getcha (10)
I'm Riding Your Shadow (Down To You) (9)
I'm Takin' You Back (14)
I'm Tired Of Giving (10)
I've Got To Find Myself A Brand New Baby (1,3)
I've Got To Make It On My Own (5,7)
I've Loved You For A Long Time ..see: Cupid
If I Knew (17)
If You Can't Be In Love (8)
If You Wanna Do A Dance (12) 49
In My Diary (1)
It's A Natural Affair (12)
It's A Shame (1,3) 14
Just As Long As We Have Love (6)
Just Can't Get You Out Of My Mind (2)
Just Let Love In (17)
Just You And Me Baby (2)
Knack For Me (16)
Lazy Susan (5)
Let's Boogie, Let's Dance (13)

Living A Little, Laughing A Little (5,7) 37
Long Live Soul Music (15)
Love Connection (Raise The Window Down) (16)
Love Don't Love Nobody - Pt. 1 (4,7) 15
Love Don't Love Nobody - Pt. 2 (7)
Love Has Gone Away (4)
Love Is Blue (medley) (1)
(Love Is) One Step Away (10)
Love Is Such A Crazy Feeling (16)
Love Or Leave (6) 36
Love Trippin' (14)
Lover Boy (17)
Magic In The Moonlight (17)
Man Just Don't Know What A Woman Goes Through (15)
Me And My Music (9)
Mighty Love (4,7,11) 20
My Lady Love (1)
My Whole World Ended (The Moment You Left Me) (1,3)
Never Thought I'd Fall In Love (16) 95
No Other Love (17)
Nothing Remains The Same ..see: Yesterday Once More
Now That We're Together (8)

Now That You're Mine Again (14)
Once You Fall In Love (12)
One Man Wonderful Band (12)
One Of A Kind (Love Affair) (2,7,11) 11
One, One, Two, Two, Boogie Woogie Avenue (Home Of The Boogie, House Of The Funk) (13)
O-o-h Child (1,3)
Painted Magic (10)
Pay Them No Mind (1)
Pipedream (14)
Plain And Simple Love Song (12)
Rubberband Man (8,11) 2
Sadie (5,7,11) 54
Send A Little Love (16)
(She's Gonna Love Me) At Sundown (1)
Since I Been Gone (4)
Sitting On Top Of The World (5)
Smile, We Have Each Other (5)
So Far Away (17)
Souly Ghost (1)
Split Decision (14)
Standing On The Rock (15)
Streetwise (14)
Superstar Medley (7)
Sweet Love Of Mine (6)

Sweet Thing (3)
Then Came You (5,7,11) 1
There's No One Like You (5)
"They Just Can't Stop It" the (Games People Play) (6,11) 5
Together We Can Make Such Sweet Music (1,3) 91
Toni My Love (8)
Truly Yours (3)
Wake Up Susan (8) 56
We Belong Together (2)
We'll Have It Made (3) 89
Winter Of Our Love (15)
With My Eyes (13)
Working My Way Back To You/Forgive Me, Girl (13) 2
Yesterday Once More/Nothing Remains The Same (15) 52
You Go Your Way (I'll Go Mine) (16)
You Got The Love That I Need (10)
You Made A Promise To Me (3)
You're All I Need In Life (8)
You're The Love Of My Life (9)
You're Throwing A Good Love Away (9) 43

SPIRAL STARECASE '69

Pop-rock group from Sacramento: Pat Upton (vocals, guitar), Harvey Kaplan (organ), Dick Lopes (sax), Bobby Raymond (bass) and Vinny Parello (drums). Kaplan is the father of **Brenda K. Starr**.

| 6/14/69 | 79 | 16 | | | | **More Today Than Yesterday** .... | | | $25 | Columbia 9852 |

Broken-Hearted Man — More Today Than Yesterday 12 — Our Day Will Come — Sweet Little Thing
For Once In My Life — — Proud Mary — This Guy's In Love With You
Judas To The Love We Knew — No One For Me To Turn To 52 — Since I Don't Have You — Thought Of Loving You

SPIRIT '69

Rock group from Los Angeles: Jay Ferguson (vocals), Randy California (guitar), John Locke (keyboards), Mark Andes (bass) and Ed Cassidy (drums). Ferguson and Andes left to form **Jo Jo Gunne** in mid-1971. Andes became an original member of **Firefall** in 1975; joined **Heart** in 1983. California drowned in Hawaii on 1/2/97 (age 45).
1)The Family That Plays Together 2)Spirit 3)Clear Spirit

4/20/68	31	32		©	1	**Spirit**			$25	Ode 44004
						also see #8 below				
1/18/69	22	21		©	2	**The Family That Plays Together**			$25	Ode 44014
						also see #6 below				
8/23/69	55	15		©	3	**Clear Spirit**			$25	Ode 44016
						also see #8 below				
12/26/70+	63	14	●	©	4	**Twelve Dreams Of Dr. Sardonicus**			$15	Epic 30267
3/18/72	63	14			5	**Feedback**			$15	Epic 31175
7/22/72	189	7			6	**The Family That Plays Together**		[R]	$15	Epic 31461
						new cover does not include the original additional flap				
7/21/73	119	12		©	7	**The Best Of Spirit**		[G]	$15	Epic 32271
8/25/73	191	4			8	**Spirit**		[R]	$20	Epic 31457 [2]
						reissue of albums #1 & 3 above				

SPIRIT — Cont'd

6/7/75	147	9			9 Spirit Of '76			$20	Mercury 804 [2]
7/31/76	179	4			10 Farther Along			$15	Mercury 1094

America, The Beautiful (medley) (9)
Animal Zoo (4,7) *97*
Apple Orchard (3,8)
Aren't You Glad (2,6)
Atomic Boogie (10)
Cadillac Cowboys (5)
Caught (3,8)
Chelsea Girls (5)
Clear (3,8)
Cold Wind (3,8)
Colossus (10)
Dark Eyed Woman (3,7,8)
Darkness (5)
Darlin' If (2,6)
Diamond Spirit (10)

Don't Lock Up Your Door (10)
Dream Within A Dream (2,6)
Drunkard, The (2,6)
Earth Shaker (5)
Elijah (1,8)
Farther Along (10)
Feeling In Time (9)
Fresh-Garbage (1,7,8)
Girl In Your Eye (1,8)
Give A Life, Take A Life (3,8)
Gramophone Man (1,8)
Great Canyon Fire In General (1,8)
Ground Hog (3,8)
Guide Me (9)
Happy (9)

Hey, Joe (9)
I Got A Line On You (2,6,7) *25*
I'm Truckin' (3,8)
Ice (3,8)
It Shall Be (2,6)
It's All The Same (2,6)
Jack Bond (Pt. I & II) (9)
Jewish (2,6)
Joker On The Run (9)
Lady Of The Lakes (9)
Life Has Just Begun (4)
Like A Rolling Stone (9)
Love Has Found A Way (4)
Maunaloa (9)
Mechanical World (1,7,8)
Mega Star (10)

Mellow Morning (5)
Morning Will Come (4,7)
Mr. Skin (4,7) *92*
My Road (9)
Nature's Way (4,7,10)
New Dope In Town (3,8)
1984 (7) *69*
Nothin' To Hide (4,7)
Once Again (9)
Once With You (10)
Phoebe (10)
Pineapple (10)
Policeman's Ball (3,8)
Poor Richard (2,6)
Puesta Del Scam (5)
Right On Time (5)

Ripe And Ready (5)
She Smiles (2,6)
Silky Sam (2,6)
So Little Time To Fly (3,8)
Soldier (4)
Space Child (4)
Star Spangled Banner (9)
Stoney Night (10)
Straight Arrow (1,8)
Street Worm (9)
Sunrise (9)
Tampa Jam (Pt. I-III) (9)
Taurus (1,8)
Thank You Lord (9)
Times, They Are A'Changing (medley) (9)

Topanga Windows (1,8)
Trancas Fog-Out (5)
Uncle Jack (1,7,8)
Urantia (9)
Veruska (9)
Victim Of Society (9)
Walking The Dog (9)
Water Woman (1,8)
What Do I Have (9)
When? (9)
When I Touch You (4)
Why Can't I Be Free (4)
Witch (5)
World Eat World Dog (10)

SPLENDER
Rock group from New York City: Wayne Boone (vocals), Jonathan Svec (guitar), James Cruz (bass) and Mike Slutsky (drums).   '00

7/29/00	200	1		©	Halfway Down The Sky			$10	Columbia 69144

Cigarette
I Apologize
I Don't Understand

I Think God Can Explain *62*
Irresponsible
London

Monotone
Space Boy
Special

Spin
Supernatural
Wallflower

Yeah, Whatever

SPLINTER
Vocal duo from England: Bill Elliott and Bob Purvis.   '74

10/26/74	81	14			The Place I Love			$12	Dark Horse 22001

produced by **George Harrison**

China Light
Costafine Town *77*

Drink All Day (Got To Find Your Own Way Home)
Elly-May
Gravy Train

Haven't Got Time
Place I Love

Situation Vacant
Somebody's City

SPLIT ENZ
Pop-rock group formed in Auckland, New Zealand: brothers Tim (vocals) and Neil (guitar, vocals) Finn, Eddie Rayner (keyboards), Noel Crombie (percussion), Nigel Griggs (bass) and Malcolm Green (drums; left in 1983). The Finns were later members of **Crowded House**.   '80

8/30/80	40	25		©	1 True Colours			$10	A&M 4822
5/23/81	45	19			2 Waiata			$10	A&M 4848
5/8/82	58	20			3 Time And Tide			$10	A&M 4894
7/21/84	137	10		©	4 Conflicting Emotions			$10	A&M 4963

Albert Of India (2)
Bon Voyage (4)
Bullet Brain And Cactus Head (4)
Choral Sea (1)
Clumsy (2)
Conflicting Emotions (4)
Devil You Know (4)

Dirty Creature (3)
Double Happy (1)
Ghost Girl (2)
Giant Heartbeat (3)
Hard Act To Follow (2)
Haul Away (3)
Hello Sandy Allen (4)
History Never Repeats (2)

How Can I Resist Her (1)
I Don't Wanna Dance (2)
I Got You (1) *53*
I Hope I Never (1)
I Wake Up Every Night (4)
I Wouldn't Dream Of It (1)
Iris (2)
Log Cabin Fever (3)

Lost For Words (3)
Make Sense Of It (3)
Message To My Girl (4)
Missing Person (1)
Never Ceases To Amaze Me (3)
No Mischief (4)
Nobody Takes Me Seriously (1)

One Step Ahead (2)
Our Day (4)
Pioneer (3)
Poor Boy (1)
Shark Attack (3)
Ships (2)
Six Months In A Leaky Boat (3)
Small World (3)

Strait Old Line (4)
Take A Walk (3)
Wail (2)
Walking Through The Ruins (2)
What's The Matter With You (1)
Working Up An Appetite (4)

SPM
Born Carlos Coy in Houston. Male rapper. SPM: South Park Mexican.   '00

9/2/00	57	8		©	1 The Purity Album			$10	Dope House 153292
12/30/00	170	3		©	2 Time Is Money			$10	Dope House 013336

Anything Goes (2)
Boys On Da Cut (2)
Burn Us Alive (2)
Child Of The Ghetto (1)
Cookie Baker (1)
Country Life (2)

Crazy Lady (1)
Don't Let Em Foolya (2)
Dope Game (1)
Follow My Lead (1)
He's A Bird, He's A Plane (2)
Hillwood Hustlaz II (2)

I Am Your Future (1)
I Wanna Know Her Name (1)
Medicine (2)
Meet Your Fate (1)
My Feria (2)
Oh My My (2)

Ooh Wee (2)
Problemas (1)
Right Now (1)
Rollin (1)
Somethin' I Would Do (2)
Styrofoam Cup (1)

Throw Away Gats (2)
Time Is Money (2)
Twice Last Night (2)
2 Joints (1)
Watch The Block Bleed (1)
We Did Dat (1)

Whatever You Do (1)
You Know My Name (1,2)

SPONGE
Rock group from Detroit: Vinnie Dombrowski (vocals), Mike Cross and Joe Mazzola (guitars), Tim Cross (bass) and Jimmy Paluzzi (drums). Charlie Grover replaced Paluzzi in early 1996.   '95

2/18/95	58	40	●	©	1 Rotting Piñata			$10	Work 57800
7/20/96	60	10		©	2 Wax Ecstatic			$10	Columbia 67578

Death Of A Drag Queen (2)
Drag Queens Of Memphis (2)
Drownin' (1)
Fields (1)

Giants (1)
Got To Be A Bore (2)
Have You Seen Mary (2)
I Am Anastasia (2)

Miles (1)
Molly (Sixteen Candles) (1) *55*
My Baby Said (2)
My Purity (2)

Neenah Menasha (2)
Pennywheels (1)
Plowed (1)
Rainin' (1)

Rotting Piñata (1)
Silence Is Their Drug (2)
Velveteen (2)

Wax Ecstatic (To Sell Angelina) (2)

SPOOKY TOOTH
Hard-rock group formed by keyboardists/vocalists **Gary Wright** and Mike Harrison. Varying personnel. Wright left from 1970-72 to recorded with the group Wonderwheel. Guitarist Luther Grosvenor left in 1972, joined **Stealers Wheel**, then changed name to Ariel Bender and joined **Mott the Hoople** and **Widowmaker**. **Mick Jones**, later of **Foreigner**, was guitarist from 1972-74.   '69

8/16/69	44	19		©	1 Spooky Two			$15	A&M 4194
3/21/70	92	14		©	2 Ceremony			$15	A&M 4225
8/15/70	84	13		©	3 The Last Puff			$15	A&M 4266
6/5/71	152	7			4 Tobacco Road		[E]	$15	A&M 4300
					reissue of their first album *It's All About...*				
5/19/73	84	14			5 You Broke My Heart So I Busted Your Jaw			$15	A&M 4385
11/10/73	99	10			6 Witness			$15	Island 9337
9/21/74	130	8		©	7 The Mirror			$15	Island 9292
4/24/76	172	4		©	8 That Was Only Yesterday		[K]	$20	A&M 3528 [2]
					GARY WRIGHT/SPOOKY TOOTH				

SPOOKY TOOTH — Cont'd

All Sewn Up (6)
As Long As The World Keeps Turning (6)
Better By You, Better Than Me (1)
Bubbles (4)
Confession (2)
Cotton Growing Man (5,8)
Don't Ever Stray Away (6)
Down River (3)
Dream Me A Mountain (6)
Evil Woman (1,8)

Fantasy Satisfier (7)
Fascinating Things (8)
Feelin' Bad (1,8)
Forget It, I've Got It (4)
Hangman Hang My Shell On A Tree (1)
Have Mercy (2)
Hell Or High Water (7)
Here I Lived So Well (4)
Higher Circles (7)
Holy Water (5,8)
Hoofer, The (7)

Hosanna (2)
I Am The Walrus (3)
I Can't See The Reason (8)
I Know (8)
I'm Alive (7)
I've Got Enough Heartaches (1)
It Hurts You So (4)
It's All About A Roundabout (4)
Jubilation (2)
Kyle (7)
Last Puff (3)
Lost In My Dream (1)

Love Really Changed Me (4)
Love To Survive (8)
Mirror, The (7)
Moriah (5)
Nobody There At All (3,8)
Ocean Of Power (6)
Offering (2)
Old As I Was Born (5)
Prayer (2)
Pyramids (6)
Self Seeking Man (5)
Sing A Song (8)

Society's Child (4)
Something To Say (3,8)
Son Of Your Father (3,8)
Stand For Our Rights (8)
Sunlight Of My Mind (6)
Sunshine Help Me (4,8)
That Was Only Yesterday (1,8)
Things Change (6)
This Time Around (5)
Times Have Changed (5)
Tobacco Road (4)
Two Faced Man (8)

Two Time Love (7)
Waitin' For The Wind (1,8)
Weight, The (4)
Wildfire (5,8)
Wings On My Heart (6)
Woman And Gold (7)
Wrong Time (3,8)

SPORTS, The　　'79

Rock group formed in Melbourne, Australia: Stephen Cummings (vocals), Andrew Pendlebury and Martin Armiger (guitars), James Niven (keyboards), Robert Glover (bass) and Paul Hitchins (drums).

DEBUT	PEAK	WKS	RIAA	CD	ARTIST — Album Title	$	Label & Number
11/24/79	194	2			Don't Throw Stones	$12	Arista 4249

Big Sleep
Don't Throw Stones

Live Work & Play
Mailed It To Your Sister

Reckless
Step By Step

Suspicious Minds
Thru The Window

Tired Of Me
Wedding Ring

Who Listens To The Radio 45
You Ain't Home Yet

SPRINGFIELD, Dusty　　'64

Born Mary O'Brien on 4/16/39 in London. Died of cancer on 3/2/99 (age 59). Pop singer. Member of **The Springfields**. Inducted into the Rock and Roll Hall of Fame in 1999.

DEBUT	PEAK	WKS	RIAA	CD	ARTIST — Album Title	Sym	$	Label & Number
6/27/64	62	13		© 1	Stay Awhile/I Only Want To Be With You		$40	Philips 600133
12/5/64	136	3		© 2	Dusty		$40	Philips 600156
7/16/66	77	10		© 3	You Don't Have To Say You Love Me		$40	Philips 600210
12/24/66	137	3		© 4	Dusty Springfield's Golden Hits	[G]	$40	Philips 600220
12/23/67+	135	7		© 5	The Look Of Love		$40	Philips 600256
3/15/69	99	14		© 6	Dusty In Memphis		$20	Atlantic 8214
2/28/70	107	13		© 7	A Brand New Me		$20	Atlantic 8249

All Cried Out (2,4) 41
All I See Is You (4) 20
Anyone Who Ever Had A Heart (1)
Bad Case Of The Blues (7)
Brand New Me (7) 24
Breakfast In Bed (6) 91
Can I Get A Witness (2)
Chained To A Memory (5)
Come Back To Me (5)
Do Re Me (Forget About The Do And Think About Me) (2)
Don't Forget About Me (6) 64
Don't Say It Baby (2)

Don't You Know (2)
Every Day I Have To Cry (1)
Give Me Time (5) 76
Guess Who? (2)
I Can't Hear You (3)
I Can't Make It Alone (6)
I Don't Want To Hear It Anymore (6)
I Had A Talk With My Man (3)
I Just Don't Know What To Do With Myself (2,4)
I Only Want To Be With You (1,4) 12
I Wish I'd Never Loved You (7)

I've Been Wrong Before (3)
If It Don't Work Out (3)
If You Go Away (5)
In The Land Of Make Believe (6)
In The Middle Of Nowhere (4)
It Was Easier To Hurt Him (3)
Joe (7)
Just A Little Lovin' (6)
Just One Smile (5)
La Bamba (3)
Let Me In Your Way (1)
Let's Get Together Soon (7)
Let's Talk It Over (7)

Little By Little (3,4)
Live It Up (2)
Long After Tonight Is All Over (3)
Look Of Love (5) 22
Losing You (4) 91
Lost (7)
Mama Said (1)
Mocking Bird (1)
My Coloring Book (2)
Never Love Again (7)
No Easy Way Down (6)
Nothing (2)
Oh No Not My Baby (3)

Silly, Silly, Fool (5) 76
Small Town Girl (5)
So Much Love (6)
Something Special (1)
Son-Of-A Preacher Man (6) 10
Star Of My Show (7)
Stay Awhile (1,4) 38
Summer Is Over (2)
Sunny (5)
Take Me For A Little While (5)
They Long To Be Close To You (5)
24 Hours From Tulsa (1)
Welcome Home (5)

What's It Gonna Be (5) 49
When The Lovelight Starts Shining Thru His Eyes (1)
Who Can I Turn To? (When Nobody Needs Me) (3)
Will You Love Me Tomorrow (1)
Windmills Of Your Mind (6) 31
Wishin' And Hopin' (1,4) 6
Won't Be Long (3)
You Don't Have To Say You Love Me (3,4) 4
You Don't Own Me (1)

★333★　SPRINGFIELD, Rick　　'82

Born Richard Springthorpe on 8/23/49 in Sydney, Australia. Pop-rock singer/songwriter/actor. Played "Noah Drake" on the TV soap opera *General Hospital*. Starred in the movie *Hard To Hold*.

DEBUT	PEAK	WKS	RIAA	CD	ARTIST — Album Title	Sym	$	Label & Number
8/12/72	35	17			1 Beginnings		$20	Capitol 11047
3/14/81	7	73	▲	©	2 Working Class Dog		$10	RCA Victor 3697
3/27/82	2³	35	▲	©	3 Success Hasn't Spoiled Me Yet	C:#4/122	$10	RCA Victor 4125
12/18/82+	159	8			4 Wait For Night	[E]	$10	RCA Victor 4235
					first released in 1976 on Chelsea 515 ($15)			
4/30/83	12	57	▲	©	5 Living In Oz		$10	RCA Victor 4660
4/7/84	16	36	▲		6 Hard To Hold	[S]	$10	RCA Victor 4935
12/8/84+	78	13		©	7 Beautiful Feelings	[E]	$10	Mercury 824107
					vocals recorded in 1978 with new music tracks added in 1984			
4/27/85	21	27	●	©	8 Tao		$10	RCA Victor 5370
2/20/88	55	16		©	9 Rock Of Life		$10	RCA 6620
5/1/99	189	1			10 Karma		$10	Platinum 9561

Act Of Faith (10)
Affair Of The Heart (5) 9
Alyson (5)
American Girl (3)
April 24, 1981 (3)
Archangel (4)
Ballad Of Annie Goodbody (1)
Beautiful Feelings (7)
Beautiful Prize (10)
Black Is Black (3)
Bop 'Til You Drop (6) 20
Brand New Feeling (7)
Bruce (7) 27
Calling All Girls (3)
Carry Me Away (2)
Celebrate Youth (8) 26
Cold Feet (7)
Come On Everybody (1)
Daddy's Pearl (2)

Dance This World Away (8)
Don't Talk To Strangers (3) 2
Don't Walk Away (6) 26
Dream In Colour (9)
Everybody's Cheating (7)
Everybody's Girl (2)
Free (10)
Goldfever (4)
Great Lost Art Of Conversation (6)
Guenevere (7)
Heart Of A Woman (4)
His Last Words (10)
Hold On To Your Dream (9)
Hole In My Heart (2)
Honeymoon In Beirut (9)
Hooky Jo (1)
How Do You Talk To Girls (9)
Human Touch (5) 18

I Can't Stop Hurting You (5)
I Didn't Mean To Love You (1)
I Get Excited (3) 32
I Go Swimming (6)
I've Done Everything For You (2) 8
(If You Think You're) Groovy (9)
In Veronica's Head (10)
Inside Silvia (2)
It'salwayssomething (10)
Jessica (4)
Jessie's Girl (2) 1
Just One Kiss (9)
Just One Look (7)
Karma (10)
Kristina (3)
Life Is A Celebration (9)
Light Of Love (2)
Like Father, Like Son (5)

Living In Oz (5)
Looking For The One (7)
Love Is Alright Tonite (2) 20
Love Somebody (6) 5
Me & Johnny (5)
Million Dollar Face (4)
Mother Can You Carry Me (1)
My Father's Chair (8)
Old Gangsters Never Die (4)
One Broken Heart (4)
One Reason (To Believe) (9)
1,000 Years (1)
Ordinary Girl (10)
Power Of Love (The Tao Of Love) (8)
Prayer (10)
Red Hot And Blue Love (2)
Religion Of The Heart (10)

Rock Of Life (9) 22
S.F.O. (6)
Shock To My System (10)
Solitary One (7)
Soul To Soul (9)
Souls (5) 23
Spanish Eyes (7)
Speak To The Sky (1) 14
Stand Up (6)
State Of The Heart (8) 22
Still Crazy For You (3)
Stranger In The House (8)
Take A Hand (4) 41
Tao Of Heaven (8)
Taxi Dancing (6) 59
Tear It All Down (9)
Tiger By The Tail (5)
Tonight (3)

Treat Me Gently In The Morning (4)
Unhappy Ending (1)
Walk Like A Man (8)
Walking On The Edge (8)
What Kind Of Fool Am I (3) 21
What Would The Children Think (1) 70
When The Lights Go Down (6)
Where's All The Love (4)
White Room (10)
Why? (1)
Woman (9)
World Start Turning (4)
Written In Rock (8)

SPRINGFIELDS, The　　'62

Folk trio from London: **Dusty Springfield**, her brother Tom Springfield and Tim Feild.

DEBUT	PEAK	WKS	RIAA	CD	ARTIST — Album Title	$	Label & Number
10/27/62	91	4			Silver Threads & Golden Needles	$40	Philips 600052

Allentown Jail
Aunt Rhody
Black Hills Of Dakota

Dear Hearts And Gentle People 95
Goodnight Irene

Gotta Travel On
Green Leaves Of Summer
Lonesome Traveller

Silver Dollar
Silver Threads And Golden Needles 20

They Took John Away
Two Brothers

SPRINGSTEEN, Bruce ★65★ '84

Born on 9/23/49 in Freehold, New Jersey. Rock singer/songwriter/guitarist. Nicknamed "The Boss." His E-Street Band: **Little Steven** Van Zant (guitar), **Clarence Clemons** (sax), Roy Bittan (keyboards), Gary Tallent (bass) and Max Weinberg (drums). Married to model/actress Julianne Phillips from 1985-89. Married backing singer Patti Scialfa on 6/8/91. Inducted into the Rock and Roll Hall of Fame in 1999.

1)Born In The U.S.A. 2)Bruce Springsteen & The E Street Band Live/1975-85 3)The River

DEBUT	PEAK	WKS	RIAA	CD		ARTIST — Album Title	Catalog	Sym	$	Label & Number
7/26/75	60	43	▲²	©	1	Greetings From Asbury Park, N.J.	C:#3/136	[E]	$20	Columbia 31903
7/26/75	59	34	▲²	©	2	The Wild, The Innocent & The E Street Shuffle	C:#27/45	[E]	$20	Columbia 32432
						above 2 originally released in 1973				
9/13/75	3	110	▲⁶	©	3	Born To Run			$15	Columbia 33795
6/17/78	5	97	▲³	©	4	Darkness on the Edge of Town			$15	Columbia 35318
11/1/80	❶⁴	108	▲³	©	5	The River			$20	Columbia 36854 [2]
10/9/82	3	29	▲	©	6	Nebraska			$10	Columbia 38358
6/23/84	❶⁷	139	▲¹⁵	©	7	Born In The U.S.A.			$10	Columbia 38653
11/29/86	❶⁷	26	▲¹³	©	8	Bruce Springsteen & The E Street Band Live/1975-85		[L]	$40	Columbia 40558 [5]
10/24/87	❶¹	45	▲³	©	9	Tunnel of Love			$10	Columbia 40999
4/18/92	2²	27	▲	©	10	Human Touch			$10	Columbia 53000
4/18/92	3	23	▲	©	11	Lucky Town			$10	Columbia 53001
3/18/95	❶²	32	▲⁴	©	12	Greatest Hits	C:#21/64	[G]	$10	Columbia 67060
12/9/95	11	14	●	©	13	The Ghost Of Tom Joad			$10	Columbia 67484
9/13/97	189	1		©	14	In Concert / MTV Plugged		[L]	$10	Columbia 68730
						recorded on 11/11/92				
11/28/98	27	7	▲	©	15	Tracks		[K]	$25	Columbia 69475 [4]
						contains unreleased songs and B-sides previously issued as singles only				
5/1/99	64	6		©	16	18 Tracks		[K]	$10	Columbia 69476
						15 of 18 songs from the above album with 3 previously unreleased tracks				
4/21/01	5	8	▲	©	17	Live In New York City		[L]	$15	Columbia 85490 [2]
						recorded on 6/29/00 at Madison Square Garden				

Across The Border (13)
Adam Raised A Cain (4,8)
Ain't Got You (9)
All Or Nothin' At All (10)
All That Heaven Will Allow (9)
American Skin (41 Shots) (17)
Angel, The (1)
Atlantic City (6,12,14,17)
Back In Your Arms (15)
Backstreets (3,8)
Badlands (4,8,12,17) *42*
Balboa Park (13)
Be True (15)
Because The Night (8)
Better Days (11,12,14) *flip*
Big Muddy (11)
Bishop Danced (15)
Blinded By The Light (1)
Blood Brothers (12)
Bobby Jean (7,8)
Book Of Dreams (11)
Born In The U.S.A. (7,8,12,15,16,17) *9*
Born To Run (3,8,12) *23*
Brilliant Disguise (9,12) *5*
Bring On The Night (15)
Brothers Under The Bridge (15,16)
Cadillac Ranch (5,8)
Candy's Room (4,8)
Car Wash (15)
Cautious Man (9)
Cover Me (7,8) *7*
Cross My Heart (10)
Crush On You (5)
Cynthia (15)
Dancing In The Dark (7,12) *2*

Darkness On The Edge Of Town (4,8,14)
Darlington County (7,8)
Does This Bus Stop At 82nd Street? (1,15)
Dollhouse (15)
Don't Look Back (15,17)
Downbound Train (7)
Drive All Night (5)
Dry Lightning (13)
E Street Shuffle (2)
Factory (4)
Fade Away (5) *20*
Fever, The (16)
57 Channels (And Nothin' On) (10) *68*
Fire (8) *46*
For You (1)
4th Of July, Asbury Park (Sandy) (2,8)
Frankie (15)
Galveston Bay (13)
Gave It A Name (15)
Ghost Of Tom Joad (13)
Give The Girl A Kiss (15)
Gloria's Eyes (10)
Glory Days (7,12) *5*
Goin' Cali (15)
Good Man Is Hard To Find (Pittsburgh) (15)
Growin' Up (1,8,15,16)
Happy (15)
Hearts Of Stone (15,16)
Highway Patrolman (6)
Highway 29 (13)
Honeymooners, The (15)
Human Touch (10,12,14) *16*

Hungry Heart (5,8,12) *5*
I Wanna Be With You (15,16)
I Wanna Marry You (5)
I Wish I Were Blind (10,14)
I'm A Rocker (5)
I'm Goin' Down (7) *9*
I'm On Fire (7,8)
Iceman (15)
If I Should Fall Behind (11,14,17)
Incident On 57th Street (2)
Independence Day (5,8)
It's Hard To Be A Saint In The City (1,8,15)
Jackson Cage (5)
Janey Don't You Lose Heart (15,16)
Jersey Girl (8)
Johnny Bye-Bye (15)
Johnny 99 (6,8)
Jungleland (3,17)
Kitty's Back (2)
Land Of Hope And Dreams (17)
Leap Of Faith (11)
Leavin' Train (15)
Light Of Day (14)
Linda Let Me Be The One (15)
Line, The (13)
Lion's Den (15,16)
Living On The Edge Of The World (15)
Living Proof (11,14)
Local Hero (11)
Long Goodbye (15)
Loose Change (15)
Loose Ends (15,16)
Lost In The Flood (1,17)

Lucky Man (15)
Lucky Town (11,14)
Man At The Top (15)
Man's Job (10,14)
Mansion On The Hill (6,17)
Mary Lou (15)
Mary Queen Of Arkansas (1,15)
Meeting Across The River (3)
Murder Incorporated (12,17)
My Beautiful Reward (11,14)
My Best Was Never Good Enough (13)
My Father's House (6)
My Hometown (7,8,12) *6*
My Love Will Not Let You Down (15,16,17)
My Lover Man (15)
Nebraska (6,8)
New Timer (13)
New York City Serenade (2)
Night (3)
No Surrender (7,8)
One Step Up (9) *13*
Open All Night (6)
Out In The Street (5,17)
Over The Rise (15)
Paradise By The "C" (8)
Part Man, Part Monkey (15,16)
Pink Cadillac (15,16)
Point Blank (5)
Pony Boy (10)
Price You Pay (5)
Promise, The (16)
Promised Land (4,8)
Prove It All Night (4,17) *33*
Racing In The Street (4,8)
Raise Your Hand (8)

Ramrod (5,17)
Real Man (10)
Real World (10)
Reason To Believe (6,8)
Red Headed Woman (14)
Rendezvous (15,16)
Restless Nights (15)
Ricky Wants A Man Of Her Own (15)
River, The (5,8,12,17)
Rockaway The Days (15)
Roll Of The Dice (10)
Rosalita (Come Out Tonight) (2,8)
Roulette (15)
Sad Eyes (15,16)
Santa Ana (15)
Seaside Bar Song (15,16)
Seeds (15)
Seven Angels (15)
She's The One (3)
Sherry Darling (5)
Shut Out The Light (15)
Sinaloa Cowboys (13)
So Young And In Love (15)
Something In The Night (4)
Soul Driver (10)
Souls Of The Departed (11)
Spare Parts (9)
Spirit In The Night (1,8)
Stand On It (15)
State Trooper (6)
Stolen Car (5,15)
Straight Time (13)
Streets Of Fire (4)
Streets Of Philadelphia (12) *9*

TV Movie (15)
Take 'Em As They Come (15)
Tenth Avenue Freeze-Out (3,8,17) *83*
This Hard Land (12,15)
This Land Is Your Land (8)
Thunder Road (3,8,12,14)
Thundercrack (15)
Ties That Bind (5)
Tougher Than The Rest (9)
Trouble In Paradise (15)
Trouble River (16)
Tunnel Of Love (9) *9*
Two Faces (9)
Two For The Road (15)
Two Hearts (5,8,17)
Used Cars (6)
Valentine's Day (9)
Wages Of Sin (15)
Walk Like A Man (9)
War (8) *8*
When The Lights Go Out (15)
When You Need Me (15)
When You're Alone (9)
Where The Bands Are (15,16)
Wild Billy's Circus Story (2)
Wish, The (15)
With Every Wish (10)
Working On The Highway (7,8)
Wreck On The Highway (5)
You Can Look (But You Better Not Touch) (5,8)
Youngstown (13,17)
Zero And Blind Terry (15)

★213★ SPYRO GYRA '80

Jazz-pop group formed in Buffalo, New York. Led by saxophonist Jay Beckenstein (born on 5/14/51). **The Brecker Brothers** (Michael and Randy) were longtime members.

1)Catching The Sun 2)Morning Dance 3)Freetime

DEBUT	PEAK	WKS	RIAA	CD		ARTIST — Album Title	Catalog	Sym	$	Label & Number
5/20/78	99	12		©	1	Spyro Gyra		[I]	$12	Amherst 1014
4/7/79	27	41	▲	©	2	Morning Dance	C:#3/213	[I]	$12	Infinity 9004
3/22/80	19	29	●	©	3	Catching The Sun		[I]	$10	MCA 5108
11/1/80	49	30		©	4	Carnaval		[I]	$10	MCA 5149
8/29/81	41	27		©	5	Freetime		[I]	$10	MCA 5238
10/23/82	46	24		©	6	Incognito		[I]	$10	MCA 5368
8/13/83	66	16		©	7	City Kids		[I]	$10	MCA 5431
7/14/84	59	19		©	8	Access All Areas		[I-L]	$15	MCA 6893 [2]
						recorded on 11/18/83 in Florida				
6/29/85	66	23		©	9	Alternating Currents		[I]	$10	MCA 5606

SPYRO GYRA — Cont'd

DEBUT	PEAK	WKS			Title		Sym	$	Label & Number
7/12/86	71	19	©	10	Breakout		[I]	$10	MCA 5753
9/26/87	84	9	©	11	Stories Without Words		[I]	$10	MCA 42046
7/16/88	104	8	©	12	Rites Of Summer		[I]	$10	MCA 6235
7/8/89	120	6	©	13	Point Of View		[I]	$10	MCA 6309
6/23/90	117	8	©	14	Fast Forward		[I]	$10	GRP 9608
7/6/91	156	2	©	15	Collection		[I-K]	$10	GRP 9642

Alexandra (14)
Alternating Currents (9)
Amber Dream (5)
Archer, The (12)
Autumn Of Our Love (3)
Awakening (4)
Ballad, A (7)
Binky's Dream No. 6 (9)
Bittersweet (4)
Bob Goes To The Store (10)
Body Wave (10)
Breakout (10,15)
Bright Lights (14)
Cafe Amore (4) *77*
Captain Karma (12)
Carnaval (4)
Carolina (13)
Cascade (1)
Cashaca (4)
Catching The Sun (3,15) *68*

Cayo Hueso (11)
Chrysalis (11)
City Kids (7)
Claire's Dream (12)
Cockatoo (3)
Conversations (7,8)
Counterpoint (13)
Daddy's Got A New Girl Now (12)
Del Corazon (11)
Dizzy (4)
Doubletake (10)
Early Light (11)
Elegy For Trane (5)
End Of Romanticism (2)
Escape Hatch (14)
Fairweather (9)
4MD (14)
Foxtrot (4)
Freefall (10)

Freetime (5)
Futurephobia (14)
Galadriel (1)
Gotcha (13)
Guiltless (10)
Hannibal's Boogie (13)
Harbor Nights (6,8,15)
Haverstraw Road (7)
Heartbeat (9)
Heliopolis (2,8)
Here Again (3)
I Believe In You (9)
Incognito (6,15)
Innocent Soul (12)
Islands In The Sky (7,8)
It Doesn't Matter (2)
Joy Ride (11)
Jubilee (2)
Laser Material (3)
Last Exit (6)

Latin Streets (8)
Leticia (15)
Limelight (12,15)
Little Linda (2)
Lovin' You (medley) (3)
Mallet Ballet (1,15)
Mardi Gras (9)
Mead (1)
Morning Dance (2,8,15) *24*
Nightlife (7)
No Man's Land (12)
Nu Sungo (11,15)
Oasis (6)
Ocean Parkway (14)
Old San Juan (6,8,15)
Opus D'Opus (1)
PG (9)
Pacific Sunrise (5)
Para Ti Latino (14,15)
Paula (medley) (1)

Paw Prints (medley) (1)
Percolator (3)
Philly (3)
Pygmy Funk (1)
Pyramid (11)
Rasul (2)
Riverwalk (11)
Safari (3)
Schu's Blues (9)
Sea Biscuit (8)
Serpent In Paradise (7,8)
Serpentine Shelly (11)
Shadow Play (14)
Shakedown (9,15)
Shaker Song (1,8) *90*
Shanghai Gumbo (12)
Silver Linings (7)
Slow Burn (13)
Soho Mojo (6)
Song For Lorraine (2)

Speak Easy (14)
Starburst (2)
String Soup (5)
Stripes (5)
Sueno (6)
Summer Strut (5)
Sunflurry (9)
Swamp Thing (13)
Sweet 'N Savvy (4)
Swept Away (10)
Swing Street (13)
Taking The Plunge (For Jennifer) (9)
Telluride (5)
Tower Of Babel (14)
Unknown Soldier (13,15)
What Exit (15)
Whirlwind (10)
Yosemite (12)
You Can Count On Me (15)

SPYS '82

Rock group from New York City: John Blanco (vocals), John DiGaudio (guitar), Al Greenwood (keyboards), Ed Gagliardi (bass) and Billy Milne (drums). Greenwood and Gagliardi were members of **Foreigner**.

DEBUT	PEAK	WKS			Title			$	Label & Number
8/14/82	138	10	©		Spys			$10	EMI America 17073

Danger
Desiree

Don't Run My Life *82*
Don't Say Goodbye

Hold On (When You Feel You're Falling)

Ice Age
Into The Night

No Harm Done
Over Her

She Can't Wait

SQUEEZE '82

Pop-rock group formed in London by vocalists/guitarists Chris Difford and Glenn Tilbrook. Originally known as UK Squeeze due to confusion with American band Tight Squeeze. **Paul Carrack** (**Ace**, **Mike & The Mechanics**) was keyboardist/vocalist in 1981 of fluctuating lineup; re-joined in 1993. Also see **Difford & Tilbrook**.

DEBUT	PEAK	WKS			Title			$	Label & Number
4/26/80	71	24	©	1	Argybargy			$10	A&M 4802
5/30/81	44	25	©	2	East Side Story			$10	A&M 4854
5/29/82	32	30	©	3	Sweets From A Stranger			$10	A&M 4899
1/8/83	47	21	▲ ©	4	Singles-45's And Under		[K]	$10	A&M 4922
9/21/85	57	20	©	5	Cosi Fan Tutti Frutti			$10	A&M 5085
10/3/87	36	29	©	6	Babylon And On			$10	A&M 5161
10/7/89	113	10	©	7	frank.			$10	A&M 5278
6/9/90	163	5	©	8	A Round And A Bout		[L]	$10	I.R.S. 82040
10/2/93	182	1	©	9	Some Fantastic Place			$10	A&M 540140

Annie Get Your Gun (4,8)
Another Nail In My Heart (1,4)
Big Beng (5)
Black Coffee In Bed (3,4,8)
Break My Heart (5)
By Your Side (5,8)
Can Of Worms (7)
Cigarette Of A Single Man (6)
Cold Shoulder (9)
Cool For Cats (4)
Dr. Jazz (7,8)
853-5937 (6) *32*
Elephant Ride (3)
Everything In The World (9)
F-Hole (2)
Farfisa Beat (1)
Footprints (6,8)

Frank (7)
Goodbye Girl (4)
Heartbreaking World (5)
Heaven (2)
Here Comes That Feeling (1)
His House Her Home (3)
Hits Of The Year (7)
Hourglass (6,8) *15*
I Can't Hold On (3)
I Learnt How To Pray (5)
I Think I'm Go Go (1)
I Won't Ever Go Drinking Again (?) (5)
I've Returned (3)
If I Didn't Love You (1,4)
If It's Love (7,8)
Images Of Loving (9)

In Quintessence (2)
In Today's Room (6)
Is It Too Late (7)
Is That Love (2,4,8)
It's Over (9)
Jolly Comes Home (9)
King George Street (5)
Labelled With Love (2,8)
Last Time Forever (5)
Love Circles (7)
Loving You Tonight (9)
Melody Motel (7)
Messed Around (2)
Misadventure (1)
Mumbo Jumbo (2)
No Place Like Home (5)
Onto The Dance Floor (3)

Out Of Touch (3)
Peyton Place (7)
Piccadilly (2)
Pinocchio (9)
Points Of View (3)
Prisoner, The (6)
Pulling Mussels (From The Shell) (1,4,8)
Rose I Said (7)
Separate Beds (1)
She Doesn't Have To Shave (7,8)
Slap And Tickle (4)
Slaughtered, Gutted And Heartbroken (7,8)
Some Americans (6)
Some Fantastic Place (9)

Someone Else's Bell (2)
Someone Else's Heart (2)
Stranger Than The Stranger On The Shore (3)
Striking Matches (6)
Take Me I'm Yours (4,8)
Talk To Him (9)
Tempted (2,4,8) *49*
There At The Top (1)
There's No Tomorrow (2)
Third Rail (9)
(This Could Be) The Last Time (7)
Tongue Like A Knife (3)
Tough Love (6)
True Colours (The Storm) (9)

Trust Me To Open My Mouth (6)
Up The Junction (4,8)
Vanity Fair (2)
Very First Dance (3)
Vicky Verky (1)
Waiting Game (6)
When The Hangover Strikes (3)
Who Are You? (2)
Woman's World (2)
Wrong Side Of The Moon (1)

SQUIER, Billy '81

Born on 5/12/50 in Wellesley Hills, Massachusetts. Hard-rock singer/songwriter/guitarist.

DEBUT	PEAK	WKS			Title			$	Label & Number
6/7/80	169	12	©	1	The Tale Of The Tape			$10	Capitol 12062
5/2/81	5	111	▲3 ©	2	Don't Say No			$10	Capitol 12146
8/7/82	5	50	▲2 ©	3	Emotions In Motion			$10	Capitol 12217
					album cover art by Andy Warhol				
8/4/84	11	29	▲ ©	4	Signs Of Life			$10	Capitol 12361
10/18/86	61	16	©	5	Enough Is Enough			$10	Capitol 12483
7/15/89	64	17	©	6	Hear & Now			$10	Capitol 48748
4/27/91	117	6	©	7	Creatures Of Habit			$10	Capitol 94303

All Night Long (4) *75*
All We Have To Give (5)
Alone In Your Dreams (Don't Say Goodbye) (4)
(Another) 1984 (4)
Big Beat (1)
Break The Silence (5)
Calley Oh (1)
Can't Get Next To You (4)
Catch 22 (3)
Come Home (5)
Conscience Point (7)

Don't Let Me Go (6)
Don't Say No (2)
Don't Say You Love Me (6) *58*
Emotions In Motion (3) *32*
Everybody Wants You (3)
Eye On You (4) *71*
Facts Of Life (7)
Fall For Love (4)
G.O.D. (6)
Hand-Me-Downs (6)
Hands Of Seduction (5)
Hollywood (7)

I Need You (2)
(I Put A) Spell On You (6)
In The Dark (2) *35*
In Your Eyes (3)
It Keeps You Rockin' (3)
Keep Me Satisfied (3)
Lady With A Tenor Sax (5)
Learn How To Live (3)
Like I'm Lovin' You (1)
Listen To The Heartbeat (3)
Lonely Is The Night (2)
Lonely One (5)

(L-O-V-E) Four Letter Word (7)
Love Is The Hero (5) *80*
Lover (7)
Mine Tonite (6)
Music's All Right (1)
My Kinda Lover (2) *45*
Nerves On Ice (7)
Nobody Knows (2)
One Good Woman (3)
Powerhouse (5)
Reach For The Sky (4)
Rich Kid (1)

Rock Me Tonite (4) *15*
Rock Out/Punch Somebody (6)
She Goes Down (7)
She's A Runner (3) *75*
Shot O' Love (5)
Strange Fire (7)
Stroke, The (2) *17*
Stronger (4)
Sweet Release (4)
Take A Look Behind Ya (4)
Tied Up (6)
Til It's Over (5)

Too Daze Gone (2)
Whadda You Want From Me (7)
Who Knows What A Love Can Do (1)
Who's Your Boyfriend (1)
Wink Of An Eye (6)
Work Song (6)
You Know What I Like (4)
You Should Be High Love (1)
Young At Heart (7)
Young Girls (1)
Your Love Is My Life (6)

SQUIRE, Chris '76
Born on 3/4/48 in London. Rock singer/bassist. Member of **Yes**.

| 1/24/76 | 69 | 12 | | | Fish Out Of Water .... | | | $12 | Atlantic 18159 |

Hold Out Your Hand | Lucky Seven | Safe (Canon Song) | Silently Falling | You By My Side

SQUIRREL NUT ZIPPERS '98
Eclectic-jazz group from Chapel Hill, North Carolina: Jim Mathus (vocals, guitar, trombone), Katharine Whalen (vocals, banjo), Ken Mosher (guitar, sax), Tom Maxwell (sax, clarinet), Je Widenhouse (trumpet), Don Raleigh (bass) and Chris Phillips (drums). Stuart Cole replaced Raleigh in 1998. Tim Smith replaced Mosher, David Wright replaced Maxwell and Reese Gray (keyboards) joined in 1999. Group name taken from a brand of candy.

2/22/97	27	51	▲	©	1 Hot ....C:#50/1			$10	Mammoth 0137
9/27/97	165	1		©	2 Sold Out .... [M]			$10	Mammoth 0177
8/22/98	18	13	●	©	3 Perennial Favorites			$10	Mammoth 980169
12/5/98	117	6		©	4 Christmas Caravan .... [X]			$10	Mammoth 980192

Christmas chart: 12/98

| 11/4/00 | 195 | 1 | | © | 5 Bedlam Ballroom .... | | | $10 | Mammoth 65502 |

Baby Wants A Diamond Ring (5) | Do What? (5) | Got My Own Thing Now (1) | Interlocutor, The (1) | Meant To Be (1) | Soon (3)
Bad Businessman (1) | Don't Fix It (5) | Hanging Up My Stockings (4) | It Ain't You (1) | Memphis Exorcism (1) | St. Louis Cemetery Blues (2)
Bedbugs (5) | Evening At Lafitte's (3) | Hell (1) | It All Depends (5) | Missing Link (5) | Stop Drop And Roll (5)
Bedlam Ballroom (2,5) | Fat Cat Keeps Getting Fatter (3) | Hot Christmas (4) | It's Over (5) | My Drag (3) | Suits Are Picking Up The Bill (3)
Bent Out Of Shape (5) | Fell To Pieces (2) | Hush (5) | Johnny Ace Christmas (4) | My Evergreen (4) | That Fascinating Thing (3)
Blue Angel (1) | Flight Of The Passing Fancy (1) | I Raise Hell (2) | Just This Side Of Blue (5) | Pallin' With Al (2,3) | Trou Macacq (1)
Carolina Christmas (4) | Ghost Of Stephen Foster (1) | I'm Coming Home For Christmas (4) | Kraken, The (3) | Prince Nez (1) | Twilight (1)
Do It This A Way (5) | Gift Of The Magi (4) | Indian Giver (4) | La Grippé (2) | Put A Lid On It (1) | Winter Weather (4)
| | | | Low Down Man (3) | Sleigh Ride (4) |

SRC '69
Psychedelic-rock group from Detroit: Scott Richardson (vocals), Steve Lyman and Gary Quackenbush (guitars), Glenn Quackenbush (organ), Robin Dale (bass) and E.G. Clawson (drums). Al Wilmont had replaced Dale by 1969.

| 9/28/68 | 147 | 4 | | © | 1 SRC .... | | | $50 | Capitol 2991 |
| 6/14/69 | 134 | 9 | | © | 2 Milestones .... | | | $50 | Capitol 134 |

Angel Song (2) | Daystar (1) | In The Hall Of The Mountain King (medley) (2) | No Secret Destination (2) | Refugeve (1)
Black Sheep (1) | Exile (1) | | Onesimpletask (1) | Show Me (2)
Bolero (medley) (2) | Eye Of The Storm (2) | Interval (1) | Our Little Secret (2) | Turn Into Love (2)
Checkmate (2) | I Remember Your Face (2) | Marionette (1) | Paragon Council (1) | Up All Night (2)

SR-71 '00
Rock group from Baltimore: Mitch Allan (vocals, guitar), Mark Beauchemin (guitar), Jeff Reid (bass) and Dan Garvin (drums).

| 7/8/00 | 81 | 19 | ● | © | Now You See Inside .... | | | $10 | RCA 67845 |

Alive | Empty Spaces | Go Away | Non-Toxic | Politically Correct | What A Mess
Another Night Alone | Fame (What She's Wanting) | Last Man On The Moon | Paul McCartney | Right Now

STABBING WESTWARD '01
Rock group from Chicago: Christopher Hall (vocals, guitar), Walter Flakus (keyboards), Jim Sellers (bass) and Andy Kubiszewski (drums).

3/9/96	67	40	●	©	1 Wither Blister Burn + Peel			$10	Columbia 66152
4/25/98	52	16	●	©	2 Darkest Days			$10	Columbia 69329
6/9/01	47	5		©	3 Stabbing Westward			$10	Koch 8204

Angel (3) | Drugstore (2) | High (3) | Only Thing (3) | So Far Away (3) | Waking Up Beside You (2)
Breathe You In (3) | Everything I Touch (2) | How Can I Hold On (2) | Perfect (3) | So Wrong (1) | Wasted (3)
Crushing Me (1) | Falls Apart (1) | I Don't Believe (1) | Save Yourself (2) | Sometimes It Hurts (2) | What Do I Have To Do? (1)
Darkest Days (2) | Goodbye (2) | I Remember (3) | Shame (1) | Television (2) | When I'm Dead (2)
Desperate Now (2) | Happy (3) | Inside You (1) | Sleep (1) | Thing I Hate (2) | Why (1)
Drowning (2) | Haunting Me (2) | On Your Way Down (2) | Slipping Away (1) | Torn Apart (2) | You Complete Me (2)

STACEY Q '86
Born Stacey Swain on 11/30/58 in Los Angeles. Dance singer.

| 9/27/86 | 59 | 39 | | © | 1 Better Than Heaven .... | | | $10 | Atlantic 81676 |
| 3/5/88 | 115 | 11 | | © | 2 Hard Machine .... | | | $10 | Atlantic 81802 |

After Hours (2) | Don't Break My Heart (1) | Favorite Things (2) | I Love You (2) | Music Out Of Bounds (1) | We Connect (1) 35
Another Chance (2) | Don't Let Me Down (1) | Good Girl (2) | Insecurity (1) | River, The (2) |
Better Than Heaven (1) | Don't Make A Fool Of Yourself (2) 66 | Hard Machine (2) | Kiss It All Goodbye (2) | Temptation (2) |
Dancing Nowhere (1) | | He Doesn't Understand (1) | Love Or Desire (1) | Two Of Hearts (1) 3 |

STACKRIDGE '75
Rock group formed in Bristol, England: Mike Slater (vocals, flute), James Warren (guitar), Andy Davis (keyboards), Jim Walter (bass) and Billy Sparkle (drums).

| 12/28/74+ | 191 | 9 | | | Pinafore Days .... | | | $12 | Sire 7503 |

Dangerous Bacon | Galloping Gaucho | Humiliation | One Rainy July Morning | Road To Venezuela
Fundamentally Yours | God Speed The Plough | Last Plimsoll | Pinafore Days | Spin Round The Room

STAFFORD, Jim '74
Born on 1/16/44 in Eloise, Florida. Singer/songwriter/guitarist. Hosted own summer TV show in 1975 and *Those Amazing Animals*. Formerly married to **Bobbie Gentry**.

| 3/16/74 | 55 | 33 | | © | Jim Stafford .... [N] | | | $12 | MGM 4947 |

I Ain't Sharin' Sharon | Mr. Bojangles (medley) | Real Good Time | **Spiders & Snakes** 3 | Visit With An Old Friend (medley)
L.A. Mamma | **My Girl Bill** 12 | 16 Little Red Noses And A Horse That Sweats | **Swamp Witch** 39 | **Wildwood Weed** 7
Last Chant | Nifty Fifties Blues | | |

STAFFORD, Jo '56
Born on 11/12/17 in Coalinga, California. Female pop singer. Member of The Pied Pipers from 1940-43. Married to **Paul Weston** from 1952-96. Hosted own TV musical series from 1954-55.

| 12/29/56 | 13 | 8 | | | Ski Trails .... | | | $50 | Columbia 910 |

Baby, It's Cold Outside | I've Got My Love To Keep Me Warm | June In January | Moonlight In Vermont | Whiffenpoof Song
By The Fireside | It Happened In Sun Valley | Let It Snow! Let It Snow! Let It Snow! | Nearness Of You | Winter Song
| | | Sleigh Ride | Winter Wonderland

STAFFORD, Terry '64
Born on 11/22/41 in Hollis, Oklahoma; raised in Amarillo, Texas. Died on 3/17/96 (age 54). Male pop singer. Appeared in the movie *Wild Wheels*.

| 5/16/64 | **81** | 11 | © | **Suspicion!** .... | $50 | Crusader 1001 |

Everybody Has Somebody   For You My Love   Invitation To A Kiss   Margarita   Pocket Full Of Rainbows   Slowly But Surely
Everything I Need   **I'll Touch A Star** *25*   Kiss Me Quick   Playing With Fire   She Wishes I Were You   **Suspicion** *3*

STAGE DOLLS '89
Rock trio from Trondheim, Norway: Torstein Flakne (vocals), Terje Storli (bass) and Steinar Krokstad (drums).

| 8/19/89 | **118** | 12 | © | **Stage Dolls** .... | $10 | Chrysalis 21716 |

Ammunition   Hanoi Waters   **Love Cries** *46*   Still In Love   Wings Of Steel
Don't Stop Believin'   Lorraine   Mystery   Waitin' For You

STAIND '01
Rock group from Boston: Aaron Lewis (vocals), Mike Mushok (guitar), Johnny April (bass) and Jon Wysocki (drums).

| 5/1/99 | **74** | 56 | ▲ © | 1 **Dysfunction** .... C:●[5]/22 | $10 | Flip 62356 |
| 6/9/01 | ●[3] | 17↑ | ▲[3] © | 2 **Break The Cycle** | $10 | Flip 62626 |

Can't Believe (2)   Fade (2)   **It's Been Awhile** (2) *7*   Open Your Eyes (2)   Safe Place (2)   Take (2)
Change (2)   Flat, A (1)   Just Go (1)   Outside (2)   Spleen (1)   Waste (2)
Crawl (1)   For You (2)   Me (1)   Pressure (2)   Suffer (2)
Epiphany (2)   Home (1)   Mudshovel (1)   Raw (1)   Suffocate (1)

STAIRSTEPS — see FIVE STAIRSTEPS, The

STALLING, Carl, Project '90
Born on 11/10/1891 in Lexington, Missouri. Died on 11/29/72 (age 81). Worked at Disney in the early 1920s where he invented the process of scoring for animation. Joined Warner Brothers in 1936 and scored over 600 cartoons in his 22 years with the company.

| 11/10/90 | **188** | 2 | © | **Music From Warner Bros. Cartoons 1936-1958** .... [I] | $10 | Warner 26027 |

Anxiety Montage (1952-1955) Medley   Dough For The Do Do (medley)   Powerhouse And Other Cuts From The Early 50's Medley   Stalling Self-Parody: Music From Porky's Preview (1941)   Various Cues From Bugs Bunny Films (1943-1956) Medley
Carl Stalling With Milt Franklyn In Session   Early WB Scores: The Depression Era (1936-1941) Medley   Putty Tat Trouble Part 6   Stalling: The War Years (1942-1946) Medley
Dinner Music For A Pack Of Hungry Cannibals (1941-1950) Medley   Good Egg (1939)   Speedy Gonzalez (1955) Meets Two Crows From Tacos (1956)   There They Go Go Go (1956)
   Hillbilly Hare (1950)   To Itch His Own (1958)
   Porky In Wackyland (medley)

STALLION '77
Pop-rock group from Denver: Buddy Stephens (vocals), Danny O'Neil (guitar), Wally Damrick (keyboards), Jorg Gonzalez (bass) and Larry Thompson (drums).

| 3/26/77 | **191** | 9 | | **Stallion** .... | $12 | Casablanca 7040 |

Fancy Francie   I Know How They Feel   Magic Of The Music   Something Just Told Me
Funny Thing   Love Is A Game   **Old Fashioned Boy (You're The One)** *37*   Woman
Glad That I Found You   Loving You

STALLONE, Sylvester — see PARTON, Dolly

STAMPEDERS '71
Pop-rock trio from Calgary, Alberta, Canada: Rick Dodson, Ronnie King and Kim Berly. All share vocals.

| 10/23/71 | **172** | 6 | © | **Sweet City Woman** .... | $20 | Bell 6068 |

Carry Me   I Didn't Love You Anyhow   Oklahoma Country   Sunday Prayin'   Train To Nowhere   With You I Got Wheels
Gator Road   Man From P.E.I.   Only A Friend   **Sweet City Woman** *8*   Tuscaloosa Women   You Got To Go

STAMPLEY, Joe — see BANDY, Moe

STAN & DOUG '70
Comedy duo from Seattle: Stan Boreson (born on 5/25/25) and Doug Setterberg.

| 12/26/70 | **19**[X] | 1 | | **Stan and Doug Yust Go Nuts at Christmas** .... [X-N] | $20 | Golden Crest 31021 |

All I Want For Christmas (Is My Upper Plate)   Ho, Ho, Ho, Don't Ever Go   Jolly Old Saint Nicholas   Uncle Sven Is Coming To Town (Santa Claus Is Coming To Town)   Yingle Bells, Yingle Bells (Jingle Bells)
Christmas Goose (Snowbird)   I Was Santa Claus At The Schoolhouse (For The PTA)   Ragnar The Flat-Nosed Reindeer (Rudolph The Red-Nosed Reindeer)   Where To Go, Where To Go, Where To Go (Let It Snow, Let It Snow, Let It Snow)
Christmas Medley   I Yust Go Nuts At Christmas
Christmas Party   I've Had A Very Merry Christmas

STANDELLS, The '66
Rock group from Los Angeles: Dick Dodd (vocals, drums), Larry Tamblyn and Tony Valentino (guitars) and Gary Lane (bass). Dodd was an original Mouseketeer of TV's *The Mickey Mouse Club*. Tamblyn is the brother of actor Russ Tamblyn.

| 7/2/66 | **52** | 16 | | **Dirty Water** .... | $60 | Tower 5027 |

Dirty Water *11*   Little Sally Tease   Pride And Devotion   **Sometimes Good Guys Don't Wear White** *43*   Why Did You Hurt Me
Hey Joe, Where You Gonna Go?   Medication   Rari   There's A Storm Coming
   19th Nervous Breakdown

STANKY BROWN GROUP, The '78
Rock group from New York City: James Brown (vocals, keyboards), Jeff Leynor (guitar), Allan Ross (sax), Richard Bunkiewicz (bass) and Jerry Cordasco (drums).

5/15/76	**192**	3		1 **Our Pleasure To Serve You**	$12	Sire 7516
3/5/77	**195**	2		2 **If The Lights Don't Get You The Helots Will**	$12	Sire 7529
4/29/78	**192**	5		3 **Stanky Brown**	$12	Sire 6053

Alone Tonight (2)   Confident Man (2)   Good To Me (2)   Masquerade (1)   She's A Taker (3)   You Be You (1)
Around Town (3)   Don't You Refuse (1)   Hundred Times Around (1)   Master Of Disguise (3)   Stop In The Name Of Love (2)   You Make It Happen For Me (1)
As A Lover I'm A Loser (2)   Faith In The Family (2)   (I Wish I Was) Back In Your Arms Again (3)   Matthew (1)   Tell Me What You Want (3)   You've Come Over Me (1)
Chains (3)   Falling Fast (3)   Let's Get To Livin' (1)   Misery (1)   Where Have They Gone (1)
Chance On Love (3)   Free And Easy (2)   Life Beyond (2)   Please Don't Be One (3)   Woman, Don't Let It Slip Away (2)
Coaltown (2)   Friday Night Without You (1)   Ravin' Beauty (1)

STANLEY, Michael, Band '81

Born Michael Stanley Gee on 3/25/48 in Cleveland. Rock singer/guitarist. Former member of **Silk**. His band: Kevin Raleigh (vocals, keyboards), Bob Pelander (keyboards), Gary Markshay (guitar), Rick Bell (sax), Mike Gismondi (bass) and Tom Dobeck (drums). Don Powers replaced Markshay in 1982.

DEBUT	PEAK	WKS		CD	Album			$	Label & Number
9/13/75	184	3		© 1	You break it...You bought it!			$15	Epic 33492
7/8/78	99	18		© 2	Cabin Fever			$12	Arista 4182
8/4/79	148	5		© 3	Greatest Hints			$12	Arista 4236
9/27/80+	86	32		© 4	Heartland			$10	EMI America 17040
8/1/81	79	15		© 5	North Coast			$10	EMI America 17056
9/4/82	136	6		© 6	MSB			$10	EMI America 17071
9/24/83	64	17		© 7	You Can't Fight Fashion			$10	EMI America 17100

All I Ever Wanted (4)
Baby If You Wanna Dance (2)
Back In My Arms Again (3)
Beautiful Lies (3)
Carolyn (5)
Chemistry (5)
Damage Is Done (7)
Dancing In The Dark (1)
Don't Lead With Your Love (3)
Don't Stop The Music (4)
Don't You Do That To Me (5)
Down To The Wire (3)
Face The Music (1)
Falling In Love Again (5) *64*
Fire In The Hole (7)

Fool's Parade (2)
Gypsy Eyes (1)
Hang Tough (6)
Hard Time (7)
He Can't Love You (4) *33*
Hearts On Fire (7)
Heaven And Hell (5)
Highlife (7)
Highway Angel (1)
Hold Your Fire (1)
How Can You Call This Love (7)
I'll Never Need Anyone More (Than I Need You Tonight) (4)
I'm Gonna Love You (1)

If You Love Me (6)
In Between The Lines (6)
In The Heartland (5)
Just A Little Bit Longer (6)
Just Give Me Tonight (7)
Just How Good (A Bad Woman Feels) (7)
Last Night (3)
Late Show (2)
Let's Hear It (5)
Lights Out (3)
Long Time (Looking For A Dream) (2)
Lost In The Funhouse (4)
Love Hurts (6)

Lover (4) *68*
Misery Loves Company (2)
My Town (7) *39*
Night By Night (6)
No Turning Back (3)
One Of Those Dreams (6)
Only A Dreamer (2)
Promises (3)
Save A Little Piece For Me (4)
Say Goodbye (4)
Slip Away (2)
Someone Like You (7) *75*
Somewhere In The Night (5)
Song For My Children (1)
Spanish Nights (6)

Step The Way (1)
Sweet Refrain (1)
Take The Time (6) *81*
Tell Me (5)
Victim Of Circumstance (5)
Voodoo (3)
Waste A Little Time On Me (1)
We Can Make It (5)
We're Not Strangers Anymore (3)
What'cha Wanna Do Tonight (2)
When I'm Holding You Tight (6) *78*
When Your Heart Says It's Right (5)

Where Have All The Clowns Gone (1)
Who's To Blame (2)
Why Should Love Be This Way (2)
Working Again (4)
You're My Love (5)

STANLEY, Paul '78

Born Paul Stanley Eisen on 1/20/52 in Queens, New York. Rock singer/guitarist. Member of **Kiss**.

DEBUT	PEAK	WKS		CD	Album			$	Label & Number
10/14/78	40	18	▲ ©	1	Paul Stanley			$20	Casablanca 7123

Ain't Quite Right
Goodbye

Hold Me, Touch Me *46*
It's Alright

Love In Chains
Move On

Take Me Away (Together As One)

Tonight You Belong To Me
Wouldn't You Like To Know Me

STANSFIELD, Lisa '90

Born on 4/11/66 in Rochdale, Manchester, England. Dance singer.

DEBUT	PEAK	WKS		CD	Album			$	Label & Number
3/10/90	9	39	▲ ©	1	Affection			$10	Arista 8554
11/30/91+	43	40	● ©	2	Real Love			$10	Arista 18679
8/16/97	55	10	©	3	Lisa Stansfield			$10	Arista 18738

Affection (1)
All Around The World (1) *3*
All Woman (2) *56*
Change (2) *27*
Don't Cry For Me (3)
First Joy (2)
Footsteps (3)
Got Me Missing You (3)
Honest (3)

I Cried My Last Tear, Last Night (3)
I Will Be Waiting (2)
I'm Leavin' (3)
It's Got To Be Real (3)
Line (3)
Little More Love (2)
Live Together (1)
Love In Me (1)

Make Love To Ya (2)
Mighty Love (1)
Never Gonna Fall (3)
Never, Never Gonna Give You Up (3) *74*
People Hold On (Bootleg Mix) (3)
Poison (1)
Real Love (2)

Real Thing (3)
Real Thing (Touch Mix) (3)
Set Your Loving Free (2)
Sincerity (1)
Somewhere In Time (3)
Soul Deep (2)
Suzanne (3)
Symptoms Of Loneliness & Heartache (2)

Tenderly (2)
This Is The Right Time (1) *21*
Time To Make You Mine (2)
Very Thought Of You (3)
Wake Up Baby (1)
Way You Want It (1)
What Did I Do To You? (1)
When Are You Coming Back? (1)

You Can't Deny It (1) *14*
You Know How To Love Me (3)

STAPLES, Mavis '70

Born in 1940 in Chicago. Leader of **The Staple Singers**. Appeared in the 1990 movie *Graffiti Bridge*.

DEBUT	PEAK	WKS		CD	Album			$	Label & Number
9/12/70	188	4		©	Only For The Lonely			$15	Volt 6010

Don't Change Me Now
Endlessly
How Many Times

I Have Learned To Do Without You *87*
It Makes Me Wanna Cry

Since I Fell For You
Since You Became A Part Of My Life

What Happened To The Real Me
You're The Fool

STAPLES, Pop — see KING, Albert

STAPLE SINGERS, The '72

R&B family group from Winoma, Mississippi: Roebuck **Pop Staples** (guitar), with his daughters Cleotha, Yvonne and **Mavis Staples** (vocals). Pop died on 12/19/2000 (age 84). Group inducted into the Rock and Roll Hall of Fame in 1999.

DEBUT	PEAK	WKS		CD	Album			$	Label & Number
3/20/71	117	11		© 1	The Staple Swingers			$20	Stax 2034
2/26/72	19	37		© 2	Bealtitude: Respect Yourself			$20	Stax 3002
8/25/73	102	21		© 3	Be What You Are			$20	Stax 3015
12/15/73	11 X	2		4	The Twenty-fifth Day Of December		[X]	$20	Fantasy 9442
					originally released in 1962 on Riverside 3513				
9/14/74	125	9		© 5	City In The Sky			$20	Stax 5515
11/1/75+	20	18		6	Let's Do It Again		[S]	$15	Curtom 5005
9/25/76	155	5		7	Pass It On			$12	Warner 2945

THE STAPLES

After Sex (6)
Almost (1)
Are You Sure (2)
Back Road Into Town (5)
Be What You Are (3) *66*
Big Mac (6)
Blood Pressure (5)
Bridges Instead of Walls (3)
Chase (6)
City In The Sky (5) *79*
Drown Yourself (3)
Funky Love (6)
Getting Too Big For Your Britches (5)
Give A Hand - Take A Hand (1)

Go Tell It On The Mountain (4)
Grandma's Hands (3)
Heaven (3)
Heavy Makes You Happy (Sha-Na-Boom Boom) (1) *27*
Holy Unto The Lord (4)
How Do You Move A Mountain (1)
I Ain't Raisin' No Sand (3)
I Like The Things About You (1)
I Want To Thank You (6)
I'll Take You There (2) *1*
I'm A Lover (1)
I'm Just Another Soldier (2)
I'm On Your Side (3)

If It Ain't One Thing It's Another (5)
If You're Ready (Come Go With Me) (3) *9*
Joy To The World (4)
Last Month Of The Year (4)
Let's Do It Again (6) *1*
Little Boy (1)
Love Comes In All Colors (3)
Love Is Plentiful (1)
Love Me Love Me, Love Me (7)
Making Love (7)
My Main Man (5) *76*
Name The Missing Word (2)
New Orleans (6) *70*

No Room At The Inn (4)
Oh Little Town Of Bethlehem (4)
Party (7)
Pass It On (7)
Precious, Precious (7)
Real Thing Inside Of Me (7)
Respect Yourself (2) *12*
Savior Is Born (4)
Silent Night (4)
Something Ain't Right (5)
Sweet Little Jesus Boy (4)
Sweeter Than The Sweet (7)
Take This Love Of Mine (7)
Take Your Own Time (7)

Tellin' Lies (3)
That's What Friends Are For (3)
There Is A God (5)
There Was A Star (4)
This Is A Perfect World (1)
This Old Town (3)
This World (2) *38*
Today Was Tomorrow Yesterday (5)
Touch A Hand, Make A Friend (3) *23*
Virgin Mary Had One Son (4)
Washington We're Watching You (5)
Wasn't That A Mighty Day (4)

We The People (2)
What's Your Thing (1)
Who (2)
Who Do You Think You Are (Jesus Christ The Superstar)? (2)
Who Made The Man (5)
Whole Lot Of Love (6)
You're Gonna Make Me Cry (1)
You've Got To Earn It (1) *97*

STARBUCK '76

Pop-rock group from Atlanta: Bruce Blackman (vocals, keyboards), Bo Wagner (marimbas), Sloan Hayes (keyboards), Tommy Strain and Ron Norris (guitars), Jim Cobb (bass) and Dave Snavely (drums). Strain, Norris and Snavely left after first album, replaced by Darryl Kutz (guitar), David Shaver (keyboards) and Ken Crysler (drums).

| 7/24/76 | 78 | 14 | | © | 1 **Moonlight Feels Right** | | | $12 | Private Stock 2013 |
| 6/11/77 | 182 | 2 | | | 2 **Rock 'n Roll Rocket** | | | $12 | Private Stock 2027 |

Bennie Bought The Big One (2)
Bordello Bordeaux (1)
Call Me (2)
City Of The Future (2)

Don't You Know How To Love A
 Lady (2)
Drop A Little Rock (1)
Everybody Be Dancin' (2) *38*

Fat Boy (2)
Fool In Line (2)
I Got To Know (1) *43*
I'm Crazy (1)

Lash LaRue (1)
Little Bird (2)
Lucky Man (1) *73*
Moonlight Feels Right (1) *3*

Rock 'N Roll Rocket (medley)
 (2)
Slower You Go (The Longer It
 Lasts) (1)

So The Night Goes (1)
Sunset Eyes (2)
Working My Heart To The Bone
 (1)

STARCASTLE '76

Progressive-rock group from Chicago: Terry Luttrell (vocals), Matthew Stewart and Stephen Hagler (guitars), Herb Schildt (keyboards), Gary Strater (bass) and Stephen Tassler (drums).

3/13/76	95	15		©	1 **Starcastle**			$12	Epic 33914
2/5/77	101	11		©	2 **Fountains Of Light**			$12	Epic 34375
11/19/77	156	3		©	3 **Citadel**			$12	Epic 34935

Can't Think Twice (3)
Change In Time (3)
Could This Be Love (3)
Dawning Of The Day (2)

Diamond Song (Deep Is The
 Light) (1)
Elliptical Seasons (1)
Evening Wind (3)

Forces (1)
Fountains (2)
Lady Of The Lake (1)
Nova (1)

Portraits (2)
Shadows Of Song (3)
Shine On Brightly (3)
Silver Winds (2)

Stargate (1)
Sunfield (1)
To The Fire Wind (1)
True To The Light (2)

Why Have They Gone (3)
Wings Of White (3)

STARGARD '78

Disco trio: Rochelle Runnells, Debra Anderson and Janice Williams. Appeared as "The Diamonds" in the movie *Sgt. Pepper's Lonely Hearts Club Band.*

| 3/4/78 | 26 | 13 | | | 1 **Stargard** | | | $12 | MCA 2321 |
| 7/4/81 | 186 | 2 | | | 2 **Back 2 Back** | | | $12 | Warner 3456 |

Back To The Funk (2)
Cat And Me (2)
Diary (2)

Disco Rufus (1) *88*
Don't Change (1)
Force, The (1)

Here Comes Love (2)
High On The Boogie (2)
I'll Always Love You (1)

It's Your Love That I'm Missin'
 (2)
Just One Love (2)

Love Is So Easy (1)
Smile (1)
Three Girls (1)

**Which Way Is Up, Theme
 Song From** (1) *21*
You're The One (2)

STARLAND VOCAL BAND '76

Pop group formed in Washington DC: Bill and wife Taffy Danoff, John Carroll and future wife Margot Chapman. Bill and Taffy had fronted the folk group Fat City (backed **John Denver** on "Take Me Home, Country Roads"). Hosted own TV variety series in 1977. Won the 1976 Best New Artist Grammy.

| 5/29/76 | 20 | 25 | | | 1 **Starland Vocal Band** | | | $12 | Windsong 1351 |
| 6/11/77 | 104 | 13 | | | 2 **Rear View Mirror** | | | $12 | Windsong 2239 |

Afternoon Delight (1) *1*
Ain't It The Fall (1)
American Tune (1)
Baby, You Look Good To Me
 Tonight (1)

Boulder To Birmingham (1)
California Day (1) *66*
Don't Say Forever (2)
Fallin' In A Deep Hole (2)

Hail! Hail! Rock And Roll!
 (1) *71*
Liberated Woman (2)
Light Of My Life (2)
Mr. Wrong (2)

Norfolk (2)
Prism (2)
Rear View Mirror (2)
St. Croix Silent Night (2)
Starland (1)

Starting All Over Again (1)
Too Long A Journey (2)
War Surplus Baby (1)

STARLITE ORCHESTRA AND SINGERS, The '97

Group of studio musicians from Canada.

| 5/3/97 | 184 | 1 | | © | **The Best Of Andrew Lloyd Webber** | | | $10 | Madacy 0331 |

All I Ask For You
Another Suitcase In Another
 Hall
Don't Cry For Me Argentina

I Don't Know How To Love Him
Jesus Christ Superstar
Love Changes Everything
Memory

Music Of The Night
Only He (Has The Power To
 Move Me)
Pie Jesu

Phantom Of The Opera
 (medley)
Take That Look Off Your Face

STARPOINT '86

R&B group from Maryland: brothers Ernesto, George, Orlando and Gregory Phillips, with Renee Diggs and Kayode Adeyemo.

5/9/81	138	8			1 **Keep On It**			$10	Chocolate City 2018
10/5/85+	60	47	●	©	2 **Restless**			$10	Elektra 60424
3/21/87	95	14		©	3 **Sensational**			$10	Elektra 60722

Another Night (3)
Baby Let Me Do It (1)
D.Y.B.O. (3)
Don't Take Your Love Away (2)
Emotions (2)

For You (1)
He Wants My Body (3) *89*
I Just Want To Be Your Lover
 (1)
I Want You Closer (1)

Keep On It (1)
More We Love (3)
Object Of My Desire (2) *25*
One More Night (2)
Prove It Tonight (3)

Restless (2) *46*
Second Chance (3)
See The Light (2)
Sensational (3)
Starpoint's Here Tonight (1)

Till The End Of Time (2)
Touch Of Your Love (3)
We're Into Love (1)
What You Been Missin' (2)

STARR, Brenda K. '88

Born Brenda Kaplan on 10/15/66 in Manhattan, New York. Singer/actress. Daughter of Harvey Kaplan (of **Spiral Starecase**).

| 5/21/88 | 58 | 24 | | © | **Brenda K. Starr** | | | $10 | MCA 42088 |

All Tied Up
Breakfast In Bed
Drive Another Girl Home

Giving You All My Love
I Still Believe *13*
Over And Over

Straight From The Heart
**What You See Is What You
 Get** *24*

You Should Be Loving Me

STARR, Edwin '70

Born Charles Hatcher on 1/21/42 in Nashville; raised in Cleveland. R&B singer.

5/17/69	73	13		©	1 **25 Miles**			$25	Gordy 940
9/5/70	52	13		©	2 **War & Peace**			$20	Gordy 948
7/31/71	178	7			3 **Involved**			$15	Gordy 956
1/20/79	80	14			4 **Clean**			$12	20th Century 559
7/28/79	115	8			5 **Happy Radio**			$12	20th Century 591

Adios Senorita (2)
All Around The World (2)
At Last (I Found A Love) (2)
Backyard Lovin' Man (1)
Ball Of Confusion (That's What
 The World Is Today) (3)
California Soul (2)
Cloud Nine (2)
Contact (4) *65*
Don't Waste Your Time (4)
Drown My Heart (5)

Funky Music Sho Nuff Turns
 Me On (3) *64*
Gonna Keep On Tryin' Till I Win
 Your Love (1)
H.A.P.P.Y. Radio (5) *79*
He Who Picks A Rose (1)
I Can't Escape Your Memory (2)
I Can't Replace My Old Love (2)
I Just Wanted To Cry (2)
I'd Rather Fight Than Switch (5)
I'm So Into You (4)

I'm Still A Struggling Man
 (3) *80*
If My Heart Could Tell The
 Story (1)
It's Called The Rock (5)
Jealous (4)
Mighty Good Lovin' (1)
Music Brings Out The Beast In
 Me (4)
My Friend (5)
My Sweet Lord (3)

Patiently (5)
Pretty Little Angel (1)
Raindrops Keep Fallin' On My
 Head (2)
Rip Me Off (5)
Running Back And Forth (2)
She Should Have Been Home
 (2)
Soul City (Open Your Arms To
 Me) (1)
Stand (3)

Stop The War Now (3) *26*
Storm Clouds On The Way (4)
Time (2)
Twenty-Five Miles (1) *6*
24 Hours (To Find My Baby) (1)
War (2,3) *1*
Way Over There (3)
Who Cares If You're Happy Or
 Not (I Do) (1)
Working Song (4)
You Beat Me To The Punch (1)

831

STARR, Fredro '01

Born in Jamaica, New York. Male rapper/actor. Member of **Onyx**. Acted in several movies.

| 3/3/01 | 76 | 7 | | © | **Firestarr** .... | | | $0 | Other Peoples M. 8180 |

America's Most Big Shots Comin' At The Game | Dat Be Dem Dyin' 4 Rap Electric Ice | I Don't Wanna One Night Perfect B!tch | Shining Through Soldierz Thug Warz | What If Who F#!k Betta

★412★ STARR, Ringo '73

Born Richard Starkey on 7/7/40 in Dingle, Liverpool, England. Played with Rory Storm and the Hurricanes before joining **The Beatles** in 1962. Acted in the movies *Candy, The Magic Christian, 200 Motels, Born To Boogie, Blindman, That'll Be The Day, Cave Man* and *Give My Regards To Broad Street*. Played "Mr. Conductor" on PBS-TV's *Shining Time Station* from 1989-91. Married actress Barbara Bach on 4/27/81.

1)Ringo 2)Goodnight Vienna 3)Sentimental Journey

5/16/70	22	14		©	1 **Sentimental Journey**			$20	Apple 3365
10/17/70	65	15		©	2 **Beaucoups of Blues**			$20	Apple 3368
11/17/73	2²	37	▲	©	3 **Ringo**			$20	Apple 3413
11/30/74+	8	25	●	©	4 **Goodnight Vienna**			$20	Apple 3417
12/6/75+	30	11		©	5 **Blast From Your Past**		[G]	$20	Apple 3422
10/16/76	28	9		©	6 **Ringo's Rotogravure**			$15	Atlantic 18193
10/15/77	162	6		©	7 **Ringo The 4th**			$15	Atlantic 19108
5/20/78	129	6		©	8 **Bad Boy**			$15	Portrait 35378
11/14/81	98	12		©	9 **Stop And Smell The Roses**			$12	Boardwalk 33246
7/4/98	61	4		©	10 **Vertical Man**			$10	Mercury 558598

All By Myself (4)
Attention (9)
Back Off Boogaloo (5,9) *9*
Bad Boy (8)
Beaucoups Of Blues (2,5) *87*
Blue, Turning Grey Over You (1)
Bye Bye Blackbird (1)
Call Me (4)
Can She Do It Like She Dances (7)
Cookin' (In The Kitchen Of Love) (6)
Cryin' (6)
Dead Giveaway (9)
Devil Woman (3)
Dose Of Rock 'N' Roll (6) *26*
Dream (1)
Drift Away (10)
Drowning In The Sea Of Love (7)

Drumming Is My Madness (9)
Early 1970 (5)
Easy For Me (4)
Fastest Growing Heartache In The West (2)
$15 Draw (2)
Gave It All Up (7)
Gypsies In Flight (7)
Hard Times (8)
Have I Told You Lately That I Love You? (1)
Have You Seen My Baby (3)
Heart On My Sleeve (8)
Hey Baby (6) *74*
Husbands And Wives (4)
I Was Walkin' (10)
I Wouldn't Have You Any Other Way (2)
I'd Be Talking All The Time (2)
I'll Be Fine Anywhere (10)
I'll Still Love You (6)

I'm A Fool To Care (1)
I'm The Greatest (3,5)
I'm Yours (10)
It Don't Come Easy (5) *4*
It's All Down To Goodnight Vienna (4) *31*
It's No Secret (7)
King Of Broken Hearts (10)
La De Da (10)
Lady Gaye (6)
Las Brisas (6)
Let The Rest Of The World Go By (1)
Lipstick Traces (On A Cigarette) (8)
Loser's Lounge (2)
Love Don't Last Long (2)
Love Is A Many-Splendored Thing (1)
Love Me Do (10)
Man Like Me (8)

Mindfield (10)
Monkey See - Monkey Do (8)
Nice Way (9)
Night And Day (1)
No No Song (4,5) *3*
Occapella (4)
Oh My My (3,5) *5*
Old Time Relovin' (8)
One (10)
Only You (4,5) *6*
Oo-Wee (4) *flip*
Out On The Streets (7)
Photograph (3,5) *1*
Private Property (9)
Puppet (10)
Pure Gold (6)
Sentimental Journey (1)
Silent Homecoming (2)
Simple Love Song (7)
Six O'Clock (3)

Sneaking Sally Through The Alley (7)
Snookeroo (4) *flip*
Spooky Weirdness (6)
Star Dust (1)
Step Lightly (3)
Stop And Take The Time To Smell The Roses (9)
Sunshine Life For Me (Sail Away Raymond) (3)
Sure To Fall (In Love With You) (9)
Tango All Night (7)
This Be Called A Song (6)
Tonight (8)
Vertical Man (10)
Waiting (2)
What In The...World (10)
Where Did Our Love Go (8)
Whispering Grass (Don't Tell The Trees) (1)

Who Needs A Heart (8)
Wine, Women And Loud Happy Songs (2)
Wings (7)
Without Her (2)
Women Of The Night (2)
Wrack My Brain (9) *38*
You Always Hurt The One You Love (1)
You And Me (Babe) (3)
You Belong To Me (9)
You Don't Know Me At All (6)
You're Sixteen (3,5) *1*

STARSHIP — see JEFFERSON AIRPLANE

STARS ON '81

Studio group assembled in Holland by producer Jaap Eggermont.

| 5/9/81 | 9 | 24 | ● | | 1 **Stars On Long Play** | | | $10 | Radio 16044 |

side 1: medley of **Beatles** songs; the singles "Stars on 45" (#1) and "Stars on 45 II" (#67) both made the *Hot 100*

| 10/31/81 | 120 | 6 | | | 2 **Stars On Long Play II** .... | | | $10 | Radio 19314 |

the single "More Stars on 45" made the *Hot 100* (#55)

| 5/8/82 | 163 | 6 | | | 3 **Stars On Long Play III** .... | | | $10 | Radio 19349 |

side 1: **Rolling Stones** medley; side 2: **Stevie Wonder** medley; the single "Stars on 45 III" made the *Hot 100* (#28)

Ain't No Mountain High Enough (2)
All Right Now (2)
And Your Bird Can Sing (1,3)
Angie (2)
As Tears Go By (3)
At The Hop (1)
Baby Love (2)
Baker Street (2)
Bang A Boomerang (2)
Bird Dog (2)
Boogie Nights (1,3)
Bread And Butter (1)
Brown Sugar (3)
Buona Sera (1)
California Dreamin' (2)
Can't Give You Anything (But My Love) (2)
Cathy's Clown (1,3)
Cracklin' Rosie (2)
Dance To The Music (2)
Day Tripper (1,3)
Do-Wah-Diddy-Diddy (2)
Do You Remember (1)
Do You Think I'm Sexy (2)
Do You Wanna Know A Secret (1,3)
Don't You Worry 'Bout A Thing (3)

Drive My Car (1,3)
Dum Dum Diddle (2)
Eight Days A Week (1,3)
Eleanor Rigby (3)
Emotional Rescue (3)
Eve Of Destruction (2)
Eve Of The War (2)
Every Little Thing (1,3)
Fernando (2)
Fingertips (3)
Fire (2)
For Once In My Life (3)
'45 Stars Get Ready (2)
Funky Town (1,3)
Get Back (1,3)
Get Off (2)
Get Off Of My Cloud (3)
Gimme! Gimme! Gimme! (A Man After Midnight) (2,3)
Gimme Shelter (3)
Golden Years Of Rock & Roll (1)
Good Day Sunshine (1,3)
Good, The Bad And The Ugly (2)
Hard Days Night (1,3)
Here Comes The Sun (1,3)
Honky Tonk Women (3)
Horse With No Name (2)

(I Can't Get No) Satisfaction (3)
I Hear A Symphony (2)
I Should Have Known Better (1,3)
I Wanna Hold Your Hand (1,3)
I Was Made To Love Her (3)
I Wish (3)
I'll Be Back (1,3)
If I Fell (1,3)
Isn't She Lovely (3)
It Won't Be Long (1,3)
It's Only Rock 'N Roll (But I Like It) (3)
Jenny, Jenny (1)
Jimmy Mack (3)
Jumpin' Jack Flash (3)
Knowing Me, Knowing You (2)
Kung-Fu-Fighting (2)
Lady Bump (2)
Lady Jane (3)
Lay All Your Love On Me (2)
Let's Go To San Francisco (2)
Let's Spend The Night Together (3)
Love Child (2)
Love Is Here And Now You're Gone (2)
Lover's Concerto (2)
Lucille (1)

M*A*S*H, Theme From (2)
Master Blaster (3)
Miss You (3)
Monday Monday (2)
Money, Money, Money (2)
My Cherie Amour (3)
My Sweet Lord (1,3)
No Reply (1,3)
Nowhere Man (1,3)
Nut Rocker (1)
On And On And On (2,3)
Only The Lonely (1,3)
Out Of Time (3)
Overture From Tommy (3)
Papa Was A Rolling Stone (2)
Place In The Sun (3)
Play With Fire (3)
Please Please Me (1,3)
Rainy Day (3)
Reach Out I'll Be There (2)
Reflections (3)
Rip It Up (1)
Ruby Tuesday (3)
Runaway (1)
S.O.S. (2)
San Francisco (2)
She's A Rainbow (3)
Sir Duke (3)
Slippin' And Slidin' (3)

Someday We'll Be Together (2)
Sound Of Silence (2)
Star Star (3)
"Star Wars" (Main Theme) (2)
Stars On 45 (medley) (3)
Stars On 45 (3)
Stars On Get Ready III (3)
Stars On Jingle (3)
Stars Will Never Stop (3)
Start Me Up (3)
Stop In The Name Of Love (2)
Sugar Baby Love (2)
Sugar, Sugar (1,3)
Summer Night City (2,3)
Sun Ain't Gonna Shine Anymore (2)
Super Trouper (2,3)
Superstition (3)
Sympathy For The Devil (3)
Take It Or Leave It (3)
Tax Man (1,3)
Tears Of A Clown (2)
Tell Me (3)
That's All Right (1)
Things We Said Today (1,3)
Ticket To Ride (1,3)
Tommy (A Rock Opera) ..see: Overture From
Under My Thumb (3)

Under The Boardwalk (3)
Uptight (Everything's Alright) (3)
Venus (1,3)
Video Killed The Radio Star (1,3)
Voulez-Vous (2)
Wait (1,3)
We Can Work It Out (1,3)
We Love You (3)
Where Did Our Love Go (2)
While My Guitar Gently Weeps (1,3)
Winner Takes It All (2)
Wooly Bully (1)
Word, The (1,3)
Y.M.C.A. (medley) (2)
Yester-Me, Yester-You, Yesterday (3)
You Are The Sunshine Of My Life (3)
You Can't Do That (1,3)
You Keep Me Hanging On (2)
You're Going To Lose That Girl (1,3)

STARZ '77

Rock group formed in New York City: Michael Lee Smith (vocals), Rich Ranno and Brendan Harkin (guitars), Peter Sweval (bass) and Joe Dube (drums). Smith is the brother of **Rex Smith**.

9/11/76	123	13		©	1 **Starz**			$12	Capitol 11539
4/16/77	89	8		©	2 **Violation**			$12	Capitol 11617
2/11/78	105	9		©	3 **Attention Shoppers!**			$12	Capitol 11730

STARZ — Cont'd

All Night Long (2)	Detroit Girls (1)	Johnny All-Alone (3)	Pull The Plug (1)	S.T.E.A.D.Y. (2)	X-Ray Spex (3)
(Any Way That You Want It)	Don't Think (3)	Live Wire (1)	Rock Six Times (2)	Subway Terror (2)	
I'll Be There (3) *79*	Good Ale We Seek (3)	Monkey Business (1)	She (3)	Tear It Down (1)	
Boys In Action (1)	**Hold On To The Night** (3) *78*	Night Crawler (1)	**(She's Just A) Fallen Angel**	Third Time's The Charm (3)	
Cherry Baby (2) *33*	Is That A Street Light Or The	Now I Can (1)	(1) *95*	Violation (2)	
Cool One (2)	Moon? (2)	Over And Over (1)	**Sing It, Shout It** (2) *66*	Waitin' On You (3)	

STATIC-X   '01

Rock group from Los Angeles: Wayne Static (vocals, guitar), Koichi Fukuda (keyboards), Tony Campos (bass) and Ken Jay (drums). Fukada left in 2000; Static took over keyboards and Tripp Rex Eisen (guitar) joined.

9/4/99+	107	43	▲	©	1 **Wisconsin Death Trip**			$10	Warner 47271
6/9/01	11	14		©	2 **Machine**			$10	Warner 47948

A Dios Alma Perdida (2)	Burn To Burn (2)	Get To The Gone (2)	Love Dump (2)	Permanence (2)	Sweat Of The Bud (1)
Bien Venidos (2)	Cold (2)	I Am (1)	Machine (2)	Push It (1)	This Is Not (2)
Black And White (2)	December (1)	I'm With Stupid (1)	Otsego Undead (2)	Stem (1)	Trance Is The Motion (1)
Bled For Days (1)	Fix (1)	...In A Bag (2)	Otsegolation (1)	Structural Defect (1)	Wisconsin Death Trip (1)

STATLER BROTHERS, The   '81

Country vocal group from Staunton, Virginia: brothers Harold and Don Reid, Phil Balsley and Lew DeWitt. In 1983, Jimmy Fortune replaced DeWitt who died from Crohn's disease on 8/15/90 (age 52). Hosted their own Nashville Network cable TV variety show.

1)Years Ago 2)The Best of The Statler Bros. 3)Flowers On The Wall

2/26/66	125	3		©	1 **Flowers On The Wall**			$30	Columbia 9249
1/30/71	126	11		©	2 **Bed Of Rose's**			$15	Mercury 61317
10/16/71	181	2			3 **Pictures Of Moments To Remember**			$15	Mercury 61349
9/13/75+	121	20	▲³	©	4 **The Best Of The Statler Bros.**		[G]	$12	Mercury 1037
6/10/78	155	9	●	©	5 **Entertainers...On And Off The Record**			$12	Mercury 5007
12/16/78	183	4	▲	©	6 **The Statler Brothers Christmas Card**		[X]	$12	Mercury 5012
7/14/79	183	2	●		7 **The Originals**			$12	Mercury 5016
2/2/80	153	11	●	©	8 **The Best Of The Statler Bros. Rides Again, Volume II**		[G]	$12	Mercury 5024
9/6/80	169	5	●	©	9 **10th Anniversary**			$12	Mercury 5027
7/11/81	103	9		©	10 **Years Ago**			$12	Mercury 6002
6/25/83	193	5	●	©	11 **Today**			$10	Mercury 812184
5/26/84	177	4		©	12 **Atlanta Blue**			$10	Mercury 818652
8/9/86	183	2			13 **Four For The Show**			$10	Mercury 826782

All I Have To Offer You Is Me (2)	Don't Wait On Me (10)	I Still Miss Someone (1)	Me And Bobby McGee (2)	Pictures (3,4)	We Got Paid By Cash (9)
Almost In Love (7)	Doodlin' Song (1)	I Wonder How The Old Folks	Memories Are Made Of This (10)	Promise (11)	We Got The Mem'ries (13)
Angel In Her Face (12)	Elizabeth (11)	Are At Home (3)	Memphis (1)	Quite A Long, Long Time (1)	Whatever Happened To
Atlanta Blue (12)	Faded Love (3)	I'll Be Home For Christmas (6)	Moments To Remember (3)	Right On The Money (11)	Randolph Scott (4)
Away In A Manger (6)	Fifteen Years Ago (2)	(I'll Even Love You) Better Than	More Like Daddy Than Me (13)	Second Thoughts (3)	When The Yankees Came
Bed Of Rose's (2,4) *58*	Flowers On The Wall (1,4) *4*	I Did Then (8)	Movies, The (8)	Silver Medals And Sweet	Home (7)
Before The Magic Turns To	For Cryin' Out Loud (13)	**I'll Go To My Grave Loving**	Mr. Autry (7)	Memories (8)	When You And I Were Young,
Memory (5)	Forever (13)	**You** (4) *93*	My Darling Hildegarde (1)	Some I Wrote (8)	Maggie (3)
Best That I Can Do (5)	Give It Your Best (12)	I'm Dyin' A Little Each Day (11)	My Only Love (12)	Some Memories Last Forever	When You Are Sixty-Five (5)
Billy Christian (1)	Guilty (3)	I'm Not Quite Through Crying (1)	My Reward (3)	(11)	Where He Always Wanted To
Carols Those Kids Used To	Here We Are Again (7,8)	If It Makes Any Difference (12)	Neighborhood Girl (2)	Something You Can't Buy (6)	Be (7)
Sing (6)	Holly Wood (12)	In The Garden (6)	New York City (2,4)	Star-Spangled Banner (7)	Whiffenpoof Song (1)
Carry Me Back (4)	How Are Things In Clay,	Jingle Bells (6)	No Love Lost (12)	Susan When She Tried (4)	White Christmas (6)
Charlotte's Web (9)	Kentucky? (9)	Junkie's Prayer (2)	Nobody Wants To Be Country	Sweet By And By (11)	Who Am I To Say (5,8)
Chet Atkins' Hand (10)	How Great Thou Art (8)	Just A Little Talk With Jesus (7)	(9)	Tender Years (3)	Who Do You Think? (6)
Christmas Medley (6)	How To Be A Country Star (7,8)	Just Someone I Used To Know	Nobody's Darlin' But Mine (4)	Thank You World (3)	Will You Be There? (13)
Christmas To Me (6)	I Believe I'll Live For Him (13)	(3)	Nothing As Original As You (7)	There Is You (11)	Years Ago (10)
Class Of '57 (4)	I Believe In Santa's Cause (6)	Kid's Last Fight (9)	Official Historian On Shirley	Things (3)	You Can't Go Home (3)
Count On Me (13)	I Don't Dream Anymore (4)	King Of The Road (1)	Jean Berrell (5,8)	This Ole House (1)	You Oughta Be Here With Me
Counting My Memories (7)	I Dreamed About You (5)	Last Goodbye (2)	Oh Baby Mine (I Get So Lonely)	This Part Of The World (2)	(13)
Dad (10)	I Forgot More Than You'll Ever	(Let's Just) Take One Night At	(11)	'Til The End (9)	You'll Be Back (Every Night In
Do You Know You Are My	Know (5)	A Time (12)	Old Cheerleaders Cry (9)	Today I Went Back (10)	My Dreams) (10)
Sunshine (5,8)	I Never Spend A Christmas	Little Farther Down The Road	One Less Day To Go (9)	Tomorrow Is Your Friend (5)	You're The First (5)
Do You Remember These (4)	That I Don't Think Of You (4)	(7)	One Size Fits All (12)	Tomorrow Never Comes (2)	Your Picture In The Paper (8)
Don't Forget Yourself (9)	I Never Want To Kiss You	Love Was All We Had (10)	One Takes The Blame (12)	We (2)	Yours Love (5)
	Goodbye (11)	Making Memories (3)	Only You (13)	We Ain't Even Started Yet (10)	

STATON, Candi   '76

Born Canzata Staton on 5/13/40 in Hanceville, Alabama. Female R&B singer. Formerly married to **Clarence Carter**.

2/27/71	188	2			1 **Stand By Your Man**			$15	Fame 4202
6/26/76	129	14			2 **Young Hearts Run Free**			$12	Warner 2948
7/28/79	129	6			3 **Chance**			$12	Warner 3333

Chance (3)	How Can I Put Out The Flame	**I'm Just A Prisoner (Of Your**	Run To Me (2)	Too Hurt To Cry (1)	You Bet Your Sweet Sweet
Destiny (2)	(When You Keep The Fire	**Good Lovin')** (1) *56*	**Stand By Your Man** (1) *24*	What A Feeling (2)	Love (2)
Freedom Is Just Beyond The	Burning) (1)	Living For You (2)	Summer Time With You (2)	What Would Become Of Me (1)	**Young Hearts Run Free** (2) *20*
Door (1)	I Ain't Got Nowhere To Go (3)	Me And My Music (3)	**Sweet Feeling** (1) *60*	When You Wake Up Tomorrow	
He Called Me Baby (1) *52*	I Know (2)	Mr. And Mrs. Untrue (1)	To Hear You Say You're Mine	(3)	
	I Live (3)	Rock (3)	(1)		

STATON, Dakota   '58

Born Aliyah Rabia on 6/3/31 in Pittsburgh. Jazz singer.

2/24/58	4	52		©	1 **The Late, Late Show**			$30	Capitol 876
10/27/58	22	1			2 **Dynamic!**			$30	Capitol 1054
6/1/59	23	9			3 **Crazy He Calls Me**			$30	Capitol 1170
11/16/59	47	3			4 **Time To Swing**			$30	Capitol 1241

Ain't No Use (1)	Cherokee (2)	Idaho (3)	Misty (1)	Summertime (1)	You Don't Know What Love Is
Angel Eyes (3)	Crazy He Calls Me (3)	If I Should Lose You (4)	Moonray (4)	They All Laughed (2)	(4)
Anything Goes (2)	Foggy Day (1)	Invitation (3)	Morning, Noon Or Night (3)	Too Close For Comfort (2)	You Showed Me The Way (1)
Avalon (4)	Give Me The Simple Life (1)	It Could Happen To You (2)	My Funny Valentine (1)	Trust In Me (1)	
Baby, Don't You Cry (4)	Gone With The Wind (4)	It Will Have To Do Until The	Night Mist (2)	What Do You Know About Love	
Best Thing For You (4)	How Does It Feel? (3)	Real Thing Comes Along (4)	No Moon At All (3)	(3)	
Broadway (3)	How High The Moon (4)	Late, Late Show (1)	Party's Over (3)	What Do You See In Her? (1)	
But Not For Me (4)	I Never Dreamt (You'd Fall In	Let Me Know (4)	Say It Ain't So, Joe (1)	When Lights Are Low (4)	
Can't Live Without 'Em	Love With Me) (3)	Let Me Off Uptown (2)	Some Other Spring (2)	When Sunny Gets Blue (2)	
Anymore (3)	I Wonder (2)	Little Girl Blue (2)	Song Is You (4)	Willow Weep For Me (4)	

STATUS QUO, The   '76

Rock group from London: Francis Michael Rossi (vocals, guitar), Rick Parfitt (guitar), Roy Lynes (organ), Alan Lancaster (bass) and John Coughlin (drums).

4/17/76 148 7 © Status Quo .... **$12** Capitol 11509

Blue For You   Is There A Better Way (1)   Mystery Song   Ring Of A Change   That's A Fact
Ease Your Mind   Mad About The Boy   Rain   Rolling Home

STEADY B   '87

Born Warren McGlone in Philadelphia. Male rapper.

10/31/87 149 7 1 What's My Name .... **$10** Jive 1060
10/22/88 193 1 © 2 Let The Hustlers Play .... **$10** Jive 1122

Believe Me Das Bad (1)   Funky Drummer (1)   I Got Cha (2)   On The Real Tip (2)   Through Thick-N-Thin (2)   What's My Name (1)
Certified Dope (2)   Gangster Rockin' (1)   Introduction (1)   Rockin' Music (1)   Turn It Loose (2)   Who's Makin' Ya Dance (2)
Do What You Wanna Do (2)   Hill Top (1)   Let The Hustlers Play (2)   Rong Ho'le (1)   Undertaker, The (2)   Ya Know My Rucka (2)
Don't Disturb This Groove (1)   Hold It Now (1)   My Benz (1)   Serious (2)   Use Me (1)

STEADY MOBB'N   '97

Male rap duo from New Orleans: Billy Bathgate and Crooked Eye.

5/24/97 29 9 © 1 Pre-Meditated Drama .... **$10** No Limit 50704
12/12/98 82 2 © 2 Black Mafia .... **$10** No Limit 50026

Animosity (1)   Check Ya Nuts (1)   Heaven Or Hell (2)   Lil N (1)   Papa Didn't Raise No Punks (2)   Trouble (1)
Block Monters (1)   Crosses Artist (2)   Hit A Lick (2)   Lil' Niggas (2)   Plead My Case (2)   Trying To Get Mine (1)
Blood Money (1)   Dice Game (1)   If I Could Change (1)   MG Theme (2)   Puff Puff Pass (1)   Turn Me Up (2)
'Bout Dat Mess (2)   Family Ties (2)   It's On (1)   Mr. Serv-On (1)   Stick Up (2)   Up To No Good (1)
Call Back (1)   4 Corners (1)   Kidnap Call (1)   Niggas Like Me (2)   Still Hustlin' (2)   West To South (1)
Carry On (2)   Ghetto Life (2)   Light Green And Remmy (2)   No One (2)   Strong Heart (1)   When Them Killas Call (2)

STEALERS WHEEL   '73

Pop-rock duo from Scotland: **Gerry Rafferty** (vocals, guitar) and Joe Egan (vocals, keyboards).

2/24/73 50 22 © 1 Stealers Wheel .... **$15** A&M 4377
4/13/74 181 3 2 Ferguslie Park .... **$15** A&M 4419

Another Meaning (1)   Gets So Lonely (1)   Next To Me (1)   Steamboat Row (2)   Wheelin' (2)
Back On My Feet Again (2)   Good Businessman (2)   Nothing's Gonna Make Me   **Stuck In The Middle With You**   You Put Something Better
Blind Faith (2)   I Get By (1)   Change My Mind (2)   (1) *6*   Inside Of Me (1)
Everyone's Agreed That   Johnny's Song (1)   Outside Looking In (1)   Waltz (You Know It Makes
Everything Will Turn Out   Jose (1)   Over My Head (2)   Sense!) (2)
Fine (2) *49*   Late Again (1)   **Star** (2) *29*   What More Could You Want (2)

STEALIN HORSES   '88

Rock-country band from Lexington, Kentucky: Kiya Heartwood (vocals), Mandy Meyer (guitar), John Durno (bass) and Kopana Terry (drums). Band name is an ancient Native American rite of passage in which young warriors stole horses from nearby tribes.

6/25/88 146 12 © Stealin Horses .... **$10** Arista 8520

Ballad Of The Pralltown Cafe   Gotta Get A Letter   Rain   Turnaround   Well, The
Dyin' By The Gun   Harriet Tubman   Tangled   Walk Away   Where All The Rivers Run

STEAM   '70

Group from Bridgeport, Connecticut. "Na Na Hey Hey Kiss Him Goodbye" was recorded by the trio of Gary DeCarlo, Paul Leka and Dale Frashur, and released as by Steam. After the song became a hit, Leka assembled an actual Steam group to record the album: Bill Steer (vocals), Jay babins and Tom Zuke (guitars), Hank Schorz (keyboards), Mike Daniels (bass) and Ray Corries (drums).

1/10/70 84 13 Steam .... **$20** Mercury 61254

Come On Back And Love Me   I'm The One Who Loves You   **I've Gotta Make You Love**   It's The Magic In You Girl   **Na Na Hey Hey Kiss Him**   New Breed, Now Generation
Come On Home Girl   I've Cried A Million Tears   **Me** *46*   Love & Affection   **Goodbye** *1*   One Good Woman

STEEL BREEZE   '82

Pop group from Sacramento, California: Ric Jacobs (vocals), Ken Goorabian and Waylin Carpenter (guitars), Rod Toner (keyboards), Vinnie Pantleoni (bass) and Barry Lowenthal (drums).

9/18/82 50 28 © Steel Breeze .... **$10** RCA Victor 4424

All I Ever Wanted To Do   Every Night   Lost In The 80's   **You Don't Want Me**
Can't Stop This Feeling   I Can't Wait   Street Talkin'   **Anymore** *16*
Dreamin' Is Easy *30*   I Think About You   Who's Gonna Love You Tonight

STEELEYE SPAN   '75

Folk group formed in London: Maddy Prior (vocals), Tim Hart and Martin Carthy (guitars), John Kilpatrick (accordian), Rick Kemp (bass) and Nigel Pegrum (drums).

12/6/75 143 6 © 1 All Around My Hat .... **$15** Chrysalis 1091
3/25/78 191 3 © 2 Storm Force Ten .... **$12** Chrysalis 1151

All Around My Hat (1)   Black Freighter (Pirate Jenny)   Dance With Me (1)   Seventeen Come Sunday (2)   Treadmill Song (2)
Awake, Awake (2)   (2)   Gamble Gold (medley) (1)   Some Rival (2)   Victory, The (2)
Batchelors Hall (1)   Black Jack Davy (1)   Hard Times Of Old England (1)   Sum Waves (Tunes) (1)   Wife Of The Soldier (2)
   Cadgwith Anthem (1)   Robin Hood (medley) (1)   Sweep, Chimney Sweep (2)   Wife Of Ushers Well (1)

STEELHEART   '91

Hard-rock group from Norwalk, Connecticut: Michael Matijevic (vocals), Chris Risola and Frank Dicostanzo (guitars), Jimmy Ward (bass) and John Fowler (drums).

9/22/90+ 40 59 ● © 1 Steelheart .... **$10** MCA 6368
6/27/92 144 7 © 2 Tangled In Reins .... **$10** MCA 10426

All Your Love (2)   Everybody Loves Eileen (1)   Like Never Before (1)   Rock 'N Roll (I Just Wanna) (1)   Take Me Back Home (2)
Can't Stop Me Loving You (1)   Gimme Gimme (1)   Loaded Mutha (2)   **She's Gone (Lady)** (1) *59*
Dancin' In The Fire (2)   **I'll Never Let You Go (Angel**   Love Ain't Easy (1)   Sheila (1)
Down N' Dirty (1)   **Eyes)** (1) *23*   Love 'Em And I'm Gone (2)   Steelheart (2)
Electric Love Child (2)   Late For The Party (2)   Mama Don't You Cry (2)   Sticky Side Up (2)

STEEL PULSE '82

Reggae group formed in Birmingham, England: David Hinds (vocals, guitar), Selwyn Brown (keyboards), Alphonso Martin (percussion), Alvin Ewen (bass) and Steve Nesbitt (drums).

DEBUT	PEAK	WKS		CD			Catalog		$	Label & Number
7/17/82	120	13	©	1	**True Democracy**				$10	Elektra 60113
3/31/84	154	12	©	2	**Earth Crisis**				$10	Elektra 60315
7/23/88	127	7	©	3	**State of...Emergency**				$10	MCA 42192

Blues Dance Raid (1)
Bodyguard (2)
Chant A Psalm (1)
Dead End Circuit (3)
Disco Drop Out (3)

Dub' Marcus Say (1)
Earth Crisis (2)
Find It...Quick! (1)
Grab Education (2)
Hijacking (3)

Leggo Beast (1)
Love This Reggae Music (3)
Man No Sober (1)
Melting Pot (3)
P.U.S.H. (3)

Rally Round (1)
Ravers (1)
Reaching Out (3)
Roller Skates (2)
Said You Was An Angel (3)

State Of Emergency (3)
Steal A Kiss (3)
Steppin' Out (2)
Throne Of Gold (3)
Tightrope (2)

Who Responsible? (1)
Wild Goose Chase (2)
Your House (1)

STEELY DAN ★131★ '77

Pop-rock/jazz-styled group formed in Los Angeles by **Donald Fagen** and Walter Becker. Group, primarily known as a studio unit, featured Fagen and Becker with various studio musicians. Duo split from 1981-92. Inducted into the Rock and Roll Hall of Fame in 2001.

1)Aja 2)Two Against Nature 3)Pretzel Logic

DEBUT	PEAK	WKS		CD			Catalog		$	Label & Number
12/2/72+	17	59	▲ ©	1	**Can't Buy A Thrill**		C:#13/181		$12	ABC 758
7/21/73	35	34	● ©	2	**Countdown To Ecstasy**		C:#20/43		$12	ABC 779
3/30/74	8	36	▲ ©	3	**Pretzel Logic**		C:#24/30		$12	ABC 808
4/12/75	13	26	▲ ©	4	**Katy Lied**		C:#19/77		$12	ABC 846
5/22/76	15	29	▲ ©	5	**The Royal Scam**		C:#22/53		$12	ABC 931
10/15/77	3	60	▲² ©	6	**Aja**		C:#2²/278		$12	ABC 1006
11/18/78+	30	22	▲ ©	7	**Greatest Hits**		[G]		$15	ABC 1107 [2]
12/6/80+	9	36	▲ ©	8	**Gaucho**		C:#11/186		$10	MCA 6102
7/3/82	115	9	● ©	9	**Gold**		[G]		$10	MCA 5324
11/4/95	40	5	©	10	**Alive In America**		[L]		$10	Giant 24634
3/18/00	6	30	▲ ©	11	**Two Against Nature**				$10	Giant 24719

2000 Grammy winner: Album of the Year

DEBUT	PEAK	WKS		CD			Catalog		$	Label & Number
4/21/01	50ᶜ	1	● ©	12	**A Decade Of Steely Dan**		[G]		$10	MCA 5570

Aja (6,10)
Almost Gothic (11)
Any Major Dude Will Tell You (3,7)
Any World (That I'm Welcome To) (4)
Babylon Sisters (8,9,10,12)
Bad Sneakers (4,7,12)
Barrytown (3)
Black Cow (6,9)
Black Friday (4,7,12) *37*
Bodhisattva (2,7,10,12)
Book Of Liars (10)
Boston Rag (2)

Brooklyn (1)
Caves Of Altamira (5)
Chain Lightning (4,9)
Change Of The Guard (1)
Charlie Freak (3)
Cousin Dupree (11)
Daddy Don't Live In That New York City No More (4)
Deacon Blues (6,9,12) *19*
Dirty Work (1)
Do It Again (1,7,12) *6*
Doctor Wu (4,7)
Don't Take Me Alive (5)

East St. Louis Toodle-oo (3,7,12)
Everyone's Gone To The Movies (4)
Everything You Did (5)
FM (No Static At All) (9,12) *22*
Fez, The (5,7) *59*
Fire In The Hole (1)
Gaslighting Abbie (11)
Gaucho (8)
Glamour Profession (8)
Green Earrings (5,9,10)
Haitian Divorce (5,7)
Here At The Western World (7)

Hey Nineteen (8,9,12) *10*
Home At Last (6)
I Got The News (6)
Jack Of Speed (11)
Janie Runaway (11)
Josie (6,7,10) *26*
Kid Charlemagne (5,7,10,12) *82*
King Of The World (2,9)
Kings (1)
Midnite Cruiser (1)
Monkey In Your Soul (3)
My Old School (2,7,12) *63*
My Rival (8)

Negative Girl (11)
Night By Night (3)
Only A Fool Would Say That (1)
Parker's Band (3)
Pearl Of The Quarter (2)
Peg (6,7,10,12) *11*
Pretzel Logic (3,7) *57*
Razor Boy (2)
Reeling In The Years (1,7,10,12) *11*
Rikki Don't Lose That Number (3,7,12) *4*
Rose Darling (4)
Royal Scam (5)

Show Biz Kids (2,7) *61*
Sign In Stranger (5,10)
Third World Man (8,10)
Through With Buzz (3)
Throw Back The Little Ones (4)
Time Out Of Mind (8) *22*
Turn That Heartbeat Over Again (1)
Two Against Nature (11)
West Of Hollywood (11)
What A Shame About Me (11)
With A Gun (3)
Your Gold Teeth (2)
Your Gold Teeth II (4)

STEINBERG, David '71

Born on 8/9/42 in Winnipeg, Manitoba, Canada. TV and movie comedian/producer/director.

DEBUT	PEAK	WKS		CD			Catalog		$	Label & Number
1/23/71	182	6			**Disguised As A Normal Person**		[C]		$15	Elektra 74065

Coast, The
Contact Lenses
Cute

Dating Game
Dr. Reuben
Jezebel

Joshua
Judy Disney
Lot

Lying
Moses
Phone Call

Sermon Introduction

STEINMAN, Jim '81

Born on 11/1/47 in New York City. Songwriter/pianist/producer. Produced songs for **Meat Loaf**, **Air Supply** and **Bonnie Tyler**.

DEBUT	PEAK	WKS		CD			Catalog		$	Label & Number
5/16/81	63	17	©		**Bad For Good**				$12	Cleveland Int'l. 36531

bonus 7" single included with album

Bad For Good
Dance In My Pants
Left In The Dark

Lost Boys And Golden Girls
Love And Death And An American Guitar

Out Of The Frying Pan (And Into The Fire)
Rock And Roll Dreams Come Through *32*

Stark Raving Love
Storm, The
Surf's Up

STEPHENSON, Van '84

Born on 11/4/53 in Hamilton, Ohio. Died of cancer on 4/8/2001 (age 47). Singer/songwriter. Member of **Blackhawk**.

DEBUT	PEAK	WKS		CD			Catalog		$	Label & Number
6/2/84	54	20			**Righteous Anger**				$10	MCA 5482

All American Boy
Cure Will Kill You

Don't Do That
Heart Over Mind

I Know Who You Are (And I Saw What You Did)

Modern Day Delilah *22*
Others Only Dream

Righteous Anger
What The Big Girls Do *45*

You've Been Lied To Before

STEPPENWOLF ★189★ '68

Hard-rock group formed in Los Angeles: **John Kay** (vocals, guitar), Mars Bonfire (guitar), Goldy McJohn (keyboards), Nick St. Nicholas (bass) and Jerry Edmonton (drums). Many personnel changes with Kay the only constant member. Edmonton died in a car crash on 11/28/93 (age 47). Group named after a Herman Hesse novel.

1)The Second 2)Steppenwolf 3)Steppenwolf 'Live'

DEBUT	PEAK	WKS			#	Title		$	Label & Number
3/9/68	6	87	●	©	1	**Steppenwolf**		$25	Dunhill/ABC 50029
10/5/68+	3	52	●	©	2	**The Second**		$25	Dunhill/ABC 50037
3/15/69	7	29		©	3	**At Your Birthday Party**		$25	Dunhill/ABC 50053
7/5/69	29	19		©	4	**Early Steppenwolf**	[E-L]	$20	Dunhill/ABC 50060
						recorded in 1967 when band was known as Sparrow			
11/15/69+	17	46	●	©	5	**Monster**		$20	Dunhill/ABC 50066
4/18/70	7	53	●	©	6	**Steppenwolf 'Live'**	[L]	$25	Dunhill/ABC 50075 [2]
11/21/70	19	17	●	©	7	**Steppenwolf 7**		$20	Dunhill/ABC 50090
3/6/71	24	36			8	**Steppenwolf Gold/Their Great Hits**	[G]	$20	Dunhill/ABC 50099
10/2/71	54	11		©	9	**For Ladies Only**		$20	Dunhill/ABC 50110
6/17/72	62	13			10	**Rest In Peace**	[K]	$20	Dunhill/ABC 50124
2/24/73	152	9	●	©	11	**16 Greatest Hits**	C:#4/254 [G]	$20	Dunhill/ABC 50135
9/21/74	47	12			12	**Slow Flux**		$15	Mums 33093
9/20/75	155	4			13	**Hour Of The Wolf**		$12	Epic 33583
9/26/87	171	4			14	**Rock & Roll Rebels**		$10	Qwil 1560

JOHN KAY & STEPPENWOLF

America (medley) (5)
Annie, Annie Over (13)
Another's Lifetime (13)
Ball Crusher (7)
Berry Rides Again (1)
Black Pit (9)
Born To Be Wild (1,6,8,11) **2**
Caroline (Are You Ready For The Outlaw World) (13)
Cat Killer (3)
Chicken Wolf (3)
Children Of Night (12)
Corina, Corina (4,6)
Desperation (1,10)
Disappointment Number (Unknown) (2)
Don't Cry (3)
Don't Step On The Grass, Sam (2,6,10)

Draft Resister (5,6)
Earschplittenloudenboomer (7)
Everybody Knows You (14)
Everybody's Next One (1,10)
Fag (5)
Faster Than The Speed Of Life (2)
Fat Jack (7)
Fishin' In The Dark (12)
Foggy Mental Breakdown (7,10)
Fool's Fantasy (12)
For Ladies Only (9,11) **64**
Forty Days And Forty Nights (7)
From Here To There Eventually (5,6)
Gang War Blues (12)
Get Into The Wind (9)
Girl I Knew (1)
Give Me Life (14)

Give Me News I Can Use (14)
God Fearing Man (3)
Happy Birthday (3)
Hard Rock Road (13)
Hey Lawdy Mama (6,8,11) **35**
Hippo Stomp (7,10)
Hodge, Podge, Strained Through A Leslie (2)
Hold On (Never Give Up, Never Give In) (14)
Hootchie Kootchie Man (1)
Howlin' For My Darlin' (4)
I'm Asking (9)
I'm Goin' Upstairs (4)
In Hopes Of A Garden (9)
It's Never Too Late (3,8,11) **51**
Jaded Strumpet (9)
Jeraboah (12)
Jupiter's Child (3,8,11)

Just For Tonight (13)
Justice Don't Be Slow (12)
Lost And Found By Trial And Error (2)
Lovely Meter (3)
Magic Carpet Ride (2,6,8,11) **3**
Man On A Mission (14)
Mango Juice (3)
Monster (5,6,11) **39**
Morning Blue (12)
Move Over (5,8,11) **31**
Mr. Penny Pincher (13)
Night Time's For You (9)
None Of Your Doing (2,10)
Ostrich, The (1,10)
Power Play (4,5,6)
Pusher, The (1,4,6,8,11)
Rage (14)
Reflections (2)

Renegade (7,10)
Replace The Face (14)
Resurrection (2)
Ride With Me (9,11) **52**
Rock & Roll Rebels (14)
Rock Me (3,8,11) **10**
Rock Steady (I'm Rough And Ready) (14)
Round And Down (3)
Screaming Night Hog (8,11) **62**
Shackles And Chains (9)
She'll Be Better (3)
Sleeping Dreaming (3)
Smokey Factory Blues (12)
Snow Blind Friend (7,11) **60**
Someone Told A Lie (13)
Sookie Sookie (1,6,8,11)
Sparkle Eyes (9)

Spiritual Fantasy (2)
Straight Shootin' Woman (12) **29**
Suicide (medley) (5)
Take What You Need (1,10)
Tenderness (9,11)
Tighten Up Your Wig (2,4,6)
Turn Out The Lights (14)
28 (2)
Twisted (6)
Two For The Love Of One (13)
What Would You Do (If I Did That To You) (5)
Who Needs Ya (7,8,11) **54**
Your Wall's Too High (1,10)

STEPS '00

Pop vocal group from England: Lisa Scott-Lee, Ian Watkins, Claire Richards, Lee Latchford-Evans and Faye Tozer.

3/4/00	79	10	©	**Step One**		$10	Jive 41688

After The Love Has Gone
Better The Devil You Know

Deeper Shade Of Blue 5, 6, 7, 8

Heartbeat
Last Thing On My Mind

Love's Got A Hold Of My Heart
One For Sorrow

Say You'll Be Mine
Stay With Me

Tragedy

STEREOLAB '97

Experimental-rock group formed in London: Laetitia Sadier and Mary Hansen (vocals), Tim Gane (guitar), Morgane Lhote (organ), Richard Harrison (bass) and Andy Ramsay (drums).

10/11/97	111	2	©	1	**Dots And Loops**		$10	Elektra 62065
10/9/99	154	1	©	2	**Cobra And Phases Group Play Voltage In The Milky Night**		$10	Elektra 62409

Blips Drips And Strips (2)
Blue Milk (2)
Brakhage (1)
Caleidoscopic Gaze (2)
Come And Play In The Milky Night (2)

Contronatura (1)
Diagonals (1)
Emergency Hisses (2)
Flower Called Nowhere (1)
Free Design (2)
Fuses (2)

Infinity Girl (2)
Italian Shoes Continuum (2)
Miss Modular (1)
Op Hop Detonation (2)
Parsec (1)
People Do It All The Time (2)

Prisoner Of Mars (1)
Puncture In The Radax Permutation (2)
Rainbo Conversation (1)
Refractions In The Plastic Pulse (1)

Spiracles, The (2)
Strobo Acceleration (2)
Ticker-Tape Of The Unconscious (1)
Velvet Water (2)

STEREO MC'S '93

Dance trio from London: Rob Birch, Nick Hallam and Owen Rossiter.

3/27/93	92	29	©	**Connected**		$10	Gee Street 514061

All Night Long
Chicken Shake
Connected 20

Creation
Don't Let Up
End, The

Everything
Fade Away
Ground Level

Playing With Fire
Pressure
Sketch

Step It Up **58**

STEREOMUD '01

Hard-rock group formed in New York City: Eric Rogers (vocals), John Fattoruso and Joey Z (guitars), Corey Lowery (bass) and Dan Richardson (drums). Joey Z and Richardson were members of **Life Of Agony**.

6/9/01	142	3	©	**Perfect Self**		$10	Loud 85483

Closer Now
Don't Be Afraid
Down From Here

Get Me Out
How We Stand
Leave (Back Up)

Lost Your Faith
Old Man
Pain

Perfect Self
Steppin Away
Sunlight

What

STEREOPHONICS '01

Rock trio from Cwmaman, South Wales: Kelly Jones (vocals, guitar), Richard Jones (bass) and Stuart Cable (drums).

5/5/01	188	1	©	**Just Enough Education To Perform**		$10	V2 27092

Caravan Holiday
Everyday I Think Of Money

Have A Nice Day
Lying In The Sun

Maybe
Mr. Writer

Nice To Be Out
Rooftop

Step On My Old Size Nines
Vegas Two Times

Watch Them Fly Sundays

STEVENS, April — see TEMPO, Nino

STEVENS, Cat ★192★   '72

Born Steven Georgiou on 7/21/47 in London. Pop-folk singer/songwriter/guitarist. Began career playing folk music at Hammersmith College in 1966. Contracted tuberculosis in 1968 and spent over a year recuperating. Adopted new style when he re-emerged. Lived in Brazil in the mid-1970s. Converted to Muslim religion in 1979; took name Yusef Islam.

1)Catch Bull At Four 2)Buddha And The Chocolate Box 3)Teaser And The Firecat

DEBUT	PEAK	WKS	RIAA	CD	#	Album Title	Catalog/Sym	$	Label & Number
2/6/71	8	79	▲³	©	1	**Tea for the Tillerman**		$15	A&M 4280
3/20/71	164	16	●	©	2	**Mona Bone Jakon**		$15	A&M 4260
						first released in 1970			
4/3/71	173	12		©	3	**Matthew & Son/New Masters**	[E]	$20	Deram 18005/10 [2]
						Matthew & Son first released in 1967 on Deram 18005 ($20) / New Masters first released in 1968 on Deram 18010 ($15)			
10/9/71	2¹	67	▲³	©	4	**Teaser And The Firecat**		$15	A&M 4313
1/8/72	94	10			5	**Very Young And Early Songs**	[E]	$15	Deram 18061
10/14/72	❶³	48	▲	©	6	**Catch Bull At Four**		$12	A&M 4365
7/28/73	3	43	●	©	7	**Foreigner**		$12	A&M 4391
4/13/74	2³	36	▲	©	8	**Buddha And The Chocolate Box**		$12	A&M 3623
7/12/75	6	45	▲⁴	©	9	**Greatest Hits**	C:#8/4 [G]	$12	A&M 4519
12/13/75+	13	19	●	©	10	**Numbers**		$12	A&M 4555
5/21/77	7	23	●	©	11	**Izitso**		$12	A&M 4702
12/23/78+	33	15		©	12	**Back To Earth**		$12	A&M 4735
12/15/84	165	8	●	©	13	**Footsteps In The Dark - Greatest Hits, Volume Two**	[K]	$10	A&M 3736
4/15/00	58	38		©	14	**The Very Best Of Cat Stevens**	[G]	$10	A&M 541387

Angelsea (6)
Another Saturday Night (9,14) *6*
Artist, The (12)
Baby, Get Your Head Screwed On (3)
Bad Brakes (12) *83*
Bad Night (5)
Bad Penny (8)
Banapple Gas (10) *41*
Bitterblue (4)
Blackness Of The Night (3)
Bonfire (11)
Boy With A Moon & Star On His Head (6)
Bring Another Bottle (3)
But I Might Die Tonight (1)
Can't Keep It In (6,9,14)
Ceylon City (3)
Changes IV (4)
Child For A Day (11)
Come On & Dance (5)
Come On Baby (5)

Crazy (11)
Daytime (12,13)
Don't Be Shy (13)
Drywood (10)
18th Avenue (6)
Father (12)
Father & Son (1,9,13,14)
Fill My Eyes (medley) (2)
First Cut Is The Deepest (3,14)
Foreigner Suite (7,14)
Freezing Steel (9)
Ghost Town (8)
Hard-Headed Woman (1,9,14)
Here Comes My Baby (3)
Here Comes My Wife (5)
Home (10)
Home In The Sky (8)
How Can I Tell You (4,13)
How Many Times (7)
Humming Bird (5)
Hurt, The (7,13) *31*
I Love My Dog (3)
I Love Them All (3)

(I Never Wanted) To Be A Star (11,13)
I See A Road (3)
I Think I See The Light (2)
I Want To Live In A Wigwam (13)
I Wish, I Wish (2)
I'm Gonna Be King (3)
I'm Gonna Get A Gun (3)
I'm So Sleepy (3)
I've Found A Love (3)
I've Got A Thing About Seeing My Grandson Grow Old (14)
If I Laugh (4)
If You Want To Sing Out, Sing Out (13)
Image Of Hell (5)
Into White (1)
It's A Super Duper Life (5)
Jesus (8)
Just Another Night (12,14)
Jzero (10)
Katmandu (2,13)

Killin' Time (11)
King Of Trees (8)
Kitty (3)
Kypros (11)
Lady (3)
Lady D'Arbanville (2,14)
Land O' Freelove & Goodbye (10)
Last Love Song (12)
Later (7)
Laughing Apple (3)
Life (11)
Lilywhite (2)
Longer Boats (1)
Lovely City (5)
Majik Of Majiks (10,14)
Matthew And Son (3,14)
Maybe You're Right (2)
Miles From Nowhere (4)
Mona Bone Jakon (2)
Monad's Anthem (10)
Moon Shadow (4,9) *30*
Moonshadow (14)

Moonstone (3)
Morning Has Broken (4,9,14) *6*
Music (8)
Nascimento (12)
Never (12)
New York Times (12)
Northern Wind (3)
Novim's Nightmare (10)
O Caritas (6)
Oh Very Young (8,9,14) *10*
On The Road To Findout (1,13)
100 I Dream (7)
Peace Train (4,9,14) *7*
Pop Star (2)
Randy (12)
Ready (8,9) *26*
(Remember The Days Of The) Old Schoolyard (11,14) *33*
Rubylove (4)
Ruins (6)
Sad Lisa (1)
School Is Out (3)

Shift That Log (3)
Silent Sunlight (6,13)
Sitting (6,9,14) *16*
Smash Your Heart (3)
Speak To The Flowers (3)
Sun/C79 (8)
Sweet Jamaica (11)
Sweet Scarlet (5)
Tea For The Tillerman (1)
Time (medley) (2)
Tramp, The (5)
Trouble (2,13)
Two Fine People (9) *33*
View From The Top (5)
Was Dog A Doughnut (11) *70*
Where Are You (5)
Where Do The Children Play (1,13,14)
Whistlestar (10)
Wild World (1,9,14) *11*
Wind, The (4,13,14)

STEVENS, Ray   '71

Born Harold Ray Ragsdale on 1/24/39 in Clarkdale, Georgia. Country-novelty singer/songwriter. Hosted own TV variety show in 1970. Also recorded as Henhouse Five Plus Too.

1)Everything Is Beautiful 2)Gitarzan 3)Ray Stevens' Greatest Hits

DEBUT	PEAK	WKS	RIAA	CD	#	Album Title	Catalog/Sym	$	Label & Number
9/15/62	135	2			1	**1,837 seconds of Humor**	[N]	$50	Mercury 60732
6/21/69	57	13		©	2	**Gitarzan**	[N]	$20	Monument 18115
6/13/70	35	19			3	**Everything Is Beautiful**		$15	Barnaby 35005
12/12/70+	141	8			4	**Ray Stevens...Unreal!!!**		$15	Barnaby 30092
9/4/71	95	8			5	**Ray Stevens' Greatest Hits**	C:#28/6 [G]	$15	Barnaby 30770
2/5/72	175	9			6	**Turn Your Radio On**		$15	Barnaby 30809
6/15/74	159	11			7	**Boogity Boogity**	[N]	$12	Barnaby 6003
6/28/75	106	14			8	**Misty**	[N]	$12	Barnaby 6012
12/27/75+	173	4			9	**The Very Best of Ray Stevens**	[G]	$12	Barnaby 6018
3/15/80	132	8			10	**Shriner's Convention**	[N]	$12	RCA Victor 3574
1/19/85	118	19	▲		11	**He Thinks He's Ray Stevens**	[N]	$10	MCA 5517
1/23/93	36ᶜ	3	●	©	12	**His All-Time Greatest Comic Hits**	[G-N]	$10	Curb 77312

Ahab, The Arab (1,2,5,9,12) *5*
All My Trials (6) *70*
Alley Oop (2)
Along Came Jones (2,5) *27*
America, Communicate With Me (4,5) *45*
Bagpipes - That's My Bag (2,7)
Bridget The Midget (The Queen Of The Blues) (5,7,12) *50*
Brighter Day (3)
Can We Get To That (4)
Coin Machine (10)
Come Around (4)
Cow-Cow Boogie (8)
Deep Purple (8)
Don't Boogie Woogie (7)
Dooright Family (10)
Dream Girl (4)
Early In The Morning (3)

Erik The Awful (11)
Everything Is Beautiful (3,5,9) *1*
Fred (11)
Freddie Feelgood (And His Funky Little Five Piece Band) (2,7,12) *91*
Further More (1,11) *91*
Get Together (3)
Gitarzan (2,5,9,12) *8*
Glory Special (6)
Happy Hour (Is The Saddest Time Of The Day) (11)
Harry The Hairy Ape (2,5) *17*
Have A Little Talk With Myself (5,6)
Heart Transplant (7)
Hermit Named Dave (1)
Hey There (10)
I'll Fly Away (6)
I'm Kissin' You Goodbye (11)

Imitation Of Life (4)
In The Mood (12) *40*
Indian Love Call (8,9) *68*
Islands (4)
Isn't It Lonely Together (5)
It's Me Again, Margaret (11,12)
Jeremiah Peabody's Poly Unsaturated Quick Dissolving Fast Acting Pleasant Tasting Green And Purple Pills (1,9) *35*
Joggin' (11)
Julius Played The Trumpet (1)
Just So Proud To Be Here (7)
Lady Of Spain (8)
Last Laugh (10)
Leaving On A Jet Plane (3)
Let Your Love Be A Light Unto The People (6)
Little Egypt (2)

Love Lifted Me (6)
Loving You On Paper (4)
Mama And A Papa (6) *82*
Martha's Atom Bomb (2)
Mississippi Squirrel Revival (11,12)
Misty (8,9) *14*
Mockingbird Hill (8)
Monkees, Theme From The (11)
Monkey See, Monkey Do (4)
Moonlight Special (7,9) *73*
Mr. Businessman (5,9) *28*
Mr. Custer (2)
Nashville (9)
Ned Nostril (And His South Seas Paradise, Puts Your Blues On Ice, Cheap At Twice The Price Band - Ikky-Ikky, Ukky-Ukky) (11)
Night People (4)

Oh, Lonesome Me (8)
Oh! Will There Be Any Stars (6)
Over The Rainbow (8)
PFC Rhythm And Blues Jones (1)
Popeye And Olive Oil (1)
Put It In Your Ear (10)
Raindrops Keep Fallin' On My Head (3)
Rita's Letter (10)
Rock And Roll Show (1)
Rockin' Boppin' Waltz (1)
Romeo And Juliet (A Time For Us), Love Theme From (3)
Saturday Night At The Movies (1)
Scratch My Back (I Love It) (1)
She Belongs To Me (3)
She Came In Through The Bathroom Window (3)
Shriner's Convention (10,12)

Sir Thanks-A-Lot (2)
Smith And Jones (7)
Something (3)
Streak, The (7,9,12) *1*
Sunset Strip (4) *81*
Sunshine (8)
Take Care Of Business (8)
Talking (4)
Turn Your Radio On (6,9) *63*
Unwind (5,9) *52*
Walk A Mile In My Shoes (3)
Watch Song (10)
Why Don't You Lead Me To That Rock (4)
Would Jesus Wear A Rolex (12)
Yakety Yak (2)
Yes, Jesus Loves Me (6)
You're Never Goin' To Tampa With Me (10)
Young Love (8) *93*

STEVENS, Steve, Atomic Playboys '89

Born in Los Angeles. Rock guitarist. Member of **Billy Idol**'s band. The Atomic Playboys: Perry McCarty (vocals), Phil Ashley (keyboards) and Thommy Price (drums).

| 9/2/89 | 119 | 12 | | © | Steve Stevens Atomic Playboys | | | $10 | Warner 25920 |

Action
Atomic Playboys

Crackdown
Desperate Heart

Evening Eye
Pet The Hot Kitty

Power Of Suggestion
Run Across Desert Sands

Slipping Into Fiction
Soul On Ice

Woman Of 1,000 Years

STEVENSON, B.W. '73

Born Louis Stevenson on 10/5/49 in Dallas. Died of heart failure on 4/28/88 (age 38). B.W. is short for Buck Wheat.

| 9/15/73 | 45 | 14 | | | My Maria | | | $15 | RCA Victor 0088 |

Be My Woman Tonight
Good Love Is Like A Good
 Song

Grab On Hold Of My Soul
I Got To Boogie
Lucky Touch

My Maria *9*
Pass This Way
Remember Me

Shambala *66*
Sunset Woman

STEVIE B '91

Born Steven Hill in Miami. Pop singer/multi-instrumentalist.

7/23/88	78	21	●	©	1 Party Your Body			$10	LMR 5500
3/11/89	75	46	●	©	2 In My Eyes			$10	LMR 5531
7/21/90+	54	43	●	©	3 Love & Emotion			$10	LMR 2307

Baby I'm A Fool For Love (1)
**Because I Love You (The
 Postman Song)** (3) *1*
Broken Hearted (3)
Children Of Tomorrow (2)

Come With Me (2)
Day N' Night (1)
Dreamin' Of Love (1) *80*
Facts Of Love (3)
Forever More (3) *96*

Girl I Am Searching For You
 (2) *56*
I Came To Rock Your Body (2)
I Need You (1)
I Wanna Be The One (2) *32*

I'll Be By Your Side (3) *12*
In My Eyes (2) *37*
Lifetime Love Affair (2)
Love And Emotion (3) *15*
Love Me For Life (2) *29*

Memories Of Loving You (3)
No More Tears (1)
Party Your Body (1)
**Spring Love (Come Back To
 Me)** (1) *43*

Stop The Love (1)
We're Jammin' Now (3)
Who's Loving You Tonight (3)

STEWART, Al '77

Born on 9/5/45 in Glasgow, Scotland. Pop singer/songwriter/guitarist.

6/1/74	133	14		©	1 Past, Present And Future			$15	Janus 3063
3/1/75	30	23		©	2 Modern Times			$15	Janus 7012
10/9/76+	5	48	▲	©	3 Year Of The Cat			$15	Janus 7022
10/7/78	10	31	▲	©	4 Time Passages			$12	Arista 4190

above 3 produced by **Alan Parsons**

| 9/13/80 | 37 | 13 | | © | 5 24 Carrots | | | $12 | Arista 9520 |
| 11/14/81 | 110 | 11 | | | 6 Live/Indian Summer | | [L] | $15 | Arista 8607 [2] |

recorded on 4/29/81 at the Roxy in Hollywood

Almost Lucy (4)
Apple Cider Re-Constitution (2)
Broadway Hotel (3)
Carol (2)
Clarence Frogman Henry (6)
Constantinople (5)
Dark And The Rolling Sea (2)
Delia's Gone (6)
Ellis Island (medley) (5)

End Of The Day (4)
Flying Sorcery (3)
Here In Angola (5)
If It Doesn't Come Naturally,
 Leave It (3,6)
Indian Summer (6)
Last Day Of June 1934 (1)
Life In Dark Water (4)
Lord Grenville (3)
Man For All Seasons (4)

Merlin's Time (5,6)
Midas Shadow (3)
Midnight Rocks (5) *24*
Modern Times (5)
Mondo Sinistro (3)
Murmansk Run (medley) (5)
Next Time (2)
Nostradamus - Part One & Two
 (1,6)
Not The One (2)

Old Admirals (1)
On The Border (3,6) *42*
One Stage Before (3)
Optical Illusion (5)
Paint By Numbers (5)
Palace Of Versailles (4)
Pandora (6)
Post World War Two Blues (1)
Princess Olivia (6)
Roads To Moscow (1,6)

Rocks In The Ocean (5)
Running Man (5,6)
Sand In Your Shoes (3)
Sirens Of Titan (5)
Soho (Needless To Say) (1,6)
Song On The Radio (4) *29*
Terminal Eyes (1)
Time Passages (4,6) *7*
Timeless Skies (4)
Valentina Way (4,6)

Warren Harding (1)
What's Going On (2)
World Goes To Riyadh
 (medley) (6)
Year Of The Cat (3,6) *8*

STEWART, Amii '79

Born in 1956 in Washington DC. Disco singer/dancer/actress. In the Broadway musical *Bubbling Brown Sugar*.

| 3/17/79 | 19 | 23 | ● | | Knock On Wood | | | $12 | Ariola 50054 |

Am I Losing You
Bring It On Back To Me

Closest Thing To Heaven
Get Your Love Back

Knock On Wood *1*
**Light My Fire/137 Disco
Heaven** *69*

Only A Child In Your Eyes
You Really Touched My Heart

STEWART, Billy '65

Born on 3/24/37 in Washington DC. Died in a car crash on 1/17/70 (age 32). R&B singer/keyboardist. Nicknamed "Fat Boy."

| 7/3/65 | 97 | 10 | | | 1 I Do Love You | | | $75 | Chess 1496 |
| 5/7/66+ | 138 | 6 | | | 2 Unbelievable | | | $75 | Chess 1499 |

Almost Like Being In Love (2)
Canadian Sunset (2)
Count Me Out (1)
Fat Boy (1)
Fat Boy Can Cry (1)

Foggy Day (2)
I Do Love You (1) *26*
I'm No Romeo (1)
Keep Lovin' (2)
Love Is Here To Stay (2)

Misty (2)
Moon River (2)
My Funny Valentine (2)
Oh My! What Can The Matter
 Be (1)

Once Again (1)
Over The Rainbow (2)
Reap What You Sow (1) *79*
Sitting In The Park (1) *24*
Strange Feeling (1) *70*

Summertime (2) *10*
Sweet Senorita (1)
Teach Me Tonight (2)
That Old Black Magic (2)
Time After Time (2)

STEWART, Gary '80

Born on 5/28/45 in Letcher County, Kentucky. Country singer/songwriter/pianist.

| 8/16/80 | 165 | 3 | | © | Cactus And A Rose | | | $12 | RCA Victor 3627 |

Are We Dreamin' The Same
 Dream
Cactus And A Rose

Ghost Train
Harlan County Highway

How Could We Come To This
 After That
Lovers' Knot

Okeechobee Purple
 Roarin'
Staring Each Other Down

We Made It As Lovers (We Just
 Couldn't Make It As Friends)

STEWART, Jermaine '86

Born on 9/7/57 in Columbus, Ohio. Died of cancer on 3/17/97 (age 39). R&B singer/dancer.

3/2/85	90	11			1 The Word Is Out			$10	Arista 8261
6/14/86	32	25		©	2 Frantic Romantic			$10	Arista 8395
4/23/88	98	12		©	3 Say It Again			$10	Arista 8455

Brilliance (1)
Call It A Miracle (3)
Dance Floor (2)
Debbie (1)
Don't Ever Leave Me (2)

Don't Have Sex With Your Ex
 (3)
Don't Talk Dirty To Me (3)
Dress It Up (3)
Eyes (3)
Frantic Romantic (2)

Get Lucky (3)
Get Over It (1)
Give Your Love To Me (2)
Got To Be Love (3)
I Like It (1)
In Love Again (1)

Is It Really Love? (3)
Jody (2) *42*
Month Of Mondays (1)
Moonlight Carnival (2)
My House (3)
Out To Punish (2)

Reasons Why (1)
Say It Again (3) *27*
She's A Teaser (3)
Spies (1)
Versatile (2)

**We Don't Have To Take Our
 Clothes Off** (2) *5*
Word Is Out (1) *41*
You (1)

STEWART, John '79

Born on 9/5/39 in San Diego. Folk-pop singer/songwriter. Member of **The Kingston Trio** from 1961-67. Brother of Mike Stewart (drummer for **We Five**).

6/21/69	193	3		©	1 California Bloodlines			$15	Capitol 203
1/15/72	195	2		©	2 The Lonesome Picker Rides Again			$15	Warner 1948
7/6/74	195	2		©	3 The Phoenix Concerts-Live		[L]	$20	RCA Victor 0265 [2]

recorded March 1974 at the Phoenix Symphony Hall

DEBUT	PEAK	WKS	RIAA	CD	ARTIST — Album Title	Catalog	Sym	$	Label & Number
5/17/75	150	6			4 Wingless Angels			$15	RCA Victor 0816
11/26/77	126	8			5 Fire In The Wind			$12	RSO 3027
5/19/79	10	28		©	6 Bombs Away Dream Babies			$12	RSO 3051
4/12/80	85	10			7 Dream Babies Go Hollywood			$12	RSO 3074

Adelita (medley) (4)
All The Brave Horses (2)
Bolinas (2)
Boston Lady (5)
California Bloodlines (1,3)
Cody (3)
Comin' Out Of Nowhere (6)
Cops (3)
Crazy (2)
Daydream Believer (2)
18 Wheels (5)
Fire In The Wind (5)
Freeway Pleasure (2)
Gold (6) *5*

Hand Your Heart To The Wind (6)
Heart Of The Dream (6)
Hollywood Dreams (7)
Hung On The Heart (Of A Man Back Home) (4)
Josie (6)
July, You're A Woman (1,3)
Just An Old Love Song (2)
Kansas (3)
Kansas Rain (3)
Lady Of Fame (7)
Last Campaign Trilogy (3)

Last Hurrah (5)
Let The Big Horse Run (4)
Little Road And A Stone To Roll (2,3)
Lonesome Picker (1)
Lost Her In The Sun (6) *34*
Love Has Tied My Wings (7)
Mazatlan (medley) (4)
Midnight Wind (6) *28*
Missouri Bird (1)
Monterey (5)
Moonlight Rider (7)
Morning Thunder (5)
Mother Country (1,3)

Never Going Back (1,3)
Nightman (7)
(Odin) Spirit Of The Water (7)
Oldest Living Son (3)
Omaha Rainbow (1)
On You Like The Wind (5)
Over The Hill (6)
Pirates Of Stone County Road (1,3)
Promise The Wind (5)
Raven, The (7)
Razorback Woman (1)
Ride Stone Blind (4)
Road Shines Bright (2)

Rock It In My Own Sweet Time (5)
Roll Away The Stone (3)
Rose Water (4)
Runaway Fool Of Love (3,6)
Runner, The (5)
Shackles And Chains (1)
She Believes In Me (1)
Some Kind Of Love (4)
Somewhere Down The Line (6)
Spinnin' Of The World (6)
Summer Child (4)
Survivors (4)
Swift Lizard (2)

Touch Of The Sun (2)
Wheatfield Lady (3)
Wheels Of Thunder (7)
Wild Horse Road (2)
Wild Side Of You (5)
Wind On The River (7)
Wingless Angels (Survivors II) (4)
Wolves In The Kitchen (2)
You Can't Look Back (1,3)

STEWART, Rod ★31★ '71

Born on 1/10/45 in London. Pop-rock singer/songwriter. Member of the **Jeff Beck** Group from 1967-69. Member of **Faces** from 1969-75. Won Grammy's Living Legends Award in 1989. Married to actress Alana Hamilton from 1979-84. Married supermodel Rachel Hunter on 12/15/90. Inducted into the Rock and Roll Hall of Fame in 1994.

1)Every Picture Tells A Story 2)Blondes Have More Fun 3)Foot Loose & Fancy Free
4)Unplugged...And Seated 5)A Night On The Town

DEBUT	PEAK	WKS	RIAA	CD	ARTIST — Album Title	Catalog	Sym	$	Label & Number
12/13/69+	139	27		©	1 The Rod Stewart Album			$25	Mercury 61237
6/20/70	27	57		©	2 Gasoline Alley			$20	Mercury 61264
6/19/71	❶⁴	52	▲	©	3 Every Picture Tells A Story	C:#45/4		$15	Mercury 609
8/12/72	2³	36	●	©	4 Never A Dull Moment			$15	Mercury 646
7/7/73	31	25	●	©	5 Sing It Again Rod		[G]	$15	Mercury 680
1/5/74	63	11		©	6 Rod Stewart/Faces Live - Coast To Coast Overture and Beginners		[L]	$15	Mercury 697
10/26/74	13	14		©	7 Smiler			$15	Mercury 1017
9/6/75	9	29		©	8 Atlantic Crossing			$12	Warner 2875
5/15/76	90	26		©	9 The Best Of Rod Stewart		[G]	$15	Mercury 7507 [2]
7/17/76	2⁵	57	▲²	©	10 A Night On The Town			$12	Warner 2938
11/26/77+	2⁶	47	▲³	©	11 Foot Loose & Fancy Free			$12	Warner 3092
12/23/78+	❶³	37	▲⁴	©	12 Blondes Have More Fun			$12	Warner 3261
11/24/79+	22	19	▲³	©	13 Rod Stewart Greatest Hits	C:#30/6	[G]	$12	Warner 3373
12/6/80	12	21	▲		14 Foolish Behaviour			$12	Warner 3485
11/21/81	11	31	▲	©	15 Tonight I'm Yours			$12	Warner 3602
11/20/82	46	13	●	©	16 Absolutely Live		[L]	$15	Warner 23743 [2]
6/25/83	30	22		©	17 Body Wishes			$10	Warner 23877
6/30/84	18	35	●	©	18 Camouflage			$10	Warner 25095
7/12/86	28	19		©	19 Rod Stewart			$10	Warner 25446
6/4/88+	20	72	▲²	©	20 Out Of Order			$10	Warner 25684
12/2/89+	54	18	▲²	©	21 Storyteller/The Complete Anthology: 1964-1990		[K]	$25	Warner 25987 [4]
3/24/90	20	27	▲²	©	22 Downtown Train: Selections From The Storyteller Anthology ...C:#15/45		[G]	$10	Warner 26158
4/13/91	10	81	●	©	23 Vagabond Heart			$10	Warner 26300
6/12/93	2⁵	63	▲³	©	24 Unplugged...And Seated		[L]	$10	Warner 45289
6/24/95	35	16	●	©	25 A Spanner In The Works			$10	Warner 45867
11/30/96	19	41	▲	©	26 If We Fall In Love Tonight		[G]	$10	Warner 46452
6/20/98	44	14		©	27 When We Were The New Boys			$10	Warner 46792
2/24/01	50	8		©	28 Human			$10	Atlantic 83411

Ain't Love A Bitch (12) *22*
All For Love (26)
All In The Name Of Rock 'N' Roll (8)
All Right Now (18) *72*
Alright For An Hour (8)
Amazing Grace (medley) (6)
Angel (4,6,9,21) *40*
Another Heartache (19) *52*
Attractive Female Wanted (12)
Baby Jane (17,21) *14*
Bad For You (18)
Balltrap, The (10)
Best Days Of My Life (12)
Better Off Dead (14)
Big Bayou (10)
Blind Prayer (1)
Blondes (Have More Fun) (12)
Body Wishes (17)
Born Loose (11)
Borstal Boys (medley) (6)
Bring It On Home To Me (medley) (7)
Broken Arrow (23,26) *20*
Camouflage (18)
Can I Get A Witness? (21)
  recorded as Steampacket

Can We Still Be Friends (18)
Charlie Parker Loves Me (28)
Cigarettes And Alcohol (27)
Cindy's Lament (1)
Country Comforts (2,5,21)
Crazy About Her (20,21) *11*
Cut Across Shorty (2,6,9,21,24)
Da Ya Think I'm Sexy? (12,13,16,21) *1*
Dancin' Alone (1)
Delicious (25)
Dirty Old Town (1)
Dirty Weekend (12)
Dixie Toot (7)
Don't Come Around Here (with Helicopter Girl) (28)
Downtown Lights (25)
Downtown Train (21,22,26) *3*
Drift Away (21)
Dynamite (20,21)
Every Beat Of My Heart (19,21) *83*
Every Picture Tells A Story (3,6,9,21,24)
Farewell (7)
First Cut Is The Deepest (10,13,21,24,26) *21*

Fool For You (10)
Foolish Behaviour (14)
For The First Time (26)
Forever Young (20,21,22) *12*
Forever Young (1996) (26)
Gasoline Alley (2,5,9,16,21)
Get Back (21)
Ghetto Blaster (17)
Gi' Me Wings (14)
Girl From The North Country (7)
Go Out Dancing (23)
Good Morning Little Schoolgirl (21)
Great Pretender (16)
Guess I'll Always Love You (16)
Had Me A Real Good Time (7)
Handbags And Gladrags (1,5,9,21,24) *42*
Hang On St. Christopher (25)
Hard Road (7)
Have I Told You Lately (23,24,26) *5*
Having A Party (24) *36*
Heart Is On The Line (18)
Here To Eternity (19)
Highgate Shuffle (24)
Hot Legs (11,13,16,21,24) *28*

Hotel Chambermaid (27)
How Long (15) *49*
Human (28)
I Ain't Superstitious (21)
I Can't Deny It (28)
I Don't Want To Talk About It (8,13,16,21,22,26) *46*
(I Know) I'm Losing You (3,5,9,21) *24*
I Was Only Joking (11,13,21) *22*
I Wish It Would Rain (6)
I Wouldn't Ever Change A Thing (1)
Killing Of Georgie (Part I And II) (10,13,21,22) *30*
Lady Day (21)
Lady Luck (25)
Last Summer (21)
Leave Virginia Alone (25) *52*
Let Me Be Your Car (7,9,21)
Lethal Dose Of Love (20)
Little Miss Understood (21)
Little Queenie (medley) (16)
Lost In You (20,21) *12*
Lost Paraguayos (4,5)
Love Touch (19,21) *6*
Loveless (28)

Is That The Thanks I Get? (12)
It Takes Two (23)
It Was Love That We Needed (28)
It's All Over Now (2,6,9,21)
It's Not The Spotlight (8)
Italian Girls (4)
Jealous (15)
Jealous Guy (21)
Jo's Lament (2)
Jodie (9)
Just Like A Woman (15)

Maggie May (3,5,9,13,16,21,24) *1*
Mama You Been On My Mind (4)
Man Of Constant Sorrow (1)
Mandolin Wind (3,5,21,24)
Mine For Me (7,9) *91*
Moment Of Glory (23)
Motown Song (23) *10*
Move Me (17)
Muddy, Sam And Otis (25)
My Girl (14)
My Heart Can't Tell You No (20,21,22,26) *4*
My Way Of Giving (2)
Never Give Up On A Dream (15)
Night Like This (19)
No Holding Back (23)
Nobody Knows You When You're Down And Out (20)
Oh God, I Wish I Was Home Tonight (14,21)
Oh! No Not My Baby (9,21) *59*
Old Raincoat Won't Ever Let You Down (1,9)
Only A Boy (15)

STEWART, Rod — Cont'd

Only A Hobo (2)
Ooh La La (27) **39**
Passion (14,16,21,22) **5**
People Get Ready (21,22,24) **48**
Pinball Wizard (5,9,21)
Pretty Flamingo (10)
Purple Heather (25)
Ready Now (17)
Reason To Believe (3,5,21) **62**
Reason To Believe [live] (24) **19**
Rebel Heart (23)
Red Hot In Black (19)
Rhythm Of My Heart (23) **5**
Rock My Plimsoul (16)
Rocks (23)
Run Back Into Your Arms (28)
Sailing (8,13,16,21) **58**
Sailor (7,9)

Satisfied (25)
Say It Ain't True (14)
Scarred And Scared (12)
Secret Heart (27)
Seems Like A Long Time (3)
Shake (21)
Shapes Of Things (21)
She Won't Dance With Me (14,16)
Shelly My Love (27)
Smitten (28)
So Far Away (26)
So Much To Say (21)
So Soon We Change (14)
Some Guys Have All The Luck (18,21) **10**
Somebody Special (14) **71**
Sometimes When We Touch (26)
Sonny (15)

Soothe Me (25)
Soul On Soul (28)
Standin' In The Shadows Of Love (12)
Stay With Me (6,16,21,22,24) **17**
Still Love You (8)
Stone Cold Sober (8,21)
Strangers Again (17)
Street Fighting Man (1,5,9,21)
Stripper, The (16)
Superstar (27)
Sweet Lady Mary (21)
Sweet Little Rock 'N Roller (7,16,21)
Sweet Surrender (17)
Sweetheart Like You (25)
Tear It Up (15,16)
Ten Days Of Rain (19)
That's All Right (3)

This (25)
This Old Heart Of Mine (8) **83**
This Old Heart Of Mine (21,22) **10**
Three Time Loser (8)
To Be With You (28)
To Love Somebody (21)
Tom Traubet's Blues (Waltzing Matilda) (24)
Tomorrow Is Such A Long Time (3)
Tonight I'm Yours (Don't Hurt Me) (15,16,21) **20**
Tonight's The Night (Gonna Be Alright) (10,13,16,21,22,24,26) **1**
Too Bad (medley) (6)
Tora, Tora, Tora (Out With The Boys) (15)
Trade Winds (10)
Trouble (18)

True Blue (4,21)
Try A Little Tenderness (20)
Twisting The Night Away (4,5,21) **80**
Weak (27)
What Am I Gonna Do (I'm So In Love With You) (17,21) **35**
What Do You Want Me To Do? (27)
What's Made Milwaukee Famous (Has Made A Loser Out Of Me) (9,21)
When A Man's In Love (23)
When I Need You (26)
When I Was Your Man (20)
When We Were The New Boys (27)
Who's Gonna Take Me Home (The Rise And Fall Of A Budding Gigolo) (19)
Wild Horse (20)

Wild Side Of Life (10)
Windy Town (25)
You Are Everything (23)
You Can Make Me Dance, Sing Or Anything (21)
You Got A Nerve (11)
You Keep Me Hangin' On (11)
(You Make Me Feel Like) A Natural Man (7)
You Send Me (medley) (7)
You Wear It Well (4,5,9,21) **13**
You're In My Heart (The Final Acclaim) (11,13,16,21,26) **4**
You're Insane (11)
You're My Girl (I Don't Want To Discuss It) (2)
You're The Star (25)
Young Turks (15,16,21,22) **5**

STEWART, Sandy   '63

Born Sandra Galitz on 7/10/37 in Philadelphia. Pop singer. Regular on the **Eddie Fisher** and **Perry Como** variety TV shows.

4/6/63	**138**	2			My Coloring Book			$25	Colpix 441

Beautiful Brown Eyes
Deep Purple
Greensleeves

Ivy Rose
Little Girl Blue
Little White Lies

My Coloring Book 20
Over The Rainbow
Red Sails In The Sunset

Scarlet Ribbons
Tangerine

Where The Blue Of The Night Meets The Gold Of The Day

STEWART, Wynn   '67

Born on 6/7/34 in Morrisville, Missouri. Died of a heart attack on 7/17/85 (age 51). Country singer/songwriter/guitarist.

7/22/67	**158**	8			It's Such A Pretty World Today			$20	Capitol 2737

Angels Don't Lie
'Cause I Have You
Half Way In Love

I Keep Forgettin' That I Forgot About You
It's Such A Pretty World Today

Let's Pretend We're Kids Again
Ol' What's Her Name
Out There Is Your World

Tourist, The
Unfaithful Arms
You Told Him

You Can Always Give Her Back To Me

STICKY FINGAZ   '01

Born Kirk Jones in New York City. Male rapper. Member of **Onyx**.

6/9/01	**44**	5		©	[Black Trash] The Autobiography Of Kirk Jones			$10	Universal 157990

Baby Brother
Cheatin'
Come On

Get It Up
Ghetto
Kirk Jones Conscience

Licken Off In Hip-Hop
Money Talks
My Dogz Iz My Gunz

Not Die'n
Oh My God
Sister I'm Sorry

State Vs. Kirk Jones
What Chu Want
What If I Was White

Why
Wonderful World

STIGERS, Curtis   '92

Born in Boise, Idaho. Pop singer/saxophonist.

11/9/91+	**101**	28		©	Curtis Stigers			$10	Arista 18660

Count My Blessings
I Guess It Wasn't Mine
I Keep Telling Myself
I Wonder Why 9

Last Time I Said Goodbye
Man You're Gonna Fall In Love With
Never Saw A Miracle

Nobody Loves You Like I Do
People Like Us
Sleeping With The Lights On 96

You're All That Matters To Me 98

★279★   STILLS, Stephen   '76

Born on 1/3/45 in Dallas. Singer/songwriter/guitarist. Member of **Buffalo Springfield** and **Crosby, Stills & Nash**. Manassas included **Chris Hillman** (guitar; **The Byrds**), Dallas Taylor (drums), Fuzzy Samuels (bass), Paul Harris (organ), Al Perkins (guitar) and Joe Lala (percussion).

1)Stephen Stills 2)Manassas 3)Stephen Stills 2

8/31/68	**12**	37	●	©	1 Super Session			$20	Columbia 9701
					MIKE BLOOMFIELD/AL KOOPER/STEVE STILLS				
11/28/70+	**3**	39	●	©	2 Stephen Stills			$15	Atlantic 7202
7/17/71	**8**	20	●	©	3 Stephen Stills 2			$15	Atlantic 7206
4/29/72	**4**	30	●	©	4 Manassas			$20	Atlantic 903 [2]
5/12/73	**26**	18		©	5 Down The Road			$15	Atlantic 7250
					STEPHEN STILLS & MANASSAS (above 2)				
7/5/75	**19**	17		©	6 Stills			$12	Columbia 33575
12/27/75+	**42**	11		©	7 Stephen Stills Live			[L] $12	Atlantic 18156
5/15/76	**31**	15		©	8 Illegal Stills			$12	Columbia 34148
10/9/76	**26**	18	●	©	9 Long May You Run			$12	Reprise 2253
					STILLS-YOUNG BAND				
1/8/77	**127**	5			10 Still Stills-The Best Of Stephen Stills			[G] $12	Atlantic 18201
11/11/78	**83**	4			11 Thoroughfare Gap			$12	Columbia 35380
9/1/84	**75**	12		©	12 Right By You			$10	Atlantic 80177

Albert's Shuffle (1)
Anyway (4)
As I Come Of Age (6)
Beaucoup Yumbo (11)
Black Coral (9)
Black Queen (2)
Bluebird Revisited (3)
Blues Man (4)
Both Of Us (Bound To Lose) (4)
Bound To Fall (1)
Business On The Street (5)
Buyin' Time (8)
Can't Get No Booty (11)
Can't Let Go (12) **67**
Change Partners (3,7,10) **43**
Cherokee (2)
Church (Part Of Someone) (2)
Circlin' (8)
City Junkies (5)
Closer To You (8)

Cold Cold World (6)
Colorado (4)
Crossroads (medley) (7)
Cuban Bluegrass (medley) (4,10)
Different Tongues (8)
Do For The Others (4)
Do You Remember The Americans (7)
Don't Look At My Shadow (4)
Down The Road (5)
Ecology Song (3)
Everybody's Talkin' At Me (7)
Fallen Eagle (4)
50/50 (12)
First Things First (6)
Fishes And Scorpions (3)
Flaming Heart (12)
Fontainebleau (9)
4 + 20 (7)

Four Days Gone (7)
Go Back Home (2,10)
Grey To Green (12)
Guaguanco De Vero (5)
Guardian Angel (9)
Harvey's Tune (1)
Hide It So Deep (4)
His Holy Modal Majesty (1)
How Far (4)
In The Way (6)
Isn't It About Time (5,10) **56**
It Doesn't Matter (4,10) **61**
It Takes A Lot To Laugh, It Takes A Train To Cry (1)
Jesus Gave Love Away For Free (4)
Jet Set (Sigh) (4,7)
Johnny's Garden (4,10)
Know You Got To Run (3)
Let It Shine (9)

Lies (5)
Loner, The (8)
Long May You Run (9)
Love Again (12)
Love Gangster (4)
Love Story (6)
Love The One You're With (2,10) **14**
Lowdown (4)
Make Love To You (9)
Man's Temptation (1)
Marianne (3,10) **42**
Midnight In Paris (8)
Midnight On The Bay (9)
Midnight Rider (11)
Move Around (4)
My Angel (6)
My Favorite Changes (6)
Myth Of Sisyphus (medley) (7)
New Mama (6)

No Hiding Place (12)
No Me Nieges (8)
No Problem (12)
Not Fade Away (11)
Nothin' To Do But Today (3)
Ocean Girl (9)
Old Times Good Times (2)
Only Love Can Break Your Heart (2)
Open Secret (2,3)
Pensamiento (5)
Really (1)
Relaxing Town (3)
Right By You (12)
Right Now (4)
Ring Of Love (8)
Rock And Roll Crazies (medley) (4,10) **92**
Rocky Mountain Way (medley) (7)

Rollin' My Stone (5)
Season Of The Witch (1)
Shuffle Just As Bad (6)
Singin' Call (3)
Sit Yourself Down (2,10) **37**
So Begins The Task (4)
So Many Times (5)
Soldier (4)
Song Of Love (4)
Special Care (7)
Stateline Blues (8)
Stop (1)
Stranger (12) **61**
Sugar Babe (3)
Thoroughfare Gap (11)
To A Flame (2)
To Mama From Christopher And The Old Man (4)
Treasure (Take One) (4)
Turn Back The Pages (6) **84**

STILLS, Stephen — Cont'd

12/8 Blues (All The Same) (9)
We Are Not Helpless (2,10)
We Will Go On (11)
What To Do (4)
What's The Game (11)
Woman Lleva (11)
Wooden Ships (7)
Word Game (3,7)
You Can't Catch Me (medley) (7)
You Can't Dance Alone (11)
You Don't Love Me (1)

★294★ STING '85

Born Gordon Sumner on 10/2/51 in Wallsend, England. Pop singer/songwriter/bassist. Lead singer of **The Police**. Acted in several movies, including *Quadrophenia*, *Dune*, *The Bride* and *Plenty*. Married actress/producer Trudie Styler in 1992. Nicknamed "Sting" because of a yellow and black jersey he liked to wear.

DEBUT	PEAK	WKS	RIAA	CD		$	Label & Number
7/13/85	2[6]	58	▲[3]	© 1	The Dream Of The Blue Turtles	$10	A&M 3750
10/31/87	9	52	▲[2]	© 2	...Nothing Like The Sun	$15	A&M 6402 [2]
2/9/91	2[1]	39	▲	© 3	The Soul Cages	$10	A&M 6405
3/27/93	2[1]	68	▲[3]	© 4	Ten Summoner's Tales	$10	A&M 540070
10/9/93	162	5		© 5	Demolition Man	[L-M] $10	A&M 540162
					recorded on 7/25/93 in Italy		
11/26/94	7	38	▲[2]	© 6	Fields Of Gold - The Best Of Sting 1984-1994	[G] $10	A&M 540269
3/30/96	5	34	▲	© 7	Mercury Falling	$10	A&M 540483
12/13/97	100	13		© 8	The Very Best Of Sting & The Police	[G] $10	A&M 540834
10/16/99+	9	90	▲[3]	© 9	Brand New Day	$10	A&M 490443

After The Rain Has Fallen (9)
All Four Seasons (7)
All This Time (3,6) *5*
Be Still My Beating Heart (2,6) *15*
Big Lie Small World (9)
Brand New Day (9)
Can't Stand Losing You (8)
Children's Crusade (1)
Consider Me Gone (1)
Day In The Life (5)
Demolition Man (5)
Desert Rose (9) *17*
Don't Stand So Close To Me (8) *10*
Dream Of The Blue Turtles (1)
Englishman In New York (2,6,8) *84*
Epilogue (Nothing 'Bout Me) (4)
Every Breath You Take (8) *1*
Every Little Thing She Does Is Magic (8) *3*
Fields Of Gold (4,6,8) *23*
Fill Her Up (9)
Fortress Around Your Heart (1,6) *8*
Fragile (2,6)
Ghost Story (9)
Heavy Cloud No Rain (4)
History Will Teach Us Nothing (2)
Hounds Of Winter (7)
I Hung My Head (7)
I Was Brought To My Senses (7)
I'm So Happy I Can't Stop Crying (7) *94*
If I Ever Lose My Faith In You (4,6,8) *17*
If You Love Somebody Set Them Free (1,6) *3*
Island Of Souls (3)
It's Probably Me (4,5)
Jeremiah Blues (Part I) (3)
King Of Pain (5)
La Belle Dame Sans Regrets (7)
Lazarus Heart (2)
Let Your Soul Be Your Pilot (7,8) *86*
Lithium Sunset (7)
Little Wing (2)
Love Is Stronger Than Justice (The Munificent Seven) (4,5)
Love Is The Seventh Wave (1) *17*
Mad About You (3)
Message In A Bottle (8) *74*
Moon Over Bourbon Street (1)
Perfect Love...Gone Wrong (9)
Rock Steady (2)
Roxanne (8) *32*
Roxanne '97 - Puff Daddy Remix (8) *59*
Russians (1,6,8) *16*
Saint Agnes And The Burning Train (3)
Saint Augustine In Hell (4)
Secret Marriage (2)
Seven Days (4)
Shadows In The Rain (1)
Shape Of My Heart (4,5)
She's Too Good For Me (4)
Sister Moon (2)
Something The Boy Said (4)
Soul Cages (3)
Straight To My Heart (2)
They Dance Alone (Gueca Solo) (2,6)
This Cowboy Song (6)
Thousand Years (9)
Tomorrow We'll See (9)
Valparaiso (7)
Walking On The Moon (8)
We Work The Black Seam (1)
We'll Be Together (2,6) *7*
When The Angels Fall (3)
When We Dance (6,8) *38*
Why Should I Cry For You? (3,6)
Wild Wild Sea (3)
You Still Touch Me (7) *60*

STITT, Sonny '67

Born Edward Stitt on 2/2/24 in Boston. Died on 7/22/82 (age 58). Jazz saxophonist.

DEBUT	PEAK	WKS				Sym	$	Label & Number
4/8/67	172	2			What's New!!!	[I]	$25	Roulette 25343

Beastly Blues
Cocktails For Two
Fever
Georgia
I've Got The World On A String
If I Didn't Care
Jumpin' With Symphony Sid
Mame
Morgan's Song
Round About Midnight
Stardust
What's New!

STONE, Angie '00

Born in Columbia, South Carolina. R&B singer/keyboardist.

DEBUT	PEAK	WKS	RIAA	CD		$	Label & Number
10/16/99+	46	34	● ©	Black Diamond		$10	Arista 19092

Black Diamonds & Blue Pearls
Bone 2 Pic (Wit U)
Coulda Been You
Everyday
Green Grass Vapors
Heaven Help
Just A Pimp
Life Story
Love Junkie
Man Loves His Money
No More Rain (In This Cloud) *56*
Trouble Man
Visions

STONE, Doug '92

Born Douglas Brooks on 6/19/56 in Marietta, Georgia. Country singer/guitarist. Starred in the 1995 movie *Gordy*.

DEBUT	PEAK	WKS	RIAA	CD		$	Label & Number
5/19/90+	97	51	▲ © 1	Doug Stone		$10	Epic 45303
8/31/91+	74	51	▲ © 2	I Thought It Was You	C:#47/1	$10	Epic 47357
8/29/92	99	34	● © 3	From The Heart		$10	Epic 52436
1/23/93	186	1	© 4	The First Christmas	[X]	$10	Epic 52844
12/4/93+	88	15	● © 5	More Love		$10	Epic 57271
12/17/94+	142	12	● © 6	Greatest Hits Volume 1	[G]	$10	Epic 66803

Addicted To A Dollar (5)
Ain't Your Memory Got No Pride At All (3)
All I Want For Christmas Is You (4)
Angel Like You (4)
Burning Down The Town (2)
Christmas Card (4)
Come In Out Of The Pain (2,6)
Crying On Your Shoulder Again (1)
Dream High (5)
Feeling Never Goes Away (2)
First Christmas (4)
(For Every Inch I've Laughed) I've Cried A Mile (2)
Fourteen Minutes Old (1)
High Weeds And Rust (1)
I Never Knew Love (5) *81*
I Thought It Was You (2,6)
I'd Be Better Off (In A Pine Box) (1,6)
If It Was Up To Me (2)
In A Different Light (1,6)
It's A Good Thing I Don't Love You Anymore (1)
Jukebox With A Country Song (2,6)
Just Put A Ribbon In Your Hair (4)
Leave Me The Radio (3)
Left, Leavin', Goin' Or Gone (3)
Little Houses (6)
Little Sister's Blue Jeans (5)
Love, You Took Me By Surprise (5)
Made For Lovin' You (3,6)
More Love (5)
My Hat's Off To Him (1)
Remember The Ride (2)
Right To Remain Silent (2)
Sailing Home For Christmas (4)
Santa's Flying A 747 Tonight (4)
She Used To Love Me A Lot (5)
She's Got A Future In The Movies (3)
Small Steps (3)
That's A Lie (5)
These Lips Don't Know How To Say Goodbye (1)
They Don't Make Many Like They Used To (2)
This Empty House (3)
Three Little Pennies (4)
Too Busy Being In Love (3,6)
Turn This Thing Around (1)
Warmest Winter (4)
Warning Labels (3,6)
We Always Agree On Love (1)
When December Comes Around (4)
Why Didn't I Think Of That (3,6)
Wishbone (5)
Workin' End Of A Hoe (3)

STONE, Kirby, Four '58

Born on 4/27/18 in New York City. His vocal group included Eddie Hall, Larry Foster and Mike Gardner.

DEBUT	PEAK	WKS		CD		$	Label & Number
8/25/58	13	9		©	Baubles, Bangles And Beads	$25	Columbia 1211

Baubles Bangles And Beads *25*
Bidin' My Time
Fugue For Tinhorns
In The Good Old Summertime
Lady Love Me
Let's Do It (Let's Fall In Love)
Lullaby Of Broadway
Rain
Swingin' Down The Lane
When My Sugar Walks Down The Street
Whispering
Zing! Went The Strings Of My Heart

STONE, Sly — see SLY & THE FAMILY STONE

STONE CITY BAND '80

Backing group for **Rick James**: Levi Ruffin (vocals), Tom McDermott (guitar), OBX and Erskine Williams (keyboards), Oscar Alston (bass) and Lanise Hughes (drums).

DEBUT	PEAK	WKS				$	Label & Number
3/22/80	122	8			In 'N' Out	$12	Gordy 991

F.I.M.A. (Funk In Mama Afrika)
Havin' You Around
In 'N' Out
Little Runaway
Party Girls
South American Sneeze
Strut Your Stuff

STONE FURY '85

Hard-rock group formed in Los Angeles: Lenny Wolf (vocals), Bruce Gowdy (guitar), Rick Wilson (bass) and Jody Cortez (drums). Wolf formed **Kingdom Come** in 1987.

| 11/24/84+ | 144 | 12 | | | Burns Like A Star .... | | | $10 | MCA 5522 |

Break Down The Wall   Don't Tell Me Why   I Hate To Sleep Alone   Mamas Love   Tease
Burns Like A Star   Hold It   Life Is Too Lonely   Shannon You Lose

STONE PONEYS — see RONSTADT, Linda

STONE ROSES, The '95

Pop-rock group from Manchester, England: Ian Brown (vocal), John Squire (guitar), Gary Mounfield (bass) and Alan Wren (drums).

| 1/20/90 | 86 | 26 | | © | 1 The Stone Roses .... | | | $10 | Silvertone 1184 |
| 2/4/95 | 47 | 13 | | © | 2 Second Coming .... | | | $10 | Geffen 24503 |

Begging You (2)   Driving South (2)   How Do You Sleep (2)   She Bangs The Drums (1)   Tears (2)   Your Star Will Shine (2)
Breaking Into Heaven (2)   Elephant Stone (1)   I Am The Resurrection (1)   Shoot You Down (1)   Ten Storey Love Song (2)
Bye Bye Bad Man (1)   Elizabeth My Dear (1)   I Wanna Be Adored (1)   (Song For My) Sugar Spun   This Is The One (1)
Daybreak (2)   Fools Gold (1)   Love Spreads (1)   Sister (1)   Tightrope (2)
Don't Stop (1)   Good Times (2)   Made Of Stone (1)   Straight To The Man (2)   Waterfall (1)

STONE TEMPLE PILOTS '94

Rock group formed in San Diego: **Scott Weiland** (vocals), brothers Dean (guitar) and Robert (bass) DeLeo, and Eric Kretz (drums). Also see **The Magnificent Bastards** and **Talk Show**.

1/9/93	3	114	▲7	©	1 Core	C:#32/4		$10	Atlantic 82418
6/25/94	❶3	64	▲6	©	2 Purple			$10	Atlantic 82607
4/13/96	4	50	▲2	©	3 Tiny Music...Songs From The Vatican Gift Shop			$10	Atlantic 82871
11/13/99	6	40	▲	©	4 No.4			$10	Atlantic 83255

Adhesive (3)   Creep (1)   Lady Picture Show (3)   Pop's Love Suicide (3)   Sin (1)   Where The River Goes (1)
And So I Know (3)   Daisy (3)   Lounge Fly (2)   Press Play (3)   **Sour Girl** (4) **78**   Wicked Garden (1)
Army Ants (2)   Dead & Bloated (1)   MC5 (4)   Pretty Penny (2)   Still Remains (2)
Art School Girl (3)   Down (4)   Meat Plow (2)   Pruno (4)   Trippin' On a Hole in a Paper
Atlanta (4)   Glide (4)   Naked Sunday (1)   Ride The Cliche (3)   Heart (3)
Big Bang Baby (3)   Heaven & Hot Rods (4)   No Memory (1)   Seven Caged Tigers (3)   Tumble In The Rough (3)
Big Empty (2)   I Got You (4)   No Way Out (4)   Sex & Violence (4)   "Unglued" (2)
Church On Tuesday (4)   Interstate Love Song (2)   Piece Of Pie (1)   Sex Type Thing (1)   Vasoline (2)
Crackerman (1)   Kitchenware & Candybars (2)   Plush (1)   Silvergun Superman (2)   Wet My Bed (1)

STOOKEY, Paul '71

Born on 12/30/37 in Baltimore. Folk singer/songwriter/guitarist. Member of **Peter, Paul & Mary**.

| 8/21/71 | 42 | 15 | | | Paul and.. .... | | | $15 | Warner 1912 |

Been On The Road Too Long   Give A Damn   Ju Les Ver Negre En Cheese   Meanings Will Change   Tiger
Gabriel's Mother's Hiway Ballad   Hey Sad Sack   (Ed's Tune)   Sebastian   **Wedding Song (There Is**
#16 Blues   John Henry Bosworth   Lucy   Tender Hands   **Love) 24**

STORIES '73

Rock group from New York City: Ian Lloyd (vocals, bass), Steve Love (guitar), Michael Brown (keyboards) and Bryan Madey (drums). Brown was a member of **Left Banke**.

| 7/1/72 | 182 | 9 | | | 1 Stories | | | $15 | Kama Sutra 2051 |
| 7/28/73 | 29 | 19 | | © | 2 About Us | | | $15 | Kama Sutra 2068 |

Believe Me (2)   Darling (2)   Hey France (2)   Love Is In Motion (2)   Step Back (1)   Winter Scenes (1)
Brother Louie (2) **1**   Don't Ever Let Me Down (2)   High And Low (2)   Nice To Have You Here (1)   Take Cover (1)   Words (2)
Changes Have Begun (2)   Down Time Blooze (2)   **I'm Coming Home** (1) **42**   Please, Please (2)   Top Of The City (2)   You Told Me (1)
Circles (2)   Hello People (1)   Kathleen (1)   Saint James (1)   What Comes After (2)

STORM, The '92

Rock group formed in San Francisco: Kevin Chalfant (vocals), Gregg Rolie (vocals, keyboards), Josh Ramos (guitar), Ross Valory (bass) and Steve Smith (drums). Rolie was a member of **Santana**. Rolie, Valory and Smith were members of **Journey**. Chalfant was a member of 707.

| 11/16/91+ | 133 | 17 | | © | The Storm .... | | | $10 | Interscope 91741 |

Call Me   I Want You Back   In The Raw   Take Me Away   You're Gonna Miss Me
Can't Live Without Love   **I've Got A Lot To Learn About**   Show Me The Way   Touch And Go
Gimme Love   **Love 26**   Still Loving You   You Keep Me Waiting

STRADLIN, Izzy, And The Ju Ju Hounds '92

Born Jeffrey Isbell on 4/8/62 in Lafayette, Indiana. Rock singer/guitarist. Former member of **Guns N' Roses**. The Ju Ju Hounds: Rick Richards (guitar), Jimmy Ashhurst (bass) and Charlie Quintana (drums). Richards was a member of the **Georgia Satellites**.

| 10/31/92 | 102 | 9 | | © | Izzy Stradlin And The Ju Ju Hounds .... | | | $10 | Geffen 24490 |

Bucket O' Trouble   Cuttin' The Rug   Pressure Drop   Somebody Knockin'   Time Gone By
Come On Now Inside   How Will It Go   Shuffle It All   Take A Look At The Guy   Train Tracks

STRAIT, George ★78★ '97

Born on 5/18/52 in Poteet, Texas. Country singer/guitarist. Starred in the movie *Pure Country*. Started his first band in 1973 while stationed with the U.S. Army in Hawaii. Moved to Nashville in the late 1970s.

1)Carrying Your Love With Me 2)One Step At A Time 3)Latest Greatest Straitest Hits
4)Easy Come, Easy Go 5)Pure Country

3/3/84	163	7	▲	©	1 Right Or Wrong			$10	MCA 5450
11/10/84	139	16	▲	©	2 Does Fort Worth Ever Cross Your Mind			$10	MCA 5518
4/20/85	157	8	▲3	©	3 Greatest Hits	C:#34/5	[G]	$10	MCA 5567
7/5/86	126	11	▲	©	4 #7			$10	MCA 5750
2/14/87	117	28	▲2	©	5 Ocean Front Property			$10	MCA 5913
9/26/87	68	31	▲3	©	6 Greatest Hits, Volume Two	C:#23/34	[G]	$10	MCA 42035
12/19/87+	17X	14		©	7 Merry Christmas Strait To You!	C:#17/13	[X]	$10	MCA 5800

Christmas charts: 24/'87, 25/'88, 17/'92, 24/'93, 29/'94

STRAIT, George — Cont'd

DEBUT	PEAK	WKS	RIAA	CD	ARTIST — Album Title	Catalog	Sym	$	Label & Number
3/19/88	87	14	▲	©	8 If You Ain't Lovin' You Ain't Livin'			$10	MCA 42114
3/4/89	92	24	▲	©	9 Beyond The Blue Neon			$10	MCA 42266
6/2/90	35	42	▲	©	10 Livin' It Up			$10	MCA 6415
4/6/91	45	49	▲	©	11 Chill Of An Early Fall			$10	MCA 10204
1/18/92	46	19	▲	©	12 Ten Strait Hits		[G]	$10	MCA 10450
5/9/92	33	24	▲	©	13 Holding My Own			$10	MCA 10532
10/3/92	6	129	▲5	©	14 Pure Country	C:#47/1	[S]	$10	MCA 10651
10/16/93	5	53	▲2	©	15 Easy Come, Easy Go			$10	MCA 10907
11/26/94	26	44	▲2	©	16 Lead On			$10	MCA 11092
9/30/95+	43	39	▲7	©	17 Strait Out Of The Box		[K]	$25	MCA 11263 [4]
5/11/96	7	57	▲2	©	18 Blue Clear Sky			$10	MCA 11428
5/10/97	❶1	57	▲3	©	19 Carrying Your Love With Me			$10	MCA 11584
5/9/98	2¹	36	▲2	©	20 One Step At A Time			$10	MCA 70020
3/20/99	6	40	▲	©	21 Always Never The Same			$10	MCA 70050
11/20/99	78	9	●	©	22 Merry Christmas Wherever You Are	C:#45/2	[X]	$10	MCA 170093
					Christmas charts: 9/'99, 26/'00				
3/25/00	2¹	34	▲	©	23 Latest Greatest Straitest Hits		[G]	$10	MCA 170100
10/7/00	7	14	●	©	24 George Strait			$10	MCA 170143

Ace In The Hole (9,12,17)
Adalida (16,23)
All I Want For Christmas (Is My Two Front Teeth) (22)
All My Ex's Live In Texas (5,6,17)
All Of Me (Loves All Of You) (8,13)
Always Never The Same (21)
Am I Blue (5,6,17)
Amarillo By Morning (3,17)
Angel, Angelina (19)
Any Old Love Won't Do (17)
Any Old Time (2)
Anything You Can Spare (11)
Away In A Manger (7)
Baby Blue (8,12,17)
Baby Your Baby (14)
Baby's Gotten Good At Goodbye (9,12,17)
Back To Bein' Me (8)
Best Day (23) *31*
Beyond The Blue Neon (9)
Big Ball's In Cowtown (17)
Big One (16,17)
Bigger Man Than Me (8,17)
Blame It On Mexico (17)
Blue Clear Sky (18,23)
Carried Away (18,23)
Carrying Your Love With Me (19,23)
Chair, The (6,17)
Check Yes Or No (17)
Chill Of An Early Fall (11,17)
Christmas Song (22)
Cow Town (4)
Cowboy Rides Away (2,6,17)
Deep Water (4)
Do The Right Thing (18)
Does Fort Worth Ever Cross Your Mind (2,6,17)
Don't Make Me Come Over There And Love You (24)
Don't Mind If I Do (8)
Down And Out (3)
Down Louisiana Way (16)
Drinking Champagne (10,12,17)
Easy Come, Easy Go (15,17) *71*
80 Proof Bottle Of Tear Stopper (1,17)
Every Time It Rains (Lord Don't It Pour) (1)

Famous Last Words Of A Fool (8,12,17)
Faults And All (13)
Fifteen Years Going Up (And One Night Coming Down) (1)
Fire I Can't Put Out (3,17)
Fireman (2,6,17)
Fly Me To The Moon (17)
Fool Hearted Memory (3,17)
For Christ's Sake, It's Christmas (7)
4 Minus 3 Equals Zero (21)
Frosty The Snowman (7)
Go On (24) *40*
Gone As A Girl Can Get (13,17)
Haven't You Heard (17)
Heartbroke (17)
Heartland (14,17)
Heaven Must Be Wondering Where You Are (10)
Her Goodbye Hit Me In The Heart (17)
Her Only Bad Habit Is Me (11)
Here We Go Again (13)
Holding My Own (13)
Hollywood Squares (9,17)
Home Improvement (24)
Home In San Antone (11)
Honky Tonk Saturday Night (2)
Hot Burning Flames (5)
I Ain't Never Seen No One Like You (18)
I Can Still Make Cheyenne (18,23)
I Can't See Texas From Here (17)
I Cross My Heart (14,17)
I Don't Want To Talk It Over Anymore (17)
I Just Can't Go On Dying Like This (17)
I Just Want To Dance With You (20) *61*
I Know She Still Loves Me (17)
I Know What I Want For Christmas (22)
I Look At You (21)
I Met A Friend Of Yours Today (16)
I Need Someone Like Me (2)
I Should Have Watched That First Step (2)
I Thought I Heard You Calling My Name (17)

I Wasn't Fooling Around (15)
I'd Just As Soon Go (18)
I'd Like To Have That One Back (15,17)
I'll Always Be Loving You (16)
I'm All Behind You Now (5)
I'm Never Gonna Let You Go (4)
I'm Satisfied With You (1)
I've Come To Expect It From You (10,12,17)
I've Convinced Everybody But Me (11)
I've Got A Funny Feeling (19)
If I Know Me (11,17)
If It's Gonna Rain (24)
If You Ain't Lovin' (You Ain't Livin') (8,12,17)
If You Can Do Anything Else (24) *51*
If You're Thinking You Want A Stranger (There's One Coming Home) (3,17)
In Too Deep (17)
Is It Already Time (11)
Is It That Time Again (8)
It Ain't Cool To Be Crazy About You (4,6,17)
It's Alright With Me (13)
It's Too Late Now (8)
Jingle Bell Rock (22)
Just Look At Me (15,17)
King Of Broken Hearts (14,17)
King Of The Mountain (18,23)
Last In Love (14)
Lead On (16,23)
Leavin's Been Comin' (For A Long, Long Time) (9)
Lefty's Gone (17)
Let It Snow, Let It Snow, Let It Snow (22)
Let's Fall To Pieces Together (1,3,17)
Let's Get Down To It (8)
Little Heaven's Rubbing Off On Me (1)
Lonesome Rodeo Cowboy (10)
Looking Out My Window Through The Pain (24)
Love Comes From The Other Side Of Town (2)
Love Without End, Amen (10,12,17)
Lovebug (15,17)

Lovesick Blues (11,17)
Man In Love With You (15,17)
Maria (20)
Marina Del Rey (3,17)
Meanwhile (21) *38*
Merry Christmas Strait To You (7)
Merry Christmas (Wherever You Are) (22)
Milk Cow Blues (11,17)
Murder On Music Row (23)
My Heart Won't Wander Very Far From You (5)
My Old Flame Is Burnin' Another Honky Tonk Down (4)
Need I Say More (18)
Neon Row (20)
Nerve, The (19)
Night's Just Right For Love (24)
No One But You (16)
Nobody Has To Get Hurt (16)
Nobody In His Right Mind Would've Left Her (4,6,17)
Noel Leon (22)
Ocean Front Property (5,6,17)
Oh Me, Oh My Sweet Baby (9)
Old Time Christmas (22)
One Night At A Time (19,23) *59*
One Of You (21)
One Step At A Time (20)
Our Paths May Never Cross (1)
Overnight Male (14,17)
Overnight Success (9,12)
Peace Of Mind (21)
Real Good Place To Start (19)
Remember The Alamo (20)
Rhythm Of The Road (4,17)
Right Or Wrong (1,3,17)
Rockin' In The Arms Of Your Memory (18)
Round About Way (19,23)
Rudolph The Red-Nosed Reindeer (22)
Santa Claus Is Coming To Town (7)
Santa's On His Way (22)
Second Chances (5)
She Knows When You're On My Mind (18)
She Lays It All On The Line (14,17)
She Loves Me (She Don't Love You) (10)

She Took The Wind From His Sails (24)
She'll Leave You With A Smile (19)
Six Pack To Go (17)
So Much Like My Dad (13,17)
Someone Had To Teach You (10)
Someone's Walkin' Around Upstairs (5)
Stay Out Of My Arms (15,17)
Stranger In My Arms (10)
Stranger Things Have Happened (4)
(That Don't Change) The Way I Feel About You (17)
That's Me (Every Chance I Get) (19)
That's The Breaks (20)
That's The Truth (21)
That's Where I Wanna Take Our Love (21)
That's Where My Baby Feels At Home (15)
There's A New Kid In Town (7)
Thoughts Of A Fool (14)
Today My World Slipped Away (19,23)
Too Much Of Too Little (9)
Trains Make Me Lonesome (13,17)
True (20,23)
Under These Conditions (8)
Unwound (3,17)
We Must Be Loving Right (15)
We Really Shouldn't Be Doing This (20,23) *44*
We're Supposed To Do That Now And Then (10)
What A Merry Christmas This Could Be (7)
What Am I Waiting For (16)
What Did You Expect Me To Do (2)
What Do You Say To That (21) *45*
What Would Your Memory Do (17)
What's Going On In Your World (9,12,17)
When Did You Stop Loving Me (14,17)
When It's Christmas Time In Texas (7)

When You're A Man On Your Own (10)
Where The Sidewalk Ends (14,17)
Which Side Of The Glass (24)
White Christmas (7)
Why Not Now (20)
Why'd You Go And Break My Heart (4)
Winter Wonderland (7)
Without Me Around (15)
Without You Here (5)
Won't You Come Home (And Talk To A Stranger) (19)
Wonderland Of Love (13,17)
You Can't Buy Your Way Out Of The Blues (5)
You Can't Make A Heart Love Somebody (16,23)
You Haven't Left Me Yet (20)
You Know Me Better Than That (11,17)
You Look So Good In Love (1,3,17)
You Still Get To Me (4)
You're Dancin' This Dance All Wrong (2)
You're Right I'm Wrong (13)
You're Something Special To Me (6,17)
You're Stronger Than Me (24)
You're The Cloud I'm On (When I'm High) (1)

STRANGE, Billy '64
Born on 9/29/30 in Long Beach, California. Session guitarist.

DEBUT	PEAK	WKS	RIAA	CD	ARTIST — Album Title	Catalog	Sym	$	Label & Number
10/24/64	135	5			1 The James Bond Theme		[I]	$20	GNP Crescendo 2004
7/3/65	146	3			2 English Hits Of '65		[I]	$20	GNP Crescendo 2009

Bernie's Tune (1)
Can't You Hear My Heartbeat? (2)
C'mon And Swim (1)
Come Stay With Me! (2)
007 Theme (1)
Eight Days A Week (2)
Game Of Love (2)
Girl From Ipanema (1)
Hard Day's Night (1)
House Of The Rising Sun (1)
I Know A Place! (1)
I'm Telling You Now (2)
In The Mood (1)
It's Not Unusual (2)
James Bond Theme (1) *58*
Last Time (2)
Memphis (2)
Mrs. Brown, You've Got A Lovely Daughter! (2)
Nobody I Know (1)
Silhouettes (2)
Ticket To Ride (2)
Tired Of Waiting (2)
Walk, Don't Run '64 (1)
Wishin & Hopin (1)

STRANGELOVES, The '65
Writers/producers Bob Feldman, Jerry Goldstein and Richard Gottehrer.

DEBUT	PEAK	WKS	RIAA	CD	ARTIST — Album Title	Catalog	Sym	$	Label & Number
11/13/65	141	2		©	I Want Candy			$100	Bang 211

Cara-Lin *39*
Hang On Sloopy
I Want Candy *11*
It's About My Baby
Just The Way You Are
New Orleans
Night Time *30*
No Jive
Rhythm Of Love
(Roll On) Mississippi
Satisfaction
Sendin' My Love

STRANGLERS, The '87

Pop-rock group formed in London: Hugh Cornwell (vocals, guitar), Dave Greenfield (keyboards), Jean-Jacques Burnel (bass) and Jet Black (drums).

DEBUT	PEAK	WKS			ARTIST — Album Title			$	Label & Number
5/2/87	172	4	©		Dreamtime			$10	Epic 40607

Always The Sun · Big In America · Dreamtime · Ghost Train · Mayan Skies · Nice In Nice · Shakin' Like A Leaf · Too Precious · Was It You? · You'll Always Reap What You Sow

STRAWBERRY ALARM CLOCK '68

Psychedelic-rock group formed in Los Angeles: Greg Munford (vocals), Ed King and Lee Freeman (guitars), Mark Weitz (keyboards), Gary Lovetro (bass) and Randy Seol (drums). King later joined **Lynyrd Skynyrd**.

| 11/4/67+ | 11 | 24 | © | | Incense And Peppermints | | | $50 | Uni 73014 |

Birds In My Tree · Hummin' Happy · Incense And Peppermints *1* · Lose To Live · Pass Time With The Sac · Paxton's Back Street Carnival · Rainy Day Mushroom Pillow · Strawberries Mean Love · Unwind With The Clock · World's On Fire

STRAWBS '75

Progressive-rock group formed in Leicester, England: David Cousins (vocals), Dave Lambert (guitar), John Hawken (keyboards), Chas Cronk (bass) and Rod Coombes (drums).

7/15/72	191	5			1 Grave New World			$15	A&M 4344
4/28/73	121	9			2 Bursting At The Seams			$15	A&M 4383
3/2/74	94	17			3 Hero and Heroine			$15	A&M 3607
3/8/75	47	13			4 Ghosts			$15	A&M 4506
10/11/75	147	6			5 Nomadness			$15	A&M 4544
10/30/76	144	5		©	6 Deep Cuts			$12	Oyster 1603
8/6/77	175	4		©	7 Burning For You			$12	Oyster 1604

Absent Friend (How I Need You) (5) · Ah Me, Ah My (1) · Alexander The Great (7) · Angel Wine (medley) (4) · Autumn Medley (3) · Back On The Farm (5) · Barcarole (For The Death Of Venice) (7) · Benedictus (1) · Beside The Rio Grande (6) · Burning For Me (7) · Carry Me Home (7) · Charmer (6) · Cut Like A Diamond (7) · Don't Try To Change Me (4) · Down By The Sea (2) · Flower And The Young Man (1) · Flying (2) · Ghosts Medley (4) · Golden Salamander (5) · Goodbye (Is Not An Easy Word To Say) (7) · Grace Darling (4) · Hanging In The Gallery (5) · Hard, Hard Winter (6) · Heartbreaker (7) · Heavy Disguise (1) · Hero And Heroine (3) · Hero's Theme (3) · Hey, Little Man...Thursday's Child (1) · Hey, Little Man...Wednesday's Child (1) · I Feel Your Loving Coming On (7) · I Only Want My Love To Grow In You (6) · Is It Today, Lord? (1) · Journey's End (1) · Just Love (3) · Keep On Trying (7) · Lady Fuschia (2) · Lay A Little Light On Me (3) · Lay Down (2) · Lemon Pie (4) · Life Auction Medley (4) · Little Sleepy (5) · Midnight Sun (3) · Mind Of My Own (5) · My Friend Peter (6) · New World (1) · On Growing Older (1) · Out In The Cold (3) · Part Of The Union (2) · Promised Land (5) · Queen Of Dreams (1) · Remembering (4) · River, The (2) · Round And Round (3) · Sad Young Man (6) · Shine On Silver Sun (3) · Simple Visions (6) · So Close And Yet So Far Away (6) · So Shall Our Love Die? (5) · Soldiers' Tale (6) · Starshine (medley) (4) · Stormy Down (2) · Tears And Pavan Medley (2) · Thank You (2) · To Be Free (5) · Tokyo Rosie (5) · Tomorrow (1) · Turn Me Round (6) · (Wasting My Time) Thinking Of You (6) · Where Do You Go (When You Need A Hole To Crawl In) (4) · Winter And The Summer (2) · You And I (When We Were Young) (4)

STRAY CATS '82

Rockabilly trio from Long Island, New York: **Brian Setzer** (vocals, guitar), Lee Rocker (bass) and Slim Jim Phantom (drums). Also see **Phantom, Rocker & Slick**.

7/3/82	2¹⁵	74	▲	©	1 Built For Speed			$10	EMI America 17070
9/10/83	14	29	●	©	2 Rant n' Rave with the Stray Cats			$10	EMI America 17102
9/27/86	122	5		©	3 Rock Therapy			$10	EMI America 17226
4/29/89	111	9		©	4 Blast Off			$10	EMI 91401

Baby Blue Eyes (1) · Beautiful Delilah (3) · Blast Off (4) · Bring It Back Again (4) · Broken Man (3) · Built For Speed (1) · Change Of Heart (3) · Dig Dirty Doggie (2) · Double Talkin' Baby (1) · 18 Miles To Memphis (3) · Everybody Needs Rock 'N' Roll (4) · Gene And Eddie (4) · Gina (4) · Hotrod Gang (2) · How Long You Wanna Live, Anyway? (4) · I Wanna Cry (3) · **I Won't Stand In Your Way** (2) *35* · I'm A Rocker (3) · Jeanie, Jeanie, Jeanie (1) · Little Miss Prissy (1) · Lonely Summer Nights (1) · **Look At That Cadillac** (2) *68* · Looking For Someone To Love (4) · Nine Lives (4) · One Hand Loose (3) · Race With The Devil (3) · Rebels Rule (2) · Reckless (3) · Rev It Up & Go (1) · Rock Therapy (3) · **Rock This Town** (1) *9* · Rockabilly Rules (4) · Rockabilly World (4) · Rockin' All Over The Place (4) · Rumble In Brighton (1) · Runaway Boys (1) · **(She's) Sexy + 17** (2) *5* · Slip, Slip, Slippin' In (4) · Something's Wrong With My Radio (2) · **Stray Cat Strut** (1) *3* · Too Hip, Gotta Go (2) · You Don't Believe Me (1)

STREEP, Meryl '85

Born on 6/22/49 in Summit, New Jersey. Leading movie actress.

| 4/20/85 | 180 | 4 | | © | The Velveteen Rabbit | | [TV] | $10 | Dancing Cat 3007 |

MERYL STREEP & GEORGE WINSTON
from the PBS-TV animated children's special

Anxious Moments · Christmas · Fairy, The · Flying · Lullaby · Nana · Rabbit Dance · Returning · Shabbiness Doesn't Matter · Skin Horse · Spring · Summer · Toys, The · Velveteen Rabbit

STREET, Janey '84

Born in New York City. Pop-rock singer.

| 11/3/84 | 145 | 6 | | | Heroes, Angels & Friends | | | $10 | Arista 8219 |

(How Long) Till My Ship Comes In · In My Mind · Jimmy (Lives In The House Down The Street) · Let's Give Into The Night · Me And My Friends · **Say Hello To Ronnie** *68* · There Ain't No Angels In The Sky · Under The Clock · Where Are The Heroes

STREETS '84

Rock group formed in Atlanta: **Steve Walsh** (vocals, keyboards), Mike Slamer (guitar), Billy Greer (bass) and Tim Gehrt (drums). Walsh was a member of **Kansas**.

| 12/3/83+ | 166 | 11 | | | 1st | | | $10 | Atlantic 80117 |

Blue Town · Cold Hearted Woman · Everything Is Changing · Fire · **If Love Should Go** *87* · Lonely Woman's Cry · Move On · One Way Street · So Far Away

844

STREISAND, Barbra ★5★   '64

Born on 4/24/42 in Brooklyn, New York. Singer/actress. Starred in several movies and Broadway shows. Married to actor Elliott Gould from 1963-71. Married actor James Brolin on 7/2/98. Won Grammy's Living Legends Award (1991) and Grammy's Lifetime Achievement Award (1995).

1)A Star Is Born 2)People 3)The Broadway Album 4)Guilty 5)Barbra Streisand's Greatest Hits, Volume 2

DEBUT	PEAK	WKS	RIAA	CD	#	ARTIST — Album Title	Sym	$	Label & Number
4/13/63	8	101	●	©	1	The Barbra Streisand Album		$25	Columbia 2007 / 8807
						1963 Grammy winner: Album of the Year			
9/14/63	2³	74	●	©	2	The Second Barbra Streisand Album		$25	Columbia 2054 / 8854
2/29/64	5	74	●	©	3	The Third Album		$25	Columbia 2154 / 8954
5/2/64	2³	51	●	©	4	Funny Girl	[OC]	$25	Capitol 2059 / 8859
						includes "Find Yourself A Man" and "If A Girl Isn't Pretty" by Danny Meehan, Kay Medford & Jean Stapleton and "Who Taught Her Everything" by Kay Medford & Danny Meehan			
10/3/64	❶⁵	84	●	©	5	People		$25	Columbia 2215 / 9015
5/22/65	2³	68	●	©	6	My Name Is Barbra	[TV]	$25	Columbia 2336 / 9136
						aired on 4/28/65			
11/6/65	2³	48	▲	©	7	My Name Is Barbra, Two...		$25	Columbia 2409 / 9209
4/9/66	3	36	●	©	8	Color Me Barbra	[TV]	$25	Columbia 2478 / 9278
						aired on 3/30/66			
11/19/66+	5	29		©	9	Je m'appelle Barbra		$25	Columbia 2547 / 9347
						title is French for "My Name Is"			
11/11/67+	12	23		©	10	Simply Streisand		$25	Columbia 2682 / 9482
9/28/68+	12	108	▲	©	11	Funny Girl	[S]	$20	Columbia 3220
						includes "If A Girl Isn't Pretty" by Mae Questal & Kay Medford			
10/12/68	30	20	●	©	12	A Happening In Central Park	[L]	$20	Columbia 9710
						recorded on 6/17/67			
9/6/69	31	17		©	13	What About Today?		$20	Columbia 9816
11/15/69+	49	33		©	14	Hello, Dolly!	[S]	$20	20th Century Fox 5103
						includes "Elegance" by **Michael Crawford**; "It Only Takes A Moment" by **Michael Crawford** & Marianne McAndrew; "It Takes A Woman" by Walter Matthau; and "Ribbons Down My Back" by Marianne McAndrew			
2/28/70	32	30	▲²	©	15	Barbra Streisand's Greatest Hits	[G]	$20	Columbia 9968
7/25/70	108	24		©	16	On A Clear Day You Can See Forever	[S]	$20	Columbia 30086
						includes "Come Back To Me," "Melinda" and "On A Clear Day (You Can See Forever)" by Yves Montand; and "On A Clear Day (You Can See Forever)" by **Nelson Riddle**			
2/6/71	186	6		©	17	The Owl and the Pussycat	[S-T]	$20	Columbia 30401
						comedy dialogue highlights from the movie; background music by **Blood, Sweat & Tears**			
2/20/71	10	29	▲	©	18	Stoney End		$15	Columbia 30378
9/18/71	11	26	●	©	19	Barbra Joan Streisand		$15	Columbia 30792
11/18/72+	19	27	▲	©	20	Live Concert At The Forum	[L]	$15	Columbia 31760
						recorded on 4/15/72			
11/24/73	64	16		©	21	Barbra Streisand...and other musical instruments	[TV]	$15	Columbia 32655
						aired on 11/2/73			
2/16/74	❶²	31	▲²	©	22	The Way We Were		$15	Columbia 32801
11/16/74+	13	24	●	©	23	ButterFly		$12	Columbia 33095
3/29/75	6	25	●	©	24	Funny Lady	[S]	$12	Arista 9004
						includes "Clap Hands, Here Comes Charley" by Ben Vereen; "It's Only A Paper Moon/I Like Her" and "Me And My Shadow" by James Caan			
11/1/75	12	20	●	©	25	Lazy Afternoon		$12	Columbia 33815
3/6/76	46	14	●	©	26	Classical Barbra	[F]	$12	Columbia 33452
12/11/76+	❶⁶	51	▲⁴	©	27	A Star Is Born	[L-S]	$12	Columbia 34403
						includes "Crippled Crow," "Hellacious Acres" and "Watch Closely Now" by **Kris Kristofferson**			
7/2/77	3	25	▲²	©	28	Streisand Superman		$12	Columbia 34830
6/17/78	12	27	▲	©	29	Songbird		$12	Columbia 35375
12/2/78+	❶³	46	▲⁵	©	30	Barbra Streisand's Greatest Hits, Volume 2	[G]	$12	Columbia 35679
7/7/79	20	18	●	©	31	The Main Event	[S]	$12	Columbia 36115
						includes "Angry Eyes" by **Loggins & Messina**; "Big Girls Don't Cry" by **The 4 Seasons**; "Body Shop" by Michalski & Oosterveen; and "Copeland Meets The Coasters/Get A Job," "I'd Clean A Fish For You," and "It's Your Foot Again" by Michael Melvoin (**The Plastic Cow**)			
11/3/79	7	26	▲	©	32	Wet		$10	Columbia 36258
10/11/80	❶³	49	▲⁵	©	33	Guilty		$10	Columbia 36750
						produced by **Barry Gibb**			
12/12/81	10	104	▲⁵	©	34	Memories	C:#44/1 [K]	$10	Columbia 37678
12/19/81+	108	5	▲⁵	©	35	A Christmas Album	C:#5/52 [X-E]	$10	Columbia 9557
						originally released in 1967; Christmas charts: 1/'67, 3/'68, 15/'69, 7/'70, 6/'71, 1/'73, 2/'83, 5/'84, 3/'85, 5/'87, 5/'88, 9/'89, 9/'90, 6/'91, 9/'92, 17/'93, 13/'94, 16/'95, 17/'96, 16/'97, 31/'98, 31/'99			
11/26/83+	9	26	▲	©	36	Yentl	[S]	$10	Columbia 39152
10/27/84	19	28	▲	©	37	Emotion		$10	Columbia 39480
11/23/85+	❶³	50	▲⁴	©	38	The Broadway Album		$10	Columbia 40092
5/9/87	9	28	▲	©	39	One Voice	[L]	$10	Columbia 40788
						recorded on 9/6/86 at her Malibu ranch			
11/12/88	10	26	▲	©	40	Till I Loved You		$10	Columbia 40880
10/21/89	26	25	▲²	©	41	A Collection Greatest Hits...And More	C:#38/8 [G]	$10	Columbia 45369
12/15/90	167	4		©	42	A Christmas Album	[X-E-R]	$10	Columbia 9557

STREISAND, Barbra — Cont'd

| 10/12/91 | 38 | 16 ▲ | © 43 | **Just For The Record**... [K] | $40 | Columbia 44111 [4] |

includes Barbra's mother on "Second Hand Rose" as part of a medley

7/17/93	❶¹	49 ▲²	© 44	**Back To Broadway**	$10	Columbia 44189
10/15/94	10	22 ▲³	© 45	**The Concert** [L]	$15	Columbia 66109 [2]
5/27/95	81	7 ●	© 46	**The Concert-Highlights** .... [L]	$10	Columbia 67100

above 2 recorded in June 1994 at Madison Square Garden in New York City

11/29/97	❶¹	27 ▲³	© 47	**Higher Ground**	$10	Columbia 66181
10/9/99	6	23 ▲	© 48	**A Love Like Ours**	$10	Columbia 69601
10/7/00	21	17 ▲	© 49	**Timeless - Live In Concert**.................. [L]	$10	Columbia 63778 [2]

contains performances from her entire career

Absent Minded Me (5)
After The Rain (32)
After You've Gone (medley) (43)
Alfie (13,49)
All I Ask Of You (40,41)
All In Love Is Fair (22,30) *63*
All That I Want (7)
All The Things You Are (10)
Am I Blue (24)
America The Beautiful (39)
Animal Crackers In My Soup (medley) (8)
Answer Me (28)
Any Place I Hang My Hat Is Home (2,43)
Apres Un Reve (26)
As If We Never Said Goodbye (44,45,46)
As Time Goes By (3,49)
Ask Yourself Why (13)
At The Same Time (47,49)
Auf Dem Wasser Zu Singen (21)
Auld Lang Syne (43,49)
Autumn (5)
Autumn Leaves (9)
Ave Maria (35,42)
Avinu Malkeinu (47)
Baby Me Baby (28)
Be My Guest (43)
Beau Soir (26)
Beautiful (19)
Before The Parade Passes By (14)
Being Alive (38,49)
Being At War With Each Other (22)
Best Gift (35,42)
Best I Could (37)
Best Thing You've Ever Done (22)
Best Things In Life Are Free (medley) (7,43)
Between Yesterday And Tomorrow (43)
Bewitched (Bothered And Bewildered) (3)
Blind Date (24)
Boy Next Door (10)
Brezairola ("Berceuse") (26)
Brother Can You Spare A Dime? (medley) (7)
By Myself (21,43)
By The Way (25,41)
C'est Si Bon (It's So Good) (8)
Cabin Fever (28)
Can You Tell The Moment? (43)
Can't Help Lovin' That Man (38,45,46)
Child Is Born (25)
Children Will Listen (44)
Christmas Song (Chestnuts Roasting On An Open Fire) (35,42)
Circle (47)
Clear Sailing (37)
Clicker Blues (49)
Clopin Clopant (9)
Come Back To Me (21)
Come Rain Or Come Shine (32)
Come To The Supermarket (In Old Peking) (1)
Comin' In And Out Of Your Life (34,41) *11*
Confrontation, The (17)
Cornet Man (4)
Cry Me A River (1,12,43,49)
Crying Time (23,43)
Dancing (14)
Dank Sei Dir, Herr (26)
Deep In The Night (29)
Deep River (medley) (47)
Didn't We (20) *82*

Ding-Dong! The Witch Is Dead (43)
Disney Medley (45)
Don't Believe What You Read (28)
Don't Ever Leave Me (21)
Don't Like Goodbyes (5,49)
Don't Rain On My Parade (4,11,15,20,21,43,45,46,49)
Down With Love (2)
Draw Me A Circle (3)
Emotion (37) *79*
(Enough Is Enough) ..see: No More Tears
(Evergreen) ..see: Star Is Born
Everybody Says Don't (44,45,46)
Everything (27)
Everything Must Change (47)
Everytime You Hear Auld Lang Syne (49)
Eyes Of Laura Mars (Prisoner), Love Theme From (30) *21*
Fight ..see: Main Event
Finale (11,14)
Fine And Dandy (5)
Flim Flam Man (18) *82*
For All We Know (45)
Free Again (9,15) *83*
Free The People (18)
Funny Face (medley) (8)
Funny Girl (11,43) *44*
Get Happy (medley) (43,49)
Give Me The Simple Life (medley) (7,43)
Glad To Be Unhappy (medley) (21)
Go To Sleep (16)
God Bless The Child (43)
Good Man Is Hard To Find (medley) (43)
Goodnight (13)
Gotta Move (2,8,15)
Grandma's Hands (43)
Guava Jelly (43)
Guilty (33,39,41,43,49) *3*
Hands Off The Man ..see: Flim Flam Man
Happy Days Are Here Again (1,12,15,20,39,43,45,46,49)
Hatikvah (43)
(Have I Stayed) Too Long At The Fair ..see: I Stayed Too Long
Have Yourself A Merry Little Christmas (35,42)
He Isn't You (16)
He Touched Me (7,12,15,43,45,46) *53*
Heart Don't Change My Mind (37)
Hello, Dolly! (14,43)
Henry Street (4)
Here We Are At Last (37,43)
Higher Ground (47)
His Love Makes Me Beautiful (4,11)
Honey Can I Put On Your Clothes (29)
Honey Pie (13)
Hooray For Love (medley) (43)
House Is Not A Home (medley) (19)
House Of Flowers (43)
How About Me (medley) (22)
How Does The Wine Taste? (5)
How Lucky Can You Get (24)
How Much Of The Dream Comes True (7)
Hurry! It's Lovely Up Here (16)
I Ain't Gonna Cry Tonight (32)
I Believe (medley) (47,49)
I Believe In Love (27)
I Can Do It (43)
I Can See It (6,12)

Ding-Dong! The Witch Is Dead
I Don't Break Easily (29)
I Don't Care Much (2)
I Don't Know Where I Stand (18)
I Finally Found Someone (medley) (49) *8*
I Found A Million Dollar Baby (In A Five & Ten Cent Store) (24)
I Found You Love (28)
I Got A Code In My Doze (24)
I Got Plenty Of Nothin' (7)
I Got Rhythm (medley) (21)
I Had Myself A True Love (3,43)
I Hate Music (43)
I Have A Love (medley) (44)
I Haved Dreamed (medley) (38)
I Know Him So Well (43)
I Like Him (medley) (24)
(I Like New York In June) How About You (medley) (43)
I Love You (medley) (8)
I Loved You (26)
I Loves You Porgy (medley) (38)
I Mean To Shine (19)
I Never Had It So Good (25)
I Never Has Seen Snow (21)
I Never Meant To Hurt You (19)
I Stayed Too Long At The Fair (2,8,43)
I Want To Be Seen With You Tonight (4)
I Wish You Love (9)
I Won't Last A Day Without You (23)
I Wonder As I Wander (35,42)
I'd Rather Be Blue Over You (Than Happy With Somebody Else) (11)
I'll Be Home (18)
I'll Know (10,45,46)
I'll Tell The Man In The Street (1)
I'm All Smiles (5)
I'm Always Chasing Rainbows (43)
I'm Five (medley) (6)
I'm Still Here (medley) (45,46)
I'm The Greatest Star (4,11,43,49)
I've Been Here (9)
I've Dreamed Of You (48,49)
I've Got A Crush On You (medley) (49)
I've Got No Strings (6)
I've Grown Accustomed To Her Face (medley) (8)
I've Never Been A Woman Before (22)
I've Never Been In Love Before (44)
If I Close My Eyes (43)
If I Could (47)
If I Didn't Love You (48)
If I Love Again (24)
If I Loved You (38,43)
If I Never Met You (48)
If You Could Read My Mind (18)
If You Ever Leave Me (48)
If You Were The Only Boy In The World (43)
In The Wee Small Hours Of The Morning (medley) (43)
In Trutina (26)
Island, The (48)
Isn't It A Pity? (48)
Isn't This Better (24)
It All Depends On You (medley) (43)
It Had To Be You (3)
It Must Be You (48)
It's A New World (39)
(It's Gonna Be A) Great Day (24)

Jenny Rebecca (6)
Jingle Bells? (35,42)
Johnny One Note (medley) (21)
Jubilation (23)
Jule Styne (43)
Just A Little Lovin' (Early In The Mornin') (18)
Just In Time (3)
Just Leave Everything To Me (14)
Just One Lifetime (48)
Keepin' Out Of Mischief Now (1,43)
Kid Again (medley) (6)
Kind Of Man A Woman Needs (43)
Kiss Me In The Rain (32) *37*
Ladies Who Lunch (medley) (38)
Lascia Ch'io Pianga (26)
Lazy Afternoon (25,45,46)
Le Mur (9)
Leading With Your Heart (47)
Left In The Dark (37) *50*
Lessons To Be Learned (47)
Let Me Go (18)
Let The Good Times Roll (23)
Let's Face The Music And Dance (medley) (8)
Let's Hear It For Me (24)
Letters That Cross In The Mail (25)
Life On Mars (23)
Life Story (33)
Like A Straw In The Wind (2)
Little Tin Soldier (13)
Look At That Face (medley) (8,43)
Lord's Prayer (35,42)
Lost Inside Of You (27,34,43)
Love (19)
Love And Learn (9)
Love Breakdown (29)
Love Comes From Unexpected Places (28)
Love In The Afternoon (23)
Love Inside (33,34)
Love Is A Bore (5)
Love Is Like A New Born Child (12)
Love Is Only Love (14)
Love Light (40)
Love Like Ours (48)
Love With All The Trimmings (16)
Lover, Come Back To Me (2,43,49)
Lover Man (45)
Lover Man (Oh, Where Can You Be?) (11)
Luck Be A Lady (44)
Lullaby For Myself (28)
Ma Premiere Chanson (9)
Main Event/Fight (31,41,49) *3*
Make Believe (3)
Make It Like A Memory (23)
Make No Mistake, He's Mine (37) *51*
Make The Man Love Me (10)
Make Your Own Kind Of Music (20,21) *94*
hit the "Hot 100" as a medley with "Sing A Song"
Man I Love (44)
Man I Loved (29)
Man That Got Away (45,46)
Martina (9)
Marty The Martian (12)
Maybe (18)
Memory (34,41) *52*
Minute Waltz (8)
Miss Marmelstein (43,49)
Moanin' Low (25)
Mondnacht (26)
Moon And I (43)

Moon River (43)
More Than You Know (10,24)
Morning After (13)
Morning After (17)
Mother (19) *79*
Move On (44)
Much More (1)
Music Of The Night (44)
Music That Makes Me Dance (4,48)
My Buddy (medley) (22)
My Coloring Book (2,15)
My Father's Song (25)
My Favorite Things (35,42)
My Funny Valentine (10)
My Heart Belongs To Me (28,30,34) *4*
My Honey's Loving Arms (1,43)
My Lord And Master (5)
My Man (6,11,15,20,43,45,46) *79*
My Melancholy Baby (3)
My Name Is Barbara (6)
My Pa (6)
Natural Sounds (12)
Nearness Of You (10)
Never Give Up (33)
Never Will I Marry (3)
New York State Of Mind (28,34)
Niagara (32)
No Easy Way Down (18)
No Matter What Happens (36)
No More Songs For Me (7)
No More Tears (Enough Is Enough) (32,34) *1*
No Wonder (Part One & Two) (36)
Nobody Knows (medley) (43)
Nobody Knows You When You're Down And Out (medley) (7)
Nobody's Heart (Belongs To Me) (43)
Non C'est Rien (8)
Not While I'm Around (38,45,46)
Nuts, Theme From ..see: Two People
O Little Town Of Bethlehem (35,42)
On A Clear Day (You Can See Forever) (20,43,45,49)
On Holy Ground (47)
On My Way To You (40)
On Rainy Afternoons (32)
Once Upon A Summertime (9)
One Hand, One Heart (44)
One Kiss (8)
One Less Bell To Answer (medley) (19)
One More Night (29)
One More Time Around (40)
One Note Samba (medley) (21)
Ordinary Miracles (45,46)
Over The Rainbow (39,43)
Overture (4,11)
Papa, Can You Hear Me? (36,39,43,45,46,49)
Pavane (Vocalise) (26)
People (4,5,11,12,15,20,21,39,43,45, 46,49) *5*
Piano Practicing (medley) (21)
Piece Of Sky (36,43,45,46,49)
Pieces Of Dreams (22)
Places You Find Love (40)
Porgy, I's Your Woman Now (Bess, You Is My Woman) (medley) (38)
Pretty Women (medley) (38)
Promises (33) *48*
Punky's Dilemma (13)
Put On Your Sunday Clothes (14)
Putting It Together (38,43,49)
Queen Bee (27)
Quiet Night (7)

Quiet Thing (medley) (43)
Rat-Tat-Tat-Tat (4)
Reunion, The (17)
Richard Rodgers (43)
Right As The Rain (2)
Roller Skate Rag (11)
Run Wild (33)
'S Wonderful (medley) (43)
Sadie, Sadie (4,11)
Sam, You Made The Pants Too Long (8,15) *98*
(Sandpiper, Love Theme From The) ..see: Shadow Of Your Smile
Second Hand Rose (7,12,15,21,43,49) *32*
Seduction, The (17)
Send In The Clowns (38,49)
Shadow Of Your Smile (7)
Shake Me, Wake Me (When It's Over) (25)
Simple Man (23)
Simple Pleasures (49)
Since I Don't Have You (23)
Since I Fell For You (19,43)
Sing (medley) (49)
Sing A Song (medley) (20) *94*
hit the "Hot 100" as a medley with "Make Your Own Kind Of Music"
Singer, The (43)
Sleep In Heavenly Peace (Silent Night) (12,35,42,43)
Sleepin' Bee (1,43,49)
Small World (medley) (8)
So Long Dearie (14)
So Long Honey Lamb (24)
Some Enchanted Evening (44)
Some Good Things Never Last (40)
Some Of These Days (medley) (43)
Someone That I Used To Love (41)
Someone To Watch Over Me (6)
Something So Right (22)
Something Wonderful (medley) (38,49)
Something's Coming (38,39,49)
Somewhere (38,39,41,45,46,49) *43*
Songbird (29,30) *25*
Soon It's Gonna Rain (19)
Space Captain (19)
Speak Low (44,49)
Speak To Me Of Love (9)
Splish Splash (32)
Spring Can Really Hang You Up The Most (43)
"Star Is Born" (Evergreen), Love Theme From A (27,30,34,39,43,45,46,49) *1*
Starting Here, Starting Now (8,20,43)
Stay Away (29)
Stoney End (18,20,30,43) *6*
Stout-Hearted Men (10) *92*
Summer Knows (19)
Summer Me, Winter Me (22)
Superman (28,30)
Supper Time (7)
Swan, The (11)
Sweet Inspiration/Where You Lead (20,30) *37*
Sweet Zoo (9)
Sweetest Sounds (21)
Taking A Chance On Love (3)
Taste Of Honey (1)
Tell Him (47,49)
That Face (medley) (8)
That's A Fine Kind O' Freedom (13)
There Won't Be Trumpets (medley) (43)

STREISAND, Barbra — Cont'd

They Didn't Believe Me (medley) (8)
(They Long To Be) Close To You (43)
This Is One Of Those Moments (36)
Till I Loved You (40) *25*
Time And Love (18) *51*
Time Machine (37)
Tomorrow (29)
Tomorrow Night (36)
Two People (40,43)
Until It's Time For You To Go (13)
Value (12,43)
Verschwiegene Liebe (26)
Wait (48)

Warm All Over (43)
Warmup, The (17)
Water Is Wide (medley) (47)
Way He Makes Me Feel (36,41) *40*
Way We Were (22,30,34,39,43,45,46,49) *1*
Way We Weren't (medley) (43)
We Kiss In A Shadow (medley) (38)
We Must Be Loving Right (48)
We're Not Makin' Love Anymore (41)
We've Only Just Begun (43)
Were Thine That Special Face (medley) (8)
Wet (32)

What About Today (13)
What Are You Doing The Rest Of Your Life? (22,43)
What Did I Have That I Don't Have (16)
What Kind Of Fool (33,39,41) *10*
What Now My Love (9)
What Were We Thinking Of (40)
What's New Pussycat? (medley) (8)
When I Dream (37)
When In Rome (I Do As The Romans Do) (5)
When Sunny Gets Blue (10)
When The Sun Comes Out (2,43)

When You Gotta Go (medley) (43)
When You're Down And Out (medley) (43)
Where Am I Going? (8) *94*
Where Is It Written? (36,45,46)
Where Is The Wonder (6)
Where Or When (8)
Where You Lead (19) *40*
Where's That Rainbow? (7)
White Christmas (35,42)
Who Are You Now? (4)
Who Will Buy? (2)
Who's Afraid Of The Big Bad Wolf (1,43)
Why Did I Choose You (6,15) *77*

Why Let It Go? (40)
Widescreen (25)
Will He Like Me (5,45,46)
Will Someone Ever Look At Me That Way? (36,45,46)
With A Little Help From My Friends (13)
With One Look (44)
With One More Look At You (medley) (27)
Woman In Love (33,41) *1*
Woman In The Moon (27)
World Is A Concerto (medley) (21)
Yesterdays (8)
You And I (25)
You And Me For Always (40)

You And The Night And The Music (medley) (43)
You Are Woman, I Am Man (4,11)
You Don't Bring Me Flowers (29,30,34,43,45,46,49) *1*
You Wanna Bet (43)
You'll Never Know (43,49)
You'll Never Walk Alone (medley) (47)
You're A Step In The Right Direction (37)
You're The Top (43)
You've Got A Friend (19)

STRIKERS, The · '81
Funk group from New York City: Ruben Faison (vocals), Robert Gilliom and Robert Rodriguez (guitars), Darryl Gibbs (sax), Howie Young (keyboards), Willie Slaughter (bass) and Milton Brown (drums).

| 8/29/81 | 174 | 3 | | © | The Strikers | | | $10 | Prelude 14100 |

Body Music
Bring Out The Devil
Give It What You Got
Hold Onto The Feeling
Inch By Inch
Strike It Up

STRING CHEESE INCIDENT, The · '01
Rock group from Boulder, Colorado: Michael Kang (vocals), Bill Nershi (guitar), Kyle Hollingsworth (keyboards), Keith Moseley (bass) and Michael Travis (drums).

| 6/2/01 | 147 | 1 | | © | Outside Inside | | | $10 | Sci Fidelity 1009 |

Black And White
Close Your Eyes
Drifting
Joyful Sound
Latinissmo
Lost
Outside And Inside
Rollover
Search
Sing A New Song
Up The Canyon

STROKE 9 · '00
Rock group from San Francisco: Luke Esterkyn (vocals), John McDermott (guitar), Greg Gueldner (bass) and Eric Stock (drums).

| 12/18/99+ | 83 | 28 | ● | © | Nasty Little Thoughts | | | $10 | Cherry 53157 |

Angels
Are You In This?
City Life
Down
Letters
Little Black Backpack
Make It Last
Not Nothin'
One Time
Tail Of The Sun
Tear Me In Two
Washin' + Wonderin'

STRUNK, Jud · '73
Born Justin Strunk on 6/11/36 in Jamestown, New York; raised in Farmington, Maine. Killed in a plane crash on 10/15/81 (age 45). Singer/songwriter. Regular on TV's *Laugh In.*

| 5/5/73 | 138 | 9 | | | Daisy A Day | | | $15 | MGM 4898 |

Bill Jones General Store
Daisy A Day *14*
Farethewell
If I Could Have My Way
Jacob Brown
Long Ride Home
Next Door Neighbor's Kid
Runaway, The
Searchers, The
This House

STRUNZ & FARAH · '91
Male flamenco guitar duo of Costa Rican Jorge Strunz (of **Caldera**) and Iranian Ardeshir Farah.

| 3/9/91 | 164 | 6 | | © | Primal Magic | | [I] | $10 | Mesa 79023 |

Amazonas
Anochecer (Nightfall)
Bola
Canto Al Sol
Huixamatli (Luna Llena)
Ida Y Vuelta
Rainmaker
Tierra Verde
Twilight At The Zuq
Zumba

STRYPER · '87
Christian hard-rock group from Los Angeles: brothers Michael (vocals) and Robert (drums) Sweet, with Oz Fox (guitar) and Tim Gaines (bass).

9/28/85	84	64	●	©	1 Soldiers Under Command			$10	Enigma 72077
8/23/86	103	30		©	2 The Yellow And Black Attack!		[E]	$10	Enigma 73207
					recordings from 1984				
11/22/86+	32	74	▲	©	3 To Hell With The Devil			$10	Enigma 73237
7/16/88	32	25	●	©	4 In God We Trust			$10	Enigma 73317
9/8/90	39	12		©	5 Against The Law			$10	Enigma 73527

Abyss (To Hell With The Devil) (3)
Against The Law (5)
All For One (5)
All Of Me (3)
Always There For You (4) *71*
Battle Hymn Of The Republic (1)
Calling On You (3)
Caught In The Middle (5)

Co'Mon Rock (2)
Come To The Everlife (4)
First Love (1)
Free (3)
From Wrong To Right (2)
Holding On (3)
Honestly (3) *23*
I Believe In You (4) *88*
In God We Trust (4)
It's Up To You (4)

Keep The Fire Burning (4)
Lady (5)
Lonely (4)
Loud 'N' Clear (2)
Loving You (2)
Makes Me Wanna Sing (1)
More Than A Man (3)
My Love I'll Always Show (2)
Not That Kind Of Guy (5)
Ordinary Man (5)

Reach Out (1)
Reason For The Season (2)
Reign, The (4)
Rock That Makes Me Roll (1)
Rock The Hell Out Of You (5)
Rock The People (5)
Rockin' The World (3)
Shining Star (5)
Sing-Along Song (3)
Soldiers Under Command (1)

Surrender (1)
To Hell With The Devil (3)
Together As One (1)
Together Forever (1)
Two Bodies (One Mind One Soul) (5)
Two Time Woman (5)
(Waiting For) A Love That's Real (1)
Way, The (3)

World Of You And I (4)
Writings On The Wall (4)
You Know What To Do (2)
You Won't Be Lonely (2)

STUART, Marty · '92
Born on 9/30/58 in Philadelphia, Mississippi. Country singer/guitarist.

5/16/92	193	1	●	©	1 Tempted			$10	MCA 10106
7/25/92	77	30	●	©	2 This One's Gonna Hurt You			$10	MCA 10596
4/2/94	141	2		©	3 Love And Luck			$10	MCA 10880
7/13/96	196	1		©	4 Honky Tonkin's What I Do Best			$10	MCA 11429

Blue Train (1)
Burn Me Down (1)
Country (4)
Country Girls (4)
Doin' My Time (2)
Down Home (2)
Get Back To The Country (1)
Half A Heart (1)
Hey Baby (2)

High On A Mountain Top (2)
Honky Tonk Crowd (2)
Honky Tonkin's What I Do Best (4)
I Ain't Giving Up On Love (3)
I Want A Woman (1)
I'll Be There For You (4)
I'm Blue, I'm Lonesome (1)
If I Give My Soul (3)

Just Between You And Me (2)
King Of Dixie (2)
Kiss Me, I'm Gone (3)
Little Things (2)
Love And Luck (3)
Marty Stuart Visits The Moon (3)
Me & Hank & Jumpin' Jack Flash (2)

Mississippi Mudcat and Sister Sheryl Crow (4)
Now That's Country (2)
Oh, What A Silent Night (4)
Paint The Town Tonight (1)
Rocket Ship (4)
Shake Your Hips (3)
Shelter From The Storm (4)
So Many People (4)

Sweet Love (4)
Tempted (1)
Thanks To You (4)
That's What Love's About (3)
That's When You'll Know It's Over (3)
This One's Gonna Hurt You (For A Long, Long Time) (2)
Till I Found You (1)

Wheels (3)
You Can Walk All Over Me (3)
You Can't Stop Love (4)

STUART, Mary '55

Born Mary Stuart Houchins on 7/4/26 in Miami; raised in Oklahoma City. Actress/singer. Played "Joanne Barron" on TV's *Search For Tomorrow* when she recorded her album below.

3/19/55	12	4			Joanne Sings	[EP]		$50	Columbia 487 [2]

with **Percy Faith** and His Orchestra

Birds' Courting Song   Hush, Little Baby   More I Cannot Wish You   Pigeon House   What Shall We Do With The
Dance Like A Lady   Lullaby And Goodnight   One More River   Baby-Oh

STUFF '77

Group of New York's top R&B session musicians: Richard Tee (keyboards), Gordon Edwards (bass), Cornell Dupree and **Eric Gale** (guitars), and Christopher Parker and Stephen Gadd (drums). Tee died of cancer on 7/21/93 (age 49). Gale died of cancer on 5/25/94 (age 55).

11/27/76	163	3			1 Stuff	[I]		$12	Warner 2968
7/30/77	61	13			2 More Stuff	[I]		$12	Warner 3061

And Here You Are (2)   (Do You) Want Some Of This   Honey Coral Rock (2)   Love Of Mine (2)   Sometimes Bubba Gets Down   This One's For You (2)
As (2)   (1)   How Long Will It Last (1)   My Sweetness (1)   (2)   Up On The Roof (medley) (1)
Dixie (medley) (1)   Foots (1)   Looking For The Juice (1)   Need Somebody (2)   Subway (2)
   Happy Farms (1)   Reflections Of Divine Love (1)   Sun Song (1)

STYLE COUNCIL, The '84

Pop duo from England: Paul Weller (vocals) and Mick Talbot (keyboards).

10/22/83	172	5		©	1 Introducing The Style Council	[M]		$10	Polydor 815277
4/7/84	56	22			2 My Ever Changing Moods			$10	Geffen 4029
6/29/85	123	11		©	3 Internationalists			$10	Geffen 24061
4/18/87	122	10		©	4 The Cost Of Loving			$10	Polydor 831443
8/13/88	174	6		©	5 Confessions Of A Pop Group			$10	Polydor 835785

All Gone Away (3)   Down In The Seine (3)   How She Threw It All Away (5)   Luck (3)   Speak Like A Child (1)   With Everything To Lose (3)
Angel (4)   Dropping Bombs On The   I Was A Doledads Toyboy (5)   Man Of Great Promise (3)   Stand Up Comic's Instructions   Woman's Song (4)
Blue Cafe (2)   Whitehouse (3)   Internationalists (3)   Mick's Blessings (2)   (3)   **You're The Best Thing** (2) 76
Boy Who Cried Wolf (3)   Fairy Tales (4)   It Didn't Matter (4)   Mick's Up (1)   Stone's Throw Away (3)
Changing Of The Guard (5)   Gardener Of Eden (A Three   It's A Very Deep Sea (5)   Money-Go-Round (1)   Story Of Someone's Shoe (5)
Come To Milton Keynes (3)   Piece Suite) Medley (5)   Life At A Top Peoples Health   **My Ever Changing Moods**   Strength Of Your Nature (2)
Confessions Of A Pop-Group (5)   Gospel, A (2)   Farm (5)   (2) 29   Waiting (4)
Confessions 1, 2 & 3 (5)   Headstart For Happiness (1,2)   Little Boy In A Castle (medley)   Paris Match (1,2)   Walking The Night (4)
Cost Of Loving (4)   Heavens Above (4)   (5)   Right To Go (4)   Walls Come Tumbling Down (3)
Dove Flew Down From The   Here's One That Got Away (2)   Lodgers, The (3)   Shout To The Top (3)   Whole Point Of No Return (3)
Elephant (medley) (5)   Homebreakers (3)   Long Hot Summer (1)   Solid Bond In Your Heart (2)   Why I Went Missing (5)

★387★ STYLISTICS, The '74

R&B vocal group from Philadelphia: Russell Thompkins Jr., Airrion Love, James Smith, James Dunn and Herbie Murrell.

1)Let's Put It All Together 2)The Stylistics 3)Round 2: The Stylistics

12/18/71+	23	38	● ©		1 The Stylistics			$15	Avco 33023
11/11/72+	32	38	● ©		2 Round 2: The Stylistics			$15	Avco 11006
11/24/73+	66	44		©	3 Rockin' Roll Baby			$15	Avco 11010
5/25/74	14	31	●		4 Let's Put It All Together			$15	Avco 69001
11/2/74	43	16			5 Heavy			$15	Avco 69004
2/22/75	41	30		©	6 The Best of The Stylistics	C:#34/21	[G]	$15	Avco 69005
6/14/75	72	13			7 Thank You Baby			$15	Avco 69008
11/8/75	99	11			8 You Are Beautiful			$15	Avco 69010
6/19/76	117	6			9 Fabulous			$12	H&L 69013
11/8/80	127	12		©	10 Hurry Up This Way Again			$12	TSOP 36470

And I'll See You No More (10)   Ebony Eyes (1)   I'm Gonna Win (7)   Make It Last (7)   Starvin' For Love (9)   **You Are Everything** (1,6) 9
Baby, Don't Change Your Mind   Found A Love You Couldn't   **I'm Stone In Love With You**   Maybe It's Because You're   Stay (7)   **You Make Me Feel Brand New**
(9)   Handle (10)   (2,6) 10   Lonely (9)   **Stop, Look, Listen (To Your**   (3,4,6) 2
Because I Love You, Girl (9)   From The Mountain (5)   If I Love You (1)   Maybe It's Love This Time (10)   **Heart)** (1) 39   You Ought To Be With Me (9)
Betcha By Golly, Wow (1,6) 3   **Funky Weekend** (8) 76   If You Are There (8)   Michael Or Me (8)   Tears And Souvenirs (7)   **You'll Never Get To Heaven (If**
Break Up To Make Up (2,6) 5   Go Now (5)   If You Don't Watch Out (2)   Miracle, The (5)   **Thank You Baby** (7) 70   **You Break My Heart)** (2) 23
Can't Give You Anything (But   **Heavy Fallin' Out** (5,6) 41   Is There Something On Your   Na-Na Is The Saddest Word (8)   That Don't Shake Me (10)   **You're A Big Girl Now** (1,6) 73
My Love) (7) 51   Hey Girl, Come And Get It (5)   Mind (10)   Only For The Children (3)   There's No Reason (3)   You're As Right As Rain (2)
Can't Help Falling In Love (9)   Honky Tonk Cafe (7)   It Started Out (10)   Pay Back Is A Dog (3)   To Save My Rock 'N' Roll Soul
Children Of The Night (2)   Hurry Up This Way Again (10)   It's So Good (9)   Peek-A-Boo (2)   (8)
Could This Be The End (3)   I Got A Letter (4)   It's Too Late (2)   **People Make The World Go**   We Can Make It Happen Again
Country Living (1)   I Got Time On My Hands (4)   Jenny (8)   **Round** (1,6) 25   (4)
Day The Clown Came To Town   I Have You, You Have Me (10)   Keeping My Fingers Crossed   Pieces (2)   We Just Can't Help It (8)
(8)   I Take It Out On You (4)   (4)   Point Of No Return (1)   What Goes Around Comes
Disco Baby (7)   I Will Love You Always (9)   Let Them Work It Out (3)   **Rockin' Roll Baby** (3,6) 14   Around (7)
Doin' The Streets (4)   I Won't Give You Up (3)   **Let's Put It All Together**   She Did A Number On Me (5)   What's Happenin', Baby? (5)
Don't Put It Down Til You Been   I'd Rather Be Hurt By You   (4,6) 18   Sing Baby Sing (7)   You And Me (2)
There (1)   (Than Be Loved By   Love Comes Easy (3)   Sixteen Bars (9)   You Are (9)
Driving Me Wild (10)   Somebody Else) (7)   Love Is The Answer (4)   **Star On A TV Show** (5) 47   **You Are Beautiful** (8) 79

STYX ★173★ '81

Pop-rock group from Chicago: **Dennis DeYoung** (vocals, keyboards), John Curulewski and James Young (guitars), and twin brothers Chuck (bass) and John (drums) Panozzo. **Tommy Shaw** replaced Curulewski in 1976. Disbanded in 1984. Reunited in 1990 with guitarist **Glen Burtnick** replacing Shaw, who joined **Damn Yankees**. John Panozzo died on 7/16/96 (age 47). Todd Sucherman (drums) joined in 1997. In Greek mythology, Styx is a river of Hades.

1)Paradise Theater 2)Cornerstone 3)Kilroy Was Here

2/9/74	192	2		©	1 The Serpent Is Rising			$20	Wooden Nickel 0287
11/9/74	154	12		©	2 Man Of Miracles			$20	Wooden Nickel 0638
1/25/75	20	19	●	©	3 Styx II	[E]		$20	Wooden Nickel 1012

originally released in 1973

12/20/75+	58	50	●	©	4 Equinox			$15	A&M 4559
10/30/76	66	18	●	©	5 Crystal Ball			$15	A&M 4604

DEBUT	PEAK	WKS	RIAA	CD		ARTIST — Album Title	Catalog	Sym	$	Label & Number

STYX — Cont'd

DEBUT	PEAK	WKS	RIAA	CD	#	Title	Catalog	$	Label & Number
7/30/77+	6	127	▲³	©	6	The Grand Illusion	C:#22/80	$12	A&M 4637
9/30/78	6	92	▲³	©	7	Pieces Of Eight		$12	A&M 4724
10/13/79	2¹	60	▲²	©	8	Cornerstone		$12	A&M 3711
1/31/81	❶³	61	▲³	©	9	Paradise Theater	C:#26/60	$12	A&M 3719
3/19/83	3	34	▲	©	10	Kilroy Was Here		$12	A&M 3734
4/21/84	31	15		©	11	Caught In The Act - Live	[L]	$15	A&M 6514 [2]
10/27/90	63	38	●	©	12	Edge Of The Century		$10	A&M 5327
9/23/95	138	5	▲	©	13	Greatest Hits	C:#5/58 [G]	$10	A&M 540387
5/24/97	139	1	●	©	14	Return To Paradise	[L]	$15	CMC Int'l. 86212 [2]
						recorded at the Rosemont Horizon in Chicago			
7/17/99	175	1		©	15	Brave New World		$10	CMC Int'l. 86275

A.D. 1928 (9)
A.D. 1958 (9)
Aku-Aku (7)
All In A Day's Work (12)
As Bad As This (1)
Babe (8,11,13,14) *1*
Back To Chicago (12)
Ballerina (medley) (5)
Best New Face (15)
Best Of Times (9,11,13,14) *3*
Best Thing (2) *82*
Blue Collar Man (Long Nights) (7,11,13,14) *21*
Boat On The River (8,14)
Born For Adventure (4)
Borrowed Time (8) *64*
Brave New World (15)
Carrie Ann (12)
Castle Walls (6)
Christopher, Mr. Christopher (2)
Clair De Lune (medley) (5)
Cold War (10)

Come Sail Away (6,11,13,14) *8*
Crystal Ball (5,11,13,14)
Day, A (3)
Dear John (14)
Don't Let It End (10,11,13) *6*
Double Life (10)
Earl Of Roseland (3)
Eddie (8)
Edge Of The Century (12)
Everything Is Cool (15)
Evil Eyes (2)
Fallen Angel (15)
Father O.S.A. (3)
First Time (8)
Fooling Yourself (The Angry Young Man) (6,11,13,14) *29*
Golden Lark (2)
Goodbye Roseland (15)
Grand Finale (6)
Grand Illusion (6,13,14)
Great Expectations (15)
Great White Hope (7)

Grove Of Eglantine (1)
Half-Penny, Two-Penny (9)
Hallelujah Chorus (1)
Haven't We Been Here Before (10)
Havin' A Ball (2)
Heavy Metal Poisoning (10)
Heavy Water (15)
High Crimes & Misdemeanors (15)
High Time (10) *48*
Homewrecker (12)
I Will Be Your Witness (15)
I'm Gonna Make You Feel It (3)
I'm O.K. (7)
Jennifer (5)
Jonas Bladder (1)
Just Fell In (15)
Just Get Through This Night (10)
Krakatoa (1)
Lady (3,13,14) *6*

Light Up (4)
Lights (8)
Little Fugue In 'G' (3)
Lonely Child (4)
Lonely People (9)
Lords Of The Ring (7)
Lorelei (4,13,14) *27*
Love At First Sight (12) *25*
Love In The Midnight (8)
Love Is The Ritual (12) *80*
Mademoiselle (5) *36*
Man In The Wilderness (6)
Man Like Me (2)
Man Of Miracles (2)
Message, The (7)
Midnight Ride (4)
Miss America (6,11,13,14)
Mother Dear (14)
Mr. Roboto (10,11,13) *3*
Music Time (11) *40*
Never Say Never (8)
Not Dead Yet (12)

Nothing Ever Goes As Planned (9) *54*
Number One (15)
On My Way (14)
Paradise (14)
Pieces Of Eight (7)
Prelude 12 (4)
Put Me On (5)
Queen Of Spades (7)
Renegade (7,13,14) *16*
Rock & Roll Feeling (2)
Rockin' The Paradise (9,11,14)
Serpent Is Rising (1)
She Cares (9)
Shooz (5)
Show Me The Way (12,13,14) *3*
Sing For The Day (7) *41*
Snowblind (9,11,14)
Song For Suzanne (2)
Southern Woman (2)
State Street Sadie (9)

Suite Madame Blue (4,11,13,14)
Superstars (6)
This Old Man (5)
Too Much Time On My Hands (9,11,13,14) *9*
22 Years (1)
What Have They Done To You (15)
While There's Still Time (15)
Why Me (8) *26*
Winner Take All (1)
Witch Wolf (1)
World Tonite (12)
You Better Ask (3)
You Need Love (3) *88*
Young Man (1)

SUAVE' '88
Born on 2/22/66 in Los Angeles. Son of Waymond Anderson (of **GQ**).

DEBUT	PEAK	WKS	CD		Title	$	Label & Number
4/23/88	101	12	©		I'm Your Playmate	$10	Capitol 48686

B And E Of The Heart
Back Stabber

Don't Rush
I Wanna Please You

Love Triangle
My Girl *20*

Now That I Fell In Love
Playmate

Shake Your Body
Stop Acting Ill

SUBLIME '97
Ska-rock group from San Francisco: Brad Nowell (vocals, guitar), Eric Wilson (bass) and Bud Gaugh (drums). Nowell died of a drug overdose on 5/25/96 (age 28).

DEBUT	PEAK	WKS	RIAA	CD	#	Title	Catalog	$	Label & Number
8/17/96+	13	104	▲³	©	1	Sublime	C:#5/146	$10	Gasoline Alley 11413
9/28/96+	140	9	▲	©	2	40 Oz. To Freedom	C:#3/124 [E]	$10	Gasoline Alley 11474
						originally released on Skunk 1 in 1992			
10/11/97	169	3		©	3	What I Got...The 7 Song EP	[M]	$10	Gasoline Alley 11678
12/13/97	28	19	●	©	4	Second-Hand Smoke		$10	Gasoline Alley 11714
7/11/98	49	10		©	5	Stand By Your Van - Live In Concert	[L]	$10	Gasoline Alley 11798
12/5/98	107	2		©	6	Acoustic - Bradley Nowell and Friends	[E]	$10	Gasoline Alley 11889
						recorded from 1993-95			
11/27/99	114	9		©	7	Greatest Hits	[G]	$10	Gasoline Alley 112125

All You Need (3,5)
April 29, 1992 (Miami) (1,4)
Badfish (2,4,5,7)
Ball And Chain (medley) (2)
Ballad Of Johnny Butt (1)
Big Salty Tears (medley) (6)
Boss D.J. (2)
Burritos (1)
Caress Me Down (1,5)
Chica Me Tipo (2)
Chick On My Tip (4)
D.J.s (2,3,5)

Date Rape (2,5,7)
Doin' Time (1,3,4,7) *87*
Don't Push (2,4,5,6)
Drunk Drivin' (4)
Ebin (2,5)
Eye Of Fatima (medley) (6)
5446 That's My Number (medley) (4)
Foolish Fool (4)
40 Oz. To Freedom (2,3,7)
Freeway Time In L.A. County Jail (6)

Garbage Grove (4)
Garden Grove (1,6)
Get Out! (4)
Get Ready (1)
Greatest Hits (5)
Had A Dat (4)
Hope (2)
It's Who You Know (6)
Jailhouse (1)
KRS-One (2,5,6)
Legal Dub (4)
Let's Go Get Stoned (2,5)

Little District (6)
Live At E's (2)
Marley Medley (6)
Mary (medley) (6)
New Realization (2)
New Song (2)
New Thrash (2,5)
Paddle Out (1)
Pawn Shop (1)
Pool Shark (6)
Poolshark (5,7)
Right Back (2,5)

Rivers Of Babylon (6)
Romeo (4)
S.T.P. (5)
Same In The End (1,3)
Santeria (1,7)
Saw Red (4,6,7)
Scarlet Begonias (2)
Seed (1)
Slow Ride (4)
Smoke Two Joints (2,7)
Superstar Punani (4)
Thanx Dub (4)

Trenchtown Rock (4)
Under My Voodoo (1)
Waiting For My Ruca (2,5)
We're Only Gonna Die For Our Arrogance (2)
What Happened (2,6)
What I Got (1,3,7)
What I Got Video (7)
What's Really Goin' Wrong (4)
Work That We Do (3,5)
Wrong Way (1,6,7)
Wrong Way Video (7)

SUBWAY '95
R&B vocal group from Chicago: Eric McNeal, Roy Jones, Keith Thomas and Trerail Puckett.

DEBUT	PEAK	WKS	CD		Title	$	Label & Number
2/11/95	101	21	©		Good Times	$10	Biv 10 0354

Better The Love
Chi-Town Ride

Fire *91*
Get Da Money

Goodtimes
Sticky Situation

This Is Not A Goodbye
This Lil' Game We Play *15*

SUGAR '94
Rock trio formed in Athens, Georgia: **Bob Mould** (vocals, guitar), David Barbe (bass) and Malcolm Travis (drums). Mould a member of **Hüsker Dü**.

DEBUT	PEAK	WKS	CD	#	Title	$	Label & Number
4/24/93	130	3	©	1	Beaster	[M]	$10	Rykodisc 50260
9/24/94	50	6	©	2	File Under: Easy Listening		$10	Rykodisc 10300
8/12/95	122	3	©	3	Besides	[K]	$15	Rykodisc 10321 [2]

After All The Roads Have Led To Nowhere (3)
And You Tell Me (3)
Anyone (3)
Armenia City In The Sky (3)
Believe What You're Saying (2,3)

Can't Help You Anymore (2)
Clownmaster (3)
Come Around (1)
Company Book (3)
Explode And Make Up (2,3)
Feeling Better (1)
Frustration (3)

Gee Angel (2)
Gift (2)
Going Home (3)
Granny Cool (2)
If I Can't Change Your Mind (3)
In The Eyes Of My Friends (3)
JC Auto (1,3)

Judas Cradle (1)
Mind Is An Island (3)
Needle Hits E (3)
Panama City Motel (2)
Slim, The (3)
Tilted (1)
Try Again (3)

Walking Away (1)
What You Want It To Be (2)
Where Diamonds Are Halos (3)
Your Favorite Thing (2)

SUGARCUBES, The '88

Rock group from Reykjavik, Iceland: **Björk** Gudmundsottir (vocals), Einar Orn Benediktsson (vocals, trumpet), Thor Eldon Jonsson (guitar), Margret Ornolfsdottir (keyboards), Bragi Olafsson (bass) and Siggi Baldursson (drums). Group began as an artist's collective called Kukl (an Icelandic term for witches). Björk and Thor were married for a time. Thor and Margret married in 1989.

6/18/88	54	29		©	1 Life's Too Good			$10	Elektra 60801
10/14/89	70	9		©	2 Here Today, Tomorrow Next Week!			$10	Elektra 60860
3/7/92	95	11		©	3 Stick Around For Joy			$10	Elektra 61123

Bee (2)
Birthday (1)
Blue Eyed Pop (1)
Chihuahua (3)
Coldsweat (1)
Day Called Zero (2)

Dear Plastic (2)
Delicious Demon (1)
Deus (1)
Dream TV (2)
Eat The Menu (2)
F***ing In Rhythm & Sorrow (1)

Gold (3)
Happy Nurse (3)
Hetero Scum (3)
Hit (3)
I'm Hungry (3)
Leash Called Love (3)

Lucky Night (3)
Mama (1)
Motorcrash (1)
Nail (2)
Planet (2)
Pump (2)

Regina (2)
Shoot Him (2)
Sick For Toys (1)
Speed Is The Key (2)
Take Some Petrol Darling (2)
Tidal Wave (2)

Traitor (1)
Vitamin (3)
Walkabout (3)
Water (2)

SUGARHILL GANG '82

Rap trio from Harlem, New York: Mike Wright, Guy O'Brien and Hank Jackson.

| 1/30/82 | 50 | 18 | | | 8th Wonder .... | | | $15 | SugarHill 249 |

Apache *53*
8th Wonder *82*

Funk Box
Giggalo

Hot Hot Summer Day
On The Money

Showdown

SUGARLOAF '70

Rock group from Denver: Jerry Corbetta (vocals, keyboards), Bob Webber (guitar), Bob Raymond (bass) and Bob MacVittie (drums). Myron Pollock replaced MacVittie in 1974.

8/15/70	24	29			1 Sugarloaf			$20	Liberty 7640
2/13/71	111	9			2 Spaceship Earth			$20	Liberty 11010
4/12/75	152	6			3 Don't Call Us-We'll Call You			$15	Claridge 1000

SUGARLOAF/JERRY CORBETTA

Bach Doors Man (medley) (1)
Chest Fever (medley) (1)
Colorado Jones (3)
Country Dawg (2)
Don't Call Us, We'll Call You (3) *9*

Gold And The Blues (1)
Green-Eyed Lady (1) *3*
Hot Water (2)
I Don't Need You Baby (3)
I Got A Song (3)
Lay Me Down (3)

Lookin' For Some Fun (3)
Mother Nature's Wine (2) *88*
Music Box (2)
Myra, Myra (3)
Rollin' Hills (2)
Round And Round (3)

Rusty Cloud (2)
Spaceship Earth (2)
Things Gonna Change Some (1)
Tongue In Cheek (2) *55*

Train Kept A-Rollin' (Stroll On) (1)
We Could Fly So High (3)
West Of Tomorrow (1)
Wild Child (3)
Woman (2)

SUGAR RAY '01

Rock group from Los Angeles: Mark McGrath (vocals), Craig Bullock (DJ), Rodney Sheppard (guitar), Murphy Karges (bass) and Stan Frazier (drums).

7/12/97	12	42	▲2	©	1 Floored			$10	Lava 83006
1/30/99	17	66	▲3	©	2 14:59			$10	Lava 83151
6/30/01	6	14↑	●	©	3 Sugar Ray			$10	Lava 83414

Abracadabra (2)
Aim For Me (2)
American Pig (1)
Answer The Phone (3)
Anyone (1)
Breathe (1)

Burning Dog (2)
Cash (1)
Disasterpiece (3)
Even Though (1)
Every Morning (2) *3*
Falls Apart (2) *29*

Fly (1)
Glory (2)
High Anxiety (1)
Invisible (1)
Just A Little (3)
Live & Direct (2)

New Direction (2)
Ode To The Lonely Hearted (2)
Ours (2)
Personal Space Invader (2)
RPM (1)
Right Direction (1)

Satellites (3)
Someday (2) *7*
Sorry Now (3)
Speed Home California (1)
Stand And Deliver (1)
Stay On (3)

Tap, Twist, Snap (1)
Under The Sun (3)
Waiting (3)
When It's Over (3) *13*
Words To Me (3)

SUGA T '96

Born in San Francisco. Female rapper. Member of **The Click**. Sister of **E-40**.

| 3/16/96 | 193 | 1 | | © | Paper Chasin' (4eva Hustlin') .... | | | $10 | Jive 41578 |

Did That
Fuckin' Around Wit' Suga

Hustlas & Tendas
Hustlin' 4 Life

If U Don't Want None
Playas Changed

Recognize
Should I...

Suga Daddy
U Don't See Wanna See Me

Wanna Get Freaky
What U Gone Do

SUICIDAL TENDENCIES '92

Hard-rock group from Venice, California: Mike Muir (vocals), Rocky George and Mike Clark (guitars), and Robert Trujillo (bass). Muir and Trujillo went on to form **Infectious Grooves**.

5/23/87	100	13		©	1 Join The Army			$10	Carol 1336
10/1/88	111	12		©	2 How Will I Laugh Tomorrow When I Can't Even Smile Today			$10	Epic 44288
10/28/89	150	5	●	©	3 Controlled By Hatred/Feel Like Shit...Deja-Vu			$10	Epic 45244
7/21/90	101	15	●	©	4 Lights...Camera...Revolution			$10	Epic 45389
7/18/92	52	10		©	5 The Art Of Rebellion			$10	Epic 48864
7/3/93	117	3		©	6 Still Cyco After All These Years			$10	Epic 46230
7/2/94	82	3		©	7 Suicidal For Life			$10	Epic 57774

Accept My Sacrifice (5)
Alone (4)
Asleep At The Wheel (medley) (5)
Can't Stop (5)
Choosing My Own Way Of Life (3)
Controlled By Hatred (3)
Cyco (1)
Depression And Anguish (7)
Disco's Out, Murder's In (4)
Don't Give A Fuck! (7)
Don't Give Me Your Nothin' (6)
Emotion No. 13 (4)

Evil (7)
Fascist Pig (6)
Feel Like Shit...Deja-Vu (3)
Feeling's Back (2)
Fucked Up Just Right! (7)
Get Whacked (4)
Give It Revolution (4)
Go'n Breakdown (4)
Gotta Kill Captain Stupid (5)
Hearing Voices (4)
How Will I Laugh Tomorrow (2,3)
I Feel Your Pain And I Survive (1)

I Saw Your Mommy (6)
I Shot The Devil (6)
I Want More (6)
I Wasn't Meant To Feel This (medley) (5)
I Wouldn't Mind (7)
I'll Hate You Better (5)
If I Don't Wake Up (2)
Institutionalized (6)
It's Going Down (5)
It's Not Easy (3)
Join The Army (1)
Just Another Love Song (3)
Little Each Day (1,6)

Looking In Your Eyes (1)
Lost Again (4)
Love Vs. Loneliness (7)
Lovely (4)
Master Of No Mercy (3)
Memories Of Tomorrow (6)
Miracle, The (2)
Monopoly On Sorrow (5)
No Bullshit (7)
No Fuck'n Problem (7)
No Name, No Words (1)
Nobody Hears (5)
One Too Many Times (2)
Pledge Your Allegiance (2)

Possessed (6)
Possessed To Skate (1)
Prisoner, The (1)
Send Me Your Money (4)
Sorry?! (2)
Subliminal (6)
Suicidal Failure (6)
Suicidal Maniac (2)
Suicide's An Alternative (6)
Suicyco Muthafucka (7)
Surf And Slam (2)
Tap Into The Power (5)
Trip At The Brain (1)
Two-Sided Politics (6)

Two Wrongs Don't Make A Right (But They Make Me Feel A Whole Lot Better) (1)
Waking The Dead (3)
War Inside My Head (1,6)
We Call This Mutha Revenge (5)
What Else Could I Do? (7)
What You Need's A Friend (7)
Where's The Truth (5)
Which Way To Free? (5)
Won't Fall In Love Today (4)
You Can't Bring Me Down (4)
You Got, I Want (1)

SUICIDE MACHINES, The '98

Rock group from Detroit: Jason Navarro (vocals), Dan Lukacinsky (guitar), Royce Nunley (bass) and Derek Grant (drums). Ryan Vandeberghe replaced Grant in 1999.

| 4/25/98 | 127 | 2 | | © | 1 Battle Hymns .... | | | $10 | Hollywood 62060 |
| 3/4/00 | 188 | 1 | | © | 2 The Suicide Machines .... | | | $10 | Hollywood 62189 |

All Out (2)
Black & White World (1)
Confused (1)
DDT (1)
Empty Room (1)
Extraordinary (2)

Face Another Day (1)
Fade Away (2)
Give (1)
Goodbye For Now (2)
Green (2)
Hating Hate (1)

High Society (1)
Hope (1)
I Hate Everything (2)
I Never Promised You A Rose Garden (2)
In The End (1)

Independence Parade (1)
No Sale (2)
Perfect Day (2)
Permanent Holiday (2)
Reasons (2)
Sides (1)

Sincerity (2)
Someone (1)
Sometimes I Don't Mind (2)
Speak No Evil (1)
Step One (1)
Strike (1)

Sympathy (1)
Too Many Words (1)
What You Say (1)

SULTON, Kasim '82
Born in 1950 in Brooklyn, New York. Rock singer/bassist. Member of **Utopia** and **Joan Jett & The Blackhearts.**

| 2/27/82 | 197 | 2 | | | Kasim .... | | | $10 | EMI America 17063 |

Don't Break My Heart | Evil | Rock And Roll | Someone To Love | This Must Be Love
Drivin' Me Mad | Just A Little Bit | Roll The Dice | Sweet Little Accident | White And Red

SUM 41 '01
Punk-rock group from New York City: Deryck Whibley (vocals, guitar), Dave Baksh (guitar), Cone McCaslin (bass) and Steve Jocz (drums).

| 5/26/01 | 13 | 19↑ ▲ © | | | All Killer No Filler .... | | | $10 | Island 548662 |

All She's Got | Fat Lip 66 | Heart Attack | Motivation | Pain For Pleasure | Summer
Crazy Amanda Bunkface | Handle This | In Too Deep | Nothing On My Back | Rhythms

SUMMER, Donna ★121★ '79
Born Adrian Donna Gaines on 12/31/48 in Boston. R&B singer. Dubbed "The Queen of Disco." Acted in European productions of *Hair, Godspell, The Me Nobody Knows* and *Porgy And Bess.* Married Bruce Sudano (of **Alive & Kicking** and **Brooklyn Dreams**) on 7/16/80.

1)Bad Girls 2)Live And More 3)On The Radio-Greatest Hits-Volumes I & II

11/1/75+	11	30	● ©	1	Love To Love You Baby			$15	Oasis 5003
3/27/76	21	27	● ©	2	A Love Trilogy			$15	Oasis 5004
11/6/76	29	26	● ©	3	Four Seasons Of Love			$12	Casablanca 7038
6/4/77	18	40	● ©	4	I Remember Yesterday			$12	Casablanca 7056
11/26/77+	26	58	● ©	5	Once Upon A Time...			$15	Casablanca 7078 [2]
9/16/78	❶[1]	75	▲ ©	6	Live And More		[L]	$15	Casablanca 7119 [2]
5/12/79	❶[6]	49	▲[2] ©	7	Bad Girls			$15	Casablanca 7150 [2]
11/3/79+	❶[1]	39	▲[2] ©	8	On The Radio-Greatest Hits-Volumes I & II		[G]	$15	Casablanca 7191 [2]
10/11/80	50	15		9	Walk Away - Collector's Edition (The Best Of 1977-1980)		[G]	$12	Casablanca 7244
11/8/80	13	18	● ©	10	The Wanderer			$10	Geffen 2000
8/14/82	20	37	● ©	11	Donna Summer			$10	Geffen 2005
7/16/83	9	32	● ©	12	She Works Hard For The Money			$10	Mercury 812265
9/22/84	40	17	©	13	Cats Without Claws			$10	Geffen 24040
10/10/87	122	6	©	14	All Systems Go			$10	Geffen 24102
5/20/89	53	20	©	15	Another Place And Time			$10	Atlantic 81987
7/10/99	43	13	©	16	VH1 Presents Donna Summer - Live & More Encore!		[L]	$10	Epic 69910

All Systems Go (14) | Forgive Me (13) | Last Dance (6,8,9,16) 3 | My Life (16) | Running For Cover (10) | Try Me, I Know We Can Make
All Through The Night (7) | Full Of Emptiness (1) | Livin' In America (11) | My Man Medley (6) | Say Something Nice (5) | It (2,6,8) 80
Autumn Changes (3) | Grand Illusion (10) | Looking Up (10) | Mystery Of Love (11) | Sentimental (15) | Unconditional Love (12) 43
Back In Love Again (4) | Happily Ever After (5) | Love Has A Mind Of Its Own | Need-A-Man Blues (1) | She Works Hard For The | Voices Cryin' Out (14)
Bad Girls (7,8,9,16) 1 | He's A Rebel (12) | (12) 70 | Nightlife (10) | Money (12,16) 3 | Walk Away (7,9) 36
Bad Reputation (14) | Heaven Knows (6,8) 4 | Love Is In Control (Finger On | No More Tears (Enough Is | Spring Affair (3,6) 47 | Wanderer, The (10) 3
Black Lady (4) | Hot Stuff (7,8,9,16) 1 | The Trigger) (11) 10 | Enough) (8,16) 1 | State Of Independence | Wasted (2)
Breakaway (15) | I Believe In Jesus (10) | Love Is Just A Breath Away | Now I Need You (5) | (11) 41 | Way We Were (6)
Breakdown (10) | I Do Believe (I Fell In Love) (12) | (11) | Oh Billy Please (13) | Stop, Look And Listen (12) | Whatever Your Heart Desires
Can't Get To Sleep At Night (7) | I Don't Wanna Get Hurt (15) | Love Is The Healer (16) | On My Honor (7) | Stop Me (10) | (15)
Can't We Just Sit Down (And | I Feel Love (4,6,8,9,16) 6 | Love Shock (14) | On The Radio (8,9,16) 5 | Summer Fever (3) | When Love Takes Over You
Talk It Over) (4) | I Love You (5,6,8) 37 | Love To Love You Baby | Once Upon A Time (5,6) | Sunset People (7,8,9) | (15)
Cats Without Claws (13) | I Remember Yesterday (4,6,8) | (1,6,8) 2 | One Night In A Lifetime (7) | Supernatural Love (13) 75 | Whispering Waves (1)
Cold Love (10) 33 | I Will Go With You (Con Te | Love Will Always Find You (7) | One Of A Kind (6) | Suzanna (13) | Who Do You Think You're
Come With Me (2) | Partiró) (16) 79 | Love's About To Change My | Only One (15) | Sweet Romance (5) | Foolin' (10) 40
Could It Be Magic (2) 52 | I'm Free (13) | Heart (15) 85 | Only One Man (6) | Take Me (4) | Winter Melody (3) 43
Dance Into My Life (5) | (If It) Hurts Just A Little (11) | Love's Unkind (4,6) | Only The Fool Survives (14) | (Theme) Once Upon A Time (5) | Woman (12)
Dim All The Lights (7,8,16) 2 | If It Makes You Feel Good (15) | Lucky (7) | Our Love (7,8,9) | There Goes My Baby (13) 21 | Woman In Me (11) 33
Dinner With Gershwin (14) 48 | If You Got It Flaunt It (5) | Lush Life (11) | Pandora's Box (11) | There Will Always Be A You (7) | Working The Midnight Shift (5)
Eyes (13) | In Another Place And Time (15) | MacArthur Park (6,8,9,16) 1 | People, People (12) | Thinkin' 'Bout My Baby (14) |
Fairy Tale High (5,6) | It's Not The Way (13) | Man Like You (5) | Prelude To Love (2) | This Time I Know It's For Real |
Fascination (14) | Jeremy (14) | Maybe It's Over (13) | Protection (11) | (15,16) 7 |
Faster And Faster To Nowhere | Journey To The Centre Of Your | Mimi's Song (6) | Queen For A Day (5) | Tokyo (12) |
(5,6) | Heart (7) | My Baby Understands (7) | Rumour Has It (5,6) 53 |

SUMMER, Henry Lee '88
Born in Brazil, Indiana. Rock singer/songwriter/guitarist.

| 3/12/88 | 56 | 23 | © | 1 | Henry Lee Summer .... | | | $10 | CBS Associated 40895 |
| 5/27/89 | 78 | 17 | © | 2 | I've Got Everything .... | | | $10 | CBS Associated 45124 |

Close Enough For Me (2) | Hands On The Radio (1) 85 | I Wish I Had A Girl (1) 20 | Louie Louie Louie (2) | Roll Me (2) | What's A Poor Boy To Do (2)
Darlin' Danielle Don't (1) 57 | Hey Baby (2) 18 | I'll Hurt For You (1) | Lovin' Man (1) | Something Is Missing (2) | Wing Tip Shoes (1)
Don't Leave (2) | I Ain't Comin' Home (1) | I've Got Everything (2) | My Louisa (2) | Still Bein' Seventeen (1) |
Got No Money (2) | I Know How You Feel (1) | Just Another Day (1) | My Turn Train (2) | Treat Her Like A Lady (1) |

SUMMERS, Andy/Robert Fripp '82
Born on 12/31/42 in Lancashire, England. Lead guitarist of **The Police.**

| 11/6/82 | 60 | 11 | © | 1 | I Advance Masked .... | | [I] | $10 | A&M 4913 |
| 10/20/84 | 155 | 5 | © | 2 | Bewitched .... | | [I] | $10 | A&M 5011 |

Aquarelle (medley) (1) | Girl On A Swing (1) | In The Cloud Forest (1) | Parade (2) | Tribe (2)
Begin The Day (2) | Guide (2) | Lakeland (medley) (2) | Seven On Seven (1) | Truth Of Skies (1)
Bewitched (2) | Hardy Country (1) | Maquillage (1) | Still Point (1) | Under Bridges Of Silence (1)
China - Yellow Leader (1) | I Advance Masked (1) | New Marimba (1) | Stultified (1) | What Kind Of Man Reads
Forgotten Steps (2) | Image And Likeness (2) | Painting And Dance (1) | Train (2) | Playboy (2)

SUMMERS, Bill, & Summers Heat '82

Born in Detroit. R&B percussionist. Formerly with **Herbie Hancock**'s Head Hunters.

| 4/4/81 | 129 | 15 | | | 1 Call It What You Want | | | $10 | MCA 5176 |
| 12/12/81+ | 92 | 16 | | | 2 Jam The Box! | | | $10 | MCA 5266 |

At The Concert (2)
Call It What You Want (1)
Come On Out (1)
Dream Of Love (2)

Dreaming (2)
Drum Affair (2)
Give Your Love To Me (2)
Go For It (2)

Having Big Fun On Saturday (2)
I Believe In You (1)
Jam The Box (2)
Jammin (1)

Love Not My Life (1)
Snatch (Is A Dance) (1)
Summer Fun (1)
T.V. (1)

Throw Down (2)
We Call It The Box (2)
You Better Turn Around (1)
Your Style Ain't The Way (1)

SUN '78

Funk group from Dayton, Ohio: Byron Byrd (vocals), Sheldon Reynolds and Anthony Thompson (guitars), Dean Francis (keyboards), Ernie Knisley (percussion), Robert Arnold, Gary King and Larry Hatchet (horns), Don Taylor (bass) and Kym Yancey (drums).

| 5/6/78 | 69 | 22 | ● | | 1 Sunburn | | | $12 | Capitol 11723 |
| 7/21/79 | 85 | 10 | | | 2 Destination: Sun | | | $12 | Capitol 11941 |

Baby I Confess (2)
Dance (Do What You Wanna Do) (1)
Deep Rooted Feeling (Stand Up) (2)

Everybody Disco Down (2)
Hallelujah Spirit (2)
I Had A Choice (1)
I Want To Be With You (Forever) (2)

Light Of The Universe (2)
Long Drawn Out Thang (1)
Pure Fire (2)
Radiation Level (2)
Sun Is Here (medley) (1)

Sun Of A Gun (1)
When You Put Your Hand In Mine (1)
You Are My Sunshine (medley) (1)

You Don't Have To Hurry (1)
You're The One (1)

SUNDAYS, The '97

Pop-rock group from London: Harriet Wheeler (vocals), David Gavurin (guitar), Paul Brindley (bass) and Patrick Hannan (drums).

5/26/90	39	23	●	©	1 Reading, Writing And Arithmetic			$10	DGC 24277
11/7/92	103	25	●	©	2 Blind			$10	DGC 24479
10/11/97	33	17		©	3 Static & Silence			$10	DGC 25131

Another Flavour (3)
Blood On My Hands (2)
Can't Be Sure (1)
Certain Someone (1)
Cry (3)
Folk Song (3)
God Made Me (2)

Goodbye (2)
Here's Where The Story Ends (1)
Hideous Towns (1)
Homeward (2)
I Can't Wait (3)
I Feel (2)

I Kicked A Boy (1)
I Won (1)
Joy (1)
Leave This City (3)
Life & Soul (2)
Love (2)
Medicine (2)

Monochrome (3)
More (2)
My Finest Hour (1)
On Earth (2)
She (3)
Skin & Bones (1)
So Much (3)

Summertime (3)
24 Hours (2)
What Do You Think? (2)
When I'm Thinking About You (3)
Wild Horses (2)

You're Not The Only One I Know (1)
Your Eyes (3)

SUNNY & THE SUNLINERS '63

Latin group from San Antonio, Texas: Sunny Ozuna, with brothers Jesse, Oscar and Ray Villanueva, Tony Tostado, Gilbert Fernandez and Alred Luna. Originally known as Sunny & The Sunglows.

| 11/2/63 | 142 | 2 | | © | 1 Talk To Me | | | $100 | Tear Drop 2000 |
| 8/14/65 | 148 | 2 | | © | 2 the original Peanuts | | [I] | $100 | Sunglow 103 |

THE SUNGLOWS

Battle Of Flowers (2)
Beer Barrel Polka (2)
Carino Nuevo (1)
Chin-Wen-Wen Chona (2)
Circus, The (2)

Colt 45 (2)
Every Week Every Month Every Year (1)
Golly Gee (1)
Got You On My Mind (1)

Happy Hippo (2)
I'm A Fool To Care (1)
Indian, The (2)
Just A Moment (1)
La Raspa (2)

Merry Go Round (2)
No One Else Will Do (1)
Not Even Judgement Day (1)
Peanuts (La Cacahuata) (2) *64*
Please Mr. Sandman (1)

Popcorn (2)
Rags To Riches (1) *45*
Rancho Grande (2)

Talk To Me (1) *11*
hit "Hot 100" as Sunny & The Sunglows
Think It Over (1)

SUNNY DAY REAL ESTATE '00

Rock trio from Seattle: Dan Hoerner (vocals, guitar), Jeff Palmer (bass) and William Goldsmith (drums).

| 10/10/98 | 132 | 1 | | © | 1 How It Feels To Be Something On | | | $10 | Sub Pop 409 |
| 7/8/00 | 97 | 2 | | © | 2 The Rising Tide | | | $10 | Time Bomb 43541 |

Days Were Golden (1)
Disappear (2)
Every Shining Time You Arrive (1)
Faces In Disguise (2)

Fool In The Photograph (1)
Guitar And Video Games (1)
How It Feels To Be Something On (1)
Killed By An Angel (1)

Ocean, The (2)
One (2)
100 Million (1)
Pillars (1)
Prophet, The (1)

Rain Song (2)
Rising Tide (2)
Roses In Water (1)
Shark's Own Private Fuck (1)
Snibe (2)

Tearing In My Heart (2)
Television (1)
Two Promises (1)

SUNSCREEM '93

Techno-pop group from England: Lucia Holm (vocals), Darren Woodford (guitar), Paul Carnell (keyboards), Rob Fricker (bass) and Sean Wright (drums).

| 3/20/93 | 141 | 5 | | © | O3 | | | $10 | Columbia 53449 |

B
Broken English
Chasing Dreams

Doved Up
Idaho
Love U More *36*

Perfect Motion
Portal
Pressure

Psycho
Release Me
Walk On

Your Hands

SUNSHINE BAND, The — see KC

SUNSHINE COMPANY, The '67

Pop group formed in Los Angeles: Mary Nance (vocals), Doug "Red" Mark and Maury Manseau (guitars), Larry Sims (bass) and Merle Brigante (drums). Mark later formed **Redeye**.

| 10/21/67 | 126 | 10 | | | Happy Is The Sunshine Company | | | $20 | Imperial 12359 |

Back On The Street Again *36*
Children Could Help Us Find The Way

Four In The Mornin'
Happy *50*
I Just Want To Be Your Friend

I Need You
Just Beyond Your Smile
Love Is A Happy Thing

Rain
Up, Up And Away
Warm In My Heart

Year Of Jaine Time

SUNZ OF MAN '98

Rap group from New York City: **Killah Priest**, 60 Second Assassin, Prodigal Sunn and Hell Razah.

| 8/8/98 | 20 | 7 | | © | The Last Shall Be First | | | $10 | Red Ant 12305 |

Battle, The
Can I See You
Cold
Collaboration '98

Five Arch Angels
Flaming Swords
For The Lust Of Money (medley)

Grandz, The (medley)
Illusions
Inmates To The Fire
Intellectuals

Israeli News
Natural High
Next Up
Not Promised Tomorrow

Plan, The
Shining Star
Tribulations

SUPERDRAG '96

Rock group from Knoxville, Tennessee: John Davis (vocals), Brandon Fisher (guitar), Tom Pappas (bass) and Don Coffey (drums).

| 8/3/96 | 158 | 5 | | © | Regretfully Yours | | | $10 | Elektra 61900 |

Carried
Cynicality
Destination Ursa Major

Garmonbozia
N.A. Kicker
Nothing Good Is Real

Phaser
Rocket
Slot Machine

Sucked Out
Truest Love
What If You Don't Fly

Whitey's Theme

SUPERNAW, Doug   '94

Born on 9/26/60 in Bryan, Texas. Country singer/songwriter/guitarist.

| 8/7/93+ | 147 | 28 | ● | © | **1 Red And Rio Grande** | | | $10 | BNA 66133 |

Carousel · Five Generations Of Rock · I Don't Call Him Daddy · Perfect Picture (To Fit My · Reno
Daddy's Girl · County Wilsons · I Would Have Loved You All · Frame Of Mind) · You're Gonna Bring Back
· Honky Tonkin' Fool · Night Long · Red And Rio Grande · Cheatin' Songs

SUPERSAX   '73

Jazz group formed in Los Angeles: Meredith Flory, Bill Perkins, Warne Marsh and Jay Migliori (saxophones), Conte Candoli (trumpet), Ron Bright (piano), Bud Clark (bass) and Jake Hanna (drums).

| 7/14/73 | 169 | 7 | | © | **1 Supersax plays Bird** | | [I] | $12 | Capitol 11177 |
| 4/6/74 | 182 | 3 | | | **2 Supersax plays Bird, Volume 2/Salt Peanuts** | | [I] | $12 | Capitol 11271 |

Be-Bop (1) · Groovin' High (2) · Lover (2) · Night In Tunisia (1) · Salt Peanuts (2)
Bird, The (2) · Hot House (1) · Lover Man (Oh Where Can You · Oh, Lady Be Good! (1) · Scrapple From The Apple (2)
Confirmation (2) · Just Friends (1) · Be) (2) · Parker's Mood (1) · Star Eyes (1)
Embraceable You (2) · Ko-Ko (1) · Moose The Mooche (1) · Repetition (1) · Yardbird Suite (2)

★335★ SUPERTRAMP   '79

Rock group formed in England: **Roger Hodgson** (vocals, guitar), Rick Davies (vocals, keyboards), John Helliwell (sax), Dougie Thomson (bass) and Bob Siebenberg (drums). Thomson is the brother of **Ali Thomson**. Hodgson left in 1983.

12/7/74+	38	76	●	©	**1 Crime Of The Century**			$12	A&M 3647
12/13/75+	44	28		©	**2 Crisis? What Crisis?**			$12	A&M 4560
4/23/77	16	49	●	©	**3 Even In The Quietest Moments**			$12	A&M 4634
3/4/78	158	5		©	**4 Supertramp**		[E]	$12	A&M 4665

recorded in 1970

| 3/31/79 | ❶[6] | 88 | ▲[4] | © | **5 Breakfast In America** | | | $12 | A&M 3708 |
| 10/11/80 | 8 | 26 | ● | © | **6 Paris** | | [L] | $15 | A&M 6702 [2] |

recorded on 11/29/79 at the Paris Pavillon

11/13/82	5	28	●	©	**7 ...famous last words...**			$10	A&M 3732
6/1/85	21	22		©	**8 Brother Where You Bound**			$10	A&M 5014
10/31/87	101	11		©	**9 Free As A Bird**			$10	A&M 5181

Ain't Nobody But Me (2,6) · C'est Le Bon (7) · Fool's Overture (3,6) · **It's Raining Again** (7) **11** · Nothing To Show (4) · **Take The Long Way Home** (5,6) **10**
And I Am Not Like Other Birds · **Cannonball** (8) **28** · Free As A Bird (9) · Just A Normal Day (2) · Oh Darling (5) · Thing For You (9)
Of Prey (medley) (4) · Casual Conversations (5) · From Now On (3,6) · Just Another Nervous Wreck (5) · Poor Boy (2) · Try Again (4)
Another Man's Woman (2) · Child Of Vision (5) · **Give A Little Bit** (3) **15** · Know Who You Are (7) · Put On Your Old Brown Shoes · Two Of Us (2,6)
Asylum (1,6) · Crazy (7) · Gone Hollywood (5) · Lady (2) · (7) · Waiting So Long (7)
Aubade (medley) (4) · Crime Of The Century (1,6) · **Goodbye Stranger** (5) **15** · **Logical Song** (5,6) **6** · Rudy (1,6) · Where I Stand (9)
Awful Thing To Waste (9) · Don't Leave Me Now (7) · Hide In Your Shell (1,6) · Lord Is It Mine (7) · School (1,6) · Words Unspoken (4)
Babaji (3) · Downstream (3) · Home Again (4) · Lover Boy (3) · Shadow Song (4) · You Never Can Tell With
Better Days (8) · **Dreamer** (1,6) **15** · I'm Beggin' You (7) · Maybe I'm A Beggar (4) · Sister Moonshine (2) · Friends (9)
Bloody Well Right (1,6) **35** · Easy Does It (2) · If Everyone Was Listening (1) · Meaning, The (2) · Soapbox Opera (2,6) · You Started Laughing (6)
Bonnie (7) · Even In The Quietest Moments · It Doesn't Matter (9) · **My Kind Of Lady** (7) **31** · Still In Love (8)
Breakfast In America (5,6) **62** · (3) · It's A Long Road (4) · No Inbetween (8) · Surely (4)
Brother Where You Bound (8) · Ever Open Door (8) · It's Alright (9) · Not The Moment (9)

SUPREMES, The   ★23★   '69

R&B vocal trio from Detroit: **Diana Ross**, Mary Wilson and Florence Ballard. Cindy Birdsong (of **Patti LaBelle**'s Blue Belles) replaced Ballard in 1967. Jean Terrell replaced Ross in late 1969. Lynda Laurence replaced Birdsong in 1972. Terrell and Laurence left in 1973. Mary Wilson re-formed group with Scherrie Payne (sister of **Freda Payne**) and Cindy Birdsong. Ballard died of heart failure on 2/22/76 (age 32). Group inducted into the Rock and Roll Hall of Fame in 1988.

1)Diana Ross and the Supremes Greatest Hits 2)The Supremes A' Go-Go 3)TCB 4)Where Did Our Love Go
5)Diana Ross & the Supremes Join the Temptations

9/19/64+	2[4]	89		©	**1 Where Did Our Love Go**			$40	Motown 621
11/28/64+	21	21		©	**2 A Bit Of Liverpool**			$40	Motown 623
3/20/65	79	8		©	**3 The Supremes sing Country Western & Pop**			$40	Motown 625
5/8/65	75	19		©	**4 We Remember Sam Cooke**			$40	Motown 629
8/21/65	6	37		©	**5 More Hits By The Supremes**			$40	Motown 627
11/13/65+	11	54		©	**6 The Supremes at the Copa**		[L]	$40	Motown 636
12/11/65	6[X]	12		©	**7 Merry Christmas**		[X]	$40	Motown 638

Christmas charts: 6/'65, 13/'66, 19/'67, 26/'70

3/19/66	8	55		©	**8 I Hear A Symphony**			$40	Motown 643
9/24/66	❶[2]	60		©	**9 The Supremes A' Go-Go**			$40	Motown 649
2/18/67	6	29		©	**10 The Supremes sing Holland-Dozier-Holland**			$40	Motown 650
6/17/67	20	19			**11 The Supremes Sing Rodgers & Hart**			$40	Motown 659

DIANA ROSS & THE SUPREMES:

9/30/67	❶[5]	89		©	**12 Diana Ross and the Supremes Greatest Hits**		[G]	$30	Motown 663 [2]
4/27/68	18	29		©	**13 Reflections**			$30	Motown 665
10/5/68+	57	18		©	**14 Live At London's Talk Of The Town**		[L]	$30	Motown 676
10/5/68	150	12			**15 Funny Girl**			$30	Motown 672
11/30/68+	2[1]	32	●	©	**16 Diana Ross & The Supremes Join the Temptations**			$30	Motown 679

DIANA ROSS & THE SUPREMES WITH THE TEMPTATIONS

| 12/14/68+ | 14 | 21 | | © | **17 Love Child** | | | $30 | Motown 670 |
| 12/28/68+ | ❶[1] | 34 | ● | © | **18 TCB** | | [TV] | $30 | Motown 682 |

DIANA ROSS & THE SUPREMES WITH THE TEMPTATIONS

| 6/21/69 | 24 | 18 | | © | **19 Let The Sunshine In** | | | $30 | Motown 689 |
| 10/25/69 | 28 | 18 | | © | **20 Together** | | | $30 | Motown 692 |

DIANA ROSS & THE SUPREMES WITH THE TEMPTATIONS

| 11/29/69+ | 33 | 20 | | © | **21 Cream Of The Crop** | | | $30 | Motown 694 |

SUPREMES, The — Cont'd

DEBUT	PEAK	WKS						$	Label & Number
12/6/69	38	12			22 On Broadway .... [TV]			$30	Motown 699

DIANA ROSS & THE SUPREMES WITH THE TEMPTATIONS

1/10/70	31	25	©		23 Diana Ross & the Supremes Greatest Hits, Volume 3 .... [G]			$25	Motown 702
5/16/70	46	18			24 Farewell .... [L]			$25	Motown 708 [2]
					recorded on 1/14/70 at the Frontier Hotel in Las Vegas				

THE SUPREMES:

6/6/70	25	19	©		25 Right On			$25	Motown 705
10/17/70	113	16	©		26 The Magnificent 7			$25	Motown 717

SUPREMES & FOUR TOPS

10/24/70+	68	17	©		27 New Ways But Love Stays			$25	Motown 720
6/26/71	85	10	©		28 Touch			$25	Motown 737
6/26/71	154	6			29 The Return Of The Magnificent Seven			$25	Motown 736
1/8/72	160	6			30 Dynamite			$25	Motown 745

SUPREMES & FOUR TOPS (above 2)

5/27/72	54	15	©		31 Floy Joy			$20	Motown 751
11/25/72+	129	13			32 The Supremes			$20	Motown 756
6/29/74	66	15	●	©	33 Anthology (1962-1969) .... [G]			$25	Motown 794 [3]

DIANA ROSS & THE SUPREMES

6/28/75	152	8			34 The Supremes			$20	Motown 828
5/22/76	42	15			35 High Energy			$20	Motown 863
4/7/84	35 C	8			36 Great Songs And Performances That Inspired The Motown 25th Anniversary Television Special			$10	Motown 5313
5/17/86	112	17			37 25th Anniversary .... [K]			$20	Motown 5381 [3]

DIANA ROSS & THE SUPREMES (above 2)

Ain't No Mountain High Enough (16)
Ain't Nothing Like The Real Thing (20,26)
Ain't That Good News (4)
All I Want (32)
Any Girl In Love (Knows What I'm Going Through) (8)
Aquarius (medley) (19,24)
Are You Sure Love Is The Name Of This Game (37)
Ask Any Girl (1,5,12,33)
Automatically Sunshine (31) 37
Baby Baby (25)
Baby Doll (3)
Baby I Need Your Loving (9)
Baby Love (1,6,12,14,18,24,33,36,37) 1
Baby, (You've Got What It Takes) (26)
Back In My Arms Again (5,6,12,33,36,37) 1
Bah-Bah-Bah (13)
Because (2)
Beginning Of The End (21)
Beyond Myself (32)
Big Spender (24)
Bigger You Love (The Harder You Fall) (30)
Bill, When Are You Coming Back (25)
Bits And Pieces (2)
Blowin' In The Wind (21)
Blue Moon (11)
Blue Room (37)
Born Of Mary (7)
Boy From Ipanema (6)
Breath Taking Guy (1,33) 75
Bridge Over Troubled Water (27)
Bring It On Home To Me (4,6)
Broadway Medley (22)
But I Love You More (25)
Call Me (29)
Can't Buy Me Love (2)
Can't Shake It Loose (17)
Can't Take My Eyes Off You (20,24)
Can't You See It's Me (21)
Chain Gang (4,6)
Change Is Gonna Come (4)
Cheap Lovin' (30)
Children's Christmas Song (7)
Color My World Blue (34)
Come And Get These Memories (9)
Come On And See Me (37)
Come On Boy (37)
Come See About Me (1,6,12,14,18,24,33,36,37) 1
Come Together (27)
Composer, The (19,23,33) 27
Cornet Man (15)
Cupid (4,6)
Dancing On The Ceiling (11)
Didn't We (24)
Discover Me (And You'll Discover Love) (19)

Do You Know The Way To San Jose (medley) (18)
Do You Love Me (2)
Do You Love Me Just A Little, Honey (30)
Does Your Mama Know About Me (17)
Doin' What Comes Natur'lly (medley) (22)
(Don't Break These) Chains Of Love (17)
Don't Let Me Lose This Dream (30)
Don't Let My Teardrops Bother You (35)
Don't Rain On My Parade (15)
Early Morning Love (34)
Eleanor Rigby (medley) (18)
Everybody's Got The Right To Love (25) 21
Everyday People (19,26)
Everything Is Good About You (8,12)
Everything's Coming Up Roses (medley) (22)
Falling In Love With You (11,24,33)
5:30 Plane (32)
For Better Or Worse (20)
For Your Love (25)
Forever Came Today (13,23,33) 28
Funky Broadway (16,22)
Funny Girl (15)
Funny How Time Slips Away (3,33)
G.I.T. On Broadway (22)
Get Ready (9)
Give Out, But Don't Give Up (34)
Going Down For The Third Time (10)
Good Lovin' Ain't Easy To Come By (30)
Hang On Sloopy (9)
Happening, The (12,14,23,33,37) 1
Happy (Is A Bumpy Road) (28)
Hard Day's Night (2,33)
Have I Lost You (28)
Havin' A Party (4)
He Holds His Own (5)
He Means The World To Me (1)
He's All I Got (8)
He's My Man (34)
He's My Sunny Boy (17)
Heart Like Mine (31)
Heigh-Ho (37)
Hello Stranger (30)
Here Comes The Sunrise (28)
Hey Jude (21)
Hey Western Union Man (19)
High Energy (35)
His Love Makes Me Beautiful (15)
Honey Bee (Keep On Stinging Me) (17)
Honey Boy (9)

House Of The Rising Sun (2)
How Do You Do It (2)
How Long Has That Evening Train Been Gone (17)
I Am Woman (6,15)
I Can't Believe You Love Me (29)
I Can't Help Myself (9)
I Can't Make It Alone (13)
I Don't Want To Lose You (medley) (35)
I Got Hurt (Trying To Be The Only Girl In Your Life) (25)
I Guess I'll Always Love You (10)
I Guess I'll Miss The Man (32) 85
I Hear A Symphony (8,12,18,33,36,37) 1
I Keep It Hid (32)
(I Love You) For Sentimental Reasons (medley) (6)
I Second That Emotion (16)
I Want To Hold Your Hand (2)
I Wish I Were Your Mirror (27)
I Wonder Where We're Going (29)
I'll Be Doggone (26)
I'll Set You Free (17)
I'll Try Not To Cry (29)
I'll Try Something New (16,33,36) 25
I'll Turn To Stone (10)
I'm Giving You, Your Freedom (1)
I'm Glad About It (29)
I'm Gonna Let My Heart Do The Walking (35) 40
I'm Gonna Make It (I Will Wait For You) (13)
I'm Gonna Make You Love Me (16,24,33,37) 2
I'm Gonna Wash That Man Right Outa My Hair (medley) (22)
I'm In Love Again (5)
I'm Livin' In Shame (19,23,33,37) 10
(I'm So Glad) Heartaches Don't Last Always (5)
I'm So Glad I Got Somebody (Like You Around) (19)
I'm The Greatest Star (15,33)
If (30)
If A Girl Isn't Pretty (15)
If I Could Build The Whole World Around You (30)
If I Ruled The World (24)
If You Could See Me Now (29)
Il Voce De Silenzio (Silent Voices) (32)
Impossible Dream (16,18,24)
In And Out Of Love (13,14,23,24,33,37) 9
Is There A Place (In His Heart For Me) (27)
It Makes No Difference Now (1)
It's All Been Said Before (34)
It's All Your Fault (37)

It's Allright With Me (24)
It's Got To Be A Miracle (This Thing Called Love) (26)
It's Impossible (30)
It's So Hard For Me To Say Good-Bye (28)
It's The Same Old Song (10)
It's Time To Break Down (27)
Johnny Raven (28)
Joy To The World (7)
Keep An Eye (17)
Knock On My Door (26)
Lady Is A Tramp (11,14,24)
Lazybones (3)
Leading Lady (medley) (22)
Let Me Go The Right Way (33) 90
Let The Music Play (19)
Let The Sunshine In (The Flesh Failures) (medley) (19,22,24)
Let's Get Away From It All (medley) (14,24)
Let's Make Love Now (29)
Little Bright Star (7)
Little Drummer Boy (7)
Long Gone Lover (1)
Love Child (17,23,24,33,36,37) 1
Love Is Here And Now You're Gone (10,12,14,23,24,33,37) 1
Love Is In Our Hearts (10)
Love Is Like A Heat Wave (10)
Love Is Like An Itching In My Heart (9,12,33,37) 9
Love It Came To Me This Time (28)
Love (Makes Me Do Foolish Things) (13)
Love The One You're With (30)
Lover (11)
Lover's Concerto (8)
Loving Country (25)
Loving You Is Better Than Ever (21)
Make Someone Happy (6)
Malteds Over Manhattan (22)
Mame (medley) (14,22)
(Man With The) Rock And Roll Banjo Band (7)
Manhattan (24)
Melodie (30)
Michelle (medley) (14)
Misery Makes Its Home In My Heart (13)
Money (That's What I Want) (9)
More (14)
Mother Dear (5)
Mother You, Smother You (10)
Mountain Greenery (11)
Mrs. Robinson (medley) (18)
Music That Makes Me Dance (15)
My Christmas Tree (7)
My Favorite Things (7)
My Funny Valentine (11)
My Guy (medley) (20)
My Heart Can't Take It No More (3)

My Heart Stood Still (11)
My Man (24)
My Romance (11)
My World Is Empty Without You (8,12,14,18,24,33,37) 5
Na Na Hey Hey Kiss Him Goodbye (27)
Nathan Jones (28) 16
No Matter What Sign You Are (19,23,33) 31
Nothing But Heartaches (5,12,33,37) 11
Nothing Can Change This Love (4)
Now The Bitter, Now The Sweet (31)
Ode To Billie Joe (13)
Oh Be My Love (31)
Once In The Morning (32)
One More Bridge To Cross (29)
Only Sixteen (4)
Only Time I'm Happy (5)
Only You (Can Love Me Like You Love Me) (35)
Ooowee Baby (7)
Over And Over (31)
Paradise (32)
Penny Pincher (37)
People (15,22)
Place In The Sun (16)
Precious Little Things (31)
Put On A Happy Face (6)
Put Yourself In My Place (9)
Queen Of The House (4)
Reach Out And Touch (Somebody's Hand) (26)
Reflections (13,14,23,24,33,37) 2
Remove This Doubt (10)
Respect (19)
Rhythm Of Life (22)
River Deep - Mountain High (26) 14
Rock-A-Bye Your Baby With A Dixie Melody (6)
Rudolph, The Red-Nosed Reindeer (7)
Run, Run, Run (1,12,33) 93
Sadie, Sadie (15)
Santa Claus Is Coming To Town (7)
Second Hand Rose (medley) (14)
Send Me No Flowers (37)
Shadows Of Society (21)
Shake (4,6)
Shake Me, Wake Me (When It's Over) (9)
Shine On Me (27)
Silver Bells (7)
Sincerely (37)
Sing A Simple Song (20)
Sleep Walk (37)
Some Things You Never Get Used To (17,23,33) 30
Someday My Prince Will Come (37)
Someday We'll Be Together (21,23,24,33,36,37) 1

Somewhere (6)
Somewhere (18)
Standing At The Crossroads Of Love (1,12,33)
Stoned Love (27) 7
Stoned Soul Picnic (26)
Stop! In The Name Of Love (5,6,12,14,18,24,33,36,37) 1
Stranger In Paradise (8,14)
Stubborn Kind Of Fellow (20)
Student Mountie (22)
Sunset (3)
Surfer Boy (33)
Sweet Inspiration (16)
T.C.B. (18,24)
Take A Closer Look At Me (25)
Taste Of Honey (26)
Tears In Vain (3)
Thank Him For Today (27)
Then (13,16)
Then I Met You (25)
Then We Can Try Again (25)
There's No Stopping Us Now (10,12)
These Boots Are Made For Walking (9)
This Can't Be Love (11)
This Guy's In Love With You (16)
This Is The Story (28)
This Is Why I Believe In You (34)
This Old Heart Of Mine (Is Weak For You) (14)
Thoroughly Modern Millie (medley) (14)
Those D.J. Shows (37)
Thou Swell (11)
Till Johnny Comes (21)
Till The Boat Sails Away (medley) (35)
Time And Love (28)
Together We Can Make Such Sweet Music (26,27)
Tossin' And Turning (32)
Touch (28) 71
Treat Me Nice John Henry (37)
Try It Baby (9)
Tumbling Tumbleweeds (23)
Twinkle Twinkle Little Me (7)
Unchained Melody (8)
Up The Ladder To The Roof (25) 10
Up, Up And Away (13)
Uptight (Everything's Alright) (20)
Wait A Minute Before You Leave Me (25)
Way You Do The Things You Do (18)
We Couldn't Get Along Without You (37)
Weight, The (20) 46
What Becomes Of The Brokenhearted (19)
What Do You Have To Do (To Stay On The Right Side Of Love) (29)

SUPREMES, The — Cont'd

What The World Needs Now Is Love (13)
When Can Brown Begin (32)
When It's To The Top (Still I Won't Stop Giving You Love) (21)
When The Lovelight Starts Shining Through His Eyes (1,12,33,37) **23**
When You Wish Upon A Star (37)
Where Did Our Love Go (1,12,33,36,37) **1**
Where Do I Go From Here (34)
Where Is It I Belong (34)

Where Or When (11)
Where Would I Be Without You, Baby (29)
Whisper You Love Me Boy (5,12)
White Christmas (7)
Who Can I Turn To (When Nobody Needs Me) (37)
Who Could Ever Doubt My Love (5)
Why (Must We Fall In Love) (20)
Will This Be The Day (19)
Wisdom Of Time (31)

With A Child's Heart (19)
With A Song In My Heart (8,14,18)
Without A Song (8,14,18)
Without The One You Love (26)
Wonderful, Wonderful (8,14)
Wonderful World (4)
World Without Love (2)
Wouldn't It Be Lovely (medley) (22)
Yesterday (8,14)
You Ain't Livin' Till You're Lovin' (17)
You Can't Do That (2)

You Can't Hurry Love (9,12,33,36,37) **1**
You Can't Stop A Girl In Love (34)
You Didn't Care (3)
You Gave Me Love (21)
You Gotta Have Love In Your Heart (29) **55**
You Keep Me Hangin' On (10,12,14,18,33,37) **1**
You Keep Me Moving On (35)
You Move Me (25)
You Need Me (33)
You Send Me (4,6,33)

You Turn Me Around (34)
You're Gone (But Always In My Heart) (10)
You're Nobody Till Somebody Loves You (6,14)
You're What's Missing In My Life (35)
You've Been So Wonderful To Me (17)
You've Really Got A Hold On Me (2)
Young Folks (21) **69**
Your Kiss Of Fire (1)

Your Wonderful, Sweet Sweet Love (31) **59**

SURFACE '89
R&B trio from New Jersey: Bernard Jackson (vocals, bass), David Townsend (guitar, keyboards) and Dave Conley (drums, sax).

DEBUT	PEAK	WKS	RIAA	CD	ARTIST — Album Title	Sym	$	Label & Number
5/30/87	55	19		©	1 **Surface**		$10	Columbia 40374
11/26/88+	56	39	▲	©	2 **2nd Wave**		$10	Columbia 44284
11/24/90+	65	34	●	©	3 **3 Deep**		$10	Columbia 46772

Ain't Givin' Up (3)
All I Want Is You (3)
Black Shades (2)
Can We Spend Some Time (3)
Closer Than Friends (2) **57**
Don't Wanna Turn You Off (3)

Feels So Good (1)
First Time (3) **1**
Girls Were Made To Love (1)
Give Her Your Love (3)
Gotta Make Love Tonight (1)
Happy (1) **20**

Hold On To Love (2)
I Missed (2)
Kid Stuff (Believe In Yourself) (3)
Lady Wants A Man (1)
Lately (1)

Let's Try Again (1)
Love X Trust (3)
Never Gonna Let You Down (3)
Shower Me With Your Love (2) **5**

"10" (3)
Tomorrow (3)
We're All Searchin' (1)
When It Comes To Love (3)
Where's That Girl (2)
Who Loves You (1)

You Are My Everything (2) **84**
You're Fine (1)
You're The One (3)

SURFARIS, The '63
Surf group from Glendora, California: Ron Wilson (drums), Jim Fuller and Bob Berryhill (guitars), Pat Connolly (bass) and Jim Pash (sax, clarinet). Wilson died of a brain aneurysm on 5/19/89 (age 44).

DEBUT	PEAK	WKS	RIAA	CD	ARTIST — Album Title	Sym	$	Label & Number
8/10/63	15	51		©	1 **Wipe Out**	[I]	$50	Dot 25535
11/30/63	94	11			2 **The Surfaris play Wipe Out and others**	[I]	$50	Decca 74470
3/7/64	120	5			3 **Hit City 64**		$50	Decca 74487

Bat Man (2)
Be True To Your School (3)
Comin' Home Baby (3)
Earthquake (3)
Green Onions (1)
Hiawatha (3)

I Wanna Take A Trip To The Islands (3)
I'm A Hog For You (2)
Jack The Ripper (2)
Little Deuce Coupe (3)
Louie Louie (3)

Memphis (1)
Misirlou (2)
Mystic Island Drums (3)
Point Panic (2) **49**
Scatter Shield (3)
Scratch (3)

Similau (2)
Sugar Shack (3)
Surf Scene (2)
Surfaris Stomp (2)
Surfer Joe (1,2) **62**
Surfing Drums (2)

Teen Beat (1)
Tequila (1)
Torquay (1)
Waikiki Run (1)
Walk, Don't Run (1)
Wax Board And Woodie (3)

Wiggle Wobble (1)
Wild Weekend (1)
Wipe Out (1,2) **2**
Yep (1)
You Can't Sit Down (1)

SURVIVOR '82
Pop-rock group formed in Chicago: Dave Bickler (vocals), Frankie Sullivan (guitar), Jim Peterik (keyboards), Stephan Ellis (bass) and Marc Droubay (drums). Peterik was lead singer for **Ides Of March**. Jimi Jamison replaced Bickler in 1983. Droubay and Ellis left in early 1988.

DEBUT	PEAK	WKS	RIAA	CD	ARTIST — Album Title	Sym	$	Label & Number
3/29/80	169	7			1 **Survivor**		$10	Scotti Brothers 7107
10/24/81	82	25		©	2 **Premonition**		$10	Scotti Brothers 37549
6/26/82	2[4]	41	▲	©	3 **Eye Of The Tiger**		$10	Scotti Brothers 38062
10/22/83	82	9		©	4 **Caught In The Game**		$10	Scotti Brothers 38791
9/29/84+	16	61	▲	©	5 **Vital Signs**		$10	Scotti Brothers 39578
11/8/86	49	24		©	6 **When Seconds Count**		$10	Scotti Brothers 40457
11/5/88	187	2		©	7 **Too Hot To Sleep**		$10	Scotti Brothers 44282

Across The Miles (7) **74**
American Heartbeat (3) **17**
As Soon As Love Finds Me (1)
Backstreet Love Affair (6)
Broken Promises (5)
Burning Bridges (7)
Can't Getcha Offa My Mind (1)
Can't Give It Up (7)
Can't Let You Go (6)
Caught In The Game (4) **77**
Chevy Nights (1)
Children Of The Night (3)

Desperate Dreams (7)
Didn't Know It Was Love (5) **61**
Ever Since The World Began (3)
Everlasting (5)
Eye Of The Tiger (3) **1**
Feels Like Love (3)
First Night (5) **53**
Freelance (1)
Half-Life (4)
Heart's A Lonely Hunter (2)

Here Comes Desire (7)
Hesitation Dance (3)
High On You (5) **8**
How Much Love (6) **51**
I Can't Hold Back (5) **13**
I Never Stopped Loving You (4)
I See You In Everyone (3)
I'm Not That Man Anymore (3)
In Good Faith (3)
Is This Love (6) **9**
It Doesn't Have To Be This Way (4)

It's The Singer Not The Song (5)
Jackie Don't Go (4)
Keep It Right Here (6)
Let It Be Now (1)
Light Of A Thousand Smiles (2)
Love Has Got Me (1)
Love Is On My Side (2)
Man Against The World (6) **86**
Nothing Can Shake Me (From Your Love) (1)
Oceans (6)

One That Really Matters (3) **74**
Poor Man's Son (2) **33**
Popular Girl (5)
Ready For The Real Thing (4)
Rebel Son (6)
Rhythm Of The City (7)
Runway Lights (2)
Santa Ana Winds (4)
Search Is Over (5) **4**
She's A Star (7)
Silver Girl (3)

Slander (4)
Somewhere In America (1) **70**
Summer Nights (2) **62**
Take You On A Saturday (2)
Tell Me I'm The One (7)
Too Hot To Sleep (7)
20/20 (1)
What Do You Really Think? (4)
Whatever It Takes (1)
When Seconds Count (6)
Whole Town's Talkin' (1)
Youngblood (1)

SUSAN '79
Rock group from Boston: brothers Charles (vocals, bass) and Mick (drums) Leland, with Ricky Byrd and Tom Dickie (guitars). Byrd later joined **Joan Jett & The Blackhearts**.

DEBUT	PEAK	WKS	RIAA	CD	ARTIST — Album Title	Sym	$	Label & Number
5/5/79	169	5			**Falling In Love Again**		$12	RCA Victor 3372

Don't Let Me Go
Falling In Love Again

I Was Wrong
Little Time

Love The Way
Marlene

Power
Really Gonna Show

Takin' It Over
Tonight You're Mine

Too Bad

SUSAN OF SESAME STREET '70
Born Loretta Long in Boston. Joined the cast of TV's *Sesame Street* in 1969.

DEBUT	PEAK	WKS	RIAA	CD	ARTIST — Album Title	Sym	$	Label & Number
8/1/70	86	13			**Susan Sings Songs From Sesame Street**		$15	Scepter 584

ABC Song
Children (Sister's Song And Brother's Song)

Counting Song (1-20)
Draw Me A Circle
Happiness

Happy Talk
Here Are Some Things That Belong Together

If You're Happy And You Know It (Clap Your Hands)
Right In The Middle Of My Face

Square Song
Three Of These Things Belong Together

What Are Little Children Made Of

SUTHERLAND, Joan '65
Born on 11/7/26 in Sydney, Australia. Legendary opera singer.

DEBUT	PEAK	WKS	RIAA	CD	ARTIST — Album Title	Sym	$	Label & Number
12/18/65	22[X]	2			**Joy Of Christmas**	[X]	$15	London 25943

with the New Philharmonia Orchestra; Richard Bonynge, conductor

Adeste Fideles
Angels We Have Heard On High
Ave Maria

Deck The Hall
Good King Wenceslas
Hark The Herald Angels Sing
Holly And The Ivy

It Came Upon The Midnight Clear
Joy To The World
O Divine Redeemer

O Holy Night
Twelve Days Of Christmas
Virgin's Slumber Song
What Child Is This

SUTHERLAND BROTHERS AND QUIVER '73

Pop-rock group formed in England: brothers Iain (vocals, guitar) and Gavin (vocals, bass) Sutherland, with their four-piece group Quiver: Tim Renwick (guitar), Pete Wood (keyboards), Bruce Thomas (bass) and Willie Wilson (drums). Quiver disbanded in 1977 and Thomas joined **Elvis Costello**'s Attractions.

8/18/73	77	17			1 Lifeboat			$15	Island 9326
5/11/74	193	3			2 Dream Kid			$15	Island 9341
5/8/76	195	2			3 Reach For The Sky			$12	Columbia 33982

Ain't Too Proud (3) — **Arms Of Mary** (3) *81* — Bad Loser (2) — Bluesy World (2) — Champion The Underdog (2) — Change The Wind (1) — Dirty City (3) — Dr. Dancer (3) — Dream Kid (3) — Flying Down To Rio (2) — Have You Had A Vision (1) — **(I Don't Want To Love You But) You Got Me Anyway** (1) *48* — I Hear Thunder (2) — Lifeboat (1) — Lonely Love (medley) (2) — Love On The Moon (3) — Mad Trail (2) — Maker (2) — Moonlight Lady (3) — Not Fade Away (1) — Reach For The Sky (3) — Real Love (1) — Rock And Roll Show (1) — Rocky Road (medley) (2) — Rollin' Away (medley) (2) — Sailing (1) — Saved By The Angel (medley) (2) — Seagull (medley) (2) — Something Special (3) — Space Hymn (1) — When The Train Comes (3) — Where Do We Go Wrong (1) — You And Me (2)

SWAN, Billy '75

Born on 5/12/42 in Cape Girardeau, Missouri. Singer/songwriter/keyboardist/guitarist. Wrote "Lover Please" for Clyde McPhatter. Produced **Tony Joe White**'s first three albums. Toured with **Kris Kristofferson** from the early '70s. Formed band Black Tie with **Randy Meisner** in 1986.

12/7/74+	21	16		©	I Can Help			$15	Monument 33279

Don't Be Cruel — **I Can Help** *1* — I'd Like To Work For You — **I'm Her Fool** *53* — Lover Please — P.M.S. (Post Mortem Sickness) — Queen Of My Heart — Shake, Rattle And Roll — Ways Of A Woman In Love — Wedding Bells

SWANSON, Brad, & His Whispering Organ Sound '69

Born in Buffalo, New York. Male organist.

10/18/69	185	2			Quentin's Theme		[I]	$15	Thunderbird 9004

Ain't She Sweet — Heart Of My Heart — Mac The Knife — Margie — My Imaginary Love — Old Piano Roll Blues — Poor Butterfly — Quentin's Theme — Stars In Your Eyes — Sweet Georgia Brown — You Are My Sunshine

SWAY & KING TECH '99

Male rap duo from San Francisco: rapper Sway and DJ King Tech.

7/3/99	107	7		©	This Or That			$10	Interscope 90292

Above The Clouds — Anthem, The — Belly Of The Beast — Canibus Freestyle — Canibus Remix — Clientele — Court Is In Session — Ego Trippin' 99 — Get You Mad — I Know You Got Soul — Improvise — Looking At The Front Door — New York Niggaz — 1-9-8-6 — Number One Crew — Rework The Angles — They Reminisce Over You (T.R.O.Y.) — 3 To The Dome — Ugly People Be Quiet — Underground Tactics — Wake Up Show Trivia

SWEAT, Keith '90

★422★

Born on 7/22/61 in Harlem, New York. R&B singer/songwriter/producer. Member of **LSG**.

1/9/88	15	67	▲³	©	1 Make It Last Forever			$10	Vintertainment 60763
6/30/90	6	62	▲²	©	2 I'll Give All My Love To You			$10	Vintertainment 60861
12/14/91	19	33	▲	©	3 Keep It Comin'			$10	Elektra 61216
7/16/94	8	23	▲	©	4 Get Up On It			$10	Elektra 61550
7/13/96	5	62	▲³	©	5 Keith Sweat			$10	Elektra 61707
10/10/98	6	27	▲	©	6 Still In The Game			$10	Elektra 62262
12/2/00	16	19	●	©	7 Didn't See Me Coming			$10	Elektra 62515

Can We Make Love (6) — Caught Up (7) — Chocolate Girl (5) — **Come And Get With Me** (6) *12* — Come Back (2) — Come Into My Bedroom (4) — **Come With Me** (5) *68* — Don't Have Me (7) — Don't Stop Your Love (1) — Feels So Good (4) — For You (You Got Everything) (4) — Freak With Me (5) — Funky Dope Lovin' (5) — Games (7) — **Get Up On It** (4) *62* — Give Me What I Want (3) — Grind On You (4) — He Say She Say (7) — How Deep Is Your Love (1) — **How Do You Like It?** (4) *48* — I Knew That You Were Cheatin (2) — I Put U On (7) — I Really Love You (3) — **I Want Her** (1) *5* — I Want To Love You Down (3) — **I'll Give All My Love To You** (2) *7* — I'll Trade (A Million Bucks) (7) — I'm Going For Mine (3) — **I'm Not Ready** (6) *16* — In The Mood (5) — In Your Eyes (6) — It Gets Better (4) — Just A Touch (5) — Just Another Day (6) — Just One Of Them Thangs (2) — **Keep It Comin'** (3) *17* — Kiss You (7) — Let Me Have My Way (6) — Let Me Love You (3) — Love Jones (6) — Love To Love You (2) — **Make It Last Forever** (1) *59* — **Make You Sweat** (2) *14* — Merry Go Round (2) — My Whole World (4) — **Nobody** (5) *3* — Only Wanna Please You (7) — Put Your Lovin' Through The Test (4) — Real Man (7) — Right And A Wrong Way (1) — Rumors (6) — Satisfy You (7) — Show U What Love Is (6) — **Something Just Ain't Right** (1) *79* — Spend A Little Time (3) — Telephone Love (4) — Tell Me It's Me You Want (1) — Ten Commandments Of Love (3) — (There You Go) Tellin' Me No Again (3) — Things (7) — Tonite (7) — **Twisted** (5) *2* — What Goes Around (6) — Whatcha Like (7) — Whatever You Want (5) — **When I Give My Love** (4) *85* — **Why Me Baby?** (3) *44* — Why U Treat Me So Cold (7) — You Know I Like (6) — Your Love (2) — **Your Love - Part 2** (2) *71* — Yumi (5)

SWEAT BAND '81

Spin-off of **George Clinton**'s Parliament/Funkadelic groups. Core members: **Bootsy** Collins, **Fred Wesley**, Maceo Parker, Bernie Worrell, Joel Johnson and Carl Smalls. Parker had been with **James Brown**. Smalls had been in The Undisputed Truth and The Dramatics.

12/13/80+	150	8			Sweat Band			$15	Uncle Jam 36857

Body Shop — Freak To Freak — Hyper Space — Jamaica — Love Munch — We Do It All Day Long

SWEET '75

Pop-rock group formed in England: Brian Connolly (vocals), Andy Scott (guitar, keyboards), Steve Priest (bass) and Mick Tucker (drums). Connolly died of kidney failure on 2/10/97 (age 52).

7/28/73	191	4		©	1 The Sweet			$20	Bell 1125
7/26/75	25	44	●	©	2 Desolation Boulevard			$15	Capitol 11395
3/6/76	27	13		©	3 Give Us A Wink			$15	Capitol 11496
5/14/77	151	4		©	4 Off The Record			$15	Capitol 11636
2/18/78	52	28		©	5 Level Headed			$15	Capitol 11744
5/12/79	151	5		©	6 Cut Above The Rest			$15	Capitol 11929

A.C.D.C. (2) — **Action** (3) *20* — Air On 'A' Tape Loop (5) — Anthem No. I & II (5) — **Ballroom Blitz** (2) *5* — Big Apple Waltz (6) — **Blockbuster** (1) *73* — **California Nights** (5) *76* — Call Me (6) — Cockroach (3) — Discophony (dis-kof-o-nee) (6) — Done Me Wrong Alright (1) — Dorian Gray (6) — Dream On (5) — Eye Games (6) — Fever Of Love (4) — Fountain (5) — 4th Of July (3) — **Fox On The Run** (2) *5* — **Funk It Up (David's Song)** (4) *88* — Hard Times (4) — Healer (3) — Hell Raiser (1) — Hold Me (6) — I Wanna Be Committed (2) — In To Night (2) — Keep It In (3) — Lady Starlight (5) — Laura Lee (4) — Lettres D'Amour (5) — Lies In Your Eyes (3) — **Little Willy** (1) *3* — Live For Today (4) — Lost Angels (4) — **Love Is Like Oxygen** (5) *8* — Man From Mecca (1) — Midnight To Daylight (4) — Mother Earth (6) — Need A Lot Of Lovin' (1) — New York Connection (1) — No You Don't (2) — Play All Night (6) — Set Me Free (2) — She Gimme Lovin' (4) — Silverbird (5) — 6-Teens (2) — Solid Gold Brass (2) — Spotlight (1) — Stairway To The Stars (4) — Stay With Me (6) — Strong Love (5) — Sweet F.A. (2) — White Mice (3) — Wig-Wam Bam (1) — Windy City (4) — Yesterday's Rain (3) — You're Not Wrong For Loving Me (1)

SWEET, Matthew '95
Born on 10/6/64 in Lincoln, Nebraska. Pop-rock singer/bassist/drummer.

2/29/92	100	29	●	©	1 Girlfriend			$10	Zoo 11015
7/31/93	75	7		©	2 Altered Beast			$10	Zoo 11050
4/1/95	65	25	●	©	3 100% Fun			$10	Zoo 11081
4/12/97	66	5		©	4 Blue Sky On Mars			$10	Volcano 31130
10/30/99	188	1		©	5 In Reverse			$10	Volcano 31154

All Over My Head (4)
Back To You (4)
Behind The Smile (4)
Beware My Love (5)
Come To California (4)
Come To Love (3)
Day For Night (1)
Devil With The Green Eyes (2)
Dinosaur Act (2)
Divine Intervention (1)
Do It Again (2)
Does She Talk? (1)
Don't Go (1)

Evangeline (1)
Evergreen (2)
Everything Changes (3)
Faith In You (5)
Falling (2)
Future Shock (5)
Get Older (3)
Girlfriend (1)
Giving It Back (3)
Heaven And Earth (4)
Hide (5)
Hollow (4)
Holy War (1)

I Almost Forgot (3)
I Should Never Have Let You Know (5)
I Wanted To Tell You (1)
I've Been Waiting (1)
If Time Permits (5)
In Too Deep (2)
Into Your Drug (4)
Knowing People (2)
Life Without You (2)
Looking At The Sun (1)
Lost My Mind (3)
Make Believe (4)

Millennium Blues (5)
Missing Time (4)
Not When I Need It (3)
Nothing Lasts (1)
Over It (4)
Reaching Out (2)
Sick Of Myself (3) 58
Smog Moon (3)
Someone To Pull The Trigger (2)
Split Personality (5)
Super Baby (3)
Thought I Knew You (1)

Thunderstorm (5)
Time Capsule (2)
Trade Places (5)
Ugly Truth (2)
Ugly Truth Rock (2)
Until You Break (4)
Untitled (1)
Walk Out (3)
We're The Same (3)
What Do You Know? (2)
What Matters (5)
Where You Get Love (4)
Winona (1)

Worse To Live (5)
Write Your Own Song (5)
You Don't Love Me (1)
Your Sweet Voice (1)

SWEET, Rachel '79
Born on 7/28/62 in Akron, Ohio. Pop singer/actress.

8/4/79	97	9			1 Fool Around			$12	Stiff 36101
3/22/80	123	11			2 Protect The Innocent			$12	Stiff 36337
9/5/81	124	7			3 ...And Then He Kissed Me			$10	ARC 37077

B-A-B-Y (1)
Baby, Let's Play House (2)
Be My Baby (medley) (3)
Billy And The Gun (3)
Cuckoo Clock (1)
Everlasting Love (3) 32

Fool's Gold (2)
Fool's Story (3)
Foul Play (2)
I Go To Pieces (1)
I've Got A Reason (2)
It's So Different Here (1)

Jealous (2)
Little Darlin' (3)
Lovers' Lane (2)
New Age (2)
New Rose (2)
Party Girl (3)

Pin A Medal On Mary (1)
Sad Song (1)
Shadows Of The Night (3)
Spellbound (2)
Stay Awhile (1)
Stranger In The House (1)

Streetheart (3)
Suspended Animation (1)
Take Good Care Of Me (2)
Then He Kissed Me (medley) (3)
Tonight (2)

Tonight Ricky (2)
Two Hearts Full Of Love (3)
Who Does Lisa Like? (1)
Wildwood Saloon (1)

SWEETBACK '97
Trio consisting of the musicians from **Sade**'s band: Stuart Matthewman (guitar, sax), Andrew Hale (keyboards) and Paul Denman (bass).

| 3/8/97 | 169 | 5 | | © | Sweetback | | [I] | $10 | Epic 67492 |

Arabesque
Au Natural

Chord
Cloud People

Come Dubbing
Gaze

Hope She'll Be Happier
Powder

Sensations
Softly Softly

Walk Of Ju
You Will Rise

SWEET F.A. '90
Hard-rock group: Steve DeLong (vocals), Jon Huffman and James Thunder (guitars), Jim Quick (bass) and Tricky Lane (drums).

| 9/15/90 | 161 | 10 | | © | Stick To Your Guns | | | $10 | MCA 6400 |

Breakin' The Law
Daily Grind

Devil's Road
Do A Little Drivin'

Heart Of Gold
I Love Women

Nothin' For Nothin'
Prince Of The City

Rhythm Of Action
Southern Comfort

Stick To Your Guns
Whiskey River

SWEET INSPIRATIONS, The '68
R&B vocal quartet: **Cissy Houston**, Estelle Brown, Sylvia Shemwell and Myrna Smith. Spent nearly six years as a studio group, primarily for Atlantic. Work included backing **Aretha Franklin** and **Elvis Presley**. Houston, mother of **Whitney Houston** and aunt of **Dionne Warwick**, recorded solo in 1970.

| 4/6/68 | 90 | 6 | | | The Sweet Inspirations | | | $20 | Atlantic 8155 |

Blues Stay Away From Me
Do Right Woman - Do Right Man

Don't Fight It
Don't Let Me Lose This Dream
Here I Am (Take Me)

I'm Blue
Knock On Wood
Let It Be Me 94

Oh! What A Fool I've Been
Reach Out For Me
Sweet Inspiration 18

Why (Am I Treated So Bad) 57

SWEET SENSATION '75
R&B group from Manchester, England: Marcel King (lead vocals), St. Clair Palmer, Vincent James and Junior Daye (backing vocals), Garry Shaughnessy (guitar), Leroy Smith (keyboards), Barry Johnson (bass) and Roy Flowers (drums).

| 5/3/75 | 163 | 7 | | | Sad Sweet Dreamer | | | $15 | Pye 12110 |

Emptiness Filled With Love
Eyes In The Back Of My Head

Fancy Woman
Mr. Cool

Please Excuse Me
Purely By Coincidence

Sad Sweet Dreamer 14
Snow Fire

That Same Old Feeling
Yes Miss, No Miss

SWEET SENSATION '89
Female dance trio from New York City: Betty LeBron, and sisters Margie and Mari Fernandez. Sheila Bega replaced Mari in 1989.

| 10/8/88+ | 63 | 32 | | © | 1 Take It While It's Hot | | | $10 | Atco 90917 |
| 4/28/90 | 78 | 23 | | © | 2 Love Child | | | $10 | Atco 91307 |

Bring It Back (2)
Destiny (2)
Each And Every Time (2) 59

He'll Never Know (2)
Heartbreak (1)
Hooked On You (1) 23

I Surrender (2)
If Wishes Came True (2) 1
Let Me Be The One (1)

Love Child (2) 13
Love Games (1)
Never Let You Go (1) 58

One Good Man (2)
Pleasure And Pain (2)
Sincerely Yours (1) 14

Take It While It's Hot (1) 57
Victim Of Love (1)

SWEET TEE '89
Born Toi Jackson in Queens, New York. Female rapper.

| 2/25/89 | 169 | 13 | | © | It's Tee Time | | | $10 | Profile 1269 |

As The Beat Goes On
I Got Da Feelin'

It's Like That Y'all
It's My Beat

Let's Dance
On The Smooth Tip

Show And Prove
Why Did It Have To Be Me

Work Out

SWEET THUNDER '78
R&B group from Youngstown, Ohio: Booker Newberry (vocals, keyboards), Charles Buie (guitar), Rudell Alexander (bass) and John Aaron (drums).

| 7/15/78 | 125 | 11 | | | Sweet Thunder | | | $12 | Fantasy 9547 |

Baby I Need Your Love Today
Everybody's Singin' Love Songs

Hot Line
I Don't Care What You Say

Joyful Noise
Keep On Growin'

Sweet Thunder

SWEETWATER '69
Folk-rock group: Nansi Nevins (vocals), R.G. Carlyle (guitar), Albert Moore (flute), Pete Cobain (conga), August Burns (cello), Alex Del Zeppo (keyboards), Fred Herrera (bass) and Alan Malarowitz (drums). The 1999 VH-1 TV movie *Sweetwater* was based on the band's career.

| 9/13/69 | 200 | 2 | | | Sweetwater | | | $20 | Reprise 6313 |

Come Take A Walk
For Pete's Sake

Here We Go Again
In A Rainbow

Motherless Child
My Crystal Spider

Rondeau
Through An Old Storybook

Two Worlds
What's Wrong

Why Oh Why

SWINGING BLUE JEANS, The   '64
Rock group from Liverpool, England: Ray Ennis (vocals, guitar), Ralph Ellis (guitar), Les Braid (bass) and Norman Kuhlke (drums).

| 5/30/64 | 90 | 9 | | | Hippy Hippy Shake .... | | | $100 | Imperial 12261 |

Angie
Do You Know

| Good Golly Miss Molly 43 | It's Too Late Now | Save The Last Dance For Me | Shakin' All Over | Think Of Me |
| Hippy Hippy Shake 24 | Now I Must Go | Shake Rattle & Roll | Shaking Feeling | Wasting Time |

SWINGIN' MEDALLIONS   '66
Rock group from Greenwood, South Carolina: John McElrath (vocals), Jimbo Dores (guitar), Brent Forston (organ), Carroll Bledsoe, Charlie Webber and Steve Caldwell (horns), Jim Perkins (bass) and Joe Morris (drums).

| 7/30/66 | 88 | 12 | | | Double Shot (Of My Baby's Love) .... | | | $50 | Smash 67083 |

Barefootin'
Double Shot (Of My Baby's Love) 17

Hang On Sloopy	Louie, Louie	She Drives Me Out Of My	What Kind Of Fool
(I Can't Get No) Satisfaction	M.T.Y.L.T.T.	**Mind** 71	Wooly Bully
Idaho Jane		That's When I Like It	You Gotta Have Faith

SWINGLE SINGERS, The   '64
Born Ward Swingle on 9/21/27 in Mobile, Alabama. Pianist/saxophonist. Formed his scat-singing group in Paris in 1960. Group won the 1963 Best New Artist Grammy Award.

10/26/63+	15	74			1 Bach's Greatest Hits	[I]		$15	Philips 600097
5/30/64	65	17			2 Going Baroque	[I]		$15	Philips 600126
2/20/65	140	6			3 Anyone For Mozart?			$15	Philips 600149

Ah! Vous Dirais Je Maman (Twinkle, Twinkle, Little Star) (3)
Badinerie (2)
Bouree (1)
Canon (1)
Cello Suite In C Major - Gigue (2)

Concerto Grosso, Op. 6, No. 4 - Allegro (2)	Fugue In D Major (1)	Partita No. 5 In G Major - Preambule (2)	Prelude No. 7 (2)
Der Fruehling (Spring) (2)	Fugue In D Minor (1)	Prelude For Organ Choral No. 1 (1)	Prelude No. 24 (2)
Eine Kleine Nacht Music (3)	Harpsichord Concerto In F Minor - Largo (2)	Prelude In C Major (1)	Sinfonia (1)
Estro Harmonico Op. 3, No.11 - Fuque (2)	Harpsichord Suite In E Major - Air (2)	Prelude In F Major (1)	Solfeggietto (2)
Fugue (3)	Invention In C Major (1)	Prelude No. 9 (1)	Sonata No. 15 (3)
Fugue In C Minor (1)		Prelude No. 19 (2)	Sonata No. 14 - Allegro (3)
			Suite In D Major - Aria (1)

SWING OUT SISTER   '88
Pop trio formed in England: Corinne Drewery (vocals), Andy Connell (keyboards) and Martin Jackson (drums). Jackson left in 1989.

8/29/87+	40	43	●	©	1 It's Better To Travel			$10	Mercury 832213
5/27/89	61	19		©	2 Kaleidoscope World			$10	Fontana 838293
9/19/92	113	11		©	3 Get In Touch With Yourself			$10	Fontana 512241

After Hours (1)
Am I The Same Girl (3) 45
Between Strangers (2)
Blue Mood (1)
Breakout (1) 6
Circulate (3)

Communion (1)	Heart For Hire (2)	It's Not Enough (1)	Surrender (1)	Who Let The Love Out (3)
Don't Say A Word (3)	I Can Hear You But I Can't See You (3)	Kaleidoscope Affair (2)	Tainted (2)	You On My Mind (2)
Everyday Crime (3)		Love Child (3)	**Twilight World** (1) 31	
Fooled By A Smile (1)	Incomplete Without You (3)	Masquerade (2)	Understand (3)	
Forever Blue (2)	It's Better To Travel, Theme From (1)	Notgonnachange (3)	**Waiting Game** (2) 86	
Get In Touch With Yourself (3)		Precious Words (2)	Where In The World (2)	

SWITCH   '79
Funk group from Mansfield, Ohio: Philip Ingram (vocals), brothers Bobby (keyboards) and Tommy (bass) DeBarge, Greg Williams and Eddie Fluellen (horns) and Jody Sims (drums). The DeBarges are brothers to the family group **DeBarge**. Bobby DeBarge died of AIDS on 8/16/95 (age 36).

9/2/78	37	33			1 Switch			$12	Gordy 980
6/2/79	37	36			2 Switch II			$12	Gordy 988
4/12/80	57	14			3 Reaching For Tomorrow			$12	Gordy 993
11/15/80+	85	17			4 This Is My Dream			$12	Gordy 999
11/21/81	174	4			5 Switch V			$12	Gordy 1007

All I Need Is You (4)
Believe In Yourself (4)
Best Beat In Town (2) 69
Best Of Love (5)
Call On Me (5)
Calling On All Girls (2)
Don't Take My Love Away (3)
Fallin' (2)

Fever (1)	I Luv It (5)	My Friend In The Sky (3)	This Is Just For You (5)	Without You In My Life (4)
Get Back With You (3)	I Wanna Be Closer (3)	Next To You (2)	This Is My Dream (4)	You And I (4)
Go On Doin' What You Feel (2)	I Wanna Be With You (1)	Power To Dance (3)	Two Wrongs Don't Make A Right (5)	You Keep Me High (5)
Honey, I Love You (3)	I'll Always Keep (5)	Push The Switch (High Energy Switch) (5)		You Pulled A Switch (1)
I Call Your Name (2) 83	It's So Real (1)	Reaching For Tomorrow (3)	We Like To Party...Come On (1)	You're The One For Me (2)
I Do Love You (5)	Just Imagine (4)	Somebody's Watchin' You (1)	What A Feeling (4)	
I Finally Found Someone New (3)	Keep Movin' On (3)	**There'll Never Be** (1) 36	Why'd You Let Love Fall (4)	
	Love Over And Over Again (4)			

SWV (Sisters With Voices)   '93
Female R&B vocal trio from New York City: Cheryl "**Coko**" Gamble, Tamara Johnson and Leanne Lyons.

1/23/93	8	71	▲3	©	1 It's About Time			$10	RCA 66074
5/28/94	92	10	●	©	2 The Remixes	[K-M]		$10	RCA 66401
5/11/96	9	25	▲	©	3 New Beginning			$10	RCA 66487
8/30/97	24	25	●	©	4 Release Some Tension			$10	RCA 67525

Anything (1,2) 18
Blak Pudd'n (1)
Can We (4) 75
Come And Get Some (4)
Coming Home (1)
Don't Waste Your Time (3)
Downtown (1,2) flip

Fine Time (3)	It's About Time (1)	Rain (4) 25	That's What I Need (1)	When This Feeling (3)
Gettin' Funky (4)	It's All About U (3) 61	Release Some Tension (4)	That's What I'm Here For (3)	When U Cry (4)
Give It To Me (1)	Lose My Cool (4)	Right Here (1) 92	Think You're Gonna Like It (1)	You Are My Love (3)
Give It Up (4)	Lose Myself (4)	Right Here/Human Nature (2) 2	Use Your Heart (3) 22	You're Always On My Mind (1,2) 54
Here For You (4)	Love Is So Amazin' (3)		Weak (1,2) 1	You're The One (3) 5
I'm So In Love (3)	Love Like This (4)	SWV (In The House) (1)	What's It Gonna Be (3)	
I'm So Into You (1,2) 6	On & On (3)	**Someone** (4) 19	Whatcha Need (3)	

SYBIL   '89
Born Sybil Lynch in Paterson, New Jersey. R&B singer.

| 10/21/89 | 75 | 24 | | © | Sybil .... | | | $10 | Next Plateau 1018 |

Bad Beats Suite
Can't Wait (On Tomorrow)
Crazy 4 U

Don't Make Me Over 20	In My Dreams	Take Me Away	We're Gonna Make It Work This Time
Give It To Me	Living For The Moment	**Walk On By** 74	
I Wanna Be Where You Are	Love's Calling		

SYKES, Keith   '80
Born in 1948 in Murray, Kentucky; raised in Memphis. Rockabilly singer/songwriter.

| 11/22/80 | 147 | 11 | | | I'm Not Strange I'm Just Like You .... | | | $12 | Backstreet 3265 |

Ain't That Some Lovin'
B.I.G.T.I.M.E.

| I'm Not Strange (I'm Just Like You) | I'm On A Roll | Makin' It Before They Got Married | Maybe I'm A Mockingbird 928 | Smack Dab In The Middle |
| | Love To Ride | | | When My Work Is Done |

SYLK-E. FYNE   '98
Born in Los Angeles. Female rapper.

| 4/11/98 | 121 | 12 | | © | Raw Sylk .... | | | $10 | RCA 67551 |

Grand Jury (Coming Through)
I Ain't Down With The System

| I Make Moves | Keep It Real | Love No More (Look Into My Eyes) | Material Girl | They'll Never Be |
| I Miss My Loved Ones | Lost In The Game | | **Romeo And Juliet** 6 | This Is The Way We Roll |

SYLVAIN, Sylvain   '80
Born Syl Mizrahi in 1953 in Cairo, Egypt; raised in Brooklyn, New York. Rock singer/guitarist. Member of the **New York Dolls** (1973-74).

| 2/16/80 | **123** | 8 | | | Sylvain Sylvain | | | $12 | RCA Victor 3475 |

Ain't Got No Home | Emily | 14th Street Beat | Teenage News | What's That Got To Do With | Without You
Deeper And Deeper | Every Boy And Every Girl | I'm So Sorry | Tonight | Rock 'N' Roll

SYLVERS, The   '76
R&B family vocal group from Memphis: Olympia-Ann, Leon, Charmaine, James, Edmund, Ricky, Angelia, Pat, Jonathon and **Foster Sylvers**. Leon formed the group **Dynasty** in 1979.

3/3/73	**180**	7			1 The Sylvers			$15	Pride 0007
8/4/73	**164**	5			2 The Sylvers II			$15	Pride 0026
2/14/76	**58**	25			3 Showcase			$12	Capitol 11465
11/20/76	**80**	18			4 Something Special			$12	Capitol 11580
11/26/77+	**134**	13			5 New Horizons			$12	Capitol 11705
9/16/78	**132**	8			6 Forever Yours			$12	Casablanca 7103

Ain't No Doubt About It (4) | Cotton Candy (3) 59 | Hot Line (4) 5 | Let It Be Me (2) | Roulette Wheel Of Love (3) | We Can Make It If We Try (2)
Ain't No Good In Good-bye (3) | Cry Of A Dreamer (2) | How Love Hurts (1) | Love Changes (6) | Shake 'Um Up (4) | Wish That I Could Talk To
Ain't Nothin' But A Party (3) | Diamonds Are Rare (6) | I Can Be For Real (3) | Love Me, Love Me Not (2) | So Close (1) | You (1) 77
Another Day To Love (5) | Disco Showdown (4) | I Don't Need To Prove Myself | Love Won't Let Me Go (6) | Star Fire (5) | Yesterday (2)
Any Way You Want Me (5) 72 | Don't Stop, Get Off (6) | (2) | Lovin' Me Back (5) | **Stay Away From Me** (2) 89 | You Bring The Sunshine (Back
Boogie Fever (3) 1 | Dressed To Kill (5) | I Know Myself (1) | Lovin' You Is Like Lovin' The | Storybook Girl (3) | Into My Life) (5)
Chaos (1) | **Fool's Paradise** (1) 94 | I Remember (2) | Wind (4) | Swept For You Baby (6)
Charisma (3) | Forever Yours (6) | I'll Never Be Ashamed (1) | Mista Guitar Man (4) | Take A Hand (1)
Clap Your Hands To The Music | Free Style (3) | I'll Never Let You Go (2) | New Horizons (5) | That's What Love Is Made Of
(3) | Got To Have You (For My Very | I'm Truly Happy (1) | Now I Want You (4) | (4)
Come Dance With Me (6) | Own) (4) | Just A Little Bit Longer (6) | Only One Can Win (1) | Through The Love In My Heart
Come On Down To My House | Handle It (2) | Keep On Keepin' On (Doin' | Party Maker (5) | (2)
(6) | **High School Dance** (4) 17 | What You Do) (3) | Play This One Last Record (6) | Touch Me Jesus (1)

SYLVERS, Foster   '73
Born on 2/25/62 in Memphis. Member of **The Sylvers**.

| 7/21/73 | **159** | 7 | | | Foster Sylvers | | | $15 | Pride 0027 |

Big Things Come In Small | Hey, Little Girl 92 | Lullaby (medley) | More Love | Uncle Albert/Admiral Halsey
Packages | I'll Get You In The End | **Misdemeanor** 22 | Only My Love Is True
Happy Face | I'm Your Puppet | Mockingbird | Swooperman

SYLVESTER   '78
Born Sylvester James on 9/6/47 in Los Angeles. Died of AIDS on 12/16/88 (age 41). Male disco singer.

8/5/78	**28**	42	●		1 Step II			$12	Fantasy 9556
4/28/79	**63**	15			2 Stars			$12	Fantasy 9579
11/24/79+	**123**	12		©	3 Living Proof		[L]	$15	Fantasy 79010 [2]
					recorded on 3/11/79 in San Francisco				
9/27/80	**147**	8			4 Sell My Soul			$12	Honey 9601
7/11/81	**156**	4		©	5 Too Hot To Sleep			$12	Honey 9607
3/19/83	**168**	5			6 All I Need			$12	Megatone 1005
2/14/87	**164**	5			7 Mutual Attraction			$10	Warner 25527

All I Need (6) | Could It Be Magic (medley) (3) | Happiness (3) | I'll Dance To That (4) | Ooo Baby Baby (5) | Tell Me (6)
Anything Can Happen (7) | Cry Me A River (4) | Hard Up (6) | In My Fantasy (I Want You, I | Sell My Soul (6) | Thinking Right (5)
Be With You (6) | **Dance (Disco Heat)** (1,3) 19 | Here Is My Love (5) | Need You) (3) | Sharing Something Perfect | Too Hot To Sleep (5)
Blackbird (3) | Do Ya Wanna Funk (6) | I Can't Believe I'm In Love (5) | Just You And Me Forever (1) | Between Ourselves (3) | Was It Something That I Said
Body Strong (2,3) | Doin' It For The Real Thing (4) | I Need Somebody To Love | Living For The City (7) | Someone Like You (7) | (1)
Can't Forget The Love (5) | Don't Stop (6) | Tonight (2) | Lover Man (Oh Where Can You | Song For You (medley) (3) | Won't You Let Me Love You (6)
Can't Stop Dancing (3) | Fever (4) | I Need You (4) | Be) (3) | Sooner Or Later (7) | You Are My Friend (3)
Can't You See (5) | Give It Up (Don't Make Me | I Took My Strength From You | Mutual Attraction (7) | Stars (2) | **You Make Me Feel (Mighty
Change Up (4) | Wait) (5) | (1) | My Life Is Loving You (4) | Summertime (7) | Real)** (1,3) 36
Cool Of The Evening (7) | Grateful (1,3) | **I (Who Have Nothing)** (2) 40 | New Beginnings (5) | Talk To Me (7)

SYLVIA   '73
Born Sylvia Vanderpool on 5/6/36 in New York City. R&B singer/songwriter/producer. Half of Mickey & Sylvia duo.

| 6/2/73 | **70** | 12 | | © | Pillow Talk | | | $20 | Vibration 126 |

Cowards Way Out | Don't Leave Me Starving | Had Any Lately | Not On The Outside | Sunday
Didn't I 70 | Give It Up In Vain | My Thing | **Pillow Talk** 3

SYLVIA   '82
Born Sylvia Kirby on 12/9/56 in Kokomo, Indiana. Country singer/songwriter.

5/9/81	**139**	11		©	1 Drifter			$10	RCA Victor 3986
8/7/82	**56**	33	●	©	2 Just Sylvia			$10	RCA Victor 4312
6/18/83	**77**	11		©	3 Snapshot			$10	RCA Victor 4672
4/28/84	**178**	4		©	4 Surprise			$10	RCA Victor 4960

Bobby's In Vicksburg (3) | I Just Don't Have The Heart (4) | Jason (3) | Missin' You (1) | So Complete (3) | Whippoorwill (1)
Boy Gets Around (3) | I Never Quite Got Back (From | Like Nothing Ever Happened | **Nobody** (2) 15 | Surprise (4) | Who's Kidding Who (3)
Cry Baby Cry (1) | Loving You) (3) | (2) | Not Tonight (2) | Sweet Yesterday (2) | Winter Heart (3)
Drifter (1) | I'll Make It Right With You (2) | Love Over Old Times (4) | On The Other Side Of Midnight | Tonight I'm Gettin' Friendly With | You Can't Go Back Home (2)
Give 'Em Rhythm (4) | I'm Going With Him (1) | Matador, The (1) | (4) | The Blues (3) | You're A Legend In Your Own
Gone But Not Forgotten (3) | Isn't It Always Love (4) | Mill Song (Everybody's Got A | One Foot On The Street (4) | Tumbleweed (3) | Mind (2)
Heart On The Mend (1) | It Don't Hurt To Dream (1) | Dream) (2) | Rainbow Rider (1) | Unguarded Moments (4)
I Feel Cheated (2) | It's Still There (4) | Mirage (2) | Snapshot (3) | Victims Of Goodbye (4)

SYNDICATE OF SOUND   '66
Garage-rock group from San Jose, California: Don Baskin (vocals), Jim Sawyers and John Sharkey (guitars), Bob Gonzalez (bass), and John Duckworth (drums).

| 8/27/66 | **148** | 2 | | © | Little Girl | | | $75 | Bell 6001 |

Almost Grown | I'm Alive | **Little Girl** 8 | **Rumors** 55 | Witch
Big Boss Man | Is You Is Or Is You Ain't My | Lookin' For The Good Times | So Alone | You
Dream Baby | Baby | (The Robot) | That Kind Of Man

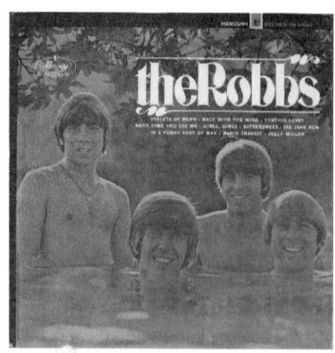

The Robbs
The Robbs ('68)

Chris Rock
Bigger & Blacker ('99)

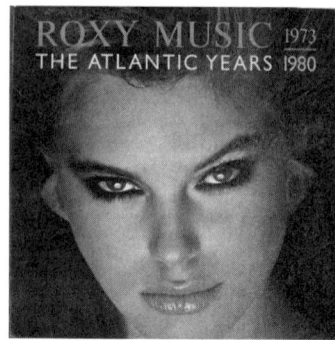

Roxy Music
The Atlantic Years 1973-1980 ('84)

Arthur Rubinstein
Heart of the Piano Concerto ('61)

Bobby Rydell
the Top Hits of 1963 ('64)

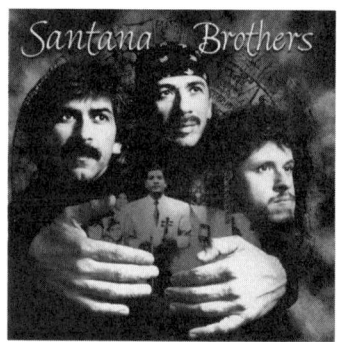

Santana Brothers
Santana Brothers ('94)

Santo & Johnny
Santo & Johnny ('60)

Savatage
Fight For The Rock ('86)

Saxon
Innocence Is No Excuse ('85)

Selena
Amor Prohibido ('94)

The Shangri-Las
Leader Of The Pack ('65)

Del Shannon
Little Town Flirt ('63)

Vonda Shepard... Heart And Soul - New
Songs From Ally McBeal ('99)

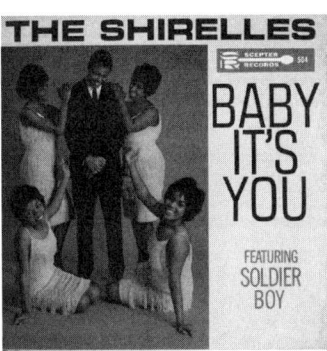

The Shirelles
Baby It's You ('62)

Hank Snow
Christmas With Hank Snow ('67)

Spinal Tap
Break Like The Wind ('92)

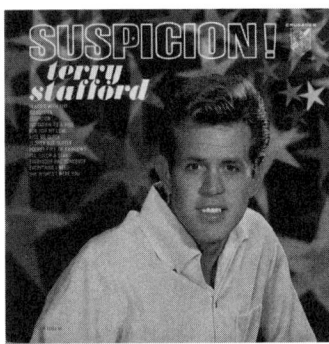

Terry Stafford
Suspicion! ('64)

The Stranglers
Dreamtime ('87)

Strawbs
Deep Cuts ('76)

Sunny and the Sunliners
Talk To Me ('63)

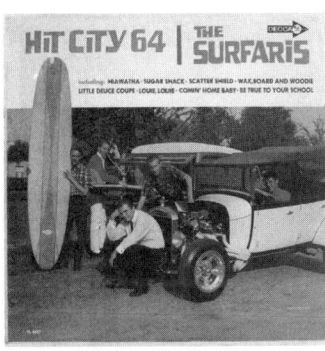

The Surfaris
Hit City 64 ('64)

Sweet Sensation
Sad Sweet Dreamer ('75)

The Swingin' Medallions
Double Shot (Of My Baby's Love) ('66)

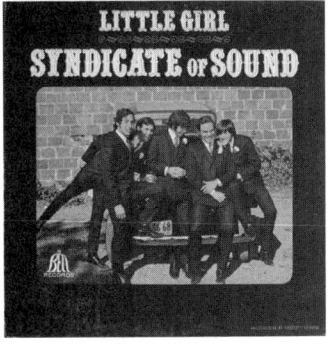

Syndicate Of Sound
Little Girl ('66)

SYNERGY '75

Electronic equipment performed and programmed by New Jersey native Larry Fast.

6/21/75	66	18	©	1	**Electronic Realizations for Rock Orchestra**	[I]	$12	Passport 98009
6/26/76	144	11	©	2	**Sequencer**	[I]	$12	Passport 98014
9/16/78	146	6	©	3	**Cords**	[I]	$12	Passport 6000

Chateau (2)
Classical Gas (2)
Cybersports (2)
Disruption In World Communications (3)

Escape ..see: S-Scape
Full Moon Flyer (3)
Legacy (1)
On Presuming To Be Modern I-III (3)

Paradox Medley (2)
Phobos And Deimos Go To Mars (3)
Relay Breakdown (1)
S-Scape (2)

(Sequence) 14 (2)
Sketches Of Mythical Beasts (3)
Slaughter On Tenth Avenue (1)
Small Collection Of Chords (3)
Synergy (1)

Terra Incognita (3)
Trellis (3)
Warriors (1)

SYREETA '80

Born Rita Wright in 1946 in Pittsburgh. RB singer/songwriter. Married to **Stevie Wonder** from 1972-74.

8/12/72	185	8		1	**Syreeta**	$15	MoWest 113
7/20/74	116	17	©	2	**Stevie Wonder presents Syreeta**	$15	Motown 808
					above 2 produced by **Stevie Wonder**		
5/17/80	73	15		3	**Syreeta**	$12	Tamla 372
8/8/81	127	9		4	**Billy Preston & Syreeta**	$12	Motown 958
1/30/82	189	3		5	**Set My Love In Motion**	$12	Tamla 376

Baby Don't Let Me Lose This (1)
Black Maybe (1)
Blame It On The Sun (3)
Can't Shake Your Love (5)
Cause We've Ended As Lovers (2)
Come And Get This Stuff (2)
Dance For Me Children (3)
Happiness (1)
He's Gone (3)
Heavy Day (2)
Here's My Love (3)

Hey You (4)
How Many Days (1)
I Know The Way To Your Heart (5)
I Love Every Little Thing About You (1)
I Love You (5)
I Must Be In Love (5)
I Wanna Be By Your Side (medley) (2)
I'm Goin' Left (2)
It's So Easy (4)
Just A Little Piece Of You (medley) (2)

Just For You (4)
Keep Him Like He Is (1)
Let Me Be The One (3)
Long And Lasting Love (4)
Love (4)
Love Fire (3)
Move It, Do It (5)
New Way To Say I Love You (4)
One More Time For Love (3)
One More Try (4)
Out Of The Box (5)
Please Stay (3)

Quick Slick (5)
Searchin' (4)
She's Leaving Home (1)
Signed, Sealed, Delivered (I'm Yours) (3)
Someone Special (4)
Spinnin' And Spinnin' (2)
There's Nothing Like A Woman In Love (5)
To Know You Is To Love You (1)
Universal Sound Of The World (Your Kiss Is Sweet) (medley) (2)

Waitin' For The Postman (medley) (2)
What Love Has Joined Together (2)
What We Did For Love (4)
When Your Daddy's Not Around (medley) (2)
Wish Upon A Star (5)
You Bring Out The Love In Me (3)
You Set My Love In Motion (5)
Your Kiss Is Sweet (2)

SYSTEM, The '87

Techno-funk duo from New York City: Mic Murphy (vocals, guitar) and David Frank (synthesizer).

3/12/83	94	23	©	1	**Sweat**	$10	Mirage 90062
3/31/84	182	5		2	**X-Periment**	$10	Mirage 90146
4/18/87	62	25	©	3	**Don't Disturb This Groove**	$10	Atlantic 81691

Bad Girl (2)
Come As You Are (Superstar) (3)
Dangerous (2)
Didn't I Blow Your Mind (3)

Don't Disturb This Groove (3) *4*
Escape (2)
Experiment ..see: X-Periment
Get Jumpin' (2)
Go For What U Know (1)

Groove (3)
Heart Beat Of The City (3)
House Of Rhythm (3)
I Can't Take Losing You (2)
I Wanna Make You Feel Good (2)

I Won't Let Go (1)
It's Passion (1)
Lollipops And Everything (2)
Modern Girl (3)
Nighttime Lover (3)

Now I Am Electric (1)
Promises Can Break (2)
Save Me (3)
Soul Boy (3)
Stand Up And Cheer (1)

Sweat (1)
X-Periment (2)
You Are In My System (1) *64*

SYSTEMATIC '01

Hard-rock group from San Francisco: Adam Ruppel (vocals, guitar), Tim Narducci (guitar), Nick St. Dennis (bass) and Shaun Bannon (drums).

6/9/01	143	1	©		**Somewhere In Between**	$10	TMC 62595

Bedsores
Beginning Of The End
Deep Colors Bleed

Dopesick
Glass Jaw
If Only

Mailbomb
Of A Lesser God
Pitch Black

Return To Zero
Slowburn
Somewhere In Between

Thick Skin

SYSTEM OF A DOWN '00

Rock group from Los Angeles: Serj Tankian (vocals), Daron Malakian (guitar), Shavo Odadjian (bass) and John Dulmayan (drums).

10/2/99+	124	33	●	©	**System Of A Down**	C:#13/10	$10	American 68924

Cubert
Darts
Ddevil

Know
Mind
Peephole

P.L.U.C.K.
Soil
Spiders

Sugar
Suggestions
Suite-Pee

War?

SZABO, Gabor '67

Born on 3/8/36 in Budapest, Hungary. Died on 2/26/82 (age 45). Jazz guitarist.

1/28/67	140	4		1	**Spellbinder**	[I]	$20	Impulse! 9123
1/13/68	194	2	©	2	**The Sorcerer**	[I-L]	$20	Impulse! 9146
					recorded on 4/14/67 at The Jazz Workshop in Boston			
6/15/68	157	3	©	3	**Bacchanal**	[I]	$20	Skye 3
8/16/69	143	7	©	4	**Gabor Szabo 1969**	[I]	$20	Skye 9
5/16/70	162	10	©	5	**Lena & Gabor**	[I]	$20	Skye 15

LENA HORNE & GABOR SZABO

Autumn Leaves (medley) (1)
Bacchanal (3)
Bang Bang (My Baby Shot Me Down) (1)
Beat Goes On (2)
Both Sides Now (4)
Cheetah (1)
Comin' Back (2)
Dear Prudence (4)

Divided City (3)
Everybody's Talkin' (5)
Fool On The Hill (5)
Gypsy Queen (1)
I've Just Seen A Face (4)
In My Life (4,5)
It Was A Very Good Year (1)
Little Boat (O Barquinho) (2)
Look Of Love (3)

Lou-ise (2)
Love Is Blue (3)
Message To Michael (5)
Michael From Mountains (4)
Mizrab (2)
My Foolish Heart (1)
My Mood Is You (5)
Nightwind (5)
Rocky Raccoon (5)

Sealed With A Kiss (4)
Some Velvet Morning (3)
Something (5)
Somewhere I Belong (4)
Space (2)
Speak To Me Of Love (medley) (1)
Spellbinder (1)
Stormy (4)

Stronger Than Us (2)
Sunshine Superman (3)
Three King Fishers (3)
Until It's Time For You To Go (4)
Valley Of The Dolls, Theme From The (3)
Walk Away Renee (4)
Watch What Happens (5)

What Is This Thing Called Love? (2)
Witchcraft (1)
Yearning (1)
Yesterday When I Was Young (5)
You Won't See Me (4)

T

TACO '83
Born Taco Ockerse in 1955 in Jaharta, Indonesia (Dutch parents). Techno-pop singer.

| 7/23/83 | 23 | 24 | © | **After Eight** | | | $10 | RCA Victor 4818 |

After Eight
Carmella

Cheek To Cheek — I Should Care — Livin' In My Dreamworld — Singin' In The Rain — Tribute To Tino
Encore (Sweet Gypsy Rose) — La Vie En Rose — **Puttin' On The Ritz 4** — Thanks A Million

TAG TEAM '93
Rap duo from Atlanta: Cecil Glenn and Steve Gibson.

| 8/7/93 | 39 | 40 | ● © | **Whoomp! (There It Is)** | | $10 | Life 78000 |

Bobyahead
Bring It On
Drop Dem

Free Style — Gettin' Phat — Kick Da Flow — Wreck Da Set
Funk Key — It's Somethin' — U Go Girl
Get Nasty — Just Call Me DC — **Whoomp! (There It Is) 2**

TAKE 6 '89
Contemporary gospel group from Alabama: Claude McKnight, Mark Kibble, Mervyn Warren, Cedric Dent, David Thomas and Alvin Chea. McKnight is older brother of **Brian McKnight**.

3/11/89	71	19	▲ ©	1 **Take 6**		$10	Reprise 25670
9/29/90	72	18	©	2 **So Much 2 Say**		$10	Reprise 25892
12/7/91+	100	6	©	3 **He Is Christmas**	C:#48/2 [X]	$10	Reprise 26665

Christmas charts: 11/'91, 23/'92

| 7/16/94 | 86 | 13 | ● © | 4 **Join The Band** | | $10 | Reprise 45497 |

All I Need (Is A Chance) (4)
Amen! (3)
Away In A Manger (3)
Biggest Part Of Me (4)
Can't Keep Goin' On And On (4)
Come Unto Me (2)
David And Goliath (1)
Even Though (4)

Get Away, Jordan (1)
God Rest Ye Merry Gentlemen (3)
Gold Mine (1)
Hark! The Herald Angels Sing (3)
Harmony (4)
He Never Sleeps (1)
[Human Body] (2)

I Believe (2)
I L-O-V-E U (2)
I'm On My Way (2)
I've Got Life (4)
If We Ever (1)
It's Gonna Rain (4)
Let The Words (1)
Little Drummer Boy (3)
Lullaby (4)

Mary (1)
Milky-White Way (1)
My Friend (4)
[Not Again!?] (2)
O Come All Ye Faithful (3)
Oh! He Is Christmas (3)
Quiet Place (1)
Silent Night (3)
So Much 2 Say (2)

Something Within Me (2)
Spread Love (1)
Sunday's On The Way (2)
Sweet Little Jesus Boy (3)
[That's The Law] (2)
Time After Time (The Savior Is Waiting) (2)
'Twas Da Nite (3)

Where Do The Children Play? (2)
Why I Feel This Way (4)
You Can Never Ask Too Much (Of Love) (4)

TAKE THAT '95
Pop vocal group from England: Gary Barlow, Howard Donald, Jason Orange, Mark Owen and **Robbie Williams**.

| 9/16/95 | 69 | 19 | | **Nobody Else** | | $10 | Arista 18800 |

Babe
Back For Good 7

Day After Tomorrow — Holding Back The Tears — Never Forget — Pray
Every Guy — Love Ain't Here Anymore — Nobody Else — Sure

★273★ TALKING HEADS '83
Pop-rock group from New York City: **David Byrne** (vocals, guitar), **Jerry Harrison** (keyboards, guitar), Tina Weymouth (bass) and Chris Frantz (drums). Husband-and-wife Weymouth and Frantz also formed **Tom Tom Club**.

1)Speaking In Tongues 2)True Stories 3)Remain In Light

10/8/77+	97	29	©	1 **Talking Heads: 77**	C:#25/25	$12	Sire 6036
8/12/78	29	42	● ©	2 **More Songs About Buildings And Food**	C:#19/18	$12	Sire 6058
9/1/79	21	30	● ©	3 **Fear Of Music**		$12	Sire 6076
11/1/80	19	27	● ©	4 **Remain In Light**		$12	Sire 6095
4/17/82	31	14		5 **The Name Of This Band Is Talking Heads**	[L]	$15	Sire 3590 [2]
6/25/83	15	51	▲ ©	6 **Speaking In Tongues**		$10	Sire 23883
9/22/84	41	118	▲² ©	7 **Stop Making Sense**	[L-S]	$10	Sire 25121

recorded December 1983 at The Pantages Theatre in Hollywood

7/6/85	20	77	▲² ©	8 **Little Creatures**		$10	Sire 25305
10/4/86	17	29	● ©	9 **True Stories**		$10	Sire 25512
4/2/88	19	21	● ©	10 **Naked**		$10	Sire 25654
10/31/92	158	2	©	11 **Popular Favorites 1976-1992: Sand In The Vaseline**	[G]	$15	Sire 26760 [2]

Air (3,5)
And She Was (8,11) **54**
Animals (3)
Artists Only (2,5)
Big Country (2,11)
Big Daddy (10)
Blind (10,11)
Book I Read (1)
Born Under Punches (The Heat Goes On) (4)
Building On Fire (5,11)
Burning Down The House (6,7,11) **9**
Cities (3)
City Of Dreams (9,11)
Clean Break (5)
Cool Water (10)
Creatures Of Love (8)

Crosseyed And Painless (4,5,11)
Democratic Circus (10)
Don't Worry About The Government (1,5,11)
Dream Operator (9)
Drugs (3,5)
Electric Guitar (3)
Facts Of Life (10)
First Week/Last Week...Carefree (1)
Found A Job (2)
Gangster Of Love (11)
Girlfriend Is Better (6,7,11)
Girls Want To Be With The Girls (2)
Give Me Back My Name (8)
Good Thing (2)

Great Curve (4,5)
Happy Day (1)
Heaven (3,11)
Hey Now (9)
Houses In Motion (4,5)
I Get Wild (medley) (6)
I Want To Live (11)
I Wish You Wouldn't Say That (11)
I Zimbra (3,5,11)
I'm Not In Love (2)
Lady Don't Mind (8)
Life During Wartime (This Ain't No Party...This Ain't No Disco...This Ain't No Foolin' Around) (3,5,7,11) **80**
Lifetime Piling Up (11)
Listening Wind (4)

Love For Sale (9,11)
Making Flippy Floppy (6)
Memories Can't Wait (3,5,11)
Mind (3)
Mommy Daddy You And I (10)
Moon Rocks (6)
Mr. Jones (10,11)
New Feeling (1,5)
No Compassion (1,11)
(Nothing But) Flowers (10,11)
Once In A Lifetime (4,7,11) **91**
Overload, The (4)
Papa Legba (9)
Paper (3)
People Like Us (9)
Perfect World (8)
Popsicle (11)
Psycho Killer (1,5,7,11) **92**

Pull Up The Roots (6)
Pulled Up (1,5)
Puzzlin' Evidence (9)
Radio Head (9)
Road To Nowhere (8,11)
Ruby Dear (10)
Sax And Violins (11)
Seen And Not Seen (4)
Slippery People (6,7)
Stay Hungry (2,5)
Stay Up Late (8,11)
Sugar On My Tongue (11)
Swamp (6,7,11)
Take Me To The River (2,5,7,11) **26**
Television Man (8)
Tentative Decisions (1)

Thank You For Sending Me An Angel (2)
This Must Be The Place (Naive Melody) (6,11) **62**
Totally Nude (10)
Uh-Oh, Love Comes To Town (1)
Walk It Down (8)
Warning Sign (2,11)
What A Day That Was (7)
Who Is It? (1)
Wild Gravity (medley) (6)
Wild Wild Life (9,11) **25**
With Our Love (2)

TALK SHOW '97
Rock group consisting of three members of **Stone Temple Pilots**: brothers Dean (guitar) and Robert (bass) DeLeo and Eric Kretz (drums), with Dave Coutts (vocals).

| 9/20/97 | 131 | 3 | © | **Talk Show** | | $10 | Atlantic 83040 |

Behind
End Of The World

Everybody Loves My Car — Hello Hello — John — Peeling An Orange — So Long
Fill The Fields — Hide — Morning Girl — Ring Twice — Wash Me Down

TALK TALK '84
Pop-rock group from England: Mark Hollis (vocals), Simon Brenner (keyboards), Paul Webb (bass) and Lee Harris (drums). Brenner left in 1983.

9/18/82	132	16	©	1 **The Party's Over**		$10	EMI America 17083
4/7/84	42	22	©	2 **It's My Life**		$10	EMI America 17113
3/22/86	58	17	©	3 **The Colour Of Spring**		$10	EMI America 17179

DEBUT	PEAK	WKS	RIAA	CD	ARTIST — Album Title	Catalog	Sym	$	Label & Number

TALK TALK — Cont'd

Another Word (1)	Does Caroline Know (2)	Have You Heard The News (1)	Life's What You Make It (3) 90	Serious (1)	Tomorrow Started (2)
April 5th (3)	Dum Dum Girl (2)	I Don't Believe In You (3)	Living In Another World (3)	**Such A Shame** (2) 89	
Call In The Night Boy (2)	Give It Up (3)	**It's My Life** (2) 31	Mirror Man (1)	**Talk Talk** (1) 75	
Candy (1)	Happiness Is Easy (3)	It's You (2)	Party's Over (1)	Time It's Time (3)	
Chameleon Day (3)	Hate (1)	Last Time (2)	Renee (2)	Today (1)	

TAMAR '00
Born Tamar Braxton in Severn, Maryland. Female R&B singer. Sister of **Toni Braxton**.

| 4/8/00 | 127 | 4 | | © | Tamar .... | | | $10 | DreamWorks 50110 |

Can't Nobody	I'm Over You	Miss Your Kiss	Once Again	Words
Get Mine	**If You Don't Wanna Love**	Money Can't Buy You Love	Tonight	You Don't Know
Get None	**Me** 89	No Disrespect	Way It Should Be	Your Room

TA MARA & THE SEEN '86
Dance group from Minneapolis: Margaret "Ta Mara" Cox (vocals), Oliver Leiber (guitar), Gina Fellicetta (keyboards), Keith Woodson (bass) and Jamie Chez (drums). Leiber is the son of songwriter Jerry Leiber (of Leiber & Stoller).

| 11/2/85+ | 54 | 25 | | | Ta Mara & The Seen .... | | | $10 | A&M 5078 |

Affection	Got To Have You	Long Cold Nights	Thinking About You
Everybody Dance 24	Lonely Heart	Summertime Love	

TAMIA '00
Born in Windsor, Ontario, Canada. Female R&B singer.

| 5/2/98 | 67 | 24 | | © | 1 | Tamia .... | | | $10 | Qwest 46213 |
| 11/11/00 | 46 | 28 | ● | © | 2 | A Nu Day .... | | | $10 | Elektra 62516 |

Can't Go For That (2) 84	Go (2)	Long Distance Love (2)	Show Me Love (1)	Un'h...To You (2)
Can't No Man (2)	Gotta Move On (1)	Love Me In A Special Way (2)	**So Into You** (1) 30	Wanna Be (2)
Careless Whisper (1)	If I Were You (2)	Loving You Still (2)	**Stranger In My House** (2) 10	Who Do You Tell? (1)
Dear John (2)	**Imagination** (1) 37	Never Gonna Let You Go (1)	Tell Me Who (2)	You Put A Move On My Heart
Falling For You (1)	Is That You? (1)	Rain On Me (1)	This Time It's Love (1)	(1)

TANGERINE DREAM '86
Progressive-rock group formed in Germany by Edgar Froese. Varying lineup also included Christopher Franke (1971-87), Peter Baumann (1972-77), Steve Jollife (1978-84), Klaus Kreiger (1978), Johannes Schmoelling (1979-84) and Paul Haslinger (1985).

7/6/74	196	2		©	1	Phaedra	[I]	$12	Virgin 13108
4/2/77	158	7		©	2	Stratosfear	[I]	$12	Virgin 34427
7/23/77	153	6		©	3	Sorcerer	[I-S]	$12	MCA 2277
12/3/77	178	2		©	4	Encore	[I-L]	$15	Virgin 35014 [2]
5/9/81	115	10			5	Thief	[I-S]	$10	Elektra 521
11/21/81	195	2		©	6	Exit	[I]	$10	Elektra 557
5/17/86	96	7		©	7	Legend	[I-S]	$10	MCA 6165

includes "Is Your Love Strong Enough" by **Bryan Ferry** and "Loved By The Sun" by **Jon Anderson**

Abyss (3)	Choronzon (6)	Dr. Destructo (5)	Kiew Mission (6)	Phaedra (1)	3 AM At The Border Of The
Beach Theme (5)	Coldwater Canyon (4)	Exit (6)	Kitchen, The (medley) (7)	Pilots Of Purple Twilight (6)	Marsh From Okefenokee (2)
Betrayal (Sorcerer Theme) (3)	Confrontation (5)	Fairies (7)	Legend, Opening Theme (7)	Rain Forest (3)	Trap Feeling (5)
Big Sleep In Search Of Hades	Cottage (7)	Goblins (7)	Monolight (4)	Remote Viewing (6)	Unicorn Theme (7)
(2)	Creation (7)	Grind (3)	Mountain Road (1)	Scrap Yard (5)	Vengeance (3)
Blue Room (7)	Dance, The (7)	Igneous (5)	Movements Of A Visionary (1)	Search (3)	
Burning Bar (5)	Darkness (7)	Impressions Of Sorcerer (3)	Mysterious Semblance At The	Sequent C' (1)	
Call, The (3)	Desert Dream (4)	Invisible Limits (3)	Strand Of Nightmares (1)	Sorcerer, Main Title (3)	
Cherokee Lane (4)	Diamond Diary (5)	Journey, The (3)	Network (6)	Stratosfear (2)	

TANGIER '89
Rock group from Philadelphia: Bill Mattson (vocals), Doug Gordon and Gari Saint (guitars), Garry Nutt (bass) and Bobby Bender (drums).

| 7/29/89 | 91 | 17 | | © | 1 | Four Winds .... | | | $10 | Atco 91251 |
| 3/16/91 | 187 | 5 | | © | 2 | Stranded .... | | | $10 | Atco 91603 |

Back In The Limelight (2)	Excited (2)	If Ya Can't Find Love (2)	**On The Line** (1) 67	Stranded (2)
Bad Girl (1)	Fever For Gold (1)	In Time (1)	Ripcord (1)	Sweet Surrender (1)
Caution To The Wind (2)	Four Winds (1)	It's Hard (2)	Since You Been Gone (2)	Takes Just A Little Time (2)
Down The Line (2)	Good Lovin' (1)	Mississippi (1)	Southbound Train (1)	You're Not The Lovin' Kind (2)

TANK '01
Born Durrell Babbs in Milwaukee. Male R&B singer.

| 3/31/01 | 7 | 25 | ● | © | Force Of Nature | | | $10 | Blackground 50404 |

Bounce & Grind	I Don't Wanna Be Lovin' You	Let It Go	Slowly	What You Want
Can't Get Down	Kill 4 You	**Maybe I Deserve** 38	Street Life	
Designated Driver	Lady On My Block	My Freak	Throw Your Hands Up	

TANNER, Marc, Band '79
Born on 8/20/52 in Hollywood. Pop-rock singer/guitarist.

| 3/3/79 | 140 | 8 | | | No Escape .... | | | $12 | Elektra 168 |

Crawlin'	**Elena** 45	In A Spotlight	Lost At Love	She's So High
Edge Of Love	Getaway	Lady In Blue	Never Again	Your Tears Don't Lie

TAÑÓN, Olga '98
Born on 4/13/67 in San Juan, Puerto Rico. Female singer. Married to pro baseball player Juan Gonzalez from 1997-99.

5/4/96	170	2	●	©	1	Nuevos Senderos	[F]	$10	WEA Latina 13667
						title is Spanish for "New Paths"			
5/24/97	175	1		©	2	Llévame Contigo	[F]	$10	WEA Latina 18733
						title is Spanish for "Bring Me With You"			
11/14/98	111	2		©	3	Te Acordarás De Mí	[F]	$10	WEA Latina 25098
						title is Spanish for "You Remembered My Name"			

Así Es El Amor (2)	Déjame Aprender (3)	Engáñame (3)	Llévame Contigo (2)	Por Amor Al Arte (2)	Te Acordarás De Mí (3)
¡Basta Ya! (1)	Despierta Corazón (2)	Escondidos (3)	Lo Que Son Las Apariencias (2)	Porque No Te Encontré (2)	Tu Amor (3)
Choque De Planetas (2)	Diálogo Mudo (3)	Hielo Y Fuego (3)	Me Subes, Me Bajas, Me	Que Bailen Los Niños (2)	Un Hombre Y Una Mujer (3)
Cómo Pude Haber Vivido Sin Ti	El Daño Que Me Haces (1)	La Magia Del Ritmo (Rhythm Is	Subes (1)	Qué Grande Es Este Amor (2)	Voy A Sacarte De Mi Mente
(3)	El Frío De Tu Adiós (2)	Magic) (3)	Mi Eterno Amor Secreto (1)	Serpiente Mala (2)	(King Of Wishful Thinking) (3)
Cuando No Puedo Verlo (2)	El Niño (3)	La Última Oportunidad (1)	Mi Perdón (1)	Siempre En Mi Corazón (2)	
Cuestión De Suerte (1)	En Ti (1)	Llegó El Amor (2)	No Te Vas (1)	Siempre Estuve Cerca (1)	

TANTRIC '01

Rock group from Louisville, Kentucky: Hugo Ferreira (vocals), Todd Whitener (guitar), Jesse Vest (bass) and Matt Taul (drums). The latter three were members of **Days Of The New**.

3/3/01	**71**	31↑		©	**Tantric**			$10	Maverick 47978

All To Myself   Breakdown   Hate Me   I'll Stay Here   Live Your Life (Down)   Paranoid
Astounded   Frequency   I Don't Care   Inside Your Head   Mourning   Revillusion

TANTRUM '80

Rock group from Canada: Barb Erber, Sandy Caulfield and Pam Bradley (vocals), Ray Sapko (guitar), Phil Balsano (keyboards), Bill Syniar (bass) and Vern Wennerstrom (drums).

1/19/80	**199**	3			**Rather Be Rockin'**			$12	Ovation 1747

Applaud The Winner   How Long   Runnin'   Searchin' For A Reason   You Are The World
Don't Turn Me Off   Rather Be Rockin'   Sammy And Susie   Take A Look   You Need Me

TAPROOT '00

Hard-rock group from Ann Arbor, Michigan: Stephen Richards (vocals), Mike DeWolf (guitar), Philip Lipscomb (bass) and Jarrod Montague (drums).

7/15/00	**160**	2		©	**Gift**			$10	Atlantic 83341

Again & Again   Comeback   Emotional Times   Impact   Mirror's Reflection   1 Nite Stand
Believed   Dragged Down   I   Mentobe   Now   Smile

TARNEY/SPENCER BAND, The '78

Pop-rock duo from Australia: Alan Tarney (vocals, guitar, keyboards) and Trevor Spencer (drums).

7/29/78	**174**	4			1 **Three's A Crowd**			$12	A&M 4692
5/12/79	**181**	4			2 **Run For Your Life**			$12	A&M 4757

Bye Bye Now My Sweet Love (1)   Easier For You (1)   I'm Alive (2)   Magic Still Runs Through Your Head (1)   Race Is Almost Run (2)   We Believe In Love (1)
Capital Shame (1)   Far Better Man (2)   **It's Really You** (1) *86*   Maybe I'm Right (1)   Run For Your Life (2)   Won'tcha Tell Me (2)
Don't (2)   Heart Will Break Tonight (2)   Lies (2)   **No Time To Lose** (2) *74*   Set The Minstrel Free (1)
   I Can Hear Love (1)   Live Again (2)   Takin' Me Back (1)

TASH '99

Born Rico Smith in Los Angeles. Male rapper. Member of **Tha Alkaholiks**.

12/11/99	**148**	2		©	**Rap Life**			$10	Loud 63836

Bermuda Triangle   G's Iz G's   Only When I'm Drunker   Ricochet   True Homies
Blackula   Game, The   Pimpin' Ain't Easy   SmokeFest 1999
Fallin' On   NightFall   Rap Life   Tash Rules

TASTE '69

Rock trio from Ireland: **Rory Gallagher** (vocals, guitar), Richard McCracken (bass) and John Wilson (drums).

8/16/69	**133**	9			**Taste**			$25	Atco 296

Blister On The Moon   Catfish   I'm Moving On   Sugar Mama
Born On The Wrong Side Of Time   Dual Carriageway Pain   Leavin' Blues
   Hail   Same Old Story

TASTE OF HONEY, A '78

Disco group from Los Angeles: Janice Johnson (vocals, guitar), Hazel Payne (vocals, bass), Perry Kibble (keyboards) and Donald Johnson (drums). By 1980, reduced to a duo Janice Johnson and Hazel Payne. Won the 1978 Best New Artist Grammy Award. Kibble died of heart failure in February 1999 (age 49).

6/17/78	**6**	27	▲	©	1 **A Taste of Honey**			$12	Capitol 11754
7/14/79	**59**	13			2 **Another Taste**			$12	Capitol 11951
8/2/80+	**36**	32		©	3 **Twice As Sweet**			$10	Capitol 12089
4/24/82	**73**	12			4 **Ladies Of The Eighties**			$10	Capitol 12173

Ain't Nothin' But A Party (3)   **Do It Good** (2) *79*   If We Loved (1)   Race (2)   Sky High (1)   We've Got The Groove (4)
Boogie Oogie Oogie (1) *1*   Don't You Lead Me On (3)   Leavin' Tomorrow (4)   Rainbow's End (2)   **Sukiyaki** (3) *3*   World Spin (1)
Dance (2)   Good-Bye Baby (3)   Let's Begin (4)   Rescue Me (3)   Superstar Superman (3)   You (1)
Diamond Real (4)   I Love You (2)   Lies (4)   Say That You'll Stay (3)   Take The Boogae Or Leave It (2)   You're In Good Hands (1)
Disco Dancin' (1)   **I'll Try Something New** (4) *41*   Midnight Snack (4)   Sayonara (4)   This Love Of Ours (1)   Your Love (2)
Distant (1)   I'm Talkin' 'Bout You (3)   Never Go Wrong (4)   She's A Dancer (3)

TAVARES '76

Family R&B vocal group from New Bedford, Massachusetts: brothers Ralph, Antone, Feliciano, Arthur and Perry Tavares. Feliciano was married to actress/singer Lola Falana.

1)Sky High! 2)In The City 3)Love Storm

2/9/74	**160**	8			1 **Check It Out**			$12	Capitol 11258
9/21/74+	**121**	23			2 **Hard Core Poetry**			$12	Capitol 11316
8/9/75	**26**	17			3 **In The City**			$12	Capitol 11396
6/12/76	**24**	31			4 **Sky High!**			$12	Capitol 11533
4/30/77	**59**	22			5 **Love Storm**			$12	Capitol 11628
10/15/77	**72**	10			6 **The Best Of Tavares**	[G]		$12	Capitol 11701
5/13/78	**115**	8			7 **Future Bound**			$12	Capitol 11719
2/3/79	**92**	11			8 **Madam Butterfly**			$12	Capitol 11874
3/8/80	**75**	7			9 **Supercharged**			$12	Capitol 12026
12/11/82+	**137**	11			10 **New Directions**			$12	RCA Victor 4357

Abra-Ca-Dabra Love You Too (10)   Ghost Of Love (7)   I Hope She Chooses Me (3)   Leave It Up To The Lady (2)   Mystery Lady (10)   Ridin' High (4)
All I See Is You (7)   Going Ups & Coming Downs (5)   I Hope You'll Be Very Unhappy Without Me (10)   Let Me Heal The Bruises (8)   Never Had A Love Like This Before (8)   **She's Gone** (2,6) *50*
Bad Times (9) *47*   Goodnight My Love (5)   Let's Make The Best Of What We Got (1)   Nothing You Can Do (3)   Skin You're In (10)
Bein' With You (4,6)   Got To Find My Way Back To You (10)   I Wanna See You Soon (5)   Little Girl (1)   One Step Away (5)   Slow Train To Paradise (7)
Can't Get Enough (9)   Got To Have Your Love (9)   I'll Never Say Never Again (1)   Love I Never Had (3,6)   One Telephone Call Away (8)   Someone To Go Home To (2)
Check It Out (1,6) *35*   Guiding Star (4)   I'm Back For More (8)   Madam Butterfly (8)   Out Of The Picture (5)   Straight From Your Heart (8)
Don't Take Away The Music (4,6) *34*   Hard Core Poetry (2)   I'm In Love (1)   Mama's Little Girl (1)   Paradise (9)   **That's The Sound That Lonely Makes** (1) *70*
Feel So Good (7)   **Heaven Must Be Missing An Angel (Part 1)** (4,6) *15*   If That's The Way You Want It (1)   Maybe We'll Fall In Love Again (10)   **Penny For Your Thoughts** (10) *33*   Timber (7)
Fool Of The Year (5)   Honey Can I (7)   In The City (3)   Mighty Power Of Love (4)   Positive Forces (8)   To Love You (3)
Fool's Hall Of Fame (3)   I Can't Go On Living Without You (9)   In The Eyes Of Love (3)   **More Than A Woman** (7) *32*   Ready, Willing And Able (3)   To The Other Man (4)
Free Ride (3) *52*   I Don't Want You Anymore (9)   **It Only Takes A Minute** (3,6) *10*   My Love Calls (8)   **Remember What I Told You To Forget** (2,6) *25*   **Too Late** (2) *59*
Games, Games (8)   Keep In Touch (5)   **My Ship** (2) *flip*   Wanna Be Close To You (10)

TAVARES — Cont'd

Watchin' The Woman's Movement (5)	We Both Tried (9)	We're Both Ready For Love (7)	Whodunit (5) 22
	We Fit To A Tee (3)	What You Don't Know (2)	Why Can't We Fall In Love (9)

Wish You Were With Me Mary (1)   Wonderful (4)

TAXXI '83

Rock trio from England: David Cumming (vocals, guitar), Colin Payne (keyboards) and Jeff Nead (drums).

12/25/82+	161	11	States Of Emergency	$15	Fantasy 9617

Cocktail Queen (Don't She Love To Rock & Roll)	Girl (New York City)	Heart Is A Lonely Hunter	I'm Leaving
	Gold Digger	I Remember	Players

Whipping Boy

TAYLOR, Alex '71

Born in 1947 in Boston. Died of a heart attack on 3/12/93 (age 46). Singer/songwriter/guitarist. Brother of **James Taylor**, **Kate Taylor** and **Livingston Taylor**.

3/20/71	190	2	With Friends And Neighbors	$15	Capricorn 860

All In Line	C Song	It's All Over Now	Southbound
Baby Ruth	Highway Song	Night Owl	Southern Kids

Take Out Some Insurance

TAYLOR, Andy '87

Born on 2/16/61 in Dolver-Hampton, England. Lead guitarist of **Duran Duran** and **The Power Station**.

3/28/87	46	17	©	Thunder	$10	MCA 5837

Bringin' Me Down	Don't Let Me Die Young	I Might Lie	Night Train
Broken Window	French Guitar	Life Goes On	Thunder

Tremblin'

TAYLOR, James ★75★ '70

Born on 3/12/48 in Boston. Singer/songwriter/guitarist. Brother of **Alex Taylor**, **Kate Taylor** and **Livingston Taylor**. Married to **Carly Simon** from 1972-83. Appeared in the movie *Two Lane Blacktop*. Recipient of *Billboard*'s Century Award in 1998. Inducted into the Rock and Roll Hall of Fame in 2000.

1)*Mud Slide Slim And The Blue Horizon* 2)*Sweet Baby James* 3)*JT*

Debut	Peak	Wks	RIAA	CD	#	Album Title	Catalog	Sym	$	Label & Number
3/14/70	3	102	▲³	©	1	Sweet Baby James			$15	Warner 1843
10/3/70	62	28		©	2	James Taylor		[E]	$30	Apple 3352
						recorded in 1968				
2/6/71	74	8		©	3	James Taylor and the original Flying Machine-1967		[E]	$20	Euphoria 2
5/8/71	2⁴	45	▲²	©	4	Mud Slide Slim And The Blue Horizon			$15	Warner 2561
11/25/72+	4	25	●	©	5	One Man Dog			$15	Warner 2660
7/13/74	13	18		©	6	Walking Man			$15	Warner 2794
5/31/75	6	27	●	©	7	Gorilla			$12	Warner 2866
7/4/76	16	24	●	©	8	In The Pocket			$12	Warner 2912
12/4/76+	23	41	▲¹¹	©	9	Greatest Hits	C:❶¹/613	[G]	$12	Warner 2979
7/9/77	4	39	▲³	©	10	JT			$12	Columbia 34811
5/12/79	10	23	▲	©	11	Flag			$12	Columbia 36058
3/21/81	10	23	▲	©	12	Dad Loves His Work			$12	Columbia 37009
11/23/85	34	30	▲	©	13	That's Why I'm Here			$10	Columbia 40052
2/13/88	25	34	▲	©	14	Never Die Young			$10	Columbia 40851
10/19/91	37	47	▲	©	15	New Moon Shine			$10	Columbia 46038
8/28/93	20	24	▲²	©	16	(Live)		[L]	$15	Columbia 47056 [2]
6/7/97	9	24	▲	©	17	Hourglass			$10	Columbia 67912
11/25/00	97	12		©	18	Greatest Hits Volume 2		[G]	$10	Columbia 85223

Ain't No Song (6)	Don't Talk Now (2)	Hymn (5)	Looking For Love On Broadway (10)	Places In My Past (4)	That's Why I'm Here (13,18)
Ananas (17)	Down In The Hole (15)	I Was A Fool To Care (7)	Love Has Brought Me Around (4)	Promised Land (6)	There We Are (10)
Angry Blues (7)	Enough To Be On Your Way (17,18)	I Was Only Telling A Lie (10)	Love Songs (7)	Rainy Day Man (2,3,11)	Traffic Jam (10,16)
Another Day (17,18)	Everybody Has The Blues (8,16)	I Will Follow (12,16)	Machine Gun Kelly (4)	Riding On A Railroad (4,16)	Turn Away (13)
Another Grey Morning (10)	Everybody Loves To Cha Cha Cha (15)	(I've Got To) Stop Thinkin' 'Bout That (15,18)	Man Who Shot Liberty Valance (13)	Rock 'N' Roll Is Music Now (6)	Up Er Mei (17)
Anywhere Like Heaven (1)	**Everyday** (13,18) **61**	If I Keep My Heart Out Of Sight (10)	Me And My Guitar (6)	Runaway Boy (14)	Up From Your Life (17)
B.S.U.R. (11)	Fading Away (6)	Instrumental I (5)	Mescalito (5)	Sarah Maria (7)	**Up On The Roof** (11,16,18) **28**
Baby Boom Baby (14)	Family Man (8)	Instrumental II (5)	**Mexico** (7,9,16) **49**	Secret O' Life (10,16,18)	Valentine's Day (14)
Back On The Street Again (5)	Fanfare (5)	Is That The Way You Look? (11)	Migration (6)	She Thinks I Still Care (16)	Walking Man (6,9,16)
Bartender's Blues (10)	**Fire And Rain** (1,9,16) **3**	Isn't It Nice To Be Home Again (4)	Millworker (11,16)	Shed A Little Light (15,16,18)	Walking My Baby Back Home (17)
Believe It Or Not (12)	First Of May (14)	Jig (5)	Mona (13)	**Shower The People** (8,9,16) **22**	Wandering (7)
Blossom (1)	Fool For You (5)	Johnnie Comes Back (11)	Money Machine (8)	Slap Leather (15,16)	Water Is Wide (15)
Blues Is Just A Bad Dream (3)	Frozen Man (15)	Jump Up Behind Me (17)	Mud Slide Slim (4)	Sleep Come Free Me (11)	Will Not Lie For You (11)
Boatman (7)	Gaia (17)	Junkie's Lament (8)	Music (7)	Slow Burning Love (8)	Woh, Don't You Know (5)
Brighten Your Night With My Day (2,3)	Going Around One More Time (13)	Knocking Round The Zoo (2,3)	Native Son (15)	Soldiers (4)	Woman's Gotta Have It (8)
Brother Trucker (11)	Golden Moments (8)	Kootch's Song (3)	**Never Die Young** (14,18) **80**	Someone (5)	Yellow And Rose (17)
Captain Jim's Drunken Dream (8)	Gorilla (7)	Let It All Fall Down (6)	New Hymn (16)	Something In The Way She Moves (2,9,16)	You Can Close Your Eyes (4)
Carolina In My Mind (2,9,16) **67**	**Handy Man** (10,16,18) **4**	Let Me Ride (4)	New Tune (5)	Something's Wrong (2,3)	You Make It Easy (7,16)
Chanson Francaise (11)	**Hard Times** (12) **72**	Letter In The Mail (14)	Night Owl (2,3)	Song For You Far Away (13,18)	**You've Got A Friend** (4,9,16) **1**
Chili Dog (5)	Hello Old Friend (6)	Lighthouse (7)	Nobody But You (5)	Stand And Fight (12)	**Your Smiling Face** (10,16,18) **20**
Circle Round The Sun (2)	**Her Town Too** (12,18) **11**	Like Everyone She Knows (15)	Nothing Like A Hundred Miles (8)	Steamroller (1,9,16)	
Company Man (11)	Hey Mister, That's Me Up On The Jukebox (4)	Limousine Driver (13)	Oh Baby, Don't You Loose Your Lip On Me (1)	Sugar Trade (7)	
Copperline (15,16,18)	Highway Song (4)	Line 'Em Up (17)	Oh Brother (15)	Suite For 20 G (1)	
Country Road (1,9,16) **37**	Home By Another Way (14)	Little David (5)	Oh, Susanna (1)	Summer's Here (12)	
Daddy's All Gone (8)	**Honey Don't Leave L.A.** (10) **61**	Little More Time With You (17,18)	**One Man Parade** (5) **67**	Sun On The Moon (14,16)	
Daddy's Baby (6)	Hour That The Morning Comes (12)	Lo And Behold (1)	One More Go Round (15)	Sunny Skies (1)	
Dance (5)	**How Sweet It Is (To Be Loved By You)** (7,9,16) **5**	London Town (12)	One Morning In May (5)	Sunshine Sunshine (2)	
Day Tripper (11)		**Long Ago And Far Away** (4) **31**	Only A Dream In Rio (13,18)	Sweet Baby James (1,9,16)	
Don't Be Sad 'Cause Your Sun Is Down (8)			Only For Me (12)	Sweet Potatoe Pie (14)	
Don't Let Me Be Lonely Tonight (5,9,16) **14**			Only One (13,16)	T-Bone (14)	
				Taking It In (2)	
				Terra Nova (10)	
				That Lonesome Road (12,16)	

★477★ TAYLOR, Johnnie   '76

Born on 5/5/38 in Crawfordsville, Arkansas. Died of a heart attack on 5/31/2000 (age 62). R&B singer. Known as the "Soul Philosopher."

1)Eargasm 2)Who's Making Love... 3)Rated Extraordinaire

DEBUT	PEAK	WKS		CD	#	Album Title	Sym	$	Label & Number
1/25/69	42	18		©	1	Who's Making Love...		$40	Stax 2005
4/26/69	126	9		©	2	Raw Blues		$25	Stax 2008
7/5/69	109	6		©	3	The Johnnie Taylor Philosophy Continues		$25	Stax 2023
12/19/70	141	5		©	4	Johnnie Taylor's Greatest Hits	[G]	$25	Stax 2032
4/17/71	112	11		©	5	One Step Beyond		$25	Stax 2030
7/14/73	54	20		©	6	Taylored In Silk		$20	Stax 3014
6/8/74	182	8		©	7	Super Taylor		$20	Stax 5509
3/13/76	5	28	●	©	8	Eargasm		$12	Columbia 33951
3/19/77	51	11			9	Rated Extraordinaire		$12	Columbia 34401
5/6/78	164	5			10	Ever Ready		$12	Columbia 35340
7/27/96	108	18		©	11	Good Love		$10	Malaco 7480
6/17/00	140	15		©	12	Gotta Get The Groove Back		$10	Malaco 7499

Ain't That Lovin' You (For More Reasons Than One) (11)
And I Panicked (9)
At Night Time (My Pillow Tells A Tale On Me) (7)
Big Head Hundreds (12)
Bittersweet Love (10)
Body Rock (11)
Can't Trust Your Neighbor (1)
Cheaper To Keep Her (6) *15*
Darling I Love You (7)
Did He Make Love To You (9)
Disco Lady (8) *1*
Don't Take My Sunshine (5)
Don't Touch Her Body (If You Can't Touch Her Mind) (8)
Ease Back Out (12)
Ever Ready (10)
Fool Like Me (5)
Free (7)
Games People Play (3)
Give Me My Baby (10)
Good Love (11)
Gotta Get The Groove Back (12)

Hello Sundown (2)
Here I Go (Through These Changes Again) (9)
Hey Mister Melody Maker (10)
Hold On This Time (1,4)
I Ain't Particular (4)
I Am Somebody Part II (5) *39*
I Believe In You (You Believe In Me) (6) *11*
I Can Read Between The Lines (6)
I Could Never Be President (3,4) *48*
I Don't Wanna Lose You (5) *86*
I Gotta Keep Groovin' You (10)
I Love To Make Love When It's Raining (10)
I Love You Lady (12)
I'd Rather Drink Muddy Water (1)
I'm From The Old School (12)
I'm Gonna Keep On Loving You (8)
I'm Just A Shoulder To Cry On (9)

I'm Not The Same Person (1,4)
I'm Trying (1)
I've Been Born Again (7) *78*
If I Had A Fight With Love (3)
If I Had It To Do Over Again (2)
In What You Do (It's How You Do It) (9)
It Don't Hurt Me Like It Used To (8)
It Don't Pay To Get Up In The Morning (1)
It's Amazing (3)
It's September (7)
It's Your Thing (3)
Jody's Got Your Girl And Gone (5) *28*
Juke Joint (12)
Just One Moment (7)
Keep On Dancing (10)
Last Two Dollars (11)
Let's Get Back On Track (12)
Love Bones (3,4) *43*
Love Is A Hurting Thing (3)
Love Is Better In The A.M. (Part 1) (9) *77*

Mr. Nobody Is Somebody Now (1,4)
Not Just Another Booty Song (9)
One In A Million (12)
One Thing Wrong With My Woman (6)
Pardon Me Lady (2)
Part Time Love (2)
Party Life (7)
Payback Hurts (1)
Pick Up The Pieces (8)
Please Don't Stop (That Song From Playing) (8)
Poor Make Believer (1)
Running Out Of Lies (8)
Sending You A Kiss (11)
Separation Line (3)
Slide On (11)
Somebody's Gettin' It (8) *33*
Somebody's Sleeping In My Bed (4) *95*
Soul Fillet (10)
Soul Heaven (12)
Starting All Over Again (6)

Steal Away (4) *37*
Stop Giving People Hard Luck Stories (9)
Stormy (9)
Take Care Of Your Homework (1,4) *20*
Talk To Me (6)
Testify (I Wonna) (3,4) *36*
That Bone (9)
That's Where It's At (2)
This Bitter Earth (6)
This Masquerade (11)
Time After Time (5)
Too Close For Comfort (12)
Too Late To Try To Do Right (11)
Too Many Memories (11)
Try Me Tonight (1)
Walk Away With Me (11)
We're Getting Careless With Our Love (6) *34*
Where Can A Man Go From Here (2)
Where There's Smoke There's Fire (2)

Who Can I Turn To (3,4)
Who's Making Love (1,4) *5*
Whole Lotta Lovin' (11)
Will You Love Me Forever (5)
Woman Across The River (1)
Woman, Don't Be Afraid (12)
Wounded In The Battle Of Love (12)
You Can't Keep A Good Man Down (2)
You Can't Win With A Losing Hand (2)
You Got Me In The Mood For Love (11)
You're Good For Me (2)
You're The Best In The World (8)
Your Love Is Rated X (9)

TAYLOR, Kate   '71

Born on 8/15/49 in Boston. Singer/songwriter/guitarist. Sister of **James Taylor**, **Alex Taylor** and **Livingston Taylor**.

3/27/71	88	8			Sister Kate		$15	Cotillion 9045

Ballad Of A Well Known Gun
Be That Way
Country Comfort

Do I Still Figure In Your Life
Handbags And Gladrags
Home Again

Jesus Is Just All Right (medley)
Lo And Behold (medley)
Look At Granny Run, Run

Sweet Honesty
Where You Lead
White Lightning

You Can Close Your Eyes

TAYLOR, Little Johnny   '63

Born Johnny Young on 2/11/43 in Memphis; raised in Los Angeles. Blues singer/harmonica player.

11/9/63	140	2			Little Johnny Taylor		$100	Galaxy 203

As Quick As I Can
Darling, Believe In Me
Part Time Love *19*

She Tried To Understand
She's Yours, She's Mine, (She's Somebody Else's, Too)

Since I Found A New Love *78*
Somewhere Down The Line
Stay Sweet

What You Need Is A Ball
You Gotta Go On
You'll Need Another Favor

You're The One (For Me)

TAYLOR, Livingston   '70

Born on 11/21/50 in Boston. Singer/songwriter/guitarist. Brother of **James Taylor**, **Alex Taylor** and **Kate Taylor**.

7/25/70	82	20		©	1	Livingston Taylor		$20	Atco 334
12/18/71+	147	10		©	2	Liv		$15	Capricorn 863
11/3/73	189	5		©	3	Over The Rainbow		$15	Capricorn 0114

Be That Way (2)
Blind (3)
Can't Get Back Home (1)
Carolina Day (1) *93*
Caroline (2)
Doctor Man (1)

Easy Prey (2)
Falling In Love With You (3)
Gentleman (2)
Get Out Of Bed (2) *97*
Good Friends (1)
Hush A Bye (1)

I Can Dream Of You (3)
I Just Can't Be Lonesome No More (2)
If I Needed Someone (3)
In My Reply (1)
Lady Tomorrow (3)

Let Me Go Down (3)
Lost In The Love Of You (1)
Loving Be My New Horizon (3)
May I Stay Around (3)
Mom, Dad (2)
Oh Hallelujah (3)

On Broadway (2)
Open Up Your Eyes (2)
Packet Of Good Times (1)
Pretty Woman (3)
Rodeo (3)
Sit On Back (1)

Six Days On The Road (1)
Somewhere Over The Rainbow (3)
Thank You Song (1)
Truck Driving Man (2)

TAYLOR, Mick   '79

Born on 1/17/48 in Hereford, England. Guitarist with **The Rolling Stones** (1969-74).

7/21/79	119	5		©	Mick Taylor		$12	Columbia 35076

A Minor (medley)
Alabama

Baby I Want You
Broken Hands

Giddy-Up
Leather Jacket

S.W.5
Slow Blues

Spanish (medley)

TAYLOR, R. Dean   '71

Born in 1939 in Toronto. Singer/songwriter.

2/20/71	198	1			I Think, Therefore I Am		$15	Rare Earth 522

Ain't It A Sad Thing *66*
Back Street
Fire And Rain

Gonna Give Her All The Love
I've Got
Gotta See Jane *67*

Indiana Wants Me *5*
Love's Your Name
Sunday Morning Coming Down

Two Of Us
Woman Alive

TAYLOR, Roger   '81

Born on 7/26/49 in Norfolk, England. Drummer of **Queen**.

5/9/81	121	10			Fun In Space		$10	Elektra 522

Airheads
Fun In Space

Future Management
Good Times Are Now

Interlude In Constantinople
Laugh Or Cry

Let's Get Crazy
Magic Is Loose

My Country - I & II
No Violins

T-BONES, The '66

Instrumental studio group: Danny Hamilton (guitar), Joe Frank Carollo (bass) and Tommy Reynolds (drums). Later recorded as **Hamilton, Joe Frank & Reynolds**. Hamilton died on 12/23/94 (age 48).

| 2/12/66 | 75 | 12 | © | No Matter What Shape (Your Stomach's In) | [I] | $25 | Liberty 7439 |

Chiquita Banana
Don't Think Twice, It's All Right
Fever
Hole In The Wall
Let's Hang On
Lies
Moment Of Softness
My Headache's Gone
No Matter What Shape (Your Stomach's In) *3*
Pizza Parlor
Sippin' 'N Chippin' *62*
What's In The Bag, Goose

TCHAIKOVSKY, Bram — see BRAM TCHAIKOVSKY

T-CONNECTION '79

Disco group from Nassau, Bahamas: brothers Theo (vocals, keyboards) and Kirk Coakley (bass), Dave Mackey (guitar) and Tony Flowers (drums).

5/14/77	109	11	©	1 Magic		$12	Dash 30004
1/21/78	139	11	©	2 On Fire		$12	Dash 30008
1/27/79	51	19	©	3 T-Connection		$12	Dash 30009
11/24/79	188	3		4 Totally Connected		$12	Dash 30014
3/21/81	138	8		5 Everything Is Cool		$10	Capitol 12128
3/20/82	123	10		6 Pure & Natural		$10	Capitol 12191

At Midnight (3) *56*
Best Of My Love (6)
Born To Boogie (4)
Choosing (4)
Coming Back For More (3)
Crazy Mixed Up World (1)
Cush (2)
Danger Zone (4)
Disco Magic (1)
Do What You Wanna Do (1) *46*
Don't Stop The Music (3)
Ecstasy (4)
Everything Is Cool (5)
Funkannection (3)
Funky Lady (3)
Girl Watching (6)
Give Me Your Love (5)
Go Back Home (1)
Goombay Time (5)
Got To See My Lady (1)
Groove City (5)
Groove To Get Down (2)
Heaven In Your Eyes (5)
I Like Funkin' With You (4)
Lady Of The Night (2)
Let Yourself Go (2)
Let's Do It Today (4)
Little More Love (6)
Love Supreme (3)
Midnight Train (3)
Might As Well Dance (6)
Monday Morning (1)
Mothers Love (1)
On Fire (2)
Paradise (5)
Party Night (6)
Peace Line (1)
Playin' Games (2)
Prisoner Of My Mind (2)
Rushing Through The Crowd (6)
Saturday Night (3)
Slippin' Away (6)
Spend The Night With Me (5)
Spinnin' (5)
That's Love (4)
Totally Connected (4)
Watching You (2)
We've Got A Good Thing (5)

TEAR DA CLUB UP THUGS '99

Rap trio from Memphis: DJ Paul, Juicy J and Lord Infamous. All are members of **Three 6 Mafia**.

| 2/20/99 | 18 | 13 | © | CrazyNDaLazDayz | | $10 | Hypnotize Minds 1716 |

All Dirty Hoes
Big Business
DaLazDayz
Elbow A Nigga
Get Buck, Get Wild
Hell Naw
Hypnotize Cash Money
Hypnotize Minds/Profit Posse
I'm Losing It
Niggas Worst Downfall
Paper Chase
Push 'Em Off
Slob On My Nob
Smoked Out
Throw Your Sets
Triple Six Clubhouse
Undercover Freaks
Wet Party
What You Lookin' For
When God Calls Time Out
Who The Crunkest

TEARDROP EXPLODES '81

Pop-rock group from England: **Julian Cope** (vocals, bass), Alan Gill (guitar), David Balfe (keyboards) and Gary Dwyer (drums).

| 2/28/81 | 156 | 6 | © | 1 Kilimanjaro | | $10 | Mercury 4016 |
| 2/6/82 | 176 | 4 | © | 2 Wilder | | $10 | Mercury 4035 |

...And The Fighting Takes Over (2)
Bent Out Of Shape (2)
Books (1)
Brave Boys Keep Their Promises (1)
Colours Fly Away (2)
Culture Bunker (2)
Falling Down Around Me (2)
Great Dominions (2)
Ha, Ha, I'm Drowning (1)
Like Leila Khaled Said (2)
Passionate Friend (2)
Poppies In The Field (1)
Pure Joy (2)
Reward (1)
Seven Views Of Jerusalem (2)
Sleeping Gas (1)
Suffocate (1)
Thief Of Baghdad (1)
Tiny Children (2)
Treason (1)
Went Crazy (1)
When I Dream (1)

TEARS FOR FEARS '85

Pop-rock group from England: Roland Orzabal (vocals, guitar, keyboards) and Curt Smith (vocals, bass). Adopted name from Arthur Janev's book *Prisoners of Pain* in 1981. Assisted by Manny Elias (drums) and Ian Stanley (keyboards). Smith left in 1992.

5/7/83	73	69	●	©	1 The Hurting		$10	Mercury 811039
3/30/85	❶⁵	83	▲⁵	©	2 Songs From The Big Chair		$10	Mercury 824300
10/7/89	8	34	▲	©	3 The Seeds Of Love		$10	Fontana 838730
4/4/92	53	13	▲	©	4 Tears Roll Down (Greatest Hits 82-92)	[G]	$10	Fontana 510939
7/10/93	45	21	●	©	5 Elemental		$10	Mercury 514875
10/28/95	79	5		©	6 Raoul And The Kings Of Spain		$10	Epic 67318

Advice For The Young At Heart (3,4) *89*
Bad Man's Song (3)
Break It Down Again (5) *25*
Brian Wilson Said (5)
Broken (2)
Change (1,4) *73*
Cold (5)
Dog's A Best Friend's Dog (5)
Don't Drink The Water (6)
Elemental (5)
Everybody Wants To Rule The World (2,4) *1*
Falling Down (6)
Famous Last Words (3)
Fish Out Of Water (6)
Gas Giants (5)
God's Mistake (6)
Goodnight Song (5)
Head Over Heels (2,4) *3*
Humdrum And Humble (6)
Hurting, The (1)
I Believe (2,4)
I Choose You (6)
Ideas As Opiates (1)
Laid So Low (Tears Roll Down) (4)
Listen (2)
Los Reyes Católicos (6)
Mad World (1,4)
Me And My Big Ideas (6)
Memories Fade (1)
Mothers Talk (2,4) *27*
Mr. Pessimist (5)
Pale Shelter (1,4)
Power (5)
Prisoner, The (1)
Raoul And The Kings Of Spain (6)
Secrets (6)
Shout (2,4) *1*
Sketches Of Pain (6)
Sorry (6)
Sowing The Seeds Of Love (3,4) *2*
Standing On The Corner Of The Third World (3)
Start Of The Breakdown (1)
Suffer The Children (1)
Swords And Knives (3)
Watch Me Bleed (1)
Woman In Chains (3,4) *36*
Working Hour (2)
Year Of The Knife (3)

TECHMASTER P.E.B. '92

Born Neil Case in Florida. Techno-bass artist.

| 2/29/92 | 132 | 30 | © | 1 Bass Computer | | $10 | Newtown 2208 |
| 8/28/93 | 186 | 2 | © | 2 It Came From Outer Bass II | [I] | $10 | Newtown 2211 |

Bad Bass Mix (1)
Bass By Numbers (1)
Bass Computer (1)
Bass Out (2)
Bassgasm (1)
Computer Love (1)
D.P.E. (1)
DSTM 2 (2)
Do You Like Technobass? (2)
Don't Stop The Bass (1)
Don't Stop The Music (1)
006 (2)
Dragon Bass (2)
Eurobass (2)
Euromusik (1)
I Like The Boom (1)
It Came From Outer Bass (2)
Keep On Scratchin' (2)
Listen To The Music (2)
Machines (2)
Outerbass Mix (1)
P.E.B. 500 (1)
Phonz (2)
Power Bass Ultra Mix (1)
Reggatek (2)
Robot Love (2)
Robot Machines (2)
Scratchin' Megabass Mix (1)
Tech'in Slow N' Low (1)
Techno Bass Beats (1)
Technohaus (2)
Time To Jam (1)
Voices (2)

TECHNOTRONIC '90

Dance studio group created by Belgian DJ/producer Thomas DeQuincey and female rapper Ya Kid K.

| 12/23/89+ | 10 | 55 | ▲ | © | Pump Up The Jam - The Album | C:#25/2 | $10 | SBK 93422 |

Come Back
Come On
Get Up! (Before The Night Is Over) *7*
Move This *6*
Pump Up The Jam *2*
Raw
Rockin' Over The Beat *95*
Take It Slow
This Beat Is Technotronic
Tough

TEDESCHI, Susan '99

Born on 11/7/70 in Norwell, Massachusetts. Singer/songwriter/guitarist.

| 2/13/99 | 181 | 4 | ● | Just Won't Burn | C:#7/5 | $10 | Tone-Cool 1164 |

Angel From Montgomery
Can't Leave You Alone
Found Someone New
Friar's Point
It Hurt So Bad
Just Won't Burn
Little By Little
Looking For Answers
Mama, He Treats Your Daughter Mean
Rock Me Right
You Need To Be With Me

TEENAGE FANCLUB '92

Pop-rock group from Glasgow, Scotland: Norman Blake (vocals, guitar), Ray McGinley (guitar), Gerry Love (bass) and Brendan O'Hare (drums).

3/7/92	137	4		©	**Bandwagonesque**			$10	DGC 24461

Alcoholiday   December   I Don't Know   Metal Baby   Satan   Star Sign
Concept, The   Guiding Star   Is This Music?   Pet Rock   Sidewinder   What You Do To Me

TEENAGERS, The — see LYMON, Frankie

TEE SET, The '70

Pop group from Delft, Holland: Peter Tetteroo (vocals), Hans Van Eijck (organ), Dill Bennink (guitar), Franklin Madjid (bass) and Joop Blom (drums).

5/16/70	158	6		©	**Ma Belle Amie**			$20	Colossus 1001

Bring A Little Sunshine   Finally In Love Again   I Don't Want To Know   Long Ago   Magic Lantern   Walk On By My Door
Charmaine   Here In My House   **If You Do Believe In Love** *81*   **Ma Belle Amie** *5*   Since I Lost Your Love   What Can I Do

TE KANAWA, Kiri '86

Born on 3/6/44 in Gisborne, New Zealand. Operatic soprano.

12/7/85+	136	16		©	**Blue Skies**			$10	London 414666

Blue Skies   Here's That Rainy Day   It Might As Well Be Spring   True Love   Yesterdays
Folks Who Live On The Hill   How High The Moon   So In Love   When I Grow Too Old To
Gone With The Wind   I Didn't Know What Time It Was   Speak Low   Dream

TELA '00

Born in Memphis. Male rapper.

11/23/96+	70	23		© 1	**Piece Of Mind**			$10	Suave House 1553
10/24/98	49	5		© 2	**Now Or Never**			$10	Rap-A-Lot 46588
10/7/00	47	7		© 3	**The World Ain't Enuff**			$10	Rap-A-Lot 49856

B.I.G.P.I.M.P.S.I.S.I (2)   Fallin' Soldiers (2)   Now Or Never (They Wanna Kill   Sho Nuff (1) *58*   Table Dance (2,3)   Twisted (1)
Blackhaven (1)   Hell Naw (3)   Me) (2)   Sho Nuff 2000 (3)   Tela (3)   U Can't Tell (1)
Bring Em Out (2)   Jetzt Oder Nie (2)   Piece Of Mind (1)   Still A Man (2)   These Hoe's (2)   Way U (1)
Bye! Bye! Hater! (3)   Let It Rain (1)   Playboy (3)   Strange (1)   Throat On A Boat (3)   World Ain't Enuff (3)
Caesar Knight (2)   Let's Be Friends (3)   Right Now (2)   Suave House (1)   Time (1)
Can't Stop Me (3)   Make A Million (2)   Roll Wit It (2)   Success (1)   Tired Of Ballin (1)
Drugs (3)   Money & The Power (2)   Set Me Free (3)   Survival (1)   Too Slick (The Movie) (2)

TEMPLE OF THE DOG '92

Gathering of Seattle musicians in tribute to Andrew Wood, lead singer of **Mother Love Bone**, who died of a drug overdose in 1990. Features Stone Gossard, Jeff Ament, Eddie Vedder and Mike McCready of **Pearl Jam**, with Chris Cornell and Matt Cameron of **Soundgarden**. Gossard and Ament were members of Mother Love Bone.

6/27/92	5	47	▲	©	**Temple Of The Dog**			$10	A&M 5350

All Night Thing   Four Walled World   Pushin Forward Back   Say Hello 2 Heaven   Wooden Jesus
Call Me A Dog   Hunger Strike   Reach Down   Times Of Trouble   Your Saviour

TEMPO, Nino, & April Stevens '64

Brother-and-sister duo from Niagara Falls, New York: Nino Tempo (born on 1/6/35) and April Stevens (born on 4/29/36).

11/23/63+	48	14			**Deep Purple**			$50	Atco 156

Baby Weemus   I've Been Carrying A Torch For   Indian Love Call   Paradise   Tears Of Sorrow
Deep Purple *1*   You So Long That I Burned A   It's Pretty Funny   Shine On Harvest Moon   True Love
   Great Big Hole In My Heart   One Dozen Roses   **Sweet And Lovely** *77*   (We'll Always Be) Together

TEMPTATIONS, The ★9★ '69

R&B vocal group from Detroit: **Eddie Kendricks**, **David Ruffin**, Paul Williams, Melvin Franklin and Otis Williams. **Dennis Edwards** replaced Ruffin in 1968. Ricky Owens and Richard Street replaced Kendricks and Paul Williams in 1971. Damon Harris replaced Owens in early 1972. Glenn Leonard replaced Harris in 1975. Edwards left group, 1977-79, replaced by Louis Price. Ali Ollie Woodson replaced Edwards from 1984-87. Lineup in 1988: Otis Williams, Franklin, Street, Edwards and Ron Tyson. Lineup in 1998: Otis Williams (the only original member remaining), Ron Tyson, Terry Weeks, Harry McGilberry and Barrington Henderson. Paul Williams died of a self-inflicted gunshot on 8/17/73 (age 34). Ruffin died of a drug overdose on 6/1/91 (age 50). Kendricks died of cancer on 10/5/92 (age 52). Franklin died of heart failure on 2/23/95 (age 52). Group inducted into the Rock and Roll Hall of Fame in 1989.

     1)TCB   2)All Directions   3)Diana Ross & the Supremes Join the Temptations   4)Cloud Nine
     5)The Temptations Greatest Hits

5/9/64	95	11		© 1	**Meet The Temptations**			$50	Gordy 911
4/3/65	35	26		© 2	**The Temptations Sing Smokey**			$40	Gordy 912
11/27/65+	11	37		© 3	**Temptin' Temptations**			$40	Gordy 914
7/9/66	12	35		© 4	**Gettin' Ready**			$40	Gordy 918
12/17/66+	5	120	▲²	© 5	**The Temptations Greatest Hits**	C:#5/0	[G]	$30	Gordy 919
4/1/67	10	51		© 6	**Temptations Live!**		[L]	$30	Gordy 921
8/12/67	7	36		© 7	**With A Lot O' Soul**			$30	Gordy 922
12/23/67+	13	44		© 8	**The Temptations in a Mellow Mood**			$30	Gordy 924
5/25/68	13	41		© 9	**Wish It Would Rain**			$30	Gordy 927
11/30/68+	2¹	32	●	© 10	**Diana Ross & The Supremes Join the Temptations**			$30	Motown 679
12/28/68+	❶¹	34	●	© 11	**TCB**		[TV]	$30	Motown 682
					DIANA ROSS & THE SUPREMES WITH THE TEMPTATIONS (above 2)				
1/4/69	15	24		© 12	**Live At The Copa**		[L]	$30	Gordy 938
3/15/69	4	40	●	© 13	**Cloud Nine**			$30	Gordy 939
8/9/69	24	16		14	**The Temptations Show**		[TV]	$30	Gordy 933
					includes "When I Lay My Burdens Down" by George Kirby				
10/11/69	5	41	●	© 15	**Puzzle People**			$30	Gordy 949
10/25/69	28	18		© 16	**Together**			$30	Motown 692
12/6/69	38	12		17	**On Broadway**		[TV]	$30	Motown 699
					DIANA ROSS & THE SUPREMES WITH THE TEMPTATIONS (above 2)				
4/4/70	9	30	●	© 18	**Psychedelic Shack**			$25	Gordy 947
8/22/70	21	18		19	**Live at London's Talk of The Town**		[L]	$25	Gordy 953

TEMPTATIONS, The — Cont'd

DEBUT	PEAK	WKS		CD	ARTIST — Album Title	Sym	$	Label & Number
9/26/70	15	70	●	© 20	Temptations Greatest Hits II	[G]	$25	Gordy 954
12/5/70+	4ˣ	7	●	© 21	The Temptations' Christmas Card	[X]	$25	Gordy 951
					Christmas charts: 7/'70, 7/'71, 4/'72			
5/8/71	16	35	●	© 22	Sky's The Limit		$25	Gordy 957
1/29/72	24	22		© 23	Solid Rock		$25	Gordy 961
8/19/72	2²	44	●	© 24	All Directions		$25	Gordy 962
3/10/73	7	28	●	© 25	Masterpiece		$25	Gordy 965
9/15/73	65	26	▲	© 26	Anthology	[G]	$25	Motown 782 [3]
12/29/73+	19	22			27 1990		$20	Gordy 966
2/8/75	13	36	●	© 28	A Song For You		$20	Gordy 969
11/29/75	40	20			29 House Party		$20	Gordy 973
4/3/76	29	20			30 Wings Of Love		$20	Gordy 971
9/11/76	53	14			31 The Temptations Do The Temptations		$20	Gordy 975
12/10/77+	113	13			32 Hear To Tempt You		$15	Atlantic 19143
5/17/80	45	14			33 Power		$15	Gordy 994
8/29/81	119	9			34 The Temptations		$15	Gordy 1006
5/1/82	37	18		© 35	Reunion		$15	Gordy 6008
3/19/83	159	9			36 Surface Thrills		$15	Gordy 6032
12/17/83	6ˣ	41	▲	© 37	Give Love At Christmas	C:#22/30 [X]	$12	Motown 2842
					first released in 1980 on Gordy 998; Christmas charts: 6/'83, 14/'87, 12/'88, 17/'89, 13/'90, 20/'92, 22/'93, 25/'94, 37/'95, 37/'96, 29/'97, 29/'98, 36/'99			
4/21/84	152	9			38 Back To Basics		$12	Gordy 6085
11/17/84+	55	34		© 39	Truly For You		$12	Gordy 6119
1/25/86	146	10			40 Touch Me		$12	Gordy 6164
5/17/86	140	16		© 41	25th Anniversary	[K]	$15	Motown 5389 [2]
8/2/86	74	33		© 42	To Be Continued...		$12	Gordy 6207
10/24/87	112	21		© 43	Together Again		$12	Motown 6246
9/5/98	44	44	▲	© 44	Phoenix Rising		$10	Motown 530937
11/21/98	7ᶜ	2	●	© 45	Great Songs And Performances That Inspired The Motown 25th Anniversary Television Special	[G]	$10	Motown 5315
11/21/98	15ᶜ	1	▲	© 46	All The Million-Sellers	[G]	$10	Motown 5212
11/21/98	137	1		© 47	The Ultimate Collection	[G]	$10	Motown 530562
6/3/00	54	12		© 48	Ear-Resistible		$10	Motown 157742

TEMPTATIONS, The — Cont'd

Set Your Love Right (39)
Shadow Of Your Love (33)
Shakey Ground (28,47) **26**
She Got Tired Of Loving Me (40)
She's All I've Got (32)
Show Me Your Love (36)
Silent Night (21,37)
Silver Bells (21)
Since I Lost My Baby (3,5,26,41,47) **17**
Since I've Lost You (15)
Sing A Simple Song (16)
Slave (15)
Slow Down Heart (1)
Smiling Faces Sometimes (22)
Smooth Sailing (From Now On) (23)
Snake In The Grass (32)
So Much Joy (41)
Somebody's Keepin' Score (14)
Someday At Christmas (21)
Someone (42)
Somewhere (8)
Song For You (28)
Sorry Is A Sorry Word (7)

Soulmate (41)
Standing On The Top-Part 1 (35) **66**
Stay (44)
Stop The War Now (23)
Stop The World Right Here (I Wanna Get Off) (38)
Struck By Lightning Twice (33)
Stubborn Kind Of Fellow (16)
Student Mountie (17)
Superstar (Remember How You Got Where You Are) (23,26) **18**
Surface Thrills (36)
Swanee (12,14)
Sweet Gypsy Jane (30)
Sweet Inspiration (10)
Sweetness In The Dark (30)
T.C.B. (11)
Take A Look Around (23) **30**
Take A Stroll Thru Your Mind (18)
Take Me In Your Arms (44)
Taste Of Honey (8,11)
Tear From A Woman's Eyes (41)

Tempt Me (44)
10 X 10 (43)
Thanks To You (41)
That's Life (8)
That's The Way Love Is (15)
That's What Friends Are For (44)
Then (10)
There's No Stopping (Til We Set The Whole World Rockin') (31)
Think For Yourself (32)
This Christmas (37)
This Guy's In Love With You (10,19)
This Is My Beloved (9)
This Is My Promise (24)
Throw A Farewell Kiss (22)
To Be Continued (42)
Too Busy Thinking About My Baby (4)
Touch Me (40)
Treat Her Like A Lady (39,41,47) **48**
Truly Yours (41)
Try It Baby (10,14)

Try To Remember (8,26)
Two Sides To Love (7)
Ungena Za Ulimwengu (Unite The World) (22) **33**
Up The Creek (Without A Paddle) (30) **94**
Uptight (Everything's Alright) (16)
War (18)
Way Over There (2)
Way You Do The Things You Do (1,2,5,11,26,47) **11**
Ways Of A Grown Up Man (29)
Weight, The (16) **46**
What A Way To Put It (36)
What Else (34)
What It Is? (23)
What Love Has Joined Together (2,6)
What Now My Love (6,8)
What You Need Most (I Do Best Of All) (29)
What's So Good About Good Bye (2)
Wherever I Lay My Hat (That's My Home) (41)

White Christmas (21)
Who Are You (And What Are You Doing The Rest Of Your Life) (31)
Who Can I Turn To (When Nobody Needs Me) (8)
Who You Gonna Run To (4)
Who's Lovin' You (2)
Why Can't You And Me Get Together (31)
Why Did She Have To Leave Me (Why Did She Have To Go) (13)
Why Did You Leave Me Darling (9)
Why (Must We Fall In Love) (16)
With These Hands (8,12)
World Of You, Love And Music (29)
Yesterday (medley) (6)
You Beat Me To The Punch (2)
You Better Beware (35)
(You Can) Depend On Me (4)
You Can't Stop A Man In Love (29)

You Don't Love Me No More (15)
You Make Your Own Heaven And Hell Right Here On Earth (18)
You Need Love Like I Do (Don't You) (18)
You'll Lose A Precious Love (2,6)
You're My Everything (7,12,14,19,20,26,47) **6**
You're Not An Ordinary Girl (4)
You're The One (42)
You're The One I Need (3)
You've Got My Soul On Fire (27) **74**
You've Got To Earn It (3)
You've Really Got A Hold On Me (2)
Your Love (48)
Your Lovin' Is Magic (34)
Your Wonderful Love (1)
Zoom (27)

10cc · '75

Art-rock group formed in Manchester, England: Eric Stewart (vocals, guitar), Lol Creme (guitar, keyboards), Graham Gouldman (bass) and Kevin Godley (drums). Stewart and Gouldman were members of **The Mindbenders**. **Godley & Creme** left in 1976, replaced by drummer Paul Burgess. Added members **Rick Fenn**, Stuart Tosh and Duncan MacKay in 1978. Gouldman later in duo **Wax**.

DEBUT	PEAK	WKS		CD			$	Label & Number
8/10/74	81	14		©	1 Sheet Music		$15	UK 53107
4/19/75	15	25		©	2 The Original Soundtrack		$15	Mercury 1029
9/13/75	161	5			3 100cc	[K]	$15	UK 53110
2/14/76	47	13		©	4 How Dare You!		$15	Mercury 1061
5/14/77	31	20		©	5 Deceptive Bends		$15	Mercury 3702
12/24/77+	146	6			6 Live And Let Live	[L]	$20	Mercury 8600 [2]
10/14/78	69	17			7 Bloody Tourists		$12	Polydor 6161
12/22/79+	188	4			8 Greatest Hits 1972-1978	[G]	$12	Polydor 6244
5/17/80	180	2			9 Look Hear?		$12	Warner 3442

Anonymous Alcoholic (7)
Art For Art's Sake (4,6,8) **83**
Baron Samedi (1)
Blackmail (2)
Brand New Day (2)
Clockwork Creep (1)
Dean And I (3,8)
Don't Hang Up (4)
Don't Send We Back (9)
Donna (3,8)
Dreadlock Holiday (7,8) **44**
Dressed To Kill (9)

Everything You've Wanted To Know About !!! (Exclamation Marks) (7)
Feel The Benefit (5,6)
Film Of My Love (2)
Flying Junk (2)
For You And I (7) **85**
Fresh Air For My Momma (2)
From Rochdale To Ocho Rios (7)
Good Morning Judge (5,6,8) **69**
Head Room (4)
Honeymoon With B Troop (5,6)

Hotel (1)
How Dare You (4)
How'm I Ever Gonna Say Goodbye (9)
I Bought A Flat Guitar Tutor (5)
I Hate To Eat Alone (9)
I Took You Home (9)
I Wanna Rule The World (9)
I'm Mandy Fly Me (4,6,8) **60**
I'm Not In Love (2,6,8) **2**
Iceberg (4)
It Doesn't Matter At All (9)
L.A. Inflatable (9)

Last Night (7)
Latin Break (medley) (5)
Lazy Ways (4)
Life Is A Minestrone (2,8)
Life Line (7)
Lovers Anonymous (9)
Marriage Bureau Rendezvous (5,6)
Modern Man Blues (5,6)
Oh! Effendi (1)
Old Mister Time (7)
Old Wild Men (1,3)
One Two Five (9)

People In Love (5,6) **40**
Reds In My Bed (7)
Reminisce And Speculation (medley) (5)
Rock 'N' Roll Lullaby (4)
Rubber Bullets (3,8) **73**
Sacro-Iliac, The (1)
Second Sitting For The Last Supper (2,6)
Ships Don't Disappear In The Night (Do They?) (6)
Shock On The Tube (Don't Want Love) (7)
Silly Love (1,3,8)

Somewhere In Hollywood (1,3)
Strange Lover (9)
Take These Chains (7)
Things We Do For Love (5,6,8) **5**
Tokyo (7)
Une Nuit A Paris Medley (2)
Wall Street Shuffle (1,3,6,8)
Waterfall (9)
Welcome To The World (9)
Worst Band In The World (1,3)
You've Got A Cold (5,6)

TENNILLE, Toni · '84

Born on 5/8/43 in Montgomery, Alabama. Half of **Captain & Tennille** duo.

DEBUT	PEAK	WKS		CD		$	Label & Number
6/9/84	142	11		©	1 More Than You Know	$10	Mirage 90162
12/26/87	198	2		©	2 All Of Me	$10	Gaia 139001

All Of Me (2)
But Not For Me (1)
Can't Help Lovin' That Man Of Mine (1)
Day Dream (1)

Do It Again (1)
Do Nothing Til You Hear From Me (1)
Dream (2)
Easy Street (2)

Guess Who I Saw Today? (1)
Happiness Is Just A Thing Called Joe (2)
Honeysuckle Rose (2)
How High The Moon (2)

I Got It Bad And That Ain't Good (1)
I'll Be Tired Of You (2)
Let's Do It (1)
Moon Glow (1)

More Than You Know (1)
Nature Boy (2)
Our Love Is Here To Stay (1)
They All Laughed (2)
Very Thought Of You (2)

10,000 MANIACS · '93

Pop group formed in Jamestown, New York: **Natalie Merchant** (vocals), Robert Buck (guitar), Dennis Drew (keyboards), Steven Gustafson (bass) and Jerome Augustyniak (drums). Mary Ramsey replaced Merchant in 1994. Buck died of liver failure on 12/19/2000 (age 42).

DEBUT	PEAK	WKS	RIAA	CD				$	Label & Number
9/19/87+	37	77	▲²	©	1 In My Tribe	C:#47/1		$10	Elektra 60738
6/3/89	13	28	▲	©	2 Blind Man's Zoo			$10	Elektra 60815
11/3/90	102	10		©	3 Hope Chest - The Fredonia Recordings 1982-1983	[E]		$10	Elektra 60962
					remixes of early songs recorded at Fredonia State University in New York				
10/17/92+	28	56	▲²	©	4 Our Time In Eden			$10	Elektra 61385
11/13/93	13	45	▲³	©	5 MTV Unplugged	[L]		$10	Elektra 61569
7/5/97	104	14		©	6 Love Among The Ruins			$10	Geffen 25009

Across The Fields (6)
All That Never Happens (6)
Anthem For Doomed Youth (3)
Because The Night (5) **11**
Big Parade (2)
Big Star (6)
Campfire Song (1)
Candy Everybody Wants (4,5) **67**
Cherry Tree (1)
Circle Dream (4)

City Of Angels (1)
Daktari (3)
Death Of Manolete (3)
Don't Talk (1,5)
Dust Bowl (2)
Eat For Two (2,5)
Eden (4)
Even With My Eyes Closed (6)
Few And Far Between (4) **95**
Girl On A Train (6)
Gold Rush Brides (4,5)

Green Children (6)
Grey Victory (3)
Groove Dub (3)
Gun Shy (1)
Hateful Hate (3)
Headstrong (2)
Hey Jack Kerouac (1,5)
How You've Grown (4)
I'm Not The Man (4,5)
If You Intend (4)
Jezebel (4,5)

Jubilee (2)
Katrina's Fair (3)
Latin One (3)
Like The Weather (1,5) **68**
Lion's Share (2)
Love Among The Ruins (2)
More Than This (6) **25**
My Mother The War (3)
My Sister Rose (1)
National Education Week (3)
Noah's Dove (4,5)

Orange (2)
Painted Desert (1)
Peace Train (1)
Pit Viper (3)
Planned Obsolescence (3)
Please Forgive Us (2)
Poison In The Well (2)
Poor De Chirico (4)
Rainy Day (6)
Room For Everything (6)
Shining Light (6)

Stockton Gala Days (4,5)
Tension (3)
These Are Days (4,5) **66**
Tolerance (4)
Verdi Cries (1)
Trouble Me (2,5) **44**
What's The Matter Here? (1,5) **80**
You Happy Puppet (2)
You Won't Find Me There (6)

TEN WHEEL DRIVE With Genya Ravan '70

Jazz-rock group: **Genya Ravan** (vocals), **Michael Zager** (keyboards), Aram Schefrin (guitar), Steve Satten, John Gatchell, Dave Liebman, John Eckert and Dennis Parisi (horns), Bob Piazza (bass) and Allen Herman (drums).

1/10/70	**151**	16	1 **Construction #1**	$15 Polydor 4008
8/1/70	**161**	8	2 **Brief Replies**	$15 Polydor 4024
6/19/71	**190**	5	3 **Peculiar Friends**	$15 Polydor 4062

Ain't Gonna Happen (1)
Brief Replies (2)
Candy Man Blues (1)
Come Live With Me (2)

Down In The Cold (3)
Eye Of The Needle (1)
Fourteenth Street (I Can't Get Together) (3)
House In Central Park (1)

How Long Before I'm Gone (2)
I Am A Want Ad (1)
I Had Him Down (3)
Lapidary (1)
Last Of The Line (2)

Love Me (3)
Morning Much Better (2) 74
Night I Got Out Of Jail (1)
No Next Time (3)
Peculiar Friends (3)

Pickpocket, The (3)
Polar Bear Rug (1)
Pulse (2)
Shootin' The Breeze (3)
Stay With Me (2)

Tightrope (1)

★337★ TEN YEARS AFTER '71

Blues-rock group from England: **Alvin Lee** (vocals, guitar), Chick Churchill (keyboards), Leo Lyons (bass) and Ric Lee (drums).
1)Cricklewood Green 2)A Space In Time 3)SSSSH

8/10/68	**115**	14	© 1 **Undead**	[L] $20	Deram 18016
2/22/69	**61**	18	© 2 **Stonedhenge**	$20	Deram 18021
8/30/69	**20**	23	© 3 **SSSSH**	$20	Deram 18029
4/18/70	**14**	30	© 4 **Cricklewood Green**	$20	Deram 18038
12/12/70+	**21**	16	© 5 **Watt**	$20	Deram 18050
8/28/71	**17**	26 ▲	© 6 **A Space In Time**	$15	Columbia 30801
4/8/72	**55**	18	© 7 **Alvin Lee & Company**	[K] $15	Deram 18064
10/14/72	**43**	25	© 8 **Rock & Roll Music To The World**	$15	Columbia 31779
6/23/73	**39**	21	© 9 **Recorded Live**	[L] $20	Columbia 32290 [2]
5/18/74	**81**	14	© 10 **Positive Vibrations**	$15	Columbia 32851
7/19/75	**174**	5	11 **Goin' Home! Their Greatest Hits**	[K] $15	Deram 18072
9/16/89	**120**	10	© 12 **About Time**	$10	Chrysalis 21722

As The Sun Still Burns Away (4)
Baby Won't You Let Me Rock 'N Roll You (6) 61
Bad Blood (12)
Bad Scene (3)
Band With No Name (5)
Boogie On (7)
Choo Choo Mama (8,9) 89
Circles (4)
Classical Thing (9)
Convention Prevention (8)
Extension On One Chord (9)
Faro (2)
50,000 Miles Beneath My Brain (4)
Going Back To Birmingham (10)
Going To Chicago (12)
Going To Try (2,11)

Gonna Run (5)
Good Morning Little Schoolgirl (3,9)
Hard Monkeys (6)
Hear Me Calling (2,11)
Help Me (9)
Here They Come (6)
Highway Of Love (12)
Hobbit (9)
Hold Me Tight (7)
I Can't Keep From Cryin' Sometimes Pt. I & II (9)
I Can't Live Without Lydia (2)
I Don't Know That You Don't Know My Name (3)
I Get All Shook Up (12)
I May Be Wrong, But I Won't Be Wrong Always (1)
I Say Yeah (5)

I Wanted To Boogie (10)
I Woke Up This Morning (3,11)
I'd Love To Change The World (6) 40
I'm Coming On (5)
I'm Going Home (1,9,11)
I've Been There Too (6)
If You Should Love Me (3)
It's Getting Harder (10)
Let The Sky Fall (6)
Let's Shake It Up (12)
Look Into My Life (10)
Look Me Straight Into The Eyes (10)
Love Like A Man (4,11) 98
Me And My Baby (4)
My Baby Left Me (5)
No Title (2,11)
Nowhere To Run (10)

Once There Was A Time (6)
One Of These Days (6,9)
Outside My Window (12)
Over The Hill (6)
Portable People (7)
Positive Vibrations (10)
Religion (6)
Rock & Roll Music To The World (8)
Rock Your Mama (7)
Sad Song (2)
Saturday Night (12)
Scat Thing (9)
Shantung Cabbage (medley) (1)
She Lies In The Morning (5)
Silly Thing (7)
Skoobly-Oobly-Doobob (2)
Slow Blues In "C" (9)

Sounds, The (7)
Speed Kills (2)
Spider In My Web (1)
Standing At The Crossroads (7)
Standing At The Station (5)
Stomp, The (3)
Stone Me (10)
Stoned Woman (3)
Sugar The Road (4)
Summertime (medley) (1)
Sweet Little Sixteen (5)
Think About The Times (5)
Three Blind Mice (1)
Tomorrow I'll Be Out Of Town (8)
Turned Off T.V. Blues (8)
Two Time Mama (3)
Uncle Jam (6)
Victim Of Circumstance (12)

Waiting For The Judgment Day (12)
Wild Is The River (12)
Without You (10)
Woman Trouble (2)
Woodchopper's Ball (1,11)
Working In A Parking Lot (12)
Working On The Road (4)
Year 3,000 Blues (4)
You Can't Win Them All (8)
You Give Me Loving (8,9)
You're Driving Me Crazy (10)

TEPPER, Robert '86

Born in Bayonne, New Jersey. Rock singer/songwriter.

4/19/86	**144**	8	© **No Easy Way Out**	$10	Scotti Brothers 40128

Angel Of The City
Domination

Don't Walk Away 85
Hopeless Romantic

If That's What You Call Lovin'
No Easy Way Out 22

Restless World
Soul Survivor

Your Love Hurts

TERMINATOR X '91

Born Norman Rogers on 8/25/66 in New York City. Male rapper. Member of **Public Enemy**.

5/25/91	**97**	11	© 1 **Terminator X & The Valley Of The Jeep Beets**	$10	P.R.O. Division 46896
7/9/94	**189**	1	© 2 **Super Bad**	$10	P.R.O. Division 523343

TERMINATOR X AND THE GODFATHERS OF THREATT

A Side Final Promo (2)
Ain't Gut Nuttin' (1)
Back To The Scene Of The Bass (1)
Blues, The (1)
Buck Whylin' (1)
Can't Take My Style (1)

DJ Is The Selector (1)
Don't Even Go There (1)
Funky Piano (1)
G'Damn Datt DJ Made My Day (2)
Godfather Promo (2)
Herc Yardman Word (2)

Herc's Message (2)
High Priest Of Turbulence (1)
Homey Don't Play Dat (1)
It All Comes Down To The Money (2)
Juvenile Delinquintz (2)
Punks From The Terror (2)

Krunchtime (2)
Learn That Poem (2)
Make Room For Thunder (2)
Mashitup (2)
Money Promo (2)
1994 Street Muthafuckas Gong Show (2)

No Further (1)
Put Cha Thang Down (2)
Run That Go-Power Thang (1)
Say My Brother (2)
Scary-Us (2)
Sticka (2)
Stylewild '94 (2)

Terminator's Back (2)
Thumpin's Goin On (2)
Under The Sun (2)
Vendetta...The Big Getback (1)
Wanna Be Dancin' (1)

TERRELL, Tammi — see GAYE, Marvin

TERROR SQUAD '99

All-star rap group: **Fat Joe**, **Big Punisher**, Cuban Link, Armageddon, Triple Seis and Prospect.

10/9/99	**22**	8	© **Terror Squad: The Album**	$10	Big Beat 83232

All Around The World
As The World Turns
Bring It On

Feelin' This
Gimme Dat
In For Life

My Kinda Girls
'99 Live
Pass The Glock

Payin' Dues
Rudeboy Salute
Tell Me What U Want

Triple Threat
www.ThatsMySh-t.com
War

Whatcha Gon Do?

TERRY, Sonny, & Brownie McGhee '73

Blues harmonica player Terry was born Saunders Terrell on 10/24/11 in Greensboro, Georgia. Blinded as a youth. Died on 3/11/86 (age 74). Blues guitarist McGhee was born Walter Brown McGhee on 11/30/15 in Knoxville, Tennessee. Died of cancer on 2/16/96 (age 80).

4/7/73	**185**	5	© **Sonny & Brownie**	$15	A&M 4379

Battle Is Over (But The War Goes On)
Big Wind (Is A' Comin')

Bring It On Home To Me
God And Man
Jesus Gonna Make It Alright

On The Road Again
People Get Ready
Sail Away

Sonny's Thing
Walkin' My Blues Away
White Boy Lost In The Blues

You Bring Out The Boogie In Me

TERRY, Tony '88

Born on 3/12/64 in Pinehurst, North Carolina; raised in Washington DC. R&B singer.

| 1/9/88 | 151 | 20 | | © | 1 Forever Yours.. | | | $10 | Epic 40890 |
| 6/22/91 | 184 | 6 | | © | 2 **Tony Terry**.. | | | $10 | Epic 45015 |

Baby Love (2)
Bad Girl (2)
Come Home With Me (2)
Day Dreaming (1)

Everlasting Love (2) *81*
Forever Yours (1) *80*
Friends And Lovers (2)
Fulltime Girl (1)

Head Over Heels (2)
Here With Me (1)
Let Me Love You (2)
Lovey Dovey (1)

Read My Mind (2)
She's Fly (1) *80*
That Kind Of Guy (2)
Tongue Tied (2)

Up & Down Love (1)
Wassup Wit U (1)
What Would It Take (1)
With You (2) *14*

Young Love (1)

TESH, John '98

Born on 7/9/52 in Garden City, New York. New Age multi-instrumentalist. Co-host of TV's *Entertainment Tonight* from 1986-96. Appeared in the movie *Shocker*. Married actress Connie Sellecca on 4/4/92.

12/12/92+	50	5	●	©	1 **A Romantic Christmas**....................................C:#2¹/18 [X-I]			$10	GTS 4569
					Christmas charts: 9/'92, 9/'93, 35/'94, 3/'95				
6/19/93	181	3		©	2 **Monterey Nights**...[I]			$10	GTS 4570
12/10/94	103	5		©	3 **A Family Christmas**....................................C:#3/5 [X-I]			$10	GTS 4575
					Christmas charts: 26/'94, 4/'95				
3/18/95	160	4		©	4 **Sax On The Beach**...[I]			$10	GTS 4578
					THE JOHN TESH PROJECT				
3/25/95	54	33	●	©	5 **Live At Red Rocks**...[I-L]			$10	GTS 4579
					with the Colorado Symphony Orchestra				
3/30/96	114	2		©	6 **Discovery**..[I]			$10	GTSP 532125
					THE JOHN TESH PROJECT				
3/22/97	55	18		©	7 **Avalon**...[I]			$10	GTSP 537112
2/14/98	45	18		©	8 **Grand Passion**..[I]			$10	GTSP 539804
2/27/99	121	7		©	9 **One World**...[I]			$10	GTSP 559673

Against All Odds (5)
April Song (2,5,8)
Avalon (7)
Avalon Shores (7)
Barcelona (5)
Bastille Day (2,5,8)
Biggest Part Of Me (4)
Bring A Torch, Jeannette, Isabella (1)
Can You Feel The Love Tonight (4)
Canta Domine (5)
Carol Of The Bells (3)
Christmas Song (Chestnuts Roasting On An Open Fire) (1)
Concetta (2,5)
Coventry Carol (1)
Day One (5)
Dear Unknown (8)

Destiny (7)
Discovery (6)
Don't Let Me Be Lonely Tonight (6)
Eleanor Rigby (6)
Ellas Danzan Solas (They Dance Alone) (3)
Emerald Bay (9)
Endless Road (2)
Fields Of Gold (5)
First Noel (1)
Flamenco Legato (9)
Forever More (I'll Be The One) (9)
Fragile (6)
Games, The (2)
Garden City (2,5)
Gesu Bambino (3)
Give Me Forever (I Do) (8)
Gloria In Excelsis Deo (1)
Gloriette (9)

God Rest Ye Merry, Gentlemen (3)
Good Christian Men Rejoice (3)
Good King Wenceslas (3)
Goodnight Marie (8)
Goodnight Moon (5)
Grand Passion (8)
Group Five (5)
Halcyon Days (7,8)
Hark! The Herald Angels Sing (3)
Have Yourself A Merry Little Christmas (3)
Heart Of The Sunrise (9)
Homecoming, The (1,8)
I Keep Forgettin' (Every Time You're Near) (4)
I'll Be Over You (4)
In A Child's Eyes (1,2,5,8)
In Your Eyes (4)
Inn On Mt. Ada (7)

It Came Upon A Midnight Clear (1)
Jesu, Joy Of Man's Desiring (1)
Joy To The World (3)
Key Of Love (2,5)
Kyrie (6)
L'Aquila (7)
Lady In Red (6)
Little Drummer Boy (3)
Love Will Follow (6)
Lullabye (Goodnight My Angel) (6)
Message In A Bottle (4)
Monterey Nights (2)
Mother I Miss You (8)
O Come, All Ye Faithful (1)
O Holy Night (1)
O Little Town Of Bethlehem (1)
O Tannenbaum (3)
On American Shores (5)
One Final Wish (3)

One World (9)
Our Love (6)
PS491 (5)
Panis Angelicus (1)
Piano In G Major (9)
Piano In The Dark (4)
Polar Express (7)
Promise Of Love (8)
Rhapsody In Love (2)
Road Rage For Animals (5)
San Panfilo (7)
September (4)
Seven Fourty Seven (7)
Shock (5)
Shower The People (4)
Siberian Allegretto (9)
Silent Night, Holy Night (1)
Sonata Di Roma (9)
Song For Prima (3,8)
Spanish Steps (7)
St. Agnes' Treasure (9)

Synchronicity II (4)
This Is It (4)
Thousand Summers (5)
Valley Of Dreams (9)
Venezia (7)
View From Here (7,8)
Walking In Memphis (6)
Waltz, The (2)
Way It Is (4)
We Three Kings Of Orient Are (1)
We Wish You A Merry Christmas (3)
What Child Is This? (3)
White Christmas (3)
Who Am I? (9)
Wishing For Home (2)
You Break It (6)

TESLA '91

Hard-rock group formed in Sacramento, California: Jeff Keith (vocals), Frank Hannon and Tommy Skeoch (guitars), Brian Wheat (bass) and Troy Luccketta (drums). Band named after the inventor of the alternating current generator, Nikola Tesla.

1/31/87	32	61	▲	©	1 **Mechanical Resonance**..			$10	Geffen 24120
2/18/89	18	67	▲²	©	2 **The Great Radio Controversy**			$10	Geffen 24224
12/1/90+	12	48	▲	©	3 **Five Man Acoustical Jam**...................................[L]			$10	Geffen 24311
					recorded on 7/2/90 at the Trocadero in Philadelphia				
9/28/91	13	56	▲	©	4 **Psychotic Supper**...			$10	Geffen 24424
9/10/94	20	10	●	©	5 **Bust A Nut**..			$10	Geffen 24713
1/20/96	197	1		©	6 **Time's Makin' Changes: The Best Of Tesla**...............[G]			$10	Geffen 24833

Action Talks (5)
Alot To Lose (5,6)
Be A Man (2)
Before My Eyes (1,3)
Call It What You Want (4)
Can't Stop (4)
Change In The Weather (4)
Changes (1,6)
Cover Queen (1)
Cry (5)
Cumin' Atcha Live (1,3)

Did It For The Money (2)
Don't De-Rock Me (4)
Down Fo' Boogie (3)
Earthmover (5)
Edison's Medicine (4,6)
Ez Come Ez Go (3)
Flight To Nowhere (2)
Freedom Slaves (4)
Games People Play (5)
Gate/Invited (5)
Gettin' Better (1,3,6)

Government Personnel (4)
Had Enough (4)
Hang Tough (2)
Heaven's Trail (No Way Out) (2,3,6)
Lady Luck (2)
Lazy Days, Crazy Nights (2)
Little Suzi (1,6) *91*
Lodi (3)
Love Me (1)
Love Song (2,3,6) *10*

Makin' Magic (2)
Mama's Fool (5,6)
Modern Day Cowboy (1,3,6)
Mother's Little Helper (3)
Need Your Lovin' (5)
Paradise (2,3,6)
Party's Over (2)
Rock Me To The Top (1)
Rubberband (5)
She Want She Want (5)
Shine Away (5)

Signs (3,6) *8*
Solution (5)
Song & Emotion (4,6)
Steppin' Over (6)
Stir It Up (4)
Time (4)
Toke About It (4)
Tommy's Down Home (3)
2 Late 4 Love (1)
Truckin' (medley) (3)
Try So Hard (5)

Way It Is (2,3,6) *55*
We Can Work It Out (3)
We're No Good Together (1)
What You Give (4,6) *86*
Wonderful World (5)
Yesterdaze Gone (2)

TESTAMENT '92

Hard-rock group formed in San Francisco: Chuck Billy (vocals), Eric Peterson and Alex Skolnick (guitars), Greg Christian (bass) and Louie Clemente (drums). Skolnick and Clemente left in 1992, replaced by Glen Abelais (guitar) and John Tempesta (drums). Abelais and Tempesta left in 1994, replaced by James Murphy (guitar) and John Dette (drums).

6/25/88	136	14		©	1 **The New Order**..			$10	Megaforce 81849
9/2/89	77	12		©	2 **Practice What You Preach**.......................................			$10	Megaforce 82009
10/27/90	73	8		©	3 **Souls Of Black**..			$10	Megaforce 82143
5/30/92	55	9		©	4 **The Ritual**..			$10	Atlantic 82392
10/22/94	122	2		©	5 **Low**...			$10	Atlantic 82645

Absence Of Light (3)
Agony (4)
All I Could Bleed (5)
As The Seasons Grey (4)
Ballad, The (2)
Beginning Of The End (3)
Blessed In Contempt (2)
Chasing Fear (4)
Confusion Fusion (2)

Day Of Reckoning (1)
Deadline (4)
Disciples Of The Watch (1)
Dog Faced Gods (5)
Eerie Inhabitants (1)
Electric Crown (4)
Envy Life (5)
Face In The Sky (3)
Falling Fast (3)

Greenhouse Effect (2)
Hail Mary (5)
Hypnosis (4)
Into The Pit (1)
Last Call (5)
Legacy, The (1)
Legions (In Hiding) (5)
Let Go Of My World (4)
Love To Hate (3)

Low (5)
Malpractice (3)
Musical Death (A Dirge) (1)
New Order (1)
Nightmare (Coming Back To You) (2)
Nobody's Fault (1)
One Man's Fate (1)
P.C. (5)

Perilous Nation (2)
Practice What You Preach (2)
Preacher, The (1)
Return To Serenity (4)
Ride (5)
Ritual, The (4)
Sermon, The (4)
Seven Days Of May (3)
Shades Of War (5)

Signs Of Chaos (4)
Sins Of Omission (3)
So Many Lies (4)
Souls Of Black (3)
Time Is Coming (2)
Trail Of Tears (5)
Trial By Fire (1)
Troubled Dreams (4)
Urotsukidoji (5)

TEX, Joe '72
Born Joseph Arrington Jr. on 8/8/33 in Rogers, Texas. Died of a heart attack on 8/13/82 (age 49). R&B singer.

DEBUT	PEAK	WKS	CD	#	Title	Sym	$	Label & Number
2/6/65	124	7	©	1	Hold What You've Got		$50	Atlantic 8106
11/27/65	142	7	©	2	The New Boss		$50	Atlantic 8115
5/7/66	108	8	©	3	The Love You Save		$50	Atlantic 8124
9/2/67	168	4		4	The Best Of Joe Tex	[G]	$25	Atlantic 8144
2/24/68	84	17		5	Live And Lively	[L]	$25	Atlantic 8156
7/27/68	154	7		6	Soul Country		$25	Atlantic 8187
7/19/69	190	5		7	Buying A Book		$25	Atlantic 8231
4/22/72	17	21		8	I Gotcha		$20	Dial 6002
5/7/77	108	9		9	Bumps & Bruises		$15	Epic 34666

Ain't Gonna Bump No More (With No Big Fat Woman) (9) 12
Any Little Bit (2)
Anything You Wanna Know (7)
Are We Ready (1)
Baby Let Me Steal You (8)
Bad Feet (8)
Be Cool (Willie Is Dancing With A Sissy) (9)
Build Your Love (On A Solid Foundation) (3)
By The Time I Get To Phoenix (6)
C.C. Rider (2)
Close The Door (3)
Dark End Of The Street (6)
Detroit City (2)
Do Right Woman - Do Right Man (5)

Don't Give Up (5)
Don't Let Your Left Hand Know (3) 95
Don't Make Your Children Pay (2)
Engine Engine Number Nine (3)
For My Woman (8)
For Your Love (2)
Fresh Out Of Tears (1)
Funny Bone (3)
Funny How Time Slips Away (6)
Get Out Of My Life, Woman (5)
Get Your Lies Together (7)
Give The Baby Anything The Baby Wants (8)
God Of Love (8)
Grandma Mary (7)
Green Green Grass Of Home (6)
Heartbreak Hotel (3)
Heep See Few Know (1)

Hold What You've Got (1,2,4) 5
Honey (6)
Hungry For Your Love (9)
I Almost Got To Heaven Once (9)
I Believe I'm Gonna Make It (4) 67
I Don't Trust Myself Around You (3)
I Gotcha (8) 2
I Mess Up Everything I Get My Hands On (9)
I Want To (Do Everything For You) (2,4) 23
I'll Never Do You Wrong (6) 59
I'm A Man (3)
I'm Not Going To Work Today (1)
I've Got To Do A Little Bit Better (4) 64

If Sugar Was As Sweet As You
It Ain't Gonna Work Baby (8)
It Ain't Sanitary (7)
Jump Bad (9)
King Of The Road (2)
Leaving You Dinner (9)
Live For Yourself (3)
Love Is A Hurtin' Thing (5)
Love Me Right Girl (9)
Love You Save (May Be Your Own) (3,4) 56
Ode To Billie Joe (6)
One Monkey Don't Stop No Show (1) 65
Only Way (7)
Papa Was Too (4,5) 44
S.Y.S.L.J.F.M. (The Letter Song) (4) 39
Same Things You Did To Get Me (7)

Set Me Free (6)
Show Me (4,5) 35
Skinny Legs And All (5) 10
Skip A Rope (6)
Stop Look And Listen (2)
Sure Is Good (7)
Sweet Woman Like You (3,4) 29
Takin' A Chance (8)
Tell Me Right Now (1)
That's Life (5)
That's The Way (7) 94
There Is A Girl (1)
There's Something Wrong (9)
Together We Stand (1)
We Can't Sit Down Now (7)
We Held On (9)
What In The World (2)
Woman Can Change A Man (2,4) 56
Woman Cares (8)

Woman's Hands (5) 63
Wooden Spoon (5)
You Better Get It (1,4) 46
You Can Stay (1)
You Got What It Takes (1,2,4,5) 51
You Said A Bad Word (8) 41
You're Gonna Thank Me, Woman (3)
You're In Too Deep (8)

TEXAS '89
Pop-rock group from Glasgow, Scotland: Sharleen Spiteri (vocals, guitar), Ally McErlaine (guitar), John McElhone (bass) and Stuart Kerr (drums). McElhone was a member of **Hipsway**. Kerr was an early member of **Love And Money**.

| 8/19/89 | 88 | 16 | © | Southside | $10 | Mercury 838171 |

Everyday Now
Fight The Feeling

Fool For Love
Future Is Promise

I Don't Want A Lover 77
One Choice

Prayer For You
Southside

Tell Me Why
Thrill Has Gone

TEXAS TORNADOS '90
All-star group: **Freddy Fender, Doug Sahm**, Augie Myers and Flaco Jimenez. Sahm and Meyers were members of the **Sir Douglas Quintet**. Sahm died of heart failure on 11/18/99 (age 58).

| 9/8/90 | 154 | 10 | © | Texas Tornados | $10 | Reprise 26251 |

Adios Mexico
Baby! Heaven Sent Me You
Dinero

(Hey Baby) Que Paso
If That's What You're Thinking
Laredo Rose

Man Can Cry
She Never Spoke Spanish To Me

Soy De San Luis
Who Were You Thinkin' Of

TEXTONES '85
Rock group: Carla Olson (vocals, guitar), George Callins (guitar), Tom Morgan (keyboards), Joe Read (bass) and **Phil Seymour** (drums). Seymour died of cancer on 8/17/93 (age 41).

| 11/24/84+ | 176 | 8 | | Midnight Mission | $10 | Gold Mountain 86010 |

Clean Cut Kid
Hands Of The Working Man

Luck Don't Last Forever
Midnight Mission

No Love In You
Number One Is To Survive

Running
See The Light

Standing In The Line
Upset Me

THE, The '87
Rock group formed in London by songwriter Matt Johnson. Changing lineup features contributing musicians headed and produced by Johnson. Guitarist Johnny Marr, earlier with **The Smiths**, is also a member of **Electronic** (since 1990) and Electrafixion (since 1995).

2/14/87	89	18	©	1	Infected		$10	Epic 40471
6/27/87	38 C	4	©	2	Soul Mining	[E]	$10	Epic 39266
					released in 1985			
7/22/89	138	12	©	3	Mind Bomb		$10	Epic 45241
2/13/93	142	4	©	4	Dusk		$10	Epic 53164

Angels Of Deception (1)
Armageddon Days Are Here (Again) (3)
August & September (3)
Beat(en) Generation (3)
Beyond Love (3)

Bluer Than Midnight (4)
Dogs Of Lust (4)
Giant (2)
Good Morning Beautiful (3)
Gravitate To Me (3)
Heartland (1)
Helpline Operator (4)

I've Been Waitin' For Tomorrow (All Of My Life) (2)
Infected (1)
Kingdom Of Rain (3)
Lonely Planet (4)
Love Is Stronger Than Death (4)

Lung Shadows (4)
Mercy Beat (1)
Out Of The Blue (Into The Fire) (1)
Perfect (2)
Sinking Feeling (2)
Slow Emotion Replay (4)

Slow Train To Dawn (1)
Sodium Light Baby (4)
Soul Mining (2)
Sweet Bird Of Truth (1)
This Is The Day (2)
This Is The Night (4)

True Happiness This Way Lies (4)
Twilight Hour (2)
Twilight Of A Champion (1)
Uncertain Smile (2)
Violence Of Truth (3)

THEE PROPHETS '69
Pop-rock group from Milwaukee: Brian Lake (vocals), Jim Anderson (guitar), Dave Leslie (bass) and Chris Michaels (drums).

| 6/28/69 | 163 | 3 | | Playgirl | $25 | Kapp 3596 |

Broken Heart
Double Life

Heartbreak Avenue
I Pretend I'm With You

It Isn't So Easy
Kind Of A Drag

Magic Island
Man Enough

Playgirl 49
Shame Shame

Some Kind-A Wonderful
They Call Her Sorrow

THEM '65
Rock group from Belfast, Northern Ireland: **Van Morrison**, brothers Jackie (piano) and Pat (drums) McAuley, Billy Harrison (guitar), Alan Henderson (bass) and **Pete Bardens** (keyboards).

7/24/65	54	23	©	1	Them		$50	Parrot 71005
4/16/66	138	6	©	2	Them Again		$50	Parrot 71008
7/22/72	154	11	©	3	Them Featuring Van Morrison	[R]	$25	Parrot 71053 [2]
					reissue (condensed) of the first 2 albums above			

Bad Or Good (2,3)
Bring 'Em On In (2,3)
Call My Name (2)
Could You Would You (2,3)
Don't Look Back (1,3)

Don't You Know (2)
Gloria (1,3) 71
Go On Home Baby (1)
Here Comes The Night (1,3) 24

How Long Baby (2,3)
I Can Only Give You Everything (2,3)
I Like It Like That (3)
I'm Gonna Dress In Black (1)

If You And I Could Be As True
It's All Over Now Baby Blue (2,3)
Little Girl (1,3)

My Lonely Sad Eyes (2,3)
Mystic Eyes (1,3) 33
One More Time (1,3)
One Two Brown Eyes (2,3)
Out Of Sight (2,3)

Route 66 (1,3)
Something You Got (2,3)
Turn On Your Lovelight (2,3)

DEBUT	PEAK	WKS	RIAA	CD	ARTIST — Album Title	Catalog	Sym	$	Label & Number

THEODORE, Mike, Orchestra '77
Disco studio group assembled by producer Mike Theodore.

| 10/1/77 | 178 | 2 | | © | Cosmic Wind | | | $12 | Westbound 305 |

Ain't Nothing To It
Belly Boogie
Brazilian Lullaby
Bull, The
Cosmic Wind
I Love The Way You Move
Moon Trek

THEO VANESS — see VANESS, Theo

THEY EAT THEIR OWN '91
Pop-rock group formed in Los Angeles: Laura B. (vocals), Kevin Dixon and Shark Darkwater (guitars), J.D. Dotson (bass) and Juno Brown (drums).

| 3/23/91 | 184 | 5 | | © | They Eat Their Own | | | $10 | Relativity 1042 |

Better Now
Cancer Food
Enemy, The
Like A Drug
Locked Up
Money Knocks
No Right To Kill
Too Many Guns
Video Martyr
Why Don't You Disagree?

THEY MIGHT BE GIANTS '94
Novelty-rock duo from Boston: John Flansburgh (guitar) and John Linnell (accordian). Group named after a George C. Scott movie.

12/24/88+	89	19		© 1	Lincoln			$10	Bar/None 72600
2/10/90	75	22	●	© 2	Flood			$10	Elektra 60907
4/11/92	99	6		© 3	Apollo 18			$10	Elektra 61257
10/1/94	61	4		© 4	John Henry			$10	Elektra 61654
10/26/96	89	2		© 5	Factory Showroom			$10	Elektra 61862
8/29/98	186	1		© 6	Severe Tire Damage		[L]	$10	Restless 72965

AKA Driver (4)
About Me (6)
Ana Ng (1,6)
Bells Are Ringing (5)
Birdhouse In Your Soul (2,6)
Cage & Aquarium (1)
Cowtown (1)
Dead (2)
Destination Moon (4)
Dig My Grave (3)
Dinner Bell (3)
Dirt Bike (4)
Doctor Worm (6)
End Of The Tour (4)
Exquisite Dead Guy (5)
Extra Savoir-Faire (4)
Fingertips (3)
First Kiss (6)
Flood, Theme From (2)
Guitar, The (3)
Hall Of Heads (3)
Hearing Aid (2)
Hot Cha (2)
How Can I Sing Like A Girl? (5)
Hypnotist Of Ladies (3)
I Can Hear You (5)
I Palindrome I (3)
I Should Be Allowed To Think (4)
I've Got A Match (1)
If I Wasn't Shy (3)
Istanbul (Not Constantinople) (2,6)
James K. Polk (5)
Kiss Me, Son Of God (1)
Letterbox (2)
Lie Still, Little Bottle (1)
Lucky Ball & Chain (2)
Mammal (3)
Meet James Ensor (4,6)
Metal Detector (5)
Minimum Wage (2)
Mr. Me (1)
My Evil Twin (3)
Narrow Your Eyes (3)
New York City (5)
No One Knows My Plan (4)
O, Do Not Forsake Me (4)
Out Of Jail (4)
Particle Man (2,6)
Pencil Rain (1)
Pet Name (5)
Piece Of Dirt (1)
Purple Toupee (1)
Road Movie To Berlin (2)
Santa's Beard (1)
Sapphire Bullets Of Pure Love (2)
See The Constellation (3)
Self Called Nowhere (4)
Severe Tire Damage Theme (6)
S-E-X-X-Y (5,6)
She's Actual Size (3,6)
She's An Angel (6)
Shoehorn With Teeth (3)
Sleeping In The Flowers (4)
Snail Shell (4)
Snowball In Hell (1)
Someone Keeps Moving My Chair (1)
Space Suit (3)
Spider (3,6)
Spiraling Shape (5)
Spy (5)
Stand On Your Own Head (1)
Statue Got Me High (3)
Stomp Box (4)
Subliminal (4)
Thermostat (4)
They Got Lost (6)
They Might Be Giants (2)
They'll Need A Crane (1)
Till My Head Falls Off (5,6)
Turn Around (3)
Twisting (2)
Unrelated Thing (4)
We Want A Rock (2)
Where Your Eyes Don't Go (1)
Which Describes How You're Feeling (3)
Whistling In The Dark (2)
Why Does The Sun Shine? (The Sun Is A Mass Of Incandescent Gas) (6)
Why Must I Be Sad? (4)
Window (4)
Women & Men (4)
World's Address (1)
XTC Vs. Adam Ant (5,6)
You'll Miss Me (4)
Your Own Worst Enemy (5)
Your Racist Friend (2)

THIN LIZZY '76
Rock group from Dublin, Ireland: Phil Lynott (vocals, bass), Brian Robertson and Scott Gorham (guitars) and Brian Downey (drums). Numerous personnel changes. **Gary Moore** was a member from 1978-79. Lynott died on 1/4/86 (age 34).

4/17/76	18	28	●	© 1	Jailbreak			$15	Mercury 1081
11/13/76	52	11		© 2	Johnny The Fox			$15	Mercury 1119
9/24/77	39	11		© 3	Bad Reputation			$15	Mercury 1186
7/22/78	84	12		© 4	Live And Dangerous		[L]	$15	Warner 3213 [2]
6/2/79	81	12		© 5	Black Rose/A Rock Legend			$12	Warner 3338
11/29/80	120	10		© 6	Chinatown			$12	Warner 3496
2/20/82	157	11		© 7	Renegade			$12	Warner 3622
5/28/83	159	5		© 8	Thunder And Lightning			$12	Warner 23831
1/28/84	185	3		© 9	'Life'-Live		[L]	$15	Warner 23986 [2]

Angel From The Coast (1)
Angel Of Death (7,9)
Are You Ready (4,9)
Baby Drives Me Crazy (4)
Baby Please Don't Go (8,9)
Bad Habits (8)
Bad Reputation (3)
Black Rose (9)
Boogie Woogie Dance (2)
Borderline (2)
Boys Are Back In Town (1,4,9) *12*
Chinatown (6)
Cold Sweat (8,9)
Cowboy Song (1,4) *77*
Cowgirls' Song (medley) (4)
Dancing In The Moonlight (It's Caught Me In Its Spotlight) (3,4)
Dear Lord (3)
Didn't I (6)
Do Anything You Want To (5)
Don't Believe A Word (2,4,9)
Downtown Sundown (3)
Emerald (1,4,9)
Fats (7)
Fight Or Fall (1)
Fool's Gold (2)
Genocide (The Killing Of The Buffalo) (6)
Get Out Of Here (5)
Got To Give It Up (5,9)
Having A Good Time (4)
Heart Attack (8)
Hey You (6)
Hollywood (Down On Your Luck) (7,9)
Holy War (8,9)
It's Getting Dangerous (7)
Jailbreak (1,4,9)
Johnny (2)
Johnny The Fox Meets Jimmy The Weed (2,4)
Killer On The Loose (6,9)
Killer Without A Cause (9)
Leave This Town (7)
Massacre (2,4)
Mexican Blood (7)
My Sarah (7)
No One Told Him (7)
Old Flame (2)
Opium Trail (3)
Pressure Will Blow (7)
Renegade (7,9)
Rocker, The (4,9)
Rocky (8)
Roisin Dubh (Black Rose) A Rock Legend (5)
Romeo And The Lonely Girl (1)
Rosalie (medley) (4)
Running Back (4)
S & M (5)
Sha-La-La (4)
Soldier Of Fortune (3)
Someday She Is Going To Hit Back (8)
Southbound (3)
Still In Love With You (4,9)
Sugar Blues (6)
Suicide (4)
Sun Goes Down (8,9)
Sweet Marie (2)
Sweetheart (6)
That Woman's Gonna Break Your Heart (5)
This Is The One (8)
Thunder And Lightning (8,9)
Toughest Street In Town (5)
Waiting For An Alibi (5,9)
Warriors (1,4)
We Will Be Strong (6)
With Love (5)

3RD BASS '91
White rap duo from Queens, New York: Pete Nash and Michael Berrin. Supported by black DJ Richard Lawson. Also see **MC Serch** and **Prime Minister Pete Nice & Daddy Rich**.

| 12/2/89+ | 55 | 30 | ● | © 1 | The Cactus Album | | | $10 | Def Jam 45415 |
| 7/6/91 | 19 | 22 | ● | © 2 | Derelicts Of Dialect | | | $10 | Def Jam 47369 |

Ace In The Hole (2)
Al'za-B-Cee'z (2)
Brooklyn-Queens (1)
Cactus, The (1)
Come In (2)
Daddy Rich In The Land Of 1210 (2)
Derelicts Of Dialect (2)
Desert Boots (1)
Episode #3 (1)
Eye Jammie (2)
Flippin' Off The Wall Like Lucy Ball (1)
French Toast (2)
Gas Face (1)
Green Eggs And Swine (2)
Herbalz In Your Mouth (2)
Hoods (1)
Jim Backus (1)
Kick Em In The Grill (2)
M.C. Disagree (1)
M.C. Disagree And The Re-animator (2)
Merchant Of Grooves (2)
Microphone Techniques (2)
Monte Hall (1)
No Master Plan No Master Race (2)
No Static At All (2)
Oval Office (1)
Pop Goes The Weasel (2) *29*
Portrait Of The Artist As A Hood (2)
Problem Child (2)
Product Of The Environment (1)
Russell Rush (1)
Sea Vessel Soliloquy (2)
Sons Of 3rd Bass (1)
Soul In The Hole (1)
Steppin' To The A.M. (1)
Stymie's Theme (1)
3 Strikes 5000 (2)
Triple Stage Darkness (1)
Who's On Third (1)
Word To The Third (1)
Wordz Of Wizdom (1)

THIRD DAY '97
Christian rock group from Marietta, Georgia: Mac Powell (vocals), Mark Lee and Brad Avery (guitars), Tai Anderson (bass) and David Carr (drums).

9/13/97	50	7		© 1	Conspiracy No. 5			$10	Reunion 10006
9/11/99	63	9		© 2	Time			$10	Essential 0528
7/29/00	66	34	●	© 3	Offerings: A Worship Album			$10	Essential 10670

THIRD DAY — Cont'd

Agnus Dei (medley) (3)
Alien (1)
All The Heavens (3)
Believe (2)
Can't Take The Pain (2)
Consuming Fire (3)

Don't Say Goodbye (2)
Give (2)
Give Me A Reason (1)
Gomer's Theme (1)
Have Mercy (1)
How's Your Head (1)

I Deserve? (1)
I've Always Loved You (2)
King Of Glory (3)
Love Song (3)
More To This (1)
My Hope Is You (1,3)

Never Bow Down (2)
Peace (1)
Saved (3)
Sky Falls Down (2)
These Thousand Hills (3)
Thief (3)

This Song Was Meant For You (1)
Took My Place (2)
What Good (2)
Who I Am (1)
Worthy (medley) (3)

You Make Me Mad (1)
You're Everywhere (3)
Your Love Endures (1)
Your Love Oh Lord (Psalm 36) (2,3)

THIRD EYE BLIND '98

Rock group from San Francisco: Stephan Jenkins (vocals), Kevin Cadogan (guitar), Arion Salazar (bass) and Brad Hargreaves (drums).

DEBUT	PEAK	WKS	RIAA	CD	#	Album	Catalog	$	Label & Number
4/26/97+	25	104	▲6	©	1	Third Eye Blind	C:#4/18	$10	Elektra 62012
12/11/99	40	53	▲	©	2	Blue		$10	Elektra 62415

Anything (2)
Background, The (1)
Burning Man (1)
Camouflage (2)
Darkness (2)

Darwin (2)
Deep Inside Of You (2) 69
Farther (2)
God Of Wine (1)
Good For You (1)

Graduate (1)
How's It Going To Be (1) 9
I Want You (1)
Jumper (1) 5
London (1)

Losing A Whole Year (1)
Motorcycle Drive By (1)
Narcolepsy (1)
Never Let You Go (2) 14
Ode To Maybe (2)

Red Summer Sun (2)
Semi-Charmed Life (1) 4
Slow Motion (2)
10 Days Late (2)
Thanks A Lot (1)

1000 Julys (2)
Wounded (2)

THIRD POWER '70

Rock trio from Detroit: Drew Abbott (guitar), Jem Targal (vocals, bass) and Jim Craig (drums). Abbott later joined Bob Seger's Silver Bullet Band.

DEBUT	PEAK	WKS				Album		$	Label & Number
7/4/70	194	2				Believe......................		$30	Vanguard 6554

Comin' Home
Crystalline Chandelier

Feel So Lonely
Gettin' Together

Like Me Love Me
Lost In A Daydream

Passed By
Persecution

Won't Beg Any More

THIRD WORLD '79

Reggae group from Jamaica: William Clarke (vocals), Stephen Coore (guitar), Michael Cooper (keyboards), Irvin Jarrett (percussion), Richard Daley (bass) and Willie Stewart (drums). Jarrett left by 1989.

DEBUT	PEAK	WKS		CD	#	Album		$	Label & Number
11/25/78+	55	24		©	1	Journey To Addis		$12	Island 9554
7/21/79	157	5		©	2	The Story's Been Told		$12	Island 9569
8/30/80	186	2		©	3	Third World, Prisoner in The Street .... [L-S]		$12	Island 9616
7/25/81	186	3		©	4	Rock The World		$10	Columbia 37402
3/20/82	63	27		©	5	You've Got The Power		$10	Columbia 37744
						produced by Stevie Wonder			
10/1/83	137	7		©	6	All The Way Strong		$10	Columbia 38687
4/13/85	119	11		©	7	Sense Of Purpose		$10	Columbia 39877
7/15/89	107	14		©	8	Serious Business		$10	Mercury 836952

African Woman (1,3)
All The Way Strong (6)
Always Around (2)
Before You Make Your Move (Melt With Everyone) (7)
Can't Get You (Outta My Mind) (7)
Children Of The World (1)
Cold Sweat (1,3)
Come On Home (6)
Come Together (2)
Cool Meditation (1)
D.J. Ambassador (8)

Dancing On The Floor (Hooked On Love) (4)
Dubb Music (4)
Forbidden Love (8)
Fret Not Thyself (1)
Girl From Hiroshima (7)
Having A Party (2)
How Can You (7)
Hug It Up (4)
I Wake Up Cryin' (4)
Inna Time Like This (5)
Irie Ites (2,3)
It's The Same Old Song (8)

Jah, Jah Children Moving Up (5)
Journey To Addis (1)
Keep Your Head To The Sky (8)
Lagos Jump (6)
Love Is Out To Get You (6)
Love Will Always Be There (4)
Low Key-Jammin' (5)
Never Say Never (8)
96 In The Shade (3)
Now That We Found Love (1,3) 47

Once There's Love (6)
One Cold Vibe (Couldn't Stop Dis Ya Boogie) (1)
One More Time (7)
One Song (Nyahbinghi) (7)
One To One (7)
Peace And Love (4)
Prisoner In The Street (3)
Reggae Ambassador (7)
Reggae Jam Boogie (7)
Rejoice (1)
Ride On (5)
Rock And Rave (6)

Rock Me (7)
Rock The World (4)
Seasons When (6)
Sense Of Purpose (7)
Serious Business (8)
Shine Like A Blazing Fire (4)
Spiritual Revolution (4)
Standing In The Rain (4)
Story's Been Told (2)
Street Fighting (3)
Swing Low (6)
Take This Song (8)
Talk To Me (2)

There's No Need To Question Why (4)
Third World Man (3)
Tonight For Me (2)
Try Jah Love (5)
Underdog, Theme From The (8)
We The People (8)
Who Gave You (Jah Rastafari) (4)
World Of Uncertainty (7)
You're Playing Us Too Close (5)
You've Got The Power (To Make A Change) (5)

★441★ 38 SPECIAL '82

Rock group formed in Jacksonville, Florida: Donnie Van Zant (vocals), Don Barnes and Jeff Carlisi (guitars), Larry Junstrom (bass), and Steve Brookins and Jack Grondin (drums). By 1988, Barnes and Brookins replaced by Danny Chauncey (guitar) and Max Carl (keyboards). Barnes returned in 1992 to replace Carl. Van Zant is the brother of Lynyrd Skynyrd's Ronnie Van Zant.

DEBUT	PEAK	WKS	RIAA	CD	#	Album	Catalog	$	Label & Number
5/28/77	148	5		©	1	38 Special	C:#36/2	$12	A&M 4638
1/5/80	57	19		©	2	Rockin' Into The Night		$10	A&M 4782
2/21/81	18	57	▲	©	3	Wild-Eyed Southern Boys		$10	A&M 4835
5/29/82	10	42	▲	©	4	Special Forces		$10	A&M 4888
12/3/83+	22	39	▲	©	5	Tour De Force		$10	A&M 4971
5/17/86	17	31	●	©	6	Strength In Numbers		$10	A&M 5115
8/22/87	35	17	▲	©	7	Flashback .... [G]		$10	A&M 3910
10/22/88+	61	41		©	8	Rock & Roll Strategy		$10	A&M 5218
8/10/91	170	7		©	9	Bone Against Steel		$10	Charisma 91640

Against The Night (6)
Around And Around (1)
Back Alley Sally (3)
Back Door Stranger (4)
Back On The Track (4)
Back To Paradise (7) 41
Back Where You Belong (5,7) 20
Bone Against Steel (9)
Breakin' Loose (4)
Bring It On (3)
Burning Bridges (9)
Can't Shake It (9)
Caught Up In You (4,7) 10
Chain Lightnin' (4)

Chattahoochee (8)
Comin' Down Tonight (8) 67
Don't Wanna Get It Dirty (9)
Fantasy Girl (3,7) 52
Firestarter (4)
First Time Around (4)
Fly Away (1)
Four Wheels (1)
Gypsy Belle (1)
Has There Ever Been A Good Goodbye (6)
Heart's On Fire (6)
Hittin' And Runnin' (3)
Hold On Loosely (3,7) 27
Honky Tonk Dancer (8)

Hot 'Lanta (8)
I Oughta Let Go (5)
If I'd Been The One (5,7) 19
Innocent Eyes (8)
Jimmy Gillum (9)
Just A Little Love (6)
Just Hang On (1)
Just Wanna Rock & Roll (1)
Last Thing I Ever Do (9)
Last Time (6)
Like No Other Night (6,7) 14
Little Sheba (8)
Long Distance Affair (5)
Long Time Gone (1)
Love Strikes (8)

Love That I've Lost (2)
Midnight Magic (8)
Money Honey (2)
Never Be Lonely (8)
Never Give An Inch (8)
Once In A Lifetime (6)
One Of The Lonely Ones (5)
One Time For Old Times (5)
Play A Simple Song (1)
Rebel To Rebel (9)
Robin Hood (2)
Rock & Roll Strategy (8) 67
Rockin' Into The Night (2,7) 43

Rough-Housin' (4,7)
Same Old Feeling (7)
Second Chance (8) 6
See Me In Your Eyes (5)
Signs Of Love (9)
Somebody Like You (6) 48
Sound Of Your Voice (9) 33
Stone Cold Believer (2,7)
Take 'Em Out (4)
Take Me Through The Night (2)
Teacher Teacher (7) 25
Tear It Up (9)
Tell Everybody (1)
Throw Out The Line (3)
Treasure (9)

Turn It On (2)
Twentieth Century Fox (5,7)
Undercover Lover (5)
What's It To Ya? (7)
Wild-Eyed Southern Boys (3,7)
You Be The Dam, I'll Be The Water (9)
You Definitely Got Me (1)
You Got The Deal (2)
You Keep Runnin' Away (4) 38
You're The Captain (2)

THOMAS, B.J. '70

Born Billy Joe Thomas on 8/7/42 in Hugo, Oklahoma; raised in Rosenberg, Texas. Pop singer.
1)Raindrops Keep Fallin' On My Head 2)Reunion 3)Most Of All

DEBUT	PEAK	WKS	RIAA	CD	#	Album	$	Label & Number
1/18/69	133	12			1	On My Way	$15	Scepter 570
11/8/69+	90	28			2	Greatest Hits, Volume 1 .... [G]	$15	Scepter 578
1/3/70	12	41	●		3	Raindrops Keep Fallin' On My Head	$15	Scepter 580
5/2/70	72	20			4	Everybody's Out Of Town	$15	Scepter 582

THOMAS, B.J. — Cont'd

DEBUT	PEAK	WKS			Title		Sym	$	Label & Number
12/12/70+	67	24		5	Most Of All			$15	Scepter 586
11/20/71	92	13		6	Greatest Hits, Volume Two		[G]	$15	Scepter 597
5/20/72	145	9		7	Billy Joe Thomas			$15	Scepter 5101
3/29/75	59	14		8	Reunion			$12	ABC 858
8/27/77	114	12		9	B.J. Thomas			$12	MCA 2286
5/21/83	193	3	©	10	New Looks			$10	Cleveland Int'l. 38561

Amour (10)
Are We Losing Touch (7)
Beautiful Things For You (8)
Billy And Sue (2) *34*
Bridge Over Troubled Water (4)
Bring Back The Time (2) *75*
Brown Eyed Woman (5)
Circle 'Round The Sun (5)
City Boys (8)
Created For Man (4)
Crying (8)
Crying In The Chapel (2)
Do What You Gotta Do (3)
Doctor God (8)
Don't Worry Baby (9) *17*
Even A Fool Would Let Go (9)
Everybody's Out Of Town (4,6) *26*
Everybody's Talking (4)
Eyes Of A New York Woman (1,2) *28*
Fine Way To Go (7)

Four Walls (1)
Gone (1)
Greatest Love (3)
Happier Than The Morning Sun (7) *100*
Hello Love (5)
Here You Come Again (9)
(Hey Won't You Play) Another Somebody Done Somebody Wrong Song (8) *1*
Hooked On A Feeling (1,2) *5*
I Can't Help It (If I'm Still In Love With You) (2) *94*
I Don't Know Any Better (5)
I Finally Got It Right This Time (8)
I Get Enthused (7)
I Just Can't Help Believing (4,6) *9*

I Just Sing (10)
I Love Us (10)
I Need You So (2)
I Saw Pity In The Face Of A Friend (1)
I'm Saving All The Good Times For You (10)
I'm So Lonesome I Could Cry (2) *8*
I've Been Down This Road Before (1)
If You Ever Leave Me (3)
If You Must Leave My Life (3)
Impressions (9)
It's Only Love (6) *45*
It's Sad To Belong (9)
Just As Gone (7)
Life (6)
Light My Fire (1)
Little Green Apples (3)
Long Ago Tomorrow (6) *61*
Love Me Tender (2)

Mama (2) *22*
Mask, The (4)
Maybe It's Time To Go (8)
Memory Machine (10)
Mighty Clouds Of Joy (6) *34*
Most Of All (5,6) *38*
Mr. Businessman (1)
Mr. Mailman (3)
My Love (9)
New Looks From An Old Lover (10)
No Love At All (5,6) *16*
Oh Me Oh My (4)
Our Love Goes Marching On (9)
Plain Jane (2)
Plastic Words (9)
Play Me A Little Traveling Music (9)
Raindrops Keep Fallin' On My Head (3,6) *1*
Rainy Day Man (5)

Rainy Night In Georgia (5)
Real Life Blues (8)
Roads (7)
Rock And Roll Lullaby (7) *15*
Rock And Roll You're Beautiful (10)
Sandman (1,4)
Sea Of Love (8)
Send My Picture To Scranton, Pa. (4)
Since I Don't Have You (2)
Smoke Gets In Your Eyes (1)
Song For My Brother (7)
Still The Lovin' Is Fun (9) *77*
Stories We Can Tell (7)
Suspicious Minds (3)
Sweet Cherry Wine (7)
Table For Two For One (5)
That's What Friends Are For (7) *74*
(They Long To Be) Close To You (5)

This Guy's In Love With You (3)
We Had It All (9)
We Have Got To Get Our Ship Together (7)
What Does It Take (4)
Whatever Happened To Old Fashioned Love (10) *93*
Who Broke Your Heart And Made You Write That Song (8)
Wind Beneath My Wings (10)
You Keep The Man In Me Happy (And The Child In Me Alive) (10)

THOMAS, Carl
Born in Chicago. R&B singer.
'00

DEBUT	PEAK	WKS			Title		Sym	$	Label & Number
5/6/00	9	49	▲ ©		Emotional			$10	Bad Boy 73025

Cold, Cold World
Come To Me
Emotional *47*

Giving You All My Love
Hey Now
I Wish *20*

Lady Lay Your Body
My Valentine
Special Lady

Summer Rain *80*
Supastar
Woke Up In The Morning

You Ain't Right

THOMAS, Carla
Born on 12/21/42 in Memphis. R&B singer. Daughter of **Rufus Thomas**.
'67

DEBUT	PEAK	WKS			Title		Sym	$	Label & Number
3/5/66	134	10	©	1	Comfort Me			$40	Stax 706
10/15/66	130	5	©	2	Carla			$40	Stax 709
4/22/67	36	31	©	3	King & Queen			$50	Stax 716
					OTIS REDDING & CARLA THOMAS				
7/1/67	133	6	©	4	The Queen Alone			$40	Stax 718
7/5/69	151	5		5	Memphis Queen			$40	Stax 2019
7/19/69	190	4		6	The Best Of Carla Thomas		[G]	$25	Atlantic 8232

All I See Is You (4)
Another Night Without My Man (1)
Any Day Now (4)
Are You Lonely For Me Baby (3)
B-A-B-Y (2,6) *14*
Baby What You Want Me To Do (medley) (2)
Bring It On Home To Me (3,6)
Comfort Me (1,6)
Dime A Dozen (6)
Don't Say No More (5)
Fate (2)
For Your Love (medley) (2)

Forever (1)
Gee Whiz (Look At His Eyes) (6) *10*
Give Me Enough (To Keep Me Going) (4)
Guide Me Well (5)
He's Beating Your Time (5)
How Can You Throw My Love Away (5)
I Fall To Pieces (2)
I Got You, Boy (2)
I Like What You're Doing (To Me) (5) *49*
I Play For Keeps (5)
I Take It To My Baby (4)

I Want To Be Your Baby (4)
I'll Always Have Faith In You (4) *85*
I'm For You (1)
I'm So Lonesome I Could Cry (2)
I've Fallen In Love (With You) (5)
It Takes Two (3)
Knock On Wood (3) *30*
Let It Be Me (1)
Let Me Be Good To You (2,3,6) *62*
Lie To Keep Me From Crying (4)

Looking Back (2)
Lover's Concerto (1)
Lovey Dovey (3,6) *60*
More Man Than I Ever Had (5)
Move On Drifter (3)
New Year's Resolution (3)
No Time To Lose (1,6)
Oh! What A Fool I've Been (6)
Ooh Carla, Ooh Otis (3)
Pick Up The Pieces (6) *68*
Precious Memories (5)
Red Rooster (3)
Something Good (Is Going To Happen To You) (4) *74*

Stop! Look What You're Doing (6) *92*
Stop Thief (4,6)
Strung Out (5)
Tell It Like It Is (3)
Tramp (3,6) *26*
Unchanging Love (4)
Unyielding (5)
What Have You Got To Offer Me (2)
What The World Needs Now (1)
When Something Is Wrong With My Baby (3)
When Tomorrow Comes (4) *99*

Where Do I Go (5) *86*
Will You Love Me Tomorrow (1)
Woman's Love (1,6) *71*
Yes, I'm Ready (1)
You Don't Have To Say You Love Me (2)

THOMAS, Irma
Born Irma Lee on 2/18/41 in Ponchatoula, Louisiana. R&B singer. Nicknamed "The Soul Queen of New Orleans."
'64

DEBUT	PEAK	WKS			Title		Sym	$	Label & Number
6/27/64	104	8			Wish Someone Would Care			$75	Imperial 12266

Another Woman's Man
Break-A-Way
I Need You So

I Need Your Love So Bad
I've Been There

Please Send Me Someone To Love
Straight From The Heart

Sufferin' With The Blues
Time Is On My Side
While The City Sleeps

Wish Someone Would Care *17*
Without Love (There Is Nothing)

THOMAS, Lillo
Born in Brooklyn, New York. Male R&B singer.
'84

DEBUT	PEAK	WKS			Title		Sym	$	Label & Number
10/6/84	186	3			All Of You			$10	Capitol 12346

All Of You
Holding On

I Like Your Style
My Girl

Never Give You Up
Settle Down

Show Me
Your Love's Got A Hold On Me

THOMAS, Ray
Born on 12/29/42 in England. Flute/harmonica player of **The Moody Blues**.
'75

DEBUT	PEAK	WKS			Title		Sym	$	Label & Number
8/9/75	68	11	©	1	From Mighty Oaks			$15	Threshold 16
8/14/76	147	5		2	Hopes Wishes & Dreams			$15	Threshold 17

Adam And I (1)
Carousel (2)
Didn't I (2)
Friends (2)

From Mighty Oaks (1)
Hey Mama Life (1)
High Above My Head (1)
I Wish We Could Fly (1)

In Your Song (2)
Keep On Searching (2)
Last Dream (2)
Love Is The Key (1)

Migration (2)
One Night Stand (2)
Play It Again (1)
Rock-A-Bye Baby Blues (1)

We Need Love (2)
Within Your Eyes (2)
You Make Me Feel Alright (1)

THOMAS, Rufus
Born on 3/26/17 in Cayce, Mississippi; raised in Memphis. R&B singer/songwriter. Father of **Carla Thomas**.
'64

DEBUT	PEAK	WKS			Title		Sym	$	Label & Number
12/28/63+	138	3	©	1	Walking The Dog			$150	Stax 704
4/3/71	147	5	©	2	Rufus Thomas Live/Doing The Push & Pull At P.J.'s		[L]	$25	Stax 2039

Boom Boom (1)
Can Your Monkey Do The Dog (1) *48*
Cause I Love You (1)

Do The Funky Chicken (2)
(Do The) Push And Pull (2)
Dog, The (1) *87*
I Want To Be Loved (1)

It's Aw'rite (1)
Land Of 1,000 Dances (1)
Mashed Potatoes (1)

Night Time Is The Right Time (2)
Old McDonald Had A Farm (1)
Ooh-Poo-Pah-Doo (1,2)

Preacher And The Bear (2)
Walking The Dog (1,2) *10*
Ya Ya (1)
You Said (1)

DEBUT	PEAK	WKS	RIAA	CD	ARTIST — Album Title	Catalog	Sym	$	Label & Number

THOMAS, Timmy '73
Born on 11/13/44 in Evansville, Indiana. R&B singer/songwriter/keyboardist.

1/20/73	53	15		©	**Why Can't We Live Together**			$20	Glades 6501

Cold Cold People
Coldest Days Of My Life
Dizzy Dizzy World
First Time Ever I Saw Your Face
Funky Me
In The Beginning
Opportunity
Rainbow Power
Take Care Of Home
Why Can't We Live Together 3

THOMPSON, Richard '85
Born on 4/3/49 in London. Singer/songwriter/guitarist. Formed **Fairport Convention** in 1969. Went solo in 1971. Married to singer Linda Peters from 1972-82.

7/30/83	186	5		©	1	**Hand Of Kindness**			$12	Hannibal 1313
3/9/85	102	13		©	2	**Across A Crowded Room**			$10	Polydor 825421
10/25/86	142	6		©	3	**Daring Adventures**			$10	Polydor 829728
11/5/88	182	5		©	4	**Amnesia**			$10	Capitol 48845
2/26/94	109	3		©	5	**Mirror Blue**			$10	Capitol 81492
5/4/96	97	1		©	6	**You? Me? Us?**			$15	Capitol 33704 [2]

Al Bowlly's In Heaven (3)
Am I Wasting My Love On You? (6)
Baby Don't Know What To Do With Herself (5)
Baby Talk (3)
Bank Vault In Heaven (6)
Beeswing (5)
Bone Through Her Nose (3)
Both Ends Burning (1)
Burns Supper (6)
Business On You (6)
Can't Win (4)
Cash Down Never Never (3)
Cold Kisses (6)
Dark Hand Over My Heart (6)
Dead Man's Handle (3)
Devon Side (1)
Don't Tempt Me (4)
Easy There, Steady Now (5)
Fast Food (5)
Fire In The Engine Room (2)
For The Sake Of Mary (5)
Ghost Of You Walks (6)
Ghosts In The Wind (2)
Gypsy Love Songs (4)
Hand Of Kindness (1)
Hide It Away (6)
How I Wanted To (1)
How Will I Ever Be Simple Again (3)
I Ain't Going To Drag My Feet No More (2)
I Can't Wake Up To Save My Life (5)
I Ride In Your Slipstream (5)
I Still Dream (4)
Jennie (4)
Jerusalem On The Jukebox (4)
King Of Bohemia (5)
Little Blue Number (2)
Long Dead Love (3)
Love In A Faithless Country (2)
Lovers' Lane (3)
MGB-GT (5)
Mascara Tears (5)
Mingus Eyes (5)
Missie How You Let Me Down (3)
Nearly In Love (3)
No's Not A Word (6)
Pharaoh (4)
Poisened Heart And A Twisted Memory (1)
Put It There Pal (6)
Razor Dance (6)
Reckless Kind (4)
Sam Jones (6)
Shane And Dixie (5)
She Cut Off Her Long Silken Hair (6)
She Steers By Lightning (6)
She Twists The Knife Again (2)
Taking My Business Elsewhere (5)
Tear Stained Letter (1)
Train Don't Leave (6)
Turning Of The Tide (4)
Two Left Feet (1)
Valerie (3)
Walking Through A Wasted Land (2)
Waltzing's For Dreamers (4)
Way That It Shows (5)
When The Spell Is Broken (2)
Woods Of Darney (6)
Wrong Heartbeat (1)
Yankee, Go Home (4)
You Don't Say (2)

THOMPSON, Robbin, Band '80
Pop-rock group from Virginia: Robbin Thompson (vocals, guitar), Velpo Robertson (guitar), Eric Heiberg (keyboards), Michael Lanning (bass) and Bob Antonelli (drums). Thompson played in **Bruce Springsteen**'s early Steel Mill band.

10/25/80	168	11			**Two B's Please**			$12	Ovation 1759

All Alone In The Endzone
Barroom Romance
Brite Eyes 66
Candy Apple Red
Even Cowgirls Get The Blues
Let It All Out
Rock & Roll Singer
Sweet Virginia Breeze
That's Alright

THOMPSON, Sue '65
Born Eva Sue McKee on 7/19/26 in Nevada, Missouri; raised in San Jose, California.

3/20/65	134	3			**Paper Tiger**			$50	Hickory 121

Bad Boy
Big Hearted Me
'Cause I Ask You To
Fan Club
I Need A Harbor
I'd Like To Know You Better
Paper Tiger 23
Suzie
True Confession
What I'm Needin' Is You
What's The Use (To Take My Lovin')
What's Wrong Bill

THOMPSON, Tony '95
Born on 9/2/75 in Waco, Texas; raised in Oklahoma City. R&B singer. Member of **Hi-Five**.

7/15/95	99	5		©	**Sexsational**			$10	Giant 24596

Break It Down
Come Over
Dance With Me
Goodbye Eyes
Handle Our Business
I Know
I Wanna Love Like That 59
My Cherie Amour
Slave
Sweat
What's Goin' On

THOMPSON TWINS '84
Pop-rock trio from England: Tom Bailey (vocals, synthesizer), Alannah Currie (xylophone, percussion) and Joe Leeway (conga, synthesizer). Leeway left in 1986.

6/26/82	148	8		©	1	**In The Name Of Love**			$10	Arista 6601
2/26/83	34	25		©	2	**Side Kicks**			$10	Arista 6607
3/17/84	10	53	▲	©	3	**Into The Gap**			$10	Arista 8200
10/19/85+	20	35	●	©	4	**Here's To Future Days**			$10	Arista 8276
4/25/87	76	14		©	5	**Close To The Bone**			$10	Arista 8449
8/27/88	175	6		©	6	**Greatest Mixes/The Best Of Thompson Twins**		[K]	$10	Arista 8542
10/21/89	143	6		©	7	**Big Trash**			$10	Warner 25921

All Fall Out (2)
Another Fantasy (1)
Big Trash (7)
Bombers In The Sky (7)
Bouncing (1)
Bush Baby (5)
Dancing In Your Shoes (5)
Day After Day (3)
Dirty Summer's Day (7)
Doctor! Doctor! (3,6) 11
Don't Mess With Doctor Dream (4)
Emperor's Clothes (Part 1) (4)
Follow Your Heart (5)
Fool's Gold (1)
Future Days (4)
Gap, The (3) 69
Get That Love (5,6) 31
Gold Fever (5)
Good Gosh (1)
If You Were Here (2)
In The Name Of Love (1)
In The Name Of Love '88 (6)
Judy Do (2)
Kamikaze (2)
King For A Day (4,6) 8
Lay Your Hands On Me (4,6) 6
Lies (2,6) 30
Living In Europe (1)
Long Goodbye (6)
Love Is The Law (4)
Love Jungle (7)
Love Lies Bleeding (2)
Love On Your Side (2,6) 45
Make Believe (1)
No Peace For The Wicked (3)
Perfect Day (5)
Perfect Game (1)
Queen Of The U.S.A. (7)
Revolution (4)
Rock This Boat (7)
Roll Over (1)
Rowe, The (1)
Runaway (1)
Salvador Dali's Car (7)
Savage Moon (5)
Sister Of Mercy (3)
Still Waters (5)
Storm On The Sea (3)
Sugar Daddy (7) 28
T.V. On (7)
Tears (2)
This Girl's On Fire (7)
Tokyo (4)
Twentieth Century (5)
Watching (2)
We Are Detective (2)
Who Can Stop The Rain (3)
Wild (7)
You Killed The Clown (4)
You Take Me Up (3) 44

THOMSON, Ali '80
Born in Glasgow, Scotland. Pop singer/songwriter. Brother of **Supertramp**'s Dougie Thomson.

7/5/80	99	15			**Take A Little Rhythm**			$12	A&M 4803

African Queen
Fools' Society
Goodnight Song
Hollywood Role
Jamie
Live Every Minute 42
Page By Page
Saturday Heartbreaker
Take A Little Rhythm 15
We Were All In Love

THORNTON, Big Mama '69
Born Willie Mae Thornton on 12/11/26 in Montgomery, Alabama. Died of heart failure on 7/25/84 (age 67). Legendary blues singer.

8/30/69	198	2			**Stronger Than Dirt**			$25	Mercury 61225

Ain't Nothin' You Can Do
Ball And Chain
Born Under A Bad Sign
Funky Broadway
Hound Dog
I Shall Be Released
Let's Go Get Stoned
Rollin' Stone
Summertime
That Lucky Old Sun

★377★ THOROGOOD, George, & The Destroyers '79

Born on 12/31/52 in Wilmington, Delaware. Blues-rock singer/guitarist. The Destroyers: Ron Smith (guitar), Billy Blough (bass) and Jeff Simon (drums). By 1980, Smith left and Hank Carter (sax) joined. Guitarist Steve Chrismar joined in 1986.

1)Born To Be Bad 2)Maverick 3)Move It On Over

12/9/78+	33	47	●	©	1	Move It On Over		$12	Rounder 3024
9/1/79	78	10			2	Better Than The Rest	[E]	$12	MCA 3091
						recorded in 1974			
11/8/80	68	12		©	3	More George Thorogood and the Destroyers		$12	Rounder 3045
8/28/82	43	48	●	©	4	Bad To The Bone		$10	EMI America 17076
3/2/85	32	42	●	©	5	Maverick		$10	EMI America 17145
8/23/86	33	42	▲	©	6	Live	[L]	$10	EMI America 17214
						recorded on 5/23/86 at the Cincinnati Gardens			
2/6/88	32	24	●	©	7	Born To Be Bad		$10	EMI-Manhattan 46973
3/16/91	77	13		©	8	Boogie People		$10	EMI 92514
8/15/92	100	20	▲	©	9	The Baddest Of George Thorogood And The Destroyers	[G]	$10	EMI 97718
8/14/93	120	10		©	10	Haircut		$10	EMI 89529

Alley Oop (6)
As The Years Go Passing By (4)
Baby Don't Go (10)
Baby Please Set A Date (1)
Back To Wentsville (4)
Bad To The Bone (4,6,9)
Blue Highway (4)
Boogie People (8)
Born In Chicago (8)
Born To Be Bad (7)
Bottom Of The Sea (3,6)
Can't Be Satisfied (8)
Cocaine Blues (1)
Cops And Robbers (10)
Crawling King Snake (5)
Dixie Fried (5)
Down In The Bottom (10)
Gear Jammer (5,9)
Get A Haircut (10)
Gone Dead Train (5)
Goodbye Baby (2,3)
Hello Little Girl (8)
Highway 49 (7)
House Of Blue Lights (3)
Howlin' For My Baby (10)
Howlin' For My Darling (2)
Huckle Up Baby (2)
I Drink Alone (5,6,9)
I Really Like Girls (7)
I'm A Steady Rollin' Man (9)
I'm Just Your Good Thing (1)
I'm Movin' On (7)
I'm Ready (2,7,10)
I'm Wanted (3)
If You Don't Start Drinkin' (I'm Gonna Leave) (8,9)
In The Night Time (2)
It Wasn't Me (1)
It's A Sin (4)
Just Can't Make It (3)
Kids From Philly (3)
Killer's Bluze (10)
(Let's) Go Go Go (5)
Long Distance Lover (8)
Long Gone (5,9)
Louie To Frisco (9)
Mad Man Blues (8)
Madison Blues (6)
Maverick (5)
Memphis, Tennessee (5)
Miss Luann (4)
Move It On Over (1,9)
My Friend Robert (10)
My Way (2)
My Weakness (2)
Nadine (2)
New Boogie Chillen (2)
New Hawaiian Boogie (1)
Night Time (3,6)
No Particular Place To Go (4)
No Place To Go (8)
Nobody But Me (4)
Oklahoma Sweetheart (8)
One Bourbon, One Scotch, One Beer (6,9)
One Way Ticket (3)
Reelin' & Rockin' (6)
Restless (3)
Shake Your Money Maker (7)
Six Days On The Road (8)
Sky Is Crying (1,6)
Smokestack Lightning (7)
So Much Trouble (1)
That Same Thing (1)
Tip On In (3)
Treat Her Right (7,9)
Want Ad Blues (10)
Wanted Man (4)
What A Price (5)
Who Do You Love (1,6,9)
Willie And The Hand Jive (5) *63*
Woman With The Blues (5)
Worried About My Baby (2)
You Can't Catch Me (7)
You Talk Too Much (7,9)
You're Gonna Miss Me (2)

THORPE, Billy '79

Born on 3/29/46 in Manchester, England. Moved to Australia in 1964. Rock singer/guitarist. Member of **Mick Fleetwood**'s Zoo.

| 5/5/79 | 39 | 23 | | | 1 | Children Of The Sun | | $12 | Polydor 6228 |
| 11/8/80 | 151 | 5 | | | 2 | 21st Century Man | | $12 | Elektra 294 |

Beginning, The (1)
Children Of The Sun (1) *41*
Dream-Maker (1)
Goddess Of The Night (1)
In My Room (2)
1991 (2)
Rise (1)
She's Alive (2)
Simple Life (1)
Solar Anthem (1)
Solar Dawn (1)
21st Century Man (2)
We Welcome You... (1)
We Were Watching You (2)
We're Leaving (1)
Wrapped In The Chains Of Your Love (1)

THP ORCHESTRA '78

Disco duo from Canada: Barbara Fry (vocals) and W. Michael Lewis (synthesizer). THP: Two Hot People.

| 2/4/78 | 65 | 19 | | | | Two Hot For Love! | | $12 | Butterfly 005 |

Carnival (Theme from Black Orpheus)
Crazy, Crazy
Dawn Patrol
Early Riser
Two Hot For Love

3 '88

Rock trio formed by **Emerson, Lake & Palmer** alumni: **Keith Emerson** and Carl Palmer (both British) with California songwriter/guitarist Robert Barry.

| 3/19/88 | 97 | 10 | | © | | To The Power Of Three | | $10 | Geffen 24181 |

Chains
Desde La Vida Medley
Eight Miles High
Lover To Lover
On My Way Home
Runaway
Talkin' Bout
You Do Or You Don't

THREE DEGREES, The '75

R&B vocal trio from Philadelphia: Fayette Pinkey, Sheila Ferguson and Valerie Holiday.

8/8/70	139	7			1	"Maybe"		$40	Roulette 42050
12/14/74+	28	15			2	The Three Degrees		$12	Philadelphia Int'l. 32406
6/21/75	99	8			3	International		$12	Philadelphia Int'l. 33162
1/17/76	199	1			4	The Three Degrees Live	[L]	$12	Philadelphia Int'l. 33840
						recorded at Bailey's in London			
12/23/78+	169	8			5	New Dimensions		$12	Ariola 50044

Another Heartache (3)
Can't You See What You're Doing To Me (2)
Collage (1)
Dirty Ol' Man (2,4)
Distant Lover (3)
Don't Let The Sun Go Down On Me (4)
Everybody Gets To Go To The Moon (4)
Falling In Love Again (5)
For The Love Of Money (medley) (4)
Free Ride (4)
Get Your Love Back (3)
Giving Up, Giving In (5)
Harlem (4)
Here I Am (3)
I Didn't Know (2)
I Like Being A Woman (2)
If And When (2)
Living For The City (medley) (4)
Lonelier Are Fools (3)
Lonely Town (1)
Long Lost Lover (3)
Looking For Love (5)
Love Train (4)
Loving Cup (3)
MacArthur Park (1)
Magic Door (1)
Magic In The Air (5)
Maybe (1) *29*
Rosegarden (1)
Runner, The (5)
Stardust (1)
Sugar On Sunday (1)
TSOP (The Sound Of Philadelphia) (3,4)
Take Good Care Of Yourself (3)
Together (3)
When Will I See You Again (2,4) *2*
Woman In Love (5)
Woman Needs A Good Man (2)
Year Of Decision (2,4)
You're The Fool (1)
You're The One (1) *77*

THREE DOG NIGHT ★164★ '71

Pop-rock vocal trio formed in Los Angeles: Danny Hutton (born on 9/10/42), Cory Wells (born on 2/5/42) and Chuck Negron (born on 6/8/42). Named for the coldest night in the Australian outback.

1)Golden Bisquits 2)Captured Live At The Forum 3)Seven Separate Fools

1/25/69	11	62	●		1	Three Dog Night		$15	Dunhill/ABC 50048
7/12/69	16	74	●	©	2	Suitable For Framing		$15	Dunhill/ABC 50058
11/29/69	6	72	●	©	3	Was Captured Live At The Forum	[L]	$15	Dunhill/ABC 50068
5/2/70	8	48	●	©	4	It Ain't Easy		$15	Dunhill/ABC 50078
12/12/70+	14	64	●	©	5	Naturally		$15	Dunhill/ABC 50088

DEBUT	PEAK	WKS	RIAA	CD	ARTIST — Album Title	Catalog	Sym	$	Label & Number

THREE DOG NIGHT — Cont'd

DEBUT	PEAK	WKS	RIAA	CD	#	Album Title	Sym	$	Label & Number
2/27/71	5	61	●		6	Golden Bisquits	[G]	$15	Dunhill/ABC 50098
10/23/71	8	34	●	©	7	Harmony		$15	Dunhill/ABC 50108
7/29/72	6	40	●	©	8	Seven Separate Fools		$15	Dunhill/ABC 50118
3/17/73	18	27	●		9	Around The World With Three Dog Night	[L]	$20	Dunhill/ABC 50138 [2]
10/20/73	26	17	●	©	10	Cyan		$15	Dunhill/ABC 50158
4/6/74	20	22	●	©	11	Hard Labor		$15	Dunhill/ABC 50168
12/21/74+	15	17	●	©	12	Joy To The World-Their Greatest Hits	[G]	$15	Dunhill/ABC 50178
6/21/75	70	12			13	Coming Down Your Way		$12	ABC 888
4/24/76	123	6			14	American Pastime		$12	ABC 928

Ain't That A Lotta Love (2)
Anytime Babe (11)
Billy The Kid (14)
Black & White (8,9,12) **1**
Can't Get Enough Of It (5)
Celebrate (2,6) **15**
Chained (8)
Change Is Gonna Come (2)
Chest Fever (1,3)
Circle For A Landing (2)
Coming Down Your Way (13)
Cowboy (4)
Dance The Night Away (14)
Don't Make Promises (1,6)
Dreaming Isn't Good For You (2)
Drive On, Ride On (14)
Easy Evil (14)
Easy To Be Hard (2,3,6) **4**

Eli's Coming (2,3,6,9) **10**
Everybody's A Masterpiece (14)
Family Of Man (7,9,12) **12**
Feeling Alright (2,3)
Find Someone To Love (1)
Fire Eater (2)
Freedom For The Stallion (8)
Going In Circles (8,9)
Good Feeling (1957) (4,9)
Good Old Feeling (13)
Good Time Living (4)
Hang On (14)
Happy Song (10)
Heaven Is In Your Mind (1,3)
Heavy Church (5)
I Can Hear You Calling (5)
I'd Be So Happy (11,12)
I'll Be Creeping (5)
I've Got Enough Heartache (1)
In Bed (8)

Into My Life (10)
It Ain't Easy (4)
It's For You (1,3)
Jam (7,9)
Joy To The World (5,9,12) **1**
King Solomon's Mines (2)
Kite Man (13)
Lady Samantha (2)
Lay Me Down Easy (10)
Lean Back, Hold Steady (13)
Let Me Go (1)
Let Me Serenade You (10,12) **17**
Liar (5,9,12) **7**
Loner, The (1)
Mama Told Me (Not To Come) (4,6,9) **1**
Mellow Down (14)
Midnight Flyer ("Eli Wheeler") (13)

Midnight Runaway (8,9)
Mind Over Matter (13)
Mistakes And Illusions (poem) (7)
Murder In My Heart For The Judge (7)
My Impersonal Life (7)
My Old Kentucky Home (Turpentine And Dandelion Wine) (2)
Never Been To Spain (7,9,12) **5**
Never Dreamed You'd Leave In Summer (7)
Night In The City (7)
Nobody (1,3,6)
Old Fashioned Love Song (7,9,12) **4**
On The Way Back Home (11)
One (1,3,6,12) **5**

One Man Band (5,6,9,12) **19**
Out In The Country (4,6,9) **15**
Peace Of Mind (7)
Pieces Of April (8,9) **19**
Play Children Play (10)
Play Something Sweet (Brickyard Blues) (11,12) **33**
Prelude (11)
Prelude To Morning (8)
Put Out The Light (11)
Ridin' Thumb (10)
Rock & Roll Widow (7)
Shambala (10,12) **3**
Show Must Go On (11,12) **4**
Singer Man (10)
Sitting In Limbo (11)
Southbound (14)
Storybook Feeling (10)
Sunlight (5)

Sure As I'm Sittin' Here (11,12) **16**
That No One Ever Hurt This Bad (1)
Til The World Ends (13) **32**
Try A Little Tenderness (1,3,6) **29**
Tulsa Turnaround (8)
When It's Over (13)
Woman (4,6)
Writings On The Wall (8)
Yellow Beach Umbrella (14)
Yo Te Quiero Hablar (Take You Down) (13)
You (7)
You Can Leave Your Hat On (13)
Your Song (4,6)

3 DOORS DOWN   '00

Rock group from Escatawpa, Mississippi: Brad Arnold (vocals), Matt Roberts (guitar), Todd Harrell (bass) and Chris Henderson (drums).

2/26/00	7	84↑▲⁵	©		The Better Life		$10	Republic 153920

Be Like That
Better Life

By My Side
Down Poison

Duck And Run
Kryptonite 3

Life Of My Own
Loser 55

Not Enough
Smack

So I Need You

311   '97

Rock-funk group from Omaha, Nebraska: Nicholas Hexum and SA Martinez (vocals), Tim Mahoney (guitar), P-Nut (bass) and Chad Sexton (drums). 311 is the police code for indecent exposure.

DEBUT	PEAK	WKS	RIAA	CD	#	Album Title	Sym	$	Label & Number
7/30/94	193	1	●	©	1	Grassroots ... C:#23/9		$10	Capricorn 42026
8/12/95+	12	72	▲³	©	2	311 ... C:#13/10		$10	Capricorn 42041
9/14/96	20ᶜ	12	●	©	3	Music	[E]	$10	Capricorn 42008
						released in 1993			
11/23/96	95	1		©	4	Enlarged To Show Detail		$10	Capricorn 010039
						music video with bonus four song EP included			
8/23/97	4	33	▲	©	5	Transistor		$10	Capricorn 536181
11/21/98	77	2		©	6	Live	[L]	$10	Capricorn 538263
10/30/99	9	13	●	©	7	Soundsystem		$10	Capricorn 546645

All Mixed Up (2)
Applied Science (1,6)
Beautiful Disaster (5,6)
Borders (5)
Brodels (2)
Can't Fade Me (7)
Color (5)
Come Original (7)
Continuous Life (5)
Creature Feature (5)
DLMD (2)
Do You Right (3)
Don't Stay Home (2)
Down (2,6)

8:16 A.M. (1)
Electricity (5)
Eons (7)
Evolution (7)
Fat Chance (3)
Feels So Good (3,6)
Firewater (4)
Flowing (7)
Freak Out (3,6)
Freeze Time (7)
Galaxy (5,6)
Gap (4)
Grassroots (1)
Guns [are for pussies] (2)

Hive (2)
Homebrew (1,6)
Hydroponic (3,6)
Inner Light Spectrum (5)
Jackolantern's Weather (2)
Jupiter (5)
Large In The Margin (7)
Leaving Babylon (7)
Let The Cards Fall (4)
Life Years (5,6)
Livin' & Rockin' (7)
Loco (2)
Lose (1)

Lucky (1)
Mindspin (5)
Misdirected Hostility (2,6)
My Stoney Baby (3)
Nix Hex (3,6)
No Control (5)
Nutsymptom (1)
Offbeat Bare-Ass (1)
Omaha Stylee (1,6)
1,2,3 (1)
Paradise (3)
Plain (5)
Prisoner (5)
Purpose (2)

Random (2)
Rub A Dub (5)
Running (5)
Salsa (1)
Sever (7)
Silver (1)
Six (1)
Starshines (5)
Stealing Happy Hours (5)
Strangers (1)
Strong All Along (7)
Sweet (2)
T & P Combo (2)
Taiyed (1)

Transistor (5)
Tribute (4,6)
Tune In (5)
Unity (3)
Use Of Time (5)
Visit (3)
Welcome (3)
What Was I Thinking (5)
Who's Got The Herb? (6)

THREE HANKS — see WILLIAMS, Hank Sr. & Jr.

3LW   '01

Female R&B vocal trio from New Jersey: Naturi Naughton, Kiely Williams and Adrienne Bailon. 3LW: 3 Little Women.

12/23/00+	29	40	▲		3LW		$10	Nine Lives 63961

Crush On You
Curious
Gettin Too Heavy

I Can't Take It
I'm Gonna Make You Miss Me
Is You Feelin' Me

More Than Friends (That's Right)

No More (Baby I'ma Do Right) 23
Not This Time

Ocean
Playas Gon' Play 81
'Til I Say So

THREE O'CLOCK, The   '85

Rock group from Los Angeles: Michael Quercio (vocals, bass), Louis Gutierrez (guitar), Mike Mariano (keyboards) and Danny Benair (drums).

5/25/85	125	10		©	Arrive Without Travelling		$10	I.R.S. 5591

Another World
Each And Every Lonely Heart

Girl With The Guitar (Says Oh Yeah)
Half The Way There

Hand In Hand
Her Head's Revolving
Knowing When You Smile

Mrs. Green
Simon In The Park (With Tentacles)

Spun Gold
Underwater

THREE 6 MAFIA   '00

Rap group from Memphis: female **Gangsta Boo** with males Jordan Houston, Crunchy Black, Paul Beauregard, Koopsta Knicca and Lord Infamous. Also see **Hypnotize Camp Posse** and **Tear Da Club Up Thugs**.

3/29/97	126	3		©	1	The End		$10	Prophet 4405
11/22/97	40	29	●	©	2	Chpt. 2: "World Domination"		$10	Relativity 1644

THREE 6 MAFIA — Cont'd

| 7/1/00 | 6 | 23 ▲ | © | 3 | **When The Smoke Clears Sixty 6, Sixty 1** | | | $10 | Loud 1732 |

includes "M.E.M.P.H.I.S." by **Hypnotize Camp Posse**

| 11/18/00 | 130 | 2 | © | 4 | **Kings Of Memphis: Underground Vol. 3** | | | $10 | Smoked Out 9997 |

TRIPLE SIX MAFIA

Act Like You Know Me (Point 'Em Out) (3)
Anyone Out There (2)
Are U Ready 4 Us (2)
Barrin' You Bitches (3)
Body Parts (1)
Bodyparts 2 (2)
Da Summa (4)
Destruction Terror (1)
End, The (1)
Flashes (2)
From Da Back (3)

F*ck What U Heard (4)
Fuck Y'all Hoes (3)
Gette'm Crunk (1)
Good Stuff (4)
Gotcha Shakin' (1)
Grab Tha Gauge (4)
Gunclaps (2)
Hit A Muthafucka (2)
I Ain't Cha Friend (2)
I Ain't Goin' (1)
I'm So Hi (3)
In-2-Deep (1,2)

Jealous AZZ B*tch (4)
Jus Like Us (3)
Just Anotha Crazy Click (3)
Land Of The Lost (2)
Last Man Standing (1)
Late Night Tip (1,2)
Life Or Death (1)
Lock Down (4)
Love To Make A Stang (4)
Mafia Niggaz (3)
M.E.M.P.H.I.S. (4)
Mindstate (4)

Money Flow (1)
Motivated (2)
Neighborhood Hoe (2)
Niggaz Down 2 Make Some Endz (4)
Pass That Junt (4)
Powder (4)
Prophet Posse (2)
Put Ya Signs (3)
Sippin' On Some Syrup (3)
Sleep (4)
Smokin On Da Dro (4)

South Memphis B*tch (4)
Spill My Blood (2)
Stomp (1)
Take A Bump (3)
Talkin (4)
Tear Da Club Up '97 (2)
3-6 In The Morning (2)
Tongue Ring (3)
Touched Wit It (3)
Walk Up 2 Yo House (1)
Watcha Do (2)
We Are Waiting (4)

Weak Azz Bitch (3)
Weed Is Got Me High (2)
Whatcha Know (3)
Where Da Cheese At (3)
Where Da Killaz Hang (1)
Where's Da Bud (1)
Who Got Dem 9's (2)
Who Run It (3)
Will Blast (2)
Wonabees (4)

THREE SUNS, The   '55

Instrumental trio from Philadelphia: brothers Al (guitar) and Morty (accordian) Nevins, with cousin Artie Dunn (organ). Al Nevins died on 1/25/65 (age 48). Morty Nevins died on 7/23/90 (age 63). Dunn died on 1/15/96 (age 73).

| 5/28/55 | 13 | 9 | © | 1 | **Soft and Sweet** | [I] | | $30 | RCA Victor 1041 |

LP: RCA Victor LPM-1041 (#13); EP: RCA Victor EPB-1041 (#13)

| 8/18/56 | 19 | 1 | | 2 | **High Fi and Wide** | [I] | | $30 | RCA Victor 1249 |
| 1/26/57 | 16 | 6 | © | 3 | **Midnight For Two** | [I] | | $30 | RCA Victor 1333 |

Ain't Misbehavin' (3)
Alouette (2)
April In Portugal (2)
Autumn Nocturne (1)
Bali Ha'i (2)
Blue Bells Of Scotland (2)
Blue Orchids (1)
Blue Tango (3)
Come Back To Sorrento (2)

Cumana (3)
Far Away Places (2)
Flamingo (1)
Galway Bay (2)
Hindustan (2)
I Don't Stand A Ghost Of A Chance (3)
In A Little Spanish Town ('Twas On A Night Like This) (2)

In A Persian Market (2)
Intermission Time (3)
It's Dawn Again (1)
Lady Of Shangri-La (2)
Let's Call The Whole Thing Off (3)
Londonderry Air (2)
Memory Lane (3)
Mexican Hat Dance (3)

Midnight For Two (3)
Moonlight In Vermont (1)
On A Little Street In Singapore (2)
River Seine (1)
Sheik Of Araby (2)
Sinner Kissed An Angel (1)
Skylark (1)
Song Of India (2)

Song Of Old Hawaii (2)
Stars Fell On Alabama (1)
Stella By Starlight (3)
There Is No Greater Love (1)
Touch Of Your Lips (1)
Velvet Moon (1)
Very Thought Of You (3)
Viennese Refrain (The Old Refrain) (2)

When Yuba Plays The Rumba On The Tuba (3)
World Is Waiting For The Sunrise (3)

3T   '96

R&B vocal trio: brothers Taryll, T.J. and Taj Jackson. Sons of Tito Jackson (of **The Jacksons**).

| 1/20/96 | 127 | 15 | © | | **Brotherhood** | | | $10 | MJJ Music 57450 |

Anything 15
Brotherhood

Give Me All Your Lovin'
Gotta Be You

I Need You
Memories

Sexual Attention
Tease Me

24/7
Why

With You
Words Without Meaning

THREE TENORS, The   '94

All-star trio of operatic tenors: **Jose Carreras**, **Placido Domingo** and **Luciano Pavarotti**.

| 10/6/90+ | 35 | 100 | ▲³ | © | 1 | **Carreras/Domingo/Pavarotti In Concert** | [L] | | $10 | London 430433 |

recorded on 7/7/90 at the Baths of Caracalla in Rome

| 12/11/93 | 127 | 4 | © | 2 | **Christmas Favorites From The World's Favorite Tenors** | C:#21/10 | [X] | $10 | Sony Master. 53725 |

Christmas charts: 29/'93, 21/'94, 36/'95

| 9/17/94 | 4 | 33 ▲ | © | 3 | **The 3 Tenors In Concert 1994** | [L] | | $10 | Atlantic 82614 |

recorded on 7/16/94 at Dodger Stadium in Los Angeles

| 9/5/98 | 83 | 10 ● | © | 4 | **The 3 Tenors - Paris 1998** | [L] | | $10 | Atlantic 83110 |

recorded on 7/10/98

| 11/25/00 | 54 | 8 | © | 5 | **The Three Tenors Christmas** | [X] | | $10 | Sony Classical 89131 |

Christmas chart: 9/00

Adeste Fideles (2,5)
Agnus Dei (2)
All I Ask Of You (medley) (3)
Amapola (medley) (1)
Amazing Grace (5)
America (medley) (3)
Amor Ti Vieta (4)
Amor, Vida De Mi Vida (3)
Ave Maria (2)
Ave Maria, Dolce Maria (5)
Ay, Ay, Ay (4)
Be My Love (medley) (3)
Because (3,4)
Brazil (medley) (3)
Caminito (medley) (1)
Cantique De Noel (O Holy Night) (2,5)
Carol Of The Drum (The Little Drummer Boy) (5)

Caruso (4)
Cielito Lindo (medley) (1)
Core 'Ngrato (1,4)
Dein Ist Mein Ganzes Herz (1)
Dicitencello Vuie (4)
Dormi, O Bambino (5)
E Lucevan Le Stelle (1)
El Cant Tels Ocells (medley) (2)
Feliz Navidad (5)
Funiculi, Funicula (medley) (3)
Granada (1,3,4)
Guten Abend, Gut' Nacht (2)
Happy Christmas/War Is Over (5)
I'll Be Home For Christmas (2,5)
Il Lamento De Federico (1)
Io Conosco Un Giardino (4)
Jingle Bells (2)

Joy To The World (medley) (2)
L'Improvviso (1)
La Donna E Mobile (3)
La Vie En Rose (medley) (1)
La Virgin Lava Panales (2,5)
Libiamo Ne' Lieti Calici (Brindisi) (3)
Lippen Schweigen (medley) (3)
Lolita (4)
Manha De Carnaval (4)
Marechiare (medley) (3)
Maria (medley) (1)
Maria, Mari (4)
Mary's Boy Child (medley) (2)
Mattinata (medley) (1)
Memoires De Danton (4)
Memory (medley) (1)
Mille Cherubini (2)
Moon River (medley) (3)

My Way (medley) (3)
Navidad (2)
Nessun Dorma (1,3,4)
No Puede Ser (1)
Non Ti Scordar Di Me (3)
O Come, All Ye Faithful ..see: Adeste Fideles
'O Paese D' 'O Sole (medley) (1)
O Paradis! (1)
'O Sole Mio (1,4)
O Souverain, O Juge, O Pere (3)
O Surdato 'Nnamurato (4)
Ochi Tchorniye (medley) (1)
Oh Tannenbaum (5)
Parlami D'Amore Mariu (4)
Pourquoi Me Reveiller (3)
Pregaria (5)

Quiero Desterrar De Tu Pecho El Temor (4)
Recondita Armonia (1)
Rondine Al Nido (1)
Santa Lucia Luntana (medley) (3)
Silent Night (5)
Singin' In The Rain (medley) (3)
Sleigh Ride (5)
Solamente Una Vez (4)
Sous Le Ciel De Paris (2)
Sous Les Ponts De Paris (medley) (3)
Ständchen (4)
Stille Nacht (Silent Night) (2)
Susani (5)
T'Estimo (4)
Te Quiero Dijiste (medley) (3)
Te Voglio Tanto Bene (4)

Those Were The Days (medley) (3)
Tonight (medley) (1)
Torero Quiero (4)
Torna A Surriento (1,3)
Tu, Ca Nun Chiagne (3,4)
Tu Scendi Dalle Stelle (5)
Un Nuevo Siglo (3)
Vesti La Giubba (4)
Voce 'E Notte (4)
White Christmas (2,5)
Wiegenlied I & II (5)
Wien, Wien, Nur Du Allein (medley) (3)
Winter Wonderland (5)
With A Song In My Heart (3)
You'll Never Walk Alone (4)

THREE TIMES DOPE   '89

Rap trio from Philadelphia: Duerwood Beale, Walter Griggs and Robert Waller.

| 4/22/89 | 122 | 18 | © | | **Original Stylin'** | | | $10 | Arista 8571 |

Believe Dat
From Da Giddy Up
Funky Dividends

Greatest Man Alive
Improvin Da Groovin
Increase The Peace (medley)

Once More You Hear The Dope Stuff
Original Stylin'

Straight Up
What's Going On (medley)
Who Is This?

3XKRAZY   '97

Rap trio from Oakland: Bart, Keek Tha Sneek and Agerman.

| 4/26/97 | 136 | 4 | © | | **Stackin Chips** | | | $10 | Noo Trybe 42961 |

Can't Fuck With This
Dem Niggas
Get 'Em

Ghetto Soldiers
In The Name Of Rame
Keep It On The Real

Next Niggas Ho
Open Your Eyes
Pistols Blazin

Rollin 100's
Sickkaluffa
Stackin Chips

Stanky Panky
Tired Of The Pain
West Coast Shit

DEBUT	PEAK	WKS	RIAA	CD	ARTIST — Album Title	Catalog	Sym	$	Label & Number

THRILLS '81

Rock group from New York City: Dave Fullerton (guitar), Tony Monaco (keyboards), Bill Gilbert (bass) and Rob Owens (drums). All share vocals.

6/27/81   199   4   **First Thrills** .... **$12**   G&P 1002

Blinded By Love	Carrie	Dream Away	Good Friends	Not Gonna Run
Breaking My Heart	Changing My Ways	Going Out	Lie For Your Love	Won't Be A Fool

THUG LIFE '94

Rap group formed and led by **2Pac**. Also includes Syke, Macadoshis, Mopreme and The Rated R. 2Pac died of gunshot wounds on 9/13/96 (age 25).

10/29/94   42   29 ● ©   **Volume 1** .... **$10**   Interscope 92360

Bury Me A G	Don't Get It Twisted	Pour Out A Little Liquor	Stay True	Street Fame
Cradle To The Grave	How Long Will They Mourn Me?	Shit Don't Stop	Str8 Ballin'	Under Pressure

THUNDER '91

Hard-rock group from England: Daniel Bowes (vocals), Luke Morley (guitar), Ben Matthews (keyboards), Mark Luckhurst (bass) and Gary James (drums).

6/1/91   114   10 ©   **Backstreet Symphony** .... **$10**   Geffen 24384

Backstreet Symphony	Distant Thunder	Englishman On Holiday	Girl's Going Out Of Her Head	Love Walked In	Until My Dying Day
Dirty Love 55	Don't Wait For Me	Gimme Some Lovin'	Higher Ground	She's So Fine	

THUNDERCLAP NEWMAN '73

Rock trio formed in England: Andy Newman (keyboards), John "Speedy" Keene (vocals) and Jimmy McCulloch (guitar). McCulloch was a member of **Paul McCartney**'s Wings from 1975-77; died of heart failure on 9/27/79 (age 26).

10/10/70+   161   10 ©   **Hollywood Dream** .... **$25**   Track 8264
produced by **Pete Townshend**

Accidents	Hollywood #1 & #2	Look Around	Open The Door, Homer	**Something In The Air 37**	Wild Country
Hollywood Dream	I Don't Know	Old Cornmill	Reason, The	When I Think	

TIERRA '81

Latin group formed in Los Angeles: brothers Steve (trombone, timbales) and Rudy (guitar) Salas, Joey Guerra (keyboards), Bobby Navarrete (reeds), Andre Baeza (congas), Steve Falomir (bass) and Phil Madayag (drums). The Salas brothers and Baeza were formerly with **El Chicano**.

12/27/80+   38   21 ©   **City Nights** .... **$12**   Boardwalk 36995

Givin' Up On Love	Latin Disco	Street Scene	**Together 18**	
Gonna Find Her	**Memories 62**	Time To Dance	Zoot Suit Boogie	

TIFFANY '88

Born Tiffany Darwish on 10/2/71 in Norwalk, California. Pop singer.

9/26/87+   ❶²   69 ▲⁴ ©   1   **Tiffany** .... **$10**   MCA 5793
12/10/88+   17   29 ▲ ©   2   **Hold An Old Friend's Hand** .... **$10**   MCA 6267

All This Time (2) 6	Hearts Never Lie (2)	I'll Be The Girl (2)	Kid On A Corner (1)	Spanish Eyes (1)
Could've Been (1) 1	Hold An Old Friend's Hand (2)	It's The Lover (Not The Love)	Oh Jackie (2)	Walk Away While You Can (2)
Danny (1)	**I Saw Him Standing There**	(2)	Promises Made (1)	We're Both Thinking Of Her (2)
Drop That Bomb (2)	(1) 7	Johnny's Got The Inside Moves	**Radio Romance** (2) 35	
Feelings Of Forever (1) 50	**I Think We're Alone Now** (1) 1	(1)	Should've Been Me (1)	

TIKARAM, Tanita '89

Born on 12/8/69 in Munster, West Germany; raised in Basingstoke, England. Female singer/songwriter.

2/11/89   59   23 ©   1   **Ancient Heart** .... **$10**   Reprise 25839
2/24/90   124   7 ©   2   **The Sweet Keeper** .... **$10**   Reprise 26091
4/20/91   142   5 ©   3   **Everybody's Angel** .... **$10**   Reprise 26486

Cathedral Song (1)	He Likes The Sun (1)	It All Came Back Today (2)	Once & Not Speak (2)	Sunface (3)	To Wish This (3)
Consider The Rain (2)	Hot Pork Sandwiches (3)	Little Sister Leaving Town (2)	Only The Ones We Love (3)	Sunset's Arrived (2)	Twist In My Sobriety (1)
Deliver Me (3)	I Love The Heaven's Solo (3)	Love Story (2)	Poor Cow (1)	Swear By Me (3)	Valentine Heart (1)
For All These Years (1)	I Love You (1)	Me In Mind (3)	Preyed Upon (1)	This Story In Me (3)	We Almost Got It Together (2)
Good Tradition (1)	I Owe All To You (2)	Mud In Any Water (3)	Sighing Innocents (1)	This Stranger (2)	World Outside Your Window (1)
Harm In Your Hands (2)	I'm Going Home (3)	Never Known (3)	Sometime With Me (3)	Thursday's Child (2)	

TILLIS, Pam '97

Born on 7/24/57 in Plant City, Florida. Country singer. Daughter of Mel Tillis.

1/25/92   69   23 ● ©   1   **Put Yourself In My Place** .... **$10**   Arista 18642
10/17/92   82   42 ▲ ©   2   **Homeward Looking Angel** .... **$10**   Arista 18649
5/14/94   51   37 ▲ ©   3   **Sweetheart's Dance** .... **$10**   Arista 18758
11/25/95   151   2 ● ©   4   **All Of This Love** .... **$10**   Arista 18799
6/21/97   47   21 ▲ ©   5   **Greatest Hits** .... [G]   **$10**   Arista 18836
3/24/01   183   1 ©   6   **Thunder & Roses** .... **$10**   Arista 67000

All Of This Love (4)	Deep Down (2)	In Between Dances (3,5)	No Two Ways About It (4)	Sweetheart's Dance (3)	You Can't Have A Good Time
All The Good Ones Are Gone	Do You Know Where Your Man	It Isn't Just Raining (6)	Off-White (6)	Tequila Mockingbird (4)	Without Me (4)
(5)	Is (2)	It's Lonely Out There (4)	One Of Those Things (1)	They Don't Break 'Em Like	
Already Fallen (1)	Don't Tell Me What To Do (1,5)	Jagged Hearts (6)	Please (6)	They Used To (3)	
Ancient History (1)	Draggin' My Chains (1)	Land Of The Living (5)	Put Yourself In My Place (1)	Thuder And Roses (6)	
Be A Man (6)	Fine, Fine, Very Fine Love (2)	Let That Pony Run (2,5)	River And The Highway (4,5)	'Til All The Lonely's Gone (3)	
Better Off Blue (3)	Homeward Looking Angel (2)	Love Is Only Human (2)	Rough And Tumble Heart (2)	Tryin' (2)	
Betty's Got A Bass Boat (4)	How Gone Is Goodbye (2)	Mandolin Rain (4)	Shake The Sugar Tree (2,5)	Waiting On The Wind (6)	
Blue Rose Is (1)	I Smile (6)	Maybe It Was Memphis (1,5)	Space (6)	We've Tried Everything Else (2)	
Calico Plains (3)	I Was Blown Away (3)	Melancholy Child (1)	Spilled Perfume (3,5)	When You Walk In The Room	
Cleopatra, Queen Of Denial	I've Seen Enough To Know (1)	Mi Vida Loca (My Crazy Life)	Sunset Red And Pale Moonlight	(3,5)	
(2,5)	If I Didn't Love You (6)	(3,5)	(4)	Which Five Years (6)	

TILLOTSON, Johnny '62

Born on 4/20/39 in Jacksonville, Florida; raised in Palatka, Florida. Pop singer. Appeared in the movie *Just For Fun*.

4/14/62   120   5   1   **Johnny Tillotson's Best** .... [G]   **$50**   Cadence 3052
7/21/62   8   31   2   **It Keeps Right On A-Hurtin'** .... **$50**   Cadence 3058
2/22/64   48   14 ©   3   **Talk Back Trembling Lips** .... **$25**   MGM 4188
2/6/65   148   3 ©   4   **She Understands Me** .... **$25**   MGM 4270

TILLOTSON, Johnny — Cont'd

All Alone Am I (3)
Another You (3)
Blowin' In The Wind (3)
Blue Velvet (3)
Busted (4)
Cutie Pie (1)
Danke Schoen (3)
Dreamy Eyes (1) *35*
Earth Angel (1) *57*
Fool #1 (2)

Four Walls (2)
Funny How Time Slips Away (2) *50*
Hello Walls (2)
I Can't Help It (If I'm Still In Love With You) (2) *24*
I Can't Stop Loving You (3)
I Fall To Pieces (2)
I'm So Lonesome I Could Cry (2) *89*

Island Of Dreams (4)
It Keeps Right On A-Hurtin' (2) *3*
Jimmy's Girl (1) *25*
Little Boy (4)
(Little Sparrow) His True Love Said Goodbye (1)
Lonely Street (2)
More Than Before (4)
Much Beyond Compare (1)

My Little World (3)
Please Don't Go Away (3)
Pledging My Love (1) *63*
Poetry In Motion (1) *2*
Princess Princess (1)
Rhythm Of The Rain (3)
Send Me The Pillow You Dream On (2) *17*
She Understands Me (4) *31*
Take Good Care Of Her (2)

Take This Hammer (4)
Talk Back Trembling Lips (3) *7*
That's Love (4)
That's When It Hurts The Most (4)
To Be A Child Again (4)
Tomorrow (4)
True True Happiness (1) *54*
What Am I Gonna Do (3)

What'll I Do (2)
Why Do I Love You So (1) *42*
Willow Tree (4)
Without You (1) *7*
Worried Guy (3) *37*
Yellow Bird (4)

'TIL TUESDAY '85

Pop group formed in Boston: **Aimee Mann** (vocals, bass), Robert Holmes (guitar), Joey Pesce (keyboards) and Michael Hausmann (drums). Michael Montes replaced Pesce in 1988.

DEBUT	PEAK	WKS	RIAA	CD	ARTIST — Album Title	$	Label & Number
4/20/85	19	31	●	©	1 **Voices Carry**	$10	Epic 39458
10/25/86	49	26	●	©	2 **Welcome Home**	$10	Epic 40314
11/19/88	124	19		©	3 **Everything's Different Now**	$10	Epic 44041

Angels Never Call (2)
(Believed You Were) Lucky (3) *95*
Coming Up Close (2) *59*
Crash And Burn (3)
David Denies (2)
Don't Watch Me Bleed (1)

Everything's Different Now (3)
Have Mercy (2)
How Can You Give Up (3)
I Could Get Used To This (1)
J For Jules (3)
Limits To Love (3)
Long Gone (Buddy) (3)

Looking Over My Shoulder (1) *61*
Love In A Vacuum (1)
Lovers' Day (2)
Maybe Monday (1)
No More Crying (1)

No One Is Watching You Now (2)
On Sunday (2)
Other End (Of The Telescope) (3)
Rip In Heaven (3)
Sleep (1)

Sleeping And Waking (2)
Voices Carry (1) *8*
What About Love (2) *26*
Why Must I (3)
Will She Just Fall Down (2)
Winning The War (1)
You Know The Rest (1)

TIMBALAND AND MAGOO '98

Rap duo from Norfolk, Virginia: Tim Mosley and Magoo.

DEBUT	PEAK	WKS	RIAA	CD	ARTIST — Album Title	$	Label & Number
11/29/97+	33	37	▲	©	1 **Welcome To Our World**	$10	Blackground 92772
12/12/98	41	15		©	2 **Tim's Bio: From The Motion Picture: Life From Da Bassment**	$10	Blackground 92813

TIMBALAND
includes "Wit' Yo' Bad Self" by **Mad Skillz**, "What Cha Know About This" by Mocha & Babe Blue, "Fat Rabbit" by **Ludacris**, "Who Am I" by **Twista**, "Talking On The Phone" by **Kelly Price** & Lil' Man, "John Blaze" by **Aaliyah** & Missy "**Misdemeanor**" Elliott, "Birthday" by **Playa**, and "3:30 In The Morning" by Virginia Williams

Beep Beep (1)
Bringin' It (2)
Can't Nobody (2)
Clock Strikes (1) *37*

Deep In Your Memory (1)
Fat Rabbit (2)
Feel It (1)
15 After Da' Hour (1)

Here We Come (2) *92*
I Get It On (2)
Joy (1)
Keep It Real (2)

Lobster & Scrimp (2)
Luv 2 Luv U (1)
Man Undercover (1)
Peepin' My Style (1)

Put 'Em On (2)
Sex Beat (Interlude) (1)
Smoke In Da' Air (1)
To My (2)

Up Jumps Da' Boogie (1) *12*
What Cha Know About This (2)
What Cha Talkin' About (2)
Writtin' Rhymes (1)

TIMBUK 3 '87

Husband-and-wife duo from Austin, Texas: Patrick and Barbara MacDonald.

DEBUT	PEAK	WKS	RIAA	CD	ARTIST — Album Title	$	Label & Number
10/4/86+	50	30		©	1 **Greetings From Timbuk 3**	$10	I.R.S. 5739
5/7/88	107	13		©	2 **Eden Alley**	$10	I.R.S. 42124

Cheap Black And White (1)
Dance Fever (2)
Easy (2)
Eden Alley (2)
Facts About Cats (1)
Friction (1)

Future's So Bright, I Gotta Wear Shades (1) *19*
Hairstyles And Attitudes (1)
I Love You In The Strangest Way (1)
I Need You (1)

Just Another Movie (1)
Life Is Hard (1)
Little People Make Big Mistakes (2)
Reckless Driver (2)

Rev. Jack & His Roamin' Cadillac Church (2)
Sample The Dog (2)
Shame On You (1)
Sinful Life (2)
Tarzan Was A Bluesman (2)

Too Much Sex, Not Enough Affection (1)
Welcome To The Human Race (2)

TIME, The '84

Funk group from Minneapolis: **Morris Day** (vocals), Jerome Benton (dancer), **Jesse Johnson** (guitar), Jimmy "Jam" Harris, Monte Moir and Paul Peterson (keyboards), Terry Lewis (bass) and Jellybean Johnson (drums). Group featured in the movie *Purple Rain*. Lewis and Harris became highly successful songwriting/production team. Peterson, Benton and Johnson formed **The Family**. Lewis married **Karyn White**.

DEBUT	PEAK	WKS	RIAA	CD	ARTIST — Album Title	$	Label & Number
9/12/81	50	32	●	©	1 **The Time**	$10	Warner 3598
9/25/82	26	33	●	©	2 **What Time Is It?**	$10	Warner 23701
7/28/84	24	57	▲	©	3 **Ice Cream Castle**	$10	Warner 25109
7/28/90	18	16	●	©	4 **Pandemonium**	$10	Paisley Park 27490

After Hi School (1)
Bird, The (3) *36*
Blondie (4)
Chili Sauce (4)
Chocolate (4)
Cooking Class (4)

Cool (Part 1) (1) *90*
Data Bank (4)
Donald Trump (Black Version) (4)
Dreamland (4)
Get It Up (1)

Gigolos Get Lonely Too (2)
Girl (1)
I Don't Wanna Leave You (2)
Ice Cream Castles (3)
If The Kid Can't Make You Come (3)

It's Your World (4)
Jerk Out (1) *9*
Jungle Love (3) *20*
My Drawers (3)
My Summertime Thang (4)
Oh, Baby (1)

Onedayi'mgonnabesomebody (2)
Pandemonium (4)
Pretty Little Women (4)
777-9311 (2) *88*
Sexy Socialites (4)

Skillet (4)
Sometimes I Get Lonely (4)
Stick, The (1)
Walk, The (2)
Wild And Loose (2)
Yount (2)

TIMES TWO '88

Male vocal duo of from Pt. Reyes, California: Shanti Jones and John Dollar.

DEBUT	PEAK	WKS	RIAA	CD	ARTIST — Album Title	$	Label & Number
4/30/88	137	11		©	**X2**	$10	Reprise 25624

Cecilia *79*
I Wantcha
Jet

L.O.D. (Love On Delivery)
Mr. D.J.

Only My Pillow Knows (For Sure)
Painted Heart

Romeo
Strange But True *21*
3 Into 2 (Don't Go)

TIMMY -T- '91

Born Timmy Torres on 9/21/67 in Fresno, California.

DEBUT	PEAK	WKS	RIAA	CD	ARTIST — Album Title	$	Label & Number
1/26/91	46	23		©	**Time After Time**	$10	Quality 15103

My Exceptional Girl
One More Try *1*

Over And Over *63*
Paradise

Please Don't Go
Time After Time *40*

Too Young To Love You
What Will I Do *96*

You're The Only One

TIN MACHINE '89

Rock group: **David Bowie** (vocals), Reeves Gabrels (guitar), Tony (bass; **Utopia, Chequered Past**) and Hunt (drums; **Utopia, Paris**) Sales. The Sales brothers are the sons of TV comedian **Soupy Sales**.

DEBUT	PEAK	WKS	RIAA	CD	ARTIST — Album Title	$	Label & Number
6/10/89	28	17		©	1 **Tin Machine**	$10	EMI 91990
9/21/91	126	3		©	2 **Tin Machine II**	$10	Victory 511216

Amazing (1)
Amlapura (2)
Baby Can Dance (1)
Baby Universal (2)

Betty Wrong (2)
Big Hurt (2)
Bus Stop (1)
Crack City (1)

Goodbye Mr. Ed (2)
Heaven's In Here (1)
I Can't Read (1)
If There Is Something (2)

One Shot (2)
Pretty Thing (1)
Prisoner Of Love (1)
Shopping For Girls (2)

Sorry (2)
Stateside (2)
Tin Machine (1)
Under The God (1)

Video Crime (1)
Working Class Hero (1)
You Belong In Rock & Roll (2)
You Can't Talk (2)

TIN TIN '71

Australian duo: Steve Kipner (keyboards) and Steve Groves (guitar). Disbanded in 1973. Kipner later co-wrote **Chicago**'s "Hard Habit To Break" and **Olivia Newton-John**'s "Physical" and "Twist Of Fate."

| 6/5/71 | 197 | 1 | | | **Tin Tin** | | | $20 | Atco 350 |

produced by Maurice Gibb (**Bee Gees**)

Come On Over Again
Family Tree
Flag (medley)
He Wants To Be A Star

Lady In Blue
Manhattan Woman
Nobody Moves Me Like You
Only Ladies Play Croquet

Put Your Money On My Dog (medley)
She Said Ride
Spanish Shepherd

Swans On The Canal
Toast And Marmalade For Tea 20
Tuesday's Dreamer

TINY TIM '68

Born Herbert Khaury on 4/12/30 in New York City. Died of heart failure on 11/30/96 (age 66). Novelty singer/ukulele player. Shot to national attention with appearances on TV's *Rowan & Martin's Laugh-In*. Married "Miss Vicki" on Johnny Carson's *Tonight Show* on 12/18/69; divorced in 1977.

| 5/4/68 | 7 | 32 | | | **God Bless Tiny Tim** | [N] | | $20 | Reprise 6292 |

Coming Home Party
Daddy, Daddy, What Is Heaven Like?
Ever Since You Told Me That You Love Me (I'm A Nut)

Fill Your Heart
I Got You, Babe
Livin' In The Sunlight, Lovin' In The Moonlight
On The Old Front Porch

Other Side
Stay Down Here Where You Belong
Strawberry Tea
Then I'd Be Satisfied With Life

This Is All I Ask
Tip-Toe Thru' The Tulips With Me 17
Viper, The
Welcome To My Dream

TIPPIN, Aaron '92

Born on 7/3/58 in Pensacola, Florida; raised in South Carolina. Country singer/songwriter.

5/25/91	153	21	●	©	1 You've Got To Stand For Something			$10	RCA 2374
3/28/92	50	60	▲	©	2 Read Between The Lines			$10	RCA 61129
8/28/93	53	39	●	©	3 Call Of The Wild			$10	RCA 66251
11/26/94+	114	13	●	©	4 Lookin' Back At Myself			$10	RCA 66420
11/11/95	63	23	●	©	5 Tool Box			$10	RCA 66740
5/3/97	97	5		©	6 Greatest Hits...And Then Some	[G]		$10	RCA 67427
8/12/00	53	26	●	©	7 People Like Us			$10	Lyric Street 65014

Ain't That A Hell Of A Note (1)
Always Was (7)
And I Love You (7)
Bayou Baby (4)
Best Love We Ever Made (7)
Big Boy Toys (4)
Call Of The Wild (3,6)
Cold Gray Kentucky Morning (6)
Country Boy's Tool Box (4,5)
Door, A (6)
Every Now And Then (I Wish Then Was Now) (7)
Everything I Own (5)
Honky-Tonk Superman (3)

How's The Radio Know (5)
I Can Help (5)
I Got It Honest (4,6)
I Miss Misbehavin' (6)
I Promised You The World (3)
I Was Born With A Broken Heart (2)
I Wonder How Far It Is Over You (1)
I Wouldn't Have It Any Other Way (2,6)
I'd Be Afraid Of Losing You (7)
I've Got A Good Memory (1)
If I Had It To Do Over (2)
If Only Your Eyes Could Lie (6)

In My Wildest Dreams (1)
Kiss This (7) 42
Let's Talk About You (3)
Lookin' Back At Myself (4)
Lost (7)
Lovin' Me Into An Early Grave (4)
Man That Came Between Us (Was Me) (1)
Many, Many, Many Beers Ago (1)
Mission From Hank (4)
My Blue Angel (4)
My Kind Of Town (3)
Night Shift (7)

Nothin' In The World (3)
People Like Us (7)
Read Between The Lines (2)
Real Nice Problem To Have (5)
She Feels Like A Brand New Man Tonight (4)
She Made A Man Out Of A Mountain Of Stone (5)
She Made A Memory Out Of Me (1)
She's Got A Way (Of Makin' Me Forget) (4)
Sky's Got The Blues (7)
Sound Of Your Goodbye (Sticks And Stones) (2)

Standin' On The Promises (4)
Ten Pound Hammer (5)
That's As Close As I'll Get To Loving You (5,6)
That's What Happens When I Hold You (6)
There Ain't Nothin' Wrong With The Radio (2,6)
These Sweet Dreams (2)
This Heart (2)
Trim Yourself To Fit The World (3)
Twenty-Nine And Holding (7)
Up Against You (1)

When Country Took The Throne (3)
Whole Lotta Love On The Line (3,6)
Without Your Love (5)
Working Man's Ph.D. (3,6)
You Are The Woman (4)
You Gotta Start Somewhere (5)
You've Always Got Me (5)
You've Got To Stand For Something (1,6)

TJADER, Cal '65

Born on 7/16/25 in St. Louis. Died on 5/5/82 (age 56). Jazz vibraphonist.

| 9/28/63 | 79 | 14 | | © | 1 Several Shades Of Jade | [I] | | $25 | Verve 8507 |
| 4/17/65 | 52 | 22 | | © | 2 Soul Sauce | [I] | | $25 | Verve 8614 |

Afro-Blue (2)
Almond Tree (1)
Borneo (1)
Cherry Blossoms (1)

China Nights (Shina No Yoru) (1)
Fakir, The (1)
Hot Sake (1)
Joao (2)

Leyte (2)
Maramoor (2)
Pantano (2)
Sahib (1)
Somewhere In The Night (2)

Song Of The Yellow River (1)
Soul Sauce (Guacha Guaro) (2) 88
Spring Is Here (2)
Tanya (2)

Tokyo Blues (1)

TKA '88

R&B vocal trio from New York City: Tony Ortiz, Louis "**K7**" Sharpe and Ralph Cruz.

| 1/30/88 | 135 | 11 | | © | 1 Scars Of Love | | | $10 | Tommy Boy 1011 |
| 4/25/92 | 131 | 9 | | © | 2 Greatest Hits | [G] | | $10 | Tommy Boy 1040 |

Come Get My Love (1,2)
Crash (Have Some Fun) (2) 80
Don't Be Afraid (1,2)

Give Your Love To Me (2)
I Can't Help It (2)
I Won't Give Up On You (2) 65

Is It Love? (2)
It's Got To Be Love (1)
Louder Than Love (2) 62

Maria (2) 44
One Way Love (1,2) 75
Scars Of Love (1,2)

Someone In The Dark (1)
Tears May Fall (1,2)
X-Ray Vision (1,2)

You Are The One (2) 91

TKO '79

Rock group from Seattle: Brad Sinsel (vocals), Rick Pierce (guitar), Tony Bortko (keyboards), Mark Seidenverg (bass) and Darryl Siguenza (drums).

| 4/21/79 | 181 | 2 | | | **Let It Roll** | | | $12 | Infinity 9005 |

Ain't No Way To Be
Bad Sister

Come A Day
Gutter Boy

Kill The Pain
Let It Roll

Only Love
Rock 'N Roll Again

What In The World

TLC '99

Female R&B vocal trio from Atlanta: Tionne "T-Boz" Watkins, Lisa "Left Eye" Lopes and Rozanda "Chilli" Thomas. Founded and managed by **Pebbles**. T-Boz married **Mack 10** on 8/19/2000.

3/14/92	14	73	▲⁴	©	1 Oooooooohhh...On The TLC Tip			$10	LaFace 26003
12/3/94+	3	99	▲¹⁰	©	2 CrazySexyCool	C:#33/1		$10	LaFace 26009
3/13/99	❶⁵	64	▲⁶	©	3 Fanmail			$10	LaFace 26055

Ain't 2 Proud 2 Beg (1) 6
Automatic (3)
Baby-Baby-Baby (1) 2
Bad By Myself (1)
Can I Get A Witness (2)
Case Of The Fake People (2)
Come On Down (3)

Conclusion (1)
Creep (2) 1
Das Day We Like 'Em (1)
Dear Lie (3) 51
Depend On Myself (1)
Diggin' On You (2) 5
Don't Pull Out On Me Yet (3)

FanMail (3)
Hat 2 Da Back (1) 30
His Story (1)
I Miss You So Much (3)
I'm Good At Being Bad (3)
If I Was Your Girlfriend (3)
If They Knew (3)

Kick Your Game (2)
Let's Do It Again (2)
Lovesick (3)
My Life (3)
No Scrubs (3) 1
Red Light Special (2) 2
Shock Dat Monkey (1)

Shout (3)
Silly Ho (3) 59
Somethin' You Wanna Know (1)
Sumthin' Wicked This Way Comes (2)
Switch (2)
Take Our Time (2)

This Is How It Should Be Done (1)
Unpretty (3) 1
Waterfalls (2) 1
What About Your Friends (1) 7

TNT '87
Hard-rock group from Norway: Tony Harnell (vocals), Ronni Le Tekro (guitar), Morty Black (bass) and Diesel Dahl (drums).

5/23/87	**100**	21		1 **Tell No Tales**	$10 Mercury 830979
3/18/89	**115**	12	©	2 **Intuition**	$10 Mercury 836777

As Far As The Eye Can See (1)　End Of The Line (2)　Intuition (2)　Northern Lights (1)　Take Me Down (Fallen Angel)　Tonight I'm Falling (2)
Caught Between The Tigers (2)　Everyone's A Star (1)　Learn To Love (2)　Ordinary Lover (2)　(2)　Wisdom (2)
Child's Play (1)　Forever Shine On (2)　Listen To Your Heart (1)　Sapphire (1)　Tell No Tales (1)
Desperate Night (1)　Incipits (1)　Nation Free (2)　Smooth Syncopation (1)　10,000 Lovers (In One) (1)

TOADIES '95
Rock group from Fort Worth, Texas: Todd Lewis (vocals, guitar), Darrel Herbert (guitar), Lisa Umbarger (bass) and Mark Reznicek (drums). Clark Vogeler replaced Herbert in 2000.

8/12/95	**56**	49	▲ ©	1 **Rubberneck**	$10 Interscope 92402
4/7/01	**130**	1		2 **Hell Below / Stars Above**	$10 Interscope 490872

Away (1)　Heel (2)　Jigsaw Girl (2)　Motivational (2)　Push The Hand (2)　Velvet (1)
Backslider (1)　Hell Below / Stars Above (2)　Little Sin (2)　Plane Crash (2)　Quitter (1)　What We Have We Steal (2)
Dollskin (2)　I Burn (1)　Mexican Hairless (1)　Possum Kingdom (1)　Sweetness (2)　You'll Come Down (2)
Happyface (1)　I Come From The Water (1)　Mister Love (1)　Pressed Against The Sky (2)　Tyler (1)

TOAD THE WET SPROCKET '94
Pop-rock group from Santa Barbara, California: Glen Phillips (vocals), Todd Nichols (guitar), Dean Dinning (bass) and Randy Guss (drums). Name taken from a **Monty Python** skit.

7/11/92	**49**	46	▲ ©	1 **Fear**	$10 Columbia 47309
6/11/94	**34**	42	▲ ©	2 **Dulcinea**	$10 Columbia 57744
11/11/95	**37**	15	● ©	3 **In Light Syrup**	$10 Columbia 67394
6/7/97	**19**	12	©	4 **Coil**	$10 Columbia 67862

All I Want (1) *15*　Brother (3)　**Fall Down** (2) *33*　Inside (2)　Pray Your Gods (1)　Throw It All Away (4)
All In All (3)　Butterflies (1)　Fly From Heaven (2)　Is It For Me (1)　Reincarnation Song (2)　**Walk On The Ocean** (1) *18*
All Right (3)　Chicken (3)　Good Intentions (3)　Janitor (3)　Rings (4)　Whatever I Fear (4)
All She Said (3)　Come Down (4)　Hobbit On The Rocks (3)　(Listen) (2)　So Alive (3)　Windmills (2)
All Things In Time (4)　Crazy Life (4)　Hold Her Down (1)　Little Buddha (4)　Something To Say (1)　Woodburning (2)
Amnesia (4)　Crowing (3)　Hope (3)　Little Heaven (3)　**Something's Always Wrong**
Are We Afraid (3)　Dam Would Break (4)　I Will Not Take These Things　Little Man Big Man (4)　(2) *41*
Before You Were Born (1)　Desire (4)　For Granted (4)　Nanci (2)　Stories I Tell (1)
Begin (2)　Don't Fade (4)　In My Ear (1)　Nightingale Song (1)　Stupid (2)

TOBY BEAU '78
Pop group from Texas: Balde Silva (vocals, harmonica), Danny McKenna (guitar), Ron Rose (banjo), Steve Zipper (bass) and Rob Young (drums).

6/10/78	**40**	23		**Toby Beau**	$12 RCA Victor 2771

Broken Down Cowboy (1)　Bulldog　Into The Night　**My Angel Baby** *13*　Watching The World Go By　Wink Of An Eye
Buckaroo　California　Moonshine　Same Old Line　Westbound Train

TODAY '89
R&B vocal group from Englewood, New Jersey: Lee Drakeford, Larry McCain, Wesley Adams and Larry Singletary.

1/14/89	**86**	22	©	1 **Today**	$10 Motown 6261
10/13/90	**132**	6		2 **The New Formula**	$10 Motown 6309

Every Little Thing About You (2)　Home Is Where You Belong (2)　Let Me Know (2)　Sexy Lady (1)　Tennis Anyone (2)　Your Love Is Not True (1)
Girl I Got My Eyes On You (1)　I Got The Feeling (2)　My Happiness (2)　Style (1)　Trying To Get Over You (2)
Gonna Make You Mine (2)　I Wanna Come Back Home (2)　No Need To Worry (2)　Take It Off (1)　Why You Get Funky On Me (2)
Him Or Me (1)　Lady (1)　Self Centered (2)　Take Your Time (1)　You Stood Me Up (1)

TOKENS, The '62
Vocal group formed in Brooklyn, New York: brothers Phil and Mitch Margo, Hank Medress and Jay Siegel. Formed own B.T. Puppy record label in 1964. The Margos and Siegel recorded as **Cross Country** in 1973.

1/27/62	**54**	16		1 **The Lion Sleeps Tonight**	$100 RCA Victor 2514
5/21/66	**148**	2		2 **I Hear Trumpets Blow**	$40 B.T. Puppy 1000
7/22/67	**134**	6		3 **Back To Back**	$40 B.T. Puppy 1002

THE TOKENS/THE HAPPENINGS
side 1: The Tokens; side 2: **The Happenings**

Barbara Ann (2)　Every Breath I Take (2)　**Lion Sleeps Tonight** (1) *1*　Speedo (2)　Wake Up Little Suzy (2)
Big Boat (1)　He's In Town (2,3) *43*　Lonesome Traveller (1)　Swing (2,3)　Water Is Over My Head (2)
Children Go Where I Send　Hindi Lullabye (1)　Michael (1)　Sylvie Sleepin' (2,3)　Water Prayer (1)
Thee (1)　**I Hear Trumpets Blow** (2,3) *30*　Riddle, The (1)　Three Bells (The Jimmy Brown　Wreck Of The John B. (1)
Don't Cry, Sing Along With The　Jamaica Farewell (1)　Saloogy (2,3)　Song) (2)
Music (2)　Laugh (3)　Shenandoah (1)　Tina (1)

TOMITA '74
Born Isao Tomita in 1932 in Tokyo. Classical keyboardist.

8/31/74	**57**	25		1 **Snowflakes Are Dancing**	[I] $12 RCA Victor 0488
5/24/75	**49**	12		2 **Moussorgsky: Pictures At An Exhibition**	[I] $12 RCA Victor 0838
2/14/76	**71**	12		3 **Firebird**	[I] $12 RCA Victor 11312
1/8/77	**67**	13		4 **Holst: The Planets**	[I] $12 RCA Victor 1919
2/18/78	**115**	10		5 **Kosmos**	[I] $12 RCA Victor 2616
3/3/79	**152**	6		6 **The Bermuda Triangle**	[I] $12 RCA Victor 2885
2/9/80	**174**	5		7 **Ravel: Bolero**	[I] $12 RCA Victor 3412

Arabesque (1)　Electromagnetic Waves　Harp Of The Ancient People　Prelude To The Afternoon Of A　Space Ship Lands Emitting
Aranjuez (5)　Descend (6)　With Songs Of Venus And　Faun (3)　Silvery Light (6)
Bolero (7)　Engulfed Cathedral (1)　Space Children (6)　Reverie (1)　Star Wars Main Title (5)
Clair De Lune (1)　Firebird Suite (3)　Hora Staccato (5)　Sea Named "Solaris" (5)　Unanswered Question (5)
Daphnis And Chloe: Suite No. 2　Footprints In The Snow (1)　Mother Goose Suite (7)　Snowflakes Are Dancing (1)　Venus In A Space Uniform
(7)　Gardens In The Rain (1)　Night On Bare Mountain (3)　Solvejg's Song (5)　Shining In Fluorescent Light
Dawn Over The Triangle And　Giant Pyramid And Its Ancient　Pacific (1)　Song Of Venus (6)　(6)
Mysterious Electric Waves (6)　People (6)　Passepied (1)　Space Children In The　Visionary Flight To The 1448
Dazzling Cylinder That Crashed　Girl With The Flaxen Hair (1)　Pavane For A Dead Princess　Underground Kingdom Called　Nebular Group Of The Bootes
In Tunguska, Siberia (6)　Golliwog's Cakewalk (1)　(7)　Agharta (6)　(6)
Earth -- A Hollow Vessel (6)　　Pictures At An Exhibition (2)　Space Fantasy (5)　World Of Different Dimensions
　　Planets, The (4)　　(6)

TOMLIN, Lily   '71

Born Mary Jean Tomlin on 9/1/39 in Detroit. Comic actress. Cast member of TV's *Laugh-In* (1970-73). Starred in several movies.

3/27/71	15	25			1 **This is a Recording**	[C]	**$15**	Polydor 4055
3/25/72	41	22			2 **And That's The Truth**	[C]	**$15**	Polydor 5023
11/12/77	120	6			3 **On Stage**	[C]	**$12**	Arista 4142

Alexander Graham Bell (1)
Awards Dinner (1)
Bordello, The (1)
Boswick 9 (1)
Do You Have Any Chewing Gum? (2)
Does This Chair Lean Back? (2)
Don't My Toes Look Pretty? (2)
Ernestine (1,3)
F.B.I., The (1)
Finish Putting The Groceries Away (1)
Glenna - A Child Of The 60's (3)
Guess This Riddle (2)
Here's My House (2)
Here's The Empty Lot (3)
Hey Lady (3)
I Always Kiss Buster (2)
I.B.M. (1)
I Can't Go To The Movies Here (2)
I Dressed Him Up (2)
I Go To Sunday School (2)
I Like Your Kitchen (2)
I Want You To Go (2)
I Will Help You Unpack (2)
Joan Crawford (1)
Lady Lady Open Up (2)
Lily And Shopping Bag Lady (3)
Look In The Sky (1)
Lud And Marie Meet Dracula's Daughter (A Tale Of Teen-Age Tyranny) (3)
Mafia And The Pope (1)
Marriage Counselor (1)
Mr. Theater Goer And Shopping Bag Lady (3)
Mr. Veedle (1)
Mrs. Judith Beasley (Unnatural Resources) (3)
Mrs. Mitchell (1)
My Sister Mary Jean (2)
Obscene Phone Call (1)
Pageant, The (1)
Peeved (1)
Repairman, The (1)
Shopping Bag Lady And UFO Guy (1)
Strike, The (1)
Tell Me Something Lady (1)
Tell Miss Sweeney Goodbye (1)

TOMMY TUTONE   '82

Rock group formed in San Francisco: Tommy Heath (vocals), Jim Keller (guitar), Jon Lyons (bass) and Victor Carberry (drums).

5/24/80	68	13		©	1 **Tommy Tutone**		**$12**	Columbia 36372
2/6/82	20	30		©	2 **Tommy Tutone-2**		**$12**	Columbia 37401
10/29/83	179	3			3 **National Emotion**		**$12**	Columbia 38425

Am I Supposed To Lie (1)
Angel Say No (1) *38*
Baby It's Alright (2)
Bernadiah (2)
Blame, The (1)
Cheap Date (1)
Dancing Girl (1)
Dumb But Pretty (3)
867-5309/Jenny (2) *4*
Fat Chance (1)
Get Around Girl (3)
Girl In The Back Seat (1)
Hide-Out (1)
I Believe (1)
I Wanna Touch Her (3)
Imaginary Heart (3)
Laverne (3)
Money Talks (3)
National Emotion (3)
No Way To Cry (2)
Not Say Goodbye (2)
Only One (2)
Rachel (1)
Shadow On The Road Ahead (2)
Someday Will Come (3)
Sounds Of A Summer Night (1)
Steal Away (2)
Sticks And Stones (3)
Tonight (2)
What'cha Doin' To Me (1)
Which Man Are You (1)
Why Baby Why (2)

TOMS, Gary, Empire   '75

Disco group from New York City: Gary Toms (keyboards), Helen Jacobs (vocals), Rick Kenny (guitar), Eric Oliver (trumpet), Les Rose (sax), Warren Tesoro (percussion), John Freeman (bass) and Rick Murray (drums).

| 9/27/75 | 178 | 3 | | | **7-6-5-4-3-2-1 Blow Your Whistle** | | **$12** | PIP 6814 |

Do Your Thing
Drive My Car *69*
Feel That Funky Groove
Jubilation (Excitation)
Love Me Right
New Empire
7-6-5-4-3-2-1 (Blow Your Whistle) *46*
Slow & Funky
Tell The People
This Crazy World
You Are The One For Me

TOM TOM CLUB   '82

Studio project formed by husband-and-wife Chris Frantz and Tina Weymouth. Both were members of **Talking Heads**.

10/24/81+	23	33	●	©	1 **Tom Tom Club**		**$10**	Sire 3628
8/20/83	73	13			2 **Close To The Bone**		**$10**	Sire 23916
4/15/89	114	11		©	3 **Boom Boom Chi Boom Boom**		**$10**	Sire 25888

As Above, So Below (1)
Atsababy! (Life Is Great) (2)
Bamboo Town (2)
Booming And Zooming (1)
Call Of The Wild (3)
Challenge Of The Love Warriors (3)
Don't Say No (3)
Femme Fatale (3)
Genius Of Love (1) *31*
I Confess (3)
Kiss Me When I Get Back (3)
L' Elephant (1)
Little Eva (3)
Lorelei (1)
Man With The 4-Way Hips (2)
Measure Up (2)
Never Took A Penny (2)
On, On, On, On... (1)
On The Line Again (2)
Pleasure Of Love (2)
Shock The World (3)
Suboceana (2)
This Is A Foxy World (2)
Tom Tom Theme (1)
Wa Wa Dance (3)
Wordy Rappinghood (1)

TONE LOC   '89

Born Anthony Smith on 3/3/66 in Los Angeles. Male rapper/actor. Appeared in several movies.

| 2/18/89 | ❶[1] | 42 | ▲[2] | © | **Loc-ed After Dark** | | **$10** | Delicious Vinyl 3000 |

Cheeba Cheeba
Cutting Rhythms
Don't Get Close
Funky Cold Medina *3*
Homies, The
I Got It Goin' On
Loc'ed After Dark
Loc'in On The Shaw
Next Episode
On Fire
Wild Thing *2*

TONEY, Oscar Jr.   '67

Born on 5/26/39 in Selma, Alabama; raised in Columbus, Georgia. R&B singer.

| 7/29/67 | 192 | 5 | | © | **For Your Precious Love** | | **$30** | Bell 6006 |

Ain't That True Love
Any Day Now
Dark End Of The Street
Do Right Woman - Do Right Man
Down In Texas
For Your Precious Love *23*
He Don't Love You (And He'll Break Your Heart)
Moon River
No Sad Song
That's All I Want From You
Turn On Your Love Light *65*

TONIC   '97

Rock group from Los Angeles: Emerson Hart (vocals, guitar), Jeff Russo (guitar), Dan Rothchild (bass) and Kevin Shepard (drums). Dan Lavery replaced Rothchild in 1998.

| 4/19/97 | 28 | 57 | ▲ | © | 1 **Lemon Parade** | | **$10** | Polydor 531042 |
| 11/27/99 | 81 | 8 | | © | 2 **Sugar** | | **$10** | Universal 542069 |

Bigot Sunshine (1)
Casual Affair (1)
Celtic Aggression (1)
Drag Me Down (2)
Future Says Run (2)
If You Could Only See (1)
Knock Down Walls (2)
Lemon Parade (1)
Love A Diamond (2)
Mean To Me (2)
Mountain (1)
Mr. Golden Deal (2)
My Old Man (1)
Open Up Your Eyes (1)
Queen (2)
Soldier's Daughter (1)
Stronger Than Mine (2)
Sugar (2)
Sunflower (2)
Thick (1)
Top Falls Down (2)
Waiting For The Light To Change (2)
Waltz With Me (2)
Wicked Soldier (2)
You Wanted More (2)

TONIGHT SHOW BAND, The — see SEVERINSEN, Doc

TONY! TONI! TONÉ!   '93

R&B-funk trio from Oakland: brothers Raphael Saadiq (vocals, bass, keyboards) and **Dwayne Wiggins** (vocals, guitar), with cousin Tim Riley (drums). Trio appeared in the movie *House Party 2*.

5/28/88	69	46	●	©	1 **Who?**		**$10**	Wing 835549
5/26/90	34	64	▲	©	2 **The Revival**		**$10**	Wing 841902
7/10/93	24	43	▲[2]	©	3 **Sons Of Soul**		**$10**	Wing 514933
12/7/96+	32	31	▲	©	4 **House Of Music**		**$10**	Mercury 534250

All My Love (2)
All The Way (2)
Annie May (4)
Anniversary (3) *10*
Baby Doll (1)
Blues, The (2) *46*
Born Not To Know (1)
Castleers (3)
Dance Hall (3)
Don't Fall In Love (4)
Don't Talk About Me (2)
Feels Good (2) *9*
For The Love Of You (1)
Fun (3)
Gangsta Groove (3)
Holy Smokes & Gee Whiz (4)
I Care (3)
I Couldn't Keep It To Myself (3)
If I Had No Loot (3) *7*
It Never Rains (In Southern California) (2) *34*
Jo-Jo (2)
(Lay Your Head On My) Pillow (3) *31*
Leavin' (3) *82*
Let Me Know (4)
Let's Get Down (4)
Let's Have A Good Time (2)
Little Walter (1) *47*
Love Struck (1)
Lovin' You (4)
My Ex-Girlfriend (3)
Not Gonna Cry For You (1)
Oakland Stroke (2)
Pain (1)
Party Don't Cry (4)
Skin Tight (2)
Sky's The Limit (2)
Slow Wine (3)
Still A Man (4)
Tell Me Mama (1)
Thinking Of You (4) *22*
Those Were The Days (2)
Til Last Summer (4)
Tonyies! In The Wrong Key (3)
Top Notch (4)
Tossin' & Turnin' (4)
261.5 (1)
What Goes Around Comes Around (3)
Whatever You Want (2) *48*
Who's Lovin' You (1)
Wild Child (4)

DEBUT	PEAK	WKS	RIAA	CD	ARTIST — Album Title	Catalog	Sym	$	Label & Number

TOOL '01
Hard-rock group from Los Angeles: Maynard James Keenan (vocals), Adam Jones (guitar), Paul D'Amour (bass) and Danny Carey (drums). Justin Chancellor replaced D'Amour in 1995. Also see **A Perfect Circle**.

7/17/93	50	62	▲²	©	1 Undertow...	C:#10/5		$10	Zoo 11052
10/19/96	2¹	104	▲²	©	2 **Aenima**	C:#5/87		$10	Volcano 31087
12/30/00	38	11		©	3 Salival...		[L]	$10	Volcano 31159
6/2/01	❶¹	18↑▲		©	4 **Lateralus**			$10	Volcano 31160
6/2/01	48ᶜ	1	●	©	5 Opiate...		[E]	$10	Volcano 31027

released in 1995

Aenima (2)
Bottom (4)
Cesaro Summability (2)
Cold And Ugly (5)
Crawl Away (1)
Die Eier Von Satan (2)
Disgustipated (1)
Disposition (4)
Eon Blue Apocalypse (4)
Eulogy (2)

Faaip De Oiad (4)
Flood (1)
Forty Six & 2 (2)
4° (1)
Grudge, The (4)
H. (2)
Hooker With A Penis (2)
Hush (5)
Intolerance (1)
(·) Ions (2)

Jerk Off (5)
Jimmy (2)
Lamc (3)
Lateralis (4)
Mantra (4)
Merkaba (3)
Message To Harry Manback (2)
Message To Harry Manback II (3)
No Quarter (3)
Opiate (5)

Parabol (4)
Parabola (4)
Part Of Me (3,5)
Patient, The (4)
Prison Sex (1)
Pushit (2,3)
Reflection (4)
Schism (4) *67*
Sober (1)
Stinkfist (2)

Swamp Song (1)
Sweat (5)
Third Eye (2,3)
Ticks & Leeches (4)
Triad (4)
Undertow (1)
You Lied (3)

★374★ TOO $HORT '96
Born Todd Shaw on 4/28/66 in Los Angeles. Male rapper.

2/25/89	37	78	▲²	©	1 Life Is...Too $hort			$10	Jive 1149
9/29/90	20	53	▲	©	2 Short Dog's In The House			$10	Jive 1348
8/1/92	6	21	▲	©	3 **Shorty The Pimp**			$10	Jive 41467
11/13/93	4	33	▲	©	4 **Get In Where You Fit In**			$10	Jive 41526
2/11/95	6	20	▲	©	5 **Cocktails**			$10	Jive 41553
6/8/96	3	25	▲	©	6 **Gettin' It (Album Number Ten)**			$10	Jive 41584
7/31/99	5	14	●	©	7 Can't Stay Away			$10	Jive 41644

includes "Nation Riders" by Slink Capone, "G-2000" & "Don't Trust Her" by Badwayz, and "In The Studio" by Quint Black

9/30/00	12	9	●	©	8 You Nasty...			$10	Jive 41711

Ain't No Bitches (7)
Ain't Nothin' But A Word To Me (2)
Ain't Nothing Like Pimpin' (5)
All My Bitches Are Gone (4)
All The Time (8)
Anything Is Possible (8)
Baby D (6)
Bad Ways (6)
Be My Dirty Love (8)
Blowjob Betty (4)
Buy You Some (6)
Call Me Daddy (8)
Can I Get A Bitch (5)
Can't Stay Away (7)
City Of Dope (1)
Cocktales (5) *69*

Coming Up $hort (5)
CussWords (1)
Dangerous Crew (4)
Dead Or Alive (2)
Don't Fight The Feelin' (1)
Don't Fuck For Free (5)
Don't Hate The Player (8)
Don't Stop Rappin' (7)
Extra Dangerous Thanks (3)
Fuck My Car (6)
Game (5)
Get In Where You Fit In (4)
Gettin' It (6) *68*
Ghetto, The (2) *42*
Giving Up The Funk (5)
Good Life (7)
Gotta Get Some Lovin' (4)

Hard On The Boulevard (2)
Here We Go (7)
Hoes (3)
Hoochie (3)
How Does It Feel (7)
I Ain't Nothin' But A Dog (3)
I Ain't Trippin' (2)
I Must Confess (6)
I Want To Be Free (That's The Truth) (3)
I've Been Watching You (Move Your Sexy Body) (6)
In The Oaktown (1)
In The Trunk (3)
Invasion Of The Flat Booty Bitches (7) *51*

It Don't Stop (3)
It's All Good (4)
It's Your Life (2)
Just Another Day (4)
Just Like Dope (8)
Life Is...Too $hort (1)
Longevity (7)
Money In The Ghetto (4) *90*
More Freaky Tales (7)
Nasty Rhymes (6)
Nation Riders Anthem (8)
Never Talk Down (6)
No Love From Oakland (3)
Nobody Does It Better (1)
Oakland Style (4)
Old School (8)
Paula & Janet (2)

Paystyle (5)
Pimp Me (6)
Pimp Shit (8)
Pimp The Ho (1)
Pimpology (4)
Playboy $hort (4)
Punk Bitch (2)
Rap Like Me (2)
Recognize Game (8)
Rhymes (1)
Sample The Funk (5)
She Know (8)
Short But Funky (2)
Short Dog's In The House (2)
So Watcha Sayin' (6)
So You Want To Be A Gangster (3)

Something To Ride To (3)
Step Daddy (3)
Survivin' The Game (6)
Take My Bitch (6)
Thangs Change (5)
That's Why (6)
Top Down (5)
2 Bitches (8)
Way Too Real (4)
We Do This (5)
What Happened To The Groupies (7)
Where They At? (8)
You Might Get G'eed (7)
You Nasty (8)

TOOTS & THE MAYTALS '76
Reggae trio from Jamaica: Fred "Toots" Hibbert, Nate Matthias and Henry Gordon.

11/1/75	164	13		©	1 Funky Kingston			$15	Island 9330
7/17/76	157	5		©	2 Reggae Got Soul			$15	Mango 9374

Country Road (1)
Everybody Needs Lovin' (2)
Funky Kingston (1)
Got To Be There (1)

I Shall Sing (2)
In The Dark (1)
Living In The Ghetto (1)
Louie Louie (1)

Love Is Gonna Let Me Down (1)
Never You Change (2)
Pomp And Pride (1)
Premature (2)

Pressure Drop (1)
Rastaman (2)
Reggae Got Soul (2)
Sail On (1)

Six And Seven Books (2)
So Bad (2)
Time Tough (1)
True Love Is Hard To Find (2)

TOP AUTHORITY '95
Rap duo of cousins from Flint, Michigan: Dia Kanyama Peacock and Diallo Sekou Peacock.

11/25/95	144	3		©	1 Rated G			$10	Trak 72668
11/8/97	192	2		©	2 Uncut - The New Yea...			$10	Wrap 8160

Buck Em Down (2)
Channel 12 Newz (1)
Coppers (1)
Dope Game (2)

Down For My Scratch (1)
Dreamin (2)
Flintown G's (1)
Freestyles (1)

Ghetto Is The Trigger (2)
Ghetto Soldier (1)
Haters (2)
It Be Real (1)

Lifestyle Of A "G" (2)
Livin' 2 Die (1)
Murda (1)
National Anthem (1)

Never Know When (2)
Playaz (2)
Smokin' (1)
So High (1)

Strange (2)
Trying So Hard (2)
World War III (2)

TORA TORA '89
Hard-rock group from Memphis: Anthony Corder (vocals), Keith Douglas (guitar), Patrick Francis (bass) and John Patterson (drums).

7/15/89	47	33		©	1 Surprise Attack...			$10	A&M 5261
6/6/92	132	6		©	2 Wild America			$10	A&M 5371

Amnesia (2)
As Time Goes By (2)
Being There (1)
City Of Kings (2)

Cold Fever (2)
Dead Man's Hand (2)
Dirty Secrets (2)
Faith Healer (2)

Guilty (2)
Hard Times (1)
Lay Your Money Down (2)
Love's A Bitch (2)

Nowhere To Go But Down (2)
One For The Road (1)
Phantom Rider (1)
Riverside Drive (1)

Shattered (2)
She's Good She's Bad (1)
28 Days (1)
Walkin' Shoes (1) *86*

Wild America (2)

TORME, Mel '92
Born Melvin Howard on 9/13/25 in Chicago. Died of a stroke on 6/5/99 (age 73). Jazz singer/songwriter/pianist/drummer/actor. Wrote "The Christmas Song." Frequently appeared as himself on TV's *Night Court.* Nicknamed "The Velvet Fog."

12/19/92	170	3		©	Christmas Songs		[X]	$10	Telarc 83315

Christmas Feeling
Christmas Medley
Christmas Song
Christmas Waltz

Christmas Was Made For Children
Christmastime Is Here
Glow Worm
God Rest Ye Merry Gentlemen

Good King Wenceslas
Happy Holiday (medley)
Have Yourself A Merry Little Christmas (medley)
It Happened In Sun Valley

Just Look Around (medley)
Let's Start The New Year Right (medley)
Silver Bells
Sleigh Ride

What Are You Doing New Year's Eve? (medley)
What Child Is This?
White Christmas

TORNADOES, The '63

Instrumental group formed in England: Alan Caddy (lead guitar), George Bellamy (rhythm guitar), Roger Jackson (keyboards), Heinz Burt (bass) and Clem Cattini (drums). Burt died of muscular dystrophy on 4/7/2000 (age 57).

| 1/5/63 | 45 | 17 | | | The Original Telstar | | [I] | $200 | London 3279 |

Breeze And I | Dreamin' On A Cloud | Jungle Fever | Popeye Twist | **Ridin' The Wind** 63 | Swinging Beefeater
Chasing Moonbeams | Earthy | Love And Fury | Red Roses And A Sky Of Blue | Summer Place, Theme From | **Telstar** 1

TORONTO '82

Rock group from Toronto: Holly Woods (vocals), Sheron Alton and Brian Allen (guitars), Scott Kreyer (keyboards) and Jim Fox (drums).

| 8/30/80 | 185 | 4 | | | 1 Lookin' For Trouble | | | $10 | A&M 4821 |
| 9/4/82 | 162 | 10 | | | 2 Get It On Credit | | | $10 | Network 60153 |

Break Down The Barricade (2) | Don't Walk Away (2) | Get Your Hands Off Me (1) | Sick N' Tired (2) | Ya Love Ta Love (2) | **Your Daddy Don't Know**
Delirious (1) | Even The Score (1) | Lookin' For Trouble (1) | Start Tellin' The Truth (2) | You Better Run (1) | (2) 77
Do Watcha; Be Watcha (1) | 5035 (1) | Run For Your Life (2) | Tie Me Down (1) | You're A Mystery To Me (2)
Don't Stop Me (1) | Get It On Credit (2) | Shot Down (1) | Why Can't We Talk? (2)

TORRANCE, Richard, & Eureka '75

Rock group: Richard Torrance (vocals, guitar), Gary Rowles (guitar), Richard Cantu (congas), Duane Scott (keyboards), Jon Lamb (bass) and Dennis Mansfield (drums).

| 3/8/75 | 107 | 17 | | | Belle Of The Ball | | | $12 | Shelter 2134 |

Don't Let Me Down Again | Jam, The | Lazy Town | Side By Each | Southern Belles | That's What I Like In My
Hard Heavy Road | Lady | North Dakota Lady | Singing Springs | Sweet Sweet Rock & Roll | Woman

TORTOISE '01

Punk-rock trio from Chicago: John Herndon (vocals, guitar), Doug McCombs (bass) and John McEntire (drums).

| 3/10/01 | 200 | 1 | | © | Standards | | [I] | $10 | Thrill Jockey 089 |

Benway | Eden 1 | Eros | Monica | Six Pack
Blackjack | Eden 2 | Firefly | Seneca | Speakeasy

TOSH, Peter '83

Born Winston Hubert MacIntosh on 10/9/44 in Jamaica. Fatally shot during a robbery on 9/11/87 (age 42). Former member of **Bob Marley & The Wailers**.

7/31/76	199	2	▲	©	1 Legalize It			$12	Columbia 34253
12/9/78+	104	20		©	2 Bush Doctor			$12	Rolling Stones 39109
8/4/79	123	10			3 Mystic Man			$12	Rolling Stones 39111
7/18/81	91	13		©	4 Wanted Dread & Alive			$10	EMI America 17055
6/18/83	59	17		©	5 Mama Africa			$10	EMI America 17095
9/22/84	152	8		©	6 Captured Live		[L]	$10	EMI America 17126

recorded at the Greek Theatre in Los Angeles

African (6) | Crystal Ball (3) | Glasshouse (5) | Mama Africa (5) | Rastafari Is (4,6) | Wanted Dread & Alive (4)
Brand New Second Hand (1) | Day The Dollar Die (3) | I'm The Toughest (2) | "Moses" - The Prophets (2) | Recruiting Soldiers (3) | Whatcha Gonna Do (1)
Buk-In-Hamm Palace (3) | Dem Ha Fe Get A Beaten (2) | Igziabeher (Let Jah Be Praised) | Mystic Man (3) | Reggae-Mylitis (4) | Where You Gonna Run (5)
Burial (1) | Downpresser Man (medley) (6) | (1) | No Sympathy (1) | Rumours Of War (3) | Why Must I Cry (1)
Bush Doctor (2,6) | Equal Rights (medley) (6) | Jah Seh No (3) | Not Gonna Give It Up (5) | Soon Come (2) | **(You Got To Walk And) Don't**
Can't You See (3) | Feel No Way (5) | Johnny B. Goode (5,6) 84 | Nothing But Love (4) | Stand Firm (2) | **Look Back** (2) 81
Cold Blood (4) | Fight On (3) | Ketchy Shuby (1) | Peace Treaty (5) | Stop That Train (5)
Coming In Hot (4,6) | Fools Die (4) | Legalize It (1) | Pick Myself Up (2) | That's What They Will Do (4)
Creation (2) | Get Up, Stand Up (6) | Maga Dog (5) | Poor Man Feel It (4) | Till Your Well Runs Dry (1)

TOTAL '96

Female R&B vocal trio from New York City: Kima Raynor, Keisha Spivey and Pam Long.

| 3/2/96 | 23 | 27 | ▲ | © | 1 Total | | | $10 | Bad Boy 73006 |
| 11/21/98 | 39 | 30 | ● | © | 2 Kima, Keisha & Pam | | | $10 | Bad Boy 73120 |

Bet She Can't (2) | Don't Ever Change (1) | Love Is All We Need (1) | Rock Track (2) | **What About Us** (2) 16
Can't You See (1) | I Don't Wanna (2) | Most Beautiful... (2) | **Sitting Home** (2) 42 | When Boy Meets Girl (1) 50
Do Something (2) | I Don't Wanna Smile (2) | Move Too Fast (2) | Someone Like You (1)
Do You Know (1) | I Tried (2) | **No One Else** (1) 22 | Spend Some Time (1)
Do You Think About Us? | If You Want Me (2) | Press Rewind (2) | Tell Me (1)
(1) 61 | **Kissin' You** (1) 12 | Rain (2) | **Trippin'** (2) 7

★411★ TOTO '82

Pop-rock group formed in Los Angeles: Bobby Kimball (vocals), Steve Lukather (guitar), David Paich and Steve Porcaro (keyboards), David Hungate (bass) and Jeff Porcaro (drums). Prominent session musicians. Steve and Jeff's brother, Mike Porcaro, replaced Hungate in 1983. Fergie Fredericksen replaced Kimball in early 1984. Joseph Williams (son of composer **John Williams**) replaced Fredericksen in early 1986. Jean-Michel Byron replaced Williams in 1990. Jeff Porcaro died of a heart attack on 8/5/92 (age 38).

10/21/78+	9	48	▲²	©	1 Toto	C:#3/42		$12	Columbia 35317
11/17/79	37	29	●	©	2 Hydra	C:#24/22		$12	Columbia 36229
2/7/81	41	10		©	3 Turn Back			$12	Columbia 36813
4/24/82	4	82	▲³	©	4 Toto IV			$10	Columbia 37728

1982 Grammy winner: Album of the Year

11/24/84	42	21	●	©	5 Isolation			$10	Columbia 38962
12/22/84+	168	8		©	6 Dune		[I-S]	$10	Polydor 823770
9/13/86	40	36	●	©	7 Fahrenheit			$10	Columbia 40273
3/19/88	64	18		©	8 The Seventh One			$10	Columbia 40873
9/22/90	153	4	▲	©	9 Past To Present 1977-1990		[G]	$10	Columbia 45368

Afraid Of Love (4) | Carmen (5) | Floating Fat Man (The Baron) | I Think I Could Stand You | Live For Today (3) | Out Of Love (9)
Africa (4,9) 1 | Change Of Heart (5) | (6) | Forever (3) | Lorraine (2) | **Pamela** (8,9) 22
All Us Boys (2) | Child's Anthem (1) | **Georgy Porgy** (1,9) 48 | **I Won't Hold You Back** | Love Has The Power (9) | Paul Kills Feyd (6)
Angel Don't Cry (5) | Could This Be Love (7) | Gift With A Golden Gun (3) | (4,9) 10 | Lovers In The Night (4) | Paul Meets Chani (6)
Angela (1) | Don't Stop Me Now (7) | Girl Goodbye (1) | **I'll Be Over You** (7,9) 11 | **Make Believe** (4) 30 | Paul Takes The Water Of Life
Animal (9) | Dune (Desert Theme) (6) | Good For You (4) | **I'll Supply The Love** (1) 45 | Mama (2) | (6)
Anna (8) | Dune, Main Title (6) | Goodbye Elenore (3) | If It's The Last Night (3) | Manuela Run (1) | Prophecy Theme (6)
Big Battle (6) | Endless (5) | **Hold The Line** (1,9) 5 | Isolation (5) | Million Miles Away (3) | Robot Fight (6)
Box, The (6) | English Eyes (3) | **Holyanna** (5) 71 | It's A Feeling (4) | Mr. Friendly (5) | Rockmaker (1)
Can You Hear What I'm Saying | Fahrenheit (7) | Home Of The Brave (8) | Lea (7) | Mushanga (8) | **Rosanna** (4,9) 2
(9) | Final Dream (6) | How Does It Feel (5) | Leto's Theme (6) | **99** (2,9) 26 | Secret Love (2)
Can't Stand It Any Longer (7) | First Attack (6) | Hydra (2) | Lion (5) | Only The Children (8) | Somewhere Tonight (7)

TOTO — Cont'd

St. George And The Dragon (2)	Stranger In Town (5) *30*	Thousand Years (8)	Waiting For Your Love (4) *73*	Without Your Love (7) *38*	
Stay Away (8)	Take My Hand (6)	Till The End (7)	We Can Make It Tonight (7)	You Are The Flower (1)	
Stop Loving You (8,9)	Takin' It Back (1)	Trip To Arrakis (6)	We Made It (4)	You Got Me (8)	
Straight For The Heart (8)	These Chains (8)	Turn Back (3)	White Sister (2)		

TOUCH, Tony   '00
Born Joseph Anthony Hernandez in 1970 in Brooklyn, New York. Male rapper.

| 5/6/00 | 57 | 9 | © | **The Piece Maker** .... | $10 | Tommy Boy 1347 |

includes "Get Back" by D-12

Abduction, The	Foundation, The	No, No, No	Return Of The Diaz Bros.	What's That? (¿Que Eso?)
Basics	I Wonder Why? (He's The	P.R. All-Stars	Set It On Fire	
Class Of '87	Greatest DJ)	Piece Maker	U Know The Rules (Mi Vida	
Club, The	Likwit Rhyming	Pit Fight	Loca)	

TOUPS, Wayne, & Zydecajun   '89
Rock group from New Orleans: Wayne Toups (vocals, accordian), Wade Richard (guitar), Rick Lagneaux (keyboards), Mark Miller (bass) and Troy Gaspard (drums).

| 3/18/89 | 183 | 4 | © | **Blast From The Bayou** .... | $10 | Mercury 836518 |

Going Back To Big Mamou	Let's Fall In Love (All Over	Secret Love	Sweet Joline	Tupelo Honey	Zydecajun Train
Johnnie Can't Dance	Again)	Sugar Bee	Tell It Like It Is	Two-Step Mamou	

★409★ TOWER OF POWER   '73
Funk group from Oakland: **Lenny Williams** (vocals), Willie Fulton (guitar), Greg Adams, Mic Gillette, Steve Kupka, Emilio Castillo and Lenny Pickett (horns). Chester Thompson (keyboards), Francis Prestia (bass) and David Garibaldi (drums).
1)Tower Of Power 2)Urban Renewal 3)Back To Oakland

4/10/71+	106	12	©	1	**East Bay Grease**	$50	San Francisco 204
6/17/72	85	20	©	2	**Bump City**	$15	Warner 2616
6/2/73	15	31	● ©	3	**Tower Of Power**	$15	Warner 2681
3/9/74	26	35	©	4	**Back To Oakland**	$15	Warner 2749
1/25/75	22	16	©	5	**Urban Renewal**	$15	Warner 2834
10/11/75	67	11	©	6	**In The Slot**	$15	Warner 2880
5/22/76	99	8	©	7	**Live And In Living Color**	[L] $15	Warner 2924
9/11/76	42	17	©	8	**Ain't Nothin' Stoppin' Us Now**	$12	Columbia 34302
4/22/78	89	8	©	9	**We Came To Play!**	$12	Columbia 34906
8/11/79	106	12	©	10	**Back On The Streets**	$12	Columbia 35784

Ain't Nothin' Stoppin' Us Now (8)	Come Back, Baby (5)	I Got The Chop (4)	Love's Been Gone So Long (4)	**So Very Hard To Go** (3) *17*	What Is Hip? (3,7) *91*
Am I A Fool (9)	Deal With It (8)	I Won't Leave Unless You Want	Lovin' You Is Gonna See Me	Social Lubrication (1)	While We Went To The Moon (8)
And You Know It (10)	Doin' Alright (8)	Me To (5)	Thru (9)	Something Calls Me (10)	Will I Ever Find A Love? (3)
As Surely As I Stand Here (5)	**Don't Change Horses (In The**	If I Play My Cards Right (6)	Make Someone Happy (8)	Somewhere Down The Road (9)	Willing To Learn (5)
Because I Think The World Of	**Middle Of A Stream)** (4) *26*	In Due Time (10)	Man From The Past (4)	Soul Of A Child (6)	Yin-Yang Thang (9)
You (8)	Down To The Nightclub	It Can Never Be The Same (5)	Maybe It'll Rub Off (5)	Soul Vaccination (3)	You Got To Funkifize (2)
Below Us, All The City Lights (4)	(2,7) *66*	It Takes Two (To Make It	Nowhere To Run (5)	Sparkling In The Sand (1,7)	**You Ought To Be Havin' Fun** (8) *68*
Bittersweet Soul Music (9)	Drop It In The Slot (6)	Happen) (10)	Oakland Stroke (4)	Squib Cakes (4)	You Strike My Main Nerve (2)
Both Sorry Over Nothin' (3)	Ebony Jam (6)	It's Not The Crime (5)	Of The Earth (2)	**This Time It's Real** (3) *65*	You're So Wonderful, So
By Your Side (8)	Essence Of Innocence (6)	It's So Nice (8)	On The Serious Side (6)	**Time Will Tell** (4) *69*	Marvelous (8)
Can't Stand To See The	Fanfare: Mantanuska (6)	Just Another Day (3)	Only So Much Oil In The	(To Say The Least) You're The	**You're Still A Young Man** (2,7) *29*
Slaughter (8)	Flash In The Pan (2)	Just Enough And Too Much (4)	Ground (5)	Most (5)	
Can't You See (You Doin' Me	Get Yo' Feet Back On The	Just Make A Move (And Be	Our Love (10)	Treat Me Like Your Man (6)	
Wrong) (4)	Ground (3)	Yourself) (10)	Price, The (1)	Vuela Por Noche (6)	
Clean Slate (3)	Give Me The Proof (5)	Just When We Start Makin' It	Rock Baby (10)	Walkin' Up Hip Street (5)	
Clever Girl (3)	Gone (2)	(4)	Share My Life (9)	We Came To Play (9)	
	Heaven Must Have Made You (10)	Knock Yourself Out (1,7)	Skating On Thin Ice (2)	What Happened To The World That Day? (1)	
	I Believe In Myself (5)	Let Me Touch You (9)	Skunk, The Goose, And The Fly (1)		
		Love Bug (9)			

★444★ TOWNSHEND, Pete   '80
Born on 5/19/45 in London. Rock singer/songwriter/guitarist. Member of **The Who**. Brother of **Simon Townshend**.
1)Empty Glass 2)White City - A Novel 3)All The Best Cowboys Have Chinese Eyes

| 11/18/72+ | 69 | 17 | © | 1 | **Who Came First** .... | $25 | Track 79189 |
| 10/15/77 | 45 | 12 | © | 2 | **Rough Mix** .... | $15 | MCA 2295 |

PETE TOWNSHEND/RONNIE LANE

5/17/80	5	30	▲ ©	3	**Empty Glass**	$12	Atco 100
7/10/82	26	26	©	4	**All The Best Cowboys Have Chinese Eyes**	$12	Atco 149
3/26/83	35	13	©	5	**Scoop**	[K] $15	Atco 90063 [2]
11/30/85+	26	29	● ©	6	**White City - A Novel**	$10	Atco 90473
10/25/86	98	9	©	7	**Pete Townshend's Deep End Live!**	[L] $10	Atco 90553
4/4/87	198	1	©	8	**Another Scoop**	[K] $15	Atco 90539 [2]
7/15/89	58	13	©	9	**The Iron Man: The Musical By Pete Townshend**	$10	Atlantic 81996

includes "Over The Top" and "I Eat Heavy Metal" by **John Lee Hooker**, "Man Machines" by **Simon Townshend**, "Dig" and "Fire" by **The Who** and "Fast Food" by **Nina Simone**

| 7/3/93 | 118 | 2 | © | 10 | **Psychoderelict** .... | $10 | Atlantic 82494 |

After The Fire (7)	Call Me Lightning (8)	Empty Glass (3)	Goin' Fishin' (5)	Keep On Working (3)	New Life (9)
All Shall Be Well (9)	Cat Snatch (8)	English Boy (10)	Gonna Get Ya (3)	Kids Are Alright (8)	North Country Girl (5)
And I Moved (3)	Cat's In The Cupboard (3)	Evolution (5)	Happy Jack (8)	La-La-La-Lies (8)	Nothing Is Everything (Let's See
Annie (2)	Catmelody (2)	Exquisitely Bored (4)	Heart To Hang On To (2)	**Let My Love Open The Door** (3) *9*	Action) (1)
April Fool (2)	Christmas (8)	Eyesight To The Blind (7)	Hiding Out (6)	Let's Get Pretentious (10)	Now And Then (10)
Ask Yourself (8)	Circles (8)	Face Dances Part Two (4)	Holly Like Ivy (8)	**Little Is Enough** (3,7) *72*	Nowhere To Run (2)
Baba O'Riley (8)	Come To Mama (6)	**Face The Face** (6) *26*	I Am Afraid (10)	Long Live Rock (3)	Outlive The Dinosaur (10)
Barefootin' (7)	Communication (4)	Fake It (10)	I Am An Animal (3)	Love Reign O'er Me (8)	Parvardigar (1)
Bargain (5)	Content (1)	Ferryman, The (8)	I Am Secure (6)	Magic Bus (5)	Pictures Of Lily (8)
Baroque Ippanese (8)	Cookin' (5)	Flame (3)	I Put A Spell On You (7)	Mary (5)	Pinball Wizard (7,8)
Begin The Beguine (8)	Crashing By Design (6)	Fool Says... (9)	I Want That Thing (10)	Meher Baba M3, M4, & M5 (10)	Politician (5)
Behind Blue Eyes (5,7)	Dirty Water (5)	Football Fugue (6)	I Won't Run Any More (9)	Melancholia (5)	Popular (5)
Body Language (5)	Don't Let Go The Coat (8)	Forever's No Time At All (1)	I'm One (7)	Misunderstood (2)	Praying The Game (8)
Brilliant Blues (6)	Don't Try To Make Me Real (10)	Friend Is A Friend (9)	Initial Machine Experiments (5)	My Baby Gives It Away (2)	Predictable (10)
Brooklyn Kids (8)	Driftin' Blues (9)	Girl In A Suitcase (8)	Jools And Jim (3)	Never Ask Me (8)	Prelude (4)
Cache, Cache (5)	Early Morning Dreams (10)	Give Blood (6)	Keep Me Turning (2)		Prelude #556 (8)

TOWNSHEND, Pete — Cont'd

Prelude, The Right To Write (8)	Save It For Later (7)	So Sad About Us/Brrr (8)	Substitute (8)	Tipperary (5)	You Better You Bet (8)
Pure And Easy (1)	Sea Refuses No River (4)	Somebody Saved Me (4)	There's A Heartache Followin'	To Barney Kessell (5)	You Came Back (5)
Quadrophenia (5)	Secondhand Love (6)	Squeezebox (5)	Me (1)	Uniforms (5)	You're So Clever (5)
Recorders (5)	Sheraton Gibson (1)	Stardom In Acton (4)	Things Have Changed (5)	Vicious Interlude (8)	Zelda (5)
Rough Boys (3) *89*	Shout, The (8)	Stop Hurting People (4,7)	Till The Rivers All Run Dry (2)	Was There Life (9)	
Rough Mix (2)	Slit Skirts (4)	Street In The City (2)	Time Is Passing (1)	White City Fighting (6)	

TOWNSHEND, Simon   '84
Born in 1963 in London. Brother of **Pete Townshend**.

12/3/83+	**169**	7			Sweet Sound..			$10	21 Records 815708

produced by **Pete Townshend**

...And More With You	Heart Stops	Mr. Sunday	Palace In The Air	Sweet Sound
Freakers	I'm The Answer	On The Scaffolding	So Real	

TOY MATINEE   '91
Pop group duo formed in Los Angeles: Kevin Gilbert (vocals) and Patrick Leonard (instruments). Gilbert formed a songwriting partnership with **Sheryl Crow**; died of accidental asphyxiation on 5/18/96 (age 29). Leonard did much songwriting and production work for **Madonna**.

1/26/91	**129**	8	©	Toy Matinee..	$10	Reprise 26235

Ballad Of Jenny Ledge	Queen Of Misery	There Was A Little Boy	Toy Matinee	We Always Come Home
Last Plane Out	Remember My Name	Things She Said	Turn It On Salvador	

TOYS, The   '66
Female vocal trio from Queens, New York: Barbara Harris, June Montiero and Barbara Parritt.

2/5/66	**92**	8		The Toys sing "A Lover's Concerto" and "Attack!"....................	$50	DynoVoice 9002

Attack *18*	Back Street	Deserted	I Got A Man	See How They Run	What's Wrong With Me Baby
Baby's Gone	Can't Get Enough Of You Baby	Hallelujah	**Lover's Concerto** *2*	This Night	Yesterday

T'PAU   '87
Pop-rock group from Shrewsbury, England: Carol Decker (vocals), Dean Howard (guitar), Mick Chetwood (keyboards), Paul Jackson (bass) and Tim Burgess (drums). Group named after a Vulcan Princess in an episode of the TV series *Star Trek*.

6/6/87	**31**	24	©	T'Pau..	$10	Virgin 90595

Bridge Of Spies	Friends Like These	I Will Be With You	Sex Talk	Valentine
China In Your Hand	**Heart And Soul** *4*	Monkey House	Thank You For Goodbye	You Give Up

TQ   '98
Born Terrance Quaites in Mobile, Alabama; raised in Los Angeles. R&B singer/songwriter.

11/28/98	**122**	10	©	They Never Saw Me Coming..	$10	ClockWork 69431

Better Days	Darlin' Mary	If The World Was Mine	RememberMelinda	When I Get Out
Bye Bye Baby	Gotta Make That Money	One More Lick	They Never Saw Me Coming	Your Sister
Comeback, The	I Get Around	Paradise	**Westside** *12*	

TRACTORS, The   '95
Country-rock group formed in Tulsa, Oklahoma: Casey Van Beek (vocals), Steve Ripley (guitar), Walt Richmond (keyboards), Ron Getman (bass) and Jamie Oldaker (drums).

9/17/94+	**19**	46	▲² ©	1	The Tractors..			$10	Arista 18728
12/2/95	**68**	7	©	2	Have Yourself A Tractors Christmas...................................	C:#40/1	[X]	$10	Arista 18805

Christmas chart: 15/95

Baby Likes To Rock It (1)	Doreen (1)	Rockin' This Christmas (2)	Santa Claus Is Comin' To Town	Shelter, The (2)	Tryin' To Get To New Orleans
Baby Wanna Be My Love (2)	Fallin' Apart (1)	**Santa Claus Boogie** (2) *91*	(2)	Silent Night, Christmas Blue (2)	(1)
Badly Bent (1)	I've Had Enough (1)	Santa Claus Comin' (In A	Santa Looked A Lot Like Daddy	Swingin' Home For Christmas	Tulsa Shuffle (1)
Blue Collar Rock (1)	Jingle My Bells (2)	Boogie Woogie Choo Choo	(2)	(2)	White Christmas (2)
Christmas Is Comin' (2)	Little Man (1)	Train) (2)	Settin' The Woods On Fire (1)	Thirty Days (1)	

★269★   TRAFFIC   '70
Rock group formed in England. Original lineup: **Steve Winwood** (keyboards, guitar), **Dave Mason** (guitar), **Jim Capaldi** (drums) and Chris Wood (flute, sax; died on 7/12/83). Varying personnel also included bassists **Rick Grech**, David Hood and Roscoe Gee, percussionist Reebop Kwaku Baah, and drummers Jim Gordon and Roger Hawkins; disbanded in 1974. Winwood and Capaldi reunited in 1994.

1)John Barleycorn Must Die 2)Shoot Out At The Fantasy Factory 3)The Low Spark Of High Heeled Boys

4/27/68	**88**	22	©	1	Mr. Fantasy...			$30	United Artists 6651
11/30/68+	**17**	26	©	2	Traffic..			$25	United Artists 6676
5/17/69	**19**	22	©	3	Last Exit...			$25	United Artists 6702
1/3/70	**48**	14	©	4	Best Of Traffic..		[G]	$25	United Artists 5500
7/11/70	**5**	38	●	5	John Barleycorn Must Die			$25	United Artists 5504
10/2/71	**26**	19	©	6	Welcome To The Canteen..		[L]	$25	United Artists 5550
					TRAFFIC, ETC.				
12/11/71+	**7**	30	▲ ©	7	The Low Spark Of High Heeled Boys	C:#24/27		$20	Island 9306
2/3/73	**6**	29	● ©	8	Shoot Out At The Fantasy Factory			$20	Island 9323
11/3/73	**29**	24	©	9	Traffic-On The Road..		[L]	$25	Island 9336 [2]
9/28/74	**9**	27	●	10	When The Eagle Flies			$15	Asylum 1020
5/3/75	**155**	3		11	Heavy Traffic..		[G]	$15	United Artists 421
9/27/75	**193**	4		12	More Heavy Traffic		[G]	$15	United Artists 526
5/21/94	**33**	9	©	13	Far From Home...			$10	Virgin 39490

Berkshire Poppies (1)	Feelin' Good (3)	House For Everyone (1)	No Face, No Name And No	Shoot Out At The Fantasy	Tragic Magic (8,9)
Blind Man (3)	Forty Thousand Headmen	John Barleycorn (5,12)	Number (1,4,12)	Factory (8,9)	Vagabond Virgin (2,12)
Coloured Rain (1,4,11)	(2,4,6,11)	Just For You (3)	No Time To Live (2)	Shouldn't Have Took More	Walking In The Wind (10)
Cryin' To Be Heard (2,12)	Freedom Rider (5,9)	Light Up Or Leave Me Alone	Nowhere Is Their Freedom (2)	Than You Gave (6)	We're A Fade, You Missed This
Dealer (1)	**Gimme Some Lovin'-Pt. 1**	(7,9)	**Paper Sun** (1,4,11) *94*	Smiling Phases (1,11)	(1)
Dear Mr. Fantasy (1,4,6,11)	(6,12) *68*	Love (10)	Pearly Queen (2,12)	Some Kinda Woman (13)	When The Eagle Flies (10)
Don't Be Sad (2)	Giving To You (1)	Low Spark Of High Heeled	Rainmaker (7)	Something New (10)	Who Knows What Tomorrow
Dream Gerrard (10)	Glad (5,9)	Boys (7,9)	Riding High (13)	Something's Got A Hold Of My	May Bring (2,12)
Empty Pages (5,11) *74*	Graveyard People (10)	Many A Mile To Freedom (7)	**Rock & Roll Stew...Part 1**	Toe (3)	Withering Tree (3)
Evening Blue (8)	Heaven Is In Your Mind (1,4,11)	Means To An End (2,12)	(7) *93*	(Sometimes I Feel So)	You Can All Join In (2,4,12)
Every Mother's Son (3)	Here Comes A Man (13)	Medicated Goo (3,4,6,11)	Roll Right Stones (8)	Uninspired (8,9)	
Every Night, Every Day (13)	Hidden Treasure (3)	Memories Of A Rock N' Roller	Sad And Deep As You (6)	State Of Grace (13)	
Far From Home (13)	Hole In My Shoe (1,4,12)	(10)	Shanghai Noodle Factory	Stranger To Himself (5)	
Feelin' Alright? (2,4,11)	Holy Ground (13)	Mozambique (13)	(3,4,11)	This Train Won't Stop (13)	

TRAGICALLY HIP, The   '90

Rock group from Kingston, Ontario, Canada: Gordon Downie (vocals), Bobby Baker and Paul Langlois (guitars), Gord Sinclair (bass) and Johnny Fay (drums).

5/12/90	170	6	©	1 **Up To Here**	$10	MCA 6310
6/1/96	134	1	©	2 **Trouble At The Henhouse**	$10	Atlantic 82899
8/1/98	143	1	©	3 **Phantom Power**	$10	Sire 31025
7/1/00	139	1	©	4 **Music @ Work**	$10	Sire 31135

Ahead By A Century (2)
Another Midnight (1)
Apartment Song (3)
As I Wind Down The Pines (4)
Bastard, The (4)
Bear, The (4)
Blow At High Dough (1)
Bobcaygeon (3)
Boots Or Hearts (1)

Butts Wigglin (2)
Chagrin Falls (3)
Coconut Cream (2)
Completists, The (4)
Don't Wake Daddy (2)
Emperor Penguin (3)
Escape Is At Hand For The Travellin' Man (3)
Everytime You Go (1)

Fireworks (3)
Flamenco (2)
Freak Turbulence (4)
Gift Shop (2)
I'll Believe In You (Or I'll Be Leaving You Tonight) (1)
Lake Fever (4)
Lets Stay Engaged (2)
Membership (3)

My Music At Work (4)
New Orleans Is Sinking (1)
Opiated (1)
Poets (3)
Put It Off (2)
Putting Down (4)
Rules, The (3)
Save The Planet (3)
700 Ft. Ceiling (2)

Sharks (4)
She Didn't Know (1)
Sherpa (2)
Something On (3)
Springtime In Vienna (2)
Stay (4)
38 Years Old (1)
Thompson Girl (3)
Tiger The Lion (4)

Toronto #4 (4)
Train Overnight (4)
Trickle Down (1)
Vapour Trails (3)
When The Weight Comes Down (1)
Wild Mountain Honey (4)

TRAIN   '01

Rock group from San Francisco: Patrick Monahan (vocals), Rob Hotchkiss and Jimmy Stafford (guitars), Charlie Colin (bass) and Scott Underwood (drums).

| 7/10/99 | 76 | 32 | ▲ | © | 1 **Train** ....C:#6/18 | $10 | Aware 38052 |
| 4/14/01 | 6 | 25↑ | ▲ | © | 2 **Drops Of Jupiter** | $10 | Aware 69888 |

Blind (1)
Days (1)
Drops Of Jupiter (Tell Me) (2) *5*

Eggplant (1)
Free (1)
Getaway (2)
Homesick (1)

Hopeless (2)
I Am (1)
I Wish You Would (1)
Idaho (1)

If You Leave (1)
It's About You (2)
Let It Roll (2)
Meet Virginia (1) *20*

Mississippi (2)
Rat (1)
Respect (2)
She's On Fire (2)

Something More (2)
Swaying (1)
Whipping Boy (2)

TRAMMPS, The   '77

Disco vocal group from Philadelphia: Jimmy Ellis, Earl Young, Harold Wade, Stanley Wade and Robert Upchurch.

7/5/75	159	4			1 **Trammps**	$15	Golden Fleece 33163
5/15/76	50	24			2 **Where The Happy People Go**	$12	Atlantic 18172
1/22/77	46	49	●	©	3 **Disco Inferno**	$12	Atlantic 18211
12/17/77+	85	13			4 **The Trammps III**	$12	Atlantic 19148
9/9/78	139	6			5 **The Best Of The Trammps** .... [G]	$12	Atlantic 19194
5/26/79	184	2			6 **The Whole World's Dancing**	$12	Atlantic 19210

Body Contact Contract (3,5)
Can We Come Together (2)
Disco Inferno (3,5) *11*
Disco Party (2,5)
Don't Burn No Bridges (3)
Down Three Dark Streets (1)
Every Dream I Dream Is You (1)
Hooked For Life (2,5)

I Feel Like I've Been Livin' (On The Dark Side Of The Moon) (3,5)
I Know That Feeling (1)
I'm So Glad You Came Along (4)
It Don't Take Much (4)
Life Ain't Been Easy (4)
Living The Life (4)
Love Epidemic (1)

Love Insurance Policy (6)
Love Is A Funky Thing (2)
Love Magnet (3)
Love Per Hour (4)
More Good Times To Remember (6)
My Love, It's Never Been Better (6)
Night The Lights Went Out (4,5)
Ninety-Nine And A Half (2)

People Of The World, Rise (4)
Save A Place (1)
Seasons For Girls (4,5)
Shout (1)
Soul Bones (6)
Soul Searchin' Time (2,5)
Starvin' (3)
Stop And Think (1)
Teaser (6)

That's Where The Happy People Go (2,5) *27*
Trammps Disco Theme (1)
Trusting Heart (1)
Where Do We Go From Here (1)
Whole World's Dancing (6)
You Touch My Hot Line (3)

TRANS-SIBERIAN ORCHESTRA   '97

Studio orchestra assembled by producer Paul O'Neill.

12/28/96+	89	3	●	©	1 **Christmas Eve And Other Stories** ....C:#3/23 [X]	$10	Lava 92736
					Christmas charts: 15/'96, 6/'97, 11/'98, 10/'99, 10/'00		
12/12/98	103	5		©	2 **The Christmas Attic** ....C:#16/7 [X]	$10	Lava 83145
					Christmas charts: 9/'98, 26/'99, 24/'00		
4/29/00	165	1		©	3 **Beethoven's Last Night**	$10	Lava 83319

After The Fall (3)
Angel Came Down (1)
Angel Returned (1)
Angel's Share (2)
Angels We Have Heard On High (medley) (3)
Appalachian Snowfall (2)
Beethoven (3)
Boughs Of Holly (2)
Christmas Canon (2)
Christmas Eve (medley) (1)

Christmas In The Air (2)
Dark, The (3)
Dream Child (A Christmas Dream) (2)
Dreams Of Candlelight (3)
Fate (3)
Final Dream (3)
Find Our Way Home (3)
First Noel (1)
First Snow (1)

Fur Elise (3)
Ghosts Of Christmas Eve (2)
God Rest Ye Merry Gentlemen (1)
Good King Joy (1)
Hark The Herald Angel (medley) (2)
I'll Keep Your Secrets (3)
Joy (medley) (2)
Last Illusion (3)
Mad Russian's Christmas (1)

March Of The Kings (medley) (2)
Mephistopheles (3)
Mephistopheles' Return (3)
Midnight (3)
Midnight Christmas Eve (2)
Misery (3)
Moment, The (3)
Mozart/Figaro (3)
Music Box (3)
Music Box Blues (2)

O Come All Ye Faithful (Instrumental) (medley) (1)
O Holy Night (Instrumental) (1)
Old City Bar (1)
Ornament (1)
Prince Of Peace (1)
Promises To Keep (1)
Requiem (The Fifth) (3)
Sarajevo (Instrumental) (medley) (1)
Silent Nutcracker (1)

Snow Came Down (2)
Star To Follow (1)
This Christmas Day (1)
This Is Who You Are (3)
Three Kings And I (What Really Happened) (2)
Vienna (1)
What Good This Deafness (3)
What Is Eternal (3)
Who Is This Child (3)
World That She Sees (2)

TRANSVISION VAMP   '88

Pop-rock group from England: Wendy James (vocals), Nick Sayer (guitar), Tex Axile (keyboards), Dave Parsons (bass) and Pol Burton (drums).

| 9/24/88 | 115 | 8 | © | **Pop Art** .... | $10 | Uni 5 |

Andy Warhol's Dead
Hanging Out With Halo Jones

I Want Your Love
Psychosonic Cindy

Revolution Baby
Sex Kick

Sister Moon
Tell That Girl To Shut Up *87*

Trash City
Wild Star

TRAPEZE   '75

Rock group from Wolverhampton, England: Glenn Hughes (vocals, bass; **Deep Purple**), Mel Galley (guitar) and Dave Holland (drums). Hughes left after first album, replaced by Pete Wright. Rob Kendrick (guitar) also joined after first album.

| 11/2/74 | 172 | 6 | | 1 **The Final Swing** .... [E-K] | $30 | Threshold 11 |
| 1/4/75 | 146 | 6 | © | 2 **Hot Wire** .... | $15 | Warner 2828 |

Back Street Love (2)
Black Cloud (1)
Coast To Coast (1)

Dat's It (1)
Feel It Inside (2)
Goin' Alone (1)

Good Love (1)
Medusa (1)
Midnight Flyer (2)

Send Me No More Letters (1)
Steal A Mile (2)
Take It On Down The Road (2)

Turn It On (2)
Wake Up, Shake Up (2)
Will Our Love End (1)

You Are The Music (1)
Your Love Is Alright (1)

TRAPP   '97

Born John Parker in Atlanta. Male rapper/producer.

| 5/10/97 | 123 | 5 | © | **Stop The Gunfight** .... | $10 | Deff Trapp 9268 |

Be The Realist
Brick House
Can I Get Your Number

Don't Drink And Drive
5th Ward
History

Monkey See Monkey Do
Recognize
Standtall

Stone Jam
Stop The Gunfight *77*
Swing That Axx

When I Come Down

TRASH CAN SINATRAS, The '91

Pop-rock group from Irvine, Scotland: brothers John (guitar) and Stephen (drums) Douglas, Frank Reader (vocals), Paul Livingston (guitar) and George McDaid (bass).

| 2/2/91 | 131 | 13 | © | | Cake... | | | $10 | Go! Discs 828201 |

Best Man's Fall — Even The Odd — January's Little Joke — Obscurity Knocks — Thrupenny Tears
Circling The Circumference — Funny — Maybe I Should Drive — Only Tongue Can Tell — You Made Me Feel

TRASHMEN, The '64

Garage-rock group from Minneapolis: Tony Andreason, Dal Winslow and Bob Reed (guitars), with Steve Wahrer (drums). Wahrer died of cancer on 1/21/89 (age 47).

| 2/15/64 | 48 | 15 | © | | Surfin' Bird... | | | $300 | Garrett 200 |

Bird Bath — It's So Easy — Kuk — Misirlou — My Woodie — **Surfin' Bird** 4
Henrietta — King Of The Surf — Malaguena — Money — Sleeper, The — Tube City

TRAVELING WILBURYS '89

Supergroup masquerading as a band of brothers. Spearheaded by Nelson (**George Harrison**), with Lucky (**Bob Dylan**), Otis (**Jeff Lynne** of **ELO**), Lefty (**Roy Orbison**) and Charlie (**Tom Petty**) Wilbury. Orbison died on 12/6/88 (age 52). For their second album, Vol. 3, the names have changed to Spike (Harrison), Muddy (Petty), Clayton (Lynne) and Boo (Dylan).

| 11/12/88+ | 3 | 53 | ▲3 | © | 1 | Volume One | | | $10 | Wilbury 25796 |
| 11/17/90 | 11 | 22 | ▲ | © | 2 | Vol. 3 | | | $10 | Wilbury 26324 |

Congratulations (1) — Handle With Care (1) 45 — Margarita (1) — 7 Deadly Sins (2) — Where Were You Last Night?
Cool Dry Place (2) — Heading For The Light (1) — New Blue Moon (2) — She's My Baby (2) — (2)
Devil's Been Busy (2) — If You Belonged To Me (2) — Not Alone Any More (1) — Tweeter And The Monkey Man — Wilbury Twist (2)
Dirty World (1) — Inside Out (2) — Poor House (2) — (1) — You Took My Breath Away (2)
End Of The Line (1) 63 — Last Night (1) — Rattled (1)

TRAVERS, Mary '71

Born on 11/7/37 in Louisville. Folk singer. Member of **Peter, Paul & Mary**.

4/17/71	71	29			1	Mary			$15	Warner 1907
4/29/72	157	5			2	Morning Glory			$15	Warner 2609
2/24/73	169	6			3	All My Choices			$15	Warner 2677
7/20/74	200	1			4	Circles			$15	Warner 2795
3/11/78	186	5			5	It's In Everyone Of Us			$12	Chrysalis 1168

Air That I Breathe (5) — Eye Of The Day (5) — I Am Your Child (4) — It's In Everyone Of Us (5) — Running (2) — That's Enough For Me (2)
All My Choices (3) — First Time Ever I Saw Your — I Guess He'd Rather Be In — Light Of Day (4) — Scarlet And The Grey (2) — Too Many Mondays (3)
Catch The Rain (4) — Face (1) — Colorado (1) — Man Song (2) — Simple Song (4) — When I Need You Most Of All
Children One And All (1) — Five Hundred Miles (3) — I Wish I Knew How It Would — Morning Glory (2) — Single Wing (5) — (2)
Circles (4) — Follow Me (1) 56 — Feel To Be Free (1) — My Love And I (2) — So Close (4) — Will We Ever Find Our Fathers
Circus (1) — Goin' Back (4) — I'll Have To Say I Love You In A — Oh, What A Feeling (3) — Song For The Asking (1) — (5)
Conscientious Objector (I Shall — Good News (For The Lady) (5) — Song (4) — On The Path Of Glory (La — Song Is Love (1) — You Turn Me Around (5)
Die) (2) — Goodbye Again (3) — If I'm Lucky (3) — Colline Au Whisky) (1) — Song Of Peace (Finlandia) (2)
Doctor My Eyes (3) — Half Of It (3) — Indian Sunset (1) — Part Of The Plan (5) — Southbound Train (3)
Erika With The Windy Yellow — Home Is Where The Hurt Is (5) — Is It Really Love At All? (4) — Rest Of The Year (2) — That Year There Was No
Hair (1) — House At Pooh Corner (4) — It Will Come To You Again (2) — Rhymes And Reasons (1) — Winter (3)

TRAVERS, Pat '80

Born on 4/12/54 in Toronto. Hard-rock singer/guitarist.

12/17/77+	70	22			1	Putting It Straight			$12	Polydor 6121
10/21/78	99	16			2	Heat In The Street			$12	Polydor 6170
7/21/79	29	22		©	3	Pat Travers Band Live! Go For What You Know		[L]	$12	Polydor 6202
4/5/80	20	25		©	4	Crash And Burn			$12	Polydor 6262

PAT TRAVERS BAND (above 2)

3/28/81	37	15			5	Radio Active			$12	Polydor 6313
11/6/82	74	13			6	Pat Travers' Black Pearl			$12	Polydor 6361
5/5/84	108	8			7	Hot Shot			$10	Polydor 821064

Amgwanna Kick Booty (6) — Feelin' In Love (5) — (I Just Wanna) Live It My Way — Killer's Instinct (2) — Night Into Day (7) — Stevie (3)
Big Event (4) — Fifth, The (6) — (5) — Life In London (1) — Off Beat Ride (1) — Tonight (7)
Boom Boom (Out Go The — Gettin' Betta (1,3) — I La La La Love You (6) — Louise (7) — One For Me And One For You — Untitled (5)
Lights) (3) 56 — Go All Night (2,3) — I Tried To Believe (2) — Love Will Make You Strong (4) — (2) — Who'll Take The Fall (6)
Born Under A Bad Sign (4) — Hammerhead (2) — I'd Rather See You Dead (6) — Lovin' You (1) — Play It Like You See It (5) — Women On The Edge Of Love
Can't Stop The Heartaches (4) — Heat In The Street (2,3) — In The Heat Of The Night (7) — Makes No Difference (3) — Prelude (2) — (7)
Crash And Burn (4) — Hooked On Music (3) — **Is This Love** (4) 50 — Makin' Magic (3) — Rockin' (6) — Your Love Can't Be Right (4)
Dedication - Part 1 & Part 2 (1) — Hot Shot (7) — It Ain't What It Seems (1) — Material Eyes (4) — Runnin' From The Future (1)
Electric Detective (5) — I Can Love You (6) — Just Try Talking (To Those — Misty Morning (6) — Snortin' Whiskey (4)
Evie (2) — I Don't Wanna Be Awake (5) — Dudes) (7) — My Life Is On The Line (5) — Speakeasy (1)
— I Gotta Fight (7) — Killer (7) — New Age Music (5) — Stand Up (6)

TRAVIS '01

Rock group from Glasgow, Scotland: Fran Healy (vocals), Andy Dunlop (guitar), Dougie Payne (bass) and Neil Primrose (drums).

| 4/22/00 | 135 | 10 | | © | 1 | The Man Who | | | $10 | Independiente 62151 |
| 6/30/01 | 39 | 7 | | © | 2 | The Invisible Band | | | $10 | Independiente 85788 |

Afterglow (2) — Driftwood (1) — Humpty Dumpty Love Song (2) — Luv (1) — Side (2) — Why Does It Always Rain On
As You Are (1) — Fear, The (1) — Indefinitely (2) — Pipe Dreams (2) — Sing (2) — Me? (1)
Cage, The (2) — Flowers In The Window (2) — Last Laugh Of The Laughter (1) — Safe (2) — Slide Show (1) — Writing To Reach You (1)
Dear Diary (2) — Follow The Light (2) — Last Train (2) — She's So Strange (1) — Turn (1)

★218★ TRAVIS, Randy '87

Born Randy Traywick on 5/4/59 in Marshville, North Carolina. Country singer/guitarist.

1)Always & Forever 2)Heroes And Friends 3)No Holdin' Back

7/19/86	85	100	▲3	©	1	Storms Of Life			$10	Warner 25435
5/30/87	19	103	▲5	©	2	Always & Forever		C:#31/8	$10	Warner 25568
7/30/88	35	43	▲2	©	3	Old 8x10			$10	Warner 25738
10/14/89	33	47	▲2	©	4	No Holdin' Back			$10	Warner 25988
12/2/89	70	7	●	©	5	An Old Time Christmas		C:#43/3 [X]	$10	Warner 25972

Christmas charts: 5/'89, 14/'90, 26/'91

TRAVIS, Randy — Cont'd

9/29/90	31	41	▲	©	6 Heroes And Friends			$10	Warner 26310
9/14/91	43	31	▲	©	7 High Lonesome			$10	Warner 26661
10/3/92	44	24	▲	©	8 Greatest Hits Volume One	[G]		$10	Warner 45044
10/3/92	67	31	▲	©	9 Greatest Hits Volume Two	[G]		$10	Warner 45045
9/11/93	121	6		©	10 Wind In The Wire	[TV]		$10	Warner 45319
5/14/94	59	21	●	©	11 This Is Me			$10	Warner 45501
8/31/96	77	4		©	12 Full Circle			$10	Warner 46328
5/9/98	49	9		©	13 You And You Alone			$10	DreamWorks 50034
10/9/99	130	3		©	14 A Man Ain't Made Of Stone			$10	DreamWorks 450119

All Night Long (6)
Allergic To The Blues (7)
Ants On A Log (12)
Anything (2)
Are We In Trouble Now (12)
Before You Kill Us All (11)
Better Class Of Losers (7)
Beyond The Reef (10)
Birth Of The Blues (6)
Blue Mesa (10)
Blues In Black And White (3)
Box, The (11)
Card Carryin' Fool (4)
Christmas Song (5)
Come See About Me (6)
Cowboy Boogie (10)
Day One (14)
Deeper Than The Holler (3,8)
Diggin' Up Bones (1,9)
Do I Ever Cross Your Mind (6)
Don't Take Your Love Away From Me (12)
Down At The Old Corral (10)
Easy To Love You (13)
Family Bible And The Farmer's Almanac (14)
Few Ole Country Boys (6)
Forever And Ever, Amen (2,9)
Forever Together (7)

Future Mister Me (12)
God Rest Ye Merry Gentlemen (5)
Gonna Walk That Line (11)
Good Intentions (2)
Happy Trails (6)
Hard Rock Bottom Of Your Heart (4,8)
Have A Nice Rest Of Your Life (4)
He Walked On Water (4,9)
Heart Of Hearts (7)
Heartache In The Works (14)
Here In My Heart (3)
Heroes And Friends (6,8)
High Lonesome (7)
Highway Junkie (12)
Hole, The (13)
Honky Tonk Moon (3,8)
Honky Tonk Side Of Town (11)
Horse Called Music (13)
How Do I Wrap My Heart For Christmas (5)
Hula Hands (10)
Human Race (6)
I Can Almost Hear Her Wings (12)
I Did My Part (13)
I Told You So (2,8)

I Wish It Would Rain (12)
I Won't Need You Anymore (2,9)
I'd Do It All Again With You (9)
I'd Surrender All (7)
I'll Be Right Here Loving You (14)
I'm Gonna Have A Little Talk (7)
I'm Still Here, You're Still Gone (13)
If I Didn't Have You (8)
If It Ain't One Thing It's Another (12)
In A Heart Like Mine (14)
Is It Still Over? (3,9)
It's Just A Matter Of Time (4,9)
It's Out Of My Hands (3)
King Of The Road (12)
Let Me Try (7)
Little Bitty Crack In Her Heart (14)
Little Left Of Center (14)
Long On Lonely (Short On Pride) (12)
Look Heart, No Hands (9)
Man Ain't Made Of Stone (14) **82**
Meet Me Under The Mistletoe (5)

Memories Of Old Santa Fe (10)
Messin' With My Mind (1)
Mining For Coal (4)
My Heart Cracked (But It Did Not Break) (1)
My House (2)
1982 (1,8)
No Place Like Home (1,9)
No Reason To Change (14)
No Stoppin' Us Now (4)
Oh, What A Silent Night (5)
Oh, What A Time To Be Me (7)
Old Chisholm Trail (10)
Old 8x10 (3)
Old Pair Of Shoes (8)
Old Time Christmas (5)
On The Other Hand (1,8)
Once You've Heard The Truth (14)
One Word Song (13)
Only Worse (13)
Oscar The Angel (11)
Out Of My Bones (13) **64**
Paniolo Country (10)
Point Of Light (7)
Pretty Paper (5)
Price To Pay (12)
Promises (3,9)
Reasons I Cheat (1,8)

Roamin' Wyoming (10)
Runaway Train (11)
Santa Claus Is Coming To Town (5)
Satisfied Mind (13)
Send My Body (1)
Shopping For Dresses (6)
Singing The Blues (6)
Small Y'all (11)
Smokin' The Hive (6)
Somewhere In My Broken Heart (4)
Spirit Of A Boy - Wisdom Of A Man (13) **42**
Storms Of Life (1)
Stranger In My Mirror (13) **81**
Take Another Swing At Me (9)
That's Where I Draw The Line (11)
There'll Always Be A Honky Tonk Somewhere (1)
Thirteen Mile Goodbye (14)
This Is Me (11)
Tonight We're Gonna Tear Down The Walls (2)
Too Gone Too Long (2,8)
Truth Is Lyin' Next To You (2)
Waiting On The Light To Change (6)

Walk Our Own Road (6)
We Ain't Out Of Love Yet (3)
We're Strangers Again (6)
What'll You Do About Me (2)
When Your World Was Turning For Me (4)
Where Can I Surrender (14)
Whisper My Name (11)
White Christmas Makes Me Blue (3)
Wind In The Wire (10)
Winter Wonderland (5)
Would I (12)
Written In Stone (3)
You And You Alone (13)

TRAVOLTA, John   '76

Born on 2/18/54 in Englewood, New Jersey. Actor/singer. Played "Vinnie Barbarino" on the TV series *Welcome Back Kotter*. Starred in several movies. Married actress Kelly Preston on 9/5/91.

5/22/76	39	22			1 John Travolta			$12	Midland Int'l. 1563
3/12/77	66	9			2 Can't Let You Go			$12	Midland Int'l. 2211
12/23/78+	161	7			3 Travolta Fever	[R]		$15	Midsong Int'l. 001 [2]

reissue of first two albums above

All Strung Out On You (2,3) **34**
Baby I Could Be So Good At Lovin' You (1,3)
Back Doors Crying (2,3)

Big Trouble (1,3)
Can't Let You Go (2,3)
Easy Evil (2,3)
Girl Like You (1,3)
Goodnight Mr. Moon (1,3)

I Don't Know What I Like About You Baby (1,3)
It Had To Be You (1,3)
Let Her In (1,3) **10**
Moonlight Lady (2,3)

Never Gonna Fall In Love Again (1,3)
Rainbows (1,3)
Razzamatazz (1,3)
Right Time Of The Night (3)

Settle Down (2,3)
Slow Dancing (2,3)
What Would They Say (2,3)
Whenever I'm Away From You (2,3) **38**

You Set My Dreams To Music (2,3)

TREAT HER RIGHT   '88

Rock group from Boston: Mark Sandman (vocals, guitar), David Champagne (guitar), Jim Fitting (harmonica) and Billy Conway (drums). Sandman and Conway later formed **Morphine**. Sandman died of a heart attack on 7/4/99 (age 46).

4/9/88	127	18		©	Treat Her Right			$10	RCA 6884

Bringin' It All Back Home
Don't Look Back
Everglades

Honest Job
I Got A Gun
I Think She Likes Me

Jesus Everyday
Square
Trail Of Tears

Where Did All The Girls Come From?
You Don't Need Money

TREMELOES, The   '67

Pop-rock group from England: Len "Chip" Hawkes (vocals, bass), Alan Blakely and Ricky West (guitars), and Dave Munden (drums). Alan is the brother of Mike Blakely (of **Christie**). Hawkes is the father of singer Chesney Hawkes. Blakely died of cancer on 6/10/96 (age 54).

6/24/67	119	8			Here Comes My Baby			$25	Epic 26310

Even The Bad Times Are Good **36**
Good Day Sunshine

Here Comes My Baby **13**
Loving You (Is Sweeter Than Ever)

My Town
Run Baby Run (Back Into My Arms)
What A State I'm In

Shake Hands (And Come Out Crying)

When I'm With Her
You

TRESVANT, Ralph   '91

Born on 5/16/68 in Roxbury, Massachusetts. R&B singer. Member of **New Edition**.

12/8/90+	17	37	▲	©	1 Ralph Tresvant			$10	MCA 10116
1/15/94	131	6		©	2 It's Goin' Down			$10	MCA 10889

Alright Now (1)
Booty Affair (2)
Do What I Gotta Do (1)
G-Spot (2)
Girl I Can't Control It (1)

Graveyard (2)
I Love You (Just For You) (1)
It's Goin' Down (2)
Last Night (1)
Love At First Sight (2)

Love Hurts (1)
Love Takes Time (1)
My Aphrodisiac (2)
Public Figure (Ordinary Guy) (1)
Rated R (1)

Sensitivity (1) **4**
Sex Maniac (2)
Sex-O (1)
Shaky Ground (2)
She's My Love Thang (1)

Stone Cold Gentleman (1) **34**
When I Need Somebody (2)
Who's The Mack (2)
You'll Remember Me (2)
Your Touch (2)

TREVINO, Rick   '96

Born on 5/16/71 in Austin, Texas. Country singer.

3/12/94	119	18	●	©	1 Rick Trevino			$10	Columbia 53560
3/25/95	121	18		©	2 Looking For The Light			$10	Columbia 66771
8/3/96	117	7		©	3 Learning As You Go			$10	Columbia 67452

Anytime (3)
Bobbie Ann Mason (2)
Doctor Time (1)
Family Reunion (2)
Full Deck Of Cards (2)
Honky Tonk Crowd (1)

I Only Get This Way With You (3)
I Want A Girl In A Pick-up Truck (2)
I Wish He Wouldn't Treat Her That Way (3)
I'm Here For You (3)

It Only Hurts When I Laugh (1)
Just Enough Rope (1)
Learning As You Go (3)
Life Can Turn On A Dime (1)
Looking For The Light (2)
Mary's Just A Plain Jane (3)
Oh Jenny (3)

Pain, The (2)
Poor, Broke, Mixed Up Mess Of A Heart (2)
Running Out Of Reasons To Run (3)
San Antonio Rose To You (2)
Save This One For Me (3)

See Rock City (3)
Serious Love (3)
She Can't Say I Didn't Cry (1)
She Just Left Me Lounge (1)
She Used To Say That To Me (2)
Un Momento Allá (1)

Walk Out Backwards (1)
What I'll Know Then (1)
You Are To Me (2)

T. REX '72

Rock group from England: Marc Bolan (vocals, guitar), Mickey Finn (guitar), Steve Currie (bass) and Bill Legend (drums). Bolan died in a car crash on 9/16/77 (age 30).

5/1/71	188	5			1 **T-Rex**			$15	Reprise 6440
11/6/71+	32	34		©	2 **Electric Warrior**			$15	Reprise 6466
8/26/72	17	24		©	3 **The Slider**			$15	Reprise 2095
10/7/72	113	12			4 **Tyrannosaurus Rex (A Beginning)**		[E]	$20	A&M 3514 [2]
					recordings from 1968				
4/28/73	102	10		©	5 **Tanx**			$15	Reprise 2132

Afghan Woman (4)
Aznagell The Mage (4)
Baby Boomerang (3)
Baby Strange (3)
Ballrooms Of Mars (3)
Bang A Gong (Get It On) (2) *10*
Beltane Walk (1)
Born To Boogie (5)
Broken Hearted Blues (5)
Buick Mackane (3)
Chariot Choogle (3)
Chateau In Virginia Waters (4)
Child Star (4)

Childe (1)
Children Of Rarn (1)
Consesuala (4)
Cosmic Dancer (2)
Country Honey (5)
Deboraarobed (4)
Diamond Meadows (1)
Dwarfish Trumpet Blues (4)
Eastern Spell (1)
Electric Slim And The Factory Hen (5)
Friends, The (4)
Frowning Atahuallpa (4)
Girl (2)

Graceful Fat Sheba (4)
Highway Knees (5)
Hot Rod Mama (4)
Is It Love? (1)
Jeepster (2)
Jewel (1)
Juniper Suction (4)
Knight (4)
Lean Woman Blues (2)
Left Hand Luke And The Beggar Boys (5)
Life Is Strange (5)
Life's A Gas (2)
Mad Donna (5)

Main Man (3)
Mambo Sun (2)
Metal Guru (3)
Mister Mister (5)
Monolith (2)
Motivator, The (2)
Mustang Ford (4)
Mystic Lady (3)
Oh Harley (The Saltimbanques) (4)
One Inch Rock (1)
Our Wonderful Brownskin Man (4)
Planet Queen (2)

Rabbit Fighter (3)
Rapids (5)
Ride A White Swan (1) *76*
Rip Off (2)
Rock On (3)
Root Of Star (1)
Salamanda Palaganda (4)
Scenesof (4)
Scenesof Dynasty (4)
Seagull Woman (1)
Shock Rock (5)
Slider, The (3)
Spaceball Ricochet (3)
Stacey Grove (4)

Strange Orchestras (4)
Street And Babe Shadow (5)
Summer Deep (1)
Suneye (1)
Telegram Sam (3) *67*
Tenement Lady (5)
Time Of Love Is Now (1)
Traveling Tragition (4)
Trelawny Lawn (4)
Visit, The (1)
Wielder Of Words (4)
Wind Quartets (4)
Wizard, The (1)

TRIBE CALLED QUEST, A '96

Rap trio from Queens, New York: Jonathan "**Q-Tip**" Davis, Ali Shaheed Muhammad and Malik "**Phife Dawg**" Taylor.

4/28/90	91	19	●	©	1 **People's Instinctive Travels And The Paths Of Rhythm**			$10	Jive 1331
10/12/91	45	49	▲	©	2 **The Low End Theory**			$10	Jive 1418
11/27/93	8	29	▲	©	3 **Midnight Marauders**			$10	Jive 41490
8/17/96	❶¹	16	▲		4 **Beats, Rhymes And Life**			$10	Jive 41587
10/17/98	3	11	●	©	5 **The Love Movement**			$10	Jive 41638
11/13/99	81	4		©	6 **The Anthology**		[G]	$10	Jive 41679

includes "Vivrant Thing" by **Q-Tip**

After Hours (1)
Against The World (5)
Award Tour (3,6) *47*
Baby Phife's Return (4)
Bonita Applebum (1,6)
Buggin' Out (2,6)
Busta's Lament (5)
Butter (2)
Can I Kick It? (1,6)
Chase, Part II (3)
Check The Rhime (2,6)
Clap Your Hands (3)

Common Ground (Get It Goin' On) (5)
Crew (4)
Da Booty (5)
Description Of A Fool (1,6)
8 Million Stories (3)
Everything Is Fair (2)
Excursions (2)
Find A Way (5,6) *71*
Footprints (1)
4 Moms (5)
Get A Hold (4)
Give Me (5)

Go Ahead In The Rain (1)
God Lives Through (3)
Ham 'N' Eggs (1)
His Name Is Mutty Ranks (5)
Hop, The (4)
Hot 4 U (5)
Hot Sex (5,6)
I Left My Wallet In El Segundo (1,6)
If The Papes Come (6)
Infamous Date Rape (2)
Jam (4)
Jazz (We've Got) (2,5,6)
Keep It Rollin' (3)

Keeping It Moving (4,6)
Like It Like That (5)
Love, The (5)
Luck Of Lucien (1,6)
Lyrics To Go (3)
Midnight (3)
Mind Power (4)
Money Maker (5)
Motivators (4)
Mr. Muhammad (1)
Oh My God (3,5,6)
1nce Again (4)
One Two S**t (5)
Pad & Pen (5)

Phony Rappers (4)
Pressure, The (4)
Pubic Enemy (1)
Push It Along (1)
Rap Promoter (2)
Rhythm (Devoted To The Art Of Moving Butts) (1)
Rock Rock Y'all (1)
Scenario (2,5,6) *57*
Separate/Together (4)
Show Business (2)
Skypager (2)
Start It Up (5)
Steppin' It Up (5)

Steve Biko (Stir It Up) (3)
Stressed Out (4,6)
Sucka Nigga (3,6)
Verses From The Abstract (2)
Vibes And Stuff (2)
Vivrant Thing (6)
We Can Get Down (3)
What? (2)
What Really Goes On (4)
Word Play (4)
Youthful Expression(1)

TRICK DADDY '01

Born Maurice Young in Miami. Male rapper/producer.

1/30/99	30	37	●	©	1 **www.thug.com**			$10	Slip-N-Slide 2802
3/4/00	26	28	●	©	2 **Book Of Thugs: Chapter A.K., Verse 47**			$10	Slip-N-Slide 83275
4/7/01	4	26	▲	©	3 **Thugs Are Us**			$10	Slip-N-Slide 83432

America (2)
Amerika (3)
Back In The Days (1)
Bout My Money (2)
Boy (2)
Bricks & Marijuana (3)
Call From Dante (1)
Can't F**k With The South (3)

Change My Life (1)
Could It Be (2)
Duece Poppi Snippet (3)
For All My Ladies (3)
For The Thugs (1)
Get On Up (3)
Gotta Let You Have It (2)
Have My Cheese (3)

Hoe But Can't Help It (2)
Hold On (1)
Hotness, The (3)
I'll Be Your Other Man (1)
I'll Be Your Player (1)
I'm A Thug (3) *17*
K*ll Your A** (2)
Living In A World (1)

N Word (3)
Nann (1) *62*
99 Problems (3)
Noodle (3)
Pull Over Remix (3)
Run Nigga (1)
Shut Up (2) *83*
Sittin' On D's (2)

So What (1)
Somebody Shoulda Told Ya (3)
Stroke It Gently (1)
Suckin' Fuckin' (1)
Survivin' The Drought (3)
Take It To Da House (3) *50*
Tater Head (1)
Thug For Life (2)

Thug Life Again (2)
Tryin' To Stop Smokin' (2)
Walkin' Like A Hoe (2)
Where U From (3)

TRICK PONY '01

Country trio formed in Nashville: Heidi Newfield (vocals), Keith Burns (guitar) and Ira Dean (bass).

| 3/31/01 | 91 | 16↑ | | © | **Trick Pony** .... | | | $10 | Warner 47927 |

Big River
Can't Say That On The Radio
Every Other Memory

Just What I Do
More Like Me
Not Hidden Track

Now Would Be The Time
On A Night Like This
One In A Row

Party Of One
Pour Me *71*
Spent

Stay In This Moment

TRICKY '98

Born Adrian Thaws in 1964 in Bristol, England. Male techno-dance artist.

12/7/96	140	6		©	1 **Pre-Millennium Tension**			$10	Island 524302
6/20/98	84	3		©	2 **Angels With Dirty Faces**			$10	Island 524520
9/4/99	182	1		©	3 **Juxtapose**			$10	Island 546432

Analyze Me (2)
Bad Dream (1)
Bad Things (1)
Bom Bom Diggy (3)
Broken Homes (2)
Call Me (3)

Carriage For Two (2)
Christiansands (1)
Contradictive (3)
Demise (2)
For Real (3)
Ghetto Youth (1)

Hot Like A Sauna (3)
I Like The Girls (3)
Lyrics Of Fury (1)
Makes Me Wanna Die (1)
Mellow (2)
Moment I Feared (2)

Money Greedy (2)
My Evil Is Strong (1)
Piano (1)
Record Companies (2)
Scrappy Love (3)
Sex Drive (1)

She Said (3)
Singing The Blues (2)
6 Minutes (3)
Talk To Me (Angels With Dirty Faces) (2)
Tear Out My Eyes (2)

Tricky Kid (1)
Vent (1)
Wash My Soul (3)

TRINA '00

Born in Miami. Female rapper.

| 4/8/00 | 33 | 29 | ● | © | **Da Baddest B***h** .... | | | $10 | Slip-N-Slide 83212 |

Ain't S**t
Ball Wit Me
Big Lick

Da Baddest B***h
I Don't Need U
I Need

I'll Always
If U
Mama

Off Glass
Off The Chain With It
69 Ways

Take Me
Watch Yo Back

TRINERE '89
Born Trinere Veronica Farrington in Miami. Female dance singer.

| 9/23/89 | 196 | 2 | | © | Greatest Hits .... | [K] | $10 | Pandisc 8804 |

TRINERE & FRIENDS
includes "Lookout Weekend" and "When I Hear Music" by Debbie Deb and "Don't Stop The Rock," "It's Automatic" and "The Party Has Just Begun" by Freestyle

All Night | Can't Get Enough | Can't Stop The Beat | How Can We Be Wrong | I Know You Love Me | I'll Be All You Ever Need

TRIN-I-TEE 5:7 '98
Contemporary gospel female vocal trio from New Orleans: Terri Brown, Chanelle Hayes and Angel Taylor.

| 8/8/98 | 139 | 27 | ● | © | 1 Trin-I-Tee 5:7 .... | | $10 | B-Rite 90094 |
| 1/29/00 | 174 | 12 | | © | 2 Spiritual Love .... | | $10 | B-Rite 490359 |

Call His Name (1) | Good For Me (1) | I Won't Turn Back (1) | Pray For Awhile (1) | There He Is (2) | You Were There (2)
Day You Came (2) | Highway (2) | If They Only Knew (2) | Put Your Hands (1) | We Know (2)
God's Blessing (1) | Holy & Righteous (1) | Imagine That (2) | Respect Yourself (2) | With All My Heart (1)
God's Grace (1) | How You Living (2) | My Body (2) | Spiritual Love (2) | You Can Always Call His Name (1)
Gonna Get Myself Together (2) | I Promise You (2) | Oh Mary, Don't You Weep (1) | Sunshine (1)

TRIO '97
Electronic-rock trio from Sweden: Stephan Remmler, Kralle Krawinkel and Peter Behrens.

| 8/9/97 | 118 | 12 | | © | Da Da Da .... | [E] | $10 | Mercury 536205 |

recorded in 1982; title track featured in a 1997 Volkswagon commercial

Anna - Letmeinletmeout | Da Da Da I Don't Love You | Girl Girl Girl | Out In The Streets | Tooralooraloolaroo - Is It Old & | W.W.W.
Boom Boom | Don't Love Me Aha Aha Aha | Hearts Are Trump | Sunday You Need Love | Is It New
Bye Bye | Drei Mann Im Doppelbett | Ich Lieb Den Rock 'N' Roll | Monday Be Alone | Tutti Frutti

TRIPLETS, The '91
Triplet sisters Diana, Sylvia and Vicky Villegas. Born on 4/18/65 in Mexico (American mother and Mexican father).

| 4/20/91 | 125 | 5 | | © | ...Thicker Than Water .... | | $10 | Mercury 848290 |

Blood Is Thicker Than Water | If I Could Only Make You Love | Pyramids Of Pleasure | Spanish Surrender | Where Were You When I | **You Don't Have To Go Home**
Dancing In The Shadows | Me | Reminds Me Of You | Sunrise | Needed You | **Tonight** 14
 | Light A Candle | So Hard

TRIPPING DAISY '95
Pop-rock group from Dallas: Tim DeLaughter (vocals), Wes Berggren (guitar), Mark Pirro (bass) and Bryan Wakeland (drums). Berggren died on 10/27/99 (age 28).

| 7/15/95 | 95 | 13 | | | I Am An Elastic Firecracker .... | | $10 | Island 524112 |

Bang | I Got A Girl | Noose | Prick | Rocketpop | Step Behind
High | Motivation | Piranha | Raindrop | Same Dress New Day | Trip Along

★355★ TRITT, Travis '94
Born James Travis Tritt on 2/9/63 in Marietta, Georgia. Country singer/guitarist.

3/31/90+	70	99	▲²	©	1 Country Club		$10	Warner 26094
6/15/91	22	94	▲³	©	2 It's All About To Change		$10	Warner 26589
9/5/92	27	57	▲²	©	3 T-R-O-U-B-L-E		$10	Warner 45048
11/28/92+	75	8		©	4 A Travis Tritt Christmas - Loving Time Of The Year	[X]	$10	Warner 45029

Christmas chart: 13/'92

5/28/94	20	44	▲²	©	5 Ten Feet Tall And Bulletproof		$10	Warner 45603
9/30/95	21	37	▲	©	6 Greatest Hits - From The Beginning	[G]	$10	Warner 46001
9/14/96	53	29	▲	©	7 The Restless Kind		$10	Warner 46304
10/31/98	119	13		©	8 No More Looking Over My Shoulder		$10	Warner 47097
10/21/00	51	49↑	●	©	9 Down The Road I Go		$10	Columbia 62165

All I Want For Christmas Dear Is You (4) | Don't Give Your Heart To A Rambler (2) | Hundred Years From Now (3) | Looking Out For Number One (3) | Outlaws Like Us (5) | Start The Car (8)
Anymore (2,6) | Double Trouble (7) | I Heard The Bells On Christmas Day (4) | Lord Have Mercy On The Working Man (3) | Put Some Drive In Your Country (1,6) | Still In Love With You (7)
Back Up Against The Wall (7) | Down The Road I Go (9) | I Wish I Could Go Back Home (3) | Love Of A Woman (9) | Restless Kind (7) | Tell Me I Was Dreaming (5,6)
Best Of Intentions (9) **27** | Draggin' My Heart Around (7) | I Wish I Was Wrong (9) | Loving Time Of The Year (4) | Road Home (1) | Ten Feet Tall And Bulletproof (5,6)
Between An Old Memory And Me (5) | Drift Off To Dream (1,6) | I'm All The Man (8) | Mission Of Love (8) | Road To You (3) | Tougher Than The Rest (8)
Bible Belt (2) | Foolish Pride (5,6) | I'm Gonna Be Somebody (1,6) | Modern Day Bonnie And Clyde (9) | Rough Around The Edges (8) | T-R-O-U-B-L-E (3,6)
Blue Collar Man (3) | For You (8) | If Hell Had A Jukebox (2) | | Sack Full Of Stones (7) | Walkin' All Over My Heart (5)
Can I Trust You With My Heart (3,6) | Girls Like That (8) | **If I Lost You** (8) **86** | More Than You'll Ever Know (7) | Santa Looked A Lot Like Daddy (4) | When I Touch You (3)
Christmas In My Hometown (4) | Hard Times And Misery (3) | If I Were A Drinker (1) | Never Get Away From Me (9) | She's Going Home With Me (7) | Where Corn Don't Grow (7)
Christmas Just Ain't Christmas Without You (4) | Have Yourself A Merry Little Christmas (4) | If The Fall Don't Kill You (9) | No More Looking Over My Shoulder (8) | Sign Of The Times (1) | Whiskey Ain't Workin' (2,6)
Country Club (1,6) | Help Me Hold On (1,6) | **It's A Great Day To Be Alive** (9) **33** | No Vacation From The Blues (5) | Silver Bells (4) | Winter Wonderland (4)
Did You Fall Far Enough (7) | Helping Me Get Over You (7) | It's All About To Change (2) | Nothing Short Of Dying (2) | Someone For Me (2) | Wishful Thinking (5)
Dixie Flyer (1) | Here's A Quarter (Call Someone Who Cares) (2,6) | Just Too Tired To Fight It (9) | O Little Town Of Bethlehem (4) | Sometimes She Forgets (6) | Worth Every Mile (3)
 | Homesick (2) | Leave My Girl Alone (3) | Only You (And You Alone) (6) | Son Of The New South (1)
 | | Livin' On Borrowed Time (9) | | Southbound Train (9)
 | | | | Southern Justice (5)

★443★ TRIUMPH '81
Hard-rock trio formed in Toronto: Rik Emmett (vocals, guitar), Mike Levine (keyboards, bass) and Gil Moore (drums).

| 5/5/79 | 48 | 28 | | © | 1 Just A Game .... | | $12 | RCA Victor 3224 |
| 5/19/79 | 185 | 2 | | © | 2 Rock & Roll Machine ....C:#22/16 | [E] | $12 | RCA Victor 2982 |

released in 1978

3/29/80	32	18		©	3 Progressions Of Power		$10	RCA Victor 3524
9/19/81	23	59	●	©	4 Allied Forces		$10	RCA Victor 3902
1/29/83	26	27	●	©	5 Never Surrender		$10	RCA Victor 4382
12/8/84+	35	30		©	6 Thunder Seven		$10	MCA 5537
11/2/85	50	18		©	7 Stages	[L]	$15	MCA 8020 [2]
9/6/86	33	27		©	8 The Sport Of Kings		$10	MCA 5786
11/28/87	82	13		©	9 Surveillance		$10	MCA 42083

A Minor Prelude (5) | Allied Forces (4,7) | Bringing It On Home (2) | Druh Mer Selbo (7) | Fingertalkin' (3) | **Hold On** (1,7) **38**
Air Raid (4) | American Girls (1) | Carry On The Flame (9) | Embrujo (8) | **Follow Your Heart** (6,7) **88** | Hooked On You (8)
All Over Again (9) | Battle Cry (5) | Cool Down (6) | Empty Inside (7) | Fool For Your Love (4) | Hot Time (In This City Tonight) (4)
All The King's Horses (9) | Blinding Light Show (medley) (2) | Don't Love Anybody Else But Me (8) | Fantasy Serenade (1) | Hard Road (3)
All The Way (5) | | Fight The Good Fight (4,7) | Headed For Nowhere (9) | **I Can Survive** (3) **91**

TRIUMPH — Cont'd

I Live For The Weekend (3)
If Only (8)
In The Middle Of The Night (8)
In The Night (3)
Into The Forever (9)
Just A Game (1)
Just One Night (8)
Killing Time (6)
Lay It On The Line (1,7) *86*

Let The Light (Shine On Me) (9)
Little Boy Blues (6)
Long Time Gone (9)
Magic Power (4,7) *51*
Midsummer's Daydream (6,7)
Mind Games (1)
Moonchild (medley) (2)
Movin' On (1)
Nature's Child (3)

Never Say Never (9)
Never Surrender (5,7)
On And On (9)
Ordinary Man (4)
Petite Etude (4)
Play With The Fire (8)
Rock & Roll Machine (2,7)
Rock Out, Roll On (6)
Rock You Down (9)

Rocky Mountain Way (2)
Running In The Night (9)
Say Goodbye (4)
Somebody's Out There (8) *27*
Spellbound (6,7)
Stranger In A Strange Land (6)
Street Fighter (2)
Suitcase Blues (1)
Take A Stand (8)

Take My Heart (3)
Takes Time (2)
Tear The Roof Off (3)
Tears In The Rain (8)
Time Canon (6)
Time Goes By (6)
Time Goes By (6)
Too Much Thinking (5)
24 Hours A Day (2)
Waking Dream (9)

What Rules My Heart (8)
When The Lights Go Down (5,7)
Woman In Love (3)
World Of Fantasy (5,7)
Writing On The Wall (5)
Young Enough To Cry (1)

TRIUMVIRAT '75

Techno-rock group from Germany: Helmut Kollen (guitar, vocals), Jurgen Fritz (keyboards) and Hans Bathelt (drums). Kollen replaced by Barry Palmer (vocals) and Dick Frangenberg (bass) in 1976. Kollen committed suicide on 5/5/77 (age 27).

8/10/74	55	17		1 Illusions On A Double Dimple	$15	Harvest 11311
6/7/75	27	17	©	2 Spartacus	$12	Capitol 11392
8/7/76	85	8		3 Old Loves Die Hard	$12	Capitol 11551

Bad Deal (1)
Burning Sword Of Capua (2)
Capital Of Power (2)
Cold Old Worried Lady (3)
Dawning (1)

Day In A Life Medley (3)
Deadly Dream Of Freedom (2)
Dimplicity (1)
Flashback (1)
Hazy Shades Of Dawn (2)

History Of Mystery (Part One & Two) (3)
I Believe (3)
Illusions (1)
Last Dance (1)

Lucky Girl (1)
March To The Eternal City Medley (2)
Maze (1)
Million Dollars (1)

Old Loves Die Hard (2)
Panic On 5th Avenue (3)
Roundabout (1)
School Of Instant Pain Medley (2)

Schooldays (1)
Spartacus Medley (2)
Sweetest Sound Of Liberty (2)
Triangle (1)
Walls Of Doom (2)

TRIXTER '91

Hard-rock group from Paramus, New Jersey: Peter Loran (vocals), Steve Brown (guitar), P.J. Farley (bass) and Mark Scott (drums).

9/1/90+	28	54	● ©	1 Trixter	$10	MCA 6389
10/31/92	109	3	©	2 Hear!	$10	MCA 10635

Always A Victim (1)
As The Candle Burns (2)
Bad Girl (1)
Bloodrock (2)
Damn Good (2)

Give It To Me Good (1) *65*
Heart Of Steel (1)
Line Of Fire (1)
Nobody's A Hero (2)
On And On (1)

On The Road Again (2)
One In A Million (1) *75*
Only Young Once (1)
Play Rough (1)
Power Of Love (2)

Ride The Whip (1)
Road Of A Thousand Dreams (2)
Rockin' Horse (2)
Runaway Train (2)

Surrender (1) *72*
Waiting In That Line (2)
What It Takes (2)
Wild Is The Heart (2)
You'll Never See Me Cryin' (1)

TROCCOLI, Kathy '97

Contemporary Christian singer from New York City.

5/24/97	170	1		Love & Mercy	$10	Reunion 10003

All Glory To God
Baby's Prayer

Call Out To Me
Faithful To Me

He'll Never Leave Me
Help Me God

How Would I Know
I Call Him Love

Love One Another
Water Into Wine

TROGGS, The '66

Rock group from Andover, England: Reg Presley (vocals), Chris Britton (guitar), Pete Staples (bass) and Ronnie Bullis (drums). Bullis died on 11/13/92 (age 51).

9/3/66	52	16		1 Wild Thing	$50	Fontana 67556

same album charted simultaneously on Atco 193

5/18/68	109	9		2 Love Is All Around	$50	Fontana 67576

Any Way That You Want Me (2)
Cousin Jane (2)
Evil (1)
From Home (1)
Girl In Black (2)

Give It To Me (All Your Love) (2)
Gonna Make You (2)
Hi Hi Hazel (1)
I Can't Control Myself (2) *43*

I Just Sing (1)
I Want You (1)
Jingle Jangle (2)
Little Girl (2)
Lost Girl (1)

Love Is All Around (2) *7*
Night Of The Long Grass (2)
Our Love Will Still Be There (1)
66-5-4-3-2-1 (1)
When I'm With You (1)

When Will The Rain Come (2)
Wild Thing (1) *1*
With A Girl Like You (1) *29*
Your Love (1)

TROOP '90

R&B vocal group from Pasadena, California: Steve Russell, Allen McNeil, Rodney Benford, John Harreld and Reggie Warren.

9/3/88	133	9	©	1 Troop	$10	Atlantic 81851
1/13/90	73	39	● ©	2 Attitude	$10	Atlantic 82035
6/20/92	78	12	©	3 Deepa	$10	Atlantic 82393

All I Do Is Think Of You (2) *47*
Another Lover (2)
Come Back To Your Home (3)
Deepa (3)
For You (2)
Give It Up (3)

Happy Relationship (1)
Hot Water (3)
I Feel You (3)
I Like That (1)
I Will Always Love You (2)
I'm Not Gamin' (3)

I'm Not Soupped (2)
Keep You Next To Me (3)
Mamacita (1)
My Heart (1)
My Love (2)
My Music (2)

Only When I Laugh (3)
Praise (3)
Set Me Free (3)
She Blows My Mind (3)
She's My Favorite Girl (1)
Soupped Mix (2)

Spread My Wings (2)
Still In Love (1)
Strange Hotel (3)
Sweet November (3) *58*
That's My Attitude (2)
Watch Me Dance (1)

Whatever It Takes (To Make You Stay) (3) *63*
You Take My Heart With You (3)
Young Girl (1)

TROOPER '78

Rock group from Vancouver: Ra McGuire (vocals, guitar), Brian Smith (guitar), Frank Ludwig (keyboards), Doni Underhill (bass) and Tommy Stewart (drums).

8/26/78	182	4		Thick As Thieves	$12	MCA 2377

Drivin' Crazy
Gambler

Live From The Moon
Moment That It Takes

No Fun Being Alone
One Good Reason

Raise A Little Hell *59*
Roll With It

Round, Round We Go
Say Goodnight

TROPEA '76

Born John Tropea in Florida. Jazz guitarist.

3/20/76	138	7		1 Tropea	[I] $12	Marlin 2200
5/14/77	149	7		2 Short Trip To Space	[I] $12	Marlin 2204

Blue Too (2)
Bratt, The (1)
Can't Hide Love (2)
Cisco Disco (1)

Dreams (1)
Funk You See, Is The Funk You Do! (2)
Jingle, The (1)

Just Blue (1)
Love's Final Moment (2)
Muff (1)
7th Heaven (2)

Short Trip To Space (2)
Southside (2)
Tambourine (1)
Twist Of The Wrist (2)

You Can't Have It All (2)

TROUBADOURS DU ROI BAUDOUIN '69

Choir and percussionists consisting of 45 boys and 15 teachers from the Kamina School in the Congo.

8/2/69	184	5		Missa Luba	[F] $20	Philips 600606

Agnus Dei
Banana (Soldiers Song)
Benedictus
Credo

Dibwe Diambula Kabanda (Marriage Song)
Ebu Bwale Kemai (Marriage Ballad)

Gloria
Katumbo (Dance)
Kyrie

Lutuku Y A Bene Kanyoka (Emergence From Grief)
Sanctus

Seya Wa Mama Ndalamba (Marital Celebration)
Twai Tshinaminai (Work Song)

TROUBLE FUNK '82

Funk group from Washington DC: Robert Reed (vocals), Tony Fisher, James Avery, Taylor Reed, Tim David, Mack Carey, Emmett Nixon, Alonzo Robinson, Dean Harris, David Rudd and Chester Davis.

| 5/8/82 | 121 | 14 | © | **Drop The Bomb** .... | $12 | SugarHill 266 |

Don't Try To Use Me   Drop The Bomb   Get On Up   Hey Fellas   Let's Get Hot   Pump Me Up

★297★ TROWER, Robin '74

Born on 3/9/45 in London. Rock guitarist. Original member of **Procol Harum**. James Dewar was his lead singer from 1973-83, replaced by Davey Pattison in 1986.

1)For Earth Below 2)Bridge Of Sighs 3)Robin Trower Live!

5/12/73	106	24	©	1	**Twice Removed From Yesterday**	$12	Chrysalis 1039
4/20/74	7	31	● ©	2	**Bridge Of Sighs**	$12	Chrysalis 1057
3/1/75	5	17	● ©	3	**For Earth Below**	$12	Chrysalis 1073
3/27/76	10	20	©	4	**Robin Trower Live!** [L]	$12	Chrysalis 1089

recorded on 2/3/75 at the Stockholm Concert Hall

10/9/76	24	19	● ©	5	**Long Misty Days**	$12	Chrysalis 1107
10/1/77	25	19	● ©	6	**In City Dreams**	$12	Chrysalis 1148
8/26/78	37	17	©	7	**Caravan To Midnight**	$12	Chrysalis 1189
3/1/80	34	15	©	8	**Victims Of The Fury**	$12	Chrysalis 1215
3/21/81	37	16	©	9	**B.L.T.**	$10	Chrysalis 1324

JACK BRUCE/BILL LORDAN/ROBIN TROWER

| 1/30/82 | 109 | 6 | © | 10 | **Truce** | $10 | Chrysalis 1352 |

JACK BRUCE/ROBIN TROWER

10/1/83	191	2	©	11	**Back It Up**	$10	Chrysalis 41420
12/27/86+	100	25	©	12	**Passion**	$10	GNP Crescendo 2187
5/21/88	133	10	©	13	**Take What You Need**	$10	Atlantic 81838

About To Begin (2)
Alethea (3,4)
Back It Up (11)
Bad Time (12)
Ballerina (12)
Benny Dancer (11)
Birthday Boy (7)
Black To Red (11)
Bluebird (6)
Bridge Of Sighs (2)
Caledonia (5) *82*
Captain Midnight (11)
Caravan To Midnight (7)
Careless (13)
Carmen (9)
Caroline (12)
Confessin' Midnight (3)
Day Of The Eagle (2)
Daydream (1,4)

End Game (9)
Fall In Love (10)
Falling Star (6)
Farther Up The Road (6)
Fat Gut (10)
Feel The Heat (9)
Fine Day (3)
Fly Low (8)
Fool (7)
Fool And Me (2)
For Earth Below (3)
Gone Too Far (10)
Gonna Be More Suspicious (3)
Gonna Shut You Down (10)
Hannah (1)
Hold Me (5)
I Can't Live Without You (5)
I Can't Stand It (1)
I Can't Wait Much Longer (1,4)

I Want You Home (13)
I'm Out To Get You (7)
If Forever (12)
In City Dreams (6)
In This Place (2)
Into Money (9)
Into The Flame (6)
Islands (11)
It's For You (7)
It's Only Money (3)
It's Too Late (9)
Jack And Jill (8)
King Of The Dance (7)
Lady Love (2,4)
Last Train To The Stars (11)
Life On Earth (9)
Little Bit Of Sympathy (2,4)
Little Boy Lost (10)
Little Girl (6)

Long Misty Days (5)
Lost In Love (7)
Love Attack (13)
Love Won't Wait Forever (13)
Love's Gonna Bring You Round (6)
Madhouse (8)
Man Of The World (1)
Messin The Blues (5)
My Love (Burning Love) (7)
Night (12)
No Island Lost (9)
No Time (12)
None But The Brave (11)
Once The Bird Has Flown (9)
One More Word (12)
Only Time (8)
Over You (13)
Passion (12)

Pride (5)
Ready For The Taking (8)
Ring, The (8)
River (11)
Roads To Freedom (8)
Rock Me Baby (1,4)
S.M.O. (5)
Sail On (7)
Sailing (5)
Same Rain Falls (5)
Second Time (13)
Secret Doors (12)
Settling The Score (11)
Shadows Touching (10)
Shame The Devil (3)
Shattered (13)
Shout, The (8)
Sinner's Song (1)
Smile (6)

Somebody Calling (6)
Sweet Wine Of Love (6)
Take Good Care Of Yourself (10)
Take What You Need (From Me) (13)
Tale Untold (3)
Tear It Up (13)
Thin Ice (10)
Time Is Short (11)
Too Rolling Stoned (2,4)
Twice Removed From Yesterday (1)
Victims Of The Fury (8)
What It Is (9)
Won't Even Think About You (12)
Won't Let You Down (9)

TRU '99

Rap group from New Orleans: brothers **Master P**, **Silkk The Shocker** and **C-Murder**, with **Mia X** and **Mo B Dick**. TRU: The Real Untouchables.

| 3/8/97 | 8 | 48 | ▲² © | 1 | **Tru 2 Da Game** | $15 | No Limit 50660 [2] |
| 6/19/99 | 5 | 21 | © | 2 | **Da Crime Family** | $15 | No Limit 50010 [2] |

Bounce (2)
Bounce To This (2)
Buss That (2)
Dangerous In My City (2)
Don't F--- With Tru (2)
Don't Judge Me (2)
FEDz (1)
Final Ride (2)
Freak Hoes (1)
Gangstas Make The World (1)

Ghetto Cheeze (1)
Ghetto Is A Struggle (2)
Ghetto Thang (1)
Hail Mary (2)
Hard N's (2)
Heaven 4 A Gangsta (1)
Hoody Hooo (2)
I Always Feel Like (Somebody's Watching Me) (1) *71*

I Don't Want You No More (2)
I Got Candy (1)
It's A Beautiful Thing (2)
It's My Time (1)
Livin' Like A Hustler (2)
Lord Is Testin Me (2)
Miller Boyz (2)
Never (2)
No Limit Army (2)
No Limit Soldiers (1)

1nce Upon A Time (1)
Pop Goes My 9 (1)
Prayer For A G (2)
Rip Kevin (2)
Run Away Slaves (2)
Smoking Green (1)
Soldier Till I Die (2)
Stay Real (2)
Suppose To Be My Friend (2)
Swamp Aggin (1)

Tank Goes On (2)
There Dey Go (1)
They Can't Stop Us! (1)
Torcher Chamber (1)
Tru - The Beginning (2)
Tru Homies (2)
TRU ?'s (1)
TRU 2 Da Game (1)
We Riders (2)
What They Call Us? (1)

World Is Yours (2)
You'll Never Change (2)

TRUE, Andrea, Connection '76

Born in Nashville. Female disco singer/actress. Appeared in several X-rated movies in the 1970s.

| 6/19/76 | 47 | 17 | | | **More, More, More** .... | $12 | Buddah 5670 |

Call Me   Fill Me Up (Heart To Heart)   Keep It Up Longer   **More, More, More Pt. 1** *4*   Party Line *80*

TRUE VIBE '01

Christian vocal group from Cincinnati: Jason Barton, Nathan Gaddis, Jonathan Lippmann and Jordan Roe.

| 6/2/01 | 178 | 2 | © | | **True Vibe** .... | $10 | Essential 10619 |

Give You More   Jump, Jump, Jump   Now And Forever   What Do We Wish On Now   You Are The Way
I Live For You   Never Again   Sweet Jesus   Without Love   You Found Me

TRUTH, The '87

Rock duo from England: Dennis Greaves and Mick Lister.

| 5/30/87 | 115 | 8 | © | | **Weapons Of Love** .... | $10 | I.R.S. 5981 |

Another New Day   Cover Up My Face   Respect   This Way Forever   **Weapons Of Love** *65*
Come On Back To Me   Edge Of Town   Soul Deep Fascination   Until It Burns   Winterland

TRYTHALL, Gil '70

Born Richard Trythall on 7/25/39 in Knoxville, Tennessee. Moog synthesizer player.

| 2/7/70 | 157 | 6 | | | **Switched On Nashville/Country Moog** .... [I] | $15 | Athena 6003 |

Cattle Call   Folsom Prison Blues   Harper Valley P.T.A.   Little Green Apples   Walkin' The Floor Over You   Yakety Moog
Foggy Mountain Breakdown   Gentle On My Mind   Last Date   Orange Blossom Special   Wildwood Flower

TSOL '87

Hard-rock group formed in Los Angeles: Joe Wood (vocals), Ron Emory (guitar), Mike Roche (bass) and Mitch Dean (drums). TSOL: True Sounds Of Liberty.

| 7/4/87 | 184 | 2 | | © | Hit And Run .... | | | $10 | Enigma 73263 |

Dreamer | Hit And Run | Name Is Love | Road Of Gold | Stay With Me | You Can Try
Good Mornin' Blues | It's Too Late | Not Alone Anymore | Sixteen | Where Did I Go Wrong

TUBES, The '83

Pop-rock group from San Francisco: **Fee Waybill** (vocals), Bill Spooner and Roger Steen (guitars), Michael Cotton and Vince Welnick (keyboards), Rick Anderson (bass) and Prairie Prince (drums). Welnick joined the **Grateful Dead** in 1990.

8/2/75	113	18		© 1	The Tubes			$12	A&M 4534
5/15/76	46	15		© 2	Young And Rich			$12	A&M 4580
5/28/77	122	6		3	Now...			$12	A&M 4632
3/11/78	82	8		4	What Do You Want From Live		[L]	$15	A&M 6003 [2]

recorded November 1977 at the Hammersmith Odeon in London

3/31/79	46	18		© 5	Remote Control			$12	A&M 4751
5/30/81	36	27		© 6	The Completion Backward Principle			$10	Capitol 12151
8/29/81	148	6		© 7	T.R.A.S.H. (Tubes Rarities And Smash Hits)................		[K]	$10	A&M 4870
4/2/83	18	34		© 8	Outside Inside			$10	Capitol 12260
3/23/85	87	10		© 9	Love Bomb			$10	Capitol 12381

Amnesia (6)
Attack Of The Fifty Foot Woman (6)
Be Mine Tonight (5)
Bora Bora 2000 (medley) (9)
Boy Crazy (1,4)
Brighter Day (2)
Cathy's Clone (3)
Come As You Are (9)
Crime Medley (4)
Don't Touch Me There (2,4,7) **61**
Don't Want To Wait Anymore (6) **35**
Drivin' All Night (7)
Drum Solo (4)

Drums (8)
Eyes (9)
Fantastic Delusion (8)
Feel It (9)
For A Song (9)
Getoverture (5)
Glass House (8)
God-Bird-Change (3,4)
Golden Boy (3)
Got Yourself A Deal (9)
Haloes (1)
Hit Parade (5)
I Saw Her Standing There (4)
I Want It All Now (5)
I Was A Punk Before You Were A Punk (4)

I'm Just A Mess (3,7)
Let's Make Some Noise (6)
Love Bomb (medley) (9)
Love Will Keep Us Together (7)
Love's A Mystery (I Don't Understand) (5)
Madam I'm Adam (medley) (2)
Malaguena Salerosa (1)
Matter Of Pride (6)
Mondo Bondage (1,4,7)
Monkey Time (8) **68**
Mr. Hate (6)
Muscle Girls (9)
My Head Is My Only House Unless It Rains (3)
Night People (9)

No Mercy (5)
No Not Again (8)
No Way Out (5)
One Good Reason (9)
Only The Strong Survive (5,7)
Out Of The Business (8)
Outside Lookin' Inside (9)
Overture (4)
Piece By Piece (9) **87**
Pimp (2)
Poland Whole (medley) (2)
Pound Of Flesh (3)
Power Tools (6)
Prime Time (5,7)
Proud To Be An American (2)
Say Hey (Part 1 & 2) (9)

She's A Beauty (8) **10**
Show Me A Reason (4)
Slipped My Disco (2,7)
Smoke (La Vie En Fumer) (3,4)
Space Baby (1)
Special Ballet (4)
Stand Up And Shout (2,4)
Stella (9)
Strung Out On Strings (3)
Summer Place, Theme From A (9)
Sushi Girl (6)
TV Is King (5)
Talk To Ya Later (6)
Telecide (5)
Theme Park (8)

Think About Me (6)
This Town (3)
Tip Of My Tongue (8) **52**
Tubes World Tour (2)
Turn Me On (5,7)
Up From The Deep (1)
What Do You Want From Life (1,4,7)
White Punks On Dope (1,4,7)
Wild Women Of Wongo (8)
Wooly Bully (medley) (9)
You're No Fun (3,4)
Young And Rich (2)

TUCK & PATTI '89

Husband-and-wife duo: Tuck Andress (guitar) Patti Cathcart (vocals). Married in 1981.

| 6/24/89 | 162 | 11 | | © 1 | Love Warriors .... | | | $10 | Windham Hill 116 |
| 5/18/91 | 186 | 1 | | © 2 | Dream .... | | | $10 | Windham Hill 0130 |

All The Love (2)
As Time Goes By (2)
Cantador (Like A Lover) (1)
Castles Made Of Sand (medley) (1)

Dream (2)
Europa (1)
Friends In High Places (2)
From Now On (We're One) (2)
Glory Glory (1)

High Heel Blues (2)
Hold Out, Hold Up And Hold On (1)
Honey Pie (1)
I Wish (2)

If It's Magic (1)
Little Wing (medley) (1)
Love Warriors (1)
On A Clear Day (1)
One Hand, One Heart (2)

Sitting In Limbo (2)
They Can't Take That Away From Me (1)
Togetherness (2)
Voodoo Music (2)

TUCKER, Louise '83

Born in England. Classical-styled vocalist.

| 8/6/83 | 127 | 10 | | © | Midnight Blue .... | | | $10 | Arista 8088 |

Gettin' Older | Hush | **Midnight Blue** **46** | Shadows | Waiting For Hugo
Graveyard Angel | Jerusalem | Only For You | Voices In The Wind

TUCKER, Tanya '92

Born on 10/10/58 in Seminole, Texas; raised in Wilcox, Arizona. Country singer.

1)What Do I Do With Me 2)Can't Run From Yourself 3)TNT

3/30/74	159	6	●	© 1	Would You Lay With Me (In A Field Of Stone)...............			$15	Columbia 32744
5/17/75	113	7	●	2	Tanya Tucker			$12	MCA 2141
12/2/78+	54	22	●	© 3	TNT			$12	MCA 3066
12/1/79	121	8		4	Tear Me Apart			$12	MCA 5106
8/1/81	180	3		5	Should I Do It			$12	MCA 5228
7/20/91+	48	70	▲	© 6	What Do I Do With Me			$10	Capitol 95562
10/24/92	51	39	▲	© 7	Can't Run From Yourself			$10	Liberty 98987
5/15/93	65	15	▲	© 8	Greatest Hits 1990-1992		[G]	$10	Liberty 81367
11/6/93	87	19	●	© 9	Soon			$10	Liberty 89048
4/8/95	169	5		© 10	Fire To Fire.			$10	Liberty 28943
4/12/97	124	12		© 11	Complicated..			$10	Capitol 36885

All I Have To Offer You Is Love (11)
Angel From Montgomery (3)
Baptism Of Jesse Taylor (1)
Bed Of Roses (1)
Better Late Than Never (4)
Between The Two Of Them (10)
Bidding America Goodbye (The Auction) (6)
Blind Love (4)
Blue Guitar (9)
Brown Eyed Handsome Man (3)
By Day By Day (4)
By The Way (1)
Can't Run From Yourself (7)
Come In Out Of The World (10)
Come On Honey (9)
Complicated (11)
Crossfire Of Desire (4)
Danger Ahead (7)
Don't Go Out (8)

Don't Let My Heart Be The Last To Know (7)
Down To My Last Teardrop (6,8)
Everything That You Want (6)
Find Out What's Happenin' (10)
Fire To Fire (10)
Half The Moon (7)
Hangin' In (9)
He Was Just Leaving (6)
Heartache #3 (5)
Heartbreak Hotel (3)
How Can I Tell Him (1)
I Believe The South Is Gonna Rise Again (1)
I Bet She Knows (10)
I Don't Believe That's How You Feel (11)
I Left My Heart In San Francisco (medley) (4)
I Love You Anyway (9)

I Oughta Let Go (5)
I'll Take The Memories (10)
I'll Take Today (10)
I'm Not Lisa (2)
I'm The Singer, You're The Song (3)
I've Learned To Live (7)
I've Never Said No Before (4)
If You Feel It (3)
If Your Heart Ain't Busy Tonight (6,8)
It Hurts Like Love (11)
It Won't Be Me (8)
It's A Little Too Late (7,8)
It's Nice To Be With You (3)
King Of Country Music (2)
Lay Back In The Arms Of Someone (4)
Let Me Be There (1)
Let The Good Times Roll (9)
Little Things (11)

Lizzie And The Rainman (2) **37**
Love Of A Rolling Stone (2)
Love Thing (11)
Love Will (10)
Love You Gave To Me (10)
Lover Goodbye (3)
Lucky Enough For Two (5)
Man That Turned Me Mama On (1) **86**
No Man's Land (1)
Nobody Dies From A Broken Heart (10)
Not Fade Away (3) **70**
Oh What It Did To Me (8)
Old Dan Tucker's Daughter (1)
Rainbow Rider (7)
Ridin' Out The Heartache (11)
Right About Now (6)
River And The Wind (3)
Rodeo Girls (5)
San Antonio Stroll (2)

San Francisco (Be Sure To Wear Some Flowers In Your Hair) (medley) (4)
Serenade That We Played (2)
Shady Streets (4)
Should I Do It (5)
Shoulder To Shoulder (5)
Silence Is King (9)
Sneaky Moon (3)
Some Kind Of Trouble (6,8)
Somebody Must Have Loved You Right Last Night (4)
Someday Soon (2)
Son-Of-A-Preacher Man (2)
Soon (9)
Stormy Weather (5)
Tear Me Apart (4)
Tell Me About It (7)
Texas (When I Die) (3)
Time And Distance (6)
Trail Of Tears (6)
Traveling Salesman (2)

Two Sparrows In A Hurricane (7,8)
Walking Shoes (8)
We Don't Have To Do This (9)
We're Playing Games Again (5)
What Do They Know (7)
What If We Were Running Out Of Love (1)
What Your Love Does For Me (11)
When Will I Be Loved (2)
Why Me, Lord (1)
Wishin' It All Away (11)
(Without You) What Do I Do With Me (6,8)
Would You Lay With Me (In A Field Of Stone) (1) **46**
You Don't Do It (11)
You Don't Have To Say You Love Me (5)
You Just Watch Me (9)

DEBUT	PEAK	WKS	RIAA	CD	ARTIST — Album Title	Catalog	Sym	$	Label & Number

TUFF DARTS '78
Rock group from New York City: Tommy Frenzy (vocals), Jeff Salen and Bobby Butani (guitars), John DeSalvo (bass) and John Morelli (drums). **Robert Gordon** was a member until 1976.

| 3/18/78 | 156 | 6 | | | Tuff Darts! | | | $15 | Sire 6048 |

All For The Love Of Rock & Roll
Fun City
Head Over Heels

Here Comes Trouble
Love And Trouble

My Guitar Lies Bleeding In My Arms
Phone Booth Man (P.B.M.)

Rats
She's Dead
Slash

Who's Been Sleeping Here?
(Your Love Is Like) Nuclear Waste

TURK '01
Born in New Orleans. Male rapper. Member of **Cash Money Millionaires** and **Hot Boy$**.

| 6/23/01 | 9 | 9 | | © | Young & Thuggin' | | | $10 | Cash Money 860926 |

All Night
At The Same Time
Bout To Go Down

Finna Records
Freak Da Hoes
Growing Up

Hallways & Cuts
It's In Me
One Saturday Night

Project
Soldierette
Trife Livin'

Untamed Guerrilla
Wanna Be Down
What Would You Do

Yes We Do

TURNER, Ike & Tina '71
Husband-and-wife R&B duo: guitarist Ike Turner (born on 11/5/31 in Clarksdale, Mississippi) and singer **Tina Turner** (born on 11/26/38 in Brownsville, Tennessee). Married from 1958-76. Duo inducted into the Rock and Roll Hall of Fame in 1991.
1)*Live At Carnegie Hall/What You Hear Is What You Get* 2)*Workin' Together* 3)*Outta Season*

| 2/6/65 | 126 | 6 | | | 1 Live! The Ike & Tina Turner Show | | [L] | $40 | Warner 1579 |

includes "Down In The Valley" by Jimmy Thomas, "Good Time Tonight" by Vanetta Fields and "My Man, He's A Lovin' Man" by Jessie Smith

| 4/19/69 | 91 | 12 | | | 2 Outta Season | | | $20 | Blue Thumb 5 |
| 7/19/69 | 142 | 9 | | | 3 In Person | | [L] | $20 | Minit 24018 |

recorded at the Basin Street West in San Francisco

| 9/27/69 | 102 | 8 | © | | 4 River Deep-Mountain High | | | $25 | A&M 4178 |

recorded in 1966

11/22/69	176	3			5 The Hunter			$20	Blue Thumb 11
5/16/70	130	19	©		6 Come Together			$15	Liberty 7637
12/5/70+	25	38	©		7 Workin' Together			$15	Liberty 7650
7/10/71	25	22	● ©		8 Live At Carnegie Hall/What You Hear Is What You Get		[L]	$20	United Artists 9953 [2]
11/20/71	108	10			9 'Nuff Said			$15	United Artists 5530
7/22/72	160	9			10 Feel Good			$15	United Artists 5598
12/22/73+	163	6	©		11 Nutbush City Limits			$15	United Artists 180
5/11/85	189	2			12 Get Back!		[G]	$10	Liberty 51156

African Boo's (medley) (3)
All I Could Do Was Cry (medley) (3)
(As Long As I Can) Get You When I Want You (7)
Baby-Get It On (12) **88**
Baby I Love You (medley) (3)
Baby (What You Want Me To Do) (9)
Black Coffee (10)
Bold Soul Sister (5) **59**
Bolic (10)
Can't You Hear Me Callin' (9)
Chopper (10)
Club Manhattan (11)
Come Together (6) **57**
Contact High (6)
Crazy 'Bout You Baby (2)
Daily Bread (11)
Doin' It (6)
Doin' The Tina Turner (8)
Drift Away (11)
Dust My Broom (2)
Early In The Morning (5)
Every Day I Have To Cry (4)

Everyday People (3,8)
Evil Man (6)
Fancy Annie (11)
Feel Good (10)
Finger Poppin' (1)
Five Long Years (2)
Fool In Love (3,4,12) **27**
Funkier Than A Mosquita's Tweeter (7)
Funky Street (3)
Game Of Love (7)
Get Back (7,12)
Get It Out Of Your Mind (11)
Gimme Some Lovin' (medley) (3)
Good Times (1)
Goodbye, So Long (3,7)
Grumbling (2)
High Heel Sneakers (Tight Pants) (1)
Hold On Baby (4)
Honest I Do (2)
Honky Tonk Women (6,8,12)
Hunter, The (5) **93**
I Am A Motherless Child (2)

I Can't Stop Loving You (1)
I Heard It Through The Grapevine (3)
I Idolize You (4) **82**
I Know (You Don't Want Me No More) (1,5)
I Like It (10)
I Love Baby (9)
I Love What You Do To Me (8)
I Smell Trouble (5,8)
I Want To Take You Higher (6,8,12) **34**
I'll Never Need More Than This (4)
I've Been Loving You Too Long (2,8) **68**
If I Knew Then (What I Know Now) (10)
If You Can Hully Gully (I Can Hully Gully Too) (10)
Ike's Tune (8)
It Ain't Right (Lovin' To Be Lovin') (6)
It's Gonna Work Out Fine (4) **14**

Kay Got Laid (Joe Got Paid) (10)
Keep On Walkin' (Don't Look Back) (6)
Let It Be (7)
Let's Spend The Night Together (12)
Love Like Yours (Don't Come Knocking Every Day) (4,8)
Make 'Em Wait (4)
Make Me Over (11)
Mean Old World (2)
Moving Into Hip Style-A Trip Child! (9)
My Babe (2)
Nutbush City Limits (11,12) **22**
Oh Baby! (Things Ain't What They Used To Be) (4)
Ooh Poo Pah Doo (7,8,12) **60**
Pick Me Up (Take Me Where Your Home Is) (9)
Piece Of My Heart (8)
Please Love Me (2)

Please, Please, Please (medley) (3)
Proud Mary (7,8,12) **4**
Reconsider Baby (2)
Respect (3,8)
River Deep-Mountain High (4,11,12) **88**
Rock Me Baby (2)
Save The Last Dance For Me (4)
She Came In Through The Bathroom Window (10)
Something's Got A Hold On Me (1)
Son Of A Preacher Man (3)
Such A Fool For You (4)
Sumit, The (medley) (3)
Sweet Flustrations (9)
Sweet Soul Music (3,8)
Tell The Truth (1,9)
That's My Purpose (11)
There Was A Time (medley) (3)
Things I Used To Do (5)
3 O'Clock In The Morning Blues (2)

Too Much Woman (For A Henpecked Man) (6)
Twist And Shout (1)
Unlucky Creature (4)
Way You Love Me (7)
What You Don't See (Is Better Yet) (9)
Why Can't We Be Happy (6)
Workin' Together (7)
You Are My Sunshine (1,11)
You Better Think Of Something (10)
You Can Have It (7)
You Don't Love Me (Yes I Know) (5)
You Got Me Running (5)
You're Still My Baby (5)
Young And Dumb (6)

TURNER, Joe Lynn '85
Born in New Jersey. Rock singer/guitarist. Member of **Rainbow** and **Deep Purple**.

| 11/2/85 | 143 | 12 | | | Rescue You | | | $10 | Elektra 60449 |

Endlessly
Eyes Of Love

Feel The Fire
Get Tough

Losing You
On The Run

Race Is On
Rescue You

Soul Searcher
Young Hearts

TURNER, Ruby '90
Born in 1958 in Jamaica; raised in Birmingham, England. R&B singer.

| 3/31/90 | 194 | 2 | © | | Paradise | | | $10 | Jive 1298 |

Everytime I Breathe
It's A Cryin' Shame

It's Gonna Be Alright
It's You My Heart Beats For

Leaves In The Wind
Paradise

See Me
Sexy

Surrender
There's No Better Love

TURNER, Spyder '67
Born Dwight Turner in 1947 in Beckley, West Virginia. R&B singer.

| 3/25/67 | 158 | 3 | | | Stand By Me | | | $30 | MGM 4450 |

Don't Hold Back
Dream Lover
For Your Precious Love

Hold On, I'm Coming
I Can't Make It Anymore **95**

I Can't Wait To See My Baby's Face
I Don't Want To Cry

I'm Alive With A Lovin' Feeling
Moon River
Morning, Morning

Stand By Me **12**

★386★ TURNER, Tina '84
Born Anna Mae Bullock on 11/26/38 in Brownsville, Tennessee. R&B singer/actress. Half of **Ike & Tina Turner** duo. Married to Ike from 1958-76. Acted in the movies *Tommy* and *Mad Max-Beyond Thunderdome*. Her autobiography, *What's Love Got To Do With It*, was made into a movie in 1993.

9/20/75	155	5		©	1 Acid Queen			$15	United Artists 495
6/16/84	3	106	▲5	©	2 Private Dancer			$10	Capitol 12330
9/27/86	4	52	▲	©	3 Break Every Rule			$10	Capitol 12530

TURNER, Tina — Cont'd

DEBUT	PEAK	WKS	RIAA	CD	ARTIST — Album Title	Catalog	Sym	$	Label & Number
4/9/88	86	9		© 4	Tina Live In Europe		[L]	$15	Capitol 90126 [2]
10/7/89	31	21	●	© 5	Foreign Affair			$10	Capitol 91873
11/9/91	113	17	▲	© 6	Simply The Best	C:#41/1	[G]	$10	Capitol 97152
7/3/93	17	30	▲	© 7	What's Love Got To Do With It		[S]	$10	Virgin 88189
9/21/96	61	27		© 8	Wildest Dreams			$10	Virgin 41920
2/19/00	21	16	●	© 9	Twenty Four Seven			$10	Virgin 23180

Absolutely Nothing's Changed (9)
Acid Queen (1)
Addicted To Love (4)
Afterglow (3)
All Kinds Of People (8)
All The Woman (3)
Ask Me How I Feel (5)
Baby-Get It On (1)
Back Where You Started (3)
Be Tender With Me Baby (5)
Best, The (5,6) *15*
Better Be Good To Me (2,4,6) *5*
Bootsey Whitelaw (1)
Break Every Rule (3,4) *74*
Change Is Gonna Come (4)
Confidential (8)

Dancing In My Dreams (8)
(Darlin') You Know I Love You (7)
Difference Between Us (8)
Disco Inferno (7)
Do What You Do (8)
Don't Leave Me This Way (9)
Falling (9)
Falling Like Rain (5)
Fool In Love (7)
Foreign Affair (5)
Girls (3)
Go Ahead (9)
Goldeneye (8)
Help (4)
I Can See For Miles (1)
I Can't Stand The Rain (2,4,6)

I Don't Wanna Fight (7) *9*
I Don't Wanna Lose You (5,6)
I Might Have Been Queen (Soul Survivor) (2,7)
I Want You Near Me (6)
I Will Be There (9)
I'll Be Thunder (3)
In The Midnight Hour (4)
In Your Wildest Dreams (8)
It Take Two (6)
It's Gonna Work Out Fine (7)
It's Only Love (4)
Land Of 1,000 Dances (4)
Let's Dance (4)
Let's Spend The Night Together (1)
Let's Stay Together (2,4,6) *26*
Look Me In The Heart (5,6)

Love Thing (6)
Missing You (8) *84*
1984 (2)
Not Enough Romance (5)
Nutbush City Limits (4,7)
Nutbush City Limits (The 90's Version) (6)
On Silent Wings (8)
Overnight Sensation (3)
Paradise Is Here (3,4)
Pick Me Tonight (1)
Private Dancer (2,4,6) *7*
Proud Mary (4,7)
River Deep - Mountain High (6)
Rock Me Baby (7)
Rockin' And Rollin' (1)
Show Some Respect (2,4) *37*
634-5789 (4)

Something Beautiful Remains (8)
Stay Awhile (7)
Steamy Windows (5,6) *39*
Steel Claw (2)
Talk To My Heart (9)
Tearing Us Apart (4)
Thief Of Hearts (8)
Till The Right Man Comes Along (3)
Tonight (4)
Twenty Four Seven (9)
Two People (3,4) *30*
Typical Male (3,4,6) *2*
Under My Thumb (1)
Undercover Agent For The Blues (7)
Unfinished Sympathy (8)

Way Of The World (6)
We Don't Need Another Hero (Thunderdome) (4,6) *2*
What You Get Is What You See (3,4,6) *13*
What's Love Got To Do With It (2,4,6,7) *1*
Whatever You Need (9)
Whatever You Want (6)
When The Heartache Is Over (9)
Whole Lotta Love (1)
Why Must We Wait Until Tonight? (7) *97*
Without You (9)
You Can't Stop Me Loving You (5)
You Know Who (Is Doing You Know What) (5)

★452★   TURRENTINE, Stanley   '75

Born on 4/5/34 in Pittsburgh. Died of a stroke on 9/12/2000 (age 66). Jazz fusion tenor saxophonist. Member of **Fuse One**.

1)West Side Highway   2)In The Pocket   3)Pieces Of Dreams

DEBUT	PEAK	WKS			ARTIST — Album Title	Catalog	Sym	$	Label & Number
1/7/67	149	2		© 1	Rough 'N Tumble		[I]	$20	Blue Note 84240
11/2/68	193	3		2	The Look Of Love		[I]	$20	Blue Note 84286
3/20/71	182	3		© 3	Sugar		[I]	$15	CTI 6005
10/19/74	69	21		© 4	Pieces Of Dreams		[I]	$15	Fantasy 9465
11/16/74	185	7		5	The Baddest Turrentine		[I-K]	$15	CTI 6048
3/8/75	110	13		6	The Sugar Man		[I-K]	$15	CTI 6052
5/10/75	65	14		7	In The Pocket		[I]	$12	Fantasy 9478
11/1/75	76	16		8	Have You Ever Seen The Rain		[I]	$12	Fantasy 9493
6/12/76	100	14		© 9	Everybody Come On Out		[I]	$12	Fantasy 9508
11/27/76+	96	14		10	The Man With The Sad Face		[I]	$12	Fantasy 9519
9/10/77	84	9		11	Nightwings		[I]	$12	Fantasy 9534
3/18/78	63	12		12	West Side Highway		[I]	$12	Fantasy 9548
9/16/78	106	13		13	What About You!		[I]	$12	Fantasy 9563
10/10/81	162	3		14	Tender Togetherness		[I]	$12	Elektra 534

After The Love Is Gone (14)
Airport Love Theme (9)
All By Myself (9)
And Satisfy (1)
Ann, Wonderful One (12)
Baptismal (1)
Beautiful Friendship (2)
Birdland (11)
Black Lassie (7)
Blanket On The Beach (4)
Blues For Stan (2)
Cabin In The Sky (2)
Cherubim (14)
Deep In Love (4)
Disco Dancing (13)
Don't Give Up On Us (11)
Don't Mess With Mister T (5)
Emily (2)

Everybody Come On Out (9)
Evil (4)
Evil Ways (10)
Feel The Fire (13)
Feeling Good (1)
Have It Your Way, Sandy (7)
Have You Ever Seen The Rain (8)
Havin' Fun With Mr. T. (14)
Here There And Everywhere (2)
Heritage (13)
Hermanos (14)
Hope That We Can Be Together Soon (9)
Hudson Parkway (West Side Highway) (12)
I Know It's You (4)
I Want You (10)

I'll Give You My Love (14)
I'm Always Drunk In San Francisco (2)
I'm In Love (4)
I'm Not In Love (9)
If You Don't Believe (11)
Impressions (3)
In The Pocket (7)
Joao (1)
Just As I Am (6)
Ligia (10)
Look Of Love (2)
Love Hangover (10)
Loving You Is Sweeter Than Ever (7)
MacArthur Park (2)
Make Me Rainbows (6)
Man With The Sad Face (10)

Manhattan Skyline (13)
Many Rivers To Cross (9)
Midnight And You (4)
Mighty High (10)
More (Theme from Mondo Cane) (6)
My Wish For You (13)
Naked As The Day I Was Born (7)
Nightwings (11)
Only You And Me (14)
Over To Where You Are (7)
Papa "T" (11)
Peace Of Mind (12)
Pieces Of Dreams (4,6)
Reasons (8)
Salt Song (5)
Shake (1)

Smile (2)
Spaced (7)
Speedball (5)
Stairway To Heaven (9)
Stan's Thing (12)
Stretch, The (6)
Sugar (3,5,12)
Sunshine Alley (3)
T's Dream (8)
Tamarac (14)
That's The Way Of The World (8)
There Is A Place (Rita's Theme) (9)
There's Music In The Air (11)
This Guy's In Love With You (2)
Tommy's Tune (3)
Touching You (8)

Vera Cruz (6)
Walk On By (1)
Walkin' (12)
What Could I Do Without You (1)
Whatever Possess'd Me (10)
Wind And The Sea (13)
World Chimes (14)
You (8)
You Are The Melody Of My Life (7)
You'll Never Find Another Love Like Mine (10)
You're My Baby (7)

TURTLES, The   '68

Pop-rock group formed in Los Angeles: Mark Volman and Howard Kaylan (vocals), Jim Tucker (guitar), Al Nichol (keyboards), Chuck Portz (bass) and Don Murray (drums). Volman and Kaylan (under the names Flo and Eddie) later joined **The Mothers Of Invention**. Murray died on 3/22/96 (age 50).

DEBUT	PEAK	WKS			ARTIST — Album Title	Catalog	Sym	$	Label & Number
10/23/65+	98	19		© 1	It Ain't Me Babe			$40	White Whale 7111
4/29/67	25	22		© 2	Happy Together			$40	White Whale 7114
11/18/67+	7	39	●	3	The Turtles! Golden Hits		[G]	$40	White Whale 7115
11/16/68	128	12		© 4	The Turtles Present The Battle of the Bands			$40	White Whale 7118
11/1/69	117	9		© 5	Turtle Soup			$40	White Whale 7124
4/11/70	146	9		6	The Turtles! More Golden Hits		[G]	$40	White Whale 7127
12/21/74	194	7		7	The Turtles' Greatest Hits/Happy Together Again		[G]	$20	Sire 3703 [2]

Bachelor Mother (5)
Battle Of The Bands (4,7)
Buzzsaw (4)
Can I Get To Know You Better (3,7) *89*
Can I Go On (7)
Can't You Hear The Cows (7)
Cat In The Window (6)
Chicken Little Was Right (4)
Come Over (5)
Dance This Dance (4)
Earth Anthem (4)
Elenore (4,6,7) *6*
Eve Of Destruction (1) *100*

Food (4)
Gas Money (7)
Glitter And Gold (1)
Grim Reaper Of Love (3,7) *81*
Guide For The Married Man (2,7)
Happy Together (2,3,7) *1*
Hot Little Hands (5,6)
House On The Hill (5)
How You Loved Me (5)
I'm Chief Kamanawanalea (We're The Royal Macadamia Nuts) (3)
Is It Any Wonder (3)

It Ain't Me Babe (1,3,7) *8*
It Was A Very Good Year (7)
John & Julie (5)
Lady-O (5,7) *78*
Last Laugh (7)
Last Thing I Remember (4)
Let Me Be (1,3,7) *29*
Let The Cold Winds Blow (1)
Like A Rolling Stone (1)
Like It Or Not (7)
Like The Seasons (2)
Love In The City (5,6,7) *91*
Love Minus Zero (1)
Makin' My Mind Up (2)

Me About You (2,7)
Oh, Daddy! (4)
Outside Chance (3,7)
Person Without A Care (2)
Rugs Of Woods & Flowers (2)
Santa And The Sidewalk Surfer (7)
She Always Leaves Me Laughing (5)
She'd Rather Be With Me (2,3,7) *3*
She's My Girl (6,7) *14*
So Goes Love (3)
Somewhere Friday Night (5,7)

Sound Asleep (6,7) *57*
Story Of Rock And Roll (6,7) *48*
Surfer Dan (4)
Teardrops (7)
There You Sit Lonely (7)
Think I'll Run Away (2)
Too Much Heartsick Feeling (4)
Too Young To Be One (2)
Torn Between Temptations (5)
Walk In The Sun (1)
Walking Song (2)
Wanderin' Kind (1)

We Ain't Gonna Party No More (6)
Who Would Ever Think That I Would Marry Margaret (6)
You Baby (3,7) *20*
You Don't Have To Walk In The Rain (5,6,7) *51*
You Know What I Mean (3,7) *12*
You Showed Me (4,6,7) *6*
You Want To Be A Woman (7)
Your Maw Said You Cried In Your Sleep Last Night (1)

TUTONE, Tommy — see TOMMY

TUXEDO JUNCTION '78
Female disco group: Jamie Edlin, Marilyn Jackson, Sue Allen and Marti McCall.

2/18/78 **56** 32 **Tuxedo Junction** .... $12 Butterfly 007

Chattanooga Choo Choo *32*   I Didn't Know About You   Rainy Night In Rio   Volga Boatman
Fox Trot   Moonlight Serenade   Tuxedo Junction

TWAIN, Shania '96
Born Eileen Edwards on 8/28/65 in Windsor, Ontario; raised in Timmins, Ontario, Canada. Country singer/songwriter. Married record producer Robert John "Mutt" Lange on 12/28/93.

3/18/95+ **5** 107 ▲12 © 1 **The Woman In Me**   C:❶1/155 $10 Mercury 522886
2/24/96 **35**C 9 ▲ © 2 **Shania Twain** .... [E] $10 Mercury 514422
    released in 1993
11/22/97 **2**2 151 ▲18 © 3 **Come On Over**   C:#21/51 $10 Mercury 536003

Any Man Of Mine (1) *31*   God Ain't Gonna Getcha For   I'm Holdin' On To Love (To   **Love Gets Me Every Time**   There Goes The Neighborhood   You Lay A Whole Lot Of Love
Black Eyes, Blue Tears (3)   That (2)   Save My Life) (3)   (3) *25*   (2)   On Me (2)
Come On Over (3) *58*   **God Bless The Child** (1) *75*   If It Don't Take Two (1)   **Man! I Feel Like A Woman!**   What Made You Say That (2)   You Win My Love (1)
Crime Of The Century (2)   Got A Hold On Me (2)   If You Wanna Touch Her, Ask!   (3) *23*   Whatever You Do! Dont! (3)   **You're Still The One** (3) *2*
Dance With The One That   Home Ain't Where His Heart Is   (3)   No One Needs To Know (1)   When (3)   **You've Got A Way** (3) *49*
   Brought You (2)   (Anymore) (1)   **(If You're Not In It For Love)**   Raining On Our Love (1)   When He Leaves You (2)
Don't Be Stupid (You Know I   Honey, I'm Home (3)   **I'm Outta Here!** (1) *74*   Rock This Country! (3)   **Whose Bed Have Your Boots**
   Love You) (3) *40*   I Won't Leave You Lonely (3)   Is There Life After Love? (1)   Still Under The Weather (2)   **Been Under?** (1) *87*
Forget Me (2)   Leaving Is The Only Way Out (1)   **That Don't Impress Me Much**   Woman In Me (Needs The
From This Moment On (3) *4*   (3) *7*   Man In You) (1)

T.W.D.Y. '99
Rap production presented by **Ant Banks**. T.W.D.Y.: The Who Damn Yey.

5/8/99 **135** 9 © **Derty Werk** .... $10 Thump Street 9986

Cross Me Up   Gameless Mortals   On The Reala   **Players Holiday** *90*   Squeeze Onem
Drinks On Me   Gotta Have Heart   Out 2 Get Mo   Ride Wit Me   Stragglas
Game, The   I Can't Change   Pervin   Shook Niggas

12 GAUGE '94
Born Isiah Pinkney in Augusta, Georgia. Male rapper.

4/2/94 **141** 8 © **12 Gauge** .... $10 Street Life 75439

Bend Over (Ooh Lord)   **Dunkie Butt** *28*   Freestyle   Grip Ya Hips   Lay You Down   U Go Girl
Brother's Keeper   Freak It   Ghetto Freakin   I Got A Thing For You   Rump

TWENNYNINE FEATURING LENNY WHITE '80
Funk group from New York City: Donald Blackman (vocals), Eddie Martinez and Nick Moroch (guitars), Denzil Miller (keyboards), Barry Johnson (bass) and **Lenny White** (drums).

12/8/79+ **54** 16 1 **Best Of Friends** .... $12 Elektra 223
11/1/80 **106** 8 2 **Twennynine with Lenny White** .... $12 Elektra 304
12/5/81 **162** 5 3 **Just Like Dreamin'** .... $12 Elektra 551

All I Want (3)   Citi Dancin' (1)   It's Music, It's Magic (2)   Morning Sunrise (1)   **Peanut Butter** (1) *83*   Twennynine (The Rap) (3)
All Over Again (3)   Don't Look Back (3)   Just Like Dreamin' (3)   Movin' On (3)   Rhythm (3)   We Had To Break Away (2)
Back To You (2)   11th Fanfare (3)   Just Right For Me (2)   My Melody (2)   Slip Away (2)
Best Of Friends (1)   Fancy Dancer (2)   Kid Stuff (3)   Need You (3)   Take Me Or Leave Me (1)
Betta (1)   Find A Love (3)   Love And Be Loved (2)   Oh, Sylvie (1)   Tropical Nights (1)

24-7 SPYZ '89
Black hard-rock group from the Bronx, New York: Peter Forest (vocals), Jimi Hazel (guitar), Rick Skatore (bass) and Anthony Johnson (drums).

6/17/89 **113** 16 © 1 **Harder Than You** .... $10 In-Effect 3006
7/14/90 **135** 11 © 2 **Gumbo Millennium** .... $10 In-Effect 3014

Ballots Not Bullets (1)   Dude U Knew (2)   John Connelly's Theory (2)   Racism (2)   Spyz Dope (1)   We'll Have Power (2)
Culo Posse (2)   Grandma Dynamite (1)   Jungle Boogie (1)   Social Plague (1)   Spyz On Piano (2)
Deathstyle (2)   Heaven And Hell (2)   New Drug (1)   Some Defenders' Memories (1)   Tango Skin Polka (2)
Don't Break My Heart! (1)   I Must Go On (1)   New Super Hero Worship (2)   Spill My Guts (1)   Valdez 27 Million? (2)
Don't Push Me (2)   Jimi'z Jam (1)   Pillage (1)   Sponji Reggae (1)   We Got A Date (2)

20/20 '81
Pop-rock group from Tulsa, Oklahoma: Steve Allen (vocals, guitar), Chris Silagyi (keyboards), Ron Flynt (bass) and Mike Gallo (drums).

11/3/79 **138** 13 © 1 **20/20** .... $12 Portrait 36205
6/20/81 **127** 12 © 2 **Look Out!** .... $12 Portrait 37050

Action Now (1)   Cheri (1)   Mobile Unit 245 (2)   Remember The Lightning (1)   Tell Me Why (Can't Understand
Alien (2)   Girl Like You (2)   Night I Heard A Scream (2)   She's An Obsession (1)   You) (1)
American Dream (2)   Jet Lag (1)   Nuclear Boy (2)   Sky Is Falling (1)   Tonight We Fly (1)
Backyard Guys (1)   Leaving Your World Behind (1)   Out Of My Head (2)   Strange Side Of Love (2)   Yellow Pills (1)
Beat City (2)   Life In The U.S.A. (2)   Out Of This Time (1)

TWILLEY, Dwight '84
Born on 6/6/51 in Tulsa, Oklahoma. Rock singer/songwriter/pianist. Formed the Dwight Twilley Band with **Phil Seymour** (bass, drums) in 1974.

7/31/76 **138** 14 1 **Sincerely** .... $12 Shelter 52001
10/8/77 **70** 13 2 **Twilley Don't Mind** .... $12 Arista 4140
      DWIGHT TWILLEY BAND (above 2)
3/24/79 **113** 9 3 **Twilley** .... $12 Arista 4214
3/13/82 **109** 11 4 **Scuba Divers** .... $10 EMI America 17064
2/18/84 **39** 21 5 **Jungle** .... $10 EMI America 17107

Alone In My Room (3)   Don't You Love Her (5)   I Wanna Make Love To You (3)   **Little Bit Of Love** (5) *77*   Runaway (3)   Three Persons (1)
Baby Let's Cruise (3)   England (1)   I'm Back Again (4)   Long Lonely Nights (5)   Sincerely (1)   To Get To You (5)
Betsy Sue (3)   Falling In Love Again (4)   I'm Losing You (4)   Looking For The Magic (2)   Sleeping (4)   Touchin' The Wind (4)
Chance To Get Away (2)   Feeling In The Dark (1)   **I'm On Fire** (1) *16*   Max Dog (4)   Somebody To Love (4)   Trying To Find My Baby (2)
Could Be Love (1)   Girls (5) *16*   Invasion (2)   Nothing's Ever Gonna Change   Standin' In The Shadow Of Love (3)   Twilley Don't Mind (3)
Cry Baby (5)   Got You Where I Want You (3)   It Takes Alot Of Love (3)   So Fast (4)   TV (1)   Why You Wanna Break My
Cryin' Over Me (4)   Here She Come (2)   Jungle (4)   Out Of My Hands (3)   10,000 American Scuba Divers   Heart (5)
Darlin' (3)   I Found The Magic (4)   Just Like The Sun (1)   Release Me (1)   Dancin' (4)   You Can Change It (5)
Dion Baby (4)   I Think It's That Girl (4)   Later That Night (4)   Rock And Roll '47 (2)   That I Remember (2)   You Were So Warm (1)

901

TWIN HYPE '89

Rap duo from New Jersey: twin brothers Glennis and Lennis Brown.

| 8/26/89 | 140 | 11 | | © | Twin Hype .... | | | $10 | Profile 1281 |

Do It To The Crowd · For Those Who Like To Groove · My Metaphors · Smooth · Tales Of The Twins
Fanatics · Lori · Serious Attitude · Suckers Never Change · Twin Hype

TWINZ '95

Rap duo from Long Beach, California: identical twins Deon and DeWayne Williams.

| 9/9/95 | 36 | 9 | | © | Conversation .... | | | $10 | G Funk 527883 |

Don't Get It Twisted · 1st Round Draft Pick · Good Times · Journey Wit Me · Pass It On · Sorry I Kept You
Eastside LB · 4 Eyes 2 Heads · Hollywood · Jump Ta This · **Round & Round 84**

TWISTA '98

Born in Chicago. Male rapper.

| 7/12/97 | 77 | 17 | ● | © 1 | Adrenaline Rush... | | | $10 | Creator's Way 92757 |
| 10/24/98 | 34 | 6 | | © 2 | Mobstability .... | | | $10 | Creator's Way 83142 |

TWISTA & THE SPEEDKNOT MOBSTAZ

| 3/24/01 | 150 | 9 | | © 3 | Twista Presents: New Testament 2K Street Scriptures Compilation ...... [K] | | | $10 | Legit Ballin' 0001 |

Adrenaline Rush (1) · Get Her In Tha Mood (1) · Korrupt World (1) · Motive 4 Murder (2) · Round Here (3) · Wee Straight (3)
Ball Wit Us (3) · **Get It Wet** (1) 96 · Legit Ballers (2,3) · No Remorse (1) · Run (3) · Why (3)
Crook County (2) · Getty Up (3) · Loyalty (2) · Overdose (1) · Smoke Wit You (2) · Would U Mind (3)
Death Before Dishonor (1) · He Lay (3) · Mash & Bang (3) · Party Hoes (2) · Stick Up Part Two (3)
Dirty Game (3) · How To Ball (3) · Mob Niggas Don't Die (3) · Peace Of Mind (3) · Stories (3)
Dreams (2) · In Your World (2) · Mob Up (2) · Pray For Me (3) · U Don't Know Me (3)
Emotions (1) · It Feels So Good (1) · Mobstability (2) · Put That Thang On Me (3) · Unsolved Mystery (1)
Front Porch (2) · Kill Murder (3) · Mobster's Anthem (1) · Rock Y'all Spot (2) · Warm Embrace (2)

TWISTED SISTER '84

Hard-rock group from Long Island, New York: Dee Snider (vocals), Jay French (guitar) and Eddie Ojeda (guitars), Mark Mendosa (bass), and A.J. Pero (drums). Joey Franco replaced Pero in 1987.

8/27/83+	130	14	●	© 1	You Can't Stop Rock 'N' Roll..			$10	Atlantic 80074
7/7/84	15	51	▲³	© 2	Stay Hungry			$10	Atlantic 80156
7/6/85	125	11		© 3	Under The Blade			[E]	$10	Atlantic 81256

remixed edition of their first album plus bonus track

| 12/21/85+ | 53 | 17 | ● | © 4 | Come Out And Play... | | | $10 | Atlantic 81275 |
| 8/1/87 | 74 | 11 | | © 5 | Love Is For Suckers .... | | | $10 | Atlantic 81772 |

Bad Boys (Of Rock 'N' Roll) (3) · Horror-Teria (The Beginning) · I'll Take You Alive (1) · One Bad Habit (5) · Tear It Loose (3) · Yeah Right! (5)
Be Chrool To Your Scuel (4) · Medley (2) · I'm So Hot For You (5) · Out On The Streets (4) · Tonight (5) · You Are All That I Need (5)
Beast, The (2) · Hot Love (5) · I've Had Enough (1) · Power And The Glory (1) · Under The Blade (3) · You Can't Stop Rock 'N' Roll (1)
Burn In Hell (2) · I Am (I'm Me) (1) · Kids Are Back (1) · Price, The (2) · Wake Up (The Sleeping Giant) · You Want What We Got (4)
Come Out And Play (4) · I Believe In Rock 'N' Roll (4) · Kill Or Be Killed (4) · Ride To Live, Live To Ride (1) · (5) · You're Not Alone (Suzette's
Day Of The Rocker (3) · I Believe In You (4) · Leader Of The Pack (4) 53 · Run For Your Life (3) · We're Gonna Make It (1) · Song) (1)
Destroyer (3) · **I Wanna Rock** (2) 68 · Like A Knife In The Back (1) · S.M.F. (2) · **We're Not Gonna Take It**
Don't Let Me Down (2) · I Want This Night (To Last · Lookin' Out For #1 (4) · Shoot 'Em Down (3) · (2) 21
Fire Still Burns (4) · Forever) (5) · Love Is For Suckers (5) · Sin After Sin (3) · What You Don't Know (Sure
· I'll Never Grow Up, Now! (3) · Me And The Boys (5) · Stay Hungry (2) · Can Hurt You) (3)

TWITTY, Conway '71

Born Harold Jenkins on 9/1/33 in Friars Point, Mississippi; raised in Helena, Arkansas. Died of an abdominal aneurysm on 6/5/93 (age 59). Legendary country singer. Appeared in the movies *Sexpot Goes To College* and *College Confidential*. Switched from pop to country music in 1965.

1)Hello Darlin' 2)We Only Make Believe 3)How Much More Can She Stand

8/16/69	161	3		1	I Love You More Today			$20	Decca 75131
7/4/70	65	26	●	© 2	Hello Darlin'			$20	Decca 75209
1/23/71	140	7		3	Fifteen Years Ago..			$20	Decca 75248
3/13/71	78	14	●		4	We Only Make Believe			$20	Decca 75251

CONWAY TWITTY & LORETTA LYNN

5/22/71	91	9		5	How Much More Can She Stand			$20	Decca 75276
9/18/71	142	8		6	I Wonder What She'll Think About Me Leaving			$20	Decca 75292
3/4/72	106	13	●		7	Lead Me On			$20	Decca 75326

CONWAY TWITTY & LORETTA LYNN

| 4/8/72 | 130 | 9 | | 8 | I Can't See Me Without You.. | | | $20 | Decca 75335 |
| 8/25/73 | 153 | 9 | | 9 | Louisiana Woman-Mississippi Man............................... | | | $15 | MCA 335 |

CONWAY TWITTY & LORETTA LYNN

9/15/73	134	9	●		10	You've Never Been This Far Before/Baby's Gone			$15	MCA 359
2/13/82	144	15		11	Southern Comfort...			$10	Elektra 60005
6/26/93	15 C	11	▲	© 12	The Very Best Of Conway Twitty .... [G]			$10	MCA 31238
6/26/93	43 C	1		© 13	The Best Of The Best Of Conway Twitty .... [G]			$10	Federal 6502
6/26/93	44 C	1		© 14	Greatest Hits Volume III .... [G]			$10	MCA 6391
9/18/93	135	7		© 15	Final Touches			$10	MCA 10882

Above And Beyond (The Call Of · Bring It On Home (To Your · Georgia Keeps Pulling On My · (I Can't Believe) She Gives It All · I Wish I Was Still In Your · If You Touch Me, (You've Got
Love) (10) · Woman) (10) · Ring (12) · To Me (12) · Dreams (14) · To Love Me) (9)
After The Fire Is Gone (4) 56 · Bye Bye Love (9) · Get Some Loving Done (7) · I Can't Believe That You've · I Wonder If You Told Her About · It Turns Me Inside Out (11)
Ain't She Something Else (13) · Clown, The (11) · Goodbye Time (14) · Stopped Loving Me (3) · Me (7) · It's A Cryin' Shame (8)
Amos Moses (5) · Crazy Arms (1) · Hangin' On (4) · I Can't See Me Without You (8) · I Wonder What She'll Think · It's Been One Heck Of A Day
As Good As A Lonely Girl Can · Darling Days (3) · Hank Williams Medley (5) · I Didn't Lose Her (I Threw Her · About Me Leaving (6) · (8)
Be (9) · Don't Call Him A Cowboy (13) · Heartache Just Walked In (6) · Away) (8) · I'd Rather Love You (6) · **It's Only Make-Believe**
Baby's Gone (10) · **Don't Cry Joni** (12) 63 · Heartache Tonight (13) · I Don't Love You (15) · I'll Come Running (3) · (4,12,13) 1
Back Street Affair (3,7) · Don't It Make You Lonely (15) · Heartaches By The Number (1) · I Fall To Pieces (6) · I'll Get Over Losing You (2) · Johnny B. Goode (1)
Before Your Time (9) · Don't Tell Me You're Sorry (4) · **Hello Darlin'** (2,12,13) 60 · I Hurt For You (5) · I'll Never Make It Home Tonight · Joy To The World (6)
Between Blue Eyes And Jeans · Easy Loving (7) · Help Me Make It Through The · I Love You More In Memory · (8) · Julia (14)
(13) · Everyday Family Man (5) · Night (5) · (10) · I'll Share My World With You (1) · Just Like A Stranger (5)
Blue Eyes Crying In The Rain · **Fifteen Years Ago** (3) 81 · Hey! Baby (3) · I Love You More Today (1) · I'm So Used To Loving You · Kiss An Angel Good Morning
(2) · Final Touches (15) · House On Old Lonesome Road · I Never Once Stopped Loving · (2,4) · (8)
Born To Lose (10) · Fit To Be Tied Down (14) · (14) · You (2) · I'm The Only Thing (I'll Hold · Last One To Touch Me (5)
Bottle In The Hand (Is Much · For Heavens Sake (9) · How Far Can We Go (7) · I Want To Know You Before We · Against You) (15) · Lead Me On (7)
Stronger Than The Man) (1) · Games People Play (1) · How Much More Can She · Make Love (14) · I've Already Loved You In My · Legend And The Man (13)
Boy Next Door (11) · · Stand (5) · I Was The First (11) · Mind (12) · Let Me Be The Judge (5)

TWITTY, Conway — Cont'd

Letter And A Ring (6)
Likes Of Me (15)
Linda On My Mind (12) *61*
Little Girl Cried (3)
Living Together Alone (9)
Looking Thru My Glass (4)
Louisiana Woman, Mississippi Man (9)
Love And Only Love (11)
Memory Of Your Sweet Love (5)
My Heart Won't Listen To My Mind (6)
My Love For You Is Stronger (Than The Weakness In Me) (6)
Never Ending Song Of Love (7)

Old Memory Like Me (15)
One For The Money (1)
One I Can't Live Without (4)
One More Sunrise (8)
One More Time (6)
Our Conscience You And Me (9)
Pickin' Wild Mountain Berries (4)
Play Guitar Play (12)
Playing House Away From Home (7)
Proud Mary (1)
Release Me (9)
Rocky Top (2)
Rose (2)
Rueben James (2)

Sand Covered Angels (3)
Saturday Night Special (14)
Seasons Of My Heart (10)
She Can Only See The Good In Me (3)
She Knows What She's Crying About (8)
She Only Meant To Use Him (11)
She's All I Got (8)
She's Got A Single Thing In Mind (14)
Slow Hand (11)
Slowly (3)
Something Strange Got Into Her Last Night (11)
Southern Comfort (11)

Star Spangled Heaven (1)
Take Me (4)
That's My Job (14)
This Road That I Walk (8)
This Time I've Hurt Her More (Than She Loves Me) (12)
Three Times A Lady (13)
'Til The Pain Outwears The Shame (11)
Two Timin' Two Stepper (11)
Up Comes The Bottle (Down Goes The Man) (2)
We've Closed Our Eyes To Shame (4)
Weakness In Your Man (10)
What Are We Gonna Do About Us (9)

When I Turn Off My Lights (Your Memory Turns On) (7)
When Love Was Something Else (11)
When The Final Change Is Made (11)
Who'll Turn Out The Lights (In Your World Tonight) (9)
Who's Gonna Know (14)
Wild Mountain Rose (3)
Will You Visit Me On Sunday (2,4)
Wine Me Up (6)
Working Girl (4)
World Of Forgotten People (1)
You And Your Sweet Love (2)
You Are To Me (15)

You Blow My Mind (7)
You Lay So Easy On My Mind (9)
(You Make It Hard) To Take The Easy Way Out (10)
You Ought To Try It Sometime (15)
You're The Reason (7)
You've Never Been This Far Before (10,12,13) *22*

TWIZTID '00
White male rap duo from Detroit: Jamie Madrox and Monoxide Child.

7/10/99	**149**	1	© 1 Mostasteless	$10	Psychopathic 042099
11/18/00	**51**	2	© 2 Freek Show	$10	Psychopathic 548179

All I Ever Wanted (2)
Bagz (2)
Blink (1)
Broken Wingz (2)
Bury Me Alive (1)

Diemuthafuckadie! (1)
Different (2)
Do You Really Know? (2)
$85 Bucks An Hour (1)
Empty (2)

Fall Apart (2)
1st Day Out (1)
Fuck On The 1st Date (2)
Hound Dogs (1)
How Does It Feel? (1)

I Wanna Be... (2)
I'm Alright (2)
Leave Me Alone (2)
Maniac Killa (2)
Mutant X (2)

People Are Strange (1)
Renditions Of Reality (1)
Rock The Dead (1)
2nd Hand Smoke (1)
Spin The Bottle (1)

We Don't Die (2)
Whatthefuck!?!? (1)
Where Itz Goin Down (2)
Wut Tha Dead Like (2)

TWO '98
Rock group formed in Phoenix: Rob **Halford** (vocals; **Judas Priest**; **Fight**), John Lowery (guitar), James Woolley (keyboards), Ray Reandeau (bass) and Sid Riggs (drums).

3/28/98	**176**	1	© Voyeurs	$10	Nothing 90155

Bed Of Rust
Deep In The Ground

Gimp
Hey, Sha La La

I Am A Pig
If

Leave Me Alone
My Ceiling's Low

Stutter Kiss
Wake Up

Water's Leaking

II D EXTREME '93
R&B vocal trio from Washington DC: D'Extra Wiley, Randy Gill (brother of **Johnny Gill**) and his cousin Jermaine Mickey.

11/27/93	**115**	4	II D Extreme	$10	Gasoline Alley 10958

Cry No More *48*
Falling In Love
Finally

I Need Your Lovin'
Let Me Love You
No Way

Outstanding
Tell Me
Thinkin'

Thinkin' Bout Cha
To Love Someone
Up On The Roof

Yummy

2GE+HER '00
Male vocal group formed for the same-named MTV series: Evan Farmer ("Jerry O'Keefe"), Michael Cuccione ("Jason McKnight"), Alex Solovitz ("Mickey Parke"), Noah Bastian ("Chad Linus") and Kevin Farley ("Doug Linus"). Farley is the younger brother of the late comedian Chris Farley. Cuccione died of respiratory failure on 1/13/2001 (age 16).

3/11/00	**35**	11	© 1 2Ge+her	[TV]	$10	TVT 6800
9/16/00	**15**	8	© 2 2Ge+her Again	[TV]	$10	TVT 6840

Awesum Luvr (2)
Before We Say Goodbye (1)
Breaking All The Rules (1)
Every Minute, Every Hour (2)

5Gether (2)
Hardest Part Of Breaking Up (Is Getting Back Your Stuff) (2)
I Gave My 24-7 To You (2)

I Wanna Know Your Name (2)
Regular Guy (2)
Right Where It Counts (2)
Rub One Out (1)

Say It (Don't Spray It) (1)
Sister (2)
That's When I'll Be Gone (1)
2Gether (1)

U & U & Me (2)
U + Me = Us (Calculus) (1)
Visualize (1)
Way You Do Me (2)

You're My Baby Girl (1)
You're The Only One That's Real (2)

---

2 IN A ROOM '91
Dance duo from Washington Heights, New York: rapper Rafael Vargas and remixer Roger Pauletta.

12/22/90+	**151**	9	© Wiggle It	$10	Cutting 91594

Body To Body
Booty Hump

Bring It On Down
Do What You Want

Got 'Em On The Run
House Junkie

Hype Stuff
Rock Bottom

Rock The House
She's Got Me Going Crazy

Soul Train
Wiggle It *15*

---

2 LIVE CREW, The '90
Rap group from Miami: Luther "**Luke**" Campbell, David Hobbs, Chris Wong Won and Mark Ross. By 1994, group consisted of Campbell, Wong Won and Larry Dobson; changed name to **The New 2 Live Crew**. Luke went solo in 1996; Hobbs, Wong Won and Ross reunited as **The 2 Live Crew**.

4/11/87	**128**	33	● © 1 The 2 Live Crew "is what we are"		$10	Luke Skyywalker 100
6/4/88	**68**	42	● © 2 Move Somethin'		$10	Luke Skyywalker 101
7/29/89+	**29**	81	▲ © 3 As Nasty As They Wanna Be		$15	Luke Skyywalker 107 [2]
8/11/90	**21**	22	● © 4 Banned In The U.S.A.		$10	Luke 91424
1/19/91	**92**	12	© 5 Live In Concert	[L]	$10	Effect 3003
10/26/91	**22**	30	● © 6 Sports Weekend (As Nasty As They Wanna Be Part II)		$10	Luke 91720
2/19/94	**52**	14	© 7 Back At Your Ass For The Nine-4		$10	Luke 207

THE NEW 2 LIVE CREW

8/24/96	**145**	2	© 8 Shake A Lil' Somethin'	$10	Lil' Joe 215

Ain't No Pussy Like... (6)
Anotha Pussy Caper (8)
Arrest In Effect (4)
Baby Baby Please (Just A Little More Head) (6)
Bad Ass Bitch (3)
Banned In The U.S.A. (4,5)
Bass 9-1-7 (4)
Be My Private Dancer (8)
Beat Box (1)
Break It On Down (3)
Bulldozer Stole My Bitch (8)
Caper Reprise (8)
Capt. D-ck And Dolemite (7)
Check It Out Yall (1)
C'mon Babe (3,5)
Coolin' (3)
Cut It Up (1)

Dem A Talk (7)
Dick Almighty (3)
Dirty Nursery Rhymes (3)
Do The Bart (4)
Do The Damn Thing (8)
Do Wah Diddy (2)
Drop The Bomb (3)
Face Down A-- Up (4,5)
Feel Alright Yall (2)
Fraternity Joint (6)
Fraternity Record (3)
Freaky Behavior (6)
F--k A Gang (4)
F-ck 'Em (4)
Fuck Is A Fuck (6)
F-ck Martinez (4)
F-ck Nigga (7)
Fuck Shop (3,5)

Get It Girl (1)
Get Loose Now (3)
Get The Fuck Out Of My House (3)
Ghetto Bass II (2)
H-B-C (5)
Head, Booty, And Cock (2)
Hell, Yeah (7)
Here I Come (6)
I Ain't Bullshittin' (3)
I Ain't Bullshittin' Part 2 (4)
I Ain't Bullshittin' III (6)
I Like It, I Love It (6)
If You Believe In Having Sex (3,5)
Initiation, The (7)
Introduction (2)
Jam Session I (8)

Mamolenga (4)
Man, Not A Myth (4)
Me So Horny (3,5) *26*
Mega Mix (4)
Mega Mix 6 (8)
Mega Mixx II (2)
Mega Mixx III (3)
Mega Mixx IV (4)
Mega Mixx V (6)
Move Somethin' (2,5)
Mr. Mixx Turntable Show (Part I & II) (5)
Mr. Mixx On The Mix!! (1)
My Seven Bizzos (3)
One And One (2,5)
PSK'95 (8)
Pop That Pussy (6)
P-ssy And D-ck Thing (7)

Pussy Ass Nigga (2)
Pussy Caper (6)
Pussy (Reprise) For Those Who Like To Fuck (6)
Put Her In The Buck (3)
Reggae Joint (3)
S & M (3)
Savage In The Sack (8)
Sex, I Like -- I Love (5)
Shake A Lil' Somethin' (8) *72*
Skeeta Man (8)
So Funky (4)
Some Hot Head (4)
Strip Club (4)
Suck My D-ck (1)
Table Dance (8)
This Is To Luke From The Posse (4)

Throw The D (1,5)
Trick, The (7)
2 Live Blues (3)
2 Live Freestyle (7)
2 Live Is What We Are (Word) (1)
Ugly As Fuck (6)
We Want Some Pussy (1,5)
We Want Some P-ssy II (7)
When We Get Them Hoes (8)
Who's Fuckin' Who (6)
With Your Bad Self (2)
Word II (2)
Work That P-ssy (7)
You Go Girl (7)

2 LIVE JEWS, The '90

Parody of rap group **The 2 Live Crew**: Eric "MC Moisha" Lambert and Joe "Easy Irving" Stone.

| 9/15/90 | 150 | 9 | | © | As Kosher As They Wanna Be .... | | [N] | $10 | Kosher 3328 |

Accountant Suckers / Ballad Of Moisha & Irving / J.A.P. Rap / Matchmaka' Game / Shake Your Tuchas
As Kosher As They Wanna Be / Beggin' For A Bargain / Jokin' Jews / Oui! It's So Humid / Young Jews Be Proud

2 LOW '94

Born Cedric White on 3/10/70 in Houston. Male rapper.

| 2/12/94 | 176 | 6 | | © | Funky Lil Brotha .... | | | $10 | Rap-A-Lot 53884 |

Boo Ya / Da Hood / Groove With Mr. Scarface / Growing Up Ain't Easy / Send Ya Fa Ya Mama
Class Clown / Everyday Thang / (Strictly For The Funk Lovers / Here We Go / Throw Ya Hands In The Air
Comin' Up / Funky Lil Brother / Pt. 2) / Pain

2PAC ★190★ '95

Born Tupac Amaru Shakur on 6/16/71 in New York City. Died on 9/13/96 (age 25) of wounds suffered on 9/7/96 in a shooting in Las Vegas. Rapper/actor. Member of **Digital Underground** in 1991. Appeared in the movies *Nothing But Trouble, Juice* and *Poetic Justice*. Also recorded as **Makaveli**. Also see **Thug Life**.

1)*Me Against The World* 2)*All Eyez On Me* 3)*The Don Killuminati - The 7 Day Theory*

2/29/92	64	23	●	©	1	2Pacalypse Now	C:#3/9		$10	Interscope 91767
3/6/93	24	60	▲	©	2	Strictly 4 My N.I.G.G.A.Z...	C:#2³/9		$10	Interscope 92209
4/1/95	❶⁴	65	▲²	©	3	Me Against The World	C:#12/40		$10	Interscope 92399
3/2/96	❶²	100	▲⁹	©	4	All Eyez On Me	C:#13/49		$15	Death Row 524204 [2]
11/23/96	❶¹	63	▲⁴	©	5	The Don Killuminati - The 7 Day Theory	C:#24/3		$10	Death Row 90039
						MAKAVELI				
12/13/97	2¹	26	▲⁴	©	6	R U Still Down? [Remember Me]		[E]	$15	Amaru 41628 [2]
8/8/98	112	11		©	7	In His Own Words		[T]	$10	Mecca 8807
						includes "Mourn You Till I Join Me" by **Naughty By Nature**				
12/12/98+	3	76	▲⁹	©	8	Greatest Hits	C:#15/33	[G]	$15	Amaru 490301 [2]
1/8/00	6	20	▲	©	9	Still I Rise			$10	Interscope 490413
						2PAC + OUTLAWZ				
5/6/00	178	1		©	10	The Lost Tapes		[E]	$10	Herb 'N Soul 54377
						recorded in 1989				
4/14/01	❶¹	25↑	▲³	©	11	Until The End Of Time			$15	Amaru 490840 [2]

Against All Odds (5) · Death Around The Corner (3) · Holla At Me (4) · Life Of An Outlaw (5) · R U Still Down? [Remember · To Live & Die In L.A. (5,8)
Ain't Hard 2 Find (4) · Definition Of A Thug Nigga (6) · Holler If Ya Hear Me (2) · Lil' Homies (11) · Me] (6) · Toss It Up (5,8)
All About U (8) · Do For Love (6) *21* · Homeboyz (9) · Lord Knows (3) · Ratha Be Ya Nigga (4) · Tradin War Stories (4)
All Bout U (4) · Enemies With Me (6) · **How Do U Want It** (4,8) *1* · Lunatic, Tha' (1) · Ready 4 Whatever (6) · Trapped (1,8)
All Eyez On Me (4) · Everything They Owe (11) · How Long Will They Mourn Me? · M.O.B. (11) · Rebel Of The Underground (4) · Trouble Followed (7)
All Out (11) · Evolution Of A Thug (7) · (8) · Mad Trouble (7) · Redemption (6) · Troublesome '96 (8)
Ambitionz Az A Ridah (4) · Fake Ass Bitches (6) · I Ain't Mad At Cha (4,8) · Me Against The World (3,8) · Representin' 93 (2) · 2 Of Amerikaz Most Wanted
As The World Turns (9) · Final Projects (7) · I Don't Give A Fuck (1) · Me And My Girlfriend (5) · Run Tha Streetz (4) · (4,8)
Baby Don't Cry (Keep Ya · 5 Deadly Venomz (4) · **I Get Around** (2,8) *11* · Minnie The Moocher (10) · Runnin On E (11) · U Can Be Touched (4)
Head Up II) (9) *72* · Fuck All Y'all (6) · **I Wonder If Heaven Got A** · My Burnin' Heart (10) · Secretz Of War (9) · Unconditional Love (8)
Ballad Of A Dead Soulja (11) · Fuck Friendz (11) · **Ghetto** (6) *67* · My Closest Roaddogz (11) · Shorty Wanna Be A Thug (4) · **Until The End Of Time** (11) *52*
Be The Realist (7) · Fuck The World (3) · I'm Gettin Money (6) · My Enemies (7) · 16 On Death Row (6) · Violent (1)
Black Jesuz (9) · Fuckin Wit The Wrong Nigga · I'm Losin It (4) · Never Be Beat (10) · Skandalouz (4) · What Happened (7)
Black Starry Night (interlude) · (11) · If I Die 2Nite (3) · Niggaz Nature (11) · **So Many Tears** (3,8) *44* · What'z Ya Phone # (4)
(6) · God Bless The Dead (8) · If My Homie Calls (1) · No More Pain (4) · Something Wicked... (1) · When I Get Free (6,11)
Blasphemy (5) · Good Die Young (9) · In His Own Words (7) · No Peace Treaty (7) · Soulja's Story (11) · When Thugz Cry (11)
Bomb First (My Second Reply) · Good Life (11) · It Ain't Easy (3) · Nothin But Love (6) · Souljah's Revenge (2) · When We Ride (4)
(5) · Got My Mind Made Up (4) · Just Like Daddy (5) · Nothing To Lose (6) · Static Mix I & II (10) · White Man'z World (5)
Breathin (11) · Guess Who's Back (2) · **Keep Ya Head Up** (2,8) *12* · **Old School** (3) *flip* · Still I Rise (9) · Why U Turn Me On (1)
Brenda's Got A Baby (1,8) · Hail Mary (5) · Killuminati (9) · Only Fear Of Death (6) · **Stop The Gunfire** (7) *77* · Wonda Why They Call U Bytch
California Love (4,8) *6* · Happy Home (11) · Krazy (5) · Only God Can Judge Me (4) · Streetz R Deathrow (2) · (4)
Can U Get Away (3) · Heartz Of Men (4,8) · Last Days (7) · Open Fire (6) · Strictly 4 My N.I.G.G.A.Z... (2) · Words Of Wisdom (1)
Can't C Me (4) · Heaven Ain't Hard 2 Find (4) · Last Wordz (2) · Outlaw (3) · Strugglin' (2) · Words 2 My First Born (11)
Case Of The Misplaced Mic · Heavy In The Game (3) · Lastonesleft (11) · Panther Power (10) · Tattoo Tears (9) · World Wide Mob Figgaz (11)
(10) · Hell 4 A Hustler (9) · Let Em Have It (11) · **Papa'z Song** (2) *87* · Teardrops And Closed Caskets · Y'All Don't Know Us (9)
Changes (8) *32* · Hellrazor (6) · Let Knowledge Drop (10) · Part Time Mutha (2) · (9) · U Don't Have 2 Worry (11)
Check Out Time (4) · High Speed (9) · Let Them Thangs Go (6) · Peep Game (2) · **Temptations** (3,8) *68* · Young Black Male (1)
Crooked Ass Nigga (1) · Hit 'Em Up (8) · Letter 2 My Unborn (11) · People Made Me (7) · This Ain't Livin' (11) · Young Niggaz (3)
Darkness Comes To Light (7) · Hold On Be Strong (6) · Letter To The President (9) · Picture Me Rollin' (4,8) · Thug N U Thug N Me (11)
Day In The Life (10) · Hold Ya Head (5) · Lie To Kick It (9) · Point The Finga (2) · Thug Passion (4)
Dear Mama (3,8) *9* · · Life Goes On (4,8) · Practice What You Preach (7) · Thug Style (6)

TWO TONS O' FUN '80

Disco duo: **Martha Wash** and Izora Rhodes. Later recorded as The Weather Girls.

| 5/17/80 | 91 | 11 | | | Two Tons O' Fun .... | | | $12 | Honey 9584 |

Do You Wanna Boogie, Hunh? / Gone Away / Just Us / Make Someone Feel Happy / One-Sided Love Affair
Earth Can Be Just Like Heaven / I Got The Feeling / Today / Taking Away Your Space

II TRU '97

Female rap duo from Cleveland: Jhaz and Brina. Part of the **Mo Thugs Family**.

| 10/18/97 | 194 | 1 | | © | A New Breed Of Female .... | | | $10 | Mo Thugs 1582 |

Are You Ready / Ballers Flossin / I Got Yo Back / New Breed Of Female / Shyste / Summer Time
Backdoor / Before I Die / Mothers Reminisce / Promises / So High / Two Hits And Pass

2 UNLIMITED '96

Techno-house duo from Amsterdam: Ray Slijngaard and Anita Dells.

| 10/17/92 | 197 | 1 | ● | © | 1 | Get Ready .... | | | $10 | Radikal 15407 |
| 3/9/96 | 107 | 8 | | © | 2 | Hits Unlimited .... | | [G] | $10 | Radikal 15446 |

2 UNLIMITED — Cont'd

Contrast (1)	Eternally Yours (1)	Jump For Joy (2)	Maximum Overdrive (2)	Pacific Walk (1)	Tribal Dance (2)
Delight (1)	Faces (2)	Let The Beat Control Your Body	No Limit (2)	Real Thing (2)	**Twilight Zone** (1,2) *49*
Desire (1)	**Get Ready For This** (1,2) *38*	(2)	No One (2)	Rougher Than The Average (1)	Workaholic (1,2)
Do What's Good For Me (2)	Here I Go (2)	Magic Friend (1,2)	Nothing Like The Rain (2)	Spread Your Love (2)	

TYCOON '79
Pop-rock group from New York City: Norman Mershon (vocals), Jon Gordon (guitar), Mark Rivera (sax), Michael Fonfara (keyboards), Mark Kreider (bass) and Richard Steinberg (drums).

3/31/79	41	17		©	**Tycoon**			$12	Arista 4215

Count On Me	Don't You Cry No More	How Long (Can We Go On)	Slow Down Boy	Too Late (New York City)
Don't Worry	Drunken Sailor	Out In The Cold	Such A Woman *26*	Way That It Goes

TYLER, Bonnie '83
Born Gaynor Hopkins on 6/8/53 in Swansea, Wales. Female singer known for her raspy vocals.

6/3/78	16	17	●		1 **It's A Heartache**			$12	RCA Victor 2821
2/17/79	145	5			2 **Diamond Cut**			$12	RCA Victor 3072
8/6/83	4	32	▲	©	3 **Faster Than The Speed Of Night**			$10	Columbia 38710
4/26/86	106	8		©	4 **Secret Dreams And Forbidden Fire**			$10	Columbia 40312

Baby Goodnight (1)	Faster Than The Speed Of	Hey Love (It's A Feelin') (1)	It's A Jungle Out There (3)	No Way To Treat A Lady (4)	Total Eclipse Of The Heart
Baby I Just Love You (2)	Night (3)	**Holding Out For A Hero** (3) *34*	Living For The City (1)	Ravishing (4)	(3) *1*
Band Of Gold (4)	Getting So Excited (3)	I'm A Fool (2)	Louisiana Rain (2)	Rebel Without A Clue (4)	What A Way To Treat My Heart
Blame Me (1)	Goin' Through The Motions (3)	If I Sing You A Love Song (3)	Lovers Again (4)	Straight From The Heart (3)	(2)
Bye Bye Now My Sweet Love	Have You Ever Seen The Rain?	If You Ever Need Me Again (2)	Loving You's A Dirty Job But	Take Me Back (3) *46*	Words Can Change Your Life
(2)	(3)	**If You Were A Woman (And I**	Somebody's Gotta Do It (4)	Tears (3)	(2)
Eyes Of A Fool (2)	Heaven (1)	**Was A Man)** (4) *77*	My Guns Are Loaded (1)	Too Good To Last (2)	Yesterday Dreams (1)
	Here Am I (1)	**It's A Heartache** (1) *3*	Natural Woman (1)		

TYMES, The '63
R&B vocal group from Philadelphia: George Williams, George Hilliard, Donald Banks, Albert Berry and Norman Burnett.

8/3/63	15	20			1 **So Much In Love**			$50	Parkway 7032
12/21/63+	117	10			2 **The Sound Of The Wonderful Tymes**			$50	Parkway 7038
3/7/64	122	4			3 **Somewhere**			$50	Parkway 7039

includes 7" bonus single ("Isle Of Love"/"I'm Always Chasing Rainbows")

Address Unknown (2)	Come With Me To The Sea	Isle Of Love (3)	One Little Kiss (2)	There Is Love (3)	**Wonderful! Wonderful!** (1,2) *7*
Alone (2)	(2,3)	Lamp Is Low (3)	Sleep Tight My Darling (3)	Till The End Of Time (3)	Words Written On Water (2)
And That Reminds Me (2)	Goodnight My Love (1)	Let's Fall In Love Tonight (3)	**So Much In Love** (1) *1*	Twelfth Of Never (1)	You Asked Me To Be Yours (1)
Anymore (3)	Hello Young Lovers (2)	Let's Make Love Tonight (1)	**Somewhere** (3) *19*	Way Beyond Today (1)	
Autumn Leaves (1)	I Thank You (2)	Moonlight Cocktails (3)	Stranger In Paradise (3)	Way You Look Tonight (2)	
Blue Velvet (2)	I'm Always Chasing Rainbows	My Summer Love (1)	Summer Day (1)	Why Should I Cry (3)	
Chances Are (2)	(3)	Night (3)	That Old Black Magic (1)	Will You Wait For Me (3)	

TYNER, McCoy '79
Born on 12/11/38 in Philadelphia. Jazz pianist.

6/14/75	161	5		©	1 **Atlantis**	[I-L]		$15	Milestone 55002 [2]
					recorded on 8/31/74 at the Keystone Korner in San Francisco				
1/3/76	198	2		©	2 **Trident**	[I]		$12	Milestone 9063
6/12/76	128	11		©	3 **Fly With The Wind**	[I]		$12	Milestone 9067
1/22/77	187	3		©	4 **Focal Point**	[I]		$12	Milestone 9072
7/9/77	167	5		©	5 **Supertrios**	[I]		$15	Milestone 55003 [2]
1/28/78	171	8		©	6 **Inner Voices**	[I]		$12	Milestone 9079
10/14/78	170	3			7 **The Greeting**	[I-L]		$12	Milestone 9085
					recorded on 3/17/78 at the Great American Music Hall in San Francisco				
5/26/79	66	11		©	8 **Together**	[I]		$12	Milestone 9087

Atlantis (1)	Elvin (Sir) Jones (2)	I Mean You (5)	Mode For Dulcimer (4)	Parody (4)	Stella By Starlight (5)
Ballad For Aisha (8)	Festival In Bahia (6)	Impressions (2)	Moment's Notice (5)	Pictures (7)	Uptown (6)
Bayou Fever (8)	Fly With The Wind (3,7)	In A Sentimental Mood (1)	My One And Only Love (1)	Prelude To A Kiss (5)	Wave (5)
Beyond The Sun (3)	For Tomorrow (6)	Indo-Serenade (4)	Naima (7)	Pursuit (1)	You Stepped Out Of A Dream
Blues For Ball (5)	Four By Five (5)	Land Of The Lonely (2)	Nana, Theme For (4)	Rolem (1)	(3)
Blues On The Corner (5)	Greeting, The (5,7)	Love Samba (1)	Nubia (8)	Rotunda (6)	
Celestial Chant (2)	Hand In Hand (7)	Lush Life (3)	Once I Loved (2)	Ruby, My Dear (2)	
Consensus (5)	Highway One (8)	Makin' Out (1)	One Of Another Kind (8)	Salvadore De Samba (3)	
Departure (4)	Hymn-Song (5)	Mes Trois Fils (4)	Opus (6)	Shades Of Light (3)	

TYPE O NEGATIVE '99
Hard-rock group from New York City: Peter Steele (vocals, bass), Kenny Hickey (guitar), Josh Silver (keyboards) and Johnny Kelly (drums).

1/14/95	166	11	▲	©	1 **Bloody Kisses**			$10	Roadrunner 9100
9/7/96	42	8	●	©	2 **October Rust**			$10	Roadrunner 8874
10/9/99	39	6		©	3 **World Coming Down**			$10	Roadrunner 8660
11/18/00	99	1			4 **The Least Worst Of**	[K]		$10	Roadrunner 8510

All Hallows Eve (3)	Can't Lose You (1)	Fay Wray Come Out And Play	Hey Pete (4)	Pyretta Blaze (3)	Unsuccessfully Coping With
Be My Druidess (2)	Christian Woman (1,4)	(1)	In Praise Of Bacchus (2)	Red Water (Christmas	The Natural Beauty Of
Black No. 1 (1,4)	Cinnamon Girl (2,4)	Glorious Liberation Of The	It's Never Enough (4)	Mourning) (2)	Infidelity (4)
Black Sabbath (From The	Creepy Green Light (3)	People's Technocratic	Kill All The White People (1)	Set Me On Fire (1)	We Hate Everyone (1)
Satanic Perspective) (4)	Day Tripper (medley) (1)	Republic Of Vinnland By The	Love You To Death (2,4)	Stay Out Of My Dreams (4)	White Slavery (3)
Blood & Fire (1)	Die With Me (2)	Combined Forces Of The	Misinterpretation Of Silence	Summer Breeze (4)	Who Will Save The Sane? (3)
Bloody Kisses (A Death In The	Everyone I Love Is Dead (3,4)	United Territories Of Europe	And Its Disastrous	3.0.I.F. (1)	Wolf Moon (Including
Family) (1)	Everything Dies (3,4)	(3)	Consequences (4)	Too Late: Frozen (1)	Zoanthropic Paranoia) (2)
Burnt Flowers Fallen (2)		Green Man (2)	My Girlfriend's Girlfriend (2,4)	12 Black Rainbows (4)	World Coming Down (3)
		Haunted (2)			

TYRESE '01
Born Tyrese Gibson on 12/30/78 in Los Angeles. Male R&B singer/actor. Played "Jody" in the movie *Baby Boy*.

11/14/98+	17	36	▲	©	1 **Tyrese**			$10	RCA 66901
6/9/01	10	17↑	●	©	2 **2000 Watts**			$10	RCA 68039

Ain't Nothin' Like A Jones (1)	Get Up On It (2)	**I Like Them Girls** (2) *48*	**Nobody Else** (1) *36*	Taste My Love (1)
Bring You Back My Way (2)	Give Love A Try (1)	I'm Sorry (2)	Off The Heezy (2)	Tell Me, Tell Me (1)
Do You Need (1)	Housekeepin' (2)	**Just A Baby Boy** (2) *90*	Promises (2)	There For Me (Baby) (2)
Fling (2)	I Ain't The One (2)	**Lately** (1) *56*	Stay In Touch (1)	What Am I Gonna Do (2)
For Always (2)	I Can't Go On (1)	Make Up Your Mind (2)	**Sweet Lady** (1) *12*	You Get Yours (1)

TYZIK '84

Born Jeff Tyzik in Hyde Park, New York. Jazz trumpeter.

| 9/8/84 | 172 | 6 | © | Jammin' In Manhattan .... | | | $10 | Polydor 821605 |

Better And Better   Jammin' In Manhattan   Melange   When I Look In Your Eyes   You're My Woman, You're My
Echoes   Killer Joe   New York Woman   Lady

U

★399★ UB40 '93

Reggae group formed in Birmingham, England: brothers Ali (vocals) and Robin (guitar, vocals) Campbell, Terence "Astro" Wilson (vocals), Norman Hassan (percussion), Michael Virtue (keyboards), Brian Travers (sax), Earl Falconer (bass) and James Brown (drums). Name taken from British unemployment form.

| 11/26/83+ | 14 | 63 | ▲ | © | 1 Labour Of Love ....C:#24/10 | | | $10 | A&M 4980 |

originally peaked at #39 in 1984; re-entered and reached new peak in 1988

11/10/84	60	26		©	2 Geffery Morgan...			$10	A&M 5033
8/17/85	40	25		©	3 Little Baggariddim			$10	A&M 5090
8/30/86	53	17		©	4 Rat In The Kitchen			$10	A&M 5137
8/29/87	121	8		©	5 CCCP: Live In Moscow .... [L]			$10	A&M 5168
8/20/88	44	27		©	6 UB40			$10	A&M 5213
1/13/90+	30	111	▲	©	7 Labour Of Love II ....C:#18/10			$10	Virgin 91324
8/14/93	6	41	▲	©	8 Promises And Lies			$10	Virgin 88229
7/19/97	176	2		©	9 Guns In The Ghetto			$10	Virgin 44402

All I Want To Do (4,5)   Dance With The Devil (6)   Homely Girl (7)   Lisa (9)   Rat In Me Kitchen (4,5)   Version Girl (1)
Always There (9)   Desert Sand (9)   Hurry Come Up (9)   Looking Down At My Reflection   Red Red Wine (1) 1   Watchdogs (4,5)
As Always You Were Wrong   Don't Blame Me (4,5)   I Got You Babe (3,5) 28   (4)   Reggae Music (8)   Way You Do The Things You
  Again (2)   Don't Break My Heart (3,5)   I Love It When You Smile (9)   Many Rivers To Cross (1)   Riddle Me (2)   Do (7) 6
Baby (7)   D.U.B. (2)   I Really Can't Say (9)   Matter Of Time (6)   Seasons (2)   Wear You To The Ball (7)
Breakfast In Bed (6)   Elevator, The (4)   I Would Do For You (6)   Mi Spliff (3)   She Caught The Train (1)   Wedding Day (7)
Bring Me Your Cup (8)   Friendly Fire (9)   I'm Not Fooled So Easily (2)   Music So Nice (6)   Sing Our Own Song (4,5)   Where Did I Go Wrong (6)
C'est La Vie (8)   Groovin' (7) 90   I've Been Missing You (9)   Nkomo A Go Go (2)   Sorry (8)   You Could Meet Somebody (4)
Can't Help Falling In Love   Guilty (1)   If It Happens Again (2,5)   Now And Then (8)   Sweet Sensation (1)   You're Always Pulling Me Down
  (8) 1   Guns In The Ghetto (9)   Impossible Love (7)   One In Ten (3)   Tears From My Eyes (7)   (6)
'Cause It Isn't True (6)   Here I Am (Come And Take   It's A Long Long Way (8)   Oracabessa Moonshine (9)   Tell It Like It Is (4,5)   You're Not An Army (2)
Cherry Oh Baby (1,5)   Me) (7) 7   Johnny Too Bad (1,5)   Pillow, The (2)   Tell Me Is It True (9)   Your Eyes Were Open (2)
Come Out To Play (6)   Higher Ground (8) 45   Keep On Moving (1,5)   Please Don't Make Me Cry (1,5)   Things Ain't Like They Used To
Contaminated Minds (6)   Hip Hop Lyrical Robot (3)   Kingston Town (7)   Promises And Lies (8)   Be (8)

UBIQUITY '78

Backing group for Roy Ayers: Sylvia Cox (vocals), Greg Moore (vocals, guitar), Philip Woo (keyboards), Justo Almario (sax), John Mosley (trumpet), Chano Oferral (congas), Kerry Turman (bass) and Ricky Lawson (drums).

| 4/8/78 | 146 | 4 | | | Starbooty .... | | | $12 | Elektra 120 |

Can You Be Yourself   If You Wanna See The   Love Is Love   Simple And Sweet   Starbooty
Five Flies   Sunshine   Midnight After Dark   Spread It

UFO '77

Hard-rock group formed in England by Phil Mogg (vocals) and Michael Schenker (guitar). Numerous personnel changes.

1)Lights Out 2)Obsession 3)Strangers In The Night

8/9/75	71	13		©	1 Force It			$12	Chrysalis 1074
6/19/76	169	4		©	2 No Heavy Petting..			$12	Chrysalis 1103
6/11/77	23	24		©	3 Lights Out			$12	Chrysalis 1127
7/29/78	41	18		©	4 Obsession			$12	Chrysalis 1182
2/3/79	42	15		©	5 Strangers In The Night .... [L]			$15	Chrysalis 1209 [2]
1/19/80	51	13			6 No Place To Run..			$12	Chrysalis 1239
1/31/81	77	11		©	7 The Wild The Willing And The Innocent			$12	Chrysalis 1307
2/20/82	82	14		©	8 Mechanix			$12	Chrysalis 1360
4/30/83	153	5		©	9 Making Contact			$12	Chrysalis 41402
4/5/86	106	19		©	10 Misdemeanor			$10	Chrysalis 41518

Ain't No Baby (4)   Chains Chains (7)   Heaven's Gate (10)   Love To Love (3,5)   Only Ones (10)   Too Hot To Handle (3,5)
All Over You (9)   Cherry (4)   High Flyer (1)   Makin Moves (7)   Only You Can Rock Me (4,5)   Too Much Of Nothing (1)
Alone Again Or (3)   Couldn't Get It Right (7)   Highway Lady (7)   Martian Landscape (2)   Out In The Street (1,5)   Try Me (3)
Alpha Centauri (6)   Dance Your Life Away (1)   Hot 'N' Ready (4)   Meanstreets (10)   Pack It Up (And Go) (4)   Way The Wild Wind Blows (9)
Anyday (6)   Diesel In The Dust (9)   I'm A Loser (2,5)   Money, Money (6)   Profession Of (7)   We Belong To The Night (8)
Arbory Hill (4)   Doctor Doctor (5)   It's Killing Me (7)   Mother Mary (1,5)   Push, It's Love (9)   When It's Time To Rock (9)
Back Into My Life (8)   Doing It All For You (8)   Just Another Suicide (3)   Mystery Train (6)   Reasons Love (2)   Wild The Willing And The
Belladonna (2)   Dream The Dream (10)   Let It Rain (8)   Name Of Love (10)   Rock Bottom (5)   Innocent (7)
Between The Walls (medley)   Dreaming (8)   Let It Roll (1,5)   Natural Thing (2,5)   Shoot Shoot (1,5)   Wreckless (10)
  (1)   Electric Phase (3)   Lettin' Go (6)   Night Run (10)   Something Else (8)   Writer, The (8)
Blinded By A Lie (9)   Feel It (8)   Lights Out (3,5)   No Getaway (9)   Take It Or Leave It (6)   You And Me (9)
Blue (10)   Fool For Love (9)   Lonely Heart (7)   No Place To Run (6)   Terri (8)   You Don't Fool Me (4)
Born To Lose (4)   Fool In Love (2)   Long Gone (7)   On With The Action (2)   This Fire Burns Tonight (6)   You'll Get Love (8)
Call My Name (9)   Gettin' Ready (3)   Lookin' Out For No. 1 (4)   One Heart (10)   This Kid's (1,5)   Youngblood (6)
Can You Roll Her (2)   Gone In The Night (6)   Love Lost Love (1)   One More For The Rodeo (4)   This Time (10)

UGK — see UNDERGROUND KINGZ

UGLY KID JOE '92

Rock group from Isla Vista, California: Whitfield Crane (vocals), Klaus Eichstadt and Roger Lahr (guitars), Cordell Crockett (bass), and Mark Davis (drums).

2/8/92	4	34	▲	©	1 As Ugly As They Want To Be .... [M]			$10	Stardog 868823
9/26/92+	27	51	▲²	©	2 America's Least Wanted..			$10	Stardog 512571
7/1/95	178	1			3 Menace To Sobriety			$10	Mercury 526997

Busy Bee (2)   Come Tomorrow (2)   Goddamn Devil (2)   Mr. Recordman (2)   Suckerpath (3)   Whiplash Liquor (1)
C.U.S.T. (3)   Don't Go (2)   Heavy Metal (1)   Neighbor (2)   Sweet Leaf (medley) (1)
Candle Song (3)   Everything About You (1,2) 9   I'll Keep Tryin' (2)   Oompa (2)   10/10 (3)
Cats In The Cradle (2) 6   Funky Fresh Country Club   Jesus Rode A Harley (3)   Panhandlin' Prince (2)   Tomorrow's World (2)
Cloudy Skies (3)   (medley) (1)   Madman (3)   Same Side (2)   Too Bad (1)
Clover (3)   God (3)   Milkman's Son (3)   So Damn Cool (2)   V.I.P. (3)

U-GOD '99
Born Lamont Hawkins in Staten Island, New York. Male rapper. Member of **Wu-Tang Clan**.

| 11/6/99 | 58 | 3 | © | Golden Arms Redemption .... | $10 | Wu-Tang 50086 |

Bizarre
Dat's Gangsta
Enter U-God

Glide
Hungry
Knockin At Your Door

Lay Down
Night The City Cried
Pleasure Or Pain

Rumble
Shell Shock
Soul Dazzle

Stay In Your Lane
Turbo Charge
Turbulence

U.K. '79
Art-rock group formed in England: John Wetton (vocals, bass; **Family**, **King Crimson**, **Uriah Heep**, **Asia**), Allan Holdsworth (guitar), **Bill Bruford** (percussion; **Yes**) Eddie Jobson (keyboards; **Roxy Music**) and Terry Bozzio (drums; **Frank Zappa**, **Roxy Music**, **Missing Persons**). Holdsworth and Bruford left after first album.

5/20/78	65	15	©	1 U.K.	$12	Polydor 6146
3/24/79	45	11	©	2 Danger Money	$12	Polydor 6194
10/20/79	109	6	©	3 Night After Night .... [L]	$12	Polydor 6234

recorded June 1979 in Tokyo

Alaska (1,3)
As Long As You Want Me Here (3)

By The Light Of Day (1)
Caesar's Palace Blues (2,3)
Carrying No Cross (2)

Danger Money (2)
In The Dead Of Night (1,3)
Mental Medication (1)

Nevermore (1)
Night After Night (3)
Nothing To Lose (2,3)

Only Thing She Needs (2)
Presto Vivace (1,3)
Rendezvous (2,3)

Thirty Years (1)
Time To Kill (1,3)

U-KREW, The '90
Rap group from Portland, Oregon: Kevin Morse, Larry Bell, Lavell Alexander, James McClendon and Hakim Muhammad.

| 2/17/90 | 93 | 23 | © | The U-Krew .... | $10 | Enigma 73524 |

All Night Lover
Angel

Feel It
Get Ready

If U Were Mine 24
Let Me Be Your Lover 68

Pick Up The Pieces
Pump Me Up

Rock That Shit
Ugly

ULLMAN, Tracey '84
Born on 12/30/59 in Buckinghamshire, England. Actress/singer/comedienne. Hosted own TV show from 1987-90. Acted in several movies.

| 3/24/84 | 34 | 20 | © | You Broke My Heart In 17 Places .... | $10 | MCA 5471 |

Bobby's Girl
Break-A-Way 70
I Close My Eyes And Count To Ten

(Life Is A Rock) But The Radio Rolled Me
Long Live Love
Move Over Darling

Oh, What A Night
Shattered
They Don't Know 8

You Broke My Heart In 17 Places
Your Presence

ULTIMATE '79
Disco studio group assembled by producers Juliano Salerni and Bruce Weeden.

| 3/3/79 | 157 | 11 | © | Ultimate .... | $12 | Casablanca 7128 |

Dancing In The Night

Love Is The Ultimate

Music In My Heart

Ritmo De Brazil

Take Me To Chinatown

Touch Me Baby 82

ULTIMATE SPINACH '68
Psychedelic-rock group from Boston: Ian Bruce-Douglas (vocals, keyboards), Barbara Hudson (vocals, guitar), Geoffrey Winthrop (guitar), Richard Nese (bass) and Keith Lahteinen (drums).

| 2/24/68 | 34 | 24 | © | 1 Ultimate Spinach .... | $30 | MGM 4518 |
| 11/9/68 | 198 | 2 | © | 2 Behold & See .... | $30 | MGM 4570 |

(Ballad Of The) Hip Death Goddess (1)
Baroque #1 (1)
Dove In Hawk's Clothing (1)
Ego Trip (1)

Fifth Horseman Of The Apocalypse (2)
Fragmentary March Of Green (2)
Funny Freak Parade (1)

Genesis Of Beauty ..see: Suite
Gilded Lamp Of The Cosmos (2)
Hung-Up Minds (medley) (1)
Jazz Thing (2)

Mind Flowers (2)
Pamela (1)
Plastic Raincoats (medley) (1)
Sacrifice Of The Moon (1)

Suite: Genesis Of Beauty (In Four Parts) (2)
Visions Of Your Reality (2)
Where You're At (2)
Your Head Is Reeling (1)

ULTRAVOX '83
Electronic-rock group from England: **Midge Ure** (vocals, guitar), Billy Currie (keyboards), Chris Cross (bass) and Warren Cann (drums). Ure and Currie also recorded in **Visage**.

9/13/80	164	9	©	1 Vienna	$10	Chrysalis 1296
10/24/81	144	6	©	2 Rage In Eden	$10	Chrysalis 1338
3/12/83	61	17	©	3 Quartet	$10	Chrysalis 1394
5/19/84	115	9	©	4 Lament	$10	Chrysalis 41459

Accent On Youth (2)
All Stood Still (1)
Ascent, The (2)
Astradyne (1)
Cut And Run (3)
Dancing With Tears In My Eyes (4)

Friend I Call Desire (4)
Heart Of The Country (4)
Hymn (3)
I Remember (Death In The Afternoon) (2)
Lament (4)
Man Of Two Worlds (4)

Mine For Life (3)
Mr. X (1)
New Europeans (1)
One Small Day (4)
Passing Strangers (1)
Private Lives (1)
Rage In Eden (2)

Reap The Wild Wind (3) **71**
Serenade (3)
Sleepwalk (1)
Song (We Go) (3)
Stranger Within (2)
Thin Wall (1)
Vienna (1)

Visions In Blue (3)
Voice, The (2)
We Came To Dance (3)
We Stand Alone (1)
Western Promise (1)
When The Scream Subsides (3)
When The Time Comes (4)

White China (4)
Your Name Has Slipped My Mind Again (2)

UNCLE KRACKER '01
Born Matthew Shafer on 6/6/74 in Mount Clemens, Michigan. White DJ/rapper. Member of **Kid Rock**'s posse.

| 7/1/00+ | 7 | 37↑● | © | Double Wide | $10 | Lava 83279 |

Aces & 8's
Better Days

Follow Me 5
Heaven

Steaks 'N Shrimp
What 'Chu Lookin' At?

Whiskey & Water
Who's Your Uncle?

Yeah, Yeah, Yeah
You Can't Take Me

UNCLE SAM '98
Born Sam Turner in Detroit. R&B singer.

| 1/17/98 | 68 | 21 | © | Uncle Sam .... | $10 | Stonecreek 67731 |

Baby You Are
Can You Feel It

I Don't Ever Want To See You Again 6
Leave Well Enough Alone

Someone Like You
Stop Foolin' Around
Tender Love

Think About Me
Throw Your Hands In The Air
Without Lovin' You

You Make Me Feel Like

UNDERGROUND KINGZ '96
Male rap duo: Pimp C and Bun B.

| 9/17/94 | 95 | 10 | © | 1 Super Tight... | $10 | Jive 41524 |
| 8/17/96 | 15 | 13 | ● © | 2 Ridin' Dirty | $10 | Jive 41586 |

UGK

Diamonds & Wood (2)
Feds In Town (1)
Front, Back & Side To Side (1)
F*** My Car (2)

Good Stuff (2)
Hi Life (2)
I Left It Wet For You (1)
It's Supposed To Bubble (1)

Murder (2)
One Day (2)
Pinky Ring (2)
Pocket Full Of Stones, Pt. 2 (1)

Protect & Serve (1)
Pussy Got Me Dizzy (1)
Return (1)
Ridin' Dirty (2)

Stoned Junkee (1)
That's Why I Carry (2)
3 In The Mornin' (2)
Three Sixteens (1)

Touched (2)
Underground (1)

UNDERGROUND SUNSHINE '69
Rock group from Montello, Wisconsin: brothers Egbert (vocals, bass) and Frank (drums) Kohl, with John Dahlberg (guitar) and Jane Little (keyboards).

| 11/8/69 | 161 | 3 | | | Let There Be Light.. | | | $30 | Intrepid 74003 |

All I Want Is You   **Birthday** *26*   Don't Shut Me Out   Proud Mary
Bad Moon Rising   Don't Let Me Down   Gimme Some Lovin'   Take Me, Break Me

UNDERTONES, The '80
Pop-rock group from Ireland: **Feargal Sharkey** (vocals), brothers Damian and John O'Neill (guitars), Mickey Bradley (bass) and Billy Doherty (drums).

| 1/26/80 | 154 | 7 | | © | The Undertones.. | | | $12 | Sire 6081 |

Billy's Third   Get Over You   I Gotta Getta   Jump Boys   (She's A) Runaround   Wrong Way
Casbah Rock   Girls Don't Like It   I Know A Girl   Listenin In   Teenage Kicks
Family Entertainment   Here Comes The Summer   Jimmy Jimmy   Male Model   True Confessions

UNDERWORLD '88
Rock group from England: Karl Hyde (vocals, guitar), Alfie Thomas (guitar), Rick Smith (keyboards), Baz Allen (bass) and Pascal Console (drums). By 1999, group reduced to trio of Karl Hyde, Darren Emerson and Rick Smith.

3/19/88	139	19		©	1	Underneath The Radar..			$10	Sire 25627
5/1/99	93	5		©	2	Beaucoup Fish			$10	V2 27042
9/30/00	192	1		©	3	Everything, Everything		[L]	$10	V2 27078

Born Slippy Nuxx (3)   Glory! Glory! (1)   Kittens (2)   Push Downstairs (2,3)   Shudder/King Of Snake (2,3)
Bright White Flame (1)   God Song (1)   Miracle Party (1)   Push Upstairs (2,3)   Skym (2)
Bruce Lee (2)   I Need A Doctor (1)   Moaner (2)   Rez/Cowgirl (3)   Something Like A Mama (2)
Call Me No. 1 (1)   Juanita/Kiteless (3)   Pearls Girl (3)   Rubber Ball (Space Kitchen) (1)   **Underneath The Radar** (1) *74*
Cups (2,3)   Jumbo (2,3)   Pray (1)   Show Some Emotion (1)   Winjer (2)

UNDISPUTED TRUTH, The '71
R&B vocal trio from Detroit: Joe Harris, Billie Calvin and Brenda Evans.

7/24/71	43	18			1	The Undisputed Truth			$25	Gordy 955
2/5/72	114	12			2	Face To Face With The Truth			$20	Gordy 959
8/18/73	191	2			3	Law Of The Land			$20	Gordy 963
6/21/75	186	2			4	Cosmic Truth			$20	Gordy 970
11/22/75	173	4			5	Higher Than High			$20	Gordy 972
1/29/77	66	17			6	Method To The Madness			$15	Whitfield 2967

Ain't No Sun Since You've Been   Friendship Train (medley) (2)   I'm In The Red Zone (5)   Love And Happiness (3)   **Smiling Faces Sometimes**   Ungena Za Ulimwengu (Unite
   Gone (1)   Girl You're Alright (3)   If I Die (3)   Ma (5)   (1) *3*   The World) (medley) (2)
Aquarius (1)   Got To Get My Hands On Some   Just My Imagination (Running   Mama I Gotta Brand New Thing   Spaced Out (4)   Walk On By (3)
Ball Of Confusion (That's What   Lovin' (4)   Away With Me) (3)   (Don't Say No) (3)   Squeeze Me, Tease Me (4)   We've Got A Way Out Love (1)
   The World Is Today) (1)   **Help Yourself** (5) *63*   Killing Me Softly With His Song   Method To The Madness (6)   Sunshine (6)   **What It Is** (2) *71*
Boogie Bump Boogie (5)   Higher Than High (5)   (3)   Overload (5)   Superstar (Remember How You   What's Going On (2)
California Soul (1)   Hole In The Wall (6)   Law Of The Land (3)   1990 (4)   Got Where You Are) (2)   With A Little Help From My
Cosmic Contact (5)   I Heard It Through The   **Let's Go Down To The Disco**   **Papa Was A Rollin' Stone**   Take A Vacation From Life (And   Friends (3)
Don't Let Him Take Your Love   Grapevine (2)   (6) *flip*   (3) *63*   Visit Your Dreams) (6)   You Got The Love I Need (1)
   From Me (2)   (I Know) I'm Losing You (4)   Life Ain't So Easy (5,6)   Poontang (5)   Take Me In Your Arms And   **You Make Your Own Heaven**
Down By The River (4)   I Saw You When You Met Her   Like A Rolling Stone (1)   Save My Love For A Rainy Day   Love Me (2)   **And Hell Right Here On**
Earthquake Shake (4)   (5)   Lil' Red Ridin' Hood (4)   (1)   This Child Needs Its Father (3)   **Earth** (2) *72*
Feelin' Alright (3)   Loose (6)   Since I've Lost You (1)   UFO's (4)   **You + Me = Love** (6) *48*

UNFORGIVEN, The '86
Rock group from Los Angeles: John Henry Jones (vocals), John Hickman, Just Jones and Todd Ross (guitars), Mike Finn (bass) and Alan Waddington (drums).

| 8/9/86 | 185 | 2 | | | The Unforgiven .... | | | $10 | Elektra 60461 |

All Is Quiet On The Western   Gauntlet, The   Hang 'Em High   Preacher, The
   Front   Ghost Dance   I Hear The Call   Roverpack
Cheyenne   Grace   Loner, The   With My Boots On

UNICORN '74
Art-rock group from England: Pete Perrier (vocals, drums), Kevin Smith (guitar), Kenny Baker (keyboards) and Pat Martin (bass).

| 10/26/74 | 129 | 5 | | | Blue Pine Trees .... | | | $12 | Capitol 11334 |

produced by **David Gilmour**

Autumn Wine   Electric Night   Holland   Just Wanna Hold You   Ooh! Mother   Sleep Song
Blue Pine Trees   Farmer, The   In The Gym   Nightingale Crescent   Rat Race

UNION GAP, The — see PUCKETT, Gary

UNION UNDERGROUND, The '00
Rock group from San Antonio: Bryan Scott (vocals, guitar), Patrick Kennison (guitar), John Moyer (bass) and Josh Memelo (drums).

| 8/26/00 | 130 | 16 | | © | ...An Education In Rebellion.. | | | $10 | Portrait 67778 |

Bitter   Education In Rebellion   Killing The Fly   Revolution Man   Trip With Jesus   Until You Crack
Drivel   Friend Song   Natural High   South Texas Deathride   Turn Me On "Mr. Deadman"

UNITED STATES AIR FORCE BAND, The '63
Conducted by Colonel George S. Howard. Formed in 1942 at the direction of President Roosevelt.

| 6/29/63 | 102 | 6 | | | The United States Air Force Band .... | | [I] | $15 | RCA Victor 2686 |
| | | | | | | | | | U.S. Air Force Blue |

American Salute   Bullets And Bayonets   Falcons' Victory March   Oh, Men Who Fly   Star Spangled Banner
Boys Of The Old Brigade   Fairest Of The Fair   Liberty Bell   Seventy Six Trombones   U.S. Air Force

UNITED STATES MARINE BAND, The '63
Directed by Lieutenant Colonel Albert F. Schoepper. Formed in 1798 at the direction of President Adams.

| 6/15/63 | 22 | 9 | | | The United States Marine Band .... | | [I] | $15 | RCA Victor 2687 |

America The Beautiful   Chimes Of Liberty   March Of The Women Marines   Semper Fidelis
American Patrol   Commando March   Marines' Hymn (From The Halls   Star Spangled Banner
Bugler's Holiday   March Of The Olympians   Of Montezuma)   Stars And Stripes Forever

UNITED STATES NAVY BAND, The '63
Directed by Commander Anthony A. Mitchell. Formed in 1925 at the direction of President Coolidge.

| 6/15/63 | 38 | 7 | | | The United States Navy Band .... [I] | | | $15 | RCA Victor 2688 |

Allies On The March Medley — El Capitan — John F. Kennedy Center March — National Emblem — Star-Spangled Banner — U.S. Navy March
Anchors Aweigh — Jack Tar March — King Cotton March — Pledge Of Allegiance — Thunderer, The — Washington Post March

UNITED STATES OF AMERICA, The '68
Electronic-rock group from Los Angeles: Dorothy Moskowitz (vocals), Gordon Marron (violin), Joseph Byrd (keyboards), Rand Forbes (bass) and Craig Woodson (drums).

| 5/4/68 | 181 | 9 | | © | The United States Of America.. | | | $50 | Columbia 9614 |

American Metaphysical Circus — Cloud Song — Garden Of Earthly Delights — I Won't Leave My Wooden Wife — Love Song For The Dead Che — Where Is Yesterday
American Way Of Love Medley — Coming Down — Hard Coming Love — For You, Sugar — Stranded In Time

UNKLE '98
Experimental hip-hop trio from England: James Lavelle, Tim Goldsworthy and Kudo.

| 10/17/98 | 107 | 2 | | © | Psyence Fiction .... | | | $10 | Mo Wax 540970 |

Bloodstain — Getting Ahead In The Lucrative — Guns Blazing (Drums Of Death — Lonely Soul — Unkle (Main Title Theme)
Celestial Annihilation — Field Of Artist Management — Part 1) — Nursery Rhyme — Unreal
Chaos — Knock (Drums Of Death Part 2) — Rabbit In Your Headlights

UNLIMITED TOUCH '81
R&B group from Brooklyn, New York: Audrey Wheeler and Stephanie James (vocals), Philip Hamilton (guitar), Galen Underwood (keyboards), Samuel Anderson (bass) and Tony Cintron (drums).

| 6/20/81 | 142 | 7 | | | Unlimited Touch .... | | | $12 | Prelude 12184 |

Carry On — Happy Ever After — In The Middle — Private Party
Feel The Music — I Hear Music In The Streets — Love To Share — Searching To Find The One

UNTOUCHABLES, The '89
Funk group from Los Angeles: Jerry Miller and Chuck Askerneese (vocals), Clyde Grimes (guitar), Brewster (keyboards), Derek Breakfield (bass) and Willie McNeil (drums).

| 4/1/89 | 162 | 9 | | © | Agent Double O Soul .... | | | $10 | Restless 72342 |

Agent Double O Soul — Cold City — Let's Get Together — Stripped To The Bone — Under The Boardwalk
Airplay — Education — Shama Lama — Sudden Attack — World Gone Crazy

UNV '93
R&B vocal group from Detroit: brothers John and Shawn Powe, with John Clay and Demetrius Peete. UNV: Universal Nubian Voices.

| 7/17/93 | 59 | 13 | | © 1 | Something's Goin' On .... | | | $10 | Maverick 45287 |
| 7/15/95 | 161 | 3 | | © 2 | Universal Nubian Voices .... | | | $10 | Maverick 45839 |

All I Have (2) — First Time (2) — Make Up Your Mind (2) — So In Love With You (2) 65 — 2 B Or Not 2 B (1) — Who Will It Be? (1)
Bone (2) — Gonna Give U What U Want (1) — No One Compares To You (1) — Something's Goin' On (1) 29 — UNV Thang (1) — You Are The Sunshine (2)
Bring Your Body To Me (2) — Hold On (1) — One More Try (2) — Straight From My Heart (1) — What's It Like (2)
Close Tonight (1) — How Can You Walk Away (1) — Peach Cobbler (2) — Tempted (1) — When Will I Know (1)

UP WITH PEOPLE '66
A "sing-out" musical production featuring various young singing talent.

| 7/23/66 | 61 | 14 | | | Up With People! .... | | | $15 | Pace 1101 |

Ballad Of Joan Of Arc — Freedom Isn't Free — Ride Of Paul Revere — Somewhere — What Color Is God's Skin — You Can't Live Crooked And
Design For Dedication — Happy Song — Run And Catch The Wind — Spirit Of The Green — Which Way America? — Think Straight
Don't Stand Still — New Tomorrow — Showboat-Go Boat (medley) — Up With People

URBAN, Keith '01
Born on 10/26/67 in Caboolture, Queensland, Australia. Country singer.

| 8/26/00+ | 145 | 27 | ● © | | Keith Urban.. | | | $10 | Capitol 97591 |

But For The Grace Of God 37 — I Thought You Knew — If You Wanna Stay — Little Luck Of Our Own — Rollercoaster — You're The Only One
Don't Shut Me Out — I Wanna Be Your Man (Forever) — It's A Love Thing — Out On My Own — Where The Blacktop Ends 35 — Your Everything 51

URBAN DANCE SQUAD '91
Rap-dance group from Amsterdam: Patrick Remington, Magic Stick, DNA, Silly Sil and Tres Manos.

| 8/25/90+ | 54 | 39 | | © | Mental Floss For The Globe .... | | | $10 | Arista 8640 |

Big Apple — Devil, The — God Blasts The Queen — No Kid — Struggle For Jive
Brainstorm On The U.D.S. — Famous When You're Dead — Man On The Corner — Piece Of Rock
Deeper Shade Of Soul 21 — Fastlane — Mental Floss For The Glove — Prayer For My Demo

URE, Midge '89
Born James Ure on 10/10/53 in Glasgow, Scotland. Rock singer/guitarist. Member of **Ultravox** and **Visage**.

| 2/11/89 | 88 | 16 | | © | Answers To Nothing .... | | | $10 | Chrysalis 41649 |

Answers To Nothing — Hell To Heaven — Just For You — Lied — Sister And Brother
Dear God 95 — Homeland — Leaving (So Long) — Remembrance Day — Take Me Home

URGE, The '98
Ska-rock group from St. Louis: Steve Ewing (vocals), Jerry Jost (guitar), Bill Reiter, Matt Kwiatkowski and Todd Painter (horns), Karl Grable (bass) and John Pessoni (drums).

| 5/9/98 | 111 | 2 | | © 1 | Master Of Styles .... | | | $10 | Immortal 69152 |
| 8/5/00 | 200 | 1 | | © 2 | Too Much Stereo .... | | | $10 | Immortal 49498 |

Closer (1) — Gene Machine (1) — If I Were You (1) — My Apology (1) — Say A Prayer (2) — Warning Warning (2)
Divide And Conquer (1) — Going Down (1) — Jump Right In (1) — Played Out (1) — S.L.O.B. (1) — Welcome To Gunville (2)
Four Letters And Two Words — I Go Home (2) — Liar Liar (2) — Prayer For Rain (1) — Straight To Hell (1) — What Do They Know (2)
(2) — Identity Crisis (1) — Living On The Surface (2) — Push On Like Flintstone (2) — Too Much Stereo (2) — What Is This (2)

URGE OVERKILL '95
Rock trio from Chicago: Nash Kato (guitar), "Eddie" King Roeser (bass) and Blackie Onassis (drums). All share vocals.

| 9/18/93 | 146 | 9 | | © 1 | Saturation .... | | | $10 | Geffen 24529 |
| 10/14/95 | 129 | 1 | | © 2 | Exit The Dragon .... | | | $10 | Geffen 24818 |

And You'll Say (2) — Digital Black Epilogue (2) — Jaywalkin' (1) — Nite And Grey (1) — Take Me (2) — View Of The Rain (2)
Back On Me (1) — Dropout (1) — Last Night (medley) (2) — Positive Bleeding (1) — Tequila Sundae (1) — Woman 2 Woman (1)
Bottle Of Fur (1) — Erica Kane (1) — Mistake, The (2) — Sister Havana (1) — This Is No Place (2)
Break, The (2) — Heaven 90210 (1) — Monopoly (2) — Somebody Else's Body (2) — Tin Foil (2)
Crackbabies (1) — Honesty Files (2) — Need Some Air (2) — Stalker, The (1) — Tomorrow (medley) (2)

URIAH HEEP '73

★353★

Hard-rock group from England. Core members: David Byron (vocals; later with **Rough Diamond**), Mick Box (guitar), **Ken Hensley** (keyboards; later with **Blackfoot**), Gary Thain (bass) and Keith Baker (drums). Thain died of a drug overdose on 3/19/76 (age 27). Byron died on 2/28/85 (age 38).

1)Demons And Wizards 2)The Magician's Birthday 3)Sweet Freedom

DEBUT	PEAK	WKS	RIAA	CD	No	Album Title	Sym	$	Label & Number
10/3/70	186	4		©	1	Uriah Heep		$15	Mercury 61294
1/30/71	103	9		©	2	Salisbury		$15	Mercury 61319
9/25/71	93	20		©	3	Look At Yourself		$12	Mercury 614
6/17/72	23	38	●	©	4	Demons And Wizards		$12	Mercury 630
12/2/72+	31	22	●	©	5	The Magician's Birthday		$12	Mercury 652
5/5/73	37	30	●	©	6	Uriah Heep Live	[L]	$15	Mercury 7503 [2]
10/6/73	33	23	●	©	7	Sweet Freedom		$12	Warner 2724
7/6/74	38	15		©	8	Wonderworld		$12	Warner 2800
8/2/75	85	10		©	9	Return To Fantasy		$12	Warner 2869
3/20/76	145	6			10	The Best Of Uriah Heep	[G]	$12	Mercury 1070
6/26/76	161	3		©	11	High And Mighty		$12	Warner 2949
4/30/77	166	3		©	12	Firefly		$12	Warner 3013
11/4/78	186	5		©	13	Fallen Angel		$12	Chrysalis 1204
8/7/82	56	16		©	14	Abominog		$10	Mercury 4057
6/4/83	159	10		©	15	Head First		$10	Mercury 812313

All My Life (4)
Beautiful Dream (9)
Been Away Too Long (12)
Bird Of Prey (1,10)
Blind Eye (5) *97*
Can't Keep A Good Band Down (11)
Can't Stop Singing (11)
Chasing Shadows (14)
Circle Of Hands (4,6)
Circus (7)
Come Away Melinda (1)
Come Back To Me (13)
Confession (11)
Devil's Daughter (9)
Do You Know (12)
Dreamer (7)
Dreammare (1)
Dreams (8)
Easy Livin (4,6,10) *39*

Easy Road (8)
Echoes In The Dark (5)
Fallen Angel (13)
Falling In Love (13)
Firefly (12)
Footprints In The Snow (11)
Gypsy (1,6,10)
Hanging Tree (12)
High Priestess (2)
Hot Night In A Cold Town (14)
Hot Persuasion (14)
I Wanna Be Free (3)
I Won't Mind (8)
I'll Keep On Trying (1)
I'm Alive (13)
If I Had The Time (7)
July Morning (3,6,10)
Lady In Black (2,10)
Lonely Nights (15)
Look At Yourself (3,6,10)

Love Is Blind (15)
Love Machine (3,6)
Love Or Nothing (13)
Magician's Birthday (5,6)
Make A Little Love (11)
Midnight (11)
Misty Eyes (11)
On The Rebound (14)
One Day (7)
One More Night (Last Farewell) (13)
One Way Or Another (11)
Other Side Of Midnight (15)
Paradise (medley) (13)
Park, The (2)
Pilgrim (7)
Poet's Justice (4)
Prima Donna (9)
Prisoner (14)
Put Your Lovin' On Me (13)

Rain (5)
Rainbow Demon (4)
Real Turned On (1)
Red Lights (15)
Return To Fantasy (9)
Rock 'N Roll Medley (6)
Roll-Overture (15)
Rollin' On (12)
Rollin' The Rock (15)
Running All Night (With The Lion) (14)
Salisbury (2)
Save It (13)
Sell Your Soul (14)
Seven Stars (7)
Shadows And The Wind (8)
Shadows Of Grief (3)
Shady Lady (9)
Showdown (9)
Simon The Bullet Freak (2)

So Tired (8)
Something Or Nothing (8)
Spell, The (medley) (4)
Spider Woman (5)
Stay On Top (15)
Stealin' (7) *91*
Straight Through The Heart (15)
Suicidal Man (8)
Sunrise (5,6,10)
Sweet Freedom (7)
Sweet Lorraine (5,6,10) *91*
Sweet Talk (15)
Sympathy (12)
Tales (5)
Tears In My Eyes (3,6)
That's The Way That It Is (14)
Think It Over (14)
Time To Live (2)
Too Scared To Run (14)
Traveller In Time (4,6)

Wake Up (Set Your Sights) (1)
Walking In Your Shadow (1)
We Got We (8)
Weekend Warriors (15)
Weep In Silence (11)
Whad'ya Say (13)
What Should Be Done (3)
Who Needs Me (12)
Why Did You Go (9)
Wise Man (12)
Wizard, The (4,10)
Woman Of The Night (13)
Woman Of The World (11)
Wonderworld (8)
Year Or A Day (9)
Your Turn To Remember (9)

USA-EUROPEAN CONNECTION '78

Female disco vocal trio: Leza Holmes, Renne Johnson and Sharon Williams.

DEBUT	PEAK	WKS				Album Title		$	Label & Number
4/8/78	66	19				Come Into My Heart		$12	Marlin 2212

Baby Love (medley) Come Into My Heart (medley) Good Loving (medley) Love's Coming (medley)

USA FOR AFRICA '85

USA: United Support of Artists. Collection of top artists formed to help starving people in Africa.

DEBUT	PEAK	WKS				Album Title		$	Label & Number
4/20/85	❶³	22	▲³	©		We Are The World		$10	Columbia 40043

4 The Tears In Your Eyes [Prince]
Good For Nothing [Chicago]

If Only For The Moment, Girl [Steve Perry]
Just A Little Closer [Pointer Sisters]

Little More Love [Kenny Rogers]
Tears Are Not Enough [Northern Lights]

Total Control [Tina Turner]
Trapped [Bruce Springsteen]
Trouble In Paradise [Huey Lewis & The News]

We Are The World *1*

USHER '98

Born Usher Raymond on 10/14/78 in Chattanooga, Tennessee. R&B singer/actor. Played "Jeremy" on TV's *Moesha*. Acted in several movies.

DEBUT	PEAK	WKS	RIAA	CD	No	Album Title	Sym	$	Label & Number
9/17/94	167	12		©	1	Usher		$10	LaFace 26008
10/4/97+	4	79	▲⁶	©	2	My Way		$10	LaFace 26043
4/10/99	73	9	●	©	3	Live	[L]	$10	LaFace 26059

Bedtime (2,3)
Can U Get Wit It (1) *59*
Come Back (2,3)
Crazy (1)
Every Little Step (3)

Final Goodbye (1)
I Will (2)
I'll Make It Right (1)
I'll Show You Love (1)
Just Like Me (2,3)

Love Was Here (1)
Many Ways (1)
My Way (2,3) *2*
Nice & Slow (2,3) *1*
One Day You'll Be Mine (2)

Pianolude (3)
Rock Wit'cha (3)
Roni (3)
Slow Jam (2)
Slow Love (1)

Smile Again (1)
Tender Love (3)
Think Of You (1,3) *58*
Whispers (1)
You Make Me Wanna... (2,3) *2*

You Took My Heart (1)

US3 '94

Jazz/rap collaboration by London producers Mel Simpson (keyboards) and Geoff Wilkinson (samples). Samples of recordings on the Blue Note jazz record label serve as the backdrop for new rap solos and jazz playing by some of Britain's top players.

DEBUT	PEAK	WKS	RIAA	CD		Album Title		$	Label & Number
1/8/94	31	33	▲	©		Hand On The Torch		$10	Blue Note 80883

Cantaloop *9*
Cruisin'
Darkside, The

Different Rhythms Different People
Eleven Long Years

I Go To Work
I Got It Goin' On
It's Like That

Just Another Brother
Knowledge Of Self
Lazy Day

Make Tracks
Tukka Yoot's Riddim

UTAH SAINTS '93

Techno-rave duo from England: Jez Willis and Tim Garbutt.

DEBUT	PEAK	WKS		CD	No	Album Title		$	Label & Number
11/14/92	182	4		©	1	Something Good		$10	London 869843
1/23/93	165	4		©	2	Utah Saints		$10	London 828374

Anything Can Happen (1)
I Want You (2)
Kinetic Synthetic (2)

My Mind Must Be Free (2)
New Gold Dream (81-82-83-84) (2)

Something Good (1,2) *98*
Soulution (2)
States Of Mind (2)

Too Much To Swallow (Part I) (2)
Trance Atlantic Flight (1)

Trance Atlantic Glide (2)
Trans Europe Caress (1)
What Can You Do For Me (1,2)

UTFO '87

Rap group from Brooklyn, New York: Shawn Fequiere, Fred Reeves, Jeff Campbell and Maurice Bailey. UTFO: Un-Touchable Force Organization.

6/15/85	80	20	©	1	UTFO	$10	Select 21614
8/9/86	142	8	©	2	Skeezer Pleezer	$10	Select 21616
10/3/87	67	20	©	3	Lethal	$10	Select 21619
6/10/89	143	4	©	4	Doin' It!	$10	Select 21629

All About Technic (4)
Ask Yo Mama (3)
Bad Luck Barry (2)
Battle Of The Sexes (4)
Beats And Rhymes (1)
Bite It (1)
Bits And Pieces (1)
Burning Bed (3)
Calling Her A Crab (1)
Cold Abrasive (4)
Diss (3)
Doin' It! (4)
Don't You Hate It When... (4)
Fairy Tale Lover (1)
Hanging Out (1)
House Will Rock (1)
Just Watch (2)
Kangol & Doc (2)
Leader Of The Pack (1)
Let's Get It On (3)
Lethal (3)
Lisa Lips (1)
Master - Baby (3)
Master Of The Mix (4)
Mo' Bass (3)
My Cut's Correct (4)
Pick Up The Pace (2)
Real Roxanne (1)
Ride, The (3)
Rough And Rugged (4)
Roxanne, Roxanne (1) 77
So Be It (3)
Split Personality (2)
S.W.A.T. (Get Down) (3)
Wanna Rock (3)
We Work Hard (2)
Where Did You Go? (2)
Ya Cold Wanna Be With Me (3)

★488★ UTOPIA '80

Pop-rock group: **Todd Rundgren** (vocals, guitar), Roger Powell (keyboards), **Kasim Sulton** (bass) and John Wilcox (drums).

1)Adventures In Utopia 2)Todd Rundgren's Utopia 3)Deface The Music

11/9/74	34	15	©	1	Todd Rundgren's Utopia	$12	Bearsville 6954
11/15/75	66	9	©	2	Todd Rundgren's Utopia/Another Live	[L] $12	Bearsville 6961
2/26/77	79	7	©	3	RA	$12	Bearsville 6965
9/24/77	73	8	©	4	Oops! Wrong Planet	$12	Bearsville 6970
1/26/80	32	21	©	5	Adventures In Utopia	$12	Bearsville 6991
10/25/80	65	9	©	6	Deface The Music	$12	Bearsville 3487
3/20/82	102	10	©	7	Swing To The Right	$12	Bearsville 3666
10/16/82	84	19	©	8	Utopia	$15	Network 60183 [2]
2/11/84	74	12	©	9	Oblivion	$10	Passport 6029
3/16/85	161	6	©	10	POV	$10	Passport 6044

Abandon City (4)
All Smiles (6)
Alone (6)
Always Late (6)
Another Life (2)
Back On The Street (4)
Bad Little Actress (6)
Bring Me My Longbow (9)
Burn Three Times (8)
Call It What You Will (8)
Caravan (5)
Chapter And Verse (6)
Communion With The Sun (3)
Crazy Lady Blue (4)
Crybaby (9)
Crystal Ball (6)
Do Ya (2)
Eternal Love (3)
Everybody Else Is Wrong (6)
Fahrenheit 451 (7)
Feel Too Good (6)
Feet Don't Fail Me Now (8) 82
For The Love Of Money (7)
Forgotten But Not Gone (8)
Freak Parade (1)
Freedom Fighters (1)
Gangrene (4)
Hammer In My Heart (8)
Heavy Metal Kids (2)
Hiroshima (3)
Hoi Poloi (6)
I Just Want To Touch You (6)
I Will Wait (9)
I'm Looking At You But I'm Talking To Myself (8)
If I Didn't Try (9)
Ikon, The (1)
Infrared And Ultraviolet (8)
Itch In My Brain (9)
Jealousy (3)
Junk Rock (Million Monkeys) (7)
Just One Victory (2)
Last Dollar On Earth (7)
Last Of The New Wave Riders (5)
Libertine (8)
Life Goes On (6)
Love Alone (4)
Love In Action (4)
Love Is The Answer (4)
Love With A Thinker (9)
Lysistrata (7)
Magic Dragon Theatre (3)
Marriage Of Heaven And Hell (4)
Martyr, The (4)
Mated (10)
Maybe I Could Change (9)
Mimi Gets Mad (10)
Mister Triscuits (2)
More Light (10)
My Angel (4)
Mystified (10)
Neck On Up (8)
One World (7)
Only Human (7)
Play This Game (10)
Princess Of The Universe (8)
Private Heaven (8)
Rape Of The Young (4)
Road To Utopia (5)
Rock Love (5)
Say Yeah (8)
Second Nature (5)
Secret Society (10)
Set Me Free (5) 27
Seven Rays (2)
Shinola (1)
Shot In The Dark (5)
Silly Boy (6)
Singring And The Glass Guitar (3)
Something's Coming (2)
Stand For Something (10)
Style (10)
Sunburst Finish (3)
Swing To The Right (7)
Take It Home (6)
That's Not Right (6)
There Goes My Inspiration (8)
Too Much Water (9)
Trapped (4)
Up, The (7)
Utopia (1)
Very Last Time (5) 76
Welcome To My Revolution (9)
Wheel, The (2)
Where Does The World Go To Hide (6)
Wildlife (10)
Windows (4)
Winston Smith Takes It On The Jaw (7)
You Make Me Crazy (5)
Zen Machine (10)

U2 ★71★ '87

Rock group formed in Dublin, Ireland: Paul "Bono" Hewson (vocals), Dave "The Edge" Evans (guitar), Adam Clayton (bass) and Larry Mullen Jr. (drums). Released concert tour documentary movie *Rattle And Hum* in 1988. Also see **Passengers**.

1)The Joshua Tree 2)Rattle And Hum 3)Zooropa

3/14/81	63	47	▲	©	1	Boy	$10	Island 9646
11/7/81	104	38	▲	©	2	October	$10	Island 9680
3/19/83	12	179	▲⁴	©	3	War	C:#23/33 $10	Island 90067
12/10/83+	28	180	▲³	©	4	Under A Blood Red Sky	C:#4/66 [L-M] $10	Island 90127
10/20/84	12	132	▲³	©	5	The Unforgettable Fire	C:#39/3 $10	Island 90231
6/29/85	37	23	▲	©	6	Wide Awake In America	[L-M] $10	Island 90279
						side A: live; side B: outtakes from #5 above		
4/4/87	❶⁹	103	▲¹⁰	©	7	The Joshua Tree	C:#9/240 $10	Island 90581
						1987 Grammy winner: Album of the Year		
10/29/88	❶⁶	38	▲⁵	©	8	Rattle And Hum	C:#39/9 [S] $15	Island 91003 [2]
12/7/91	❶¹	97	▲⁸	©	9	Achtung Baby	$10	Island 10347
7/24/93	❶²	40	▲²	©	10	Zooropa	$10	Island 518047
3/22/97	❶¹	28	▲	©	11	Pop	$10	Island 524334
11/21/98	2¹	17	▲²	©	12	The Best Of 1980-1990/The B-Sides	[G] $15	Island 524612 [2]
11/28/98	45	42	▲	©	13	The Best Of 1980-1990	C:#5/41 [G] $10	Island 524613
11/18/00	3	46↑	▲²	©	14	All That You Can't Leave Behind	$10	Interscope 524653

Acrobat (9)
All Along The Watchtower (8)
All I Want Is You (8,12,13) 83
Cat Dubh (1)
Angel Of Harlem (8,12,13) 14
Another Time, Another Place (1)
Babyface (10)
Bad (5,6,12,13)
Bass Trap (12)
Beautiful Day (14) 21
Bullet The Blue Sky (7,8)
Daddy's Gonna Pay For Your Crashed Car (10)
Dancing Barefoot (12)
Day Without Me (1)
Desire (8,12,13) 3
Dirty Day (10)
Discotheque (11) 10
Do You Feel Loved (11)
Drowning Man (3)
Electric Co. (1,4)
Elevation (14)
11 O'Clock Tick Tock (4)
Elvis Presley And America (5)
Endless Deep (12)
Even Better Than The Real Thing (12)
Everlasting Love (12)
Exit (7)
Fire (2)
First Time (10)
Fly, The (9) 61
40 (3,4)
4th Of July (5)
Freedom For My People (8)
Gloria (2,4)
God Part II (8)
Gone (11)
Grace (14)
Hallelujah Here She Comes (12)
Hawkmoon 269 (8)
Heartland (8)
Helter Skelter (8)
I Fall Down (2)
I Still Haven't Found What I'm Looking For (7,8,12,13) 1
I Threw A Brick Through A Window (2)
I Will Follow (1,4,12,13) 81
If God Will Send His Angels (11)
If You Wear That Velvet Dress (11)
In A Little While (14)
In God's Country (7) 44
Indian Summer Sky (5)
Into The Heart (1)
Is That All? (2)
Kite (1)
Last Night On Earth (11) 57
Lemon (10)
Like A Song... (3)
Love Comes Tumbling (6,12)
Love Is Blindness (9)

U2 — Cont'd

Love Rescue Me (8)
Luminous Times (Hold On To Love) (12)
MLK (5)
Miami (11)
Mofo (11)
Mothers Of The Disappeared (7)
Mysterious Ways (9) *9*
New Year's Day (3,4,12,13) *53*
New York (14)
Numb (10)
Ocean, The (1)
October (2)
One (9) *10*

One Tree Hill (7)
Out Of Control (1)
Party Girl (4)
Peace On Earth (14)
Playboy Mansion (11)
Please (11)
Pride (In The Name Of Love) (5,8,12,13) *33*
Promenade (5)
Red Hill Mining Town (7)
Red Light (3)
Refugee, The (3)
Rejoice (8)
Room At The Heartbreak Hotel (12)

Running To Stand Still (7)
Scarlet (2)
Seconds (3)
Shadows And Tall Trees (1)
Silver And Gold (8,12)
So Cruel (9)
Some Days Are Better Than Others (10)
Sort Of Homecoming (5,6)
Spanish Eyes (12)
Star Spangled Banner (8)
Staring At The Sun (11) *26*
Stay (Faraway, So Close!) (10) *61*
Stories For Boys (1)

Stranger In A Strange Land (2)
Stuck In A Moment You Can't Get Out Of (14)
Sunday Bloody Sunday (3,4,12,13)
Surrender (3)
Sweetest Thing (12,13) *63*
Three Sunrises (6,12)
Tomorrow (2)
Trash, Trampoline And The Party Girl (12)
Trip Through Your Wires (7)
Tryin' To Throw Your Arms Around The World (9)
Twilight (1)

Two Hearts Beat As One (3)
Ultra Violet (Light My Way) (9)
Unchained Melody (12)
Unforgettable Fire (5,12,13)
Until The End Of The World (9)
Van Diemen's Land (8)
Wake Up Dead Man (11)
Walk On (14)
Walk To The Water (12)
Wanderer, The (10)
When I Look At The World (14)
When Love Comes To Town (8,12,13) *68*
Where The Streets Have No Name (7,12,13) *13*

Who's Gonna Ride Your Wild Horses (9) *35*
Wild Honey (14)
Wire (5)
With A Shout (2)
With Or Without You (7,12,13) *1*
Zoo Station (9)
Zooropa (10)

V

VAI, Steve　'90

Born on 6/6/60 in Long Island, New York. Rock guitarist. With **Frank Zappa**'s band (1979-84), **Alcatrazz** (1985), **David Lee Roth**'s band (1986-88) and **Whitesnake** (1989). Formed **Vai** in 1992 which featured vocalist Devin Townsend and fluctuating band members. Former guitar student of **Joe Satriani**.

DEBUT	PEAK	WKS	CD	#	Title	Sym	$	Label & Number
6/9/90	18	25	● ©	1	**Passion And Warfare**	[I]	$10	Relativity 1037
8/14/93	48	8	©	2	**Sex & Religion** — VAI		$10	Relativity 1132
4/8/95	125	2	©	3	**Alien Love Secrets**		$10	Relativity 1245
10/5/96	106	2	©	4	**Fire Garden**		$10	Epic 67776
6/21/97	108	3	©	5	**G3 - Live In Concert** — JOE SATRIANI/ERIC JOHNSON/STEVE VAI	[I-L]	$10	Epic 67920
9/25/99	121	1	©	6	**The Ultra Zone**	[I]	$10	Epic 69817

Aching Hunger (4)
Alien Water Kiss (1)
All About Eve (4)
Animal, The (1)
Answers (1,5)
Asian Sky (6)
Attitude Song (5)
Audience Is Listening (1)
Bad Horsie (3)
Ballerina 12/24 (1)
Bangkok (4)
Blood & Tears (6)

Blowfish (4)
Blue Powder (1)
Boy From Seattle (3)
Brother (4)
Crying Machine (4)
Damn You (4)
Die To Live (3)
Dirty Black Hole (2)
Down Deep Into The Pain (2)
Dyin' Day (4)
Earth Dweller's Return (2)
Erotic Nightmares (1)

Fever Dream (6)
Fire Garden Suite (4)
For The Love Of God (1,5)
Frank (6)
Genocide (4)
Going Down (5)
Greasy Kid's Stuff (1)
Hand On Heart (4)
Here & Now (2)
Here I Am (6)
I Would Love To (1)
I'll Be Around (6)

In My Dreams With You (2)
Jibboom (6)
Juice (3)
Kill The Guy With The Ball (3)
Liberty (1)
Little Alligator (4)
Love Secrets (1)
Lucky Charms (6)
My Guitar Wants To Kill Your Mama (5)
Mysterious Murder Of Christian Tiera's Lover (4)

OOOO (6)
Pig (2)
Red House (5)
Rescue Me Or Bury Me (2)
Riddle, The (1)
Road To Mt. Calvary (4)
Sex & Religion (2)
Silent Within (6)
Sisters (1)
State Of Grace (2)
Still My Bleeding Heart (2)
Survive (2)

Tender Surrender (3)
There's A Fire In The House (4)
Touching Tongues (2)
Ultra Zone (6)
Voodoo Acid (6)
Warm Regards (4)
When I Was A Little Boy (4)
Windows To The Soul (6)
Ya-Yo Gakk (3)

VAIN　'89

Hard-rock group from San Francisco: Davy Vain (vocals), Danny West and James Scott (guitars), Ashley Mitchell (bass) and Tom Rickard (drums).

DEBUT	PEAK	WKS	CD	#	Title	$	Label & Number
8/26/89	154	8	©		**No Respect**	$10	Island 91272

Aces
Beat The Bullet

Down For The 3rd Time
Icy

Laws Against Love
No Respect

Ready
Secrets

Smoke And Shadows
1000 Degrees

Who's Watching You
Without You

★229★　VALE, Jerry　'63

Born Genaro Vitaliano on 7/8/32 in the Bronx, New York. Pop ballad singer.

1)The Language Of Love　2)Be My Love　3)Till The End Of Time　4)Have You Looked Into Your Heart　5)Arrivederci, Roma

DEBUT	PEAK	WKS	CD	#	Title	Sym	$	Label & Number
8/25/62+	60	48		1	**I Have But One Heart**		$15	Columbia 1797 / 8597
2/23/63	34	25		2	**Arrivederci, Roma**		$15	Columbia 1955 / 8755
9/7/63	22	35	©	3	**The Language Of Love**		$15	Columbia 2043 / 8843
2/22/64	28	18	©	4	**Till The End Of Time**		$15	Columbia 2116 / 8916
8/29/64	26	22	©	5	**Be My Love**		$15	Columbia 2181 / 8981
12/19/64	14 [X]	10	©	6	**Christmas Greetings From Jerry Vale**	[X]	$15	Columbia 2225 / 9025
					Christmas charts: 14/'64, 51/'65, 36/'67, 22/'68			
1/30/65	55	18	©	7	**Standing Ovation!**	[L]	$15	Columbia 2273 / 9073
					recorded on 5/30/64 at Carnegie Hall			
3/6/65	30	23	©	8	**Have You Looked Into Your Heart**		$15	Columbia 2313 / 9113
10/16/65	42	17		9	**There Goes My Heart**		$15	Columbia 2387 / 9187
2/12/66	38	17		10	**It's Magic**		$15	Columbia 2444 / 9244
7/2/66	111	4		11	**Great Moments On Broadway**		$15	Columbia 2489 / 9289
3/18/67	117	23		12	**The Impossible Dream**		$15	Columbia 2583 / 9383
9/16/67	128	6		13	**Time Alone Will Tell**		$15	Columbia 2684 / 9484
3/16/68	163	7		14	**You Don't Have To Say You Love Me**		$15	Columbia 2774 / 9574
8/10/68	135	20		15	**This Guy's In Love With You**		$15	Columbia 9694
2/15/69	90	12	©	16	**Till**		$15	Columbia 9757
7/5/69	180	4		17	**Where's The Playground Susie?**		$15	Columbia 9838
11/1/69	193	2		18	**With Love, Jerry Vale**	[K]	$15	Columbia 16 [2]
2/14/70	196	2		19	**Jerry Vale Sings 16 Greatest Hits Of The 60's**		$12	Columbia 9982
6/27/70	189	4		20	**Let It Be**		$12	Columbia 1021
2/12/72	200	2	©	21	**Jerry Vale Sings The Great Hits Of Nat King Cole**		$12	Columbia 31147

Abraham, Martin And John (16)
Al Di La (2)
All (13)
All I Have To Do Is Dream (20)
All The Way (5,18)
Always In My Heart (8)

Andiamo (2)
Anema E Core (2)
Answer Me, My Love (21)
Arrivederci, Roma (3)
Ashamed (10)

Auf Wiederseh'n, Sweetheart (3)
Baby Won't You Please Come Home (7)
Be Anything (But Be Mine) (10)
Be My Love (5)

Because (5)
Because Of You (5,18)
Because You're Mine (5)
Big Wide World (10)
Blossom Fell (21)
Blue Christmas (6)

Blue Velvet (19)
Born Free (13,19)
Bridge Over Troubled Water (20)
By The Time I Get To Phoenix (15)

Camelot (11)
Can't Take My Eyes Off You (15,19)
Can't You See I'm Sorry (9)

VALE, Jerry — Cont'd

Christmas Song (Chestnuts Roasting On An Open Fire) (6)
Ciao, Ciao, Bambina (2)
Come Back To Sorrento (1,7)
Day That We Said Goodbye (13)
Do You Know The Way To San Jose (15)
Dr. Zhivago ..see: Somewhere, My Love
Dommage, Dommage (Too Bad, Too Bad) (12) *93*
Don't Tell My Heart To Stop Loving You (15)
Don't You Know? (4)
Easy Come, Easy Go (20)
Ebb Tide (14)
Eternally (14)
First Noel (6)
For Me (10)
From The Bottom Of My Heart (2)
Full Moon And Empty Arms (4)
Galveston (17)
Games That Lovers Play (13)
Gigi (12)
Goodnight My Love (Pleasant Dreams) (17)
Granada (7)
Happy Heart (17)
Have You Ever Been Lonely (Have You Ever Been Blue) (8)
Have You Looked Into Your Heart (8) *24*
Have Yourself A Merry Little Christmas (6)
Hello, Dolly! (19)
Hey, Look Me Over (7)
Honey (I Miss You) (15)
How Are Things In Glocca Morra? (18)

I Can't Get You Out Of My Heart (1)
I Can't Help It (9)
I Can't Stop Loving You (18)
I Dream Of You (8)
I Feel A Song Comin' On (7)
I Have But One Heart (1)
I Left My Heart In San Francisco (7)
I Love How You Love Me (16)
I Love You Much Too Much (3,18)
I Understand (9)
I Won't Cry Anymore (13)
I'll Be Home For Christmas (6)
I'll Get By (18)
I'll Never Fall In Love Again (20)
I'll Never Forgive You (8)
I'm Always Chasing Rainbows (7)
I'm Yours (8)
If I Had You (7)
If I Loved You (11)
If It Isn't In Your Heart (10)
Impossible Dream (12,19)
Is It Asking Too Much (10)
It Came Upon The Midnight Clear (6)
It Had To Be You (18)
It's Magic (10)
Jean (20)
Just Friends (18)
Just One More Chance (9)
Just Say I Love Her (1,18)
La Vie En Rose (3)
Lara's Theme ..see: Somewhere, My Love
Leaving On A Jet Plane (20)
Les Bicyclettes De Belsize (16)
Let It Be (20)
Let It Be Me (17)
Little Green Apples (16,19)
Lonesome Road (7)

Look Homeward Angel (16)
Look Of Love (15)
Love Goddess (8)
Love Grows (Where My Rosemary Goes) (20)
Love Is A Many-Splendored Thing (5)
Love Is Blue (19)
Love Me With All Your Heart (13)
Lover's Roulette (14)
Lulu's Back In Town (7)
Luna Rossa (2)
Mac Arthur Park (16)
Mala Femmina (1,7)
Mama (Mamma) (1,7)
Man Without Love (15)
Maria (11)
Maria Elena (3,18)
Mona Lisa (5,21)
Moon Love (4)
Moon River (19)
More (Theme from Mondo Cane) (12,19)
Moulin Rouge (Where Is Your Heart), Song From (3)
My Cup Runneth Over (13)
My Foolish Heart (12)
My Heart Reminds Me (4,18)
My Love, Forgive Me (13)
My Melancholy Baby (10)
My Prayer (1)
My Reverie (4)
My Special Angel (16)
My Way (17)
Nature Boy (21)
No One Will Ever Know (9)
Non Dimenticar (2)
Now (3)
O Little Town Of Bethlehem (6)
'O Sole Mio (My Sunshine) (1,7)
Oh Come, All Ye Faithful (Adeste Fideles) (6)

Oh Holy Night (6)
(Oh, My Wonderful One) Tell Me You're Mine (1)
Old Cape Cod (8)
On A Clear Day (You Can See Forever) (11)
On And On (4)
On The Street Where You Live (11)
One More Blessing (9)
Palermo (1)
Piscatore 'E Pusilleco (2)
Poor Butterfly (18)
Pretend (18,21)
Prisoner Of Love (18)
Promises, Promises (16)
Put Your Head On My Shoulder (16)
Raindrops Keep Fallin' On My Head (20)
Ramblin' Rose (21)
Red Sails In The Sunset (10)
Release Me (14)
Return To Me (1)
Roman Guitar (1)
Sandpiper, Love Theme From The ..see: Shadow Of Your Smile
Santa Lucia (Me And Maria) (2)
Seattle (17)
Secret Love (5)
Shadow Of Your Smile (12,19)
She Gives Me Love (La, La, La) (15)
Silent Night, Holy Night (6)
Silver Bells (6)
Sleepy Time Gal (18)
Smile (12,21)
So In Love (11)
So Near...Yet So Far (4)
Sogni D'Oro (Dreams Of Gold) (9)
Solitude (10)

Some Enchanted Evening (11)
Somebody Else Is Taking My Place (9)
Something (20)
Somewhere Along The Way (21)
Somewhere, My Love (12)
Song Is You (7)
Spanish Eyes (19)
Stay Awhile (20)
Story Of A Starry Night (4)
Stranger In Paradise (11)
Strangers In The Night (12,18,19)
Summertime In Venice (2)
Sunny (19)
Sunrise, Sunset (11)
Tears (For Souvenirs) (10)
Tears Keep On Falling (8) *96*
Tell Me That You Love Me (1)
There Are Such Things (8)
There Goes My Heart (9,18)
There Must Be A Way (9)
There's A Kind Of Hush (All Over The World) (14)
Things I Love (4)
This Day Of Days (4)
This Guy's In Love With You (15,19)
This Is My Song (13)
Those Were The Days (16)
Three Coins In The Fountain (12)
Ti Adoro (8)
Till (16)
Till The End Of Time (4)
Till There Was You (14)
Time Alone Will Tell (13)
To Each His Own (14)
To Know You Is To Love You (17)
To Love Again (4)
Too Many Tomorrows (11)

Too Young (5,21)
Traces (17)
Two Different Worlds (3,18)
Unchained Melody (5)
Unforgettable (21)
Vaya Con Dios (5)
Very Thought Of You (18)
Volare (Nel Blu Dipinto Di Blu) (2)
Walkin' My Baby Back Home (21)
Way It Used To Be (7)
What A Wonderful World (14)
What Kind Of Fool Am I (11,19)
What Now My Love (12)
(Where Is Your Heart) ..see: Moulin Rouge
Where's The Playground Susie? (17)
White Christmas (6)
Why Don't You Believe Me (5)
With A Song In My Heart (7)
With Pen In Hand (15)
Without Saying A Word (9)
Wonderful One (3)
Yellow Days (14)
Yesterday (19)
You Alone (Solo Tu) (1)
You Belong To My Heart (3)
You Don't Have To Say You Love Me (14)
You Gave Me A Mountain (17)
You Have To Believe In Someone (14)
You Were Mine For A While (9)
You're Breaking My Heart (2)
You're My Everything (18)
Young Girl (15)
Your Love Is Mine (3)
Yours (3)

VALENS, Ritchie   '59

Born Richard Valenzuela on 5/13/41 in Pacoima, California. Killed in the plane crash that also took the lives of **Buddy Holly** and the Big Bopper on 2/3/59 (age 17). Latin-rock singer/songwriter/guitarist. Appeared in the movie *Go Johnny Go*. The 1987 movie *La Bamba* was based on his life. Inducted into the Rock and Roll Hall of Fame in 2001.

4/6/59	23	6		① **Ritchie Valens**		**$200**	Del-Fi 1201
8/29/87	100	10	©	② **The Best Of Ritchie Valens** .... [G]		**$10**	Rhino 70178

Bluebirds Over The Mountain (1,2)
Boney-Maronie (1)
Come On, Let's Go (1,2) *42*
Donna (1,2) *2*
Dooby-Dooby-Wah (1)
Fast Freight (2)
Framed (1)
Hi-Tone (1)
Hurry Up (2)
In A Turkish Town (1,2)
La Bamba (1,2) *22*
Little Girl (2) *92*
Malaguena (2)
Ooh! My Head (1,2)
Paddi-Wack Song (2)
Stay Beside Me (2)
That's My Little Suzie (1,2) *55*
We Belong Together (1,2)

VALENTIN, Dave   '81

Born in 1954 in New York City. Jazz flutist. Member of **Fuse One**.

10/25/80	194	2		① **Land Of The Third Eye** .... [I]		**$12**	GRP 5009
8/8/81	184	4		② **Pied Piper** .... [I]		**$12**	GRP 5505

Astro-March (1)
Dragon Fly (2)
Fantasy (1)
Land Of The Third Eye (1)
Los Altos (2)
Open Your Eyes (1)
Pana Fuerte (Strong Friendship) (1)
Pied Piper (Man Of Song) (2)
Sambiano (2)
Seven Stars (2)
Shamballa (2)
Sidra's Dream (1)
Tellers, The (1)
This Time (2)

VALJEAN   '62

Born Valjean Johns on 11/19/34 in Shattuck, Oklahoma. Male pianist.

7/28/62	113	5		**The Theme From Ben Casey** .... [I]		**$25**	Carlton 143

Alcoa Premiere, Theme From
Bell Telephone Hour (Waltz), Theme From The
Ben Casey, Theme From *28*
Bonanza, Theme From
Checkmate, Theme From
Dr. Kildare, Theme From
G.E. Theatre, Theme From The
Gunsmoke, Theme From
Naked City, Theme From
Perry Como Show (Dream Along With Me), Theme From
Peter Gunn, Theme From
Wagon Train (Wagons Ho!), Theme From

VALLI, Frankie   '67

Born Francis Castelluccio on 5/3/37 in Newark, New Jersey. Lead singer of **The 4 Seasons**.

7/22/67	34	23	©	① **Frankie Valli-Solo**		**$30**	Philips 600247
8/10/68	176	5	©	② **Timeless**		**$25**	Philips 600274
6/13/70	190	2		③ **Half & Half**		**$20**	Philips 600341
				half the cuts by Frankie Valli, half by **The 4 Seasons** (see 4 Seasons for tracks)			
3/29/75	51	28		④ **Closeup**		**$15**	Private Stock 2000
12/13/75+	107	8		⑤ **Our Day Will Come**		**$15**	Private Stock 2006
12/20/75+	132	8		⑥ **Frankie Valli Gold** .... [G]		**$15**	Private Stock 2001
8/26/78	160	7		⑦ **Frankie Valli...Is The Word**		**$12**	Warner/Curb 3233

By The Time I Get To Phoenix (2)
Can't Take My Eyes Off You (1,6) *2*
Carrie (I Would Marry You) (5)
Circles In The Sand (4)
Closest Thing To Heaven (5)
Donnybrook (2)
Eleanor Rigby (2)
Elise (5)
Emily (3)
Expression Of Love (2)
For All We Know (2)
Fox In A Bush (2,6)
Girl I'll Never Know (Angels Never Fly This Low) (3,6) *52*
Grease (7) *1*
He Sure Blessed You (4)
Heart Be Still (5)
How'd I Know That Love Would Slip Away (4)
I Can't Live A Dream (4)
I Got Love For You, Ruby (4)
I Make A Fool Of Myself (6) *18*
In My Eyes (4)
Ivy (1)
Make The Music Play (2)
Morning After Loving You (3,6)
My Eyes Adored You (4,6) *1*
My Funny Valentine (1)
My Mother's Eyes (1)
Needing You (7)
No Love At All (7)
Our Day Will Come (5) *11*
Over Me (7)
Proud One (1,6) *68*
Save Me, Save Me (7)
Secret Love (1)
September Rain (Here Comes The Rain) (2,6)
Sometimes Love Songs Make Me Cry (7)
Stop And Say Hello (2)
Sun Ain't Gonna Shine (Anymore) (1,6)
Sunny (2)
Swearin' To God (4) *6*
Sweet Sensational Love (5)
Tear Can Tell (7)
To Give (The Reason I Live) (2,6) *29*
To Make My Father Proud (3)
Trouble With Me (1)
Waking Up To Love (4)
Walk Away Renee (5)
Watch Where You Walk (2)
Why (4)
Without Your Love (7)
You Better Go (7)
You Can Bet (I Ain't Goin' Nowhere) (5)
You Can Do It (7)
(You're Gonna) Hurt Yourself (1,6) *39*
You're Ready Now (1)

913

VANDENBERG '83

Born on 1/31/54 in Holland. Hard-rock guitarist. His group: Bert Heerink (vocals), Dick Kemper (bass) and Jos Zoomer (drums). Vandenberg later joined **Whitesnake**.

1/8/83	65	18			1 **Vandenberg**			$10	Atco 90005
1/28/84	169	7			2 **Heading For A Storm**			$10	Atco 90121

Back On My Feet (1) — Friday Night (2) — Lost In A City (1) — Ready For You (1) — Time Will Tell (2) — Waiting For The Night (2)
Burning Heart (1) *39* — Heading For A Storm (2) — Nothing To Lose (1) — Rock On (2) — Too Late (1) — Welcome To The Club (2)
Different Worlds (2) — I'm On Fire (2) — Out In The Streets (1) — This Is War (2) — Wait (1) — Your Love Is In Vain (1)

VANDROSS, Luther ★159★ '91

Born on 4/20/51 in New York City. R&B singer/songwriter/producer. Prolific session singer (including the groups **Chic** and **Change**). Apeared in movie *The Meteor Man*. His older sister Patricia was a member of The Crests.

1)*Songs* 2)*Never Let Me Go* 3)*Power Of Love*

9/19/81	19	36	▲²	©	1 **Never Too Much**			$10	Epic 37451
10/16/82	20	36	▲	©	2 **Forever, For Always, For Love**			$10	Epic 38235
12/24/83+	32	41	▲	©	3 **Busy Body**			$10	Epic 39196
4/6/85	19	56	▲²	©	4 **The Night I Fell In Love**			$10	Epic 39882
10/18/86+	14	53	▲²	©	5 **Give Me The Reason**			$10	Epic 40415
10/22/88	9	33	▲	©	6 **Any Love**			$10	Epic 44308
11/4/89+	26	51	▲³	©	7 **The Best Of Luther Vandross...The Best Of Love** .... C:#10/61	[G]		$15	Epic 45320 [2]
5/18/91	7	60	▲²	©	8 **Power Of Love**			$10	Epic 46789
6/19/93	6	28	▲	©	9 **Never Let Me Go**			$10	Epic 53231
10/8/94	5	37	▲²	©	10 **Songs**			$10	Epic 57775
11/25/95	28	8	●	©	11 **This Is Christmas** .... C:#8/9	[X]		$10	Epic 57795
10/19/96	9	28	▲	©	12 **Your Secret Love**			$10	Epic 67553
10/18/97	44	24	●	©	13 **One Night With You - The Best Of Love Volume 2**	[G]		$10	Epic 68220
8/29/98	26	15	●	©	14 **I Know**			$10	Virgin 46089

Christmas charts: 4/95, 11/96, 25/97

Ain't No Stoppin' Us Now (10) — Evergreen (10) — I Can't Wait No Longer (Let's Do This) (12) — Kiss For Christmas (11) — O' Come All Ye Faithful (11) — **Superstar/Until You Come Back To Me (That's What I'm Gonna Do)** (3,7) *87*
All The Woman I Need (10) — Every Year, Every Christmas (11) — I Gave It Up (When I Fell In Love) (5) — Knocks Me Off My Feet (12) — Once You Know How (2)
Always And Forever (10,13) *58* — For The Sweetness Of Your Love (3) — I Know (14) — Lady, Lady (9) — One Night With You (Everyday Of Your Life) (13) — **There's Nothing Better Than Love** (5,7) *50*
Any Love (6,7) *44* — For You To Love (6) — I Know You Want To (6) — **Little Miracles (Happen Every Day)** (9,13) *62* — Other Side Of The World (4) — This Time I'm Right (12)
Anyone Who Had A Heart (5) — Forever, For Always, For Love (2) — I Listen To The Bells (11) — Love Don't Love Nobody (medley) (9) — Please Come Home For Christmas (11) — 'Til My Baby Comes Home (4,7) *29*
Are You Gonna Love Me (6) — Get It Right (14) — I Really Didn't Mean It (5,7) — Love Don't Love You Anymore (12,13) — **Power Of Love/Love Power** (8,13) *4* — Too Far Down (9)
Are You Mad At Me? (14) — **Give Me The Reason** (5,7) *57* — I Want The Night To Stay (8) — Love Is On The Way (Real Love) (9) — Promise Me (2,7) — Too Proud To Beg (12)
Are You Using Me? (14) — Goin' Out Of My Head (12) — I Wanted Your Love (3) — Love Me Again (9) — Reflections (10) — Treat You Right (7)
Bad Boy/Having A Party (2,7) *55* — Going In Circles (10) *95* — I Who Have Nothing (8) — **Love The One You're With** (10,13) *95* — Religion (14) — Wait For Love (4)
Because It's Really Love (5) — Have Yourself A Merry Little Christmas (11) — I Won't Let You Do That To Me (13) — Love Won't Let Me Wait (6,7) — **Rush, The** (8) *73* — What The World Needs Now (10)
Best Things In Life Are Free (13) — **Heaven Knows** (9) *94* — I Wonder (6) — Make Me A Believer (3) — Searching (7) — When I Need You (14)
Better Love (2) — Hello (10) — I'll Let You Slide (9) — MistleTOE JAM (Everybody Kiss Somebody) (11) — Second Time Around (6) — When You Call On Me/Baby That's When I Come Runnin' (13)
Busy Body (3) — **Here And Now** (7) *6* — I'm Gonna Start Today (8) — My Favorite Things (11,13) — See Me (5)
Can't Be Doin' That Now (9) — House Is Not A Home (1,7) — I'm Only Human (14) — My Sensitivity (Gets In The Way) (4) — She Doesn't Mind (8) — Whether Or Not The World Gets Better (12)
Come Back (6) — How Deep Is Your Love (medley) (9) — I've Been Working (1) — Never Let Me Go (medley) (9) — She Loves Me Back (2)
Crazy Love (12) — **How Many Times Can We Say Goodbye** (3) *27* — If Only For One Night (4,7) — **Never Too Much** (1,7) *33* — **She Won't Talk To Me** (6) *30* — With A Christmas Heart (11)
Creepin' (4,7) — Hustle (1) — If This World Were Mine (7) — Night I Fell In Love (4) — She's A Super Lady (1) — You Stopped Loving Me (1)
Don't Want To Be A Fool (8,13) *9* — **I Can Make It Better** (12,13) *80* — Impossible Dream (10) — Nights In Harlem (14) — Since I Lost My Baby (2,7) — You're The Sweetest One (2)
Don't You Know That? (1) — I Can Tell You That (8) — Isn't There Someone (14) — Nobody To Love (12) — Since You've Been Gone (10) — **Your Secret Love** (12,13) *52*
Dream Lover (14) — It's All About You (13) — Now That I Have You (14) — So Amazing (5,7)
Emotion Eyes (9) — It's Hard For Me To Say (12) — Sometimes It's Only Love (8)
Emotional Love (8) — It's Over Now (4) — **Stop To Love** (5,7) *15*
Endless Love (10,13) *2* — Keeping My Faith In You (14) — Sugar And Spice (I Found Me A Girl) (1)
Killing Me Softly (10)

VAN DYK, Paul '00

Born on 12/16/71 in Eisenhuttenstadt, East Germany. Dance DJ/producer.

7/8/00	192	1		©	**Out There And Back**			$10	Mute 9127 [2]

All I Need — Columbia — Namistai — Santos — Travelling
Another Way — Face To Face — Out There And Back — Tell Me Why (The Riddle) — Vega
Avenue — Love From Above — Pikes — Together We Will Conquer — We Are Alive

VANESS, Theo '79

Born on 6/9/46 in Zoeterwoude, Holland. Male singer.

6/16/79	145	6			**Bad Bad Boy**			$12	Prelude 12165

As Long As It's Love — I'm A Bad Bad Boy — Keep On Dancin' (medley) — Love Me Now — No Romance (medley) — Sentimentally It's You

VANGELIS '82

Born Evangelos Papathanassiou on 3/29/43 in Valos, Greece. Keyboardist/songwriter. Also see **Jon & Vangelis**.

10/17/81+	❶⁴	57	▲	©	1 **Chariots Of Fire**	[I-S]		$10	Polydor 6335
12/13/86+	42	39		©	2 **Opera Sauvage**	[E-I]		$10	Polydor 829663

title is French for "Wild Opera"

Abraham's Theme (1) — Eric's Theme (1) — Hymne (2) — L'Enfant (2) — Reve (2)
Chariots Of Fire - Titles (1) *1* — Five Circles (1) — Irlande (2) — Mouettes (2) — Titles (1)
Chromatique (2) — Flamants Roses (2) — Jerusalem (medley) (1) — 100 Metres (medley) (1)

VAN HALEN ★104★   '88

Hard-rock group formed in Pasadena, California: **David Lee Roth** (vocals), Eddie Van Halen (guitar), Michael Anthony (bass) and Alex Van Halen (drums). The Van Halen brothers were born in Nijmegen, Holland; moved to Pasadena in 1968. **Sammy Hagar** replaced Roth as lead singer in 1985. Eddie married actress Valerie Bertinelli on 4/11/81. Hagar left in June 1996. Gary Cherone (**Extreme**) joined as lead singer in September 1996; left after one album. Roth briefly rejoined group in 1997.

1)OU812 2)For Unlawful Carnal Knowledge 3)5150

DEBUT	PEAK	WKS	RIAA	CD		ARTIST — Album Title	Catalog	$	Label & Number
3/11/78	19	169	▲10	©	1	Van Halen	C:#19/8	$10	Warner 3075
4/14/79	6	47	▲4	©	2	Van Halen II		$10	Warner 3312
4/19/80	6	31	▲3	©	3	Women And Children First	C:#10/21	$10	Warner 3415
5/30/81	5	23	▲2	©	4	Fair Warning		$10	Warner 3540
5/8/82	3	65	▲4	©	5	Diver Down		$10	Warner 3677
1/28/84	2⁵	77	▲10	©	6	1984 (MCMLXXXIV)		$10	Warner 23985
4/12/86	❶³	64	▲5	©	7	5150	C:#42/1	$10	Warner 25394
6/18/88	❶⁴	48	▲3	©	8	OU812		$10	Warner 25732
7/6/91	❶³	74	▲3	©	9	For Unlawful Carnal Knowledge		$10	Warner 26594
3/13/93	5	23	▲2		10	LIVE: Right here, right now.	[L]	$15	Warner 45198 [2]
2/11/95	❶¹	41	▲2		11	Balance		$10	Warner 45760
11/9/96	❶¹	52	▲2		12	Best Of Volume 1	[G]	$10	Warner 46332
4/4/98	4	12	●	©	13	Van Halen 3		$10	Warner 46662

A.F.U. (Naturally Wired) (8)
Aftershock (11)
Ain't Talkin' 'Bout Love (1,10,12)
Amsterdam (11)
And The Cradle Will Rock... (3,12) *55*
Atomic Punk (1)
Ballot Or The Bullet (13)
Baluchitherium (11)
Beautiful Girls (2) *84*
Best Of Both Worlds (7,10)
Big Bad Bill (Is Sweet William Now) (5)
Big Fat Money (11)
Black And Blue (8) *34*
Bottoms Up! (2)
Cabo Wabo (8,10)
Can't Get This Stuff No More (12)
Can't Stop Lovin' You (11,12) *30*
Cathedral (5)

Could This Be Magic? (2)
D.O.A. (2)
Dance The Night Away (2,12) *15*
Dancing In The Street (5) *38*
Dirty Movies (4)
Dirty Water Dog (13)
Doin' Time (11)
Don't Tell Me (What Love Can Do) (11)
Dream Is Over (9)
Dreams (7,10,12) *22*
Drop Dead Legs (6)
Drum Solo (10)
Eruption (1,12)
Everybody Wants Some!! (3)
Feel Your Love Tonight (1)
Feelin' (11)
Feels So Good (8) *35*
5150 (7)
Finish What Ya Started (8,10) *13*

Fire In The Hole (13)
Fools (3)
From Afar (13)
Full Bug (5)
Get Up (7)
Girl Gone Bad (6)
Give To Live (10)
Good Enough (7)
Hang 'Em High (5)
Happy Trails (5)
Hear About It Later (4)
Hot For Teacher (6) *56*
House Of Pain (4)
How Many Say I (13)
Humans Being (12)
I'll Wait (6) *13*
I'm The One (1)
Ice Cream Man (1)
In A Simple Rhyme (3)
In 'N' Out (9,10)
Inside (7)
Intruder (7)

Jamie's Cryin' (1)
Josephina (13)
Judgement Day (9,10)
Jump (6,10,12) *1*
Light Up The Sky (2)
Little Dreamer (1)
Little Guitars (5)
Loss Of Control (3)
Love Walks In (7,10) *22*
Man On A Mission (9,10)
Me Wise Magic (12)
Mean Street (4)
Mine All Mine (8)
Neworld (13)
1984 (6)
Not Enough (11) *97*
(Oh) Pretty Woman (5) *12*
On Fire (1)
Once (13)
One Foot Out The Door (4)
One I Want (13)
One Way To Rock (10)

Outta Love Again (2)
Panama (6,10,12) *13*
Pleasure Dome (9,10)
Poundcake (9,10,12)
Primary (13)
Right Now (9,10,12) *55*
Romeo Delight (3)
Runaround (9,10)
Runnin' With The Devil (1,12) *84*
Secrets (5)
Seventh Seal (11)
Sinner's Swing! (4)
So This Is Love? (4)
Somebody Get Me A Doctor (2)
Source Of Infection (8)
Spanish Fly (2)
Spanked (9,10)
Strung Out (11)
Sucker In A 3 Piece (8)
Summer Nights (7)

Sunday Afternoon In The Park (4)
Take Me Back (Deja Vu) (11)
Take Your Whiskey Home (3)
316 (9,10)
Top Jimmy (6)
Top Of The World (9,10) *27*
Tora! Tora! (3)
Ultra Bass (10)
Unchained (4,12)
When It's Love (8,10,12) *5*
Where Have All The Good Times Gone! (5)
Why Can't This Be Love (7,10,12) *3*
Without You (13)
Women In Love...... (2)
Won't Get Fooled Again (10)
Year To The Day (13)
You Really Got Me (1,10) *36*
You're No Good (2)

VANILLA FUDGE   '67

Psychedelic-rock group formed in New York City: Mark Stein (vocals, keyboards), Vinnie Martell (guitar), **Tim Bogert** (bass) and **Carmine Appice** (drums).

DEBUT	PEAK	WKS	RIAA	CD		ARTIST — Album Title	Sym	$	Label & Number
9/16/67	6	80	●	©	1	Vanilla Fudge		$25	Atco 224
3/2/68	17	33		©	2	The Beat Goes On		$25	Atco 237
7/13/68	20	33		©	3	Renaissance		$25	Atco 244
3/1/69	16	27		©	4	Near the Beginning	[L]	$25	Atco 278
10/25/69	34	13		©	5	Rock & Roll		$25	Atco 303

Bang Bang (1)
Beat Goes On (2)
Break Song (4)
Church Bells Of St. Martins (5)
Eleanor Rigby (1)
Faceless People (3)
Fur Elise (medley) (2)

Game Is Over (medley) (2)
I Can't Make It Alone (5)
If You Gotta Make A Fool Of Somebody (5)
Illusions Of My Childhood - Parts One-Three (1)
Lord In The Country (5)

Merchant (medley) (2)
Moonlight Sonata (medley) (2)
Need Love (5)
Paradise (3)
People Get Ready (1)
Season Of The Witch, Pt. 1 (3) *65*

She's Not There (1)
Shotgun (4) *68*
Sketch (2)
Sky Cried - When I Was A Boy (1) *38*
Some Velvet Morning (4)
Spell That Comes After (3)

Street Walking Woman (5)
Take Me For A Little While (1) *38*
That's What Makes A Man (3)
Thoughts (3)
Ticket To Ride (1)

Variations On A Theme By Mozart Medley (2)
Voices In Time (2)
Where Is Happiness (4)
Windmills Of Your Mind (5)
You Keep Me Hangin' On (1) *6*

VANILLA ICE   '90

Born Robert Van Winkle on 10/31/68 in Miami Lakes, Florida. White rapper. Starred in the movie *Cool As Ice*.

DEBUT	PEAK	WKS	RIAA	CD		ARTIST — Album Title	Sym	$	Label & Number
9/22/90	❶¹⁶	67	▲⁷	©	1	To The Extreme		$10	SBK 95325
6/22/91	30	30	●	©	2	Extremely Live	[L]	$10	SBK 96648
11/2/91	89	15		©	3	Cool As Ice	[S]	$10	SBK 97722

includes "Gonna Catch You" by Lonnie Gordon, "You've Got To Look Up" by Derek B, "Love 2 Love U" by Partners In Kryme, "Forever" by D'New, "Faith" by Rozalla, and "Drop That Zero" by **Stanley Clarke**

Cool As Ice (Everybody Get Loose) (3) *81*
Dancin' (1)
Get Wit' It (3)

Go III (1)
Havin' A Roni (1,2)
Hooked (1,2)
I Like It (2)

I Love You (1,2) *52*
Ice Cold (1)
Ice Ice Baby (1,2) *1*
Ice Is Workin' It (1,2)

It's A Party (1)
Life Is A Fantasy (1,2)
Move (2)
Never Wanna Be Without You (3)

People's Choice (3)
Play That Funky Music (1,2) *4*
Rasta Man (1)
Road To My Riches (2)

Rollin' In My 5.0 (2)
Satisfaction (3)
Stop That Train (1,2)
V.I.P. Posse One By One (2)

VANITY   '82

Born Denise Mathews on 1/3/63 in Niagara, Canada. R&B model/actress. Appeared in several movies.

DEBUT	PEAK	WKS	RIAA	CD		ARTIST — Album Title	$	Label & Number
10/2/82	45	31	●	©	1	Vanity 6	$10	Warner 23716
9/22/84	62	23			2	Wild Animal	$10	Motown 6102
3/22/86	66	20			3	Skin On Skin	$10	Motown 6167

Animals (3)
Bite The Beat (1)
Confidential (3)
Crazy Maybe (2)
Drive Me Wild (1)

Flippin' Out (2)
Gun Shy (3)
He's So Dull (1)
If A Girl Answers (Don't Hang Up) (1)

In The Jungle (1)
Make-Up (1)
Manhunt (3)
Mechanical Emotion (2)
Nasty Girl (1)

Ouch (3)
Pretty Mess (2) *75*
Romantic Voyage (3)
Samuelle (2)
Skin On Skin (3)

Strap On "Robbie Baby" (2)
3 x 2 = 6 (1,2)
Under The Influence (3) *56*
Wet Dream (1)
Wild Animal (2)

VANNELLI, Gino '78
Born on 6/16/52 in Montreal. Pop singer/songwriter.

DEBUT	PEAK	WKS			Album		$	Label & Number
9/28/74	60	30	©	1	Powerful People		$12	A&M 3630
7/19/75	66	23	©	2	Storm At Sunup		$12	A&M 4533
8/14/76	32	22	©	3	The Gist of The Gemini		$12	A&M 4596
11/19/77+	33	16	©	4	A Pauper In Paradise		$12	A&M 4664
9/30/78	13	35	▲ ©	5	Brother To Brother	C:#50/2	$12	A&M 4722
4/11/81	15	26	©	6	Nightwalker		$10	Arista 9539
9/19/81	172	2	©	7	The Best Of Gino Vannelli	[G]	$10	A&M 3729
6/29/85	62	25	©	8	Black Cars		$10	HME 40077
5/23/87	160	7	©	9	Big Dreamers Never Sleep		$10	CBS Associated 40337

Appaloosa (5,7)
Black And Blue (4)
Black Cars (8) *42*
Brother To Brother (5)
Crazy Life (7)
Down With Love (9)
Evil Eye (5)
Father And Son (2)
Feel Like Flying (5)
Felicia (1)
Fly Into This Night (3,7)
Gettin' High (2)
Here She Comes (8)
How Much (8)
Hurts To Be In Love (8) *57*
I Believe (6)
I Just Wanna Stop (5,7) *4*
Imagination (8)
In The Name Of Money (9)
It's Over (8)
Jack Miraculous (1)
Jo Jo (1)
Just A Motion Away (8)
Keep On Walking (2)
King For A Day (9)
Lady (1)
Living Inside Myself (6) *6*
Love & Emotion (5)
Love Is A Night (2)
Love Me Now (2,7)
Love Of My Life (3) *64*
Mama Coco (2,7)
Mardi Gras (4)
New Fix For '76 (3)
Nightwalker (6) *41*
Omens Of Love (3)
One Night With You (4,7)
Other Man (8)
Pauper In Paradise (In Four Movements) (4)
People Gotta Move (1,7) *22*
People I Belong To (5)
Persona Non Grata (9)
Poor Happy Jimmy (Tribute To Jim Croce) (1)
Powerful People (1,7)
Put The Weight On My Shoulders (6)
River Must Flow (5)
Sally (She Says The Sweetest Things) (6)
Santa Rosa (6)
Seek And You Will Find (6)
Shape Me Like A Man (9)
Something Tells Me (9)
Son Of A New York Gun (1)
Song And Dance (4)
Stay With Me (6)
Storm At Sunup (2)
Surest Things Can Change (4)
Time Out (9)
Total Stranger (8)
Ugly Man (3)
Valleys Of Valhalla (4)
War Suite Medley (3)
Wheels Of Life (5,7) *78*
Where Am I Going (2)
Wild Horses (5) *55*
Work Verse (1)
Young Lover (9)

VAN SHELTON, Ricky — see SHELTON

VANWARMER, Randy '79
Born Randall Van Wormer on 3/30/55 in Indian Hills, Colorado. Singer/songwriter/guitarist.

DEBUT	PEAK	WKS			Album		$	Label & Number
6/2/79	81	10			Warmer		$12	Bearsville 6988

Call Me
Convincing Lies
Deeper And Deeper
Forever Loving You
Gotta Get Out Of Here
I Could Sing
Just When I Needed You Most *4*
Losing Out On Love
One Who Loves You
Your Light

VAN ZANDT, Miami Steve — see LITTLE STEVEN

VANZANT, Iyanla '99
Born in Philadelphia. Female self-help author.

DEBUT	PEAK	WKS			Album		$	Label & Number
10/2/99	128	6	©		In The Meantime - The Music That Tells The Story		$10	Harmony 1799

Ain't No Way [Kelly Price]
As Long As I Know [Terry Bradford]
Do You Want To Be Free?
Free [Tulani Kinard]
Fully Present
Have We Forgotten
How Do You Measure
In The Meantime [Howard Hewett]
Is It Time
Is This Love [Maxi Priest]
Just A Prayer Away [Yolanda Adams]
Leaving Just Isn't Easy
Love Is Simple
Neither One Of Us [Montell Jordan & Monifah]
Never Knew Love Like This [Angelo & Veronica]
Right Back Where I Started [Faith Evans]
There Will Come A Time (medley)
Wherever I Am [Tulani Kinard]
Who Do You Think You're Not
You Haven't Lived [Donnie McClurkin & Nancey Jackson]

VAN ZANT, Johnny, Band '80
Born in 1960 in Jacksonville, Florida. Rock singer. Brother of Ronnie (**Lynyrd Skynyrd**) and Donnie (**38 Special**) Van Zant. His band: Robbie Gay and Erik Lundgren (guitars), Danny Clausman (bass) and Robbie Morris (drums).

DEBUT	PEAK	WKS			Album		$	Label & Number
9/6/80	48	15		1	No More Dirty Deals		$10	Polydor 6289
6/13/81	119	10		2	Round Two		$10	Polydor 6322
9/18/82	159	6		3	The Last Of The Wild Ones		$10	Polydor 6355
5/4/85	170	8		4	Van-Zant		$10	Geffen 24059
8/11/90	108	11	©	5	Brickyard Road		$10	Atlantic 82110

JOHNNY VAN ZANT

Bad 4 U (5)
Brickyard Road (5)
Can't Live Without Your Love (3)
Cold Hearted Woman (2)
Coming Home (1)
Danger Zone (3)
Does A Fool Ever Learn (4)
Drive My Car (2)
Good Girls Turning Bad (3)
Hard Luck Story (1)
Heart To The Flame (4)
Hearts Are Gonna Roll (5)
I'm A Fighter (4)
Inside Looking Out (3)
It's You (3)
Just A Little Bit Of Love (5)
Keep On Rollin' (1)
Keep Our Love Alive (3)
Last Of The Wild Ones (3)
Let There Be Music (2)
Lonely Girls (4)
Love Can Be So Cruel (4)
Love Is Not Enough (5)
Midnight Sensation (4)
Never Too Late (1)
Night Time Lady (2)
No More Dirty Deals (1)
One And Only (3)
Only The Strong Survive (1)
Party In The Parking Lot (5)
Play My Music (2)
Put My Trust In You (1)
Right On Time (4)
She's Out With A Gun (4)
Shotdown (2)
634-5789 (1)
Stand Your Ground (1)
Standing In The Darkness (1)
Standing In The Falling Rain (2)
Still Hold On (3)
Take Every Beat Of My Heart (5)
Three Wishes (5)
Together Forever (3)
2+2 (4)
Two Strangers (4)
(Who's) Right Or Wrong (2)
Yesterday's Gone (2)
You've Got To Believe In Love (4)
Young Girls (5)

VAPORS, The '80
Pub-rock group from Guildford, Surrey, England: David Fenton (vocals), Ed Bazalgette (guitar), Steve Smith (bass) and Howard Smith (drums).

DEBUT	PEAK	WKS			Album		$	Label & Number
8/16/80	62	28	©	1	New Clear Days		$10	United Artists 1049
4/4/81	109	9	©	2	Magnets		$10	Liberty 1090

Bunkers (1)
Can't Talk Anymore (2)
Civic Hall (1)
Daylight Titans (2)
Isolated Case (2)
Jimmie Jones (2)
Johnny's In Love (Again) (2)
Lenina (2)
Letter From Hiro (1)
Live At The Marquee (2)
Magnets (2)
News At Ten (1)
Prisoners (1)
Silver Machines (2)
Sixty Second Interval (1)
Somehow (1)
Spiders (2)
Spring Collection (1)
Trains (1)
Turning Japanese (1) *36*
Waiting For The Weekend (1)

VAST '00
Group is actually solo guitarist Jon Crosby. VAST: Visual Audio Sensory Theater.

DEBUT	PEAK	WKS			Album		$	Label & Number
9/30/00	142	2	©		Music For People		$10	Elektra 62511

Better Place
Blue
Free
Gates Of Rock 'N' Roll
I Don't Have Anything
Lady Of Dreams
Land Of Shame
Last One Alive
My TV And You
Song Without A Name
We Will Meet Again
What Else Do I Need

VAUGHAN, Jimmie '90
Born on 3/20/51 in Dallas. Rock singer/guitarist. Member of **The Fabulous Thunderbirds**. Brother of **Stevie Ray Vaughan**. Acted in the movie *Great Balls Of Fire*. Recorded with Stevie Ray as **The Vaughan Brothers**.

DEBUT	PEAK	WKS			Album		$	Label & Number
10/13/90	7	38	▲ ©	1	Family Style		$10	Epic 46225
					THE VAUGHAN BROTHERS			
4/30/94	127	4	©	2	Strange Pleasure		$10	Epic 57202

Baboom (medley) (1)
Boom-Bapa-Boom (2)
Brothers (1)
D/FW (1)
Don't Cha Know (2)
(Everybody's Got) Sweet Soul Vibe (2)
Flamenco Dancer (1)
Good Texan (1)
Hard To Be (1)
Hey-Yeah (2)
Hillbillies From Outerspace (1)
Just Like Putty (2)
Long Way From Home (1)
Love The World (2)
Mama Said (medley) (1)
Six Strings Down (2)
Strange Pleasure (Modern Backporch Duende) (2)
Telephone Song (1)
Tick Tock (1) *65*
Tilt A Whirl (2)
Two Wings (2)
White Boots (1)

VAUGHAN, Sarah '57

Born on 3/27/24 in Newark, New Jersey. Died of cancer on 4/3/90 (age 66). Jazz singer. Nicknamed "The Divine One." Won Grammy's Lifetime Achievement Award in 1989.

DEBUT	PEAK	WKS		CD	#	Title			$	Label & Number
11/24/56	20	2		©	1	Linger Awhile			$40	Columbia 914
12/1/56	21	1			2	Sassy			$40	EmArcy 36089
4/13/57	14	9		©	3	Great Songs From Hit Shows			$40	Mercury 100 [2]
8/19/57	14	9		©	4	Sarah Vaughan sings George Gershwin			$40	Mercury 101 [2]
7/1/72	173	12		©	5	Sarah Vaughan/Michel Legrand			$15	Mainstream 361

All The Things You Are (3)
Aren't You Kinda Glad We Did (4)
Autumn In New York (3)
Bewitched (3)
Bidin' My Time (4)
Blue, Green, Grey And Gone (5)
Blues Serenade (1)
Boy Next Door (2)
Brian's Song (5)
But Not For Me (3)
Comes Love (3)
Dancing In The Dark (3)
Do It Again (4)
Don't Be Afraid (1)
Foggy Day (4)

Hands Of Time ..see: Brian's Song
He Loves And She Loves (4)
He's Only Wonderful (3)
His Eyes, Her Eyes (5)
Homework (3)
How Long Has This Been Going On (4)
I Confess (1)
I Loved Him (2)
I Was Born In Love With You (Theme From Wuthering Heights) (3)
I Will Say Goodbye (5)
I Won't Say I Will (4)
I'll Build A Stairway To Paradise (4)

I'm Afraid The Masquerade Is Over (2)
I'm Crazy To Love You (1)
I'm The Girl (2)
I've Got A Crush On You (4)
I've Got Some Crying To Do (2)
If This Isn't Love (3)
Isn't It A Pity (4)
It Never Entered My Mind (3)
It's Got To Be Love (3)
Just A Moment More (1)
Let's Call The Whole Thing Off (4)
Let's Take An Old Fashioned Walk (3)
Linger Awhile (1)
Little Girl Blue (3)

Lonely Girl (1)
Lonely Woman (2)
Looking For A Boy (4)
Lorelei (4)
Lost In The Stars (3)
Love Walked In (4)
Lover's Quarrel (1)
Lucky In Love (3)
Lush Life (2)
Man I Love (4)
Mighty Lonesome Feelin' (1)
My Darling, My Darling (3)
My Heart Stood Still (3)
My Man's Gone Now (4)
My One And Only (What Am I Gonna Do) (4)
My Romance (2)

My Ship (3)
My Tormented Heart (1)
Of Thee I Sing (4)
Old Folks (2)
Once You've Been In Love (3)
Only You Can Say (2)
Pieces Of Dreams (5)
Poor Butterfly (3)
September Song (3)
Shake Down The Stars (2)
Ship Without A Sail (3)
Sinner Kissed An Angel (2)
Sinner Or Saint (1)
Someone To Watch Over Me (4)
Summer Knows (Theme From Summer Of '42) (5)

Summer Me, Winter Me (5)
Summertime (4)
These Things I Offer You (For A Lifetime) (1)
They All Laughed (4)
They Say It's Wonderful (3)
Things Are Looking Up (4)
Touch Of Your Hand (3)
Tree In The Park (3)
What Are You Doing The Rest Of Your Life (5)

★242★ VAUGHAN, Stevie Ray, and Double Trouble '90

Born on 10/3/54 in Dallas. Died in a helicopter crash on 8/27/90 (age 35). Blues-rock singer/guitarist. Brother of **Jimmie Vaughan**. Double Trouble: Reese Wynans (keyboards), Tommy Shannon (bass) and Chris Layton (drums). Recorded with Jimmie as **The Vaughan Brothers**.

1)Family Style 2)The Sky Is Crying 3)Couldn't Stand The Weather

DEBUT	PEAK	WKS	RIAA	CD	#	Title	Catalog	Sym	$	Label & Number
7/23/83	38	33	▲²	©	1	Texas Flood	C:#26/5		$12	Epic 38734
6/23/84	31	38	▲²	©	2	Couldn't Stand The Weather	C:#40/1		$12	Epic 39304
10/12/85	34	39	▲	©	3	Soul To Soul			$12	Epic 40036
12/20/86+	52	25	▲	©	4	Live Alive		[L]	$15	Epic 40511 [2]
7/1/89	33	47	▲²	©	5	In Step			$10	Epic 45024
10/13/90	7	38	▲	©	6	Family Style			$10	Epic 46225
						THE VAUGHAN BROTHERS				
11/23/91	10	48	▲²	©	7	The Sky Is Crying		[K]	$10	Epic 47390
						recordings from 1984-89				
10/24/92	58	12		©	8	In The Beginning		[L]	$10	Epic 53168
						recorded on 4/1/80 in Austin, Texas				
11/18/95	39	35	▲²	©	9	Greatest Hits	C:#33/18	[G]	$10	Epic 66217
8/16/97	40	12	●	©	10	Live At Carnegie Hall		[E-L]	$10	Epic 68163
						recorded on 10/4/84				
4/10/99	53	17	●	©	11	The Real Deal: Greatest Hits Volume 2		[G]	$10	Epic 65873
4/22/00	80	8		©	12	Blues At Sunrise		[K]	$10	Legacy 63842
12/9/00	148	5	●	©	13	SRV		[K]	$25	Legacy 65714 [4]

Ain't Gone 'N' Give Up On Love (3,4,11,12)
All Your Love I Miss Loving (8,13)
Ask Me No Questions (13)
Baboom (medley) (6)
Blues At Sunrise (12)
Boilermaker (13)
Boot Hill (7)
Brothers (6)
C.O.D. (10)
Change It (3,4,9,13)
Chitlins Con Carne (7,12)
Close To You (7)
Cold Shot (2,4,9,10,13)
Collins' Shuffle (13)
Come On (Part III) (3,13)

Couldn't Stand The Weather (2,9,13)
Crosscut Saw (13)
Crossfire (5,9,13)
D/FW (6)
Dirty Pool (1,10,12,13)
Don't Lose Your Cool (13)
Don't Stop By The Creek, Son (13)
Empty Arms (3,7,11,13)
Goin' Down (13)
Gone Home (3)
Good Texan (6)
Hard To Be (6)
Hillbillies From Outerspace (6)
Honey Bee (2,10)
House Is Rockin' (5,9,13)
Hug You, Squeeze You (13)

I'm Cryin' (1,13)
I'm Leavin' You (Commit A Crime) (13)
I'm Leaving You (Commit A Crime) (4)
Iced Over (10)
If You Have To Know (13)
In The Open (8)
Leave My Girl Alone (5,11,12,13)
Lenny (1,10,11,13)
Let Me Love You Baby (5,13)
Letter To My Girlfriend (10,13)
Life By The Drop (7,11)
Life Without You (3,4,9)
Little Wing (7,9,13)
Live Another Day (8)
Long Way From Home (6,13)

Look At Little Sister (3,4,11,13)
Lookin' Out The Window (3,13)
Love Me Darlin' (5)
Love Struck Baby (1,4,8,10,11,13)
Mama Said (medley) (6)
Manic Depression (13)
Mary Had A Little Lamb (1,4,13)
May I Have A Talk With You (7,12,13)
Pipeline (11,13)
Pride And Joy (1,4,9,10,13)
Riviera Paradise (5,11)
Rude Mood (1,10,13)
Say What! (3,4)
Scratch-N-Sniff (5)
Scuttle Buttin' (2,10,11,13)
Shake For Me (8,11)

Shake 'N Bake (13)
Sky Is Crying (7,12,13)
Slide Thing (8)
So Excited (7)
Stang's Swang (2)
Superstition (4,11)
Taxman (9)
Telephone Song (6,11)
Tell Me (1,8)
Testify (1,13)
Testifyin' (10)
Texas Flood (1,4,9,12,13)
These Blues Is Killing Me (13)
They Call Me Guitar Hurricane (8,13)
Things (That) I Used To Do (2,10,12,13)

Third Stone From The Sun (medley) (13)
Thunderbird (13)
Tick Tock (6) *65*
Tightrope (5,9,13)
Tin Pan Alley (2,8,12)
Travis Walk (5)
Voodoo Chile (Slight Return) (2,4,11,13)
Wall Of Denial (5,11,13)
Wham (7)
White Boots (6)
Willie The Wimp (4,11,13)
You'll Be Mine (3)
You're Gonna Miss Me Baby (13)

VAUGHN, Billy ★40★ '60

Born Richard Vaughn on 4/12/19 in Glasgow, Kentucky. Died of cancer on 9/26/91 (age 72). Orchestra leader. Member of The Hilltoppers vocal group. Musical director for Dot Records.

1)Theme from A Summer Place 2)Sail Along Silv'ry Moon 3)Look For A Star 4)Theme from The Sundowners 5)Blue Hawaii

DEBUT	PEAK	WKS		CD	#	Title		Sym	$	Label & Number
4/21/58+	5	68		●	1	Sail Along Silv'ry Moon		[I]	$20	Dot 3100
10/13/58+	15	47			2	Billy Vaughn Plays The Million Sellers		[I]	$20	Dot 3119
5/4/59	20	3			3	Billy Vaughn Plays		[I]	$20	Dot 3156
5/25/59	7	108		●	4	Blue Hawaii		[I]	$20	Dot 3165
1/18/60	36	1			5	Golden Saxophones		[I]	$20	Dot 3205
3/21/60	❶²	62		●	6	Theme from A Summer Place		[I]	$20	Dot 3276
8/15/60	5	33			7	Look For A Star		[I]	$20	Dot 3322
12/19/60+	5	23			8	Theme from The Sundowners		[I]	$20	Dot 3349

DEBUT	PEAK	WKS	RIAA	CD	ARTIST — Album Title	Catalog	Sym	$	Label & Number
					VAUGHN, Billy — Cont'd				
4/24/61	11	43			9 Orange Blossom Special and Wheels	[I]		$20	Dot 3366
10/9/61	17	25			10 Golden Waltzes	[I]		$20	Dot 3280
12/4/61+	20	18			11 Berlin Melody	[I]		$20	Dot 3396
3/24/62	18	12			12 Greatest String Band Hits	[I]		$20	Dot 3409
6/2/62	14	16			13 Chapel By The Sea	[I]		$20	Dot 3424
9/15/62	10	27			14 A Swingin' Safari	[I]		$20	Dot 3458
12/29/62	145	1			15 Christmas Carols	[X-I]		$20	Dot 3148
					released in 1958; Christmas chart: 101/67				
2/16/63	17	32			16 1962's Greatest Hits	[I]		$15	Dot 25497
6/15/63	15	16			17 Sukiyaki and 11 Hawaiian Hits	[I]		$15	Dot 25523
11/9/63	94	8			18 Number 1 Hits, Vol. #1	[I]		$15	Dot 25540
2/1/64	51	17			19 Blue Velvet & 1963's Great Hits	[I]		$15	Dot 25559
6/20/64	144	4			20 Forever	[I]		$15	Dot 25578
8/29/64	141	3			21 Another Hit Album!	[I]		$15	Dot 25593
1/2/65	18	29			22 Pearly Shells	[I]		$15	Dot 25605
4/24/65	45	15			23 Mexican Pearls	[I]		$15	Dot 25628
10/9/65	31	29			24 Moon Over Naples	[I]		$15	Dot 25654
2/12/66	56	14			25 Michelle	[I]		$15	Dot 25679
7/23/66	149	2			26 Great Country Hits	[I]		$15	Dot 25698
10/22/66+	44	35			27 Alfie	[I]		$15	Dot 25751
3/18/67	114	20			28 Sweet Maria			$15	Dot 25782
					THE BILLY VAUGHN SINGERS				
5/13/67	130	7			29 That's Life & Pineapple Market	[I]		$15	Dot 25788
7/29/67	147	2			30 Josephine	[E-I]		$15	Dot 25796
8/12/67	161	5			31 I Love You			$15	Dot 25813
					THE BILLY VAUGHN SINGERS				
9/23/67	159	8			32 Golden Hits/The Best Of Billy Vaughn	[G-I]		$15	Dot 25811
10/28/67	200	2			33 Ode To Billy Joe	[I]		$15	Dot 25828
9/28/68	198	3			34 A Current Set Of Standards	[I]		$15	Dot 25882
5/17/69	95	16			35 The Windmills Of Your Mind	[I]		$15	Dot 25937
3/14/70	188	2			36 Winter World Of Love	[I]		$15	Dot 25975

Adeste Fideles (15)
Again (22)
Alabama Jubilee (12)
Alamo, Theme From The ..see:
　Green Leaves Of Summer
Alfie (27)
All The Way (6)
Aloha Oe (4)
Alone (14)
Always Mademoiselle (36)
Am I That Easy To Forget (26)
Anniversary Song (24)
Any Time (24)
Apartment, Theme From The (7)
Are You Lonesome Tonight (9)
Around The World (2)
Auf Wiedershen, My Dear (5)
Autumn Love Song (11)
Baby Face (12)
Ballerina (18)
Be My Love (18)
Beautiful Ohio (10)
Because They're Young (7)
Berlin Melody (11) *61*
Beyond The Reef (4)
Beyond The Sunset (7)
Blue Eyes Crying In The Rain (26)
Blue Flame (14)
Blue Hawaii (4,32) *37*
Blue Moon (3,11)
Blue Orchids (23)
Blue Tomorrow (11) *84*
Blue Velvet (19)
Blueberry Hill (3)
Bluebird Of Happiness (25)
Bonanza (13)
Boogie Woogie (30)
Born To Be With You (14)
Born To Lose (16)
Breeze (Blow My Baby Back To Me) (5)
Burning Memories (21)
Busted (19)
Bye Bye Blackbird (12)
C'est Si Bon (9)
Can't Help Falling In Love (13)
Canadian Sunset (2)
Caravan (22)
Careless (33)
Carolina In The Morning (12)
Chapel By The Sea (13) *69*
Chattanoogie Shoe Shine Boy (21)
Cherish (28)
Chim Chim Cheree (25)
Chinatown, My Chinatown (12)

Church's One Foundation (8)
Cimarron (Roll On) (3) *44*
Clair De Lune (11)
Climb Every Mountain (6)
Cocktails For Two (33)
Cocoanut Grove (4,30)
CoCo (36)
Come Saturday Morning (36)
Come September (11) *73*
Cross-Eyed Cyclops (34)
Crying In The Chapel (26)
Cuando Calienta El Sol ..see:
　Love Me With All Your Heart
Danke Schoen (19)
Dark At The Top Of The Stairs, Theme From (8)
Dark Moon (26)
Days Of Wine And Roses (27)
Dear Heart (23)
Dear Lonely Hearts (16)
Dear Old Girl (20)
Deck The Halls (15)
Dis-Advantages Of You (29)
Dr. Zhivago ..see: Somewhere, My Love
Dominique (34)
Don't Break The Heart That Loves You (19)
(Down At) Papa Joe's (19)
Drifting And Dreaming (3)
Early In The Morning (36)
Elaine (25)
Elmer's Tune (5)
Everybody Loves Somebody (22)
Everybody's Somebody's Fool (8)
Exodus (13)
Faith Of Our Fathers (15)
Fallen Star (26)
Fancy (36)
Fascination (2)
First Noel (15)
Foggy River (26)
Fool Such As I (14)
For Me And My Gal (22)
Forever (20)
Four Walls (21)
French Song (21)
Full Moon And Empty Arms (2)
Games That Lovers Play (28)
Girl From Ipanema (22)
Girl Of My Dreams (10)
Glad She's A Woman (35)
Glow Worm March (14)
Go Away, Little Girl (16)
God Rest Ye Merry, Gentlemen (15)

Goldfinger (24)
Green Grass Of Texas (9)
Green, Green Grass Of Home (29)
Green Leaves Of Summer (8)
Greenfields (7)
Groovin' (31)
Guantanamera (28)
Guitar Polka (26)
Happy Days Are Here Again (12)
Harbor Lights (3)
Hark! The Herald Angels Sing (15)
Have I Told You Lately That I Love You (5)
Hawaiian Paradise (4)
Hawaiian Sunset (4)
Hawaiian War Chant (4) *89*
Hawaiian Wedding Song (4)
He'll Have To Go (7)
Heart And Soul (23)
Heartaches (30)
Heaven (35)
Help Yourself (35)
Here In My Heart (18)
Here We Go Again (33)
High Noon (2)
Holiday For Strings (2)
Holly Holy (36)
Honey (34)
Hunger, Theme From (36)
I Almost Lost My Mind (5)
I Can't Stop Loving You (16)
I Could Have Danced All Night (25)
I Cried For You (22)
I Got Rhythm (31)
I Left My Heart In San Francisco (24)
I Love You And You Love Me (31)
I Will (25)
I Will Wait For You (27)
I'll Catch The Sun (34)
I'm Getting Sentimental Over You (1)
I'm Leaving It Up To You (19)
I'm Looking Over A Four Leaf Clover (12,30)
I'm Movin' (21)
I'm Sorry (18)
If You Go Away (28)
In A Shanty In Old Shanty Town (12)
In The Chapel In The Moonlight (14,25)
In The Gloaming (20)

In The Mood (2)
Indian Lake (34)
Indian Love Call (3)
Indian Summer (5)
Isle Of Capri (3)
It Came Upon A Midnight Clear (15)
It Happened In Adano (11)
It's A Sin (26)
It's A Lonesome Old Town (9)
It's Easy To Remember (23)
It's Just A Matter Of Time (31)
(It's No) Sin (14)
Japanese Sandman (12)
Jealous (1)
Jealous Heart (3)
Jingle Bells (15)
Josephine (30)
Joy To The World (15)
June In January (33)
Just A Closer Walk With Thee (7,21)
Just A Wearyin' For You (10)
Just One More Chance (23)
Kalua (17)
King's Serenade (17)
La Montana (7)
La Paloma (32) *20*
Lady-O (36)
Lara's Theme ..see: Somewhere, My Love
Laura (30)
Lazy River (9)
Let Me Call You Sweetheart (10)
Little Brown Gal (4)
Little Dutch Mill (5)
Little Green Apples (34)
Lonely Bull (16)
Lonely Is The Name (34)
Look For A Star (7) *19*
Look Of Love (34)
Love (24)
Love Birds (33)
Love In Bloom (2)
Love Is A Many-Splendored Thing (8)
Love Letters (23)
Love Letters In The Sand (1)
Love Me With All Your Heart (19,20)
Love's Old Sweet Song (20)
Lovely Hula Lands (17)
Lucky Duck (20)
Lullaby From Rosemary's Baby (34)
Make The World Go Away (26)

Make Your Own Kind Of Music (36)
Mame (27)
Man And A Woman (28)
Man Without Love (34)
Mapuana (17)
Marie (9)
Maybe (22)
Meditation (20)
Meet Me Tonight In Dreamland (10)
Melody From The Sky (23)
Melody Of Love (10,32) *2*
Memphis (21)
Mexican Pearls (23) *94*
Mexican Shuffle (25)
Mexico (11)
Michael (11)
Michelle (25) *77*
Midnight In Moscow (13)
Missouri Waltz (10)
Mister Sandman (18)
Molly Darling (17)
Mona Lisa (7)
Moon Of Manakoora (17)
Moon Over Miami (1)
Moon Over Naples (24,32)
Moon River (13,16)
Moonglow and Theme From "Picnic" (2)
Moonlight And Roses (3)
Moonlight And Shadows (22)
Moonlight Bay (3)
More (19)
More And More (33)
Mr. Lucky, Theme From (8)
Mrs. Robinson (34)
Music To Watch Girls By (29)
My Buddy (10)
My Dear (9)
My Happiness (3)
My Isle Of Golden Dreams (4)
My Little Grass Shack (4)
My Love, Forgive Me (24)
My Special Angel (26)
My Tane (17)
Nature Boy (18)
Near You (5)
Nearness Of You (23)
Never On Sunday (8)
No Matter What Shape (Your Stomach's In) (29)
No One Will Ever Know (26)
O Come, All Ye Faithful ..see: Adeste Fideles
O Holy Night (15)

O Little Town Of Bethlehem (15)
O Sole Mio (8)
O Tannenbaum (15)
Ode To Billy Joe (33)
Oh! You Beautiful Doll (1)
Old Cape Cod (8)
On The Beach At Waikiki (17)
One Has My Name (25)
One Of Those Songs (27)
One Rose (That's Left In My Heart) (20)
Only I (31)
Orange Blossom Special (9,32) *63*
Organ Grinder's Swing (25)
Out Of Limits (19)
Out Of Nowhere (33)
Over The Rainbow (22)
Pagan Love Song (17)
Painted, Tainted Rose (19)
Paper Roses (7)
Peace In The Valley (21)
Pearly Shells (22)
Peg O' My Heart (22,30)
People (21)
Perfect Song (30)
Petite Fleur (13)
Pineapple Market (29)
Please (24)
Popsicles And Icicles (19)
Promises, Promises (35)
Put On Your Old Grey Bonnet (12)
Que Sera, Sera (6)
Rag Mop (18)
Raindrops Keep Fallin' On My Head (36)
Ramblin' Rose (14)
Raunchy (1) *10*
Red Roses For A Blue Lady (24)
Red Sails In The Sunset (3)
Release Me (16)
Remember When (8)
Roses Are Red (16)
Route 66 Theme (13)
Ruby (2)
Sail Along Silvery Moon (1,32) *5*
San Antonio Rose (30)
Sayonara (6)
Second Hand Rose (27)
See See Rider (3)
Sentimental Journey (1)
Sentimental Me (5)
September Song (30)
Serenade Of The Bells (11)

VAUGHN, Billy — Cont'd

Shadow Of Your Smile (27)
Shangri-La (20)
Shifting Whispering Sands (Parts 1 & 2) (32) *5*
Shine On Harvest Moon (3)
Silent Night (15)
Silver Moon (10)
Silver Threads Among The Gold (20)
Sixteen Tons (21)
Sleepy Time Gal (1)
Slow Poke (30)
Smiles (12)
Snowfall (31)
So Rare (2)
Some Enchanted Evening (6)
Somethin' Stupid (31)
Somewhere, My Love (27)
Song Of The Islands (4)
Sorrento (9)
Soulful Strut (35)
Sound Of Music (6,24)
Spanish Pearls (34)

Stella By Starlight (23)
Stranger On The Shore (16)
Strangers In The Night (27)
Stripper, The (16)
Sugar Town (28)
Sukiyaki (17)
Summer Place, Theme From A (6,32)
Summertime (9)
Sunday In Madrid (14)
Sunday Will Never Be The Same (31)
Sundowners, The (8) *51*
Sunrise Serenade (1)
Sunrise, Sunset (27)
Sweet Georgia Brown (1)
Sweet Leilani (4)
Sweet Maria (28)
Sweet Someone (17)
Swingin' Safari (14,32) *13*
Tammy (6)
Taste Of Honey (22)
Tears And Roses (21)

Telstar (16)
Tennessee Waltz (5,10)
Terry Theme From Limelight (6)
That Lucky Old Sun (18)
That's Life (29)
There Goes My Everything (28)
There's A Long, Long Trail (20)
There's No Love (No Hay Amore) (29)
This Guy's In Love With You (34)
This Is My Song (2)
Three O'Clock In The Morning (10)
Three Penny Opera (Moritat) (6)
Throw Another Log On The Fire (14)
Till I Waltz Again With You (11)
Till The End Of Time (2)
Time Of The Season (35)
Tiny Bubbles (24)
To Each His Own (30)

To You Sweetheart Aloha (17)
Together (11)
Tonight (24)
Tonight We Love (2)
Too Young (18)
Traces (35)
Traci's Tracks (35)
Tracy's Theme (6)
Trade Winds (4)
True Love (6)
Tuff (13)
Tumbling Tumbleweeds (1) *30*
Twilight Time (1)
Twist, The (14)
Two Sleepy People (33)
Until Tomorrow (1)
Up-Up And Away (31)
Volare (Nel Blu Dipinto Di Blu) (8)
Wabash Blues (5)
Walk, Don't Run (8)
Walk In The Black Forest (24)

Walking On Wilshire (29)
Waltz You Saved For Me (10)
Washington Square (19)
Watermelon Man (25)
Way Of Love (33)
Way That I Live (35)
Wheel Of Fortune (18)
Wheel Of Hurt (28)
Wheels (9,32) *28*
When The Saints Go Marching In (14)
Where Will The Words Come From (28)
Whiffenpoof Song (9)
White Christmas (15)
Who's Afraid (27)
Wichita Lineman (35)
Wiederseh'n (2)
Willow Weep For Me (23)
Winchester Cathedral (29)
Windmills Of Your Mind (35)
Winter World Of Love (36)
Wish Me A Rainbow (28)

Wonderland By Night (13)
Wooden Heart (11)
World I Used To Know (21)
World We Knew (Over And Over) (33)
Worried Mind (26)
Yellow Roses Mean Goodbye (31)
Yester-Me, Yester-You, Yesterday (36)
You Belong To Me (18)
You Belong To My Heart (5)
You Call Everybody Darling (18)
You Can't Be True, Dear (3)
You Gave Me A Mountain (35)

★435★

VEE, Bobby '61

Born Robert Velline on 4/30/43 in Fargo, North Dakota. Pop singer. Appeared in the movies *Swingin' Along*, *It's Trad, Dad*, *Play It Cool*, *C'mon Let's Live A Little* and *Just For Fun*.

1)Bobby Vee 2)Bobby Vee's Golden Greats 3)Bobby Vee Meets The Crickets

DEBUT	PEAK	WKS			ARTIST — Album Title		$	Label & Number
3/20/61	18	15	©	1	Bobby Vee		$50	Liberty 7181
10/30/61	85	8	©	2	Bobby Vee sings Hits Of The Rockin' '50's		$50	Liberty 7205
2/3/62	91	14	©	3	Take Good Care Of My Baby		$50	Liberty 7211
7/21/62	42	23	©	4	Bobby Vee Meets The Crickets		$50	Liberty 7228
7/21/62	121	6	©	5	A Bobby Vee Recording Session		$40	Liberty 7232
11/3/62+	24	44		6	Bobby Vee's Golden Greats	[G]	$40	Liberty 7245
12/15/62	136	3	©	7	Merry Christmas From Bobby Vee	[X]	$40	Liberty 7267
					also see #12 below			
4/13/63	102	5	©	8	The Night Has A Thousand Eyes		$40	Liberty 7285
6/1/63	91	8	©	9	Bobby Vee Meets The Ventures		$40	Liberty 7289
6/27/64	146	2		10	Bobby Vee sings The New Sound From England!		$30	Liberty 7352
10/7/67	66	12	©	11	Come Back When You Grow Up		$30	Liberty 7534
12/9/67	68[X]	4		12	The Christmas Album	[X]	$25	Sunset 5186
					BOBBY VEE WITH THE JOHNNY MANN SINGERS reissue of #7 above (minus 2 tracks)			
4/27/68	187	7	©	13	Just Today		$25	Liberty 7554

Angels In The Sky (1)
Anonymous Phone Call (9)
Any Other Girl (10)
Beautiful People (13) *37*
Before You Go (11)
Blue Christmas (7,12)
Bo Diddley (4)
Brown Eyed Handsome Man (10)
Candy Man (9)
Caravan (9)
Christmas Vacation (7)
Christmas Wish (7)
Come Back When You Grow Up (11) *3*
Come Go With Me (2)
Devil Or Angel (1,6) *6*
Do You Wanna Dance (2)
Don't You Believe Them (10)
Donna (2)
Double Good Feeling (11)
Dry Your Eyes (8)
Earth Angel (2)
Everyday (6)
Foolish Tears (1)
Forever Kind Of Love (5)

Forget Me Not (5)
From Me To You (10)
Get Ready (13)
Get The Message (11)
Ginger (10)
Girl Can't Help It (4)
Girl I Left Behind Me (13)
Girl Of My Best Friend (4)
Go Away Little Girl (8)
Go On (3)
Goodnight Irene (9)
Guess Who (5)
Happy Happy Birthday Baby (2)
Hark, Is That A Cannon I Hear (3)
He Will Break Your Heart (3)
Hold On To Him (11)
Honeycomb (3)
How Many Tears (6) *63*
I Can't Say Goodbye (5) *92*
I Gotta Know (4)
I May Be Back (11)
I'll Be Home For Christmas (7,12)
I'll Make You Mine (10) *52*
I'll String Along With You (10)

I'm Gonna Sit Right Down And Write Myself A Letter (9)
If I'm Right Or Wrong (9)
If She Were My Girl (9)
In My Baby's Eyes (5)
It Couldn't Happen To A Nicer Guy (8)
It Might As Well Rain Until September (8)
Jingle-Bell Rock (7,12)
Just Keep It Up (And See What Happens) (13)
Lavender Blue (2)
Linda Lu (9)
Little Flame (3)
Little Queenie (4)
Little Star (2)
Lollipop (2)
Long Lonely Nights (1)
Lookin' For Love (4)
Love, Love, Love (1)
Lover's Goodbye (8)
Lucille (2)
Maybe Just Today (13) *46*
Mission Accomplished (11)
Mister Sandman (1)
More Than I Can Say (1,6) *61*

My Christmas Love (7,12)
My Girl/Hey Girl (13) *35*
My Golden Chance (5)
Night Has A Thousand Eyes (8) *3*
Nobody's Home To Go Home To (13)
Not So Merry Christmas (7,12)
Objects Of Gold (11)
One Last Kiss (1,6)
Peggy Sue (4)
Please Don't Ask About Barbara (5,6) *15*
Poetry In Motion (1)
Pretty Girls Everywhere (9)
Punish Her (6) *20*
Raining In My Heart (3)
Remember Me, Huh (3)
Rose Grew In The Ashes (11)
Rubber Ball (1,6) *6*
Run To Him (3,6) *2*
School Days (2)
Sealed With A Kiss (13)
Sharing You (5,6) *15*
She Loves You (10)
She's Sorry (10)

Silent Night (7,12)
Silent Partner (8)
Silver Bells (7,12)
Sixteen Candles (2)
So You're In Love (3)
Someday (When I'm Gone From You) (4,6) *99*
Stayin' In (1,6) *33*
Summertime Blues (2)
Sunrise Highway (13)
Suspicion (10)
Suzie Baby (6) *77*
Sweet Little Sixteen (4)
Take A Walk, Johnny (10)
Take Good Care Of My Baby (3,6) *1*
Talk To Me, Talk To Me (1)
Teardrops Fall Like Rain (5)
Tenderly Yours (5)
Theme For A Dream (8)
(There's No Place Like) Home For The Holidays (7,12)
This Is Where Friendship Ends (9)
Tiffany Rings (13)
Walk Right Back (9)

Walkin' With My Angel (3,6) *53*
Way You Do The Things You Do (13)
Well...All Right (4)
What About Me (8)
What Else Is New (9)
What's Your Name (4)
When You're In Love (4)
White Christmas (7,12)
Who Am I? (3)
Wild Night (9)
Will You Love Me Tomorrow (3)
Winter Wonderland (7,12)
Wisdom Of A Fool (2)
World Down On Your Knees (11)
You Better Move On (5)
You Can Count On Me (1)
You Can't Lie To A Liar (10)
You Won't Forget Me (8)
You're A Big Girl Now (11)

VEGA, Suzanne '87

Born on 8/12/59 in New York City. Singer/songwriter/guitarist. Married record producer Mitchell Froom (of **Gamma**) on 3/17/95.

DEBUT	PEAK	WKS			ARTIST — Album Title		$	Label & Number
6/15/85	91	31	©	1	Suzanne Vega		$10	A&M 5072
5/16/87	11	32	▲ ©	2	Solitude Standing		$10	A&M 5136
5/5/90	50	13	©	3	days of open hand		$10	A&M 5293
9/26/92	86	21	● ©	4	99.9 F°		$10	A&M 540005
9/28/96	92	5	©	5	Nine Objects Of Desire		$10	A&M 540583

As A Child (4)
As Girls Go (4)
Bad Wisdom (4)
Big Space (3)
Birth-day (love made real) (5)
Blood Makes Noise (4)
Blood Sings (4)
Book Of Dreams (3)
Calypso (3)
Caramel (5)
Casual Match (5)

Cracking (1)
Fancy Poultry (medley) (2)
Fat Man & Dancing Girl (4)
Fifty-Fifty Chance (4)
Freeze Tag (1)
Gypsy (2)
Headshots (5)
Honeymoon Suite (5)
(If You Were) In My Movie (5)
In Liverpool (4)
In The Eye (2)

Institution Green (3)
Ironbound (medley) (2)
Knight Moves (1)
Language (3)
Lolita (5)
Luka (2) *3*
Marlene On The Wall (1)
Men In The Ashes (4)
My Favorite Plum (5)
Neighborhood Girls (1)
Night Vision (2)

99.9 F° (4)
No Cheap Thrill (5)
Pilgrimage (3)
Predictions (3)
Queen And The Soldier (1)
Rock In This Pocket (Song Of David) (4)
Room Off The Street (3)
Rusted Pipe (3)
Small Blue Thing (1)
Solitude Standing (2) *94*

Some Journey (1)
Song Of Sand (4)
Stockings (5)
Straight Lines (4)
Thin Man (5)
Those Whole Girls (Run In Grace) (5)
Tired Of Sleeping (4)
Tom's Diner (2)
Tombstone (5)
Undertow (4)

When Heroes Go Down (4)
Wooden Horse (Caspar Hauser's Song) (4)
World Before Columbus (5)

VEGA, Tata '79
Born Carmen Rosa Vega on 10/7/51 in Queens, New York. Gospel singer.

4/21/79 170 8 Try My Love .... **$12** Tamla 360

Come On And Try My Love   Gonna Do My Best To Love   I Just Keep Thinking About You   I Need You Now   In The Morning   Whopper Bopper Show Stopper
Get It Up For Love   You   Baby   If Love Must Go   Magic Feeling

VELASQUEZ, Jaci '00
Born in 1979 in Houston. Female Christian singer.

5/10/97	142	16	▲	©	1 **Heavenly Place**			**$10**	Word 67823
6/20/98	56	20	●	©	2 **Jaci Velasquez**			**$10**	Word 69311
9/23/00	49	16		©	3 **Crystal Clear**			**$10**	Word 61073

Adore (3)   Come As You Are (3)   God So Loved The World (2)   Little Voice Inside (2)   Show You Love (2)   We Can Make A Difference (1)
Al Mundo Dios Amó (2)   Crystal Clear (3)   He's My Savior (3)   Look What Love Has Done (2)   Speak For Me (2)   We Will Overcome (1)
Baptize Me (1)   Escuchame (Listen To Me) (3)   I Promise (1)   Made My World (2)   Sweet Surrender (2)   You (2)
Center Of Your Love (3)   Everytime I Fall (3)   If This World (1)   On My Knees (1)   Thief Of Always (1)   You Don't Miss A Thing (3)
Child Of Mine (I Have Come)   Flower In The Rain (1)   Imagine Me Without You (3)   Paper Tigers (2)   Un Lugar Celestial (A Heavenly   You're Not There (3)
(2)   Glory (2)   Just A Prayer Away (3)   Shelter (1)   Place) (1)

VELEZ, Martha '76
R&B singer/actress. Starred in the Broadway production of *Hair*.

5/15/76 153 17 Escape From Babylon .... **$15** Sire 7515
produced by **Bob Marley**

Bend Down Low   Disco Night   Happiness   There You Are
Come On In   Get Up Stand Up   Money Man   Wild Bird

VELVET UNDERGROUND, The '85
Experimental-rock group formed in New York City: **Lou Reed** (vocals, guitar), **John Cale** (keyboards), Sterling Morrison (bass) and Maureen Tucker (percussion). Andy Warhol managed the group from 1965-67. Recorded first album with female singer Nico (born Christa Paffgen on 10/16/39 in Cologne, Germany; died of a brain hemorrhage on 7/18/88, age 48). Morrison died of cancer on 8/30/95 (age 53). Group inducted into the Rock and Roll Hall of Fame in 1996.

| 5/13/67 | 171 | 13 | | © | 1 **The Velvet Underground & Nico** | | | **$200** | Verve 5008 |

produced by Andy Warhol

| 3/16/68 | 199 | 2 | | © | 2 **White Light/White Heat** | | | **$100** | Verve 5046 |
| 3/9/85 | 85 | 13 | | © | 3 **VU** | | [K] | **$10** | Verve 823721 |

collection of previously unreleased material from 1968-69

| 4/20/85 | 197 | 2 | | © | 4 **The Velvet Underground** | | [E] | **$12** | Verve 815454 |

first released in 1969 on MGM 4617 ($50)

| 11/13/93 | 180 | 1 | | © | 5 **Live MCMXCIII** | | [L] | **$10** | Sire 45465 |

recorded on 6/15/93 at L'Olympia Theater in Paris

Afterhours (4,5)   Femme Fatale (1)   I'm Set Free (4)   One Of These Days (3)   Sunday Morning (1)   White Light/White Heat (2)
All Tomorrow's Parties (1,5)   Foggy Notion (3)   I'm Sticking With You (3)   Pale Blue Eyes (4,5)   Sweet Jane (5)
Andy's Chest (3)   Gift, The (2,5)   I'm Waiting For The Man (1,5)   Rock 'N' Roll (5)   Temptation Inside Your Heart
Beginning To See The Light (4)   Here She Comes Now (2)   Jesus (4)   Run, Run, Run (1)   (3)
Black Angel's Death Song (1)   Heroin (1,5)   Lady Godiva's Operation (2)   She's My Best Friend (3)   That's The Story Of My Life (4)
Candy Says (4)   I Can't Stand It (3)   Lisa Says (3)   Sister Ray (2)   There She Goes Again (1)
European Son To Delmore   I Heard Her Call My Name (2)   Murder Mystery (4)   Some Kinda Love (4,5)   Venus In Furs (1,5)
   Schwartz (1)   I'll Be Your Mirror (1)   Ocean (3)   Stephanie Says (3)   What Goes On (4)

VENGABOYS '99
Dance group assembled by Spanish producers Danski and DJ Delmundo: Kim, Robin, Deniece and Roy.

| 4/24/99 | 86 | 30 | ● | | **The Party Album!** | | | **$10** | Groovilicious 100 |

Boom, Boom, Boom,   Movin' Around   To Brazil!   Vengabeat, The   You And Me
   Boom!! *84*   Paradise...   Up & Down   **We Like To Party!** *26*
Ho Ho Vengaboys!   Superfly Slick   Vengababes From Outer Space   We're Going To Ibiza

VENTURES, The ★37★ '63
Instrumental group from Seattle: guitarists Nokie Edwards, Bob Bogle and Don Wilson, with drummer Howie Johnson. Johnson suffered serious injuries in a 1961 car accident; replaced by Mel Taylor. Johnson died in January 1988 (age 50). Taylor died of cancer on 8/11/96 (age 62).

1)The Ventures play Telstar, The Lonely Bull   2)Hawaii Five-O   3)Walk Don't Run   4)The Ventures a go-go
5)Walk, Don't Run, Vol. 2

12/5/60+	11	37		©	1 **Walk Don't Run**		[I]	**$50**	Dolton 8003
6/26/61	39	14		©	2 **Another Smash!!!**		[I]	**$50**	Dolton 8006
9/18/61	105	14		©	3 **The Ventures**		[I]	**$50**	Dolton 8004
10/2/61	94	17		©	4 **The Colorful Ventures**		[I]	**$50**	Dolton 8008
1/20/62	24	29		©	5 **Twist With The Ventures**		[I]	**$50**	Dolton 8010
5/19/62	40	11		©	6 **The Ventures' Twist Party, Vol. 2**		[I]	**$50**	Dolton 8014
8/11/62	45	12		©	7 **Mashed Potatoes And Gravy**		[I]	**$50**	Dolton 8016
11/24/62	93	8		©	8 **Going To The Ventures Dance Party!**		[I]	**$50**	Dolton 8017
1/5/63	8	40	●	©	9 **The Ventures play Telstar, The Lonely Bull**		[I]	**$50**	Dolton 8019
5/4/63	30	28		©	10 **"Surfing"**		[I]	**$50**	Dolton 8022
6/1/63	91	8		©	11 **Bobby Vee Meets The Ventures**			**$40**	Liberty 7289
6/8/63	101	14		©	12 **The Ventures Play The Country Classics**		[I]	**$40**	Dolton 8023
8/31/63	30	33		©	13 **Let's Go!**		[I]	**$40**	Dolton 8024
1/25/64	27	18		©	14 **(The) Ventures In Space**		[I]	**$40**	Dolton 8027
7/18/64	32	19		©	15 **The Fabulous Ventures**		[I]	**$40**	Dolton 8029
10/10/64	17	24		©	16 **Walk, Don't Run, Vol. 2**		[I]	**$40**	Dolton 8031
2/13/65	31	24		©	17 **The Ventures Knock Me Out!**		[I]	**$40**	Dolton 8033
6/19/65	27	30		©	18 **The Ventures On Stage**		[I-L]	**$40**	Dolton 8035

DEBUT	PEAK	WKS	RIAA	CD	ARTIST — Album Title	Catalog	Sym	$	Label & Number
					VENTURES, The — Cont'd				
8/7/65	96	13		© 19	Play Guitar with the Ventures		[I-T]	$30	Dolton 16501
9/25/65	16	35		© 20	The Ventures a go-go		[I]	$30	Dolton 8037
12/11/65	9ˣ	9		© 21	The Ventures' Christmas Album		[X-I]	$30	Dolton 8038
					Christmas charts: 9/'65, 32/'66, 32/'67, 15/'69				
2/12/66	33	22		© 22	Where The Action Is		[I]	$30	Dolton 8040
3/5/66	42	21		© 23	The Ventures/Batman Theme		[I]	$30	Dolton 8042
6/11/66	39	25		© 24	Go With The Ventures!		[I]	$30	Dolton 8045
9/17/66	33	26		© 25	Wild Things!		[I]	$30	Dolton 8047
2/18/67	57	26		© 26	Guitar Freakout		[I]	$30	Dolton 8050
6/3/67	69	15		© 27	Super Psychedelics		[I]	$25	Liberty 8052
9/2/67	50	44	●	© 28	Golden Greats By The Ventures		[I]	$25	Liberty 8053
12/23/67+	55	21		© 29	$1,000,000.00 Weekend		[I]	$25	Liberty 8054
5/25/68	169	6		© 30	Flights Of Fantasy		[I]	$25	Liberty 8055
8/24/68	128	9		© 31	The Horse		[I]	$25	Liberty 8057
1/18/69	157	14		© 32	Underground Fire		[I]	$25	Liberty 8059
5/10/69	11	24	●	© 33	Hawaii Five-O		[I]	$20	Liberty 8061
12/13/69+	81	12		© 34	Swamp Rock		[I]	$20	Liberty 8062
3/14/70	154	5		© 35	More Golden Greats		[I]	$20	Liberty 8060
10/10/70	91	21		© 36	The Ventures 10th Anniversary Album		[I]	$25	Liberty 35000 [2]
1/15/72	195	3		© 37	Theme From Shaft		[I]	$15	United Artists 5547
3/18/72	146	3		© 38	Joy/The Ventures play the classics		[I]	$15	United Artists 5575

Action (22)
Action Plus (22)
Ad-Venture (24)
Apache (9,28)
Apache '65 (18)
Aquarius (medley) (33)
(Baby) Hully Gully (7)
Bach's Prelude (38)
Bad Moon Rising (medley) (36)
Ballad Of Bonnie And Clyde (30)
Barefoot Adventure (10)
Bat, The (14)
Batman Theme (23)
Besame Mucho (6)
Beyond The Reef (2)
Bird Rockers (17)
Blowin' In The Wind (medley) (36)
Blue Christmas (21)
Blue Moon (4) **54**
Blue Skies (4)
Blue Star (16)
Blue Tail Fly (6)
Blue Tango (3)
Bluebird (6)
Bluer Than Blue (4)
Born To Be Wild (32)
Born To Lose (12)
Bridge Over Troubled Water (36)
Bulldog (2)
Bumble Bee (18)
Bumble Bee Twist (5)
By The Time I Get To Phoenix (36)
Calcutta (9)
California Dreamin' (24)
Candy Man (11)
Cape, The (23)
Caravan (1,11,18)
Carry Me Back (34)
Catfish Mud Dance (34)
Changing Tides (10)
Cherries Jubilee (31)
Cherry Pink And Apple Blossom White (4)
Choo Choo Train (31)
Classical Gas (37)
Come September, Theme From (8)
Cookout Freakout On Lookout Mountain (26)
Counterpoint (5)
Country Funk And The Canned Head (32)
Crazy Horse (31)
Creeper, The (16)
Cruel Sea (15)
Cruncher (10)
Cry Like A Baby (30)
Dark Eyes Twist (6)
Deep, Deep In The Water (37)
Delilah (9)
Detour (5)
Diamond Head (16) **70**
Diamonds (10)
Dizzy (33)
Don't Give In To Him (33)
Don't Think Twice, It's All Right (medley) (36)

00-711 (23)
Down On Me (32)
Driving Guitars (5,18)
Eight Miles High (24)
El Watusi (13)
Eleanor Rigby (36)
Eleventh Hour (15)
Elise (38)
Embers In E Minor (32)
Endless Dream (27)
Escape (24)
Everybody's Talkin' (36)
Exploration In Terror (14)
Fear (14)
Fever (22)
Fire (32)
Flights Of Fantasy (30)
Fly Away (30)
Fourth Dimension (14)
Frankie And Johnny (24)
Frosty The Snowman (21)
Fugitive (15)
Fuzzy And Wild (25)
Gallop, The (31)
Galveston (33)
Games People Play (33)
Gandy Dancer (8)
Georgy Girl (29)
Get Smart Theme (23)
(Ghost) Riders In The Sky (2)
Gimme Some Lovin' (37)
Ginchy (2)
Ginza Lights (24)
Go (24)
Go Go Dancer (20)
Go Go Guitar (20)
Go Go Slow (20)
Gone, Gone, Gone (17)
Good Lovin' (24)
Good Morning Starshine (36)
Good, The Bad, And The Ugly (35)
Good Thing (26)
Goodnight Irene (11)
Gravy (For My Mashed Potatoes) (7)
Grazing In The Grass (31,35)
Green Grass (24)
Green Hornet "66" (23)
Green Leaves Of Summer (4)
Green Light (30)
Green Onions (9,35)
Green River (34)
Greenfields (4)
Gringo (5)
Groovin' (29)
Guitar Freakout (26)
Guitar Psychedelics (27)
Guitar Twist (5)
Gully-Ver (8)
Gumbo (34)
Gypsys, Tramps And Thieves (37)
Hang On Sloopy (My Girl Sloopy) (22)
Hanky Panky (25)
Happy Together (27)
Harlem Nocturne (3)
Hawaii Five-O (33,35) **4**
Hawaiian War Chant (3)

He Never Came Back (14)
Heavies, The (10)
Here Comes The Judge (34)
Hernando's Hideaway (7)
Hey Jude (36)
High And Dry (26)
Higher Than Thou (32)
Home (1)
Honeycomb (11)
Honky Tonk (1,28)
Honky Tonk Women (34)
Horse, The (31)
Horse Power (31)
Hot Line (23)
Hot Pastrami (13)
Hot Summer (Asian Mashed) (7)
House Of The Rising Sun (16,35)
How Now Wild Cow (25)
I Can Hear Music (33)
(I Can't Get No) Satisfaction (20)
I Can't Stop Loving You (12)
I Feel Fine (17)
I Like It Like That (20)
I Walk The Line (12)
I'm A Believer (26)
I'm A Man (37)
I'm Gonna Sit Right Down And Write Myself A Letter (11)
If I'm Right Or Wrong (11)
In A Persian Market (38)
"In" Crowd (36)
Indian Sun (37)
Innermotion Faze (30)
Instant Guitars (6)
Instant Mashed (7)
Intruder, The (8)
Jambalaya (34)
Jingle Bell Rock (21)
Jingle Bells (21)
Joker's Wild (23)
Josie (2)
Journey To The Stars (15,18)
Joy (Jesu Joy Of Man's Desiring) (38)
Jumpin' Jack Flash (31)
Kandy Koncoction (27)
Kicking Around (6)
La Bamba (29)
Land Of 1,000 Dances (medley) (31)
Last Date (2)
Last Night (9)
Let It Be (36)
Let The Sunshine In (The Flesh Failures) (medley) (33)
Let There Be Drums (9)
Let's Go (13,28)
Let's Twist Again (5)
Letter, The (33)
Licking Stick-Licking Stick (31)
Lies (22)
Light My Fire (32)
Limbo Rock (8)
Linda Lu (11)
Little Bit Me, A Little Bit You (27)
Little Bit Of Action (22)

Loco-Motion (8)
Lolita Ya-Ya (8) **61**
Lonely Bull (9,28)
Lonely Girl (17)
Lonely Heart (2)
Lonely Sea (10)
Lonesome Town (3)
Louie Louie (20)
Love Goddess Of Venus (14)
Love Is Blue (35)
Love Potion Number Nine (17)
Love Shower (30)
Lovesick Blues (12)
Lovin' Things (33)
Lucille (7)
Lullaby Of The Leaves (2,18) **69**
MacArthur Park (36)
Man From U.N.C.L.E. (23)
Mariner No. 4 (14)
Mashed Potato Time (7)
McCoy, The (1)
Meet Mister Callahan (2)
Melody Of Joy (38)
Memphis (13,19,28)
Mexico (9)
Michelle (36)
Mighty Quinn (Quinn, The Eskimo) (30)
Mission: Impossible (35)
Mod East (24)
Monday, Monday (24)
Moon Child (14)
Moon Dawg (2)
Moon Of Manakoora (3)
More (13,35)
Morgen (1)
Movin' & Groovin' (5)
Mozart Forty (38)
Mozart's Minuet (38)
Mr. Moto (1)
Muddy Mississippi Line (34)
Music To Watch Girls By (29)
My Bonnie Lies (6)
My Own True Love (Tara's Theme) (1)
Needles And Pins (15)
Never My Love (36,37)
Never On Sunday (9)
New Orleans (13)
Night Drive (8)
Night Stick (20)
Night Train (1,16)
Night Walk (16)
Niki Hoeky (34)
1999 A.D. (27)
Ninth Wave (10)
No Matter What Shape (Your Stomach's In) (22)
No Tresspassing (1)
Nutty (2)
Ode To Billie Joe (29)
Off In The 93rds (26)
Oh, Lonesome Me (12)
Oh, Pretty Woman (17)
One Fine Day (Un Bel Di) (38)
One Mint Julep (16)
Only The Young (15)
Opus Twist (3)
Orange Fire (4)

Out Of Limits (14,28)
Over The Mountain Across The Sea (13)
Panhandle Rag (12)
Paper Airplane (26)
Party In Laguna (10)
Pavane (38)
Peace Train (37)
Peach Fuzz (16)
Pedal Pusher (16,18)
Penetration (14)
Percolator (14)
Perfidia (3,18) **15**
Peter And The Wolf (38)
Pied Piper (25)
Pink Panther Theme (15)
Pipeline (10,28)
Plaquemines Parish (34)
Poison Ivy (7)
Pretty Girls Everywhere (11)
Proud Mary (34)
Psyched-Out (27)
Psychedelic Venture (27)
Raindrops Keep Fallin' On My Head (36)
Ram-Bunk-Shush (1) **29**
Rap City (16)
Raunchy (1,19,35)
Ravin' Blue (15)
Raw-Hide (2)
Rebel-Rouser (28)
Red River Rock (9)
Red Top (4)
Red Wing Twist (6)
Reflections (36)
Respect (29)
Road Runner (2)
Rudolph The Red Nosed Reindeer (21)
Runaway (3)
Runnin' Wild (15)
San Antonio Rose (12)
Santa Claus Is Comin' To Town (21)
Scarborough Fair/Canticle (30)
Scratch (7)
Scratchin' (15)
Scrooge (21)
Sea Of Grass (32)
Sealed With A Kiss (29)
Secret Agent Man (23) **54**
Sha La La (17)
Shaft, Theme From (37)
Shanghied (3)
She's Just My Style (22)
She's Not There (17)
Shuck, The (3)
Silver Bells (21)
Silver City, Theme From (4) **83**
Slaughter On Tenth Avenue (17,18) **35**
Sleep Walk (1)
Sleigh Ride (21)
Sloop John B (37)
Snoopy Vs. The Red Baron (26)
Snow Flakes (21)
So Fine (13)
Solar Race (14)
Sonata In C# Minor (38)

Soul Breeze (31)
Soul Coaxing (Ame Caline) (30)
Sounds Of Silence (36)
Spinning Wheel (36)
Spooky (medley) (33)
Spudnik (7)
Standing In The Shadows Of Love (26)
Steel Guitar Rag (12)
Stop Action (22)
Stormy (medley) (33)
Stranger On The Shore (16)
Strangers In The Night (36)
Strawberry Fields Forever (27)
Sugar, Sugar (34)
Sugarfoot Rag (12)
Sukiyaki (3)
Summer In The City (25)
Summer Place, Theme From A (33) **83**
Summertime (7)
Summertime Blues (5)
Sunny (29)
Sunny River (5)
Sunshine Of Your Love (32)
Surf Rider (10)
Suspicious Minds (34)
Swamp Rock (34)
Swan Lake (38)
Swanee River Twist (6)
Sweet And Lovely (8)
Sweet Caroline (Good Times Never Seemed So Good) (36)
Sweet Pea (25)
Swingin' Creeper (20)
Switch, The (1)
Tall Cool One (5)
Taste Of Honey (22,35)
Telstar (9,28)
Ten Over (10)
Tequila (9,19,28)
These Boots Are Made For Walkin' (24)
This Is Where Friendship Ends (11)
Those Were The Days (36)
3's A Crowd (22)
Thunder Cloud (37)
Tight Fit (37)
Tip-Toe Thru' The Tulips With Me (31)
To Sir, With Love (29)
Tomorrow's Love (17)
Torquay (3,35)
Traces (medley) (33)
Trambone (2)
Twilight Zone (14)
Twist, The (5)
Twisted (6)
Two Divided By Love (37)
Twomp, The (6)
Underground Fire (32)
Up, Up, And Away (23,36)
Up, Up And Down (2)
Ups 'n Downs (3)
Uptight (Everything's Alright) (29)
Vampcamp (23)
Venus (8)
Vibrations (27)

VENTURES, The — Cont'd

Wabash Cannonball (12)
Wack Wack (26)
Wah-Watusi (7)
Wailin' (3)
Walk--Don't Run (1,18,19,28,31) *2*
Walk-Don't Run '64 (16) *8*
Walk Right Back (11)

Walk Right In (13)
Walkin' With Pluto (15)
Walking The Carpet (30)
War Of The Satellites (14)
We Wish You A Merry Christmas (21)
Weight, The (32)
Western Union (27)

What Else Is New (11)
What Now My Love (29)
Wheels (2)
When You Walk In The Room (17)
White Christmas (21)
White Silver Sands (4)
Whittier Blvd. (20)

Who'll Stop The Rain (medley) (36)
Wild And Wooly (25)
Wild Angels, Theme From The (26)
Wild Child (25)
Wild Night (11)
Wild Thing (25)

Wild Trip (25)
Wildcat (25)
Wildwood Flower (12)
Windy (29)
Windy And Warm (10)
Wipe Out (13,18,28)
Wooly Bully (20)
Work Song (25)

Ya Ya Wobble (8)
Yellow Bird (4)
Yellow Jacket (4,18)
Yesterday (29)
You Are My Sunshine (12)
Zocko (23)

VERA, Billy, & The Beaters '87

Born William McCord on 5/28/44 in Riverside, California; raised in Westchester County, New York. Pop singer/songwriter. Acted in the movies *Buckaroo Banzai* and *The Doors*.

5/16/81	118	10		1 Billy & The Beaters		[L] $12	Alfa 10001

recorded on 1/15/81 at the Roxy in Hollywood

12/6/86+	15	26 ● ©	2 By Request (The Best Of Billy Vera & The Beaters)		[E-L] $10	Rhino 70858

At This Moment (1,2) *1*
Corner Of The Night (1,2)

Here Comes The Dawn Again (1,2)
Hopeless Romantic (2)

I Can Take Care Of Myself (1,2) *39*
Millie, Make Some Chili (1,2)

Peanut Butter (2)
Someone Will School You, Someone Will Cool You (1,2)

Strange Things Happen (1,2)
Strollin' With Bones (1)

VERLAINE, Tom '81

Born Thomas Miller on 12/13/49 in Mt. Morris, New Jersey. Rock singer.

10/10/81	177	3 ©	Dreamtime		$12	Warner 3539

Always
Blue Robe

Down On The Farm
Fragile

Future In Noise
Mary Marie

Mr Blur
Penetration

There's A Reason
Without A Word

VERTICAL HORIZON '00

Rock group from Boston: Matt Scannell (vocals), Keith Kane (guitar), Sean Hurley (bass) and Ed Toth (drums).

1/22/00	40	71 ▲² ©	Everything You Want		$10	RCA 67818

All Of You
Best I Ever Had (grey sky morning) *58*

Everything You Want *1*
Finding Me
Give You Back

Miracle
Send It Up
Shackled

We Are
You Say
You're A God *23*

VERUCA SALT '97

Rock group from Chicago: **Nina Gordon** and Louise Post (vocals, guitars), with Steven Lack (bass) and Jim Shapiro (drums). Name taken from a character in the children's book *Charlie and The Chocolate Factory*.

11/5/94+	69	23 ● ©	1 American Thighs		$10	Minty Fresh 7
3/1/97	55	24 ©	2 Eight Arms To Hold You		$10	Outpost 30001
6/3/00	171	1 ©	3 Resolver		$10	Velveteen 78103

All Dressed Up (3)
All Hail Me (1)
Awesome (2)
Benjamin (2)
Best You Can Get (3)
Born Entertainer (3)
Celebrate You (1)

Disconnected (3)
Don't Make Me Prove It (2)
Earthcrosser (2)
Fly (1)
Forsythia (1)
Get Back (1)
Hellraiser (3)

Imperfectly (3)
Loneliness Is Worse (2)
Morning Sad (2)
Number One Blind (1)
Officially Dead (3)
One Last Time (2)
Only You Know (3)

Pretty Boys (3)
Same Person (3)
Seether (1)
Shutterbug (2)
Sleeping Where I Want (1)
Sound Of The Bell (2)
Spiderman '79 (1)

Stoneface (2)
Straight (2)
25 (1)
Twinstar (1)
Used To Know Her (3)
Venus Man Trap (2)
Victrola (1)

Volcano Girls (2)
Wet Suit (3)
With David Bowie (2)
Wolf (1)
Yeah Man (3)

VERVE, The '98

Rock group from Wigan, England: **Richard Ashcroft** (vocals), Nick McCabe (guitar), Simon Jones (bass) and Peter Salisbury (drums).

10/18/97+	23	46 ▲ ©	Urban Hymns		$10	Virgin 44913

Bitter Sweet Symphony *12*
Catching The Butterfly
Come On

Drugs Don't Work
Lucky Man
Neon Wilderness

One Day
Rolling People
Sonnet

Space And Time
This Time
Velvet Morning

Weeping Willow

VERVE PIPE, The '97

Rock group from East Lansing, Michigan: brothers Brian (vocals) and Brad (bass) Vander Ark, A.J. Dunning (guitar), Doug Corella (keyboards) and Donny Brown (drums).

4/13/96+	24	48 ▲ ©	1 Villains		$10	RCA 66809
8/14/99	158	1 ©	2 The Verve Pipe		$10	RCA 67664

Barely (if at all) (1)
Cattle (1)
Cup Of Tea (1)
Drive You Mild (1)
F Word (2)

Freshmen, The (1) *5*
Generations (2)
Half A Mind (2)
Headlines (2)
Hero (2)

In Between (2)
Kiss Me Idle (2)
La La (2)
Myself (1)
Ominous Man (1)

Penny Is Poison (1)
Photograph (1)
Real (1)
Reverend Girl (1)
She Has Faces (2)

She Loves Everybody (2)
Supergig (2)
Television (2)
Veneer (1)
Villains (1)

VESTA '89

Born Vesta Williams in Coshocton, Ohio; raised in Los Angeles. Female R&B singer.

9/2/89	131	10 ©	Vesta 4 U		$10	A&M 5223

All On You
Best I Ever Had

Congratulations *55*
4 U

Here/Say
How You Feel

Hunger
Running Into Memories

Sweet, Sweet Love

VICIOUS BASE '91

Rap duo: D.J. Lace and M.C. Madness.

1/26/91	153	22 ● ©	Back To Haunt You!		$10	Cheetah 9404

VICIOUS BASE Featuring D.J. MAGIC MIKE!

All Wild D.J.'s He Will Tame
Are You Ready
Back To Haunt You
Break, The

Comin On Strong
Get Laid, Get Funked
Hard To Keep A Good Rhyme Down
Nice & Nasty

It's Automatic
Magic Meets Lace
Meeting, The

No Stop To The Madness
Party With Peace Of Mind
Royalty's Arrived
Sorry, Wrong Beat

Vicious Groove
You Want Bass

VICTOR '96

Studio project formed by **Rush** guitarist Alex Lifeson. Features various studio musicians/vocalists.

1/27/96	99	3 ©	Victor		$10	Atlantic 82852

At The End
Big Dance

Don't Care
I Am The Spirit

Mr. X
Promise

Sending Out A Warning
Shut Up Shuttin' Up

Start Today
Strip And Go Naked

Victor

VICTORY '89

Hard-rock group from Germany: Fernando Garcia (vocals), Herman Frank and Tommy Newton (guitars), Peter Knorn (bass) and Fritz Randow (drums).

5/6/89	182	5 ©	Culture Killed The Native		$10	Rhino 70844

Always The Same
Don't Tell No Lies

Let It Rock On
Lost In The Night

More And More
Never Satisfied

On The Loose
Power Strikes The Earth

So They Run
Standing On The Edge Of Time

Warning, The

VILLAGE PEOPLE '79

Disco vocal group from New York City: Victor Willis (policeman), Randy Jones (cowboy), David Hodo (construction worker), Felipe Rose (indian), Glenn Hughes (leather man) and Alexander Briley (army man). Group appeared in the movie *Can't Stop The Music*. Hughes died of cancer on 3/4/2001 (age 50).

10/1/77+	54	86	●	©	1 Village People		$12	Casablanca 7064
3/25/78	24	69	▲	©	2 Macho Man		$12	Casablanca 7096
10/21/78+	3	45	▲	©	3 Cruisin'		$12	Casablanca 7118
4/14/79	8	21	▲	©	4 Go West		$12	Casablanca 7144
10/20/79	32	20	●	©	5 Live And Sleazy	[L]	$15	Casablanca 7183 [2]

record 1: live; record 2: studio

6/21/80	47	12		©	6 Can't Stop The Music	[S]	$12	Casablanca 7220

includes "Give Me A Break" and "Sophistication" by **The Ritchie Family**, and "Samantha" and "Sound Of The City" by David London

8/1/81	138	4		©	7 Renaissance		$10	RCA Victor 4105

Action Man (7)
Big Mac (7)
Can't Stop The Music (6)
Citizens Of The World (4)
Diet (7)
(Do You Wanna) Spend The Night (7)

Fire Island (1,5)
Fireman (7)
5 O'Clock In The Morning (7)
Food Fight (7)
Get Away Holiday (4)
Go West (4) *45*
Hot Cop (3,5)
I Ain't Got Nobody (medley) (4)

I Am What I Am (2)
I Love You To Death (6)
I Wanna Shake Your Hand (4)
I'm A Cruiser (medley) (3)
In Hollywood (Everybody Is A Star) (medley) (1,5)
In The Navy (4,5) *3*
Jungle City (7)

Just A Gigolo (medley) (2)
Key West (2)
Liberation (6)
Macho Man (2,5) *25*
Magic Night (6)
Manhattan Woman (4)
Milkshake (6)
My Roomate (3)

Ready For The 80's (5) *52*
Rock & Roll Is Back Again (5)
San Francisco (You've Got Me) (medley) (1,5)
Save Me (5)
Sleazy (5)
Sodom And Gomorrah (2)
Ups And Downs (7)

Village People (1)
Women, The (medley) (3)
Y.M.C.A. (3,5,6) *2*

VILLAGE STOMPERS, The '63

Dixieland-styled band from Greenwich Village, New York City: Dick Brady, Ralph Casale, Don Coates, Frank Hubbell, Mitchell May, Joe Muranyi, Al McManus and Lenny Pogan.

11/2/63	5	30		©	1 Washington Square	[I]	$20	Epic 26078
4/25/64	139	3		©	2 More Sounds of Washington Square	[I]	$20	Epic 26090

Bei Mir Bist Du Schon (2)
Blowin' In The Wind (1)
Blue Grass (1)
Bridges Of Budapest (2)
Cold Steel Canyons (1)

Dominique (2)
Don't Think Twice, It's All Right (2)
Follow The Drinkin' Gourd (1)
Frankie And Johnny (1)

Goodnight, Irene (2)
Gotta Travel On (2)
Green, Green (1)
Haunted House Blues (2)
If I Had A Hammer (1)

La-Dee-Da Song (2)
Melodie D'Amour (2)
Midnight In Moscow (1)
Mountain Greenery (2)
Poet And The Prophet (1)

Saints, The (2)
Tie Me Kangaroo Down, Sport (1)
Walk Right In (1)
Washington Square (1) *2*

We Can't Stop Singin' (1)

VINCENT, Gene, and His Blue Caps '56

Born Vincent Eugene Craddock on 2/11/35 in Norfolk, Virginia. Died of a bleeding ulcer on 10/12/71 (age 36). Rock singer/songwriter/guitarist. Formed the Blue Caps in Norfolk in 1956. Appeared in the movies *The Girl Can't Help It* and *Hot Rod Gang*. Injured in car crash that killed Eddie Cochran in 1960. Inducted into the Rock and Roll Hall of Fame in 1998.

9/29/56	16	2		©	Bluejean Bop!		$400	Capitol 764

Ain't She Sweet
Bluejean Bop *49*

Bop Street
I Flipped

Jezebel
Jump Back, Honey, Jump Back

Jumps, Giggles And Shouts
Peg O' My Heart

That Old Gang Of Mine
Up A Lazy River

Waltz Of The Wind
Who Slapped John

VINCENT, Vinnie, Invasion '86

Born on 8/5/52 in New York City. Rock guitarist. Member of **Kiss** from 1982-83. His group: Bob Fleischman (vocals), Dana Strum (bass) and Bob Rock (drums). Mark Slaughter replaced Fleischman after first album. Strum and Slaughter left in 1989 to form **Slaughter**.

9/20/86	64	29		©	1 Vinnie Vincent Invasion		$10	Chrysalis 41529
5/21/88	64	15		©	2 All Systems Go		$10	Chrysalis 41626

Animal (1)
Ashes To Ashes (2)
Baby-O (1)
Back On The Streets (1)

Boyz Are Gonna Rock (1)
Breakout (2)
Burn (2)
Deeper And Deeper (2)

Dirty Rhythm (2)
Do You Wanna Make Love (1)
Ecstasy (2)
Heavy Pettin (2)

I Wanna Be Your Victim (1)
Invasion (1)
Let Freedom Rock (2)
Love Kills (1)

Naughty Naughty (2)
No Substitute (1)
Shoot U Full Of Love (1)
That Time Of Year (2)

Twisted (1)

VINTON, Bobby ★123★ '62

Born Stanley Robert Vinton on 4/16/35 in Canonsburg, Pennsylvania. Pop singer. Nickamed "The Polish Prince." Hosted own musical variety TV series from 1975-78.

1)*Roses Are Red* 2)*There! I've Said It Again* 3)*Blue Velvet* 4)*Bobby Vinton's Greatest Hits*
5)*Melodies Of Love*

8/4/62	5	27		©	1 Roses Are Red		$25	Epic 26020
1/5/63	137	2			2 Bobby Vinton sings the Big Ones		$25	Epic 26035
8/10/63	10	33			3 Blue Velvet		$25	Epic 26068
2/1/64	8	28			4 There! I've Said It Again		$25	Epic 26081
7/25/64	31	12			5 Tell Me Why		$20	Epic 26113
10/3/64+	12	38	●	©	6 Bobby Vinton's Greatest Hits	[G]	$20	Epic 26098
12/5/64	13[X]	4		©	7 A Very Merry Christmas	[X]	$20	Epic 26122
1/16/65	18	13		©	8 Mr. Lonely		$20	Epic 26136
7/3/65	116	5		©	9 Bobby Vinton Sings for Lonely Nights		$20	Epic 26154
2/12/66	110	5			10 Satin Pillows and Careless		$20	Epic 26182
12/16/67+	41	33			11 Please Love Me Forever		$20	Epic 26341
6/15/68	164	8			12 Take Good Care Of My Baby		$20	Epic 26382
1/4/69	21	24			13 I Love How You Love Me		$20	Epic 26437
6/14/69	69	12			14 Vinton		$20	Epic 26471
1/17/70	138	8			15 Bobby Vinton's Greatest Hits Of Love	[K]	$20	Epic 26517
4/11/70	90	6			16 My Elusive Dreams		$20	Epic 26540
4/8/72	72	15			17 Ev'ry Day Of My Life		$15	Epic 31286
7/29/72	77	14			18 Sealed With A Kiss		$15	Epic 31642
11/25/72+	119	16			19 Bobby Vinton's All-Time Greatest Hits	[G]	$20	Epic 31487 [2]
11/30/74+	16	22	●		20 Melodies Of Love		$12	ABC 851
12/7/74	109	5			21 With Love	[K]	$12	Epic 32921

VINTON, Bobby — Cont'd

6/28/75	**154**	5			22 Bobby Vinton Sings The Golden Decade Of Love	[K]		$15	Epic 33468 [2]
7/19/75	**108**	5			23 Heart Of Hearts			$12	ABC 891
12/27/75+	**161**	7			24 The Bobby Vinton Show			$12	ABC 924
6/11/77	**183**	2			25 The Name Is Love			$12	ABC 981
12/19/87	**20**ˣ	3			26 Santa Must Be Polish/And Other Christmas Sounds Of Today	[X]		$10	Tapestry 1001
					Christmas charts: 20/'87, 22/'88				
4/13/96	**199**	1		©	27 16 Most Requested Songs	[G]		$10	Epic/Legacy 47855

Adios Amigo (23)
After Loving You (11)
Ain't That Lovin' You (25)
All Alone Am I (9)
All My Todays (25)
All The King's Horses (And All The King's Men) (10)
Always, Always (Yesterday's Love Song) (8)
Always In My Heart (1)
Am I Blue (3)
Am I Losing You (20)
And I Love You So (17,21,24)
Are You Sincere (14)
Autumn Leaves (2)
Baby I'm Yours (16)
Baby Take Me In Your Arms (16)
Baby, When It Comes To Loving You (25)
Bad Bad Leroy Brown (24)
Be My Love (2)
Because Of You (2)
Beer Barrel Polka (23) *33*
Bell That Couldn't Jingle (7)
Bitter Teardrops (10)
Blue, Blue Day (3)
Blue Hawaii (3)
Blue Moon (3)
Blue On Blue (3,6,19,27) *8*
Blue Skies (3)
Blue Velvet (3,6,19,27) *1*
Blueberry Hill (3)
Bouquet Of Roses (11)
Build Me Up Buttercup (24)
Careless (23)
Charlie (23)
Christmas Angel (7)
Christmas Chopsticks (7)
Christmas In Killarney (7)
Christmas Tree (7)
Clinging Vine (21) *17*
Come Softly To Me (18)
Coming Home Soldier (19,27) *11*
Crying (1)
Days Of Sand And Shovels (14,15,19) *34*
Dearest Santa (7)
Deck The Halls (26)
Dick And Jane (20) *flip*
Do You Hear What I Hear (7)
Earth Angel (Will You Be Mine) (22)
End Of The World (18,22)

Every Day Of My Life (17,19) *24*
Everyone's Gone To The Moon (10)
Feelings (23)
First Time Ever (I Saw Your Face) (18)
For All We Know (15)
For Once In My Life (13)
Forever Yours I Remain (8)
Forget Me Not (2)
Godfather (Speak Softly Love), Love Theme From The (18)
Going Steady With A Heartache (10)
Gone (From My Heart) (12,22)
Goodnight My Love (Pleasant Dreams) (2)
Grass Is Always Greener (8)
Great Pretender (22)
Greatest Gift (7)
Greenfields (18)
Halfway To Paradise (13,15,19,27) *23*
Have I Told You Lately That I Love You? (1)
Have You Ever Been Lonely (Have You Ever Been Blue?) (9)
He'll Have To Go (2)
Heaven's Gonna Miss You (12)
Hello Loneliness (9)
Help Me Make It Through The Night (24)
Her Name Is Love (25)
Here In My Heart (20)
Hold Me, Thrill Me, Kiss Me (25)
Hurt (21)
I Apologize (12)
I Can Dream, Can't I? (4)
I Can't Believe That It's All Over (21)
I Can't Help It (1)
I Can't Stop Loving You (1)
I Fall To Pieces (1)
I Honestly Love You (20)
I Love How You Love Me (13,15,19,27) *9*
I Love You Much Too Much (5)
I Love You The Way You Are (2,6,21) *38*
I Remember Loving You (25)
I Remember You (2)
I Wanna Be Loved (5)

I Want To Spend My Life With You (12)
I Will Follow You (16)
I Won't Cry Anymore (17)
I Won't Give Up (23)
I'll Be Loving You (16)
I'll Make You My Baby (17,19)
I'll Never Fall In Love Again (16)
I'll Never Smile Again (8)
I'll Remember ..see: In The Still Of The Night
I'll Walk Alone (9)
I'm Comin' Home, Girl (17)
I'm Gettin' Sentimental Over You (2)
I'm Leaving It Up To You (18)
I'm Walkin' (24)
If (4)
If Ever I Would Leave You (16)
If I Didn't Care (13)
If I Give My Heart To You (1)
If You Love Me, Really Love Me (5)
Imagination Is A Magic Dream (5)
In The Still Of The Night (9,22)
It's A Sin To Tell A Lie (14)
It's All In The Game (11,22)
It's Better To Have Loved (8)
It's No Sin (13)
It's The Talk Of The Town (11)
Jingle Bells (26)
Just A Dream (22)
Just A Little Lovin' (Early In The Mornin') (17)
Just As Much As Ever (11,15,27) *24*
Killing Me Softly With His Song (24)
Laughing On The Outside (Crying On The Inside) (8)
Lavender Blue (4)
Leaving On A Jet Plane (16)
Let's Kiss And Make Up (6) *38*
Let's Sing A Song (17)
Life Goes On (8)
Little Barefoot Boy (12)
Little Miss Blue (3)
L-O-N E-L-Y (9,27) *22*
Lonely Street (9)
Long Lonely Nights (9,19) *17*
Love Makes Everything Better (25)
Love Me With All Your Heart (11)

Lovely Lady (23)
May You Always (14)
Maybe You'll Be There (5)
Middle Of The Night (14)
Misty Blue (17)
Moody (1)
Most Beautiful Girl (20)
Mr. Blue (3,22)
Mr. Lonely (1,6,8,19,27) *1*
My Blue Heaven (3)
My Christmas Prayer (7)
My Elusive Dreams (16,19) *46*
My Foolish Heart (4)
My Gypsy Love (20)
My Heart Belongs To Only You (4,6,19,27) *9*
My Heart Cries For You (2)
My Melody Of Love (20) *3*
My Song (23)
My Song Of Love (11)
My Special Angel (22)
My Way Of Life (4)
Never Ending Song Of Love (20)
Night Life (9)
No Arms Can Ever Hold You (14,19) *93*
Oh, How I Miss You Tonight (9)
Once More With Feeling (25)
Only Love Can Break A Heart (25) *99*
Only You (And You Alone) (22)
Our Day Will Come (18)
Over The Mountain (Across The Sea) (6,19,22,27) *21*
P.S. I Love You (11)
Peppermint Stick Parade (7)
Perfect Woman (16)
Petticoat White (Summer Sky Blue) (10) *81*
Please Help Me, I'm Falling (1)
Please Love Me Forever (11,15,19,27) *6*
Polka Pose (23)
Pretty Girl Is Like A Melody (5)
Rain Rain Go Away (2,6,19) *12*
Raindrops Keep Fallin' On My Head (16)
Ramblin' Rose (2)
Roses Are Red (My Love) (1,6,19,27) *1*
Runaway (24)
Santa Claus Is Coming To Town (26)

Santa Must Be Polish (26)
Satin (8)
Satin Pillows (10) *23*
Saturday Night (Is The Loneliest Night Of The Week) (9)
Save The Last Dance For Me (13)
Sealed With A Kiss (18,21) *19*
Seasons In The Sun (21)
Sentimental Me (1,12,15)
Serenade Of The Bells (12)
Shangri-La (13)
She Loves Me (17)
She's Gotta Be A Saint (21)
Silent Night (26)
Silhouettes (22)
Sincerely (22)
So Many Lonely Girls (9)
Some Kind Of Wonderful (18)
Some Of These Days (5)
Somebody's Breakin' My Heart (18)
Someday (You'll Want Me To Want You) (10)
Someone I Used To Know (8)
Something (16)
Somewhere Along The Way (5)
Song Sung Blue (19)
St. Louis Blues (3)
Stand By Your Man (14)
Take Good Care Of My Baby (12,15,27) *33*
Teardrops (22)
Tears On My Pillow (22)
Tell Me Why (5,6,19,27) *13*
There Goes My Heart (5)
There Goes That Song Again (5)
There! I've Said It Again (4,6,19,27) *1*
Thing Called Sadness (8)
This Guy's In Love With You (14)
Those Were The Days (13)
Thousand Miles Away (22)
Three Wise Men, Wise Men Three (7)
Till (13,22)
Tina (1)
To Be Alone (12)
To Each His Own (4)
To Know You Is To Love You (14,15,19,27) *34*

To Think You've Chosen Me (12)
Together (13)
Too Young (4)
Traces (16)
Travelin' Band (24)
Trouble Is My Middle Name (6) *33*
True Love (1)
Try A Little Tenderness (14)
Trying (4)
Twelfth Of Never (2,22)
Two Purple Shadows (10)
Unchained Melody (4)
United We Stand (24)
Wanted (15)
Warm And Tender (4)
Way We Were (24)
When I Fall In Love (14,15)
When I Lost You (5)
When Will I Be Loved (24)
When You Love (21)
(Where Do I Begin) Love Story (24)
Where Were You All Of My Life (25)
White Christmas (7)
Who's Sorry Now (11)
Whose Garden Was This (17)
Why Can't I Get Over You (23)
Why Don't You Believe Me (13)
Wooden Heart (23) *58*
You Are Love (25)
You Can Do It To Me Anytime (17)
You Own My Heart (10)
You Were Only Fooling (1)
You'll Never Know (20)
You're Nobody 'Til Somebody Loves You (4)
You've Got Your Momma's Eyes (23)
Young Love (11)

VIO-LENCE
Hard-rock group from San Francisco: Sean Killian (vocals), Phil Demmel and Robb Flynn (guitars), Deen Dell (bass) and Perry Strickland (drums).

										'88
8/20/88	**154**	6		©	Eternal Nightmare				$10	Mechanic 42187

Bodies On Bodies
Calling In The Coroner

Eternal Nightmare
Kill On Command

Phobophobia
Serial Killer

T.D.S. (Take It As You Will)

VIOLENT FEMMES
Punk-folk trio from Milwaukee: Gordon Gano (vocals, guitar), Brian Ritchie (bass) and Victor DeLorenzo (drums). Guy Hoffman replaced DeLorenzo in 1992.

									'86
2/15/86	**84**	24	©	1 The Blind Leading The Naked			$10	Slash 25340
2/4/89	**93**	13	©	2 3			$10	Slash 25819
5/18/91	**141**	5	©	3 Why Do Birds Sing?			$10	Slash 26476
8/3/91	**171**	7 ▲ ©	4 Violent Femmes	C:#30/68	[E]	$10	Slash 23845
				released in 1982				
10/2/93	**146**	3 ● ©	5 Add It Up (1981-1993)	[K]		$10	Slash 45403
6/4/94	**90**	4	©	6 New Times			$10	Elektra 61553

Add It Up (4,5)
Agamemnon (6)
America Is (5)
American Music (3,5)
Black Girls (5)
Blister In The Sun (4,5)
Breakin' Hearts (1)
Breakin' Up (6)
Candlelight Song (1)
Children Of The Revolution (1)
Cold Canyon (1)
Confessions (1)
Country Death Song (5)

Dance, Motherfucker, Dance! (5)
Dating Days (2)
Degradation (5)
Do You Really Want To Hurt Me (3)
Don't Start Me On The Liquor (6)
Faith (5)
Fat (5)
Flamingo Baby (3)
Fool In The Full Moon (2)
4 Seasons (6)
Gimme The Car (4,5)

Girl Trouble (3)
Gone Daddy Gone (4,5)
Good Feeling (4)
Good Friend (1)
Gordon's Message (1)
He Likes Me (3)
Heartache (1)
Hey Nonny, Nonny (3)
I Hate The TV (5)
I Held Her In My Arms (1,5)
I Saw You In The Crowd (6)
I'm Free (5)
I'm Nothing (6)

Jesus Of Rio (6)
Jesus Walking On The Water (5)
Johnny (5)
Just Like My Father (2)
Key Of 2 (6)
Kiss Off (4,5)
Lack Of Knowledge (6)
Lies (2,5)
Life Is A Scream (3)
Look Like That (3)
Love & Me Make Three (1)
Machine (6)

Mirror Mirror (I See A Damsel) (6)
More Money Tonight (3)
Mother Of A Girl (2)
New Times (6)
Nightmares (2)
No Killing (1)
Nothing Worth Living For (2)
Old Mother Reagan (1,5)
Out The Window (3,5)
Outside The Palace (1)
Please Do Not Go (4)
Promise (4)
Prove My Love (4)

See My Ships (2)
Special (1)
Telephone Book (2)
36-24-36 (1)
This Island Life (6)
To The Kill (4)
Two People (1)
Ugly (4)
Used To Be (3)
Vancouver (5)
Waiting For The Bus (1)
When Everybody's Happy (6)
World We're Living In (2)

VISAGE '81
Dance-rock group from England: Steve Strange (vocals), **Midge Ure** and John McGeoch (guitars), Billy Currie (voilin), Dave Formula (keyboards) and Rusty Egan (drums). Ure and Currie were members of **Ultravox**.

8/8/81	178	4		©	Visage..		[M]	$10	Polydor 501

Blocks On Blocks   Fade To Grey   Frequency 7   Tar   We Move

VISCOUNTS, The '66
Instrumental group from New Jersey: Harry Haller (sax), brothers Bobby (guitar) and Joe (bass) Spievak, Larry Vecchio (organ) and Clark Smith (drums).

1/29/66	144	2			Harlem Nocturne..		[I]	$50	Amy 8008

Along The Navajo Trail   **Harlem Nocturne** 39   September Song   Touch, The   When The Saints Go Marching
Chug A Lug   I Cover The Waterfront   Sophisticated Lady   Viscount Rock   In
Dig   Opus #1   Summertime

VITALE, Joe '81
Born in Dundalk, Maryland. Rock singer/drummer.

7/4/81	181	3			Plantation Harbor..			$12	Asylum 529

Bamboo Jungle   I'm Flyin'   Laugh-Laugh   Never Gonna Leave You Alone   Plantation Harbor
Cabin Weirdos, Theme From   Lady On The Rock   Man Gonna Love You   (Crazy 'Bout You Baby)   Sailor Man

VITAMIN C '00
Born Colleen Fitzpatrick on 7/20/72 in New Jersey. Former lead singer of Eve's Plum. Played "Amber Von Tussle" in the 1988 movie *Hairspray*.

9/18/99+	29	29	▲	©	1 Vitamin C..			$10	Elektra 62406
2/17/01	122	1		©	2 More..			$10	Elektra 62584

Where's The Party (2)
About Last Night (1)   Do What You Want To Do (1)   I Can't Say No (2)   Money (1)   **Smile** (1) 18
As Long As You're Loving Me   Fear Of Flying (1)   I Got You (1)   Not That Kind Of Girl (1)   Special (2)
(2)   Girls Against Boys (1)   I Know What Boys Like (2)   Real Life (1)   That Was Then, This Is Now (2)
Busted (2)   **Graduation (Friends Forever)**   **Itch, The** (2) 45   Sex Has Come Between Us (2)   Turn Me On (1)
Dangerous Girl (2)   (1) 38   Me, Myself And I (1)   She Talks About Love (2)   Unhappy Anniversary (1)

VITAMIN Z '85
Pop group from Sheffield, England: Geoff Barradale (vocals), Neil Hubbard and David Rhodes (guitars), Nick Lockwood (keyboards, bass) and Jerry Marotta (drums).

8/10/85	183	3			Rites Of Passage..			$10	Geffen 24057

Angela   **Burning Flame** 73   Circus Ring   Hi Hi Friend
Anybody Out There?   Casablanca   Every Time That I See You   Something We Can Do

VIXEN '89
Female hard-rock group formed in Los Angeles: Janet Gardner (vocals, guitar), Jan Kuehnemund (guitar), Share Pedersen (bass) and Roxy Petrucci (drums). Pedersen later joined **Contraband**.

10/1/88+	41	40	●	©	1 Vixen...			$10	EMI-Manhattan 46991
8/18/90	52	16		©	2 Rev It Up...			$10	EMI 92923

Waiting (1)
American Dream (1)   Desperate (1)   Hard 16 (2)   It Wouldn't Be Love (2)   One Night Alone (1)   Wrecking Ball (2)
Bad Reputation (2)   **Edge Of A Broken Heart**   Hellraisers (1)   **Love Is A Killer** (2) 71   Only A Heartbeat Away (2)
Cruisin' (1)   (1) 26   **How Much Love** (2) 44   Love Made Me (1)   Rev It Up (2)
Cryin' (1) 22   Fallen Hero (2)   I Want You To Rock Me (1)   Not A Minute Too Soon (2)   Streets In Paradise (2)

VOGUES, The '68
Vocal group formed in Turtle Creek, Pennsylvania: Bill Burkette, Hugh Geyer, Chuck Blasko and Don Miller.

2/12/66	137	7			1 Five O'Clock World..................................			$50	Co & Ce 1230
9/7/68	29	30			2 Turn Around, Look At Me			$20	Reprise 6314
2/15/69	30	23			3 Till...			$20	Reprise 6326
9/27/69	115	9			4 Memories...			$20	Reprise 6347
1/10/70	148	9			5 The Vogues' Greatest Hits.......................		[G]	$20	Reprise 6371

Come Into My Arms Again (2)   Humpty Dumpty (1)   Let's Hang On (1)   No Sun Today (2)   She Was Too Good To Me (3)   Till (3,5) 27
Dream Baby (How Long Must I   I Keep It Hid (2)   Love Is A Many-Splendored   On Broadway (3)   Since I Don't Have You (4)   Time After Time (4)
Dream) (2)   I Will (3)   Thing (4)   Once In A While (4)   So This Is Love (2)   **Turn Around, Look At Me**
Earth Angel (Will You Be   I'll Know My Love (By The Way   **Magic Town** (5) 21   One More Sunrise (1)   Standing On The Corner (4)   (2,5) 7
Mine) (4,5) 42   She Talks) (3)   Make The World Go Away (1)   Over And Over Again (1)   Sun Shines Out Of Your Shoes   **Woman Helping Man** (3,5) 47
Everyone's Gone To The Moon   I've Got My Eyes On You (3)   **Moments To Remember**   P.S. I Love You (4)   (3)   **You're The One** (5) 4
(1)   If I Loved You (4)   (4,5) 47   Run Baby Run (1)   Sunday And Me (1)
Five O'Clock World (1,5) 4   Impossible Dream (2)   **My Special Angel** (2,5) 7   See That Girl? (5)   Taste Of Honey (3)
Goodnight My Love (1)   It's Getting Better (2)   My Troubles Are Not At End (1)   Shangri-La (4)   Then (2)
Green Fields (5) 92   Just Say Goodbye (1)   **No, Not Much** (3,5) 34   She Is Today (2)   Thousand Miles Away (1)

VOICES OF EAST HARLEM, The '70
Black choir from Harlem, New York.

10/10/70	191	3			Right On Be Free..			$15	Elektra 74080

For What It's Worth   Let It Be Me   No No No   Proud Mary   Run Shaker Life
Gotta Be A Change   Music In The Air   Oh Yeah   Right On Be Free   Simple Song Of Freedom

VOIVOD '90
Hard-rock group from Jonquiere, Quebec: Denis Belanger (vocals), Denis D'Amour (guitar), Jean-Yves Theriault (bass) and Michel Langevin (drums).

12/16/89+	114	16		©	Nothingface..			$10	Mechanic 6326

Astronomy Domine   Into My Hypercube   Nothingface   Sub-Effect   X-Ray Mirror
Inner Combustion   Missing Sequence   Pre-Ignition   Unknown Knows

VOLLENWEIDER, Andreas '89
Born in 1953 in Zurich, Switzerland. Electro-acoustic harpist.

12/1/84+	121	18	●	©	1 ...Behind The Gardens-Behind The Wall-Under The Tree...		[I]	$10	CBS 37793
12/15/84+	149	15	●	©	2 Caverna Magica (...Under The Tree-In The Cave...)		[I]	$10	CBS 37827
3/2/85	76	39	●	©	3 White Winds...		[I]	$10	FM/CBS 39963
8/2/86	60	39	●	©	4 Down To The Moon...................................		[I]	$10	FM/CBS 42255
4/15/89	52	19		©	5 Dancing With The Lion		[I]	$10	Columbia 45154
2/29/92	117	5		©	6 Book Of Roses..		[I]	$10	Columbia 48601

VOLLENWEIDER, Andreas — Cont'd

Afternoon (1)
Ahgoh! (1)
And The Long Shadows (5)
Ascent From The Circle (5)
Behind The Gardens-Behind The Wall-Under The Tree (1)
Belladonna (2)
Birds Of Tilmun (6)
Book Of Roses (6)
Brothership (3)
Canopy Choir (medley) (2)
Caverna Magica (2)
Chanson De L'Heure Bleue (6)
Con Chiglia (medley) (2)
Czippa And The Ursanian Girl (6)

Dance Of The Masks (5)
Dancing With The Lion (5)
Down To The Moon (4)
Drown In Pale Light (4)
Five Curtains (6)
Five Planets (medley) (3)
Flight Feet & Root Hands (3)
Garden Of My Childhood (5)
Geastrum Coronatum (medley) (2)
Glass Hall (Choose The Crystal) (medley) (3)
Grand Ball Of The Duljas (6)
Hall Of The Mosaics (Meeting You) (medley) (3)
Hall Of The Stairs (medley) (3)

Hands And Clouds (1)
Hippolyte (5)
Hirzel (6)
Huiziopochtli (2)
Hush - Patience At Bamboo Forest (4)
In Doga Gamee (6)
In The Woods Of Kroandal (4)
Jours D'Amour (5)
Jugglers In Obsidian (6)
La Lune Et L'Enfant (4)
La Paix Verde (medley) (2)
La Strega (Her Journey To The Grand Ball) (6)
Letters To A Young Rose (6)
Lion And Sheep (1)

Lunar Pond (2)
Mandragora (2)
Manto's Arrow And The Sphinx (6)
Micro-Macro (1)
Moon Dance (4)
Moonlight, Wrapped Around Us (1)
Morning At Boma Park (6)
Night Fire Dance (4)
Passage To Promise (6)
Pearls & Tears (5)
Phases Of The Three Moons (3)
Play Of The Five Balls (medley) (3)

Pyramid-In The Wood-In The Bright Light (1)
Quiet Observer (4)
Schajah Saretosh (2)
Secret, The Candle, And Love (4)
See, My Love... (5)
Sena Stanjena? (2)
Silver Dew, Golden Grass (5)
Silver Wheel (4)
Sisterseed (4)
Skin And Skin (1)
Steam Forest (4)
Still Life (5)
Stone (Close-Up) (3)
Sunday (1)

Three Silver Ladies Dance (4)
Trilogy (At The Water Magic Gardens) (medley) (3)
Unto The Burning Circle (5)
Water Moon (4)
White Boat (First View) (medley) (3)
White Winds (medley) (3)
Woman And The Stone (3)

VOUDOURIS, Roger '79

Born on 12/29/54 in Sacramento, California. Pop singer/songwriter/guitarist.

| 7/7/79 | 171 | 3 | | | Radio Dream .... | | | $12 | Warner 3290 |

Anything From Anyone
Does Our Love (Depend On The Night)

Get Used To It 21
Just What It Takes
Next Time Around

Radio Dream
We Can't Stay Like This Forever

We Only Dance 'Cause We Have To

VOYAGE '78

Disco group from Europe: Sylvia Mason (vocals), Slim Pezin (guitar), Marc Chantereau (keyboards), Sauver Mallin (bass) and Pierre-Alain Dahan (drums).

| 4/8/78 | 40 | 21 | | | 1 Voyage .... | | | $12 | Marlin 2213 |
| 12/16/78+ | 47 | 27 | | | 2 Fly Away .... | | | $12 | Marlin 2225 |

Bayou Village (1)
Eastern Trip (2)
From East To West (1)

Golden Eldorado (2)
Gone With The Music (2)
Kechak Fantasy (2)

Lady America (1)
Latin Odyssey (1)
Let's Fly Away (2)

Orient Express (1)
Point Zero (1)
Scotch Machine (1)

Souvenirs (2) 41
Tahiti, Tahiti (2)

V.S.O.P. '77

All-star jazz group: **Herbie Hancock** (piano), **Freddie Hubbard** (trumpet), **Wayne Shorter** (sax), **Ron Carter** (bass) and **Tony Williams** (drums). V.S.O.P.: Very Special Onetime Performance.

| 11/12/77 | 123 | 5 | © | | The Quintet .... | | [I-L] | $15 | Columbia 34976 [2] |

Byrdlike
Darts

Dolores
Jessica

Lawra
Little Waltz

One Of A Kind
Third Plane

W

WAGNER, Jack '85

Born on 10/3/59 in Washington, Missouri. Actor/singer. Played "Frisco Jones" on the TV soap opera *General Hospital* (1983-87).

9/22/84+	44	29			1 All I Need.....................		[M]	$10	Qwest 25089
10/19/85	150	15			3 Lighting Up The Night			$10	Qwest 25318
5/2/87	151	8	©		2 Don't Give Up Your Day Job			$10	Qwest 25562

All I Need (1) 2
Back Home Again (3)
Common Man (3)
Easy Way Out (3)
I Never Said Goodbye (2)
I'll Be There (2)

If She Loves Like She Looks (2)
Island Fever (3)
It's Been A Long Time (3)
It's What We Don't Say (3)
Just Tell Her (2)
Keep Holdin' On (2)

Let's Start All Over (2)
Lighting Up The Night (2)
Love Can Take Us All The Way (2)
Love...Find It (3)
Lovers In The Night (3)

Make Me Believe It (1)
Premonition (1)
Sneak Attack (1)
Sneakin' Suspicions (3)
Tell Him (That You Won't Go) (1)

Too Young (2) 52
Weatherman Says (3) 67
With Your Eyes (2)

WAGONER, Porter '70

Born on 8/12/27 in West Plains, Missouri. Country singer. Hosted own TV variety show from 1960-79.

7/1/67	199	1			1 The Cold Hard Facts Of Life.....................			$20	RCA Victor 3797
3/15/69	161	8			2 The Carroll County Accident			$20	RCA Victor 4116
					PORTER WAGONER & DOLLY PARTON:				
3/22/69	184	4			3 Just The Two Of Us.....................			$20	RCA Victor 4039
8/16/69	162	5			4 Always, Always			$20	RCA Victor 4186
4/4/70	137	7			5 Porter Wayne And Dolly Rebecca			$20	RCA Victor 4305
5/16/70	190	2			6 You Got-ta Have A License			$20	RCA Victor 4286
					PORTER WAGONER				
10/10/70	191	2			7 Once More			$20	RCA Victor 4388
3/13/71	142	3	©		8 Two Of A Kind			$20	RCA Victor 4490

Afraid To Love Again (3)
All I Need Is You (8)
Always, Always (4)
Anything's Better Than Nothing (4)
Banks Of The Ohio (2)
Barefoot Nellie (2)
Before Our Weakness Gets Too Strong (7)
Black Jack's Bar (2)
Carroll County Accident (2) 92
Closer By The Hour (3)
Cold Hard Facts Of Life (1)
Curse Of The Wild Weed Flower (8)
Daddy Was An Old Time Preacher Man (3)
Dark End Of The Street (3)

Each Season Changes You (5)
Fairchild (6)
Fallen Leaves (2)
Fight And Scratch (7)
Fighting Kind (8)
First Mrs. Jones (1)
Flame, The (8)
Forty Miles From Poplar Bluff (5,6)
Good As Gold (4)
Good Understanding (7)
Holding On To Nothin' (3)
House Where Love Lives (4)
Hundred Dollar Funeral (1)
I Can (3)
I Don't Believe You've Met My Baby (4)
I Just Can't Let You Say Goodbye (1)

I Know You're Married But I Love You Still (7)
I Lived So Fast And Hard (2)
I Washed My Face In The Morning Dew (3)
I'll Get Ahead Some Day (1)
I'm Wasting Your Time And You're Wasting Mine (1)
If I Could Only Start Over (1)
Is It Real (8)
It Might As Well Be Me (5)
Jeannie's Afraid Of The Dark (3)
Julie (1)
Just Someone I Used To Know (5)
Just The Two Of Us (3)
King Of The Cannon County Hills (2)

Let's Live For Tonight (7)
Little Boy's Prayer (6)
Malena (4)
Mendy Never Sleeps (3)
Milwaukee, Here I Come (4)
My Hands Are Tied (4)
My Special Prayer Request (6)
No Love Left (5)
No Reason To Hurry Home (4)
Oh, The Pain Of Loving You (8)
Once More (7)
One Day At A Time (7)
Party, The (3)
Possum Holler (3)
Ragged Angel (7)
Rocky Top (2)
Roses Out Of Season (6)
Run That By Me One More Time (5)

Shopworn (1)
Silver Sandals (2)
Sing Me Back Home (2)
Sleep (1)
Slip Away Today (3)
Somewhere Between (3)
Sorrow Overtakes The Wine (2)
Southern Bound (6)
Stranger's Story (6)
There Never Was A Time (4)
There'll Be Love (8)
Thoughtfulness (7)
Today, Tomorrow And Forever (8)
Tomorrow Is Forever (5)
Tragic Romance (1)
Try Being Lonely (1)
Two Of A Kind (8)
Walk On Fool (6)

Way He Said Your Name (6)
We Can't Let This Happen To Us (5)
We'll Get Ahead Someday (3)
When You're Hot You're Hot (6)
Why Don't You Haul Off & Love Me (4)
Words And Music (1)
World Needs A Washin' (2)
You Got-ta Have A License (6)
Your Mother's Eyes (2)
Yours Love (4)

WAIKIKIS, The   '65
Instrumental group from Belgium.

| 1/16/65 | 93 | 9 | | | Hawaii Tattoo | | [I] | $20 | Kapp 3366 |

Aloha Parade   **Hawaii Tattoo** *33*   Honolulu Rag   I'll Remember Sweet Hawaii   Mauna Loa   Tahiti Tamoure
Carnival Of Venice   Hilo Kiss   Honolulu Rose   March Of The Beachcombers   Pacific Punch   Tiki Tiki Puka

WAILERS, The   '64
Group from Tacoma, Washington: John Greek and Rich Dangel (guitars), Mark Marush (sax), Kent Morrill (piano) and Mike Burk (drums).

| 6/27/64 | 127 | 6 | © | | Tall Cool One | | | $100 | Imperial 12262 |

Doin' The Seaside   Hokey   Louie Louie   Party Time U.S.A.   Shake Down   Tough Walk
Frenzy   Isabella   Mashi   Seattle   Tall Cool One   We're Going Surfin'

WAILERS, The — see MARLEY, Bob

WAINWRIGHT, Loudon III   '73
Born on 9/5/46 in Chapel Hill, North Carolina. Folk singer/songwriter/guitarist. Father of **Rufus Wainwright**.

3/3/73	102	13	©	1	Album III			$15	Columbia 31462
3/15/75	156	5	©	2	Unrequited			$15	Columbia 33369
6/19/76	188	4		3	T Shirt			$12	Arista 4063

Absence Makes The Heart   **Dead Skunk** (1) *16*   Just Like President Thieu (3)   New Paint (1)   Say That You Love Me (1)   Unrequited To The Nth Degree
  Grow Fonder (3)   Drinking Song (1)   Kick In The Head (2)   Old Friend (2)   Smokey Joe's Cafe (1)   (2)
At Both Ends (3)   East Indian Princess (1)   Kings And Queens (2)   On The Rocks (2)   Summer's Almost Over (3)   Untitled (2)
B Side (1)   Guru (2)   Lowly Tourist (2)   Prince Hal's Dirge (3)   Sweet Nothings (2)   Whatever Happened To Us (2)
Bicentennial (3)   Hey Packy (3)   Mr. Guilty (2)   Reciprocity (3)   Talking Big Apple '75 (3)   Wine With Dinner (3)
California Prison Blues (3)   Hollywood Hopeful (3)   Muse Blues (1)   Red Guitar (1)   Trilogy (Circa 1967) (1)
Crime Of Passion (2)   Hometeam Crowd (1)   Needless To Say (1)   Rufus Is A Tit Man (2)

WAINWRIGHT, Rufus   '01
Born in 1974 in Montreal. Singer/songwriter. Son of **Loudon Wainwright III**.

| 6/23/01 | 117 | 1 | © | | Poses | | | $10 | DreamWorks 450237 |

California   Consort, The (1)   Greek Song   In A Graveyard   Poses   Shadows
Cigarettes And Chocolate Milk   Evil Angel   Grey Gardens   One Man Guy   Rebel Prince   Tower Of Learning

WAITE, John   '84
Born on 7/4/55 in Lancashire, England. Lead singer of **The Babys** and **Bad English**.

7/17/82	68	23	©	1	Ignition			$12	Chrysalis 1376
7/14/84	10	43	● ©	2	No Brakes			$10	EMI America 17124
8/31/85	36	16	©	3	Mask Of Smiles			$10	EMI America 17164
7/11/87	77	12	©	4	Rover's Return			$10	EMI America 17227

Act Of Love (4)   Desperate Love (1)   Going To The Top (1)   **Missing You** (2) *1*   Sometimes (4)   Wild Life (1)
Ain't That Peculiar (3)   **Don't Lose Any Sleep** (4) *81*   I'm Still In Love (1)   Mr. Wonderful (1)   **Tears** (2) *37*   Wild One (4)
Be My Baby Tonight (1)   Dreamtime (medley) (2)   Just Like Lovers (3)   No Brakes (3)   Temptation (1)   Woman's Touch (4)
Big Time For Love (4)   Encircled (4)   Laydown (3)   **Restless Heart** (2) *59*   These Times Are Hard For   You're The One (3)
Change (1) *54*   Euroshima (2)   Love Collision (2)   Saturday Night (2)   Lovers (4) *53*
Choice, The (3)   **Every Step Of The Way** (3) *25*   Lust For Life (3)   Shake It Up (medley) (2)   Welcome To Paradise (3) *85*
Dark Side Of The Sun (2)   For Your Love (2)   Make It Happen (1)   She's The One (4)   White Heat (1)

WAITRESSES, The   '82
Pop-rock group from Akron, Ohio: Patty Donahue (vocals), Chris Butler (guitar), Dan Klayman (keyboards), Mars Williams (sax), Tracy Wormworth (bass) and Billy Ficca (drums; Television). Donahue died of cancer on 12/9/96 (age 40).

2/6/82	41	24		1	Wasn't Tomorrow Wonderful?			$10	Polydor 6346
12/18/82+	128	10		2	I Could Rule The World If I Could Only Get The Parts		[M]	$10	Polydor 507
6/4/83	155	5		3	Bruiseology			$10	Polydor 810980

Bread And Butter (2)   Go On (1)   Jimmy Tomorrow (1)   Pussy Strut (1)   They're All Out Of Liquor, Let's
Bruiseology (3)   Heat Night (1)   Luxury (3)   Quit (1)   Find Another Party (3)
Christmas Wrapping (2)   I Could Rule The World If I   Make The Weather (3)   Redland (1)   Thinking About Sex Again (3)
Everything's Wrong If My Hair Is   Could Only Get The Parts (2)   No Guilt (1)   Smartest Person I Know (2)   Wasn't Tomorrow Wonderful?
  Wrong (3)   **I Know What Boys Like** (1) *62*   Open City (3)   Spin (3)   (1)
Girl's Gotta Do (3)   It's My Car (1)   Pleasure (3)   Square Pegs (2)   Wise Up (1)

WAITS, Tom   '99
Born on 12/7/49 in Pomona, California. Gravelly-voiced song stylist/actor. Appeared in several movies.
1)Mule Variations 2)Small Change 3)Heartattack And Vine

11/29/75	164	6	©	1	Nighthawks At The Diner		[L]	$15	Asylum 2008 [2]
11/6/76	89	5	©	2	Small Change			$12	Asylum 1078
10/22/77	113	8	©	3	Foreign Affairs			$12	Asylum 1117
11/18/78	181	4	©	4	Blue Valentine			$12	Asylum 162
10/4/80	96	10	©	5	Heartattack And Vine			$12	Asylum 295
10/29/83	167	7	©	6	Swordfishtrombones			$10	Island 90095
11/16/85	181	7	©	7	Rain Dogs			$10	Island 90299
9/26/87	115	10	©	8	Franks Wild Years			$10	Island 90572
10/8/88	152	6	©	9	Big Time		[L]	$10	Island 90987
9/26/92	176	3	©	10	Bone Machine			$10	Island 512580
11/20/93	130	2	©	11	The Black Rider			$10	Island 518559
5/15/99	30	9	©	12	Mule Variations			$10	Epitaph 86547

All Stripped Down (10)   Black Rider (11)   Cemetery Polka (7)   Dave The Butcher (6)   Eyeball Kid (12)   Gospel Train (11)
Anywhere I Lay My Head (7)   Black Wings (10)   Chocolate Jesus (12)   Diamonds & Gold (7)   Falling Down (9)   Gun Street Girl (7,9)
Bad Liver And A Broken Heart   Blind Love (7)   Christmas Card From A Hooker   Dirt In The Ground (10)   Filipino Box Spring Hog (12)   Hang Down Your Head (7)
  (2)   Blow Wind Blow (8)   In Minneapolis (4)   Down, Down, Down (6)   Flash Pan Hunter (11)   Hang On St. Christopher (8)
Barber Shop (3)   Blue Valentines (4)   Cinny's Waltz (3)   Downtown (5)   Foreign Affair (3)   Heartattack And Vine (5)
Better Off Without A Wife (1)   Briar And The Rose (11)   Clap Hands (7)   Downtown Train (7)   Frank's Wild Years (6)   Hold On (12)
Big Black Mariah (7,9)   Bride Of Rain Dog (7)   Cold Cold Ground (8,9)   Earth Died Screaming (10)   Franks Theme (8)   House Where Nobody Lives
Big In Japan (12)   Burma Shave (3)   Cold Water (12)   Eggs And Sausage (In A   Georgia Lee (12)   (12)
Big Joe And Phantom 309 (1)   California Here I Come   Come On Up To The House   Cadillac With Susan   Get Behind The Mule (12)   I Can't Wait To Get Off Work (2)
Black Box Theme (11)   (medley) (3)   (12)   Michelson) (1)   Gin Soaked Boy (6)   I Don't Wanna Grow Up (10)
Black Market Baby (12)   Carnival (11)   Crossroads (11)   Emotional Weather Report (1)   Goin' Out West (10)   I Never Talk To Strangers (3)

927

WAITS, Tom — Cont'd

I Wish I Was In New Orleans (2)
I'll Be Gone (8)
I'll Shoot The Moon (11)
I'll Take New York (8)
In Shades (5)
In The Colosseum (10)
In The Neighborhood (4)
Innocent When You Dream (8)
Invitation To The Blues (2)
Jack & Neal (medley) (3)
Jersey Girl (5)
Jesus Gonna Be Here (10)
Jitterbug Boy (2)
Jockey Full Of Bourbon (7)
Johnsburg, Illinois (6)

Just Another Sucker On The Vine (6)
Just The Right Bullets (11)
Kentucky Avenue (4)
Last Rose Of Summer (11)
Let Me Get Up On It (10)
Little Rain (10)
Lowside Of The Road (12)
Lucky Day (11)
Midtown (7)
More Than Rain (8)
Mr. Siegal (5)
Murder In The Red Barn (10)
Muriel (5)
Nighthawk Postcards (From Easy Street) (1)
9th & Hennepin (7)

Nobody (2)
November (11)
Ocean Doesn't Want Me (10)
Oily Night (11)
On A Foggy Night (1)
On The Nickel (11)
One That Got Away (2)
Pasties And A G-String (2)
Piano Has Been Drinking (2)
Picture In A Frame (12)
Please Wake Me Up (8)
Pony (12)
Potter's Field (3)
Putnam County (1)
Rain Dogs (7,9)
Rainbirds (4)
Red Shoes (9)

Red Shoes By The Drugstore (4)
Romeo Is Bleeding (4)
Ruby's Arms (5)
Russian Dance (11)
Saving All My Love For You (5)
Shore Leave (6)
Sight For Sore Eyes (3)
Singapore (7)
16 Shells From A Thirty-Ought-Six (6,9)
Small Change (7)
Soldier's Things (6)
Somewhere (4)
Spare Parts I & II (1)
Step Right Up (2)
Straight To The Top (8)

Strange Weather (9)
Such A Scream (10)
Sweet Little Bullet From A Pretty Blue Gun (4)
Swordfishtrombone (6)
T'Ain't No Sin (11)
Take It With Me (12)
Tango Till They're Sore (7)
Telephone Call From Istanbul (8,9)
Temptation (8)
That Feel (10)
That's The Way (11)
'Til The Money Runs Out (5)
Time (7,9)
Tom Traubert's Blues (2)
Town With No Cheer (6)

Train Song (8,9)
Trouble's Braids (6)
$29.00 (4)
Underground (6)
Union Square (7)
Walking Spanish (7)
Warm Beer And Cold Women (1)
Way Down In The Hole (8,9)
What's He Building? (12)
Whistle Down The Wind (10)
Whistlin' Past The Graveyard (4)
Who Are You (10)
Wrong Side Of The Road (4)
Yesterday Is Here (8)

WAKEMAN, Rick   '74

Born on 5/18/49 in London. Rock keyboardist. Member of **Strawbs** and **Yes**.

DEBUT	PEAK	WKS		CD	ARTIST — Album Title	Sym	$	Label & Number
3/24/73	30	45	●	©	1 **The Six Wives Of Henry VIII**	[I]	$12	A&M 4361
6/15/74	3	27	●	©	2 **Journey To The Centre Of The Earth**	[L]	$12	A&M 3621
					recorded on 1/18/74 at the Royal Festival Hall			
4/19/75	21	15		©	3 **The Myths and Legends of King Arthur and the Knights of the Round Table**		$12	A&M 4515
5/15/76	67	8			4 **No Earthly Connection**		$12	A&M 4583
2/26/77	126	7			5 **White Rock**	[I-S]	$12	A&M 4614
12/17/77+	128	8			6 **Rick Wakeman's Criminal Record**	[I]	$12	A&M 4660
7/21/79	170	5			7 **Rhapsodies**	[I]	$15	A&M 6501 [2]

After The Ball (5)
Animal Showdown (Yes We Have No Bananas) (7)
Anne Boleyn 'The Day Thou Gavest Lord Hath Ended' (1)
Anne Of Cleves (7)
Arthur (7)
Battle, The (2)
Big Ben (7)

Birdman Of Alcatraz (6)
Bombay Duck (7)
Breathalyser, The (6)
Catherine Howard (1)
Catherine Of Aragon (1)
Catherine Parr (1)
Chamber Of Horrors (6)
Crime Of Passion (6)
Flacons De Neige (7)
Flasher, The (7)

Forest, The (2)
Front Line (7)
Guinevere (3)
Half Holiday (7)
Ice Run (5)
Jane Seymour (1)
Journey, The (2)
Judas Iscariot (6)
Lady Of The Lake (3)
Last Battle (3)

Lax'x (5)
Loser, The (5)
Lost Cycle (4)
March Of The Gladiators (7)
Merlin The Magician (3)
Montezuma's Revenge (5)
Music Reincarnate Medley (4)
Palais (7)
Pedra Da Gavea (7)
Prisoner, The (4)

Pulse, The (7)
Recollection (2)
Rhapsody In Blue (7)
Sea Horses (7)
Searching For Gold (5)
Shoot, The (5)
Sir Galahad (3)
Sir Lancelot And The Black Knight (3)
Stand-By (7)

Statue Of Justice (6)
Summertime (7)
Swan Lager (7)
White Rock (5)
Wooly Willy Tango (7)

WALDEN, Narada Michael   '80

Born Michael Walden on 4/23/52 in Kalamazoo, Michigan. R&B singer/songwriter/drummer/producer. With **John McLaughlin**'s Mahavishnu Orchestra from 1974-76.

DEBUT	PEAK	WKS		CD	ARTIST — Album Title		$	Label & Number
3/10/79	103	16		©	1 **Awakening**		$12	Atlantic 19222
1/5/80	74	19		©	2 **The Dance Of Life**		$12	Atlantic 19259
10/18/80	103	8			3 **Victory**		$12	Atlantic 19279
6/5/82	135	6			4 **Confidence**		$12	Atlantic 19351

Alone Without You (3)
Awakening, The (1)
Awakening Suite Part I (1)
Blue Side Of Midnight (4)
Carry On (2)
Confidence (4)

Crazy For Ya (2)
Dance Of Life (2)
Full & Satisfied (1)
Get Up! (3)
Give Your Love A Chance (1)
Holiday (4)

I Don't Want Nobody Else (To Dance With You) (1) 47
I Shoulda Loved Ya (2) 66
I Want You (3)
I'm Ready (4)
Listen To Me (1)

Love Me Only (1)
Lovin' You Madly (2)
Lucky Fella (3)
Real Thang (3)
Safe In My Arms (4)
Summer Lady (4)

Take It To The Bossman (3)
They Want The Feeling (1)
Tonight I'm Alright (2)
Victory Suite Medley (3)
Why Did You Turn Me On (2)
Will You Ever Know (1)

You Ought To Love Me (4)
You Will Find Your Way (3)
You're #1 (4)
You're Soo Good (2)

WALKER, Clay   '97

Born on 8/19/69 in Beaumont, Texas. Country singer/songwriter/guitarist.

DEBUT	PEAK	WKS	RIAA	CD	ARTIST — Album Title	Sym	$	Label & Number
9/4/93+	52	57	▲	©	1 **Clay Walker**		$10	Giant 24511
10/15/94+	42	43	▲	©	2 **If I Could Make A Living**		$10	Giant 24582
11/4/95	57	34	▲	©	3 **Hypnotize The Moon**		$10	Giant 24640
4/26/97	32	46	▲	©	4 **Rumor Has It**		$10	Giant 24674
6/27/98	41	19	●	©	5 **Greatest Hits**	[G]	$10	Giant 24700
9/11/99	55	21	●	©	6 **Live, Laugh, Love**		$10	Giant 24717
4/14/01	129	3		©	7 **Say No More**		$10	Giant 24759

Boogie Till The Cows Come Home (2)
Bury The Shovel (3)
Chain Of Love (6) 40
Cold Hearted (7)
Could I Ask You Not To Dance (7)
Country Boy And City Girl (4)
Cowboy's Toughest Ride (4)
Down By The Riverside (2)
Dreaming With My Eyes Open (1,5)
Hand Me Down Heart (3)
Heart Over Head Over Heels (4)

Heartache Highway (2)
Holding Her And Loving You (6)
How To Make A Man Lonesome (1)
Hypnotize The Moon (3,5)
I Don't Know How Love Starts (1)
I Love It (7)
I Need A Margarita (4)
I Won't Have The Heart (3)
I'd Say That's Right (4)
If A Man Ain't Thinking ('Bout His Woman) (6)
If I Could Make A Living (2,5)

If You Ever Feel Like Lovin' Me Again (7)
It Ain't Called Heartland (For Nothin') (6)
La Bamba (5)
Let Me Take The Heartache (Off Your Hands) (3)
Live, Laugh, Love (6) 74
Live Until I Die (1,5)
Lose Some Sleep Tonight (6)
Lose Your Memory (2)
Love Me Like You Love Me (3)
Loving You Comes Naturally To Me (3)

Melrose Avenue Cinema Two (2)
Money Ain't Everything (2)
Money Can't Buy (The Love We Had) (1)
My Heart Will Never Know (2)
Next Step In Love (1)
Once In A Lifetime Love (6)
One, Two, I Love You (4)
Only On Days That End In "Y" (3,5)
Ordinary People (5)
Real (7)
Rough Around The Edges (7)
Rumor Has It (4,5)

Say No More (7)
She's Always Right (6) 74
She's Easy To Hold (7)
Silence Speaks For Itself (1)
So Much More (7)
Texas Swing (7)
That's Us (4)
Then What (4,5) 65
Things I Should Have Said (1)
This Time Love (6)
This Woman And This Man (2,5)
Watch This (4,5)
What Do You Want For Nothin' (2)

What's It To You (1,5) 73
Where Do I Fit In The Picture (1,5)
Where Were You (3)
White Palace (1)
Who Needs You Baby (3,5)
Woman Thing (6)
You Deliver Me (7)
You Make It Look So Easy (2)
You'll Never Hear The End Of It (4)
You're Beginning To Get To Me (5) 39

WALKER, David T.   '76

Born in Los Angeles. R&B singer/songwriter/guitarist. Member of **Paul Humphrey's Cool Aid Chemists** and **Afrique**.

DEBUT	PEAK	WKS			ARTIST — Album Title	Sym	$	Label & Number
2/9/74	187	8			1 **Press On**	[I]	$12	Ode 77020
9/4/76	166	5			2 **On Love**		$12	Ode 77035

Brother, Brother (1)
Didn't I Blow Your Mind This Time (1)
Feeling Feeling (2)
I Get High On You (2)

I Got Work To Do (1)
I Who Have Nothing (1)
I Wish You Love (2)
If That's The Way You Feel (1)
If You Let Me (1)

Kinda Sorta (2)
Let Me In Your Life (2)
Lovin' You (2)
On Love (2)
Our Lives (2)

Press On (1)
Save You Love For Me (1)
Superstition (1)
Windows Of The World (2)

With A Little Help From My Friends (1)
Work To Do ..see: I Got Work To Do

WALKER, Hezekiah '99
Born in 1962 in Brooklyn, New York. Pastor of the Love Fellowship Church in Brooklyn.

6/7/97	182	2		© 1	**Live In London At Wembley** .... [L]	$10	Verity 43023
					recorded on 11/15/96		
11/27/99	151	2		© 2	**Family Affair**	$10	Verity 43132

HEZEKIAH WALKER & THE LOVE FELLOWSHIP CRUSADE CHOIR (above 2)

Ain't Nobody Like Jesus (2)
Finally (2)
Get On Up (medley) (1)
Give'em Your Life (2)
He Can (2)
Hold Out (1)
I Can Make It (medley) (1)
I'm Waiting (1)
I've Got A Reason (Draper's Legacy) (2)
It Shall Come To Pass (1)
Jesus Is My Help (1)
Job's Song (Blessed) (1)
Let's Dance (2)
More Like Him (2)
Never Leave Me Alone (2)
Oh I Feel Jesus (2)
Oh My Brother, Be Encouraged (1)
Patiently Waiting (2)
Power Belongs To God (2)
To Be Like Jesus (1)
Try Christ (1)
We've Got The Victory (1)
Will Of God (2)
Wonderful Is Your Name (2)

WALKER, Jerry Jeff '77
Born Ronald Clyde Crosby on 3/16/42 in Oneonta, New York. Country-rock singer/songwriter.

12/15/73+	160	11	●	© 1	**Viva Terlingua!**	$12	MCA 382
1/11/75	141	8		2	**Walker's Collectibles**	$12	MCA 450
10/4/75	119	7		© 3	**Ridin' High**	$12	MCA 2156
7/4/76	84	10		4	**It's A Good Night For Singin'**	$12	MCA 2202
5/28/77	60	21		© 5	**A Man Must Carry On**	$15	MCA 6003 [2]
7/1/78	111	9		6	**Contrary To Ordinary**	$12	MCA 3041
7/19/80	185	3		7	**The Best Of Jerry Jeff Walker** .... [G]	$12	MCA 5128
6/20/81	188	3		8	**Reunion**	$12	SouthCoast 5199

Backsliders Wine (1)
Bittersweet (8)
Carry Me Away (6)
Contrary To Ordinary (6)
Couldn't Do Nothin' Right (4)
Dear John Letter Lounge (4)
Deeper Than Love (6)
Derby Day (5)
Desperados Waiting For The Train (1,7)
Don't It Make You Wanna Dance? (1)
First Showboat (2)
For Little Jessie (She Knows Her Daddy Sings) (8)
Get It Out (1)
Gettin' By (1,7)
Goodbye Easy Street (3)
Got Lucky Last Night (8)
Head Full Of Nothin' (4)
Hill Country Rain (7)
His Heart Was So Full Of Mischief (5)
Honky Tonk Music (5)
I Like To Sleep Late In The Morning (2)
I Love You (3,7)
I Spent All My Money Lovin' You (5)
It Shall Be A Midnight Music (5)
It's A Good Night For Singing (4)
Jaded Lover (3)
L.A. Freeway (5,7) *98*
Leavin' Texas (5,7)
Leroy (4)
Like A Coat From The Cold (3)
Like Some Song You Can't Unlearn (5)
Little Bird (4)
London Homesick Blues (1)
Long Afternoons (5)
(Looking For) The Heart Of Saturday Night (4)
Luckenbach Moon (5)
Maybe Mexico (8)
Mississippi You're On My Mind (5)
Morning Song To Sally (8)
Mr. Bojangles (5,7) *77*
My Buddy (5)
My Old Man (2)
Night Rider's Lament (3)
O.D. Corral (2)
Old Five And Dimers Like Me (4)
One Too Many Mornings (5)
Pick Up The Tempo (3,8)
Pissin' In The Wind (3)
Pot Can't Call The Kettle Black (3,7)
Public Domain (3)
Railroad Lady (5)
Rock Me Roll Me (2)
Rockin' Chair (5)
Ro-Deo-Deo Cowboy (5)
Roll On Down The Road (5)
Sailing (8)
Salvation Army Band (2)
Sangria Wine (1,7)
Saturday Night Special (6)
Sea Cruise Medley (5)
She Left Me Holdin' (2,8)
Some Day I'll Get Out Of These Bars (4)
Some Go Home (The Train Song) (8)
Song For The Life (5)
Standin' At The Big Hotel (4)
Stereo Chickens (5)
Stoney (4)
Stranger (He Was The Kind) (5)
Suckin' A Big Bottle Of Gin (6)
Takin' It As It Comes (6)
Till I Gain Control Again (6)
Tryin' To Hold The Wind Up With A Sail (6)
Up Against The Wall Red Neck (1,5,7)
Very Short Time (4)
We Were Kinda Crazy Then (6)
Well Of The Blues (2)
What Are We Doing? (6)
Wheel (1)
Will The Circle Be Unbroken? (5)
Will There Be Any (2)
Wingin' It Home To Texas (2)
Won't You Give Me One More Chance (4)

WALKER, Jimmie '75
Born on 6/25/49 in New York City. Actor/comedian. Played "J.J. Evans" on TV's *Good Times*.

5/31/75	130	12			**Dyn-O-Mite** .... [C]	$12	Buddah 5635

Apollo, The
Autographs
Black Prince Has Arrived
Caucasians And Other White Folk
Ghetto, The
Great Black Myth
Prince And The Public
Progress
S-Cool Daze
Show Biz
Suburbia

WALKER, Jr., & The All Stars '69
Born Autry DeWalt Walker on 6/14/31 in Blythesville, Arkansas. Died of cancer on 11/23/95 (age 64). R&B singer/saxophonist. The All Stars: Willie Woods (guitar), Vic Thomas (keyboards) and James Graves (drums). Woods died on 5/27/97 (age 60).
1)Greatest Hits 2)Road Runner 3)Rainbow Funk

7/10/65	108	35		© 1	**Shotgun**	$50	Soul 701
4/9/66	130	7		2	**Soul Session** .... [I]	$50	Soul 702
9/3/66	64	13		© 3	**Road Runner**	$50	Soul 703
10/7/67	119	11		© 4	**"Live!"** .... [L]	$50	Soul 705
					includes "Heart Break" by Earl Van Dyke		
2/8/69	172	4		© 5	**Home Cookin'**	$40	Soul 710
6/28/69	43	18		6	**Greatest Hits** .... [G]	$40	Soul 718
1/17/70	92	22		7	**What Does It Take To Win Your Love**	$40	Soul 721
10/3/70	110	5		8	**A Gasssss**	$25	Soul 726
7/24/71	91	14		9	**Rainbow Funk**	$25	Soul 732
1/8/72	142	16		10	**Moody Jr.**	$25	Soul 733

Ain't That The Truth (1)
Ame' Cherie (Soul Darling) (3,4,7)
And When I Die (8)
Anyway You Wannta' (3)
At A Saturday Matinee (8)
Baby Ain't You Shame (5)
Baby You Know You Ain't Right (3)
Brainwasher (2)
Bristol's Way (10)
Carry Your Own Load (8)
Cleo's Back (1,4) *43*
Cleo's Mood (1,6,7) *50*
Clinging To The Thought That She's Coming Back (7)
Come See About Me (5,6) *24*
Decidedly (2)
Do The Boomerang (1) *36*
Do You See My Love (For You Growing) (8) *32*
Don't Blame The Children (10)
Eight Hour Drag (2)
Everybody Get Together (2)
Fanny Mae (5)
Feeling Alright (9)
Good Rockin' (2)
Gotta Hold On To This Feeling (7) *21*
Groove And Move (8)
Groove Thang (10)
Hewbie Steps Out (2)
Hey Jude (8)
Hip City - Pt. 1 (5)
Hip City - Pt. 2 (5,6) *31*
Holly Holy (8) *75*
Home Cookin (5,6) *42*
Honey Come Back (8)
Hot Cha (1,4,7)
How Sweet It Is (To Be Loved By You) (3,4,6,7) *18*
I Don't Want To Do Wrong (10)
I Was Made To Love Her (8)
(I'm A) Road Runner (1,3,4,6) *20*
I've Got To Find A Way To Win Maria Back (7)
Last Call (3)
Mark Anthony (Speaks) (2)
Me And My Family (10)
Money (That's What I Want) Part 1 (5) *52*
Monkey Jump (1)
Moody Junior (10)
Moonlight In Vermont (2,4)
Mutiny (3)
Never Can Say Goodbye (10)
Pieces Of A Man (9)
Proud Mary (7)
Psychedelic Shack (9)
Pucker Up Buttercup (3,6) *31*
Riding High On Love (8)
Right On Brothers And Sisters (9)
San-Ho-Zay (3,7)
Satan's Blues (2)
Shake And Fingerpop (1,4,6) *29*
Shake Everything (2)
Shoot Your Shot (1,6) *44*
Shotgun (1,4,6) *4*
Shut Up, Don't Interrupt Me (8)
Something (8)
Still Water Medley (10)
Sweet Daddy Deacon (5)
Sweet Soul (5,7)
Take Me Girl, I'm Ready (9) *50*
Tally Ho (1)
Teach Them To Pray (9)
These Eyes (7) *16*
These Things Will Keep Me Loving You (9)
Things I Do For You (5)
Three Four Three (2)
Tune Up (1,4)
Twist Lackawanna (3)
Us (2)
Walk In The Night (10) *46*
Way Back Home (9,10) *52*
What Does It Take (To Win Your Love) (5,6,7) *4*

WALKER, Tommy '01
Born in Los Angeles. Christian singer/songwriter/guitarist.

1/27/01	153	1		©	**Never Gonna Stop**	$10	Hosanna! 1846

Give Us The Sounds
He Knows My Name
He Saved Us To Show His Glory
How Could I But Love You
How Good And Pleasant
I Fix My Eyes On You
I Hide Myself In Thee
Jerry's Story
Jesus, That Name
Let's Think About Our God
Never Gonna Stop
Only A God Like You
When All Is Said And Done
Where You Are

WALLACE, Jerry — '64
Born on 12/15/28 in Guilford, Missouri; raised in Glendale, Arizona. Pop-country singer/guitarist.

| 11/7/64 | 96 | 7 | | | 1 **In The Misty Moonlight** | | | $25 | Challenge 619 |
| 3/3/73 | 179 | 8 | | | 2 **Do You Know What It's Like To Be Lonesome?** | | | $15 | MCA 301 |

Am I That Easy To Forget (1) — Do You Know What It's Like To — Greatest Feeling (2) — Move Over (When True Love Walks By) (1) — There She Goes (1) 26 — You'll Never Know (1)
Angel On My Shoulder (1) — Be Lonesome? (2) — Hot Line (2) — Until You (2)
Auf Wiedersehen (1) — Empty Arms Again (1) — In The Misty Moonlight (1) 19 — Song That Nobody Sings (2) — Where Did He Come From?
(Ballad Of Hec Ramsey) ..see: — Even The Bad Times Are Good — Just Walkin' In The Rain (1) — Sound Of Goodbye (2) — (The Ballad Of Hec Ramsey)
Where Did He Come From? — (1,2) — Love Song Of The Year (2) — Standing Ovation (2) — (2)

WALLER, Robert James — '93
Born in 1939 in Rockford, Iowa. Novelist/songwriter/singer/guitarist.

| 8/28/93 | 200 | 1 | | © | **The Ballads Of Madison County** | | | $10 | Atlantic 82511 |

Autumn Leaves (Les Feuilles — Dutchman, The — Idaho Rain — Rollin' Out Of Roanoke — Tangerine
Mortes) — Girl From The North Country — Madison County Waltz — (medley) — Wabash Cannonball (medley)
Blue Suspenders — Golden Apples Of The Sun — Steamer

WALLFLOWERS, The — '97
Pop-rock group: Jakob Dylan (vocals), Michael Ward (guitar), Rami Jaffe (keyboards), Greg Richling (bass) and Mario Calire (drums). Dylan is the son of **Bob Dylan**.

| 7/20/96+ | 4 | 98 | ▲⁴ | © | 1 **Bringing Down The Horse** | C:#21/10 | | $10 | Interscope 90055 |
| 10/28/00 | 13 | 15 | ● | © | 2 **(Breach)** | | | $10 | Interscope 490745 |

Angel On My Bike (1) — God Don't Make Lonely Girls (1) — Invisible City (1) — Mourning Train (2) — **Sleepwalker** (2) 73 — Witness (2)
Birdcage (1) — Hand Me Down (2) — Josephine (1) — Murder (1) — Some Flowers Bloom Dead (2)
Bleeders (1) — I Wish I Felt Nothing (1) — Laughing Out Loud (1) — One Headlight (1) — Three Marlenas (1)
Difference, The (1) — I've Been Delivered (2) — Letters From The Wasteland (2) — 6th Avenue Heartache (1) — Up From Under (2)

WALL OF VOODOO — '83
Electronic-rock group formed in Los Angeles: **Stan Ridgway** (vocals), Marc Moreland (guitar), Chas Gray (bass) and Joe Nanini (drums).

| 10/17/81 | 177 | 2 | | © | 1 **Dark Continent** | | | $12 | I.R.S. 70022 |
| 1/15/83 | 45 | 23 | | © | 2 **Call Of The West** | | | $12 | I.R.S. 70026 |

Animal Day (1) — Crack The Bell (1) — Hands Of Love (2) — **Mexican Radio** (2) 58 — They Don't Want Me (1) — Two Minutes Till Lunch (1)
Back In Flesh (1) — Factory (2) — Look At Their Way (2) — On Interstate 15 (2) — This Way Out (1)
Call Box (1-2-3) (1) — Full Of Tension (1) — Lost Weekend (2) — Red Light (1) — Tomorrow (1)
Call Of The West (2) — Good Times (1) — Me And My Dad (1) — Spy World (2) — Tse Tse Fly (1)

★331★ WALSH, Joe — '73
Born on 11/20/47 in Wichita, Kansas. Rock singer/songwriter/guitarist. Member of **The James Gang** and the **Eagles**.
1)The Smoker You Drink, The Player You Get 2)But Seriously, Folks... 3)So What

10/21/72+	79	29		©	1 **Barnstorm**			$15	Dunhill/ABC 50130
6/23/73	6	54	●	©	2 **The Smoker You Drink, The Player You Get**			$15	Dunhill/ABC 50140
1/4/75	11	22	●	©	3 **So What**			$15	Dunhill/ABC 50171
4/10/76	20	18			4 **You Can't Argue With A Sick Mind**		[L]	$12	ABC 932
6/10/78	8	27	▲	©	5 **But Seriously, Folks...**			$12	Asylum 141
10/28/78	71	7		©	6 **The Best Of Joe Walsh**		[G]	$12	ABC 1083
5/23/81	20	18		©	7 **There Goes The Neighborhood**			$10	Asylum 523
7/9/83	48	14			8 **You Bought It-You Name It**			$10	Warner 23884
6/1/85	65	19		©	9 **The Confessor**			$10	Warner 25281
8/1/87	113	8		©	10 **Got Any Gum?**			$10	Warner 25606
5/18/91	112	17		©	11 **Ordinary Average Guy**			$10	Pyramid 47384

All-Night Laundry-Mat Blues (3) — Dear John (9) — Here We Go (1) — Love Letters (8) — Rivers (Of The Hidden Funk) — Told You So (8)
All Of A Sudden (11) — Down On The Farm (7) — Home (1) — Made Your Mind Up (7) — (7) — Tomorrow (5)
Alphabetical Order (11) — Dreams (2) — "I.L.B.T.'s" (8) — Malibu (10) — Rockets (1) — **Turn To Stone** (1,3,4,6) 93
At The Station (5) — Falling Down (3) — I Broke My Leg (9) — Meadows (2,4,6) 89 — **Rocky Mountain Way** — Two Sides To Every Story (11)
Birdcall Morning (1) — 15 Years (9) — I Can Play That Rock & Roll (8) — Memory Lane (10) — (2,4,6) 23 — Up All Night (11)
Boat Weirdos, Theme From (5) — Fun (10) — I'll Tell The World About You (1) — Midnight Moodies (2) — Rosewood Bitters (9) — Up To Me (10)
Bones (7) — **Funk #49** (6) 59 — I'm Actin' Different (11) — Midnight Visitor (1) — School Days (11) — Welcome To The Club (3)
Book Ends (2) — Gamma Goochee (11) — In My Car (10) — Mother Says (1,6) — Second Hand Store (5) — Where I Grew Up (Prelude To
Bubbles (9) — Giant Bohemoth (1) — Indian Summer (5) — No Peace In The Jungle (10) — Shadows (8) — School Days) (11)
Class Of '65 (8) — Good Man Down (9) — Inner Tube (3) — One And One (1) — Slow Dancing (9) — Wolf (2)
Comin' Down (1) — Got Any Gum? (10) — Island Weirdos, Theme From — Ordinary Average Guy (11) — Song For Emma (3) — Worry Song (8)
Confessor, The (9) — Half Of The Time (10) — (8) — Over And Over (5) — Space Age Whiz Kids (8) 52 — You Might Need Somebody
County Fair (3,6) — Happy Ways (2) — Life Of Illusion (7) 34 — Pavane (3) — Things (7) — (11)
(Day Dream) Prayer (2) — Help Me Thru The Night (3,4,6) — **Life's Been Good** (5) 12 — Problems (9) — Time (10) — You Never Know (7)
Days Gone By (2) — Here We Are Now (8) — Look At Us Now (11) — Radio Song (10) — Time Out (3,4,6) — **Walk Away** (4,6) 51

WALSH, Steve — '80
Born in 1951 in St. Joseph, Missouri. Rock singer/keyboardist. Member of **Kansas** and **Streets**.

| 2/16/80 | 124 | 6 | | | **Schemer-Dreamer** | | | $12 | Kirshner 36320 |

Every Step Of The Way — Just How It Feels — So Many Nights — Wait Until Tomorrow
Get Too Far — Schemer-Dreamer (medley) — That's All Right (medley) — You Think You Got It Made

WALTER & SCOTTY — '93
R&B vocal duo: twin brothers Walter and Wallace "Scotty" Scott. Born on 9/3/43 in Fort Worth, Texas. Members of **The Whispers**.

| 5/22/93 | 151 | 7 | | | **My Brother's Keeper** | | | $10 | Capitol 92958 |

Dirty Dancin' (Slow Motion) — I Know You're My Baby — My Love — Sticks And Stones — With All My Heart
Fool For You (Baby) — I Want To Know Your Name — Open Door — Thank You (Falletin Me Be Mice
Heaven — Move Your Body — Rest My Lips — Elf Agin)

WALTERS, Jamie — '95
Born on 6/13/69 in Boston. Male singer/actor. Former lead singer of **The Heights**. Played "Roy Pruit" on TV's Beverly Hills 90210.

| 3/11/95 | 70 | 18 | | © | **Jamie Walters** | | | $10 | Atlantic 82600 |

Comfort Of Strangers — Drive Me — I Know The Game — No Rhyme, No Reason — Release Me
Distance, The — **Hold On** 16 — Neutral Ground — Perfect World — Why

WANDERLEY, Walter   '66
Born on 5/12/32 in Recife, Brazil. Died of cancer on 9/4/86 (age 54). Samba organist.

9/3/66	22	41		©	Rain Forest	[I]	$20	Verve 8658	

Beach Samba · Call Me · Cry Out Your Sadness · Great Love · Rain · Summer Samba (So Nice) 26
Beloved Melancholy · Cried, Cried · Girl From Ipanema · It's Easy To Say Good-bye · Song Of The Jet · Taste Of Sadness

WANG CHUNG   '84
Pop-rock group from London: Jack Hues (vocals, guitar, keyboards), Nick Feldman (bass, keyboards) and Darren Costin (drums). Costin left in 1985.

2/25/84	30	37	©	1	Points On The Curve		$10	Geffen 4004
11/2/85	85	18	©	2	To Live And Die In L.A.	[S]	$10	Geffen 24081
11/1/86	41	36	● ©	3	Mosaic		$10	Geffen 24115
6/10/89	123	6	©	4	The Warmer Side Of Cool		$10	Geffen 24222

At The Speed Of Life (4) · Don't Be My Enemy (1) 86 · Flat Horizon (3) · Lullaby (2) · To Live And Die In L.A. (2) 41 · What's So Bad About Feeling Good? (4)
Betrayal (3) · Don't Let Go (3) · Fool And His Money (3) · Praying To A New God (4) 63 · True Love (1) · When Love Looks Back At You (4)
Big World (4) · Even If You Dream (1) · Games Of Power (4) · Red Stare (2) · Wait (1,2) · World In Which We Live (3)
Black-Blue-White (2) · Every Big City (2) · Hypnotize Me (3) 36 · Snakedance (4) · Wake Up, Stop Dreaming (2)
City Of The Angels (2) · Everybody Have Fun Tonight (3) 2 · Let's Go! (3) 9 · Swing (4) · Warmer Side Of Cool (4)
Dance Hall Days (1) 16 · Logic And Love (4) · Talk It Out (1) · Waves, The (1)
Devoted Friends (1) · Eyes Of The Girl (3) · Look At Me Now (1) · Tall Trees In A Blue Sky (4)

WANSEL, Dexter   '78
Born in Philadelphia. R&B keyboardist/producer/arranger.

4/30/77	168	3	©	1	What The World Is Coming To		$12	Philadelphia Int'l. 34487
4/1/78	139	6	©	2	Voyager		$12	Philadelphia Int'l. 34985

All Night Long (2) · Dreams Of Tomorrow (1) · Holdin' On (1) · Latin Love (Let Me Know) (2) · Solutions (2) · What The World Is Coming To (1)
Dance With Me Tonight (1) · First Light Of The Morning (1) · I Just Want To Love You (2) · Ode Infinitum (1) · Time Is The Teacher (2)
Disco Lights (1) · Going Back To Kingston Town (1) · I'm In Love (2) · Prelude #1 (1) · Voyager (2)

WAR ★162★   '73
Latin group from Long Beach, California: Howard Scott (guitar), Lee Oskar (harmonica), Lonnie Jordan (keyboards), Charles Miller (sax), Thomas Allen (percussion), Morris Dickerson (bass) and Harold Brown (drums). All share vocals. Eric Burdon's backup band until 1971. Alice Tweed Smyth (vocals) added in 1978. By 1979, Luther Rabb replaced Dickerson; Pat Rizzo (horns) and Ron Hammond (percussion) joined. Rabb and Hammond were members of Ballin' Jack. Smyth left group in 1982. Lineup by 1994: Jordan, Scott, Brown and Hammond with Rae Valentine (music programmer), Charles Green and Kerry Campbell (saxophones), Tetsuya Nakamura (harmonica) and Sal Rodriguez (percussion). Miller was shot to death in June 1980 (age 41). Allen died on 8/30/88 (age 57).

1)The World Is A Ghetto 2)Greatest Hits 3)Deliver The Word

5/16/70	18	27	©	1	Eric Burdon Declares "War"		$20	MGM 4663
12/26/70+	82	9	©	2	The Black-Man's Burdon		$25	MGM 4710 [2]
					ERIC BURDON AND WAR (above 2)			
4/24/71	190	6	©	3	War		$15	United Artists 5508
11/20/71+	16	49	● ©	4	All Day Music		$15	United Artists 5546
11/18/72+	❶²	68	● ©	5	The World Is A Ghetto		$15	United Artists 5652
9/1/73	6	36	● ©	6	Deliver The Word		$15	United Artists 128
3/23/74	13	35	● ©	7	War Live!	[L]	$20	United Artists 193 [2]
7/5/75	8	31	● ©	8	Why Can't We Be Friends?		$12	United Artists 441
9/4/76	6	21	▲ ©	9	Greatest Hits	[G]	$12	United Artists 648
12/25/76+	140	5	©	10	Love Is All Around	[E]	$12	ABC 988
					WAR FEATURING ERIC BURDON			
					recorded 1969-70			
7/23/77	23	14	● ©	11	Platinum Jazz	[K]	$15	Blue Note 690 [2]
12/3/77+	15	23	● ©	12	Galaxy		$12	MCA 3030
8/19/78	69	6	©	13	Youngblood	[S]	$12	United Artists 904
4/14/79	41	16	● ©	14	The Music Band		$12	MCA 3085
12/8/79	111	13	©	15	The Music Band 2		$12	MCA 3193
3/20/82	48	27	©	16	Outlaw		$12	RCA Victor 4208
7/23/83	164	4	©	17	Life (Is So Strange)		$12	RCA Victor 4598
5/30/87	156	10	▲ ©	18	The Best Of War.....And More	C.#18/9	[G]	$10	Priority 9467
7/23/94	200	1	©	19	Peace Sign		$10	Avenue 71706

All Around The World (14) · All Day Music (4,7,9,18) 35 · Angel (19) · Baby Brother (4) · Baby Face (She Said Do Do Do Do) (12) · Baby It's Cold Outside (16) · Back Home (3) · Ballero (7) 33 · Bare Back Ride (2) · Beautiful New Born Child (2) · Beetles In The Bog (5) · Bird & The Squirrel (2) · Birth (1) · Black Bird (2) · Black On Black In Black (2) · Blisters (6) · Cinco De Mayo (16) · Cisco Kid (5,7,9,18) 2 · City, Country, City (5,11,18) · Corns & Callouses (Hey Dr. Shoals) (14) · Da Roof (19) · Danish Pastry (1) · Day In The Life (10)

Dedication (1) · Deliver The Word (6,11) · Don't Let No One Get You Down (8) · Don't Take It Away (15) · East L.A. (19) · Fidel's Fantasy (3) · Flying Machine (The Chase) (13) · Four Cornered Room (5,11) · Galaxy (12,18) 39 · Get Down (4,7) · Good, Good Feelin' (4) · Gun (2) · Gypsy Man (6,9) 8 · H Overture (6,11) · Happiness (17) · Heartbeat (medley) (8) · Hey Senorita (12) · Home Cookin' (2) · Home Dream (10) · Homeless Hero (19) · I Got You (1) · I Have A Dream (1) · I'll Be Around (15)

I'll Take Care Of You (15) · I'm About Somebody (16) · I'm The One Who Understands (14,19) · In Mazatlan (8) · In Your Eyes (8) · Introduction (7) · Jimbo (2) · Jungle Medley (16) · Junk Yard (13) · Just Because (16) · Keep On Doin' (13) · Kingsmen Jig (13) · L.A. Sunshine (11) 45 · La Fiesta (8) · Lament (8) · Laurel & Hardy (2) · Leroy's Latin Lament (medley) (8) · Let Me Tell You (19) · Life (Is So Strange) (17) · Livin' In The Red (18) · Lonely Feelin' (3,7) · Lonnie Dreams (8) · Lotus Blossom (8)

Love Is All Around (10) · Low Rider (8,9,18) 7 · Magic Mountain (10) · Me And Baby Brother (6,9,18) 15 · Millionaire (2) · Mother Earth (1) · Mr. Charlie (1) · Music Band (14) · Music Band 2 (We Are The Music Band) (15) · Nappy Head (4,11) · Night People (15) · Nights In White Satin I & II (2) · Nuts, Seeds & Life (2) · Out Of Nowhere (2) · P.C. 3 (2) · Paint It Black (2,10) · Peace Sign (19) · Pintelo Negro II (2) · Platinum Jazz (11) · Pretty Colors (2) · River Niger (11) · Roll On Kirk (1)

Searching For Youngblood & Rommel (13) · Seven Tin Soldiers (12) · Shake It Down (17) · Sing A Happy Song (13) · Slippin' Into Darkness (4,7,9,18) 16 · Slippin' Part 2 (7) · Slowly We Walk Together (11) · Smile For Me (19) · Smile Happy (8,11) · Smuggler, The (19) · So (8) · Southern Part Of Texas (6,9) · Spill The Wine (1,18) 3 · Spirit (2) · Summer (9,18) 7 · Summer Dreams (17) · Sun/Moon (2) · Sun On Sun (3) · Superdude (13) · Sweet Fighting Lady (12) · That's What Love Will Do (4) · There Must Be A Reason (4)

They Can't Take Away Our Music (2) 50 · This Funky Music Makes You Feel Good (13) · Tobacco Road (1,10) · U B O.K. (19) · U-2 Medley (17) · Vibeka (2) · W.W. III Medley (17) · Walking To War (13) · War Drums (2) · War Is Coming! War Is Coming (13) · Way We Feel (8) · What If (19) · Where Was You At (5) · Whose Cadillac Is That (18) · Why Can't We Be Friends? (8,9,18) 6 · Wild Rodriguez (19) · World Is A Ghetto (5,9,15) 7 · You Got The Power (16) 66 · You're No Stranger (1) · Youngblood & Sybil (13) · Youngblood (Livin' In The Streets) (13)

WARD, Anita '79
Born on 12/20/57 in Memphis. Disco singer.

| 5/26/79 | **8** | 19 | | | **Songs Of Love** | | | **$12** | Juana 200,004 |

I Won't Stop Loving You   If I Could Feel That Old Feeling Again   Make Believe Lovers   **Ring My Bell** *1*   Spoiled By Your Love   Sweet Splendor   There's No Doubt About It   You Lied

WARINER, Steve '99
Born on 12/25/54 in Noblesville, Indiana. Country singer/songwriter/guitarist.

10/17/87	**187**	2		©	1 **Greatest Hits**	[G]		**$10**	MCA 42032
11/16/91	**180**	7	●	©	2 **I Am Ready**			**$10**	Arista 18691
5/9/98	**41**	15	●	©	3 **Burnin' The Roadhouse Down**			**$10**	Capitol 94482
5/22/99	**35**	12	●	©	4 **Two Teardrops**			**$10**	Capitol 96139

Big Ol' Empty House (3)   Big Tops (3)   Burnin' The Roadhouse Down (3)   Closer I Get To You (3)   Crash Course In The Blues (2)   Cry No More (4)   Every Little Whisper (3)   Everything's Gonna Be Alright (2)   For The First Time (4)   Gone Out Of My Mind (2)   Hands Of Time (4)   Harry Shuffle (4)   Heart Trouble (1)   Holes In The Floor Of Heaven (3)   I Don't Know How To Fix It (3)   I'll Always Have Denver (4)   **I'm Already Taken** (4) *42*   I've Been In That Movie (4)   If You Don't Know By Now (4)   Leave Him Out Of This (2)   Life's Highway (1)   Like A River To The Sea (2)   Love Me Like You Love Me (3)   Lynda (1)   My, How The Time Don't Fly (2)   On My Heart Again (2)   Road Trippin' (3)   Since You Walked Away (4)   Six Pack Ago (3)   Small Town Girl (1)   Smoke From An Old Flame (3)   So Much (4)   Some Fools Never Learn (1)   Starting Over Again (1)   Talk To Her Heart (4)   Tattoos Of Life (4)   That's How You Know When Love's Right (3)   That's Love For You (4)   Tips Of My Fingers (2)   **Two Teardrops** (4) *30*   Weekend, The (1)   What I Didn't Do (1)   **What If I Said** (3) *59*   When Will I Let Go (2)   Woman Loves (2)   You Be My Everything (4)   You Can Dream Of Me (1)

WARING, Fred, And The Pennsylvanians '57
Born on 6/9/1900 in Tyrone, Pennsylvania. Died on 7/29/84 (age 84). Orchestra leader.

9/9/57	**25**	1			1 **Fred Waring And The Pennsylvanians In Hi-Fi**			**$25**	Capitol 845
12/23/57	**6**	3		©	2 **Now Is The Caroling Season**		[X]	**$25**	Capitol 896
12/22/58+	**19**	3		©	3 **Now Is The Caroling Season**		[X-R]	**$25**	Capitol 896
5/30/64	**116**	7			4 **America, I Hear You Singing**			**$20**	Reprise 2020

FRANK SINATRA/BING CROSBY/FRED WARING

| 12/12/64 | **9**ˣ | 3 | | | 5 **12 Songs Of Christmas** | | [X] | **$20** | Reprise 2022 |

BING CROSBY/FRANK SINATRA/FRED WARING

| 12/24/66 | **71**ˣ | 3 | | | 6 **A Caroling We Go** | | [X] | **$15** | Decca 74809 |

Christmas charts: 71/'66, 74/'67

America, I Hear You Singing! (medley) (4)   Angels From The Realms Of Glory (2,3)   Angels We Have Heard On High (2,3,6)   Away In A Manger (medley) (6)   Battle Hymn Of The Republic (1)   Be Joyful, Be Merry (6)   Bright, Bright The Holly Berries (6)   Bring A Torch, Jeanette, Isabella (2)   Carol, Brothers, Carol (6)   Caroling, Caroling (6)   Caroling We Go (6)   Christmas Candles (5)   Christmas Roundelay (medley) (6)   Christmas Song (Merry Christmas To You) (2,3)   Christmas Was Meant For Children (2,3)   Cigarette Sweet Music And You (1)   Come, Dear Children (medley) (6)   Do You Hear What I Hear (5)   Dry Bones (1)   Early American (4)   Give Me Your Tired, Your Poor (1,4)   Go Tell It On The Mountain (5)   Heigh Ho The Holly (2,3)   Here We Come Awassailing (2,3)   Hills Of Home (4)   Hit The Road To Dreamland (1)   Home In The Meadow (4)   Hora Staccato (1)   House I Live In (4)   I Hear Music (1)   I Heard The Bells On Christmas Day (2,3,5)   I Wonder As I Wander (6)   In Sweetest Jubilee (2,3)   In The Still Of The Night (1)   It Was A Night Of Wonder (2,3,6)   It's Christmas Time Again (5)   Jubilate Deo (medley) (6)   King Herod's Black Decree (6)   Let Us Break Bread Together (4)   Little Drummer Boy (5)   Lolly Too Dum Dey (1)   March Of The Kings (2,3)   Mary's Baby (6)   Masters In This Hall (2,3)   Now Is The Caroling Season (2,3)   O Christmas Tree (2,3)   O Come, O Come Emmanuel (2,3,6)   O Listen To The Angels' Song (6)   Ol' Man River (1)   Old-Fashioned Christmas (5)   Season's Greetings (medley) (6)   Secret Of Christmas (5)   Silver Bells (2,3)   Sleep (1)   Sleigh Ride (medley) (2,3)   Smoke Gets In Your Eyes (1)   So Beats My Heart For You (1)   Some Children See Him (6)   Sometimes I Feel Like A Motherless Child (1)   Stars And Stripes Forever (4)   This Is A Great Country (medley) (4)   This Land Is Your Land (4)   Twelve Days Of Christmas (2,3,5)   Way Back Home (1)   We Three Kings (2,3)   We Wish You The Merriest (5)   What Child Is This? (medley) (6)   When Angels Sang Of Peace (5)   Whiffenpoof Song (Baa! Baa! Baa!) (1)   White Christmas (2,3,5)   Winter Wonderland (2,3)   You Never Had It So Good (4)   You'll Never Walk Alone (1)   You're A Lucky Fellow, Mr. Smith (4)

WARLOCK '88
Hard-rock group from Dusseldorf, Germany: **Doro** (vocals), Peter Szigeti and Rudy Graf (guitars), Frank Rittel (bass) and Michael Eurich (drums).

| 12/19/87+ | **80** | 27 | | © | **Triumph And Agony** | | | **$10** | Mercury 832804 |

All We Are   Cold, Cold World   East Meets West   Fur Immer   I Rule The Ruins   Kiss Of Death   Make Time For Love   Metal Tango   Three Minute Warning   Touch Of Evil

WARNES, Jennifer '77
Born on 3/3/47 in Seattle; raised in Orange County, California. Pop singer.

2/26/77	**43**	18			1 **Jennifer Warnes**			**$12**	Arista 4062
6/9/79	**94**	23			2 **Shot Through The Heart**			**$12**	Arista 4217
2/14/87	**72**	21		©	3 **Famous Blue Raincoat**			**$10**	Cypress 661111

Ain't No Cure For Love (3)   Bird On A Wire (3)   Bring Ol' Maggie Back Home (1)   Came So Far For Beauty (3)   Coming Back To You (3)   Daddy Don't Go (1)   Don't Lead Me On (1)   **Don't Make Me Over** (1) *67*   Famous Blue Raincoat (3)   First We Take Manhattan (3)   Frankie In The Rain (2)   Hard Times, Come Again No More (2)   **I Know A Heartache When I See One** (2) *19*   **I'm Dreaming** (1) *50*   I'm Restless (2)   Joan Of Arc (3)   Love Hurts (1)   Mama (1)   O God Of Loveliness (1)   **Right Time Of The Night** (1) *6*   Round And Round (1)   Shine A Light (1)   Shot Through The Heart (2)   Sign On The Window (2)   Singer Must Die (3)   Song Of Bernadette (3)   Tell Me Just One More Time (2)   **When The Feeling Comes Around** (2) *45*   You Remember Me (2)   You're The One (1)

WARRANT '90
Male hard-rock group from Los Angeles: Jani Lane (vocals), Erik Turner and Joey Allen (guitars), Jerry Dixon (bass) and Steven Sweet (drums).

3/4/89	**10**	65	▲²	©	1 **Dirty Rotten Filthy Stinking Rich**			**$10**	Columbia 44383
9/29/90	**7**	60	▲²	©	2 **Cherry Pie**			**$10**	Columbia 45487
9/12/92	**25**	13	●	©	3 **Dog Eat Dog**			**$10**	Columbia 52584

All My Bridges Are Burning (3)   Andy Warhol Was Right (3)   April 2031 (3)   Bed Of Roses (2)   **Big Talk** (1) *93*   Bitter Pill (3)   **Blind Faith** (2) *88*   Bonfire (3)   **Cherry Pie** (2) *10*   Cold Sweat (1)   D.R.F.S.R. (1)   **Down Boys** (1) *27*   **Heaven** (1) *2*   Hole In My Wall (3)   Hollywood (So Far, So Good) (3)   **I Saw Red** (2) *10*   In The Sticks (1)   Inside Out (3)   Let It Rain (3)   Love In Stereo (2)   Machine Gun (3)   Mr. Rainmaker (2)   Ode To Tipper Gore (2)   Quicksand (3)   Ridin' High (1)   Sad Theresa (3)   So Damn Pretty (Should Be Against The Law) (1)   **Sometimes She Cries** (1) *20*   Song And Dance Man (2)   Sure Feels Good To Me (2)   32 Pennies (1)   Train, Train (2)   **Uncle Tom's Cabin** (2) *78*   You're The Only Hell Your Mama Ever Raised (2)

★458★ WARREN, Rusty '61

Born Ilene Goldman in 1930 in New York City; raised in Milton, Massachusetts. Female novelty singer of adults-only songs.

DEBUT	PEAK	WKS		CD				$	Label & Number
11/7/60+	8	181		©	1 Knockers Up!		[C]	$25	Jubilee 2029
5/8/61	55	40		©	2 Songs For Sinners		[C]	$25	Jubilee 2024
5/22/61	21	51			3 Sin-Sational		[C]	$25	Jubilee 2034
12/18/61+	31	50			4 Rusty Warren Bounces Back		[C]	$25	Jubilee 2039
11/3/62+	22	32			5 Rusty Warren In Orbit		[C]	$25	Jubilee 2044
10/19/63	52	18			6 Banned In Boston?		[C]	$25	Jubilee 2049
1/1/66	124	7			7 More Knockers Up!		[C]	$25	Jubilee 2059

no track titles listed on albums #2, 4-7

Frankie And Johnny (1)　In The Family Way (1)　Life Is Just A Bowl Of Cherries　Red River Sally (1)　You're Nobody Til Somebody
Good Man Is Hard To Find (3)　It's Mine... (3)　　(3)　Rusty For President? (3)　Loves You (1)
Growing Pains (3)　Knockers Up! (1)　Mother-Daughter Talk "Don't Do　Those Stairs Are Killing Me! (3)
I Like It Girls (3)　Let Me Entertain You (3)　It!" (3)

WARREN G '94

Born Warren Griffin in Long Beach, California. Male rapper.

DEBUT	PEAK	WKS	RIAA	CD				$	Label & Number
6/25/94	2[1]	53	▲3	©	1 Regulate...G Funk Era			$10	Violator 523364
4/12/97	11	16	●	©	2 Take A Look Over Your Shoulder (Reality)			$10	Def Jam 537254
10/30/99	21	10	●	©	3 I Want It All			$10	Restless 73710

And Ya Don't Stop (1)　G-Spot (3)　If We Give You A Chance (3)　Runnin' Wit No Breaks (1)　Transformers (2)　You Never Know (3)
Annie Mae (2)　Game Don't Wait (3)　My Momma (Ola Mae) (3)　Smokin' Me Out (2) 35　We Brings Heat (2)　Young Fun (2)
Back Up (2)　Gangsta Love (3)　'94 Ho Draft (1)　So Many Ways (1)　We Got That (3)
Can You Feel It (2)　Gangsta Sermon (1)　Reality (2)　Super Soul Sis (1)　What We Go Through (2)
Do You See (1) 42　Havin' Things (3)　Recognize (1)　This D.J. (1) 9　What's Next (1)
Dollars Makes Sense (3)　I Shot The Sheriff (2) 20　Regulate (1) 2　This Is The Shack (1)　Why Oh Why (3)
Dope Beat (3)　I Want It All (3) 23　Relax Ya Mind (2)　To All D.J.'s (2)　World Wide Ryders (3)

WARWICK, Dionne ★49★ '68

Born Marie Dionne Warwick on 12/12/40 in East Orange, New Jersey. R&B singer. Niece of Cissy Houston (of **Sweet Inspirations**) and cousin of **Whitney Houston**. Added an "e" to her last name for a time in the 1970s. Co-hosted TV's **Solid Gold** from 1980-81 and 1985-86.

1)Valley of the Dolls 2)Dionne Warwick's Golden Hits, Part One 3)Soulful 4)Friends 5)Dionne

DEBUT	PEAK	WKS		CD				$	Label & Number
9/12/64	68	20			1 Make Way For Dionne Warwick			$25	Scepter 523
3/6/65	107	9			2 The Sensitive Sound of Dionne Warwick			$25	Scepter 528
1/1/66	45	29			3 Here I Am			$20	Scepter 531
4/16/66	76	11			4 Dionne Warwick in Paris		[L]	$20	Scepter 534
					recorded on 1/18/66 at the Olympia Theater				
1/7/67	18	66	●		5 Here Where There is Love			$20	Scepter 555
5/13/67	169	9			6 On Stage and in The Movies			$20	Scepter 559
9/16/67	22	31			7 The Windows of The World			$20	Scepter 563
11/18/67	10	69			8 Dionne Warwick's Golden Hits, Part One		[G]	$20	Scepter 565
3/9/68	6	48	●		9 Valley of the Dolls			$20	Scepter 568
12/14/68+	18	39			10 Promises, Promises			$20	Scepter 571
4/5/69	11	28			11 Soulful			$20	Scepter 573
8/16/69	31	24	●		12 Dionne Warwick's Greatest Motion Picture Hits		[K]	$20	Scepter 575
11/1/69	28	28			13 Dionne Warwick's Golden Hits, Part 2		[G]	$20	Scepter 577
5/2/70	23	39			14 I'll Never Fall In Love Again			$20	Scepter 581
12/12/70+	37	24			15 Very Dionne			$20	Scepter 587
					DIONNE WARWICKE:				
10/30/71	48	17	●		16 The Dionne Warwicke Story		[L]	$20	Scepter 596 [2]
1/29/72	54	14			17 Dionne			$15	Warner 2585
4/8/72	169	5			18 From Within		[K]	$20	Scepter 598 [2]
2/3/73	178	8			19 Just Being Myself			$15	Warner 2658
3/8/75	167	6			20 Then Came You			$15	Warner 2846
					DIONNE WARWICK:				
12/6/75+	137	15			21 Track of the Cat			$15	Warner 2893
2/19/77	49	13			22 A Man And A Woman		[L]	$20	HBS 996 [2]
					ISAAC HAYES & DIONNE WARWICK				
7/2/77	188	7			23 Only Love Can Break A Heart		[K]	$12	Musicor 2501
6/9/79	12	54	▲	©	24 Dionne			$12	Arista 4230
					produced by **Barry Manilow**				
8/9/80	23	25			25 No Night So Long			$12	Arista 9526
6/13/81	72	14		©	26 Hot! Live and Otherwise		[L]	$15	Arista 8605 [2]
					3 of 4 sides are live recordings				
5/22/82	83	12			27 Friends In Love			$10	Arista 9585
10/30/82+	25	28	●	©	28 Heartbreaker			$10	Arista 9609
					produced by **Barry Gibb**				
10/29/83	57	17			29 How Many Times Can We Say Goodbye			$10	Arista 8104
					produced by **Luther Vandross**				
3/2/85	106	11		©	30 Finder Of Lost Loves			$10	Arista 8262
12/21/85+	12	26	●	©	31 Friends			$10	Arista 8398
8/22/87	56	27		©	32 Reservations For Two			$10	Arista 8446
12/23/89+	177	7		©	33 Greatest Hits 1979-1990		[G]	$10	Arista 8540

WARWICK, Dionne — Cont'd

8/18/90   **155**   9   © 34 **Dionne Warwick Sings Cole Porter** .... **$10**   Arista 8573

After You (24) *65*
Alfie (5,12,16,26) *15*
All Kinds Of People (medley) (18)
All Of You (34)
All The Love In The World (28)
All The Time (24,33)
Another Chance To Love (32)
Another Night (7) *49*
Any Old Time Of Day (8)
Anyone Who Had A Heart (8,16,26) *8*
Anything Goes (34)
Anything You Can Do (6)
April Fools (12) *37*
Aquarius (16)
Are You There (With Another Girl) (3,13) *39*
As Long As He Needs Me (5,12)
As Long As There's An Apple Tree (9)
Balance Of Nature (17)
Battle Hymn Of The Republic (18)
Baubles, Bangles & Beads (6)
Be Aware (17)
Bedroom Eyes (30)
Begin The Beguine (34)
Beginning Of Loneliness (7) *79*
Betcha By Golly Wow (27)
Blowing In The Wind (5)
Body Language (22)
By The Time I Get To Phoenix (medley) (22)
C'est Si Bon (4)
Can't Hide Love (22,27)
Check Out Time (15)
Chocolate Chip (22)
Close Enough (32)
Close To You (17)
Come Back (19)
Come Live With Me (22)
Come Together (medley) (16)
Cry On Me (32)
Dedicate This Heart (26)
Deja Vu (24,26,33) *15*
Didn't We (14,23)
Do Right Woman - Do Right Man (11,18)
Do You Know The Way To San Jose (9,13,16,26) *10*
Don't Burn The Bridge (That Took You Across) (19)
Don't Go Breaking My Heart (19)
Don't Let My Teardrops Bother You (19)
Don't Make Me Over (8,16,26) *21*
Don't Say I Didn't Tell You So (2)
Easy Love (25,26) *62*
Even A Fool Would Let Go (26)
Everyday People (18)
Extravagant Gestures (31)
Feeling Old Feelings (24)
Feelings (medley) (22)
Finder Of Lost Loves (30)
For All We Know (23)
For Everything You Are (32)

For Once In My Life (16)
For The Rest Of My Life (9)
For You (27)
Forever My Love (2,13)
Friends In Love (27,33) *38*
Games People Play (18)
Get Down Tonight (medley) (22)
Get Rid Of Him (1)
Get Together (medley) (16)
Getting In My Way (20)
Give A Damn (18)
Go With Love (5)
Going Out Of My Head (15,16)
Good Life (4)
Got A Date (29)
Got You Where I Want You (27)
Grace (18)
Green Grass Starts To Grow (15) *43*
Hard Day's Night (11)
Hasbrook Heights (17)
Have You Never Been Mellow (medley) (22)
He (She) Loves Me (6)
Heartbreak Of Love (32)
Heartbreaker (28,33) *10*
Here I Am (3,12) *65*
Here Where There Is Love (5)
Here's That Rainy Day (15)
Hey Jude (11)
His House And Me (21)
House Is Not A Home (1,4,12,16,26) *71*
How Can I Hurt You (3)
How Can I Tell Him (20)
How Long? (3)
How Many Days Of Sadness (2)
How Many Times Can We Say Goodbye (29,33) *27*
How You Once Loved Me (25)
Hurts So Bad (18)
I Always Get Caught In The Rain (19)
I Believe In You (6)
I Can Let Go Now (29)
I Can't See Anything (But You) (28)
I Can't Wait To See My Baby's Face (20)
I Concentrate On You (34)
I Do It 'Cause I Like It (29)
I Don't Need Another Love (33)
I Get A Kick Out Of You (34)
I Got Love (15,23)
I Just Don't Know What To Do With Myself (5,13,16,22) *26*
I Just Have To Breathe (17)
I Love Music (medley) (22)
I Love Paris (4,34)
I Loves You, Porgy (3)
(I Never Knew) What You Were Up To (5)
I Say A Little Prayer (7,13,16,22) *4*
I Smiled Yesterday (1,8)
I Think You Need Love (19)
I Wish You Love (5)
I'll Never Fall In Love Again (14,16) *6*

I'll Never Love This Way Again (24,26,33) *5*
(I'm) Just Being Myself (19)
I'm Putting Me In Your Hands (16)
I'm Your Puppet (11,18)
I've Been Loving You Too Long (11,18)
I've Got You Under My Skin (34)
If I Ever Make You Cry (3)
If I Ruled The World (23)
If We Only Have Love (17) *84*
If You Let Me Make Love To You Then Why Can't I Touch You (18)
If You Never Say Goodbye (17)
Impersonation Medley (16)
Impossible Dream (medley) (16)
In A World Such As This (32)
In Between The Heartaches (3,13)
In The Stone (medley) (26)
In Your Eyes (24)
Is There Another Way To Love You (2)
It Makes No Difference (28)
It's All Right With Me (34)
It's Love (30)
It's Love That Really Counts (8)
It's Magic (20)
It's The Falling In Love (25)
It's You (30)
Jealousy (21)
Jesus Will (18)
Just One More Night (28)
Just One Of Those Things (34)
Knowing When To Leave (14)
La Vie En Rose (4)
Land Of Make Believe (1)
Last One To Be Loved (1)
Let It Be Me (23)
Let Me Be Lonely (9) *71*
Let Me Go To Him (14) *32*
Letter, The (24)
Little Green Apples (10)
Loneliness Remembers What Happiness Forgets (14)
Lonely In My Heart (10)
Long Day, Short Night (3)
Look Of Love (12,16,26)
Looking With My Eyes (3) *64*
Love (7)
Love At Second Sight (31)
Love Doesn't Live Here Anymore (33)
Love Me One More Time (21)
Love Of My Man (18)
Love Power (32,33) *12*
Love So Right (27)
Love Song (17)
Love Will Keep Us Together (medley) (22)
Loving You Is Sweeter Than Ever (18)
MacArthur Park (18)
Make It Easy On Yourself (8,15,16,26) *37*
Make The Night A Little Longer (1)

Message To Michael (4,13,16,26) *8*
Misunderstood (28)
Moments Aren't Moments (31)
Monday, Monday (23)
More Than Fascination (27)
Move Me No Mountain (20)
My Everlasting Love (24)
My Eyes Adored You (medley) (22)
My Favorite Things (6)
My First Night Alone Without You (17)
My Love (22)
My Ship (6)
My Way (14)
Never Gonna Let You Go (27)
Night And Day (34)
No Night So Long (25,26,33) *23*
No One In The World (30,32)
No One There (To Sing Me A Love Song) (31)
Now We're Starting Over Again (26)
Oh Yeah Yeah Yeah (4,16)
Once In A Lifetime (3)
Once You Hit The Road (21,22) *79*
One Hand, One Heart (6,12)
One In A Million You (26)
One Less Bell To Answer (17)
Only Love Can Break A Heart (23)
Only The Strong, Only The Brave (2)
Our Ages Or Our Hearts (18)
Our Day Will Come (28)
Out Of My Hands (24)
Paper Mache (14,16) *43*
People (1,12)
People Get Ready (11,18)
People Got To Be Free (11,18)
Promises, Promises (10,16,26) *19*
Put A Little Love In Your Heart (medley) (16)
Raindrops Keep Falling On My Head (14,16)
Reach Out And Touch (medley) (18)
Reach Out For Me (1,8,16) *20*
Reaching For The Sky (25)
Remember Your Heart (31)
Reservations For Two (32) *62*
Ronnie Lee (21)
Run To Me (30)
She Loves Me ..see: He
Silent Voices (9)
Slaves (12,18)
So Amazing (29)
So In Love (medley) (34)
Some Changes Are For Good (26) *65*
Somebody Bigger Than You And I (18)
Somebody's Angel (25)
Someday We'll Be Together (18)
Something (14)
Something Wonderful (6)

Somewhere (7,12,16)
Stand (18)
Stay Devoted (31)
Steal Away (18)
Stronger Than Before (31)
Summertime (6,18)
Sure Thing (20)
Sweetie Pie (25)
Take Good Care Of You And Me (33)
Take It From Me (20)
Take The Short Way Home (28) *41*
Taking A Chance On Love (16)
Thank Heaven For Little Girls (medley) (16)
That's Not The Answer (2)
That's The Way I Like It (medley) (22)
That's What Friends Are For (31,33) *1*
Then Came You (20,22,26) *1*
There's A Long Road Ahead Of Us (26)
(There's) Always Something There To Remind Me (7,8,26) *65*
They Don't Give Medals To Yesterday's Heroes (15)
They Long To Be Close To You (1,26)
They Say It's Wonderful (23)
This Empty Place (8) *84*
This Girl's In Love With You (10,16) *7*
This Is Love (21)
This Little Light (3,18)
This Will Be (An Everlasting Love) (medley) (22)
To Be Young, Gifted And Black (18)
Track Of The Cat (21)
Trains And Boats And Planes (5,13,26) *22*
Try To Remember (16)
Two Ships Passing In The Night (29)
Unchained Melody (2,13,18)
Unity (22)
Up, Up And Away (9)
Valley Of The Dolls, Theme From (9,12,16,26) *2*
Walk Away (33)
Walk Little Dolly (7)
Walk On By (1,4,8,16,22,26) *6*
Walk The Way You Talk (15)
Walking Backwards Down The Road (9)
Wanting Things (10)
Way I Want To Touch You (medley) (22)
Way You Look Tonight (6)
We Can Work It Out (11,18)
We Had This Time (25)
We Never Said Goodbye (25,26)
We'll Burn Our Bridges Behind Us (20)
We've Only Just Begun (15)
Weakness (30)
Weight, The (18)

What Can A Miracle Do (29)
What Is This (27)
What Is This Thing Called Love? (medley) (34)
What The World Needs Now Is Love (5,13,16,26)
What You Won't Do For Love (medley) (26)
What'd I Say (4,16)
What's Good About Goodbye (7,16)
When The World Runs Out Of Love (25)
Where Am I Going (10)
Where Can I Go Without You (2)
Where Is Love (10)
Where Would I Go (9)
Whisper In The Dark (31) *72*
Who Can I Turn To (2,13,16) *62*
Who Gets The Guy (23) *57*
Who Is Gonna Love Me? (10) *33*
Who Knows (20)
Who, What, When, Where, Why (24)
Whoever You Are, I Love You (10)
Will You Still Love Me Tomorrow (29)
Window Wishing (3)
Windows Of The World (7,13) *32*
Wine Is Young (14)
Wishin' And Hopin' (1,8)
With A Touch (27)
With These Hands (6,12)
Without Your Love (30)
Wives And Lovers (2,12,16)
World Of My Dreams (21)
Yesterday (15)
Yesterday I Heard The Rain (10)
You And The Night And The Music (16)
You Are My Love (28)
You Are The Heart Of Me (19)
You Can Have Him (2) *75*
You Made Me So Very Happy (16)
You Made Me Want To Love Again (30)
You'll Never Get To Heaven (If You Break My Heart) (1,4,8,16,26) *34*
You'll Never Walk Alone (6,18)
You're All I Need To Get By (11,18)
You're Gonna Hear From Me (7,16)
You're Gonna Need Me (19)
You're My Hero (32)
You're My World (9,23)
You're The Top (34)
You've Lost That Lovin' Feeling (11,18) *16*
Yours (28)

WASH, Martha   '93

Born on 12/28/53 in San Francisco. R&B singer. Member of **Two Tons O' Fun**.

3/13/93   **169**   2   ©   **Martha Wash** .... **$10**   RCA 66052

Carry On
Give It To You *90*

Hold On (Part I & II)
Just Us

Leave A Light On
Now That You're Gone

Runaround
So Whatcha Gonna Do

Someone Who Believes In You
Things We Do For Love

When It's My Heart

WASHINGTON, Dinah   '61

Born Ruth Lee Jones on 8/29/24 in Tuscaloosa, Alabama. Died of an alcohol/pill overdose on on 12/14/63 (age 39). R&B singer. Inducted into the Rock and Roll Hall of Fame in 1993 as an early influence.

2/1/60	**34**	22	© 1	**What A Diff'rence A Day Makes!**	**$30**	Mercury 20479
1/23/61	**10**	14	© 2	**Unforgettable**	**$30**	Mercury 20572
12/18/61+	**56**	15	3	**September In The Rain**	**$30**	Mercury 20638
6/23/62	**33**	25	4	**Dinah '62**	**$25**	Roulette 25170
10/20/62	**78**	9	5	**Drinking Again**	**$25**	Roulette 25183
11/17/62	**131**	4	6	**I Wanna Be Loved**	**$25**	Mercury 20729
2/23/63	**61**	12	© 7	**Back To The Blues**	**$25**	Roulette 25189
4/4/64	**130**	6	8	**A Stranger On Earth**	**$25**	Roulette 25253

Alone (2)
As Long As I'm In Your Arms (3)
Ask A Woman Who Knows (2)

Baby Won't You Please Come Home (5)
Bad Case Of The Blues (2)
Blue Gardenia (6)

Blues Ain't Nothin' But A Woman Cryin' For Her Man (7,8)
Coquette (4)

Cry Me A River (1)
Destination Moon (4)
Do Nothin' 'Til You Hear From Me (8)

Don't Come Running Back To Me (7)
Don't Explain (6)
Drinking Again (4,5)

Duck Before You Drown (7)
Everybody Loves Somebody (2)
Everybody's Somebody's Fool (6)

WASHINGTON, Dinah — Cont'd

For All We Know (5) *88*
God Bless The Child (6)
Handful Of Stars (4)
How Long, How Long Blues (7)
I Can't Believe That You're In Love With Me (3)
I Can't Face The Music (6)
I Don't Know You Anymore (5)
I Remember You (1)
I Thought About You (1)
I Understand (2)
I Wanna Be Loved (6)
I Was Telling Him About You (3)
I Won't Cry Anymore (1)

I'll Be Around (5)
I'll Come Back For More (3)
I'll Drown In My Tears (8)
I'll Never Kiss You Goodbye (3)
I'm Gonna Laugh You Out Of My Life (5)
I'm Thru With Love (1)
I've Got My Love To Keep Me Warm (3)
If I Never Get To Heaven (7)
Invitation (6)
Is You Is Or Is You Ain't My Baby (4)
It's A Mean Old Man's World (7,8)

It's Magic (1)
Just Friends (5)
Key To The Highway (7)
Let Me Be The First To Know (7)
Let's Fall In Love (6)
Love, I Found You Gone (5)
Lover Man (5)
Man Only Does (What A Woman Makes Him Do) (2)
Man That Got Away (5,8)
Manhattan (1)
Me And My Gin (8)
Miss You (4)
No Hard Feelings (7)

Nobody Knows The Way I Feel This Morning (7,8)
Nothing In The World (Could Make Me Love You More Than I Do) (1)
On The Street Of Regret (5)
Red Sails In The Sunset (4)
Romance In The Dark (7)
Say It Isn't So (5)
September In The Rain (3) *23*
Softly (3)
Sometimes I'm Happy (6)
Somewhere Along The Line (2)
Song Is Ended (But The Melody Lingers On) (2)

Soulville (8) *92*
Stranger In Town (6)
Stranger On Earth (8)
Sunday Kind Of Love (1)
Take Your Shoes Off Baby (4)
Tell Love Hello! (3)
That's All There Is To That (1)
This Bitter Earth (2) *24*
This Heart Of Mine (3)
This Love Of Mine (2)
Time After Time (1)
Unforgettable (2) *17*
What A Diff'rence A Day Makes (1) *8*
When I Fall In Love (2)

When Your Lover Has Gone (6)
Where Are You (4) *36*
With A Song In My Heart (3)
Without A Song (3)
You're Crying (6)
You're Nobody 'Til Somebody Loves You (4) *87*
You've Been A Good Old Wagon (7,8)

WASHINGTON, Grover Jr. ★157★ '75

Born on 12/12/43 in Buffalo, New York. Died on 12/17/99 (age 56). Jazz-R&B saxophonist. Joined first band, the Four Clefs, at age 16. Much session work in Philadelphia.

1)Winelight 2)Mister Magic 3)Feels So Good

DEBUT	PEAK	WKS	RIAA	CD			ARTIST — Album Title	Sym	$	Label & Number
1/1/72	62	25		©	1	Inner City Blues		[I]	$15	Kudu 03
9/9/72	111	17		©	2	All The King's Horses		[I]	$15	Kudu 07
7/14/73	100	14		©	3	Soul Box		[I]	$20	Kudu 1213 [2]
3/8/75	10	34		©	4	Mister Magic		[I]	$15	Kudu 20
11/15/75	10	30		©	5	Feels So Good		[I]	$15	Kudu 24
1/15/77	31	16		©	6	A Secret Place		[I]	$15	Kudu 32
1/7/78	11	32		©	7	Live At The Bijou		[I-L]	$20	Kudu 3637 [2]
						recorded May 1977 at the Bijou Cafe in Philadelphia				
10/21/78	35	23		©	8	Reed Seed		[I]	$12	Motown 910
						backed by the jazz ensemble Locksmith				
4/28/79	24	19		©	9	Paradise		[I]	$12	Elektra 182
3/8/80	24	22			10	Skylarkin'		[I]	$12	Motown 933
9/13/80	96	10			11	Baddest		[I-K]	$15	Motown 940 [2]
11/15/80+	5	52	▲	©	12	Winelight		[I]	$12	Elektra 305
10/24/81	149	7			13	Anthology		[I-K]	$15	Motown 961 [2]
12/12/81+	28	27		©	14	Come Morning		[I]	$12	Elektra 562
12/11/82+	50	25		©	15	The Best Is Yet To Come		[I]	$12	Elektra 60215
11/10/84	79	23		©	16	Inside Moves		[I]	$12	Elektra 60318
8/29/87	66	16		©	17	Strawberry Moon		[I]	$10	Columbia 40510
5/16/92	149	11		©	18	Next Exit		[I]	$10	Columbia 48530
10/12/96	187	2		©	19	Soulful Strut		[I]	$10	Columbia 57505

Ain't No Sunshine (1,11)
Ain't Nobody's Business If I Do (medley) (7)
All The King's Horses (2)
Answer In Your Eyes (9)
Asia's Theme (9)
Aubrey (9)
Be Mine (Tonight) (14) *92*
Best Is Yet To Come (15)
Black Frost (4,11)
Body And Soul (Montage) (2)
Bordertown (9)
Brazilian Memories (15)
Bright Moments (10)
Can You Dig It (15)
Can You Stop The Rain (19)
Cassie's Theme (1)
Caught A Touch Of Your Love (17)
Check Out Grover (18)
Come Morning (14)
Dawn Song (16)

Days In Our Lives (medley) (7)
Do Dat (8,11)
Dolphin Dance (6)
Don't Explain (3)
Earth Tones (4)
Easy Living (medley) (3)
Easy Loving You (10)
Feel It Comin' (9)
Funkfoot (7)
Georgia On My Mind (1)
Get On Up (18)
Greene Street (18)
Headman's Haunt (19)
Hydra (5)
I Can Count The Times (19)
I Can't Help It (10)
I Loves You, Porgy (1)
I Miss Home (18)
I Will Be Here For You (17)
I'll Be With You (15)
I'm All Yours (14)
Icey (9)

In The Name Of Love (12)
Inner City Blues (1,13)
Inside Moves (16)
It Feels So Good (5,11,13)
Jamming (14)
Jet Stream (16)
Juffure (7)
Just The Two Of Us (12) *2*
Just The Way You Are (8)
Keep In Touch (17)
Knucklehead (5)
Lean On Me (2,11)
Let It Flow ("For Dr. J") (12)
Little Black Samba (14)
Lock It In The Pocket (4)
Look Of Love (17)
Loran's Dance (8)
Love (10)
Love Like This (18)
Love Makes It Better (6)
Love Song 1700 (2)
Lover Man (2)
Maddie's Blues (17)

Make Me A Memory (Sad Samba) (12)
Making Love To You (14)
Man And A Boy (Better Days), Theme From (1)
Maracas Beach (9)
Masterpiece (3,11,13)
Mercy Mercy Me (The Ecology) (1,13)
Mister Magic (4,7,11,13) *54*
Mixty Motions (15)
Monte Carlo Nights (17)
Moonstreams (5)
More Than Meets The Eye (15)
Mystical Force (19)
Next Exit (18)
No Tears In The End (2)
Not Yet (6)
On The Cusp (16)
Only For You (Siempre Para D'Sera) (18)
Open Up Your Mind (Wide) (10)
Paradise (9)

Passion Flower (4)
Play That Groove For Me (19)
Poacher Man (19)
Reaching Out (14)
Reed Seed (Trio Tune) (8)
Santa Cruzin (8,13)
Sassy Stew (16)
Sausalito (7)
Sea Lion (3)
Secret Place (6,11,13)
Secret Sounds (16)
Shana (9)
Shivaree Ride (17)
Snake Eyes (10,13)
Soulful Strut (19)
Step'N' Thru (8)
Strawberry Moon (17)
Summer Chill (18)
Summer Nights (17)
Summer Song (7,11,13)
Take Five (Take Another Five) (18)
Take Me There (12)

Taurian Matador (3)
Tell Me About It Now (9)
Things Are Getting Better (15)
Till You Return To Me (18)
Trouble Man (3,13)
Until It's Time For You To Go (1)
Uptown (19)
Village Groove (19)
Watching You Watching Me (16)
When I Look At You (16)
Where Is The Love (2,13)
Winelight (19)
You Are The Sunshine Of My Life (3)
You Make Me Dance (7)
Your Love (18)

WASHINGTON, Keith '91

Born in Detroit. R&B singer.

DEBUT	PEAK	WKS		CD			ARTIST — Album Title	$	Label & Number
5/4/91	48	25	●	©	1	Make Time For Love	$10	Qwest 26528
10/9/93	100	7		©	2	You Make It Easy	$10	Qwest 45336
3/28/98	125	8		©	3	KW	$10	Silas 11744

All Night (1)
Are You Still In Love With Me (1)
Before I Let Go (medley) (2)
Believe That (2)
Bring It On (3) *63*

Closer (1)
Do What You Like (2)
Don't Leave Me In The Dark (2)
I Can't Put You Down (3)
I Don't Mind (3)
I Love You (3)

I Warned You (3)
I'll Be There (1)
Kissing You (1) *40*
Let Me Make Love To You (2)
Long Ago (3)
Lovers After All (1)

Make Time For Love (1)
No Matter (3)
No One (2)
Only You (3)
Ready, Willing And Able (1)
Smile (3)

Stay In My Corner (2)
Tell Me (Are You With It) (3)
Trippin' (2)
We Need To Talk (medley) (2)
What It Takes (2)
When It Comes To You (1)

When You Love Somebody (1)
You Always Gotta Go (2)
You Let Me Down (3)
You Make It Easy (2)
You Sure Love To Ball (3)

WAS (NOT WAS)   '89

R&B-pop group from Detroit. Fronted by composer/bassist Don Fagenson ("Don Was") and lyricist/flutist David Weiss ("David Was"). Includes vocalists Sweet Pea Atkinson and Sir Harry Bowens. Group appeared in the movie *The Freshman*.

10/15/83	134	9		© 1	Born To Laugh At Tornadoes			$10	Geffen 4016
10/15/88+	43	37		© 2	What Up, Dog?			$10	Chrysalis 41664
8/18/90	99	11		© 3	Are You Okay?			$10	Chrysalis 21778

Anything Can Happen (2) **75**
Anytime Lisa (2)
Are You Okay? (3)
Betrayal (1)
Bow Wow Wow Wow (1)
Boy's Gone Crazy (2)
Dad I'm In Jail (2)
Dressed To Be Killed (3)

Earth To Doris (2)
11 MPH (2)
Elvis' Rolls Royce (3)
How The Heart Behaves (3)
I Blew Up The United States (3)
I Feel Better Than James Brown (3)
In K Mart Wardrobe (3)

Just Another Couple Broken Hearts (3)
Knocked Down, Made Small (Treated Like A Rubber Ball) (1)
Look What's Back (3)
Love Can Be Bad Luck (2)
Man Vs. The Empire Brain Building (1)

Maria Novarro (3)
Out Come The Freaks (2)
Papa Was A Rollin' Stone (3)
Party Broke Up (1)
Professor Night (1)
(Return To The Valley Of) Out Come The Freaks (1)
Shadow & Jimmy (3)

Shake Your Head (Let's Go To Bed) (1)
Smile (1)
Somewhere In America There's A Street Named After My Dad (2)
Spy In The House Of Love (2) 16
Walk The Dinosaur (2) 7

What Up Dog? (2)
You! You! You! (3)
Zaz Turned Blue (1)

W.A.S.P.   '89

Hard-rock group from Los Angeles: Blackie Lawless (vocals), Chris Holmes (guitar), Johnny Rod (bass) and Steve Riley (drums).

10/6/84	74	31	● © 1	W.A.S.P.				$10	Capitol 12343
11/23/85	49	23	● © 2	The Last Command				$10	Capitol 12435
11/8/86	60	19	© 3	Inside The Electric Circus				$10	Capitol 12531
10/10/87	77	14	© 4	Live...In The Raw	[L]			$10	Capitol 48053
				recorded at California Theatre (San Diego) & Long Beach Arena (LA)					
4/22/89	48	13	© 5	The Headless Children				$10	Capitol 48942

B.A.D. (1)
Ballcrusher (2)
Big Welcome (3)
Blind In Texas (2,4)
Cries In The Night (2)
Easy Living (3)
Fistful Of Diamonds (2)
Flame, The (1)

Forever Free (5)
Harder Faster (4)
Headless Children (5)
Hellion (1)
Heretic (The Lost Child) (5)
I Don't Need No Doctor (3,4)
I Wanna Be Somebody (1,4)
I'm Alive (3)

Inside The Electric Circus (3,4)
Jack Action (2)
King Of Sodom And Gomorrah (3)
Last Command (2)
L.O.V.E. Machine (1,4)
Maneater (5)
Manimal, The (4)

Mantronic (3)
Mean Man (5)
Mephisto Waltz (5)
Neutron Bomber (5)
9.5.-N.A.S.T.Y. (3,4)
On Your Knees (1)
Real Me (5)
Rebel In The F.D.G. (5)

Restless Gypsy (3)
Rock Rolls On (3)
Running Wild In The Streets (2)
School Daze (1)
Scream Until You Like it (4)
Sex Drive (2)
Shoot From The Hip (3)
Sleeping (In The Fire) (1,4)

Sweet Cheetah (3)
Thunderhead (5)
Tormentor (1)
Torture Never Stops (1)
WidowMaker (2)
Wild Child (2,4)

WATERBOYS, The   '89

Rock group formed in London by Mike Scott (vocals, guitar) and Anthony Thistlethwaite (mandolin, sax). Numerous personnel changes. Keyboardist Karl Wallinger left in 1985 to form **World Party**.

12/10/88+	76	26	© 1	Fisherman's Blues				$10	Chrysalis 41589
10/27/90	180	4	© 2	Room To Roam				$10	Chrysalis 21768
6/12/93	171	2	© 3	Dream Harder				$10	Geffen 24476

And A Bang On The Ear (1)
Bigger Picture (2)
Corn Circles (3)
Dunford's Fancy (1)
Fisherman's Blues (1)
Further Up, Further In (2)
Glastonbury Song (3)
Good News (3)

Has Anybody Here Seen Hank? (1)
How Long Will I Love You? (2)
In Search Of A Rose (2)
Islandman (2)
Kaliope House (2)
Life Of Sundays (2)
Love And Death (3)

Man Is In Love (2)
Natural Bridge Blues (2)
New Life (3)
Preparing To Fly (3)
Raggle Taggle Gypsy (2)
Return Of Jimi Hendrix (3)
Return Of Pan (3)
Room To Roam (2)

Something That Is Gone (2)
Song From The End Of The World (2)
Spiritual City (3)
Spring Comes To Spiddal (2)
Star And The Sea (2)
Stolen Child (2)
Strange Boat (1)

Suffer (3)
Sweet Thing (1)
Trip To Broadford (2)
Upon The Wind And The Waves (2)
We Will Not Be Lovers (1)
When Will We Be Married? (1)
When Ye Go Away (1)

Winter Winter (3)
Wonders Of Lewis (3)
World Party (1)

WATERFRONT   '89

Male pop-rock duo from Cardiff, Wales: Chris Duffy (vocals) and Phil Cillia (guitar).

5/20/89	103	13	©	Waterfront				$10	Polydor 837970

Broken Arrow
Cry 10

Dancing With Strangers
Move On

Nature Of Love 70
Platinum Halo

Set You Free
Soul Survivor

Tightrope
Waterfront

WATERS, Crystal   '91

Born in 1964 in Philadelphia. R&B-dance singer.

7/20/91	197	3	© 1	Surprise				$10	Mercury 848894
10/8/94	199	1	● © 2	Storyteller				$10	Mercury 522105

Daddy Do (2)
Deepest Of Hearts (1)
Ghetto Day (2)
Good Lovin (1)

Gypsy Woman (She's Homeless) (1) 8
I Believe I Love You (2)
Is It For Me (2)

Listen For My Beep (2)
Lover Lay Low (2)
Makin' Happy (1)
100% Pure Love (2) 11

Regardless (2)
Relax (2)
Small Cry (1)
Storyteller (2)

Surprise (1)
Tell Me (1)
Twisted (1)
What I Need (2) 82

WATERS, Muddy   '69

Born McKinley Morganfield on 4/4/15 in Rolling Fork, Mississippi. Died of a heart attack on 4/30/83 (age 68). Legendary blues singer/guitarist/harmonica player. Inducted into the Rock and Roll Hall of Fame in 1987. Won Grammy's Lifetime Achievement Award in 1992.

11/9/68	127	8	© 1	Electric Mud				$25	Cadet Concept 314
9/27/69	70	10	2	Fathers And Sons	[L]			$30	Chess 127 [2]
				record 2: live					
2/19/77	143	7	© 3	Hard Again				$15	Blue Sky 34449
2/25/78	157	6	© 4	I'm Ready				$15	Blue Sky 34928
5/16/81	192	2	© 5	King Bee				$15	Blue Sky 37064

above 3 produced by **Johnny Winter**

All Aboard (2)
Baby Please Don't Go (2)
Blow Wind Blow (2)
Blues Had A Baby And They Named It Rock And Roll (#2) (3)
Bus Driver (3)
Can't Lose What You Ain't Never Had (2)
Champagne & Reefer (5)

Copper Brown (4)
Crosseyed Cat (3)
Deep Down In Florida (3)
Deep Down In Florida #2 (5)
Forever Lonely (5)
Forty Days And Forty Nights (2)
Good Morning Little School Girl (4)
Got My Mojo Working (Part I & II) (2)

Herbert Harper's Free Press (1)
Honey Bee (2)
I Can't Be Satisfied (3)
I Feel Like Going Home (5)
I Just Want To Make Love To You (1)
I Want To Be Loved (3)
I'm A King Bee (5)
I'm A Man ..see: Mannish Boy
I'm Ready (2,4)

I'm Your Hoochie Coochie Man (1,4)
Jealous Hearted Man (3)
Let's Spend The Night Together (1)
Little Girl (3)
Long Distance Call (2)
Mamie (4)
Mannish Boy (1,3)
Mean Disposition (2)

Mean Old Frisco Blues (5)
(My Eyes) Keep Me In Trouble (5)
No Escape From The Blues (5)
Rock Me (4)
Sad Sad Day (5)
Same Thing (4)
Screamin' And Cryin' (4)
She's All Right (1)
Standin' Round Cryin' (4)

Sugar Sweet (2)
33 Years (4)
Tom Cat (1)
Too Young To Know (5)
Twenty-Four Hours (2)
Walkin' Thru The Park (2)
Who Do You Trust (4)

WATERS, Roger '92

Born George Roger Waters on 9/6/44 in Cambridgeshire, England. Former leader/bassist of **Pink Floyd**. Went solo in 1983.

DEBUT	PEAK	WKS		CD	#	Album	Catalog	$	Label & Number
5/19/84	31	18	●	©	1	The Pros And Cons Of Hitch Hiking		$10	Columbia 39290
7/4/87	50	19		©	2	Radio K.A.O.S.		$10	Columbia 40795
9/22/90	56	10		©	3	The Wall - Live In Berlin	[L]	$15	Mercury 846611 [2]
						recorded on 7/21/90			
9/19/92	21	10		©	4	Amused To Death		$10	Columbia 47127
12/23/00	136	1		©	5	In The Flesh - Live	[L]	$15	Columbia 85235 [2]

Amused To Death (4,5)
Another Brick In The Wall, Part 2 (5)
Another Brick In The Wall (Parts 1-3) (3)
Apparently They Were Travelling Abroad (1)
Arabs With Knives And West German Skies (1)
Ballad Of Bill Hubbard (4)
Brain Damage (5)
Bravery Of Being Out Of Range (4,5)
Breathe (In The Air) (5)

Bring The Boys Back Home (3)
Comfortably Numb (3,5)
Dogs (5)
Don't Leave Me Now (3)
Dunroamin, Duncarin, Dunlivin (1)
Each Small Candle (5)
Eclipse (5)
Empty Spaces (3)
Every Strangers Eyes (1)
For The First Time Today, Part 1 & 2 (1)
Four Minutes (2)
Get Your Filthy Hands Off My Desert (5)

Go Fishing (1)
Goodbye Blue Sky (3)
Goodbye Cruel World (3)
Happiest Days Of Our Lives (3,5)
Hey You (3)
Home (2)
In The Flesh? (3,5)
Is There Anybody Out There? (3)
It's A Miracle (4,5)
Late Home Tonight, Part I & II (4)
Me Or Him (2)
Moment Of Clarity (1)

Money (5)
Mother (3,5)
Nobody Home (3)
One Of My Turns (3)
Perfect Sense, Part I & II (4,5)
Pigs On The Wing, Part 1 (5)
Powers That Be (2)
Pros And Cons Of Hitch Hiking (1,5)
Radio Waves (2)
Remains Of Our Love (1)
Run Like Hell (5)
Running Shoes (1)
Set The Controls For The Heart Of The Sun (5)

Sexual Revolution (1)
Shine On You Crazy Diamond (Parts 1-8) (5)
Southampton Dock (5)
Stop (3)
Sunset Strip (2)
Thin Ice (3)
Three Wishes (4)
Tide Is Turning (2,3)
Time (5)
Too Much Rope (4)
Trial, The (3)
Vera (3)
Waiting For The Worms (3)
Watching TV (4)

Welcome To The Machine (5)
What God Wants, Parts I-III (4)
Who Needs Information (2)
Wish You Were Here (5)
Young Lust (3)

WATLEY, Jody '87

Born on 1/30/59 in Chicago. R&B singer. Member of **Shalamar** (1977-84). Won the 1987 Best New Artist Grammy Award.

DEBUT	PEAK	WKS	RIAA	CD	#	Album	Sym	$	Label & Number
3/21/87	10	74	▲	©	1	Jody Watley		$10	MCA 5898
4/15/89	16	40	●	©	2	Larger Than Life		$10	MCA 6276
12/2/89	86	13		©	3	You Wanna Dance With Me?	[K]	$10	MCA 6343
12/21/91+	124	9		©	4	Affairs Of The Heart		$10	MCA 10355
11/27/93	164	2		©	5	Intimacy		$10	MCA 10947

Affairs Of The Heart (4)
Always And Forever (4)
Are You The One? (5)
Best Of Me (5)
Call On Me (4)
Come Into My Life (2)
Commitment Of Love (4)
Dance To The Music (4)

Do It To The Beat (1)
Don't You Want Me (1,3) *6*
Ecstasy (5)
Everything (2) *4*
For Love's Sake (2)
For The Girls (1)
Friends (2,3) *9*
I Want You (4) *61*

I'm The One You Need (4) *19*
It All Begins With You (4)
Learn To Say No (1)
Lifestyle (2)
Looking For A New Love (1,3) *2*
Love Injection (1)
L.O.V.E.R. (2,3)

Most Of All (1,3) *60*
Once You Leave (2)
Only You (2)
Precious Love (2) *87*
Real Love (2,3) *2*
Some Kind Of Lover (1,3) *10*
Something New (2)
Still A Thrill (1,3) *56*

Stolen Moments (4)
Strange Way (4)
Take Me In Your Arms (5)
To Be With You (5)
Together (5)
Too Shy To Say (5)
Until The Last Goodbye (4)

What 'Cha Gonna Do For Me (2,3)
When A Man Loves A Woman (5)
Workin' On A Groove (5)
Your Love Keeps Working On Me (5) *100*

WATSON, Doc '75

Born Arthel Watson on 3/2/23 in Deep Gap, North Carolina. Country banjo player.

DEBUT	PEAK	WKS	CD		Album	$	Label & Number
8/30/75	193	3	©		Memories	$20	United Artists 423 [2]

Blues Stay Away From Me
Columbus Stockade
Curly Headed Baby
Don't Tell Me Your Troubles

Double File & Salt Creek
Hang Your Head In Shame
In The Jailhouse Now
Keep On The Sunny Side

Make Me A Pallet
Mama Don't Allow No Music
Miss The Mississippi & You
Moody River

My Rose Of Old Kentucky
Peartree
Rambling Hobo
Shady Grove

Steel Guitar Rag
Thoughts Of Never
Wabash Cannonball
Wake Up, Little Maggie

Walking Boss
You Don't Know My Mind Blues

WATSON, Johnny "Guitar" '77

Born on 2/3/35 in Houston. Died of a heart attack on 5/17/96 (age 61). R&B singer/songwriter/guitarist.

DEBUT	PEAK	WKS	RIAA	CD	#	Album	$	Label & Number
8/7/76	52	22	●	©	1	Ain't That A Bitch	$12	DJM 3
4/16/77	20	27	●	©	2	A Real Mother For Ya	$12	DJM 7
12/24/77+	84	14		©	3	Funk Beyond The Call Of Duty	$12	DJM 714
4/15/78	154	4			4	Master Funk	$12	DJM 13
						WATSONIAN INSTITUTE		
10/28/78	157	7		©	5	Giant	$12	DJM 19
7/5/80	115	14		©	6	Love Jones	$12	DJM 31
6/27/81	177	3		©	7	Johnny "Guitar" Watson And The Family Clone	$12	DJM 501

Ain't Movin' (7)
Ain't That A Bitch (1)
Asante Sana (4)
Baby Face (She Said Do Do Do Do) (5)
Barn Door (3)
Booty Ooty (6)
Children Of The Universe (6)
Clone Information (7)
Close Encounters (6)

Come And Dance With Me (7)
Coming Around (4)
De John's Delight (4)
Family Clone (7)
Forget The Joneses (7)
Funk Beyond The Call Of Duty (3)
Funk If I Know (4)
Gangster Of Love (5)
Give Me My Love (3)

Going Up In Smoke (6)
Guitar Disco (5)
I Need It (1)
I Wanna Thank You (2)
I Want To Ta-Ta You Baby (1)
I'm Gonna Get You Baby (3)
Institute, The (4)
It's A Damn Shame (3)
It's About The Dollar Bill (3)
Jet Plane (6)

Lady Voo Doo (4)
Lone Ranger (6)
Love Jones (6)
Love That Will Not Die (3)
Lover Jones (2)
Master Funk (4)
Miss Frisco (Queen Of The Disco) (5)
Nothing Left To Be Desired (2)
Real Deal (2)

Real Mother For Ya (2) *41*
Rio Dreamin' (7)
Since I Met You Baby (1)
Superman Lover (1)
Tarzan (2)
Telephone Bill (6)
Tu Jours Amour (5)
Virginia's Pretty Funky (4)
Voodoo What You Do (7)
We're No Exception (1)

What Is Love? (7)
Won't You Forgive Me Baby (1)
Wrapped In Black Mink (5)
You Can Stay But The Noise Must Go (5)
Your Love Is My Love (2)

WATSON, Russell '01

Born in 1973 in England. Operatic tenor.

DEBUT	PEAK	WKS	CD		Album	$	Label & Number
5/5/01	90	15↑	©		The Voice	$10	Decca 468695

Amor Ti Vieta
Barcelona (Friends Until The End)

Bridge Over Troubled Water
Caruso
Funiculí Funiculá

La Donna È Mobile
Miserere
Nella Fantasia

Nessun Dorma!
Non Ti Scordar Di Me
Panis Angelicus

Ricordo Ancor (Pelagia's Song)
Saylon Dola
Someone Like You

Vienna

WATT, Mike '95

Born on 12/20/57 in Portsmouth, Virginia. Hard-rock singer/bassist. Joined **Porno For Pyros** in 1995.

DEBUT	PEAK	WKS	CD		Album	$	Label & Number
3/18/95	129	4	©		Ball-Hog Or Tugboat?	$10	Columbia 67086

Against The 70's
Big Train
Chinese Firedrill
Coincidence Is Either Hit Or Miss

Drove Up From Pedro
E-Ticket Ride
Forever - One Reporter's Opinion
Heartbeat

Intense Song For Madonna To Sing
Maggot Brain
Max And Wells
Piss-Bottle Man

Sexual Military Dynamics
Sidemouse Advice
Song For Igor
Tell 'Em, Boy!
Tuff Gnarl

WATTS, Ernie '82

Born on 10/23/45 in Norfolk, Virginia. R&B saxophonist.

DEBUT	PEAK	WKS		Album	Sym	$	Label & Number
2/20/82	161	12		Chariots Of Fire	[I]	$12	Qwest 3637

Abraham's Theme
Chariots Of Fire (Theme)

Five Circles
Gigolo

Hold On
Lady

Valdez In The Country

WATTS 103rd STREET RHYTHM BAND — see WRIGHT, Charles

WA WA NEE '87
Pop group from Australia: brothers Paul (vocals, keyboards) and Mark (bass) Gray, with Steve Williams (guitar) and Chris Sweeney (drums).

11/7/87	123	17	©	**Wa Wa Nee**	$10	Epic 40858

Gone · Love Reaction · One And One (Ain't I Good Enough) · **Sugar Free** *35*
I Could Make You Love Me · Manchild · **Stimulation** *86* · Teacher
Jelly Baby · · · When The World Is A Home

WAX '86
Pop duo: **Andrew Gold** and Graham Gouldman (of **10cc**).

4/26/86	101	11	©	**Magnetic Heaven**	$10	RCA Victor 9546

Ball And Chain · Hear No Evil · Marie Claire · **Right Between The Eyes** *43* · Shadows Of Love
Breakout · Magnetic Heaven · Only A Visitor · Rise Up · Systematic

WAYBILL, Fee '84
Born John Waldo on 9/17/50 in Omaha, Nebraska. Lead singer of **The Tubes**.

11/10/84	146	6	©	**Read My Lips**	$10	Capitol 12369

Caribbean Sunsets · I Don't Even Know Your Name (Passion Play) · Nobody's Perfect · Star Of The Show · Who Loves You Baby · You're Still Laughing
I Could've Been Somebody · · Saved My Life · Thrill Of The Kill · Who Said Life Would Be Pretty

WAYLON & WILLIE — see JENNINGS, Waylon / NELSON, Willie

WAYNE, John '73
Born Marion Morrison on 5/26/07 in Winterset, Iowa. Died of cancer on 6/11/79 (age 72). Legendary movie actor. Nicknamed "The Duke."

3/3/73	66	16		**America, Why I Love Her**	[T]	$25	RCA Victor 4828

a narrative tribute (with orchestra and chorus) to America

American Boy Grows Up · Good Things · Mis Raices Estan Aqui (My Roots Are Buried Here) · People, The · Taps · Why I Love Her
Face The Flag · Hyphen, The · · Pledge Of Allegiance · Why Are You Marching, Son?

WAYSTED '87
Hard-rock group: Danny vaughn (vocals), Paul Chapman (guitar), Pete Way (bass) and John DiTeodoro (drums). Chapman and Way were with **UFO**.

3/21/87	185	2		**Save Your Prayers**	$10	Capitol 12538

Black And Blue · Hell Comes Home · How The West Was Won · Singing To The Night · Walls Fall Down
Heaven Tonight · Heroes Die Young · Out Of Control · So Long · Wild Night

WC AND THE MAAD CIRCLE '98
Born in Los Angeles. Male rapper. Member of **Westside Connection**. The MAAD Circle: Big G and DJ Crazy Toons.

10/21/95	85	3	©	1	**Curb Servin'**	$10	Payday 828650
5/16/98	19	11	©	2	**The Shadiest One**	$10	Red Ant 828957

WC
Autobiography, The (2) · Cheddar (2) · Hog (2) · Keep Hustlin' (2) · Put On Tha Set (1) · Wet Dream (1)
Bank Lick (2) · Creator, The (1) · Homesick (1) · Kill A Habit (1) · Rich Rollin' (2) · Where Y'all From (2)
Better Days (2) *64* · Curb Servin' (1) · In A Twist (1) · Like That (2) · Shadiest One (2) · Worldwide Gunnin' (2)
Call It What You Want (2) · Feel Me (1) · It's All Bad (2) · One, The (1) · Taking Ova (1)
Can't Hold Back (2) · Fuckin' Wit Uh House Party (2) · **Just Clownin'** (2) *56* · Outcome, The (2) · **West Up!** (1) *88*

WEATHERLY, Jim '74
Born on 3/17/43 in Pontotoc, Mississippi. Pop-country singer/songwriter.

9/28/74	94	14		**The Songs Of Jim Weatherly**	$15	Buddah 5608

California Memory · I'll Still Love You *87* · Living Every Man's Dream · **Need To Be** *11* · Where Do I Put Her Memory
Coming Apart · Like Old Times Again · My First Day Without Her · Roses And Love Songs · You Are A Song

★343★ WEATHER REPORT '77
Jazz-fusion group formed by Austrian-born Josef Zawinul (keyboards) and **Wayne Shorter** (sax). Zawinul was a member of **Cannonball Adderley**'s combo for nine years. Various personnel included **Jaco Pastorius** from 1976-82. Zawinul formed the Zawinul Syndicate in 1988.

1)Heavy Weather 2)Tale Spinnin' 3)Black Market

7/24/71	191	4	©	1	**Weather Report**	[I]	$12	Columbia 30661
7/15/72	147	6	©	2	**I Sing The Body Electric**	[I-L]	$12	Columbia 31352

side 2: recorded live in Tokyo

5/26/73	85	17	©	3	**Sweetnighter**	[I]	$12	Columbia 32210
6/22/74	46	23	©	4	**Mysterious Traveller**	[I]	$12	Columbia 32494
6/7/75	31	14	©	5	**Tale Spinnin'**	[I]	$12	Columbia 33417
4/17/76	42	12	©	6	**Black Market**	[I]	$12	Columbia 34099
4/2/77	30	22	▲ ©	7	**Heavy Weather**	C:#33/18	[I]	$12	Columbia 34418
10/28/78	52	14	©	8	**Mr. Gone**	[I]	$12	ARC 35358
10/6/79	47	11	©	9	**8:30**	[I-L]	$15	ARC 36030 [2]
12/13/80+	57	14	©	10	**Night Passage**	[I]	$12	ARC 36793
2/20/82	68	11	©	11	**Weather Report**	[I]	$12	ARC 37616
3/19/83	96	10	©	12	**Procession**	[I]	$10	Columbia 38427
3/24/84	136	8	©	13	**Domino Theory**	[I]	$10	Columbia 39147
4/27/85	191	3	©	14	**Sportin' Life**	[I]	$10	Columbia 39908
8/23/86	195	2	©	15	**This Is This**	[I]	$10	Columbia 40280

Adios (3) · Boogie Woogie Waltz (3,9) · Current Affairs (11) · Eurydice (1) · Havona (7) · Lusitanos (5)
American Tango (4) · Brown Street (9) · D Flat Waltz (13) · Face On The Barroom Floor (14) · Herandnu (6) · Madagascar (10)
And Then (8) · Can It Be Done (13) · Dara Factor One & Two (11) · Face The Fire (15) · Hot Cargo (14) · Man In The Green Shirt (5)
Badia (5,9) · Cannon Ball (6) · Directions (2) · Fast City (14) · I'll Never Forget You (15) · Man With The Copper Fingers (15)
Barbary Coast (6) · China Blues (15) · Dr. Honoris Causa (medley) (2) · Five Short Stories (5) · Ice-Pick Willy (14) · Manolete (3)
Between The Thighs (5) · Confians (14) · Domino Theory (13) · Forlorn (15) · In A Silent Way (9) · Milky Way (1)
Birdland (7,9) · Consequently (15) · Dream Clock (10) · Freezing Fire (5) · Indiscretions (14) · Molasses Run (12)
Black Market (6,9) · Corner Pocket (14) · 8:30 (9) · Gibraltar (6) · Juggler, The (7) · Moors, The (2)
Blackthorn Rose (4) · Crystal (2) · Elders, The (8) · Harlequin (7) · Jungle Book (4) · Morning Lake (1)
Blue Sound - Note 3 (13) · Cucumber Slumber (4) · Elegant People (6) · · Jungle Stuff, Part I (15) ·

WEATHER REPORT — Cont'd

Mr. Gone (8)
Mysterious Traveller (4)
N.Y.C. Medley (11)
Night Passage (10)
Non-Stop Home (3)
Nubian Sundance (4)
125th Street Congress (3)
Orange Lady (1)
Orphan, The (9)

Palladium (7)
Pearl On The Half-Shell (14)
Peasant, The (13)
Pinocchio (8)
Plaza Real (12)
Port Of Entry (10)
Predator (13)
Procession (12)
Punk Jazz (8)

Pursuit Of The Woman With
  The Feathered Hat (8)
Remark You Made (7,9)
River People (8)
Rockin' In Rhythm (10)
Rumba Mama (7)
Scarlet Woman (4,9)
Second Sunday In August (2)
Seventh Arrow (1)

Sightseeing (9)
Slang (9)
Speechless (11)
Surucucu (2)
Swamp Cabbage (13)
T.H. (medley) (2)
Tears (1)
Teen Town (7,9)
Thanks For The Memory (9)

This Is This (15)
Three Clowns (6)
Three Views Of A Secret (10)
Two Lines (12)
Umbrellas (1)
Unknown Soldier (2)
Update (15)
Vertical Invader (medley) (2)
Volcano For Hire (11)

Waterfall (1)
Well, The (12)
What's Going On (14)
When It Was Now (11)
Where The Moon Goes (12)
Will (3)
Young And Fine (8)

WEAVER, Dennis   '72
Born on 6/4/24 in Joplin, Missouri. Actor/singer. Starred in TV's *McCloud*, *Gentle Ben* and *Gunsmoke*.

| 5/13/72 | 191 | 2 | | | **Dennis Weaver** .... | | | $15 | Im'press 1614 |

Another Way
I Still Sing "Jesus Loves Me"
I'd Rather Be With You Than
  Anyone

Learn To Love
Lonesome To The Lonely
No Name

Ode To A Critter (Fish, Bird &
  Cow Song)
Time

20th Century Man (Our Man Is
  Coming)
Where Have The Wild
  Blackberries Gone

Work Through My Hands, Lord

WEAVERS, The   '61
Legendary folk group: **Pete Seeger**, Lee Hays, Fred Hellerman and female lead Ronnie Gilbert. Revived and popularized folk music in the early 1950s. Hays died on 8/26/61 (age 68).

1/23/61	126	13		©	1 **The Weavers at Carnegie Hall, Vol. 2**	[L]		$50	Vanguard 9075
					recorded on 4/1/60				
3/13/61	24	7		©	2 **The Weavers at Carnegie Hall**	[L]		$50	Vanguard 9010
					recorded on 12/24/55				

Amazing Grace (1)
Around The World (2)
Below The Gallows Tree (1)
Bill Bailey Come Home (1)
Born In East Virginia (1)
Buttermilk Hill (1)
Darling Corey (1)
Follow The Drinking Gourd (2)

Go Where I Send Thee (2)
Good Old Bowling Green (1)
Goodnight Irene (2)
Greensleeves (2)
Hush Little Baby (2)
I Know Where I'm Going (2)
I've Got A Home In That Rock

In That New Jerusalem (1)
Kisses Sweeter Than Wine (2)
Last Night I Had The Strangest
  Dream (1)
Lonesome Traveller (2)
Marching To Pretoria (1)
On My Journey (1)
Pay Me My Money Down (2)

Rock Island Line (2)
Run Come See (1)
Shalom Chaverim (2)
Sinking Of The Reuben James
  (1)
Sixteen Tons (2)
Stewball (1)
Subo (1)

Suliram (I'll Be There) (2)
Tapuach Hineni (1)
There Once Was A Young Man
  Who Went To The City (1)
Universal Folk Song (1)
Venga Jaleo (2)
Virgin Mary (1)

When The Saints Go Marching
  In (2)
Wimoweh (2)
Woody's Rag And 900 Miles (2)

WEBB, Jack   '55
Born on 4/2/20 in Santa Monica, California. Died of a heart attack on 12/23/82 (age 62). Actor/TV producer. Creator/director/star ("Joe Friday") of TV's *Dragnet* and the movie *Pete Kelly's Blues*. Married to **Julie London** from 1945-53.

| 9/3/55 | 2² | 15 | | | **Pete Kelly's Blues** | [I-T] | | $50 | RCA Victor 1126 |
| | | | | | LP: RCA Victor LPM-1126 (#2); EP: RCA Victor EPB-1126 (#1) | | | | |

Breezin' Along With The Breeze
Bye, Bye Blackbird
Hard Hearted Hannah

I Never Knew
I'm Gonna Meet My Sweetie
  Now

Oh Didn't He Ramble
Pete Kelly's Blues
Smiles

Somebody Loves Me
Sugar

What Can I Say After I Say I'm
  Sorry

WEBBER, Andrew Lloyd   '91
Born on 3/22/48 in London. Legendary musical composer. Creator of *Jesus Christ Superstar*, *Evita*, *Cats*, *Phantom Of The Opera*, *Joseph and The Amazing Technicolor Dreamcoat* and *Requiem*. Collaborated with lyricist Tim Rice. Formerly married to **Sarah Brightman**. Won Grammy's Living Legends Award in 1989. Knighted by Queen Elizabeth II.

5/25/91	130	14	▲	©	1 **The Premiere Collection** ....C:#23/45	[K]		$10	MCA 6284
4/3/93	191	6		©	2 **The Premiere Collection Encore**	[K]		$10	Polydor 517336
12/21/96+	155	7		©	3 **The Very Best Of Andrew Lloyd Webber - The Broadway Collection**	[K]		$10	Polydor 533064

All I Ask Of You [Cliff Richard &
  Sarah Brightman] (1)
Amigos Para Siempre [José
  Carreras & Sarah Brightman]
  (2)
Another Suitcase In Another
  Hall [Barbara Dickson] (1)
Any Dream Will Do [Jason
  Donovan] (2)
Any Dream Will Do [Michael
  Damian] (3)
Anything But Lonely [Sarah
  Brightman] (2)
Argentine Melody (Cancion De
  Argentina) [San Jose feat.
  Rodriguez Argentina] (2)
As If We Never Said Goodbye
  [Barbra Streisand] (3)

By Jeeves [Original London
  Cast] (3)
Close Every Door [Philip
  Schofield] (2)
Close Every Door [Donny
  Osmond] (3)
Don't Cry For Me Argentina
  [Julie Covington] (1)
Don't Cry For Me Argentina
  [Sarah Brightman] (2)
Everything's Alright [Sarah
  Brightman] (2)
First Man You Remember
  [Michael Ball & Diana
  Morrison] (2)
Gus: The Theatre Cat [Sarah
  Brightman with Sir John
  Gielgud] (3)

High Flying, Adored [Mandy
  Patinkin & Patti Lupone] (3)
Hosanna [Plácido Domingo] (2)
I Am The Starlight [Lon Satton
  & Ray Shell] (2)
I Don't Know How To Love Him
  [Yvonne Elliman] (1)
Jellicle Ball [Royal Philharmonic
  Orchestra] (2)
Love Changes Everything
  [Michael Ball] (2,3)
Magical Mr. Mistoffelees [Paul
  Nicholas] (1)
Memory [Elaine Paige] (1)
Memory [Barbra Streisand] (2)
Memory [Betty Buckley] (3)

Mr. Mistoffelees [Original
  Broadway Cast] (1)
Music Of The Night [Michael
  Crawford] (1,3)
Oh What A Circus [David
  Essex] (2)
Phantom Of The Opera [Steve
  Harley & Sarah Brightman] (1)
Phantom Of The Opera
  [Michael Crawford & Sarah
  Brightman] (3)
Pie Jesu [Sarah Brightman &
  Paul Miles Kingston] (1,3)
Point Of No Return [Michael
  Crawford & Sarah Brightman]
  (2)
Seeing Is Believing [Michael
  Ball & Ann Crumb] (2)

Starlight Express [Ray Shell] (1)
Sunset Boulevard [Alan
  Campbell] (3)
Superstar [Murray Head] (1,3)
Take That Look Off Your Face
  [Marti Webb] (1)
Tell Me On A Sunday [Marti
  Webb] (1)
Variations 1-4 [Julian Lloyd
  Webber] (1)
Wishing You Were Somehow
  Here Again [Sarah Brightman]
  (2,3)
With One Look [Glenn Close]
  (3)

WECHTER, Julius — see BAJA MARIMBA BAND

WEEN   '00
Rock duo from Lambertville, New Jersey: Mickey Melchiondo ("Dean Ween") and Aaron Freeman ("Gene Ween").

| 7/12/97 | 159 | 1 | | © | 1 **The Mollusk** .... | | | $10 | Elektra 62013 |
| 5/20/00 | 121 | 1 | | © | 2 **White Pepper** .... | | | $10 | Elektra 62449 |

Back To Basom (2)
Bananas And Blow (2)
Blarney Stone (1)
Buckingham Green (1)
Cold Blows The Wind (1)

Even If You Don't (2)
Exactly Where I'm At (2)
Falling Out (2)
Flutes Of Chi (2)
Golden Eel (1)

Grobe, The (2)
I'll Be Your Jonny On The Spot
  (1)
I'm Dancing In The Show
  Tonight (1)

Ice Castles (2)
It's Gonna Be (Alright) (1)
Mollusk, The (1)
Mutilated Lips (1)
Ocean Man (1)

Pandy Fackler (2)
Pink Eye (On My Leg) (1)
Polka Dot Tail (1)
She Wanted To Leave (1)
She's Your Baby (2)

Stay Forever (2)
Stroker Ace (2)
Waving My Dick In The Wind
  (1)

WEEZER   '01
Rock group from Los Angeles: Rivers Cuomo (vocals, guitar), Brian Bell (guitar), Matt Sharp (bass) and Patrick Wilson (drums).

8/27/94+	16	76	▲³	©	1 **Weezer** ....C:#4/24			$10	DGC 24629
10/12/96	19	16	●	©	2 **Pinkerton** ....C:#35/2			$10	DGC 25007
6/2/01	4	18	↑▲	©	3 **Weezer**			$10	Geffen 493045

Across The Sea (2)
Buddy Holly (1)
Butterfly (2)
Crab (3)
Don't Let Go (3)
El Scorcho (2)

Falling For You (2)
Getchoo (2)
Glorious Day (3)
Good Life (2)
Hash Pipe (3)
Holiday (1)

In The Garage (1)
Island In The Sun (3)
Knock-down Drag-out (3)
My Name Is Jonas (1)
No One Else (1)
No Other One (2)

O Girlfriend (3)
Only In Dreams (1)
Photograph (3)
Pink Triangle (2)
Say It Ain't So (1)
Simple Pages (3)

Smile (3)
Surf Wax America (1)
Tired Of Sex (2)
Undone - The Sweater Song
  (1) *57*
Why Bother? (2)

World Has Turned And Left Me
  Here (1)

WE FIVE '65

Pop group from San Francisco: Beverly Bivens (vocals), Bob Jones and Jerry Burgan (guitars), Pete Fullerton (bass) and Mike Stewart (drums). Stewart is the brother of **John Stewart**.

| 10/16/65 | **32** | 30 | | © | 1 **You Were On My Mind** | | | $25 | A&M 4111 |
| 1/27/68 | **172** | 6 | | © | 2 **Make Someone Happy** | | | $25 | A&M 4138 |

Can't Help Falling In Love (1) — I Can Never Go Home Again (1) — Love Me Not Tomorrow (1) — Small World (1) — Tonight (1)
Cast Your Fate To The Wind (1) — I Got Plenty O' Nuttin' (1) — Make Someone Happy (2) — Softly As I Leave You (1) — What Do I Do Now? (2)
First Time (2) — If I Were Alone (1) — My Favorite Things (1) — Somewhere (2) — What's Goin' On (2)
Five Will Get You Ten (2) — Inch Worm (2) — Our Day Will Come (2) — Somewhere Beyond The Sea — You Let A Love Burn Out (2)
High Flying Bird (2) — Let's Get Together (2) 31 — Poet (2) — (1) — You Were On My Mind (1) 3

WEILAND, Scott '98

Born on 10/27/67 in Santa Cruz, California. Lead singer of **Stone Temple Pilots**.

| 4/18/98 | **42** | 5 | | © | 12 Bar Blues | | | $10 | Atlantic 83084 |

About Nothing — Date, The — Jimmy Was A Stimulator — Mockingbird Girl — Where's The Man
Barbarella — Desperation #5 — Lady, Your Roof Brings Me — Opposite Octave Reaction
Cool Kiss — Divider — Down — Son

WEIR, Bob '78

Born Robert Hall on 10/16/47 in San Francisco. Rock singer/guitarist. Co-founder of the **Grateful Dead**. Later formed **Kingfish** and **Bobby & The Midnites**.

| 6/17/72 | **68** | 15 | | © | 1 **Ace** | | | $30 | Warner 2627 |
| 2/11/78 | **69** | 16 | | © | 2 **Heaven Help The Fool** | | | $12 | Arista 4155 |

Black-Throated Wind (1) — Easy To Slip (2) — I'll Be Doggone (2) — One More Saturday Night (1) — Shade Of Grey (2) — Wrong Way Feelin' (2)
Bombs Away (2) 70 — Greatest Story Ever Told (1) — Looks Like Rain (1) — Playing In The Band (1) — This Time Forever (2)
Cassidy (1) — Heaven Help The Fool (2) — Mexicali Blues (1) — Salt Lake City (2) — Walk In The Sunshine (1)

WEISBERG, Tim '78

Born on 4/26/43 in Los Angeles. Jazz-pop flutist.

1)Twin Sons Of Different Mothers 2)Tim Weisberg 4 3)Listen To The City

| 12/29/73+ | **160** | 4 | | | 1 **Dreamspeaker** | [I-L] | | $12 | A&M 3045 |

side 1: live; side 2: studio

11/23/74	**100**	13			2 **Tim Weisberg 4**	[I]		$12	A&M 3658
10/11/75	**105**	7			3 **Listen To The City**	[I]		$12	A&M 4545
10/2/76	**148**	7			4 **Live At Last!**	[I-L]		$12	A&M 4600

recorded on 6/12/76 at the Troubador in Hollywood

8/20/77	**108**	12			5 **The Tim Weisberg Band**	[I]		$12	United Artists 773
5/6/78	**159**	6			6 **Rotations**	[I]		$12	United Artists 857
9/16/78	**8**	35	▲	©	7 **Twin Sons Of Different Mothers**			$12	Full Moon 35339

DAN FOGELBERG & TIM WEISBERG

4/14/79	**114**	11			8 **Night-Rider!**	[I]		$12	MCA 3084
6/9/79	**169**	4		©	9 **Smile!/The Best Of Tim Weisberg**	[G-I]		$12	A&M 4749
8/2/80	**171**	7			10 **Party Of One**	[I]		$12	MCA 5125

All Tied Up (6) — Dion Blue (2,9) — High Rise (3,9) — Mercy, Mercy, Mercy (5) — Rainbow City (3,4) — Travesty (2,9)
Amber (10) — Discovery (3,4) — Hurtwood Alley (7) — Midsummer's Dream (8) — Rush Hour (Friday, P.M.) (3,9) — Twins Theme (7)
Angelic Smile (2,9) — Do Dah (1,4,9) — I'm The Lucky One (10) — Moonchild (8) — Scrabble X, Y, & Z (1) — Visit, The (2,9)
Aspen (5) — Don't Keep Me Waiting, Girl — Intimidation (7) — Night For Crying (1,9) — Shadows In The Wind (8) — Weekend (3)
Blitz, The (5) — (10) — Invisible Messenger (2) — Night Rider (8) — Shellie's Rainbow (5) — Westchester Faire (8)
Bruiser, The (2,9) — Dreamspeaker (1) — Just For You (6) — Night Watch (1) — Since You've Asked (7) — What's Going On (10)
Bullfrog (7) — Everyone Loves A Mystery (10) — Katie (10) — Nightsongs (8) — Six O'Clock In The Morning (1) — Winged Invitation (2)
California Memories Medley — Everytime I See Your Smile (6) — Killing Me Softly With His Song — Nikki's Waltz (2) — So Good To Me (6) — Wings Of Fire (8)
(2,4) — Flight Of The Phoenix (2) — (1) — Page One (1) — Someday My Prince Will Come — Won't Be Comin' Back (8)
Canterbury Tales (8) — Friends (8) — Lahaina Luna (7) — Paris Nocturne (7) — (2) — Yesterday's Dreams (8)
Cascade (5) — Gene, Jean (5) — Lazy Susan (7) — Party Of One (10) — Southern Lights (5) — Your Smiling Eyes (4)
Castile (1,4) — Gentle Storm (5) — Listen To The City (3,4,9) — Passing, The (5) — Street Party (3,9)
Catch The Breeze (6) — Glide Away (6) — Lord Vanity (7) — Power Flower (10) — Sudden Samba (6)
Chase, The (3,4,9) — Good Life (3,4,9) — Love Maker (3) — **Power Of Gold** (7) 24 — Tell Me To My Face (7)
Conception (3) — Good News (2) — Lunchbreak (3) — Power Pocket (6) — There Is A Mountain (6)
Dealer, The (3) — Guitar Etude No. 3 (7) — Magic Lady (10) — Premonition (2) — Touchstone (8)

WEISSBERG, Eric '73

Bluegrass guitarist. Prolific session musician.

| 1/27/73 | **❶**3 | 25 | | ● | 1 **Dueling Banjos** | [I] | | $15 | Warner 2683 |

ERIC WEISSBERG & STEVE MANDELL

| 10/20/73 | **196** | 2 | | | 2 **Rural Free Delivery** | | | $15 | Warner 2720 |

ERIC WEISSBERG & DELIVERANCE

Blessed Is The Man (2) — Eight More Miles To Louisville — Hard Ain't It Hard (1) — Opening Day (2) — Scalded Cat (2) — 'Til The End Of The World Rolls
Buffalo Gals (1) — (1) — Hard Hearted (2) — Pony Express (1) — Shuckin' The Corn (1) — Around (2)
Bugle Call Rag (1) — Eighth Of January (1) — Lend Me Your Heart (2) — Rawhide (1) — Somewhere In Time (2) — Uncle Pen (2)
Concrete Canyon Boogie (2) — End Of A Dream (1) — Little Maggie (1) — Reuben's Train (1) — Thanks For Bein' You And
Dueling Banjos (1) 2 — Farewell Blues (1) — Mountain Dew (1) — Ride In The Country (2) — Lovin' Me (2)
Earl's Breakdown (1) — Fire On The Mountain (1) — Old Joe Clark (1) — Riding The Waves (1)

WELCH, Bob '78

Born on 7/31/46 in Los Angeles. Pop-rock singer/guitarist. Member of **Fleetwood Mac** (1971-74) and **Paris**.

10/8/77+	**12**	46	▲	©	1 **French Kiss**			$12	Capitol 11663
3/10/79	**20**	17	●	©	2 **Three Hearts**			$12	Capitol 11907
12/1/79	**105**	8		©	3 **The Other One**			$12	Capitol 12017
10/11/80	**162**	5		©	4 **Man Overboard**			$12	Capitol 12107

B666 (4) — Don't Let Me Fall (3) — Ghost Of Flight 401 (2) — Little Star (2) — Oh Jenny (2) — Spanish Dancers (3)
Carolene (1) — Don't Rush The Good Things — Girl Can't Stop (4) — Lose My Heart (1) — Old Man Of 17 (3) — Straight Up (3)
China (2) — (4) — Here Comes The Night (2) — Lose Your... (1) — Oneonone (3) — Those Days Are Gone (4)
Church (2) 73 — Don't Wait Too Long (2) — Hideaway (3) — Lose Your Heart (1) — Outskirts (1) — 3 Hearts (2)
Come Softly To Me (2) — Easy To Fall (1) — **Hot Love, Cold World** (1) 31 — Love Came 2X (3) — **Precious Love** (2) 19 — Watch The Animals (3)
Danchiva (1) — Ebony Eyes (1) 14 — I Saw Her Standing There (2) — Man Overboard (4) — Reason (4)
Dancin' Eyes (1) — Fate Decides (4) — Jealous (4) — Mystery Train (1) — Rebel Rouser (3)
Devil Wind (2) — Future Games (3) — Justine (4) — Nightmare (4) — **Sentimental Lady** (1) 8

WELCH, Gillian '98
Born in 1968 in Los Angeles. Female singer/songwriter/guitarist.

| 8/15/98 | 181 | 1 | | © | Hell Among The Yearlings.. | | | $10 | Almo Sounds 80021 |

Caleb Meyer   Good Til Now   I'm Not Afraid To Die   My Morphine   Rock Of Ages   Winter's Come And Gone
Devil Had A Hold Of Me   Honey Now   Miner's Refrain   One Morning   Whiskey Girl

WELK, Lenny '64
Born on 5/15/38 in Asbury Park, New Jersey. Smooth R&B singer.

| 2/1/64 | 73 | 10 | | | 1 Since I Fell For You.. | | | $40 | Cadence 3068 |
| 1/1/66 | 147 | 2 | | | 2 Since I Fell For You.. | | [R] | $25 | Columbia 9230 |

new cover features same photo as original with new artwork

Are You Sincere (1,2)   I Need Someone (1,2)   Mama, Don't You Hit That Boy   Stranger In Paradise (1,2)   You Don't Know Me (1,2) 45
Darlin' (1)   I'm In The Mood For Love (1,2)   (1,2)   Taste Of Honey (1,2)
Ebb Tide (1,2) 25   It's Just Not That Easy (1,2)   **Since I Fell For You** (1,2) 4   You Can Have Her (1,2)

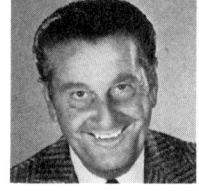

WELK, Lawrence ★18★ '61
Born on 3/11/03 in Strasburg, North Dakota. Died of pneumonia on 5/17/92 (age 89). Accordian player/polka bandleader since the mid-1920s. Band's style labeled as "champagne music." Hosted own TV musical variety show from 1955-82.

1)Calcutta! 2)Yellow Bird 3)Last Date 4)Moon River 5)Lawrence Welk and His Sparkling Strings

1/28/56	5	11			1 Lawrence Welk and His Sparkling Strings	[I]		$20	Coral 57011
3/31/56	13	2			2 TV Favorites...			$20	Coral 57025
3/31/56	18	2			3 Shamrocks and Champagne...			$20	Coral 57036
5/12/56	6	17			4 Bubbles In The Wine..			$20	Coral 57038
8/18/56	10	30			5 Say It With Music..	[I]		$20	Coral 57041
8/25/56	17	4			6 Champagne Pops Parade..			$20	Coral 57078
10/20/56	18	1			7 Moments To Remember..	[I]		$20	Coral 57068
12/22/56	8	3			8 Merry Christmas..	[X]		$20	Coral 57093
3/16/57	20	1			9 Pick-a-Polka!..	[I]		$20	Coral 57067
5/20/57	17	5			10 Waltz with Lawrence Welk..	[I]		$20	Coral 57119
10/21/57+	19	2			11 Lawrence Welk plays Dixieland	[I]		$20	Coral 57146
12/23/57	18	3			12 Jingle Bells..	[X]		$20	Coral 57186
12/19/60+	4	29			13 Last Date..	[I]		$15	Dot 3350
1/30/61	❶[11]	64	●		14 Calcutta!...	[I]		$15	Dot 3359
8/7/61	2[1]	49			15 Yellow Bird...	[I]		$15	Dot 3389
1/6/62	4	48			16 Moon River...	[I]		$15	Dot 3412
1/6/62	100	3			17 Silent Night and 13 other best loved Christmas songs	[X-I]		$15	Dot 3397
					Christmas charts: 13/'63, 61/'66, 61/'67				
5/26/62	6	20			18 Young World..	[I]		$15	Dot 3428
9/15/62	9	15			19 Baby Elephant Walk and Theme From The Brothers Grimm	[I]		$15	Dot 3457
12/29/62	140	1			20 Silent Night and 13 other best loved Christmas songs	[X-I-R]		$15	Dot 3397
3/9/63	34	25			21 Waltz Time...	[I]		$15	Dot 25499
4/6/63	20	28			22 1963's Early Hits..	[I]		$15	Dot 25510
8/10/63	33	28			23 Scarlett O'Hara..	[I]		$15	Dot 25528
12/7/63+	29	26			24 Wonderful! Wonderful!...	[I]		$15	Dot 25552
4/11/64	37	19			25 Early Hits Of 1964..	[I]		$15	Dot 25572
4/25/64	127	5			26 A Tribute To The All-Time Greats...................................	[I]		$15	Dot 25544
8/8/64	73	16			27 The Lawrence Welk Television Show 10th Anniversary			$15	Dot 25591
1/9/65	115	6			28 The Golden Millions..	[I]		$15	Dot 25611
4/3/65	108	12			29 My First Of 1965...	[I]		$15	Dot 25616
4/17/65	57	12			30 Apples & Bananas...	[I]		$15	Dot 25629
1/29/66	93	6			31 Today's Great Hits..	[I]		$15	Dot 25663
3/26/66	106	5			32 Champagne On Broadway..	[I]		$15	Dot 25688
12/3/66+	12	41	●		33 Winchester Cathedral..	[I]		$15	Dot 25774
4/15/67	72	18			34 Lawrence Welk's "Hits Of Our Time"..............................	[I]		$15	Dot 25790
10/14/67	130	12			35 Golden Hits/The Best Of Lawrence Welk..........................	[G-I]		$15	Dot 25812
4/6/68	130	12			36 Love Is Blue..	[I]		$12	Ranwood 8003
2/8/69	173	8			37 Memories..	[I]		$12	Ranwood 8044
4/19/69	55	20			38 Galveston...	[I]		$12	Ranwood 8049
9/13/69	176	4			39 Lawrence Welk plays I Love You Truly and other songs of love	[I]		$12	Ranwood 8053
11/15/69	145	7			40 Jean...	[I]		$12	Ranwood 8060
12/12/70+	133	17			41 Candida...			$12	Ranwood 8083
12/23/72+	149	10			42 Reminiscing...	[I-K]		$15	Ranwood 5001 [2]

Addams Family, Theme From The (29)
Adeste Fideles (17,20)
(also see: Come All Ye Faithful)
(also see: Come All Ye Faithful)
Alamo, Theme From The ..see: Green Leaves Of Summer
Alice Blue Gown (medley) (10)
Alice In Wonderland (22)

All I Have To Do Is Dream (22)
Alley Cat (29,42)
Always (39)
Am I That Easy To Forget (36)
And We Were Lovers (34)
Anniversary Song (37,39)
Anniversary Waltz (7,39)
Anything Goes (medley) (5)
Anything That's Part Of You (18)

Apples And Bananas (30,35) 75
April In Portugal (14)
April Love (18)
Are You Lonesome Tonight (19)
Around The World (16)
As Long As She Needs Me (29)
Autumn Nocturne (1)
Baby Elephant Walk (19,35) 48
Ball Of Fire (4)

Ballerina (26)
Barnyard Blues (11)
Be My Love (26)
Beat Goes On (34)
Beautiful Love (7)
Because (39)
Because Of You (19)
Beer Barrel Polka (Roll Out The Barrel) (9)
Begorrah! (2)
Bewitched, Theme From (29)

Beyond The Blue Horizon (medley) (5)
Blame It On The Bossa Nova (22)
Blue (And Broken Hearted) (2)
Blue Moods (11)
Blue Room (medley) (5)
Blue Skies (medley) (5)
Blue Tango (14)
Blue Velvet (24,30,42)
Blues Serenade (1)

Bombay (14)
Born Free (33)
Breakwater (23) 100
Bridal Chorus (39)
Brothers Grimm, Theme From The (19)
Bubbles In The Wine (4,35,42)
By The Time I Get To Phoenix (38)
Calcutta (14,35) 1
Call Me (30,42)

WELK, Lawrence — Cont'd

Can't Get Used To Losing You (23)
Can't Take My Eyes Off You (36)
Canadian Sunset (30)
Candida (41)
Carolina In The Morning (42)
Cecilia (medley) (5)
Champagne Polka (9)
Champagne Waltz (1)
Chances Are (13)
Charmaine (medley) (5,10)
Chicken Polka (9)
Chihuahua Polka (9)
China Boy (Go Sleep) (11)
Christmas Comes But Once A Year (8)
Christmas Dreaming (A Little Early This Year) (8)
Christmas Island (8)
Christmas Song (Merry Christmas To You) (12)
Christmas Toy (8)
Christmas Waltz (12)
Cinco Robles (37)
Clarinet Polka (9)
Close To You (41)
Come All Ye Faithful (medley) (12)
Copy Cat (33)
Corrine Corrina (14)
Cracklin' Rosie (41)
Cry Me A River (28)
Cuando (33)
Cuban Love Song (medley) (10)
Dance Aroun' A Stack Of Barley (3)
Danube Waves (21)
Darktown Strutters' Ball (4)
Days Of Wine And Roses (22)
Dear Heart (29,42)
Deck The Halls (12,17,20)
Deep Purple (24)
Diane (medley) (5,10)
Dill Pickles (2)
Do You Know The Way To San Jose (18)
Dolores (21)
Don't Break The Heart That Loves You (18)
Don't Think Twice, It's All Right (24)
Don't Worry (15)
Doodle Doo Doo (medley) (5)
18 Yellow Roses (23)
Emily (9)
Emperor Waltz (21)
End Of The World (22)
Endlessly (5)
Estrellita (42)
Everybody Loves Somebody (29)
Exactly Like You (medley) (5)
Exodus (16)
Family Affair, Theme From (33)
Fascination (37)
Fiesta (24)
First Noel (12,17,20)
Flirtation Waltz (4)
Florena Polka (9)
Fool Never Learns (25)
Fools Rush In (24)
For You (25)
Galveston (38)
Galway Bay (27)
Gentle On My Mind (38)
Georgia On My Mind (13)
Georgy Girl (34)
Get Me To The Church On Time (32)
Getting To Know You (32)
Giannina Mia (medley) (5)
Gigi (19)
Girl From Barbados (25)
Go 'Way, Go 'Way (4)
God Rest Ye Merry Gentlemen (12,17,20)
Goin' Out Of My Head (36)
Going Home (37)

Gold And Silver (21)
Good King Wenceslas (12,17,20)
Good Life (23)
Good Luck Charm (18)
Good News (25)
Goodbye, Charlie (29)
Goodnight, Irene (15)
Graduation Day (6)
Granada (27)
Green Leaves Of Summer (13,42)
Green Tambourine (36)
Gypsy In My Soul (medley) (5)
Happy Heart (40)
Harbor Lights (15)
Hark! The Herald Angels Sing (12,17,20)
Hawaiian Wedding Song (39)
Heart You Break (May Be Your Own) (2)
Heartaches By The Number (31,42)
Heartbreak Hotel (15)
Helena Polka (9,42)
Hello, Dolly! (25,27)
Hey Jude (38)
Hey There (28)
High On The House Top (8)
Hold Me, Thrill Me, Kiss Me (31)
Hold My Hand (30)
Holiday Waltz (21)
Honey (38)
Honolulu Eyes (medley) (10)
Hot Pretzels (9)
How Little It Matters How Little We Know (6)
Humoresque Boogie (14)
Hurt So Bad (40)
Hush...Hush, Sweet Charlotte (31)
I Can Dream, Can't I? (28)
I Can't Believe It's True (medley) (5)
I Could Have Danced All Night (6,16)
I Found A Million Dollar Baby (In A Five And Ten Cent Store) (medley) (5)
I Left My Heart In San Francisco (27)
I Love Thee (39)
I Love You (7)
I Love You Because (23)
I Love You More And More Every Day (25)
I Love You Truly (27,39)
I Really Don't Want To Know (22)
I Wanna Do More Than Whistle (Under The Mistletoe) (8)
I Went To Your Wedding (27)
I Whistle A Happy Tune (32)
I Will Wait For You (34)
I Wish We Were Sweethearts Again (2)
I'd Love To Live In Loveland (medley) (10)
I'll Always Be In Love With You (7)
I'll Be Home For Christmas (17,20)
I'll Never Smile Again (26)
I'll See You Again (37,42)
I'm Forever Blowing Bubbles (42)
(I'm In Heaven When I See You Smile) ..see: Diane
I've Grown Accustomed To Her Face (6,32)
If I Loved You (32,42)
Impossible Dream (38)
In A Little Spanish Town (10,42)
"In" Crowd (31)
In The Arms Of Love (34)
In The Year 2525 (40)
Ireland Must Be Heaven For My Mother Came From There (3)
Irish Alphabet (3)
Irish Soldier Boy (3)

It Came Upon The Midnight Clear (12,17,20)
It Happened In Monterey (medley) (10)
It Might As Well Be Spring (32)
It's A Sin To Tell A Lie (medley) (10)
It's All In The Game (19,25,42)
It's Almost Tomorrow (4)
It's Not For Me To Say (19)
Java (25)
Jean (40)
Jeannine (I Dream Of Lilac Time) (1)
Jenny Lind (9)
Jingle Bells (12)
Jolly Coppersmith (9)
Josephine (27,42)
Joy To The World (12,17,20)
Juanita (15)
Just Because (42)
Kazoo Song (30)
Kiss Polka (9)
L'Amour Toujours L'Amour (Love Everlasting) (medley) (5)
La Bamba (31)
Land Of Dreams (30)
Last Date (13,35) **21**
Let It Snow! Let It Snow! Let It Snow! (8)
Let Me Go, Lover! (28)
Let's Have An Old-Fashioned Christmas (12)
Lisbon Antigua (4)
Little Bit Of Heaven (Shure They Call It Ireland) (3)
Little Green Apples (38)
Little Sir Echo (medley) (5)
Little Things Mean A Lot (28)
Loch Lomond (15)
Lola O'Brien The Irish Hawaiian (2)
Longing (30)
Look Back And Laugh (2)
Look What They've Done To My Song Ma (41)
Love Is A Many-Splendored Thing (16)
Love Is Blue (36)
Love Is The Sweetest Thing (7)
Love Letters (31)
Love Letters In The Sand (26)
Love Me Tender (19)
Love Those Eyes (15)
Love's Own Sweet Song (medley) (10)
Luxembourg Polka (2)
Mam'selle (14)
Marcheta (medley) (5)
Maria (32)
Maria Elena (24,42)
Marianne (15)
Mas Que Nada (Pow-Pow-Pow) (33)
McNamara's Band (3)
Melodie D'Amour (13)
Melody Of Love (37)
Memories (37)
Merry Christmas From Our House - To Your House (12)
Merry Widow Waltz (21)
Mexicali Rose (27)
Misty (32)
Mockin' Bird Hill (15)
Moments To Remember (7)
Mona Lisa (19)
Mood Indigo (medley) (5)
Moon River (16,35)
Moonglow and Theme From "Picnic" (6)
Moonlight And Roses (Bring Mem'ries Of You) (31)
Moonlight Cocktail (1)
More (27)
More I Love You (Lo Mucho Que Te Quiero) (38)
Moritat (A Theme From "The Threepenny Opera") (4) **17**
Mountain King (14)
Musette (1)

Music To Watch Girls By (34)
My Blue Heaven (5,27)
My Darling (7)
My Dear (medley) (10)
My Heart Danced An Irish Jig (3)
My Heart Has A Mind Of Its Own (13)
My Little Angel (6)
My Love For You (15)
My North Dakota Home (42)
My Song (2)
My Three Sons, Theme From (35) **55**
My Wonderful One (7)
Nature Boy (26)
Need You (30,42)
Never On Sunday (29)
Night Life (24)
Night Theme (13)
No Other Love (26)
O Come, All Ye Faithful ..see: Adeste Fideles / Come All Ye Faithful
O Come, All Ye Faithful ..see: Adeste Fideles / Come All Ye Faithful
O Little Town Of Bethlehem (12,17,20)
O Promise Me (39)
Oh, Happy Day (4,27)
Oh, Lady Be Good (medley) (5)
On A Clear Day You Can See Forever (32)
On The Street Where You Live (6,32) **96**
One Rose (medley) (10)
Other Man's Grass Is Always Greener (36)
Our Day Will Come (29)
Our Winter Love (22)
Out Of A Clear Blue Sky (30,42)
Over The Waves (21)
Pagan Love Song (medley) (10)
Paradise (18)
Pennsylvania Polka (9)
People (29)
People Will Say We're In Love (32)
Perfidia (14)
Pete's Tail-Fly (11)
Picnic ..see: Moonglow
Pipeline (23)
Play Fiddle Play (medley) (10)
Please (medley) (5)
Please Help Me, I'm Falling (13)
Poeme (37)
Poodle Walk (27)
Poor People Of Paris (4) **17**
Practice, Practice, What You Preach (6)
President Kennedy March (27)
Pretend (19)
Pretty Baby (medley) (5)
Prisoner Of Love (26)
Puff (The Magic Dragon) (23)
Quentin's Theme (40)
Rain (medley) (5)
Rain On The Roof (medley) (5)
Ramona (medley) (10)
Rhythm Of The Rain (22,42)
Ring Those Christmas Bells (12)
Rock 'N' Roll Ruby (6)
Romance (medley) (5)
Romeo & Juliet, Love Theme From (40)
Ruby (14)
Rudolph, The Red-Nosed Reindeer (17,20)
Runaway (15,35) **56**
Rustic Dance (4)
'S Wonderful (5,11)
Sailor (Your Home Is The Sea) (14)
Sam, The Old Accordion Man (2)
San Antonio Rose (11)
Santa Claus Is Comin' To Town (8)
Santa Claus Is Here Again (12)

Santa From Santa Fe (12)
Save The Last Dance For Me (14)
Say It With Music (medley) (5)
Secret Love (18)
Send Me The Pillow You Dream On (31)
September Song (5,26)
Shamrocks, Shillelaghs And Shenanigans (3)
She's Got You (18)
Silent Night (12,17,20)
Silver Bells (12)
Silver Moon (37)
Singin' In The Rain (medley) (5)
Sixteen Reasons (28)
Sleep (10,13)
Sleepy Time Gal (medley) (5)
Sleigh Ride (12)
Snowbird (41)
Some Enchanted Evening (16,32)
Somebody Loves Me (medley) (5)
Something (41)
Something To Remember You By (7)
Somewhere My Love (34)
Song Of Love (medley) (10)
Sonny Boy (26)
Sophia Mia (30)
Sound Of Music (16,32)
Southern Roses (21)
Southtown, U.S.A. (29)
Spinning Wheel (40)
Spooky (36)
Stand By Your Man (41)
Standing On The Corner (6)
Stars In My Eyes (1)
Stay As Sweet As You Are (7)
Stockholm (25) **91**
Story Of Kevin Barry (3)
Strangers In The Night (34)
Strike Up The Band (11)
Suddenly There's A Valley (28)
Sugar Shack (24)
Sukiyaki (23)
Summer Nights (31)
Summer Samba (33)
Summer Wind (31,33)
Sunrise Serenade (1)
Sweet Caroline (40)
Sweetest Sounds (29)
Sweethearts On Parade (11)
Sympathy (medley) (5)
Tales From The Vienna Woods (21)
Talk To The Animals (36)
Taste Of Honey (31)
Tea For Two (medley) (5)
Tea 'N Trumpets (11)
Temptation (13)
Tenderly (medley) (10)
Thanks For Christmas (8,17,20)
That Sunday, That Summer (24)
That's My Desire (26)
Then You Can Tell Me Goodbye (34)
There! I've Said It Again (25)
There Is No Greater Love (2) (They Long To Be) Close To You ..see: Close To You
They Remind Me Too Much Of You (22)
3rd Man Theme (medley) (5)
Thomas Crown Affair, Theme From The ..see: Windmills Of Your Mind
Those Lazy, Hazy, Crazy Days Of Summer (23)
Those Were The Days (38)
Thou Swell (5,11)
Three Coins In The Fountain (19)
Three O'Clock In The Morning (10,37)
Through The Years (39)

Tie Me Kangaroo Down, Sport (23)
Tijuana (33)
Till I Waltz Again With You (28)
Till There Was You (16)
Till Of Thy Fingers (23)
'Tis The Luck Of The Irish (3)
To Each His Own (13)
Tonight (16)
Too Young (18)
Tree In The Meadow (28)
True Love (39)
Twelve Gifts Of Christmas (8)
Twilight Time (1)
Twilight Time In Tennessee (1)
Unchained Melody (31)
Vaya Con Dios (19)
Very Thought Of You (7)
Vienna Echoes (21)
Wabash Blues (medley) (5)
Wake The Town And Tell The People (4)
Walk Right In (22)
Walking On New Grass (33)
Waltz You Saved For Me (1)
Was That The Human Thing To Do (medley) (5)
Washington Square (24)
Watch What Happens (36)
Wayward Wind (6)
We Can Fly (36)
We Can Make Music (41)
We've Only Just Begun (41)
Wedding March (39)
Wedding Of The Winds (21)
What A Heavenly Night For Love (6)
What Will Mary Say (22)
What's A Wrong (2)
When I Grow Too Old To Dream (37)
When Irish Eyes Are Smiling (3)
When It's Sleepy Time Down South (26)
When My Baby Smiles At Me (42)
When My Sugar Walks Down The Street (11)
When The Organ Played At Twilight (1)
When Your Hair Has Turned To Silver (medley) (10)
Where The Blue Of The Night Meets The Gold Of The Day (26)
White Christmas (8,17,20)
Why Don't You Believe Me (28)
Wild Colonial Boy (3)
Winchester Cathedral (33)
Windmills Of Your Mind (40)
Winter Wonderland (8)
Wish Me A Rainbow (34)
Wish You Were Here (16)
Wives And Lovers (24)
Wonderful! Wonderful! (24)
Wonderful World Of The Young (18)
Yearning (Just For You) (medley) (5)
Yellow Bird (15,35) **71**
Yes Sir, That's My Baby (medley) (5)
Yesterday (31)
Yesterday, When I Was Young (40)
You And You (21)
You Belong To Me (28)
You Don't Own Me (25)
You Gave Me Wings (16)
You'll Never Walk Alone (16)
You're My Everything (7)
You're The Only Star (medley) (10)
You're The Reason (2)
You're The Reason I'm Living (22)
Young At Heart (18,42)
Young Love (18)
Young World (18)

WELLER, Freddy   '69

Born on 9/9/47 in Atlanta. Pop-country singer/guitarist. Member of **Paul Revere & The Raiders** (1967-71).

| 8/16/69 | 144 | 7 | | | Games People Play/These Are Not My People | | | $20 | Columbia 9904 |

Birmingham — Games People Play — Home — My, My Momma — One Woman Can't Hold Me — You Never Knew Julie
Freeborn Man — Goodnight Sandy — Louisiana Redbone — Oakridge Tennessee — These Are Not My People

WELLES, Orson '70
Born on 5/6/15 in Kenosha, Wisconsin. Died of a heart attack on 10/10/85 (age 70). Legendary movie actor/writer/director.

| 8/22/70 | 66 | 16 | | | **The Begatting of The President** .... [C] | $20 | Mediarts 41-2 |

Ascension, The   Burn, Pharaoh, Burn   Defoliation Of Eden   Pacification Of Goliath   Raising Of Richard
Book Of Hubert   Coming Of Richard   L.B. Jenesis   Paradise Bossed

WELLS, Mary '64
Born on 5/13/43 in Detroit. Died of cancer on 7/26/92 (age 49). R&B singer.

3/16/63	49	8	©	1	**Two Lovers and other great hits**	$100	Motown 607
5/16/64	42	16	©	2	**Together**	$50	Motown 613
					MARVIN GAYE & MARY WELLS		
5/30/64	18	37	©	3	**Greatest Hits** .... [G]	$50	Motown 616
7/25/64	111	12	©	4	**Mary Wells Sings My Guy**	$50	Motown 617
5/1/65	145	4		5	**Mary Wells**	$50	20th Century Fox 4171

After The Lights Go Down Low (2)   He's The One I Love (4)   Looking Back (1)   Stop Right Here (1)   What's Easy For Two Is So Hard For One (3) 29   You Lost The Sweetest Boy (3) 22
Ain't It The Truth (5) 45   How Can I Forget Him (5)   My Baby Just Cares For Me (4)   **Stop Takin' Me For Granted** (5) 88   What's The Matter With You Baby (2) 17   Your Old Stand By (3) 40
At Last (2)   How (When My Heart Belongs To You) (4)   **My Guy** (3,4) 1   Time After Time (5)   Whisper You Love Me Boy (4)
Bye Bye Baby (3) 45   (I Guess There's) No Love (1)   My Mind's Made Up (5)   Together (2)   Why Don't You Let Yourself Go (5)
Deed I Do (2)   (I Love You) For Sentimental Reasons (2)   My 2 Arms - You = Tears (1)   **Two Lovers** (1,3) 7   **You Beat Me To The Punch** (3) 9
Does He Love Me (4)   I Only Have Eyes For You (4)   Oh Little Boy (What Did You Do To Me) (3)   Until I Met You (2)   You Came A Long Way From St. Louis (2)
Everlovin' Boy (5)   If You Love Me, Really Love Me (4)   Old Love (Let's Try It Again) (3)   **Use Your Head** (5) 34   You Do Something To Me (4)
Goody, Goody (1)   It Had To Be You (4)   **One Who Really Loves You** (3) 8   Was It Worth It (1)
Guess Who (1)   Late Late Show (2)   Operator (1)   We're Just Two Of A Kind (5)
He Holds His Own (4)   **Laughing Boy** (1,3) 15   Squeeze Me (2)   What Love Has Joined Together (3)
He's A Lover (5) 74
He's Good Enough For Me (5)

WENDY AND LISA '87
Pop duo from Los Angeles: Wendy Melvoin (born on 1/26/64) and Lisa Coleman (born on 6/8/60). Formerly with **Prince**'s band The Revolution. Wendy is daughter of Mike Melvoin (**The Plastic Cow**); sister of Susannah Melvoin (of **The Family**) and Jonathan Melvoin (of **Smashing Pumpkins**).

9/19/87	88	13	©	1	**Wendy And Lisa**	$10	Columbia 40862
4/8/89	119	8	©	2	**Fruit At The Bottom**	$10	Columbia 44341
							White (1)

Always In My Dreams (2)   Everyday (2)   Honeymoon Express (1)   Lolly Lolly (2)   Song About (1)
Are You My Baby (2)   Everything But You (1)   I Think It Was December (2)   Satisfaction (2)   Stay (1)
Blues Away (1)   From Now On (We're One) (2)   Life, The (1)   Sideshow (1)   Tears Of Joy (2)
Chance To Grow (1)   Fruit At The Bottom (2)   Light (1)   Someday I (2)   **Waterfall** (1) 56

WERNER, David '79
Born in Pittsburgh. Rock singer/guitarist.

| 9/1/79 | 65 | 11 | | | **David Werner** .... | $12 | Epic 36126 |

Can't Imagine   Eye To Eye   Hold On Tight   She Sent Me Away   What Do You Need To Love
Every New Romance   High Class Blues   Melanie Cries   Too Late To Try   What's Right

WESLEY, Fred, & The Horny Horns '77
Born in 1944 in Mobile, Alabama. Funk trombonist. Member of **James Brown**'s band. Also see **The JB's**.

| 4/30/77 | 181 | 5 | © | | **A Blow For Me, A Toot To You** .... | $15 | Atlantic 18214 |

Between Two Sheets   Blow For Me, A Toot For You   Four Play   Peace Fugue   Up For The Down Stroke   When In Doubt: Vamp

WEST, Dottie '79
Born Dorothy Marsh on 10/11/32 in McMinnville, Tennessee. Died in a car crash on 9/4/91 (age 58). Country singer.

4/14/79	82	23	▲	1	**Classics**	$12	United Artists 946
1/5/80	186	3	●	2	**Every Time Two Fools Collide**	$12	United Artists 864
					KENNY ROGERS & DOTTIE WEST (above 2)		
4/11/81	126	15		3	**Wild West**	$10	Liberty 1062

All I Ever Need Is You (1)   Goodbye (1)   Let It Be Me (1)   Sorry Seems To Be The Hardest Word (3)   **What Are We Doin' In Love** (3) 14   You've Lost That Lovin' Feelin' (1)
Anyone Who Isn't Me Tonight (2)   (Hey Won't You Play) Another Somebody Done Somebody Wrong Song (1)   Let's Take The Long Way Around The World (1)   That's The Way It Could Have Been (2)   What's Wrong With Us Today (2)
Are You Happy Baby? (3)   I Wish That I Could Hurt That Way Again (3)   Loving Gift (2)   'Til I Can Make It On My Own (1)   Why Don't We Go Somewhere And Love (2)
Baby I'm-A Want You (2)   Make Us A Plan (3)   Together Again (1)   You And Me (2)
Beautiful Lies (2)   (I'm Gonna) Put You Back On The Rack (3)   Midnight Flyer (1)   We Love Each Other (2)   You Needed Me (1)
Choosin' Means Losin' (3)   Just The Way You Are (1)   Please Remember Me (3)
Every Time Two Fools Collide (2)   Right Or Wrong (3)

WEST, Leslie '69
Born Leslie Weinstein on 10/22/45 in New York City. Male rock singer/guitarist. Founder of **Mountain** and **West, Bruce & Laing**.

| 9/6/69 | 72 | 14 | © | 1 | **Mountain** .... | $15 | Windfall 4500 |
| 4/19/75 | 168 | 6 | | 2 | **The Great Fatsby** .... | $15 | Phantom 0954 |

Baby, I'm Down (1)   Blood Of The Sun (1)   E.S.P. (2)   I'm Gonna Love You Thru The Night (2)   Little Bit Of Love (2)   Storyteller Man (1)
Because You Are My Friend (1)   Doctor Love (2)   High Roller (2)   If I Still Had You (2)   Long Red (1)   This Wheel's On Fire (1)
Better Watch Out (1)   Don't Burn Me (2)   Honky Tonk Women (2)   If I Were A Carpenter (2)   Look To The Wind (1)
Blind Man (1)   Dreams Of Milk & Honey (1)   House Of The Rising Sun (2)   Southbound Train (1)

WEST, Mae '66
Born Mary Jane West on 8/17/1893 in Brooklyn, New York. Died of a stroke on 11/22/80 (age 87). Legendary movie actress.

| 7/23/66 | 116 | 5 | | | **Way Out West** .... | $50 | Tower 5028 |
| | | | | | backing band (and pictured on album cover): **Gary Lewis And The Playboys** | | |

Boom Boom   If You Gotta Go   Mae Day   Shakin' All Over   Twist And Shout   You Turn Me On
Day Tripper   Lover, Please Don't Fight   Nervous   Treat Him Right   When A Man Loves A Woman

WEST, BRUCE & LAING '73
All-star rock trio: **Leslie West** (vocals, guitar), **Jack Bruce** (bass) and Corky Laing (drums). West and Laing were with **Mountain**. Bruce was with **Cream**.

11/4/72+	26	20	©	1	**Why Dontcha**	$15	Windfall 31929
7/28/73	87	10		2	**Whatever Turns You On**	$15	Windfall 32216
5/11/74	165	6		3	**Live 'N' Kickin'** .... [L]	$15	Windfall 33899

WEST, BRUCE & LAING — Cont'd

Backfire (2)	Love Is Worth The Blues (1)	Pleasure (1)	Rock 'N' Roll Machine (2)	Sifting Sand (2)	Turn Me Over (1)
Dirty Shoes (2)	November Song (2)	Politician (3)	Scotch Crotch (2)	Slow Blues (2)	While You Sleep (1)
Doctor, The (1,3)	Out Into The Fields (1)	Pollution Woman (1)	Shake Ma Thing (Rollin Jack)	Third Degree (1)	Why Dontcha (1)
Like A Plate (2)	Play With Fire (3)	Powerhouse Sod (3)	(1)	Token (2)	

WEST COAST BAD BOYZ   '97

Gathering of various rap artists from California.

| 2/15/97 | 8 | 16 | © | 1 | West Coast Bad Boyz II | | | $10 | No Limit 50658 |
| 8/9/97 | 33^C | 2 | © | 2 | West Coast Bad Boyz I | | | $10 | No Limit 50695 |

Another Level (2)	Datz What I Said (1)	Mobbin' Thru The Town (2)	Roll Yo Voges (1)	Tryin' To Make A Dollar Out Of	What We Known Fo (2)
Bad Boyz On A Mission (1)	Deep (2)	Mr. Dayton (1)	Steady Mobbin' (1)	15 Cents (2)	Would You Take A Bullet For
Bangin' (1)	Got Tha Best Hand (1)	Paper Chasing (1)	Stressed Out (2)	Tryin 2 Make Ends (1)	Your Homie (2)
Born Hustlaz (2)	Hands On My Four 5 (1)	Playin' For Keeps (1)	Survival 1st (1)	Unexpected, The (1)	You Do Your Thang (2)
Breakin' Skrill (1)	Headin' 4 The Jack (2)	Puttin' In Work (2)	Tell Me Something Good (2)	Up's And Down's (1)	
Call It What You Want (1)	IMG (1)	R.I.P. Tupac (1)	Total Insanity (1)	What Cha Like (1)	

WEST COAST RAP ALL-STARS, The   '90

All-star rap group: **Above The Law**, **Digital Underground**, **Eazy-E**, **Ice-T**, **J.J. Fad**, **King Tee**, **M.C. Hammer**, **Michel'le**, **N.W.A.**, **Oaktown's 3-5-7**, **Tone Loc** and **Young MC**.

| 7/7/90 | 60 | 12 | | | We're All In The Same Gang | [V] | $10 | Warner 26241 |

Black In America	Keep Funkin' It	Soul Sista	We Came To Dance	
Get Up And Dance	Let's Have Some Fun	Tumba La Casa (Rock The	**We're All In The Same**	
I Got Style	Livin' In South Central L.A.	House)	**Gang 35**	

WESTERBERG, Paul   '93

Born on 12/31/60 in Minneapolis. Rock singer/guitarist. Member of **The Replacements**.

7/3/93	44	10	©	1	14 Songs			$10	Sire 45255
5/18/96	50	5	©	2	Eventually			$10	Reprise 46176
3/13/99	104	1	©	3	Suicaine Gratifaction			$10	Capitol 59004

Actor In The Street (3)	Born For Me (3)	First Glimmer (1)	Love Untold (1)	Someone I Once Knew (1)	Time Flies Tomorrow (2)
Ain't Got Me (2)	Century (2)	Fugitive Kind (3)	MamaDaddyDid (2)	Something Is Me (1)	Trumpet Clip (2)
Angels Walk (2)	Dice Behind Your Shades (1)	Good Day (2)	Mannequin Shop (1)	Sunrise Always Listens (3)	Whatever Makes You Happy (3)
Best Thing That Never	Down Love (1)	Hide N Seekin' (2)	Once Around The Weekend (2)	Tears Rolling Up Our Sleeves	World Class Fad (1)
Happened (3)	Even Here We Are (1)	It's A Wonderful Lie (3)	Runaway Wind (1)	(3)	You've Had It With You (2)
Black Eyed Susan (1)	Few Minutes Of Silence (3)	Knockin On Mine (1)	Self-Defense (3)	These Are The Days (1)	
Bookmark	Final Hurrah (3)	Lookin' Out Forever (3)	Silver Naked Ladies (1)	Things (1)	

WESTLIFE   '00

Male vocal group from Dublin, Ireland: Nicky Byrne, Shane Filan, Kian Egan, Mark Feehily and Bryan McFadden.

| 5/6/00 | 129 | 17 | © | | Westlife | | | $10 | Arista 14642 |

Can't Lose What You Never	Fool Again	If I Let You Go	My Private Movie	**Swear It Again 20**
Had	I Don't Wanna Fight	Miss You	No No	We Are One
Flying Without Wings	I Need You	More Than Words	Open Your Heart	

WESTON, Paul   '56

Born Paul Wetstein on 3/12/12 in Springfield, Massachusetts. Died on 9/20/96 (age 84). Conductor/arranger. Married to **Jo Stafford** from 1952-96. Won Grammy's Trustees Award in 1971.

| 10/29/55 | 15 | 2 | © | 1 | Mood For 12 | [I] | $20 | Columbia 693 |
| 9/1/56 | 12 | 5 | © | 2 | Solo Mood | [I] | $20 | Columbia 879 |

Autumn In New York (1)	Emaline (1)	I'm Confessin' (That I Love You)	Memories Of You (1)	Skylark (1)
Between The Devil And The	Foggy Day (2)	(1)	My Funny Valentine (1)	Sweet Lorraine (2)
Deep Blue Sea (1)	Georgia On My Mind (1)	It's The Talk Of The Town (1)	Nice Work If You Can Get It (1)	When It's Sleepy Time Down
Body And Soul (2)	Honeysuckle Rose (2)	Judy (1)	One I Love (Belongs To	South (2)
Dancing On The Ceiling (He	Hundred Years From Today (2)	Louisiana (1)	Somebody Else) (2)	You Are Too Beautiful (2)
Dances On My Ceiling) (2)	I'm Comin' Virginia (1)	Lullaby In Rhythm (2)	Rockin' Chair (2)	

WESTSIDE CONNECTION   '96

All-star rap trio: **Ice Cube**, **Mack 10** and WC (of **WC and The MAAD Circle**).

| 11/9/96 | 2¹ | 45 | ▲ © | | Bow Down | | | $10 | Priority 50583 |

All The Critics In New York	Do You Like Criminals?	**Gangstas Make The World Go**	King Of The Hill	World Domination
Bow Down 21	Gangsta, The Killa And The	**Round 40**	3 Time Felons	
Cross 'Em Out And Put A 'K	Dope Dealer	Hoo'Bangin'	Westward Ho	

WESTWIND ENSEMBLE, The   '96

Studio group from California.

| 12/28/96+ | 82 | 3 | © | | A Christmas Tribute To Mannheim Steamroller | C:#26/6 | [X-I] | $10 | Brentwood 353 |

Christmas charts: 12/96, 17/'97

Angels We Have Heard On	Deck The Halls	Greensleeves	Jingle Bells	O Little Town Of Bethlehem
High	God Rest Ye Merry Gentlemen	Hark The Herald Angels Sing	Joy To The World	Silent Night
Coventry Carol	Good King Wenceslas	I Saw Three Ships	O Holy Night	We Three Kings

WET WET WET   '88

Pop group from Glasgow, Scotland: Marti Pellow (vocals), Neil Mitchell (keyboards), Graeme Clark (bass) and Tom Cunningham (drums).

| 7/16/88 | 123 | 7 | © | | Popped In Souled Out | | | $10 | Uni 5000 |

Angel Eyes (Home And Away)	I Can Give You Everything	I Remember	Sweet Little Mystery	**Wishing I Was Lucky 58**
East Of The River	I Don't Believe (Sonny's Letter)	Moment You Left Me	Temptation	

WET WILLIE   '74

Pop-rock group from Mobile, Alabama: brothers Jack (bass) and **Jimmy Hall** (vocals), Rick Hirsch (guitar), John Anthony (keyboards) and Lewis Ross (drums). Michael Duke (keyboards, vocals) joined in late 1975.

| 5/12/73 | 189 | 4 | © | 1 | Drippin' Wet!/Live | [L] | $15 | Capricorn 0113 |

recorded on 12/31/72 at the Warehouse in New Orleans

6/1/74	41	24	©	2	Keep On Smilin'		$15	Capricorn 0128
3/8/75	114	7	©	3	Dixie Rock		$15	Capricorn 0149
4/3/76	133	7	©	4	The Wetter The Better		$15	Capricorn 0166
6/4/77	191	2	©	5	Left Coast Live	[L]	$15	Capricorn 0182

recorded at the Roxy in Hollywood

WET WILLIE — Cont'd

DEBUT	PEAK	WKS			ARTIST — Album Title			$	Label & Number
1/21/78	118	8		6	Manorisms			$12	Epic 34983
3/18/78	158	6	©	7	Greatest Hits		[G]	$12	Capricorn 0200
6/9/79	172	11		8	Which One's Willie?			$12	Epic 35794

Ain't He A Mess (3)
Airport (1,7)
Alabama (2)
Baby Fat (4,7)
Comic Book Hero (4)
Country Side Of Life (2,7) *66*
Dixie Rock (3,7) *96*
Doin' All The Right Things (The Wrong Way) (6)
Don't Let The Green Grass Fool You (medley) (8)

Don't Turn Me Away (6)
Don't Wait Too Long (2)
Everybody's Stoned (4)
Everything That 'Cha Do (Will Come Back To You) (4,5,7) *66*
Hard Way (8)
He Set Me Free (3)
How 'Bout You (6)
I'd Rather Be Blind (1)
In Our Hearts (2)

It's Gonna Stop Rainin' Soon (3)
Jailhouse Moan (3)
Keep On Smilin' (2,5,7) *10*
Leona (3,7) *69*
Let It Shine (6)
Lucy Was In Trouble (2,5)
Macon Hambone Blues (1)
Make You Feel Love Again (6) *45*
Mama Didn't Raise No Fools (3)
Mr. Streamline (8)

No Good Woman Blues (1)
No, No, No (4,5)
One Track Mind (6)
Poor Judge Of Character (3)
Rainman (6)
Ramona (8)
Red Hot Chicken (1,7)
Ring You Up (4)
She Caught The Katy (And Left Me A Mule To Ride) (1)
She's My Lady (3)
Shout Bamalama (1,7)

Smoke (8)
So Blue (6)
Soul Jones (2)
Soul Sister (2)
Spanish Moss (2)
Stop And Take A Look (At What You've Been Doing) (medley) (8)
Street Corner Serenade (6) *30*
Take It To The Music (3)
Teaser (4,5)
That's All Right (1)

This Time (8)
Tired Dreams (8)
Trust In The Lord (2)
Walkin' By Myself (1)
We Got Lovin' (6)
Weekend (8) *29*
You Don't Know What You Mean To Me (8)

WHALUM, Kirk '88

Born on 7/11/58 in Memphis. Jazz tenor saxophonist.

DEBUT	PEAK	WKS			ARTIST — Album Title			$	Label & Number
3/19/88	142	10	©		And You Know That!		[I]	$10	Columbia 40812

Don't Look At Me (In That Tone Of Voice)
Give Me Your Love
Glow

Seryna
Through The Fire

Wave, The
Where I Come From

WHAM! — see MICHAEL, George

WHAT IS THIS '85

Pop-rock trio: Alain Johannes (vocals, guitar), Chris Hutchinson (bass) and Jack Irons (drums; **Red Hot Chili Peppers**, **Pearl Jam**).

DEBUT	PEAK	WKS			ARTIST — Album Title			$	Label & Number
9/14/85	187	4			What Is This			$10	MCA 5598

produced by **Todd Rundgren**

Big Raft
Breathing

Chasing Your Ghost
Dreams Of Heaven

I'll Be Around *62*
Stuck

Touch The Flame
Waves In The Sand

Whisper (To Natasha)
Wool Over My Eyes

WHEATUS '00

Rock group from Long Island, New York: brothers Brendan (vocals, guitar) and Peter (drums) Brown, with Phil Jimenez (guitar) and Rich Leigey (bass).

DEBUT	PEAK	WKS			ARTIST — Album Title			$	Label & Number
9/2/00	76	9	©		Wheatus			$10	Columbia 62146

Hey, Mr. Brown
Hump'em N' Dump'em

Leroy
Little Respect

Love Is A Mutt From Hell
Punk Ass Bitch

Sunshine
Teenage Dirtbag

Truffles
Wannabe Gangstar

WHEELER, Billy Edd '65

Born on 12/9/32 in Whitesville, West Virginia. Folk singer/songwriter.

DEBUT	PEAK	WKS			ARTIST — Album Title			$	Label & Number
2/13/65	132	3			Memories Of America/Ode To The Little Brown Shack Out Back			$20	Kapp 3425

After Taxes
Anne
Bachelor, The

Blistered
Coal Tattoo
Desert Pete

Hot Dog Heart
Jackson

Ode To The Little Brown Shack Out Back *50*
Reverend Mr. Black

Sister Sara
Winter Sky

WHEELER, Caron '90

Born on 1/19/63 in London (Jamaican parents). Female R&B singer. Featured vocalist with **Soul II Soul**.

DEBUT	PEAK	WKS			ARTIST — Album Title			$	Label & Number
10/27/90	133	7	©		UK Blak			$10	EMI 93497

Blue (Is The Colour Of Pain)
Don't Quit
Enchanted

Jamaica
Kama Yo
Livin' In The Light *53*

Never Lonely
No Regrets
Proud

Somewhere
Song For You
This Is Mine

UK Blak

WHEN IN ROME '89

Electro-pop trio from England: Clive Farrington and Andrew Mann (vocals), with Michael Floreale (keyboards).

DEBUT	PEAK	WKS			ARTIST — Album Title			$	Label & Number
10/15/88+	84	24	©		When In Rome			$10	Virgin 90994

Child's Play
Everything

Heaven Knows *95*
I Can't Stop

If Only
Promise, The *11*

Sight Of Your Tears
Something Going On

Total Devotion
Wide Wide Sea

WHISKEYTOWN '01

Rock duo from Jacksonville, North Carolina: Ryan Adams (male vocals, guitar) and Caitlin Cary (female vocals, fiddle).

DEBUT	PEAK	WKS			ARTIST — Album Title			$	Label & Number
6/9/01	158	1	©		Pneumonia			$10	Lost Highway 170199

Ballad Of Carol Lynn
Bar Lights
Crazy About You

Don't Be Sad
Don't Wanna Know Why
Easy Hearts

Jacksonville Skyline
Mirror, Mirror
My Hometown

Paper Moon
Reasons To Lie
Sit & Listen To The Rain

Under Your Breath
What The Devil Wanted

WHISPERS, The '80

★290★

R&B vocal group from Los Angeles: twin brothers Walter and Wallace Scott, with Leaveil Degree, Marcus Hutson and Nicholas Caldwell. The Scotts also recorded as **Walter & Scotty**.

1)The Whispers 2)Just Gets Better With Time 3)Imagination

DEBUT	PEAK	WKS			ARTIST — Album Title			$	Label & Number
5/13/72	186	2		1	The Whispers' Love Story			$50	Janus 3041
8/28/76	189	6		2	One For The Money			$15	Soul Train 1450
7/16/77	65	10	©	3	Open Up Your Love			$15	Soul Train 2270
5/27/78	77	28		4	Headlights			$12	Solar 2774
4/14/79	146	9		5	Whisper In Your Ear			$12	Solar 3105
1/5/80	6	35	▲ ©	6	The Whispers			$12	Solar 3521
1/17/81	23	27	● ©	7	Imagination			$12	Solar 3578
10/3/81	100	9		8	This Kind Of Lovin'			$12	Solar 3976
1/23/82	35	25	● ©	9	Love Is Where You Find It			$10	Solar 27
3/13/82	180	5		10	The Best Of The Whispers		[G]	$10	Solar 4242
4/2/83	37	29	©	11	Love For Love			$10	Solar 60216
12/1/84+	88	26	©	12	So Good			$10	Solar 60356
5/30/87	22	37	▲ ©	13	Just Gets Better With Time			$10	Solar 72554
12/19/87	18ˣ	3	©	14	Happy Holidays To You		[X]	$10	Solar 72558

first released in 1979 on Solar 3489; Christmas charts: 18/'87, 19/'88

DEBUT	PEAK	WKS			ARTIST — Album Title			$	Label & Number
8/18/90	83	24	● ©	15	More Of The Night			$10	Capitol 92957
4/8/95	92	8	©	16	Toast To The Ladies			$10	Capitol 30270

WHISPERS, The — Cont'd

And The Beat Goes On (6,10) 19
Are You Going My Way (12)
Babes (15)
Better Watch Your Heart (16)
Bright Lights And You Girl (4)
Can You Do The Boogie (6)
Can't Do Without Love (5)
Can't Help But Love You (1)
Can't Stop Loving You Baby (8)
Can't Stop Talkin' (1)
Children Of Tomorrow (4)
Chocolate Girl (3)
Christmas Song (14)
Come On Home (16)
Contagious (12)
Continental Shuffle (7)
Crowd Of 1 (16)
Cruisin' In (9)
Disco Melody (4)
Do They Turn You On (11)
Don't Be Late For Love (15)
Don't Keep Me Waiting (12)
Emergency (9)

Every Little Thing You Do (16)
Fantasy (7)
Forever Lover (15)
Funky Christmas (14)
Girl Don't Make Me Wait (15)
Girl I Need You (7)
Give It To Me (13)
Got To Get Away (8)
Had It Not Been For You (11)
Happy Holidays To You (14)
Headlights (1)
Heaven (15)
Help Them See The Light (15)
Hey, Who Really Cares? (1)
Homemade Lovin' (5)
Hopeless Situation (1)
I Can Make It Better (7,10)
I Fell In Love Last Night (At The Disco) (3)
I Love You (6)
I Only Meant To Wet My Feet (1)
I Want 2B The 1 4U (15)
I Want You (13)
I'm Gonna Love You More (8)

I'm Gonna Make You My Wife (3)
I'm The One For You (8)
I've Got A Feeling (2)
If I Don't Get Your Love (5)
If You (1)
Imagination (7)
In My Heart (2)
In The Mood (13)
In The Raw (9)
Innocent (15) 55
Is It Good To You (15)
It's A Love Thing (7,10) 28
Jump For Joy (5)
Just Gets Better With Time (13)
Keep On Lovin' Me (11)
Keep Your Love Around (11)
Lady (6,10) 28
Lay It On Me (11)
(Let's Go) All The Way (4)
Living Together (In Sin) (2,10)
Love At Its Best (5)
Love For Love (11)
Love Is A Dream (3)
Love Is Where You Find It (9)

Love's Calling (13)
Make It With You (3,10) 94
Make Sweet Love To Me (16)
Mind Blowing (15)
Misunderstanding (15)
More Of The Night (15)
My Funny Valentine (16)
My Girl (6)
My Heart Your Heart (15)
Never Too Late (12)
No Pain, No Gain (13)
(Olivia) Lost And Turned Out (4,10)
On Impact (12)
One For The Money (Part 1) (2,10) 88
Only You (9)
Open Up Your Love (3)
Out The Box (6)
Pissed Off (Baby Come Back) (16)
Planets Of Life (4)
Pretty Lady (5)
Put Me In The News (2)
Rock Steady (13) 7

Santa Claus Is Coming To Town (14)
Say Yes (9)
Say You (Would Love For Me Too) (7)
Small Talkin' (9)
So Good (12)
Some Kinda Lover (12)
Song For Donny (6)
Sounds Like A Love Song (2)
Special F/X (13)
Suddenly (12)
Sweet Sensation (12)
There's A Love For Everyone (1)
This Christmas (14)
This Kind Of Lovin' (8)
This Time (11)
This Time Of Year (14)
Toast To The Ladies (16)
Tonight (11) 84
Try And Make It Better (4)
Try It Again (11)
Turn Me Out (9)
Up On Soul Train (7)

Very Special Holiday (14)
Welcome Into My Dream (6)
What Will I Do (8)
Whisper In Your Ear (5)
Whisperin (16)
White Christmas (14)
World Of A Thousand Dreams (8)
You Are Number One (3)
You Are The One (15)
You Fill My Life With Music (1)
You Never Miss Your Water ('Til Your Well Runs Dry) (3)
You'll Never Get Away (5)
(You're A) Special Part Of My Life (4)
You're Driving Me Crazy (16)
You're Only As Good As You Think You Are (2)
You're So Good To Me (16)
You're What's Been Missin' From My Life (1)
You've Chosen Me (1)
Your Love Is So Doggone Good (1) 93

WHITCOMB, Ian   '65
Born on 7/10/41 in Woking, England. Pop singer/songwriter/author.

| 7/10/65 | 125 | 13 | | © | You Turn Me On! | | | $30 | Tower 5004 |

Be My Baby
Fizz
N-E-R-V-O-U-S! 59
No Tears For Johnny
Poor But Honest
River Of No Return
Sugar Babe
That's Rock N' Roll
This Sporting Life 100
Too Many Cars On The Road
You Turn Me On (Turn On Song) 8

WHITE, Barry ★144★   '74
Born on 9/12/44 in Galveston, Texas; raised in Los Angeles. R&B singer/songwriter/keyboardist. Formed **Love Unlimited** in 1969, which included future wife Glodean James. Leader of 40-piece **Love Unlimited Orchestra**.

1)Can't Get Enough 2)Barry White Sings For Someone You Love 3)I've Got So Much To Give
4)Just Another Way To Say I Love You 5)The Icon Is Love

DEBUT	PEAK	WKS	RIAA	CD	#	Album Title	Catalog	Sym	$	Label & Number
4/21/73	16	63	●	©	1	I've Got So Much To Give			$12	20th Century 407
11/17/73+	20	37	●	©	2	Stone Gon'			$12	20th Century 423
9/7/74	❶¹	38	●	©	3	Can't Get Enough			$12	20th Century 444
4/12/75	17	17	●	©	4	Just Another Way To Say I Love You			$12	20th Century 466
11/15/75	23	25	▲	©	5	Barry White's Greatest Hits	C:#8/49	[G]	$12	20th Century 493
2/14/76	42	15		©	6	Let The Music Play			$12	20th Century 502
11/27/76	125	9		©	7	Is This Whatcha Wont?			$12	20th Century 516
9/17/77	8	33	▲	©	8	Barry White Sings For Someone You Love			$12	20th Century 543
10/28/78	36	28	▲	©	9	Barry White The Man			$12	20th Century 571
4/28/79	67	9	●	©	10	The Message Is Love			$12	Unlimited Gold 35763
8/18/79	132	6		©	11	I Love To Sing The Songs I Sing			$12	20th Century 590
7/26/80	85	11		©	12	Barry White's Sheet Music			$12	Unlimited Gold 36208
10/2/82	148	6		©	13	Change			$12	Unlimited Gold 38048
11/21/87	159	17		©	14	The Right Night & Barry White			$10	A&M 5154
5/19/90	143	12		©	15	The Man Is Back!			$10	A&M 5256
11/2/91	96	10		©	16	Put Me In Your Mix			$10	A&M 5377
10/22/94	20	46	▲²	©	17	The Icon Is Love			$10	A&M 540115
2/6/96	2²ᶜ	63	▲	©	18	All-Time Greatest Hits		[G]	$10	Mercury 522459
8/14/99	43	19		©	19	Staying Power			$10	Private Music 82185
5/13/00	148	4		©	20	The Ultimate Collection		[G]	$15	UTV 542291 [2]

All Because Of You (4)
Any Fool Could See (You Were Meant For Me) (10)
Baby Blues (20)
Baby, We Better Try To Get It Together (6,18) 92
Baby's Home (17)
Break It Down With You (16)
Bring Back My Yesterday (1)
Call Me, Baby (11)
Can't Get Enough Of Your Love, Babe (3,5,18,20) 1
Change (13)
Come On (17,20) 87
Dark And Lovely (You Over There) (16)
Don't Let Go (15)
Don't Make Me Wait Too Long (7,18,20)
Don't Play Games (19)
Don't Tell Me About Heartaches (13)
Don't You Want To Know? (17)
Early Years (9)
Follow That And See (Where It Leads Y'all) (15)

For Real Chill (16)
For Your Love (I'll Do Most Anything) (14)
Get Up (19)
Ghetto Letto (12)
Girl It's True, Yes I'll Always Love You (2)
Girl, What's Your Name (11)
Good Night My Love (medley) (15)
Hard To Believe That I Found You (2)
Heavenly, That's What You Are To Me (4)
Honey Please, Can't Ya See (2,5,18,20) 44
How Did You Know It Was Me? (11)
Hung Up In Your Love (10)
I Believe In Love (12)
I Can't Believe You Love Me (3)
I Can't Leave You Alone (11)
I Don't Know Where Love Has Gone (6)
I Found Love (10)
I Get Off On You (19)

I Like You, You Like Me (13)
I Love To Sing The Songs I Sing (11)
I Love You More Than Anything (In This World Girl) (3)
I Never Thought I'd Fall In Love With You (8)
I Only Want To Be With You (17)
I Wanna Do It Good To Ya (15)
I Wanna Lay Down With You (7)
I'll Do For You Anything You Want Me To (4,18,20) 40
I'm Gonna Love You Just A Little More Baby (1,5,18,20) 3
I'm On Fire (10)
I'm Qualified To Satisfy You (7,18,20)
I'm Ready For Love (14)
I'm So Blue And You Are Too (6)
I've Found Someone (1,5)
I've Got So Much To Give (1,5,18,20) 32

I've Got That Love Fever (13)
If You Know, Won't You Tell Me (6)
It's All About Love (13)
It's All Right, Babe (Until You Give It) (10,20)
It's Ecstasy When You Lay Down Next To Me (8,18,20) 4
It's Getting Harder All The Time (15)
It's Only Love Doing Its Thing (9)
Just The Way You Are (9,18,20)
L.A. My Kinda Place (15)
Lady, Sweet Lady (12)
Let Me Live My Life Lovin' You Babe (4)
Let The Music Play (6,18,20) 32
Let's Get Busy (16)
Let's Make Tonight (An Evening To Remember) (13)
Longer We Make Love (19)
Look At Her (9)
Love Ain't Easy (10)

Love Is Good With You (16)
Love Is In Your Eyes (14)
Love Is The Icon (17)
Love Makin' Music (12,20)
Love Serenade (4,5,20)
Love Will Find Us (16)
Love's Theme (18,20) 1
Loves Interlude (medley) (15)
Low Rider (19)
Mellow Mood (Pt. I & II) (3)
Midnight And You (20)
My Sweet Summer Suite (20) 48
Never, Never Gonna Give Ya Up (2,5,18,20) 7
Never I'm Gonna Make Love To You (7)
Of All The Guys In The World (8)
Oh Love, Well We Finally Made It (3)
Oh Me, Oh My (I'm Such A Lucky Guy) (11)
Oh What A Night For Dancing (8,18,20) 24

Once Upon A Time (You Were A Friend Of Mine) (11)
Passion (13)
Playing Your Game, Baby (8,18,20)
Practice What You Preach (17,20) 18
Put Me In Your Mix (16,20)
Responsible (16)
Right Night (14)
Rum And Coke (Rum And Coca-Cola) (12)
Satin Soul (18,20) 22
September When I First Met You (9)
Sexy Undercover (17)
Sha La La Means I Love You (9)
Share (14)
She's Everything To Me (12)
Sheet Music (12)
Sho' You Right (14,20)
Slow Your Roll (19)
Sometimes (19)
Standing In The Shadows Of Love (1,5)

WHITE, Barry — Cont'd

Staying Power (19,20)
Super Lover (15)
Thank You (19)
There It Is (17)
There's A Place (Where Love Never Ends) (14)
Time Is Right (17)

Turnin' On, Tunin' In (To Your Love) (13)
Volare (16)
We're Gonna Have It All (16)
What Am I Gonna Do With You (4,5,18,20) **8**

Whatever We Had, We Had (17)
When Will I See You Again (15)
Which Way Is Up (19)
Who You Giving Your Love To (16)
Who's The Fool (14)

You See The Trouble With Me (6,18,20)
You Turned My Whole World Around (8)
You're My Baby (2)
You're So Good You're Bad (8)

You're The First, The Last, My Everything (3,5,18,20) **2**
You're The One I Need (10)
Your Love -- So Good I Can Taste It (7)
Your Sweetness Is My Weakness (9,18,20) **60**

WHITE, Bryan '97

Born on 2/17/74 in Lawton, Oklahoma; raised in Oklahoma City. Country singer/songwriter/guitarist. Married actress Erika Page on 10/14/2000.

8/19/95+	88	42	▲ ©	1 **Bryan White**	$10	Asylum 61642
4/13/96	52	63	▲ ©	2 **Between Now And Forever**	$10	Asylum 61880
10/11/97	41	23	● ©	3 **The Right Place**	$10	Asylum 62047
9/11/99	81	3	©	4 **How Lucky I Am**	$10	Asylum 62278

Bad Day To Let You Go (3)
Between Now And Forever (2)
Blindhearted (2)
Call Me Crazy (3)
Eugene You Genius (1)
Everywhere I Turn (4)
God Gave Me You (4)
Going, Going, Gone (1)

Heaven Sent (4)
Helpless Heart (1)
How Lucky I Am (4)
Hundred And One (2)
I'm Not Supposed To Love You Anymore (2)
Leave My Heart Out Of This (3)
Look At Me Now (1)

Love Happens Just Like That (4)
Love Is The Right Place (3)
Love Me Like You Mean It (4)
Me And The Moon (1)
Natural Thing (3)
Never Get Around To It (3)
Nickel In The Well (2)

Nothing Less Than Love (1)
On Any Given Night (2)
One Small Miracle (4)
Rebecca Lynn (1)
Shari Ann (1)
Sittin' On Go (2)
So Much For Pretending (2)
Someone Else's Star (1)

Stayin', The (4)
Still Life (2)
That Good (4)
That's Another Song (2)
This Town (1)
Tree Of Hearts (3)
Two In A Million (4)
We Could Have Been (3)

What Did I Do (To Deserve You) (3)
You Know How I Feel (1)
You'll Always Be Loved (By Me) (4)
You're Still Beautiful To Me (4)

WHITE, Karyn '89

Born on 10/14/65 in Los Angeles. R&B singer. Married to producer Terry Lewis (of **The Time**).

10/15/88+	19	54	▲ ©	1 **Karyn White**	$10	Warner 25637
9/28/91	53	24	● ©	2 **Ritual Of Love**	$10	Warner 26320
10/15/94	99	7	©	3 **Make Him Do Right**	$10	Warner 45400

Beside You (2)
Can I Stay With You (3) **81**
Do Unto Me (2)
Don't Mess With Me (1)
Family Man (1)
Hard To Say Goodbye (2)

Here Comes The Pain Again (3)
Hooked On You (2)
How I Want You (3)
Hungah (3) **78**
I'd Rather Be Alone (3)
I'm Your Woman (3)

Love Saw It (1)
Love That's Mine (2)
Make Him Do Right (3)
Nobody But My Baby (3)
One Heart (3)
One Minute (3)

One Wish (1)
Ritual Of Love (2)
Romantic (2) **1**
Secret Rendezvous (1) **6**
Simple Pleasures (1)
Slow Down (1)

Superwoman (1) **8**
Tears Of Joy (2)
Tell Me Tomorrow (1)
Thinkin' 'Bout Love (1)
Walkin' The Dog (2)
Way I Feel About You (2) **12**

WHITE, Lari '95

Born on 5/13/65 in Dunedin, Florida. Country singer.

1/21/95	125	19	● ©	**Wishes**	$10	RCA 66395

Go On
If I'm Not Already Crazy

If You Only Knew
It's Love

Now I Know
Somebody's Fool

That's How You Know (When You're In Love)

That's My Baby
When It Rains

Wishes

WHITE, Lenny '76

Born on 12/19/49 in New York City. R&B drummer. Member of **Return To Forever** and **Twennynine**.

1/31/76	177	3	©	**Venusian Summer**	[I]	$15	Nemperor 435

Away Go Troubles Down The Drain

Chicken-Fried Steak
Mating Drive

Prelude To Rainbow Delta
Prince Of The Sea

Venusian Summer Suite
Medley

WHITE, Maurice '85

Born on 12/19/41 in Memphis. Percussionist with **Ramsey Lewis** from 1966-71. Founder and co-lead vocalist of **Earth, Wind & Fire**.

10/5/85	61	19	©	**Maurice White**	$10	Columbia 39883

Alpha Dance
Believe In Magic

Children Of Afrika
I Need You 95

Invitation
Jamboree

Lady Is Love
Sea Of Glass

Sleeping Flame
Stand By Me 50

Switch On Your Radio

WHITE, Tony Joe '69

Born on 7/23/43 in Goodwill, Louisiana. Singer/songwriter.

7/26/69	51	16		1 **Black And White**	$20	Monument 18114
11/22/69	183	3		2 **...Continued**	$20	Monument 18133
3/6/71	167	4		3 **Tony Joe White**	$15	Warner 1900

Aspen Colorado (1)
Black Panther Swamps (3)
Change, The (3)
Copper Kettle (3)
Daddy, The (3)
Don't Steal My Love (1)

Elements And Things (2)
Five Summers For Jimmy (3)
For Le Ann (2)
I Just Walked Away (3)
I Thought I Knew You Well (2)
I Want You (2)

Little Green Apples (1)
Look Of Love (1)
Migrant, The (2)
My Kind Of Woman (3)
Night In The Life Of A Swamp Fox (3)

Old Man Willis (2)
Polk Salad Annie (1) **8**
Rainy Night In Georgia (2)
Roosevelt And Ira Lee (Night Of The Mossacin) (2) **44**
Scratch My Back (1)

Soul Francisco (1)
They Caught The Devil And Put Him In Jail In Eudora, Arkansas (3)
Traveling Bone (3)
Voodoo Village (3)

Who's Making Love (1)
Whompt Out On You (1)
Wichita Lineman (1)
Willie And Laura Mae Jones (1)
Woman With Soul (2)
Woodpecker (2)

WHITE LION '88

Rock group formed in Brooklyn, New York: Mike Tramp (vocals), Vito Bratta (guitar), James Lomenzo (bass) and Greg D'Angelo (drums). Lomenzo and D'Angelo left in 1991, replaced by Tommy Caradonna and Jimmy DeGrasso (of **Y&T**).

9/26/87+	11	86	▲² ©	1 **Pride**	$10	Atlantic 81768
4/16/88	151	14	©	2 **Fight To Survive**	[E]	$10	Grand Slam 1
7/1/89	19	27	● ©	3 **Big Game**	$10	Atlantic 81969
4/27/91	61	13	©	4 **Mane Attraction**	$10	Atlantic 82193

All Burn In Hell (2)
All Join Our Hands (1)
All The Fallen Men (2)
All You Need Is Rock N Roll (1)
Baby Be Mine (3)
Blue Monday (4)
Broken Heart (2,4)

Broken Home (3)
Cherokee (3)
Cry For Freedom (3)
Don't Give Up (1)
Don't Say It's Over (3)
El Salvador (2)

Farewell To You (4)
Fight To Survive (2)
Goin' Home Tonight (3)
Hungry (1)
If My Mind Is Evil (3)
In The City (2)
It's Over (1)

Kid Of 1000 Faces (2)
Lady Of The Valley (4)
Leave Me Alone (4)
Let's Get Crazy (3)
Lights And Thunder (4)
Little Fighter (3) **52**
Living On The Edge (3)

Lonely Nights (1)
Love Don't Come Easy (4)
Out With The Boys (4)
Radar Love (3) **59**
Road To Valhalla (4)
She's Got Everything (4)
Sweet Little Loving (1)

Tell Me (1) **58**
Till Death Do Us Part (4)
Wait (1) **8**
Warsong (4)
When The Children Cry (1) **3**
Where Do We Run (2)
You're All I Need (1)

WHITEMAN, Paul '57

Born on 3/28/1890 in Denver. Died of a heart attack on 12/29/67 (age 77). Legendary orchestra leader.

1/19/57	20	1		**Paul Whiteman/50th Anniversary**	$25	Grand Award 901 [2]

Autumn Leaves
Basin Street Blues
Christmas Night In Harlem

How High The Moon
It Happened In Monterey
It's The Dreamer In Me

Jeepers Creepers
Lazy River
Limehouse Blues

Lover
Mississippi Mud
My Romance

Night Is Young & You're So Beautiful
Ramona

Rhapsody In Blue
Washboard Blues
When Day Is Done

WHITE PLAINS '70

Studio group from England. Featuring Tony Burrows (vocals), who was also with **The Brotherhood Of Man**, Edison Lighthouse, First Class and **The Pipkins**.

| 8/22/70 | 166 | 4 | | | **My Baby Loves Lovin'** | | | $20 | Deram 18045 |

I've Got You On My Mind   Show Me Your Hand   Taffeta Rose   When Tomorrow Comes
In A Moment Of Madness   Summer Morning   Today I Killed A Man I Didn't   Tomorrow
My Baby Loves Lovin' *13*   Sunny Honey Girl   Know   You've Got Your Troubles

WHITESNAKE '87

Former **Deep Purple** vocalist David **Coverdale**, who recorded solo as Whitesnake in 1977, formed British hard-rock group in 1978. Coverdale fronted everchanging lineup. Early members included his Deep Purple bandmates: keyboardist Jon Lord (1978-84) and drummer Ian Paice (1979-81). Players in 1987 included John Sykes (guitar), Neil Murray (bass) and Aynsley Dunbar (former **Jefferson Starship** drummer). Sykes left in 1988 to form **Blue Murder**. Ex-**Dio** guitarist Vivian Campbell was a member from 1987-88, later with Riverdogs, Shadow King and Def Leppard. Lineup in 1989 included guitarists **Steve Vai** (**David Lee Roth**'s band) and Adrian **Vandenberg**, Rudy Sarzo (bass) and Tommy Aldridge (drums). Lineup in 1994: Coverdale, Vandenberg, Sarzo, Warren De Martini (guitar; **Ratt**), Paul Mirkovich (keyboards) and Denny Carmassi (drums; **Heart**). Coverdale was married to actress Tawny Kitaen from 1989-92.

8/16/80	90	16			1 **Ready An' Willing**			$12	Mirage 19276
12/27/80+	146	12		©	2 **Live....In The Heart Of The City**		[L]	$12	Mirage 19292
					recorded at the Hammersmith Odeon in London				
5/30/81	151	6		©	3 **Come An' Get It**			$12	Mirage 16043
5/19/84	40	85	▲²	©	4 **Slide It In**	C:#4/70		$10	Geffen 4018
4/18/87	2¹⁰	76	▲⁸	©	5 **Whitesnake**			$10	Geffen 24099
11/25/89	10	34	▲	©	6 **Slip Of The Tongue**			$10	Geffen 24249
8/6/94	161	2	▲	©	7 **Whitesnake's Greatest Hits**		[G]	$10	Geffen 24620

Ain't Gonna Cry No More (1)   Children Of The Night (5)   Gambler (4)   Judgment Day (6,7)   She's A Woman (1)   Sweet Talker (1,2)
Ain't No Love In The Heart Of   Come An' Get It (3)   Girl (3)   Kittens Got Claws (6)   Slide It In (4,7)   Take Me With You (2)
   The City (2)   Come On (2)   **Give Me All Your Love** (5) *48*   Lonely Days, Lonely Nights (3)   Slip Of The Tongue (6)   Till The Day I Die (3)
All Or Nothing (4)   Crying In The Rain (5,7)   Give Me More Time (4)   Looking For Love (7)   Slow An' Easy (4,7)   Walking In The Shadow Of The
Bad Boys (5)   **Deeper The Love** (6,7) *28*   Guilty Of Love (4)   Love Ain't No Stranger (4,7)   Slow Poke Music (6)   Blues (2)
Black And Blue (1)   Don't Break My Heart Again (3)   **Here I Go Again** (5,7) *1*   Love Hunter (2)   Spit It Out (4)   Wine, Women An' Song (3)
Blindman (1)   Don't Turn Away (5)   Hit An' Run (3)   Love Man (1)   Standing In The Shadow (4)   Wings Of The Storm (6)
Carry Your Load (1)   **Fool For Your Loving**   Hot Stuff (3)   **Now You're Gone** (6,7) *96*   **Still Of The Night** (5,7) *79*   Would I Lie To You (3)
Cheap An' Nasty (6)   (1,2,7) *53*   Hungry For Love (4)   Ready An' Willing (1)   Straight For The Heart (5)   You're Gonna Break My Heart
Child Of Babylon (3)   **Fool For Your Loving** (6) *37*   **Is This Love** (5,7) *2*   Sailing Ships (6)   Sweet Lady Luck (2)   Again (7)

WHITE TOWN '97

Born Jyoti Mishra on 7/30/66 in Rourkela, India; raised in England. Male singer/multi-instrumentalist.

| 3/15/97 | 84 | 20 | | © | **Women In Technology** | | | $10 | Chrysalis 56129 |

Death Of My Desire   Once I Flew   Theme For An Early Evening   Undressed   White Town
Function Of The Orgasm   Shape Of Love   American Sitcom   Wanted   **Your Woman** *23*
Going Nowhere Somehow   Thursday At The Blue Note   Week Next June

WHITE TRASH '91

Hard-rock group: Dave Alvin (vocals), Ethan Collins (guitar), Aaron Collins (bass) and Mike Caldarella (drums).

| 9/21/91 | 122 | 7 | | © | **White Trash** | | | $10 | Elektra 61053 |

Apple Pie   Buzz!   Judge-Me-Do   Po' White Trash   Take My Soul
Baby   Crawl, The   Lil' Nancy   Prayer B4 Pizza
Backstage Pass   Good God   Party Line   S.D.A.S.E.

WHITE WOLF '86

Hard-rock group from Canada: Don Wilk (vocals), Cam MacLeod and Rick Nelson (guitars), Les Schwartz (bass) and Loris Bolzon (drums).

| 2/16/85 | 162 | 6 | | | 1 **Standing Alone** | | | $10 | RCA Victor 8042 |
| 6/21/86 | 137 | 8 | | | 2 **Endangered Species** | | | $10 | RCA Victor 9555 |

All Alone (2)   Holding Back (2)   Metal Thunder (1)   Ride The Storm (2)   She (2)   Time Waits For No One (2)
Crying To The Wind (2)   Homeward Bound (1)   Night Rider (1)   Run For Your Life (2)   Snake Charmer (2)   Trust Me (1)
Headlines (1)   Just Like An Arrow (2)   One More Time (2)   Shadows In The Night (1)   Standing Alone (1)   What The War Will Bring (1)

WHITE ZOMBIE '95

Hard-rock group formed in New York City: **Rob Zombie** (vocals), Jay Yuenger (guitar), Sean Yseult (bass) and John Tempesta (drums). Group named after a 1932 Bela Lugosi movie.

7/17/93	26	44	▲²	©	1 **La Sexorcisto: Devil Music Volume One**	C:#23/27		$10	Geffen 24460
4/29/95	6	88	▲²	©	2 **Astro-Creep: 2000-Songs Of Love, Destruction And Other Synthetic Delusions Of The Electric Head**	C:#39/7		$10	Geffen 24806
8/31/96	17	19	●	©	3 **Supersexy Swingin' Sounds**		[K]	$10	Geffen 24976
					remixes of songs from #2 above				

Black Sunshine (1)   Creature Of The Wheel (2)   Electric Head Pt. 1 & 2 (2,3)   I Zombie (2,3)   Spiderbaby (Yeah-Yeah-Yeah)   Thunder Kiss '65 (1)
Blood, Milk And Sky (2,3)   El Phantasmo And The   Grease Paint And Monkey   I'm Your Boogie Man (3)   (1)   Warp Asylum (1)
Blur The Technicolor (2,3)   Chicken-Run Blast-O-Rama   Brains (2,3)   More Human Than Human (2,3)   Starface (1)   Welcome To Planet
Cosmic Monsters Inc. (1)   (2,3)   Grindhouse (A Go-Go) (1)   Real Solution #9 (2,3)   Super-Charger Heaven (2,3)   Motherfucker/Psychoholic
      I Am Legend (1)   Soul-Crusher (1)   Thrust! (1)   Slag (1)

WHITING, Margaret '67

Born on 7/22/24 in Detroit; raised in Los Angeles. Pop singer.

| 2/18/67 | 109 | 8 | | | **The Wheel Of Hurt** | | | $20 | London 497 |

But Why   Show Me A Man   **Wheel Of Hurt** *26*   World Inside Your Arms   You Won't Be Sorry, Baby
It Hurts To Say Goodbye   Somewhere There's Love   Where Do I Stand   You Don't Have To Say You
Nothing Lasts Forever   Time After Time   Winchester Cathedral   Love Me

WHITLEY, Keith '90

Born Jesse Keith Whitley on 7/1/55 in Sandy Hook, Kentucky. Died of alcohol abuse on 5/9/89 (age 33). Country singer/songwriter/guitarist. Married **Lorrie Morgan** in 1986.

6/3/89	121	14	●	©	1 **Don't Close Your Eyes**			$10	RCA 6494
9/2/89	115	7	●	©	2 **I Wonder Do You Think Of Me**			$10	RCA 9809
9/1/90	67	45	▲	©	3 **Greatest Hits**		[G]	$10	RCA 2277

Between An Old Memory And   Heartbreak Highway (2)   I'm No Stranger To The Rain   Lady's Choice (2)   Ten Feet Away (3)
   Me (2)   Honky Tonk Heart (1)   (1,3)   Miami, My Amy (3)   Tennessee Courage (2)
Birmingham Turnaround (1)   I Never Go Around Mirrors (1)   I'm Over You (2,3)   Some Old Side Road (1)   'Till A Tear Becomes A Rose (3)
Brother Jukebox (1)   I Wonder Do You Think Of Me   It Ain't Nothin' (2,3)   Talk To Me Texas (2,3)   Turn This Thing Around (2)
Don't Close Your Eyes (1,3)   (2,3)   It's All Coming Back To Me Now   Tell Lorrie I Love Her (3)   When You Say Nothing At All
Flying Colors (1)   (1)   (1,3)

WHITLOCK, Bobby '72
Born in 1948 in Memphis. Keyboardist with **Delaney & Bonnie** and **Derek And The Dominos**.

4/1/72	140	10			1 Bobby Whitlock			$15	Dunhill/ABC 50121
11/4/72	190	3			2 Raw Velvet			$15	Dunhill/ABC 50131

Back Home In England (1)
Back In My Life Again (1)
Bustin' My Ass (2)
Country Life (1)
Day Without Jesus (1)
Dearest I Wonder (2)
Dreams Of A Hobo (1)
Ease Your Pain (2)
Game Called Life (1)
Hello L.A., Bye Bye Birmingham (2)
I'd Rather Live "The Straight Life" (1)
If You Ever (2)
Satisfied (2)
Scenery Has Slowly Changed (1)
Song For Paula (1)
Start All Over (2)
Tell The Truth (2)
Think About It (2)
Where There's A Will There's A Way (1)
Write You A Letter (2)
You Came Along (2)

WHITMAN, Slim '80
Born Otis Whitman on 1/20/24 in Tampa, Florida. Country yodeler/guitarist.

10/25/80	175	3			1 Songs I Love To Sing			$12	Cleveland Int'l. 36768
12/13/80	184	4	©		2 Christmas with Slim Whitman		[X]	$12	Cleveland Int'l. 36847

White Christmas (2)

Away In A Manger (2)
Beautiful Dreamer (1)
Christmas (2)
First Noel (2)
I Remember You (1)
If I Could Only Dream (1)
It Came Upon The Midnight Clear (2)
Last Farewell (1)
Let There Be Peace On Earth (Let It Begin With Me) (2)
Rose Marie (1)
Secret Love (1)
Silent Night, Holy Night (2)
Since You Went Away (1)
Sleep My Child (All Through The Night) (2)
That Silver-Haired Daddy Of Mine (1)
We Three Kings (2)
When (1)
Where Do I Go From Here (1)
Where Is The Christ In Christmas (2)

WHITTAKER, Roger '75
Born on 3/22/36 in Nairobi, Kenya (British parents). Pop ballad singer.

5/3/75	31	24	● ©		1 "The Last Farewell" and other hits			$12	RCA Victor 0855
5/5/79	115	5			2 When I Need You			$12	RCA Victor 3355
12/8/79+	157	10			3 Mirrors Of My Mind			$12	RCA Victor 3501
2/9/80	154	12			4 Voyager			$12	RCA Victor 3518
11/29/80	175	2			5 With Love			$12	RCA Victor 3778
6/13/81	177	3	©		6 Live In Concert		[L]	$15	RCA Victor 4057 [2]

All I Have To Do Is Dream (6)
All Of My Life (4)
Annie's Song (5)
Berceuse Pour Mon Amour (6)
Blow Gentle Breeze (3)
Both Sides Now (1)
Call My Name (3)
Carry Me (Dreams On A Roof) (3)
Chengalip (6)
Day In The Life Of A Lucky Man (6)
Dirty Old Town (6)
Don't Fight (5)
Durham Town (The Leavin') (1,6)
Early One Morning (6)
Family (5)
For I Loved You (5)
Good Morning Starshine (1)
Goodbye (5)
Goodnight Ruby (3)
Halfway Up A Mountain (1)
Here I Am (4)
Home Lovin' Man (2)
I Am But A Small Voice ('Ako' Y Munting Tinig') (5)
I Don't Believe In If Anymore (1,6)
I Knew You Sunset (3)
I See You In The Sunrise (4)
I Was Born (4)
I Would If I Could (5)
I'll Be There (4)
Image To My Mind - Parts 1-4 (6)
It Takes A Lot (3)
Kentucky Song Bird (3)
Kilgary Mountain (6)
Last Farewell (1,6) 19
Lighthouse (4)
Love Is A Cold Wind (4)
Love Will (5)
Lyin' Eyes (2)
Man Without Love (5)
Mexican Whistler (6)
Miss You Nights (2)
Morning Has Broken (6)
My Son (5)
New African Whistler (6)
New World In The Morning (1,6)
Newport Belle (5)
On My Own Again (4)
One Another (5)
Paper Bird (4)
Please Come To Boston (5)
Ride A Country Road (6)
Sail Away (4)
See You Shine (5)
She (2)
Skye Boat Song (6)
Solitaire (2)
Song For The Captain (4)
Sunrise, Sunset (1)
Tall Dark Stranger (5)
That's Life (6)
This Moment (5)
Time In A Bottle (2)
Water Boy (1)
Weekend In New England (2)
What Love Is (6)
When I Need You (2)
Whistle Stop (1)
Why? (6)
Wishes (3)
Yele (4)
You Are My Miracle (3)
Your Song (5)

WHO, The ★53★ '70

Rock group formed in London: **Roger Daltrey** (vocals), **Pete Townshend** (guitar, vocals), **John Entwistle** (bass) and **Keith Moon** (drums). Group starred in the movies *Tommy*, *Quadrophenia* and *The Kids Are Alright*. Moon died of a drug overdose on 9/7/78 (age 31), replaced by Kenney Jones (formerly with **Small Faces**). Eleven fans trampled to death at group's concert in Cincinnati on 12/3/79. Disbanded in 1982. Regrouped at "Live Aid" in 1986. Daltrey, Townshend and Entwistle reunited with an ensemble of 15 for a U.S. tour in 1989. Jones formed **The Law** with **Paul Rodgers** in 1991. Group inducted into the Rock and Roll Hall of Fame in 1990.

1)*Who Are You* 2)*Quadrophenia* 3)*Face Dances* 4)*Live At Leeds* 5)*Tommy*

5/20/67	67	22	©		1 Happy Jack			$50	Decca 74892
					album released in England as *A Quick One*; also see #10 below				
1/6/68	48	23	©		2 The Who Sell Out			$50	Decca 74950
					also see #10 below				
10/26/68	39	10	©		3 Magic Bus-The Who On Tour		[K]	$50	Decca 75064
6/7/69+	4	126	▲² ©		4 Tommy			$40	Decca 7205 [2]
5/30/70	4	44	▲² ©		5 Live At Leeds	C:#2³/210	[L]	$30	Decca 79175
8/14/71	4	41	▲³ ©		6 Who's Next	C:●¹⁶/270		$30	Decca 79182
11/20/71	11	21	▲ ©		7 Meaty Beaty Big And Bouncy	C:●²/91	[G]	$30	Decca 79184
11/10/73	2¹	40	▲ ©		8 Quadrophenia			$25	MCA 10004
					also see #14 below				
10/26/74	15	15	● ©		9 Odds & Sods			$25	Track 2126
					previously unreleased recordings from 1964-72				
12/21/74	185	4			10 A Quick One (Happy Jack)/The Who Sell Out		[R]	$30	Track 4067 [2]
					reissue of albums #1 and #2 above				
10/25/75	8	25	▲ ©		11 The Who By Numbers			$15	MCA 2161
9/9/78	2²	30	▲² ©		12 Who Are You	C:●⁴/251		$15	MCA 3050
6/30/79	8	25	▲ ©		13 The Kids Are Alright		[L-S]	$20	MCA 11005 [2]
10/13/79	46	16	©		14 Quadrophenia		[S]	$20	Polydor 6235 [2]
					also see #8 above; side 4 includes: "Night Train" by **James Brown**, "Louie Louie" by **The Kingsmen**, "Green Onions" by **Booker T. & The MG's**, "Rhythm Of The Rain" by **The Cascades**, "He's So Fine" by **The Chiffons**, "Be My Baby" by **The Ronettes** and "Da Doo Ron Ron" by **The Crystals**				
4/4/81	4	20	▲ ©		15 Face Dances			$12	Warner 3516
10/17/81	52	19	● ©		16 Hooligans		[K]	$15	MCA 12001 [2]
					recordings from 1965-78				
9/25/82	8	32	● ©		17 It's Hard			$12	Warner 23731
5/21/83	94	13	▲² ©		18 Who's Greatest Hits	C:#17/97	[G]	$12	MCA 5408
12/1/84+	81	14	©		19 Who's Last		[L]	$15	MCA 8018 [2]

WHO, The — Cont'd

DEBUT	PEAK	WKS	CD	ARTIST — Album Title	$	Label & Number
12/28/85+	116	8	© 20	Who's Missing .... [K]	$12	MCA 5641

contains rare B-sides and previously unreleased selections from 1965-72

4/14/90	188	2	© 21	Join Together .... [L]	$15	MCA 19501 [2]
7/23/94	170	1	© 22	Thirty Years Of Maximum R&B .... [K]	$40	MCA 11020 [4]
11/16/96	194	1	© 23	Live At The Isle Of Wight Festival 1970 .... [E-L]	$15	Columbia 65084 [2]
3/4/00	101	3	© 24	BBC Sessions .... [E-L]	$10	MCA 111960

recorded from 1965-73

Acid Queen (4,21,22,23)
Amazing Journey (4,21,23)
Another Tricky Day (15)
Anytime You Want Me (20)
Anyway, Anyhow, Anywhere (7,13,22,24)
Armenia City In The Sky (2,10,22)
Athena (17) **28**
Baba O'Riley (6,13,16,19,22)
Barbara Ann (20)
Bargain (6,16,20,22)
Behind Blue Eyes (6,16,19,21,22) **34**
Bell Boy (8,14,22)
Blue Red And Grey (11,22)
Bony Moronie (22)
Boris The Spider (1,7,10,19,22,24)
Bucket T. (3)
Cache Cache (15)
Call Me Lightning (3,22) **40**
Christmas (4,21,23)
Cobwebs And Strange (1,10)
Cooks County (17)
Cousin Kevin (4,21)
Cry If You Want (17)
Cut My Hair (8)
Daddy Rolling Stone (22)
Daily Records (15)
Dancing In The Street (24)
Dangerous (17)
Did You Steal My Money (15)
Dig (21)
Dirty Jobs (8)
Disguises (3,22,24)
Do You Think It's Alright (4,21,23)

Doctor, Doctor (3)
Dr. Jekyll & Mr. Hyde (3)
Dr. Jimmy (8,14,19)
Dogs (22)
Don't Let Go The Coat (15) **84**
Don't Look Away (1,10)
Dreaming From The Waist (11,22)
Drowned (8,16)
Early Morning Cold Taxi (22)
Eminence Front (17,21,22) **68**
Eyesight For The Blind (4,21,23)
Face The Face (21)
Faith In Something Bigger (9)
Fiddle About (4,23)
5:15 (8,14,16,18,21,22) **45**
Fortune Teller (22)
Four Faces (14)
Get Out And Stay Out (14)
Gettin' In Tune (6)
Girl's Eyes (22)
Glow Girl (9)
Go To The Mirror! (23)
Go To The Mirror Boy (4,21)
Goin' Mobile (6)
Good Lovin' (24)
Good's Gone (24)
Guitar And Pen (12,22)
Had Enough (12,16)
Happy Jack (1,7,10,13,18,22,24) **24**
Heat Wave (10)
Heaven And Hell (20,22,23)
Heinz Baked Beans (2,10)
Helpless Dancer (8,14)
Here For More (20)
Here 'Tis (22)
Hi Heel Sneakers (14)

How Can You Do It Alone (15)
How Many Friends (11)
However Much I Booze (11)
I Am The Sea (8,14)
I Can See For Miles (2,7,10,13,16,21,22) **9**
I Can't Explain (7,13,16,19,22,23) **93**
I Can't Reach You (2,3,10,22)
I Don't Even Know Myself (20,23)
I Need You (1,10)
I'm A Boy (7,20,22,24)
I'm A Man (22)
I'm Free (4,21,22,23,24) **37**
I'm One (8,14)
I'm The Face (22)
I've Had Enough (8,14)
I've Known No War (17)
Imagine A Man (11)
In A Hand Or A Face (11)
Is It In My Head (8)
It's A Boy (4,23)
It's Hard (17)
It's Your Turn (17)
Jaguar (22)
Join Together (13,16,21,22) **17**
Joker James (14)
Just You And Me, Darling (24)
Kids Are Alright (7,22)
La La La Lies (24)
Leaving Here (20,22,24)
Legal Matter (7,22)
Let's See Action (22)
Little Billy (9,22)
Little Is Enough (21)
Long Live Rock (9,13,19,22,24) **54**
Love Ain't For Keepin' (6)

Love Is Coming Down (12)
Love, Reign O'er Me (8,14,18,19,21,22) **76**
Lubie (Come Back Home) (10)
Magic Bus (3,5,7,13,18,19,22,23) **25**
Man Is A Man (17)
Mary-Anne With The Shaky Hands (2,10,22)
Medac (2,10)
Melancholia (22)
Miracle Cure (4,21,23)
Music Must Change (12,22)
My Generation (5,7,13,18,19,22,23,24) **74**
My Wife (6,13,18,22)
Naked Eye (9,22)
New Song (12)
905 (12)
1921 (21,23)
(Nothing Is Everything) Let's See Action (16)
Now I'm A Farmer (9)
Odorono (2,10)
One At A Time (17)
One Life's Enough (17)
Our Love Was (22)
Our Love Was, Is (2,3,10)
Overture (21,22,23)
Ox, The (22)
Pictures Of Lily (3,7,22,24) **51**
Pinball Wizard (4,7,13,16,18,19,21,22,23) **19**
Postcard (9)
Punk Meets The Godfather (8,14)
Pure And Easy (9,22)
Put The Money Down (9)
Quadrophenia (8)

Quick One While He's Away (1,10,13,22,24)
Quiet One (15)
Rael (2,10,22)
Real Me (8,14,16,22) **92**
Relax (2,10)
Relay, The (16,18,22,24) **39**
Roadrunner (medley) (13)
Rock, The (8)
Rough Boys (21)
Run Run Run (1,3,10,24)
Sally Simpson (4,21)
Saturday Night's Alright (For Fighting) (22)
Sea And Sand (8)
See Me, Feel Me (13,19,22) **12**
See My Way (1,10,24)
Seeker, The (7,18,22,24) **44**
Sensation (4,21)
Shakin' All Over (5,22,23,24)
Shout And Shimmy (20)
Silas Stingy (2,10)
Sister Disco (12,16,22)
Slip Kit (11,16,22)
Smash The Mirror (4,21,23)
So Sad About Us (1,10,22)
Someone's Coming (3)
Song Is Over (6,16,22)
Sparks (4,13,21,23)
Spoonful (medley) (23)
Spotted Henry ...see: Medac
Squeeze Box (11,16,18,22) **16**
Substitute (5,7,18,19,22,23,24)
Success Story (11)
Summertime Blues (5,16,19,22,23) **27**
Sunrise (2,10,22)
Tattoo (2,10,22)

There's A Doctor I've Found (4,21,23)
They Are All In Love (11)
(This Could Be) The Last Time (22)
Tommy Can You Hear Me (4,13,21,23)
Tommy's Holiday Camp (4,21,23)
Too Much Of Anything (22)
Trick Of The Light (12,21)
Twist And Shout (19,22,23)
Uncle Ernie (21)
Underture (22)
Water (23)
We're Not Gonna Take It (4,21,23)
Welcome (4)
When I Was A Boy (20)
Whiskey Man (1,10)
Who Are You (12,16,18,19,22) **14**
Why Did I Fall For That (17)
Won't Get Fooled Again (6,13,18,19,21,22) **15**
You (15)
You Better You Bet (15,21,22) **18**
You Didn't Hear It (4)
Young Man Blues (5,13,22,23)
Zoot Suit (14,22)
recorded as the High Numbers

WHODINI '85

Rap trio from New York City: Jalil Hutchins, John Fletcher and Grandmaster Dee.

DEBUT	PEAK	WKS	RIAA	CD	ARTIST — Album Title	$	Label & Number
11/24/84+	35	48	▲	© 1	Escape	$10	Jive 8251
5/17/86	35	39	●	© 2	Back In Black	$10	Jive 8407
10/17/87	30	22	●	© 3	Open Sesame	$10	Jive 8494

Be Yourself (3)
Big Mouth (1)
Cash Money (3)
Early Mother's Day Card (3)
Echo Scratch (2)
Escape (I Need A Break) (1)
Featuring Grandmaster Dee (1)

Five Minutes Of Funk (1) *flip*
For The Body (3)
Freaks Come Out At Night (1)
Friends (1) **87**
Fugitive (2)
Funky Beat (2)
Good Part (2)

Growing Up (2)
Hooked On You (3)
I'm A Ho (3)
I'm Def (Jump Back And Kiss Myself) (3)
Last Night (I Had A Long Talk With Myself) (3)

Life Is Like A Dance (1)
One Love (2)
Out Of Control (1)
Remember Where You Came From (3)
Rock You Again (Again & Again) (3)

We Are Whodini (1)
You Brought It On Yourself (3)
You Take My Breath Away (3)

WICHITA TRAIN WHISTLE, The '68

A gathering of the top session players in Los Angeles.

DEBUT	PEAK	WKS		ARTIST — Album Title	$	Label & Number
8/3/68	144	7		Mike Nesmith Presents/The Wichita Train Whistle Sings .... [I]	$30	Dot 25861

produced by **Mike Nesmith** (of **The Monkees**)

Carlisle Wheeling
Don't Call On Me

Don't Cry Now
Nine Times Blue

Papa Gene's Blue
Sweet Young Thing

Tapioca Tundra
While I Cried

You Just May Be The One
You Told Me

WIDESPREAD PANIC '97

Rock group from Athens, Georgia: John Bell (vocals, guitar), Michael Houser (guitar), John Hermann (keyboards), Domingo Ortiz (percussion), Dave Schools (bass) and Todd Nance (drums).

DEBUT	PEAK	WKS	CD	ARTIST — Album Title	$	Label & Number
4/10/93	184	1	© 1	Everyday	$10	Capricorn 42013
9/24/94	85	3	© 2	Ain't Life Grand	$10	Capricorn 42027
2/22/97	50	6	© 3	Bombs & Butterflies	$10	Capricorn 534396
5/9/98	67	2	© 4	Light Fuse Get Away .... [L]	$15	Capricorn 558145 [2]
8/14/99	68	4	© 5	'Til The Medicine Takes	$10	Capricorn 546203
6/10/00	161	1	© 6	Another Joyous Occasion .... [L]	$10	Widespread 0012

WIDESPREAD PANIC Featuring The Dirty Dozen Brass Band

Ain't Life Grand (2)
Airplane (2)
All Time Low (5)
Arleen (2)
Aunt Avis (3)
Barstools & Dreamers (4)
Bear's Gone Fishin' (5)
Beehive Jam (6)
Better Off (1)
Big Chief (6)
Blackout Blues (2)

Blue Indian (5)
Can't Get High (2)
Christmas Katie (5,6)
Climb To Safety (5)
Coconuts (6)
Conrad (4)
Diner (1,4)
Disco (4)
Dream Song (1)
Drums (4,6)
Dyin' Man (5)

Fishwater (2,6)
Fishwater Reprise (6)
Gimme (4)
Glory (4)
Gradle (3)
Greta (3,4)
Happy (3)
Hatfield (1)
Henry Parsons Died (1)
Heroes (2)
Hope In A Hopeless World (3)

I Walk On Guilded Splinters (6)
Impossible/Jam (4)
Jack (2)
Junior (2)
L.a. (2)
Little Kin (2)
Love Tractor (4)
Nobody's Loss (5)
One Arm Steve (5)
Papa Legba (4)
Papa's Home (1)

Party At Your Mama's House (5)
Pickin' Up The Pieces (1,4)
Pigeons (4)
Pilgrims (1,4)
Pleas (1)
Porch Song (4)
Postcard (1)
Radio Child (3)
Raise The Roof (2)
Rebirtha (3,4)

Rock (4)
Space Wrangler (4)
Superstition (6)
Surprise Valley (5)
Tall Boy (3)
Travelin' Light (4)
Waker, The (5)
Weight Of The World (5)
Wondering (1,4)
You Got Yours (3)
You'll Be Fine (5)

WIDOWMAKER '77

Hard-rock group from England: John Butler (vocals), Ariel Bender and Huw Lloyd-Langton (guitars), Bob Daisley (bass) and Paul Nicholls (drums). Bender was also with **Spooky Tooth** and **Mott The Hoople**.

| 6/11/77 | 150 | 9 | | | **Too Late To Cry** .... | | | $12 | United Artists 723 |

Here Comes The Queen
Hustler, The

Mean What You Say
Pushin' 'N' Pullin'

Sign The Papers
Sky Blues

Something I Can Do Without
Too Late To Cry

What A Way To Fall

WIEDLIN, Jane '88

Born on 5/20/58 in Oconomowoc, Wisconsin; raised in California. Pop-rock singer/guitarist. Member of the **Go-Go's**.

| 10/26/85 | 127 | 6 | | | 1 **Jane Wiedlin** .... | | | $10 | I.R.S. 5638 |
| 5/28/88 | 105 | 21 | | © | 2 **Fur** .... | | | $10 | EMI-Manhattan 48683 |

Blue Kiss (1) *77*
East Meets West (1)
End Of Love (2)
Forever (1)
Fur (2)

Give! (2)
Goodbye Cruel World (1)
Homeboy (2)
I Will Wait For You (1)
Inside A Dream (2) *57*

Lover's Night (2)
Modern Romance (1)
My Traveling Heart (1)
One Heart One Way (2)

One Hundred Years Of Solitude (1)
Rush Hour (2) *9*
Somebody's Going To Get Into This House (1)

Sometimes You Really Get On My Nerves (1)
Song Of The Factory (1)
Whatever It Takes (1)
Where We Can Go (1)

WIER, Rusty '75

Born in Austin, Texas. Country singer/songwriter/guitarist.

| 7/19/75 | 103 | 14 | | | 1 **Don't It Make You Wanna Dance?** .... | | | $12 | 20th Century 469 |
| 1/17/76 | 131 | 9 | | | 2 **Rusty Wier** .... | | | $12 | 20th Century 495 |

Aqua Dulce (1)
Basic Lady (2)
Blue Haze (1)
Cloudy Days (1)
Dixie Lynn (2)

Don't It Make You Wanna Dance? (1) *82*
Fly Away (2)
I Believe In The Way That You Love Me (1)

I Don't Want To Lay This Guitar Down (1)
I Heard You Been Layin' My Old Lady (Apologies To Susie) (1)
Just One More Time (2)

Listen To My Song (2)
Long And Lonesome Highway Blues (2)
Pass The Buck (2)
Queen Of My Dreams (2)

Relief (1)
Sally Mae (1)
Seminole Jail (2)
Sing Me (1)
Sophia (2)

Trouble (1)
Tulsa Turnaround (1)

WIGGINS, Dwayne '00

Born on 2/14/63 in Oakland. R&B singer. Member of **Tony, Toni, Toné**.

| 5/20/00 | 197 | 1 | | © | **Eyes Never Lie** .... | | | $10 | Motown 157594 |

Don't Sleep
Eyes Never Lie
Flower

Fly Me To The Moon
Let's Make A Baby
Move With Me

Music Is Power
Pushin' On
R & B Singer

Rollin' Mountain
Tribecca

What's Really Going On (Strange Fruit)

WILBURN BROTHERS '70

Country duo from Hardy, Arkansas: brothers Doyle (born on 7/7/30; died on 10/16/82, age 52) and Teddy (born on 11/30/31) Wilburn.

| 3/28/70 | 143 | 2 | | | **Little Johnny From Down The Street** .... | | | $30 | Decca 75173 |

All We Had Going Is Gone
I Will Never Be Happy (Until You're Happy Too)

I'm A Long Gone
I'm So Afraid Of Losing You Again

Lilacs In Winter
Little Johnny From Down The Street

Make My Heart Die Away
Signs Are Everywhere
Try A Little Kindness

Vision At The Peace Table
Which Side's The Wrong Side

WILCO '96

Rock group from Chicago: Jeff Tweedy (vocals, guitar), Jay Bennett (guitar), John Stirratt (bass) and Ken Coomer (drums).

11/16/96	73	3		©	1 **Being There**			$15	Reprise 46236 [2]
7/11/98	90	7		©	2 **Mermaid Avenue**			$10	Elektra 62204
					BILLY BRAGG & WILCO				
3/27/99	78	3		©	3 **Summerteeth**			$10	Reprise 47282
6/17/00	88	4		©	4 **Mermaid Avenue Vol. II**			$10	Elektra 62522
					BILLY BRAGG & WILCO				

Aginst Th' Law (4)
Airline To Heaven (4)
All You Fascists (4)
Another Man's Done Gone (2)
At My Window Sad And Lonely (2)
Birds And Ships (2)
Black Wind Blowing (4)
Blood Of The Lamb (4)
California Stars (2)
Can't Stand It (3)
Christ For President (2)

Dreamer In My Dreams (1)
ELT (3)
Eisler On The Go (2)
Far, Far Away (1)
Feed Of Man (4)
Forget The Flowers (1)
Hesitating Beauty (2)
Hoodoo Voodoo (2)
Hot Rod Hotel (4)
Hotel Arizona (1)
How To Fight Loneliness (3)

I Got You (At The End Of The Century) (1)
I Guess I Planted (2)
I Was Born (4)
I'm Always In Love (3)
In A Future Age (3)
Ingrid Bergman (2)
Joe Dimaggio Done It Again (4)
Kingpin (1)
Lonely 1 (1)
Meanest Man (4)
Misunderstood (1)

Monday (1)
My Darling (3)
My Flying Saucer (4)
Nothing'severgonnastandinmy-way(again) (3)
One By One (3)
Outta Mind (Outta Sight) (1)
Outtasite (Outta Mind) (1)
Pieholden Suite (3)
Red-Eyed And Blue (1)
Remember The Mountain Bed (4)

Say You Miss Me (1)
Secret Of The Sea (4)
She Came Along To Me (2)
She's A Jar (3)
Shot In The Arm (3)
Someday Some Morning Sometime (4)
Someday Soon (3)
Someone Else's Song (1)
Stetson Kennedy (4)
Summer Teeth (3)
Sunken Treasure (1)

Unwelcome Guest (2)
Via Chicago (3)
Walt Whitman's Niece (2)
(Was I) In Your Dreams (1)
Way Over Yonder In The Minor Key (2)
We're Just Friends (3)
What's The World Got In Store (1)
When You Wake Up Feeling Old (3)
Why Would You Wanna Live (1)

WILCOX, David '94

Born on 3/9/58 in Mentor, Ohio. Singer/songwriter/guitarist.

| 2/26/94 | 165 | 1 | | © | **Big Horizon** .... | | | $10 | A&M 540060 |

All The Roots Grow Deeper When It's Dry
Big Mistake

Block Dog
Break In The Cup
Farthest Shore

Hold It Up To The Light
It's The Same Old Song
Make It Look Easy

Missing You
New World
Please Don't Call

Show The Way
Someday Soon
Strong Chemistry

That's What The Lonely Is For

WILD CHERRY '76

White funk group from Steubenville, Ohio: Robert Parissi (vocals, guitar), Bryan Bassett (guitar), Mark Avsec (keyboards), Allen Wentz (bass) and Ron Beitle (drums).

7/24/76	5	29	▲	©	1 **Wild Cherry**			$12	Sweet City 34195
4/2/77	51	9			2 **Electrified Funk**			$12	Sweet City 34462
2/18/78	84	9			3 **I Love My Music**			$12	Sweet City 35011

Are You Boogieing Around On Your Daddy (2)
Baby Don't You Know (2) *43*
Closest Thing To My Mind (2)
Dancin' Music Band (2)
Don't Go Near The Water (1)

Don't Stop, Get Off (3)
Electrified Funk (2)
Fools Fall In Love (3)
Get It Up (1)
Hold On (1,2) *61*
Hole In The Wall (2)

Hot To Trot (2) *95*
I Feel Sanctified (1)
I Love My Music (3) *69*
If You Want My Love (3)
It's All Up To You (2)
It's The Same Old Song (3)

Lady Wants Your Money (3)
Lana (3)
99 1/2 (1)
No Way Out Love Affair (3)
Nowhere To Run (1)
1 2 3 Kind Of Love (3)

Play That Funky Music (1) *1*
Put Yourself In My Shoes (2)
This Old Heart Of Mine (Is Weak For You) (3)
Try One More Time (3)

What In The Funk Do You See (1)

WILDE, Danny '88

Born in Maine; raised in California. Pop-rock singer/songwriter/guitarist. Member of **The Rembrandts**.

| 3/26/88 | 176 | 9 | | © | **Any Man's Hunger** .... | | | $10 | Geffen 24179 |

Ain't I Good Enough
Any Man's Hunger

Bitter Moon
Contradiction

Every Goodbye
In A Bordertown

Set Me Free
Time Runs Wild

Too Many Years Gone By
Wouldn't Be The First Time

WILDE, Eugene
Born Ronald Broomfield in Miami. R&B singer/songwriter.
'85

| 1/26/85 | 97 | 15 | © | Eugene Wilde | $10 | Philly World 90239 |

Chey Chey Kule | Gotta Get You Home | Just Be Good To Me | Let Her Feel It | Rainbow
Gold | Tonight *83* | Lately | Personality

WILDE, Kim
Born Kim Smith on 11/18/60 in Chiswick, England. Pop-rock singer. Daughter of singer Marty Wilde.
'87

6/5/82	86	22	©	1	Kim Wilde	$12	EMI America 17065
2/9/85	84	10	©	2	Teases & Dares	$10	MCA 5550
4/4/87	40	26	©	3	Another Step	$10	MCA 5903
10/1/88	114	6	©	4	Close	$10	MCA 42230

Another Step (Closer To You) (3) | Falling Out (1) | Janine (2) | **Say You Really Want Me** (3) *44* | Thrill Of It (3) | You'll Never Be So Wrong (1)
Bladerunner (2) | Fit In (2) | **Kids In America** (1) *25* | Schoolgirl (3) | Touch, The (2) | Young Heroes (1)
Brothers (3) | Four Letter Word (4) | Love In The Natural Way (4) | Shangri-La (2) | Tuning In Tuning On (1)
Chequered Love (1) | **Go For It** (2) *65* | Love's A No (4) | She Hasn't Got Time For You (3) | 2-6-5-8-0 (1)
Don't Say Nothing's Changed (3) | Hey Mister Heartache (4) | Lucky Guy (4) | | Water On Glass (1)
European Soul (4) | Hit Him (3) | Missing (3) | Stone (4) | **You Came** (4) *41*
Everything We Know (1) | How Do You Want My Love (3) | Never Trust A Stranger (4) | Suburbs Of Moscow (2) | **You Keep Me Hangin' On** (3) *1*
| I've Got So Much Love (3) | Our Town (1) | Thought It Was Goodbye (2) | You'll Be The One Who'll Lose (4)
| Is It Over (2) | Rage To Love (2) |

WILDER, Matthew
Born on 1/24/53 in Manhattan, New York. Singer/songwriter/keyboardist.
'84

| 1/7/84 | 49 | 16 | © | I Don't Speak The Language | $10 | Private I 39112 |

Break My Stride *5* | Dreams Keep Bringing You Back | I Don't Speak The Language | **Kid's American** *33* | Love Above The Ground Floor
| | I Was There | Ladder Of Lovers | World Of The Rich And Famous

WILD MAN STEVE
Born Steve Gallon in Boston. Black DJ/comedian for WILD radio in Boston.
'70

11/1/69	185	6		1	My Man! Wild Man!	[C] $20	Raw 7000
6/6/70	179	2		2	Wild! Wild! Wild! Wild!	[C] $20	Raw 7001
					no track titles listed on above 2 albums

WILD ONES, The
Rock group from New York City: Chuck Alden, Tom Trick, Jordan Christopher, Ed Wright and Tom Graves.
'65

| 11/20/65 | 149 | 2 | | The Arthur Sound | [L] $30 | United Artists 3450 |

Around The Corner | I Can't Help Myself | My Little Red Book (All I Do Is | Satisfaction | You've Lost That Lovin' Feelin'
Dancing In The Streets | It's Not Unusual | Talk About You) | What's New Pussycat?
Foolish Pride | My Girl | People Sure Act Funny | Wild Way Of Living

WILD ORCHID
Female vocal trio from Los Angeles: Stacy Ferguson, Stefanie Ridel and Renee Sandstrom. Both Ferguson (1984-89) and Sandstrom (1984-87) were regulars on the TV show Kids Incorporated.
'97

| 4/12/97 | 153 | 4 | © | Wild Orchid | $10 | RCA 66894 |

At Night I Pray *63* | He's Alright | Life | My Tambourine | **Supernatural** *70* | You Don't Own Me
Follow Me | I Won't Play The Fool | Love Will Wait | River, The | **Talk To Me** *48*

WILD TURKEY
*Rock group from England: Gary Pickford-Hopkins (vocals), Tweke Lewis and Jon Blackmore (guitars), Glenn Cornick (bass; **Jethro Tull**) and Jeff Jones (drums).*
'72

| 5/6/72 | 193 | 3 | © | Battle Hymn | $15 | Reprise 2070 |

Battle Hymn | Easter Psalm | Sanctuary | Twelve Streets Of Cobbled
Butterfly | Gentle Rain | Sentinel | Black
Dulwich Fox | One Sole Survivor | To The Stars

WILKINSONS, The
Country vocal trio from Belleville, Ontario, Canada: father Steve with children Amanda and Tyler Wilkinson.
'00

| 8/29/98 | 133 | 19 | ● © | 1 | Nothing But Love | $10 | Giant 24699 |
| 4/22/00 | 114 | 3 | © | 2 | Here And Now | $10 | Giant 24736 |

Back On My Feet (1) | Hypothetically (2) | 1999 (2) | Only Rose (2) | Williamstown (1)
Boy Oh Boy (1) | I'll Know Love (2) | Nothing But Love (Standing In | Shame On Me (2) | Word, The (1)
Don't I Have A Heart (1) | It Was Only A Kiss (2) | The Way) (1) | Then There's You (1) | Yodelin' Blues (1)
Don't Look At Me Like That (2) | Jimmy's Got A Girlfriend (2) | One Faithful Heart (1) | Till You Let Go (2)
Fly (the angel song) (1) *53* | Me, Myself And I (2) | One Of Us Is In Love (2) | 26¢ (1) *55*

WILL AND THE KILL
*Rock group from Austin, Texas: Will Sexton (vocals, guitar), David Grissom (guitar), Alex Napier (bass) and Jeff Boaz (drums). Sexton is the brother of **Charlie Sexton**.*
'88

| 4/9/88 | 129 | 8 | © | Will And The Kill | $10 | MCA 42054 |

All Just To Get To You | Hard To Please | I Thought I Heard A Heartbeat | Restless To Reckless | Teach The Teacher
Breakin' All The Rules | Heart Of Steel | No Sleep | Rocks In My Pillow | Their Game

WILLIAMS, Andy ★17★   '63

Born Howard Andrew Williams on 12/3/28 in Wall Lake, Iowa. Pop singer. Hosted own TV variety show from 1962-71. Appeared in the movie *I'd Rather Be Rich*. Married to **Claudine Longet** from 1962-67.

1)Days of Wine and Roses 2)Moon River & Other Great Movie Themes 3)Love Story 4)Dear Heart
5)The Academy Award Winning "Call Me Irresponsible"

DEBUT	PEAK	WKS				ARTIST — Album Title	$	Label & Number
1/25/60	38	4		©	1	Lonely Street	$25	Cadence 3030
3/3/62	19	36			2	"Danny Boy" and other songs I love to sing	$20	Columbia 1751 / 8551
4/7/62+	59	44		©	3	Andy Williams' Best	[G] $20	Cadence 3054
						also see #14 below		
5/12/62+	3	176	●	©	4	Moon River & Other Great Movie Themes	$20	Columbia 1809 / 8609
10/20/62+	16	44			5	Warm And Willing	$20	Columbia 1879 / 8679
1/12/63	54	43			6	Million Seller Songs	[K] $20	Cadence 3061
4/20/63	❶16	107	●	©	7	Days of Wine and Roses	$15	Columbia 2015 / 8815
11/30/63	❶9X	34	●	©	8	The Andy Williams Christmas Album	[X] $15	Columbia 2087 / 8887
						Christmas charts: 1/'63, 1/'64, 1/'65, 60/'66, 6/'67, 17/'68, 30/'69, 4/'70, 4/'71, 8/'72, 6/'73		
1/25/64	9	24	●		9	The Wonderful World Of Andy Williams	$15	Columbia 2137 / 8937
5/9/64	5	63	●		10	The Academy Award Winning "Call Me Irresponsible"	$15	Columbia 2171 / 8971
9/26/64	5	33	●		11	The Great Songs From "My Fair Lady" and other Broadway hits	$15	Columbia 2205 / 9005
4/10/65	4	65	●	©	12	Dear Heart	$15	Columbia 2338 / 9138
5/22/65	61	18		©	13	Hawaiian Wedding Song	[E] $15	Columbia 2323 / 9123
						reissue of 1959 album To You Sweetheart, Aloha *on Cadence 3029 ($25)*		
7/3/65	112	6			14	Canadian Sunset	[R] $15	Columbia 2324 / 9124
						reissue of album #3 above		
12/18/65+	❶3X	20	●	©	15	Merry Christmas	[X] $15	Columbia 2420 / 9220
						Christmas charts: 5/'65, 1/'66, 20/'67, 4/'68, 1/'69, 19/'70		
2/5/66	23	23			16	Andy Williams' Newest Hits	[K] $15	Columbia 2383 / 9183
5/14/66	6	54	●	©	17	The Shadow of Your Smile	$15	Columbia 2499 / 9299
1/21/67	21	22		©	18	In The Arms Of Love	$15	Columbia 2533 / 9333
5/13/67	5	79	●	©	19	Born Free	$15	Columbia 2680 / 9480
11/18/67+	8	36	●	©	20	Love, Andy	$15	Columbia 2766 / 9566
6/8/68	9	40	●	©	21	Honey	$15	Columbia 9662
2/1/69	139	7			22	The Andy Williams Sound of Music	[K] $20	Columbia 5 [2]
5/17/69	9	23	●	©	23	Happy Heart	$15	Columbia 9844
11/8/69	27	21	●		24	Get Together With Andy Williams	$15	Columbia 9922
3/7/70	42	20	●	©	25	Andy Williams' Greatest Hits	[G] $15	Columbia 9979
6/13/70	43	19			26	Raindrops Keep Fallin' On My Head	$15	Columbia 9896
11/14/70	81	17			27	The Andy Williams Show	[L] $12	Columbia 30105
2/20/71	3	33	▲	©	28	Love Story	$12	Columbia 30497
8/28/71	54	12			29	You've Got A Friend	$12	Columbia 30797
1/8/72	123	5			30	The Impossible Dream	[K] $15	Columbia 31064 [2]
4/8/72	29	26	●		31	Love Theme From "The Godfather"	$12	Columbia 31303
9/30/72	86	18			32	Alone Again (Naturally)	$12	Columbia 31625
7/7/73	174	5		©	33	Andy Williams' Greatest Hits, Vol. 2	[G] $12	Columbia 32384
11/17/73	185	6			34	Solitaire	$12	Columbia 32383
12/28/74+	150	2			35	You Lay So Easy On My Mind	$12	Columbia 33234
12/17/94	137	2		©	36	The New Andy Williams Christmas Album ....C:#32/5	[X] $10	LaserLight 12326
						Christmas charts: 40/'94, 38/'95, 31/'96		

WILLIAMS, Andy — Cont'd

(In The Summer Time) ..see:
You Don't Want My Love
In The Wee Small Hours Of The
Morning (1)
It Could Happen To You (2)
It Had To Be You (12)
It Might As Well Be Spring (4)
It's A Most Unusual Day (7)
It's All In The Game (6)
It's Impossible (28)
It's Over (26)
It's The Most Wonderful Time
Of The Year (8,36)
It's Too Late (29)
Jimmy Bishop Christmas
Column (36)
Joanne (27)
Joy To The World (medley) (36)
Ka-Lu-A (13)
Kay Thompson's Jingle Bells
(8,36)
Kisses Sweeter Than Wine (20)
Lara's Theme ..see:
Somewhere, My Love
Last Tango In Paris (34)
Last Time I Saw Her (30)
Laura (10)
Leaving On A Jet Plane (27)
Let It Be Me (9,22)
Let It Snow! Let It Snow! Let It
Snow! (15,36)
Let The Sunshine In (medley)
(24)
Little Altar Boy (15)
Little Boy (medley) (26)
Little Drummer Boy (8)
Little Green Apples (23)
Lonely Street (1,3,14,33) 5
Long And Winding Road (32)
Long Long Time (30)
Long Time Blues (26)
Look Of Love (20)
Love Is A Many-Splendored
Thing (4)
Love Is Blue (21,30)

Love Is Here To Stay (5)
Love Letters (10)
Love Letters In The Sand (6)
Love Song Of Kalua (13)
Love Story ..see: (Where Do I
Begin)
MacArthur Park (31,33)
Madrigal (10)
Make It Easy For Me (34)
Make It With You (27)
Mam'selle (6,22)
Man And A Woman (18,30)
Maria (4)
Mary's Little Boy Child (15)
May Each Day (7,16,22,25,36)
Meditation (17)
Memories (23)
Michelle (17)
Misty (2)
Mona Lisa (10)
Moon Of Manakoora (13)
Moon River (4,25)
More (10,25)
More I See You (20)
More Than You Know (5)
More Today Than Yesterday
(24)
Moulin Rouge (Where Is Your
Heart), Song From (10)
Music From Across The Way
(31,33)
Music To Watch Girls By
(19,33) **34**
My Carousel (12)
My Cherie Amour (24,30)
My Coloring Book (7)
My Elusive Dreams (35)
My Favorite Things (15)
My Love (34)
My One And Only Love (5)
My Sweet Lord (28,30)
My Way (23)
Never Can Say Goodbye (29)

Never My Love (27)
Never On Sunday (4)
Noelle (9,16)
O Come All Ye Faithful
(medley) (36)
O Holy Night (8,36)
Old Fashioned Love Song (31)
**On The Street Where You
Live** (11,16,22) **28**
Once Upon A Time (11)
Our Last Goodbye (21)
Peg O' My Heart (17)
Pennies From Heaven (9)
People (11,22)
Picnic (6)
Pieces Of April (32)
Precious And Few (31)
Pretty Butterfly (18)
Put A Little Love In Your Heart
(24)
Quentin's Theme (Shadows Of
The Night) (24)
Quiet Nights Of Quiet Stars
(16,22) **92**
Raindrops Keep Fallin' On My
Head (26)
Rainy Days And Monday (29)
Reason To Believe (26)
Red Roses For A Blue Lady
(12,16)
Remember (18,34)
Romeo & Juliet (A Time For
Us), Love Theme From
(24,30)
Rose Garden (28)
Sand And Sea (18)
Sand Pebbles (And We Were
Lovers), Theme From The
(18)
Say It Isn't So (1,22)
Scarborough Fair/Canticle (21)
Second Time Around (4)
Secret Love (2)
September Song (9)
Shadow Of Your Smile (17)

Sherry! (19)
Show Me (11)
Silent Night, Holy Night (8,36)
Silver Bells (15)
Simple Thing As Love (26)
Sing A Rainbow (9)
Sleigh Ride (15,36)
Snowbird (27)
So Nice (Summer Samba) (18)
So Rare (6)
Softly, As I Leave You (9)
Solitaire (34)
Some Children See Him (15)
Someone Who Cares (30)
Somethin' Stupid (20)
Something (28)
Somewhere (17)
Somewhere, My Love (19,30)
Song And A Christmas Tree
(The Twelve Days Of
Christmas) (8)
Song For You (29,33) **82**
Song Of Old Hawaii (13)
Song Of The Islands (13)
Song Sung Blue (32)
Sound Of Music (22)
Spanish Eyes (19)
Spanish Harlem (27,30)
(Speak Softly Love) ..see:
Godfather
Spooky (21)
Stranger On The Shore (5) **38**
Strangers In The Night (19)
Suddenly There's A Valley (6)
Summer Love (1,14)
Summer Of '42, Theme From
(31)
Summer Of Our Love (17,22)
Summer Place (4)
Summertime (2)
Sunny (19)
Sweet Caroline (24)
Sweet Leilani (15)
Sweet Little Jesus Boy (8)

Sweet Memories (26) **75**
Sweetest Sounds (11)
Tammy (2)
Taste Of Honey (17)
Tender Is The Night (4)
That Is All (34)
That Old Feeling (17,22)
Then You Can Tell Me
Goodbye (19)
There Will Never Be Another
You (20)
They Long To Be Close To You
(27,30)
This Is All I Ask (9)
This Is My Song (21)
Three Bells (6)
Three Coins In The Fountain (4)
Till (12)
To You Sweetheart Aloha (13)
Today Medley (35)
Tonight (4)
Touch Of Your Lips (5,22)
Try To Remember (17,22)
Twelfth Of Never (2)
Twilight Time (6) **86**
Unchained Melody (1)
Until It's Time For You To Go
(31)
Up, Up And Away (21)
Valley Of The Dolls, Theme
From (21)
Very Thought Of You (18,22)
Village Of St. Bernadette
(3,14,33) **7**
Walk Right Back (34)
Warm All Over (5)
Warm And Willing (5)
Watch What Happens (20)
Way You Look Tonight (5)
We've Only Just Begun (28)
What Are You Doing The Rest
Of Your Life? (27)
What Kind Of Fool Am I? (7)
What Now My Love (20,30)
When I Look In Your Eyes (20)

When You're Smiling (The
Whole World Smiles With
You) (7)
When Your Lover Has Gone
(1,22)
**(Where Do I Begin) Love
Story** (28,33) **9**
Where Is The Love (32)
(Where Is Your Heart) ..see:
Moulin Rouge
Where Or When (11)
Where's The Playground
Susie? (23)
White Christmas (8,36)
Who Can I Turn To (When
Nobody Needs Me) (12)
Wichita Lineman (23)
Willow Weep For Me (1)
Windy (21)
Winter Wonderland (15)
Without You (31)
Wives And Lovers (9)
**Wonderful World Of The
Young** (16) **99**
Wouldn't It Be Lovely (11)
Yesterday (17)
Yesterday When I Was Young
(24)
You Are (24)
You Are My Sunshine (7)
You Are The Sunshine Of My
Life (34)
You Are Where Everything Is
(19)
You Don't Know What Love Is
(1,22)
You Don't Want My Love
(3,14) **64**
You Lay So Easy On My Mind
(35)
You're Nobody 'Til Somebody
Loves You (12)
You've Got A Friend (29)
Your Song (28)

WILLIAMS, Christopher

Born in Harlem, New York. R&B singer. Nephew of **Ella Fitzgerald**.   **'93**

| 1/16/93 | 63 | 25 | | © | 1 Changes .... | | | $10 | Uptown 10751 |
| 3/18/95 | 104 | 5 | | © | 2 Not A Perfect Man .... | | | $10 | Giant 24564 |

All I See (1)
Changes (1)
Come Go With Me (1)
Dance 4 Me (2)

Don't U Wanna Make Love (1)
Down On My Knees (2)
Dreamin' (1)
Every Little Thing U Do (1) **75**

Good Luvin' (1)
If You Say (2)
Learning To Love Again (2)
Let's Get Right (1)
Lonely (2)

Never Stop (2)
Not A Perfect Man (2)
Oh Girl (2)
Please, Please, Please (1)
R U Ready (2)

Solidarity (2)
We Don't Know How To Say
Goodbye (2)
When A Fool Becomes A Man
(1)

Where Are U Now (1)
Where Is The Love (1)

WILLIAMS, Danny

Born on 1/7/42 in Port Elizabeth, South Africa. Smooth R&B singer.   **'64**

| 6/13/64 | 122 | 5 | | | White On White .... | | | $25 | United Artists 3359 |

Charade
Comedy Has Ended
Doreen

Forget Her
I Talk To The Trees
Impossible

Lonely
My Heart Tells Me
Story Of A Starry Night

We Will Never Be As Young As
This Again

Weaver Of Dreams
White On White **9**

WILLIAMS, Dar

Born in 1967 in Mount Kisco, Massachusetts. Female singer/songwriter.   **'00**

| 8/2/97 | 169 | 1 | | © | 1 End Of The Summer .... | | | $10 | Razor & Tie 82830 |
| 9/9/00 | 143 | 1 | | © | 2 The Green World .... | | | $10 | Razor & Tie 82856 |

After All (2)
And A God Descended (2)
Another Mystery (2)
Are You Out There (1)

Better Things (2)
Bought And Sold (1)
Calling The Moon (2)
End Of The Summer (1)

I Had No Right (2)
I Won't Be Your Yoko Ono (2)
If I Wrote You (1)
It Happens Every Day (2)

It's A War In There (1)
My Friends (1)
Party Generation (1)
Playing To The Firmament (2)

Road Buddy (1)
Spring Street (2)
Teenagers, Kick Our Butts (1)
We Learned The Sea (2)

What Do You Hear In These
Sounds (1)
What Do You Love More Than
Love (2)

★500★ WILLIAMS, Deniece

Born Deniece Chandler on 6/3/51 in Gary, Indiana. R&B singer/songwriter.   **'78**

10/30/76+	33	36	●	©	1 This is Niecy			$12	Columbia 34242
11/19/77+	66	20		©	2 Song Bird			$12	Columbia 34911
7/29/78	19	16	●	©	3 That's What Friends Are For			$12	Columbia 35435
					JOHNNY MATHIS & DENIECE WILLIAMS				
8/18/79	96	8			4 When Love Comes Calling			$12	ARC 35568
4/4/81	74	32		©	5 My Melody			$12	ARC 37048
4/17/82	20	22			6 Niecy			$12	ARC 37952
6/4/83	54	19			7 I'm So Proud			$10	Columbia 38622
6/9/84	26	19		©	8 Let's Hear It For The Boy			$10	Columbia 39366

Are You Thinking? (4)
Baby, Baby My Love's All For
You (2)
Be Good To Me (2)
Black Butterfly (8)
Blind Dating (8)
Boy I Left Behind (2)
Cause You Love Me Baby (1)
Do What You Feel (7)

Don't Tell Me We Have Nothing
(8)
Free (1) **25**
God Is Amazing (2)
God Knows (4)
Haunting Me (8)
Heaven In Your Eyes (7)
Heaven Must Have Sent You
(3)
How Does It Feel (6)

How'd I Know That Love Would
Slip Away (1)
I Believe In Miracles (6)
I Found Love (4)
I Just Can't Get Over You (3)
I Want You (8)
I'm Glad It's You (7)
I'm So Proud (7)
I've Got The Next Dance
(4) **73**

If You Don't Believe (1)
It's Gonna Take A Miracle
(6) **10**
It's Important To Me (1)
It's Okay (7)
It's Your Conscience (5)
Just The Way You Are (3)
Let's Hear It For The Boy (8) **1**
Like Magic (4)
Love Notes (6)

Love, Peace And Unity (7)
Me For You, You For Me (3)
My Melody (5)
My Prayer (7)
Next Love (8) **81**
Now Is The Time For Love (6)
Paper, The (7)
Part Of Love (6)
Picking Up The Pieces (8)

Ready Or Not (3)
Season (2)
Silly (5) **53**
So Deep In Love (7)
Strangers (5)
Suspicious (5)
Sweet Surrender (5)
That's What Friends Are For
(1,3)
They Say (7)

WILLIAMS, Deniece — Cont'd

Time (2)
Touch Me Again (4)
Touching Me With Love (3)
Turn Around (4)

Until You Come Back To Me
(That's What I'm Gonna Do)
(3)
Waiting (6)

Waiting By The Hotline (6)
Watching Over (1)
We Have Love For You (2)
What Two Can Do (5)

When Love Comes Calling (4)
Whiter Than Snow (8)
Why Can't We Fall In Love? (4)
Wrapped Up (8)

You're A Special Part Of My
Life (3)
You're All I Need To Get By
(3) *47*

You're All That Matters (5)

WILLIAMS, Don   '80

Born on 5/27/39 in Floydada, Texas. Country singer/songwriter/guitarist. Member of the **Pozo-Seco Singers**.

DEBUT	PEAK	WKS	RIAA	CD	#	Album Title		Sym	$	Label & Number
1/27/79	161	7			1	Expressions			$12	ABC 1069
10/4/80	57	31	▲	©	2	I Believe In You			$10	MCA 5133
7/25/81	109	11		©	3	Especially For You			$10	MCA 5210
5/1/82	166	8			4	Listen To The Radio			$10	MCA 5306

Ain't It Amazing (2)
All I'm Missing Is You (1)
Don't Stop Loving Me Now (4)
Especially You (3)
Fairweather Friends (3)
Falling Again (2)
Fool, Fool Heart (4)
Give It To Me (1)

Help Yourselves To Each Other
(4)
I Believe In You (2) *24*
I Can't Get To You From Here
(4)
I Don't Want To Love You (3)
I Keep Putting Off Getting Over
You (2)
I Want You Back Again (2)

I Would Like To See You Again
(1)
I've Got You To Thank For That
(3)
If Hollywood Don't Need You (4)
If I Needed You (3)
If She Just Helps Me Get Over
You (4)
It Must Be Love (1)

It's Good To See You (2)
Just Enough Love (For One
Woman) (2)
Lay Down Beside Me (1)
Listen To The Radio (4)
Lord, I Hope This Day Is Good
(3)
Miracles (3)
Mistakes (4)

Not A Chance (1)
Now And Then (3)
Only Love (4)
Rainy Nights And Memories (4)
Simple Song (2)
Smooth Talking Baby (3)
Standin' In A Sea Of Teardrops
(4)

Tears Of The Lonely (1)
Tulsa Time (1)
When I'm With You (4)
Years From Now (3)
You've Got A Hold On Me (1)

WILLIAMS, Hank   '65

Born Hiram King Williams on 9/17/23 in Mount Olive, Alabama. Died of alcohol/drug abuse on 1/1/53 (age 29). Legendary country singer/songwriter/guitarist. Father of **Hank Williams, Jr.** Won Grammy's Lifetime Achievement Award in 1987. Inducted into the Rock and Roll Hall of Fame in 1987 as an early influence. George Hamilton portrayed Hank in the movie biography *Your Cheatin' Heart*.

DEBUT	PEAK	WKS	RIAA	CD	#	Album Title		Sym	$	Label & Number
8/7/65	139	3		©	1	Father & Son			$25	MGM 4276
						HANK WILLIAMS, SR. & HANK WILLIAMS, JR.				
8/7/82	27[C]	2		©	2	Hank Williams, Sr./Live At The Grand Ole Opry		[L]	$25	MGM 5019
1/23/93	179	1		©	3	The Best Of Hank & Hank		[G]	$10	Curb 77552
						HANK WILLIAMS, SR. & HANK WILLIAMS, JR.				
6/29/96+	30[C]	3	▲	©	4	24 Of Hank Williams' Greatest Hits		[G]	$15	Polydor 823293 [2]
10/12/96	167	1		©	5	Men With Broken Hearts		[G]	$10	Curb 77868

THREE HANKS (Hank Sr., Hank Jr. and Hank III)
includes the solo "'Neath A Cold Gray Tomb Of Stone" by Hank III

| 10/17/98 | 41[C] | 1 | | © | 6 | 20 Of Hank Williams' Greatest Hits | | [G] | $10 | Mercury 536029 |

Baby, We're Really In Love
(4,6)
Cold, Cold Heart (2,4,6)
Crazy Heart (1)
Dear John (2)
Half As Much (4,6)
Hey, Good Lookin' (2,4,6)
Honky Tonk Blues (1,4,5,6)
Honky Tonkin' (4,6)

I Can't Help It (If I'm Still In Love
With You) (4,6)
(I Heard That) Lonesome
Whistle (1)
I Just Don't Like This Kind Of
Livin' (1,2)
I Won't Be Home No More (1,5)
I'm A Long Gone Daddy (5)
I'm So Lonesome I Could Cry
(4,6)

Jambalaya (On The Bayou)
(3,4,6)
Kaw-Liga (3,4,6)
Long Gone Lonesome Blues (2)
Lost Highway (1,5)
Lovesick Blues (1,2,4,6)
May You Never Be Alone (1,4)
Men With Broken Hearts (5)
Mind Your Own Business (1,4)
Moanin' The Blues (2,5)

Move It On Over (1,4,5,6)
My Heart Would Know (4,6)
Nobody's Lonesome For Me (2)
Ramblin' Man (4,6)
Settin' The Woods On Fire (4)
Take These Chains From My
Heart (4,6)
There'll Be No Teardrops
Tonight (4,6)
There's A Tear In My Beer (3)

They'll Never Take Her Love
From Me (2)
Wedding Bells (1,4)
Where The Soul Of Man Never
Dies (5)
Why Don't You Love Me
(1,2,3,4,6)
Window Shopping (4,6)
You Win Again (4,6)

You're Gonna Change (Or I'm
Gonna Leave) (2)
Your Cheatin' Heart (4,6)

WILLIAMS, Hank Jr. ★111★   '65

Born Randall Hank Williams on 5/26/49 in Shreveport, Louisiana; raised in Nashville. Country singer/songwriter/guitarist. Son of **Hank Williams**. Nicknamed "Bocephus." Richard Thomas starred as Hank in the 1983 biographical TV movie *Living Proof: The Hank Williams Story*.

1)*Your Cheatin' Heart* 2)*Born To Boogie* 3)*Pure Hank* 4)*Maverick* 5)*Wild Streak*

DEBUT	PEAK	WKS	RIAA	CD	#	Album Title		Sym	$	Label & Number
1/2/65	16	37	●	©	1	Your Cheatin' Heart		[S]	$25	MGM 4260
8/7/65	139	3		©	2	Father & Son			$25	MGM 4276
						HANK WILLIAMS, SR. & HANK WILLIAMS, JR.				
11/2/68	189	3			3	A Time To Sing		[S]	$25	MGM 4540
						includes "Next Time I Say Goodbye I'm Leaving" by Shelley Fabares				
6/21/69	164	4			4	Songs My Father Left Me			$20	MGM 4621
10/18/69	187	2			5	Live At Cobo Hall, Detroit		[L]	$20	MGM 4644
6/21/80	154	17	●	©	6	Habits Old And New			$10	Elektra/Curb 278
2/21/81	82	15	●	©	7	Rowdy			$10	Elektra/Curb 330
9/5/81	76	23	▲	©	8	The Pressure Is On			$10	Elektra/Curb 535
5/8/82	123	20	●	©	9	High Notes			$10	Elektra/Curb 60100
11/13/82+	107	70	▲[4]	©	10	Hank Williams, Jr.'s Greatest Hits	C:#25/47	[G]	$10	Elektra/Curb 60193
4/23/83	64	16	●	©	11	Strong Stuff			$10	Elektra/Curb 60223
11/19/83	116	13	●	©	12	Man Of Steel			$10	Warner/Curb 23924
6/9/84	100	19	▲	©	13	Major Moves			$10	Warner/Curb 25088
5/18/85	72	22	●	©	14	Five-O			$10	Warner/Curb 25267
1/11/86	183	8	▲	©	15	Greatest Hits - Volume 2		[G]	$10	Warner/Curb 25328
7/19/86	93	18	●	©	16	Montana Cafe			$10	Warner/Curb 25412
2/14/87	71	24	▲	©	17	Hank "Live"		[L]	$10	Warner/Curb 25538
8/1/87	28	47	▲	©	18	Born To Boogie			$10	Warner/Curb 25593
7/16/88	55	19	●	©	19	Wild Streak			$10	Warner/Curb 25725
2/25/89	61	35	▲	©	20	Greatest Hits III		[G]	$10	Warner/Curb 25834
2/24/90	71	18	●	©	21	Lone Wolf			$10	Warner/Curb 26090
11/3/90	116	14	●	©	22	America (The Way I See It)		[K]	$10	Warner/Curb 26453
5/11/91	50	19	●	©	23	Pure Hank			$10	Warner/Curb 26536
3/7/92	55	20	●	©	24	Maverick			$10	Curb/Capricorn 26806

WILLIAMS, Hank Jr. — Cont'd

1/23/93	179	1	©	25	**The Best Of Hank & Hank** .... [G]			$10	Curb 77552
					HANK WILLIAMS, SR. & HANK WILLIAMS, JR.				
3/27/93	121	4	©	26	**Out Of Left Field**			$10	Curb/Capricorn 45225
2/11/95	91	14	©	27	**Hog Wild**			$10	Curb 77690
10/12/96	167	1	©	28	**Men With Broken Hearts**			$10	Curb 77868
					THREE HANKS (Hank Sr., Hank Jr. and Hank III)				
					includes the solo "'Neath A Cold Gray Tomb Of Stone" by Hank III				
10/9/99	162	1	©	29	**Stormy**			$10	Curb 77953

Ain't Makin' No Headlines (Here Without You) (9)
Ain't Misbehavin' (14,20)
Ain't Much More (7)
Ain't Nobody's Business (21)
Air That I Breathe (12)
All In Alabama (6)
All Jokes Aside (29)
All My Rowdy Friends Are Coming Over For Monday Night Football (22)
All My Rowdy Friends Are Coming Over Tonight (13,15)
All My Rowdy Friends (Have Settled Down) (8,10,17)
Almost Persuaded (21)
American Dream (10)
American Way (6,22)
Angels Are Hard To Find (23)
Are You Lonely Too (4)
Are You Sure Hank Done It This Way (7)
Attitude Adjustment (13,15)
Ballad Of Hank Williams (8)
Be Careful Who You Love (Arthur's Song) (23)
Between Heaven And Hell (27)
Big Mamou (21)
Blue Jean Blues (11)
Blue Lady In A Red Mercedes (26)
Blues Man (6)
Born To Boogie (18,20)
Both Sides Of Goodbye (26)
Buck Naked (18)
Cajun Baby (4)
Coalition To Ban Coalitions (8,22)
Cold, Cold Heart (1)
Come On Over To The Country (24)
Conversation, The (15,17,25)
Count Song (24)
Country Boy Can Survive (8,10,17,22)
Country Relaxin' (13)
Country State Of Mind (16,20)
Crazy Heart (2)
Cut Bank, Montana (24)
Darling, You Know I Wouldn't Lie (5)

Daytona Nights (27)
Detroit City (5)
Diamond Mine (26)
Dinosaur (6)
Dirty Mind (26)
Dixie On My Mind (7,10)
Don't Give Us A Reason (22)
Early In The Morning And Late At Night (19)
Everything Comes Down To Money And Love (24)
Everytime I Hear That Song (8)
Eyes Of Waylon (27)
Family Tradition (10,17,25)
Fat Friends (16)
Fax Me A Beer (24)
Finders Are Keepers (20)
Foggy Mountain Breakdown (5)
Footlights (7)
For Me There Is No Place (4)
Games People Play (9)
Gibbonsville Gold (29)
Girl On The Front Row At Fort Worth (1)
Give A Damn (7,22)
Give Me The Hummingbird Line (3)
Gonna Go Huntin' Tonight (11,15)
Good Friends, Good Whiskey, Good Lovin' (21)
Greeted In End (27)
Hand Me Down (28)
Hank (25)
Hank Hill Is The King (29)
Harvest Moon (medley) (16)
Heaven Can't Be Found (18,20)
Here I Am Fallin' Again (6)
Hey, Good Lookin' (1,17)
Hide And Seek (26)
High And Pressurized (9)
Hog Wild (27)
Hold Up Your Head (medley) (13)
Hold What You've Got (26)
Hollywood Honeys (23)
Homecoming Queen (11)
Homesick (4)
Honky Tonk Blues (2,28)
Honky Tonk Train (23)
Honky Tonk Women (18)

Honky Tonkin' (9,15)
Hot To Trot (21)
Hotel Whiskey (24)
House Of The Rising Sun (17)
I Ain't Going Peacefully (27)
I Can't Change My Tune (9)
I Can't Help It (If I'm Still In Love With You) (1)
I Don't Care (If Tomorrow Never Comes) (8)
I Got A Right To Be Wrong (7)
(I Heard That) Lonesome Whistle (2)
I Just Don't Like This Kind Of Livin' (2)
I Know What You've Got Up Your Sleeve (24)
I Like It When It's Stormy (29)
I Mean I Love You (21)
I Really Like Girls (14,17)
I Saw The Light (1,5)
I Won't Be Home No More (2,28)
I'd Love To Knock The Hell Out Of You (29)
I'm A Long Gone Daddy (28)
I'm For Love (14,17,20)
I'm Just A Man (19)
I'm Just Crying 'Cause I Care (4)
I'm So Lonesome I Could Cry (1,5)
I'm Tired (26)
I've Been Around (14)
I've Been Down (9)
(I've Got My) Future On Ice (23)
I've Got Rights (22)
If Heaven Ain't A Lot Like Dixie (9,17)
If It Will It Will (23)
If The South Woulda Won (19)
If You Don't Like Hank Williams (6,17,25)
If You Wanna Get To Heaven (9)
In The Arms Of Cocaine (11)
Iron Horse (27)
Is This Goodbye (4)
It Just Don't Get It No More (12)
It's A Start (27)
It's All Over But The Crying (3)

Jambalaya (On The Bayou) (1,5)
Just Me And My Broken Heart (4)
Just To Satisfy You (23)
Kaw-Liga (1,6,10)
Keep Your Hands To Yourself (18)
Kiss Mother Nature Goodbye (23)
Knoxville Courthouse Blues (13)
La Grange (11,17)
Lawyers, Guns And Money (14)
Leave Them Boys Alone (11,15)
Little Less Talk And A Lot More Action (24)
Lone Wolf (21)
Long Gone Lonesome Blues (1) *67*
Lost Highway (2)
Love M.D. (19)
Lovesick Blues (2,12)
Loving Instructor (16)
Low Down Blues (24)
Lyin' Jukebox (24)
Made In The Shade (11)
Major Moves (3)
Man Is On His Own (3)
Man Of Steel (12,15,17)
Man To Man (2)
May You Never Be Alone (2)
Memphis Belle (23)
Men With Broken Hearts (28)
Midnight Rider (12)
Mind Your Own Business (2,16,20)
Money Can't Buy Happiness (3)
Montana Cafe (16)
Move It On Over (2,6,28)
Mr. Lincoln (13,22)
My Girl Don't Like My Cowboy Hat (12)
My Heart Won't Let Me Go (4)
My Name Is Bocephus (16,17,20)
My Starter Won't Start This Morning (medley) (13)
Naked Women And Beer (29)
Nashville Scene (14)

Never Again (Will I Knock On Your Door) (28)
New Orleans (14)
Norwegian Wood (This Bird Has Flown) (9)
Now I Know How George Feels (12)
Old Before My Time (3)
Old Habits (6,10)
One Kind Favor (medley) (13)
Orange Blossom Special (12)
Out Of Left Field (26)
Outlaw's Reward (14)
Practice What I Preach (18,22)
Pressure Is On (8)
Promises (3)
Queen Of My Heart (12,15)
Ramblin' In My Shoes (8)
Ramblin' Man (1,7)
Ride, The (17)
Rock In My Shoe (3)
Shadow Face (18)
She Had Me (12)
She Thinks I Still Care (5)
Short Haired Woman (medley) (17)
Simple Man (23)
Social Call (19)
Something To Believe In (14)
Sometimes I Feel Like Joe Montana (29)
South's Gonna Rattle Again (9)
Southern Thunder (29)
St Louis Blues (medley) (16)
Standing In The Shadows (5)
Stoned At The Jukebox (21)
Sweet Home Alabama (17)
Tennessee River (7)
Tennessee Stud (8)
Texas Women (7,10)
Thanks A Lot (18)
There's A Tear In My Beer (20,25)
There's Gotta Be Much More To Life Than You (3)
They All Want To Go Wild (And I Want To Go Home) (29)
This Ain't Dallas (14,20)
Time To Sing (3)
Tobacco Road (27)

Trouble In Mind (medley) (13,17)
Tuesday's Gone (19)
Two Old Cats Like Us (15)
Twodot Montana (11)
U.S.A. Today (21,22)
Video Blues (13)
Warm In Dallas (26)
Weatherman (8)
Wedding Bells (2)
What It Boils Down To (18)
What You Don't Know (Won't Hurt You) (19)
When Something Is Good (Why Does It Change) (16)
Where Do I Go From Here (4)
Where The Soul Of Man Never Dies (28)
Where Would We Be Without Yankees (29)
Whiskey Bent And Hell Bound (10)
Whiskey On Ice (9)
Whole Lot Of Hank (11)
Why Don't You Love Me (2)
Wild And Blue (19)
Wild Streak (19)
Wild Thing (2)
Wild Weekend (24)
Woman On The Run (12)
Women I've Never Had (10)
Won't It Be Nice (6)
Workin' For MCA (17)
You Brought Me Down To Earth (19)
You Can't Find Many Kissers (7)
You Can't Judge A Book (By Looking At The Cover) (18)
You Can't Take My Memories Of You (4)
You Win Again (1,5,25)
You're Gonna Be A Sorry Man (19)
Young Country (18,20)
Your Cheatin' Heart (1,5,25)
Your Turn To Cry (4)

WILLIAMS, Hank III— see WILLIAMS, Hank

WILLIAMS, John — see BOSTON POPS ORCHESTRA

WILLIAMS, Lenny   '78

Born in February 1945 in Little Rock, Arkansas; raised in Oakland. Lead singer of **Tower Of Power** from 1972-75.

8/6/77	99	26			1 **Choosing You**			$12	ABC 1023
7/22/78	87	25	●	©	2 **Spark Of Love**			$12	ABC 1073
7/7/79	108	9			3 **Love Current**			$12	MCA 3155
11/15/80	185	2			4 **Let's Do It Today**			$12	MCA 5147

'Cause I Love You (2)
Changes (2)
Choosing You (1)
Doing The Loop De Loop (3)
Don't Stop Me Now (4)
Half Past Love (2)
Here's To The Lady (3)

I Still Reach Out (2)
I've Been Away From Love Too Long (1)
If You Don't Want My Love (4)
If You're In Need (3)
Last Night I Dreamed (3)
Let's Do It Today (4)

Let's Talk It Over (3)
Look Up With Your Mind (1)
Looks Like You Made It (4)
Love Came And Rescued Me (2)
Love Hurt Me, Love Healed Me (3)

Messing With My Mind (4)
Midnight Girl (2)
Ooh Child (4)
Play With Me, Stay With Me (Lay With Me) (4)
Please Don't Tempt Me (1)
Problem Solver (1)

Riding The High Wire (1)
Shoo Doo Fu Fu Ooh! (1)
Suspicions (4)
Sweet Ecstasy (3)
Think What We Have (2)
Though We Loved Once (3)
Trust In Me (1)

When I'm Dancin' (3)
You Got Me Running (2)

WILLIAMS, Lucinda   '01

Born on 1/26/53 in Lake Charles, Louisiana. Female singer/songwriter.

7/18/98	65	20	●	©	1 **Car Wheels On A Gravel Road**			$12	Mercury 558338
6/23/01	28	11		©	2 **Essence**			$10	IDJMG 170197

Are You Down (2)
Blue (2)
Broken Butterflies (2)
Bus To Baton Rouge (2)
Can't Let Go (1)

Car Wheels On A Gravel Road (1)
Concrete And Barbed Wire (1)
Drunken Angel (1)
Essence (2)

Get Right With God (2)
Greenville (1)
I Envy The Wind (2)
I Lost It (1)
Jackson (1)

Joy (1)
Lake Charles (1)
Lonely Girls (2)
Metal Firecracker (1)
Out Of Touch (2)

Reason To Cry (2)
Right In Time (1)
Steal Your Love (1)
Still I Long For Your Kiss (1)
2 Kool 2 Be 4-Gotten (1)

WILLIAMS, Mason   '68

Born on 8/24/38 in Abilene, Texas. Folk guitarist. Comedy writer for **The Smothers Brothers** Comedy Hour (1967-69) and *Saturday Night Live* (1980).

6/29/68	14	34		©	1 **The Mason Williams Phonograph Record**			$15	Warner 1729
12/28/68+	164	8			2 **The Mason Williams Ear Show**			$15	Warner 1766

WILLIAMS, Mason — Cont'd

5/10/69	**44**	17		3 Music By Mason Williams	**$15** Warner 1788
12/19/87+	**118**	19	● ©	4 Classical Gas	[I] **$10** American Gram. 800

MASON WILLIAMS & MANNHEIM STEAMROLLER

All The Time (1) · **Baroque-A-Nova** (1,2,4) **96** · Brothers Theme (3) · Bucko's Memoirs (3) · Cinderella-Rockefella (2) · Come To Me (3) · Country Idyll (4) · Cowboy Buckaroo (3) · Doot-Doot (4) · Dylan Thomas (1) · Generatah-Oscillatah (2) · Gift Of Song (3) · **Greensleeves** (3,4) **90** · Here Am I (1) · J. Edgar Swoop (3) · Katydid's Ditty (4) · La Chanson De Claudine (3,4) · Last Great Waltz (2) · Life Song (1) · Long Time Blues (1) · Love Are Wine (2) · Major Thang (3) · McCall (4) · One Minute Commercial (2) · Overture (1) · Prince's Panties (1) · Road Song (2) · Samba Beach (4) · **Saturday Night At The World** (2,4) **99** · Shady Dell (4) · She's Gone Away (1) · Sunflower (1,3,4) · $13 Stella (2) · Vancouver Island (4) · Wanderlove (1) · (Whistle) Hear (2)

WILLIAMS, Paul   '74

Born on 9/19/40 in Omaha. Singer/songwriter/actor. Appeared in several movies.

12/25/71+	**141**	21		1 Just An Old Fashioned Love Song	**$12** A&M 4327
12/2/72+	**159**	14		2 Life Goes On	**$12** A&M 4367
3/2/74	**165**	10		3 Here Comes Inspiration	**$12** A&M 3606
11/23/74	**95**	9		4 A Little Bit Of Love	**$12** A&M 3655
12/13/75+	**146**	6		5 Ordinary Fool	**$12** A&M 4550
8/6/77	**155**	8		6 Classics	[K] **$12** A&M 4701

Born To Fly (3) · California Roses (4) · Day Of The Locust, Theme From ..see: Lonely Hearts · Don't Call It Love (5) · Dream Away (3) · Driftwood (3) · Even Better Than I Know Myself (5) · Evergreen (Love Theme From A Star Is Born) (6) · Family Of Man (4) · Flash (5) · Gone Forever (1) · I Never Had It So Good (1) · I Won't Last A Day Without You (2,6) · If We Could Still Be Friends (3) · In The Beginning (3) · Inspiration (3) · Lady Is Waiting (2) · Let Me Be The One (1) · Life Goes On (2) · Lifeboat (3) · Little Bit Of Love (4) · Little Girl (2) · Lone Star (5) · Loneliness (4,6) · Lonely Hearts (5) · Margarita (4) · My Love And I (1) · Nice To Be Around (4) · Nilsson Sings Newman (3) · Old Fashioned Love Song (1,6) · Old Souls (5) · Ordinary Fool (5) · Out In The Country (2) · Park Avenue (2) · Perfect Love (1) · Rainy Days And Mondays (3,6) · Rose (2) · Sad Song (4) · She Sings For Free (4) · Simple Man (1) · Sleep Warm (4) · Soul Rest (5) · Sunday (4) · That Lucky Old Sun (2) · That's Enough For Me (1,6) · That's What Friends Are For (3) · Then I'll Be Home (4) · Time And Tide (5) · Traveling Boy (2) · **Waking Up Alone** (1,6) **60** · We've Only Just Begun (1,6) · What Would They Say (3) · When I Was All Alone (1) · Where Do I Go From Here (2) · With One More Look At You (6) · You And Me Against The World (3,6) · You Know Me (3)

WILLIAMS, Robbie   '99

Born on 2/13/74 in Port Vale, England. Former member of **Take That**.

5/22/99	**63**	28	● ©	1 The Ego Has Landed	**$10** Capitol 97726
10/21/00	**110**	4	©	2 Sing When You're Winning	**$10** Capitol 29024

Angels (1) **53** · Better Man (2) · By All Means Necessary (2) · Forever Texas (2) · If It's Hurting You (2) · Jesus In A Camper Van (1) · Karma Killer (1) · Kids (2) · Killing Me (1) · Knutsford City Limits (2) · Lazy Days (1) · Let Love Be Your Energy (2) · Let Me Entertain You (1) · Love Calling Earth (2) · Man Machine (1) · **Millennium** (1) **72** · No Regrets (1) · Old Before I Die (1) · One Of God's Better People (1) · Road To Mandalay (2) · Rock DJ (2) · She's The One (1) · Singing For The Lonely (2) · Strong (1) · Supreme (1) · Win Some Lose Some (1)

WILLIAMS, Robin   '79

Born on 7/21/52 in Chicago. Actor/comedian. Starred in several movies and TV's *Mork & Mindy*.

7/21/79	**10**	22	●	1 Reality...What A Concept	[C] **$12** Casablanca 7162
4/2/83	**119**	9		2 Throbbing Python Of Love	[C] **$10** Casablanca 811150

Babies (2) · Back Home (2) · Cats (2) · Christopher (2) · Come Inside My Mind (1) · Devil's Dandruff (2) · Elmer Fudd Sings Bruce Springsteen (Fire) (2) · Falklands, The (2) · Grandpa Funk (1) · Hollywood Casting Session (1) · Jack (2) · Kindergarten Of The Stars (1) · Newsboy (2) · Nicholson (2) · Nicky Lenin (1) · Pop Goes The Weasel (1) · Reverend Earnest Angry (1) · Richard Simmons (2) · Roots People (1) · Shake Hands With Mr. Happy (2) · Shakespeare (A Meltdowner's Nightmare) (1) · Tank You, Boyce (1) · Throbbing Python Of Love (2) · Touch Of Fairfax (1) · Wines (2)

WILLIAMS, Roger   ★34★   '60

Born Louis Weertz on 10/1/24 in Omaha, Nebraska. Learned to play piano by age three. Educated at Drake University, Idaho State University, and Juilliard School of Music. Took lessons from Lenny Tristano and Teddy Wilson. Win on Arthur Godfrey's TV show led to recording contract.

1)Till 2)Temptation 3)Songs Of The Fabulous Fifties 4)Born Free 5)With These Hands

3/31/56	**19**	2		1 Roger Williams	[I] **$20** Kapp 1012
				album also released as *Autumn Leaves*	
8/25/56	**19**	3		2 Daydreams	[I] **$15** Kapp 1031
10/27/56	**16**	2		3 Roger Williams plays the wonderful Music of the Masters	[I] **$15** Kapp 1040
3/23/57	**6**	65	●	4 Songs Of The Fabulous Fifties	[I] **$20** Kapp 5000 [2]
10/7/57	**20**	5		5 Almost Paradise	[I] **$15** Kapp 1063
11/4/57+	**19**	4		6 Songs Of The Fabulous Forties	[I] **$20** Kapp 5003 [2]
3/31/58	**4**	93	●	7 Till	[I] **$15** Kapp 1081
2/23/59+	**9**	70		8 Near You	[I] **$15** Kapp 1112
6/15/59	**11**	24	●	9 More Songs Of The Fabulous Fifties	[I] **$15** Kapp 1130
				also see #23 below	
10/26/59+	**8**	34		10 With These Hands	[I] **$15** Kapp 1147
12/28/59+	**12**	2	©	11 Christmas Time	[X-I] **$15** Kapp 1164
				Christmas charts: 20/'64, 26/'65, 18/'66, 28/'67	
4/4/60	**25**	22		12 Always	[I] **$15** Kapp 1172
				also see #23 below	
12/19/60+	**5**	39		13 Temptation	[I] **$15** Kapp 1217
9/11/61	**49**	15		14 Yellow Bird	[I] **$15** Kapp 1244
10/2/61	**35**	11		15 Songs Of The Soaring '60s	[I] **$15** Kapp 1251
12/25/61+	**105**	3	©	16 Christmas Time	[X-I-R] **$15** Kapp 1164
2/3/62	**44**	23	●	17 Greatest Hits	[G-I] **$15** Kapp 3260
3/17/62	**9**	46		18 Maria	[I] **$15** Kapp 3266

DEBUT	PEAK	WKS	RIAA	CD	ARTIST — Album Title	Catalog	Sym	$	Label & Number

WILLIAMS, Roger — Cont'd

9/15/62	27	30			19 Mr. Piano		[I]	$15	Kapp 3290
4/20/63	122	13			20 Country Style		[I]	$15	Kapp 3305
10/12/63	59	12			21 For You		[I]	$15	Kapp 3336
2/8/64	27	19			22 The Solid Gold Steinway		[I]	$15	Kapp 3354
4/4/64	108	8			23 10th Anniversary/Limited Edition		[R]	$20	Kapp 1 [3]

reissue of albums #9 and 12 above, plus *Roger Williams plays Gershwin*

9/5/64	126	9			24 Academy Award Winners		[I]	$12	Kapp 3406
4/10/65	118	6			25 Roger Williams plays The Hits		[I]	$12	Kapp 3414
10/9/65	63	18			26 Summer Wind		[I]	$12	Kapp 3434
12/25/65+	130	7			27 Autumn Leaves-1965		[I]	$12	Kapp 3452
3/26/66	24	67			28 I'll Remember You		[I]	$12	Kapp 3470
12/10/66+	7	69	●		**29 Born Free**		[I]	$12	Kapp 3501
5/13/67	51	27			30 Roger!		[I]	$12	Kapp 3512
9/9/67	87	29			31 Roger Williams/Golden Hits		[G-I]	$12	Kapp 3530
3/2/68	164	5			32 More Than A Miracle		[I]	$12	Kapp 3550
1/25/69	131	10			33 Only For Lovers		[I]	$12	Kapp 3565
5/31/69	60	11			34 Happy Heart		[I]	$12	Kapp 3595
8/9/69	145	10			35 Love Theme From "Romeo & Juliet"		[I]	$12	Kapp 3610
3/6/71	112	13			36 Love Story		[I]	$12	Kapp 3645
9/18/71	187	3			37 Summer of '42		[I]	$12	Kapp 3650
4/8/72	187	8			38 Love Theme from "The Godfather"		[I]	$12	Kapp 3665

WILLIAMS, Roger — Cont'd

This Guy's In Love With You (34)
This Is My Prayer (28)
Those Were The Days (34)
Three Coins In The Fountain (4)
Three O'Clock In The Morning (26)
(Three Stars Will Shine Tonight) ..see: Dr. Kildare
Threepenny Opera (Moritat), Theme From The (9,23)
Tico-Tico (27)
Till (7,31) *22*

Till The End Of Time (12,23)
Time For Love Is Anytime (36)
Tiny Bubbles (30)
To A Wild Rose (12,23)
To Be The One You Love (The Anonymous Venetian), Theme From (38)
To Each His Own (6)
To Love Again (Chopin E Flat Nocturne) (22)
To Sir With Love (32)
Toccata (22)
Tom Dooley (9,23)
Tonight (18)

Too Young (4)
Traumerei (12,23)
True Love (4)
Try To Remember (25) *97*
Tumbling Tumbleweeds (5) *60*
Two Different Worlds (10,14)
Unchained Melody (4)
Until It's Time For You To Go (38)
Up-Up And Away (33)
Vaya Con Dios (4)
Very Thought Of You (medley) (22)

Volare (Nel Blu Dipinto Di Di) (8)
Walk In The Black Forest (26)
Walking Alone (21)
Wanderin' Star (36)
Wanting You (1,17) *38*
Warsaw Concerto (6)
Water Boy (20)
Way Of Love (38)
Way You Look Tonight (18)
We Three Kings Of Orient Are (medley) (11,16)
We've Got To Get It On Again (38)

What Lies Over The Hill? (13)
When I Grow Too Old To Dream (2)
When It's Springtime In The Rockies (23)
(Where Is Your Heart) ..see: Moulin Rouge
Whiffenpoof Song (27)
Whirlaway (18)
White Christmas (11,16)
Willow Weep For Me (25)
Winter Wonderland (11,16)
Wish You Were Here (4)
With These Hands (10)

World Outside (8) *71*
Yellow Bird (10,14,26)
Yesterday (28,31)
You'll Never Know (6,24)
You'll Never Walk Alone (26)
Young And Warm And Wonderful (8)
Young At Heart (4)
Your Loves Return (37)
Your Song (36)
Zip-A-Dee-Doo-Dah (6,24)
Zorba The Greek, Theme From (28)

WILLIAMS, Tony '79
Born on 12/12/45 in Chicago. Died of a heart attack on 2/23/97 (age 51). Jazz-fusion drummer. Also see **V.S.O.P.**

5/12/79	113	7		©	**The Joy Of Flying**			**$12**	Columbia 35705

Coming Back Home
Eris
Going Far
Hip Skip
Hittin' On 6
Morgan's Motion
Open Fire
Tony

WILLIAMS, Vanessa '92
Born on 3/18/63 in Tarrytown, New York. R&B singer/actress. In 1983, became the first black woman to win the Miss America pageant; relinquished crown after *Penthouse* magazine scandal. Acted in several movies and Broadway shows.

7/9/88+	38	55	●	©	1 **The Right Stuff**			**$10**	Wing 835694
9/7/91+	17	91	▲³	©	2 **The Comfort Zone**			**$10**	Wing 843522
12/24/94+	57	31	▲	©	3 **The Sweetest Days**			**$10**	Wing 526172
11/23/96	36	9	●	©	4 **Star Bright**	C:#12/11	[X]	**$10**	Mercury 532827

includes "Sleep Well Little Children" by The Claremont School Singers; Christmas charts: 5/'96, 17/'97, 33/'98

9/13/97	53	9		©	5 **Next**			**$10**	Mercury 536060

Am I Too Much? (1)
And If I Ever (5)
And My Heart Goes (5)
Angels We Have Heard On High (4)
Baby, It's Cold Outside (4)
Be A Man (1)
Betcha Never (1)
Better Off Now (2)
Can This Be Real? (1)
Comfort Zone (2) *62*
Constantly (3)

Crazy 'Bout You (5)
Darlin' I (1) *88*
Do You Hear What I Hear (medley) (4)
Dreamin' (1) *8*
Easiest Thing (5)
Ellamental (3)
First Noel (4)
First Thing On Your Mind (5)
Freedom Dance (Get Free!) (2)
Go Tell It On The Mountain (medley) (4)

Goodbye (2)
Gracious Good Shepherd (4)
Happiness (5)
Hark The Herald Angels Sing (Shout) (4)
(He's Got) The Look (1)
Higher Ground (3)
I Wonder As I Wander (4)
I'll Be Home For Christmas (4)
I'll Be The One (1)
If You Really Love Him (1)
Just For Tonight (2) *26*

Little Drummer Boy (medley) (4)
Long Way Home (3)
Lost Without You (5)
Mary Had A Baby (medley) (4)
Moonlight Over Paris (3)
Oh How The Years Go By (5)
One Reason (2)
Right Stuff (1) *44*
Running Back To You (2) *18*
Save The Best For Last (2) *1*
Security (1)
Sister Moon (3)

Someone Like You (5)
Star Bright (4)
Star Bright (5)
Still In Love (2)
Strangers Eyes (2)
Surrender (5)
Sweetest Days (3) *18*
2 Of A Kind (2)
Way That You Love (3) *67*
What Child Is This (4)
What Will I Tell My Heart (2)
Whatever Happens (1)

Who Were You Thinkin' 'Bout? (5)
Work To Do (2)
You Can't Run (3)
You Don't Have To Say You're Sorry (3)
You Gotta Go (2)

WILLIAMS, Vesta — see VESTA

WILLIE AND THE POOR BOYS '85
All-star rock group: Andy Fairweather Low and Mickey Gee (guitars), Geraint Watkins (keyboards), **Bill Wyman** (bass) and Charlie Watts (drums). Wyman and Watts are members of **The Rolling Stones**.

5/25/85	96	12		©	**Willie And The Poor Boys**			**$12**	Passport 6047

All Night Long
Baby Please Don't Go
Can You Hear Me?
Chicken Shack Boogie
Let's Talk It Over
Poor Boy Boogie
Revenue Man (White Lightening)
Saturday Night
Slippin' And Slidin'
Sugar Bee
These Arms Of Mine
You Never Can Tell

WILLIE D '92
Born Willie Dennis on 11/1/66 in Houston. Male rapper. Member of **The Geto Boys**.

10/3/92	88	8		©	1 **I'm Goin' Out Lika Soldier**			**$10**	Rap-A-Lot 57188
11/11/00	124	3		©	2 **Loved By Few, Hated By Many**			**$10**	Rap-A-Lot 50022

Backstage (1)
Campaign 92' (1)
Clean Up Man (1)
Dear God (2)
Dem Boys (2)
Die (1)

Fearing Nothing But God (2)
Freaky Deaky (2)
Go Back 2 School (1)
Gun Talk (2)
Hearse Cadillac (2)
I'll Make U Famous (2)

I'm Goin' Out Lika Soldier (1)
If I Was White (2)
It Ain't Easy (2)
Lil' Killaz (2)
Little Hooker (1)
My Alibi (2)

Pass Da Piote (1)
Profile Of A Criminal (1)
Pusscndclick (2)
Rodney K. (1)
She Likes 2 Ball (2)
Sickness, The (2)

Slippers Go (2)
Trenchcoats-N-Ganksta Hats (1)
U Ain't No Ganksta (1)
U Special (2)
Wet 'M (2)

What's Up Aggin (1)
Yo P My D (1)
You Still A Aggin (1)

WILLIS, Bruce '87
Born on 3/19/55 in Penns Grove, New Jersey. Starred in several movies and TV's *Moonlighting*. Married to actress Demi Moore from 1987-2000.

2/14/87	14	29	●	©	**The Return Of Bruno**			**$10**	Motown 6222

Comin' Right Up
Down In Hollywood
Flirting With Disaster
Fun Time
Jackpot (Bruno's Bop)
James Bond Is Back (medley)
Lose Myself
Respect Yourself *5*
Secret Agent Man (medley)
Under The Boardwalk *59*
Young Blood *68*

WILLS, Mark '00
Born on 8/8/73 in Cleveland, Tennessee; raised in Blue Ridge, Georgia. Country singer.

5/30/98	74	56	▲	©	1 **Wish You Were Here**			**$10**	Mercury 536317
1/29/00	23	29	●	©	2 **Permanently**			**$10**	Mercury 546296

Almost Doesn't Count (2)
Anywhere But Memphis (1)
Back At One (2) *36*
Because I Love You (2)
Don't Laugh At Me (1) *73*

Don't Think I Won't (1)
Emily Harper (1)
Everything There Is To Know About You (1)
Forget About Love (2)

Help Me Fall (1)
I Do [Cherish You] (1) *72*
In My Arms (2)
It's Working (1)
Last Memory (1)

Love Is Alive (1)
Perfect Conversation (2)
Permanently (2)
Rich Man (2)
Right Here (2)

She's In Love (1) *60*
Still Waiting (2)
This Can't Be Love (2)
Time Machine (2)
Wish You Were Here (1) *34*

WILL TO POWER '88
Pop-dance trio from Florida: Bob Rosenberg, Maria Mendez and Dr. J. Rosenberg is the son of singer Gloria Mann. By 1990, reduced to a duo of Rosenberg and Elin Michaels. Group name taken from the work of 19th-century German philosopher Frederich Nietzsche.

9/10/88	68	29		©	1 **Will To Power**			**$10**	Epic 40940
2/2/91	178	4		©	2 **Journey Home**			**$10**	Epic 46051

Also Sprach Zarathustra ..see: Zarathustra
Anti-Social (1)

Baby I Love Your Way/Freebird Medley (Free Baby) (1) *1*
Best Friend's Girl (2)
Boogie Nights (2)

Clock On The Wall (2)
Don't Like It (2)
Dreamin' (1) *50*
Fading Away (1) *65*
Fly Bird (2)

I'm Not In Love (2) *7*
It's My Life (2)
Journey Home (2)
Koyaanisqatsi (2)
Say It's Gonna Rain (1) *49*

Searchin' (2)
Show Me The Way (1)
Somebody Told Me (1)
Strangers (1)
Zarathustra (1)

WILMER AND THE DUKES '69

R&B-rock group led by Wilmer Alexander.

| 8/16/69 | 173 | 3 | © | **Wilmer & The Dukes** | | | $20 | Aphrodisiac 6001 |

Count On Me   Get Out Of My Life, Woman   Heavy Time   I'm Free   Love-itis (medley)   St. James Infirmary
Get It   **Give Me One More Chance** 80   I Do Love You   Living In The U.S.A.   Show Me (medley)

WILSON, Al '74

Born on 6/19/39 in Meridian, Mississippi. R&B singer/drummer.

12/22/73+	70	17		1 **Show And Tell**			$15	Rocky Road 3601
10/19/74	171	7		2 **La La Peace Song**			$15	Rocky Road 3700
7/10/76	185	2		3 **I've Got A Feeling**			$12	Playboy 410

Ain't Nothin' New Under The Sun (3)   Goin' Through The Motions (2)   I'm A Weak Man (2)   Love Me Gentle, Love Me Blind (1)   Song For You (1)   You're The One Thing (Keeps Me Goin') (2)
Baby I Want Your Body (3)   Having A Party (3)   I'm Out To Get You (1)   Moonlightin' (1)   Stay With Me (3)
Broken Home (1)   Honoring (3)   **I've Got A Feeling (We'll Be Seeing Each Other Again)** (3) 29   My Song (1)   Stones Throw (2)
Differently (3)   How's Your Love Life (3)   Passport (2)   **Touch And Go** (1) 57
Fifty-Fifty (3)   **I Won't Last A Day Without You/Let Me Be The One** (2) 70   Queen Of The Ghetto (1)   What You See (1)
For Cryin' Out Loud (1)   **La La Peace Song** (3) 30   **Show And Tell** (1) 1   Willoughby Brook (2)
Longer We Stay Together (2)   You Did It For Me (3)

WILSON, Brian '88

Born on 6/20/42 in Hawthorne, California. Pop singer/songwriter. Leader of **The Beach Boys**. His daughters, **Carnie & Wendy Wilson**, formed the trio **Wilson Phillips** with Chynna Phillips in 1989.

| 7/30/88 | 54 | 13 | © | 1 **Brian Wilson** | | | $10 | Sire 25669 |
| 7/4/98 | 88 | 2 | © | 2 **Imagination** | | | $10 | Paladin 24703 |

Baby Let Your Hair Grow Long (1)   Keep An Eye On Summer (2)   Love And Mercy (1)   One For The Boys (1)   Sunshine (2)
Cry (1)   Lay Down Burden (2)   Meet Me In My Dreams Tonight (1)   Rio Grande (1)   There's So Many (1)
Dream Angel (2)   Let Him Run Wild (2)   She Says That She Needs Me (2)   Walkin' The Line (1)
Happy Days (2)   Let It Shine (1)   Melt Away (1)   South American (2)   Where Has Love Been? (2)
Little Children (1)   Night Time (1)   Your Imagination (2)

WILSON, Carl '81

Born on 6/21/46 in Hawthorne, California. Died of cancer on 2/6/98 (age 51). Guitarist of **The Beach Boys**.

| 5/2/81 | 185 | 2 | | **Carl Wilson** | | | $12 | Caribou 37010 |

Bright Lights   Heaven   Hurry Love   Seems So Long Ago   What You Gonna Do About Me?
Grammy, The   Hold Me   Right Lane

WILSON, Carnie & Wendy — see WILSON PHILLIPS

WILSON, Cassandra '96

Born on 12/4/55 in Jackson, Mississippi. Jazz singer.

| 3/23/96 | 141 | 5 | © | 1 **New Moon Daughter** | | | $10 | Blue Note 32861 |
| 4/10/99 | 158 | 5 | © | 2 **Traveling Miles** | | | $10 | Blue Note 54123 |

Death Letter (1)   Little Warm Death (1)   Right Here, Right Now (1)   Solomon Sang (1)   Until (1)
Find Him (1)   Love Is Blindness (1)   Run The VooDoo Down (2)   Someday My Prince Will Come (2)   When The Sun Goes Down (2)
Harvest Moon (1)   Memphis (1)   Seven Steps (2)
I'm So Lonesome I Could Cry (1)   Never Broken (ESP) (2)   Sky And Sea (Blue In Green) (2)   Strange Fruit (1)
Last Train To Clarksville (1)   Piper (2)   Skylark (1)   Time After Time (2)
Resurrection Blues (Tutu) (2)   Traveling Miles (2)

WILSON, Charlie '01

Born in Tulsa, Oklahoma. Lead singer of **The Gap Band**.

| 2/10/01 | 152 | 10 | © | **Bridging The Gap** | | | $10 | Major Hits 490371 |

Absolutely   Can I Take You Home   For Your Love   Sweet Love   Would You Mind
Another Man   Charlie's Angel   Him Or Me   Without You
Big Pimpin'   Come Back My Way   Now Ya Sayin' Bye   Wonderful One

WILSON, Dennis '77

Born on 12/4/44 in Inglewood, California. Drowned on 12/28/83 (age 39). Drummer of **The Beach Boys**.

| 9/10/77 | 96 | 8 | © | **Pacific Ocean Blue** | | | $15 | Caribou 34353 |

Dreamer   Farewell My Friend   Moonshine   Rainbows   Thoughts Of You   What's Wrong
End Of The Show   Friday Night   Pacific Ocean Blues   River Song   Time   You And I

WILSON, Flip '70

Born Clerow Wilson on 12/8/33 in Jersey City, New Jersey. Died of cancer on 11/25/98 (age 64). Black comedian. Hosted own TV variety show (1970-74). Also recorded as his female alter ego, Geraldine.

8/26/67+	34	63		1 **Cowboys & Colored People**		[C]	$15	Atlantic 8149
6/1/68	147	7		2 **You Devil You**		[C]	$15	Atlantic 8179
2/28/70	17	54	●	3 **"The Devil made me buy this dress"**		[C]	$15	Little David 1000
1/2/71	45	15		4 **"Flip" - The Flip Wilson Show**		[C]	$15	Little David 2000
5/13/72	63	15		5 **Geraldine/Don't Fight The Feeling**		[C]	$15	Little David 1001

Bat, The (2)   Cowboys & Colored People (1)   Flip Wilson Show (4)   Herman's Berry (2)   Midgets (1)   Seeing Ed Eat A Chittlin' On Network Television (3)
Big Hand (1)   Creamed Chipped Beef (4)   Gardener, The (2)   I Wanted To Be A Singer (2)   Millionaire, The (2)
Blues, The (4)   David And Goliath (1)   Geraldine Honey (5)   I'm Not Flip Wilson (2)   Miss Johnson (3)   Shadow, The (2)
Bunny Club (5)   Days Of The Knights (2)   Geraldine Visits David Frost (3)   Ice (3)   Muhammad Ali (4)   Staying On Too Long (1)
Cheap Hotel (1)   Devil Made Me Buy This Dress (3)   Gold Story (3)   Joey Bishop Show (2)   Paid To Die (3)   Trala (2)
Chicken Delicious (5)   Go-Rilla, The (3)   Kids (1)   Perfect Secretary (5)   Twenty Minutes Of Silence (2)
Christopher Columbus (1)   Dr. Freddie (2)   Great Motor Bike And Tennis Shoe Race, Honey (3)   Killer (5)   Pet Shop (3)   Ugly Baby (2)
Church On Sunday (1)   Doctors Have More Fun (3)   Land Of Opportunity (2)   Reverend Leroy (4)   Ugly Girl (2)
Complaint Department (5)   Don't Fight The Feeling (5)   Great Quotations (3)   Lemonade Stand (3)   Riot Suit (1)   Ugly People (1)
Confidential Survey (1)   Drive-In Movie (3)   Haunted House (4)   Lulu (2)   Ruby Begonia (3)   Wardrobe Lady Part I & II (3)

WILSON, Hank — see RUSSELL, Leon

WILSON, J. Frank, and The Cavaliers '64

Born on 12/11/41 in Lufkin, Texas. Died on 10/4/91 (age 49). The Cavaliers: Sid Holmes (guitar), Lewis Elliott (bass) and Ray Smith (drums).

| 11/14/64 | 54 | 14 | | **Last Kiss** | | | $100 | Josie 4006 |

Day Before Our Wedding   Kiss And Run   Only The Lonely   School Days   Speak To Me   That'll Be The Day
Ding Go The Chimes   **Last Kiss** 2   Over The Mountain   Sea Of Love   Tell Laura I Love Her   Young Love

WILSON, Jackie '63

Born on 6/9/34 in Detroit. Died on 1/21/84 (age 49). Male R&B singer. Collapsed after suffering a stroke on stage on 9/25/75 at the Latin Casino in Cherry Hill, New Jersey; spent rest of his life in nursing homes. Inducted into the Rock and Roll Hall of Fame in 1987.

DEBUT	PEAK	WKS	CD	#	Title	Sym	$	Label & Number
11/24/62	137	2	©	1	Jackie Wilson At The Copa	[L]	$100	Brunswick 754108
4/27/63	36	21	©	2	Baby Workout		$100	Brunswick 754110
11/30/63	6ˣ	4		3	Merry Christmas from Jackie Wilson	[X]	$50	Brunswick 754112
					Christmas charts: 6/'63, 46/'64			
1/14/67	108	7	©	4	Whispers		$40	Brunswick 754122
11/25/67	163	4	©	5	Higher And Higher		$50	Brunswick 754130
6/1/68	195	3	©	6	Manufacturers Of Soul		$20	Brunswick 754134

JACKIE WILSON/COUNT BASIE

Adeste Fideles (O Come All Ye Faithful) (3)
And This Is My Beloved (1)
Baby Workout (2) 5
Body And Soul (medley) (1)
Chain Gang (6) 84
Deck The Hall (3)
Even When You Cry (6)
Fairest Of Them All (4)
First Noel (3)
For Your Precious Love (6) 49
Funky Broadway (6)
God Rest Ye Merry, Gentlemen (3)

I Apologize (medley) (1)
I Can Do Better (4)
I Don't Need You Around (5)
I Don't Want To Lose You (4) 84
(I Feel Like I'm In) Paradise (2)
I Love Them All Medley - Part I & II (1)
I Need Your Loving (5)
I Never Loved A Woman (The Way I Love You) (6)
I Was Made To Love Her (6)
I'll Be Home For Christmas (3)
I'm The One To Do It (5)

I've Gotta Talk To You (4)
I've Lost You (5) 82
In The Midnight Hour (6)
It Came Upon The Midnight Clear (3)
It's All My Fault (2)
Joy To The World (3)
Just Be Sincere (4) 91
Kickapoo (2)
Love For Sale (1)
Love Train (2)
My Girl (6)
My Heart Is Calling (4)
Now That I Want Her (2)

O Holy Night (Cantique de Noel) (3)
O Little Town Of Bethlehem (3)
Ode To Billy Joe (6)
Only Your Love Can Save Me (4)
Open The Door To Your Heart (5)
Perfect Day (1)
Respect (6)
Say You Will (2)
Shake! Shake! Shake! (2) 33
Silent Night (3)
Silver Bells (3)

(So Many) Cute Little Girls (2)
Somebody Up There Likes You (5)
Soulville (3)
St. James Infirmary (1)
Tears Will Tell It All (4)
Those Heartaches (5)
To Make A Big Man Cry (4)
Tonight (1)
(Too Much) Sweet Loving (4)
Uptight (Everything's Alright) (6)
Way I Am (1)
What Good Am I Without You (2)

When Will Our Day Come (5)
Whispers (Gettin' Louder) (4) 11
White Christmas (3)
Who Am I (4)
Yeah! Yeah! Yeah! (1)
You Can Count On Me (5)
You Only Live Once (2)
(Your Love Keeps Lifting Me) Higher And Higher (5) 6

WILSON, Nancy ★59★ '64

Born on 2/20/37 in Chillicothe; raised in Columbus, Ohio. R&B/jazz-styled singer. Started as regular singer at Rusty Bryant's Carolyn Club in Columbus. First recorded for Dot in 1956. Moved to New York City in 1959.

1)How Glad I Am 2)Yesterday's Love Songs/Today's Blues 3)Today-My Way 4)Today, Tomorrow, Forever 5)Hollywood-My Way

DEBUT	PEAK	WKS	CD	#	Title	Sym	$	Label & Number
5/5/62	30	21	©	1	Nancy Wilson/Cannonball Adderley		$30	Capitol 1657
9/15/62+	49	18		2	Hello Young Lovers		$25	Capitol 1767
4/6/63	18	46		3	Broadway-My Way		$20	Capitol 1828
					also see #23 below			
8/17/63	11	58		4	Hollywood-My Way		$20	Capitol 1934
					also see #23 below			
1/25/64	4	42	©	5	Yesterday's Love Songs/Today's Blues		$20	Capitol 2012
5/30/64	10	30	©	6	Today, Tomorrow, Forever		$20	Capitol 2082
9/5/64	4	31		7	How Glad I Am		$20	Capitol 2155
2/6/65	24	29		8	The Nancy Wilson Show!	[L]	$20	Capitol 2136
					recorded at the Cocoanut Grove in Los Angeles			
6/5/65	7	21		9	Today-My Way		$20	Capitol 2321
8/28/65	17	24		10	Gentle Is My Love		$20	Capitol 2351
2/5/66	44	18		11	From Broadway With Love		$20	Capitol 2433
5/28/66	15	33	©	12	A Touch Of Today		$20	Capitol 2495
8/27/66	35	23		13	Tender Loving Care		$20	Capitol 2555
1/28/67	35	21		14	Nancy-Naturally		$20	Capitol 2634
6/3/67	40	15		15	Just For Now		$20	Capitol 2712
9/2/67	46	19	©	16	Lush Life		$20	Capitol 2757
					also see #27 below			
2/3/68	115	17	©	17	Welcome To My Love		$15	Capitol 2844
6/1/68	51	24		18	Easy		$15	Capitol 2909
8/31/68	145	14		19	The Best Of Nancy Wilson	[G]	$15	Capitol 2947
10/12/68	122	7		20	The Sound Of Nancy Wilson		$15	Capitol 2970
2/8/69	117	14		21	Nancy		$15	Capitol 148
7/5/69	122	15		22	Son Of A Preacher Man		$15	Capitol 234
8/23/69	193	2		23	Close-Up	[R]	$20	Capitol 256 [2]
					reissue of albums #3 and #4 above			
11/8/69+	92	18		24	Hurt So Bad		$15	Capitol 353
3/28/70	155	6		25	Can't Take My Eyes Off You		$15	Capitol 429
11/28/70+	54	21		26	Now I'm A Woman		$15	Capitol 541
6/12/71	185	3		27	The Right To Love	[R]	$15	Capitol 763
					reissue (new title) of album #16 above			
7/17/71	185	5	©	28	But Beautiful		$15	Capitol 798
12/25/71+	151	6		29	Kaleidoscope		$15	Capitol 852
9/28/74	97	18		30	All In Love Is Fair		$12	Capitol 11317
7/26/75	119	10		31	Come Get To This		$12	Capitol 11386
5/1/76	126	13		32	This Mother's Daughter		$12	Capitol 11518
7/30/77	198	1		33	I've Never Been To Me		$12	Capitol 11659
9/8/84	144	9	©	34	The Two Of Us		$12	Columbia 39326

RAMSEY LEWIS & NANCY WILSON

Ages Ago (24)
(Ah, The Apple Trees) When The World Was Young (16,27)
Ain't No Sunshine (29)
Ain't That Lovin' You (14)

Alfie (15)
All By Myself (33)
All In Love Is Fair (30)
All My Love Comes Down (31)
All My Tomorrows (5)

Almost In Your Arms (4)
Almost Persuaded (22)
Alone With My Thoughts Of You (20)
Alright, Okay, You Win (14)

And I Love Him (12)
And Satisfy (9)
Angel Eyes (17)
As Long As He Needs Me (3,23)

As You Desire Me (13)
At Long Last Love (10)
Back In Your Own Backyard (2)
Before The Rain (12)
Below, Above (20)

Best Is Yet To Come (5)
Bewitched (5)
Black Is Beautiful (20)
Blue Prelude (5)
Boogeyin' All The Way (31)

WILSON, Nancy — Cont'd

Born Free (15)
Boy From Ipanema (7)
Brand New Me (25)
Bridge Over Troubled Water (26)
But Beautiful (28)
By Myself (20)
By The Time I Get To Phoenix (22)
Call Me (1)
Call Me Irresponsible (6)
Can't Take My Eyes Off You (24,25) *52*
Car Of Love (33)
Changes (33)
China (32)
Close Your Eyes (13)
Come Back To Me (24)
Come Get To This (31)
Days Of Wine And Roses (4,19,23)
Dear Heart (9)
Dearly Beloved (4,23)
Did I Remember (4,23)
Do It Again (28)
Do You Know Why (24)
Don't Come Running Back To Me (9) *58*
Don't Go To Strangers (13)
Don't Let Me Be Lonely Tonight (31)
Don't Rain On My Parade (7,19)
Don't Take Your Love From Me (8)
Don't Talk, Just Sing (8)
Everyone Knows (29)
Face It Girl, It's Over (18,19) *29*
Fireworks (8)
Flying High (33)
For Heaven's Sake (28)
For Once In My Life (17)
Free Again (16,27)
From You To Me To You (32)
Funnier Than Funny (10)
Gee Baby, Ain't I Good To You (13)
Gentle Is My Love (10,19)
Gentle On My Mind (18)
Getting To Know You (3,23)
Glad To Be Unhappy (28)
Go Away, Little Boy (6)
Goin' Out Of My Head (12)
Good Life (6)
Good Man Is Hard To Find (2)
Got It Together (22)
Grass Is Greener (7,19)
Greatest Performance Of My Life (29)

Guess Who I Saw Today (8,19)
Happiness Is A Thing Called Joe (28)
Happy Talk (1)
Happy Tears (31)
Have A Heart (12)
He Called Me Baby (31)
He Loves Me (11)
He Never Had It So Good (32)
Hello Dolly (11)
Hello, Young Lovers (2)
Here It Comes (33)
Here's That Rainy Day (11)
Hey There (11)
Hotel, Theme From (17)
Houdini Of The Midnite Hour (31)
How Insensitive (18)
How Many Broken Wings (26)
Hurt So Bad (24)
Husbands And Wives (22)
I Believe In You (3,23)
I Can't Stop Loving You (6)
I Don't Want A Sometimes Man (32)
I Had A Ball (11)
I Left My Heart In San Francisco (6)
I Made You This Way (22)
(I Stayed) Too Long At The Fair (16,27)
I Thought About You (28)
I Wanna Be With You (7) *57*
I Want To Talk About You (13)
I Wish I Didn't Love You So (14)
I'll Get Along Somehow (29)
I'll Know (3,23)
I'll Make A Man Of The Man (15)
I'll Never Stop Loving You (4)
I'll Only Miss Him When I Think Of Him (11)
I'll Walk Alone (28)
I'm All Smiles (9)
I'm Always Drunk In San Francisco (And I Don't Drink At All) (17)
I'm Beginning To See The Light (8)
I'm Your Special Fool (21)
I've Got Your Number (11)
I've Never Been To Me (33)
If Ever I Would Leave You (10)
If He Walked Into My Life (15)
If I Ever Lose This Heaven (31)
If I Ruled The World (9)
If I Were Your Woman (29)
If Love Is Good To Me (10)

If We Only Have Love (21)
In A Long White Room (21)
In The Dark (14)
In The Heat Of The Night (17)
It Never Entered My Mind (17)
It Only Takes A Moment (20)
Joe (26)
Joey, Joey, Joey (3,23)
Just For A Thrill (14)
Just For Now (15)
Let It Be Me (29)
Let's Fall In Love All Over (26)
Let's Make The Most Of A Beautiful Thing (24)
Like A Circle Never Stops (31)
Like Someone In Love (13)
Listen, Little Girl (2)
Little Girl Blue (2)
Little Green Apples (22)
Lonely, Lonely (26)
Long And Winding Road (26)
Look Of Love (18)
Looking Back (21)
Lot Of Livin' To Do (3,23)
Love Can Do Anything (15)
Love Has Many Faces (9)
Love Has Smiled On Us (32)
Love Is Alive (33)
Love Is Blue (18)
Love-Wise (13)
Lush Life (16,27)
Make It With You (26)
Make Me A Present Of You (18)
Make Me Rainbows (18)
Make Someone Happy (3,23)
Make The World Go Away (22)
Makin' Whoopee (11)
Masquerade Is Over (1)
May I Come In? (17)
Mercy, Mercy, Mercy (15)
Middle Of The Road (29)
Midnight Rendezvous (34)
Midnight Sun (16,27)
Miss Otis Regrets (2)
Mixed-Up Girl (25)
Moments (33)
Moon River (4,23)
More (10)
Mr. Bojangles (29)
Mr. Walker, It's All Over (22)
Music That Makes Me Dance (8)
My Babe (14)
My Love (30)
My Love, Forgive Me (Amore, Scusami) (9)
My One And Only Love (10)
My Shining Hour (4,23)
My Ship (3,23)

Never Less Than Yesterday (7)
Never Let Me Go (5)
Never Wanna Say Goodnight (34)
Never Will I Marry (1)
Nina Never Knew (2)
No One Else But You (12)
Nobody (33)
Now (32)
Now I'm A Woman (26) *93*
Ocean Of Love (30)
Ode To Billie Joe (17)
Oh! Look At Me Now (28)
Old Country (1)
On Broadway (6)
On The Other Side Of The Tracks (20)
Once In My Lifetime (29)
One Like You (18)
One Note Samba (6)
One Soft Night (24)
Only Love (21)
Only The Young (16,27)
Our Day Will Come (6)
Out Of This World (20)
Over The Weekend (16,27)
Patience My Child (33)
Peace Of Mind (20) *55*
People (7)
Player Play On (21)
Please Send Me Someone To Love (5)
Prelude To A Kiss (28)
Prisoner Of My Eyes (21)
Put On A Happy Face (2)
Quiet Nights Of Quiet Stars (Corcovado) (7)
Quiet Soul (21)
Rain Sometimes (15)
Raindrops Keep Fallin' On My Head (25)
Reach Out For Me (9)
Real Me (26)
Right To Love (Reflections) (16,27)
River Shallow (16,27)
Rules Of The Road (20)
Saga Of Bill Bailey (9)
Sandpiper, Love Theme From The ..see: Shadow Of Your Smile
Satin Doll (5)
Save Your Love For Me (1)
Second Time Around (4,23)
Secret Love (23)
Send Me Yesterday (5)
Shadow Of Your Smile (12)
Show Goes On (7)
Since I Fell For You (14)

Sleepin' Bee (1)
Slippin' Away (34)
Someone To Watch Over Me (5)
Somewhere (11)
Son Of A Preacher Man (22)
Song Is You (5)
Sophisticated Lady (2)
Spinning Wheel (24)
Stay Tuned (22)
Streetrunner (30)
Suffering With The Blues (5)
Sunny (16)
Supper Time (28)
Suzanne (25)
Sweetest Sounds (3,23)
Take What I Have (9)
Tell The Truth (30)
Ten Good Years (8)
Ten Years Of Tears (14)
Tender Loving Care (13)
That's Life (15)
There Will Never Be Another You (10)
There'll Always Be Forever (30) (They Long To Be) Close To You (26)
This Bitter Earth (20)
This Dream (11)
This Girl Is A Woman Now (25)
This Mother's Daughter (32)
This Time Last Summer (31)
Time After Time (10)
To Be The One You Love (29)
To Make It Easier On You (30)
Tonight May Have To Last Me All My Life (6)
Too Late Now (13)
Tree Of Life (32)
Trip With Me (35)
Trouble In Mind (22)
Try A Little Tenderness (13)
Try It, You'll Like It (30)
Two Of Us (34)
Unchain My Heart (6)
Uptight (Everything's Alright) (12,19) *84*
Very Thought Of You (5)
Waitin' For Charlie To Come Home (25)
Walk Away (18)
Wasn't It Wonderful (12)
Watch What Happens (14)
Wave (18)
We Could Learn Together (21)
Welcome To My Love (17)
Welcome, Welcome (9)
West Coast Blues (7)
What Do You See In Her? (21)

What Kind Of Fool Am I? (6)
What Now My Love (15)
When A Woman Loves A Man (2)
When Did You Leave Heaven? (4,19,23)
When He Makes Music (10)
When I Look In Your Eyes (18)
When Sunny Gets Blue (2)
When The Sun Comes Out (20)
When We Were One (32)
Who Can I Turn To (When Nobody Needs Me) (10)
Why Try To Change Me Now (17)
Wild Is The Wind (23)
Willie And Laura Mae Jones (24)
Willow Weep For Me (14)
Winchester Cathedral (15)
Wives And Lovers (6)
Words And Music (25)
Yesterday (12)
You Can Have Him (3,8,19,23)
(You Don't Know) How Glad I Am (7,19) *11*
You Don't Know Me (17)
You Don't Know What Love Is (2)
You'd Be So Nice To Come Home To (4,23)
You'd Better Go (21)
You'd Better Love Me (11)
You're All I Need To Get By (24)
You're As Right As Rain (30)
You're Gonna Hear From Me (12)
You've Changed (16,27)
You've Got Your Troubles (12)
You've Lost That Lovin' Feelin' (9)
You've Made Me So Very Happy (25)
Young And Foolish (11)
Your Name Is Love (13)

WILSON, Shanice — see SHANICE

WILSON PHILLIPS '90

Vocal trio formed in Los Angeles: sisters **Carnie & Wendy Wilson**, with Chynna Phillips. Carnie and Wendy's father is **Brian Wilson** (of **The Beach Boys**). Chynna, the daughter of Michelle and **John Phillips** (of **The Mamas & The Papas**), acted in the movie *Caddyshack II* and married actor Billy Baldwin on 9/9/95. Carnie hosted own TV talk show in 1995.

DEBUT	PEAK	WKS	RIAA	CD	#	Title	Sym	$	Label & Number
4/14/90	2[10]	125	▲5	©	1	**Wilson Phillips**		$10	SBK 93745
6/20/92	4	33	▲	©	2	**Shadows And Light**		$10	SBK 98924
12/25/93	116	3		©	3	**Hey Santa!** .... [X]		$10	SBK 27113

CARNIE & WENDY WILSON
Christmas chart: 25/'93

All The Way From New York (2)
Alone (2)
Don't Take Me Down (2)
Dream Is Still Alive (1) *12*
Eyes Like Twins (1)
First Noel (medley) (3)
Flesh And Blood (2)
Fueled For Houston (2)

Give It Up (2) *30*
Goodbye, Carmen (2)
Have Yourself A Merry Little Christmas (3)
Hey Santa! (3)
Hold On (1) *1*
I Saw Mommy Kissing Santa Claus (3)

Impulsive (1) *4*
It's Only Life (2)
Jingle Bell Rock (3)
Let It Snow, Let It Snow, Let It Snow (3)
Little Drummer Boy (3)
Next To You (Someday I'll Be) (1)

Ooh You're Gold (1)
Over And Over (1)
Reason To Believe (1)
Release Me (1) *1*
Rudolph The Red Nosed Reindeer (3)
Silent Night (medley) (3)
Silver Bells (3)

This Doesn't Have To Be Love (2)
We Three Kings Of Orient Are (medley) (3)
Where Are You (2)
Winter Wonderland (3)
You Won't See Me Cry (2) *20*
You're In Love (1) *1*

WINANS, BeBe '00

Born Benjamin Winans in 1962 in Detroit. Gospel singer.

DEBUT	PEAK	WKS	RIAA	CD	#	Title	Sym	$	Label & Number
11/15/97	125	7		©	1	**BeBe Winans**		$10	Atlantic 83041
9/16/00	30	12		©	2	**Love And Freedom**		$10	Motown 159405

BeBe

Brand New Dance (2)
Coming Back Home (2)
Did You Know (1)
Everyday (2)
Everything To Me (2)

For The Rest Of My Life (2)
How Do We (2)
I Wanna Be The Only One (1)
I'm In Love With You (2)
If You Say (1)

In Harm's Way (1) *83*
In The Midst Of The Rain (1)
Jesus Children Of America (2)
Love And Freedom (2)
Love Is The Reason (1)

Love's Coming (1)
My Heart (2)
Oh Happy Day (1)
Seeing For The Very First Time (1)

So In Love (1)
Stand (2)
Thank You (1)
This Song (1)
Tonight Tonight (2)

What About It (2)
With All Of My Heart (1)

WINANS, BeBe & CeCe '91

Brother-and-sister gospel duo from Detroit.

DEBUT	PEAK	WKS	RIAA	CD	#	Album Title	Catalog	Sym	$	Label & Number
3/4/89	95	25	●	©	1	Heaven			$10	Capitol 90959
7/20/91	74	51	▲	©	2	Different Lifestyles			$10	Capitol 92078
12/25/93+	163	2		©	3	First Christmas		[X]	$10	Capitol 89757
10/8/94	111	10	●	©	4	Relationships			$10	Capitol 28216

Addictive Love (2)
All Because (3)
Better Place (2)
Blood, The (2)
Both Night & Day (4)
Bridge Over Troubled Water (1)
Can't Take This Away (2)
Celebrate New Life (1)
Count It All Joy (4)
Depend On You (3)
Don't Cry (1)
Don't Let Me Walk This Road Alone (4)
First Noel (3)
For Unto Us (A Child Is Born) (3)
Give Me A Star (3)
Hark The Herald Angels Sing (3)
He's Always There (4)
Heaven (1)
Hold Up The Light (1)
I Love You (3)
If Anything Ever Happened To You (4)
I'll Take You There (2) 90
(If I Was Only) Welcomed In (4)
It's O.K. (2)
Jingle Bells (3)
Joy To The World (3)
Lost Without You (1)
Love Of My Life (1)
Meantime (1)
Ooh Child (3)
Right Away (4)
Searching For Love (It's Real) (2)
Silent Night, Holy Night (3)
Silver Bells (3)
Stay With Me (4)
Supposed To Be (2)
These What Abouts (4)
Trust Him (1)
Two Different Lifestyles (2)
Wanna Be More (1)
We Can Make A Difference (4)
White Christmas (3)
You (1)
You Know And I Know (2)

WINANS, CeCe '98

Born Priscilla Winans in 1954 in Detroit. Gospel singer.

DEBUT	PEAK	WKS	RIAA	CD	#	Album Title	Catalog	Sym	$	Label & Number
10/28/95+	124	9	●	©	1	Alone In His Presence			$10	Sparrow 51441
4/4/98	107	13		©	2	Everlasting Love			$10	Pioneer 92793
11/21/98+	27 X	2		©	3	His Gift		[X]	$10	Pioneer 92810
11/6/99	129	7	●	©	4	Alabaster Box			$10	Sparrow 51711

Alabaster Box (4)
Alone In The Presence (1)
Away In A Manger (3)
Because Of You (1)
Blessed Assurance (1)
Blessed, Broken, & Given (4)
Blood Medley (1)
Christmas Star (3)
Come On Back Home (2)
Comforter (2)
Do You Hear What I Hear? (3)
Everlasting Love (2)
Every Time (1)
Feel The Spirit (2)
Fill My Cup (4)
Glory To The King (3)
Go Tell It On The Mountain (3)
Great Is Thy Faithfulness (1)
He's Always There (1)
He's Brought Joy To The World (3)
He's Not On His Knees Yet (4)
Healing Part (2)
Higher Place Of Praise (4)
His Strength Is Perfect (1)
I Am (2)
I Surrender All (1)
It Wasn't Easy (4)
Just Come (2)
King Of Kings (He's A Wonder) (4)
Let's Celebrate Christmas (3)
Life (2)
Listen With Your Heart (2)
Love Of My Heart (4)
Oh, Holy Night (3)
On That Day (2)
One And The Same (4)
Praise Medley (1)
Slippin' (2)
We Wish You A Merry Christmas (3)
Well, Alright (2)
What A Child (3)
What About You (2)
Wind, The (2)
Without Love (4)

WINANS, The '90

Family gospel group from Detroit: brothers Michael, Ronald, Marvin and Carvin Winans. Marvin and Carvin are twins. All are brothers of **BeBe & CeCe Winans**.

DEBUT	PEAK	WKS	RIAA	CD	#	Album Title	Catalog	Sym	$	Label & Number
9/26/87	109	11		©	1	Decisions			$10	Qwest 25510
5/19/90	90	10	●	©	2	Return			$10	Qwest 26161

Ain't No Need To Worry (1)
Breaking Of Day (1)
Don't Leave Me (2)
Don't Let The Sun Go Down On Me (1)
Everyday The Same (2)
Free (2)
Friend, A (2)
Give Me You (1)
Gonna Be Alright (2)
How Can You Live Without Christ? (1)
It's Time (1)
Love Has No Color (1)
Millions (1)
Right, Left In A Wrong World (2)
This Time It's Personal (2)
Together We Stand (2)
What Can I Say? (1)
When You Cry (2)
Wherever I Go (2)

WINANS PHASE2 '99

Family gospel group from Detroit consisting of sons of **The Winans**: Juan and Carvin Jr. (sons of Carvin Winans), Michael Jr. (son of Michael Winans) and Marvin Jr. (son of Marvin Winans).

DEBUT	PEAK	WKS	RIAA	CD	#	Album Title	Catalog	Sym	$	Label & Number
9/25/99	168	2		©		We Got Next			$10	Myrrh 69881

Always For You
Come On Over
Everyday Away
I'm A Winans Too
It's Alright (Send Me)
Just For A Day
Let Him In
Real Love
Thank You Lord
Too Much Heaven (Phase 2)
Who Do You Love

WINBUSH, Angela '87

Born in St. Louis. R&B singer/songwriter. Half of **Rene & Angela** duo.

DEBUT	PEAK	WKS	RIAA	CD	#	Album Title	Catalog	Sym	$	Label & Number
11/7/87	81	28		©	1	Sharp			$10	Mercury 832733
11/11/89	113	17		©	2	The Real Thing			$10	Mercury 838866
4/2/94	96	14		©	3	Angela Winbush			$10	Elektra 61591

Angel (1)
Baby Hold On (3)
C'est Toi (It's You) (1)
Dream Lover (3)
Hello Beloved (1)
Hot Summer Love (3)
I'll Never Be The Same (2)
I'm The Kind Of Woman (3)
I've Learned To Respect (The Power Of Love) (2)
Imagination Of The Heart (1)
Inner City Blues (3)
It's The Real Thing (2)
Keep Turnin' Me On (3)
Lay Your Troubles Down (2)
Menage 'A Trois (2)
No More Tears (2)
No One Has Ever Cared (Like You) (1)
Please Bring Your Love Back (2)
Precious (2)
Run To Me (1)
Sensitive Heart (2)
Sensual Lover (1)
Sharp (1)
Thank You Love (2)
Too Good To Let You Go (3)
Treat U Rite (3)
You Had A Good Girl (1)
You're My Everything (3)

WINCHESTER, Jesse '77

Born on 5/17/44 in Shreveport, Louisiana. Pop singer/songwriter/guitarist.

DEBUT	PEAK	WKS	RIAA	CD	#	Album Title	Catalog	Sym	$	Label & Number
12/30/72+	193	5		©	1	Third Down, 110 To Go			$15	Bearsville 2102
5/28/77	115	16		©	2	Nothing But A Breeze			$12	Bearsville 6968
8/26/78	156	7		©	3	A Touch On The Rainy Side			$12	Bearsville 6984
6/27/81	188	2		©	4	Talk Memphis			$12	Bearsville 6989

All Of Your Stories (1)
Baby Blue (4)
Bowling Green (2)
Candida (3)
Dangerous Fun (1)
Do It (1)
Do La Lay (1)
Easy Way (1)
Full Moon (1)
Gilding The Lily (2)
Glory To The Day (1)
God's Own Jukebox (1)
High Ball (3)
Holly (3)
Hoot And Holler (4)
I Love You No End (4)
I'm Looking For A Miracle (3)
If Only (4)
Isn't That So? (1)
It Takes A Young Girl (2)
Just Now It Feels So Right (3)
Leslie (4)
Let Go (4)
Little Glass Of Wine (3)
Lullaby For The First Born (1)
Midnight Bus (1)
My Songbird (3)
North Star (1)
Nothing But A Breeze (2) 86
Pourquoi M'Aimes-tu Pas? (2)
Reckon On Me (4)
Rhumba Man (2)
Sassy (3)
Say What (4) 32
Seems Like Only Yesterday (2)
Showman's Life (3)
Silly Heart (1)
Sure Enough (4)
Talk Memphis (4)
Touch On The Rainy Side (3)
Twigs And Seeds (2)
Wintry Feeling (3)
You Remember Me (2)

WINDING, Kai '63

Born on 5/18/22 in Aarhus, Denmark. Died on 5/6/83 (age 60). Jazz trombonist.

DEBUT	PEAK	WKS	RIAA	CD	#	Album Title	Catalog	Sym	$	Label & Number
8/10/63	67	24				More!!!		[I]	$25	Verve 8551

China Nights
Comin' Home Baby
Gravy Waltz
Hearse Ride
Hero
More 8
Pipeline
Soul Surfin'
Spinner
Sukiyaki
Surf Bird
Tube Wail

WIND IN THE WILLOWS, The '68

Folk-rock group: **Debbie Harry** (vocals; **Blondie**), Paul Klein (vocals, guitar), Peter Brittain (guitar), Wayne Kirby (keyboards), Ida Andrews (flute), Steve DePhillips (bass) and Anton Carysforth (drums).

DEBUT	PEAK	WKS	RIAA	CD	#	Album Title	Catalog	Sym	$	Label & Number
8/17/68	195	3		©		The Wind In The Willows			$50	Capitol 2956

Djini Judy
Friendly Lion
Little People
Moments Spent
My Uncle Used To Love Me But She Died
Park Avenue Blues
She's Fantastic And She's Yours
So Sad (To Watch Good Love Go Bad)
There Is But One Truth, Daddy
Uptown Girl
Wheel Of Changes

DEBUT	PEAK	WKS	RIAA	CD	ARTIST — Album Title	Catalog	Sym	$	Label & Number

WING AND A PRAYER FIFE AND DRUM CORPS., The   '76
Studio group assembled by producer Harold Wheeler. Vocals by Linda November, Vivian Cherry, Arlene Martell and Helen Miles.

| 2/14/76 | 47 | 16 | | | **Babyface** .... | | | $12 | Wing & A Prayer 3025 |

Baby Face 14
Charleston

Eleanor Rigby
I Hear A Symphony

Just An Old Fashioned Medley   Those Were The Days
Show Medley

WINGER   '90
Hard-rock group formed in New York City: Kip Winger (vocals, bass), Reb Beach (guitar), Paul Taylor (keyboards; left in 1992) and Rod Morgenstein (drums). Kip was a member of **Alice Cooper**'s band. Morgenstein was a member of **Dixie Dregs**.

9/17/88+	21	64	▲	©	1 **Winger**			$10	Atlantic 81867
8/11/90	15	42	▲	©	2 **In The Heart Of The Young**			$10	Atlantic 82103
6/5/93	83	5		©	3 **Pull**			$10	Atlantic 82485

Baptized By Fire (2)
Blind Revolution Mad (3)
Can't Get Enuff (2) 42
Down Incognito (3)
Easy Come Easy Go (2) 41
Hangin On (1)

Headed For A Heartbreak (1) 19
Hungry (1) 85
In For The Kill (3)
In My Veins (3)
In The Day We'll Never See (2)

In The Heart Of The Young (2)
Junkyard Dog (Tears On Stone) (3)
Like A Ritual (3)
Little Dirty Blonde (2)
Loosen Up (3)

Lucky One (3)
Madalaine (1)
Miles Away (2) 12
No Man's Land (3)
Poison Angel (1)
Purple Haze (1)

Rainbow In The Rose (2)
Seventeen (1) 26
Spell I'm Under (3)
State Of Emergency (1)
Time To Surrender (1)
Under One Condition (2)

Who's The One (3)
Without The Night (1)
You Are The Saint, I Am The Sinner (2)

WINGFIELD, Pete   '75
Born on 5/7/48 in Kiphook, Hampshire, England. Singer/keyboardist/producer.

| 12/6/75 | 165 | 5 | | | **Breakfast Special** .... | | | $15 | Island 9333 |

Anytime
Eighteen With A Bullet 15
Hold Me Closer

Kangaroo Dip
Lovin' As You Wanna Be
Number One Priority

Please
Shadow Of A Doubt
Shining Eyes

Whole Pot Of Jelly (For A Little Slice Of Toast)

WINGS — see McCARTNEY, Paul

| | ★483★ | | | | ## WINSTON, George   '84 |
Born in 1949 in Michigan. New Age pianist. Founded Dancing Cat Records in 1983.
1)December 2)Summer 3)Forest

| 3/12/83+ | 54 | 135 | ▲³ | © | 1 **December** .... | C:#7/42 | [X-I] | $10 | Windham Hill 1025 |

Christmas charts: 5/'85, 3/'87, 2/'88, 6/'89, 6/'90, 5/'91, 10/'92, 18/'93, 23/'94, 30/'95, 38/'96, 38/'97, 29/'00

| 5/12/84 | 127 | 32 | ▲ | © | 2 **Winter Into Spring** .... | | [E-I] | $10 | Windham Hill 1019 |

recorded March 1982

| 6/2/84+ | 139 | 44 | ▲ | © | 3 **Autumn** .... | | [E-I] | $10 | Windham Hill 1012 |

recorded June 1980

| 4/20/85 | 180 | 4 | | © | 4 **The Velveteen Rabbit** .... | | [TV] | $10 | Dancing Cat 3007 |

MERYL STREEP & GEORGE WINSTON
from the PBS-TV animated children's special

11/29/86+	85	15		©	5 **December**		[X-I-R]	$10	Windham Hill 1025
12/12/87+	89	10		©	6 **December**		[X-I-R]	$10	Windham Hill 1025
12/17/88+	111	5		©	7 **December**		[X-I-R]	$10	Windham Hill 1025
12/16/89+	101	6		©	8 **December**		[X-I-R]	$10	Windham Hill 1025
12/8/90	106	7		©	9 **December**		[X-I-R]	$10	Windham Hill 1025
10/26/91	55	24	●	©	10 **Summer**		[I]	$10	Windham Hill 11107
10/29/94	62	19	●	©	11 **Forest**		[I]	$10	Dancing Cat 11157
10/5/96	55	22	●	©	12 **Linus & Lucy - The Music Of Vince Guaraldi**		[I]	$10	Dancing Cat 11184
4/11/98	137	8		©	13 **All The Seasons Of George Winston - Piano Solos**		[I-K]	$10	Windham Hill 11266
10/16/99	76	17		©	14 **Plains**		[I]	$10	Windham Hill 11465

Alone (4)
Angel (14)
Anxious Moments (4)
Before Barbed Wire (14)
Black Stallion (10)
Blossom (medley) (2)
Bon Voyage (12)
Building The Snowman (11)
Carol Of The Bells (1,5,6,7,8,9)
Cast Your Fate to the Wind (12,13)
Charlie Brown and His All-Stars (12)
Charlie Brown Thanksgiving (12)
Christmas (4)
Cloudburst (14)
Cloudy This Morning (11)
Colors (medley) (3,13)
Corrina, Corrina (10,13)
Cradle, The (11,13)
Dance (medley) (3,13)

Dance, The (14)
Dubuque (14)
Early Morning Range (10)
Eight Five Five (12)
Fairy, The (4)
February Sea (2)
Flying (4)
Forbidden Forest (11)
Fragrant Fields (10)
Frangenti (14)
Garden, The (10)
Give Me Your Hand (medley) (14)
Goodbye Montana (Part 1 & 2) (10)
Graceful Ghost (11)
Graduation (14)
Great Pumpkin Waltz (12)
Holly And The Ivy (1,5,6,7,8,9)
Hummingbird (10,13)
Ike la Ladana Queen's Jubilee (14)

January Stars (2)
Japanese Music Box (Itsuki No Komoriuta) (11)
Jesus, Jesus, Rest Your Head (1,5,6,7,8)
Joy (1,5,6,7,8,9)
La Valse Pour Les Petites Jeunes Filles (medley) (14)
Lament (medley) (12)
Last Lullaby Here (11)
Lights In The Sky (11)
Linus & Lucy (12)
Living In The Country (10,13)
Living Without You (10)
Longing (medley) (3,13)
Loreta And Desiree's Bouquet (Part 1 & 2) (10)
Love (medley) (3,13)
Love Song To A Ballerina (11)
Lullaby (4,10)
Masked Marvel (12)
Meadow (medley) (2)

Merry Go Round (14)
Miles City Train (13)
Mon Enfant (My Child) (11)
Monterey (12)
Moon (3)
Muliwai (14)
Nana (4)
Night Medley (1,5,6,7,8,9)
Night Sky (11)
No Ke Ano Ahiahi (In The Evening Time) (14)
Northern Plains (13)
Ocean Waves (O Mar) (2)
Peace (1,5,6,7,8,9)
Peppermint Patty (12)
Plains (Eastern Montana Blues) (14)
Prelude (1,5,6,7,8,9)
Rabbit Dance (4)
Rain Dance (2)
Rainsong (Fortune's Lullaby) (14)

Reflection (2)
Remembrance (12)
Returning (4,11)
Road (3)
Sandman (13)
Sase (Sassy) (14)
Sea (3)
Shabbiness Doesn't Matter (4)
Skating (12)
Skin Horse (4)
Sleep Baby Mine (13)
Snowman's Music Box Dance (11,13)
Some Children See Him (1,5,6,7,8,9)
Spring (4)
Spring Creek (10)
Stars (3)
Summer (4)
Swan, The (14)
Tamarack Pines (11)
Teach Me Tonight (14)

Thanksgiving (1,5,6,7,8,9,13)
Theme to Grace (medley) (12)
Toys, The (4)
Treat Street (12,13)
Troubadour (11)
Variations On The Kanon By Johann Pachelbel (1,5,6,7,8,9,13)
Velveteen Rabbit (4)
Venice Dreamer (2,13)
Walking In The Air (11)
Waltz For The Lonely (14)
Where Are You Now (10)
Woods (3)
You're in Love, Charlie Brown (12)
Young Man's Fancy (12)

WINSTONS, The   '69
R&B group from Washington DC: Richard Spencer (vocals), Quincy Mattison (guitar), Ray Maritano (sax), Phil Tolotta (organ), Sonny Peckrol (bass) and G.C. Coleman (drums).

| 8/2/69 | 78 | 12 | | | **Color Him Father** .... | | | $50 | Metromedia 1010 |

Amen, Brother
Birds Of A Feather

Chokin' Kind
Color Him Father 7

Days Of Sand And Shovels
Everyday People

Greatest Love
Handful Of Friends

I've Gotta Be Me
Only The Strong Survive

Traces

WINTER, Edgar, Group   '73
Born on 12/28/46 in Beaumont, Texas. Rock singer/keyboardist/saxophonist. Brother of **Johnny Winter**. His group included **Dan Hartman** (1972-76), Ronnie **Montrose** (1972-74) and **Rick Derringer** (1974-76).

| 6/27/70 | 196 | 2 | | © | 1 **Entrance** .... | | | $15 | Epic 26503 |

EDGAR WINTER

| 5/1/71 | 111 | 19 | | © | 2 **Edgar Winter's White Trash** .... | | | $15 | Epic 30512 |
| 3/25/72 | 23 | 25 | ● | © | 3 **Roadwork** .... | | [L] | $20 | Epic 31249 [2] |

EDGAR WINTER'S WHITE TRASH (above 2)

WINTER, Edgar, Group — Cont'd

DEBUT	PEAK	WKS		CD	ARTIST — Album Title	$	Label & Number
12/9/72+	3	80	▲² ©	4	They Only Come Out At Night	$15	Epic 31584
5/25/74	13	23	● ©	5	Shock Treatment	$15	Epic 32461
6/21/75	69	10	©	6	Jasmine Nightdreams	$12	Blue Sky 33483

EDGAR WINTER

| 10/18/75 | 124 | 8 | | 7 | The Edgar Winter Group With Rick Derringer | $12 | Blue Sky 33798 |
| 6/19/76 | 89 | 9 | | 8 | Together | [L] $12 | Blue Sky 34033 |

JOHNNY & EDGAR WINTER

All Out (6)
Alta Mira (4)
Animal (5)
Autumn (4)
Baby, Whatcha Want Me To Do (8)
Back In The Blues (1)
Back In The U.S.A. (3)
Can't Tell One From The Other (7)
Chainsaw (7)
Cool Dance (7)
Cool Fool (3)
Diamond Eyes (7)
Different Game (1)
Do Like Me (1)
Do Yourself A Favor (3)

Dying To Live (2)
Easy Street (5) *83*
Entrance (1)
Fire And Ice (1)
Fly Away (2)
Frankenstein (4) *1*
Free Ride (4) *14*
Give It Everything You Got (2)
Good Morning Music (2)
Good Shot (2)
Hangin' Around (4) *65*
Harlem Shuffle (8)
Hello Mellow Feelin' (6)
How Do You Like Your Love (6)
Hung Up (1)
I Always Wanted You (6)

I Can't Turn You Loose (3) *81*
I've Got News For You (2)
Infinite Peace In Rhythm (7)
J.A.P. (Just Another Punk) (7)
Jimmy's Gospel (1)
Jive, Jive, Jive (3)
Jump Right Out (1)
Keep On Burnin' (6)
Keep Playin' That Rock 'N' Roll (2) *70*
Let The Good Times Roll (8)
Let's Do It Together Again (1)
Let's Get It On (2)
Little Brother (7)
Maybe Some Day You'll Call My Name (5)
Mercy, Mercy (8)

Miracle Of Love (5)
Modern Love (7)
Nothin' Good Comes Easy (7)
One Day Tomorrow (6)
Outa Control (6)
Paradise (medley) (7)
Peace Pipe (1)
People Music (7)
Queen Of My Dreams (5)
Re-Entrance (1)
Rise To Fall (1)
River's Risin' (5) *33*
Rock 'N' Roll Boogie Woogie Blues (4)
Rock And Roll, Hoochie Koo (3)
Rock And Roll Medley 2 (8)

Rock & Roll Woman (5)
Round & Round (4)
Save The Planet (2,3)
Shuffle-Low (6)
Sides (medley) (7)
Sky Train (6)
Solar Strut (6)
Some Kinda Animal (5)
Someone Take My Heart Away (5)
Soul Man (8)
Still Alive And Well (3)
Sundown (5)
Tell Me In A Whisper (6)
Tobacco Road (1,3)
Turn On Your Lovelight (3)

Undercover Man (4)
We All Had A Real Good Time (4)
When It Comes (4)
Where Have You Gone (1)
Where Would I Be (2)
You Were My Light (2)
You've Lost That Lovin' Feelin' (8)

★323★ **WINTER, Johnny**   '69
Born on 2/23/44 in Leland, Mississippi. Blues-rock singer/guitarist. Brother of **Edgar Winter**.
1)Still Alive And Well 2)Johnny Winter 3)Live/Johnny Winter And

DEBUT	PEAK	WKS		CD	ARTIST — Album Title	$	Label & Number
4/12/69	40	20	©	1	The Progressive Blues Experiment	$25	Imperial 12431
5/10/69	24	23	©	2	Johnny Winter	$20	Columbia 9826
9/27/69	111	6		3	The Johnny Winter Story	[E] $20	GRT 10010
12/6/69	55	17	©	4	Second Winter	$25	Columbia 9947 [2]
					a 3-sided album (4th side is blank)		
9/26/70	154	4		5	Johnny Winter And	$15	Columbia 30221
3/13/71	40	27	● ©	6	Live/Johnny Winter And	[L] $15	Columbia 30475
4/7/73	22	24	©	7	Still Alive And Well	$15	Columbia 32188
2/23/74	42	16	©	8	Saints & Sinners	$15	Columbia 32715
12/7/74	78	12		9	John Dawson Winter III	$12	Blue Sky 33292
3/6/76	93	12	©	10	Captured Live!	[L] $12	Blue Sky 33944
6/19/76	89	9		11	Together	[L] $12	Blue Sky 34033

JOHNNY & EDGAR WINTER

7/23/77	146	8	©	12	Nothin' But The Blues	$12	Blue Sky 34813
8/26/78	141	4		13	White, Hot & Blue	$12	Blue Sky 35475
8/4/84	183	4	©	14	Guitar Slinger	$10	Alligator 4735
10/19/85	156	10	©	15	Serious Business	$10	Alligator 4742

Ain't Nothing To Me (7)
Ain't That A Kindness (5)
All Tore Down (7)
Am I Here? (5)
Baby, Whatcha Want Me To Do (11)
Back Door Friend (2)
Bad Luck And Trouble (1)
Bad Luck Situation (8)
Be Careful With A Fool (2)
Black Cat Bone (1)
Bladie Mae (12)
Blinded By Love (8)
Bony Moronie (8,10)
Boot Hill (14)
Broke And Lonely (3)
Broke Down Engine (1)
By The Light Of The Silvery Moon (1)
Can't You Feel It (7)
Cheap Tequila (7)
Creepy (3)
Crying In My Heart (3)
Dallas (2)

Divin' Duck (13)
Don't Take Advantage Of Me (14)
Drinkin' Blues (12)
E-Z Rider (13)
Ease My Heart (3)
Everybody's Blues (12)
Fast Life Rider (4)
Feedback On Highway 101 (8)
Five After Four A.M. (3)
Forty-Four (1)
Funky Music (5)
Gangster Of Love (3)
Give It Back (15)
Golden Olden Days Of Rock & Roll (9)
Good Love (4)
Good Morning Little School Girl (2,6)
Good Time Woman (15)
Guess I'll Go Away (5)
Guy You Left Behind (3)
Harlem Shuffle (11)
Help Me (1)

Highway 61 Revisited (4,10)
Honest I Do (13)
Hurtin' So Bad (8)
Hustled Down In Texas (4)
I Can't Believe You Want To Leave (3)
I Got Love If You Want It (1)
I Hate Everybody (4)
I Love Everybody (4)
I Smell Trouble (14)
I'll Drown In My Tears (2)
I'm Not Sure (4)
I'm Yours And I'm Hers (2)
Iodine In My Coffee (14)
It Ain't Your Business (15)
It Was Rainin' (12)
It's All Over Now (10)
It's My Life, Baby (14)
It's My Own Fault (1,6)
Johnny B. Goode (4,6) *92*
Jumpin' Jack Flash (6) *89*
Kiss Tomorrow Goodbye (14)
Last Night (13)
Lay Down Your Sorrows (9)

Leave My Woman (Wife) Alone (3)
Leland Mississippi Blues (2)
Let It Bleed (7)
Let The Good Times Roll (11)
Let The Music Play (5)
Lights Out (14)
Look Up (5)
Love Song To Me (9)
Mad Blues (12)
Mad Dog (14)
Master Mechanic (15)
Mean Mistreater (2)
Mean Town Blues (1,6)
Memory Pain (4)
Mercy, Mercy (11)
Messin' With The Kid (13)
Mind Over Matter (9)
Miss Ann (4)
Murdering Blues (15)
My Soul (14)
My Time After Awhile (15)
Nickel Blues (13)
No Time To Live (5)

Nothing Left (5)
Oh My Darling (3)
On The Limb (5)
One Step At A Time (13)
Pick Up On My Mojo (9)
Prodigal Son (5)
Raised On Rock (9)
Riot In Cell Block #9 (8)
Road Runner (3)
Rock & Roll (7)
Rock And Roll, Hoochie Koo (5)
Rock And Roll Medley 1 (6)
Rock And Roll Medley 2 (11)
Rock And Roll People (9,10)
Rock Me Baby (7)
Roll With Me (9,10)
Rollin' And Tumblin' (1)
Rollin' 'Cross The Country (8)
Route 90 (15)
Self-Destructive Blues (14)
Serious As A Heart Attack (15)
Shed So Many Tears (3)
Silver Train (7)
Slidin' In (13)

Slippin' And Slidin' (4)
Soul Man (11)
Sound The Bell (15)
Still Alive & Well (7)
Stone County (8)
Stranger (9)
Stray Cat Blues (8)
Sweet Love And Evil Women (12)
Sweet Papa John (9,10)
TV Mama (12)
That's What Love Does (3)
Thirty Days (8)
Tired Of Tryin' (12)
Too Much Seconal (7)
Tribute To Muddy (1)
Trick Bag (14)
Unseen Eye (15)
Walkin' By Myself (13)
Walking Thru The Park (12)
When You Got A Good Friend (2)
You've Lost That Lovin' Feelin' (11)

WINTER, Paul   '63
Born on 8/31/39 in Altoona, Pennsylvania. Jazz saxophonist.

DEBUT	PEAK	WKS		CD	ARTIST — Album Title	$	Label & Number
12/29/62+	109	4	©	1	Jazz Meets The Bossa Nova	[I] $20	Columbia 8725

PAUL WINTER SEXTET

| 5/3/86 | 138 | 11 | © | 2 | Canyon | [I] $10 | Living Music 6 |

Adeus, Passaro Preto (Bye Bye, Blackbird) (1)
Air (2)
Anguish Of Longing (1)

Bedrock Cathedral (2)
Bright Angel (2)
Con Alma (1)
Don't Play Games With Me (1)

Elves' Chasm (2)
Foolish One (1)
Grand Canyon Sunrise (2)
Grand Canyon Sunset (2)

Journey To Recife (1)
Little Boat (1)
Longing For Bahia (1)
Maria Nobody (1)

Morning Echoes (2)
Only You And I (1)
Raven Dance (2)
River Run (2)

Sad Eyes, Song Of The (1)
Sockdolager (2)
Spell Of The Samba (1)

WINTERS, Jonathan   '60
Born on 11/11/25 in Dayton, Ohio. Improvisational comedian. Appeared in several movies and TV shows.

DEBUT	PEAK	WKS		CD	ARTIST — Album Title	$	Label & Number
2/1/60	18	53		1	The Wonderful World Of Jonathan Winters	[C] $25	Verve 15009
9/19/60	25	23		2	Down To Earth	[C] $25	Verve 15011
5/29/61	19	42		3	Here's Jonathan	[C] $25	Verve 15025
9/1/62	127	3		4	Another Day, Another World	[C] $25	Verve 15032

DEBUT	PEAK	WKS	RIAA	CD	ARTIST — Album Title	Catalog	Sym	$	Label & Number

WINTERS, Jonathan — Cont'd

| 3/21/64 | 145 | 2 | | | 5 Jonathan Winters' Mad, Mad, Mad, Mad World | [C] | $25 | Verve 15041 |
| 12/19/64 | 148 | 2 | | | 6 Whistle Stopping with Jonathan Winters | [C] | $25 | Verve 15037 |

Airline Pilots (1)
Amateur Show (2)
American Farmer - Elwood P. Suggins (6)
American Housewife - Sally Sweetwater (6)
American Indian - Chief Crying Trout (6)
American Labor Leader - Billy Bigbody (6)
American Teenager - Melvin Gohard (6)

Billy The Kid (3)
Broadway Musical (2)
California (4)
Chief Running Fox (5)
Child Psychiatrist (3)
Civil War (4)
Commercials (2)
Driving On The Turnpike - Thoughts Of A Turtle (3)
Extreme Liberal - Lance Lovegard (6)

Flying Saucer (1)
Football Game (1,5)
Grand Old Man - Price Boothcourt (4)
Great White Hunter (2,5)
Hip Robin Hood (1,5)
Horror Movies (2)
Human Torpedo (4)
Igor And The Monster (4)
Interviews (2)
Lost Island (4)

Marine Corps (1,5)
Moby Dick & Captain Arnold (5)
Moon Map and Ivy Leaguer (4)
My School Days (4,5)
New Flying Saucer (3)
New Frontiers (4)
Old Age Speaks Out - Maude Frickert (6)
Oldest Airline Stewardess - Maude Frickert (3,5)
Opening (3)

Portugese Pirate Ship (3)
Presidential Nominee - Daniel Douglas Diddle (6)
Prison Scene (2,5)
Sail Cat (4)
Scratchy (2)
Super Service Station (1)
TV Commercials and American In Paris (4)
Test Flight (3)

Ultra-Conservative - Mr. Tick Bitterford (6)
Used Pet Shop (1,5)
Western (1)

WINTERS, Robert, & Fall '81
Born in Detroit. R&B singer/keyboardist. His group Fall featured lead singer Walter Turner.

| 5/9/81 | 71 | 8 | | | Magic Man | | | $12 | Buddah 5732 |

Face The Music
Happiness

How Can Love Be Wrong
Into My World

Magic Man
She Believes In Me

Touched By You
Watchin' You

When Will My Love Be Right

★306★ WINWOOD, Steve '88
Born on 5/12/48 in Birmingham, England. Rock singer/keyboardist/guitarist. Lead singer of **Spencer Davis Group**, **Blind Faith** and **Traffic**.
1)Roll With It 2)Back In The High Life 3)Arc Of A Diver

5/29/71	93	8			1 Winwood	[K]		$25	United Artists 9950 [2]
					STEVIE WINWOOD				
8/21/76	60	12			2 Go			$12	Island 9387
					STOMU YAMASHTA/STEVE WINWOOD/MICHAEL SHRIEVE				
7/16/77	22	17		©	3 Steve Winwood			$12	Island 9494
1/17/81	3	43	▲	©	4 Arc Of A Diver			$12	Island 9576
8/21/82	28	25		©	5 Talking Back To The Night			$12	Island 9777
7/19/86	3	86	▲³	©	6 Back In The High Life			$10	Island 25448
11/21/87+	26	26	▲	©	7 Chronicles	[K]		$10	Island 25660
7/9/88	❶¹	45	▲²	©	8 Roll With It			$10	Virgin 90946
11/24/90	27	20	●	©	9 Refugees of the Heart			$10	Virgin 91405
6/21/97	123	4		©	10 Junction Seven			$10	Virgin 44059

Air Over (2)
And I Go (5)
Angel Of Mercy (10)
Another Deal Goes Down (9)
Arc Of A Diver (4,7) **48**
Back In The High Life Again (6) **13**
Big Girls Walk Away (5)
Carnival (2)
Coloured Rain [Traffic] (1)
Come Out And Dance (9)
Cross Roads [Powerhouse] (1)
Crossing The Line (2)
Dealer [Traffic] (1)
Dear Mr. Fantasy [Traffic] (1)
Don't You Know What The Night Can Do? (8) **6**
Dust (4)
Empty Pages [Traffic] (1) **74**

Every Day (Oh Lord) (9)
Family Affair (10)
Fill Me Up (10)
Finer Things (6) **8**
Forty Thousand Headmen [Traffic] (1)
Freedom Overspill (6) **20**
Freedom Rider [Traffic] (1)
Ghost Machine (2)
Gimme Some Lovin' [Spencer Davis Group] (1) **7**
Goodbye Stevie [Spencer Davis Group] (1)
Gotta Get Back To My Baby (10)
Hearts On Fire (8) **53**
Heaven Is In Your Mind [Traffic] (1)
Help Me Angel (5,7)

Higher Love (6,7) **1**
Hold On (3)
Holding On (8) **11**
I Can't Get Enough Of It [Spencer Davis Group] (1)
I Will Be Here (9)
I'm A Man [Spencer Davis Group] (1) **10**
In The Light Of Day (9)
It Was Happiness (5)
Just Wanna Have Some Fun (10)
Keep On Running [Spencer Davis Group] (1) **76**
Let Me Make Something In Your Life (3)
Let Your Love Come Down (10)
Lord Of The Street (10)
Luck's In (3)

Man Of Leo (2)
Medicated Goo [Traffic] (1)
Midland Maniac (3)
Morning Side (8)
My Love's Leavin' (6,7)
Nature (2)
Night Train (4)
One And Only Man (9) **18**
One More Morning (8)
Paper Sun [Traffic] (1) **94**
Plenty Lovin' (10)
Put On Your Dancing Shoes (8)
Real Love (10)
Roll With It (8) **1**
Running On (9)
Sea Of Joy [Blind Faith] (1)
Second-Hand Woman (4)
Shining Song (4)
Slowdown Sundown (4)

Smiling Phases [Traffic] (1)
Solitude (2)
Somebody Help Me [Spencer Davis Group] (1) **47**
Someone Like You (10)
Space Requiem (2)
Space Song (2)
Space Theme (2)
Spanish Dancer (4,7)
Split Decision (6)
Spy In The House Of Love (10)
Stellar (2)
Stevie's Blues [Spencer Davis Group] (1)
Still In The Game (5) **47**
Stranger To Himself [Traffic] (1)
Surfspin (2)
Take It As It Comes (6)

Talking Back To The Night (5,7) **57**
There's A River (5)
Time Is Here (2)
Time Is Running Out (3)
Vacant Chair (3,7)
Vagabond Virgin [Traffic] (1)
Valerie (5) **70**
Valerie (7) **9**
Wake Me Up On Judgment Day (6,7)
While There's A Candle Burning (5)
While You See A Chance (4,7) **7**
Winner/Loser (2)
You'll Keep On Searching (9)

WIRE '89
Rock group from London: Colin Newman (vocals, guitar), Bruce Gilbert (guitar), Graham Lewis (bass) and Mark Field (drums).

| 7/8/89 | 135 | 10 | | © | It's Beginning To And Back Again | | | $10 | Enigma 73516 |

Boiling Boy
Eardrum Buzz

Finest Drops
German Shepherds

Illuminated
It's A Boy

Over Theirs
Public Place

WIRE TRAIN '84
Rock group formed in San Francisco: Kevin Hunter (vocals), Jeff Trott (guitar), Anders Rundblad (bass) and Brian MacLeod (drums).

| 2/18/84 | 150 | 9 | | © | 1 ...In A Chamber | | | $10 | Columbia 38998 |
| 5/2/87 | 181 | 4 | | © | 2 Ten Women | | | $10 | Columbia 40387 |

Breakwater Days (2)
Certainly No One (2)
Chamber Of Hellos (1)
)

Diving (2)
Everything's Turning Up Down Again (1)
Hollow Song (2)

I Forget It All (When I See You) (1)
I Gotta Go (1)
I'll Do You (1)

Like (1)
Love Against Me (1)
Mercy Mercy (2)
Never (1)

She Comes On (2)
She's A Very Pretty Thing (2)
She's Got You (2)
She's On Fire (1)

Slow Down (1)
Take Me Back (2)
Too Long Alone (2)

WISHBONE ASH '73
Progressive-rock group from Devonshire, England: Andy Powell and Ted Turner (vocals, guitar), Martin Turner (bass) and Steve Upton (drums). Male guitarist Laurie Wisefield replaced Ted Turner in 1974.
1)Wishbone Four 2)Live Dates 3)There's The Rub

9/11/71	174	7		©	1 Pilgrimage			$20	Decca 75295
6/24/72	169	13		©	2 Argus			$20	Decca 75437
4/28/73	44	15		©	3 Wishbone Four			$15	MCA 327
12/1/73	82	18		©	4 Live Dates	[L]		$20	MCA 8006 [2]
11/30/74	88	13		©	5 There's The Rub			$15	MCA 464
3/27/76	136	9			6 Locked In			$12	Atlantic 18164
12/18/76+	154	9			7 New England			$12	Atlantic 18200
11/5/77	166	4		©	8 Front Page News			$12	MCA 2311
3/29/80	179	2			9 Just Testing			$12	MCA 3221
1/23/82	192	4			10 Hot Ash	[K-L]		$12	MCA 5283

WISHBONE ASH — Cont'd

Alone(1)
Baby What You Want Me To Do (4)
Bad Weather Blues (10)
Ballad Of The Beacon (3,4)
Blowin' Free (2,4,10)
Candle-Light (7)
Come In From The Rain (8)
Day I Found Your Love (8)
Diamond Jack (8)
Doctor (3,10)
Don't Come Back (5)

Everybody Needs A Friend (3)
F*U*B*B* (5)
Front Page News (8)
Goodbye Baby Hello Friend (8,10)
Half Past Lovin' (4)
Haunting Me (9)
Heart Beat (8)
Helpless (9,10)
Hometown (5)
(In All Of My Dreams) You Rescue Me (7)

Insomnia (9)
It Started In Heaven (6)
Jail Bait (1,4)
King Will Come (2,4)
Lady Jay (5)
Lady Whiskey (4)
Leaf And Stream (2)
Lifeline (9)
Living Proof (9,10)
Lonely Island (7)
Lorelei (7)
Lullabye (1)

Master Of Disguise (9)
Midnight Dancer (8)
Moonshine (6)
Mother Of Pearl (7)
New Rising Star (9)
No Easy Road (3,10)
No Water In The Well (6)
Outward Bound (7)
Pay The Price (9)
Persephone (5)
Phoenix (4)
Pilgrim, The (1,4)

Prelude (7)
Rest In Peace (6)
Right Or Wrong (8)
Rock 'N Roll Widow (3,4)
Runaway (7)
Say Goodbye (6)
714 (8)
She Was My Best Friend (6)
Silver Shoes (5)
Sing Out The Song (3)
So Many Things To Say (3)
Sometime World (2)

Sorrel (3)
Surface To Air (8)
Throw Down The Sword (2,4)
Time Was (2)
Trust In You (6)
Valediction (1)
Vas Dis (1)
Warrior (2,4)
Way Of The World (10)
When You Know Love (7)
Where Were You Tomorrow (1)

WITCHDOCTOR '98
Born in Atlanta. Male rapper.

| 5/9/98 | 157 | 1 | © | | ...A S.W.A.T Healin' Ritual .... | | | $10 | Organized Noize 90146 |

A.T.L. The Great Big Lick
Ancient Sahore
D.F.

Dez Only 1
4 In The Temple
Georgia Plains (Holy Grounds)

Heaven Comin'
Holiday (medley)
Hurtin'

Island Koneelalee
Lil' Mama's Gone
Remedy

Ritual, The
Serengetti, The (medley)
7th Floor (medley)

Smooth Shit
Spells
12 Scanner (medley)

WITCH QUEEN '79
Studio disco group produced by Peter Alves and **Gino Soccio.**

| 4/28/79 | 158 | 6 | | | Witch Queen .... | | | $12 | Roadshow 3312 |

All Right Now
Bang A Gong *68*
Got The Time
Witch Queen

WITHERS, Bill '72
Born on 7/4/38 in Slab Fork, West Virginia. R&B singer/songwriter/guitarist.
1)Still Bill 2)Just As I Am 3)Menagerie

6/26/71	39	33		1	Just As I Am			$15	Sussex 7006
5/20/72	4	43	●	2	Still Bill			$15	Sussex 7014
4/21/73	63	21	©	3	Bill Withers Live At Carnegie Hall		[L]	$20	Sussex 7025 [2]
4/6/74	67	21		4	+'Justments			$15	Sussex 8032
5/17/75	182	2		5	The Best Of Bill Withers		[G]	$15	Sussex 8037
11/8/75+	81	15		6	Making Music			$12	Columbia 33704
11/6/76	169	4		7	Naked & Warm			$12	Columbia 34327
10/29/77+	39	26	●	8	Menagerie			$12	Columbia 34903
3/17/79	134	9		9	'Bout Love			$12	Columbia 35596
5/16/81	183	3	©	10	Bill Withers' Greatest Hits		[G]	$10	Columbia 37199
5/25/85	143	9	©	11	Watching You Watching Me			$10	Columbia 39887

Ain't No Sunshine (1,3,5,10) *3*
All Because Of You (9)
Another Day To Run (2)
Best You Can (6)
Better Off Dead (1,3)
City Of The Angels (7)
Close To Me (7)
Cold Baloney (medley) (3)
Dedicated To You My Love (9)
Do It Good (1)
Don't It Make It Better (9)
Don't Make Me Wait (11)
Don't You Want To Stay? (6)
Dreams (7)
Everybody's Talkin' (1,5)
Family Table (6)

For My Friend (3)
Friend Of Mine (3) *80*
Grandma's Hands (1,3,5,10) *42*
Green Grass (4)
Harlem (1,3,5)
Heart In Your Life (11)
Heartbreak Road (4) *89*
Hello Like Before (6,10)
Hope She'll Be Happier (1,3)
I Can't Write Left Handed (3)
I Don't Know (2)
I Don't Want You On My Mind (2)
I Love You Dawn (6)
I Want To Spend The Night (8,10)

I Wish You Well (6)
I'll Be With You (7)
I'm Her Daddy (1)
If I Didn't Mean You Well (7)
In My Heart (1)
It Ain't Because Of Me Baby (8)
Just The Two Of Us (10) *2*
Kissing My Love (2,5) *31*
Lean On Me (2,3,5,10) *1*
Let It Be (1)
Let Me Be The One You Need (8)
Let Me In Your Life (2,3)
Let Us Love (3) *47*
Liza (4)
Lonely Town, Lonely Street (4)

Look To Each Other For Love (9)
Love (9)
Love Is (9)
Lovely Day (8,10) *30*
Lovely Night For Dancing (8)
Make A Smile For Me (4)
Make Love To Your Mind (6) *76*
Memories Are That Way (9)
Moanin' And Groanin' (1)
My Imagination (7)
Naked & Warm (Heaven! Oh! Heaven!) (7)
Oh Yeah! (11)
Paint Your Pretty Picture (6)
Railroad Man (4)

Ruby Lee (4)
Same Love That Made Me Laugh (4,5) *50*
She Wants To (Get On Down) (8)
She's Lonely (6)
Something That Turns You On (11)
Sometimes A Song (6)
Soul Shadows (10)
Steppin' Right Along (11)
Stories (4)
Sweet Wanomi (11)
Take It All In And Check It All Out (2)
Tender Things (8)
Then You Smile At Me (8)

Use Me (2,3,5,10) *2*
Watching You Watching Me (11)
We Could Be Sweet Lovers (11)
Whatever Happens (11)
Where You Are (7)
Who Is He And What Is He To You? (2,5,10)
Wintertime (8)
World Keeps Going Around (3)
You (4,5)
You Got The Stuff (9)
You Just Can't Smile It Away (11)
You Try To Find A Love (11)

WITHERSPOON, Jimmy '75
Born on 8/8/23 in Gurdon, Arkansas. Died on 9/18/97 (age 74). Blues singer/bassist.

| 3/8/75 | 176 | 2 | © | | Love Is A Five Letter Word .... | | | $12 | Capitol 11360 |

Aviation Man
Buried Alive In The Blues

Fool's Paradise
I Was Lost (But Now I'm Found)

Landlord, Landlord
Love Is A Five Letter Word

No Money Down
Nothing's Changed

Other Side Of Love
Reflection

Spoon Tang
What's Going Down

WOLF, Peter '84
Born Peter Blankfield on 3/7/46 in the Bronx, New York. Lead singer of the **J. Geils Band.** Married to actress Faye Dunaway from 1974-79. Not to be confused with the producer of the same name.

8/11/84	24	26	©	1	Lights Out			$10	EMI America 17121
4/18/87	53	15	©	2	Come As You Are			$10	EMI America 17230
3/31/90	111	7	©	3	Up To No Good!			$10	MCA 6349

Arrows And Chains (3)
Baby Please Don't Let Me Go (1)
Billy Bigtime (1)
Blue Avenue (2)
Can't Get Started (2) *75*

Come As You Are (2) *15*
Crazy (1)
Daydream Getaway (3)
Drive All Night (3)
Flame Of Love (2)
Gloomy Sunday (1)

Go Wild (3)
Here Comes That Hurt (1)
I Need You Tonight (1) *36*
Lights Out (1) *12*
Lost In Babylon (3)
Once On Ice (2)

Magic Moon (2)
Mamma Said (2)
Mars Needs Women (1)
Never Let It Go (3)
99 Worlds (3) *78*
Oo-Ee-Diddley-Bop! (1) *61*

Poor Girl's Heart (1)
Pretty Lady (Tell Me Why) (1)
River Runs Dry (3)
Run Silent Run Deep (2)
Shades Of Red--Shades Of Blue (3)

Thick As Thieves (2)
2 Lane (2)
Up To No Good (3)
When Women Are Lonely (3)
Wind Me Up (2)

WOLFMAN JACK — see VARIOUS ARTIST COMPILATIONS

★385★ WOMACK, Bobby '73
Born on 3/4/44 in Cleveland. R&B singer/songwriter/guitarist. Nicknamed "The Preacher."
1)The Poet 2)Facts Of Life 3)Understanding

12/28/68	174	2		1	Fly Me To The Moon			$30	Minit 24014
4/17/71	188	5	©	2	The Womack "Live"		[L]	$20	Liberty 7645
12/4/71+	83	17	©	3	Communication			$15	United Artists 5539
6/24/72	43	48	©	4	Understanding			$15	United Artists 5577

WOMACK, Bobby — Cont'd

DEBUT	PEAK	WKS	CD		ARTIST — Album Title	Sym	$	Label & Number
1/13/73	50	20	©	5	Across 110th Street	[S]	$15	United Artists 5225

includes "Harlem Clavinette," "Hang On In There," "Harlem Love Theme," "Across 110th Street" and "(If You Don't Want My Love) Give It Back" by J.J. Johnson

7/7/73	37	21	©	6	Facts Of Life		$15	United Artists 043
2/9/74	85	19	©	7	Lookin' For A Love Again		$15	United Artists 199
12/14/74+	142	7		8	Bobby Womack's Greatest Hits	[G]	$15	United Artists 346
5/24/75	126	4	©	9	I Don't Know What The World Is Coming To		$15	United Artists 353
1/17/76	147	11	©	10	Safety Zone		$15	United Artists 544
12/26/81+	29	23	©	11	The Poet		$12	Beverly Glen 10000
4/7/84	60	14	©	12	The Poet II		$12	Beverly Glen 10003

with guest vocalist **Patti LaBelle**

| 9/21/85 | 66 | 19 | | 13 | So Many Rivers .... | | $10 | MCA 5617 |

Across 110th Street (5) *56*
All Along The Watchtower (6)
American Dream (7)
And I Love Her (4)
Baby! You Oughta Think It Over (1)
California Dreamin' (1,2) *43*
Can't Stop A Man In Love (4)
Check It Out (9,13) *91*
Come L'Amore (3)
Communication (3)
Copper Kettle (7)
Daylight (10)
Do It Right (8)
Doing It My Way (7)
Don't Let Me Down (7)
Everybody's Talkin' (2)
Everything Is Beautiful (3)
Everything's Gonna Be Alright (10)
Fact Of Life (medley) (6)
Fire And Rain (3)
Fly Me To The Moon (1,8) *52*

Games (11)
Git It (9)
Got To Be With You Tonight (13)
Got To Get You Back (4)
Gypsy Woman (13)
Hang On In There (5)
Harry Hippie (4,8) *31*
He'll Be There When The Sun Goes Down (medley) (8)
Holdin' On To My Baby's Love (medley) (8)
I Can Understand It (4,8)
I Don't Know (Interlude #1 & 2) (9)
I Don't Wanna Be Hurt By Ya Love Again (7)
I Feel A Groove Comin' On (10)
I Wish He Didn't Trust Me So Much (13)
I Wish I Had Someone To Go Home To (12)
I Wish I Would Rain (10)
I'm A Midnight Mover (1,2)

I'm Gonna Forget About You (8)
I'm In Love (1)
I'm Through Trying To Prove My Love To You (6)
If You Can't Give Her Love Give Her Up (6)
(If You Don't Want My Love) Give It Back (3,5)
If You Think You're Lonely Now (11)
(If You Want My Love) Put Something Down On It (9)
It Takes A Lot Of Strength To Say Goodbye (12)
It's All Over Now (9)
Jealous Love (9)
Just My Imagination (11)
Laughing And Clowning (2)
Lay Some Lovin' On Me (11)
Let It Hang Out (7)
Let It Out (2)
Let Me Kiss It Where It Hurts (13)
Lillie Mae (1)

Look Of Love (6)
Lookin' For A Love (7,8) *10*
Love Ain't Something You Can Get For Free (10)
Love Has Finally Come At Last (12) *88*
Love, The Time Is Now (1)
Moonlight In Vermont (1)
More Than I Can Stand (2,8) *90*
Natural Man (6)
No Money In My Pocket (1)
Nobody (medley) (6)
Nobody Wants You When You're Down And Out (6,8) *29*
Oh How I Miss You Baby (2)
Only Survivor (13)
Point Of No Return (7)
Preacher, The (2,8)
Quicksand (5)
Ruby Dean (4)
Secrets (11)
Simple Man (4)

So Baby, Don't Leave Home Without It (13)
So Many Rivers (13)
So Many Sides Of You (11)
Somebody Special (1)
Something (2)
Something You Got (10)
Stand Up (11)
Superstar (9)
Surprise Surprise (12)
Sweet Caroline (Good Times Never Seemed So Good) (4,8) *51*
Take Me (1)
Tell Me Why (12)
That's Heaven To Me (6)
That's The Way I Feel About Cha (3,8) *27*
That's Where It's At (13)
There's One Thing That Beats Failing (7)
(They Long To Be) Close To You (3)
Thing Called Love (4)

Through The Eyes Of A Child (12)
Trust In Me (10)
Tryin' To Get Over You (12)
What Is This (1)
What's Your World (9)
Whatever Happened To The Times? (13)
Where Do We Go From Here (11)
Where There's A Will, There's A Way (10)
Who's Foolin' Who (12)
Woman's Gotta Have It (4,8) *60*
Yes, Jesus Loves Me (9)
Yield Not To Temptation (3)
You're Messing Up A Good Thing (7)
You're Welcome, Stop On By (7,8) *59*

WOMACK, Lee Ann   '01

Born on 8/19/66 in Jacksonville, Texas. Country singer.

5/31/97	106	23	▲	©	1	Lee Ann Womack	$10	Decca 11585
10/10/98	136	12	●	©	2	Some Things I Know	$10	Decca 70040
6/10/00+	16	69↑	▲²	©	3	I Hope You Dance	$10	MCA 170099

After I Fall (3)
Am I The Only Thing That You've Done Wrong (1)
Ashes By Now (3) *45*
Buckaroo (1)
Do You Feel For Me (1)
Does My Ring Burn Your Finger (3)

Don't Tell Me (2)
Fool, The (1)
Get Up In Jesus' Name (1)
Healing Kind (3)
I Feel Like I'm Forgetting Something (3)
I Hope You Dance (3) *14*
I Keep Forgetting (2)

I Know Why The River Runs (3)
I'd Rather Have What We Had (2)
I'll Think Of A Reason Later (2) *38*
If You're Ever Down In Dallas (2)
Little Past Little Rock (2) *43*

Lonely Too (3)
Lord I Hope This Day Is Good (3)
Make Memories With Me (1)
Man Who Made My Mama Cry (2)
Man With 18 Wheels (1)
Montgomery To Memphis (3)

Never Again, Again (1)
(Now You See Me) Now You Don't (2) *72*
Preacher Won't Have To Lie (2)
Some Things I Know (2)
Stronger Than I Am (3)
Thinkin' With My Heart Again (3)

Trouble's Here (1)
When The Wheels Are Coming Off (2)
Why They Call It Falling (3) *78*
You've Got To Talk To Me (1)

WOMENFOLK, The   '64

Female folk group from Pasadena: Elaine Gealer, Joyce James, Leni Ashmore, Babs Cooper and Judy Fine.

| 5/2/64 | 118 | 6 | | The Womenfolk .... | $20 | RCA Victor 2832 |

Don't You Rock 'Em Daddy-O
Good Old Mountain Dew
Green Mountain Boys
Little Boxes *83*
Little Rag Doll
Love Come A-Tricklin' Down
Old Maid's Lament
One Man's Hands
Para Bailar La Bamba
Rickety Tickety Tin
Skip To My Lou
Whistling Gypsy Rover

WONDER, Stevie ★39★   '76

Born Steveland Morris on 5/13/50 in Saginaw, Michigan. R&B singer/songwriter/keyboardist. Blind since birth. Signed to Motown in 1960, did backup work. First recorded in 1962, named "Little Stevie Wonder" by Berry Gordy. Married to **Syreeta** Wright from 1970-72. Appeared in the movies *Bikini Beach* and *Muscle Beach Party*. Inducted into the Rock and Roll Hall of Fame in 1989. Won Grammy's Lifetime Achievement Award in 1996.

1)*Songs In The Key Of Life* 2)*Fulfillingness' First Finale* 3)*Little Stevie Wonder* 4)*Hotter Than July* 5)*Talking Book*

7/13/63	❶¹	20	©	1	Little Stevie Wonder/The 12 Year Old Genius	[L]	$100	Tamla 240
6/18/66	33	25	©	2	Up-Tight Everything's Alright		$40	Tamla 268
1/28/67	92	7		3	Down To Earth		$40	Tamla 272
9/30/67	45	13	©	4	I Was Made To Love Her		$40	Tamla 279
12/23/67	81ˣ	2	©	5	Someday At Christmas	[X]	$40	Tamla 281
4/27/68	37	29	©	6	Greatest Hits	[G]	$30	Tamla 282
1/11/69	50	18	©	7	For Once In My Life		$30	Tamla 291
10/11/69	34	20	©	8	My Cherie Amour		$30	Tamla 296
4/11/70	81	15		9	Stevie Wonder Live	[L]	$30	Tamla 298
8/29/70	25	16	©	10	Signed Sealed & Delivered		$30	Tamla 304
5/8/71	62	27	©	11	Where I'm Coming From		$30	Tamla 308
11/20/71+	69	12	©	12	Stevie Wonder's Greatest Hits, Vol. 2	[G]	$30	Tamla 313
3/25/72	21	35	©	13	Music Of My Mind		$30	Tamla 314
11/18/72+	3	109	©	14	Talking Book		$20	Tamla 319
8/18/73	4	89	©	15	Innervisions		$20	Tamla 326

1973 Grammy winner: Album of the Year

Ai No, Sono (19)
Ain't No Lovin' (7)
Ain't That Asking For Trouble (2,18)
Alfie (9,18) **66**
All I Do (20)
All In Love Is Fair (15)
Angel Baby (Don't You Ever Leave Me) (3)
Angie Girl (8,18)
Another Star (17) **32**
Anything You Want Me To Do (10)
As (17) **36**
As If You Read My Mind (20)
At Last (8)
Ave Maria (5)
Baby Don't You Do It (4)
Bang Bang (3)
Be Cool, Be Calm (And Keep Yourself Together) (5)
Bedtime For Toys (5)
Big Brother (14)
Bird Of Beauty (16)
Black Man (17)
Black Orchid (19)
Blame It On The Sun (14)
Blowin In The Wind (2,6,9,18) **9**
Boogie On Reggae Woman (16,21) **3**
By The Time I Get To Phoenix (9)
Ca' Purange (9)
Can I Get A Witness (4)
Cash In Your Face (20)
Castles In The Sand (6,18) **52**
Chemical Love (25)
Christmas Song (Merry Christmas To You) (5)
Christmastime (5)
Cold Chill (26)
Come Back As A Flower (19)
Contract On Love (2,6,18)
Contusion (17)
Conversation Peace (26)
Creepin' (16)
Cryin' Through The Night (24)
Dark 'N' Lovely (24)
Day That Love Began (5)
Did I Hear You Say You Love Me (20)
Do I Do (21) **13**

Do I Love Her (7)
Do Like You (20)
Do Yourself A Favor (11,18)
Don't Drive Drunk (22)
Don't Wonder Why (10)
Don't You Know (1)
Don't You Worry 'Bout A Thing (15) **16**
Down To Earth (3,9,18)
Drown In My Own Tears (1)
Each Other's Throat (25)
Earth's Creation (19)
Ecclesiastes (19)
Edge Of Eternity (26)
Every Time I See You I Go Wild (4)
Everybody Needs Somebody (I Need You) (4)
Everybody's Talking (9)
Evil (13)
Finale (19)
Fingertips - Pt 2 (1,6,18) **1**
First Garden (19)
Fool For You (4)
For Once In My Life (7,9,12,18) **2**
For Your Love (26) **53**
Free (24)
Front Line (21)
Fun Day (25)
Galaxy Paradise (24)
Get It (24) **80**
Girl Blue (13)
Give Your Love (8)
Go Home (23) **10**
God Bless The Child (7)
Golden Lady (15)
Gotta Have You (25) **92**
Hallelujah I Love Her So (1)
Happier Than The Morning Sun (13)
Happy Birthday (20)
Have A Talk With God (17)
He's Misstra Know-It-All (15)
Heaven Help Us All (10,12,18) **9**
Heaven Is 10 Zillion Light Years Away (16)
Hello Young Lovers (8)
Hey Harmonica Man (6,18) **29**
Hey Love (3,6,18) **90**
High Heel Sneakers (18) **59**
Higher Ground (15,21) **4**

Hold Me (2)
House On The Hill (7)
I Ain't Gonna Stand For It (20) **11**
I Believe (When I Fall In Love It Will Be Forever) (14)
I Can't Let My Heaven Walk Away (10)
I Don't Know Why (7,18) **39**
I Go Sailing (25)
I Gotta Have A Song (10,18)
I Just Called To Say I Love You (22) **1**
I Love Every Little Thing About You (13)
I Love You Too Much (23)
I Pity The Fool (4)
I Wanna Make Her Love Me (7)
I Wanna Talk To You (11)
I Want My Baby Back (2)
I Was Made To Love Her (4,6,18) **2**
I Wish (17,21) **1**
I'd Be A Fool Right Now (7,18)
I'd Cry (4,18)
(I'm Afraid) The Masquerade Is Over (1)
I'm More Than Happy (I'm Satisfied) (7)
I'm New (26)
I'm Wondering (6,18) **12**
I've Got You (8)
I've Gotta Be Me (medley) (9)
If I Ruled The World (9)
If She Breaks Your Heart (25)
If You Really Love Me (11,12,18) **8**
In Your Corner (24)
Isn't She Lovely (17,21)
It Ain't No Use (16)
It's More Than You (22)
It's Wrong (Apartheid) (23)
It's You (22)
Jesus Children Of America (15)
Joy Inside My Tears (17)
Joy (Takes Over Me) (10)
Jungle Fever (25)
Keep On Running (13) **90**
Kesse Ye Lolo De Ye (19)
Knocks Me Off My Feet (17)
La La La La La (1)
Land Of La La (23) **86**

Lately (20) **64**
Light My Fire (8)
Lighting Up The Candles (25)
Little Drummer Boy (5)
Living For The City (15,21) **8**
Lonesome Road (3)
Look Around (11)
Lookin' For Another Pure Love (14)
Love A Go Go (2)
Love Having You Around (13)
Love Light In Flight (22) **17**
Love's In Need Of Love Today (17)
Make Sure You're Sure (25)
Master Blaster (Jammin') (20,21) **5**
Maybe Your Baby (14)
More Than A Dream (18)
Mr. Tambourine Man (3)
Music Talk (2)
My Cherie Amour (8,9,12,18) **4**
My Girl (4)
My Love Is With You (26)
My World Is Empty Without You (3)
Never Dreamed You'd Leave In Summer (11,12,18) **78**
Never Had A Dream Come True (10,12,18) **26**
Never In Your Sun (23)
Ngiculela-Es Una Historia - I Am Singing (17)
Nothing's Too Good For My Baby (2,6,18) **20**
Once In A Lifetime (medley) (9)
One Little Christmas Tree (5)
One Of A Kind (24)
Ordinary Pain (17)
Outside My Window (19) **52**
Overjoyed (23) **24**
Part-Time Lover (23) **1**
Pastime Paradise (17)
Pearl (8)
Place In The Sun (3,6,9,18) **9**
Please Don't Go (16)
Please, Please, Please (4)
Power Flower (19)
Pretty Little Angel (3)
Pretty World (9)
Queen In The Black (25)
Race Babbling (19)
Rain Your Love Down (26)

Respect (4)
Ribbon In The Sky (21) **54**
Rocket Love (20)
Romeo & Juliet (A Time For Us), Love Theme From (9)
Same Old Story (19)
Seasons (19)
Secret Life Of Plants (19)
Seed's A Star (medley) (19)
Seems So Long (13)
Send One Your Love (19,21) **4**
Sensuous Whisper (26)
Shadow Of Your Smile (8)
Shoo-Be-Doo-Be-Doo-Da-Day (7,9,12,18) **9**
Signed, Sealed, Delivered I'm Yours (10,12,18) **3**
Silver Bells (5)
Sir Duke (17,21) **1**
Sixteen Tons (3)
Skeletons (24) **19**
Smile Please (16)
Somebody Knows, Somebody Cares (8)
Someday At Christmas (5)
Something Out Of The Blue (11,18)
Something To Say (10)
Sorry (26)
Soul Bongo (1)
Spiritual Walkers (23)
Stranger On The Shore Of Love (23)
Sugar (10)
Summer Soft (17)
Sunny (7,9)
Sunshine In Their Eyes (11)
Superstition (14,21) **1**
Superwoman (Where Were You When I Needed You) (13,21) **33**
Sweet Little Girl (13)
Sylvia (3,18)
Taboo To Love (8)
Take The Time Out (26)
Take Up A Course In Happiness (11)
Teach Me Tonight (2)
Thank You (For Loving Me All The Way) (18)
Thank You (3,9,18)
That Girl (21) **4**

These Three Words (25)
They Won't Go When I Go (16)
Think Of Me As Your Soldier (11)
Tomorrow Robins Will Sing (26)
Too High (15)
Too Shy To Say (16)
Travlin' Man (12,18) **32**
Treat Myself (26)
Tree (19)
Tuesday Heartbreak (14)
Twinkle Twinkle Little Me (5)
Until You Come Back To Me (That's What I'm Gonna Do) (18)
Uptight (Everything's Alright) (2,6,18) **3**
Venus' Flytrap And The Bug (19)
Village Ghetto Land (17)
Visions (15)
Voyage To India (19)
Warm Little Home On A Hill (5)
We Can Work It Out (10,12) **13**
Weakness (22)
What Christmas Means To Me (5)
Whereabouts (23)
With A Child's Heart (2)
With Each Beat Of My Heart (24)
Woman In Red (22)
Workout Stevie, Workout (6,18) **33**
Yester-Me, Yester-You, Yesterday (8,9,12,18) **7**
You And I (14)
You And Me (8)
You Are The Sunshine Of My Life (14,21) **1**
You Can't Judge A Book By It's Cover (10)
You Haven't Done Nothin (16,21) **1**
You Met Your Match (7,12,18) **35**
You Will Know (24) **77**
You've Got It Bad Girl (14)

Best Thing I Ever Had
Birdman
Come Here Girl

Gimme Little Sign 9
I Like The Way You Love Me

I Think You've Got Your Fools Mixed Up
I'm The One Who Knows

Little Bit Of Love
Oogum Boogum Song 34
Psychotic Reaction

Runnin' Wild
Take A Chance

Big Bayou (1)
Breakin' My Heart (2)
Breathe On Me (1)
Buried Alive (2)
Caribbean Boogie (1)
Come To Realise (2)

Delia (2)
Don't Worry (2)
Down To The Ground (3)
F.U.C. Her (2)
Fountain Of Love (3)
I Can Say She's Allright (1)

I Can't Stand The Rain (1)
I Got A Feeling (1)
I Got Lost When I Found You (1)
If You Don't Want My Love (1)
Infekshun (2)

It's Unholy (1)
Lost And Lonely (2)
Now Look (1)
1234 (3)
Outlaws (3)
Priceless (3)

Redeyes (3)
Seven Days (2)
She Never Told Me (3)
She Was Out There (3)
Sweet Baby Mine (1)
We All Get Old (2)

Wind Howlin' Through (3)
Worry No More (2)

WOOD, Roy '73
Born Ulysses Wood on 11/8/46 in Birmingham, England. Co-founder/cello player of **The Move** and **Electric Light Orchestra**.

| 11/3/73 | 176 | 6 | © | **Boulders** .... | $15 | United Artists 168 |

All The Way Over The Hill (medley)
Dear Elaine
Irish Loafer (And His Hen) (medley)
Miss Clarke And The Computer
Nancy Sing Me A Song
Rock Down Low
Rock Medley
Songs Of Praise
Wake Up
When Gran'ma Plays The Banjo

WOODBURY, Woody '60
Born in 1927 in Fort Lauderdale, Florida. Adult comedy storyteller.

| 3/7/60 | 10 | 78 | 1 | Woody Woodbury Looks At Love And Life | [C] $25 | Stereoddities 1 |
no track titles listed on this album

| 6/13/60 | 16 | 59 | 2 | **Woody Woodbury's Laughing Room** .... | [C] $25 | Stereoddities 2 |
| 1/20/62 | 46 | 21 | 3 | **Woody Woodbury's Saloonatics** .... | [C] $25 | Stereoddities 4 |

Allergic (3)
Blue Side (2)
Bright Side (2)
I'm Returning All Your Presents (3)

WOODENTOPS, The '86
Rock group from Northampton, England: Rolo McGinty (vocals), Simon Mawby (guitar), Alice Thompson (keyboards), Frank DeFreitas (bass) and Benny Staples (drums).

| 9/20/86 | 185 | 6 | © | **Giant** .... | $10 | Columbia 40468 |

Everything Breaks
Get It On
Give It Time
Good Thing
Hear Me James
History
Last Time
Love Affair With Everyday Livin'
Love Train
Shout
So Good Today
Travelling Man

WOODS, Stevie '82
Born in Columbus, Ohio. Male R&B singer/songwriter. Son of jazz great Rusty Bryant.

| 12/5/81+ | 153 | 25 | | **Take Me To Your Heaven** .... | $12 | Cotillion 5229 |

Fly Away 84
Gotcha
Just Can't Win 'Em All 38
Read Between The Lines
Steal The Night 25
Take Me To Your Heaven
Through The Years
Throw A Little Bit Of Love My Way
Wanna' Be Close To You

WOOLLEY, Bruce, & The Camera Club '80
Pop-rock group from England: Bruce Woolley (vocals), David Birch (guitar), **Thomas Dolby** (keyboards), Matthew Selingman (bass) and Rod Johnson (drums).

| 3/8/80 | 184 | 2 | | **Bruce Woolley & The Camera Club** .... | $12 | Columbia 36301 |

Clean/Clean (medley)
Dancing With The Sporting Boys
English Garden
Flying Man
Get Away William
Goodbye To Yesterday
Johnny
No Surrender
Video Killed The Radio Star
W.W. 9 (medley)
You Got Class
You're The Circus (I'm The Clown)

WORLD PARTY '87
Group is actually rock singer/keyboardist Karl Wallinger (born on 10/19/57 in Prestatyn, Wales). Wallinger was also a member of **The Waterboys**.

12/27/86+	39	31	©	1	**Private Revolution**	$10	Chrysalis 41552
6/2/90	73	23	©	2	**Goodbye Jumbo**	$10	Ensign 21654
5/8/93	126	8	©	3	**Bang!**	$10	Ensign 21991
7/5/97	167	1	©	4	**Egyptology**	$10	Chrysalis 56482

Ain't Gonna Come Till I'm Ready (2)
All Come True (1)
All I Gave (3)
All I Really Want To Do (1)
Always (4)
And God Said... (3)
And I Fell Back Alone (2)
Ballad Of The Little Man (1)
Beautiful Dream (4)
Call Me Up (4)
Curse Of The Mummy's Tomb (4)
Dance Of The Hoppy Lads (1)
Give It All Away (3)
God On My Side (2)
Hawaiian Island World (1)
Hercules (2)
Hollywood (3)
Is It Like Today? (3)
Is It Too Late? (2)
It Can Be Beautiful (Sometimes) (1)
It Is Time (4)
It's All Mine (1)
Kingdom Come (3)
Love Is Best (4)
Love Street (2)
Making Love (To The World) (1)
Piece Of Mind (4)
Private Revolution (1)
Put The Message In The Box (2)
Radio Days (3)
Rescue Me (3)
Rolling Off A Log (4)
She's The One (4)
Ship Of Fools (Save Me From Tomorrow) (1) 27
Show Me To The Top (2)
Sooner Or Later (3)
Strange Groove (4)
Sunshine (3)
Sweet Soul Dream (2)
Take It Up (2)
Thank You World (2)
This World (4)
Vanity Fair (4)
Way Down Now (2)
What Is Love All About? (3)
When The Rainbow Comes (2)
Whole Of The Night (4)
World Party (1)

WRABIT '82
Rock group from Canada: Lou Nadeau (vocals), David Aplin and John Albani (guitars), Les Paulhus (keyboards), Chris Brockway (bass) and Scott Jefferson Steck (drums).

| 2/6/82 | 157 | 8 | | **Wrabit** .... | $10 | MCA 5268 |

Anyway Anytime
Back Home
Can't Be Wrong
Don't Say Goodnite To Rock And Roll
Here I'll Stay
How Does She Do It
Just Go Away
Pushin' On
Tell Me What To Do
Too Many Years

WRATHCHILD AMERICA '89
Hard-rock group from Baltimore: Brad Divens (vocals, bass; **Kix**), Jay Abbene and Terry Carter (guitars) and Shannon Larkin (drums).

| 9/30/89 | 190 | 6 | © | **Climbin' The Walls** .... | $10 | Atlantic 81889 |

Candy From A Madman
Climbin' The Walls
Day Of The Thunder
Hell's Gates
Hernia
London After Midnight
No Deposit, No Return
Silent Darkness (Smothered Life)
Time

WRAY, Link, & His Ray Men '71
Born on 5/2/35 in Dunn, North Carolina. Rock guitarist. Also see **Robert Gordon**.

| 7/24/71 | 186 | 4 | | **Link Wray** .... | $20 | Polydor 4064 |
recorded at Wray's 3-track shack in Maryland

Black River Swamp
Crowbar
Fallin' Rain
Fire And Brimstone
God Out West
Ice People
Juke Box Mama
La De Da
Rise And Fall Of Jimmy Stokes
Tail Dragger
Take Me Home Jesus

WRECKX-N-EFFECT '93
Male rap duo: Aqil Davidson and Markell Riley (brother of Teddy Riley).

| 1/13/90 | 103 | 11 | © | 1 | **Wrecks-N-Effect** .... | $10 | Motown 6281 |
| 12/12/92+ | 9 | 34 | ▲ © | 2 | Hard Or Smooth | $10 | MCA 10566 |

Club Head (1)
Deep (1)
Ez Come Ez Go (What Goes Up Must Come Down) (2)
Friends To The End (1)
Hard (Short) (2)
Here We Come (2)
Juicy (1)
Knock-N-Boots (2) 72
Leave The Mike Smokin' (1)
My Cutie (2)
New Jack Swing (1)
New Jack Swing II (2)
Peanut Butter (1)
Rock Steady (1)
Rump Shaker (2) 2
Smooth (Short) (2)
Soul Man (1)
Tell Me How You Feel (2)
V-Man (1)
WRECKX-N-Effect (2)
WRECKX Shop (2)
Wipe Your Sweat (1)

WRIGHT, Bernard — '81
Born in 1965 in New York City. R&B singer/keyboardist.

| 3/14/81 | 116 | 14 | | | 'Nard .... | | | $12 | GRP 5011 |

Bread Sandwiches — Haboglabotribin' — Master Rocker — Solar — We're Just The Band
Firebolt Hustle — Just Chillin' Out — Music Is The Key — Spinnin'

WRIGHT, Betty — '78
Born on 12/21/53 in Miami. R&B singer.

2/26/72	123	6		1	I Love The Way You Love			$15	Alston 388
6/17/78	26	36	©	2	Betty Wright Live		[L]	$12	Alston 4408
6/2/79	138	6	©	3	Betty Travelin' In The Wright Circle			$12	Alston 4410
4/23/88	127	13	©	4	Mother Wit			$10	Ms. B 3301

After The Pain (4) — I Found That Guy (1) — Let's Get Married Today (medley) (2) — Me And Mrs. Jones (medley) (2) — Open The Door To Your Heart (medley) (3) — Tonight Is The Night (2)
Ain't No Sunshine (1) — I Love The Way You Love (1) — Let's Not Rush Down The Road Of Love (1) — Miami Groove (4) — Pillow Talk (medley) (2) — Unsolicited Advice (4)
All Your Kissin' Sho' Don't Make True Lovin' (1) — I'll Love You Forever Heart And Soul (1) — Listen To The Music (Dance) (3) — Midnight At The Oasis (medley) (2) — Pure Love (1) — Where Is The Love (2) 96
Child Of The Man (3) — I'm Gettin' Tired Baby (1) — Love Days (4) — Mr. Melody (medley) (2) — Say It Again (4) — (You Are My) Sunshine (medley) (2)
Clean Up Woman (1,2) 6 — I'm Telling You Now (3) — Love Train (medley) (3) — Ms. Time (4) — Shoot It From The Hip (4) — You Can't See For Lookin' (2)
Don't Let It End This Way (1) — If You Love Me Like You Say You Love Me (1) — Lovin' Is Really My Game (2) — My Love Is (3) — Song For You (2) — You Got The Love (medley) (2)
Fakin' Moves (4) — — — No Pain (No Gain) (4) — Thank You For The Many Things You've Done (3) — You're Just What I Need (3)
I Believe It's Love (3)

WRIGHT, Charles — '69
Born in 1942 in Clarksdale, Mississippi. R&B singer/guitarist/pianist.

4/19/69	140	5		1	Together			$20	Warner 1761
10/18/69	145	4	©	2	In The Jungle, Babe			$20	Warner 1801
					THE WATTS 103RD STREET RHYTHM BAND (above 2)				
8/8/70	182	10	©	3	Express Yourself			$15	Warner 1864
5/15/71	147	11		4	You're So Beautiful			$15	Warner 1904
					CHARLES WRIGHT AND THE WATTS 103RD STREET RHYTHM BAND (above 2)				

Comment (2) — Giggin' Down 103rd (1) — I'm Aware (3) — Must Be Your Thing (2) — Settle My Nerves (4) — Twenty-Five Miles (2)
Dance, A Kiss And A Song (1) — High As Apple Pie - Slice I & II (3) — Joker (On A Trip Through The Jungle) (2) — My Summer's Gone (1) — 65 Bars And A Taste Of Soul (1) — What Can You Bring Me? (4)
Do Your Thing (1) 11 — (I Can't Get No) Satisfaction (1) — Knock On Wood (1) — Oh Happy Gabe (Sometimes Blue) (2) — Something You Got (1) — You're So Beautiful (4)
Everyday People (2) — I Got Love (3,4) — Let's Make Love Not War (4) — Papa's Got A Brand New Bag (1) — Sorry Charlie (1) — Your Love (Means Everything To Me) (4) 73
Express Yourself (3) 12 — I Wake Up Crying (1) — Light My Fire (2) — Phuncky Bill (1) — Stormy Monday (1) — —
Express Yourself II (4) — I'm A Midnight Mover (2) — Love Land (2,3) 16 — — Till You Get Enough (2) 67 — —
Get Ready (1)

WRIGHT, Chely — '99
Born on 10/25/70 in Kansas City. Country singer.

| 10/4/97 | 171 | 7 | © | 1 | Let Me In .... | | | $10 | MCA 70003 |
| 6/5/99 | 124 | 5 | ● © | 2 | Single White Female .... | | | $10 | MCA 70052 |

Before You Lie (1) — Fire, The (2) — Just Another Heartache (1) — Rubbin' It In (2) — Single White Female (2) 36 — Why Do I Still Want You (2)
Emma Jean's Guitar (1) — I Already Do (2) — Let Me In (1) — She Went Out For Cigarettes (2) — Some Kind Of Somethin' (2) — Your Woman Misses Her Man (1)
Feelin' Single And Seein' Double (1) — Is It Love Yet? (1) — Love That We Lost (2) — Shut Up And Drive (1) — 10 Lb. Heart (1) — —
— It Was (2) 64 — Picket Fences (2) — — Unknown (2)

WRIGHT, Gary — '76
Born on 4/26/43 in Creskill, New Jersey. Pop-rock singer/songwriter/keyboardist. Appeared in *Captain Video* TV series in 1950. Member of Spooky Tooth.

8/23/75+	7	75	▲² ©	1	The Dream Weaver			$12	Warner 2868
4/24/76	172	4	©	2	That Was Only Yesterday		[K]	$20	A&M 3528 [2]
					GARY WRIGHT/SPOOKY TOOTH				
1/22/77	23	15		3	The Light Of Smiles			$12	Warner 2951
12/10/77+	117	9		4	Touch And Gone			$12	Warner 3137
3/17/79	147	5		5	Headin' Home			$12	Warner 3244
6/27/81	79	19		6	The Right Place			$12	Warner 3511

Are You Weepin' (3) — Fascinating Things (2) — I'm Alright (3) — Love It Takes (4) — Really Wanna Know You (6) 16 — Stay Away (4)
Blind Feeling (1) — Feel For Me (1) — I'm The One Who'll Be By Your Side (5) — Love To Survive (2) — Right Place (6) — Sunshine Help Me (2)
Can't Find The Judge (1) — Feelin' Bad (3) — Keep Love In Your Soul (5) — Love's Awake Inside (5) — Silent Fury (3) — That Was Only Yesterday (2)
Can't Get Above Losing You (4) — Follow Next To You (5) — Let It Out (1) — Made To Love You (1) 79 — Sing A Song (2) — Time Machine (3)
Child Of Light (3) — Got The Feelin' (6) — Let Me Feel Your Love Again (5) — Moonbeams (5) — Sky Eyes (4) — Touch And Gone (4) 73
Close To You (6) — Heartbeat (6) — Light Of Smiles (3) — More Than A Heartache (6) — Something To Say (2) — Two Faced Man (2)
Comin' Apart (6) — Holy Water (2) — Lost In My Emotions (4) — Much Higher (1) — Something Very Special (4) — Waitin' For The Wind (2)
Cotton Growing Man (2) — I Am The Sky (3) — Love Is A Rose (6) — Night Ride (4) — Son Of Your Father (2) — Water Sign (1)
Dream Weaver (1) 2 — I Can Feel You Cryin' (5) — Love Is Alive (1) 2 — Nobody There At All (2) — Stand (5) — Who Am I (3)
Empty Inside (3) — I Can't See The Reason (1) — Love Is Why (5) — Phantom Writer (3) 43 — Stand For Our Rights (2) — Wildfire (2)
Evil Woman (2) — I Know (2) — — Positive Feelins (6) — Starry Eyed (4) — Wrong Time (2)
— — — Power Of Love (1) — — You Don't Own Me (5)

WRIGHT, Michelle — '92
Born on 7/1/61 in Morpeth, Ontario, Canada. Country singer.

| 6/13/92 | 126 | 14 | © | | Now & Then .... | | | $10 | Arista 18685 |

Change, The — Fastest Healing Wounded Heart — He Would Be Sixteen — Little More Comfortable — One Time Around
Don't Start With Me — Guitar Talk — If I'm Ever Over You — Now & Then — Take It Like A Man

WRIGHT, Steven — '85
Born on 12/6/55 in New York City. Comedian/actor. Known for his "deadpan" delivery.

| 11/23/85 | 192 | 2 | © | | I Have A Pony .... | | [C] | $10 | Warner 25335 |

Ants — Book Store — Hitchhiking — Jiggs Casey — Water
Apt. — Cross Country — Ice — Rachel — Winny
Babies And Skiing — Dog Stay — Introduction — 7's And Museums — Pup

W'S, The — '98
Christian ska-rock group: Andrew Schar (vocals, guitar), Valentine Hellman, Bret Barker and James Carter (horns), Todd Gruener (bass) and Brian Morris (drums).

| 8/15/98 | 147 | 2 | © | | Fourth From The Last .... | | | $10 | Sarabellum 25204 |

Alarm Clock — Dexter — Frank — J.P. — Open Minded
Devil Is Bad — Flower Tattoo — Hui — Jason E — Pup

WU-SYNDICATE '99
Male rap duo from New York City: Myalansky and Joe Mafia.

5/8/99	61	3		©	**Wu-Syndicate**			$10	Wu-Tang 50056

Ask Son	Ghetto Syringe	Hit, The	Metropolis	Thug War	Where Was Heaven
Bust A Slug	Global Politics	Ice Age	Muzzle Toe	VA Cats	Wings Of Life
Crime Syndicate	Golden Sands	Lutunza	Pointin' Fingers	Weary Eyes	Young Brothas

WU-TANG CLAN '97
Rap group from Staten Island, New York: Gary Grice (**Genius/GZA**), Clifford Smith (**Method Man**), Russell Jones (**Ol Dirty Bastard**), Corey Woods (**Raekwon**), Jason Hunter (**Inspectah Deck**), Dennis Coles (**Ghostface Killah**), Lamont Hawkins (**U-God**), Robert Diggs (**RZA**) and Elgin Turner (Masta Killa). Diggs was also a member of **Gravediggaz**.

11/27/93	41	42	▲	© 1	**Enter The Wu-Tang (36 Chambers)** ....C:#19/23			$10	Loud 66336
6/21/97	❶[1]	41	▲[4]	© 2	**Wu-Tang Forever**			$15	Loud 66905 [2]
12/9/00	5	17	▲	© 3	**The W**			$10	Wu-Tang 62193

As High As Wu-Tang Get (2)	City, The (2)	Duck Seazon (2)	Jah World (3)	Projects, The (2)	Shame On A Nigga (1)
Bells Of War (2)	Clan In Da Front (1)	For Heavens Sake (2)	Let My Niggas Live (3)	Protect Ya Neck (1)	Tearz (1)
Better Tomorrow (2)	Conditioner (3)	Gravel Pit (3)	Little Ghetto Boys (2)	Protect Ya Neck (The Jump Off)	Triumph (2)
Black Shampoo (2)	C.R.E.A.M. (1) 60	Heaterz (2)	M.G.M., The (2)	(3)	Visionz (2)
Bring Da Ruckus (1)	Da Mystery Of Chessboxin' (1)	Hellz Wind Staff (2)	Maria (2)	Redbull (3)	Wu-Revolution (2)
Can It Be All So Simple (1)	Deadly Melody (2)	Hollow Bones (2)	Method Man (1) 69	Reunited (2)	Wu-Tang Clan Ain't Nuthing Ta
Careful (Click, Click) (3)	Do You Really (Thang, Thang)	I Can't Go To Sleep (3)	Monument, The (3)	Scary Hours (medley) (2)	F' Wit (1)
Cash Still Rules (medley) (2)	(3)	Impossible (2)	Older Gods (2)	Second Coming (2)	Wu-Tang: 7th Chamber - Part I
Chamber Music (3)	Dog Sh*t (2)	It's Yourz (2)	One Blood Under W (3)	Severe Punishment (2)	& II (1)

WU-TANG KILLA BEES '98
Rap group from New York City. Features **Wu-Tang Clan** members **RZA**, **Method Man**, **Ghostface Killah**, **Raekwon**, **Inspectah Deck** and Masta Killa, with **Cappadonna**, **Killarmy** and **Sunz Of Man**.

8/8/98	4	10	●	●	**The Swarm**			$10	Wu-Tang 50013

And Justice For All	Co-Defendant	Execute Them	Never Again	Punishment
Bastards	Cobra Clutch	Fatal Sting	'97 Mentality	S.O.S.
Bronx War Stories	Concrete Jungle	Legacy, The	On The Strength	Where Was Heaven

WYMAN, Bill '74
Born William Perks on 10/24/36 in London. Bass guitarist of **The Rolling Stones** from 1962-92.

6/15/74	99	11		© 1	**Monkey Grip**			$15	Rolling Stones 59102
3/27/76	166	5		© 2	**Stone Alone**			$15	Rolling Stones 79103

Apache Woman (2)	Get It On (2)	If You Wanna Be Happy (2)	No More Foolin' (2)	Soul Satisfying (2)	Wine & Wimmen (2)
Crazy Woman (1)	Gimme Just One Chance (2)	It's A Wonder (1)	Peanut Butter Time (2)	What A Blow (1)	
Every Sixty Seconds (2)	I Wanna Get Me A Gun (1)	Mighty Fine Time (1)	Pussy (1)	What's The Point (1)	
Feet (2)	I'll Pull You Thro' (1)	Monkey Grip Glue (1)	Quarter To Three (2)	White Lightnin' (1)	

WYNETTE, Tammy ★392★ '69
Born Virginia Wynette Pugh on 5/5/42 in Itawamba County, Mississippi. Died of a blood clot on 4/6/98 (age 55). Dubbed "The First Lady of Country Music." Married to **George Jones** from 1969-75.

1)Tammy's Greatest Hits 2)Honky Tonk Angels 3)Stand By Your Man

9/7/68+	147	15		© 1	**D-I-V-O-R-C-E**			$20	Epic 26392
2/8/69	43	21		© 2	**Stand By Your Man**			$20	Epic 26451
5/24/69	189	3		3	**Inspiration**			$20	Epic 26423
9/6/69	37	61	▲	© 4	**Tammy's Greatest Hits**		[G]	$20	Epic 26486
2/21/70	83	11		5	**The Ways To Love A Man**			$20	Epic 26519
5/16/70	85	17		6	**Tammy's Touch**			$20	Epic 26549
8/15/70	145	2		7	**The World Of Tammy Wynette**		[K]	$20	Epic 503 [2]
10/31/70	119	14		8	**The First Lady**			$20	Epic 30213
12/26/70	30[X]	1		9	**Christmas With Tammy**		[X]	$20	Epic 30343
5/22/71	115	10		10	**We Sure Can Love Each Other**			$20	Epic 30658
9/18/71	118	8	●	11	**Tammy's Greatest Hits, Volume II**		[G]	$20	Epic 30733
11/13/71	169	6		12	**We Go Together**			$20	Epic 30802

TAMMY WYNETTE & GEORGE JONES

4/8/72	133	9		13	**Bedtime Story**			$20	Epic 31285
11/20/93	42	16	●	© 14	**Honky Tonk Angels**			$10	Columbia 53414

DOLLY PARTON, LORETTA LYNN, TAMMY WYNETTE

7/8/95	117	13		© 15	**One**			$10	MCA 11248

GEORGE JONES & TAMMY WYNETTE

After Closing Time (12)	Don't Come Home A Drinkin'	He's Still My Man (8)	If You Think I Love You Now	Let Her Fly (14)	Never Grow Cold (12)
All I Have To Offer You Is Me	(With Lovin' On Your Mind) (7)	Honey (I Miss You) (1,7)	(10)	Let's Put Christ Back Into	O Little Town Of Bethlehem (9)
(15)	Don't Liberate Me (Love Me)	How Great Thou Art (3)	It Came Upon The Midnight	Christmas (9)	Ode To Billie Joe (7)
All Night Long (1)	(10)	I Believe (3,7)	Clear (9)	Lifetime Left Together (12)	One (15)
Almost Persuaded (4)	Don't Make Me Go To School	I Don't Wanna Play House (4)	It Is No Secret (What God Can	Lighter Shade Of Blue (6)	One Happy Christmas (9)
Apartment #9 (4)	(2)	I Dreamed Of A Hillbilly Heaven	Do) (3,7)	Livin' On Easy Street (12)	Only Time I'm Really Me (11)
Away In A Manger (9)	Don't Touch Me (7)	(14)	It Keeps Slipping My Mind (2)	Lonely Christmas Call (9)	Our Last Night Together (6,11)
Baby, Come Home (10)	Enough Of A Woman (5)	I Forgot More Than You'll Ever	It Wasn't God Who Made Honky	Lonely Days (And Nights More	Playin' Around With Love (8)
Battle Hymn Of The Republic	Forever Yours (2)	Know (14)	Tonk Angels (14)	Lonely) (6)	Please Help Me I'm Falling (In
(3)	Gentle On My Mind (1)	I Got Me A Man (13)	It's An Old Love Thing (15)	Lonely Street (1)	Love With You) (14)
Bedtime Story (13) 86	Gentle Shepherd (9)	I Know (5)	It's Just A Matter Of Time (6)	Longing To Hold You Again	Put It Off Until Tomorrow (14)
Blue Christmas (9)	Good (7)	I Never Once Stopped Loving	It's My Way (2,7)	(10)	Reach Out Your Hand (13)
Bring Him Safely Home To Me	Good Lovin' (Makes It Right)	You (8)	It's So Sweet (12)	Love Me, Love Me (6)	Run, Angel, Run (4)
(10)	(11)	I Stayed Long Enough (2,7)	Joey (3)	Love's The Answer (13)	**Run, Woman, Run** (8,11) 92
Buy Me A Daddy (8)	Have A Little Faith (10)	I Wish I Had A Mommy Like	Joy Of Being A Woman (10)	Lovesick Blues (6)	Safe In These Lovin' Arms Of
Cold Lonely Feeling (6)	He (3)	You (8)	Joy To The World (9)	Lovin' Kind (8)	Mine (8)
Come On Home (1)	He Knows All The Ways To	I'll See Him Through	Just A Closer Walk With Thee	Make Me Your Kind Of Woman	Sally Trash (8)
Count Your Blessings Instead	Love (10)	(6,11)	(3)	(10)	(She's Just) An Old Love
Of Sheep (9)	**He Loves Me All The Way**	I'll Share My World With You (3)	Just As Soon As I Get Over	May The Good Lord Bless And	Turned Memory (15)
Cry (7)	(6,11) 97	I'm Gonna Keep On Loving Him	Loving You (13)	Keep You (3)	Silent Night, Holy Night (9)
Cry, Cry Again (2,7)	He Thinks I Love Him (6)	(13)	Just Look What We've Started	(Merry Christmas) We Must Be	Silver Threads And Golden
Crying In The Chapel (3,7)	He'll Never Take The Place Of	I've Learned (2)	Again (15)	Having One (9)	Needles (14)
D-I-V-O-R-C-E (1,4) 63	You (5)	If God Met You (15)	Kiss Away (1)	My Arms Stay Open Late (2,7)	**Singing My Song** (4,5) 75
Divorce Sale (6)	He's Got The Whole World In	If I Were A Little Girl (2)	Legend Of Bonnie And Clyde	My Daddy Doll (9)	
	His Hands (3)	If This Is Our Last Time (13)	(1,7)	**My Elusive Dreams** (4) 89	

DEBUT	PEAK	WKS	RIAA	CD		ARTIST — Album Title	Catalog	Sym	$	Label & Number

WYNETTE, Tammy — Cont'd

Sittin' On The Front Porch Swing (14)
Solid As A Rock (15)
Someone I Used To Know (12)
Something To Brag About (12)
Stand By Your Man (2,4) *19*
Still Around (5,11)
Sweet Dreams (1)
Take Me (12)

Take Me Home And Love Me (13)
Take Me To Your World (4)
That's The Way It Should Have Been (14)
That's When I Feel It (13)
There Goes My Everything (7)
These Two (5)
They're Playing Our Song (15)

Tonight My Baby's Coming Home (13)
Too Far Gone (4)
True And Lasting Love (8)
Twelfth Of Never (5)
Walk Through This World With Me (7)
Ways To Love A Man (5,11) *81*
We Go Together (12)

We Sure Can Love Each Other (10,11)
What Ever Happened To Us (15)
When There's A Fire In Your Heart (1)
When True Love Steps In (12)
Where Could You Go (But To Her) (5,7)
White Christmas (9)

Will You Travel Down This Road With Me (15)
Wings Of A Dove (14)
Wonders You Perform (11)
Wouldn't It Be Great (14)
Yearning (To Kiss You) (5)
Yesterday (1,7)
You Can't Hang On (Lookin' On) (11)

You Make My Skies Turn Blue (6)
You'll Never Walk Alone (3)
You're Everything (12)
Your Good Girl's Gonna Go Bad (4)
Your Love's Been A Long Time Coming (13)

WYNONNA '92
Born Christina Ciminella on 5/30/64 in Ashland, Kentucky. Country singer. Half of **The Judds** duo with her mother, Naomi. Sister of actress Ashley Judd.

DEBUT	PEAK	WKS	RIAA	CD	#	Album	$	Label
4/18/92	4	86	▲5	©	1	Wynonna	$10	Curb/MCA 10529
5/29/93	5	54	▲	©	2	Tell Me Why	$10	Curb/MCA 10822
						WYNONNA JUDD (above 2)		
3/2/96	9	26	▲	©	3	Revelations	$10	Curb/MCA 11090
4/26/97	72	10		©	4	Collection [G]	$10	Curb/MCA 11583
11/8/97	38	19	●	©	5	The Other Side	$10	Curb 53061
2/19/00	40	7		©	6	New Day Dawning	$15	Curb 541067 [2]

All Of That Love From Here (1)
Always Will (5)
Can't Nobody Love You (Like I Do) (6)
Chain Reaction (6)
Change The World (3)
Come Some Rainy Day (5)
Dance! Shout! (3)
Don't Look Back (3)
Don't You Throw That Mojo On Me (5)

Father Sun (2)
Free Bird (3)
Girls With Guitars (2,4)
Going Nowhere (6)
He Rocks (4)
Heaven Help My Heart (3,4)
I Can't Wait To Meet You (6)
I Just Drove By (2)
I Saw The Light (1,4)
I've Got Your Love (6)

Is It Over Yet (2,4)
It's Never Easy To Say Goodbye (1)
Just Like New (2)
Kind Of Fool Love Makes (5)
Learning To Live With Love Again (6)
Let's Make A Baby King (2)
Little Bit Of Love (Goes A Long, Long Way) (1)
Live With Jesus (1)

Lost Without You (6)
Love By Grace (3)
Love Like That (5)
Love's Funny That Way (5)
My Angel Is Here (3)
My Strongest Weakness (1,4)
New Day Dawning (6)
No One Else On Earth (1,4) *83*
Old Enough To Know Better (3)
Only Love (2,4)
Other Side (5)

Rock Bottom (2,4)
She Is His Only Need (1,4)
Somebody To Love You (3)
Tell Me Why (2,4) *77*
That Was Yesterday (2)
To Be Loved By You (3,4)
Troubled Heart And A Troubled Mind (1)
Tuff Enuff (6)
We Can't Unmake Love (5)
What It Takes (1)

When I Reach The Place I'm Goin' (1)
When Love Starts Talkin' (5) *98*
Who Am I Trying To Fool (6)
Why Now (5)
Wyld Unknown (5)

X

X '82
Rock group formed in Los Angeles: Exene Cervenka (vocals), Billy Zoom (guitar), **John Doe** (bass) and Don Bonebrake (drums). Zoom was replaced by Tony Gilkyson (son of Canadian singer Terry Gilkyson) in early 1987. Cervenka and Doe were married for a time.

DEBUT	PEAK	WKS	CD	#	Album	$	Label
6/6/81	165	5	©	1	Wild Gift	$15	Slash 107
7/17/82	76	15	©	2	Under The Big Black Sun	$12	Elektra 60150
10/8/83	86	23	©	3	More Fun In The New World	$12	Elektra 60283
					above 3 produced by Ray Manzarek		
8/17/85	89	14	©	4	Ain't Love Grand	$12	Elektra 60430
7/11/87	107	11	©	5	See How We Are	$12	Elektra 60492
5/14/88	175	5	©	6	Live At The Whiskey A Go-Go On The Fabulous Sunset Strip [L]	$15	Elektra 60788 [2]

Adult Books (1)
All Or Nothing (4)
Anyone Can Fill Your Shoes (5)
Around My Heart (4,6)
Back 2 The Base (1)
Because I Do (2,6)
Beyond And Back (1)
Blue Spark (2,6)
Breathless (3)
Burning House Of Love (4,6)
Call Of The Wreckin' Ball (6)
Come Back To Me (2)
Cyrano De Berger's Back (5)

Dancing With Tears In My Eyes (2)
Devil Doll (3,6)
Drunk In My Past (3)
4th Of July (5)
Have Nots (2)
Holiday Story (5)
Hot House (3)
House I Call Home (6)
How I (Learned My Lesson) (2)
Hungry Wolf (2,6)
I Must Not Think Bad Thoughts (3)

I See Red (3)
I'll Stand Up For You (4)
I'm Coming Over (1)
I'm Lost (5)
In The Time It Takes (5,6)
In This House That I Call Home (1)
It's Who You Know (1)
Johny Hit & Run Pauline (6)
Just Another Perfect Day (6)
Left & Right (5)
Little Honey (4)
Los Angeles (6)

Love Shack (4)
Make The Music Go Bang (3)
Motel Room In My Bed (2)
My Goodness (4,6)
My Soul Cries Your Name (4)
New World (3,6)
Once Over Twice (1)
Painting The Town Blue (3)
Poor Girl (1)
Real Child Of Hell (2)
Riding With Mary (2,6)
See How We Are (5)
Skin Deep Town (6)

So Long (6)
Some Other Time (1)
Supercharged (4)
Surprise Surprise (5,6)
True Love (3,6)
True Love Pt. #2 (3)
Under The Big Black Sun (2)
Unheard Music (6)
Universal Corner (1)
Watch The Sun Go Down (4)
We're Desperate (1)
We're Having Much More Fun (3)

What's Wrong With Me... (4)
When It Rains... (5)
When Our Love Passed Out On The Couch (1)
White Girl (1,6)
World's A Mess (6)
Year 1 (1,6)
You (5)

XAVIER '82
Funk group from Hartford, Connecticut: Ernest "Xavier" Smith (guitar, vocals), Ayanna Little, Emonie Branch and Chuck Hughes (vocals), Jeff Mitchell (guitar), Lyburn Downing (percussion), Ralph Hunt (bass) and Tim Williams (drums).

DEBUT	PEAK	WKS	#	Album	$	Label
4/24/82	129	7		Point Of Pleasure	$10	Liberty 51116

Dial The Love Man (634-5789)
Do It To The Max

Love Is On The One
Rock Me, Sock Me

Truly Devoted
What Goes Around

Work That Sucker To Death

X-CLAN '92
Rap group from New York City: Professor X, **Inspectah Deck**, Sugar Shaft and Architect Paradise. Inspectah Deck joined **Wu-Tang Clan**. Sugar Shaft died of AIDS on 9/1/95 (age 25).

DEBUT	PEAK	WKS	CD	#	Album	$	Label
6/2/90	97	25	©	1	To The East, Blackwards	$10	4th & B'way 4019
6/6/92	31	12	©	2	Xodus-The New Testament	$10	Polydor 513225

A.D.A.M. (2)
Cosmic Ark (2)
Day Of Outrage, Operation Snatchback (1)
Earth Bound (1)

F.T.P. (2)
Fire & Earth (100% Natural) (2)
Foreplay (2)
Funk Liberation (2)
Funkin' Lesson (1)

Grand Verbalizer, What Time Is It? (1)
Heed The Word Of The Brother (1)
Holy Rum Swig (2)

In The Ways Of The Scales (1)
Ooh Baby (2)
Raise The Flag (1)
Rhythem Of God (2)
Shaft's Big Score (1)

Tribal Jam (1)
Verbal Milk (1)
Verbal Papp (2)
Verbs Of Power (1)
Xodus (2)

XSCAPE '93
Female R&B vocal group from Atlanta: sisters LaTocha and Tamika Scott, with **Kandi** Burruss and Tameka Cottle.

DEBUT	PEAK	WKS	RIAA	CD	#	Album	$	Label
10/30/93	17	36	▲	©	1	Hummin' Comin' At 'Cha	$10	So So Def 57107
8/5/95	23	42	▲	©	2	Off The Hook	$10	So So Def 67022
5/30/98	28	33	▲	©	3	Traces Of My Lipstick	$10	So So Def 68042

All About Me (3)
All I Need (3)
Am I Dreaming (3) *31*
Arms Of The One Who Loves You (3) *7*
Can't Hang (2) *56*

Do Like Lovers Do (2)
Do You Know (3)
Do You Want To (2) *50*
Do Your Thang (2)
Feels So Good (2) *32*
Hard To Say Goodbye (2)

Hip Hop Barber Shop Request Line (2)
Hold On (3)
I Will (3)
Is My Living In Vain (1)
Just Kickin' It (1) *2*

Keep It On The Real (2)
Let Me Know (1)
Love On My Mind (1) *46*
Love's A Funny Thing (2)
My Little Secret (3) *9*
One Of Those Love Songs (3)

Pumpin' (1)
Runaround, The (3)
Softest Place On Earth (3)
Tonight (1)
Understanding (1) *8*
W.S.S. Deez Nuts (1)

What Can I Do (2)
Who Can I Run To (2) *8*
With You (1)
Work Me Slow (2)
Your Eyes (3)

XTC '81

Rock group formed in Wiltshire, England: Andy Partridge (guitar), Dave Gregory (keyboards), Colin Moulding (bass) and Terry Chambers (drums). All share vocals. Chambers left in 1986.

1)Black Sea 2)Oranges & Lemons 3)English Settlement

1/26/80	176	8	©	1	**Drums And Wires**	$12	Virgin 13134
11/22/80+	41	24	©	2	**Black Sea**	$12	Virgin 13147
3/20/82	48	20	©	3	**English Settlement**	$10	Epic 37943
2/25/84	145	5	©	4	**Mummer**	$10	Geffen 4027
11/10/84	178	5	©	5	**The Big Express**	$10	Geffen 24054
1/24/87	70	29	©	6	**Skylarking**	$10	Geffen 24117

later pressings substitute the track "Mermaid Smiled" with "Dear God"

3/18/89	44	21	©	7	**Oranges & Lemons**	$15	Geffen 24218 [2]
5/16/92	97	11	©	8	**Nonsuch**	$10	Geffen 24474
3/13/99	106	3	©	9	**Apple Venus Volume 1**	$10	TVT 3250
6/10/00	108	2	©	10	**Wasp Star (Apple Venus Volume 2)**	$10	TVT 3260

Across This Antheap (7)
All Of A Sudden (It's Too Late) (3)
All You Pretty Girls (5)
Another Satellite (6)
Ball And Chain (4)
Ballad Of Peter Pumpkinhead (8)
Ballet For A Rainy Day (6)
Beating Of Hearts (4)
Big Day (6)
Boarded Up (10)
Books Are Burning (8)
Bungalow (8)
Burning With Optimism's Flames (2)
Chalkhills And Children (7)
Church Of Women (10)
Complicated Game (1)
Crocodile (8)
Cynical Days (7)
Dear God (6)
Dear Madam Barnum (8)
Deliver Us From The Elements (4)
Disappointed (8)
Dying (6)
Earn Enough For Us (6)
Easter Theatre (9)
English Roundabout (3)
Everyday Story Of Smalltown (5)
Frivolous Tonight (9)
Fruit Nut (9)
Funk Pop A Roll (4)
Garden Of Earthly Delights (7)
Generals And Majors (2)
Grass (6)
Great Fire (4)
Green Man (9)
Harvest Festival (9)
Helicopter (1)
Here Comes President Kill Again (4)
Hold Me My Daddy (7)
Holly Up On Poppy (8)
Human Alchemy (4)
Humble Daisy (8)
I Bought Myself A Liarbird (9)
I Can't Own Her (9)
I Remember The Sun (5)
I'd Like That (9)
I'm The Man Who Murdered Love (10)
In Another Life (10)
In Loving Memory Of A Name (4)
It's Nearly Africa (3)
Jason And The Argonauts (3)
King For A Day (7)
Knights In Shining Karma (9)
Ladybird (4)
Last Balloon (9)
Life Begins At The Hop (1)
Living Through Another Cuba (2)
Love At First Sight (2)
Love On A Farmboy's Wages (4)
Loving, The (7)
Making Plans For Nigel (1)
Man Who Sailed Around His Soul (6)
Mayor Of Simpleton (7) *72*
Me And The Wind (4)
Meeting Place (6)
Melt The Guns (3)
Merely A Man (7)
Mermaid Smiled (6)
Millions (1)
Miniature Sun (7)
My Bird Performs (8)
My Brown Guitar (10)
No Language In Our Lungs (2)
No Thugs In Our House (3)
Omnibus (8)
One Of The Millions (5)
1000 Umbrellas (6)
Outside World (1)
Paper And Iron (Notes And Coins) (2)
Pink Thing (7)
Playground (10)
Poor Skeleton Steps Out (7)
Real By Reel (1)
Reign Of Blows (5)
Respectable Street (2)
River Of Orchids (9)
Roads Girdle The Globe (1)
Rocket From A Bottle (2)
Rook (8)
Runaways (3)
Sacrificial Bonfire (6)
Scarecrow People (7)
Scissor Man (1)
Seagulls Screaming Kiss Her, Kiss Her (5)
Season Cycle (6)
Senses Working Overtime (3)
Sgt. Rock (Is Going To Help Me) (2)
Shake You Donkey Up (5)
Smartest Monkeys (8)
Snowman (3)
Standing In For Joe (10)
Stupidly Happy (10)
Summer's Cauldron (6)
Ten Feet Tall (1)
That Is The Way (1)
That Wave (8)
That's Really Super, Supergirl (6)
Then She Appeared (8)
This World Over (5)
Towers Of London (2)
Train Running Low On Soul Coal (5)
Travels In Nihilon (2)
Ugly Underneath (8)
Wake Up (5)
War Dance (8)
We're All Light (10)
Wheel And The Maypole (10)
When You're Near Me I Have Difficulty (1)
Wonderland (4)
Wounded Horse (10)
Wrapped In Grey (8)
You And The Clouds Will Still Be Beautiful (10)
You're The Wish You Are I Had (5)
Your Dictionary (9)

XYMOX '89

Pop trio from Amsterdam, Holland: Ronny Moorings (vocals, guitar, keyboards), Pieter Nooten (keyboards) and Anka Wolbert (bass, vocals, keyboards).

| 6/3/89 | 165 | 10 | © | 1 | **Twist Of Shadows** .... | $10 | Wing 839233 |
| 5/11/91 | 163 | 2 | © | 2 | **Phoenix** .... | $10 | Wing 848516 |

At The End Of The Day (2)
Believe Me Sometimes (2)
Blind Hearts (1)
Clementina (1)
Craving (1)
Crossing The Water (2)
Dancing Barefoot (2)
Evelyn (1)
Imagination (1) *85*
In A City (1)
Mark The Days (2)
Million Things (1)
Obsession (1)
Phoenix Of My Heart (medley) (2)
River, The (1)
Shore Down Under (2)
Smile Like Heaven (2)
Tonight (1)
Wild Thing Outro (medley) (2)
Wonderland (2)
Written In The Stars (2)

XYZ '90

Hard-rock group from Los Angeles: Terry Ilous (vocals), Marc Diglio (guitar), Pat Fontaine (bass) and Paul Monroe (drums).

| 12/16/89+ | 99 | 24 | © | | **XYZ** .... | $10 | Enigma 73525 |

After The Rain
Come On N' Love Me
Follow The Night
Inside Out
Maggy
Nice Day To Die
Souvenirs
Take What You Can
Tied Up
What Keeps Me Loving You

XZIBIT '01

Born in Detroit; raised in New Mexico. Male rapper.

11/2/96	74	4	©	1	**At The Speed Of Life**	$10	Loud 66816
9/12/98	58	5	©	2	**40 Dayz & 40 Nightz**	$10	Loud 67578
12/30/00+	12	28	▲	©	3	**Restless**	$10	Loud 1885

Alkaholik (3)
At The Speed Of Life (1)
Been A Long Time (3)
Best Of Things (3)
Bird's Eye View (1)
Carry The Weight (3)
Chamber Music (2)
D.N.A. (Drugs-N-Alkahol) (3)
Deeper (2)
Don't Approach Me (3)
Don't Hate Me (1)
Double Time (3)
Enemies & Friends (1)
Eyes May Shine (1)
Focus (3)
Foundation, The (1)
Front 2 Back (3)
Fuckin' You Right (3)
Get Your Walk On (3)
Grand Opening (1)
Handle Your Business (2)
Hit & Run (Part II) (1)
Inside Job (2)
Just Maintain (1)
Kenny Parker Show 2001 (3)
Last Words (1)
Let It Rain (2)
Los Angeles Times (2)
Loud & Clear (3)
Mrs. Crabtree (1)
Nobody Sound Like Me (2)
Paparazzi (1) *83*
Plastic Surgery (1)
Positively Negative (1)
Pu**y Pop (2)
Recycled Assassins (2)
Rimz & Tirez (2)
Shroomz (2)
Sorry I'm Away So Much (3)
3 Card Molly (2)
U Know (3)
What U See Is What U Get (2) *50*
X (3) *76*

Y

YACHTS '79

Rock group from Liverpool, England: Martin Watson (guitar), Henry Priestman (keyboards), Martin Dempsey (bass) and Bob Bellis (drums). All share vocals.

| 10/20/79 | 179 | 3 | | | **S.O.S.** .... | $12 | Polydor 6220 |

Box 202
Heads Will Turn
I Can't Stay Long
In A Second
Look Back In Love
Love You, Love You
Mantovani's Hits
Semaphore Love
Suffice To Say
Tantamount To Bribery
Then And Now
Yachting Type

YAMASHTA, Stomu '76

Born on 3/15/47 in Kyoto, Japan. Eclectic composer/percussionist.

| 8/21/76 | 60 | 12 | | 1 | **Go** | $12 | Island 9387 |

STOMU YAMASHTA/STEVE WINWOOD/MICHAEL SHRIEVE

| 10/15/77 | 156 | 6 | © | 2 | **Go Too** .... | $12 | Arista 4138 |

YAMASHTA, Stomu — Cont'd

Air Over (1)
Beauty (2)
Carnival (1)
Crossing The Line (1)
Ecliptic (2)
Ghost Machine (1)
Madness (2)
Man Of Leo (1)
Mysteries Of Love (2)
Nature (1)
Prelude (2)
Seen You Before (2)
Solitude (1)
Space Requiem (1)
Space Song (1)
Space Theme (1)
Stellar (1)
Surfspin (1)
Time Is Here (1)
Wheels Of Fortune (2)
Winner/Loser (1)
You And Me (2)

Y&T '84

Hard-rock group from San Francisco: Dave Meniketti (vocals, guitar), Joey Alves (guitar), Philip Kennemore (bass) and Leonard Haze (drums). Haze was replaced by Jimmy DeGrasso in 1986. Alves was replaced by Stef Burns in 1989. Band name stands for Yesterday & Today.

DEBUT	PEAK	WKS		CD	#	Title		$	Label & Number
9/10/83	103	12			1	Mean Streak		$10	A&M 4960
8/18/84	46	17		©	2	In Rock We Trust		$10	A&M 5007
7/20/85	70	17			3	Open Fire	[L]	$10	A&M 5076
11/23/85	91	12		©	4	Down For The Count		$10	A&M 5101
7/11/87	78	13		©	5	Contagious		$10	Geffen 24142
6/2/90	110	8		©	6	Ten		$10	Geffen 24283

All American Boy (4)
Anything For Money (4)
Anytime At All (4)
Armed And Dangerous (5)
Barroom Boogie (3)
Bodily Harm (5)
Break Out Tonight! (2)
Breaking Away (1)
City (6)
Come In From The Rain (6)
Contagious (5)
Don't Be Afraid Of The Dark (6)
Don't Stop Runnin' (2)
Don't Tell Me What To Wear (4)
Down And Dirty (1)
Eyes Of A Stranger (5)
Face Like An Angel (4)
Fight For Your Life (5)
Forever (3)
Girl Crazy (6)
Go For The Throat (3)
Goin' Off The Deep End (6)
Hands Of Time (4)
Hang 'Em High (1)
Hard Times (6)
I Believe In You (3)
I'll Cry For You (5)
I'll Keep On Believin' (Do You Know) (2)
In The Name Of Rock (4)
Kid Goes Crazy (4)
L.A. Rocks (5)
Let It Out (6)
Life, Life, Life (2)
Lipstick And Leather (2)
Lonely Side Of Town (1)
Looks Like Trouble (1)
Lucy (6)
Masters And Slaves (2)
Mean Streak (1)
Midnight In Tokyo (1)
Open Fire (5)
Red Hot & Ready (6)
Rescue Me (3)
Rhythm Or Not (5)
Rock & Roll's Gonna Save The World (2)
Sentimental Fool (1)
She's A Liar (2)
She's Gone (6)
Straight Thru The Heart (1)
Summertime Girls (3,4) 55
Surrender (6)
Take You To The Limit (1)
Temptation (5)
Ten Lovers (6)
This Time (2)
25 Hours A Day (3)
(Your Love Is) Drivin' Me Crazy (2)
Your Mama Don't Dance (4)

★413★ YANKOVIC, "Weird Al" '96

Born on 10/23/59 in Lynwood, California. Novelty singer/accordionist. Specializes in song parodies. Starred in the movie *UHF*.

1)Bad Hair Day 2)Running With Scissors 3)Off The Deep End

DEBUT	PEAK	WKS		CD	#	Title		$	Label & Number
5/21/83	139	8		©	1	"Weird Al" Yankovic	[N]	$10	Rock 'n' Roll 38679
3/17/84	17	23	▲	©	2	"Weird Al" Yankovic In 3-D	[N]	$10	Rock 'n' Roll 39221
7/13/85	50	16	●	©	3	Dare To Be Stupid	[N]	$10	Rock 'n' Roll 40033
11/15/86	177	4		©	4	Polka Party!	[N]	$10	Rock 'n' Roll 40520
5/7/88	27	26	▲	©	5	Even Worse	[N]	$10	Rock 'n' Roll 44149
8/19/89	146	4		©	6	UHF/Original Motion Picture Soundtrack And Other Stuff	[N-S]	$10	Rock 'n' Roll 45265
5/2/92	17	27	●	©	7	Off The Deep End	[N]	$10	Scotti Brothers 75256
10/23/93	46	24	●	©	8	Alapalooza	[N]	$10	Scotti Brothers 75415
12/17/94	198	1		©	9	Greatest Hits Volume II	[G-N]	$10	Scotti Brothers 75456
3/30/96	14	56	▲	©	10	Bad Hair Day	[N]	$10	Rock 'n' Roll 75500
7/17/99	16	32	▲	©	11	Running With Scissors	[N]	$10	Way Moby 32118

Achy Breaky Song (8,9)
Addicted To Spuds (4)
Airline Amy (7)
Albuquerque (11)
Alimony (5)
Alternative Polka (10)
Amish Paradise (10) 53
Another One Rides The Bus (1)
Attack Of The Radioactive Hamsters From A Planet Near Mars (6)
Bedrock Anthem (8,9)
Biggest Ball Of Twine In Minnesota (6)
Bohemian Polka (8)
Brady Bunch (2)
Buckingham Blues (1)
Buy Me A Condo (2)
Cable TV (3)
Callin' In Sick (10)
Cavity Search (10)
Check's In The Mail (1)
Christmas At Ground Zero (4,9)
Dare To Be Stupid (3)
Dog Eat Dog (4)
Don't Wear Those Shoes (4)
Eat It (2)
Everything You Know Is Wrong (10)
Fat (5) 99
Frank's 2000" TV (8)
Fun Zone (6)
Gandhi II (6)
Generic Blues (6)
George Of The Jungle (3)
Germs (5)
Girls Just Want To Have Lunch (3)
Good Enough For Now (4)
Good Old Days (5)
Gotta Boogie (1)
Grapefruit Diet (11)
Gump (10)
Happy Birthday (1)
Harvey The Wonder Hamster (8)
Headline News (9)
Here's Johnny (2)
Hooked On Polkas Medley (3)
Hot Rocks Polka (6)
I Can't Watch This (7)
I Lost On Jeopardy (2) 81
I Love Rocky Road (1)
I Remember Larry (10)
I Think I'm A Clone Now (5)
I Want A New Duck (3)
I Was Only Kidding (7)
I'll Be Mellow When I'm Dead (1)
I'm So Sick Of You (10)
Isle Thing (6)
It's All About The Pentiums (11)
Jerry Springer (11)
Jurassic Park (8,9)
King Of Suede (2) 62
Lasagna (5)
Let Me Be Your Hog (6)
Like A Surgeon (3) 47
Livin' In The Fridge (8)
Living With A Hernia (4)
Melanie (5)
Midnight Star (4)
Money For Nothing/Beverly Hillbillies (6,9)
Mr. Frump In The Iron Lung (1)
Mr. Popeil (2)
My Baby's In Love With Eddie Vedder (11)
My Bologna (1)
Nature Trail To Hell (2)
Night Santa Went Crazy (10)
One More Minute (3)
One Of Those Days (4)
Phony Calls (10)
Plumbing Song (7)
Polka Party! (4)
Polka Power! (11)
Polka Your Eyes Out (7,9)
Polkas On 45 (2)
Pretty Fly For A Rabbi (11)
(This Song's Just) Six Words Long (3)
Ricky (1) 63
Rocky XIII, Theme From (2)
Saga Begins (11)
She Drives Like Crazy (6)
She Never Told Me She Was A Mime (8)
Since You've Been Gone (10)
Slime Creatures From Outer Space (3)
Smells Like Nirvana (7,9) 35
Spam (6)
Spatula City (8)
Stop Draggin' My Car Around (1)
Stuck In A Closet With Vanna White (7)
Such A Groovy Guy (1)
Syndicated Inc. (10)
Taco Grande (7)
Talk Soup (8)
That Boy Could Dance (2)
This Is The Life (3,9)
Toothless People (4)
Traffic Jam (8)
Trigger Happy (7)
Truck Drivin' Song (11)
Twister (5)
UHF (6,9)
Velvet Elvis (5)
Waffle King (8)
Weird Al Show Theme (11)
When I Was Your Age (7)
White Stuff (3)
Yoda (3)
You Don't Love Me Anymore (7,9)
You Make Me (5)
Young, Dumb & Ugly (8)
Your Horoscope For Today (11)

★253★ YANNI '94

Born Yiannis Chryssolmalis on 11/14/54 in Kalamata, Greece. New Age keyboardist.

1)Live At The Acropolis 2)In The Mirror 3)If I Could Tell You

DEBUT	PEAK	WKS		CD	#	Title		$	Label & Number
8/4/90+	29	93	▲²	©	1	Reflections Of Passion	C:#3/71 [I-K]	$10	Private Music 2067
11/30/91+	60	17	●	©	2	In Celebration Of Life	C:#14/3 [I-K]	$10	Private Music 2093

above 2 feature selections from albums released from 1986-89

3/28/92	32	35	▲	©	3	Dare To Dream	C:#5/80 [I]	$10	Private Music 82096
4/24/93	24	73	▲	©	4	In My Time	[I]	$10	Private Music 82106
3/19/94	5	114	▲⁴	©	5	Live At The Acropolis	[I-L]	$10	Private Music 82116

recorded on 9/25/93 in Athens, Greece

5/3/97	17	19	●	©	6	In The Mirror	[I-K]	$10	Private Music 82150
5/24/97	142	2		©	7	Port Of Mystery	[I-K]	$10	Windham Hill 11241
9/13/97	42	22	●	©	8	Devotion: The Best Of Yanni	[I-K]	$10	Private Music 82153
11/22/97	21	33	▲	©	9	Tribute	[I-L]	$10	Virgin 44981
5/1/99	98	8		©	10	Love Songs	[I]	$10	Private Music 82167
10/21/00	20	22	●	©	11	If I Could Tell You	[I]	$10	Virgin 49893

Acroyali (1,5)
Adagio In C Minor (9)
After The Sunrise (7)
Almost A Whisper (1,10)
Aria (3,6,8)
Before I Go (4,6,10)
Butterfly Dance (7)
Chasing Shadows (9)
Dance With A Stranger (9)
Deliverance (9)
Desire (3)
Enchantment (4,6,10)
End Of August (4,6,8)
Face In The Photograph (3,6)
Farewell (1,7)
Felitsa (3,4,10)
First Touch (1,10)
Flame Within (11)
Flight Of Fantasy (1,8)
Forbidden Dreams (6)
Highland (11)
If I Could Tell You (11)
In The Mirror (3,4,6,10)
In The Morning Light (4,6,10)
In Your Eyes (11)
Keys To Imagination (2,5)
Looking Glass (2,7)
Love For Life (3,6,8)
Love Is All (9)
Magus, The (7)

YANNI — Cont'd

Marching Season (2,8)	November Sky (11)	Rain Must Fall (1,5)	Someday (2)	To The One Who Knows	Whispers In The Dark (4,10)
Mermaid, The (1)	On Sacred Ground (11)	Reason For Rainbows (11)	Song For Antarctica (2,8)	(3,8,10)	Wishing Well (11)
Midnight Hymn (11)	Once Upon A Time (3,6,8)	Reflections Of Passion (1,5,8)	Southern Exposure (9)	Tribute (9)	With An Orchid (11)
Nice To Meet You (3,8)	One Man's Dream (4,5,6)	Renegade (9)	Sphynx, The (7)	True Nature (1)	Within Attraction (2,5,6,8)
Night To Remember (3,8)	Only A Memory (4,8)	Sand Dance (2)	Standing In Motion (2,5)	Until The Last Moment (4,5)	Word In Private (1)
Nightingale (9)	Port Of Mystery (7)	Santorini (2,5,8)	Street Level (7)	Walk In The Rain (11)	You Only Live Once (3,7)
Niki Nana (We're One) (9)	Prelude (9)	Secret Vows (1,10)	Swept Away (1,5)	Walkabout (2)	
Nostalgia (1,5)	Quiet Man (1,6)	So Long My Friend (3,6,10)	To Take...To Hold (4,8,10)	Waltz In 7/8 (9)	

YARBROUGH, Glenn   '65
Born on 1/12/30 in Milwaukee. Folk singer. Lead singer of **The Limeliters** (1959-63).

1)Baby The Rain Must Fall 2)The Lonely Things 3)It's Gonna Be Fine

DEBUT	PEAK	WKS	CD	#	Title		$	Label & Number
9/19/64	142	4		1	One More Round		$20	RCA Victor 2905
5/8/65	112	8		2	Come Share My Life		$20	RCA Victor 3301
6/12/65	35	24	©	3	Baby The Rain Must Fall		$15	RCA Victor 3422
11/6/65	75	12	©	4	It's Gonna Be Fine		$15	RCA Victor 3472
6/25/66	61	24		5	The Lonely Things		$15	RCA Victor 3539
11/5/66	85	9		6	Live At The Hungry i	[L]	$15	RCA Victor 3661
5/27/67	159	14		7	For Emily, Whenever I May Find Her		$15	RCA Victor 3801
9/16/67	141	18		8	Honey & Wine		$15	RCA Victor 3860
11/9/68	188	2		9	Each Of Us Alone (the words and music of Rod McKuen)		$15	Warner 1736
5/10/69	189	5		10	Glenn Yarbrough Sings The Rod McKuen Songbook	[K]	$15	RCA Victor 6018 [2]

Above The Wave (9)	Gently Here Beside Me (7)	Kind Of Loving (5)	Only Love (6,10)	Things Men Do (6,10)
Ain't You Glad You're Livin', Joe	Goin' Down The Track (900	Listen To The Warm (9)	People Change (5)	Times Gone By (10)
(8,10)	Miles) (6)	Lonely Things (5)	Pleasures Of The Harbor (7)	Tomorrow Is A Long Time (7)
Alamo Junction (10)	Golden Under The Sun (7)	Lonesome (3)	Rain Drops (1)	Until It's Time For You To Go
All The Time (8)	Half A World Away (4,10)	Long Time Blues (3)	Ring Of Bright Water (4)	(7)
Baby, I'm Gone Again (1)	Happy Birthday To Me (8,10)	Love Come A-Tricklin' Down (2)	Rose (6,10)	Walk On Little Boy (3)
Baby The Rain Must Fall	Happy Whistler (2)	Love, Let Me Not Hunger (3,10)	Rusting In The Rain (3,10)	Walking On Air (8)
(3) *12*	Hello (5)	Love's Been Good To Me (1)	She (3,10)	Warm And Gentle Girls (2,10)
Beautiful Strangers (9)	Her Lover (1)	Lovers, The (1)	She's Too Far Above Me (3)	Way The World Would Be (1)
Billy Goat Hill (3)	Here Am I (8)	Mattie Down (2)	Single Man (9)	What The World Needs Now (4)
Brownstone (5)	Honey And Wine (8)	Me And My Dog (Old Blue) (6)	So Long, San Francisco (5)	What You Gonna Do? (6)
Bull Frog Song (3)	Hotel Room (9)	Mermaid, The (6)	So Many Others (8)	When Flora Was Mine (10)
Channing Way, 2 (5)	How Deep Is Down (6,10)	More I Cannot Wish You (2)	Some Trust In Chariots (6,10)	When Summer Ends (2,10)
Cloudy Summer Afternoon (1)	Hummingbird (2)	Music Of The World A Turnin'	Sometimes (4,10)	Where Are We Now? (9)
Come Share My Life (2)	I Hate To See The Sun Go	(6)	Stanyan Street (2,10)	Where Are You Going With The
Comes And Goes (7)	Down (4)	Never Let Her Go (4)	Stanyan Street, Revisited (5)	Rain (6)
Crucifixion (7)	I Wonder (1)	New "Frankie And Johnnie"	Summer Sunshine (4)	Where Does Love Go (4)
Down In The Jungle (4)	I'll Catch The Sun (9)	Song (1)	Summer's Long (6,10)	Women, The (5)
Each Of Us Alone (9)	I'll Remember You (8)	Night Song (5)	Summertime Of Days (5)	Word Before Goodbye (5)
Everybody's Rich But Us (3,10)	I'm Strong But I Like Roses (9)	No One To Talk My Troubles	Ten O'Clock, All Is Well (The	Worry Is A Rockin' Chair (1)
Everybody's Wrong (7)	I've Been To Town (3)	To (2)	Town Crier's Song) (1)	Young Girl (2)
Fields Of Wonder (8,10)	Island Of The Mind (4,10)	Now That They're Playing A	Thank You (6,10)	
For Emily, Whenever I May	Isle In The Water (1,10)	Love Song (4,10)	That's The Way It's Gonna Be	
Find Her (7)	**It's Gonna Be Fine** (4) *54*	One Day Soon (6,10)	(2)	
French Girl (7)	It's Raining (9)	One More Round (1)	They Are Gone (8)	

YARBROUGH & PEOPLES   '81
Male-female R&B vocal duo from Dallas: Cavin Yarbrough and Alisa Peoples.

DEBUT	PEAK	WKS		#	Title		$	Label & Number
12/27/80+	16	24	●	1	The Two Of Us		$12	Mercury 3834
4/14/84	90	16		2	Be A Winner		$10	Total Experience 5700

Be A Winner (2)	Don't Waste Your Time (2) *48*	Only Love You (2)	Let Me Have It (From The Start)	Two Of Us (1)
Come To Me (1)	Easy Tonight (1)	I Want You Back Again (1)	(2)	Who Said That (2)
Crazy (1)	I Believe I'm Falling In Love (1)	I'll Be There (2)	Power, The (2)	You're My Song (1)
Don't Stop The Music (1) *19*	I Gave My All (To You) (2)	I'm Ready To Jam (2)	Third Degree (1)	

YARDBIRDS, The   '67
Rock group formed in England: Keith Relf (vocals, harmonica), **Eric Clapton** and Chris Dreja (guitars), Paul Samwell-Smith (bass, keyboards) and Jim McCarty (drums). **Jeff Beck** replaced Clapton after first album. Samwell-Smith left in 1966; Dreja switched to bass and **Jimmy Page** (guitar) was added. Beck left in December 1966. Group disbanded in July 1968. Page formed the New Yardbirds in October 1968, which evolved into **Led Zeppelin**. Relf died from electrocution on 5/14/76 (age 33). Group inducted into the Rock and Roll Hall of Fame in 1992.

DEBUT	PEAK	WKS	CD	#	Title		$	Label & Number
7/31/65	96	11	©	1	For Your Love		$200	Epic 26167
12/18/65+	53	33		2	Having a Rave Up with The Yardbirds		$100	Epic 26177
8/27/66	52	16		3	Over Under Sideways Down		$100	Epic 26210
4/29/67	28	37		4	The Yardbirds' Greatest Hits	[G]	$75	Epic 26246
8/12/67	80	8	©	5	Little Games		$75	Epic 26313
10/3/70	155	6		6	The Yardbirds/Featuring Performances By Jeff Beck, Eric Clapton, Jimmy Page	[K]	$60	Epic 30135 [2]

Certain Girl (1,6)	Got To Hurry (1,6)	I Can't Make Your Way (3)	No Excess Baggage (5)	Still I'm Sad (2,4)
Drinking Muddy Water (5,6)	**Happenings Ten Years Time**	I Wish You Would (1,6)	Only The Black Rose (5,6)	Sweet Music (1)
Ever Since The World Began	**Ago** (4) *30*	I'm A Man (2,4) *17*	Over Under Sideways Down	Tinker, Tailor, Soldier, Sailor
(3,6)	He's Always There (3)	I'm Not Talking (1,4)	(3,4) *13*	(5,6)
Evil Hearted You (2)	Heart Full Of Soul (2,4) *9*	Jeff's Boogie (3,6)	Putty (In Your Hands) (1)	Train Kept A-Rollin' (2,6)
Farewell (3,6)	Here 'Tis (2,6)	**Little Games** (5,6) *51*	Respectable (6)	Turn Into Earth (3,6)
For Your Love (1,4) *6*	Hot House Of Omagarashid	Little Soldier Boy (5)	**Shapes Of Things** (4) *11*	What Do You Want (3,6)
Glimpses (5)	(3,6)	Lost Woman (3,6)	Smile On Me (5,6)	White Summer (5,6)
Good Morning Little Schoolgirls	I Ain't Done Wrong (1,6)	My Girl Sloopy (1)	Smokestack Lightning (2,4)	You're A Better Man Than I (2)
(1)	I Ain't Got You (1,6)	New York City Blues (4)	Stealing, Stealing (5)	

YARROW, Peter   '72
Born on 5/31/38 in New York City. Folk singer/songwriter/guitarist. Member of **Peter, Paul & Mary**.

DEBUT	PEAK	WKS			Title		$	Label & Number
3/4/72	163	8			Peter		$15	Warner 2599

Beautiful City	Goodbye Josh	Plato's Song	Take Off Your Mask	Wings Of Time
Don't Ever Take Away My	Greenwood	River Of Jordan	Tall Pine Trees	
Freedom *100*	Mary Beth	Side Road	Weave Me The Sunshine	

YAZ '82

Pop duo from England: **Alison Moyet** and Vince Clarke (formerly of **Depeche Mode**). Duo formerly named **Yazoo**. Clarke later formed **Erasure**.

| 10/2/82 | 92 | 32 ▲ | © | 1 Upstairs At Eric's | C:#12/79 | $10 | Sire 23737 |

YAZOO

| 8/13/83 | 69 | 13 | © | 2 You And Me Both | $10 | Sire 23903 |

And On (2)
Anyone (2)
Bad Connection (1)
Bring Your Love Down (Didn't I) (1)

Don't Go (1)
Good Times (2)
Goodbye Seventies (1)
I Before E Except After C (1)
In My Room (1)

Midnight (1)
Mr. Blue (1)
Nobody's Diary (2)
Ode To Boy (2)
Only You (1) 67

Situation (1) 73
Softly Over (2)
State Farm (2)
Sweet Thing (2)
Too Pieces (1)

Unmarked (2)
Walk Away From Love (2)
Winter Kills (1)

★330★ YEARWOOD, Trisha '97

Born on 9/19/64 in Monticello, Georgia. Country singer. Married to Robert Reynolds (of **The Mavericks**) from 1994-99.
1)Songbook - A Collection Of Hits 2)Real Live Woman 3)Inside Out

7/20/91	31	83	▲² ©	1 Trisha Yearwood	$10	MCA 10297
9/19/92	46	46	▲ ©	2 Hearts In Armor	$10	MCA 10641
11/13/93	40	20	▲ ©	3 The Song Remembers When	$10	MCA 10911
12/10/94	105	6	● ©	4 The Sweetest Gift	C:#46/1 [X]	$10	MCA 11091

Christmas charts: 17/'94, 37/'99, 39/'00

3/4/95	28	24	▲ ©	5 Thinkin' About You	$10	MCA 11201
9/14/96	52	16	©	6 Everybody Knows	$10	MCA 11477
9/13/97	4	54	▲⁴ ©	7 Songbook - A Collection Of Hits	[G]	$10	MCA 70011
8/1/98	33	25	▲ ©	8 Where Your Road Leads	$10	MCA 70023
4/15/00	27	12	● ©	9 Real Live Woman	$10	MCA 70102
6/23/01	29	15↑	©	10 Inside Out	$10	MCA 70200

Away In A Manger (4)
Believe Me Baby (I Lied) (6)
Better Your Heart Than Mine (3)
Bring Me All Your Lovin' (8)
Christmas Song (Chestnuts Roasting On An Open Fire) (4)
Come Back When It Ain't Rainin' (9)
Down On My Knees (2,7)
Everybody Knows (6)
Fairytale (5)
Fools Like Me (1)
For A While (10)
For Reasons I've Forgotten (2)
Hard Promises To Keep (3)
Harmless Heart (10)
Heart Like A Sad Song (8)

Hearts In Armor (2)
Hello, I'm Gone (6)
Here Comes Temptation (3)
How Do I Live (7) 23
I Did (9)
I Don't Fall In Love So Easy (3)
I Don't Paint Myself Into Corners (10)
I Don't Want To Be The One (8)
I Need You (6)
I Wanna Go Too Far (3)
I Want To Live Again (6)
I Would've Loved You Anyway (10) 45
I'll Still Love You More (8) 65
I'm Still Alive (9)
If I Ain't Got You (3)
In Another's Eyes (7)
Inside Out (10)
It Wasn't His Child (4)

It's Alright (6)
Let It Snow! Let It Snow! Let It Snow! (4)
Like We Never Had A Broken Heart (1,7)
Little Hercules (6)
Lonesome Dove (1)
Love Alone (10)
Love Let Go (10)
Love Me Or Leave Me Alone (10)
Love Wouldn't Lie To Me (8)
Lover Is Forever (6)
Lying To The Moon (3)
Maybe It's Love (6)
Melancholy Blue (10)
Mr. Radio (3)
Nearest Distant Shore (2)
Never Let You Go Again (8)
Nightingale, The (3)

O Mexico (5)
Oh Lonesome You (2)
On A Bus To St. Cloud (5)
One In A Row (3)
One Love (9)
Perfect Love (6)
Powerful Thing (8) 50
Real Live Woman (9) 81
Reindeer Boogie (4)
Restless Kind (5)
Sad Eyes (9)
Santa Claus Is Back In Town (4)
Second Chance (10)
Seven Year Ache (10)
She's In Love With The Boy (1,7)
Some Days (9)
Song Remembers When (3,7) 82

Sweet Little Jesus Boy (4)
Sweetest Gift (4)
Take A Walk Through Bethlehem (4)
That Ain't The Way I Heard It (8)
That's What I Like About You (1)
There Goes My Baby (8) 93
There's A New Kid In Town (4)
Thinkin' About You (5,7)
Those Words We Said (5)
Till I Get It Right (9)
Too Bad You're No Good (9)
Try Me Again (9)
Under The Rainbow (6)
Victim Of The Game (1)
Walkaway Joe (2,7)
When A Love Song Sings The Blues (9)

When Goodbye Was A Word (1)
When We Were Still In Love (10)
Where Are You Now (9)
Where Your Road Leads (8)
Whisper Of Your Heart (1)
Wild For You Baby (9)
Woman Before Me (1,7)
Woman Walk The Line (3)
Wouldn't Any Woman (8)
Wrong Side Of Memphis (2,7)
XXX's And OOO's (An American Girl) (5,7)
You Can Sleep While I Drive (5)
You Don't Have To Move That Mountain (2)
You Done Me Wrong (And That Ain't Right) (1)
You Say You Will (2)

YELLA '96

Born Antoine Carraby in Los Angeles. Male rapper. Member of **N.W.A.**

| 4/13/96 | 82 | 4 | © | One Mo Nigga Ta Go | $10 | Street Life 75488 |

Ain't No Luv
Dat's How I'm Livin

4 Tha E
Neva Had A Chance

Not Long Ago
Send 4 Me

So In Luv
Streets Won't Let Me Go

2Two Face
Westside Story

YELLO '87

Computer/synthesizer duo from Zurich, Switzerland: Dieter Meier and Boris Blank.

7/16/83	184	4	©	1 You Gotta Say Yes To Another Excess	$12	Elektra 60271
9/26/87	92	10	©	2 One Second	$10	Mercury 832765
4/15/89	152	9	©	3 Flag	$10	Mercury 836426

Alhambra (3)
Blazing Saddles (3)
Call It Love (2)
Crash Dance (1)
Dr Van Steiner (3)
Goldrush (2)

Great Mission (1)
Hawaiian Chance (2)
Heavy Whispers (2)
I Love You (1)
La Habanera (2)
Le Secret Farida (2)

Lost Again (1)
Moon On Ice (2)
No More Words (1)
Of Course I'm Lying (3)
Oh Yeah (2) 51
Otto Di Catania (3)

Pumping Velvet (1)
Race, The (3)
Rhythm Divine (2)
Salut Mayoumba (1)
Santiago (3)
Si Senor The Hairy Grill (2)

Smile On You (1)
Swing (1)
3rd Of June (3)
Tied Up (3)
Tied Up In Gear (3)

You Gotta Say Yes To Another Excess (1)

YELLOWJACKETS '83

Pop-jazz group formed in Los Angeles in 1980 as **Robben Ford**'s backing band: Russell Ferrante (keyboards), Marc Russo (sax), Jimmy Haslip (bass) and Ricky Lawson (drums). Haslip was a member of **Blackjack**.

5/28/83	145	10	©	1 Mirage A Trois	[I]	$10	Warner 23813
4/13/85	179	4	©	2 Samurai Samba	[I]	$10	Warner 25204
9/6/86	195	2	©	3 Shades	[I]	$10	MCA 5752

And You Know That (3)
Black Tie (3)
Booby Trap, Theme From ..see: Oasis
Claire's Song (1)

Daddy's Gonna Miss You (2)
Deat Beat (2)
Elamar (1)
Goin' Home (1)
Homecoming (2)

I Got Rhythm (1)
Lonely Weekend (2)
Los Mambos (2)
Man In The Moon (1)
New Shoes (3)

Nimbus (1)
Oasis (3)
One Family (3)
Pass It On (1)
Regular Folks (3)

Revelation (3)
Samurai Samba (2)
Silverlake (2)
Sonja's Sanfona (3)
Sylvania (3)

Top Secret (1)

YELLOW MAGIC ORCHESTRA '80

Electronic trio from Japan: Ryuichi Sakamoto, Yukihiro Takahashi and Haruomi Hosono.

| 1/26/80 | 81 | 21 | © | 1 Yellow Magic Orchestra | [I] | $12 | Horizon 736 |
| 9/20/80 | 177 | 2 | © | 2 X Multiplies | $12 | A&M 4813 |

Behind The Mask (2)
Bridge Over Troubled Music (1)
Citizens Of Science (2)

Computer Game "Theme From The Circus" (1) 60
Computer Game (Theme from The Invader) (1)

Cosmic Surfin' (1)
Day Tripper (2)
Firecracker (1)
La Femme Chinoise (1)

Mad Pierrot (1)
Multiplies (2)
Nice Age (2)
Rydeen (2)

Simoon (1)
Solid State Survivor (2)
Technopolis (2)
Yellow Magic (Tong Poo) (1)

YES ★95★ '72

Progressive-rock group formed in London: **Jon Anderson** (vocals), Peter Banks (guitar), Tony Kaye (keyboards), **Chris Squire** (bass) and **Bill Bruford** (drums). Banks, who went on to form **Flash** and **After The Fire**, replaced by **Steve Howe** in 1971. Kaye (joined **Badfinger** in 1978) replaced by **Rick Wakeman** in 1971. Bruford left to join **King Crimson**, replaced by Alan White in late 1972. Wakeman replaced by **Patrick Moraz** in 1974, re-joined in 1976 when Moraz left. Wakeman and Anderson left in 1980, replaced by **The Buggles'** Trevor Horne (guitar) and Geoff Downes (keyboards). Group disbanded in 1980. Howe and Downes joined **Asia**. Re-formed in 1983 with Anderson, Kaye, Squire, White and South African guitarist **Trevor Rabin**. Anderson left group in 1988. **Anderson, Bruford, Wakeman, Howe** formed self-named group in early 1989. Yes reunited in 1991 with Anderson, Bruford, Wakeman, Howe, Kaye, Squire, White and Rabin. Bruford, Wakeman and Howe had left group by 1994. Lineup in 1996: Anderson, Howe, Squire, Wakeman and White. Billy SHerwood replaced Wakeman in 1997.

1)Close To The Edge 2)Fragile 3)90125 4)Relayer 5)Tales From Topographic Oceans

DEBUT	PEAK	WKS	RIAA	CD	ARTIST — Album Title	Catalog	Sym	$	Label & Number
5/8/71+	40	50	▲	© 1	The Yes Album	C:#25/12		$15	Atlantic 8283
1/22/72	4	46	▲²	© 2	Fragile	C:#5/30		$15	Atlantic 7211
10/7/72	3	32	▲	© 3	Close To The Edge	C:#25/12		$15	Atlantic 7244
5/26/73	12	32	▲	© 4	Yessongs		[L]	$25	Atlantic 100 [3]
2/2/74	6	27	●	© 5	Tales From Topographic Oceans			$20	Atlantic 908 [2]
12/28/74+	5	16	●	© 6	Relayer			$12	Atlantic 18122
3/22/75	17	12		© 7	Yesterdays		[K]	$12	Atlantic 18103
7/30/77	8	21	●	© 8	Going For The One			$12	Atlantic 19106
10/14/78	10	14	▲	© 9	Tormato			$12	Atlantic 19202
9/13/80	18	19		© 10	Drama			$12	Atlantic 16019
12/20/80+	43	12			11	Yesshows		[L]	$15	Atlantic 510 [2]
1/9/82	142	5	▲	© 12	Classic Yes		[K]	$10	Atlantic 19320
7/24/82	36ᶜ	2		© 13	Yes		[E]	$10	Atlantic 8243
					released in 1969				
12/3/83+	5	53	▲³	© 14	90125			$10	Atco 90125
					title refers to label number				
11/30/85	81	11			15	9012Live - The Solos		[L]	$10	Atco 90474
10/17/87	15	30	▲	© 16	Big Generator			$10	Atco 90522
7/1/89	30	16	●	© 17	Anderson, Bruford, Wakeman, Howe			$10	Arista 90126
5/18/91	15	19	●	© 18	Union			$10	Arista 8643
11/13/93	164	2		© 19	Symphonic Music Of Yes		[I]	$10	RCA Victor 61938
4/9/94	33	8		© 20	Talk			$10	Victory 480033
11/16/96	99	1		© 21	Keys To Ascension		[L]	$15	CMC Int'l. 86208 [2]
					recorded on 3/4/96 at the Fremont Theatre in San Luis Obispo, California				
12/13/97	151	1		© 22	Open Your Eyes			$10	Beyond 3074
10/16/99	99	2		© 23	The Ladder			$10	Beyond 78046

All Good People (medley) (1,4)
Almost Like Love (16)
Amazing Grace (15)
America (7,21) 46
Ancient, The (5)
And You And I Medley (3,4,12) 42
Angkor Wat (18)
Arriving UFO (9)
Astral Traveller (7)
Awaken (8,21)
Be The One (21)
Beyond And Before (13)
Big Generator (16)
Birthright (17)
Brother Of Mine Medley (17)
Calling, The (20)
Can I? (23)
Cans And Brahms (2)
Changes (14,15)
Cinema (14)
Circus Of Heaven (9)
City Of Love (14)
Clap, The (1)
Close To The Edge (19)

Close To The Edge Medley (3,4)
Dangerous (Look In The Light Of What You're Searching For) (18)
Dear Father (7)
Does It Really Happen? (10)
Don't Kill The Whale (9,11)
Endless Dream (18)
Evensong (18)
Every Little Thing (13)
Face To Face (23)
Final Eyes (16)
Finally (23)
Fish (Schindleria Praematurus) (2,4,12)
Fist Of Fire (17)
Five Per Cent For Nothing (2)
Fortune Seller (22)
From The Balcony (22)
Future Times (medley) (9)
Gates Of Delirium (4)
Going For The One (8,11)
Harold Land (13)
Heart Of The Sunrise (2,4,12,19)

Hearts (14)
Hold On (14,15)
Holding On (18)
Holy Lamb (Song For Harmonic Convergence) (16)
Homeworld (The Ladder) (23)
I Am Waiting (20)
I See You (13)
I Would Have Waited Forever (18)
I'm Running (16)
I've Seen All Good People (19)
If Only You Knew (23)
Into The Lens (10)
It Can Happen (14) 51
It Will Be A Good Day (The River) (23)
Leave It (14) 24
Let's Pretend (17)
Lift Me Up (18) 86
Lightning Strikes (23)
Long Distance Runaround (2,4,12)
Looking Around (7,13)
Love Shine (23)
Love Will Find A Way (16) 30

Machine Messiah (10)
Madrigal (9)
Man In The Moon (22)
Masquerade (18)
Meeting, The (17)
Messenger, The (23)
Miracle Of Life (18)
Mood For A Day (2,4,19)
More We Live - Let Go (18)
New Language (23)
New State Of Mind (22)
Nine Voices (Longwalker) (23)
No Way We Can Lose (22)
On The Silent Wings Of Freedom (9)
Onward (9,21)
Open Your Eyes (22)
Order Of The Universe Medley (17)
Our Song (14)
Owner Of A Lonely Heart (14,19) 1
Parallels (8,11)
Perpetual Change (1,4)
Quartet Medley (17)
Real Love (20)
Rejoice (medley) (9)

Release, Release (9)
Remembering (5)
Revealing Science Of God (5,21)
Rhythm Of Love (16) 40
Ritual (5,11)
Roundabout (2,4,19,21) 13
Run Through The Light (10)
Saving My Heart (18)
Shock To The System (18)
Shoot High Aim Low (16)
Siberian Khatru (3,4,21)
Silent Talking (18)
Six Wives Of Henry VIII, Excerpts From The (4)
Solly's Beard (15)
Solution, The (22)
Somehow, Someday (22)
Soon (15,19)
Sound Chaser (6)
South Side Of The Sky (2)
Starship Trooper Medley (1,4,12,19,21)
State Of Play (20)
Survival (7,13,19)
Sweet Dreams (7)

Sweetness (13)
Take The Water To The Mountain (18)
Teakbois (17)
Tempus Fugit (10)
That, That Is (21)
Themes Medley (17)
Then (7)
Time And A Word (7,11)
To Be Alive (Hep Yadda) (23)
To Be Over (6)
Turn Of The Century (8)
Universal Garden (22)
Venture, A (1)
Walls (20)
We Have Heaven (2)
Where Will You Be (20)
White Car (10)
Whitefish (15)
Without Hope You Cannot Start The Day (18)
Wonderlove (22)
Wonderous Stories (8,11,12,19)
Yesterday And Today (13)
Your Move (medley) (1,4) 40
Yours Is No Disgrace (1,4,12)

YIPES!! '79

Rock group from Milwaukee: Pat McCurdy (vocals), Andy Bartel and Mike Hoffmann (guitars), Pete Strand (bass) and Teddy Freese (drums).

DEBUT	PEAK	WKS	RIAA	CD	ARTIST — Album Title	$	Label & Number
10/6/79	177	4			Yipes!!	$12	Millennium 7745

Ballad Of Roy Orbison
East Side Kids

Girls Get In Trouble
Good Boys

Hangin' Around
Last Of The Angry Young Men

Me And My Face
Out In California

Russian Roll
This Is Your Life

★288★ YOAKAM, Dwight '93

Born on 10/23/56 in Pikeville, Kentucky. Country singer/songwriter/actor. Appeared in several movies.

1)This Time 2)Gone 3)Hillbilly Deluxe

DEBUT	PEAK	WKS	RIAA	CD	ARTIST — Album Title	Sym	$	Label & Number
4/19/86	61	65	▲²	© 1	Guitars, Cadillacs, Etc., Etc.		$10	Reprise 25372
5/16/87	55	28	▲	© 2	Hillbilly Deluxe		$10	Reprise 25567
8/20/88	68	15	▲	© 3	Buenas Noches From A Lonely Room		$10	Reprise 25749
10/14/89	68	10	▲	© 4	Just Lookin' For A Hit	[G]	$10	Reprise 25989
11/17/90+	96	75	▲	© 5	If There Was A Way		$10	Reprise 26344
4/10/93	25	81	▲³	© 6	This Time		$10	Reprise 45241
6/10/95	56	13	●	© 7	Dwight Live	[L]	$10	Reprise 45907
11/18/95	30	14	●	© 8	Gone		$10	Reprise 46051

YOAKAM, Dwight — Cont'd

8/2/97	92	7		© 9	Under The Covers			$10	Reprise 46690
6/27/98	60	11		© 10	A Long Way Home			$10	Reprise 46918
6/5/99	80	19	●	© 11	Last Chance For A Thousand Years - Dwight Yoakam's Greatest Hits From The 90's		[G]	$10	Reprise 47389
6/17/00	195	1		© 12	dwightyoakamacoustic.net			$10	Reprise 47714
11/18/00	68	4		© 13	Tomorrow's Sounds Today			$10	Reprise 47827

Ain't That Lonely Yet (6,11)
Alright I'm Wrong (13)
Always Late With Your Kisses (2)
Baby Don't Go (9)
Baby Why Not (8)
Buenas Noches From A Lonely Room (She Wore Red Dresses) (3,12)
Bury Me (1,12)
Claudette (9)
Crazy Little Thing Called Love (11) *64*
Curse, The (10)
Dangerous Man (5)
Distance Between You And Me (5,12)
Don't Be Sad (8)
Dreams Of Clay (13)
Fast As You (6,7,11,12) *70*
Floyd County (3)
For Love's Sake (13)

Free To Go (13)
Gone (That'll Be Me) (8)
Good Time Charlie's Got The Blues (9)
Guitars, Cadillacs (1,4,12)
Heart Of Stone (8)
Heart That You Own (5,7,11)
Heartaches Are Free (13)
Heartaches By The Number (1)
Here Comes The Night (9)
Hold On To God (3)
Home For Sale (6,12)
Home Of The Blues (9)
Honky Tonk Man (1,4)
I Don't Need It Done (5)
I Got You (3,4)
I Hear You Knockin' (3)
I Sang Dixie (3,4)
I Want You To Want Me (13)
I Was There (13)
I Wouldn't Put It Past Me (10)
I'll Be Gone (1,12)

I'll Go Back To Her (11)
I'll Just Take These (10)
If There Was A Way (5)
It Only Hurts When I Cry (5,7,11,12)
It Won't Hurt (1,12)
Johnson's Love (2,12)
King Of Fools (9)
Last Time (9)
Let's Work Together (5)
Listen (10)
Little Sister (2,4,7,12)
Little Ways (2,4,7,12)
Lonesome Roads (6,7,12)
Long Way Home (10,12)
Long White Cadillac (4,7)
Love Caught Up To Me (13)
Maybe You Like It, Maybe You Don't (10)
Miner's Prayer (1,7)
Near You (4)
Never Hold You (8)

North To Alaska (9)
Nothing (8,11)
Nothing's Changed Here (5,7,12)
One More Name (3)
One More Night (8)
Only Want You More (10)
Place To Cry (13)
Playboy (9)
Please, Please Baby (2,4,7,12)
Pocket Of A Clown (6,11)
Promise You Can't Keep (13)
Readin', Rightin', Rt. 23 (2,12)
Ring Of Fire (1)
Rocky Road Blues (7)
Sad, Sad Music (5,12)
Sad Side Of Town (13)
Same Fool (10)
Send A Message To My Heart (5)
Send Me The Pillow (3)
Sin City (4)

Since I Started Drinkin' Again (5)
Smoke Along The Track (2)
Sorry You Asked? (8,11)
South Of Cincinnati (1)
Streets Of Bakersfield (3,4,7)
Suspicious Minds (7,11)
Takes A Lot To Rock You (5)
That's Okay (10)
These Arms (10)
Things Change (10,12)
Things We Said Today (9)
Thinking About Leaving (11)
This Drinkin' Will Kill Me (2,12)
This Much I Know (8)
This Time (5,12)
1,000 Miles (2,12)
Thousand Miles From Nowhere (6,7,11,12)
Throughout All Time (2,12)
Time Spent Missing You (13)
Tired Of Waiting For You (9)

Train In Vain (9)
Traveler's Lantern (10)
Try Not To Look So Pretty (6)
Turn It On, Turn It Up, Turn Me Loose (5,11)
Twenty Years (1)
Two Doors Down (6,7,12)
What Do You Know About Love (13)
What I Don't Know (3)
Wichita Lineman (9)
Wild Ride (6,7)
World Of Blue (13)
Yet To Succeed (10)
You're The One (5,11)

YO LA TENGO '00
Rock duo from New Jersey: Ira Kaplan (vocals, guitar) and Georgia Hubley (drums).

3/11/00	138	2		©	And Then Nothing Turned Itself Inside-Out			$10	Matador 371

Cherry Chapstick
Crying Of Lot G
Everyday

From Black To Blue
Last Days Of Disco

Let's Save Tony Orlando's House
Madeline

Night Falls On Hoboken
Our Way To Fall
Saturday

Tears Are In Your Eyes
Tired Hippo
You Can Have It All

YOST, Dennis — see CLASSICS IV

YOUNG, Barry '66
Pop singer.

1/1/66	67	12			One Has My Name			$20	Dot 25672

I Gotta Have My Baby Back
I Miss You So

I Still Need You
I'll Never Smile Again

In The Chapel In The Moonlight
Laughing On The Outside (Crying On The Inside)

One Has My Name (The Other Has My Heart) *13*
Show Me The Way

Since You Have Gone From Me
Why
Yesterday

You'll Never Know

YOUNG, Jesse Colin '74
Born Perry Miller on 11/11/44 in New York City. Folk-rock singer/bassist. Leader of **The Youngbloods**.

3/25/72	157	6		© 1	Together			$15	Raccoon 2588
10/6/73	51	44		© 2	Song For Juli			$12	Warner 2734
2/9/74	172	6		© 3	The Soul Of A City Boy		[E]	$12	Capitol 11267
					first released in 1964 on Capitol 2070 ($50)				
4/20/74	37	29		© 4	Light Shine			$12	Warner 2790
3/22/75	26	14		© 5	Songbird			$12	Warner 2845
3/27/76	34	15		© 6	On The Road		[L]	$12	Warner 2913
4/2/77	64	9		© 7	Love On The Wing			$12	Warner 3033
12/9/78	165	2			American Dreams			$12	Elektra 157

Again (5)
American Dreams Suite Medley (8)
Barbados (4)
Before You Came (5)
Black Eyed Susan (3)
Born In Chicago (1)
California Cowboy (7)
California Suite Medley (4)
Corinna (1)
Country Home (2)
Creole Belle (1)

Cuckoo, The (4)
Daniel (7)
Do It Slow (7)
Drift Away (7)
Drifter's Blues (3)
Evenin' (2)
Fool (7)
Four In The Morning (3)
Good Times (1)
Have You Seen My Baby (6)
Hey, Good Lookin' (7)
Higher & Higher (7)

I Think I'll Take To Whiskey (3)
It's A Lovely Day (1)
Jambalaya (On The Bayou) (medley) (2)
Josianne (5)
Knock On Wood (8)
Lafayette Waltz (medley) (2)
Louisiana Highway (7)
Love On The Wing (7)
Maui Sunrise (4)
Mercy Mercy Me (The Ecology) (medley) (6)

Miss Hesitation (2,6)
Morning Sun (2)
Motorcycle Blues (2)
Motorhome (5)
Pastures Of Plenty (1)
Peace Song (1,6)
Pretty And The Fair (4)
Rave On (8)
Reveal Your Dreams (8)
Ridgetop (2,6)
Rye Whiskey (3)
Same Old Man (3)

Six Days On The Road (1)
6000 Miles (1)
Slick City (5)
Slow And Easy (8)
Song For Juli (2)
Songbird (5)
Stranger Love (3)
Sugar Babe (5)
Sunlight (6)
Susan (4)
Susanne (3)
Sweet Little Child (1)

Sweet Little Sixteen (1)
T-Bone Shuffle (2,6)
Talk To Me (3)
'Til You Come Back Home (5)
Together (1)
Walkin' Off The Blues (6)
What's Going On (medley) (6)
Whoa Baby (3)
Workin' (7)
You Gotta Fix It (3)
You Lovin' Hobo (7)

YOUNG, John Paul '79
Born on 6/21/50 in Glasgow, Scotland; raised in Sydney, Australia. Pop singer/songwriter/pianist.

11/11/78+	119	18			Love Is In The Air			$12	Scotti Brothers 7101

Day That My Heart Caught Fire
Fool In Love

Lazy Days
Lost In Your Love *55*

Love Is In The Air *7*
Lovin' In Your Soul

Open Doors
Things To Do

12 Celsius

YOUNG, Neil ★35★ '72
Born on 11/12/45 in Toronto. Rock singer/songwriter/guitarist. Member of **Buffalo Springfield** and **Crosby, Stills, Nash & Young**. Appeared in the 1987 movie *Made In Heaven*. Inducted into the Rock and Roll Hall of Fame in 1995.

1)Harvest 2)Mirror Ball 3)Comes A Time 4)After The Gold Rush 5)Rust Never Sleeps

6/21/69+	34	98	▲	© 1	Everybody Knows This Is Nowhere			$15	Reprise 6349
					NEIL YOUNG & CRAZY HORSE				
9/19/70	8	66	▲²	© 2	After The Gold Rush			$15	Reprise 6383

DEBUT	PEAK	WKS	RIAA	CD	ARTIST — Album Title	Catalog	Sym	$	Label & Number
					YOUNG, Neil — Cont'd				
3/4/72	❶²	41	▲⁴	© 3	**Harvest**	C:#17/22		$15	Reprise 2032
11/25/72+	45	21		© 4	Journey Through The Past		[S]	$20	Warner 6480 [2]
10/27/73	22	18	●	© 5	Time Fades Away		[L]	$12	Reprise 2151
8/3/74	16	18		© 6	On The Beach			$12	Reprise 2180
7/12/75	25	12		© 7	Tonight's The Night			$12	Reprise 2221
11/29/75+	25	21	●	© 8	Zuma			$12	Reprise 2242
					NEIL YOUNG & CRAZY HORSE				
10/9/76	26	18	●	© 9	Long May You Run			$12	Reprise 2253
					STILLS-YOUNG BAND				
7/2/77	21	15	●	10	American Stars 'N Bars			$12	Reprise 2261
					NEIL YOUNG, CRAZY HORSE & THE BULLETS				
11/26/77	43	18	▲	© 11	Decade		[K]	$20	Reprise 2257 [3]
10/21/78	7	30	●	© 12	**Comes A Time**			$12	Reprise 2266
7/21/79	8	39	▲	© 13	**Rust Never Sleeps**			$12	Reprise 2295
12/8/79+	15	24	▲	© 14	Live Rust		[L]	$15	Reprise 2296 [2]
					NEIL YOUNG & CRAZY HORSE (above 2)				
11/22/80	30	16		© 15	Hawks & Doves			$12	Reprise 2297
11/21/81	27	17			16 Re-ac-tor			$12	Reprise 2304
					NEIL YOUNG & CRAZY HORSE				
1/22/83	19	17			17 Trans			$10	Geffen 2018
8/20/83	46	15		© 18	Everybody's Rockin'			$10	Geffen 4013
					NEIL & THE SHOCKING PINKS				
9/7/85	75	12		© 19	Old Ways			$10	Geffen 24068
8/16/86	46	16		© 20	Landing On Water			$10	Geffen 24109
7/25/87	75	11		© 21	Life			$10	Geffen 24154
					NEIL YOUNG & CRAZY HORSE				
4/30/88	61	18		© 22	This Note's For You			$10	Reprise 25719
					NEIL YOUNG & THE BLUENOTES				
10/21/89	35	28	●	© 23	Freedom			$10	Reprise 25899
9/29/90	31	25		© 24	Ragged Glory			$10	Reprise 26315
11/9/91	154	4		© 25	Weld		[L]	$20	Reprise 26746 [3]
					NEIL YOUNG & CRAZY HORSE (above 2)				
11/14/92	16	42	▲²	© 26	Harvest Moon			$10	Reprise 45057
7/3/93	23	18	●	© 27	Unplugged		[L]	$10	Reprise 45310
					recorded on 2/7/93				
9/3/94	9	12	●	© 28	**Sleeps With Angels**			$10	Reprise 45749
					NEIL YOUNG & CRAZY HORSE				
7/15/95	5	13	●	© 29	**Mirror Ball**			$10	Reprise 45934
7/20/96	31	8		© 30	Broken Arrow			$10	Reprise 46291
7/5/97	57	5		© 31	Year Of The Horse		[L]	$15	Reprise 46652 [2]
					NEIL YOUNG & CRAZY HORSE (above 2)				
5/13/00	22	13		© 32	Silver & Gold			$10	Reprise 47305
12/23/00	169	1		© 33	Road Rock V 1		[L]	$10	Reprise 48036

Act Of Love (29)
After The Gold Rush (2,11,14)
Alabama (3,4)
Albuquerque (7)
All Along The Watchtower (33)
Already One (12)
Ambulance Blues (6)
Arc (25)
Are There Any More Real Cowboys? (19)
Are You Ready For The Country? (3,4)
Around The World (21)
Baby What You Want Me To Do (30)
Bad News Beat (20)
Barstool Blues (8,31)
Betty Lou's Got A New Pair Of Shoes (18)
Big Green Country (29)
Big Time (30,31)
Birds (2)
Bite The Bullet (10)
Black Coral (9)
Blowin' In The Wind (25)
Blue Eden (28)
Borrowed Tune (7)
Bound For Glory (19)
Bridge, The (5)
Bright Lights, Big City (18)
Broken Arrow (11)
Buffalo Springfield Again (32)
Burned (11)
California Sunset (19)
Campaigner (11)
Can't Believe Your Lyin' (22)
Captain Kennedy (15)
Change Your Mind (28)
Changing Highways (30)
Cinnamon Girl (1,11,14,25) **55**
Coastline (15)
Come On Baby Let's Go Downtown (7)

Comes A Time (12,14)
Comin' Apart At Every Nail (15)
Computer Age (17)
Computer Cowboy (AKA Syscrusher) (17)
Cortez The Killer (8,11,14,25)
Country Home (24)
Coupe De Ville (22)
Cowgirl In The Sand (1,11,33)
Crime In The City (23,25)
Cripple Creek Ferry (2)
Cry, Cry, Cry (18)
Cryin' Eyes (21)
Daddy Went Walkin' (32)
Danger Bird (8,31)
Days That Used To Be (24)
Deep Forbidden Lake (11)
Distant Camera (32)
Don't Be Denied (5)
Don't Cry (23)
Don't Cry No Tears (8)
Don't Let It Bring You Down (2)
Down By The River (1,11)
Down To The Wire (11)
Downtown (29)
Dream That Can Last (28)
Dreamin' Man (26)
Drifter (7)
Drive Back (8)
Driveby (28)
Eldorado (23)
Everybody Knows This Is Nowhere (1)
Everybody's Rockin' (18)
Expecting To Fly (11)
Fallen Angel (29)
Farmer John (24,25)
Field Of Opportunity (12)
Find The Cost Of Freedom (4)
Fontainebleau (9)
Fool For Your Love (13)
For The Turnstiles (6,11)
For What It's Worth (medley) (4)

Four Strong Winds (12) **61**
From Hank To Hendrix (26,27)
F*!#in' Up (24,25)
Get Back On It (16)
Get Back To The Country (19)
God Bless America (medley) (4)
Goin' Back (12)
Good To See You (32)
Great Divide (32)
Guardian Angel (9)
Handel's Messiah (4)
Hangin' On A Limb (23)
Hard Luck Stories (20)
Harvest (3,11)
Harvest Moon (26,27)
Hawks & Doves (15)
Heart Of Gold (3,11) **1**
Helpless (11,27)
Hey Babe (10)
Hey Hey (22)
Hippie Dream (20)
Hold Back The Tears (10)
Hold On To Your Love (17)
Homegrown (10)
Horseshoe Man (32)
Human Highway (12,31)
I Am A Child (11,14)
I Believe In You (2,11)
I Got A Problem (20)
I'm The Ocean (29)
Inca Queen (21)
Jellyroll Man (13)
Journey Thru The Past (5)
Kinda Fonda Wanda (18)
King Of Kings Theme (4)
L.A. (5)
Last Dance (5)
Let It Shine (9)
Let Me Call You Sweetheart (4)
Let's Go Away For Awhile (4)
Life In The City (13)
Like A Hurricane (10,11,14,25,27)

Like An Inca (17)
Little Thing Called Love (17)
Little Wing (15)
Loner, The (11,14)
Long May You Run (9,11,27)
Long Walk Home (21)
Look Out For My Love (12,27)
Lookin' For A Love (8)
Lookout Joe (7)
Loose Change (30)
Losing End (When You're On) (1)
Lost In Space (15)
Lotta Love (12,14)
Love And Only Love (24,25)
Love In Mind (5)
Love Is A Rose (11)
Love To Burn (24,25)
Make Love To You (9)
Man Needs A Maid (3,11)
Mansion On The Hill (24,25)
Married Man (22)
Mellow My Mind (7)
Mideast Vacation (21)
Midnight On The Bay (9)
Misfits (19)
Mother Earth (Natural Anthem) (24)
Motion Pictures (6)
Motor City (16)
Motorcycle Mama (12,33)
Mr. Soul (4,11,17,27,31)
Music Arcade (30)
My Boy (19)
My Heart (28)
My My, Hey Hey (Out Of The Blue) (13,14)
Mystery Train (18)
Natural Beauty (26)
Needle And The Damage Done (3,11,14,27)
New Mama (7)
No More (23)

Ocean Girl (9)
Oh, Lonesome Me (2)
Ohio (4,11)
Old Country Waltz (10)
Old Homestead (15)
Old King (26)
Old Laughing Lady (11,27)
Old Man (3,11) **31**
Old Ways (19)
On Broadway (23)
On The Beach (6)
Once An Angel (19)
One Of These Days (26)
One Thing (22)
Only Love Can Break Your Heart (2) **33**
Opera Star (16)
Out On The Weekend (3)
Over And Over (24)
Pardon My Heart (8)
Payola Blues (18)
Peace And Love (29)
Peace Of Mind (12,33)
People On The Street (20)
Piece Of Crap (28)
Pocahontas (13,27,25)
Powderfinger (13,14,25)
Pressure (20)
Prime Of Life (28)
Prisoners Of Rock 'N' Roll (21,31)
Rainin' In My Heart (18)
Rapid Transit (16)
Razor Love (32)
Red Sun (32)
Relativity Invitation (4)
Revolution Blues (6)
Ride My Llama (13)
Rock & Roll Woman (4)
Rockin' In The Free World (23,25)
Roll Another Number (For The Road) (7,25)

Round & Round (It Won't Be Long) (1)
Running Dry (Requiem For The Rockets) (1)
Rust Never Sleeps (Hey Hey, My My [Into The Black]) (13,14,25) **79**
Saddle Up The Palomino (10)
Safeway Cart (28)
Sail Away (13)
Sample And Hold (17)
Scattered [Let's Think About Livin'] (30,31)
Scenery (29)
Sedan Delivery (13,14,31)
See The Sky About To Rain (6)
Shots (18)
Silver & Gold (32)
Sleeps With Angels (28)
Slip Away (30,31)
Soldier (4,11)
Someday (7)
Song X (29)
Southern Man (2,4,11)
Southern Pacific (16) **70**
Speakin' Out (7)
Star Of Bethlehem (10,11)
Stayin' Power (15)
Stringman (27)
Stupid Girl (8)
Such A Woman (26)
Sugar Mountain (11,14)
Sunny Inside (22)
Surfer Joe And Moe The Sleaze (16)
T-Bone (13)
Tell Me Why (2)
Ten Men Workin' (21)
There's A World (3)
This Note's For You (22)
This Town (30)
Thrasher (13)
Through My Sails (8)

980

DEBUT	PEAK	WKS	RIAA	CD	ARTIST — Album Title	Catalog	Sym	$	Label & Number

YOUNG, Neil — Cont'd

Throw Your Hatred Down (29)
Till The Morning Comes (2)
Time Fades Away (5)
Tired Eyes (7,11)
Tonight's The Night (Part I & II) (7,11,14,25,33)
Too Far Gone (23)

Too Lonely (21)
Touch The Night (20)
Train Of Love (28)
Trans Am (28)
Transformer Man (17,27)
Truth Be Known (29)
12/8 Blues (All The Same) (9)
Twilight (22)

Union Man (15)
Unknown Legend (26,27)
Vampire Blues (6)
Violent Side (20)
Walk On (6,11,33) *69*
War Of Man (1)
Ways Of Love (23)
Wayward Wind (19)

We Never Danced (21)
We R In Control (17)
Weight Of The World (20)
Welfare Mothers (13,25)
Western Hero (28)
What Happened Yesterday (29)
When You Dance I Can Really Love (2,14,31) *93*

When Your Lonely Heart Breaks (21,31)
Where Is The Highway Tonight? (19)
White Line (24)
Will To Love (10)
Winterlong (11)
Without Rings (32)

Wonderin' (18)
Words (33)
Words (Between The Lines Of Age) (3,4)
World On A String (7,27)
Wrecking Ball (23)
Yonder Stands The Sinner (5)
You And Me (26)

YOUNG, Paul   '85
Born on 1/17/56 in Bedfordshire, England. Pop-rock singer.

4/14/84	79	23		© 1	No Parlez			$10	Columbia 38976

title is French for "You Don't Talk"

5/25/85	19	43	● © 2	The Secret Of Association		$10	Columbia 39957
11/22/86	77	17	© 3	Between Two Fires		$10	Columbia 40543
8/11/90	142	13	© 4	Other Voices		$10	Columbia 46755

Between Two Fires (3)
Bite The Hand That Feeds (2)
Broken Man (1)
Calling You (4)
Certain Passion (3)
Come Back And Stay (1) *22*
Everything Must Change (2) *56*

Everytime You Go Away (2) *1*
Heaven Can Wait (4)
Hot Fun (2)
I Was In Chains (2)
I'm Gonna Tear Your Playhouse Down (2) *13*
In The Long Run (3)
Iron Out The Rough Spots (1)

It's What She Didn't Say (4)
Ku-Ku Kurama (1)
Little Bit Of Love (4)
Love Of The Common People (1) *45*
Love Will Tear Us Apart (1)
No Parlez (1)
Oh Girl (1) *8*

Oh Women (1)
One Step Forward (2)
Our Time Has Come (4)
Prisoner Of Conscience (3)
Right About Now (4)
Sex (1)
Softly Whispering I Love You (4)

Soldier's Things (2)
Some People (3) *65*
Standing On The Edge (2)
Stop On By (4)
Tender Trap (1)
This Means Anything (2)
Together (4)
Tomb Of Memories (2)

War Games (3)
Wasting My Time (3)
Wedding Day (3)
Wherever I Lay My Hat (That's My Home) (1) *70*
Why Does A Man Have To Be Strong? (3)
Wonderland (3)

YOUNG AMERICANS, The   '69
A 36-member chorus of teenagers and young adults. **Vicki Lawrence** was a member from 1964-67.

4/19/69	178	3		Time For Livin'			$15	ABC 659

Blackberry Organ
Bowling Green

For Emily, Whenever I May Find Her

Gotham City Municipal Swing Band At County Fair
Here's That Rainy Day

Little Green Apples
Little Joy
On The Blue Cloud Sea

Scarborough Fair
Singing In The Rain
Time For Livin'

YOUNG & RESTLESS   '90
Rap duo from Miami: Charles Trahan and Leon Johnson.

5/5/90	104	14		©	Something To Get You Hyped			$10	Pandisc 8809

"B" Girls *54*
Cold Get Ill

Funky Az Bass Line
Gimme Them Guts

It Just Wasn't Our Day
Louie, Louie

Poison Ivy
Something To Get You Hyped

YOUNG BLACK TEENAGERS   '93
White rap group from New York: Firstborn, Kamron, A.T.A. and **DJ Skribble**.

2/20/93	158	8		©	Dead Enz Kidz Doin' Lifetime Bidz			$10	Soul 10733

Blowin' Up The Spot
First True Love Affair

Looney Toonz
On The DL (Down Low)

Outta My Head
Plead The Fifth

Roll W/The Flavor
Soul Wide Open

Sweatin' Me
Tap The Bottle *55*

Time To Make The Dough Nutz
Y.B. Teenagers

YOUNG BLEED   '98
Born in New Orleans. Male rapper.

2/7/98	10	15	● © 1	All I Have In This World, Are...My Balls And My Word		$10	No Limit 50738
2/19/00	61	6	© 2	My Own		$10	Priority 50018

All They Lef' Me Wuz' Da' Streets (2)
Better Than Last Time (1)
Bless Em' All (2)
Bounce, Mob, Skate (2)

Bring The Noise (1)
Confedi (1)
Da Last Outlaw (1)
Day They Make Me Boss (1)
Ghostrider (1)

Give And Take (2)
How Ya Do Dat (1)
Husla', A (2)
I Couldn't C' It (2)
Keep It Real (1)

Lil Poppa Got A Brand New Bag (1)
Minute Ta' Breathe (2)
Mo Money (1)
My Own (2)

No Disrespect (2)
Offer U Can't Refuse (1)
Pull It Off (1)
Time And Money (2)
Times So Hard (1)

To Be A Soldier (2)
Trecherous (2)
We Don't Stop (1)

YOUNGBLOOD, Sydney   '90
Born Sydney Ford in San Antonio, Texas. R&B singer.

10/20/90	185	3		©	Sydney Youngblood			$10	Arista 8651

Ain't No Sunshine
Congratulations

Don't Keep Me Waiting
Feeling Free

Good Times Bad Times
I'd Rather Go Blind *46*

If Only I Could
Kiss And Say Goodbye

Not Just A Lover But A Friend
Sit And Wait

YOUNGBLOODS, The   '70
Folk-rock group formed in Boston: **Jesse Colin Young** (vocals, bass), Lowell Levinger and Jerry Corbitt (guitars) and Joe Bauer (drums). Corbitt left after first album. Bassist Michael Kane joined in 1971. Group disbanded in 1973. Bauer died in 1982.

3/25/67+	131	8	© 1	The Youngbloods			$25	RCA Victor 3724
5/10/69	118	29	© 2	Elephant Mountain			$20	RCA Victor 4150
9/5/70	144	10	© 3	The Best Of The Youngbloods	[G]	$20	RCA Victor 4399
10/31/70	80	13	4	Rock Festival	[L]	$15	Raccoon 1878
7/24/71	157	8	© 5	Ride The Wind	[L]	$15	Raccoon 2563

produced by **Charlie Daniels**

8/7/71	186	3	6	Sunlight	[K]	$15	RCA Victor 4561
12/4/71	160	5	7	Good And Dusty		$15	Raccoon 2566
12/9/72+	185	10	8	High On A Ridge Top		$15	Raccoon 2653

Ain't That Lovin' You, Baby (1,6)
All Over The World (La-La) (8)
Beautiful (2,5)
Black Mountain Breakdown (2)
C.C. Rider (1,3)
Circus Face (7)
Darkness, Darkness (2,3) *86*
Dolphin, The (5)
Don't Let The Rain Get You Down (2)
Donna (8)
Double Sunlight (2)

Dreamboat (8)
Dreamer's Dream (6)
Drifting And Drifting (7)
Euphoria (3)
Faster All The Time (1)
Fiddler A Dram (4)
Foolin' Around (The Waltz) (1,6)
Four In The Morning (1)
Get Together (1,3,5) *5*
Going By The River (8)
Good And Dusty (7)
Grizzly Bear (1,3) *52*
Hippie From Olema #5 (7)

I Can Tell (6)
I Shall Be Released (8)
I'm A Hog For You Baby (7)
Ice Bag (4)
It's A Lovely Day (4)
Josiane (4)
Kind Hearted Woman (8)
La Bamba (8)
Let The Good Times Roll (7)
Light Shine (7)
Long & Tall (6)
Misty Roses (4)
Moonshine Is The Sunshine (7)

On Beautiful Lake Spenard (4)
On Sir Francis Drake (2,6)
One Note Man (1,6)
Other Side Of This Life (1)
Peepin' 'N' Hidin' (Baby, What You Want Me To Do) (4)
Pontiac Blues (7)
Quicksand (2,3)
Reason To Believe (8)
Ride The Wind (2,5)
Running Bear (8)
Sea Cow Boogie (4)
Sham (2,3)

She Came In Through The Bathroom Window (8)
She Caught The Katy & Left Me A Mule To Ride (8)
Smug (2)
Speedo (8)
Stagger Lee (7)
Statesboro Blues (1,6)
Sugar Babe (3,5)
Sunlight (2,3,5,6)
Tears Are Falling (1)
That's How Strong My Love Is (7)

Trillium (2)
Turn It Over (2)
Will The Circle Be Unbroken (7)
Willie And The Hand Jive (7)
Wine Song (3)

Little Johnny Taylor
Little Johnny Taylor ('63)

Third World
Prisoner In The Street ('80)

The Toys
A Lover's Concerto and Attack! ('66)

The Trashmen
Surfin' Bird ('64)

Robin Trower
B.L.T. ('81)

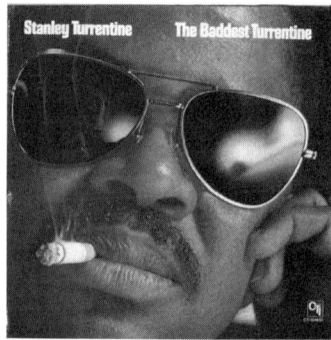

Stanley Turrentine
The Baddest Turrentine ('74)

The Tymes
Somewhere ('64)

U2
The Best Of 1980-1990 ('98)

Sarah Vaughan
Great Songs From Hit Shows ('57)

The Ventures
The Ventures' Christmas Album ('65)

John Wayne
America, Why I Love Her ('73)

Lenny Welch
Since I Fell For You ('64)

Mary Wells
Mary Wells ('65)

Mae West
Way Out West ('66)

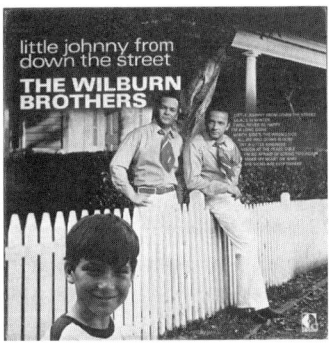

The Wilburn Brothers
Little Johnny From Down The Street ('70)

Hank Williams Jr
Hog Wild ('95)

Jackie Wilson
Higher And Higher ('67)

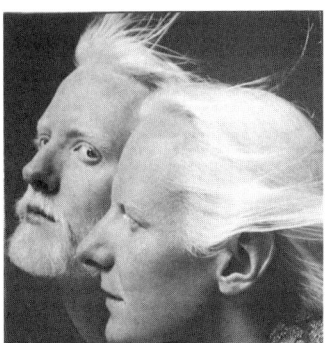

Johnny & Edgar Winter
Together ('76)

The Womenfolk
The Womenfolk ('64)

The Young Holt Trio
Wack Wack ('67)

Timi Yuro
Hurt!!!!!!! ('61)

John Zacherle
Monster Mash ('62)

Frank Zappa
Sheik Yerbouti ('79)

ZZ Top
XXX ('99)

YOUNGBLOODZ '99
Rap duo from Atlanta: Sean Paul and J-Bo.

| 10/30/99 | 92 | 17 | | © | **Against Da Grain** | | | $10 | LaFace 26054 |

Booty Club Playa
Down Heya (In The South)
85

87 Fleetwood
Get It How We Get It
Hot Heat

It's The Money
Just A Dream
Pop, Pop, Pop

Shakem' Off
6 To 14 In 12
Thangs Movin' Slow

U-Way (How We Do It)

YOUNG-HOLT UNLIMITED '69
R&B instrumental group from Chicago: Eldee Young (bass), Isaac "Red" Holt (drums) and Don Walker (piano). Both Young and Holt were members of the **Ramsey Lewis Trio**. Walker left by 1968.

| 1/14/67 | 132 | 6 | | | 1 **Wack Wack** | | | [I] | $25 | Brunswick 754121 |

THE YOUNG HOLT TRIO

| 1/4/69 | 9 | 30 | | | 2 **Soulful Strut** | | | [I] | $20 | Brunswick 754144 |
| 8/16/69 | 185 | 6 | | | 3 **Just A Melody** | | | [I] | $20 | Brunswick 754150 |

Ain't There Something Money Can't Buy (2)
Baby Your Light Is Out (2)
Be By My Side (2)
By The Time I Get To Phoenix (3)
Funky Is As Funky Does (2)

Girl Talk (1)
Give It Away (3)
Gotta Find Me A Lover (24 Hours A Day) (3)
I Heard It Through The Grapevine (3)
I Wish You Love (3)

Just A Melody (3)
Just Ain't No Love (2)
Light My Fire (3)
Little Green Apples (2)
Love Makes A Woman (2)
Monday, Monday (1)
My Whole World Ended (3)

Please Sunrise, Please (2)
Red Sails In The Sunset (1)
Song For My Father (1)
Soulful Strut (2) *3*
Strangers In The Night (1)
Sunny (1)
This Little Light Of Mine (1)

Wack Wack (1) *40*
What Now My Love (2)
When I'm Not Around (3)
Who's Making Love (2) *57*
Yesterday (1)
You Know That I Love You (1)
Young And Holtful (3)

YOUNG M.C. '89
Born Marvin Young on 5/10/67 in London; raised in Queens, New York. Male rapper.

| 9/23/89 | 9 | 48 | ▲ | © | 1 **Stone Cold Rhymin'** | | | $10 | Delicious Vinyl 91309 |
| 8/31/91 | 66 | 7 | ● | © | 2 **Brainstorm** | | | $10 | Capitol 96337 |

After School (2)
Album Filler (2)
Bust A Move (1) *7*
Do You Feel Like I Do (2)
Fastest Rhyme (1)

Got More Rhymes (1)
I Come Off (1) *75*
I Let 'Em Know (1)
Inside My Head (2)
Just Say No (1)

Keep It In Your Pants (2)
Keep Your Eyes On The Prize (2)
Know How (1)
Life In The Fast Lane (2)
Pick Up The Pace (1)

Listen To The Beat Of The Music (2)
My Name Is Young (1)
Non Stop (1)

Principal's Office (1) *33*
Right One (2)
Roll With The Punches (1)
Stone Cold Buggin' (1)

That's The Way Love Goes (2) *54*
Um Dee Dum Song (2)
Use Your Head (2)

YOUNGSTOWN '00
Male vocal trio from Youngstown, Ohio: Sammy Lopez, James Dallas and David Yeager.

| 3/4/00 | 96 | 10 | | © | **Let's Roll** | | | $10 | Hollywood 62192 |

Angel
Don't Worry
Early Frost

Forever In Love
I'll Be Your Everything *71*
It's Not What You Think

Jamie Lee
Lose My Cool
Pedal To The Steel

Prince You Charmed
Remember
Through Your Eyes

Whenever You Need Me

YO-YO '91
Born Yolanda Whitaker on 8/4/71 in Los Angeles. Female rapper.

4/13/91	74	21		©	1 **Make Way For The Motherlode**			$10	EastWest 91605
7/11/92	145	2		©	2 **Black Pearl**			$10	EastWest 92120
7/10/93	107	5		©	3 **You Better Ask Somebody**			$10	EastWest 92252

Ain't Nobody Better (1)
Black Pearl (2)
Bonnie And Clyde Theme (3) *72*
Can You Handle It? (1)
Cleopatra (2)
Cube Gets Played (1)

Dedication (1)
Few Good Men (2)
Girl, Don't Be No Fool (1)
Girls Got A Gun (3)
Givin' It Up (3)
Hoes (2)
Home Girl Don't Play Dat (1)

I Can't Take No More (2)
I Got Played (1)
I.B.W.C. National Anthem (1)
IBWin' Wit My Crewin' (3) *flip*
It's A Long Way Home (2)
Letter To The Pen (3)
Mackstress (3)

Make Way For The Motherlode (1)
More Of What Can I Do (1)
Pass It On (3)
Put A Lid On It (1)
Sisterland (1)
So Funky (2)

Stand Up For Your Rights (1)
Stompin' To Tha 90's (1)
They Shit Don't Stink (3)
Tonight's The Night (1)
20 Sack (3)
Westside Story (3)
What Can I Do? (1)

Will You Be Mine (2)
Woman To Woman (2)
You Better Ask Somebody (3)
You Can't Play With My Yo-Yo (1) *36*
You Should Have Listened (2)

YUKMOUTH '99
Born Jerold Ellis in Oakland. Male rapper. Member of **Luniz**.

| 3/13/99 | 40 | 7 | | © | 1 **Thugged Out: The Albulation** | | | $15 | Rap-A-Lot 46720 [2] |
| 4/21/01 | 71 | 8 | | © | 2 **Thug Lord: The New Testament** | | | $10 | Rap-A-Lot 10042 |

Baller Mode (1)
Ballers Feud (1)
Bumbell (1)
City Of Dope (1)
Clap Yo Hands (2)
Do It Right (2)
Do Yo Thug Thang (1)

Extortion (1)
Falling (1)
Father Like Son (1)
Gangsta Bitch (1)
Godzilla (1)
Hater (1)
Hi Maintenance (2)

Ice Cream Man (1)
It's In My Blood Part II (1)
Mackin Vs. Pimpin' (1)
Menage A Trois (1)
My Buddy (1)
Oh Boy! (1)
Ooh! Ooh! (2)

Pop Da Collar (1)
Puffin Lab (2)
Rap-A-Lot Mafia (1)
Regime Killers 2001 (2)
Revelationz (1)
Ridaz (1)
Rolex Rulez (1)

Sacrifice My Life (1)
Sad Millionaire (1)
Secret Indictment (1)
Smile (1)
So Ignorant (2)
Stallion (1)
Still Ballin' (1)

Thug Lord (2)
Thug Money (1)
Thugged Out (1)
U Love 2 Hate (1)
We Gone Ride (2)
World's Most Hated (2)

YURO, Timi '61
Born Rosemarie Timothy Yuro on 8/4/40 in Chicago. Female singer.

| 9/18/61 | 51 | 13 | | | **Hurt!!!!!!!** | | | $40 | Liberty 3208 |

And That Reminds Me
Cry

For You
Hurt *4*

I Apologize *72*
I Should Care

I Won't Cry Anymore
I'm Confessin' (That I Love You)

Just Say I Love Him
Little Bird Told Me

Trying
You'll Never Know

YUTAKA '81
Born Yutaka Yokokura in Tokyo. Male jazz-pop keyboardist.

| 7/11/81 | 174 | 4 | | | **Love Light** | | | [I] | $12 | Alfa 10004 |

Breath Of Night
Dragonfly

Evening Star
Haiku

Love Light *81*
Oriental Express

Rest Of My Life

Z

ZAA, Charlie '97
Born in Colombia, South America. Latin singer/songwriter.

| 9/20/97 | 185 | 2 | ▲ | © | 1 **Sentimientos** | | | [F] | $10 | Sonolux 82136 |

title is Spanish for "Feelings"

| 7/4/98 | 193 | 1 | | © | 2 **Un Segundo Sentimiento** | | | [F] | $10 | Sonolux 82706 |

title is Spanish for "A Second Feeling"

Amores (2)
Anhelos (2)
Añoranzas (1)
Desengaños (2)

Deseos (1)
Esperanzas (1)
Evocaciones (1)
Ilusiones (1)

Melancolias (1)
Nostalgias (1)
Pasiones (1)
Pensamientos (2)

Promesas (2)
Quimeras (1)
Recuerdos (2)
Sensaciones (2)

Sentimientos (1)
Sueños (2)
Tentaciones (2)
Traiciones (2)

Verdades (2)

ZACHERLE, John, "The Cool Ghoul" '62
Born on 9/26/18 in Philadelphia. Hosted horror movies on TV during the 1950s.

11/10/62 **44** 10 **Monster Mash** .... [N] **$75** Parkway 7018

Bat, The
Dinner With Drac Part 1 *6*
Gravy (With Some Cynide)
Ha-Ha-Ha

Hurry Bury Baby
I'm The Ghoul From Wolverton
Mountain

Let's Twist Again (Mummy Time Is Here)
Limb From Limbo Rock
Monster Mash

Pistol Stomp
Popeye (The Gravedigger)
Weird Watusi

ZADORA, Pia '86
Born Pia Schipani on 5/4/54 in Hoboken, New Jersey. Singer/actress. Appeared in several movies.

3/8/86 **113** 20 © **Pia & Phil** .... **$10** CBS Associated 40259
with the London Philharmonic Orchestra

All My Tomorrows
Boy Next Door
But Not For Me

Come Rain Or Come Shine
East Of The Sun (And West Of The Moon)

Embraceable You
I Thought About You
It Had To Be You

Man That Got Away
Maybe This Time

Smile (Though Your Heart Is Breaking)
When The Sun Comes Out

ZAGER, Michael, Band '78
Born on 1/3/43 in Passaic, New Jersey. Disco keyboardist/producer. Member of **Ten Wheel Drive** from 1968-73.

4/22/78 **120** 13 **Let's All Chant** .... **$12** Private Stock 7013
Soul To Soul

Dancin' Disney Medley
Freak

Let's All Chant *36*

Love Express

Music Fever

ZAGER & EVANS '69
Folk-rock duo from Lincoln, Nebraska: Denny Zager and Rick Evans (both sing and play guitar).

8/2/69 **30** 13 **2525 (Exordium & Terminus)** .... **$20** RCA Victor 4214

Bayoan
Cary Lynn Javes
Fred

I Remember Heide
In The Land Of Green

In The Year 2525 (Exordium & Terminus) *1*
Less Than Tomorrow

Self
Taxi Man
Woman

ZAPP '80
Funk group from Dayton, Ohio: brothers **Roger** (vocals, guitar), Larry (percussion), Tony (bass) and Lester (drums) Troutman. Roger was shot to death by Larry in a murder-suicide on 4/25/99. Roger was age 47 and Larry was age 54.

9/27/80	**19**	19	●	©	1	**Zapp**			**$12**	Warner 3463
8/14/82	**25**	19	●	©	2	**Zapp II**			**$10**	Warner 23583
9/3/83	**39**	22			3	**Zapp III**			**$10**	Warner 23875
11/23/85+	**110**	26	●	©	4	**The New Zapp IV U**			**$10**	Warner 25327
10/7/89	**154**	4		©	5	**Zapp V**			**$10**	Reprise 25807
11/13/93	**39**	29	▲	©	6	**All The Greatest Hits**	C:#26/1	[G]	**$10**	Reprise 45143

ZAPP & ROGER

Ain't The Thing To Do (5)
Back To Bass-Iks (5)
Be Alright (1,6)
Been This Way Before (5)
Brand New Pplayer (1)
Cas-Ta-Spellome (4)
Come On (2)
Coming Home (1)
Computer Love (4,6)
Curiosity '93 (6)

Dance Floor (2,6)
Do It Roger (6)
Do You Really Want An Answer? (2)
Doo Wa Ditty (Blow That Thing) (2,3,6)
Fire (5)
Freedom (1)
Funky Bounce (1)
Heartbreaker (Part I & II) (3,6)

I Can Make You Dance (3,6)
I Heard It Through The Grapevine (Part 1) (6) *79*
I Only Have Eyes For You (4)
I Play The Talk Box (5)
I Want To Be Your Man (6) *3*
In The Mix (6)
It Doesn't Really Matter (4)
Itchin' For Your Twitchin' (4)
Ja Ready To Rock (4)

Jake E Stanstill (5)
Jesse Jackson (5)
Make Me Feel Good (4)
Mega Medley (6) *54*
Midnight Hour (6)
More Bounce To The Ounce - Part I (1,6) *86*
Night And Day (6)
Ooh Baby Baby (5)
Play Some Blues (3)

Playin' Kinda Ruff (2)
Radio People (4)
Rock 'N' Roll (4)
Rock Star (5)
Sad-Day Moaning (5)
Slow And Easy (6) *43*
So Ruff, So Tuff (6)
Spend My Whole Life (3)
Stop That (5)

Touch Of Jazz (Playin' Kinda Ruff Part II) (2)
Tut-Tut (Jazz) (3)
We Need The Buck (3)

ZAPPA, Frank ★80★ '74
Born on 12/21/40 in Baltimore, Maryland; raised in California. Died of cancer on 12/4/93 (age 52). Rock music's leading satirist. Singer/songwriter/guitarist/activist. Formed **The Mothers Of Invention** in 1965. In the movies *200 Motels* and *Baby Snakes*. Father of Dweezil and Moon Unit Zappa. Inducted into the Rock and Roll Hall of Fame in 1995.

1)Apostrophe (') 2)Sheik Yerbouti 3)Ship arriving too late to save a drowning witch
4)One Size Fits All 5)Joe's Garage, Act I

2/11/67	**130**	23	©	1	**Freak Out!**		**$100**	Verve 5005 [2]
7/8/67	**41**	22	©	2	**Absolutely Free**		**$100**	Verve 5013
3/16/68	**30**	19	©	3	**We're Only In It For The Money**		**$100**	Verve 5045
					THE MOTHERS OF INVENTION (above 3)			
6/8/68	**159**	5	©	4	**Lumpy Gravy**	[I]	**$75**	Verve 8741
					THE ABNUCEALS EMUUKHA ELECTRIC SYMPHONY ORCHESTRA AND CHORUS			
12/21/68+	**110**	12	©	5	**Cruising with Ruben & The Jets**		**$75**	Verve 5055
4/5/69	**151**	9		6	**Mothermania/The Best Of The Mothers**	[K]	**$75**	Verve 5068
					selections from the first 3 albums above			
5/3/69	**43**	11	©	7	**Uncle Meat**	[I]	**$50**	Bizarre 2024 [2]
					THE MOTHERS OF INVENTION (above 3)			
11/29/69	**173**	6	©	8	**Hot Rats**	[I]	**$50**	Bizarre 6356
3/14/70	**94**	8	©	9	**Burnt Weeny Sandwich**	[I]	**$50**	Bizarre 6370
9/26/70	**189**	3	©	10	**Weasels Ripped My Flesh**	[L]	**$50**	Bizarre 2028
					THE MOTHERS OF INVENTION (above 2)			
11/21/70	**119**	14	©	11	**Chunga's Revenge**		**$50**	Bizarre 2030
8/21/71	**38**	15	©	12	**The Mothers/Fillmore East-June 1971**	[L]	**$50**	Bizarre 2042
10/30/71	**59**	13	©	13	**Frank Zappa's 200 Motels**	[S]	**$50**	United Artists 9956 [2]
4/22/72	**85**	9	©	14	**Just Another Band From L.A.**	[L]	**$50**	Bizarre 2075
					THE MOTHERS			
					recorded on 8/7/71 at UCLA in Los Angeles			
9/9/72	**152**	7	©	15	**Waka/Jawaka - Hot Rats**	[I]	**$30**	Reprise 2094
10/6/73	**32**	50	● ©	16	**Over-nite Sensation**		**$25**	DiscReet 2149
					THE MOTHERS			

DEBUT	PEAK	WKS	RIAA	CD	ARTIST — Album Title	Catalog	Sym	$	Label & Number
					ZAPPA, Frank — Cont'd				
4/20/74	10	43	●	© 17	Apostrophe (')			$25	DiscReet 2175
10/5/74	27	18		© 18	Roxy & Elsewhere		[L]	$30	DiscReet 2202 [2]
					ZAPPA/MOTHERS				
7/19/75	26	12		© 19	One Size Fits All			$20	DiscReet 2216
					FRANK ZAPPA AND THE MOTHERS OF INVENTION				
11/1/75	66	8		© 20	Bongo Fury		[L]	$20	DiscReet 2234
					FRANK ZAPPA/CAPTAIN BEEFHEART/THE MOTHERS				
					recorded on 5/20/75 in Austin, Texas				
11/27/76	61	13		© 21	Zoot Allures			$15	Warner 2970
4/15/78	57	8		© 22	Zappa In New York		[L]	$20	DiscReet 2290 [2]
10/21/78	147	6		© 23	Studio Tan		[I]	$15	DiscReet 2291
2/17/79	175	4		© 24	Sleep Dirt		[I]	$15	DiscReet 2292
3/24/79	21	23		© 25	Sheik Yerbouti			$15	Zappa 1501 [2]
6/2/79	168	4		© 26	Orchestral Favorites		[I]	$15	DiscReet 2294
9/22/79	27	25		© 27	Joe's Garage, Act I			$12	Zappa 1603
12/15/79+	53	12		© 28	Joe's Garage, Acts II & III			$15	Zappa 1502 [2]
5/30/81	66	11		© 29	Tinsel Town Rebellion		[L]	$15	Barking P. 37336 [2]
10/3/81	93	7		© 30	You Are What You Is			$15	Barking P. 37537 [2]
6/12/82	23	22		© 31	Ship arriving too late to save a drowning witch ...			$12	Barking Pumpkin 38066
4/16/83	153	5		© 32	The Man From Utopia			$12	Barking Pumpkin 38403
1/18/86	153	6		© 33	Frank Zappa Meets The Mothers Of Prevention ...			$12	Barking Pumpkin 74203

Absolutely Free (3)
Advance Romance (20)
Aerobics In Bondage (33)
Air, The (7)
Alien Orifice (33)
America Drinks & Goes Home (2,6)
Amnesia Vivace (2)
Andy (19)
Any Downers? (30)
Any Way The Wind Blows (1,5)
Anything (5)
Apostrophe' (17)
Are You Hung Up (3)
Aybe Sea (9)
Baby Snakes (25)
Bamboozled By Love (29)
Be-Bop Tango (Of The Old Jazzmen's Church) (18)
Beauty Knows No Pain (30)
Big Leg Emma (22)
Big Swifty (15)
Billy The Mountain (14)
Black Napkins (21)
Black Page #1 & 2 (22)
Blue Light (29)
Bobby Brown (25)
Bogus Pomp (26)
Bow Tie Daddy (3)
Broken Hearts Are For Assholes (25)
Brown Shoes Don't Make It (2,6,29)
Burnt Weeny Sandwich, Theme From (9)
Bwana Dik (12)
Call Any Vegetable (2,6,14)
Camarillo Brillo (16)
Can't Afford No Shoes (19)
Carolina Hard-Core Ecstasy (20)
Catholic Girls (27)
Centerville (13)
Central Scrutinizer (27)
Charlie's Enormous Mouth (30)
Cheap Thrills (5)
Cheepnis (18)
Chrome Plated Megaphone Of Destiny (4)
Chunga's Revenge (11)
City Of Tiny Lites (25)
Clap, The (11)
Cocaine Decisions (32)
Concentration Moon (3)
Conehead (23)
Cosmik Debris (17)
Crew Slut (27)
Cruising For Burgers (7)
Cucamonga (20)
Daddy, Daddy, Daddy (13)
Dance Contest (29)
Dance Of The Just Plain Folks (13)
Dance Of The Rock & Roll Interviewers (13)
Dancin' Fool (25) *45*
Dangerous Kitchen (32)
Debra Kadabra (20)

Dental Hygiene Dilemma (13)
Deseri (5)
Dew On The Newts We Got (13)
Didja Get Any Onya (10)
Dinah - Moe Humm (16)
Directly From My Heart To You (10)
Dirty Love (16)
Disco Boy (21)
Do You Like My New Car? (12)
Does This Kind Of Life Look Interesting To You? (13)
Dog Breath (7,14)
Doing Work For Yuda (28)
Don't Eat The Yellow Snow (17) *86*
Don't You Ever Wash That Thing? (18)
Doreen (30)
Drafted Again (30)
Drowning Witch (31)
Duke Of Prunes (2,6,26)
Duke Regains His Chops (2)
Dumb All Over (30)
Dummy Up (18)
Dwarf Nebula Processional March & Dwarf Nebula (10)
Easy Meat (29)
Echidna's Arf (Of You) (18)
Eddie, Are You Kidding? (14)
Electric Aunt Jemina (7)
Envelopes (31)
Eric Dolphy Memorial Barbecue (10)
Evelyn, A Modified Dog (19)
Excentrifugal Forz (17)
Father O'Blivion (17)
Fifty - Fifty (16)
Filthy Habits (24)
Find Her Finer (21)
Fine Girl (29)
Flakes (25)
Flambay (24)
Florentine Pogen (19)
Flower Punk (3)
For The Young Sophisticate (29)
Fountain Of Love (5)
Friendly Little Finger (21)
Get A Little (10)
Girl Wants To Fix Him Some Broth (13)
Girl's Dream (13)
Go Cry On Somebody Else's Shoulder (1)
Goblin Girl (30)
God Bless America (7)
Greggery Peccary (23)
Gumbo Variations (8)
Half A Dozen Provocative Squats (13)
Happy Together (12)
Harder Than Your Husband (30)
Harry, You're A Beast (3)
He Used To Cut The Grass (28)
Heavenly Bank Account (30)
Holiday In Berlin, Full Blown (9)

Honey, Don't You Want A Man Like Me? (22)
Hot Poop (3)
How Could I Be Such A Fool (1,5)
Hungry Freaks, Daddy (1,6)
I Ain't Got No Heart (1,29)
I Come From Nowhere (31)
I Have Been In You (25)
I Promise Not To Come In Your Mouth (22)
I'm A Beautiful Guy (30)
I'm Not Satisfied (1,5)
I'm So Cute (25)
I'm Stealing The Towels (13)
I'm The Slime (16)
Ian Underwood Whips It Out (7)
Idiot Bastard Son (3,6)
If Only She Woulda (24)
If We'd All Been Living In California (7)
Igor's Boogie, Phase One & Two (9)
Illinois Enema Bandit (22)
In Memoriam, Edgar Varese (medley) (1)
Inca Roads (19)
Invocation & Ritual Dance Of The Young Pumpkin (2)
It Can't Happen Here (1,6)
It Just Might Be A One-Shot Deal (15)
It Must Be A Camel (8)
Janet's Big Dance Number (13)
Jazz Discharge Party Hats (32)
Jelly Roll Gum Drop (5)
Jewish Princess (25)
Joe's Garage (27)
Jones Crusher (25)
Jumbo Go Away (30)
Keep It Greasey (28)
King Kong (7)
Lad Searches The Night For His Newts (13)
Later That Night (5)
Latex Solar Beef (12)
Legend Of The Golden Arches (7)
Let Me Take You To The Beach (23)
Let's Make The Water Turn Black (3)
Little Beige Sambo (33)
Little Green Rosetta (28)
Little Green Scratchy Sweaters & Courduroy Ponce (13)
Little House I Used To Live In (9,12)
Little Umbrellas (8)
Lonely Little Girl (3)
Lonesome Cowboy Burt (13)
Lonesome Electric Turkey (12)
Louie Louie (7)
Love Of My Life (5,29)
Lucille Has Messed My Mind Up (27)
Lucy's Seduction Of A Bored Violinist (13)
Lumpy Gravy - Part I & II (4)

Magdalena (14)
Magic Fingers (13)
Man From Utopia Meets Mary Lou (32)
Man With The Woman Head (20)
Manx Needs Women (22)
Meek Shall Inherit Nothing (30)
Moggio (32)
Mom & Dad (3)
Montana (16)
More Trouble Every Day (18)
Mother People (3,6)
Motherly Love (1)
Motorhead's Midnight Ranch (13)
Mr. Green Genes (7)
Ms. Pinky (21)
Mud Shark (12)
Mudd Club (30)
Muffin Man (20)
My Guitar Wants To Kill Your Mama (10)
Mysterioso (13)
Mystery Roach (13)
Nancy & Mary Music - Part 1, 2, & 3 (11)
Nanook Rubs It (17)
Nasal Rententive Caliope Music (3)
Naval Aviation In Art (26)
9 Types Of Industrial Pollution (7)
No No No (3)
No Not Now (31)
Now You See It - Now You Don't (29)
Nun Suit Painted On Some Old Boxes (13)
Ocean Is The Ultimate Solution (24)
Oh No (10)
Okay To Tap Dance (medley) (1)
Orange County Lumber Truck (10)
Our Bizarre Relationship (7)
Outside Now (28)
Overture To A Holiday In Berlin (9)
Packard Goose (28)
Panty Rap (29)
Peaches En Regalia (8,12)
Peaches III (29)
Pedro's Dowry (26)
Penguin In Bondage (18)
Penis Dimension (13)
Pick Me, I'm Clean (29)
Plastic People (2,6)
Po-Jama People (19)
Poofter's Froth Wyoming Plans Ahead (20)
Porn Wars (33)
Pound For A Brown On The Bus (7)
Preamble (18)
Prelude To The Afternoon Of A Sexually Aroused Gas Mask (10)

Project X (7)
Purple Lagoon (22)
Pygmy Twylyte (18)
Radio Is Broken (32)
Rat Tomago (25)
Redneck Eats (13)
Redunzl (23)
Regyptian Strut (24)
Return Of The Son Of Monster Magnet Medley (1)
Revised Music For Guitar And Low Budget Orchestra (23)
Road Ladies (11)
Rubber Shirt (25)
Rudy Wants To Buy Yez A Drink (11)
Sam With The Showing Scalp Flat Top (20)
San Ber'dino (19)
Sealed Tuna Bolero (13)
Semi-Fraudulent/Direct-From-Hollywood (13)
Sex (32)
Sharleena (11)
She Painted Up Her Face (13)
Sheik Yerbouti Tango (25)
Shove It Right In (13)
Sleep Dirt (24)
Sleeping In A Jar (7)
Society Pages (30)
Sofa No. 1 & 2 (19,22)
Soft-Sell Conclusion (2)
Son Of Mr. Green Genes (7)
Son Of Orange County (18)
Son Of Suzy Creamcheese (3)
Spider Of Destiny (24)
St. Alfonzo's Pancake Breakfast (17)
Status Back Baby (2)
Stick It Out (28)
Stick Together (32)
Stink-Foot (17)
Strictly Genteel (13,26)
Stuff Up The Cracks (5)
Suicide Chump (30)
Sy Borg (28)
Take Your Clothes Off When You Dance (3)
Tears Began To Fall (12)
Teen-age Prostitute (31)
Teenage Wind (30)
Tell Me You Love Me (11,29)
3rd Movement Of Sinister Footwear, Theme From The (30)
This Town Is A Sealed Tuna Sandwich (13)
Time Is Money (24)
Tink Walks Amok (32)
Tinsel Town Rebellion (29)
Titties & Beer (22)
Toad-O Line (27)
Toads Of The Short Forest (10)
Token Of My Extreme (28)
Torture Never Stops (21)
Touring Can Make You Crazy (13)
Transylvania Boogie (11)
Trouble Comin' Every Day (1)

Tryin' To Grow A Chin (25)
Tuna Fish Promenade (13)
Twenty Small Cigars (11)
200 Years Old (20)
Uncle Bernie's Farm (2)
Uncle Meat (7)
Uncle Remus (17)
Valarie (2)
Valley Girl (31) *32*
Village Of The Sun (18)
Voice Of Cheese (7)
WPLJ (The Four Deuces) (9)
Waka/Jawaka (15)
Watermelon In Easter Hay (28)
We Are Not Alone (32)
We Can Shoot You (7)
We Gotta Get Into Something Real (25)
We're Turning Again (33)
Weasels Ripped My Flesh (10)
Wet T-Shirt Nite (27)
What Ever Happened To All The Fun In The World (25)
What Kind Of Girl Do You Think We Are? (12)
What Will This Evening Bring Me This Morning (13)
What's New In Baltimore? (33)
What's The Ugliest Part Of Your Body? (13)
Who Are The Brain Police? (1,6)
Who Needs The Peace Corps (3)
Why Does It Hurt When I Pee? (27)
Wild Love (25)
Willie The Pimp - Part One & Two (8,12)
Wind Up Workin' In A Gas Station (27)
Wonderful Wino (21)
Would You Go All The Way? (11)
Would You Like A Snack? (13)
Wowie Zowie (1)
Yo Cats (33)
Yo' Mama (25)
You Are What You Is (30)
You Didn't Try To Call Me (1,5)
You're Probably Wondering Why I'm Here (1,6)
Your Mouth (15)
Zolar Czakl (2)
Zomby Woof (16)
Zoot Allures (21)

ZEBRA '83
Rock trio from New Orleans: Randy Jackson (vocals, guitar), Felix Hanemann (bass) and Guy Gelso (drums).

| 5/14/83 | 29 | 28 | ● | © | 1 **Zebra** | | | $10 | Atlantic 80054 |
| 9/22/84 | 84 | 11 | | © | 2 **No Tellin' Lies** | | | $10 | Atlantic 80159 |

As I Said Before (1)
Bears (2)
But No More (2)
Don't Walk Away (1)

Drive Me Crazy (2)
I Don't Care (2)
I Don't Like It (2)
La La Song (1)

Little Things (2)
Lullaby (2)
No Tellin' Lies (2)
One More Chance (1)

Slow Down (1)
Take Your Fingers From My Hair (1)
Takin' A Stance (2)

Tell Me What You Want (1)
Wait Until The Summer's Gone (2)
When You Get There (1)

Who's Behind The Door? (1) *61*

ZEBRAHEAD '00
Rock-rap group from Los Angeles: Justin Mauriello (vocals), Ali Tabatabee (rap vocals), Greg Bergdorf (guitar), Ben Osmundson (bass) and Ed Udhus (drums).

| 9/9/00 | 127 | 2 | | © | **Playmate Of The Year** | | | $10 | Columbia 63817 |

E Generation
Go

Hell That Is My Life
I Am

I'm Money
In My Room

Livin' Libido Loco
Now Or Never

Playmate Of The Year
Subtract You

Wasted
What's Goin' On?

ZENO '86
Hard-rock trio from Germany: Michael Flexig (vocals, drums), Zeno Roth (guitar) and U. Winsomie Ritgen (bass). Roth's brother Uli is a member of **Scorpions**.

| 5/10/86 | 107 | 10 | | | **Zeno** | | | $10 | Manhattan 53025 |

Circles Of Dawn
Don't Tell The Wind

Eastern Sun
Emergency

Far Away
Heart On The Wing

Little More Love
Love Will Live

Sent By Heaven
Signs On The Sky

Sunset

ZENTNER, Si, And His Orchestra '62
Born Simon Zentner on 6/13/17 in New York City. Died of leukemia on 1/31/2000 (age 82). Jazz trombonist.

12/18/61+	65	8		©	1 **Big Band Plays The Big Hits**		[I]	$20	Liberty 7197
3/17/62	107	12		©	2 **Up A Lazy River (Big Band Plays The Big Hits: Vol. 2)**		[I]	$20	Liberty 7216
9/1/62	108	6			3 **The Stripper And Other Big Band Hits**		[I]	$20	Liberty 7247
2/9/63	139	5			4 **Desafinado**		[I]	$20	Liberty 7273

title is Spanish for "Out Of Tune"

African Waltz (1)
Apache (1)
Asia Minor (1)
Autumn Leaves (2)
Because They're Young (1)
Bernie's Tune (4)
Blue Moon (2)
Blue Tango (2)
Calcutta (1)
Canadian Sunset (3)

Caravan (4)
Come Closer To Me (4)
Desafinado (4)
Goza Goza (4)
Heart And Soul (2)
Hollywood Twist (2)
Honky Tonk (Part 2) (2)
Hot Toddy (3)
I'll See You In My Dreams (4)
Lisbon Antigua (4)

Manhattan Spiritual (3)
Maria (4)
Midnight In Moscow (3)
Midnight Sun (4)
Moon River (4)
Moonglow/Theme From Picnic (3)
Never On Sunday (2)
Nice 'N Easy (2)
One Mint Julep (3)

Oso Blanco (4)
Perfidia (2)
Petite Fleur (3)
Picnic ..see: Moonglow
Quizas, Quizas, Quizas (Perhaps, Perhaps, Perhaps) (4)
Raindrops (1)
Save The Last Dance For Me (1)

Shadrack (3)
Speak Low (4)
Star Eyes (4)
Stranger On The Shore (3)
Stripper, The (3)
Take Five (2)
Tenderly (1)
Up A Lazy River (1,2) *43*
Walk - Don't Run (1)
Walk On The Wild Side (3)

Will You Love Me Tomorrow (1)
Wonderland By Night (1)
Yellow Bird (2)

ZEPHYR '70
Rock group formed in Denver: Candy Givens (vocals), her brother David Givens (bass), **Tommy Bolin** (guitar; **Deep Purple**, **The James Gang**), John Faris (keyboards) and Robbie Chamberlain (drums). Bolin died of a drug overdose on 12/4/76 (age 26). Givens died of a drug overdose on 1/27/84 (age 37).

| 12/20/69+ | 48 | 26 | | © | **Zephyr** | | | $50 | Probe 4510 |

Boom-Ba-Boom
Cross The River

Hard Chargin' Woman
Huna Buna

Raindrops
Sail On

Somebody Listen
St. James Infirmary

Sun's A-Risin'

ZEVON, Warren '78
Born on 1/24/47 in Chicago. Rock singer/songwriter/pianist. Also see **Hindu Love Gods**.

| 8/28/76 | 189 | 2 | | © | 1 **Warren Zevon** | C:#45/4 | | $15 | Asylum 1060 |
| 2/25/78 | 8 | 28 | ▲ | © | 2 **Excitable Boy** | C:#10/14 | | $12 | Asylum 118 |

above 2 produced by **Jackson Browne**

3/8/80	20	16		©	3 **Bad Luck Streak In Dancing School**			$12	Asylum 509
1/17/81	80	10			4 **Stand In The Fire**		[L]	$12	Asylum 519
8/14/82	93	13			5 **The Envoy**			$12	Asylum 60159
6/27/87	63	18		©	6 **Sentimental Hygiene**			$10	Virgin 90603
5/1/93	198	1		©	7 **Learning To Flinch**		[L]	$10	Giant 24493
2/12/00	173	1		©	8 **Life'll Kill Ya**			$10	Artemis 751003

Accidentally Like A Martyr (2)
Ain't That Pretty At All (5)
Back In The High Life Again (6)
Backs Turned (Looking Down The Path) (1)
Bad Karma (6)
Bad Luck Streak In Dancing School (3)
Bed Of Coals (3)
Bill Lee (3)
Bo Diddley (medley) (4)
Bo Diddley's A Gunslinger (medley) (4)
Boom Boom Mancini (6,7)
Carmelita (1)
Certain Girl (3) *57*

Charlie's Medicine (5)
Desperados Under The Eaves (1)
Detox Mansion (6)
Dirty Little Religion (8)
Don't Let Us Get Sick (8)
Empty-Handed Heart (3)
Even A Dog Can Shake Hands (6)
Excitable Boy (2,4,7)
Factory, The (6)
Fistful Of Rain (8)
For My Next Trick I'll Need A Volunteer (8)
Frank And Jesse James (1)

French Inhaler (1,7)
Gorilla, You're A Desperado (3)
Hasten Down The Wind (1,7)
Heartache, The (6)
Hostage-O (4)
Hula Hula Boys (5)
I Was In The House When The House Burned Down (8)
I'll Sleep When I'm Dead (1,4)
I'll Slow You Down (8)
Indifference Of Heaven (7)
Jeannie Needs A Shooter (3,4)
Jesus Mentioned (5)
Johnny Strikes Up The Band (2)
Join Me In L.A. (1)
Jungle Work (3,7)

Lawyers, Guns And Money (2,4,7)
Leave My Monkey Alone (6)
Let Nothing Come Between You (5)
Life'll Kill Ya (8)
Looking For The Next Best Thing (5)
Mama Couldn't Be Persuaded (1)
Mohammed's Radio (1,4)
Mr. Bad Example (7)
My Shit's Fucked Up (8)
Never Too Late For Love (5)
Nighttime In The Switching Yard (2)
Ourselves To Know (8)

Overdraft, The (5)
Piano Fighter (7)
Play It All Night Long (3,7)
Poor Poor Pitiful Me (1,4,7)
Porcelain Monkey (8)
Reconsider Me (6)
Roland Chorale (7)
Roland The Headless Thompson Gunner (2,7)
Searching For A Heart (7)
Sentimental Hygiene (6)
Sin, The (4)
Splendid Isolation (7)
Stand In The Fire (4)
Tenderness On The Block (2)
Trouble Waiting To Happen (6)

Veracruz (2)
Werewolves Of London (2,4,7) *21*
Wild Age (3)
Worrier King (7)

ZHANÉ '94
Female R&B vocal duo from Philadelphia: Reneé Neufville and Jean Norris.

| 2/26/94 | 37 | 31 | ▲ | © | 1 **Pronounced Jah-Nay** | | | $10 | Motown 6369 |
| 5/10/97 | 41 | 9 | | © | 2 **Saturday Night** | | | $10 | Illtown 0751 |

Changes (1)
Color (2)
Confusion (2)
Crush (2)
For A Reason (1)

For The Longest Time (2)
Good Times (2)
Groove Thang (1) *17*
Hey Mr. D.J. (1) *6*
Just Like That (2)

Kindness For Granted (2)
La, La, La (1)
Last Dance (2)
Love Me Today (1)
My Word Is Bond (2)

Off My Mind (1)
Piece It Together (2)
Rendez-vous (2)
Request Line (2) *39*
Saturday Night (2)

Sending My Love (1) *40*
So Badd (2)
Sweet Taste Of Love (1)
Temporary Thing (2)
This Song Is For You (2)

Vibe (1)
You're Sorry Now (1)

ZODIAC MINDWARP & THE LOVE REACTION   '88
Born Mark Manning in England. Rock singer.

3/26/88	132	15	©	**Tattooed Beat Messiah**		$10	Vertigo 832729

Back Seat Education — Driving On Holy Gasoline — Let's Break The Law — Prime Mover — Spasm Gang — Tattooed Beat Messiah
Bad Girl City — Kid's Stuff — Planet Girl — Skull Spark Joker — Speech — Untamed Stare

ZOEGIRL   '01
Christian vocal trio: Alisa Girard, Chrissy Conway and Kristin Swinford.

| 4/28/01 | 173 | 1 | © | **Zoegirl** .... | $10 | Sparrow 51734 |

Anything Is Possible — Give Me One Reason — Little Did I Know — Living For You — Stop Right There — Upside Down
Constantly — I Believe — Live Life — No You — Suddenly

ZOMBIE, Rob   '98
Born Robert Cummings on 1/12/66 in Haverhill, Massachusetts. Founder of **White Zombie**.

| 9/12/98 | 5 | 66 | ▲³ © 1 | **Hellbilly Deluxe** .... | | $10 | Geffen 25212 |
| 11/13/99 | 38 | 6 | © 2 | **American Made Music To Strip By** .... | [K] | $10 | Geffen 490349 |

Ballad Of Resurrection Joe And — Call Of The Zombie (1) — How To Make A Monster (1,2) — Perversion 99 (1) — Spookshow Baby (1,2) — What Lurks On Channel X?
 Rosa Whore (1,2) — Demonoid Phenomenon (1,2) — Living Dead Girl (1,2) — Return Of The Phantom — Superbeast (1,2) — (1,2)
Beginning Of The End (1) — Dragula (1,2) — Meet The Creeper (1,2) — Stranger (1,2)

ZOMBIES, The   '65
Rock group from Hertfordshire, England: Colin Blunstone (vocals), Paul Atkinson (guitar), Rod **Argent** (keyboards), Chris White (bass) and Hugh Grundy (drums).

| 2/27/65 | 39 | 17 | 1 | **The Zombies** .... | | $50 | Parrot 71001 |
| 3/15/69 | 95 | 13 | © 2 | **Odessey & Oracle** .... | | $30 | Date 4013 |

Beechwood Park (2) — Care Of Cell (2) — I Want Her She Wants Me (2) — **She's Not There** (1) 2 — **Time Of The Season** (2) 3 — You've Really Got A Hold On
Brief Candles (2) — Changes (2) — I've Got My Mojo Working (1) — Sometimes (1) — What More Can I Do (1) — Me (1)
Butchers Tale (Western Front — Friends Of Mine (2) — It's Alright With Me (1) — Summertime (1) — Woman (1)
 1914) (2) — Hung Up On A Dream (2) — Maybe After He's Gone (2) — **Tell Her No** (1) 6 — Work 'N' Play (1)
Can't Nobody Love You (1) — I Don't Want To Know (1) — Rose For Emily (2) — This Will Be Our Year (2)

ZYDECO, Buckwheat — see BUCKWHEAT

ZZ TOP ★150★   '85
Rock trio formed in Houston: Billy Gibbons (vocals, guitar), Dusty Hill (vocals, bass) and Frank Beard (drums). Group appeared in the movie *Back To The Future III*.

1)Afterburner 2)Recycler 3)Tres Hombres

5/6/72	104	10	© 1	**Rio Grande Mud**		$15	London 612
8/4/73+	8	81	● © 2	**Tres Hombres**	C:#34/6	$15	London 631
				title is Spanish for "Three Men"			
5/17/75	10	47	● © 3	**Fandango!**	[L]	$15	London 656
				side 1: live; side 2: studio			
1/22/77	17	24	● © 4	**Tejas**		$15	London 680
12/17/77+	94	19	▲² © 5	**The Best Of ZZ Top**	[G]	$15	London 706
11/24/79+	24	43	▲ © 6	**Deguello**		$12	Warner 3361
8/8/81	17	22	● © 7	**El Loco**		$12	Warner 3593
4/23/83	9	183	▲¹⁰ © 8	**Eliminator**	C:#42/3	$10	Warner 23774
11/16/85	4	70	▲⁵ © 9	**Afterburner**		$10	Warner 25342
11/3/90	6	37	▲ © 10	**Recycler**		$10	Warner 26265
5/2/92	9	73	▲³ © 11	**Greatest Hits**	C:#13/68 [G]	$10	Warner 26846
2/5/94	14	23	▲ © 12	**Antenna**		$10	RCA 66317
10/5/96	29	11	© 13	**Rhythmeen**		$10	RCA 66956
10/16/99	100	4	© 14	**XXX**		$10	RCA 67850

Antenna Head (12) — Concrete And Steel (10) — **Give It Up** (10,11) 79 — Just Got Paid (1,5) — Party On The Patio (7) — Ten Foot Pole (7)
Apologies To Pearly (1) — Cover Your Rig (12) — Got Me Under Pressure (8,11) — Ko Ko Blue (1) — Pearl Necklace (7,11) — 36-22-36 (14)
Arrested For Driving While — Crucifixx-A-Flatt (14) — Groovy Little Hippie Pad (7) — **La Grange** (2,5,11) 41 — Penthouse Eyes (10) — Thug (8)
 Blind (4) 91 — Deal Goin' Down (12) — Gun Love (11) — **Legs** (8,11) 8 — Pincushion (12) — Thunderbird (3)
Asleep In The Desert (4) — Decision Or Collision (10) — Hairdresser (13) — Leila (7) 77 — Planet Of Women (9,11) — Trippin' (14)
Avalon Hideaway (4) — Delirious (9) — Have You Heard? (7) — (Let Me Be Your) Teddy Bear — Poke Chop Sandwich (14) — Tube Snake Boogie (7,11)
Backdoor Love Affair (4) — Dipping Low (In The Lap Of — Heard It On The X (3,5) — (14) — Precious And Grace (2) — **Tush** (3,5,11) 20
Backdoor Medley (3) — Luxury) (9) — Heaven, Hell Or Houston (7) — Lizard Life (12) — Prettyhead (13) — 2000 Blues (10)
Bad Girl (8) — Dirty Dog (8) — Hey Mr. Millionaire (14) — Loaded (13) — Rhythmeen (13) — **Velcro Fly** (9) 35
Balinese (3) — Don't Tease Me (7) — Hi Fi Mama (6) — Lovething (10) — **Rough Boy** (9,11) 22 — Vincent Price Blues (13)
Bang Bang (13) — **Doubleback** (10,11) 50 — Hot, Blue And Righteous (2) — Lowdown In The Street (6) — **Sharp Dressed Man** (8,11) 56 — Viva Las Vegas (11)
Bar-B-Q (1) — Down Brownie (1) — Hummbucking, Part 2 (13) — Made Into A Movie (14) — She Loves My Automobile (6) — Waitin' For The Bus (2,5)
Beatbox (14) — Dreadmonboogaloo (14) — I Got The Message (9) — Manic Mechanic (6) — She's A Heartbreaker (4) — What's Up With That (13)
Beer Drinkers & Hell Raisers — Dust My Broom (6) — I Got The Six (8) — Master Of Sparks (2) — She's Just Killing Me (13) — Whiskey'n Mama (1)
 (2,5) — El Diablo (4) — I Need You Tonight (8) — Mexican Blackbird (3) — Shiek (2) — Woke Up With Wood (9)
Belt Buckle (14) — Enjoy And Get It On (4) — **I Thank You** (6) 34 — Move Me On Down The Line (2) — Sinpusher (14) — World Of Swirl (14)
Black Fly (13) — Esther Be The One (6) — I Wanna Drive You Home (7) — Mushmouth Shoutin' (1) — **Sleeping Bag** (9,11) 8 — Zipper Job (13)
Blue Jean Blues (3,5) — Fearless Boogie (14) — I'm Bad, I'm Nationwide (6,11) — My Head's In Mississippi — Snappy Kakkie (4)
Breakaway (12) — Fool For Your Stockings (6) — If I Could Only Flag Her Down — (10,11) — **Stages** (9) 21
Burger Man (10) — Francene (1,5) 69 — (8) — My Mind Is Gone (13) — Sure Got Cold After The Rain
Can't Stop Rockin' (9) — Fuzzbox Voodoo (12) — **It's Only Love** (4) 44 — Nasty Dogs And Funky Kings — Fell (1)
Cheap Sunglasses (6,11) 89 — **Gimme All Your Lovin** — It's So Hard (7) — (3) — TV Dinners (8)
Cherry Red (12) — (8,11) 37 — Jailhouse Rock (3) — PCH (12) — Tell It (10)
Chevrolet (1) — Girl In A T-Shirt (12) — Jesus Just Left Chicago (2,5) — Pan Am Highway Blues (4) — Ten Dollar Man (1)

ALBUMS BY CATEGORY

The following categories list charted albums that are not listed in the Main Artist section. The albums within these categories are listed alphabetically by album title.

THE CATEGORIES

Movie Soundtracks (& Movie Soundtrack Compilations)
Original Casts
Television Soundtracks
Christmas (Various Artists)
Various Artist Compilations

CROSS REFERENCES

Many albums are cross referenced in their respective sections and refer back to an artist in the Main Artist section of this book A Movie Soundtrack or Original Cast album is listed in the Main Artist section if one artist contributed a major portion of the album's cuts.

CUTS INDEX GUIDELINES

If various artists contributed songs to an album, then the contributing artist is listed in brackets after the cut title.

Original versions of *Hot 100* hits appear in bold type with their peak position listed to the right. Keep in mind that many "oldie" hits charted years before their appearance on an album.

The following are unique to Movie Soundtrack, Original Cast and/or Television Soundtrack albums:

LETTER(S) IN BRACKETS AFTER ALBUM TITLES

Most symbols used in these sections correspond to the symbols used in the Main Artist section (see User's Guide on page xviii). In addition, the following three letter symbols are unique to these sections:

M: Musical   **O:** Oldies   **V:** Various Artists

Two or more letters within brackets separated by a "+" indicate that the symbols apply to different cuts. For example, **[I+V]** means that some of the cuts are Instrumental and the remaining are by Various Artists.

ABBREVIATIONS IN THE TITLE NOTES

cp: Composer	ly: Lyricist	pf: Performer
cd: Conductor	mu: Music writer	sw: Songwriter (music and lyrics)

MOVIE SOUNDTRACK/ORIGINAL CAST STARS

The Movie Soundtrack and Original Cast stars are listed below their respective titles. This information is also included below the Movie Soundtrack and Original Cast cross references.

DEBUT	PEAK	WKS	RIAA	CD	ARTIST — Album Title	Catalog	Sym	$	Label & Number

MOVIE SOUNDTRACKS

7/26/86 | **72** | 14 | | | **1 About Last Night...** .... [V] **$10** EMI America 17210
Rob Lowe/Demi Moore/James Belushi/Elizabeth Perkins/George DiCenzo

If Anybody Had A Heart [John Waite] **76**	Natural Love [Sheena Easton] (She's The) Shape Of Things To Come [John Oates]	Step By Step [J.D. Souther] 'Til You Love Somebody [Michael Henderson]
If We Can Get Through The Night [Paul Davis]	**So Far So Good** [Sheena Easton] **43**	Trials Of The Heart [Nancy Shanks]
Living Inside My Heart [Bob Seger]		True Love [Del Lords]

Words Into Action [Jermaine Jackson]

4/9/94 | **2**[1] | 36 | ▲2 | © | **2 Above The Rim** .... [V] **$10** Death Row 92359
Duane Martin/Leon/**2Pac**/Marlon Wayans/Bernie Mac

Afro Puffs [Lady Of Rage] **57**	Didn't Mean To Turn You On [2nd II None]	Hoochies Need Too [Paradise]
Anything [SWV] **18**	Dogg Pound 4 Life [Dogg Pound]	**I'm Still In Love With You** [Al B. Sure!]
Big Pimpin' [Dogg Pound]	Doggie Style [D.J. Rogers]	It's Not Deep Enough [Jewell]
Blowed Away [B Rezell]	Gonna Give It To Ya [Jewell & Aaron Hall]	Jus So Ya No [CPO-Boss Hog]
Crack 'Em [O.F.T.B.]		**Old Time's Sake** [Sweet Sable] **93**

Part Time Lover [H-Town] **57**
Pour Out A Little Liquor [Thug Life]
Regulate [Warren G. & Nate Dogg] **2**
U Bring Da Dog Out [Rhythm & Knowledge]

4/12/86 | **62** | 13 | | © | **3 Absolute Beginners** .... [V] **$10** EMI America 17182
Eddie O'Connell/Patsy Kensit/**David Bowie**/Ray Davies (**The Kinks**)/Sade

Absolute Beginners [David Bowie] **53**	Having It All [Eighth Wonder]	Rodrigo Bay [Working Week]
Have You Ever Had It Blue [Style Council]	Killer Blow [Sade]	Selling Out [Slim Gaillard]
	Quiet Life [Ray Davies]	That's Motivation [David Bowie]
	Riot City [Jerry Dammers]	Va Va Voom [Gil Evans]

Across 110th Street - see WOMACK, Bobby
Anthony Quinn/Yaphet Kotto/Anthony Franciosa/Antonio Fargas/Burt Young

Advance To The Rear - see NEW CHRISTY MINSTRELS, The
Glenn Ford/Stella Stevens/Melvyn Douglas/Jim Backus/Joan Blondell

7/14/90 | **66** | 9 | | © | **4 Adventures Of Ford Fairlane, The** .... [V] **$10** Elektra 60952
Andrew Dice Clay/Wayne Newton/Priscilla Presley/**Morris Day**/Lauren Holly

Can't Get Enough [Tone Loc]	Glad To Be Alive [Teddy Pendergrass & Lisa Fisher]	Last Time In Paris [Queensryche]
Cradle Of Love [Billy Idol] **2**	I Ain't Got You [Andrew Dice Clay]	Rock 'N Roll Junkie [Mötley Crüe]
Funky Attitude [Sheila E.]		Sea Cruise [Dion]

Unbelievable (Theme) [Yello]
Wind Cries Mary [Richie Sambora]

9/17/94 | **106** | 10 | | © | **5 Adventures Of Priscilla: Queen Of The Desert, The** ...... [O-V] **$10** Mother 516937
Terance Stamp/Hugo Weaving/Guy Pearce/Bill Hunter/Julia Cortez

Billy Don't Be A Hero [Paper Lace] **96**	Go West [Village People] **45**	I've Never Been To Me [Charlene] **3**
Can't Help Lovin' That Man [Trudy Richards]	I Don't Care If The Sun Don't Shine [Patti Page]	**Mamma Mia** [Abba] **32**
Finally [Ce Ce Peniston] **5**	**I Love The Nightlife (Disco 'Round)** [Alicia Bridges] **5**	My Baby Loves Lovin' [White Plains] **13**
Fine Romance [Lena Horne]	I Will Survive [Gloria Gaynor] **1**	

Save The Best For Last [Vanessa Williams] **1**
Shake Your Groove Thing [Peaches & Herb] **5**
Take A Letter Maria [R.B. Greaves] **2**

3/31/84 | **12** | 22 | ● | © | **6 Against All Odds** .... [I+V] **$10** Atlantic 80152
Rachel Ward/Jeff Bridges/James Woods/Alex Karras/Richard Widmark; cp/pf: **Larry Carlton** and Michel Colombier

Against All Odds (Take A Look At Me Now) [Phil Collins] **1**	For Love Alone	My Male Curiosity [Kid Creole & The Coconuts]
Balcony [Big Country]	Making A Big Mistake [Mike Rutherford]	Race, The
El Solitario	Murder Of A Friend	Rock And Roll Jaguar

Search, The (Main Theme)
Violet And Blue [Stevie Nicks]
Walk Through The Fire [Peter Gabriel]

8/20/94 | **157** | 3 | | © | **7 Airheads** .... [V] **$10** Fox 11014
Brendan Fraser/Steve Buscemi/**Adam Sandler**/Chris Farley/Joe Mantegna

Bastardizing Jellikit [Primus]	Degenerated [Lone Rangers]	I'll Talk My Way Out Of It [Stuttering John]
Born To Raise Hell [Motorhead]	Feed The Gods [White Zombie]	I'm The One [4 Non Blondes]
Can't Give In [Candlebox]	Fuel [Stick]	Inheritance [Prong]
Curious George Blues [Dig]		

London [Anthrax]
No Way Out [DGeneration]
We Want The Airwaves [Ramones]

4/18/70 | **104** | 19 | | © | **8 Airport** .... [I] **$30** Decca 79173
Burt Lancaster/**Dean Martin**/George Kennedy/Helen Hayes/Maureen Stapleton; cp/cd: Alfred Newman

Ada Quonsett, Stowaway!	Airport! (Main Title)	Inez - Lost Forever
Airport (End Title)	Emergency Landing!	Inez' Theme
Airport Love Theme	Guerrero's Goodbye	Joe Patroni (medley)

Mel And Tanya
Plane Or Plows? (medley)
Triangle!

11/28/92+ | **6** | 74 | ▲3 | © | **9 Aladdin** .... [M] **$10** Disney 60846
animated movie, voices by: **Robin Williams**/Lea Salonga/Bruce Adler; cp: Alan Menken; ly: Tim Rice/Howard Ashman

Aladdin's Word	Friend Like Me	Legend Of The Lamp
Arabian Nights	Happy End In Agrabah	Marketplace
Battle, The	Jafar's Hour	On A Dark Night
Cave Of Wonders	Jasmine Runs Away	One Jump Ahead
Ends Of The Earth	Kiss, The	Prince Ali

Street Urchins
To Be Free
Whole New World (cast version)
Whole New World [Peabo Bryson & Regina Belle] **1**

12/5/60+ | **7** | 47 | | © | **10 Alamo, The** .... [I+V] **$30** Columbia 1558 / 8358
John Wayne/Richard Widmark/Laurence Harvey/**Frankie Avalon**/Chill Wills; cp/cd: Dimitri Tiomkin

Ballad Of The Alamo [Marty Robbins] **34**	David Crockett's Speech [John Wayne]	General Santa Anna
Charge Of Santa Anna (medley)	De Guella (medley)	**Green Leaves Of Summer** [Brothers Four] **65**
David Crockett [John Wayne]	Death Of David Crockett (medley)	Green Leaves Of Summer (instrumental)
David Crockett Arrives	Final Assault (medley)	

Here's To The Ladies
Raid For Cattle
Tennessee Babe (Oh, Lisa!)

Alice's Restaurant - see GUTHRIE, Arlo
Arlo Guthrie/Pat Quinn/James Broderick/**Pete Seeger**/Lee Hays

7/7/79 | **113** | 8 | | © | **11 Alien** .... [I] **$15** 20th Century 593
Tom Skerritt/Sigourney Weaver/John Hurt/Harry Dean Stanton/Yaphet Kotto; cp: Jerry Goldsmith; cd: Lionel Newman

Acid Test	Droid, The	Landing, The
Alien Planet	End Title	Main Title
Breakaway	Face Hugger	Recovery, The

Shaft, The

3/22/80 | **36** | 23 | | | **12 All That Jazz** .... [M] **$12** Casablanca 7198
Roy Scheider/Jessica Lange/Ann Reinking/Ben Vereen/Max Wright; cd: Ralph Burns

After You've Gone	Everything Old Is New Again [Peter Allen]	Michelle
Bye Bye Love	Going Home Now	**On Broadway** [George Benson] **7**
Concert In G	Main Title	Ponte Vecchio
		Some Of These Days

South Mt. Sinai Parade
Take Off With Us
There'll Be Some Changes Made
Who's Sorry Now

SOUNDTRACKS

DEBUT	PEAK	WKS	RIAA	CD	ARTIST — Album Title	Catalog	Sym	$	Label & Number

12/3/83+ **165** 7 — **13 All The Right Moves** .... [V] $10 Casablanca 814449
Tom Cruise/Lea Thompson/Craig T. Nelson/Chris Penn/Mel Winkler

All The Right Moves [Jennifer Warnes/Chris Thompson] **85**	Hold Me Close To You [Stephanie Mills]	Last Stand [Doug Kahan]	This Could Be Our Last Chance [Danny Spanos]
Blue Skies Forever [Frankie Miller]	I Don't Wanna Go Down [Roach]	Love Theme [David Campbell] Mr. Popularity [Winston Ford]	Unison [Junior]

11/27/76 **48** 9 — **14 All This And World War II** .... [V] $25 20th Century 522 [2]
documentary movie; features **John Lennon** and **Paul McCartney** songs and a book of lyrics

Because [Lynsey DePaul]	Golden Slumbers (medley) [Bee Gees]	**Magical Mystery Tour** [Ambrosia] **39**	Strawberry Fields Forever [Peter Gabriel]
Carry That Weight (medley) [Bee Gees]	Help [Henry Gross]	Maxwell's Silver Hammer [Frankie Laine]	Sun King [Bee Gees]
Come Together [Tina Turner]	Hey, Jude [Brothers Johnson]	Michelle [Richard Cocciante]	We Can Work It Out [Four Seasons]
Day In The Life [Frankie Valli]	I Am The Walrus [Leo Sayer]	Nowhere Man (medley) [Jeff Lynne]	When I'm Sixty-Four [Keith Moon]
End, The [London Symphony Orchestra]	Let It Be [Leo Sayer]	Polythene Pam [Roy Wood]	With A Little Help From My Friends (medley) [Jeff Lynne]
Fool On The Hill [Helen Reddy]	Long And Winding Road [Leo Sayer]	She Came In Through The Bathroom Window [Bee Gees]	Yesterday [David Essex]
Get Back [Rod Stewart]	Lovely Rita [Roy Wood]	She's Leaving Home [Bryan Ferry]	You Never Give Me Your Money [Wil Malone & Lou Reizner]
Getting Better [Status Quo]	**Lucy In The Sky With Diamonds** [Elton John] **1**		

9/30/00 **43** 29 ● © **15 Almost Famous** .... [O-V] $10 Dreamworks 50279
Frances McDormand/Kate Hudson/Jason Lee/Patrick Fugit/Philip Seymour Hoffman

America [Simon & Garfunkel] **97**	I've Seen All Good People (medley) [Yes]	**One Way Out** [Allman Brothers Band] **86**	That's The Way [Led Zeppelin]
Every Picture Tells A Story [Rod Stewart]	It Wouldn't Have Made Any Difference [Todd Rundgren]	Simple Man [Lynyrd Skynyrd]	**Tiny Dancer** [Elton John] **41**
Feel Flows [Beach Boys]	Lucky Trumble [Nancy Wilson]	**Slip Away** [Clarence Carter] **6**	Wind, The [Cat Stevens]
Fever Dog [Stillwater]	**Mr. Farmer** [Seeds] **86**	Something In The Air [Thunderclap Newman] **37**	Your Move (medley) [Yes]
I'm Waiting For The Man [David Bowie]		Sparks [Who]	

Amadeus - see MARRINER, Neville
Tom Hulce/F. Murray Abraham/Elizabeth Berridge/Simon Callow/Jeffrey Jones

7/5/86 **91** 12 — **16 American Anthem** .... [V] $10 Atlantic 81661
Mitch Gaylord/Janet Jones/Michele Phillips/R.J. Williams/Michael Pataki

Angel Eyes [Andy Taylor]	Julie's Theme [Alan Silvestri]	Run To Her [Mr. Mister]	Two Hearts [John Parr]
Arthur's Theme [Alan Silvestri]	Love And Loneliness [Chris Thompson]	Same Direction [INXS]	Wings Of Love [Andy Taylor]
Battle Of The Dragon [Stevie Nicks]		**Take It Easy** [Andy Taylor] **24**	Wings To Fly [Graham Nash]

3/1/80 **7** 25 ● © **17 American Gigolo** [I+V] $12 Polydor 6259
Richard Gere/Lauren Hutton/Hector Elizondo/Bill Duke/Carol Bruce; cp/pf: **Giorgio Moroder**

Apartment, The	Hello Mr. W.A.M. (Finale)	Night Drive	Seduction, The (Love Theme)
Call Me [Blondie] **1**	Love And Passion [Cheryl Barnes]	Palm Springs Drive	

9/1/73+ **10** 60 ▲³ © **18 American Graffiti** [O-V] $25 MCA 8001 [2]
Richard Dreyfuss/Ron Howard/Cindy Williams/Charles Martin Smith/Harrison Ford

Ain't That A Shame [Fats Domino] **10**	Goodnight Sweetheart, Goodnite [Spaniels]	**Party Doll** [Buddy Knox] **1**	**Surfin' Safari** [Beach Boys] **14**
All Summer Long [Beach Boys]	Great Pretender [Platters] **1**	**Peppermint Twist** [Joey Dee & The Starliters] **1**	**Teen Angel** [Mark Dinning] **1**
Almost Grown [Chuck Berry] **32**	**Green Onions** [Booker T. & The MG's] **3**	**Rock Around The Clock** [Bill Haley] **1**	**That'll Be The Day** [Crickets] **1**
At The Hop [Flash Cadillac & The Continental Kids]	(He's) The Great Impostor [Fleetwoods] **30**	**Runaway** [Del Shannon] **1**	**Thousand Miles Away** [Heartbeats] **53**
Barbara-Ann [Regents] **13**	**Heart And Soul** [Cleftones] **18**	See You In September [Tempos] **23**	**To The Aisle** [Five Satins] **25**
Book Of Love [Monotones] **5**	I Only Have Eyes For You [Flamingos] **11**	She's So Fine [Flash Cadillac & The Continental Kids]	**Why Do Fools Fall In Love** [Frankie Lymon & The Teenagers] **6**
Chantilly Lace [Big Bopper] **6**	**Johnny B. Goode** [Chuck Berry] **8**	**Since I Don't Have You** [Skyliners] **12**	**Ya Ya** [Lee Dorsey] **7**
Come Go With Me [Dell-Vikings] **4**	**Little Darlin'** [Diamonds] **2**	**16 Candles** [Crests] **2**	**You're Sixteen** [Johnny Burnette] **8**
Crying In The Chapel [Orioles]	**Love Potion No. 9** [Clovers] **23**	**Smoke Gets In Your Eyes** [Platters] **1**	
Do You Want To Dance [Bobby Freeman] **5**	**Maybe Baby** [Crickets] **17**	**Stroll, The** [Diamonds] **4**	
Fanny Mae [Buster Brown] **38**	**Only You (And You Alone)** [Platters] **5**		
Get A Job [Silhouettes] **1**			

4/8/78 **31** 11 — **19 American Hot Wax** .... [O-V] $25 A&M 6500 [2]
Tim McIntire/Fran Drescher/Laraine Newman/Jay Leno/Hamilton Camp

Goodnight Sweetheart, Goodnite [Spaniels]	Maybe [Delights]	**Sincerely** [Moonglows] **20**	**There Goes My Baby** [Drifters] **1**
Great Balls Of Fire [Jerry Lee Lewis]	Mr. Blue [Timmy & The Tulips]	**Splish Splash** [Bobby Darin] **3**	**Tutti Frutti** [Little Richard] **17**
Hey Little Girl [Clark Otis]	Mr. Lee [Delights]	**Stay** [Maurice Williams] **1**	**When You Dance** [Turbans] **33**
Hot Wax Theme [Big Beat Band]	**Rave On** [Buddy Holly] **37**	**Sweet Little Sixteen** [Chuck Berry] **2**	Whole Lotta Shakin' Goin' On [Jerry Lee Lewis]
Hushabye [Mystics] **20**	Reelin' And Rockin' [Chuck Berry]	That Is Rock And Roll [Chesterfields]	Why Do Fools Fall In Love [Chesterfields]
I Put A Spell On You [Screamin' Jay Hawkins]	Rock And Roll Is Here To Stay [Prof. LaPlano & The Planotones]	**That's Why (I Love You So)** [Jackie Wilson] **13**	Zoom [Cadillacs]
Little Star [Elegants] **1**	Roll Over Beethoven [Chuck Berry] Sea Cruise [Frankie Ford] **14**		

7/17/99 **50** 22 ● © **20 American Pie** .... [V] $10 Universal 53269
Jason Biggs/Chris Klein/Tara Reid/Mena Suvari/Eugene Levy

Find Your Way Back Home [Dishwalla]	Man With The Hex [Atomic Fireballs]	Stranger By The Day [Shades Apart]	Sway [Big Runga]
Glory [Sugar Ray]	Mutt [Blink 182]	Summertime [Bachelor Number One]	Vintage Queen [Goldfinger]
Good Morning Baby [Dan Wilson & Big Runga]	New Girl [Third Eye Blind]	Super Down [Super Transatlantic]	Wishen [Loose Nuts] You Wanted More [Tonic]

1/31/87 **42** 19 © **21 American Tail, An** .... [M] $10 MCA 39096
animated movie, voices by: Dom DeLuise/Christopher Plummer/ Madeline Kahn/Laura Carson; cp/cd: James Horner

Cossack Cats	Great Fire	Releasing The Secret Weapon	Somewhere Out There (cast version)
Duo, A	Main Title	Reunited	Storm, The
Flying Away	Market Place	**Somewhere Out There** [Linda Ronstadt & James Ingram] **2**	There Are No Cats In America
Give Me Your Tired, Your Poor	Never Say Never		

1/3/98 **80** 6 © **22 American Werewolf In Paris, An** .... [V] $10 Hollywood 62131
Tom Everett Scott/Julie Delpy/Vince Vieluf/Phil Buckman/Julie Bowen

Adrenaline [Phunk Junkeez]	If I Could (What I Would Do) [Vanessa Daou]	Never Gonna Give You Up [Cake]	Theme from "An American Werewolf In Paris" [Wilbert Hirsch]
Break The Glass [Suicide Machines]	Loverbeast In Paris [Smooe Diamonds]	Normal Town [Better Than Ezra]	Turned Blue [Caroline's Spine]
Downtime [Fat]	Mouth [Bush]	Psychosis [Refreshments]	
Hardset Head [Skinny Puppy]		Sick Love [Redd Kross]	
Human Torch [Fastball]		Soup Kitchen [Eva Trout]	

992

DEBUT	PEAK	WKS	RIAA	CD	ARTIST — Album Title	Catalog	Sym	$	Label & Number

11/22/97 · 41 · 32 · ● · © 23 · Anastasia .... [M] $10 Atlantic 83053
animated movie, voices by: Meg Ryan/John Cusack/Angela Lansbury; ly: Lynn Ahrens; mu: Stephen Flaherty; cp/cd: David Newman

At The Beginning [Donna Lewis & Richard Marx] **45**	Kidnap And Reunion	Once Upon A December	Rumor In St. Petersburg
In The Dark Of The Night	Learn To Do It	Paris Holds The Key (To Your Heart)	Speaking Of Sophie
Journey To The Past	Learn To Do It (Waltz Reprise)		Viaje Tiempo Atrás (Journey To The Past) [Thalia]
	Nightmare, The	Reminiscing With Grandma	

9/30/95 · 96 · 3 · © 24 · Angus .... [V] $10 Reprise 45960
George C. Scott/Charlie Talbert/Kathy Bates/Ariana Richards/Rita Moreno

Ain't That Unusual [Goo Goo Dolls]	Enough [Dance Hall Crashers]	Jack Names The Planets [Ash]	You Gave Your Love To Me Softly [Weezer]
Am I Wrong [Love Spit Love]	Funny Face [Muffs]	Kung Fu [Ash]	
Back To You [Riverdales]	J.A.R. (Jason Andrew Relva) [Green Day]	Mrs. You And Me [Smoking Popes]	
Deep Water [Pansy Division]		White Homes [Tilt]	

9/2/78 · 71 · 18 · © 25 · Animal House .... C:#14/89 [O-V] $15 MCA 3046
John Belushi/Tim Matheson/John Vernon/Tom Hulce/Donald Sutherland

Animal House [Stephen Bishop] **73**	Let's Dance [Chris Montez] **4**	Shama Lama Ding Dong [Lloyd Williams]	**Twistin' The Night Away** [Sam Cooke] **9**
Dream Girl [Stephen Bishop]	**Louie, Louie** [John Belushi] **89**	Shout [Lloyd Williams]	**Wonderful World** [Sam Cooke] **12**
Faber College Theme [Elmer Berstein]	Money (That's What I Want) [John Belushi]	**Tossin' And Turnin'** [Bobby Lewis] **1**	
Hey Paula [Paul & Paula] **1**			

5/29/82 · 35 · 31 · ▲ · 26 · Annie .... [M] $12 Columbia 38000
Aileen Quinn/Carol Burnett/Albert Finney/Tim Curry; mu: Charles Strouse; ly: Martin Charnin; cd: Ralph Burns

Dumb Dog	I Think I'm Gonna Like It Here	Maybe	We Got Annie
Easy Street	It's The Hard-Knock Life	Sandy	You're Never Fully Dressed Without A Smile
I Don't Need Anything But You (medley)	Let's Go To The Movies	Sign	
	Little Girls	Tomorrow	

Annie Get Your Gun - see "Those Glorious MGM Musicals"
Betty Hutton/Howard Keel/Louis Calhern/J. Carol Naish/Keenan Wynn

1/22/00 · 28 · 11 · © 27 · Any Given Sunday .... [V] $10 Warner Sunset 83272
Al Pacino/Cameron Diaz/Dennis Quaid/James Woods/Jamie Foxx

Any Given Sunday [Jamie Foxx]	Move Right Now [Swizz Beatz]	Shut 'Em Down [LL Cool J]	Whatever It Takes [P.O.D.]
Be A Man [Hole]	My Ni**as [DMX]	**Shut Up** [Trick Daddy] **83**	Who You Gonna Call [Missy "Misdemeanor" Elliott]
F**k That [Kid Rock]	Never Goin' Back [Mobb Deep]	Sole Sunday [Goodie Mob]	Why [Godsmack]
Jump [Mystikal]	Reunion [Capone-N-Noreaga]	Stompbox [Overseer]	

1/17/81 · 141 · 9 · 28 · Any Which Way You Can .... [V] $12 Warner 3499
Clint Eastwood/Sondra Locke/Geoffrey Lewis/Ruth Gordon/William Smith

Acapulco [Johnny Duncan]	Beers To You [Ray Charles & Clint Eastwood]	Good Guys And The Bad Guys [John Durrill]	Too Loose [Sondra Locke]
Any Way You Want Me [Gene Watson]	Cotton-Eyed Clint [Texas Opera Company]	One Too Many Women In Your Life [Sondra Locke]	Whiskey Heaven [Fats Domino]
Any Which Way You Can [Glen Campbell]	Cow Patti [Jim Stafford]	Orangutan Hall Of Fame [Cliff Crofford]	You're The Reason God Made Oklahoma [David Frizzell & Shelly West]

1/9/61 · 18 · 15 · 29 · Apartment, The .... [I] $50 United Artists 3105
Jack Lemmon/Shirley MacLaine/Fred MacMurray/Ray Walston/Jack Kruschen; cp: Adolph Deutsch; cd: Mitchell Powell

Apartment, The (Theme)	Kicked In The Head	Ring A Ding Ding	Where Are You Fran
Blue Christmas	Little Brown Jug	So Fouled Up	
Career March	Lonely Room	Tavern In Town	
Hong Kong Blues	Office Workers	This Night	

7/15/95 · 90 · 8 · © 30 · Apollo 13 .... [I+O] $10 MCA 11241
Tom Hanks/Ed Harris/Kevin Bacon/Kathleen Quinlan/Gary Sinise; cp: James Horner; cd: Sandy DeCrescent

All Systems Go	House Cleaning	**Night Train** [James Brown] **35**	**Somebody To Love** [Jefferson Airplane] **5**
Blue Moon [Mavericks]	Houston, We Have A Problem	One Small Step	**Spirit In The Sky** [Norman Greenbaum] **3**
Darkside Of The Moon (medley)	**I Can See For Miles** [Who] **9**	Out Of Time	Waiting For Disaster
End Titles	Into The LEM (medley)	Privilege, A	Welcome To Apollo 13
Failure Is Not An Option	Launch, The	**Purple Haze** [Jimi Hendrix] **65**	What's Going On
Groovin' [Young Rascals] **1**	Main Title (medley)	Re-Entry & Splashdown	
Honky Tonkin' [Hank Williams]	Master Alarm (medley)	Shut Her Down	

3/14/98 · 175 · 2 · © 31 · Apostle, The .... [V] $10 Rising Tide 53058
Robert Duvall/Farrah Fawcett/Billy Bob Thornton/Miranda Richardson/June Carter Cash

I Love To Tell The Story [Emmylou Harris/Robert Duvall]	I'm A Soldier In The Army Of The Lord [Lyle Lovett]	There Ain't No Grave (Gonna Hold My Body Down) [Russ Taff]	Two Coats [Patty Loveless]
I Will Not Go Quietly [Steven Curtis Chapman]	In The Garden [Johnny Cash]	There Is A River [Gaither Vocal Band]	Victory Is Mine [Sounds Of Blackness]
I'll Fly Away [Gary Chapman/Wynonna]	Softly & Tenderly [Rebecca Lynn Howard]	There Is Power In The Blood [Lari White]	Waitin' On The Far Side Banks Of Jordan [Carter Family]
	Softly & Tenderly [Dino Kartsonakis]		

April Love - see BOONE, Pat
Pat Boone/Shirley Jones/Dolores Michaels/Arthur O'Connell/Matt Crowley

Arabesque - see MANCINI, Henry
Gregory Peck/Sophia Loren/Alan Badel/Kieron Moore/Carl Duering

1/23/71 · 137 · 10 · © 32 · Aristocats, The .... C:#17/5 [M] $15 Disneyland 3995
animated movie, voices by: Phil Harris/Sterling Holloway/Paul Winchell/Scatman Crothers/Nancy Kulp

Aristocats, The	Scales And Arpeggios	Thomas O'Malley Cat	
Ev'rybody Wants To Be A Cat	She Never Felt Alone		

7/11/98 · ❶² · 56 · ▲⁴ · © 33 · Armageddon .... [V] $10 Columbia 69440
Bruce Willis/Liv Tyler/Billy Bob Thornton/Ben Affleck/Steve Buscemi

Animal Crackers [Steven Tyler]	Leaving On A Jet Plane [Chantal Kreviazuk]	Starseed [Our Lady Peace]	What Kind Of Love Are You On [Aerosmith]
Come Together [Aerosmith] **23**	Mister Big Time [Jon Bon Jovi]	**Sweet Emotion** [Aerosmith] **36**	When The Rainbow Comes [Shawn Colvin]
I Don't Want To Miss A Thing [Aerosmith] **8**	Remember Me [Journey]	Theme From Armageddon [Trevor Rabin]	Wish I Were You [Patty Smyth]
La Grange [ZZ Top] **41**	**Roll Me Away** [Bob Seger] **27**		

4/13/57 · ❶¹⁰ · 88 · © 34 · Around The World In 80 Days .... [I] $40 Decca 79046
David Niven/Cantinflas/Noel Coward/Robert Newton/Shirley MacLaine; cp/cd: Victor Young

Around The World (Main Theme) **13**	India Country Side	Paris Arrival	Temple Of Dawn
Entrance Of The Bull March (medley)	Invitation To A Bull Fight (medley)	Passepartout	
	Land Ho	Prairie Sail Car	
	Pagoda Of Pillagi	Sky Symphony	

SOUNDTRACKS

DEBUT	PEAK	WKS	RIAA	CD	ARTIST — Album Title	Catalog	Sym	$	Label & Number

10/21/57 · 8 · 4 · 35 · Around The World In 80 Days [I] $30 Stereo-Fidelity 2800
pf: New World Theatre Orchestra; not the original soundtrack (see version above)

Around The World - Pt. 1 & 2	India Country Side	Paris Arrival
Around The World - Pt. II	Invitation To A Bull Fight (medley)	Passepartout
Entrance Of The Bull March (medley)	Land Ho	Prairie Sail Car
	Pagoda Of Pillagi	Sky Symphony

Temple Of Dawn

9/5/81 · 32 · 22 · 36 · Arthur (The Album) [I+V] $12 Warner 3582
Dudley Moore/**Liza Minnelli**/John Gielgud/Geraldine Fitzgerald/Jill Eikenberry; cp: **Burt Bacharach**

Arthur's Theme (Best That You Can Do) [Christopher Cross] 1	Arthur's Theme (Best That You Can Do) (instrumental)	It's Only Love [Stephen Bishop]
	Fool Me Again [Nicolette Larson]	Money
		Moving Pictures

Poor Rich Boy [Ambrosia]
Touch

5/31/97 · 184 · 4 · © · 37 · Austin Powers - International Man Of Mystery ...... C:#14/6 [V] $10 Hollywood 62112
Mike Myers/Elizabeth Hurley/Michael York/Mimi Rogers/Robert Wagner

Austin Powers [Wondermints]	Carnival [Cardigans]	Magic Piper (Of Love) [Edwyn Collins]
Austin's Theme [James Taylor Quartet]	Female Of The Species [Space]	**Mas Que Nada** [Sergio Mendes & Brasil '66] 47
BBC [Ming Tea]	**I Touch Myself** [Divinyls] 4	"Shag-adelic" Austin Powers Score Medley [George Clinton]
Book Lovers [Broadcast]	**Incense And Peppermints** [Strawberry Alarm Clock] 1	
Call Me [Mike Flowers Pops]	Look Of Love [Susanna Hoffs]	

Soul Bossa Nova [Quincy Jones]
These Days [Luxury]
What The World Needs Now Is Love [Burt Bacharach & The Posies]
You Showed Me [Lightning Seeds]

6/19/99 · 5 · 28 · ▲ · © · 38 · Austin Powers - The Spy Who Shagged Me [V] $10 Maverick 47348
Mike Myers/Heather Graham/Verne Troyer/Michael York/Robert Wagner

Alright [Lucy Nation]	Buggin' [Flaming Lips]	I'll Never Fall In Love Again [Burt Bacharach & Elvis Costello]
American Woman [Lenny Kravitz] 49	Draggin' The Line [R.E.M.]	Just The Two Of Us [Dr. Evil]
Beautiful Stranger [Madonna] 19	Espionage [Green Day]	**My Generation** [Who] 74

Soul Bossa Nova [Quincy Jones]
Time Of The Season [Big Blue Missile]
Word Up [Melanie G]

11/13/99 · 145 · 11 · © · 39 · Austin Powers - The Spy Who Shagged Me, More Music From ...... [V] $10 Maverick 47538

Am I Sexy? [Lords Of Acid]	Austin Powers Shagaphonic Medley [George Clinton]	**Beautiful Stranger** [Madonna] 19
American Woman [Guess Who] 1	Bachelor Pad [Fantastic Plastic Machine]	Crash! [Propellerheads]
Austin Meets Felicity		Dr. Evil [They Might Be Giants]
		Get The Girl [Bangles]

I'm A Believer [Monkees] 1
Let's Get It On [Marvin Gaye] 1
Magic Carpet Ride [Steppenwolf] 3
Time Of The Season [Zombies] 3

1/20/62 · 57 · 18 · 40 · Babes In Toyland ...... [M] $40 Buena Vista 4022
Tommy Sands/Annette Funicello/Ray Bolger/Ed Wynn/Ann Jillian

Castle In Spain	Just A Toy	Never Mind Bo-Peep
Floretta	Just A Whisper Away	Slowly He Sank To The Bottom Of The Sea
Forest Of No Return	Lemonade (medley)	Tom And Mary (Finale)
Go To Sleep	March Of The Toys	Toyland
I Can't Do The Sum	Mother Goose Village (medley)	

We Won't Be Happy Till We Get It
Workshop Song

9/5/87 · 188 · 2 · © · 41 · Back To The Beach ...... [V] $10 Columbia 40892
Frankie Avalon/Annette Funicello/Lori Laughlin/Connie Stevens/Demian Slade

Absolute Perfection [Private Domain]	Jamaica Ska [Annette Funicello & Fishbone]	Sign Of Love [Aimee Mann]
California Sun [Frankie Avalon]	Pipeline [Stevie Ray Vaughan & Dick Dale]	Sun, Sun, Sun, Sun, Sun [Marti Jones]
Catch A Ride [Eddie Money]		Surfin' Bird [Pee-wee Herman]

Wipe Out [Herbie Hancock]
Wooly Bully [Dave Edmunds]

7/27/85 · 12 · 32 · ● · © · 42 · Back To The Future ...... [V] $10 MCA 6144
Michael J. Fox/Christopher Lloyd/Lea Thompson/Crispin Glover/Thomas F. Wilson

Back In Time [Huey Lewis & The News]	Heaven Is One Step Away [Eric Clapton]	Night Train [Marvin Berry & The Starlighters]
Back To The Future [Alan Silvestri]	Johnny B. Goode [Marty McFly & The Starlighters]	**Power Of Love** [Huey Lewis & The News] 1
Earth Angel (Will You Be Mine) [Marvin Berry & The Starlighters]		

Time Bomb Town [Lindsey Buckingham]
Wallflower (Dance With Me Henry) [Etta James]

5/7/94 · 190 · 1 · © · 43 · BackBeat ...... [M] $10 Virgin 39386
Sheryl Lee/Stephen Dorff/Ian Hart/Gary Bakewell/Chris O'Neill; based on the early career of **The Beatles**; pf: Greg Dulli, Don Fleming, Dave Grohl (**Nirvana**), Mike Mills (**R.E.M.**), Thurston Moore (**Sonic Youth**) and Dave Pirner (**Soul Asylum**)

Bad Boy	Good Golly Miss Molly	Please Mr. Postman
Carol	Long Tall Sally	Roadrunner
C'mon Everybody	Money	Rock 'N' Roll Music

Slow Down
20 Flight Rock
Twist And Shout

4/8/95 · 26 · 21 · ▲ · 44 · Bad Boys ...... [V] $10 Work 67009
Martin Lawrence/Will Smith/Tea Leoni/Theresa Randle/Joe Pantoliano

Bad Boys Reply ('95) [Inner Circle]	Five O, Five O (Here They Come) [69 Boyz]	Me Against The World [2Pac]
Boom Boom Boom [Juster]	I've Got A Little Something For You [MN8]	Never Find Someone Like You [Keith Martin]
Call The Police [Ini Kamoze]	Juke-Joint Jezebel [KMFDM]	**Shy Guy** [Diana King] 13
Clouds Of Smoke [Call O' Da Wild]		So Many Ways [Warren G]
Da B Side [Da Brat]		

Someone To Love [Jon B] 10
Theme From Bad Boys [Mark Mancina]
Work Me Slow [Xscape]

12/7/68 · 183 · 5 · 45 · Barbarella ...... [I+M] $50 DynoVoice 31908
Jane Fonda/Milo O'Shea/David Hemmings/John Phillip Law/Marcel Marceau; ly/pf: **Bob Crewe**; mu: Charles Fox

Angel Is Love	Entrance Into Sogo	Labyrinth, The
Barbarella	Fight In Flight	Love, Love, Love Drags Me Down
Black Queen's Beads	Goodnight Alfie	Pill, The
Chamber Of Dreams	Hello Pretty Pretty	Pygar Finds Barbarella
Dead Duck	Hungry Dolls	Pygar's New Wings
Destruction Of Sogo	I Love All The Love In You	Pygar's Persecution

Sex Machine
Ski Ride
Smoke (Viper Vapor)
Spaceship Out Of Control

4/25/98 · 136 · 1 · © · 46 · Barney's Great Adventure - The Movie ...... [V] $10 Barney 9418
Bob West/George Hearn/Shirley Douglas/Trevor Morgan/Diana Rice

All The Pretty Ponies [Jane Siberry]	I Love You [Take 6/Sheena Easton/Jeffrey Osborne]	Let Me Call You Sweetheart (Reprise) [Valerie Carter]
Barney-The Song (Main Title Song) [Bernadette Peters]	If All The Raindrops [Peabo Bryson]	Let's Sing All The Way Home [Jennifer Warnes]
Count The Stars [Roberta Flack]	If You're Happy And You Know It	Old MacDonald
Dream (Twinken's Tune) [Peabo Bryson]	Imagine	Rainbows Follow The Rain [Collin Boyd]
Frere Jacques [Jennifer Rush]	Lavender's Blue [Jane Siberry]	
Goodnight [Sheena Easton]	Let Me Call You Sweetheart	

Twinkle, Twinkle Little Star [Johnny Van Zant]
We're Gonna Find A Way
Who's Inside It?
You Can [Jennifer Warnes]
You Can Do Anything [Stephen Bishop]

2/14/76 · 132 · 15 · 47 · Barry Lyndon ...... [I] $15 Warner 2903
Ryan O'Neal/Marisa Berenson/Patrick Magee/Gay Hamilton/Murray Melvin; cd: Leonard Rosenman

Adagio from Concerto For Two Harpsicords And Orchestra In C-Minor	Cavatina from "Il Barbiere Di Siviglia"	Hohenfriedberger March
British Grenadiers	Cello Concerto E-Minor (Third Movement)	Lilliburlero
	German Dance No. 1 In C-Major	March From Idomeneo
		Piano Trio In E-Flat, Op. 100 (Second Movement)

Piper's Maggot Jig
Sarabande Main Title
Sea-Maiden, The
Tin Whistles
Women Of Ireland

DEBUT	PEAK	WKS	RIAA	CD	ARTIST — Album Title	Catalog Sym	$	Label & Number

5/20/95 — **184** — **1** — © 48 — **Basketball Diaries, The** .... [V] **$10** Island 524093
Leonardo DiCaprio/Bruno Kirby/Mark Wahlberg (**Marky Mark**)/Lorraine Bracco/Ernie Hudson

Blind Dogs [Soundgarden]	Dizzy [Green Apple Quick Step]	It's Been Hard [Graeme Revell w/Jim Carroll]
Catholic Boy [Jim Carroll w/Pearl Jam]	Down By The Water [PJ Harvey]	People Who Died [Jim Carroll Band]
Coming Right Along [Posies]	Dream Massacre [Graeme Revell]	Riders On The Storm [Doors] 14
Devil's Toe [Graeme Revell w/Jim Carroll]	I Am Alone [Graeme Revell w/Jim Carroll]	Star [Cult]
	I've Been Down [Flea]	

Strawberry Wine [Massive Internal Complications]
What A Life [Rockers HiFi]

Batman - see ELFMAN, Danny / PRINCE
Michael Keaton/Jack Nicholson/Kim Basinger/Robert Wuhl/Pat Hingle

6/28/97 — **5** — **22** ▲ — © 49 — **Batman & Robin** .... [V] **$10** Warner Sunset 46620
Arnold Schwarzenegger/George Clooney/Chris O'Donnell/Uma Thurman/Alicia Silverstone

Batman Overture [Elliot Goldenthal]	End Is The Beginning Is The End [Smashing Pumpkins]	House On Fire [Arkana]
Beginning Is The End Is The Beginning [Smashing Pumpkins]	Foolish Games [Jewel] 7	Lazy Eye [Goo Goo Dolls]
Breed [Lauren Christy]	Fun For Me [Moloko]	Look Into My Eyes [Bone Thugs-N-Harmony] 4
Bug, The [Soul Coughing]	Gotham City [R. Kelly] 9	Moaner [Underworld]

Poison Ivy [Me'shell Ndegéocello]
Revolution [R.E.M.]
True To Myself [Eric Benét]

6/24/95 — **5** — **34** ▲2 — © 50 — **Batman Forever** .... [V] **$10** Atlantic 82759
Val Kilmer/Tommy Lee Jones/Jim Carrey/Nicole Kidman/Chris O'Donnell

Bad Days [Flaming Lips]	Hunter Gets Captured By The Game [Massive Attack]	One Time Too Many [PJ Harvey]
Crossing The River [Devlins]	Kiss From A Rose [Seal] 1	Passenger, The [Michael Hutchence]
8 [Sunny Day Real Estate]	Nobody Lives Without Love [Eddi Reader]	Riddler, The [Method Man] 56
Hold Me, Thrill Me, Kiss Me, Kill Me [U2] 16		Smash It Up [Offspring]

Tell Me Now [Mazzy Star]
There Is A Light [Nick Cave]
Where Are You Now? [Brandy]

Batman Returns - see ELFMAN, Danny
Michael Keaton/Michelle Pfeiffer/Danny DeVito/Christopher Walken/Michael Gough

2/19/00 — **78** — **6** — © 51 — **Beach, The** .... [V] **$10** London 31079
Leonardo DiCaprio/Tilda Swinton/Virginie Ledoyen/Robert Carlyle/Daniel York

Beached [Angelo Badalamenti & Orbital]	On Your Own [Blur]	Richard, It's Business As Usual [Barry Adamson]
Brutal [New Order]	Porcelain [Moby]	Snakeblood [Leftfield]
8 Ball [Underworld]	Pure Shores [All Saints]	Spinning Away [Sugar Ray]
Lonely Soul [Unkle]	Return Of Django [Asian Dub Foundation]	Voices [Dario G]

Woozy [Faithless]
Yeke Yeke [Mory Kante]

Beach Party - see ANNETTE
Annette Funicello/**Frankie Avalon**/Robert Cummings/Harvey Lembeck/Morey Amsterdam

Beaches - see MIDLER, Bette
Bette Midler/Barbara Hershey/John Heard/Lainie Kazan/Mayim Bialik

6/2/84 — **14** — **21** ● — © 52 — **Beat Street, Volume 1** .... [V] **$10** Atlantic 80154
Rae Dawn Chong/Guy Davis/John Chardiet/Leon Grant/Lee Chamberlin

Baptize The Beat [System]	Beat Street Strut [Juicy]	Strangers In A Strange World [Jenny Burton & Patrick Jude] 54
Beat Street Breakdown - Part 1 [Grandmaster Melle Mel & The Furious Five] 86	Breaker's Revenge [Arthur Baker]	This Could Be The Night [Cindy Mizelle]
	Frantic Situation [Afrika Bambaataa & The Soul Sonic Force]	

Tu Carino/Carmen's Theme [Ruben Blades]
Us Girls [Sharon Green, Lisa Counts & Debbie D.]

9/29/84 — **137** — **9** — 53 — **Beat Street, Volume 2** .... [V] **$10** Atlantic 80158

Battle Cry [Rockers Revenge]	It's Alright By Me [Jenny Burton]	Phony Four MC's-Wappin' (Bubblehead) [Ralph Rolle]
Give Me All [Juicy]	Nothin's Gonna Come Easy [Tina B]	Santa's Rap [Treacherous Three]
Into The Night [La La]		

Son Of Beat Street [Jazzy Jay]
Tu Carino/Carmen's Theme

3/2/96 — **95** — **5** — © 54 — **Beautiful Girls** .... [V] **$10** Elektra 61888
Matt Dillon/Lauren Holly/Timothy Hutton/**Rosie O'Donnell**/Mira Sorvino

Be For Real [Afghan Whigs]	Could It Be I'm Falling In Love [Spinners] 4	Me And Mrs. Jones [Billy Paul] 1
Beautiful Girl [Pete Droge & The Sinners]	Easy To Be Stupid [Howlin' Maggie]	Stroll, The [Diamonds] 4
Beth [Kiss] 7	Graduation Day [Chris Isaak]	Suffering [Satchel]
Can't Get Enough Of Your Love Babe [Afghan Whigs]	Groove Me [King Floyd] 6	Sweet Caroline (Good Times Never Seemed So Good) [Neil Diamond] 4
	I'll Miss You [Ween]	

That's How Strong My Love Is [Roland Gift]

12/7/91+ — **19** — **76** ▲2 — © 55 — **Beauty And The Beast** .... [M] **$10** Walt Disney 60618
animated movie, voices by: Robby Benson/Jesse Corti/ Angela Lansbury/Paige O'Hara; cp: Alan Menken; ly: Howard Ashman

Battle On The Tower	Beauty And The Beast [Celine Dion & Peabo Bryson] 9	Belle
Be Our Guest	Beauty And The Beast (cast version)	Gaston
Beast Lets Belle Go		Mob Song
		Something There

To The Fair
Transformation
West Wing

12/6/97 — **144** — **3** — © 56 — **Beauty And The Beast - The Enchanted Christmas** .... [X-M] **$10** Walt Disney 60948
animated movie, voices by: Paige O'Hara/Angela Lansbury/Tim Curry; mu: Rachel Portman; ly: Don Black; cd: Michael Starobin; Christmas chart: 14/'97

As Long As There's Christmas	Cut Above The Rest	First Noel
As Long As There's Christmas (End Title)	Deck The Halls	Joy To The World (medley)
As Long As There's Christmas (Reprise)	Do You Hear What I Hear	O Christmas Tree
Belle's Magical Gift	Don't Fall In Love	O Come, O Come, Emmanuel (medley)
	Enchanted Christmas Finale	Silent Night
	Fife's Yuletide Theme	

Stories
Twelve Days Of Christmas
We Wish You A Merry Christmas
What Child Is This

11/23/96+ — **20** — **21** ● — © 57 — **Beavis And Butt-Head Do America** .... [V] **$10** Geffen 25002
animated movie, voices by: Mike Judge/Robert Stack/Demi Moore/**Bruce Willis**/David Letterman

Ain't Nobody [LL Cool J] 46	Lord Is A Monkey [Butthole Surfers]	Ratfinks, Suicide Tanks And Cannibal Girls [White Zombie]
Gone Shootin' [AC/DC]	Love Rollercoaster [Red Hot Chili Peppers]	Snakes [No Doubt]
I Wanna Riot [Rancid]	Pimp'n Ain't EZ [Madd Head]	Two Cool Guys [Isaac Hayes]
Lesbian Seagull [Engelbert Humperdinck]		Walk On Water [Ozzy Osbourne]

White Trash [Southern Culture On The Skids]

5/9/64 — **147** — **3** — 58 — **Becket** .... [I] **$50** Decca 79117
Richard Burton/Peter O'Toole/John Gielgud/Gino Cervi/Donald Wolfit; cp: Laurence Rosenthal; cd: Muir Mathieson

Becket's Martyrdom	Escape To The Court Of King Louis (medley)	King Henry's Arrival At Canterbury Cathedral (medley)
Consecration At Canterbury	Gwendolen	Main Title (medley)
Days Of Youth	Hunt, The	Meeting On The Beach
End Title		

Trial (medley)
Triumph In France

DEBUT	PEAK	WKS	RIAA	CD	ARTIST — Album Title	Catalog	Sym	$	Label & Number

2/17/96 · 91 · 16 · © 59 · Bed Of Roses .... [I+V] **$10** Milan 35739
Christian Slater/Mary Stuart Masterson/Pamela Segall/Josh Brolin/Debra Monk; cp: Michael Convertino; cd: Artie Kane

Amelia and the King of Plants	I Looked Up	Killing Time [Daniel O'Brien]
Boom	Ice Cream [Sarah McLachlan]	Nervous Heart [Borrowers]
Dream	In Winter	Snow Fell On Walter
Family	Independent Love Song [Scarlet]	Too Much Perfection

Tuesday
Wait

Beetlejuice - see ELFMAN, Danny
Michael Keaton/Alec Baldwin/Geena Davis/Jeffrey Jones/Winona Ryder

11/21/98 · 5 · 12 ● · © 60 · Belly .... [V] **$10** Def Jam 558925
Nas/DMX/Method Man/Taral Hicks/Tyrin Turner

Crew Love [Jay-Z]	Movin' Out [Mya]	Sometimes [Noreaga]
Devil's Pie [D'Angelo]	Never Dreamed You'd Leave In	Story To Tell [Ja Rule]
Grand Finale [DMX/Method	Summer [Jerome]	Tommy's Theme [Made Men]
Man/Nas/Ja Rule]	No Way In, No Way Out [Lady]	Top Shotter [DMX/Sean Paul/Mr.
I Wanna Live [Braveheart]	Pre-Game [Sauce Money]	Vegas]
Militia Remix [Gang Starr]	Some Niggaz [Half-A-Mil]	Two Sides [Hot Totti]

We All Can Get It On [Drag-On]
What About [Sparkle]
Windpipe [Wu-Tang Clan]

4/25/60 · 6 · 98 · © 61 · Ben-Hur .... [I] **$50** MGM 1
Charlton Heston/Hugh Griffith/Haya Harareet/Stephen Boyd/Sam Jaffe; cp: Miklos Rozsa; cd: Carlo Savina; includes a full-color book about the movie

Adoration Of The Magi	Love Theme	Procession To Calvary
Burning Desert	Miracle, The (Finale)	Return To Judea
Friendship	Mother's Love	Roman March
Lepers' Search For The Christ	Naval Battle	Rowing Of The Galley Slaves

Victory Parade

5/29/93 · 45 · 18 · © 62 · Benny & Joon .... [I] **$10** Milan 35644
Johnny Depp/Mary Stuart Masterson/Aidan Quinn/Julianne Moore/Oliver Platt; mu: Rachel Portman

Balloon	**I'm Gonna Be (500 Miles)**	Love Theme
Benny & Joon	**[Proclaimers] 3**	On The Bus
Hubcaps	In The Park	Raisins (medley)
	Joon's Medicine	Sam And Joon

Sam Is Kicked Out
Sam's New Home (medley)
Snorkel Mask
Swinging

Benny Goodman Story, The - see GOODMAN, Benny
Steve Allen/Donna Reed/Herbert Anderson/Hy Averback/Sammy Davis Sr.

8/7/82 · 63 · 15 · © 63 · Best Little Whorehouse In Texas, The .... [M] **$12** MCA 6112
Burt Reynolds/**Dolly Parton**/Dom DeLuise/Charles Durning/**Jim Nabors**; sw: Carol Hall/**Dolly Parton**

Aggie Song	**I Will Always Love You** [Dolly	Sneakin' Around
Courtyard Shag	Parton] **53**	Texas Has A Whorehouse In It
Hard Candy Christmas	Lil' Ole Bitty Pissant Country Place	(medley)
	Sidestep, The	20 Fans

Watchdog Report (medley)

10/30/99 · 16 · 29 ▲ · © 64 · Best Man, The .... [V] **$10** Columbia 69924
Taye Diggs/Nia Long/Morris Chestnut/Harold Perrineau/Sanaa Lathan

After All Is Said and Done [Beyoncé	**Best Man I Can Be** [Ginuwine, R.I.,	Poetry Girl [Eric Benét]
& Marc Nelson]	Tyrese, Case] **77**	Turn Your Lights Down Low [Lauryn
As My Girl [Maxwell]	Hit It Up [Sporty Thievz]	Hill & Bob Marley]
Beautiful Girl [Kenny Lattimore]	Let's Not Play The Game [Maxwell]	Untitled [Me'Shell Ndegéocello]
Best Man [Faith Evans]	Liar, Liar [Latocha Scott]	What You Want [Roots]

When The Shades Go Down [Allure]
Wherever You Go [Sygnature]

1/12/85 · ❶² · 62 ▲² · © 65 · Beverly Hills Cop .... [V] **$10** MCA 5547
Eddie Murphy/Judge Reinhold/Lisa Eilbacher/John Ashton/Ronny Cox

All Revved Up	Do You Really (Want My Love?)	Gratitude [Danny Elfman]
Axel F [Harold Faltermeyer] **3**	[Junior]	**Heat Is On** [Glenn Frey] **2**
BHC (I Can't Stop) [Rick James]	Don't Get Stopped In Beverly Hills	**Neutron Dance** [Pointer Sisters] **6**
	[Shalamar]	**New Attitude** [Patti LaBelle] **17**

Rock 'N Roll Me Again [System]
Stir It Up [Patti LaBelle] 41

6/13/87 · 8 · 26 ▲ · © 66 · Beverly Hills Cop II .... [V] **$10** MCA 6207
Eddie Murphy/Judge Reinhold/Brigitte Nielsen/Ronny Cox/Gilbert Gottfried

All Revved Up [Jermaine Jackson]	**Cross My Broken Heart** [Jets] **7**	In Deep [Charlie Sexton]
Axel-F	Hold On [Corey Hart]	Keep The Peace
Be There [Pointer Sisters] **42**	I Can't Stand It [Sue Ann]	Leavin'
Better Way [James Ingram]	**I Want Your Sex** [George	Love/Hate [Pebbles]
Come See About Me	Michael] **2**	Right Thing, Wrong Way

Shakedown [Bob Seger] **1**
36 Lovers [Ready For The World]

6/11/94 · 158 · 3 · © 67 · Beverly Hills Cop III .... [V] **$10** MCA 11021
Eddie Murphy/Judge Reinhold/Hector Elizondo/Theresa Randle/Alan Young

All Revved Up	Heat Is On	**Place Where You Belong** [Shai] **34**
Axel-F [Nile Rodgers feat. Richard	Keep The Peace [INXS]	Right Kinda Lover [Patti LaBelle]
Hilton]	Leavin' [Tony Toni Toné]	Right Thing, Wrong Way [Terence
Come See About Me [Supremes] **1**	Luv 4 Dem Gangsta'z [Eazy-E]	Trent D'Arby]
Gratitude	Mood [Chanté Moore]	Rock 'N Roll Me Again

Stir It Up
Summer Jamming [Inner Circle]

11/12/66+ · 102 · 13 · 68 · Bible, The .... [I] **$40** 20th Century Fox 4184
George C. Scott/Ava Gardner/John Huston/**Richard Harris**/Peter O'Toole; cp: Toshiro Mayuzumi; cd: Franco Ferrara

Abraham (Scene of Love)	Creation, The	40 Days And 40 Nights
Bible, Theme From The	Creation Of Adam	New Beginning
Cain And Abel	Creation Of Eve	Noah's Ark

Sodom
Tower Of Babel

10/22/83+ · 17 · 161 ▲⁶ · © 69 · Big Chill, The .... C:#6/8 [O-V] **$10** Motown 6062
William Hurt/Glenn Close/Jobeth Williams/Jeff Goldblum/Kevin Kline

Ain't Too Proud To Beg	**I Second That Emotion** [Smokey	Natural Woman (You Make Me
[Temptations] **13**	Robinson & The Miracles] **4**	Feel Like) [Aretha Franklin] **8**
Good Lovin' [Young Rascals] **1**	**Joy To The World** [Three Dog	Tell Him [Exciters] **4**
I Heard It Through The Grapevine	Night] **1**	Tracks Of My Tears [Miracles] **16**
[Marvin Gaye] **1**	**My Girl** [Temptations] **1**	

Whiter Shade Of Pale [Procol
Harum] 5

4/28/84 · 85 · 49 ▲ · 70 · Big Chill, The (More Songs From The Original Soundtrack) .... [O-V] **$10** Motown 6094

Bad Moon Rising [Creedence	Gimme Some Lovin' [Spencer	Quicksilver Girl [Steve Miller Band]
Clearwater Revival] **2**	Davis Group] **7**	Too Many Fish In The Sea
Dancing In The Street [Martha &	In The Midnite Hour [Rascals]	[Marvelettes] **25**
The Vandellas] **2**	**It's The Same Old Song** [Four	Weight, The [Band] **63**
	Tops] **5**	What's Going On [Marvin Gaye] **2**

When A Man Loves A Woman
[Percy Sledge] 1
Wouldn't It Be Nice [Beach Boys] 8

DEBUT	PEAK	WKS	RIAA	CD	ARTIST — Album Title	Catalog	Sym	$	Label & Number

7/10/99 · **55** · 8 · © · 71 · **Big Daddy** .... [V] **$10** American 69947
Adam Sandler/Joey Lauren Adams/Jon Stewart/Rob Schneider/Josh Mostel

Babe *[Styx]* **1**	Just Like This *[Limp Bizkit]*	Overtime	Sweet Child O' Mine *[Sheryl Crow]*
Ga Ga *[Melanie C]*	Kangaroo Song *[Tim Herlihy]*	**Passin' Me By** *[Pharcyde]* **52**	What Is Life *[Shawn Mullins]*
Hooters	Kiss, The	Peace Out	When I Grow Up *[Garbage]*
If I Can't Have You *[Yvonne Elliman]* **1**	Only Love Can Break Your Heart *[Everlast & The White Folx]*	**Rush** *[Big Audio Dynamite II]* **32**	
Instant Pleasure *[Rufus Wainwright]*	Ooh La La *[Wise Guys]*	Sid	
		Smelly Kid	

10/24/87 · **107** · 9 · © · 72 · **Big Easy, The** .... [V] **$10** Antilles 7087
Dennis Quaid/Ellen Barkin/Ned Beatty/John Goodman/Gailard Sartain

Closer To You *[Dennis Quaid]*	**Iko, Iko** *[Dixie Cups]* **20**	Saviour, Pass Me Not *[Swan Silvertones]*	Tipitina *[Professor Longhair]*
Colinda *[Zachary Richard]*	Ma 'Tit Fille *[Buckwheat Zydeco]*	Tell It Like It Is *[Aaron Neville & The Neville Brothers]*	Zydeco Gris Gris *[Beausoleil]*
Hey, Hey (Indians Comin') *[Wild Tchoupitoulas]*	Oh Yeh Yai *[Terrance Simien & The Mallet Playboys]*		

6/17/00 · **41** · 13 · © · 73 · **Big Momma's House** .... [V] **$10** So So Def 61076
Martin Lawrence/Nia Long/Paul Giamatti/Terrence Howard/Cedric The Entertainer

Big Momma's Theme *[Da Brat & Vita]*	I Still Got To Have It *[Jermaine Dupri & Nas]*	Ooh Big Momma *[Lil Jon & The Eastside Boyz]*	Treated Like Her *[Latocha Scott & Chanté Moore]*
Bounce With Me *[Lil Bow Wow]* **20**	I Want To Kiss You *[Devin]*	Radio *[Kurupt, R.O.C & Phats Bossi]*	What I'm Gon' Do To You *[Kandi]*
Get Up *[Jessica]*	I've Got To Have It *[Jermaine Dupri & Nas]*	**That's What I'm Looking For** *[Da Brat]* **56**	You Can Always Go *[Jagged Edge & Blaque]*
I Like Dem *[Lil Jon & The Eastside Boyz]*	Love's Not Love *[Marc Nelson]*		

7/27/91 · **28** · 14 · © · 74 · **Bill & Ted's Bogus Journey** .... [V] **$10** Interscope 91725
Keanu Reeves/Alex Winter/William Sadler/**George Carlin**/Pam Grier

Battle Stations *[Winger]*	Go To Hell *[Megadeth]*	Perfect Crime *[Faith No More]*	Showdown *[Love On Ice]*
Dream Of A New Day *[Richie Kotzen]*	God Gave Rock And Roll To You II *[Kiss]*	Reaper, The *[Steve Vai]*	Tommy The Cat *[Primus]*
Drinking Again *[Neverland]*	Junior's Gone Wild *[King's X]*	Reaper Rap *[Steve Vai]*	
		Shout It Out *[Slaughter]*	

4/8/89 · **170** · 4 · © · 75 · **Bill & Ted's Excellent Adventure** .... [V] **$10** A&M 3915
Keanu Reeves/Alex Winter/**George Carlin**/Bernie Casey/**Jane Wiedlin**

Boys And Girls Are Doing It *[Vital Signs]*	Dancing With A Gypsy *[Tora Tora]*	In Time *[Robbie Robb]*	Two Heads Are Better Than One *[Power Tool]*
Breakaway *[Big Pig]* **60**	Dangerous *[Shark Island]*	Not So Far Away *[Glen Burtnick]*	Walk Away *[Bricklin]*
	Father Time *[Shark Island]*	Play With Me *[Extreme]*	

Bill Cosby "Himself" - see COSBY, Bill

10/9/71 · **135** · 7 · 76 · **Billy Jack** .... [I+V] **$25** Warner 1926
Tom Laughlin/Delores Taylor/Julie Webb/Howard Hesseman/Clark Howat; cp/cd: Mundell Lowe

All Forked Tongue Talk Alike	Indian Dance	**One Tin Soldier, The Legend Of Billy Jack** *[Coven]* **26**	Say Goodbye, Cause You're Leavin'
Ceremonial Dance	It's All She Left Me	One Tin Soldier, The Legend Of Billy Jack (End Title)	Thy Loving Hand
Challenge, The	Johnnie *[Teresa Kelly]*		When Will Billy Love Me *[Lynn Baker]*
Flick Of The Wrist	Look, Look To The Mountain *[Teresa Kelly]*	Rainbow Made Of Children *[Lynn Baker]*	You Shouldn't Do That
Freedom Over Me *[Gwen Smith]*	Most Beautiful Day	Ring Song *[Katy Moffatt]*	
Hello Billy Jack	Old And The New		
I Think You Always Knew			

1/5/74 · **167** · 5 · 77 · **Billy Jack** .... [R] **$15** Warner 1001
see above album for tracks; new cover features solo photo of Billy Jack

1/5/63 · **33** · 22 · © · 78 · **Billy Rose's Jumbo** .... [M] **$30** Columbia 2260
Doris Day/Stephen Boyd/**Jimmy Durante**/Martha Raye/Dean Jagger; mu: Richard Rodgers; ly: Lorenz Hart; cd: George Stoll

Circus On Parade	My Romance	Sawdust Spangles And Dreams (Finale)	Why Can't I?
Little Girl Blue	Over And Over Again	This Can't Be Love	
Most Beautiful Girl In The World			

11/12/88 · **169** · 3 · © · 79 · **Bird** .... [I] **$10** Columbia 44299
Forest Whitaker/Diane Venora/Sam Wright; features Charlie "Bird" Parker's original solos with instrumental backing

All Of Me	I Can't Believe That You're In Love	Laura	Ornithology
April In Paris	With Me	Lester Leaps In	Parker's Mood
Cool Blues	Ko Ko	Now's The Time	This Time The Dream's On Me

Birdy - see GABRIEL, Peter
Matthew Modine/Nicolas Cage/Bruno Kirby/Sandy Baron/John Harkins

4/15/00 · **124** · 3 · © · 80 · **Black And White** .... [V] **$10** Loud 62197
Robert Downey Jr./Jared Leto/**Raekwon**/Brooke Shields/Ben Stiller

Dem Crazy *[Dead Prez]*	It's Not A Game *[American Cream Team]*	Stand For Something *[Chip Banks]*	You'll Never Be Better Than Me *[Queen Pen]*
Don't Be A Follower *[Prodigy of Mobb Deep]*	Life's A Bitch *[Everlast]*	Wake Up *[Raekwon]*	You're A Big Girl Now *[LV]*
Dramacide *[X-ecutioners]*	Middle Finger Attitude *[American Cream Team]*	Year 2000 *[Xzibit]*	
Free *[Michael Fredo]*		You *[Samuel Christian]*	

Black And White Night Live, A - see ORBISON, Roy
Black Caesar - see BROWN, James
Fred Williamson/Art Lund/Julius Harris/Gloria Hendry/James Dixon

7/31/99 · **176** · 2 · © · 81 · **Black Gangster** .... [V] **$10** Black Hand 54329
soundtrack to the novel by Donald Goines

Black Hand Letter *[Killa]*	I Hope That It's You *[Donell Jones]*	Represent *[Ja Rule]*	Will You Die For It (Money)? *[Mysonne]*
Enterprise (Ride With Me) *[Jane Blaze]*	Mission (Ruby's Theme) *[Matx]*	Save The Game *[Mac Mall]*	You Ain't No Gangster *[Fifty-Cent]*
Give It Up *[Mac Dre]*	Money Tree (Nickels & Dimes) *[Kasual]*	Story, The *[DMX]*	
Hustle All Day *[Darcsyde]*	Pimpin Aint Easy *[Freddie Foxxx]*	This Life Forever *[Jay-Z]*	
		Wanna Be Down *[Ghetto Mafia]*	

9/5/98 · **36** · 22 · ● · © · 82 · **Blade** .... [V] **$10** TVT Soundtrax 8210
Wesley Snipes/Stephen Dorff/**Kris Kristofferson**/Udo Kier/Traci Lords

Blade *[DJ Krush]*	Dig This Vibe *[DJ Krush]*	Playing With Lightning *[Expansion Union]*	Wrek Tha Discotek *[Roger S]*
Blade 4 Glory *[Majesty]*	Edge Of The Blade *[Mystikal]*	Reservations *[P.A.]*	
Confusion *[New Order]*	Fightin' A War *[Down 2 Earth]*	Strictly Business *[Mantronik Vs. EPMD]*	
Deadly Zone *[Bounty Killer]* **79**	Gangsta Bounce *[Wolfpak]*	Things Ain't The Same *[Kasino]*	
Dealing With The Roster *[Junkie XL]* 1/2 & 1/2 *[Gang Starr]*			

11/27/71 · **176** · 10 · 83 · **Bless The Beasts & Children** .... [I+V] **$30** A&M 4322
Bill Mumy/Barry Robins/Miles Chapin/Jesse White/Ken Swofford; cp/cd: **Barry DeVorzon** & Perry Botkin, Jr.

Bless The Beasts And Children *[Carpenters]* **67**	Cotton's Dream	Journey's End	Stampede
Bless The Beasts And Children (instrumental)	Down The Line	Lost *[Renee Armand]*	
	Free	Requiem	

DEBUT	PEAK	WKS	RIAA	CD	ARTIST — Album Title	Catalog	Sym	$	Label & Number

5/2/87 — **198** — 1 — © 84 — **Blind Date** .... [V] **$10** Rhino 70705
Kim Basinger/**Bruce Willis**/John Larroquette/Phil Hartman/William Daniels

Anybody Seen Her? [Billy Vera & The Beaters]	Let You Get Away [Billy Vera & The Beaters]	Simply Meant To Be [Henry Mancini]
Crash, Bang, Boom [Hubert Tubbs]	Oh, What A Nite [Billy Vera & The Beaters]	Simply Meant To Be [Gary Morris & Jennifer Warnes]

Something For Nash [Henry Mancini]
Talked About Lover [Keith L'Neire]
Treasures [Stanley Jordan]

4/28/01 — **150** — 4 — © 85 — **Blow** .... [O-V] **$10** Virgin 10044
Johnny Depp/Penelope Cruz/Ray Liotta/Rachel Griffiths/Paul Reubens

All The Tired Horses [Bob Dylan]	Can't You Hear Me Knocking [Rolling Stones]	**Keep It Comin' Love** [KC & The Sunshine Band] **2**
Black Betty [Ram Jam] **18**	Can't You See [Marshall Tucker Band] **75**	Let's Boogaloo [Willie Rosario]
Blinded By The Light [Manfred Mann's Earth Band] **1**	Glad And Sorry [Faces]	Push & Pull [Nikka Costa]
		Rumble [Link Wray] **16**

Strange Brew [Cream]
That Smell [Lynyrd Skynyrd]
Yellow World [J Girls]

Blow-Up - see HANCOCK, Herbie
Vanessa Redgrave/David Hemmings/Sarah Miles/John Castle/Jane Birkin

Blue Hawaii - see PRESLEY, Elvis
Elvis Presley ("Chad Gates")/Joan Blackman/Angela Lansbury/Nancy Walters/Roland Winters

9/18/99 — **31** — 10 — ● — © 86 — **Blue Streak** .... [V] **$10** Epic 63615
Martin Lawrence/Luke Wilson/Dave Chappelle/Peter Greene/Tamala Jones

All Eyes On Me (Revisiting Cold Blooded) [Strings]	Damn (Should've Treated U Right) [So Plush]	I Put You On [Keith Sweat]
Blue Diamond [Raekwon]	Get Away [TQ & Krayzie Bone]	Na Na Be Like [Foxy Brown]
Criminal Mind [Tyrese]	Gimme My Money [Rehab]	Playboy Like Me [Playa]
Da Freak [Da Shortiez]	**Girl's Best Friend** [Jay-Z] **52**	Please Don't Forget About Me [Ruff Endz]

Rock Ice [Hot Boys]
While You Were Gone [Kelly Price]

Blues Brothers, The - see BLUES BROTHERS
John Belushi/Dan Aykroyd/Carrie Fisher/**James Brown**/Cab Calloway

Blues Brothers 2000 - see BLUES BROTHERS
Dan Aykroyd/John Goodman/Joe Morton/J. Evan Bonifant/**James Brown**

Bodyguard, The - see HOUSTON, Whitney
Whitney Houston/Kevin Costner/Gary Kemp (**Spandau Ballet**)/Bill Cobbs/Ralph Waite

4/6/68 — **12** — 21 — 87 — **Bonnie And Clyde** .... [I] **$40** Warner 1742
Warren Beatty/Faye Dunaway/Gene Hackman/Estelle Parsons/Gene Wilder; cp: Charles Strouse

Ambush (medley)	Bonnie's Poem (The Story Of Bonnie And Clyde)	Buck Falls
Bonnie And Clyde [Barrow Gang]	Buck And Blanche Meet Up With Bonnie And Clyde (Can't We Be Friends)	Captain Hamer Spits At Bonnie
Bonnie Meets Clyde (Sometimes I'm Happy)		End Title (medley)
Bonnie Wounded (medley)		Family Reunion
		Foggy Mountain Breakdown

I Ain't Much Of A Lover Boy
I Ain't No Rich Man
Law's Outside! (Lucky Day)
Okies, The (medley)

11/8/97 — **84** — 18 — © 88 — **Boogie Nights** .... [O-V] **$10** Capitol 55631
Mark Wahlberg (**Marky Mark**)/Julianne Moore/Burt Reynolds/William H. Macy/Heather Graham

Ain't No Stoppin' Us Now [McFadden & Whitehead] **13**	Brand New Key [Melanie] **1**	Livin' Thing [ELO] **13**
Best Of My Love [Emotions] **1**	God Only Knows [Beach Boys] **39**	Machine Gun [Commodores] **22**
Big Top [Michael Penn & Patrick Warren]	Got To Give It Up (Part 1) [Marvin Gaye] **1**	Magnet & Steel [Walter Egan] **8**
	Jungle Fever [Chakachas] **8**	Sister Christian [Night Ranger] **5**

Spill The Wine [War w/Eric Burdon] **3**

7/18/92 — **4** — 54 — ▲³ — © 89 — **Boomerang** .... [V] **$10** LaFace 26006
Eddie Murphy/Halle Berry/Robin Givens/David Alan Grier/**Martin Lawrence**

Don't Wanna Love You [Shanice]	Give U My Heart [Babyface] **29**	Love Shoulda Brought You Home [Toni Braxton] **33**
End Of The Road [Boyz II Men] **1**	Hot Sex [Tribe Called Quest]	Reversal Of A Dog [LaFace Cartel]
Feels Like Heaven [Kenny Vaughan & The Art Of Love]	**I'd Die Without You** [PM Dawn] **3**	7 Day Weekend [Grace Jones]
	It's Gonna Be Alright [Aaron Hall]	

There U Go [Johnny Gill]
Tonight Is Right [Keith Washington]

3/15/97 — **24** — 28 — ▲ — © 90 — **Booty Call** .... [V] **$10** Jive 41604
Jamie Foxx/Tommy Davidson/Vivica A. Fox/Bernie Mac/Tamala Jones

Baby, Baby, Baby, Baby... [R. Kelly]	Don't Blame It On Me [E-40 & B-Legit]	Fire & Desire [Johnny Gill & Coko]
Call Me [Too $hort & Lil' Kim] **90**	Don't Stop, Don't Quit [1 Accord]	Hold That Thought [Gerald Levert]
Can We [SWV] **75**	**Don't Wanna Be A Player** [Joe] **21**	(I'll Be You') Huckleberry [D-Shot]
Chocolate [L.a. Ganz]	Feel Good [Silk]	If You Stay [Backstreet Boys]
		Let Me See You Squirrel [Squirrel]

Looking For Love [Whitey Don]
Plan Up Your Family [KRS-One]
When I Rise [Crooked]

7/30/66 — **42** — 48 — © 91 — **Born Free** .... [I] **$25** MGM 4368
Virginia McKenna/Bill Travers/Geoffrey Keen/Peter Lukoye/Omar Chambati; cp/cd: John Barry

Born Free [Matt Monro]	Fight Of The Lioness	Hunt, The
Death Of Pati	Flirtation	Killing At Kiunga
Elsa At Play	Holiday With Elsa	Main Title

Reunion (medley)
Waiting For You
Warthog Hunt

1/20/90 — **32** — 15 — © 92 — **Born On The Fourth Of July** .... [I+V] **$10** MCA 6340
Tom Cruise/Kyra Sedgwick/Raymond J. Barry/Jerry Levine; side A: various artists; side B: instrumental; cp/cd: John Williams

American Pie [Don McLean] **1**	**Brown Eyed Girl** [Van Morrison] **10**	Hard Rain's A Gonna Fall [Edie Brickell & New Bohemians]
Born On The Bayou [Broken Homes]	Cua Viet River, Vietnam, 1968	Homecoming
Born On The Fourth Of July	Early Days, Massapequa, 1957	**Moon River** [Henry Mancini] **11**

My Girl [Temptations] **1**
Shooting Of Wilson
Soldier Boy [Shirelles] **1**
Venus [Frankie Avalon] **1**

12/2/00 — **124** — 3 — © 93 — **Bounce** .... [V] **$10** Arista 14661
Ben Affleck/Gwyneth Paltrow/Jennifer Grey/David Paymer/Natasha Henstridge

Central Reservation [Beth Orton]	Lose Your Way [Sophie B. Hawkins]	Never Gonna Come Back Down [BT]
Divided [Tara MacLean]	Love [Sixpence None The Richer]	Only Thing That's Real [Sister Seven]
Here With Me [Dido]	My Baby And Me [Nick Garrisi]	Our Affair [Carly Simon]
Hush [Angie Aparo]	Need To Be Next To You [Leigh Nash]	
I'm No Ordinary Girl [Anika Paris]		

Rome Wasn't Built In A Day [Morcheeba]
Silence [Delerium]

2/18/95 — **17** — 29 — ▲² — © 94 — **Boys On The Side** .... [V] **$10** Arista 18748
Whoopi Goldberg/Mary-Louise Parker/Drew Barrymore/Matthew McConaughey/Estelle Parsons

Crossroads [Jonell Mosser]	I Take You With Me [Melissa Etheridge]	Power Of Two [Indigo Girls]
Dreams [Cranberries]	Keep On Growing [Sheryl Crow]	Somebody Stand By Me [Stevie Nicks]
Everyday Is Like Sunday [Pretenders]	Ol' 55 [Sarah McLachlan]	**Why** [Annie Lennox] **34**

Willow [Joan Armatrading]
You Got It [Bonnie Raitt] **33**
You Got It [Whoopi Goldberg]

DEBUT	PEAK	WKS	RIAA	CD	ARTIST — Album Title	Catalog	Sym	$	Label & Number

7/27/91 · **12** · 18 · ● · © 95 · **Boyz N The Hood** ...... [V] **$10** Qwest 26643
Ice Cube/Cuba Gooding Jr./Morris Chestnut/Laurence Fishburne/Nia Long
Black On Black Crime [Stanley Clarke] — How To Survive In South Central [Ice Cube] — **Just Ask Me To** [Tevin Campbell] **88** — Spirit (Does Anybody Care?) [Force One Network]
Every Single Weekend [KAM] — It's Your Life [Too $hort] — Mama Don't Take No Mess [Yo-Yo] — Too Young [Hi-Five]
Growin' Up In The Hood [Comptons Most Wanted] — Just A Friendly Game Of Baseball [Main Source] — Me And You [Tony! Toni! Toné!] — Work It Out [Monie Love]
Hangin' Out [2 Live Crew] — — Setembro [Quincy Jones] —

3/18/95 · **137** · 4 · © 96 · **Brady Bunch Movie, The** ...... [V] **$10** Milan 35698
Shelley Long/Gary Cole/Michael McKean/Christine Taylor/David Graf
Beast Is Out Of Hand [Mudd Pagoda] — I Wish I Could Be Like You [Mudd Pagoda] — It's A Sunshine Day [Original Brady Bunch Kids] — Till I Met You [Christopher Daniel Barnes]
Brady Bunch Girl [Davy Jones] — I'm Feeling Nothing [dada] — Keep On [Original Brady Bunch Kids] — **Venus** [Shocking Blue] **1**
Have A Nice Day [Barry Coffing & Zachary Throne] — I'm Looking Around [Generation Why] — **Supermodel (You Better Work)** [RuPaul] **45** — Whatever [Zak]

Bram Stoker's Dracula - see Dracula

6/10/95+ · **45** · 64 · ▲ · © 97 · **Braveheart** ......C:#7/4 [I] **$10** London 448295
Mel Gibson/Sophie Marceau/Patrick McGoohan; cp/cd: James Horner; pf: **London Symphony Orchestra**
Attack On Murron — Falkirk — Main Title — Secret Wedding
Bannockburn (medley) — For The Love Of A Princess — Making Plans (medley) — Sons Of Scotland
Battle Of Stirling — Freedom (medley) — Mornay's Dream — Wallace Courts Murron
Betrayal & Desolation — Gathering The Clans (medley) — Murron's Burial
End Credits — Gift Of A Thistle — Princess Pleads For Wallace's Life
Execution, The (medley) — Legend Spreads — Revenge

Breakfast At Tiffany's - see MANCINI, Henry
Audrey Hepburn/George Peppard/Patricia Neal/Buddy Ebsen/Martin Balsam

3/9/85 · **17** · 26 · ● · © 98 · **Breakfast Club, The** ...... [V] **$10** A&M 5045
Molly Ringwald/Anthony Michael Hall/Emilio Estevez/Judd Nelson/Ally Sheedy
Didn't I Tell You [Joyce Kennedy] — Fire In The Twilight [Wang Chung] — Love Theme [Keith Forsey]
Don't You (Forget About Me) [Simple Minds] **1** — Heart Too Hot To Hold [Jesse Johnson & Stephanie Spruill] — Reggae, The [Keith Forsey] — Waiting [Elizabeth Daily]
Dream Montage [Gary Chang] — I'm The Dude [Keith Forsey] — We Are Not Alone [Karla DeVito]

6/2/84 · **8** · 23 · ▲ · © 99 · **Breakin'** ...... [V] **$10** Polydor 821919
Lucinda Dickey/Adolfo Quinones/Michael Chambers/Ben Lokey/Chris McDonald
Ain't Nobody [Rufus & Chaka Khan] **22** — **Breakin'...There's No Stopping Us** [Ollie & Jerry] **9** — Freakshow On The Dance Floor [Bar-Kays] **73** — Reckless [Chris Taylor, David Storrs & Ice-T]
Body Work [Hot Streak] — Cut-It [Re-Flex] — Heart Of The Beat [3-V] — Showdown [Ollie & Jerry]
— — **99 1/2** [Carol Lynn Townes] **77** — Street People [Fire Fox]

1/12/85 · **52** · 13 · ©100 · **Breakin' 2 Electric Boogaloo** ...... [V] **$10** Polydor 823696
Lucinda Dickey/Adolfo Quinones/Michael Chambers/Susie Bono/Harry Caesar
Believe In The Beat [Carol Lynn Townes] — Gotta Have The Money [Steve Donn] — Oye Mamacita [Rags & Riches] — Trommeltanz (Din Daa Daa) [George Kranz]
Electric Boogaloo [Ollie & Jerry] — I Don't Wanna Come Down [Mark Scott] — Radiotron [Firefox] — When I.C.U. [Ollie & Jerry]
— — Set It Out [Midway] —
— — Stylin', Profilin' [Firefox] —

6/17/95 · **47** · 11 · ● · ©101 · **Bridges Of Madison County, The** ...... [V] **$10** Malpaso 45949
Clint Eastwood/**Meryl Streep**/Annie Corley/Victor Slezak/Jim Haynie
Baby, I'm Yours [Barbara Lewis] **11** — Easy Living [Johnny Hartman] — I'll Close My Eyes [Dinah Washington] — It's A Wonderful World [Irene Kral]
Blue Gardenia [Dinah Washington] — For All We Know [Johnny Hartman] — It Was Almost Like A Song [Johnny Hartman] — Soft Winds [Dinah Washington]
Doe Eyes — I See Your Face Before Me [Johnny Hartman] — — This Is Always [Irene Kral]

4/28/01 · **36** · 12 · ©102 · **Bridget Jones's Diary** ...... [V] **$10** Island 548797
Renée Zellweger/Hugh Grant/Colin Firth/Gemma Jones/Jim Broadbent
All By Myself [Jamie O'Neal] — It's Only A Diary [Patrick Doyle] — Love [Rosey] — Someone Like You [Dina Carroll]
Dreamsome [Shelby Lynne] — It's Raining Men [Geri Halliwell] — Not Of This Earth [Robbie Williams] — Stop, Look, Listen (To Your Heart) [Diana Ross & Marvin Gaye]
Have You Met Miss Jones? [Robbie Williams] — Just Perfect [Tracy Bonham] — Out Of Reach [Gabrielle] —
I'm Every Woman [Chaka Khan] **21** — Killin' Kind [Shelby Lynne] — Pretender Got My Heart [Alisha's Attic]
— Kiss That Girl [Sheryl Crow] — —

4/2/88 · **67** · 11 · ©103 · **Bright Lights, Big City** ...... [V] **$10** Warner 25688
Michael J. Fox/Kiefer Sutherland/Phoebe Cates/Dianne Wiest/Swoosie Kurtz
Century's End [Donald Fagen] **83** — Ice Cream Days [Jennifer Hall] — Obsessed [Noise Club] — **Pump Up The Volume** [M/A/R/R/S] **13**
Divine Emotions [Narada] — **Kiss And Tell** [Bryan Ferry] **31** — Pleasure, Little Treasure [Depeche Mode] — **True Faith** [New Order] **32**
Good Love [Prince] — Love Attack [Konk] — —

9/9/00 · **119** · 16 · ©104 · **Bring It On** ...... [V] **$10** Play-Tone 61431
Kirsten Dunst/Eliza Dushku/Jesse Bradford/Gabrielle Union/Claire Kramer
Anywhere USA [P.Y.T.] — Freakin' You [Jungle Brothers] — See Ya [Atomic Kitten] — What's A Girl To Do [Sister2Sister]
As If [Blaque] — Jump Up (If You Feel Alright) [Da Beat Bros.] — 'Til I Say So [3LW]
Bring It All To Me [Blaque] **5** — — 2 Can Play That Game [Sygnature]
Cheer For Me [95 South] — Mickey [B*Witched] — U.G.L.Y. [Daphne & Celeste]

7/5/80 · **123** · 6 · 105 · **Bronco Billy** ...... [I+V] **$12** Elektra 512
Clint Eastwood/Sondra Locke/Geoffrey Lewis/Scatman Crothers/Bill McKinney; cp/cd: Steve Dorff
Bar Room Buddies [Merle Haggard & Clint Eastwood] — Bronco Billy [Ronnie Milsap] — Misery And Gin [Merle Haggard] — Stars And Stripes Forever
Bayou Lullaby [Penny DeHaven] — Cowboys And Clowns [Ronnie Milsap] — Not So Great Train Robbery — Thunderer's March
— — Stardust Cowboy [Reinsmen] —

4/7/01 · **32** · 9 · ©106 · **Brothers, The** ...... [V] **$10** Warner 48058
Morris Chestnut/D.L. Hughley/Bill Bellamy/**Tatyana Ali**/Shemar Moore
Forever [Dave Hollister] — I'm Through [Cassie] — Love Don't Love Me [Eric Benét] — Two Of A Kind [Eddie Levert Sr.]
Good Love [RL] — Josephine [DL] — Love Theme [Marcus Miller] — Wheel Of Fortune [Lil' Johnny]
Happy [AB] — Lay It Down [Jermaine Dupri & R.O.C.] — Remember Us [No Question] —
Hi 2 U [Snoop Dogg] — Let It Go [Jaheim] — Teach Each Other [Maze] —
I Put It Down [Duganz] — — 2night [Somethin' For The People] —

SOUNDTRACKS

DEBUT	PEAK	WKS	RIAA	CD	ARTIST — Album Title	Catalog	Sym	$	Label & Number

7/22/78 · 86 · 13 · ©107 · Buddy Holly Story, The .... [M] $15 Epic 35412
Gary Busey/Don Stroud/Charles Martin Smith/Maria Richwine/Conrad Janis

Clear Lake Medley	It's So Easy	Rave On
Everyday	Listen To Me	Roller Rink Medley
I'm Gonna Love You Too	Maybe Baby	True Love Ways

Well All Right
Whole Lotta Shakin' Goin' On

8/6/88 · 157 · 6 · ©108 · Bull Durham .... [V] $10 Capitol 90586
Kevin Costner/Susan Sarandon/Tim Robbins/Trey Wilson/Robert Wuhl

All Night Dance [Bennie Wallace/Dr. John with Stevie Ray Vaughan]	**Centerfield** [John Fogerty] **44**	Middle Of Nowhere [House Of Shock]
Born To Be Bad [George Thorogood]	I Got Loaded [Los Lobos]	So Long Baby, Goodbye [Blasters]
Can't Tear It Up Enuff [Fabulous Thunderbirds]	Love Ain't No Triple Play [Bennie Wallace/Dr. John with Bonnie Raitt]	Try A Little Tenderness [Bennie Wallace/Dr. John]
		Woman Loves A Man [Joe Cocker]

You Done Me Wrong [Pat McLaughlin]

9/21/96 · 85 · 7 · ©109 · Bulletproof .... [V] $10 MCA Sound. 11498
Damon Wayans/**Adam Sandler**/James Farentino/James Caan/Kristen Wilson

Champagne [Salt-N-Pepa]	Plant A Seed [Mr. Cheeks & Freaky Tah]	Tres Delinquents [Delinquent Habits]
Chocolate (Cuties And Condoms) [Cydal]	Reverend Black Grape [Black Grape]	2 Of Us [DTTX]
How Could You [K-Ci & JoJo] **53**	Show, Tha [Wreckx-N-Effect]	Until The Day [Nonchalant]
I Wanna Know Your Name [Tasha]		Where I'm From [Passion]

Where You Are [Rahsaan Patterson]

5/9/98 · 10 · 27 · ● · ©110 · Bulworth .... [V] $10 Interscope 90160
Warren Beatty/Halle Berry/Sean Astin/Paul Sorvino/Oliver Platt

Bitches Are Hustlers Too [D-Fyne]	Eve Of Destruction [Eve]	How Come [Canibus & Youssou N'Dour]
Bulworth (They Talk About It While We Live It) [Method Man/KRS-One/Prodigy/KAM]	Freak Out [Nutta Butta]	Joints & Jams [Black Eyed Peas]
Chase, The [RZA]	**Ghetto Supastar (That Is What You Are)** [Pras Michel] **15**	Kill Em Live [Public Enemy]
	Holiday/12 Scanner [Witchdoctor]	Lunatics In The Grass [B Real]

Maniac In The Brainiac [Mack 10 & Ice Cube]
Run [Cappadonna]
Zoom [Dr. Dre & LL Cool J]

10/15/88+ · 54 · 23 · ● · ©111 · Buster .... [V] $10 Atlantic 81905
Phil Collins/Julie Walters/Larry Lamb/Stephanie Lawrence/Ellen Beaven

Big Noise [Phil Collins]	**I Got You Babe** [Sonny & Cher] **1**	**Keep On Running** [Spencer Davis Group] **76**
Groovy Kind Of Love [Phil Collins] **1**	I Just Don't Know What To Do With Myself [Dusty Springfield]	Loco In Acapulco [Four Tops]
How Do You Do It? [Gerry & The Pacemakers] **9**	**Just One Look** [Hollies] **44**	Robbery, The [Anne Dudley]
		Sweets For My Sweet [Searchers]

Two Hearts [Phil Collins] **1**
Will You Still Be Waiting? [Anne Dudley]

Bustin' Loose - see FLACK, Roberta
Richard Pryor/Cicely Tyson/Alphonso Alexander/Kia Cooper/Edwin DeLeon

11/29/69+ · 16 · 74 · ● · ©112 · Butch Cassidy And The Sundance Kid .... [I+V] $20 A&M 4227
Paul Newman/Robert Redford/Katharine Ross/Strother Martin/Henry Jones; cp/cd: **Burt Bacharach**

Come Touch The Sun	On A Bicycle Built For Joy [B.J. Thomas]	Raindrops Keep Fallin' On My Head (instrumental)
Not Goin' Home Anymore	**Raindrops Keep Fallin' On My Head** [B.J. Thomas] **1**	South American Getaway
Old Fun City		

Sundance Kid

4/27/63 · 2² · 55 · ©113 · Bye Bye Birdie .... [M] $30 RCA Victor 1081
Ann-Margret/Jesse Pearson/Janet Leigh/Dick Van Dyke; mu: Charles Strouse; ly: Lee Adams; cd: Johnny Green

Bye Bye Birdie (medley)	Hymn For A Sunday Evening	One Boy
Honestly Sincere	Kids	One Last Kiss
How Lovely To Be A Woman	Lot Of Livin' To Do	Put On A Happy Face

Rosie (medley)
Telephone Hour

3/18/72+ · 25 · 72 · ● · 114 · Cabaret .... [M] $25 ABC 752
Liza Minnelli/Michael York/Joel Grey/Helmut Griem/Marisa Berenson; mu: John Kander; ly: Fred Ebb

Cabaret	Maybe This Time	Sitting Pretty
Heiraten (Married)	Mein Herr	Tiller Girls
If You Could See Her	Money, Money	Tomorrow Belongs To Me

Two Ladies
Willkommen

6/8/96 · 41 · 12 · ©115 · Cable Guy, The .... [V] $10 Work 67654
Jim Carrey/Matthew Broderick/Leslie Mann/**George Segal**/Jack Black

Blind [Silverchair]	**Hey Man, Nice Shot** [Filter] **76**	Satellite Of Love [Porno For Pyros]
Download [Expanding Man]	Last Assassin [Cypress Hill]	Somebody To Love [Jim Carrey]
End Of The World Is Coming [David Hilder]	Leave Me Alone [Jerry Cantrell]	Standing Outside A Broken Phone Booth With Money In My Hand [Primitive Radio Gods]
Get Outta My Head [Cracker]	Oh! Sweet Nuthin' [$10,000 Gold Chain]	

This Concludes Our Broadcast Day [John Ottman]
This Is [Ruby]
Unattractive [Toadies]

8/23/80 · 78 · 12 · 116 · Caddyshack .... [V] $15 Columbia 36737
Chevy Chase/Bill Murray/**Rodney Dangerfield**/Ted Knight/Michael O'Keefe

Any Way You Want It [Journey] **23**	I'm Alright [Kenny Loggins] **7**	Marina [Johnny Mandel]
Big Bang [Johnny Mandel]	Lead The Way [Kenny Loggins]	Mr. Night [Kenny Loggins]
Divine Intervention [Johnny Mandel]	Make The Move [Kenny Loggins]	

Something On Your Mind [Hilly Michaels]
There She Goes [Beat]

11/11/67+ · 11 · 87 · ▲ · ©117 · Camelot .... [M] $30 Warner 1712
Richard Harris/Vanessa Redgrave/David Hemmings; mu: Frederick Loewe; ly: Alan Jay Lerner; cd: Alfred Newman

C'est Moi	Guenevere	If Ever I Would Leave You
Camelot (medley)	How To Handle A Woman	Lusty Month Of May
Children's Chorus (medley)	I Loved You Once In Silence	Overture (medley)
Finale Ultimo	I Wonder What The King Is Doing Tonight	Prelude (medley)
Follow Me (medley)		Simple Joys Of Maidenhood

Take Me To The Fair
Wedding Ceremony (medley)
What Do The Simple Folk Do?

6/20/98 · 25 · 27 · ● · ©118 · Can't Hardly Wait .... [V] $10 Elektra 62201
Ethan Embry/Charlie Korsmo/Lauren Ambrose/Jennifer Love Hewitt/Seth Green

Can't Get Enough Of You Baby [Smash Mouth]	Flashlight [Parliament]	I Walked In [Brougham]
Can't Hardly Wait [Replacements]	Graduate [Third Eye Blind]	It's Tricky [Run-D.M.C.]
Dammit [Blink 182]	High [Feeder]	Paradise City [Guns N' Roses]
Farther Down [Matthew Sweet]	Hit 'Em Wit Da Hee [Missy "Misdemeanor" Elliott]	Swing My Way [K.P. & Envyi]

Tell Me What To Say [Black Lab]
Turn It Up/Fire It Up [Busta Rhymes] **10**
Umbrella [Dog's Eye View]

Can't Stop The Music - see VILLAGE PEOPLE
Village People/Valerie Perrine/Bruce Jenner/Steve Guttenberg/Jack Weston

DEBUT	PEAK	WKS	RIAA	CD	ARTIST — Album Title	Catalog	Sym	$	Label & Number

5/2/60 | **3** | 68 | ©119 | **Can-Can** ... [M] **$30** Capitol 1301
Frank Sinatra/Shirley MacLaine/Maurice Chevalier/Louis Jourdan/Juliet Prowse; sw: Cole Porter; cd: **Nelson Riddle**;
Original Cast version charted in 1953 (#3) on Capitol 452

C'est Magnifique / Live And Let Live / You Do Something To Me
I Love Paris / Maidens Typical Of France
Can-Can / It's All Right With Me / Main Title (medley)
Come Along With Me / Just One Of Those Things / Montmart' (medley)
Entr'acte / Let's Do It

2/1/69 | **49** | 16 | | 120 | **Candy** ... [I+V] **$30** ABC 9
Ewa Aulin/Richard Burton/Marlon Brando/**Ringo Starr**/Charles Aznavour; cp/cd: **Dave Grusin**

Ascension To Virginity / Child Of The Universe [Byrds] / It's Always Because Of This: A / Opening Night: By Surgery
Birth By Descent / Constant Journey / Deformity / **Rock Me [Steppenwolf] 10**
Border Town Blues: A Blunt / Every Mother's Daughter / **Magic Carpet Ride [Steppenwolf] 3** / Spec-Rac-Tac-Para-Comm
Instrument / Marlon & His Sacred Bird

Car Wash - see ROSE ROYCE
Richard Pryor/Franklin Ajaye/Ivan Dixon/**George Carlin**/Sully Boyar

2/8/64 | **100** | 9 | ©121 | **Cardinal, The** ... [I] **$60** RCA Victor 1084
Tom Tryon/John Huston/Carol Lynley/Robert Morse/Ossie Davis; cp/cd: Jerome Moross

Alleluia / Cardinal's Decision / Monks At Casamari / Way Down South
Annemarie / Cardinal's Faith / Stonebury
Cardinal In Vienna / Dixieland-Tango / They Haven't Got The Girls In The
Cardinal Themes / Main Title / U.S.A.

2/25/56 | **2[1]** | 57 | ▲ | ©122 | **Carousel** ... [M] **$50** Capitol 694
Gordon MacRae/Shirley Jones/Cameron Mitchell; mu: Richard Rodgers; ly: Oscar Hammerstein II; cd: Alfred Newman

Blow High, Blow Low / June Is Bustin' Out All Over / Soliloquy / When The Children Are Asleep
Carousel Waltz / Mister Snow / Stonecutters Cut It On Stone / You'll Never Walk Alone
If I Loved You / Real Nice Clambake / What's The Use Of Wondrin' / You're A Queer One, Julie Jordan!

9/5/64 | **141** | 3 | | 123 | **Carpetbaggers, The** ... [I] **$40** Ava 45
George Peppard/Alan Ladd/Carroll Baker/Bob Cummings/Martha Hyer; cp/cd: Elmer Bernstein

Carpetbagger Blues / Jonas Hits Bottom / New Star
Carpetbaggers, The / Love Theme / Producer Asks For A Divorce
Forbidden Room / Main Title / Speak Of The Devil

Carry It On - see BAEZ, Joan

5/13/67 | **22** | 21 | ©124 | **Casino Royale** ... [I] **$100** Colgems 5005
Peter Sellers/David Niven/Ursula Andress/**Woody Allen/Orson Welles**; cp/cd: **Burt Bacharach**

Big Cowboys And Indians Fight At / First Stop Berlin (medley) / Le Chifre's Torture Of The Mind / Money Penny Goes For Broke
Casino Royale (medley) / Flying Saucer (medley) / Little French Boy / Sir James' Trip To Find Mata
**Casino Royale [Herb Alpert & The / Hi There Miss Goodthighs / Look Of Love [Dusty / Venerable Sir James Bond
Tijuana Brass] 27** / Home James, Don't Spare The / Springfield] 22
Dream On James, You're Winning / Horses / Look Of Love (instrumental)

4/17/82 | **47** | 14 | ©125 | **Cat People** ... [I] **$12** Backstreet 6107
Nastassia Kinski/Malcolm McDowell/John Heard/Annette O'Toole/John Larroquette; cp: **Giorgio Moroder**

Autopsy, The / **Cat People (Putting Out Fire)** / Leopard Tree Dream / Paul's Theme (Jogging Chase)
Bring The Prod / **[David Bowie] 67** / Myth, The / To The Bridge
Irena's Theme / Night Rabbit / Transformation Seduction

3/14/98 | **30** | 5 | ©126 | **Caught Up** ... [V] **$10** Noo Trybe 45451
Bokeem Woodbine/Cynda Williams/Tony Todd/**Snoop Doggy Dogg/LL Cool J**

All In The Club [Do Or Die] / I Like [Shiro] / R.U. Down [Somethin' For The / U Should Know Me [Joe]
Cross My Heart [Killah Priest] / Made Man [O] / People] / Work [Gang Starr]
Ey-Yo! (The Reggae Virus) / My Buddy [Luniz] / Ride On/Caught Up! [Snoop Doggy / You Don't Want None [Mack 10 &
[KRS-One/Mad Lion/Shaggy] / Ordinary Guy [Lost Boyz] / Dogg & Kurupt] / Road Dawgs]
Girl [Luniz] / Rock Me [AZ]

3/20/93 | **41** | 10 | ©127 | **CB4** ... [V] **$10** MCA 10803
Chris Rock/Allen Payne/Phil Hartman/Chris Elliott/Khandi Alexander

Baby Be Mine [Blackstreet] / Livin' In A Zoo [Public Enemy] / Rapper's Delight [CB4] / Sweat Of My Balls [CB4]
Black Cop [Boogie Down / May Day On The Front Line [MC / Sneaking Up On Ya
Productions] / Ren] / [FU-Schnickens']
It's Alright [Tracie Spencer] / Nocturnal Is In The House [PM / Stick 'Em Up [Hurricane]
Lifeline [Parental Advisory] / Dawn] / Straight Out Of Locash [CB4]

5/27/00 | **120** | 8 | ©128 | **Center Stage** ... [V] **$10** Epic 63969
Amanda Schull/Zoe Saldana/Susan May Pratt/Peter Gallagher/Donna Murphy

Canned Heat [Jamiroquai] / Don't Get Lost In The Crowd / Girl Can Dream [P.Y.T.] / If I Was The One [Ruff Endz]
Come Baby Come [Elvis Crespo & / [Ashley Ballard] / Higher Ground [Red Hot Chili / **Way You Make Me Feel [Michael
Gizelle D'Cole] / First Kiss [International Five] / Peppers] / Jackson] 1**
Cosmic Girl [Jamiroquai] / Friends Forever [Thunderbugs] / **I Wanna Be With You [Mandy / We're Dancing [P.Y.T.]
Get Used To This [Cyrena] / Moore] 24

Charade - see MANCINI, Henry
Cary Grant/Audrey Hepburn/Walter Matthau/James Coburn/George Kennedy

Chariots Of Fire - see VANGELIS
Ian Charleson/Ben Cross/Nigel Havers/Nick Farrell/Ian Holm

11/11/00 | **7** | 36 | ▲ | ©129 | **Charlie's Angels** ... [O-V] **$10** Columbia 61064
Cameron Diaz/Drew Barrymore/Lucy Liu/Bill Murray

Angel's Eye [Aerosmith] / Charlie's Angels 2000 [Apollo Four / **Groove Is In The Heart / Tangerine Speedo [Caviar]**
Baby Got Back [Sir Mix-A-Lot] 1 / Forty] / **[Deee-Lite] 4** / **True [Spandau Ballet] 4**
Barracuda [Heart] 11 / Dot [Destiny's Child] / **Heaven Must Be Missing An / Turning Japanese [Vapors] 36**
**Brandy (You're A Fine Girl) / Got To Give It Up (Part I) [Marvin / Angel [Tavares] 15 / Ya Mama [Fatboy Slim]
[Looking Glass] 1** / Gaye] 1 / **Independent Women Part I / You Make Me Feel Like Dancing
[Destiny's Child] 1 / [Leo Sayer] 1**

Children Of Sanchez - see MANGIONE, Chuck
Anthony Quinn/Dolores Del Rio/Katy Jurado/Lupita Ferrer/Lucia Mendez

11/9/68+ | **58** | 28 | ©130 | **Chitty Chitty Bang Bang** ... [M] **$25** United Artists 5188
Dick Van Dyke/Sally Ann Howes/Lionel Jeffries/Gert Frobe/Benny Hill; sw: Richard M. Sherman and Robert B. Sherman

Chitty Chitty Bang Bang / Hushabye Mountain / Posh! / Truly Scrumptious
Chu-Chi Face / Lovely, Lonely Man / Roses Of Success / You Two
Doll On A Music Box (medley) / Me Ol' Bam-Boo / Toot Sweets

SOUNDTRACKS

3/3/01 — **147** — 7 — ©131 — **Chocolat** .... [I] **$10** Miramax 89472
Juliette Binoche/Judi Dench/Alfred Molina/Lena Olin/Johnny Depp; cp: Rachel Portman; cd: David Snell

Ashes To The Wind (medley)	Guillaume's Confession	Party Preparations	Three Woman
Boycott Immorality	Main Titles	Passage Of Time	Vianne Confronts The Comte
Caravan	Mayan Bowl Breaks	Roux Returns (medley)	Vianne Gazes At The River
Chocolate Sauce	Minor Swing	Story Of Grandmere	Vianne Sets Up Shop
Fire	Other Possibilities	Taste Of Chocolate	

12/28/85+ — **77** — 12 — 132 — **Chorus Line, A - The Movie** .... [M] **$10** Casablanca 826306
Michael Douglas/Terrence Mann/Alyson Reed/Cameron English; mu: **Marvin Hamlisch**; ly: Edward Kleban; cd: Ralph Burns

At The Ballet	I Hope I Get It	One	Who Am I Anyway?
Dance: Ten; Looks: Three	Let Me Dance For You	Surprise, Surprise	
I Can Do That	Nothing	What I Did For Love	

Christiane F. - see BOWIE, David
Natja Brunkhorst/Thomas Haustein

1/21/84 — **177** — 5 — ©133 — **Christine** .... [O-V] **$12** Motown 6086
Keith Gordon/John Stockwell/Alexandra Paul/Harry Dean Stanton/Robert Prosky

Bad To The Bone [George Thorogood]	Harlem Nocturne [Viscounts] 52	Little Bitty Pretty One [Thurston Harris] 6	Rock 'N' Roll Is Here To Stay [Danny & The Juniors] 19
Bony Moronie [Larry Williams] 14	I Wonder Why [Dion & The Belmonts] 22	Not Fade Away [Buddy Holly]	We Belong Together [Robert & Johnny] 32
Christine Attacks [John Carpenter & Alan Howarth]	Keep A Knockin' [Little Richard] 8	Pledging My Love [Johnny Ace] 17	

10/28/95 — **176** — 3 — ©134 — **Cinderella** .... [V] **$10** Walt Disney 60886
animated movie, voices by: Ilene Woods/William Phipps/Verna Felton; includes the 1950 movie's original score (#1 album in 1950 on RCA Victor 399) and remakes of songs by contemporary artists

Bibbidi-Bobbidi-Boo (The Magic Song)	Cinderella: Prologue	King's Plans (medley)	So This Is Love [James Ingram]
Cat and Mice (medley)	Dream Is a Wish Your Heart Makes [Linda Ronstadt]	Midnight Chase	So This Is Love: Waltz
Cinderella	Dress Building (medley)	Palace at Evening (medley)	Un Precioso Sueno (A Dream Is a Wish Your Heart Makes) [Linda Ronstadt]
Cinderella Medley	Dress for the Ball (medley)	Perfect Fit	
Cinderella: Finale	Entanglements (medley)	Royal Fanfare and Reception at the Palace	Work Song [Take 6]

4/18/98 — **❶³** — 77 — ▲⁵ — ©135 — **City Of Angels** .... C:#35/1 [V] **$10** Warner Sunset 46867
Nicolas Cage/Meg Ryan/Dennis Franz/Andre Braugher

Angel [Sarah McLachlan] 4	Further On Up The Road [Eric Clapton]	If God Will Send His Angels [U2]	Red House [Jimi Hendrix]
Angel Falls [Gabriel Yared]	I Grieve [Peter Gabriel]	Iris [Goo Goo Dolls] 9	Spreading Wings [Gabriel Yared]
City Of Angels [Gabriel Yared]	I Know [Jude]	Mama, You Got A Daughter [John Lee Hooker]	Unfeeling Kiss [Gabriel Yared]
Feelin' Love [Paula Cole]			Uninvited [Alanis Morissette]

Clambake - see PRESLEY, Elvis
Elvis Presley ("Scott Heywood")/**Shelley Fabares**/Will Hutchins/Bill Bixby/James Gregory

Claudine - see KNIGHT, Gladys/Pips
James Earl Jones/Diahann Carroll/Lawrence Hilton-Jacobs/Roxie Roker

6/22/63 — **2³** — 27 — ©136 — **Cleopatra** .... [I] **$50** 20th Century Fox 5008
Elizabeth Taylor/Richard Burton/Rex Harrison/Roddy McDowall/Martin Landau; cp/cd: Alex North

Antony And Cleopatra	Cleopatra Enters Rome	Gift For Caesar	Taste Of Death
Antony--Wait...	Cleopatra's Barge	Grant Me An Honorable Way To Die	
Caesar And Cleopatra	Dying Is Less Than Love	Love And Hate	
Caesar's Assassination	Fire Burns, The Fire Burns	My Love Is My Master	

8/18/73 — **109** — 10 — 137 — **Cleopatra Jones** .... [I+V] **$20** Warner 2719
Tamara Dobson/Bernie Casey/Shelley Winters/Antonio Fargas/Esther Rolle; cp/cd: J.J. Johnson

Airport Flight	Cleopatra Jones, Theme From (instrumental)	Go Chase Cleo	Wrap Up
Cleo And Reuben		Goin' To The Chase	Wrecking Yard
Cleopatra Jones, Theme From [Joe Simon] 18	Desert Sunrise	Hurts So Good [Millie Jackson] 24	
	Emdee	Love Doctor [Millie Jackson]	

2/5/72 — **34** — 31 — ©138 — **Clockwork Orange, A** .... [I] **$20** Warner 2573
Malcolm McDowell/Patrick Magee/Michael Bates/Warren Clarke; cp/cd: **Walter Carlos**

Clockwork Orange, Theme From A	Ninth Symphony, Second Movement	Pomp And Circumstance March No. I	Timesteps
I Want To Marry A Lighthouse Keeper	Overture To The Sun	Singin' In The Rain [Gene Kelly]	Title Music
Ninth Symphony, Fourth Movement		Thieving Magpie	William Tell Overture

1/7/78 — **17** — 16 — ● — ©139 — **Close Encounters Of The Third Kind** .... [I] **$15** Arista 9500
Richard Dreyfuss/Teri Garr/Francois Truffaut/Melinda Dillon/Bob Balaban; cp/cd: **John Williams**

Abduction Of Barry	**Close Encounters Of The Third Kind, Theme From** 13	Main Title (medley)	Resolution
Appearance Of The Visitors		Mountain Visions (medley)	
Arrival Of Sky Harbor	Conversation, The	Night Seige	
Climbing Devil's Tower	I Can't Believe It's Real	Nocturnal Pursuit	

Club Paradise - see CLIFF, Jimmy
Robin Williams/Peter O'Toole/Rick Moranis/**Jimmy Cliff**/Twiggy

8/5/95 — **49** — 43 — ▲ — ©140 — **Clueless** .... [V] **$10** Capitol 32617
Alicia Silverstone/Wallace Shawn/Brittany Murphy/Paul Rudd/Stacey Dash

All The Young Dudes [World Party]	Ghost In You [Counting Crows]	My Forgotten Favorite [Velocity Girl]	Supermodel [Jill Sobule]
Alright [Supergrass]	Here [Luscious Jackson]	Need You Around [Smoking Popes]	Where'd You Go? [Mighty Mighty Bosstones]
Change [Lightning Seeds]	Kids In America [Muffs]	Rollin' With My Homies [Coolio]	
Fake Plastic Trees [Radiohead]	Mullet Head [Beastie Boys]	Shake Some Action [Cracker]	

3/29/80 — **40** — 20 — ● — ©141 — **Coal Miner's Daughter** .... **$15** MCA 5107
Sissy Spacek/Tommy Lee Jones/Beverly D'Angelo/**Levon Helm**

Amazing Grace	Crazy	One's On The Way	You Ain't Woman Enough To Take My Man
Back In Baby's Arms	Great Titanic	Sweet Dreams	
Blue Moon Of Kentucky	I Fall To Pieces	There He Goes	You're Lookin' At Country
Coal Miner's Daughter	I'm A Honky Tonk Girl	Walking After Midnight	

6/28/86 — **100** — 6 — ©142 — **Cobra** .... [V] **$10** Scotti Brothers 40325
Sylvester Stallone/Brigitte Nielsen/Reni Santoni/David Rasche/Andrew Robinson

Angel Of The City [Robert Tepper]	Hold On To Your Vision [Gary Wright]	Skyline [Sylvester Levay]	**Voice Of America's Sons** [John Cafferty] 62
Chase [Sylvester Levay]		Suave [Miami Sound Machine]	
Cobra [Sylvester Levay]	Loving On Borrowed Time (Love Theme) [Gladys Knight & Bill Medley]	Two Into One [Bill Medley & Carmen Twillie]	
Feel The Heat [Jean Beauvoir] 73			

DEBUT	PEAK	WKS	RIAA	CD	ARTIST — Album Title	Catalog	Sym	$	Label & Number

8/13/88+   **2**[1]   61 ▲⁴ ©143 **Cocktail**   [V] $10   Elektra 60806
Tom Cruise/Bryan Brown/Elisabeth Shue/Gina Gershon/Lisa Barnes
All Shook Up [Ry Cooder]	Hippy Hippy Shake [Georgia	Powerful Stuff [Fabulous	Since When [Robbie Nevil]
Don't Worry, Be Happy [Bobby	Satellites] 45	Thunderbirds] 65	Tutti Frutti [Little Richard] 17
McFerrin] 1	Kokomo [Beach Boys] 1	Rave On [John Cougar	Wild Again [Starship] 73
	Oh, I Love You So [Preston Smith]	Mellencamp]	

7/27/85   **188**   4   ©144 **Cocoon**   [I] $12   Polydor 827041
Don Ameche/Wilford Brimley/Hume Cronyn/Jessica Tandy/Brian Dennehy; cp/cd: James Horner
Ascension, The	Cocoon (Theme)	Gravity	Rose's Death
Boys Are Out	Discovered In The Poolhouse!	Lovemaking, The	Sad Goodbyes
Chase, The	First Tears	Returning To The Sea	Through The Window

11/15/86   **81**   15   ©145 **Color Of Money, The**   [V] $10   MCA 6189
Paul Newman/Tom Cruise/Mary Elizabeth Mastrantonio/Helen Shaver/John Turturro
Don't Tell Me Nothin' [Willie Dixon]	Main Title [Robbie Robertson]	Standing On The Edge Of Love	Who Owns This Place [Don Henley]
It's In The Way That You Use It	Modern Blues [Robbie Robertson]	[B.B. King]	
[Eric Clapton]	My Baby's In Love With Another	Two Brothers And A Stranger [Mark	
Let Yourself In For It [Robert	Guy [Robert Palmer]	Knopfler]	
Palmer]		Werewolves Of London [Warren	
		Zevon] 21	

3/8/86   **79**   13   ©146 **Color Purple, The**   [I] $15   Qwest 25389 [2]
Whoopi Goldberg/Danny Glover/Margaret Avery/Oprah Winfrey; cd: **Quincy Jones**
Body And Soul (medley) [Coleman	Corrine And Olivia	Junk Bucket Blues [Get Happy	My Heart (Will Always Lead Me
Hawkins]	Dirty Dozens [Tata Vega]	Band]	Back To You) [Louis Armstrong]
Bus Pulls Out	Don't Make Me No Never Mind	Katutoka Corrine	Nettie Teaches Celie
Careless Love [Tata Vega]	[John Lee Hooker]	Letter Search	Nettie's Letters
Celie And Harpo Grow Up (medley)	First Letter	Main Title	Proud Theme (medley)
Celie Cooks Shug Breakfast	Heaven Belongs To You	Maybe God Is Tryin' To Tell You	Reunion (Finale)
Celie Leaves With Mr.	High Life (medley)	Somethin'	Scarification Ceremony (medley)
Celie Shaves Mr. (medley)	I'm Here	Miss Celie's Blues (Sister) [Tata	Separation, The
Celie's New House (medley)	J.B. King	Vega]	Sophia Leaves Harpo
Champagne Train		Mr. Dresses To See Shug (medley)	Three On The Road

5/14/88   **31**   19 ● ©147 **Colors**   [V] $10   Warner 25713
Sean Penn/Robert Duvall/Maria Conchita Alonso/Don Cheadle/Glenn Plummer
Butcher Shop [Kool G. Rap]	Go On Girl [Roxanne Shante]	Mind Is A Terrible Thing To Waste	Six Gun [Decadent Dub Team]
Colors [Ice-T] 70	Let The Rhythm Run [Salt-N-Pepa]	[M.C. Shan]	
Everywhere I Go (Colors) [Rick	Mad Mad World [7A3]	Paid In Full [Eric B. & Rakim]	
James]		Raw [Big Daddy Kane]	

9/23/72   **198**   2   148 **Come Back Charleston Blue**   [I] $25   Atco 7010
Godfrey Cambridge/Raymond St. Jacques/Adam Wade/Jonelle Allen; cp/cd/pf: **Donny Hathaway**
Basie	Furniture Truck	Little Ghetto Boy
Bossa Nova (medley)	Gravedigger Jones & Coffin Ed's	Main Theme
Come Back Basie (medley)	Funeral (medley)	Scratchy Record (medley)
Come Back Charleston Blue	Harlem Dawn (medley)	String Segue
(medley) [Donny Hathaway &	Hearse To Graveyard (medley)	Tim's High
Margie Joseph]	Liberation (medley)	Vegetable Wagon (medley)

7/30/88   **177**   2   ©149 **Coming To America**   [V] $10   Atco 90958
Eddie Murphy/Arsenio Hall (**Chunky A**)/James Earl Jones/John Amos/Eriq LaSalle
Addicted To You [Levert]	Better Late Than Never [Cover	Comin' Correct [J.J. Fad]	Livin' The Good Life [Sister Sledge]
All Dressed Up (Ready To Hit The	Girls]	Coming To America (Part One)	That's The Way It Is [Mel & Kim]
Town) [Chico DeBarge]	Come Into My Life [Laura Branigan	[System] 91	Transparent [Nona Hendryx]
	& Joe Esposito]	I Like It Like That [Michael Rodgers]	

Commitments, The - see COMMITMENTS
Andrew Strong/Angeline Ball/Robert Arkins/Maria Doyle/Bronagh Gallagher

6/12/82   **162**   5   ©150 **Conan The Barbarian**   [I] $12   MCA 6108
Arnold Schwarzenegger/James Earl Jones/Max Von Sydow/Sandahl Bergman; cp/cd: Basil Poledouris
Anvil Of Crom	Civilization (medley)	Orphans Of Doom (medley)	Theology (medley)
Atlantean Sword	Funeral Pyre	Riddle Of Steel (medley)	Wheel Of Pain
Awakening, The (medley)	Gift Of Fury	Riders Of Doom (medley)	Wifeing (Love Theme)
Battle Of The Mounds	Orgy, The	Search, The	

8/7/93   **162**   6   ©151 **Coneheads**   [V] $10   Warner 45345
Dan Aykroyd/Jane Curtin/Chris Farley/Michelle Burke/Jason Alexander
Can't Take My Eyes Off You	Fight The Power [Barenaked	Magic Carpet Ride [Slash & Michael	Tainted Love [Soft Cell] 8
[Morten Harket]	Ladies]	Monroe]	
Chale Jao [Babble]	It's A Free World Baby [R.E.M.]	No More Tears (Enough Is Enough)	
Conehead Love [Beldar & Prymaat]	Kodachrome [Paul Simon] 2	[k.d. lang & Andy Bell]	
	Little Renee [Digable Planets]	Soul To Squeeze [Red Hot Chili	
		Peppers] 22	

Cool As Ice - see VANILLA ICE
Vanilla Ice/Kristin Minter/Michael Gross/Naomi Campbell/Dody Goodman

10/30/93+   **111**   32 ● ©152 **Cool Runnings**   [V] $10   Chaos 57553
Leon/Doug E. Doug/Rawle Lewis/Malik Yoba/John Candy
Cool Me Down [Tiger]	I Can See Clearly Now [Jimmy	Love You Want [Wailing Souls]	Walk Home [Hans Zimmer]
Countrylypso [Hans Zimmer]	Cliff] 18	Picky Picky Head [Wailing Souls]	Wild Wild Life [Wailing Souls]
Dolly My Baby [Super Cat]	Jamaican Bobsledding Chant	Stir It Up [Diana King]	
	[Worl-A-Girl]	Sweet Jamaica [Tony Rebel]	

8/1/92   **89**   6   ©153 **Cool World, Songs From The**   [V] $10   Warner 45009
Kim Basinger/Gabriel Byrne/Brad Pitt
Ah-Ah [Moby]	Her Sassy Kiss [My Life With The	N.W.O. [Ministry]	Real Cool World [David Bowie]
Disappointed [Electronic]	Thrill Kill Kult]	Next Is The E [Moby]	Sex On Wheelz [My Life With The
Do That Thang [Da Juice]	Industry And Seduction [Tom	Papua New Guinea [Future Sound	Thrill Kill Kult]
Greedy [Pure]	Bailey]	Of London]	Under [Brian Eno]
	Mindless [Mindless]	Play With Me [Thompson Twins]	Witch, The [Cult]

Cornbread, Earl And Me - see BLACKBYRDS, The
Moses Gunn/Bernie Casey/Keith Wilkes/Madge Sinclair/Laurence Fishburne

DEBUT	PEAK	WKS	RIAA	CD	ARTIST — Album Title	Catalog	Sym	$	Label & Number

9/17/94 173 2 ©154 **Corrina, Corrina** .... [V] **$10** RCA 66443
Whoopi Goldberg/Ray Liotta/Tina Majorino/Joan Cusack/**Don Ameche**
- Corrina, Corrina [Ted Hawkins]
- **Corrina, Corrina** [Big Joe Turner] **41**
- **Finger Poppin' Time** [Hank Ballard & The Midnighters] **7**
- Home Movies [Thomas Newman]
- I Only Have Eyes For You [Niki Haris & Peter Cox]
- It Don't Mean A Thing If It Ain't Got That Swing [Duke Ellington/Ivie Anderson]
- **Little Bitty Pretty One** [Thurston Harris] **6**
- Over The Rainbow [Jevetta Steele]
- Pennies From Heaven [Billie Holiday]
- **'Reet Petite** [Jackie Wilson] **62**
- They Can't Take That Away From Me [Sarah Vaughan]
- This Little Light Of Mine [Steeles]
- We Will Find A Way [Oleta Adams & Brenda Russell]
- **What A Difference A Day Makes** [Dinah Washington] **8**
- You Go To My Head [Louis Armstrong & Oscar Peterson]

3/27/99 44 6 ©155 **Corruptor, The** .... [V] **$10** Jive 41671
Chow Yun-Fat/Mark Wahlberg (**Marky Mark**)/Ric Young/Paul Ben-Victor/Byron Mann
- Allustrious [Mobb Deep]
- Be My Dirty Love [Too $hort]
- Corruptor (Main Title)
- Corruptor's Execution [E-40/B-Legit/Pimp C/Bun B]
- Feel The Rush [Mic Vandalz]
- 5 Boroughs [KRS-One]
- Good Girl Goes Bad [Spice I]
- Have You Heard Of Me? [Murda Mil]
- I Ain't Playin' [Mystikal]
- I Got You Faded [Night & Day]
- Men Of Respect [Kasino]
- More Money, More Cash, More Hoes [Jay-Z]
- Reminisce [Caffeine]
- Slap Somebody [Keith Murray]
- Slow Down [Jane Blaze]
- Take It Off [UGK]
- What You Think All The Guns Is For? [Truck Turner]

1/19/85 93 10 ©156 **Cotton Club, The** .... [I] **$12** Geffen 24062
Richard Gere/Gregory Hines/Bob Hoskins/Nicolas Cage/**Tom Waits**; cd: Bob Wilder
- Best Beats Sandman (medley)
- Copper Colored Gal
- Cotton Club Stomp #1
- Cotton Club Stomp #2
- Creole Love Call
- Daybreak Express Medley
- Depression Hits (medley)
- Dixie Kidnaps Vera
- Drop Me Off In Harlem
- East St. Louis Toodle-O
- Ill Wind
- Minnie The Moocher
- Mooche, The
- Mood Indigo
- Ring Dem Bells
- Truckin'

12/1/84+ 120 15 ©157 **Country** .... [I] **$12** Windham Hill 1039
Jessica Lange/Sam Shepard/Wilford Brimley/Matt Clark; cp/cd: Charles Gross
- Aftermath
- Auction, The
- Chants
- Country Night
- Epilog (medley)
- Harvest Field
- Home
- Homecoming
- Hymn, A
- Iowa Chill
- Parting Friends
- Sunday
- Winter Mantra

8/19/00 10 59↑▲² ©158 **Coyote Ugly** [V] **$10** Curb 78703
Piper Perabo/Adam Garcia/Maria Bello/Melanie Lynskey/Tyra Banks
- All She Wants To Do Is Dance [LeAnn Rimes]
- Boom Boom Boom [Rare Blend]
- But I Do Love You [LeAnn Rimes]
- **Can't Fight The Moonlight** [LeAnn Rimes] **71**
- **Devil Went Down To Georgia** [Charlie Daniels Band] **3**
- Didn't We Love [Tamara Walker]
- **Need You Tonight** [INXS] **1**
- Please Remember [LeAnn Rimes]
- **Power, The** [Snap] **2**
- Right Kind Of Wrong [LeAnn Rimes]
- Unbelievable
- We Can Get There [Mary Griffin]

5/18/96 98 8 ©159 **Craft, The** .... [V] **$10** Columbia 67626
Fairuza Balk/Robin Tunney/Neve Campbell/Rachel True/Skeet Ulrich
- All This And Nothing [Sponge]
- Bells, Books And Candles [Graeme Revell]
- Dangerous Type [Letters To Cleo]
- Dark Secret [Matthew Sweet]
- Horror, The [Spacehog]
- How Soon Is Now? [Love Spit Love]
- I Have The Touch [Heather Nova]
- Jump Into The Fire [Tripping Daisy]
- Spastica [Elastica]
- Tomorrow Never Knows [Our Lady Peace]
- Under The Water [Jewel]
- Warning [All Too Much]
- Witches Song [Juliana Hatfield]

5/28/94 59 8 ©160 **Crooklyn** .... [O-V] **$10** 40 Acres 11036
Alfre Woodard/Delroy Lindo/Spike Lee/Zelda Harris
- **ABC** [Jackson 5] **1**
- **Crooklyn** [Crooklyn Dodgers] **60**
- El Pito (I'll Never Go Back To Georgia) [Joe Cuba]
- **Everyday People** [Sly & The Family Stone] **1**
- **Mighty Love** [Spinners] **20**
- **Mr. Big Stuff** [Jean Knight] **2**
- **Oh Girl** [Chi-Lites] **1**
- **Ooh Child** [Five Stairsteps] **8**
- Pass The Peas [JB's] **95**
- People Make The World Go Round [Marc Dorsey]
- Pusher Man [Curtis Mayfield]
- **Respect Yourself** [Staple Singers] **12**
- **Thin Line Between Love And Hate** [Persuaders] **15**
- **Time Has Come Today** [Chambers Brothers] **11**

Crossroads - see COODER, Ry
Ralph Macchio/Joe Seneca/Jami Gertz/**Steve Vai**/Allan Arbus

1/27/01 69 17 ©161 **Crouching Tiger, Hidden Dragon** .... [I] **$10** Sony Classical 89347
Michelle Yeoh/Chow Yun-Fat/Zhang Zi Yi/Chang Cheng; cp/cd: Tan Dun
- Crouching Tiger, Hidden Dragon
- Desert Capriccio
- Encounter, The
- Eternal Vow
- Farewell
- In The Old Temple
- Love Before Time (English)
- Love Before Time (Mandarin)
- Night Fight
- Silk Road
- Sorrow
- Through The Bamboo Forest
- To The South
- Wedding Interrupted
- Yearning Of The Sword

4/16/94 ❶¹ 44 ▲³ ©162 **Crow, The** .... [V] **$10** Atlantic 82519
Brandon Lee/Ernie Hudson/Rochelle Davis/Michael Wincott/David Patrick Kelly
- After The Flesh [My Life With The Thrill Kill Kult]
- Badge, The [Pantera]
- Big Empty [Stone Temple Pilots]
- Burn [Cure]
- Color Me Once [Violent Femmes]
- Darkness [Rage Against The Machine]
- Dead Souls [Nine Inch Nails]
- Ghostrider [Rollins Band]
- Golgotha Tenement Blues [Machines Of Loving Grace]
- It Can't Rain All The Time [Jane Siberry]
- Milktoast [Helmet]
- Slip Slide Melting [For Love Not Lisa]
- Snakedriver [Jesus And Mary Chain]
- Time Baby III [Medicine]

8/17/96 8 24 ▲ ©163 **Crow - City Of Angels, The** [V] **$10** Miramax 62047
Vincent Perez/Mia Kirshner/Richard Brooks/**Iggy Pop**/Thomas Jane
- City Of Angels [Above The Law]
- Gold Dust Woman [Hole]
- I Wanna Be Your Dog [Iggy Pop]
- I'm Your Boogie Man [White Zombie]
- In A Lonely Place [Bush]
- Jurassitol [Filter]
- Knock Me Out [Linda Perry]
- Lil' Boots [Pet]
- Naked Cousin [PJ Harvey]
- Paper Dress [Toadies]
- Sean Olson [Korn]
- Shelf Life [Seven Mary Three]
- Spit [NY Loose]
- Teething [Deftones]
- Tonite Is A Special Nite [Tricky vs. The Gravediggaz]

4/15/00 104 4 ©164 **Crow - Salvation, The** .... [V] **$10** Koch 8070
Kirsten Dunst/Eric Mabius/Jodi Lyn O'Keefe/William Atherton/Fred Ward
- Antihistamine [Tricky]
- Bad Brother [Infidels]
- Best Things [Filter]
- Big God [Monster Magnet]
- Burning Inside [Static X]
- Everything Sucks (Again) [Pitchshifter]
- Independent Slaves [Days Of The New]
- It's All Over Now, Baby Blue [Hole]
- Living Dead Girl [Rob Zombie]
- Now Is The Time [Crystal Method]
- Painful [Sin]
- Rusted Wings [New American Shame]
- Underbelly Of The Beast [Danzig]
- Waking Up Beside You [Stabbing Westward]
- Warm Winter [Kid Rock]
- What You Want [Flys]

3/20/99 60 15 ● ©165 **Cruel Intentions** .... [V] **$10** Virgin 47174
Ryan Phillippe/Sarah Michelle Gellar/Reese Witherspoon/Selma Blair/Louise Fletcher
- Addictive [Faithless]
- Bedroom Dancing [Day One]
- Bitter Sweet Symphony [Verve]
- Coffee & TV [Blur]
- Colorblind [Counting Crows]
- Comin' Up From Behind [Marcy Playground]
- Every You Every Me [Placebo]
- Ordinary Life [Kristen Barry]
- Praise You [Fatboy Slim]
- Secretly [Skunk Anansie]
- This Love [Craig Armstrong]
- Trip On Love [Abra Moore]
- You Blew Me Off [Bare Jr.]
- You Could Make A Killing [Aimee Mann]

DEBUT	PEAK	WKS	RIAA	CD	ARTIST — Album Title	Catalog	Sym	$	Label & Number

3/13/93 · 60 · 13 · ©166 · Crying Game, The .... [I+V] **$10** SBK 89024
Stephen Rea/Miranda Richardson/Jaye Davidson/Forest Whitaker; cp: Anne Dudley (**Art Of Noise**)
- Assassination, The
- **Crying Game** [Boy George] 15
- Dies Irae
- I'm Thinking Of Your Man
- It's In My Nature
- Let The Music Play [Carroll Thompson]
- Live For Today (Orchestral) [Cicero]
- March To The Execution
- Soldier's Tale
- Soldier's Wife
- Stand By Your Man [Lyle Lovett]
- Transformation, The
- **When A Man Loves A Woman** [Percy Sledge] 1
- White Cliffs Of Dover [Blue Jays]

12/1/58 · 21 · 1 · ©167 · Damn Yankees .... [M] **$50** RCA Victor 1047
Tab Hunter/Gwen Verdon/Ray Walston/Jean Stapleton/Russ Brown; sw: Richard Adler and Jerry Ross
- Goodbye, Old Girl
- Heart
- Little Brains, A Little Talent
- Shoeless Joe From Hannibal, Mo.
- Six Months Out Of Every Year
- There's Something About An Empty Chair
- Those Were The Good Old Days
- Two Lost Souls
- Whatever Lola Wants
- Who's Got The Pain

8/29/98 · 54 · 13 · ©168 · Dance With Me .... [F-V] **$10** Epic 68905
Vanessa Williams/Chayanne/**Kris Kristofferson**/Joan Plowright/Jane Krakowski
- Atrevete (No Puedes Conmigo) [DLG]
- Echa Pa'Lante [Thalia]
- Eres Todo En Mí (You're My Everything) [Ana Gabriel]
- Fiesta Pa'Los Rumberos [Albita]
- **Heaven's What I Feel** [Gloria Estefan] 27
- Jazz Machine [Black Machine]
- Jibaro [Electra]
- Magalenha [Sergio Mendes]
- Pantera En Libertad [Mónica Naranjo]
- Patria [Rubén Blades]
- Refugio De Amor (You Are My Home) [Vanessa Williams & Chayanne]
- Suavemente [Elvis Crespo]
- Tres Deseos (Three Wishes) [Gloria Estefan]
- Want You, Miss You, Love You [Jon Secada]
- You Are My Home [Vanessa Williams & Chayanne]

12/22/90+ · 48 · 69 · ▲ · ©169 · Dances With Wolves .... C:#24/2 [I] **$10** Epic 46982
Kevin Costner/Mary McDonnell/Graham Greene/Rodney Grant/Robert Pastorelli; cp/cd: John Barry
- Buffalo Hunt
- Death Of Cisco
- Death Of Timmons
- Farewell (End Title)
- John Dunbar Theme
- Journey To Fort Sedgewick
- Journey To The Buffalo Killing Ground
- Kicking Bird's Gift
- Looks Like A Suicide (medley)
- Loss Of The Journal (medley)
- Love Theme
- Main Title (medley)
- Pawnee Attack
- Rescue Of Dances With Wolves
- Return To Winter Camp (medley)
- Ride To Fort Hays
- Stands With A Fist Remembers
- Two Socks--The Wolf Theme
- Two Socks At Play

3/1/97 · 20 · 7 · ©170 · Dangerous Ground .... [V] **$10** Jive 41590
Ice Cube/Elizabeth Hurley/Ving Rhames
- Buddup Bap [Whitey Don]
- Chocolate Chips [Lil Doe Doe]
- Count On Me [L.A. Ganz]
- Dangerous Ground [Keith Murray]
- Fa-Sho [K-Dee]
- Ghetto Smile [B-Legit]
- It's Alright [Too $hort]
- Keep On Pushin' [MC Lyte]
- Mr. Shit Talker [Mystikal]
- Murder [Crooked]
- Only Way [Celly Cel]
- Perhaps She'll Die [KRS-One]
- Struggled & Strived [Click]
- 2 Hands And A Razor [Spice 1]
- World Is Mine [Ice Cube]
- You're Only A Customer [Jay-Z]

8/12/95 · ❶⁴ · 52 · ▲³ · ©171 · Dangerous Minds .... [V] **$10** MCA 11228
Michelle Pfeiffer/George Dzundza/Courtney Vance/Robin Bartlett
- Curiosity [Aaron Hall]
- Don't Go There [24-K]
- **Feel The Funk** [Immature] 46
- **Gangsta's Paradise** [Coolio] 1
- Gin & Juice [DeVante]
- Havin Thangs [Big Mike]
- It's Alright [Sista]
- Message For Your Mind [Rappin' 4-Tay]
- Problems [Rappin' 4-Tay]
- Put Ya Back Into It [Tre Black]
- This Is The Life [Wendy & Lisa]
- True O.G. [Mr. Dalvin & Static]

8/1/70 · 113 · 7 · 172 · Darling Lili .... [M] **$25** RCA Victor 1000
Julie Andrews/Rock Hudson/Jeremy Kemp/Lance Percival/Mike Witney; cp/cd: **Henry Mancini**
- Can-Can Cafe
- Darling Lili
- Girl In No Man's Land
- Gypsy Violin
- I'll Give You Three Guesses
- Little Birds (Les P'tits Oiseaux)
- Skal (Let's Have Another On Me)
- Smile Away Each Rainy Day
- Whistling Away The Dark
- Your Good-Will Ambassador

7/14/90 · 27 · 16 · ● · ©173 · Days Of Thunder .... [V] **$10** DGC 24294
Tom Cruise/Robert Duvall/Randy Quaid/Nicole Kidman/Michael Rooker
- Break Through The Barrier [Tina Turner]
- Deal For Life [John Waite]
- Gimme Some Lovin' [Terry Reid]
- **Hearts In Trouble** [Chicago] 75
- Knockin' On Heaven's Door [Guns N' Roses]
- Last Note Of Freedom [David Coverdale]
- Long Live The Night [Joan Jett]
- Show Me Heaven [Maria McKee]
- Thunder Box [Apollo Smile]
- Trail Of Broken Hearts [Cher]
- **You Gotta Love Someone** [Elton John] 43

10/30/93+ · 70 · 71 · ▲ · ©174 · Dazed And Confused .... C:#32/23 [O-V] **$10** Medicine 24533
Jason London/Rory Cochrane/Wiley Wiggins/Milla Jovovich/Matthew McConaughey
- Cherry Bomb [Runaways]
- **Fox On The Run** [Sweet] 5
- Highway Star [Deep Purple]
- **Jim Dandy** [Black Oak Arkansas] 25
- Love Hurts [Nazareth] 8
- Low Rider [War] 7
- Paranoid [Black Sabbath] 61
- **Rock And Roll All Nite** [Kiss] 68
- **Rock And Roll, Hoochie Coo** [Rick Derringer] 23
- School's Out [Alice Cooper] 7
- Slow Ride [Foghat] 20
- Stranglehold [Ted Nugent]
- Tuesday's Gone [Lynyrd Skynyrd]
- **Tush** [ZZ Top] 20

2/11/84 · 181 · 4 · 175 · D.C. Cab .... [V] **$12** MCA 6128
Mr. T/Gary Busey/Anne DeSalvo/Max Gail/Adam Baldwin
- **D.C. Cab** [Peabo Bryson]
- Deadline U.S.A. [Shalamar]
- **Dream (Hold On To Your Dream)** [Irene Cara] 37
- Knock Me On My Feet [Champaign]
- Knock Me On My Feet (instrumental) [Giorgio Moroder]
- One More Time Around The Block
- Ophelia [Gary U.S. Bonds]
- Party Me Tonight [Stephanie Mills]
- Single Heart [DeBarge]
- Squeeze Play [Karen Kamon]
- World Champion [Leon Sylvers III]

1/27/96 · 61 · 13 · ©176 · Dead Man Walking .... [V] **$10** Columbia 67522
Susan Sarandon/Sean Penn/Robert Prosky/Raymond J. Barry/R. Lee Ermey
- Dead Man Walkin' [Bruce Springsteen]
- Dead Man Walking (A Dream Like This) [Mary Chapin Carpenter]
- Ellis Unit One [Steve Earle]
- Face Of Love [Nusrat Fateh Ali Khan with Eddie Vedder]
- Fall Of Troy [Tom Waits]
- In Your Mind [Johnny Cash]
- Long Road [Eddie Vedder with Nusrat Fateh Ali Khan]
- Promises [Lyle Lovett]
- Quality Of Mercy [Michelle Shocked]
- Walk Away [Tom Waits]
- Walkin Blind [Patti Smith]
- Woman On The Tier (I'll See You Through) [Suzanne Vega]

10/14/95 · 14 · 18 · ● · ©177 · Dead Presidents .... [O-V] **$10** Underworld 32438
Larenz Tate/Keith David/Chris Tucker/N'Bushe Wright/Bokeem Woodbine
- Dead Presidents Theme [Danny Elfman]
- Do Right Woman, Do Right Man [Aretha Franklin]
- **(Don't Worry) If There's A Hell Below We're All Going To Go** [Curtis Mayfield] 29
- Get Up And Get Down [Dramatics] 78
- **I Miss You (Part I)** [Harold Melvin & The Blue Notes] 58
- I'll Be Around [Spinners] 3
- If You Want Me To Stay [Sly & The Family Stone] 12
- Look Of Love [Isaac Hayes] 79
- Love Train [O'Jays] 1
- Never, Never Gonna Give You Up [Barry White] 7
- Payback - Part I, The [James Brown] 26
- Tired Of Being Alone [Al Green] 11
- Walk On By [Isaac Hayes] 30
- Where Is The Love [Jesse & Trina]

Death Wish II - see PAGE, Jimmy
Charles Bronson/Jill Ireland/Vincent Gardenia/Anthony Franciosa/J.D. Cannon

7/2/77 · 70 · 10 · 178 · Deep, The .... [I+V] **$15** Casablanca 7060
Nick Nolte/Jacqueline Bisset/Robert Shaw/Louis Gossett/Eli Wallach; cp/cd: John Barry
- Disco Calypso [Beckett]
- Return To The Sea - 2033 A.D.
- Theme From The Deep (Down, Deep Inside) [Donna Summer]
- Theme From The Deep (Instrumental)

SOUNDTRACKS

DEBUT	PEAK	WKS	RIAA	CD	ARTIST — Album Title	Catalog	Sym	$	Label & Number

5/9/92 · 166 · 7 · ©179 · Deep Cover .... [V] **$10** Solar 75330
Laurence Fishburne/Jeff Goldblum/Gregory Sierra/Clarence Williams III/Charles Martin Smith

Deep Cover [Dr. Dre]	John And Betty's Theme [Michel Colombier]	Mr. Loverman [Shabba Ranks] 40
Digits [Deele]	Love Or Lust [Jewell]	Nickel Slick Nigga [Ko-Kane]
Down With My Nigga [Paradise]	Minute You Fall In Love [3rd Avenue]	Sex Is On [Po', Broke & Lonely?]
I See Ya Jay [Ragtime]		Sound Of One Hand Clapping [Calloway]

Typical Relationship [Times 3]
Way (Is In The House) [Calloway]
Why You Frontin' On Me [Emmage]

1/22/55 · 4 · 18 · ©180 · Deep In My Heart [M] **$50** MGM 3153
Jose Ferrer/Merle Oberon/Walter Pidgeon/Jim Backus/Russ Tamblyn; cd: Adolph Deutsch; LP: MGM E-3153 (#4); EP: MGM X-276 (#5)

Auf Wiedersehn	Leg Of Mutton (Some Smoke)	Softly As In A Morning Sunrise
Deep In My Heart (medley)	Lover Come Back To Me	Stout-Hearted Men (medley)
Desert Song (medley)	Mr. And Mrs. (medley)	When I Grow Too Old To Dream (medley)
I Love To Go Swimmin' With Wimmen (medley)	One Kiss (medley)	Will You Remember (medley)
It	Road To Paradise (medley)	
	Serenade	

Will You Remember (Sweetheart) (medley)
You Will Remember Vienna
Your Land And My Land

8/23/97 · 7 · 11 · ● · ©181 · Def Jam's How To Be A Player [V] **$10** Def Jam 537973
Bill Bellamy/Natalie Desselle/Bernie Mac/Lark Voorhies/Gilbert Gottfried

Big Bad Mamma [Foxy Brown] **53**	I Gotta Know [Playa]	Never Wanna Let You Go [Absolute]
Don't Ever [Black Azz Chill]	If U Stay Ready [Suga Free]	Say What [Dymon]
Down Wit Us [Redman]	In The Wind [Eightball & MJG]	Street 2 Street [Jayo Felony]
Hard To Get (Revisited) [Rick James & Richie Rich]	It's A Cold Day [Too $hort]	Troublesome [2 Pac]
How To Be A Playa [Master P]	Never Seen Before [EPMD]	Usual Suspects [Mic Geronimo]

When The Playas Live [Crucial Conflict]
Young Casanovas [Junior M.A.F.I.A.]

2/4/95 · 157 · 3 · ©182 · Demon Knight .... [V] **$10** Atlantic 82725
Billy Zane/William Sadler/Jada Pinkett/Thomas Haden Church/CCH Pounder

Beaten [Biohazard]	Fall Guy [Rollins Band]	My Misery (Demon Knight) [Machine Head]
Cemetery Gates [Pantera]	Hey Man Nice Shot [Filter]	1-800-Suicide [Gravediggaz]
Diadems [Megadeth]	Instant Larry [Melvins]	

Policia [Sepultura]
Tonight We Murder [Ministry]

9/9/95 · 53 · 11 · ©183 · Desperado .... [V] **$10** Epic Soundtrax 67294
Antonio Banderas/Joaquim Almeida/Salma Hayek/Steve Buscemi/Cheech Marin (**Cheech & Chong**)

Back To The House That Love Built [Tito & Tarantula]	Cancion Del Mariachi (Morena De Mi Corazon) [Los Lobos w/Antonio Banderas]	Manifold de Amour [Latin Playboys]
Bar Fight	Forever Night Shade Mary [Latin Playboys]	Mariachi Suite
Bella [Carlos Santana]	Jack The Ripper [Link Wray & His Ray Men]	Navajas Attacks (medley)
Bucho's Gracias (medley)	Let Love Reign [Los Lobos]	Pass The Hatchet [Roger & The Gypsies]
Bulletproof		Phone Call
		Quedate Aqui [Salma Hayek]

Rooftop Action
Six Blade Knife [Dire Straits]
Strange Face Of Love [Tito & Tarantula]
White Train (Showdown) [Tito & Tarantula]

8/21/99 · 68 · 5 · ©184 · Detroit Rock City .... [O-V] **$10** Mercury 546389
Edward Furlong/Giuseppe Andrews/James DeBello/Shannon Tweed/**Kiss**

Boys Are Back In Town [Everclear]	Iron Man [Black Sabbath] **52**	Rebel Rebel [David Bowie] **64**
Cat Scratch Fever [Pantera]	Jailbreak [Thin Lizzy]	Runnin' With The Devil [Van Halen] **84**
Detroit Rock City [Kiss] **flip**	Little Willy [Sweet] **3**	School Days [Runaways]
Highway To Hell [Marilyn Manson]	Nothing Can Keep Us From You [Kiss]	**Shout It Out Loud** [Kiss] **31**

Strutter [Donnas]
Surrender [Cheap Trick] **62**
20th Century Boy [Drain sth]

Devil's Angels - see ALLAN, Davie
John Cassavetes/Beverly Adams/Mimsy Farmer/Salli Sachse/Maurice McEndree

1/8/72 · 74 · 12 · ©185 · Diamonds Are Forever .... [I] **$25** United Artists 5220
Sean Connery/Jill St. John/**Jimmy Dean**/Charles Gray/Lana Wood; cp/cd: John Barry

Bond Meets Bambi And Thumper	**Diamonds Are Forever** [Shirley Bassey] **57**	007 And Counting
Bond Smells A Rat	Diamonds Are Forever (instrumental)	Moon Buggy Ride
Circus, Circus		Q's Trick
Death At The Whyte House		Tiffany Case

To Hell With Blofeld

6/30/90 · 108 · 5 · ©186 · Dick Tracy .... [V] **$10** Sire 26236
Warren Beatty/Al Pacino/**Madonna**/Glenne Headley/Charlie Korsmo

Blue Nights [Tommy Page]	Looking Glass Sea [Erasure]	Rompin' & Stompin' [Al Jarreau]
Confidence Man [Patti Austin]	Mr. Fix-It [Darlene Love]	Slow Rollin' Mama [LaVern Baker]
Dick Tracy [Ice-T]	Pep, Vim And Verve [Jeff Vincent & Andy Paley]	Some Lucky Day [Andy Paley]
It Was The Whiskey Talkin' (Not Me) [Jerry Lee Lewis]	Ridin' The Rails [k.d. lang & Take 6]	Wicked Woman, Foolish Man [August Darnell]

You're In The Doghouse Now [Brenda Lee]

8/19/00 · 175 · 1 · ©187 · Dinosaur .... [I] **$10** Walt Disney 860672
animated movie, voices by D.B. Sweeney/Alfre Woodard/Ossie Davis/Max Casella/Julianna Marguiles; cp/cd: James Newton Howard

Across The Desert	Courtship, The	It Comes With A Pool
Aladar And Neera	Egg Travels	Kron & Aladar Fight
Breakout	End Of Our Island	Neera Rescues The Orphans
Carnotaur Attack	Finding Water	Nesting Grounds (medley)
Cave, The	Inner Sanctum (medley)	Raptors (medley)

Stand Together (medley)
They're All Gone

9/19/87 · ❶18 · 96 · ▲11 · ©188 · Dirty Dancing C:#16/21 [O-V] **$10** RCA Victor 6408
Patrick Swayze/Jennifer Grey/Cynthia Rhodes (**Animotion**)/Jerry Orbach/Jack Weston

Be My Baby [Ronettes] **2**	In The Still Of The Night [Five Satins] **24**	She's Like The Wind [Patrick Swayze feat. Wendy Fraser] **3**
Hey! Baby [Bruce Channel] **1**	Love Is Strange [Mickey & Sylvia] **11**	Stay [Maurice Williams] **1**
Hungry Eyes [Eric Carmen] **4**	Overload [Zappacosta]	Where Are You Tonight [Tom Johnston]
(I've Had) The Time Of My Life [Bill Medley & Jennifer Warnes] **1**		

Yes [Merry Clayton] **45**
You Don't Own Me [Blow Monkeys]

3/19/88 · 3 · 52 · ▲4 · ©189 · Dirty Dancing, More [O-V] **$10** RCA 6965

Baby's Walk [John Morris Orch.]	Johnny's Mambo [Michael Lloyd & Le Disc]	Merengue [Michael Lloyd & Le Disc]
Big Girls Don't Cry [4 Seasons] **1**	Kellerman's Anthem [Emile Bergstein Chorale]	**Some Kind Of Wonderful** [Drifters] **32**
Cry To Me [Solomon Burke] **44**	Lifts In The Lake Theme (Finale) [John Morris Orch.]	**These Arms Of Mine** [Otis Redding] **85**
De Todo Un Poco [Michael Lloyd & Le Disc]	Love Man [Otis Redding] **72**	Trot The Fox [Michael Lloyd & Le Disc]
Do You Love Me [Contours] **3**		

Will You Love Me Tomorrow [Shirelles] **1**
Wipe Out [Surfaris] **2**

8/14/99 · 198 · 1 · ©190 · Dirty Dancing - The Collector's Edition .... [R] **$15** RCA 67786 [2]
includes the soundtracks Dirty Dancing and More Dirty Dancing with the songs of each in sequence with the movie

DEBUT	PEAK	WKS	RIAA	CD	ARTIST — Album Title	Catalog	Sym	$	Label & Number

9/12/87 | **99** | 8 | | 191 | **Disorderlies** .... [V] | **$10** | | | Polydor 833274

The Fat Boys/Ralph Bellamy/Tony Plana/Anthony Geary/**Helen Reddy**

Baby, You're A Rich Man [Fat Boys]	Don't Treat Me Like This [Anita]	**I Heard A Rumour** [Bananarama] 4
Big Money [Ca$hflow]	Edge Of A Broken Heart [Bon Jovi]	Roller One [Art Of Noise]
Disorderly Conduct [Latin Rascals]	Fat Off My Back [Gwen Guthrie]	Tryin' To Dance [Tom Kimmel]

Work Me Down [Laura Hunter]

8/15/98 | **169** | 2 | | ©192 | **Disturbing Behavior** .... [V] | **$10** | | | Trauma 74007

James Marsden/Katie Holmes/Nick Stahl/Bruce Greenwood/Steve Railsback

Blown [F.O.S.]	Every Little Thing Counts [Janus Stark]	Hello [Once Upon A Time]
Drivetime Radio [Eva Trout]		Hole In My Soul [Hutt]
Ever She Flows [Treble Charger]	Got You (Where I Want You) [Flys]	Million Rappers [Phunk Junkeez]
Hail Mary [Skold]		Monster Side [Addict]

Psycho Clogs [Jack Drag]
Sometimes [Driver]

Divine Madness - see MIDLER, Bette

7/22/89 | **68** | 14 | | ©193 | **Do The Right Thing**.. [V] | **$10** | | | Motown 6272

Danny Aiello/Ossie Davis/Ruby Dee/Spike Lee/John Turturro

Can't Stand It [Steel Pulse]	Fight The Power [Public Enemy]	**My Fantasy** [Teddy Riley] 62
Don't Shoot Me [Take 6]	Hard To Say [Lori Perry & Gerald Alston]	Never Explain Love [Al Jarreau]
Feel So Good [Perri]		Party Hearty [E.U.]

Prove To Me [Perri]
Tu Y Yo [Ruben Blades]
Why Don't We Try [Keith John]

10/14/67+ | **55** | 44 | ● | ©194 | **Doctor Dolittle** .... [M] | **$30** | | | 20th Century Fox 5101

Rex Harrison/Samantha Eggar/Anthony Newley/Richard Attenborough/Peter Bull; sw: Leslie Bricusse; cd: Lionel Newman

After Today	Fabulous Places	My Friend The Doctor
At The Crossroads	I Think I Like You	Something In Your Smile
Beautiful Things	I've Never Seen Anything Like It	Talk To The Animals
Doctor Dolittle	Like Animals	Vegetarian, The

When I Look In Your Eyes
Where Are The Words

7/4/98 | **4** | 37 | ▲² | ©195 | **Dr. Dolittle** [V] | **$10** | | | Blackground 83113

Eddie Murphy/Ossie Davis/Oliver Platt/Peter Boyle/Jeffrey Tambor

Ain't Nothin' But A Party [Sugarhill Gang]	Dance [Robin S]	Let's Ride [Montell Jordan] 2
Are You That Somebody? [Aaliyah] 21	Do Little Things [Changing Faces]	Lovin' You So [Jody Watley]
	In Your World [Twista & The Speed Knot Mobsters]	Push 'Em Up [Eddie Kane & DeVille]
Da Funk [Timbaland]	Lady Marmalade [All Saints]	Rock Steady [Dawn Robinson]

Same Ol' G [Ginuwine]
That's Why I Lie [Ray J.]
Woof Woof [69 Boyz] 31
Your Dress [Playa]

7/27/63 | **82** | 10 | | ©196 | **Dr. No** .... [I] | **$50** | | | United Artists 5108

Sean Connery/Ursula Andress/Joseph Wiseman/Jack Lord/Bernard Lee; cp/cd: Monty Norman

Audio Bongo	Island Speaks	James Bond Theme
Boy Chase	Jamaica Jazz	Jump Up
Dr. No's Fantasy	Jamaican Rock	Kingston Calypso

Love At Last
Twisting With James
Under The Mango Tree

11/25/00 | **52** | 9 | | ©197 | **Dr. Seuss' How The Grinch Stole Christmas**... [X-V] | **$10** | | | Interscope 490765

Jim Carrey/Molly Shannon/Jeffrey Tambor/Taylor Momsen/Christine Baranski; Christmas chart: 5/'00

Better Do It Right [Smash Mouth]	Christmas, Why Can't I Find You?	He Carves The Roast Beast
Big Heist	Does Cindy Lou Really Ruin Christmas?	Kids Today (dialogue)
Change Of The Heart		Lonely Christmas Eve [Ben Folds]
Christmas Is Going To The Dogs [Eels]	Green Christmas [Barenaked Ladies]	Memories Of A Green Childhood
Christmas Means More (dialogue)	Grinch Schedule (dialogue)	Reindeer (dialogue)
Christmas Of Love [Little Isidor & The Inquisitors]	Grinch 2000 [Busta Rhymes/Jim Carrey]	Shape Of Things To Come
		Sleigh Of Presents
		Stealing Christmas

Where Are You Christmas? [Faith Hill] 65
Whoville Medley [Trans-Siberian Orchestra]
You Don't Have To Be Alone ['N Sync]
You're A Mean One, Mr. Grinch [Jim Carrey]

3/19/66 | **❶¹** | 157 | ● | ©198 | **Doctor Zhivago** [I] | **$25** | | | MGM 6

Omar Sharif/Julie Christie/Rod Steiger/Alec Guinness/Ralph Richardson; cp/cd: Maurice Jarre

At The Student Cafe	Lara Leaves Yuri	Revolution
Funeral, The	Lara's Theme	Sventyski's Waltz
Komarovsky And Lara's Rendezvous	Main Title	Tonya Arrives At Varykino
	Overture	Yuri Escapes

Yuri Writes A Poem For Lara

2/19/72 | **173** | 5 | | 199 | **Dollar ($)** .... [I+V] | **$20** | | | Reprise 2051

Warren Beatty/Goldie Hawn/Gert Frobe/Robert Webber; cp/cd: **Quincy Jones**

Brooks' 50 Cent Tour [Little Richard & Roberta Flack]	Kitty With The Bent Frame	Redeye Runnin' Train [Doug Kershaw]
Candy Man	Money Is [Little Richard]	Rubber Ducky
Do It - To It [Little Richard]	**Money Runner** 57	Shady Lady
	Passin' The Buck	

Snow Creatures
When You're Smiling (The Whole World Smiles With You) [Roberta Flack]

5/6/95 | **61** | 30 | ● | ©200 | **Don Juan DeMarco**.. [I] | **$10** | | | A&M 540357

Johnny Depp/Marlon Brando/Faye Dunaway; cp: Michael Kamen

Arabia	Don Octavio Del Flores	Habanera
Don Alfonso	Dona Ana	**Have You Ever Really Loved A Woman?** [Bryan Adams] 1
Don Juan	Dona Julia	

I Was Born In Mexico
Love At First Sight (Mother And Father)

1/27/96 | **18** | 19 | ● | ©201 | **Don't Be A Menace To South Central While Drinking Your Juice In The Hood** .... [V] | **$10** | | | Island 524146

Shawn Wayans/Marlon Wayans/Tracey Jones/Chris Spencer

All The Things (Your Man Won't Do) [Joe] 11	Funky Sounds [Lil Bud & Tizone]	Maintain [Erick Sermon]
Can't Be Wasting My Time [Mona Lisa] 65	Give It Up [Jodeci]	**Renee** [Lost Boyz] 33
	It's Time [Blue Raspberry]	Suga Daddy [Suga-T]
Don't Give Up [Island Inspirational All-Stars]	**Let's Lay Together** [Isley Brothers] 93	Tempo Slow [R. Kelly]
Freak It Out! [Doug E. Fresh]	Live Wires Connect [UGK]	Time To Shine [Lil Kim]
		Up North Trip [Mobb Deep]

We Got More [Shock G]
Winter Warz [Ghostface Killah]

Don't Knock The Twist - see CHECKER, Chubby
Chubby Checker/Gene Chandler/**Vic Dana**/Linda Scott/Frank Albertson

Doors, The - see DOORS
Val Kilmer/Meg Ryan/Kevin Dillon/Kyle MacLachlan/Frank Whaley

Double Trouble - see PRESLEY, Elvis
Elvis Presley ("Guy Lambert")/Annette Day/John Williams/Yvonne Romain/Leon Askin

4/5/86 | **68** | 7 | | ©202 | **Down And Out In Beverly Hills** [I+V] | **$10** | | | MCA 6160

Nick Nolte/**Bette Midler**/Richard Dreyfuss/Tracy Nelson; cp: **Andy Summers**

California Girls [David Lee Roth] 3	El Tecalitleco [Mariachi Vargas de Tecalitlan]	I Love L.A. [Randy Newman]
Down And Out In Beverly Hills Theme	**Great Gosh A'Mighty! (It's A Matter Of Time)** [Little Richard] 42	Jerry's Suicide Attempt
		Mission Blues
		Nouvelle Cuisine

Search For Kerouac
Tutti Frutti [Little Richard] 17
Wave Hands Like Clouds

SOUNDTRACKS

DEBUT	PEAK	WKS	RIAA	CD	ARTIST — Album Title	Catalog	Sym	$	Label & Number

3/3/01 | **71** | 6 | | ©203 **Down To Earth** .... [V] **$10** Epic 61599
Chris Rock/Regina King/Eugene Levy/Frankie Faison/Chazz Palminteri

Angel *[Kelly Rowland]*	Gin And Juice *[Snoop Doggy Dogg]* **8**	Never Let Go *[3LW]*
Can You Tell It's Me *[Ginuwine]*	Glitches *[Roots & Amel Larrieux]*	One Time *[Jill Scott]*
Dreamed You *[Jagged Edge]*	I Think I Like You *[Jordan Brown]*	Someone To Love You *[Ruff Endz]*
Everything Is Everything *[Lauryn Hill]* **35**	**Just Another Girl** *[Monica]* **64**	Thug Music Play On *[Bone Thugs-N-Harmony]*

Up Against The Wall *[Layzie Bone]* / What If I Was White *[Sticky Fingaz]* / With You *[Son By Four]*

12/12/92 | **94** | 6 | | ©204 **Dracula, Bram Stoker's** .... [I] **$10** Columbia 53165
Gary Oldman/Winona Ryder/Anthony Hopkins/Keanu Reeves/Sadie Frost; cp: Wojciech Kilar; cd: Anton Coppola

Ascension	Hunt Builds	Love Song For A Vampire *[Annie Lennox]*
Brides, The	Hunters Prelude	Ring Of Fire
Dracula - The Beginning	Love Eternal	Lucy's Party	Storm, The
End Credits	Love Remembered	Mina/Dracula	Vampire Hunters
Green Mist		Mina's Photo

12/30/00+ | **81** | 9 | | ©205 **Dracula 2000** .... [V] **$10** Columbia 61585
Gerard Butler/Jonny Lee Miller/Justine Waddell/Christopher Plummer/Omar Epps

Avoid The Light *[Pantera]*	Day By Day *[Taproot]*	One Step Closer *[Linkin Park]*
Blind World *[Flybanger]*	Heads Explode *[Monster Magnet]*	Ostego Undead *[Static-X]*
Bloodline *[Slayer]*	Malice *[Endo]*	Sober *[Half Cocked]*
Break You Down *[Godhead]*	Metro *[System Of A Down]*	Swan Dive *[(Hed)P.E.]*

Ultra Mega *[Powerman 5000]* / Welcome Burden *[Disturbed]* / Your Disease *[Saliva]*

7/18/87 | **137** | 6 | | ©206 **Dragnet** .... [I+V] **$10** MCA 6210
Dan Aykroyd/Tom Hanks/Christopher Plummer/Dabney Coleman/Harry Morgan; cp: Ira Newborn

City Of Crime *[Dan Aykroyd & Tom Hanks]*	Danger Ahead (medley)	Joe Gets Fired
Dairy Apologies	Dragnet *[Art Of Noise]*	Just The Facts *[Patti LaBelle]*
Dance Or Die *[Peter Aykroyd & Pat Thrall]*	Dragnet March (medley)	Kill Me Instead
	End Credits	Looking For Muzz
	Helplessly In Love *[New Edition]*	Pagan Fight

Pagan Tension / Tank, The / This Is The City (medley)

4/8/89 | **94** | 10 | | ©207 **Dream A Little Dream** .... [V] **$10** Cypress 0125
Jason Robards/Corey Feldman/Piper Laurie/Meredith Salenger/Harry Dean Stanton

Dream A Little Dream Of Me *[Mickey Thomas]*	Dreams Come True (Stand Up And Take It) *[Lone Justice]*	**It's The End Of The World As We Know It (And I Feel Fine)** *[R.E.M.]* **69**
Dream A Little Dream Of Me *[Mel Torme & Mickey Thomas]*	**I've Got Dreams To Remember** *[Otis Redding]* **41**	Never Turn Away *[Chris Thompson]*
	Into The Mystic *[Van Morrison]*	**Rock On** *[Michael Damian]* **1**

Time Runs Wild *[Danny Wilde]* / Whenever There's A Night *[Mike Reno]* / You'd Better Wait *[Fee Waybill]*

10/16/99 | **44** | 7 | | ©208 **Drive Me Crazy** .... [V] **$10** Jive 41692
Melissa Joan Hart/Adrian Grenier/Stephen Collins/Mark Webber/Mark Metcalf

Faith In You *[Matthew Sweet]*	Is This Really Happening To Me? *[Phantom Planet]*	Original *[Silage]*
Hammer To The Heart *[Tamperer]*	**It's All Been Done** *[Barenaked Ladies]* **44**	Regret *[Mukala]*
Help Save The Youth Of America From Exploding *[Less Than Jake]*	Keep On Loving You *[Donnas]*	Stranded *[Plumb]*
I Want It That Way *[Backstreet Boys]*	One For Sorrow *[Steps]*	Sugar *[Don Philip]*
		Unforgetful You *[Jars Of Clay]*

(You Drive Me) Crazy *[Britney Spears]* **10**

5/19/01 | **124** | 2 | | ©209 **Driven** .... [V] **$10** Curb 78715
Sylvester Stallone/Burt Reynolds/Kip Pardue/Gina Gershon/Stacy Edwards

Break On Through *[Steve Holy]*	Good Time *[Leroy]*	I'm Not Driving Anymore *[Rob Dougan]*
Breakdown *[Tantric]*	Green Light Girl *[Doyle Bramhall II & Smokestack]*	Mother *[Era]*
Burn *[Jo Dee Messina]* **42**	Hang On *[Hank III]*	Poison Well *[Insolence]*
Falling For Me *[Tamara Walker]*	I Wanna Get Back With You *[Mary Griffin]*	Satellite *[BT]*
For The Love Of Money *[Rare Blend]*		Soon *[LeAnn Rimes]*

Take Me Away From Here *[Tim McGraw]*

4/16/94 | **105** | 7 | | ©210 **D2: The Mighty Ducks** .... [V] **$10** Hollywood 61603
Emilio Estevez/Michael Tucker/Jan Rubes/Kathryn Erbe/Carsten Norgaard

Mighty Ducks Suite	Rock The Pond *[John Bisaha]*	**Whoomp! (There It Is)** *[Tag Team]* **2**
Mr. Big Stuff *[Martha Wash]*	**We Are The Champions** *[Queen]* **4**	Wild Thing *[Troggs]* **1**
Rock And Roll Part 2 *[Gary Glitter]* **7**	**We Will Rock You** *[Queen]* **52**	

You Ain't Seen Nothin' Yet *[Poorboys]* / Zamboni *[Gear Daddies]*

9/30/00 | **102** | 22 | | ©211 **Duets** .... [V] **$10** Hollywood 62241
Huey Lewis/Gwyneth Paltrow/Paul Giamatti/Andre Braugher/Angie Dickinson

Beginnings/Endings *[David Newman]*	Cruisin' *[Gwyneth Paltrow & Huey Lewis]*	I Can't Make You Love Me *[Maria Bello]*
Bette Davis Eyes *[Gwyneth Paltrow]*	Feeling Alright *[Huey Lewis]*	Just My Imagination (Running Away With Me) *[Babyface & Gwyneth Paltrow]*
Copacabana *[John Pinette]*	Free Bird *[Arnold McCuller]*	
	Hello, It's Me *[Paul Giamatti]*	

Lonely Teardrops *[Huey Lewis]* / Sweet Dreams (Are Made Of This) *[Maria Bello]* / Try A Little Tenderness *[Paul Giamatti & Arnold McCuller]*

1/7/95 | **62** | 29 | ● | ©212 **Dumb And Dumber** .... [V] **$10** RCA 66523
Jim Carrey/Jeff Daniels/Lauren Holly/Karen Duffy/Teri Garr

Ballad Of Peter Pumpkinhead *[Crash Test Dummies]*	Hurdy Gurdy Man *[Butthole Surfers]*	Take *[Lupins]*
Bear Song *[Green Jelly]*	If You Don't Love Me (I'll Kill Myself) *[Pete Droge]*	Too Much Of A Good Thing *[Sons]*
Crash - the '95 Mix *[Primitives]*	Insomniac *[Echobelly]*	Where I Find My Heaven *[Gigolo Aunts]*
Get Ready *[Proclaimers]*	**New Age Girl** *[Deadeye Dick]* **27**	

Whiney, Whiney (What Really Drives Me Crazy) *[Willi One Blood]* **62** / You Sexy Thing *[Deee-Lite]*

Dune - see TOTO
Brad Dourif/Kyle MacLachlan/Kenneth McMillan/Linda Hunt/Sting

7/20/91 | **50** | 14 | | ©213 **Dying Young** .... [I] **$10** Arista 18692
Julia Roberts/Campbell Scott/Vincent D'Onofrio/Colleen Dewhurst; cp/cd: James Newton Howard

All The Way *[King Curtis]*	Driving North (medley) *[Kenny G & James Newton Howard]*	I'll Never Leave You (Love Theme) *[Kenny G & James Newton Howard]*
All The Way *[Jeffrey Osborne]*	Dying Young (Theme) *[Kenny G]*	Love Montage
Bluff, The	Hillary's Theme *[Kenny G & James Newton Howard]*	Maze, The
Clock, The		

Moving In (medley) *[Kenny G & James Newton Howard]* / San Francisco / Victor / Victor Teaches Art

Easter Parade - see "Those Glorious MGM Musicals"
Judy Garland/Fred Astaire/Peter Lawford/Ann Miller/Jules Munshin

9/6/69+ | **6** | 72 | ● | ©214 **Easy Rider** .... [V] **$30** Dunhill/ABC 50063
Peter Fonda/Dennis Hopper/Jack Nicholson/Karen Black/Robert Walker

Ballad Of Easy Rider *[Roger McGuinn]*	If Six Was Nine *[Jimi Hendrix Experience]*	It's Alright, Ma (I'm Only Bleeding) *[Roger McGuinn]*
Born To Be Wild *[Steppenwolf]* **2**	If You Want To Be A Bird *[Holy Modal Rounders]*	Kyrie Eleison *[Electric Prunes]*
Don't Bogart Me *[Fraternity Of Man]*		Pusher, The *[Steppenwolf]*

Wasn't Born To Follow *[Byrds]* / Weight, The *[Smith]*

DEBUT	PEAK	WKS	RIAA	CD	ARTIST — Album Title	Catalog	Sym	$	Label & Number

6/15/96 119 4 ©215 Eddie .... [V] **$10** Island 524243
Whoopi Goldberg/Frank Langella/Dennis Farina/Richard Jenkins

After Last Night [Jodeci]	**It's All The Way Live (Now)**	Say It Again [Nneka]	Skills [Stanley Clarke]
Ain't No Love [40 Thevz]	[Coolio] **29**	Say That You're Ready [J'son]	Step Up To The Line [Mighty Reel]
Da Dribbol [N.B. Hey]	Punch Drunk [House Of Pain]	**Scarred** [Luke] **64**	**Tell Me** [Dru Hill] **18**
	Rain Falls [Darcus]	Sistas [Myron]	Where You At [ILL Al Skratch]

Eddie And The Cruisers - see CAFFERTY, John
Michael Pare/Tom Berenger/Ellen Barkin

5/26/56 ❶¹ 99 ©216 Eddy Duchin Story, The [I] **$40** Decca 8289
Tyrone Power/Kim Novak/James Whitmore/Victoria Shaw/Jack Albertson; pf: Carmen Cavallaro

Brazil (Aquarela Do Brasil)	It Must Be True (You Are Mine, All	On The Sunny Side Of The Street	To Love Again (Finale) (Based On
Chopsticks	Mine)	Shine On Harvest Moon	Chopin's E Flat Nocturne)
Dizzy Fingers	La Vie En Rose	To Love Again	Whispering
	Manhattan		You're My Everything

Edward Scissorhands - see ELFMAN, Danny
Johnny Depp/Winona Ryder/Dianne Wiest/Anthony Michael Hall/Vincent Price

2/5/94 33 18 ▲ ©217 8 Seconds .... [V] **$10** MCA 10927
Luke Perry/Stephen Baldwin/Cynthia Geary/Carrie Snodgress/Renee Zellweger

Burnin' Up The Road [John	No More Cryin' [McBride & The	Ride 'Em High, Ride 'Em Low	When Will I Be Loved [Vince Gill]
Anderson]	Ride]	[Brooks & Dunn]	You Hung The Moon [Patty Smyth]
If I Had Only Known [Reba	Once In A While [Billy Dean]	Standing Right Next To Me [Karla	
McEntire]	Pull Your Hat Down Tight [Pam	Bonoff]	
Just Once [David Lee Murphy]	Tillis]	Texas Is Bigger Than It Used To Be	
Lane's Theme [Bill Conti]		[Mark Chesnutt]	

8/4/62 35 13 ©218 El Cid .... [I] **$50** MGM 3977
Charlton Heston/Sophia Loren/Raf Vallone/Gary Raymond; cp/cd: Miklos Rozsa

Battle Of Valencia	Fight For Calahorra	Palace Music
Cid's Death	Intermezzo: The El Cid March	13 Knights
Farewell	Legend, The	Twins, The

10/20/73 194 2 219 Electra Glide In Blue .... [I+V] **$40** United Artists 062
Robert Blake/Billy Green Bush; cp: James William Guercio; includes a booklet of pictures and 2 posters

Chase, The	Meadow Mountain Top [Mark	Morning	Song Of Sad Bottles [Mark
Free From The Devil [Madura]	Spolestra]	Most Of All [Marcels]	Spolestra]
Jolene's Dance	Monument Valley		Tell Me

9/1/84 94 9 220 Electric Dreams .... [V] **$10** Virgin 39600
Lenny Von Dohlen/Virginia Madsen/Maxwell Caulfield/Bud Cort/Don Fellows

Chase Runner [Heaven 17]	Electric Dreams [P.P. Arnold]	Madeline's Theme [Giorgio	Together In Electric Dreams
Dream, The [Culture Club]	Let It Run [Jeff Lynne]	Moroder]	[Giorgio Moroder & Philip Oakey]
Duel, The [Giorgio Moroder]	Love Is Love [Culture Club]	Now You're Mine [Helen Terry]	**Video!** [Jeff Lynne] **85**

Electric Horseman, The - see NELSON, Willie
Robert Redford/**Jane Fonda**/Willie Nelson/Valerie Perrine/Allan Arbus

Elvis-That's The Way It Is - see PRESLEY, Elvis

2/13/88 150 5 ©221 Empire Of The Sun .... [I] **$10** Warner 25668
Christian Bale/John Malkovich/Miranda Richardson/Nigel Havers/Ben Stiller; cp/cd: **John Williams**

British Grenadiers	Jim's New Life	Pheasant Hunt	Suo Gan
Cadillac Of The Skies	Liberation: Exsultate Justi	Return To The City	Toy Planes, Home And Hearth
Exsultate Justi	Lost In The Crowd	Seeing The Bomb (medley)	
Imaginary Air Battle	No Road Home (medley)	Streets Of Shanghai	

9/9/95 63 20 ● ©222 Empire Records .... [V] **$10** A&M 540384
Anthony LaPaglia/Maxwell Caulfield/Debi Mazar/Liv Tyler/Renee Zellweger

Ballad Of El Goodo [Evan Dando]	Free [Martinis]	Liar [Cranberries]	**Til I Hear It From You** [Gin
Bright As Yellow [Innocence	**Girl Like You** [Edwyn Collins] **32**	Nice Overalls [Lustre]	Blossoms] **11**
Mission]	Here It Comes Again [Please]	Ready, Steady, Go [Meices]	What You Are [Drill]
Circle Of Friends [Better Than Ezra]	I Don't Want To Live Today [Ape	Sugarhigh [Coyote Shivers]	Whole Lotta Trouble [Cracker]
Crazy Life [Toad The Wet Sprocket]	Hangers]		

5/17/80 4 28 ● ©223 Empire Strikes Back, The [I] **$25** RSO 4201 [2]
Mark Hamill/Harrison Ford/Carrie Fisher/Billy Dee Williams/Alec Guinness; cp/cd: **John Williams**

Asteroid Field	Han Solo And The Princess	Lando's Palace	Yoda And The Force
Battle In The Snow	Heroics Of Luke And Han	Magic Tree	Yoda's Theme
City In The Clouds	Hyperspace	Rebels At Bay	
Departure Of Boba Fett	Imperial March (Darth Vader's	Star Wars (Main Theme)	
Duel, The	Theme)	Training Of A Jedi Knight	

9/6/80 178 4 224 Empire Strikes Back, The/The Adventures Of Luke Skywalker .... [T] **$20** RSO 3081
storyline excerpts from the movie (no track titles listed); narrated by Malachi Throne

2/15/97 60 9 ©225 Empire Strikes Back, The .... [I-R] **$15** RCA Victor 68747 [2]
complete score in sequence with previously unreleased music issued in conjunction with the 1997 release of The Empire Strikes Back
Special Edition movie in theaters

Aboard The Executor (medley)	Darth Vader's Trap (medley)	Imperial Probe (medley)	Rebel Fleet (medley)
Arrival On Dagobah	Deal With The Dark Lord	Imperial Starfleet Deployed	Rescue From Cloud City (medley)
Asteroid Field	Departure Of Boba Fett (medley)	(medley)	Snowspeeders Take Flight (medley)
Attacking A Star Destroyer	End Title (medley)	Jedi Master Revealed (medley)	Training Of A Jedi Knight (medley)
Battle Of Hoth	Han Solo And The Princess	Lando's Palace	20th Century Fox Fanfare
Betrayal At Bespin	Hyperspace (medley)	Luke's Nocturnal Visitor	Vision Of Obi-Wan (medley)
Carbon Freeze (medley)	Ice Planet Hoth (medley)	Magic Tree (medley)	Wampa's Lair (medley)
City In The Clouds (medley)	Imperial March (Darth Vader's	Main Title (medley)	Yoda And The Force
Clash Of Lightsabers	Theme)	Mynock Cave (medley)	Yoda's Theme

6/13/92 130 5 ©226 Encino Man .... [V] **$10** Hollywood 61330
Sean Astin/Pauly Shore/Brendan Fraser/Megan Ward/Rose McGowan

Cool Hand Loc [Tone Loc]	Leave My Curl Alone [Hi-C]	Why'd You Want Me? [Jesus &	You're Invited But Your Friend Can't
Feed The Monkey [Infectious	Luxury Cruiser [T-Ride]	Mary Chain]	Come [Vince Neil]
Grooves]	Mama Said Knock You Out	Wild Thing [Cheap Trick]	Young And Dumb [Scream]
Frankenstein [Edgar Winter	[Scatterbrain]	Wooly Bully [Smithereens]	
Group] **1**	Stone Cold Crazy [Queen]	You Turn Me On [Crystal Waters]	
Get The Hell Out Of Here [Steve	Treaty [Yothu Yindi]		
Vai]			

DEBUT	PEAK	WKS	RIAA	CD	ARTIST — Album Title	Catalog	Sym	$	Label & Number
11/27/99	20	14 ▲		©227	**End Of Days**		[V]	$10	Geffen 490508

Arnold Schwarzenegger/Gabriel Byrne/Kevin Pollak/Robin Tunney/Rod Steiger

Bad Influence [Eminem]	I Wish I Had [Stroke]	Poison [Prodigy]	Sugar Kane [Sonic Youth]
Camel Song [Korn]	Nobody's Real [Powerman 5000]	Slow [Professional Murder Music]	Superbeast [Rob Zombie]
Crushed [Limp Bizkit]	Oh My God [Guns N' Roses]	So Long [Everlast]	Wrong Way [Creed]

DEBUT	PEAK	WKS	RIAA	CD	ARTIST — Album Title	Catalog	Sym	$	Label & Number
8/1/81	9	20 ●		©228	**Endless Love**		[I+V]	$12	Mercury 2001

Brooke Shields/Martin Hewitt/Shirley Knight/Don Murray; cp: Jonathan Tunick/**Lionel Richie**

Ann Sees David And Jade Making Love	Dreaming [Cliff Richard] 10	Endless Love [Diana Ross & Lionel Richie] 1	I Was Made For Lovin' You [Kiss] 11
David At The Institution	Dreaming Of You [Diana Ross & Lionel Richie]	Endless Love Theme	
David Goes To Jade's House	Dreaming Of You (instrumental)	Heart Song	

Endless Summer, The - see SANDALS, The

DEBUT	PEAK	WKS	RIAA	CD	ARTIST — Album Title	Catalog	Sym	$	Label & Number
2/8/97	133	5		©229	**English Patient, The**		[I]	$10	Fantasy 16001

Ralph Fiennes/Juliette Binoche/Willem Dafoe/Kristin Scott Thomas; cp: Gabriel Yared; cd: Harry Rabinowitz

Am I K. In Your Book?	Convento Di Sant' Anna	Let Me Come In!	Szerelem, Szerelem [Muzsikas feat. Marta Sebestyen]
Aria From The Goldberg Variations [Julie Steinberg]	En Csak Azt Csodalom (Lullaby For Katharine)	Let Me Tell You About Winds	Wang Wang Blues [Benny Goodman]
As Far As Florence	English Patient	One O'Clock Jump [Benny Goodman]	What Else Do You Love?
Ask Your Saint Who He's Killed	Hana's Curse	Read Me To Sleep	Where Or When [Shepheard's Hotel Jazz Orchestra]
Black Nights	Herodotus	Retreat, A	Why Picton?
Cave Of Swimmers	I'll Always Go Back To That Church	Rupert Bear	
Cheek To Cheek [Fred Astaire]	I'll Be Back	Swoon, I'll Catch You	
Cheek To Cheek [Ella Fitzgerald]	Kip's Lights		

DEBUT	PEAK	WKS	RIAA	CD	ARTIST — Album Title	Catalog	Sym	$	Label & Number
8/10/96	80	6		©230	**Escape From L.A.**		[V]	$10	Lava 92714

Kurt Russell/Stacy Keach/Steve Buscemi/Peter Fonda/Cliff Robertson

Blame [Gravity Kills]	Escape From The Prison Planet [Clutch]	Foot On The Gas [Sexpod]	Professional Widow [Tori Amos]
Can't Even Breathe [Deftones]	Et Tu Bruté? [CIV]	One, The [White Zombie]	Sweat [Tool]
Cut Me Out [Toadies]	Fire In The Hole [Orange 9mm]	Paisley [Ministry]	10 Seconds Down [Sugar Ray]
Dawn [Stabbing Westward]		Pottery [Butthole Surfers]	

DEBUT	PEAK	WKS	RIAA	CD	ARTIST — Album Title	Catalog	Sym	$	Label & Number
7/3/82	37	33 ●		©231	**E.T. - The Extra-Terrestrial**		[I]	$10	MCA 6109

Henry Thomas/Peter Coyote/Dee Wallace/Drew Barrymore/Robert MacNaughton; cp/cd: **John Williams**

Abandoned And Pursued	E.T. Phone Home	Over The Moon
Adventure On Earth	E.T.'s Halloween	Three Million Light Years From Earth
E.T. And Me	Flying	

Even Cowgirls Get The Blues - see LANG, K.D.

Uma Thurman/Rain Phoenix/John Hurt/Pat Morita/Keanu Reeves

DEBUT	PEAK	WKS	RIAA	CD	ARTIST — Album Title	Catalog	Sym	$	Label & Number
8/22/98	100	7		©232	**Ever After**		[I]	$10	London 460581

Drew Barrymore/Anjelica Huston/Dougray Scott/Jeanne Moreau; cp/cd: George Fenton

Cinderella	Going To The Ball	Proposal, The	Trying To Relate
Danielle's Wings	Happily Ever After	Put Your Arms Around Me [Texas]	Utopia
Ever After Main Title	Homecoming, The	Rescuing Maurice	Walking On Water
First Kiss	Marguerite	Royal Wedding	"Your Highness - What A Surprise"
Girls, The Prince And The Painting	Market, The	Ruins, The	
Glass Slipper	Prince's Decision	Sweet Revenge	

DEBUT	PEAK	WKS	RIAA	CD	ARTIST — Album Title	Catalog	Sym	$	Label & Number
1/20/79	78	15		233	**Every Which Way But Loose**		[V]	$12	Elektra 503

Clint Eastwood/Sondra Locke/Ruth Gordon/Geoffrey Lewis/Beverly D'Angelo; cd: Steve Dorff

Behind Closed Doors [Charlie Rich] 15	Eastwood's Alley Walk	I'll Wake You Up When I Get Home [Charlie Rich]	Send Me Down To Tucson [Mel Tillis]
Biker's Theme	**Every Which Way But Loose** [Eddie Rabbitt] 30	Monkey See, Monkey Do [Cliff Crofford]	Six Pack To Go [Hank Thompson]
Coca-Cola Cowboy [Mel Tillis]	I Can't Say No To A Truck Drivin' Man [Carol Chase]	Red Eye Special [Larry Collins]	Under The Double Eagle
Don't Say You Don't Love Me No More [Sondra Locke & Phil Everly]	I Seek The Night [Sondra Locke]	Salty Dog Blues	

Evita -- see MADONNA

Madonna/Antonio Banderas/Jonathan Pryce/Jimmy Nail

DEBUT	PEAK	WKS	RIAA	CD	ARTIST — Album Title	Catalog	Sym	$	Label & Number
4/7/01	8	14↑		©234	**Exit Wounds**		[V]	$10	Blackground 10192

Steven Seagal/**DMX**/Bill Duke/Tom Arnold

Bust Your Gun [Lox]	Hey Ladies [Lady Luck]	1-2-3 [Memphis Bleek]	They Don't Fuck Wit U [Three 6 Mafia]
Dog 4 Life [Iceberg]	Incense Burning [Playa]	Party [Sincere]	Walk With Me [Big Stan]
Fo' All Y'all [Caviar]	It's On Me [Ideal]	State To State [Black Child]	We Got [Trick Daddy feat. Trina]
Gangsta Tears [Nas]	No Sunshine [DMX]	Steady Grinding [Mack 10]	
Hell Yeah [Outsiderz 4 Life]	Off Da Chain Daddy [Drag-On]		

DEBUT	PEAK	WKS	RIAA	CD	ARTIST — Album Title	Catalog	Sym	$	Label & Number
1/16/61	❶[14]	89 ●		©235	**Exodus**		[I]	$30	RCA Victor 1058

Paul Newman/Eva Marie Saint/Ralph Richardson/Peter Lawford/Lee J. Cobb; cp/cd: Ernest Gold

Ari	Escape	In Jerusalem	Valley Of Jezreel
Brothers, The	Exodus (Theme)	Karen	
Conspiracy	Fight For Peace	Prison Break	
Dawn	Fight For Survival	Summer In Cyprus	

Experiment In Terror - see MANCINI, Henry

Glenn Ford/Lee Remick/Stefanie Powers/Roy Poole/Ned Glass

DEBUT	PEAK	WKS	RIAA	CD	ARTIST — Album Title	Catalog	Sym	$	Label & Number
8/12/78	124	9		236	**Eyes Of Laura Mars**		[I+V]	$15	Columbia 35487

Faye Dunaway/Tommy Lee Jones/Raul Julia/Brad Dourif/Rene Auberjonois; cp/cd: Artie Kane

Burn [Michalski & Oosterveen]	Prisoner (Disco Instrumental) (medley)	**Let's All Chant** [Michael Zager Band] 36	**Native New Yorker** (medley) [Odyssey] 21
Elaine		Love And Pity	**(Shake, Shake, Shake) Shake Your Booty** (medley) [KC & The Sunshine Band] 1
Eyes Of Laura Mars (Prisoner), Love Theme From [Barbra Streisand] 21	Laura & Neville (Instrumental)	Lulu And Michelle	
	Laura Nightmare		
	Laura - Warehouse		

DEBUT	PEAK	WKS	RIAA	CD	ARTIST — Album Title	Catalog	Sym	$	Label & Number
7/31/99	133	3		©237	**Eyes Wide Shut**		[V]	$10	Warner Sunset 47450

Tom Cruise/Nicole Kidman/Sydney Pollack/Marie Richardson

Baby Did A Bad Bad Thing [Chris Isaak]	I Got It Bad (And That Ain't Good) [Oscar Peterson Trio]	Musica Ricercata, II [Dominic Harlan]	Strangers In The Night [Peter Hughes Orch.]
Blame It On My Youth [Brad Mehldau]	If I Had You [Roy Gerson]	Musica Ricercata, II (Reprise) [Dominic Harlan]	Waltz 2 from Jazz Suite [Royal Concertgebouw Orch.]
Dream, The [Jocelyn Pook]	Masked Ball [Jocelyn Pook]	Naval Officer [Jocelyn Pook]	When I Fall In Love [Victor Silvester Orch.]
Grey Clouds [Dominic Harlan]	Migrations [Jocelyn Pook]		

Fabulous Baker Boys, The - see GRUSIN, Dave

Jeff Bridges/Michelle Pfeiffer/Beau Bridges/Jennifer Tilly

DEBUT	PEAK	WKS	RIAA	CD	ARTIST — Album Title	Catalog	Sym	$	Label & Number
1/9/99	47	11		©238	**Faculty, The**		[V]	$10	Columbia 69762

Famke Janssen/Bebe Neuwirth/**Usher**/Robert Patrick/Elijah Wood

Another Brick In The Wall (Part 2) [Class Of '99]	Helpless [D Generation]	Maybe Someday [Flick]	Stay Young [Oasis]
Changes [Shawn Mullins]	I'm Eighteen [Creed]	Medication [Garbage]	
Haunting Me [Stabbing Westward]	It's Over Now [Neve]	Resuscitation [Sheryl Crow]	
	Kids Aren't Alright [Offspring]	School's Out [Soul Asylum]	

Falcon And The Snowman, The - see METHENY, Pat, Group
Timothy Hutton/Sean Penn/Lori Singer/Pat Hingle/Dorian Harewood

| 6/13/64 | 147 | 2 | | ©239 | **Fall Of The Roman Empire, The** .... | | [I] | $75 | Columbia 2460 |

Sophia Loren/Stephen Boyd/James Mason/Alec Guinness/Christopher Plummer; cp/cd: Dimitri Tiomkin

Addio	Fall Of Rome	Pax Romana	Resurrection
Ballomar's Barbarian Attack	Lucilla's Sorrow	Persian Battle	Roman Forum
Dawn Of Love	Morning	Profundo	Tarantella
Fall Of Love	Notturno	Prophecy, The	

| 6/7/80 | 7 | 82 | ▲ | ©240 | **Fame** | | [M] | $12 | RSO 3080 |

Irene Cara/Eddie Barth/Maureen Teefy/Lee Curreri

Dogs In The Yard	I Sing The Body Electric	Out Here On My Own [Irene Cara] 19	**Red Light** [Linda Clifford] 41
Fame [Irene Cara] 4	Is It Okay If I Call You Mine?		
Hot Lunch Jam	Never Alone	Ralph And Monty (Dressing Room Piano)	

| 9/25/61 | 88 | 13 | | 241 | **Fanny** .... | | [I] | $40 | Warner 1416 |

Leslie Caron/Maurice Chevalier/**Charles Boyer**/Lionel Jeffries; cp: Harold Rome; cd: Morris Stoloff

Fanny	Love Is A Very Light Thing	Panisse And Son	Welcome Home
I Have To Tell You	Never Too Late For Love	Restless Heart	
I Like You	Oysters, Cockles & Mussels	To My Wife	

| 11/17/90 | 190 | 2 | ▲ | ©242 | **Fantasia, Walt Disney's** ....C:#33/5 | | [I] | $15 | Buena Vista 60072 [2] |

50th anniversary celebration of the release of the animated movie; cd: Leopold Stokowski; pf: **The Philadelphia Orchestra**

Ave Maria	Night On Bald Mountain	Rite Of Spring	Symphony No. 6, Op. 68
Dance Of The Hours	Nutcracker Suite	Sorcerer's Apprentice	Toccata and Fugue in D Minor

| 6/13/92 | 89 | 9 | | ©243 | **Far And Away** .... | | [I] | $10 | MCA 10628 |

Tom Cruise/Nicole Kidman/Thomas Gibson/Robert Prosky/Barbara Babcock; cp/cd: **John Williams**

Am I Beautiful?	Duel Scene (medley)	Joseph And Shannon	Reunion, The
Big Match	End Credits	Joseph's Dream	Settling With Steven (medley)
Blowing Off Steam	Fighting Donellys	Land Race	Shannon Is Shot
Book Of Days [Enya]	Fighting For Dough	Leaving Home	
Burning The Manor House	Inside The Mansion	Oklahoma Territory	
County Galway, June 1892	Joe Sr.'s Passing (medley)	Race To The River (medley)	

| 6/23/01 | 7 | 15↑ | ● | ©244 | **Fast And The Furious, The** | | [V] | $10 | Murder Inc. 548832 |

Vin Diesel/Paul Walker/Michelle Rodriguez

Cali Diseaz [Shade Sheist]	Hustlin' [Fat Joe]	**Put It On Me** [Ja Rule] 8	Take My Time Tonight [R. Kelly]
Didn't I [Petey Pablo]	Justify My Love [Vita]	Race Against Time [Tank]	Tudunn Tudunn Tudunn (Make U Jump) [Funkmaster Flex]
Freestyle [Bone & Gotti]	Life Ain't A Game [Ja Rule]	**Rollin' (Urban Assault Vehicle)** [Limp Bizkit] 65	When A Man Does Wrong [Ashanti]
Furious [Ja Rule]	Pov City Anthem [Caddillac Tah]	Suicide [Scarface]	
Good Life [Faith Evans]	Prayer, The [Black Child]		

| 8/28/82 | 54 | 20 | | ©245 | **Fast Times At Ridgemont High** .... | | [V] | $15 | Full Moon 60158 [2] |

Sean Penn/Phoebe Cates/Jennifer Jason Leigh/Judge Reinhold/Ray Walston

Don't Be Lonely [Quarterflash]	I Don't Know (Spicoli's Theme) [Jimmy Buffett]	Never Surrender [Don Felder]	**Somebody's Baby** [Jackson Browne] 7
Fast Times At Ridgement High [Sammy Hagar]	I'll Leave It Up To You [Poco]	Raised On The Radio [Ravyns]	Speeding [Go-Go's]
Fast Times (The Best Years Of Our Lives) [Billy Squier]	Look In Your Eyes [Gerard McMahon]	She's My Baby (And She's Outta Control) [Dave Palmer & Phil Jost]	Uptown Boys [Louise Goffin]
Goodbye, Goodbye [Oingo Boingo]	Love Is The Reason [Graham Nash]	Sleeping Angel [Stevie Nicks]	Waffle Stomp [Joe Walsh]
Highway Runner [Donna Summer]	Love Rules [Don Henley]	**So Much In Love** [Timothy B. Schmit] 59	

| 6/13/98 | 174 | 1 | | ©246 | **Fear And Loathing In Las Vegas** .... | | [O-V] | $10 | Geffen 25218 |

Johnny Depp/Benicio Del Toro/Mark Harmon/Christina Ricci/Gary Busey

Combination Of The Two [Big Brother & The Holding Company]	For Your Love [Yardbirds] 6	One Toke Over The Line [Brewer & Shipley] 10	Time Is Tight [Booker T. & The MG's] 6
Drug Score - Parts 1-3 [Tomoyasu Hotei & Ray Cooper]	Get Together [Youngbloods] 5	She's A Lady [Tom Jones] 2	Viva Las Vegas [Dead Kennedys]
Expecting To Fly [Buffalo Springfield] 98	Magic Moments [Perry Como] 4	Stuck Inside Of Mobile With The Memphis Blues Again [Bob Dylan]	**White Rabbit** [Jefferson Airplane] 8
	Mama Told Me Not To Come [Three Dog Night] 1	Tammy [Debbie Reynolds] 1	

Ferry Cross The Mersey - see GERRY AND THE PACEMAKERS
Gerry and The Pacemakers/Cilla Black/Jimmy Saville

| 10/30/71+ | 30 | 90 | ▲ | ©247 | **Fiddler On The Roof** .... | | [M] | $25 | United Artists 10900 [2] |

Topol/Norma Crane/Leonard Frey/Molly Picon; mu: Jerry Bock; ly: Sheldon Harnick; cd: **John Williams**

Anatevka	Far From The Home I Love	Miracle Of Miracles	To Life
Bottle Dance (medley)	If I Were A Rich Man	Sabbath Prayer	Wedding Celebration (medley)
Chavet Ballet Sequence	Main Title	Sunrise, Sunset	
Do You Love Me?	Matchmaker	Tevye's Dream	

| 6/7/97 | 99 | 6 | | ©248 | **Fifth Element, The** .... | | [I] | $10 | Virgin 44203 |

Bruce Willis/Gary Oldman/Ian Holm/Chris Tucker/Milla Jovovich; cp/cd/pf: Eric Serra

Aknot! Wot?	Human Nature	Little Light Of Love (End Titles Version)	Pictures Of War
Akta	Koolen	Lucia Di Lammermoor	Plavalaguna
Badaboom	Korben Dallas	Mangalores	Protect Life
Bomb In The Hotel	Lakta Ligunai	Mina Hinoo	Radiowaves
Diva Dance	Leeloo	Mondoshawan	Ruby Rap
Five Millenia Later	Leeloominai	No Cash No Trash	Timecrash
Heat	Little Light Of Love		

| 9/12/98 | 77 | 5 | | ©249 | **54 - Volume 1** .... | | [O-V] | $10 | Tommy Boy 1293 |

Ryan Phillippe/Salma Hayek/Sela Ward/Mike Myers/Neve Campbell

Boss, The [Diana Ross] 19	**Keep On Dancin'** [Gary's Gang] 41	Que Sera Mi Vida [Gibson Brothers]	**You Make Me Feel (Mighty Real)** [Sylvester] 36
Contact [Edwin Starr] 65	Knock On Wood [Mary Griffin]	Relight My Fire (medley) [Dan Hartman]	
Dance Dance Dance (Yowsah Yowsah Yowsah) [Chic] 6	Let's Start The Dance [Bohannon]	Studio 54 [54 Allstars]	**Young Hearts Run Free** [Candi Staton] 20
I Got My Mind Made Up [Instant Funk] 20	**Love Machine (Part I)** [Miracles] 1	Vertigo (medley) [Dan Hartman]	
	Move On Up [Destination]	Wishing On A Star [Rose Royce]	
	Native New Yorker [Odyssey] 21		

DEBUT	PEAK	WKS	RIAA	CD	ARTIST — Album Title	Catalog	Sym	$	Label & Number

9/12/98   **74**   6   ©250 **54 - Volume 2**.. [O-V] **$10** Tommy Boy 1294

Cherchez La Femme/Se Si Bon *[Dr. Buzzard's Original Savannah Band]* **27**
Come To Me *[France Joli]* **15**
Disco Nights (Rock-Freak) *[GQ]* **12**
Don't Leave Me This Way *[Thelma Houston]* **1**
Don't Let Me Be Misunderstood *[Santa Esmeralda]* **15**
Fly Robin Fly *[Silver Convention]*
Found A Cure *[Ashford & Simpson]* **36**
Galaxy *[War]* **39**
Haven't Stopped Dancing Yet *[Gonzalez]* **26**
Heart Of Glass *[Blondie]* **1**
Heaven Must Have Sent You *[Bonnie Pointer]* **11**
I Need A Man *[Grace Jones]*
If You Could Read My Mind *[Ultra Naté/Amber/Jocelyn Enriquez]* **52**
Loving Is Really My Game *[Brainstorm]*
Spank *[Jimmy "Bo" Horne]*
Take Your Time (Do It Right) *[S.O.S. Band]* **3**

8/23/86   **183**   3   251 **Fine Mess, A**.. [V] **$10** Motown 6180

Ted Danson/**Howie Mandel**/Richard Mulligan/Stuart Margolin/Paul Sorvino
Can't Help Falling In Love *[Christine McVie]*
Easier Said Than Done *[Chico DeBarge]*
Fine Mess *[Temptations]*
I'm Gonna Be A Wheel Someday *[Los Lobos]*
Love's Closing In *[Nick Jameson]*
Moving So Close *[Keith Burston & Darryl Littlejohn]*
Slow Down *[Billy Vera & The Beaters]*
Stan And Ollie *[Henry Mancini]*
Walk Like A Man *[Mary Jane Girls]* **41**
Wishful Thinking *[Smokey Robinson]*

10/5/68+   **90**   26   252 **Finian's Rainbow**.. [M] **$30** Warner 2550

Fred Astaire/**Petula Clark**/Tommy Steele/Keenan Wynn; ly: E.Y. Harburg; mu: Burton Lane; cd: **Ray Heindorf**
Begat, The
How Are Things In Glocca Morra?
If This Isn't Love
Look To The Rainbow
Main Title
Necessity
Old Devil Moon
Rain Dance Ballet
Something Sort Of Grandish
That Great Come-And-Get-It Day
This Time Of The Year
When I'm Not Near The Girl I Love
When The Idle Poor Become The Idle Rich

7/24/93   **131**   4   ©253 **Firm, The** .... [I+V] **$10** MCA/GRP 2007

Tom Cruise/Jeanne Tripplehorn/Ed Harris/Holly Hunter/Hal Holbrook; cp: **Dave Grusin**
Blues: The Death Of Love & Trust
Dance Class *[Dave Samuels]*
Firm - Main Title
How Could You Lose Me? - End Title
Memphis Stomp
Mitch & Abby
M-O-N-E-Y *[Lyle Lovett]*
Mud Island Chase
Never Mind *[Nanci Griffith]*
Plan, The
Ray's Blues
Stars On The Water *[Jimmy Buffett]*
Start It Up *[Robben Ford & The Blue Line]*

10/5/96   **90**   7   ©254 **First Wives Club, The** .... [V] **$10** Work 67814

Bette Midler/Goldie Hawn/Diane Keaton/Maggie Smith/Dan Hedaya
Beautiful Morning *[Rascals]* **3**
Game Of Love *[Brownstone]*
Heartbreak Road *[Dionne Farris]*
I Will Survive *[Chantay Savage]* **24**
I'm Still Standing *[Martha Wash]*
Love Is On The Way *[Billy Porter]*
Moving On Up *[M People]* **34**
Over And Over *[Puff Johnson]*
Piece Of My Heart *[Diana King]*
Sisters Are Doin' It For Themselves *[Eurythmics & Aretha Franklin]* **18**
Think *[Aretha Franklin]* **7**
Wives & Lovers *[Dionne Warwick]*
You Don't Own Me *[Bette Midler, Goldie Hawn & Diane Keaton]*

6/24/67   **107**   28   ©255 **Fistful Of Dollars, A** .... [I] **$30** RCA Victor 1135

Clint Eastwood/Marianne Koch/Carol Brown/Mario Brega; cp/cd: Ennio Morricone
Almost Dead
Chase, The
Fistful Of Dollars (Theme)
Fistful Of Dollars Suite
Result, The
Square Dance
Titoli
Without Pity

4/27/91   **58**   13 ●   ©256 **Five Heartbeats, The**.. [V] **$10** Virgin 91609

Robert Townsend/Michael Wright/Leon/Harry Lennix/Tico Wells
Are You Ready For Me *[Flash & The Ebony Sparks]*
Baby Stop Running Around *[Bird & The Midnight Falcons]*
Bring Back The Days *[U.S. Male]*
Heart Is A House For Love *[Dells]*
I Feel Like Going On *[Eddie, Baby Doll and The L.A. Mass Choir]*
In The Middle *[Flash & The Five Heartbeats]*
Nights Like This *[After 7]* **24**
Nothing But Love *[Five Heartbeats]*
Stay In My Corner *[Dells]* **10**
We Haven't Finished Yet *[Patti LaBelle]*

10/12/59   **22**   10   257 **Five Pennies, The** .... [M] **$50** Dot 29500

Danny Kaye/**Louis Armstrong**/Barbara Bel Geddes/Tuesday Weld/Bob Crosby
After You've Gone
Back Home Again In Indiana
Battle Hymn Of The Republic
Bill Bailey, Won't You Please Come Home
Carnival Of Venice
College Montage (medley)
Five Pennies
Five Pennies Saints
Follow The Leader (medley)
Good Night, Sleep Tight Medley
Indiana Radio Montage
Jingle Bells
Just The Blues
Lullaby In Ragtime
Main Title
Music Goes 'Round And 'Round
Wail Of The Winds

Flame - see SLADE

2/16/85   **130**   8   258 **Flamingo Kid, The**... [O-V] **$10** Motown 6131

Matt Dillon/Richard Crenna/Hector Elizondo/Jessica Walter/Fisher Stevens
Boys Will Be Boys *[Maureen Steele]*
Breakaway *[Jesse Frederick]*
Finger Poppin' Time *[Hank Ballard & The Midnighters]* **7**
Get A Job *[Silhouettes]* **1**
Good Golly, Miss Molly *[Little Richard]* **10**
He's So Fine *[Chiffons]* **1**
Heat Wave *[Martha & The Vandellas]* **4**
It's All Right *[Impressions]* **4**
Money (That's What I Want) *[Barrett Strong]* **23**
One Fine Day *[Chiffons]* **5**
Runaround Sue *[Dion]* **1**
Stranger On The Shore *[Mr. Acker Bilk]* **1**

Flash Gordon - see QUEEN

Sam Jones/Max Von Sydow/Melody Anderson/Topol/Timothy Dalton

4/30/83   **❶**²   78 ▲⁶   ©259 **Flashdance**   [V] **$10** Casablanca 811492

Jennifer Beals/Michael Nouri/Marine Johan/Lilia Skala
Flashdance...What A Feeling *[Irene Cara]* **1**
He's A Dream *[Shandi]*
I'll Be Here Where The Heart Is *[Kim Carnes]*
Imagination *[Laura Branigan]*
Lady, Lady, Lady *[Joe "Bean" Esposito]* **86**
Love Theme *[Helen St. John]*
Manhunt *[Karen Kamon]*
Maniac *[Michael Sembello]* **1**
Romeo *[Donna Summer]*
Seduce Me Tonight *[Cycle V]*

7/27/85   **160**   4   260 **Fletch** .... [I+V] **$10** MCA 6142

Chevy Chase/Dana Wheeler-Nicholson/Joe Don Baker/Tim Matheson/George Wendt; cp/cd: Harold Faltermeyer
Bit By Bit *[Stephanie Mills]* **78**
Diggin' In
Exotic Skates
Fletch, Get Outta Town *[Dan Hartman]*
Fletch Theme
Is It Over *[Kim Wilde]*
Letter To Both Sides *[Fixx]*
Name Of The Game *[Dan Hartman]*
Running For Love *[John Farnham]*
Running For Love (instrumental)

5/28/94   **73**   8   ©261 **Flintstones, The: Music From Bedrock** .... [V] **$10** MCA 11045

John Goodman/Rick Moranis/Elizabeth Perkins/**Rosie O'Donnell**/Halle Berry
Anarchy In The U.K. *[Green Jelly]*
Bedrock Anthem *["Weird Al" Yankovic]*
Bedrock Twitch *[BC-52's]*
Hit & Run Holiday *[My Life With The Thrill Kill Kult]*
Human Being (Bedrock Steady) *[Stereo MC's]*
I Showed A Caveman How To Rock *[US3 Feat. Def Jef]*
I Wanna Be A Flintstone *[Screaming Blue Messiahs]*
In The Days Of The Caveman *[Crash Test Dummies]*
(Meet) The Flintstones *[BC-52's]* **33**
Mesozoic Music *[David Newman]*
Prehistoric Daze *[Shakespears Sister & The Holy Ghost]*
Rock With The Caveman *[Big Audio Dynamite]*
Walk The Dinosaur *[Was Not Was]* **7**

12/25/61+   **15**   35   262 **Flower Drum Song** .... [M] **$30** Decca 79098

Nancy Kwan/James Shigeta/Miyoshi Umeki; mu: Richard Rodgers; ly: Oscar Hammerstein II; cd: Alfred Newman
Chop Suey
Don't Marry Me
Dream Ballet
Fan Tan Fanny (medley)
Gliding Through My Memoree (medley)
Grant Avenue
Hundred Million Miracles
I Am Going To Like It Here
I Enjoy Being A Girl
Love Look Away
Main Title
Other Generation
Sunday
You Are Beautiful

DEBUT	PEAK	WKS	RIAA	CD	ARTIST — Album Title	Catalog	Sym	$	Label & Number

5/6/78 | **5** | 24 ▲ | ©263 | **FM** | [V] | **$15** | MCA 12000 [2]

Michael Brandon/Eileen Brennan/Alex Karras/**Martin Mull**/Cleavon Little

Bad Man [Randy Meisner]
Breakdown [Tom Petty] **40**
Cold As Ice [Foreigner] **6**
Do It Again [Steely Dan] **6**
FM (No Static At All) [Steely Dan] **22**
Fly Like An Eagle [Steve Miller] **2**

It Keeps You Runnin' [Doobie Brothers] **37**
Just The Way You Are [Billy Joel] **3**
Lido Shuffle [Boz Scaggs] **11**
Life In The Fast Lane [Eagles] **11**
Life's Been Good [Joe Walsh] **12**

Livingston Saturday Night [Jimmy Buffett] **52**
More Than A Feeling [Boston] **5**
Night Moves [Bob Seger] **4**
Poor Poor Pitiful Me [Linda Ronstadt]

There's A Place In The World For A Gambler [Dan Fogelberg]
Tumbling Dice [Linda Ronstadt]
We Will Rock You [Queen] **flip**
Your Smiling Face [James Taylor] **20**

Follow The Boys - see FRANCIS, Connie
Connie Francis/Paula Prentiss/Ron Randell/Janis Paige/Russ Tamblyn

4/10/99 | **32** | 7 ● | ©264 | **Foolish** | [V] | **$10** | No Limit 50053

Master P/Eddie Griffin/**Andrew Dice Clay**/Marla Gibbs/Bill Duke

Aqua Boogie (A Psychoalphadiscobetabioquadoloop) [Parliament] **89**
Don't Be Foolish [Snoop Dogg/Daz/Kurupt]
Foolish [Master P/Mo B. Dick/Magic]

For Money [Silkk The Shocker]
For The Love Of Money [O'Jays]
Get Yo Mob On [Crooked Eye]
Jungle Boogie [Kool & The Gang] **4**
Let's Get It On [Marvin Gaye] **1**

Like A Jungle [C-Murder]
N**** [Ghetto Commission]
Nothing Stays The Same [O'Dell & Porsha]
Put 'Em Up [Mr. Serv-On]
Runnin' From The Police [C-Murder]

School On Lock [Lil' Soldiers]
That's That Shit [Mystikal]
They Don't Hear Me [Fiend]
Whatchanogood [Mia X]
Yes Indeed [Kane & Abel]

2/18/84 | **❶**[10] | 61 ▲[9] | ©265 | **Footloose** | C:#27/25 [V] | **$10** | Columbia 39242

Kevin Bacon/Lori Singer/John Lithgow/Dianne Wiest/Chris Penn

Almost Paradise...Love Theme From Footloose [Mike Reno & Ann Wilson] **7**

Dancing In The Sheets [Shalamar] **17**
Footloose [Kenny Loggins] **1**
Girl Gets Around [Sammy Hagar]

Holding Out For A Hero [Bonnie Tyler] **34**
I'm Free (Heaven Helps The Man) [Kenny Loggins] **22**

Let's Hear It For The Boy [Deniece Williams] **1**
Never [Moving Pictures]
Somebody's Eyes [Karla Bonoff]

9/14/68 | **192** | 2 | | 266 | **For Love Of Ivy** | [I+V] | **$30** | ABC 7

Sidney Poitier/Abbey Lincoln/Beau Bridges/**Carroll O'Connor**; cp/cd: **Quincy Jones**

B. B. Jones [B.B. King]
Black Pearl
Don't You Believe It [Cashman, Pistilli & West]

End Title [Shirley Horn]
For Love Of Ivy
Little Hippy Dippy
Main Title

Messy But Good [B.B. King]
My Side Of The Sky [Cashman, Pistilli & West]
Somethin' Strange

Soul Motion
Wheelin' And Dealin'
You Put It On Me [B.B. King] **82**

10/2/99 | **72** | 5 | | ©267 | **For Love Of The Game** | [V] | **$10** | MCA 112068

Kevin Costner/Kelly Preston/John C. Reilly/Jena Malone/Brian Cox

Baby Love [Joan Osborne]
Come Around [Kim Richey]
For The Love Of The Game [Semisonic]
Fun Of Your Love [Jennifer Day]
Hope [Shaggy]

I See You In A Different Light [Chanté Moore]
Just One Breath [Mulberry Lane]
Lover Man [Kami Lyle]
Loving You Makes Me A Better Man [Vince Gill]

Only One [Roy Orbison]
Paint It Black [Jonny Lang]
Reeling In The Years [Steely Dan] **11**
Something So Right [Trisha Yearwood]

Suite, The [Basil Poledouris]
Summer Wind [Lyle Lovett]

For The Boys - see MIDLER, Bette
Bette Midler/James Caan/**George Segal**/Chris Rydell/Patrick O'Neal

For The First Time - see LANZA, Mario
Mario Lanza/Zsa Zsa Gabor/Kurt Kasznar/Hans Sohnker

7/25/81 | **84** | 19 | | ©268 | **For Your Eyes Only** | [I] | **$12** | Liberty 1109

Roger Moore/Carole Bouquet/Topol/Lynn-Holly Johnson/Julian Glover; cp/cd: Bill Conti

Cortina
Drive In The Country
For Your Eyes Only [Sheena Easton] **4**

For Your Eyes Only (instrumental)
Gonzales Takes A Dive
Make It Last All Night [Rage]
Melina's Revenge

P.M. Gets The Bird (medley)
Runaway
St. Cyril's Monastery
Submarine

Take Me Home

6/17/95 | **182** | 1 | | ©269 | **Forget Paris** | [I+V] | **$10** | Elektra 61825

Billy Crystal/Debra Winger/Joe Mantegna/Julie Kavner/Richard Masur; cp: Marc Shaiman

April In Paris
April In Paris [Ella Fitzgerald & Louis Armstrong]
Come Rain Or Come Shine [David Sanborn]
Craig and Lucy

For All We Know [Billie Holiday]
It Don't Mean A Thing If It Ain't Got That Swing (medley)
Lazy River [Louis Prima]
Love Is Here To Stay [Billie Holiday]
Marriage, The

My Melancholy Baby
Nice Work If You Can Get It
Paris Suite
Swish
Tea For Two (medley)

When You Love Someone [Anita Baker & James Ingram]
When You Love Someone (instrumental)

7/23/94 | **2**[5] | 94 ▲[12] | ©270 | **Forrest Gump** | C:#23/1 [O-V] | **$15** | Epic 66329 [2]

Tom Hanks/Robin Wright/Gary Sinise/Mykelti Williamson/Sally Field

Against The Wind [Bob Seger & The Silver Bullet Band] **5**
Aquarius/Let The Sunshine In [5th Dimension] **1**
Blowin' In The Wind [Joan Baez]
Break On Through (To The Other Side) [Doors]
But I Do [Clarence "Frogman" Henry] **4**
California Dreamin' [Mamas And The Papas] **4**
Everybody's Talkin' [Harry Nilsson] **6**

For What It's Worth (Stop, Hey What's That Sound) [Buffalo Springfield] **7**
Forrest Gump Suite [Alan Silvestri]
Fortunate Son [Creedence Clearwater Revival] **14**
Get Together [Youngbloods] **5**
Hound Dog [Elvis Presley] **1**
I Can't Help Myself [Four Tops] **1**
I've Got To Use My Imagination [Gladys Knight & The Pips] **4**
It Keeps You Runnin' [Doobie Brothers] **37**
Joy To The World [Three Dog Night] **1**

Land Of 1000 Dances [Wilson Pickett] **6**
Mr. President (Have Pity On The Working Man) [Randy Newman]
Mrs. Robinson [Simon & Garfunkel] **1**
On The Road Again [Willie Nelson] **20**
Raindrops Keep Falling On My Head [B.J. Thomas] **1**
Rainy Day Women #12 & 35 [Bob Dylan] **2**
Rebel Rouser [Duane Eddy] **6**
Respect [Aretha Franklin] **1**

San Francisco (Be Sure To Wear Some Flowers In Your Hair) [Scott McKenzie] **4**
Sloop John B [Beach Boys] **3**
Stoned Love [Supremes] **7**
Sweet Home Alabama [Lynyrd Skynyrd] **8**
Turn! Turn! Turn! (To Everything There Is A Season) [Byrds] **1**
Volunteers [Jefferson Airplane] **65**
Walk Right In [Rooftop Singers] **1**
What The World Needs Now Is Love [Jackie DeShannon] **7**

9/2/78 | **102** | 7 | | 271 | **Foul Play** | [I+V] | **$12** | Arista 9501

Goldie Hawn/Chevy Chase/Burgess Meredith/Dudley Moore/Billy Barty; cp/cd: Charles Fox

Beware Of The Dwarf
Copacabana (At The Copa) [Barry Manilow] **8**
Foul Play

Get Me To The Opera On Time
Gloria Escapes
Gloria Falls For Trap
Help

Houseboat (Love Theme)
Ready To Take A Chance Again [Barry Manilow] **11**

Ready To Take A Chance Again (instrumental)
Scarface

Foxy Brown - see HUTCH, Willie
Pam Grier/Peter Brown/Terry Carter/Antonio Fargas/Sid Haig

Frankie And Johnny - see PRESLEY, Elvis
Elvis Presley ("Johnny")/Donna Douglas ("Frankie")/Nancy Kovack/Harry Morgan

SOUNDTRACKS

DEBUT	PEAK	WKS	RIAA	CD	ARTIST — Album Title	Catalog	Sym	$	Label & Number

7/31/93 — **47** — 35 — ● — ©272 **Free Willy** .... [V] **$10** MJJ Music 57280
Jason James Richter/Lori Petty/Jayne Atkinson/Michael Madsen

Audition	Friends Montage	Keep On Smilin' [NKOTB]
Connection	Gifts, The	Main Title
Didn't Mean To Hurt You [3T]	How Can You Leave Me Now	**Right Here/Human Nature** [SWV] 2
Farewell Suite Medley	[Funky Poets]	

Will You Be There [Michael Jackson] 7

6/3/95 — **170** — 3 — ©273 **French Kiss** .... [V] **$10** Mercury 528136
Meg Ryan/Kevin Kline/Timothy Hutton

C'est Trop Beau [Tino Rossi]	I Want You (Love Theme From	Les Yeux De Ton Pere [Les
Feels Like A Woman [Zucchero]	"French Kiss")	Negresses Vertes]
I Love Paris	La Mer [Kevin Kline]	Les Yeux Ouverts [Beautiful South]
I Love Paris [Ella Fitzgerald]	La Vie En Rose [Louis Armstrong]	Someone Like You [Van Morrison]

Verlaine [Charles Trenet]
Via Con Me [Paolo Conte]

4/29/95 — **❶²** — 73 — ▲² — ©274 **Friday** [V] **$10** Priority 53959
Ice Cube/Chris Tucker/Nia Long/Tiny Lister/John Witherspoon

Blast If I Have To [E-A-Ski]	**I Heard It Through The Grapevine**	Lettin' Niggas Know [Threat]
Coast II Coast [Alkaholiks]	**(Part 1)** [Roger] 79	**Mary Jane** [Rick James] 41
Friday [Ice Cube]	**I Wanna Get Next To You** [Rose	Roll It Up, Light It Up, Smoke It Up
Friday Night [Scarface]	Royce] 10	[Cypress Hill]
Hoochie Mama [2 Live Crew]	**Keep Their Heads Ringin'** [Dr.	Superhoes [Funkdoobiest]
	Dre] 10	Take A Hit [Mack 10]

Tryin' To See Another Day [Isley Brothers]
You Got Me Wide Open [Bootsy Collins & Bernie Worrell]

2/29/92 — **181** — 3 — ©275 **Fried Green Tomatoes** .... [V] **$10** MCA 10461
Kathy Bates/Jessica Tandy/Mary-Louise Parker/Mary Stuart Masterson/Gailard Sartain

Barbeque Bess [Patti LaBelle]	Cool Down Yonder [Marion	Ghost Train (Main Title) [Thomas
Charge To Keep I Have [Thomas	Williams]	Newman]
Newman feat. Marion Williams]	Danger Heartbreak Dead Ahead	I'll Remember You [Grayson Hugh]
Cherish [Jodeci]	[Taylor Dayne]	If I Can Help Somebody [Aaron Hall]

Rooster Blues [Peter Wolf]
Visiting Ruth [Thomas Newman]
What Becomes Of The Broken Hearted [Paul Young] 22

Friends - see JOHN, Elton
Sean Bury/Anicee Alvina/Ronald Lewis/Toby Robins/Pascale Roberts

2/10/96 — **89** — 6 — ©276 **From Dusk Till Dawn** .... [V] **$10** Los Hooligans 67523
Harvey Keitel/George Clooney/Quentin Tarantino/Juliette Lewis/Cheech Marin (**Cheech & Chong**)

After Dark [Tito & Tarantula]	Everybody Be Cool	Mexican Standoff [Graeme Revell]
Angry Cockroaches (Cucarachas	Foolish Heart [Mavericks]	Sex Machine Attacks [Graeme
Enojadas) [Tito & Tarantula]	Kill The Band	Revell]
Chet's Speech	Mary Had A Little Lamb [Stevie Ray	She's Just Killing Me [ZZ Top]
Dark Night [Blasters]	Vaughan & Double Trouble]	Texas Funeral [Jon Wayne]
Dengue Woman Blues [Jimmie	Mexican Blackbird [ZZ Top]	Torquay [Leftovers]
Vaughan]		

Willie The Wimp [Stevie Ray Vaughan & Double Trouble]
Would You Do Me A Favor?

5/2/64 — **27** — 34 — ©277 **From Russia With Love** .... [I] **$25** United Artists 5114
Sean Connery/Daniela Bianchi/Lotte Lenya/Robert Shaw/Pedro Armendariz; cp/cd: John Barry

Bond Meets Tania	From Russia With Love	James Bond With Bongos
Death Of Grant	Girl Trouble	Leila Dances
Death Of Kerim	Golden Horn	Man Overboard (medley)
007	Guitar Lament	Meeting In St. Sophia
007 Takes The Lektor	Gypsy Camp	Opening Titles

Smersh In Action (medley)
Spectre Island
Stalking
Tania Meets Klebb

10/4/97+ — **99** — 19 — ● — ©278 **Full Monty, The** .... [V] **$10** RCA Victor 68904
Robert Carlyle/Tom Wilkinson/Mark Addy/Leslie Sharp/Emily Woof

Flashdance...What A Feeling '95	Lunchbox Has Landed	**Rock And Roll, Part 2** [Gary
[Irene Cara]	Make Me Smile (Come Up And See	Gliter] 7
Full Monty	Me) [Steve Harley & Cockney	Stripper, The [Joe Loss & His Orch.]
Hot Stuff [Donna Summer] 1	Rebel]	**We Are Family** [Sister Sledge] 2
Land Of A 1,000 Dances [Wilson	**Moving On Up** [M People] 34	You Can Leave Your Hat On [Tom
Pickett] 6		Jones]

You Sexy Thing [Hot Chocolate] 3
Zodiac, The [David Lindup]

Fun In Acapulco - see PRESLEY, Elvis
Elvis Presley ("Mike Windgren")/Ursula Andress/Elsa Cardenas/Paul Lukas/Alejandro Rey

Funny Girl - see STREISAND, Barbra
Barbra Streisand/Omar Sharif/Kay Medford/Anne Francis/Walter Pidgeon

Funny Lady - see STREISAND, Barbra
Barbra Streisand/James Caan/Omar Sharif/Roddy McDowall/Ben Vereen

4/30/83 — **168** — 3 — 279 **Gandhi** .... [I] **$12** RCA Victor 4557
Ben Kingsley/Candice Bergen/John Gielgud/Trevor Howard; cp/cd: George Fenton; pf: **Ravi Shankar**

Bands Of The Raj Medley	Intermission	Raghupati Raghava Raja Ram
Discovery Of India	Massacre At Amritsar And The	(medley)
End Of The Fast	Aftermath	Reflections Of Early Days (medley)
For All Mankind	Partition	Remember This Always

Salt
South Africa - The Beginning
31st January 1948
Villages Of Bihar

10/25/97 — **2¹** — 20 — ▲² — ©280 **Gang Related** [V] **$15** Death Row 53509 [2]
James Belushi/**2Pac**/Lela Rochon/Dennis Quaid/James Earl Jones

Change To Come [J-Flexx]	Get Yo Bang On [Mack 10]	Loc'd Out Hood [Kurupt]
Devotion [Paradise]	Greed [Ice Cube]	Lost Souls [2Pac]
Feelin A Good Thang [2DV]	Hollywood Bank Robbery [Gang]	Made Niggaz [2Pac]
Freak Somethin' [Roland]	I Can't Fix It [Jackers]	Mash For Our Dreams [Storm]
Free 'Em All [J-Flexx]	Keep Your Eyes Open [O.F.T.B.]	Questions [Tech9ne]
Gang Related [WC, CJ Mac, Daz	Lady [6 Feet]	Staring Through My Rearview
Dillinger, Tray Deee]	Life's So Hard [2Pac]	[2Pac]

Take A Nigga Like Me [Young Soldierz]
These Days [Nate Dogg]
Way Too Major [Daz Dillinger]
What Have You Done? [B.G.O.T.I.]
What's Ya Fantasy [Outlawz]

8/16/97 — **196** — 1 — ©281 **George Of The Jungle** .... [V] **$10** Walt Disney 60806
Brendan Fraser/Leslie Mann/Thomas Haden Church/Holland Taylor/Richard Roundtree

Aba Daba Honeymoon	George Of The Jungle [Presidents	George To The Rescue
Dela (I Know Why The Dog Howls	of the United States of America]	Go Ape
At The Moon) [Johnny Clegg &	George Of The Jungle ["Weird Al"	Jungle Band
Savuka]	Yankovic]	Little Monkey
	George Of The Jungle (Main Title)	Man On The Flying Trapeze

My Way [John Cleese]
Rumble In The Jungle
Wipe Out [Surfaris]

DEBUT	PEAK	WKS	RIAA	CD	ARTIST — Album Title	Catalog	Sym	$	Label & Number

11/2/96 · **184** · 2 · ©282 · **Get On The Bus** .... [V] · **$10** · 40 Acres 90089

Charles S. Dutton/Ossie Davis/Bernie Mac/Richard Belzer/Andre Braugher

Ayindé's Speech [Ayindé Jean-Baptiste]	Destiny Is Calling [Guru]	My Life Is In Your Hands [God's Property]
Coming Home To You [BLACKstreet]	Girl You Need A Change Of Mind [D'Angelo]	New World Order [Curtis Mayfield]
Cruisin' [Earth, Wind & Fire]	I Love My Woman [Marvin Davis]	Over A Million Strong [Neville Brothers]

Redemption Song [Stevie Wonder]
Remedy, The [Tribe Called Quest]
Shabooyah (Roll Call) [Bus Crew]
Tonite's The Nite [Doug E. Fresh]
Welcome [Marc Dorsey]

11/18/95 · **170** · 2 · ©283 · **Get Shorty** .... [I+V] · **$10** · Antilles 529310

John Travolta/Gene Hackman/Rene Russo/Danny DeVito/Dennis Farina; cp: John Lurie; cd: Steven Bernstein

Bo at Airport	Chilli Hot [US3]	I Had My Chance [Morphine]
Bo's Veranda [Morphine]	Chubb Sub [Medeski Martin & Wood]	Nose Punch
Can't Be Still [Booker T. & the MG's]	**Green Onions** [Booker T. & The MG's] **3**	Panacea [Greyboy]
Chilli and Karen at Sunset		Romantic Walk
Chili at Airport (Parts I & II)		Stink

To Be Alive and in a Convertible
Vesuvio's

9/1/90 · **8** · 64 ▲ · ©284 · **Ghost** .... [I] · **$10** · Varese Sarabande 5276

Patrick Swayze/Demi Moore/Whoopi Goldberg/Tony Goldwyn/Rick Aviles; cp/cd: Maurice Jarre

Carl	Ghost	**Unchained Melody** [Righteous Brothers] **4**
Ditto	Molly	
End Credits	Sam	Unchained Melody (instrumental)

7/7/84 · **6** · 34 ▲ · ©285 · **Ghostbusters** .... [V] · **$10** · Arista 8246

Bill Murray/Dan Aykroyd/Sigourney Weaver/Harold Ramis/Rick Moranis

Cleanin' Up The Town [Bus Boys] **68**	**Ghostbusters** [Ray Parker, Jr.] **1**	I Can Wait Forever [Air Supply]
Dana's Theme [Elmer Bernstein]	Ghostbusters (instrumental)	In The Name Of Love [Thompson Twins]
	Hot Night [Laura Branigan]	

Magic [Mick Smiley]
Main Title Theme [Elmer Bernstein]
Savin' The Day [Alessi]

7/1/89 · **14** · 19 ● · ©286 · **Ghostbusters II** .... [V] · **$10** · MCA 6306

Bill Murray/Dan Aykroyd/Sigourney Weaver/Harold Ramis/Rick Moranis

Flesh 'N Blood [Oingo Boingo]	Higher And Higher [Howard Huntsberry]	Promised Land [James "J.T." Taylor]
Flip City [Glenn Frey]	Love Is A Cannibal [Elton John]	Spirit [Doug E. Fresh & The Get Fresh Crew]
Ghostbusters [Run-D.M.C.]	On Our Own [Bobby Brown] **2**	

Supernatural [New Edition]
We're Back [Bobby Brown]

4/29/00 · **84** · 3 · ©287 · **Ghost Dog: The Way Of The Samurai** .... [V] · **$10** · Epic 63794

Forest Whitaker/John Tormey/Cliff Gorman/Henry Silva/Victor Argo

Cakes [Kool G Rap]	Fast Shadow [Wu Tang Clan]	Stay With Me [Melodie & 12 O'Clock]
Don't Test/Wu Stallion [Suga Bang Bang]	4 Sho Sho [North Star]	Strange Eyes [Sunz Of Man, 12 O'Clock & Blue Raspberry]
East New York Stamp [Jeru & Afu Ra]	Man, The [Masta Killah & Superb]	
	Samurai Code Quote	
	Samurai Showdown [RZA]	

Walk The Dogs [Royal Fam & La The Darkman]
Walking Through The Darkness [Tekitha]
Zip Code [Black Knights]

12/29/56+ · **16** · 7 · ©288 · **Giant** .... [I] · **$75** · Capitol 773

Elizabeth Taylor/Rock Hudson/James Dean/Jane Withers/Sal Mineo; cp/cd: Dimitri Tiomkin

Angel's Return (medley)	Home In Reata	Main Title (Giant Theme)
Christmas Morning (medley)	Hunt Scene	Road To Reata
Eyes Of Texas Are Upon You	Jett Rink, Oil Baron	Romantic Interludes
First Love	Jett Rink Theme	

There's Never Been Anyone Else But You (Love Theme)
Toy Trumpet March (medley)
Yellow Rose Of Texas

G.I. Blues - see PRESLEY, Elvis
Elvis Presley ("Tulsa McCauley")/Juliet Prowse/James Douglas/Robert Ivers/Leticia Roman

6/23/58 · ❶[10] · 172 ● · ©289 · **Gigi** .... [M] · **$50** · MGM 3641

Leslie Caron/Maurice Chevalier/Louis Jordan/Eva Gabor; ly: Alan Jay Lerner; mu: Frederick Loewe; cd: **Andre Previn**

Gigi (Gaston's Soliloquy)	It's A Bore	Say A Prayer For Me Tonight
I Remember It Well	Night They Invented Champagne	Thank Heaven For Little Girls
I'm Glad I'm Not Young Anymore	Parisians, The	

Waltz At Maxim's (She Is Not Thinking Of Me)

Girl 6 - see PRINCE
Theresa Randle/Isaiah Washington/Spike Lee/Debi Mazar

Girl Happy - see PRESLEY, Elvis
Elvis Presley ("Rusty Wells")/**Shelley Fabares**/Gary Crosby/Jackie Coogan

Girls! Girls! Girls! - see PRESLEY, Elvis
Elvis Presley ("Ross Carpenter")/Stella Stevens/Laurel Goodwin/Jeremy Slate

Give My Regards To Broad Street - see McCARTNEY, Paul
Paul McCartney/Bryan Brown/**Ringo Starr**/Tracey Ullman/Barbara Bach

5/20/00 · **66** · 24 ● · ©290 · **Gladiator** .... [I] · **$10** · Decca 467094

Russell Crowe/Joaquin Phoenix/Connie Nielsen/Oliver Reed/**Richard Harris**; cp/cd: Hans Zimmer

Am I Not Merciful?	Emperor Is Dead	Progeny
Barbarian Horde	Honor Him	Reunion
Battle, The	Might Of Rome	Slaves To Rome
Earth	Now We Are Free	Sorrow
Elysium	Patricide	Strength And Honor

To Zucchabar
Wheat, The

3/17/90 · **190** · 2 · ©291 · **Glory** .... [I] · **$10** · Virgin 91329

Matthew Broderick/Denzel Washington/Cary Elwes/Morgan Freeman/Cliff DeYoung; cp/cd: James Horner

After Antietam	Call To Arms	Epitaph
Brave Words, Braver Deeds	Charging Fort Wagner	Forming The Regiment
Burning The Town Of Darien	Closing Credits	Lonely Christmas

Preparations For Battle
Whipping
Year Of Jubilee

4/17/99 · **67** · 18 · ©292 · **Go** .... [V] · **$10** · Work 69851

Katie Holmes/Breckin Meyer/Jay Mohr/Sarah Polley/Scott Wolf

Believer [BT]	Magic Carpet Ride [Philip Steir]	**Steal My Sunshine** [Len] **9**
Cha Cha Cha [Jimmy Luxury]	New [No Doubt]	Swords [Leftfield]
Fire Up The Shoesaw [Lionrock]	Shooting Up In Vain [Eagle-Eye Cherry]	Talisman [Air French Band]
Gangster Tripping [Fatboy Slim]	Song For Holly [Esthero]	To All The Lovely Ladies [Goldo]
Good To Be Alive [DJ Rap]		

Troubled By The Way We Came Together [Natalie Imbruglia]

4/8/72 · **21** · 35 · ©293 · **Godfather, The** .... [I] · **$25** · Paramount 1003

Marlon Brando/Al Pacino/James Caan/Robert Duvall/Diane Keaton; cp: Nino Rota; cd: Carlo Savina

Apollonia	**Godfather, Love Theme From The** **66**	I Have But One Heart [Al Martino]
Baptism, The	Godfather Waltz	New Godfather
Connie's Wedding	Halls Of Fear	Pickup, The
Finale		Sicilian Pastorale

SOUNDTRACKS

DEBUT	PEAK	WKS	RIAA	CD	ARTIST — Album Title	Catalog	Sym	$	Label & Number

3/8/75 | **184** | 2 | ©294 **Godfather, Part II, The**... [I] **$20** ABC 856

Al Pacino/Robert DeNiro/Robert Duvall/Diane Keaton/Lee Strasberg; cp: Nino Rota and Carmine Coppola; cd: Carmine Coppola

After The Party (medley)	Godfathers At Home	Michael Comes Home	Senza Mamma
Brothers Mourn	Immigrant, The (medley)	Murder Of Don Fanucci	Vito And Abbandando
End Title	Kay	New Carpet	
Ev'ry Time I Look In Your Eyes (medley)	Main Title (medley)	Ninna Nanna A Michele	
	Marcia Stilo Italiano	Remember Vito Andolini	

1/12/91 | **102** | 7 | ©295 **Godfather, Part III, The**... [I] **$10** Columbia 47078

Al Pacino/Diane Keaton/Talia Shire/Andy Garcia/Sofia Coppola; cp/cd: Carmine Coppola and Nino Rota

Altobello	Immigrant, The (medley)	Preghiera	Sicilian Medley
Casa Amiche	Main Title	Preludio And Siciliana	To Each His Own [Al Martino]
Godfather Intermezzo	Marcia Religioso	Promise Me You'll Remember (Love Theme)	Vincent's Theme
Godfather Waltz	Michael's Letter		

4/14/73 | **50** | 51 | ©296 **Godspell**... [M] **$20** Bell 1118

Victor Garber/David Haskell/Robin Lamont; cp: Stephen Schwartz

Alas For You	Beautiful City	Day By Day	Prepare Ye (The Way Of The Lord)
All For The Best	Bless The Lord	Light Of The World	Save The People
All Good Gifts	By My Side	On The Willows	Turn Back, O Man

6/6/98 | **2**[1] | 26 | ▲ | ©297 **Godzilla** | [V] **$10** Epic 69338

Matthew Broderick/Jean Reno/Hank Azaria/Harry Shearer/Vicki Lewis

A320 [Foo Fighters]	Deeper Underground [Jamiroquai]	No Shelter [Rage Against The Machine]	Running Knees [Days Of The New]
Air [Ben Folds Five]	Heroes [Wallflowers]		Undercover [Joey DeLuxe]
Brain Stew [Green Day]	Looking For Clues [David Arnold]	Opening Titles [David Arnold]	Untitled [Silverchair]
Come With Me [Puff Daddy] 4	Macy Day Parade [Michael Penn]	Out There [Fuzzbubble]	Walk The Sky [Fuel]

Goin' Coconuts - see OSMOND, Donny & Marie

Donny & Marie Osmond/Kenneth Mars/Ted Cassidy/Herb Edelman/Harold Sakata

1/24/87 | **126** | 7 | ©298 **Golden Child, The**... [I+V] **$10** Capitol 12544

Eddie Murphy/Charlotte Lewis/Charles Dance/Victor Wong/Randall "Tex" Cobb; cp/cd: Michel Colombier

Best Man In The World [Ann Wilson] 61	Confrontation	(Let Your Love Find) The Chosen One [Marlon Jackson]	Sardo And The Child
Body Talk [Ratt]	Deeper Love [Meli'sa Morgan]		Shame On You [Martha Davis]
Chosen One [Robbie Buchanan]	Golden Love	Love Goes On (Love Theme) [Ashford & Simpson]	Wisdom Of The Ages [John Barry]

12/2/95 | **180** | 2 | ©299 **GoldenEye**... [I] **$10** Virgin 41048

Pierce Brosnan/Sean Bean/Izabella Scorupco/Famke Janssen/Joe Don Baker; cp/pf: Eric Serra

Dish Out Of Water	GoldenEye [Tina Turner]	Our Lady Of Smolensk	Severnaya Suite
Experience Of Love [Eric Serra]	GoldenEye Overture	Pleasant Drive In St. Petersburg	That's What Keeps You Alone
Fatal Weakness	Ladies First	Run, Shoot, and Jump	We Share The Same Passions
For Ever, James	Little Surprise For You	Scale To Hell	Whispering Statues

12/12/64+ | **❶**[3] | 70 | ©300 **Goldfinger** | [I] **$25** United Artists 5117

Sean Connery/Gert Frobe/Honor Blackman/Harold Sakata/Tania Mallet; cp/cd: John Barry

Alpine Drive (medley)	Bond's Journey Home	Gassing The Gangsters	Teasing The Korean
Arrival Of The Bomb (medley)	Count Down (medley)	**Goldfinger** [John Barry] 72	
Auric's Factory (medley)	Dawn Raid On Fort Knox	**Goldfinger** [Shirley Bassey] 8	
Bond Back In Action Again	Death Of Goldfinger	Oddjob's Pressing Engagement	

7/1/00 | **69** | 13 | ©301 **Gone In 60 Seconds**... [V] **$10** Island 542793

Nicolas Cage/Angelina Jolie/Giovanni Ribisi/Delroy Lindo/Robert Duvall

Better Days (And The Bottom Drops Out) [Citizen King] 25	Flower [Moby]	Painted On My Heart [Cult]	Stop The Rock [Apollo Four Forty]
Boost Me [Trevor Rabin]	Leave Home [Chemical Brothers]	**Party Up (Up In Here)** [DMX] 27	Sugarless [Caviar]
Da Rockwilder [Method Man/Redman]	Machismo [Gomez]	Rap [Groove Armada]	Too Sick To Pray [A3]
	Never Gonna Come Back Down [BT]	Roll All Day [Ice Cube]	

7/3/61 | **64** | 13 | ©302 **Gone With The Wind**... [I] **$25** RCA Camden 625

new recording of movie soundtrack; cp/cd: Max Steiner; originally charted in 1954 (#10) on RCA Victor 3227; also see original soundtrack below

Ashley	Bonnie's Theme	Oath, The	Scarlet O'Hara
Ashley And Melanie (Love Theme)	Gone With The Wind	Prayer, The	Scarlet's Agony
Bonnie Blue Flag	Invitation To The Dance	Return To Tara	Tara
Bonnie's Death	Melanie's Theme	Rhett Butler	War

10/14/67+ | **24** | 36 | ©303 **Gone With The Wind**... [I] **$25** MGM 10

Clark Gable/Vivien Leigh/Leslie Howard/Olivia DeHavilland/Hattie McDaniel; taken directly from the movie soundtrack (premiered in 1939); cp/cd: Max Steiner

Ashley & Scarlett	Bonnie's Fatal Pony Ride	Mammy	Scarlett Makes Her Demands Of Rhett
Ashley Return To Tara From The War Prison	Christmas During The War In Atlanta	Reconstruction	Scarlett's Fall Down The Staircase
Atlanta In Flames	Main Title	Scarlett & Rhett Rebuild Tara	
		Scarlett & Rhett's First Meeting	

8/9/97 | **101** | 5 | ©304 **Good Burger**... [V] **$10** Capitol 57955

Kel Mitchell/Kenan Thompson/Sinbad/Abe Vigoda/Dan Schneider

All I Want [702] 35	I'll Be There For You [Tracie Spencer]	Man [Presidents of the United States of America]	So-Cal V8 [Redd Kross]
Do Fries Go With That Shake? [Trulio Disgracias]	Keep On [Pharcyde]	(Not The) Greatest Rapper [1000 Clowns]	That's The Way (It's Goin' Down) [Mint Condition]
Friends [Warren G]	Knee Deep [George Clinton]	Roxanne [Spearhead]	We're All Dudes [Less Than Jake]

2/6/88 | **10** | 35 | ▲ | ©305 **Good Morning, Vietnam** | [O-V] **$10** A&M 3913

Robin Williams/Forest Whitaker/Tung Thanh Tran/Bruno Kirby/Robert Wuhl

Baby Please Don't Go [Them]	**Game Of Love** [Wayne Fontana & The Mindbenders] 1	Liar, Liar [Castaways] 12	**What A Wonderful World** [Louis Armstrong] 32
California Sun [Rivieras] 5		**Nowhere To Run** [Martha & The Vandellas] 8	
Danger Heartbreak Dead Ahead [Marvelettes] 61	**I Get Around** [Beach Boys] 1		
Five O'Clock World [Vogues] 4	**I Got You (I Feel Good)** [James Brown] 3	**Sugar And Spice** [Searchers] 44	
		Warmth Of The Sun [Beach Boys]	

2/10/68 | **4** | 52 | ● | ©306 **Good, The Bad And The Ugly, The** | [I] **$20** United Artists 5172

Clint Eastwood/Lee Van Cleef/Eli Wallach/Mario Brega; cp/cd: Ennio Morricone

Carriage Of The Spirits	Good, The Bad And The Ugly (Main Title)	Story Of A Soldier	
Death Of A Soldier		Strong, The	
Desert, The	Marcia	Sundown, The	
Ecstasy Of Gold	Marcia Without Hope	Trio, The	

DEBUT	PEAK	WKS	RIAA	CD	ARTIST — Album Title	Catalog	Sym	$	Label & Number

Good Times - see SONNY & CHER
Sonny & Cher/George Sanders/Norman Alden

| 2/7/98 | 91 | 11 | | ©307 | **Good Will Hunting** .... | | [V] | $10 | Capitol 23338 |

Robin Williams/Matt Damon/Ben Affleck/Minnie Driver

Angeles [Elliott Smith]
As The Rain [Jeb Loy Nichols]
Baker Street [Gerry Rafferty] **2**
Between The Bars [Elliott Smith]

Between The Bars (Orchestral) [Elliott Smith]
Boys Better [Dandy Warhols]
Fisherman's Blues [Waterboys]

How Can You Mend A Broken Heart [Al Green]
Miss Misery [Elliott Smith]
No Name #3 [Elliott Smith]
Say Yes [Elliott Smith]

Somebody's Baby [Andru Donalds]
Weepy Donuts [Danny Elfman]
Why Do I Lie? [Luscious Jackson]
Will Hunting (Main Titles) [Danny Elfman]

Goodbye, Columbus - see ASSOCIATION, The
Richard Benjamin/Jack Klugman/Ali MacGraw

| 12/6/69 | 164 | 5 | | 308 | **Goodbye, Mr. Chips** .... | | [M] | $25 | MGM 19 |

Peter O'Toole/**Petula Clark**/Michael Redgrave; sw: Leslie Bricusse; cd: **John Williams**

And The Sky Smiled
Apollo
Entr'acte (medley)
Fill The World With Love

London Is London
Schooldays
Walk Through The World
What A Lot Of Flowers!

What Shall I Do With Today (medley)
When I Am Older
When I Was Younger

Where Did My Childhood Go?
You And I!

| 6/29/85 | 73 | 10 | | ©309 | **Goonies, The** .... | | [V] | $10 | Epic 40067 |

Sean Astin/Josh Brolin/Jeff Cohen/Corey Feldman/Ke Huy Quan

Eight Arms To Hold You [Goon Squad]
14K [Teena Marie]
Goonies (Theme) [Dave Grusin]

Goonies 'R' Good Enough [Cyndi Lauper] **10**
I Got Nothing [Bangles]
Love Is Alive [Philip Bailey]

Save The Night [Joseph Williams]
She's So Good To Me [Luther Vandross]
What A Thrill [Cyndi Lauper]

Wherever You're Goin' (It's Alright) [REO Speedwagon]

Graduate, The - see SIMON & GARFUNKEL
Dustin Hoffman/Anne Bancroft/Katharine Ross/William Daniels/Murray Hamilton

Graffiti Bridge - see PRINCE
Prince/Morris Day/Ingrid Chavez/Jerome Benton

| 3/18/67 | 76 | 28 | | ©310 | **Grand Prix** .... | | [I] | $25 | MGM 8 |

James Garner/Eva Marie Saint/Yves Montand/Toshiro Mifune/Brian Bedford; cp/cd: Maurice Jarre

Clermont Race
Grand Prix, Theme From

In The Garden
Lonely Race Track (Finale)

Sarti's Love Theme
Scott & Pat — Sarti & Louise

Scott's Theme
Zandvoort Race (Scott's Comeback)

| 5/20/78 | ❶¹² | 77 | ▲⁸ | ©311 | **Grease** .... | C:❶⁵²/242 | [M] | $15 | RSO 4002 [2] |

John Travolta/Olivia Newton-John/Stockard Channing/Jeff Conaway/Didi Conn

Alone At A Drive-In Movie [Bill Oakes]
Beauty School Dropout [Frankie Avalon]
Blue Moon [Sha-Na-Na]
Born To Hand-Jive [Sha-Na-Na]
Freddy My Love [Cindy Bullens]
Grease [Frankie Valli] **1**
Greased Lightnin' [John Travolta] **47**

Hopelessly Devoted To You [Olivia Newton-John] **3**
Hound Dog [Sha-Na-Na]
It's Raining On Prom Night [Cindy Bullens]
Look At Me, I'm Sandra Dee [Stockard Channing]
Look At Me, I'm Sandra Dee [Olivia Newton-John]

Love Is A Many Splendored Thing [Bill Oakes]
Mooning [Louis St. Louis & Cindy Bullens]
Rock 'N' Roll Is Here To Stay [Sha-Na-Na]
Rock 'N' Roll Party Queen [Louis St. Louis]
Sandy [John Travolta]

Summer Nights [John Travolta & Olivia Newton-John] **5**
Tears On My Pillow [Sha-Na-Na]
There Are Worse Things I Could Do [Stockard Channing]
Those Magic Changes [Sha-Na-Na]
We Go Together [John Travolta & Olivia Newton-John]
You're The One That I Want [John Travolta & Olivia Newton-John] **1**

| 6/19/82 | 71 | 13 | | ©312 | **Grease 2** .... | | [M-V] | $12 | RSO 3803 |

Maxwell Caulfield/Michelle Pfeiffer/Adrian Zmed/Lorna Luft

Back To School Again [Four Tops] **71**
Charades
Cool Rider

Do It For Our Country
Girl For All Seasons
(Love Will) Turn Back The Hands Of Time

Prowlin'
Reproduction
Rock-A-Hula-Luau (Summer Is Coming)

Score Tonight
We'll Be Together
Who's That Guy?

Great Balls Of Fire! - see LEWIS, Jerry Lee
Dennis Quaid/Winona Ryder/Alec Baldwin/Trey Wilson/**Mojo Nixon**

| 9/21/63 | 50 | 21 | ● | ©313 | **Great Escape, The** .... | | [I] | $50 | United Artists 5107 |

Steve McQueen/James Garner/Richard Attenborough/James Coburn/Charles Bronson; cp/cd: Elmer Bernstein

Betrayal
Blythe
Chase, The

Cooler And Mole
Discovery
Hendley's Risk

Main Title
More Action
On The Road

Premature Plans
Road's End
Various Troubles

| 1/24/98 | 25 | 16 | ● | ©314 | **Great Expectations** .... | | [V] | $10 | Atlantic 83058 |

Ethan Hawke/Gwyneth Paltrow/Anne Bancroft/Robert DeNiro/Hank Azaria

Bésame Mucho [Cesaria Evora]
Breakable [Fisher]
Finn [Tori Amos]
Her Ornament [Verve Pipe]

Lady, Your Roof Brings Me Down [Scott Weiland]
Life In Mono [Mono] **70**
Like A Friend [Pulp]
Resignation [Reef]

Siren [Tori Amos]
Slave [David Garza]
Success [Iggy Pop]
Sunshower [Chris Cornell]
Today [Poe]

Uncle John's Band [Grateful Dead]
Walk This Earth Alone [Lauren Christy]
Wishful Thinking [Duncan Sheik]

| 4/20/74 | 85 | 16 | | 315 | **Great Gatsby, The** .... | | [I+V] | $20 | Paramount 3001 [2] |

Robert Redford/Mia Farrow/Bruce Dern/Karen Black/Scott Wilson; cd: **Nelson Riddle**

Ain't We Got Fun (medley)
Alice Blue Gown
Beale Street Blues
Charleston
Daisy (What'll I Do)
Daisy's Tango

Five Four Two, Eyes Of Blue [Nick Lucas]
I'm Gonna Charleston Back To Charleston [Nick Lucas]
It Had To Be You
Jordan's Tango
Kitten On The Keys

Long Time Ago
My Favorite Beau (What'll I Do)
Myrtle's Theme
Ring (What'll I Do)
Sheik Of Araby
Summer's Almost Over
Tom And Myrtle

We've Met Before (What'll I Do)
What'll I Do [Bill Atherton]
When You And I Were Seventeen [Nick Lucas]
Whispering
Who?
Yes, Sir, That's My Baby

| 7/11/81 | 66 | 11 | | 316 | **Great Muppet Caper, The** .... | | [M] | $12 | Atlantic 16047 |

Jim Henson/Frank Oz/Jerry Nelson/Richard Hunt/Dave Goelz

Apartment, The
Big Red Bus
Couldn't We Ride
First Time It Happens

Great Muppet Caper Medley
Happiness Hotel
Hey A Movie!
Homeward Bound

Lady Holiday
Main Title
Night Life
Piggy's Fantasy ("Miss Piggy")

Steppin' Out With A Star

Great Race, The - see MANCINI, Henry
Tony Curtis/Jack Lemmon/Natalie Wood/Peter Falk/Keenan Wynn

| 5/18/96 | 93 | 5 | | ©317 | **Great White Hype, The** .... | | [V] | $10 | Hudlin Bros. 67636 |

Samuel L. Jackson/Jeff Goldblum/Peter Berg/Jon Lovitz/**Jamie Foxx**

And I Love You [Marcus Miller]
Baller's Lady [Passion]
Bring The Pain [Method Man] **45**
Chicken Huntin' [Insane Clown Posse]

Coolie High [Camp Lo]
I've Got You Under My Skin [Lou Rawls & Biz Markie]
If It's Alright With You [Cappadonna]

Knocked Nekked (From The Waist Down) [Jamie Foxx]
Movin' On [D.J. U-Neek]
Running Song [Ambersunshower]

Shoot 'Em Up [Bone Thugs-N-Harmony]
We Got It [Premier]
Who's The Champion [Ghostface Killer]

SOUNDTRACKS

DEBUT	PEAK	WKS	RIAA	CD	ARTIST — Album Title	Catalog	Sym	$	Label & Number
6/25/77	166	8		318	**Greatest, The**..		[I+V]	$15	Arista 7000

Muhammad Ali (**Cassius Clay**)/Ernest Borgnine/Robert Duvall/James Earl Jones; cp: Michael Masser
Ali Bombaye (Parts 1 & 2)	**Greatest Love Of All** [George	I Always Knew I Had It In Me
Ali's Theme	Benson] **24**	[George Benson]
	Greatest Love Of All (instrumental)	Variations On Theme

| 4/17/65 | 82 | 13 | ©319 | **Greatest Story Ever Told, The**.. | | [I] | $40 | United Artists 5120 |

Charlton Heston/Sidney Poitier/Angela Lansbury/Robert Loggia/Claude Rains; cp/cd: Alfred Newman
Come Unto Me	Into Thy Hands	Prophecy, A	Triumph Of The Spirit
Great Journey	Jesus Of Nazareth (Main Theme)	There Shall Come A Time To Enter	Voice In The Wilderness
Hour Has Come	New Commandment	Time Of Wonders	

| 7/7/84 | 143 | 7 | | 320 | **Gremlins**.. | | [I+V] | $10 | Geffen 24044 |

Zach Galligan/Phoebe Cates/**Hoyt Axton**/Polly Holliday/Judge Reinhold; cp/cd: Jerry Goldsmith
Gift, The	Gremlins...Mega Madness [Michael	Mrs. Deagle
Gizmo	Sembello]	Out Out [Peter Gabriel]
Gremlin Rag	Make It Shine [Quarterflash]	

| 2/15/97 | ❶¹ | 12 | ● ©321 | **Gridlock'd** | | [V] | $10 | Death Row 90114 |

2Pac/Tim Roth/Thandie Newton/Charles Fleischer/Howard Hesseman
Body And Soul [O.F.T.B.]	It's Over Now [Danny Boy]	Off The Hook [Snoop Doggy Dogg]	Wanted Dead Or Alive [2PAC &
Deliberation [Anonymous]	Lady Heroin [J. Flex]	Out The Moon (Boom, Boom,	Snoop Doggy Dogg]
Don't Try To Play Me Homey [Dat	Life Is A Traffic Jam [Eight Mile	Boom) [Snoop Doggy Dogg]	Why [Nate Dogg]
Nigga Daz]	Road]	Sho Shot [Lady Of Rage]	Will I Rize [Storm]
I Can't Get Enough [Danny Boy]	Never Had A Friend Like Me [2PAC]	Tonight It's On [BGOTI]	

| 4/26/97 | 31 | 13 | ● ©322 | **Grosse Pointe Blank**... | | [V] | $10 | London 828867 |

John Cusack/Minnie Driver/Alan Arkin/Dan Aykroyd/Joan Cusack
Absolute Beginners [Jam]	El Matador [Los Fabulosos	Let My Love Open The Door [Pete	Pressure Drop [Specials]
Armagideon Time [Clash]	Cadillacs]	Townshend]	Rudie Can't Fail [Clash]
Blister In The Sun [Violent Femmes]	I Can See Clearly Now [Johnny	Live & Let Die [Guns N' Roses]	Under Pressure [David Bowie &
Blister 2000 [Violent Femmes]	Nash]	Mirror In The Bathroom [English	Queen]
		Beat]	We Care A Lot [Faith No More]

| 4/27/68 | 177 | 3 | | 323 | **Guess Who's Coming To Dinner** .... | | [I] | $30 | Colgems 108 |

Spencer Tracy/Katharine Hepburn/Sidney Poitier/Beah Richards/Isabel Sanford; cp/cd: Frank DeVol
Dear Old Dad	Groovy Delivery Boy	Guess Who's Coming To Dinner	Sentimental Suitcase
Drive In	Guess Who's Coming To Dinner	(Vocal)	Sunset And Glory (End Title)
Glory Of Love [Billy Hill]	(Theme)	Happy Child	Two's A Majority

| 9/25/61 | 48 | 14 | ©324 | **Guns Of Navarone, The** .... | | [I] | $50 | Columbia 8455 |

Gregory Peck/David Niven/Anthony Quinn/**James Darren**; cp/cd: Dimitri Tiomkin
Anna	Guns Of Navarone [Mitch Miller]	Mission Accomplished	Sea Scene (medley)
Climbing The South Cliff	Finale	Odyssey Begins (medley)	Wedding Music
Death Of Young Pappadimos	Legend Of Navarone	Preparation For Guns	Yassu

| 12/15/62+ | 10 | 32 | | 325 | **Gypsy** | | [M] | $40 | Warner 1480 |

Rosalind Russell/Natalie Wood/Karl Malden/Ann Jillian/Harvey Korman; mu: Jule Styne; ly: Stephen Sondheim
All I Need Is The Girl	If Mama Was Married	Rose's Turn	You Gotta Have A Gimmick
Baby June And Her Newsboys	Let Me Entertain You	Small World	You'll Never Get Away From Me
Dainty June And Her Farmboys	Little Lamb	Some People	
Everything's Coming Up Roses	Mr. Goldstone, I Love You	Together Wherever We Go	

| 4/7/79 | 65 | 16 | ● ©326 | **Hair** .... | | [M] | $20 | RCA Victor 3274 [2] |

John Savage/Treat Williams/Beverly D'Angelo; mu/cd: Galt MacDermot; ly: Gerome Ragni and James Rado
Abie Baby (medley)	**Easy To Be Hard** [Cheryl	Hare Krishna	Party Music
Ain't Got No (medley)	Barnes] **64**	Hashish (medley)	Sodomy
Air	Electric Blues (medley)	I Got Life	Somebody To Love
Aquarius	Flesh Failures/Let The Sunshine In	I'm Black (medley)	3-5-0-0
Black Boys	Fourscore (medley)	L.B.J. (Initials)	Walking In Space
Colored Spade	Frank Mills	Manchester	What A Piece Of Work Is Man
Don't Put It Down	Good Morning Starshine	My Conviction	Where Do I Go?
Donna (medley)	Hair	Old Fashioned Melody (medley)	White Boys

| 4/2/88 | 114 | 6 | ©327 | **Hairspray** .... | | [O-V] | $10 | MCA 6228 |

Sonny Bono (**Sonny & Cher**)/Ruth Brown/Divine/**Debbie Harry**/ Ricki Lake
Bug, The [Jerry Dallman & The	I'm Blue (The Gong-Gong Song)	Nothing Takes The Place Of You	Town Without Pity [Gene
Knightcaps]	[Ikettes] **19**	[Toussaint McCall] **52**	Pitney] **13**
Foot Stomping - Part 1 [Flares] **25**	**Madison Time - Part 1** [Ray Bryant	Roach (Dance) [Gene & Wendell]	You'll Lose A Good Thing
Hairspray [Rachel Sweet]	Combo] **30**	**Shake A Tail Feather** [Five	[Barbara Lynn] **8**
I Wish I Were A Princess [Little	**Mama Didn't Lie** [Jan Bradley] **14**	Du-Tones] **51**	
Peggy March] **32**			

| 8/17/68 | 193 | 4 | ©328 | **Hang 'Em High** .... | | [I] | $30 | United Artists 5179 |

Clint Eastwood/Inger Stevens/Ed Begley/Pat Hingle/Arlene Golonka; cp/cd: Dominic Frontiere
| Bordello | I'll Get 'Em Myself | Rachel (Love Theme) | Tumbleweed Wagon |
| Hang 'Em High | It's No Deal | They Took Me | |

| 3/3/01 | 129 | 3 | ©329 | **Hannibal** .... | | [I] | $10 | Decca 467696 |

Anthony Hopkins/Julianne Moore/Gary Oldman/Ray Liotta/Giancarlo Giannini; cp: Hans Zimmer; cd: Gavin Greenaway
Aria Da Capo	Capponi Library	For A Small Stipend	To Every Captive Soul
Avarice	Dear Clarice	Gourmet Valse Tartare	Vide Cor Meum
Burning Heart	Firenze Di Notte	Let My Home Be My Gallows	Virtue

| 3/23/68 | 166 | 9 | | 330 | **Happiest Millionaire, The** .... | | [M] | $25 | Buena Vista 5001 |

Fred MacMurray/Tommy Steele/Greer Garson; sw: Richard M. Sherman and Robert B. Sherman; cd: Jack Elliott
Are We Dancing	I Believe In This Country	There Are Those	When A Man Has A Daughter
Bye-Yum Pum Pum	I'll Always Be Irish	Valentine Candy	
Detroit	Let's Have A Drink On It	Watch Your Footwork	
Fortuosity	Strengthen The Dwelling	What's Wrong With That	

Hard Day's Night, A - see BEATLES, The
The Beatles/Wilfrid Brambell

Hard To Hold - see SPRINGFIELD, Rick
Rick Springfield/Janet Eilber/Patti Hansen/Bill Mumy/Albert Salmi

Harder They Come, The - see CLIFF, Jimmy
Jimmy Cliff/Janet Barkley/Carl Bradshaw

DEBUT	PEAK	WKS	RIAA	CD	ARTIST — Album Title	Catalog	Sym	$	Label & Number

Harum Scarum - see PRESLEY, Elvis
Elvis Presley ("Johnny Tyronne")/Mary Ann Mobley/Fran Jeffries/Jay Novello/Billy Barty

Hatari! - see MANCINI, Henry
John Wayne/Red Buttons/Hardy Kruger

Having A Wild Weekend - see CLARK, Dave, Five
Dave Clark Five/Barbara Ferris

7/4/98 · 39 · 8 · ©331 · HavPlenty .... [V] $10 Yab Yum 69356
Christopher Scott Cherot/Chenoa Maxwell/Hill Harper/Betty Vaughn

Any Other Night [Chico DeBarge]	I Can't Help It [Shya]	Tears Away [Faith Evans]	Whatcha Gonna Do [Jayo Felony]
Fire [Babyface & Des'ree]	I Wanna Be Where You Are [SWV]	What I've Been Missin' [Changing Faces]	Ye Yo [Erykah Badu]
Heat [Absolute]	Keep It Real [Jon B. & Coko]		
I Can't Get You (Out Of My Mind) [Blackstreet]	Rock The Body [Queen Pen & Tracey Lee]	What The Hell Do You Want [Az Yet]	

11/19/66+ · 85 · 16 · 332 · Hawaii .... [I] $30 United Artists 5143
Julie Andrews/Richard Harris/Max Von Sydow/**Carroll O'Connor**/Gene Hackman; cp/cd: Elmer Bernstein

Abner (medley)	Hawaiian Welcome	Malama's Death	Quiet Harbor
Abner And Jerusha	Keoki's Tragedy	Pastoral Letter	Sailors And Women
Hawaii	Main Title	Promise Kept	Wishing Doll (medley)

He Got Game - see PUBLIC ENEMY
Denzel Washington/Ray Allen/Milla Jovovich/Ned Beatty

Head - see MONKEES, The
The Monkees/Victor Mature/**Annette** Funicello/Vito Scotti/**Frank Zappa**

10/29/88 · 176 · 2 · ©333 · Heartbreak Hotel .... [V] $10 RCA 8533
David Keith/Charlie Schlatter/Tuesday Weld

Burning Love [Elvis Presley] 2	**Eighteen** [Alice Cooper] 21	If I Can Dream [Elvis Presley] 12	Soul On Fire [Charlie Schlatter]
Can't Help Falling In Love [David Keith]	Heartbreak Hotel [David Keith & Charlie Schlatter]	Love Me [David Keith]	
		One Night [Elvis Presley] 4	
Drift Away [Dobie Gray] 5	**Heartbreak Hotel** [Elvis Presley] 1	Ready Teddy [Elvis Presley]	

8/8/81 · 12 · 28 · ● · ©334 · Heavy Metal .... C:#28/2 [V] $25 Asylum 90004 [2]
animated movie, voices by: John Candy/Joe Flaherty/Harold Ramis/Richard Romanus/Eugene Levy

All Of You [Don Felder]	**Heavy Metal (Takin' A Ride)** [Don Felder] 43	Prefabricated [Trust]	Veteran Of The Psychic Wars [Blue Oyster Cult]
Blue Lamp [Stevie Nicks]		Queen Bee [Grand Funk Railroad]	**Working In The Coal Mine** [Devo] 43
Crazy [Nazareth]	I Must Be Dreamin' [Cheap Trick]	Radar Rider [Riggs]	
Heartbeat [Riggs]	Mob Rules [Black Sabbath]	Reach Out [Cheap Trick]	
Heavy Metal [Sammy Hagar]	**Open Arms** [Journey] 2	True Companion [Donald Fagen]	

5/6/00 · 101 · 4 · ©335 · Heavy Metal 2000 .... [V] $10 Restless 73717
animated movie, voices by **Billy Idol**/Michael Ironside/Julie Strain/Arthur Holden

Alcoholocaust [Machine Head]	F.A.K.K. U	Inside The Pervert Mound [Zilch]	Storaged [System Of A Down]
Buried Alive [Billy Idol]	Green Iron Fist [Full Devil Jacket]	Missing Time [MDFMK]	Tirale [Puya]
Dirt Ball [Insane Clown Posse]	Hit Back [Hate Dept.]	Psychosexy [Sinisstar]	Wishes [Coal Chamber]
Dog's A Vapour [Bauhaus]	Immortally Insane [Pantera]	Rough Day [Days Of The New]	
Dystopia [Apartment 26]	Infinity [Queens Of The Stone Age]	Silver Future [Monster Magnet]	

2/3/58 · 25 · 1 · ©336 · Helen Morgan Story, The .... $100 RCA Victor 1030
Ann Blyth/Paul Newman/Alan King/Gene Evans; vocals performed by Gogi Grant; cd: **Ray Heindorf**

April In Paris	Do Do Do (medley)	Love Nest	Someone To Watch Over Me (medley)
Avalon (medley)	Don't Ever Leave Me	Man I Love	Something To Remember You By
Bill	I Can't Give You Anything But Love	More Than You Know	Speak To Me Of Love
Body And Soul	I'll Get By (medley)	My Melancholy Baby	Why Was I Born
Breezin' Along With The Breeze (medley)	I've Got A Crush On You (medley)	On The Sunny Side Of The Street	
Can't Help Lovin' That Man	If You Were The Only Girl In The World (medley)	One I Love Belongs To Somebody Else	
Deep Night (medley)	Just A Memory (medley)		

10/11/69 · 184 · 3 · 337 · Hell's Angels '69 .... [I+V] $30 Capitol 303
Tom Stern/Conny Van Dyke/Jeremy Slate/G.D. Spradlin/Sonny Barger; cp/cd: Tony Bruno

Al And Alice [Stream Of Consciousness]	Chase Of Death	Lazy [Sonny Valdez]	Till You're Through [Stream Of Consciousness]
Bass Lake Run	Goofin'	Say Girl [Wendy Cole]	What's His Is His [Sonny Valdez]
	Hang On Tight		

Hello, Dolly! - see STREISAND, Barbra
Barbra Streisand/Walter Matthau/**Michael Crawford**

9/30/67 · 165 · 2 · 338 · Hells Angels On Wheels .... [I] $30 Smash 67094
Adam Roarke/Jack Nicholson/Sabrina Scharf/Jana Taylor/John Garwood; cp/cd: Stu Phillips

Bike Ballet	Hells Angels On Wheels	Skip To My Mary J.	Tea Party
Flowers	Poet	Study In Motion #1 [Poor]	
Four, Five, Sex	Poet Scores	Sunday Art And Football	

Help! - see BEATLES, The
The Beatles/Leo McKern/Eleanor Bron/Victor Spinetti

6/14/97 · 37 · 15 · ● · ©339 · Hercules .... [M] $10 Walt Disney 60864
animated movie, voices by: Danny DeVito/Tate Donovan/James Woods; mu/cp: Alan Menken; ly: David Zippel

All Time Chump	Go The Distance (Reprise)	Long Ago...	Rodeo
Big Olive	Gospel Truth (medley)	Main Titles (medley)	Speak Of The Devil
Cutting The Thread	Gospel Truth II	Meg's Garden	Star Is Born
Destruction Of The Agora	Gospel Truth III	Oh Mighty Zeus	True Hero (medley)
Go The Distance	Hercules' Villa	One Last Hope	Zero To Hero
Go The Distance [Michael Bolton] 24	Hydra Battle	Phil's Island	
	I Won't Say (I'm In Love)	Prophecy, The	

4/15/00 · 198 · 1 · ©340 · Here On Earth .... [V] $10 Columbia 63596
Chris Klein/Leelee Sobieski/Josh Hartnett/Bruce Greenwood

Birches	If You Sleep [Tal Bachman]	Tic Tocs [Tim James]	**Where You Are** [Jessica Simpson] 62
Don't Need A Reason [Beth Orton]	Pick A Part That's New [Stereophonics]	We Have Forgotten [Sixpence None The Richer]	
Here On Earth Score Suite	SkyFall [Neve]	Whatever Turns You On [Devin]	
I Need Love [Sixpence None The Richer]	1,000 Oceans [Tori Amos]		

Hey Boy! Hey Girl! - see PRIMA, Louis / SMITH, Keely
Louis Prima/**Keely Smith**/James Gregory/Henry Slate/Kim Charney

Hey, Let's Twist - see DEE, Joey, & The Starliters
Joey Dee & The Starliters/Teddy Randazzo/Jo Ann Campbell/Kay Armen/Allan Arbus

SOUNDTRACKS

DEBUT	PEAK	WKS	RIAA	CD	ARTIST — Album Title	Catalog	Sym	$	Label & Number

12/5/87+ 146 13 ©341 **Hiding Out** .... [V] $10 Virgin 90661
Jon Cryer/Annabeth Gish/Keith Coogan/Gretchen Cryer/Oliver Cotton
Bang Your Head [Lolita Pop] · **Live My Life** [Boy George] 40 · Run! Hide! [All That Jazz]
Catch Me (I'm Falling) [Pretty · Max For President Rap [Lee · Seattle [P.I.L.]
Poison] 8 · Anthony Briston/David L. · So Different Now [Felix Cavaliere]
Crying [Roy Orbison & k.d. lang] · Robinson/Daryl Smith] · **You Don't Know** [Scarlett &
I Refuse [Hue & Cry] · Real Life [Black Britain] · Black] 20

4/22/00 135 4 ©342 **High Fidelity** .... [V] $10 Hollywood 62188
John Cusack/Jack Black/Lisa Bonet/Joelle Carter/Joan Cusack
Always See Your Face [Love] · Fallen For You [Sheila Nicholls] · Let's Get It On [Jack Black] · Shipbuilding [Elvis Costello & The
Cold Blooded Old Times [Smog] · I Believe (When I Fall In Love It Will · Lo Boob Oscillator [Stereolab] · Attractions]
Dry The Rain [Beta Band] · Be Forever) [Stevie Wonder] · Most Of The Time [Bob Dylan] · Who Loves The Sun [Velvet
Everybody's Gonna Be Happy · I'm Wrong About Everything [John · Oh! Sweet Nuthin' [Velvet · Underground]
[Kinks] · Wesley Harding] · Underground] · **You're Gonna Miss Me** [Thirteenth
· Inside Game [Royal Trux] · Floor Elevators] 55

9/28/96 20 12 ● ©343 **High School High** .... [V] $10 Big Beat 92709
Jon Lovitz/Tia Carrere/Louise Fletcher/Makhi Phifer
Bohemian Rhapsody [Braids] 42 · I Got Somebody Else [Changing · Rap World [Large Professor & Pete · Why You Wanna Funk? [Spice
C'mon N' Ride It (The Train-Part · Faces] · Rock] · 1/E-40 & The Click]
II) [Quad City DJ's] 3 · I Just Can't [Faith Evans] · Semi-Automatic: Full Rap Metal · **Wu-Wear: The Garment**
Get Down For Mine [Real Live] · Next Spot [Sadat X & Grand Puba] · Jacket [Inspectah Deck & U-God] · **Renaissance** [RZA] 60
Good, The Bad And The Desolate · Peace, Prosperity & Paper [Tribe · Skrilla [Scarface] · Your Precious Love [D'Angelo &
[Roots] · Called Quest] · **So Many Ways** [Braxtons] 83 · Erykah Badu]
High School Rock [KRS-One] · Queen B@$#H [Lil' Kim] · Ultimate (You Know The Time)
I Can't Call It [De La Soul] · [Artifacts]

8/25/56 5 28 ©344 **High Society** [M] $50 Capitol 750
Bing Crosby/Grace Kelly/**Frank Sinatra**; sw: Cole Porter
High Society Calypso · Mind If I Make Love To You · **True Love** [Bing Crosby & Grace · Who Wants To Be A Millionaire
High Society (Overture) · **Now You Has Jazz** [Bing Crosby & · Kelly] 3 · **You're Sensational** [Frank
I Love You, Samantha · Louis Armstrong] 88 · **Well Did You Evah?** [Bing Crosby · Sinatra] 52
Little One · & Frank Sinatra] 92

1/21/95 39 17 ©345 **Higher Learning** .... [V] $10 550 Music 66944
Jennifer Connelly/**Ice Cube**/Omar Epps/Laurence Fishburne
Ask Of You [Raphael Saadiq] 19 · Higher Learning/Time For Change · Phobia [OutKast] · Year Of The Boomerang [Rage
Butterfly [Tori Amos] · [Brand New Heavies] · Situation: Grimm [Mista Grimm] · Against The Machine]
By Your Side [Zhané] · Learning Curve [Stanley Clarke] · Something To Think About [Ice
Don't Have Time [Liz Phair] · Losing My Religion [Tori Amos] · Cube]
Eye [Eve's Plum] · My New Friend [Cole Hauser & · Soul Searchin' (I Wanna Know If It's
Higher [Ice Cube] · Michael Rapaport] · Mine) [Me'Shell Ndegéocello]

Hold On! - see HERMAN'S HERMITS
Peter Noone (**Herman's Hermits**)/**Shelley Fabares**/Sue Ane Langdon

12/12/92 98 5 ©346 **Home Alone 2 - Lost In New York** .... [X-V] $10 Fox 11000
Macaulay Culkin/Joe Pesci/Daniel Stern/**Tim Curry**/Brenda Fricker; Christmas chart: 15/'92
All Alone On Christmas [Darlene · It's Beginning To Look A Lot Like · My Christmas Tree [Home Alone · Sleigh Ride [TLC]
Love] 83 · Christmas [Johnny Mathis] · Children's Choir] · Somewhere In My Memory [Bette
Christmas Star [John Williams] · **Jingle Bell Rock** [Bobby Helms] 6 · O Come All Ye Faithful [Lisa · Midler]
Cool Jerk [Capitols] 7 · Merry Christmas, Merry Christmas · Fischer]
Holly Jolly Christmas [Alan Jackson] · [John Williams] · Silver Bells [Atlantic Starr]

Home Of The Brave - see ANDERSON, Laurie

8/29/92 18 38 ▲ ©347 **Honeymoon In Vegas** .... [V] $10 Epic Soundtrax 52845
James Caan/Nicolas Cage/Sarah Jessica Parker/Pat Morita/Anne Bancroft
All Shook Up [Billy Joel] 92 · Burning Love [Travis Tritt] · Jailhouse Rock [John Mellencamp] · Wear My Ring Around Your Neck
Are You Lonesome Tonight? [Brian · Can't Help Falling In Love [Bono] · Love Me Tender [Amy Grant] · [Ricky Van Shelton]
Ferry] · Heartbreak Hotel [Billy Joel] · Suspicious Minds [Dwight Yoakam] · (You're The) Devil In Disguise
Blue Hawaii [Willie Nelson] · Hound Dog [Jeff Beck & Jed Leiber] · That's All Right [Vince Gill] · [Trisha Yearwood]

Honeysuckle Rose - see NELSON, Willie
Willie Nelson/Dyan Cannon/Amy Irving/Slim Pickens

8/30/97 94 6 ©348 **Hoodlum** .... [V] $10 Loud 90131
Laurence Fishburne/Tim Roth/Vanessa Williams/Andy Garcia
Basin Street Blues [L.V.] · Gangsta Partna [Cool Breeze] · I Can't Believe [112] · **So Good** [Davina] 60
Certainly [Erykah Badu] · Harlem Is Home [Tony Rich] · Lucky Dayz [Adriana Evans] · Street Life [Rahsaan Patterson]
Dirty The Moocher [Wu-Tang Clan] · Hoodlum [Mobb Deep] · No Guarantee [Chico DeBarge] · Zoom [Big Bub]

1/18/92 182 2 ©349 **Hook** .... [I] $10 Epic 48888
Dustin Hoffman/**Robin Williams**/Julia Roberts/Bob Hoskins; cp/cd: **John Williams**; ly: Leslie Briscusse
Arrival Of Tink (medley) · From Mermaids To Lost Boys · Presenting The Hook · When You're Alone
Banning Back Home · Granny Wendy · Remembering Childhood · You Are The Pan
Banquet, The · Hook-Napped · Smee's Plan
Farewell Neverland · Lost Boy Chase · Ultimate War
Flight To Neverland (medley) · Never-Feast · We Don't Wanna Grow Up

6/6/98 4 59 ▲² ©350 **Hope Floats** [V] $10 Capitol 93402
Sandra Bullock/**Harry Connick Jr.**/Gena Rowlands/Mae Whitman/Michael Pare
All I Get [Mavericks] · Paper Wings [Gillian Welch] · To Make You Feel My Love [Garth · When You Love Someone [Bryan
Chances Are [Bob Seger & Martina · Smile [Lyle Lovett] · Brooks] · Adams]
McBride] · Stop In The Name Of Love [Jonell · What Makes You Stay [Deana · Wither, I'm A Flower [Whiskeytown]
Honest I Do [Rolling Stones] · Mosser] · Carter]
In Need [Sheryl Crow] · To Get Me To You [Lila McCann]

5/16/98 91 8 ©351 **Horse Whisperer, The** .... [V] $10 MCA 70025
Robert Redford/Kristin Scott Thomas/Sam Neill/Dianne Wiest
Big Ball's In Cowtown [Don Walser] · Leaving Train [Gillian Welch] · Soft Place To Fall [Allison Moorer] · Still I Long For Your Kiss [Lucinda
Cattle Call [Dwight Yoakam] · Me And The Eagle [Steve Earle] · South Wind Of Summer · Williams]
Cowboy Love Song [Don Edwards] · Red River Valley [George Strait] · [Flatlanders] · Whispering Pines [Iris DeMent]
Dream River [Mavericks] · Slow Surprise [Emmylou Harris]

DEBUT	PEAK	WKS	RIAA	CD	ARTIST — Album Title	Catalog	Sym	$	Label & Number

4/7/90 104 9 ©352 **House Party** .... [V] $10 Motown 6296
Kid 'N Play/Full Force/**Martin Lawrence**/Robin Harris/Tisha Campbell
| | | |
Funhouse [Kid 'N Play] · Jive Time Sucker [Force MD's] · This Is Love [Kenny Vaughan & The Art Of Love] · Why You Get Funky On Me? [Today]
House Party [Full Force] · Kid Vs. Play (The Battle) [Kid 'N Play] · To Da Break Of Dawn [L.L. Cool J]
I Ain't Going Out Like That [Zan] · Surely [Arts & Crafts] · What A Feeling [Arts & Crafts]
I Can't Do Nothin' For You, Man [Flavor Flav]

11/9/91 55 12 ©353 **House Party 2** .... [V] $10 MCA 10397
Kid 'N Play/Full Force/**Martin Lawrence**/Tisha Campbell/Iman
Ain't Gonna Hurt Nobody [Kid 'N Play] **51** · House Party (I Don't Know What You Come To Do) [Tony! Toni! Toné!] · It's So Hard To Say Goodbye To Yesterday [Flex] · What's On Your Mind [Eric B & Rakim]
Big Ol' Jazz [M.C. Trouble] · I Like Your Style [Bubba] · Let Me Know Something?! [Bell Biv DeVoe] · Yo, Baby, Yo! [Ralph Tresvant]
Candlelight & You [Keith Washington] · I Lust 4 U [London Jones] · Ready Or Not [Wrecks 'N' Effect]

8/29/98 8 22 ● ©354 **How Stella Got Her Groove Back** [V] $10 Flyte Tyme 11806
Angela Bassett/Taye Diggs/Regina King/Whoopi Goldberg
Art Of Seduction [Maxi Priest] · Jazzie B. Intro [Jazzie B.] · Make My Body Hot [Diana King] · Never Say Never Again [K-Ci & JoJo]
Beautiful [Mary J. Blige] · Jazzie's Groove [Jazzie B.] · Makes Me Sweat [Big Punisher & Beenie Man] · Your Home Is In My Heart (Stella's Love Theme) [Boyz II Men]
Dance For Me [Kevin Ford] · Let Me Have You [Me'Shell Ndegéocello] · Mastablasta '98 [Stevie Wonder & Wyclef Jean]
Escape To Jamaica [Lady Saw] · **Luv Me, Luv Me** [Shaggy] **76**
Free Again [Soul II Soul]

4/20/63 4 84 ● ©355 **How The West Was Won** $25 MGM 5
Gregory Peck/Henry Fonda/James Stewart/**Debbie Reynolds**/Lee J. Cobb; cd: Alfred Newman
Bereavement And Fulfillment · Come Share My Life · Home In The Meadow · Raise A Ruckus
Cheyennes · Entr'acte · Main Title · River Pirates
Cleve And The Mule · Finale · Marriage Proposal · What Was Your Name In The States?
Climb A Higher Hill · He's Linus' Boy · No Goodbye

How To Beat The High Cost Of Living - see KLUGH, Earl / LAWS, Hubert
Susan St. James/Jane Curtin/Jessica Lange/Richard Benjamin/Fred Willard

4/22/67 146 4 ©356 **How To Succeed In Business Without Really Trying** .... [M] $30 United Artists 5151
Robert Morse/Michele Lee/Rudy Vallee/Anthony Teague; sw: Frank Loesser; cd: **Nelson Riddle**
Been A Long Day · Company Way · Overture · Secretary Is Not A Toy
Brotherhood Of Man · Grand Old Ivy · Paris Original (medley)
Coffee Break · I Believe In You · Rosemary

6/15/96 11 18 ▲ ©357 **Hunchback Of Notre Dame, The** .... [M] $10 Walt Disney 60893
animated movie, voices by: Tom Hulce/Heidi Mollenhauer/Jason Alexander; mu/cp: Alan Menken; ly: Stephen Schwartz; cd: Michael Starobin
And He Shall Smite the Wicked (Score) · God Help the Outcasts · Hellfire (medley) · Sanctuary! (Score)
Bell Tower (Score) · God Help the Outcasts [Bette Midler] · Humiliation (Score) · **Someday** [All-4-One] **30**
Bells of Notre Dame · Guy Like You · Into the Sunlight (Score) · Topsy Turvy
Court of Miracles · Heaven's Light (medley) · Out There
 · · Paris Burning (Score)

4/22/67 153 2 358 **Hurry Sundown** .... [I] $50 RCA Victor 1133
Michael Caine/**Jane Fonda**/Diahann Carroll/Faye Dunaway; cp/cd: **Hugo Montenegro**
Breakfast In Bed · Homecoming · Loser, The · Playing With Dynamite
Charlie's Trip · Hurry Sundown · Love Me Vivian
Cool It Julie · Hurry Sundown Blues · Love Theme
End Title (medley) · Interlude (medley) · Main Title

I Could Go On Singing - see GARLAND, Judy
Judy Garland/Dirk Bogarde/Jack Klugman

4/25/98 3 18 ▲ ©359 **I Got The Hook-Up!** [V] $10 No Limit 50745
Master P/A.J. Johnson/Gretchen Palmer/Tiny Lister
Bang Or Ball [Mack 10] · From What I Was Told [Soulja Slim] · Itch Or Scratch [Master P] · We Got It [Mr. Serv-On]
Bump And Grill [U.G.K.] · Ghetto Vet [Ice Cube] · Keep It Real [Mechalie Jamison] · What The Game Made Me [Jay-Z]
Call It What You Want [Steady Mobbin'] · Hook It Up [Master P] · Let's Ride [Eight-Ball & MJG] · What You Need [Commission]
Down With You [Master P] · Hooked [Snoop Doggy Dogg] · Shake Somethin' [Mystikal] · Who Rock This [Ol' Dirty Bastard]
Drama [Skull Dugrey] · I Don't Want To Go [Mo B. Dick] · Tell Me What You're Lookin' For [Kane & Abel] · Would You Hesitate [C-Murder]
 · **I Got The Hook-Up!** [Master P] **16**

11/1/97 125 5 ©360 **I Know What You Did Last Summer - The Album** .... [V] $10 Columbia 68696
Jennifer Love Hewitt/Sarah Michelle Gellar/Ryan Phillippe/Freddie Prinze Jr.
Clumsy [Our Lady Peace] · Hey Bulldog [Toad The Wet Sprocket] · My Baby's Got The Strangest Ways [Southern Culture On The Skids] · This Ain't The Summer Of Love [L7]
D.U.I. [Offspring] · Hush [Kula Shaker] · One Hundred Days [Flick] · 2Wicky [Hooverphonic]
Don't Mean Anything [Adam Cohen] · Kid [Green Apple Quick Step] · Proud [Korn] · Waterfall [Din Pedals]
Great Life [Goatboy] · Losin' It [Soul Asylum] · Summer Breeze [Type O Negative]

I Walk The Line - see CASH, Johnny
Gregory Peck/Tuesday Weld/Estelle Parsons/Ralph Meeker

I Want To Live! - see MULLIGAN, Gerry
Susan Hayward/Simon Oakland/Theodore Bikel

6/7/97 4 25 ● ©361 **I'm Bout It** [V] $10 No Limit 50643
Master P/Anthony Boswell/Moon Jones/Tracy Philpott/**Mack 10**
Before I Die [Mr. Serv-On] · For Realz [Kane & Abel] · Meal Ticket [Master P] · That Thing Is On [Mo B. Dick]
Come On [E-40 & B-Legit] · Game Tight [J.T. The Bigga Figga & The Fast One] · Much Love [Mia X] · What Cha Think [Mystikal]
Cops Runnin' After Ya [Prime Suspects] · Heat [Skull Drugery] · Murder Murder [Ghetto Twins] · Who's Who [C-Loc]
Don't Mess Around [Fiend] · How Ya Do Dat [Master P] · **Pushin' Inside You** [Sons Of Funk] **97** · Why They Wanna See Me Dead [Gambino Family]
Down & Dirty [Tru] · If I Could Change [Master P & Steady Mobb'n] **60** · Ride 4U [Mr. Jinks]
Faces Of Death [E-A-Ski] · Lock Down [Mac] · Situation On Dirty [Brotha Lynch Hung]

4/21/79 174 5 ©362 **Ice Castles** ....**C:**#35/2 [I] $12 Arista 9502
Robby Benson/Lynn-Holly Johnson/Colleen Dewhurst/Tom Skerritt; cp/cd: **Marvin Hamlisch**
Deborah's Rock · Ice Castles (Through The Eyes Of Love), Theme From (instrumental) · Scarlotti Suite · Voyager [Alan Parsons Project]
Ice Castles (Through The Eyes Of Love), Theme From [Melissa Manchester] **76** · Learning Again · They Threw Flowers ·
 · · Touch

SOUNDTRACKS

DEBUT	PEAK	WKS	RIAA	CD	ARTIST — Album Title	Catalog	Sym	$	Label & Number

12/20/80+ 130   9   363 **Idolmaker, The** .... [V] **$12**   A&M 4840
Ray Sharkey/Tovah Feldshuh/Peter Gallagher/Paul Land/Olympia Dukakis; sw: Jeff Barry

Baby *[Peter Gallagher]*	However Dark The Night *[Peter Gallagher]*	I Can't Tell *[Colleen Fitzpatrick]*
Boy And A Girl *[Sweet Inspirations & London Fog]*	I Believe It Can Be Done *[Ray Sharkey]*	I Know Where You're Goin' *[Nino Tempo]*
Come And Get It *[Nino Tempo]*	I Believe It Can Be Done (instrumental) *[Nino Tempo]*	Ooh-Wee Baby *[Darlene Love]*
Here Is My Love *[Jesse Frederick]*		Sweet Little Lover *[Jesse Frederick]*

Imagine: John Lennon - see **LENNON, John**

1/21/95 63   18   ●   ©364 **Immortal Beloved** .... [I] **$10**   Sony Classical 66301
Gary Oldman/Jeroen Krabbe/Isabella Rossellini; cp: Ludwig Van Beethoven; cd: Sir Georg Solti; pf: **London Symphony Orchestra**

Fur Elise	Piano Sonata No. 14 in C-Sharp Minor, Op. 27, No. 2 "Moonlight"	Symphony No. 9 in D Minor, Op. 125	Symphony No. 3 in E-Flat Major, Op. 55 "Eroica"
Missa Solemnis in D Major, Op. 123			
Piano Concerto No. 5 in E-Flat Major, Op. 73 "Emperor"	Piano Trio No. 4 in D Major, Op. 70, No. 1 "Ghost"	Symphony No. 7 in A Major, Op. 92	Violin Concerto in D Major, Op. 61
Piano Sonata No. 8 in C Minor, Op. 13 "Pathetique"	Symphony No. 5 in C Minor, Op. 67	Symphony No. 6 in F Major, Op. 68 "Pastoral"	Violin Sonata in A Major, Op. 47 "Kreutzer"

9/30/67 153   11   ©365 **In The Heat Of The Night** .... [I+V] **$25**   United Artists 5160
Sidney Poitier/Rod Steiger/Warren Oates/Lee Grant/Scott Wilson; cp/cd: **Quincy Jones**

Blood & Roots	Give Me Until Morning	Nitty Gritty Time	Where Whitey Ain't Around
Bowlegged Polly *[Glen Campbell]*	**In The Heat Of The Night** *[Ray Charles]* **33**	No You Won't	Whipping Boy
Chief's Drive To Mayor		On Your Feet, Boy!	
Cotton Curtain	It Sure Is Groovy! *[Gil Bernal]*	Peep-Freak Patrol Car	
Foul Owl *[Boomer & Travis]*	Mama Caleba's Blues *[Ray Charles]*	Shag Bag, Hounds & Harvey	

2/12/94 114   10   ©366 **In The Name Of The Father** .... [V] **$10**   Island 518841
Daniel Day-Lewis/Emma Thompson/Pete Poslethwaite/John Lynch

Billy Boola *[Gavin Friday & Bono]*	Interrogation *[Trevor Jones]*	Voodoo Child (Slight Return) *[Jimi Hendrix Experience]*	You Made Me The Thief Of Your Heart *[Sinéad O'Connor]*
Dedicated Follower Of Fashion *[Kinks]* **36**	Is This Love *[Bob Marley & the Wailers]*	Walking The Circle *[Trevor Jones]*	
In The Name Of The Father *[Bono & Gavin Friday]*	Passage Of Time *[Trevor Jones]*	Whiskey In The Jar *[Thin Lizzy]*	

9/4/99 28   8   ©367 **In Too Deep** .... [V] **$10**   Columbia 69934
Omar Epps/**LL Cool J**/Nia Long/Stanley Tucci/Pam Grier

Bleeding From The Mouth *[Capone & Noreaga, & The Lox]*	Give Me A Reason *[Dave Hollister]*	Quiet Storm *[Mobb Deep]*	Tear It Off *[Method Man & Redman]*
Bust A Nut *[Product G&B]*	How To Rob *[50 Cent]*	Rowdy Rowdy *[50 Cent]*	Thug Money *[Trick Daddy]*
Dreamin' *[Jill Scott]*	In Too Deep *[Nas & Nature]*	Somethin' About Love *[Imajin]*	Use To Me Spending *[R. Kelly]*
	Keys To The Range *[Jagged Edge]*	Specialist, The *[Ali Vegas]*	Where Ya Heart At *[Mobb Deep]*

5/1/93 137   6   ©368 **Indecent Proposal** .... [V] **$10**   MCA 10795
Robert Redford/Demi Moore/Woody Harrelson/Oliver Platt/Seymour Cassel

I'm Not In Love *[Pretenders]*	In All The Right Places *[Lisa Stansfield]*	Nearness Of You *[Sheena Easton]*	Will You Love Me Tomorrow *[Bryan Ferry]*
If I'm Not In Love With You *[Dawn Thomas]*	Instrumental Suite *[John Barry]*	Out Of The Window *[Seal]*	
	Love So Beautiful *[Roy Orbison]*	What Do You Want The Girl To Do *[Vince Gill]*	

7/20/96 73   8   ©369 **Independence Day** .... [I] **$10**   RCA Victor 68564
Will Smith/Bill Pullman/Jeff Goldblum/Mary McDonnell/Judd Hirsch; cp: David Arnold; cd: Nicholas Dodd

Aftermath	Day We Fight Back	Fire Storm	President's Speech
Base Attack	El Toro Destroyed	International Code	S.E.T.I.-Radio Signal
Canceled Leave	End Titles	Jolly Roger	
Darkest Day	Evacuation	1969-We Came In Peace	

6/16/84 42   10   370 **Indiana Jones And The Temple Of Doom** .... [I] **$10**   Polydor 821592
Harrison Ford/Kate Capshaw/Ke Huy Quan; cp/cd: **John Williams**

Anything Goes	Fast Streets Of Shanghai	Nocturnal Activities	Slave Children's Crusade
Bug Tunnel And Death Trap	Finale	Shortround's Theme	Temple Of Doom
Children In Chains	Mine Car Chase	Slalom On Mt. Humol	

10/19/68 136   5   371 **Interlude** .... [I] **$50**   Colgems 5007
Oskar Werner/Barbara Ferris/Donald Sutherland/John Cleese

Bittersweet Interlude	Excerpts from Symphony No. 1--2nd Movement	Excerpts from Symphony No. 2--3rd Movement	Interlude Triangle
Excerpts from Carnival Overture			Must It Happen Once To Everyone?
Excerpts from Symphony No. 5--Finale	Excerpts from Symphony No. 3--1st Movement	Interlude *[Timi Yuro]*	
		Interlude (Instrumental)	

12/31/94 118   6   ©372 **Interview With The Vampire** .... [I] **$10**   Geffen 24719
Tom Cruise/Brad Pitt/Antonio Banderas/Stephen Rea/Kirsten Dunst; cp: Elliot Goldenthal; cd: Jonathan Sheffer

Abduction & Absolution	Escape To Paris	Louis' Revenge	Scent Of Death
Armand Rescues Louis	Forgotten Lore	Madeleine's Lament	**Sympathy For The Devil** *[Guns N' Roses]* **55**
Armand's Seduction	Lestat's Recitative	Marche Funebre	
Born To Darkness Part I & II	Lestat's Tarantella	Plantation Pyre	Theatre Des Vampires
Claudia's Allegro Agitato	Libera Me	Santiago's Waltz	

4/13/85 118   8   373 **Into The Night** .... [V] **$10**   MCA 5561
Jeff Goldblum/Michelle Pfeiffer/Richard Farnsworth/Dan Aykroyd/Irene Papas

Century City Chase *[Joel Peskin]*	**I Can't Help Myself** *[Four Tops]* **1**	Keep It Light *[Thelma Houston]*	
Don't Make Me Sorry *[Patti LaBelle]*	In The Midnight Hour *[B.B. King]*	**Let's Get It On** *[Marvin Gaye]* **1**	
Enter Shaheen *[B.B. King]*	Into The Night *[B.B. King]*	My Lucille *[B.B. King]*	

11/13/65 133   2   374 **Ipcress File, The** .... [I] **$40**   Decca 79124
Michael Caine/Nigel Green/Sue Lloyd; cp/cd: John Barry

Alone Blues	Goodbye Harry	Main Title	
Alone In Three-Quarter Time	If You're Not Clean - I'll Kill You	Man Alone	
Death Of Carswell	Jazz Along Alone	Meeting With Grantby And Fight	

9/14/63 69   11   ©375 **Irma La Douce** .... [I] **$40**   United Artists 5109
Jack Lemmon/Shirley MacLaine/**Lou Jacobi**/Herschel Bernardi; cp/cd: **Andre Previn**

But That's Another Story	I'm Sorry Irma	Market, The	This Is The Story
Don't Take All Night	In The Tub With Fieldglasses	Meet Irma	Wedding Ring
Easy Living The Hard Way	Juke Box: Let's Pretend Love	Nestor, The Honest Policeman	
Escape	Juke Box: Look Again	Our Language Of Love	
Goodbye Lord X	Main Title	Return Of Lord X	

DEBUT	PEAK	WKS	RIAA	CD	ARTIST — Album Title	Catalog	Sym	$	Label & Number

2/15/86 54 11 ©376 Iron Eagle .... [V] **$10** Capitol 12499
Louis Gossett Jr./Jason Gedrick/David Suchet/Tim Thomerson
Hide In The Rainbow *[Dio]*	It's Too Late *[Helix]*	**One Vision** *[Queen]* **61**	This Raging Fire *[Jon Butcher Axis]*
Intense *[George Clinton]*	Love Can Make You Cry *[Urgent]*	Road Of The Gypsy *[Adrenalin]*	
Iron Eagle (Never Say Die) *[King Kobra]*	Maniac House *[Katrina & The Waves]*	These Are The Good Times *[Eric Martin]*	

It Happened At The World's Fair - see PRESLEY, Elvis
Elvis Presley ("Mike Edwards")/Joan O'Brien/Gary Lockwood

12/21/63+ 101 11 ©377 It's A Mad, Mad, Mad, Mad World .... [I] **$30** United Artists 5110
Spencer Tracy/Sid Caesar/Milton Berle/**Jonathan Winters**/Buddy Hackett; cp/cd: Ernest Gold
Adios Santa Rosita	Great Pursuit	Living End	You Satisfy My Soul
Away We Go	Gullible Otto Meyer	Main Title	
Big W	Instant Chase	Retribution	
Follow The Leader	It's A Mad, Mad, Mad, Mad World	Thirty One Flavors	

11/22/80 137 11 378 It's My Turn .... [I+V] **$12** Motown 947
Jill Clayburgh/Michael Douglas/Charles Grodin/Beverly Garland/Steven Hill; cp/cd: Patrick Williams
| Honest Talk | It's My Turn (instrumental) | Main Title (medley) | Walk On *[Ozone]* |
| **It's My Turn** *[Diana Ross]* **9** | Love Begins (medley) | This Is My Love *[Tony Travalini]* | |

1/17/98 73 7 ©379 Jackie Brown .... [O-V] **$10** Maverick 46841
Pam Grier/Samuel L. Jackson/Robert Forster/Bridget Fonda/Robert DeNiro
Across 110th Street *[Bobby Womack]* **56**	(Holy Matrimony) Letter To The Firm *[Foxy Brown]*	Melanie, Simone And Sheronda	Strawberry Letter 23 *[Brothers Johnson]* **5**
Beaumont's Lament	**Inside My Life** *[Minnie Riperton]* **74**	**Midnight Confessions** *[Grass Roots]* **5**	**Street Life** *[Crusaders]* **36**
Detroit 9000	Just Ask Melanie	Monte Carlo Nights *[Elliot Easton's Tiki Gods]*	Tennessee Stud *[Johnny Cash]*
Didn't I (Blow Your Mind This Time) *[Delfonics]* **10**	Lions And The Cucumber *[Vampire Sound Inc.]*	**Natural High** *[Bloodstone]* **10**	Who Is He (And What Is He To You) *[Bill Withers]*
	Long Time Woman *[Pam Grier]*		

Janis - see JOPLIN, Janis

10/15/94 17 32 ▲ ©380 Jason's Lyric .... [V] **$10** Mercury 522915
Forest Whitaker/Allen Payne/Jada Pinkett/Bokeem Woodbine
Brothers And Sistas *[Jayo Felony]*	If Trouble Was Money *[Mint Condition]*	Love Is The Key *[LSD]*	This City Needs Help *[Buddy Guy]*
Candyman *[LL Cool J]*	**If You Think You're Lonely Now** *[K-Ci Hailey]* **17**	Many Rivers To Cross *[Oleta Adams]*	**U Will Know** *[B.M.U. (Black Men United)]* **28**
Crazy Love *[Brian McKnight]* **45**	Jesse James *[Scarface]*	Nigga Sings The Blues *[Spice 1]*	Up And Down *[J. Quest]*
First Round Draft Pick *[Twinz]*	Just Like My Papa *[Tony Toni Toné]*	No More Love *[DRS]*	Walk Away *[Five Footer Crew]*
Forget I Was A G *[Whitehead Brothers]*	Love Is Still Enough *[Savory]*	Rodeo Style *[Jamecia]*	
		That's How It Is *[Ahmad]*	

7/26/75 30 17 ©381 Jaws .... [I] **$15** MCA 2087
Roy Scheider/Richard Dreyfuss/Robert Shaw/Lorraine Gary/Murray Hamilton; cp/cd: John Williams
Chrissie's Death	Indianapolis Story	One Barrel Chase	Promenade (Tourists On The Menu)
End Title	**Main Title 32**	Out To Sea	Sea Attack Number One
Hand To Hand Combat	Night Search	Preparing The Cage	Underwater Siege

Jazz Singer, The - see DIAMOND, Neil
Neil Diamond/Laurence Olivier/Lucie Arnaz/Franklin Ajaye/Sully Boyar

2/11/95 79 8 ©382 Jerky Boys, The .... [V] **$10** Select 82708
Johnny Brennan/Kamal Ahmed/Alan Arkin/William Hickey/Vincent Pastore
Accordions & Keyboards *[Johnny Brennan]*	Beef Jerky *[House Of Pain]*	Gel *[Collective Soul]*	2,000 Light Years Away *[Green Day]*
Are You Gonna Go My Way *[Tom Jones]*	Dial A Jam *[Coolio & The 40 Thevz]*	Hangin' On The Telephone *[L7]*	(You Got Me) Sick As A Dog *[Jerky Boys]*
	Dirty Dancing *[Wu-Tang Clan]*	Shallow End *[Superchunk]*	
	Four Fly Guys *[Hurricane]*	Symptom Of The Universe *[Helmet]*	

1/4/97 49 36 ▲ ©383 Jerry Maguire .... [V] **$10** Epic Soundtrax 67910
Tom Cruise/Cuba Gooding Jr./Renee Zellweger/Kelly Preston/Jonathan Lipnicki
Gettin' In Tune *[Who]*	Pocketful Of Rainbows *[Elvis Presley]*	Shelter From The Storm *[Bob Dylan]*	We Meet Again *[Nancy Wilson]*
Horses, The *[Rickie Lee Jones]*	Sandy *[Nancy Wilson]*	Singalong Junk *[Paul McCartney]*	Wise Up *[Aimee Mann]*
Magic Bus *[Who]* **25**	**Secret Garden** *[Bruce Springsteen]* **19**	Sitting Still Moving Still Staring Outlooking *[His Name Is Alive]*	World On A String *[Neil Young]*
Momma Miss America *[Paul McCartney]*			

6/30/73 21 39 ▲ ©384 Jesus Christ Superstar .... [M] **$20** MCA 11000 [2]
Ted Neeley/**Yvonne Elliman**/Carl Anderson/Barry Dennen; mu: **Andrew Lloyd Webber**; ly: Tim Rice
Arrest, The	Heaven On Their Minds	Peter's Denial	Temple, The
Blood Money (medley)	Hosanna	Pilate And Christ	Then We Are Decided
Could We Start Again Please?	I Don't Know How To Love Him	Pilate's Dream	This Jesus Must Die
Crucifixion, The	John Nineteen: Forty-One	Poor Jerusalem	Trial Before Pilate
Damned For All Time (medley)	Judas' Death	Simon Zealotes	What's That Buzz
Everything's Alright	King Herod's Song	Strange Thing Mystifying	
Gethsemane (I Only Want To Say)	Last Supper	Superstar	

12/28/85+ 55 17 ©385 Jewel Of The Nile, The .... [V] **$10** Jive 8406
Michael Douglas/Kathleen Turner/Danny DeVito
African Breeze *[Hugh Masekela & Jonathan Butler]*	I'm In Love *[Ruby Turner]*	Love Theme *[Jack Nitzsche]*	Plot Thickens *[Jack Nitzsche]*
Freaks Come Out At Night *[Whodini]*	Jewel Of The Nile *[Precious Wilson]*	Nubian Dance *[Nubians]*	**When The Going Gets Tough, The Tough Get Going** *[Billy Ocean]* **2**
	Legion (Here I Come) *[Mark Shreeve]*	Party (No Sheep Is Safe Tonight) *[Willesden Dodgers]*	

Jimi Hendrix - see HENDRIX, Jimi

Jonathan Livingston Seagull - see DIAMOND, Neil / HARRIS, Richard
James Franciscus/Juliet Mills

4/14/01 16 18 ● ©386 Josie And The Pussycats .... [M] **$10** Play-Tone 85683
Rachael Leigh Cook/Tara Reid/Rosario Dawson/Parker Posey/Alan Cumming
Backdoor Lover *[DuJour]*	Josie And The Pussycats	Shapeshifter	You're A Star
Come On	Money	Spin Around	
Dujour Around The World *[DuJour]*	Pretend To Be Nice	3 Small Words	
I Wish You Well	Real Wild Child	You Don't See Me	

Journey Through The Past - see YOUNG, Neil

DEBUT	PEAK	WKS	RIAA	CD	ARTIST — Album Title	Catalog	Sym	$	Label & Number

10/2/93 · 17 · 20 · ● · ©387 **Judgment Night** .... [V] **$10** Immortal 57144
Emilio Estevez/Cuba Gooding Jr./**Denis Leary**/Jeremy Piven/**Everlast**
Another Body Murdered *[Faith No More & Boo-Yaa T.R.I.B.E.]* — Freak Momma *[Mudhoney & Sir Mix-A-Lot]* — Just Another Victim *[Helmet & House Of Pain]* — Real Thing *[Pearl Jam & Cypress Hill]*
Come And Die *[Therapy? & Fatal]* — I Love You Mary Jane *[Sonic Youth & Cypress Hill]* — Me, Myself & My Microphone *[Living Colour & Run D.M.C.]*
Disorder *[Slayer & Ice-T]* — Judgment Night *[Biohazard & Onyx]* — Missing Link *[Dinosaur Jr. & Del The Funky Homosapien]*
Fallin' *[Teenage Fanclub & De La Soul]*

1/18/92 · 17 · 29 · ● · ©388 **Juice**.. [V] **$10** MCA 10462
Omar Epps/Jermaine Hopkins/Khalil Kain/**2Pac**/Cindy Herron (**En Vogue**)
Does Your Man Know About Me *[Rahiem]* — It's Going Down *[EPMD]* — Sex, Money & Murder *[M.C. Pooh]* — What Could Be Better Bitch *[Son Of Bazerk]*
Don't Be Afraid *[Aaron Hall]* 44 — **Juice (Know The Ledge)** *[Eric B. & Rakim]* 96 — Shoot 'Em Up *[Cypress Hill Crew]*
Flipside *[Juvenile Committee]* — Nuff' Respect *[Big Daddy Kane]* — So You Want To Be A Gangster *[Too $hort]*
He's Gamin' On Ya *[Salt-N-Pepa]* — People Get Ready *[Brand New Heavies]* — Uptown Anthem *[Naughty By Nature]*
Is It Good To You *[Teddy Riley]*

11/22/86 · 159 · 4 · · ©389 **Jumpin' Jack Flash** .... [V] **$10** Mercury 830545
Whoopi Goldberg/Carol Kane/Stephen Collins/Annie Potts
Breaking The Code *[Thomas Newman]* — **Jumpin' Jack Flash** *[Rolling Stones]* 3 — Rescue Me *[Gwen Guthrie]* — Window To The World *[Face To Face]*
Hold On *[Billy Branigan]* — Love Music *[Thomas Newman]* — Set Me Free *[Rene & Angela]* — You Can't Hurry Love *[Supremes]* 1
Misled *[Kool & The Gang]* 10 — Trick Of The Night *[Bananarama]* 76

2/3/68 · 19 · 34 · · ©390 **Jungle Book, The**..C:#21/2 [M] **$25** Disneyland 3948
animated movie, voices by: Phil Harris/Sebastian Cabot/ **Louis Prima**; sw: Richard M. Sherman and Robert B. Sherman
Bare Necessities — I Wan'na Be Like You — That's What Friends Are For
Colonel Hathi's March — My Own Home — Trust In Me

Jungle Fever - see WONDER, Stevie
Wesley Snipes/Annabella Sciorra/Spike Lee/Ossie Davis/Ruby Dee

6/12/93 · 36 · 26 · ● · ©391 **Jurassic Park** .... [I] **$10** MCA 10859
Sam Neill/Laura Dern/Jeff Goldblum/Richard Attenborough/Wayne Knight; cp/cd: **John Williams**
Dennis Steals The Embryo — High-Wire Stunts — Jurassic Park Gate — Remembering Petticoat Lane
End Credits — Incident At Isla Nublar — My Friend, The Brachiosaurus — T-Rex Rescue & Finale
Eye To Eye — Journey To The Island — Opening Titles — Tree For My Bed
Hatching Baby Raptor — Jurassic Park, Theme From — Raptor Attack — Welcome To Jurassic Park

7/21/84 · 114 · 12 · · 392 **Karate Kid, The** .... [V] **$12** Casablanca 822213
Ralph Macchio/Pat Morita/Elisabeth Shue/Martin Kove
(Bop Bop) On The Beach *[Flirts w/Jan & Dean]* — (It Takes) Two To Tango *[Paul Davis]* — Rhythm Man *[St. Regis]* — Young Hearts *[Commuter]*
Desire *[Gang Of Four]* — **Moment Of Truth** *[Survivor]* 63 — Tough Love *[Shandi]*
Feel The Night *[Baxter Robertson]* — No Shelter *[Broken Edge]* — You're The Best *[Joe "Bean" Esposito]*

7/12/86 · 30 · 17 · · 393 **Karate Kid Part II, The** .... [V] **$10** United Artists 40414
Ralph Macchio/Pat Morita/Tony O'Dell/Danny Kamekona
Earth Angel *[New Edition]* 21 — Love Theme *[Bill Conti]* — Rock 'N' Roll Over You *[Moody Blues]* — **This Is The Time** *[Dennis DeYoung]* 93
Fish For Life *[Mancrab]* — Rock Around The Clock *[Paul Rodgers]* — Storm, The *[Bill Conti]* — Two Looking At One *[Carly Simon]*
Glory Of Love *[Peter Cetera]* 1
Let Me At 'Em *[Southside Johnny]*

Kids Are Alright, The - see WHO, The

7/21/56 · ❶[1] · 277 · ● · ©394 **King And I, The** .... [M] **$40** Capitol 740
Yul Brynner/Deborah Kerr/Rita Moreno; mu: Richard Rodgers; ly: Oscar Hammerstein; cd: Alfred Newman
Getting To Know You — March Of Siamese Children — Shall I Tell You What I Think Of You? — Song Of The King
Hello, Young Lovers — My Lord And Master — We Kiss In A Shadow
I Have Dreamed — Puzzlement, A — Shall We Dance?
I Whistle A Happy Tune — Something Wonderful

King Creole - see PRESLEY, Elvis
Elvis Presley ("Danny Fisher")/Carolyn Jones/Walter Matthau/Dean Jagger

1/8/77 · 123 · 8 · · 395 **King Kong** .... [I] **$20** Reprise 2260
Jeff Bridges/Jessica Lange/Charles Grodin/John Randolph/Rene Auberjonois; cp/cd: John Barry
Arrival On The Island — End, The — How About Buying Me A Drink (medley) — Opening, The
Arthusa — End Is At Hand — Sacrifice - Hail To The King
Blackout In New York (medley) — Full Moon Domain - Beauty Is A Beast — Incomprehensible Captivity
Breakout To Captivity — Kong Hits The Big Apple
Climb To Skull Island — Maybe My Luck Has Changed

4/16/83 · 162 · 6 · · 396 **King Of Comedy, The** .... [V] **$12** Warner 23765
Robert DeNiro/**Jerry Lewis**/Tony Randall/Sandra Bernhard/Shelley Hack
Back On The Chain Gang *[Pretenders]* 5 — Come Rain Or Come Shine *[Ray Charles]* — Rainbow Sleeve *[Rickie Lee Jones]* — 'Tain't Nobody's Bizness (If I Do) *[B.B. King]*
Between Trains *[Robbie Robertson]* — Finer Things *[David Sanborn]* — Steal The Night *[Ric Ocasek]* — Wonderful Remark *[Van Morrison]*
King Of Comedy *[Bob James]* — Swamp *[Talking Heads]*

11/6/61+ · 10 · 39 · · ©397 **King Of Kings** .... [I] **$50** MGM 2
Jeffrey Hunter/Sibohan McKenna/Rip Torn; cp/cd: Miklos Rozsa; includes a full-color book about the movie
Christ's Entry Into Jerusalem (medley) — Miracles Of Christ — Resurrection (Finale) — Virgin Mary
Holy Of Holies — Mount Galilee (medley) — Salome's Dance — Way Of The Cross
John The Baptist — Nativity — Scourging Of Christ
King Of Kings Theme (Prelude) — Pontius Pilate's Arrival Into Jerusalem — Sermon On The Mount (medley)
Mary At The Sepulcher — Prayer Of Our Lord — Tempest In Judea (medley)
— Temptation Of Christ

4/21/01 · 61 · 10 · · ©398 **Kingdom Come** .... [V] **$10** Gospo Centric 70035
LL Cool J/Jada Pinkett/Vivica A. Fox/Loretta Devine/**Toni Braxton**
Daddy's Song *[Carl Thomas, Natalie Wilson & SOP]* — It's Alright *[Trin-I-Tee 5:7]* — Thank You *[Kirk Franklin & Mary Mary]*
Every Woman *[AZ Yet]* — Kingdom Come *[Kirk Franklin & Jill Scott]* — Thy Will Be Done *[Deborah Cox]*
God's Got It All In Control *[Kurt Carr]* — Someday *[Crystal Lewis]* — Try Me *[Tamar Braxton & One Nation Crew]*
— Stand *[Shawn Stockman]*

DEBUT	PEAK	WKS	RIAA	CD	ARTIST — Album Title	Catalog	Sym	$	Label & Number

Kissin' Cousins - see PRESLEY, Elvis
Elvis Presley ("Josh Morgan" & "Jodie Tatum")/Arthur O'Connell/Jack Albertson

| 5/26/01 | 42 | 9 | | ©399 | **Knight's Tale, A** .... [O-V] | | | $10 | Columbia 85648 |

Boys Are Back In Town *[Thin Lizzy]* 12 — Further On Up The Road *[Eric Clapton]* — I Want To Take You Higher *[Sly & The Family Stone]* 38 — Takin' Care Of Business *[Bachman-Turner Overdrive]* 12
Crazy On You *[Heart]* 35 — Get Ready *[Rare Earth]* 4 — Low Rider *[War]* 7 — We Are The Champions *[Robbie Williams & Queen]*
Eye Conqueror *[Third Eye Blind]* — Golden Years *[David Bowie]* 10 — One Of Your Own *[Carter Burwell]* — We Will Rock You *[Queen]* 52
Pieces *[Dan Powell]*

| 10/26/85 | 79 | 20 | | 400 | **Krush Groove** .... [V] | | | $12 | Warner 25295 |

Sheila E./Run-DMC/The Fat Boys/Kurtis Blow
All You Can Eat *[Fat Boys]* — If I Ruled The World *[Kurtis Blow]* — Krush Groovin' *[Fat Boys, Run-D.M.C., Sheila E. & Kurtis Blow]* — Tender Love *[Force M.D.'s]* 10
Feel The Spin *[Debbie Harry]* — (Krush Groove) Can't Stop The Street *[Chaka Khan]*
Holly Rock *[Sheila E.]* — Love Triangle *[Gap Band]*
I Can't Live Without My Radio *[L.L. Cool J]* — She's On It *[Beastie Boys]*

La Bamba - see LOS LOBOS
Lou Diamond Phillips/Esai Morales/Rosana DeSoto/Elizabeth Pena

Labyrinth - see BOWIE, David
David Bowie/Jennifer Connelly

| 8/6/55 | 14 | 4 | | 401 | **Lady and The Tramp** .... [EP] | | | $50 | Capitol 3056 [2] |

animated movie, voices by Daws Butler/June Foray/Larry Roberts/Barbara Luddy; no track titles listed; includes a full-color book of scenes from the movie

Lady Sings The Blues - see ROSS, Diana
Diana Ross/Billy Dee Williams/Richard Pryor

| 6/23/01 | 32 | 10 | ● | ©402 | **Lara Croft: Tomb Raider** .... [V] | | | $10 | Elektra 62665 |

Angelina Jolie/Jon Voight/Iain Glen/Noah Taylor
Absurd *[Fluke]* — Edge Hill *[Groove Armada]* — Illuminati *[Fatboy Slim]* — Speedballin' *[OutKast]*
Ain't Never Learned *[Moby]* — Elevation *[U2]* — Revolution, The *[BT]* — Terra Firma *[Delerium]*
Deep *[Nine Inch Nails]* — Galaxy Bounce *[Chemical Brothers]* — Satellite *[Bosco]* — Where's Your Head At *[Basement Jaxx]*
Devil's Nightmare *[Oxide & Neutrino]* — Get Ur Freak On *[Missy Elliott]* 7 — Song Of Life *[Leftfield]*

| 6/26/93 | 7 | 21 | ▲ | ©403 | **Last Action Hero** | | | [V] $10 | Columbia 57127 |

Arnold Schwarzenegger/Austin O'Brien/F. Murray Abraham/Art Carney/Anthony Quinn
Angry Again *[Megadeth]* — Jack And The Ripper *[Michael Kamen]* — Poison My Eyes *[Anthrax]* — Two Steps Behind *[Def Leppard]* 12
Big Gun *[AC/DC]* 65 — — Real World *[Queensryche]* — What The Hell Have I *[Alice In Chains]*
Cock The Hammer *[Cypress Hill]* — Last Action Hero *[Tesla]* — Swim *[Fishbone]* —
Dream On *[Aerosmith]* 6 — Little Bitter *[Alice In Chains]* — —

| 3/30/85 | 58 | 15 | | ©404 | **Last Dragon, The** .... [V] | | | $10 | Motown 6128 |

Taimak/Julius J. Carry III/Chris Murney/Leo O'Brien/**Vanity**
Fire *[Charlene]* — Glow, The *[Willie Hutch]* — Last Dragon (Title Song) *[Dwight David]* — 7th Heaven *[Vanity]*
First Time On A Ferris Wheel (Love Theme) *[Smokey Robinson & Syreeta]* — Inside You *[Willie Hutch & The Temptations]* — Peeping Tom *[Rockwell]* — Star *[Alfie]*
 — — **Rhythm Of The Night** *[DeBarge]* 3 — Upset Stomach *[Stevie Wonder]*

| 2/27/88 | 152 | 10 | | ©405 | **Last Emperor, The** .... [I-V] | | | $10 | Virgin 90690 |

John Lone/Joan Chen/Peter O'Toole/Ying Ruocheng
Baby (Was Born Dead) — Last Emperor (Theme Variation 1) — Picking A Bride *[David Byrne]* — Red Guard Dance *[Girls Red Guard Dancers]*
Bed *[David Byrne]* — Lunch *[Cong Su]* — Picking Up Brides — Where Is Armo?
Emperor's Waltz *[Ball Orchestra of Vienna]* — Main Title Theme *[David Byrne]* — Rain (I Want A Divorce) — Wind, Rain And Water *[David Byrne]*
First Coronation — Open The Door — Red Guard *[Red Guard Accordion Band]* —
 — Paper Emperor *[David Byrne]* — —

| 10/24/92 | 42 | 65 | ▲ | ©406 | **Last Of The Mohicans, The** .... [I] | | | $10 | Morgan Creek 20015 |

Daniel Day-Lewis/Madeleine Stowe; cp: Trevor Jones/Randy Edelman; cd: Daniel A. Carlin/Randy Edelman
British Arrival — Elk Hunt — Main Title — Promontory
Canoes (medley) — Fort Battle — Massacre (medley) — River Walk (medley)
Cora — Glade Part II, The — Munro's Office (medley) — Stockade (medley)
Courier, The — I Will Find You *[Clannad]* — Parlay — Top Of The World
Discovery (medley) — Kiss, The — Pieces Of A Story —

Last Tango In Paris - see BARBIERI, Gato
Marlon Brando/Maria Schneider

Last Temptation Of Christ, The - see GABRIEL, Peter
Willem Dafoe/Harvey Keitel/Barbara Hershey/Harry Dean Stanton

Last Waltz, The - see BAND, The

| 3/2/63 | 2² | 86 | | ©407 | **Lawrence Of Arabia** | | | [I] $50 | Colpix 514 |

Peter O'Toole/Alec Guinness/Anthony Quinn/Omar Sharif; cp/cd: Maurice Jarre; pf: **London Philharmonic Orchestra**
Arrival At Auda's Camp — End Title — Miracle — Sun's Anvil
Bringing Gasim Into Camp (medley) — Lawrence & Body Guard — Nefud Mirage — That Is The Desert
Continuation Of The Miracle — Main Title — Rescue Of Gasim (medley) — Voice Of The Guns

| 7/25/92 | 159 | 6 | | ©408 | **League Of Their Own, A** .... [V] | | | $10 | Columbia 52919 |

Tom Hanks/Geena Davis/**Madonna**/Lori Petty/Jon Lovitz
All American Girls Professional Baseball League Song *[Rockford Peaches]* — Final Game *[Hans Zimmer]* — It's Only A Paper Moon *[James Taylor]* — On The Sunny Side Of The Street *[Manhattan Transfer]*
 — Flying Home *[Doc's Rhythm Cats]* — Life Goes On *[Hans Zimmer]* — Two Sleepy People *[Art Garfunkel]*
Choo Choo Ch'Boogie *[Manhattan Transfer]* — I Didn't Know What Time It Was *[James Taylor]* — Now And Forever *[Carole King]* —
 — In A Sentimental Mood *[Billy Joel]* — —

| 2/17/96 | 124 | 13 | | ©409 | **Leaving Las Vegas** .... [I+V] | | | $10 | Pangaea 36071 |

Nicolas Cage/Elisabeth Shue/Julian Sands/Richard Lewis/Valeria Golino; cp: Mike Figgis
Angel Eyes *[Sting]* — Blues For Ben — Intro Dialogue — Sera Invites Ben To Stay
Are You Desirable? — Bossa Vega — It's A Lonesome Old Town *[Sting]* — Sera Talks To The Cab Driver
Ben & Bill — Burlesque — Leaving Las Vegas — Sera's Dark Side
Ben And Sera — Come Rain Or Come Shine *[Don Henley]* — Mara — She Really Loved Him
Ben Pawns His Rolex/Sera Talks To Her Shrink — Get Out — My One And Only Love *[Sting]* —
Ben's Hell — I Won't Be Going South For A While *[Palladinos]* — On The Street —
Biker Bar — — Reunited —
 — — Ridiculous —

SOUNDTRACKS

DEBUT	PEAK	WKS	RIAA	CD	ARTIST — Album Title	Catalog	Sym	$	Label & Number

11/18/00 · **174** · 1 · ©410 · **Left Behind** .... [V] **$10** · Reunion 10022
Kirk Cameron/Brad Johnson/Chelsea Noble/Gordon Currie
- After All - Rayford's Song [Bob Carlisle]
- All The Way To Heaven [V-enna]
- Believer - Buck's Song [Jake]
- Can't Wait For You To Return [Fred Hammond]
- Come Quickly Lord [Rebecca St. James]
- Fly - Chloe's Song [Larue]
- Hide My Soul [Avalon]
- I Believe In You [Joy Williams]
- I Need A Miracle [Plus One]
- Left Behind - Main Theme [Bryan Duncan]
- Live For The Lord - Irene's Song [Kathy Troccoli]
- Midnight Cry - Closing Theme [Various Artists]
- Never Been Unloved - Bruce's Song [Michael W. Smith]
- No Fear - Panic In The City [Clay Crosse]
- Sky Falls Down - Israel Is Attacked [Third Day]

Legend - see TANGERINE DREAM
Tom Cruise/Mia Sara/**Tim Curry**/Arnon Milchan

2/4/95 · **147** · 7 · ©411 · **Legends Of The Fall** .... [I] **$10** · Epic Soundtrax 66462
Brad Pitt/Anthony Hopkins/Aidan Quinn/Henry Thomas/Julia Ormand; cp/cd: James Horner
- Alfred Moves To Helena
- Alfred, Tristan, The Colonel, The Legend...
- Changing Seasons, Wild Horses, Tristan's Return
- Farewell/Descent Into Madness
- Goodbyes
- Isabel's Murder, Recollections Of Samuel
- Legends Of The Fall
- Ludlows, The
- Off To War
- Revenge
- Samuel's Death
- To The Boys...
- Wedding, The

1/18/75 · **180** · 3 · ©412 · **Lenny** .... [C] **$20** · United Artists 359
Dustin Hoffman/Valerie Perrine; cp/cd: Ralph Burns; based on life of **Lenny Bruce**
- Aurenthology
- Blah Blah
- Dikes
- Dirty
- Flic-Flac
- Honeycomb
- It Never Entered My Mind [Miles Davis]
- Lament
- Lenny (Theme)
- Myrtle's Tune
- Nan's Dream
- Niggers
- Time Does It Again
- To Come
- Valerie
- We're All The Same Schmucks, Part I & II

12/5/87+ · **31** · 23 · ● · ©413 · **Less Than Zero** .... [V] **$10** · Def Jam 44042
Robert Downey Jr./Andrew McCarthy/Jami Gertz/James Spader
- Are You My Woman? [Black Flames]
- Bring The Noise [Public Enemy]
- **Going Back To Cali** [L.L. Cool J] **31**
- **Hazy Shade Of Winter** [Bangles] **2**
- How To Love Again [Oran "Juice" Jones]
- In-A-Gadda-Da-Vida [Slayer]
- Life Fades Away [Roy Orbison]
- Rock And Roll All Nite [Poison]
- Rocking Pneumonia And The Boogie Woogie Flu [Aerosmith]
- She's Lost You [Joan Jett]
- You & Me (Less Than Zero) [Glen Danzig & The Power & Fury Orch.]

Let It Be - see BEATLES, The
Let The Good Times Roll - see VARIOUS ARTISTS COMPILATIONS
Let's Do It Again - see STAPLE SINGERS, The
Sidney Poitier/**Bill Cosby**/Jimmie Walker/John Amos

9/2/89 · **164** · 3 · ©414 · **Lethal Weapon 2** .... [I+V] **$10** · Warner 25985
Mel Gibson/Danny Glover/Joe Pesci/Joss Ackland; cp/pf: **Eric Clapton** and **David Sanborn**
- Cheer Down [George Harrison]
- Embassy, The
- Goodnight Rika
- Knockin' On Heaven's Door [Randy Crawford feat. Eric Clapton & David Sanborn]
- Leo
- Riggs
- Riggs And Roger
- Shipyard, The (medley)
- **Still Cruisin'** [Beach Boys] **93**
- Stilt House

6/27/92 · **101** · 3 · ©415 · **Lethal Weapon 3** .... [I+V] **$10** · Reprise 26989
Mel Gibson/Danny Glover/Joe Pesci/Rene Russo; cp/cd: Michael Kamen/**Eric Clapton**/**David Sanborn**
- Armour Piercing Bullets
- Darryl Dies
- God Judges Us By Our Scars
- Grab The Cat
- It's Probably Me [Sting with Eric Clapton]
- Leo Getz Goes To The Hockey Game
- Lorna - A Quiet Evening By The Fire
- Riggs And Rog
- Roger's Boat
- Runaway Train [Elton John & Eric Clapton]

4/3/99 · **10** · 21 · ▲ · ©416 · **Life** .... [V] **$10** · Rock Land 90314
Eddie Murphy/Martin Lawrence/Bernie Mac/Ned Beatty
- Discovery [Brian McKnight]
- Every Which Way [Talent]
- Follow The Wind [Trisha Yearwood]
- **Fortunate** [Maxwell] **4**
- It's Gonna Rain [Kelly Price]
- It's Like Everyday [DJ Quik]
- **Life** [K-Ci & JoJo] **60**
- Lovin' You [Sparkle]
- New Day [Wyclef Jean]
- Speechless [Isley Brothers]
- Stimulate [Destiny's Child]
- 25 To Life [Xzibit]
- What Goes Around [Khadejia]
- **What Would You Do?** [City High] **8**
- Why Should I Believe You? [Mya]

4/10/99 · **200** · 1 · ©417 · **Life Is Beautiful (La Vita È Bella)** .... [I] **$10** · Virgin 46428
Roberto Benigni/Nicoletta Braschi; cp/cd: Nicola Piovani
- Abbiamo Vinto
- Arriva Il Carro Armato
- Barcarolle
- Buon Giorno Principessa
- Grand Hotel Fox
- Grand Hotel Valse
- Guido E Ferruccio
- Il Gioco Di Giosué
- Il Treno Nel Buio
- Krautentang
- L'Uovo Di Struzzo-Danza Etiope
- La Notte Di Favola
- La Notte Di Fuga
- La Vita È Bella
- Le Uova Nel Cappello
- Valse Larmoyante
- Viva Giosué

11/1/97 · **102** · 4 · ©418 · **Life Less Ordinary, A** .... [V] **$10** · Innerstate 540809
Ewan McGregor/Cameron Diaz/Holly Hunter/Delroy Lindo/Ian Holm
- Always On My Mind [Elvis Presley]
- **Beyond The Sea** [Bobby Darin] **6**
- Deadweight [Beck]
- Deeper River [Dusted]
- Don't Leave [Faithless]
- Full Throttle [Prodigy]
- It's War [Cardigans]
- Kingdom Of Lies [Folk Implosion]
- Leave [R.E.M.]
- Life Less Ordinary [Ash]
- Love Is Here [Luscious Jackson]
- Oh [Underworld]
- Peace In The Valley [A3]
- Put A Lid On It [Squirrel Nut Zippers]
- Velvet Divorce [Sneaker Pimps]

Life Of Brian - see MONTY PYTHON
Graham Chapman/John Cleese/Eric Idle/Michael Palin

11/27/99 · **19** · 9 · ● · ©419 · **Light It Up** .... [V] **$10** · Yab Yum 62410
Usher/Forest Whitaker/Judd Nelson/**Vanessa Williams**
- Anything [112]
- Burgundy [Shya]
- Catz Don't Know [DMX]
- First One Hit [Amil & Solé]
- Free To Believe [Jack Herrera]
- Ghetto's A Battlefield [Blaze & Firestarr]
- Here [Beverly]
- High Schoolin' [OutKast]
- How Many Wanna [Ja Rule]
- If Only In Heaven's Eyes ['N Sync]
- Light It Up [Master P]
- That's Real [AZ & Beanie Sigel]
- Waiting In Vain [Jon B.]

3/14/87 · **82** · 10 · ©420 · **Light Of Day** .... [V] **$10** · Blackheart 40654
Michael J. Fox/**Joan Jett**/Gena Rowlands/Michael McKean/Jason Miller
- Cleveland Rocks [Ian Hunter]
- Elegy [Rick Cox, Chas Smith, Jon C. Clarke & Michael Boddicker]
- **Light Of Day** [Barbusters] **33**
- **Only Lonely** [Bon Jovi] **54**
- It's All Coming Down Tonight [Barbusters]
- Rabbit's Got The Gun [Hunzz]
- Rude Mood [Barbusters]
- Stay With Me Tonight [Dave Edmunds]
- This Means War [Barbusters]
- Twist It Off [Fabulous Thunderbirds]
- You Got No Place To Go [Michael J. Fox]

5/30/64 · **110** · 6 · 421 · **Lilies Of The Field** .... [I] **$50** · Epic 26094
Sidney Poitier/Lilia Skala/Lisa Mann; cp/cd: Jerry Goldsmith
- Amen
- Breakfast (medley)
- Contractor, The
- Drive To Mass (medley)
- End Cast (medley)
- End Title (medley)
- Feed The Slaves (medley)
- Homer Awakes (medley)
- Homer Returns
- Lots Of Bricks
- Main Title
- No Hammer
- Out Of Bricks
- Roof, The

DEBUT	PEAK	WKS	RIAA	CD	ARTIST — Album Title	Catalog	Sym	$	Label & Number

5/3/69 — **182** — 7 — ©422 **Lion In Winter, The** .... [I] $25 Columbia 3250
Peter O'Toole/Katharine Hepburn/Timothy Dalton/Anthony Hopkins; cp/cd: John Barry
Allons Gai Gai Gai	God Damn You	Media Vita In Morte Sumus (In The	We're Jungle Creatures
Chinon - Eleanor's Arrival	Herb Garden	Midst Of Life We Are In Death)	
Christmas Wine	How Beautiful You Make Me	To Rome	
Eya, Eya, Nova Gaudia	Main Title	To The Chapel	

6/18/94 — ❶¹⁰ — 88 — ▲¹⁰ ©423 **Lion King, The** [M] $10 Walt Disney 60858
animated movie, voices by: Jonathan Taylor Thomas/Jeremy Irons/James Earl Jones; mu: **Elton John**; ly: Tim Rice
Be Prepared	Circle Of Life [Elton John] 18	I Just Can't Wait To Be King (cast	Under The Stars
Can You Feel The Love Tonight	Circle Of Life (cast version)	version)	
[Elton John] 4	Hakuna Matata	King Of Pride Rock	
Can You Feel The Love Tonight	I Just Can't Wait To Be King [Elton	This Land	
(cast version)	John]	...To Die For	

11/8/75 — **145** — 6 — 424 **Lisztomania** .... [M] $15 A&M 4546
Roger Daltrey/Rick Wakeman/**Ringo Starr**; cp: Franz List; ly: **Roger Daltrey** and Rick Wakeman
Chopsticks Fantasia (medley)	Funerailles	Master Race	Rienzi (medley)
Dante Period	Hell	Orpheus Song	
Excelsior Song	Hibernation	Peace At Last	
Free Song (Hungarian Rhapsody)	Love's Dream	Rape, Pillage & Clap	

12/16/89+ — **32** — 48 — ▲³ ©425 **Little Mermaid, The** ....C:#2¹/23 [M] $10 Disney 018
animated movie, voices by: Jodi Benson/Pat Carroll/Samuel E. Wright; mu: Alan Menken; ly: Howard Ashman
Bedtime	Fathoms Below	Kiss The Girl	Storm, The
Daughters Of Triton	Fireworks	Les Poissons	Tour Of The Kingdom
Destruction Of The Grotto	Flotsam And Jetsam	Main Titles	Under The Sea
Eric To The Rescue	Happy Ending	Part Of Your World	Wedding Announcement
Fanfare	Jig	Poor Unfortunate Souls	

11/18/00 — **95** — 8 — ©426 **Little Nicky** .... [V] $10 Maverick 47856
Adam Sandler/Patricia Arquette/Harvey Keitel/**Rodney Dangerfield**/Tiny Lister
Be Quiet And Drive (Far Away)	Change (In The House Of Flies)	Pardon Me [Incubus]	Stupify [Disturbed]
[Deftones]	[Deftones]	Points Of Authority [Linkin Park]	Take A Picture [Filter]
Cave [Muse]	Natural High [Insolence]	(Rock) Superstar [Cypress Hill]	When Worlds Collide [Powerman
	Nothing [Unloco]	School Of Hard Knocks [P.O.D.]	5000]

1/17/87 — **47** — 17 — ©427 **Little Shop Of Horrors** .... [M] $10 Geffen 24125
Rick Moranis/Ellen Greene/Vincent Gardenia/**Steve Martin**; mu: Alan Menken; ly: Howard Ashman
Da-Doo	Grow For Me	Meek Shall Inherit	Suddenly, Seymour
Dentist!	Little Shop Of Horrors	Skid Row (Downtown)	Suppertime
Don't Feed The Plants	Mean Green Mother From	Some Fun Now	
Feed Me (Git It)	Outerspace	Somewhere That's Green	

7/28/73 — **17** — 15 — ©428 **Live And Let Die** .... [I] $25 United Artists 100
Roger Moore/Jane Seymour/Yaphet Kotto/Clifton James; cp/cd: **George Martin**
Baron Samedi's Dance Of Death	If He Finds It, Kill Him	New Second Line (medley)	Whisper Who Dares
Bond Drops In	James Bond Theme	Sacrifice	
Bond Meets Solitaire	Just A Closer Walk With Thee	San Monique	
Fillet Of Soul - Harlem (medley)	(medley)	Snakes Alive	
Fillet Of Soul - New Orleans	**Live And Let Die** [Wings] 2	Solitaire Gets Her Cards	
(medley)	Live And Let Die (medley)	Trespassers Will Be Eaten	

1/27/68 — **188** — 7 — ©429 **Live For Life** .... [I] $25 United Artists 5165
Yves Montand/Candice Bergen/Annie Girardot; cp/cd: Francis Lai
| All At Once It's Love | Now You Want To Be Loved | Theme To Catherine | Zoom |
| Live For Life | Theme To Candice | Theme To Robert | |

9/22/62 — **63** — 6 — ©430 **Lolita** .... [I] $30 MGM 4050
Peter Sellers/Sue Lyon/Shelley Winters/James Mason; cp/cd: **Nelson Riddle**
Arrival In Town	Lolita (Love Theme)	Quilty's Theme	Two Beat Society
Discovery Of Diary	Lolita Ya Ya	School Dance	
Humbert Contemplates Killing Wife	Mother And Humbert At Dinner	Thoughts Of Lolita	

Looking For Love - see FRANCIS, Connie
Connie Francis/Jim Hutton/Susan Oliver

11/26/77 — **134** — 8 — 431 **Looking For Mr. Goodbar** .... [V] $15 Columbia 35029
Diane Keaton/Richard Gere/William Atherton/Tuesday Weld
Back Stabbers [O'Jays] 3	Don't Ask To Stay Until Tomorrow	**Machine Gun** [Commodores] 22	Theme From "Looking For Mr.
Could It Be Magic [Donna	(Theme) [Marlena Shaw]	Prelude To Love [Donna Summer]	Goodbar" (Don't Ask To Stay Until
Summer] 52	**Don't Leave Me This Way** [Thelma	She Wants To (Get On Down) [Bill	Tomorrow)
Don't Ask To Stay Until Tomorrow	Houston] 1	Withers]	**Try Me I Know We Can Make It**
(Theme) [Artie Kane]	**Love Hangover** [Diana Ross] 1	She's Lonely [Bill Withers]	[Donna Summer] 80
	Lowdown [Boz Scaggs] 3		

3/27/65 — **123** — 5 — 432 **Lord Jim** .... [I] $50 Colpix 521
Peter O'Toole/James Mason/Curt Jurgens/Eli Wallach; cp: Bronislau Kaper; cd: **Muir Mathieson**
Color Of Love	Fire, The	Intermission	Patna
Compassion	Four Generations	Lord Jim Theme	River Journey
Father And Son	Girl From Patusan	Man In Search	Sunrise, Victory And Celebration

12/9/78+ — **39** — 12 — ©433 **Lord Of The Rings, The** .... [I] $20 Fantasy 1 [2]
animated movie, voices by: Christopher Guard/William Squire/John Hurt; cp/cd: Leonard Rosenman
Attack Of The Orcs	Encounter With The Ringwraiths	Gandalf Remembers	Mines Of Moria
Balrog, The (medley)	(medley)	Helm's Deep	Mithrandir
Battle In The Mines (medley)	Escape To Rivendell	History Of The Ring	Riders Of Rohan
Dawn Battle (medley)	Following The Orcs	Journey Begins (medley)	Theoden's Victory (medley)
	Frodo Disappears	Lord Of The Rings (Theme)	Voyage To Mordor (medley)

8/1/87 — **15** — 39 — ● ©434 **Lost Boys, The** ....C:#41/1 [V] $10 Atlantic 81767
Kiefer Sutherland/Dianne Wiest/Jami Gertz/Jason Patric/Barnard Hughes
Beauty Has Her Way [Mummy	Don't Let The Sun Go Down On Me	Laying Down The Law [INXS &	People Are Strange [Echo & The
Calls]	[Roger Daltrey]	Jimmy Barnes]	Bunnymen]
Cry Little Sister (Theme) [Gerard	**Good Times** [INXS & Jimmy	Lost In Shadows (The Lost	Power Play [Eddie & The Tide]
McMann]	Barnes] 47	Boys) [Lou Gramm]	To The Shock Of Miss Louise
	I Still Believe [Tim Cappello]		[Thomas Newman]

SOUNDTRACKS

DEBUT	PEAK	WKS	RIAA	CD	ARTIST — Album Title	Catalog	Sym	$	Label & Number
3/8/97	7	18	●	©435	**Lost Highway**		[V]	$10	Nothing 90090

Bill Pullman/Patricia Arquette/Balthazar Getty/Robert Blake

Apple Of Sodom [Marilyn Manson]
Driver Down [Trent Reznor]
Dub Driving [Angelo Badalamenti]
Eye [Smashing Pumpkins]
Fats Revisited [Angelo Badalamenti]
Fred & Renee Make Love [Angelo Badalamenti]
Fred's World [Angelo Badalamenti]
Haunting & Heartbreaking [Angelo Badalamenti]
Hierate Mich [Rammstein]
Hollywood Sunset [Barry Adamson]
I Put A Spell On You [Marilyn Manson]
I'm Deranged [David Bowie]
Insensatez [Antonio Carlos Jobim]
Mr. Eddy's Theme 1 [Barry Adamson]
Mr. Eddy's Theme 2 [Barry Adamson]
Perfect Drug [Nine Inch Nails] 46
Police [Angelo Badalamenti]
Rammstein [Rammstein]
Red Bats With Teeth [Angelo Badalamenti]
Something Wicked This Way Comes [Barry Adamson]
This Magic Moment [Lou Reed]
Videodrones; Questions [Trent Reznor]

| 2/3/73 | 58 | 21 | | ©436 | **Lost Horizon** | | [M] | $20 | Bell 1300 |

Peter Finch/Liv Ullmann/**Charles Boyer**/John Gielgud; mu/cd: **Burt Bacharach**; ly: Hal David

I Come To You
I Might Frighten Her Away
If I Could Go Back
Living Together, Growing Together
Lost Horizon [Shawn Phillips] 63
Question Me An Answer
Reflections
Share The Joy
Things I Will Not Miss
Where Knowledge Ends (Faith Begins)
World Is A Circle

| 4/18/98 | 107 | 4 | | ©437 | **Lost In Space** | | [I] | $10 | TVT Soundtrax 8180 |

Gary Oldman/William Hurt/Matt LeBlanc/Mimi Rogers/Heather Graham; cp/cd: Bruce Broughton

Bang On! [Propellerheads]
Busy Child [Crystal Method]
Everybody Needs A 303 [Fatboy Slim]
I'm Here...Another Planet [Juno Reactor & The Creatures]
Lost In Space [Space]
Lost In Space (Theme) [Apollo Four Forty]
Song For Penny [Death In Vegas]
Will & Penny's Theme [Apollo Four Forty]

| 6/7/97 | 88 | 4 | | ©438 | **Lost World: Jurassic Park, The** | | [I] | $10 | MCA Soundtrax 11628 |

Jeff Goldblum/Julianne Moore/Pete Postlethwaite/Arliss Howard; cp/cd: John Williams

Compys Dine
Finale and Jurassic Park Theme
Finding Camp Jurassic
Hammond's Plan
Hunt, The
Island Prologue
Lost World
Ludlow's Demise
Malcolm's Journey
Raptors Appear
Rescuing Sarah
Stegosaurus, The
Trek, The
Visitor In San Diego

| 5/6/00 | 45 | 12 | | ©439 | **Love & Basketball** | | [V] | $10 | Overbrook 9001 |

Omar Epps/Sanaa Lathan/Alfre Woodard/Dennis Haysbert

Complete Beloved [Black Eyed Peas]
Dance Tonight [Lucy Pearl] 36
Fool Of Me [Meshell Ndegéocello]
Holding Back The Years [Angie Stone]
I Like [Guy] 70
I Want To Be Your Man [Roger] 3
I'll Go [Donell Jones]
It Takes Two [Rob Base & DJ EZ Rock] 36
Love And Happiness [Al Green]
Lyte As A Rock [MC Lyte]
Soul Sista [Bilal]
Sweet Thing [Rufus feat. Chaka Khan] 5

| 3/29/97 | 16 | 32 | ▲ | ©440 | **Love Jones - The Music** | | [V] | $10 | Columbia 67917 |

Larenz Tate/Nia Long/Isaiah Washington/Lisa Nicole Carson

Can't Get Enough [Kenny Lattimore]
Girl [Cassie]
Hopeless [Dionne Farris]
I Got A Love Jones For You [Refugee Camp All-Stars]
I Like It [Brand New Heavies]
In A Sentimental Mood [Duke Ellington & John Coltrane]
In The Rain [Xscape]
Inside My Love [Trina Broussard]
Jelly, Jelly [Lincoln Center Jazz Orch.]
Never Enough [Groove Theory]
Rush Over [Marcus Miller & Me'Shell Ndegéocello]
Sumthin' Sumthin' [Maxwell]
Sweetest Thing [Refugee Camp All-Stars]
You Move Me [Cassandra Wilson]

| 8/28/71 | 172 | 6 | | 441 | **Love Machine, The** | | [I] | $20 | Scepter 595 |

Dyan Cannon/John Phillip Law/Robert Ryan/Jackie Cooper/David Hemmings; cp/cd: Artie Butler

Amanda [Dionne Warwicke] 83
Amanda And Robin In Love
Backstage: The Christie Lane Show
Farewell Amanda
He's Moving On (Theme) [Dionne Warwicke]
House Party, Part I & II
Love Clown Love
New Threads On Parade
White Fox
White Fox Returns

Love Me Or Leave Me - see DAY, Doris
Doris Day/James Cagney/Cameron Mitchell
Love Me Tender - see PRESLEY, Elvis
Elvis Presley ("Clint Reno")/Richard Egan/Debra Paget

| 1/2/71 | 2[6] | 39 | ● | 442 | **Love Story** | | [I] | $20 | Paramount 6002 |

Ali MacGraw/Ryan O'Neal/Ray Milland/John Marley; cp/cd: Francis Lai

Bozo Barrett
Christmas Trees
Concerto No. 3 In D Major (Allegro)
I Love You, Phil
Long Walk Home
Love Story, Theme From [Francis Lai] 31
Search For Jenny
Skating In Central Park
Snow Frolic
Sonata In F Major (Allegro)

Loving You - see PRESLEY, Elvis
Elvis Presley ("Deke Rivers")/Lizabeth Scott/Delores Hart

| 11/26/94 | 70 | 13 | ● | ©443 | **Low Down Dirty Shame, A** | | [V] | $10 | Hollywood 41536 |

Keenan Ivory Wayans/Charles S. Dutton/Jada Pinkett/Salli Richardson

Birthday Girl [Hi-Five]
Cray-Z [FU-Schnickens]
Down 4 Whateva [Nuttin' Nyce] 92
Front, Back & Side To Side [UGK]
Get The Girl, Grab The Money And Run [Souls Of Mischief]
Ghetto Style [Smooth]
Gotta Get Yo' Groove On [Tevin Campbell]
Homie, Lover, Friend [R. Kelly]
How's That [Keith Murray]
I Can Go Deep [Silk] 71
In Front Of The Kids [Extra Prolific]
Later On [Casual]
Let's Organize [Organized Konfusion]
Shame [Zhané] 28
Stroke You Up [Changing Faces]
Thing I Like [Aaliyah]
Turn It Up [Raja-Nee]
U Rong 4 That [Mz. Kilo]

Mack, The - see HUTCH, Willie
Max Julien/**Richard Pryor**/Don Gordon
Mackintosh & T.J. - see JENNINGS, Waylon
Roy Rogers/Clay O'Brien/Joan Hackett
Mad Dogs & Englishmen - see COCKER, Joe

| 7/1/95 | 164 | 1 | | ©444 | **Mad Love** | | [V] | $10 | Zoo 11111 |

Chris O'Donnell/Drew Barrymore/Matthew Lillard/Robert Nadir

As Long As You Hold Me [Kirsty MacColl]
Fallout [Fluorescein]
Glazed [Rocket from the Crypt]
Here Comes My Girl [Throneberry]
Icy Blue [7 Year Bitch]
Mockingbirds [Grant Lee Buffalo]
Mona Lisa Overdrive [Head Candy]
Scratch, The [7 Year Bitch]
Slowly, Slowly [Magnapop]
Ultra Anxiety (Teenage Style) [Madder Rose]

| 8/24/85 | 39 | 13 | | ©445 | **Mad Max Beyond Thunderdome** | | [I] | $12 | Capitol 12429 |

Mel Gibson/**Tina Turner**/Angelo Rossitto/Helen Buday/Bruce Spence; cp/cd: Maurice Jarre

Bartertown
Children, The
Coming Home
One Of The Living [Tina Turner] 15
We Don't Need Another Hero (Thunderdome) [Tina Turner] 2
We Don't Need Another Hero (Thunderdome) (instrumental)

| 6/19/93 | 196 | 2 | | ©446 | **Made In America** | | [V] | $10 | Elektra 61498 |

Whoopi Goldberg/Ted Danson/**Will Smith**/Nia Long/Paul Rodriguez

Colors Of Love [Lisa Fischer]
Dance Or Die [DJ Jazzy Jeff & The Fresh Prince]
Does He Do It Good [Keith Sweat & Silk]
Go Away [Gloria Estefan]
I Know I Don't Walk On Water [Laura Satterfield & Ephraim Lewis]
If You Need A Miracle [Ben E. King]
Made In America [Del Tha Funkee Homosapien]
Made In Love [Mark Isham]
Smoke On The Water [Deep Purple] 4
Stand [Y.T. Style]
What Is This? [Sergio Mendes]

DEBUT	PEAK	WKS	RIAA	CD	ARTIST — Album Title	Catalog	Sym	$	Label & Number

3/21/70 — 106 — 12 — 447 — Magic Christian, The .... [I] $30 Commonwealth 6004
Peter Sellers/**Ringo Starr**/Raquel Welch; cp/cd: Ken Thorne

Carry On To Tomorrow [Badfinger]	Hamlet Scene	Magic Christian Waltz
Come And Get It [Badfinger] 7	Hunting Scene	Newsreel Music March
Come And Get It (instrumental)	Lilli Marlene	Rock Of Ages [Badfinger]
Day In The Life	Mad About The Boy	

Something In The Air
[Thunderclap Newman] 37

Magical Mystery Tour - see BEATLES, The

Magnolia - see MANN, Aimee
Tom Cruise/William H. Macy/Jason Robards/Philip Seymour Hoffman

11/8/75+ — 19 — 26 — ©448 — Mahogany .... [I] $15 Motown 858
Diana Ross/Billy Dee Williams/Anthony Perkins/Beah Richards; cp/cd: Lee Holdridge

After You	**Mahogany (Do You Know Where**	Mahogany (Do You Know Where
Cat Fight	**You're Going To), Theme From**	You're Going To), Theme From
Erucu	[Diana Ross] 1	(instrumental)
Feeling Again		Mahogany Suite
Let's Go Back To Day One		My Hero Is A Gun

She's The Ideal Girl
Sweets (And Other Things)
Tracy
You Don't Ever Have To Be Alone

Main Event, The - see STREISAND, Barbra
Barbra Streisand/Ryan O'Neal/Paul Sand/Whitman Mayo/Rory Calhoun

12/5/92 — 130 — 3 — ©449 — Malcolm X .... [V] $10 Qwest 45130
Denzel Washington/Angela Bassett/Albert Hall/Spike Lee/Delroy Lindo

Alabama [John Coltrane]	Big Stuff [Billie Holiday]	**Revolution** [Arrested
Arabesque Cookie [Duke Elllington]	Don't Cry Baby [Erskine Hawkins]	Development] 90
Azure [Ella Fitzgerald]	Flying Home [Lionel Hampton]	Roll 'Em Pete [Joe Turner]
Beans And Cornbread [Louis	My Prayer [Ink Spots]	**Shotgun** [Jr. Walker & The
Jordan]		All-Stars] 4

Someday We'll Be Free [Aretha
Franklin]
That Lucky Old Sun [Ray
Charles] 20

11/4/95 — 151 — 2 — ©450 — Mallrats .... [V] $10 MCA Soundtrax 11294
Shannen Doherty/Jason Lee/Jeremy London/Michael Rooker

Broken [Belly]	Guilty [All]	Mission Impossible #1
Bubbles [Bush]	Hated It [Thrush Hermit]	Mission Impossible #2
Build Me Up Buttercup [Goops]	Kryptonite Condoms	Post Coital Techno Boogie
Cousin Walter	Last Words	Seventeen [Sponge]
Cruise Your New Baby Fly Self	Line Up [Elastica]	Smoke Two Joints [Sublime]
[Girls Against Boys]	Love and Sharks	Social [Squirtgun]
Freeing One's Mind	Mallrats [Wax]	Stoned [Silverchair]

Susanne [Weezer]
Taken With A Grain Of Salt
That Ski Trip
Very Uncomfortable Place
Web In Front [Archers Of Loaf]

3/14/92 — 50 — 14 — ● — ©451 — Mambo Kings, The .... [F-V] $10 Elektra 61240
Armand Assante/Antonio Banderas/Cathy Moriarty/Maruschka Detmers

Accidental Mambo [Mambo	Cuban Pete [Tito Puente]	Melao De Cana (Moo La Lah) [Celia
All-Stars]	Guantanamera [Celia Cruz]	Cruz]
Beautiful Maria Of My Soul [Mambo	La Dicha Mia [Celia Cruz]	Para Los Rumberos [Tito Puente]
All-Stars]	Mambo Caliente [Arturo Sandoval]	Perfidia [Linda Ronstadt]
Como Fue [Beny More]		Quiereme Mucho [Linda Ronstadt]

Ran Kan Kan [Tito Puente]
Sunny Ray [Mambo All-Stars]
Tanga, Rumba-Afro-Cubana
[Mambo All-Stars]
Tea For Two [Mambo All-Stars]

4/13/74 — 196 — 3 — 452 — Mame .... [M] $15 Warner 2773
Lucille Ball/Beatrice Arthur/Bruce Davison/Robert Preston; sw: Jerry Herman

Bosom Buddies	It's Today	Main Title
Gooch's Song	Letter, The	Mame
If He Walked Into My Life	Loving You	Man In The Moon

My Best Girl
Open A New Window
We Need A Little Christmas

11/19/66+ — 10 — 93 — ● — 453 — Man And A Woman, A .... [I] $25 United Artists 5147
Jean-Louis Trintignant/Anouk Aimee/Simone Paris; cp/cd: Francis Lai

In Our Shadow	124 Miles An Hour	Stronger Than Us
Man And A Woman	Samba Saravah	Today It's You

12/9/72+ — 76 — 17 — ©454 — Man Of La Mancha .... [M] $20 United Artists 9906
Peter O'Toole/Sophia Loren/James Coco; mu: Mitch Leigh; ly: Joe Darion; cd: Laurence Rosenthal

Aldonza	Golden Helmet Of Mambrino	Impossible Dream (The Quest)
Barber's Song (medley)	(medley)	It's All The Same
Dubbing, The	I Really Like Him	Life As It Really Is (Soliloquy)
Dulcinea	I'm Only Thinking Of Him	(medley)

Little Bird, Little Bird
Little Gossip
Man Of La Mancha (I, Don Quixote)
Psalm, The

1/1/00 — 109 — 7 — ©455 — Man On The Moon .... [V] $10 Warner 47483
Jim Carrey/Danny DeVito/Courtney Love (**Hole**)/Paul Giamatti

Andy Gets Fired	Lynne & Andy	Miracle
Angela (Theme From Taxi) [Bob	**Man On The Moon** [R.E.M.] 30	One More Song For You [Andy
James]	Man On The Moon [Orchestral]	Kaufman]
Great Beyond [R.E.M.] 57	Mighty Mouse Theme (Here I Come	Rose Marie [Andy Kaufman]
I Will Survive [Tony Clifton]	To Save The Day) [Sandpipers]	This Friendly World [R.E.M., Andy &
Kiss You All Over [Exile] 1	Milk & Cookies	Tony]

Tony Thrown Out

3/24/56 — 2⁴ — 17 — 456 — Man With The Golden Arm, The .... [I] $50 Decca 78257
Frank Sinatra/Eleanor Parker/Kim Novak/Darren McGavin; cp/cd: Elmer Bernstein

Audition	Cure, The	Frankie Machine
Breakup	Desperation	Molly
Clark Steet	Fix, The	Sunday Morning

Zosh

7/28/79 — 94 — 11 — ©457 — Manhattan .... [I] $12 Columbia 36020
Woody Allen/Diane Keaton/**Meryl Streep**/Mariel Hemingway; cp: **George Gershwin**; cd: **Zubin Mehta**

Blue, Blue, Blue (medley)	He Loves And She Loves (medley)	Love Is Sweeping The Country
Bronco Busters (medley)	I've Got A Crush On You (medley)	(medley)
But Not For Me (medley)	Land Of The Gay Caballero	Mine
Do, Do, Do (medley)	(medley)	Oh, Lady Be Good (medley)
Embraceable You (medley)	Love Is Here To Stay	Rhapsody In Blue

'S Wonderful (medley)
Someone To Watch Over Me
(medley)
Strike Up The Band (medley)
Sweet And Low-Down (medley)

10/1/88 — 197 — 3 — ©458 — Married To The Mob .... [V] $10 Reprise 25763
Michelle Pfeiffer/Matthew Modine/Dean Stockwell/Mercedes Ruehl/Alec Baldwin

Bizarre Love Triangle [New Order]	Jump In The River [Sinéad	Suspicion Of Love [Chris Isaak]
Devil Does Your Dog Bite? [Tom	O'Connor]	Time Bums [Ziggy Marley & The
Tom Club]	Liar, Liar [Debbie Harry]	Melody Makers]
Goodbye Horses [Q. Lazzarus]	Queen Of Voudou [Voodooist Corp.]	Too Far Gone [Feelies]

You Don't Miss Your Water [Brian
Eno]

DEBUT	PEAK	WKS	RIAA	CD	ARTIST — Album Title	Catalog	Sym	$	Label & Number

10/3/64+ ❶¹⁴ 114 ● ©459 **Mary Poppins** **[M]** **$20** Buena Vista 4026

Julie Andrews/Dick Van Dyke/David Tomlinson/Glynis Johns; sw: Richard M. Sherman and Robert B. Sherman; cd: Irwin Kostal

British Bank	Jolly Holiday	Perfect Nanny
Chim Chim Cheree	Let's Go Fly A Kite	Sister Suffragette
Feed The Birds (Tuppence A Bag)	Life I Lead	Spoonful Of Sugar
Fidelity Fiduciary Bank	Man Has Dreams	Stay Awake
I Love To Laugh	Pavement Artist	Step In Time

Super-cali-fragil-istic-expi-ali-doci ous *[Julie Andrews & Dick Van Dyke]* 66

8/4/73 141 8 460 **Mary Poppins** .... **[R]** **$15** Buena Vista 5005

see above album for tracks; new blue cover features new artwork

7/11/70 120 16 ©461 **M*A*S*H** **[I]** **$20** Columbia 3520

Elliott Gould/Donald Southerland/Tom Skerritt/Sally Kellerman/Robert Duvall; cp: Johnny Mandel

Duke And Hawkeye Arrive At M.A.S.H.	Going Home	M*A*S*H Theme *[Ahmad Jamal]*
Football Game	Hot Lips Shows Her True Colors	Moments To Remember
	Major Houlihan And Major Burns	Operating Theater

Painless' Suicide, Funeral And Resurrection

8/20/94 80 12 ©462 **Mask, The** .... **[V]** **$10** Chaos 66207

Jim Carrey/Peter Riegert/Peter Greene/Amy Yasbeck/Richard Jeni

Bounce Around *[Tony Toni Toné]*	Hey Pachuco *[Royal Crown Revue]*	Let The Good Times Roll *[Fishbone]*
Cuban Pete *[Jim Carrey]*	Hi De Ho *[K7]*	Straight Up *[Brian Setzer Orchestra]*
Gee Baby, Ain't I Good To You *[Susan Boyd]*	**(I Could Only) Whisper Your Name** *[Harry Connick, Jr.]* 67	This Business Of Love *[Domino]*
		Who's That Man *[Xscape]*

You Would Be My Baby *[Vanessa Williams]*

8/1/98 87 6 ©463 **Mask Of Zorro, The** .... **[I]** **$10** Sony Classical 60627

Antonio Banderas/Anthony Hopkins/Catherine Zeta-Jones; cp/cd: James Horner

Confession, The	Fencing Lesson	Plaza Of Execution
Diego's Goodbye	I Want To Spend My Lifetime Loving You *[Marc Anthony & Tina Arena]*	Ride, The
Elena And Esperanza	Mine (Montero's Vision)	Stealing The Map
Elena's Truth		Tornado In The Barracks

Zorro's Theme

4/17/99 7 55 ▲ ©464 **Matrix, The** **[V]** **$10** Maverick 47390

Keanu Reeves/Laurence Fishburne/Carrie-Anne Moss/Hugo Weaving

Bad Blood *[Ministry]*	Leave You Far Behind *[Lunatic Calm]*	My Own Summer (Shove It) *[Deftones]*
Clubbed To Death *[Rob D]*	Look To Your Orb For The Warning *[Monster Magnet]*	Prime Audio Soup *[Meat Beat Manifesto]*
Dragula *[Rob Zombie]*	Mindfields *[Prodigy]*	Rock Is Dead *[Marilyn Manson]*
Du Hast *[Rammstein]*		

Spybreak! (Short One) *[Propellerheads]*
Ultrasonic Sound *[Hive]*
Wake Up *[Rage Against The Machine]*

6/4/94 35 16 ● ©465 **Maverick** .... **[V]** **$10** Atlantic 82595

Mel Gibson/Jodie Foster/James Garner/Graham Greene/James Coburn

Amazing Grace *[Maverick Choir]*	Maverick *[Restless Heart]*	Ride Gambler Ride *[Randy Newman]*
Dream On Texas Ladies *[John Michael Montgomery]*	Ophelia *[Vince Gill]*	Solitary Travelers *[Hal Ketchum]*
Good Run Of Bad Luck *[Clint Black]*	Rainbow Down The Road *[Patty Loveless/Radney Foster]*	Something Already Gone *[Carlene Carter]*
Ladies Love Outlaws *[Confederate Railroad]*	Renegades, Rebels And Rogues *[Tracy Lawrence]*	

You Don't Mess Around With Me *[Waylon Jennings]*

Maximum Overdrive - see AC/DC

Emilio Estevez/Pat Hingle/Laura Harrington/Yeardley Smith

McVicar - see DALTREY, Roger

Roger Daltrey/Adam Faith/Cheryl Campbell

7/8/00 134 4 ©466 **Me, Myself & Irene** .... **[V]** **$10** Elektra 62512

Jim Carrey/Renee Zellweger/Robert Forster

Any Major Dude Will Tell You *[Wilco]*	Breakout *[Foo Fighters]*	Do It Again *[Smash Mouth]*
Bad Sneakers *[Push Stars]*	Can't Find The Time To Tell You *[Hootie & The Blowfish]*	Only A Fool Would Say That *[Ivy]*
Barrytown *[Ben Folds Five]*	Deep Inside Of You *[Third Eye Blind]*	Razor Boy *[Billy Goodrum]*
Bodhisattva *[Brian Setzer Orch.]*		Reelin' In The Years *[Marvelous 3]*
		Strange Condition *[Pete Yorn]*

Totalimmortal *[Offspring]*
Where He Can Hide *[Tom Wolfe]*
World Ain't Slowin' Down *[Ellis Paul]*

8/18/79 170 5 467 **Meatballs** .... **[V]** **$12** RSO 3056

Bill Murray/Chris Makepeace/Kate Lynch/Jack Blum/Harvey Atkin; mu: Elmer Bernstein

Are You Ready For The Summer? *[Camp North Star Kids Chorus]*	**Good Friend** *[Mary McGregor]* 39	Moondust *[Terry Black]*
C.I.T. Song	**Makin' It** *[David Naughton]* 5	Olympiad
	Meatballs *[Rick Dees]*	Rudy And Tripper

Rudy Wins The Race

7/19/97 ❶² 43 ▲³ ©468 **Men In Black - The Album** **[V]** **$10** Columbia 68169

Tommy Lee Jones/Will Smith/Linda Fiorentino/Vincent D'Onofrio/Rip Torn

Chanel No. Fever *[De La Soul]*	I'm Feelin' You *[Ginuwine]*	M.I.B. Main Theme *[Danny Elfman]*
Dah Dee Dah (Sexy Thing) *[Alicia Keys]*	Just Cruisin' *[Will Smith]*	Make You Happy *[Trey Lorenz]*
Erotik City *[Emoja]*	Killing Time *[Destiny's Child]*	Men In Black *[Will Smith]*
Escobar '97 *[Nas]*	M.I.B. Closing Theme *[Danny Elfman]*	'Notic, The *[Roots]*
		Same Ol' Thing *[Tribe Called Quest]*

Some Cow Fonque (More Tea, Vicar?) *[Buckshot LeFonque]*
Waiting For Love *[3T]*
We Just Wanna Party With You *[Snoop Doggy Dogg]*

6/12/93 11 35 ▲ ©469 **Menace II Society** .... **[V]** **$10** Jive 41509

Tyrin Turner/Larenz Tate/Jada Pinkett/Bill Duke/Charles S. Dutton

All Over A Ho *[Mz. Kilo]*	Guerillas Ain't Gangstas *[Da Lench Mob]*	"P" Is Still Free *[Boogie Down Productions]*
Can't Fuck Wit A Nigga *[DJ Quik]*	Lick Dem Muthaphuckas *[Brand Nubian]*	Packin' A Gun *[Ant Banks]*
Death Becomes You *[Pete Rock & C.L. Smooth]*	Only The Strong Survive *[Too $hort]*	Pocket Full Of Stone *[UGK]*
		Stop Lookin' At Me *[Cutthroats]*

Streiht Up Menace *[MC Eiht]* 72
Top Of The World *[Kenya Gruv]*
Trigga Gots No Heart *[Spice 1]*
Unconditional Love *[Hi-Five]* 92
You Been Played *[Smooth]*

1/12/91 65 24 ©470 **Mermaids** .... **[O-V]** **$10** Geffen 24310

Cher/Bob Hoskins/Winona Ryder/Christina Ricci

Baby I'm Yours *[Cher]*	**It's My Party** *[Lesley Gore]* 1	Love Is Strange *[Mickey & Sylvia]* 11
Big Girls Don't Cry *[4 Seasons]* 1	**Johnny Angel** *[Shelley Fabares]* 1	**Shoop Shoop Song (It's In His Kiss)** *[Cher]* 33
If You Wanna Be Happy *[Jimmy Soul]* 1	**Just One Look** *[Doris Troy]* 10	

Sleep Walk *[Santo & Johnny]* 1
You've Really Got A Hold On Me *[Miracles]* 8

2/27/99 39 9 ©471 **Message In A Bottle** .... **[V]** **$10** Atlantic 83163

Kevin Costner/Robin Wright Penn/John Savage/Paul Newman

Carolina *[Sheryl Crow]*	I Love You *[Sarah McLachlan]*	Message In A Bottle *[Gabriel Yared]*
Dear Catherine *[Gabriel Yared]*	I Will Know Your Love *[Beth Nielsen Chapman]*	No Mermaid *[Sinéad Lohan]*
Don't *[Yve.n.Adam]*	I'll Still Love You Then *[Anna Nordell]*	One More Time *[Laura Pausini]*
Fallen Angels *[Marc Cohn]*	Let Me Let Go *[Faith Hill]*	Only Lonely *[Hootie & The Blowfish]*
I Could Not Ask For More *[Edwin McCain]* 37		Somewhere In The Middle *[Nine Sky Wonder]*

Theresa & Garret *[Gabriel Yared]*
What Will I Do *[Clannad]*

DEBUT	PEAK	WKS	RIAA	CD	ARTIST — Album Title	Catalog	Sym	$	Label & Number

8/25/84 **110** 13 ©472 **Metropolis**.. [V] **$12** Columbia 39526
Gustav Froelich/Brigitte Helm; 1926 movie restored and presented with a contemporary score; cp: **Giorgio Moroder**

Blood From A Stone [Cycle V] | Here She Comes [Bonnie Tyler] 76 | Love Kills [Freddie Mercury] 69 | What's Going On [Adam Ant]
Cage Of Freedom [Jon Anderson] | Here's My Heart [Pat Benatar] | Machines [Giorgio Moroder]
Destruction [Loverboy] | Legend Of Babel [Giorgio Moroder] | On Your Own [Billy Squier]

1/11/97 **53** 16 ©473 **Michael**.. [V] **$10** Revolution 24666
John Travolta/Andie MacDowell/William Hurt/Bob Hoskins/Jean Stapleton

Bright Side Of The Road [Van Morrison] | I Don't Care If You Love Me Anymore [Mavericks] | Spider And The Fly [Kenny Wayne Shepherd] | What A Wonderful World [Willie Nelson]
Chain Of Fools [Aretha Franklin] 2 | Love God (And Everyone Else) [Al Green] | Spirit In The Sky [Norman Greenbaum] 3
Feels Like Home [Bonnie Raitt] | Sittin' By The Side Of The Road [Andie MacDowell] | Through Your Hands [Don Henley]
Heaven Is My Home [Randy Newman]

8/9/69 **19** 57 ● ©474 **Midnight Cowboy**.. [I+V] **$20** United Artists 5198
Dustin Hoffman/Jon Voight/Sylvia Miles/Brenda Vaccaro/Barnard Hughes; mu: John Barry

Everybody's Talkin' [Nilsson] 6 | Fun City | Jungle Gym At The Zoo [Elephants Memory] | Old Man Willow [Elephants Memory]
Famous Myth [Groop] | He Quit Me Man [Leslie Miller] | Midnight Cowboy | Science Fiction
Florida Fantasy | Joe Buck Rides Again | | Tears And Joys [Groop]

11/25/78+ **59** 26 ©475 **Midnight Express**.. [I] **$12** Casablanca 7114
Brad Davis/John Hurt/Randy Quaid/Bo Hopkins; cp/cd: **Giorgio Moroder**

Cacaphoney | Istanbul Blues | Love's Theme | Wheel, The
Chase [Giorgio Moroder] 33 | Istanbul Opening | (Theme From) Midnight Express

12/13/97 **161** 5 ©476 **Midnight In The Garden Of Good And Evil**................................. [V] **$10** Warner 46829
Kevin Spacey/John Cusack/Alison Eastwood/Lady Chablis/Jude Law

Ac-Cent-Tchu-Ate The Positive [Clint Eastwood] | Dream [Brad Mehldau] | Laura [Kevin Mahogany] | Too Marvelous For Words [Joe Williams]
Autumn Leaves [Paula Cole] | Fools Rush In (Where Angels Fear To Tread) [Rosemary Clooney] | Midnight Sun [Diana Krall]
Come Rain Or Come Shine [Alison Eastwood] | I Wanna Be Around [Tony Bennett] 14 | Skylark [K.D. Lang]
Days Of Wine And Roses [Cassandra Wilson] | I'm An Old Cowhand (From The Rio Grande) [Joshua Redman] | That Old Black Magic [Kevin Spacey]
| | This Time The Dream's On Me [Alison Krauss]

Mighty Ducks - see D2: The Mighty Ducks

7/8/95 **98** 6 ©477 **Mighty Morphin Power Rangers: The Movie**.............................. [V] **$10** Atlantic 82777
Karan Ashley/Johnny Yong Bosch/Steve Cardenas

Are You Ready?! [Devo] | Firebird [Graeme Revell] | Higher Ground [Red Hot Chili Peppers] | SenSurround [They Might Be Giants]
Ayeyaiyai (Alpha Song) [Power Jet] | Free Ride [Dan Hartman] | Kung Fu Dancing [Fun Tomas Feat. Carl Douglas] | Trouble [Shampoo]
Cross My Line [Aaron Waters (The Mighty Raw)] | Go Go Power Rangers [Power Rangers Orchestra] | Power, The [Snap] 2
Dreams [Van Halen] 7

Mike's Murder - see JACKSON, Joe
Debra Winger/Mark Keyloun/Darrell Larson/Paul Winfield

4/1/00 **104** 2 ©478 **Million Dollar Hotel, The**.. [V] **$10** Interscope 542395
Jeremy Davies/Milla Jovovich/Jimmy Smits/Peter Stormare/Mel Gibson

Amsterdam Blue (Cortege) [Jon Hassell] | Dancin' Shoes [Bono & The MDH Band] | Funny Face [MDH Band] | Stateless [U2]
Anarchy In The USA [Tito Larriva & The MDH Band] | Ground Beneath Her Feet [U2] | Tom Tom's Dream [MDH Band]
Bathtub [MDH Band] | Falling At Your Feet [Bono & Daniel Lanois] | Never Let Me Go [Bono & The MDH Band] | Tom Tom's Room [Brad Mehldau]
| First Time [U2] | Satellite Of Love [Milla Jovovich]

1/13/01 **30ˣ** 2 ©479 **Miracle On 34th Street**.. [X-V] **$10** Arista 44980
Richard Attenborough/Elizabeth Perkins/Dylan McDermott/J.T. Walsh

Bellevue Carol | It's Beginning To Look A Lot Like Christmas [Dionne Warwick] | Santa Claus Is Back In Town [Elvis Presley] | Song For A Winter's Night [Sarah McLachlan]
Have Yourself A Merry Little Christmas [Kenny G] | Jingle Bells [Natalie Cole] | Santa Claus Is Comin' To Town [Ray Charles]
| Joy To The World [Aretha Franklin]

11/30/96 **16** 22 ▲ ©480 **Mirror Has Two Faces, The**.. [I] **$10** Columbia 67887
Barbra Streisand/Jeff Bridges/Pierce Brosnan; cp: **Marvin Hamlisch** & Barbra Streisand; cd: **Marvin Hamlisch**

Ad? | Got Any Scotch? | Mirror, The | Rose Dumps Alex
Alex Hurts Rose | Greg Claims Rose | My Intentions? | Rose Leaves Greg
All Of My Life [Barbra Streisand] | Greg Falls For Rose | Picnic In The Park | Rose Sees Rose
Apology, The (medley) | I Finally Found Someone [Barbra Streisand & Bryan Adams] 8 | Power Inside Of Me [Richard Marx] | Ruby
Dating Montage | In A Sentimental Mood | In Questa Reggia (medley) | Try A Little Tenderness [David Sanborn]
Funny Kind Of Proposal | Main Title (medley) | Nessun Dorma (medley) | You Picked Me!
Going Back To Mom | | Rocking In The Chair

2/21/87 **132** 13 ● ©481 **Mission, The**.. [I] **$12** Virgin 90567
Robert DeNiro/Jeremy Irons/Liam Neeson/Aidan Quinn; cp/cd: Ennio Morricone

Alone | Climb | Mission, The | River
Asuncion | Falls | On Earth As It Is In Heaven | Sword, The
Ave Maria Guarani | Gabriel's Oboe | Penance | Te Deum Guarani
Brothers | Guarani | Refusal | Vita Nostra
Carlotta | Miserere | Remorse

6/1/96 **16** 14 ● ©482 **Mission: Impossible**.. [V] **$10** Mother 531682
Tom Cruise/Jon Voight/Henry Czerny/Emmanuelle Beart/Jean Reno

Alright | Impossible Mission [Danny Elfman] | On & On [Longpigs] | Trouble [Danny Elfman]
Claire [Danny Elfman] | Mission: Impossible Theme (Mission Accomplished) [Adam Clayton & Larry Mullen] | So [Salt] | Weak [Skunk Anansie]
Dreams [Cranberries] | | Spying Glass [Massive Attack] | You, Me And World War III [Gavin Friday]
Headphones [Björk] | No Government [Nicolette] | Theme From Mission: Impossible [Larry Mullen & Adam Clayton] 7
I Spy [Pulp]

5/27/00 **2¹** 32 ▲ ©483 **Mission: Impossible 2**.. [V] **$10** Hollywood 62244
Tom Cruise/Dougray Scott/Thandie Newton/Ving Rhames/Anthony Hopkins

Alone [Buckcherry] | Have A Cigar [Foo Fighters & Brian May] | Mission 2000 [Chris Cornell] | Scum Of The Earth [Rob Zombie]
Backwards [Apartment 26] | I Disappear [Metallica] 76 | My Kinda Scene [Powderfinger] | Take A Look Around (Theme From "M:I-2") [Limp Bizkit]
Carnival [Tori Amos] | Immune [Tinfed] | Nyah [Hans Zimmer] | They Came In [Butthole Surfers]
Going Down [Godsmack] | Karma [Diffuser] | Rocket Science [Pimps] | What U Lookin' At? [Uncle Kracker]

Mo' Better Blues - see MARSALIS, Branford
Denzel Washington/Spike Lee/Wesley Snipes/Giancarlo Esposito

SOUNDTRACKS

DEBUT	PEAK	WKS	RIAA	CD	ARTIST — Album Title	Catalog	Sym	$	Label & Number

7/11/92 · **6** · 19 ▲ · ©484 **Mo' Money** .... [V] **$10** Perspective 1004
Damon Wayans/Marlon Wayans/Stacey Dash/Joe Santos/John Diehl

Best Things In Life Are Free [Luther Vandross & Janet Jackson] **10** · Brother Will [Harlem Yacht Club] · **Forever Love** [Color Me Badd] **15** · Get Off My Back [Public Enemy] · I Adore You [Caron Wheeler] · Ice Cream Dream [MC Lyte] · Job Ain't Nuthin' But Work [Big Daddy Kane] · Joy [Sounds Of Blackness] · Let's Get Together (So Groovy Now) [Krush] · Let's Just Run Away [Johnny Gill] · **Money Can't Buy You Love** [Ralph Tresvant] **54** · My Dear [Mint Condition] · New Style [Jam & Lewis]

4/17/99 · **184** · 1 · ©485 **Mod Squad, The** .... [V] **$10** Elektra 62364
Claire Danes/Omar Epps/Giovanni Ribisi/Dennis Farina/Josh Brolin

Action Speaks Louder Than Words [Chocolate Milk] **69** · Alarm Call [Björk] · Can't Find My Way Home [Alana Davis] · Collage [Breeders] · Ends [Everlast] · Goin' Crazy [SX10] · Hello It's Me [Gerald Levert] · Here But I'm Gone (Part II) [Curtis Mayfield] · Keep A Lid On Things [Crash Test Dummies] · Messin' Around [Ivan Matias] · My Favorite Things [Skerik & The Keefus Trio] · Party Is Goin' On Over Here [Busta Rhymes] · You're An Artist [Morphine]

7/20/63 · **15** · 74 · ©486 **Mondo Cane** .... [I] **$25** United Artists 5105
documentary depicting various cultures around the world; cp/cd: Riz Ortolani and Nino Oliviero

Breakfast At The Colony (medley) · Cargo Cult (Finale) · China Tarantella · Damned Island · Dog Heat · Festival Of The Bull · Fisherman Of Ragjput (medley) · Free Way · Girls And Sailors · Hong Kong Cha Cha Cha (medley) · House Of Death · Last Flight · Models In Blue · More · Pergatory · Repabhan Street · Sharks, The (medley)

9/6/97 · **37** · 17 ● · ©487 **Money Talks - The Album** .... [V] **$10** Arista 18975
Chris Tucker/Charlie Sheen/Heather Locklear/Paul Sorvino

Avenues [Refugee Camp All Stars] **35** · Back In You Again [Rick James] · Dream, A [Mary J. Blige] · Everyday [Angie Stone & Devox] · Feel So Good [Mase] **5** · Keep It Bubblin' [Brand Nubian] · Money Talks [Lil' Kim] · My Everything [Barry White & Faith Evans] · No Way Out [Puff Daddy] · Penetration [Next & Naughty By Nature] · Real Thing [Lisa Stansfield] · Teaching, The [Me'Shell Ndegéocello] · Tell Me How You Want It [SWV] · **Thing Just Ain't The Same** [Deborah Cox] **56** · **You're The First, The Last, My Everything** [Barry White] **2**

Monterey Pop - see HENDRIX, Jimi / REDDING, Otis

Monty Python & The Holy Grail - see MONTY PYTHON
Graham Chapman/John Cleese/Eric Idle/Carol Cleveland

8/18/79 · **159** · 4 · ©488 **Moonraker** .... [I] **$12** United Artists 971
Roger Moore/Lois Chiles/Richard Kiel/Michel Lonsdale; cp/cd: John Barry

Boat Chase (medley) · Bond Arrives In Rio (medley) · Bond Lured To Pyramid · Bond Smells A Rat · Cable Car (medley) · Centrifuge (medley) · Corrinne Put Down (medley) · End Title [Shirley Bassey] · Flight Into Space · Main Title [Shirley Bassey] · Miss Goodhead Meets Bond · Snake Fight (medley) · Space Lazer Battle

More - see PINK FLOYD
Mimsi Farmer/Klaus Grunberg

8/11/79 · **84** · 12 · 489 **More American Graffiti** .... [O-V] **$20** MCA 11006 [2]
Ron Howard/Candy Clark/Bo Hopkins/Cindy Williams

Ballad Of The Green Berets [SSGT Barry Sadler] **1** · **Beechwood 4-5789** [Marvelettes] **17** · **Cool Jerk** [Capitols] **7** · Hang On Sloopy [McCoys] **1** · **Heat Wave** [Martha & The Vandellas] **4** · I Feel Like I'm Fixin' To Die Rag [Country Joe & The Fish] · I'm A Man [Doug Sahm] · **Just Like A Woman** [Bob Dylan] **33** · **Like A Rolling Stone** [Bob Dylan] **2** · Moon River [Andy Williams] · **Mr. Lonely** [Bobby Vinton] **1** · **Mr. Tambourine Man** [Byrds] **1** · My Boyfriend's Back [Angels] **1** · **My Guy** [Mary Wells] **1** · **96 Tears** [? (Question Mark) & The Mysterians] **1** · **Pipeline** [Chantay's] **4** · Respect [Aretha Franklin] **1** · Season Of The Witch [Donovan] · **She's Not There** [Zombies] **2** · Since I Fell For You [Lenny Welch] **4** · **Sounds Of Silence** [Simon & Garfunkel] **1** · **Stop! In The Name Of Love** [Supremes] **1** · Strange Brew (Cream) · When A Man Loves A Woman [Percy Sledge] **1**

More Songs For Sleepless Nights - see VARIOUS ARTISTS COMPILATIONS

9/9/95 · **10** · 46 ▲ · ©490 **Mortal Kombat** .... [V] **$10** TVT 6110
Christopher Lambert/Linden Ashby/Robin Shou/Bridgette Wilson

Blood & Fire [Type O Negative] · Burn [Sister Machine Gun] · Control [Traci Lords] · Demon Warriors/Final Kombat · Goodbye [Gravity Kills] · Goro Vs. Art · Halcyon + On + On [Orbital] · I Reject [Bile] · Invisible, The [Geezer (GZR)] · Juke-Joint Jezebel [KMFDM] · Taste Of Things To Come · Theme From Mortal Kombat [Utah Saints] · Theme From Mortal Kombat [Immortals] · Twist The Knife (Slowly) [Napalm Death] · Unlearn [Psykosonik] · What U See/We All Bleed Red [Mutha's Day Out] · Zero Signal [Fear Factory]

11/15/97 · **69** · 13 · ©491 **Mortal Kombat: Annihilation** .... [V] **$10** TVT Soundtrax 8200
Robin Shou/Talisa Soto/Brian Thompson/Sandra Hess/James Remar

Almost Honest [Megadeth] · Anomaly (Calling Your Name) [Libra Presents Taylor] · Back On A Mission [Cirrus] · Brutality [Urban Voodoo] · Conga Fury [Juno Reactor] · Death Is The Only Way Out [Joseph Bishara] · Engel [Rammstein] · Fire [Scooter] · Genius [Pitchshifter] · I Won't Lie Down [Face To Face] · Leave U Far Behind [Lunatic Calm] · Megalomaniac [KMFDM] · Panik Kontrol [Psykosonik] · Ready Or Not [Manbreak] · Theme From Mortal Kombat [Kasz & Beal] · Theme From Mortal Kombat (Encounter The Ultimate) [Immortals] · Two Telephone Calls And An Air Raid [Shaun Imrei] · We Have Explosive [Future Sound Of London] · X-Squad [George Clinton]

5/26/01 · **3** · 19 ↑▲ · ©492 **Moulin Rouge** .... [V] **$10** Interscope 493035
Nicole Kidman/Ewan McGregor/John Leguizamo/Jim Broadbent

Because We Can [Fatboy Slim] · Children Of The Revolution [Bono/Gavin Friday/Maurice Seezer] · Come What May [Nicole Kidman & Ewan McGregor] · Complainte De La Butte [Rufus Wainwright] · Diamond Dogs [Beck] · El Tango De Roxanne [Ewan McGregor/Jose Feliciano/Jacek Koman] · Elephant Love Medley [Nicole Kidman/Ewan McGregor/Jamie Allen] · Hindi Sad Diamonds [Nicole Kidman/John Leguizamo/Alka Yagnik] · **Lady Marmalade** [Christina Aguilera/Lil' Kim/Mya/Pink] **1** · Nature Boy [David Bowie] · Nature Boy [David Bowie & Massive Attack] · One Day I'll Fly Away [Nicole Kidman] · Rhythm Of The Night [Valeria] · Sparkling Diamonds [Nicole Kidman/Jim Broadbent/Caroline O'Connor/Natalie Mendoza/Lara Mulcahy] · Your Song [Ewan McGregor & Allessandro Safina]

DEBUT	PEAK	WKS	RIAA	CD	ARTIST — Album Title	Catalog	Sym	$	Label & Number

2/10/96 **42** 15 ● ©493 **Mr. Holland's Opus** .... [O-V] **$10** London 529508

Richard Dreyfuss/Glenne Headly/Jay Thomas/Olympia Dukakis

American Symphony (Mr. Holland's Opus) [London Metropolitan Orchestra]	I Got A Woman [Ray Charles]	1-2-3 [Len Barry] 2	**Uptight (Everything's Alright)** [Stevie Wonder] 3
Beautiful Boy (Darling Boy) [John Lennon & Yoko Ono]	**Imagine** [John Lennon & The Plastic Ono Band] 3	**Pretender, The** [Jackson Browne] 58	**Visions Of A Sunset** [Shawn Stockman] 45
Cole's Song [Julian Lennon]	**Keep On Running** [Spencer Davis Group] 76	Someone To Watch Over Me [Julia Fordham]	
	Lover's Concerto [Toys] 2		

Mrs. Brown, You've Got A Lovely Daughter - see HERMAN'S HERMITS

Herman's Hermits/Stanley Holloway/Mona Washbourne

6/20/98 **24** 23 ● ©494 **Mulan** .... [M] **$10** Walt Disney 60631

animated movie, voices by Ming-Na Wen/**Eddie Murphy**/Harvey Fierstein/B.D. Wong; mu: **Matthew Wilder**; ly: David Zippel; cp/cd: Jerry Goldsmith

Attack At The Wall	Girl Worth Fighting For	I'll Make A Man Out Of You	Reflection (Pop Version)
Blossoms	Honor To Us All	Mulan's Decision	Suite From Mulan
Burned-Out Village	Huns Attack	Reflection	True To Your Heart

12/26/92 **189** 1 ©495 **Muppet Christmas Carol, The** .... [X-M] **$10** Jim Henson 30017

Michael Caine/Brian Henson/Frank Oz; sw: **Paul Williams** and Miles Goodman

Bless Us All	Christmas Scat	One More Sleep 'Til Christmas	When Love Is Gone (cast version)
Chairman Of The Board	Fozziwig's Party	Room In Your Heart	When Love Is Gone [Martina McBride]
Christmas Future	Good King Wenceslas	Scrooge	
Christmas Morning	It Feels Like Christmas	Thankful Heart	
Christmas Past	Marley And Marley	When Love Is Found (medley)	

7/21/79 **32** 34 ● ©496 **Muppet Movie, The** .... [M] **$12** Atlantic 16001

Jim Henson/Frank Oz/Jerry Nelson

America	I Hope That Somethin' Better Comes Along	Magic Store	**Rainbow Connection** [Kermit] 25
Animal...Come Back Animal	I'm Going To Go Back There Someday	Movin' Right Along	
Can You Picture That		Never Before, Never Again	

11/5/94 ❶² 34 ▲² ©497 **Murder Was The Case** .... [V] **$10** Death Row 92484

Snoop Doggy Dogg/Charlie Murphy

Come Up To My Room [Jodeci]	Horny [B-Rezell]	21 Jumpstreet [Snoop Doggy Dogg & Tray Deee]	Who Got Some Gangsta Shit? [Snoop Doggy Dogg]
Come When I Call [Danny Boy]	Murder Was The Case [Snoop Doggy Dogg]	U Better Recognize [Sam Sneed]	**Woman To Woman** [Jewell] 72
Dollars & Sense [D.J. Quik]	Natural Born Killaz [Dr. Dre & Ice Cube]	What Would U Do? [Tha Dogg Pound]	
Eastside-Westside [Young Soldierz]	One More Day [Nate Dogg]		
Eulogy, The [Slip Capone & CPO]			
Harvest For The World [Jewell]			

4/22/95 **177** 2 ©498 **Muriel's Wedding** .... [O-V] **$10** Polydor 527493

Toni Collette/Bill Hunter/Rachel Griffiths

Bean Bag [Wedding Band]	**I Do, I Do, I Do, I Do, I Do** [Abba] 15	Lonely Hearts [Wedding Band]	**Waterloo** [Abba] 6
Bridal Dancing Queen [Wedding Band]	I Go To Rio [Peter Allen]	Muriel's Wedding [Wedding Band]	**We've Only Just Begun** [Carpenters] 2
Dancing Queen [Abba] 1	I Just Don't Know What To Do With Myself [Dusty Springfield]	**Sugar Baby Love** [Rubettes] 37	
Happy Together [Turtles] 1		**T-Shirt & Jeans** [Razorbrain]	
		Tide Is High [Blondie] 1	

8/11/62 **2**⁶ 56 ● ©499 **Music Man, The** .... [M] **$30** Warner 1459

Robert Preston/Shirley Jones/Buddy Hackett/Ron Howard; cp: Meredith Willson; cd: **Ray Heindorf**

Being In Love	Iowa Stubborn (medley)	Pick-A-Little, Talk-A-Little	Sincere
Gary, Indiana	Lida Rose (medley)	Rock Island (medley)	Till There Was You
Goodnight My Someone	Main Title (medley)	Sadder But Wiser Girl	Wells Fargo Wagon
If You Don't Mind My Saying So (medley)	Marian The Librarian	Seventy Six Trombones (medley)	Will I Ever Tell You? (medley)
	Piano Lesson (medley)	Shipoopi	Ya Got Trouble

10/2/99 **51** 8 ● ©500 **Music Of The Heart** .... [V] **$10** Miramax 67861

Meryl Streep/Aidan Quinn/Angela Bassett/**Gloria Estefan**/Cloris Leachman

Baila [Jennifer Lopez]	Love Will Find You [Jaci Velasquez]	One Night With You [C Note]	
Concerto In D Minor For Two Violins	**Music Of My Heart** [*NSYNC & Gloria Estefan] 2	Revancha De Amor [Gizelle D'Cole]	
Do Something [Macy Gray]	Nothing Else [Julio Iglesias, Jr.]	Seventeen [Tre-O]	
Groove With Me Tonight [MDO]		Turn The Page [Aaliyah]	

1/5/63 **14** 19 501 **Mutiny On The Bounty** .... [I] **$50** MGM 4

Marlon Brando/Trevor Howard/**Richard Harris**; cp: Bronislau Kaper; cd: Robert Armbruster; includes a full-color souvenir book

Arrival In Tahiti	Mutiny, The	Native Festival Music Medley	Storm At Sea
Christian's Death	Mutiny On The Bounty (Follow Me),	Outrigger Chase	
Girls And Sailors	Love Song From	Pitcairn Island	
Leaving Harbor	Mutiny On The Bounty (Theme)	Portsmouth Harbor	

7/5/97 **14** 66 ▲² ©502 **My Best Friend's Wedding** .... [V] **$10** Work 68166

Julia Roberts/Dermot Mulroney/Cameron Diaz/Rupert Everett/Philip Bosco

Always You [Sophie Zelmani]	I'll Be Okay [Amanda Marshall]	Suite From "My Best Friend's Wedding" [James Newton Howard]	**What The World Needs Now Is Love** [Jackie DeShannon] 7
I Just Don't Know What To Do With Myself [Nicky Holland]	I'll Never Fall In Love Again [Mary Chapin Carpenter]	Tell Him [Exciters] 4	Wishin' And Hopin' [Ani DiFranco]
I Say A Little Prayer [Diana King] 38	**If You Wanna Be Happy** [Jimmy Soul] 1	Way You Look Tonight [Tony Bennett]	You Don't Know Me [Jann Arden]
I Say A Little Prayer [Cast]			

10/10/64+ **4** 111 ● ©503 **My Fair Lady** .... [M] **$25** Columbia 8000 / 2600

Audrey Hepburn/Rex Harrison/Stanley Holloway; mu: Frederick Loewe; ly: Alan Jay Lerner; cd: **Andre Previn**

Ascot Gavotte	I'm Just An Ordinary Man	On The Street Where You Live	With A Little Bit Of Luck
Get Me To The Church On Time	I've Grown Accustomed To Her Face	Rain In Spain	Without You
Hymn To Him	Just You Wait	Show Me	Wouldn't It Be Loverly
I Could Have Danced All Night		Why Can't The English?	You Did It

1/4/92 **104** 10 ©504 **My Girl** .... [O-V] **$10** Epic 48732

Dan Aykroyd/Jamie Lee Curtis/Macauley Culkin/Anna Chlumsky/Richard Masur

Bad Moon Rising [Creedence Clearwater Revival] 2	**Hot Fun In The Summertime** [Sly & The Family Stone] 2	**If You Don't Know Me By Now** [Harold Melvin & The Blue Notes] 3	My Girl (Theme) [James Newton Howard]
Do Wah Diddy Diddy [Manfred Mann] 1	**I Only Have Eyes For You** [Flamingos] 11	**More Today Than Yesterday** [Spiral Starecase] 12	**Saturday In The Park** [Chicago] 3
Good Lovin' [Young Rascals] 1	**I Saw The Light** [Todd Rundgren] 16	**My Girl** [Temptations] 1	**Wedding Bell Blues** [5th Dimension] 1

DEBUT	PEAK	WKS	RIAA	CD	ARTIST — Album Title	Catalog	Sym	$	Label & Number

7/19/75 · 80 · 13 · ©505 · Nashville .... [M] $15 ABC 893

Henry Gibson/**Lily Tomlin**/Shelley Duvall/**Keith Carradine**/Ned Beatty

Bluebird	**I'm Easy** *[Keith Carradine]* **17**	Memphis
Dues	It Don't Worry Me	My Idaho Home
For The Sake Of The Children	Keep A-Goin'	One, I Love You

Rolling Stone
Tapedeck In His Tractor
200 Years

9/10/94 · 19 · 31 · ● · ©506 · Natural Born Killers .... [V] $10 Nothing 92460

Woody Harrelson/Juliette Lewis/Robert Downey Jr./Tommy Lee Jones/**Rodney Dangerfield**

Allah, Mohammed, Char, Yaar	Fall Of The Rebel Angels *[Sergio*	Rock N Roll Nigger *[Patti Smith]*
Back In Baby's Arms *[Patsy Cline]*	*Cervetti]*	Route 666 *["BB Tone" Brian*
Batonga In Batongaville	Forkboy *[Lard]*	*Berdan]*
Born Bad *[Juliette Lewis]*	Future, The *[Leonard Cohen]*	Sex Is Violent
Burn *[Nine Inch Nails]*	History Repeats Itself *[A.O.S.]*	Shitlist *[L7]*
Day The Niggaz Took Over *[Dr.*	Hungry Ants	Something I Can Never Have *[Nine*
Dre]	I Will Take You Home *[Russel*	*Inch Nails]*
Drums A Go-Go *[Hollywood*	*Means]*	Sweet Jane *[Cowboy Junkies]*
Persuaders]	Moon Over Green County *[Dan*	Taboo *[Peter Gabriel/Nusrat Fateh*
	Zanes]	*Ali Khan]*

Totally Hot
Trembler, The *[Duane Eddy]*
Waiting For The Miracle *[Leonard Cohen]*
Warm Place *[Nine Inch Nails]*
What Would U Do? *[Dogg Pound]*
You Belong To Me *[Bob Dylan]*

4/24/99 · 161 · 3 · ©507 · Never Been Kissed .... [V] $10 Capitol 98505

Drew Barrymore/David Arquette/Michael Vartan/Leelee Sobieski

At My Most Beautiful *[R.E.M.]*	**Don't Worry Baby** *[Beach Boys]* **24**	Lucky Denver Mint *[Jimmy Eat*
Candy In The Sun *[Swirl 360]*	Erase/Rewind *[Cardigans]*	*World]*
Catch A Falling Star *[Block]*	Girl Named Happiness (Never Been	Never You Mind *[Semisonic]*
Closer To Myself *[Kendall Payne]*	Kissed) *[Jeremy Jordan]*	Please, Please, Please, Let Me Get
Cumbia De Los Muertos *[Ozomatli]*	Innocent Journey *[Sonichrome]*	What I Want *[Smiths]*

Problem *[Remy Zero]*
Standing By *[Willis]*
Until You Loved Me *[Moffatts]*
Watching The Wheels *[John Lennon]* **10**

1/30/61 · 2⁵ · 74 · ©508 · Never On Sunday .... [I] $30 United Artists 5070

Melina Mercouri/Jules Dassin/Tito Vandis; cp/cd: Manos Hadjidakis

Betrayed	Danse Yorgo	Lantern, The
Bouzoukia	End Title	Main Title
Charms Of Ilya	Hasapico	Organ Grinder
Children Of Athens	Ilya	Speak Softly

Taki

3/23/91 · 2¹ · 38 · ▲ · ©509 · New Jack City .... [V] $10 Giant 24409

Wesley Snipes/**Ice-T**/**Chris Rock**/Mario Van Peebles/Judd Nelson

Facts Of Life *[Danny Madden]*	**I Wanna Sex You Up** *[Color Me*	In The Dust *[2 Live Crew]*
For The Love Of Money (medley)	*Badd]* **2**	Living For The City (medley)
[Troop/Levert/Queen Latifah]	**I'm Dreamin'** *[Christopher*	*[Troop/Levert/Queen Latifah]*
Get It Together (Black Is A Force)	*Williams]* **89**	Lyrics 2 The Rhythm *[Essence]*
[F.S. Effect]	I'm Still Waiting *[Johnny Gill]*	New Jack City *[Guy]*

New Jack Hustler (Nino's Theme)
[Ice-T] **67**
(There You Go) Tellin' Me No Again
[Keith Sweat]

4/15/95 · 22 · 15 · ● · ©510 · New Jersey Drive Vol. 1 .... [V] $10 Tommy Boy 1114

Sharron Corley/Gabriel Casseus/Saul Stein/Gwen McGee

Ain't Nuttin' But Killin *[MC Eiht]*	**Can't You See** *[Total]* **13**	Jersey *[Queen Latifah]*
All About My Fetti *[Young Lay]*	Check It Out *[Heavy D]*	Love Slave *[Undacova]*
Before I Let Go *[Maze]*	Do What U Want *[Blak Panta]*	Old Thing *[Isabelle]*
Benz Or Beamer *[Outkast]*	Don't Shut Down On A Player *[ILL*	One And Only *[Smooth]*
Burn Rubber *[Lords Of The*	*Al Skratch]*	Thru The Window *[Coolio]*
Underground]	East Left *[Keith Murray]*	

21 In The Ghetto *[Poets Of Darkness]*
Where Am I? *[Redman]*

4/29/95 · 58 · 4 · ©511 · New Jersey Drive Vol. 2 .... [V] $10 Tommy Boy 1130

Connections *[Naughty By Nature]*	Funky Piano *[E. Bros]*	Invasion *[Jeru The Damaja]*
Flip Squad's In Da House *[Flip*	Headz Ain't Ready *[Black Moon &*	Nobody Beats The Biz *[Biz Markie]*
Squad Allstars]	*Smif 'N' Wessun]*	Own Destiny *[Mad Lion]*

You Won't Go Far *[O.C. & Organized Konfusion]*

7/16/77 · 50 · 14 · 512 · New York, New York .... [M] $20 United Artists 750 [2]

Liza Minnelli/Robert DeNiro/Lionel Stander/Mary K. Place; sw: John Kander and Fred Ebb; cd: Ralph Burns

Blue Moon	Happy Endings	Man I Love
Bobby's Dream	Hazoy	Once Again Right Away
But The World Goes 'Round	Honeysuckle Rose	Once In A While
Don't Be That Way	It's A Wonderful World	Opus Number One
Flip The Dip	Just You, Just Me	Theme From New York, New York
Game Over	Main Title	There Goes The Ball Game

V. J. Stomp
You Are My Lucky Star
You Brought A New Kind Of Love To Me

5/2/92 · 149 · 1 · ©513 · Newsies .... [M] $10 Disney 60832

Christian Bale/Max Casella/Bill Pullman/Robert Duvall/**Ann-Margret**; mu: Alan Menken; ly: Jack Feldman

Carrying The Banner	High Times, Hard Times	Once And For All
Escape From Snyder	King Of New York	Rooftop
Fightin' Irish: Strike Action	My Lovey-Dovey Baby	Santa Fe

Seize The Day
World Will Know

3/11/00 · 34 · 8 · ©514 · Next Best Thing, The .... [V] $10 Maverick 47595

Rupert Everett/**Madonna**/Lynn Redgrave/Illeana Douglas

American Pie *[Madonna]* **29**	Forever And Always *[Gabriel Yared]*	Stars All Seem To Weep *[Beth*
Bongo Bong *[Manu Chao]*	I'm Not In Love *[Olive]*	*Orton]*
Boom Boom Ba *[Metisse]*	If Everybody Looked The Same	Swayambhu *[Solar Twins]*
Don't Make Me Love You ('Til I'm	*[Groove Armada]*	This Life *[Mandalay]*
Ready) *[Christina Aguilera]*		Time Stood Still *[Madonna]*

Why Does My Heart Feel So Bad? *[Moby]*

1/1/00 · 19 · 27 · ● · ©515 · Next Friday .... [V] $10 Priority 23123

Ice Cube/Mike Epps/John Witherspoon/Tamala Jones

Chin Check *[N.W.A.]*	Hot *[Toni Estes]*	Make Your Body Sing *[Isley*
Friday *[Krayzie Bone]*	**I Don't Wanna** *[Aaliyah]* **35**	*Brothers]*
Fried Day *[Bizzy Bone]*	Livin It Up *[Pharoahe Monch]*	Mamacita
Good Friday *[Big Tymers]*	Low Income *[Wyclef Jean]*	*[Frost/Kurupt/Soopafly/Don Cisco]*
		Money Stretch *[Lil' Zane]*

Murder Murder *[Eminem]*
Shoalin Worldwide *[Wu-Tang Clan]*
We Murderers Baby *[Vita]*
You Can Do It *[Ice Cube]* **35**

10/17/98 · 95 · 22 · ● · ©516 · Night At The Roxbury, A .... [V] $10 DreamWorks 50033

Will Ferrell/Chris Kattan/Dan Hedaya/Molly Shannon/Richard Grieco

Bamboogie *[Bamboo]*	Da Ya Think I'm Sexy *[N-Trance]*	**Little Bit Of Ecstasy** *[Jocelyn*
Be My Lover *[La Bouche]* **6**	Disco Inferno *[Cyndi Lauper]*	*Enriquez]* **55**
Beautiful Life *[Ace Of Base]* **15**	Insomnia *[Faithless]*	Make That Money *[Robi Rob's Club*
Careless Whisper *[Tamia]*		*World]*

Pop Muzik *[3rd Party]*
This Is Your Night *[Amber]* **24**
What Is Love *[Haddaway]* **11**
Where Do You Go *[No Mercy]* **5**

DEBUT	PEAK	WKS	RIAA	CD	ARTIST — Album Title	Catalog	Sym	$	Label & Number

8/22/81 — 189 — 5 — 517 — Night The Lights Went Out In Georgia, The .... [V] $12 — Mirage 16051

Kristy McNichol/Dennis Quaid/Mark Hamill

Amanda [Dennis Quaid]	I Need You Strong For Me [Kristy McNichol]	Little Gettin' Used To [George Jones]
Hangin' Up The Gun [Kristy McNichol & Dennis Quaid]	Imaginary Arms [Tammy Wynette]	Melody's Melody [David Shire]
I Love My Truck [Glen Campbell] 94	It's So Easy [Billy Preston & Syreeta]	Night The Lights Went Out In Georgia [Tanya Tucker]

Rodeo Girl [Tanya Tucker]

Nighthawks - see EMERSON, Keith

3/29/86 — 59 — 15 — ©518 — 9 1/2 Weeks .... [V] $10 — Capitol 12470

Sylvester Stallone/Rutger Hauer/Billy Dee Williams/Nigel Davenport/Persis Khambatta
Mickey Rourke/Kim Basinger/Christine Baranski/Margaret Whitten

Best Is Yet To Come [Luba]	Eurasian Eyes [Corey Hart]	Slave To Love [Bryan Ferry]
Black On Black [Dalbello]	**I Do What I Do... (Theme for 9 1/2 Weeks)** [John Taylor] 23	This City Never Sleeps [Eurythmics]
Bread And Butter [Devo]	Let It Go [Luba]	You Can Leave Your Hat On [Joe Cocker]
Cannes [Stewart Copeland]		

8/5/95 — 166 — 5 — ©519 — Nine Months .... [I+V] $10 — Milan 35726

Hugh Grant/Julianne Moore/Tom Arnold/**Robin Williams**/Joan Cusack; cp: Hans Zimmer; cd: Nick Glennie-Smith

Baby, Baby	It's A Boy	Time Of Your Life [Little Steven]
Baby's Room	**Let's Get It On** [Marvin Gaye] 1	**Turn Back The Hands Of Time** [Tyrone Davis] 3
From Russia...	Open Your Eyes	We Can Work It Out

Voodoo Woman

12/27/80+ — 77 — 15 — 520 — 9 To 5 .... [I] $12 — 20th Century 627

Jane Fonda/Lily Tomlin/**Dolly Parton**/Dabney Coleman/Sterling Hayden; cp/cd: Charles Fox

Ajax Warehouse	Hart Tries To Escape	Office Montage
Charlie's Bar	Intruder, The	Pillow Fight
Dora Lee's Fantasy	Judy's Fantasy	Violet Steals Body
Easy Time	**9 To 5** [Dolly Parton] 1	Violet's Fantasy

Violet's Poisoned The Boss

1984 - see EURYTHMICS

12/17/88+ — 186 — 6 — ©521 — 1969 .... [O-V] $10 — Polydor 837362

John Hurt/Richard Burton/Suzanna Hamilton/Cyril Cusack
Robert Downey Jr./Kiefer Sutherland/Bruce Dern/Mariette Hartley

All Along The Watchtower [Jimi Hendrix Experience] 20	Going Up The Country [Canned Heat] 11	**Tuesday Afternoon (Forever Afternoon)** [Moody Blues] 24
Can't Find My Way Home [Blind Faith]	Green River [Creedence Clearwater Revival] 2	When I Was Young [Eric Burdon & The Animals] 15
Get Together [Jesse Colin Young]	Time Of The Season [Zombies] 3	White Room [Cream] 6

Windows Of The World [Pretenders]
Wooden Ships [Crosby, Stills & Nash]

Norwood - see CAMPBELL, Glen

9/20/86 — 190 — 3 — ©522 — Nothing In Common .... [V] $12 — Arista 8438

Glen Campbell/Kim Darby/Joe Namath/Carol Lynley/Pat Hingle
Tom Hanks/**Jackie Gleason**/Eva Marie Saint/Hector Elizondo/Barry Corbin

Burning Of The Heart [Richard Marx]	Instrumental Theme [Pat Leonard]	No One's Gonna Love You [Real To Reel]
Don't Forget To Dance [Kinks] 29	Loving Stranger (David's Theme) [Christopher Cross]	**Nothing In Common** [Thompson Twins] 54
If It Wasn't Love [Carly Simon]		

Over The Weekend [Nick Heyward]
Seven Summers [Cruzados]
Until You Say You Love Me [Aretha Franklin]

7/19/97 — 12 — 13 — ● — ©523 — Nothing To Lose .... [V] $10 — Tommy Boy 1169

Martin Lawrence/Tim Robbins/John C. McGinley/Kelly Preston

C U When U Get There [Coolio]	In A Magazine [911]	Poppin' That Fly [Oran "Juice" Jones]
Crazy Maze [Des'ree]	**It's Alright** [Queen Latifah] 76	Put The Monkey In It [Dat Nigga Daz & Soopafly]
Everlasting [OutKast]	**Not Tonight** [Lil' Kim] 6	Route 69 [Quad City DJ's]
Get Down With Me [Amari]	Nothin' To Lose [Naughty By Nature]	Thug Paradise [Capone-N-Noreaga]
Go Stetsa I [Stetsasonic]		
Hit 'Em Up [Master P]		

Way 2 Saucy [Mac & A.K.]
What's Going On [Black Caesar]

6/5/99 — 19 — 40 — ▲ — ©524 — Notting Hill .... [V] $10 — Island 546196

Julia Roberts/Hugh Grant/Hugh Bonneville/Emma Chambers/James Dreyfus

Ain't No Sunshine [Bill Withers] 3	**Gimme Some Lovin'** [Spencer Davis Group] 7	No Matter What [Boyzone]
Ain't No Sunshine [Lighthouse Family]	How Can You Mend A Broken Heart [Al Green]	Notting Hill [Trevor Jones]
Everything About You [Steve Poltz]	**I Do (Cherish You)** [98°] 13	She [Elvis Costello]
From The Heart [Another Level]		When You Say Nothing At All [Ronan Keating]

Will And Anna [Trevor Jones]
You've Got A Way [Shania Twain] 49

11/11/95+ — 103 — 35 — ● — ©525 — Now And Then .... [O-V] $10 — Columbia 67380

Christina Ricci/Thora Birch/**Rosie O'Donnell**/Melanie Griffith/Demi Moore

All Right Now [Free] 4	**I'll Be There** [Jackson 5] 1	**No Matter What** [Badfinger] 8
Band Of Gold [Freda Payne] 3	**I'm Gonna Make You Love Me** [Diana Ross & The Supremes w/The Temptations] 2	Now And Then [Susanna Hoffs]
Daydream Believer [Monkees] 1		**Signed, Sealed, Delivered I'm Yours** [Stevie Wonder] 3
Hitchin' A Ride [Vanity Fare] 5	**Knock Three Times** [Tony Orlando & Dawn] 1	**Sugar, Sugar** [Archies] 1
I Want You Back [Jackson 5] 1		

6/22/96 — 8 — 21 — ▲ — ©526 — Nutty Professor, The .... [V] $10 — Def Jam 531911

Eddie Murphy/Jada Pinkett/James Coburn/Dave Chappelle/Larry Miller

Ain't No Nigga [Jay-Z] 50	Doin' It Again [L.L. Cool J]	My Crew Can't Go For That [Trigger Tha Gambler]
Ain't Nobody [Monica] **flip**	**I Like** [Montell Jordan] 28	Nasty Immigrants [12 O'Clock]
Breaker 1, Breaker 2 [Def Squad]	**Last Night** [Az Yet] 9	Pillow [Richie Rich]
Come Around [Dos Of Soul]	Love You Down [Da Bassment]	

Touch Me Tease Me [Case] 14
We Want Yo Hands Up [Warren G]

7/29/00 — 4 — 18 — ▲ — ©527 — Nutty Professor II: The Klumps .... [V] $10 — Def Jam 542522

Eddie Murphy/Janet Jackson/Larry Miller/John Ales/Anna Maria Horsford

Do You Remember (Once Upon A Time) [Montell Jordan]	Get With Me [Shorty 101]	Just A Touch [R. Kelly]
Doesn't Really Matter [Janet] 1	Here With Me [Jazz]	**Just Friends (Sunny)** [Musiq] 31
Even If [Method Man]	**Hey Papi** [Jay-Z] 76	Let Me Be [Eve]
	I'm Gonna Crawl [DMX]	Missing You [Case]

No You Didn't Say [Kandice Love]
Off The Wall [Redman & Eminem]
Thinkin' 'Bout Me [Brian McKnight]
Thong Song [Sisqo] 3

DEBUT	PEAK	WKS	RIAA	CD	ARTIST — Album Title	Catalog	Sym	$	Label & Number

1/13/01 11 38↑▲² ©528 O Brother, Where Art Thou? .... **[V] $10** Mercury 170069
George Clooney/John Turturro/Tim Blake Nelson/John Goodman/Charles Durning

Angel Band [Stanley Brothers]	I Am A Man Of Constant Sorrow [Soggy Bottom Boys]	I'll Fly Away [Alison Krauss & Gillian Welch] Po Lazarus [James Carter & the Prisoners]
Big Rock Candy Mountain [Harry McClintock]	I Am A Man Of Constant Sorrow [Norman Blake]	In The Highways [Sarah, Hannah & You Are My Sunshine [Norman Leah Peasall] Blake]
Didn't Leave Nobody But The Baby [Emmylou Harris, Alison Krauss & Gillian Welch]	I Am A Man Of Constant Sorrow [John Hartford]	In The Jailhouse Now [Soggy Bottom Boys]
Down To The River To Pray [Alison Krauss]	I Am A Man Of Constant Sorrow [Soggy Bottom Boys]	Indian War Whoop [John Hartford] Keep On The Sunny Side [Whites]
Hard Time Killing Floor Blues [Chris Thomas King]	I Am Weary (Let Me Rest) [Cox Family]	Lonesome Valley [Fairfield Four] O Death [Ralph Stanley]

O Lucky Man! - see PRICE, Alan
Malcolm McDowell/Rachel Roberts/Ralph Richardson

7/16/83 137 5 ©529 Octopussy .... **[I] $12** A&M 4967
Roger Moore/Maud Adams/Louis Jourdan/Vijay Amritraj; cp/cd: John Barry

All Time High [Rita Coolidge] 36	Bond Look-Alike	Death Of Vijay (medley)	Palace Fight
Arrival At The Island Of Octopussy	Bond Meets Octopussy	009 Gets The Knife (medley)	That's My Little Octopussy
Bond At The Monsoon Palace	Chase Bomb Theme	Gobinda Attacks (medley)	Yo-Yo Fight (medley)

7/27/68 190 2 530 Odd Couple, The .... **[I] $25** Dot 25862
Jack Lemmon/Walter Matthau/John Fiedler/Herb Edelman; cp/cd: **Neal Hefti**

Clean Poker	Domestic Quarrel	Man Chases Man	Oscar Blows Up
Curse Of The Cat People	Down With The Lights	Metropole	Tomatoes
Dirty Poker	End Title	Odd Couple	

10/30/82 38 23 ©531 Officer And A Gentleman, An .... **[V] $12** Island 90017
Richard Gere/Debra Winger/David Keith/Lou Gossett Jr.

Be Real [Sir Douglas Quintet]	Main Title [Jack Nitzsche]	Tunnel Of Love [Dire Straits]
Hungry For Your Love [Van Morrison]	Morning After Love Theme [Jack Nitzsche]	Tush [ZZ Top] 20
Love Theme [Lee Ritenour]	Treat Me Right [Pat Benatar] 18	Up Where We Belong [Joe Cocker & Jennifer Warnes] 1

9/17/55+ ❶⁴ 305 ▲² ©532 Oklahoma! .... **[M] $40** Capitol 595
Gordon MacRae/Shirley Jones/Rod Steiger; mu: Richard Rodgers; ly: Oscar Hammerstein II; cd: Jay Blackton; LP: Capitol SAO-595 (#1); EP: Capitol SDM-595 (#4); Original Cast version charted in 1945 (#4) on Decca 359

All Er Nothin'	Kansas City	Oklahoma	Poor Jud Is Dead
Farmer And The Cowman	Many A New Day	Out Of My Dreams	Surrey With The Fringe On Top
I Cain't Say No	Oh, What A Beautiful Mornin'	People Will Say We're In Love	

12/28/68+ 20 91 ● ©533 Oliver! .... **[M] $20** Colgems 5501
Mark Lester/Ron Moody/Jack Wild/Oliver Reed; sw: Lionel Bart; cd: John Green

As Long As He Needs Me	Food, Glorious Food (medley)	Oom-Pah-Pah	Who Will Buy?
Be Back Soon	I'd Do Anything	Pick A Pocket Or Two	
Boy For Sale	It's A Fine Life	Reviewing The Situation	
Consider Yourself	Oliver! (medley)	Where Is Love?	

1/7/89 170 7 ©534 Oliver & Company .... C:#10/4 **[M] $10** Disney 64101
animated movie, voices by: **Joey Lawrence/Bette Midler/Billy Joel**; cp/cd: J.A.C. Redford

Bedtime Story	Good Company [Myhanh Tran]	Perfect Isn't Easy [Bette Midler]	Streets Of Gold [Ruth Pointer]
Buscando Guayaba [Ruben Blades]	Once Upon A Time In New York City [Huey Lewis]	Pursuit Through The Subway	Sykes
End Title		Rescue, The	Why Should I Worry? [Billy Joel]

On A Clear Day You Can See Forever - see STREISAND, Barbra
Barbra Streisand/Yves Montand/**Bob Newhart**/Jack Nicholson

2/27/82 147 11 535 On Golden Pond .... **[I] $12** MCA 6106
Henry Fonda/Katharine Hepburn/**Jane Fonda**/Doug McKeon/Dabney Coleman; cp/cd: **Dave Grusin**

Career Opportunities/Back Porch	Epilogue	Illicit Sex Question	New Hampshire Hornpipe
Confessional	Father-Daughter Relationship	Lake-Song	Purgatory Cove
Early Bird	First Call	Main Theme	Season's End

2/7/70 103 13 ©536 On Her Majesty's Secret Service .... **[I+V] $20** United Artists 5204
George Lazenby/Diana Rigg/**Telly Savalas**; cp/cd: John Barry

Battle At Piz Gloria	Journey To Blowfeld's Hideaway	This Never Happened To The Other	We Have All The Time In The World
Do You Know How Christmas Trees Are Grown? [Nina]	Main Theme	Feller	[Louis Armstrong]
James Bond Theme (medley)	Over & Out	Try	
	Ski Chase		

1/4/97 57 25 ● ©537 One Fine Day .... **[V] $10** Columbia 67916
Michelle Pfeiffer/George Clooney/Mae Whitman/Charles Durning/**Robert Klein**

Boy From New York City [Ad Libs] 8	Isn't It Romantic [Ella Fitzgerald]	One Fine Day [Chiffons] 5	What A Diff'rence A Day Made [Tony Bennett]
For The First Time [Kenny Loggins]	Just Like You [Keb' Mo']	Someone Like You [Shawn Colvin]	
Glory Of Love [Keb' Mo']	Love's Funny That Way [Tina Arena]	Suite From "One Fine Day" [James Newton Howard]	
Have I Told You Lately? [Van Morrison]	Mama Said [Shirelles]	This Guy's In Love With You [Harry Connick, Jr.]	
	One Fine Day [Natalie Merchant]		

4/17/76 158 7 ©538 One Flew Over The Cuckoo's Nest .... **[I] $20** Fantasy 9500
Jack Nicholson/Louise Fletcher/Will Sampson/Scatman Crothers/Danny DeVito; cp: Jack Nitzsche

Act Of Love	Charmaine	Medication Valse	Play The Game
Aloha Los Pescadores	Cruising	One Flew Over The Cuckoo's Nest (opening theme)	Trolling
Bus Ride To Paradise	Last Dance		

101 - see DEPECHE MODE
One On One - see SEALS & CROFTS
Robby Benson/Annette O'Toole/G.D. Spradlin/Gail Strickland/Melanie Griffith
One-Trick Pony - see SIMON, Paul
Paul Simon/Blair Brown/Rip Torn/Joan Hackett/**Lou Reed**

5/18/96 41 6 ©539 Original Gangstas .... **[V] $10** Noo Trybe 41533
Fred Williamson/Jim Brown/Pam Grier/Paul Winfield/Isabel Sanford

Ain't No Fun [Dino]	How Many [N.O. Joe]	Slugs [Spice 1]	Who Wanna Be The Villain [MC Ren]
Flowamatic 9 [3X Crazy]	Inner City Blues [Ideal]	War's On [Almighty RSO]	World Is A Ghetto [Geto Boys] 82
Good Stuff [Smooth]	On The Grind [Click]	White Chalk Part II [Junior M.A.F.I.A.]	X.O. [Luniz]
How Does It Feel [Ice T]	Rivals [Facemob]		

DEBUT	PEAK	WKS	RIAA	CD	ARTIST — Album Title	Catalog	Sym	$	Label & Number
9/9/00	50	6		©540	Original Kings Of Comedy, The		[C]	$10	Universal 159306

Steve Harvey/D.L. Hughley/Bernie Mac/Cedric The Entertainer

Ain't You Big Poppa [Cedric The Entertainer]	I Love My Job [D.L. Hughley]	#1 Stunna [Big Tymers]	Titanic [Steve Harvey]
Airplanes [D.L. Hughley]	I Say What You Scared To Say [Bernie Mac]	Post Tiger Renaissance [Cedric The Entertainer]	We Run [Cedric The Entertainer]
Big Momma [D.L. Hughley]	I'll Eat Anything [D.L. Hughley]	Racists [D.L. Hughley]	What Blacks Do For Excitement [D.L. Hughley]
Church All The Time [Steve Harvey]	Indecent Proposal [D.L. Hughley]	Section 8 Island [D.L. Hughley]	What's Up Wit That [Juvenile & Lil Wayne]
Delicious [Cedric The Entertainer]	Jesus Was Black [D.L. Hughley]	Something Got To Be Wrong In Cuba [Steve Harvey]	
Dysfunctional Black Family [D.L. Hughley]	Mother *#!%@$ [Bernie Mac]	Summer In The City [St. Lunatics]	
Ghetto [Sticky Fingaz]	My Sister's Kids [Bernie Mac]	Time Out [D.L. Hughley]	
	Na Na [Monifah]		

DEBUT	PEAK	WKS	RIAA	CD	ARTIST — Album Title	Catalog	Sym	$	Label & Number
3/20/99	109	5		©541	Other Sister, The		[V]	$10	Hollywood 62180

Juliette Lewis/Diane Keaton/Tom Skerritt/Giovanni Ribisi

Animal Song [Savage Garden] **19**	Come Rain Or Come Shine [Juliette Lewis]	Loving You Is All I Know [Pretenders]	She Comes 'Round [Fastball]
At Last [Joan Osborne]	Follow If You Lead [Idina Menzel]	Me [Paula Cole]	**When You Say Nothing At All** [Alison Krauss] **53**
Carla & Danny's Theme [Rachel Portman]	**I'm Free** [Soup Dragons] **79**	Mrs. Robinson [Lemonheads]	

DEBUT	PEAK	WKS	RIAA	CD	ARTIST — Album Title	Catalog	Sym	$	Label & Number
3/19/66	118	5		©542	Our Man Flint		[I]	$50	20th Century Fox 4179

James Coburn/Lee J. Cobb/Gila Golan; cp/cd: Jerry Goldsmith

All I Have To Do Is Take A Bite Of Your Apple?	Galaxy A Go Go! -or- Leave It To Flint	Man Does Not Live By Bread Alone	Take Some Risks, Mr. Flint?
Doing As The Romans Did	In Like Flint	Never Mind, You'd Love It	Tell Me More About That Volcano
	It's Gotta Be A World's Record	Our Man Flint	You're A Foolish Man, Mr. Flint
		Stall! Stall! Flint's Alive	

DEBUT	PEAK	WKS	RIAA	CD	ARTIST — Album Title	Catalog	Sym	$	Label & Number
2/1/86	38	22	●	©543	Out Of Africa	C:#22/2	[I]	$12	MCA 6158

Meryl Streep/Robert Redford/Klaus Maria Brandauer/Michael Gough; cp/cd: John Barry

Alone On The Farm	I Had A Compass From Deny's (Karen's Theme II)	If I Know A Song Of Africa (Karen's Theme III)	Siyawe (medley)
Concerto For Clarinet And Orchestra In A (K. 622)	I Had A Farm In Africa (Main Title)	Karen's Journey (medley)	You Are Karen (End Title)
Flying Over Africa	I'm Better At Hello (Karen's Theme I)	Let The Rest Of The World Go By	
Have You Got A Story For Me?		Safari	

DEBUT	PEAK	WKS	RIAA	CD	ARTIST — Album Title	Catalog	Sym	$	Label & Number
3/7/87	120	8		©544	Over The Top		[V]	$10	Columbia 40655

Sylvester Stallone/Robert Loggia/Susan Blakely/David Mendenhall/Terry Funk

All I Need Is You [Big Trouble]	Gypsy Soul [Asia]	**Meet Me Half Way** [Kenny Loggins] **11**	Take It Higher [Larry Greene]
Bad Nite [Frank Stallone]	I Will Be Strong [Eddie Money]	Mind Over Matter [Larry Greene]	**Winner Takes It All** [Sammy Hagar] **54**
Fight, The [Giorgio Moroder]	In This Country [Robin Zander]		

Owl and the Pussycat, The - see STREISAND, Barbra
Barbra Streisand/George Segal/Robert Klein/Roz Kelly

DEBUT	PEAK	WKS	RIAA	CD	ARTIST — Album Title	Catalog	Sym	$	Label & Number
10/25/69	28	56	●	©545	Paint Your Wagon		[M]	$25	Paramount 1001

Lee Marvin/Clint Eastwood/Jean Seberg/Ray Walston; mu: Frederick Loewe; ly: Alan Jay Lerner; cd: **Nelson Riddle**; Original Cast version charted in 1952 (#7) on RCA Victor 1006

Best Things	Hand Me Down That Can O' Beans	Million Miles Away Behind The Door	Whoop-Ti-Ay! (Shivaree)
First Thing You Know	I Still See Elisa	There's A Coach Comin' In	
Gold Fever	I Talk To The Trees	They Call The Wind Maria	
Gospel Of No Name City	I'm On My Way (Main Title)	Wand'rin Star	

DEBUT	PEAK	WKS	RIAA	CD	ARTIST — Album Title	Catalog	Sym	$	Label & Number
9/23/57	9	14		©546	Pajama Game, The		[M]	$50	Columbia 5210

Doris Day/John Raitt/Carol Haney/Reta Shaw; sw: Richard Adler and Jerry Ross; cd: **Ray Heindorf**; Original Cast version charted in 1954 (#4) on Columbia 4840

Hernando's Hideaway	I'm Not At All In Love	Racing With The Clock (medley)	Steam Heat
Hey There	Once-A-Year Day!	Seven-And-A-Half Cents	There Once Was A Man
I'll Never Be Jealous Again	Pajama Game (medley)	Small Talk	

Pal Joey - see SINATRA, Frank
Frank Sinatra/Rita Hayworth/Kim Novack

DEBUT	PEAK	WKS	RIAA	CD	ARTIST — Album Title	Catalog	Sym	$	Label & Number
5/20/95	37	8	●	©547	Panther		[V]	$10	Mercury 525479

Kadeem Hardison/Bokeem Woodbine/Tyrin Turner/Joe Don Baker

Black People [Funkadelic feat. George Clinton & Belita Woods]	**Freedom (Theme From The Panther)** [Various Artists] **45**	Points, The [Various Artists]	Ultimate Sacrifice [William Kidd]
Don't Give Me No Broccoli And Tell Me It's Greens (What Happened To Our Rhythm) [Last Poets]	Head Nod [Hodge]	Slick Partner [Bobby Brown]	We Shall Not Be Moved [Sounds Of Blackness feat. Black Sheep]
Express Yourself [Joe]	If I Were Your Woman [Shanice]	Stand [Tony Toni Toné]	We'll Meet Again [BLACKstreet]
	Let's Straighten It Out [Monica & Usher]	Stand (You Got To) [Aaron Hall]	World Is A Ghetto [Da Lench Mob]
	Natural Woman [Female]	Star Spangled Banner [Brian McKnight & The Boys Choir of Harlem]	

DEBUT	PEAK	WKS	RIAA	CD	ARTIST — Album Title	Catalog	Sym	$	Label & Number
8/4/73	154	12		548	Paper Moon		[O-V]	$20	Paramount 1012

Ryan O'Neal/Tatum O'Neal/Madeline Kahn/John Hillerman

About A Quarter To Nine [Ozzie Nelson]	I Found A Million Dollar Baby [Victor Young/Boswell Sisters]	Just One More Chance [Bing Crosby]	On The Banks Of The Ohio [Blue Sky Boys]
After You've Gone [Tommy Dorsey]	(It Will Have To Do) Until The Real Thing Comes Along [Leo Reisman]	Let's Have Another Cup Of Coffee [Enric Madriguera]	One Hour With Me [Jimmie Grier]
Flirtation Walk [Dick Powell]		My Mary [Jimmie Davis]	Picture Of Me Without You [Paul Whiteman/Ken Darby/Ramona]
Georgia On My Mind [Hoagy Carmichael]	It's Only A Paper Moon [Paul Whiteman]	Object Of My Affection [Jimmie Grier]	Sunnyside Up [Johnny Hamp's Kentucky Serenaders]

Paradise, Hawaiian Style - see PRESLEY, Elvis
Elvis Presley ("Rick Richards")/Suzanne Leigh/James Shigeta

DEBUT	PEAK	WKS	RIAA	CD	ARTIST — Album Title	Catalog	Sym	$	Label & Number
10/23/61	92	8		549	Parent Trap!, The		[I+V]	$50	Buena Vista 3309

Hayley Mills/Brian Keith/Maureen O'Hara; cd: Tutti Camarata

Alice In Wonderland	**Let's Get Together** [Hayley Mills] **8**	Parent Trap [Tommy Sands & Annette]	Swiss Family Robinson Theme (My Heart Was An Island)
Cobbler Cobbler [Hayley Mills]	Love Theme From Sleeping Beauty	Sleeping Beauty Overture	Whistling At The Boys [School Belles]
For Now For Always	Maggie's Theme		
Intermezzo			

DEBUT	PEAK	WKS	RIAA	CD	ARTIST — Album Title	Catalog	Sym	$	Label & Number
2/13/99	180	4		©550	Parent Trap, The		[V]	$10	Hollywood 62167

Dennis Quaid/Natasha Richardson/Lindsay Lohan/Polly Holliday

Bad To The Bone [George Thorogood & The Destroyer]	Groovin' [Pato Banton & The Reggae Revolution]	Let's Get Together [Nobody's Angel]	Suite from The Parent Trap [Alan Silvestri]
Do You Believe In Magic [Lovin' Spoonful] **9**	Happy Club [Bob Geldof]	**L-O-V-E** [Nat King Cole] **5**	**There She Goes** [La's] **49**
Dream Come True [Ta-Gana]	Here Comes The Sun [Bob Khaleel]	Never Let You Go [Jakaranda]	**This Will Be** [Natalie Cole] **6**
	I Love You For Sentimental Reasons [Linda Ronstadt]	**Soulful Strut** [Young Holt Unlimited] **3**	Top Of The World [Shonen Knife]

SOUNDTRACKS

DEBUT	PEAK	WKS	RIAA	CD	ARTIST — Album Title	Catalog	Sym	$	Label & Number

9/25/61 · 45 · 12 · 551 Parrish .... [I] **$75** Warner 1413
Troy Donahue/Claudette Colbert/Karl Malden/Dean Jagger/Connie Stevens; cp/cd: Max Steiner
| Allison's Theme | Lucy's Theme | Someday, I'll Meet You Again | Tara's Theme |
| Ellen's Theme | Paige's Theme | Summer Place, Theme From A | Tobacco Theme |

2/5/83 · 169 · 6 · 552 Party Party .... [V] **$12** A&M 3212
Daniel Peacock/Phoebe Nicholls/Karl Howman/Perry Fenwick/Sean Chapman
Auld Lang Syne [Chas & Dave]	Little Town Flirt [Altered Images]	No Feelings [Bananarama]	Run Rudolph Run [Dave Edmunds]
Band Of Gold [Modern Romance]	Man Who Sold The World [Midge Ure]	No Woman, No Cry [Pauline Black]	Tutti Frutti [Sting]
Driving In My Car [Madness]	Need Your Love So Bad [Sting]	Party Party [Elvis Costello & The Attractions]	Yakety Yak [Bad Manners]
Elizabethan Reggae [Bad Manners]			

Pat Garrett & Billy The Kid - see DYLAN, Bob
James Coburn/**Bob Dylan**/Kris Kristofferson/Jason Robards

1/23/99 · 180 · 2 · ©553 Patch Adams .... [V] **$10** Universal 53245
Robin Williams/Monica Potter/Philip Seymour Hoffman/Bob Gunton
Bell Bottom Blues [Derek & The Dominoes]	Children's Ward	Let It Rain [Eric Clapton]	People Got To Be Free [Rascals]
Butterfly (medley)	Faith Of The Heart [Rod Stewart]	Look Beyond The Finger	Ranch Reveal
Carry On [Crosby, Stills, Nash & Young]	Front Porch	Main Title	Ruling, The (medley)
Children's Reprise (medley)	Good Lovin' [Rascals]	Noodle Pool (medley)	Speech (medley)
	Graduation (medley)	Only You Know And I Know [Dave Mason]	Stand [Sly & The Family Stone]
	Hello		Weight, The [Band]

7/15/00 · 129 · 3 · ©554 Patriot, The .... [I] **$0** Hollywood 62258
Mel Gibson/Heath Ledger/Joely Richardson/Rene Auberjonois; cp/cd: **John Williams**
Ann And Gabriel	Family Farm	Patriot	Tavington's Trap
Ann Recruits The Parishoners	First Ambush And Remembering	Preparing For Battle	To Charleston
Burning Of The Plantation	The Wilderness	Redcoats At The Farm And The Death Of Thomas	Yorktown And The Return Home
Colonial Cause	Martin Vs. Tavington		
Facing The British Lines	Parish Church Aflame	Susan Speaks	

5/22/71 · 117 · 8 · 555 Patton .... [I] **$20** 20th Century Fox 4208
George C. Scott/Karl Malden/Michael Bates/Edward Binns; cp/cd: Jerry Goldsmith
Attack	Funeral, The	No Assignment	Winter March
Battleground, The	German Advance	Patton March	
End Title Speech	Hospital, The	Patton Speech	
First Battle	Main Title	Payoff, The	

6/9/01 · 14 · 17↑● · ©556 Pearl Harbor .... [I] **$10** Hollywood 48113
Ben Affleck/Josh Hartnett/Kate Beckinsale/Cuba Gooding Jr.; cp: Hans Zimmer; cd: Gavin Greenaway
...And Then I Kissed Him	December 7th	Tennessee	
Attack	Heart Of A Volunteer	**There You'll Be** [Faith Hill] **10**	
Brothers	I Will Come Back	War	

1/23/82 · 188 · 2 · 557 Pennies From Heaven .... [O-V] **$15** Warner 3639 [2]
Steve Martin/Bernadette Peters/Christopher Walken
Clouds Will Soon Roll By [Elsie Carlisle]	I'll Never Have To Dream Again [Connie Boswell]	Let's Put Out The Lights And Go To Sleep [Rudy Vallee]	Roll Along Prairie Moon [Fred Latham]
Did You Ever See A Dream Walking? [Bing Crosby]	It's A Sin To Tell A Lie [Dolly Dawn]	Life Is Just A Bowl Of Cherries [Walt Harrah/Gene Merlino/Vern Rowe]	Serenade In The Night [Ronnie Hill]
Fancy Our Meeting [Jack Buchanan & Elsie Randolph]	It's The Girl [Boswell Sisters]	Love Is Good For Anything That Ails You [Ida Sue McCune]	Yes, Yes! [Sam Browne]
Glory Of Love [Lew Stone]	Let's Face The Music And Dance [Fred Astaire]	Pennies From Heaven [Arthur Tracy]	
I Want To Be Bad [Helen Kane]	Let's Misbehave [Irving Aaronson]		

6/29/85 · 45 · 12 · ©558 Perfect .... [V] **$10** Arista 8278
John Travolta/Jamie Lee Curtis/Marilu Henner/Laraine Newman/Jann Wenner
All Systems Go [Pointer Sisters]	I Sweat (Going Through The Motions) [Nona Hendryx]	Masquerade [Berlin]	Wear Out The Grooves [Jermaine Stewart]
(Closest Thing To) Perfect [Jermaine Jackson] **67**	**Lay Your Hands On Me** [Thompson Twins] **6**	Shock Me [Jermaine Jackson & Whitney Houston]	Wham Rap (Enjoy What You Do)! [Wham!]
Hot Hips [Lou Reed]		Talking To The Wall [Dan Hartman]	

12/24/77+ · 131 · 10 · 559 Pete's Dragon .... [M] **$12** Capitol 11704
Helen Reddy/Jim Dale/Mickey Rooney/Red Buttons; sw: Al Kasha and Joel Hirschhorn; cd: Irwin Kostal
Bill Of Sale	Brazzle Dazzle Day	Happiest Home In These Hills	Main Title
Boo Bop BopBop Bop (I Love You, Too)	Candle On The Water	I Saw A Dragon	Passamashloddy
	Every Little Piece	It's Not Easy	There's Room For Everyone

2/23/63 · 88 · 7 · 560 Phaedra .... [I] **$30** United Artists 5102
Melina Mercouri/Anthony Perkins; cp/cd: Mikis Theodorakis
Agapimou	London's Fog	Phaedra (Love Theme) [Melina Mercouri]	Rendezvous
Candlelight	One More Time		Rodostimo
Fling, The	Only You	Phaedra (Love Theme) (instrumental)	Ship To Shore
Goodbye John Sebastian			

3/1/75 · 194 · 1 · 561 Phantom Of The Paradise .... [M] **$15** A&M 3653
Paul Williams/William Finley/Jessica Harper; sw: **Paul Williams**
Beauty And The Beast (Phantom's Theme)	Goodbye Eddie, Goodbye	Old Souls	Special To Me (Phoenix Audition Song)
Faust	Hell Of It	Somebody Super Like You (Beef Construction Song)	Upholstery
	Life At Last		

7/20/96 · 12 · 43 ▲ · ©562 Phenomenon .... [V] **$10** Reprise 46360
John Travolta/Kyra Sedgwick/Forest Whitaker/Robert Duvall
Change The World [Eric Clapton] **5**	Dance With Life (The Brilliant Light) [Bryan Ferry]	I Have The Touch [Peter Gabriel]	Para Donde Vas [Iguanas]
Corinna [Taj Mahal]		Misty Blue [Dorothy Moore]	Piece Of Clay [Marvin Gaye]
Crazy Love [Aaron Neville]	Have A Little Faith In Me [Jewel]	Orchard, The [Thomas Newman]	Thing Going On [J.J. Cale]

1/22/94 · 12 · 36 ▲ · ©563 Philadelphia .... [V] **$10** Epic Soundtrax 57624
Tom Hanks/Denzel Washington/Jason Robards/Mary Steenburgen/Antonio Banderas
Have You Ever Seen The Rain? [Spin Doctors]	Ibo Lele (Dreams Come True) [Ram]	Lovetown [Peter Gabriel]	**Streets Of Philadelphia** [Bruce Springsteen] **9**
I Don't Wanna Talk About It [Indigo Girls]	It's In Your Eyes [Pauletta Washington]	Philadelphia [Neil Young]	
	La Mamma Morta [Maria Callas]	Please Send Me Someone To Love [Sade]	
		Precedent [Howard Shore]	

Piano, The - see NYMAN, Michael
Holly Hunter/Harvey Keitel/Sam Neill/Anne Paquin

DEBUG	PEAK	WKS	RIAA	CD	ARTIST — Album Title	Catalog	Sym	$	Label & Number

5/5/56 — **6** — 18 — ©564 — **Picnic** — [I] $50 — Decca 78320

William Holden/Kim Novak/Rosalind Russell/Cliff Robertson; cp: George Duning; cd: Morris Stoloff

Culmination (medley)	Hal's Turmoil (medley)	**Moonglow and Theme From**
Flo And Madge	It's A Blue World (medley)	**"Picnic"** [Morris Stoloff] 1
Hal's Boots	Madge Decides (medley)	Owens Family
Hal's Escape (medley)	Millie (medley)	Rosemary Alone (medley)
Hal's Theme		Rosemary Pleads (medley)

That Owens Girl (medley)
Torn Shirt (Part 1) (medley)
You Love Me (medley)

Pink Panther, The - see MANCINI, Henry
Peter Sellers/David Niven/Robert Wagner/Capucine

Pipe Dreams - see KNIGHT, Gladys/Pips
Gladys Knight/Barry Hankerson/Bruce French/Sherry Bain

8/28/82 — **166** — 6 — 565 — **Pirate Movie, The** — [M] $15 — Polydor 9503 [2]

Kristy McNichol/Christopher Atkins/Ted Hamilton/Bill Kerr

Chase, The	Happy Ending	Modern Major General's Song
Chinese Battle	Hold On	Pirate Movie Medley
Come Friends Who Plough The Sea	**How Can I Live Without Her**	Pirates, Police & Pizza
Duel, The	[Christopher Atkins] 71	Pumpin' & Blowin'
First Love	I Am A Pirate King	Sister's Song

Stand Up And Sing
Tarantara
Victory
We Are The Pirates

7/27/68 — **195** — 3 — ©566 — **Planet Of The Apes** — [I] $30 — Project 3 5023

Charlton Heston/Roddy McDowall/Kim Hunter/Maurice Evans/James Whitmore; cp/cd: Jerry Goldsmith

Bid For Freedom	Forbidden Zone	New Mate
Cave, The	Main Title	No Escape
Clothes Snatchers	New Identity	Revelation, The

Search, The

4/4/87 — **75** — 13 — ©567 — **Platoon** — [O-V] $10 — Atlantic 81742

Tom Berenger/Willem Dafoe/Charlie Sheen/Forest Whitaker/John C. McGinley

Adagio For Strings [Vancouver	**Groovin'** [Young Rascals] 1	**Respect** [Aretha Franklin] 1
Symphony Orchestra]	**Hello, I Love You** [Doors] 1	**(Sittin' On) The Dock Of The Bay**
Barnes Shoots Elias [Vancouver	**Okie From Muskogee** [Merle	[Otis Redding] 1
Symphony Orchestra]	Haggard] 41	Tracks Of My Tears [Miracles] 16

When A Man Loves A Woman
[Percy Sledge] 1
White Rabbit [Jefferson Airplane] 8

4/4/98 — **10** — 25 ▲ — ©568 — **Players Club, The** — [V] $10 — A&M 540886

Bernie Mac/Monica Calhoun/Lisa Raye/**Ice Cube/Jamie Foxx**

Don't Play Me Wrong [Brownstone]	My Loved One [Ice Cube]	Under Pressure [Kurupt]
Don't Worry (My Shorty) [Rufus	Same Tempo [Changing Faces]	We Be Clubbin' [Ice Cube]
Blaq]	Shake Whatcha Mama Gave Ya	What A Woman Feels [Public
Dreamin' [Emmage]	(But Make Sho Your Niggas Pay	Announcement]
From Marcy To Hollywood [Jay-Z]	Ya) [Mia X]	Who Are You Lovin' [Ice Cube]
Get Mine [Mr. Dalvin]	Splackavellie [Pressha]	

You Delinquent [Mack 10 &
Scarface]
You Know I'm A Ho [Master P & Ice
Cube]

6/17/95 — **❶**[1] — 48 ▲[3] — ©569 — **Pocahontas** — [V] $10 — Walt Disney 60874

animated movie, voices by: Irene Bedard/Judy Kuhn/Mel Gibson; mu: Alan Menken; ly: Stephen Schwartz

Colors Of The Wind (cast version)	Grandmother Willow	Listen With Your Heart II
Colors Of The Wind [Vanessa	I'll Never See Him Again	Mine, Mine, Mine
Williams] 4	If I Never Knew You [Jon Secada &	Percy's Bath
Council Meeting	Shanice]	Picking Corn
Execution	John Smith Sneaks Out	Pocahontas
Farewell	Just Around The Riverbend	Ratcliffe's Plan
Getting Acquainted	Listen With Your Heart I	River's Edge

Savages (Part 1)
Savages (Part 2)
Ship At Sea
Skirmish
Steady As The Beating Drum
Virginia Company
Warriors Arrive

7/17/93 — **23** — 15 ● — ©570 — **Poetic Justice** — [V] $10 — Epic Soundtrax 57131

Janet Jackson/**2Pac**/Tyra Ferrell/Regina King/Joe Torry

Call Me A Mack [Usher Raymond]	I've Been Waiting [Terri & Monica]	Niggas Don't Give A Fuck [Dogg
Cash In My Hands [Nice & Smooth]	**Indo Smoke** [Mista Grimm] 56	Pound]
Definition Of A Thug Nigga [2Pac]	Justice's Groove [Stanley Clarke]	Nite & Day [Cultural Revolution]
Get It Up [TLC] 42	Never Dreamed You'd Leave In	One In A Million [Pete Rock & C.L.
I Wanna Be Your Man [Chaka	Summer [Stevie Wonder]	Smooth]
Demus & Pliers]		

Poor Man's Poetry [Naughty By
Nature]
Waiting For You [Tony! Toni! Toné!]
Well Alright [Babyface]

11/27/99 — **8** — 24 ▲[2] — ©571 — **Pokémon - The First Movie** — [V] $10 — Atlantic 83261

animated movie, voices by Veronica Taylor/Philip Bartlett/Rachael Lillis/Eric Stuart

Brother My Brother [Blessid Union	(Have Some) Fun With The Funk	It Was You [Ashley Ballard]
Of Souls]	[Aaron Carter]	Lullaby [Mandah]
Catch Me If You Can [Angela Via]	(Hey You) Free Up Your Mind	Makin' My Way (Any Way That I
Don't Say You Love Me [M2M] 21	[Emma Bunton]	Can) [Billie]
Fly With Me [98°]	If Only Tears Could Bring You Back	Pokémon Theme [Billy Crawford]
Get Happy [B*witched]	[Midnight Sons]	Soda Pop [Britney Spears]

Somewhere Someday ['N Sync]
Vacation [Vitamin C]
We're A Miracle [Christina Aguilera]

8/5/00 — **85** — 7 — ©572 — **Pokémon The Movie 2000: The Power Of One** — [V] $10 — Atlantic 83370

animated movie, voices by Veronica Taylor/Ted Lewis/Stan Hart

Blah, Blah, Blah [Devotion 2 Music]	Extra Mile [Laura Pausini]	Pokémon World [Youngstown]
Chosen One [B-52's]	Flying Without Wings [Westlife]	Polkamon ["Weird Al" Yankovic]
Comin' To The Rescue [O-Town]	Legend Comes To Life	Power Of One [Donna Summer]
Dance Of The Bellossom	One [Denisse Lara]	They Don't Understand [Dream
Dreams [Alysha]	One Heart [O-Town]	Street]

With All Your Heart [Plus One]
Wonderland [Angela Via]

7/17/82 — **168** — 5 — ©573 — **Poltergeist** — [I] $12 — MGM 5408

JoBeth Williams/Craig T. Nelson/Heather O'Rourke/Beatrice Straight; cp/cd: Jerry Goldsmith

Carol Ann's Theme	Light, The	Night Of The Beast
Escape From Suburbia	Neighborhood-Day	Night Visitor

Rebirth
Twisted Abduction

12/27/80+ — **115** — 10 — 574 — **Popeye** — [M] $12 — Boardwalk 36880

Robin Williams/Shelley Duvall/Ray Walston/Paul Dooley; sw: **Nilsson**

Blow Me Down	He's Large	I'm Popeye The Sailor Man
Din' We	I Yam What I Yam	It's Not Easy Being Me
He Needs Me	I'm Mean	Kids

Sailin'
Swee'pea's Lullaby
Sweethaven

7/13/59 — **8** — 96 ● — ©575 — **Porgy And Bess** — [M] $25 — Columbia 2016

Sidney Poitier/Dorothy Dandridge; mu: **George Gershwin**; ly: DuBose Heyward and Ira Gershwin; cd: **Andre Previn**

Bess, You Is My Woman Now	I Got Plenty O' Nuttin'	My Man's Gone Now
Catfish Row (medley)	I Loves You, Porgy	Oh, Where's My Bess?
Clara, Clara	I'm On My Way	Red Headed Woman
I Ain't Got No Shame	It Ain't Necessarily So	Street Cries Medley
I Can't Sit Down	Morning (medley)	Summertime

There's A Boat That's Leavin' Soon
For New York
Wake Medley
What You Want With Bess?
Woman Is A Sometime Thing

SOUNDTRACKS

DEBUT	PEAK	WKS	RIAA	CD	ARTIST — Album Title	Catalog	Sym	$	Label & Number

4/13/85 | **122** | 8 | ©576 **Porky's Revenge!** .... [V] **$12** Columbia 39983
Dan Monahan/Wyatt Knight/Tony Ganios/Mark Herrier/Kaki Hunter

Blue Suede Shoes *[Carl Perkins/Slim Jim Phantom/Lee Rocker]*
Do You Want To Dance *[Dave Edmunds]*
High School Nights *[Dave Edmunds]* **91**
I Don't Want To Do It *[George Harrison]*
Love Me Tender *[Willie Nelson]*
Peter Gunn Theme *[Clarence Clemons]*
Philadelphia Baby *[Crawling King Snakes]*
Porky's Revenge *[Dave Edmunds]*
Queen Of The Hop *[Dave Edmunds]*
Sleepwalk *[Jeff Beck]*
Stagger Lee *[Fabulous Thunderbirds]*

5/29/93 | **178** | 2 | ©577 **Posse** .... [V] **$10** A&M 540081
Mario Van Peebles/**Tone Loc**/**Big Daddy Kane**/Blair Underwood/Stephen Baldwin

Cruel Jim Crow (Posse Don't Play That) *[Melvin Van Peebles]*
Free At Last *[David + David]*
Freemanville (Homecoming) *[Sounds Of Blackness]*
I Think To Myself *[Top Choice Clique]*
If I Knew You At All *[Salli Richardson]*
Jesse *[Michel Colombier]*
Let That Hammer Fall *[Neville Brothers]*
One Night Of Freedom *[B.B.O.T.I. (Badd Boyz Of The Industry)]*
Posse Love *[Tone Loc]*
Posse (Shoot 'Em Up) *[Intelligent Hoodlum]*
Ride Of Your Life *[Vesta]*
Tell Me *[Vesta]*

4/13/96 | **182** | 1 | ©578 **Postman (Il Postino), The** .... [I+T] **$10** Miramax 62029
Massimo Troisi/Philippe Noiret/Maria Grazia Cucinotta; cp/cd: Luis Bacalov

Adonic Angela (poem)
And Now You're Mine (Love Sonnet LXXXI) (poem)
Beatrice
Bicycle
Fable of the Mermaid and the Drunks (poem)
I Like For You To Be Still (poem)
If You Forget Me (Madonna)
Integrations (poem)
Leaning into the Afternoons... (poem)
Loved By Women
Madreselva *[Carlos Gardel]*
Madreselva (instrumental)
Metaphors
Milonga Del Poeta
Morning (Love Sonnet XXVII) (poem)
Ode to a Beautiful Nude (poem)
Ode To The Sea (poem)
Pablito
Poetry (poem)
Poor Fellows (poem)
Postman Poet
Postman (Titles)
Postman, The
Postman's Dreams
Sounds of The Island Theme
Tonight I Can Write... (poem)
Walking Around (poem)

10/31/98 | **36** | 22 | ©579 **Practical Magic** .... [V] **$10** Warner Sunset 47140
Sandra Bullock/Nicole Kidman/Dianne Wiest/Stockard Channing

Always On My Mind *[Elvis Presley]*
Black Eyed Dog *[Nick Drake]*
Case Of You *[Joni Mitchell]*
Coconut *[Harry Nilsson]* **8**
Convening The Coven *[Michael Nyman Orch.]*
Crystal *[Stevie Nicks]*
Everywhere *[Bran Van 3000]*
Got To Give It Up (Pt. 1) *[Marvin Gaye]* **1**
If You Ever Did Believe *[Stevie Nicks]*
Is This Real? *[Lisa Hall]*
Maria Owens *[Michael Nyman Orch.]*
Nowhere And Everywhere *[Michelle Lewis]*
This Kiss *[Faith Hill]* **7**

Preacher's Wife, The - see HOUSTON, Whitney
Denzel Washington/**Whitney Houston**/Gregory Hines/Courtney Vance

3/1/86 | **5** | 27 | ● | ©580 **Pretty In Pink** | [V] **$12** A&M 3901
Molly Ringwald/Jon Cryer/Andrew McCarthy/Harry Dean Stanton/Annie Potts

Bring On The Dancing Horses *[Echo & The Bunnymen]*
Do Wot You Do *[INXS]*
Get To Know Ya *[Jesse Johnson]*
If You Leave *[Orchestral Manoeuvres In The Dark]* **4**
Left Of Center *[Suzanne Vega/Joe Jackson]*
Please Please Please Let Me Get What I Want *[Smiths]*
Pretty In Pink *[Psychedelic Furs]* **41**
Round, Round *[Belouis Some]*
Shell-Shock *[New Order]*
Wouldn't It Be Good *[Danny Hutton Hitters]*

4/7/90 | **4** | 91 | ▲3 | ©581 **Pretty Woman** | C:#44/1 [V] **$10** EMI 93492
Richard Gere/Julia Roberts/Ralph Bellamy/Jason Alexander/Laura San Giacomo

Fallen *[Lauren Wood]*
Fame 90 *[David Bowie]*
It Must Have Been Love *[Roxette]* **1**
King Of Wishful Thinking *[Go West]* **8**
Life In Detail *[Robert Palmer]*
No Explanation *[Peter Cetera]*
Oh Pretty Woman *[Roy Orbison]* **1**
Real Wild Child (Wild One) *[Christopher Otcasek]*
Show Me Your Soul *[Red Hot Chili Peppers]*
Tangled *[Jane Wiedlin]*
Wild Women Do *[Natalie Cole]* **34**

12/5/98+ | **25** | 20 | ▲ | ©582 **Prince Of Egypt, The** .... [V] **$10** DreamWorks 50041
animated movie, voices by: Val Kilmer/Ralph Fiennes/Michelle Pfeiffer/Jeff Goldblum; cp: Hans Zimmer; sw: Stephen Schwartz

All I Ever Wanted *[Amick Byram & Linda Dee Shayne]*
Burning Bush
Cry *[Ofra Haza]*
Death Of The First Born
Deliver Us *[Ofra Haza & Eden Riegel]*
Following Tzipporah
Goodbye Brother *[Ofra Haza]*
Humanity
I Will Get There *[Boyz II Men]* **32**
Plagues, The *[Ralph Fiennes & Amick Byram]*
Playing With The Big Boys *[Steve Martin & Martin Short]*
Prince Of Egypt ..see: When You Believe
Rally
Red Sea
Reprimand, The
River Lullaby *[Amy Grant]*
Through Heaven's Eyes *[Brian Stokes Mitchell]*
Through Heaven's Eyes *[K-Ci & JoJo]*
When You Believe *[Whitney Houston & Mariah Carey]* **15**
When You Believe *[Michelle Pfeiffer & Sally Dworsky]*

1/11/92 | **84** | 12 | ©583 **Prince Of Tides, The** .... [I] **$10** Columbia 48627
Barbra Streisand/Nick Nolte/Blythe Danner/Kate Nelligan; cp: James Newton Howard; cd: Marty Paich

Bloodstain, The
Daddy's Home
End Credits
Fishmarket, The
For All We Know *[Barbra Streisand]*
For All We Know (instrumental)
Hallway (Love Theme)
Home Movies
Lila's Theme
Love Montage
Main Title
New York Willies
Outdoors, The
Places That Belong To You *[Barbra Streisand]*
Reunion, The
Savannah Awakes
So Cruel
Street, The
Teddy Bears
They Love You Dad
To New York
Tom Comes Home
Tom's Breakdown
Village Walk

10/31/87 | **180** | 1 | ©584 **Princess Bride, The** .... [I] **$10** Warner 25610
Cary Elwes/Robin Wright/**Mandy Patinkin**/**Billy Crystal**/Andre The Giant; cp: **Mark Knopfler**

Cliffs Of Insanity
Fireswamp And The Rodents Of Unusual Size
Florin Dance
Friend's Song
Guide My Sword
Happy Ending
I Will Never Love Again
Morning Ride
Once Upon A Time...Storybook Love
Revenge
Storybook Love *[Willy DeVille]*
Swordfight

3/15/97 | **❶1** | 9 | ▲ | ©585 **Private Parts** | [V] **$10** Warner 46477
Howard Stern/Robin Quivers/Fred Norris/Mary McCormack/Paul Giamatti

Cat Scratch Fever *[Ted Nugent]* **30**
Great American Nightmare *[Rob Zombie]*
Hard Charger *[Porno For Pyros]*
I Make My Own Rules *[LL Cool J]*
I Want You To Want Me *[Cheap Trick]*
Jamie's Cryin' *[Van Halen]*
Pictures Of Matchstick Men *[Ozzy Osbourne]*
Pinhead *[Ramones]*
Smoke On The Water *[Deep Purple]* **4**
Suck For Your Solution *[Marilyn Manson]*
Tired Of Waiting For You *[Green Day]*
Tortured Man *[Howard Stern & The Dust Brothers]*
You Shook Me All Night Long *[AC/DC]* **35**

10/29/94 | **21** | 107 | ▲3 | ©586 **Pulp Fiction** ....C:#31/8 [O-V] **$10** MCA 11103
John Travolta/Samuel L. Jackson/Uma Thurman/**Bruce Willis**/Tim Roth

Bullwinkle Part II *[Centurians]*
Bustin' Surfboards *[Tornadoes]*
Comanche *[Revels]*
Flowers On The Wall *[Statler Brothers]* **4**
Girl, You'll Be A Woman Soon *[Urge Overkill]* **59**
If Love Is A Red Dress (Hang Me In Rags) *[Maria McKee]*
Jungle Boogie *[Kool & The Gang]* **4**
Let's Stay Together *[Al Green]* **1**
Lonesome Town *[Ricky Nelson]* **7**
Misirlou *[Dick Dale & His Del-Tones]*
Son Of A Preacher Man *[Dusty Springfield]* **10**
Surf Rider *[Lively Ones]*
You Never Can Tell *[Chuck Berry]* **14**

1040

DEBUT	PEAK	WKS	RIAA	CD	ARTIST — Album Title	Catalog	Sym	$	Label & Number

9/8/90 — **50** — 34 — ● — ©587 — **Pump Up The Volume** .... [V] **$10** MCA 8039
Christian Slater/Scott Paulin/Ellen Greene/Samantha Mathis

Everybody Knows [Concrete Blonde]	I've Got A Secret Miniature Camera [Peter Murphy]	Me And The Devil Blues [Cowboy Junkies]	Titanium Expose [Sonic Youth]
Freedom Of Speech [Above The Law]	Kick Out The Jams [Bad Brains & Henry Rollins]	Stand [Liquid Jesus]	Wave Of Mutilation (U.K. Surf) [Pixies]
Heretic [Soundgarden]		Tale O' The Twister [Chagall Guevara]	Why Can't I Fall In Love [Ivan Neville]

Pure Country - see STRAIT, George
George Strait/Lesley Ann Warren/Isabel Glasser

Purple Rain - see PRINCE
Prince/Apollonia/Morris Day/Clarence Williams III

Quadrophenia - see WHO, The
Phil Daniels/Leslie Ash/Sting

5/30/98 — **117** — 5 — ©588 — **Quest For Camelot** .... [V] **$10** Curb 83097
animated movie, voices by: Pierce Brosnan/Gabriel Byrne/Cary Elwes/Eric Idle/**Don Rickles**

Battle, The	If I Didn't Have You [Eric Idle & Don Rickles]	Looking Through Your Eyes [Corrs & Bryan White]	Prayer, The [Celine Dion]
Dragon Attack (medley)		Looking Through Your Eyes (instrumental)	Prayer, The [Andrea Bocelli]
Forbidden Forest (medley)	**Looking Through Your Eyes** [LeAnn Rimes] 18		Ruber [Gary Oldman]
I Stand All Alone [Bryan White]		On My Father's Wings [Corrs]	United We Stand [Steve Perry]
I Stand Alone [Steve Perry]			

4/17/82 — **154** — 6 — ©589 — **Quest For Fire** .... [I] **$12** RCA Victor 4274
Everett McGill/Rae Dawn Chong/Ron Perlman; cp: Philippe Sarde

Bear Fight	Creation Of Fire	Mammoths	Village Of Painted People
Beginning Of Future	Kzamns	Noah's Distress	Wagabous
Birth Of Love	Last Ander	Sabre-Teeth Lions	
Cave Attack	Love Theme	Small Blue Female	

3/1/86 — **140** — 5 — ©590 — **Quicksilver** .... [V] **$12** Atlantic 81631
Kevin Bacon/Jami Gertz/Paul Rodriguez/Laurence Fishburne

Casual Thing [Fiona]	Quicksilver Lightning [Roger Daltrey]	Shortcut To Somewhere [Fish & Tony Banks]	Through The Night (Love Song) [John Parr & Marilyn Martin]
Motown Song [Larry John McNally]	Quicksilver Suite Medley [Tony Banks]	Suite Streets From Quicksilver [Thomas Newman]	
Nothing At All [Peter Frampton]			
One Sunny Day (medley) 96			

1/23/82 — **134** — 9 — 591 — **Ragtime** .... [I] **$12** Elektra 565
James Cagney/Howard Rollins/Elizabeth McGovern/Moses Gunn; cp/cd: **Randy Newman**

Atlantic City	Delmonico Polka	Morgan Library Takeover	Sarah's Funeral
Change Your Way	Denouement Medley	Newsreel	Sarah's Responsibility
Clef Club (Parts 1 & 2)	I Could Love A Million Girls	One More Hour	Tateh's Picture Book
Coalhouse And Sarah	Lower East Side	Ragtime (Main Title)	Train Ride
Coalhouse's Prayer	Main Title	Rhinelander Waldo	Waltz For Evelyn

7/4/81 — **62** — 13 — ©592 — **Raiders Of The Lost Ark** .... [I] **$12** Columbia 37373
Harrison Ford/Karen Allen/John Rhys-Davies/Denholm Elliott; cp/cd: **John Williams**

Basket Game	Map Room: Dawn	Raiders March	
Desert Chase	Marion's Theme	Raiders Of The Lost Ark	
Flight From Peru	Miracle Of The Ark	Well Of The Souls	

3/11/89 — **31** — 16 — ©593 — **Rain Man** .... [V] **$10** Capitol 91866
Dustin Hoffman/Tom Cruise/Valeria Golino/Bonnie Hunt/Barry Levinson

At Last [Etta James] 47	Las Vegas [Hans Zimmer]	Nathan Jones [Bananarama]	Stardust [Rob Wasserman with Aaron Neville]
Beyond The Blue Horizon [Lou Christie] 80	Leaving Wallbrook (medley) [Hans Zimmer]	On The Road (medley) [Hans Zimmer]	
Dry Bones [Delta Rhythm Boys]	Lonely Avenue [Ian Gillan & Roger Glover]	Scatterlings Of Africa [Johnny Clegg]	
Iko Iko [Belle Stars] 14			

Rainbow Bridge - see HENDRIX, Jimi

Rattle And Hum - see U2

12/31/94+ — **29** — 18 — ● — ©594 — **Ready To Wear (Pret-A-Porter)** .... [V] **$10** Columbia 66791
Juliet Roberts/Tim Robbins/Sophia Loren/Marcello Mastroianni

Close To You [Brand New Heavies]	Jump On Top Of Me [Rolling Stones]	Martha [Deep Forest]	Supermodel Sandwich [Terence Trent D'Arby]
Get Wild [New Power Generation]	Keep Givin' Me Your Love [Ce Ce Peniston]	My Girl Josephine [Supercat]	These Boots Are Made For Walkin' [Sam Phillips]
Here Comes The Hotstepper [Ini Kamoze] 1		Natural Thing [M People]	
Here We Come [Salt-N-Pepa]	Lemon [U2]	Pretty [Cranberries]	
		70's Love Groove [Janet Jackson]	

2/26/94 — **13** — 52 — ▲² — ©595 — **Reality Bites** .... [V] **$10** RCA 66364
Winona Ryder/Ethan Hawke/Ben Stiller/Janeane Garofalo/Steve Zahn

All I Want Is You [U2]	Locked Out [Crowded House]	**Spinning Around Over You** [Lenny Kravitz] flip	When You Come Back To Me [World Party]
Baby I Love Your Way [Big Mountain] 6	**My Sharona** [Knack] 91	**Stay (I Missed You)** [Lisa Loeb & Nine Stories] 1	
Bed Of Roses [Indians]	Revival [Me Phi Me]		
Going, Going, Gone [Posies]	**Spin The Bottle** [Juliana Hatfield Three] 97	Tempted [Squeeze]	
I'm Nuthin' [Ethan Hawke]		Turnip Farm [Dinosaur Jr.]	

10/21/00+ — **49** — 34 — ©596 — **Remember The Titans** .... [O-V] **$10** Walt Disney 60687
Denzel Washington/Will Patton/Wood Harris/Ryan Hurst

Act Naturally [Buck Owens]	Hard Rain's A-Gonna Fall [Leon Russell]	**Na Na Hey Hey Kiss Him Goodbye** [Steam] 1	**Spirit In The Sky** [Norman Greenbaum] 3
Ain't No Mountain High Enough [Marvin Gaye & Tammi Terrell] 19	I Want To Take You Higher [Ike & Tina Turner] 34	Peace Train [Cat Stevens] 7	Titans Spirit (Score)
Express Yourself [Charles Wright] 12	**Long Cool Woman (In A Black Dress)** [Hollies] 2	Spill The Wine [Eric Burdon & War] 3	Up Around The Bend [Creedence Clearwater Revival] 4

3/11/95 — **24**ᶜ — 33 — ©597 — **Reservoir Dogs** .... [O-V] **$10** MCA 10541
Harvey Keitel/Tim Roth/Chris Penn/Steve Buscemi/Quentin Tarantino

Coconut [Nilsson] 8	**Hooked On A Feeling** [Blue Swede] 1	Little Green Bag [George Baker Selection] 21	**Stuck In The Middle With You** [Stealers Wheel] 6
Fool For Love [Sandy Rogers]	I Gotcha [Joe Tex] 2	Magic Carpet Ride [Bedlam]	
Harvest Moon [Bedlam]			

6/11/83 — **20** — 17 — ©598 — **Return Of The Jedi** .... [I] **$15** RSO 811767
Mark Hamill/Harrison Ford/Carrie Fisher/Billy Dee Williams; cp/cd: **John Williams**

Emperor, The	Han Solo Returns (At The Court Of Jabba The Hutt)	Lapti Nek (Jabba's Palace Band)	Parade Of The Ewoks
Ewok Celebration	Into The Trap	Luke And Leia	Rebel Briefing
Forest Battle		Main Title (The Story Continues)	Return Of The Jedi

SOUNDTRACKS

DEBUT	PEAK	WKS	RIAA	CD	ARTIST — Album Title	Catalog	Sym	$	Label & Number

3/29/97 · **51** · **4** · ©599 · **Return Of The Jedi** .... [I-R] **$15** · RCA Victor 68748 [2]

complete score in sequence with previously unreleased music issued in conjunction with the 1997 release of the *Return Of The Jedi* Special Edition movie in theaters

Alliance Assembly	Emperor Arrives (medley)	Jedi Rocks	Part Of The Tribe (medley)
Approaching The Death Star (medley)	Emperor's Throne Room	Land Of The Ewoks (medley)	Pit Of Carkoon (medley)
Battle Of Endor I (Medley)	End Title (medley)	Leia's News (medley)	Sail Barge Assault (medley)
Battle Of Endor II (Medley)	Ewok Battle (medley)	Levitation, The (medley)	Sail Barge Assault (Alternate)
Battle Of Endor III (Medley)	Ewok Feast (medley)	Light Of The Force (medley)	Sarlacc Sentence (medley)
Bounty For A Wookiee	Father And Son (medley)	Lightsaber, The (medley)	Shuttle Tydirium Approaches Endor
Brother And Sister (medley)	Fleet Enters Hyperspace (medley)	Luke And Leia	Speeder Bike Chase (medley)
Death Of Yoda (medley)	Forest Battle (Concert Suite)	Luke Confronts Jabba (medley)	Tatooine Rendezvous (medley)
Den Of The Rancor (medley)	Han Solo Returns	Main Title (medley)	Threepio's Bedtime Story (medley)
Droids Are Captured	Heroic Ewok (medley)	Obi-Wan's Revelation (medley)	20th Century Fox Fanfare
	Jabba's Baroque Recital	Parade Of The Ewoks	Victory Celebration (medley)

Rhinestone - see PARTON, Dolly
Sylvester Stallone/Dolly Parton/Richard Farnsworth/Ron Leiman

2/1/97 · **16** · **13** · ● · ©600 · **Rhyme & Reason** .... [V] **$10** · Priority 50635

concert movie/documentary

Bogus Mayn [Crucial Conflict]	Liquor Store Run [Volume 10]	Reason For Rhyme [Eight Ball & MJG]
Bring It Back [KRS-ONE]	Niggaz Don't Want It [Lost Boyz]	Represent [MC Eiht]
Business First [Nyoo & DeCoca]	No Identity [Delinquent Habits]	Tragedy [RZA]
Every Year [E-40]	**Nothin' But The Cavi Hit** [Mack 10 & Tha Dogg Pound] **38**	Uni-4-Orm [Ras Kass, Heltah Skeltah & Cannibus]
Is There A Heaven 4 A Gangsta? [Master P]		
		Way It Iz [Guru, Kai:Bee & Lil' Dap]
		Wild Hot [Busta Rhymes & A Tribe Called Quest]

7/28/73 · **117** · **9** · 601 · **Richard Nader/Let The Good Times Roll** .... [L] **$20** · Bell 9002 [2]

Richard Nader's Rock and Roll Revival show

At The Hop [Danny & The Juniors]	Hey Bo Diddley [Bo Diddley]	My Blue Heaven [Fats Domino]	Shake, Rattle, & Roll [Bill Haley]
Blueberry Hill [Fats Domino]	I'll Be Seeing You [5 Satins]	Poison Ivy [Coasters]	Sincerely (medley) [Five Satins]
Charlie Brown [Coasters]	I'm A Man [Bo Diddley]	Pony Time [Chubby Checker]	Soldier Boy [Shirelles]
Earth Angel (medley) [Five Satins]	In The Still Of The Nite (medley)	Rip It Up [Little Richard]	Twist, The [Chubby Checker]
Everybody Loves A Lover [Shirelles]	[Five Satins]	Rock Around The Clock [Bill Haley]	
Good Golly Miss Molly [Little Richard]	Let's Twist Again [Chubby Checker]	Save The Last Dance For Me (medley) [Five Satins]	
	Lucille [Little Richard]		

Richard Pryor Live On The Sunset Strip - see PRYOR, Richard
Richard Pryor: Here And Now - see PRYOR, Richard

3/7/98 · **54** · **7** · ©602 · **Ride** .... [V] **$10** · Tommy Boy 1227

Malik Yoba/Melissa De Sousa/John Witherspoon/Fredro Starr (**Onyx**)

Blood Money (Part 2) [Noreaga]	Higher [Sexions]	No One [Somethin' For The People]	Worst, The [Wu-Tang & Onyx]
Callin' [Amari]	Jam On It [Cardan]	Outta Sight [Rufus Blaq]	
Can't Get Enough [Raphael Saadiq]	**Mourn You Till I Join You**	Soldier Funk [Mia X]	
Feels So Good [Eastsiders]	[Naughty By Nature] **51**	Symptoms, The [Black Caesar]	
Game, The [Mack 10/Big Mike/D.J. U-Neek]	Never Say Goodbye [Adriana Evans]	Weekend, The [Dave Hollister]	
		Why [Eric Benet & The Roots]	

Ride The Wild Surf - see JAN & DEAN
Tab Hunter/**Fabian**/**Shelley Fabares**/Barbara Eden

Right On! - see LAST POETS
David Nelson/Felipe Luciano/Gylan Kain

6/3/89 · **67** · **10** · ©603 · **Road House** .... [V] **$10** · Arista 8576

Patrick Swayze/Ben Gazzara/Kelly Lynch/Sam Elliott/Terry Funk

Blue Monday [Bob Seger]	Hoochie Coochie Man [Jeff Healey Band]	Raising Heaven (In Hell Tonight) [Patrick Swayze]	**These Arms Of Mine** [Otis Redding] **85**
Cliff's Edge [Patrick Swayze]	I'm Tore Down [Jeff Healey Band]	Roadhouse Blues [Jeff Healey Band]	When The Night Comes Falling From The Sky [Jeff Healey Band]
Good Heart [Kris McKay]	Rad Gumbo [Little Feat]		

Road To El Dorado, The - see JOHN, Elton
animated movie, voices by Kevin Kline/Kenneth Branagh/Rosie Perez

6/21/80 · **125** · **8** · 604 · **Roadie** .... [V] **$15** · Warner 3441 [2]

Meat Loaf/Art Carney/Kaki Hunter/Gailard Sartain

American Way [Hank Williams, Jr.]	**Drivin' My Life Away** [Eddie Rabbitt]	Man Needs A Woman [Jay Ferguson]	**That Lovin' You Feeling Again** [Roy Orbison & Emmylou Harris] **55**
Brainlock [Joe Ely Band]	**Everything Works If You Let It** [Cheap Trick] **44**	Pain [Alice Cooper]	**You Better Run** [Pat Benatar] **42**
Can't We Try [Teddy Pendergrass] **52**	(Hot Damn) I'm A One Woman Man [Jerry Lee Lewis]	Ring Of Fire [Blondie]	Your Precious Love [Stephen Bishop & Yvonne Elliman]
Crystal Ball [Styx]		Road Rats [Alice Cooper]	
Double Yellow Line [Sue Saad & The Next]		Texas, Me And You [Asleep At The Wheel]	

7/18/64 · **56** · **14** · ©605 · **Robin And The 7 Hoods** .... [M] **$75** · Reprise 2021

Frank Sinatra/Dean Martin/Bing Crosby/Sammy Davis, Jr.; sw: Sammy Cahn and James Van Heusen; cd: **Nelson Riddle**

All For One And One For All	Don't Be A Do-Badder	Mister Booze
Any Man Who Loves His Mother	Give Praise! Give Praise! Give Praise!	My Kind Of Town
Bang! Bang!		Robin And The 7 Hoods (Overture)
Charlotte Couldn't Charleston	I Like To Lead When I Dance	Style

7/20/91 · **5** · **45** · ▲ · ©606 · **Robin Hood: Prince Of Thieves** · [I] **$10** · Morgan Creek 20004

Kevin Costner/Mary Elizabeth Mastrantonio/Morgan Freeman/Christian Slater/Alan Rickman; cp/cd: Michael Kamen

Abduction (medley)	Final Battle At The Gallows (medley)	Marian At The Waterfall	Sheriff and His Witch
Escape To Sherwood (medley)	Little John And The Band In The Forest	Overture (medley)	Sir Guy Of Gisborne (medley)
(Everything I Do) I Do It For You [Bryan Adams] **1**		Prisoner Of The Crusades (medley)	Training (medley)
	Maid Marian	Robin Hood, Prince Of Thieves (medley)	Wild Times [Jeff Lynne]

6/2/79 · **118** · **6** · 607 · **Rock 'N' Roll High School** .... [V] **$15** · Sire 6070

P.J. Soles/Vincent Van Patten/Dey Young/**Ramones**

Come Back Jonee [Devo]	I Want You Around [Ramones]	**School Day** [Chuck Berry] **3**	Teenage Depression [Eddie & The Hot Rods]
Come On Let's Go [Paley Brothers & Ramones]	Ramones Medley [Ramones]	**School's Out** [Alice Cooper] **7**	
Dream Goes On Forever [Todd Rundgren] **69**	Rock 'N' Roll High School [Ramones]	**Smokin' In The Boy's Room** [Brownsville Station] **3**	
Energy Fools The Magician [Eno]	Rock 'N' Roll High School [P.J. Soles]	So It Goes [Nick Lowe]	

DEBUT	PEAK	WKS	RIAA	CD	ARTIST — Album Title	Catalog	Sym	$	Label & Number

3/9/57 · **16** · 9 · **608** · **Rock, Pretty Baby** .... **[M]** · **$150** · Decca 8429
Sal Mineo/John Saxon/Luana Patten; cp: **Henry Mancini**; pf: Jimmy Daley & The Ding-A-Lings
Big Band Rock And Roll	Happy Is A Boy Named Me	Picnic By The Sea	Saints Rock 'N Roll
Can I Steal A Little Love	Hot Rod	Rock, Pretty Baby	Teen Age Bop
Dark Blue	Juke Box Rock	Rockabye Lullaby Blues	What's It Gonna Be
Free And Easy	Most, The	Rockin' Boogie	Young Love

3/5/77 · **4** · 34 · ▲ · ©**609** · **Rocky** · **[I]** · **$15** · United Artists 693
Sylvester Stallone/Talia Shire/Carl Weathers/Burgess Meredith/Burt Young; cp/cd: Bill Conti
Alone In The Ring	First Date	Philadelphia Morning	Yankee Doodle (medley)
Butkus	Going The Distance	Reflections	You Take My Heart Away
Fanfare For Rocky	**Gonna Fly Now** [Bill Conti] 1	Rocky's Reward	
Final Bell	Marine's Hymn (medley)	Take You Back	

8/25/79 · **147** · 5 · ©**610** · **Rocky II** .... **[I]** · **$12** · United Artists 972
Sylvester Stallone/Talia Shire/Carl Weathers/Burgess Meredith/Burt Young; cp/cd: Bill Conti
| All Of My Life | Gonna Fly Now | Two Kinds Of Love |
| Conquest | Redemption (Theme) | Vigil |

7/10/82 · **15** · 19 · ● · ©**611** · **Rocky III** .... **[I+V]** · **$12** · Liberty 51130
Sylvester Stallone/Talia Shire/Mr. T/Burt Young/Burgess Meredith; cp/cd: Bill Conti
Adrian	**Eye Of The Tiger** [Survivor] 1	Pushin' [Frank Stallone]	Take You Back (includes 2
Conquest	Gonna Fly Now	Reflections	versions) [Frank Stallone]
Decision	Mickey		

11/16/85+ · **10** · 30 · ▲ · ©**612** · **Rocky IV** · **[V]** · **$10** · Scotti Brothers 40203
Sylvester Stallone/Talia Shire/Dolph Lundgren/Burt Young/Brigitte Nielsen
Burning Heart [Survivor] 2	**Eye Of The Tiger** [Survivor] 1	**No Easy Way Out** [Robert	Sweetest Victory [Touch]
Double Or Nothing [Kenny Loggins	Heart's On Fire [John Cafferty] 76	Tepper] 22	Training Montage [Vince DiCola]
& Gladys Knight]	Living In America [James Brown] 4	One Way Street [Go West]	War [Vince DiCola]

4/15/78 · **49** · 58 · ● · ©**613** · **Rocky Horror Picture Show** ....**C:#45/1** · **[M]** · **$20** · Ode 21653
Tim Curry/Susan Sarandon/Barry Bostwick/**Meat Loaf**; sw: Richard O'Brien
Damn It Janet	I Can Make You A Man	Rose Tint My World	Sweet Transvestite
Eddie	I'm Going Home	Science Fiction Double Feature	Time Warp
Hot Patootie-Bless My Soul	Over At The Frankenstein Place	Super Heroes	Touch-A, Touch-A, Touch Me

8/23/75 · **156** · 6 · **614** · **Rollerball** .... **[I]** · **$15** · United Artists 470
James Caan/John Houseman/Maud Adams/John Beck/Moses Gunn; cd: **Andre Previn**
Adagio	Excerpt from Symphony No. 5	Executive Party Dance
Excerpt from Symphony No. 8 (First	(Third Movement))	Toccata In D Minor
Movement)	Executive Party	Waltz from "Sleeping Beauty"

6/16/62 · **5** · 28 · **615** · **Rome Adventure** · **[I]** · **$25** · Warner 1458
Troy Donahue/Suzanne Pleshette/Angie Dickinson; cp: Max Steiner
Al Di La' [Emilio Pericoli] 6	Lovers Must Learn	Prudence	Serenade
Arrivederci, Roma	Mattinata	Rome Adventure	Tarantella
Come Back To Sorrento	Oh, Marie	Santa Lucia	Volare (Nel Blu Di Pinto Di Blu)

2/8/69 · **2²** · 74 · ▲ · ©**616** · **Romeo & Juliet** · **$20** · Capitol 2993
Leonard Whiting/Olivia Hussey/Michael York/Pat Heywood/John McEnery; cp/cd: Nino Rota
All Are Punished	**Farewell Love Scene** 86	In Capulet's Tomb (Death of Romeo	Romeo & Juliet Are Wed
Balcony Scene	Feast At The House Of Capulet	& Juliet)	Romeo's Foreboding (medley)
Death Of Mercutio And Tybalt	(medley)	Likeness Of Death	

11/16/96+ · **2²** · 48 · ▲³ · ©**617** · **Romeo & Juliet** · **[V]** · **$10** · Capitol 37715
Claire Danes/Leonardo DiCaprio/John Leguizamo/Paul Sorvino/Pete Postlethwaite
Angel [Gavin Friday]	Local God [Everclear]	Talk Show Host [Radiohead]	Young Hearts Run Free [Kym
Everybody's Free (To Feel Good)	Lovefool [Cardigans]	To You I Bestow [Mundy]	Mazelle]
[Quindon Tarver]	#1 Crush [Garbage]	Whatever (I Had A Dream) [Butthole	
Kissing You [Des'ree]	Pretty Piece Of Flesh [One Inch	Surfers]	
Little Star [Stina Nordenstam]	Punch]	You And Me Song [Wannadies]	

4/26/97 · **27** · 18 · ● · ©**618** · **Romeo & Juliet Volume 2** .... **[I]** · **$10** · Capitol 55567
Balcony Scene	Gas Station Scene	Mantua	Slow Movement
Challenge, A	Introduction To Romeo	Mercutio's Death	Tybalt Arrives
Death Scene	Juliet's Requiem	Montague Boys	When Dove's Cry
Drive Of Death	Kissing You (Love Theme from	Morning Breaks	Young Hearts Run Free (Ballroom
Escape From Mantua	Romeo + Juliet)	O Verona	Version)
Fight Scene	Liebestod	Queen Mab Interlude	

4/15/00 · **3** · 29 · ▲ · ©**619** · **Romeo Must Die** · **[V]** · **$10** · Blackground 49052
Jet Li/**Aaliyah**/Russell Wong/**DMX**/Delroy Lindo
Are You Feelin' Me? [Aaliyah]	Perfect Man [Destiny's Child]	Simply Irresistible [Ginuwine]	Thugz [Mack 10]
Come Back In One Piece [Aaliyah]	Pump The Brakes [Dave Hollister]	Somebody Gonna Die Tonight	**Try Again** [Aaliyah] 1
Come On [Blade]	Revival [Non-A-Miss]	[Dave Bing]	We At It Again [Timbaland &
I Don't Wanna [Aaliyah] 35	Rollin' Raw [BG]	Swung On [Stanley Clarke]	Magoo]
It Really Don't Matter [Confidential]	Rose In A Concrete World [Joe]	This Is A Test [Chanté Moore]	Woozy [Playa]

5/17/97 · **64** · 17 · ©**620** · **Romy And Michele's High School Reunion** .... **[O-V]** · **$10** · Hollywood 62098
Mira Sorvino/Lisa Kudrow/Janeane Garofalo/Alan Cumming
Always Something There To	**Everybody Wants To Rule The**	I Want Candy [Bow Wow Wow] 62	Venus [Bananarama] 1
Remind Me [Naked Eyes] 8	**World** [Tears For Fears] 1	Karma Chameleon [Culture Club] 1	We Got The Beat [Go-Go's] 2
Blood And Roses [Smithereens]	**Heaven Is A Place On Earth**	Our Lips Are Sealed [Go-Go's] 20	
Dance Hall Days [Wang Chung] 16	[Belinda Carlisle] 1	Turning Japanese [Vapors] 36	

Rose, The - see MIDLER, Bette
Bette Midler/Alan Bates/Frederic Forrest/Harry Dean Stanton

1/24/87 · **196** · 3 · ©**621** · **Round Midnight** .... **[I]** · **$10** · Columbia 40464
Dexter Gordon/Francois Cluzet/Gabrielle Haker/Lonette McKee; cp/cd: **Herbie Hancock**
Berangere's Nightmare	Fair Weather	Minuit Aux Champs-Elysees	Round Midnight
Body And Soul	How Long Has This Been Going	Peacocks, The	Still Time
Chan's Song (Never Said)	On?	Rhythm-A-Ning	Una Noche Con Francis

Roustabout - see PRESLEY, Elvis
Elvis Presley ("Charlie Rogers")/Barbara Stanwyck/Joan Freeman/Pat Buttram

DEBUT	PEAK	WKS	RIAA	CD	ARTIST — Album Title	Catalog	Sym	$	Label & Number

10/31/70 — **148** — 6 — 622 — **R.P.M.** .... [I+V] — **$20** — Bell 1203
Anthony Quinn/**Ann-Margret**/Gary Lockwood/Paul Winfield; sw: **Barry DeVorzon** and Perry Botkin Jr.

All Night Long [Chris Morgan]	Paco's Farewell	Stop! I Don't Wanna' Hear It
All Night Long (instrumental)	Riot, The	Anymore (instrumental)
I Wanna' Spend Some Time With	Stop! I Don't Wanna' Hear It	Transistor Q
You [Christopher]	Anymore [Melanie]	We Don't Know Where We're Goin'
		[Melanie]

We Don't Know Where We're Goin'
(instrumental)
When I Get Home To You
[Christopher]

11/25/00 — **48** — 16 — ● — ©623 — **RugRats In Paris: The Movie** .... [V] — **$10** — Maverick 47850
animated movie, voices by Susan Sarandon/E.G. Daily/Christine Cavanaugh/Cheryl Chase

Bad Girls [Angelica & The Sumos]	I Want A Mom That Will Last	Life Is A Party [Aaron Carter]
Chuckie Chan (Martial Arts Expert	Forever [Cyndi Lauper]	My Getaway [T-Boz]
Of Reptarland) [Isaac Hayes]	I'm Telling You This [No Authority]	These Boots Are Made For Walkin'
Excuse My French [2BE3]	L'histoire D'une Fee, C'est...	[Geri Halliwell]
Final Heartbreak [Jessica Simpson]	[Mylene Farmer]	When You Love [Sinéad O'Connor]

Who Let The Dogs Out [Baha
Men] **40**
You Don't Stand A Chance
[Amanda]

11/21/98+ — **19** — 26 — ▲ — ©624 — **RugRats Movie, The** .... [V] — **$10** — Interscope 90181
animated movie, voices by: E.G. Daily/Melanie Chartoff/Whoopi Goldberg/**Busta Rhymes**

All Day [Lisa Loeb]	On Your Marks, Get Set, Ready,	Take The Train [Rakim & Danny
Baby Is A Gift From A Bob [Cheryl	Go! [Busta Rhymes]	Saber]
Chase & Cree Summer]	One Way Or Another [Cheryl	This World Is Something New To
Dil-A-Bye [E.G. Daily]	Chase]	Me [Various Artists]
I Throw My Toys Around [No Doubt]	**Take Me There** [Blackstreet &	Wild Ride [Kevi of 1000 Clowns
	Mya] **14**	feat. Lisa Stone]

Witch Doctor [Devo]
Yo Ho Ho And A Bottle Of Yum!
[E.G. Daily/Christine Cavanaugh &
Kath Soucie]

Rumble Fish - see COPELAND, Stewart
Matt Dillon/Mickey Rourke/Diane Lane/Dennis Hopper/Diana Scarwid

8/14/99 — **4** — 33 — ▲ — ©625 — **Runaway Bride** — [V] — **$10** — Columbia 69923
Julia Roberts/Richard Gere/Joan Cusack/Hector Elizondo/Rita Wilson

And That's What Hurts [Daryl Hall &	**I Love You** [Martina McBride] **24**	Maneater [Daryl Hall & John
John Oates]	**I Still Haven't Found What I'm**	Oates] **1**
Before I Fall In Love [Coco Lee]	**Looking For** [U2] **1**	Never Saw Blue Like That [Shawn
Blue Eyes Blue [Eric Clapton]	It Never Entered My Mind [Miles	Colvin]
From My Head To My Heart [Evan	Davis]	**Ready To Run** [Dixie Chicks] **39**
& Jaron]		

Where Were You (On Our Wedding
Day)? [Billy Joel]
You Can't Hurry Love [Dixie Chicks]
You Sang To Me [Marc Anthony] **2**
You're The Only One For Me
[Allure]

7/5/86 — **43** — 15 — ©626 — **Running Scared** .... [V] — **$12** — MCA 6169
Gregory Hines/**Billy Crystal**/Steven Bauer/Jimmy Smits

El Chase [Rod Temperton]	**Man Size Love** [Klymaxx] **15**	Once In A Lifetime Groove [New
I Just Wanna Be Loved [Ready For	Never Too Late To Start [Rod	Edition]
The World]	Temperton]	Running Scared [Fee Waybill]
I Know What I Want [Patti LaBelle]		

Say You Really Want Me [Kim
Wilde] **44**
Sweet Freedom [Michael
McDonald] **7**

Rush - see CLAPTON, Eric
Jason Patric/Jennifer Jason Leigh/**Gregg Allman**/Sam Elliott/Max Perlich

10/3/98 — **5** — 33 — ▲ — ©627 — **Rush Hour** — [V] — **$10** — Def Jam 558663
Jackie Chan/Chris Tucker/Tom Wilkinson/Chris Penn/Elizabeth Peña

And You Don't Stop [Wu-Tang Clan]	Faded Pictures [Case & Joe] **10**	N.B.C. [Charli Baltimore]
Bitch Betta Have My Money [Ja	Glad That We Loved [Jon B.]	Nasty Girl [Kasino]
Rule]	**How Deep Is Your Love** [Dru Hill] **3**	No Love [Imajin]
Can I Get A... [Jay-Z] **19**	If I Die Tonight [Montell Jordan]	Rush Hour Main Title Theme [Lalo
Disco [Grenique]	Impress The Kid [Slick Rick]	Schifrin]

Tell The Feds [Too $hort]
Terror Squadians [Terror Squad]
Way Too Crazy [Tray Deee]
You'll Never Miss Me 'Til I'm Gone
[Terry Dexter]

3/13/99 — **191** — 1 — ©628 — **Rushmore** .... [O-V] — **$10** — London 556074
Jason Schwartzman/Olivia Williams/Bill Murray/Brian Cox

Blinuet [Zoot Sims]	Nothing In This World Can Stop Me	Quick One While He's Away [Who]
Concrete & Clay [Unit 4 + 2] **28**	Worrin' About That Girl [Kinks]	Rue St. Vincent [Yves Montand]
Here Comes My Baby [Cat Stevens]	Oh Yoko [John Lennon]	"Snowflake Music" From
Making Time [Creation]	Ooh La La [Faces]	Bottlerocket [Mark Mothersbaugh]

Summer Song [Chad & Jeremy] **7**
Wind, The [Cat Stevens]

7/5/86 — **20** — 16 — ● — ©629 — **Ruthless People** .... [V] — **$10** — Epic 40398
Danny DeVito/**Bette Midler**/Judge Reinhold/Helen Slater/Anita Morris

Dance Champion [Kool & The	**Give Me The Reason** [Luther	Neighborhood Watch [Michel
Gang]	Vandross]	Colombier]
Don't You Want My Love [Nicole]	**Modern Woman** [Billy Joel] **10**	No Say In It [Machinations]
		Ruthless People [Mick Jagger] **51**

Stand On It [Bruce Springsteen]
Waiting To See You [Dan Hartman]
**Wherever I Lay My Hat (That's My
Home)** [Paul Young] **70**

12/19/70+ — **199** — 4 — ©630 — **Ryan's Daughter** .... [I] — **$30** — MGM 27
Robert Mitchum/Sarah Miles/Trevor Howard; cp/cd: Maurice Jarre

It Was A Good Time (Rosy's	Michael Shows Randolph His	Ride Through The Woods
Theme)	Strange Treasure	Rosy And The Schoolmaster
Main Title	Michael's Theme	Rosy On The Beach
	Obsession	Shakes, The

Song Of The Irish Rebels
Where Was I When The Parade
Went By? (The Major)
You Don't Want Me Then?

4/12/97 — **24** — 16 — ©631 — **Saint, The** .... [V] — **$10** — Virgin 42959
Val Kilmer/Elisabeth Shue/Rade Serbedzija

Atom Bomb [Fluke]	Dead Man Walking [David Bowie]	Oil 1 [Moby]
Before Today [Everything But The	Dream Within A Dream [Dreadzone]	Out Of My Mind [Duran Duran]
Girl]	In The Absence Of Sun [Duncan	Pearl's Girl [Underworld]
Da Funk [Daft Punk]	Sheik]	Polaroid Millenium [Superior]

Roses Fade [Luscious Jackson]
Saint Theme [Orbital]
Setting Sun [Chemical Brothers]
6 Underground [Sneaker Pimps]

Saint ..see: St.

6/25/88 — **112** — 6 — ©632 — **Salsa** .... [V] — **$10** — MCA 6232
Robby Rosa/Rodney Harvey/Magali Alvarado/Tito Puente

Cali Pachanguero [Grupo Niche]	Good Lovin' [Kenny Ortega]	Oye Como Va (Give It All You Got)
Chicos Y Chicas [Mavis Vegas	I Know [Marisela]	[Tito Puente]
Davis]	Margarita [Wilkins]	Puerto Rico [Bobby Caldwell]

Spanish Harlem [Ben E. King]
Under My Skin [Robby Rosa]
Your Love [Laura Branigan]

10/23/65 — **89** — 15 — 633 — **Sandpiper, The** .... [I] — **$50** — Mercury 61032
Elizabeth Taylor/Richard Burton/Eva Marie Saint/Charles Bronson; cp: Johnny Mandel; cd: Robert Armbruster

Art Gallery	Desire	San Simeon
Baby Sandpiper	End Title	Seduction
Bird Bath	Main Title	Shadow Of Your Smile

Weekend Montage

DEBUT	PEAK	WKS	RIAA	CD	ARTIST — Album Title	Catalog	Sym	$	Label & Number

10/24/92 · 200 · 1 · ©634 · Sarafina! The Sound Of Freedom .... [M] **$10** Qwest 45060
Whoopi Goldberg/Leleti Khumalo/**Miriam Makeba**/John Kani; cp: Mbongeni Ngema and **Hugh Masekela**

Freedom Is Coming Tomorrow	Nkonyane Kandaba	Safa Saphel' Isizwe	Thank You Mama
Lizobuya	One More Time [James Ingram]	Sarafina!	Vuma Dlozi Lami
Lord's Prayer	Sabela	Sechaba	

Saturday Night Fever - see BEE GEES
John Travolta/Karen Gorney/Donna Pescow/Barry Miller/Sal Bisoglio

1/13/01 · 3 · 38↑▲ · ©635 · Save The Last Dance .... [V] **$10** Hollywood 162288
Julia Stiles/Sean Patrick Thomas/Fredro Starr (**Onyx**)

All Or Nothing [Athena Cage]	Move It Slow [Kevon Edmonds]	Shining Through [Fredro Starr & Jill Scott]	You Can Do It [Ice Cube] 35
Bonafide [X-2-C]	**Murder She Wrote** [Chaka Demus & Pliers] 57	**U Know What's Up** [Donell Jones] 7	You Make Me Sick [Pink] 33
Crazy [K-Ci & JoJo] 11	My Window [Soulbone]	You [Lucy Pearl]	
Get It On...Tonite [Montell Jordan] 4	Only You [112] 13		

5/6/89 · 62 · 14 · ©636 · Say Anything... .... [V] **$10** WTG 45140
John Cusack/Ione Skye/John Mahoney/Lili Taylor/Eric Stoltz

All For Love [Nancy Wilson]	Keeping The Dream Alive [Freiheit]	Taste The Pain [Red Hot Chili Peppers]
Cult Of Personality [Living Colour] 13	One Big Rush [Joe Satriani]	Within Your Reach [Replacements]
In Your Eyes [Peter Gabriel] 26	Skankin' To The Beat [Fishbone]	You Want It [Cheap Trick]
	Stripped [Depeche Mode]	

4/9/94 · 45 · 7 ● · ©637 · Schindler's List .... [I] **$10** MCA 10969
Liam Neeson/Ben Kingsley/Ralph Fiennes/Caroline Goodall; cp/cd: **John Williams**

Auschwitz-Birkenau	Jewish Town (Krakow Ghetto - Winter '41)	Remembrances	Yeroushalaim Chel Zahav (Jerusalem Of Gold)
Give Me Your Names	Making The List	Schindler's Workforce	
I Could Have Done More	Nacht Aktion (medley)	Stolen Memories	
Immolation (With Our Lives, We Give Life)	OYF'N Pripetshok (medley)	Theme From Schindler's List	

3/19/88 · 81 · 17 · ©638 · School Daze .... [V] **$10** EMI-Manhattan 48680
Laurence Fishburne/Giancarlo Esposito/Tisha Campbell/Spike Lee

Be Alone Tonight [Rays]	I Can Only Be Me [Keith John]	Straight And Nappy [Kyme & Tisha Campbell]	We've Already Said Goodbye (Before We Said Hello) [Pieces Of A Dream]
Be One [Phyllis Hyman]	One Little Acorn [Kenny Baron & Terence Blanchard]	Wake Up Suite [Natural Spiritual Orchestra]	
Building Me A Home [Tracy Coley]	Perfect Match [Tech]		
Da'Butt [E.U.] 35			

12/20/97+ · 50 · 10 ● · ©639 · Scream 2 .... [V] **$10** Capitol 21911
David Arquette/Neve Campbell/Courteney Cox/Sarah Michelle Gellar/Laurie Metcalf

Dear Lover [Foo Fighters]	One More Chance [Kelly]	Right Place Wrong Time [Jon Spencer Blues Explosion]	She's Always In My Hair [D'Angelo]
Eyes Of Sand [Tonic]	Race, The [Ear2000]	Rivers [Sugar Ray]	Suburban Life [Kottonmouth Kings]
Help Myself [Dave Matthews Band]	Red Right Hand [Nick Cave & The Bad Seeds]	Scream [Master P]	Swing, The [Everclear]
I Think I Love You [Less Than Jake]		She Said [Collective Soul]	Your Lucky Day In Hell [eels]

2/12/00 · 32 · 14 ● · ©640 · Scream 3 .... [V] **$10** Wind-Up 13056
David Arquette/Neve Campbell/Courtney Cox Arquette/Patrick Dempsey

Automatic [American Pearl]	Dissention [Orgy]	Spiders [System Of A Down]	Wait And Bleed [Slipknot]
Click Click [Ear2000]	Fall [Sevendust]	Suffocate [Finger Eleven]	Wanna' Be Martyr [Full Devil Jacket]
Crawl [Staind]	Get On, Get Off [Powerman 5000]	Sunburn [Fuel]	What If [Creed]
Crowded Elevator [Incubus]	Is This The End [Creed]	Time Bomb [Godsmack]	
Debonaire [Dope]	So Real [Static-X]	Tyler's Song [Coal Chamber]	

12/26/70+ · 95 · 8 · 641 · Scrooge .... [X-M] **$30** Columbia 30258
Albert Finney/Alec Guinness/Edith Evans; sw: Leslie Bricusse; cd: Ian Fraser; Christmas chart: 13/70

Beautiful Day	December The 25th	I Hate People	See The Phantoms
Christmas Carol	Father Christmas	I Like Life	Thank You Very Much
Christmas Children	Happiness	I'll Begin Again	You...You

12/3/88+ · 93 · 9 · ©642 · Scrooged .... [V] **$10** A&M 3921
Bill Murray/Karen Allen/John Forsythe/Bobcat Goldthwait/Carol Kane

Brown Eyed Girl [Buster Poindexter]	Get Up 'N' Dance [Kool Moe Dee]	Sweetest Thing [New Voices Of Freedom]
Christmas Must Be Tonight [Robbie Robertson]	Love You Take [Dan Hartman & Denise Lopez]	We Three Kings Of Orient Are [Miles Davis/Larry Carlton/Paul Shaffer]
Christmas Song (Chestnuts Roasting On An Open Fire) [Natalie Cole]	**Put A Little Love In Your Heart** [Annie Lennox & Al Green] 9	Wonderful Life [Mark Lennon]

6/13/87 · 131 · 8 · ©643 · Secret Of My Success, The .... [V] **$10** MCA 6205
Michael J. Fox/Helen Slater/Richard Jordan/Margaret Whitton

Don't Ask The Reason Why [Restless Heart]	I Burn For You [Danny Peck & Nancy Shanks]	**Secret Of My Success** [Night Ranger] 64	3 Themes [David Foster]
Gazebo [David Foster]	Price Of Love [Roger Daltrey]	Sometimes The Good Guys Finish First [Pat Benatar]	Water Fountain [David Foster]
Heaven And The Heartaches [Taxxi]	Riskin' A Romance [Bananarama]		

Serenade - see LANZA, Mario
Mario Lanza/Joan Fontaine/Vincent Price/**Vincent Edwards**

10/12/96 · 4 · 38 ▲ · ©644 · Set It Off .... [V] **$10** EastWest 61951
Jada Pinkett/**Queen Latifah**/Vivica A. Fox/Kimberly Elise

Angel [Simply Red]	**Don't Let Go (Love)** [En Vogue] 2	Live To Regret [Busta Rhymes]	Sex Is On My Mind [Blulight]
Angelic Wars [Goodie Mob]	From Yo Blind Side [X-Man]	**Missing You** [Brandy, Tamia, Gladys Knight & Chaka Khan] 25	
Come On [Billy Lawrence] 44	Heist, The [Da 5 Footaz]	Name Callin' [Queen Latifah]	
Days Of Our Livez [Bone Thugs-N-Harmony]	Hey Joe [Seal]	Set It Off [Organized Noize]	
	Let It Go [Ray J.] 25		

Seven Hills Of Rome - see LANZA, Mario
Mario Lanza/Renato Roscel/Marisa Allasio

12/30/72+ · 163 · 11 · 645 · 1776 .... [M] **$25** Columbia 31741
William Daniels/Howard DaSilva/Ken Howard/David Ford/Blythe Danner; sw: Sherman Edwards

But, Mr. Adams	Lees Of Old Virginia	Piddle, Twiddle And Resolve (medley)	Till Then (medley)
Egg, The	Molasses To Rum	1776 (Overture)	Yours, Yours, Yours
He Plays The Violin	Momma Look Sharp	Sit Down, John	
Is Anybody There?			

SOUNDTRACKS

DEBUT	PEAK	WKS	RIAA	CD	ARTIST — Album Title	Catalog	Sym	$	Label & Number
10/17/64	148	3		646	**7th Dawn, The**		[I]	$50	United Artists 5115

William Holden/Susannah York/Capucine; cp/cd: Riz Ortolani

Battle In The Jungle	Ferris Meets Candace (medley)	Night In Malaya
Closing Theme	Fire In The Native Village	Opening Titles
Dhana's Torment	Governor's Ball	Paradise Club
Duel, The	Jungle Attack (medley)	Prison Prayer

Seventh Dawn
Seventh Dawn (Love Theme)
Seventh Dawn Variations
Trial, The

DEBUT	PEAK	WKS	RIAA	CD	ARTIST — Album Title	Catalog	Sym	$	Label & Number
8/12/78	5	28	▲	©647	**Sgt. Pepper's Lonely Hearts Club Band**	[M]		$15	RSO 4100 [2]

Peter Frampton/Bee Gees/George Burns/Steve Martin; sw: **John Lennon** and **Paul McCartney**

Because	Golden Slumbers (medley)	Maxwell's Silver Hammer
Being For The Benefit Of Mr. Kite	Good Morning, Good Morning	Mean Mr. Mustard
Carry That Weight (medley)	**Got To Get You Into My Life**	Nowhere Man (medley)
Come Together [Aerosmith] **23**	[Earth, Wind & Fire] **9**	**Oh! Darling** [Robin Gibb] **15**
Day In The Life	Here Comes The Sun	Polythene Pam (medley)
Fixing A Hole	I Want You (She's So Heavy)	Sgt. Pepper's Lonely Hearts Club
Get Back [Billy Preston] **86**	Long And Winding Road	Band
Getting Better	Lucy In The Sky With Diamonds	

She Came In Through The
Bathroom Window (medley)
She's Leaving Home
Strawberry Fields Forever
When I'm Sixty-Four
With A Little Help From My Friends
(medley)
You Never Give Me Your Money

Shaft - see HAYES, Isaac

Richard Roundtree/Moses Gunn/Gwenn Mitchell

DEBUT	PEAK	WKS	RIAA	CD	ARTIST — Album Title	Catalog	Sym	$	Label & Number
7/1/00	22	12	●	©648	**Shaft**		[V]	$10	LaFace 26080

Samuel L. Jackson/**Vanessa Williams**/Jeffrey Wright/Christian Bale

Ain't Gonna See Tomorrow	Do What I Gotta Do [Donell Jones]	Pimp Sh*t [Too $hort]
[Mystikal]	Fix Me [Parle]	Rock Wit U [Alicia Keys]
Automatic [Sleepy Brown]	How You Want It? [Mil]	Serenata Negra [Fulanito]
Bad Man [R. Kelly]	My Lovin' Will Give You Something	**Summer Rain** [Carl Thomas] **80**
Cheatin' [Liberty City]	[Angie Stone]	Theme From Shaft [Isaac Hayes]

Tough Guy [OutKast]
2 Glock 9's [T.I.P.]
Up And Outta Here [R. Kelly]
We Servin' [Big Gipp]

DEBUT	PEAK	WKS	RIAA	CD	ARTIST — Album Title	Catalog	Sym	$	Label & Number
7/21/73	147	9		649	**Shaft In Africa**		[I]	$20	ABC 793

Richard Roundtree/Vonetta McGee/Frank Finlay; cp/cd: Johnny Pate

Aleme Finds Shaft	Are You Man Enough (Main Title)	Shaft In Africa (Addis)
Aleme's Theme	El Jardia	Truck Stop
Are You Man Enough [Four	Headman	You Can't Even Walk In The Park
Tops] **15**	Jazar's Theme	(Opening Theme)

DEBUT	PEAK	WKS	RIAA	CD	ARTIST — Album Title	Catalog	Sym	$	Label & Number
8/26/72	100	16		650	**Shaft's Big Score!**		[I]	$20	MGM 36

Richard Roundtree/Moses Gunn/Joe Santos; cp: Gordon Parks; cd: Dick Hazard

Asby - Kelly Man	First Meeting	Smart Money
Blowin' Your Mind [O.C. Smith]	Move On In [O.C. Smith]	Symphony For Shafted Souls
Don't Misunderstand [O.C. Smith]	Other Side	Medley

DEBUT	PEAK	WKS	RIAA	CD	ARTIST — Album Title	Catalog	Sym	$	Label & Number
1/23/82	171	8		651	**Sharky's Machine**		[V]	$12	Warner 3653

Burt Reynolds/Rachel Ward/Bernie Casey/Brian Keith

Before You [Sarah Vaughan & Joe	8 To 5 I Lose [Joe Williams]	My Funny Valentine [Chet Baker]
Williams]	High Energy [Doc Severinsen]	My Funny Valentine [Julie London]
Dope Bust [Flora Purim & Buddy	Let's Keep Dancing [Peggy Lee]	**Route 66** [Manhattan Transfer] **78**
DeFranco]	Love Theme [Sarah Vaughan]	Sexercise [Doc Severinsen]

Sharky's Theme [Eddie Harris]
Street Life [Crusaders] **36**

DEBUT	PEAK	WKS	RIAA	CD	ARTIST — Album Title	Catalog	Sym	$	Label & Number
3/12/88	92	8		©652	**She's Having A Baby**		[V]	$10	I.R.S. 6211

Kevin Bacon/Elizabeth McGovern/Alec Baldwin/Dennis Dugan

Apron Strings [Everything But The	Full Of Love [Dr. Calculus]	She's Having A Baby [Dave
Girl]	Happy Families [XTC]	Wakeling]
Crazy Love [Bryan Ferry]	Haunted When The Minutes Drag	This Woman's Work [Kate Bush]
Desire (Come And Get It) [Gene	[Love & Rockets]	You Just Haven't Earned It Yet
Loves Jezebel]	It's All In The Game [Carmel]	Baby [Kirsty MacColl]

She's The One - see PETTY, Tom, And The Heartbreakers

Jennifer Aniston/Maxine Bahns/Edward Burns/Cameron Diaz

DEBUT	PEAK	WKS	RIAA	CD	ARTIST — Album Title	Catalog	Sym	$	Label & Number
10/9/65	147	2		653	**Shenandoah**		[I]	$50	Decca 79125

James Stewart/Patrick Wayne/Doug McClure; cp: Frank Skinner; cd: Joseph Gershenson

Bridal Suite	Legend Of Shenandoah [James	Memorium
Dead And The Living	Stewart]	Ripe For Pickin'
End Title	Main Title	Roll Call
Horse Play	Martha's Namesake	War Is Hell

We're Ridin' Out Tonight
Young Captives

DEBUT	PEAK	WKS	RIAA	CD	ARTIST — Album Title	Catalog	Sym	$	Label & Number
1/18/97	59	15		©654	**Shine**		[I]	$10	Philips 454710

Armin Mueller-Stahl/Noah Taylor/Geoffrey Rush/Lynn Redgrave; cp: David Hirschfelder; cd: Ricky Edwards; pf: **David Helfgott**

As If There Was No Tomorrow	Goodnight Daddy	Polonaise
Back Stage	Hungarian Rhapsody No. 2	Prelude In C # Minor
Bath To Daisy Beryl	La Campalesson	Punished For The Rest Of Your Life
Complicato In Israel	La Campanella	Rach. 3
Did He Win?	Letters To Katharine	Rach. 3 Reborn
Familiar Faces (medley)	Loud Bit Of Ludwig's 9th	Rach. 3 Encore (medley)
1st Movement Cadenza From The	Moments Of Genius	Raindrop Prelude
Rach. 3	Night Practice/Parcel From	Raindrop Reprise
Flight Of The Bumble Bee	Catherine	Scales To America
Gloria	Nulla In Mundo Pax Sincera	

Scenes From Childhood - "Almost
Too Serious"
Sospiro
Tell Me A Story, Katharine
These People Are A Disgrace
What's The Matter,
David/Appassionata
Will You Teach Me?
With The Help Of God, Shine
Your Father Your Family

DEBUT	PEAK	WKS	RIAA	CD	ARTIST — Album Title	Catalog	Sym	$	Label & Number
11/18/89	97	12		©655	**Shocker (No More Mr. Nice Guy) The Music**		[V]	$10	SBK 93233

Michael Murphy/Peter Berg/Cami Cooper/Mitch Pileggi

Awakening, The [Voodoo X]	Different Breed [Dead On]	Shockdance [Dudes Of Wrath]
Demon Bell (The Ballad Of Horace	Love Transfusion [Iggy Pop]	Shocker [Dudes Of Wrath]
Pinker) [Dangerous Toys]	No More Mr. Nice Guy [Megadeth]	Sword And Stone [Bonfire]

Timeless Love [Saraya] **85**

DEBUT	PEAK	WKS	RIAA	CD	ARTIST — Album Title	Catalog	Sym	$	Label & Number
9/2/95	4	21	●	©656	**Show, The**	[L-V]		$10	Def Jam 529021

concert movie/documentary

Domino's In The House [Domino]	Hip Hop Is... [Kid Creole, Kid Capri,	Me And My Bitch (Live From Philly)
Droppin Bombz [Tray D/So.	Ecstasy]	[Notorious B.I.G.]
Sentrelle]	**How High** [Redman/Method	Move On... [Slick Rick]
Everyday It Rains [Mary J. Blige]	Man] **13**	My Block [2Pac]
Everyday Thang [Bone	It's All I Had [Notorious B.I.G.]	Nuttin' But A Drumbeat... [Russell
Thugs-N-Harmony]	It's Entertainment... [Dr. Dre]	Simmons]
Glamour And Glitz [Tribe Called	It's What I Feel Inside... [Kid Creole,	Ol' Skool [Isaac 2 Isaac]
Quest]	Ecstasy]	Papa Luv It [L.L. Cool J]
Headbanger Boogie [Method Man]	Kill Dem All [Kali Ranks]	Save Yourself [Snoop Doggy Dogg]
	Live!!! [Onyx]	Show Theme [Stanley Clarke]

Sowhatusayin [South Central Cartel
Productions]
Still Can't Fade It [Warren G
Productions]
Summertime In The LBC [Dove
Shack] **54**
West Coast... [Treach]
What's Up Star? [Suga]
Zoom Zooms And Wam Wam [Jayo
Felony]

DEBUT	PEAK	WKS	RIAA	CD	ARTIST — Album Title	Catalog	Sym	$	Label & Number

Show Boat - see "Those Glorious MGM Musicals"
Kathryn Grayson/Howard Keel/Ava Gardner/Joe E. Brown

| 6/2/01 | 28 | 18↑● | | ©657 | **Shrek** .... | | [V] | $10 | DreamWorks 450305 |

animated movie, voices by Mike Myers/Cameron Diaz/John Lithgow/**Eddie Murphy**
All Star [Smash Mouth] 4 — Hallelujah [Rufus Wainwright] — I'm On My Way [Proclaimers] — My Beloved Monster [Eels]
Bad Reputation [Halfcocked] — I'm A Believer [Smash Mouth] 25 — It Is You (I Have Loved) [Dana Glover] — Stay Home [Self]
Best Years Of Our Lives [Baha Men] — I'm A Believer (Reprise) [Eddie Murphy] — Like Wow! [Leslie Carter] — True Love's First Kiss
You Belong To Me [Jason Wade]

Silencers, The - see MARTIN, Dean
Dean Martin/Stella Stevens/Daliah Lavi/**Victor Buono**

| 4/29/89 | 196 | 1 | | ©658 | **Sing** .... | | [V] | $10 | Columbia 45086 |

Lorraine Bracco/Peter Dobson/Jessica Steen/Louise Lasser
Birthday Suit [Johnny Kemp] 36 — Romance (Love Theme) [Paul Carrack & Terri Nunn] — Total Concentration [Patti LaBelle] — You Don't Have To Ask Me Twice [Nia Peeples]
(Everybody's Gotta) Face The Music [Kevin Cronin] — Sing [Mickey Thomas] — We'll Never Say Goodbye [Art Garfunkel]
One More Time [Michael Bolton] — Somethin' To Believe In [Bill Champlin] — What's The Matter With Love? [Laurnea Wilkerson]

Sing Boy Sing - see SANDS, Tommy
Tommy Sands/Lili Gentle/Edmond O'Brien

Singin' In The Rain - see ....ose Glorious MGM Musicals
Gene Kelly/Donald O'Connor/**Debbie Reynolds**

Singing Nun, The - see REYNOLDS, Debbie
Debbie Reynolds/Ricardo Montalban/Greer Garson

| 7/18/92 | 6 | 69 | ▲ | ©659 | **Singles** | | [V] | $10 | Epic 52476 |

Matt Dillon/Bridget Fonda/Campbell Scott/Kyra Sedgwick
Battle Of Evermore [Lovemongers] — Crown Of Thorns (medley) [Mother Love Bone] — Nearly Lost You [Screaming Trees] — Waiting For Somebody [Paul Westerberg]
Birth Ritual [Soundgarden] — Drown [Smashing Pumpkins] — Overblown [Mudhoney] — Would? [Alice In Chains]
Breath [Pearl Jam] — Dyslexic Heart [Paul Westerberg] — Seasons [Chris Cornell]
Chloe Dancer (medley) [Mother Love Bone] — May This Be Love [Jimi Hendrix] — State Of Love And Trust [Pearl Jam]

| 6/27/92 | 40 | 54 | ● | ©660 | **Sister Act** .... | | [I+V] | $10 | Hollywood 61334 |

Whoopi Goldberg/Maggie Smith/Mary Wickes/Kathy Najimi/Harvey Keitel; cp/cd: Marc Shaiman
Deloris Is Kidnapped — I Will Follow Him [Deloris & The Ronelles] — Lounge Medley [Deloris & The Ronelles] — **Rescue Me** [Fontella Bass] 4
Getting Into The Habit — If My Sister's In Trouble [Lady Soul] — Murder, The — Roll With Me Henry [Etta James]
Gravy (For My Mashed Potatoes) [Dee Dee Sharp] 9 — **Just A Touch Of Love** [C & C Music Factory] 50 — My Guy (My God) [Deloris & The Sisters] — Shout [Deloris & The Sisters & The Ronelles]
Hail Holy Queen [Deloris & The Sisters] — Nuns To The Rescue

| 12/25/93+ | 74 | 14 | ● | ©661 | **Sister Act 2: Back In The Habit** .... | | [V] | $10 | Hollywood 61562 |

Whoopi Goldberg/Kathy Najimy/James Coburn/Maggie Smith/Mary Wickes
Ain't No Mountain High Enough [Whoopi & The Cast] — **Deeper Love** [Aretha Franklin] 63 — Joyful, Joyful [St. Francis Choir] — Pay Attention [Valeria Andrews & Ryan Toby]
Ball Of Confusion (That's What The World Is Today) [Whoppi & The Sisters] — Get Up Offa That Thing (medley) [Whoopi & The Sisters] — **Never Should've Let You Go** [Hi-Five] 30 — Wandering Eyes [Nuttin' Nyce]
Dancing In The Street (medley) [Whoopi & The Sisters] — Greatest Medley Ever Told [Whoopi & The Ronelles] — O Happy Day [St. Francis Choir]
His Eye Is On The Sparrow [Tanya Blount & Lauryn Hill] — Ode To Joy [Chapman College Choir]

| 10/31/98 | 84 | 3 | | ©662 | **Slam** .... | | [V] | $10 | Immortal 69587 |

Saul Williams/Sonja Sohn/Bonz Malone/Beau Sia/Lawrence Wilson
Ain't No Stoppin' [Most Wanted] — I Dare You [Black Rob] — Sellin' D.O.P.E. (Drugs Oppress People Everyday) [dead prez] — Thug Poetry [Noreaga]
Feel My Gat Blow [Mobb Deep] — Ocean Within [KRS-One] — Sex, Money & Drugs [Big Punisher] — Time Is Running Out [Brand Nubian]
Galactic Funk [DJ Spooky] — Park, The [Ol' Dirty Bastard & Coolio] — Take A Walk In My Shoes [Flipmode Squad] — World I Know [Goodie Mob & Esthero]
Hey [Q-Tip]
I Can See [Tekitha & Cappadonna]

Slaughter's Big Rip-Off - see BROWN, James
Jim Brown/Brock Peters/Ed McMahon/Art Metrano/Don Stroud

| 7/10/93 | ❶¹ | 79 | ▲⁴ | ©663 | **Sleepless In Seattle** | C:#18/6 | [V] | $10 | Epic Soundtrax 53764 |

Tom Hanks/Meg Ryan/**Rosie O'Donnell**/Bill Pullman/Rob Reiner
As Time Goes By [Jimmy Durante] — In The Wee Small Hours Of The Morning [Carly Simon] — Make Someone Happy [Jimmy Durante] — **Stardust** [Nat King Cole] 79
Affair To Remember — Kiss To Build A Dream On [Louis Armstrong] — Makin' Whoopee [Dr. John] — **When I Fall In Love** [Celine Dion & Clive Griffin] 23
Back In The Saddle Again [Gene Autry] — **Stand By Your Man** [Tammy Wynette] 9 — Wink And A Smile [Harry Connick, Jr.]
Bye Bye Blackbird [Joe Cocker]

| 6/19/93 | 23 | 23 | ● | ©664 | **Sliver** .... | | [V] | $10 | Virgin 88064 |

Sharon Stone/William Baldwin/Tom Berenger/Martin Landau
Can't Help Falling In Love [UB40] 1 — Move With Me [Neneh Cherry] — Slave To The Vibe [Aftershock] — Wild At Heart [Bigod 20]
Carly's Loneliness [Enigma] — **Oh Carolina** [Shaggy] 59 — Slid [Fluke]
Carly's Song [Enigma] — Penthouse And Pavement [Heaven 17] — Star Sail [Verve]
Most Wonderful Girl [Lords Of Acid] — Skinflowers [Young Gods] — Unfinished Sympathy [Massive Attack]

| 7/25/98 | 103 | 5 | | ©665 | **Small Soldiers** .... | | [O-V] | $10 | DreamWorks 50051 |

Kirsten Dunst/Gregory Smith/Jay Mohr/Phil Hartman/**Denis Leary**
Another One Bites The Dust [Queen] 1 — Love Removal Machine [Cult] — Stroke, The [Billy Squier] 17 — War [Edwin Starr] 1
My City Was Gone [Pretenders] — Surrender [Cheap Trick] 62
Love Is A Battlefield [Pat Benatar] 5 — Rock And Roll (Part 2) [Gary Glitter] 7 — Tom Sawyer [Rush] 44
War [Bone Thugs-N-Harmony]

| 9/6/80 | 103 | 11 | | 666 | **Smokey And The Bandit 2** .... | | [V] | $12 | MCA 6101 |

Burt Reynolds/Sally Field/**Jackie Gleason**/Jerry Reed
Again And Again [Brenda Lee] — **Let's Do Something Cheap And Superficial** [Burt Reynolds] 88 — Ride Concrete Cowboy, Ride [Roy Rogers] — Tulsa Time [Don Williams]
Charlotte's Web [Statler Brothers] — Texas Bound And Flyin' [Jerry Reed] — Wildwood Flower [Bandit Band]
Do You Know You Are My Sunshine [Statler Brothers] — Pecos Promenade [Tanya Tucker] — To Be Your Man [Don Williams]
Here's Lookin' At You [Mel Tillis] — Pickin' Lone Star Style [Bandit Band]

DEBUT	PEAK	WKS	RIAA	CD	ARTIST — Album Title	Catalog	Sym	$	Label & Number

2/10/01 · 143 · 4 · ©667 · Snatch .... [V] $10 TVT Soundtrax 6950

Benicio Del Toro/Dennis Farina/Brad Pitt/Vinnie Jones

Angel *[Massive Attack]*	Disco Science *[Mirwais]*	Ghost Town *[Specials]*
Are You There *[Klint]*	**Don't You Just Know It** *[Huey*	Golden Brown *[Stranglers]*
Cross The Tracks (We Better Go	*'Piano' Smith & The Clowns]* 9	Hava Nagila *[John Murphy]*
Back) *[Maceo & The Macks]*	**Dreadlock Holiday** *[10cc]* 44	Hernando's Hideaway *[Johnston*
Diamond *[Klint]*	F**kin' In The Bushes *[Oasis]*	*Brothers]*

Hot Pants (I'm Coming, Coming, I'm Coming) *[Bobby Byrd]* 85
Lucky Star *[Madonna]* 4
Sensual Woman *[Herbaliser]*
Supermoves *[Overseer]*

3/4/00 · 183 · 2 · ©668 · Snow Day .... [V] $10 Geffen 490598

Chris Elliott/Mark Webber/Jean Smart/Chevy Chase

Another Dumb Blonde *[Hoku]* 27	Noise Brigade *[Mighty Mighty*	Still *[98°]*
Come On Come On *[Smash Mouth]*	*Bosstones]*	**There She Goes** *[Sixpence None*
Lifetime Affair *[Mytown]*	Picture Of You *[Boyzone]*	*The Richer]* 32
My Heart's Saying Now *[Jordan*	Reason Why *[LFO]*	**Waiting For A Girl Like You**
Knight]	Say You Love Me *[Dina Carroll]*	*[Foreigner]* 2

Wasting My Life *[Hippos]*

8/14/93 · 88 · 7 · ©669 · So I Married An Axe Murderer .... [V] $10 Chaos 57303

Mike Myers/Nancy Travis/Anthony LaPaglia/Amanda Plummer/Brenda Fricker

Break, The *[Soul Asylum]*	Maybe Baby *[Sun-60]*	Saturday Night *[Ned's Atomic*
Brother *[Toad The Wet Sprocket]*	My Insatiable One *[Suede]*	*Dustbin]*
Long Day In The Universe *[Darling*	**Rush** *[Big Audio Dynamite II]* 32	Starve To Death *[Chris Whitley]*
Buds]		There She Goes *[Boo Radleys]*

There She Goes *[La's]* 49
Two Princes *[Spin Doctors]* 7

3/21/87 · 57 · 13 · ©670 · Some Kind Of Wonderful .... [V] $10 MCA 6200

Lea Thompson/Eric Stoltz/Mary Stuart Masterson/Craig Sheffer

Brilliant Mind *[Furniture]*	Cry Like This *[Blue Room]*	I Go Crazy *[Flesh For Lulu]*
Can't Help Falling In Love *[Lick The*	Do Anything *[Pete Shelley]*	Miss Amanda Jones *[March Violets]*
Tins]	Hardest Walk *[Jesus & Mary Chain]*	She Loves Me *[Stephen Duffy]*

Shyest Time *[Apartments]*
Turn To The Sky *[March Violets]*

12/6/80 · 187 · 2 ▲ · ©671 · Somewhere In Time .... [I] $12 MCA 5154

Christopher Reeve/Jane Seymour/Teresa Wright; cp/cd: John Barry

Day Together	Journey Back In Time	Old Woman
Is He The One	Man Of My Dreams	Return To The Present

Rhapsody On A Theme Of Paganini
Somewhere In Time

Son Of Dracula - see NILSSON

Nilsson/Ringo Starr/Rosanna Lee

1/23/71 · 95 · 8 · 672 · Song Of Norway .... [M] $20 ABC 14

Florence Henderson/Toralv Maurstad/Edward G. Robinson; cp: Edvard Grieg

At Christmastime	I Love You	Norwegian National Anthem
Be A Boy Again	John Heggerstrom	(medley)
Finale	Life Of A Wife Of A Sailor	Rhyme And A Reason (medley)
Freddy And His Fiddle	Little House	Ribbons And Wrappings
Hill Of Dreams	Midsummer's Eve - Hand In Hand	Solitary Wanderer
Hymn Of Betrothal		Solvejg's Song (medley)

Song Of Norway
Strange Music
Three There Were
Welcome Toast
When We Wed (medley)
Wrong To Dream

Song Remains The Same, The - see LED ZEPPELIN

SongWriter - see KRISTOFFERSON, Kris / NELSON, Willie

Willie Nelson/Kris Kristofferson/Melinda Dillon

Sorcerer - see TANGERINE DREAM

Roy Scheider/Bruno Cremer/Francisco Rabal

10/4/97 · 4 · 35 ▲² · ©673 · Soul Food .... [V] $10 LaFace 26041

Vanessa Williams/Vivica A. Fox/Nia Long/Mekhi Phifer

Baby I *[Tenderoni]*	Don't Stop What You're Doing *[Puff*	Let's Do It Again *[Xscape]*
Boys And Girls *[Tony Toni Toné]*	*Daddy]*	September *[Earth, Wind & Fire]*
Call Me *[Blackstreet]*	**I Care 'Bout You** *[Milestone]* 23	Slow Jam *[Monica & Usher]*
	In Due Time *[OutKast]*	Song For Mama *[Boyz II Men]*

We're Not Making Love No More *[Dru Hill]* 13
What About Us *[Total]* 16
You Are The Man *[En Vogue]*

10/4/97 · 73 · 3 · ©674 · Soul In The Hole .... [L-V] $10 Loud 67531

concert movie/documentary

Against The Grain *[Sauce Money]*	High Expectations *[Common]*	Rare Species (Modus Operandi)
Child Is Born *[Brand Nubian]*	Late Night Action *[Organized*	*[Mobb Deep]*
Diesel *[Wu-Tang Clan]*	*Konfusion]*	Ride *[M.O.P.]*
Game Of Life *[dead prez]*	Los Angeles Times *[Xzibit]*	Soul In The Hole *[Wu All-Stars]*
	Main Aim *[Dwellas]*	Visions Of Blur *[Darc Mind]*

Won On Won *[Cocoa Brovaz]*
You Ain't A Killer *[Big Punisher]*
Your Life *[O.C.]*

11/15/86 · 138 · 9 · ©675 · Soul Man .... [V] $10 A&M 3903

C. Thomas Howell/Rae Dawn Chong/Arye Gross/James Sikking

Bang Bang Bang (Who's On The	Eek-Ah-Bo-Static Automatic *[Sly*	Love And Affection *[Martha Davis &*
Phone) *[Ricky]*	*Stone]*	*Sly Stone]*
Black Girls *[Rae Dawn Chong]*	Evolution *[Models]*	Outside *[Nu Shooz]*
		Soul Man *[Sam Moore & Lou Reed]*

Suddenly It's Magic *[Vesta Williams]*
Sweet Sarah *[Tom Scott]*
Totally Academic *[Brenda Russell]*

9/25/71 · 112 · 10 · 676 · Soul To Soul .... [L-V] $20 Atlantic 7207

concert movie shot in Ghana, West Africa

Are You Sure (medley) *[Staple*	He's Alright (medley) *[Staple*	Land Of 1000 Dances *[Wilson*
Singers]	*Singers]*	*Pickett]*
Freedom Song *[Roberta Flack]*	Heyjorler *[Eddie Harris & Les*	Run Shaker Life *[Voices Of East*
Funky Broadway *[Wilson Pickett]*	*McCann]*	*Harlem]*
	I Smell Trouble *[Ike & Tina Turner]*	Soul To Soul *[Ike & Tina Turner]*

Soul To Soul *[Voices Of East Harlem]*
Tryin' Times *[Roberta Flack]*

3/20/65 · ❶² · 233 ● · ©677 · Sound Of Music, The .... [M] $25 RCA Victor 2005

Julie Andrews/Christopher Plummer/Eleanor Parker; mu: Richard Rodgers; ly: Oscar Hammerstein II; cd: Irwin Kostal

Climb Ev'ry Mountain	Lonely Goatherd	Preludium (Dixit Dominus)
Do-Re-Mi	Maria	Processional
Edelweiss	Morning Hymn - Alleluia	Sixteen Going On Seventeen
I Have Confidence	My Favorite Things	So Long, Farewell

Something Good
Sound Of Music

6/12/82 · 168 · 12 · 678 · Soup For One .... [V] $12 Mirage 19353

Saul Rubinek/Marcia Strassman/Gerrit Graham; sw: Bernard Edwards and Nile Rodgers (**Chic**)

Dream Girl *[Teddy Pendergrass]*	Jump, Jump *[Deborah Harry]*	Soup For One *[Chic]* 80
I Want Your Love *[Chic]* 7	Let's Go On Vacation *[Sister*	Tavern On The Green *[Chic]*
I Work For A Livin' *[Fonzi Thornton]*	*Sledge]*	**Why** *[Carly Simon]* 74

DEBUT	PEAK	WKS	RIAA	CD	ARTIST — Album Title	Catalog	Sym	$	Label & Number
3/31/58	**❶**[31]	262	●	©679	**South Pacific**		[M]	$30	RCA Victor 1032

Rossano Brazzi/Mitzi Gaynor/John Kerr; mu: Richard Rodgers; ly: Oscar Hammerstein II; cd: Alfred Newman; Original Cast version charted in 1949 (#1 for a record 69 weeks) on COlumbia 4180

Bali Ha'i
Bloody Mary
Carefully Taught
Cockeyed Optimist
Dites-Moi
Happy Talk
Honey Bun
I'm Gonna Wash That Man Right Outa My Hair
I'm In Love With A Wonderful Guy
My Girl Back Home
Overture
Some Enchanted Evening (medley)
There Is Nothin' Like A Dame
This Nearly Was Mine
Twin Soliloquies (medley)
Younger Than Springtime

| 7/10/99 | 28 | 11 | ● | ©680 | **South Park: Bigger, Longer & Uncut**............... | | [M] | $10 | Atlantic 83199 |

animated movie, voices by: Trey Parker/Matt Stone/Mary Kay Bergman/**Isaac Hayes**

Blame Canada
Eyes Of A Child
Good Love [Isaac Hayes]
I Can Change
I Swear It (I Can Change) [Violent Femmes]
I'm Super
It's Easy, Mmmkay
Kyle's Mom's A Big Fat B**ch [Joe C.]
Kyle's Mom's A B**ch
La Resistance (Medley)
Mountain Town
Mountain Town (Reprise)
O Canada [Geddy Lee & Alex Lifeson]
Riches To Rags (Mmmkay) [Nappy Roots]
Shut Yo Face (Uncle F**ka) [Trick Daddy]
Super [RuPaul]
Uncle F**ka
Up There
What Would Brian Boitano Do?
What Would Brian Boitano Do? Pt. II [D.V.D.A]

| 11/30/96+ | 2[1] | 82 | ▲[6] | ©681 | **Space Jam** | | [V] | $10 | Warner Sunset 82961 |

Michael Jordan/Bill Murray/Wayne Knight

All Of My Days [Changing Faces] 65
Basketball Jones [Barry White & Chris Rock]
Buggin' [Bugs Bunny]
Fly Like An Eagle [Seal] 10
For You I Will [Monica] 4
Givin' U All That I've Got [Robin S.]
Hit 'Em High [B Real/Busta Rhymes/Coolio/LL Cool J/Method Man]
I Believe I Can Fly [R. Kelly] 2
I Found My Smile Again [D'Angelo]
I Turn To You [All-4-One]
Space Jam [Quad City DJ's] 37
That's The Way (I Like It) [Spin Doctors]
Upside Down ('Round-N-'Round) [Salt-N-Pepa]
Winner, The [Coolio]

Sparkle - see FRANKLIN, Aretha
Irene Cara/Philip Thomas/Lonette McKee

| 8/16/97 | 7 | 25 | ● | ©682 | **Spawn - The Album** | | [V] | $10 | Immortal 68494 |

John Leguizamo/Michael Jai White/Martin Sheen/Theresa Randle

(Can't You) Trip Like I Do [Filter & The Crystal Method]
Familiar [Incubus & D.J. Greyboy]
For Whom The Bell Tolls (The Irony Of It All) [Metallica & DJ Spooky]
Kick The P.A. [Korn & The Dust Brothers]
Long Hard Road Out Of Hell [Marilyn Manson & Sneaker Pimps]
No Remorse (I Wanna Die) [Slayer & Atari Teenage Riot]
One Man Army [Prodigy & Tom Morello]
Plane Scraped Its Belly On A Sooty Yellow Moon [Soul Coughing & Roni Size]
Satan [Orbital & Kirk Hammett]
Skin Up Pin Up [Mansun & 808 State]
Spawn [Silverchair & Vitro]
T-4 Strain [Henry Rollins & Goldie]
Tiny Rubberband [Butthole Surfers & Moby]
Torn Apart [Stabbing Westward & Wink]

| 10/29/94 | 176 | 1 | | ©683 | **Specialist, The**.................... | | [V] | $10 | Crescent Moon 66384 |

Sylvester Stallone/Sharon Stone/James Woods/Rod Steiger/Eric Roberts

All Because Of You [MSM (Miami Sound Machine)]
Did You Call Me [John Barry & The Royal Philharmonic Orchestra]
El Amor [Azucar Moreno]
El Bale De La Vela [Cheito]
El Duro Soy Yo [Tony Tatis & Su Merengue Sound]
Jambala [MSM (Miami Sound Machine)]
Love Is The Thing [Donna Allen]
Mental Picture [Jon Secada] 29
Que Manera De Quererte [Albita]
Real [Donna Allen]
Shower Me With Love [Lagaylia]
Slip Away [Lagaylia]
Specialist, The [John Barry & The Royal Philharmonic Orchestra]
Turn The Beat Around [Gloria Estefan] 13

Speedway - see PRESLEY, Elvis
Elvis Presley ("Steve Grayson")/**Nancy Sinatra**/Bill Bixby/Gale Gordon

Spinout - see PRESLEY, Elvis
Elvis Presley ("Mike McCoy")/**Shelley Fabares**/Diane McBain

| 5/17/97 | 89 | 10 | | ©684 | **Sprung** .... | | [V] | $10 | Qwest 46541 |

Tisha Campbell/Rusty Cundieff/Paula Jai Parker/Joe Torry

2 Nite's The Nite [Mr. Dalvin]
Bounce [Noggin Nodders]
Don't Ask My Neighbor [Tisha Campbell & Tichina Arnold]
Freak [Money Boss Players]
Goal Tendin' [E-40]
Group Home Family [Canibus]
I Don't Know [Next Level]
I Still Love You [Monifah]
I Want Your Love [Stanley Clarke]
If It Ain't Love [Keystone]
Let Me Know [Keystone]
Let's Get It Started [G-Ratz]
Move On (I'm Leaving) [Forte]
One In A Million [Aaliyah]
Secret Garden [Quincy Jones]
Since You've Gone Away (The Lockdown Anthem) [Bonnie & Clyde]
Who You Wit [Jay-Z] 84

| 8/27/77 | 40 | 16 | | ©685 | **Spy Who Loved Me, The** .... | | [I] | $12 | United Artists 774 |

Roger Moore/Barbara Bach/Richard Kiel/Curt Jurgens; cp/cd: **Marvin Hamlisch**

Anya
Bond 77
Eastern Lights
Mojave Club
Nobody Does It Better [Carly Simon] 2
Nobody Does It Better (instrumental)
Pyramids, The
Ride To Atlantis
Tanker, The

| 7/13/85 | 21 | 37 | ● | ©686 | **St. Elmo's Fire** .... | | [V] | $10 | Atlantic 81261 |

Emilio Estevez/Rob Lowe/Andrew McCarthy/Demi Moore/Judd Nelson

Georgetown [David Foster]
If I Turn You Away [Vikki Moss]
Love Theme From St. Elmo's Fire [David Foster] 15
Love Theme (Just For A Moment) [David Foster/Donny Gerrard/Amy Holland]
Saved My Life [Fee Waybill]
Shake Down [Billy Squier]
St. Elmo's Fire (Man In Motion) [John Parr] 1
Stressed Out (Close To The Edge) [Airplay]
This Time It Was Really Right [Jon Anderson]
Young And Innocent [Elefante]

St. Louis Blues - see COLE, Nat "King"
Nat "King" Cole/Eartha Kitt/Pearl Bailey/Cab Calloway

| 9/20/86 | 31 | 45 | ● | ©687 | **Stand By Me** .... | | [O-V] | $10 | Atlantic 81677 |

Wil Wheaton/River Phoenix/Corey Feldman/Jerry O'Connell/Richard Dreyfuss

Come Go With Me [Dell-Vikings] 4
Everyday [Buddy Holly]
Get A Job [Silhouettes] 1
Great Balls Of Fire [Jerry Lee Lewis] 2
Let The Good Times Roll [Shirley & Lee] 20
Lollipop [Chordettes] 2
Mr. Lee [Bobbettes] 6
Stand By Me [Ben E. King] 9
Whispering Bells [Dell-Vikings] 9
Yakety Yak [Coasters] 1

| 10/26/68+ | 98 | 20 | | 688 | **Star!** .... | | [M] | $20 | 20th Century Fox 5102 |

Julie Andrews/Richard Crenna/Michael Craig/Robert Reed

Burlington Bertie From Bow
Dear Little Boy (Dear Little Girl)
Do, Do, Do
Has Anybody Seen Our Ship?
In My Garden Of Joy
Jenny
Limehouse Blues
My Ship
'N' Everything
Oh, It's A Lovely War
Overture (Medley)
Parisian Pierrot
Physician, The
Piccadilly
Someday I'll Find You
Someone To Watch Over Me
Star!

Star Is Born, A - see STREISAND, Barbra
Barbra Streisand/Kris Kristofferson/Gary Busey/Oliver Clark

SOUNDTRACKS

DEBUT	PEAK	WKS	RIAA	CD	ARTIST — Album Title	Catalog	Sym	$	Label & Number

1/5/80 — **50** — 11 — ● — ©689 — **Star Trek - The Motion Picture** — [I] — **$15** — Columbia 36334
William Shatner/**Leonard Nimoy**/DeForest Kelley/James Doohan/Persis Khambatta; cp/cd: Jerry Goldsmith

Cloud, The	Ilia's Theme	Main Title (medley)	Vejur Flyover
End Title	Klingon Battle (medley)	Meld, The	
Enterprise, The	Leaving Drydock	Spock Walk	

7/17/82 — **61** — 9 — ©690 — **Star Trek II - The Wrath Of Khan** — [I] — **$12** — Atlantic 19363
William Shatner/**Leonard Nimoy**/Ricardo Montalban/DeForest Kelley; cp/cd: James Horner

Battle In The Mutara Nebula	Epilogue (medley)	Kirk's Explosive Reply	Surprise Attack
End Title (medley)	Genesis Countdown	Main Title	
Enterprise Clears Moorings	Khan's Pets	Spock	

6/23/84 — **82** — 8 — ©691 — **Star Trek III - The Search For Spock** — [I] — **$12** — Capitol 12360
William Shatner/DeForest Kelley/Christopher Lloyd; cp/cd: James Horner; includes bonus 12" single "The Search For Spock"

Bird Of Prey Decloaks	Klingons	Prologue (medley)	Stealing The Enterprise
End Titles	Main Title (medley)	Returning To Vulcan	
Katra Ritual	Mind-Meld	Search For Spock (Theme)	

1/4/92 — **171** — 1 — ©692 — **Star Trek VI - The Undiscovered Country** — [I] — **$10** — MCA 10512
William Shatner/**Leonard Nimoy**/DeForest Kelley/James Doohan; Kim Cattrall; cp/cd: Cliff Eidelman

Assassination	Death Of Gorkon	Incident, An	Sign Off
Battle For Peace	Dining On Ashes	Revealed	Star Trek VI Suite
Clear All Moorings	Escape From Rura Penthe	Rura Penthe	Surrender For Peace

6/18/77 — **2³** — 53 — ▲ — ©693 — **Star Wars** — [I] — **$20** — 20th Century 541 [2]
Mark Hamill/Harrison Ford/Carrie Fisher/Alec Guinness; cp/cd: **John Williams**

Ben's Death (medley)	Imperial Attack	Mouse Robot (medley)	Robot Auction (medley)
Blasting Off (medley)	Inner City	Princess Appears	**Star Wars (Main Title)** 10
Cantina Band	Land Of The Sandpeople	Princess Leia's Theme	Throne Room (medley)
Desert, The (medley)	Last Battle	Rescue Of The Princess	Tie Fighter Attack (medley)
End Title (medley)	Little People Work	Return Home	Walls Converge

12/17/77+ — **36** — 10 — ● — 694 — **Star Wars, The Story Of** — [T] — **$15** — 20th Century 550
storyline excerpts from the movie (no track titles listed); narrator: Roscoe Lee Browne

2/1/97 — **49** — 11 — ● — ©695 — **Star Wars: A New Hope** — [I-R] — **$15** — RCA Victor 68746 [2]
complete score in sequence with previously unreleased music issued in conjunction with the 20th anniversary release of the *Star Wars* Special Edition movie in theaters

Attack Of The Sand People (medley)	Death Star (medley)	Jawa Sandcrawler (medley)	Shootout In The Cell Bay (medley)
Battle Of Yavin	Destruction Of Alderaan	Landspeeder Search (medley)	Stormtroopers, The (medley)
Ben Kenobi's Death (medley)	Detention Block Ambush (medley)	Learn About The Force (medley)	Tales Of A Jedi Knight (medley)
Binary Sunset	Dianoga (medley)	Main Title (medley)	Throne Room (medley)
Burning Homestead	Dune Sea Of Tatooine (medley)	Millennium Falcon (medley)	Tie Fighter Attack (medley)
Cantina Band	End Title (medley)	Moisture Farm	Tractor Beam (medley)
Cantina Band #2	Hologram, The (medley)	Mos Eisley Spaceport	Trash Compactor
Chasm Crossfire (medley)	Imperial Attack	Princess Leia's Theme	20th Century Fox Fanfare
	Imperial Cruiser Pursuit (medley)	Rebel Blockade Runner (medley)	Wookiee Prisoner (medley)

5/22/99 — **3** — 16 — ▲ — ©696 — **Star Wars Episode I - The Phantom Menace** — [I] — **$10** — Sony Classical 61816
Liam Neeson/Ewan McGregor/Natalie Portman/Jake Lloyd/Samuel L. Jackson; cp/cd: **John Williams**

Anakin Defeats Sebulba	Droid Battle (medley)	Kids At Play (medley)	Sith Spacecraft (medley)
Anakin's Theme	Droid Invasion (medley)	Naboo Palace (medley)	Star Wars Main Title (medley)
Appearance Of Darth Maul (medley)	Duel Of The Fates	Panaka And The Queen's	Swim To Otoh Gunga (medley)
Arrival At Naboo (medley)	End Credits (medley)	Protectors	Trip To The Naboo Temple
Arrival At Tatooine (medley)	Flag Parade (medley)	Passage Through The Planet Core	Watto's Deal (medley)
Audience With Boss Nass (medley)	He Is The Chosen One	Queen Amidala (medley)	
Augie's Great Municipal Band (medley)	High Council Meeting (medley)	Qui-Gon's Funeral (medley)	
	Jar Jar's Introduction (medley)	Qui-Gon's Noble End	

5/12/62 — **12** — 19 — ©697 — **State Fair** — [M] — **$50** — Dot 29011
Pat Boone/**Ann-Margret**/Bobby Darin; mu: Richard Rogers; ly: Oscar Hammerstein II; cd: Alfred Newman

Finale	It's A Grand Night For Singing	Never Say No To A Man	This Isn't Heaven
Isn't It Kinda Fun	Little Things In Texas	Overture (Main Title)	Willing And Eager
It Might As Well Be Spring	More Than Just A Friend	That's For Me	

Staying Alive - see BEE GEES
John Travolta/Cynthia Rhodes (**Animotion**)/Sarah Miles/Julie Bovasso

9/6/97 — **185** — 1 — ©698 — **Steel** — [V] — **$10** — Qwest 46678
Shaquille O'Neal/Annabeth Gish/Richard Roundtree/Judd Nelson

Alone In The Crowd [Maria Christina]	Free To Be Me [Gina Breedlove]	Mobb Of Steel [Mobb Deep]	
Anything For Your Love [Jon B]	**Men Of Steel** [Shaquille O'Neal/Ice Cube/B Real/Peter Gunz/KRS-One] 82	No More Fighting [Tevin Campbell]	
Breakout [Jia]	Mind On My Money [Spice 1]	Nothing Compares [AZ Yet]	
Coming Home To You [Blackstreet]		Strait Playin' [Shaquille O'Neal]	
		We've Got Heart [S.H.E.]	

6/6/70 — **200** — 2 — ©699 — **Sterile Cuckoo, The** — [I] — **$25** — Paramount 5009
Liza Minnelli/Wendell Burton/Tim McIntire; cp/cd: Fred Karlin

Come Saturday Morning [Sandpipers] 17	Jerry	Pookie Adams	You're Absolutely Whacky
End Walk [Sandpipers]	Jerry & Pookie	Pookie Leaves	
	Montage [Sandpipers]	Weirdos, The	

Sting, The - see HAMLISCH, Marvin
Paul Newman/Robert Redford/Robert Shaw/Charles Durning/Ray Walston

Stop Making Sense - see TALKING HEADS

Straight Talk - see PARTON, Dolly
Dolly Parton/James Woods/Griffin Dunne/Michael Madsen

11/4/95 — **135** — 1 — ©700 — **Strange Days** — [V] — **$10** — Lightstorm 67226
Ralph Fiennes/Angela Bassett/Juliette Lewis/Tom Sizemore

Coral Lounge [Deep Forest]	Feed [Skunk Anansie]	Overcome [Tricky]	While The Earth Sleeps [Peter Gabriel & Deep Forest]
Dance Me To The End Of Love [Hate Gibson]	Hardly Wait [Juliette Lewis]	Real Thing [Lords Of Acid]	
Fall In The Light [Lori Carson & Graeme Revell]	Here We Come [Me Phi Me/Jeriko One]	Selling Jesus [Skunk Anansie]	
	No White Clouds [Strange Fruit]	Strange Days [Prong]	
		Walk In Freedom [Satchel]	

DEBUT	PEAK	WKS	RIAA	CD	ARTIST — Album Title	Catalog	Sym	$	Label & Number
10/17/98	185	1		©701	**Strangeland**		[V]	$10	TVT Soundtrax 8270

Dee Snider (**Twisted Sister**)/Elizabeth Peña/Kevin Gage/Robert Englund

Absent [Snot]	Fxxk Off [Kid Rock]	Inconclusion [Dee Snider]
Awake [Clay People]	Heroes Are Hard To Find [Twisted	Marmalade [System Of A Down]
Breathe [Sevendust]	Sister]	Not Living [Coal Chamber]
Captain Howdy [Crisis]	I'm The Man [Nashville Pussy]	P & V [Anthrax]
Eye For An Eye [Soulfly]	In League [Bile]	Secret Place [Megadeth]

Serpent Boy [(hed)p.e.] · Street Justice [dayinthelife...] · Sweet Tooth [Marilyn Manson] · Where You Come From [Pantera]

DEBUT	PEAK	WKS	RIAA	CD	ARTIST — Album Title	Catalog	Sym	$	Label & Number
9/12/70	91	9		©702	**Strawberry Statement, The**		[V]	$30	MGM 14 [2]

Bruce Davison/Kim Darby/James Coco

Circle Game [Buffy Sainte-Marie]	Fishin' Blues [Red Mountain Jug	Loner, The [Neil Young]
Coit Tower [Ian Freebairn-Smith]	Band]	Long Time Gone [Crosby, Stills &
Concerto In D Minor	Give Peace A Chance [cast]	Nash]
Cyclatron [Ian Freebairn-Smith]	Helpless [Crosby, Stills, Nash &	Market Basket [Ian Freebairn-Smith]
Down By The River [Neil Young]	Young]	Pocket Band [Ian Freebairn-Smith]

Something In The Air [Thunderclap Newman] 37 · "2001" A Space Odyssey [Berlin Philharmonic] 90

DEBUT	PEAK	WKS	RIAA	CD	ARTIST — Album Title	Catalog	Sym	$	Label & Number
1/14/95	135	4		©703	**Street Fighter**		[V]	$10	Priority 53948

Jean-Claude Van Damme/Raul Julia/**Kylie Minogue**

Come Widdit [Ahmad/Ras	Life As... [L.L. Cool J]	Rumbo N Da Jungo [Public Enemy]
Kass/Saafir]	One On One [Nas]	Something Kinda Funky [Rally Ral]
Do You Have What It Takes? [Craig	Pandemonium [Pharcyde]	Something There [Chage & Aska]
Mack]	Rap Commando [Anotha Level]	Straight To My Feet [Hammer/Deion
It's A Street Fight [B.U.M.S.]		Sanders]

Street Fighter [Ice Cube] · Street Soldier [Paris] · Worth Fighting For [Angelique Kidjo]

DEBUT	PEAK	WKS	RIAA	CD	ARTIST — Album Title	Catalog	Sym	$	Label & Number
5/30/98	27	12		©704	**Streets Is Watching**		[V]	$10	Roc-A-Fella 558132

Jay-Z/Dame Dash/Kareem Burke

Celebration [Team Roc]	**It's Alright** [Memphis Bleek &	My Nigga Hill Figga [M.O.P.]
Crazy [Usual Suspects]	Jay-Z] 61	Only A Customer [Jay-Z]
Doe, The [Diamonds In Da Rough]	**Love For Free** [Rell Feat. Jay-Z] 86	Pimp This Love [Christion]
In My Lifetime [Jay-Z]	Murdergram [Murder, Inc.]	Thugs R Us [DJ Clue]

Your Love [Christion]

DEBUT	PEAK	WKS	RIAA	CD	ARTIST — Album Title	Catalog	Sym	$	Label & Number
6/16/84	32	21		©705	**Streets Of Fire**		[V]	$12	MCA 5492

Michael Pare/Diane Lane/Rick Moranis/Amy Madigan

Blue Shadows [Blasters]	Hold That Snake [Ry Cooder]	Nowhere Fast [Fire Inc.]
Countdown To Love [Greg	**I Can Dream About You** [Dan	One Bad Stud [Blasters]
Phillinganes]	Hartman] 6	Sorcerer [Marilyn Martin]
Deeper And Deeper [Fixx]	Never Be You [Maria McKee]	

Tonight Is What It Means To Be Young [Fire Inc.] 80

DEBUT	PEAK	WKS	RIAA	CD	ARTIST — Album Title	Catalog	Sym	$	Label & Number
7/20/96	152	2		©706	**Striptease**		[O-V]	$10	EMI 52498

Demi Moore/Armand Assante/Ving Rhames/Robert Patrick/Burt Reynolds

Expressway To Your Heart [Soul	**Green Onions** [Booker T. & The	Love Child (Halaila) [Laladin]
Survivors] 4	MG's] 3	Mony Mony [Billy Idol]
**Get Outta My Dreams, Get Into	**I Hate Myself For Loving You**	**Return To Me** [Dean Martin] 4
My Car** [Billy Ocean] 1	[Joan Jett & The Blackhearts] 8	**Sweet Dreams (Are Made Of This)**
Gimme Some Lovin' [Spencer	I Live For You [Chynna Phillips]	[Eurythmics] 1
Davis Group] 7	If I Was Your Girlfriend [Prince] 67	Tide Is High [Blondie] 1

You've Really Got A Hold On Me [Smokey Robinson & The Miracles] 8

DEBUT	PEAK	WKS	RIAA	CD	ARTIST — Album Title	Catalog	Sym	$	Label & Number
4/27/96	90	5		©707	**Substitute, The**		[V]	$10	Priority 50576

Tom Berenger/Ernie Hudson/Diane Venora/Glenn Plummer/**Marc Anthony**

All Of Puerto Rico [Afro-Rican]	Danger [Road Dawgs]	Hood Life [Lil 1/2 Dead]
Bang'Em Up [Tru]	Head Up [Young Murder Squad]	I Got That Cream [Master P]
Bring It On [Organized Konfusion]	Hoo-Bangin' [Mack 10]	Licorice Stiks [Intense Method]

Miami Life [Ras Kass] · Money, Power & Women [G-Spot-Geez]

DEBUT	PEAK	WKS	RIAA	CD	ARTIST — Album Title	Catalog	Sym	$	Label & Number
3/19/94	169	3		©708	**Sugar Hill**		[V]	$10	Beacon 11016

Wesley Snipes/Michael Wright/Theresa Randle/Clarence Williams III

Afro-Desiac [Afro-Plane]	Money [Snoman]	Roemello's Theme [Terence
Gonna Love You Right [After 7] 87	Park Bench People [Freestyle	Blanchard Quintet]
Hit The Boomz [DBC]	Fellowship]	War Council [Terence Blanchard
Khadijah [Dirt Nation]	**Play My Funk** [Simple E] 72	Quintet]
Miles Blowin' [Chaka Khan]		What Are You Under [Definition Of
		Sound]

Worries [Screechy Dan]

DEBUT	PEAK	WKS	RIAA	CD	ARTIST — Album Title	Catalog	Sym	$	Label & Number
8/28/82	152	7		709	**Summer Lovers**		[V]	$12	Warner 23695

Peter Gallagher/Daryl Hannah/Valerie Quennessen/Barbara Rush

Crazy In The Night [Tina Turner]	If Love Takes You Away [Stephen	Just Can't Get Enough [Depeche
Do What Ya Wanna Do [Cage &	Bishop]	Mode]
Nona Hendryx]	Johnny And Mary [Tina Turner]	Play To Win [Heaven 17]
Hard To Say I'm Sorry [Chicago] 1		Sea Cave [Basil Poledouris]

Search For Lina [Basil Poledouris] · Summer Lovers [Michael Sembello] · Take Me Down To The Ocean [Elton John]

DEBUT	PEAK	WKS	RIAA	CD	ARTIST — Album Title	Catalog	Sym	$	Label & Number
9/11/71	52	34		710	**Summer Of '42**		[I]	$20	Warner 1925

Jennifer O'Neill/Gary Grimes/Jerry Houser; cp/cd: **Michel LeGrand**

And All The Time	Dancer, The	La Guerre
Awakening Awareness	Entrance To Reality	Lonely Two
Bacchanal, The	Full Awakening (medley)	Los Manos De Muerto
But Not Picasso (medley)	High I.Q.	Summer Knows

Summer Of '42 (Theme) · Summer Song

DEBUT	PEAK	WKS	RIAA	CD	ARTIST — Album Title	Catalog	Sym	$	Label & Number
7/24/99	195	1		©711	**Summer Of Sam**		[O-V]	$10	Hollywood 62190

John Leguizamo/Adrien Brody/Mira Sorvino/Jennifer Esposito

Baba O'Riley [Who]	**Don't Leave Me This Way** [Thelma	Got To Give It Up [Marvin Gaye] 1
Best Of My Love [Emotions] 1	Houston] 1	La Vie En Rose [Grace Jones]
Dance With Me [Peter Brown] 8	**Everybody Dance** [Chic] 38	Let No Man Put Asunder [First
Dancing Queen [Abba] 1	**Fooled Around And Fell In Love**	Choice]
	[Elvin Bishop] 3	Running Away [Roy Ayers]

There But For The Grace Of God Go I [Machine] 77

Sunday In New York - see NERO, Peter
Cliff Robertson/Rod Taylor/**Jane Fonda**/Robert Culp

DEBUT	PEAK	WKS	RIAA	CD	ARTIST — Album Title	Catalog	Sym	$	Label & Number
5/11/96	4	13	▲	©712	**Sunset Park**	•	[V]	$10	Flavor Unit 61904

Rhea Perlman/Carol Kane/**Fredro Starr**

All Uv It [Big Mike]	Elements I'm Among [Queen	Hoop N Yo Face [69 Boyz] 95
Are You Ready [Aaliyah]	Latifah]	It's Alright [Groove Theory]
Back At You [Mobb Deep]	For The Funk [Adina Howard]	Just Doggin' [Dogg Pound]
	High 'Til I Die [2Pac]	**Keep On, Keepin' On** [MC Lyte] 10

Motherless Child [Ghostface Killer] · Shorty's Game [Miles Goodman] · Thangz Changed [Onyx] · We Don't Need It [Junior M.A.F.I.A.]

Superfly - see MAYFIELD, Curtis
Ron O'Neal/Carl Lee/Julius Harris

Super Fly T.N.T. - see OSIBISA
Ron O'Neal/Roscoe Lee Browne/Sheila Frazier

SOUNDTRACKS

DEBUT	PEAK	WKS	RIAA	CD	ARTIST — Album Title	Catalog	Sym	$	Label & Number

8/17/96 — 133 — 5 — ©713 — Supercop .... [V] **$10** Interscope 90088
Jackie Chan/Michelle Khan/Maggie Cheung/Ken Tsang/Yuen Wah

Caged In A Rage [Dimebag Darrell]	I'll Do It [Dogg Pound]	On A Rope [Rocket From The Crypt]
Great Life [Goatboy]	Kung Fu Fighting [Tom Jones]	Open The Gate [No Doubt]
Harry The Dog [Black Grape]	Made Niggas [2Pac]	Pubstar [Pur]
Head Like A Hole [Devo]	Main Title [Joel McNeely]	Scorched Youth Policy [Polara]

Stayin' Alive [Siobhan Lynch]
Supercop [Devo]
What's Love Got To Do With It [Warren G] *32*

1/13/79 — 44 — 13 — ©714 — Superman - The Movie .... [I] **$15** Warner 3257 [2]
Christopher Reeve/Margot Kidder/Marlon Brando/Gene Hackman/Ned Beatty; cp/cd: **John Williams**

Can You Read My Mind (medley)	Fortress Of Solitude	March Of The Villains
Chasing Rockets	Growing Up	Planet Krypton
Destruction Of Krypton	Leaving Home	Super Rescues
End Title	Lex Luthor's Lair	Superfeats
Flying Sequence (medley)	Love Theme	Turning Back The World

Superman, Theme From (Main Title) *81*
Trip To Earth

7/4/81 — 133 — 9 — 715 — Superman II .... [I] **$12** Warner 3505
Christopher Reeve/Margot Kidder/Gene Hackman/Jackie Cooper/Ned Beatty; cp/cd: Ken Thorne

Aerial Battle (medley)	Honeymoon Hotel	Lovers Fly North
Clark Exposed As Superman	Lex & Miss Teschmacher To Fortress	Main Title March
Clark Fumbles Rescue	Lex Escapes	Mother's Advice
Clark To Fortress (medley)	Lift Into Space (medley)	Release Of Villains (medley)
End Title March		Sad Return

Superman Saves Spire (medley)
T.V. President Resigns (medley)
Ursa Flies Over Moon

7/2/83 — 163 — 3 — 716 — Superman III .... [I+V] **$12** Warner 23879
Christopher Reeve/**Richard Pryor**/Annette O'Toole; cp: **John Williams**/Ken Thorne/**Giorgio Moroder**

Acid Test (medley)	Main Title March	Saving The Factory (medley)
Final Victory (medley)	No See, No Cry [Chaka Khan]	Streets Of Metropolis (Main Title)
Love Theme [Helen St. John]	Rock On [Marshall Crenshaw]	Struggle Within (medley)

They Won't Get Me [Roger Miller]
Two Faces Of Superman

3/8/69 — 72 — 22 — ©717 — Sweet Charity .... [M] **$25** Decca 71502
Shirley MacLaine/**Sammy Davis Jr.**/Ricardo Montalban; mu: Cy Coleman; ly: Dorothy Fields

Big Spender	It's A Nice Face	Rhythm Of Life
I Love To Cry At Weddings	My Personal Property	Sweet Charity
I'm A Brass Band	Overture	There's Gotta Be Something Better Than This
If My Friends Could See Me Now	Pompeii Club (Rich Man's Frug)	

Where Am I Going?

Sweet Dreams - see CLINE, Patsy
Jessica Lange/Ed Harris/Ann Wedgeworth

2/24/01 — 66 — 10↑ — ©718 — Sweet November .... [V] **$10** Warner Sunset 47944
Keanu Reeves/Charlize Theron/Jason Isaacs/Frank Langella

Baby Workout [Jackie Wilson] *5*	Heart Door [Paula Cole with Dolly Parton]	Only Time [Enya]
Cellophane [Amanda Ghost]	My Number [Tegan & Sara]	Other Half Of Me [Bobby Darin]
Consequences Of Falling [K.D. Lang]	Off The Hook [Barenaked Ladies]	Rock DJ [Robbie Williams]
		Shame [BT]

Touched By An Angel [Stevie Nicks]
Wherever You Are [Celeste Prince]
You Deserve To Be Loved [Tracy Dawn]

7/3/71 — 139 — 19 — 719 — Sweet Sweetback's Baadasssss Song .... [I-V] **$30** Stax 3001
Melvin Van Peebles/Rhetta Hughes/John Amos; cp: Melvin Van Peebles

Come On Feet	Mojo Woman	Sweetback Getting It Uptight And Preaching It So Hard The
Hoppin John	Reggins Hanging On In There As Best They Can	Bourgeois Reggin Angel
Man Tries Running His Usual Game	Sanra Z	Sweetback Losing His Cherry
But Sweetback's Jones Is So Strong He Waste		Sweetback's Theme

Won't Bleed Me

8/16/97 — 168 — 9 — ©720 — Swingers .... [V] **$10** Hollywood 62091
Jon Favreau/Vince Vaughn/Ron Livingston/Patrick Van Horn

Car Train [Jazz Jury]	I'm Beginning To See The Light [Bobby Darin]	**Pick Up The Pieces** [Average White Band] *1*
Go Daddy-O [Big Bad Voodoo Daddy]	King Of The Road [Roger Miller] *4*	Pictures [Jazz Jury]
Groove Me [King Floyd] *6*	Knock Me A Kiss [Louis Jordan]	She Thinks I Still Care [George Jones]
I Wan'na Be Like You [Big Bad Voodoo Daddy]	Mucci's Jag M.K.II [Joey Altruda]	Wake Up [Jazz Jury]
	Paid For Loving [Love Jones]	

With Plenty Of Money And You [Count Basie & Tony Bennett]
You & Me & The Bottle Makes 3 Tonight (Baby) [Big Bad Voodoo Daddy]
You're Nobody 'Til Somebody Loves You [Dean Martin] *25*

Swordfish - see OAKENFOLD, Paul
John Travolta/Halle Berry/Hugh Jackman/Don Cheadle

1/29/00 — 198 — 1 — ©721 — Talented Mr. Ripley, The .... [V] **$10** Sony Classical 51337
Matt Damon/Gwyneth Paltrow/Jude Law/Cate Blanchett/Jack Davenport

Champ, The [Dizzy Gillespie]	Lullaby For Cain [Sinéad O'Connor]	Pent-Up House [Guy Barker, etc.]
Crazy Tom [Guy Barker, etc.]	Mischief	Promise
Four [Guy Barker, etc.]	Moanin' [Guy Barker International Quintet]	Proust
Guaglione [Marino Marini]	My Funny Valentine [Matt Damon]	Ripley
Italia	Nature Boy [Miles Davis]	Stabat Mater [Clifford Gurdin]
Ko-Ko [Charlie Parker]		Syncopes

Tu Vuo' Fa L'Americano [Matt Damon/Jude Law/Fiorello]
You Don't Know What Love Is [John Martyn & The Guy Barker International Quintet]

5/27/95 — 16 — 11 — ● — ©722 — Tales From The Hood .... [V] **$10** MCA Sound. 11243
Corbin Bernsen/David Alan Grier/Wings Hauser/Clarence Williams III

Born II Die [Spice 1]	From The Dark Side [Gravediggaz]	Hot Ones Echo Thru The Ghetto [Click]
Death Represents My Hood [Bokie Loc]	Grave, The [N.G.N.]	I'm Talkin' To Myself [NME & Grench The Mean 1]
Face Mob [Face Mob]	Hood Got Me Feelin' The Pain [Havoc & Prodeje]	

Let Me At Them [Wu-Tang Clan]
Ol' Dirty's Back [Ol Dirty Bastard]
One Less Nigga [MC Eiht]
Tales From The Hood [Domino]

4/15/95 — 72 — 10 — ©723 — Tank Girl .... [V] **$10** Elektra 61760
Lori Petty/**Ice-T**/Naomi Watts/Malcolm McDowell

Army Of Me [Björk]	Drown Soda [Hole]	Mockingbird Girl [Magnificent Bastards]
Aurora [Veruca Salt]	Girl U Want [Devo]	Ripper Side [Stomp]
Big Gun [Ice-T]	Let's Do It [Joan Jett & Paul Westerberg]	Roads [Portishead]
Bomb [Bush]		

Shove [L7]
Thief [Belly]

3/11/89 — 166 — 4 — ©724 — Tap .... [V] **$10** Epic 45084
Gregory Hines/Suzzanne Douglas/Joe Morton/**Sammy Davis Jr.**

All I Want Is Forever [James "J.T." Taylor & Regina Belle]	Bad Boy [Teena Marie]	Free [Gwen Guthrie]
Baby What You Want Me To Do [Etta James]	Can't Escape The Rhythm [Gregory Hines]	Lover's Intuition [Amy Keys]
	Forget The Girl [Tony Terry]	Max's Theme [Stanley Clarke]

Somebody Like You [Melissa Rowan]
Strong As Steel [Gregory Abbott]

DEBUT	PEAK	WKS	RIAA	CD	ARTIST — Album Title	Catalog	Sym	$	Label & Number
6/5/99	5	67	▲²	©725	**Tarzan**		[M]	$10	Walt Disney 60645

Tarzan — animated movie, voices by: Tony Goldwyn/Minnie Driver/Glenn Close/**Rosie O'Donnell**; sw: **Phil Collins**; cp: Mark Mancina

Gorillas, The (Score)
Moves Like An Ape, Looks Like A Man (Score)
One Family (Score)
Son Of Man
Strangers Like Me
Trashin' The Camp
Trashin' The Camp [Phil Collins & 'N Sync]
Two Worlds
Two Worlds [Phil Collins]
Two Worlds Finale
Two Worlds (Reprise)
Wondrous Place (Score)
You'll Be In My Heart
You'll Be In My Heart [Phil Collins] 21

| 10/27/84 | 34 | 16 | ● | ©726 | **Teachers** .... | | [V] | $10 | Capitol 12371 |

Teachers — Nick Nolte/JoBeth Williams/Judd Hirsch/Ralph Macchio/Lee Grant

Cheap Sunglasses [ZZ Top] 89
Edge Of A Dream [Joe Cocker] 69
Fooling Around [Freddie Mercury]
I Can't Stop The Fire [Eric Martin & Friends]
(I'm The) Teacher [Ian Hunter]
In The Jungle (Concrete Jungle) [Motels]
Interstate Love Affair [Night Ranger]
One Foot Back In Your Door [Roman Holliday] 76
Teacher Teacher [38 Special] 25
Understanding [Bob Seger & The Silver Bullet Band] 17

| 4/21/90 | 13 | 24 | ▲ | ©727 | **Teenage Mutant Ninja Turtles** .... | | [V] | $10 | SBK 91066 |

Teenage Mutant Ninja Turtles — Judith Hoag/Elias Koteas/Ray Serra/Josh Pais

Every Heart Needs A Home [St. Paul]
Family [Riff]
Let The Walls Come Down [Johnny Kemp]
9.95 [Spunkadelic]
Shredder's Suite [John Du Prez]
Spin That Wheel [Hi Tek 3] 69
Splinter's Tale (Parts I & II) [John Du Prez]
This Is What We Do [M.C. Hammer]
Turtle Power! [Partners In Kryme] 13
Turtle Rhapsody [Orchestra On The Half Shell]

| 4/13/91 | 30 | 22 | ● | ©728 | **Teenage Mutant Ninja Turtles II - The Secret Of The Ooze** .... | | [V] | $10 | SBK 96204 |

Teenage Mutant Ninja Turtles II - The Secret Of The Ooze — Paige Turco/David Warner/Ernie Reyes/Kenn Troum

Awesome (You Are My Hero) [Ya Kid K]
Back To School [Fifth Platoon]
Cowabunga [Orchestra On The Half Shell]
Creatures Of Habit [Spunkadelic]
Find The Key To Your Life [Cathy Dennis & David Morales]
Moov! [Tribal House]
Ninja Rap [Vanilla Ice]
(That's Your) Consciousness [Dan Hartman]
This World [Magnificent VII]
Tokka & Rahzar: The Monster Mix [Orchestra On The Half Shell]

| 4/10/93 | 123 | 6 | | ©729 | **Teenage Mutant Ninja Turtles III** .... | | [V] | $10 | SBK 89016 |

Teenage Mutant Ninja Turtles III — Elias Koteas/Paige Turco/Vivian Wu/Sab Shimono/Stuart Wilson

Can't Stop Rockin' [ZZ Top]
Conga [Barrio Boyzz]
Fighter [Definition Of Sound]
Rockin' Over The Beat [Technotronic feat. Ya Kid K] 95
Tarzan Boy [Baltimora] 51
Turtle Jam [Psychedelic Dust]
Turtle Power [Partners In Kryme]
Yoshi's Theme [John Du Prez & Ocean Music]

| 1/5/80 | 80 | 9 | | 730 | **"10"** | | [I] | $12 | Warner 3399 |

"10" — Bo Derek/Dudley Moore/**Julie Andrews**/Robert Webber/Brian Dennehy; cp/cd: **Henry Mancini**

Don't Call It Love
Get It On
He Pleases Me
Hot Sand Mexican Band
I Have An Ear For Love
It's Easy To Say
Keyboard Harmony
Ravel's Bolero
Something For Jenny

| 4/24/99 | 52 | 27 | ● | ©731 | **10 Things I Hate About You** .... | | [V] | $10 | Hollywood 62216 |

10 Things I Hate About You — Julia Stiles/Heath Ledger/Joseph Gordon-Levitt/Larisa Oleynik

Atomic Dog [George Clinton]
Cruel To Be Kind [Letters To Cleo]
Dazz [Brick] 3
Even Angels Fall [Jessica Riddle]
FNT [Semisonic]
I Know [Save Ferris]
I Want You To Want Me [Letters To Cleo]
New World [Leroy]
One More Thing [Richard Gibbs]
Saturday Night [Ta-Gana]
War [Cardigans]
Weakness In Me [Joan Armatrading]
Wings Of A Dove [Madness]
Your Winter [Sister Hazel]

| 1/21/89 | 101 | 13 | | ©732 | **Tequila Sunrise** .... | | [V] | $10 | Capitol 91185 |

Tequila Sunrise — Mel Gibson/Michelle Pfeiffer/Kurt Russell/Raul Julia/J.T. Walsh

Beyond The Sea [Bobby Darin] 6
Dead On The Money [Andy Taylor]
Do You Believe In Shame? [Duran Duran] 72
Don't Worry Baby [Everly Brothers & The Beach Boys]
Give A Little Love [Ziggy Marley & The Melody Makers]
Jo Ann's Song [Dave Grusin & David Sanborn]
Recurring Dream [Crowded House]
Surrender To Me [Ann Wilson & Robin Zander] 6
Tequila Dreams [Dave Grusin & Lee Ritenour]
Unsubstantiated [Church]

| 8/31/91 | 70 | 6 | | ©733 | **Terminator 2: Judgment Day** .... | | [I] | $10 | Varese Sarabande 5335 |

Terminator 2: Judgment Day — Arnold Schwarzenegger/Linda Hamilton/Robert Patrick/Edward Furlong; cp: Brad Fiedel

Attack On Dyson (Sarah's Solution)
Cameron's Inferno
Desert Suite
Escape From The Hospital (And T1000)
Hasta La Vista, Baby (T1000 Freezes)
Helicopter Chase
I'll Be Back
Into The Steel Mill
It's Over (Good-Bye)
Main Title (Theme)
Our Gang Goes To Cyberdyne
Sarah On The Run
Sarah's Dream (Nuclear Nightmare)
Swat Team Attacks
T1000 Terminated
Tanker Chase
Terminator Impaled
Terminator Revives
Trust Me

| 4/21/84 | 111 | 10 | | ©734 | **Terms Of Endearment** .... | | [I+V] | $12 | Capitol 12329 |

Terms Of Endearment — Shirley MacLaine/Debra Winger/Jack Nicholson/Jeff Daniels/John Lithgow; cp: Michael Gore

Anything Goes [Ethel Merman]
Aurora's Night Music
End Credits
Gee, Officer Krupke! [Eddie Roll/Grover Dale/Jets]
I'll Miss You, Momma
Last Look
Main Title
Pleasure Dome
Rock-A-Bye Your Baby With A Dixie Melody [Judy Garland]
Terms Of Endearment, Theme From [Michael Gore] 84
This Is My Moment (Garrett & Aurora's Love Theme)
Three Scenes From A Marriage
Wake, The

| 5/13/78 | 10 | 27 | ▲ | ©735 | **Thank God It's Friday** | | [V] | $20 | Casablanca 7099 [2] |

Thank God It's Friday — Jeff Goldblum/Valerie Landsburg/Debra Winger; includes bonus 12" single

After Dark [Pattie Brooks]
Disco Queen [Paul Jabara]
Do You Want The Real Thing [D.C. Larue]
Find My Way [Cameo]
Floyd's Theme [Natural Juices]
I Wanna Dance [Marathon]
Je T'Aime (Moi Non Plus) [Donna Summer]
Last Dance [Donna Summer] 3
Leatherman's Theme [Wright Bros. Flying Machine]
Love Masterpiece [Thelma Houston]
Lovin', Livin' And Givin' [Diana Ross]
Sevilla Nights [Santa Esmeralda]
Take It To The Zoo [Sunshine]
Thank God It's Friday [Love And Kisses] 22
Too Hot Ta Trot [Commodores] 24
Trapped In A Stairway [Paul Jabara]
With Your Love [Donna Summer]
You're The Most Precious Thing In My Life [Love And Kisses]

| 10/12/96 | 21 | 30 | ● | ©736 | **That Thing You Do!** .... | | [V] | $10 | Play-Tone 67828 |

That Thing You Do! — Tom Hanks/Tom Everett Scott/Liv Tyler/Johnathon Schaech/Steve Zahn

All My Only Dreams [Wonders]
Dance With Me Tonight [Wonders]
Drive Faster [Vicksburgs]
Hold My Hand, Hold My Heart [Chantrellines]
I Need You (That Thing You Do) [Wonders]
Little Wild One [Wonders]
Lovin' You Lots And Lots [Norm Wooster Singers]
Mr. Downtown [Freddy Fredrickson]
My World Is Over [Diane Dane]
She Knows It [Heardsmen]
Shrimp Shack [Cap'n Geech & The Shrimp Shack Shooters]
That Thing You Do! [Wonders] 41
That Thing You Do! (Live At The Hollywood Television Showcase) [Wonders]
Time To Blow [Del Paxton]
Voyage Around The Moon [Saturn 5]

DEBUT	PEAK	WKS	RIAA	CD	ARTIST — Album Title	Catalog	Sym	$	Label & Number

6/22/74 | **128** | **14** | | ©737 | **That's Entertainment** .... [M] **$25** | MCA 11002 [2]

musical highlights from MGM's greatest musicals (1929-58)

Aba Daba Honeymoon
American In Paris (medley)
Be My Love
Broadway Ballet (medley)
Broadway Melody
By Myself
Easy To Love (medley)
Get Happy
Gigi Medley
Going Hollywood

Hallelujah
Heigh Ho, The Gang's All Here
Honeysuckle Rose
I Guess I'll Have To Change My Plans
I've Got A Feeling For You
It's A Most Unusual Day
Make 'Em Laugh
Mickey Rooney - Judy Garland Medley

On The Atchison, Topeka & Santa Fe
Pretty Girl Is Like A Melody
Putting On The Ritz (medley)
Rosalie
Showboat Medley
Singin' In The Rain
Song's Gotta Come From The Heart
That's Entertainment

They Can't Take That Away From Me
Thou Swell
Under The Bamboo Tree
Varsity Drag
Wizard Of Oz Medley
You Made Me Love You (Dear Mr. Gable)

That's The Way Of The World - see EARTH, WIND & FIRE

Harvey Keitel/Ed Nelson/Cynthia Bostwick/Bert Parks

6/15/91 | **54** | **12** | | ©738 | **Thelma & Louise** .... [V] **$10** | MCA 10239

Susan Sarandon/Geena Davis/Harvey Keitel/Brad Pitt/Chris McDonald

Badlands [Charlie Sexton]
Ballad of Lucy Jordan [Marianne Faithfull]
Better Not Look Down [B.B. King]

House of Hope [Toni Childs]
I Can't Untie You From Me [Grayson Hugh]
Kick The Stones [Chris Whitley]

Little Honey [Kelly Willis]
Part Of You, Part Of Me [Glenn Frey] **55**
Tennessee Plates [Charlie Sexton]

Thunderbird [Hans Zimmer]
Wild Nights [Martha Reeves]

1/22/55 | **6** | **8** | | ©739 | **There's No Business Like Show Business** [M] **$50** | Decca 8091

Ethel Merman/Donald O'Connor/Dan Dailey/**Marilyn Monroe**; sw: Irving Berlin; LP: Decca DL-8091 (#6); EP: Decca ED-828 (#9)

After You Get What You Want, You Don't Want It
Alexander's Ragtime Band

If You Believe
Lazy
Man Chases A Girl (Until She Catches Him)

Play A Simple Melody
Sailor's Not A Sailor ('Til A Sailor's Been Tattooed)

There's No Business Like Show Business
When The Midnight Choo-Choo Leaves For Alabam'

Heat Wave

8/15/98 | **132** | **7** | | ©740 | **There's Something About Mary** .... [V] **$10** | Capitol 95737

Cameron Diaz/Matt Dillon/Ben Stiller/Lee Evans/Chris Elliott

Build Me Up Buttercup [Foundations] **3**
Every Day Should Be A Holiday [Dandy Warhols]
Everything Shines [Push Stars]
History Repeating [Propellerheads]

How To Survive A Broken Heart [Ben Lee]
If I Could Talk I'd Tell You [Lemonheads]
Is She Really Going Out With Him [Joe Jackson] **21**

Let Her Go Into The Darkness [Jonathan Richman]
Margo's Waltz [Lloyd Cole]
Mary's Prayer [Danny Wilson] **23**
Speed Queen [Zuba]

There's Something About Mary [Jonathan Richman]
This Is The Day [Ivy]
True Love Is Not Nice [Jonathan Richman]

10/23/99 | **64** | **5** | | ©741 | **Thicker Than Water** .... [V] **$15** | Hoo Bangin' 50016 [2]

Mack 10/Fat Joe/MC Eiht/Kidada Jones/**Ice Cube**

Belly Of The Beast [Eightball & Big Duke]
Blue Liquid [Beefy]
Do You Wanna Get With This [Soultre]
Drug Lord [Childrin Of Da Ghetto]
Flagrant [Choclair]
Flex With You [Michalie Jamison]
Freeze [MMO]

Gang Bang S*** [Road Dawgs]
Gangsta Gangsta [Mack 10]
Half A Million [Soultre]
Hate [CJ Mac]
I Don't Wanna Die [King T]
It's Time To Roll [Childrin Of Da Ghetto]
King Of L.A. [CJ Mac]
LB 2000 [Techniec]

Let It Reign [Westside Connection]
Live Life 2 Tha Fullest [Memphis Bleek]
Mashin'-N-Smashin [Boo Kapone & Techniec]
Me & My B**** [MC Eiht]
Partners In Crime [Mr. Mike]
Planet Rock [Tech N9ne]

Police Rush The Spot [Thugged Out]
Survival Of The Fittest [Dresta]
Thicker Than Blood [Fat Joe]
Thicker Than Water [MC Eiht]
U Know [Gangsta]
Wanna Be Gangsta [Comrads]
Who Got Some Gangsta S*** [Mack 10]

Thief - see TANGERINE DREAM

James Caan/Tuesday Weld/**Willie Nelson**

12/22/84+ | **179** | **4** | | ©742 | **Thief Of Hearts** .... [I+V] **$12** | Casablanca 822942

Steven Bauer/Barbara Williams/John Getz/George Wendt; cp/cd: Harold Faltermeyer

Collage
Final Confrontation
Just Imagine (Way Beyond Fear) [Beth Anderson & Joe "Bean" Esposito]

Love In The Shadows [Elizabeth Daily]
Love Theme
Passion Play [Annabella]
Stolen Secrets

Tear Me Up [Darwun]
Thief Of Hearts [Melissa Manchester] **86**
Thief Of Hearts (instrumental)

3/2/96 | **22** | **18** | ● | ©743 | **Thin Line Between Love & Hate, A** .... [V] **$10** | Jac-Mac 46134

Martin Lawrence/Lynn Whitfield/Regina King/**Bobby Brown**/Della Reese

Beware My Crew [L.B.C. Crew] **75**
Chocolate City [Roger Troutman]
Come Over [Sandra St. Victor]
Damned If I Do [Somethin' For The People]

Freak Tonight [R. Kelly]
I Don't Hang [Soopafly]
It's Ladies Night At Chocolate City [Dark Complexion]
Knocks Me Off My Feet [Tevin Campbell]

Let's Stay Together [Eric Benet]
Love Got My Mind Trippin' [Ganjah K]
Playa Fo Real [Dru Down]
Ring My Bell [Luniz]
Thin Line [Drawz]

Thin Line Between Love & Hate [H-Town] **37**
Way Back When [Smooth]

Third World, Prisoner in The Street - see THIRD WORLD

This Is Elvis - see PRESLEY, Elvis

This Is Spinal Tap - see SPINAL TAP

Christopher Guest/Michael McKean/Harry Shearer

8/31/68 | **182** | **6** | | ©744 | **Thomas Crown Affair, The** .... [I] **$25** | United Artists 5182

Steve McQueen/Faye Dunaway/Paul Burke/Jack Weston; cp/cd: Michel LeGrand

Boston Wrangler
Cash And Carry
Chess Game
Crowning Touch

His Eyes, Her Eyes
Man's Castle
Playing The Field
Room Service

Windmills Of Your Mind [Noel Harrison]
Windmills Of Your Mind (instrumental)

4/15/67 | **16** | **48** | ● | ©745 | **Thoroughly Modern Millie** .... [M] **$25** | Decca 71500

Julie Andrews/Mary Tyler Moore/Carol Channing/John Gavin; cd: Andre Previn

Baby Face
Do It Again
Exit Music
Intermission Medley

Jazz Baby
Jewish Wedding Song (Trinkt Le Chaim)
Jimmy

Poor Butterfly
Prelude
Rose Of Washington Square
Tapioca, The

9/15/73 | **184** | **6** | | 746 | **Those Glorious MGM Musicals: Show Boat/Annie Get Your Gun** .... [M] **$25** | MGM 42 [2]

Anything You Can Do
Bill
Can't Help Lovin' Dat Man
Doin' What Comes Natur'lly
Girl That I Marry

I Might Fall Back On You
I've Got The Sun In The Morning
Life Upon The Wicked Stage
Make Believe
My Defenses Are Down

Ol' Man River
There's No Business Like Show Business
They Say It's Wonderful
Why Do I Love You

You Are Love
You Can't Get A Man With A Gun

DEBUT	PEAK	WKS	RIAA	CD	ARTIST — Album Title	Catalog	Sym	$	Label & Number

9/15/73 — **185** — **7** — **747** — **Those Glorious MGM Musicals: Singin' In The Rain/Easter Parade** .... [M] — **$25** — MGM 40 [2]

- All I Do Is Dream Of You
- Better Luck Next Time
- Broadway Ballet
- Couple Of Swells
- Easter Parade
- Fella With An Umbrella
- Fit As A Fiddle
- Good Morning
- I Love A Piano (medley)
- It Only Happens When I Dance With You
- Make 'Em Laugh
- Moses
- Shaking The Blues Away
- Singin' In The Rain
- Snooky Ookums (medley)
- Steppin' Out With My Baby
- When The Midnight Choo Choo Leaves For Alabam' (medley)
- You Are My Lucky Star
- You Were Meant For Me

12/4/93+ — **101** — **14** — ©**748** — **Three Musketeers, The** ... [I] — **$10** — Hollywood 61581

Charlie Sheen/Kiefer Sutherland/Chris O'Donnell/Oliver Platt; cp/cd: Michael Kamen
- All For Love [Bryan Adams, Rod Stewart & Sting] 1
- Athos, Porthos And Aramis
- Cannonballs
- Cardinal's Couch
- Cavern Of Cardinal Richelieu
- D'Artagnan
- Fourth Musketeer
- Louis XIII, Queen Anne And Constance - Lady In Waiting
- M'Lady De Winter
- Sword Fight

3/18/00 — **190** — **1** — ©**749** — **3 Strikes** ... [V] — **$10** — Priority 50118

Brian Hooks/N'Bushe Wright/Faizon Love/David Alan Grier
- Been A Long Time [C-Murder]
- Chart Climbin' [Sauce Money]
- Crave [E-40]
- G'd Up [Eastsidaz] 47
- Gotta Hold On Me [Nio Renee]
- I'm Straight [E-40]
- Let's Ride [Choclair]
- West Coast Mentality [Ras Kass]
- Where Da Paper At [Likwit Crew]
- Where Dey At [Silkk The Shocker]
- Where I Come From [Solo & Kam]
- Worldwide Renegades [Da Howg]

Three Tough Guys - see HAYES, Isaac

Isaac Hayes/Fred Williamson/Lino Ventura

4/23/94 — **49** — **10** — ©**750** — **Threesome** ... [V] — **$10** — Epic Soundtrax 57881

Lara Flynn Boyle/Stephen Baldwin/Josh Charles/Alexis Arquette
- Bizarre Love Triangle [New Order]
- Boom Shack-A-Lak [Apache Indian]
- Buttercup [Brad]
- Dancing Barefoot [U2]
- He's My Best Friend [Jellyfish]
- I'll Take You There [General Public] 22
- Is Your Love Strong Enough? [Bryan Ferry]
- Like A Virgin [Teenage Fanclub]
- Make Me Smile (Come Up And See Me) [Duran Duran]
- New Star [Tears For Fears]
- That Was The Day [The]
- What Does Sex Mean To Me? [Human Sexual Response]

12/11/65+ — **10** — **28** — ©**751** — **Thunderball** — [I] — **$40** — United Artists 5132

Sean Connery/Claudine Auger/Adolfo Celi; cp/cd: John Barry
- Bomb, The
- Bond Below Disco Volante
- Cafe Martinique
- Chateau Flight
- Death Of Fiona
- 007
- Mr. Kiss Kiss Bang Bang
- Search For Vulcan
- Spa, The
- Switching The Body
- Thunderball [Tom Jones] 25
- Thunderball (instrumental)

Time To Sing, A - see WILLIAMS, Hank Jr.

Hank Williams Jr./Shelley Fabares/Ed Begley

9/27/80 — **37** — **17** — **752** — **Times Square** ... [V] — **$15** — RSO 4203 [2]

Tim Curry/Trini Alvarado/Robin Johnson
- Babylon's Burning [Ruts]
- Damn Dog [Robin Johnson]
- Down In The Park [Gary Numan]
- Flowers In The City [David Johansen & Robin Johnson]
- Grinding Halt [Cure]
- Help Me! [Marcy Levy & Robin Gibb] 50
- I Wanna Be Sedated [Ramones]
- Innocent, Not Guilty [Garland Jeffreys]
- Life During Wartime [Talking Heads] 80
- Night Was Not [Desmond Child & Rouge]
- Pissing In The River [Patti Smith Group]
- Pretty Boys [Joe Jackson]
- Rock Hard [Suzi Quatro]
- Same Old Scene [Roxy Music]
- Take This Town [XTC]
- Talk Of The Town [Pretenders]
- Walk On The Wild Side [Lou Reed] 16
- You Can't Hurry Love [D.L. Byron]
- Your Daughter Is One [Robin Johnson & Trini Alvarado]

9/7/96 — **82** — **6** — ©**753** — **Tin Cup** ... [V] — **$10** — Epic Soundtrax 67609

Kevin Costner/Rene Russo/Cheech Marin (**Cheech & Chong**)/Don Johnson
- Back To Salome [Shawn Colvin]
- Big Stick [Bruce Hornsby]
- Character Flaw [Joe Ely]
- Cool Lookin' Woman [Jimmie Vaughan]
- Crapped Out Again [Keb' Mo']
- Double Bogey Blues [Mickey Jones]
- Every Minute, Every Hour, Every Day [James House]
- I Wonder [Chris Isaak]
- Just One More [George Jones]
- Let Me Into Your Heart [Mary Chapin Carpenter]
- Little Bit Is Better Than Nada [Texas Tornados]
- Nobody There But Me [Bruce Hornsby]
- This Could Take All Night [Amanda Marshall]
- Where Are You Boy [Patty Loveless]

7/8/00 — **127** — **2** — ©**754** — **Titan A.E.** ... [V] — **$10** — Java 25275

animated moie, voices by Matt Damon/Bill Pullman/Nathan Lane/Janeane Garofalo
- Cosmic Castaway [Electrasy]
- Down To Earth [Luscious Jackson]
- End Is Over [Powerman 5000]
- Everybody's Going To The Moon [Jamiroquai]
- Everything Under The Stars [Fun Lovin' Criminals]
- It's My Turn To Fly [Urge]
- Karma Slave [Splashdown]
- Like Lovers (Holding On) [Texas]
- Not Quite Paradise [Bliss]
- Over My Head [Lit]
- Renegade Survivor [Wailing Souls]

12/27/97+ — **❶**[16] — **71** — ▲[11] — ©**755** — **Titanic** — [I] — **$10** — Sony Classical 63213

Leonardo DiCaprio/Kate Winslet/Billy Zane/Gloria Stuart/Kathy Bates; cp/cd: James Horner
- Death Of Titanic
- Distant Memories
- "Hard To Starboard"
- Hymn To The Sea
- Leaving Port
- Life So Changed
- My Heart Will Go On (Love Theme From Titanic) [Celine Dion] 58
- Never An Absolution
- Ocean Of Memories
- Promise Kept
- Rose
- Sinking, The
- Southampton
- "Take Her To Sea, Mr. Murdoch"
- Unable To Stay, Unwilling To Leave

9/12/98 — **2**[1] — **23** — ▲ — ©**756** — **Titanic, Back To** — [I] — **$10** — Sony Classical 60691

additional music from the movie *Titanic*
- Alexander's Ragtime Band [I Salonisti]
- Building Panic
- Come Josephine, In My Flying Machine [Máire Brennan]
- Epilogue - The Deep And Timeless Sea
- Irish Party In Third Class [Gaelic Storm]
- Jack Dawson's Luck
- Lament
- My Heart Will Go On [Celine Dion]
- Nearer My God To Thee [I Salonisti]
- Nearer My God To Thee [Eileen Ivers]
- Portrait, The [James Horner]
- Shore Never Reached
- Titanic Suite

To Live and Die in L.A. - see WANG CHUNG

William L. Peterson/Willem Dafoe/John Turturro/Dean Stockwell

9/23/67 — **16** — **22** — ©**757** — **To Sir, With Love** ... [I+V] — **$30** — Fontana 67569

Sidney Poitier/Judy Geeson/Christian Roberts/**Lulu**; cp/cd: Ron Grainer
- Classical Lesson
- Funeral, The
- It's Getting Harder All The Time [Mindbenders]
- Off And Running [Mindbenders]
- Perhaps I Could Tidy Your Desk
- Potter's Loss Of Temper In Gym
- Stealing My Love From Me [Lulu]
- Thackeray And Denham Box In Gym
- Thackeray Loses Temper, Gets An Idea
- Thackeray Meets Faculty, Then Alone
- Thackeray Reads Letter About Job
- To Sir With Love [Lulu] 1

9/23/95 — **108** — **4** — ©**758** — **To Wong Foo, Thanks For Everything! Julie Newmar** ... [V] — **$10** — MCA Sound. 11231

Patrick Swayze/Wesley Snipes/John Leguizamo/Stockard Channing
- Brick House [Commodores] 5
- Do What You Wanna Do [Charisse Arrington]
- Free Yourself [Chaka Khan]
- Hey Now (Girls Just Want To Have Fun [Cyndi Lauper] 87
- I Am The Body Beautiful [Salt-N-Pepa]
- Nobody's Body [Monifah]
- Over The Rainbow [Patti LaBelle]
- She's A Lady [Tom Jones] 2
- To Wong Foo Suite [Rachel Portman]
- Turn It Out [LaBelle]
- Who Taught You How [Crystal Waters]

SOUNDTRACKS

DEBUT	PEAK	WKS	RIAA	CD	ARTIST — Album Title	Catalog	Sym	$	Label & Number

Together Brothers - see LOVE UNLIMITED ORCHESTRA
Anthony Wilson/Ahmad Nurradin/Glynn Turman/Owen Pace

3/21/64 · **38** · 23 · 759 · **Tom Jones** .... [I] **$30** · United Artists 5113
Albert Finney/Susannah York/Hugh Griffith/David Tomlinson; cp/cd: John Addison

Born For Trouble	I Love You, Sophie Western	Love Theme	Tom Jones Strut
Britannia Rules	If He Swing By The String	Main Title	Tom Strikes Again
End Title	Ladies Are Irresistible	Squire Steps In	Trying Times
Grim Guardians Of Justice	Lean Days	Sylvan Misadventures	Wine And Women

3/29/75 · **2**[1] · 35 · ● · ©760 · **Tommy** [M] **$25** · Polydor 9502 [2]
Roger Daltrey/**Ann-Margret**/Oliver Reed/**Elton John**/**Tina Turner**; sw: **Pete Townshend**

Acid Queen	Extra, Extra, Extra	Mother And Son	TV Studio
Amazing Journey	Eyesight To The Blind	1951 (medley)	There's A Doctor
Bernie's Holiday Camp	Fiddle About	Pinball Wizard	Tommy Can You Hear Me
Captain Walker (medley)	Go To The Mirror	Sally Simpson	Tommy's Holiday Camp
Champagne	I'm Free	See Me, Feel Me (medley)	We're Not Gonna Take It
Christmas	It's A Boy (medley)	Sensation	Welcome
Cousin Kevin	Listening To You (medley)	Smash The Mirror	What About The Boy? (medley)
Do You Think It's Alright	Miracle Cure	Sparks	

1/17/98 · **197** · 1 · ©761 · **Tomorrow Never Dies** .... [I] **$10** · A&M 540830
Pierce Brosnan/Jonathan Pryce/Michelle Yeoh/Teri Hatcher; cp: David Arnold; cd: Nicholas Dodd

Backseat Driver	Hamburg Break Out	Sinking Of The Devonshire	Underwater Discovery
Company Car	James Bond Theme [Moby]	Station Break	White Knight
Doctor Kaufman	Last Goodbye	Surrender [k.d. lang]	
Hamburg Break It	Paris And Bond	Tomorrow Never Dies [Sheryl Crow]	

2/26/83 · **144** · 12 · 762 · **Tootsie** .... [I] **$12** · Warner 23781
Dustin Hoffman/Jessica Lange/Charles Durning/Bill Murray/Sydney Pollack; cp/cd: **Dave Grusin**

Actor's Life (Main Title)	**It Might Be You** [Stephen	Metamorphosis Blues	Tootsie [Stephen Bishop]
Don't Let It Get You Down	Bishop] **25**	Out Of The Rain	Working Girl March
	Media Zap [Stephen Bishop]	Sandy's Song	

6/7/86 · **❶**[5] · 93 · ▲[9] · ©763 · **Top Gun** C:#8/175 [V] **$10** · Columbia 40323
Tom Cruise/Kelly McGillis/Val Kilmer/Anthony Edwards/Tom Skerritt

Danger Zone [Kenny Loggins] **2**	Hot Summer Nights [Miami Sound	**Playing With The Boys** [Kenny	Top Gun Anthem [Harold
Destination Unknown [Marietta]	Machine]	Loggins] **60**	Faltermeyer & Steve Stevens]
Heaven In Your Eyes	Lead Me On [Teena Marie]	**Take My Breath Away** [Berlin] **1**	Through The Fire [Larry Greene]
[Loverboy] **12**	Mighty Wings [Cheap Trick]		

1/9/65 · **150** · 2 · 764 · **Topkapi** .... [I] **$30** · United Artists 5118
Melina Mercouri/Peter Ustinov/Maximilian Schell/Robert Morley; cp: Manos Hadjidakis

Belly Dance	Master Thief	Searchlight, The	Wrestling Tournament
Emeralds, The	Museum Roof	Success!	
In Prison	Palace Museum	Sultan's Dagger	
Lincoln Automobile	Screwball Inventor	Turkish Security	

2/1/75 · **158** · 3 · 765 · **Towering Inferno, The** .... [I] **$15** · Warner 2840
Paul Newman/Steve McQueen/William Holden/Faye Dunaway/Fred Astaire; cp/cd: **John Williams**

Architect's Dream	Main Title	Susan And Doug	**We May Never Love Like This**
Helicopter Explosion	Planting The Charges	Trapped Lovers	**Again** [Maureen McGovern] **83**
Lisolette And Harlee	Something For Susan		

12/16/95+ · **94** · 10 · ©766 · **Toy Story** .... [I] **$10** · Walt Disney 60883
animated movie, voices by: Tom Hanks/Tim Allen/**Don Rickles**/Jim Varney/Wallace Shawn; cp/pf: **Randy Newman**

Andy's Birthday	I Will Go Sailing No More	Presents	Woody And Buzz
Big One	Infinity And Beyond	Sid	Woody's Gone
Buzz	Mutants	Soldier's Mission	You've Got A Friend In Me
Hang Together	On The Move	Strange Things	

12/4/99 · **111** · 6 · ©767 · **Toy Story 2** .... [I] **$10** · Walt Disney 60647
animated movie, voices by: Tom Hanks/Tim Allen/Joan Cusack/Kelsey Grammer/**Don Rickles**; cp/pf: **Randy Newman**

Al's Toy Barn	Let's Save Woody	When She Loved Me [Sarah	You've Got A Friend In Me [Robert
Chicken Man	Off To The Museum	McLachlan]	Goulet]
Cleaner, The	Ride Like The Wind	Woody's A Star	Zurg's Planet
Emperor Zurg vs. Buzz	Talk To Jessie	Woody's Been Stolen	
Jessie And The Roundup Gang	Use Your Head	Woody's Dream	
Jessie's In Trouble	Wheezy And The Yard Sale	Woody's Roundup [Riders In The	
		Sky]	

1/16/93 · **161** · 4 · ©768 · **Toys** .... [V] **$10** · Geffen 24505
Robin Williams/Michael Gambon/Joan Cusack/**L.L. Cool J**

Alsatia's Lullaby	General, The	Let Joy And Peace Prevail [Grace	Welcome To The Pleasuredome
Battle Introduction [Robin Williams]	Happy Worker [Tori Amos]	Jones]	[Frankie Goes To Hollywood]
Closing Of The Year (medley)	Happy Workers (Reprise) (medley)	Mirror Song [Thomas Dolby/Robin	Winter Reveries
Closing Of The Year (Main Theme)	Let Joy And Innocence Prevail [Pat	Williams/Joan Cusack]	Workers
Ebudae [Enya]	Metheny]		

8/10/96 · **48** · 26 · ● · ©769 · **Trainspotting** .... [V] **$10** · Capitol 37190
Ewan McGregor/Ewen Bremner/Jonny Lee Miller/Kevin McKidd

Atomic [Sleeper]	Final Hit [Leftfield]	Nightclubbing [Iggy Pop]	Trainspotting [Primal Scream]
Born Slippy [Underworld]	For What You Dream Of [Bedrock]	Perfect Day [Lou Reed]	2:1 [Elastica]
Closet Romantic [Damon Albarn]	Lust For Life [Iggy Pop]	Sing [Blur]	
Deep Blue Day [Brian Eno]	Mile End [Pulp]	Temptation [New Order]	

12/12/92+ · **82** · 10 · ©770 · **Trespass** .... [V] **$10** · Sire 26978
Bill Paxton/**Ice-T**/William Sadler/**Ice Cube**

Depths Of Hell [Ice-T]	Gotta Get Over (Taking Loot) [Gang	I'm Gonna Smoke Him [Donald D]	Quick Way Out [W.C. & The Maad
Don't Be A 304 [AMG]	Starr]	King Of The Street [Ry Cooder &	Circle]
Gotta Do What I Gotta Do [Public	I Check My Bank [Sir Mix-A-Lot]	Jim Keltner]	Trespass [Ice-T & Ice Cube]
Enemy]	I'm A Playa (Bitch) [Penthouse	On The Wall [Black Sheep]	You Know What I'm About [Lord
	Players Clique]		Finesse]

DEBUT	PEAK	WKS	RIAA	CD	ARTIST — Album Title	Sym	$	Label & Number
12/21/74+	130	8		771	Trial Of Billy Jack, The	[I+V]	$15	ABC 853

Tom Laughlin/Delores Taylor/Victor Izay; cp/cd: Elmer Bernstein

Billy And Jean Reunion
Danny's Song (I Saw Three Ships) [Michael Bolland]
Dreaming And Hoping [Teresa Laughlin]
Freedom School Massacre
Freedom School Parade
Give Peace A Chance
Golden Lady (Farewell To Jean) [Lynn Baker]
How I Need You (Theme) [Michelle Wilson]
Indian Vision
Karate Fight
My Lai Massacre
Shed A Tear (Billy's Home Coming) [Teresa Laughlin]

Tribute To Jack Johnson, A - see DAVIS, Miles

Trick Or Treat - see FASTWAY
Marc Price/Tony Fields/**Gene Simmons**

DEBUT	PEAK	WKS	RIAA	CD	ARTIST — Album Title	Sym	$	Label & Number
7/31/82	135	5		772	Tron	[I]	$12	CBS 37782

Jeff Bridges/Bruce Boxleitner/David Warner/Barnard Hughes; cp: **Walter Carlos**; cd: Douglas Gamley

Anthem
Creation Of Tron
Ending Titles
Light Sailer
Love Theme
Magic Landings
Miracle And Magician
New Tron And The MCP
1990's Theme
Only Solutions
Ring Game And Escape
Sea Of Simulation
Tower Music - Let Us Pray
Tron (Theme)
Tron Scherzo
Water Music And Tronaction
We've Got Company
Wormhole

Trouble Man - see GAYE, Marvin
Robert Hooks/Paul Winfield/Ralph Waite/Paula Kelly

Truck Turner - see HAYES, Isaac
Isaac Hayes/Yaphet Kotto/Nichelle Nichols/Scatman Crothers

DEBUT	PEAK	WKS	RIAA	CD	ARTIST — Album Title	Sym	$	Label & Number
8/2/69	77	12		©773	True Grit	[I]	$30	Capitol 263

John Wayne/Glen Campbell/Kim Darby/Robert Duvall; cp/cd: Elmer Bernstein

Big Trail
Chen Lee And The General
Cogburn Country
Dastardly Deed
Mattie And Little Blackie
Papa's Things
Rooster
True Grit [Glen Campbell] 35
True Grit (instrumental)

DEBUT	PEAK	WKS	RIAA	CD	ARTIST — Album Title	Sym	$	Label & Number
9/19/92	173	1		©774	Twin Peaks - Fire Walk With Me	[I]	$10	Warner 45019

Sheryl Lee/Kyle MacLachlan/**David Bowie/Chris Isaak**; cp: Angelo Badalamenti/David Lynch

Best Friends
Black Dog Runs At Night [Thought Gang]
Don't Do Anything (I Wouldn't Do)
Moving Through Time
Pine Float
Pink Room
Questions In A World Of Blue [Julee Cruise]
Real Indication [Thought Gang]
Sycamore Trees [Jimmy Scott]
Twin Peaks - Fire Walk With Me (Theme)
Twin Peaks Montage
Voice Of Love

DEBUT	PEAK	WKS	RIAA	CD	ARTIST — Album Title	Sym	$	Label & Number
1/21/89	162	12		©775	Twins	[V]	$10	WTG 45036

Arnold Schwarzenegger/Danny DeVito/Kelly Preston/Chloe Webb

Brother To Brother [Spinners]
Going To Santa Fe [Randy Edelman]
I Only Have Eyes For You [Marilyn Scott]
I'd Die For This Dance [Jeff Beck feat. Nicolette Larson]
It's Too Late [Nayobe]
Main Title Theme [Georges Delerue]
No Way Of Knowin' [Henry Lee Summer]
Train Kept A-Rollin' [Jeff Beck feat. Andrew Roachford]
Turtle Shoes [Bobby McFerrin & Herbie Hancock]
Twins [Philip Bailey & Little Richard]
Yakety Yak [2 Live Crew]

DEBUT	PEAK	WKS	RIAA	CD	ARTIST — Album Title	Sym	$	Label & Number
5/25/96	28	20	●	©776	Twister	[V]	$10	Warner Sunset 46254

Helen Hunt/Bill Paxton/Jami Gertz/Cary Elwes

Broken [Belly]
Darling Pretty [Mark Knopfler]
How [Lisa Loeb & Nine Stories]
Humans Being [Van Halen]
Long Way Down [Goo Goo Dolls]
Love Affair [k.d. lang]
Melancholy Mechanics [Red Hot Chili Peppers]
Miss This [Soul Asylum]
Moments Like This [Alison Krauss & Union Station]
No One Needs To Know [Shania Twain]
Respect The Wind [Edward & Alex Van Halen]
Talula [Tori Amos]
Twisted [Stevie Nicks & Lindsey Buckingham]
Virtual Reality [Rusted Root]

Two For The Road - see MANCINI, Henry
Audrey Hepburn/**Albert Finney**/Eleanor Bron/William Daniels

DEBUT	PEAK	WKS	RIAA	CD	ARTIST — Album Title	Sym	$	Label & Number
3/20/99	154	2		©777	200 Cigarettes	[O-V]	$10	Mercury 538738

Ben Affleck/Dave Chappelle/Courtney Love/Jay Mohr/Christina Ricci

Boogie Wonderland [Girls Against Boys]
Cruel To Be Kind [Nick Lowe] 12
I Don't Care [Ramones]
I Want Candy [Bow Wow Wow] 62
In The Flesh [Blondie]
It's Different For Girls [Joe Jackson]
Just What I Needed [Cars] 27
Ladies Night [Kool & The Gang] 8
Maria (medley) [Blondie]
More Than This [Roxy Music]
No Exit (medley) [Blondie]
Nowhere Girl [B-Movie]
Our Lips Are Sealed [Go-Go's] 20
Rapture (medley) [Blondie]
Romeo & Juliet [Dire Straits]
Save It For Later [Harvey Danger]
(What's So Funny 'Bout) Peace, Love And Understanding [Elvis Costello]

DEBUT	PEAK	WKS	RIAA	CD	ARTIST — Album Title	Sym	$	Label & Number
12/3/83+	26	20	▲	©778	Two Of A Kind	[V]	$12	MCA 6127

John Travolta/Olivia Newton-John/Charles Durning/Beatrice Straight/Scatman Crothers

Ask The Lonely [Journey]
Catch 22 (2 Steps Forward, 3 Steps Back) [Steve Kipner]
It's Gonna Be Special [Patti Austin] 82
Livin' In Desperate Times [Olivia Newton-John] 31
Night Music [David Foster]
Perfect One [Boz Scaggs]
Prima Donna [Chicago]
Shaking You [Olivia Newton-John]
Take A Chance [Olivia Newton-John & John Travolta]
Twist Of Fate [Olivia Newton-John] 5

200 Motels - see ZAPPA, Frank
Frank Zappa/Ringo Starr/Theodore Bikel

DEBUT	PEAK	WKS	RIAA	CD	ARTIST — Album Title	Sym	$	Label & Number
7/13/68	24	120	●	©779	2001: A Space Odyssey	[I]	$20	MGM 13

Gary Lockwood/Keir Dullea/William Sylvester/Daniel Richter; features classical music by various orchestras

Atmospheres
Blue Danube Waltz
Gayane Ballet Suite (Adagio)
Lux Aeterna
Requiem For Soprano, Mezzo Soprano, Two Mixed Choirs And Orchestra
"2001" A Space Odyssey [Berlin Philharmonic] 90

DEBUT	PEAK	WKS	RIAA	CD	ARTIST — Album Title	Sym	$	Label & Number
10/10/70	147	7		780	2001: A Space Odyssey (Volume Two)	[I]	$20	MGM 4722

Berceuse From "Gayne Ballet Suite"
Coppelia
Entflieht Auf Leichten Kahnen
Lontano
Margarethe
String Quartet (5th Movement)
"2001" A Space Odyssey [Berlin Philharmonic] 90
Volumina
Waltzes From "Der Rosenkavalier"

DEBUT	PEAK	WKS	RIAA	CD	ARTIST — Album Title	Sym	$	Label & Number
2/2/85	173	5		©781	2010	[I]	$12	A&M 5038

Roy Scheider/John Lithgow/Helen Mirren/Bob Balaban/Keir Dullea; cp: David Shire

Also Sprach Zarathustra (medley)
Bowman
Countdown (medley)
Earth (medley)
Earth Fallout (medley)
New Worlds (Theme)
Nova (medley)
Probe
Reactivating Discovery
Space (medley)
Space Linkup (medley)
2010 [Andy Summers]
Visitation (medley)

UHF - see YANKOVIC, "Weird Al"
"Weird Al" Yankovic/Kevin McCarthy/Michael Richards/Victoria Jackson

Under The Cherry Moon - see PRINCE
Prince/Jerome Benton/Kristin Scott Thomas/Steven Berkoff

SOUNDTRACKS

DEBUT	PEAK	WKS	RIAA	CD	ARTIST — Album Title	Catalog	Sym	$	Label & Number

7/18/64 · **11** · 33 · ©782 · **Unsinkable Molly Brown, The** .... **[M]** · **$25** · MGM 4232
Debbie Reynolds/Harve Presnell/Harvey Lembeck; sw: Meredith Willson; cd: Robert Armbruster

Belly Up To The Bar, Boys	Dolce Far Niente	I Ain't Down Yet	Leadville Johnny Brown (Soliloquy)
Colorado, My Home	He's My Friend	I'll Never Say No	Up Where The People Are

2/1/92 · **114** · 9 · ©783 · **Until The End Of The World** .... **[V]** · **$10** · Warner 26707
William Hurt/Solveig Dommartin/Rüdiger Vogler/Sam Neill

Adversary, The [Crime & The City Solution]	Humans From Earth [T-Bone Burnett]	Last Night Sleep [Can]	Summer Kisses, Winter Tears [Julee Cruise]
Calling All Angels [Jane Siberry]	(I'll Love You) Till The End Of The World [Nick Cave & The Bad Seeds]	Love Theme [Graeme Revell]	Until The End Of The World [U2]
Claire's Theme [Graeme Revell]		Move With Me [Neneh Cherry]	What's Good [Lou Reed]
Days [Elvis Costello]		Opening Titles [Graeme Revell]	
Death's Door [Depeche Mode]	It Takes Time [Patti Smith & Fred Smith]	Sax And Violins [Talking Heads]	
Fretless [R.E.M.]		Sleeping In The Devil's Bed [Daniel Lanois]	

Up In Smoke - see CHEECH & CHONG
Cheech Marin/Tommy Chong (**Cheech & Chong**)/Stacy Keach

5/12/84 · **185** · 3 · 784 · **Up The Creek** .... **[V]** · **$12** · Pasha 39333
Tim Matheson/Jennifer Runyon/Dan Monahan/Stephen Furst

Chasin' The Sky [Beach Boys]	Great Expectations (You Never Know What To Expect) [Ian Hunter]	Passion In The Dark (One Track Heart) [Danny Spanos]	Two Hearts On The Loose [Randy Bishop]
Get Ready Boy [Shooting Star]		Take It [Shooting Star]	Up The Creek [Cheap Trick]
	Heat, The [Heart]	30 Days In The Hole [Kick Axe]	

Uptight - see BOOKER T. & THE MG'S
Raymond St. Jacques/Ruby Dee/Frank Silvera

5/17/80 · **3** · 47 ▲ · ©785 · **Urban Cowboy** .... **[V]** · **$15** · Asylum 90002 [2]
John Travolta/Debra Winger/Scott Glenn/Madolyn Smith/Barry Corbin

All Night Long [Joe Walsh] 19	Don't It Make Ya Wanna Dance [Bonnie Raitt]	Here Comes The Hurt Again [Mickey Gilley]	Nine Tonight [Bob Seger]
Cherokee Fiddle [Johnny Lee]	Falling In Love For The Night [Charlie Daniels Band]	**Look What You've Done To Me** [Boz Scaggs] 14	Orange Blossom Special/Hoedown [Gilley's Urban Cowboy Band]
Could I Have This Dance [Anne Murray] 33	Hearts Against The Wind [Linda Ronstadt/J.D. Souther]	**Lookin' For Love** [Johnny Lee] 5	**Stand By Me** [Mickey Gilley] 22
Darlin' [Bonnie Raitt]		Love The World Away [Kenny Rogers] 14	Times Like These [Dan Fogelberg]
Devil Went Down To Georgia [Charlie Daniels Band] 3	Hello Texas [Jimmy Buffett]	**Lyin' Eyes** [Eagles] 2	

1/10/81 · **134** · 6 · 786 · **Urban Cowboy II** .... **[V]** · **$12** · Full Moon 36921
more music from the original soundtrack

Cotton-Eyed Joe [Bayou City Beats]	Mammas Don't Let Your Babies Grow Up To Be Cowboys [Mickey Gilley/Johnny Lee]	Orange Blossom Special [Charlie Daniels Band]	Rode Hard And Put Up Wet [Johnny Lee]
Honky Tonk Wine [Mickey Gilley]		Rockin' My Life Away [Mickey Gilley]	**Texas** [Charlie Daniels Band] 91
Jukebox Argument [Mickey Gilley]	Moon Just Turned Blue [J.D. Souther]		

2/17/01 · **101** · 3 · ©787 · **Valentine** .... **[V]** · **$10** · Warner Sunset 47943
David Boreanaz/Denise Richards/Marley Shelton/Jessica Capshaw

Breed [Snake River Conspiracy]	God Of The Mind [Disturbed]	Pushing Me Away [Linkin Park]	Superbeast [Rob Zombie]
Fall Again [Professional Murder Music]	Love Dump [Static-X]	Rx Queen [Deftones]	**Take A Picture** [Filter] 12
Filthy Mind [Amanda Ghost]	1 A.M. [Beautiful Creatures]	Smartbomb [BT]	Valentine's Day [Marilyn Manson]
	Opticon [Orgy]	Son Song [Soulfly]	

Valley, The - see PINK FLOYD
Bulle Ogier/Jean-Pierre Kalfon

3/12/94 · **155** · 5 · ©788 · **Valley Girl** .... **[V]** · **$10** · Rhino 71590
Deborah Foreman/Nicholas Cage/Michael Bowen/Elizabeth Daily; selections from the original U.S. and British soundtracks, plus songs featured in the 1983 movie but not included on either album

Angst In My Pants [Sparks]	I La La La Love You [Pat Travers' Black Pearl]	Jukebox (Don't Put Another Dime) [Flirts]	School Is In [Josie Cotton]
Everywhere At Once [Plimsouls]		Love My Way [Psychedelic Furs] 44	She Talks In Stereo [Gary Myrick & The Figures]
Eyes Of A Stranger [Payola]	**I Melt With You** [Modern English] 76		**Who Can It Be Now?** [Men At Work] 1
Fanatic, The [Felony] 42		**Million Miles Away** [Plimsouls] 82	
He Could Be The One [Josie Cotton] 74	Johnny, Are You Queer? [Josie Cotton]	Oldest Story In The World [Plimsouls]	

2/3/68 · **11** · 27 · ©789 · **Valley Of The Dolls** .... **[M]** · **$50** · 20th Century Fox 4196
Barbara Parkins/**Patty Duke**/Sharon Tate/Susan Hayward; sw: Dory & **Andre Previn**; cd: Johnny Williams

Ann At Lawrenceville	Gillian Girl Commercial	It's Impossible	Neely's Career Montage
Chance Meeting	Give A Little More	Jennifer's French Movie	Valley Of The Dolls (Theme)
Come Live With Me	I'll Plant My Own Tree	Jennifer's Recollection	

1/30/99 · **19** · 23 ● · ©790 · **Varsity Blues** .... **[V]** · **$10** · Hollywood 62177
James Van Der Beek/Jon Voight/Paul Walker/Ron Lester/Scott Caan

Are You Ready For The Fallout? [Fastball]	Fly [Loudmouth]	My Hero [Foo Fighters]	Thunderstruck [Sprung Monkey]
	Horror Show [Third Eye Blind]	Nice Guys Finish Last [Green Day]	Two Faces [Days Of The New]
Black Eye [Black Lab]	**Hot For Teacher** [Van Halen] 56	**Run** [Collective Soul] 76	Varsity Blue [Caroline's Spine]
Every Little Thing Counts [Janus Stark]	Kick Out The Jams [Monster Magnet]	Ship Jumper [Simon Says]	
		Teen Competition [Redd Kross]	

6/5/82 · **174** · 4 · ©791 · **Victor/Victoria** .... **[M]** · **$25** · MGM 5407
Julie Andrews/James Garner/Robert Preston/Alex Karras; mu/cd: **Henry Mancini**; ly: Leslie Bricusse

Alone In Paris	Crazy World	Le Jazz Hot	
Cat And Mouse	Gay Paree	Shady Dame From Seville	
Chicago, Illinois	King's Can-Can	You And Me	

1/4/64 · **145** · 3 · 792 · **Victors, The** .... **[I]** · **$50** · Colpix 516
George Peppard/George Hamilton/Eli Wallach; cp/cd: Sol Kaplan

French Woman	Magda's Theme	No Other Man	Signora Maria
Have Yourself A Merry Little Christmas	Main Title	Off Limits	Sweet Talk And Death Fight
	March Of The Victors	Olive Grove	Wolf Pack
Jean Pierre	My Special Dream	Overture	

DEBUT	PEAK	WKS	RIAA	CD	ARTIST — Album Title	Catalog	Sym	$	Label & Number

6/29/85 • 38 • 15 • 793 • View To A Kill, A .... [I] **$12** Capitol 12413

Roger Moore/Tanya Roberts/Christopher Walken/**Grace Jones**; cp/cd: John Barry

Airship To Silicon Valley	Destroy Silicon Valley	May Day Jumps
Bond Escapes Roller	Golden Gate Fight	Pegasus' Stable
Bond Meets Stacey	He's Dangerous	Snow Job
Bond Underwater	May Day Bombs Out	Tibbett Gets Washed Out

View To A Kill [Duran Duran] **1**
Wine With Stacey

Virgin Suicides, The - see AIR
Kirsten Dunst/James Woods/Kathleen Turner/Scott Glenn

3/2/85 • 11 • 23 ▲ • ©794 • Vision Quest .... [V] **$12** Geffen 24063

Matthew Modine/Linda Fiorentino/Michael Schoeffling/Ronny Cox

Change [John Waite] **54**	**Hot Blooded** [Foreigner] **3**	I'll Fall In Love Again [Sammy Hagar] 43
Crazy For You [Madonna] **1**	Hungry For Heaven [Dio]	Lunatic Fringe [Red Rider]
Gambler [Madonna]		

Only The Young [Journey] **9**
She's On The Zoom [Don Henley]
Shout To The Top [Style Council]

12/2/95+ • ❶⁵ • 49 ▲⁷ • ©795 • Waiting To Exhale .... [V] **$10** Arista 18796

Whitney Houston/Angela Bassett/Lela Rochon/Loretta Devine

All Night Long [SWV]	How Could You Call Her Baby [Shanna]	My Funny Valentine [Chaka Khan]
And I Gave My Love To You [Sonja Marie]	It Hurts Like Hell [Aretha Franklin]	My Love, Sweet Love [Patti LaBelle]
Count On Me [Whitney Houston & CeCe Winans] **8**	**Kissing You** [Faith Evans] **flip**	**Not Gon' Cry** [Mary J. Blige] **2**
Exhale (Shoop Shoop) [Whitney Houston] **1**	**Let It Flow** [Toni Braxton] **flip**	**Sittin' Up In My Room** [Brandy] **2**
	Love Will Be Waiting At Home [For Real]	This Is How It Works [TLC]
		Wey U [Chanté Moore]

Why Does It Hurt So Bad [Whitney Houston] **26**

6/30/62 • 33 • 19 • ©796 • Walk On The Wild Side .... [I] **$50** Ava 4

Laurence Harvey/**Jane Fonda**/Capucine/Anne Baxter/Barbara Stanwyck; cp/cd: Elmer Bernstein

Doll House	Kitty	Rejected
Dove	Night Theme	Reminiscence
Hallies Jazz	Oliver	Somewhere In The Used To Be

Terasina
Walk On The Wild Side

8/17/68 • 189 • 3 • 797 • War And Peace .... [I] **$50** Melodiya 2918

Ludmilla Savelyeva/Vyacheslav Tikhonov/Sergei Bondarchuk; cp: Vyacheslav Ovchinnikov

Approach Of The French Army (medley)	Battle Of Schon Grabern	Intermezzo (medley)
At The Hunting Lodge	Bolkonsky's Hope Reborn	Natasha's Waltz
Battle Of Borodino	Entrance Of Tsar Alexander I (Polonaise)	Petya And The French Drummer Boy

Soldiers' Chorus
Soldiers' Hymn To The Virgin

5/5/79 • 125 • 8 • 798 • Warriors, The .... [V] **$12** A&M 4761

Michael Beck/Thomas Waites/James Remar/Deborah Van Valkenburg/Mercedes Ruehl

Baseball Furies Chase [Barry DeVorzon]	In Havana [Kenny Vance]	Love Is A Fire [Genya Ravan]
Echoes In My Mind [Mandrill]	In The City [Joe Walsh]	Nowhere To Run [Arnold McCuller]
Fight, The [Barry DeVorzon]	Last Of An Ancient Breed [Desmond Child]	Warriors (Theme) [Barry DeVorzon]

You're Movin' Too Slow [Johnny Vastano]

11/28/98 • 109 • 7 • ©799 • Waterboy, The .... [V] **$10** Hollywood 62157

Adam Sandler/Kathy Bates/Fairuza Balk/**Jerry Reed**/Henry Winkler

Always On The Run [Lenny Kravitz]	Doin' My Thang [Lifelong]	More Today Than Yesterday [Goldfinger]
Boom Boom [Big Head Todd & The Monsters]	Feed It [Candyskins]	New Year's Eve [Joe Walsh]
Born On The Bayou [Creedence Clearwater Revival]	Glowing Soul [Candlebox]	No One To Run With [Allman Brothers]
	Let's Groove [Earth, Wind & Fire] **3**	

Peace Frog [Doors]
Small Town [John Mellencamp] **6**
Tom Sawyer [Rush] **44**

2/17/73 • 28 • 17 ● • ©800 • Wattstax: The Living Word .... [L-V] **$20** Stax 3010 [2]

live concert held in August 1972 in Los Angeles

Ain't No Sunshine [Isaac Hayes]	Feel It (medley) [Bar-Kays]	I Like The Things About Me (medley) [Carla Thomas]
Angel Of Mercy (medley) [Albert King]	Gee Whiz (medley) [Carla Thomas]	I Like What You're Doing (To Me) (medley) [Carla Thomas]
Breakdown, The (medley) [Rufus Thomas]	Hearsay (medley) [Soul Children]	I'll Play The Blues For You (medley) [Albert King]
Do The Funky Chicken (medley) [Rufus Thomas]	I Can't Turn You Loose (medley) [Albert King]	I'll Take You There (medley) [Staple Singers]
Do The Funky Penguin (medley) [Rufus Thomas]	I Don't Know What This World Is Coming To (medley) [Soul Children]	Killing Floor (medley) [Albert King]
	I Have A God Who Loves (medley) [Carla Thomas]	

Knock On Wood (medley) [Eddie Floyd]
Lay Your Loving On Me (medley) [Eddie Floyd]
Oh La De Da (medley) [Staple Singers]
Respect Yourself (medley)
Son Of Shaft (medley) [Bar-Kays]

9/15/73 • 157 • 5 • 801 • Wattstaxx 2: The Living Word .... [L-V] **$20** Stax 3018 [2]

more songs from the concert

Ain't That Loving You (For More Reasons Than One) (medley) [David Porter]	I May Not Be What You Want [Mel & Tim]	Old Time Religion [Golden 13]
Arrest (medley) [Richard Pryor]	Jody's Got Your Girl And Gone (medley) [Johnnie Taylor]	Peace Be Still [Emotions]
Backroom (medley) [Richard Pryor]	Lift Every Voice And Sing [Kim Weston]	Reach Out And Touch (medley) [David Porter]
Blue Note (medley) [Richard Pryor]	Line Up (medley) [Richard Pryor]	Rolling Down A Mountainside [Isaac Hayes]
Can't See You When I Want To (medley) [David Porter]	Lying On The Truth [Rance Allen Group]	Saturday Night (medley) [Richard Pryor]
Finale (medley)	Negroes [Richard Pryor]	Show Me How (medley) [Emotions]
Handshake [Richard Pryor]	Niggers [Richard Pryor]	So I Can Love You (medley) [Emotions]

Someone Greater Than You And I [Jimmy Jones]
Steal Away (medley) [Johnnie Taylor]
Stop Doggin' Me (medley) [Johnnie Taylor]
Walking The Backstreets And Crying [Little Milton]
Whatcha See Is Whatcha Get [Dramatics]
Wino Get A Job [Richard Pryor]

2/16/74 • 20 • 15 ● • ©802 • Way We Were, The .... [I] **$15** Columbia 32830

Barbra Streisand/Robert Redford/Bradford Dillman/Sally Kirkland/James Woods; cp: Marvin Hamlisch

Did You Know It Was Me?	Look What I've Got	**Way We Were** [Barbra Streisand] **1**
In The Mood	Red Sails In The Sunset	Way We Were (Finale)
Katie	Remembering	Way We Were (instrumental)
Like Pretty	River Stay Way From My Door	

Wrap Your Troubles In Dreams (And Dream Your Troubles Away)

3/7/92 • ❶² • 47 ▲² • ©803 • Wayne's World .... [V] **$10** Reprise 26805

Mike Myers/Dana Carvey/Rob Lowe/Tia Carrere/Lara Flynn Boyle

Ballroom Blitz [Tia Carrere]	**Foxey Lady** [Jimi Hendrix] **67**	Sikamikanico [Red Hot Chili Peppers]
Bohemian Rhapsody [Queen] **2**	Hot And Bothered [Cinderella]	Time Machine [Black Sabbath]
Dream Weaver [Gary Wright] **2**	Loving Your Lovin' [Eric Clapton]	Wayne's World Theme [Wayne & Garth]
Feed My Frankenstein [Alice Cooper]	Ride With Yourself [Rhino Bucket]	
	Rock Candy [BulletBoys]	

Why You Wanna Break My Heart [Tia Carrere]

SOUNDTRACKS

DEBUT	PEAK	WKS	RIAA	CD	ARTIST — Album Title	Catalog	Sym	$	Label & Number

1/1/94 **78** 9 — ©804 **Wayne's World 2** .... [V] **$10** Reprise 45485
Mike Myers/Dana Carvey/Tia Carrere/Christopher Walken/Chris Farley

Can't Get Enough [Bad Company] 5	I Love Rock 'N Roll [Joan Jett & The Blackhearts] 1	Out There [Dinosaur Jr.]
Dude (Looks Like A Lady) [Aerosmith] 14	Idiot Summer [Gin Blossoms]	Radar Love [Golden Earring] 13
Frankenstein [Edgar Winter] 1	Louie, Louie [Robert Plant]	Shut Up And Dance [Aerosmith]
	Mary's House [4 Non Blondes]	Spirit In The Sky [Norman Greenbaum] 3

Superstar [Superfan]
Y.M.C.A. [Village People] 2

2/21/98 **5** 63 ▲ ©805 **Wedding Singer, The** .... [O-V] **$10** Maverick 46840
Adam Sandler/Drew Barrymore/Christine Taylor/Allen Covert/Steve Buscemi

Blue Monday [New Order]	Everyday I Write The Book [Elvis Costello] 36	Pass The Dutchie [Musical Youth] 10
China Girl [David Bowie] 10	Hold Me Now [Thompson Twins] 3	Rapper's Delight (Medley) [Ellen Dow & Sugarhill Gang]
Do You Really Want To Hurt Me [Culture Club] 2	How Soon Is Now? [Smiths]	Somebody Kill Me [Adam Sandler]
Every Little Thing She Does Is Magic [Police] 3	Love My Way [Psychedelic Furs] 44	

Video Killed The Radio Star [Presidents Of The United States Of America]
White Wedding [Billy Idol] 36

8/8/98 **22** 35 ● ©806 **Wedding Singer Volume 2, The** .... [O-V] **$10** Maverick 46984

Grow Old With You [Adam Sandler]	Love Stinks [J. Geils Band] 38	Space Age Love Song [Flock Of Seagulls] 30
Holiday [Madonna] 16	Money (That's What I Want) [Flying Lizards] 50	Too Shy [Kajagoogoo] 5
It's All I Can Do [Cars] 41	Private Idaho [B-52's] 74	True [Spandau Ballet] 4
Just Can't Get Enough [Depeche Mode]		

You Make My Dreams [Hall & Oates] 5
You Spin Me Round (Like A Record) [Dead Or Alive] 11

8/31/85 **105** 11 — 807 **Weird Science** .... [V] **$12** MCA 6146
Anthony Michael Hall/Ilan Mitchell-Smith/Kelly LeBrock/Bill Paxton

Circle, The [Max Carl]	Do Not Disturb (Knock, Knock) [Broken Homes]	Method To My Madness [Lords Of The New Church]
Deep In The Jungle [Wall Of Voodoo]	Eighties [Killing Joke]	Private Joy [Cheyne]
	Forever [Taxxi]	Turn It On [Kim Wilde]

Weird Romance [Ira & The Geeks]
Weird Science [Oingo Boingo] 45
Why Don't Pretty Girls (Look At Me) [Wild Men Of Wonga]

10/23/61+ **❶54** 198 ▲³ ©808 **West Side Story** .... [M] **$30** Columbia 2070
Natalie Wood/Richard Beymer/Rita Moreno/George Chakiris; mu: **Leonard Bernstein**; ly: Steephen Sondheim; cd: Johnny Green

America	Gee, Officer Krupke!	Maria
Boy Like That (medley)	I Feel Pretty	One Hand, One Heart
Cool	I Have A Love (medley)	Quintet
Dance At The Gym Medley	Jet Song	Rumble, The

Something's Coming
Somewhere
Tonight

What Did You Do In The War, Daddy? - see MANCINI, Henry
James Coburn/Dick Shawn/Aldo Ray/**Carroll O'Connor**

12/30/00+ **30** 25 ● ©809 **What Women Want** .... [O-V] **$10** Columbia 61595
Mel Gibson/Helen Hunt/Marisa Tomei/Lauren Holly/Alan Alda

Best Is Yet To Come [Nancy Wilson]	I Won't Dance [Frank Sinatra]	Mack The Knife [Bobby Darin] 1
Bitch [Meredith Brooks] 2	I've Got The World On A String [Peggy Lee]	Night And Day [Temptations]
Everything About You [Alan Silvestri]	I've Got You Under My Skin [Frank Sinatra]	Nobody But Me [Lou Rawls]
Good Life [Tony Bennett] 18	If I Had You [Nnenna Freelon]	Something's Gotta Give [Sammy Davis, Jr.] 9

Too Marvelous For Words [Frank Sinatra]
What A Girl Wants [Christina Aguilera] 1

What's Love Got To Do With It - see TURNER, Tina
Angela Bassett/Laurence Fishburne/Jenifer Lewis/Khandi Alexander

8/7/65 **14** 22 ©810 **What's New Pussycat?** .... [I+V] **$30** United Artists 5117
Peter Sellers/Peter O'Toole/Capucine/**Woody Allen**; mu: **Burt Bacharach**; ly: Hal David

Bookworm (medley)	Here I Am [Dionne Warwick] 65	My Little Red Book [Manfred Mann]
Catch As Catch Can	Here I Am (medley)	Pussy Cats On Parade
Chateau Chantel	High Temperature, Low Resistance	School For Anatomy (medley)
Downhill And Shady	Marriage, French Style	Stripping Really Isn't Sexy, Is It?

Walk On The Wild Wharf
What's New Pussycat? [Tom Jones] 3

6/16/01 **38** 10 — ©811 **What's The Worst That Could Happen?** .... [V] **$10** NY.LA 493069
Martin Lawrence/Danny DeVito/John Leguizamo/Glenne Headly

Bang Ta Dis [Benzino]	I Got Duvs On It [Boss Town]	Shoot 'Em Up [Doggy's Angels]
Everywhere You Go [Queen Latifah]	Ladies Are U Wit Me [Dyme]	Stick 'Em [Cha Cha]
F**k What They Say [Snoop Dogg]	Music [Erick Sermon] 22	That's The Way Love Goes [Nina]
Happy Feelin's [Sam Logan]	My Love Your Love [Lejit]	What's The Worst That Could Happen? [Supafriendz]
Hit The Road Jo [Jo Doja]	No Job [Sara Jane]	

Whatever Jo Wants (Jo Gets) [Jo Doja]
Wooden Horse [Craig Mack]

What's Up, Tiger Lily? - see LOVIN' SPOONFUL
Woody Allen/China Lee/Louise Lasser

6/4/94 **133** 6 — ©812 **When A Man Loves A Woman** .... [I] **$10** Hollywood 61606
Andy Garcia/Meg Ryan/Lauren Tom/Ellen Burstyn; cp/cd: Zbigniew Preisner

Alice & Michael	El Gusto (Son Huasteco) [Los Lobos]	Homecoming
Crazy Love [Brian Kennedy]	Garbage Compulsion	I Hit Her Hard
Dressing Casey	Gary	Main Title
		Michael Decides

When A Man Loves A Woman [Percy Sledge] 1

When Harry Met Sally - see CONNICK, Harry Jr.
Billy Crystal/Meg Ryan/Carrie Fisher/Bruno Kirby

When The Boys Meet The Girls - see FRANCIS, Connie
Connie Francis/Harve Presnell/**Herman's Hermits**

5/13/00 **126** 6 — ©813 **Where The Heart Is** .... [V] **$10** RCA 67963
Natalie Portman/Ashley Judd/Stockard Channing/Joan Cusack

Beyond The Blue [Emmylou Harris & Patty Griffin]	Grow Young With You [Coley McCabe]	Only You (And You Alone) [Lonestar]
Completely [Jennifer Day]	Just Might Change Your Life [3 Of Hearts]	Rowdy Booty Time [Joan Osborne & Tommy Sims]
Few And Far Between [Shannon Curfman]	Let It Slip Away [John Hiatt]	Shake My Soul [Beth Nielsen Chapman]

So Young [Corrs]
That's The Beat Of A Heart [Warren Brothers]
There You Are [Martina McBride]
What'd I Say [Lyle Lovett]

4/11/92 **92** 8 — ©814 **White Men Can't Jump** .... [V] **$10** EMI 98414
Wesley Snipes/Woody Harrelson/Rosie Perez/Tyra Ferrell

Can You Come Out And Play [O'Jays]	I'm Going Up [Bebe & Cece Winans]	Just A Closer Walk With Thee [Venice Beach Boys]
Don't Ever Let 'Em See You Sweat [Go West]	If I Lose [Aretha Franklin]	Let Me Make It Up To You Tonight [Jody Watley]
Hook, The [Queen Latifah]	Jump For It [Jesse Johnson]	Sympin Ain't Easy [Boyz II Men]

Watch Me Do My Thang [Lipstick]
White Men Can't Jump [Riff] 90

DEBUT	PEAK	WKS	RIAA	CD	ARTIST — Album Title	Catalog	Sym	$	Label & Number

11/2/85+ · **17** · 26 · ● · ©815 · **White Nights** .... · [V] · **$12** · Atlantic 81273

Mikhail Baryshnikov/Gregory Hines/Geraldine Page/Helen Mirren

Far Post [Robert Plant]	People Have Got To Move [Jenny Burton]	**Separate Lives** [Phil Collins & Marilyn Martin] **1**
My Love Is Chemical [Lou Reed]	People On A String [Roberta Flack]	Snake Charmer [John Hiatt]
Other Side Of The World [Chaka Khan]	**Prove Me Wrong** [David Pack] **95**	Tapdance [David Foster]

This Is Your Day [Sandy Stewart & Nile Rodgers]

White Rock - see WAKEMAN, Rick

8/7/99 · **145** · 3 · · ©816 · **Whiteboys** .... · [V] · **$10** · Offline 8310

Danny Hoch/Dash Mihok/Mark Webber/Bonz Malone/**Snoop Dogg**

Come Get It [DJ Hurricane]	Hell Ya [Soopafly]	Perfect Murda [Do Or Die]
Don't Come My Way [Slick Rick & Common]	I Can Relate [Black Child]	Pimps VIP [12 Gauge]
For The Thugs [Trick Daddy]	Intrigued [Cocoa Brovas]	Real Hustlers [Gotta Boyz]
Get Rowdy [WhoRidas]	Paper Chasers (Up North) [Tommy Finger]	Respect Power [Raekwon]

Watch Who You Beef Wid [Canibus]
What's Up Jack [Wildlife Society]
White Boyz [Snoop Dogg]
Who Is A Thug [Big Punisher]
Wanna Be's [Three 6 Mafia]

9/3/66 · **119** · 5 · · ©817 · **Who's Afraid Of Virginia Woolf?** .... · [I] · **$50** · Warner 1656

Elizabeth Taylor/Richard Burton/**George Segal**/Sandy Dennis; cp/cd: Alex North

Bergin	Martha	Prologue - Act II
Colloquy	Moon Music	Sad, Sad, Sad
Fleece	Party Is Over	Snap (medley)

Sunday, Tomorrow All Day
Virginia Woolf Rock (medley)

Who's That Girl - see MADONNA

Madonna/Griffin Dunne/Haviland Morris/John McMartin

5/8/93 · **32** · 8 · · ©818 · **Who's The Man?** .... · [V] · **$10** · Uptown 10794

Doctor Dre/Ed Lover/**Denis Leary**/Bill Bellamy/**Ice-T**

Ease Up [3rd Eye & The Group Home]	Hotness [Heavy D & Buju Banton]	Pimp Or Die [Father M.C.]
Hello, It's Me [Spark 950 & Timbo King]	**Let's Go Through The Motions** [Jodeci] **65**	What's Next On The Menu? [Pete Rock & C.L. Smooth]
Hittin' Switches [Erick Sermon]	Lovin' You [Crystal J. Johnson]	**Who's The Man?** [House Of Pain] **96**
	Part And Bullshit [Big]	

You Don't Have To Worry [Mary J. Blige] **63**

9/26/98 · **55** · 4 · · ©819 · **Why Do Fools Fall In Love** .... · [V] · **$10** · EastWest 62265

Halle Berry/Vivica A. Fox/Lela Rochon/Larenz Tate/**Little Richard**

About You [Mista]	Get On The Bus [Destiny's Child]	**No Fool No More** [En Vogue] **57**
Crazy Love [Envyi]	He Be Back [Coko]	Splash [Next]
Five Minutes [Lil' Mo]	I Want You Back [Melanie B.]	What The Dealio [Total]
Get Contact [Missy "Misdemeanor" Elliott & Busta Rhymes]	Keep A Knockin' [Little Richard]	Why Do Fools Fall In Love [Gina Thompson]
	Love Is For Fools [Mint Condition]	

Without You [Nicole]

Wild Angels, The - see ALLAN, Davie

Peter Fonda/**Nancy Sinatra**/Bruce Dern/Dianne Ladd; cp/cd: **Mike Curb**

10/18/69 · **192** · 2 · · 820 · **Wild Bunch, The** .... · [I] · **$100** · Warner 1814

William Holden/Ernest Borgnine/Robert Ryan/Warren Oates/Strother Martin; cp/cd: Jerry Fielding

Adelita	Aurora Mi Amor	Drinking Song
Adventures On The High Road	Bodega El Bodega De Bano	End Credits (La Golondrina)
Assault On The Train And Escape	Dirge	Main Title

Wild Bunch (Song)

7/6/68 · **12** · 32 · · 821 · **Wild In The Streets** .... · · **$30** · Tower 5099

Christopher Jones/Diana Varsi/Shelley Winters/**Richard Pryor**; sw: Barry Mann/Cynthia Weil; cd: **Mike Curb**

Fifty Two Per Cent [Max Frost & The Troopers]	Free Lovin' [Max Frost & The Troopers]	Love To Be Your Man [Max Frost & The Troopers]
Fourteen Or Fight [Max Frost & The Troopers]	Listen To The Music [Second Time]	Psychedelic Senate [Senators]
	Sally Le Roy [Second Time]	

Shape Of Things To Come [Max Frost & The Troopers] **22**
Shelly In Camp [Gurus]
Wild In The Streets [Jerry Howard]

7/3/99 · **4** · 18 · ▲² · ©822 · **Wild Wild West** .... · [V] · **$10** · Overbrook 90344

Will Smith/Kevin Kline/Kenneth Branagh/Salma Hayek/Ted Levine

Bad Guys Always Die [Dr. Dre & Eminem]	Chocolate Form [Neutral]	Hero [Breeze]
Bailamos [Enrique Iglesias] **1**	Confused [Blackstreet]	I Sparkle [Slick Rick]
Best, The [Guy]	8 Minutes To Sunrise [Common]	I'm Wanted [Kel Spencer]
	Getting Closer [Tatyana Ali]	Keep It Movin' [MC Lyte]

Lucky Day [Tra-Knox]
Mailman [Faith Evans]
Stick Up [Lil' Bow Wow]
Wild Wild West [Will Smith] **1**

5/14/94 · **120** · 6 · · ©823 · **With Honors** .... · [V] · **$10** · Maverick 45549

Joe Pesci/Brendan Fraser/Moira Kelly/Patrick Dempsey/Josh Hamilton

Blue Skies [Lyle Lovett]	**I'll Remember** [Madonna] **2**	Run Shithead Run [Mudhoney]
Cover Me [Candlebox]	It's Not Unusual [Belly]	She Sells Sanctuary [Cult]
Forever Young [Pretenders]	On The Wrong Side [Lindsey Buckingham]	Thank You [Duran Duran]
Fuzzy [Grant Lee Buffalo]		Tribe [Babble]

Your Ghost [Kristin Hersh]

10/21/78 · **40** · 17 · ● · ©824 · **Wiz, The** .... · [M] · **$20** · MCA 14000 [2]

Diana Ross/Michael Jackson/**Lena Horne**/Nipsey Russell/**Richard Pryor**; sw: Charlie Smalls; cd: **Quincy Jones**

Be A Lion	**Ease On Down The Road** [Diana Ross & Michael Jackson] **41**	Home (medley)
Believe In Yourself	Emerald City Medley	(I'm A) Mean Ole Lion
Brand New Day (Everybody Rejoice)	End Of The Yellow Brick Road	Is This What Feeling Gets? (Dorothy's Theme)
Can I Go On?	Feeling That We Have	Liberation Agitato
Don't Nobody Bring Me No Bad News	Glinda's Theme	Liberation Ballet (medley)
	Good Witch Glinda	Main Title
	He's The Wizard (medley)	March Of The Munchkins (medley)

Now Watch Me Dance (medley)
Poppy Girls
Slide Some Oil To Me (medley)
So You Wanted To See The Wizard
Soon As I Get Home (medley)
What Would I Do If I Could Feel?
You Can't Win (Part 1) [Michael Jackson] **81**

Woman in Red, The - see WONDER, Stevie

Gene Wilder/Charles Grodin/Judith Ivey/**Gilda Radner**

3/11/00 · **155** · 5 · · ©825 · **Wonder Boys** .... · [V] · **$10** · Columbia 63849

Michael Douglas/Tobey Maguire/Frances McDormand/Katie Holmes

Buckets Of Rain [Bob Dylan]	No Regrets [Tom Rush]	Shooting Star [Bob Dylan]
Child's Claim To Fame [Buffalo Springfield]	Not Dark Yet [Bob Dylan]	**Slip Away** [Clarence Carter] **6**
Need Your Love So Bad [Little Willie John]	**Old Man** [Neil Young] **31**	Things Have Changed [Bob Dylan]
	Philosophers Stone [Van Morrison]	Waiting For The Miracle [Leonard Cohen]
	Reason To Believe [Tim Hardin]	

Watching The Wheels [John Lennon] **10**

Wonderwall - see HARRISON, George

SOUNDTRACKS

DEBUT	PEAK	WKS	RIAA	CD	ARTIST — Album Title	Catalog	Sym	$	Label & Number

5/23/98 · **52** · 7 · ©826 · **Woo** .... [V] $10 Untertainment 69364
Jada Pinkett Smith/Tommy Davidson/Dave Chappelle/**LL Cool J**

Bouncin' [Lost Boyz]	If You Love Me [Stokley]	Niggas Dun Started Sumthin' [DMX, The Lox, Mase]
Drama In My Life [Eightball]	J-A-N-E Meets N.O.R.E. [Jane Blaze]	Superman [Chico DeBarge]
Get'n It On [Mona Lisa]	Let It Be [Allure Feat. .50 Cents]	T Shirt & Panties [Adina Howard]
I Know You Love Her [Too $hort]	Money [Charli Baltimore]	Take A Ride [Heavy D]
I Will [Simone Hines]		**Nobody Does It Better [Nate Dogg] 18**
		357 [Cam'ron]
		Searching (For Your Love) [Brownstone]
		Woo Woo (Freak Out) [M.C. Lyte]

7/31/99 · **16** · 23 · ● · ©827 · **Wood, The** .... [V] $10 Jive 41686
Taye Diggs/Omar Epps/Richard T. Jones/Sean Nelson

Back In The Day [Ahmad]	Hood (It's All Good) [Cash Money Millionaires]	It's All Good [R. Kelly]
Belts To Match [UGK]		Jane's Law [Jane Blaze]
Crave [Marc Dorsey]	I Can I Can [DMX]	Love Letter [Imajin]
Dante's Girl [Night & Day]	**I Wanna Know [Joe] 4**	Make The Music With Your Mouth Biz [Biz Markie]
Freaks Come Out At Night [Whodini]	If This World Were Mine [Luther Vandross & Cheryl Lynn]	Neck Uv Da Woods [Mystikal & OutKast]
		Still Strugglin' [Too $hort]
		Think About You [Blackstreet]
		24-7 [Liberty City Fla.]
		Ya' All Know Who! [Roots]

6/6/70 · **❶**[4] · 68 · ▲[2] · ©828 · **Woodstock** .... [L-V] $25 Cotillion 500 [3]
movie of historic rock festival near Woodstock, New York, on August 15-17, 1969

At The Hop [Sha-Na-Na]	Going Up The Country [Canned Heat]	Music Lover (medley) [Sly & The Family Stone]
Coming Into Los Angeles [Arlo Guthrie]	I-Feel-Like-I'm-Fixin'-To-Die Rag (medley) [Country Joe & The Fish]	Purple Haze (medley) [Jimi Hendrix]
Dance To The Music (medley) [Sly & The Family Stone]	I Had A Dream [John Sebastian]	Rainbows All Over Your Blues [John Sebastian]
Drug Store Truck Drivin' Man [Joan Baez feat. Jeffrey Shurtleff]	I Want To Take You Higher (medley) [Sly & The Family Stone]	Rock & Soul Music [Country Joe & The Fish]
Fish Cheer (medley)	I'm Going Home [Ten Years After]	Sea Of Madness [Crosby, Stills, Nash & Young]
Freedom [Richie Havens]	Joe Hill [Joan Baez]	Soul Sacrifice [Santana]
	Love March [Butterfield Blues Band]	Star Spangled Banner (medley) [Jimi Hendrix]
		Suite: Judy Blue Eyes [Crosby, Stills & Nash]
		Volunteers [Jefferson Airplane]
		We're Not Gonna Take It [Who]
		With A Little Help From My Friends [Joe Cocker]
		Wooden Ships [Crosby, Stills, Nash & Young]

4/10/71 · **7** · 17 · ● · ©829 · **Woodstock Two** .... [L-V] $20 Cotillion 400 [2]
more songs from the 1969 festival

Birthday Of The Sun [Melanie]	4 + 20 [Crosby, Stills, Nash & Young]	Imaginary Western, Theme For An [Mountain]
Blood Of The Sun [Mountain]	Get My Heart Back Together [Jimi Hendrix]	Izabella [Jimi Hendrix]
Eskimo Blue Day [Jefferson Airplane]	Guinnevere [Crosby, Stills, Nash & Young]	Jam Back At The House [Jimi Hendrix]
Everything's Gonna Be Alright [Butterfield Blues Band]		Marrakesh Express [Crosby, Stills, Nash & Young]
		My Beautiful People [Melanie]
		Saturday Afternoon (medley) [Jefferson Airplane]
		Sweet Sir Galahad [Joan Baez]
		Won't You Try (medley) [Jefferson Airplane]
		Woodstock Boogie [Canned Heat]

3/11/89 · **45** · 14 · ©830 · **Working Girl** .... [V] $10 Arista 8593
Melanie Griffith/Harrison Ford/Sigourney Weaver/Joan Cusack/Alec Baldwin

Carlotta's Heart [Carly Simon]	**Let The River Run [Carly Simon] 49**	Man That Got Away [Rob Mounsey/George Young/Chip Jackson/Grady Tate]
I'm So Excited [Pointer Sisters] 9	Looking Through Katherine's House [Carly Simon]	Poor Butterfly [Sonny Rollins]
In Love [Carly Simon]		Scar, The [Carly Simon]
Lady In Red [Chris DeBurgh] 3		

6/20/98 · **26** · 10 · ● · ©831 · **X-Files, The** .... [V] $10 Elektra 62200
David Duchovny/Gillian Anderson/Martin Landau/Blythe Danner/Armin Mueller-Stahl

Beacon Light [Ween]	Flower Man [Tonic]	One [Filter]
Black [Sarah McLachlan]	Hunter [Björk]	One More Murder [Better Than Ezra]
Crystal Ship [X]	Invisible Sun [Sting & Aswad]	Teotihuacan [Noel Gallagher]
Deuce [Cardigans]	More Than This [Cure]	Walking After You [Foo Fighters]
	16 Horses [Soul Coughing]	X-Files Theme [Dust Brothers]

Xanadu - see NEWTON-JOHN, Olivia / ELECTRIC LIGHT ORCHESTRA
Olivia Newton-John/Michael Beck/Gene Kelly

8/7/65 · **82** · 10 · 832 · **Yellow Rolls-Royce, The** .... [I] $30 MGM 4292
Ingrid Bergman/Rex Harrison/Shirley MacLaine/Omar Shariff; cp/cd: Riz Ortolani

David's Square In Florence	Forget Domani [Katyna Ranieri]	Mae
Eloise	Going To Soriano	Main Title
		Now And Then
		Pisa

Yellow Submarine - see BEATLES, The
Yentl - see STREISAND, Barbra
Barbra Streisand/Mandy Patinkin/Amy Irving
Yes, Giorgio - see PAVAROTTI, Luciano
Luciano Pavarotti/Kathryn Harrold/Eddie Albert

10/29/77 · **17** · 15 · ● · 833 · **You Light Up My Life** .... [I] $15 Arista 4159
Didi Conn/Joe Silver/Melanie Mayron; cp/cd: Joseph Brooks

California Daydreams	Morning Of My Life	Rolling The Chords
Do You Have A Piano	Phone Call	**You Light Up My Life [Kacey Cisyk] 80**
It's A Long Way From Brooklyn	Ride To Chris's House	You Light Up My Life (instrumental)

7/15/67 · **27** · 26 · ©834 · **You Only Live Twice** .... [I] $30 United Artists 5155
Sean Connery/Donald Pleasence/Akiko Wakabayashi/Mie Hama; cp/cd: John Barry

Bond Averts World War Three	Drop In The Ocean	Mountains And Sunsets
Capsule In Space	Fight At Kobe Dock (medley)	Tanaka's World
Countdown For Blofeld	Helga (medley)	Wedding, The
Death Of Aki	James Bond - Astronaut?	**You Only Live Twice [Nancy Sinatra] 44**

You're A Big Boy Now - see LOVIN' SPOONFUL
Peter Kastner/Rip Torn/Geraldine Page/Julie Harris

12/26/98+ · **44** · 20 · ● · ©835 · **You've Got Mail** .... [O-V] $10 Atlantic 83153
Tom Hanks/Meg Ryan/Parker Posey/Jean Stapleton/Dave Chappelle

Anyone At All [Carole King]	**I'm Gonna Sit Right Down And Write Myself A Letter [Billy Williams] 3**	**Remember [Harry Nilsson] 53**
Dream [Roy Orbison]		**Rockin' Robin [Bobby Day] 2**
Dreams [Cranberries] 42		**Signed Sealed Delivered I'm Yours [Stevie Wonder] 3**
Dummy Song [Louis Armstrong]	Lonely At The Top [Randy Newman]	**Splish Splash [Bobby Darin] 3**
I Guess The Lord Must Be In New York City [Sinead O'Connor]	Over The Rainbow [Harry Nilsson]	You Made Me Love You [Jimmy Durante]
	Puppy Song [Harry Nilsson]	'You've Got Mail' Suite [George Fenton]

Young At Heart - see DAY, Doris
Doris Day/Frank Sinatra/Gig Young/Ethel Barrymore

DEBUT	PEAK	WKS	RIAA	CD	ARTIST — Album Title	Catalog	Sym	$	Label & Number
3/22/75	128	8		©836	**Young Frankenstein**		[T]	$20	ABC 870

Gene Wilder/Peter Boyle/Marty Feldman/Teri Garr/Cloris Leachman

Frau Blucher	Main Title *[John Morris]*	Riot Is An Ugly Thing
Grandfather's Private Library	Monster Talks	That's Fron-Kon-Steen!
He Was My Boyfriend	My Name Is Frankenstein!	Young Frankenstein (Theme)
He's Broken Loose	Puttin' On The Ritz *[Gene Wilder &*	*[Rhythm Heritage]*
It's Alive!	*Peter Boyle]*	

Train Ride To Transylvania/The
  Doctor Meets Igor
Wedding Night

Young Guns II - see BON JOVI, Jon
Emilio Estevez/Kiefer Sutherland/Lou Diamond Phillips

DEBUT	PEAK	WKS	RIAA	CD		Catalog	Sym	$	Label & Number
3/1/86	166	6		©837	**Youngblood**		[V]	$12	RCA Victor 7172

Rob Lowe/Ed Lauter/Cynthia Gibb/Patrick Swayze

Cut You Down To Size *[Starship]*	Opening Score *[William Orbit]*	**Something Real (Inside Me/Inside**
Footsteps *[Nick Gilder]*	Soldier Of Fortune *[Marc Jordan]*	**You)** *[Mr. Mister]* **29**
I'm A Real Man *[John Hiatt]*		Stand In The Fire *[Mickey Thomas]*

Talk Me Into It *[Glenn Jones]*
Winning Is Everything *[Autograph]*

Youngblood - see WAR
Lawrence Hilton-Jacobs/Bryan O'Dell/Ren Woods

Your Cheatin' Heart - see WILLIAMS, Hank Jr.
George Hamilton/Susan Oliver/Red Buttons/Arthur O'Connell

DEBUT	PEAK	WKS	RIAA	CD		Catalog	Sym	$	Label & Number
4/11/70	128	8		838	**Z**		[I]	$30	Columbia 3370

Yves Montand/Irene Papas; cp: Mikis Theodorakis; cd: Bernard Gerard

Arrival Of Helen	Finale	Main Title (O Andonis)
Batucada	Idep Otsaley Ot	Pios Den Mila Yia Ti Lambri
Cafe Rock	La Course De Manuel (Chase)	Safti Gitonia

To Palikari Echi Kaimo
To Yelasto Pedi

Ziggy Stardust - The Motion Picture - see BOWIE, David

DEBUT	PEAK	WKS	RIAA	CD		Catalog	Sym	$	Label & Number
5/1/65	26	79		839	**Zorba The Greek**		[I]	$25	20th Century Fox 4167

Anthony Quinn/Irene Papas/Alan Bates; cp/cd: Mikis Theodorakis

Always Look For Trouble	Free	One Unforgiveable Sin
Clever People And Grocers	Full Catastrophe	Questions Without Answers
Fire Inside	Life Goes On	That's Me - Zorba!

Zorba The Greek (Theme)
Zorba's Dance

DEBUT	PEAK	WKS	RIAA	CD	ARTIST — Album Title	Catalog	Sym	$	Label & Number

MOVIE SOUNDTRACK COMPILATIONS

4/3/99 82 12 ● © 1 All Time Greatest Movie Songs, The .... **$10** Sony 69879

As I Lay Me Down [Sophie B. Hawkins] 6
For The First Time [Kenny Loggins]
Go The Distance [Michael Bolton] 24
Heart Of A Hero [Luther Vandross]
Heaven's What I Feel [Gloria Estefan] 27

I Finally Found Someone [Barbra Streisand & Bryan Adams] 8
I Say A Little Prayer [Diana King] 38
I Want To Spend My Lifetime Loving You [Marc Anthony & Tina Arena]
I'm Kissing You [Des'ree]
Men In Black [Will Smith]

Modern Woman [Billy Joel] 10
My Heart Will Go On (Love Theme From 'Titanic') [Celine Dion] 1
Streets Of Philadelphia [Bruce Springsteen] 9
Sweetest Thing [Refugee Camp All-Stars]

Whole New World [Peabo Bryson & Regina Belle] 1
Will You Be There [Michael Jackson] 7
You Were There [Babyface]

2/8/69 198 2 2 Best Of The Soundtracks .... **$30** Tower 5148

Billy Jack's Theme [Sidewalk Sounds]
Blue's Theme [Davie Allan & The Arrows] 37
Listen To The Music [Second Time]

Devil's Angels [David Allan & The Arrows] 97
Hell Rider [Mike Curb Congregation]

Love Children [Ron Stein]
Psych-Out [Ron Stein]
Shape Of Things To Come [Max Frost & The Troopers] 22

Wild Angels, Theme From The [Davie Allan & The Arrows] 99
Wild Orgy [Hands Of Time]

4/22/95 95 46 ▲ © 3 Classic Disney Volume I - 60 Years Of Musical Magic .... **C**:#25/11 **$10** Walt Disney 60865

Beauty And The Beast [Angela Lansbury]
Chim Chim Cher-ee [Dick Van Dyke & Julie Andrews]
Circle Of Life [Carmen Twillie]
Colonel Hathi's March [J. Pat O'Malley]
Dance Of The Reed Flutes [Leopold Stokowski]

Dream Is A Wish Your Heart Makes [Ilene Woods]
Hakuna Matata [Nathan Lane & Ernie Sabella]
I Just Can't Wait To Be King [Jason Weaver]
Jolly Holiday [Dick Van Dyke & Julie Andrews]
Kiss The Girl [Samuel E. Wright]
Let's Get Together [Hayley Mills] 8

Love Is A Song [Donald Novis]
Minnie's Yoo Hoo!
Monkey's Uncle [Annette Funicello w/The Beach Boys]
Poor Unfortunate Souls [Pat Carroll]
Some Day My Prince Will Come [Adriana Caselotti]
Spectrum Song [Paul Frees]
Spoonful Of Sugar [Julie Andrews]
Ugly Bug Ball [Burl Ives]

Under The Sea [Samuel E. Wright]
Whale Of A Tale [Kirk Douglas]
Whole New World [Brad Kane & Lea Salonga]
Work Song [Mouse Chorus]
You Can Fly! You Can Fly! You Can Fly! [Bobby Driscoll & Kathryn Beaumont]
Zip-A-Dee-Doo-Dah [James Baskett]

4/29/95 143 15 ▲ © 4 Classic Disney Volume II - 60 Years Of Musical Magic .... **$10** Walt Disney 60866

Age Of Not Believing [Angela Lansbury]
Bare Necessities [Phil Harris & Bruce Reitherman]
Be Our Guest [Jerry Orbach & Angela Lansbury]
Best Of Friends [Pearl Bailey]
Bibbidi-Bobbidi-Boo [Verna Felton & James MacDonald]
Can You Feel The Love Tonight [Joseph Williams & Sally Dworsky]

Candle On The Water [Helen Reddy]
Ev'rybody Has A Laughing Place [James Baskett]
Feed The Birds (Tuppence A Bag) [Julie Andrews]
Gaston [Richard White & Jesse Corti]
Heigh-Ho [Dwarf Chorus]
It's A Small World (After All) [Disneyland Chorus]

Let's Go Fly A Kite [David Tomlinson & Dick Van Dyke]
Main Street Electrical Parade
Mickey Mouse Club March [Mouseketeers]
On The Front Porch [Burl Ives]
One Jump Ahead [Brad Kane]
Part Of Your World [Jodi Benson]
Second Star To The Right [Jud Conlon Chorus]
So This Is Love [Ileen Woods & Mike Douglas]

Something There [Paige O'Hara & Robby Benson]
Supercalifragilisticexpialidocious [Julie Andrews & Dick Van Dyke]
Tiki, Tiki, Tiki Room [Wally Boag & Fulton Burley]
When You Wish Upon A Star [Cliff Edwards]
Who's Afraid Of The Big Bad Wolf? [Pinto Colvig & Mary Moder]

8/17/96 178 11 ● © 5 Classic Disney Volume III - 60 Years Of Musical Magic .... **$10** Walt Disney 60907

Are We Dancing [John Davidson & Leslie Ann Warren]
Ballad Of Davy Crockett [Wellingtons]
Be Prepared [Jeremy Irons]
Bella Notte [George Givot & Bill Thompson]
Colors Of The Wind [Judy Kuhn]
Family [Original Cast]

Following The Leader [Bobby Driscoll & Paul Collins]
Heffalumps And Woozles [Disney Chorus]
I Wan'na Be Like You [Louis Prima]
I'm Professor Ludwig Von Drake [Paul Frees]
Jacks' Lament [Danny Elfman]
Les Poissons [Rene Auberjonois]
Little April Shower [Disney Chorus]

Mine, Mine, Mine [David Ogden Stiers & Mel Gibson]
Mob Song [Original Cast]
My Name Is James [Paul Terry]
Once Upon A Dream [Mary Costa & Bill Shirley]
Oo-De-Lally [Roger Miller]
Out There [Tony Jay & Tom Hulce]
Pink Elephants On Parade [Disney Chorus]

Portobello Road [David Tomlinson & Angela Lansbury]
Silly Song (Dwarfs' Yodel Song [Dwarf Chorus]
Stay Awake [Julie Andrews]
Trust In Me [Sterling Holloway]
You've Got A Friend In Me [Randy Newman]

1/23/61 2³ 81 6 Great Motion Picture Themes .... **[I] $25** United Artists 3122

Apartment, Theme From The [Ferrante & Teicher] 10
Big Country, Theme From The [Jerome Moross]
Diggin' In The Morning [Elmer Bernstein]
Exodus [Ferrante & Teicher] 2

Green Leaves Of Summer [Nick Perito]
Horse Soldiers, Theme From The [David Buttolph]
I Want To Live [Gerry Mulligan]
Magnificent Seven [Al Caiola] 35
Never On Sunday [Don Costa] 19

On The Beach [Mitchell Powell]
Smile [Alfred Newman]
Solomon And Sheba, Theme From [Mario Nascimbene]
Some Like It Hot [Adolph Deutsch]
Unforgiven (The Need For Love), Theme From The [Don Costa] 27

Vikings, Theme From The [Mario Nascimbene]
Wonderful Country, Theme From The [Alex North]

9/25/61 129 5 7 Great Motion Picture Themes (More Original Sound Tracks And Hit Music) .... **[I] $25** United Artists 3158

Bonanza [Al Caiola] 19
Diggin' In The Morning [Elmer Bernstein]
Elmer Gantry, Main Title From [Andre Previn]
Gone With The Wind, Theme From [Ferrante & Teicher]

Goodbye Again, Theme From [Ferrante & Teicher] 85
Houseboat, Love Song From [Don Costa]
I Wanna Be Loved By You [Marilyn Monroe]
Misfits, Theme From The [Don Costa]

Moulin Rouge (Where Is Your Heart), Theme From [Don Costa]
Naked Maja, Theme From The [Mitchell Powell]
Never On Sunday [Melina Mercouri]
Odds Against Tomorrow [Modern Jazz Quartet]

One Eyed Jacks, Love Theme From [Ferrante & Teicher] 37
Porgy And Bess, Theme From [Bill Potts]
Take The A Train [Louis Armstrong]

12/28/96+ 155 9 © 8 Movie Luv - The Ultimate Movie Soundtrack Collection .... **$10** EMI-Capitol 54555

Can You Feel The Love Tonight [Elton John] 4
Colors Of The Wind [Vanessa Williams] 4
Gangsta's Paradise [Coolio feat. L.V.] 1

I Don't Wanna Fight [Tina Turner] 9
I'd Die Without You [PM Dawn] 3
I'm Gonna Be (500 Miles) [Proclaimers] 3

(I've Had) The Time Of My Life [Bill Medley & Jennifer Warnes] 1
It Must Have Been Love [Roxette] 1
Stay (I Missed You) [Lisa Loeb & Nine Stories] 1

Take My Breath Away [Berlin] 1
Unchained Melody [Righteous Brothers] 4
Whole New World (Aladdin's Theme) [Peabo Bryson & Regina Belle] 1

3/13/65 72 27 9 Music To Read James Bond By .... **$25** United Artists 6415

Black On Pink [Sir Julian]
007 [John Barry]
Elegant Venus [Dick Ruedebusch]
From Russia With Love [Al Caiola]

Girl Trouble [John Barry]
Golden Girl [LeRoy Holmes]
Goldfinger [Shirley Bassey] 8
Goldfinger [Perez Prado]

Jamaica Jump Up [Monty Norman]
James Bond Theme [Ferrante & Teicher]
Living It Up [Leasebreakers]

Underneath The Mango Tree [La Playa]

5/19/62 31 16 10 Original Motion Picture Hit Themes .... **$25** United Artists 3197

Blue Hawaii (medley) [Alfred Newman]
El Cid [Ferrante & Teicher]
Fanny [Ferrante & Teicher]
Guns Of Navarone [Al Caiola]
Happy Thieve's Theme [Nick Perito]

King Of Kings [Ferrante & Teicher]
Let's Get Together [Tutti Camarata]
Lili Marleen [Ralph Marterie]
Love Look Away (medley) [Alfred Newman]
Maria [Ferrante & Teicher]

Moon River [Ferrante & Teicher]
One, Two, Three Waltz [Roger Wayne]
Pocketful Of Miracles [Walter Scharf]

Take The "A" Train [Louis Armstrong]
Tonight [Ferrante & Teicher] 8
Town Without Pity [Gene Pitney] 13

DEBUT	PEAK	WKS	RIAA	CD	ARTIST — Album Title	Catalog	Sym	$	Label & Number

ORIGINAL CASTS

9/23/78 **161** 5 © **1 Ain't Misbehavin'** .... **$20** RCA Victor 2965 [2]
Ken Page/Nell Carter/Andre DeShields; cp: Fats Waller

Ain't Misbehavin'	Honeysuckle Rose	Lookin' Good But Feelin' Bad
Black And Blue	How Ya Baby	Lounging At The Waldorf
Cash For Your Trash	I've Got A Feeling I'm Falling	Mean To Me
Entr'acte	Jitterbug Waltz	Off-Time
Fat And Greasy	Joint Is Jumpin'	Reefer Song
Find Out What They Like	Keepin' Out Of Mischief Now	Spreadin' Rhythm Around
Handful Of Keys	Ladies Who Sing With The Band	Squeeze Me

'Tain't Nobody's Biz-ness If I Do
That Ain't Right
Viper's Drag
When The Nylons Bloom Again
Yacht Club Swing
Your Feet's Too Big

4/21/62 **21** 16 © **2 All American** .... **$50** Columbia 2160
Ray Bolger/Eileen Herlie/Ron Husmann; mu: Charles Strouse; ly: Lee Adams

Fight Song (medley)	I've Just Seen Her (As Nobody Else	Nightlife
Have A Dream	Has Seen Her)	Once Upon A Time
I Couldn't Have Done It Alone	If I Were You	Our Children
I'm Fascinating	It's Fun To Think	Physical Fitness (medley)
	Melt Us (medley)	Real Me

We Speak The Same Language
What A Country! (medley)
Which Way?

6/18/77 **81** 39 ▲ © **3 Annie** .... **$15** Columbia 34712
Andrea McArdle/Reid Shelton/Danielle Brisebois; mu: Charles Strouse; ly: Martin Charnin

Annie	Little Girls	Tomorrow
Easy Street	Maybe	We'd Like To Thank You Herbert
Hard-Knock Life	N.Y.C.	Hoover
I Don't Need Anything But You	New Deal For Christmas	You Won't Be An Orphan For Long
I Think I'm Gonna Like It Here	Something Was Missing	

You're Never Fully Dressed Without
A Smile

12/30/57+ **12** 5 **4 Annie Get Your Gun** .... **$50** Capitol 913
Mary Martin/John Raitt; sw: Irving Berlin; produced by NBC for a TV presentation; Original Cast version with Ethel Merman charted in 1946 (#2) on Decca 468

Anything You Can Do	I Got The Sun In The Morning	My Defenses Are Down
Doin' What Comes Natur'lly	I'm A Bad, Bad Man	There's No Business Like Show
Girl That I Marry	I'm An Indian Too	Business
I Got Lost In His Arms	Moonshine Lullaby	They Say It's Wonderful

You Can't Get A Man With A Gun

8/6/66 **113** 7 © **5 Annie Get Your Gun** .... **$20** RCA Victor 1124
Ethel Merman/Bruce Yarnell; sw: Irving Berlin

Anything You Can Do	I Got The Sun In The Morning	Old Fashioned Wedding
Colonel Buffalo Bill	I'm A Bad, Bad Man	There's No Business Like Show
Doin' What Comes Natur'lly	I'm An Indian Too	Business
Girl That I Marry	Moonshine Lullaby	There's No Business Like Show
I Got Lost In His Arms	My Defenses Are Down	Business (Reprise)

They Say It's Wonderful
You Can't Get A Man With A Gun

5/23/70 **168** 7 © **6 Applause** .... **$25** ABC 11
Lauren Bacall/Robert Mandan/Bonnie Franklin/Brandon Maggert; mu: Charles Strouse; ly: Lee Adams

Applause	Fasten Your Seat Belts	One Of A Kind
Backstage Babble	Good Friends	She's No Longer A Gypsy
Best Night Of My Life	Hurry Back	Something Greater
But Alive	One Hallow'een	Think How It's Gonna Be

Welcome To The Theater
Who's That Girl

12/17/66+ **113** 9 © **7 Apple Tree, The** .... **$30** Columbia 3020
Barbara Harris/Larry Blyden/Alan Alda/**Robert Klein**; mu: Jerry Bock; ly: Sheldon Harnick

Apple Tree (Forbidden Fruit)	Go To Sleep, Whatever You Are	It's A Fish
Beautiful, Beautiful World	Gorgeous	Lady Or The Tiger? (medley)
Eve	Here In Eden (medley)	Make Way (medley)
Feelings	I Know and Wealth	Oh, To Be A Movie Star (medley)
Forbidden Love (In Gaul)	I'll Tell You A Truth (medley)	Tiger, Tiger
Friends	I've Got What You Want	What Makes Me Love Him?

Which Door (medley)
Who Is She?
You Are Not Real

2/20/65 **143** 2 © **8 Bajour** .... **$40** Columbia 2700
Chita Rivera/Nancy Dussault/**Herschel Bernardi**/Paul Sorvino; sw: Walter Marks

Bajour	I Can	Mean
Guarantees (medley)	Living Simply	Move Over, America
Haggle, The	Love Is A Chance (medley)	Move Over, New York
Honest Man	Love-Line	Must It Be Love?

Soon
Where Is The Tribe For Me?
Words, Words, Words

5/8/65 **138** 4 **9 Baker Street (A Musical Adventure Of Sherlock Holmes)** .... **$30** MGM 7000
Fritz Weaver/Inga Swenson; sw: Marian Grudeff and Raymond Jessel

Cold Clear World	I'm In London Again	Letters
Finding Words For Spring	It's So Simple	Married Man
I Shall Miss You	Jewelry	Pursuit
I'd Do It Again	Leave It To Us, Guv	Roof Space

What A Night This Is Going To Be

2/9/57 **20** 1 © **10 Bells Are Ringing** .... **$50** Columbia 5170
Judy Holliday/Sydney Chaplin; mu: Jule Styne; ly: Betty Comden and Adolph Green

Bells Are Ringing	I'm Goin' Back	Just In Time
Drop That Name	Is It A Crime?	Long Before I Knew You
Hello, Hello There!	It's A Perfect Relationship	Midas Touch
I Met A Girl	It's A Simple Little System	Mu-Cha-Cha

On My Own
Party's Over
Salzburg

12/26/64+ **132** 8 © **11 Ben Franklin In Paris** .... **$40** Capitol 2191
Robert Preston/Ulla Sallert; mu: Mark Sandrich Jr.; ly: Sidney Michaels

Balloon Is Ascending	Hic Haec Hoc	Look For Small Pleasure (medley)
Diane (medley)	How Laughable It Is	To Be Alone With You
God Bless The Human Elbow	I Invented Myself	Too Charming
Half The Battle	I Love The Ladies	We Sail The Seas

Whatever Became Of Old Temple?
When I Dance With The Person I
Love
You're In Paris

12/15/62+ **73** 20 © **12 Beyond The Fringe** .... **$40** Capitol 1792
Dudley Moore/Alan Bennett/Peter Cook/Jonathan Miller

Aftermth Of War	Deutscher Chansons	Sadder And Wiser Beaver
And The Same To You	End Of The World	Sitting On The Bench
Bollard	Portrait From Memory	So That's The Way You Like It

Take A Pew

6/14/69 **195** 3 **13 Boys In The Band, The** .... **$30** A&M 6001 [2]
Kenneth Nelson/Peter White; no track titles listed

ORIGINAL CASTS

DEBUT	PEAK	WKS	RIAA	CD	ARTIST — Album Title	Catalog	Sym	$	Label & Number
7/18/60+	12	61		© 14	**Bye Bye Birdie**			$30	Columbia 5510

Chita Rivera/Dick Van Dyke/Kay Medford/Dick Gautier; mu: Charles Strouse; ly: Lee Adams

Baby, Talk To Me | Hymn For A Sunday Evening | One Boy | Spanish Rose
English Teacher | Kids | One Last Kiss | Telephone Hour
Honestly Sincere | Lot Of Livin' To Do | Put On A Happy Face | What Did I Ever See In Him?
How Lovely To Be A Woman | Normal American Boy | Rosie |

DEBUT	PEAK	WKS	RIAA	CD	ARTIST — Album Title	Catalog	Sym	$	Label & Number
1/7/67	37	39		© 15	**Cabaret**			$25	Columbia 3040

Joel Grey/Jill Haworth/Jack Gilford/Bert Convy/Lotte Lenya; mu: John Kander; ly: Fred Ebb

Cabaret | It Couldn't Please Me More | So What? | Why Should I Wake Up?
Don't Tell Mama | Married | Telephone Song | Willkommen
Entr'acte | Meeskite | Tomorrow Belongs To Me |
If You Could See Her (The Gorilla Song) | Money Song | Two Ladies |
 | Perfectly Marvelous | What Would You Do? |

DEBUT	PEAK	WKS	RIAA	CD	ARTIST — Album Title	Catalog	Sym	$	Label & Number
1/23/61	❶⁶	265	●	© 16	**Camelot**			$30	Columbia 2031

Richard Burton/**Julie Andrews**/**Robert Goulet**; mu: Frederick Loewe; ly: Alan Jay Lerner

Before I Gaze At You Again | Guenevere | If Ever I Would Leave You | Simple Joys Of Maidenhood
C'est Moi | How To Handle A Woman | Lusty Month Of May | Then You May Take Me To The Fair
Camelot | I Loved You Once In Silence | Overture (medley) | What Do The Simple Folks Do
Fie On Goodness! | I Wonder What The King Is Doing | Parade |
Follow Me | Tonight (medley) | Seven Deadly Virtues |

DEBUT	PEAK	WKS	RIAA	CD	ARTIST — Album Title	Catalog	Sym	$	Label & Number
4/19/69	171	4		© 17	**Canterbury Tales**			$25	Capitol 229

George Rose/Hermione Baddeley/Martyn Green; mu: Richard Hill and John Hawkins; ly: Nevill Coghill

April Love (medley) | Darling, Let Me Teach You How To Kiss | If She Has Never Loved Before (medley) | Pilgrim Riding Music (medley)
Beer Is Best (medley) | Goodnight Hymn (medley) | It Depends On What You're At | Song Of Welcome (medley)
Canterbury Day (medley) | Hymen, Hymen (medley) | Love Will Conquer All | There's The Moon
Chaucer's Epilogue (medley) | I Am All A-Blaze | Mug Dance (medley) | What Do Women Want
Chaucer's Prologue (medley) | I Have A Noble Cock | Overture (medley) | Where Are The Girls Of Yesterday
Come On And Marry Me, Honey | I'll Give My Love A Ring | Pear Tree Quintet |

DEBUT	PEAK	WKS	RIAA	CD	ARTIST — Album Title	Catalog	Sym	$	Label & Number
5/29/61	❶¹	67		© 18	**Carnival**			$25	MGM 3946

Anna Maria Alberghetti/James Mitchell/Kaye Ballard; sw: Bob Merrill

Beautiful Candy | I Hate Him (medley) | Mira (Can You Imagine That?) | Very Nice Man
Everybody Likes You | I've Got To Find A Reason | Opening - Direct From Vienna | Yes, My Heart
Grand Imperial Cirque De Paris | It Was Always You | Rich, The (medley) | Yum, Ticky, Ticky, Tum, Tum (medley)
Her Face | Love Makes The World Go Around (Theme) | She's My Love |
Humming | | Sword, The Rose And The Cape |

DEBUT	PEAK	WKS	RIAA	CD	ARTIST — Album Title	Catalog	Sym	$	Label & Number
11/10/62	12	19			19 **Carousel**			$25	Command 843

version of the Rodgers & Hammerstein musical; produced by **Enoch Light** and featuring vocalists Alfred Drake and Roberta Peters; Original Cast version charted in 1945 (#1) on Decca 400

Blow High, Blow Low | If I Loved You | Soliloquy | You'll Never Walk Alone
Carousel Waltz | June Is Bustin' Out All Over | Stonecutters (medley) |
Geraniums In The Winder (medley) | Mr. Snow | What's The Use Of Wond'rin' |
Highest Judge Of All | Real Nice Clambake | When The Children Are Asleep |

Catherine Wheel, The - see BYRNE, David

DEBUT	PEAK	WKS	RIAA	CD	ARTIST — Album Title	Catalog	Sym	$	Label & Number
11/6/82+	86	22		© 20	**Cats**			$15	Geffen 2017 [2]

Wayne Sleep/Paul Nicholas/Elaine Paige; original London cast; sw: **Andrew Lloyd Webber**

Ad-dressing Of Cats | Growltiger's Last Stand (medley) | Macavity | Old Deuteronomy
Ballad Of Billy McCaw (medley) | Gus: The Theatre Cat | Memory | Old Gumbie Cat (medley)
Bustopher Jones | Invitation To The Jellicle Ball (medley) | Moments Of Happiness | Prologue: Jellicle Songs For Jellicle Cats
Grizabella | Jellicle Ball | Mr. Mistoffelees | Rum Tum Tugger
Grizabella, The Glamour Cat (medley) | Journey To The Heaviside Layer | Mungojerrie And Rumpleteazer | Skimbleshanks The Railway Cat
 | | Naming Of Cats |

DEBUT	PEAK	WKS	RIAA	CD	ARTIST — Album Title	Catalog	Sym	$	Label & Number
2/26/83	113	64	▲	© 21	**Cats**			$15	Geffen 2031 [2]

Ken Page/Betty Buckley/Timothy Scott/Reed Jones; original Broadway cast

Ad-dressing Of Cats | Invitation To The Jellicle Ball | Moments Of Happiness | Old Gumbie Cat
Bustopher Jones | Jellicle Ball | Mr. Mistoffelees | Prologue: Jellicle Songs For Jellicle Cats
Grizabella, The Glamour Cat | Journey To The Heaviside Layer | Mungojerrie And Rumpleteazer | Rum Tum Tugger
Growltiger's Last Stand | Macavity | Naming Of Cats | Skimbleshanks The Railway Cat
Gus: The Theatre Cat | Memory | Old Deuteronomy |

DEBUT	PEAK	WKS	RIAA	CD	ARTIST — Album Title	Catalog	Sym	$	Label & Number
2/26/83	131	14		© 22	**Cats**			$12	Geffen 2026

selections from the original Broadway cast

Ad-dressing Of Cats | Macavity | Old Gumbie Cat | Solo Dance
Grizabella, The Glamour Cat | Memory | Prologue: Jellicle Songs For Jellicle Cats |
Gus: The Theatre Cat | Mr. Mistoffelees | Rum Tum Tugger |
Jellicle Ball | Mungojerrie And Rumpleteazer | Skimbleshanks The Railway Cat |
Journey To The Heaviside Layer | Old Deuteronomy |

DEBUT	PEAK	WKS	RIAA	CD	ARTIST — Album Title	Catalog	Sym	$	Label & Number
8/23/75	73	10			23 **Chicago**			$15	Arista 9005

Gwen Verdon/Chita Rivera/Jerry Orbach; mu: John Kander; ly: Fred Ebb

All I Care About | I Can't Do It Alone | My Own Best Friend | We Both Reached For The Gun
Cell Block Tango | Little Bit Of Good | Nowadays | When Velma Takes The Stand
Class | Me And My Baby | Razzle Dazzle | When You're Good To Mama
Funny Honey | Mr. Cellophane | Roxie |

DEBUT	PEAK	WKS	RIAA	CD	ARTIST — Album Title	Catalog	Sym	$	Label & Number
2/15/97	131	2		© 24	**Chicago - The Musical**			$10	RCA Victor 68727

Ann Reinking/Bebe Neuwirth/James Naughton/Joel Grey; mu: John Kander; ly: Fred Ebb

All I Care About | Hot Honey Rag | Mr. Cellophane | We Both Reached For The Gun
All That Jazz | I Can't Do It Alone | My Own Best Friend | When Velma Takes The Stand
Cell Block Tango | I Know A Girl | Nowadays | When You're Good To Mama
Class | Little Bit Of Good | Razzle Dazzle |
Funny Honey | Me And My Baby | Roxie |

DEBUT	PEAK	WKS	RIAA	CD	ARTIST — Album Title	Catalog	Sym	$	Label & Number
8/16/75	98	49	▲²	© 25	**Chorus Line, A**			$15	Columbia 33581

Pamela Blair/Wayne Cilento/Priscilla Lopez/Donna McKechnie; mu: Marvin Hamlisch; ly: Edward Kleban

At The Ballet | I Can Do That | One |
Dance: Ten; Looks: Three | I Hope I Get It | Sing! |
Hello Twelve, Hello Thirteen, Hello Love | Music And The Mirror | What I Did For Love |
 | Nothing |

DEBUT	PEAK	WKS	RIAA	CD	ARTIST — Album Title	Catalog	Sym	$	Label & Number

4/29/57 | **15** | 1 | | 26 **Cinderella** .... | | | **$40** Columbia 5190

Julie Andrews; mu: Richard Rodgers; ly: Oscar Hammerstein II; a special CBS-TV production (March 31, 1957)

Do I Love You Because You're	Impossible! (medley)	March: Where Is Cinderella?	Stepsisters' Lament
Beautiful	In My Own Little Corner	Prince Is Giving A Ball	Ten Minutes Ago
Gavotte	It's Possible! (medley)	Royal Dressing Room Scene	Waltz For A Ball
Godmother's Song (medley)	Lovely Night	Search, The	Wedding, The

6/20/70 | **178** | 2 | © 27 **Company** .... | | | **$20** Columbia 3550

Dean Jones/Barbara Barrie; sw: Stephen Sondheim

Another Hundred People	Getting Married Today	Poor Baby (medley)	Tick Tock (medley)
Barcelona	Have I Got A Girl For You (medley)	Side By Side By Side	You Could Drive A Person Crazy
Being Alive	Ladies Who Lunch	Someone Is Waiting (medley)	
Company	Little Things You Do Together	Sorry-Grateful	

6/13/92 | **165** | 2 | © 28 **Crazy For You** .... | | | **$10** Angel 54618

Harry Groener/Jodi Benson/Joel Goodness/Ida Henry; mu: George Gershwin; ly: Ira Gershwin

Bidin' My Time	I Got Rhythm	Shall We Dance?	Things Are Looking Up
But Not For Me	K-ra-zy For You	Slap That Bass	Tonight's The Night
Could You Use Me?	Naughty Baby	Someone To Watch Over Me	What Causes That?
Embraceable You	New York Interlude (Concerto in F)	Stiff Upper Lip	
Entrance To Nevada Medley	Nice Work If You Can Get It	They Can't Take That Away From	
I Can't Be Bothered Now	Real American Folk Song (Is A Rag)	Me	

8/2/69 | **195** | 2 | © 29 **Dames At Sea** .... | | | **$20** Columbia 3330

Bernadette Peters/David Christmas/Tamara Long/Sally Stark; mu: Jim Wise; ly: George Haimsohn and Robin Miller

Beguine, The	Echo Waltz	Raining In My Heart	That Mister Man Of Mine
Broadway Baby	Good Times Are Here To Stay	Sailor Of My Dreams	There's Something About You
Choo-Choo Honeymoon	It's You	Singapore Sue	Wall Street
Dames At Sea	Let's Have A Simple Wedding	Star Tar	

6/11/55 | **6** | 12 | © 30 **Damn Yankees** .... | | | **$30** RCA Victor 1021

Gwen Verdon/Stephen Douglass/Ray Walston; sw: Richard Adler and Jerry Ross; LP: RCA Victor LOC-1021 (#6); EP: RCA Victor EOC-1021 (#11)

Game, The	Near To You	Six Months Out Of Every Year	Whatever Lola Wants
Goodbye, Old Girl	Overture (medley)	(medley)	Who's Got The Pain?
Little Brains-A Little Talent	Shoeless Joe From Hannibal, Mo.	Those Were The Good Old Days	You've Got To Have Heart
Man Doesn't Know		Two Lost Souls	

4/5/69 | **128** | 8 | © 31 **Dear World** .... | | | **$20** Columbia 3260

Angela Lansbury/Milo O'Shea/Carmen Mathews/Ted Agress; sw: Jerry Herman

And I Was Beautiful	Finale - Reprises	I've Never Said I Love You	Spring Of Next Year
Dear World	Garbage	Kiss Her Now	Tea Party Medley
Each Tomorrow Morning	I Don't Want To Know	One Person	

8/24/59 | **44** | 2 | © 32 **Destry Rides Again** .... | | | **$50** Decca 79075

Andy Griffith/Dolores Gray/Scott Brady/Stuart Damon; sw: Harold Rome

Anyone Would Love You	Fair Warning	Ladies	Respectability (medley)
Are You Ready, Gyp Watson?	Hoop-Dee-Dingle	Not Guilty	Rose Lovejoy Girls (medley)
Ballad Of The Gun	I Hate Him	Once Knew A Fella	Rose Lovejoy Of Paradise Alley
Bottleneck	I Know Your Kind	Only Time Will Tell	That Ring On The Finger
Every Once In A While	I Say Hello	Overture	Tomorrow Morning

5/22/65 | **81** | 9 | © 33 **Do I Hear A Waltz?** .... | | | **$25** Columbia 2770

Elizabeth Allen/**Sergio Franchi**/Carol Bruce; mu: Richard Rodgers; ly: Stephen Sondheim

Bargaining	No Understand	Stay	This Week Americans
Do I Hear A Waltz?	Perfectly Lovely Couple	Take The Moment	We're Gonna Be All Right
Here We Are Again	Someone Like You	Thank You So Much (Finale)	What Do We Do? We Fly!
Moon In My Window	Someone Woke Up	Thinking	

3/20/61 | **12** | 22 | © 34 **Do Re Mi** .... | | | **$50** RCA Victor 2002

Phil Silvers/Nancy Walker/Nancy Dussault; mu: Jule Styne; ly: Betty Comden and Adolph Green

Adventure	Asking For You	It's Legitimate	Waiting, Waiting
All Of My Life	Cry Like The Wind	Late, Late Show	What's New At The Zoo
All You Need Is A Quarter	Fireworks	Make Someone Happy	
Ambition	I Know About Love	Take A Job	

7/31/61 | **58** | 9 | 35 **Donnybrook!** .... | | | **$30** Kapp 8500

Eddie Foy/Art Lund/Joan Fagan; sw: Johnny Burke

Day The Snow Is Meltin'	For My Own	Loveable Irish	Sez I
Dee-lightful Is The Word	He Makes Me Feel I'm Lovely	Mr. Flynn	Toast To The Bride
Donnybrook	I Have My Own Way	Quiet Life	Wisha Wurra
Ellen Roe	I Wouldn't Bet One Penny	Sad Was The Day	

5/22/82 | **11** | 29 | ● © 36 **Dreamgirls** .... | | | **$12** Geffen 2007

Jennifer Holliday/Loretta Devine/Cleavant Derricks; mu: Henry Krieger; ly: Tom Eyen

Ain't No Party	Fake Your Way To The Top	I Meant You No Harm	Rap, The
And I Am Telling You I'm Not	Family	I Miss You Old Friend	Steppin' To The Bad Side
Going [Jennifer Holliday] 22	Firing Of Jimmy	Move (You're Steppin' On My Heart)	When I First Saw You
Cadillac Car	Hard To Say Goodbye, My Love	One Night Only	
Dreamgirls	I Am Changing	Press Conference	

Evening With Mike Nichols And Elaine May, An - see NICHOLS, Mike, & Elaine May

8/23/80 | **105** | 19 | ▲ © 37 **Evita** .... | | | **$20** MCA 11007 [2]

Patti LuPone/**Mandy Patinkin**/Bob Gunton; mu: **Andrew Lloyd Webber**; ly: Tim Rice

Actress Hasn't Learned The Lines	Cinema In Buenos Aires, 26 July	High Flying, Adored	On This Night Of A Thousand Stars
(You'd Like To Hear)	1952	I'd Be Surprisingly Good For You	(medley)
And The Money Kept Rolling In	Dice Are Rolling	(medley)	Peron's Latest Flame
(And Out)	Don't Cry For Me Argentina	Lament	Rainbow High
Another Suitcase In Another Hall	(medley)	Montage	Rainbow Tour
Art Of The Possible	Eva And Magaldi (medley)	New Argentina	Requiem For Evita (medley)
Buenos Aires	Eva Beware Of The City (medley)	Oh What A Circus (medley)	Santa Evita
Charity Concert (medley)	Eva's Final Broadcast	On The Balcony Of The Casa	She Is A Diamond
	Goodnight And Thank You	Rosada (medley)	Waltz For Eva And Che

DEBUT	PEAK	WKS	RIAA	CD	ARTIST — Album Title	Catalog	Sym	$	Label & Number

7/25/64   **96**   8   38 **Fade Out-Fade In** .... $40   ABC-Paramount 3
Carol Burnett/Jack Cassidy/**Lou Jacobi**; mu: Jule Styne; ly: Betty Comden/Adolph Green

Call Me Savage	Fear	It's Good To Be Back Home
Close Harmony	Fiddler And The Fighter (medley)	L.Z. In Quest Of His Youth (medley)
Dangerous Age (medley)	Go Home Train	Lila Tremaine
Fade Out-Fade In	I'm With You	My Fortune Is My Face

My Heart Is Like A Violin (medley)
Oh Those Thirties
Usher From The Mezzanine
You Mustn't Be Discouraged

1/22/55   **6**   2   © 39 **Fanny** $30   RCA Victor 1015
Ezio Pinza/Walter Slezak/Florence Henderson; sw: Harold Rome; EP: RCA Victor EOC-1015 (#6); LP: RCA Victor LOC-1015 (#7)

Be Kind To Your Parents	I Have To Tell You	Octopus Song
Birthday Song	I Like You	Other Hands, Other Hearts
Cold Cream Jar Song	Love Is A Very Light Thing	Panisse And Son
Fanny	Montage	Restless Heart
Finale Act 1	Never Too Late For Love	Shika Shika

Thought Of You
To My Wife
Wedding Dance
Welcome Home
Why Be Afraid To Dance

8/3/63   **117**   6   © 40 **Fantasticks, The** ....
Kenneth Nelson/Jerry Orbach/Rita Gardner; mu: Harvey Schmidt; ly: Tom Jones $25   MGM 3872

Happy Ending (medley)	Much More	Round And Round
I Can See It	Never Say No	Soon It's Gonna Rain
It Depends On What You Pay	Plant A Radish	There Is A Curious Paradox
Metaphor	Rape Ballet (medley)	They Were You

This Plum Is Too Ripe
Try To Remember
You Wonder How These Things
  Begin

10/31/64+   **7**   206   ▲²   © 41 **Fiddler On The Roof** ....
Zero Mostel/Maria Karnilova/Bea Arthur/Bert Convy; mu: Jerry Bock; ly: Sheldon Harnick $25   RCA Victor 1093

Anatevka	Matchmaker, Matchmaker	Sunrise, Sunset
Do You Love Me?	Miracle Of Miracles	Tevye's Dream (The Tailor Motel
Far From The Home I Love	Now I Have Everything	Kamzoil)
If I Were A Rich Man	Sabbath Prayer	To Life

Tradition

1/11/60   **7**   89   © 42 **Fiorello!**
Tom Bosley/Patricia Wilson/Ellen Hanley/Howard da Silva; mu: Jerry Bock; ly: Sheldon Harnick $25   Capitol 1321

Bum Won	Little Tin Box	Politics And Poker
Gentleman Jimmy	Marie's Law	'Til Tomorrow
Home Again	Name's La Guardia	Unfair
I Love A Cop	On The Side Of The Angels	Very Next Man

When Did I Fall In Love

7/3/65   **111**   8   43 **Flora, The Red Menace** ....
Liza Minnelli/Bob Dishy/Robert Kaye/Danny Carroll; mu: John Kander; ly: Fred Ebb $40   RCA Victor 1111

All I Need (Is One Good Break)	Hello Waves	Prologue (medley)
Dear Love	Knock Knock	Quiet Thing
Express Yourself	Not Every Day Of The Week	Sign Here
Flame, The	Palomino Pal	Sing Happy

Unafraid (medley)
You Are You

1/12/59   **❶³**   151   ●   © 44 **Flower Drum Song**
Miyoshi Umeki/Larry Blyden/Pat Suzuki; mu: Richard Rodgers; ly: Oscar Hammerstein II $30   Columbia 2009

Chop Suey	Gliding Through My Memoree	I Enjoy Being A Girl
Don't Marry Me	(medley)	Like A God
Entr'acte	Grant Avenue	Love, Look Away
Fan Tan Fanny (medley)	Hundred Million Miracles	Other Generation
Finale (medley)	I Am Going To Like It Here	Sunday

Wedding Parade (medley)
You Are Beautiful

6/5/71   **172**   3   © 45 **Follies** ....
Alexis Smith/Gene Nelson/Yvonne De Carlo/Dorothy Collins; sw: Stephen Sondheim $20   Capitol 761

Ah, Paris! (medley)	God-Why-Don't-You-Love-Me Blues	Love Will See Us Through (medley)
Beautiful Girls	I'm Still Here	Right Girl
Broadway Baby (medley)	In Buddy's Eyes	Road You Didn't Take
Could I Leave You?	Live, Laugh, Love (Finale)	Story Of Lucy And Jessie
Don't Look At Me	Losing My Mind	Too Many Mornings

Waiting For The Girls Upstairs
Who's That Woman?
You're Gonna Love Tomorrow
  (medley)

1/25/86   **181**   6   © 46 **Follies - In Concert** ....
Carol Burnett/George Hearn/Lee Remick/**Mandy Patinkin**; sw: Stephen Sondheim $15   RCA Victor 7128 [2]

Ah, Paree!	Finale	Loveland
Beautiful Girls	I'm Still Here	One More Kiss
Broadway Baby	In Buddy's Eyes	Rain On The Roof
Buddy's Blues	Live, Laugh, Love	Right Girl
Could I Leave You?	Losing My Mind	Road You Didn't Take
Don't Look At Me	Love Will See Us Through (medley)	Story Of Lucy And Jessie

Too Many Mornings
Waiting For The Girls Upstairs
Who's That Woman?
You're Gonna Love Tomorrow
  (medley)

1/17/81   **120**   11   © 47 **42nd Street** ....
Tammy Grimes/Jerry Orbach/Stan Page/Carole Cook; mu: Harry Warren; ly: Al Dubin $12   RCA Victor 3891

About A Quarter To Nine	42nd Street	Overture (medley)
Audition (medley)	Getting Out Of Town	Shadow Waltz
Dames	Go Into Your Dance	Shuffle Off To Buffalo
Finale	Lullaby Of Broadway	Sunny Side To Every Situation

We're In The Money
You're Getting To Be A Habit With
  Me
Young And Healthy

7/7/62   **60**   14   48 **Funny Thing Happened On The Way To The Forum, A** ....
Zero Mostel/Jack Gilford/David Burns/John Carradine; sw: Stephen Sondheim $25   Capitol 1717

Bring Me My Bride	Free	Impossible
Comedy Tonight	Funeral Sequence	Love, I Hear
Everybody Ought To Have A Maid	I'm Calm	Lovely

Pretty Little Picture
That Dirty Old Man
That'll Show Him

2/24/62   **81**   9   49 **Gay Life, The** ....
Walter Chiari/Barbara Cook/Jules Munshin; sw: Howard Dietz and Arthur Schwartz $50   Capitol 1560

Bloom Is Off The Rose	I Wouldn't Marry You (medley)	Oh, Mein Liebchen
Bring Your Darling Daughter	I'm Glad I'm Single	Something You Never Had Before
Come A-Wandering With Me	Label On The Bottle	This Kind Of A Girl
For The First Time (medley)	Magic Moment	What A Charming Couple
I Never Had A Chance	Now I'm Ready For A Frau	Who Can? You Can

Why Go Anywhere At All
You Will Never Be Lonely
You're Not The Type

5/25/68   **161**   6   © 50 **George M!** ....
Joel Grey/Betty Ann Grove/**Bernadette Peters** $25   Columbia 3200

All Aboard For Broadway (medley)	Give My Regards To Broadway	Oh, You Wonderful Boy (medley)
All Our Friends	Harrigan (medley)	Over There (medley)
Billie (medley)	Mary	Popularity (medley)
Down By The Erie (medley)	Musical Comedy Man	Push Me Along In My Push Cart
Finale	Musical Moon (medley)	(medley)
Forty-Five Minutes From Broadway	My Town	Ring To The Name Of Rose
(medley)	Nellie Kelly I Love You (medley)	(medley)

So Long, Mary (medley)
Twentieth Century Love
Yankee Doodle Dandy (medley)
You're A Grand Old Flag (medley)

DEBUT	PEAK	WKS	RIAA	CD	ARTIST — Album Title	Catalog	Sym	$	Label & Number

1/25/64 · **33** · 14 · © 51 · **Girl Who Came To Supper, The** .... · **$50** Columbia 2420
Jose Ferrer/Florence Henderson; sw: **Noel Coward**

Carpathian National Anthem (medley)	Here And Now	Lonely
Coconut Girl Medley	How Do You Do, Middle Age?	My Family Tree (medley)
Coronation Chorale	I'll Remember Her	Sir Or Ma'am
Curt, Clear and Concise	I've Been Invited To A Party	Soliloquies
	London Medley	This Time It's True Love

When Foreign Princes Come To Visit Us

8/7/71+ · **34** · 79 · ● · © 52 · **Godspell** .... · **$20** Bell 1102
Stephen Nathan/Robin Lamont; sw: Stephen Schwartz

Alas For You	By My Side	On The Willows
All For The Best	**Day By Day** *13*	Prepare Ye The Way Of The Lord
All Good Gifts	Learn Your Lessons Well	Save The People
Bless The Lord	Light Of The World	Turn Back, O Man

We Beseech Thee

12/19/64+ · **36** · 16 · © 53 · **Golden Boy** .... · **$40** Capitol 2124
Sammy Davis Jr./Billy Daniels/Cindy Robbins; mu: Charles Strouse; ly: Lee Adams

Can't You See It	Gimme Some	Night Song
Colorful	Golden Boy	No More
Don't Forget 127th Street	I Want To Be With You	Stick Around
Everything's Great	Lorna's Here	This Is The Life

While The City Sleeps
Workout

1/1/66 · **118** · 4 · 54 · **Great Waltz, The** .... · **$40** Capitol 2426
Giorgio Tozzi/Jean Fenn; cp: Johann Strauss

Artist's Life	Gypsy Told Me	Of Men And Violins
At Dommayer's	I'm In Love With Vienna	Philosophy Of Life
Birthday Song	Love And Gingerbread	Radetsky March (medley)
Blue Danube (Finale)	Music!	State Of The Dance (medley)
Enchanted Wood	No Two Ways	Teeter-Totter Me

Two By Two
Waltz With Wings

8/1/92 · **109** · 5 · © 55 · **Guys And Dolls** .... · **$10** RCA Victor 61317
Peter Gallagher/Nathan Lane/Faith Prince; mu: Frank Loesser; Original Cast version charted in 1951 (#1) on Decca 8036

Adelaide's Lament	Guys And Dolls	Luck Be A Lady
Bushel And A Peck	Havana	Marry The Man Today
Crapshooters' Dance	I'll Know	More I Cannot Wish You
Follow The Fold	I've Never Been In Love Before	My Time Of Day
Fugue For Tinhorns	If I Were A Bell	Oldest Established

Runyonland
Sit Down, You're Rockin' The Boat
Sue Me
Take Back Your Mink

7/20/59 · **13** · 116 · © 56 · **Gypsy** .... · **$30** Columbia 2017
Ethel Merman/Jack Klugman/Sandra Church; mu: Jule Styne; ly: Stephen Sondheim

All I Need Is The Girl	If Mama Was Married	Rose's Turn
Baby June And Her Newsboys	Let Me Entertain You	Small World
Dainty June And Her Farmboys	Little Lamb	Some People
Everything's Coming Up Roses	Mr. Goldstone, I Love You	Together Wherever We Go

You Gotta Have A Gimmick
You'll Never Get Away From Me

8/3/68+ · ❶[13] · 151 · ● · © 57 · Hair · **$20** RCA Victor 1150
Gerome Ragni/James Rado/Lynn Kellogg; mu: Galt MacDermot; ly: Gerome Ragni and James Rado

Abie Baby	Don't Put It Down	Hair
Ain't Got No (medley)	Donna (medley)	Hashish (medley)
Air	Easy To Be Hard	I Got Life
Aquarius	Flesh Failures (Let The Sunshine In)	I'm Black (medley)
Be In		Initials
Black Boys (medley)	Frank Mills	Manchester England
Colored Spade	Good Morning Starshine	My Conviction

Sodomy
Three-Five-Zero-Zero (medley)
Walking In Space
What A Piece Of Work Is Man (medley)
Where Do I Go?
White Boys (medley)

5/10/69 · **186** · 4 · 58 · **Hair** .... · **$30** Atco 7002
Paul Nicholas/Oliver Tobias; original London cast

Abie Baby	Coloured Spade (medley)	Frank Mills (medley)
Ain't Got No (medley)	Donna	Good Morning Starshine (medley)
Air	Easy To Be Hard (medley)	Hair
Aquarius	Electric Blues	I Got Life
Bed, The (medley)	Flesh Failures (Let The Sunshine In)	My Conviction (medley)
Black Boys (medley)		Sodomy (medley)

Three-Five-Zero-Zero (medley)
Walking In Space
What A Piece Of Work Is Man (medley)
Where Do I Go
White Boys (medley)

6/12/65 · **103** · 14 · © 59 · **Half A Sixpence** .... · **$30** RCA Victor 1110
Tommy Steele/Polly James/Norman Allen/John Cleese; sw: David Heneker

All In The Cause Of Economy	I Know What I Am	Money To Burn
Flash, Bang, Wallop!	If The Rain's Got To Fall	Party's On The House
Half A Sixpence	Long Ago	Proper Gentleman

She's Too Far Above Me

8/15/64 · **128** · 13 · 60 · **Hamlet** .... · **$40** Columbia 702 [4]
Richard Burton/Hume Cronyn/Alfred Drake/Eileen Herlie; 4-album set of dialogue from Shakespeare's play

7/3/61 · **84** · 6 · 61 · **Happiest Girl In The World, The** .... · **$50** Columbia 2050
Cyril Ritchard/Janice Rule; mu: Jacques Offenbach; ly: E.Y. Harburg

Adrift On A Star	Glory That Is Grace (medley)	Never Be-devil The Devil
Entrance Of The Courtesans	Greek Marine	Never Trust A Virgin
Eureka	Happiest Girl In The World	Oath, The
Finale, Act I	How Soon, Oh Moon?	Overture (medley)
Five Minutes Of Spring	Love-sick Serenade	Shall We Say Farewell?

That'll Be The Day
Vive La Virtue
Whatever That May Be

2/22/64 · ❶[1] · 90 · ● · © 62 · Hello, Dolly! · **$25** RCA Victor 1087
Carol Channing/David Burns/Eileen Brennan/Charles Nelson Reilly/Mary Jo Catlett; sw: Jerry Herman

Before The Parade Passes By	Hello, Dolly!	It Takes A Woman
Dancing	I Put My Hand In	Motherhood
Elegance	It Only Takes A Moment	Put On Your Sunday Clothes

Ribbons Down My Back
So Long Dearie

11/16/63+ · **38** · 16 · © 63 · **Here's Love** .... · **$50** Columbia 2400
Janis Paige/Craig Stevens; sw: Meredith Willson

Arm In Arm	Here's Love	My State
Big Clown Balloons (medley)	Look, Little Girl	My Wish
Bugle, The	Love Come Take Me Again	Overture (medley)
Expect Things To Happen (medley)	(medley)	Parade (medley)

Pine Cones And Holly Berries
She Hadda Go Back
That Man Over There
You Don't Know

DEBUT	PEAK	WKS	RIAA	CD	ARTIST — Album Title	Catalog	Sym	$	Label & Number

5/16/64 — PEAK **76** — WKS **20** — © 64 — **High Spirits** — $40 — ABC-Paramount 1
Beatrice Lillie/Tammy Grimes/Edward Woodward; sw: Hugh Martin and Timothy Gray
Bicycle Song	Home Sweet Heaven	Something Tells Me	Where Is The Man I Married?
Faster Than Sound	I Know Your Heart	Talking To You	You'd Better Love Me
Forever And A Day	If I Gave You	Was She Prettier Than I?	
Go Into Your Trance	Something Is Coming To Tea	What In The World Did You Want?	

11/27/61+ — PEAK **19** — WKS **47** — © 65 — **How To Succeed In Business Without Really Trying** — $30 — RCA Victor 1066
Robert Morse/Rudy Vallee/Bonnie Scott/Charles Nelson Reilly; sw: Frank Loesser
Been A Long Day	Coffee Break	Happy To Keep His Dinner Warm	Paris Original
Brotherhood Of Man	Company Way	I Believe In You	Rosemary
Cinderella, Darling	Grand Old Ivy	Love From A Heart Of Gold	Secretary Is Not A Toy

7/21/62 — PEAK **125** — WKS **5** — © 66 — **I Can Get It For You Wholesale** — $40 — Columbia 2180
Lillian Roth/Jack Kruschen/Elliott Gould/**Barbra Streisand**; sw: Harold Rome
Ballad Of The Garment Trade	Have I Told You Lately?	Sound Of Money	When Gemini Meets Capricorn
Eat A Little Something	I'm Not A Well Man (medley)	Too Soon	Who Knows?
Family Way	Miss Marmelstein	Way Things Are	
Funny Thing Happened	Momma, Momma, Momma	What Are They Doing To Us Now?	
Gift Today	Overture (medley)	What's In It For Me?	

1/14/67 — PEAK **84** — WKS **16** — © 67 — **I Do! I Do!** — $25 — RCA Victor 1128
Mary Martin/Robert Preston; mu: Harvey Schmidt; ly: Tom Jones
All The Dearly Beloved (medley)	I Do! I Do! (medley)	Roll Up The Ribbons	Well Known Fact
Father Of The Bride	I Love My Wife	Someone Needs Me	What Is A Woman?
Flaming Agnes	Love Isn't Everything	Something Has Happened	When The Kids Get Married
Goodnight	My Cup Runneth Over	This House	Where Are The Snows?
Honeymoon Is Over	Nobody's Perfect	Together Forever (medley)	

1/30/65 — PEAK **126** — WKS **8** — 68 — **I Had A Ball** — $30 — Mercury 6210
Buddy Hackett/Richard Kiley; sw: Jack Lawrence and Stan Freeman
Addie's At It Again	Coney Island, U.S.A.	Garside The Great (medley)	Other Half Of Me
Affluent Society	Dr. Freud	I Had A Ball	Overture (medley)
Almost	Faith	I've Got Everything I Want	Think Beautiful
Can It Be Possible?	Fickle Finger Of Fate	Neighborhood Song	You Deserve Me

6/17/67 — PEAK **177** — WKS **8** — 69 — **Illya Darling** — $25 — United Artists 9901
Melina Mercouri/Orson Bean; mu: Manos Hadjidakis; ly: Joe Darion
After Love	Heaven Help The Sailors On A	Illya Darling	Overture (Entracte)
Bouzouki Nights	Night Like This	Love, Love, Love	Piraeus, My Love
Dear Mr. Schubert	I Think She Needs Me	Medea Tango	Ya Chara
Golden Land	I'll Never Lay Down Anymore	Never On Sunday	Yorgo's Dance (Zebekiko)

3/26/88 — PEAK **126** — WKS **6** — © 70 — **Into The Woods** — $10 — RCA 6796
Bernadette Peters/Joanna Gleason/Chip Zien/Tom Aldredge; sw: Stephen Sondheim
Agony	Giants In The Sky (medley)	Lament	On The Steps Of The Palace
Any Moment (medley)	Hello, Little Girl	Last Midnight (medley)	So Happy
Children Will Listen	I Guess This Is Goodbye (medley)	Maybe They're Magic (medley)	Stay With Me
Cinderella At The Grave	I Know Things Now	Moments In The Woods (medley)	Very Nice Prince (medley)
Ever After	Into The Woods	No More	Your Fault (medley)
First Midnight (medley)	It Takes Two	No One Is Alone	

12/5/60+ — PEAK **9** — WKS **33** — © 71 — **Irma La Douce** — $30 — Columbia 2029
Elizabeth Seal/Keith Michell/Clive Revill; mu: Marguerite Monnot; ly: Alexandre Breffort
Arctic Ballet (medley)	Freedom Of The Seas (medley)	Our Language Of Love	There Is Only One Paris For That
Bridge Of Caulaincourt	From A Prison Cell	She's Got The Lot	(medley)
But	Irma-La-Douce	Sons Of France	Valse Milieu
Christmas Child	Le Grisbi Is Le Root Of Le Evil In	That's A Crime	Wreck Of A Mec
Dis-Donc, Dis-Donc	Man		

1/4/64 — PEAK **87** — WKS **5** — © 72 — **Jennie** — $50 — RCA Victor 1083
Mary Martin/George Wallace/Robin Bailey; mu: Arthur Schwartz; ly: Howard Dietz
Before I Kiss The World Goodbye	I Believe In Takin' A Chance	Over Here	When You're Far Away From New
Born Again	I Still Look At You That Way	Sauce Diable	York Town
For Better Or Worse	Lonely Nights	See Seattle	Where You Are
High Is Better Than Low	Night May Be Dark	Waitin' For The Evening Train	

1/8/72 — PEAK **31** — WKS **10** — © 73 — **Jesus Christ Superstar** — $25 — Decca 1503
Ben Vereen/Jeff Fenbolt/**Yvonne Elliman**/Bob Bingham; mu: **Andrew Lloyd Webber**; ly: Tim Rice
Could We Start Again Please	Hosanna	King Herod's Song	Trial Before Pilate
Everything's Alright	I Don't Know How To Love Him	Pilate's Dream	
Gethsemane (I Only Want To Say)	John Nineteen: Forty-One	Superstar	
Heaven On Their Minds	Judas' Death	This Jesus Must Die	

8/7/82 — PEAK **47**[C] — WKS **2** — © 74 — **Joseph And The Amazing Technicolor Dreamcoat** — $12 — MCA 399
Bill Hutton/Stephen Hope/Laurie Beechman/Barry Tarallo; sw: **Andrew Lloyd Webber**
Any Dream Will Do	Jacob And Sons	Pharaoh Story	Stone The Crows
Benjamin Calypso	Jacob In Egypt	Pharaoh's Dreams Explained	Those Canaan Days
Brothers Come To Egypt (medley)	Joseph All The Time	Poor, Poor Joseph	Who's The Thief?
Close Every Door	Joseph's Coat (medley)	Poor, Poor Pharaoh (medley)	
Go, Go, Go Joseph	Joseph's Dreams	Potiphar	
Grovel, Grovel (medley)	One More Angel In Heaven	Song Of The King (medley)	

3/14/70 — PEAK **187** — WKS **4** — 75 — **Joy** — $25 — RCA Victor 1166
Oscar Brown Jr./Jean Pace/Sivuca; sw: various
Afro Blue	If I Only Had	Nothing But A Fool	What Is A Friend
Brown Baby	Mother Africa's Day	Sky And Sea	Wimmen's Ways
Funky World	Much As I Love You	Time	
Funny Feelin'	New Generation	Under The Sun	

12/25/61+ — PEAK **80** — WKS **12** — 76 — **Kean** — $50 — Columbia 2120
Alfred Drake/Lee Venora; sw: Robert Wright and George Forrest
Apology	King Of London (medley)	Penny Plain, Twopence Colored	Swept Away
Chime In!	Let's Improvise	(medley)	To Look Upon My Love (medley)
Civilized People	Man And Shadow (medley)	Queue At Drury Lane (medley)	Willow, Willow, Willow
Elena	Mayfair Affair (medley)	Service For Service	
Fog And The Grog	Overture (medley)	Sweet Danger	

DEBUT	PEAK	WKS	RIAA	CD	ARTIST — Album Title	Catalog	Sym	$	Label & Number
10/24/92	135	4		© 77	**King And I, The**............			$10	Philips 438007

musical score performed in the studio, not on stage; mu: Richard Rogers; ly: Oscar Hammerstein II; cd: John Mauceri; pf: **Julie Andrews**/Ben Kingsley/Lea Salonga/**Peabo Bryson**; Original Cast version charted in 1951 (#2) on Decca 9008

Anna Unpacks	Hello, Young Lovers	My Lord And Master	Song Of The King
Banquet Scene	Home, Sweet Home	Puzzlement, A	Temple Scene
Finale Ultimo	I Have Dreamed	Shall I Tell You What I Think Of	We Kiss In A Shadow
Garden Scene	I Whistle A Happy Tune	You?	Welcome To Bangkok
Getting To Know You	Main Title	Shall We Dance?	
Harbour	March Of The Siamese Children	Something Wonderful	

Kismet - see MANTOVANI
Alfred Drake/Doretta Morrow/Richard Kiley

3/24/62	139	3		© 78	**Kwamina**			$75	Capitol 1645

Sally Ann Howes/Terry Carter; sw: Richard Adler

Another Time, Another Place	Nothing More To Look Forward To	Seven Sheep, Four Red Shirts And	Welcome Home
Cocoa Bean Song	One Wife	A Bottle Of Gin	What Happened To Me Tonight?
Did You Hear That?	Ordinary People	Something Big	What's Wrong With Me?
Man Can Have No Choice		Sun Is Beginning To Crow	You're As English As

9/24/83	52	15	●	© 79	**La Cage Aux Folles**			$12	RCA Victor 4824

George Hearn/Gene Barry/David Cahn/Linda Haberman; sw: Jerry Herman

Best Of Times	I Am What I Am	Look Over There	We Are What We Are
Cocktail Counterpoint	La Cage Aux Folles	Masculinity	With Anne On My Arm
Finale	Little More Mascara	Song On The Sand (La Da Da Da)	With You On My Arm

4/11/87	106	15	▲	© 80	**Les Miserables**			$15	Relativity 8140 [2]

Colm Wilkinson/Roger Allam/Rebecca Caine/Patti LuPone; original London cast; mu: Claude-Michel Schonberg; ly: Herbert Kretzmer

At The End Of The Day	Do You Hear The People Sing?	In My Life (medley)	One Day More
Attack, The	Dog Eats Dog	Javert's Suicide	Red And Black
Beggars At The Feast (medley)	Drink With Me	Little Fall Of Rain	Stars
Bring Him Home	Empty Chairs At Empty Tables	Little People	Wedding Chorale
Castle On A Cloud	Finale (medley)	Look Down	Who Am I?
Come To Me (Fantine's Death)	Heart Full Of Love (medley)	Lovely Ladies	
(medley)	I Dreamed A Dream	Master Of The House	
Confrontation (medley)	I Saw Him Once (medley)	On My Own	

6/20/87	117	10	▲⁴	© 81	**Les Miserables** ....C:#21/43			$15	Geffen 24151 [2]

Colm Wilkinson/Terrence Mann/Judy Kuhn/Randy Graff; Broadway cast; mu: Claude-Michel Schonberg; ly: Herbert Kretzmer

At The End Of The Day	Drink With Me	Little Fall Of Rain	Red And Black
Beggars At The Feast (medley)	Empty Chairs At Empty Tables	Little People (medley)	Stars
Bring Him Home	First Attack	Look Down	Thenadier Waltz Of Treachery
Castle On A Cloud	Heart Full Of Love	Lovely Ladies	Turning
Come To Me (Fantine's Death)	I Dreamed A Dream	Master Of The House	Wedding Chorale (medley)
Confrontation	In My Life	On My Own	Who Am I?
Do You Hear The People Sing?	Javert At The Barricade (medley)	One Day More	
Dog Eats Dog	Javert's Suicide	Plumet Attack	

1/11/92	184	1	●	© 82	**Les Miserables: Highlights From The Complete Symphonic**			$10	First Night 1099
					International Cast Record ....C:#42/1				

features performers drawn from worldwide productions of musical; mu: Claude-Michel Schonberg; ly: Alain Boublil & Herbert Kretzmer

ABC Cafe (medley)	Do You Hear The People Sing?	Javert's Suicide	Stars
At The End Of The Day	Drink With Me	Master Of The House	Trial, The (medley)
Bring Him Home	Empty Chairs At Empty Tables	On My Own	Who Am I? (medley)
Come To Me (Fantine's Death)	Heart Full Of Love	One Day More	
Confrontation	I Dreamed A Dream	Red And Black (medley)	

12/29/56	19	3		© 83	**Li'l Abner**			$50	Columbia 5150

Edith Adams/Peter Palmer/Howard St. John/Stubby Kaye; mu: Gene de Paul; ly: Johnny Mercer

Country's In The Very Best Of	Jubilation T. Cornpone	Oh, Happy Day	Typical Day
Hands	Love In A Home	Progress Is The Root Of All Evil	Unnecessary Town
I'm Past My Prime	Matrimonial Stomp	Put 'Em Back	
If I Had My Druthers	Namely You	Rag Offen The Bush	

12/6/97	162	10	●	© 84	**Lion King, The**			$10	Walt Disney 60802

John Vickery/Samuel E. Wright/Geoff Hoyle; mu: Elton John; ly: Tim Rice

Be Prepared	Grasslands Chant	Lion Sleeps Tonight	Rafiki Mourns
Can You Feel The Love Tonight	Hakuna Matata	Lioness Hunt	Shadowland
Chow Down	He Lives In You	Madness Of King Scar	Simba Confronts Scar
Circle Of Life	I Just Can't Wait To Be King	Morning Report	Stampede, The
Endless Night	King Of Pride Rock	One By One	They Live In You

1/19/63	44	10		© 85	**Little Me**			$30	RCA Victor 1078

Sid Caesar/Virginia Martin/Nancy Andrews; mu: Cy Coleman; ly: Carolyn Leigh

Be A Performer!	Goodbye (The Prince's Farewell)	Little Me	Truth, The
Boom-Boom	Here's To Us	Other Side Of The Tracks	
Deep Down Inside	I Love You	Poor Little Hollywood Star	
Dimples	I've Got Your Number	Real Live Girl	

5/5/73	94	12		© 86	**Little Night Music, A**			$15	Columbia 32265

Glynis Johns/Len Cariou/Hermione Gingold; sw: Stephen Sondheim

Every Day A Little Death	Later (medley)	Overture (medley)	Sun Won't Set
Finale	Liaisons	Perpetual Anticipation	Weekend In The Country
Glamorous Life	Miller's Son	Remember?	You Must Meet My Wife
In Praise Of Women	Night Waltz (medley)	Send In The Clowns	
It Would Have Been Wonderful	Now (medley)	Soon (medley)	

3/22/97	116	11		© 87	**Lord Of The Dance**		[I]	$10	Philips 533757

music from the Irish dance production starring world champion dancer Michael Flatley; cp: Ronan Hardiman

Breakout	Gypsy	Our Wedding Day	Suil A Ruin
Celtic Dream	Lament	Siamsa	Victory
Cry Of The Celts	Lord Of The Dance	Spirit In The New World	Warriors
Fiery Nights	Nightmare	Stolen Kiss	

DEBUT	PEAK	WKS	RIAA	CD	ARTIST — Album Title	Catalog	Sym	$	Label & Number

1/11/69 · 185 · 2 · 88 · Maggie Flynn .... **$30** RCA Victor 2009

Shirley Jones/Jack Cassidy; sw: Hugo Peretti/Luigi Creatore (**Hugo & Luigi**)/George David Weiss

Game Of War	Learn How To Laugh	Pitter Patter
How About A Ball?	Look Around Your Little World	Pitter Patter (Reprise)
I Won't Let It Happen Again	Maggie Flynn	Thank You Song
I Wouldn't Have You Any Other	Mr. Clown	They're Never Gonna Make Me
Way	Nice Cold Mornin'	Fight

Why Can't I Walk Away

7/2/66 · 23 · 66 · ● © · 89 · Mame .... **$25** Columbia 3000

Angela Lansbury/Bea Arthur/Ron Young/Margaret Hall; sw: Jerry Herman

Bosom Buddies	It's Today	Man In The Moon
Gooch's Song	Letter, The	My Best Girl
If He Walked Into My Life	Mame	Open A New Window

St. Bridget
That's How Young I Feel
We Need A Little Christmas

1/22/66+ · 31 · 167 · ● © · 90 · Man Of La Mancha .... **$25** Kapp 4505

Richard Kiley/Irving Jacobson/Joan Diener; mu: Mitch Leigh; ly: Joe Darion

Abduction, The	Dulcinea	It's All The Same
Aldonza	Golden Helmet (medley)	Little Bird, Little Bird
Barber's Song (medley)	I Really Like Him	Little Gossip
Dubbing (Knight Of The Woeful	I'm Only Thinking Of Him	Man Of La Mancha (I, Don Quixote)
Countenance)	Impossible Dream (The Quest)	

To Each His Dulcinea (To Every
Man His Dream)
What Do You Want Of Me?

10/17/64 · 137 · 4 · 91 · Merry Widow, The .... **$30** RCA Victor 1094

Patrice Munsel/Bob Wright; sw: Franz Lehar

Finale Act I	I Love You So (The Merry Widow	Riding On A Carousel
Finale Act II	Waltz)	Romance
Girls At Maxim's	Maxim's	Villa
	Respectable Wife (medley)	When In France (medley)

Who Knows The Way To My Heart?
Women

11/20/61+ · 10 · 41 · © · 92 · Milk And Honey .... **$40** RCA Victor 1065

Robert Weede/Mimi Benzell/Molly Picon; sw: Jerry Herman

As Simple As That	I Will Follow You	Like A Young Man
Chin Up, Ladies	Independence Day Hora	Milk And Honey
Hymn To Hymie	Let's Not Waste A Moment	Shalom

That Was Yesterday
There's No Reason In The World
Wedding, The

3/10/90 · 122 · 11 · ▲ © · 93 · Miss Saigon .... **$15** Geffen 24271 [2]

Jonathan Pryce/Claire Moore/Lea Salonga/Simon Bowman; original London cast; mu: Claude-Michel Schonberg and Alain Boublil; ly: Richard Maltby Jr. and Alain Boublil

American Dream	Heat Is On In Saigon	Morning Of The Dragon
Bui-Doi	Her Or Me	Movie In My Mind
Ceremony (Dju Vui Vai)	I Still Believe	Please
Confrontation, The	I'd Give My Life For You	Revelation, The
Dance, The	If You Want To Die In Bed	Room 317
Deal, The	Last Night Of The World	Sacred Bird
Fall Of Saigon	Let Me See His Western Nose	Sun And Moon

Telephone Song
This Is The Hour
This Money's Yours
What A Waste
What's This I Find
Why God Why?

8/4/56 · 11 · 4 · © · 94 · Most Happy Fella, The .... **$30** Columbia 2330

Robert Weede/Jo Sullivan/Art Lund/Susan Johnson; sw: Frank Loesser

Abbondanza	I Like Ev'rybody	My Heart Is So Full Of You
Big "D"	I Made A Fist	Ooh, My Feet (medley)
Don't Cry	Joey, Joey, Joey	Overture (medley)
Happy To Make Your Acquaintance	Mama, Mama	Rosabella
How Beautiful The Days	Most Happy Fella	Somebody Somewhere

Song Of A Summer Night
Sposalizio
Standing On The Corner
Warm All Over

12/1/62 · 14 · 24 · © · 95 · Mr. President .... **$30** Columbia 2270

Robert Ryan/Nanette Fabray; sw: Irving Berlin

Don't Be Afraid Of Romance	In Our Hide-Away	Meat And Potatoes
Empty Pockets Filled With Love	Is He The Only Man In The World	Overture (medley)
First Lady	It Gets Lonely In The White House	Pigtails And Freckles
Glad To Be Home	Laugh It Up	Secret Service (medley)
I'm Gonna Get Him	Let's Go Back To The Waltz	Song For Belly Dancer
I've Got To Be Around (medley)	(medley)	They Love Me

This Is A Great Country
Washington Twist
You Need A Hobby

2/24/58 · ❶ 12 · 245 · ▲ © · 96 · Music Man, The .... **$25** Capitol 990

Robert Preston/Barbara Cook; sw: Meredith Willson

Gary, Indiana	Lida Rose (medley)	Pick-A-Little, Talk-A-Little (medley)
Goodnight Ladies (medley)	Marian The Librarian	Rock Island (medley)
Goodnight My Someone	My White Knight	Sadder-But-Wiser Girl For Me
Iowa Stubborn	Overture (medley)	Seventy Six Trombones
It's You	Piano Lesson	Shipoopi

Sincere
Till There Was You
Wells Fargo Wagon
Will I Ever Tell You (medley)
Ya Got Trouble

4/28/56 · ❶ 15 · 480 · ▲³ © · 97 · My Fair Lady .... **$30** Columbia 5090

Rex Harrison/**Julie Andrews**/Stanley Holloway/Robert Coote; mu: Frederick Loewe; ly: Alan Jay Lerner

Ascot Gavotte	I've Grown Accustomed To Her	Rain In Spain
Get Me To The Church On Time	Face	Show Me
Hymn To Him	Just You Wait	Why Can't The English? (medley)
I Could Have Danced All Night	On The Street Where You Live	With A Little Bit Of Luck
I'm An Ordinary Man	Overture (medley)	Without You

Wouldn't It Be Loverly
You Did It

6/28/86 · 150 · 6 · © · 98 · Mystery Of Edwin Drood, The .... **$12** Polydor 827969

Betty Buckley/**Cleo Laine**/George Rose; sw: **Rupert Holmes**

Both Sides Of The Coin	Man Could Go Quite Mad	No Good Can Come From Bad
Ceylon	Moonfall	Off To The Races
Don't Quit While You're Ahead	Moonfall Quartet	Out On A Limerick
Garden Path To Hell	Name Of Love (medley)	Perfect Strangers
Jasper's Confession	Never The Luck	Puffer's Confession

Setting Up The Score
There You Are
Two Kinsmen
Wages Of Sin
Writing On The Wall (Finale)

8/5/57 · 17 · 3 · © · 99 · New Girl In Town .... **$50** RCA Victor 1027

Gwen Verdon/Thelma Ritter/George Wallace; sw: Bob Merrill

Anna Lilla	Flings	On The Farm
At The Check Apron Ball	If That Was Love	Roll Yer Socks Up
Chess And Checkers	It's Good To Be Alive	Sunshine Girl
Did You Close Your Eyes?	Look At 'Er	There Ain't No Flies On Me

Ven I Valse
Yer My Friend Ain'tcha?

3/13/71 · 61 · 19 · © · 100 · No, No, Nanette .... **$15** Columbia 30563

Ruby Keeler/Jack Gilford/Bobby Van/Helen Gallagher; mu: Vincent Youmans; ly: Irving Caesar and Otto Harbach

Call Of The Sea	I've Confessed To The Breeze	Tea For Two
Finaletto Act II	No, No, Nanette	Telephone Girlie
I Want To Be Happy	Take A Little One-Step (Finale)	Too Many Rings Around Rosie

Waiting For You
Where-Has-My-Hubby-Gone Blues
You Can Dance With Any Girl

DEBUT	PEAK	WKS	RIAA	CD	ARTIST — Album Title	Catalog	Sym	$	Label & Number

4/21/62 — PEAK **5** — WKS **62** — ©101 **No Strings** — **$40** Capitol 1695

Richard Kiley/Diahann Carroll/Alvin Epstein/Polly Rowles; sw: Richard Rodgers

Be My Host	La La La	Maine
Eager Beaver	Loads Of Love	Man Who Has Everything
Finale	Look No Further	No Strings
How Sad	Love Makes The World Go	Nobody Told Me

Orthodox Fool / Sweetest Sounds / You Don't Tell Me

11/3/62 — PEAK **4** — WKS **99** ● — ©102 **Oliver!** — **$25** RCA Victor 2004

Clive Revill/Georgia Brown/Bruce Prochnik; sw: Lionel Bart

As Long As He Needs Me	Food, Glorious Food	Oliver
Be Back Soon	I Shall Scream	Oom-Pah-Pah
Boy For Sale (medley)	I'd Do Anything	Reviewing The Situation
Consider Yourself	It's A Fine Life	Where Is Love? (medley)
Finale	My Name	Who Will Buy?

You've Got To Pick A Pocket Or Two

12/11/65+ — PEAK **59** — WKS **32** — ©103 **On A Clear Day You Can See Forever** — **$25** RCA Victor 2006

Barbara Harris/John Cullum/Tito Vandis; mu: Burton Lane; ly: Alan Jay Lerner

Come Back To Me	Melinda	On The S.S. Bernard Cohn
Don't Tamper With My Sister	On A Clear Day (You Can See	She Wasn't You
Hurry! It's Lovely Up Here!	Forever)	Tosy And Cosh

Wait Till We're Sixty-Five / What Did I Have That I Don't Have? / When I'm Being Born Again

1/4/64 — PEAK **37** — WKS **15** — ©104 **110 In The Shade** — **$40** RCA Victor 1085

Robert Horton/Inga Swenson/Stephen Douglass; mu: Harvey Schmidt; ly: Tom Jones

Everything Beautiful Happens At	Is It Really Me?	Melisande
Night	Little Red Hat	Old Maid
Finale	Lizzie's Comin' Home	Poker Polka
Gonna Be Another Hot Day	Love, Don't Turn Away	Rain Song
Hungry Men	Man And A Woman	Raunchy

Simple Little Things / You're Not Foolin' Me

Over Here! - see ANDREWS SISTERS

Patty Andrews/Maxene Andrews/**John Travolta**; sw: Richard M. Sherman/Robert B. Sherman

9/10/94 — PEAK **103** — WKS **2** — ©105 **Passion** — **$10** Angel 55251

Marin Mazzie/Donna Murphy/Jere Shea/Gregg Edelman; sw: Stephen Sondheim

Farewell Letter	Garden Sequence	Loving You
First Letter	Happiness	No One Has Ever Loved Me
Flashback	I Read	Second Letter
Forty Days	I Wish I Could Forget You	Soldiers' Gossip
Fourth Letter	Is This What You Call Love?	Sunrise Letter

Third Letter / Transition / Trio

4/2/55 — PEAK **4** — WKS **10** — ©106 **Peter Pan** — **$50** RCA Victor 1019

Mary Martin/**Cyril Ritchard**; mu: Mark Charlap and Jule Styne; ly: Carolyn Leigh/Betty Comden/Adolph Green; LP: RCA Victor LOC-1019 (#4); EP: RCA Victor EOC-1019 (#5)

Distant Melody	I'm Flying	Oh My Mysterious Lady
Hook's Tango	I've Gotta Crow	Pirate Song
Hook's Waltz	Indians	Tarantella
I Won't Grow Up	Never, Never Land	Tender Shepherd

Ugg-A-Wugg / Wendy

5/23/87+ — PEAK **33** — WKS **255** ▲⁴ — ©107 **Phantom Of The Opera, The** — C:#12/87 — **$15** Polydor 831273 [2]

Michael Crawford/Sarah Brightman/Steve Barton; original London cast; mu: **Andrew Lloyd Webber**; ly: Charles Hart

All I Ask Of You	Masquerade	Prima Donna
Angel Of Music	Mirror (Angel Of Music)	Raoul, I've Been There (medley)
Down Once More (medley)	Music Of The Night	Stranger Than You Dreamt It
Entr'acte	Notes	Think Of Me
I Remember	Phantom Of The Opera	Track Down This Murderer (medley)
Little Lotte	Point Of No Return	Twisted Every Way
Magical Lasso	Poor Fool, He Makes Me Laugh	Wandering Child

Why Have You Brought Me Here (medley) / Why So Silent / Wishing You Were Somehow Here Again

3/10/90+ — PEAK **46** — WKS **331** ▲⁴ — ©108 **Phantom Of The Opera, Highlights From The** — C:#23/24 — **$10** Polydor 831563

second volume released from the London stage production

All I Ask Of You	Masquerade	Point Of No Return
Angel Of Music	Mirror (Angel Of Music)	Prima Donna
Down Once More (medley)	Music Of The Night	Think Of Me
Entr'acte	Phantom Of The Opera	Track Down This Murderer (medley)

Wishing You Were Somehow Here Again

1/13/73 — PEAK **129** — WKS **10** — ©109 **Pippin** — **$15** Motown 760

Ben Vereen/Jill Clayburgh/Irene Ryan; sw: Stephen Schwartz

Corner Of The Sky	Kind Of Woman	No Time At All
Extraordinary	Love Song	On The Right Track
Glory	Magic To Do	Simple Joys
I Guess I'll Miss The Man	Morning Glow	Spread A Little Sunshine

War Is A Science / With You

6/6/81 — PEAK **178** — WKS **3** — ©110 **Pirates Of Penzance, The** — **$15** Elektra 601 [2]

Kevin Kline/Estelle Parsons/**Linda Ronstadt/Rex Smith**; ly: W.S. Gilbert; mu: Arthur Sullivan

All Is Prepared	No, I Am Brave	Poor Wandering One
Away, Away! My Heart's On Fire	Now For The Pirates' Lair!	Pour, O Pour The Pirate Sherry
Climbing Over Rocky Mountain	Oh, Better Far To Live And Die	Rollicking Band Of Pirates We
Hold, Monsters!	Oh, Dry The Glistening Tear	Sighing Softly To The River
How Beautifully Blue The Sky	Oh, False One, You Have Deceived	Sorry Her Lot
Hush, Hush! Not A Word	Me!	Stay, Frederic, Stay!
I Am The Very Model Of A Modern	Oh, Is There Not One Maiden	Stay, We Must Not Lose Our
Major-General	Breast	Senses
My Eyes Are Fully Open	Oh, Men Of Dark And Dismal Fate	Stop, Ladies, Pray!

Then Frederic / What Ought We To Do? / When A Felon's Not Engaged In His Employment / When Frederic Was A Little Lad / When The Foeman Bares His Steel / When You Had Left Our Pirate Fold / With Cat-Like Tread, Upon Our Prey We Steal

5/5/01 — PEAK **139** — WKS **10** — ©111 **Producers, The** — **$10** Sony Classical 89646

Nathan Lane/Matthew Broderick/Roger Bart/Gary Beach/Cady Huffman; sw: **Mel Brooks**

Along Came Bialy	I Wanna Be A Producer	Opening Night (Reprise)
Betrayed	In Old Bavaria	Prisoners Of Love (Leo & Max)
Der Guten Tag Hop-Clop	Keep It Gay	Springtime For Hitler
Goodbye!	King Of Broadway	That Face
Haben Sie Gehört Das	Opening Night	'Til Him

We Can Do It / When You Got It, Flaunt It / Where Did We Go Right? / You Never Say Good Luck On Opening Night

1/25/69 — PEAK **95** — WKS **12** — ©112 **Promises, Promises** — **$20** United Artists 9902

Jerry Orbach/Jill O'Hara/Edward Winter; mu: **Burt Bacharach**; ly: Hal David

Christmas Day	Knowing When To Leave	Turkey Lurkey Time
Fact Can Be A Beautiful Thing	Our Little Secret	Upstairs
Grapes Of Roth	Overture (medley)	Wanting Things
Half As Big As Life (medley)	Promises, Promises	Where Can You Take A Girl?
I'll Never Fall In Love Again	She Likes Basketball	Whoever You Are

You'll Think Of Someone / Young Pretty Girl Like You

ORIGINAL CASTS

DEBUT	PEAK	WKS	RIAA	CD	ARTIST — Album Title	Catalog	Sym	$	Label & Number

6/13/70 — **138** — WKS 5 — CD 113 — **Purlie** .... **$40** Ampex 40101
Cleavon Little/**Melba Moore**/Sherman Hemsley/Helen Martin; mu: Gary Geld; ly: Peter Udell

Barrels Of War (medley)	God's Alive	I Got Love
Big Fish, Little Fish	Great White Father	New Fangled Preacher Man
Down Home	Harder They Fall	Purlie
First Thing Monday Mornin'	He Can Do It	Skinnin' A Cat

Unborn Love (medley)
Walk Him Up The Stairs
World Is Comin' To A Start

5/25/59 — **47** — WKS 1 — ©114 — **Redhead** .... **$40** RCA Victor 1048
Gwen Verdon/Richard Kiley/Leonard Stone; mu: Albert Hague; ly: Dorothy Fields

Behave Yourself	Just For Once	Right Finger Of My Left Hand
Chase (medley)	Look Who's In Love	She's Just Not Enough Woman For
Erbie Fitch's Twitch	Merely Marvelous	Me
Finale (medley)	My Girl Is Just Enough Woman For	Simpson Sisters' Door
I'll Try	Me	Two Faces In The Dark
I'm Back In Circulation	Pick-Pocket Tango	Uncle Sam Rag

We Loves Ya, Jimey

9/14/96 — **19** — WKS 22 ▲ — ©115 — **Rent** .... **$15** DreamWorks 50003 [2]
Adam Pascal/Anthony Rapp/Daphne Rubin-Vega; sw: Jonathan Larson

Another Day	La Vie Boheme	Seasons Of Love [feat. Stevie
Christmas Bells	La Vie Boheme B	Wonder]
Contact	Life Support	Seasons Of Love B
Finale B	Light My Candle	Take Me Or Leave Me
Goodbye Love	On The Street	Tango: Maureen
Halloween	One Song Glory	Today 4 U
Happy New Year	Out Tonight	Tune Up #1
Happy New Year B	Over The Moon	Tune Up #2
I Should Tell You	Rent	Tune Up #3
I'll Cover You	Santa Fe	Voice Mail #1
I'll Cover You Reprise	Seasons Of Love	Voice Mail #2

Voice Mail #3
Voice Mail #4
Voice Mail #5
We're Okay
What You Own
Will I?
Without You
You Okay Honey?
You'll See
Your Eyes

3/30/96+ — **48** — WKS 27 ▲ — ©116 — **Riverdance - Music From The Show** .... **$10** Celtic Heartbeat 82816
traditional Irish music from the music and dance revue production; sw: Bill Whelan

American Wake (The Nova Scotia	Firedance	Macedonian Morning
Set)	Harvest, The	Marta's Dance (medley)
Andalucia	Heart's Cry	Reel Around The Sun
Caoineadh Cu Chulainn (Lament)	Home And The Heartland	Riverdance
Countess Cathleen (medley)	Lift The Wings	Riverdance (Dance Reprise)

Russian Dervish (medley)
Shivna
Slip Into Spring
Women Of The Sidhe (medley)

4/10/65 — **54** — WKS 34 — ©117 — **Roar Of The Greasepaint, The-The Smell Of The Crowd** .... **$25** RCA Victor 1109
Anthony Newley/**Cyril Ritchard**; sw: Anthony Newley and Leslie Bricusse

Beautiful Land	My First Love Song	That's What It Is To Be Young
Feeling Good	My Way	Things To Remember
It Isn't Enough	Nothing Can Stop Me Now!	This Dream
Joker, The	Put It In The Book	What A Man!
Look At That Face	Sweet Beginning (medley)	Where Would You Be Without Me?

Who Can I Turn To (When Nobody
 Needs Me)
With All Due Respect
Wonderful Day Like Today

11/27/61+ — **36** — WKS 22 — ©118 — **Sail Away** .... **$40** Capitol 1643
Elaine Stritch/James Hurst/Grover Dale/Evelyn Russell; sw: **Noel Coward**

Beatnik Love Affair	Go Slow, Johnny	Sail Away
Come To Me	Later Than Spring	Something Very Strange
Customer's Always Right	Little Ones' ABC	Useful Phrases
Don't Turn Away From Love	Passenger's Always Right	When You Want Me

Where Shall I Find Him?
Why Do The Wrong People Travel?
You're A Long, Long Way From
 America

2/24/01 — **191** — WKS 1 — ©119 — **Seussical: The Musical** .... **$10** Decca Broad. 159792
Kevin Chamberlin/Janine LaManna/Michele Pawk/Anthony Blair Hall; mu: Stephen Flaherty; ly: Lynn Ahrens

All For You	Egg, Nest And Tree	Horton Sits On The Egg/Act 1
Alone In The Universe	Finale/Oh, The Thinks You Can	Finale
Alone In The Universe (Reprise)	Think	How Lucky You Are
Amazying Gertrude	Green Eggs And Ham (Curtain Call)	How Lucky You Are (Mayzie's
Amayzing Mayzie	Havin' A Hunch	Reprise)
Biggest Blame Fool	Here On Who	How To Raise A Child
Chasing The Whos	Horton Hears A Who	It's Possible (McElligot's Pool)
Day For The Cat In The Hat		Mayzie In Palm Beach

Military, The
Monkey Around
Notice Me, Horton
Oh, The Thinks You Can Think
One Feather Tail Of Miss Gertrude
 McFuzz
People Versus Horton The Elephant
Solla Sollew

5/17/69 — **174** — WKS 6 — ©120 — **1776** .... **$20** Columbia 3310
William Daniels/Ken Howard/Howard da Silva; sw: Sherman Edwards

But, Mr. Adams	Is Anybody There?	Piddle, Twiddle And Resolve
Cool, Cool, Considerate Men	Lees Of Old Virginia	(medley)
Egg, The	Molasses To Rum	1776 (Overture)
He Plays The Violin	Momma Look Sharp	Sit Down, John

Till Then (medley)
Yours, Yours, Yours

6/22/63 — **15** — WKS 17 — ©121 — **She Loves Me** .... **$50** MGM 4118 [2]
Barbara Cook/Daniel Massey/Barbara Baxley/Jack Cassidy; mu: Jerry Bock; ly: Sheldon Harnick

Days Gone By	I Resolve	Romantic Atmosphere
Dear Friend	Ice Cream	She Loves Me
Good Morning, Good Day	Ilona	Sounds While Selling
Goodbye, Georg	No More Candy	Tango Tragique
Grand Knowing You	Overture To Act II	Three Letters
I Don't Know His Name	Perspective	Tonight At Eight

Trip To The Library
Try Me
Twelve Days To Christmas
Where's My Shoe?
Will He Like Me?

9/15/62 — **95** — WKS 6 — ©122 — **Show Boat** .... **$25** Columbia 2220
John Raitt/Barbara Cook/William Warfield/Anita Darian; mu: Jerome Kern; ly: Oscar Hammerstein II

After The Ball	Finale Act I	Ol' Man River
Bill	Finale Act II (medley)	Opening Act II
Can't Help Lovin' Dat Man	Life Upon The Wicked Stage	Where's The Mate For Me?
Cotton Blossom	Make Believe (medley)	(medley)

Why Do I Love You?
You Are Love

4/16/55 — **9** — WKS 6 — ©123 — **Silk Stockings** .... **$50** RCA Victor 1016
Hildegarde Neff/**Don Ameche**/Gretchen Wyler/Leon Belasco; sw: Cole Porter

All Of You (medley)	It's A Chemical Reaction, That's All	Satin And Silk
As On Through The Seasons We	Josephine	Siberia
Sail	Paris Loves Lovers	Silk Stockings
Hail Bibinski	Red Blues	Stereophonic Sound

Too Bad
Without Love

DEBUT	PEAK	WKS	RIAA	CD	ARTIST — Album Title	Catalog	Sym	$	Label & Number
1/8/66	128	8		©124	**Skyscraper**			$30	Capitol 2422

Julie Harris/Peter Marshall/Charles Nelson Reilly; mu: James Van Heusen; ly: Sammy Cahn

Don't Worry / Haute Couture / Local 403 / Run For Your Life
Everybody Has The Right To Be / I'll Only Miss Her When I Think Of / More Than One Way / Spare That Building
Wrong / Her / Occasional Flight Of Fancy
Gaiety, The / Just The Crust / Opposites

| 12/21/59+ | ❶16 | 276 | ● | ©125 | **Sound Of Music, The** | | | $30 | Columbia 2020 |

Mary Martin/Theodore Bikel; mu: Richard Rodgers; ly: Oscar Hammerstein II

Climb Ev'ry Mountain / Laendler / No Way To Stop It / Sixteen Going On Seventeen
Do-Re-Me / Lonely Goatherd / Ordinary Couple / So Long, Farewell
Edelweiss / Maria / Preludium / Sound Of Music
How Can Love Survive / My Favorite Things / Processional

| 11/24/62+ | 3 | 76 | | ©126 | **Stop The World-I Want To Get Off** | | | $25 | London 88001 |

Anthony Newley/Anna Quayle; sw: Leslie Bricusse and Anthony Newley

A.B.C. Song (medley) / I Wanna Be Rich (medley) / Once In A Lifetime / **What Kind Of Fool Am I** [Anthony
All American / Lumbered / Overture (medley) / Newley] 85
Family Fugue (medley) / Meilinki Meilchick (medley) / Someone Nice Like You
Glorious Russian (medley) / Mumbo Jumbo / Typically English
Gonna Build A Mountain / Nag! Nag! Nag! (medley) / Typische Deutsche

| 4/7/62 | 81 | 11 | | 127 | **Subways Are For Sleeping** | | | $50 | Columbia 2130 |

Sydney Chaplin/Carol Lawrence/Orson Bean; mu: Jule Styne; ly: Betty Comden and Adolph Green

Be A Santa / I Just Can't Wait / Ride Through The Night (medley) / Swing Your Projects
Comes Once In A Lifetime / I Said It And I'm Glad / Strange Duet / What Is This Feeling In The Air?
Girls Like Me / I Was A Shoo-In / Subway Directions (medley) / Who Knows What Might Have
How Can You Describe A Face? / I'm Just Taking My Time / Subways Are For Sleeping / Been?

| 8/25/84 | 149 | 11 | | ©128 | **Sunday In The Park With George** | | | $15 | RCA Victor 5042 [2] |

Mandy Patinkin/Bernadette Peters/Brent Spiner/Judith Moore; sw: Stephen Sondheim

Beautiful / Day Off / It's Hot Up Here / Putting It Together (medley)
Children And Art / Everybody Loves Louis / Lesson #8 / Sunday
Chromolume #7 (medley) / Finishing The Hat / Move On / Sunday In The Park With George
Color And Light / Gossip / No Life / We Do Not Belong Together

| 11/20/93 | 170 | 1 | | ©129 | **Sunset Boulevard - The Andrew Lloyd Webber Musical** | | | $15 | Polydor 519767 [2] |

Patti LuPone/Kevin Anderson/Daniel Benzali/Meredith Braun; mu: **Andrew Lloyd Webber**

As If We Never Said Goodbye / Greatest Star Of All / Perfect Year / This Time Next Year
Eternal Youth Is Worth A Little / Lady's Paying / Salome / Too Much In Love To Care
Suffering / Let's Have Lunch / Sunset Boulevard / With One Look
Girl Meets Boy / New Ways To Dream / Surrender

| 10/1/94 | 191 | 1 | | ©130 | **Sunset Boulevard, Andrew Lloyd Webber's - American Premiere Recording** | | | $15 | Really Useful 3507 [2] |

Glenn Close/Alan Campbell/Judy Kuhn/George Hearn; mu: **Andrew Lloyd Webber**

As If We Never Said Goodbye / Every Movie's A Circus / New Year's Eve (Back At The / There's Been A Call/Journey To
At The House On Sunset / Final Scene / House On Sunset) / Paramount
Back At The House On Sunset / Girl Meets Boy / Overture/I Guess It Was 5 A.M. / This Time Next Year
Betty's Office At Paramount / Greatest Star Of All / Paramount Conversation / Too Much In Love To Care
Car Chase / Lady's Paying / Perfect Year / Who's Betty Schaefer?
Completion Of The Script / Let's Have Lunch / Phone Call / With One Look
Entr'acte / New Ways To Dream / Salome
Eternal Youth Is Worth A Little / New Year's Eve / Sunset Boulevard
Suffering / Surrender

| 6/9/79 | 78 | 11 | | ©131 | **Sweeney Todd-The Demon Barber Of Fleet Street** | | | $20 | RCA Victor 3379 [2] |

Angela Lansbury/Len Cariou/Victor Garber/Edmund Lyndeck; sw: Stephen Sondheim

Ah, Miss (medley) / Green Finch And Linnet Bird / Lift Your Razor High, Sweeney! / Prelude (medley)
Attend The Tale Of Sweeney Todd / (medley) / (medley) / Pretty Women (medley)
(medley) / His Hands Were Quick, His Fingers / Little Priest / Sweeney Pondered And Sweeney
Barber And His Wife (medley) / Strong (medley) / My Friends (medley) / Planned (medley)
By The Sea / Johanna / No Place Like London (medley) / Sweeny'd Waited Too Long Before
Contest, The (medley) / Kiss Me (medley) / Not While I'm Around / (medley)
Epiphany (medley) / Ladies In Their Sensitivities / Parlor Songs / Wait (medley)
Final Sequence (medley) / (medley) / Pirelli's Miracle Elixir (medley) / Wigmaker Sequence (medley)
God, That's Good! / Letter, The (medley) / Poor Thing / Worst Pies In London

| 3/12/66 | 92 | 16 | | ©132 | **Sweet Charity** | | | $25 | Columbia 2900 |

Gwen Verdon/John McMartin/Thelma Oliver/Ruth Buzzi; mu: Cy Coleman; ly: Dorothy Fields

Baby Dream Your Dream / I'm A Brass Band / Sweet Charity / You Should See Yourself
Big Spender / I'm The Bravest Individual / There's Gotta Be Something Better
Charity's Soliloquy / If My Friends Could See Me Now / Than This
Charity's Theme / Rhythm Of Life / Too Many Tomorrows
I Love To Cry At Weddings / Rich Man's Frug / Where Am I Going?

| 1/16/61 | 15 | 34 | | ©133 | **Tenderloin** | | | $50 | Capitol 1492 |

Maurice Evans/Ron Husmann/Wayne Miller/Eileen Rodgers; mu: Jerry Bock; ly: Sheldon Harnick

Army Of The Just / Dr. Brock / My Gentle Young Johnny / Tommy, Tommy
Artificial Flowers / Good Clean Fun / My Miss Mary / Trial, The
Bless This Land / How The Money Changes Hands / Picture Of Happiness / What's In It For You?
Dear Friend / Little Old New York / Reform

| 3/24/79 | 167 | 6 | | ©134 | **They're Playing Our Song** | | | $12 | Casablanca 7141 |

Robert Klein/Lucie Arnaz; mu: **Marvin Hamlisch**; ly: **Carole Bayer Sager**

Entr'acte / I Still Believe In Love / Right / When You're In My Arms
Fallin' / If He Really Knew Me / They're Playing Our Song (The / Workin' It Out
Fill In The Words / Just For Tonight / Bows)

| 8/6/66 | 145 | 2 | | 135 | **Time For Singing, A** | | | $60 | Warner 1639 |

Ivor Emmanuel/Tessie O'Shea/Shani Wallis; mu: John Morris; ly: Gerald Freedman and John Morris

Come You Men / I've Nothing To Give You (medley) / Peace Come To Every Heart / Three Ships
Far From Home / Let Me Love You (medley) / (medley) / Time For Singing
Gone In Sorrow (medley) / Mountains Sing Back / Someone Must Try / What A Good Day Is Saturday
How Green Was My Valley / Oh, How I Adore Your Name / Tell Her / When He Looks At Me
I Wonder If / Old Long John / That's What Young Ladies Do / Why Would Anyone Want To Get
I'm Always Wrong / / There Is Beautiful You Are / Married

ORIGINAL CASTS

DEBUT	PEAK	WKS	RIAA	CD	ARTIST — Album Title	Catalog	Sym	$	Label & Number

7/19/97 | **158** | 1 | | ©136 **Titanic - A New Musical** .... | | | **$10** | RCA Victor 68834

David Costabile/John Cunningham/David Garrison; sw: Maury Yeston

Autumn/Finale	1st Class Roster	Mr. Andrews' Vision
Barrett's Song	Godspeed Titanic	Night Was Alive
Blame, The	How Did They Build Titanic?	No Moon
Doing The Latest Rag (medley)	Hymn (medley)	Overture/Prologue: In Every Age
Dressed In Your Pyjamas In The	I Have Danced	Proposal, The (medley)
Grand Salon	I Must Get On That Ship	Still
Epilogue: In Every Age/Finale	Lady's Maid	There She Is

To Be A Captain
To The Lifeboats
We'll Meet Tomorrow
What A Remarkable Age This Is!

7/31/93 | **114** | 2 | | ©137 **Tommy, The Who's** .... | | | **$15** | RCA Victor 61874 [2]

Michael Cerveris/Marcia Mitzman/Jonathan Dokuchitz/Paul Kandel; sw: **Pete Townshend**

Acid Queen	Go to the Mirror (medley)	See Me, Feel Me (medley)
Amazing Journey	I Believe My Own Eyes	Sensation
Captain Walker	I'm Free	Smash The Mirror
Christmas (medley)	It's A Boy	Sparks
Courtroom Scene	Listening to You (medley)	Streets Of London 1961-63: Miracle
Cousin Kevin	Pinball Wizard	Cure
Eyesight To The Blind	Sally Simpson	There's a Doctor (medley)
Fiddle About	Sally Simpson's Question	Tommy, Can You Hear Me?

Tommy's Holiday Camp
Twenty-One
Underture (Entr'acte)
We're Not Gonna Take It
We've Won
Welcome

7/27/63 | **64** | 11 | | ©138 **Tovarich** .... | | | **$40** | Capitol 1940

Vivian Leigh/Jean Pierre Aumont/Alexander Scourby; mu: Lee Pockriss; ly: Anne Croswell

All For You	Make A Friend	Say You'll Stay
I Go To Bed	Nitchevo	Small Cartel
I Know The Feeling	No! No! No!	Stuck With Each Other
It Used To Be	Only One	That Face

Uh-Oh!
Wilkes-Barre, Pa.
You Love Me

5/8/76 | **200** | 2 | | 139 **Treemonisha** .... | | | **$20** | DG 2707 [2]

Carmen Balthrop/Betty Allen/Curtis Rayam; sw: **Scott Joplin**; cd: Gunther Schuller

Afternoon | Evening | Morning

12/26/60+ | **6** | 48 | | ©140 **Unsinkable Molly Brown, The** | | | **$40** | Capitol 1509

Tammy Grimes/Harve Presnell; sw: Meredith Willson

Are You Sure?	Denver Police	I May Never Fall In Love With You
Bea-u-ti-ful People Of Denver	Dolce Far Niente (medley)	(medley)
Belly Up To The Bar, Boys	Happy Birthday, Mrs. J.J. Brown	I'll Never Say No
Bon Jour (The Language Song)	I Ain't Down Yet	I've A'ready Started In
Chick-A-Pen		If I Knew

Keep-A-Hoppin' (medley)
Leadville Johnny Brown (Soliloquy)
(medley)
My Own Brass Bed
Up Where The People Are

3/17/58+ | **5** | 191 | ● | ©141 **West Side Story** | | | **$30** | Columbia 5230

Carol Lawrence/Larry Kert/Chita Rivera/Art Smith; mu: **Leonard Bernstein**; ly: Stephen Sondheim

America	Gee, Officer Krupke!	Maria
Boy Like That (medley)	I Feel Pretty	One Hand, One Heart
Cool	I Have A Love (medley)	Prologue (medley)
Dance At The Gym	Jet Song (medley)	Rumble, The

Something's Coming
Somewhere
Tonight

4/4/64 | **28** | 14 | | 142 **What Makes Sammy Run?** .... | | | **$50** | Columbia 2440

Steve Lawrence/Sally Ann Howes/Robert Alda; sw: Ervin Drake

Friendliest Thing	Lites! Camera! Platitude!	Room Without Windows (medley)
I Feel Humble	Maybe Some Other Time	Some Days Everything Goes Wrong
I See Something	My Hometown	Something To Live For
Kiss Me No Kisses	New Pair Of Shoes	Tender Spot

Wedding Of The Year
You Can Trust Me (medley)
You Help Me
You're No Good

1/30/61 | **6** | 41 | | ©143 **Wildcat** | | | **$50** | RCA Victor 1060

Lucille Ball/Keith Andes; mu: Cy Coleman; ly: Carolyn Leigh

Corduroy Road	Oil!	Tippy Tippy Toes
El Sombrero	One Day We Dance	What Takes My Fancy
Give A Little Whistle	Tall Hope	Wildcat
Hey, Look Me Over!	That's What I Want For Janie	You're A Liar!

You've Come Home

5/3/75 | **43** | 16 | ● | ©144 **Wiz, The** .... | | | **$15** | Atlantic 18137

Stephanie Mills/Tiger Haynes/Ted Ross/Hinton Battle; sw: Charlie Smalls

Be A Lion	Feeling We Once Had	I'm A Mean Ole Lion
Don't Nobody Bring Me No Bad	He's The Wizard	If You Believe
News	Home (Finale)	Slide Some Oil To Me
Ease On Down The Road	I Was Born On The Day Before	So You Wanted To See The Wizard
Everybody Rejoice	Yesterday	Soon As I Get Home

Tornado
What Would I Do If I Could Feel
Y'all Got It!

6/27/81 | **196** | 2 | | ©145 **Woman Of The Year** .... | | | **$12** | Arista 8303

Lauren Bacall/Harry Guardino/Rex Everhart; mu: John Kander; ly: Fred Ebb

Grass Is Always Greener	It Isn't Working	Shut Up Gerald
Happy In The Morning	One Of The Boys	So What Else Is New?
I Told You So	Poker Game	Sometimes A Day Goes By
I Wrote The Book	See You In The Funny Papers	Table Talk

We're Gonna Work It Out
When You're Right; You're Right
Woman Of The Year

7/1/67 | **165** | 5 | | ©146 **You're A Good Man, Charlie Brown** .... | | | **$25** | MGM 9

Gary Burghoff/Bob Balaban/Bill Hinnant/Reva Rose; sw: Clark Gesner

Book Report	Little Known Facts	Red Baron
Dr. Lucy	My Blanket & Me	Schroeder
Happiness	Peanuts Potpourri	Snoopy
Kite	Queen Lucy	Suppertime

T-E-A-M (Baseball Game)
You're A Good Man, Charlie Brown

1/25/69 | **177** | 7 | | ©147 **Zorba** .... | | | **$25** | Capitol 118

Herschel Bernardi/Maria Karnilova; mu: John Kander; ly: Fred Ebb

Bend Of The Road (medley)	First Time	I Am Free (medley)
Butterfly, The	Goodbye, Canavaro	Life Is
Crow, The (medley)	Grandpapa (medley)	No Boom Boom
Entr'acte	Happy Birthday (medley)	Only Love (medley)

Top Of The Hill
Why Can't I Speak?
Y'assou
Zorba's Dance (medley)

DEBUT	PEAK	WKS	RIAA	CD	ARTIST — Album Title	Catalog	Sym	$	Label & Number

TELEVISION SOUNDTRACKS

The stars of the show are listed directly below the title.

11/20/71+ **8** 22 ● 1 **All In The Family** [C] **$15** Atlantic 7210
Carroll O'Connor/Jean Stapleton/Rob Reiner/Sally Struthers; comedy excerpts from the show

Archie's Hangup	Jury Duty	Sweety Pie Roger
Bacon Souffle & Women's Lib	No Ribs?	Those Were The Days [Carroll
Do You Love Me?	Shove Yours	O'Connor & Jean Stapleton] 43
God Is Black	Station Wagon Filled With Nuns	Transplants

VD Day
Why God Made Hands

12/30/72+ **129** 8 2 **All In The Family - 2nd Album** [C] **$15** Atlantic 7232
more comedy excerpts from the show

Archie And Maude	Breasts	Hog Jowls
Archie In Jail	Change Of Life	Man In The Street
Archie Meets Mike	Elevator, The	Sammy's Visit

1/11/97 **134** 6 © 3 **All That - The Album**.................. [V] **$10** Loud 67423
Keenan Thompson/Kel Mitchell/Amanda Bynes

Age Ain't Nothing But A Number [Aaliyah] 75	Clap Yo' Hands [Naughty By Nature]	(Good Burger/Good Weenie)
All That - Outro Theme Song [TLC]	(Coach Kreeton)	He's Mine [MoKenStef] 7
All That Theme Song [TLC]	(Earboy & Pizza Face)	(Loud Librarian)
Baby [Brandy] 4	(Ed & Coolio)	(Miss Fingerly V. Bacteria)
Candy Rain [Soul For Real] 2	Fantastic Voyage [Coolio] 3	(Superdude)
(5 Minutes)		(Vital Information I)
		(Vital Information II)

Watch Me Do My Thing [Immature Feat. Smooth & Ed from Good Burger] 32
We Got It [Immature] 37
You Used To Love Me [Faith Evans] 24

Ally McBeal - see SHEPARD, Vonda
Calista Flockhart/Peter MacNicol/Lisa Nicole Carson/Jane Krakowski

11/27/99 **175** 1 © 4 **Annie**.......................... [M] **$10** Sony Classical 89008
Alicia Morton/Kathy Bates/Alan Cumming/Victor Garber

Easy Street	I Don't Need Anything But You	Maybe/Tomorrow (Reprise)
Finale/I Don't Need Anything But You	I Think I'm Gonna Like It Here	NYC
	Little Girls	NYC Reprise/Lullaby
Hard-Knock Life	Little Girls (Reprise)	Something Was Missing
Hard-Knock Life (Reprise)	Maybe	Tomorrow

You're Never Fully Dressed Without A Smile (Radio Version)
You're Never Fully Dressed Without A Smile (Cast Version)

9/18/93 **9** 47 ▲³ © 5 **Barney's Favorites - Volume 1** C:#34/11 [M] **$10** SBK 27114
Bob West/Julie Johnson/Patty Wirtz/Brice Armstrong/Todd Duffey

A-Camping We Will Go	B-I-N-G-O	Itsy Bitsy Spider
Alphabet Song	Clean Up	Kookaburra
And The Green Grass Grows All Around	Do Your Ears Hang Low?	Looby Loo
	Down On Grandpa's Farm	Me And My Teddy
Ants Go Marching	Hurry, Hurry, Drive The Firetruck	Mr. Knickerbocker
Apples And Bananas	I Love You	My Family's Just Right For Me
Barney Theme Song	If All The Raindrops	Old Brass Wagon

Peanut Butter
Sally The Camel
Sarasponda
Sister Song
Six Little Ducks
Stranger Song
There Are Seven Days

9/17/94 **66** 20 ▲ © 6 **Barney's Favorites - Volume 2**.......... [M] **$10** EMI 28338
pf: Bob West/Julie Johnson/shows cast members; songs from the popular children's PBS series

Airplane Song	Good Manners	Just Imagine
BJ's Song	Growing	Mister Sun
Barney Bag	Happy Wanderer	My Aunt Came Back
Barney Theme Song	If I Lived Under The Sea	My Yellow Blankey
Buckle Up My Seatbelt	It's Nice Just To Be Me	Please And Thank You
Everyone Is Special	John Jacob Jingleheimer Schmidt	Pop Goes The Weasel
Friendship Song	Jungle Adventure	Rainbow Song

Sea Medley
Tinkerputt's Song
Wheels On The Bus
When I Grow Up

4/23/66 **112** 8 7 **Batman**........................... [I+T] **$50** 20th Century Fox 4180
Adam West/Burt Ward; cd: Nelson Riddle; music and dialogue excerpts from the show

Batman Blues	Batman Thaws Mr. Freeze -or-	Gotham City
Batman Pows The Penguin -or- (Aha, My Fine-Feathered Finks!)	(That's The Way The Ice-Cube Crumbles!)	Holy Flypaper
Batman Riddles The Riddler! -or-	Batman Theme	Holy-Hole-In-The-Doughnut -or- (Robin, You've Done It Again!)
(Hi Diddle Riddle)	Batusi A-Go! Go! -or- (I Shouldn't Wish To Attract Attention)	To The Batmobile

Two Perfectly Ordinary People -or- (!!!!)
Zelda Tempts Batman -or- (Must He Go It Alone???)

10/21/78 **144** 6 © 8 **Battlestar Galactica**................... [I] **$15** MCA 3051
Lorne Greene/Richard Hatch/Dirk Benedict; cp/cd: Stu Phillips

Adama's Theme	Dash To The Elevator	Fighter Launch
Boxey's Problem (medley)	Destruction Of Peace	It's Love, Love, Love (The Casino On Carillon)
Cassiopia And Starbuck	End Of The Atlantia	Let's Go Home (End Title)
Cylon Base Ship (Imperious Leader)	Escape From The Ovion Mines	Main Title
Cylon Trap	Exploration (medley)	

Red Nova
Serena's Illness (medley)
Suffering

6/17/89 **157** 10 © 9 **Beauty And The Beast / Of Love And Hope**.......... [I+T] **$10** Capitol 91583
Linda Hamilton/Ron Perlman; cp/cd: Lee Holdridge; includes poetry readings by Perlman

Angel's Theme	Devin's Theme (I Arise From The Dreams Of Thee)	Journey's End (Sonnet #CXVI)
Beauty And The Beast (Acquainted With The Night)	Father Remembers (Composed On Westminster Bridge)	Laura's Theme
Broken Dreams		Margaret's Theme (Longing)
Catherine's Lullaby (Somewhere I Have Never Travelled)	Fear (You Darkness)	Night Of Beauty
	First Time I Loved Forever	On Her Own (She Walks In Beauty)
Dancing Light (Sonnet #XXIX)	Happy Life (This Is The Creature)	Promise Remembered
		Quest (Letters To A Young Poet)

Return, The
Riches, Not Gold
Single Night (Love-Song)
To Cast All Else Aside

12/11/93 **5** 23 ▲² © 10 **Beavis & Butt-head Experience, The** C:#40/1 [V] **$10** Geffen 24613
animated series, voices by Mike Judge/Tracy Grandstaff/Adam Welch

Bounce [Run-D.M.C.]	I Got You Babe [Cher w/Beavis & Butt-Head]	Mental *@%#! [Jackyl]
Come To Butt-Head [Beavis & Butt-Head]	I Hate Myself And Want To Die [Nirvana]	Monsta Mack [Sir Mix-A-Lot]
Deuces Are Wild [Aerosmith]		99 Ways To Die [Megadeth]
I Am Hell [White Zombie]	Looking Down The Barrel Of A Gun [Anthrax]	Poetry And Prose [Primus]

Search And Destroy [Red Hot Chili Peppers]

Ben Casey - see VALJEAN
Vincent Edwards/Sam Jaffe/Harry Landers/Jeanne Bates

TELEVISION SOUNDTRACKS

DEBUT	PEAK	WKS	RIAA	CD	ARTIST — Album Title	Catalog	Sym	$	Label & Number

11/7/92+ — PEAK **76** — WKS **34** — ● © 11 **Beverly Hills, 90210 - The Soundtrack** .... [V] **$10** Giant 24465
Luke Perry/Jason Priestly/Shannon Doherty/Jennie Garth

Action Speaks Louder Than Words [Tara Kemp]	Beverly Hills, 90210 (Theme) [John Davis]	Let Me Be Your Baby [Geoffrey Williams]
All The Way To Heaven [Jody Watley]	Got To Have You [Color Me Badd]	Love Is [Vanessa Williams & Brian McKnight] 3
Bend Time Back Around [Paula Abdul]	Just Wanna Be Your Friend [Puck & Natty]	Right Kind Of Love [Jeremy Jordan] 14

Saving Forever For You [Shanice] 4
Time To Be Lovers [Michael McDonald & Chaka Khan]
Why [Cathy Dennis w/D-Mob]

11/24/62+ — PEAK **49** — WKS **9** — 12 **Bonanza** .... [M] **$50** RCA Victor 2583
Lorne Greene/Michael Landon/Dan Blocker/Pernell Roberts; songs performed by each of the stars

Bonanza	Happy Birthday	Place Where I Worship (Is The Wide Open Spaces)
Careless Love	In The Pines	Ponderosa
Early One Morning	Miss Cindy	Shenandoah
Hangin' Blues	My Sons, My Sons	

Skip To My Lou
Sky Ball Paint
Sourwood Mountain

Brady Bunch - see Main Artist Section

11/6/99 — PEAK **51** — WKS **4** — © 13 **Buffy The Vampire Slayer** .... [V] **$10** TVT Soundtrax 8300
Sarah Michelle Gellar/Seth Green/Nicholas Brendon/Alyson Hannigan

Already Met You [Superfine]	Devil You Know (God Is A Man) [Face To Face]	Lucky [Bif Naked]
Buffy The Vampire Slayer Theme [Nerf Herder]	I Quit [Hepburn]	Nothing But You [Kim Ferron]
Charge [Splendid]	It Doesn't Matter [Alison Krauss & Union Station]	Over My Head [Furslide]
Close Your Eyes [Christophe Beck]	Keep Myself Awake [Black Lab]	Pain [Four Star Mary]
		Strong [Velvet Chain]

Teenage FBI [Guided By Voices]
Temptation Waits [Garbage]
Transylvanian Concubine [Rasputina]
Virgin State Of Mind [K's Choice]
Wild Horses [Sundays]

12/12/98 — PEAK **16** — WKS **21** — ▲ © 14 **Chef Aid: The South Park Album** .... [V] **$10** American 69377
animated show, voices by Trey Parker/Matt Stone/Mary Kay Bergman/**Isaac Hayes**

Brad Logan [Rancid]	Hot Lava [Perry Farrell & D.V.D.A.]	Mephisto And Kevin [Primus]
Bubblegoose [Wyclef Jean]	Huboon Stomp [Devo]	No Substitute [Chef]
Chocolate Salty Balls (P.S. I Love You) [Chef]	It's A Rockin' World [Joe Strummer]	Nowhere To Run [Ozzy Osbourne/DMX/Ol' Dirty Bastard]
Come Sail Away [Eric Cartman]	Kenny's Dead [Master P]	Rainbow, The [Ween]
Feel Like Makin' Love [Ned Gerblansky]	Love Gravy [Rick James & Ike Turner]	Simultaneous [Chef]
Horny [Mousse T. Vs. Hot 'N' Juicy]	Mentally Dull [Vitro]	South Park Theme [Primus]

Tonight Is Right For Love [Chef & Meat Loaf]
Wake Up Wendy [Elton John]
Will They Die 4 You [Mase/Puffy/Lil' Kim/System Of A Down]

12/22/90+ — PEAK **76** — WKS **15** — ● © 15 **Civil War, The** .... [I+V] **$10** Elektra N. 79256
from the documentary series produced by public television; pf: Jay Ungar/Jacqueline Schwab/New American Brass Band

All Quiet On The Potomac	Dixie	Marching Through Georgia
Angel Band	Drums Of War	Oliver Wendell Holmes
Ashokan Farewell	Flag Of Columbia	Palmyra Schottische
Battle Cry Of Freedom	Hail Columbia	Parade
Battle Hymn Of The Republic	Johnny Has Gone For A Soldier	Shenandoah
Bonnie Blue Flag (medley)	Kingdom Coming	Sullivan Ballou Letter (medley)
Cheer Boys Cheer	Lorena	We Are Climbing Jacob's Ladder

Weeping Sad And Lonely
When Johnny Comes Marching Home
Yankee Doodle

3/1/86 — PEAK **125** — WKS **7** — © 16 **Cosby Show, Music From The - A House Full Of Love** .... [I] **$12** Columbia 40270
Bill Cosby/Phylicia Rashad/Lisa Bonet/Malcolm-Jamal Warner; sw: **Bill Cosby** & Stu Gardner; pf: **Grover Washington, Jr.**

Camille	Huxtable Kids	Love In Its Proper Place
Clair (Phylicia)	Kitchen Jazz	Outstretched Hands (Gloria)
House Full Of Love	Look At This	Poppin'

Resthatherian

5/9/81 — PEAK **136** — WKS **13** — © 17 **Cosmos, The Music Of** .... [I] **$15** RCA Victor 4003
selections from PBS television series hosted by Carl Sagan; cp/cd: various

Affirmation	Exploration	Life
Cataclysm	Harmony Of Nature	Space/Time Continuum

Dallas - see CRAMER, Floyd
Larry Hagman/Victoria Principal/Patrick Duffy/Barbara Bel Geddes/Charlene Tilton

8/2/69 — PEAK **18** — WKS **19** — 18 **Dark Shadows** .... [I] **$50** Philips 314
Jonathan Frid/David Selby/Joan Bennett/Kate Jackson; cp/cd: Robert Cobert

Back At The Blue Whale	I, Barnabas	#1 At The Blue Whale
Collinwood (medley)	I'll Be With You, Always	Old House
Dark Shadows (medley)	Josette's Theme	Seance
Darkness At Collinwood	Meditations	Secret Room
Epitaph	Night Of The Pentagram	

Shadows Of The Night (Quentin's Theme)
When I Am Dead

5/15/99 — PEAK **7** — WKS **17** — ● © 19 **Dawson's Creek** .... [V] **$10** Columbia 69853
James Van Der Beek/Katie Holmes/Michelle Williams/Joshua Jackson/Kerr Smith

Any Lucky Penny [Nikki Hassman]	I Don't Want To Wait [Paula Cole] 11	Life's A Bitch [Shooter]
Cry Ophelia [Adam Cohen]	Kiss Me [Sixpence None The Richer] 2	London Rain (Nothing Heals Me Like You Do) [Heather Nova]
Did You Ever Love Somebody [Jessica Simpson]	Letting Go [Sozzi]	Lose Your Way [Sophie B. Hawkins]
Feels Like Home [Chantal Kreviazuk]		Ready For A Fall [PJ Olsson]

Shimmer [Shawn Mullins]
Stay You [Wood]
To Be Loved [Curtis Stigers]

10/21/00 — PEAK **59** — WKS **6** — © 20 **Dawson's Creek Volume 2, Songs From** .... [V] **$10** Columbia 85149

Broken Boy [Michal]	I Think God Can Explain [Splender]	If I Am [Nine Days]
Crazy For This Girl [Evan & Jaron]	I Think I'm In Love With You [Jessica Simpson]	Just Another [Pete Yorn]
Daydream Believer [Mary Beth Maziarz]	I'm Gonna Make You Love Me [Jayhawks]	Never Saw Blue Like That [Shawn Colvin]
Givin' Up On You [Lara Fabian]		Respect [Train]

Show Me Heaven [Jessica Andrews]
Superman [Five For Fighting]
Teenage Dirtbag [Wheatus]

1/13/01 — PEAK **36**[X] — WKS **1** — © 21 **Dr. Seuss' How The Grinch Stole Christmas! & Horton Hears A Who!** ... [X] **$12** Rhino 75969
includes the original TV soundtracks for 2 Dr. Seuss classics: How The Grinch Stole Christmas! (narrated by Boris Karloff-1966) and Horton Hears A Who! (narrated by Hans Conreid-1969)

Be Kind To Your Small Person	I Must Stop Christmas	Tomorrow Is Christmas, It's Practically Here
Friends	Mrs. Toucanella Told Me	
Doctor Hoovey, You Were Right	Old Doc Hoovey	Trim Up The Tree
Horton The Elephant's Going To Be Caged	Quarter Of Dawn	We Are Here
		Welcome Christmas

Who-Ville Aloft
Wickersham Brothers Song
You're A Mean One, Mr. Grinch
You're A Mean One, Mr. Grinch (Reprise)

4/17/82 — PEAK **93** — WKS **14** — © 22 **Dukes Of Hazzard, The** .... [M] **$12** Scotti Brothers 37712
John Schneider/Tom Wopat/Sorrell Booke/James Best/Catherine Bach; includes songs and narration by cast members

Ballad Of The General Lee [Doug Kershaw]	Duelin' Dukes	In The Driver's Seat
Cover Girl Eyes [Doug Kershaw]	Flash	Keep Between Them Ditches [Doug Kershaw]
Down Home American Girl	General Lee [Johnny Cash]	Laughing All The Way To The Bank
	Good Ol' Boys	

Up On Cripple Creek

DEBUT	PEAK	WKS	RIAA	CD	ARTIST — Album Title	Catalog	Sym	$	Label & Number

Fame - see KIDS FROM "FAME"
Debbie Allen/Lee Curreri/Albert Hague

| 5/29/99 | 97 | 5 | | © 23 | **Felicity** .... | | [V] | $10 | Hollywood 62228 |

Keri Russell/Scott Speedman/Amanda Foreman/Scott Foley

All I Need [Air French Band] — Everyday Down [Joan Jones] — Here Comes The Flood [Peter Gabriel] — She Will Have Her Way [Neil Finn]
Angels [Joe Henry] — Felicity Theme — Hermes Bird [Remy Zero] — Slingshots [Morley]
Bridge Over Troubled Water [Aretha Franklin] **6** — **Good Enough** [Sarah McLachlan] **77** — I've Got A Feeling [Ivy] — This Woman's Work [Kate Bush]
Day Before Yesterday [Scout] — Heart And Shoulder [Heather Nova] — Puddle Of Grace [Amy Jo Johnson]

Flying Nun, The - see FIELD, Sally
Sally Field/Alejandro Rey/Marge Redmond/Madeleine Sherwood

| 10/14/95 | 41 | 29 | ▲ | © 24 | **Friends**.................... | | [V] | $10 | Reprise 46008 |

Jennifer Aniston/Courteney Cox/Lisa Kudrow/Matt LeBlanc/Matthew Perry/David Schwimmer

Angel Of The Morning [Pretenders] — I Go Blind [Hootie & The Blowfish] — It's A Free World Baby [R.E.M.] — Sunshine [Paul Westerberg]
Big Yellow Taxi [Joni Mitchell] — **I'll Be There For You** [Rembrandts] **17** — Sexuality [k.d. lang] — You'll Know You Were Loved [Lou Reed]
Good Intentions [Toad The Wet Sprocket] — In My Room [Grant Lee Buffalo] — Shoe Box [Barenaked Ladies] — Stain Yer Blood [Paul Westerberg]

Gypsy - see MIDLER, Bette
Bette Midler/Peter Riegert/Cynthia Gibb/Edward Asner

| 5/23/70 | 196 | 4 | | 25 | **Hee Haw, The Stars Of** .... | | [V] | $20 | Capitol 437 |

Buck Owens/Roy Clark/Archie Campbell/Grandpa Jones/Junior Samples

Big Mama's Medicine Show [Buddy Alan] — Gotta Get To Oklahoma ('Cause California's Gettin' To Me) [Hagers] — Maybe If I Close My Eyes (It'll Go Away) [Susan Raye] — We're Gonna Get Together [Buck Owens & Susan Raye]
Biggest Storm Of All [Doyle Holly & The Buckaroos] — How Long Will My Baby Be Gone [Buck Owens & The Buckaroos] — Nobody But You [Don Rich & The Buckaroos] — When The Wind Blows In Chicago [Roy Clark]
Buckaroo [Buck Owens & The Buckaroos] **60** — Overdue Blues [Roy Clark]

Here's Johnny - see Tonight Show

| 12/5/92 | 137 | 2 | | © 26 | **Jacksons: An American Dream, The** .... | | [V] | $10 | Motown 6356 |

Lawrence Hilton-Jacobs/Billy Dee Williams/**Vanessa Williams**/Angela Bassett/Jason Weaver

ABC (medley) [Jackson 5] — I Want You Back (medley) [Jackson 5] — Love You Save (medley) [Jackson 5] — Walk On (medley) [Jackson 5]
Dancing Machine [Jackson 5] **2** — **I'll Be There** [Jackson 5] **1** — Never Can Say Goodbye [Jackson 5] **2** — Who's Lovin' You [Jackson 5]
Dream Goes On [Jermaine Jackson] — **In The Still Of The Night** [Boyz II Men] **3** — Stay With Love [Jermaine Jackson & Syreeta Wright] — You Are The Ones [3T]
I Wanna Be Where You Are [Jason Weaver] — Kansas City [Jason Weaver]

| 4/15/00 | 79 | 14 | | © 27 | **Jesus - The Epic Mini-Series** .... | | [V] | $10 | Sparrow 51730 |

Jeremy Sisto/Jacqueline Bisset/Armin Mueller-Stahl/Gary Oldman

City By A River [Hootie & The Blowfish] — Jesus, He Loves Me [Edwin McCain] — Love That You've Been Looking For [98°] — Shining Star [Yolanda Adams]
Fly To You [Avalon] — Love Can Change Your Mind [Lonestar] — Nobody Ever (Only You) [Steven Curtis Chapman] — Spirit In The Sky [DC Talk]
I Need You [LeAnn Rimes] **11** — Pie Jesu [Sarah Brightman] — When You Walked Into My Life [Jaci Velasquez]
Jesus [Patrick Williams]

| 1/27/01 | 99 | 7 | | © 28 | **Ken Burns Jazz, The Best Of** .... | | [O-V] | $10 | Legacy 61439 |

Begin The Beguine [Artie Shaw] — Groovin' High [Dizzy Gillespie Sextet] — Mooche, The [Duke Ellington] — Straight, No Chaser [Thelonious Monk]
Cotton Tail [Duke Ellington] — Hotter Than 'Ell [Fletcher Henderson] — Singin' The Blues [Frankie Trumbauer] — Take Five [Dave Brubeck Quartet]
Dead Man Blues [Jelly Roll Morton's Red Hot Peppers] — Jumpin' At The Woodside [Count Basie] — So What [Miles Davis Sextet] — Take The "A" Train [Lincoln Center Jazz Orchestra]
Dear Old Southland [Noble Sissle] — King Porter Stomp [Benny Goodman] — Solitude [Billie Holiday with Eddie Heywood] — They Can't Take That Away From Me [Sarah Vaughan]
Doodlin' [Horace Silver & The Jazz Messengers] — St. Louis Blues [Louis Armstrong]
Giant Steps [John Coltrane Quartet] — Star Dust [Louis Armstrong]

| 1/27/01 | 113 | 6 | ▲ | © 29 | **Ken Burns Jazz - The Story Of America's Music** .... | | [O-V] | $50 | Legacy 61432 [5] |

A-Tisket A-Tasket [Chick Webb feat. Ella Fitzgerald] — For Dancers Only [Jimmie Lunceford] — Mooche, The [Duke Ellington] — Soon One Mornin' (Death Comes-A-Creepin' In My Room) [Mississippi Fred McDowell]
Acknowledgement [John Coltrane Quartet] — Get Happy [Bud Powell Trio] — Mood Indigo [Jungle Band] — Spanish Key [Miles Davis]
Ain't Misbehavin' [Louis Armstrong] — Giant Steps [John Coltrane Quartet] — Moon Dreams [Miles Davis Nonet] — St. Louis Blues [Louis Armstrong]
Back Water Blues [Bessie Smith] — God Bless The Child [Billie Holiday with Eddie Heywood] — Moten Swing [Bennie Moten] — St. Thomas [Sonny Rollins]
Begin The Beguine [Artie Shaw] — Groovin' High [Dizzy Gillespie] — Oh, Lady, Be Good! [Jones-Smith Incorporated] — Star Dust [Louis Armstrong]
Birdland [Weather Report] — Harlem Congo [Chick Webb] — Original Faubus Fables [Charles Mingus] — Straight, No Chaser [Thelonious Monk]
Black Beauty [Duke Ellington] — Heebie Jeebies [Louis Armstrong] — Pearls, The [Jelly Roll Morton] — Strange Fruit [Billie Holiday]
Body And Soul [Coleman Hawkins] — **Hello, Dolly!** [Louis Armstrong] **1** — Potato Head Blues [Louis Armstrong] — Sugar Foot Stomp [Fletcher Henderson]
Cake Walkin' Babies (From Home) [Clarence Williams's Blue Five] — Hotter Than 'Ell [Fletcher Henderson] — Rebecca [Pete Johnson & "Big" Joe Turner] — **Take Five** [Dave Brubeck Quartet] **25**
Charleston [James P. Johnson] — I Get A Kick Out Of You [Clifford Brown & Max Roach] — Rick Kick Shaw [Cecil Taylor Trio] — Take The "A" Train [Duke Ellington]
Chimes Blues [King Oliver's Creole Jazz Band] — I Got Rhythm [Ethel Waters] — Riverboat Shuffle [Frankie Trumbauer feat. Bix Beiderbecke] — Take The "A" Train [Lincoln Center Jazz Orchestra]
Chronology [Ornette Coleman] — In A Sentimental Mood [John Coltrane & Duke Ellington] — Rockin' Chair [Louis Armstrong] — Tanya [Dexter Gordon]
Cotton Tail [Duke Ellington] — In The Mood [Glenn Miller] — **Rockit** [Herbie Hancock] **71** — There Ain't No Sweet Man (Worth The Salt Of My Tears) [Paul Whiteman feat. Bix Beiderbecke]
Dead Man Blues [Jelly Roll Morton's Red Hot Peppers] — It Don't Mean A Thing (If It Ain't Got That Swing) [Duke Ellington] — Rose Room [Benny Goodman]
Dear Old Southland [Noble Sissle] — Jumpin' At The Woodside [Count Basie] — Salt Peanuts [Dizzy Gillespie] — They Can't Take That Away From Me [Sarah Vaughan]
Death Letter [Cassandra Wilson] — Just Friends [Charlie Parker] — Scrapple From The Apple [Charlie Parker Quintet] — Three Little Words [Art Tatum]
Desafinado [Stan Getz & Charlie Byrd] **15** — King Porter Stomp [Benny Goodman] — Sent For You Yesterday And Here You Come Today [Count Basie] — Tourist Point Of View [Duke Ellington]
Django [Modern Jazz Quartet] — Ko-Ko [Charlie Parker's Re-Boppers] — Shine [Django Reinhardt] — Un Ange En Danger [Ron Carter & M.C. Solaar]
Doodlin' [Horace Silver & The Jazz Messengers] — Lester Leaps In [Count Basie] — Sing, Sing, Sing (With A Swing) [Benny Goodman] — Walkin' Shoes [Chet Baker & Gerry Mulligan]
Drum Boogie [Gene Krupa] — Livery Stable Blues [Original Dixieland Jazz Band] — Singin' The Blues [Frankie Trumbauer feat. Bix Beiderbecke] — Well, Git It! [Tommy Dorsey]
E.S.P. [Miles Davis Quintet] — Manteca [Dizzy Gillespie] — So What [Miles Davis Sextet] — West End Blues [Louis Armstrong]
East St. Louis Toodle-Oo [Duke Ellington] — Memphis Blues [Lieut. Jim Europe's 369th Infantry Band] — Solitude [Billie Holiday with Eddie Heywood] — Wild Cat Blues [Clarence Williams's Blue Five]
Echoes Of Harlem [Duke Ellington] — **Mister Magic** [Grover Washington, Jr.] **54** — Soon All Will Know [Wynton Marsalis] — Without Your Love [Billie Holiday]
Embraceable You [Charlie Parker Quintet]
Epistrophy [Thelonious Monk]
Fine And Mellow [Billie Holiday]

DEBUT	PEAK	WKS	RIAA	CD	ARTIST — Album Title	Catalog	Sym	$	Label & Number

10/19/68+ | **105** | 17 | | © 30 | **Laugh-In** .... | [C] | | $20 | Epic 15118

Dan Rowan/Dick Martin/Arte Johnson/Judy Carne/Goldie Hawn

Cocktail Party	Goodnight Dick!	New Talent
Cuckoo Laugh-In World	Half Time	News--Past, Present And Future
Cuckoos, The	Here Come The Judge	Other Cocktail Party
Etcetera	Mod Mod World	Personality Of The Week

Sock It To Me--Potpourri

4/5/69 | **88** | 10 | | 31 | **Laugh-In '69** .... | [C] | | $15 | Reprise 6335

second cast album featuring comedy highlights

American Institution	Chamber Of Commerce	Mecca
Big Cocktail Party	Children Of Laugh-in	News, The
Broncos	Down Town	Swingers
Bus Stop	Dum Dums	Trading Center
By Henry Gibson	Laugh-in Strikes Again	Up Town

Vacation In
Well, Ring My Chimes!

2/14/98 | **178** | 1 | | © 32 | **Long Journey Home** .... | [V] | | $10 | Unisphere 68963

from the PBS documentary series *The Irish In America: Long Journey Home*

American Theme	Long Journey Home (Anthem) [Elvis	O'Donnell's Lament (medley)
Bard Of Armagh (medley) [Vince	Costello w/Anúna]	[Eileen Ivers]
Gill]	Main Theme	Paddy's Lamentation (medley)
Bean Pháidín [Kevin Conneff]	Muldoon, The Solid Man (medley)	[Mary Black]
Emigration Theme	[Mick Moloney]	Raibh Tú Ag An Gcarraig? (Were
Famine Theme	Night That Larry Was Stretched-Jig	You At The Rock?) [Sissel]
Grandfather's Tune (medley) [Mick	[Chieftains & Friends]	Reel With The Beryle (medley)
Moloney]	O'Carolan's Farewell To Music	[Eileen Ivers]

Shenandoah [Van Morrison & The
Chieftains]
Ships Are Sailing (medley) [Mary
Black]
Skibbereen [Sinéad O'Connor]
Streets Of Laredo (medley) [Vince
Gill]
White Potatoes [Liam Ó Maonlai]

2/24/01 | **148** | 2 | | © 33 | **Malcolm In The Middle** .... | | | $10 | Restless 73743

Frankie Muniz/Jane Kaczmarek/Bryan Cranston/Justin Berfield/Erik Per Sullivan

Been Here Once Before [Eagle-Eye	Drunk Is Better Than Dead [Push	Older [They Might Be Giants]
Cherry]	Stars]	Right Place, Wrong Time [Screamin'
Bizarro [Citizen King]	Falling For The First Time	Cheetah Wheelies]
Boss Of Me [They Might Be Giants]	[Barenaked Ladies]	Smile [Hanson]
Cotton Eye Joe [Rednex] **25**	Good Life [Getaway People]	Tune In (Round Window) [Flak]
Don't Push It, Don't Force It	Heaven Is A Halfpipe [OPM]	Washin' + Wonderin' [Stroke 9]
[Gordon]	I Just Don't Care [Dust Brothers]	

We Are Monkeys [Travis]
You All Dat [Baha Men]

Man From U.N.C.L.E., The - see MONTEGRO, Hugo

Robert Vaughn/**David McCallum**/Leo Carroll

10/12/85 | ❶[11] | 34 | ▲[4] | © 34 | **Miami Vice** | [V] | | $10 | MCA 6150

Don Johnson/Philip Michael Thomas/Edward James Olmos

Better Be Good To Me [Tina	Evan [Jan Hammer]	**Miami Vice Theme** [Jan Hammer] **1**
Turner] **5**	Flashback [Jan Hammer]	**Own The Night** [Chaka Khan] **57**
Chase [Jan Hammer]	**In The Air Tonight** [Phil Collins] **19**	**Smuggler's Blues** [Glenn Frey] **12**

Vice [Grandmaster Melle Mel]
You Belong To The City [Glenn
Frey] **2**

12/6/86+ | **82** | 12 | | © 35 | **Miami Vice II** .... | | | $10 | MCA 6192

second album of songs featured on the show

Crockett's Theme [Jan Hammer]	Lives In The Balance [Jackson	Miami Vice Theme [Jan Hammer]
In Dulce Decorum [Damned]	Browne]	New York Theme [Jan Hammer]
Last Unbroken Heart [Patti LaBelle	Lover [Roxy Music]	Send It To Me [Gladys Knight & The
& Bill Champlin]	Mercy [Steve Jones]	Pips]

Take Me Home [Phil Collins] **7**
When The Rain Comes Down
[Andy Taylor] **73**

5/3/75 | **51** | 13 | | | 36 | **Mickey Mouse Club** .... | [M] | | $15 | Disneyland 1362

Jimmie Dodd/**Annette**/Spin & Marty/Mouseketeers

Anything Can Happen	Hi To You	Mickey Mouse Theme (Alma Mater)
Cowboy Needs A Horse	How Will I Know My Love	Mousekartoon Time
Do Mi So	I'm No Fool (As A Pedestrian)	Mousekedance, The
Don't Jump To Conclusions	Meetin' At The Malt Shop	Pussy Cat Polka
Fun With Music	Mickey Mouse Mambo	Simple Simon
Happy Mouse	Mickey Mouse March	Stop, Look And Listen

Talent Roundup
Today Is Tuesday
Triple R Song

7/23/66 | **120** | 15 | | | 37 | **Mickie Finn's - America's No.1 Speakeasy** .... | [L] | | $20 | Dunhill/ABC 50009

San Diego night club specializing in *Gay '90s* music; featuring pianist Fred Finn and his wife Mickie (banjo)

Alley Cat	K.C. Jerk	Mickie Finn Theme
Beer Barrel Polka	King Of The Road	Side By Side
Bye, Bye Blackbird	Let Me Call You Sweetheart	Swinging On A Star (medley)
It's A Sin To Tell A Lie (medley)	Liebestraum	When The Saints Come Marching In

You've Gotta See Your Mama Every
Night

Mission: Impossible - see SCHIFRIN, Lalo

Peter Graves/Greg Morris/Martin Landau

8/8/87 | **50** | 14 | | © 38 | **Moonlighting** .... | [O-V] | | $10 | MCA 6214

Cybill Shepherd/**Bruce Willis**/Allyce Beasley/Curtis Armstrong

Blue Moon [Cybill Shepherd]	**Limbo Rock** [Chubby Checker] **2**	Someone To Watch Over Me [Linda
Good Lovin' [Bruce Willis]	**Moonlighting** [Al Jarreau] **23**	Ronstadt]
I Told Ya I Love Ya, Now Get Out!	Since I Fell For You [Bob James &	Stormy Weather [Billie Holiday]
[Cybill Shepherd]	David Sanborn]	

**This Old Heart Of Mine (Is Weak
For You)** [Isley Brothers] **12**
When A Man Loves A Woman
[Percy Sledge] **1**

Mr. Lucky - see MANCINI, Henry

John Vivyan/Ross Martin/Pippa Scott

1/21/78 | **153** | 5 | | | 39 | **Muppet Show, The** .... | [M] | | $12 | Arista 4152

Frank Oz/Jim Henson/Jerry Nelson/Richard Hunt/Dave Goelz

Bein' Green	I'm In Love With A Big Blue Frog	Muppaphone
Cottleston Pie	Lydia The Tattooed Lady	Muppet Show Theme
Flight Of The Bumble Bee	Mah-Na-Mah-Na	Sax And Violence
Fozzie's Monologue	Mississippi Mud	Simon Smith And His Amazing
Halfway Down The Stairs	Mr. Bassman	Dancing Bear

Tenderly
Tit Willow
Trees
Veterinarian's Hospital
What Now My Love

Native Americans, Music For The - see ROBERTSON, Robbie

10/7/95 | **73** | 6 | | © 40 | **New York Undercover** .... | [V] | | $10 | Uptown 11342

Michael DeLorenzo/Malik Yoba/Patti D'Arbanville-Quinn

Beautiful [K-Ci & JoJo - The Hailey	Good Morning Heartache [Gladys	I'll Take You There [Mavis Staples]
Brothers]	Knight]	Inside My Love [Chanté Moore]
Dom Perignon [Little Shawn]	**I Miss You (Come Back Home)**	**Jeeps, Lex Coups, Bimaz & Benz**
Erase The Dayz (Come Home) [Al	[Monifah] **56**	[Lost Boyz] **67**
B. Sure!]	I Will Go [Anthony Hamilton Feat.	L.I.F.E. [Tyme]
	Terri Robinson]	

Tell Me What You Like [Guy]
Theme From New York Undercover
(You Make Me Feel Like A)
Natural Woman [Mary J. Blige] **95**

DEBUT	PEAK	WKS	RIAA	CD	ARTIST — Album Title	Catalog	Sym	$	Label & Number
2/26/94	83	5		© 41	One Life To Live - The Best Of Love		[V]	$10	SBK 28336

Erica Slezak/Robin Strasser/Phil Carey/Robert S. Woods/Clint Ritchie

All I Know [Amy Holland & Michael McDonald] / From This Day On [Brenda Russell & Howard Hewitt] / I Still Believe In You [Cliff Richard] / Way That You Love Me [Wendy Moten]
For Your Precious Love [Jerry Butler (with the Impressions)] 11 / Goodbye [Warren Wiebe] / New Fire From An Old Flame [Stephanie Mills] / (You're My) Soul And Inspiration [Darlene Love & Bill Medley]
Here We Are My Friend [Billy Dean] / Teach Me How To Dream [Chris Walker]

| 5/9/60 | 30 | 2 | | © 42 | One Step Beyond, Music From .... | | [I] | $40 | Decca 8970 |

from the Alcoa Presents TV series hosted by John Newland; cd: Harry Lubin; pf: Berlin Symphony Orchestra

Bullfight / Island Off Spain / Paris / Weird
Bygone Memories / Jungle Aire / Pathetique / You Are My Love
Fear / On The Terrace / Trip To The Far East

| 1/27/01 | 42 | 10 | | © 43 | Oz .... | | [V] | $10 | Avatar 10007 |

Ernie Hudson/Terry Kinney/Rita Moreno/B.D. Wong

Ain't No Sunshine [East Side Cult] / Incarcerated [Magic, Blaxuede & Fiend] / Shackled Up [Krayzie Bone] / War Wit Us [Three 6 Mafia]
Behind The Walls [Kurupt Feat. Nate Dogg] / Land Of Oz [Snoop Dogg] / Some Niggas [Styles & Jadakiss] / What Is The Law [Pharoahe Monch]
Can I Live [Cypress Hill] / Locked Up [Master P] / Thug Niggas Don't Live That Long [Trick Daddy] / What Ya Gonna Do [Tez & Tajiee]
Can't Wait [Devin The Dude] / Oz Theme 2000 [Kool G Rap, Lord Jamar & Talib Kweli] / Tonight [Drag-On] / What You In Fo' [Wu-Tang Clan Feat. Method Man, RZA, Raekwon]

Peter Gunn - see MANCINI, Henry
Craig Stevens/**Herschel Bernardi**/Lola Albright

| 4/17/99 | 86 | 7 | | © 44 | PJs, The .... | | [V] | $10 | Hollywood 62170 |

animated series, voices by **Eddie Murphy**/Janet DuBois/Loretta Divine

Always Been You [Imajin] / Hat Low [Goodie Mob] / Life In The Projects [Snoop Dogg] / Til It's Over [Krumb Snatchas]
Get Involved [Raphael Saadiq & Q-Tip] 67 / Here I Go [Infamous Syndicate] / No More Rainy Days [Destiny's Child] / Way 2 Strong [Bizzy B.O.N.E.]
Ghetto, The [Krayzie B.O.N.E. ft. O] / Holiday [Earth, Wind & Fire ft. Marie Antoinette] / PJs [George Clinton] / What I Am [Sy Smith]
Giant Size [Raekwon & American Cream Team] / It's Nothing [Jermaine Dupri & Da Brat ft. R.O.C.] / Rapid Fire [O] / Talkin' Trash [Timbaland ft. Bassy]

| 5/5/01 | 152 | 3 | | © 45 | Queer As Folk .... | | [V] | $10 | RCA Victor 63769 |

Randy Harrison/Gale Harold/Hal Sparks/Sharon Gless

Crying At The Discoteque [Alcazar] / High School Confidential [Carole Pope] / Shake Me [Mint Royale] / Summerfire [B-U]
Dive In The Pool [Barry Harris feat. Pepper Mashay] / Let's Hear It For The Boy [Katty B.] / Start Rockin' [Antiloop] / You Think You're A Man [Full Frontal]
Do Ya (Feel The Love) [Love Inc.] / Lovin' You [Kristine W] / Straight To...Number One [Touch and Go]
Proud [Heather Small] / Suffering [Jay-Jay Johanson]

| 9/18/93 | 156 | 18 | | © 46 | Ren & Stimpy: You Eediot! .... | | [M] | $10 | Nickelodeon 57400 |

animated series, voices by Billy West/Cheryl Chase/Vincent Waller

Better Than No One / Filthy's Dance / Log Theme (medley) / Space Madness (medley)
Big House Blues / Firedogs / Muddy Mudskipper Theme / Sven Blues
Captain's Log (medley) / Happy, Happy, Joy, Joy / Nose Goblins / Sven Theme
Dizzy Monkees / I'm Gonna Be A Monkey / Ren's Pecs / Whistler, The
Dog Pound Hop / Jungle Boogie / Royal Canadian Kilted Yaksmen
Don't Whiz On The Electric Fence / Log Blues (medley) / Smokin'

Roaring 20's, The - see PROVINE, Dorothy
Dorothy Provine/Donald May/Rex Reason
Roots - see JONES, Quincy
LeVar Burton/John Amos/Leslie Uggams/Ben Vereen

| 11/14/98 | 71 | 16 | ● | © 47 | Sabrina The Teenage Witch .... | | [V] | $10 | Geffen 25220 |

Melissa Joan Hart/Caroline Rhea/Beth Broderick/Nick Bakay

Abracadabra [Sugar Ray] / Hey, Mr. DJ (Keep Playin' This Song) [Backstreet Boys] / Magnet & Steel [Matthew Sweet] / Smash [Murmurs]
Amnesia [Chumbawamba] / One Way Or Another [Melissa Joan Hart] / So I Fall Again [Phantom Planet]
Blah, Blah, Blah [Cardigans] / I Know What Boys Like [Pure Sugar] / Soda Pop [Britney Spears]
Doctor Jones [Aqua] / Kate [Ben Folds Five] / **Show Me Love** [Robyn] 7 / Walk Of Life [Spice Girls]
Giddy Up ['N Sync] / Slam Dunk (Da Funk) [Five]

Sanford and Son - see FOXX, Redd
Redd Foxx/Demond Wilson/LaWanda Page/Whitman Mayo

| 12/25/76+ | 38 | 13 | | © 48 | Saturday Night Live .... | | [C] | $15 | Arista 4107 |

John Belushi/Dan Aykroyd/Chevy Chase/Jane Curtin/**Gilda Radner**

Anna Freud / Fluckers / Monologue / Weatherman
Bedtime Story / Fondue / News For The Hard Of Hearing / Weekend Update
Bees On Parade / Gerald Ford / Shimmer / Word Association
Chevy's Girls / Goodbyes / Speed
Dueling Brandos / Gun Control / Spud
Emily Litella / Jimmy Carter / Uvula

| 10/16/99 | 183 | 1 | | © 49 | Saturday Night Live - The Musical Performances Volume 1 .... | | [L-TV] | $10 | DreamWorks 50205 |

Are You Gonna Go My Way [Lenny Kravitz] / I Love L.A. [Randy Newman] / Round Here [Counting Crows] / Who Will Save Your Soul [Jewel]
Casey Jones [Grateful Dead] / If I Ever Lose My Faith In You [Sting] / Scary Monsters (And Super Creeps) [David Bowie] / Why [Annie Lennox]
Diamonds On The Soles Of Her Shoes [Paul Simon] / Only The Good Die Young [Billy Joel] / Secret O' Life [James Taylor] / Wonderful Tonight [Eric Clapton]
Honey Bee [Tom Petty] / Radio, Radio [Elvis Costello] / What Would You Say [Dave Matthews Band]

| 7/25/70 | 23 | 54 | ● | 50 | Sesame Street Book & Record, The .... | | [M] | $15 | Columbia 1069 |

Bob McGrath/Loretta Long/Jim Henson/Frank Oz/Carroll Spinney

ABC-DEF-GHI / Green / Number 5 / Sesame Street
Everybody Wash / I Love Trash / One Of These Things / Somebody Come And Play
Face, A / I've Got Two / People In Your Neighborhood / Up And Down
Five People In My Family / J-Jump / Rub Your Tummy / What Are Kids Called
Goin' For A Ride / Nearly Missed / **Rubber Duckie** [Ernie] 16

| 12/11/71+ | 78 | 10 | | 51 | Sesame Street 2 .... | | [M] | $15 | Warner 2569 |

Circles / High Middle Low / Play Along / What Do I Do When I'm Alone?
Everyone Makes Mistakes / I'm Pretty / Sesame Street / Word Family Song
Garden, The / Mad! / Sing
Grouch Song / Over Under Around And Through / Someday, Little Children
Has Anybody Seen My Dog? / Picture A World / Stop!

TELEVISION SOUNDTRACKS

DEBUT	PEAK	WKS	RIAA	CD	ARTIST — Album Title	Catalog	Sym	$	Label & Number

5/6/00   **42**   5   © 52   **'70s, The** .... [O-V]   **$10**   Island 542473
Brad Rowe/Guy Torry/Vinessa Shaw/Amy Smart/Kathryn Harrold

All Right Now [Free] 4	Hot Stuff [Donna Summer] 1	Nothing From Nothing [Billy Preston] 1
Can't Get Enough Of Your Love, Babe [Barry White] 1	Hustle, The [Van McCoy] 1	Three Little Birds [Bob Marley & The Wailers]
Don't Let The Sun Go Down On Me [Elton John] 2	Jessica [Allman Brothers Band] 65	What's Going On [Marvin Gaye] 2
Heart Of Glass [Blondie] 1	Joy To The World [Three Dog Night] 1	Papa Was A Rolling Stone [Temptations] 1
	Miracles [Jefferson Starship] 3	Peace Train [Cat Stevens] 7
		Superstition [Stevie Wonder] 1

4/20/59   **3**   28   53   **77 Sunset Strip**   [I]   **$50**   Warner 1289
Efrem Zimbalist, Jr./Roger Smith/Ed Byrnes; musical director: Warren Barker

Blue Night On The Strip	I Get A Kick Out Of You	Late At Bailey's Pad	Stu Bailey Blues
Caper At The Coffee House	If I Could Be With You	Lover Come Back To Me	Swingin' On The Strip
Cleo's Theme	Kookie's Caper	77 Sunset Strip	You Took Advantage Of Me

10/4/80   **115**   6   54   **Shogun** .... [I]   **$12**   RSO 3088
Richard Chamberlain/Toshiro Mifune/Yoko Shimada; cp/cd: Maurice Jarre

Anjiro	Despair And Madness	Mariko	Tea And Jealousy
Blackthorne	Escape From Osaka	Nocturne	To The Galley!
Ceremonial	Japans, The	Shogun	Toranaga

Simpsons Sing The Blues - see SIMPSONS
animated series, voices by Dan Castellaneta/Julie Kavner/Nancy Cartwright/Yeardley Smith/Hank Azaria/Harry Shearer

2/13/99   **22**   8   © 55   **'60s, The** .... [O-V]   **$10**   PolyGram TV 538743
Julia Stiles/Bill Smitrovich/Jerry O'Connell/Josh Hamilton

Can I Get A Witness [Marvin Gaye] 22	Do Wah Diddy Diddy [Manfred Mann] 1	Feelin' Alright [Traffic]	Somebody To Love [Jefferson Airplane] 5
Chicago [Graham Nash] 35	Do You Believe In Magic [Lovin' Spoonful] 9	My Boyfriend's Back [Angels] 1	Sunshine Of Your Love [Cream] 5
Chimes Of Freedom [Bob Dylan with Joan Osborne]	Don't Worry Baby [Beach Boys] 24	My Girl [Temptations] 1	Weight, The [Band] 63
	Draft Morning [Byrds]	Say It Loud, I'm Black And I'm Proud (Part 1) [James Brown] 10	Winds Of Change [Eric Burdon & The Animals]

1/22/00   **54**   26   ●   © 56   **Sopranos, The** .... [V]   **$10**   Play-Tone 63911
James Gandolfini/Lorraine Bracco/Nancy Marchand/Edie Falco/**Little Steven**

Beast In Me [Nick Lowe]	Gotta Serve Somebody [Bob Dylan] 24	Inside Of Me [Little Steven & The Disciples Of Soul]	Mystic Eyes [Them Feat. Van Morrison] 33
Blood Is Thicker Than Water [Wyclef Jean Feat. G&B]	I Feel Free [Cream]	It Was A Very Good Year [Frank Sinatra] 28	State Trooper [Bruce Springsteen]
Complicated Shadows [Elvis Costello & The Attractions]	I'm A Man [Bo Diddley]	It's Bad You Know [R.L. Burnside]	Viking [Los Lobos]
	I've Tried Everything [Eurythmics]		Woke Up This Morning [A3]

5/26/01   **38**   7   ●   © 57   **Sopranos: Peppers & Eggs, The** .... [V]   **$15**   Play-Tone 85453 [2]

Affection [Lost Boys]	Dialogue From "The Sopranos"	I (Who Have Nothing) [Ben E. King] 29	Return To Me [Bob Dylan]
Battle Flag [Pigeonhed]	Every Breath You Take (medley)	I've Got A Feeling [Campbell Brothers w/Katie Jackson]	Shuck Dub [R.L. Burnside]
Baubles, Bangles And Beads [Frank Sinatra]	Frank Sinatra [Cake]	Living On A Thin Line [Kinks]	Space Invader [Pretenders]
Black Books [Nils Lofgren]	Girl [Vue]	Make No Mistake [Keith Richards]	Sposa Son Dispressata [Cecilia Bartoli]
Captain, The [Kasey Chambers]	Gloria [Van Morrison]	My Lover's Prayer [Otis Redding] 61	Theme From Peter Gunn (medley)
Certamente [Madreblu]	High Fidelity [Elvis Costello & The Attractions]	Piove [Lorenzo Jovanotti]	Thru And Thru [Rolling Stones]
Core 'Ngrato [Dominic Chianese]			Tiny Tears [Tindersticks]

1/20/01   **147**   4   © 58   **Soul Food: The Series - The Best R&B Of 2000** .... [V]   **$10**   Def Soul 548156
Rockmond Dunbar/Irma Hall/Aaron Meeks/Darrin Dewitt Henson

All That I Can Say [Mary J. Blige] 44	I Don't Wanna [Aaliyah] 35	Sweet November [Case, Jazz of Dru Hill, Musiq, Montell Jordan & R.L.]	When A Woman's Fed Up [R. Kelly] 22
As We Lay [Kelly Price] 65	I Wish [Carl Thomas with LL Cool J] 20	Thong Song [Sisqó Feat. Foxy Brown] 3	Where I Wanna Be [Donell Jones] 29
Get It On...Tonite [Montell Jordan] 4	No Scrubs [TLC] 1	Through The Storm [Yolanda Adams]	
Happily Ever After [Case] 15	Separated [Avant] 23	Way Love Goes [Al Green]	
He Wasn't Man Enough [Toni Braxton] 2	Shackles (Praise You) [Mary Mary] 28		

12/1/73+   **34**   23   59   **Sunshine** .... [M]   **$15**   MCA 387
Cliff DeYoung/Christina Raines/Brenda Vaccaro/Meg Foster/Bill Mumy; cp: **John Denver**

Day Dreams	Goodbye, Sam & Jill	My Sweet Lady [Cliff DeYoung] 17	Winter
Diary	Hello Tape Recorder	My Sweet Lady (Instrumental)	
Flashback	I'm Gonna Miss You, Sam & Jill	Sunshine	
Goodbye Again	If I Had A Piano	Take Me Home, Country Roads	

Taxi - see JAMES, Bob
Judd Hirsch/Tony Danza/Marilu Henner/Danny DeVito/Andy Kaufman

12/21/74+   **30**   11   ●   60   **Tonight Show, Here's Johnny - Magic Moments From The** .... [C]   **$20**   Casablanca 1296 [2]
actual musical and comedy excerpts from the TV show hosted by Johnny Carson from October 1, 1962-May 22, 1992

All In The Family [Lucille Ball & Desi Arnaz, Jr.]	Copper Capers [Peter Falk & Jack Webb]	Lullabye Of Broadway (medley) [Bette Midler]	Singing In The Rain [Sammy Davis, Jr.]
Anniversary Salute [Dean Martin]	Discovery, The [Lenny Bruce]	Man That Got Away [Judy Garland]	Stars And Stripes Forever [Richard Nixon & John Twomey]
Art Fern & The Teatime Movies	Father's Day [Groucho Marx]	Morningside Heights [George Carlin]	Them There Eyes [Billie Holliday]
Beginning, The	Fiddler On The Bus [Jack Benny]	Mr. Warmth [Don Rickles]	Tonto, Tonto [Jay Silverheels]
Bleep That... [Buddy Hackett & Dean Martin]	Free For All [Jerry Lewis & Joey Bishop]	Ode To Billy Joe [Doc Severinsen]	Until You Come Back To Me (That's What I'm Gonna Do) [Aretha Franklin]
Boil That Cabbage Down [Smothers Brothers]	Indiana [Glen Campbell]	Our Love Is Here To Stay [Pearl Bailey]	What A Band
Boogie Woogie Bugle Boy (medley) [Bette Midler]	It's Gonna Work Out Fine [Ike & Tina Turner]	See Saw [Luci Arnaz]	

11/21/98   **16**   27   ▲   © 61   **Touched By An Angel - The Album** .... [V]   **$10**   550 Music 68971
Roma Downey/Della Reese/John Dye

Believe In You [Amanda Marshall]	Independence Day [Imani Coppola]	Somebody's Out There Watching [Kinleys]	When You Cry [Faith Hill]
Colour Everywhere [Deana Carter]	Little Bits Of Lightning [Martina McBride]	Testify To Love [Wynonna]	You Were Loved [Wynonna]
Dignity [Bob Dylan]	Love Can Move Mountains [Celine Dion with God's Property]	Walk With You [Della Reese & The Verity All-Stars]	
Follow Me Up [Keb' Mo']		When I See You Smile [Uncle Sam]	
God Loves You [Jaci Velasquez]	Shine All Your Light [Amy Grant]		
I Don't Know Why [Shawn Colvin]			

DEBUT	PEAK	WKS	RIAA	CD	ARTIST — Album Title	Catalog	Sym	$	Label & Number
12/4/99	86	7	©	62	**Touched By An Angel - The Christmas Album**		[X-V]	$10	550 Music 69710

Christmas chart: 9/'99

Breath Of Heaven (Mary's Song) *[Amy Grant]*	God Rest Ye Merry Gentlemen *[Randy Travis]*	If I Can Dream *[Della Reese]*
Christmas Spirit *[Donna Summer]*	God's With Us *[Ashley Robles]*	Irish Blessing *[Roma Downey/Phil Coulter]*
For Such A Time As This *[Wayne Watson]*	I Still Believe *[Crystal Lewis feat. Kirk Franklin]*	Jingle Bell Jamboree *[Keb' Mo]*
		Miracles *[Kenny Lattimore]*

O Holy Night *[Collin Raye]*
One Silent Night *[Jaci Velasquez]*
Panis Angelicus *[Charlotte Church]*

| 9/29/90 | 22 | 25 | ● © | 63 | **Twin Peaks**... | | [I] | $10 | Warner 26316 |

Kyle McLachlan/Michael Ontkean/Joan Chen/Sherilyn Fenn/Piper Laurie; cp/cd: Angelo Badalamenti

Audrey's Dance	Falling *[Julee Cruise]*	Laura Palmer's Theme
Bookhouse Boys	Freshly Squeezed	Love Theme
Dance Of The Dream Man	Into The Night *[Julee Cruise]*	Night Life In Twin Peaks

Nightingale, The *[Julee Cruise]*
Twin Peaks Theme

Velveteen Rabbit, The - see STREEP, Meryl / WINSTON, George

| 11/10/58+ | 2⁴ | 89 | | 64 | **Victory At Sea, Vol. 2** | | [I] | $25 | RCA Victor 2226 |

Allies On The March	Fire On The Waters	Mediterranean Mosaic
Danger Down Deep	Magnetic North	Peleliu

Sound Of Victory
Voyage Into Fate

| 9/11/61 | 7 | 32 | | 65 | **Victory At Sea, Vol. 3** | | [I] | $25 | RCA Victor 2523 |

above 2 are orchestral suites from the NBC-TV series which featured actual footage of World War II naval battles; cp: Richard Rodgers; cd: Robert Russell Bennett

Full Fathom Five	Ships That Pass	Turkey Shoot
Rings Around Rabaul	Symphonic Scenario	Turning Point

Two If By Sea

Waltons, The - see CHRISTMAS (Various Artists)

Richard Thomas/Ralph Waite/Michael Lerned/Will Geer/Ellen Corby

| 4/13/96 | 47 | 10 | © | 66 | **X-Files: Songs In The Key Of X, The**... | | [V] | $10 | Warner 46079 |

David Duchovny/Gillian Anderson/Mitch Pileggi/William B. Davis

Deep *[Danzig]*	Man Of Steel *[Frank Black]*	Star Me Kitten *[William S. Burroughs & R.E.M.]*
Down In The Park *[Foo Fighters]*	My Dark Life *[Elvis Costello w/Brian Eno]*	Thanks Bro *[Filter]*
Frenzy *[Screamin' Jay Hawkins]*	On The Outside *[Sheryl Crow]*	Time Jesum Transeuntum Et Non Riverentum
Hands Of Death (Burn Baby Burn) *[Rob Zombie & Alice Cooper]*	Red Right Hand *[Nick Cave & The Bad Seeds]*	Unexplained *[Meat Puppets]*
If You Never Say Goodbye *[P.M. Dawn]*		

Unmarked Helicopters *[Soul Coughing]*
X-Files Theme
X-Files Theme (Main Title) *[Mark Snow]*
X-Files Theme (P.M. Dawn Remix)

DEBUT	PEAK	WKS	RIAA	CD	ARTIST — Album Title	Catalog	Sym	$	Label & Number

CHRISTMAS (Various Artists)

12/16/00 — PEAK **145** — WKS **3** — © — **1 All-Star Christmas** .... **$10** Epic 85113
Christmas chart: 25/'00

Amazing Grace *[Jeff Beck]*	Every Year, Every Christmas *[Luther Vandross]*	I'll Be Home For Christmas *[Al Green]*
Christmas Song (Chestnuts Roasting On An Open Fire) *[Celine Dion]*	**Grandma Got Run Over By A Reindeer** *[Elmo & Patsy]* **87**	It's The Most Wonderful Time Of The Year *[Donny Osmond]*
Christmas Through Your Eyes *[Gloria Estefan]*	Have Yourself A Merry Little Christmas *[Babyface]*	Jingle Bell Jamboree *[Keb' Mo']*
Deck The Halls *[Millennia]*	(I Long To Feel The) Christmas Spirit *[Donna Summer]*	Last Christmas *[Wham!]*
Early Christmas Morning *[Cyndi Lauper]*		Little Drummer Boy *[Charlotte Church]*
		Love On Layaway *[Gloria Estefan]*

Rudolph The Red Nosed Reindeer *[Billy Gilman w/Ray Benson & Asleep At The Wheel]*
Silent Night (medley) *[Ottmar Liebert]*
Snow White (medley) *[Ottmar Liebert]*

11/20/82 — PEAK **96** — WKS **9** — © — **2 Annie's Christmas** .... **$12** Columbia 38361
children's story with music, narration and dialogue; Annie: Robin Ignico; narrator: William Woodson

Angels We Have Heard On High (medley)	Deck The Halls With Boughs Of Holly (medley)	Jolly Old St. Nicholas (medley)

We Wish You A Merry Christmas (medley)

1/20/01 — PEAK **22**ˣ — WKS **1** — © — **3 Arthur's Perfect Christmas** .... [TV] **$10** Rounder 8097
music from the PBS Kids animated TV special, plus 18 more holiday favorites

Angels We Have Heard On High	Fum, Fum, Fum	Nu Är Det Jul Igen
Baxter Day	Here We Come A'Wassailing	O Little Town Of Bethlehem
Boogie Woogie Christmas	I'm Not Scared Of Santa	O Tannenbaum
Bring A Torch, Jeanette, Isabella	It Came Upon A Midnight Clear	Perfect Christmas
Chanukah Blessing	It's Kwanzaa Time!	Perfect Christmas Reprise
Chanukah, Oh Chanukah	Jingle Bells	Sankta Lucia
First Noël	Joy To The World	Sevivon

Silent Night
We Three Kings
What Child Is This?
What's The Use Of Presents?

12/23/89+ — PEAK **24**ˣ — WKS **11** — ● — © — **4 Billboard Greatest Christmas Hits (1935-1954)** .... C:#37/11 **$10** Rhino 70637
Christmas charts: 28/'89, 25/'90, 24/'91, 35/'97

All I Want For Christmas (Is My Two Front Teeth) *[Spike Jones]*	**Christmas Song (Merry Christmas To You)** *[Nat "King" Cole]* **65**	I Saw Mommy Kissing Santa Claus *[Jimmy Boyd]*
Christmas Island *[Andrews Sisters & Guy Lombardo]*	Here Comes Santa Claus (Down Santa Claus Lane) *[Gene Autry]*	Let It Snow! Let It Snow! Let It Snow! *[Vaughn Monroe]*

Rudolph, The Red-Nosed Reindeer *[Gene Autry]* **70**
Santa Baby *[Eartha Kitt]*
Silent Night *[Bing Crosby]* **54**
White Christmas *[Bing Crosby]* **7**

12/23/89+ — PEAK **15**ˣ — WKS **59** — ▲ — © — **5 Billboard Greatest Christmas Hits (1955-Present)** .... C:#13/41 **$10** Rhino 70636
Christmas charts: 19/'89, 21/'90, 15/'91, 17/'92, 22/'93, 25/'94, 25/'95, 23/'96, 32/'97, 32/'99, 31/'00

Blue Christmas *[Elvis Presley]*	**Jingle Bell Rock** *[Bobby Helms]* **6**	**Nuttin' For Christmas** *[Barry Gordon]* **6**
Chipmunk Song *[Chipmunks w/David Seville]* **1**	**Little Drummer Boy** *[Harry Simeone Chorale]* **13**	**Please Come Home For Christmas** *[Charles Brown]* **76**
Grandma Got Run Over By A Reindeer *[Elmo 'N Patsy]* **87**	**Mary's Boy Child** *[Harry Belafonte]* **12**	

Rockin' Around The Christmas Tree *[Brenda Lee]* **14**
White Christmas *[Drifters]* **80**

12/21/63+ — PEAK **15**ˣ — WKS **3** — © — **6 Bonanza - Christmas on the Ponderosa** .... [TV] **$40** RCA Victor 2757
Christmas charts: 26/'63, 15/'64

Christmas Is A-Comin' (May God Bless You)	Hark! The Herald Angels Sing	Merry Christmas Neighbor
Deck The Halls	Jingle Bells	New Born King
First Christmas Trees	Merry Christmas And Goodnight (Silent Night)	O Come, All Ye Faithful
		Oh Fir Tree Dear

Santa Got Lost In Texas
Stuck In The Chimney
Why We Light Candles On The Christmas Tree

12/26/92 — PEAK **196** — WKS **1** — © — **7 Carnegie Hall Christmas Concert, A** .... [L] **$10** Sony Classical 48235
cd: **Andre Previn**; pf: **Kathleen Battle**, Frederica von Stade and **Wynton Marsalis**; recorded in New York City on 12/8/91

Alleluia	Evening Prayer	Lo, How A Rose E'er Blooming
American Songs Medley	Gesu Bambino	Maria Wiegenlied
Christmas Song (medley)	Have Yourself A Merry Little Christmas (medley)	Mary's Little Boy Chile
Christmas Songs Medley	Joy To The World!	My Favorite Things

Silent Night
Twelve Days Of Christmas
We Three Kings Of Orient Are
Winter Wonderland

12/14/96 — PEAK **113** — WKS **5** — © — **8 Carols Of Christmas, The** .... [I] **$10** Windham Hill 11193
Christmas chart: 22/'96

Angels We Have Heard On High (medley) *[Nightnoise]*	Do You Hear What I Hear? *[Jim Brickman]*	Hark! The Herald Angels Sing (medley) *[Nightnoise]*
Ave Maria *[Will Galison & Toninho Horta]*	Dona Nobis Pacem *[Richard Stoltzman]*	Have Yourself A Merry Little Christmas *[Brian Keane]*
Carol Of The Bells *[Steve Morse & Manuel Barruecco]*	Emmanuel *[Will Ackerman]*	O Holy Night *[David Darling]*
Christmas Time Is Here *[George Winston]*	First Noel *[John Boswell]*	Oh Little Town Of Bethlehem *[Tracy Silverman]*
	God Rest Ye Merry Gentlemen *[Michael Manring]*	Silent Night *[Ray Lynch]*

Simple Gifts *[Liz Story]*
We Three Kings *[Marion Meadows]*
What Child Is This? *[Michael Hedges]*

12/2/95 — PEAK **97** — WKS **6** — © — **9 Celtic Christmas** .... C:#36/3 [I] **$10** Windham Hill 11178
Christmas chart: 15/'95

Christmas Eve (medley) *[Kevin Burke & Micheal O Domhnaill]*	Nollaig Na Mban *[Cormac Breatnach]*	Snow On High Ground *[Nightnoise]*
Ciara *[Luka Bloom]*	On A Cold Winter's Day (medley) *[Kevin Burke & Micheal O Domhnaill]*	Soillse Na Nollag *[Altan]*
Galician Carol *[Carlos Nunez]*	Snow *[Loreena McKennitt]*	Solus *[Triona Ni Dhomhnaill]*
King Holly, King Oak *[Johnny Cunningham]*		Third Carol For Christmas Day *[Maighread Ni Dhomhnaill & Donal Lunny]*

We Follow A Star *[Jeff Johnson & Brian Dunning]*
When The Snow Melts *[Phil Cunningham & Manus Lunny]*
Winter's End *[Liam O'Flynn]*

11/30/96 — PEAK **96** — WKS **7** — © — **10 Celtic Christmas II** .... [I] **$10** Windham Hill 11192
Christmas chart: 14/'96

After Aughrim's Great Disaster *[Triona Ní Dhomhnaill]*	Dove's Return *[Áine Minogue]*	Lament *[Brian Dunning & Jeff Johnson]*
Amanecer (Dawn) *[Carlos Nunez]*	I'll Rock You To Rest *[James Galway]*	Listen To The River *[Luka Bloom]*
Bríd Óg Ní Mháille *[Nightnoise]*	Jenny's Chicken's (medley) *[Kevin Burke & Micheál Ó Dhomhnaill]*	Marbhna Luimní *[Deiseal]*
Chanonry Point *[Phil Cunningham & Manus Lunny]*	Johnny Seoighe *[Maighread Ní Dhomhnaill]*	Muladach Mi Is Mi Air M'aineol *[Capercaillie]*
Day's Last Light *[Seamus Egan]*		

Star Of The County Down (medley) *[Kevin Burke & Micheál Ó Domhnaill]*
Sweeney's Buttermilk *[Kevin Burke & Micheál Ó Domhnaill]*
Wexford Carol *[James Galway]*

11/29/97 — PEAK **103** — WKS **6** — © — **11 Celtic Christmas III** .... [I] **$10** Windham Hill 11233
Christmas charts: 13/'97, 34/'98

Angels In The Snow *[David Arkenstone]*	Coinnle An Linoh Iosa *[Seamus Begley & Stephen Cooney]*	Raven In The Snow *[Brian Dunning & Jeff Johnson]*
Black Is The Colour *[James McNally]*	Home *[Lisa Lynne]*	Sails Of Galway *[Snuffy Walden]*
Circle Of Joy *[Lisa Lynne]*	Lament *[Patrick Cassidy]*	Snows, The *[Maighread & Tríona Ní Dhomhnaill]*
	Lully Lullay *[Nightnoise]*	

South Wind *[Paddy Glackin & Micheál Ó Domhnaill]*
Wexford Carol *[David Agnew & David Downes]*

DEBUT	PEAK	WKS	RIAA	CD	ARTIST — Album Title	Catalog	Sym	$	Label & Number

11/21/98   **27**[X]   5   © 12   **Celtic Christmas IV** .... [I]   **$10**   Windham Hill 11367

Christmas chart: 27/'98

Airdí Cuan	Cradle Song	Morning Star
Droichead (The Bridge)	December Rain	Sior-Uaine (Evergreen)
Ar Droim Na Gaothe	Derdriu	St. Stephen's Green
Christmas Time's A Comin'	Kitty Magennis	Sweeney's Buttermilk

Whiter Than Snow

12/9/72   **7**[X]   12   13   **Christmas Album, The**   **C:#17/6**   **$20**   Columbia 30763 [2]

Christmas charts: 7/'72, 10/'73, 19/'91, 28/'92; also see #14 below

Christmas Bells [Patti Page]	Have Yourself A Merry Little	**Little Drummer Boy** [Johnny	Sleigh Ride [Johnny Mathis w/Percy
Christmas Song (Chestnuts	Christmas [Robert Goulet]	Cash] **63**	Faith]
Roasting On An Open Fire) [Tony	It Came Upon The Midnight Clear	O Come, All Ye Faithful [Jim	We Wish You A Merry Christmas
Bennett]	[Burl Ives]	Nabors]	[Andre Kostelanetz]
Deck The Hall With Boughs Of Holly	It's The Most Wonderful Time Of	O Little Town Of Bethlehem [Marty	White Christmas [Frank Sinatra]
[Mormon Tabernacle Choir/N.Y.	The Year [Andy Williams]	Robbins]	Winter Wonderland [Mitch Miller &
Philharmonic]	Jingle Bells? [Barbra Streisand]	Silent Night, Holy Night [Mahalia	The Gang]
First Noel [Anita Bryant]	Joy To The World [Percy Faith]	Jackson]	
Greensleeves (What Child Is This)	Let It Snow! Let It Snow! Let It	Silver Bells [Jerry Vale]	
[Ray Conniff Singers]	Snow! [Doris Day]		

12/19/87+   **26**[X]   5   14   **Christmas Album, A** ....   **$10**   Columbia 39466

all 11 tracks taken from #13 above; Christmas charts: 27/'87, 26/'88

Christmas Song (Chestnuts	Have Yourself A Merry Little	Joy To The World [Percy Faith	We Wish You A Merry Christmas
Roasting On An Open Fire)	Christmas [Robert Goulet]	Orch.]	[Andre Kostelanetz]
Deck The Hall With Boughs Of	It's The Most Wonderful Time Of	O Come, All Ye Faithful [Jim	White Christmas [Frank Sinatra]
Holly [Mormon Tabernacle	The Year [Andy Williams]	Nabors]	Winter Wonderland [Mitch Miller]
Choir/New York Philharmonic]	Jingle Bells? [Barbra Streisand]	Sleigh Ride [Johnny Mathis w/Percy	
		Faith Orch.]	

11/20/99   **40**[X]   1   © 15   **Christmas: All-Time Greatest Records, Volume 2** ....   **$10**   Curb 77515

first released in 1991

Christmas Song [Osmond Brothers]	I Saw Mommy Kissing Santa Claus	**Rockin' Around The Christmas**	Sleigh Ride [Jack Jones]
God Rest Ye Merry Gentlemen	[Andy Williams]	**Tree** [Brenda Lee] **14**	What Are You Doing New Years
[Bobby Vinton]	I'll Be Home For Christmas [Wayne	Santa Claus Is Coming To Town	Eve [Donny Osmond]
Have Yourself A Merry Little	Newton]	[Andrews Sisters]	White Christmas [Don McLean]
Christmas [Judy Garland]	**Jingle Bell Rock** [Bobby Helms] **6**	Silver Bells [Bing Crosby]	

12/14/63   **13**[X]   3   16   **Christmas Gift For You (From Philles Records), A** ....   **$150**   Philles 4005

Bells Of St. Mary [Bob B. Soxx &	Here Comes Santa Claus [Bob B.	Parade Of The Wooden Soldiers	Silent Night [Phil Spector & Artists]
The Blue Jeans]	Soxx & The Blue Jeans]	[Crystals]	Sleigh Ride [Ronettes]
Christmas (Baby Please Come	I Saw Mommy Kissing Santa Claus	Rudolph, The Red-Nosed Reindeer	White Christmas [Darlene Love]
Home) [Darlene Love]	[Ronettes]	[Crystals]	Winter Wonderland [Darlene Love]
Frosty The Snowman [Ronettes]	Marshmallow World [Darlene Love]	Santa Claus Is Coming To Town	
		[Crystals]	

12/19/87+   **22**[X]   10   © 17   **Christmas Gift For You (From Phil Spector), A** .... [R]   **$15**   Rhino 70235

reissue of A Christmas Gift For You (Philles/1963); Christmas charts: 25/'87, 22/'88, 30/'90

Bells Of St. Mary [Bob B. Soxx &	Here Comes Santa Claus [Bob B.	Parade Of The Wooden Soldiers	Silent Night [Phil Spector & Artists]
The Blue Jeans]	Soxx & The Blue Jeans]	[Crystals]	Sleigh Ride [Ronettes]
Christmas (Baby Please Come	I Saw Mommy Kissing Santa Claus	Rudolph The Red-Nosed Reindeer	White Christmas [Darlene Love]
Home) [Darlene Love]	[Ronettes]	[Crystals]	Winter Wonderland [Darlene Love]
Frosty The Snowman [Ronettes]	Marshmallow World [Darlene Love]	Santa Claus Is Coming To Town	
		[Crystals]	

12/1/73   **7**[X]   4   © 18   **Christmas Greetings From Nashville**   **$15**   RCA Victor 0262

Blue Christmas [Browns] **97**	Christmas Time's A-Coming	I Heard The Bells On Christmas	Old Christmas Card [Jim Reeves]
Christmas Song (Chestnuts	[Skeeter Davis]	Day [Chet Atkins]	Silent Night [Eddy Arnold]
Roasting On An Open Fire)	Frosty The Snowman [Porter	Jingle Bell Rock [Floyd Cramer]	You Are My Christmas, Carol [Dottie
[Danny Davis]	Wagoner]	Little Stranger (In A Manger) [Hank	West]
		Snow]	

12/23/67   **98**[X]   2   19   **Christmas in Germany** .... [F]   **$15**   Capitol 10095

10 of 14 songs performed by the 120+ children's choir "Bielefelder Kinderchor"; first released in 1957

Alle Jahre Wieder (medley)	Heil'ge Nacht, Nacht Der	Kling, Glöckchen, Kling	Stille Nacht, Heilige Nacht
Es Ist Ein Ros' Entsprungen	Unendlichen Liebe	Leise Rieselt Der Schnee	Süsser Die Glocken Hie Klingen
(medley)	Heil'ge Nacht, O Giesse Du	O Du Fröhliche (medley)	Von Himmel Hoch (medley)
	Ihr Kinderlein Kommet (medley)	O Tannenbaum (medley)	Weisse Weihnacht

---

12/16/95   **161**   3   © 20   **Christmas Of Hope** ....   **$10**   Columbia 67407

Bells Of St. Mary's [Aaron Neville]	Let It Snow! Let It Snow! Let It	**Please Come Home For**	Step Into Christmas [Elton John]
I'll Be Home For Christmas [Reba	Snow! [Wynton Marsalis]	**Christmas** [Eagles] **18**	Teddi's Song (When Christmas
McEntire]	Merry Christmas, Baby [James	Santa Claus Is Comin' To Town	Comes) [John Mellencamp]
Joy To The World [Aretha Franklin]	Brown]	[Bruce Springsteen]	
	New Year's Day [U2] **53**	Silent Night [Mariah Carey]	

12/28/96   **155**   2   © 21   **Christmas On Death Row** ....   **$10**   Death Row 90108

Christmas chart: 35/'96

Be Thankful [Nate Dogg]	Have Yourself A Merry Little	Party 4 Da Homies [Sean Barney	Silent Night [B.G.O.T.I./6 Feet
Christmas Everyday [Guess]	Christmas [6 Feet Deep]	Thomas]	Deep/Guess]
Christmas In The Ghetto [Operation	I Wish [Dogg Pound]	Peaceful Christmas [Danny Boy]	Silver Bells [Michel'le]
From The Bottom]	O Holy Night [B.G.O.T.I.]	Santa Claus Goes Straight To The	This Christmas [Danny Boy]
Christmas Song [Danny Boy]	On This Glorious Day ["816"]	Ghetto [Snoop Doggy Dogg]	White Christmas [Guess]
Frosty The Snowman [6 Feet Deep]			

12/12/87+   **130**   8   © 22   **Christmas Rap** ....   **$10**   Profile 1247

Christmas charts: 4/'87, 4/'88

Chillin' With Santa [Derek B]	Dana Dane Is Coming To Town	Let The Jingle Bells Rock [Sweet	That's What I Want For Christmas
Christmas In Hollis [Run-D.M.C.]	[Dana Dane]	Tee]	[Showboys]
Christmas In The City [King Sun-D	Ghetto Santa [Spyder-D]	Surf M.C. New Year [Surf M.C.'s]	
Moet]	He's Santa Claus [Disco 4]		

CHRISTMAS (Various Artists)

DEBUT	PEAK	WKS	RIAA	CD	ARTIST — Album Title	Catalog	Sym	$	Label & Number

11/23/96 · 28ˣ · 4 · © 23 · Christmas: 16 Most Requested Songs .... $10 · Columbia/Legacy 48947
Christmas charts: 28/'96, 34/'99

- Christmas Song (Chestnuts Roasting On An Open Fire) [Mel Tormé]
- Frosty The Snow Man [Gene Autry]
- Have Yourself A Merry Little Christmas [Robert Goulet]
- Here Comes Santa Claus [Doris Day]
- I Saw Mommy Kissing Santa Claus [Jimmy Boyd]
- I'll Be Home For Christmas [Johnny Mathis]
- Joy To The World [Mahalia Jackson]
- **Rudolph The Red-Nosed Reindeer [Gene Autry] 70**
- Santa Claus Is Coming To Town [Patti Page]
- Silent Night, Holy Night [Julie Andrews]
- Silver Bells [Ray Conniff Singers]
- Sleigh Ride [Andy Williams]
- Twelve Days Of Christmas [Mitch Miller]
- We Need A Little Christmas [Angela Lansbury/Frankie Michaels/Jane Connell/Sab Shimono]
- White Christmas [Tony Bennett]
- Winter Wonderland [Rosemary Clooney]

12/19/98 · 186 · 2 · © 24 · Colors Of Christmas, The .... $10 · Windham Hill 11368
Christmas chart: 32/'98

- Born On Christmas Day [Peabo Bryson]
- Breath Of Heaven (Mary's Song) [Melissa Manchester]
- Christmas Song [Oleta Adams]
- Gift, The [Roberta Flack & Peabo Bryson]
- Have Yourself A Merry Little Christmas [Melissa Manchester]
- It's The Most Wonderful Time Of The Year [Peabo Bryson]
- Lord's Prayer [Sheena Easton]
- O' Come All Ye Faithful [Roberta Flack]
- Place Where We Belong [Sheena Easton & Jeffrey Osborne]
- Silent Night [Philip Bailey]
- This Christmas [Jeffrey Osborne]
- Who Would Imagine A King [Philip Bailey]

11/25/95 · 173 · 1 · © 25 · Contemporary Gospel Christmas, A .... C:#3/13 · $10 · Regency 20026
Christmas charts: 20/'95, 5/'96, 15/'99

- Auld Lang Syne [Derrick Lee & Ralph Lofton]
- Away In A Manger [Tomaz Vinson]
- Go, Tell It On The Mountain [Jackie Reddick]
- Hark! The Herald Angels Sing [Beverly Crawford & Mike-E]
- It Came Upon A Midnight Clear [Z-da James]
- Joy To The World [Francine Belcher]
- O Holy Night [Bob Bailey]
- Silent Night [Kelli Williams]
- What Child Is This? [Mark Baldwin & Mark Douthit]

12/25/82+ · 172 · 4 · 26 · Country Christmas, A .... $12 · RCA Victor 4396
- Christmas In Dixie [Alabama]
- Christmas Is Just A Song For Us This Year [Louise Mandrell/RC Bannon]
- Every Time I Hear Blue Christmas (I Get The Christmas Blues) [Leon Everette]
- Fall Softly Snow [Jim Ed Brown/Helen Cornelius]
- Let It Snow, Let It Snow, Let It Snow [Charley Pride]
- Noel, Noel [Steve Wariner]
- Peace On Earth (A Song For All Seasons) [Razzy Bailey]
- Pretty Paper [Willie Nelson]

12/20/97 · 159 · 2 · © 27 · Country Cares For Kids .... $10 · BNA 67518
Christmas chart: 28/'97

- Angels Among Us [Alabama]
- Butterfly Kisses [Bob Carlisle]
- Christmas For Every Boy And Girl [Clint Black]
- Christmas Song [John Berry]
- Christmas Time's A Comin' [Sammy Kershaw]
- I'll Be Home For Christmas [Lonestar]
- Let's Talk About Love [Mindy McCready]
- Loving Time Of The Year [Travis Tritt]
- Make A Miracle [Various Artists]
- O Holy Night [Martina McBride]
- Take A Walk Through Bethlehem [Ray Vega]
- Up On Santa Claus Mountain [Lorrie Morgan]
- We Three Kings (Star Of Wonder) [Blackhawk]
- When You Wish Upon A Star [Bryan White]

11/29/97 · 96 · 6 · © 28 · Country Superstar Christmas, A .... $10 · Hip-O 40066
Christmas chart: 13/'97

- Angels Cried [Alan Jackson with Alison Krauss]
- Away In A Manger [Reba McEntire]
- Christmas Like Mama Used To Make It [Tracy Byrd]
- Christmas Song (Chestnuts Roasting On An Open Fire) [Trisha Yearwood]
- Let There Be Peace On Earth [Vince Gill with Jenny Gill]
- Let's Make A Baby King [Wynonna]
- Merry Christmas Strait To You [George Strait]
- O Holy Night [Lorrie Morgan]
- O Little Town Of Bethlehem [Alabama]
- Please Come Home For Christmas [Gary Allan]
- Santa Claus Is Back In Town [Mavericks]
- Santa Claus Is Comin' (In A Boogie Woogie Choo Choo Train) [Tractors]
- Santa Claus Is Coming To Town [Vince Gill]
- Santa's Reindeer Ride [Amy Grant]

12/12/98 · 152 · 3 · © 29 · Country Superstar Christmas II, A .... $10 · Hip-O 40124
Christmas chart: 27/'98

- Cabin In The Valley [Brooks & Dunn]
- Christmas Won't Be Christmas Without You [Sammy Kershaw]
- God Bless The Child [Shania Twain]
- I'll Be Home For Christmas [Vince Gill]
- It's The Most Wonderful Time Of The Year [Amy Grant]
- Little Drummer Boy [Collin Raye]
- No Room [Rhett Akins]
- Nothing But A Child [Lee Ann Womack]
- On Christmas Morning [Steve Wariner]
- Slow As Christmas [Clint Black]
- Two Steppin' Around The Christmas Tree [Suzy Bogguss]
- When It's Christmas Time In Texas [George Strait]
- Wrap Me In Your Love [Joe Diffie]

12/16/00 · 185 · 2 · © 30 · Country Superstar Christmas III, A .... $10 · Hip-O 541831
Christmas chart: 40/'00

- Christmas Cookies [George Strait]
- Christmas In Dixie [Alabama]
- Christmas Rock [Toby Keith]
- Holly Jolly Christmas [Alan Jackson]
- I'll Be Home For Christmas [Martina McBride]
- Let It Snow! Let It Snow! Let It Snow! [Chely Wright]
- New Star Shining [Mark Wills]
- O Come All Ye Faithful [Vince Gill]
- Pretty Paper [Randy Travis]
- Silent Night [Reba McEntire]
- What Child Is This? [Alecia Elliott]
- Winter Wonderland [Sammy Kershaw]

12/7/91 · 25ˣ · 3 · © 31 · Disney presents A Family Christmas .... $10 · Disneyland 005
Christmas charts: 25/'91, 28/'92

- Away In A Manger
- Deck The Halls
- First Noel
- From All Of Us To All Of You
- Frosty The Snow Man
- Here Comes Santa Claus
- Here We Come A-Caroling
- Jingle Bells
- Jolly Old Saint Nicholas
- Joy To The World
- O Christmas Tree
- Rudolph, The Red-Nosed Reindeer
- Silent Night
- Silver Bells
- Sleigh Ride
- Twelve Days Of Christmas
- We Wish You A Merry Christmas
- Winter Wonderland

11/30/96 · 192 · 1 · © 32 · Disney's Christmas Collection .... C:#5/25 · $10 · Walt Disney 60887
Christmas charts: 17/'96, 10/'97, 3/'98, 33/'99, 24/'00

- Away In A Manger
- From All Of Us To All Of You
- Hark The Herald Angels Sing (medley)
- Here We Come A-Caroling
- Jingle Bells
- O Christmas Tree
- O Come All Ye Faithful (medley)
- O Little Town of Bethlehem (medley)
- Silent Night
- 'Twas The Night Before Christmas
- We Wish You A Merry Christmas

12/2/95 · 119 · 5 · © 33 · Disney's Christmas Sing Along .... $10 · Walt Disney 60882
Christmas chart: 22/'95

- Deck The Halls
- Frosty The Snowman
- Here We Come A-Caroling
- Jingle Bells
- Jolly Old St. Nicholas
- Joy To The World
- O Christmas Tree
- Rudolph The Red-Nosed Reindeer
- Silent Night
- We Wish You A Merry Christmas

12/5/98 · 187 · 3 · ● © 34 · Disney's Favorite Christmas Songs .... $10 · Walt Disney 60987

- Deck The Halls
- Here Comes Santa Claus
- Jingle Bells
- Jolly Old St. Nicholas
- Joy To The World
- Rare Old Christmas
- Silent Night
- Sleigh Ride
- We Wish You A Merry Christmas
- What Child Is This?

DEBUT	PEAK	WKS	RIAA	CD	ARTIST — Album Title	Catalog	Sym	$	Label & Number

12/6/97 — **32**[X] — **2** — © 35 — **Disney's Season Of Song: A Traditional Holiday Collection** .... [I] — **$10** — Walt Disney 60843

Away In A Manger	Good King Wenceslas	Joy To The World (medley)
Bring A Torch	Hark! The Herald Angels Sing	Let There Be Peace On Earth
Carol Of The Bells	Have Yourself A Merry Little	Little Drummer Boy
Dance Of The Sugar-Plum Fairies	Christmas	March Of The Toy Soldiers (medley)
Gloria In Excelsis Deo	It Came Upon A Midnight Clear	Messiah Majesty
God Rest Ye Merry Gentlemen	Jingle Bells	O Come All Ye Faithful
(medley)	Jolly Old St. Nicholas	O Holy Night

Right column: Rudolph The Red-Nosed Reindeer / Russian Dance / Santa Claus Is Coming To Town / Up On The Housetop / What Child Is This? / Winter Wonderland

12/7/91 — **8**[X] — **10** — © 36 — **50 All Time Christmas Favorites** — C:#11/15 — **$15** — Madacy 3289 [2]

all songs performed by Canadian studio vocalists and musicians; Christmas charts: 8/'91, 16/'92, 39/'94

Adeste Fideles	Deck The Halls	I Wonder As I Wander
Amen	Ding Dong Merrily On High	Infant King
Angels From The Realms	First Noel	It Came Upon A Midnight Clear
Angels We Have Heard On High	For On To Us A Child Is Born	Jingle Bells
As With Gladness Men Of Old	From Heaven On High I Come	Jolly Old St. Nicholas
Auld Lang Syne	Gloria In Excelsis Deo	Joy To The World
Ave Maria	Go Tell It On The Mountain	Lo How A Rose
Away In A Manger	God Rest Ye Merry Gentlemen	O Christmas Tree
Christians Awake	Good Christian Men Rejoice	O Come All Ye Faithful
Christmas Song	Good King Wenceslas	O Holy Night
Coventry Carol	Hallelujah	O Little Town Of Bethlehem
Dance Of The Reed Flutes	Hark The Herald Angels Sing	O Tannenbaum
Dance Of The Sugar Plum Fairy	Holly And The Ivy	Oh Thou Joyful Day

Far right column: Once In Royal David's City / Patapan / Silent Night, Holy Night / Silver Bells / Twelve Days Of Christmas / Up On The Housetop / We Three Kings Of Orient Are / We Wish You A Merry Christmas / What Child Is This? / While Shepherd's Watched Their Flocks By Night / White Christmas

12/25/99 — **179** — **2** — © 37 — **Gift Of Christmas, A** .... — **$10** — Foundation 99681

Christmas chart: 39/'99

Adeste Fideles [James Galway]	Carol Of The Bells [George Winston]	Greensleeves [Kenny G]
Angels We Have Heard On High [Robert Shaw Chorale]	**Christmas Song (Chestnuts Roasting On An Open Fire)** [Nat King Cole] 65	Hark! The Herald Angels Sing [Mannheim Steamroller]
Ave Maria [Placido Domingo]		I Saw Three Ships A Sailing [Chieftains w/Marianne Faithfull]
Blue Christmas [Elvis Presley]	Gift, [Jim Brickman]	It's Christmas [*N Sync]

Right column: Merry Christmas Baby [Etta James] / Merry Christmas Wherever You Are [Judy Collins] / Miracle Of Love [Eurythmics] / Wonderful Christmastime [Paul McCartney & Wings]

11/29/97 — **35**[X] — **1** — © 38 — **God With Us: A Celebration Of Christmas Carols & Classics** .... — **$10** — Sparrow 51642

All Is Well Tonight [CeCe Winans]	Child Of Peace [Sandi Patty]	I'll Be Home For Christmas [Clay Crosse]
Angels We Have Heard On High [Avalon]	First Noel [Steve Green]	Joy To The World [Anointed]
Anthem For Christmas [Michael W. Smith]	Go Tell It On The Mountain [Larnelle Harris]	O Come, O Come, Emmanuel [Steven Curtis Chapman]

Right column: O Holy Night [Out Of The Grey] / Silent Night [Twila Paris] / Still Her Little Child [Ray Boltz] / Sweet Little Jesus Boy [Chris Willis] / What Child Is This [Cheri Keaggy]

1/7/89 — **140** — **2** — ● © 39 — **GRP Christmas Collection, A** .... — **$10** — GRP 9574

Christmas charts: 5/'88, 5/'89, 11/'90

Carol Of The Bells [David Benoit]	Have Yourself A Merry Little Christmas [Tom Scott]	Silent Night [Special EFX]
Christmas Song [Diane Schuur]	Little Drummer Boy [Daryl Stuermer]	Sleigh Ride [Eddie Daniels]
God Rest Ye Merry Gentlemen [Chick Corea Elektric Band]	Santa Claus Is Coming To Town [Dave Valentin]	Some Children See Him [Dave Grusin]
		This Christmas [Yutaka]

Right column: What Child Is This? (Greensleeves) [Mark Egan] / White Christmas [Lee Ritenour]

1/6/90 — **162** — **1** — ● © 40 — **GRP Christmas Collection, A** .... [R] — **$10** — GRP 9574

see album above for tracks

12/14/91 — **137** — **4** — © 41 — **GRP Christmas Collection Vol. II, A** .... — **$10** — GRP 9650

Christmas chart: 17/'91

Angels We Have Heard On High [Don Grusin]	First Noel [George Howard]	Let It Snow! Let It Snow! Let It Snow! [Nelson Rangell]
Blue Christmas [Laima]	I Wonder As I Wander [New York Voices]	Let There Be Peace On Earth [Voyceboxing]
Christmas Time Is Here [Patti Austin]	I'll Be Home For Christmas [Spyro Gyra]	O Come All Ye Faithful [Arturo Sandoval]
Earl Of Salisbury Pavane [Acoustic Alchemy]	Jesu, Joy Of Man's Desiring [Russ Freeman]	O Holy Night [Carl Anderson]

Right column: We Three Kings Of Orient Are [Deborah Henson-Conant]

12/25/93 — **185** — **1** — © 42 — **GRP Christmas Collection Vol. III, A** .... [I] — **$10** — GRP 9728

Deck The Halls [Billy Taylor]	Hark The Herald Angels Sing [Ramsey Lewis]	Joy To The World [Kim Pensyl]
Feliz Navidad [Tom Scott]	I'll Be Home For Christmas [Diane Schuur]	Lo, How A Rose E'er Blooming [Dave Grusin]
Go Tell It On The Mountain [Yellowjackets]		Merry Christmas Baby [B.B. King]

Right column: O' Little Town Of Bethlehem [David Benoit] / There's No Place Like Home For The Holidays [Sergio Salvatore]

12/5/92 — **82** — **6** — © 43 — **Handel's Messiah - A Soulful Celebration** .... — **$10** — Reprise 26980

Christmas chart: 12/'92

And He Shall Purify [Tramaine Hawkins]	Comfort Ye My People [Vanessa Bell Armstrong & Daryl Coley]	Hallelujah!
And The Glory Of The Lord [Dianne Reeves]	Every Valley Shall Be Exalted [Lizz Lee & Chris Willis]	I Know That My Redeemer Liveth [Tevin Campbell]
Behold, A Virgin Shall Conceive [Howard Hewitt]	For Unto Us A Child Is Born [Core Cotton/Jamecia Bennett/James Wright/Carrie Harrington/Pat Lacey]	Lift Up Your Heads, O Ye Gates [Commissioned & The Clark Sisters]
Behold The Lamb Of God [Yellowjackets]		O Thou That Tellest Good Tidings To Zion [Stevie Wonder & Take 6]
But Who May Abide The Day Of His Coming [Patti Austin]	Glory To God [Boys Choir Of Harlem]	Partial History Of Black Music Medley

Right column: Rejoice Greatly, O Daughter Of Zion [Richard Smallwood Singers] / Why Do The Nations So Furiously Rage? [Al Jarreau]

11/29/97 — **150** — **5** — © 44 — **Happy Holidays Love, Barney** .... — **$10** — Barney 9517

Christmas chart: 11/'97

Deck The Halls	I Love You	Let It Snow! Let It Snow! Let It Snow!
Frosty The Snow Man	It's Snowing!	My Dreidel
Habari Gani	It's Twinkle Time	Over The River And Through The Woods
Hey, Santa Claus	Jingle-Bell Rock	Rudolph The Red-Nosed Reindeer
Holly Jolly Christmas	Jingle Bells	
I Love The Holidays		

Right column: Sleigh Ride / Suzy Snowflake / Twelve Days Of Christmas / Up On The House-Top / We Wish You A Merry Christmas / Winter Wonderland

12/9/67 — **54**[X] — **4** — 45 — **Have A Jewish Christmas...?** .... [C] — **$15** — Tower 5081

Lennie Weinrib narrates comedy sketches

Christmas Cards	Party, The	Shut Up Irving
Christmas Machers	Problem, The	Tanta And The Tree
Christmas Trees	Santa Claus	

CHRISTMAS (Various Artists)

DEBUT	PEAK	WKS	RIAA	CD	ARTIST — Album Title	Catalog	Sym	$	Label & Number
12/9/95	95	5		© 46	**Jazz To The World**	C:#36/2	[I]	$10	Blue Note 32127

Angels We Have Heard On High *[Steps Ahead]*
Baby, It's Cold Outside *[Dianne Reeves & Lou Rawls]*
Christmas Blues *[Holly Cole]*
Christmas Song *[Anita Baker]*
Christmas Waltz *[Brecker Brothers w/Steve Khan]*
Have Yourself A Merry Little Christmas *[Diana Krall]*
I'll Be Home For Christmas *[Herbie Hancock & Eliane Elias]*
Il Est Ne, Le Divin Enfant *[Dr. John]*
It Came Upon A Midnight Clear *[Fourplay]*
Let It Snow! Let It Snow! Let It Snow! *[Michael Franks]*
Little Drummer Boy *[Cassandra Wilson]*
O Come O Come Emmanuel *[John McLaughlin]*
O Tannenbaum *[Stanley Clarke, George Duke & Everette Harp]*
What Child Is This? *[Chick Corea]*
Winter Wonderland *[Herb Alpert & Jeff Lorber]*
Winter Wonderland *[Dave Koz]*

DEBUT	PEAK	WKS	RIAA	CD	ARTIST — Album Title	Catalog	Sym	$	Label & Number
12/10/88	28[X]	2		© 47	**Jingle Bell Jazz**		[I]	$10	Columbia 36803

originally issued in 1962 on Columbia 8693 (The Dukes of Dixieland's "Frosty The Snowman" replaced by Herbie Hancock's "Deck The Halls")

Blue Xmas (To Whom It May Concern) *[Miles Davis]*
Christmas Song (Chestnuts Roasting On An Open Fire) *[Carmen McRae]*
Deck The Halls *[Herbie Hancock]*
Deck Us All With Boston Charlie *[Lambert, Hendricks & Ross]*
If I Were A Bell *[Manhattan Jazz All Stars]*
Jingle Bells *[Duke Ellington]*
Rockin' Around The Christmas Tree *[Marlowe Morris]*
Rudolph, The Red-Nosed Reindeer *[Pony Poindexter]*
Santa Claus Is Comin' To Town *[Dave Brubeck Quartet]*
We Three Kings Of Orient Are *[Paul Horn]*
White Christmas *[Lionel Hampton]*
Winter Wonderland *[Chico Hamilton]*

DEBUT	PEAK	WKS	RIAA	CD	ARTIST — Album Title	Catalog	Sym	$	Label & Number
1/1/94	186	2		© 48	**LaFace Family Christmas, A**			$10	LaFace 26011

Christmas chart: 28/'93

All I Want For Christmas *[TLC]*
Christmas Song *[Toni Braxton]*
Have Yourself A Merry Little Christmas *[McArthur]*
Merry Christmas My Dear *[Few Good Men]*
Player's Ball *[OutKast]* **37**
Silver Bells *[Few Good Men]*
Sleigh Ride *[TLC]*
This Christmas *[Usher]*

DEBUT	PEAK	WKS	RIAA	CD	ARTIST — Album Title	Catalog	Sym	$	Label & Number
12/24/66	76[X]	1			**Littlest Angel, The**			$25	Decca 8009

a Charles Tazewell story (written in 1946), narrated by Loretty Young; B-side is also a Tazewell story, narrated by Gregory Peck; first released in 1950

Littlest Angel *[Loretta Young]*
Lullaby Of Christmas *[Gregory Peck]*

DEBUT	PEAK	WKS	RIAA	CD	ARTIST — Album Title	Catalog	Sym	$	Label & Number
12/27/69+	14[X]	4		© 50	**Littlest Angel, The**		[TV]	$25	Mercury 603

original cast album from the Hallmark Hall of Fame TV special starring Johnnie Whitaker and Fred Gwynne;
Christmas charts: 25/'69, 14/'70

Heavenly Ever After *[Cab Calloway & Chorus]*
I Bring You Good Tidings *[Angel Chorus]*
I Have Saved *[Johnnie Whitaker & Chorus]*
I Have Saved (Reprise) *[Johnnie Whitaker]*
I'm Master Of All I Survey *[Johnnie Whitaker & Chorus]*
May It Bring Him Pleasure *[Angel Chorus]*
Once Upon Another Time *[Fred Gwynne]*
What Do You Do (When You Say You're Doin' Nothin') *[Fred Gwynne]*
Where Am I *[Johnnie Whitaker & Chorus]*
Where Is Blue *[Johnnie Whitaker & Fred Gwynne]*
You Can Fly *[Connie Stevens & Angel Chorus]*
You're Not Real *[Tony Randall & Corinna Manetto]*

DEBUT	PEAK	WKS	RIAA	CD	ARTIST — Album Title	Catalog	Sym	$	Label & Number
12/30/57+	19	3		51	**Merry Christmas From The Ames Brothers - Don Cornell - Eileen Barton - Johnny Desmond**		[EP]	$50	Coral EC 82003 [2]

7" double-packet EP (originally released as a 10" LP in 1952 on Coral 56080)

Christmas Is A Time (That Will Never Change) *[Johnny Desmond]*
I've Got The Christmas Spirit *[Don Cornell]*
Let's Have An Old Fashioned Christmas *[Don Cornell]*
Little Match Girl *[Eileen Barton]*
Night Before Christmas Song *[Eileen Barton]*
Sing A Song Of Santa Claus *[Ames Brothers]*
Winter's Here Again *[Ames Brothers]*
(You Can Just Feel) Christmas In The Air *[Johnny Desmond]*

DEBUT	PEAK	WKS	RIAA	CD	ARTIST — Album Title	Catalog	Sym	$	Label & Number
12/28/68	24[X]	1		52	**Merry Christmas from Motown**			$30	Motown 681

reissued in 1970 as *Christmas Gift Rap* on Motown 725

Ave Maria *[Stevie Wonder]*
Christmas Everyday *[Smokey Robinson & The Miracles]*
Christmas Lullaby *[Smokey Robinson & The Miracles]*
God Rest Ye Merry Gentlemen *[Smokey Robinson & The Miracles]*
My Christmas Tree *[Diana Ross & The Supremes]*
One Little Christmas Tree *[Stevie Wonder]*
Rudolph, The Red-Nosed Reindeer *[Temptations]*
Santa Claus Is Comin' To Town *[Diana Ross & The Supremes]*
Silent Night *[Temptations]*
Silver Bells *[Diana Ross & The Supremes]*
What Christmas Means To Me *[Stevie Wonder]*
White Christmas *[Temptations]*

DEBUT	PEAK	WKS	RIAA	CD	ARTIST — Album Title	Catalog	Sym	$	Label & Number
11/25/00+	12[X]	6		© 53	**Most Wonderful Time Of The Year, The**	C:#12/10		$15	LaserLight 55610 [3]

3 CD albums: *Merry Christmas from Pat Boone...* (LaserLight 15469 in 1992), *Home For Christmas* (LaserLight 12345 in 1994), and *The Most Wonderful Time of the Year* (LaserLight 12507 in 1995)

Ave Maria *[Vikki Carr]*
Away In A Manger *[Debbie Reynolds]*
Bells Of St. Mary's *[Vic Damone]*
Christmas Song *[Vikki Carr]*
Deck The Halls *[Boots Randolph]*
Deck The Halls *[Bing Crosby]*
First Noël *[Tony Orlando]*
First Noel *[Johnny Cash]*
God Rest Ye Merry Gentlemen *[Joe Pass]*
Hark! The Herald Angels Sing *[Pat Boone]*
Have Yourself A Merry Little Christmas *[Diahann Carroll]*
I'll Be Home For Christmas *[Johnny Cash]*
It Came Upon A Midnight Clear *[Patti Page]*
It Came Upon A Midnight Clear *[Janie Fricke]*
It Must Have Been The Mistletoe *[Vikki Carr]*
It's The Most Wonderful Time Of The Year *[Andy Williams]*
Jingle Bells *[Boots Randolph]*
Joy To The World *[Joe Williams]*
Let It Snow! Let It Snow! Let It Snow! *[Debbie Reynolds]*
O' Christmas Tree *[Impressions]*
O Come All Ye Faithful *[Tony Orlando]*
O' Come All Ye Faithful *[Boots Randolph]*
O Little Town Of Bethlehem *[Pat Boone]*
Silent Night *[Pat Boone]*
Silent Night *[Mahalia Jackson]*
We Wish You A Merry Christmas *[Boots Randolph]*
White Christmas *[Pat Boone]*
Winter Wonderland *[Glen Campbell]*

DEBUT	PEAK	WKS	RIAA	CD	ARTIST — Album Title	Catalog	Sym	$	Label & Number
12/8/73	❶[1X]	4		© 54	**Motown Christmas, A**			$30	Motown 795 [2]

Christmas charts: 1/'73, 26/'87

Ave Maria *[Stevie Wonder]*
Bring A Torch, Jeannette, Isabella (medley) *[Smokey Robinson & The Miracles]*
Children's Christmas Song *[Diana Ross & The Supremes]*
Christmas Song (Merry Christmas To You) *[Jackson 5]*
Deck The Halls (medley) *[Smokey Robinson & The Miracles]*
Frosty The Snowman *[Jackson 5]*
Give Love On Christmas Day *[Jackson 5]*
God Rest Ye Merry Gentlemen *[Smokey Robinson & The Miracles]*
Have Yourself A Merry Little Christmas *[Jackson 5]*
I Saw Mommy Kissing Santa Claus *[Jackson 5]*
It's Christmas Time *[Smokey Robinson & The Miracles]*
Jingle Bells *[Smokey Robinson & The Miracles]*
Joy To The World *[Diana Ross & The Supremes]*
Little Christmas Tree *[Michael Jackson]*
Little Drummer Boy *[Temptations]*
My Christmas Tree *[Temptations]*
My Favorite Things *[Diana Ross & The Supremes]*
One Little Christmas Tree *[Stevie Wonder]*
Rudolph, The Red-Nosed Reindeer *[Temptations]*
Santa Claus Is Comin' To Town *[Jackson 5]*
Silent Night *[Temptations]*
Silver Bells *[Diana Ross & The Supremes]*
Someday At Christmas *[Stevie Wonder]*
What Christmas Means To Me *[Stevie Wonder]*
White Christmas *[Diana Ross & The Supremes]*

DEBUT	PEAK	WKS	RIAA	CD	ARTIST — Album Title	Catalog	Sym	$	Label & Number
12/18/99	138	4		© 55	**Mr. Hankey's Christmas Classics**		[TV]	$10	American 62224

Mr. Hankey is an animated character from TV's *South Park*; Christmas Chart: 23/'99

Carol Of The Bells
Christmas Time In Hell
Dead, Dead, Dead
Dreidel, Dreidel, Dreidel
Hark The Herald Angels Sing
Have Yourself A Merry Little Christmas
I Saw Three Ships
It Happened In Sun Valley
Lonely Jew On Christmas
Merry F**king Christmas
Most Offensive Song Ever
Mr. Hankey The Christmas Poo
O Holy Night
O Tannenbaum
Santa Claus Is On His Way
Swiss Colony Beef Log
We Three Kings
What The Hell Child Is This?

DEBUT	PEAK	WKS	RIAA	CD	ARTIST — Album Title	Catalog	Sym	$	Label & Number

12/24/88+ · **12**[X] · 11 · © 56 · **Narada Christmas Collection** .... [I] **$10** Narada 63902
Christmas charts: 14/'88, 12/'89, 24/'90
- Away In A Manger [David Darling]
- God Rest Ye Merry Gentlemen [John Doan]
- I Saw Three Ships [David Arkenstone]
- It Came Upon A Midnight Clear [Eric Tingstad/Nancy Rumbel]
- Joy To The World [Bruce Mitchell]
- Man From Ceasaria [Friedemann]
- Noël Nouvelet (medley)
- O Holy Night [David Lanz & Paul Speer]
- Patapan (medley) [Nancy Rumbel]
- Return Of The Magi [William Ellwood]
- Ukranian Carol [Spencer Brewer]
- What Child Is This [Peter Buffett]

12/19/92 · **166** · 2 · © 57 · **Narada Christmas Collection Volume 2** .... [I] **$10** Narada 63909
Christmas chart: 23/'92
- Christmas Eve [Ira Stein]
- Christmas Song (Chestnuts Roasting On An Open Fire) [Doug Cameron]
- Coventry Carol (medley) [Bob Read]
- First Noel [Spencer Brewer]
- From Heaven Above [Ralf Illenberger]
- Gloria [Nando Lauria]
- Hark (Rock) The Herald Angels [David Lanz & Paul Speer]
- Il Est Ne (He Is Born) [Michael Gettel]
- Joseph, Dearest Joseph Mine [Simon Wynberg]
- Lo, How A Rose E'er Blooming [Sheldon Mirowitz]
- Noel Nouvelet (medley) [Bob Read]
- O Come, O Come, Emmanuel [Wayne Gratz]
- O Holy Night [Peter Buffett]
- Song Of The Evergreen [Kostia]
- Unto Us A Boy Is Born [Michael Jones]
- We Three Kings [David Arkenstone]

1/19/91 · **19**[X] · 1 · © 58 · **Narada Nutcracker, The** .... [I] **$10** Narada 63904
- Arabian Dance
- Children's Galop
- Chinese Dance
- Dance Of The Mirlitons
- Dance Of The Sugar-Plum Fairy
- Kingdom Of Sweets
- March
- Mother Gigogne
- Pas De Deux
- Pine Forest
- Russian Dance
- Spanish Dance
- Tarantella
- Waltz Of The Flowers
- Waltz Of The Snowflakes

1/15/00 · **27**[X] · 1 · © 59 · **Nutcracker & Messiah Highlights** .... **$20** LaserLight 24829 [2]
2 CD albums: The Nutcracker Highlights by the Berlin Symphony Orchestra (LaserLight 15146 in 1989) and Handel's Messiah by The Oratorio Society Of New York (LaserLight 12346 in 1998)
- And He Shall Purify
- And The Glory Of The Lord Shall Be Revealed
- Behold, A Virgin Shall Conceive
- But Who May Abide The Day Of His Coming
- Chocolate (Spanish Dance) (medley)
- Closing Waltz and Grand Finale
- Clown, The (medley)
- Coffee (Arabian Dance) (medley)
- Comfort Ye My People
- Dance Of The Toy Flutes (medley)
- Ev'ry Valley Shall Be Exalted
- For Behold, Darkness Shall Cover
- For Unto Us A Child Is Born
- Glory To God In The Highest
- Grave - Allegro Moderato
- Hallelujah!
- He Shall Feed His Flock
- His Yoke Is Easy, His Burden Is Light
- No. 13 Waltz Of The Flowers
- No. 14 Pas De Deux
- No. 2 March
- No. 4 Dance Scene
- No. 5 Scene and the Grandfather Dance
- No. 6 Scene
- No. 7 Scene
- No. 8 Scene
- O Thou That Tellest Good Tidings
- People That Walked In Darkness
- Pifa
- Rejoice Greatly, O Daughter Of Zion
- Tea (Chinese Dance) (medley)
- Then Shall The Eyes Of The Blind
- There Were Shepherds Abiding In The Fields
- Thus Saith The Lord Of Hosts
- Trepak (Russian Dance) (medley)

11/29/97 · **22**[X] · 7 · © 60 · **Nutcracker Christmas** .... C:#28/4 **$10** Intersound 1631
- Arabian Dance
- Away In A Manger
- Babes In Toyland: March
- Carol Of The Bells
- Chinese Dance
- Dance Of The Mirlitons
- Dance Of The Sugar-Plum Fairy
- Fantasy On 'Greensleeves'
- Four Seasons: Winter
- Joy To The World
- L'Arlesienne: Carillon
- Miniature Overture
- Nutcracker Suite: March
- Russian Dance
- Snowdrops Waltz
- Waltz Of The Flowers

12/25/93+ · **40**[C] · 5 · © 61 · **Nutcracker Highlights, The** .... **$10** LaserLight 15146
- Chocolate (Spanish Dance) (medley)
- Clown, The (medley)
- Coffee (Arabian Dance) (medley)
- Dance Of The Toy Flutes (medley)
- No. 13 Waltz Of The Flowers
- No. 14 Pas De Deux
- No. 15 Closing Waltz and Grand Finale
- No. 2 March
- No. 4 Dance Scene
- No. 5 Scene and the Grandfather Dance
- No. 6 Scene
- No. 7 Scene
- No. 8 Scene
- Tea (Chinese Dance) (medley)
- Trepak (Russian Dance) (medley)

12/5/70 · **7**[X] · 4 · © 62 · **Peace On Earth** **$20** Capitol 585 [2]
- Adeste Fidelis [Tennessee Ernie Ford]
- Angels We Have Heard On High [Roger Wagner Chorale]
- Ave Maria [Hollywood Pops Orchestra]
- Deck The Hall [Douglas Leedy]
- Do You Hear What I Hear? [Sonny James]
- First Noel [Ella Fitzgerald]
- God Rest Ye Merry, Gentlemen [Eddie Dunstedter]
- Hark! The Herald Angels Sing [Frank Sinatra]
- It Came Upon The Midnight Clear [Guy Lombardo & The Royal Canadians]
- Joy To The World [Eddie Dunstedter]
- Little Altar Boy [Glen Campbell]
- Little Drummer Boy [Wayne Newton]
- O Come All Ye Faithful [Al Martino]
- O Holy Night (Cantique De Noël) [Tennessee Ernie Ford]
- O Little Town Of Bethlehem [Nat King Cole]
- Silent Night [Lettermen]
- Sleep, My Little Jesus [Ella Fitzgerald]
- Star Carol [Fred Waring & The Pennsylvanians]
- Susa-Ninna [Sandler & Young]
- We Three Kings Of Orient Are [Beach Boys]

12/23/72 · **6**[X] · 4 · 63 · **Phil Spector's Christmas Album** [R] **$30** Apple 3400
reissue of A Christmas Gift For You (Philles/1963); Christmas charts: 6/'72, 8/'73
- Bells Of St. Mary's [Bob B. Soxx & The Blue Jeans]
- Christmas (Baby Please Come Home) [Darlene Love]
- Frosty The Snowman [Ronettes]
- Here Comes Santa Claus [Bob B. Soxx & The Blue Jeans]
- I Saw Mommy Kissing Santa Claus [Ronettes]
- Marshmallow World [Darlene Love]
- Parade Of The Wooden Soldiers [Crystals]
- Rudolph The Red-Nosed Reindeer [Crystals]
- Santa Claus Is Coming To Town [Crystals]
- Silent Night [Phil Spector]
- Sleigh Ride [Ronettes]
- White Christmas [Darlene Love]
- Winter Wonderland [Darlene Love]

12/2/00 · **32** · 7 · ▲ · © 64 · **Platinum Christmas** .... **$10** Arista 41741
Christmas chart: 3/'00
- Christmas Day [Dido]
- Christmas Song [Dave Matthews]
- Christmas Song (Chestnuts Roasting On An Open Fire) [Toni Braxton]
- Christmas Time [Backstreet Boys]
- Grown-Up Christmas List [Monica]
- I Don't Wanna Spend One More Christmas Without You [*NSYNC]
- Little Drummer Boy [Jars Of Clay]
- Merry X-mas Everybody [Steps]
- My Gift To You [Donell Jones]
- My Only Wish (This Year) [Britney Spears]
- Posada (Pilgrimage To Bethlehem) [Santana]
- Silent Night/Noche De Paz [Christina Aguilera]
- Sleigh Ride [TLC]
- This Christmas [Joe]
- Who Would Imagine A King [Whitney Houston]
- World Christmas [R. Kelly]

11/21/98 · **9**[X] · 1 · © 65 · **Renaissance Holiday** [I] **$15** American Gram. 298
festive music and Christmas carols that have their roots in the 15th, 16th, and 17th centuries
- Ballet
- Bateman's Masque
- Bouree
- Cos Colo Odo Sa
- Coventry Carol
- Ding Dong! Merrily On High
- En Avois Tant Que Vivray
- Gagliarda
- Gigue
- God Rest Ye (medley)
- Greensleeves
- I Saw Three Ships
- In Dulci Jubilo
- Intrada
- Joseph Dearest, Joseph Mine
- Kings Mistresse
- Lachrimae Antiquae
- Laura Suave
- Lo, How A Rose E'er Blooming
- M. George Whitehead His Almand
- Malle Sijmon
- Merry Bells Of Speyer
- New Yeeres Gift
- Nymph's Dance (medley)
- Patapan (medley)
- Second Of Grays Inn (medley)
- There Is No Rose Of Such Virtue
- Volte
- Wolseys Wilde

DEBUT	PEAK	WKS	RIAA	CD	ARTIST — Album Title	Catalog	Sym	$	Label & Number

12/21/96 189 2 © 66 Rudolph, Frosty And Friends Favorite Christmas Songs .... $10 Sony Wonder 67766
Christmas chart: 40/'97
First Toymaker To The King [Joan Gardner] — Little Drummer Boy [Vienna Boys' Choir] — Put One Foot In Front Of The Other [Mickey Rooney & Keenan Wynn] — There's Always Tomorrow [Janet Orenstein]
Frosty The Snowman [Jimmy Durante] — Most Wonderful Day Of The Year [Chorus] — Rudolph The Red-Nosed Reindeer [Burl Ives] — We're A Couple Of Misfits [Billie Richards & Paul Soles]
Holly Jolly Christmas [Burl Ives & Chorus] — No More Toymakers To The King [Paul Frees] — Santa Claus Is Comin' To Town [Fred Astaire] — Silver And Gold [Burl Ives]
Jingle, Jingle, Jingle [Stan Francis]

12/9/67 17ˣ 4 67 Santa's Own Christmas .... $15 Capitol 2836
Santa (Walt Jacobs) sings and tells stories for children
Finale: Holiday On Ice — Jolly Old Saint Nicholas — Story Of Small One
Introduction: Holiday On Ice — Santa's Night Before Christmas — Up On The House Top
Jingle Bells — Stories About The North Pole — What Santa Wants For Christmas

12/25/65 37ˣ 1 68 Season's Greetings/A Christmas Festival Of Stars! .... $20 Columbia 1394 / 8189
first released in 1959
Auld Lang Syne [Mitch Miller] — Hallelujah Chorus [Percy Faith Orch.] — Secret Of Christmas [Bing Crosby w/Frank DeVol Orch.] — Wassail, Wassail, All Over The Town (medley) [Norman Luboff Choir]
Christmas Song (Merry Christmas To You) [Johnny Mathis w/Percy Faith Orch.] — Hark! The Herald Angels Sing (medley) [Norman Luboff Orch.] — Silent Night, Holy Night [Percy Faith Orch.] — What Child Is This [Johnny Mathis w/Percy Faith Orch.]
First Noel (medley) [Norman Luboff Choir] — O Come, All Ye Faithful (Adeste Fideles) [Mitch Miller] — Star Carol [Hi-Lo's] —
God Rest Ye Merry, Gentlemen (medley) [Norman Luboff Choir] — Season's Greetings [Mitch Miller] — Twelve Days Of Christmas [Ed Kenny w/Luther Henderson Orch.]

1/16/99 29ˣ 1 © 69 Sleigh Ride / The Joy of Christmas .... $10 Reader's Digest 9114
Christmas Needs Love To Be Christmas [Andy Williams] — Hark! The Herald Angels Sing [Mormon Tabernacle Choir] — Silent Night [Floyd Cramer] — Sleigh Ride [London Symphony Orch.]
Do You Hear What I Hear? [Glen Campbell] — It's Beginning To Look A Lot Like Christmas [London Festival Orch.] — Silver Bells [Romantic Strings Orch. & Voices] — Winter Wonderland [London Festival Orch.]
Gather Around The Christmas Tree (medley) — Little Drummer Boy [Vienna Boys' Choir] — Skaters' Waltz [New Symphony Orch. Of London]

12/21/68+ 8ˣ 8 70 Soul Christmas .... $30 Atco 269
Christmas charts: 13/'68, 8/'69, 8/'70
Back Door Santa [Clarence Carter] — Gee Whiz, It's Christmas [Carla Thomas] — Merry Christmas Baby [Otis Redding] — What Are You Doing New Year's Eve [King Curtis]
Christmas Song [King Curtis] — I'll Make Every Day Christmas (For My Woman) [Joe Tex] — Presents For Christmas [Solomon Burke] — White Christmas [Otis Redding]
Every Day Will Be Like A Holiday [William Bell] — Jingle Bells [Booker T. & The MG's] — Silver Bells [Booker T. & The MG's]

11/29/97 43 7 © 71 Superstar Christmas .... C:#10/13 $10 Epic 68750
Christmas charts: 5/'97, 18/'98, 36/'99, 35/'00
Christmas Song (Chestnuts Roasting On An Open Fire) [Celine Dion] — Happy Xmas (War Is Over) [John Lennon & Yoko Ono] — Lord's Prayer [Barbra Streisand] — What If Jesus Comes Back Like That [Collin Raye]
Christmas Through Your Eyes [Gloria Estefan] — Have Yourself A Merry Little Christmas [Luther Vandross] — Merry Christmas Baby [Bruce Springsteen & The E Street Band] — Merry Christmas [Plácido Domingo]
Early Christmas Morning [Cyndi Lauper] — I'll Be Home For Christmas [Amy Grant] — O Holy Night [Mariah Carey] — Winter Wonderland [Tony Bennett]
Let It Snow, Let It Snow, Let It Snow [Frank Sinatra] — Santa Claus Is Coming To Town [Michael Bolton] — Silent Night [Boyz II Men] — You Make It Feel Like Christmas [Neil Diamond]

12/23/95 182 1 © 72 Superstars Of Christmas 1995 .... $10 Capitol 35347
Adeste Fideles (O, Come All Ye Faithful) [Nat King Cole] — I'll Be Home For Christmas [Frank Sinatra] — Santa Claus Is Comin' To Town [Peggy Lee] — You'll Never Be Alone [Richard Marx]
First Noel [Ella Fitzgerald] — Little Saint Nick [Beach Boys] — Silent Night [Diana Ross]
Happy Xmas (War Is Over) [John & Yoko/Plastic Ono Band] — O Holy Night [Jon Secada] — Wonderful Christmastime [Paul McCartney]
Pretty Paper [Willie Nelson]

12/5/98 71 6 ● © 73 Ultimate Christmas .... C:#4/15 $10 Arista 19019
Christmas charts: 8/'98, 11/'99, 12/'00
Blue Christmas [Elvis Presley] — It's Beginning To Look Like Christmas [Dionne Warwick] — O Come All Ye Faithful [Luther Vandross] — Song For A Winter's Night [Sarah McLachlan]
Cantique De Noël (O Holy Night) [Luciano Pavarotti] — Jingle Bells [Herb Alpert & The Tijuana Brass] — Santa Baby [Eartha Kitt] — White Christmas [Bing Crosby] 7
Christmas Song [Nat King Cole] 65 — Joy To The World [Whitney Houston/Georgia Mass Choir] — Silent Night [Boyz II Men] — Winter Wonderland [Aretha Franklin]
Frosty The Snow Man [Ella Fitzgerald] — Night Before Christmas [Carly Simon] — Silver Bells [Kenny G]
Have Yourself A Merry Little Christmas [Judy Garland] — Sleigh Ride [Johnny Mathis]

12/17/94 139 4 © 74 Ultimate Christmas Album, The .... $10 Collectables 2511
compiled by Joe McCoy of WCBS-FM, an oldies station in New York; Christmas chart: 31/'94
Another Lonely New Year's Eve [Jimmy Beaumont & The Skyliners] — I Saw Mommy Kissing Santa Claus [Jimmy Boyd] — Rockin' Around The Christmas Tree [Brenda Lee] 14 — This Christmas [Donny Hathaway]
Baby's First Christmas [Connie Francis] 26 — I'll Be Home For Christmas [Fats Domino] — Rudolph The Red-Nosed Reindeer [Gene Autry] 70 — This Time Of The Year [Brook Benton] 81
Chipmunk Song [Alvin & The Chipmunks] 1 — It's Christmas Once Again [Frankie Lymon] — Rudolph The Red-Nosed Reindeer [Cadillacs] — What Christmas Means To Me [Stevie Wonder]
Christmas Ain't Christmas (Without The One You Love) [O'Jays] — Jingle Bell Rock [Bobby Helms] 6 — Run Rudolph Run [Chuck Berry] 69 — White Christmas [Drifters]
Christmas Auld Lang Syne [Bobby Darin] 51 — Little Drummer Boy [Harry Simeone Chorale] 13 — Santa Claus Is Coming To Town [Four Seasons] 23 — You're My Christmas Present [Jimmy Beaumont & The Skyliners]
Christmas Serenade [Johnny Maestro & The Brooklyn Bridge] — Merry Merry Christmas Baby [Margo Sylvia & The Tune Weavers] — Silent Night [Temptations] —
Please Come Home For Christmas [Dion] — Silver Bells [Diana Ross & The Supremes]

12/23/95 147 2 © 75 Ultimate Christmas Album Volume II, The .... $10 Collectables 2512
After New Year's Eve [Heartbeats] — Grandma Got Run Over By A Reindeer [Elmo & Patsy] 87 — It's The Most Wonderful Time Of The Year [Andy Williams] — Pretty Paper [Roy Orbison] 15
Christmas Long Ago (Jingle Jingle) [Echelons] — Happy New Year Baby [Jo Ann Campbell] — Let It Snow! Let It Snow! Let It Snow! [Dean Martin] — Rudolph The Red-Nosed Reindeer [Melodeers] 71
Christmas Song [Duprees] — Have Yourself A Merry Little Christmas [Johnny Maestro & The Brooklyn Bridge] — Little Saint Nick [Beach Boys] — Sleigh Ride [Johnny Mathis]
Dominick The Donkey [Lou Monte] — Here Comes Santa Claus [Gene Autry] — Merry Christmas All [Denise Montana & The Salsoul Orchestra] — Someday At Christmas [Stevie Wonder]
Donde Esta Santa Claus [Augie Rios] 47 — Holly Jolly Christmas [Burl Ives] — Merry Christmas Baby [Dion] — White Christmas [Diana Ross & The Supremes]
Frosty The Snowman [Beach Boys] — It's Beginning To Look A Lot Like Christmas [Bing Crosby] — Merry Christmas Darling [Carpenters] —
Give Love On Christmas Day [Jackson Five] — Nuttin' For Christmas [Barry Gordon] 6

DEBUT	PEAK	WKS	RIAA	CD	ARTIST — Album Title	Catalog	Sym	$	Label & Number

11/14/87 | **20** | 13 | ▲⁴ | © 76 | **Very Special Christmas, A** ....**C:❶**¹/59 | **$10** | A&M 3911

Christmas charts: 1/'87, 1/'88, 4/'89, 5/'90, 3/'91, 5/'92, 9/'93, 9/'94, 9/'95, 12/'96, 14/'97, 21/'98, 34/'99, 34/'00

Back Door Santa [Bon Jovi]
Christmas (Baby Please Come Home) [U2]
Christmas In Hollis [Run-D.M.C.]
Coventry Carol [Alison Moyet]

Do You Hear What I Hear [Whitney Houston]
Gabriel's Message [Sting]
Have Yourself A Merry Little Christmas [Pretenders]

I Saw Mommy Kissing Santa Claus [John Cougar Mellencamp]
Little Drummer Boy [Bob Seger]
Merry Christmas Baby [Bruce Springsteen]
Run Rudolph Run [Bryan Adams]

Santa Baby [Madonna]
Santa Claus Is Coming To Town [Pointer Sisters]
Silent Night [Stevie Nicks]
Winter Wonderland [Eurythmics]

12/17/88+ | **57** | 5 | ▲⁴ | © 77 | **Very Special Christmas, A** .... [R] | **$10** | A&M 3911
12/9/89+ | **55** | 7 | ▲⁴ | © 78 | **Very Special Christmas, A** .... [R] | **$10** | A&M 3911
12/8/90+ | **58** | 6 | ▲⁴ | © 79 | **Very Special Christmas, A** .... [R] | **$10** | A&M 3911

see first chart entry in 1987 for tracks of above 3 re-entries

11/14/92 | **7** | 11 | ▲ | © 80 | **Very Special Christmas 2, A** ....**C:#3/34** | **$10** | A&M 540003

Christmas charts: 2/'92, 6/'93, 8/'94, 12/'95, 18/'96, 23/'97, 39/'98

Birth Of Christ [Boyz II Men]
Blue Christmas [Ann & Nancy Wilson]
Christmas All Over Again [Tom Petty & The Heartbreakers]
Christmas Is [Run D.M.C.]
Christmas Song [Luther Vandross]

Christmas Time Again [Extreme]
I Believe In You [Sinead O'Connor]
Jingle Bell Rock [Randy Travis]
Merry Christmas Baby [Bonnie Raitt & Charles Brown]
O Christmas Tree [Aretha Franklin]
O Holy Night [Tevin Campbell]

Please Come Home For Christmas [Jon Bon Jovi]
Rockin' Around The Christmas Tree [Ronnie Spector/Darlene Love]
Santa Claus Is Coming To Town [Frank Sinatra/Cyndi Lauper]
Silent Night [Wilson Phillips]
Sleigh Ride [Debbie Gibson]

What Child Is This? [Vanessa Williams]
What Christmas Means To Me [Paul Young]
White Christmas [Michael Bolton]

11/8/97 | **31** | 10 | ● | © 81 | **Very Special Christmas 3, A** ....**C:#3/14** | **$10** | A&M 540764

Christmas charts: 2/'97, 7/'98, 34/'99, 33/'00

Ave Maria [Chris Cornell with Eleven]
Blue Christmas [Sheryl Crow]
Children Go Where I Send Thee [Natalie Merchant]
Christmas [Blues Traveler]

Christmas In The City [Mary J. Blige feat. Angie Martinez]
Christmas Is Now Drawing Near At Hand [Steve Winwood]
Christmas Song [Hootie & The Blowfish]

Christmas Song [Dave Matthews & Tim Reynolds]
Christmastime [Smashing Pumpkins]
I Saw Three Ships [Sting]
O Holy Night [Tracy Chapman]
Oi To The World [No Doubt]

Oiche Chiun (Silent Night) [Enya]
Santa Baby [Rev Run & The Christmas All Stars]
Santa Claus Is Back In Town [Jonny Lang]
We Three Kings [Patti Smith]

12/4/99 | **100** | 7 | | © 82 | **Very Special Christmas Live: From Washington, D.C., A** ....**C:#38/1** | [L] | **$10** | A&M 490484

Christmas charts: 17/'99, 11/'00

Christmas (Baby Please Come Home) [Jon Bon Jovi]
Christmas Blues [John Popper w/Eric Clapton]
Christmas In Hollis [Run-D.M.C.]

Christmas Tears [Eric Clapton]
Give Me One Reason [Tracy Chapman & Eric Clapton]
Merry Christmas Baby [Sheryl Crow w/Eric Clapton]

O Holy Night [Tracy Chapman]
Please Come Home For Christmas [Jon Bon Jovi]
Rockin' Around The Christmas Tree [Mary J. Blige & Sheryl Crow]

Santa Claus Is Coming To Town [All]
What Child Is This? [Vanessa Williams]

12/5/98 | **162** | 1 | | © 83 | **Very Veggie Christmas, A**..**C:#18/4** | **$10** | Lyrick 9456

Christmas charts: 11/'98, 22/'99

Angels We Have Heard On High
Away In A Manger
Big Medley!
Boar's Head Carol

Can't Believe It's Christmas
8 Polish Foods Of Christmas
Feliz Navidad
Go Tell It On The Mountain

Grumpy Kids
He Is Born, The Holy Child
Oh Santa!
Ring, Little Bells

While By My Sheep

12/23/67 | **83ˣ** | 2 | | 84 | **Walt Disney presents 30 Favorite Songs Of Christmas with Chimes And Chorus** .... | **$15** | Disneyland 1239

first released in 1963

Angels From The Realms Of Glory (medley)
As With Gladness (medley)
Away In A Manger (medley)
Come All Ye Faithful (medley)
Coventry Carol (medley)
Deck The Halls With Boughs Of Holly (medley)
Fantasyland Christmas Tree
First Noel (medley)

From All Of Us To All Of You
God Rest Ye Merry Gentlemen (medley)
Good Christian Men Rejoice (medley)
Good King Wenceslas (medley)
Hark The Herald Angels Sing (medley)
Here We Come A Wassailing (medley)

It Came Upon A Midnight Clear (medley)
Jingle Bells (medley)
Jolly Old Saint Nick (medley)
Joy To The World (medley)
Kris Kringle
Oh Christmas Tree (medley)
Oh Little Town Of Bethlehem (medley)
Oh Sanctissima (medley)

Pat A Pan (medley)
Silent Night (medley)
Up On A House Top (medley)
We Three Kings (medley)
We Wish You A Merry Christmas (medley)
Westminster Carol (medley)
What Child Is This (medley)
While Shepherds Watch Their Flocks (medley)

12/21/74 | **125** | 2 | | 85 | **Waltons' Christmas Album, The** .... | **$20** | Columbia 33193

album cover pictures TV's The Waltons; songs performed by The Holiday Singers; narration by Earl Hamner (creator of The Waltons)

First Noel
God Rest Ye Merry Gentlemen
Grandpa's Christmas Wish

Hark! The Herald Angels Sing
It Came Upon A Midnight Clear
Joy To The World

O Come All Ye Faithful
O Little Town Of Bethlehem
Silent Night

Spirit Of Christmas
Waltons' Theme

12/4/99 | **131** | 6 | © | 86 | **Winter Solstice On Ice** .... | [I] | **$15** | Windham Hill 11459 [2]

Christmas charts: 12/'99, 21/'00

Bittersweet [Jim Brickman]
Black Diamond [Rippingtons feat. Russ Freeman]
Christmas Wish [Tuck & Patti]
Esawayo [Samite]
First Noel [Sean Harkness]
Gift, The [Roberta Flack & Peabo Bryson]
I Wish I Could [Peabo Bryson]

Ice Palace [David Arkenstone]
Joy Ride [Mark Snow]
Joy To The World [Liz Story]
Little Drummer Boy [Schönertz & Scott]
Magic Forest [Ensemble]
Mr. Moto's Penguin [Mark Isham]
Nigh Bethlehem [George Winston]
O Holy Night [Angels Of Venice]

Santorini [Yanni]
Silent Night [Hiroshima]
Skating [George Winston]
Snow Is Lightly Falling [Nightnoise]
Stars To Share [Samite]
Sweeney's Buttermilk [Micheál Ó Domhnaill & Paddy Glackin]
This Christmas [Jeffrey Osborne]

Twinkle Twinkle Little Star [L.A. Guitar Quartet]
We Three Kings [Janis Ian]
What Child Is This [Michael Hedges]
White Spirit [Uman]
Winter [Phil Perry]
Yesterday's Rain [W.G. Snuffy Walden]
Your Love [Jim Brickman]

12/5/98 | **30ˣ** | 2 | © | 87 | **Winter Solstice Reunion, A** .... | [I] | **$10** | Windham Hill 11369

Babe Is Born (medley)
Christmas Wish [Tuck & Patti]
Dreamtime
El Noi De La Mare (Son Of Mary) (medley)

Enter The Stable Gently (medley)
I Saw Three Ships
Impending Death Of The Virgin Spirit
It Came Upon A Midnight Clear

Keiki's Dream
La Nit De Nadal (Christmas Night) (medley)
Rain Into Snow
Snowfall Lullaby

Song Before Spring
20° Below
What Are The Signs
Year's End

12/7/85+ | **77** | 14 | ● | © 88 | **Winter's Solstice, A**... | [I] | **$10** | Windham Hill 1045

Christmas charts: 15/'87, 17/'88, 16/'89, 13/'90, 22/'91

Bourree [Darol Anger & Mike Marshall]
Engravings II [Ira Stein & Russel Walder]
Greensleeves [Liz Story]

High Plains (Christmas On The High-Line) [Philip Aaberg]
Jesu, Joy Of Man's Desiring [David Qualey]

New England Morning [William Ackerman]
Nollaig [Billy Oskay & Micheál O Domhnaill]

Northumbrian Lullabye [Malcolm Dalglish]
Petite Aubade [Shadowfax]
Tale Of Two Cities [Mark Isham]

12/20/86+ | **172** | 5 | ● | © 89 | **Winter's Solstice, A** .... | [I-R] | **$10** | Windham Hill 1045

see above entry for tracks

CHRISTMAS (Various Artists)

DEBUT	PEAK	WKS	RIAA	CD	ARTIST — Album Title	Catalog	Sym	$	Label & Number
12/10/88+	108	7		© 90	**Winter's Solstice II, A** ....C:#39/1		[I]	$10	Windham Hill 1077

Christmas charts: 8/'88, 14/'89, 19/'90, 16/'91

Abide The Winter [Will Ackerman]
Bring Me Back A Song [Nightnoise]
By The Fireside [William Allaudin Mathieu]
Chorale #220 [Turtle Island String Quartet]
Come Life Shaker Life [Malcolm Dalglish]
Dadme Albricias Hijos D'Eva (medley) [Modern Mandolin Quartet]
E'en So, Lord Jesus Quickly Come (medley) [Modern Mandolin Quartet]
Flute Sonata In Em, 3rd Movement [Barbara Higbie & Emily Klion]
Gift, The [Philip Aaberg]
Medieval Memory II [Ira Stein & Russel Walder]
Prelude To Cello Suite #1 In G Major [Michael Hedges]
Salve Regina [Therese Schroeder-Sheker]
17th Century Canon [Paul McCandless/James Matheson/Robin May]
Simple Psalm [Fred Simon]
Sung To Sleep [Michael Manring]
This Rush Of Wings [Metamora]

DEBUT	PEAK	WKS	RIAA	CD	ARTIST — Album Title	Catalog	Sym	$	Label & Number
12/1/90	90	8	●	© 91	**Winter's Solstice III, A** ....C:#32/5		[I]	$10	Windham Hill 1098

Christmas charts: 8/'90, 11/'91, 29/'92

Christmas Bells [John Gorka]
Christmas Song [Steve Erquiaga]
Coventry Carol [Paul McCandless]
Earth Abides [Philip Aaberg]
Hopeful [Michael Manring]
In Dulci Jubilo (Good Christian Men Rejoice) [Michael Hedges]
In The Bleak Midwinter [Pierce Pettis]
Little Drummer Boy [Schonherz & Scott]
Lullay, Lully [Barbara Higbie]
Of The Father's Love Begotten [Tim Story]
Pavane [Liz Story]
Sleepers Awake [Andy Narell]
Snow Is Lightly Falling [Nightnoise]
Trepak [Modern Mandolin Quartet]
Veni Emmanuel [Turtle Island String Quartet]

DEBUT	PEAK	WKS	RIAA	CD	ARTIST — Album Title	Catalog	Sym	$	Label & Number
11/27/93	55	7	●	© 92	**Winter's Solstice IV, A** ....C:#20/7		[I]	$10	Windham Hill 11134

Christmas charts: 11/'93, 17/'94

Angels We Have Heard On High [Darol Anger & Mike Marshall]
Asleep The Snow Came Flying [Tim Story]
Carol Of The Bells [Windham Hill Artists]
Christmas Hymn [Billy Childs]
Crystal Palace [Oystein Sevag]
Dona Nobis Pacem [Michael Manring]
Four Seasons - Rain, The [Turtle Island String Quartet]
Just Before Dawn [Will Ackerman]
Sheep May Safely Graze [Modern Mandolin Quartet]
Silent Night [Steve Erquiaga]
Three Candles [Schonherz & Scott]
Trumpet Tune [Alex de Grassi]
We Three Kings [Barbara Higbie]
Wexford Carol [Nightnoise]
Winter Bourne [Paul McCandless]

DEBUT	PEAK	WKS	RIAA	CD	ARTIST — Album Title	Catalog	Sym	$	Label & Number
12/2/95	85	6		© 93	**Winter's Solstice V, A**		[I]	$10	Windham Hill 11174

Christmas charts: 13/'95, 33/'96

Angels We Have Heard On High [Windham Hill Artists]
Doo'lit'Saa'Da (Another Silent Night) [Douglas Spotted Eagle]
First Noel [Tracy Silverman & Thea Suits-Silverman]
God Rest You Merry, Gentlemen [Steve Erquiaga]
Holly And The Ivy [Alex de Grassi]
Joy To The World [Jim Brickman]
Light And Song [Will Ackerman]
My Heart Is Always Moving [Oystein Sevag]
O Come Little Children (medley) [Liz Story]
Poli'Ahu-The Snow Goddess Of Mauna Kea [Keola Beamer with George Winston]
Shepherds' Rocking Carol [Philip Aaberg]
Simple Birth [Barbara Highie]
Snow In The Prairies [Torcuato Mariano]
Sussex Carol [Nightnoise]
We'll Dress The House (medley) [Liz Story]

DEBUT	PEAK	WKS	RIAA	CD	ARTIST — Album Title	Catalog	Sym	$	Label & Number
12/13/97	139	4		© 94	**Winter's Solstice VI, A**		[I]	$10	Windham Hill 11220

Christmas chart: 21/'97

In The Winter's Pale [Tim Story]
January Stars [George Winston]
Joyful Times [Marion Meadows]
Northern Lights [Lisa Lynne]
Quiet Time [Jim Brickman]
Secret Places [Todd Cochran]
Simple Praise [Joanie Madden]
Snow Dance [David Arkenstone]
Snowfall [Liz Story]
Sonata For Two Clarinets (2nd Movement) [Richard Stoltzman]
This Clearness Of Light [Will Ackerman]
Ursa Major [Michael Hedges]
Western Sky [Brian Keane/Michael Manring/Paul McCandless/Lou Soloff]
Winkus McGinkus [Sean Harkness]
Yesterday's Rain [W.G. Snuffy Walden]

DEBUT	PEAK	WKS	RIAA	CD	ARTIST — Album Title	Catalog	Sym	$	Label & Number
1/15/00	28 [X]	1		© 95	**Yule B-Swingin'**			$10	Hip-O 440117

first released in 1998

Cool Yule [Louis Armstrong & The Commanders]
Dig That Crazy Santa Claus [Ralph Marterie]
(Everybody's Waitin' For) The Man With The Bag [Kay Starr]
Have Yourself A Merry Little Christmas [Ella Fitzgerald]
I've Got My Love To Keep Me Warm [Dean Martin]
Jingle Bells [Glenn Miller]
Jingle Bells (medley) [Pete Fountain]
Let It Snow! Let It Snow! Let It Snow! [Les Brown]
Merry Christmas, Baby [Lionel Hampton]
Ring Those Christmas Bells [Peggy Lee]
Santa Claus Is Comin' To Town (medley) [Pete Fountain]
Sleigh Ride [Johnny Desmond]
Swingle Jingle [Lionel Hampton]
What Are You Doing New Year's Eve? [Nancy Wilson]
What Will Santa Claus Say (When He Finds Everybody Swinging?) [Louis Prima]

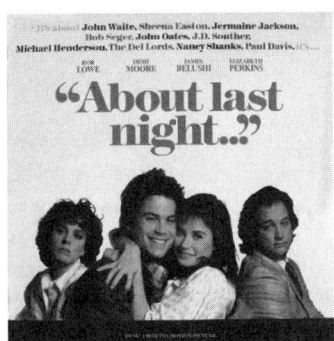

Soundtrack
About Last Night... ('86)

Soundtrack
The Cable Guy ('96)

Soundtrack
Coneheads ('93)

Soundtrack
Dr. No ('63)

Soundtrack
Good Will Hunting ('98)

Soundtrack
Light Of Day ('87)

Soundtrack
My Girl ('92)

Soundtrack
One Flew Over The Cuckoo's Nest ('76)

Soundtrack
Parrish ('61)

Soundtrack
Picnic ('56)

Soundtrack
Rain Man ('89)

Soundtrack
Robin And The 7 Hoods ('64)

Original Cast
Destry Rides Again ('59)

Original Cast
Illya Darling ('67)

Original Cast
Jennie ('64)

Television Soundtrack
Batman ('66)

Christmas (Various Artists)... Bonanza -
Christmas on the Ponderosa ('63)*

Various Artists
If I Were A Carpenter ('94)

Various Artists
Mad 'Twists' Rock 'N' Roll ('62)

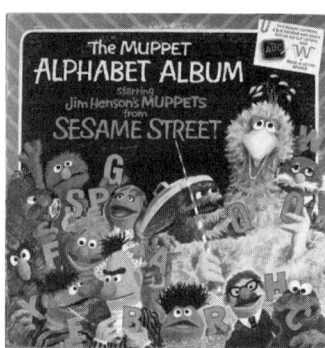

Various Artists
Muppet Alphabet Album ('71)

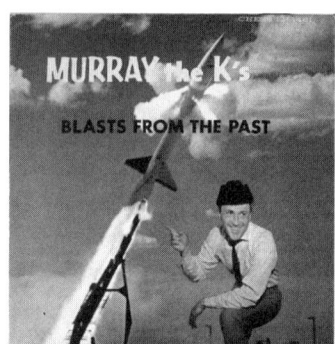

Various Artists... Murray The K's
Blasts From The Past ('61)*

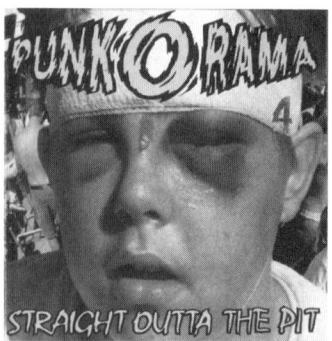

Various Artists
Punk-O-Rama 4 ('99)

Various Artists
Pure Reggae ('98)

Various Artists
Zodiac: Cosmic Sounds ('67)

DEBUT	PEAK	WKS	RIAA	CD	ARTIST — Album Title	Catalog	Sym	$	Label & Number

VARIOUS ARTIST COMPILATIONS

4/3/99 — **75** — 11 — © — 1 **Absolute Hits, The**.. **$10** Atlantic 83158

Are You That Somebody? [Aaliyah] 21	Hold My Hand [Hootie & The Blowfish] 10	I'll Be [Edwin McCain] 5	3 AM [Matchbox 20]
Barely Breathing [Duncan Sheik] 16	I Can Love You Like That [All-4-One] 5	Mania [Babel Fish]	World I Know [Collective Soul] 19
Fly [Sugar Ray Feat. Super Cat]	I Love You Always Forever [Donna Lewis] 7	Missing [Everything But The Girl] 2	
Foolish Games [Jewel] 7	I Wanna Be Down [Brandy] 6	Not Tonight [Lil' Kim] 6	
For You I Will [Monica] 4		Return Of The Mack [Mark Morrison] 2	

2/17/62 — **99** — 7 — — — 2 **Alan Freed's Memory Lane**.. **$100** End 314

Crying In The Chapel [Orioles]	I'll Be Home [Flamingos]	Sincerely [Moonglows]	We Belong Together [Robert & Johnny] 32
Eddie My Love [Teen Queens] 14	In The Still Of The Nite [Five Satins] 24	16 Candles [Crests] 2	Why Don't You Write Me? [Jacks] 82
For Your Precious Love [Jerry Butler & The Impressions] 11	Oh What A Night [Dells]	Tears On My Pillow [Little Anthony & The Imperials] 4	
Goodnight My Love [Jesse Belvin]	Silhouettes [Rays] 3	Tonite, Tonite [Mello-Kings] 77	

8/5/78 — **151** — 6 — — — 3 **Alivemutherforya**.. [I–L] **$12** Columbia 35349

| "Anteres" - The Star [Billy Cobham] | On A Magic Carpet Ride [Billy Cobham] | Shadows [Tom Scott] | Spindrift [Tom Scott] |
| Bahama Mama [Alphonso Johnson] | | Some Punk Funk [Steve Khan] | |

4/1/95 — **40[C]** — 1 — © — 4 **All The Best From Ireland**... **$10** Madacy 71

Cockles And Mussels	I'll Take You Home Again Kathleen	Kerry Dance	Wearing O' The Green
Danny Boy	If You're Irish Come Into The Parlour	Little Bit Of Irish	When Irish Eyes Are Smiling
Dear Little Shamrock	Irish Washerwoman	Mother Macree	With My Shillelagh Under My Arm
Dear Old Donegal	It's A Great Day For The Irish	Mountains Of The Mourne	
Eileen Alannah	Kathleen Marvourneen	Phil The Fluter's Ball	
Galway Bay		Rose Of Tralee	

11/24/62 — **110** — 7 — — — 5 **All The Hits By All The Stars**... **$50** Parkway 7013

Bristol Stomp [Dovells] 2	Hucklebuck, The [Chubby Checker] 14	Mashed Potato Time [Dee Dee Sharp] 2	Volare [Bobby Rydell] 4
Bristol Twistin' Annie [Dovells] 27	I'll Be True [Orlons]	Pony Time [Chubby Checker] 1	Wah Watusi [Orlons] 2
Gravy (For My Mashed Potatoes) [Dee Dee Sharp] 9		Twist, The [Chubby Checker] 1	We Got Love [Bobby Rydell] 6
			Wild One [Bobby Rydell] 2

5/18/91 — **187** — 1 — © — 6 **Alligator Records 20th Anniversary Collection, The** ...... **$15** Alligator 105/6 [2]

Big Chief [Professor Longhair]	Eyeballin' [Lonnie Brooks]	I've Got Dreams To Remember [Delbert McClinton]	Serves Me Right To Suffer [Jimmy Johnson]
Black Cat Bone [Albert Collins & Johnny Copeland]	Fannie Mae [Elvin Bishop]	If I Hadn't Been High [Detroit Junior]	Strike Like Lightning [Lonnie Mack]
Blues After Hours [Pinetop Perkins]	Full Moon On Main Street [Kinsey Report]	Leavin' [Siegel-Schwall Band]	That's Why I'm Crying [Koko Taylor]
Boot Hill [Johnny Winter]	Give Me Back My Wig [Hound Dog Taylor]	Leaving Your Town [Charlie Musselwhite]	These Blues Is Killing Me [A.C. Reed w/Stevie Ray Vaughan]
Born In Louisiana [Clarence "Gatemouth" Brown]	Going Back Home [Son Seals]	Look But Don't Touch [Kenny Neal]	300 Pounds Of Heavenly Joy [Big Twist & The Mellow Fellows]
Brick [Albert Collins]	Going Down To Big Mary's [Paladins]	Middle Aged Blues Boogie [Saffire]	Trouble In Mind [Big Walter Horton]
Crow Jane [Sonny Terry]	I'm Free [Lucky Peterson]	No Cuttin' Loose [James Cotton]	You Don't Exist Any More [Lil' Ed & The Blue Imperials]
Double Eyed Whammy [Tinsley Ellis]	I'm The Zydeco Man [Clifton Chenier]	Pussycat Moan [Katie Webster]	You Don't Know What Love Is [Fenton Robinson]
Drowning On Dry Land [Roy Buchanan]		Rain [Little Charlie & The Nightcats]	
		Second Hand Man [Carey Bell & Junior Wells]	

2/19/94 — **167** — 3 — © — 7 **Alternative NRG**.. [L] **$10** Hollywood 61449

Cold [Annie Lennox]	JC [Sonic Youth]	New Kind Of Kick [Jesus And Mary Chain]	Sweetmeat [Soup Dragons]
Drive [R.E.M.]	Looking Through Patient Eyes [PM Dawn]	Ring The Bells [James]	Tell Me The Truth [Midnight Oil]
Everyday Life Has Become A Health Risk [Disposable Heroes Of Hiphoprisy]	New Damage [Soundgarden/Brian May]	Search And Destroy [EMF]	Until The End Of The World [U2]
Fam Bam [Boo-Yaa T.R.I.B.E.]		Shitlist [L7]	Yolngu Boy [Yothu Yindi]
		Sing Our Own Song [UB40]	

9/23/95 — **198** — 2 — ● © — 8 **Amazing Grace: A Country Salute To Gospel** .... **$10** Sparrow 51445

Amazing Grace [Lari White]	I'd Rather Have Jesus [Alison Krauss & The Cox Family Feat. Suzanne Cox]	Kneel At The Cross [Charlie Daniels Band]	Peace In The Valley [John Anderson]
Beulah Land [Shenandoah]		Mansion Over The Hilltop [Paul Overstreet]	Precious Memories [Emmylou Harris]
Blessed Assurance [John Berry]	In The Garden [Billy Dean & Susan Ashton]		
How Great Thou Art [Martina McBride]			

11/22/69 — **197** — 1 — — — 9 **Amazing Mets, The**... **$30** Buddah 1969

featuring the singing voices of the New York Mets; 1969 World Series Champs (note label number)

God Bless America	La La La La	Mets Ball Game	We're Gonna Win The Series
Green Grass Of Shea	Locker Room Chatter	Mets - Hallelujah	We've Got The Whole World Watching Us
Heart	Mets Are Here To Stay	Song For The '69 Mets	

7/13/96 — **51** — 5 — © — 10 **America Is Dying Slowly**.. **$10** Red Hot 61925

America [Wu-Tang Clan]	Hustle, The [De La Soul & Da Beatminerz]	No Rubber, No Backstage Pass [Biz Markie, Chubb Rock & Prince Paul]	Street Life [Mobb Deep, L.E.S. & A.C.D.]
Blood [Goodie Mob]	I Breaks 'Em Off [Coolio]		Suckas P.H. [Mac Mall]
Check Ya Self [Spice 1, Celly Cel, 187-Fac, Ant Banks & Gangsta P]	(Lately) I've Been Thinking [Common & Sean Lett]	Sport That Raincoat [Domino]	What I Represent [O.C. & Buckwild]
Decisions [Organized Konfusion]	Listen To Me Now [Eightball & MJG]	Yearn, The [Pete Rock & The Lost Boyz]	
Games [Money Boss Players]		(Stay Away From Me) Nasty Hoes [Sadat X, Fat Joe & Diamond D.]	

5/31/97 — **198** — 1 — © — 11 **...And Then There Was Bass**... **$10** Tony Mercedes 26038

Ahh Haa [L.A. Sno feat. Stylz]	Get Ready [Southsyde B.O.I.Z.]	I Want To Ball [Southern Playas]	MyBabyDaddy [B-Rock & The Bizz]
As We Lay [Dana Harris]	Have I Never [Few Good Men feat. 69 Boyz & K-Nock]	Keep It Crunk [Thump Squad]	Swing Low [Stylz & The J.I.Z.]
Dat's Real [Big Kenny & The Ghetto Crew]	Hola Mami [Kinani feat. DJ Laz & Danny D.]	Let's Ride [Luke]	U Like Piña Colada [Da Real One]
Fired Up [Deep Scandal]		Make A Playa Rich [J.T. Money feat. Verb]	Wall 2 Wall Booty [N.C. feat. Kid Money]

12/28/68 — **200** — 2 — — — 12 **Anthology Of British Blues Vol. 2, An**.................................. **$30** Immediate 52014

Choker [Eric Clapton & Jimmy Page]	Freight Loader [Eric Clapton & Jimmy Page]	On Top Of The World [John Mayall/Bluesbreakers]	True Blue [Savoy Brown Blues Band]
Dealing With The Devil [Dharma Blues Band]	I Can't Quit You Baby [Savoy Brown Blues Band]	Roll 'Em Pete [Dharma Blues Band]	When You Got A Good Friend [T. S. McPhee]
Draggin' My Tail [Eric Clapton & Jimmy Page]	Look Down At My Woman [Jeremy Spencer]	Someone To Love Me [T. S. McPhee]	Who's Knocking At Your Door [Jeremy Spencer]

4/13/96 — **130** — 1 — © — 13 **Antonio Vivaldi, The Four Seasons**............................... [I] **$10** Digital Master. 71847

| Autumn / concerto no. 24 in F major RV 293 | Spring / concerto no. 22 in E major RV 269 | Summer / concerto no. 23 in G minor RV 315 | Winter / concerto no. 25 in F minor RV 297 |

VARIOUS ARTISTS COMPILATIONS

DEBUT	PEAK	WKS	RIAA	CD	ARTIST — Album Title	Catalog	Sym	$	Label & Number
9/6/69	185	5		14	**Apollo 11: Flight To The Moon**			$15	Bell 1100

actual voice transmissions of America's space missions; narrated by astronaut Wally Schirra

Alan Shepard...America's First Manned Flight	Apollo 10...Approaching The Lunar Surface
Apollo 8...First Orbiting Of The Moon	Ed White...Walks In Space
Gemini 6 & 7...Rendezvous Above The Earth	Return To Earth
John Glenn...Orbits The Earth On The Lunar Surface	Scott Carpenter...Reentry Into Earth's Atmosphere
	To The Moon

DEBUT	PEAK	WKS	RIAA	CD	ARTIST — Album Title	Catalog	Sym	$	Label & Number
2/22/64	43	17		15	**Apollo Saturday Night**			$50	Atco 159

recorded on 11/16/63 at the Apollo Theater in New York City

Alabama Bound [Falcons] — Misty [Doris Troy] — Speedo's Back In Town [Coasters] — Walking The Dog [Rufus Thomas]
Don't Play That Song [Ben E. King] — Pain In My Heart [Otis Redding] — Stand By Me [Ben E. King] — What'd I Say [Falcons/Otis Redding/Doris Troy/Rufus Thomas/Coasters/Ben E. King]
Groovin' [Ben E. King] — Rockin' Chair [Rufus Thomas] — T'ain't Nothin' To Me [Coasters]
I Found A Love [Falcons] — Say Yeah [Doris Troy] — These Arms Of Mine [Otis Redding]

DEBUT	PEAK	WKS	RIAA	CD	ARTIST — Album Title	Catalog	Sym	$	Label & Number
3/26/94	184	3	©	16	**Art Laboe's Dedicated To You Vol. 4**			$10	Original Sound 9304

Between The Sheets [Isley Brothers] — Firma Hina [Proper Dos] — **Let's Stay Together** [Al Green] 1 — **Payback - Part I** [James Brown] 26
Break Up To Make Up [Stylistics] — **Forever Mine** [O'Jays] 28 — Never Give You Up [Jerry Butler] 28 — Smile Now, Cry Later [Sunny & The Sunliners]
Break Your Promise [Delfonics] 35 — It's Gonna Take A Miracle [Deniece Williams] 10 — Oh Honey [Delegation] 45 — Take Me Back [Little Anthony & The Imperials] 16
Distant Lover [Marvin Gaye] 28 — It's Okay [Sunglows] — Oh My Angel [Bertha Tillman] 61

DEBUT	PEAK	WKS	RIAA	CD	ARTIST — Album Title	Catalog	Sym	$	Label & Number
2/28/70	180	3		17	**Astromusical House Of..., The**	[I]		$15	Astro 1001/1012

series of 12 albums, each named after a zodiac sign; music selected is supposed to reflect the character of the sign

DEBUT	PEAK	WKS	RIAA	CD	ARTIST — Album Title	Catalog	Sym	$	Label & Number
12/29/62+	47	12		18	**At Home With That Other Family**	[C]		$20	Roulette 25203

Booking Agent — Mr. K's Diet — Nick And Chou En-Lai — To Tell The Truth
Boris, The Hairdresser — Mrs. K's Styles — Nick And Dick — Tour Of The Kremlin
Cosmonaut's Wife — Mrs. K's Troubles — Nick And Jack
It's A White Tornado — Nervous Nick — Overcoat, The
Knock-Knock — Nick And Ben — Premier's Press Conference

DEBUT	PEAK	WKS	RIAA	CD	ARTIST — Album Title	Catalog	Sym	$	Label & Number
7/20/63	99	6		19	**At The Hootenanny**	[L]		$20	Kapp 3330

Baby, Where You Been So Long [Samplers] — Hang On The Bell, Nellie [Chad Mitchell Trio] — Muleskinner Blues [David Hill] — Rum By Gum [Chad Mitchell Trio]
Daddy Roll 'Em [David Hill] — I Never Will Marry [Jo March] — Native Minstrel Song [Marais & Miranda] — Willie, Oh, Willie [Betty & The Duke]
Green Grow The Lilacs [Terry Gilkyson & The South Coasters] — Kisses Sweeter Than Wine [Jo March] — Pull Off Your Old Coat [Samplers]
 — Queen Bee [Marais & Miranda]

DEBUT	PEAK	WKS	RIAA	CD	ARTIST — Album Title	Catalog	Sym	$	Label & Number
10/31/98	51	7 ●	©	20	**Bad Boy Greatest Hits Volume 1**			$10	Bad Boy 73022

Can't Nobody Hold Me Down [Puff Daddy & The Family feat. Mase] 1 — Flava In Ya Ear [Craig Mack ft. Notorious B.I.G./Rampage/LL Cool J/Busta Rhyme] 9 — Mad Rapper Interlude — Only You [112 feat. Notorious B.I.G. & Mase] 13
Can't You See [Total feat. Notorious B.I.G.] 13 — It's All About The Benjamins [Puff Daddy ft. Notorious B.I.G./Lil' Kim/Lox] 2 — Mad Rapper Outro — Too Old For Me [Jerome]
Feel So Good [Mase] 5 — Mad Rapper Intro — Money, Power & Respect [Lox feat. DMX & Lil' Kim] 17 — You Used To Love Me [Faith Evans] 24
 — — One More Chance/Stay With Me [Notorious B.I.G.] 2

DEBUT	PEAK	WKS	RIAA	CD	ARTIST — Album Title	Catalog	Sym	$	Label & Number
8/1/92	32	12	©	21	**Barcelona Gold**			$10	Warner 26974

Barcelona [Freddie Mercury/Montserrat Caballe] — Go Out Dancing [Rod Stewart] — Love Is Here To Stay [Natalie Cole] — **This Used To Be My Playground** [Madonna] 1
Don't Tread On Me [Damn Yankees] — Heart To Climb The Mountain [Randy Travis] — No Se Tu [Luis Miguel] — Wonderful Tonight [Eric Clapton]
Free Your Mind [En Vogue] 8 — Higher Baby [D.J. Jazzy Jeff & The Fresh Prince] — **Not Enough Time** [INXS] 28
Friends For Life [Jose Carreras/Sarah Brightman] — How Fast How Far [Anita Baker] — Old Soldier [Marc Cohn]
 — **Keep It Comin'** [Keith Sweat] 17 — One Song [Tevin Campbell]
 — — Texas Flyer [Travis Tritt]

DEBUT	PEAK	WKS	RIAA	CD	ARTIST — Album Title	Catalog	Sym	$	Label & Number
10/12/96+	107	26	©	22	**Best Of Country Sing The Best Of Disney, The**			$10	Walt Disney 60902

Baby Mine [Alison Krauss] — Colors Of The Wind [Pam Tillis] — Some Day My Prince Will Come [Tanya Tucker] — Whole New World [Collin Raye]
Beauty And The Beast [Diamond Rio] — If I Never Knew You [Hal Ketchum & Shelby Lynne] — Someday [Lee Roy Parnell] — You've Got A Friend In Me [George Jones & Kathy Mattea]
Can You Feel The Love Tonight [Larry Stewart] — Kiss The Girl [Little Texas] — When You Wish Upon A Star [Bryan White]
 — Part Of Your World [Faith Hill]

DEBUT	PEAK	WKS	RIAA	CD	ARTIST — Album Title	Catalog	Sym	$	Label & Number
2/7/98	82	8	©	23	**Best Of Love - 16 Great Soft Rock Hits**			$10	Macady 6806

Almost Paradise [Mike Reno & Ann Wilson] 7 — **I Want To Know What Love Is** [Foreigner] 1 — **Maggie May** [Rod Stewart] 1 — Two Out Of Three Ain't Bad [Meat Loaf] 11
Endless Love [Diana Ross & Lionel Richie] 1 — I'm Not In Love [Will To Power] 7 — Oh Girl [Paul Young] 8 — Separate Lives [Phil Collins & Marilyn Martin] 1 — **You're In Love** [Wilson Phillips] 1
Here And Now [Luther Vandross] 6 — **Keep On Loving You** [REO Speedwagon] 1 — So Far Away [Carole King] 14 — You've Lost That Lovin' Feelin' [Righteous Brothers] 1
How Much I Feel [Ambrosia] 3 — Longer [Dan Fogelberg] 2 — Still [Commodores] 1

DEBUT	PEAK	WKS	RIAA	CD	ARTIST — Album Title	Catalog	Sym	$	Label & Number
10/23/99	178	3	©	24	**Best Of Rap City**			$10	Fully Loaded 48291

Bet Ya Man Can't [Triz] [Fat Joe] — Discipline [Gang Starr Feat. Total] — It Ain't My Fault 2 [Silkk The Shocker feat. Mystikal] 18 — Tell Me [Beenie Man Feat. Angie Martinez]
Break Ups 2 Make Ups [Method Man Feat. D'Angelo] 98 — Ha [Juvenile] 68 — Make 'Em Say Uhh [Master P] 16 — What's It Gonna Be?! [Busta Rhymes Feat. Janet] 3
Cheapskate [Sporty Thieves] — Hand In Hand [DJ Quik Feat. 2nd II None] — My Name Is [Eminem] 36 — Who Dat [JT Money Feat. Solé] 5
Da Art Of Story Telling (Pt. I) [OutKast Feat. Slick Rick] — **Hot Spot** [Foxy Brown] 91 — Nas Is Like [Nas] 86
 — In Decatur [Ghetto Mafia Feat. Silk] — Superthug [Noreaga] 36

DEBUT	PEAK	WKS	RIAA	CD	ARTIST — Album Title	Catalog	Sym	$	Label & Number
8/14/99	136	1	©	25	**Best Opera Album In The World...Ever!, The**	[F]		$15	Virgin 42203 [2]

Au Fond Du Temple Saint [Nicolai Gedda/Ernest Blanc] — Ebben? Ne Andro Lontana [Maria Callas] — Mon Coeur S'Ouvre A Ta Voix [Maria Callas] — Soave Sia Il Vento [Margaret Marshall/Jose Van Dam/Anges Baltsa]
Barcarolle [Schwartzkopf/Jeannine] — Io Son L'Umile Ancella [Dame Kiri Te Kanawa] — Nessun Dorma [Jose Carreras] — Suzel, Bon Di [Luciano Pavarotti/Mirella Freni]
Che Gelida Manina [Roberto Alagna] — L'Amour Est Un Oiseau Rebelle [Victoria de los Angeles] — Non Piu Andrai [Thomas Allen] — Un Bel Di Vedremo [Renata Scotto]
Chi Il Bel Sogno Di Doretta [Montserrat Caballe] — La Donna E Mobile [Roberto Alagna] — O Mio Babbino Caro [Victoria de los Angeles] — Va, Pensiero [Chorus of the Royal Opera House]
Der Holle Rache [Edita Gruberova] — La Mamma Morta [Maria Callas] — Pourquoi Me Reveiller? [Roberto Alagna] — Vedi! Le Fosche Notturne [Chorus of the Royal Opera House]
Der Vogelfanger Bin Ich Ja [Walter Berry] — La Fleur Que Tu M'Avais Jetee [Roberto Alagna] — Recondita Armonia [Placido Domingo] — Vesti La Giubba [Jose Carreras]
Dove Sono [Elisabeth Schwartzkopf] — Largo Al Factotum [Thomas Hampson] — Se Quel Guerrier Io Fossi! [Placido Domingo] — Viens, Mallika [Mady Mesple/Danielle Millet]
Dvorak: Song To The Moon [Lucia Popp] — Libiamo Ne'lieti Calici [Alfredo Kraus/Renata Scotto] — Si, Mi Chiamano Mimi [Mirella Freni] — Vissi D'Arte [Maria Callas]
E Lucevan Le Stelle [Placido Domingo] — M'Apparai [Roberto Alagna] — Signore, Ascolta! [Montserrat Caballe] — Voi, Che Sapete [Ann Murray]
 — Mild Und Leise [Helge Dernesch] — — Votre Toast [Robert Massard]

DEBUT	PEAK	WKS	RIAA	CD	ARTIST — Album Title	Catalog	Sym	$	Label & Number

8/14/99 · 130 · 1 · © 26 · Best Soul Album In The World...Ever!, The .... **$10** Virgin 47421

- Hangin' On A String (Contemplating) [Loose Ends] 43
- Hyperbolicsyllabicsesquedalymistic [Isaac Hayes]
- I Can't Stand The Rain [Ann Peebles] 38
- Let's Get It On [Marvin Gaye] 1
- Me And Mrs. Jones [Billy Paul] 1
- My Girl [Temptations] 1
- Nightshift [Commodores] 3
- People Get Ready [Impressions] 14
- Piece Of My Heart [Erma Franklin] 62
- Rainy Night In Georgia [Randy Crawford]
- Respect Yourself [Staple Singers] 12
- Rock Me Tonight (For Old Times Sake) [Freddie Jackson] 18
- Something Beautiful Remains [Tina Turner]
- Soul Man [Sam & Dave] 2
- Tired Of Being Alone [Al Green] 11
- Woman To Woman [Shirley Brown] 22
- Woman's Gotta Have It [Bobby Womack] 60

4/10/99 · 102 · 10 · © 27 · BET - Best Of Planet Groove .... **$10** Fully Loaded 47109

- Anytime [Brian McKnight]
- Arms Of The One Who Loves You [Xscape] 7
- Be Careful [Sparkle Feat. R. Kelly]
- Breakdown [Mariah Carey Feat. Krayzie Bone & Wish Bone]
- Butta Love [Next] 16
- I Can Love You [Mary J. Blige Feat. Lil' Kim] 28
- I Get Lonely [Janet] 3
- It's All About Me [Mya Feat. Sisqo] 6
- Let's Ride [Montell Jordan Feat. Master P & Silk The Shocker] 2
- My Body [LSG] 4
- No Guarantee [Chico Feat. Joe]
- Rain [SWV] 25
- Song For Mama [Boyz II Men] 7
- They Don't Know [Jon B.] 7
- Tyrone [Erykah Badu]

8/5/00 · 137 · 1 · © 28 · BET On Jazz Presents: For The Love Of Jazz .... **$10** NARM 50004

- Dear Miss Lucy [Dave's True Story]
- Descargasses [Roberto Carassés]
- Desert Skies [Dwight Sills]
- Heart And Mind [Jay Beckenstein]
- Her Song [D.D. Jackson]
- Hidden Light [Gregory Tardy]
- I Can't Believe [Mary Pearson]
- Kisses In The Rain [John Pizzarelli]
- Lament [James Hardway]
- Panama Hat [Acoustic Alchemy]
- Prelude To A Kiss [Claudia Acuña]
- Toe To Toe [Peggy Stern]
- Whale Song [Scott Wilkie]

1/11/69 · 190 · 6 · 29 · Beware Of Greeks Bearing Gifts .... [C] **$20** Musicor 3173

- Big Fix
- Bride To Be
- Chairman Of The Board
- Dinner, The
- Disagreement, The
- Games People Play
- Getting Ready For The Wedding
- Gratitude
- Man Of Action
- Momma
- My Husband, The Captain
- Paparazzi, The
- Press Conference
- Quiet Evening At Home
- Sisters
- Tailor, The
- Telephone Call
- Typical Morning
- Visit To New York
- Wedding, The

8/8/70 · 197 · 2 · 30 · Big Hits Now, The .... **$20** Dunhill/ABC 50085

- Baby Hold On [Grass Roots] 35
- Can I Change My Mind [Tyrone Davis] 5
- Celebrate [Three Dog Night] 15
- Eli's Coming [Three Dog Night] 10
- Heaven Knows [Grass Roots] 24
- Hey Lawdy Mama [Steppenwolf] 35
- Hey There Lonely Girl [Eddie Holman] 2
- Jam Up Jelly Tight [Tommy Roe] 8
- New World Coming [Mama Cass Elliot] 42
- So Excited [B.B. King] 54
- Take A Look Around [Smith] 43
- Thrill Is Gone [B.B. King] 15

12/14/63+ · 27 · 18 · 31 · Big Sounds Of The Drags!, The .... **$25** Capitol 2001

actual sounds of drag racing at a quarter-mile track; no track titles listed on this album

4/8/72 · 191 · 4 · 32 · Big Sur Festival/One Hand Clapping .... [L] **$20** Columbia 31138

- Corinna [Taj Mahal]
- Hello In There [Kris Kristofferson & Joan Baez]
- Jesse Younger [Kris Kristofferson]
- Love Is Just A Four Letter Word [Joan Baez]
- Lucretia Mac Evil [Blood, Sweat & Tears]
- Me And Bobby McGee [Big Sur Choir]
- Nobody's Business But My Own [Taj Mahal]
- Oh Happy Day [Joan Baez]
- Pilgrim - Chapter 33 [Kris Kristofferson]
- San Francisco Mabel Joy [Mickey Newbury & Joan Baez]
- Song Of The French Partisan [Joan Baez]
- Thirty-Third Of August [Mickey Newbury]

4/10/99 · 199 · 1 · © 33 · Blue's Big Treasure - A Musical Adventure .... **$10** Kid Rhino 75626

- Blue's Big Treasure
- Blue's Big Treasure (Extended Version)
- Can You Help Me Today?
- Hi, Out There!
- Listen For A Pawprint
- Mailtime
- Things I Love To Do
- Time To Play Blue's Clues
- We Are Going To Play Blue's Clues
- We Just Figured Out Blue's Clues
- Whose Treasure Is This?
- You Sure Are Smart

9/11/93 · 40 · 11 · ● © 34 · Bob Dylan - The 30th Anniversary Concert Celebration .... [L] **$15** Columbia 53230 [2]

recorded on 10/16/92 at Madison Square Garden in New York City

- Absolutely Sweet Marie [George Harrison]
- All Along The Watchtower [Neil Young]
- Blowin' In The Wind [Stevie Wonder]
- Don't Think Twice, It's All Right [Eric Clapton]
- Emotionally Yours [O'Jays]
- Foot Of Pride [Lou Reed]
- Girl Of The North Country [Bob Dylan]
- Highway 61 Revisited [Johnny Winter]
- I Shall Be Released [Chrissie Hynde]
- I'll Be Your Baby Tonight [Kris Kristofferson]
- It Ain't Me, Babe [June Carter Cash/Johnny Cash]
- It's Alright, Ma (I'm Only Bleeding) [Bob Dylan]
- Just Like A Woman [Richie Havens]
- Just Like Tom Thumb's Blues [Neil Young]
- Knockin' On Heaven's Door [Bob Dylan & Friends]
- Leopard-Skin Pill-Box Hat [John Mellencamp]
- License To Kill [Tom Petty & The Heartbreakers]
- Like A Rolling Stone [John Mellencamp]
- Masters Of War [Eddie Vedder]
- Mr. Tambourine Man [Roger McGuinn]
- My Back Pages [Bob Dylan & Friends]
- Rainy Day Women #12 & 35 [Tom Petty & The Heartbreakers]
- Seven Days [Ron Wood]
- Times They Are A-Changin' [Tracy Chapman]
- What Was It You Wanted [Willie Nelson]
- When I Paint My Masterpiece [Band]
- When The Ship Comes In [Clancy Brothers/Robbie O'Connell/Tommy Makem]
- You Ain't Goin' Nowhere [Mary-Chapin Carpenter/Rosanne Cash/Shawn Colvin]

4/17/99 · 92 · 8 · © 35 · Body + Soul: Love Serenade .... C:#3/11 **$15** Time Life 33972 [2]

- After The Love Has Gone [Earth, Wind & Fire] 2
- Always And Forever [Heatwave] 18
- Betcha By Golly, Wow [Stylistics] 3
- Can You Stop The Rain [Peabo Bryson] 52
- Cruisin' [Smokey Robinson] 4
- Float On [Floaters] 2
- Here And Now [Luther Vandross] 6
- How 'Bout Us [Champaign] 12
- I've Got Love On My Mind [Natalie Cole] 5
- If You Don't Know Me By Now [Harold Melvin & the Blue Notes] 3
- Let Me Make Love To You [O'Jays] 75
- Love You Down [Ready For The World] 9
- Make It Like It Was [Regina Belle] 43
- Me And Mrs. Jones [Billy Paul] 1
- Oh Girl [Chi-Lites] 1
- Rock Me Tonight (For Old Times Sake) [Freddie Jackson] 18
- Sexual Healing [Marvin Gaye] 3
- Shake You Down [Gregory Abbott] 1
- Shining Star [Manhattans] 5
- Shower Me With Your Love [Surface] 5
- Three Times A Lady [Commodores] 1
- Tonight, I Celebrate My Love [Peabo Bryson w/Roberta Flack] 16
- Too Much, Too Little, Too Late [Johnny Mathis & Deniece Williams] 1
- You Are My Starship [Norman Connors] 27

4/18/98 · 119 · 5 · © 36 · Boom! - 17 Explosive Hits .... **$10** Beast 54112

- All Cried Out [Allure] 4
- Bitch [Meredith Brooks] 2
- Boom Intro!
- Breaking All The Rules [She Moves] 32
- Call Me [Le Click] 35
- Can U Feel It [3rd Party] 43
- Da Da Da (I Don't Love You You Don't Love Me Ah Aha Aha) [Trio]
- How Bizarre [OMC]
- I Like It [Blackout Allstars] 25
- Love You Down [INOJ] 25
- My Boo [Ghostown DJ's] 31
- On My Own [Peach Union] 39
- Please Don't Go [No Mercy] 21
- Rhythm Of Love [DJ Company] 53
- Space Cowboy [Jamiroquai]
- Spin Spin Sugar [Sneaker Pimps]
- Tubthumping [Chumbawamba] 87

4/19/97 · 93 · 20 · © 37 · Booty Mix 2 .... **$10** Intersound 9510

- Bass Mechanic [M.C.A.D.E.]
- Booty Bounce [Goon Sqwad]
- Can't Stop The Rock [D.J. Kizzy Rock]
- Dickey Ride [Southern Playas]
- Get Retarded [K.J. & Da Fellas]
- Give It All You Got [Afro-Rican]
- Hear What I Hear [Kilo]
- Heiny Heiny [95 South]
- Run Forrest Run [Get Some Crew]
- Scarred [Luke] 64
- Shake A Lil' Somethin' [2 Live Crew] 74
- Shake Whatcha Mama Gave Ya [Poison Clan]
- 2 Much Booty (In The Pants) [Soundmaster T]
- Tootsie Roll [69 Boyz] 8
- Work It Out [M.C. Shy-D]

VARIOUS ARTISTS COMPILATIONS

DEBUT	PEAK	WKS	RIAA	CD	ARTIST — Album Title	Catalog	Sym	$	Label & Number

4/25/98 · 182 · 2 · © 38 · Booty Mix 3 - Wiggle Patrol .... **$15** Intersound 9526 [2]

Bass Train [M.C. A.D.E.]
Break It Down [Ant D & The Puppies]
Can't Stop No Playa [Da Organization]
Crank It [M.C. A.D.E.]
Crank This [DJ Kizzy Rock]
Da' Dip [Freak Nasty] **15**
Get It [DJ Uncle AL]
Grits & Eggs [Breakdown]
Hold Up! Wait A Minute [DJ Smurf & P.M.H.I.]
I'm Gonna Luv U [Summer Junkies]
Keep Doin' It [MC Shy D]
Let Me Ride [12 Gauge]
(Let Me See Ya) Booty Drop [DJ Spin & Fresh Kid]
MyBabyDaddy [B-Rock & The Bizz] **10**
1-2-3-4-5-6 Bass [Beat Dominator]
Pullit All The Way Down [Beatmaster Clay D. & Prince Rahiem]
Reckless [Chris Taylor/David Storrs]
Scrub Da Ground [Splack Pack]
Show Me Love [Kilo Ali]
Splash Down [Danny D]
That Moon Pie [Afro-Rican]
True That [MC Shy D]
Who U Wit [Lil Jon & The East Side Boyz]
Wiggle Wiggle [Disco & The City Boyz]

4/22/89 · 178 · 4 · © 39 · Brazil Classics 1 Beleza Tropical .... [F] **$10** Fly 25805

Andar Com Fe [Gilberto Gil]
Anima [Milton Nascimento]
Cacada [Chico Buarque]
Caixa De Sol [Nazare Pereira]
Fio Maravilha [Jorge Ben]
O Leaozinho [Caetano Veloso]
Ponta De Lanca Africano (Umbarauma) [Jorge Ben]
Queixa [Caetano Veloso]
Quilombo, O El Dorado Negro [Gilberto Gil]
San Vicente [Milton Nascimento]
So Quero Um Xodo [Gilberto Gil]
Sonho Meu [Maria Bethania E Gal Costa]
Terra [Caetano Veloso]
Um Canto De Afoxe Para O Bloco Do Ile (Ile Aye) [Caetano Veloso]

3/22/69 · 105 · 9 · 40 · Bubble Gum Music Is The Naked Truth .... **$25** Buddah 5032

Chewy Chewy [Ohio Express] **15**
Down At Lulu's [Ohio Express] **33**
Goody Goody Gumdrops [1910 Fruitgum Co.] **37**
Green Tambourine [Lemon Pipers] **1**
I'm In Love With You [Kasenetz-Katz Super Cirkus]
Jelly Jungle (Of Orange Marmalade) [Lemon Pipers] **51**
May I Take A Giant Step (Into Your Heart) [1910 Fruitgum Co.] **63**
1, 2, 3, Red Light [1910 Fruitgum Co.] **5**
Quick Joey Small (Run Joey Run) [Kasenetz-Katz Singing Orchestral Circus] **25**
Rice Is Nice [Lemon Pipers] **46**
Shake [Shadows Of Knight] **46**
Simon Says [1910 Fruitgum Co.] **4**
We Can Work It Out [Kasenetz-Katz Super Cirkus]
Yummy Yummy Yummy [Ohio Express] **4**

1/16/99 · 187 · 1 · 41 · Bug's Life Sing-Along, A .... **$10** Walt Disney 60971

includes a 22-page book and songs from the movie; available only on cassette

Flea-Ring Circus
Grasshopper
He's A Kick! That Walking Stick
High Hopes
I Just Wanna Fly
I.N.S.E.C.T.
Ladybug
Roly-Poly Rock 'n' Rolly Pill Bugs
Star Of The Show
Ugly Bug Ball

8/26/95 · 91 · 1 · © 42 · Buy-Product - A Tasty Sample Of Choice Cuts From 16 Artists .... **$10** DGC 24824

Datskat [Roots]
Dress [Hardvark]
El Camino [Rake's Progress]
Good Times [Stone Roses]
More Human Than Human [White Zombie]
N20 [Skiploader]
Not Going Back There Again [Bivouac]
Nothing Lies Still Long [Pell Mell]
Ono Soul [Thurston Moore]
Scuba Diving [St. Johnny]
Silently [that dog]
Sincerely Jasper [Jasper & the Prodigal Suns]
Sparky's Dream [Teenage Fanclub]
Teen Age Riot [Sonic Youth]
Waking Up [Elastica]
White Trash [Southern Culture On The Skids]

7/22/78 · 84 · 10 · © 43 · California Jam 2 .... [L] **$20** Columbia 35389 [2]

recorded on 3/18/78 in Ontario, California

Chip Away The Stone [Aerosmith]
Dance Sister Dance [Santana]
Draw The Line [Aerosmith]
Free-For-All [Ted Nugent]
I'm A King Bee [Frank Marino & Mahogany Rush]
Johnny B. Goode [Frank Marino & Mahogany Rush]
Jugando [Santana]
Let It Go, Let It Flow [Dave Mason]
Little Queen [Heart]
Love Alive [Heart]
Never Gonna Leave [Rubicon]
Oxygene (Part 5) [Jean Michel Jarre]
Same Old Song And Dance [Aerosmith]
Snakeskin Cowboys [Ted Nugent]
Too Hot To Handle [Rubicon]
We Just Disagree [Dave Mason]

11/13/82 · 63 · 19 · © 44 · Casino Lights .... [L] **$12** Warner 23718

recorded at the Montreux Jazz Festival in Switzerland

Casino Lights [Neil Larsen & Buzz Feiten]
Hideaway [David Sanborn]
Imagine [Randy Crawford & Yellowjackets]
Love Is Not Enough, Theme From [David Sanborn]
Monmouth College Fight Song [Yellowjackets]
Sure Enough [Al Jarreau & Randy Crawford]
Who's Right, Who's Wrong [Al Jarreau & Randy Crawford]
Your Precious Love [Al Jarreau & Randy Crawford]

4/13/96 · 121 · 4 · © 45 · Cell Block Compilation .... **$10** Cell Block 50556

Can You Swing It [Devin]
Crooked [FM-Blue]
Deep Shit [Bad-n-fluenz]
80 Oz. [Richie Rich]
Expect The Unexpected [Mr.III/FM-Blue/Bad-n-fluenz]
Flossn [Father Dom]
Fucked In The Game [3X Krazy]
Game Time [Too $hort]
Gettin' High [A.M.W.]
It's Goin' Down In Oakland [Gangsta P.]
Keep It Real [Delinquents]
Oakland So Saucy [Half Pint]
1-800-FED-UP [Mr.III/Shorty B.]
Out To Be The Boss [Seagram]
Out To Get Rich [J. Dubb]
3 Hills Of Suga [Mr. III]

2/24/01 · 8[C] · 3 · © 46 · Celtic Moods .... **$10** Virgin 44951

Blackbird [Sharon Shannon]
Caide Sin Don Té Sin? [Altan]
Call To Dance Medley [Leahy]
Carmel Mahoney Mulhaire's (medley) [Matt Maloy]
Crib Of Perches (medley) [Matt Maloy]
Gaelic Reels [Capercaillie]
Heroine [Edge & Sinéad O'Connor]
Invisible To You [Mary Coughlan]
Island, The [Paul Brady]
No Frontier [Mary Black]
Only A Woman's Heart [Eleanor McEvoy]
Ride On [Christy Moore]
Samain Night [Loreena McKennitt]
Sleepy Maggie [Ashley MacIsaac]
Strange Boat [Waterboys]
Theme From Harry's Game [Clannad]
Woodbrook [Micheál O'Súilleabháin]

3/16/85 · 47 · 21 · © 47 · Chess .... **$15** RCA Victor 5340 [2]

American And Florence (medley)
Anthem
Argument
Chess
Deal (No Deal)
Embassy Lament
Endgame
Florence Quits
Heaven Help My Heart
I Know Him So Well
Merano
Mountain Duet
Nobody's Side (medley)
One Night In Bangkok [Murray Head] **3**
Opening Ceremony
Pity The Child
Quartet (A Model Of Decorum And Tranquillity)
Russian And Molokov (medley)
Story Of Chess (medley)
Where I Want To Be (medley)
You And I (medley)

6/5/71 · 148 · 9 · 48 · Child's Garden Of Grass (A Pre-Legalization Comedy), A .... [C] **$20** Elektra 75012

Acquiring Marijuana, General Effects
Creativity
Eating Food
Funniness
Getting Hung-Up
History Of Marijuana
Listening To Music
Making Love
Meditation
Physical And Intellectual Games
Physical Effects
Psychological Effects
Time And Space

DEBUT	PEAK	WKS	RIAA	CD	ARTIST — Album Title	Catalog	Sym	$	Label & Number

5/22/99 11 9 © 49 Chronic 2000 .... **$15** Death Row 51161 [2]

Beautiful Lady [Danny Boy feat. K-Ci] — Gotta Love Gangsta's [Realest feat. Scarface & Richie Rich] — Like It Or Not [Soopafly] — Mr. Officer [Michel'le feat. Captain Save M' & El Dorado] — They Wanna Be Like Us [Realest feat. Top Dogg & Doobie]
Because Of You Girl [Daz Dillinger & Kurupt feat. Realest] — I Thought You Knew [Mac-Shawn feat. E-40 & Daz Dillinger] — Now What [Capricorn] — Things Your Man Won't Do [VK]
Chronic 2000 [VK feat. Treach] — I Wanna Be Loved By You [Kelmar, Ruby & Strothart] — Og To Bg [Soopafly, Daz Dillinger & Kurupt] — Top Dogg Cindafella [Top Dogg]
Curiosity [VK] — I'm Comin' Home [Realest feat. Jewell] — Presenting Miilkbone [Miilkbone & Naji] — Wanna Be Loved [Michel'le feat. VK]
Don't Forget Where You Came From [Swoop G] — I'm Country [Doobie] — Ride Or Get Rode On [Bad Habitz] — We Don't Love Em' [Top Dogg]
Drinks On Me [Captain Save M' & Ant Banks] — It's Goin Down [Mac-Shawn feat. Daz Dillinger & Tha Realest] — Roll Wit' Us [Daz Dillinger & Kurupt] — Who Do You Believe In [2Pac feat. Yaka Kadafi]
Easy To Be A Soldier When There Ain't No War [Realest, Swoop G & Lil' C-Style] — Late Night [2Pac feat. DJ Quik & Outlawz] — Stand Strong [Realest feat. Danny Boy & Jewell]

9/9/00 148 9 © 50 City On A Hill - Songs Of Worship And Praise .... **$10** Essential 10607

City On A Hill [Third Day] — I Remember You [Mac Powell w/ Gene Eugene] — Precious Jesus [The Choir w/Leigh Nash] — Where You Are [FFH]
Covenant Song [Caedmon's Call] — Marvelous Light [Gene Eugene w/All Artists] — Stone, The [Jars Of Clay] — With Every Breath [Leigh Nash & Dan Haseltine]
God Of Wonders [Mac Powell & Cliff & Danielle Young] — Merciful Rain [FFH] — This Road [Jars Of Clay] — You're Here [Sixpence None The Richer]
— — Unified [SonicFlood w/Peter Furler]

10/7/95 142 14 © 51 Club Mix 95 V. 2 .... **$10** Coldfront 6186

Back & Forth [Aaliyah] 5 — Get Ready For This [2 Unlimited] 38 — Tootsee Roll [69 Boyz] 8 — What Hope Have I [Sphinx]
Cotton Eye Joe [Rednex] 25 — Lick It [Roula] 72 — Total Eclipse Of The Heart [Nicki French] 2 — Yolanda [Reality] 72
Fatboy [Max-A-Million] 69 — Mr. Personality [Gillette] 42 — Wanna Get Busy [Reality] —

2/17/96 51 38 ● © 52 Club Mix '96 - Volume 1 .... **$10** Cold Front 6218

Bomb, The [Bucketheads] 49 — Groove Thang [Zhané] 17 — Party Girl [Ultra Naté] — Tonight Is The Night [Le Click] 68
Do You Wanna Get Funky [C & C Music Factory] 40 — Love & Devotion [Joi Cardwell] — Scatman (Third-Level) [Scatman John] 60 — Too Many Fish [Frankie Knuckles Feat. Adeva]
Everybody Be Somebody [Ruffneck Feat. Yavahn] 82 — Macarena [Los Del Mar] 71 — Sexual Healing [Max-A-Million] 60 — —
— Magic Carpet Ride [Mighty Dub Kats] 58 — Stay Together [Barbara Tucker] — —

9/21/96 188 3 © 53 Club Mix '96 - Volume 2 .... **$10** Cold Front 6236

Bang Da Bush [Fresh Fish] — Freedom (Make It Funky) [Black Magic] — Make The World Go Round [Sandy B] — StopGo [D'still'd]
Can't Stop Love [Soul Solution] — I Want You (She's So Heavy) [Groove Collective] — Mind Fluid [Nuyorican Soul] — Sunday Afternoons [Vanessa Daou]
Don't Turn Around [Ace Of Base] 4 — — Say A Prayer [Taylor Dayne] — What A Sensation [Kenlou III]
— — Set U Free [Planet Soul] 26 — You Got To Pray [Joi Cardwell]

3/8/97 36 36 ▲ © 54 Club Mix '97 .... **$15** Cold Front 6242 [2]

Are You Ready For Some More? [Reel 2 Real] — Crossroads, Tha [Bone thugs-n-harmony] 1 — Keep On Jumpin' [Todd Terry Presents Martha Wash & Jocelyn Brown] — Theme From "Mission Impossible" [FC 7]
Bohemian Rhapsody [Braids] 42 — DJ Girl [Katalina] 86 — Total Eclipse Of The Heart [Nicki French] 2
Boom Boom Boom [Outhere Brothers] 65 — Feels So Good (Show Me Your Love) [Lina Santiago] 35 — Macarena [Los Del Mar] 71 — Walking On Sunshine [Jah Boyz feat. Chralie Cassanova & Ian Starr]
Come And Get Your Love [Real McCoy] 19 — I Wanna Be With U [Fun Factory] 45 — Move Your Body [Ruffneck feat. Yavahn] — One More Try [Kristine W] 78
Come Go With Me [Exposé] 5 — If Madonna Calls [Junior Vasquez] — Roof Is On Fire [Too Kool Chris] — Your Loving Arms [Billie Ray Martin] 46
C'mon 'N Ride It (The Train) [Quad City DJ's] 3 — Jazz It Up [Erick Morillo Project] — Sweet Dreams [La Bouche] 13
— Jellyhead [Crush] 72 — Tell Me [Groove Theory] 5

11/1/97 64 25 ▲ © 55 Club Mix '98 .... **$15** Cold Front 6254 [2]

Can't Get You Out Of My Mind [Lil' Suzy] 79 — Dub-I-Dub [Me & My] — Land Of The Living [Kristine W] — Say...If You Feel Alright [Crystal Waters] 40
Child (Inside) [Qkumba Zoo] 69 — Falling In Love [La Bouche] — Little Bit Of Ecstacy [Jocelyn Enriquez] 55 — That Girl [Maxi Priest feat. Shaggy] 20
Colour Of Love [Amber] 74 — Hey You [Smooth] — Make The World Go Round [Sandy B.] — Where Do You Go [No Mercy] 5
Da' Dip [Freak Nasty] 15 — I Believe I Can Fly [R. Kelly] 2 — — Where Have All The Cowboys Gone? [Paula Cole] 8
Dance Hall Days [Wang Chung] 16 — I'm Not Feeling You [Yvette Michele] 44 — Only Words [Deborah Gibson]
Don't Speak [Clueless] — In My Nature [Nuttin' Nyce] 83 — Power, The [Snap! feat. Einstein] 2
Don't Wanna Be A Player [Joe] 21 — Just Be Good To Me [Deborah Cox] — Quit Playing Games (With My Heart) [Backstreet Boys] 2

6/20/98 107 9 © 56 Club Mix '98 - Volume 2 .... **$15** Cold Front 6340 [2]

As Long As You Love Me [Backstreet Boys] — Do You Know (What It Takes) [Robyn] 7 — Like A Playa [L.A. Ganz] — Please Don't Go [No Mercy] 21
Busy Child [Crystal Method] — Feel What You Want [Kristine W.] — Like I Do [For Real] 72 — Point Of No Return [Exposé] 5
Call Me [Le Click] 35 — Free [Ultra Naté] 75 — Love Scene [Joe] — She's Playing Hard To Get [Hi-Five] 5
Can We [SWV Feat. Missy "Misdemeanor" Elliott] 75 — Gotham City [R. Kelly] 9 — Never Make A Promise [Dru Hill] 7 — Space Jam [Quad City DJ's] 37
D.J. Keep Playin' (Get Your Music On) [Yvette Michele] 84 — How Do I Live [Debra Michaels] — Never, Never Gonna Give You Up [Lisa Stansfield] 74 — Supernatural [Wild Orchid] 70
— I Belong To You (Every Time I See Your Face) [Rome] 6 — One More Night [Amber] 58 — You're Not Alone [Olive] 56
— — One More Time [Real McCoy] 27

11/21/98+ 152 7 ● © 57 Club Mix 99 .... **$15** Cold Front 6366 [2]

Cetch Da Monkey [Atomic Babies] — I Like The Way (The Kissing Game) [Hi-Five] 1 — My Love Is The Shhh! [Somethin' For The People] 4 — Strictly Business [Mantronik vs. EPMD]
Coco Jamboo [Mr. President] 21 — I'll Be There For You [Solid Harmonie] — No Tengo Dinero [Los Umbrellos] 42 — Thank God It's Friday [R. Kelly]
Don't Go [Le Click feat. Kayo] 62 — Legend Of A Cowgirl [Imani Coppola] 36 — One And One [Robert Miles] 54 — Walkin' On The Sun [Smash Mouth]
Everybody (Backstreet's Back) [Backstreet Boys] 4 — Love Is Alive [3rd Party] 61 — Outlaw [Olive] — Where Do We Go [Wamdue Project]
Everybody Dance [Barbara Tucker] — MyBabyDaddy [B-Rock & The Bizz] 10 — Rain [SWV] 20 — You Only Have To Say You Love Me [Hannah Jones] 65
Found A Cure [Ultra Naté] — My Heart Will Go On [Deja Vu] 58 — Shorty (You Keep Playin' With My Mind) [Imajin] 25
Get Ready To Bounce [Brooklyn Bounce] 95 — — Show Me Love [Robyn] 7

5/25/91 38 19 ● © 58 Club MTV Party To Go - Volume One .... **$10** Tommy Boy 1037

At The Club [Joe Boys] — Humpty Dance [Digital Underground] 11 — Personal Jesus [Depeche Mode] 28 — Think [Information Society] 28
Don't Wanna Fall In Love [Jane Child] 2 — Knocked Out [Paula Abdul] 41 — Play That Funky Music [Vanilla Ice] 4 — Tom's Diner [D.N.A. feat. Suzanne Vega] 5
Feels Good [Tony! Toni! Toné!] 9 — Knockin' Boots [Candyman] 9 — Poison [Bell Biv DeVoe] 3 — Turn This Mutha Out [M.C. Hammer]

4/22/95 90 11 © 59 Come Together - America Salutes The Beatles .... **$10** Liberty 31712

All My Loving [Suzy Bogguss & Chet Atkins] — I'll Follow The Sun [David Ball] — Nowhere Man [Randy Travis] — We Can Work It Out [Phil Keaggy & PFR]
Can't Buy Me Love [Shenandoah] — If I Fell [Sammy Kershaw] — Oh! Darling [Huey Lewis] — Yesterday [Billy Dean]
Come Together [Delbert McClinton] — In My Life [Susan Ashton & Gary Chapman] — One After 909 [Willie Nelson]
Get Back [Steve Wariner] — Let It Be [Collin Raye] — Paperback Writer [Kris Kristofferson]
Help! [Little Texas] — Long And Winding Road [John Berry] — Something [Tanya Tucker]

VARIOUS ARTISTS COMPILATIONS

DEBUT	PEAK	WKS	RIAA	CD	ARTIST — Album Title	Catalog	Sym	$	Label & Number

10/30/93 — 3 — 55 — ▲³ — © 60 — Common Thread: The Songs Of The Eagles — $10 — Giant 24531

- Already Gone [Tanya Tucker]
- Best Of My Love [Brooks & Dunn]
- Desperado [Clint Black]
- Heartache Tonight [John Anderson]
- I Can't Tell You Why [Vince Gill]
- Lyin' Eyes [Diamond Rio]
- New Kid In Town [Trisha Yearwood]
- Peaceful Easy Feeling [Little Texas]
- Sad Cafe [Lorrie Morgan]
- Saturday Night [Billy Dean]
- Take It Easy [Travis Tritt]
- Take It To The Limit [Suzy Bogguss]
- Tequila Sunrise [Alan Jackson]
- (also see: You Got Me Over)

Concert For Bangla Desh, The - see HARRISON, George

4/18/81 — 36 — 12 — 61 — Concerts For The People Of Kampuchea .... [L] — $15 — Atlantic 7005 [2]
recorded in December 1979 in London

- Armagideon Time [Clash]
- Baba O'Riley [Who]
- Behind Blue Eyes [Who]
- Coming Up [Paul McCartney & Wings]
- Crawling From The Wreckage [Rockpile]
- Every Night [Paul McCartney & Wings]
- Got To Get You Into My Life [Paul McCartney & Wings]
- Hit Me With Your Rhythm Stick [Ian Dury & The Blockheads]
- Imposter, The [Elvis Costello & The Attractions]
- Let It Be [Rockestra]
- Little Sister [Rockpile w/Robert Plant]
- Lucille [Rockestra]
- Monkey Man [Specials]
- Now I'm Here [Queen]
- Precious [Pretenders]
- Rockestra Theme [Rockestra]
- See Me, Feel Me [Who]
- Sister Disco [Who]
- Tattooed Love Boys [Pretenders]
- Wait, The [Pretenders]

6/13/70 — 175 — 4 — 62 — Core of Rock, The .... — $20 — MGM 4669

- Come To The Sunshine [Van Dyke Parks]
- Flute Thing [Blues Project]
- Handsome Johnny [Richie Havens]
- If I Were A Carpenter [Tim Hardin]
- Just Like A Woman [Richie Havens]
- Mojo Woman [Enemys]
- Number Nine [Van Dyke Parks]
- Reason To Believe [Tim Hardin]
- Society's Child (Baby I've Been Thinking) [Janis Ian] 14
- Too Much Monkey Business [Enemys]
- You Can't Catch Me [Blues Project]

11/18/00 — 143 — 2 — © 63 — Damizza Presents...Where I Wanna Be .... — $10 — Baby Ree 31149

- Bounce [Shade Sheist Feat. TQ]
- Get Ur Head Out Ur Ass Playboy [Shade Sheist]
- Have A Nice Day [Caz feat. Shade Sheist & Damizza]
- If You Were Mine [Shade Sheist feat. Tatum Tots]
- Is It Me? [Damon Sharpe feat. Krayzie Bone]
- Let Me Do My Thang [Damon Sharpe]
- Life Ain't A Game [Ja Rule]
- Lord What Have I Done? [Krayzie Bone, Layzie Bone feat. Shade Sheist]
- Used To [TQ]
- Where I Wanna Be [Shade Sheist feat. Nate Dogg & Kurupt]

6/27/64 — 102 — 6 — 64 — Dance Discotheque .... — $25 — Decca 74556

- Compadre Pedro Juan [Tommy Dorsey Orch./Warren Covington]
- Desafinado [Discotheque Orchestra]
- El Leoncito [Discotheque Orchestra]
- Fly Me To The Moon (In Other Words) [Discotheque Orchestra]
- Hello, Dolly! [Discotheque Orchestra]
- Hot Pastrami With Mashed Potatoes [Discotheque Orchestra]
- If I Had A Hammer [Discotheque Orchestra]
- Mack The Knife [Discotheque Orchestra]
- Make Someone Happy [Peter Duchin]
- Mi Guantanamera [Emilio Reyes]
- Roll Over Beethoven [Discotheque Orchestra]
- Yesterdays [Discotheque Orchestra]

9/14/96 — 60 — 24 — © 65 — Dance Hits '96 Supermix .... — $10 — Popular 12001

- Beautiful Life [Ace Of Base] 15
- Captain Jack [Captain Jack]
- Come Go With Me [Exposé] 5
- Everybody [Clock]
- Get Ready For This [2 Unlimited] 38
- I Wanna Be With You [Fun Factory] 45
- Let Me Be [Apex]
- Macarena [Los Del Mar] 71
- Magic Carpet Ride [Mighty Dub Kats] 58
- Me & You [Alexia]
- Missing [Everything But The Girl] 2
- Mover La Colita [Artie The One Man Party] 45
- Reach [Judy Cheeks]
- Rhythm Of The Night [Corona] 11
- Run Away [Real McCoy] 3
- Stayin' Alive [N-Trance] 62
- Summer Is Magic [Playahitty]
- Total Eclipse Of The Heart [Nicki French] 2
- You & I [JK]
- Zombie [A.D.A.M. Feat. Amy]

5/17/97 — 144 — 11 — © 66 — Dance Hits Supermix 2 .... — $10 — Popular 12013

- Because You Loved Me [Lost]
- Child (Inside) [Qkumba Zoo] 69
- Close To You [Fun Factory] 46
- Cry India [Umboza]
- Dabadabiaboo [Bizz Nizz]
- Do What's Good For Me [2 Unlimited]
- Do You Miss Me [Jocelyn Enriquez] 49
- Don't Cry For Me Artentina [M.A.C.]
- Feels So Good [Lina Santiago] 35
- I Love You, Always Forever [Rochelle]
- I Luv U Baby [Original] 66
- Jellyhead [Crush] 72
- Let Me Be Free [Samantha Fox]
- Maria [Ricky Martin] 88
- Sunshine After The Rain [Berri]
- Sweet Dreams [La Bouche] 13
- This Is Your Night [Amber] 24
- Tonight Is The Night [Le Click] 68
- Touch [France Joli]
- Where Do You Go [No Mercy] 5

3/5/94 — 167 — 16 — ● — © 67 — Dance Mix USA .... — $10 — Radikal 6705

- Ain't 2 Proud 2 Beg [TLC] 6
- Everybody's Free (To Feel Good) [Rozalla] 37
- Gonna Make You Sweat (Everybody Dance Now) [C & C Music Factory] 1
- Gypsy Woman (She's Homeless) [Crystal Waters] 8
- Jump! [Movement] 53
- Let The Beat Hit 'Em [Lisa Lisa & Cult Jam] 37
- Let's Talk About Sex [Salt-N-Pepa] 13
- Living In Ecstacy [BKS]
- Move This [Technotronic] 2
- Please Don't Go [Double You]
- Rhythm Is A Dancer [Snap!] 5
- Run To You [Rage]
- Strike It Up [Black Box] 8
- Summer Of Love [Claudja B.]
- Touch Me (All Night Long) [Cathy Dennis] 2
- Tribal Dance [2 Unlimited]
- Twilight Zone [2 Unlimited] 49

9/3/94 — 127 — 12 — © 68 — Dance Mix USA Vol. 2 .... — $10 — Radikal 6712

- Ditty [Paper Boy] 10
- Finally [Ce Ce Peniston] 5
- Forget Me Nots [Ava Cherry]
- Give It Up [Goodmen] 71
- Happy [Legacy Of Sound] 68
- I'm Gonna Get You [Bizarre Inc.] 47
- Informer [Snow] 1
- Key, The Secret [Urban Cookie Collective]
- More & More [Captain Hollywood] 17
- No Limit [2 Unlimited] 4
- Shoop [Salt-N-Pepa] 4
- Show Me Love [Robin S] 5
- Supermodel [RuPaul] 45
- Take Me In Your Arms [Lil Suzy] 67
- Talkin About Love [BKS]
- This Is It [Dannii Minogue]
- Whoomp! There It Is [Tag Team] 2

5/6/95 — 71 — 19 — © 69 — Dance Mix USA Vol. 3 .... — $10 — Radikal 6727

- Can't Get Enough Of Your Love [Taylor Dayne] 20
- Come Baby Come [K7] 18
- Good Time [Sound Factory]
- Hey Mr. D.J. [Zhané] 6
- High On A Happy Vibe [Urban Cookie Collective]
- Hip Hop Hooray [Naughty By Nature] 8
- I Like To Move It [Reel 2 Real Feat. The Mad Stuntman] 89
- I Must Be Free [Kym Sims]
- Mr. Vain [Culture Beat] 17
- No More [Maxx]
- 100% Pure Love [Crystal Waters] 38
- Real Thing [2 Unlimited]
- Real Thing (If I Can't Have You) [Tony Dibart]
- Return To Innocence [Enigma] 4
- Sweat (A La La La La Long) [Inner Circle] 16
- What Is Love [Haddaway] 11
- Whiggle In Line [Black Duck]

4/6/96 — 37 — 29 — © 70 — Dance Mix USA Vol. 4 .... — $10 — Radikal 6747

- All I Wanna Do [Joanne Farrell]
- Another Night [Real McCoy] 3
- Bomb, The [Bucketheads] 49
- Close To You [Fun Factory] 46
- Cotton Eye Joe [Rednex] 25
- Don't Turn Around [Ace Of Base] 4
- Dreamer [Livin' Joy] 72
- Find Me [Jam & Spoon]
- Get-A-Way [Maxx]
- Get Ready For This [2 Unlimited] 38
- Movin' On Up [M People] 34
- Rhythm Of The Night [Corona] 11
- Saturday Night [Whigfield]
- Set U Free [Planet Soul] 26
- Set You Free [N-Trance]
- Stay Together [Barbara Tucker]
- Take Control [BKS]
- This Is How We Do It [Montell Jordan] 1
- Tonight Is The Night [Le Click] 68

10/26/96 — 101 — 15 — © 71 — Dance Mix USA Vol. 5 .... — $10 — Radikal 6750

- America (I Love America) [Full Intention]
- Beautiful Life [Ace Of Base] 15
- Boom, Boom, Boom [Outhere Brothers] 65
- Boombastic [Shaggy] 3
- Everybody Be Somebody [Ruffneck feat. Yavahn] 82
- Feel The Music [Planet Soul] 73
- Feels So Good (Show Me Your Love) [Lina Santiago] 35
- Got Myself Together [Bucketheads]
- If Madonna Calls [Junior Vasquez]
- Inside Out [Culture Beat]
- Macarena [Wil Veloz]
- Magic Carpet Ride [Mighty Dub Kats] 58
- Missing [Everything But The Girl] 2
- Release Me [Angelina] 52
- Runaway [Real McCoy] 3
- Say A Prayer [Taylor Dane]
- Your Loving Arms [Billy Ray Martin] 46

DEBUT	PEAK	WKS	RIAA	CD	ARTIST — Album Title	Catalog	Sym	$	Label & Number

3/29/97 · **125** · 8 · © 72 · **Dance Mix USA Vol. 6** .... · **$10** Quality 6760

Child (Inside) [Qkumba Zoo] 69
Children [Robert Miles] 21
C'mon N' Ride It (The Train) [Quad City DJ's] 3
Do You Miss Me [Jocelyn Enriquez] 49
Fired Up! [Funky Green Dogs] 80
I Don't Need Your Love [Angelina] 69
I Love You Always Forever [Donna Lewis] 2
I Luv U Baby [Original] 66
I Wanna B With U [Fun Factory] 45
I'm In Love [Georgie Porgie]
Jellyhead [Crush] 72
One More Try [Kristine W] 78
Snapshot [RuPaul] 95
Stand Up [Love Tribe] 89
Sweet Dreams [La Bouche] 13
Take Me On [John Anthony]
This Is Your Night [Amber] 24

5/11/91 · **24** · 16 · © 73 · **Deadicated** .... · **$10** Arista 8669

Bertha [Los Lobos]
Casey Jones [Warren Zevon w/David Lindley]
Cassidy [Suzanne Vega]
China Doll [Suzanne Vega]
Deal [Dr. John]
Estimated Prophet [Burning Spear]
Friend Of The Devil [Lyle Lovett]
Jack Straw [Bruce Hornsby & The Range]
Ripple [Jane's Addiction]
Ship Of Fools [Elvis Costello]
To Lay Me Down [Cowboy Junkies]
Truckin' [Dwight Yoakam]
U.S. Blues [Marshed Mellows]
Uncle John's Band [Indigo Girls]
Wharf Rat [Midnight Oil]

12/14/96 · **35** · 24 · ▲ · © 74 · **Death Row - Greatest Hits** .... · **$15** Death Row 50677 [2]

Afro Puffs [Lady Of Rage] 57
Ain't No Fun [Snoop Doggy Dogg]
Come Up To My Room [Jodeci feat. Tha Dogg Pound]
Come When I Call [Danny Boy]
Daydreaming [Michel'le]
Dear Mama [2Pac] 9
Doggy Dogg World [Snoop Doggy Dogg feat. Tha Dogg Pound & The Dramatics]
F--- Wit Dre Day [Jewell]
Gin & Juice [includes 2 versions] [Snoop Doggy Dogg] 8
Hit 'Em Up [2Pac feat. the Outlawz]
I Get Around [2Pac] 11
Keep Their Heads Ringin' [Dr. Dre] 10
Keep Ya Head Up [2Pac] 12
Let Me Ride [Dr. Dre] 34
Lil' Ghetto Boy [includes 2 versions] [Dr. Dre]
Lodi Dodi [Snoop Doggy Dogg]
Me Against The World [2Pac feat. Dramacycal]
Me In Your World [Dat Nigga Daz]
Murder Was The Case [Snoop Doggy Dogg]
Natural Born Killaz [Dr. Dre & Ice Cube]
No Vaseline [Ice Cube]
Nuthin' But A G Thang [includes 2 versions] [Dr. Dre] 2
Pour Out A Little Liquor [Thug Life feat. 2Pac]
Shiznit, The [Snoop Doggy Dogg]
Smile For Me Now [2Pac & Scarface]
Stranded On Death Row [Dr. Dre]
What Would You Do [Dogg Pound]
What's My Name? [includes 2 versions] [Snoop Doggy Dogg] 8
Who Been There, Who Done That? [J-Flex]

3/17/01 · **104** · 5 · © 75 · **Def Jam 1985-2001: The History Of Hip Hop, Volume 1** .... · **$10** Def Jam 542951

Can I Get A... [Jay-Z Feat. Amil] 19
Children's Story [Slick Rick]
Crossover [EPMD] 42
Da Rockwilder [Method Man/Redman]
Fight For Your Right [Beastie Boys]
Fight The Power [Public Enemy]
Get Me Home [Foxy Brown Feat. BLACKstreet]
Getto Jam [Domino] 7
Holla Holla [Ja Rule] 35
I Can't Live Without My Radio [LL Cool J]
I'll Be There For You/You're All I Need To Get By [Method Man Feat. Mary J. Blige] 3
Party Up (Up In Here) [DMX] 27
Pop Goes The Weasel [3rd Bass] 29
Rain, The [Oran "Juice" Jones] 9
Regulate [Warren G & Nate Dogg] 2
Slam [Onyx] 4
Sometimes I Rhyme Slow [Nice & Smooth] 44

11/14/98 · **84** · 3 · © 76 · **Def Jam Survival Of The Illest Live From 125 N.Y.C.** .... [L] · **$10** Def Jam 538176

Affirmative Action [Cormega feat. Foxy Brown]
Dead Man Walking [Cormega]
F'n' Wit' D
4,3,2,1 [DMX feat. Method Man & Redman]
Freestyle [Erick Sermon]
Full Cooperation [Def Squad]
Get At Me Dog [DMX]
Get Lifted [Keith Murray]
How High [Method Man & Redman]
I Shot Ya [Def Squad]
Last Dayz [Onyx]
Money, Power, Respect [DMX feat. The Lox]
Most Beautifullest Thing In This World [Keith Murray]
Pick It Up [Redman]
Poem [DMX]
Raze It Up [Onyx]
React [Onyx]
Ruff Ryders' Anthem [DMX]
Shut 'Em Down [Onyx]
Slam [Onyx]
Slow Down [Cormega feat. Foxy Brown]
Stop Being Greedy [DMX]
Throw Ya Gunz [Onyx]
Whateva Man [Redman]
X-Is Coming [DMX]

7/23/94 · **139** · 10 · © 77 · **DGC Rarities Vol. 1** .... · **$10** DGC 24704

Allegory [Murray Attaway]
Beautiful Son [Hole]
Bogusflow [Beck]
Compilation Blues [Sonic Youth]
Don't Tell Your Mother [Sundays]
Einstein On The Beach (For An Eggman) [Counting Crows]
Grunge Couple [that dog]
Jamie [Weezer]
Mad Dog 20/20 [Teenage Fanclub]
Never Too High [Cell]
Open Every Window [Posies]
Pay To Play [Nirvana]
Stove/Smother [Sloan]
Wild Goose Chasing [St. Johnny]

10/18/97 · **36** · 5 · © 78 · **Diana Princess Of Wales 1961-1997** .... [L] · **$10** BBC/London 460000

the BBC recording of the funeral service held at London's Westminster Abbey on 9/6/97

Air from County Derry
Alleluia [John Tavener]
Bidding, The
Candle In The Wind [Elton John]
Commendation, The
Funeral Sentences
Hymn: Guide Me O Thou Great Redeemer
Hymn: I Vow To Thee, My Country
Hymn: Make Me A Channel Of Your Peace
Hymn: The King Of Love My Shepherd Is
Introduction: William Harris: Prelude
Libera Me
Lord's Prayer
National Anthem
Prayers
Reading by Lady Jane Fellowes
Reading by Lady Sarah McCorquodale
Reading the Right Honourable Tony Blair MP
Tribute by The Earl Spencer

12/20/97 · **15** · 11 · ▲ · © 79 · **Diana, Princess Of Wales - Tribute** .... · **$15** Columbia 69012 [2]

All That Matters [Cliff Richard]
Angel [Annie Lennox]
Ave Maria [Michael Bolton/Plácido Domingo]
Because You Loved Me [Celine Dion] 1
Don't Dream It's Over [Neil Finn]
Don't Wanna Lose You [Gloria Estefan] 1
Every Nation [Red Hot R+B All Stars]
Everybody Hurts [R.E.M.] 29
Gone Too Soon [Michael Jackson]
Hero [Mariah Carey]
How Could An Angel Break My Heart [Toni Braxton with Kenny G]
Hymn To Her [Pretenders]
I Am In Love With The World [Chicken Shed]
I'll Be Missing You [Puff Daddy] 1
I'll Fly Away [Aretha Franklin]
In The Sun [Peter Gabriel]
Little Willow [Paul McCartney]
Love Is A Beautiful Thing [Tina Turner]
Love Minus Zero/No Limit [Rod Stewart]
Love Theme From "A Star Is Born" (Evergreen) [Barbra Streisand] 1
Make Me A Channel Of Your Peace [Sinéad O'Connor]
Mama [Spice Girls]
Miss Sarajevo [Passengers/Pavarotti]
Missing You [Diana Ross] 10
Pavane [Lesley Garrett]
Prayer For The Dying [Seal] 21
Shakespeare's Sonnet No. 18 [Bryan Ferry]
Stars [Simply Red] 44
Streets Of Philadelphia [Bruce Springsteen] 9
Tears In Heaven [Eric Clapton] 2
Watermark [Enya]
Who Wants To Live Forever [Queen]
Wish You Were Here [Bee Gees]
You Gotta Be [Des'ree] 5
You Have Been Loved [George Michael]
You Were Loved [Whitney Houston]

7/14/73 · **27** · 18 · ● · 80 · **Dick Clark/20 Years Of Rock N' Roll** .... · **$20** Buddah 5133 [2]

All I Have To Do Is Dream [Everly Brothers] 1
Blue Suede Shoes [Carl Perkins] 2
Brown Eyed Girl [Van Morrison] 10
Crimson And Clover [Tommy James & The Shondells] 1
Crying In The Chapel [Orioles]
Do You Believe In Magic [Lovin' Spoonful] 9
Good Lovin' [Young Rascals] 1
Hang On Sloopy [McCoys] 1
I Walk The Line [Johnny Cash] 17
I'm Walkin' [Fats Domino] 4
Lay Down (Candles In The Rain) [Melanie] 6
Leader Of The Pack [Shangri-Las] 1
Louie Louie [Kingsmen] 2
Nice To Be With You [Gallery] 4
Oh Happy Day [Edwin Hawkins' Singers] 4
Peppermint Twist - Part 1 [Joey Dee & the Starliters] 1
Put Your Head On My Shoulder [Paul Anka] 2
Rebel-'Rouser [Duane Eddy] 6
Rock Around The Clock [Bill Haley] 1
Runaround Sue [Dion] 1
Sh-Boom [Crew Cuts] 2
(Sittin' On) The Dock Of The Bay [Otis Redding] 1
So You're Leaving [Al Green]
Soldier Boy [Shirelles] 1
Superfly [Curtis Mayfield] 8
Sweet Nothin's [Brenda Lee] 4
Whole Lot Of Shakin' Going On [Jerry Lee Lewis] 3
Why [Frankie Avalon] 1
Wooly Bully [Sam The Sham & The Pharoahs] 2
You've Lost That Lovin' Feeling [Righteous Brothers] 1

DEBUT	PEAK	WKS	RIAA	CD	ARTIST — Album Title	Catalog	Sym	$	Label & Number

3/13/71 **85** 7 81 **Different Strokes** .... **$20** Columbia 12

All This Paradise [Fraser & DeBolt] — Found A Child [Ballin' Jack] — Mr. Natural [Big Brother & The Holding Company] — Saturday Miles [Miles Davis]
Big Bird [Flock] — Going To The Mill [Chambers Brothers] — New York [Dreams] — Soapstone Mountain [It's A Beautiful Day]
Blackpatch [Laura Nyro]
Don't Fight It (Feel It) [Elvin Bishop Group] — Maggie [Redbone] **45** — Nothing At All [Bill Puka] — Too Young To Be Married [Hollies]
Man Like Me [Poco] — Out-Bloody-Rageous [Soft Machine]
Fields Of Joy [New York Rock Ensemble] — Merrimac County [Tom Rush] — Rock And Roll, Hoochie Koo [Johnny Winter]
Morning Will Come [Spirit]

3/21/98 **192** 3 © 82 **Digital Empire - Electronica's Best** .... **$15** Cold Front 6321 [2]

Absurd [Fluke] — Cop Car [Joey Beltram] — Going Out Of My Head [Fatboy Slim] — Refuse To Fight [Frankie Bones]
Block Rockin' Beats [Chemical Brothers] — Flaming June [BT] — Roots [Mark Verbos]
414 [Doormouse] — Hipgnosis [Electric Skychurch] — Shnowed In [Hawke]
Born Slippy [Underworld] — Fructose [Joey Jupiter] — Majick [Keoki] — Smiles [Atomic Babies]
Busy Child [Crystal Method] — Funky Back Home [Dubtribe Sound System] — No Good (Start The Dance) [Prodigy] — Subconscious [Rabbit In The Moon]
Choose Life [PF Project Feat. Ewan McGregor] — Take California [Propellerheads]
Get Yourself Organised [Headrillaz] — Nude Photo [Derrick May]
Ciao [Empirion] — One 4 Da Head [Buzz Fiend]

12/24/77+ **115** 11 © 83 **Disco Boogie** .... **$20** Salsoul 0101 [2]

Dance, Dance, Dance [Claudja Barry] — Magic Bird Of Fire [Salsoul Orchestra] — Salsoul Hustle [Salsoul Orchestra] **76** — This Will Be A Night To Remember [Eddie Holman] **90**
Doctor Love [First Choice] **41** — More [Carol Williams] — Spring Rain [Silvetti] **39** — We're Getting Stronger (The Longer We Stay Together) [Loleatta Holloway]
Getaway [Salsoul Orchestra] — My Love Is Free [Double Exposure] — Sweet Dynamite [Claudja Barry]
Helplessly [Moment Of Truth] — Nice 'N' Naasty [Salsoul Orchestra] **30** — Tale Of Three Cities [Salsoul Orchestra] — You Got Me Hummin' [Moment Of Truth]
Hit And Run [Loleatta Holloway] — Run Away [Salsoul Orchestra/Loleatta Holloway] — Tangerine [Salsoul Orchestra] **18** — You're Just The Right Size [Salsoul Orchestra] **88**
Love Is Still Blue [Paul Mauriat]
Love Is You [Carol Williams] — Ten Percent [Double Exposure] **54**

7/26/75 **153** 5 84 **Disco Gold** .... **$12** Scepter 5120

Ain't No Love Lost [Patti Jo] — Make Me Believe In You [Patti Jo] — Wan Tu Wah Zuree [George Tindley] — We're On The Right Track [Ultra High Frequency]
Arise And Shine [Independents] — Needing You [Clara Lewis]
I Love You, Yes I Do [Independents] — Pity The Poor Man [George Tindley]

7/15/78 **115** 12 85 **Disco Party** .... **$15** Marlin 2207/8 [2]

Best Disco In Town [Ritchie Family] **17** — Do Ya Wanna Get Funky With Me? [Peter Brown] **18** — Kiss Me (The Way I Like It) [George McCrae] — Superman [Celi Bee & The Buzzy Bunch] **41**
Calypso Breakdown [Ralph MacDonald] — Get Down Tonight [KC & The Sunshine Band] **1** — Lady Luck [Ritchie Family] — Where Is The Love [Betty Wright] **96**
Disco Magic [T-Connection] — Get Off Your Aahh And Dance [Foxy] — Love Chant [Eli's Second Coming]
Do What You Wanna Do [T-Connection] **46** — Rock Your Baby [George McCrae] **1**
Gimme Some [Jimmy 'Bo' Horne]

4/28/79 **159** 5 86 **Disco Spectacular Inspired By The Film "Hair"** .... **$12** RCA Victor 3356

all star group: Evelyn "Champagne" King/Vicki Sue Robinson/Revelation/The Brothers
Aquarius (medley) — Good Morning Starshine — Where Do I Go?
Easy To Be Hard — Let The Sunshine In (medley)

2/14/70 **95** 13 87 **DisinHAIRited** .... **$15** RCA Victor 1163

songs written for, but not included in the musical Hair
Bed, The — Going Down — Mr. Berger — So Sing The Children On The Avenue
Climax — Hello There — Oh Great God Of Power (medley)
Dead End — I Dig — One Thousand Year-Old Man — Washing The World
Electric Blues — I'm Hung — Reading The Writing (medley) — You Are Standing On My Bed
Exanaplanatooch — Manhattan Beggar — Sentimental Ending (medley)
Eyes Look Your Last (medley) — Mess O'Dirt — Sheila Franklin (medley)

10/8/94+ **18**C 58 © 88 **Disney Children's Favorites 1** .... **$10** Walt Disney 60605

Animal Fair — Home On The Range — Mary Had A Little Lamb — Take Me Out To The Ball Game
Bicycle Built For Two — I'm A Policeman — Oh, Susanna! — Ten Little Indians
Blue-Tail Fly (Jimmy Crack Corn) — I've Been Working On The Railroad — Old MacDonald — This Old Man (Knick-Knack, Patty-Whack)
Dixie — In The Good, Old Summertime — Pop! Goes The Weasel
Friends Lullaby — It Ain't Gonna Rain No More — Row, Row, Row Your Boat — Three Blind Mice
Green Grass Grew All Around — Mail Must Go Through — She'll Be Comin' Round The Mountain — Twinkle, Twinkle, Little Star
Hokey Pokey — Man On The Flying Trapeze — When I Go To School

3/31/01 **181** 2 © 89 **Disney's Greatest Volume 1** .... **$10** Walt Disney 860693

Beauty And The Beast — I Wan'na Be Like You (The Monkey Song) — Out There — You Can Fly! You Can Fly! You Can Fly!
Bella Notte — Reflection
Bibbidi-Bobbidi-Boo — I Won't Say (I'm In Love) — Strangers Like Me — You've Got A Friend In Me
Circle Of Life — Just Around The Riverbend — Supercalifragilisticexpialidocious — Zip-A-Dee-Doo-Dah
Cruella De Vil — Kiss The Girl — When You Wish Upon A Star
Heigh-Ho — Once Upon A Dream — Whole New World

10/12/96 **193** 1 © 90 **Disney's Music From The Park** .... **$10** Walt Disney 60915

commemorating the 25th Anniversary of Walt Disney World
Ballad Of Davy Crockett [Tim Curry] — Grim Grinning Ghosts [Barenaked Ladies] — Mickey Mouse March (medley) [Disney Big Band] — When You Wish Upon A Star [Etta James]
Can You Feel The Love Tonight (medley) [Richard Page] — Hakuna Matata (medley) [Rembrandts] — Part Of Your World [Olivia Newton-John] — Yo Ho (A Pirate's Life For Me) [Pointer Sisters]
Circle Of Life (medley) [Richard Page] — I Just Can't Wait To Be King (medley) [Rembrandts] — Remember The Magic (Theme Song) [Brian McKnight] — Zip-A-Dee-Doo-Dah [Patti Austin]
Dream Is A Wish Your Heart Makes [Linda Ronstadt] — It's A Small World (medley) [Etta James] — SpectroMagic Medley [David Benoit] — Zip-A-Dee-Doo-Dah (medley)

4/11/98 **130** 5 © 91 **D.J. Magic Mike Presents Bootyz In Motion** .... **$10** Jake 90188

Baby Got Back [Sir Mix-A-Lot] **1** — Give It All You Got [Afro-Rican] — Planet Rock [Afrika Bambataa & Soul Sonic Force] **48** — Whoomp There It Is [Tag Team] **2**
Booty Hop [Kinsu] — I Wanna Rock [Luke] **73** — Shake It [MC Shy D] — Whoot There It Is [95 South] **11**
Crossroad, The [Bone thugs-n-harmony] **1** — Me So Horny [2 Live Crew] **26** — Tootsie Roll [69 Boyz] **8** — Work It Out [D.J. Magic Mike]
Da Dip [Freak Nasty] **15** — Ooh Lawd (Party People) [D.J. Smurf/P.M.H.I.] — Whatz Up, Whatz Up 2 [A. Town Players]
Dazzey Dukes [Duice] **12**

8/10/96 **168** 5 © 92 **D.J. Mix '96 Volume 1** .... **$10** Beast 5300

Do Fries Go With That Shake? [Gillette] — Every Little Thing I Do [Soul For Real] **17** — Look Who's Talking [Dr. Alban] — Set U Free [Planet Soul] **26**
Lover That You Are [Pulse] — Stayin' Alive [N-Trance] **62**
Esa Nena Linda [Artie The 1 Man Party] **74** — Froggy Style [Nuttin' Nyce] **63** — Moving On Up [M People] **34** — You Oughta Know [U.D.S. Boyz]
I Found It [Daphne] — Release Me [Angelina] **52** — You Should Be Dancing [E-Sensual]

DEBUT	PEAK	WKS	RIAA	CD	ARTIST — Album Title	Catalog	Sym	$	Label & Number
5/17/97	87	13	©	93	**D.J. Mix '97 Vol. 2**			$10	Beast 53112

Bang Bump *[Pump House Gang]* | Feels So Good (Show Me Your Love) *[Lina Santiago]* 35 | I Luv U Baby *[Original]* 66 | Luchini aka (This Is It) *[Camp Lo]* 50
Be My Lover *[La Bouche]* 6 | It's All About U *[SWV]* 61 | Snapshot *[RuPaul]* 95
D.J. Mix '97 Vol. 2 Theme | Fired Up! *[Funky Green Dogs]* 80 | Keep Pushin' *[Boris D'Lugosch]* | Soul To Bare *[Joi Cardwell]*
Da' Dip *[Freak Nasty]* 15 | Heartbroken *[Althea McQueen]* | La La La Hey Hey *[Outhere Brothers]* | That Girl *[Maxi Priest]* 20
Do The Damn Thang *[2 Live Crew]* | I Don't Need Your Love *[Angelina]* 69 | | This Is Your Night *[Amber]* 24

| 10/25/97 | 178 | 3 | © | 94 | **D.J. Mix '98 Vol. 1** | | | $10 | Beast 53332 |

Big Daddy *[Heavy D.]* 18 | I Can't Sleep Baby (If I) *[R. Kelly]* 5 | MyBabyDaddy *[B-Rock & The Bizz]* 10 | Things'll Never Change *[E-40]* 29
Block Rockin' Beats *[Chemical Brothers]* | I'm Still In Love With You *[New Edition]* 7 | On & On *[Erykah Badu]* 12 | This Is Your Night *[Amber]* 24
Da' Dip *[Freak Nasty]* 15 | Love Is All We Need *[Mary J. Blige]* | Only You *[112]* 13 | Too Hot *[Coolio]* 24
Don't Stop Movin' *[Livin' Joy]* 67 | | Runaway *[Nuyorican Soul]* | Your Woman *[White Town]* 23

| 1/16/99 | 189 | 1 | © | 95 | **D.J. Mix 99** | | | $20 | Beast 54422 [3] |

Are You Jimmy Ray *[Jimmy Ray]* 13 | Estasy *[Rhythm Ritual]* | No Tengo Dinero *[Los Umbrellos]* 42 | Sugar Cane *[Space Monkeys]* 58
Babe *[Disguy]* | Give Me Love *[Fussy Cussy]* | Party, The *[Mother Ship Connection]* | Superhero *[Daze]* 88
Be Good To Me *[Christine]* | Gone Till November *[Wyclef Jean feat. Canibus]* 7 | Party Continues *[Jermaine Dupri feat. Da Brat & Usher]* 29 | Take Me Out *[Azure Pekan]*
Can't Keep My Hands Off You *[React]* | Hungry *[Common]* | | This Is How We Party *[S.O.A.P.]* 51
DJ Mix '99 Outro | Imagine To Be With You *[Jo-Jo]* | Romeo And Juliet *[Sylk-E. Fyne feat. Chill]* 6 | Ti Queiro *[Majestica]*
Deja Vu (Uptown Baby) *[Lord Tariq & Peter Gunz]* 9 | Jungle Lion *[Daktary]* | Rub A Dub Love *[Mo-Reece]* | Torn *[Natalie Browne]*
Ding-A-Ling *[Hi-Town DJs]* 56 | Love & Devotion *[M&M]* | Say It *[Voices Of Theory]* 10 | Treat Me Right *[Kim Richardson]*
Do Your Thing *[7 Mile]* 50 | Ninety Nine (Flesh The Message) *[John Forté]* 59 | (Sex U UP) The Way You Like It *[LFO]* | We Come To Party *[N-Tyce]*
Don't Leave Me *[Blackstreet]* | No, No, No (Part 2) *[Destiny's Child feat. Wyclef Jean]* 3 | Someday *[Laurell]* | Whatcha Gonna Do *[Link]* 23
Dream Of A Child *[Groove Factory]* | | | Y'everybody *[MC Rive]*
| | | | You Only Have To Say You Love Me *[Hannah Jones]* 65

| 8/31/96 | 197 | 1 | © | 96 | **DMA Dance - Vol. 2: Eurodance** | | | $10 | Interhit 20152 |

Anybody *[Masterboy]* | Into The Night *[Ondina]* | Lovedream *[Rotate]* | Right Type Of Mood *[Herbie]*
Be My Lover *[La Bouche]* 6 | It's My Life *[Dr. Alban]* 88 | Memories *[Netzwerk]* | Take A Chance *[Dream Project]*
Call It Love *[Deuce]* | Let Me Be Free *[2 Bros. On The 4th Floor]* | Miracles *[Cartouche]* | When I Fall In Love *[Lil Suzy]*
Dancing With An Angel *[Double You]* | Love Message *[Love Message]* | No One *[2 Unlimited]*
| | One Of Us *[Outta Control]*

| 11/18/95 | 139 | 1 | ● © | 97 | **Down South Hustlers Bouncin' And Swingin' Tha Value Pack Compilation** | | | $15 | No Limit 53993 [2] |

Backstreets *[20-2 Life]* | Fright Night *[Tre-8]* | Lot Auh Nuttin *[Chico & 187]* | So Much Pain *[Tre-8 Feat. Mia X & Master P]*
Bounce That Ass *[Gangsta T/King George/Silk/Master P]* | G's Stay Real *[Niggas Out The Ghetto]* | Murder Weapon *[Hounds from Gert-Town]* | South, The *[E.S.G.]*
Can't Trust No Man *[Mia X]* | Gettin' High *[Fire]* | My Mind Went Blank Screwed *[Pointt Blankk & DJ Screw]* | Stick N Move *[Dayton Family]*
Darkside *[Skull Dugrey]* | Got It Sowed Up *[P.K.O.]* | My Woman *[Coop MC]* | Way Down South *[Joe Blakk]*
Don't Underestimate Me *[Sir True]* | Handle Your Business *[Mr. Serv On]* | | Who Am I? *[C-Loc]*
Down South Thugs *[Polo]* | Hustlin' *[C. Murder/Master P/Partners In Crime]* | Playaz From The South *[UGK/Master P/Silk]* | You Got It *[Magnolia Slim]*
F' Dem N' *[Eightball & MJG]* | | RIP *[CCG Feat. Master P & Silk]*

| 11/29/75 | 198 | 2 | | 98 | **Dr. Demento's Delights** [N] | | | | Warner 2855 |

Ballad Of Ben Gay *[Ben Gay & The Silly Savages]* | Friendly Neighborhood Narco Agent *[Jef Jaisun]* | If You're A Viper *[Jim Kweskin's Jug Band]* | Ya Wanna Buy A Bunny *[Spike Jones & His City Slickers]*
Boobs A Lot *[Holy Modal Rounders]* | Get A Load Of This *[R. Crumb & His Cheap Suit Serenaders]* | They're Coming To Take Me Away, Ha-Haaa! *[Napoleon XIV]* 3
Cockroach That Ate Cincinnati *[Possum]* | Hello Muddah, Hello Fadduh! (A Letter From Camp) *[Allan Sherman]* 2 | Who Put The Benzedrine In Mrs. Murphy's Ovaltine *[Harry "The Hipster" Gibson]*
Eleanor Rigby *[Doodles Weaver]*

| 12/14/96 | 6 | 13 | ▲ © | 99 | **Dr. Dre Presents...The Aftermath** | | | $10 | Aftermath 90044 |

Aftermath (The Intro) | Choices *[Kim Summerson]* | Got Me Open *[Hands-On]* | Please *[Maurice Wilcher]*
As The World Keeps Turning *[Miscellaneous]* | Do 4 Love *[Jheryl Lockhart]* | L.A.W. (Lyrical Assault Weapon) *[Sharief]* | Sexy Dance *[RC]*
Been There Done That *[Dr. Dre]* | East Coast/West Coast Killas *[Group Therapy]* | Nationowl *[NOWL]* | Sh**tin' On The World *[Mel-Man]*
Blunt Time *[RBX]* | Fame *[RC]* | No Second Chance *[Whoz Who]* | Str-8 Gone *[King T]*

| 12/5/64 | 129 | 3 | | 100 | **Dracula's Greatest Hits** [N] | | | $50 | RCA Victor 2977 |

parodies of popular songs by Dracula (Gene Moss)

Carry Me Back To Transylvania | Ghoul Days | Little Black Bag | Monster Hootenanny
Drac The Knife | I Want To Bite Your Hand | Monster Bossa Nova | New Frankenstein & Johnny Song
Frankenstein | King Kong Stomp | Monster Goose Rhymes | Surf Monster

| 11/15/97+ | 16 C | 3 | © | 101 | **Drew's Famous Halloween Party Music** | | | $10 | Turn Up 1023 |

Bad Moon Rising | Hot Hot Hot | Purple People Eater | Stayin' Alive
Disco Inferno | Let's Go Dancin' | Rock Lobster | Super Freak
Don't Leave Me This Way | Macho Man | Soul Man | Time Warp
Ghostbusters | Monster Mash | Spooky | Twilight Zone

| 4/29/95 | 137 | 8 | | 102 | **D-Shot Presents Boss Ballin' Compilation Album - The Best In The Business** | | | $10 | Shot 7000 |

Act Like You Know *[A.M.W.]* | I Puts Its Down *[Prodigy & Havok]* | Still On Parole *[Gov]* | Time To Get My Serve *[RBL Posse]*
Do Now *[Emgee]* | Late Night *[Delinquents]* | Straight Killer *[C-BO]* | Top Notch *[Sean T]*
Hit The Gas *[3 Times Krazy]* | She's So Tight *[Conscious Daughters]* | Streets Made Me *[D-Shot Feat. Spice 1]* | Weak Moves *[Dru Down]*
Hoes Be Trippin' *[D.M.S.]* | | | Were They At *[Mac Mall]*

| 1/16/71 | 185 | 3 | | 103 | **Earle Doud Presents Spiro T. Agnew Is A Riot!** [C] | | | $20 | Cadet Concept 1 |

Diplomacy | Goodnight | Joke, The | PTA
Doomsday Machine | I'm Sorry | Monument, The | Polish Ambassador
Fight, The | Jack Frost (Parts 1-6) | Oath Of Office | Silent Majority

| 2/6/82 | 105 | 11 | | 104 | **Echoes Of An Era** | | | $12 | Elektra 60021 |

all-star group: **Chaka Khan/Freddie Hubbard/Joe Henderson/Chick Corea/Lenny White**

All Of Me | I Love You Porgy | Spring Can Really Hang You Up The Most | Them There Eyes
Hire Wire - The Aerialist | I Mean You | Take The A Train
I Hear Music

| 11/14/98 | 191 | 1 | © | 105 | **ECW: Extreme Music** | | | $10 | Slab 86262 |

Big Balls *[Muscadine]* | Heard It On The X *[Tres Diablos]* | Phantom Lord *[Anthrax]* | Trust *[Megadeth]*
El Phantasmo And The Chicken Run Blast-O-Rama *[White Zombie]* | Huka Blues *[Harry Slash & The Slashtones]* | Snap Your Fingers, Snap Your Neck *[Grinspoon]* | Walk *[Kilgore]*
| Kick Out The Jams *[Monster Magnet]* | This Is Extreme! (ECW Theme) *[Harry Slash & The Slashtones]* | Zoo, The *[Bruce Dickinson]*
Enter Sandman *[Motorhead]*

VARIOUS ARTISTS COMPILATIONS

DEBUT	PEAK	WKS	RIAA	CD	ARTIST — Album Title	Catalog	Sym	$	Label & Number

5/12/01 111 3 ©106 8Ball Presents... The Slab .... **$10** JCOR 860924

All In A Day-Hood	Down And Dirty	Kill Em All
Big Trick	Fuck Wit Me	Like Me
Buc Wid It	G-Type	Niggas & Bitches
Creeses & Pieces	Keep On Pimpin	Something 2 Say

2 All My Niggas
2 Much
Top Notch
U Can't Fuk Wit It

9/8/84 147 9 107 Electric Breakdance .... **$12** Dominion 2320

Clock On The Wall [Double Vision]	Jam On It [Newcleus] 56	Play That Beat Mr. D.J. [G.L.O.B.E.
Electric Kingdom [Twilight 22] 79	Magic's Wand [Whodini]	& Whiz Kid]
It's Like That [Run-D.M.C.]		Rockit [B.T. & The City Slickers]

White Lines (Don't Don't Do It)
[Grandmaster Flash & Melle Mel]
You're The One For Me ["D" Train]

3/21/98 166 5 ©108 Elmopalooza! .... **$10** Sony Wonder 63432

Caribbean Amphibian [Jimmy	I Don't Want To Live On The Moon	Just Happy To Be Me [Fugees]
Buffett, Kermit the Frog and the	[Shawn Colvin and Ernie]	Mambo I, I, I [Gloria Estefan]
All-Amphibian Band]	I Love Trash [Steven Tyler]	Nearly Missed [Rosie O'Donnell and
Happy To Meet You [Celine Dion,	I Want A Monster To Be My Friend	Elmo]
Herry Monster, Elmo and Big Bird]	[En Vogue]	

One Small Voice [Kenny Loggins
and the Kids]
Songs [Elmo and the Kids]
Zig Zag Dance [Mighty Mighty
Bosstones and The Count]

4/10/99 41 7 ● ©109 Elton John And Tim Rice's Aida .... **$10** Rocket 524628

Amneris' Letter [Shania Twain]	Gods Love Nubia [Kelly Price]	My Strongest Suit [Spice Girls]
Another Pyramid [Sting]	How I Know You [James Taylor]	Not Me [Boyz II Men]
Easy As Life [Tina Turner]	I Know The Truth [Elton John &	Orchestral Finale
Elaborate Lives [Heather Headley]	Janet Jackson]	Step Too Far [Elton John/Heather
Enchantment Passing Through [Dru	Like Father Like Son [Lenny Kravitz]	Headley/Sherie Scott]
Hill]	Messenger, The [Elton John & Lulu]	

Written In The Stars [Elton John &
LeAnn Rimes] 29

11/12/94 125 1 ©110 Elvira Presents Monster Hits .... **$10** Rhino 71778

Addams Family [Joey Gaynor]	Here Comes The Bride (The Bride	Monsta' Rap [Elvira]
Feed My Frankenstein [Alice	Of Frankenstein) [Elvira]	Monster Mash [Bobby "Boris"
Cooper]	Little Demon [Screamin' Jay	Pickett] 1
	Hawkins]	

Nightmare On My Street [D.J.
Jazzy Jeff & The Fresh Prince] 15

11/30/96 124 6 ©111 Emmanuel - A Musical Celebration Of The Life Of Christ .... **$10** Sparrow 51556

Christmas chart: 16/'96

And It Came To Pass In Those	Emmanuel [Michael W. Smith/Amy	Glory To God In The Highest [Gary
Days - Recitative [Michael	Grant]	Chapman/Susan Ashton]
Anderson]	Emmanuel Theme	Glory To God On The Highest -
And They Shall Look Upon The One	Emmanuel Theme - Reprise [Sandi	Reprise [Sandi Patty/Larnelle
Whom They Have Pierced -	Patty/Larnelle Harris]	Harris]
Recitative	Follow The Star [Point Of	Is This Not The Carpenter? [Sandi
Behold, A King Shall Reign [Sandi	Grace/Clay Crosse]	Patty/Susan Ashton]
Patty/BeBe Winans]	For Unto Us	Man Of Sorrows [Larnelle Harris]
Daughter Of Zion [Margaret Becker]	From The Fullness Of His Love	One Who Comes From Heaven
	[Twila Paris/Chris Willis]	

Punishment Of Our Peace -
Recitative
Rejoice Emmanuel [Larnelle Harris]
Though He Was Rich [Sandi
Patty/Larnelle Harris]
We Beheld His Glory [Sandi
Patty/Larnelle Harris]
Word Was Made Flesh [Anointed]

8/2/80 168 5 112 Empire Jazz .... [!] **$12** RSO 3085

adaptation of *The Empire Strikes Back*; all-star group: **Ron Carter/Bob James/Billy Cobham/Ralph MacDonald**

Asteroid Field	Han Solo And The Princess (Love	Imperial March (Darth Vader's
	Theme)	Theme)

Lando's Palace
Yoda's Theme

4/8/95 17 19 ● ©113 Encomium: A Tribute To Led Zeppelin .... **$10** Atlantic 82731

Custard Pie [Helmet w/David Yow]	Four Sticks [Rollins Band]	Hey Hey What Can I Do [Hootie &
D'yer Mak'er [Sheryl Crow]	Going To California [Never The	The Blowfish]
Dancing Days [Stone Temple Pilots]	Bride]	Misty Mountain Hop [4 Non
Down By The Seaside [Robert Plant	Good Times Bad Times [Cracker]	Blondes]
& Tori Amos]		Out On The Tiles [Blind Melon]

Tangerine [Big Head Todd & The
Monsters]
Thank You [Duran Duran]

9/9/67 197 1 114 England's Greatest Hits .... **$30** Fontana 67570

Bend It [Dave Dee, Dozy, Beaky,	My Boy Lollipop [Millie Small] 2	Sun Ain't Gonna Shine (Anymore)
Mick & Tich]	Semi-Detached Suburban Mr.	[Walker Bros.] 13
Game Of Love [Wayne Fontana &	James [Manfred Mann]	Wild Thing [Troggs] 1
The Mindbenders] 1	Silver Threads And Golden	Winchester Cathedral [New
Groovy Kind Of Love	Needles [Springfields] 20	Vaudeville Band] 1
[Mindbenders] 2		

You Don't Have To Say You Love
Me [Dusty Springfield] 4
You've Got To Hide Your Love
Away [Silkie] 10

8/12/95 30 104 ▲² ©115 ESPN Presents Jock Jams Volume 1 .... C:#6/75 **$10** Tommy Boy 1137

Come Baby Come [K7] 18	Hip Hop Hooray [Naughty By	Pump Up The Jam
Get Ready 4 This [2 Unlimited] 38	Nature] 8	[Technotronic] 2
Gonna Make You Sweat	It Takes Two [Rob Base] 36	Pump Up The Volume
(Everybody Dance Now) [C & C	Let's Get Ready To Rumble!	[M/A/R/R/S] 13
Music Factory] 1	Old Ballgame	Rock And Roll Part 2 [Gary
Gridiron Groove...	Power, The [Snap] 2	Glitter] 7
	Pump It Up, Go 'Head, Go 'Head	Strike It Up [Black Box] 8

Tootsee Roll [69 Boyz] 8
Twilight Zone [2 Unlimited] 49
Uh, Ungawaa!
Unbelievable [EMF] 1
Whoomp! There It Is [Tag Team] 2
YMCA [Village People] 2

9/7/96 10 63 ▲² ©116 ESPN Presents Jock Jams Volume 2 .... **$10** Tommy Boy 1163

Action, Boys, Action	Get Down Tonight [KC & The	Macarena [Los Del Mar] 71
Bomb (These Sounds Fall Into My	Sunshine Band] 1	Macho Man [Village People] 25
Mind) [Bucketheads] 49	Give It Up [Goodmen] 71	No Limit [2 Unlimited]
Boom Boom Boom [Outhere	Groovin' In The Bleachers	1,2,3,4 (Sumpin' New) [Coolio] 5
Brothers] 65	Happy And You Know It	Party [Dis N' Dat]
Everybody Everybody [Black	Hey, Hey You	Set It Off [Strafe]
Box] 8	I Like To Move It [Reel 2 Real] 89	

This Is How We Do It [Montell
Jordan] 1
This Is Your Night [Amber] 30
We Got A Love Thang [Ce Ce
Peniston] 20
Welcome To The Big Show
What's Up [D.J. Miko] 58

9/27/97 23 41 ▲ ©117 ESPN Presents Jock Jams Volume 3 .... **$10** Tommy Boy 1214

Chant, The	Don't Stop Movin' [Livin' Joy] 67	Let Me Clear My Throat [DJ
Chicken Dance	Fired Up [Funky Green Dogs] 80	Kool] 30
C'mon & Ride It (The Train) [Quad	I Like It Like That [Tito Nieves]	Let's Go
City DJ's] 3	It's Awesome Baby	No Diggity [BLACKstreet] 1
Cotton Eye Joe [Rednex] 25	Jellyhead [Crush] 72	Ready To Go [Republica] 56
Da' Dip [Freak Nasty] 15	Jock Jam 31	Robi Rob's Boriqua Anthem [C & C
Don't Stop, Get It, Get It!!	Jump! [Movement] 53	Music Factory]

R.O.W.D.I.E.
Supersonic [Sabrina Sang]
That's The Way I Like It [KC & The
Sunshine Band] 1
Tribal Dance [2 Unlimited]

DEBUT	PEAK	WKS	RIAA	CD	ARTIST — Album Title	Catalog	Sym	$	Label & Number
9/12/98	20	35	●	©118	**ESPN Presents Jock Jams Volume 4**			$10	Tommy Boy 1266

ESPN Presents Jock Jams Volume 4
Be Aggressive
Beautiful Day [Hypertrophy]
Can U Feel It [3rd Party] 43
Everybody (Backstreet's Back) [Backstreet Boys] 4
Get Ready To Bounce [Brooklyn Bounce] 95
Gettin' Jiggy Wit It [Will Smith] 1
Going Out Of My Head [Fatboy Slim]
Good Night
Hear The Organ Get Wicked
Jump Around [House Of Pain] 3
Mo Money, Mo Problems [Notorious B.I.G. feat. Puff Daddy & Mase] 1
Mueve La Cadera (Move Your Body) [Reel 2 Real]
No One Pushes Us Around
One More Night [Amber] 58
Push It [Salt 'N Pepa] 19
Raise The Roof [Luke] 26
Seventh Inning Stretch
Son Of Jock Jam [Jock Jam All Stars]
Space Jam [Quad City DJ's] 37
Tubthumping [Chumbawamba] 6
Unlimited Megajam [2 Unlimited]
Watch Out We're Here
Yeah Baby!!

| 7/10/99 | 78 | 10 | | ©119 | **ESPN Presents Jock Rock 2000** | | | $10 | Tommy Boy 1332 |

Bleacher Creatures
Block Rockin' Beats [Chemical Brothers]
Can't Wait One More Minute [CIV]
Down For The Count [Mills Lane]
Firestarter [Prodigy] 30
Flagpole Sitta [Harvey Danger]
Go, Fight, Win!
It's All About The Benjamins [Puff Daddy & The Family] 2
Let's Get It On! [Mills Lane]
Machinehead [Bush] 43
Oh Yeah, All Right [Local H]
One Week [Barenaked Ladies] 1
Peppyrock [BTK]
Pump It Up [Elvis Costello]
Put Your Hands Together!
Ready To Go [Republica] 56
Rockafeller Skank [Fatboy Slim] 76
Semi-Charmed Life [Third Eye Blind] 4
Sportscenter Mega Mix
Walk This Way [Run-D.M.C. Feat. Aerosmith] 4
Zoot Suit Riot [Cherry Poppin' Daddies]

| 11/12/94+ | 79 | 30 | ● | ©120 | **ESPN Presents Jock Rock Volume 1** | C:#32/3 | | $10 | Tommy Boy 1100 |

And That's The End Of The Ballgame!
And The Home Of The...
Bang The Drum All Day [Todd Rundgren] 63
Blitzkrieg Bop ("Hey Ho! Let's Go") [Ramones]
Born To Be Wild [Steppenwolf] 2
Charge!
Dance To The Music [Sly & The Family Stone] 8
Dee-fense!
ESPN Sportscenter Theme ("Da Da Da")
He Shoots! He Scores!
I Got You (I Feel Good) [James Brown] 3
Let's Go!
Make Some Noise!
Mony, Mony [Tommy James & The Shondells] 3
Na Na Hey Hey Kiss Him Goodbye [Steam] 1
Rock And Roll Part 2 [Gary Glitter] 7
Shotgun [Jr. Walker & The All Stars] 4
Shout [Isley Brothers] 47
Takin' Care Of Business [Bachman-Turner Overdrive] 12
Tequila [Champs] 1
Three Point Goal!
We Will Rock You [Queen] 52
What I Like About You [Romantics] 49
Who Wants A Hotdog!

| 11/4/95 | 121 | 18 | | ©121 | **ESPN Presents Jock Rock Volume 2** | | | $10 | Tommy Boy 1136 |

Addams Family Theme
Cool Jerk [Capitols] 7
Devil With The Blue Dress On & Good Golly Miss Molly [Mitch Ryder] 4
En Fuego
Final Countdown
Get Ready [Rare Earth] 4
Great Balls Of Fire [Jerry Lee Lewis] 2
He Could Go All The Way
Hold On! I'm Comin' [Sam & Dave] 21
Homecoming Game
I Want You Back [Jackson 5] 1
Louie, Louie [Kingsmen] 2
Low Rider [War] 7
Nobody But Me [Human Beinz] 8
Respect [Aretha Franklin] 1
Rock And Roll All Nite [Kiss] 68
Sirius [Alan Parsons Project]
Stadium Beat
300 Game
Twist & Shout [Isley Brothers] 17
We Are The Champions [Queen] 4
William Tell Overture
Wooly Bully [Sam The Sham & The Pharaohs] 2

| 6/15/96 | 49 | 14 | | ©122 | **ESPN Presents X Games - Music From The Edge** | | | $10 | Tommy Boy 1173 |

Are You Gonna Go My Way [Lenny Kravitz]
Blind [Korn]
Epic [Faith No More] 9
Go [Sexpod]
Go To... [Drill]
Guilty [Gravity Kills] 86
Higher Ground [Red Hot Chili Peppers]
Jerry Was A Race Car Driver [Primus]
Jesus Built My Hot Rod [Ministry]
My My [Seven Mary Three]
Only One Performed [Goo Goo Dolls]
Paranoid [Megadeth]
Possum Kingdom [Toadies]
Ratamahatta [Sepultura]
Shamrocks And Shenanigans [House Of Pain]
Tainted Love [Shades Apart]
(You Gotta) Fight For Your Right (To Party!) [Beastie Boys] 7

| 6/28/97 | 102 | 8 | | ©123 | **ESPN Presents X Games - The Soundtrack Album** | | | $10 | Tommy Boy 1202 |

Adrenaline [Phunk Junkeez]
Circles Of Sin [Psycho Realm feat. B. Real]
Dog [Fat]
Exactly What You Wanted [Helmet]
Insomniac [Chronic Future]
Johnny, Kick A Hole In The Sky [Red Hot Chili Peppers]
No Regrets [Vibrolush]
Old [Bush]
Party At Ground Zero [Fishbone]
Protect Ya Neck [Wu Tang Clan]
RPM [Sugar Ray]
Shout It [CIV]
Step Right In [Dog Eat Dog feat. The RZA]
Superman [Goldfinger]
Voodoo People [Prodigy]
Welcome To The Terrordome [Public Enemy]
What I Got [Sublime]

| 7/8/00 | 182 | 2 | | ©124 | **Everlasting Love Songs** | | | $10 | UTV 170137 |

All This Time [Reba McEntire]
Baby Blue [George Strait]
Butterfly Kisses [Raybon Bros.] 22
From This Moment On [Shania Twain] 4
Give My Heart To You [Billy Ray Cyrus]
I Already Do [Chely Wright]
I Do (Cherish You) [Mark Wills] 72
I Honestly Love You [Olivia Newton-John] 67
Keeper Of The Stars [Tracy Byrd] 68
Look At Us [Vince Gill]
Love Of My Life [Sammy Kershaw] 85
Loving You [Mavericks]
Me Too [Toby Keith]
Now That I've Found You [Terri Clark] 72
Sending Me Angels [Kathy Mattea]
Some Things I Know [Chely Wright]
Your Love Is A Miracle [Mark Chesnutt]

| 10/13/84 | 75 | 10 | | ©125 | **Every Man Has A Woman** | | | $12 | Polydor 823490 |

all songs written by Yoko Ono
Dogtown [Alternating Boxes]
Dream Love [Nilsson]
Every Man Has A Woman Who Loves Him [John Lennon]
Goodbye Sadness [Roberta Flack]
I'm Moving On [Eddie Money]
It's Alright [Sean Ono Lennon]
Loneliness [Nilsson]
Nobody Sees Me Like You Do [Rosanne Cash]
Now Or Never [Spirit Choir]
Silver Horse [Nilsson]
Wake Up [Trio]
Walking On Thin Ice [Elvis Costello]

| 7/22/72 | 178 | 6 | | 126 | **Everything You Always Wanted To Know About The Godfather - But Don't Ask** | [C] | | $15 | Columbia 31608 |

Another Favor
Arrangement, An
At Home
At The Employment Agency
At The I.R.S.
At The Psychiatrist
At The Restaurant
Bad News
Commercial Message
Complaint, The
Contract, The
Day In The Life
Favor, The
For Better Or For Worse
Protocol
Special Announcement
This Is Your Life
Treaty, The
Trial, The
Wiretap, The

| 6/20/98 | 131 | 4 | | ©127 | **Exodus** | | | $10 | Word 69349 |

Agnus Dei [Third Day]
Brighten My Heart [Sixpence None The Richer]
Draw Me Close [Katinas]
I See You [Michael W. Smith]
Make Us One [Cindy Morgan]
My Will [DC Talk]
Needful Hands [Jars Of Clay]
Nothin' [Chris Rice]
Salvation Belongs To Our God [Crystal Lewis]

| 6/27/81 | 51 | 9 | | 128 | **Exposed/A Cheap Peek At Today's Provocative New Rock** | | | $15 | CBS 37124 [2] |

Baby, Better Start Turnin' Em Down [Rosanne Cash]
Breaking The Law [Judas Priest]
Cellophane City [Steve Forbert]
Christabelle [Sorrows]
Dog Eat Dog [Adam & The Ants]
Elephants Graveyard [Boomtown Rats]
First In Line [Romantics]
Heading Out To The Highway [Judas Priest]
Hold On [Ian Gomm] 18
I Don't Like It Like That [Sorrows]
Jump Jump [Garland Jeffreys]
Keep It Up [Boomtown Rats]
Kid Is Hot Tonite [Loverboy] 55
Killer In The Home [Adam & The Ants]
Lady Of The 80's [Loverboy]
Man On A Mountain [Ian Gomm]
Phases Of Travel [Ellen Foley]
True Confessions [Garland Jeffreys]
21 And Over [Romantics]
We Belong To The Night [Ellen Foley]
What Kinda Girl? [Loverboy]
You Cannot Win If You Do Not Play [Steve Forbert]

VARIOUS ARTISTS COMPILATIONS

DEBUT	PEAK	WKS	RIAA	CD	ARTIST — Album Title	Catalog	Sym	$	Label & Number

12/5/81 | 124 | 5 — **129 Exposed II** .... **$15** CBS 37601 [2]

- Bates Motel [Hitmen]
- Cheap Date [Tommy Tutone]
- Cool World [Karla DeVito]
- Electricity [Orchestral Manoeuvres In The Dark]
- Every Morning [Whitford/St. Holmes Band]
- Guess Who [Hitmen]
- Hit And Run [Jo Jo Zep & The Falcons]
- I'm Not A Number [Gary Myrick & The Figures]
- Innocence [Harlequin]
- Just The Way I Like It [Billy Thorpe]
- Let Me Outta Here [Billy Thorpe]
- Messages [Orchestral Manoeuvres In The Dark]
- Pretty In Pink [Psychedelic Furs]
- Rock Against Romance [Holly & The Italians]
- She Talks In Stereo [Gary Myrick & The Figures]
- Sister Europe [Psychedelic Furs]
- Sweet Honey Sweet [Jo Jo Zep & The Falcons]
- Tell That Girl To Shut Up [Holly & The Italians]
- Thinking Of You [Harlequin]
- Which Man Are You [Tommy Tutone]
- Whiskey Woman [Whitford/St. Holmes Band]
- Work [Karla DeVito]

2/17/68 | 194 | 4 — **130 Family Portrait** .... **$20** A&M 19002

- Baja Humbug [Baja Marimba Band]
- Cross My Heart [Phil Ochs]
- Debutante's Ball [Liza Minnelli]
- Dolphin [Tamba 4]
- Early In The Morning [Merry-Go-Round]
- Flea Bag [Herb Alpert]
- Fly Me To The Moon [Sandpipers]
- Foolin' Around [Chris Montez]
- Girl, I'm Out To Get You [Tommy Boyce & Bobby Hart]
- House Of The Risin' Sun [Herbie Mann]
- I Say A Little Prayer [Burt Bacharach]
- Like A Lover [Sergio Mendes & Brasil '66]
- Triste [Antonio Carlos Jobim]
- Wanderlove [Claudine Longet]
- **Windy** [Wes Montgomery] **44**
- You Pass Me By [Jimmie Rodgers]

4/17/99 | 7 | 20 | ● | ©131 Family Values Tour '98 .... [L] **$10** Immortal 69904

- Blue Monday [Orgy]
- Cambodia [Limp Bizkit]
- Check Yo Self [Ice Cube]
- Dissention [Orgy]
- Du Hast [Rammstein]
- Faith [Limp Bizkit]
- Freak On A Leash [Korn]
- Fuck Tha Police (medley) [Ice Cube]
- Gender [Orgy]
- Got The Life [Korn]
- Interlude #1
- Interlude #2
- Interlude #3
- Interlude #4
- Interlude #5
- Jump Around [Limp Bizkit]
- Natural Born Killaz [Ice Cube]
- New Skin [Incubus]
- Shot Liver Medley
- Straight Outta Compton (medley) [Ice Cube]
- Twist/Chi [Korn]

6/10/00 | 32 | 33 | | ©132 Family Values Tour 1999, The .... [L] **$10** Flawless 490641

- A.D.I.D.A.S. [Korn]
- Break Stuff [Limp Bizkit]
- Falling Away From Me [Korn]
- Good God (medley) [Korn]
- Hey Man, Nice Shot [Filter]
- I Would For You [Limp Bizkit]
- Keep Hope Alive [Crystal Method]
- Lacquer Head [Primus]
- Mudshovel [Staind]
- My Name Is Mud [Primus]
- Nookie [Limp Bizkit]
- Outside [Aaron Lewis & Fred Durst]
- Rearranged [Limp Bizkit]
- Rockwilder [Method Man & Redman]
- Welcome To The Fold [Filter]

4/13/96 | 126 | 1 | | ©133 Famous Overtures III .... [I] **$10** Digital Master. 71855

- Boccaccio: Overture
- Cosi Fan Tutte: Overture
- Fierabras: Overture
- La Gazza Ladra: Overture
- Spanish Comic Overture
- Vom Himmel Hoch: Christmas Overture
- William Tell Overture

3/24/01 | 187 | 1 | | ©134 Fat Music Volume 5: Live Fat, Die Young .... **$10** Fat Wreck Chords 613

- Alison's Disease [Lagwagon]
- Always [Good Riddance]
- Bad Place [Tilt]
- Dear James [Consumed]
- Down This Road [Zero Down]
- Flesh And Bones [Fabulous Disaster]
- Hats Off To Larry [Me First & The Gimme Gimmes]
- Hearing Aid [Bracket]
- I Believe [Sick Of It All]
- I Follow [Swingin' Utters]
- Join The Ranks [Rise Against]
- Let Me Down [No Use For A Name]
- Novacain [Strung Out]
- Prognosis: Fuck You [Frenzal Rhomb]
- R.A.F. [Wizo]
- San Francisco Fat [NOFX]
- Seattle Was A Riot [Anti-Flag]
- Shut The Door [Mad Caddies]
- War Is Peace, Slavery Is Freedom, May All Your Interventions Be Humanitarian [Propagandhi]
- Who's Asking [Snuff]

7/15/72 | 40 | 16 | | ©135 Fillmore: The Last Days .... [L] **$40** Fillmore 31390 [3]

- Baby's Callin' Me Home [Boz Scaggs]
- Back On The Streets Again [Tower Of Power]
- Casey Jones [Grateful Dead]
- Fresh Air [Quicksilver Messenger Service]
- Hello [John Walker]
- Hello Friends [Lamb]
- Henry [New Riders Of The Purple Sage]
- I Just Want To Make Love To You [Cold Blood]
- In A Silent Way [Santana]
- Incident At Neshabur [Santana]
- Johnny B. Goode [Grateful Dead]
- Keep Your Lamps Trimmed And Burnin' [Hot Tuna]
- Long And Tall [Taj Mahal/Elvin Bishop/Boz Scaggs]
- Mojo [Quicksilver Messenger Service]
- Pana [Malo]
- Party Till The Cows Come Home [Elvin Bishop Group]
- Passion Flower [Stoneground]
- Poppa Can Play [Sons Of Champlin]
- So Fine [Elvin Bishop Group]
- We Gonna Rock [Taj Mahal/Elvin Bishop/Boz Scaggs]
- White Bird [It's A Beautiful Day]

9/18/71 | 47 | 9 — **136 First Great Rock Festivals Of The Seventies: Isle Of Wight/Atlanta Pop Festival** .... **$30** Columbia 30805 [3]

Isle Of Wight was held August 26-31, 1970 in England; Atlanta Pop Festival was held July 3-5, 1970

- Blame It On The Stones (medley) [Kris Kristofferson]
- Call It Anythin' [Miles Davis]
- Foxy Lady (medley) [Jimi Hendrix]
- Grand Junction [Poco]
- I Can't Keep From Cryin' Sometime [Ten Years After]
- Kind Woman [Poco]
- Love, Peace And Happiness [Chambers Brothers]
- Mean Mistreater [Johnny Winter]
- Midnight Lightning (medley) [Jimi Hendrix]
- Mr. Bojangles [David Bromberg]
- No Need To Worry (medley) [Cactus]
- Parchman Farm (medley) [Cactus]
- Pilgrim - Chapter 33 (medley) [Kris Kristofferson]
- Power To Love (medley) [Jimi Hendrix]
- Salty Dog [Procol Harum]
- Stand! (medley) [Sly & The Family Stone]
- Statesborough Blues [Allman Brothers]
- Stormy Monday [Mountain]
- Tonight Will Be Fine [Leonard Cohen]
- Whippen Post [Allman Brothers]
- You Can Make It If You Try (medley) [Sly & The Family Stone]

7/11/64 | 96 | 14 — **137 First Nine Months Are The Hardest!, The** .... [C] **$20** Capitol 2034

- Breaking The News
- Breast Feeding
- Due Date
- Honesty
- Insurance
- It's Kicking
- It's Time
- Lovely To Look At
- Morning Sickness
- Naming The Baby
- Nurse Or My Mother?
- Overdue
- Superstitions

9/17/88 | 70 | 10 | | ©138 Folkways: A Vision Shared - A Tribute To Woody Guthrie And Leadbelly .... **$10** Columbia 44034

- Bourgeois Blues [Taj Mahal]
- Do Re Mi [John Mellencamp]
- East Texas Red [Arlo Guthrie]
- Goodnight Irene [Brian Wilson]
- Gray Goose [Sweet Honey In The Rock]
- Hobo's Lullaby [Emmylou Harris]
- I Ain't Got No Home [Bruce Springsteen]
- Jesus Christ [U2]
- Philadelphia Lawyer [Willie Nelson]
- Pretty Boy Floyd [Bob Dylan]
- Rock Island Line [Little Richard w/Fishbone]
- Sylvie [Sweet Honey In The Rock]
- This Land Is Your Land [Pete Seeger/Sweet Honey In The Rock/Doc Watson]
- Vigilante Man [Bruce Springsteen]

10/19/63 | 87 | 10 — **139 Fool Britannia** .... [C] **$20** Acappella 1

- Common Market
- Eugenius!
- House That Mac Built
- Is There A Doctor In The House?
- Mightier Than The Sword
- There Goes That Song Again
- There's No Business Like No Business
- They Only Fade Away
- Twelve Randy Men
- Two Old Ladies Locked In Conversation
- Vice Italian Style
- Whatever Happened To John And Marsha?
- Wry On The Rocks

6/15/91 | 31 | 30 | ● | ©140 For Our Children .... **$10** Disney 60616

- Autumn To May [Ann & Nancy Wilson]
- Ballad Of Davy Crockett [Stephen Bishop]
- Blanket For A Sail [Harry Nilsson]
- Blueberry Pie [Bette Midler]
- Chicken Lips And Lizard Hips [Bruce Springsteen]
- Child Is Born [Barbra Streisand]
- Child Of Mine [Carole King]
- Country Feelin's [Brian Wilson]
- Cushie Butterfield [Sting]
- Gartan Mother's Lullaby [Meryl Streep]
- Getting To Know You [James Taylor]
- Give A Little Love [Ziggy Marley & the Melody Makers]
- Golden Slumbers [Jackson Browne & Jennifer Warnes]
- Good Night, My Love (Pleasant Dreams) [Paula Abdul]
- Itsy Bitsy Spider [Little Richard]
- Mary Had A Little Lamb [Paul McCartney]
- Medley Of Rhymes [Debbie Gibson]
- Pacifier [Elton John]
- Tell Me Why [Pat Benatar]
- This Old Man [Bob Dylan]

DEBUT	PEAK	WKS	RIAA	CD	ARTIST — Album Title	Catalog	Sym	$	Label & Number

10/5/96 144 4 ©141 For Our Children Too! .... **$10** Kid Rhino 72494

Angel's Lullaby [Richard Marx]
Both Sides Now [Natalie Cole]
Brahms' Lullaby [Celine Dion]
Brown Baby [Toni Braxton]
Come Take A Trip In My Airship [Natalie Merchant]
Dream Is A Wish Your Heart Makes [Cher]
Greatest Discovery [Elton John]
If [Babyface]
If I Had A Hammer [Luther Vandross]
Love Lights The World [David Foster/Celine Dion/Peabo Bryson/Color Me Badd]
Mockingbird [Carly Simon & James Taylor]
My Buddy [Amy Grant]
Over The Rainbow (Faith Hill)
Puff (The Magic Dragon) [Seal]
Snowflakes [Vanessa Williams]
You Are My Sunshine [Bryan White]

8/22/98 69 4 ©142 For The Masses .... **$10** A&M 540919

Black Celebration [Monster Magnet]
Enjoy The Silence [Failure]
Everything Counts [Meat Beat Manifesto]
Fly On The Windscreen [God Lives Underwater]
I Feel You [Apollo Four Forty]
Master And Servant [Locust]
Monument [Gus Gus]
Never Let Me Down Again [Smashing Pumpkins]
Policy Of Truth [Dishwalla]
Shake The Disease [Hooverphonic]
Shame [Self]
Somebody [Veruca Salt]
Stripped [Rammstein]
To Have And To Hold [Deftones]
Waiting For The Night [Rabbit In The Moon]
World In My Eyes [Cure]

3/24/01 173 1 ©143 Fred Hammond Presents: "In Case You Missed It...And Then Some" .... **$10** F Hammond 43154

Heart Of Mine [Darrin Patterson]
Heart Towards You [Donald Hayes]
I Anoint Myself [PamKenyon M. Donald]
Let Me Tell It [Fred Hammond & Keith Staten]
Let Me Tell It (Interlude)
Life That Shows [Resurrection]
Love U With The Rest Of My Life [Charles Laster & Candace Laster-Jones]
More, More, More [Joann Rosario]
My Deliverer [Jonathan Dunn]
My Heart Depends On You [Shea Norman]
Pour Out Your Holy Spirit [Singletons]
Save Me Now [Howard Smith & Lisa Scott-Bailey]
When Jesus Sings [Duawne Starling & Tiffany Palmer]
When Jesus Sings (Interlude)
Who Do Men Say I Am? [Brian J. Pratt/Frederick J. Purifoy II/Marcus Cole, Keith Staten/Fred Hammond]
Who Do Men Say I Am? (Interlude)
Yeah, Yeah [Bridgette Campbell]

1/6/73+ 68 58 ● ©144 Free To Be...You And Me .... **$15** Bell 1110

Atalanta [Alan Alda & Marlo Thomas]
Boy Meets Girl [Mel Brooks & Marlo Thomas]
Don't Dress Your Cat In An Apron [Billy De Wolfe]
Dudley Pippin And His No-Friend [Bobby Morse & Marlo Thomas]
Dudley Pippin And The Principal [Billy De Wolfe/Bobby Morse/Marlo Thomas]
Free To Be...You And Me [New Seekers]
Girl Land [Jack Cassidy & Shirley Jones]
Glad To Have A Friend Like You [Marlo Thomas]
Grandma [Diana Sands]
Helping [Tom Smothers]
Housework [Carol Channing]
It's All Right To Cry [Rosey Grier]
Ladies First [Marlo Thomas]
My Dog Is A Plumber [Dick Cavett]
Parents Are People [Harry Belafonte & Marlo Thomas]
Sisters And Brothers [Sisters & Brothers]
When We Grow Up [Diana Ross]
William's Doll [Alan Alda & Marlo Thomas]

5/26/56 9 9 145 Gentlemen, Be Seated! .... **$30** Epic 3238

recreation of a complete minstrel show

Camptown Races (medley)
Can't You Hear Me Callin' Caroline
Hello! Ma Baby (medley)
Honeymoon (medley)
I Wish't I Was In Peoria
I Wonder What's Become Of Sally?
I Wonder Who's Kissing Her Now
In The Evening By The Moonlight (medley)
Lassus Trombone
Mandy Lee (medley)
My Lady Love (medley)
Oh By Jingo, Oh By Gee, You're The Only Girl For Me
Old Folks At Home (medley)
Ole Dan Tucker (medley)
Shine On Harvest Moon
There'll Be A Hot Time In The Old Town Tonight (medley)
Waitin' For The Robert E. Lee (medley)
When The Bell In The Lighthouse Rings

8/16/97 183 1 ©146 Give 'Em The Boot .... **$10** Hellcat 80402

Barroom Heroes [Dropkick Murphy's]
Beautiful Girl [Gadjits]
Brothels, The [Rancid]
Can't Wait [Hepcat]
Does He Love You [Skinnerbox]
Fifteenth And T [Swingin' Utters]
Heart Like A Lion [Pressure Point]
Infested [Choking Victim]
Jaks [U.S. Bombs]
Latin Goes Ska [Skatalites]
Los Hombres No Lloran [VooDoo Glow Skulls]
New Breed [Pietasters]
No Time [F-Minus]
Open Season [Stubborn Allstars]
Playtime [Dave Hillyard Rocksteady 7]
Policeman [Silencers]
Roots Radicals [Union 13]
17 @ 17 [Upbeat]
Spirit Of The Streets [Business]
Watch This [Slackers]

10/15/94 192 1 ©147 Glory Of Gershwin, The .... **$10** Mercury 526091

But Not For Me [Elvis Costello]
Embraceable You [Oleta Adams]
How Long Has This Been Going On [Jon Bon Jovi]
I Got Rhythm [Robert Palmer]
I'll Build A Stairway To Paradise [Issy Van Randwyck]
I've Got A Crush On You [Carly Simon]
It Ain't Necessarily So [Cher]
Man I Love [Kate Bush]
My Man's Gone Now [Sinéad O'Connor]
Nice Work If You Can Get It [Sting]
Our Love Is Here To Stay [Elton John]
Rhapsody In Blue [Larry Adler & George Martin]
Somebody Loves Me [Meat Loaf]
Someone To Watch Over Me [Elton John]
Summertime [Peter Gabriel]
They Can't Take That Away From Me [Lisa Stansfield]

2/10/01 28 31 ● ©148 Goin' South .... **$10** Razor & Tie 89033

Amie [Pure Prairie League] 27
Bad To The Bone [George Thorogood & The Destroyers]
Black Betty [Ram Jam] 18
Black Water [Doobie Brothers] 1
Devil Went Down To Georgia [Charlie Daniels Band] 3
Dixie Chicken [Little Feat]
Flirtin With Disaster [Molly Hatchet] 42
Heard It In A Love Song [Marshall Tucker Band] 14
Hold On Loosely [38 Special] 27
Keep Your Hands To Yourself [Georgia Satellites] 2
Mississippi Queen [Mountain] 21
My Maria [B.W. Stevenson] 9
Night They Drove Old Dixie Down [Band]
Ramblin' Man [Allman Brothers] 2
Rocky Mountain Way [Joe Walsh] 23
Sweet Home Alabama [Lynyrd Skynyrd] 8
Tuff Enuff [Fabulous Thunderbirds] 10

7/27/63 97 6 149 Golden Goodies, Vol. 1 .... **$25** Roulette 25207

Cry Like I Cried [Harptones]
Darling, How Long [Heartbeats]
Ding Dong [Echoes]
Don't Say Goodnight [Valentines]
Glory Of Love [Angels]
Masquerade Is Over [Harptones]
Out In The Cold Again [Frankie Lymon]
Paper Castles [Frankie Lymon]
People Are Talking [Heartbeats]
Rip Van Winkle [Devotions] 36
Shrine Of St. Cecila [Harptones]
Wedding Bells [Tiny Tim & The Hits]
Your Way [Heartbeats]

7/20/63 89 5 150 Golden Goodies, Vol. 2 .... **$25** Roulette 25210

Chapel Of Dreams [Dubs] 74
Charlie Brown [Coasters] 2
Crying In The Chapel [Orioles]
For Sentimental Reasons [Cleftones] 60
Gee [Crows]
I Only Have Eyes For You [Flamingos] 11
Little Girl Of Mine [Cleftones] 57
Look In My Eyes [Chantels] 14
Priscilla [Eddie Cooley] 20
Tears On My Pillow [Little Anthony & The Imperials] 4
Thousand Miles Away [Heartbeats] 53
Why Do Fools Fall In Love [Frankie Lymon & The Teenagers] 6

8/3/63 112 4 151 Golden Goodies, Vol. 3 .... **$25** Roulette 25218

Barbara [Temptations] 29
Bim Bam Boom [Eldorados]
Goodnight Sweetheart, Goodnite [Flamingos]
I Love You So [Chantels] 42
I Shot Mr. Lee [Bobbettes] 52
I'll Be Home [Flamingos]
Long Lonely Nights [Lee Andrews & The Hearts] 45
Maybe [Chantels] 15
See Saw [Moonglows] 25
16 Candles [Crests] 2
Speedo [Cadillacs] 17
There Goes My Baby [Drifters] 2

7/27/63 124 4 152 Golden Goodies, Vol. 5 .... **$25** Roulette 25215

Book Of Love [Monotones] 5
Closer You Are [Channels]
Dance, Dance, Dance [Dells]
Five Hundred Miles To Go [Heartbeats]
Joe Joe [Dells]
Just You [Dion & The Belmonts]
So Far Away [Pastels]
So Fine [Fiestas] 11
Story Untold [Nutmegs]
Ten Commandments Of Love [Harvey & The Moonglows] 22
You Gave Me Peace Of Mind [Spaniels]
Zoom [Cadillacs]

VARIOUS ARTISTS COMPILATIONS

DEBUT	PEAK	WKS	RIAA	CD	ARTIST — Album Title	Catalog	Sym	$	Label & Number

8/3/63 · 86 · 3 · 153 · Golden Goodies, Vol. 6 .... **$25** Roulette 25216
- Everyone's Laughing [Spaniels] 69
- Goodnight Sweetheart, Goodnite [Spaniels]
- I'm Confessin' [Chantels]
- In The Still Of The Nite [Five Satins] 24
- Lovers Never Say Goodbye [Flamingos] 52
- Most Of All [Moonglows]
- Oh What A Night [Dells]
- Ship Of Love [Nutmegs]
- There's Our Song Again [Chantels]
- Up On The Mountain [Magnificents]
- We Belong Together [Robert & Johnny] 32
- When You Dance [Turbans] 33

10/14/67 · 177 · 4 · 154 · Golden Instrumentals .... **[I] $25** Dot 25820
- Bongo Rock [Preston Epps] 14
- Happy Organ [Dave "Baby" Cortez] 1
- Hot Pastrami [Dartells] 11
- Memphis [Lonnie Mack] 5
- Pipeline [Chantay's] 4
- Red River Rock [Johnny & The Hurricanes] 5
- Sleep Walk [Santo & Johnny] 1
- Teen Beat [Sandy Nelson] 4
- Tequila [Champs] 1
- Topsy II [Cozy Cole] 3
- Torquay [Fireballs] 39
- Wipe Out [Surfaris] 2

2/25/95 · 26 · 11 · ©155 · Grammy Nominees 1995 .... **$10** Grammy 67043
- All I Wanna Do [Sheryl Crow] 2
- Can You Feel The Love Tonight [Elton John] 4
- He Thinks He'll Keep Her [Mary Chapin Carpenter]
- Hero [Mariah Carey] 1
- I'll Make Love To You [Boyz II Men] 1
- Longing In Their Hearts [Bonnie Raitt]
- Love Sneakin' Up On You [Bonnie Raitt] 19
- Love The One You're With [Luther Vandross] 95
- Ordinary Miracles [Barbra Streisand]
- Power Of Love [Celine Dion] 1
- Prayer For The Dying [Seal] 21
- Said I Loved You...But I Lied [Michael Bolton] 6
- Streets Of Philadelphia [Bruce Springsteen] 9

2/24/96 · 16 · 13 · ▲ · 156 · Grammy Nominees 1996 .... **$10** Grammy 67565
- Any Man Of Mine [Shania Twain] 31
- Baby [Brandy] 4
- Gangsta's Paradise [Coolio feat. L.V.] 1
- I Can Love You Like That [All-4-One] 5
- Kiss From A Rose [Seal] 1
- Let Her Cry [Hootie & The Blowfish] 9
- One Of Us [Joan Osborne] 4
- One Sweet Day [Mariah Carey & Boyz II Men] 1
- Waterfalls [TLC] 1
- You Are Not Alone [Michael Jackson] 1
- You Oughta Know [Alanis Morissette]

3/1/97 · 14 · 20 · ● · ©157 · Grammy Nominees 1997 .... **$10** Grammy 553292
- Because You Loved Me [Celine Dion] 1
- Change The World [Eric Clapton] 5
- Get Out Of This House [Shawn Colvin]
- Give Me One Reason [Tracy Chapman] 3
- Ironic [Alanis Morissette] 4
- My Baby [LeAnn Rimes]
- 1979 [Smashing Pumpkins] 12
- Nobody Knows [Tony Rich Project] 2
- Reach [Gloria Estefan] 42
- Spiderwebs [No Doubt]
- Stupid Girl [Garbage] 24
- Un-Break My Heart [Toni Braxton] 1
- Who Will Save Your Soul [Jewel] 11

2/28/98 · 11 · 12 · ● · ©158 · Grammy Nominees 1998 .... **$10** Grammy 11752
- Anybody Seen My Baby? [Rolling Stones]
- Criminal [Fiona Apple] 21
- Don't Speak [No Doubt]
- Everyday Is A Winding Road [Sheryl Crow] 11
- I Believe I Can Fly [R. Kelly] 2
- MMMBop [Hanson] 1
- On & On [Erykah Badu] 12
- Silver Springs [Fleetwood Mac]
- Sunny Came Home [Shawn Colvin] 7
- Virtual Insanity [Jamiroquai]
- Where Have All The Cowboys Gone? [Paula Cole] 8

2/27/99 · 8 · 16 · ● · ©159 · Grammy Nominees 1999 .... **$10** Grammy 62381
songs by Backstreet Boys, Celine Dion, Dixie Chicks, Lauryn Hill, Shania Twain, and others
- Amor Ti Vieta [Andrea Bocelli]
- Anytime [Brian McKnight]
- Boy Is Mine [Brandy & Monica] 1
- Doo Wop (That Thing) [Lauryn Hill] 1
- Everybody (Backstreet's Back) [Backstreet Boys] 4
- Iris [Goo Goo Dolls] 9
- Lullaby [Shawn Mullins] 7
- My Father's Eyes [Eric Clapton]
- My Heart Will Go On [Celine Dion] 1
- Ray Of Light [Madonna] 5
- Save Tonight [Eagle-Eye Cherry] 5
- Torn [Natalie Imbruglia] 42
- Wide Open Spaces [Dixie Chicks] 41
- You Were Meant For Me [Sting]
- You're Still The One [Shania Twain] 2

2/26/00 · 9 · 20 · ▲ · ©160 · Grammy Nominees 2000 .... **$10** Grammy 67945
- ...Baby One More Time [Britney Spears] 1
- Bawitdaba [Kid Rock]
- Brand New Day [Sting]
- Do Something [Macy Gray]
- Genie In A Bottle [Christina Aguilera] 1
- I Need To Know [Marc Anthony] 3
- I Want It That Way [Backstreet Boys] 6
- It Hurt So Bad [Susan Tedeschi]
- Livin' La Vida Loca [Ricky Martin] 1
- Mambo No. 5 (A Little Bit Of...) [Lou Bega] 3
- No Scrubs [TLC] 1
- Smooth [Santana feat. Rob Thomas] 1
- Sogno [Andrea Bocelli]

2/24/01 · 12 · 12 · ● · ©161 · Grammy Nominees 2001 .... **$10** Grammy 31520
- Beautiful Day [U2] 21
- Both Sides Now [Joni Mitchell]
- Breathless [Corrs]
- Bye Bye Bye ['N Sync] 4
- Cousin Dupree [Steely Dan]
- I Try [Macy Gray] 5
- Music [Madonna] 1
- Oops!...I Did It Again [Britney Spears] 9
- Say My Name [Destiny's Child] 1
- Sexx Laws [Beck]
- Pinch Me [Barenaked Ladies] 15
- Real Slim Shady [Eminem] 4
- Save Me [Aimee Mann]
- Show Me The Meaning Of Being Lonely [Backstreet Boys] 6
- What A Girl Wants [Christina Aguilera] 1
- You're The One [Paul Simon]

2/27/99 · 54 · 11 · ©162 · Grammy Rap Nominees 1999 .... **$10** Grammy 62380
songs by Big Punisher, Busta Rhymes, Jermaine Dupri, Mase, Will Smith, and others
- Dangerous [Busta Rhymes] 9
- Deja Vu (Uptown Baby) [Lord Tariq & Peter Gunz] 4
- Find A Way [Tribe Called Quest] 71
- Gettin' Jiggy Wit It [Will Smith] 1
- Ghetto Supastar [Pras Michel Feat. Ol' Dirty Bastard & Mya] 15
- Gone Till November [Wyclef Jean] 7
- Intergalactic [Beastie Boys] 28
- Lookin' At Me [Mase Feat. Puff Daddy] 8
- Lost Ones [Lauryn Hill]
- Money Ain't A Thang [Jermaine Dupri Feat. Jay-Z] 52
- Rosa Parks [OutKast] 55
- Sweetheart [Jermaine Dupri & Mariah Carey]
- You Came Up [Big Punisher Feat. Noreaga]

3/11/00 · 151 · 2 · ©163 · Grammy Rap Nominees 2000 .... **$10** Grammy 67944
- Gimme Some More [Busta Rhymes]
- Guilty Conscience [Eminem & Dr. Dre]
- My Name Is [Eminem] 36
- Nas Is Like [Nas] 86
- Next Movement [Roots]
- She's A Bitch [Missy "Misdemeanor" Elliott] 90
- Still D.R.E. [Dr. Dre Feat. Snoop Dogg] 93
- What's It Gonna Be?! [Busta Rhymes Feat. Janet Jackson] 3
- Wild Wild West [Will Smith Feat. Dru Hill & Kool Mo Dee] 1
- You Got Me [Roots Feat. Erykah Badu] 39

2/24/01 · 43 · 9 · ©164 · Grammy Rap/R&B Nominees 2001 .... **$10** Grammy 31647
- Alive [Beastie Boys]
- As We Lay [Kelly Price] 65
- Bag Lady [Erykah Badu] 6
- Gettin' In The Way [Jill Scott]
- He Wasn't Man Enough [Toni Braxton] 2
- (Hot S**t) Country Grammar [Nelly] 7
- I Wanna Know [Joe] 4
- I Wish [Kelly Price]
- Light, The [Common] 44
- Next Episode [Dr. Dre feat. Snoop Dogg] 23
- Party Up (Up In Here) [DMX] 27
- Real Slim Shady [Eminem] 4
- Shake Ya Ass [Mystikal] 13
- Stay Or Let It Go [Brian McKnight] 76
- Thong Song [Sisqó] 3
- Try Again [Aaliyah] 1
- Untitled (How Does It Feel) [D'Angelo] 25

4/25/64 · 70 · 15 · 165 · Great Voices Of The Century .... **$20** Angel 4
- Ah! Dispar, Vision [Tito Schipa]
- Ah! I Am Suffocating [Feodor Chaliapin]
- Beau Soir [Maggie Teyte]
- Mattinata [Nellie Melba]
- Mein Herr, Was Dachten Sie [Lotte Lehmann]
- Nacht Und Traume [Elisabeth Schumann]
- Questa O Quella [Enrico Caruso]
- Tristan and Isolde [Frida Leider & Lauritz Melchoir]
- Vesti La Giubba [Beniamino Gigli]
- Voi Lo Sapete [Claudia Muzio]
- Where'er You Walk [John McCormack]

5/13/67 · 87 · 18 · 166 · Greatest Hits From England, The .... **$25** Parrot 71010
- Black Is Black [Los Bravos] 4
- Concrete And Clay [Unit Four plus Two] 28
- Everyone's Gone To The Moon [Jonathan King] 17
- Gloria [Them] 71
- Go Now! [Moody Blues] 10
- It's Good News Week [Hedgehoppers Anonymous] 48
- It's Not Unusual [Tom Jones] 10
- She's Not There [Zombies] 2
- Tobacco Road [Nashville Teens] 14
- Way Of Love [Kathy Kirby] 88
- You've Got Your Troubles [Fortunes] 7
- Young Girl [Noel Harrison] 51

1108

DEBUT	PEAK	WKS	RIAA	CD	ARTIST — Album Title	Catalog	Sym	$	Label & Number
9/27/69	189	2		167	**Greatest Hits From Memphis, The**			$20	Hi 32049

Cottonfields *[Ace Cannon]* 67 — Don't Be Cruel *[Bill Black's Combo]* 11 — Haunted House *[Gene Simmons]* 11 — Let The Four Winds Blow *[Jerry Jaye]* — Long Tall Texan *[Murry Kellum]* 51 — My Girl Josephine *[Jerry Jaye]* 29 — Smokie - Part 2 *[Bill Black's Combo]* 17 — Soul Serenade *[Willie Mitchell]* 23 — Tuff *[Ace Cannon]* 17 — 20-75 *[Willie Mitchell]* 31 — White Silver Sands *[Bill Black's Combo]* 9

DEBUT	PEAK	WKS	RIAA	CD	ARTIST — Album Title	Catalog	Sym	$	Label & Number
5/3/97	129	15	©	168	**Greatest Sports Rock And Jams**			$15	Cold Front 6245 [2]

Addams Family: Main Theme *[Vic Mizzy]* — Born To Be Wild *[Steppenwolf]* 2 — Bullfight — Celebration *[Kool & The Gang]* 1 — Charge! — Clap, The — Everybody Everybody *[Black Box]* 8 — Get Ready For This *[2 Unlimited]* 38 — Hot, Hot, Hot *[Buster Poindexter]* 45 — (I Wanna) Be Like Mike *[Teknoe]* — I Wanna Have Some Fun *[Samantha Fox]* 8 — I'm Gonna Get You *[Bizarre Inc. feat. Angie Brown]* 47 — Louie, Louie *[Kingsmen]* 2 — Macarena *[Los Del Mar]* 71 — Na, Na, Hey, Hey, Kiss Him Goodbye *[Steam]* 1 — Power, The *[Snap!]* 2 — Pump Up The Volume *[M/A/R/R/S]* 13 — Rock And Roll Part 2 *[Gary Glitter]* 7 — Shout *[Otis Day & The Knights]* — Sirius *[Alan Parsons Project]* — Strikeout — Surfin' Bird *[Trashmen]* 4 — Tequila *[Champs]* 1 — Twilight Zone *[2 Unlimited]* 49 — Twist, The *[Chubby Checker]* 1 — Whoomp! There It Is *[Tag Team]* 2 — Wiggle It *[2 In A Room]* 15 — Wild Thing *[Tone Loc]* 2 — Wild, Wild West *[Escape Club]* 1 — Willie & The Hand Jive *[Johnny Otis]* 9 — Woodchopper's Ball

DEBUT	PEAK	WKS	RIAA	CD	ARTIST — Album Title	Catalog	Sym	$	Label & Number
10/4/97	192	4	©	169	**Greatest Sports Rock And Jams Volume 2**			$15	Cold Front 6255 [2]

Bad To The Bone *[George Thorogood & The Destroyers]* — Bang The Drum All Day *[Todd Rundgren]* 63 — Beer Barrel Polka — Bust A Move *[Young MC]* 7 — Charge! — Everybody Have Fun Tonight *[Wang Chung]* 16 — Good Vibrations *[Marky Mark & The Funky Bunch feat. Loleatta Holloway]* 1 — Hava Nagilia — Heart Of Rock & Roll *[Huey Lewis & The News]* 6 — Heat Is On *[Glenn Frey]* 2 — Hi Yo Silver — Hippy Hippy Shake *[Swinging Blue Jeans]* 24 — Hit Me With Your Best Shot *[Pat Benatar]* 9 — I Think I Can Beat Mike Tyson *[DJ Jazzy Jeff & The Fresh Prince]* 58 — I'm So Excited *[Pointer Sisters]* 9 — "Jaws" Theme — Let's Hear It For The Boy *[Deniece Williams]* 1 — Mony Mony *[Billy Idol]* 1 — Pump Up The Jam *[Technotronic]* 2 — Rhythm Is A Dancer *[Snap!]* 5 — Rock & Roll Part 2 *[Gary Glitter]* 7 — Rock This Town *[Stray Cats]* 9 — Some Like It Hot *[Power Station]* 6 — Twist And Shout *[Isley Brothers]* 17 — Walking On Sunshine *[Katrina & The Waves]* 9 — War Chant — What I Like About You *[Romantics]* 49 — When The Going Gets Tough, The Tough Get Going *[Billy Ocean]* 2 — Wipe Out *[Surfaris]* 2 — You Ain't Seen Nothing Yet *[Bachman-Turner Overdrive]* 1

DEBUT	PEAK	WKS	RIAA	CD	ARTIST — Album Title	Catalog	Sym	$	Label & Number
7/15/89	68	24	©	170	**Greenpeace/Rainbow Warriors**			$15	Geffen 24236 [2]

City Of Dreams *[Talking Heads]* — Don't Stop The Dance *[Bryan Ferry]* — Heaven Is A Place On Earth *[Belinda Carlisle]* 1 — I Will Be Your Friend *[Sade]* — It's The End Of The World As We Know It (And I Feel Fine) *[R.E.M.]* 69 — Last Great American Whale *[Lou Reed]* — Lay Your Hands On Me *[Thompson Twins]* — Let's Go Forward *[Terence Trent D'Arby]* — Look Out Any Window *[Bruce Hornsby & The Range]* 35 — Love Is The Seventh Wave *[Sting]* 17 — Middle Of The Road *[Pretenders]* 19 — Miles Away *[Basia]* — Pride (In The Name Of Love) *[U2]* — Red Rain *[Peter Gabriel]* — Set Them Free *[Aswad]* — Ship Of Fools (Save Me From Tomorrow) *[World Party]* 27 — Small World *[Huey Lewis & The News]* 25 — Somebody *[Bryan Adams]* 11 — This Time *[INXS]* 81 — Throwing Stones *[Grateful Dead]* — Waterfront *[Simple Minds]* — We Are The People *[John Cougar Mellencamp]* — When Tomorrow Comes *[Eurythmics]* — Whole Of The Moon *[Waterboys]* — Wholly Humble Heart *[Martin Stephenson & The Daintees]* — Why Worry *[Dire Straits]* — You're The Voice *[John Farnham]* 82

DEBUT	PEAK	WKS	RIAA	CD	ARTIST — Album Title	Catalog	Sym	$	Label & Number
4/29/00	122	3	©	171	**Guerra De Estados Pesados**		[F]	$10	Lideres 950016

Cargamento Del Chivero *[El Original]* — Clave 7 *[Chuy Vega]* — El Elotero *[Los Gatilleros De Durango]* — El Imagen *[El Jilguero Y El Original]* — El Yoyo *[Los Comandantes De Durango]* — 454 *[Los Herederos Del Norte]* — La Bella Juanita *[Chuy Vega]* — La Fuga Del Moreno *[El Marquez De Sinaloa]* — Lreina De Reinas *[Los Gatilleros De Durango]* — Mil Kilos *[Los Comandantes De Durango]* — 100% Cabron *[Los Herederos Del Norte]* — Regalo Caro *[Chuy Vega]* — Reten De La Sierra *[El Original]* — Sinaloense De Corazon *[Los Herederos Del Norte]*

DEBUT	PEAK	WKS	RIAA	CD	ARTIST — Album Title	Catalog	Sym	$	Label & Number
12/17/88	171	8	©	172	**Guitar Speak**		[I]	$10	I.R.S. 42240

Blood Alley 152 *[Ronnie Montrose]* — Captain Zlogg *[Hank Marvin]* — Danjo *[Pete Haycock]* — Let Me Out'a Here *[Leslie West]* — No Limit *[Alvin Lee]* — Prisoner, The *[Randy California]* — Sharp On Attack *[Steve Howe]* — Sloe Moon Rising *[Rick Derringer]* — Sphinx *[Phil Manzanera]* — Strut A Various *[Robby Krieger]* — Urban Strut *[Steve Hunter]* — Western Flyer *[Eric Johnson]*

DEBUT	PEAK	WKS	RIAA	CD	ARTIST — Album Title	Catalog	Sym	$	Label & Number
11/16/91	190	1	©	173	**Halloween Hits**		C:#18/1	$10	Rhino 70535

Addams Family (Main Title) *[Vic Mizzy]* — Attack Of The Killer Tomatoes *[Lewis Lee]* — Blob, The *[Five Blobs]* 33 — Ghostbusters *[Ray Parker Jr.]* 1 — Haunted House *[Gene Simmons]* 11 — I Put A Spell On You *[Screamin' Jay Hawkins]* — Martian Hop *[Ran-Dells]* 16 — Monster Mash *[Bobby "Boris" Pickett]* 1 — Purple People Eater *[Sheb Wooley]* 1 — Twilight Zone *[Neil Norman]*

DEBUT	PEAK	WKS	RIAA	CD	ARTIST — Album Title	Catalog	Sym	$	Label & Number
10/11/97	73	14	©	174	**Halloween Songs & Sounds**		C:#20/4	$10	Walt Disney 60625

Dungeon, The — Encounter in the Fog — Haunted House — Heffalumps and Woozles — I Wanna Scare Myself — Mad Scientist's Laboratory — Night Creatures — Shake Your Bones — They Don't Scare Me — Werewolf Song — Which Witch Is Which? — Witches, The

DEBUT	PEAK	WKS	RIAA	CD	ARTIST — Album Title	Catalog	Sym	$	Label & Number
10/21/00	176	3	©	175	**Halloween Sound Effects**			$10	LaserLight 21375

Alien Invasion — Big One — Bone Breaking — Bones Crackling — Calm Before The Storm — Choking — Comical Laughs — Crazy Group Laugh — Creepy Chimes — Dentist Drill Of Death — Diminished Aahs — Door Creek (long) — Door Creeks — Door Shut — Downward Spiral — Emergency! — Evil Laughs — Evil Laughs II — Footsteps — Gateway To Hell — Ghost Sounds — Gunshots — Heartbeat — Heavy Breather — Heavy Breather II — Help Me — Help Me II — Helpless — Jaws Strings — Lurking In The Dark — Mad Organ — Mad Science — Misc. Sound FX — Misc. Sound FX II — More Laughs — Outer Space — "Prepare To Die" — Psychotic Strings — Punched Out — Rabid Dogs — Revelation — Sawing A Body In Half — Sleep Little Baby — Spirits In The Attic — Terror Screams — Terror's On Its Way — Thrown Off A Cliff — Thunderstorm — "Tonight You Die" — Total Terror — UFO Has Landed — Vertigo — Vortex — Watch Out... — "Welcome" — "Welcome To My House" — Whipped Senseless — "Why Don't You Come In?" — Wind — Witch, The

DEBUT	PEAK	WKS	RIAA	CD	ARTIST — Album Title	Catalog	Sym	$	Label & Number
11/11/89	65	21	©	176	**Happy Anniversary, Charlie Brown!**			$10	GRP 9596

Benjamin *[Dave Brubeck]* — Breadline Blues *[Kenny G.]* — Charlie Brown Theme *[Amani A.W.-Murray]* — Christmas Time Is Here *[Patti Austin]* — Great Pumpkin Waltz *[Chick Corea]* — History Lesson *[Dave Grusin]* — Joe Cool *[B.B. King]* — Linus & Lucy (with the Peanuts Gang) *[David Benoit]* — Little Birdie *[Joe Williams]* — Rain, Rain, Go Away *[Gerry Mulligan]* — Red Baron *[Lee Ritenour]*

DEBUT	PEAK	WKS	RIAA	CD	ARTIST — Album Title	Catalog	Sym	$	Label & Number

11/20/99 · 105 · 4 · ©177 Hard + The Heavy Volume One, The .... **$15** Redline 75997 [2]

Anarchy In The U.K. [Megadeth]
Avon [Queens Of The Stone Age]
Bad Blood [Ministry]
Big Truck [Coal Chamber]
Black [Sevendust]
Breathe Out [Nothingface]
Choke [Sepultura]
Counterfeit [Limp Bizkit]
Detached [Spineshank]
Divinity [Amorphis]
Edgecrusher [Fear Factory]
Eye For An Eye [Soulfly]
Fake [Puya]
From This Day [Machine Head]
Gimme Danger [Monster Magnet]
Hollywood [P.O.D.]
I Am The Bullgod [Kid Rock]
I Am The Dog [Nevermore]
Isolation [Grip Inc.]
Living Dead Girl [Rob Zombie]
Over The Edge [Fu Manchu]
Overnight Sensation [Motorhead]
Raw [Staind]
Son Of X-51 [Powerman 5000]
Spit It Out [Slipknot]
Stuck Between A Rock And A White Face [One Minute Silence]
Ty Jonathan Down [Videodrone]
Under The Surface [Neurosis]
When You Lie [Orange 9MM]
Wisconsin Death Trip [Static-X]

11/11/00 · 152 · 1 · ©178 Haunted House CD, The .... **$10** Laserlight 21376

Circus Raucous
Dance Of Sacrifice
Ghost Of Dr. Zigo
Haunted Highway (Help Me)
Is Anybody There?
Monster Mash
Mystery
Prelude To Horror
Theme From The X-Files
Torture Chamber
Welcome To My House

6/15/91 · 198 · 1 · ©179 Hearts Of Gold - The Classic Rock Collection .... **$10** Foundation 96647

Badlands [Bruce Springsteen] 42
Can't Get Enough [Bad Company] 5
Carry On Wayward Son [Kansas] 11
Free Bird [Lynyrd Skynyrd] 19
Hot Blooded [Foreigner] 3
I Shot The Sheriff [Eric Clapton] 1
I Want You To Want Me [Cheap Trick] 7
Let's Go [Cars] 14
Love The One You're With [Stephen Stills] 1
Money [Pink Floyd] 13
Ramblin' Man [Allman Brothers Band] 2
Smoke On The Water [Deep Purple] 4

9/20/97 · 161 · 2 · ©180 Heat .... **$10** Boss 70012

Brand Nu Playa [N2Deep/Baby Beesh]
Fatha Figure [Snoop Doggy Dogg/J.T. The Bigga Figure]
535% [Mac Mall/Dubee]
Give It Up [11/5 & Big Mac]
Gladiator Tank [B-Legit/Kaveo]
Gorilla Milk [E-40/Don P./The Mossie/Silky]
Heart Break [Don P.]
Keep Thuggin' Alive [Rappin 4 Tay/Self Tha Gaffla]
Layout Your Suits [Fast 1]
Put That On Something [Dru Down/Young Dre]
Raise Up Off These Nuts [Tupac/Dwayne Wiggins/Silky]
Thick N' Thin [Jay Tee The Bigga Figga]
Throw Your Hands Up High [Rodney-O/Suga T]
Tip Toe [Celly Cel/Levitti]

8/9/69 · 151 · 2 · 181 Heavy Hits! .... **$20** Columbia 9840

Eight Miles High [Byrds] 14
I Can't Quit Her [Blood, Sweat & Tears]
Omaha [Moby Grape] 88
Piece Of My Heart [Big Brother & The Holding Company] 12
Stoned Soul Picnic [Laura Nyro]
Sunny [Electric Flag]
Suzanne [Leonard Cohen]
Time Has Come Today [Chambers Brothers] 11
Weight, The [Mike Bloomfield & Al Kooper]
White Rabbit [Great Society with Grace Slick]
You Don't Miss Your Water ('Til Your Well Runs Dry) [Taj Mahal]

2/28/70 · 128 · 3 · 182 Heavy Sounds .... **$20** Columbia 9952

Albert's Shuffle [Mike Bloomfield-Al Kooper]
Ball And Chain [Big Brother & The Holding Company]
Cold Sweat [Mongo Santamaria]
Diving Duck Blues [Taj Mahal]
God Bless The Child [Blood, Sweat & Tears]
I'll Drown In My Tears [Johnny Winter]
Killing Floor [Electric Flag]
Lay Lady Lay [Byrds]
Listen [Chicago]
Sweet Blindness [Laura Nyro]
White Bird [It's A Beautiful Day]

7/26/97 · 191 · 1 · ©183 Hercules Sing-Along .... **$10** Walt Disney 60925

Go The Distance
I Won't Say (I'm In Love)
One Last Hope
Star Is Born
Zero To Hero

4/28/73 · 160 · 8 · 184 History Of British Blues, Volume One .... **$20** Sire 3701 [2]

Baby What's Wrong [Yardbirds]
Blue Guitar [John Lee's Groundhogs]
Cobwebs [Aynsley Dunbar Retaliation]
Come Back Baby [Mike Vernon]
Country Line Special [Cyril Davis Rhythm & Blues All Stars]
Crazy 'Bout You Baby [Christine Perfect]
Funk Pedal [Gordon Smith]
Homework [Fleetwood Mac]
How Long Blues [Alexis Korner Blues Inc.]
I Be's Troubled [T.S. McPhee]
I've Been Down So Long [Gordon Smith]
It's Okay With Me Baby [Chicken Shack]
Long Tall Shorty [Graham Bond Organization]
Mean Old Frisco [Spencer Davis R & B Quartet]
Nothing In Rambling [Jo Ann Kelly]
Rockin' Pneumonia And The Boogie Woogie Flu [Jellybread]
Someday After Awhile [John Mayall's Bluesbreakers]
Stone Crazy [Aynsley Dunbar Retaliation]
Sugar Beet [Duster Bennett]
Take Out Some Insurance [Climax Blues Band]
That Did It [Key Largo]
Things Are Changing [Duster Bennett]
Tiger In Your Tank [Downliners]
True Blue [Savoy Brown]

6/1/74 · 198 · 2 · 185 History Of British Rock .... **$20** Sire 3702 [2]

Blue Turns To Grey [Cliff Richard]
Catch The Wind [Donovan] 23
Do Wah Diddy Diddy [Manfred Mann] 1
Don't Bring Me Down [Pretty Things]
Easy Livin [Uriah Heep] 39
Game Of Love [Wayne Fontana & The Mindbenders] 1
Glad All Over [Dave Clark Five] 6
Groovy Kind Of Love [Mindbenders] 2
Have I The Right? [Honeycombs] 5
Hippy Hippy Shake [Swinging Blue Jeans] 24
Hitchin' A Ride [Vanity Fare] 5
I Can't Let Go [Hollies] 42
I Like It [Gerry & The Pacemakers] 17
I Only Want To Be With You [Dusty Springfield] 12
I'm Telling You Now [Freddie & The Dreamers] 1
In The Summertime [Mungo Jerry] 3
Itchycoo Park [Small Faces] 16
Little Children [Billy J. Kramer With The Dakotas] 7
Maggie May [Rod Stewart] 1
Needles And Pins [Searchers] 13
New York Mining Disaster 1941 (Have You Seen My Wife, Mr. Jones) [Bee Gees] 14
Pictures Of Matchstick Men [Status Quo] 12
Sorrow [Merseys]
Sun Ain't Gonna Shine (Anymore) [Walker Bros.] 13
Wild Thing [Troggs] 1
World Without Love [Peter & Gordon] 1
You Really Got Me [Kinks] 7
You've Got To Hide Your Love Away [Silkie] 10

12/21/74+ · 141 · 11 · 186 History Of British Rock, Vol. 2 .... **$20** Sire 3705 [2]

Ain't She Sweet [Beatles] 19
All Day And All Of The Night [Kinks] 7
Bad To Me [Billy J. Kramer With The Dakotas] 9
Bits And Pieces [Dave Clark Five] 4
Brown Eyed Girl [Van Morrison] 10
Bus Stop [Hollies] 5
Call Me Lightning [Who] 40
Colours [Donovan] 61
Come And Get It [Badfinger] 7
Ferry Cross The Mersey [Gerry & The Pacemakers] 6
Fire [Crazy World Of Arthur Brown] 2
Girl Don't Come [Sandie Shaw] 42
Hush [Deep Purple] 4
I Go To Pieces [Peter & Gordon] 9
Lady Samantha [Elton John]
Lazy Sunday [Small Faces] (Lights Went Out In)
Massachusetts [Bee Gees] 11
Little Miss Understood [Rod Stewart]
Love Potion Number Nine [Searchers] 3
Mighty Quinn (Quinn The Eskimo) [Manfred Mann] 10
Silence Is Golden [Tremeloes] 11
Something In The Air [Thunderclap Newman] 37
Summer Song [Chad & Jeremy] 7
Sunshine Of Your Love [Cream] 5
This Wheel's On Fire [Julie Driscoll & Brian Auger]
Wishin' And Hopin' [Dusty Springfield] 6
With A Girl Like You [Troggs] 29
You're My World [Cilla Black] 26

11/22/75+ · 145 · 10 · 187 History Of British Rock, Volume 3 .... **$20** Sire 3712 [2]

Anyone For Tennis [Cream] 64
Because [Dave Clark Five] 3
Can't Help Thinkin' About Me [David Bowie & The Lower Third]
Concrete And Clay [Unit Four plus Two] 28
Day After Day [Badfinger] 4
Do You Want To Know A Secret [Billy J. Kramer & The Dakotas]
Here Comes The Night [Them] 24
How Do You Do It? [Gerry & The Pacemakers] 9
I've Gotta Get A Message To You [Bee Gees] 8
If Not For You [Olivia Newton-John] 25
In A Broken Dream [Python Lee Jackson] 56
Kentucky Woman [Deep Purple] 38
Layla [Derek & The Dominoes] 10
Long Tall Sally [Kinks]
Look Through Any Window [Hollies] 32
Love Is All Around [Troggs] 7
My Bonnie (My Bonnie Lies Over The Ocean) [Beatles w/Tony Sheridan]
Out Of Time [Chris Farlowe]
Pretty Flamingo [Manfred Mann] 29
Rock & Roll Madonna [Elton John]
San Franciscan Nights [Eric Burdon & The Animals] 9
She's Not There [Zombies] 2
Those Were The Days [Mary Hopkin] 2
Universal Soldier [Donovan] 53
When You Walk In The Room [Searchers] 35
Woman [Peter & Gordon] 14
Woodstock [Matthews' Southern Comfort] 23
You Don't Have To Say You Love Me [Dusty Springfield] 4

DEBUT	PEAK	WKS	RIAA	CD	ARTIST — Album Title	Catalog	Sym	$	Label & Number

4/6/68 · 187 · 3 · 188 · History Of Rhythm & Blues, Volume 1/The Roots 1947-52 · $20 · Atlantic 8161

Anytime, Anyplace, Anywhere [Laurie Tate & Joe Morris Orch.]
Chains Of Love [Joe Turner]
Cole Slaw [Frank Cully]
Don't You Know I Love You [Clovers]
Drinkin' Wine Spo-Dee-O-Dee ["Stick" McGhee]
5-10-15 Hours [Ruth Brown]
Goodnight Irene [Leadbelly]
Heavenly Father [Edna McGriff]
If You See The Tears In My Eyes [Delta Rhythm Boys]
It's Too Soon To Know [Orioles]
Ol' Man River [Ravens]
One Mint Julep [Clovers]
Shouldn't I Know [Cardinals]
Wheel Of Fortune [Cardinals]

3/30/68 · 173 · 5 · 189 · History Of Rhythm & Blues, Volume 2/The Golden Years 1953-55 · $20 · Atlantic 8162

Adorable [Drifters]
Beggar For Your Kisses [Diamonds]
Blue Velvet [Clovers]
Close Your Eyes [Five Keys]
Greenbacks [Ray Charles]
Honey Love [Drifters]
I've Got A Woman [Ray Charles]
Jam Up [Tommy Ridgeley]
Mama, He Treats Your Daughter Mean [Ruth Brown]
Money Honey [Drifters]
Sh-Boom [Chords]
Shake, Rattle & Roll [Joe Turner]
Tweedlee Dee [LaVern Baker] 14
Yes It's You [Clovers]

4/6/68 · 189 · 3 · 190 · History Of Rhythm & Blues, Volume 3/Rock & Roll 1956-57 · $20 · Atlantic 8163

C. C. Rider [Chuck Willis] 12
Corrine Corrina [Joe Turner] 41
Devil Or Angel [Clovers]
Down In The Alley [Clovers]
Fools Fall In Love [Drifters] 69
Jim Dandy [LaVern Baker] 17
Just To Hold My Hand [Clyde McPhatter] 26
Long Lonely Nights [Clyde McPhatter] 49
Ruby Baby [Drifters]
Searchin' [Coasters] 3
Since I Met You Baby [Ivory Joe Hunter] 12
Smokey Joe's Cafe [Robins] 79
Treasure Of Love [Clyde McPhatter] 16
Young Blood [Coasters] 8

4/6/68 · 180 · 4 · 191 · History Of Rhythm & Blues, Volume 4/The Big Beat 1958-60 · $20 · Atlantic 8164

Charlie Brown [Coasters] 2
Dance With Me [Drifters] 15
Gee Whiz (Look At His Eyes) [Carla Thomas] 10
I Count The Tears [Drifters] 17
I Cried A Tear [LaVern Baker] 6
(If You Cry) True Love, True Love [Drifters] 33
Lover's Question [Clyde McPhatter] 6
Poison Ivy [Coasters] 7
Save The Last Dance For Me [Drifters] 1
Spanish Harlem [Ben E. King] 10
Splish Splash [Bobby Darin] 3
There Goes My Baby [Drifters] 2
This Magic Moment [Drifters] 16
What'd I Say (Part I) [Ray Charles] 6
Yakety Yak [Coasters] 1

1/18/97 · 188 · 2 · ©192 · Hot Luv - The Ultimate Dance Songs Collection · $10 · EMI-Capitol 54547

Be My Lover [La Bouche] 6
Boombastic [Shaggy] 3
Get Ready For This [2 Unlimited] 38
Here Comes The Hotstepper [Ini Kamoze] 1
Macarena [Los Del Mar] 71
Missing [Everything But The Girl] 2
100% Pure Love [Crystal Waters] 11
Rhythm Of The Night [Corona] 11
Run Away [Real McCoy] 3
Sign, The [Ace Of Base] 1
This Is How We Do It [Montell Jordan] 1
Total Eclipse Of The Heart [Nicki French] 2

2/15/64 · 138 · 3 · 193 · Hot Rod Hootenanny [N] · $50 · Capitol 2010

Chopped Nash
Dragnutz
Eefen It Don't Go Chrome It
Fastest Shift Alive
Hot Rod Hootenanny
Mad'vette
Mr. Gasser
My Coupe Eefen Talks
Termites In My Woody
1320
Weirdo Wiggle
You Ain't Nothing But A Honda

12/14/63+ · 62 · 15 · 194 · Hot Rod Rally · $50 · Capitol 1997

'54 Corvette [Super Stocks]
Flash Falcon [Shutdown Douglas]
426 Superstock [Super Stocks]
Hot Rod City [Super Stocks]
Little Nifty Fifty [Super Stocks]
Little Stick Nomad [Super Stocks]
Little Street Machine [Hot Rod Rog]
Night Rod [Shutdown Douglas]
Repossession Blues [Hot Rod Rog]
Twin Cut Outs [Shutdown Douglas]
Wheel Man [Super Stocks]
Woody Walk [Shutdown Douglas]

5/24/97 · 113 · 2 · ©195 · House Connection Volume 1 · $10 · Aqua Boogie 0003

Be True To Your School [D.J. Appollo]
Big O Booty [Fast Eddie]
Butta [Pampa & DA]
Down With It [Mercury Man]
Feel The Rhythm [Gruv Station]
Get Down [Tony, Toni, Toné]
Get Up [Byron Stingley]
Grace, The [DJ Lonz Luv]
Horns [Dj Louis Love & DJ EDD]
I Found Something Real [Sandra Stephens]
In Love With Love [Kelly M]
Jazz It Up [Reel 2 Reel]
Keep Pushin' [Boris Dlugosch]
Let's Go Disco [Southern Comfort]
Mami [Artie The 1 Man Party Feat. Vienna]
Music Is My Life [Gee Zone]
Music Is Pumpin' [Underground People]
No One Can Love You More Than Me [Hahnah]
Nobody To Love [Dynamic Duo]
Now This [Dem Rats]
Ohh Baby [Steve Spinnin Santovo]
Party, The [Cassanovas]
Pump [SP-1200]
Restricted [CZR]
Rock The Beat [Tony B!]
Runaway [Nu Yorican Soul]
Sax Manis [Mijangos]
Somebody Knew [Rick Garcia]
Spark Da Meth [Da Mongoloids]
Stand Up [Love Tribe]
Sugar Is Sweeter [CJ Bolland]
That Sound [Pump Friction]
To The Three [SP-1200]
Way You Touch Me [D.J. Juanito Feat. Sunshine]
We Can Make It [Moné]
Wishing On A Star [88.3 Feat. Lisa May]
Work That Body [DJ Funk]
You Used To Hold Me [Xavier Gold]

1/19/63 · 56 · 19 · 196 · How To Strip For Your Husband [I] · $25 · Roulette 25186

instrumentals by Sonny Lester, with booklet How To Strip For Your Husband by strip-teaser Ann Corio
Blues To Strip By
Bumps & Grinds
Easter Parade
For Strippers Only
Lament
Lonely Little G-String
Pretty Girl Is Like A Melody
Raid, The
Seduction Of The Virgin Princess
Shivas Regal
Turkish
Walkin' & Strippin'

7/6/96 · 180 · 4 · ● · ©197 · Hunchback Of Notre Dame Sing-Along, The · $10 · Walt Disney 60894

features original cast recordings from The Hunchback Of Notre Dame movie and a 22-page, illustrated songbook with lyrics
Bells Of Notre Dame
Guy Like You
Heaven's Light
Out There
Topsy Turvy

4/10/76 · 177 · 2 · 198 · Hustle Hits! · $15 · De-Lite 2019

Dreaming A Dream [Crown Heights Affair] 43
Drive My Car [Gary Toms Empire] 69
Every Beat Of My Heart [Crown Heights Affair] 83
Girl From Ipanema [Zakariah]
Hustle Wit Every Muscle [Kay-Gees]
Mother Earth [Kool & The Gang]
7-6-5-4-3-2-1 (Blow Your Whistle) [Gary Toms Empire] 46
Spirit Of The Boogie [Kool & The Gang] 35
Sunny [Yambu]

9/16/00+ · 144 · 6 · ● · ©199 · I Could Sing Of Your Love Forever: 25 Modern Worship Songs · $15 · Worship 20282 [2]

Better Is One Day [Passion]
Come, Now Is The Time To Worship [Noel Richards]
Did You Feel The Mountains Tremble? [Matt Redman]
Every Move I Make [Passion]
Happy Song [Delirious?]
Heart Of Worship [Matt Redman w/Martin Smith]
I Could Sing Of Your Love Forever [SonicFlood]
I Will Exalt Your Name [Passion]
Jesus, Friend Of Sinners [Paul Oakley]
Jesus, Lover Of My Soul [Passion]
Joy [Tim Hughes]
Lord, Reign In Me [Brenton Brown]
Once Again [Matt Redman]
Open The Eyes Of My Heart [Praise Band]
Pour Out Your Spirit [Tom Lane]
Set Me On Fire [Burn Service]
Shout To The Lord [Matt Redman]
Shout To The North [Delirious?]
Thank You For The Blood [Matt Redman]
Trading My Sorrows [Darrell Evans]
We Fall Down [Passion]
We Want To See Jesus Lifted High [Noel Richards]
What A Friend I've Found [Stoneleigh Band]
You Are Merciful To Me [Ian White]
You're Worthy Of My Praise [Passion]

7/9/55 · 5 · 10 · 200 · I Like Jazz! [K] · $30 · Columbia 1

Four-Twenty, A.M. [Pete Rugolo]
Got Dem Blues [Turk Murphy]
Home Cooking [Eddie Condon]
I'll Never Be The Same [Teddy Wilson & Billie Holiday]
Jam Session [Original Benny Goodman Orchestra]
Jazz Lips [Louis Armstrong]
Makin' Time [Dave Brubeck]
Maple Leaf Rag [Wally Rose]
Merry-Go-Round [Duke Ellington]
Put It Right Here (Or Keep It Out There) [Bessie Smith]
Sensation Rag [Phil Napoleon]
Sentimental Baby [Bix Beiderbecke]

9/30/95 · 104 · 8 · ©201 · Idiot's Guide To Classical Music, The [I] · $10 · RCA Victor 62641

99 snippets of recognizable classical themes by 55 composers such as Bach, Beethoven, Chopin, Handel, Mendelssohn, Mozart, Pachelbel, Rachmaninoff, Ravel, Rossini, Schubert, Tchaikovsky, Verdi, Vivaldi and Wagner

VARIOUS ARTISTS COMPILATIONS

DEBUT	PEAK	WKS	RIAA	CD	ARTIST — Album Title	Catalog	Sym	$	Label & Number

10/1/94 · **70** · 8 · ©202 · **If I Were A Carpenter** .... · **$10** A&M 540258

Bless The Beasts And Children *[4 Non Blondes]*
Calling Occupants Of Interplanetary Craft *[Babes In Toyland]*
For All We Know *[Bettie Serveert]*
Goodbye To Love *[American Music Club]*
Hurting Each Other *[Johnette Napolitano w/Marc Moreland]*
It's Going To Take Some Time *[Dishwalla]*
Let Me Be The One *[Matthew Sweet]*
Rainy Days And Mondays *[Cracker]*
Solitaire *[Sheryl Crow]*
Superstar *[Sonic Youth]*
(They Long To Be) Close To You *[Cranberries]*
Top Of The World *[Shonen Knife]*
We've Only Just Begun *[Grant Lee Buffalo]*
Yesterday Once More *[Redd Kross]*

1/10/81 · **156** · 5 · ©203 · **In Harmony - A Sesame Street Record** .... · **$12** Sesame Street 3481

Be In Harmony *[Carly Simon]*
Blueberry Pie *[Bette Midler]*
Friend For All Seasons *[George Benson & Pauline Wilson]*
I Have A Song *[Lucy Simon]*
I Want A Horse *[Linda Ronstadt & Wendy Waldman]*
In Harmony *[Kate Taylor & The Simon-Taylor Family]*
Jelly Man Kelly *[James Taylor]*
One Good Turn *[Al Jarreau]*
Pajamas *[Livingston Taylor]*
Sailor And The Mermaid *[Libby Titus & Dr. John]*
Share *[Ernie & Cookie Monster]*
Wynken, Blynken And Nod *[Doobie Brothers]* 76

11/21/81 · **129** · 10 · · 204 · **In Harmony 2** .... · **$12** Columbia 37641

Ginny The Flying Girl *[Janis Ian]*
Here Comes The Rainbow *[Crystal Gayle]*
Maryanne *[Carly & Lucy Simon]*
Nobody Knows But Me *[Billy Joel]*
Owl And The Pussycat *[Lou Rawls & Deniece Williams]*
Reach Out And Touch (Somebody's Hand) *[Teddy Pendergrass]*
Santa Claus Is Comin' To Town *[Bruce Springsteen]*
Some Kitties Don't Care *[Kenny Loggins]*
Splish Splash *[Dr. John]*
Sunny Skies *[James Taylor]*

12/13/97 · **15** · 19 · ● · ©205 · **In Tha Beginning...There Was Rap** .... · **$10** Priority 50639

Big Ole Butt *[Sean "Puffy" Combs]*
Dopeman *[Mack 10]*
Freaky Tales *[Snoop Doggy Dogg]*
F--- Tha Police *[Bone thugs-n-harmony]*
I Need A Freak *[Too $hort]*
I'm Still #1 *[Cypress Hill]*
Knick Knack Patty Wack *[Tha Dogg Pound]*
Money (Dollar Bill Y'all) *[Coolio]*
Rapper's Delight *[Erick Sermon/Keith Murray/Redman]*
Show, The *[Roots]*
6 'N Tha Mornin' *[Master P]*
Sucker M.C.'s *[Wu-Tang Clan]*

11/4/95 · **106** · 3 · ©206 · **Inner City Blues - The Music Of Marvin Gaye** .... · **$10** Motown 0452

God Is Love (medley) *[Sounds Of Blackness]*
I Want You *[Madonna w/Massive Attack]*
Inner City Blues (Make Me Wanna Holler) *[Nona Gaye]*
Just To Keep You Satisfied *[Lisa Stansfield]*
Let's Get It On *[Boyz II Men]*
Like Marvin Gaye Said (What's Going On) *[Speech]*
Marvin, You're The Man *[Digable Planets]*
Mercy Mercy Me (medley) *[Sounds Of Blackness]*
Save The Children *[Bono]*
Stubborn Kind Of Fellow *[Stevie Wonder]*
Trouble Man *[Neneh Cherry]*

5/11/96 · **53** · 4 · ©207 · **Insomnia - The Erick Sermon Compilation Album** .... · **$10** Interscope 90060

As The... *[Passion]*
Beez Like That (Sometimes) *[Jamal & Calif]*
Fear *[Tommy Gunn]*
Funkorama *[Redman]*
I Feel It *[L.O.D.]*
It's That Hit *[Keith Murray]*
On The Regular *[Duo]*
Ready For War *[Domo]*
Reign *[Erick Sermon]*
Up Jump The Boogie *[Wixtons]*
Vibe, The *[Xross-Breed]*

12/26/87+ · **180** · 6 · ©208 · **Island Story, 1962-1987: 25th Anniversary, The** .... · **$15** Island 90684 [2]

Addicted To Love *[Robert Palmer]* 1
Adventures In Success *[Will Powers]*
All Right Now *[Free]* 4
Boops (Here To Go) *[Sly & Robbie]*
Broken English *[Marianne Faithfull]*
Cuba *[Gibson Brothers]* 81
Do Anything You Wanna Do *[Eddie & The Hot Rods]*
Eighteen With A Bullet *[Pete Wingfield]* 15
Forgotten Town *[Christians]*
Funky Kingston *[Toots & The Maytals]*
Harder They Come *[Jimmy Cliff]*
Innocent When You Dream (Bar Room) *[Tom Waits]*
Israelites *[Desmond Dekker & The Aces]* 9
Keep On Running *[Spencer Davis Group]* 76
Love Hurts *[Jim Capaldi]* 97
Montego Bay *[Amazulu]* 90
My Boy Lollipop *[Millie Small]* 2
Night Train *[Steve Winwood]*
No Woman No Cry *[Bob Marley & The Wailers]*
Now That We Found Love *[Third World]* 47
Padlock *[Gwen Guthrie]*
Paper Sun *[Traffic]* 94
Pull Up To The Bumper *[Grace Jones]*
Relax *[Frankie Goes To Hollywood]* 10
Si Tu Dois Partir *[Fairport Convention]*
Sinsemilla *[Black Uhuru]*
This Town Ain't Big Enough For The Both Of Us *[Sparks]*
Up Where We Belong *[Joe Cocker & Jennifer Warnes]* 1
Video Killed The Radio Star *[Buggles]* 40
With Or Without You *[U2]* 1
World Shut Your Mouth *[Julian Cope]* 84

10/23/99 · **58** · 5 · ©209 · **J Prince Presents Realest Niggaz Down South** .... · **$15** Rap-A-Lot 50119 [2]

Armageddon Comes *[3-6 Mafia]*
Catch Up *[Ludacris f/Fate & Infamous 2-0]*
Crank It Up *[5th Ward Boyz]*
Dirty MF *[C-Loc & K.B.]*
Do You Wanna Ride *[ESG f/Pimp Tyte]*
Good N' *[Goodie Mob]*
Got 2 Be A Thug *[Doracell]*
Homies & Thuggs *[Scarface f/Master P & Doracell]*
If U Only Knew *[Fat Pat]*
It Goes Down *[OCB]*
Live To Hustle *[Big Mike]*
Mind On My Money *[DJ Screw]*
Mo Problems *[Tela]*
One *[Scarface]*
P' In The Click *[Willie D]*
Paper *[Hoodlumz f/Tela]*
Payin' For P' *[Devin f/Jugg Mugg]*
Rap-A-Lot Worldwide *[Driza]*
Realest, The *[Scarface]*
Southern Comfort *[Big Mike f/Mystikal]*
Stop Playin *[Scarface f/Roy Jones, Jr.]*
Throw It Up *[Ace Deuce]*
U Don't Wanna *[Hot Boyz]*
Us B' *[Ghetto Twinz]*
Wanna Taste *[MC Breed f/Young La]*
Why U *[Tela f/Jermaine Dupri]*
Woodwheel *[UGK]*

12/22/90+ · **131** · 11 · ©210 · **Jam Harder - The A&M Underground Dance Compilation** .... · **$10** A&M 5339

Coming Back For More (Back Off Girl) *[La Mix]*
Feel The Rhythm *[Jazzi P]*
Got 2 B Free *[New Life]*
Groove Me *[Seduction]*
Hip House Party *[Overweight Pooch]*
I'm The One *[Steve Harvey]*
Tom's Diner *[D.N.A. feat. Suzanne Vega]* 5
Won't Stop Loving You *[Certain Ratio]*

12/18/65+ · **93** · 9 · · 211 · **James Blonde, Secret Agent 006.95, "The Man From T.A.N.T.E."** .... [C] · **$20** Colpix 495 / Weinstein's Apartment

Alone With Sissy Alot
At The Stage Delicatessen
Athletic Club
Goldflaker Bakery
Homeward Bound
In The Weapons Room
"M's" Office In London
On Fire Island With Dr. Nu?
President's Press Conference

2/19/00 · **181** · 2 · ©212 · **Jazz For A Rainy Afternoon** .... [I] · **$10** 32 Jazz 32061

Blue In Green *[Wallace Roney]*
Everything Must Change *[David "Fathead" Newman]*
I Can't Get Started *[Warren Vaché]*
Imagination *[Woody Shaw]*
My Ideal *[Sonny Criss]*
'Round Midnight *[Charles Brown]*
Ruby My Dear *[Hank Jones]*
Spring Can Really Hang You Up *[Houston Person]*
The Most *[Houston Person & Ron Carter]*
St. Louis Blues *[Johnny Lytle]*
Talk Of The Town *[Houston Person]*
Tribute To A Rose *[Jimmy Ponder]*

11/21/70+ · **❶3** · 101 · ● · ©213 · **Jesus Christ Superstar** .... · **$25** Decca 7206 [2]

Arrest, The
Blood Money (medley)
Crucifixion
Damned For All Time (medley)
Everything's Alright *[Yvonne Elliman]* 92
Gethsemane (I Only Want To Say)
Heaven On Their Minds
Hosanna
I Don't Know How To Love Him *[Yvonne Elliman]* 28
John Nineteen Forty-One
Judas' Death
King Herod's Song (Try It And See)
Last Supper
Peter's Denial
Pilate And Christ
Pilate's Dream
Poor Jerusalem (medley)
Simon Zealotes (medley)
Strange Thing Mystifying (medley)
Superstar *[Murray Head]* 14
Temple, The
This Jesus Must Die
Trial Before Pilate
What's The Buzz (medley)

11/6/71 · **183** · 7 · · 214 · **Jewish American Princess, The** .... [C] · **$15** Bell 6063

Allergy Doctor
Back From The Honeymoon
Boy Friends
Care And Feeding Of Judy Ann Pearlman
Engaged To Be Married
Enrollment, The
Everything You Have Always Wanted To Know About The Jewish American Princess
Guess Who's Coming To Dinner
Her First Home Away From Home
"In" Places
Jewish American Princess
Night Before The Wedding
Panic In The House
Peace March
Wedding Night

1112

DEBUT	PEAK	WKS	RIAA	CD	ARTIST — Album Title	Catalog	Sym	$	Label & Number

8/1/98 — **170** — **4** — ©215 **Jim Brickman's Visions Of Love** .... — **$10** Windham Hill 11342

After All These Years *[Anne Cochran]*
Getting Over You *[Janis Ian]*
Gift, The *[Jim Brickman w/Collin Raye & Susan Ashton]*
Like Love *[Phillip Ingram & Marilyn Harris]*
My Heart Belongs To You *[Peabo Bryson]*
One Heart One Love *[Phil Perry]*
Partners In Crime *[Jim Brickman & Dave Koz]*
Shower The People *[Amanda Upchurch]*
Still In Love *[Larry Stewart]*
That's What I'm Here For *[David Grow]*
We Live For Love *[Stephen Bishop]*
Your Love *[Michelle Wright]*

9/11/99 — **51** — **13** — ©216 **Jock Jams Volume 5** .... — **$10** Tommy Boy 1364

All I Have To Give *[Backstreet Boys]* 5
Burnin' Up *[Cevin Fisher]*
Can You Feel It!
Deep To Right Field!
Feel It *[Tamperer]*
Got To Be Real *[Cheryl Lynn]* 12
Hit The Showers
I'm Gonna Get You *[Bizarre Inc.]* 47
Mexican Hat Dance
Miami *[Will Smith]* 17
Nice And Slow *[Usher]* 1
Nobody's Supposed To Be Here *[Deborah Cox]* 2
Ray Of Light *[Madonna]* 5
Reach Up *[Perfecto All-Stars]*
Suavemente *[Elvis Crespo]* 84
Too Close *[Next]* 1
Turn It Up/Fire It Up *[Busta Rhymes]* 10
We Came To Play!
We Like To Party *[Vengaboys]* 26
Woof Woof *[69 Boyz]* 31
You Ugly

4/13/96 — **195** — **1** — ©217 **Johannes Brahms, Piano Concerto No. 1 - 16 Waltzes Op. 39** .... [I] **$10** Digital Master. 71812

Concerto for piano and orchestra no. 1 in D minor
16 waltzes op. 39

4/3/71 — **84** — **12** — ©218 **Joseph And The Amazing Technicolor Dreamcoat** .... **$15** Scepter 588

no individual song titles listed

5/13/95 — **145** — **8** — ● — ©219 **Keith Whitley - A Tribute Album** .... **$10** BNA 66416

All I Ever Loved Was You *[Ricky Skaggs & Shenandoah]*
Charlotte's In North Carolina *[Keith Whitley]*
Comeback Kid *[Keith Whitley]*
Don't Close Your Eyes *[Alan Jackson]*
I Just Want You *[Keith Whitley & Lorrie Morgan]*
I Never Go Around Mirrors *[Mark Chesnutt]*
I'm Gonna Hurt Her On The Radio *[Keith Whitley]*
I'm No Stranger To The Rain *[Joe Diffie]*
I'm Over You *[Tracy Lawrence]*
Little Boy Lost *[Daron Norwood]*
Ten Feet Away *[Diamond Rio]*
Voice Still Rings True *[Various Artists]*
When You Say Nothing At All *[Alison Krauss & Union Station]* 53

7/9/94 — **19** — **12** — ● — ©220 **Kiss My Ass: Classic Kiss Regrooved** .... **$10** Mercury 522123

Black Diamond *[Yoshiki]*
Calling Dr. Love *[Shandi's Addiction]*
Christine Sixteen *[Gin Blossoms]*
Detroit Rock City *[Mighty Mighty Bosstones]*
Deuce *[Lenny Kravitz]*
Goin' Blind *[Dinosaur Jr.]*
Hard Luck Woman *[Garth Brooks]*
Plaster Caster *[Lemonheads]*
Rock And Roll All Nite *[Toad The Wet Sprocket]*
She *[Anthrax]*
Strutter *[Extreme]*

9/1/90 — **92** — **8** — ©221 **Knebworth - The Album** .... [L] **$15** Polydor 84702 [2]

recorded on 6/30/90 in England
Badman's Song *[Tears For Fears]*
Comfortably Numb *[Pink Floyd]*
Coming Up *[Paul McCartney]*
Dirty Water *[Status Quo]*
Do You Wanna Dance *[Cliff Richard & The Shadows]*
Everybody Wants To Rule The World *[Tears For Fears]*
Hey Jude *[Paul McCartney]*
Hurting Kind *[Robert Plant]*
(I Can't Get No) Satisfaction (medley) *[Genesis]*
In The Midnight Hour (medley) *[Genesis]*
Liars Dance *[Robert Plant]*
Mama *[Genesis]*
On The Beach *[Cliff Richard & The Shadows]*
Pinball Wizard (medley) *[Genesis]*
Reach Out I'll Be There (medley) *[Genesis]*
Rockin' All Over The World *[Status Quo]*
Run Like Hell *[Pink Floyd]*
Sad Songs (Say So Much) *[Elton John]*
Saturday Night's All Right (For Fighting) *[Elton John]*
Somebody To Love (medley) *[Genesis]*
Sunshine Of Your Love *[Eric Clapton]*
Sussudio *[Phil Collins]*
Tall Cool One *[Robert Plant]*
Think I Love You Too Much *[Dire Straits]*
Turn It On Again (medley) *[Genesis]*
Twist And Shout (medley) *[Genesis]*
Wearing And Tearing *[Robert Plant]*
Whatever You Want *[Status Quo]*
You've Lost That Lovin' Feeling (medley) *[Genesis]*

8/14/99 — **152** — **8** — ©222 **Latin Mix USA 2** .... [F] **$10** Sony Discos 69989

Ciega Sordomuda *[Shakira]*
Como Baila *[Grupo Mania]*
Diselo Con Flores *[Fey]*
Groove With Me Tonight *[MDO]*
In The Zone *[Ivy Queen Feat. Wyclef Jean]*
Livin' La Vida Loca *[Ricky Martin]* 1
Magdalena, Mi Amor *[DLG]*
Miami *[Will Smith]* 17
No Me Ames *[Jennifer Lopez & Marc Anthony]*
Que Tu Tienes *[Jennifer Delgado]*
Salomé *[Chayanne]*
Suavemente *[Elvis Crespo]* 84

10/4/97 — **169** — **1** — ©223 **Lawhouse Experience Volume One** .... **$10** Street Life 75525

Arch Angels *[Ras Kass Feat. Xzibit]*
Entrance *[Coolio/Kokane]*
Exit *[Kokane]*
Give It Up *[W.C.]*
I Just Wanna Play *[L.V.]*
Legal Paper *[Ice Cube]*
Lil' Sumpin' *[Kausion]*
Live Yo Life *[Luniz Feat. Dru Down]*
One Way In *[Go Mack]*
Phalosmode *[Phalos]*
Spank That Ass *[Phat Freddie]*
Westcyde 242 *[Da Pharcyde]*
World Wide *[K-Dee]*
You Might Get Stuck *[Above The Law]*
Your Hustle Ain't On *[Ice-T]*

4/11/98 — **86** — **7** — ©224 **Legacy: A Tribute To Fleetwood Mac's Rumours** .... **$10** Lava 83054

Chain, The *[Shawn Colvin]*
Don't Stop *[Elton John]*
Dreams *[Corrs]*
Go Your Own Way *[Cranberries]*
Gold Dust Woman *[Sister Hazel]*
I Don't Want To Know *[Goo Goo Dolls]*
Never Going Back Again *[Matchbox 20]*
Oh Daddy *[Tallulah]*
Second Hand News *[Tonic]*
Songbird *[Duncan Sheik]*
You Make Loving Fun *[Jewel]*

12/6/80 — **154** — **13** — ©225 **Legend Of Jesse James, The** .... **$12** A&M 3718

Death Of Me *[Johnny Cash & Levon Helm]*
Have You Heard The News? *[Albert Lee]*
Heaven Ain't Ready For You Yet *[Emmylou Harris]*
Help Him, Jesus *[Johnny Cash]*
High Walls *[Levon Helm]*
Hunt Them Down *[Albert Lee]*
Northfield: The Disaster *[Charlie Daniels]*
Northfield: The Plan *[Levon Helm]*
Old Clay County *[Charlie Daniels & Levon Helm]*
One More Shot *[Levon Helm]*
Plot, The *[Paul Kennerley]*
Quantrill's Guerillas *[Levon Helm]*
Ride Of The Redlegs *[Rodney Crowell/Jody Payne/Levon Helm/Rosanne Cash]*
Riding With Jesse James *[Charlie Daniels]*
Six Gun Shooting *[Johnny Cash]*
Wish We Were Back In Missouri *[Emmylou Harris]*

8/6/77 — **121** — **9** — 226 **Let's Clean Up The Ghetto** .... **$12** Philadelphia Int. 34659

Big Gangster *[O'Jays]*
Everybody's Talkin' *[Harold Melvin & The Blue Notes]*
Let's Clean Up The Ghetto *[Philadelphia International All Stars]* 91
New Day, New World Comin' *[Billy Paul]*
Now Is The Time To Do It *[Teddy Pendergrass]*
Old People *[Archie Bell & The Drells]*
Ooh Child *[Dee Dee Sharp Gamble]*
Save The Children *[Intruders]*
Trade Winds *[Lou Rawls]*
Year Of Decision *[Three Degrees]*

5/8/99 — **172** — **2** — ©227 **Life In The Fat Lane - Fat Music Vol. IV** .... **$10** Fat Wreck Chords 585

Coming Too Close *[No Use For A Name]*
Do You Wanna Fight Me *[Frenzal Rhomb]*
Dummy Up *[Screeching Weasel]*
Exumation Of Virginia Madison *[Strung Out]*
Heresy, Hypocrisy And Revenge *[Good Riddance]*
Keep The Beat *[Snuff]*
May 16 *[Lagwagon]*
My Favorite Things *[Me First & The Gimme Gimme's]*
Old School Pig *[Tilt]*
Part Time SF Ecologist *[Goober Patrol]*
Pass The Buck *[Sick Of It All]*
Plan, The *[NOFX]*
Promise To Distinction *[Swingin' Utters]*
Quadret Im Kreis *[Wizo]*
Road Rash *[Mad Caddies]*
San Dimas High School Football Rules *[Ataris]*
Taken *[Avail]*
Twat Called Maurice *[Consumed]*

VARIOUS ARTISTS COMPILATIONS

DEBUT	PEAK	WKS	RIAA	CD	ARTIST — Album Title	Catalog	Sym	$	Label & Number

5/16/98 — 24 — 15 ▲ — ©228 — Lilith Fair: A Celebration Of Women In Music [L] $15 — Arista 19007 [2]
songs by Paula Cole, Emmylou Harris, Lisa Loeb, Sarah McLachlan, Suzanne Vega, and others
- Been It [Cardigans]
- Building A Mystery [Sarah McLachlan]
- Cain [Patty Griffin]
- Charm [Wild Colonials]
- El Payande [Lhasa]
- Eternal Flame [Susanna Hoffs]
- Falling In Love [Lisa Loeb]
- Four Leaf Clover [Abra Moore]
- Going Back To Harlan [Emmylou Harris]
- Hold Me Jordan [Tara MacLean]
- I Don't Want To Think About It [Wild Strawberries]
- I Want [Dayna Manning]
- Ladder [Joan Osborne]
- Lama Dorje Chang [Yungchen Lhamo]
- Loneliness Of The Long Distance Runner [September 67]
- Mississippi [Paula Cole]
- One, The [Tracy Bonham]
- Periwinkle Sky [Victoria Williams]
- Rock In This Pocket (Song Of David) [Suzanne Vega]
- Scooter Boys [Indigo Girls]
- Sur Tes Pas [Autour de Lucie]
- Trouble [Shawn Colvin]
- Wash My Hands [Meredith Brooks]
- Water Is Wide [Indigo Girls/Jewel/Sarah McLachlan]
- What Do You Hear In These Sounds [Dar Williams]

6/5/99 — 87 — 2 — ©229 — Lilith Fair: A Celebration Of Women In Music Volume 2 [L] $10 — Arista 19079
- Angel [Sarah McLachlan w/Emmylou Harris]
- Elmo [Holly McNarland]
- Fire On Babylon [Sinéad O'Connor]
- I Do [Lisa Loeb]
- In The Ghetto [Natalie Merchant]
- Island [Heather Nova]
- Life [Queen Latifah]
- Meat Hook [Tracy Bonham]
- Miles From Our Home [Cowboy Junkies]
- Never Know [Angelique Kidjo]
- New Thing Now [Shawn Colvin]
- Sea, The [Morcheeba]
- Sway [Bic Runga]
- Trampoline [Wild Strawberries]

6/5/99 — 98 — 2 — ©230 — Lilith Fair: A Celebration Of Women In Music Volume 3 [L] $10 — Arista 19081
- Black & White [Sarah McLachlan]
- Deeper Well [Emmylou Harris]
- Get Out The Map [Indigo Girls]
- Kiss Me [Sixpence None The Richer]
- Little Black Girl [Rebekah]
- Luka [Suzanne Vega]
- Naked Eye [Luscious Jackson]
- Never Said [Liz Phair]
- Not An Addict [K's Choice]
- Onion Girl [Holly Cole]
- Soul Record [Me'Shell Ndegéocello]
- Spit Of Love [Bonnie Raitt]
- Surrounded [Chantal Kreviazuk]
- Underneath A Red Moon [N'Dea Davenport]

7/2/94 — 40 — 53 ▲ — 231 — Lion King Sing-Along, The $10 — Walt Disney 60857
features original cast recordings from The Lion King movie and a 20-page, illustrated lyric book; available only on cassette
- Be Prepared
- Can You Feel The Love Tonight
- Circle Of Life
- Hakuna Matata
- I Just Can't Wait To Be King

10/25/69 — 200 — 2 — 232 — Live At Bill Graham's Fillmore West [L] $20 — Columbia 9893
- Blues On A Westside [Nick Gravenites]
- Carmelita Skiffle [Mike Bloomfield]
- It Takes Time [Nick Gravenites]
- It's About Time [Nick Gravenites]
- Love Got Me [Bob Jones]
- Oh Mama [Mike Bloomfield]
- One More Mile To Go [Taj Mahal]

6/7/86 — 105 — 7 — 233 — Live! For Life [L] $10 — I.R.S. 5731
- Ages Of You [R.E.M.]
- Hero Takes A Fall [Bangles]
- Howling Man [Alarm]
- I Been Down So Long [Sting]
- Lively Up Yourself [Bob Marley & The Wailers]
- Love Lessons [Stewart Copeland & Derek Holt]
- Take Your Medicine [Oingo Boingo]
- Tempted [Squeeze]
- Tenderness [General Public]
- We Got The Beat [Go-Go's]

5/6/00 — 175 — 2 — ©234 — Loaded With Hits $15 — Foundation 99715 [2]
- Anytime [Brian McKnight]
- As Long As You Love Me [Backstreet Boys]
- Beautiful Skin [Goodie Mob]
- **Blue On Black** [Kenny Wayne Shepherd] 78
- **Building A Mystery** [Sarah McLachlan] 13
- **C'est La Vie** [B*Witched] 9
- **Come And Get With Me** [Keith Sweat] 12
- Do You Really Want Me (Show Respect) [Robyn]
- Don't Drink The Water [Dave Matthews Band]
- **Freshmen, The** [Verve Pipe] 5
- **Home Alone** [R. Kelly] 65
- **I Do** [Lisa Loeb] 17
- **I Want You Back** [*NSYNC] 13
- **I'm Not A Player** [Big Punisher] 57
- Immortality [Celine Dion]
- **Inside Out** [Eve 6] 28
- **Jackie's Strength** [Tori Amos] 54
- **Just The Two Of Us** [Will Smith] 20
- Love For All Seasons [Christina Aguilera]
- **Make It Hot** [Nicole] 5
- **Maria** [Blondie] 82
- **My All** [Mariah Carey] 1
- My Own Prison [Creed]
- **Save Tonight** [Eagle Eye Cherry] 5
- **Step Into A World (Rapture's Delight)** [KRS-One] 70
- **Stop** [Spice Girls] 16
- **Torn** [Natalie Imbruglia] 42
- Urgently In Love [Billy Crawford Feat. Nona Hendryx]
- **When The Lights Go Out** [Five] 10

9/23/00 — 108 — 4 — ©235 — Loud Rocks $10 — Loud 62201
- Caribbean Connection [Shootyz Groove/Big Pun]
- For Heaven's Sake 2000 [Ozzy Osbourne & Tony Iommi]
- Hip Hop [Static-X/Dead Prez]
- How Bout Some Hardcore [Butch Vig/M.O.P.]
- Los Angeles Times [Endo/Xzibit]
- Make Room [Sugar Ray/Tha Alkaholiks]
- Only When I'm Drunk [Crazy Town/Tha Alkaholiks]
- Shame [System Of A Down/Wu-Tang Clan]
- Shook Ones Part II [Everlast/Mobb Deep]
- Still Not A Player [Incubus/Big Pun]
- Survival Of The Fittest [Sick Of It All/Mobb Deep]
- What U See Is What U Get [Sevendust/Xzibit]
- Wu-Tang Clan Ain't Nothing Ta F*** Wit [Tom Morello & Chad Smith/Wu-Tang Clan]

4/13/96 — 174 — 1 — ©236 — Ludwig Van Beethoven, Symphony No. 5 - Violin Romances No. 2+1 [I] $10 — Digital Master. 71805
- Romance for Violin and Orchestra no. 2 in F major op. 50
- Romance for Violin and Orchestra no. 1 in G major op. 40
- Symphony no. 5 in C minor op. 67

1/20/68 — 176 — 5 — 237 — Lyndon Johnson's Lonely Hearts Club Band [C] $20 — Atco 230
featuring the actual recorded voices of political leaders
- Governor Ronald Reagan
- Mrs. Ladybird Johnson
- President Lyndon B. Johnson
- Senator Barry Goldwater
- Senator Everett Dirksen
- Senator Robert Kennedy
- Vice President Hubert Humphrey
- Vice President Richard Nixon

5/23/98 — 167 — 2 — ©238 — Lyricist Lounge Volume One [L] $15 — Open Mic 1129 [2]
- Action Guaranteed [O.C. & Ras Kass]
- After The Show
- All In My Own [Mike Zoot]
- Bathroom Cipher [Hazadus/J-Treds/Thirstin Howl III/Kwest/I.G. Off]
- Be OK [Bahamadia & Rah Digga]
- Blood [Sarah Jones]
- Body Rock [Mos Def]
- Bring Hip-Hop Back [Cipher Complete]
- C.I.A. (Criminals In Action) [KRS-One/Zack De La Rocha/Last Emperor]
- Da Cipher [Punch & Words]
- Famous Last Words [Word A'Mouth]
- Holy Water [Lord Have Mercy More & D.V. alias Khrist]
- Jayou [Jurassic 5]
- Keep Pouring [Diaz Brothers]
- Live from the D.J. Stretch Armstrong Show
- Lyrics [A.L. (All Lyrics)]
- Maifesto [Talib Kweli]
- Mayday [Natural Elements]
- No Matter [Prime]
- Ohm [Saul Williams]
- Outside The Lounge
- Phone Call (skit)
- Society [Problemz]
- Street Promoters (skit)
- Weight [Indelible MCs]

12/16/00 — 33 — 15 — ©239 — Lyricist Lounge Volume Two [L] $10 — Rawkus 26131
- Battle [Erick Sermon feat. Sy Scott]
- Get That Dough [Beanie Sigel]
- Get Up [Cocoa Brovaz]
- Grimy Ways [Big Noyd & Prodigy]
- I've Committed Murder [Macy Gray]
- Legendary Street Team [Kool G Rap & M.O.P.]
- Let's Grow [Royce Da 5'9"]
- Makin' It Blend [Q-Tip & Words]
- Ms. Fat Booty 2 [Mos Def & Ghostface Killah]
- Oh No [Mos Def & Pharoahe Monch feat. Nate Dogg]
- Right And Exact [Dilated Peoples]
- Sharp Shooters [Talib Kweli & Dead Prez]
- 16 Bars [Notorious B.I.G.]
- Still Here [Big L feat. C-Town]
- W.K.Y.A. [Saukrates feat. Redman]
- Watcha [Master Fúol feat. JT Money & Pastor Troy]

7/27/96 — 65 — 20 ● — ©240 — Macarena Club Cutz $10 — RCA 66745
- Can You Feel It [Matrix]
- Don't Stop Me Now [Loft]
- Everything [Hysterix]
- Gotta Find Love [Layla]
- I Was Made For Loving You [Chill]
- Let Me In Your Heart [Lisa Nilsson]
- Lookin' Up [Michelle Gayle]
- Love Me The Right Way [Rapination]
- **Macarena** [Los Del Rio] 1
- Movin' Up [Dreamworld]
- **Scatman (Ski-Ba-Bop-Ba-Dop-Bop)** [Scatman John] 60
- Wait (For Our Love To Find Us) [Legacy Of Sound]

7/27/96 — 85 — 13 — ©241 — Macarena Mix [F] $10 — BMG 31388
- All My Loving [Los Manolos]
- Amigos Para Siempre [Los Manolos]
- La Señal [Sandalo]
- **Macarena** [Los Del Rio] 1
- Pedro Navaja [El Lupe]
- Ritmo De La Noche [Secados]
- Te Informo [Sandalo]
- Una Aventura [Los Manolos]

DEBUT	PEAK	WKS	RIAA	CD	ARTIST — Album Title	Catalog	Sym	$	Label & Number
7/28/62	108	14		242	**Mad "Twists" Rock 'n' Roll**	[N]		$100	Big Top 1305

Agnes — High School Basketball Game — Nose Job — Pretzel
Blind Date — I'll Always Remember Being Young — Pimples Turned To Dimples — Serious Teenager In Love
Boys' Bathroom Wall — My Johnny's Hub Cap — Please, Betty Jane — Somebody Else's Dandruff

| 12/16/89+ | 87 | 15 | ©243 | | **Make A Difference Foundation: Stairway To Heaven/Highway To Hell** ... | [L] | | $10 | Mercury 842093 |

recorded on 8/12/89 at the Moscow Music Peace Festival
Blue Suede Shoes (medley) [Bon Jovi & Cinderella] — Hound Dog [Bon Jovi & Cinderella] — Moby Dick [Drum Madness] — Rock And Roll [Skid Row & Motley Crue]
Boys Are Back In Town [Bon Jovi] — I Can't Explain [Scorpions] — Move Over [Cinderella]
Holidays In The Sun [Skid Row] — Long Tall Sally (medley) [Scorpions & Gorky Park] — My Generation [Gorky Park] — Teaser [Motley Crue]
— Purple Haze [Ozzy Osbourne]

| 10/7/72 | 186 | 7 | | 244 | **Mar Y Sol** .... | [L] | | $20 | Atco 705 [2] |

recorded on 4/1/72 in Puerto Rico
Ain't Wastin' Time No More [Allman Brothers Band] — Looking For A Love [J. Geils Band] — Sometimes In The Morning [Jonathan Edwards] — Wang Dang Doodle [Dr. John]
Bedroom Mazurka [Cactus] — Lucky Man (medley) [Emerson, Lake & Palmer] — Take A Pebble (medley) [Emerson, Lake & Palmer] — Why I Sing The Blues [B.B. King]
Bring My Baby Back [John Baldry] — Noonward Race [Mahavishnu Orchestra w/John McLaughlin] — Texas Blues (medley) [Nitzinger]
Do You Know [Osibisa] — Respect Yourself [Herbie Mann] — Train Of Glory [Jonathan Edwards]
Jelly Roll (medley) [Nitzinger]

| 7/10/99 | 97 | 6 | ©245 | | **Marvin Is 60 - A Tribute Album** .... | | | $10 | Motown 549520 |

songs by Erykah Badu, El DeBarge, Will Downing, Brian McKnight, and others
Distant Lover [Brian McKnight] — Just To Keep Her Satisfied [Kenny Lattimore] — Soon I'll Be Loving You Again [Joe] — Your Precious Love [Erykah Badu & D'Angelo]
Got To Give It Up [Zhané] — Let's Get It On [Gerald Levert] — Til Tomorrow [Chico DeBarge]
I Want You [Montell Jordan] — Mercy Mercy Me [Jon B.] — What's Going On [Profyle]
If This World Were Mine [Grenique & Tony Rich] — Sexual Healing [El DeBarge] — You Sure Love To Ball [Will Downing]

| 6/12/99 | 62 | 5 | ©246 | | **Master P Presents: No Limit All Stars - Who U Wit?** .... | | | $10 | No Limit 50106 |

B-Ball — Give Me The Rock [Ghetto Commission] — **It Ain't My Fault 2** [Silkk The Shocker & Mystikal] — Smash & Ball [Mr. Serv-On]
B-Ballin On My Block [C-Murder] — Hoop Dreams (He Got Game) [Snoop Dogg] — Pass The Ball [2 for 1] — Such A Bad Girl [Mia X]
Bring It 2 U [Lil Soldiers] — I'm Hot [Big Ed] — Put Me In Tha Game [Mac] — **Woof** [Snoop Dogg/Mystikal/Fiend] **62**
Cold Wit It [Fiend] — Shake 'Em Off [Reginelli & P'heno] — You Ain't A Baller [Magic]

| 12/11/99 | 82 | 1 | ©247 | | **McCaughey Septuplets: Sweet Dreams, The** .... | | | $10 | Word 63922 |

Dreamland [Cindy Morgan] — Loving You Eternally [Michael W. Smith] — Oh What Dreams [Chris Rice] — 'Tis So Sweet [Kenny & Bobbi McCaughey]
Goodnight Emily [Steve Green] — My Dream Come True [Geoff Moore] — Over And Under [Cindy Morgan] — Up To The Moon [Kathie Lee Gifford]
He'll Take Care Of You [Kim Hill] — Peace Be Still [Sandi Patty]
Hush My Dear [Ginny Owens] — Sleepytime Suites 1-4

| 10/17/98 | 9 | 7 | ● ©248 | | **Mean Green - Major Players Compilation** | | | $10 | No Limit 53505 |

Ashes And Dust [Gambino Family] — Dying In My City [C-Murder/Snoop Dogg/Magic] — Luv 4 Me [Mr. Serv-On & Full Blooded] — Mirror Don't Lie [2 For 1]
Better Player [Too $hort] — For Ya Troubles [Prime Suspects] — M G Theme [Steady Mobb'n] — Sucka Repellent [E-40 & Suga T]
Bigga Than... [B-Legit & C-Murder] — Gotta Have Cash [Mack 10 & The Comrads] — Major Players [Master P/Mia X/Silkk The Shocker/Porsha] — Tell Me When [Mo B. Dick]
Close 2 You [Lil' Soldiers] — Mean Green (Intro Commercial) — That's The Nigga [Mystikal]
Devil's Playground [Commission] — Tossed Up [UGK]
Don't Be Mad [Passion] — We... [Fiend & Mac]

| 7/15/72 | 176 | 7 | | 249 | **Metropolitan Opera Gala Honoring Sir Rudolf Bing** .... | [L] | | $15 | DG 2530 260 |

Die Fledermaus [Regina Resnik] — Gia Nella Notte Densa [Teresa Zylis-Gara & Franco Corelli] — Salome: Final Scene [Brigit Nilsson] — Tu, Tu, Amore? Tu? [Montserrat Caballe/Placido Domingo]
Dove Sono [Leontyne Price] — Invano Alvaro [Richard Tucker & Robert Merrill] — Tacea La Notte Placida [Martina Arroyo]

| 4/12/80 | 35 | 27 | ▲ ©250 | | **Mickey Mouse Disco** .... | | | $12 | Disneyland 2504 |

Chim Chim Cher-ee — It's A Small World — Watch Out For Goofy
Disco Mickey Mouse — Macho Duck — Welcome To Rio
Greatest Band — Mousetrap — Zip-A-Dee-Doo-Dah

| 12/3/94 | 173 | 4 | ©251 | | **Mickey Unrapped** .... | | | $10 | Walt Disney 60627 |

Bowww To The Beat [Whoopi Goldberg] — Ducks In The 'Hood — Mickey Mouse Club Mix — **Whoomp! (There It Went)** [Tag Team] **97**
Color Of Music [Color Me Badd] — Ice Ice Mickey — Minnie Mouse In The House
D.J. Goof — Little Red Rappinghood — U Can't Botch This
— M.C. Mickey — Whatta Mouse

| 1/27/79 | 122 | 8 | ©252 | | **Milestone Jazzstars In Concert** .... | [I-L] | | $20 | Milestone 55006 [2] |

all-star group: **McCoy Tyner/Ron Carter**/Sonny Rollins/Al Foster
Alone Together — Don't Stop The Carnival — N.O. Blues
Continuum — In A Sentimental Mood — Nubia
Cutting Edge — Little Pianissimo — Willow Weep For Me

| 3/20/99 | 195 | 2 | ©253 | | **Millennium Classic Rock Party** .... | | | $10 | Rhino 75628 |

American Woman [Guess Who] **1** — Free Bird [Lynyrd Skynyrd] **19** — No More Mr. Nice Guy [Alice Cooper] **25** — **Smoke On The Water** [Deep Purple] **4**
Aqualung [Jethro Tull] — **Hocus Pocus** [Focus] **9** — Radar Love [Golden Earring] **13** — **25 Or 6 To 4** [Chicago] **4**
China Grove [Doobie Brothers] **15** — **Hot Blooded** [Foreigner] **3** — Ramblin Man [Allman Brothers Band] **2** — We Will Rock You [Queen] **52**
Do You Feel Like We Do [Peter Frampton] **10** — Joy To The World [Three Dog Night] **1** — Rock'n Me [Steve Miller] **1** — You Ain't Seen Nothing Yet [Bachman Turner Overdrive] **1**
Don't Stop [Fleetwood Mac] **3** — More Than A Feeling [Boston] **5** — Sister Golden Hair [America] **1**
Fame [David Bowie] **1**

| 11/13/99 | 179 | 1 | ©254 | | **Millennium '80s New Wave Party** .... | | | $10 | Rhino 75923 |

Cars [Gary Numan] **9** — I Ran (So Far Away) [Flock Of Seagulls] **9** — Mickey [Toni Basil] **1** — **Sweet Dreams (Are Made Of This)** [Eurythmics] **1**
Come On Eileen [Dexy's Midnight Runners] **1** — I Want Candy [Bow Wow Wow] **62** — Our House [Madness] **7** — **Tainted Love** [Soft Cell] **8**
Everybody Have Fun Tonight [Wang Chung] **2** — In The Name Of Love [Thompson Twins] — Rock Lobster [B-52's] **56** — Take On Me [A-Ha] **1**
I Melt With You [Modern English] **78** — **Just What I Needed** [Cars] **27** — Rock This Town [Stray Cats] **9** — Valley Girl [Frank & Moon Zappa] **2**
— Love Plus One [Haircut One Hundred] **37** — Safety Dance [Men Without Hats] **3** — **Whip It** [Devo] **14**
— — She Blinded Me With Science [Thomas Dolby] **5**

VARIOUS ARTISTS COMPILATIONS

DEBUT	PEAK	WKS	RIAA	CD	ARTIST — Album Title	Catalog	Sym	$	Label & Number

8/1/98 — **124** — 12 — ©255 — **Millennium Funk Party** — **$10** Rhino 75467
- Atomic Dog [George Clinton]
- Best Of My Love [Emotions] 1
- Brick House [Commodores] 5
- Dazz [Brick] 3
- Do It ('Til You're Satisfied) [B.T. Express] 2
- Fantastic Voyage [Lakeside] 55
- I'll Take You There [Staple Singers] 1
- Jungle Boogie [Kool & The Gang] 4
- Love Rollercoaster [Ohio Players] 1
- More Bounce To The Ounce Part I [Zapp] 86
- Pick Up The Pieces [AWB] 5
- Play That Funky Music [Wild Cherry] 1
- Rapper's Delight [Sugarhill Gang] 36
- Serpentine Fire [Earth, Wind & Fire] 13
- Slide [Slave] 32
- Superfly [Curtis Mayfield] 8
- Tear The Roof Off The Sucker (Give Up The Funk) [Parliament] 15
- Tell Me Something Good [Rufus] 3
- What Is Hip? [Tower Of Power] 91
- You Dropped A Bomb On Me [Gap Band] 31

5/22/99 — **63** — 45 — ● — ©256 — **Millennium Hip-Hop Party** — **$10** Rhino 75699
- Around The Way Girl [L.L. Cool J] 9
- Baby Got Back [Sir Mix-A-Lot] 1
- Bust A Move [Young MC] 7
- Funky Cold Medina [Tone Loc] 3
- Good Vibrations [Marky Mark & The Funky Bunch] 1
- Hip Hop Hooray [Naughty By Nature] 8
- Humpty Dance [Digital Underground] 11
- It Takes Two [Rob Base & D.J. E-Z Rock] 36
- Jump Around [House Of Pain] 3
- Now That We Found Love [Heavy D. & The Boys] 11
- Nuthin' But A "G" Thang [Dr. Dre] 2
- Parents Just Don't Understand [D.J. Jazzy Jeff & The Fresh Prince] 12
- Set Adrift On Memory Bliss [PM Dawn] 1
- Tennessee [Arrested Development] 6
- U Can't Touch This [M.C. Hammer]
- Walk This Way [Run-D.M.C.] 4
- What's My Name? [Snoop Doggy Dogg] 8
- White Lines (Don't Don't Do It) [Grandmaster & Melle Mel]

1/20/01 — **47**[C] — 1 — ©257 — **Mob Hits** — **$15** Triage 96401 [2]
- Al-Di-La [Jerry Vale]
- Angelina (medley) [Louis Prima]
- Buona Sera [Louis Prima]
- Domani (Tomorrow) [Julius La Rosa] 13
- Eh Cumpari [Julius La Rosa]
- Godfather Waltz
- I Have But One Heart [Al Martino]
- Innamorata [Dean Martin] 27
- Lazy Mary [Lou Monte] 12
- Love Me The Way I Love You [Jerry Vale]
- Mambo Italiano [Rosemary Clooney]
- My Way [Paul Anka]
- Non Dimentica [Jerry Vale]
- Oh Marie [Louis Prima]
- On An Evening In Roma [Dean Martin] 59
- Pretend You Don't See Her [Jerry Vale]
- Return To Me [Dean Martin] 4
- Roman Guitar [Lou Monte]
- Speak Softly Love [Al Martino] 80
- That's Amore [Dean Martin]
- Volare (Nel Blu Di Pinto Di Blu) [Dean Martin] 12
- Zooma Zooma (medley) [Louis Prima]

7/20/96 — **98** — 6 — ©258 — **MOM - Music For Our Mother Ocean** — **$10** Surfdog 90062
- Army Of Me [Helmet]
- Bad Fish [Sublime]
- Bali Eyes [Porno For Pyros]
- Blackwing [Seven Mary Three]
- California Sun [Ramones]
- Good Times [Sprung Monkey]
- Gremmie Out Of Control [Pearl Jam]
- Hateful [Everclear]
- Honky Tonk [Brian Setzer Orchestra]
- I Can't Surf [Reverend Horton Heat]
- Mama Nature [Pato Banton & The Reggae Revolution]
- Mr. Know It All [Primus]
- My Wave [Soundgarden]
- Netty's Girl [Beastie Boys]
- Never Give Up [Common Sense]
- Quiet Warrior [Jewel]
- Sailin' On [No Doubt]
- Surfin' Bird [Silverchair]
- Surfin' USA [Pennywise]
- Waggy [Blink-182]
- Wipeout [Gary Hoey with Donavon Frankenreiter]

7/17/99 — **27** — 39 — ▲ — ©259 — **Monster Ballads** — **$10** Razor & Tie 89024
- Almost Paradise [Mike Reno & Ann Wilson] 7
- Carrie [Europe] 3
- Don't Close Your Eyes [Kix] 11
- Don't Know What You Got Til It's Gone [Cinderella] 12
- Headed For A Heartbreak [Winger] 19
- Heaven [Warrant] 2
- High Enough [Damn Yankees] 3
- I'll Never Let You Go (Angel Eyes) [Steelheart] 23
- Is This Love [Whitesnake] 2
- More Than Words [Extreme] 1
- Something To Believe In [Poison] 4
- To Be With You [Mr. Big] 1
- When I Look Into Your Eyes [Firehouse] 8
- When I See You Smile [Bad English] 1
- When I'm With You [Sheriff] 1
- Wind Of Change [Scorpions] 4

3/10/01 — **110** — 6 — ©260 — **Monster Ballads Volume 2** — **$10** Razor & Tie 89035
- Amanda [Boston] 1
- Ballad Of Jayne [L.A. Guns] 33
- Can't Fight This Feeling [REO Speedwagon] 1
- Eyes Without A Face [Billy Idol] 4
- Honestly [Stryper] 23
- House Of Pain [Faster Pussycat] 28
- I Won't Forget You [Poison] 13
- Love Is On The Way [Saigon Kick] 12
- Love Of A Lifetime [Firehouse] 5
- Miles Away [Winger] 12
- More Than Words Can Say [Alias] 2
- Only Time Will Tell [Nelson] 28
- Price Of Love [Bad English] 5
- Sometimes She Cries [Warrant] 20
- This Could Be The Night [Loverboy] 10
- When The Children Cry [White Lion] 3

4/21/01 — **95** — 9 — ©261 — **Monster Booty** — **$10** Razor & Tie 89034
- Baby Got Back [Sir Mix-A-Lot] 1
- Boom Boom Boom [Outhere Brothers] 65
- Booti Call [BLACKstreet] 34
- Bump 'N Grind [R. Kelly] 1
- Da Booty [Tribe Called Quest]
- Da Butt [E.U.] 35
- Da Dip [Freak Nasty] 15
- Dazzey Dukes [Duice] 12
- Do Me! [Bell Biv DeVoe] 3
- Flex [Mad Cobra] 13
- I Like To Move It [Reel To Reel] 89
- Pull Up To The Bumper [Patra] 60
- Rump Shaker [Wreckx-N-Effect] 2
- Shake Your Thang [Salt-N-Pepa]
- Tic Tac Toe [Kyper] 14
- Whoomp! (There It Is) [Tag Team] 2
- Wiggle It [2 In A Room] 15

3/11/00 — **171** — 5 — ©262 — **Monster '80s** — **$10** Razor & Tie 89026
- Broken Wings [Mr. Mister] 1
- Dancing With Myself [Billy Idol]
- Der Kommissar [After The Fire] 5
- Do You Really Want To Hurt Me [Culture Club] 2
- Goody Two Shoes [Adam Ant] 12
- Hazy Shade Of Winter [Bangles] 2
- Hungry Like The Wolf [Duran Duran] 3
- If This Is It [Huey Lewis & The News] 6
- Jessie's Girl [Rick Springfield] 1
- Mickey [Toni Basil] 1
- She Blinded Me With Science [Thomas Dolby] 5
- Stray Cat Strut [Stray Cats] 3
- Sunglasses At Night [Corey Hart] 7
- Take On Me [A-Ha] 1
- Too Shy [Kajagoogoo] 5
- True [Spandau Ballet] 4
- Who Can It Be Now? [Men At Work] 1

5/6/00 — **89** — 10 — ©263 — **Monster Madness** — **$10** Razor & Tie 89028
- Bang Your Head (Metal Health) [Quiet Riot] 31
- Dr. Feelgood [Mötley Crüe] 6
- Don't Treat Me Bad [Firehouse] 41
- Easy Come, Easy Go [Winger] 41
- Epic [Faith No More] 9
- Hole Hearted [Extreme] 4
- I Remember You [Skid Row] 6
- I Saw Red [Warrant] 10
- I Wanna Rock [Twisted Sister] 68
- I'll See You In My Dreams [Giant] 20
- In My Dreams [Dokken] 77
- Kiss Me Deadly [Lita Ford] 12
- Silent Lucidity [Queensryche] 9
- Unskinny Bop [Poison] 3
- Up All Night [Slaughter] 27
- Wait [White Lion] 8

10/18/97 — **20**[C] — 6 — ©264 — **Monster Mash** — **$10** Holly Music 19157
- Alley Cat
- Chicken Dance
- Electric Slide
- Hands Up
- Hokey Pokey
- Hot Hot Hot
- Limbo
- Monster Mash
- Twist, The
- YMCA

11/13/99 — **12**[C] — 1 — ©265 — **Monster Mash And Other Songs Of Horror** — **$10** Madacy 0028
- Batman/Robin Hood
- Clap For The Wolfman
- Ghostbusters
- I Put A Spell On You
- In The Midnight hour
- Love Potion No. 9
- Monster Mash
- Psycho: Suite For Strings
- Purple People Eater
- Spiders And Snakes
- Spooky
- Twilight Zone (Movie Theme)

8/12/00 — **52** — 13 — ©266 — **Monsters Of Rap** — **$10** Razor & Tie 89031
- Baby Got Back [Sir Mix-A-Lot] 1
- Bust A Move [Young MC] 7
- Get Up! (Before The Night Is Over) [Technotronic] 7
- I Got A Man [Positive K] 14
- Ice Ice Baby [Vanilla Ice] 1
- Joy & Pain [Rob Base & DJ E-Z Rock] 58
- Parents Just Don't Understand [DJ Jazzy Jeff & The Fresh Prince] 12
- Pop Goes The Weasel [3rd Bass] 29
- Power, The [Snap] 2
- Rump Shaker [Wreckx-N-Effect] 2
- Scenario [Tribe Called Quest] 57
- Slam [Onyx] 4
- Things That Make You Go Hmmm [C+C Music Factory] 4
- U Can't Touch This [MC Hammer] 8
- Walk This Way [Run-DMC] 4
- Wild Thing [Tone Loc] 2
- You Can't Play With My Yo-Yo [Yo-Yo] 36

DEBUT	PEAK	WKS	RIAA	CD	ARTIST — Album Title	Catalog	Sym	$	Label & Number

6/27/98 — 112 — 58 ▲ — ©267 Monsters Of Rock .... **$10 Razor & Tie 89004**

Cherry Pie [Warrant] 10
Cult Of Personality [Living Colour] 13
Cum On Feel The Noize [Quiet Riot] 5
Every Rose Has Its Thorn [Poison] 1
Final Countdown [Europe] 8
Here I Go Again [Whitesnake] 1
Hold On Loosely [38 Special] 27
Nobody's Fool [Cinderella] 13
Once Bitten, Twice Shy [Great White] 5
Poison [Alice Cooper] 7
Round And Round [Ratt] 12
Seventeen [Winger] 26
Sister Christian [Night Ranger] 5
Turn Up The Radio [Autograph] 29
We're Not Gonna Take It [Twisted Sister] 21
You've Got Another Thing Comin' [Judas Priest] 67

3/11/00 — 145 — 5 — ©268 Monsters Of Rock Volume 2 .... **$10 Razor & Tie 89027**

Bang Bang [Danger Danger] 49
(Can't Live Without Your) Love And Affection [Nelson] 1
Edge Of A Broken Heart [Vixen] 26
Fantasy [Aldo Nova] 23
Fly High Michelle [Enuff Z'Nuff] 47
Fly To The Angels [Slaughter] 19
Girlschool [Britny Fox]
Give It To Me Good [Trixter] 65
Heat Of The Moment [Asia] 4
(I Just) Died In Your Arms [Cutting Crew] 1
Love Of A Lifetime [Firehouse] 5
Owner Of A Lonely Heart [Yes] 1
Stone Cold [Rainbow] 40
Warrior, The [Scandal] 7
When The Children Cry [White Lion] 3
Your Love [Outfield] 6

12/11/93+ — 124 — 13 — ©269 More Songs For Sleepless Nights .... **$10 Epic Soundtrax 57682**

collection of songs inspired by the movie Sleepless In Seattle starring Tom Hanks and Meg Ryan

Affair To Remember (Our Love Affair) [Vic Damone] 16
But I Do [Clarence Henry] 4
Down In The Depths [Ethel Merman]
I Want To Be Loved By You [Sinéad O'Connor]
I'll See You In My Dreams [Jimmy Durante]
Just In Time [Tony Bennett] 46
Mockingbird [Carly Simon & James Taylor] 5
My Funny Valentine [Carly Simon]
Someday I'll Find You [Doris Day] 1
Sonny Boy [Al Jolson]
Stars Fell On Alabama [Jimmy Buffett]
These Foolish Things [Bryan Ferry]
When I Fall In Love [Nat King Cole]

7/26/97 — 179 — 1 — ©270 More Sun Splashin' - 16 Hot Summer Hits! .... **$10 Madacy 6804**

California Girls [David Lee Roth] 3
Electric Avenue [Eddy Grant] 2
59th Street Bridge Song (Feelin' Groovy) [Harpers Bizarre] 13
Follow Your Daughter Home [Guess Who] 61
Freeway Of Love [Aretha Franklin] 3
Gonna Make You Sweat (Everybody Dance Now) [C & C Music Factory] 1
Good Vibrations [Beach Boys] 1
Groovin' [Rascals] 1
Heat Is On [Glenn Frey] 2
La Bamba [Los Lobos] 1
Listen To The Music [Doobie Brothers] 11
Sugar Magnolia [Grateful Dead] 91
Summer In The City [Lovin' Spoonful] 1
Tide Is High [Blondie] 1
Wild, Wild West [Escape Club] 1
Wonderful World, Beautiful People [Jimmy Cliff] 25

6/8/63 — 47 — 14 — 271 Motor-Town Review, Vol. 1, The .... **[L] $30 Motown 609**

recorded at the Apollo Theatre in New York City

Bye Bye Baby [Mary Wells]
Don't You Know [Little Stevie Wonder]
Let Me Go The Right Way [Supremes]
Someday, Someway (medley) [Marvelettes]
Strange I Know (medley) [Marvelettes]
Stubborn Kind Of Fellow [Marvin Gaye]
Two Lovers [Mary Wells]
Way Over There [Miracles]
What Kind Of Fool Am I [Marvin Gaye]
Whole Lotta Woman [Contours]
You've Really Got A Hold On Me [Miracles]

5/30/64 — 102 — 5 — 272 Motor-Town Review, Vol. 2, The .... **[L] $30 Motown 615**

recorded at the Fox Theatre in Detroit

Days Of Wine And Roses [Marvin Gaye]
Dream Come True [Temptations]
He's Alright [Kim Weston]
Heat Wave [Martha & The Vandellas]
I Call It Pretty Music, But The Old People Call It The Blues [Stevie Wonder]
I Want A Love I Can See [Temptations]
It's Alright [Martha & The Vandellas]
Just Loving You [Kim Weston]
Love Me All The Way [Kim Weston]
Mickey's Monkey [Miracles]
Moon River [Stevie Wonder]
Playboy (medley) [Marvelettes]
Please Mr. Postman (medley) [Marvelettes]
Pride And Joy [Marvin Gaye]
Quicksand [Martha & The Vandellas]
Someday, Someway (medley) [Marvelettes]
Strange I Know (medley) [Marvelettes]
What's Easy For Two Is So Hard For One [Mary Wells]
You Lost The Sweetest Boy [Mary Wells]

12/18/65+ — 111 — 7 — 273 Motortown Review In Paris .... **[L] $25 Tamla 264**

recorded at Olympia Music Hall in Paris, France

Baby Love [Supremes]
Dancing In The Street [Martha & The Vandellas]
Fingertips [Stevie Wonder]
Funny How Time Slips Away [Stevie Wonder]
High Heel Sneakers [Stevie Wonder]
If I Had A Hammer [Martha & The Vandellas]
Mickey's Monkey [Miracles]
Nowhere To Run [Martha & The Vandellas]
Ooo Baby Baby [Miracles]
Somewhere [Supremes]
Stop! In The Name Of Love [Supremes]
Too Many Fish In The Sea [Earl Van Dyke & The Soul Brothers]

8/23/69 — 177 — 5 — 274 Motortown Review Live .... **[L] $20 Motown 688**

recorded at the Fox Theatre in Detroit

Ain't No Sun Since You've Been Gone [Gladys Knight & The Pips]
Cloud Nine [Temptations]
Does Your Mama Know About Me [Bobby Taylor]
For Once In My Life [Stevie Wonder]
I Can't Turn You Loose [Blinky]
I Heard It Through The Grapevine [Gladys Knight & The Pips]
I Wish It Would Rain [Gladys Knight & The Pips]
I Wouldn't Change The Man He Is [Blinky]
(I'm Afraid) The Masquerade Is Over [Gladys Knight & The Pips]
Malinda [Bobby Taylor]
Shoo-Be-Doo-Be-Doo-Da-Day [Stevie Wonder]
Sing A Simple Song [Originals]
Uptight (Everything's Alright) [Stevie Wonder]
Who's Making Love [Bobby Taylor]

4/11/70 — 105 — 4 — 275 Motown At The Hollywood Palace .... **[L] $20 Motown 703**

Ain't No Sun Since You've Been Gone [Gladys Knight & The Pips]
Can You Remember (medley) [Jackson 5]
Can't Take My Eyes Off You [Mary Wilson]
Don't Know Why I Love You [Stevie Wonder]
For Once In My Life [Stevie Wonder & Diana Ross]
Good Morning Starshine (medley) [Diana Ross & The Supremes]
I Want You Back [Jackson 5]
I'm Gonna Make You Love Me [Stevie Wonder & Diana Ross]
Nitty Gritty [Gladys Knight & The Pips]
Sing A Simple Song (medley) [Jackson 5]
Someday We'll Be Together [Diana Ross & The Supremes]
Where Do I Go (medley) [Diana Ross & The Supremes]

3/7/98 — 65 — 12 — ©276 Motown 40 Forever .... **$15 Motown 0849 [2]**

ABC [Jackson 5] 1
Ain't Nothing Like The Real Thing [Marvin Gaye & Tammi Terrell] 8
All Night Long (All Night) [Lionel Richie] 1
All This Love [DeBarge] 17
Baby I'm For Real [Originals] 72
Dancing In The Street [Martha & The Vandellas] 2
Don't Look Any Further [Dennis Edwards] 72
Fire & Desire [Teena Marie & Rick James]
Heat Wave [Martha & The Vandellas] 4
Him Or Me [Today]
I Can't Help Myself [Four Tops] 1
I Love Your Smile [Shanice] 2
I Want You Back '98 [Jackson 5 feat. Black Rob]
I'll Be There [Jackson 5] 1
I'll Make Love To You [Boyz II Men] 1
I'm Coming Out [Diana Ross] 5
Just My Imagination (Running Away With Me) [Temptations] 1
Keep On Truckin' [Eddie Kendricks] 1
Let It Whip [Dazz Band] 5
Let's Get It On [Marvin Gaye] 1
Let's Get Serious [Jermaine Jackson] 9
My Cherie Amour [Stevie Wonder] 4
My Girl [Temptations] 1
My Guy [Mary Wells] 1
Neither One Of Us (Wants To Be The First To Say Goodbye) [Gladys Knight/Pips] 2
Papa Was A Rollin' Stone [Temptations] 1
Please Mr. Postman [Marvelettes] 1
Rub You The Right Way [Johnny Gill] 3
Shop Around [Smokey Robinson & The Miracles] 2
Somebody's Watching Me [Rockwell] 2
Someday We'll Be Together [Diana Ross & The Supremes] 1
Stop! In The Name Of Love [Supremes] 1
Super Freak [Rick James] 16
Superstition [Stevie Wonder] 1
Tears Of A Clown [Smokey Robinson] 1
Three Times A Lady [Commodores] 1
War [Edwin Starr] 1
What Becomes Of The Brokenhearted [Jimmy Ruffin] 7
What's Going On [Marvin Gaye] 2
When You Tell Me You Love Me [Diana Ross]

DEBUT	PEAK	WKS	RIAA	CD	ARTIST — Album Title	Catalog	Sym	$	Label & Number

7/9/83   **114**   9   ©277   **Motown Story: The First Twenty-Five Years, The** .... **$30**   Motown 6048 [5]
narrated by Lionel Richie and Smokey Robinson

Baby, Baby Don't Cry [Smokey Robinson & The Miracles] 8
Baby I Need Your Loving [Four Tops] 11
Baby, I'm For Real [Originals] 14
Beauty Is Only Skin Deep [Temptations] 3
Can I Get A Witness [Marvin Gaye] 22
Cloud Nine [Temptations] 6
Cruisin' [Smokey Robinson] 4
Dancing In The Street [Martha & The Vandellas] 2
Dancing Machine [Jackson 5] 2
Endless Love [Diana Ross & Lionel Richie] 1
Every Little Bit Hurts [Brenda Holloway] 13
Fingertips - Pt 2 [Little Stevie Wonder] 1
For Once In My Life [Stevie Wonder] 2

Heat Wave [Martha & The Vandellas] 4
How Sweet It Is To Be Loved By You [Marvin Gaye] 6
I Can't Help Myself [Four Tops] 1
I Hear A Symphony [Supremes] 1
I Heard It Through The Grapevine [Marvin Gaye] 1
I Second That Emotion [Smokey Robinson & The Miracles] 4
I Was Made To Love Her [Stevie Wonder] 2
I Wish It Would Rain [Temptations] 4
I'll Be Doggone [Marvin Gaye] 8
I'm Gonna Make You Love Me [Diana Ross & The Supremes w/The Temptations] 2
Jimmy Mack [Martha & The Vandellas] 10
Keep On Truckin' (Part 1) [Eddie Kendricks] 1
Let It Whip [Dazz Band] 5

Let Me Tickle Your Fancy [Rick James] 16
Love Child [Diana Ross & The Supremes] 1
Love Machine (Part 1) [Miracles] 1
My Girl [Temptations] 1
My Guy [Mary Wells] 1
Nowhere To Run [Martha & The Vandellas] 8
Papa Was A Rollin' Stone [Temptations] 1
Please Mr. Postman [Marvelettes] 1
Reflections [Diana Ross & The Supremes] 2
Shop Around [Miracles] 2
Someday We'll Be Together [Diana Ross & The Supremes] 1
Stop! In The Name Of Love [Supremes] 1
Stubborn Kind Of Fellow [Marvin Gaye] 46

Super Freak (Part 1) [Rick James] 16
Three Times A Lady [Commodores] 1
Tracks Of My Tears [Miracles] 16
Truly [Lionel Richie] 1
Two Lovers [Mary Wells] 7
Way You Do The Things You Do [Temptations] 11
What Becomes Of The Brokenhearted [Jimmy Ruffin] 7
What Does It Take (To Win Your Love) [Jr. Walker & The All Stars] 4
Where Did Our Love Go [Supremes] 1
You Can't Hurry Love [Supremes] 1
You're All I Need To Get By [Marvin Gaye & Tammi Terrell] 7
You've Really Got A Hold On Me [Miracles] 8

2/22/69   **159**   4   278   **Motown Winners' Circle/No. 1 Hits, Vol. 1** .... **$20**   Gordy 835

Baby I Need Your Loving [Four Tops] 11
Dancing In The Street [Martha & The Vandellas] 2

Fingertips - Pt 2 [Stevie Wonder] 1
Playboy [Marvelettes] 7
Pride And Joy [Marvin Gaye] 10
Shop Around [Miracles] 2

Shotgun [Jr. Walker & The All Stars] 4
Way You Do The Things You Do [Temptations] 11

Where Did Our Love Go [Supremes] 1
You Beat Me To The Punch [Mary Wells] 9

2/22/69   **135**   5   279   **Motown Winners' Circle/No. 1 Hits, Vol. 2** .... **$20**   Gordy 836

Do You Love Me [Contours] 3
Every Little Bit Hurts [Brenda Holloway] 13
Heat Wave [Martha & The Vandellas] 4

I Can't Help Myself [Four Tops] 1
I Second That Emotion [Smokey Robinson & The Miracles] 4
Money (That's What I Want) [Barrett Strong] 1

My Girl [Temptations] 1
My Guy [Mary Wells] 1
Stop! In The Name Of Love [Supremes] 1

Uptight (Everything's Alright) [Stevie Wonder] 3

5/11/96   **75**   20   ©280   **MTV Buzz Bin: Volume 1** .... **$10**   Mammoth 92672

Cantaloop [US3] 9
Creep [Radiohead] 34
Everything Zen [Bush]
Hey Jealousy [Gin Blossoms] 25

Hey Man, Nice Shot [Filter] 76
Low [Cracker] 64
More Human Than Human [White Zombie]

Mother [Danzig] 43
No Rain [Blind Melon] 20
Plush [Stone Temple Pilots]

What Would You Say? [Dave Matthews Band]
Zombie [Cranberries]

11/15/97   **180**   2   ©281   **MTV Grind Volume One** .... **$10**   Tommy Boy 1207

Fired Up! [Funky Green Dogs] 80
Free [Ultra Naté] 75
It's No Good [Depeche Mode] 38
Little Bit Of Ecstacy [Jocelyn Enriquez] 55

Nightmare [Brainbug]
One More Night [Amber] 58
Ooh Aah...Just A Little Bit [Gina G] 12
Runaway [Nuyorican Soul]

Samba De Janeiro [Felizia]
Spin Spin Sugar [Sneaker Pimps] 87
Stupid Girl [Garbage] 24
Sugar Is Sweeter [CJ Bolland]

Virtual Insanity [Jamiroquai]
Wannabe [Spice Girls] 1
Your Woman [White Town] 23

12/13/97+   **50**   21   ●   ©282   **MTV: Party To Go '98** .... **$10**   Tommy Boy 1234

Been There, Done That [Dr. Dre]
Block Rockin' Beats [Chemical Brothers]
I'll Be [Foxy Brown Feat. Jay-Z] 7
If Your Girl Only Knew [Aaliyah] 11
In My Bed [Dru Hill] 4

No Diggity [BLACKstreet Feat. Dr. Dre] 1
Not Tonight [Lil' Kim] 6
On And On [Erykah Badu] 12
Ooh La La [Coolio] 6
Pony [Ginuwine] 6

Quit Playing Games (With My Heart) [Backstreet Boys] 2
Return Of The Mack [Mark Morrison] 2
Snoop's Upside Your Head [Snoop Doggy Dogg]
Steelo [702] 32

You're All I Need To Get By ..see:
I'll Be There For You

12/12/98+   **60**   16   ●   ©283   **MTV: Party To Go '99** .... **$10**   Tommy Boy 1268

As Long As You Love Me [Backstreet Boys]
Butta Love [Next] 16
Da Rain (Supa Dupa Fly) [Missy "Misdemeanor" Elliott]
Deja Vu (Uptown Baby) [Lord Tariq & Peter Gunz] 1

Fly [Sugar Ray]
Let's Ride [Montell Jordan Feat. Master P & Silkk The Shocker] 2
Make 'Em Say Uhh! [Master P] 16
My Heart Will Go On (Love Theme From Titanic) [Deja Vu] 58

No, No, No Part 2 [Destiny's Child Feat. Wyclef Jean] 3
Put Your Hands Where My Eyes Could See [Busta Rhymes]
Shorty (You Keep Playin' With My Mind) [Imajin Feat. Keith Murray] 25

Show Me Love [Robyn] 7
Still Not A Player Feat. Joe] 24
Superthug [Noreaga] 36
You're All I Need To Get By ..see:
I'll Be There For You

12/25/99+   **86**   9   ©284   **MTV: Party To Go 2000** .... **$10**   Tommy Boy 1365

Are You That Somebody [Aaliyah] 21
Come Correct [Before Dark]
Crush [Jennifer Paige] 3

Everybody (Backstreet's Back) [Backstreet Boys] 4
First Night [Monica] 1
5,6,7,8 [Steps]
Hardest Thing [98°] 5

Here We Go ['N Sync]
How Do I Deal [Jennifer Love Hewitt] 59
How Do I Live [LeAnn Rimes] 2
Sexual [Amber] 42

Stay The Same [Joey McIntyre] 10
Thinkin' About You [Britney Spears]
Where My Girls At? [702] 4

10/24/98   **100**   7   ©285   **MTV: Party To Go Platinum Mix** .... **$10**   Tommy Boy 1267

California Love [2 Pac feat. Dr. Dre] 6
Creep [TLC] 1
Express Yourself [Madonna] 2
Here Comes The Hotstepper [Ini Kamoze] 1

Love Will Never Do (Without You) [Janet Jackson] 1
Now That We Found Love [Heavy D. & The Boyz] 11
Nuthin' But A "G" Thang [Dr. Dre feat. Snoop Doggy Dogg] 2

O.P.P. [Naughty By Nature] 6
Real Love [Mary J. Blige] 7
Scenario [Tribe Called Quest] 57
Shoop [Salt 'N Pepa] 4

Summertime [DJ Jazzy Jeff & The Fresh Prince] 4
This Is How We Do It [Montell Jordan] 1
Woo Haa!! Got You All In Check [Busta Rhymes] 8

6/20/92   **19**   41   ▲   ©286   **MTV: Party To Go Volume 2** .... **$10**   Tommy Boy 1053

All 4 Love [Color Me Badd] 1
Good Vibrations [Marky Mark & The Funky Bunch Feat. Loleatta Holloway] 1
Here We Go [C & C Music Factory] 3

Let's Talk About Sex [Salt-N-Pepa] 13
Motownphilly [Boyz II Men] 3
Now That We Found Love [Heavy D & The Boyz] 11
O.P.P. [Naughty By Nature] 6

Playground [Another Bad Creation] 10
Sadeness Part I [Enigma] 5
Set Adrift On Memory Bliss [PM Dawn] 1

Summertime [D.J. Jazzy Jeff & The Fresh Prince] 4
3 AM Eternal [KLF] 5

7/10/93   **29**   25   ●   ©287   **MTV: Party To Go Volume 3** .... **$10**   Tommy Boy 1074

Baby Got Back [Sir Mix-A-Lot] 1
Come & Talk To Me [Jodeci] 11
Deeper And Deeper [Madonna] 7

End of the Road [Boyz II Men] 1
Finally [Ce Ce Peniston] 5
I Got A Man [Positive K] 14

I'm Too Sexy [Right Said Fred] 1
Jump Around [House Of Pain] 3
Mr. Loverman [Shabba Ranks] 40

Real Love [Mary J. Blige] 7

DEBUT	PEAK	WKS	RIAA	CD	ARTIST — Album Title	Catalog	Sym	$	Label & Number

7/10/93 — **35** — 23 — ● — ©288 — **MTV: Party To Go Volume 4** .... — **$10** — Tommy Boy 1075
- Baby-Baby-Baby [TLC] 2
- Back To The Hotel [N2Deep] 14
- Give It Away [Red Hot Chili Peppers] 73
- Hip Hop Hooray [Naughty By Nature] 8
- Jump [Kris Kross] 1
- My Lovin' [En Vogue] 2
- Please Don't Go [KWS] 6
- Rhythm Is A Dancer [Snap] 5
- Supermodel (You Better Work) [RuPaul] 45
- They Want EFX [DAS EFX] 25

6/18/94 — **36** — 24 — ● — ©289 — **MTV: Party To Go Volume 5** .... — **$10** — Tommy Boy 1097
- Anniversary [Tony Toni Toné] 10
- Boom! Shake The Room [Jazzy Jeff & Fresh Prince] 13
- Come Baby Come [K7] 11
- Hey Mr. DJ [Zhané] 6
- I Get Around [2Pac] 11
- Informer [Snow] 1
- Knockin' Da Boots [H-Town] 3
- Let Me Ride [Dr. Dre] 34
- Slam [Onyx] 4
- Weak [SWV] 1
- What Is Love [Haddaway] 11
- Whoomp! (There It Is) [Tag Team] 2

12/10/94+ — **54** — 25 — ● — ©290 — **MTV: Party To Go Volume 6** .... — **$10** — Tommy Boy 1109
- All That She Wants [Ace Of Base] 2
- Award Tour [Tribe Called Quest] 47
- Back & Forth [Aaliyah] 5
- Can We Talk [Tevin Campbell] 9
- Cantaloop [US3] 9
- Fantastic Voyage [Coolio] 3
- Getto Jam [Domino] 7
- I Swear [All-4-One] 1
- Move It Like This [K7] 54
- 100% Pure Love [Crystal Waters] 11
- Regulate [Warren G & Nate Dogg] 2
- Shoop [Salt-N-Pepa] 4
- Your Body's Callin' [R. Kelly] 13

11/18/95 — **54** — 25 — ● — ©291 — **MTV: Party To Go Volume 7** .... — **$10** — Tommy Boy 1138
- Can't You See [Total feat. The Notorious B.I.G.] 13
- Candy Rain [Soul For Real] 2
- Dear Mama [2 Pac] 9
- Freak Like Me [Adina Howard] 2
- Freek'n You [Jodeci] 14
- Here Comes The Hotstepper [Ini Kamoze] 1
- Human Nature [Madonna] 46
- I Wanna Be Down [Brandy] 6
- I'll Make Love To You [Boyz II Men] 1
- Short Short Man [20 Fingers] 14
- This Is How We Do It [Montell Jordan] 1
- Thuggish Ruggish Bone [Bone Thugs-N-Harmony] 22

12/9/95+ — **47** — 31 — ● — ©292 — **MTV: Party To Go Volume 8** .... — **$10** — Tommy Boy 1139
- Big Poppa [Notorious B.I.G.] 6
- Boombastic/Summer Time 3
- Bounce It Y'all [DJ Kizzy Rock]
- Can't Cry Anymore [Sheryl Crow] 36
- Feel Me Flow [Naughty By Nature] 17
- 1st Of Tha Month [Bone Thugs-N-Harmony] 14
- Gangsta's Paradise [Coolio feat. L.V.] 1
- I Wish [Skee-Lo] 13
- I'll Be There For You/You're All I Need To Get By [Method Man & Mary J. Blige] 3
- If You Love Me [Brownstone] 8
- Rhythm Of The Night [Corona] 11

7/27/96 — **28** — 16 — ● — ©293 — **MTV: Party To Go Volume 9** .... — **$10** — Tommy Boy 1164
- Baby [Brandy] 4
- Beautiful Life [Ace Of Base] 15
- Get On Up [Jodeci] 22
- Hey Lover [L.L. Cool J] 3
- Missing [Everything But The Girl] 2
- One More Chance/Stay With Me [Notorious B.I.G.] 2
- 1,2,3,4 (Sumpin' New) [Coolio] 5
- Runaway [Real McCoy] 3
- Set U Free [Planet Soul] 26
- Tell Me [Groove Theory] 5
- Throw Your Hands Up [L.V.] 63
- You Remind Me Of Something [R. Kelly] 4

11/16/96 — **40** — 18 — ● — ©294 — **MTV: Party To Go Volume 10** .... — **$10** — Tommy Boy 1168
- Ain't Nobody [Monica feat. Treach] flip
- Be My Lover [La Bouche] 6
- California Love [2 PAC] 6
- Crossroads, Tha [Bone Thugs-N-Harmony] 1
- Do You Miss Me [Jocelyn Enriquez] 49
- It's All The Way Live (Now) [Coolio] 24
- Lady [D'Angelo feat. AZ] 10
- Macarena [Los Del Mar] 71
- This Is Your Night [Amber] 24
- Tonite's Tha Night [Kris Kross] 12
- You're The One [SWV] 5
- Your Loving Arms [Billie Ray Martin] 46

3/14/98 — **152** — 2 — — ©295 — **MTV Presents: Hip Hop Back In The Day** .... — **$10** — Priority 51070
- Breaks, The [Kurtis Blow] 87
- Bridge, The [MC Shan]
- Fat Boys [Fat Boys]
- Freaks Come Out At Night [Whodini]
- Funky Cold Medina [Tone Loc] 3
- Message, The [Grandmaster Flash & The Furious Five] [includes 2 versions] 62
- Overweight Lovers In The House [Heavy D. & The Boyz]
- Planet Rock [Afrika Bambaataa & Soulsonic Force] 48
- Rock The Bells [LL Cool J]
- Roxanne, Roxanne [UTFO] 77
- Show, The [Doug E. Fresh & The Get Fresh Crew]
- South Bronx [Boogie Down Productions]

7/1/00 — **42** — 11 — — ©296 — **MTV: The Return Of The Rock** .... — **$10** — Roadrunner 8536
- Blunt Force Trauma [Liquid Gang]
- Brackish [Kittie]
- Crash [Methods Of Mayhem]
- Denial [Sevendust]
- Do It Again [Boiler Room]
- Everything Sucks [Dope]
- From This Day [Machine Head]
- F#@K That [Kid Rock]
- Infest [Papa Roach]
- Just Go [Staind]
- Make Me Bad [Korn]
- Not Living [Coal Chamber]
- Pardon Me [Incubus]
- S.O.M. [Static-X]
- Southtown [P.O.D.]
- Spit It Out [Slipknot]
- Stain [Full Devil Jacket]
- Suite-Pee [System Of A Down]
- When Worlds Collide [Powerman 5000]

11/25/00 — **75** — 10 — — ©297 — **MTV: The Return Of The Rock Volume 2** .... — **$10** — Roadrunner 8509
- Back To The Primitive [Soulfly]
- Change (In The House Of Flies) [Deftones]
- Down [Fuel]
- Freestyle [P.O.D.]
- God Of The Mind [Disturbed]
- Godless [U.P.O.]
- Goin' Down [Godsmack]
- Just Got Wicked [Cold]
- Leader Of Men [Nickelback]
- Legacy [Papa Roach]
- Mechanical Animals [Marilyn Manson]
- One Step Closer [Linkin Park]
- Show Me What You Got [Limp Bizkit]
- Spectrum, The [Orgy]
- Synthetic [Spineshank]
- Waiting To Die [(Hed) Planet Earth]

5/24/97 — **63** — 12 — — ©298 — **MTV's Amp** .... — **$10** — Astralwerks 7550
- Are You There? [Josh Wink]
- Atom Bomb [Fluke]
- Block Rockin' Beats [Chemical Brothers]
- Box, The [Orbital]
- Busy Child [Crystal Method]
- Girl/Boy Song [Aphex Twin]
- Inner City Life [Goldie]
- Ni Ten Ichi Ryu [Photek]
- Pearl's Girl [Underworld]
- Sick To Death [Atari Teenage Riot]
- Voodoo People [Prodigy]
- We All Want To Be Free [Tranquility Bass]
- We Have Explosive [Future Sound Of London]

7/11/98 — **181** — 3 — — ©299 — **MTV's Amp²** .... — **$10** — Astralwerks 7558
- Abandon Ship (Sharks And Mermaids) [Hardkiss]
- Bang On! [Propellerheads]
- Battleflag [Pigeonhed]
- Brown Paper Bag [Roni Size/Reprazent]
- Circles [Adam F]
- Digital [Goldie feat. KRS One]
- Genius [Pitchshifter]
- Jungle Brother [Jungle Brothers]
- Release Yo' Delf [Method Man] 98
- Rockafeller Skank [Fatboy Slim] 76
- Sexy Boy [Air]
- War [Chuck D of Public Enemy vs. Ticc-Tacc]

6/30/01 — **138** — 1 — — ©300 — **MTV's Hip Hopera: Carmen** .... — **$10** — Music World 85846
- Black & Blue [Mos Def/Mekhi Phifer]
- B.L.A.Z.E. [Casey Lee/Rah Digga/Joy Bryant]
- Blaze Finale [Casey Lee]
- Boom [Royce Da 5'9"]
- Bootylicious [Destiny's Child]
- Cards Never Lie [Beyoncé Knowles/Wyclef Jean/Ray Digga]
- If Looks Could Kill (You Would Be Dead) [Beyoncé Knowles/Mos Def/Sam Sarpong]
- Last Great Seduction [Beyoncé Knowles/Mekhi Phifer]
- Stop That! [Beyoncé Knowles/Mekhi Phifer]
- Survivor [Destiny's Child Feat. Da Brat]
- What We Gonna Do [Rah Digga]

3/2/85 — **91** — 12 — — 301 — **MTV's Rock 'N Roll To Go** .... — **$12** — Elektra 60399
- Are We Ourselves? [Fixx] 15
- Dance Hall Days [Wang Chung]
- Drive [Cars] 3
- Hell Is For Children [Pat Benatar]
- Hold Me Now [Thompson Twins] 3
- King Of Pain [Police] 3
- Lick It Up [Kiss] 66
- Lucky Star [Madonna] 4
- Oh Sherrie [Steve Perry] 3
- Rebel Yell [Billy Idol] 46
- Round And Round [Ratt] 12
- Say It Isn't So [Hall & Oates] 2
- She Bop [Cyndi Lauper] 3
- What's Love Got To Do With It [Tina Turner] 1

12/25/71+ — **189** — 4 — — 302 — **Muppet Alphabet Album, The** .... — **$20** — Columbia 25503
includes blackboard, chalk and a set of letters
- C Is For Cookie
- Dee Dee Dee
- Four Furry Friends
- Ha Ha
- Herb's Silly Poem
- J Friends
- Just Because
- La La La
- Lecture
- Mmm Monster Meal
- My Favorite Letter
- National Association Of W Lovers
- Noodle Story
- Oscar's B Sandwich
- Question Song
- R Machine
- Sammy The Snake
- Sound Of The Letter A
- Stand Up Straight And Tall
- Tale Of Tom Tattertall Tuttletut
- Two G Sounds
- Very Very Special Letter
- What's My Letter?
- Would You Like To Buy An O?
- X Marks The Spot
- Zizzy Zoomers

DEBUT	PEAK	WKS	RIAA	CD	ARTIST — Album Title	Catalog	Sym	$	Label & Number

11/30/63 | **148** | 2 — **303 Murray The K - Live From The Brooklyn Fox** .... [L] **$40** KFM 1001
Be My Baby *[Ronettes]* — I (Who Have Nothing) *[Ben E. King]* — Shop Around *[Miracles]* — You Can't Sit Down *[Dovells]*
Denise *[Randy & The Rainbows]* — Linda *[Jan & Dean]* — So Much In Love *[Tymes]*
Everybody Loves A Lover *[Shirelles]* — My Boyfriend's Back *[Angels]* — There Goes My Baby *[Drifters]*
He's So Fine *[Chiffons]* — She Cried *[Jay & The Americans]* — Town Without Pity *[Gene Pitney]*

12/25/61+ | **26** | 15 — **304 Murray The K's Blasts From The Past** .... **$40** Chess 1461
Been So Long *[Pastels]* 24 — (Do The) Mashed Potatoes (Part — Sho Doo Be Doo *[Moonlighters]* — Vow, The *[Flamingos]*
Blue Velvet *[Moonglows]* — 1) *[Nat Kendrick]* 84 — So Fine *[Fiestas]* 11 — We Go Together *[Moonglows]*
Bo Diddley *[Bo Diddley]* — He's Gone *[Chantels]* 71 — Sweet Little Sixteen *[Chuck — You're Everything To Me *[Orchids]*
La Bamba *[Ritchie Valens]* 22 — Berry]* 2

8/4/62 | **124** | 13 — **305 Murray The K's Gassers For Submarine Race Watchers** .... **$40** Chess 1470
Dedicated To The One I Love — Life Is But A Dream *[Harptones]* — So Far Away *[Pastels]* — Tonight I Fell In Love *[Tokens]* 15
[Shirelles] 3 — Maybe *[Chantels]* 15 — Sunday Kind Of Love *[Harptones]* — Will You Love Me Tomorrow
Everyday Of The Week *[Students]* — My Memories Of You *[Harptones]* — Tears On My Pillow *[Little Anthony — [Shirelles]* 1
In My Diary *[Moonglows]* — My Vow To You *[Students]* — & The Imperials]* 4

7/20/63 | **69** | 10 — **306 Murray The K's Nineteen-Sixty Two Boss Golden Gassers** .... **$40** Scepter 510
Any Day Now (My Wild Beautiful — Duke Of Earl *[Gene Chandler]* 1 — Rama Lama Ding Dong — Twist And Shout *[Isley
Bird) [Chuck Jackson]* 23 — It Keeps Right On A-Hurtin' — *[Edsels]* 21 — Brothers]* 17
Baby It's You *[Shirelles]* 8 — *[Johnny Tillotson]* 3 — Soldier Boy *[Shirelles]* 1 — What's Your Name *[Don & Juan]* 7
Don't Play That Song (You Lied) — Let Me In *[Sensations]* 4 — Something's Got A Hold On Me — You Belong To Me *[Duprees]* 7
[Ben E. King] 11 — *[Etta James]* 37

10/9/61 | **63** | 29 | ©**307 Murray The K's Sing Along With The Original Golden Gassers** .... **$40** Roulette 25159
Beep Beep *[Playmates]* 4 — Gee *[Crows]* — Little Girl Of Mine *[Cleftones]* 57 — Why Do Fools Fall In Love
Closer You Are *[Channels]* — Honeycomb *[Jimmie Rodgers]* 1 — Party Doll *[Buddy Knox]* 1 — *[Frankie Lymon & The
Crying In The Chapel *[Orioles]* — I'm Stickin' With You *[Jimmy — Thousand Miles Away — Teenagers]* 6
Dear Lord *[Continentals]* — Bowen]* 14 — *[Heartbeats]* 53 — You Talk Too Much *[Joe Jones]* 3

8/18/79 | **171** | 4 — **308 Music for UNICEF Concert/A Gift Of Song, The** .... [L] **$15** Polydor 6214
recorded on 1/9/79 at the United Nations Hall
Chiquitita *[Abba]* — I Go For You *[Andy Gibb]* — Rhymes And Reasons *[John — That's The Way Of The World
Da Ya Think I'm Sexy? *[Rod — Key, The *[Olivia Newton-John]* — Denver]* — (medley) *[Earth, Wind & Fire]*
Stewart]* — Mimi's Song *[Donna Summer]* — September (medley) *[Earth, Wind & — Too Much Heaven *[Bee Gees]*
Fallen Angels *[Kris Kristofferson & — Rest Your Love On Me *[Andy Gibb — Fire]*
Rita Coolidge]* — & Olivia Newton-John]*

3/18/72 | **165** | 6 — **309 Music People, The** .... **$30** Columbia 31280 [3]
Abalone Dream *[Pamela Polland]* — Grand Coulee Dam *[Bob Dylan]* — Magnificent Sanctuary Band *[David — Sleepless Nights *[Wayne Cochran &
Baby Won't You Let Me Rock 'N — Hallelujah *[Sweathog]* 33 — Clayton-Thomas]* — The C. C. Riders]*
Roll You *[Ten Years After]* 61 — Hello Mary Lou (Goodbye Heart) — Monkey Time *[Boz Scaggs & Band]* — So Many People *[Chase]*
Bugler *[Byrds]* — *[New Riders Of The Purple Sage]* — My Impersonal Life *[Blue Rose]* — Stealin' *[Taj Mahal]*
Calico *[Dreams]* — High Priest Of Memphis *[Bell + Arc]* — Nest, The *[Jimmie Spheeris]* — Sun Never Shines On The Lonely
Celebration Of Life *[Chambers — Hoe Down *[Poco]* — No Word For Glad *[It's A Beautiful — *[Redbone]*
Brothers]* — Holy Smoke Doo Dah Band *[Mylon]* — Day]* — To Make A Woman Feel Wanted
Chelsea Girls *[Spirit]* — I Call That True Love *[Dr. Hook & — 157 Riverside Avenue *[R.E.O. — *[Kenny Loggins & Jim Messina]*
Cool Fool *[Edgar Winter's White — The Medicine Show]* — Speedwagon]* — Too Many Mondays *[Barry Mann]*
Trash]* — I'm Funky *[Grootna]* — Para Los Rumberos *[Santana]* — What Kind Of Man Are You *[Genya
Country Song *[Compost]* — I'm On The Lamb But I Ain't No — She Loves The Way They Love Her — Ravan]*
Dawn *[Mahavishnu Orchestra — Sheep *[Blue Oyster Cult]* — *[Colin Blunstone]* — While The Sun Still Shines *[Fields]*
w/John McLaughlin]* — Jumpin' Jack Flash *[Johnny — Silence *[Jake Holmes]* — White Lies *[Grin]* 75
Go Down Gamblin' *[Blood, Sweat — Winter]* 89 — Situation *[Jeff Beck Group]*
& Tears]* 32 — Little Girl Lost *[Kris Kristofferson]*

9/9/95 | **99** | 18 | ● | ©**310 My Utmost For His Highest** .... **$10** Myrrh 83410
God Of All Of Me *[Sandi Patty]* — Man After Your Own Heart *[Gary — Shine On Us *[Phillips, Craig & — Where He Leads Me *[Twila Paris]*
Heart Like Mine *[Bryan Duncan]* — Chapman]* — Dean]* — You Are Holy *[4 Him]*
Hold On To Me *[Point Of Grace]* — Move In Me *[Michael W. Smith]* — Sometimes He Comes In The — You'll Be There *[Cindy Morgan]*
Lover Of My Soul *[Amy Grant]* — Clouds *[Steven Curtis Chapman]*

10/13/90 | **125** | 14 | ©**311 Narada Wilderness Collection, The** .... [I] **$10** Narada 63905
Break Of Day *[Bernardo Rubaja]* — Glacier And Flower *[Jim Jacobsen]* — Ocala *[Wayne Gratz]* — White Water *[Doug Cameron]*
Early Moon And Firelight *[Carol — Lament For Hetch Hetchy *[Alasdair — Return To Emerald Forest *[Richard — Wildflowers *[Michael Jones]*
Nethen]* — Fraser]* — Souther]* — Wonderland *[Spencer Brewer]*
Fragile Majesty *[Eric — Madre De La Tierra *[David Lanz]* — Sahara Sunrise *[Ralf Illenberger]* — Woodland Mission *[William Ellwood]*
Tingstad/Nancy Rumbel]* — Northern Morning *[Peter Buffett]* — Tal *[Trapezoid]* — Yosemite *[David Arkenstone]*

4/29/95 | **90** | 11 | ©**312 NASCAR - Runnin' Wide Open** .... **$10** Columbia 67020
Cadillac Ranch *[Rick Trevino]* — Fastest Horse In A One Horse Town — Oh King Richard *[Kyle Petty]* — Wall, The *[Collin Raye]*
Dedicated NASCAR Fans *[T. — *[Billy Ray Cyrus]* — Racing With My Heart *[Sammy — You Could Be A NASCAR Fan If...
Graham Brown]* — Fuel To The Fire *[Ken Mellons]* — Kershaw]* — *[Jeff Foxworthy]*
Junk Cars *[Ricky Van Shelton]* — Runnin' Wide Open *[Joe Diffie]*

10/22/94 | **50** | 9 | ● | ©**313 Nativity In Black: A Tribute To Black Sabbath** .... **$10** Columbia 66335
After Forever *[Biohazard]* — Iron Man *[Ozzy Osbourne — Paranoid *[Megadeth]* — Sympton Of The Universe
Black Sabbath *[Type O Negative]* — w/Therapy]* — Sabbath Bloody Sabbath *[Bruce — *[Sepultura]*
Children Of The Grave *[White — Lord Of This World *[Corrosion Of — Dickinson w/Godspeed]* — War Pigs *[Faith No More]*
Zombie]* — Conformity]* — Supernaut *[1,000 Homo DJ's]* — Wizard, The *[Bullring Brummies]*
N.I.B. *[Ugly Kid Joe]*

6/24/00 | **95** | 3 | ©**314 Nativity In Black II: A Tribute To Black Sabbath** .... **$10** Divine 26095
Behind The Wall Of Sleep *[Static-X]* — Into The Void *[Monster Magnet]* — Never Say Die *[Megadeth]* — Under The Sun *[Soulfly]*
Electric Funeral *[Pantera]* — Iron Man (This Means War) *[Busta — Sabbra Cadabra *[Hed(pe)]*
Hand Of Doom *[Slayer]* — Rhymes]* — Snowblind *[System Of A Down]*
Hole In The Sky *[Machine Head]* — N.I.B. *[Primus with Ozzy]* — Sweet Leaf *[Godsmack]*

12/17/66+ | **72** | 10 — **315 New First Family, 1968, The** .... [C] **$15** Verve 15054
Acting School — Inauguration, The — Meet The New Cabinet — Showdown With The Soviets
Critic, The — Job For The Secret Service — 91st Congress — State Dinner
Election Of The President, 1968 — Meanwhile, Back At The White — Panic In The White House
Epilogue, The — House — Secret Luncheon

DEBUT	PEAK	WKS	RIAA	CD	ARTIST — Album Title	Catalog	Sym	$	Label & Number

5/13/00 · 100 · 11 · ©316 · New Millennium Hip-Hop Party · $10 · Rhino 79824

Back To The Hotel [N2Deep] 14 · Ditty [Paperboy] 10 · Gangsta's Paradise [Coolio feat. L.V.] 1 · (I Know I Got) Skillz [Shaquille O'Neal] 35 · Informer [Snow] 1 · Joy And Pain [Rob Base & D.J. E-Z Rock] 58 · Juicy [Notorious B.I.G.] 27 · Me Myself And I [De La Soul] 34 · Mentirosa [Mellow Man Ace] 14 · Message, The [Grand Master Flash & The Furious Five] 62 · Method Man [Wu-Tang Clan] 69 · O.P.P. [Naughty By Nature] 6 · People Everyday [Arrested Development] 8 · Pray [M.C. Hammer] 2 · Scenario [Tribe Called Quest] 57 · Summertime [DJ Jazzy Jeff & The Fresh Prince] 4 · Wild Thing [Tone Loc] 2 · You Be Illin' [Run-D.M.C.] 29

2/17/01 · 170 · 3 · ©317 · New Millennium Love Songs · $10 · Rhino 76699

Baby, Come To Me [Patti Austin with James Ingram] 1 · Barely Breathing [Duncan Sheik] 16 · Don't Know Much [Linda Ronstadt feat. Aaron Neville] 2 · Drive [Cars] 3 · Glory Of Love [Peter Cetera] 1 · Hard Habit To Break [Chicago] 3 · Hold My Hand [Hootie & The Blowfish] 10 · Hold On My Heart [Genesis] 12 · Holding Back The Years [Simply Red] 1 · I Don't Want To Wait [Paula Cole] 11 · I Love You Always Forever [Donna Lewis] 2 · I Want To Know What Love Is [Foreigner] 1 · I'll Be [Edwin McCain] 5 · Never Tear Us Apart [INXS] 7 · Romeo And Juliet [Dire Straits] · Time After Time [Cyndi Lauper] 1 · Tonight, I Celebrate My Love [Peabo Bryson & Roberta Flack] 16 · You're All I Need To Get By [Aretha Franklin] 19

3/7/70 · 200 · 1 · 318 · New Spirit Of Capitol, The · $15 · Capitol 6

Astronomy Domine [Pink Floyd] · Boy Soldier [Edgar Broughton Band] · Broke An' Hungry [Guitar, Jr.] · Games People Play [Joe South] 12 · Innervenus Eyes [Bob Seger System] · It's Time [Sons] · Jamie [Hedge & Donna] · July, You're A Woman [John Stewart] · Little Girl [Steve Miller Band] · Little Girl Lost [David Axelrod] · Please Don't Worry [Grand Funk Railroad] · Red Cross Store [Mississippi Fred McDowell] · Silver Threads And Golden Needles [Linda Ronstadt]

12/9/00+ · 93 · 22 · ©319 · New York City Underground Party Vol. 3 · $10 · E-lastik 5002

Blackout [Mada & Moody] · Castles In The Sky [Ian Vandahl] · Dive In The Pool [Barry Harris] · Don't Want Another Man [Dynamix] · Final Chapter [Mike Macaluso] · I Turn To You [Melanie C] · Kernkraft 400 [Zombie Nation] · Kiss [DJ Sugar Kid & Bad Boy Joe] · New York City Underground Party Vol. 3 Medley [Bad Boy Joe] · Outa Space [Mellow Trax] · Pitchin [High Gate] · Plan B [Blue Harvest] · Sandstorm [Darude] · Someone [Ascension] · Spente Le Stelle [Emma Shapplin] · Take Your Time [Love Bite] · You See The Trouble With Me [Black Legend]

11/23/91+ · 170 · 10 · ©320 · New York Rock And Soul Revue - Live At The Beacon, The · [L] · $10 · Giant 24423

recorded on 3/1/91 in New York City

At Last [Phoebe Snow] · Chain Lightning [Donald Fagen] · Driftin' Blues [Charles Brown] · Drowning In The Sea Of Love [Boz Scaggs] · Green Flower Street [Donald Fagen] · Groovin' [Eddie & David Brigati] · Knock On Wood [Michael McDonald & Phoebe Snow] · Lonely Teardrops [Michael McDonald] · Madison Time [Donald Fagen] · Minute By Minute [Michael McDonald] · People Got To Be Free [New York Rock & Soul Revue] · Pretzel Logic [Donald Fagen & Michael McDonald] · Shakey Ground [Phoebe Snow]

9/26/98 · 105 · 18 · ©321 · Next Generation Swing · $10 · Beast 56532

Blue Suit Boogie [Indigo Swing] · Checkbook Daddy-O [Swingtips] · Daddy-O [Dave's True Story] · Datin' With No Dough [Royal Crown Revue] · Don't Let Go [Mighty Blue Kings] · Hey Kat [Speak Easy Spies] · I Get A Kick Out Of You [Wally's Swing World] · Jump, Jive, An' Wail [Louis Prima] · Jumpin' At The Green Mill [Mighty Blue Kings] · Oak Tree [Alien Fashion Show] · Rascal King [Mighty Mighty Bosstones] · Route 66 [Brian Setzer Orchestra] · Sing Sing Sing [Lee Press-on & The Nails] · Zoot Suit Riot [Chill Pill Dancers]

7/28/79 · 21 · 25 · ● · 322 · Night At Studio 54, A · $15 · Casablanca 7161 [2]

Disco Nights (Rock-Freak) [GQ] 12 · Got To Be Real [Cheryl Lynn] 12 · Hot Jungle Drums And Voodoo Rhythm [D.C. LaRue] · Hot Shot [Karen Young] 67 · I Found Love (Now That I Found You) [Love & Kisses] · I Got My Mind Made Up (You Can Get It Girl) [Instant Funk] 20 · I Love America [Patrick Juvet] · I Love The Nightlife (Disco 'Round) [Alicia Bridges] 5 · In The Bush [Musique] 58 · Instant Replay [Dan Hartman] 29 · Last Dance [Donna Summer] 3 · Le Freak [Chic] 1 · Let's All Chant [Michael Zager Band] 36 · Shake Your Groove Thing [Peaches & Herb] 5 · Souvenirs [Voyage] 41 · Take Me Home [Cher] 8 · Y.M.C.A. [Village People] 2

10/30/99 · 142 · 1 · ©323 · Night In Rocketown, A · [L] · $10 · Rocketown 63746

Big Enough [Chris Rice] · Cartoons [Chris Rice] · Closer Still [Wilshire] · Deep Enough To Dream [Chris Rice] · Ginny's Story · Gloria [Watermark] · I Wanna Be Moved [Ginny Owens] · If You Want Me To [Ginny Owens] · In This Moment [Wilshire] · Make Us One [Cindy Morgan] · Praise The King [Cindy Morgan] · Sometimes Love [Chris Rice] · Take Me There [Watermark] · What Manner Of Love [Watermark] · Worship Medley

9/24/88 · 31 · 17 · ● · ©324 · 1988 Summer Olympics Album/One Moment In Time · $10 · Arista 8551

Fight (No Matter How Long) [Bunburys] · Harvest For The World [Christians] · Indestructible [Four Tops] 35 · Olympic Joy [Kashif] · Olympic Spirit [John Williams] · One Moment In Time [Whitney Houston] 5 · Peace In Our Time [Jennifer Holliday] · Reason To Try [Eric Carmen] 87 · Shape Of Things To Come [Bee Gees] · That's What Dreams Are Made Of [Odds & Ends] · Willpower [Taylor Dayne]

11/27/93 · 56 · 12 · ©325 · No Alternative · $10 · Arista 18737

All Your Jeans Were Too Tight [American Music Club] · Bitch [Goo Goo Dolls] · Brittle [Straitjacket Fits] · Can't Fight It [Bob Mould] · Effigy [Uncle Tupelo] · For All To See [Buffalo Tom] · Glynis [Smashing Pumpkins] · Heavy 33 [Verlaines] · Hold On [Sarah McLachlan] · Iris [Breeders] · It's The New Style [Beastie Boys] · Joed Out [Barbara Manning] · Memorial Tribute [Patti Smith] · Sexual Healing [Soul Asylum] · Show Me [Soundgarden] · Superdeformed [Matthew Sweet] · Take A Walk [Urge Overkill] · Unseen Power Of The Picket Fence [Pavement]

7/3/99 · 18 · 21 · ©326 · No Boundaries - A Benefit For The Kosovar Refugees · $10 · Epic 63653

Baba [Alanis Morissette] · Black Paintings [Peter Gabriel] · Come Down [Bush] · Freak On A Leash [Korn] · Ghost Of Tom Joad [Rage Against The Machine] · Go [Indigo Girls] · Last Kiss [Pearl Jam] 2 · Leather Jacket [Ben Folds Five] · Mary [Sarah McLachlan] · Merman [Tori Amos] · Psycho Man [Black Sabbath] · Soldier Of Love [Pearl Jam] · Take Me Away [Oasis] · Used To Be Lucky [Wallflowers] · War Of Man [Neil Young] · Wolf In Sheep's Clothing [Jamiroquai]

12/26/98 · 19 · 14 · ©327 · No Limit Soldier Compilation - We Can't Be Stopped · $10 · No Limit 50724

Assassin [Big Ed feat. Master P] · Break Something [Fiend] · Bring My Burners [Freedom] · Gangsta Move [Snoop Dogg] · Ghost In Da Dark II [Ghetto Commission] · Girl Power [Mia X] · Heaven 4 A Thug [Magic & Mac] · Hound Out [Full Blooded & the Hounds] · I Ain't Playin' [Mystikal] · It's A Riot [Kane & Abel] · My City [Mr Serv-On] · New Orleans Threats [Gotti/Q.B./Pheno] · No Limit Soldiers II [Master P/C-Murder/Fiend/Magic/Mr. Serv-On/Mia X/Mystikal] · Real Niggaz Gon Ride [C-Murder & Magic] · Red Rum [Steady Mobb'n] · Straight From Da Heart [Prime Suspects] · Where Da Lil Soldiers At? [Lil' Soldiers]

VARIOUS ARTISTS COMPILATIONS

DEBUT	PEAK	WKS	RIAA	CD	ARTIST — Album Title	Catalog	Sym	$	Label & Number

12/22/79+ | 19 | 18 | ● | ©328 | **No Nukes/The MUSE Concerts For A Non-Nuclear Future** .... [L] | **$25** Asylum 801 [3]

benefit concerts recorded in September 1979 at Madison Square Garden in New York City

Angel From Montgomery [Bonnie Raitt]
Before The Deluge [Jackson Browne]
Captain Jim's Drunken Dream [James Taylor]
Cathedral [Graham Nash]
Crow On The Cradle [Jackson Browne & Graham Nash]
Cry To Me [Tom Petty & The Heartbreakers]
Dependin' On You [Doobie Brothers]
Devil With The Blue Dress (medley) [Bruce Springsteen & The E Street Band]
Get Together [Jesse Colin Young]
Good Golly, Miss Molly (medley) [Bruce Springsteen & The E Street Band]
Heart Of The Night [Poco]
Honey Don't Leave L.A. [James Taylor]
Jenny Take A Ride (medley) [Bruce Springsteen/Jackson Browne/E Street Band]
Little Sister [Ry Cooder]
Long Time Gone [Crosby, Stills & Nash]
Lotta Love [Nicolette Larson & The Doobie Brothers]
Mockingbird [James Taylor & Carly Simon]
Once You Get Started [Chaka Khan]
Plutonium Is Forever [John Hall]
Power [Doobie Brothers/John Hall/James Taylor]
Runaway [Bonnie Raitt]
Stay [Bruce Springsteen/Jackson Browne/E Street Band]
Takin' It To The Streets [Doobie Brothers & James Taylor]
Teach Your Children [Crosby, Stills & Nash]
Times They Are A-Changin' [James Taylor/Carly Simon/Graham Nash]
We Almost Lost Detroit [Gil Scott-Heron]
Woman, A [Sweet Honey In The Rock]
You Can't Change That [Raydio]
You Don't Have To Cry [Crosby, Stills & Nash]

8/11/90 | 79 | 9 | | ©329 | **Nobody's Child - Romanian Angel Appeal** .... | **$10** Warner 26280

Ain't That Peculiar [Mike & The Mechanics]
Big Day Little Boat [Edie Brickell & New Bohemians]
Civil War [Guns N' Roses]
Feeding Off The Love Of The Land [Stevie Wonder]
Goodnight Little One [Ric Ocasek]
Homeward Bound [Paul Simon & George Harrison]
How Can You Mend A Broken Heart? [Bee Gees]
Lovechild [Billy Idol]
Medicine Man [Elton John]
Nobody's Child [Traveling Wilburys]
That Kind Of Woman [Eric Clapton]
This Week [Dave Stewart & The Spiritual Cowboys]
Trembler, The [Duane Eddy]
With A Little Help From My Friends [Ringo Starr & His All Star Band]
Wonderful Remark [Van Morrison]

2/24/96 | 119 | 2 | | ©330 | **Not Fade Away (Remembering Buddy Holly)** .... | **$10** Decca 11260

Crying, Waiting, Hoping [Marty Stuart & Steve Earle]
It Doesn't Matter Anymore [Suzy Bogguss w/Dave Edmunds]
Learning The Game [Waylon Jennings w/Mark Knopfler]
Maybe Baby [Nitty Gritty Dirt Band]
Midnight Shift [Los Lobos]
Not Fade Away [Band & The Crickets]
Oh Boy! [Joe Ely & Todd Snider]
Peggy Sue Got Married [Buddy Holly & The Hollies]
Think It Over [Tractors]
True Love Ways [Mavericks]
Well...All Right [Nanci Griffith w/The Crickets]
Wishing [Mary Chapin Carpenter & Kevin Montgomery]

11/14/98+ | 10 | 33 | ▲ | ©331 | **Now** .... | **$10** Virgin 46795

All My Life [K-Ci & JoJo] 1
Anytime [Brian McKnight]
As Long As You Love Me [Backstreet Boys]
Barbie Girl [Aqua] 7
Flagpole Sitta [Harvey Danger]
Fly Away [Lenny Kravitz] 12
I Will Buy You A New Life [Everclear]
If You Could Only See [Tonic]
Karma Police [Radiohead]
MMMBop [Hanson] 1
Never Ever [All Saints] 4
Say You'll Be There [Spice Girls] 3
Sex And Candy [Marcy Playground] 8
Shorty (You Keep Playing With My Mind) [Imajin] 25
Together Again [Janet] 1
Way, The [Fastball]
Zoot Suit Riot [Cherry Poppin' Daddies]

8/14/99 | 3 | 29 | ▲2 | ©332 | **Now 2** .... | **$10** Virgin 47910

...Baby One More Time [Britney Spears] 1
Because Of You [98°] 3
Closing Time [Semisonic]
Everybody's Free (To Wear Sunscreen) [Baz Luhrmann] 45
Father Of Mine [Everclear] 70
Goodbye [Spice Girls] 11
Hard Knock Life [Jay-Z] 15
I Think I'm Paranoid [Garbage]
I'll Never Break Your Heart [Backstreet Boys] 35
Millennium [Robbie Williams] 72
My Favorite Mistake [Sheryl Crow] 20
Never There [Cake] 78
Praise You [Fatboy Slim] 36
Sweetest Thing [U2] 63
Take Me There [BLACKstreet & Mya] 14
What I Got [Sublime]
When A Woman's Fed Up [R. Kelly] 22
You Get What You Give [New Radicals] 36

12/25/99+ | 4 | 37 | ▲2 | ©333 | **Now 3** .... | **$10** Universal 545417

All I Have To Give [Backstreet Boys] 5
All Star [Smash Mouth] 4
American Woman [Lenny Kravitz] 49
Bailamos [Enrique Iglesias] 1
Chanté's Got A Man [Chanté Moore] 10
Get Gone [Ideal] 13
Happily Ever After [Case] 15
Hardest Thing [98°] 5
Hey Leonardo (She Likes Me For Me) [Blessid Union Of Souls] 33
If I Could Turn Back The Hands Of Time [R. Kelly] 12
Nookie [Limp Bizkit] 80
Out Of My Head [Fastball] 20
Rockafeller Skank [Fatboy Slim] 76
Sometimes [Britney Spears] 21
Special [Garbage] 52
Tell Me It's Real [K-Ci & JoJo] 2
What's My Age Again? [Blink 182] 58
Why I'm Here [Oleander]

8/5/00 | ❶3 | 43 | ▲2 | ©334 | **Now 4** .... | **$10** Universal 524772

All The Small Things [Blink 182] 6
Blue (Da Ba Dee) [Eiffel 65] 6
Candy [Mandy Moore] 41
Get It On Tonite [Montell Jordan] 4
I Belong To You [Lenny Kravitz] 71
I Knew I Loved You [Savage Garden] 1
I Need To Know [Marc Anthony] 3
I Try [Macy Gray] 5
I Wanna Know [Joe] 4
It Feels So Good [Sonique] 8
Larger Than Life [Backstreet Boys] 25
Meet Virginia [Train] 20
Steal My Kisses [Ben Harper & The Innocent Criminals]
Then The Morning Comes [Smash Mouth] 11
This Time Around [Hanson] 20
Try Again [Aaliyah] 1
Waiting For Tonight [Jennifer Lopez] 8
(You Drive Me) Crazy [Britney Spears] 10

12/2/00 | 22 | 42 | ▲4 | ©335 | **Now 5** .... | **$10** Sony 85206

Aaron's Party (Come Get It) [Aaron Carter] 35
Absolutely (Story Of A Girl) [Nine Days] 6
Back Here [BBMak] 13
Case Of The Ex [Mya] 2
Doesn't Really Matter [Janet] 1
Don't Think I'm Not [Kandi] 24
Faded [Souldecision] 22
Give Me Just One Night (Una Noche) [98°] 2
I Think I'm In Love With You [Jessica Simpson] 21
I Wanna Be With You [Mandy Moore] 24
Incomplete [Sisqó] 1
It's Gonna Be Me [*NSYNC] 1
It's My Life [Bon Jovi] 33
Jumpin' Jumpin' [Destiny's Child] 3
Kryptonite [3 Doors Down] 3
Lucky [Britney Spears] 23
Shake Ya Ass [Mystikal] 13
Show Me The Meaning Of Being Lonely [Backstreet Boys] 6
Wonderful [Everclear] 11

4/21/01 | ❶3 | 24↑ | ▲3 | ©336 | **Now 6** .... | **$10** Sony 85663

AM Radio [Everclear]
Again [Lenny Kravitz] 4
Around The World (La La La La La) [ATC] 28
Beautiful Day [U2] 21
Bye Bye Bye [*NSYNC] 4
Crazy [K-Ci & JoJo] 11
Crazy For This Girl [Evan & Jaron] 15
Drive [Incubus] 9
Gotta Tell You [Samantha Mumba] 4
Hemorrhage (In My Hands) [Fuel] 30
I Wish [R. Kelly] 14
Independent Women Part I [Destiny's Child] 1
It Wasn't Me [Shaggy] 1
Love Don't Cost A Thing [Jennifer Lopez] 3
No More (Baby I'ma Do Right) [3LW] 23
Shape Of My Heart [Backstreet Boys] 9
Stronger [Britney Spears] 11
With Arms Wide Open [Creed] 1
Yellow [Coldplay] 48

8/12/00 | 155 | 4 | | ©337 | **Nuthin' But A Gangsta Party** .... | **$10** Priority 23916

B-Please [Snoop Dogg Feat. Xzibit]
Backyard Boogie [Mack 10] 37
Big Thangs [Ant Banks Feat. Too $hort & Ice Cube]
Bop Gun (One Nation) [Ice Cube Feat. George Clinton] 23
Everybody Knows [Kurupt Feat. Fred Wreck]
Friday [Ice Cube]
Girls All Pause [Kurupt]
I Love Cali [Roscoe]
I Want It All [Warren G Feat. Mack 10] 23
Just Clownin' [W.C.] 56
Keep Their Heads Ringin' [Dr. Dre] 10
Let It Reign [Westside Connection]
Pay Ya Dues [Low Profile]
Players Holiday [Ant Banks Presents T.W.D.Y. Feat. Too $hort & Mac Mall]
2 Of Amerikaz Most Wanted [2 Pac Feat. Snoop Doggy Dogg]
We Be Puttin' It Down! [Bad Azz Feat. Snoop Dogg]
What U See Is What U Get [Xzibit]
Where My Thugs At [Krayzie Bone]

1122

DEBUT	PEAK	WKS	RIAA	CD	ARTIST — Album Title	Catalog	Sym	$	Label & Number

4/10/99 · 77 · 8 · ● · ©338 · N.W.A. Legacy Volume 1 1988-1998, The .... **$15** Priority 51111 [2]

Alwayz Into Somethin' [N.W.A.]
Bow Down [Westside Connection] 21
Boyz-N-Tha Hood [Eazy-E]
California Love [2Pac Feat. Dr. Dre & Roger Troutman] 6
Color Blind [Ice Cube]
Dead Homiez [Ice Cube]
Final Frontier [MC Ren]
Fuck Tha Police [N.W.A.]
Gangsta, The Killa And The Dope Dealer [Westside Connection]
Guerillas In Tha Mist [Da Lench Mob]
In California [Daz Dillinger]
It Was A Good Day [Ice Cube] 15
Keep Their Heads Ringin' [Dr. Dre] 10
Last Song [Above The Law]
Let Me Ride [Dr. Dre] 34
Murder Was The Case [Snoop Doggy Dogg]
Natural Born Killaz [Dr. Dre/Ice Cube]
No One Can Do It Better [D.O.C.]
Nothin' But The Cavi Hit [Mack 10 & Tha Dogg Pound] 38
Only In California [Mack 10 Feat. Ice Cube & Snoop Doggy Dogg]
Steady Mobbin' [Ice Cube]
Straight Outta Compton [N.W.A.]
Trust No Bitch [Penthouse Players Clique]
We Want Eazy [Eazy-E]
Westside Slaughterhouse [Mack 10 Feat. Ice Cube & WC]
Westsyde Radio Megamix [N.W.A. & Eazy-E]

12/19/98 · 142 · 2 · ©339 · N.W.A. - Straight Outta Compton - 10th Anniversary Tribute .... **$10** Priority 53532

Compton's N The House [Dr. Dre & MC Ren]
Dopeman [Mack 10]
8 Ball [Jayo Felony]
Express Yourself [Silkk The Shocker]
Fuck Tha Police [Bone thugs-n-harmony]
Gangsta Gangsta [Snoop Dogg & C-Murder]
I Ain't Tha 1 [Mr. Mike]
If It Ain't Ruff [WC]
Parental Discretion Iz Advised [Comrads/Allfrumtha I/Boo Kapone]
Quiet On Tha Set [Big Punisher/Fat Joe/Cuban Link]
Something Like That [J-Dubb & Ant Banks]
Straight Outta Compton [King T/MC Eiht/Dre'sta]

7/14/84 · 92 · 13 · 340 · Official Music Of The XXIIIrd Olympiad Los Angeles 1984, The .... **$15** Columbia 39322 [2]

Bugler's Dream [Felix Slatkin]
Chance For Heaven [Christopher Cross] 76
Courtship [Bob James]
Grace [Quincy Jones]
Junku [Herbie Hancock]
Moodido (The Match) [Toto]
Nothing's Gonna Stop You Now [Loverboy]
Olympian-Lighting Of The Torch [Philip Glass]
Olympic Fanfare And Theme [John Williams]
Power [Bill Conti]
Reach Out [Giorgio Moroder] 81
Street Thunder [Foreigner]

2/5/94 · 123 · 19 · ● · ©341 · Old School .... **$10** Thump 4010

All Night Long [Mary Jane Girls]
Atomic Dog [George Clinton]
Cutie Pie [One Way] 61
Double Dutch Bus [Frankie Smith] 30
Five Minutes Of Funk [Whodini] 87
Flashlight [Parliament] 16
Friends [Whodini] 87
Funkin For Jamaica [Tom Browne]
It Takes Two [Rob Base] 36
Mr. Groove [One Way]
Smerphies Dance [Spyder-D]
Square Biz [Teena Marie] 50
You Dropped A Bomb On Me [Gap Band] 31
Your The One For Me [D-Train]

6/18/94 · 147 · 5 · ©342 · Old School Volume 2 .... **$10** Thump 4020

Bounce, Rock, Skate, Roll [Vaughn Mason & Crew] 81
Burn Rubber (Why You Wanna Hurt Me) [Gap Band] 84
Dazz [Brick] 3
Got To Be Real [Cheryl Lynn] 12
I Feel Good [James Brown] 3
Juicy Fruit [Mtume] 45
Let It Whip [Dazz Band] 5
Love Rollercoaster [Ohio Players] 1
Mary Jane [Rick James] 41
Oh Sheila [Ready For The World] 1
Pop It [One Way]
Pull Fancy Dancer/Pull [One Way]
Push It [Salt-N-Pepa] 19
Strawberry Letter 23 [Brothers Johnson] 5

9/21/59 · 12 · 183 · 343 · Oldies But Goodies .... **$50** Original Sound 5001

Confidential [Sonny Knight] 17
Convicted [Oscar McLollie]
Dance With Me Henry [Etta James]
Earth Angel (Will You Be Mine) [Penguins] 8
Eddie My Love [Teen Queens] 14
Heaven And Paradise [Don Julian & The Meadowlarks]
In The Still Of The Nite [Five Satins] 24
Let The Good Times Roll [Shirley & Lee] 20
Letter, The [Medallions]
Stranded In The Jungle [Cadets] 15
Tonite, Tonite [Mello-Kings] 77
Way You Look Tonight [Jaguars]

8/14/61 · 12 · 54 · 344 · Oldies But Goodies, Vol. 3 .... **$30** Original Sound 5004

At My Front Door [El Dorados] 17
Bongo Rock [Preston Epps] 14
Come Go With Me [Dell-Vikings] 4
Don't You Just Know It [Huey (Piano) Smith] 9
For Your Precious Love [Jerry Butler & The Impressions] 11
Long Tall Sally [Little Richard] 6
Lovers Never Say Goodbye [Flamingos] 52
Oh, What A Night [Dells]
Sea Cruise [Frankie Ford] 14
This Is My Story [Gene & Eunice]
Two People In The World [Little Anthony & The Imperials]
You Cheated [Shields] 12

6/16/62 · 15 · 39 · 345 · Oldies But Goodies, Vol. 4 .... **$30** Original Sound 5005

Blue Suede Shoes [Carl Perkins] 2
Casual Look [Six Teens] 25
Could This Be Magic [Dubs] 23
Love Is Strange [Mickey & Sylvia] 11
Money (That's What I Want) [Barrett Strong] 23
Plea, The [Chantels]
Silhouettes [Rays] 3
Teen Age Prayer [Gloria Mann] 19
Teen Beat [Sandy Nelson] 4
Tell Me Why [Norman Fox & The Rob-Roys]
To The Aisle [Five Satins] 25
Whole Lot Of Shakin' Going On [Jerry Lee Lewis] 3

6/1/63 · 16 · 31 · 346 · Oldies But Goodies, Vol. 5 .... **$25** Original Sound 5007

Alley-Oop [Hollywood Argyles] 1
Angel Baby [Rosie & The Originals] 5
Bongo Bongo Bongo [Preston Epps] 78
Closer You Are [Channels]
Daddy's Home [Shep & The Limelites] 2
Diamonds And Pearls [Paradons] 18
Hearts Of Stone [Jewels]
Little Star [Elegants] 1
Rock-in Robin [Bobby Day] 2
Since I Don't Have You [Skyliners] 12
Sixty-Minute Man [Dominoes]
Stay [Maurice Williams] 1

1/25/64 · 31 · 11 · 347 · Oldies But Goodies, Vol. 6 .... **$25** Original Sound 5011

Duke Of Earl [Gene Chandler] 1
Every Beat Of My Heart [Pips] 6
Honky Tonk (Parts 1 & 2) [Bill Doggett] 2
Image Of A Girl [Safaris] 6
Mashed Potato Time [Dee Dee Sharp] 2
Quarter To Three [U.S. Bonds] 1
Raindrops [Dee Clark] 2
Teenager In Love [Dion & The Belmonts] 5
This I Swear [Skyliners] 26
Those Oldies But Goodies (Remind Me Of You) [Little Caesar & The Romans] 9
You Were Mine [Fireflies] 21

1/9/65 · 121 · 9 · 348 · Oldies But Goodies, Vol. 7 .... **$25** Original Sound 5012

Bumble Boogie [B. Bumble & the Stingers] 21
Donna [Ritchie Valens] 2
Handy Man [Jimmy Jones] 2
He Will Break Your Heart [Jerry Butler] 7
I Know (You Don't Love Me No More) [Barbara George] 3
I Love How You Love Me [Paris Sisters] 5
It's All In The Game [Tommy Edwards] 1
New Orleans [U.S. Bonds] 6
Once In A While [Chimes] 11
Runaround Sue [Dion] 1
Teen Angel [Mark Dinning] 1
Tequila [Champs] 1

4/25/98 · 145 · 6 · ©349 · One And Only Love Album, The .... **$15** Polydor 555610 [2]

All Out Of Love [Air Supply] 2
Baby, I Love Your Way [Peter Frampton] 12
Endless Love [Diana Ross & Lionel Richie] 1
Fernando [Abba] 13
Get Here [Oleta Adams] 5
How Can You Mend A Broken Heart [Bee Gees] 1
How Much I Feel [Ambrosia] 3
I Want To Know What Love Is [Foreigner] 1
I'd Really Love To See You Tonight [England Dan & John Ford Coley] 2
I'll Stand By You [Pretenders] 16
I'm Not In Love [10 cc] 2
Make It With You [Bread] 1
More Than Words [Extreme] 1
Never Knew Love Like This Before [Stephanie Mills] 6
Never My Love [Association] 2
Nights In White Satin [Moody Blues] 2
Reason To Believe [Rod Stewart] 19
Reunited [Peaches & Herb] 1
Save The Best For Last [Vanessa Williams] 1
True [Spandau Ballet] 4
Up Where We Belong [Joe Cocker & Jennifer Warnes] 1
Without You [Harry Nilsson] 1
Wonderful Tonight [Eric Clapton] 16
Your Song [Elton John] 8

12/21/96 · 160 · 3 · 350 · 101 Dalmatians Sing-Along .... **$10** Walt Disney 60910

available only on cassette
Cruella De Vil
Dalmatian Plantation
He's A Tramp
(How Much Is) That Doggie In The Window?
Kanine Krunchies Kommercial
Oh Where, Oh Where Has My Little Dog Gone?
One Hundred And One Dalmatians
Pongo

VARIOUS ARTISTS COMPILATIONS

DEBUT	PEAK	WKS	RIAA	CD	ARTIST — Album Title	Catalog	Sym	$	Label & Number

6/16/01 — 162 — 1 — ©351 — 100 Songs For Kids — $20 — Time Life 00831 [4]

Aiken Drum / Aunt Rhodie / Baa-Baa Black Sheep / Big Ship Sails On The Ali-Ali-O / Billy Boy / Bingo / Bluetail Fly (Jimmy Crack Corn) / Bobby Shafto / Boys And Girls Come Out To Play / Bye Baby Bunting / Clementine / Cockles And Mussels (Molly Marlone) / Daddy Wouldn't Buy Me A Bow-Wow / Daisy Daisy / Do You Ken John Peel? / Do Your Ears Hang Low? / Farmer In The Dell / Five Green Bottles / For He's A Jolly-Good Fellow / Frère Jacques / God Bless The Moon / Goosey Goosey Gander / Grand Olde Duke Of York / Grandfather Clock / Happy Birthday / Happy Wanderer / Here We Go Luby-Loo / Here We Go Round The Mulberry Bush / Hickory Dickory Dock / Home On The Range / Hot Cross Buns / How Many Miles To Babylon? / How Much Is That Doggy In The Window? / Humpty Dumpty / Hush Little Baby / I Had A Little Nut Tree / I Saw Three Ships / I Was Working On The Railroad / I'm A Little Teapot / I'm H-A-P-P-Y / Incy-Wincy Spider / Jack And Jill / John Brown's Baby / Lavender's Blue / Little Bo Peep / Little Boy Blue / Little Brown Jug / Little Jack Horner / Little Miss Muffet / London Bridge Is Falling Down / London's Burning / Lucy Locket / Lullaby And Goodnight / Mary Had A Little Lamb / Michael Finigan / Muffin Man / My Bonny Lies Over The Ocean / North Wind Doth Blow / Oh Dear What Can The Matter Be? / Oh Where, Oh Where Has My Little Dog Gone / Old Grey Mare / Old MacDonald Had A Farm / On Top Of Old Smokey / One Man Went To Mow / Oranges And Lemons / Pat-A-Cake Pat-A-Cake / Peas Pudding / Polly Put The Kettle On / Polly Wally Doodle / Pop Goes The Weasel / Ride A Cock-Horse To Banbury Cross / Ring-A-Ring-A-Roses / Rock-A-Bye Baby / Row Row Row Your Boat / Rub-A-Dub Dub Three Men In A Tub / See-Saw Margery Daw / She'll Be Coming Round The Mountain / Simple Simon / Sing A Song Of Sixpence / Six In A Bed / Skip To My Lou / Sky Boat Song / T'was On A Monday Morning / Take Me Out To The Ball Game / There Was A Crooked Man / There's A Hole In My Bucket / This Is The Way The Ladies Ride / This Little Pig / This Old Man (Knick-Knack Paddy Wack) / Three Blind Mice / Three Little Kittens / Three Little Pigs / To Market To Market / Tom Tom The Piper's Son / Twinkle Twinkle Little Star / Waltzing Matilda / Winkum Winkum / Yankee Doodle / Yellow Rose Of Texas / You Are My Sunshine

10/11/97 — 193 — 1 — ©352 — One Step Up/Two Steps Back: The Songs Of Bruce Springsteen — $15 — Right Stuff 59780 [2]

All Or Nothin' At All [Marshall Crenshaw] / Atlantic City [Kurt Neumann] / Darkness On The Edge Of Town [Martin Zellar] / Don't Look Back [Knack] / Downbound Train [Smithereens] / Fever, The [Southside Johnny & The Asbury Jukes] / 4th Of July, Asbury Park (Sandy) [Ben E. King] / Guilty [Robbin Thompson] / Human Touch [Joe Cocker] / If I Was The Priest [Allan Clarke] / It's Hard To Be A Saint In The City [David Bowie] / Jackson Cage [John Wesley Harding] / Janey, Don't You Lose Heart [Mrs. Fun/Tina & The B-Side Movement] / Johnny 99 [John Hiatt] / Light Of Day [Joe Grushecky & The Houserockers] / Love's On The Line [Gary U.S. Bonds] / Meeting Across The River [Syd Straw] / One Step Up [Paul Cebar] / Protection [Donna Summer] / Restless Nights [Rocking Chairs] / Savin' Up [Clarence Clemons & The Red Bank Rockers] / Seaside Bar Song [Little Bob Story] / Seeds [Dave Alvin] / Something In The Night [Aram] / Stolen Car [Elliott Murphy] / Streets Of Philadelphia [Richie Havens] / Tiger Rose [Sonny Burgess] / Wreck On The Highway [Nils Lofgren]

10/8/66 — 49 — 21 — 353 — Opening Nights At The Met — $25 — RCA Victor 6171 [3]

historic recordings by opera stars who performed at New York's old Metropolitan Opera House from 1883-1965

Barber of Seville: Trio [Peters/Valletti/Merrill] / Bell Song [Lily Pons] / Ciel! Mio Padre; Su, Dunque! [Elisabeth Rethberg/Giuseppe De Luca] / Death Of Boris [Ezio Pinza] / Death Of Otello [Vinay/Assandri/Moscona/Newman] / Deh Vieni Non Tardar [Bidu Sayao] / Dite Alla Giovine [Amelita Galli-Curci/Giuseppe De Luca] / Euch Luften, Die Mein Klagen [Helen Traubel] / Forse La Soglia Attinse [Jan Peerce] / Iago's Creed [Antonio Scotti] / Il Balen Del Suo Sorriso [Leonard Warren/Nicola Moscona] / Je Viens Celebrer La Victoire [Caruso/Homer] / Jewel Song [Nellie Melba] / Juliet's Waltz Song [Emma Eames] / Le Roi De Thule [Emma Eames] / Mir Ist Die Ehre / Non Pensateci Piu Ora E Per Sempre Addio [Martinelli/Tibbett] / O Patria Mia [Emmy Destinn] / Ora Stammi A Sentir [Geraldine Farrar] / Plebe, Patrizi [Tibbett/Martinelli/Bampton/Nicholson] / Qual Pallor! [Jussi Bjoerling/Robert Merrill] / Rachel! Quand Du Seigneur [Enrico Caruso] / Rigoletto: Quartet [Caruso/Sembrich/Scotti/Severina] / Ritorna Vincitor [Zinka Milanov] / Sempre Libera [Lucrezia Bori] / Stella Del Marinar [Louise Homer] / Suicidio! [Rosa Ponselle] / Temple Scene [Ezio Pinza/Giovanni Martinelli/Grace Anthony] / Tristan And Isolde [Kirsten Flagstad/Lauritz Melchior] / Vissi D'Arte [Maria Jeritza]

12/13/69+ — 166 — 5 — 354 — Original Hits Of Right Now, The — $20 — Dunhill/ABC 50070

Baby It's You [Smith] 5 / Ballad Of Easy Rider [Odetta] / **Easy To Be Hard** [Three Dog Night] 4 / I Wasn't Born To Follow [Robbs] / **I'd Wait A Million Years** [Grass Roots] 15 / It's Getting Better [Mama Cass] 30 / **Make Your Own Kind Of Music** [Mama Cass Elliot] 36 / **Move Over** [Steppenwolf] 31 / One [Three Dog Night] 5 / **River Is Wide** [Grass Roots] 31 / **Rock Me** [Steppenwolf] 10 / Weight, The [Smith]

8/31/63 — 128 — 4 — 355 — Original Hootenanny, The — $25 — Crestview 806

Bonnie Ship The Diamond [Judy Collins] / If I Had A Hammer [Limeliters] / John Henry [Josh White] / Josie [Ed McCurdy] / Katy Cruel [Travelers 3] / La Bamba [Bud & Travis] / Reuben's Train [Dillards] / Rising Of The Moon [Theodore Bikel] / Squid Jiggin' Ground [Oscar Brand] / Three Jovial Huntsmen [Will Holt] / Wade In The Water [Judy Henske] / You Can Tell The World [Bob Gibson]

12/29/62+ — 27 — 13 — 356 — Other Family, The — [C] $20 — Laurie 5000

Another Saturday Night / Bedtime Story / In The Department Store / In The Shop / Phone Call / Press Conference / Radio Commercial / T.V. Show / Talent Show / Visit, The

9/10/66 — 40 — 14 — 357 — Our Wedding Album or The Great Society Affair — [C] $20 — Jamie 3028

Birds And The Bees / Daughter's Hand / End, The / Great Society Affair / Guest List / In-Laws / News, The / Parents Of The Bride / Proposal, The / Sister And The Movie Star / Stag Party / Tape Recording / Wedding Gown

5/17/97 — 192 — 1 — ©358 — OzzFest — [L] $10 — Red Ant 7000

Angel Of Death [Slayer] / Attitude [Sepultura] / Broken Foundation [Earth Crisis] / Loco [Coal Chamber] / Locust Star [Neurosis] / Organized [Powerman 5000] / Perry Mason [Ozzy Osbourne] / Replica [Fear Factory] / Ride Thy Neighbor [Cellophane] / These Eyes [Biohazard]

4/14/01 — 144 — 2 — ©359 — OzzFest - Second Stage Live — [L] $15 — Divine 28860 [2]

Angel Of Death [Slayer] / Attitude [Sepultura] / Big Fuck You [Primer 55] / Broken Foundation [Earth Crisis] / Eye For An Eye [Soulfly] / I Don't Know [Ozzy Osbourne] / Keep It Clean [Pitchshifter] / Loco [Coal Chamber] / Locust Star [Neurosis] / Mirror's Reflection [Taproot] / Ode To Clarissa [Queens Of The Stone Age] / Organized [Powerman 5000] / Pain [Soulfly] / Perry Mason [Ozzy Osbourne] / Pushing Me [Slaves On Dope] / Replica [Fear Factory] / Suck [Kittie] / These Eyes [Biohazard] / Voices [Disturbed]

DEBUT	PEAK	WKS	RIAA	CD	ARTIST — Album Title			Catalog	Sym	$	Label & Number
2/21/98	105	6		©360	**Party Over Here 98**					$10	Elektra 62088

Party Over Here 98
Big Daddy [Heavy D] 18 — Love, Peace & Nappiness [Lost Boyz] — Rain (Supa Dupa Fly) [Missy "Misdemeanor" Elliott] — Take It To The Streets [Rampage Feat. Billy Lawrence] 34
Cold Rock A Party [MC Lyte Feat. Missy "Misdemeanor" Elliott] 11 — No Diggity [BLACKstreet Feat. Dr. Dre] 1 — Return Of The Mack [Mark Morrison] 2 — Twisted [Keith Sweat] 2
Come On [Billy Lawrence Feat. MC Lyte] 44 — Put Your Hands Where My Eyes Could See [Busta Rhymes] — Steelo [702 Feat. Missy "Misdemeanor" Elliott] 32 — Whatever [En Vogue] 16
Let It Go [Ray J] 25

| 1/18/64 | 80 | 8 | | 361 | **Pick Hits Of The Radio Good Guys** | | | | | $30 | Laurie 2021 |

Denise [Randy & The Rainbows] 10 — Little Bit Of Soap [Jarmels] 12 — Over The Rainbow [Demensions] 16 — Runaround Sue [Dion] 1
He's So Fine [Chiffons] 1 — New Orleans [U.S. Bonds] 6 — Please Write [Tokens] — Wanderer, The [Dion] 1
Hushabye [Mystics] 20 — One Fine Day [Chiffons] 5
Just To Be With You [Passions] 69 — Quarter To Three [U.S. Bonds] 1

| 10/17/87 | 123 | 20 | | 362 | **Piledriver: The Wrestling Album II** | | | [N] | | $10 | Epic 40889 |

Crank It Up [Jimmy Hart] — Honky Tonk Man [Honky Tonk Man] — Rock And Roll Hoochie Koo [Gene Okerlund & Rick Derringer] — Waking Up Alone [Hillbilly Jim & Gertrude]
Demolition [Rick Derringer] — If You Only Knew [Wrestlers] — Stand Back [Vince McMahon]
Girls In Cars [Robbie Dupree & Strike Force] — Jive Soul Bro [Slick]
Piledriver [Koko B. Ware]

| 9/23/00 | 59 | 8 | | ©363 | **Platinum Hits 2000** | | | | | $10 | Columbia 61586 |

Bounce With Me [Lil Bow Wow] 20 — Don't Give Up [Chicane feat. Bryan Adams] — I Think God Can Explain [Splender] 62 — Maria [Ricky Martin] 88
Bring It All To Me [Blaque] 5 — Doo Wop (That Thing) [Lauryn Hill] 1 — I Wanna Love You Forever [Jessica Simpson] 3 — Puro Dolor [Son By 4] 26
Crash And Burn [Savage Garden] 24 — Fortunate [Maxwell] 4 — Let's Get Married [Jagged Edge] 11 — Say My Name [Destiny's Child] 1
Don't Call Me Baby [Madison Avenue] 88 — Freakin' It [Will Smith] 99 — Lullaby [Shawn Mullins] 7 — Shackles (Praise You) [Mary Mary] 28
You Sang To Me [Marc Anthony] 2

| 6/17/95 | 46 | 16 | ▲ | 364 | **Pocahontas Sing-Along** | | | | | $10 | Walt Disney 60876 |

available only on cassette
Colors Of The Wind — Listen With Your Heart — Steady As The Beating Drum
Just Around The Riverbend — Mine, Mine, Mine — Virginia Company

| 7/17/99 | 90 | 25 | ● | ©365 | **Pokémon - 2.B.A. Master** | | | | | $10 | Koch 8901 |

Double Trouble (Team Rocket) — Pokémon — Time Has Come (Pikachu's Goodbye) — Viridian City
Everything Changes — Pokémon Theme — 2B A Master — What Kind Of Pokémon Are You?
Misty's Song — PokéRAP — Together Forever — You Can Do It (If You Really Try)
My Best Friends

| 10/15/55 | 8 | 9 | | 366 | **Pop Shopper** | | | | | $30 | RCA Victor 12-13 |

EP: RCA Victor SPC 7-13 (#8); LP: RCA Victor SPL 12-13 (#9)
Aupres de Ma Blonde (medley) [George Melachrino Orch.] — Hey Jacque [Eartha Kitt] — Jack's Kinda Swing [Al Cohn's Natural Seven] — Solo For Joe [Sauter-Finegan Orch.]
Corrine Corrina [Chet Atkins] — Il Etait Une Bergere (medley) [George Melachrino Orch.] — Le Reve Passe (medley) [George Melachrino Orch.] — They All Laughed [Jaye P. Morgan]
Cuba Rhumba [Hank Snow] — It's A Good Day [Perry Como] — Rivers [Harry Geller & His Orch.] — Voodoo Suite-Part 1 [Perez Prado]
Fump [Milton Hinton] — Wayfaring Stranger [Eddy Arnold]

| 1/18/97 | 51 | 14 | | ©367 | **Power Of Love** | | | | | $10 | Madacy 6803 |

Arthur's Theme (Best That You Can Do) [Christopher Cross] 1 — Everytime You Go Away [Paul Young] 1 — Lady In Red [Chris DeBurgh] 3 — Tonight I Celebrate My Love [Peabo Bryson/Roberta Flack] 16
At This Moment [Billy Vera & The Beaters] 1 — Her Town Too [James Taylor/J.D. Souther] 11 — Never Gonna Let You Go [Sergio Mendes] 4 — Unchained Melody [Righteous Brothers] 4
Baby, Come To Me [Patti Austin/James Ingram] 1 — I Can Dream About You [Dan Hartman] 6 — One More Night [Phil Collins] 1
Don't Know Much [Linda Ronstadt/Aaron Neville] 2 — I'll Always Love You [Taylor Dayne] 3 — Power Of Love [Jennifer Rush] 57
— Power Of Love/Love Power [Luther Vandross] 4
— Slow Hand [Pointer Sisters] 2

| 8/12/00 | 181 | 2 | | ©368 | **Powerpuff Girls: Heroes & Villains, The** | | | | | $10 | Rhino 75848 |

B.L.O.S.S.O.M. [Komeda] — Don't Look Down [Sugarplastic] — Go Monkey Go [Devo] — Signal In The Sky (Let's Go) [Apples In Stereo]
Bubbles [Dressy Bessy] — Fight, The [Cornelius] — Powerpuff Girls (End Theme) [Bis] — Walk & Chew Gum [Optiganally Yours]
Buttercup (I'm A Super Girl) [Shonen Knife] — Fight The Power [Bis] — Powerpuff Girls (Main Theme) [Bis]
— Friends Win [The Bill Doss] — Pray For The Girls [Frank Black]

| 1/12/63 | 35 | 13 | | 369 | **President Strikes Back!, The** | | | [C] | | $20 | Kapp 1322 |

Big Men — Fan Mail — TV Commercial — U.N. Meeting
Cabinet Meeting — International Competition — Taxi Ride
Cuber — "President" Strikes Back — Theatrical Agent
Face To Face — Press Conference — Typical Day At The White House

| 12/5/98+ | 73 | 15 | ● | ©370 | **Prince Of Egypt - Inspirational, The** | | | [V] | | $10 | DreamWorks 50050 |

songs inspired by the movie
As Long As You're With Me [Trini-I-Tee 5:7] — Father [Brian McKnight] — Let Go, Let God [Tyrone Tribbett & Greater Anointing] — My Deliverer [DC Talk]
Destiny [Take 6] — God Will Take Care Of Me [Carman] — Let My People Go [Kirk Franklin] — Power [Fred Hammond & Radical For Christ]
Didn't I [Christian] — I Am [Donnie McClurkin] — Moses The Deliverer [Shirley Caesar] — River, The [CeCe Winans]
Everything In Between [Jars Of Clay] — I Will Get There [Boyz II Men] 32 — Most High Interlude, Part 1-3 — Stay With Me [BeBe Winans]
— I Will Get There (A Cappella)

| 12/5/98+ | 85 | 11 | ● | ©371 | **Prince Of Egypt - Nashville, The** | | | [V] | | $10 | DreamWorks 50045 |

songs inspired by the movie
Could It Be Me [Charlie Daniels] — I Give You To His Heart [Alison Krauss] — Moving Of The Mountain [Mac McAnally] — Somewhere Down The Road [Faith Hill]
Freedom [Wynonna] — I Will Be There For You [Jessica Andrews] — Once In Awhile [Vince Gill] — Voice, The [Alabama]
Godspeed [Beth Nielsen Chapman] — Make It Through [Randy Travis & Linda Davis] — Please Be The One [Reba McEntire] — Walk In Glory [Mindy McCready]
Heartbeat Of Hope [Steven Curtis Chapman] — Milk And Honey [Pam Tillis] — Slavery, Deliverance And Faith [Clint Black] — You Are My Light [Gary Chapman]
I Can't Be A Slave [Toby Keith]

| 6/6/87 | 194 | 3 | | ©372 | **Prince's Trust 10th Anniversary Birthday Party, The** | | | [L] | | $10 | A&M 3906 |

recorded on 6/20/86 at Wembley Arena in London
Better Be Good To Me [Tina Turner] — I'm Still Standing [Elton John] — Money For Nothing [Dire Straits] — Sailing [Rod Stewart]
Call Of The Wild [Midge Ure] — In The Air Tonight [Phil Collins] — No One Is To Blame [Howard Jones] — Something About You [Level 42]
Fields Of Fire [Big Country] — Marlene On The Wall [Suzanne Vega] — Reach Out [Joan Armatrading]
Get Back [Paul McCartney]

| 4/24/99 | 136 | 2 | | ©373 | **Prodigy Present The Dirtchamber Sessions Volume One** | | | | | $10 | Beggars Banquet 128 |

no track titles listed

VARIOUS ARTISTS COMPILATIONS

DEBUT	PEAK	WKS	RIAA	CD	ARTIST — Album Title	Catalog	Sym	$	Label & Number

7/18/98 — 80 — 8 — ©374 — Punk-O-Rama 3 — **$10** — Epitaph 86534

A.D.D. [Ten Foot Pole]
Alright [Osker]
Bad Seed [Wayne Kramer]
Defiled [New Bomb Turks]
Delinquent Song [Voodoo Glow Skulls]
Everready [H2O]
Everybodies Girl [Dwarves]
Gotta Go [Agnostic Front]
Greed Motivates [Straight Faced]
Haulass Hyena [Cramps]
If [Pulley]
Lozin' Must [Millencolin]
Never Connected [Union 13]
No Equalizer [Down By Law]
Ordinary Fight [I Against I]
Poison Steak [Red Aunts]
Rats In The Hallway [Rancid]
Rotten Egg [Gas Huffer]
Say Anything [Bouncing Souls]
Steel-Toed Sneakers [Humpers]
Telepath Boy [Zeke]
Wake Up [Pennywise]
We Threw Gasoline On The Fire And Now We Have Stumps ForArmsAndNoEyebrows [NOFX]
World's On Heroin [All]
You [Bad Religion]

7/10/99 — 113 — 8 — ©375 — Punk-O-Rama 4 — **$10** — Epitaph 86563

Big In Japan [Tom Waits]
Don't Panic [Gas Huffer]
Faster Than The World [H2O]
Fight It [Pennywise]
Generator [Bad Religion]
Getaway, The [Ten Foot Pole]
Hopeless Romantic [Bouncing Souls]
I Will Deny [Dwarves]
It's My Life [Agnostic Front]
Kids Of The K Hole [NOFX]
Let's Do This [Straight Faced]
Life's Story [Union 13]
Lucky [Osker]
Mr. Clean [Millencolin]
1998 [Rancid]
Picture This [98 Mute]
Second Best [Pulley]
Snap Decision [New Bomb Turks]
Someone To Love? [Gentleman Jack Grisham]
Summerholiday Vs. Punkroutine [Refused]
They Always Come Back [Voodoo Glow Skulls]
Think The World [All]
Twisted [Zeke]
Weakend Revolution [59 Times The Pain]
Will The Message [Bombshell Rocks]

7/8/00 — 71 — 9 — ©376 — Punk-O-Rama 5 — **$10** — Epitaph 86588

Automatic Teller [New Bomb Turks]
Badge Of Pride [Pennywise]
Better Be Women [Dwarves]
Close Minded [Vision]
Evil Dead [Zeke]
Game, The [Union 13]
Gone [Pulley]
Good Rats [Dropkick Murphys]
Guilty By Association [H2O]
Happy [Straight Faced]
Hives - Introduce The Metric System In Time [Hives]
Hold It Down [Madball]
Kid [Bouncing Souls]
Lookin' Out For #1 [Death By Stereo]
No Cigar [Millencolin]
1.80 Down [Bombshell Rocks]
Panic [Osker]
Poison [Rancid]
Problematic [All]
Pump Up The Valuum [NOFX]
Refused Are Fucking Dead [Refused]
Riot, Riot Upstart [Agnostic Front]
Secure Horizons [Guttermouth]
Slow Motion Riot [98 Mute]
Smash It Up [The (International) Noise Conspiracy]
Stranded In The Jungle [Voodoo Glow Skulls]
We Have To Figure It Out Tonight [Beatsteaks]
What Ever [Satanic Surfers]

6/23/01 — 80 — 10 — ©377 — Punk-O-Rama 6 — **$10** — Epitaph 86615

Bath Of Least Resistance [NOFX]
Blackeye [Millencolin]
Can I Borrow Some Ambition? [Guttermouth]
Come With Me [Deviates]
Different But The Same [Raised Fist]
Gauntlet, The [Dropkick Murphys]
Holding 60 Dollars On A Burning Bridge [Death By Stereo]
I Want To Conquer The World [Bad Religion]
Innocence [Union 13]
It's Quite Alright [Rancid]
Jack Of All Trades [Hot Water Music]
Let Me In [Beatsteaks]
Only Lovers Left Alive [T(i)nc]
Original Me [Descendents]
Pure Trauma [downset.]
Runaway [Pulley]
Say Goodnight [Voodoo Glow Skulls]
She Broke My Dick [All]
Strangled [Osker]
Takers & Users [Business]
Tonight I'm Burning [Bombshell Rocks]
True Believers [Bouncing Souls]
We're Desperate [Pennywise w/Exene]

5/5/01 — 161 — 1 — ©378 — Pure Blues — **$10** — UTV 556176

Big Boss Man [Jimmy Reed] 78
Born Under A Bad Sign [Albert King]
Flood Down In Texas [Stevie Ray Vaughan & Double Trouble]
Good Morning Little School Girl [Jonny Lang]
Have You Ever Loved A Woman [Freddy King]
Hound Dog [Big Mama Thornton]
(I'm Your) Hoochie Coochie Man [Muddy Waters]
Just Won't Burn [Susan Tedeschi]
Let Me Love You Baby [Buddy Guy]
Little Red Rooster [Luther Allison]
Mean Old World [Eric Clapton & Duane Allman]
One Bourbon, One Scotch, One Beer [John Lee Hooker]
Shame, Shame, Shame [Kenny Wayne Shepherd]
Smoking Gun [Robert Cray] 22
Spoonful [Howlin' Wolf]
Statesboro Blues [Allman Brothers Band]
Tell Mama [Etta James] 23
Thrill Is Gone [B.B. King] 15
Turn On Your Love Light [Bobby "Blue" Bland] 28
Wang Dang Doodle [Koko Taylor] 58

10/11/97 — 125 — 7 — ©379 — Pure Dance 1998 — **$10** — Polygram 553847

Da' Dip [Freak Nasty] 15
Discotheque [U2] 10
Don't Speak [Clueless]
Encore Une Fois [Sash]
Fired Up [Funky Green Dogs] 80
Get Up [Byron Stingily]
How Bizarre [OMC]
In De Ghetto [Bad Yard Club Feat. Crystal Waters]
Jellyhead [Crush] 72
Let's Get Down [Tony, Toni, Toné]
Lovefool [Cardigans]
Lover That You Are [Pulse]
My Baby Daddy [B-Rock & The Bizz] 10
Say...If You Feel Alright [Crystal Waters] 40
Talk To Me [Wild Orchid] 48
This Is Your Night [Amber] 24
Wind Up Your Body [David Morales Feat. Delta]

12/14/96+ — 83 — 57 — ▲ — ©380 — Pure Disco — C:#37/1 — **$10** — Polydor 535877

Best Disco In Town [Ritchie Family] 17
Celebration [Kool & The Gang] 1
Cuba [Gibson Brothers] 81
Dancing Queen [Abba] 1
Don't Leave Me This Way [Thelma Houston] 1
Flashback [Imagination]
Funkytown [Lipps, Inc.] 1
Got To Give It Up (Part One) [Marvin Gaye] 1
Grease Megamix [John Travolta & Olivia Newton-John]
Hot Stuff [Donna Summer] 1
I Don't Believe You Want To Get Up And Dance (Oops!) [Gap Band]
I Feel Love [Donna Summer] 6
I Love The Nightlife [Alicia Bridges] 5
I Need Your Lovin' [Teena Marie] 37
I Will Survive [Gloria Gaynor] 1
If I Can't Have You [Yvonne Elliman] 1
Knock On Wood [Amii Stewart] 1
Love Hangover [Diana Ross] 1
That's The Way (I Like It) [K.C. & The Sunshine Band] 1
Y.M.C.A. [Village People] 2
You're The First, The Last, My Everything [Barry White] 2

11/8/97+ — 71 — 46 — ● — ©381 — Pure Disco 2 — **$10** — Polydor 555120

Can't Get Enough Of Your Love, Babe [Barry White] 1
Diva Megamix [Various Artists]
Everlasting Love [Carl Carlton] 6
Flashdance...What A Feeling [Irene Cara] 1
Fly, Robin, Fly [Silver Convention] 1
Gimme! Gimme! Gimme! (A Man After Midnight) [Abba]
Hustle, The [Van McCoy] 1
I Just Want To Be Your Everything [Andy Gibb] 1
I Will Survive [Gloria Gaynor] 1
It's Raining Men [Weather Girls] 46
Last Dance [Donna Summer] 3
Love Rollercoaster [Ohio Players] 1
Love's Theme [Love Unlimited Orchestra] 1
Macho Man [Village People] 25
Play That Funky Music [Wild Cherry] 1
Ring My Bell [Anita Ward] 1
Rock The Boat [Hues Corporation] 1
(Shake, Shake, Shake) Shake Your Booty [KC & The Sunshine Band] 1
Turn The Beat Around [Vicki Sue Robinson] 10
Upside Down [Diana Ross] 1
We Are Family [Sister Sledge] 2

10/17/98 — 150 — 5 — ©382 — Pure Disco 3 — **$10** — PolyGram TV 565357

Boogie Oogie Oogie [Taste Of Honey] 1
Come To Me [France Joli] 15
Could It Be Magic [Donna Summer] 52
December, 1963 (Oh, What A Night) [4 Seasons] 1
Disco Inferno [Trammps] 11
Forget Me Nots [Patrice Rushen] 23
Get Up & Boogie [Silver Convention] 2
He's The Greatest Dancer [Sister Sledge] 9
Heart Of Glass [Blondie] 1
In The Navy [Village People] 3
Ladies Night [Kool & The Gang] 8
Lay All Your Love On Me [Abba]
Le Freak [Chic] 1
Love Machine [Miracles] 1
Never Can Say Goodbye [Gloria Gaynor] 9
Shadow Dancing [Andy Gibb] 1
Shake Your Groove Thing [Peaches & Herb] 5
Then Came You [Dionne Warwicke & Spinners] 1
When Will I See You Again [Three Degrees] 2
You Make Me Feel (Mighty Real) [Sylvester] 36
You're The One That I Want [John Travolta & Olivia Newton-John] 1

8/28/99 — 113 — 10 — ©383 — Pure 80's — **$10** — UTV 564809

Addicted To Love [Robert Palmer] 1
Centerfold [J. Geils Band] 1
Come On Eileen [Dexy's Midnight Runners] 1
Everybody Have Fun Tonight [Wang Chung] 2
Everybody Wants To Rule The World [Tears For Fears] 1
Higher Love [Steve Winwood] 1
Hold Me Now [Thompson Twins] 3
Hungry Like The Wolf [Duran Duran] 3
Jessie's Girl [Rick Springfield] 1
Karma Chameleon [Culture Club] 1
Obsession [Animotion] 6
Everybody Have Fun Tonight [Fixx] 4
Our House [Madness] 7
Relax [Frankie Goes To Hollywood] 1
Rock This Town [Stray Cats] 9
Something About You [Level 42] 7
Sweet Dreams (Are Made Of This) [Eurythmics] 1
Tainted Love [Soft Cell] 8
Tempted [Squeeze] 49
Video Killed The Radio Star [Buggles] 40

DEBUT	PEAK	WKS	RIAA	CD	ARTIST — Album Title	Catalog	Sym	$	Label & Number

3/31/01 — 184 — 1 — ● — ©384 — Pure 80's Hits — $10 — UTV 560784

Breakout [Swing Out Sister] 6
Don't Forget Me (When I'm Gone) [Glass Tiger] 2
Don't You (Forget About Me) [Simple Minds] 1
Head Over Heels [Tears For Fears] 3
Heat Of The Moment [Asia] 4
Human Touch [Rick Springfield] 18
I Can Dream About You [Dan Hartman] 6
Kids In America [Kim Wilde] 25
Lessons In Love [Level 42] 12
Million Miles Away [Plimsouls] 82
Missing You [John Waite] 1
Need You Tonight [INXS] 1
No More Words [Berlin] 23
Notorious [Duran Duran] 1
Shattered Dreams [Johnny Hates Jazz] 2
Sister Christian [Night Ranger] 5
Some Like It Hot [Power Station] 6
You Make My Dreams [Hall & Oates] 5
Your Love [Outfield] 6

5/23/98 — 51 — 29 — ● — ©385 — Pure Funk — $10 — PolyGram TV 558299

Brick House [Commodores] 5
Car Wash [Rose Royce] 1
Don't Stop The Music [Yarbrough & Peoples] 19
Early In The Morning [Gap Band] 24
(Every Time I Turn Around) Back In Love Again [L.T.D.] 4
Fire [Ohio Players] 1
Flash Light [Parliament] 16
Forget Me Nots [Patrice Rushen] 23
Good Times [Ohio]
Jungle Boogie [Kool & The Gang] 4
Kung Fu Fighting [Carl Douglas] 1
Lady Marmalade [LaBelle] 1
Mr. Big Stuff [Jean Knight] 2
Pick Up The Pieces [Average White Band] 1
Shining Star [Earth, Wind & Fire] 1
Super Freak [Rick James] 16
Superfly [Curtis Mayfield] 8
Tell Me Something Good [Rufus Feat. Chaka Khan] 3
Theme From Shaft [Isaac Hayes] 1
Word Up [Cameo] 6

5/29/99 — 147 — 2 — ©386 — Pure Funk Volume 2 — $10 — PolyGram TV 565550

Ain't Nobody [Rufus & Chaka Khan] 22
Another One Bites The Dust [Queen] 1
Cut The Cake [Average White Band] 10
Get Down On It [Kool & The Gang] 10
Give It To Me Baby [Rick James] 40
Got To Give It Up (Part 1) [Marvin Gaye] 1
I Gotcha [Joe Tex] 2
I'm Gonna Love You Just A Little More Baby [Barry White] 3
It's A Love Thing [Whispers] 28
It's Your Thing [Isley Brothers] 2
Keep On Truckin' (Part 1) [Eddie Hendricks] 1
Let It Whip [Dazz Band] 5
Mama Used To Say [Junior] 30
Outstanding [Gap Band]
Payback, The [James Brown] 26
She's A Bad Mama Jama [Carl Carlton] 22
Street Life [Crusaders] 36
Use Me [Bill Withers] 2
You Sexy Thing [Hot Chocolate] 3
You're The One For Me ["D" Train]

1/27/01 — 68 — 10 — ©387 — Pure Jazz — $10 — UTV 520191

April In Paris [Count Basie] 28
At Last [Etta James] 47
Everything Happens To Me [Chet Baker]
Girl From Ipanema [Stan Getz & Astrud Gilberto] 5
God Bless The Child [Billie Holiday]
In The Mood [Glenn Miller]
Mack The Knife [Ella Fitzgerald] 27
Misty [Sarah Vaughan]
My Baby Just Cares For Me [Nina Simone]
Night Train [Oscar Peterson]
Peel Me A Grape [Diana Krall]
'Round Midnight [Miles Davis]
Sing Sing Sing [Benny Goodman]
Summertime [Ella Fitzgerald & Louis Armstrong]
Take Five [Dave Brubeck] 25
Unforgettable [Nat King Cole]
What A Wonderful World [Louis Armstrong] 32
What A Diff'rence A Day Makes [Dinah Washington] 8

2/19/00 — 136 — 3 — ©388 — Pure Love — $10 — UTV 541225

Anytime [Brian McKnight]
I Believe In You And Me [Four Tops]
I Don't Want To Wait [Paula Cole] 11
I Miss You [Klymaxx] 5
I Still Believe [Brenda K. Starr] 13
I'll Make Love To You [Boyz II Men] 1
Just Once [Quincy Jones] 17
Lady In Red [Chris DeBurgh] 3
Let's Get It On [Marvin Gaye] 1
More Than Words [Extreme] 1
Reason To Believe [Rod Stewart] 1
Right Here Waiting [Richard Marx] 1
Sara Smile [Hall & Oates] 4
Secret Lovers [Atlantic Starr] 3
Still [Commodores] 1
Strong Enough [Sheryl Crow] 5
Sweetest Days [Vanessa Williams] 18
With You I'm Born Again [Billy Preston & Syreeta] 4

5/17/97 — 10 — 48 — ▲2 — ©389 — Pure Moods — $10 — Virgin 42186

Adiemus [Adiemus]
Crockett's Theme [Jan Hammer]
Lily Was Here [David A. Stewart feat. Candy Dulfer] 11
Main Title Theme (The Last Emperor) [David Byrne]
Makambo [Geoffrey Oryema]
My Wife With Champagne Shoulders [Mark Isham]
Orinoco Flow (Sail Away) [Enya] 24
Oxygene Part IV [Jean Michele Jarre]
Promise, The [Michael Nyman]
Return To Innocence [Enigma] 4
Sadeness [Enigma] 5
Sweet Lullaby [Deep Forest] 78
Theme From "The Mission" [Ennio Morricone]
Theme From Twin Peaks - Fire Walk With Me [Angelo Badalamenti]
Tubular Bells [Mike Oldfield] 7
X-Files Theme [DJ Dado]
Yeha-Noha (Wishes Of Happiness & Prosperity) [Sacred Spirits]

12/5/98+ — 154 — 13 — ©390 — Pure Moods II — $10 — Virgin 46796

Beyond The Invisible [Enigma]
Breezin' [George Benson] 63
Chariots Of Fire [Vangelis] 1
Cradlesong (Da Wa) [Sacred Spirit feat. Cherokee Rose]
Emily [Dave Koz]
Euphoria (Firefly) [Delerium]
Life In A Northern Town [Dream Academy] 7
Montezuma [Cusco]
Mummers' Dance [Loreena McKennitt] 18
Mystic's Dream [Loreena McKennitt]
Nightingale [Yanni]
Teardrop [Massive Attack]
Theme From Harry's Game [Clannad]
2 The Night [Ottmar Liebert]
Weatherstorm [Craig Armstrong]
Zarabanda (Saraband) [Adiemus III]

2/24/01 — 66 — 10 — ©391 — Pure Moods III — $10 — Virgin 50836

Cristofori's Dream [David Lanz]
Dela Dela [Sacred Spirit]
Deliver Me [Sarah Brightman]
Ever So Lonely/Eyes/Ocean [Sheila Chandra]
Games Without Frontiers [Peter Gabriel] 48
Gravity Of Love [Enya]
Land Of Anaka [Geoffrey Oryema/Brian Eno]
Life In Mono [Mono] 70
Merry Christmas, Mr. Lawrence [Ryuichi Sakamoto]
On Sacred Ground [Yanni]
Only If [Enya] 88
Porcelain [Moby]
Silk Road [Kitaro]
Synaesthetic [Blue Man Group]
Velocity Of Love [Suzanne Ciani]
Virtue [Jesse Cook]

8/15/98 — 150 — 8 — ©392 — Pure Reggae — $10 — PolyGram TV 565122

Baby, I Love Your Way [Big Mountain]
Bad Boys [Inner Circle] 8
Boom Shakalak [Apache Indian]
Don't Turn Around [Aswad]
Electric Avenue [Eddy Grant] 2
Exodus [Bob Marley & The Wailers]
Hot Hot Hot [Arrow]
I Shot The Sheriff [Eric Clapton] 1
Israelites [Desmond Dekker] 9
Kingston Town [Lord Creator]
Many Rivers To Cross [Jimmy Cliff]
Montego Bay [Freddie Notes & The Rudies]
My Boy Lollipop [Millie Small] 2
Now That We Found Love [Third World] 47
Rivers Of Babylon [Melodians]
Stir It Up [Bob Marley & The Wailers]
Tease Me [Chaka Demus & Pliers]
You Don't Love Me (No, No, No) [Dawn Penn] 58

6/21/97 — 124 — 5 — ©393 — Pure Soul — $10 — Polygram 553641

All The Things (Your Man Won't Do) [Joe] 11
Falling [Montell Jordan] 18
Freek 'n You [Jodeci] 14
He's Mine [MoKenStef] 7
It's Your Body [Johnny Gill feat. Roger Troutman] 43
Lady [D'Angelo] 10
Let's Get Down [Tony Toni Toné]
Practice What You Preach [Barry White] 18
Spirit [Sounds Of Blackness feat. Craig Mack]
Steelo [702] 32
Sugar Honey Ice Tea [Goodfellaz] 64
Things That You Do [Gina Thompson] 41
Vibin' [Boyz II Men] 56
What Kind Of Man Would I Be [Mint Condition] 17
Where Do U Want Me To Put It [Solo] 50
You Put A Move On My Heart [Quincy Jones feat. Tamia] 98

3/18/00 — 92 — 12 — ©394 — Radio Disney Jams Vol. 2 — $10 — Walt Disney 60980

Boogie Shoes [KC & The Sunshine Band] 35
Boom Da Boom [Goldo]
Disney Mambo #5 (A Little Bit Of...) [Lou Bega]
Girl You Shine [Aaron Carter]
I'll Be Your Everything [Youngstown] 71
I'll Never Break Your Heart [Backstreet Boys] 35
Just The Two Of Us [Will Smith] 20
Let's Go [I-8-Paste]
Lovin' You Lovin' Me [Jason Raize]
One For Sorrow [Steps]
Reflection [Christina Aguilera]
Saga Begins ["Weird Al" Yankovic]
Sodapop [Britney Spears]
True To Your Heart [98° & Stevie Wonder]
We Are Family [Sister Sledge] 2
We Are The Champions [Queen] 4
We Will Rock You [Queen] 52
YMCA [Village People] 2

3/3/01 — 109 — 7 — ©395 — Radio Disney Jams Vol. 3 — $10 — Walt Disney 860692

All Star [Smash Mouth] 4
Back Here [BBMak] 13
Dance With Me [Debeleh Morgan] 8
Dancing In The Street [Myra]
Don't Say You Love Me [M2M] 21
Hampsterdance Song [Hampton The Hampster]
How Do I Feel (The Burrito Song) [Hoku]
If You Wanna Dance [Nobody's Angel]
Jumpin', Jumpin' [Destiny's Child] 3
Mamma Mia [A*Teens]
Thinkin' About You [Britney Spears]
Upside Down [Tik 'N Tak]
Vacation [Vitamin C]
Valentino [Bowling For Soup]
We Like To Party [Vengaboys] 26

VARIOUS ARTISTS COMPILATIONS

DEBUT	PEAK	WKS	RIAA	CD	ARTIST — Album Title	Catalog	Sym	$	Label & Number

11/8/86+ 114 17 ● ©396 Rap's Greatest Hits .... **$10** Priority 9466
Fat Boys *[Fat Boys]* — Howie's Teed Off *[Real Roxanne w/Howie Tee]* — Roof Is On Fire *[Rockmaster Scott/Dynamic Three]*
Fly Girl *[Boogie Boys]* — King Of Rock *[Run-D.M.C.]* — Roxanne, Roxanne *[UTFO]* 77
Friends *[Whodini]* 87 — Pee-Wee's Dance *[Joeski Love]* — **Rumors** *[Timex Social Club]* 8
Show, The *[Doug E. Fresh/Get Fresh Crew]*

5/2/87 167 4 397 Rap's Greatest Hits, Volume 2 .... **$10** Priority 9468
Bridge, The *[M.C. Shan]* — Eric B. Is President *[Eric B. Feat. Rakim]* — Make The Music With Your Mouth, Biz *[Biz Markie]*
Coast To Coast *[Word Of Mouth]* — I'm Chillin' *[Kurtis Blow]* — One Love *[Whodini]*
Dream Team Is In The House *[L.A. Dream Team]* — Split Personality *[UTFO]*
Together Forever *[Run-D.M.C.]* — Woppit *[B. Fats]*

8/29/92 136 14 ©398 Rave 'Til Dawn .... **$10** SBK 80070
Can You Feel The Passion *[Blue Pearl]* — **Get Ready For This** *[2 Unlimited]* 76 — Injected With A Poison *[Praga Khan]*
Dreamer, Dream *[Code Red]* — Green Man *[Shut Up & Dance]* — Jump! *[Movement]* 53
Fuck You *[Ottorongo]* — Million Colors *[Channel X]*
O Fortuna *[Apotheosis]* — Stylophonia *[Two Little Boys]* — Take Control *[Lords Of Acid]*

6/5/99 30 7 ©399 Rawkus Presents Soundbombing II .... **$10** Rawkus 50069
Any Man *[Eminem]* — Every Rhyme I Write *[Shabaam Sahdeeq f/Cocoa Brovaz]* — 1-9-9-9 *[Common f/Sadat X]*
B-Boy Document 99 *[High & Mighty f/Mos Def & Mad Skillz]* — Mayor *[Pharoahe Monch]* — On Mission *[Reflection Eternal]*
Brooklyn Hard Rock *[Thirstin Howl III]* — Message From J-Live & Prince Paul — Patriotism *[Company Flow]*
Chaos *[Reflection Eternal f/Bahamadia]* — Message From Mos Def & The Beat Junkies — 7XL *[Sir Menelik f/Grand Puba & Sadat X]*
Crosstown Beef *[Medina Green]* — Next Universe *[Mos Def]* — Soundbombing *[Dilated Peoples & Tash]*
Stanley Kubrick *[R.A. The Rugged Man]* — WWIII *[Pharoahe Monch & Shabaam Sahdeeq]* — When It Pours It Rains *[Diamond]*

11/17/90+ 38 24 ©400 Red Hot + Blue .... **$10** Chrysalis 21799
After You *[Jody Watley]* — From This Moment On *[Jimmy Somerville]* — It's All Right With Me *[Tom Waits]*
Begin The Beguine *[Salif Keita]* — I Get A Kick Out Of You *[Jungle Brothers]* — Just One Of Those Things (medley) *[Kirsty MacColl & The Pogues]*
Do I Love You? *[Aztec Camera]* — I Love Paris *[Les Negresses Vertes]* — Love For Sale *[Fine Young Cannibals]*
Don't Fence Me In *[David Byrne]* — I've Got U Under My Skin *[Neneh Cherry]* — Miss Otis Regrets (medley) *[Kirsty MacColl & The Pogues]*
Down In The Depths *[Lisa Stansfield]* — In The Still Of The Night *[Neville Brothers]* — Night And Day *[U2]*
Ev'ry Time We Say Goodbye *[Annie Lennox]* — So In Love *[k.d. lang]*
Too Darn Hot *[Erasure]* — Well, Did You Evah! *[Debbie Harry & Iggy Pop]* — Who Wants To Be A Millionaire? *[Thompson Twins]* — You Do Something To Me *[Sinead O'Connor]*

10/1/94 183 1 ©401 Red Hot + Country .... **$10** Mercury 522639
Blind Bartimus (medley) *[Marty Stuart w/Jerry & Tammy Sullivan]* — Goodbye Comes Hard For Me *[Mark Chesnutt]* — Rock Me On The Water *[Kathy Mattea w/Jackson Browne]*
Close Up The Honky Tonks *[Radney Foster]* — If These Old Walls Could Speak *[Nanci Griffith w/Jimmy Webb]* — T.B. Is Whipping Me *[Wilco w/Syd Straw]*
Crazy *[Jimmy Dale Gilmore w/Willie Nelson]* — Keep On The Sunny Side *[Randy Scruggs w/Earl Scruggs & Doc Watson]* — Teach Your Children *[Suzy Bogguss/Alison Krause/Kathy Mattea/Crosby, Stills & Nash]*
Fire And Rain *[Sammy Kershaw]* — Matchbox *[Carl Perkins, Duane Eddy & The Mavericks]* — Up Above My Head (medley) *[Marty Stuart w/Jerry & Tammy Sullivan]*
Folsom Prison Blues *[Brooks & Dunn w/Johnny Cash]* — Pictures Don't Lie *[Billy Ray Cyrus]*
When I Reach The Place I'm Going *[Patty Loveless]* — Willie Short *[Mary-Chapin Carpenter]* — You Gotta Be My Baby *[Dolly Parton]*
Forever Young *[Johnny Cash]*

7/25/92 52 11 ©402 Red Hot + Dance .... **$10** Columbia 52826
Apparently Nothin' *[Young Disciples]* — Do You Really Want To Know *[George Michael]* — Red Hot + Dance, Theme From *[tomandandy]*
Change *[Lisa Stansfield]* 27 — **Gypsy Woman** *[Crystal Waters]* 8 — Set Adrift On Memory Bliss *[PM Dawn]* 1
Crazy *[Seal]* 7 — Happy *[George Michael]* — Supernatural *[Madonna]*
Peace *[Sabrina Johnston]*
Thank You (Falettin Me Be Mice Elf Agin) *[Sly & The Family Stone]* 1 — **Too Funky** *[George Michael]* 10 — **Unbelievable** *[EMF]* 1

7/5/97 192 2 ©403 Reggae Gold 1997 .... **$10** VP 1509
Call On The Father *[Beres Hammond]* — Ghetto People Song *[Everton Blender]* — Love Sponge *[Buju Banton]*
Don't Ask My Neighbor *[Benjy Myaz]* — Girls Dem Sugar *[Beenie Man]* — Mission Impossible *[Taxi Gang]*
Fudgie *[Goofy]* — Healing *[Lady Saw & Beenie Man]* — Pure Gal *[Harry Todler]*
If Jah *[Tony Rebel]* — Put Down The Weapon *[Capleton & Yami Bolo]*
Romie *[Beenie Man]* — Rubbers *[Frisco Kid]* — Worthless Bwoy *[Bounty Killer]* — Yuh Nuh Ready Fi Dis Yet *[Tanya Stephens]*

6/6/98 147 8 ©404 Reggae Gold 1998 .... **$10** VP 1529
Babylon Ah Listen *[Sizzla]* — Destiny *[Buju Banton]* — Going Away *[Sanchez & Beenie Man]*
Bad Man Nuh Dress Like Girl *[Harry Toddler]* — Don't Follow Rumours *[Shabba Ranks & Carlton Livingston]* — Heads High *[Mr. Vegas]*
Boom Boom *[Degree]* — Gal Pon De Side *[Frisco Kid]* — Hold On *[Beres Hammond]*
Cry For Die For *[Bounty Killer]* — Infiltrate *[Sean Paul]*
She Nuh Ready Yet *[Spragga Benz]* — Sweep Over My Soul *[Luciano]* — Tell Me *[Beenie Man]* — Tight Up Skirt *[Red Rat]* — We Nuh Like *[Spragga Benz]*

6/5/99 131 5 ©405 Reggae Gold 1999 .... **$10** VP 1559
Always Be True To You *[Sanchez]* — From This Moment On *[Fiona & Brian Gold]* — Haters *[Ward 21]*
Better Learn *[Beenie Man]* — Good Times *[Luciano]* — Heads High (Kill Dem Wid It) *[Mr. Vegas]*
Big Phat Fish *[Machel Montano]* — Haffi Get Da Gal Yah *[Sean Paul & Mr. Vegas]* — Jah Blessing *[Luciano & Sizzla]*
Big Up Yu Status *[Tanto Metro & Devonte]* — Hardcore Lover *[Lady Saw & T.O.K.]* — Jah Jah City *[Capelton]*
Don't Haffi Dread *[Morgan Heritage]* — Psyco Med *[Bounty Killer]*
Pull It Up *[Beres Hammond & Buju Banton]* — Soconuma Clash *[Buccaneer]* — Unfair *[Zebra]* — Wave *[Mr. Vegas]*

6/10/00 153 10 ©406 Reggae Gold 2000 .... **$15** VP 1599 [2]
Back At One *[Sanchez]* — Hot Gal Today *[Sean Paul & Mr Vegas]* — Nuh Play Chess *[Madd Anju]*
Call U *[Lexxus & Lady Saw]* — Keep Them Coming *[Wayne Wonder]* — One Of These Days *[Glen Washington]*
Cook *[Lexxus]* — Look *[Bounty Killer]* — Psalms 23 *[Buju Banton Feat. Gramps]*
Down By The River *[Heritage]* — Magnet *[Richie Stephens feat. Bounty Killer]* — Satan Strong *[Professor Nuts]*
Ganja Farm *[Beenie Man]*
Good In Her Clothes *[Capleton]*
Stalag Y2K *[Tenor Saw/General Echo/Buju Banton/Candy Man/Sister Nancy]* — They Gonna Talk *[Beres Hammond]* — War Forever *[Baby Cham]* — What Ah Gal *[Delly Ranks & Rik Rock]*

6/16/01 196 2 ©407 Reggae Gold 2001 .... **$15** VP 1629 [2]
Ain't It Good To Know *[Beres Hammond & Buju Banton]* — Gimmi The Woman *[Capleton]* — Man & Man *[Baby Cham]*
All Out War *[Bounty Killer]* — **Girls Dem Sugar** *[Beenie Man Feat. Mya]* 54 — Peace Cry *[Various Artists]*
Boom Draw *[Jr.Kelly]* — God Is Standing By *[George Nooks]* — Pretty Girl *[Sanchez]*
Changez *[Cecile]* — Kushungpeng *[Shabba Ranks & Mikey Spice]* — Shake Your Bam Bam *[Tok]*
Chi-Chi Man *[Tok]* — Son Of A B!t@h *[Lady Saw & Marsha]*
Spy *[Lexxus Feat. Zavia]* — Take Up Your Cross *[Morgan Heritage]* — Taking Over *[Sizzla]* — Wrong Application *[Elephant Man]*

DEBUT	PEAK	WKS	RIAA	CD	ARTIST — Album Title	Catalog	Sym	$	Label & Number

4/6/85 — **77** — 14 — 408 — **Requiem** .... **$12** Angel 38218
- Dies Irae
- Hosanna
- Kyrie (medley)
- Libera Me (medley)
- Lux Aeterna (medley)
- Pie Jesu
- Offertorium
- Requiem (medley)

3/24/90 — **166** — 5 — ©409 — **Requiem For The Americas - Songs From The Lost World** .... **$10** Enigma 73354
- Born In The Dreamtime
- Chant Movement
- Du He Kah (The Healer)
- Far Far Cry
- Father And Son
- Follow In My Footsteps
- I've Not Forgotten You
- Invisible Man
- Journey, The
- Talk With Grandfather
- Within The Lost World

7/31/99 — **185** — 1 — ©410 — **Return Of The Grievous Angel - A Tribute To Gram Parsons** .... **$10** Almo Sounds 80024
- Hickory Wind [Gillian Welch]
- High Fashion Queen [Chris Hillman & Steve Earl]
- Hot Burrito #1 [Mavericks]
- In My Hour Of Darkness [Rolling Creekdippers]
- Juanita [Sheryl Crow & Emmylou Harris]
- One Hundred Years From Now [Wilco]
- $1,000 Wedding [Evan Dando & Julianna Hatfield]
- Ooh Las Vegas [Cowboy Junkies]
- Return Of The Grievous Angel [Lucinda Williams & David Crosby]
- She [Pretenders & Emmylou Harris]
- Sin City [Beck & Emmylou Harris]
- Sleepless Nights [Elvis Costello]
- Song For You [Whiskeytown]

3/19/94 — **18** — 31 — ▲ — ©411 — **Rhythm Country And Blues** .... **$10** MCA 10965
- Ain't Nothing Like The Real Thing [Vince Gill & Gladys Knight]
- Chain Of Fools [Clint Black & Pointer Sisters]
- Funny How Time Slips Away [Al Green & Lyle Lovett]
- I Fall To Pieces [Aaron Neville & Trisha Yearwood]
- Patches [George Jones & B.B. King]
- Rainy Night In Georgia [Sam Moore & Conway Twitty]
- Since I Fell For You [Natalie Cole & Reba McEntire]
- Somethin' Else [Little Richard & Tanya Tucker]
- Southern Nights [Chet Atkins & Allen Toussaint]
- Weight, The [Staple Singers & Marty Stuart]
- When Something Is Wrong With My Baby [Patti LaBelle & Travis Tritt]

8/10/96 — **138** — 3 — ©412 — **Rhythm Of The Games - 1996 Olympic Games Album** .... **$10** LaFace 26026
- Champions Theme [Kenny G]
- Dreamin' [Usher]
- Everlasting Love [Mary J. Blige]
- Imagine [Corey Glover]
- Impossible Dream [Tevin Campbell]
- Reach [Gloria Estefan] 42
- Reaching For My Goal [Brian McKnight]
- Star Spangled Banner [Boyz II Men]
- What Am I Doing Here [Jordan Hill]
- Wild Flower [K Ci Hailey]
- You Gotta Believe In Love [Soul For Real feat. Monifah]
- You're A Winner [Tony Rich]

3/18/95 — **23** — 23 — ©413 — **Rhythm Of The Pride Lands** .... **$10** Walt Disney 60871
- Busa [Lebo M]
- Hakuna Matata [Jimmy Cliff feat. Lebo M]
- He Lives In You [Lebo M]
- It's Time [Lebo M]
- Kube [Lebo M]
- Lala [Lebo M]
- Lea Halalela [Khululiwe Sithole]
- Lion Sleeps Tonight [Lebo M]
- Noyana [Lebo M]
- One By One [Lebo M]
- Warthog Rhapsody [Nathan Lane & Ernie Sabella]

11/24/56 — **20** — 2 — 414 — **Rock & Roll Forever** .... **$150** Atlantic 1239
- Bop-Ting-A-Ling [LaVern Baker]
- 5-10-15 Hours [Ruth Brown]
- Flip, Flop & Fly [Joe Turner]
- Good Lovin' [Clovers]
- Hide & Seek [Joe Turner]
- Honey Love [Drifters]
- I've Got A Woman [Ray Charles]
- It Should've Been Me [Ray Charles]
- Mama, He Treats Your Daughter Mean [Ruth Brown]
- Money Honey [Drifters]
- One Mint Julep [Clovers]
- Shake, Rattle & Roll [Joe Turner]
- T-Bone Shuffle [T-Bone Walker]
- **Tweedlee Dee** [LaVern Baker] 14

1/24/87 — **121** — 11 — ©415 — **Rock For Amnesty** .... **$10** Mercury 830617
- Biko [Peter Gabriel]
- Brothers In Arms [Dire Straits]
- Ghost Dancing [Simple Minds]
- I Believe [Tears For Fears]
- **No One Is To Blame** [Howard Jones] 4
- Passengers [Elton John]
- **Pink Houses** [John Cougar Mellencamp] 8
- Pipes Of Peace [Paul McCartney]
- Strange Fruit [Sting]
- Tonight [Bryan Adams]

7/5/69 — **182** — 7 — 416 — **Rock's Greatest Hits** .... **$25** Columbia 11 [2]
- **Distant Shores** [Chad & Jeremy] 30
- **Down In The Boondocks** [Billy Joe Royal] 9
- 8:05 [Moby Grape]
- I Can't Stand It [Chambers Brothers]
- **If You Don't Want My Love** [Robert John] 49
- **Let's Fall In Love** [Peaches & Herb] 21
- Louie, Louie [Paul Revere & The Raiders]
- **Mercy, Mercy, Mercy** [Buckinghams] 5
- People [Tymes] 39
- **Red Rubber Ball** [Cyrkle] 2
- **Ruby Baby** [Dion] 2
- Suzanne [Leonard Cohen]
- **Symphony For Susan** [Arbors] 51
- Take A Look [Aretha Franklin]
- That's Life [O. C. Smith]
- **Three Window Coupe** [Rip Chords] 28
- **Turn! Turn! Turn! (To Everything There Is A Season)** [Byrds] 1
- **Watermelon Man** [Mongo Santamaria] 10
- We Could Be Happy [Cryan' Shames]
- **Woman, Woman** [Union Gap feat. Gary Puckett] 4

6/5/93 — **135** — 1 — ©417 — **Roll Wit Tha Flava** .... **$10** Flavor Unit 53615
- Badd Boyz [Almighty R.S.O.]
- Bring It On [Naughty By Nature]
- Bring Tha Flava, La [Queen Latifah]
- Enough Is Enough [Rottin Razkals]
- Freak Out [Nikki D.]
- Gimme Head [Leshaun]
- **Hey Mr. D.J.** [Zhané] 6
- Keep It Real [Apache]
- Let Yourself Go [Latee]
- On The Bone Again [Brooklyn Assault Team]
- **Roll Wit Tha Flava** [Flavor Unit MCs] 86
- Rough Enough [Freddie Foxxx]
- Since You Asked [Groove Garden]
- Sounds Of Fatness [Bigga Sistas]
- Uuh [D. Nice]

3/5/94 — **175** — 1 — ©418 — **Romantic Classics - Intimate Moments** .... [I] **$10** Madacy 0330
- Blue Danube Waltz
- Bolero
- Dreamings
- Eine Kleine Nachtmusic
- Erotic
- For Eliza
- 4 Seasons (Allegro)
- 4 Seasons (Spring)
- Liebestraum
- Moment Musical
- Moonlight Sonata
- Prelude OP 28
- Reverie
- Venetian Gondola Song
- Waltz

12/9/00 — **89** — 4 — ©419 — **Rose That Grew From Concrete Vol. 1, The** .... **$10** Amaru 490813
- And Still I Love You [Red Rat]
- Can U C The Pride In The Panther (male & female versions) [Mos Def]
- Family Tree [Lamar Antwon Robinson]
- Fear In The Heart Of A Man [Q-Tip]
- God [Reverend Run]
- If There Be Pain [Providence & RasDaveed El Harar]
- In The Event Of My Demise [Outlawz]
- Lady Liberty Needs Glasses [Malcolm Jamal Warner]
- One 4 The Righteous [Rha Goddess]
- River That Flows Forever [Danny Glover, Afeni Shakur & the Cast of the Lion King]
- Rose That Grew From Concrete [Nikki Giovanni]
- Sometimes I Cry [Dan Rockett]
- Starry Night [Quincy Jones, Mac Mall & Rashida Jones]
- Sun & The Moon [Chief Okena Littlehawk]
- Tears Of A Teenage Mother [Jasmine Guy]
- Thug Blues [Lamar Antwon Robinson & Tina Thomas Bayyan]
- U R Ripping Us Apart!!! [Dead Prez]
- Wake Me When I'm Free [Batatunde Olatunji & Sikiru Adepoju]
- What Of A Love Unspoken [Tre' from Pharcyde]
- What Of Fame? [Russell Simmons]
- When Ure Heart Turns Cold [Sonia Sanchez]
- Why Must U Be Unfaithful [Sarah Jones]
- Wife 4 Life [4th Avenue Jones]

10/27/90 — **140** — 11 — ©420 — **Rubaiyat - Elektra's 40th Anniversary** .... **$15** Elektra 60940 [2]
- Almost Saturday Night (medley) [Georgia Satellites]
- Apricot Brandy [Danny Gatton]
- Blacksmith, The [Linda Ronstadt]
- Born In Chicago [Pixies]
- Both Sides Now [Michael Feinstein]
- Bottle Of Wine [Havalinas]
- First Girl I Loved [Jackson Browne]
- Get Ourselves Together [Phoebe Snow]
- Going Down [Lynch Mob]
- Going Going Gone [Bill Frisell/Robin Holcomb/Wayne Horvitz]
- Hello, I Am Your Heart [Sara Hickman]
- Hello I Love You [Cure]
- Hotel California [Gipsy Kings]
- House Of The Rising Sun [Tracy Chapman]
- I Can't Tell You Why [Howard Hewett]
- I'd Like To Teach The World To Sing [Jevetta Steele]
- Inbetween Days [John Eddie]
- Kick Out The Jams [Big F]
- Let's Go [Ernie Isley]
- Little Bit Of Rain [Ambitious Lovers]
- Love Wars [Beautiful South]
- Make It With You [Teddy Pendergrass]
- Marquee Moon [Kronos Quartet]
- Motorcycle Mama [Sugarcubes]
- Mt. Airy Groove [Leaders Of The New School]
- One Meatball [Shinehead]
- One More Parade [They Might Be Giants]
- Road To Cairo [Howard Jones]
- Rockin' All Over The World (medley) [Georgia Satellites]
- Seven & Seven Is [Billy Bragg]
- Stone Cold Crazy [Metallica]
- T.V. Eye [John Zorn]
- These Days [10,000 Maniacs]
- Tokoloshe Man [Happy Mondays]
- Union Man [Shaking Family]
- Werewolves Of London [Black Velvet Band]
- You Belong To Me [Anita Baker]
- You Brought The Sunshine [Shirley Murdock]
- You're So Vain [Faster Pussycat]

VARIOUS ARTISTS COMPILATIONS

DEBUT	PEAK	WKS	RIAA	CD	ARTIST — Album Title	Catalog	Sym	$	Label & Number

DEBUT	PEAK	WKS	RIAA	CD	ARTIST — Album Title	Sym	$	Label & Number
4/11/98	119	2		©421	**Ruthless Records Tenth Anniversary Compilation - Decade Of Game**		$15	Ruthless 68766 [2]

Alwayz Into Somethin' *[N.W.A.]*
Black Nigga Killa *[Eazy-E]*
Black Superman *[Above The Law]*
Boyz-N-The Hood *[Eazy-E]*
Dopeman *[N.W.A.]*
8 Ball *[N.W.A.]*
Final Frontier *[MC Ren]*
Formula, The *[D.O.C.]*
Fuck What Ya Heard *[MC Ren]*
Grand Finale *[D.O.C.]*
Great Tazte - Less Fillaz *[H.W.A.]*
I Ain't No Lady *[H.W.A.]*
It's Funky Enough *[D.O.C.]*
Murder Rap *[Above The Law]*
Nicety *[Michel'le] 29*
Real Muthaphuckkin' G's *[Eazy-E] 42*
Same Ol' Shit *[MC Ren] 90*
Something In My Heart *[Michel'le] 31*
Supersonic *[JJ Fad] 30*
24 HRS To Live *[Eazy-E]*
Untouchable *[Above The Law]*

DEBUT	PEAK	WKS	RIAA	CD	ARTIST — Album Title	Sym	$	Label & Number
7/10/99	61	5		©422	**RZA Hits, The**		$10	Razor Sharp 69610

songs by Method Man, Ol Dirty Bastard, Raekwon, Wu-Tang Clan, and others

All I Need *[Method Man]*
All That I Got Is You *[Ghostface Killah]*
Bring The Pain *[Method Man] 45*
Brooklyn Zoo *[Ol' Dirty Bastard] 54*
C.R.E.A.M. *[Wu-Tang Clan] 60*
Ice Cream *[Raekwon] 37*
Incarcerated Scarfaces *[Raekwon] 71*
Liquid Swords *[GZA] 48*
Method Man *[Wu-Tang Clan] 69*
Protect Ya Neck *[Wu-Tang Clan]*
Shimmy Shimmy Ya *[Ol' Dirty Bastard] 62*
Winter Warz *[Ghostface Killah]*
Wu-Tang Clan Ain't Nuthing Ta F' Wit *[Wu-Tang Clan]*
Wu Wear, The Garment Renaissance *[RZA] 60*

DEBUT	PEAK	WKS	RIAA	CD	ARTIST — Album Title	Sym	$	Label & Number
6/22/96	197	1		©423	**Sanctuary: 20 Years Of Windham Hill**	[I]	$15	Windham Hill 11180 [2]

Aerial Boundaries *[Michael Hedges]*
Asleep The Snow Came Flying *[Tim Story]*
Blue Kiss *[Ray Obiedo]*
Children's Dance *[Alex de Grassi]*
Daydreams *[Schönherz & Scott]*
Dolphins *[Mike Marshall & Darol Anger]*
Every Deep Dream *[Philip Aaberg]*
Fionnghuala (Mouth Music) *[Nightnoise]*
Hand Picked Rose Of A Fading Dream *[Billy Childs]*
House Made Of Dawn Light *[Billy Childs]*
Hummingbird *[George Winston]*
Intermezzo From Carmen *[Tracy Silverman & Thea Suits-Silverman]*
Ivory *[Ray Lynch]*
Manhattan Underground *[Scott Cossu]*
Night In That Land *[Nightnoise]*
Night Slip *[William Ackerman]*
Pittsburgh 1901 (Theme From Mrs. Soffel) *[Mark Isham]*
Rameau's Nephew *[Philippe Saisse]*
Redonda *[Modern Mandolin Quartet]*
Rocket To The Moon *[Jim Brickman]*
Siri's Arrival *[Metamora]*
Tears Of Joy *[Tuck & Patti]*
There's A Monk In My Garden *[Øystein Sevåg]*
Thousand Teardrops *[Shadowfax]*
To Be *[Montreux]*
Transit *[Ira Stein & Russel Walder]*
Turning Twice *[Turtle Island String Quartet]*
Very Special Place *[Torcuato Mariano]*
View Of You *[Fred Simon]*
We Kinda Music *[Andy Narell]*
Wedding Rain *[Liz Story]*
Wide Asleep *[Michael Manring]*

DEBUT	PEAK	WKS	RIAA	CD	ARTIST — Album Title	Sym	$	Label & Number
12/23/95+	67	17	●	©424	**Saturday Morning Cartoons' Greatest Hits**		$10	MCA 11348

Bugaloos, The *[Collective Soul]*
Eep Opp Ork Ah-Ah (Means I Love You) *[Violent Femmes]*
Fat Albert Theme *[Dig]*
Friends (medley) *[Tripping Daisy]*
Gigantor *[Helmet]*
Go Speed Racer Go *[Sponge]*
Goolie Get-Together *[Toadies]*
H. R. Pufnstuf *[Murmurs]*
Happy, Happy, Joy, Joy *[Wax]*
Hong Kong Phooey *[Sublime]*
I'm Popeye The Sailor Man *[Face to Face]*
Jonny Quest (medley) *[Reverend Horton Heat]*
Josie And The Pussycats *[Juliana Hatfield & Tanya Donelly]*
Open Up Your Heart And Let The Sun Shine In *[Frente!]*
Scooby-Doo, Where Are You? *[Matthew Sweet]*
Sigmund And The Seamonsters (medley) *[Tripping Daisy]*
Spider-Man *[Ramones]*
Stop That Pigeon (medley) *[Reverend Horton Heat]*
Sugar Sugar *[Mary Lou Lord w/Semisonic]*
Tra La La Song (One Banana, Two Banana) *[Liz Phair w/Material Issue]*
Underdog *[Butthole Surfers]*

DEBUT	PEAK	WKS	RIAA	CD	ARTIST — Album Title	Sym	$	Label & Number
11/7/64	95	8		425	**Saturday Night At The Uptown**	[L]	$30	Atlantic 8101

recorded at the Uptown Theatre in Philadelphia

Can't You Hear The Beat *[Carltons]*
Down The Aisle *[Patti LaBelle & The Blue Belles]*
I'm Gonna Cry *[Wilson Pickett]*
If You Need Me *[Wilson Pickett]*
Mixed Up, Shook Up, Girl *[Patty & The Emblems]*
My Girl Sloopy *[Vibrations]*
Oh! Baby (We Got A Good Thing Goin') *[Barbara Lynn]*
On Broadway *[Drifters]*
There Goes My Baby *[Drifters]*
Under The Boardwalk *[Drifters]*
Watusi, The *[Vibrations]*

DEBUT	PEAK	WKS	RIAA	CD	ARTIST — Album Title	Sym	$	Label & Number
4/27/96	70	13		©426	**Schoolhouse Rock! Rocks**		$10	Lava 92681

Conjunction Junction *[Better Than Ezra]*
Electricity, Electricity *[Goodness]*
Energy Blues *[Biz Markie]*
I'm Just A Bill *[Deluxx Folk Implosion]*
Interplanet Janet *[Man Or Astro-Man?]*
Little Twelvetoes *[Chavez]*
Lolly, Lolly, Lolly, Get Your Adverbs Here *[Buffalo Tom]*
My Hero, Zero *[Lemonheads]*
No More Kings *[Pavement]*
Schoolhouse Rocky (Original Theme Music) *[Bob Dorough & Friends]*
Shot Heard 'Round The World *[Ween]*
Tale Of Mr. Morton *[Skee-Lo]*
Three Is A Magic Number *[Blind Melon]*
Unpack Your Adjectives *[Daniel Johnston]*
Verb: That's What's Happening *[Moby]*

DEBUT	PEAK	WKS	RIAA	CD	ARTIST — Album Title	Sym	$	Label & Number
5/23/81	106	12		427	**Secret Policeman's Ball/The Music, The**	[L]	$12	Island 9630

Bourree *[John Williams]*
Cavatina *[John Williams]*
Drowned *[Pete Townshend]*
Glad To Be Gay *[Tom Robinson]*
1967 (So Long Ago) *[Tom Robinson]*
Pinball Wizard *[Pete Townshend]*
Spontaneous *[Neil Innes]*
Won't Get Fooled Again *[Pete Townshend & John Williams]*

DEBUT	PEAK	WKS	RIAA	CD	ARTIST — Album Title	Sym	$	Label & Number
3/20/82	29	16		©428	**Secret Policeman's Other Ball/The Music, The**	[L]	$12	Island 9698

above 2 are benefit concerts for Amnesty International

Catch The Wind *[Donovan]*
'Cause We've Ended As Lovers *[Jeff Beck & Eric Clapton]*
Crossroads *[Jeff Beck & Eric Clapton]*
Farther Up The Road *[Jeff Beck & Eric Clapton]*
I Don't Like Mondays *[Bob Geldof & Johnny Fingers]*
I Shall Be Released *[Secret Police]*
In The Air Tonight *[Phil Collins]*
Message In A Bottle *[Sting]*
Roof Is Leaking *[Phil Collins]*
Roxanne *[Sting]*
Universal Soldier *[Donovan]*

DEBUT	PEAK	WKS	RIAA	CD	ARTIST — Album Title	Sym	$	Label & Number
9/9/78	75	10	●	429	**Sesame Street Fever**		$12	Sesame Street 79005

C Is For Cookie
Doin' The Pigeon
Has Anybody Seen My Dog?
Rubber Duckie
Sesame Street Fever
Trash

DEBUT	PEAK	WKS	RIAA	CD	ARTIST — Album Title	Sym	$	Label & Number
6/19/99	191	1		©430	**Short Music For Short People**		$10	Fat Wreck Chords 591

no track titles listed

DEBUT	PEAK	WKS	RIAA	CD	ARTIST — Album Title	Sym	$	Label & Number
6/6/98	38	10	●	©431	**$hort Records - Nationwide - Independence Day: The Compilation**		$15	$hort 46100 [2]

Abstract Hustle *[38 Deep & Kat]*
All About It *[Too $hort & Pimp C of UGK]*
Are You Ready For This *[Badwayz]*
Couldn't Be A Better Player *[Lil' Jon & The Eastside Boyz Feat. Too $hort]*
Don't Stop *[Lyrical Giants]*
Cet All Your Change *[Too $hort Feat. Biz Zack & Trauma Black]*
Get Your Hustle On *[Baby D Feat. Too $hort]*
Hellbound *[Slink Capone]*
I Ain't Gonna Forget This *[Badwayz Feat. Jamal]*
If I Wasn't High *[Studd]*
Independence Day *[Too $hort w/Keith Murray]*
Keep It Real *[Sylk-E. Fyne Feat. Too $hort]*
Killa Team *[Joe Riz Feat. George Clinton]*
Lady Luv *[Zu]*
Paper Chase *[Al Block]*
Pimpin' Ain't Easy *[Polyester Playas]*
Playa Hatin' Hoes *[Playa Playa]*
Same Old Song *[Father Dom]*
Short Dog - Hit 'Em Up *[Too $hort]*
Spread Your Love *[Murda One]*
Time After Time *[Casual & Dollar Will]*
Whatever Man *[Redman]*
When You See Me *[G-Side]*
Who Loves Ya *[Jay-O Felony]*
Wreckognize *[Mddl Fngz]*

DEBUT	PEAK	WKS	RIAA	CD	ARTIST — Album Title	Sym	$	Label & Number
8/22/98	24^C	1		©432	**Shout To The Lord**		$10	Hosanna! 68965

All The Power You Need
Father Of Creation
I Believe The Presence
I Will Never Be
Jesus, Jesus
Jesus, Lover Of My Soul
Let The Peace Of God Reign
People Just Like Us
Power Of Your Love
Shout To The Lord
Show Me Your Ways
This Kingdom

DEBUT	PEAK	WKS	RIAA	CD	ARTIST — Album Title	Sym	$	Label & Number
1/30/99	156	3		©433	**Shout To The Lord 2000**	[L]	$10	Word 69789

All Things Are Possible
Breathe On Me
Can't Stop Talking
Eagle's Wings
Friends In High Places
Glory To The King
God Is Good
God Is In The House
Hear Our Praises
Jesus Is Alive
Love You So Much
My Heart Will Trust
My Redeemer Lives
Potter's Hand
Shout To The Lord
That's What We Came Here For

DEBUT	PEAK	WKS	RIAA	CD	ARTIST — Album Title	Catalog	Sym	$	Label & Number
1/27/01	168	3		©434	**Shout To The Lord: The Platinum Collection**			$15	Hosanna! 1867 [2]

All Things Are Possible
And That My Soul Knows Very Well
Can't Stop Talking
Church On Fire
Dwelling Places
Eagles Wings
God Is In The House
Great Southland
(He's Real) All The Power You Need
Hear Our Praises
Holy Spirit Rain Down
I Believe The Promise
I Give You My Heart
I Will Run To You
Jesus, Lover Of My Soul
Jesus What A Beautiful Name
Jesus, You Gave It All
Joy In The Holy Ghost
Love You So Much
My Redeemer Lives
People Just Like Us
Potter's Hand
Power Of Your Love
Shout To The Lord
Show Me Your Ways
So You Would Come
That's What We Came Here For
This Is How We Overcome
Touching Heaven, Changing Earth
What The Lord Has Done In Me
You Said
Your Love Keeps Following Me

DEBUT	PEAK	WKS	RIAA	CD	ARTIST — Album Title	Catalog	Sym	$	Label & Number
7/13/63	7	46		435	**Shut Down**			$50	Capitol 1918

Ballad Of Thunder Road [Robert Mitchum] 62
Black Denim Trousers [Cheers] 6
Brontosaurus Stomp [Piltdown Men] 75
Car Trouble [Eligibles]
Cheater Slicks [Super Stocks]
Chicken [Cheers]
409 [Beach Boys] 76
Four On The Floor [Super Stocks]
Hot Rod Race [Jimmy Dolan]
Shut Down [Beach Boys] 23
Street Machine [Super Stocks]
Wide Track [Super Stocks]

DEBUT	PEAK	WKS	RIAA	CD	ARTIST — Album Title	Catalog	Sym	$	Label & Number
12/6/69+	147	15			**Signs Of The Zodiac**			$15	A&M 4211-22

series of 12 albums about the signs of the zodiac

DEBUT	PEAK	WKS	RIAA	CD	ARTIST — Album Title	Catalog	Sym	$	Label & Number
10/19/91	160	12		©437	**Simply Mad About The Mouse**			$10	Columbia 46019

Bare Necessities [Harry Connick, Jr.]
Dream Is A Wish Your Heart Makes [Michael Bolton]
I've Got No Strings [Gipsy Kings]
Kiss The Girl [Soul II Soul]
Mad About The Wolf [Kirk Whalum]
One Song (medley)
Siamese Cat Song [Bobby McFerrin]
Someday My Prince Will Come (medley)
When You Wish Upon A Star [Billy Joel]
Who's Afraid Of The Big Bad Wolf [L.L. Cool J]
Zip-A-Dee-Doo-Dah [Ric Ocasek]

DEBUT	PEAK	WKS	RIAA	CD	ARTIST — Album Title	Catalog	Sym	$	Label & Number
7/17/99	200	1		©438	**Sing America**			$10	Warner 47245

Amazing Grace [Judy Collins] 15
America [Neil Diamond] 8
America The Beautiful (medley) [O'Landa Draper's Associates]
Back In The U.S.A. [Linda Ronstadt] 16
Blowin' In The Wind [Bob Dylan]
Centerfield [John Fogerty] 44
City Of New Orleans [Arlo Guthrie] 18
Fanfare For The Common Man [Leonard Bernstein/NY Philharmonic]
God Bless America [LeAnn Rimes]
Graceland [Paul Simon] 81
House I Live In [Frank Sinatra]
If I Can Dream [Elvis Presley] 12
Living In The Promiseland [Willie Nelson]
Oh, Susanna [James Taylor]
Sing, America [Denyce Graves]
Sir Duke [Stevie Wonder] 1
Star Spangled Banner [Cher]
Summertime [Ella Fitzgerald & Louis Armstrong]
Take Me Home, Country Roads [John Denver] 2
This Is My Country [Impressions]
This Land Is Your Land [Peter, Paul & Mary]
We Shall Overcome (medley) [O'Landa Draper's Associates]

DEBUT	PEAK	WKS	RIAA	CD	ARTIST — Album Title	Catalog	Sym	$	Label & Number
4/11/64	84	11		439	**16 Original Big Hits**			$25	Motown 614

Beechwood 4-5789 [Marvelettes] 17
Come And Get These Memories [Martha & The Vandellas] 29
Contract On Love [Little Stevie Wonder]
Do You Love Me [Contours] 3
Jamie [Eddie Holland] 30
Love Me All The Way [Kim Weston] 88
Money (That's What I Want) [Barrett Strong] 23
One Who Really Loves You [Mary Wells] 8
Please Mr. Postman [Marvelettes] 1
Pride And Joy [Marvin Gaye] 10
Shop Around [Miracles] 2
Stubborn Kind Of Fellow [Marvin Gaye] 46
Sunset [Little Stevie Wonder]
You Beat Me To The Punch [Mary Wells] 9
You've Really Got A Hold On Me [Miracles] 8
Your Heart Belongs To Me [Supremes] 95

DEBUT	PEAK	WKS	RIAA	CD	ARTIST — Album Title	Catalog	Sym	$	Label & Number
1/15/66	108	5		440	**16 Original Big Hits, Volume 4**			$25	Motown 633

Baby I Need Your Loving [Four Tops] 11
Baby Love [Supremes] 1
Can You Jerk Like Me [Contours] 47
Devil With The Blue Dress [Shorty Long]
Hot Cha [Jr. Walker & The All Stars]
I'll Be In Trouble [Temptations] 33
I'm Crazy 'Bout My Baby [Marvin Gaye] 77
In My Lonely Room [Martha & The Vandellas] 44
Let Me Go The Right Way [Supremes] 90
My Guy [Mary Wells] 1
Once Upon A Time [Marvin Gaye & Mary Wells] 19
That's What Love Is Made Of [Miracles] 35
Too Many Fish In The Sea [Marvelettes] 25
Try It Baby [Marvin Gaye] 15
Two Lovers [Mary Wells] 7
What's The Matter With You Baby [Marvin Gaye & Mary Wells] 17

DEBUT	PEAK	WKS	RIAA	CD	ARTIST — Album Title	Catalog	Sym	$	Label & Number
11/5/66	57	19		441	**16 Original Big Hits, Volume 5**			$25	Motown 651

Come See About Me [Supremes] 1
First I Look At The Purse [Contours] 57
High Heel Sneakers [Stevie Wonder] 59
How Sweet It Is To Be Loved By You [Marvin Gaye] 6
I Can't Help Myself [Four Tops] 1
I'll Be Doggone [Marvin Gaye] 8
I'll Keep Holding On [Marvelettes] 34
It's Growing [Temptations] 18
Love (Makes Me Do Foolish Things) [Martha & The Vandellas] 70
My Girl [Temptations] 1
Nowhere To Run [Martha & The Vandellas] 8
Shotgun [Jr. Walker & The All Stars] 4
Take Me In Your Arms (Rock Me A Little While) [Kim Weston] 50
Tracks Of My Tears [Miracles] 16
When I'm Gone [Brenda Holloway] 25
Where Did Our Love Go [Supremes] 1

DEBUT	PEAK	WKS	RIAA	CD	ARTIST — Album Title	Catalog	Sym	$	Label & Number
2/25/67	95	25		442	**16 Original Big Hits, Volume 6**			$25	Motown 655

Ain't That Peculiar [Marvin Gaye] 8
As Long As There Is L-O-V-E Love [Jimmy Ruffin]
Don't Mess With Bill [Marvelettes] 7
Going To A Go-Go [Miracles] 11
Helpless [Kim Weston] 56
I Can't Believe You Love Me [Tammi Terrell] 72
It's The Same Old Song [Four Tops] 5
Just A Little Misunderstanding [Contours] 85
My Baby [Temptations] 13
My Baby Loves Me [Martha & The Vandellas] 22
Needle In A Haystack [Velvelettes] 45
Shake And Fingerpop [Jr. Walker & The All Stars] 29
Stop! In The Name Of Love [Supremes] 1
This Old Heart Of Mine (Is Weak For You) [Isley Brothers] 12
Truly Yours [Spinners]
Uptight (Everything's Alright) [Stevie Wonder] 3

DEBUT	PEAK	WKS	RIAA	CD	ARTIST — Album Title	Catalog	Sym	$	Label & Number
10/14/67	81	18		443	**16 Original Big Hits, Volume 7**			$25	Motown 661

Ain't Too Proud To Beg [Temptations] 13
Back In My Arms Again [Supremes] 1
Come On And See Me [Tammi Terrell] 80
Darling Baby [Elgins] 72
Function At The Junction [Shorty Long] 97
How Sweet It Is (To Be Loved By You) [Jr. Walker & The All Stars] 18
Hunter Gets Captured By The Game [Marvelettes] 13
I Hear A Symphony [Supremes] 1
I'll Be Doggone [Marvin Gaye] 8
I'm Ready For Love [Martha & The Vandellas] 9
It Takes Two [Marvin Gaye & Kim Weston] 14
My Girl Has Gone [Miracles] 14
Place In The Sun [Stevie Wonder] 9
Pucker Up Buttercup [Jr. Walker & The All Stars] 31
Shake Me, Wake Me (When It's Over) [Four Tops] 18
What Becomes Of The Brokenhearted [Jimmy Ruffin] 7

DEBUT	PEAK	WKS	RIAA	CD	ARTIST — Album Title	Catalog	Sym	$	Label & Number
12/30/67+	163	7		444	**16 Original Big Hits, Volume 8**			$25	Motown 666

Beauty Is Only Skin Deep [Temptations] 3
(Come 'Round Here) I'm The One You Need [Miracles] 17
Gonna Give Her All The Love I've Got [Jimmy Ruffin] 29
Greetings (This Is Uncle Sam) [Monitors] 100
Heaven Must Have Sent You [Elgins] 50
I Guess I'll Always Love You [Isley Brothers] 61
(I Know) I'm Losing You [Temptations] 8
(I'm A) Road Runner [Jr. Walker & The All Stars] 20
Jimmy Mack [Martha & The Vandellas] 10
Loving You Is Sweeter Than Ever [Four Tops] 45
My World Is Empty Without You [Supremes] 5
Shoot Your Shot [Jr. Walker & The All Stars] 44
Take Me In Your Arms And Love Me [Gladys Knight & The Pips] 98
Travlin' Man [Stevie Wonder] 32
You Can't Hurry Love [Supremes] 1
Your Unchanging Love [Marvin Gaye] 33

DEBUT	PEAK	WKS	RIAA	CD	ARTIST — Album Title	Catalog	Sym	$	Label & Number
11/16/68+	173	9		445	**16 Original Big Hits, Volume 9**			$25	Motown 668

Ain't No Mountain High Enough [Marvin Gaye & Tammi Terrell] 19
All I Need [Temptations] 8
Bernadette [Four Tops] 4
Come See About Me [Jr. Walker & The All Stars] 24
Don't You Miss Me A Little Bit Baby [Jimmy Ruffin] 68
Everybody Needs Love [Gladys Knight & The Pips] 39
Honey Chile [Martha Reeves & The Vandellas] 11
I Second That Emotion [Smokey Robinson & The Miracles] 4
I Was Made To Love Her [Stevie Wonder] 2
(Loneliness Made Me Realize) It's You That I Need [Temptations] 14
Love Is Here And Now You're Gone [Supremes] 1
More Love [Smokey Robinson & The Miracles] 23
My Baby Must Be A Magician [Marvelettes] 17
Reach Out I'll Be There [Four Tops] 1
You Keep Me Hangin' On [Supremes] 1
Your Precious Love [Marvin Gaye & Tammi Terrell] 5

VARIOUS ARTISTS COMPILATIONS

DEBUT	PEAK	WKS	RIAA	CD	ARTIST — Album Title	Catalog	Sym	$	Label & Number
11/30/59+	2[7]	78	●	446	**60 Years Of Music America Loves Best**			$30	RCA Victor 6074 [2]
10/31/60	6	59		447	**60 Years Of Music America Loves Best, Volume II**			$30	RCA Victor 6088 [2]
9/4/61	5	40		448	**60 Years Of Music America Loves Best, Volume III (Popular)**			$25	RCA Victor 1509
9/4/61	6	18		449	**60 Years Of Music America Loves Best, Volume III (Red Seal)**			$25	RCA Victor 2574
11/12/94	56	12	●	©450	**Skynyrd Frynds**			$10	MCA 11097
2/13/99	111	10		©451	**Slammin' Wrestling Hits**			$10	Beast 54582
9/9/00	110	3		©452	**Smooth Grooves: The Essential Collection**			$10	Rhino 79885
7/6/96	32	33	●	©453	**So So Def Bass All-Stars**			$10	So So Def 67532
7/12/97	71	23		©454	**So So Def Bass All-Stars Volume II**			$10	So So Def 67998
10/24/98	129	3		©455	**So So Def Bass All-Stars Volume III**			$10	So So Def 69346
3/19/66	107	19		456	**Solid Gold Soul**			$25	Atlantic 8116

60 Years Of Music America Loves Best (446):
And The Angels Sing [Benny Goodman]; Ave Maria [Marian Anderson]; Banana Boat (Day-O) [Harry Belafonte] 5; Be My Love [Mario Lanza]; Begin The Beguine [Artie Shaw]; Blue Danube Waltz [Leopold Stokowski]; Bluebird Of Happiness [Jan Peerce]; Bouquet Of Roses [Eddy Arnold]; **Canadian Sunset** [Hugo Winterhalter/Eddie Heywood] 2; Carmen [Vladimir Horowitz]; **Cherry Pink And Apple Blossom White** [Perez Prado] 1; Hora Staccato [Jascha Heifetz]; Indian Love Call [Jeanette MacDonald & Nelson Eddy]; Jalousie (Jealousy) [Arthur Fiedler/Boston Pops]; Liebesfreud (Love's Joy) [Fritz Kreisler]; Lohengrin: Act III, Prelude [Arturo Toscanini]; Minuet In G, Op. 14, No. 1 [Ignace Paderewski]; **Naughty Lady Of Shady Lane** [Ames Brothers] 3; Peg O' My Heart [Three Suns]; Piano Concerto No. 1 [Freddy Martin]; Polonaise In A-Flat, Op. 53, No. 6 [Jose Iturbi]; Prelude In C-Sharp Minor, Op. 3. No. 2 [Sergei Rachmaninoff]; Prisoner Of Love [Perry Como]; Ramona [Gene Austin]; Ritual Fire Dance [Artur Rubinstein]; Sunrise Serenade [Glenn Miller]; Take The "A" Train [Duke Ellington]; There Are Such Things [Tommy Dorsey & Frank Sinatra]; Vesti La Giubba [Enrico Caruso]; Whispering [Paul Whiteman]

60 Years Of Music America Loves Best, Volume II (447):
Air For The G String [Mischa Elman]; Beer Barrel Polka [Will Glahe]; Boogie Woogie [Tommy Dorsey]; Ciribiribin [Grace Moore]; Cocktails For Two [Spike Jones]; Dipsy Doodle [Larry Clinton]; Donkey Serenade [Allan Jones]; Habanera [Rise Stevens]; Holiday For Strings [David Rose]; Il Bacio (The Kiss) [Lucrezia Bori]; In The Mood [Glenn Miller]; Josephine [Wayne King]; Louise [Maurice Chevalier]; Matilda, Matilda! [Harry Belafonte]; Meditation [Fritz Kreisler]; Oh! My Pa-Pa (O Mein Papa) [Eddie Fisher]; Prelude To Act I Of "La Traviata" [Arturo Toscanini]; Riders In The Sky (A Cowboy Legend) [Vaughn Monroe]; Sabre Dance [Arthur Fiedler/Boston Pops Orch.]; Star Dust [Artie Shaw]; Stars And Stripes Forever [John Philip Sousa]; Swan (Le Cygne) [Pablo Casals]; Sweethearts On Parade [Guy Lombardo]; Tales From The Vienna Woods [Leopold Stokowski]; Till The End Of Time [Perry Como]; Toreador Song [Leonard Warren]; Troika En Traineaux (In A Three-Horse Sleigh) [Sergei Rachmaninoff]; Verdi: Bella Figlia Dell' Amore [Caruso/Galli-Curci/Perini/De Luca]; Vesti La Giubba [Mario Lanza]; Whiffenpoof Song [Robert Merrill]

60 Years Of Music America Loves Best, Volume III (Popular) (448):
Chattanooga Choo Choo [Glenn Miller/Tex Beneke/Modernaires]; Frenesi [Artie Shaw]; Goodnight My Love [Benny Goodman & Ella Fitzgerald]; Got A Date With An Angel [Hal Kemp]; Heartaches [Ted Weems]; I Can't Get Started [Bunny Berigan]; Just A Gigolo [Bing Crosby]; Marie [Tommy Dorsey]; Night And Day [Frank Sinatra]; Prisoner's Song [Vernon Dalhart]; Scarlet Ribbons (For Her Hair) [Harry Belafonte]; Wee Deoch An' Doris [Harry Lauder]

60 Years Of Music America Loves Best, Volume III (Red Seal) (449):
Caprice Viennois [Fritz Kreisler]; Caro Nome [Lily Pons]; Che Gelida Manina [Jussi Bjoerling]; Dance Of The Hours [Arturo Toscanini]; Deh, Vieni Alla Finestra [Ezio Pinza]; Go Down Moses [Marian Anderson]; Hamlet: Soliloquy [John Barrymore]; Ho-Yo-Yo-Ho! [Kirsten Flagstad]; La Donna E Mobile [Enrico Caruso]; Moonlight Sonata: First Movement [Vladimir Horowitz]; Serenade For Strings: Waltz [Serge Koussevitzky]; Song Fest [Arthur Fiedler/Boston Pops]

Skynyrd Frynds (450):
Call Me The Breeze [Mavericks]; Don't Ask Me No Questions [Travis Tritt]; Free Bird [Wynonna]; I Know A Little [Sammy Kershaw]; One More Time [Charlie Daniels]; Saturday Night Special [Terry McBride & The Ride]; Simple Man [Confederate Railroad]; Sweet Home Alabama [Alabama]; Tuesday's Gone [Hank Williams, Jr.]; What's Your Name [Steve Earle]

Slammin' Wrestling Hits (451):
Al Snow Theme; Bill Goldberg Theme; Dude Love Theme; Edge Theme; Gangrel Theme; Goldust Theme; Ken Shamrock Theme; Lex Luger Theme; Mankind Theme; N.W.O. Theme; Ric Flair Theme; Sable Theme; Stone Cold Steve Austin Theme; Undertaker Theme; Val Venis Theme

Smooth Grooves: The Essential Collection (452):
Always And Forever [Heatwave] 18; Best Thing That Ever Happened To Me [Gladys Knight & The Pips] 3; Cherish [Kool & The Gang] 2; Could It Be I'm Falling In Love [Spinners] 4; Didn't I (Blow Your Mind This Time) [Delfonics] 10; Float On [Floaters] 2; (If Loving You Is Wrong) I Don't Want To Be Right [Luther Ingram] 3; In The Rain [Dramatics] 5; It's Ecstasy When You Lay Down Next To Me [Barry White] 4; Let's Get It On [Marvin Gaye] 1; Let's Stay Together [Al Green] 1; Me And Mrs. Jones [Billy Paul] 1; Natural High [Bloodstone] 10; Oh Girl [Chi-Lites] 1; Reunited [Peaches & Herb] 1; Sideshow [Blue Magic] 8; Solid [Ashford & Simpson] 12; What You Won't Do For Love [Bobby Caldwell] 9; You Are Everything [Stylistics] 9; You'll Never Find Another Love Like Mine [Lou Rawls] 2

So So Def Bass All-Stars (453):
Body Hop (Oh My Goodness) [T'Baby]; City Boy Bounce [City Boyz]; Edward J Bass Test [Edward J]; Koochie Kuterz [Playa Poncho]; Let It Burn [Playa Poncho]; Mega Mix [Bass Allstars]; **My Boo** [Ghost Town DJ's] 31; Sexiest [Don Yute]; Shakedown [Trigga Man]; So So Def Bass Contest [Raheem The Dream]; Thyow [Zoe]; Whatz Up, Whatz Up [Playa Poncho & LA Sno]

So So Def Bass All-Stars Volume II (454):
Apple Pie [Virgo]; Bass [Edward J feat. Poon Daddy & Lil Jon]; Booty Time [Zae feat. Sonji]; Eastside Side To The Westside [Edward J]; Es Verano [Corina]; Freak It [Lathun]; Hard Core Wuk [Don Yute feat. DJ Uncle Al]; Love You Down [INOJ] 25; Mega Mix II [Bass All-Stars]; My Boo [Ghostown DJ's]; Preface [Afroman & Skeeter Rock]; Sally (That Girl) [Gucci Crew II]; Slick Partna [Virgo]; So So Def Quad [Luke feat. Kandi (of Xscape)]; **Summertime Summertime** [Corina] 86; Uh Uhh [Bo Hagon]

So So Def Bass All-Stars Volume III (455):
Bounce Around [June Dog Feat. DJ Kizzy Rock]; Drop Dem Boes [Bo Hagon Feat. Lil Jon & The Eastside Boyz]; Drop Don't Stop [McAde Feat. DJ Smurf]; Es Verano; Gimmie What I Want [Lathun Feat. Katrina.]; Let It Go [Butter]; Mega Mix III [Bass All-Stars]; Six Eight [Katrina.]; Time After Time [INOJ] 6; True City Thugs [Ying Yang Twins]; Uhh Uhh Uhh [Lil Chris]; What It Is? [Virgo]; What The F$@k [V.I.P. Squad]; What's Goin' On [TBM Feat. Mark Twayne]; When Will I See You Smile Again? [Ricky Bell]

Solid Gold Soul (456):
Don't Fight It [Wilson Pickett] 53; Don't Play That Song (You Lied) [Ben E. King] 11; Got To Get You Off My Mind [Solomon Burke] 22; Hold What You've Got [Joe Tex] 5; I Want To (Do Everything For You) [Joe Tex] 23; I've Been Loving You Too Long (To Stop Now) [Otis Redding] 21; In The Midnight Hour [Wilson Pickett] 21; Just Out Of Reach (Of Two Open Arms) [Solomon Burke] 24; Mercy, Mercy [Don Covay] 35; Mr. Pitiful [Otis Redding] 41; Seesaw [Don Covay] 44; Stand By Me [Ben E. King] 4

DEBUT	PEAK	WKS	RIAA	CD	ARTIST — Album Title	Catalog Sym	$	Label & Number

4/22/00 — **94** — 7 — ©457 — **Solid Gold Soul - Deep Soul**.. — **$10** Rhino 79779

Any Day Now (My Wild Beautiful Bird) [Chuck Jackson] 23 · Cry Baby [Garnet Mimms & The Enchanters] 4 · Cry, Cry, Cry [Bobby Bland] 71 · Cry To Me [Betty Harris] 23 · Dark End Of The Street [James Carr] 77 · Doggin' Around [Jackie Wilson] 15 · Eight Men, Four Women [O.V. Wright] 80 · I Found A Love [Wilson Pickett] 32 · I'd Rather Go Blind [Clarence Carter] · I've Been Loving You Too Long (To Stop Now) [Otis Redding] 21 · (If Loving You Is Wrong) I Don't Want To Be Right [Luther Ingram] 3 · If You Need Me [Solomon Burke] 37 · It's A Man's Man's Man's World [James Brown] 8 · Piece Of My Heart [Erma Franklin] 62 · Stand By Me [Ben E. King] 4 · Tell It Like It Is [Aaron Neville] 2 · That's How Strong My Love Is [Otis Redding] 74 · Thrill Is Gone [B.B. King] 15 · Time Is On My Side [Irma Thomas] · When A Man Loves A Woman [Percy Sledge] 1 · When Something Is Wrong With My Baby [Sam & Dave] 42 · (You Make Me Feel Like) A Natural Woman [Aretha Franklin] 8

7/20/63 — **72** — 12 — — 458 — **Songs For A Summer Night**... — **$25** Columbia 2 [2]

Bend In The River [Marty Robbins] · By The Light Of The Silvery Moon [Julie Andrews] · Dat Dere [Oscar Brown, Jr.] · God Bless The Child [Aretha Franklin] · Green Leaves Of Summer [Mahalia Jackson] · Guess I Should Have Loved Him More [Eydie Gorme] · I Know Where I'm Goin' [New Christy Minstrels] · I Was Just Walkin' Out The Door [Jimmy Dean] · If You Love Her Tell Her So [Steve Lawrence] · In The Chapel In The Moonlight [Anita Bryant] · In The Good Old Summertime (medley) [Mitch Miller] · In The Shade Of The Old Apple Tree (medley) [Mitch Miller] · Just A Simple Melody [Patti Page] · Loneliest Man In The World [Dion] · May Each Day [Andy Williams] · Moon Was Yellow [Robert Goulet] · Moonlight Gambler [Frankie Laine] · My Coloring Book [Barbra Streisand] · Oh What A Beautiful Dream [Doris Day] · Rising Of The Moon [Clancy Brothers & Tommy Makem] · Some Enchanted Evening [Earl Wrightson] · Stella By Starlight [Tony Bennett] · Summer Days Alone [Brothers Four] · Summertime [Leslie Uggams] · Summertime In Venice [Jerry Vale]

10/31/98 — **151** — 2 — ©459 — **Songs 4 Life - Embrace His Grace!**.......................................C:#15/1 — **$15** Time Life 80403 [2]

Every Time [CeCe Winans] · Friends [Michael W. Smith] · Glory To You [Steve Green] · Great Adventure [Steven Curtis Chapman] · Great Lengths [PFR] · He Is [Aaron Jeoffrey] · Here In My Heart [Susan Ashton] · Light Your World [Newsong] · Look A Little Closer [Helen Baylor] · Love Takes Time [Bryan Duncan] · Nothing's Gonna Keep Me From You [Out Of The Grey] · One More Broken Heart [Point Of Grace] · Robe, The [Wes King] · Serve The Lord [Carman] · Takin' My Time [Ashton, Becker, Dente] · Thy Word [Amy Grant] · Undivided [First Call] · Watercolour Ponies [Wayne Watson] · We Shall Behold Him [Sandi Patti] · We Will Stand [Russ Taff] · When I Let It Go [Sierra] · You Put This Love In My Heart [Keith Green]

10/3/98+ — **43** — 19 — ● — ©460 — **Songs 4 Life - Feel The Power!**..C:#9/3 — **$15** Time Life 80401 [2]

Another Time, Another Place [Sandi Patti & Wayne Watson] · Awesome God [Rich Mullins] · Basics Of Life [4Him] · Between You And Me [DC Talk] · Crucified With Christ [Phillips, Craig & Dean] · El Shaddai [Amy Grant] · Go Light Your World [Kathy Troccoli] · God Is In Control [Twila Paris] · Great Divide [Point Of Grace] · Heaven [BeBe & CeCe Winans] · I Believe [Wes King] · I Surrender All [Clay Crosse] · I Will Be Here [Steven Curtis Chapman] · Love Crucified Arose [Michael Card] · Love Song For A Savior [Jars Of Clay] · Man After Your Own Heart [Gary Chapman] · Man Of God [Audio Adrenaline] · On My Knees [Jaci Velasquez] · Place In This World [Michael W. Smith] · Revive Us O Lord [Carman] · Thank You [Ray Boltz] · Trumpet Of Jesus [Imperials]

10/17/98 — **131** — 2 — ©461 — **Songs 4 Life - Lift Your Spirit!**...C:#13/1 — **$15** Time Life 80402 [2]

Addictive Love [BeBe & CeCe Winans] · Build My World Around You [Sandi Patti] · Call, The [Anointed] · Fear Not My Child [Carman] · Find Us Faithful [Steve Green] · Flood [Jars Of Clay] · Friend Of A Wounded Heart [Wayne Watson] · Heart Like Mine [Bryan Duncan] · Heaven In The Real World [Steven Curtis Chapman] · I Pledge Allegiance To The Lamb [Ray Boltz] · I Will Be Here For You [Michael W. Smith] · I'm Not Ashamed [Newsboys] · In Christ Alone [Michael English] · Keep The Candle Burning [Point Of Grace] · Listen To Our Hearts [Geoff Moore] · My Heart's Already There [Newsong] · Sing Your Praise To The Lord [Amy Grant] · Stand [Susan Ashton] · Sweet Glow Of Mercy [Gary Chapman] · Un Lugar Celestial [Jaci Velasquez] · Warrior Is A Child [Twila Paris] · Where There Is Faith [4Him]

11/21/98 — **189** — 1 — ©462 — **Songs 4 Life - Renew Your Heart!**...C:#12/1 — **$15** Time Life 80404 [2]

All We Need [Out Of The Grey] · Count It All Joy [BeBe & CeCe Winans] · Find A Way [Amy Grant] · Flesh Of My Flesh [Leon Patillo] · For Future Generations [4Him] · For The Sake Of The Call [Steven Curtis Chapman] · He Is Exalted [Twila Paris] · I Call Your Name [Clay Crosse] · I'll Be Believing [Point Of Grace] · I'll Lead You Home [Michael W. Smith] · I've Just Seen Jesus [Larnelle Harris & Sandi Patti] · In Heaven's Eyes [Sandi Patti] · Joy In The Journey [Michael Card] · Mansion Builder [2nd Chapter Of Acts] · Mercy Came Running [Phillips, Craig & Dean] · People Get Ready...Jesus Is Comin' [Crystal Lewis] · People Need The Lord [Steve Green] · Seize The Day [Carolyn Arends] · Sometimes By Step [Rich Mullins] · Sweet Jesus [Gary Chapman] · Waiting For Your Love [Susan Ashton] · What If I Stumble? [DC Talk]

6/2/01 — **91** — 10 — ©463 — **Songs 4 Worship - Be Glorified**... — **$15** Integrity 61003 [2]

Be Exalted O God [Jeff Hamlin] · Be Glorified [Ron Kenoly] · Blessed Be The Name Of The Lord [Don Moen] · Come Let Us Worship And Bow Down [Maranatha Singers] · Father I Adore You [Maranatha Singers] · He Is Lord [Maranatha Singers] · Here In Your Presence [Charlie LeBlanc] · I Stand In Awe [Bob Fitts] · I Will Come And Bow Down [Leann Albrecht] · I Will Praise Your Name [Bob Fitts] · In His Time [Maranatha Singers] · In Moments Like These [Maranatha Singers] · Isn't He [Terry Clark] · Jesus Lover Of My Soul [Darlene Zschech] · O Come Let Us Adore Him (medley) [Maranatha Singers] · Oh The Glory Of Your Presence [Steve Fry] · Only By Grace [Graham Kendrick] · Surely The Presence Of The Lord [Brentwood Singers] · There Is None Like You [Lenny LeBlanc] · Thou Art Worthy (medley) [Maranatha Singers] · We Bow Down [Twila Paris] · Yes We All Agree [Tommy Walker] · You Are My Hiding Place [Maranatha Singers]

5/5/01 — **122** — 10 — ● — ©464 — **Songs 4 Worship - Holy Ground**.. — **$15** Integrity 61002 [2]

As The Deer [Maranatha Singers] · Change My Heart, Oh God [Roby Duke] · Come Into His Presence [Joseph Garlington] · Come Now Is The Time To Worship [Brian Doerksen] · Glorify Thy Name [Maranatha Singers] · God Will Make A Way [Don Moen] · He Who Began A Good Work [Steve Green] · Holy And Anointed One [Randy Butler] · Holy Ground [Geron Davis] · I Love You, Lord [Maranatha Singers] · I Worship You, Almighty God [Kent Henry] · In The Presence [Eugene Greco] · Jesus, Name Above All Names [Charlie LeBlanc] · More Precious Than Silver [LaMar Boschman] · Oh Lord, You're Beautiful [Keith Green] · Open Your Eyes [Maranatha Singers] · Seek Ye First [Maranatha Singers] · Spirit Of The Living God [Brentwood Singers] · We Will Glorify [Twila Paris] · We Worship And Adore Thee [Maranatha Singers] · When I Look Into Your Holiness [Maranatha Singers] · You Are My All In All [Dennis Jernigan]

3/10/01 — **51** — 30↑▲ — ©465 — **Songs 4 Worship - Shout To The Lord**...................................... — **$15** Integrity 61001 [2]

All Hail King Jesus [Kent Henry] · Awesome God [Rich Mullins] · Blessed Be The Lord God Almighty [David Butterbaugh] · Celebrate Jesus [Charlie LeBlanc] · Give Thanks [Don Moen] · He Has Made Me Glad [Maranatha Singers] · He Is Exalted [Twila Paris] · I Could Sing Of Your Love Forever [Delirious?] · I Exalt Thee [Pete Sanchez] · I Will Call Upon The Lord [Marty Nystrom] · I Will Celebrate [Paul Baloche] · Lord, I Lift Your Name On High [Maranatha Singers] · Majesty [Ron Kenoly] · Mighty Is Our God [J. Daniel Smith] · My Life Is In You, Lord [Joseph Garlington] · Praise The Name Of Jesus [Kent Henry] · Shine, Jesus, Shine [Graham Kendrick] · Shout To The Lord [Darlene Zschech] · There Is A Redeemer [Keith Green] · This Is The Day [Ed Gungor] · Thy Word [Amy Grant] · What A Mighty God We Serve [Don Moen]

VARIOUS ARTISTS COMPILATIONS

DEBUT	PEAK	WKS	RIAA	CD	ARTIST — Album Title	Catalog	Sym	$	Label & Number

3/27/71 | 176 | 8 | | ©466 Songs Of The Humpback Whale .... **$15** Capitol 620
actual recorded sounds of Whales near Bermuda
Distant Whale | Solo Whale | Tower Whales
Slowed-Down Solo Whale | Three Whale Trip

2/17/96 | 65 | 11 | ● | ©467 Songs Of West Side Story, The .... **$10** RCA Victor 62707
America [Natalie Cole, Patti LaBelle & Sheila E.] | Eye" Lopes/Jerky Boys/Paul Rodriguez] | One Hand, One Heart [Tevin Campbell] | Something's Coming [All-4-One]
Boy Like That [Selena] | I Feel Pretty [Little Richard] | Prelude To Somewhere [Orchestra] | Somewhere [Aretha Franklin]
Cool [Patti Austin, Mervyn Warren & Bruce Hornsby] | I Have A Love [Trisha Yearwood] | Prelude To The Rumble [Chick Corea] | Somewhere [Phil Collins]
Gee, Officer Krupke [Salt-N-Pepa/Def Jef/Lisa "Left | Jet Song [Brian Setzer] | Maria [Michael McDonald, James Ingram & David Pack] | Rumble, The [Chick Corea's Electric Band vs. Steve Vai's Monsters] | Tonight [Kenny Loggins & Wynonna]

3/22/97 | 20 | 9 | | ©468 Soul Assassins - Chapter I .... **$10** Columbia 66820
Battle Of 2001 [Cypress Hill] | It Could Happen To You [Mobb Deep] | Move Ahead [KRS-One] | Time Has Come
Decisions, Decisions [Goodie Mob] | John 3:16 [Wyclef from Refugee Camp] | New York Undercover [Call O' Da Wild]
Devil In A Blue Dress [LA The Darkman] | Life Is Tragic [Infamous Mobb] | Puppet Master [Dr. Dre & B Real]
Heavy Weights [MC Eiht] | | Third World [RZA/GZA/Genius]

4/5/69 | 172 | 3 | | 469 Soul Explosion .... **$25** Stax 2007 [2]
Book Of Love [Carla Thomas] | Hot Hips [Bar-Kays] | Long Walk To D.C. [Staple Singers] | Soul Clap '69 [Booker T. & The M.G.'s]
Booker's Theme [Booker T. & The M.G.'s] | I Got A Sure Thing [Ollie & The Nightingales] 73 | Mercy, Mercy, Mercy [Southwest F.O.B.] | Soul-Limbo [Booker T. & The M.G.'s] 17
Bring It On Home To Me [Eddie Floyd] 17 | I Like Everything About You [Jimmy Hughes] | Peeped Around Yonder's Bend [Jimmy Hughes] | These Old Memories [Mad Lads]
Cold Feet [Albert King] 67 | I've Never Found A Girl (To Love Me Like You Do) [Eddie Floyd] 40 | Private Number [Judy Clay & William Bell] 75 | Twenty Years From Today [Johnnie Taylor]
Copy Kat [Bar-Kays] | It's Me [Judy Clay] | Save Your Love For Me [Johnnie Taylor] | Where Do I Go [Carla Thomas] 86
Hang 'Em High [Booker T. & The M.G.'s] 9 | It's Wrong To Be Loving You [Eddie Floyd] | Smell Of Incense [Southwest F.O.B.] 56 | Who's Making Love [Johnnie Taylor] 5
Hear My Call [Staple Singers] | Left Hand Woman (Get Right With Me) [Albert King] | So Nice [Mad Lads]
Heartache Mountain [Ollie & The Nightingales]

5/11/63 | 39 | 8 | | 470 Sound of Genius, The .... **$25** Columbia SGS 1 [2]
Capriccio Espagnol [Leonard Bernstein] | Love For Three Oranges: March [Thomas Schippers] | Quartet In G Minor: Scherzo [Budapest Quartet] | Symphonic Variations: Finale [Eugene Ormandy]
Clair De Lune [Philippe Entremont] | Marriage Of Figaro: Overture [Bruno Walter] | Song Of The Birds [Pablo Casals] | Tonight [Richard Tucker]
Concerto No. 5: Arioso [Glenn Gould] | Mi Chiamano Mimi [Eileen Farrell] | Song Without Words (medley) [Rudolf Serkin] | Violin Concerto In D Major: Finale [Isaac Stern]
Danse Russe [Igor Stravinsky] | Polonaise [Alexander Brailowsky] | Spinning Song (medley) [Rudolf Serkin] | Violin Concerto In E Minor: Finale [Zino Francescatti]
Lord's Prayer [Mormon Tabernacle Choir] | Prince Of Denmark's March [E. Power Biggs] | Swan Lake: Final Scene [Eugene Ormandy]

9/4/99 | 53 | 11 | | ©471 Source Hip-Hop Music Awards 1999 - The Album, The .... **$10** UTV 564891
Break Ups 2 Make Ups [Method Man Feat. D'Angelo] 98 | 5 Mics [Kurupt Feat. El Drex & The Committee] | It's On [DJ Clue Feat. DMX] | Skew It On The Bar-B [OutKast Feat. Raekwon]
Can I Get A... [Jay-Z Feat. Amil & Ja Rule] 19 | Ha [Juvenile] 68 | Joints & Jam [Black Eyed Peas] | Superthug [Noreaga] 36
Deja Vu (Uptown Baby) [Lord Tariq & Peter Gunz] 9 | I'll Bee Dat! [Redman] | Militia [Gang Starr Feat. Big Shug & Freddie Foxxx] | Thug Girl [Master P]
Find A Way [Tribe Called Quest] | Is It You? (Deja Vu) [Made Men Feat. Master P] | My Name Is [Eminem] 36 | You Got Me [Roots Feat. Erykah Badu] 39
| It Ain't My Fault 2 [Silkk The Shocker Feat. Mystikal] 18 | Party Is Goin' On Over Here [Busta Rhymes]

9/2/00 | 17 | 21 | ● | ©472 Source Hip-Hop Music Awards 2000 - The Album, The .... **$10** Def Jam 542829
Back That Thang Up [Juvenile] 19 | Cold Hearted [Made Men] | Jigga My Nigga [Jay-Z] 28 | What's My Name [DMX] 67
Bitch Please [Snoop Dogg feat. Xzibit] | Da Rockwilder [Method Man/Redman] | Ms. Fat Booty [Mos Def] | Whoa! [Black Rob] 43
Bling Bling [B.G.] 36 | Forgot About Dre [Dr. Dre feat. Eminem] 25 | Quiet Storm [Mobb Deep feat. Lil' Kim] | Wild Out [Lox]
Cherchez LaGhost [Ghostface Killah] 98 | Got Beef [Eastsidaz] 99 | Truth, The [Beanie Sigel] | You Owe Me [Nas feat. Ginuwine] 59
| | Vivrant Thing [Q-Tip] 26

1/3/98 | 38 | 32 | | ©473 Source Presents Hip Hop Hits - Volume 1, The .... **$10** PolyGram TV 536204
Big Bad Mamma [Foxy Brown Feat. Dru Hill] 53 | Can't Nobody Hold Me Down [Puff Daddy Feat. Mase] 1 | Hay [Crucial Conflict] 18 | Mary Jane [Scarface]
Bout It, Bout It [Master P] | Crush On You [Lil' Kim & Lil' Ceas] | Hell On Earth [Mobb Deep] | Phenomenon [LL Cool J] 55
Bow Down [Westside Connection] 21 | Da Joint [EPMD] | Hypnotize [Notorious B.I.G.] 1 | Triumph [Wu-Tang Clan]
| Elevators [OutKast] 12 | I'll Be [Foxy Brown & Jay-Z] 7 | We Trying To Stay Alive [Wyclef Jean/Refugee All-Stars] 45
| Firm Biz [Firm] | Look Into My Eyes [Bone Thugs-N-Harmony] 4 | Whateva Man [Redman] 42

11/28/98+ | 46 | 23 | ● | ©474 Source Presents Hip Hop Hits - Volume 2, The .... **$10** PolyGram TV 565668
Deja Vu (Uptown Baby) [Lord Tariq & Peter Gunz] 9 | Gone Till November [Wyclef Jean] 7 | It's Alright [Memphis Bleek & Jay-Z] 61 | Party Ain't A Party [Queen Pen] 74
Do For Love [2Pac] 21 | Hope I Don't Go Back [E-40] | Luv 2 Luv U [Timbaland & Magoo] | Still A G Thing [Snoop Dogg] 19
4,3,2,1 [LL Cool J feat. Redman/Method Man/Canibus/DMX] 75 | Horse & Carriage [Cam'ron feat. Mase] 41 | Money Ain't A Thang [Jermaine Dupri feat. Jay-Z] 52 | Still Not A Player [Big Punisher feat. Joe] 24
Get At Me Dog [DMX feat. Sheek of The Lox] 39 | I Got The Hook-Up! [Master P & Sons Of Funk] 16 | Money, Power & Respect [Lox feat. DMX & Lil' Kim] 17 | Turn It Up/Fire It Up [Busta Rhymes] 10
| | N.O.R.E. [Noreaga] | Whatcha Gonna Do [Jayo Felony feat. Method Man & DMX]

12/18/99+ | 45 | 19 | | ©475 Source Presents Hip Hop Hits - Volume 3, The .... **$10** UTV 545440
Guilty Conscience [Eminem] | Holla Holla [Ja Rule] 35 | Simon Says [Pharoahe Monch] 97 | Watch Out For The Hook [Cool Breeze]
He [Juvenile feat. Jay-Z] 68 | Hoody Hooo [Tru feat. Master P] | Slippin' [DMX] | Watch Out Now [Beatnuts] 84
Hard Knock Life (Ghetto Anthem) [Jay-Z] 15 | Jamboree [Naughty By Nature feat. Zhané] 10 | Tear It Off [Redman & Method Man] | What Ya Want [Eve & Nokio] 29
Hate Me Now [Nas feat. Puff Daddy] 62 | Nann [Trick Daddy] 62 | Tommy's Theme [Made Men feat. The Lox] | Who Dat [JT Money feat. Solé] 5
| Quiet Storm [Mobb Deep]

12/30/00+ | 43 | 20 | ● | ©476 Source Presents Hip-Hop Hits - Volume 4, The .... **$10** Def Jam 520062
Bad Boyz [Shyne Feat. Barrington Levy] 57 | It's So Hard [Big Pun] 75 | Oooh [De La Soul Feat. Redman] | What'chu Like [Da Brat Feat. Tyrese] 26
Holla Back (Holla Boston) [Made Men] | Light, The [Common] 44 | Party Up (Up In Here) [DMX] 27 | Wobble Wobble [504 Boyz] 17
(Hot S**t) Country Grammar [Nelly] 7 | Next Episode [Dr. Dre Feat. Snoop Dogg] 23 | Real Slim Shady [Eminem] 4 | Y.O.U. [Method Man/Redman]
Imagine That [LL Cool J] 98 | No Matter What They Say [Lil' Ki] 60 | Shut Up [Trick Daddy] 83
| #1 Stunna [Big Tymers] | Sippin' On Some Syrup [Three-6 Mafia Feat. UGK & Project Pat]

DEBUT	PEAK	WKS	RIAA	CD	ARTIST — Album Title	Catalog	Sym	$	Label & Number

7/30/77 — **142** — 11 — 477 — **South's Greatest Hits, The** .... — $12 — Capricorn 0187

- Doraville [Atlanta Rhythm Section] 35
- Fire On The Mountain [Marshall Tucker Band] 38
- Fooled Around And Fell In Love [Elvin Bishop] 6
- Keep On Smilin' [Wet Willie] 10
- Midnight Rider [Gregg Allman] 19
- Ramblin' Man [Allman Brothers Band] 2
- Right Place, Wrong Time [Dr. John] 9
- South's Gonna Do It [Charlie Daniels Band] 29
- Sweet Home Alabama [Lynyrd Skynyrd] 8
- There Goes Another Love Song [Outlaws] 34
- Third Rate Romance [Amazing Rhythm Aces] 14

9/13/97 — **23** — 6 — ©478 — **Southwest Riders** .... — $15 — Sick Wid' It 45009 [2]

- About My Money [Calvin-T]
- After Dollars No Cents [Master P feat. Silkk The Shocker]
- Ain't Fuckin' Around [SKA-Face Al Kapone]
- Bad Bitches [Suga T. w/Conscious Daughters]
- Big Bank [Mr. Malik]
- Call The Coroner [3X Krazy]
- Capable [Luniz]
- Cop Stories [Graveyard Shift]
- Dis Year [Tela]
- Evil Ways [Komacauszy feat. The Lost Mob]
- Flashin' [Cydal feat. Swoop G]
- Get Cha Mind Right [Mystikal]
- Getto Tales [Coughnut & Baldhead]
- Hiside [UGK]
- Load Unload [Chilla feat. Dope Spot]
- N.S.R. [Mossie]
- Niggas Talk Shit [Eight Ball & MJG]
- On Top Of The World [Comrads]
- Paystyle [918]
- Playa Haters [San Quinn & Messy Marv]
- Represent [A-1]
- Respect It [Celly Cel]
- Threesixafix [Three 6 Mafia]
- Tremendous [Brotha Lynch Hung feat. Sicx]
- Walk With Me [W.C.]
- Who Do I Trust [D-Shot feat. The Mossie]
- Y'all My Nugz [Twista]
- Yay Deep [E-40/B-Legit/Richie Rich]

6/5/61 — **❶⁹** — 40 — 479 — **Stars For A Summer Night** — $30 — Columbia 1 [2]

- Bouquet [Percy Faith Strings]
- By The Campfire [Andre Kostelanetz]
- Can-Can [New York Philharmonic Orch.]
- Clair De Lune [Philippe Entremont]
- Fantasia On Greensleeves [Strings Of The Philadelphia Orch.]
- Hoe Down [Leonard Bernstein]
- In The Evening By The Moonlight (medley) [Frank DeVol]
- It's A Wonderful World [Les Brown]
- Jeannie With The Light Brown Hair [Dave Brubeck Quartet]
- Just Friends [Billy Butterfield]
- Lazy Afternoon [Les & Larry Elgart]
- Liebestraum [Ivan Davis]
- Like Love [Andre Previn]
- Listen To The Mocking Bird (medley) [Frank DeVol]
- Londonderry Air [Mormon Tabernacle Choir]
- March from "The Love For Three Oranges" [Thomas Schippers]
- Nutcracker Suite, Op. 71A-Waltz Of The Flowers [Leonard Bernstein]
- One Fine Day (Un Bel Di) [Eileen Farrell]
- Ramona [Jerry Murad's Harmonicats]
- Russian Sailors' Dance [Eugene Ormandy]
- Stairway To The Stars [Bobby Hackett]
- Star Eyes [Art Van Damme Quintet]
- Stars Were Shining (E Lucevan Le Stelle) [Richard Tucker]
- Summertime [Ray Conniff]
- Symphonie Espagnole (Second Movement) [New York Philharmonic]
- Waltz No. 7 In C-Sharp Minor, Op. 64, No. 2 [A. Brailowsky]
- While Strolling Through The Park One Day (medley) [Frank DeVol]

9/2/67 — **145** — 4 — ©480 — **Stax/Volt Revue - Live In London, The** .... [L] — $25 — Stax 721

- B-A-B-Y [Carla Thomas]
- Green Onions [Booker T. & The MG's]
- Hold On! I'm A Comin' [Sam & Dave]
- I Take What I Want [Sam & Dave]
- If I Had A Hammer [Eddie Floyd]
- Knock On Wood [Eddie Floyd]
- Philly Dog [Mar-Keys]
- Shake [Otis Redding]
- When Something Is Wrong With My Baby [Sam & Dave]
- Yesterday [Carla Thomas]

11/12/88 — **119** — 15 — ©481 — **Stay Awake: Various Interpretations Of Music from Vintage Disney Films** ..... — $10 — A&M 3918

- Baby Mine [Bonnie Raitt & Was (Not Was)]
- Blue Shadows On The Trail (medley) [Syd Straw]
- Castle In Spain (medley) [Buster Poindexter]
- Cruella De Ville (medley) [Replacements]
- Desolation Theme (medley) [Ken Nordine]
- Feed The Birds (medley) [Natalie Merchant/Michael Stipe/Roches]
- Heigh Ho (The Dwarfs Marching Song) [Tom Waits]
- Hi Diddle Dee Dee (An Actor's Life For Me) (medley) [Ken Nordine]
- I Wan'na Be Like You (The Monkey Song) (medley) [Los Lobos]
- I Wonder (medley) [Yma Sumac]
- I'm Wishing (medley) [Betty Carter]
- Little April Shower (medley) [Natalie Merchant/Michael Stipe/Roches]
- Little Wooden Head (medley) [Bill Frisell & Wayne Horvitz]
- Mickey Mouse March [Aaron Neville]
- Pink Elephants On Parade (medley) [Sun Ra]
- Second Star To The Right (medley) [James Taylor]
- Someday My Prince Will Come [Sinead O'Connor]
- Stay Awake (medley) [Suzanne Vega]
- When You Wish Upon A Star (medley) [Ringo Starr]
- Whistle While You Work (medley) [NRBQ]
- Zip-A-Dee-Doo-Dah (medley) [Nilsson]

10/31/98 — **170** — 4 — ©482 — **Steve Austin's Stone Cold Metal** .... — $10 — Mars 44004

- Balls To The Wall [Accept]
- Breaking The Chains [Dokken]
- Detroit Rock City [Kiss] **flip**
- Dreams I'll Never See [Molly Hatchet]
- God Of Thunder [Kiss]
- No One Like You [Scorpions] 65
- On Through The Night [Def Leppard]
- Perfect Strangers [Deep Purple]
- Rain [Cult]
- Rainbow In The Dark [Dio]
- Rock You Like A Hurrican [Scorpions] 25
- Slow Ride [Foghat] 20
- Stone Cold [Rainbow] 40
- Stranglehold [Ted Nugent]

10/25/97 — **150** — 3 — ©483 — **Stone Country: Country Artists Perform The Songs Of The Rolling Stones** ..... — $10 — Beyond Music 3055

- Angie [Sammy Kershaw]
- Beast Of Burden [Little Texas]
- Brown Sugar [Collin Raye]
- Honky Tonk Women [Travis Tritt]
- Jumpin' Jack Flash [Rodney Crowell]
- Last Time [Tractors]
- No Expectations [Nanci Griffith]
- Paint It Black [Tracy Lawrence]
- Ruby Tuesday [Deana Carter]
- Time Is On My Side [George Jones]
- Wild Horses [BlackHawk]

11/27/93 — **28** — 19 — ● — ©484 — **Stone Free: A Tribute To Jimi Hendrix** .... — $10 — Reprise 45438

- Are You Experienced? [Belly]
- Bold As Love [Pretenders]
- Crosstown Traffic [Living Colour]
- Fire [Nigel Kennedy]
- Hey Baby (Land Of The New Rising Sun) [M.A.C.C.]
- Hey Joe [Body Count]
- I Don't Live Today [Slash & Paul Rodgers]
- Manic Depression [Seal & Jeff Beck]
- Purple Haze [Cure]
- Red House [Buddy Guy]
- Spanish Castle Magic [Spin Doctors]
- Stone Free [Eric Clapton]
- Third Stone From The Sun [Pat Metheny]
- You Got Me Floatin' [P.M. Dawn]

12/2/00 — **72** — 11 — ©485 — **Stoned Immaculate -- The Music Of The Doors** .... — $10 — Elektra 62475

- Break On Through [Stone Temple Pilots]
- Children Of Night [Perry Farrell & Exene]
- Cosmic Movie [Doors]
- End, The [Days Of The New]
- Hello I Love You [Oleander]
- Is Everybody In? [William S. Burroughs]
- L.A. Woman [Days Of The New]
- Light My Fire [Train]
- Love Her Madly [Bo Diddley]
- Love Me Two Times [Aerosmith]
- Peace Frog [Smash Mouth]
- Riders On The Storm [Creed]
- Roadhouse Blues [John Lee Hooker & Jim Morrison]
- Roadhouse Rap [Jim Morrison]
- Touch Me [Ian Astbury of The Cult]
- Under Waterfall [Doors]
- Wild Child [Cult]

2/19/94 — **129** — 1 — ©486 — **Straight From Da Streets Volume 1** .... — $10 — Priority 53885

proceeds benefit the Knowledge is Power Fund for the building of a performing arts center and training complex

- Atomic Dog [George Clinton]
- Baby Got Back [Sir Mix-A-Lot] 1
- Back To The Hotel [N2Deep] 14
- Can't Truss It [Public Enemy] 50
- Choice Is Yours [Black Sheep] 57
- Dazzey Duks [Duice] 12
- Ditty, The [Paperboy] 10
- I Get Around [2PAC] 11
- It Was A Good Day [Ice Cube] 15
- Jump Around [House Of Pain] 3
- Let Me Ride [Dr. Dre] 34
- One Nation Under A Groove [Funkadelic] 28
- Rebirth Of Slick (Cool Like Dat) [Digable Planets] 15
- They Want EFX [DAS EFX] 25
- U Don't Hear Me Tho' [Rodney O & Joe Cooley] 93
- We Out [Power 106]
- Whoomp! (There It Is) [Tag Team] 2

9/14/91 — **95** — 11 — ©487 — **Straight From The Hood** .... — $10 — Priority 7063

- Alwayz Into Somethin' [N.W.A.]
- Behind Closed Doors [WC & The Maad Circle]
- Boyz-N-The-Hood [Eazy-E]
- Jackin' For Beats [Ice Cube]
- Lifestyle As A Gangsta [415]
- Mind Playing Tricks On Me [Geto Boys] 23
- Playing It Cool [O.G. Style]
- Psycho [KMC]
- So Wat Cha Sayin' [EPMD]
- This Is For The Convicts [Convicts]

11/25/00 — **56** — 7 — ©488 — **Strait Up** .... — $10 — Immortal 50365

- Absent [Snot]
- Angel's Son [Lajon of Sevendust]
- Catch A Spirit [Max of Soulfly]
- Divided (An Argument For The Soul) [Brandon of Incubus]
- Forever [Fred of Limp Bizkit]
- Funeral Flights [Dex of Coal Chamber]
- I Know Where You're At [M.C.U.D. of (hed)p.e.]
- Reaching Out [Mark of Sugar Ray]
- Requiem [Corey of Slipknot]
- Sad Air (spoken word) [Lynn Strait of Snot]
- Starlit Eyes [Serj of System Of A Down]
- Take It Back [Jonathan of Korn]
- Until Next Time [Jason of R.K.L.]

VARIOUS ARTISTS COMPILATIONS

6/19/99 · **167** · 3 · ©489 · **Streams** ....
Abigail [Irish Film Orchestra] · Don't Give Up [Máire Brennan & Michael McDonald] · Forever On And On [Point Of Grace] · $10 · Word 69875
Breathe [Sixpence None The Richer] · Find Me In The River [Delirious? w/Amy Grant] · From Above [Burlap To Cashmere] · Job [Cindy Morgan] · Only Thing I Need [4Him w/Jon Anderson]
Delaney McDowell [Irish Film Orchestra] · For Cova [Irish Film Orchestra] · Hold On [Michelle Tumes] · I Will Rest In You [Jaci Valesquez] · Sanctuary [Chris Rodriguez] · Streams [Irish Film Orchestra]

8/23/97 · **26** · 7 · ©490 · **Suave House** .... · $10 · Suave House 1585
Death Notes [Fedz] · Just Like Candy [8-Ball & MJG] · Questions [Thorough Of South Circle] · Starships and Rockets [Eightball Feat. Randy]
Dusk Til Dawn [Fedz] · Life Is Crying [NOLA Feat. Nina Creque] · Rider [Tela] · Trapped [NOLA]
Getto Madness [South Circle]
Heat Of The Night [Fedz]

7/8/00 · **158** · 1 · ©491 · **Suave House: Off Da Chain** .... · $10 · Suave House 751030
Bad Muthafucka [Mr. Charlie] · For Da Luv [Eightball & Gillie Da Kid] · Money, Sex & Drugs [Gillie Da Kid feat. AB Luva] · Something To Bounce To [Gillie Da Kid]
Do It Like That [Gillie Da Kid feat. AB Luva] · Get Money [Clinic] · Shake If Off [Eightball & MJG feat. Chico DeBarge & Joe] · We Got Them Things For You [Eightball]
Do You Wanna Ride [Toni Hickman] · Life Got A Loaded Gun [Toni Hickman] · Shine [Lil' Noah]
Done That [Lil' Noah]
Evil & Innocence [PsychoDrama]

5/5/01 · **145** · 3 · ©492 · **Suddenly '70s** .... · $10 · Razor & Tie 89036
Afternoon Delight [Starland Vocal Band] 1 · Don't Pull Your Love [Hamilton, Joe Frank & Reynolds] 4 · Knock Three Times [Dawn] 1 · Saturday Night [Bay City Rollers] 1
Bad Blood [Neil Sedaka] 1 · Go All The Way [Raspberries] 5 · Let Her In [John Travolta] 10 · Stuck In The Middle With You [Stealers Wheel] 6
Billy Don't Be A Hero [Bo Donaldson & The Hyewoods] 1 · Hooked On A Feeling [Blue Swede] 1 · My Maria [B.W. Stevenson] 9 · Welcome Back [John Sebastian] 1
Brandy (You're A Fine Girl) [Looking Glass] 1 · I Am Woman [Helen Reddy] 1 · Play That Funky Music [Wild Cherry] 1
Brother Louie [Stories] 1 · Joy To The World [Three Dog Night] 1 · Rock The Boat [Hues Corporation] 1

6/16/62 · **24** · 14 · 493 · **Summer Festival** .... · $25 · RCA Victor 6097 [2]
Ah! Lo Vedi [Renata Tebaldi/Jussi Bjoerling] · Concerto No. 1: Finale [Sviatoslav Richter/Charles Munch] · Mi Chiamano Mimi [Anna Moffo] · Sleeping Beauty: Waltz [Pierre Monteux]
Barber Of Seville: Overture [Erich Leinsdorf] · Concerto No. 2: Scherzo [Van Cliburn] · On The Trail [Morton Gould] · Thunder And Lightning Polka [Arthur Fiedler/Boston Pops]
Barcarolle [Georg Solti] · Guitar Concerto: Finale [Julian Bream] · Roman Carnival: Overture [Charles Munch] · Un Bel Di [Leontyne Price]
Blow The Man Down [Robert Shaw Chorale] · Hungarian Rhapsody No. 2 [Leopold Stokowski] · Russlan And Ludmilla: Overture [Fritz Reiner] · West Side Story (Excerpt) [Robert Russell Bennett]
Come Prima [Mario Lanza] · I Love Thee [Birgit Nilsson] · Scherzando [Henryk Szeryng/Walter Hendl]

7/6/96 · **66** · 14 · ©494 · **Sun Splashin' - 16 Hot Summer Hits!** .... · $10 · Madacy 26927
Brown Eyed Girl [Van Morrison] 10 · Hot Fun In The Summertime [Sly & The Family Stone] 2 · Macarena [D.S.B.] · Walking On Sunshine [Katrina & The Waves] 9
Celebration [Kool & The Gang] 1 · Hot, Hot, Hot [Buster Poindexter & His Banshees Of Blue] 45 · Montego Bay [Amazulu] 90 · Wild World [Maxi Priest] 25
Coconut [Nilsson] 8 · One Love [Bob Marley & The Wailers]
Don't Worry, Be Happy [Bobby McFerrin] 1 · I Can See Clearly Now [Johnny Nash] 1 · Reggae Night [Jimmy Cliff]
Escape (The Pina Colada Song) [Rupert Holmes] 1 · Kokomo [Beach Boys] 1 · Summer Breeze [Seals & Crofts] 6

3/1/69 · **178** · 5 · 495 · **Super Groups, The** .... · $20 · Atco 279
Bluebird [Buffalo Springfield] 58 · How Can I Be Sure [Young Rascals] 4 · In-A-Gadda-Da-Vida [Iron Butterfly] 30 · Take Me For A Little While [Vanilla Fudge] 38
Come On Up [Young Rascals] 43 · I Can't See Nobody [Bee Gees] · Mr. Soul [Buffalo Springfield] · Words [Bee Gees] 15
Eleanor Rigby [Vanilla Fudge] · I Feel Free [Cream] · Strange Brew [Cream]

8/5/67 · **12** · 60 · 496 · **Super Hits, The** .... · $20 · Atlantic 501
B-A-B-Y [Carla Thomas] 14 · Hip Hug-Her [Booker T. & The MG's] 37 · In The Midnight Hour [Wilson Pickett] 21 · Respect [Aretha Franklin] 1
Baby, I'm Yours [Barbara Lewis] 11 · Hold On! I'm A Comin' [Sam & Dave] 21 · Knock On Wood [Eddie Floyd] 28 · S.Y.S.L.J.F.M. (The Letter Song) [Joe Tex] 39
Good Lovin' [Young Rascals] 1 · Mustang Sally [Wilson Pickett] 23 · When A Man Loves A Woman [Percy Sledge] 1
Philly Dog [Mar-Keys] 89

7/20/68 · **76** · 33 · 497 · **Super Hits, Vol. 2, The** .... · $20 · Atlantic 8188
Baby I Love You [Aretha Franklin] 4 · Chain Of Fools [Aretha Franklin] 2 · Funky Broadway [Wilson Pickett] 8 · Skinny Legs And All [Joe Tex] 10
Beat Goes On [Sonny & Cher] 6 · For What It's Worth (Stop, Hey What's That Sound) [Buffalo Springfield] 7 · Groovin' [Young Rascals] 1 · Soul Finger [Bar-Kays] 17
Bottle Of Wine [Fireballs] 9 · (Sittin' On) The Dock Of The Bay [Otis Redding] 1 · Soul Man [Sam & Dave] 2
To Love Somebody [Bee Gees] 17

11/23/68+ · **68** · 19 · 498 · **Super Hits, Vol. 3, The** .... · $20 · Atlantic 8203
Beautiful Morning [Rascals] 3 · I'm A Midnight Mover [Wilson Pickett] 24 · (Sweet Sweet Baby) Since You've Been Gone [Aretha Franklin] 5 · Tighten Up [Archie Bell & The Drells] 1
Funky Street [Arthur Conley] 14 · Sunshine Of Your Love [Cream] 5 · Take Time To Know Her [Percy Sledge] 11 · You Keep Me Hangin' On [Vanilla Fudge] 6
Groovin' [Booker T. & The MG's] 21 · Sweet Inspiration [Sweet Inspirations] 18 · Think [Aretha Franklin] 7
I Thank You [Sam & Dave] 9

7/19/69 · **164** · 10 · 499 · **Super Hits, Vol. 4, The** .... · $20 · Atlantic 8224
Can I Change My Mind [Tyrone Davis] 5 · I Can't Stop Dancing [Archie Bell & The Drells] 9 · People Got To Be Free [Rascals] 1 · Too Weak To Fight [Clarence Carter] 13
Fire [Crazy World Of Arthur Brown] 2 · I Say A Little Prayer [Aretha Franklin] 10 · See Saw [Aretha Franklin] 14 · White Room [Cream] 6
Hey Jude [Wilson Pickett] 23 · I Started A Joke [Bee Gees] 6 · Slip Away [Clarence Carter] 6
Son-Of-A-Preacher Man [Dusty Springfield] 10

6/29/68 · **130** · 9 · 500 · **Super Oldies/Vol. 3** .... · $20 · Capitol 2910 [2]
Birds Of A Feather [Joe South] 96 · Gentle On My Mind [Glen Campbell] 39 · If I Loved You [Chad & Jeremy] 23 · Michelle [David & Jonathan] 18
By The Time I Get To Phoenix [Glen Campbell] 26 · Get That Feeling [Curtis Knight & Jimi Hendrix] · Knight In Rusty Armour [Peter & Gordon] 15 · Nobody But Me [Human Beinz] 8
Dead End Street [Lou Rawls] 29 · Goin' Out Of My Head/Can't Take My Eyes Off You [Lettermen] 7 · Lady Godiva [Peter & Gordon] 6 · Ode To Billie Joe [Bobbie Gentry] 1
Different Drum [Stone Poneys feat. Linda Ronstadt] 13 · Love Is A Hurtin' Thing [Lou Rawls] 13 · Time Won't Let Me [Outsiders] 5
Elvira [Dallas Frazier] 72 · Help Me Girl [Outsiders] 37 · Mercy, Mercy, Mercy [Cannonball Adderley] 11 · Turn On Your Love Light [Human Beinz] 80
I Love You [People] 14

DEBUT	PEAK	WKS	RIAA	CD	ARTIST — Album Title	Catalog	Sym	$	Label & Number

7/12/69   **196**   2   501   **Super Oldies/Vol. 5** ....   **$20**   Capitol 216 [2]

- Don't Touch Me [Bettye Swann] 38
- For The First Time [Crystal Mansion]
- Galveston [Glen Campbell] 4
- Georgy Girl [Seekers] 2
- I'm Telling You Now [Freddie & The Dreamers] 1
- Lady Godiva [Peter & Gordon] 6
- Let It Be Me [Glen Campbell & Bobbie Gnetry] 36
- Papa, Won't You Let Me Go To Town With You [Bobbie Gentry]
- Queen Of The House [Jody Miller] 12
- Ramblin' Rose [Nat King Cole] 2
- Sukiyaki [Kyu Sakamoto] 1
- Summer Place, Theme From A [Lettermen] 16
- Summer Song [Chad & Jeremy] 7
- Superlove [David & The Giants]
- Taking Inventory [Vic Waters & The Entertainers]
- These Are Not My People [Joe South]
- Universal Soldier [Glen Campbell] 45
- Way You Look Tonight [Lettermen] 13
- Where Have All The Flowers Gone [Kingston Trio] 21
- World Of Our Own [Seekers] 19

11/14/70   **197**   2   502   **Super Rock** ....   **$20**   Columbia 30121 [2]

- Bombay Calling [It's A Beautiful Day]
- Do You Believe In Love? [Hollies]
- Drop Down Mama [Tom Rush]
- I Can't Turn You Loose [Chambers Brothers] 37
- Jailhouse Rock [Jeff Beck]
- Jesus Is Just Alright [Byrds] 97
- Jingo [Santana] 56
- Johnny B. Goode [Johnny Winter] 92
- Pickin' Up The Pieces [Poco]
- Questions 67 And 68 [Chicago] 24
- Rocket Number 9 [NRBQ]
- Smiling Phases [Blood, Sweat & Tears]
- Spanish Key [Miles Davis]
- Staggolee [Pacific Gas & Electric]
- Time And Love [Laura Nyro]
- Tired Of Waiting [Flock]
- Try (Just A Little Bit Harder) [Janis Joplin]
- You Can Make It If You Try [Sly & The Family Stone]
- You Never Know Who Your Friends Are [Al Kooper]
- You're Gonna Need Somebody On Your Bond [Taj Mahal]

3/30/96   **95**   1   ©503   **Surrender To The Air** .... [I]   **$10**   Elektra 61905

- And Furthermore
- Down
- Out
- We Deflate

7/24/93   **131**   15   ©504   **Sweet Relief: A Benefit For Victoria Williams** ....   **$10**   Thirsty Ear 57134

- Animal Wild [Shudder To Think]
- Big Fish [Giant Sand]
- Crazy Mary [Pearl Jam]
- Frying Pan [Evan Dando]
- Holy Spirit [Michelle Shocked]
- Lights [Jayhawks]
- Main Road [Lucinda Williams]
- Merry Go Round [Buffalo Tom]
- Opelousas (Sweet Relief) [Maria McKee]
- Summer Of Drugs [Soul Asylum]
- Tarbelly And Featherfoot [Lou Reed]
- This Moment [Matthew Sweet]
- Weeds [Michael Penn]
- Why Look At The Moon [Waterboys]

8/24/96   **115**   2   ©505   **Sweet Relief II: Gravity Of The Situation - The Songs Of Vic Chesnutt** ....   **$10**   Columbia 67573

- Dodge [dog's eye view]
- Florida [Mary Margaret O'Hara]
- Free Of Hope [Indigo Girls]
- God Is Good [Vic Chesnutt & Victoria Williams]
- Gravity Of The Situation [Nanci Griffith w/Hootie & The Blowfish]
- Guilty By Association [Joe Henry & Madonna]
- Kick My Ass [Garbage]
- Panic Pure [Kristin Hersh]
- Sad Peter Pan [Smashing Pumpkins & Red Red Meat]
- Sponge [R.E.M.]
- Supernatural [Live]
- West Of Rome [Sparklehorse]
- When I Ran Off & Left Her [Soul Asylum]
- Withering [Cracker]

8/29/98   **146**   7   ©506   **Swing This, Baby!** ....   **$10**   Slimstyle 78000

- Bill's Bounce [Bill Elliott Swing Orchestra]
- Black And White [Bellevue Cadillac]
- Boogie Man [Red & The Red Hots]
- Datin' With No Dough [Royal Crown Revue]
- Ding Dong Daddy Of The D-Car Line [Cherry Poppin' Daddies]
- (Everytime I Hear) That Mellow Saxophone [Brian Setzer Orchestra]
- Jumpin' Jack [Big Bad Voodoo Daddy]
- Knockin' At Your Door [New Morty Show]
- Lost For Words [Crescent City Maulers]
- Mr. Zoot Suit [Flying Neutrinos]
- Night Out [Blue Plate Special]
- Pick Up The Phone [Swingerhead]
- Rumpus Room Honeymoon [Steve Lucky & The Rhumba Bums]
- We Still Talk The Way Lovers Do [Johnny Favourite Swing Orchestra]
- We The Boys Will Rock Ya! [Big Six]

11/11/00   **195**   1   ©507   **Take A Bite Outta Rhyme: A Rock Tribute To Rap** ....   **$10**   Republic 158301

- Boyz-N-The Hood [Dynamite Hack]
- Bring The Noise [Staind]
- Bring The Pain [Mindless Self Indulgence]
- Going Back To Cali [Sevendust]
- Insane In The Brain [Factory 81]
- It's Tricky [Bloodhound Gang]
- Microphone Fiend [Fun Lovin' Criminals]
- My Mind Playin' Tricks On Me [Kottonmouth Kings]
- New Jack Hustler [Dope]
- Posse On Broadway [Insane Clown Posse]
- Sucker M.C.'s [Lordz Of Brooklyn w/Everlast & Stoned Soul]
- Tribute, The [Nonpoint]
- White Lines (Don't Do It) [Driver]

11/18/95   **158**   6   ●   ©508   **Take My Hand - Songs From The 100 Acre Wood** ....   **$10**   Walt Disney 60863

- All Good Things (A Pooh Perspective)
- Friends Around The World
- Just For A Taste Of Honey
- Kanga-roo Hop [Kathie Lee Gifford & The Roo-ettes]
- Little Black Rain Cloud (medley) [Maureen McGovern]
- My Balloon [Kathie Lee Gifford]
- Never Alone (Eeyore's Lullaby) [Tyler Collins] 48
- Owl's Song
- Perfect Place To Hide
- Special Bear [Chieftains]
- Sunny Skies (medley) [Maureen McGovern]
- That's What Tiggers Do Best [Owls]
- We're Gonna Catch A Heffalump
- Winnie The Pooh [Chieftains]

4/20/91   **165**   5   ©509   **Tame Yourself** ....   **$10**   R.N.A. 70772

- Across The Way [Aleka's Attic]
- Asleep Too Long [Goosebumps]
- Bless The Beasts And The Children [Belinda Carlisle]
- Born For A Purpose [Pretenders]
- Damned Old Dog [k.d. lang]
- Do What I Have To Do [Exene Cervenka]
- Don't Be Part Of It [Howard Jones]
- Don't Kill The Animals [Nina Hagen & Lene Lovich]
- Fur [Jane Wiedlin]
- I'll Give You My Skin [Indigo Girls & Michael Stipe]
- Quiche Lorraine [B-52's]
- Rage [Erasure & Lene Lovich]
- Slaves [Fetchin Bones]
- Tame Yourself [Raw Youth]

9/26/98   **111**   5   ©510   **Tammy Wynette Remembered** ....   **$10**   Asylum 62277

- Apartment #9 [Melissa Etheridge]
- D-I-V-O-R-C-E [Rosanne Cash]
- Golden Ring [Emmylou Harris w/Linda Ronstadt/Anna & Kate McGarrigle]
- I Don't Wanna Play House [Sara Evans]
- In My Room [Tammy Wynette & Brian Wilson]
- Stand By Your Man [Elton John]
- Take Me To Your World [George Jones]
- 'Til I Can Make It On My Own [Faith Hill]
- 'Til I Get It Right [Trisha Yearwood]
- Woman To Woman [Wynonna]
- You And Me [Lorrie Morgan]
- Your Good Girl's Gonna Go Bad [K.T. Oslin]

11/18/95+   **53**   22   ●   ©511   **Tapestry Revisited - A Tribute To Carole King** ....   **$10**   Lava 92604

- Beautiful [Richard Marx]
- Home Again [Curtis Stigers]
- I Feel The Earth Move [Eternal]
- It's Too Late [Amy Grant]
- Smackwater Jack [Manhattan Transfer]
- So Far Away [Rod Stewart]
- Tapestry [All-4-One]
- Way Over Yonder [Blessid Union Of Souls]
- Where You Lead [Faith Hill]
- Will You Love Me Tomorrow? [Bee Gees]
- (You Make Me Feel Like) A Natural Woman [Celine Dion]
- You've Got A Friend [BeBe & CeCe Winans Feat. Aretha Franklin]

7/3/99   **152**   4   512   **Tarzan Read & Sing Along** ....   **$10**   Walt Disney 60991

- available only on cassette
- Strangers Like Me
- You'll Be In Your Heart

9/9/00   **164**   3   ©513   **Teen Riot!** ....   **$10**   Razor & Tie 89030

- All 4 Love [Color Me Badd] 1
- Cool It Now [New Edition] 4
- Girlfriend [Pebbles] 5
- Hold Me [Menudo] 62
- I Like It [Dino] 7
- I Think We're Alone Now [Tiffany] 1
- Ice Ice Baby [Vanilla Ice] 1
- If Wishes Came True [Sweet Sensation] 1
- Never Gonna Give You Up [Rick Astley] 1
- Only In My Dreams [Debbie Gibson] 4
- Point Of No Return [Exposé] 5
- Rocket 2 U [Jets] 6
- Sending All My Love [Linear] 5
- Touch Me (I Want Your Body) [Samantha Fox] 4
- Toy Soldiers [Martika] 1
- Two Of Hearts [Stacey Q] 3
- You Got It (The Right Stuff) [New Kids On The Block] 3

DEBUT	PEAK	WKS	RIAA	CD	ARTIST — Album Title	Catalog	Sym	$	Label & Number
6/10/89	159	18		©514	**TeeVee Toons: The Commercials**..			**$10**	TVT 1400
11/9/85+	82	34		©515	**Television's Greatest Hits**			**$15**	TeeVee T. 1100 [2]
11/15/86	149	16		©516	**Television's Greatest Hits, Volume II**			**$15**	TeeVee T. 1200 [2]

TeeVee Toons: The Commercials (©514)

Ajax Cleanser
Ajax Laundry Detergent
Alka Seltzer Effervescent Antacid (Plop Plop Fizz Fizz)
Alka Seltzer Effervescent Antacid (The Shape Your Stomach's In)
Armour Hot Dogs
Ballantine Premium Lager Beer (Add A Ring)
Ballantine Premium Lager Beer (Hey Get Your Cold Beer)
Bosco
Brylcreem
Budweiser Beer
Chevrolet Motors
Chiquita Bananas
Chock Full O'Nuts Coffee
Coca Cola (I'd Like To Buy The World A Coke)
Coca Cola (It's The Real Thing)
Coca Cola (Things Go Better With Coke)
Colt 45 Malt Liquor
Cracker Jack
Dippity Do Styling Gel
Dr. Pepper
Fab Laundry Detergent
Gillette Blue Blades (How're You Fixed For Blades)
Gillette Blue Blades (Look Sharp March)
Good & Plenty
Hawaiian Punch Fruit Punch
Health PSA
Hershey's Chocolate Bars
Kellogg's Rice Krispies
Ken-L Ration Dog And Puppy Food
Kent Cigarettes
Lowenbrau Beer
Magnificent Seven (The Marlboro Song)
Marshmallow Fluff
Meow Mix Cat Food
Miller High Life
Mounds And Almond Joy Candy Bars
Mr. Clean All Purpose Cleaner
Muriel Cigars (Hey Big Spender)
Muriel Cigars (Pick One Up And Smoke It Sometime)
NYS Department Of Safety
Nestles Quik Chocolate Flavor
Noxzema Shave Cream
Old Spice Long Lasting Cologne
Oreo Chocolate Sandwich Cookies
Pepsi Cola
Polaroid Swinger
Rheingold Extra Dry Beer
Rice-A-Roni
Salem Cigarettes
Sara Lee
Schaefer Beer
Schlitz Beer
Slinky
Texaco
Winston Cigarettes

Television's Greatest Hits (©515)

Adam 12
Addams Family
Adventures Of Rin Tin Tin
Alfred Hitchcock Presents
Andy Griffith Show
Batman
Beverly Hillbillies (Ballad Of Jed Clampett)
Bonanza
Branded
Bugs Bunny Show (This Is It)
Captain Kangaroo (Puffin' Billy)
Casper, The Friendly Ghost
Combat
Daniel Boone
Dennis The Menace
Dick Van Dyke Show
Donna Reed Show
Dragnet
F Troop
F.B.I., The
Felix The Cat
Fireball XL-5
Flintstones (Meet The Flintstones)
Flipper
Get Smart
Gilligan's Island
Green Acres
Hawaii Five-O
Howdy Doody
I Dream Of Jeannie
I Love Lucy
Ironside
Jetsons
Late Late Show (The Syncopated Clock)
Leave It To Beaver (The Toy Parade)
Little Rascals (Good Old Days)
Lone Ranger (William Tell Overture)
Lost In Space
Magilla Gorilla Show
Man From U.N.C.L.E.
Mannix
Many Loves Of Dobie Gillis
McHale's Navy
Mission: Impossible
Mister Ed
Mod Squad
Munsters
My Three Sons
News Medley (We Interrupt This Program)
Patty Duke Show
Peer Gynt-WTVT Sign On
Perry Mason
Petticoat Junction
Popeye
Rifleman
Roy Rogers Show (Happy Trails)
Secret Agent Man
77 Sunset Strip
Star Trek
Superman
Surfside 6
Technical Difficulties (Please Stand By)
Test Of The Emergency Broadcast System-Duck And Cover
Tonight Show (Johnny's Theme)
Top Cat
Twilight Zone
WTVT Sign Off-The Star Spangled Banner
Wild Wild West
Woody Woodpecker Show
Yogi Bear

Television's Greatest Hits, Volume II (©516)

ABC's Wide World Of Sports
Adventures Of Robin Hood
Avengers
Bat Masterson
Ben Casey
Bewitched
Brady Bunch
Car 54, Where Are You?
Courageous Cat & Minute Mouse
Courtship Of Eddie's Father (My Best Friend)
Daktari
Dark Shadows
George Of The Jungle
Gidget
Gomer Pyle, U.S.M.C.
Green Hornet
Have Gun Will Travel (The Ballad Of Paladin)
Hawaiian Eye
Hogan's Heroes
Honeymooners (You're My Greatest Love)
Huckleberry Hound
I Married Joan
I Spy
It's About Time
Jackie Gleason Show (Melancholy Serenade)
Jeopardy (Think Music)
Jonny Quest
Looney Tunes (The Merry-Go-Round Breaks Down)
Love, American Style
Mary Tyler Moore (Love Is All Around)
Maverick
Medical Center
Merrie Melodies (Merrily We Roll Along)
Mighty Mouse
Mister Roger's Neighborhood (Won't You Be My Neighbor?)
Monkees
Monty Python's Flying Circus
My Favorite Martian
My Mother The Car
NBC Mystery Movie
Odd Couple
Outer Limits
Partridge Family (Come On Get Happy)
Peanuts Theme (Linus & Lucy)
Peter Gunn
Pink Panther
Rat Patrol
Rawhide
Rebel
Road Runner
Rocky & Bullwinkle
Route 66
Saint, The
Sea Hunt
Smothers Brothers Comedy Hour
Spider-Man
Tarzan
That Girl
Three Stooges
Time Tunnel
Twelve O'Clock High
Underdog
Virginian
Voyage To The Bottom Of The Sea
Wagon Train

DEBUG	PEAK	WKS	RIAA	CD	ARTIST — Album Title	Catalog	Sym	$	Label & Number
3/1/69	**31**	17		517	**Themes Like Old Times**			**$20**	Viva 36018 [2]

features 180 of the most famous original radio themes

Abbott & Costello Show
Adventures Of Archie Andrews
Adventures Of Frank Merriwell
Adventures Of Jungle Jim
Adventures Of Ozzie & Harriet
Adventures Of Philip Marlowe
Adventures Of Sam Spade, Detective
Adventures Of Sherlock Holmes
Adventures Of The Saint
Against The Storm
Air Adventures Of Jimmy Allen
Aldrich Family
Amos 'N' Andy
Answer Man
Armour Star Jester
Backstage Wife
Believe It Or Not
Benny Goodman's Swing School
Big Sister
Bill Stern Sports Newsreel
Black Castle
Black Hood
Blondie
Bobby Benson And The B-Bar-B Riders
Bold Venture
Boston Blackie
Brave Tomorrow
Brighter Day
Buck Rogers In The Twenty Fifth Century
Bulldog Drummond
Buster Brown Gang
Campana Serenade
Can You Top This?
Canary Pet Show
Captain Midnight
Carters Of Elm Street
Chamber Music Society Of Lower Basin Street
Chandu The Magician
Charlie McCarthy Show
Chick Carter, Boy Detective
Coast To Coast On A Bus
Coke Club
Counterspy
Crime Does Not Pay

David Harum
Dick Tracy
Dr. Christian (The Vaseline Program)
Dr. I. Q.
Dr. Kildare, Story Of
Double Or Nothing
Duffy's Tavern
Easy Aces
Ed Wynn Show
Eddie Cantor Show
Escape
FBI In Peace And War
Falcon, The
Fat Man
Fibber McGee And Molly
Firstnighter Program
Fitch Bandwagon
Front Page Farrell
Gabriel Heatter's News Of The World
Gangbusters
Goldbergs, The
Grand Central Station
Great Gildersleeve
Green Hornet
Guiding Light
Gunsmoke
Hal Kemp On The Air For Griffin
Hardy Family
Helping Hand
Here's Morgan
Hermit's Cave
Hoofbeats, Starring Buck Jones
Hop Harrigan
House Of Mystery
I Love A Mystery
Information Please
Inner Sanctum Mysteries
It Pays To Be Ignorant
Jack Armstrong
Jergen's Journal
Jimmy Durante Show
Jimmy Fiddler In Hollywood
Joe Penner Show
John's Other Wife
Just Plain Bill
Kaltenborn Edits The News

Kay Fairchild, Stepmother
Lassie
Let Yourself Go
Let's Pretend
Life Can Be Beautiful
Life With Luigi
Lifeboy Program
Lights Out
Linda's First Love
Lone Ranger
Lorenzo Jones
Lucky Strike Program
Lum 'N' Abner Show
Lux Radio Theatre
Ma Perkins
Magic Detective
Major Bowes' Original Amateur Hour
Mandrake The Magician
Manhattan Merry-Go-Round
March Of Time
Mark Trail
Marlin Hurt And Beulah Show
Maxwell House Coffee Time
Melody Ranch
Mercury Theatre On The Air
Michael Shayne
Molle Mystery Theatre
Mr. District Attorney
Murder At Midnight
My Friend Irma
Myrt And Marge
Mysterious Traveller
National Barn Dance
New Adventures Of The Thin Man
Nick Carter, Master Detective
Norge Kitchen Committee
Official Detective
One Man's Family
Pepper Young's Family
Pepsodent Show
Phil Harris-Alice Faye Show
Philco Radio Time
Philip Morris Playhouse
Raleigh And Kool Cigarette Program
Red Ryder
Red Skelton Program

Richard Diamond, Private Eye
Right To Happiness
Road Of Life
Romance Of Helen Trent
Scattergood Baines
Second Mrs. Burton
Sergeant Preston Of The Yukon
Shadow, The
Shadow Of Fu Manchu
Songs By Sinatra
Spike Jones Show
Stagedoor Canteen
Stella Dallas
Straight Arrow
Strange Romance Of Evelyn Winters
Superman
Suspense
Tarzan
Taystee Breadwinner
Ted Lewis, The High-Hatted Tragedian Of Song
Tennessee Jed
Terry And The Pirates
This Is Nora Drake
This Life Is Mine
Tom Corbett, Space Cadet
Tom Mix Ralston Straight Shooters
Town Hall Tonight
Troman Harper, Rumor Detective
True Detective Mysteries
Uncle Don
Valiant Lady
Vaughn DeLeath Show
Vic And Sade
What Was The Name Of That Shave Cream He Used To Sell?
When A Girl Marries
Whispering Jack Smith
Whistler, The
Wild Bill Elliot
Witch's Tale
Woody Herman Show
X Minus One
Young Dr. Malone
Young Widder Brown
Your Hit Parade

10/17/98	**156**	1	©518		**This Is Alice Music Volume 2**			**$10**	Alice 32

album compiled by San Francisco radio station Alice 97.3

Brick [Ben Folds Five]
Building A Mystery [Sarah McLachlan] *13*
Closing Time [Semisonic]
Earthbound [Billy Mann]

How's It Going To Be [Third Eye Blind] *9*
I Do [Lisa Loeb] *17*
I'll Be [Edwin McCain] *5*
Jealousy [Natalie Merchant] *23*

Kiss Me [Sixpence None The Richer] *2*
Meet Virginia [Train] *20*
Never Is A Promise [Fiona Apple]
Raining On The Sky [Naked]
Summer Of Love [B-52's]

Sunny Came Home [Shawn Colvin] *7*
Way, The [Fastball]
What Would Happen [Meredith Brooks] *46*

3/16/68	**146**	22		519	**This Is Soul**			**$25**	Atlantic 8170

Cool Jerk [Capitols] *7*
Hold What You've Got [Joe Tex] *5*
I Never Loved A Man (The Way I Love You) [Aretha Franklin] *9*

If You Need Me [Solomon Burke] *37*
Land Of 1000 Dances [Wilson Pickett] *6*
Mercy, Mercy [Don Covay] *35*

On Broadway [Drifters] *9*
Release Me [Esther Phillips] *8*
Spanish Harlem [Ben E. King] *10*
Sweet Soul Music [Arthur Conley] *2*

What'd I Say (Part I) [Ray Charles] *6*
When A Man Loves A Woman [Percy Sledge] *1*

12/27/75+	**192**	3		520	**Threads Of Glory - 200 Years Of America In Words & Music**			**$40**	London Phase 4 14000 [6]

6 volume boxed set tracing America's history using music, sound effects and many famous guest narrators

Also Sprach Zarathustra [Henry Lewis]
America [Eric Rogers]
America, The Beautiful [Eric Rogers]
American Revolutionary War Medley [Bob Sharples]
Apollo 11 Moon Landing [Daws Butler]
Battle Hymn Of The Republic [Eric Rogers]
Casablanca Medley [Stanley Black]
Col. William Travis [Forrest Tucker]
Columbia, The Gem Of The Ocean [Eric Rogers]
Constitution and The Bill Of Rights [Ronald & Nancy Reagan]
Dixie [Eric Rogers]
Dorothea Lynde Dix [Anne Baxter]
Dr. Martin Luther King [Roscoe Lee Browne]
Elizabeth Cady Staton [Rosalind Russell]
Entertainer, The [Ronnie Aldrich]

Fanfare [London Festival Brass]
General Douglas MacArthur [Efren Zimbalist, Jr.]
General Robert E. Lee [Lloyd Bowman]
George Washington [Lloyd Nolan]
Hail To The Chief [Eric Rogers]
Hoe Down Medley [Stanley Black]
Jefferson Davis [George Hamilton]
Lady Of Liberty [Joan Foster]
Let's Dance [Ted Heath]
Margaret Fuller [Virginia Gregg]
Massachusetts Patriot [Rosalind Russell]
National Emblem [Bob Sharples]
Patrick Henry [Burt Lancaster]
President Abraham Lincoln [Walter Pidgeon]
President Andrew Jackson [Jonathan Winters]
President Chester Arthur [William Bakewell]
President Dwight D. Eisenhower [Fred MacMurray]

President Franklin D. Roosevelt [Lorne Greene]
President George Washington [Lloyd Nolan]
President Gerald Ford [Lee Sharples]
President Harry S Truman [Ernest Borgnine]
President James Buchanan [Richard Carlson]
President James Monroe [John Forsythe]
President James Polk [Cesar Romero]
President John F. Kennedy [Henry Fonda]
President Lyndon B. Johnson [Hugh O'Brian]
President Thomas Jefferson [Richard Carlson]
President Woodrow Wilson [John Forsythe]
Rhapsody In Blue [Frank Chacksfield]

Shenandoah [Frank Chacksfield]
Spokesman Of The South [Lee Bowman]
Star-Spangled Banner [Bob Sharples]
Stars And Stripes Forever [Bob Sharples]
Thomas Jefferson [Richard Carlson]
Thomas Paine [Lee Bowman]
Voice Of The Indians [Cesar Romero]
Washington Post March [Bob Sharples]
We Shall Overcome [Bob Sharples]
When The Saints Go Marching In [Eric Rogers]
William Lloyd Garrison [William Bakewell]
World War One Medley [Bob Sharples]
Zimmerman Note [Daws Butler]

DEBUT	PEAK	WKS	RIAA	CD	ARTIST — Album Title	Catalog	Sym	$	Label & Number
11/22/97	181	1		©521	Tibetan Freedom Concert [L]			$25	Grand Royal 59110 [3]
5/1/93	125	8		©522	Today's Hit Country			$10	K-Tel 6068
1/23/93	177	1		©523	Today's Hot Country			$10	K-Tel 6063
12/18/93+	179	4		©524	Today's Top Country			$10	K-Tel 6099
11/18/00+	16[C]	15	●	©525	Toddler Favorites			$10	Rhino 75262
12/9/72+	5	38	●	©526	Tommy			$20	Ode 99001 [2]
10/21/00	171	3		©527	Too Gangsta For Radio			$10	Death Row 2018
9/11/99	197	1		©528	Too $hort Mix Tape Volume 1 - Nation Riders			$10	$hort 46106
12/9/95	191	1		©529	Too $hort Presents The Dangerous Crew - Don't Try This At Home			$10	Dangerous 41573
11/27/99	14	36	▲	©530	Totally Hits			$10	Arista 14625
6/17/00	13	19	▲	©531	Totally Hits 2			$10	Warner 62529
12/2/00	25	19	▲	©532	Totally Hits 3			$10	Arista 83412

©521 Tibetan Freedom Concert — Grand Royal 59110 [3]
About A Boy [Patti Smith]; Ajo Sotop [Chaksam-pa]; Asshole [Beck]; Beetlebum [Blur]; Birthday Cake [Cibo Matto]; Black Cop (medley) [KRS-1]; Blues Explosion Man [Jon Spencer Blues Explosion]; Bridge Is Over (medley) [KRS-1]; Bulls On Parade [Rage Against The Machine]; Cast No Shadow [Noel Gallagher]; Celebration, The [Nawang Khechog]; Closing Prayers [Monks]; Electrolite [Michael Stipe & Mike Mills]; Fake Plastic Trees [Radiohead]; Fu Gee La [Fugees]; Ground On Down [Ben Harper]; Gyi Ma Gyi [Dadon]; Harder They Come [Rancid]; Heads Of Government [Lee Perry]; Hyper-Ballad [Björk]; Me, Myself & I [De La Soul]; Meija [Porno For Pyros]; Nobody Beats The Biz (medley) [Biz Markie]; Noise Brigade [Mighty Mighty Bosstones]; Oh My God [Tribe Called Quest]; Om Mani Padme Hung [Yungchen Lhamo]; One [U2]; Opening Prayers; Root Down [Beastie Boys]; She Caught The Katy [Taj Mahal & The Phantom Blues Band]; South Bronx Medley [KRS-1]; Star Spangled Banner (medley) [Biz Markie]; This Is A Call [Foo Fighters]; Type Slowly [Pavement]; Wake Up [Alanis Morissette]; Wildflower [Sonic Youth]; Yellow Ledbetter [Eddie Vedder & Mike McCready]

©522 Today's Hit Country — K-Tel 6068
Brand New Man [Brooks & Dunn]; Brother Jukebox [Mark Chesnutt]; Down Home [Alabama]; Look At Us [Vince Gill]; Love Can Build A Bridge [Judds]; Maybe It Was Memphis [Pam Tillis]; Mirror Mirror [Diamond Rio]; Seminole Wind [John Anderson]; Something In Red [Lorrie Morgan]; There Ain't Nothin' Wrong With The Radio [Aaron Tippin]

©523 Today's Hot Country — K-Tel 6063
Alcohol Of Fame [Wood Brothers]; Bing Bang Boom [Highway 101]; Don't Tell Me What To Do [Pam Tillis]; Down At The Twist And Shout [Mary-Chapin Carpenter]; Feed Jake [Pirates Of The Mississippi]; I Am A Simple Man [Ricky Van Shelton]; I'm That Kind Of Girl [Patty Loveless]; Love, Me [Collin Raye]; Meet In The Middle [Diamond Rio]; Pocket Full Of Gold [Vince Gill]; Straight Tequila Night [John Anderson]

©524 Today's Top Country — K-Tel 6099
Better Class Of Losers [Randy Travis]; Born Country [Alabama]; Born To Roam [Paul Hale]; Bubba Shot The Jukebox [Mark Chesnutt]; Even The Man In The Moon Is Cryin' [Mark Collie]; Love Without End, Amen [Randy Travis]; Never Knew Lonely [Vince Gill]; Norma Jean Riley [Diamond Rio]; Now That's Country [Marty Stuart]; Take It Like A Man [Michelle Wright]; Woman Before Me [Trisha Yearwood]

©525 Toddler Favorites — Rhino 75262
Alphabet Song; Baa Baa Black Sheep; Down By The Station (medley); Engine Number Nine; Frere Jacques; Fuzzy Wuzzy; Happy Birthday To You; I'm A Little Teapot; If You're Happy And You Know It; It's Raining (medley); Itsy Bitsy Spider (medley); Little Red Caboose (medley); Mary Had A Little Lamb; Monkeys On The Bed; More We Get Together; Old MacDonald Had A Farm; Peas, Porridge Hot; Ring-Around-The-Rosy; 7, 8, 9 Joke; Skip To My Lou; This Little Pig; This Old Man; Twinkle Twinkle Little Star; Wheels On The Bus; Where Is Thumbkin

©526 Tommy — Ode 99001 [2]
Acid Queen; Amazing Journey; Christmas; Cousin Kevin; Do You Think It's Alright; Eyesight To The Blind; Fiddle About; Go To The Mirror Boy; I'm Free; It's A Boy; Miracle Cure; 1921; Pin Ball Wizard; Sally Simpson; See Me, Feel Me; Sensation; Smash The Mirror; Sparks; There's A Doctor I've Found; Tommy Can You Hear Me?; Tommy's Holiday Camp; Underture; We're Not Gonna Take It; Welcome

©527 Too Gangsta For Radio — Death Row 2018
Coff, The [G.P.]; Death Rizzo [Crooked I]; Everywhere We Go [Above The Law]; Funeral [Tupac]; Fuck Dre [Tha Realest/Swoop G/Twista/Lil C Style]; Fuck Hollywood [Tha Realest]; Gangsta Rap [Crooked I]; Gangsta'd Out [K-9]; Give It Up For Compton [Dre'sta]; I Ain't Fuckin' Wit Cha [C.J. Mac]; In Too Deep [Ruff Ryders]; Murda For Life [Ja Rule]; Projects [Swoop G]; Real Type Gangsta [Mac-Shawn]; This Is The Thanks You Get [Relativez]; Thug Nature [Tupac]; Too Gangsta [Dre'sta]

©528 Too $hort Mix Tape Volume 1 - Nation Riders — $hort 46106
songs by Baby DC, Slink Capone, Murda One, Keith Murray, Too $hort, and others
All 4 Keeps [Jezabell]; At Cha Neck [Zu]; Crazy World [G-Side]; Funkin' Over Nuthin' Pt. 1 & 2 [Too $hort]; Here We Go [Too $hort]; I'm A Player Bitch [Murda One & Slink Capone]; It's Goin' Down [Paper View]; Jackin' Rich Rappers [Nation Riders]; Keep It Tight [Quint Black & Keith Murray]; Live In The Blue Basement [Nation Riders]; No Fear [Al Block]; One Time Shot [Dolla Will]; Poppa Was A Soldier [Baby DC]; Save Me [Playa Playa]; Stand In My Way [Slink Capone]; Tell The Feds [Too $hort]; We're Nation Riders [Murda One & Too $hort]

©529 Too $hort Presents The Dangerous Crew - Don't Try This At Home — Dangerous 41573
Buy You Some [Erick Sermon/Too $hort]; Can I Get Loose [Baby-D]; Don't Try This At Home [Shorty B]; Freddy B [Freddy B]; Funk Session [Shock G/Too $hort]; Gone With The Wind [Pee Wee]; I Was Only Tryin' To Get Mine [Blacked Up]; Joe Riz [Joe Riz]; Leave It Alone [Too $hort]; Moan [About Face]; Out For The Props [Shorty B]; Pimpin's Just In Me [Doo Doo Brown]; Rumors [Father Dom]; Trouble (Scared To Blast) [Spice 1/Too $hort/J-Dubb]; Weed Break [MC Breed]; Welcome To The Bay [Shorty B/Collision]; You Crossed Me [Goldy]

©530 Totally Hits — Arista 14625
Almost Doesn't Count [Brandy] 16; Angel [Sarah McLachlan] 4; Angel Of Mine [Monica] 1; Bawitdaba [Kid Rock]; Believe [Cher] 1; (God Must Have Spent) A Little More Time On You ['N Sync] 8; Heartbreak Hotel [Whitney Houston Feat. Faith Evans & Kelly Price] 2; Jumper [Third Eye Blind] 5; No Scrubs [TLC] 1; Nobody's Supposed To Be Here [Deborah Cox] 2; One Week [Barenaked Ladies] 1; Ray Of Light [Madonna] 5; Smooth [Santana Feat. Rob Thomas] 1; Someday [Sugar Ray] 7; Summer Girls [LFO] 3; This Kiss [Faith Hill] 7; When The Lights Go Out [Five] 10; You Make Me Wanna... [Usher] 2

©531 Totally Hits 2 — Warner 62529
Amazed [Lonestar] 1; Beautiful Stranger [Madonna] 19; Dear Lie [TLC] 51; Falls Apart [Sugar Ray] 29; Genie In A Bottle [Christina Aguilera] 1; Girl On TV [LFO] 10; Great Beyond [R.E.M.] 57; Hot Boyz [Missy Elliott] 5; I Drive Myself Crazy ['N Sync] 67; I Will Remember You [Sarah McLachlan] 14; Mambo No. 5 (A Little Bit Of...) [Lou Bega] 3; Maria Maria [Santana Feat. The Product G&B] 1; My Love Is Your Love [Whitney Houston] 4; Natural Blues [Moby]; Never Let You Go [Third Eye Blind] 14; Right Here Waiting [Monica Feat. 112] 1; Take A Picture [Filter] 12; U Know What's Up [Donell Jones] 7

©532 Totally Hits 3 — Arista 83412
Bent [Matchbox Twenty] 1; Breathless [Corrs] 34; Dance With Me [Debelah Morgan] 8; Deep Inside Of You [Third Eye Blind] 69; Everything You Want [Vertical Horizon] 1; Fine [Whitney Houston]; Graduation (Friends Forever) [Vitamin C] 38; He Wasn't Man Enough [Toni Braxton] 2; Here With Me [Dido]; Little Girl [John Michael Montgomery] 35; Most Girls [Pink] 4; Music [Madonna] 1; Pinch Me [Barenaked Ladies] 15; Tell Me How You Feel [Joy Enriquez]; Way You Love Me [Faith Hill] 6; What A Girl Wants [Christina Aguilera] 1; Wifey [Next] 7

DEBUT	PEAK	WKS	RIAA	CD	ARTIST — Album Title	Catalog	Sym	$	Label & Number
10/14/95	198	1		©533	**Tower Of Song - The Songs Of Leonard Cohen**			$10	A&M 540259
1/18/97	151	1		©534	**Toy Story Sing-Along**			$10	Walt Disney 60922
7/26/69	144	7		535	**Treasury Of Great Contemporary Hits, A**			$15	Dunhill/ABC 50057
3/12/94	56	14		©536	**Tribute To Curtis Mayfield, A**			$10	Warner 45500
8/24/96	47	10	●	©537	**Tribute To Stevie Ray Vaughan, A**		[L]	$10	Epic 67599
4/29/72	183	2		©538	**Tribute To Woody Guthrie - Part One, A**		[L]	$15	Columbia 31171
4/29/72	189	2		©539	**Tribute To Woody Guthrie - Part Two, A**		[L]	$15	Warner 2586
12/18/71+	185	7		540	**Truth Of Truths - A Contemporary Rock Opera**			$20	Oak 1001 [2]
2/27/61	19	23		541	**12 + 3 = 15 Hits**			$75	End 310
6/4/83	42	28	●	©542	**25 #1 Hits From 25 Years**	C:#12/42		$15	Motown 5308 [2]
6/11/83	107	9		©543	**25 Years Of Grammy Greats**	C:#45/4		$12	Motown 5309
3/20/65	44	18		544	**20 Original Winners Of 1964**			$25	Roulette 25293

Tower Of Song - The Songs Of Leonard Cohen (533):
Ain't No Cure For Love [Aaron Neville] · Bird On A Wire [Willie Nelson] · Coming Back To You [Trisha Yearwood] · Coming Back To You [Martin Gore] · Everybody Knows [Don Henley] · Famous Blue Raincoat [Tori Amos] · Hallelujah [Bono] · I'm Your Man [Elton John] · If It Be Your Will [Jann Arden] · Light As The Breeze [Billy Joel] · Sisters Of Mercy [Sting & The Chieftains] · Story Of Isaac [Suzanne Vega] · Suzanne [Peter Gabriel]

Toy Story Sing-Along (534):
Cadence · Claw, The · I Think I'd Be Perfect For You · I Will Go Sailing No More · Pig Rap · Short People · Strange Things · You've Got A Friend In Me

Treasury Of Great Contemporary Hits, A (535):
Born To Be Wild [Steppenwolf] 2 · California Dreamin' [Mamas & The Papas] 4 · Dedicated To The One I Love [Mamas & The Papas] 2 · Dream A Little Dream Of Me [Mama Cass] 12 · Eve Of Destruction [Barry McGuire] 1 · Let's Live For Today [Grass Roots] 8 · MacArthur Park [Richard Harris] 2 · Magic Carpet Ride [Steppenwolf] 3 · Midnight Confessions [Grass Roots] 5 · Monday, Monday [Mamas & The Papas] 1 · Try A Little Tenderness [Three Dog Night] 29

Tribute To Curtis Mayfield, A (536):
Amen [Elton John & Sounds Of Blackness] · Billy Jack [Lenny Kravitz] · Choice Of Colors [Gladys Knight] · (Don't Worry) If There's A Hell Below, We're All Going To Go [Narada Michael Walden] · Fool For You [Branford Marsalis & The Impressions] · Gypsy Woman [Bruce Springsteen] · I'm So Proud [Isley Brothers] · I'm The One Who Loves You [Stevie Wonder] · I've Been Trying [Phil Collins] · It's All Right! [Steve Winwood] · Keep On Pushin' [Tevin Campbell] · Let's Do It Again [Repercussions & Curtis Mayfield] · Look Into Your Heart [Whitney Houston] · Makings Of You [Aretha Franklin] · People Get Ready [Rod Stewart] · Woman's Got Soul [B.B. King] · You Must Believe Me [Eric Clapton]

Tribute To Stevie Ray Vaughan, A (537):
recorded on 5/11/95 at the Austin City Limits Studio in Austin, Texas
Ain't Gone 'N Give Up On Your Love [Eric Clapton] · Cold Shot [Dr. John] · Long Way From Home [Buddy Guy] · Love Struck Baby [Robert Cray] · Pride And Joy [Bonnie Raitt] · SRV Shuffle [Various Artists] · Six Strings Down [Various Artists] · Telephone Song [B.B. King] · Texas Flood [Jimmie Vaughan] · Tick Tock [Various Artists]

Tribute To Woody Guthrie - Part One, A (538):
Curley Headed Baby [Pete Seeger] · Dear Mrs. Roosevelt [Bob Dylan] · Do Re Mi [Arlo Guthrie] · Grand Coulee Dam [Bob Dylan] · I Ain't Got No Home [Bob Dylan] · Oklahoma Hills [Arlo Guthrie] · Pastures Of Plenty [Tom Paxton] · Rambling 'Round Your City (Ramblin' 'Round) [Odetta] · So Long It's Been Good To Know Yuh (Dusty Old Dust) [Judy Collins] · Vigilante Man [Richie Havens]

Tribute To Woody Guthrie - Part Two, A (539):
above 2 albums used proceeds to benefit Huntington's Disease Research
Biggest Thing Man Has Ever Done (Great Historical Bum) [Tom Paxton] · Deportee (Plane Wreck At Los Gatos) [Judy Collins] · Hobo's Lullaby [Joan Baez] · Howdido [Jack Elliott] · Jackhammer John [Richie Havens & Pete Seeger] · Jesus Christ [Arlo Guthrie] · Mail Myself To You [Earl Robinson] · 1913 Massacre [Jack Elliott] · Roll On Columbia [Judy Collins] · This Land Is Your Land [Odetta, Arlo Guthrie & Company] · Union Maid [Judy Collins & Pete Seeger] · Why Oh Why [Odetta] · Woman At Home [Country Joe McDonald]

Truth Of Truths - A Contemporary Rock Opera (540):
Creation · Cross, The · David To Bathsheba · Fall, The · Forty Days And Forty Nights · God Called On To Abraham · He Will Come Again · He's The Light Of The World · Hosanna · I Am What I Say I Am · Jesus Of Nazareth · John The Baptist · Joseph Beloved Son Of Israel · Last Supper · Let My People Go · My Life Is In Your Hands · Prophecies Of The Coming Messiah · Prophecies Of The Coming Of The End Of The World · Resurrection · Road, The · Sodom And Gomorrah Were The Cities Of Sin · Song Of The Children Of Israel · Ten Commandments · Tower Of Babel · Trial, The · Turn Back To God

12 + 3 = 15 Hits (541):
Barbara [Temptations] 29 · Chapel Of Dreams [Dubs] 74 · Could This Be Magic [Dubs] 23 · Dedicated To The One I Love [Shirelles] 3 · I Only Have Eyes For You [Flamingos] 11 · I Shot Mr. Lee [Bobbettes] 52 · Maybe [Chantels] 15 · Mio Amore [Flamingos] 74 · Nobody Loves Me Like You [Flamingos] 30 · Shimmy, Shimmy, Ko-Ko-Bop [Little Anthony & The Imperials] 24 · Tears On My Pillow [Little Anthony & The Imperials] 4 · That's My Desire [Channels] · Wait A Minute [Jo Ann Campbell] · When You Wish Upon A Star [Little Anthony & The Imperials] · Whoever You Are [Chantels]

25 #1 Hits From 25 Years (542):
ABC [Jackson 5] 1 · Ain't No Mountain High Enough [Diana Ross] 1 · Baby Love [Supremes] 1 · Don't Leave Me This Way [Thelma Houston] 1 · Endless Love [Diana Ross & Lionel Richie] 1 · Give It To Me Baby [Rick James] 40 · Got To Give It Up (Pt. 1) [Marvin Gaye] 1 · I Can't Help Myself [Four Tops] 1 · I Heard It Through The Grapevine [Marvin Gaye] 1 · I Want You Back [Jackson 5] 1 · I'll Be There [Jackson 5] 1 · Just My Imagination (Running Away With Me) [Temptations] 1 · Keep On Truckin' (Part 1) [Eddie Kendricks] 1 · Let's Get It On [Marvin Gaye] 1 · My Girl [Temptations] 1 · Papa Was A Rollin' Stone [Temptations] 1 · Please Mr. Postman [Marvelettes] 1 · Reach Out I'll Be There [Four Tops] 1 · Still [Commodores] 1 · Superstition [Stevie Wonder] 1 · Tears Of A Clown [Smokey Robinson & The Miracles] 1 · Three Times A Lady [Commodores] 1 · What's Going On [Marvin Gaye] 2 · You Are The Sunshine Of My Life [Stevie Wonder] 1 · You Can't Hurry Love [Supremes] 1

25 Years Of Grammy Greats (543):
Cloud Nine [Temptations] 6 · Don't Leave Me This Way [Thelma Houston] 1 · Endless Love [Diana Ross & Lionel Richie] 1 · Heat Wave [Martha & The Vandellas] 4 · I Second That Emotion [Smokey Robinson & The Miracles] 4 · Keep On Truckin' (Part 1) [Eddie Kendricks] 1 · Let It Whip [Dazz Band] 5 · Let's Get Serious [Jermaine Jackson] 9 · Papa Was A Rollin' Stone [Temptations] 1 · Touch Me In The Morning [Diana Ross] 1

20 Original Winners Of 1964 (544):
California Sun [Rivieras] 5 · C'mon And Swim [Bobby Freeman] 5 · Have I The Right? [Honeycombs] 5 · I Stand Accused [Jerry Butler] 61 · I Want You To Be My Boy [Exciters] 98 · Just Be True [Gene Chandler] 19 · (Just Like) Romeo & Juliet [Reflections] 6 · Leader Of The Laundromat [Detergents] 19 · Mixed-Up, Shook-Up, Girl [Patty & The Emblems] 37 · My Boy Lollipop [Millie Small] 2 · My Guy [Mary Wells] 1 · Puppy Love [Barbara Lewis] 38 · Quicksand [Martha & The Vandellas] 8 · Sand In My Shoes [Drifters] · Shoop Shoop Song (It's In His Kiss) [Betty Everett] 6 · Steal Away [Jimmy Hughes] 17 · Under The Boardwalk [Drifters] 4 · What A Guy [Raindrops] 41 · You're A Wonderful One [Marvin Gaye] 15 · You've Really Got A Hold On Me [Miracles] 8

VARIOUS ARTISTS COMPILATIONS

DEBUT	PEAK	WKS	RIAA	CD	ARTIST — Album Title	Catalog	Sym	$	Label & Number
4/12/80	150	6		545	20/20 - Twenty No. 1 Hits From Twenty Years At Motown			$15	Motown 937 [2]

Ain't No Mountain High Enough [Diana Ross] 1 / Ben [Michael Jackson] 1 / Got To Give It Up (Pt. 1) [Marvin Gaye] 1 / I Want You Back [Jackson 5] 1 / I'll Be There [Jackson 5] 1 / Keep On Truckin' (Part 1) [Eddie Kendricks] 1 / Let's Get It On [Marvin Gaye] 1 / Love Hangover [Diana Ross] 1 / Love Machine (Part 1) [Miracles] 1 / Mahogany (Do You Know Where You're Going To), Theme From [Diana Ross] 1 / Never Can Say Goodbye [Jackson 5] 2 / Papa Was A Rollin' Stone [Temptations] 1 / Signed, Sealed, Delivered I'm Yours [Stevie Wonder] 3 / Someday We'll Be Together [Diana Ross & The Supremes] 1 / Still [Commodores] 1 / Superstition [Stevie Wonder] 1 / Tears Of A Clown [Smokey Robinson & The Miracles] 1 / Three Times A Lady [Commodores] 1 / What's Going On [Marvin Gaye] 2 / You Are The Sunshine Of My Life [Stevie Wonder] 1

DEBUT	PEAK	WKS	RIAA	CD	ARTIST — Album Title	Catalog	Sym	$	Label & Number
11/9/91+	18	32	▲	©546	Two Rooms - Celebrating The Songs Of Elton John & Bernie Taupin			$10	Polydor 845750

Bitch Is Back [Tina Turner] / Border Song [Eric Clapton] / Burn Down The Mission [Phil Collins] / Come Down In Time [Sting] / Crocodile Rock [Beach Boys] / Daniel [Wilson Phillips] / Don't Let The Sun Go Down On Me [Oleta Adams] / Levon [Jon Bon Jovi] / Madman Across The Water [Bruce Hornsby] / Philadelphia Freedom [Daryl Hall & John Oates] / Rocket Man (I Think It's Going To Be A Long, Long Time) [Kate Bush] / Sacrifice [Sinéad O'Connor] / Saturday Night's Alright For Fighting [Who] / Sorry Seems To Be The Hardest Word [Joe Cocker] / Tonight [George Michael] / Your Song [Rod Stewart] 48

DEBUT	PEAK	WKS	RIAA	CD	ARTIST — Album Title	Catalog	Sym	$	Label & Number
9/30/00	125	3		©547	2000 Latin Grammy Nominees [F]			$10	Epic 85133

Puro Dolor [Son By Four] / Al Despertar [Mercedes Sosa] / Corazón Espinado [Santana] / Da La Vuelta [Marc Anthony] / Dímelo (I Need To Know) [Marc Anthony] / El Niagara En Bicicleta [Juan Luis Guerra] / Fruta Fresca [Carlos Vives] / Genio Atrapado [Christina Aguilera] / Livin' La Vida Loca [Ricky Martin] / Llegar A Ti [Jaci Velásquez] / Meu Erro [Zizi Possi] / No Me Dejes De Querer [Gloria Estefan] / Ojos Así [Shakira] / Tiempos [Ruben Blades]

DEBUT	PEAK	WKS	RIAA	CD	ARTIST — Album Title	Catalog	Sym	$	Label & Number
8/1/98	83	14	●	©548	Ultimate Country Party			$10	Arista 18850

Baby Likes To Rock It [Tractors] / Better Man [Clint Black] / Blame It On Your Heart [Patty Loveless] / Boot Scootin' Boogie [Brooks & Dunn] 50 / Chattahoochee [Alan Jackson] 46 / Cherokee Boogie [BR5-49] / Cleopatra, Queen Of Denial [Pam Tillis] / Daddy's Money [Ricochet] / Going Through The Big D [Mark Chesnutt] / How Your Love Makes Me Feel [Diamond Rio] / If The House Is Rockin' [Lee Roy Parnell] / No News [Lonestar] / One More Last Chance [Vince Gill] / She Lays It All On The Line [George Strait] / (This Ain't) No Thinkin' Thing [Trace Adkins] / Watermelon Crawl [Tracy Byrd] 81 / What Part Of No [Lorrie Morgan] / Whose Bed Have Your Boots Been Under [Shania Twain] 87

DEBUT	PEAK	WKS	RIAA	CD	ARTIST — Album Title	Catalog	Sym	$	Label & Number
5/6/00	141	5		©549	Ultimate Country Party 2			$10	Arista 18890

Better Things To Do [Terri Clark] / Bubba Shot The Jukebox [Mark Chesnutt] / Country Club [Travis Tritt] / Guys Do It All The Time [Mindy McCready] 72 / Honky Tonk Song [BR5-49] / I Left Something Turned On At Home [Trace Adkins] / Little Bitty [Alan Jackson] 58 / Little Red Rodeo [Collin Raye] / Mi Vida Loca (My Crazy Life) [Pam Tillis] / My Maria [Brooks & Dunn] 79 / Texas Size Heartache [Joe Diffie] / There Ain't Nothin' Wrong With The Radio [Aaron Tippin] / There You Have It [Blackhawk] 41 / Thinkin' Problem [David Ball] 40 / Too Much Fun [Daryle Singletary] / Unbelievable [Diamond Rio] 36 / Wink [Neal McCoy] 91 / You Ain't Much Fun [Toby Keith]

DEBUT	PEAK	WKS	RIAA	CD	ARTIST — Album Title	Catalog	Sym	$	Label & Number
11/30/96+	17	50	▲	©550	Ultimate Dance Party 1997			$10	Arista 18943

Another Night [Real McCoy] 3 / Be My Lover [La Bouche] 6 / Beautiful Life [Ace Of Base] 15 / Boom Boom Boom [Outhere Brothers] 65 / Children [Robert Miles] 21 / C'mon N' Ride It (The Train) [Quad City D.J.'s] 3 / Deeper Love [Aretha Franklin] 63 / Dreamer [Livin' Joy] 72 / I Like To Move It [Reel 2 Real] 89 / Macarena [Los Del Mar] 71 / Missing [Everything But The Girl] 2 / No More "I Love You's" [Annie Lennox] 23 / Tell It To My Heart [Taylor Dayne] 7 / This Is Your Night [Amber] 24 / Total Eclipse Of The Heart [Nicki French] 2 / Where Do You Go [No Mercy] 5 / Who Do U Love [Deborah Cox] 17

DEBUT	PEAK	WKS	RIAA	CD	ARTIST — Album Title	Catalog	Sym	$	Label & Number
11/15/97	38	31	●	©551	Ultimate Dance Party 1998			$10	Arista 18988

Block Rockin' Beats [Chemical Brothers] / Bomb (These Sounds Fall Into My Mind) [Bucketheads] 49 / Child (Inside) [Qkumba Zoo] 69 / I Luv U Baby [Original] 66 / Insomnia [Faithless] 62 / Jellyhead [Crush] 72 / Kiss You All Over [No Mercy] 80 / Mo Money Mo Problems [Notorious B.I.G. Feat. Puff Daddy & Mase] 1 / 100% Pure Love [Crystal Waters] 11 / One More Time [Real McCoy] 27 / Ooh Aah...Just A Little Bit [Gina G] 12 / People Hold On [Lisa Stansfield] / Return Of The Mack [Mark Morrison] 2 / Step By Step [Whitney Houston] 15 / Sweet Dreams [La Bouche] 13 / Things Just Ain't The Same [Deborah Cox] 56 / Un-Break My Heart [Toni Braxton] 1 / What Is Love [Haddaway] 11

DEBUT	PEAK	WKS	RIAA	CD	ARTIST — Album Title	Catalog	Sym	$	Label & Number
11/14/98	69	21	●	©552	Ultimate Dance Party 1999			$10	Arista 19026

Cruel Summer [Ace Of Base] 10 / Everybody (Backstreet's Back) [Backstreet Boys] 4 / Feel It [Tamperer Feat. Maya] / First Night [Monica] 1 / Free [Ultra Naté] 75 / I Say A Little Prayer [Diana King] 38 / I'm Leavin' [Lisa Stansfield] / It's Like That [Run-D.M.C. vs. Jason Nevins] / Kiss The Rain [Billie Myers] 15 / Nobody's Supposed To Be Here [Deborah Cox] 2 / One More Night [Amber] 58 / Put Your Hands Where My Eyes Could See [Busta Rhymes] / Rose Is Still A Rose [Aretha Franklin] 26 / Shorty (You Keep Playin' With My Mind) [Imajin Feat. Keith Murray] 25 / Still Not A Player [Big Punisher] 24 / Too Close [Next] 1 / Walkin' On The Sun [Smash Mouth]

DEBUT	PEAK	WKS	RIAA	CD	ARTIST — Album Title	Catalog	Sym	$	Label & Number
6/24/00	70	14		©553	Ultimate Dance Party 2000			$10	Arista 14647

Ain't That A Lot Of Love [Simply Red] / Anywhere [112 Feat. Lil' Zane] 15 / Bodyrock [Moby] / Central Reservation [Beth Orton] / Give Me Tonight [Shannon] / I Do Both Jay & Jane [La Rissa] / I Love You [Sarah McLachlan] / I Never Knew [Deborah Cox] / I'll Fly With You (L'Amour Toujours) [Gigi D'Agostino] / It's Not Right But It's Okay [Whitney Houston] 4 / Maria Maria [Santana Feat. The Product G&B] 1 / New York City Boy [Pet Shop Boys] / Sexual (Li Da Di) [Amber] 42 / Share The Love [Andrea Martin] / Sun Is Shining [Bob Marley] / There You Go [Pink] 7 / Unpretty [TLC] 1 / Void (I Need You) [Catapila]

DEBUT	PEAK	WKS	RIAA	CD	ARTIST — Album Title	Catalog	Sym	$	Label & Number
6/26/99	174	1		©554	Ultimate Divas			$10	Arista 19066

Broken Hearted Melody [Sarah Vaughan] 7 / I Have Nothing [Whitney Houston] 4 / I'll Never Love This Way Again [Dionne Warwick] 5 / If Only You Knew [Patti LaBelle] 46 / Midnight Train To Georgia [Gladys Knight & The Pips] 1 / My Funny Valentine [Chaka Khan] / My Man (Mon Homme) [Billie Holiday] / Nessun Dorma [Aretha Franklin] / Not Gon' Cry [Mary J. Blige] 2 / Over The Rainbow [Judy Garland] / Someone To Watch Over Me [Ella Fitzgerald] / Stormy Weather [Lena Horne] / Touch Me In The Morning [Diana Ross] 1 / Un-Break My Heart [Toni Braxton] 1 / What A Difference A Day Makes [Dinah Washington] 8 / What's Love Got To Do With It [Tina Turner] 1 / Why [Annie Lennox] 34

DEBUT	PEAK	WKS	RIAA	CD	ARTIST — Album Title	Catalog	Sym	$	Label & Number
9/13/97	46	27	●	©555	Ultimate Hip Hop Party 1998			$10	Arista 18977

C.R.E.A.M. [Wu-Tang Clan] 60 / Doin It [LL Cool J] 9 / Don't Take It Personal (just one of dem days) [Monica] 2 / Down Low (Nobody Has To Know) [R. Kelly] 4 / Get Money [Junior M.A.F.I.A.] 17 / Lady [D'Angelo] 10 / Let's Get Down [Tony Toni Toné Feat. DJ Quik] / No One Else [Total] 22 / No Time [Lil' Kim Feat. Puff Daddy] 18 / One More Chance/Stay With Me [Notorious B.I.G.] 2 / Only You [112 Feat. The Notorious B.I.G. & Mase] 13 / Sentimental [Deborah Cox] 27 / Sittin' Up In My Room [Brandy] 2 / Stressed Out [Tribe Called Quest Feat. Faith Evans] / Touch Me Tease Me [Case] 14 / You Used To Love Me [Faith Evans] 24

DEBUT	PEAK	WKS	RIAA	CD	ARTIST — Album Title	Catalog	Sym	$	Label & Number
9/13/97	124	10		©556	**Ultimate New Wave Party 1998**			$10	Arista 18985

Dancing With Myself [Billy Idol] | In The Name Of Love [Thompson Twins] | Rock Lobster [B-52's] 56 | Take My Breath Away [Berlin Feat. Terri Nunn] 1
Heart Of Glass [Blondie] 1 | Just What I Needed [Cars] 27 | She Blinded Me With Science [Thomas Dolby] 5 | What I Like About You [Romantics] 49
Hungry Like The Wolf [Duran Duran] 3 | Let's Dance [David Bowie] 1 | She Drives Me Crazy [Fine Young Cannibals] 1
I Melt With You [Modern English] 78 | Look Of Love (Part 1) [ABC] 18 | Sweet Dreams (Are Made Of This) [Eurythmics] 1
I Ran (So Far Away) [Flock Of Seagulls] 9 | Love Plus One [Haircut 100] 37 | Tainted Love [Soft Cell] 8
| | Our House [Madness] 7 | |

DEBUT	PEAK	WKS	RIAA	CD	ARTIST — Album Title	Catalog	Sym	$	Label & Number
9/27/69	196	2		557	**Underground Gold**			$20	Liberty 7625

Amphetamine Annie [Canned Heat] | Dust My Broom [Canned Heat] | Make Me A Pallet On Your Floor [Jo-Ann Kelly] | Pushin' [Albert Collins]
Black Cat Bone [Johnny Winter] | Feelin' Alright? [Traffic] | Mean Woman Blues [Spencer Davis Group] | Rollin' And Tumblin' [Jo-Ann Kelly]
Do The Sissy [Albert Collins] | I Got Love If You Want It [Johnny Winter] | Paper Sun [Traffic] 94
Drown In My Own Tears [Spencer Davis Group]

DEBUT	PEAK	WKS	RIAA	CD	ARTIST — Album Title	Catalog	Sym	$	Label & Number
11/11/00	43	15		©558	**Universal Smash Hits**			$10	Universal 158299

All For You [Sister Hazel] 11 | Blue (Da Ba Dee) [Eiffel 65] 6 | Kryptonite [3 Doors Down] 3 | Where My Girls At [702] 4
Back At One [Brian McKnight] 2 | (Hot S**t) Country Grammar [Nelly] 7 | Little Black Backpack [Stroke 9] | Why I'm Here [Oleander]
Back That Thang Up [Juvenile] 19 | I Do (Cherish You) [98°] 13 | Summer In The City [St. Lunatics Feat. Nelly & Cedric The Entertainer] | You Know My Name [SPM]
Bad Touch [Bloodhound Gang] 52 | If You Could Only See [Tonic] | Wanna Be A Baller [Lil' Troy] 70
Better Off Alone [Alice Deejay] 27 | It Feels So Good [Sonique] 8
Bling Bling [B.G.] 36

DEBUT	PEAK	WKS	RIAA	CD	ARTIST — Album Title	Catalog	Sym	$	Label & Number
12/24/94	97	10	●	©559	**Unplugged Collection Volume One, The** .... [L]			$10	Warner 45774

Are You Gonna Go My Way [Lenny Kravitz] | Come Rain Or Come Shine [Don Henley] | Don't Talk [10,000 Maniacs] | Pride And Joy [Stevie Ray Vaughan]
Barefoot [k.d. lang] | Deep Dark Truthful Mirror [Elvis Costello & The Rude 5] | Gasoline Alley [Rod Stewart] | Somebody To Shove [Soul Asylum]
Before You Accuse Me [Eric Clapton] | Don't Let The Sun Go Down On Me [Elton John] | Graceland [Paul Simon] | We Can Work It Out [Paul McCartney]
| | Half A World Away [R.E.M.] | Why [Annie Lennox]
| | Like A Hurricane [Neil Young]
| | Pink Houses [John Mellencamp]

DEBUT	PEAK	WKS	RIAA	CD	ARTIST — Album Title	Catalog	Sym	$	Label & Number
6/19/93	71	16		©560	**Uptown MTV Unplugged** .... [L]			$10	Uptown 10858

All I See [Christopher Williams] | Forever My Lady [Jodeci] | Is It Good To You [Heavy D & The Boyz] | One Nite Stand [Father MC]
Blue Funk [Heavy D & The Boyz] | I Don't Want To Do Anything [Mary J. Blige] | Lately [Jodeci] 4 | Reminisce [Mary J. Blige]
Come & Talk To Me [Jodeci] | Interlude [Heavy D & The Boyz] | Next Stop Uptown [Uptown All-Stars] | Stay [Jodeci]
Come Go With Me [Christopher Williams] | | | Sweet Thing [Mary J. Blige]

DEBUT	PEAK	WKS	RIAA	CD	ARTIST — Album Title	Catalog	Sym	$	Label & Number
8/23/97	184	3		©561	**Urbal Beats**			$10	Polygram 553764

Before Today [Everything But The Girl] | Busy Child [Crystal Method] | Poison [Prodigy] | Toxygene [Orb]
Big Ditch [DJ Icey] | Caterpillar [Keoki] | Saint, The [Orbital] | We Have Explosive [Future Sound Of London]
Block Rockin Beats [Chemical Brothers] | Higher State Of Consciousness [Wink] | Share The Fall [Reprazent feat. Roni Size]
Born Slippy [Underworld] | Inner City Life [Goldie] | Sour Times [Portishead]
| O.B.E. [Rabbit In The Moon] | Sugar Is Sweeter [CJ Bolland]

DEBUT	PEAK	WKS	RIAA	CD	ARTIST — Album Title	Catalog	Sym	$	Label & Number
6/6/98	193	1		©562	**Urbal Beats 2: The Definitive Guide To Electronic Music**			$15	Polygram 555840 [2]

B-Boy Stance [Freestylers] | Go [Moby] | Renegade Master [Wildchild] | Treat Infamy [Rest Assured]
Charly [Prodigy] | Going Out Of My Head [Fatboy Slim] | Rock The Funky Beat [Natural Born Chillers] | Ultrasonic Sound [Hive]
Chime [Orbital] | Keep Hope Alive [Crystal Method] | Salsa Life [Rhythim Is Rhythim] | Voodoo Ray [Guy Called Gerald]
City Of Groove [DJ Icey] | Mother Earth [Dubtribe] | Smack My B···· Up | What Does Your Soul Look Like [DJ Die vs. DJ Shadow]
Clear [Cybotron] | My Mate Paul [David Holmes] | Something Good [Utah Saints]
Cubik [808 State] | Over [Portishead] | Subfusion [Rabbit In The Moon]
Energy Flash [Joey Beltram] | Release Yo' Delf [Method Man] | Temper, Temper [Goldie]
Freakz, The [Uberzone]

DEBUT	PEAK	WKS	RIAA	CD	ARTIST — Album Title	Catalog	Sym	$	Label & Number
9/26/81	173	3		©563	**Urgh! A Music War** .... [L]			$15	A&M 6019 [2]

Ain't This The Life [Oingo Boingo] | Down In The Park [Gary Numan] | Model Worker [Magazine] | Sign Of The Cross [Skafish]
Back In Flesh [Wall Of Voodoo] | Driven To Tears [Police] | Nothing Means Nothing Anymore [Alley Cats] | Tear It Up [Cramps]
Bad Reputation [Joan Jett & The Blackhearts] | Enola Gay [Orchestral Manoeuvres In The Dark] | Offshore Banking Business [Members] | Total Eclipse [Klaus Nomi]
Beyond And Back [X] | Foolish I Know [Jools Holland] | Puppet, The [Echo & The Bunnymen] | Uncontrollable Urge [Devo]
Birdies [Pere Ubu] | He'd Send In The Army [Gang Of Four] | Respectable Street [XTC] | We Got The Beat [Go-Go's]
Cheryl's Going Home [John Otway] | Homicide [999] | Shadow Line [Fleshtones] | Where's Captain Kirk [Athletico Spizz]
Come Again [Au Pairs] | Ku Klux Klan [Steel Pulse]
Dance [Toyah Wilcox]

DEBUT	PEAK	WKS	RIAA	CD	ARTIST — Album Title	Catalog	Sym	$	Label & Number
4/25/98+	14ᶜ	32		©564	**Veggie Tunes**			$10	Word 8438

Busy, Busy | Hairbrush Song | Oh, No! What We Gonna' Do? | We Are The Grapes Of Wrath
Fear Not, Daniel | I Can Be Your Friend | Some Veggies Went To Sea | We've Got Some News, King Darius
Forgiveness Song | King Darius Suite | Veggie Tales Theme | What Have We Learned?
God Is Bigger | Love Your Neighbor | Water Buffalo Song | You Were In His Hand

DEBUT	PEAK	WKS	RIAA	CD	ARTIST — Album Title	Catalog	Sym	$	Label & Number
7/18/98	161	4		©565	**Veggie Tunes 2**			$10	Word 5874

Big Things Too | It's Laura's Fault | New Improved Bunny Song | Stand
Bunny Song (Reprise) | Keep Walking | Pirates Who Don't Do Anything | Stand (Reprise)
Dance Of The Cucumber | Larry-Boy | Promised Land | Think Of Me
Good Morning George | Lord Has Given | Promised Land (Reprise) | VeggieTales Theme Song
I Love My Lips | Lord Has Given (Reprise) | Song Of The Cebú | What We Have Learned

DEBUT	PEAK	WKS	RIAA	CD	ARTIST — Album Title	Catalog	Sym	$	Label & Number
10/21/00	177	4		©566	**Very Scary Music: Classic Horror Themes**			$10	Laserlight 21378

Dracula Main Title | Nightmare On Elm Street | Theme From Jaws | This Is Halloween
Exorcist, The | Psycho Suite | Theme From Poltergeist | Twilight Zone
Halloween Main Title | Theme From Friday The 13th | Theme From The X-Files

DEBUT	PEAK	WKS	RIAA	CD	ARTIST — Album Title	Catalog	Sym	$	Label & Number
10/24/98	21	20	●	©567	**VH1 Divas Live** .... [L]			$10	Epic 69600

recorded on 4/14/98 in New York City

Chain Of Fools [Aretha Franklin & Mariah Carey] | Megamix | Reason, The [Celine Dion & Carole King] | Turn The Beat Around [Gloria Estefan]
Heaven's What I Feel [Gloria Estefan] | My All [Mariah Carey] | River Deep, Mountain High [Celine Dion] | You're Still The One [Shania Twain]
Make It Happen [Mariah Carey] | My Heart Will Go On [Celine Dion] | Testimony [Celine Dion/Gloria Estefan/Aretha Franklin/Shania Twain/Carole King] | You've Got A Friend [Celine Dion/Gloria Estefan/Shania Twain/Carole King]
Man! I Feel Like A Woman! [Shania Twain] | Natural Woman [Celine Dion/Gloria Estefan/Aretha Franklin/Shania Twain/Mariah Carey]

VARIOUS ARTISTS COMPILATIONS

DEBUT	PEAK	WKS	RIAA	CD	ARTIST — Album Title	Catalog	Sym	$	Label & Number

11/20/99 · 90 · 5 · ● · ©568 · VH1 Divas Live/99 .... **[L] $10 Arista 14604**

Ain't No Way *[Whitney Houston & Mary J. Blige]*
Almost Doesn't Count (medley) *[Brandy]*
Best, The *[Tina Turner]*
Bitch Is Back *[Tina Turner & Elton John]*
(Everything I Do) I Do It For You *[Brandy & Faith Hill]*
Have You Ever? (medley) *[Brandy]*
How Do I Live *[Leann Rimes]*
I Will Always Love You *[Whitney Houston]*
I'm Every Woman *[Whitney Houston & Chaka Khan]*
I'mEveryWoman(Reprise) *[WhitneyHouston/ChakaKhan/FaithHill/Brandy/LeannRimesMaryJ*
I'm Still Standing *[Elton John]*
If I Could Turn Back Time *[Cher]*
Proud Mary *[Tina Turner, Elton John & Cher]*
This Kiss *[Faith Hill]*

9/6/97 · 174 · 2 · ©569 · VH1 More Of The Big 80's .... **[TV] $10 Rhino 72820**

Come On Eileen *[Dexys Midnight Runners]* 1
Cry *[Godley & Creme]* 16
Der Kommissar *[After The Fire]* 5
Doctor! Doctor! *[Thompson Twins]* 11
Everybody Have Fun Tonight *[Wang Chung]* 2
I Ran (So Far Away) *[Flock Of Seagulls]* 9
Major Tom (Coming Home) *[Peter Schilling]* 14
Mickey *[Toni Basil]* 1
Obsession *[Animotion]* 6
She's A Beauty *[Tubes]* 10
Stray Cat Strut *[Stray Cats]* 3
They Don't Know *[Tracey Ullman]* 8
Tuff Enuff *[Fabulous Thunderbirds]* 10
What I Like About You *[Romantics]* 49
Whip It *[Devo]* 14
Words *[Missing Persons]* 42

5/13/00 · 160 · 3 · ©570 · VH1 Storytellers .... **[L] $10 Interscope 490511**

Back On The Chain Gang *[Pretenders]*
Carnival *[Natalie Merchant]*
China Girl *[David Bowie]*
Crash *[Dave Matthews feat. Tim Reynolds]*
Edge Of Seventeen *[Stevie Nicks]*
Here Comes The Rain Again *[Eurythmics]*
How Deep Is Your Love *[Bee Gees]*
Jack & Diane *[John Mellencamp]*
Just A Memory *[Elvis Costello]*
Mexico *[James Taylor]*
Rain King *[Counting Crows]*
Regarding Steven *[John Popper]*
Stay *[Lisa Loeb]*
Strong Enough *[Sheryl Crow feat. Stevie Nicks]*
Who Will Save Your Soul *[Jewel]*

8/21/99 · 195 · 1 · ©571 · VH1 The Big 80's - Big Hair .... **[TV] $10 Rhino 75842**

Burning Like A Flame *[Dokken]* 72
Cherry Pie *[Warrant]* 10
Cryin' *[Vixen]* 22
Cum On Feel The Noize *[Quiet Riot]* 5
Feel It Again *[Honeymoon Suite]* 34
Headed For A Heartbreak *[Winger]* 19
Here I Go Again *[Whitesnake]* 1
Last Mile *[Cinderella]* 36
Mutha (Don't Wanna Go To School Today) *[Extreme]*
Once Bitten Twice Shy *[Great White]* 5
Rock You Like A Hurricane *[Scorpions]* 25
Round And Round *[Ratt]* 12
Summertime Girls *[Y&T]* 55
Talk Dirty To Me *[Poison]* 9
Up All Night *[Slaughter]* 27
We're Not Gonna Take It *[Twisted Sister]* 21

8/28/99 · 8 · 14 · ● · ©572 · Violator - The Album .... **$10 Violator 558941**

Beatnuts Forever *[Beatnuts]*
Bus-A-Bus Remix *[Busta Rhymes]*
Do What Playas Do *[Mysone, Mase & Eightball]*
First Degree *[Da Franchise & Ja Rule]*
Heavy Weights *[Fat Joe, Big Pun & Eightball]*
I Wanna F*** You *[Noreaga & Scarlett]*
Nobody *[Next & Mysonne]*
Nobody Likes Me *[Mobb Deep]*
Ohh Wee *[Cru]*
Say What *[LL Cool J]*
S*** That He Said *[Big Noyd]*
Thugged Out N**** *[Noreaga/Capone/Scarlett/Maze/etc.]*
Truth, The *[Mysonne]*
Violators *[L Boogie/Sonya Blade/Noreaga/Mysonne/Prodigy/Busta Rhymes]*
Vivrant Thing *[Q-Tip]* 26
What My N**** Want *[Cam'ron & Busta Rhymes]*
Whatcha Come Around Here For *[Flipmode Squad]*
Who Can I Trust *[Cormega & Hot Boys]*

7/24/76 · 153 · 6 · 573 · Volunteer Jam .... **[L] $15 Capricorn 0172**

recorded on 9/9/75 in Murfreesboro, Tennessee
Birmingham Blues *[Charlie Daniels Band]*
Mountain Dew *[Charlie Daniels Band]*
South's Gonna Do It *[Charlie Daniels Band]*
Sweet Mama *[Dickey Betts]*
Thrill Is Gone *[Marshall Tucker Band]*
Whiskey *[Charlie Daniels Band]*

7/19/80 · 104 · 9 · 574 · Volunteer Jam VI .... **[L] $15 Epic 36438 [2]**

recorded on 1/12/80 at the Nashville Municipal Auditorium
Amazing Grace (medley) *[Charlie Daniels Band & Bobby Jones]*
Carol *[Ted Nugent]*
Do The Funky Chicken *[Rufus Thomas]*
Down Home Blues *[Papa John Creach]*
Funky Junky *[Charlie Daniels Band]*
Keep On Smilin' *[Wet Willie]*
Lady Luck *[Grinderswitch]*
New Orleans Ladies *[Louisiana's LeRoux]*
Night They Drove Old Dixie Down *[Dobie Gray]*
Rich Kids *[Winters Brothers Band]*
Same Old Story (Same Old Song) *[Crystal Gayle]*
So Long *[Henry Paul Band]*
Will The Circle Be Unbroken (medley) *[Charlie Daniels Band & Bobby Jones]*

7/25/81 · 149 · 4 · ©575 · Volunteer Jam VII .... **[L] $12 Epic 37178**

recorded on 1/17/81 at the Nashville Municipal Auditorium
Around And Around *[Ted Nugent]*
Can't You See *[Charlie Daniels Band]*
Change Is Gonna Come *[Dobie Gray]*
Falling In Love For The Night *[Crystal Gayle/Charlie Daniels Band]*
Marie La Veau *[Bobby Bare]*
Mississippi Queen *[Molly Hatchet w/Ted Nugent]*
Standing On Shakey Ground *[Delbert McClinton]*
Sweet Home Alabama *[Charlie Daniels Band]*
(Your Love Has Lifted Me) Higher And Higher *[Jimmy Hall]*

8/12/78 · 98 · 25 · ©576 · War Of The Worlds, The .... **$20 Columbia 35290 [2]**

Artilleryman And The Fighting Machine
Brave New World
Dead London
Eve Of The War
Forever Autumn *[Justin Hayward]* 47
Horsell Common And The Heat Ray
Red Weed (Parts 1 & 2)
Spirit Of Man
Thunder Child

6/23/73 · 62 · 18 · 577 · Watergate Comedy Hour, The .... **[C] $15 Hidden 11202**

Agnew Interview
Break-In, The
Dick Cravett Show
Hello UPI No. 1
Hello UPI No. 2
Investigation, The
Meeting, The
Plan, The
President's Prayer
Reverend And The President
Ron Ziegler Meets The Press
Special Investigator
Watergate Comedy Hour

10/16/71 · 181 · 4 · 578 · Way To Become The Sensuous Woman By "J", The .... **$15 Atlantic 7209**

no track titles listed

12/4/99 · 40 · 8 · ● · ©579 · WCW Mayhem The Music .... **$10 Tommy Boy 1353**

American Made
Bailando *[Nitro Girls]*
Blast *[Kid Rock]*
Bone Crusher *[Lyrical Giants]*
Bow, Wow, Wow
Buff Daddy
Count That Man Out
Crush 'Em *[Megadeth]*
Faith *[Limp Bizkit feat. Everlast]*
Fist Full *[Cypress Hill & Defari]*
Give It Up *[Screwball]*
Got Him In The Corner
Here Comes The Pain *[Slayer]*
Invasion
Kevin Nash/Wolfpac Theme
Loose *[Primer 55]*
Make Some Noise *[DJ Ran]*
Make The Crowd Roar *[Big Punisher & Fat Joe]*
Pay Per View *[Ruff Ryders]*
Rap Is Crap *[Curt Hennig & The West Texas Rednecks]*
Seek And Destroy *[Metallica]*
Self High Five
Sting Theme
Take It *[Insane Clown Posse]*
WCW Monday Nitro Theme
What Up Mach

11/27/65 · 3 · 25 · ● · 580 · Welcome to the LBJ Ranch! .... **[C] $15 Capitol 2423**

featuring the actual recorded voices of political leaders
Governor Nelson Rockefeller
Mrs. Ladybird Johnson
President Dwight D. Eisenhower
President Lyndon B. Johnson
Senator Barry Goldwater
Senator Everett Dirksen
Senator Robert Kennedy
Vice President Richard Nixon

6/1/59 · 3 · 3 · 581 · What's New? On Capitol Stereo, Vol. 1 .... **$30 Capitol SN-1**

Cha Cha Cacciatore *[Guy Lombardo]*
Coffee House Rag *[Ray Bauduc & Nappy Lamare]*
Conquest *[Alfred Newman]*
Gal That Got Away *[Four Freshmen]*
I Dig Chicks! *[Jonah Jones Quartet]*
My Heart's Treasure *[Nat "King" Cole]*
One Minute To One *[Mavis Rivers]*
River Kwai March *[Jack Marshall]*
September In The Rain *[George Shearing Quintet]*
Tenderly *[Paul Weston]*
That's All There Is, There Isn't Any More *[Judy Garland]*
Voodoo Dreams *[Les Baxter]*

DEBUT	PEAK	WKS	RIAA	CD	ARTIST — Album Title	Catalog	Sym	$	Label & Number

4/2/66 — **22** — 18 — ©582 — **When You're In Love The Whole World Is Jewish** .... [C] — **$15** Kapp 4506
Ballad Of Irving *[Frank Gallop]* 34 / Great Bank Robbery / Schtick / When You're In Love The Whole
Bar Mitzvah / Hobby, The / Shoe Repair Shop / World Is Jewish
Call From Greenwich Village / Kidnapping, The / Things Might Have Been Different / Would You Believe It?
Discussion In The Airplane / Miami Beach / Voyage To The Bottom Of The Sea
Divorce, Kosher Style / My Husband, The Monster

7/22/78 — **181** — 4 — ©583 — **White Mansions** .... — **$12** A&M 6004
Bad Man / King Has Called Me Home / Praise The Lord / Union Mare & The Confederate
Bring Up The Twelve Pounders / Last Dance & The Kentucky / Southern Boys / Grey
Dixie, Hold On / Racehorse / Southland's Bleeding / White Trash
Dixie, Now You're Done / No One Would Believe A Summer / Story To Tell (Preface)
Join Around The Flag / Could Be So Cold / They Laid Waste To Our Land

12/21/85+ — **167** — 12 — ©584 — **Windham Hill Records Piano Sampler** .... [I] — **$10** Windham Hill 1040
Amy's Song *[Peggy Stern]* / In This Small Spot *[Tim Story]* / Lou Ann *[Philip Aaberg]* / Morning With The Roses *[Richard
Consolation *[Rick Peller]* / Listening To Evening *[Allaudin / Messenger Of The Son *[Cyrille / Dworsky]*
In Flight *[Michael Harrison]* / Mathieu]* / Verdeaux]* / Out To Play *[Paul Dondero]*

10/20/84 — **108** — 25 — ©585 — **Windham Hill Records Sampler '84** .... [I] — **$10** Windham Hill 1035
Aerial Boundaries *[Michael Hedges]* / On The Threshold Of Liberty *[Mark / Shadowdance *[Shadowfax]* / Western *[Alex de Grassi]*
Cricket's Wicket *[Billy Oskay & / Isham]* / Thanksgiving *[George Winston]*
Micheal O Domhnaill]* / Oristana Sojourn *[Scott Cossu]* / Ventana *[Will Ackerman]*

3/29/86 — **102** — 18 — ©586 — **Windham Hill Records Sampler '86** .... [I] — **$10** Windham Hill 1048
Another Country *[Shadowfax]* / Engravings *[Ira Stein & Russel / Marias River Breakdown *[Philip / Pittsburgh, 1901 (Theme from Mrs.
Devotion *[Liz Story]* / Walder]* / Aaberg]* / Soffel) *[Mark Isham]*
Dolphins *[Mike Marshall & Darol / Gwenlaise *[Scott Cossu w/Eugene / Near Northern *[Darol Anger/Barbara / Welcoming *[Michael Manring]*
Anger]* / Friesen]* / Higbie Quintet]*
Hot Beach *[Interior]* / New Waltz *[Malcolm Dalglish]*

2/27/88 — **134** — 16 — ©587 — **Windham Hill Records Sampler '88** .... [I] — **$10** Windham Hill 1065
Angel Steps *[Scott Cossu]* / Climbing In Geometry *[William / Indian Woman *[Rubaja & / Toys Not Ties *[Nightnoise]*
Because It's There *[Michael / Ackerman]* / Hernandez]* / Unseen Rain *[W.A. Mathieu]*
Hedges]* / Close Cover *[Wim Mertens]* / Road To Hanna *[Shadowfax]* / Wishing Well *[Schonherz & Scott]*
/ / To Be *[Montreux]* / Woman At The Well *[Tim Story]*

4/15/89 — **176** — 4 — ©588 — **Windham Hill Records Sampler '89** .... [I] — **$10** Windham Hill 1082
Credo Of Ballymacoda *[Therese / Life In The Trees *[Michael Manring]* / Sojourner *[Paul McCandless]* / Walking Through Walls *[Philip
Schroeder-Sheker]* / Manhattan Underground *[Scott / Through The Woods *[Metamora]* / Aaberg]*
Floyd's Ghost *[Will Ackerman]* / Cossu]* / Usually/Always *[Fred Simon]*
Hugh *[Nightnoise]* / Rameau's Nephew *[Philippe Saisse]* / Visiting Card *[Wim Mertens]*

9/6/80 — **69** — 7 — 589 — **Winners** .... — **$12** I&M 017
And The Beat Goes On / **Don't Let Go** *[Isaac Hayes]* 18 / **Shake Your Body (Down To The** / **Turn Off The Lights** *[Teddy
[Whispers] 19 / **I Do Love You** *[G.Q.]* 20 / **Ground)** *[Jacksons]* 7 / Pendergrass]* 48
Cruisin' *[Smokey Robinson]* 4 / **I'll Never Love This Way Again** / **Special Lady** *[Ray, Goodman &* / **Working My Way Back To**
Dance With You *[Carrie Lucas]* 70 / *[Dionne Warwick]* 5 / *Brown]* 5 / **You/Forgive Me, Girl** 2
Do You Love What You Feel / **Second Time Around** *[Shalamar]* 8 / **Still** *[Commodores]* 1 / **You Can't Change That** *[Raydio]* 9
[Rufus & Chaka Khan] 30 / / **Too Hot** *[Kool & The Gang]* 5

3/9/96 — **122** — 7 ● — 590 — **Winnie The Pooh Sing Along** .... — **$10** Walt Disney 60889
available only on cassette
Heffalumps And Woozles / It's So Much More Friendly With / Rain, Rain, Rain Came Down, / Up, Down, And Touch The Ground
Hip, Hip, Pooh-Ray / Pooh / Down, Down / Winnie The Pooh
It Really Was A Woozle, Yes It Was / Little Black Rain Cloud / Rather Blustery Day / Wonderful Thing About Tiggers
/ Pooh, Pooh, The Birthday Bear / Rumbly In My Tumbly

4/13/96 — **175** — 1 — ©591 — **Wolfgang Amadeus Mozart, Piano Concertos No. 22 and No. 24** .... [I] — **$10** Digital Master. 71832
Concerto for piano and orchestra / Concerto for piano and orchestra
no. 22 in E flat major / no. 24 in C minor KV 491

4/13/96 — **196** — 1 — ©592 — **Wolfgang Amadeus Mozart, Violin Concertos No. 1, 2 + 3** .... [I] — **$10** Digital Master. 71825
Concerto for violin and orchestra no. / Concerto for violin and orchestra no. / Concerto for violin and orchestra no.
1 in B flat major KV 207 / 2 in D major KV 211 / 3 in G major KV 216

4/5/75 — **84** — 10 — 593 — **Wolfman Jack/More American Graffiti** .... — **$20** MCA 8007 [2]
Bony Moronie *[Larry Williams]* 14 / **It Might As Well Rain Until** / **Peggy Sue** *[Buddy Holly]* 3 / **Teenager In Love** *[Dion & The
Could This Be Magic *[Dubs]* 23 / **September** *[Carole King]* 22 / **Poison Ivy** *[Coasters]* 7 / Belmonts]* 5
Duke Of Earl *[Gene Chandler]* 1 / **Loco-Motion** *[Little Eva]* 1 / **Ready Teddy** *[Little Richard]* 44 / **Tutti-Frutti** *[Little Richard]* 17
Gee *[Crows]* / **Louie Louie** *[Kingsmen]* 2 / **See You Later, Alligator** *[Bill / **Twilight Time** *[Platters]* 1
Happy, Happy Birthday Baby / **Maybe** *[Chantels]* 15 / *Haley]* 6 / **Will You Love Me Tomorrow**
[Tune Weavers] 5 / **My Heart Is An Open Book** *[Carl / **Shoop Shoop Song (It's In His** / *[Shirelles]* 1
He Will Break Your Heart *[Jerry / Dobkins Jr.]* 3 / **Kiss)** *[Betty Everett]* 6
Butler]* 7 / **Oh, Boy!** *[Crickets]* 10 / **Speedo** *[Cadillacs]* 17
I'm Sorry *[Brenda Lee]* 1 / **One Summer Night** *[Danleers]* 7 / **Stagger Lee** *[Lloyd Price]* 1

VARIOUS ARTISTS COMPILATIONS

DEBUT	PEAK	WKS	RIAA	CD	ARTIST — Album Title	Catalog	Sym	$	Label & Number

8/27/94 | 186 | 1 | ©594 Woodstock: Three Days Of Peace And Music - Twenty-Fifth Anniversary Collection .... [L] **$30** Atlantic 82636 [4]

recorded from August 15-17, 1969

At The Hop *[Sha Na Na]*
Ball & Chain *[Janis Joplin]*
Beautiful People *[Melanie]*
Blood Of The Sun *[Mountain]*
Coming Into Los Angeles *[Arlo Guthrie]*
Commotion *[Creedence Clearwater Revival]*
Dance To The Music (medley) *[Sly & The Family Stone]*
Drug Store Truck Drivin' Man *[Joan Baez]*
Find The Cost Of Freedom *[Crosby, Stills & Nash]*
Fish Cheer (medley) *[Country Joe McDonald]*
4 + 20 *[Crosby, Stills, Nash & Young]*
Freedom *[Richie Havens]*
Going Up The Country *[Canned Heat]*
Green River *[Creedence Clearwater Revival]*
Guinnevere *[Crosby, Stills, Nash & Young]*
Handsome Johnny *[Richie Havens]*
I-Feel-Like-I'm-Fixin'-To-Die Rag (medley) *[Country Joe McDonald]*
I Had A Dream *[John B. Sebastian]*
I Put A Spell On You *[Creedence Clearwater Revival]*
I Want To Take You Higher (medley) *[Sly & The Family Stone]*
I'm Going Home *[Ten Years After]*
If I Were A Carpenter *[Tim Hardin]*
Joe Hill *[Joan Baez]*
Leaving This Town *[Canned Heat]*
Let's Go Get Stoned *[Joe Cocker]*
Long Black Veil *[Band]*
Love March *[Paul Butterfield Blues Band]*
Loving You Is Sweeter Than Ever *[Band]*
Marrakesh Express *[Crosby, Stills, Nash & Young]*
Mean Town Blues *[Johnny Winter]*
Music Lover (medley) *[Sly & The Family Stone]*
Ninety-Nine And A Half (Won't Do) *[Creedence Clearwater Revival]*
Purple Haze *[Jimi Hendrix]*
Rainbows All Over Your Blues *[John B. Sebastian]*
Rock & Soul Music *[Country Joe & The Fish]*
Saturday Afternoon (medley) *[Jefferson Airplane]*
Sea Of Madness *[Crosby, Stills, Nash & Young]*
Somebody To Love *[Jefferson Airplane]*
Soul Sacrifice *[Santana]*
Star Spangled Banner *[Jimi Hendrix]*
Stepping Stone (medley) *[Jimi Hendrix]*
Suite: Judy Blues Eyes *[Crosby, Stills & Nash]*
Sweet Sir Galahad *[Joan Baez]*
Theme For An Imaginary Western *[Mountain]*
Try *[Janis Joplin]*
Uncle Sam Blues *[Jefferson Airplane]*
Volunteers *[Jefferson Airplane]*
Voodoo Chile (Slight Return) (medley) *[Jimi Hendrix]*
Walking Down The Line *[Arlo Guthrie]*
We're Not Gonna Take It *[Who]*
Weight, The *[Band]*
White Rabbit *[Jefferson Airplane]*
With A Little Help From My Friends *[Joe Cocker]*
Won't You Try (medley) *[Jefferson Airplane]*
Work Me Lord *[Janis Joplin]*

11/26/94 | 50 | 12 | ▲ | ©595 Woodstock 94 .... [L] **$15** A&M 540289 [2]

recorded from August 12-14, 1994

Arrow *[Candlebox]*
Biko *[Peter Gabriel]*
Blood Sugar Sex Magik *[Red Hot Chili Peppers]*
But Anyway *[Blues Traveler]*
Come Together *[Neville Brothers]*
Dance, M.F., Dance! - Kiss Off *[Violent Femmes]*
Deja Vu *[Crosby, Stills & Nash]*
Draw The Line (medley) *[Aerosmith]*
Dreams *[Cranberries]*
Feelin' Alright *[Joe Cocker]*
F.I.N.E. (medley) *[Aerosmith]*
For Whom The Bell Tolls *[Metallica]*
Happiness In Slavery *[Nine Inch Nails]*
Headed For Destruction *[Jackyl]*
Highway 61 *[Bob Dylan]*
How I Could Just Kill A Man *[Cypress Hill]*
Hunter, The *[Paul Rodgers]*
I'm The Only One *[Melissa Etheridge]*
Pearly Queen *[Traffic]*
Porno For Pyros *[Porno For Pyros]*
Right Here Too Much *[Rollins Band]*
Run, Baby, Run *[Sheryl Crow]*
Selling The Drama *[Live]*
Shine *[Collective Soul]*
Shoop *[Salt-N-Pepa]*
Soup *[Blind Melon]*
Those Damned Blue-Collar Tweekers *[Primus]*
When I Come Around *[Green Day]*

11/6/99 | 32 | 6 | ● | ©596 Woodstock 99 .... [L] **$15** Epic 63770 [2]

recorded from July 23-25, 1999

Adrenaline *[Roots]*
Airport Song *[Guster]*
Alison *[Elvis Costello]*
Bawitdaba *[Kid Rock]*
Bitch *[Sevendust]*
Black Capricorn Day *[Jamiroquai]*
Blind *[Korn]*
Block Rockin' Beats *[Chemical Brothers]*
Bulls On Parade *[Rage Against The Machine]*
Cold Beverage *[G. Love & Special Sauce]*
Creeping Death *[Metallica]*
Down So Long *[Jewel]*
Ecstacy *[Rusted Root]*
Ends *[Everlast]*
Everything Zen *[Bush]*
Fire *[Red Hot Chili Peppers]*
Four *[Lit]*
I Alone *[Live]*
If It Makes You Happy *[Sheryl Crow]*
Keep Away *[Godsmack]*
Kids Aren't Alright *[Offspring]*
Lip Up *[Buckcherry]*
Resting Place *[Bruce Hornsby]*
Roadhouse Blues *[Creed]*
Rock This Town *[Brian Setzer Orchestra]*
Santa Monica (Watch The World Die) *[Everclear]*
Secret Place *[Megadeth]*
Show Me What You Got *[Limp Bizkit]*
So Pure *[Alanis Morissette]*
Stop Being Greedy *[DMX]*
Superman's Dead *[Our Lady Peace]*
Tripping Billies *[Dave Matthews Band]*

10/28/95 | 94 | 3 | | ©597 Working Class Hero - A Tribute To John Lennon .... **$10** Hollywood 62015

Cold Turkey *[Cheap Trick]*
Grow Old With Me *[Mary Chapin Carpenter]*
How Do You Sleep? *[Magnificent Bastards]*
I Don't Wanna Be A Soldier *[Mad Season]*
I Found Out *[Red Hot Chili Peppers]*
Imagine *[Blues Traveler]*
Instant Karma! *[Toad The West Sprocket]*
Isolation *[Sponge]*
Jealous Guy *[Collective Soul]*
Mind Games *[George Clinton]*
Nobody Told Me *[Flaming Lips]*
Power To The People *[Minus 5]*
Steel And Glass *[Candlebox]*
Well, Well, Well *[Super 8]*
Working Class Hero *[Screaming Trees]*

7/10/65 | 107 | 7 | | 598 World Of Country Music, The .... **$20** Capitol 5 [2]

All Of The Monkeys Ain't In The Zoo *[Tommy Collins]*
Blackboard Of My Heart *[Hank Thompson]*
Half Of This, Half Of That *[Wynn Stewart]*
He Believes Me *[Mary Taylor]*
Hello Walls *[Faron Young]* **12**
I Don't Love Nobody *[Leon McAuliffe]*
I Don't Love You Anymore *[Charlie Louvin]*
I Dreamed Of A Hill-Billy Heaven *[Tex Ritter]* **20**
Kickin' Mule *[Walter Hensley]*
Minute You're Gone *[Sonny James]* **95**
My Baby's Gone *[Wanda Jackson]*
My Heart Skips A Beat *[Buck Owens]* **94**
My Past Is Present *[Bobby Durham]*
Second Fiddle *[Jean Shepard]*
Summer, Winter, Spring, And Fall *[Glen Campbell]*
Sweet Temptation *[Merle Travis]*
Take Your Hands Off My Heart *[Ray Pillow]*
There's A Grand Ole Opry Show Playing Somewhere *[Red Johnson]*
Tia Lisa Lynn *[Rose Maddox]*
Timber, I'm Falling *[Ferlin Husky]*
Tips Of My Fingers *[Roy Clark]* **45**
When The Moon Comes Over The Mountain *[Mac Wiseman]*
Yodel, Sweet Molly *[Ira Louvin]*
Your Name's Become A Household Word *[Neal Merritt]*

4/8/00 | 8 | 17 | ● | ©599 World Wrestling Federation - Aggression .... **$10** Priority 50120

Big *[Mack 10/K Mac/Boo Kapone]*
Big Red Machine *[Eastsidaz]*
Break Down The Walls *[RA The Rugged Man]*
Game *[Mystikal & Ras Kass]*
Hell Yeah *[Snoop Dogg & W.C.]*
I Won't Stop *[C-Murder feat. Magic]*
Kings, The *[Run-DMC]*
Know Your Role *[Method Man]*
Ministry *[Dame Grease Presents Meeno]*
No Chance *[Redman & Rock of Heltah Skeltah]*
Pimpin' Ain't Easy *[Ice-T]*
Wreck *[Kool Keith & O.D.B.]*
You Ain't Hard *[Bad Azz & Techniec]*

10/26/96 | 184 | 2 | | ©600 World Wrestling Federation - Full Metal .... **$10** Edel America 8689

Angel
Bad Boy
Diesel Blues
Goldust
Graveyard Symphony
Hart Attack
Lyin' King
1-2-3
Psycho-Dance
Sexy Boy
Smokin'
Thorn In Your Eye
We're All Together Now
With My Baby Tonight

3/7/98 | 165 | 17 | ● | ©601 World Wrestling Federation - The Music Volume 2 .... **$10** Koch 8709

Can't Get Enough
Dangerous
Dark Side
Destiny
Dude Love
Hell Frozen Over
I Know You Want Me
Mastodon
Nation Of Domination
Ode To Freud
Pearl River Rip
Sexy Boy
Snap
Wild Cat
You Start The Fire

1/23/99 | 10 | 30 | ▲ | ©602 World Wrestling Federation - The Music Volume 3 .... **$10** Koch 8803

D-Generation X
Dude Love
Edge
Gangrel/The Brood
Kane
Ken Shamrock
New Age Outlaws
Oddities
Rock, The
Sable
Stone Cold Steve Austin
Undertaker
Val Venis
X-Pac

DEBUT	PEAK	WKS	RIAA	CD	ARTIST — Album Title	Catalog	Sym	$	Label & Number

11/20/99 | 4 | 22 | ▲ | ©603 — World Wrestling Federation - The Music Volume 4 — $10 | Koch 8808

AssMan	Danger At The Door	No Chance In Hell
Big	Know Your Role	Oh Hell Yeah
Blood Brother	Ministry	On The Edge
Break Down The Wall	My Time	Sexual Chocolate

This Is A Test
Wreck

3/10/01 | 2¹ | 15 | ● | ©604 — World Wrestling Federation - The Music Volume 5 — $10 | Smack Down! 8830

Bad Man	It Just Feels Right	Pie
Game, The	Latino Heat	Rowdy
I've Got It All	Medal	Shooter
If You Dare	Out Of The Fire	Turn It Up

What About Me?
Who I Am

12/9/95 | 144 | 14 | ▲ | ©605 — WOW 1996 — $15 | Sparrow 51516 [2]

Anchor Holds [Ray Boltz]	Count It All Joy [BeBe & CeCe Winans]	Great Lengths [PFR]
Biggest Part Of Me [Take 6]	Cry For Love [Michael W. Smith]	Heaven In The Real World [Steven Curtis Chapman]
Brother's Keeper [Rich Mullins]	Deep Calling Deep [Margaret Becker]	His Love Is Comin' Over Me [Clay Crosse]
Build My World Around You [Sandi Patty]	Don't Look Away [Bryan Duncan]	Home Run [Geoff Moore & The Distance]
Children Of The World [Amy Grant]	For Future Generations [4 Him]	I Wish We'd All Been Ready [DC Talk]
Class Of '95 [Wayne Watson]	Go Light Your World [Kathy Troccoli]	No Doubt [Petra]
Common Creed [Wes King]	God Is In Control [Twila Paris]	Send Out A Prayer [Anointed]
Concert Of The Age [Phillips, Craig & Dean]	Great Divide [Point Of Grace]	

Shine [Newsboys]
Stand [Susan Ashton]
Step Of Faith [Carman]
Sweet Days Of Grace [Cindy Morgan]
Taking My Time [Ashton, Becker, Denté]
True Believers [Phil Keaggy]
When Love Comes To Life [Out Of The Grey]

11/16/96 | 71 | 32 | ▲ | ©606 — WOW 1997 — $15 | Sparrow 51562 [2]

After The Rain [Aaron Jeoffrey]	Keep The Candle Burning [Point Of Grace]	Melodies From Heaven [Kirk Franklin and the Family]
After This Day Is Gone [Bryan Duncan]	Listen [Cindy Morgan]	Mercy Came Running [Phillips, Craig & Dean]
All Kinds Of People [Susan Ashton]	Lord Of The Dance [Steven Curtis Chapman]	Message, The [4 Him]
Anything [PFR]	Love Song For A Savior [Jars Of Clay]	More Than Gold [Geoff Moore & The Distance]
Between You And Me [DC Talk]	Love's Been Following You [Twila Paris]	Nothing At All [Third Day]
Every Time [CeCe Winans]	Man After Your Own Heart [Gary Chapman]	One Drop Of Blood [Ray Boltz]
God [Rebecca St. James]		Right Place [Petra]
I Know You Know [Sierra]		R.I.O.T. (Righteous Invasion Of Truth) [Carman]
I'll Lead You Home [Michael W. Smith]		

Sing Your Praise To The Lord [Rich Mullins]
Take Me To Your Leader [Newsboys]
Through It All [Wayne Watson]
Time To Believe [Clay Crosse]
True Devotion [Margaret Becker]
Under The Influence [Anointed]
Walk On Water [Audio Adrenaline]

11/22/97 | 52 | 30 | ▲ | ©607 — WOW 1998 — $15 | Sparrow 51629 [2]

Abba (Father) [Rebecca St. James]	Just One [Phillips, Craig & Dean]	My Utmost For His Highest [Twila Paris]
Adore You [Anointed]	Let Us Pray [Steven Curtis Chapman]	On My Way To Paradise [Bob Carlisle]
Breathe On Me [Sandi Patty]	Man Of God [Audio Adrenaline]	One Of Two [Gary Chapman]
Carry You [Amy Grant]	Measure Of A Man [4Him]	Overjoyed [Jars Of Clay]
Circle Of Friends [Point Of Grace]	Missing Person [Michael W. Smith]	People Get Ready...Jesus Is Comin' [Crystal Lewis]
Colored People [dc Talk]	Mission 3:16 [Carman]	Reality [Newsboys]
Disappear [Out Of The Grey]	More Than You Know [Out Of Eden]	Saving The World [Clay Crosse]
Give It Up [Avalon]	My Hope Is You [Third Day]	
Hope To Carry On [Caedmon's Call]		
I Call Him Love [Kathy Troccoli]		

Up Where We Belong [BeBe & CeCe]
We Can Make A Difference [Jaci Velasquez]
We Need Jesus [Petra]
Whisper Heard Around The World [Bryan Duncan]
You Move Me [Susan Ashton]

11/7/98 | 51 | 42 | ▲² | ©608 — WOW 1999 — $15 | Sparrow 51686 [2]

Agnus Dei [Third Day]	He Will Make A Way [Kathy Troccoli]	Little Man [Supertones]
Anything Genuine [Smalltown Poets]	Healing Waters [Michelle Tumes]	Lord I Believe In You [Crystal Lewis]
Can't Get Past The Evidence [4Him]	His Cheeseburger [Veggietales]	Lord Of The Eternity [Fernando Ortega]
Chevette [Audio Adrenaline]	I Will Not Go Quietly [Steven Curtis Chapman]	Love Me Good [Michael W. Smith]
Crazy Times [Jars Of Clay]	If You Really Knew [Out Of Eden]	Never Be [Carman]
Deeper [Delirious?]	In The Hands Of Jesus [Bob Carlisle]	Power Of A Moment [Chris Rice]
Devil Is Bad [The W's]	Into Jesus [DC Talk]	Pray [Rebecca St. James]
Entertaining Angels [Newsboys]	Light On The Hill [Máire Brennan]	Somewhere Down The Road [Amy Grant]
God So Loved [Jaci Velasquez]		Steady On [Point Of Grace]

Strollin' On The Water [Bryan Duncan]
Testify To Love [Avalon]
That Where I Am, There You... [Rich Mullins]
There Is A God [Natalie Grant]
To Know You [Nichole Nordeman]
Undo Me [Jennifer Knapp]
What Would Jesus Do? [Big Tent Revival]

8/7/99 | 84 | 19 | ▲ | ©609 — WOW - The 90s — $15 | Word 69975 [2]

Adonai [Avalon]	God So Loved The World [Jaci Velasquez]	Keep The Candle Burning [Point Of Grace]
Another Time, Another Place [Sandi Patti w/Wayne Watson]	Great Adventure [Steven Curtis Chapman]	Liquid [Jars Of Clay]
Awesome God [Rich Mullins]	Great Divide [Point Of Grace]	Lover Of My Soul [Amy Grant]
Basics Of Life [4Him]	I Surrender All [Clay Crosse]	My Will [DC Talk]
Crucified With Christ [Phillips, Craig & Dean]	I Will Be Here [Steven Curtis Chapman]	On My Knees [Jaci Velasquez]
Deep Enough To Dream [Chris Rice]	I Will Be Here For You [Michael W. Smith]	People Get Ready...Jesus Is Comin' [Crystal Lewis]
Everything Changes [Kathy Troccoli]	In Christ Alone [Michael English]	Place In This World [Michael W. Smith]
God Is In Control [Twila Paris]	Jesus Freak [DC Talk]	Serve The Lord [Carman]

Shine [Newsboys]
Sometimes By Step [Rich Mullins]
That's What Love Is For [Amy Grant]
Under The Influence [Anointed]
When God's People Pray [Wayne Watson]
Where There Is Faith [4Him]

11/13/99 | 29 | 37 | ▲² | ©610 — WOW 2000 — $15 | Sparrow 51703 [2]

Always And Forever [Raze]	For The Glory Of Your Name [Michelle Tumes]	I've Always Loved You [Third Day]
Away From You [O.C. Supertones]	Get Down [Audio Adrenaline]	It's Alright (Send Me) [Winans Phase2]
Basic Instructions [Burlap To Cashmere]	Gravity [Delirious?]	Little More [Jennifer Knapp]
Breathe [Sixpence None The Richer]	I Want To Know You (In The Secret) [Sonicflood]	Love Liberty Disco [Newsboys]
Can't Live A Day [Avalon]	I Will Be Your Friend [Michael W. Smith]	Nobody Loves Me Like You [Jars Of Clay]
Cartoons [Chris Rice]	I Will Follow Christ [Clay Crosse feat. BeBe Winans & Bob Carlisle]	Omega [Rebecca St. James]
Consume Me [DC Talk]		One Of These Days [FFH]
		Revive Us [Anointed]

River [Out Of Eden]
Rumor Weed Song [W's]
Run To You [Twila Paris]
Saving Grace [Point Of Grace]
Show You Love [Jaci Velasquez]
Speechless [Steven Curtis Chapman]
Stranded [Plumb]
Takes A Little Time [Amy Grant]
Thankful [Caedmon's Call]

VARIOUS ARTISTS COMPILATIONS

DEBUT	PEAK	WKS	RIAA	CD	ARTIST — Album Title	Catalog	Sym	$	Label & Number

11/18/00 — 36 — 36 ▲ — ©611 — WOW 2001 — $15 — Sparrow 51779 [2]

Alabaster Box [CeCe Winans] / Always Have, Always Will [Avalon] / America [Passion] / Beautiful Sound [Newsboys] / Crystal Clear [Jaci Velasquez] / Dive [Steven Curtis Chapman] / Don't Look At Me [Stacie Orrico] / Every Season [Nichole Nordeman] / Follow Your Dreams [Raze] / Free [Ginny Owens] / Gather At The River [Point Of Grace] / God Of Wonders [City On A Hill] / God You Are My God [Delirious?] / Hands And Feet [Audio Adrenaline] / I Am The Way [Mark Schultz] / Into You [Jennifer Knapp] / King Of Glory [Third Day] / Live For You [Rachael Lampa] / More Than You'll Ever Know [Watermark] / Only One [Caedmon's Call] / Reborn [Rebecca St. James] / Red Letters [DC Talk] / Redeemer [Nicole C. Mullen] / Set Your Eyes To Zion [P.O.D.] / Shackles (Praise You) [MaryMary] / This Good Day [Fernando Ortega] / This Is Your Time [Michael W. Smith] / Unforgetful You [Jars Of Clay] / When I Praise [FFH] / Written On My Heart [Plus One]

7/8/00 — 111 — 11 ● — ©612 — WOW Gold — $15 — Provident 10533 [2]

Awesome God [Rich Mullins] / Basics Of Life [4Him] / Beyond Belief [Petra] / Butterfly Kisses [Bob Carlisle] / Call, The [Anointed] / Champion, The [Carman] / Easter Song [2nd Chapter Of Acts] / Flood [Jars Of Clay] / For The Sake Of The Call [Steven Curtis Chapman] / Friends [Michael W. Smith] / God [Rebecca St. James] / He Is Exalted [Twila Paris] / I Could Sing Of Your Love Forever [Delirious?] / I'm Not Ashamed [Newsboys] / Love Bruke Thru [Phil Keaggy] / Love Takes Time [Bryan Duncan] / My Tribute [Andrae Crouch & The Disciples] / Praise The Lord [Imperials] / Rise Again [Dallas Holm & Praise] / Stomp [Kirk Franklin] / Testify To Love [Avalon] / Thank You [Ray Boltz] / Thy Word [Amy Grant] / To Hell With The Devil [Stryper] / Undivided [First Call] / We Shall Behold Him [Sandi Patty] / We Will Stand (You're My Brother, You're My Sister) [Russ Taff] / What If I Stumble? [DC Talk] / Why Should The Devil Have All The Good Music? [Larry Norman] / You Put This Love In My Heart [Keith Green]

2/14/98 — 100 — 16 ▲ — ©613 — WOW Gospel 1998 — $15 — Verity 43109 [2]

Battle Is The Lord's [Yolanda Adams] / Be Encouraged [William Becton & Friends] / Beyond The Veil [Daryl Coley] / Call, The [Anointed] / Crucified With Christ [Commissioned] / Every Time [CeCe Winans] / Glad I've Got Jesus [Canton Spirituals] / God Cares [Sounds Of Blackness] / Gotta Feelin' [O'Landa Draper & The Associates] / Greatest Part Of Me [Virtue] / He's An On Time God [Dottie Peoples] / Heaven [Shirley Caesar] / Helen's Testimony [Helen Baylor] / Holy Is The Lamb [Oleta Adams] / I've Got A Testimony [Rev. Clay Evans And The AARC Mass Choir] / Jesus Is My Help [Hezekiah Walker & The Love Fellowship Crusade Choir] / Jesus Paid It All [Mississippi Mass Choir Feat. Rev. James Moore] / Mother Sherman Story (We'll Understand It Better By And By) [Carlton Pearson] / No Weapon [Fred Hammond & Radical For Christ] / Not The Time, Not The Place [Marvin Sapp] / Order My Steps [GMWA Women Of Worship] / Shout [Rev. Milton Brunson & The Thompson Community Singers] / Speak To My Heart [Donnie McClurkin] / Stand! [Victory In Praise Music And Arts Seminar Mass Choir] / Stir Up '98 [Colorado Mass Choir Feat. Joe Pace] / Stomp [God's Property] / Stranger [Donald Lawrence And The Tri-City Singers] / Thank You Lord (He Did It All) [New Life Community Choir Feat. John P. Kee] / Total Praise [Richard Smallwood With Vision] / You Don't Have To Be Afraid [Take 6]

3/13/99 — 94 — 12 ● — ©614 — WOW Gospel 1999 — $15 — Verity 43125 [2]

Angels Watching Over Me [Virtue] / Balm In Gilead [Karen Clark-Sheard] / Clean Up [Canton Spirituals] / Don't Give Up On Jesus [Daryl Coley feat. Vanessa Bell Armstrong] / Follow Me [Maurette Brown Clark] / For Every Mountain [Kurt Carr Singers] / Give It Up [O'Landa Draper & The Associates] / Hold On (Change Is Comin') [Sounds Of Blackness] / I Believe [Angie & Debbie Winans] / I Will Bless The Lord [Pastor Hezekiah Walker Presents The LFT Church Choir] / I Will Love You [Oleta Adams] / I'm Too Close [Williams Brothers feat. Stevie Wonder] / If It Had Not Been For The Lord On My Side [Helen Baylor] / In Harm's Way [BeBe Winans] / Jesus I Won't Forget [Rev. Milton Brunson's Thompson Community Singers] / Just As Soon (I'll Be Shouting) [Beverly Crawford] / Let The Praise Begin [Fred Hammond & Radical For Christ] / Long As I Got King Jesus (Don't Need Nobody Else) [Vickie Winans] / Need To Know [Dawkins & Dawkins] / Only Believe [Yolanda Adams] / So Good [Colorado Mass Choir feat. Joe Pace] / Stand Up On Your Feet [Lamar Campbell & Spirit Of Praise] / Strength [New Life Community Choir feat. John P. Kee] / Testify [Dottie Peoples] / Under The Influence [Anointed] / Vision, The [Patrick Love & The A.L. Jinwright Mass Choir] / Well, Alright [CeCe Winans] / What A Friend [Bobby Jones & New Life] / When Will We Sing The Same Song? [Victory In Praise Music&ArtsSeminarMassChoir] / Worship Christ [New Direction] / You're Next In Line For A Miracle [Shirley Caesar] / You're The One [Darwin Hobbs]

2/26/00 — 93 — 11 ▲ — ©615 — WOW Gospel 2000 — $15 — Word 43149 [2]

Awesome God [Helen Baylor] / Caravan Of Love [Bob Carlisle/Marvin Sapp/Kirk Whalum] / Give Thanks [Marvin Sapp] / God Can [Dottie Peoples] / Goodtime [Brent Jones & The T.P. Mobb] / Hark The Herald Angels Sing [Donnie McClurkin] / Healing [Richard Smallwood w/Vision] / I Come To You More Than I Give [Kim Burrell] / I Know The Lord (medley) [Carlton Pearson] / I Made It [Canton Spirituals] / I'd Rather Have Jesus [Dallas Fort Worth Mass Choir] / In Your Will [Men Of Standard] / It's All About The Love [Lamar Campbell & Spirit Of Praise] / Jesus Is All [Fred Hammond] / Lighthouse [New Direction] / Mighty God [New Life Community Choir] / Never Seen The Righteous [Tri-City Singers] / Oh Happy Day [BeBe Winans] / Oh What A Friend [Montrel Darrett] / Power Belongs To God [Hezekiah Walker] / Put Your War Clothes On [Virtue] / Real With U [Tonéx] / Reminding The Saints Of The Hope (medley) [Carlton Pearson] / Revive Us [Anointed] / Safe In His Arms [Vickie Winans] / Secret Place [Darwin Hobbs] / Strong Man [Shirley Caesar] / Testify [Commissioned] / Unconditional Love [Tarralyn Ramsey] / We Worship You [Joe Pace] / Who Do You Love [Winans Phase 2] / Word Iz Bond [B.B.Jay] / Wrapped Up [Dawkins & Dawkins]

2/24/01 — 75 — 14 ● — ©616 — WOW Gospel 2001 — $15 — EMI 43163 [2]

Alabaster Box [CeCe Winans] / At The Table [Richard Smallwood] / Battlefield [Norman Hutchins] / Better Days [Wordd] / Closer [Lamar Campbell & Spirit Of Praise] / Everyday [Darwin Hobbs Feat. Michael McDonald] / Fall Down 2000 [Kelli Williams] / God's Favor [Tri-City Singers] / God's Got It [Joe Pace & The Colorado Mass Choir] / His Love [B.B. Jay] / Holy Place [Ricky Dillard & New G] / I Anoint Myself [PamKenyon M. Donald] / I Came To Jesus [New Direction] / I Want My Destiny [Fred Hammond & RFC] / I'll Keep Holding On [Kim Burrell] / If It Had Not Been For The Lord On My Side [Helen Baylor] / It's Alright (Send Me) [Winans Phase 2] / Let's Dance [Hezekiah Walker] / Mary Don't You Weep [Aaron Neville] / Memories (When Will I See You Again?) [Canton Spirituals] / Nothing Else Matters [Marvin Sapp] / Once [Londa Larmond] / Personal Jesus [Tonéx] / Real [Tommies] / Rejoice [Shirley Caesar] / Right Here [New Life Community Choir Feat. John P. Kee] / Shackles (Praise You) [Mary Mary] / Still I Rise [Yolanda Adams] / Tell It [Tarralyn Ramsey] / That'll Do It [Anointed] / Walk Right [Commissioned] / We Fall Down [Donnie McClurkin]

7/3/99 — 70 — 89 ▲² — ©617 — WOW Worship — $15 — Integrity 69974 [2]

Ancient Of Days / Blessed Be The Lord God Almighty / Blessed Be The Name Of The Lord / Change My Heart, Oh God / Come Into His Presence / Come Let Us Worship And Bow Down / Come, Now Is The Time To Worship / Father, I Adore You / Give Thanks / Heart Of Worship / I Could Sing Of Your Love Forever / I Love You Lord / I Will Celebrate / In His Time / Isn't He / Jesus Name Above All Names / Let It Rise / Let The River Flow / Lord, I Lift Your Name On High / Mighty Is Our God / More Love, More Power / More Precious Than Silver / My Life Is In You, Lord / Open Our Eyes / Open The Eyes Of My Heart / Refiner's Fire / River Is Here / Shout To The Lord / Take My Life / We Will Embrace Your Move

DEBUT	PEAK	WKS	RIAA	CD	ARTIST — Album Title	Catalog	Sym	$	Label & Number

4/7/01 · 78 · 20 · ©618 · WOW Worship Green ...... [ ] **$15** Integrity 19552 [2]

Agnus Dei [Michael W. Smith]
All Things Are Possible [Darlene Zschech]
Awesome In This Place [Dave Billington]
Breathe [Marie Barnett]
Come Just As You Are [Joseph Sabolick]
Cry Of My Heart [Terry Butler]
Doxology [Ken Thomas]
Draw Me Close [Kelly Carpenter]
Every Move I Make [David Ruis]
Fuel [Tom Wuest]
Good To Me [Craig Musseau]
Great Is The Lord [Michael W. Smith & Deborah Smith]
Hallelujah (Your Love Is Amazing) [Brenton Brown & Brian Doerksen]
He Is Exalted [Twila Paris]
He Knows My Name [Tommy Walker]
Hosanna [Carl Tuttle]
I Worship You Almighty God [Sondra Corbett Wood]
Jesus, Draw Me Close [Rick Founds]
Lord Reign In Me [Brenton Brown]
My Redeemer Lives [Reuben Morgan]
Power Of Your Love [Geoff Bullock]
Rise Up And Praise Him [Paul Baloche & Gary Sadler]
Seek Ye First [Karen Lafferty]
Shout To The North [Martin Smith]
That's Why We Praise Him [Tommy Walker]
Think About His Love [Walt Harrah]
This Is Love [Terry Butler & Mike Young]
To Him Who Sits On The Throne [Debbye Graafsma]
Trading My Sorrows [Darrell Evans]
Unashamed Love [Lamont Hiebert]
We Fall Down [Chris Tomlin]
Worthy, You Are Worthy [Don Moen]
You're Worthy Of My Praise [David Ruis]

4/15/00 · 65 · 33 · ▲ · ©619 · WOW Worship Orange ...... **$15** Integrity 63840 [2]

Above All [Lenny LeBlanc]
As The Deer [Maranatha! Singers]
Awesome God [Praise Band]
Better Is One Day [Charlie Hall]
Celebrate Jesus [Alleluia Singers]
Did You Feel The Mountain Tremble [Delirious?]
Glorify Thy Name [Maranatha! Singers]
God Is Good (All The Time) [Don Moen]
God Will Make A Way [Don Moen]
He Is Able [Praise Band]
Holy And Anointed One [Randy Butler]
Holy Ground [Geron Davis]
Hungry (Falling On My Knees) [Kathryn Scott]
I Believe In Jesus [Keith Matten]
I See The Lord [Chris Falson]
I Walk By Faith [Praise Band]
I Will Celebrate [Maranatha! Singers]
I Will Not Forget You [Praise Band]
In That Day [Praise Band]
In The Secret [Sonic Flood]
Jesus Is Alive [Ron Kenoly]
Jesus, Lover Of My Soul [Darlene Zschech]
Light The Fire Again [Brian Doerksen]
Redeemer, Savior, Friend [Dave Brooks]
Rock Of Ages [Praise Band]
Shine, Jesus, Shine [Graham Kendrick]
There Is None Like You [Lenny LeBlanc]
Victory Chant [Bob Fitts]
We Want To See Jesus Lifted High [Noel Richards]
We Will Dance [David Ruis]
When I Look Into Your Holiness [Kent Henry]
Worship You [Jami Smith]
You Are God [Scott Underwood]

11/30/85+ · 84 · 19 · ©620 · Wrestling Album, The ...... [N] **$10** Epic 40223

Captain Lou's History Of Music [Captain Lou Albano]
Cara Mia [Nikolai Volkoff]
Don't Go Messin' With A Country Boy [Hillbilly Jim]
Eat Your Hart Out Rick Springfield [Jimmy Hart]
For Everybody ["Rowdy" Roddy Piper]
Grab Them Cakes [Junk Yard Dog]
Hulk Hogan's Theme [WWF All Stars]
Land Of 1,000 Dances?!!? [Wrestlers]
Real American [Rick Derringer]
Tutti Frutti ["Mean" Gene Okerlund]

4/10/99 · 25 · 9 · ©621 · Wu-Tang Records Presents: Wu-Chronicles ...... **$10** Wu-Tang 51143

songs by Killarmy, Mobb Deep, Notorious B.I.G., Raekwon, and others
Black Trump [Cocoa Brovaz]
Cold World [Genius] **97**
End, The [Ras Kass]
4th Chamber [Genius]
Gunz 'N Onez [Heltah Skeltah]
Hip Hop Drunkies [Alkaholiks] **66**
Latunza Hit [Wu-Syndicate]
'96 Recreation [Cappadonna/RZA/Ol' Dirty Bastard]
Right Back At You [Mobb Deep]
Semi-Automatic: Full Rap Metal Jacket [Inspectah Deck/U-God/Streetlife]
Tragedy [RZA]
Wake Up [Killarmy]
What, The [Notorious B.I.G. & Method Man] flip
Whatever Happened (The Birth) [AZ]
Wu-Gambinos [Raekwon]
Young Godz [Shyheim]

12/13/97 · 182 · 2 · ©622 · WWJD ...... **$10** ForeFront 25183

Bag Lady [Audio Adrenaline]
Breathe [Newsboys]
Consequences [Considering Lily]
Downtown [Sarah Masen]
Epidermis Girl [Bleach]
Go And Sin No More [Rebecca St. James]
If You Let Me Love You [SmallTown Poets]
In Betweens [Geoff Moore & the Distance]
Only Natural [Steven Curtis Chapman]
Pain [Grammatrain]
Put The Blame On Me [Waiting]
Two Sets Of Jones' [Big Tent Revival]
What If I Stumble? [dc Talk]
What Would Jesus Do? [Big Tent Revival]
Whirlwind [Skillet]

10/14/67 · 165 · 5 · 623 · Yiddish Are Coming! The Yiddish Are Coming!, The ...... [C] **$15** Verve 15058

American In Paris
Back To School
Battle In The Desert
Command Headquarters
Commanding Officer
Gypsy Fortune Teller
Hello, Mama
Hello, Papa
Last Wish
Man With The Black Patch On His Eye
Meeting At The White House
Military Decision
Military Patrol
Mission Possible
Opening, The
Pvt. Goldberg, Volunteer
Sheldon, Sheldon, Sheldon
Tsuriss
Visit From The Press
Yiddish Are Coming! The Yiddish Are Coming!

10/23/99 · 173 · 2 · ©624 · YM Hot Tracks Vol. 1 ...... **$10** Damian 12227

As Long As You Love Me [Backstreet Boys]
Baby Can I Hold You [Boyzone]
Because We Want To [Billie]
Hardest Thing [98°] **5**
Harmless [Mulberry Lane] **99**
It's The Things You Do [Five] **53**
Keep My Heart In Mind [Don Philip]
Kiss Me [Sixpence None The Richer] **3**
Love U More [Steps]
My First Night With You [Mya] **28**
Nobody Else [Tyrese] **36**
Sailing [*NSync]
Until You Loved Me [Moffats]
We Like To Party! [Vengaboys] **26**
When I Close My Eyes [Shanice] **12**

7/12/97 · 88 · 8 · ©625 · Yo! MTV Raps ...... **$10** Def Jam 534746

C.R.E.A.M. [Wu-Tang Clan] **60**
Crossroads, Tha [Bone thugs-n-harmony] **1**
Elevators [OutKast] **12**
Get Me Home [Foxy Brown Feat. BLACKstreet]
Get Money [Junior M.A.F.I.A.] **17**
I Get Around [2 Pac] **11**
Jeeps, Lex Coups, Bimaz & Benz [Lost Boyz] **67**
Loungin [LL Cool J] **3**
No Time [Lil' Kim Feat. Puff Daddy] **18**
1nce Again [Tribe Called Quest]
Riddler, The [Method Man] **56**
Runnin' [Pharcyde] **55**

9/18/65 · 9 · 34 · ©626 · You Don't Have To Be Jewish ...... [C] **$15** Kapp 4503

Agony And The Ecstasy
Call From Long Island
Cocktail Party
Conversation In The Hotel Lobby
Convicts, The
Diamond, The
Enough Already With The Quickies
Final Discussion
Goldstein
Home From The Office
Housewarming, The
Jury, The
Luncheon, The
More Quickies
My Son, The Captain
Presidents, The
Quickies
Reading Of The Will
Secret Agent, James Bondstein
Still More Quickies

7/15/67 · 118 · 9 · 627 · Zodiac: Cosmic Sounds, The ...... **$15** Elektra 74009

Aquarius - The Lover of Life
Aries - The Fire-Fighter
Cancer - The Moon Child
Capricorn - The Uncapricious Climber
Gemini - The Cool Eye
Leo - The Lord of Lights
Libra - The Flower Child
Pisces - The Peace Piper
Sagittarius - The Versatile Daredevil
Scorpio - The Passionate Hero
Taurus - The Voluptuary
Virgo - The Perpetual Perfectionist

TOP ARTISTS

The Top 500 Album Artists Ranking From 1955-2001

Point System:

Next to each artist's name is their point total. The points are totaled through the September 29, 2001, chart. Each artist's points are accumulated according to the following formula:

1. Highest chart position each album reached on *Billboard's* main Pop Albums chart:

#1	=	200 points for its first week at #1, plus 20 points for each additional week at #1
#2	=	190 points for its first week at #2, plus 10 points for each additional week at #2
#3	=	180 points for its first week at #3, plus 5 points for each additional week at #3

#4-5	=	170 points	#91-100	=	110 points
#6-10	=	160 points	#101-110	=	100 points
#11-15	=	155 points	#111-120	=	90 points
#16-20	=	150 points	#121-130	=	80 points
#21-30	=	145 points	#131-140	=	70 points
#31-40	=	140 points	#141-150	=	60 points
#41-50	=	135 points	#151-160	=	50 points
#51-60	=	130 points	#161-170	=	40 points
#61-70	=	125 points	#171-180	=	30 points
#71-80	=	120 points	#181-190	=	20 points
#81-90	=	115 points	#191-200	=	10 points

2. Highest chart position each album reached on *Billboard's* Top Pop Catalog Albums chart and special Christmas Albums chart <u>exclusively</u> (not included if album also made *Billboard's* main Pop Albums chart):

$$\#1 \quad = \quad \text{50 points for its first week at \#1, plus 5 points for each additional week at \#1}$$

$$\#2 \quad = \quad \text{45 points for its first week at \#2, plus 3 points for each additional week at \#2}$$

$$\#3 \quad = \quad \text{40 points for its first week at \#3, plus 2 points for each additional week at \#3}$$

#4-5	=	35 points	#21-30	=	15 points
#6-10	=	30 points	#31-40	=	10 points
#11-15	=	25 points	#41-50	=	5 points
#16-20	=	20 points	#51-75	=	3 points

3. Total weeks charted (includes <u>all</u> weeks charted on the Top Pop Catalog Albums chart; does <u>not</u> include weeks charted on the special Christmas Albums chart if the album also made the Top 200 Albums chart).

Christmas albums are awarded points for their peak position for their <u>first</u> chart appearance only. Their seasonal re-entries are awarded points for their weeks charted only.

In the case of a tie, the artist listed first is determined by the following tie-breaker rules:

1) Most charted albums   2) Most Top 40 albums   3) Most Top 10 albums

When two artists combine for a hit album, such as Kenny Rogers and Dolly Parton, the full point value is given to both artists. Duos, such as Simon & Garfunkel, Hall & Oates, and Brooks & Dunn, are considered regular recording teams, and their points are not shared by either artist individually.

Headings And Special Symbols:

Old Rank: Artist ranking in *Top Pop Albums 1955-1996* book

New Rank: Artist ranking in *Top Pop Albums 1955-2001* book

● **Deceased Solo Artist**

■ **Deceased Group Member**
The total number of square symbols indicates the total number of deceased members.

★ **Hot Artist**
Hot artists charted a Top 10 Album since the previous edition.
(Greatest Hits, Compilations, Catalog and Christmas albums do not qualify.)

+ Subject to change since an album is still charted as of the 9/29/01 cut-off date.

Old Rank	New Rank		Points
(184)	118.	Lynyrd Skynyrd ■■■■■	3,062
(192)	119.	Bob Marley ●	3,055
(139)★	120.	Cher	3,054
(116)	121.	Donna Summer	3,027
(115)	122.	Olivia Newton-John	3,025
(108)	123.	Bobby Vinton	3,023
(107)	124.	Percy Faith ●	3,009
(104)	125.	Alice Cooper	3,004
(137)	126.	Bette Midler	3,003
(106)	127.	Connie Francis	3,002
(177)★	128.	John Cougar Mellencamp	3,002
(132)	129.	Black Sabbath	2,978
(109)	130.	Peter, Paul & Mary	2,969
(266)★	131.	Steely Dan	2,953
(118)	132.	George Benson	2,944
(113)	133.	Jimmy Smith	2,942
(143)	134.	Natalie Cole	2,938
(114)	135.	Al Hirt ●	2,912
(180)★	136.	R.E.M.	2,905
(125)	137.	The O'Jays ■	2,904
(136)	138.	Heart	2,896
(157)★	139.	B.B. King	2,893
(117)	140.	Grand Funk Railroad	2,860
(123)	141.	Lou Rawls	2,839
(237)★	142.	Mariah Carey	2,834
(164)	143.	Emmylou Harris	2,822
(156)	144.	Barry White	2,810
(122)	145.	Chubby Checker	2,809
(126)	146.	The Doobie Brothers ■	2,779
(149)	147.	Simon & Garfunkel	2,773
(128)	148.	Kool & The Gang	2,765
(129)	149.	Commodores	2,760
(159)	150.	ZZ Top	2,759
(130)	151.	Deep Purple ■	2,741
(244)★	152.	Reba McEntire	2,738
(131)	153.	Tom Jones	2,736
(194)	154.	Def Leppard ■	2,727
(221)★	155.	Whitney Houston	2,727
(217)★	156.	Bon Jovi	2,722
(134)	157.	Grover Washington, Jr. ●	2,720
(276)★	158.	Kenny G	2,711
(208)★	159.	Luther Vandross	2,701
(135)	160.	Bob James	2,690
(416)★	161.	Pearl Jam	2,674
(140)	162.	War ■■	2,655
(161)	163.	The Righteous Brothers	2,648
(141)	164.	Three Dog Night	2,631
(160)	165.	Al Green	2,620
(145)	166.	George Harrison	2,602
(165)	167.	Bonnie Raitt	2,600
(142)	168.	Dave Brubeck	2,598
(144)	169.	Roberta Flack	2,584
(234)	170.	Dan Fogelberg	2,577
(151)	171.	Bert Kaempfert ●	2,575
(146)	172.	Poco	2,575
(182)	173.	Styx ■	2,568
(152)	174.	Pat Boone	2,565
(155)	175.	Electric Light Orchestra	2,550
(174)	176.	Quincy Jones	2,543
(185)	177.	Crosby, Stills & Nash (& Young)	2,541

Old Rank	New Rank		Points
(150)	178.	Donovan	2,536
(235)	179.	Gloria Estefan	2,525
(179)	180.	Ozzy Osbourne	2,499
(204)	181.	Paul Simon	2,490
(153)	182.	Engelbert Humperdinck	2,482
(154)	183.	REO Speedwagon	2,480
(166)	184.	Smokey Robinson	2,450
(163)	185.	Brenda Lee	2,441
(264)	186.	Phil Collins	2,437
(258)	187.	Jeff Beck	2,432
(187)	188.	Carpenters ■	2,420
(197)	189.	Steppenwolf ■	2,416
— ★	190.	2Pac ●	2,413 +
(158)	191.	The Band ■■	2,411
(190)	192.	Cat Stevens	2,408
(193)	193.	Miles Davis ●	2,396
(199)	194.	The Police	2,395
(162)	195.	Judy Collins	2,394
(383)★	196.	Alan Jackson	2,390 +
(167)	197.	Joe Cocker	2,377
(172)	198.	Jackie Gleason ●	2,373
(168)	199.	Lou Reed	2,371
(176)	200.	Robert Goulet	2,358
(169)	201.	J. Geils Band	2,342
(211)	202.	Duran Duran	2,341
(171)	203.	Johnny Rivers	2,336
(238)	204.	Patti LaBelle/LaBelle	2,335
(170)	205.	Peter Nero	2,333
(363)★	206.	Beastie Boys	2,330
(173)	207.	The 5th Dimension ■	2,328
(175)	208.	The Crusaders	2,302
(178)	209.	America	2,300
(181)	210.	Ohio Players ■	2,290
(183)	211.	The Byrds ■■■	2,254
(186)	212.	Sergio Mendes/Brasil '66	2,243
(227)	213.	Spyro Gyra	2,241
(191)	214.	Ricky Nelson ●	2,237
(195)	215.	Pat Benatar	2,237
(188)	216.	Earl Klugh	2,235
(189)	217.	Herbie Mann	2,233
(239)	218.	Randy Travis	2,231
(281)	219.	Michael Bolton	2,231
(243)	220.	Iron Maiden	2,219
(225)	221.	Cheap Trick	2,201
(312)★	222.	Mötley Crüe	2,200
— ★	223.	Celine Dion	2,196
(247)	224.	The Guess Who ■	2,190
(196)	225.	Pointer Sisters	2,188
(228)	226.	Jackson Browne	2,181
(200)	227.	Emerson, Lake & Palmer	2,170
(207)	228.	Foreigner	2,167
(205)	229.	Jerry Vale	2,164
(198)	230.	Trini Lopez	2,161
(203)	231.	Eddy Arnold	2,159
(283)	232.	Kenny Loggins	2,146
(231)	233.	Bad Company	2,145
(201)	234.	Otis Redding ●	2,143
(202)	235.	Cameo	2,138
(222)	236.	Teddy Pendergrass	2,137

Old Rank	New Rank		Points
(184)	118.	Lynyrd Skynyrd ■■■■■	3,062
(192)	119.	Bob Marley ●	3,055
(139)★	120.	Cher	3,054
(116)	121.	Donna Summer	3,027
(115)	122.	Olivia Newton-John	3,025
(108)	123.	Bobby Vinton	3,023
(107)	124.	Percy Faith ●	3,009
(104)	125.	Alice Cooper	3,004
(137)	126.	Bette Midler	3,003
(106)	127.	Connie Francis	3,002
(177)★	128.	John Cougar Mellencamp	3,002
(132)	129.	Black Sabbath	2,978
(109)	130.	Peter, Paul & Mary	2,969
(266)★	131.	Steely Dan	2,953
(118)	132.	George Benson	2,944
(113)	133.	Jimmy Smith	2,942
(143)	134.	Natalie Cole	2,938
(114)	135.	Al Hirt ●	2,912
(180)★	136.	R.E.M.	2,905
(125)	137.	The O'Jays ■	2,904
(136)	138.	Heart	2,896
(157)★	139.	B.B. King	2,893
(117)	140.	Grand Funk Railroad	2,860
(123)	141.	Lou Rawls	2,839
(237)★	142.	Mariah Carey	2,834
(164)	143.	Emmylou Harris	2,822
(156)	144.	Barry White	2,810
(122)	145.	Chubby Checker	2,809
(126)	146.	The Doobie Brothers ■	2,779
(149)	147.	Simon & Garfunkel	2,773
(128)	148.	Kool & The Gang	2,765
(129)	149.	Commodores	2,760
(159)	150.	ZZ Top	2,759
(130)	151.	Deep Purple ■	2,741
(244)★	152.	Reba McEntire	2,738
(131)	153.	Tom Jones	2,736
(194)	154.	Def Leppard ■	2,727
(221)★	155.	Whitney Houston	2,727
(217)★	156.	Bon Jovi	2,722
(134)	157.	Grover Washington, Jr. ●	2,720
(276)★	158.	Kenny G	2,711
(208)★	159.	Luther Vandross	2,701
135)	160.	Bob James	2,690
116)★	161.	Pearl Jam	2,674
40)	162.	War ■■	2,655
61)	163.	The Righteous Brothers	2,648
41)	164.	Three Dog Night	2,631
50)	165.	Al Green	2,620
5)	166.	George Harrison	2,602
5)	167.	Bonnie Raitt	2,600
?)	168.	Dave Brubeck	2,598
)	169.	Roberta Flack	2,584
)	170.	Dan Fogelberg	2,577
	171.	Bert Kaempfert ●	2,575
	172.	Poco	2,575
	173.	Styx ■	2,568
	174.	Pat Boone	2,565
	175.	Electric Light Orchestra	2,550
	176.	Quincy Jones	2,543
	177.	Crosby, Stills & Nash (& Young)	2,541

Old Rank	New Rank		Points
(150)	178.	Donovan	2,536
(235)	179.	Gloria Estefan	2,525
(179)	180.	Ozzy Osbourne	2,499
(204)	181.	Paul Simon	2,490
(153)	182.	Engelbert Humperdinck	2,482
(154)	183.	REO Speedwagon	2,480
(166)	184.	Smokey Robinson	2,450
(163)	185.	Brenda Lee	2,441
(264)	186.	Phil Collins	2,437
(258)	187.	Jeff Beck	2,432
(187)	188.	Carpenters ■	2,420
(197)	189.	Steppenwolf ■	2,416
— ★	190.	2Pac ●	2,413 +
(158)	191.	The Band ■■	2,411
(190)	192.	Cat Stevens	2,408
(193)	193.	Miles Davis ●	2,396
(199)	194.	The Police	2,395
(162)	195.	Judy Collins	2,394
(383)★	196.	Alan Jackson	2,390 +
(167)	197.	Joe Cocker	2,377
(172)	198.	Jackie Gleason ●	2,373
(168)	199.	Lou Reed	2,371
(176)	200.	Robert Goulet	2,358
(169)	201.	J. Geils Band	2,342
(211)	202.	Duran Duran	2,341
(171)	203.	Johnny Rivers	2,336
(238)	204.	Patti LaBelle/LaBelle	2,335
(170)	205.	Peter Nero	2,333
(363)★	206.	Beastie Boys	2,330
(173)	207.	The 5th Dimension ■	2,328
(175)	208.	The Crusaders	2,302
(178)	209.	America	2,300
(181)	210.	Ohio Players ■	2,290
(183)	211.	The Byrds ■■■	2,254
(186)	212.	Sergio Mendes/Brasil '66	2,243
(227)	213.	Spyro Gyra	2,241
(191)	214.	Ricky Nelson ●	2,237
(195)	215.	Pat Benatar	2,237
(188)	216.	Earl Klugh	2,235
(189)	217.	Herbie Mann	2,233
(239)	218.	Randy Travis	2,231
(281)	219.	Michael Bolton	2,231
(243)	220.	Iron Maiden	2,219
(225)	221.	Cheap Trick	2,201
(312)★	222.	Mötley Crüe	2,200
— ★	223.	Celine Dion	2,196
(247)	224.	The Guess Who ■	2,190
(196)	225.	Pointer Sisters	2,188
(228)	226.	Jackson Browne	2,181
(200)	227.	Emerson, Lake & Palmer	2,170
(207)	228.	Foreigner	2,167
(205)	229.	Jerry Vale	2,164
(198)	230.	Trini Lopez	2,161
(203)	231.	Eddy Arnold	2,159
(283)	232.	Kenny Loggins	2,146
(231)	233.	Bad Company	2,145
(201)	234.	Otis Redding ●	2,143
(202)	235.	Cameo	2,138
(222)	236.	Teddy Pendergrass	2,137

Old Rank	New Rank		Points
(206)	237.	The Animals ■	2,134
(230)	238.	Alan Parsons Project	2,130
(214)	239.	Chet Atkins	2,121
(233)	240.	Pat Metheny Group	2,117
(209)	241.	Ted Nugent	2,114
(378)	242.	Stevie Ray Vaughan ●	2,111
(218)	243.	Boston Pops Orchestra	2,105
(210)	244.	Gordon Lightfoot	2,102
(212)	245.	Chuck Mangione	2,097
(213)	246.	Leon Russell	2,089
(215)	247.	Spinners ■	2,081
(350)	248.	Vince Gill	2,081
(219)	249.	Peggy Lee	2,080
—	★250.	Dave Matthews Band	2,079 +
(220)	251.	Herbie Hancock	2,074
(216)	252.	Kris Kristofferson	2,073
—	253.	Yanni	2,072
(224)	254.	Roy Orbison ●	2,070
(232)	255.	"Tennessee" Ernie Ford ●	2,063
(355)	★256.	Depeche Mode	2,063
(229)	257.	Paul Revere And The Raiders ■	2,061
(223)	258.	Dave Clark Five	2,055
(242)	259.	John Gary ●	2,036
(336)	★260.	Janet Jackson	2,035 +
(226)	261.	Paul Anka	2,032
(344)	262.	Guns N' Roses	2,026
(241)	263.	Charley Pride	2,025
(267)	264.	Joe Jackson	2,018
(236)	265.	John Mayall	2,009
(304)	266.	The Cure	1,995
(240)	267.	Bobby Darin ●	1,992
(246)	268.	Merle Haggard	1,991
(245)	269.	Traffic ■	1,984
(249)	270.	Jack Jones	1,969
(280)	271.	George Michael/Wham!	1,965
(260)	272.	Curtis Mayfield ●	1,963
(253)	273.	Talking Heads	1,963
(255)	274.	Blue Öyster Cult	1,957
(320)	275.	Harry Connick, Jr.	1,951
(248)	276.	Dire Straits	1,947
(261)	277.	Peter Gabriel	1,934
(259)	278.	Scorpions	1,933
(250)	279.	Stephen Stills	1,931
(251)	280.	The Marshall Tucker Band ■ ■	1,926
(252)	281.	Kansas	1,922
(256)	282.	Seals & Crofts	1,918
(296)	283.	Judas Priest	1,916
(254)	284.	Peabo Bryson	1,911
(358)	285.	Sammy Hagar	1,907
—	★286.	Brooks & Dunn	1,904 +
(305)	287.	INXS ■	1,902
(399)	288.	Dwight Yoakam	1,873
(284)	289.	Abba	1,863
(263)	290.	The Whispers	1,858
(275)	291.	Al Jarreau	1,848
(302)	292.	Donny Osmond	1,844
(268)	293.	Eydie Gorme	1,842
(362)	★294.	Sting	1,817
(262)	295.	Rick James	1,815
(272)	296.	David Sanborn	1,811
(265)	297.	Robin Trower	1,811

Old Rank	New Rank		Points
(269)	298.	Jerry Lee Lewis	1,802
(270)	299.	Dave Mason	1,798
(341)	300.	Boz Scaggs	1,790
(469)	★301.	LL Cool J	1,787
(273)	302.	Sammy Davis, Jr. ●	1,786
(271)	303.	Blood, Sweat & Tears	1,786
(289)	304.	Cream	1,783
(274)	305.	Herman's Hermits ■	1,783
(294)	306.	Steve Winwood	1,776
(300)	307.	Charlie Daniels Band	1,774
(277)	308.	The Impressions ■	1,758
(352)	309.	Bryan Adams	1,757
(278)	310.	Sonny & Cher ■	1,751
(279)	311.	Robert Palmer	1,749
(291)	312.	The New Christy Minstrels	1,746
(331)	313.	The Pretenders ■ ■	1,738
(282)	314.	The Manhattan Transfer	1,734
(285)	315.	Foghat ■	1,732
(287)	316.	The Mamas & The Papas ■ ■	1,723
(286)	317.	Peter Frampton	1,722
(455)	★318.	Ice Cube	1,715
—	319.	Enya	1,712 +
(309)	320.	Loggins & Messina	1,709
(288)	321.	Petula Clark	1,708
(452)	★322.	Amy Grant	1,707
(290)	323.	Johnny Winter	1,706
—	★324.	Megadeth	1,704
(295)	325.	Helen Reddy	1,704
(297)	326.	Rufus Featuring Chaka Khan	1,701
(292)	327.	Melissa Manchester	1,699
(460)	328.	Janis Joplin ●	1,694
(293)	329.	Bar-Kays ■ ■ ■ ■	1,692
—	330.	Trisha Yearwood	1,692 +
(298)	331.	Joe Walsh	1,688
(483)	332.	Clint Black	1,687
(332)	333.	Rick Springfield	1,685
(396)	334.	Nirvana ■	1,684
(299)	335.	Supertramp	1,683
(301)	336.	Rita Coolidge	1,680
(303)	337.	Ten Years After	1,675
(306)	338.	Judy Garland ●	1,661
—	★339.	Tim McGraw	1,656 +
(427)	340.	Queensrÿche	1,655
(307)	341.	Pete Fountain	1,654
(347)	342.	Eurythmics	1,653
(313)	343.	Weather Report	1,649
(308)	344.	Todd Rundgren	1,647
(442)	★345.	Sade	1,638
(317)	346.	Ronnie Milsap	1,637
(311)	347.	Moms Mabley ●	1,637
—	★348.	Boyz II Men	1,634
—	349.	Selena ●	1,627
(316)	350.	King Crimson	1,627
(314)	351.	The Limeliters ■	1,624
(315)	352.	Maze Featuring Frankie Beverly	1,619
(318)	353.	Uriah Heep ■ ■	1,604
(319)	354.	Wilson Pickett	1,603
(414)	355.	Travis Tritt	1,601 +
(491)	356.	Alice In Chains	1,600
(321)	357.	The Rascals	1,598

Old Rank	New Rank		Points
(440)	★358.	Stevie Nicks	1,594 +
(405)	359.	Pet Shop Boys	1,585
(328)	360.	The Cars	1,581
(323)	361.	Nilsson	1,575
(325)	362.	Ray Parker Jr./Raydio	1,574
(322)	363.	Ashford & Simpson	1,573
(326)	364.	The Hollies	1,564
(324)	365.	Procol Harum	1,564
(327)	366.	The Smothers Brothers	1,563
—	367.	Mannheim Steamroller	1,561
(389)	368.	Lionel Richie	1,559
(329)	369.	AWB (Average White Band)	1,547
(330)	370.	Sam Cooke	1,545
(377)	371.	Billy Idol	1,545
—	★372.	The Smashing Pumpkins	1,543
(333)	373.	John McLaughlin	1,540
(477)	★374.	Too $hort	1,538
(374)	375.	The B-52's	1,533
(334)	376.	Nazareth	1,530
(335)	377.	George Thorogood	1,528
(338)	378.	Bachman-Turner Overdrive	1,526
(337)	379.	Little River Band	1,522
(342)	380.	The Osmonds	1,519
(339)	381.	The Association	1,514
(340)	382.	Joan Armatrading	1,513
(402)	★383.	Robert Plant	1,510
(357)	384.	The Chipmunks	1,504
(343)	385.	Bobby Womack	1,500
(476)	386.	Tina Turner	1,499
(351)	387.	The Stylistics	1,495
(345)	388.	George Duke	1,492
(348)	389.	Bread	1,489
(346)	390.	Duane Eddy	1,487
(349)	391.	Allan Sherman	1,481
(354)	392.	Tammy Wynette	1,472
(359)	393.	Eddie Money	1,464
(353)	394.	The James Gang	1,463
(420)	395.	The Judds	1,460
(356)	396.	M.C. Hammer	1,460
—	397.	The Black Crowes	1,452
—	398.	John Michael Montgomery	1,451
(379)	399.	UB40	1,445
(360)	400.	Stephanie Mills	1,440
(361)	401.	Millie Jackson	1,439
(430)	402.	Booker T. & The MG's	1,430
—	★403.	Nine Inch Nails	1,427
(364)	404.	Little Feat	1,426
—	★405.	LeAnn Rimes	1,424
(369)	406.	Sly & The Family Stone	1,420
(365)	407.	Gene Pitney	1,419
(366)	408.	Charlie Rich	1,417
(368)	409.	Tower Of Power	1,415
—	410.	Lorrie Morgan	1,415
(392)	411.	Toto	1,415
(418)	412.	Ringo Starr	1,414
(471)	413.	"Weird Al" Yankovic	1,411
(367)	414.	Jean-Luc Ponty	1,410
(370)	415.	Eddie Harris	1,407
(371)	416.	Nitty Gritty Dirt Band	1,407
(372)	417.	Jermaine Jackson	1,406

Old Rank	New Rank		Points
(373)	418.	Dawn Featuring Tony Orlando	1,404
—	419.	EPMD	1,404
(376)	420.	Richard Pryor	1,402
(375)	421.	Con Funk Shun	1,398
—	★422.	Keith Sweat	1,398
—	★423.	Snoop Doggy Dogg	1,393
(381)	424.	Nancy Sinatra	1,390
(394)	425.	Ella Fitzgerald	1,387
—	426.	Meat Loaf	1,386
(380)	427.	Harry Chapin	1,385
(382)	428.	Bob Newhart	1,385
—	429.	John Fitzgerald Kennedy	1,383
(385)	430.	Outlaws	1,381
(384)	431.	Rainbow	1,381
—	★432.	Bone Thugs-N-Harmony	1,380
—	★433.	Red Hot Chili Peppers	1,377
(398)	434.	Ed Ames	1,374
(388)	435.	Bobby Vee	1,374
(421)	436.	Anthrax	1,373
—	437.	Indigo Girls	1,371
(386)	438.	Larry Graham/Graham Central Station	1,369
(387)	439.	Funkadelic	1,368
(403)	440.	Huey Lewis & the News	1,362
(390)	441.	38 Special	1,360
—	442.	Joe Satriani	1,357
(397)	443.	Triumph	1,353
(391)	444.	Pete Townshend	1,352
(393)	445.	Canned Heat	1,349
(467)	446.	Erasure	1,347
(395)	447.	New Kids On The Block	1,342
(400)	448.	Atlanta Rhythm Section	1,339
—	★449.	Cypress Hill	1,339
(401)	450.	Cheech & Chong	1,333
(472)	451.	Julio Iglesias	1,327
(404)	452.	Stanley Turrentine	1,324
(475)	453.	Chaka Khan	1,320
—	454.	Poison	1,318
(406)	455.	The Brothers Four	1,315
(429)	456.	José Feliciano	1,310
(407)	457.	Roy Ayers	1,309
(408)	458.	Rusty Warren	1,309
(450)	459.	Jim Nabors	1,308
(412)	460.	Vikki Carr	1,308
(413)	461.	Sheena Easton	1,308
(409)	462.	Billy Preston	1,307
(410)	463.	Manfred Mann	1,306
(411)	464.	Jan & Dean	1,305
—	465.	Blondie	1,305
(415)	466.	Jim Croce	1,296
(419)	467.	Parliament	1,294
(490)	468.	Run-D.M.C.	1,293
—	★469.	New Edition	1,293
—	470.	Melissa Etheridge	1,293
(417)	471.	Arlo Guthrie	1,289
(449)	472.	Doris Day	1,289
(439)	473.	Mario Lanza	1,285
(423)	474.	Oak Ridge Boys	1,284
(424)	475.	Humble Pie	1,282
—	476.	Collin Raye	1,282

Old Rank	New Rank		Points		Old Rank	New Rank		Points
(473)	477.	Johnnie Taylor	●......1,280		(433)	489.	Teena Marie	1,260
(422)	478.	Stanley Clarke	1,280		—	490.	Boston	1,260
(464)	479.	The Partridge Family	1,279		(435)	491.	Atlantic Starr	1,256
(425)	480.	Wes Montgomery	●.....1,278		(437)	492.	Graham Nash	1,254
(426)	481.	Rare Earth	■■■.1,278		(445)	493.	Mac Davis	1,253
(434)	482.	Boots Randolph	1,277		(478)	494.	Count Basie	●.....1,251
—	483.	George Winston	1,275		(438)	495.	Loretta Lynn	1,250
(487)	484.	Rickie Lee Jones	1,274		(441)	496.	Jerry Butler	1,245
(428)	485.	Crystal Gayle	1,271		(443)	497.	Quicksilver Messenger Service	■..1,244
(431)	486.	The Everly Brothers	1,265		(448)	498.	The Gap Band	1,244
(436)	487.	Pure Prairie League	1,263		(444)	499.	Ramones	■..1,243
(432)	488.	Utopia	1,261		(446)	500.	Deniece Williams	1,242

A-Z — TOP 500 ARTISTS

Parsons, Alan, Project	238	Rufus Featuring Chaka Khan	326	Too $hort	374
Parton, Dolly	87	Rundgren, Todd	344	Toto	411
Partridge Family, The	479	Run-D.M.C.	468	Tower Of Power	409
Pearl Jam	161	Rush	74	Townshend, Pete	444
Pendergrass, Teddy	236	Russell, Leon	246	Traffic	269
Peter, Paul & Mary	130	Sade	345	Travis, Randy	218
Pet Shop Boys	359	Sanborn, David	296	Tritt, Travis	355
Petty, Tom, And The Heartbreakers	92	Santana	60	Triumph	443
Pickett, Wilson	354	Satriani, Joe	442	Trower, Robin	297
Pink Floyd	25	Scaggs, Boz	300	Turner, Tina	386
Pitney, Gene	407	Scorpions	278	Turrentine, Stanley	452
Plant, Robert	383	Seals & Crofts	282	2Pac	190
Poco	172	Seger, Bob	107	UB40	399
Pointer Sisters	225	Selena	349	Uriah Heep	353
Poison	454	Sherman, Allan	391	Utopia	488
Police, The	194	Simon, Carly	100	U2	71
Ponty, Jean-Luc	414	Simon, Paul	181	Vale, Jerry	229
Presley, Elvis	1	Simon & Garfunkel	147	Vandross, Luther	159
Preston, Billy	462	Sinatra, Frank	2	Van Halen	104
Pretenders, The	313	Sinatra, Nancy	424	Vaughan, Stevie Ray	242
Pride, Charley	263	Sly & The Family Stone	406	Vaughn, Billy	40
Prince	27	Smashing Pumpkins, The	372	Vee, Bobby	435
Procol Harum	365	Smith, Jimmy	133	Ventures, The	37
Pryor, Richard	420	Smothers Brothers, The	366	Vinton, Bobby	123
Pure Prairie League	487	Snoop Doggy Dogg	423	Walsh, Joe	331
Queen	63	Sonny & Cher	310	War	162
Queensrÿche	340	Spinners	247	Warren, Rusty	458
Quicksilver Messenger Service	497	Springfield, Rick	333	Warwick, Dionne	49
Rainbow	431	Springsteen, Bruce	65	Washington, Grover Jr.	157
Raitt, Bonnie	167	Spyro Gyra	213	Weather Report	343
Ramones	499	Starr, Ringo	412	Welk, Lawrence	18
Randolph, Boots	482	Steely Dan	131	Whispers, The	290
Rare Earth	481	Steppenwolf	189	White, Barry	144
Rascals, The	357	Stevens, Cat	192	Who, The	53
Rawls, Lou	141	Stewart, Rod	31	Williams, Andy	17
Raye, Collin	476	Stills, Stephen	279	Williams, Deniece	500
Redding, Otis	234	Sting	294	Williams, Hank Jr.	111
Reddy, Helen	325	Strait, George	78	Williams, Roger	34
Red Hot Chili Peppers	433	Streisand, Barbra	5	Wilson, Nancy	59
Reed, Lou	199	Stylistics, The	387	Winston, George	483
R.E.M.	136	Styx	173	Winter, Johnny	323
REO Speedwagon	183	Summer, Donna	121	Winwood, Steve	306
Revere, Paul, And The Raiders	275	Supertramp	335	Womack, Bobby	385
Rich, Charlie	408	Supremes, The	23	Wonder, Stevie	39
Richie, Lionel	368	Sweat, Keith	422	Wynette, Tammy	392
Righteous Brothers, The	163	Talking Heads	273	Yankovic, "Weird Al"	413
Rimes, LeAnn	405	Taylor, James	75	Yanni	253
Rivers, Johnny	203	Taylor, Johnnie	477	Yearwood, Trisha	330
Robinson, Smokey	184	Temptations, The	9	Yes	95
Rogers, Kenny/First Edition	33	Ten Years After	337	Yoakam, Dwight	288
Rolling Stones, The	6	38 Special	441	Young, Neil	35
Ronstadt, Linda	38	Thorogood, George	377	Zappa, Frank	80
Ross, Diana	44	Three Dog Night	164	ZZ Top	150

The following 35 artists were ranked in the Top 500 Artists of our *Top Pop Albums 1955-1996* book but have now dropped out of the Top 500:

Paula Abdul	The Dramatics	Buddy Miles	Tears For Fears
Air Supply	Stan Getz	Sandy Nelson	B.J. Thomas
Anita Baker	Iron Butterfly	Buck Owens	The Tubes
The Brothers Johnson	Joan Jett	Graham Parker	Tanya Tucker
George Carlin	Gary Lewis	The Platters	UFO
The Dells	Luke/2 Live Crew	Ratt	Gino Vannelli
Deodato	Gloria Lynne	Jim Reeves	Village People
Dr. Hook	The Manhattans	Roxy Music	Bill Withers
Dokken	Melanie	Tavares	

TOP 30 ARTISTS BY DECADE
1955-1959

1.	Frank Sinatra	3,977	16.	Doris Day	910
2.	Johnny Mathis	2,955	17.	Dave Brubeck Quartet	818
3.	Elvis Presley	2,883	18.	Lester Lanin	786
4.	Harry Belafonte	2,376	19.	Louis Prima & Keely Smith	757
5.	Mantovani	2,029	20.	Ray Conniff	731
6.	Nat "King" Cole	2,024	21.	Henry Mancini	694
7.	Lawrence Welk	1,936	22.	Julie London	687
8.	Pat Boone	1,879	23.	Crazy Otto	671
9.	The Kingston Trio	1,857	24.	Ray Anthony	663
10.	Jackie Gleason	1,771	25.	Dakota Staton	660
11.	Roger Williams	1,433	26.	Ella Fitzgerald	642
12.	Mitch Miller	1,414	27.	Peggy Lee	629
13.	"Tennessee" Ernie Ford	1,303	28.	Sarah Vaughan	626
14.	Perry Como	1,296	29.	Eydie Gorme	624
15.	The Four Freshmen	981	30.	Norman Luboff	610

1960s

1.	The Beatles	7,989	16.	The Lettermen	3,730
2.	Frank Sinatra	6,844	17.	Herb Alpert	3,631
3.	Elvis Presley	6,047	18.	Enoch Light	3,578
4.	Ray Conniff	5,421	19.	The Beach Boys	3,559
5.	Ray Charles	4,857	20.	Nancy Wilson	3,467
6.	The Ventures	4,795	21.	Dean Martin	3,454
7.	Mantovani	4,770	22.	The Rolling Stones	3,342
8.	Andy Williams	4,752	23.	The Temptations	3,293
9.	Billy Vaughn	4,513	24.	James Brown	3,260
10.	Johnny Mathis	4,463	25.	Barbra Streisand	3,133
11.	Henry Mancini	4,087	26.	Mitch Miller	3,108
12.	Lawrence Welk	4,029	27.	Connie Francis	3,002
13.	The Kingston Trio	3,970	28.	Nat "King" Cole	2,974
14.	The Supremes	3,921	29.	The 4 Seasons	2,949
15.	Roger Williams	3,800	30.	Jimmy Smith	2,929

1970s

1.	Elton John	5,648	16.	Eagles	2,848
2.	Elvis Presley	5,505	17.	Jackson 5	2,802
3.	Neil Diamond	3,617	18.	James Taylor	2,763
4.	Barbra Streisand	3,508	19.	Led Zeppelin	2,743
5.	Chicago	3,269	20.	Jethro Tull	2,707
6.	David Bowie	3,198	21.	James Brown	2,654
7.	The Rolling Stones	3,108	22.	Eric Clapton	2,634
8.	Carole King	3,035	23.	Isaac Hayes	2,633
9.	Bee Gees	3,030	24.	Diana Ross	2,631
10.	John Denver	2,966	25.	Grand Funk Railroad	2,584
11.	Paul McCartney/Wings	2,942	26.	Rod Stewart	2,512
12.	The Who	2,926	27.	The Temptations	2,490
13.	Pink Floyd	2,909	28.	Stevie Wonder	2,488
14.	Fleetwood Mac	2,893	29.	Grateful Dead	2,487
15.	Bob Dylan	2,870	30.	Neil Young	2,422

1.	Willie Nelson	3,128	16.	Barbra Streisand	1,917
2.	Prince	2,849	17.	Elton John	1,895
3.	Kenny Rogers	2,795	18.	Diana Ross	1,804
4.	U2	2,571	19.	Jimmy Buffett	1,796
5.	Metallica	2,347	20.	Neil Diamond	1,781
6.	Alabama	2,279	21.	Madonna	1,780
7.	AC/DC	2,271	22.	Rush	1,743
8.	Michael Jackson	2,222	23.	John Cougar Mellencamp	1,740
9.	Billy Joel	2,177	24.	Elvis Costello	1,733
10.	Journey	2,129	25.	Tom Petty & The Heartbreakers	1,668
11.	The Rolling Stones	2,026	26.	Linda Ronstadt	1,664
12.	Pink Floyd	2,020	27.	Bruce Springsteen	1,642
13.	Aerosmith	2,006	28.	Anne Murray	1,596
14.	Hank Williams, Jr.	1,973	29.	Van Halen	1,580
15.	Pat Benatar	1,920	30.	Spyro Gyra	1,570

1990s

1.	Garth Brooks	4,601	16.	Dave Matthews Band	1,830
2.	Mariah Carey	2,834	17.	Kenny G	1,755
3.	Prince	2,760	18.	Pearl Jam	1,733
4.	George Strait	2,638	19.	Brooks & Dunn	1,712
5.	Alan Jackson	2,204	20.	Harry Connick, Jr.	1,694
6.	Reba McEntire	2,172	21.	Clint Black	1,687
7.	Metallica	2,060	22.	Nirvana	1,684
8.	Celine Dion	2,034	23.	Jimi Hendrix	1,636
9.	Eric Clapton	2,032	24.	Alabama	1,556
10.	Madonna	1,995	25.	Gloria Estefan	1,553
11.	2Pac	1,977	26.	Jimmy Buffett	1,551
12.	Vince Gill	1,934	27.	Luther Vandross	1,541
13.	Van Morrison	1,924	28.	Alice In Chains	1,538
14.	Yanni	1,900	29.	Selena	1,529
15.	Michael Bolton	1,890	30.	Bonnie Raitt	1,513

2000-2001

1.	Pearl Jam	941	16.	George Strait	398
2.	Bill & Gloria Gaither	558	17.	Blink 182	391 +
3.	Kid Rock	543	18.	The Beatles	384 +
4.	Destiny's Child	509 +	19.	Jessica Simpson	382 +
5.	Estéban	503	20.	Tool	375 +
6.	Billy Gilman	484	21.	Bon Jovi	375
7.	Jay-Z	480	22.	Big Punisher	372
8.	Incubus	460 +	23.	Moby	370
9.	Yolanda Adams	459	24.	Trick Daddy	369 +
10.	2Pac	436 +	25.	DJ Clue?	367
11.	Radiohead	432 +	26.	Bone Thugs-N-Harmony	364
12.	Tim McGraw	424 +	27.	Shaggy	358 +
13.	*NSYNC	417	28.	Snoop Dogg	356
14.	Eric Clapton	409	29.	The Black Crowes	354
15.	Eminem	407	30.	SheDaisy	345

+ Subject to change since an album by this artist is still charted as of the 9/29/01 cut-off date.

TOP ARTIST ACHIEVEMENTS

MOST CHARTED ALBUMS

1. Elvis Presley 104
2. Frank Sinatra 81
3. Johnny Mathis 72
4. Ray Conniff...........................52
5. James Brown 51
6. Mantovani 50
7. Barbra Streisand.................49
8. The Temptations.................48
9. The Beach Boys 48
10. Willie Nelson........................47
11. The Beatles 46
12. Bob Dylan 42
13. Lawrence Welk 42
14. The Rolling Stones 41
15. Neil Diamond 41
16. Aretha Franklin 41
17. Henry Mancini......................40
18. Kenny Rogers/First Edition..40
19. Elton John............................39
20. Ray Charles.........................38
21. Roger Williams 38
22. The Ventures 38
23. Johnny Cash 38
24. The Supremes 37
25. Eric Clapton 36
26. Andy Williams 36
27. Jimi Hendrix 36
28. Billy Vaughn.........................36

MOST TOP 40 ALBUMS

1. Frank Sinatra 53
2. Elvis Presley 48
3. Barbra Streisand.................41
4. The Rolling Stones 38
5. The Beatles 33
6. Bob Dylan 33
7. Elton John............................31
8. The Temptations.................28
9. Johnny Mathis 27
10. Mantovani 26
11. Ray Conniff..........................26
12. Eric Clapton 26
13. Neil Diamond 25
14. Lawrence Welk 24
15. Paul McCartney/Wings 23
16. Neil Young............................23
17. Aretha Franklin 22
18. Kiss 22
19. Rod Stewart 21
20. Jefferson Airplane/Starship..21
21. The Beach Boys 20
22. Andy Williams 19
23. The Kingston Trio 19
24. The Supremes 19
25. Prince 19
26. David Bowie 19
27. Roger Williams.....................19
28. Nat "King" Cole 19
29. Stevie Wonder 19

MOST TOP 10 ALBUMS

1. Frank Sinatra.......................34
2. The Rolling Stones..............34
3. The Beatles..........................28
4. Barbra Streisand 26
5. Elvis Presley........................25
6. Johnny Mathis 16
7. Elton John 15
8. Bob Dylan 15
9. The Kingston Trio 14
10. Paul McCartney/Wings 14
11. Mitch Miller 14
12. Neil Diamond 13
13. The Beach Boys...................13
14. Madonna 13
15. Ray Conniff 12
16. Andy Williams.......................12
17. Chicago 12
18. Garth Brooks 12
19. Van Halen 12
20. Mantovani.............................11
21. Eric Clapton 11
22. Billy Joel 11
23. Bruce Springsteen 11
24. The Temptations 10
25. Lawrence Welk 10
26. Herb Alpert/Tijuana Brass...10
27. Prince 10
28. Linda Ronstadt.....................10
29. Stevie Wonder......................10
30. Led Zeppelin 10

MOST #1 ALBUMS

1. The Beatles 19
2. Elvis Presley 9
3. The Rolling Stones 9
4. Barbra Streisand....................8
5. Elton John...............................7
6. Paul McCartney/Wings 7
7. Garth Brooks 7
8. Led Zeppelin 6
9. Frank Sinatra 5
10. The Kingston Trio 5
11. Pink Floyd 5
12. Herb Alpert/Tijuana Brass 5
13. Chicago...................................5
14. Bruce Springsteen 5
15. U2 5
16. Eagles.....................................5
17. Van Halen 5
18. Janet Jackson........................5

MOST WEEKS AT THE #1 POSITION

1. The Beatles........................ 132
2. Elvis Presley 64
3. Garth Brooks.......................50
4. Michael Jackson 49
5. The Kingston Trio 46
6. Whitney Houston 45
7. Elton John 39
8. The Rolling Stones 38
9. Fleetwood Mac 38
10. Harry Belafonte 37
11. The Monkees 37
12. Prince....................................33
13. Bee Gees 31
14. Eagles...................................29
15. Led Zeppelin 28
16. Herb Alpert/Tijuana Brass....26
17. Mariah Carey 26
18. Simon & Garfunkel...............26

MOST CONSECUTIVE #1 ALBUMS

1. The Beatles (1965-68) 8
2. Elton John (1972-75) 7
3. Paul McCartney (1973-77).....5
4. Chicago (1972-75) 5
5. U2 (1987-97)..........................5
6. Janet Jackson (1986-2001)....5
7. The Kingston Trio (1959-60)..4
8. Garth Brooks (1991-95) 4
9. Eatles (1975-79) 4
10. The Monkees (1966-67)..........4
11. Michael Jackson (1983-95)....4
12. Nirvana (1992-96) 4
13. Bee Gees (1978-80) 3
14. Led Zeppelin (1973-76)..........3
15. Metallica (1991-97) 3
16. Bruce Springsteen (1984-87). 3
17. Van Halen (1986-91)..............3
18. Donna Summer (1978-80) 3
19. Mariah Carey (1993-97).........3
20. Simon & Garfunkel (1968-70) 3

Ties are broken according to rank in the *Top 500 Artists* section. For all categories except Most Charted Albums, Christmas albums that made the Pop Albums chart are counted for their <u>first</u> chart appearance only; their seasonal re-entries are not added to the totals. Also, for all categories except Most Charted Albums, albums that made the special Christmas Albums chart and the Pop Catalog Albums chart are <u>not</u> counted.

MOST GOLD & PLATINUM ALBUMS

1. Elvis Presley 55
2. Barbra Streisand 42
3. The Beatles 38
4. The Rolling Stones 38
5. Neil Diamond 34
6. Elton John 32
7. Bob Dylan 30
8. Frank Sinatra 27
9. Kenny Rogers/First Edition . 26
10. Willie Nelson 24
11. Eric Clapton 23
12. Kiss 23
13. George Strait 23
14. Rush 22
15. Paul McCartney/Wings 21
16. Alabama 21
17. Prince 20
18. Chicago 20
19. Rod Stewart 20
20. Aerosmith 20
21. Hank Williams, Jr. 20

TOP ARTISTS WHO NEVER HIT #1

	Rank			Rank	
1.	11	Neil Diamond	19.	73	Alabama
2.	12	Ray Conniff	20.	74	Rush
3.	15	James Brown	21.	75	James Taylor
4.	16	Aretha Franklin	22.	76	Dean Martin
5.	20	Willie Nelson	23.	77	Joan Baez
6.	28	David Bowie	24.	79	Gladys Knight & The Pips
7.	34	Roger Williams	25.	80	Frank Zappa
8.	37	The Ventures	26.	87	Dolly Parton
9.	41	Grateful Dead	27.	88	Jackson 5/Jacksons
10.	46	Jimmy Buffett	28.	89	Steve Miller Band
11.	47	Kiss	29.	92	Tom Petty/Heartbreakers
12.	49	Dionne Warwick	30.	93	Tony Bennett
13.	50	Van Morrison	31.	94	Four Tops
14.	53	The Who	32.	95	Yes
15.	57	The Lettermen	33.	96	Bill Cosby
16.	59	Nancy Wilson	34.	98	Anne Murray
17.	62	Marvin Gaye	35.	99	The 4 Seasons
18.	68	The Kinks			

ARTISTS WITH LONGEST CHART CAREERS

Dates			Artist (Years/Months/Weeks)
10/1/55	-	2/24/01	Louis Armstrong (45/4/3)
3/31/56	-	11/4/00	Elvis Presley (44/7/1)
1/8/55	-	12/26/98	Frank Sinatra (43/11/3)
2/23/57	-	10/30/99	Tony Bennett (42/8/1)
12/8/58	-	11/25/00	Johnny Cash (41/11/2)
10/27/56	-	2/22/97	Pat Boone (40/3/3)
9/9/57	-	5/10/97	Johnny Mathis (39/8/0)
7/22/57	-	12/21/96	Rosemary Clooney (39/5/0)
11/24/62	-	1/13/01	The Beach Boys (38/1/3)
11/17/62	-	11/11/00	Aretha Franklin (37/11/3)
4/13/63	-	3/10/01	Barbra Streisand (37/11/0)
9/7/63	-	6/9/01	Bob Dylan (37/11/0)
2/1/64	-	9/29/01 +	The Beatles (37/8/0)
2/2/59	-	8/31/96	Boston Pops Orchestra (37/7/0)

+ still charted

ONE-HIT WONDERS

1. USA for Africa .... *We Are The World* (1[3]/'85)
2. Crazy Otto .... *Crazy Otto* (1[2]/'55)
3. Tone Loc .... *Loc-ed After Dark* (1[1]/'89)
4. Firm, The .... *The Firm – The Album* (1[1]/'97)
5. Jack Webb .... Pete Kelly's Blues (2[2]/'55)
6. Carmel Quinn .... *Arthur Godfrey presents ...Carmel Quinn* (2[2]/'55)
7. McGuire Sisters, The .... *By Request* (2[1]/'55)
8. Westside Connection .... *Bow Down* (2[1]/'96)
9. David Rose .... *The Stripper* (3[6]/'60)
10. Jerry Lewis .... *Jerry Lewis Just Sings* (3[2]/'56)
11. Joe Harnell .... *Fly Me To The Moon* (3[2]/'63)
12. Chumbawamba .... *Tubthumper* (3[2]/'97)
13. God's Property .... *God's Property* (3[1]/'97)
14. The Honeydrippers .... *Volume One* (4[4]/'55)
15. LSG .... *Levert – Sweat - Gill* (4[1]/'97)

The above artists' only chart hit reached the #1-4 position through 1997 (does not include new artists that charted since 1998). Weeks at the peak position and year charted are listed in parenthesis after the title.

THE TOP ALBUMS

The Biggest #1 Albums Ranking From 1955 through 2001

This ranking is based on the most weeks an album held the #1 position. Ties are broken according to this order: total weeks in the Top 10, total weeks in the Top 40; and, finally, total weeks charted.

> **The total weeks at No. 1 is shown below each album's cover photo, along with the year the album peaked.**

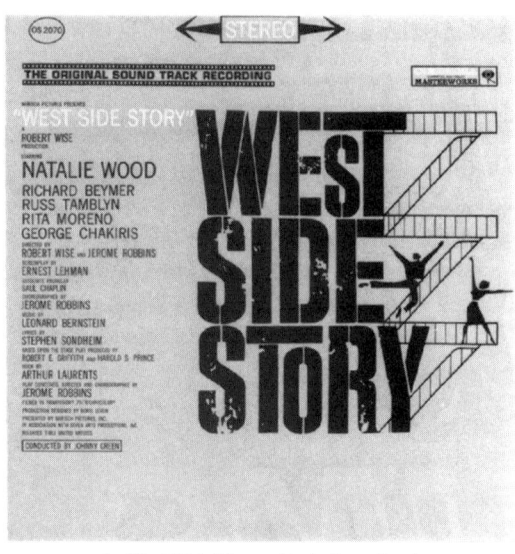

1. West Side Story...*Movie Soundtrack*
54 / 1962

2. Thriller...*Michael Jackson*
37 / 1983

3. South Pacific...*Movie Soundtrack*
31 / 1958

4. Calypso...*Harry Belafonte*
31 / 1956

5. Rumours...*Fleetwood Mac*
31 / 1977

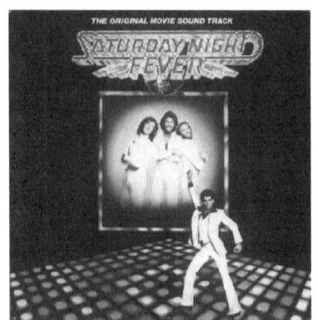

6. Saturday Night Fever...
Bee Gees/Movie Soundtrack
24 / 1978

7. Purple Rain...*Prince & The
Revolution/Movie Soundtrack*
24 / 1984

**8. Please Hammer Don't Hurt
'Em**...*M.C. Hammer*
21 / 1990

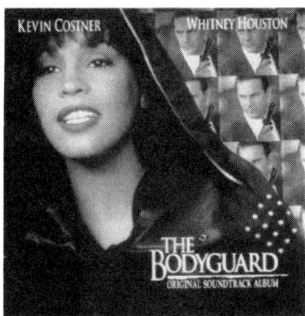

9. The Bodyguard...
Whitney Houston/Movie Soundtrack
20 / 1992

10. Blue Hawaii...
Elvis Presley/Movie Soundtrack
20 / 1961

11. Love Me Or Leave Me...
Doris Day/Movie Soundtrack
19 / 1955

12. Ropin' The Wind...
Garth Brooks
18 / 1991

13. Dirty Dancing...
Movie Soundtrack
18 / 1987

14. More Of The Monkees...
The Monkees
18 / 1967

15. Some Gave All...
Billy Ray Cyrus
17 / 1992

16. Synchronicity... The Police
17 / 1983

17. The Sound Of Music...
Original Cast
16 / 1960

18. To The Extreme... Vanilla Ice
16 / 1990

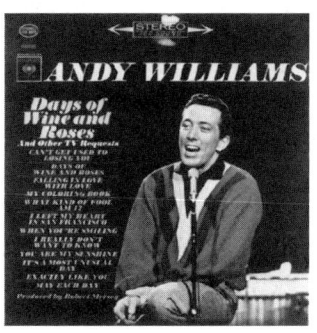

19. Days of Wine and Roses...
Andy Williams
16 / 1963

20. Titanic... Movie Soundtrack
16 / 1998

TOP 100 ALBUMS
1955-2001

PK YR	WKS CHR	WKS T40	WKS T10	WKS @ #1	RANK	TITLE	ARTIST
62	198	144	106	54	1.	West Side Story	Movie Soundtrack
83	122	91	78	37	2.	Thriller	Michael Jackson
58	262	161	90	31	3.	South Pacific	Movie Soundtrack
56	99	72	58	31	4.	Calypso	Harry Belafonte
77	134	60	52	31	5.	Rumours	Fleetwood Mac
78	120	54	35	24	6.	Saturday Night Fever	Bee Gees/Movie Soundtrack
84	72	42	32	24	7.	Purple Rain	Prince & The Revolution/Movie Soundtrack
90	108	70	52	21	8.	Please Hammer Don't Hurt 'Em	M.C. Hammer
92	141	76	40	20	9.	The Bodyguard	Whitney Houston/Movie Soundtrack
61	79	53	39	20	10.	Blue Hawaii	Elvis Presley/Movie Soundtrack
55	28	28	25	19	11.	Love Me Or Leave Me	Doris Day/Movie Soundtrack
91	132	70	50	18	12.	Ropin' The Wind	Garth Brooks
87	96	68	48	18	13.	Dirty Dancing	Movie Soundtrack
67	70	45	25	18	14.	More Of The Monkees	The Monkees
92	97	59	43	17	15.	Some Gave All	Billy Ray Cyrus
83	75	50	40	17	16.	Synchronicity	The Police
60	276	168	105	16	17.	The Sound Of Music	Original Cast
90	67	39	26	16	18.	To The Extreme	Vanilla Ice
63	107	61	23	16	19.	Days of Wine and Roses	Andy Williams
98	71	33	20	16	20.	Titanic	Movie Soundtrack
56	480	292	173	15	21.	My Fair Lady	Original Cast
71	302	68	46	15	22.	Tapestry	Carole King
67	175	63	33	15	23.	Sgt. Pepper's Lonely Hearts Club Band	The Beatles
82	90	48	31	15	24.	Business As Usual	Men At Work
59	118	43	31	15	25.	The Kingston Trio At Large	The Kingston Trio
81	101	50	30	15	26.	Hi Infidelity	REO Speedwagon
80	123	35	27	15	27.	The Wall	Pink Floyd
65	114	78	48	14	28.	Mary Poppins	Movie Soundtrack
86	162	78	46	14	29.	Whitney Houston	Whitney Houston
60	108	67	44	14	30.	The Button-Down Mind Of Bob Newhart	Bob Newhart
61	89	55	38	14	31.	Exodus	Movie Soundtrack
76	80	44	35	14	32.	Songs In The Key Of Life	Stevie Wonder
62	101	59	33	14	33.	Modern Sounds In Country And Western Music	Ray Charles
64	51	40	28	14	34.	A Hard Day's Night	The Beatles/Movie Soundtrack
60	124	105	43	13	35.	Persuasive Percussion	Enoch Light/Terry Snyder and The All-Stars
61	95	73	37	13	36.	Judy At Carnegie Hall	Judy Garland
66	78	49	32	13	37.	The Monkees	The Monkees
69	151	59	28	13	38.	Hair	Original Cast
95	113	89	72	12	39.	Jagged Little Pill	Alanis Morissette
58	245	123	66	12	40.	The Music Man	Original Cast
88	87	69	51	12	41.	Faith	George Michael
62	96	69	46	12	42.	Breakfast At Tiffany's	Henry Mancini/Movie Soundtrack
99	102	63	44	12	43.	Supernatural	Santana
60	73	42	29	12	44.	Sold Out	The Kingston Trio
78	77	39	29	12	45.	Grease	Movie Soundtrack
62	49	26	17	12	46.	The First Family	Vaughn Meader
91	113	66	49	11	47.	Mariah Carey	Mariah Carey
61	64	50	33	11	48.	Calcutta!	Lawrence Welk
87	85	51	31	11	49.	Whitney	Whitney Houston
69	129	32	27	11	50.	Abbey Road	The Beatles

TOP 100 ALBUMS (cont'd)
1955-2001

PK YR	WKS CHR	WKS T40	WKS T10	WKS @ #1	RANK	TITLE	ARTIST
64	71	27	21	11	51.	Meet The Beatles!	The Beatles
85	34	22	18	11	52.	Miami Vice	Television Soundtrack
89	175	78	64	10	53.	Forever Your Girl	Paula Abdul
57	88	88	54	10	54.	Around The World In 80 Days	Movie Soundtrack
58	172	78	54	10	55.	Gigi	Movie Soundtrack
76	97	55	52	10	56.	Frampton Comes Alive!	Peter Frampton
56	48	48	43	10	57.	Elvis Presley	Elvis Presley
59	119	47	43	10	58.	The Music From Peter Gunn	Henry Mancini
99	93	52	37	10	59.	Millennium	Backstreet Boys
81	81	52	34	10	60.	4	Foreigner
94	88	56	31	10	61.	The Lion King	Movie Soundtrack
60	111	46	29	10	62.	G.I. Blues	Elvis Presley/Movie Soundtrack
84	61	27	20	10	63.	Footloose	Movie Soundtrack
60	60	27	20	10	64.	String Along	The Kingston Trio
57	29	29	19	10	65.	Loving You	Elvis Presley/Movie Soundtrack
63	39	22	18	10	66.	The Singing Nun	The Singing Nun
70	85	24	17	10	67.	Bridge Over Troubled Water	Simon & Garfunkel
74	104	20	11	10	68.	Elton John - Greatest Hits	Elton John
85	97	55	37	9	69.	Brothers In Arms	Dire Straits
96	90	70	36	9	70.	Tragic Kingdom	No Doubt
87	103	58	35	9	71.	The Joshua Tree	U2
66	129	59	32	9	72.	What Now My Love	Herb Alpert & The Tijuana Brass
82	64	35	27	9	73.	Asia	Asia
68	69	47	26	9	74.	The Graduate	Simon & Garfunkel/Movie Soundtrack
82	106	40	22	9	75.	American Fool	John Cougar
81	58	30	22	9	76.	Tattoo You	The Rolling Stones
61	40	39	21	9	77.	Stars For A Summer Night	Various Artist Compilation
79	57	36	21	9	78.	The Long Run	Eagles
60	86	35	19	9	79.	Nice 'n' Easy	Frank Sinatra
70	69	26	19	9	80.	Cosmo's Factory	Creedence Clearwater Revival
65	71	38	16	9	81.	Beatles '65	The Beatles
65	44	33	15	9	82.	Help!	The Beatles/Movie Soundtrack
68	155	25	15	9	83.	The Beatles [White Album]	The Beatles
71	42	23	15	9	84.	Pearl	Janis Joplin
72	51	20	13	9	85.	Chicago V	Chicago
65	185	141	61	8	86.	Whipped Cream & Other Delights	Herb Alpert's Tijuana Brass
95	129	73	55	8	87.	Cracked Rear View	Hootie & The Blowfish
58	204	127	53	8	88.	Sing Along With Mitch	Mitch Miller & The Gang
86	94	60	46	8	89.	Slippery When Wet	Bon Jovi
89	78	61	41	8	90.	Girl You Know It's True	Milli Vanilli
73	103	43	36	8	91.	Goodbye Yellow Brick Road	Elton John
93	128	50	33	8	92.	Music Box	Mariah Carey
57	94	55	31	8	93.	Love Is The Thing	Nat "King" Cole
00	77	49	31	8	94.	No Strings Attached	*NSYNC
77	107	32	28	8	95.	Hotel California	Eagles
59	126	40	26	8	96.	Here We Go Again!	The Kingston Trio
80	74	27	24	8	97.	Double Fantasy	John Lennon/Yoko Ono
78	76	34	22	8	98.	52nd Street	Billy Joel
95	110	51	20	8	99.	The Hits	Garth Brooks
00	67	33	20	8	100.	The Marshall Mathers LP	Eminem

TOP 25 ALBUMS BY DECADE
1955-1959

PK YR	WKS CHR	WKS T40	WKS T10	WKS @#1	RANK	TITLE	ARTIST
58	262	161	90	31	1.	South Pacific	Movie Soundtrack
56	99	72	58	31	2.	Calypso	Harry Belafonte
55	28	28	25	19	3.	Love Me Or Leave Me	Doris Day/Movie Soundtrack
56	480	292	173	15	4.	My Fair Lady	Original Cast
59	118	43	31	15	5.	The Kingston Trio At Large	The Kingston Trio
58	245	123	66	12	6.	The Music Man	Original Cast
57	88	88	54	10	7.	Around The World In 80 Days	Movie Soundtrack
58	172	78	54	10	8.	Gigi	Movie Soundtrack
56	48	48	43	10	9.	Elvis Presley	Elvis Presley
59	119	47	43	10	10.	The Music From Peter Gunn	Henry Mancini
57	29	29	19	10	11.	Loving You	Elvis Presley/Movie Soundtrack
58	204	127	53	8	12.	Sing Along With Mitch	Mitch Miller & The Gang
57	94	55	31	8	13.	Love Is The Thing	Nat "King" Cole
59	126	40	26	8	14.	Here We Go Again!	The Kingston Trio
58	125	76	39	7	15.	Tchaikovsky: Piano Concerto No. 1	Van Cliburn
56	62	62	54	6	16.	Belafonte	Harry Belafonte
55	29	29	24	6	17.	Starring Sammy Davis, Jr.	Sammy Davis, Jr.
59	295	40	38	5	18.	Heavenly	Johnny Mathis
56	32	32	24	5	19.	Elvis	Elvis Presley
58	120	55	19	5	20.	Frank Sinatra sings for Only The Lonely	Frank Sinatra
59	63	46	19	5	21.	Exotica	Martin Denny
58	71	50	18	5	22.	Come Fly with me	Frank Sinatra
56	305	229	116	4	23.	Oklahoma!	Movie Soundtrack
55	44	33	31	4	24.	in the Wee Small Hours	Frank Sinatra
57	7	7	6	4	25.	Elvis' Christmas Album	Elvis Presley

1960s

PK YR	WKS CHR	WKS T40	WKS T10	WKS @#1	RANK	TITLE	ARTIST
62	198	144	106	54	1.	West Side Story	Movie Soundtrack
61	79	53	39	20	2.	Blue Hawaii	Elvis Presley/Movie Soundtrack
67	70	45	25	18	3.	More Of The Monkees	The Monkees
60	276	168	105	16	4.	The Sound Of Music	Original Cast
63	107	61	23	16	5.	Days of Wine and Roses	Andy Williams
67	175	63	33	15	6.	Sgt. Pepper's Lonely Hearts Club Band	The Beatles
65	114	78	48	14	7.	Mary Poppins	Movie Soundtrack
60	108	67	44	14	8.	The Button-Down Mind Of Bob Newhart	Bob Newhart
61	89	55	38	14	9.	Exodus	Movie Soundtrack
62	101	59	33	14	10.	Modern Sounds In Country And Western Music	Ray Charles
64	51	40	28	14	11.	A Hard Day's Night	The Beatles/Movie Soundtrack
60	124	105	43	13	12.	Persuasive Percussion	Enoch Light/Terry Snyder and The All-Stars
61	95	73	37	13	13.	Judy At Carnegie Hall	Judy Garland
66	78	49	32	13	14.	The Monkees	The Monkees
69	151	59	28	13	15.	Hair	Original Cast
62	96	69	46	12	16.	Breakfast At Tiffany's	Henry Mancini/Movie Soundtrack
60	73	42	29	12	17.	Sold Out	The Kingston Trio
62	49	26	17	12	18.	The First Family	Vaughn Meader
61	64	50	33	11	19.	Calcutta!	Lawrence Welk
69	129	32	27	11	20.	Abbey Road	The Beatles
64	71	27	21	11	21.	Meet The Beatles!	The Beatles
60	111	46	29	10	22.	G.I. Blues	Elvis Presley/Movie Soundtrack
60	60	27	20	10	23.	String Along	The Kingston Trio
63	39	22	18	10	24.	The Singing Nun	The Singing Nun
66	129	59	32	9	25.	What Now My Love	Herb Alpert & The Tijuana Brass

TOP 25 ALBUMS BY DECADE
1970s

PK YR	WKS CHR	WKS T40	WKS T10	WKS @#1	RANK	TITLE	ARTIST
77	134	60	52	31	1.	Rumours	Fleetwood Mac
78	120	54	35	24	2.	Saturday Night Fever	Bee Gees/Movie Soundtrack
71	302	68	46	15	3.	Tapestry	Carole King
76	80	44	35	14	4.	Songs In The Key Of Life	Stevie Wonder
78	77	39	29	12	5.	Grease	Movie Soundtrack
76	97	55	52	10	6.	Frampton Comes Alive!	Peter Frampton
70	85	24	17	10	7.	Bridge Over Troubled Water	Simon & Garfunkel
74	104	20	11	10	8.	Elton John - Greatest Hits	Elton John
79	57	36	21	9	9.	The Long Run	Eagles
70	69	26	19	9	10.	Cosmo's Factory	Creedence Clearwater Revival
71	42	23	15	9	11.	Pearl	Janis Joplin
72	51	20	13	9	12.	Chicago V	Chicago
73	103	43	36	8	13.	Goodbye Yellow Brick Road	Elton John
77	107	32	28	8	14.	Hotel California	Eagles
78	76	34	22	8	15.	52nd Street	Billy Joel
76	51	27	21	7	16.	Wings At The Speed Of Sound	Wings
79	41	28	18	7	17.	In Through The Out Door	Led Zeppelin
72	48	26	17	7	18.	American Pie	Don McLean
75	43	24	17	7	19.	Captain Fantastic And The Brown Dirt Cowboy	Elton John
71	38	22	14	7	20.	All Things Must Pass	George Harrison
70	88	40	30	6	21.	Abraxas	Santana
79	88	48	26	6	22.	Breakfast In America	Supertramp
77	51	28	18	6	23.	A Star Is Born	Barbra Streisand/Movie Soundtrack
79	55	26	18	6	24.	Spirits Having Flown	Bee Gees
79	49	26	16	6	25.	Bad Girls	Donna Summer

1980s

PK YR	WKS CHR	WKS T40	WKS T10	WKS @#1	RANK	TITLE	ARTIST
83	122	91	78	37	1.	Thriller	Michael Jackson
84	72	42	32	24	2.	Purple Rain	Prince & The Revolution/Movie Soundtrack
87	96	68	48	18	3.	Dirty Dancing	Movie Soundtrack
83	75	50	40	17	4.	Synchronicity	The Police
82	90	48	31	15	5.	Business As Usual	Men At Work
81	101	50	30	15	6.	Hi Infidelity	REO Speedwagon
80	123	35	27	15	7.	The Wall	Pink Floyd
86	162	78	46	14	8.	Whitney Houston	Whitney Houston
88	87	69	51	12	9.	Faith	George Michael
87	85	51	31	11	10.	Whitney	Whitney Houston
85	34	22	18	11	11.	Miami Vice	Television Soundtrack
89	175	78	64	10	12.	Forever Your Girl	Paula Abdul
81	81	52	34	10	13.	4	Foreigner
84	61	27	20	10	14.	Footloose	Movie Soundtrack
85	97	55	37	9	15.	Brothers In Arms	Dire Straits
87	103	58	35	9	16.	The Joshua Tree	U2
82	64	35	27	9	17.	Asia	Asia
82	106	40	22	9	18.	American Fool	John Cougar
81	58	30	22	9	19.	Tattoo You	The Rolling Stones
86	94	60	46	8	20.	Slippery When Wet	Bon Jovi
89	78	61	41	8	21.	Girl You Know It's True	Milli Vanilli
80	74	27	24	8	22.	Double Fantasy	John Lennon/Yoko Ono
84	139	96	84	7	23.	Born In The U.S.A.	Bruce Springsteen
85	123	70	31	7	24.	No Jacket Required	Phil Collins
89	63	40	27	7	25.	The Raw & The Cooked	Fine Young Cannibals

TOP 25 ALBUMS BY DECADE
1990s

PK YR	WKS CHR	WKS T40	WKS T10	WKS @#1	RANK	TITLE	ARTIST
90	108	70	52	21	1.	Please Hammer Don't Hurt 'Em	M.C. Hammer
92	141	76	40	20	2.	The Bodyguard	Whitney Houston/Movie Soundtrack
91	132	70	50	18	3.	Ropin' The Wind	Garth Brooks
92	97	59	43	17	4.	Some Gave All	Billy Ray Cyrus
90	67	39	26	16	5.	To The Extreme	Vanilla Ice
98	71	33	20	16	6.	Titanic	Movie Soundtrack
95	113	89	72	12	7.	Jagged Little Pill	Alanis Morissette
99	102	63	44	12	8.	Supernatural	Santana
91	113	66	49	11	9.	Mariah Carey	Mariah Carey
99	93	52	37	10	10.	Millennium	Backstreet Boys
94	88	56	31	10	11.	The Lion King	Movie Soundtrack
96	90	70	36	9	12.	Tragic Kingdom	No Doubt
95	129	73	55	8	13.	Cracked Rear View	Hootie & The Blowfish
93	128	50	33	8	14.	Music Box	Mariah Carey
95	110	51	20	8	15.	The Hits	Garth Brooks
92	64	35	17	7	16.	The Chase	Garth Brooks
99	103	65	50	6	17.	...Baby One More Time	Britney Spears
93	106	52	36	6	18.	janet.	Janet Jackson
95	81	49	29	6	19.	Daydream	Mariah Carey
90	52	27	16	6	20.	I Do Not Want What I Haven't Got	Sinéad O'Connor
94	99	56	43	5	21.	II	Boyz II Men
97	105	60	33	5	22.	Spice	Spice Girls
91	110	49	21	5	23.	Unforgettable With Love	Natalie Cole
96	49	30	21	5	24.	Waiting To Exhale	Movie Soundtrack
99	64	30	16	5	25.	Fanmail	TLC

2000-2001

PK YR	WKS CHR	WKS T40	WKS T10	WKS @#1	RANK	TITLE	ARTIST
00	77	49	31	8	1.	No Strings Attached	*NSYNC
00	67	33	20	8	2.	The Marshall Mathers LP	Eminem
00	44 +	27	17	8	3.	1	The Beatles
01	58 +	39	22	6	4.	Hotshot	Shaggy
00	64 +	61	25	5	5.	Country Grammar	Nelly
01	17 +	17 +	15	3	6.	Break The Cycle	Staind
01	24 +	18	11	3	7.	Now 6	Various Artist Compilation
00	43	17	9	3	8.	Now 4	Various Artist Compilation
00	48 +	40	19	2	9.	Chocolate Starfish And The Hot Dog Flavored Water	Limp Bizkit
01	20 +	20 +	14	2	10.	Survivor	Destiny's Child
01	29 +	24	7	2	11.	Everyday	Dave Matthews Band
00	42	14	6	2	12.	Black & Blue	Backstreet Boys
00	33	10	4	2	13.	Voodoo	D'Angelo
00	70 +	38	23	1	14.	Oops!...I Did It Again	Britney Spears
00	74	39	13	1	15.	...And Then There Was X	DMX
00	49 +	30	11	1	16.	Rule 3:36	Ja Rule
01	34 +	23 +	7	1	17.	J.Lo	Jennifer Lopez
01	25 +	12	7	1	18.	Until The End Of Time	2Pac
00	52 +	25	6	1	19.	Music	Madonna
01	21 +	19	6	1	20.	All For You	Janet Jackson
00	47	29	5	1	21.	Vol. 3...Life And Times Of S. Carter	Jay-Z
00	37	16	5	1	22.	Let's Get Ready	Mystikal
01	14 +	11	5	1	23.	Take Off Your Pants And Jacket	Blink 182
01	18 +	10	5	1	24.	Lateralus	Tool
00	45 +	22	4	1	25.	TP-2.com	R. Kelly

+: still charted as of 9/29/01

1172

MOST VALUABLE ALBUMS

Following is a list of all albums in this book valued at $200 or more.

YEAR		VALUE	TITLE	ARTIST...LABEL & NUMBER
64	1.	$800	The Beatles vs. The Four Seasons	The Beatles/The 4 Seasons...Vee-Jay 30
64	2.	$800	Introducing...The Beatles	The Beatles...Vee-Jay 1062
63	3.	$600	He's A Rebel	The Crystals...Philles 4001
64	4.	$500	Songs, Pictures And Stories Of The Fabulous Beatles	The Beatles...Vee-Jay 1092
64	5.	$500	Jolly What! The Beatles & Frank Ifield	The Beatles...Vee-Jay 1085
57	6.	$500	Elvis' Christmas Album	Elvis Presley...RCA Victor LOC-1035
57	7.	$500	The Teenagers featuring Frankie Lymon	The Teenagers...Gee 701
59	8.	$400	A Date With Elvis	Elvis Presley...RCA Victor LPM-2011
65	9.	$400	...presenting the fabulous Ronettes featuring Veronica	The Ronettes...Philles 4006
56	10.	$400	Bluejean Bop!	Gene Vincent...Capitol 764
62	11.	$300	You Belong To Me	The Duprees...Coed 905
63	12.	$300	The Fabulous Miracles	The Miracles...Tamla 238
65	13.	$300	Christmas With The Miracles	The Miracles...Tamla 236
56	14.	$300	Elvis Presley	Elvis Presley...RCA Victor LPM-1254
56	15.	$300	Elvis	Elvis Presley...RCA Victor LPM-1382
57	16.	$300	Loving You	Elvis Presley/Movie Soundtrack...RCA Victor LPM-1515
64	17.	$300	Surfin' Bird	The Trashmen...Garrett 200
58	18.	$250	King Creole	Elvis Presley...RCA Victor LPM-1884
59	19.	$250	For LP Fans Only	Elvis Presley...RCA Victor LPM-1990
58	20.	$250	Elvis' Golden Records	Elvis Presley...RCA Victor LPM-1707
64	21.	$250	Pain In My Heart	Otis Redding...Atco 161
68	22.	$200	The Beatles [White Album]	The Beatles...Apple 101
64	23.	$200	The Beatles with Tony Sheridan and Their Guests	The Beatles...MGM 4215
67	24.	$200	Booker T. & The MG's in the Christmas Spirit	Booker T. & The MG's...Stax 713
70	25.	$200	Charles Brown sings Christmas Songs	Charles Brown...King 775
63	26.	$200	Prisoner Of Love	James Brown...King 851
64	27.	$200	Pure Dynamite! Live At The Royal	James Brown...King 883
63	28.	$200	Live At The Apollo	James Brown...King 826
58	29.	$200	Sam Cooke	Sam Cooke...Keen 2001
59	30.	$200	The Buddy Holly Story	Buddy Holly...Coral 57279
60	31.	$200	Stormsville	Johnny & The Hurricanes...Warwick 2010
62	32.	$200	LIllloco-Motion	Little Eva...Dimension 6000
57	33.	$200	Here's Little Richard	Little Richard...Specialty 2100
63	34.	$200	The Wham Of That Memphis Man!	Lonnie Mack...Fraternity 1014
63	35.	$200	The Miracles On Stage	The Miracles...Tamla 241
64	36.	$200	doin' Mickey's Monkey	The Miracles...Tamla 245
62	37.	$200	The Original Monster Mash	Bobby "Boris" Pickett...Garpax 57001
60	38.	$200	Elvis Is Back!	Elvis Presley...RCA Victor LSP-2231
60	39.	$200	50,000,000 Elvis Fans Can't Be Wrong - Elvis' Gold Records-Volume 2	Elvis Presley ...RCA Victor LPM-2075
64	40.	$200	The Original Penetration! and other favorites	The Pyramids...Best 16501
63	41.	$200	Wild Weekend	Rockin' Rebels...Swan 509
63	42.	$200	Little Town Flirt	Del Shannon...Big Top 1308
63	43.	$200	The Original Telstar	The Tornadoes...London 3279
59	44.	$200	Ritchie Valens	Ritchie Valens...Del-Fi 1201
67	45.	$200	The Velvet Underground & Nico	Velvet Underground...Verve 5008
65	46.	$200	For Your Love	The Yardbirds...Epic 26167

VALUE: estimate of dealer-asking price for near-mint commercial copy

ALBUMS OF LONGEVITY

Albums charted 175 weeks or more.

PK YR	PK POS	PK WKS	WKS CHR	RANK	TITLE	ARTIST
73	1	1	741	1.	**The Dark Side Of The Moon**	Pink Floyd
58	1	3	490	2.	**Johnny's Greatest Hits**	Johnny Mathis
56	1	15	480	3.	**My Fair Lady**	Original Cast
92	46	1	331	4.	**Highlights From The Phantom Of The Opera**	Original Cast
56	1	4	305	5.	**Oklahoma!**	Movie Soundtrack
71	1	15	302	6.	**Tapestry**	Carole King
59	1	5	295	7.	**Heavenly**	Johnny Mathis
91	6	2	282	8.	**MCMXC A.D.**	Enigma
91	1	4	281	9.	**Metallica**	Metallica
56	1	1	277	10.	**The King And I**	Movie Soundtrack
57	2	3	277	11.	**Hymns**	Tennessee Ernie Ford
60	1	16	276	12.	**The Sound Of Music**	Original Cast
61	1	6	265	13.	**Camelot**	Original Cast
58	1	31	262	14.	**South Pacific**	Movie Soundtrack
71	2	4	259	15.	**Led Zeppelin IV (untitled)**	Led Zeppelin
88	33	1	255	16.	**The Phantom Of The Opera**	Original Cast
92	1	2	252	17.	**Nevermind**	Nirvana
92	2	4	250	18.	**Ten**	Pearl Jam
58	1	12	245	19.	**The Music Man**	Original Cast
72	4	2	243	20.	**Hot Rocks 1964-1971**	The Rolling Stones
90	41	2	242	21.	**The Best Of Van Morrison**	Van Morrison
92	17	1	238	22.	**Shepherd Moons**	Enya
65	1	2	233	23.	**The Sound Of Music**	Movie Soundtrack
59	1	1	231	24.	**Film Encores**	Mantovani and his orchestra
92	3	2	224	25.	**No Fences**	Garth Brooks
92	13	1	224	26.	**Garth Brooks**	Garth Brooks
93	2	11	214	27.	**Breathless**	Kenny G
92	11	1	207	28.	**Greatest Hits**	Queen
65	7	2	206	29.	**Fiddler On The Roof**	Original Cast
58	1	8	204	30.	**Sing Along With Mitch**	Mitch Miller & The Gang
90	3	3	202	31.	**Soul Provider**	Michael Bolton
62	1	54	198	32.	**West Side Story**	Movie Soundtrack
58	1	1	195	33.	**The Kingston Trio**	The Kingston Trio
62	5	5	191	34.	**West Side Story**	Original Cast
65	1	8	185	35.	**Whipped Cream & Other Delights**	Herb Alpert
62	1	7	185	36.	**Peter, Paul and Mary**	Peter, Paul & Mary
90	1	3	185	37.	**Nick Of Time**	Bonnie Raitt
83	9	1	183	38.	**Eliminator**	ZZ Top
59	12	2	183	39.	**Oldies But Goodies**	Various Artist Compilation
80	1	2	181	40.	**Kenny Rogers' Greatest Hits**	Kenny Rogers
61	8	1	181	41.	**Knockers Up**	Rusty Warren
59	11	1	181	42.	**The Buddy Holly Story**	Buddy Holly
84	28	3	180	43.	**Under A Blood Red Sky**	U2
83	12	1	179	44.	**War**	U2
59	2	4	178	45.	**From The Hungry I**	The Kingston Trio
89	2	3	176	46.	**Beaches**	Bette Midler/Soundtrack
63	3	1	176	47.	**Moon River & Other Great Movie Themes**	Andy Williams
67	1	15	175	48.	**Sgt. Pepper's Lonely Hearts Club Band**	The Beatles
89	1	10	175	49.	**Forever Your Girl**	Paula Abdul
74	1	3	175	50.	**John Denver's Greatest Hits**	John Denver

#1 ALBUMS

This section lists in chronological order, by peak date, all of the 557 albums which hit the #1 position on *Billboard's Top Pop Albums* chart (currently *The Billboard 200*) from 1955 through November 24, 2001. (The #1 albums listed after the June 30, 2001 research cut-off date are not listed elsewhere in this book.)

For the years 1958 through 1963, when separate stereo and monaural (mono) charts were published each week, the total number of weeks an album held the #1 spot on either or both of these charts is listed below the album. Weeks at #1 on Stereo chart and Mono chart are not totalled together; weeks at #1 is determined by total number of <u>issues</u> that an album held the #1 spot — whether it was #1 on both charts, or on either the stereo or mono chart.

Billboard has not published an issue for the last week of the year since 1976. For the years 1976 through 1991, *Billboard* considered the charts listed in the last published issue of the year to be "frozen" and all chart positions remained the same for the unpublished week. This frozen chart data is included in our tabulations. Since 1992, *Billboard* has <u>compiled</u> *The Billboard 200* chart for the last week of the year, even though an issue is <u>not published</u>. This chart is only available through *Billboard's* computerized information network (BIN). Our tabulations include this unpublished chart data.

See the introduction pages of this book for more details on researching the *Top Pop Albums* charts.

DATE: Date album first peaked at the #1 position

WKS: Total weeks album held the #1 position

   ↕: Indicates album hit #1, dropped down, and then returned to the #1 spot

   ❶: Indicates album debuted at the #1 position

> Each year's top #1 album(s) is boxed out for quick reference. The top albums are determined by the most weeks at the #1 position.

#1 ALBUMS

1955

DATE WKS

Two albums from 1954 continued into 1955 at the #1 spot: "The Student Prince" by Mario Lanza (18 wks.) and "Music, Martinis And Memories" by Jackie Gleason (2 wks.). For all of 1955 and up to 3/24/56, the LP chart was published mainly on a bi-weekly basis. The chart was considered `frozen' for a non-published week and, therefore, each position on the published chart was counted twice. In addition to these bi-weekly `frozen' charts, there were 5 other weeks of unpublished charts which did not count toward weeks at the #1 spot.

1. 5/28 **2** **Crazy Otto** *Crazy Otto*
2. 6/11 **6** **Starring Sammy Davis, Jr.**
   Sammy Davis, Jr.
3. 6/25 **4** **in the Wee Small Hours** *Frank Sinatra*
4. 7/23 **19** **Love Me Or Leave Me**
   Doris Day/Soundtrack
5. 7/23 **2** **Lonesome Echo** *Jackie Gleason*

1956

DATE WKS

Beginning with 3/24/56, Billboard published the LP chart on a weekly basis. From the first of the year to that date, there were 2 published charts, 2 frozen charts and 7 weeks of unpublished charts.

1. 1/28 **4** **Oklahoma!** *Soundtrack*
2. 3/24 **6** **Belafonte** *Harry Belafonte*
3. 5/5 **10** **Elvis Presley** *Elvis Presley*
4. 7/14 **15↕** **My Fair Lady** *Original Cast*
   peaked at #1 in 4 consecutive years: 1956 (8 weeks),
   1957 (1 week), 1958 (3 weeks) and 1959
   (3 weeks — stereo charts)
5. 9/8 **31↕** **Calypso** *Harry Belafonte*
6. 10/6 **1** **The King And I** *Soundtrack*
7. 10/13 **1** **The Eddy Duchin Story** *Carmen Cavallaro/Soundtrack*
8. 12/8 **5** **Elvis** *Elvis Presley*

1957

DATE WKS

1. 5/27 **8** **Love Is The Thing** *Nat "King" Cole*
2. 7/22 **10↕** **Around The World In 80 Days**
   Soundtrack
3. 7/29 **10** **Loving You** *Elvis Presley/Soundtrack*
4. 12/16 **4↕** **Elvis' Christmas Album** *Elvis Presley*
5. 12/30 **1** **Merry Christmas** *Bing Crosby*

1958

DATE WKS

1. 1/20 **2** **Ricky** *Ricky Nelson*
2. 2/10 **5** **Come Fly with me** *Frank Sinatra*
3. 3/17 **12↕** **The Music Man**
4. 5/19 **31↕** **South Pacific** *Soundtrack*
   includes 28 weeks at #1 on Stereo chart which began
   on 5/25/59
5. 6/9 **3↕** **Johnny's Greatest Hits** *Johnny Mathis*
6. 7/21 **10↕** **Gigi** *Soundtrack*
   includes 3 weeks at #1 in 1958, 3 weeks at #1 on solo
   chart in 1959, and 4 weeks at #1 on mono charts
   beginning on 5/25/59
7. 8/11 **7↕** **Tchaikovsky: Piano Concerto No. 1**
   Van Cliburn
8. 10/6 **8↕** **Sing Along With Mitch**
   Mitch Miller & The Gang

1958 (cont'd)

9. 10/13 **5** **Frank Sinatra sings for Only The Lonely** *Frank Sinatra*
10. 11/24 **1** **The Kingston Trio** *The Kingston Trio*
11. 12/29 **2** **Christmas Sing-Along With Mitch**
    Mitch Miller & The Gang

1959

DATE WKS

1. 2/2 **3** **Flower Drum Song** *Original Cast*
2. 2/23 **10** **The Music From Peter Gunn**
   Henry Mancini

> 5/25/59: Billboard splits solo album chart into separate
> Stereo and Monaural (Mono) charts

3. 6/22 **5** **Exotica** *Martin Denny*
   Mono: 5 weeks
4. 7/13 **1** **Film Encores** *Mantovani and his orchestra*
   Stereo: 1 week
5. 7/27 **15** **The Kingston Trio At Large**
   The Kingston Trio
   Mono: 15 weeks
6. 11/9 **5** **Heavenly** *Johnny Mathis*
   Mono: 5 weeks
7. 12/14 **8** **Here We Go Again!** *The Kingston Trio*
   Stereo: 2 weeks; Mono: 8 weeks

1960

DATE WKS

1. 1/11 **1** **The Lord's Prayer**
   Mormon Tabernacle Choir
   Stereo: 1 week
2. 1/25 **16** **The Sound Of Music** *Original Cast*
   Stereo: 15 weeks; Mono: 12
3. 4/25 **13↕** **Persuasive Percussion**
   Enoch Light/Terry Snyder and The All-Stars
   Stereo: 13 weeks
4. 5/2 **2↕** **Theme from A Summer Place**
   Billy Vaughn and his orchestra
   Mono: 2 weeks
5. 5/9 **12↕** **Sold Out** *The Kingston Trio*
   Stereo: 3 weeks; Mono: 10 weeks
6. 7/25 **14↕** **The Button-Down Mind Of Bob Newhart** *Bob Newhart*
   Mono: 14 weeks
7. 8/29 **10↕** **String Along** *The Kingston Trio*
   Stereo: 10 weeks; Mono: 5 weeks
8. 10/24 **9↕** **Nice 'n' Easy** *Frank Sinatra*
   Stereo: 9 weeks; Mono: 1 week
9. 12/5 **10↕** **G.I. Blues** *Elvis Presley/Soundtrack*
   Stereo: 2 weeks; Mono: 8 weeks

1961

DATE WKS

1. 1/9 **1** **The Button-Down Mind Strikes Back!**
   Bob Newhart
   Mono: 1 week
2. 1/16 **5↕** **Wonderland By Night**
   Bert Kaempfert and his orchestra
   Mono: 5 weeks
3. 1/23 **14↕** **Exodus** *Soundtrack*
   Stereo: 14 weeks; Mono: 3 weeks
4. 3/13 **11↕** **Calcutta!** *Lawrence Welk*
   Stereo: 11 weeks; Mono: 8 weeks

#1 ALBUMS

1961 (cont'd)

5. 6/5 **6** **Camelot** *Original Cast*
Mono: 6 weeks

6. 7/17 **9** **Stars For A Summer Night**
Various Artists
Stereo: 9 weeks; Mono: 4 weeks

7. 7/17 **1** **Carnival** *Original Cast*
Mono: 1 week

8. 8/21 **3** **Something for Everybody** *Elvis Presley*
Mono: 3 weeks

9. 9/11 **13** **Judy At Carnegie Hall** *Judy Garland*
Stereo: 9 weeks; Mono: 13 weeks

10. 11/20 **7** **Stereo 35/MM**
Enoch Light & The Light Brigade
Stereo: 7 weeks

11. 12/11 **20** **Blue Hawaii** *Elvis Presley/Soundtrack*
Stereo: 4 weeks; Mono: 20 weeks

1962

DATE	WKS	

1. 1/6 **1** **Holiday Sing Along With Mitch**
Mitch Miller And The Gang
Stereo: 1 week

2. 2/10 **12↕** **Breakfast At Tiffany's**
Henry Mancini/Soundtrack
Stereo: 12 week

3. 5/5 **54↕** **West Side Story** *Soundtrack*
Stereo: 53 weeks; Mono: 12 weeks
album with most weeks at #1 for 1955-2001 era

4. 6/23 **14** **Modern Sounds In Country And Western Music** *Ray Charles*
Stereo: 1 week; Mono: 14 weeks

5. 10/20 **7↕** **Peter, Paul and Mary** *Peter, Paul & Mary*
Mono: 6 weeks; returned to #1 spot for 1 week on solo album chart on 10/26/63

6. 12/1 **2** **My Son, The Folk Singer** *Allan Sherman*
Mono: 2 weeks

7. 12/15 **12** **The First Family** *Vaughn Meader*
Mono: 12 weeks

1963

DATE	WKS	

1. 3/9 **1** **Jazz Samba** *Charlie Byrd*
Mono: 1 week

2. 3/9 **1** **My Son, The Celebrity** *Allan Sherman*
Stereo: 1 week

3. 3/16 **5** **Songs I Sing On The Jackie Gleason Show** *Frank Fontaine*
Mono: 8 weeks

4. 5/4 **16** **Days of Wine and Roses** *Andy Williams*
Stereo: 11 weeks; Mono: 15 weeks;
Combined chart: 1 week (see below)

> 8/17/63: Billboard combines Stereo & Monaural charts into one single chart: Top LP's

5. 8/24 **1** **Little Stevie Wonder/The 12 Year Old Genius** *Stevie Wonder*

6. 8/31 **8** **My Son, The Nut** *Allan Sherman*

7. 11/2 **5** **In The Wind** *Peter, Paul & Mary*

8. 12/7 **10** **The Singing Nun** *The Singing Nun*

1964

DATE	WKS	

1. 2/15 **11** **Meet The Beatles!** *The Beatles*

2. 5/2 **5** **The Beatles' Second Album** *The Beatles*

3. 6/6 **1** **Hello, Dolly!** *Original Cast*

4. 6/13 **6** **Hello, Dolly!** *Louis Armstrong*

5. 7/25 **14** **A Hard Day's Night** *The Beatles/Soundtrack*

6. 10/31 **5** **People** *Barbra Streisand*

7. 12/5 **4** **Beach Boys Concert** *The Beach Boys*

1965

DATE	WKS	

1. 1/2 **1** **Roustabout** *Elvis Presley/Soundtrack*

2. 1/9 **9** **Beatles '65** *The Beatles*

3. 3/13 **14↕** **Mary Poppins** *Soundtrack*

4. 3/20 **3** **Goldfinger** *Soundtrack*

5. 7/10 **6** **Beatles VI** *The Beatles*

6. 8/21 **3** **Out Of Our Heads** *The Rolling Stones*

7. 9/11 **9** **Help!** *The Beatles/Soundtrack*

8. 11/13 **2** **The Sound Of Music** *Soundtrack*

9. 11/27 **8** **Whipped Cream & Other Delights**
Herb Alpert's Tijuana Brass

1966

DATE	WKS	

1. 1/8 **6** **Rubber Soul** *The Beatles*

2. 3/5 **6↕** **Going Places** *Herb Alpert And The Tijuana Brass*

3. 3/12 **5** **Ballads of the Green Berets**
SSgt Barry Sadler

4. 5/21 **1** **If You Can Believe Your Eyes And Ears** *The Mama's & The Papa's*

5. 5/28 **9↕** **What Now My Love** *Herb Alpert*

6. 7/23 **1** **Strangers In The Night** *Frank Sinatra*

7. 7/30 **5** **"Yesterday"...And Today** *The Beatles*

8. 9/10 **6** **Revolver** *The Beatles*

9. 10/22 **2** **The Supremes A' Go-Go** *The Supremes*

10. 11/5 **1** **Doctor Zhivago** *Soundtrack*

11. 11/12 **13** **The Monkees** *The Monkees*

1967

DATE	WKS	

1. 2/11 **18** **More Of The Monkees** *The Monkees*

2. 6/17 **1** **Sounds Like** *Herb Alpert & The Tijuana Brass*

3. 6/24 **1** **Headquarters** *The Monkees*

4. 7/1 **15** **Sgt. Pepper's Lonely Hearts Club Band** *The Beatles*

5. 10/14 **2** **Ode To Billie Joe** *Bobbie Gentry*

6. 10/28 **5** **Diana Ross and the Supremes Greatest Hits**
Diana Ross & The Supremes

7. 12/2 **5** **Pisces, Aquarius, Capricorn & Jones Ltd.** *The Monkees*

#1 ALBUMS

1968

	DATE	WKS	
1.	1/6	8	**Magical Mystery Tour** *The Beatles/Soundtrack*
2.	3/2	5	**Blooming Hits** *Paul Mauriat & his orchestra*
3.	4/6	9↕	**The Graduate** *Simon & Garfunkel/Soundtrack*
4.	5/25	7↕	**Bookends** *Simon & Garfunkel*
5.	7/27	2	**The Beat Of The Brass** *Herb Alpert & The Tijuana Brass*
6.	8/10	4	**Wheels Of Fire** *Cream*
7.	9/7	4↕	**Waiting For The Sun** *The Doors*
8.	9/28	1	**Time Peace/The Rascals' Greatest Hits** *The Rascals*
9.	10/12	8↕	**Cheap Thrills** *Big Brother & The Holding Company*
10.	11/16	2	**Electric Ladyland** *Jimi Hendrix Experience*
11.	12/21	5↕	**Wichita Lineman** *Glen Campbell*
12.	12/28	9↕	**The Beatles [White Album]** *The Beatles*

1969

	DATE	WKS	
1.	2/8	1	**TCB** *Diana Ross & The Supremes with The Temptations*
2.	3/29	7↕	**Blood, Sweat & Tears** *Blood, Sweat & Tears*
3.	4/26	13	**Hair** *Original Cast*
4.	8/23	4	**Johnny Cash At San Quentin** *Johnny Cash*
5.	9/20	2	**Blind Faith** *Blind Faith*
6.	10/4	4	**Green River** *Creedence Clearwater Revival*
7.	11/1	11↕	**Abbey Road** *The Beatles*
8.	12/27	7↕	**Led Zeppelin II** *Led Zeppelin*

1970

	DATE	WKS	
1.	3/7	10	**Bridge Over Troubled Water** *Simon & Garfunkel*
2.	5/16	1	**Deja Vu** *Crosby, Stills, Nash & Young*
3.	5/23	3	**McCartney** *Paul McCartney*
4.	6/13	4	**Let It Be** *The Beatles/Soundtrack*
5.	7/11	4	**Woodstock** *Soundtrack*
6.	8/8	2	**Blood, Sweat & Tears 3** *Blood, Sweat & Tears*
7.	8/22	9	**Cosmo's Factory** *Creedence Clearwater Revival*
8.	10/24	6↕	**Abraxas** *Santana*
9.	10/31	4	**Led Zeppelin III** *Led Zeppelin*

1971

	DATE	WKS	
1.	1/2	7	**All Things Must Pass** *George Harrison*
2.	2/20	3↕	**Jesus Christ Superstar** *Various Artists*
3.	2/27	9	**Pearl** *Janis Joplin*
4.	5/15	1	**4 Way Street** *Crosby, Stills, Nash & Young*
5.	5/22	4	**Sticky Fingers** *The Rolling Stones*
6.	6/19	15	**Tapestry** *Carole King*
7.	10/2	4	**Every Picture Tells A Story** *Rod Stewart*
8.	10/30	1	**Imagine** *John Lennon*
9.	11/6	1	**Shaft** *Isaac Hayes/Soundtrack*
10.	11/13	5	**Santana III** *Santana*
11.	12/18	2	**There's A Riot Goin' On** *Sly & The Family Stone*

1972

	DATE	WKS	
1.	1/1	3	**Music** *Carole King*
2.	1/22	7	**American Pie** *Don McLean*
3.	3/11	2	**Harvest** *Neil Young*
4.	3/25	2	**America** *America*
5.	4/29	5	**First Take** *Roberta Flack*
6.	6/3	2	**Thick As A Brick** *Jethro Tull*
7.	6/17	4	**Exile On Main St.** *The Rolling Stones*
8.	7/15	5	**Honky Chateau** *Elton John*
9.	8/19	9	**Chicago V** *Chicago*
10.	10/21	4	**Superfly** *Curtis Mayfield/Soundtrack*
11.	11/18	3	**Catch Bull At Four** *Cat Stevens*
12.	12/9	5	**Seventh Sojourn** *The Moody Blues*

1973

	DATE	WKS	
1.	1/13	5	**No Secrets** *Carly Simon*
2.	2/17	2	**The World Is A Ghetto** *War*
3.	3/3	2	**Don't Shoot Me I'm Only The Piano Player** *Elton John*
4.	3/17	3	**Dueling Banjos** *Eric Weissberg & Steve Mandell*
5.	4/7	2	**Lady Sings The Blues** *Diana Ross/Soundtrack*
6.	4/21	1	**Billion Dollar Babies** *Alice Cooper*
7.	4/28	1	**The Dark Side Of The Moon** *Pink Floyd*
8.	5/5	1	**Aloha from Hawaii via Satellite** *Elvis Presley*
9.	5/12	2	**Houses Of The Holy** *Led Zeppelin*
10.	5/26	1	**The Beatles/1967-1970**
11.	6/2	3	**Red Rose Speedway** *Paul McCartney & Wings*
12.	6/23	5	**Living In The Material World** *George Harrison*
13.	7/28	5↕	**Chicago VI** *Chicago*
14.	8/18	1	**A Passion Play** *Jethro Tull*
15.	9/8	5	**Brothers And Sisters** *The Allman Brothers Band*
16.	10/13	4	**Goats Head Soup** *The Rolling Stones*
17.	11/10	8	**Goodbye Yellow Brick Road** *Elton John*

1974

	DATE	WKS	
1.	1/5	1	**The Singles 1969-1973** *Carpenters*
2.	1/12	5	**You Don't Mess Around With Jim** *Jim Croce*
3.	2/16	4	**Planet Waves** *Bob Dylan*
4.	3/16	2	**The Way We Were** *Barbra Streisand*
5.	3/30	3↕	**John Denver's Greatest Hits** *John Denver*
6.	4/13	4↕	**Band On The Run** *Paul McCartney & Wings*
7.	4/27	1	**Chicago VII** *Chicago*
8.	5/4	5	**The Sting** *Marvin Hamlisch/Soundtrack*
9.	6/22	2	**Sundown** *Gordon Lightfoot*
10.	7/13	4	**Caribou** *Elton John*
11.	8/10	1	**Back Home Again** *John Denver*
12.	8/17	4	**461 Ocean Boulevard** *Eric Clapton*

#1 ALBUMS

1974 (cont'd)

13.	9/14	2	**Fulfillingness' First Finale**
14.	9/28	1	**Bad Company** *Bad Company*
15.	10/5	1	**Endless Summer** *The Beach Boys*
16.	10/12	1	**If You Love Me, Let Me Know**
17.	10/19	1	**Not Fragile** *Bachman-Turner Overdrive*
18.	10/26	1	**Can't Get Enough** *Barry White*
19.	11/2	1	**So Far** *Crosby, Stills, Nash & Young*
20.	11/9	1	**Wrap Around Joy** *Carole King*
21.	11/16	1	**Walls And Bridges** *John Lennon*
22.	11/23	1	**It's Only Rock 'N Roll** *The Rolling Stones*
23.	11/30	10	**Elton John - Greatest Hits** *Elton John*

(13. Stevie Wonder)
(16. Olivia Newton-John)

1975

DATE	WKS		
1.	2/8	1	**Fire** *Ohio Players*
2.	2/15	1	**Heart Like A Wheel** *Linda Ronstadt*
3.	2/22	1	**AWB** *Average White Band*
4.	3/1	2	**Blood On The Tracks** *Bob Dylan*
5.	3/15	1	**Have You Never Been Mellow**
			Olivia Newton-John
6.	3/22	6	**Physical Graffiti** *Led Zeppelin*
7.	5/3	2	**Chicago VIII** *Chicago*
8.	5/17	3	**That's The Way Of The World**
			Earth, Wind & Fire/Soundtrack
9.	6/7	7↕ ❶	**Captain Fantastic And The Brown Dirt Cowboy** *Elton John*
			the first album to debut at #1
10.	7/19	1	**Venus And Mars** *Wings*
11.	7/26	5	**One Of These Nights** *Eagles*
12.	9/6	4↕	**Red Octopus** *Jefferson Starship*
13.	9/13	1	**The Heat Is On** *The Isley Brothers*
14.	9/20	1	**Between The Lines** *Janis Ian*
15.	10/4	2	**Wish You Were Here** *Pink Floyd*
16.	10/18	2	**Windsong** *John Denver*
17.	11/8	3 ❶	**Rock Of The Westies** *Elton John*
18.	12/6	1	**Still Crazy After All These Years**
			Paul Simon
19.	12/13	5	**Chicago IX - Chicago's Greatest Hits**
			Chicago

1976

DATE	WKS		
1.	1/17	3	**Gratitude** *Earth, Wind & Fire*
2.	2/7	5	**Desire** *Bob Dylan*
3.	3/13	5↕	**Eagles/Their Greatest Hits 1971-1975**
			Eagles
4.	4/10	10↕	**Frampton Comes Alive!** *Peter Frampton*
5.	4/24	7↕	**Wings At The Speed Of Sound** *Wings*
6.	5/1	2	**Presence** *Led Zeppelin*
7.	5/15	4↕	**Black And Blue** *The Rolling Stones*
8.	7/31	2	**Breezin'** *George Benson*
9.	9/4	1	**Fleetwood Mac** *Fleetwood Mac*
10.	10/16	14↕ ❶	**Songs In The Key Of Life** *Stevie Wonder*

1977

DATE	WKS		
1.	1/15	8↕	**Hotel California** *Eagles*
2.	1/22	1	**Wings Over America** *Wings*
3.	2/12	6	**A Star Is Born**
			Barbra Streisand/Soundtrack
4.	4/2	31↕	**Rumours** *Fleetwood Mac*
5.	7/16	1	**Barry Manilow/Live** *Barry Manilow*
6.	12/3	5	**Simple Dreams** *Linda Ronstadt*

1978

DATE	WKS		
1.	1/21	24	**Saturday Night Fever**
			Bee Gees/Soundtrack
2.	7/8	1	**City to City** *Gerry Rafferty*
3.	7/15	2	**Some Girls** *The Rolling Stones*
4.	7/29	12↕	**Grease** *Soundtrack*
5.	9/16	2↕	**Don't Look Back** *Boston*
6.	11/4	1	**Living In The USA** *Linda Ronstadt*
7.	11/11	1	**Live And More** *Donna Summer*
8.	11/18	8↕	**52nd Street** *Billy Joel*

1979

DATE	WKS		
1.	1/6	3	**Barbra Streisand's Greatest Hits, Volume 2** *Barbra Streisand*
2.	2/3	1	**Briefcase Full Of Blues** *Blues Brothers*
3.	2/10	3	**Blondes Have More Fun** *Rod Stewart*
4.	3/3	6↕	**Spirits Having Flown** *Bee Gees*
5.	4/7	5↕	**Minute By Minute** *The Doobie Brothers*
6.	5/19	6↕	**Breakfast In America** *Supertramp*
7.	6/16	6↕	**Bad Girls** *Donna Summer*
8.	8/11	5	**Get The Knack** *The Knack*
9.	9/15	7	**In Through The Out Door** *Led Zeppelin*
10.	11/3	9	**The Long Run** *Eagles*

1980

DATE	WKS		
1.	1/5	1	**On The Radio-Greatest Hits-Volumes I & II** *Donna Summer*
2.	1/12	1	**Bee Gees Greatest** *Bee Gees*
3.	1/19	15	**The Wall** *Pink Floyd*
4.	5/3	6	**Against The Wind** *Bob Seger*
5.	6/14	6	**Glass Houses** *Billy Joel*
6.	7/26	7	**Emotional Rescue** *The Rolling Stones*
7.	9/13	1	**Hold Out** *Jackson Browne*
8.	9/20	5	**The Game** *Queen*
9.	10/25	3↕	**Guilty** *Barbra Streisand*
10.	11/8	4	**The River** *Bruce Springsteen*
11.	12/13	2	**Kenny Rogers' Greatest Hits** *Kenny Rogers*
12.	12/27	8	**Double Fantasy** *John Lennon/Yoko Ono*

#1 ALBUMS

1981

DATE	WKS	
1.	2/21	15↕	Hi Infidelity *REO Speedwagon*
2.	4/4	3↕	Paradise Theater *Styx*
3.	6/27	4	Mistaken Identity *Kim Carnes*
4.	7/25	3	Long Distance Voyager *The Moody Blues*
5.	8/15	1	Precious Time *Pat Benatar*
6.	8/22	10↕	4 *Foreigner*
7.	9/5	1	Bella Donna *Stevie Nicks*
8.	9/12	1	Escape *Journey*
9.	9/19	9	Tattoo You *The Rolling Stones*
10.	12/26	3	For Those About To Rock We Salute You *AC/DC*

1982

DATE	WKS	
1.	2/6	4	Freeze-Frame *The J. Geils Band*
2.	3/6	6	Beauty And The Beat *Go-Go's*
3.	4/17	4	Chariots Of Fire *Vangelis/Soundtrack*
4.	5/15	9↕	Asia *Asia*
5.	5/29	3	Tug Of War *Paul McCartney*
6.	8/7	5	Mirage *Fleetwood Mac*
7.	9/11	9	American Fool *John Cougar*
8.	11/13	15	Business As Usual *Men At Work*

1983

DATE	WKS	
1.	2/26	37↕	Thriller *Michael Jackson*
2.	6/25	2	Flashdance *Soundtrack*
3.	7/23	17↕	Synchronicity *The Police*
4.	11/26	1	Metal Health *Quiet Riot*
5.	12/3	3	Can't Slow Down *Lionel Richie*

1984

DATE	WKS	
1.	4/21	10	Footloose *Soundtrack*
2.	6/30	1	Sports *Huey Lewis & The News*
3.	7/7	7↕	Born In The U.S.A. *Bruce Springsteen*
4.	8/4	24	Purple Rain *Prince & The Revolution/Soundtrack*

1985

DATE	WKS	
1.	2/9	3	Like A Virgin *Madonna*
2.	3/2	3	Make It Big *Wham!*
3.	3/23	1	Centerfield *John Fogerty*
4.	3/30	7↕	No Jacket Required *Phil Collins*
5.	4/27	3	We Are The World *USA For Africa*
6.	6/1	3	Around The World In A Day *Prince & The Revolution*
7.	6/22	2	Beverly Hills Cop *Soundtrack*
8.	7/13	5↕	Songs From The Big Chair *Tears For Fears*
9.	8/10	2	Reckless *Bryan Adams*
10.	8/31	9	Brothers In Arms *Dire Straits*
11.	11/2	11↕	Miami Vice *Television Soundtrack*
12.	12/21	1	Heart *Heart*

1986

DATE	WKS	
1.	1/25	3	The Broadway Album *Barbra Streisand*
2.	2/15	2	Promise *Sade*
3.	3/1	1	Welcome To The Real World *Mr. Mister*
4.	3/8	14↕	Whitney Houston *Whitney Houston*
5.	4/26	3	5150 *Van Halen*
6.	7/5	2	Control *Janet Jackson*
7.	7/19	1	Winner In You *Patti LaBelle*
8.	7/26	5↕	Top Gun *Soundtrack*
9.	8/16	5	True Blue *Madonna*
10.	9/27	2	Dancing On The Ceiling *Lionel Richie*
11.	10/18	1	Fore! *Huey Lewis & The News*
12.	10/25	8↕	Slippery When Wet *Bon Jovi*
13.	11/1	4	Third Stage *Boston*
14.	11/29	7	❶ Bruce Springsteen & The E Street Band Live/1975-85 *Bruce Springsteen*

1987

DATE	WKS	
1.	3/7	7	Licensed To Ill *Beastie Boys*
2.	4/25	9	The Joshua Tree *U2*
3.	6/27	11	❶ Whitney *Whitney Houston*
4.	9/12	2	La Bamba *Los Lobos/Soundtrack*
5.	9/26	6	❶ Bad *Michael Jackson*
6.	11/7	1	Tunnel of Love *Bruce Springsteen*
7.	11/14	18↕	Dirty Dancing *Soundtrack*

1988

DATE	WKS	
1.	1/16	12↕	Faith *George Michael*
2.	1/23	2	Tiffany *Tiffany*
3.	6/25	4	OU812 *Van Halen*
4.	7/23	6↕	Hysteria *Def Leppard*
5.	8/6	5↕	Appetite For Destruction *Guns N' Roses*
6.	8/20	1	Roll With It *Steve Winwood*
7.	8/27	1	Tracy Chapman *Tracy Chapman*
8.	10/15	4	New Jersey *Bon Jovi*
9.	11/12	6	Rattle And Hum *U2/Soundtrack*
10.	12/24	4	Giving You The Best That I Got *Anita Baker*

1989

DATE	WKS	
1.	1/21	6↕	Don't Be Cruel *Bobby Brown*
2.	3/11	5	Electric Youth *Debbie Gibson*
3.	4/15	1	Loc-ed After Dark *Tone Loc*
4.	4/22	6	Like A Prayer *Madonna*
5.	6/3	7	The Raw & The Cooked *Fine Young Cannibals*
6.	7/22	6	Batman *Prince/Soundtrack*
7.	9/2	1	Repeat Offender *Richard Marx*
8.	9/9	2	Hangin' Tough *New Kids On The Block*
9.	9/23	8↕	Girl You Know It's True *Milli Vanilli*
10.	10/7	10↕	Forever Your Girl *Paula Abdul*
11.	10/14	2	Dr. Feelgood *Mötley Crüe*
12.	10/28	4	Janet Jackson's Rhythm Nation 1814 *Janet Jackson*
13.	12/16	1	Storm Front *Billy Joel*

#1 ALBUMS

DATE	WKS	
1.	1/6	3↕	...But Seriously *Phil Collins*
2.	4/7	3	Nick Of Time *Bonnie Raitt*
3.	4/28	6	I Do Not Want What I Haven't Got *Sinéad O'Connor*
4.	6/9	21↕	Please Hammer Don't Hurt 'Em *M.C. Hammer*
5.	6/30	1	Step By Step *New Kids On The Block*
6.	11/10	16	To The Extreme *Vanilla Ice*

1991

DATE	WKS	
1.	3/2	11	Mariah Carey *Mariah Carey*
2.	5/18	2↕	Out Of Time *R.E.M.*

5/25/91: Billboard begins compiling the pop albums chart based on actual units sold. The data is provided by SoundScan Inc. and is collected by point-of-sale scanning machines which read the UPC bar code.

3.	5/25	1	Time, Love & Tenderness *Michael Bolton*
4.	6/8	2	Spellbound *Paula Abdul*
5.	6/22	1	EFIL4ZAGGIN *N.W.A.*
6.	6/29	1	❶ Slave To The Grind *Skid Row*
7.	7/6	3	❶ For Unlawful Carnal Knowledge *Van Halen*
8.	7/27	5	Unforgettable With Love *Natalie Cole*
9.	8/31	4	❶ Metallica *Metallica*
10.	9/28	18↕	❶ Ropin' The Wind *Garth Brooks*
11.	10/5	2	❶ Use Your Illusion II *Guns N' Roses*
12.	12/7	1	❶ Achtung Baby *U2*
13.	12/14	4	❶ Dangerous *Michael Jackson*

1992

DATE	WKS	
1.	1/11	2↕	Nevermind *Nirvana*
2.	4/4	2	Wayne's World *Soundtrack*
3.	4/18	5	❶ Adrenalize *Def Leppard*
4.	5/23	2↕	Totally Krossed Out *Kris Kross*
5.	5/30	1	❶ The Southern Harmony And Musical Companion *The Black Crowes*
6.	6/13	17	Some Gave All *Billy Ray Cyrus*
7.	10/10	7↕	❶ The Chase *Garth Brooks*
8.	11/21	1	Timeless (The Classics) *Michael Bolton*
9.	12/5	1	❶ The Predator *Ice Cube*
10.	12/12	20↕	The Bodyguard *Whitney Houston/Soundtrack*

1993

DATE	WKS	
1.	3/13	3	Unplugged *Eric Clapton*
2.	4/10	1	❶ Songs Of Faith And Devotion *Depeche Mode*
3.	5/8	1	❶ Get A Grip *Aerosmith*
4.	6/5	6	❶ janet. *Janet Jackson*
5.	7/17	1	❶ Back To Broadway *Barbra Streisand*
6.	7/24	2	❶ Zooropa *U2*
7.	8/7	2	❶ Black Sunday *Cypress Hill*
8.	8/21	1	Sleepless In Seattle *Soundtrack*
9.	8/28	3	❶ River Of Dreams *Billy Joel*
10.	9/18	5↕	❶ In Pieces *Garth Brooks*

1993 (cont'd)

11.	10/9	1	❶ In Utero *Nirvana*
12.	10/30	1	Bat Out Of Hell II: Back Into Hell *Meat Loaf*
13.	11/6	5	❶ Vs. *Pearl Jam*
14.	12/11	3↕	❶ Doggy Style *Snoop Doggy Dogg*
15.	12/25	8↕	Music Box *Mariah Carey*

1994

DATE	WKS	
1.	2/12	1	❶ Jar Of Flies *Alice In Chains*
2.	2/19	1	Kickin' It Up *John Michael Montgomery*
3.	2/26	2↕	Toni Braxton *Toni Braxton*
4.	3/26	1	❶ Superunknown *Soundgarden*
5.	4/2	2↕	The Sign *Ace Of Base*
6.	4/9	1	❶ Far Beyond Driven *Pantera*
7.	4/16	1	Longing In Their Hearts *Bonnie Raitt*
8.	4/23	4	❶ The Division Bell *Pink Floyd*
9.	5/21	2	Not A Moment Too Soon *Tim McGraw*
10.	6/4	1	The Crow *Soundtrack*
11.	6/18	1	❶ III Communication *Beastie Boys*
12.	6/25	3	❶ Purple *Stone Temple Pilots*
13.	7/16	10	The Lion King *Soundtrack*
14.	9/17	5↕	❶ II *Boyz II Men*
15.	10/1	1	❶ From The Cradle *Eric Clapton*
16.	10/15	2	❶ Monster *R.E.M.*
17.	11/5	2	❶ Murder Was The Case *Soundtrack*
18.	11/19	1	❶ MTV Unplugged In New York *Nirvana*
19.	11/26	2	❶ Hell Freezes Over *Eagles*
20.	12/10	3↕	Miracles - The Holiday Album *Kenny G*
21.	12/24	1	Vitalogy *Pearl Jam*

1995

DATE	WKS	
1.	1/7	8↕	The Hits *Garth Brooks*
2.	2/11	1	❶ Balance *Van Halen*
3.	3/18	2	❶ Greatest Hits *Bruce Springsteen*
4.	4/1	4	❶ Me Against The World *2Pac*
5.	5/6	1	Throwing Copper *Live*
6.	5/13	2	Friday *Soundtrack*
7.	5/27	8↕	Cracked Rear View *Hootie & The Blowfish*
8.	6/24	1	❶ Pulse *Pink Floyd*
9.	7/8	2	❶ HIStory: Past, Present And Future - Book I *Michael Jackson*
10.	7/22	1	Pocahontas *Soundtrack*
11.	8/5	1	❶ Dreaming Of You *Selena*
12.	8/12	2	❶ E. 1999 Eternal *Bone Thugs-N-Harmony*
13.	9/2	4	Dangerous Minds *Soundtrack*
14.	10/7	12↕	Jagged Little Pill *Alanis Morissette*
15.	10/21	6↕	❶ Daydream *Mariah Carey*
16.	11/11	1	❶ Mellon Collie And The Infinite Sadness *The Smashing Pumpkins*
17.	11/18	1	❶ Dogg Food *Tha Dogg Pound*
18.	11/25	1	❶ Alice In Chains *Alice In Chains*
19.	12/2	1	❶ R. Kelly *R. Kelly*
20.	12/9	3	❶ Anthology 1 *The Beatles*

#1 ALBUMS

DATE	WKS	1996
1.	1/20	5	**Waiting To Exhale** *Soundtrack*
2.	3/2	2	❶ **All Eyez On Me** *2Pac*
3.	4/6	1	❶ **Anthology 2** *The Beatles*
4.	5/4	1	❶ **Evil Empire** *Rage Against The Machine*
5.	5/11	2	❶ **Fairweather Johnson**
			Hootie & The Blowfish
6.	5/25	4	**The Score** *Fugees (Refugee Camp)*
7.	6/22	4	❶ **Load** *Metallica*
8.	7/20	4	❶ **It Was Written** *Nas*
9.	8/17	1	❶ **Beats, Rhymes And Life**
			A Tribe Called Quest
10.	9/14	2	❶ **No Code** *Pearl Jam*
11.	9/28	1	❶ **Home Again** *New Edition*
12.	10/5	3↕	**Falling Into You** *Celine Dion*
13.	10/19	1	❶ **From The Muddy Banks Of The**
			Wishkah *Nirvana*
14.	11/2	1	❶ **Recovering The Satellites**
			Counting Crows
15.	11/9	1	❶ **Best Of Volume 1** *Van Halen*
16.	11/16	1	❶ **Anthology 3** *The Beatles*
17.	11/23	1	❶ **The Don Killuminati - The 7 Day**
			Theory *Makaveli*
18.	11/30	1	❶ **Tha Doggfather** *Snoop Doggy Dogg*
19.	12/7	2	❶ **Razorblade Suitcase** *Bush*
20.	12/21	9↕	**Tragic Kingdom** *No Doubt*

DATE	WKS	1997
1.	2/15	1	❶ **Gridlock'd** *Soundtrack*
2.	3/1	1	❶ **Unchained Melody/The Early Years**
			LeAnn Rimes
3.	3/8	1	❶ **Secret Samadhi** *Live*
4.	3/15	1	❶ **Private Parts** *Soundtrack*
5.	3/22	1	❶ **Pop** *U2*
6.	3/29	1	❶ **The Untouchable** *Scarface*
7.	4/5	1	❶ **Nine Lives** *Aerosmith*
8.	4/12	4	**Life After Death** *The Notorious B.I.G.*
9.	5/10	1	❶ **Share My World** *Mary J. Blige*
10.	5/17	1	**Carrying Your Love With Me**
			George Strait
11.	5/24	5↕	**Spice** *Spice Girls*
12.	6/21	1	❶ **Wu-Tang Forever** *Wu-Tang Clan*
13.	6/28	2	**Butterfly Kisses (Shades Of Grace)**
			Bob Carlisle
14.	7/19	1	❶ **The Fat Of The Land** *Prodigy*
15.	7/26	2	**Men In Black - The Album** *Soundtrack*
16.	8/9	4↕	❶ **No Way Out** *Puff Daddy & The Family*
17.	8/16	1	❶ **The Art Of War** *Bone Thugs-N-Harmony*
18.	9/6	1	❶ **The Dance** *Fleetwood Mac*
19.	9/20	1	**Ghetto D** *Master P*
20.	9/27	3↕	❶ **You Light Up My Life - Inspirational**
			Songs *LeAnn Rimes*
21.	10/4	1	❶ **Butterfly** *Mariah Carey*
22.	10/11	1	❶ **Evolution** *Boyz II Men*
23.	10/25	1	❶ **The Velvet Rope** *Janet Jackson*
24.	11/8	1	❶ **The Firm - The Album** *The Firm*
25.	11/15	2	❶ **Harlem World** *Mase*
26.	11/29	1	❶ **Higher Ground** *Barbra Streisand*

1997 (cont'd)

27.	12/6	1	❶ **Reload** *Metallica*
28.	12/13	5	❶ **Sevens** *Garth Brooks*

DATE	WKS	1998
1.	1/17	1	**Let's Talk About Love** *Celine Dion*
2.	1/24	16	**Titanic** *Soundtrack*
3.	5/16	1	❶ **Before These Crowded Streets**
			Dave Matthews Band
4.	5/23	2	❶ **The Limited Series** *Garth Brooks*
5.	6/6	1	❶ **It's Dark And Hell Is Hot** *DMX*
6.	6/13	3↕	**City Of Angels** *Soundtrack*
7.	6/20	2	**MP Da Last Don** *Master P*
8.	7/18	2	**Armageddon** *Soundtrack*
9.	8/1	3	❶ **Hello Nasty** *Beastie Boys*
10.	8/22	2	❶ **Da Game Is To Be Sold, Not To Be**
			Told *Snoop Dogg*
11.	9/5	1	❶ **Follow The Leader** *Korn*
12.	9/12	4↕	❶ **The Miseducation Of Lauryn Hill**
			Lauryn Hill
13.	10/3	1	❶ **Mechanical Animals** *Marilyn Manson*
14.	10/17	5	❶ **Vol. 2...Hard Knock Life** *Jay-Z*
15.	11/21	2	❶ **Supposed Former Infatuation Junkie**
			Alanis Morissette
16.	12/5	5	❶ **Double Live** *Garth Brooks*

DATE	WKS	1999
1.	1/9	3	❶ **Flesh Of My Flesh Blood Of My Blood**
			DMX
2.	1/30	6↕	❶ **...Baby One More Time** *Britney Spears*
3.	2/6	1	❶ **Made Man** *Silkk The Shocker*
4.	2/13	1	❶ **Chyna Doll** *Foxy Brown*
5.	3/13	5↕	❶ **Fanmail** *TLC*
6.	4/24	2	❶ **I Am...** *Nas*
7.	5/15	1	❶ **Ruff Ryders - Ryde Or Die Vol. I**
			Ruff Ryders
8.	5/22	1	❶ **A Place In The Sun** *Tim McGraw*
9.	5/29	1	❶ **Ricky Martin** *Ricky Martin*
10.	6/5	10↕	❶ **Millennium** *Backstreet Boys*
11.	7/10	4↕	❶ **Significant Other** *Limp Bizkit*
12.	9/11	1	❶ **Christina Aguilera** *Christina Aguilera*
13.	9/18	2	❶ **Fly** *Dixie Chicks*
14.	10/2	1	❶ **Ruff Ryders' First Lady** *Eve*
15.	10/9	1	❶ **The Fragile** *Nine Inch Nails*
16.	10/16	2	❶ **Human Clay** *Creed*
17.	10/30	12↕	**Supernatural** *Santana*
18.	11/20	1	❶ **The Battle Of Los Angeles**
			Rage Against The Machine
19.	11/27	1	❶ **Breathe** *Faith Hill*
20.	12/4	1	❶ **Issues** *Korn*
21.	12/11	3↕	**All The Way...A Decade Of Song**
			Celine Dion
22.	12/25	1	❶ **Born Again** *The Notorious B.I.G.*

#1 ALBUMS

LABEL ABBREVIATIONS

American Gram. .... American Grammaphone
Barking P. .... Barking Pumpkin
Beggars Ban. .... Beggars Banquet
Booga Base. .... Booga Basement
Canadian-Am. .... Canadian-American
CBS Assoc. .... CBS Associated
Cleveland Int'l. .... Cleveland International
CMC Int'l. .... CMC International
Commonwealth U. .... Commonwealth United
Decca Broad. .... Decca Broadway
Digital Master. .... Digital Masterworks
Disturbing Tha P. .... Disturbing Tha Peace
Documentaries Un. .... Documentaries Unlimited
Epic/Assoc. .... Epic/Associated
Exp. Hendrix .... Experience Hendrix
Midland Int'l. .... Midland International
Midsong Int'l. .... Midsong International
New York Int'l. .... New York International
Other Peoples M. .... Other Peoples Music
Philadelphia Int'l. .... Philadelphia International
Sound Of Atl. .... Sound Of Atlanta
Street Know. .... Street Knowledge
Tetragramm. .... Tetragrammaton
TeeVee T. .... TeeVee Toons
Total Exper. .... Total Experience

The Charts From Top To Bottom

When the talk turns to music, more people turn to Joel Whitburn's Record Research Collection than to any other reference source.

That's because these are the **only** books that get right to the bottom of *Billboard's* major charts, with **complete, fully accurate chart data on every record ever charted**. So they're quoted with confidence by DJ's, music show hosts, program directors, collectors and other music enthusiasts worldwide.

Each book lists every record's significant chart data, such as peak position, debut date, peak date, weeks charted, label, record number and much more, all conveniently arranged for fast, easy reference. Most books also feature artist biographies, record notes, RIAA Platinum/Gold Record certifications, top artist and record achievements, all-time artist and record rankings, a chronological listing of all #1 hits, and additional in-depth chart information.

TOP POP SINGLES 1955-1999
Over 23,000 pop singles — every "Hot 100" hit — arranged by artist. Features thousands of artist biographies and countless titles notes. Also includes the B-side title of every "Hot 100" hit. 960 pages. $79.95 Hardcover / $69.95 Softcover.

POP ANNUAL 1955-1999
A year-by-year ranking, based on chart performance, of over 23,000 pop hits. Also includes, for the first time, the songwriters for every "Hot 100" hit. 912 pages. $79.95 Hardcover / $69.95 Softcover.

HIT LIST 1955-1999
An accurate checklist of every title that appears in both our Top Pop Singles 1955-1999 and Pop Annual 1955-1999. Features a check box for each record and picture sleeve (where applicable), debut year, and record label and number on an ample 11" x 8 1/2" page format. 304 pages. Spiral-bound softcover. $39.95.

POP HITS 1940-1954
Compiled strictly from *Billboard* and divided into two easy-to-use sections — one lists all the hits artist-by-artist and the other year-by-year. Filled with artist bios, title notes, and many special sections. 414 pages. Hardcover. $44.95.

POP MEMORIES 1890-1954
Unprecedented in depth and dimension. An artist-by-artist, title-by-title chronicle of the 65 formative years of recorded popular music. Fascinating facts and statistics on over 1,600 artists and 12,000 recordings, compiled directly from America's popular music charts, surveys and record listings. 660 pages. Hardcover. $59.95.

TOP POP ALBUMS 1955-2001
An artist-by-artist history of the over 22,000 albums that ever appeared on *Billboard's* pop albums charts, with a complete A-Z listing below each artist of tracks from every charted album by that artist. Over 1200 pages. Hardcover. $99.95.

BILLBOARD HOT 100/POP SINGLES CHARTS:

THE NINETIES 1990-1999
THE EIGHTIES 1980-1989
THE SEVENTIES 1970-1979
THE SIXTIES 1960-1969
Four complete collections of the actual weekly "Hot 100" charts from each decade; black-and-white reproductions at 70% of original size. Over 550 pages each. Deluxe Hardcover. $79.95 each.

POP CHARTS 1955-1959
Reproductions of every weekly pop singles chart *Billboard* published from 1955 through 1959 ("Best Sellers," "Jockeys," "Juke Box," "Top 100" and "Hot 100"). 496 pages. Deluxe Hardcover. $59.95.

BILLBOARD POP ALBUM CHARTS 1965-1969
The greatest of all album eras...straight off the pages of *Billboard* ! Every weekly *Billboard* pop albums chart, shown in its entirety, from 1965 through 1969. Black-and-white reproductions at 70% of original size. 496 pages. Deluxe Hardcover. $59.95.

TOP COUNTRY SINGLES 1944-1997
The complete history of the most genuine of American musical genres, with an artist-by-artist listing of every "Country" single ever charted. 544 pages. Hardcover. $64.95.

COUNTRY ANNUAL 1944-1997
A year-by-year ranking, based on chart performance, of over 16,000 Country hits. 704 pages. Hardcover. $64.95.

TOP COUNTRY ALBUMS 1964-1997
First edition! A music industry first and a Record Research exclusive — features an artist-by-artist listing of every album to appear on *Billboard's* Top Country Albums chart from its first appearance in 1964 through September, 1997. Includes complete listings of all tracks from every Top 10 Country album. 304 pages. Hardcover. $49.95.

A CENTURY OF POP MUSIC
This unique book chronicles the biggest Pop hits of the past 100 years, in yearly rankings of the Top 40 songs of every year from 1900 through 1999. Includes complete artist and title sections, pictures of the top artists, top hits and top artists by decade, and more. 256 pages. Softcover. $39.95.

TOP R&B SINGLES 1942-1999
Revised edition of our R&B bestseller — loaded with new features! Every "Soul," "Black," "Urban Contemporary" and "Rhythm & Blues" charted single, listed by artist. 688 pages. Hardcover. $69.95.

TOP R&B ALBUMS 1965-1998
First edition! An artist-by-artist listing of each of the 2,177 artists and 6,940 albums to appear on *Billboard's* "Top R&B Albums" chart. Includes complete listings of all tracks from every Top 10 R&B album. 360 pages. Hardcover. $49.95.

ROCK TRACKS
Two artist-by-artist listings of the over 3,700 titles that appeared on *Billboard's* "Album Rock Tracks" chart from March, 1981 through August, 1995 and the over 1,200 titles that appeared on *Billboard's* "Modern Rock Tracks" chart from September, 1988 through August, 1995. 288 pages. Softcover. $34.95.

BUBBLING UNDER SINGLES AND ALBUMS 1998 Edition
All "Bubbling Under The Hot 100" (1959-1997) and "Bubbling Under The Top Pop Albums" (1970-1985) charts covered in full and organized artist by artist. Also features a photo section of every EP that hit *Billboard's* "Best Selling Pop EP's" chart (1957-1960). 416 pages. Softcover. $49.95.

BILLBOARD TOP 10 SINGLES CHARTS 1955-2000
A complete listing of each weekly Top 10 singles chart from *Billboard's* "Best Sellers" chart (1955-July 28, 1958) and "Hot 100" chart from its inception (August 4, 1958) through 2000. Each chart shows each single's current and previous week's positions, total weeks charted on the entire chart, original label & number, and more. 712 pages. Hardcover. $49.95.

BILLBOARD TOP 10 ALBUM CHARTS 1963-1998
This books contains more than 1,800 individual Top 10 charts from over 35 years of *Billboard's* weekly Top Albums chart (currently titled The Billboard 200). Each chart shows each album's current and previous week's positions, total weeks charted on the entire Top Albums chart, original label & number, and more. 536 pages. Hardcover. $39.95.

BILLBOARD SINGLES REVIEWS 1958
Reproductions of every weekly 1958 record review *Billboard* published for 1958. Reviews of nearly 10,000 record sides by 3,465 artists. 280 pages. Softcover. $29.95.

BILLBOARD TOP 1000 x 5 1996 Edition
Includes five complete separate rankings — from #1 through #1000 — of the all-time top charted hits of Pop & Hot 100 Singles 1955-1996, Pop Singles 1940-1954, Adult Contemporary Singles 1961-1996, R&B Singles 1942-1996, and Country Singles 1944-1996. 288 pages. Softcover. $29.95.

DAILY #1 HITS 1940-1992
A desktop calendar of a half-century of #1 pop records. Lists one day of the year per page of every record that held the #1 position on the pop singles charts on that day for each of the past 53+ years. 392 pages. Spiral-bound softcover. $24.95.

MUSIC YEARBOOKS 2000/1999/1998/1997/1996/1995/1994/1993/1992/1991/1990
A complete review of each year's charted music — as well as a superb supplemental update of our Record Research Pop Singles and Albums, Country Singles, R&B Singles, Adult Contemporary Singles, and Bubbling Under Singles books. Various page lengths. Softcover. 2000 & 1999 editions $39.95 / 1995 thru 1998 editions $34.95 each / 1990 thru 1994 editions $29.95 each.

UPCOMING BOOKS (Anticipated publication date: March, 2002)

TOP ADULT CONTEMPORARY 1961-2001
Artist-by-artist listing of the nearly 8,000 singles and over 1,900 artists that appeared on *Billboard's* "Easy Listening" and "Hot Adult Contemporary" singles charts from July 17, 1961 through December 29, 2001. Over 350 pages. Hardcover. $44.95.

ALBUM CUTS 1955-2001
A companion guide to our Top Pop Albums 1955-2001 book — an A-Z list of cut titles along with the artist name and chart debut year of the album on which the cut is first found. Over 700 pages. Hardcover. $39.95.

Order Information

Shipping/Handling Extra — If you do not order through our online Web site (see below), please contact us for shipping rates.

Order By:

☎ **U.S. Toll-Free**: 1-800-827-9810
(orders only please – Mon-Fri 8 AM-12 PM, 1 PM-5 PM CST)

Foreign Orders: 1-262-251-5408

Questions?: 1-262-251-5408 or **Email**: books@recordresearch.com

🖥 **Online at our Web site**: www.recordresearch.com

📄 **Fax** (24 hours): 1-262-251-9452

📪 **Mail**: Record Research Inc.
P.O. Box 200
Menomonee Falls, WI 53052-0200
U.S.A.

U.S. orders are shipped via UPS; please allow **7-10 business days** for delivery.

Canadian and **Foreign** orders are shipped via surface mail; please allow **8-12 weeks** for delivery. Orders must be paid in U.S. dollars and drawn on a U.S. bank.

For faster delivery, contact us for other shipping options/rates. We now offer **UPS Worldwide Express** service for Canadian and Foreign orders.

Payment methods accepted: MasterCard, VISA, American Express, Money Order, or Check (personal checks may be held up to 10 days for bank clearance).